KU-712-037

CASSELL'S DICTIONARY OF
SLANG

Jonathon Green

CASSELL&CO

EG15434

For Susan Ford

EG15434

EALING TERTIARY COLLEGE
LEARNING RESOURCE CENTRE - EALING GREEN

Cassell & Co
Wellington House
125 Strand
London
WC2R 0BB

First published 1998

First paperback edition published 2000

© Jonathon Green 1998

All rights reserved. No part of this publication may be reproduced
in any material form (including photocopying or storing it in any
medium by electronic means and whether or not transiently or
incidentally to some other use of this publication) without the
written permission of the copyright owner, except in accordance
with the provisions of the Copyright, Designs and Patents Act 1988
or under the terms of a licence issued by the Copyright Licensing
Agency, 90 Tottenham Court Road, London W1P 9HE. Applications
for the copyright owner's written permission to reproduce any part
of this publication should be addressed to Cassell.

British Library Cataloguing in Publication Data
A catalogue entry for this book is available from the British Library.

ISBN 0–304–35167–9

Typeset in Great Britain by Gem Graphics, Trenance, Cornwall
Printed and bound in Finland by WSOY

Contents

Acknowledgements

This book has been five years in the making, and if one adds on my own production of slang dictionaries and allied works, the amassing of the vocabulary here displayed has been in progress since I first began collecting slang around 1980. Like the majority, if not every slang lexicographer who has preceded me, I am, and am proud to be, a one-man band. To that end, as it is traditional to declaim, the vices as well as the virtues of the book will have to be laid at my door. But to suggest that the creation of this dictionary was a solo effort in every aspect would be not merely hubristic but quite simply wrong. There are a number of people both living and dead, to whom I am indebted, and I would like to make due acknowledgement here.

The profession of lexicography is, inevitably, a plagiaristic one, a linguistic Pacman that moves on, gobbling up its predecessors as it goes. In an ideal world such an admission would be unnecessary, but the language does not renew itself from scratch, arising fresh and untouched, so as to serve each new dictionary afresh. Modern English has been expanding for nearly a millennium, and Old and Middle English, its roots, for a millennium more. Thus one's primary acknowledgement must be to the slang collectors of the 16th century onwards, best-known among them Robert Copland, Thomas Harman, the otherwise anonymous B.E., Francis Grose, John Camden Hotten, Albert Barrère and Charles Leland, John Farmer and W.E. Henley, George Matsell and Jonathan Lighter. And above all, and most personally Eric Partridge, the exemplar of the breed and the arbiter of modern slang lexicographers, whose own works, first encountered decades ago, convinced me that here was a subject to which it might be worth devoting oneself.

On a more immediate level, I would thank my sub-editors-cum-proof-readers: Christine Cowley, Jessica Feinstein, Gill Francis, Lucy Hollingsworth, Alyson McGaw, Sam Merrell and Laura Wedgeworth. Without their efforts this would have been a lesser work. Such acknowledgement must also go to Gordon Galsworthy, whose typesetting skills are displayed on every page. And if absorption of old texts was necessary, then Karen Thomson, the country's leading dictionary dealer, has made it possible for me to read some of them in the earliest editions. I would also pay tribute to Richard Short, who assisted me with some of the most back-breaking of the work, as on occasion did my sons, Lucien and Gabriel.

Loath though I am to enter the realms of senti-mentality, I am at a loss how else to render my indebtedness to Lydia Darbyshire, sub-editor-in-chief, and to Sarah Chatwin at Cassell, who has master-minded the ever more complex compilation of the final manuscript. No-one could have been more tolerant of my failings, both lexicographical and personal than these two. No-one could have made a sometimes onerous task so palatable. Deprived of better words, I am enormously grateful to them both.

It is to my great regret that my editor Nigel Wilcockson left Cassell before publication. His role has been ably filled by Richard Milbank, who has taken on a publishing *fait accompli* with enormous sympathy, but for five years Nigel walked the same path as did I, offering encouragement, advice, endless good humour and support. In commissioning this dictionary he gave me the opportunity to fulfil my greatest professional desire, and I hope, with its publication, that I have justified his faith.

I must also thank, in his much-regretted absence, my late uncle Ezra 'Jack' Morris. The declaration that 'this would not have been possible without ...' is a tired one, but incontrovertibly true in this case. His unexpected generosity has made it possible for me to have attained most writers' dream: to work on a major project without the need for additional employment. I wish that he could see the finished product.

Finally and with respect transcending all other acknowledgements, I must thank Susan Ford, my partner. Not only has she worked on large sections of the manuscript herself, but she has lived with it and with me throughout the book's gestation. How much this has meant is not for comment here. In many ways this is as much her book as it is mine and for that reason as well as for so many others, I dedicate it to her.

Introduction

Slang is the counter-language. A jackanapes lexicon of the dispossessed. The language of the rebel, the outlaw, the despised, the marginal, the young. Above all it is the language of the city – urgent, pointed, witty, cruel, capable both of excluding and including, of mocking and confirming. Its origins lie in the Scandinavian *sleng*, which also renders standard English's *sling*, and means a slinging, a device, a strategy. Thus slang is both literally and figuratively a 'slung' or 'thrown' language, tossed cunningly, as it were, into the hearer's face and ears. At its worst it can be no more than vulgar for vulgarity's sake, stupid, depressingly obvious, the stuff of insult and obscenity. At its best it can be *à propos*, apposite, delightfully and even subtly humorous, a vibrant subset of the English language of which, like its 'neighbours' jargon, dialect and colloquialism, it provides one more part.

Reviled and proscribed by pedants and purists, it is endlessly resilient, inventive and untameable. Its age is that of speech itself. If there has always been a standard, inevitably, there has been an alternative: slang, to tease, to provoke and expand our ways of communication. It is hugely enriching, the spice in the greater linguistic dish, enhancing quotidian ingredients with its brash new flavours.

This dictionary

This dictionary represents the first brand-new attempt to codify the slang vocabulary to appear in the UK since the first edition of Partridge's *Dictionary of Slang and Unconventional English* appeared in 1937. It is not, of course, the first slang dictionary to be published since then; Partridge's own work went into eight editions (the last posthumous); there have been a variety of others of greater or lesser extent, and my own *Dictionary of Contemporary Slang* is in its third edition. All that said, this dictionary is the first in sixty years to go back to the early 16th century and make its way on from there. It also covers an unprecedentedly wide range of territory, looking at the slangs of a variety of English-speaking countries. Its 70,000 words and phrases range across the globe.

What is slang?

Among the many descriptions of slang, both positive and negative, one thing stands out: it is a good way from mainstream English. It can and does share the same vocabulary at times, but slang definitions underpin its rogue status. Whether, as one observer suggests, it is the working man of language, doing the lexicon's 'dirty work' or, as another suggests, it stands up for the disenfranchised, offering 'the poor man's poetry' or, as its many critics still proclaim, it has nothing but the most deleterious effects on 'proper speech', slang remains a law unto itself. Nor is it easy to define of itself. The official (*Oxford English Dictionary*) definition runs, 'The special vocabulary

used by any set of persons of a low or disreputable character; language of a low a vulgar type,' and adds, 'Language of a highly colloquial type, considered as below the level of standard educated speech, and consisting either of new words or of current words employed in some special sense.' All that is true, but others have essayed their opinion and I offer mine above. Between them they provide, try as they might, as much a theoretical, 'atmospheric' take on their subject as a hard, lexicographical one. Perhaps the best definition, of many, is that of John Camden Hotten, written in 1859 but equally pertinent today:

> Slang represents that evanescent, vulgar language, ever changing with fashion and taste, ... spoken by persons in every grade of life, rich and poor, honest and dishonest ... . Slang is indulged in from a desire to appear familiar with life, gaiety, town-humour and with the transient nick names and street jokes of the day ... slang is the language of street humour, of fast, high and low life ... . Slang is as old as speech and the congregating together of people in cities. It is the result of crowding, and excitement, and artificial life.

Yet stand alone as it does, the isolation of slang from its linguistic 'neighbours', and especially from colloquialism, is never cut and dried. Jargon, by which I mean 'occupational or professional slang' (rather than the obscurantisms, deliberate or otherwise, which are also described, often in relation to governmental or corporate pronouncements, as jargon) offers a relatively minor problem. Although one more *OED* definition of slang, excluded above, equates it with this occupational jargon, I would draw a hard line and, with certain exceptions, I have not listed such terminology here. I have, for instance, chosen to ignore the substantial swathes of military language, coined in two World Wars, that feature so largely in Eric Partridge's *DSUE*. Likewise, I have preferred to overlook the 'public school' and 'university' vocabularies, both collected in books by Morris Marples, that seemed to me too parochial, however fascinating. A similar fate has befallen the language of a variety of occupations, all of which I would see as jargon, pure and simple. I have, on the other hand, included campus terminology wherever used, since it is hardly restricted to the university environs and spills over into the 'normal' slang of many young people. As for criminal slang or 'cant', I have included the more common terms, many of which have been popularized through television or film, but passed over the more detailed material; the nicknames of given safes, say, or the precise mechanics of selling 'from the back of a lorry' are too specific to be anything but jargon.

Cant also calls for one major exception. The first slang collections are to be found in the 16th century and as far as they are concerned, cant is simply all we have.

It seems impossible that slang did not extend as widely through society then as it does today, but those early slang collections, more glossaries than dictionaries, concentrate purely on the villain's vocabulary, the language of the wandering, criminal beggars who thronged through Britain. That the other, general slang, existed, must be accepted, but at four centuries' distance, we have no choice but to depend on what has been preserved. Nothing else was then collected; perhaps it failed to find a lexicographical sponsor. Thus, desirous of going back as far as records permit, one has no choice but to include this early cant here.

One debatable area, which to my knowledge has never before received so substantial a coverage in a general slang dictionary is drugs. This too could be marginalized as jargon, but with literally millions of drug consumers using some subset of this large vocabulary I felt that drugs, just as was the military fifty years ago, is a topic too closely linked to contemporary society and especially to the slang-using part of it, to be ignored.

The line between slang and colloquialism, the casual language of everyday speech, is simply too close to draw with any facility. Slang slips unnoticed across that border, and while one dictionary is happy to label the distinction as it sees it, alternative lexicons may take quite the opposite viewpoint, and use their labels accordingly. Thus this dictionary contains a number of words that may be categorized by some as colloquial; I make no excuses for their presence. Certain entries have not merely moved into colloquialism but have joined standard English. As far as possible I have noted this where relevant, explaining at what stage the word progressed from slang to greater respectability.

Etymology

Slang lexicography is the collecting of the slang vocabulary and the placing of it in dictionaries, but it is not quite that simple. The nature of the vocabulary being what it is, it cannot be constrained by the same rules as govern the 'respectable' lexis of mainstream dictionary-making. For the purposes of intelligibility I have attempted to corral its more extreme vagaries, but certain idiosyncrasies have to be acknowledged. I note the problem of dating below, but slang, especially in its etymology, the explanation of the formation and roots (both linguistic and social/historical) of a word, as often plays with its basic materials as simply uses them.

In many of the etymologies that follow, the reader will have to allow for a lateral rather than a linear link between the headword and the material that underpins it. But slang is often less than forthcoming about its origins. In many cases, indeed too many as I am the first to accept, I have been forced to essay an etymology, noted thus by a '?', preferring to offer what I hope is a feasible and probable link rather than surrendering to that blank admission of failure, 'ety. unknown'. In this I may on occasion have blundered, but I hope that, bereft of more concrete background, I

have at least entered upon the right track. It is my belief that one of the greatest pleasures of a dictionary should be the 'stories' behind the words; never more so than in slang dictionaries, where the search for accurate spelling, the primary impetus of mainstream dictionary use, plays a secondary role to that for definitions and roots. Thus I have tried my best to come up as accurately and informatively as I can with those same 'stories'.

A large proportion of the entries depend on standard English words – slang either extends the standard usage or gives it a figurative or jocular twist. I have taken this to be self evident and have not noted it, so where an entry does not contain an etymology, it can be assumed that this is the case.

Dating

The dating of slang is perhaps the most problematic aspect of its collection. While it would be possible (had space not precluded the insertion of such examples) to provide a good range of citations for 19th and 20th century terminology, once one moves further backwards into history, one's choices are severely limited and the lexicographer is forced to cannibalize predecessors, taking an appearance in these earlier dictionaries as the only available proof of a word's usage. The problem, even when dealing with more recent terminology, is compounded by the nature of the slang vocabulary. All language is by its nature spoken, but slang often stays in the mouth and off the page (or for that matter the film or TV screen or any other form of medium) for far longer than does standard English. Indeed, there is an argument, embarrassing and frustrating for the slang collector, that by the time slang has made it into some form of permanence, it's already out of date. A little harsh perhaps, and much of what follows has surprising longevity, but another point to underline slang's resistance to mainstream linguistic norms. Typically too, the concept of a 'first use' is even more debatable than it might be for a mainstream term. I regret the fact, but given this situation I have too often been forced to assume a wider date range than may really be the case. More important, however, is the effect of such imprecision on etymology. Logically one links words on a chronological basis; a word coined in, say, 1790 can generally be set down as the creator of one coined a decade later; slang, if the collector adheres strictly to such dates as are available, often rejects that basic rule and readers will find that some words appear to have come from others that, according to my dates, actually emerged after that for which they are supposedly the root. I have tried to note this where possible, but it is to be borne in mind throughout.

Geography

I have included slang terms not merely from the UK, but from the United States, Canada, the anglophone islands of the Caribbean, Ireland (North and South), South Africa, Australia and New Zealand – in other words the main countries to have learned their

English, of whatever sort, through their one-time status as British colonies. I have on the whole resisted modern India, which some might see as a possible qualifier, since Indian English, that legacy of the Raj, seems to give way to the many indigenous languages of the post-independence country when it requires slang. I have, however, included a number of Raj-era entries, since these would primarily have been spoken by White Englishmen and women seconded to the subcontinent.

When checking an entry it should be assumed that I am looking first for the original use and in this the default language and usage area – thus bearing no label – is English English and the UK; if I can isolate it elsewhere, I have labelled accordingly. English may be the mother tongue, but many words and phrases remain permanent orphans. Obviously many terms are used in England and America, the Antipodes and so on; I have not, however, attempted to list every relevant country if the default stands. As will be seen, dialect features in many etymologies, and it is my belief that a large amount of slang was generated simply by the arrival of country-dwellers in the new towns and cities of the industrial era. Their local usage came with them, but, deprived of its nurturing environment, lost its roots. No longer dialect, an essentially rural phenomenon, and certainly not qualified for standard English, it became slang, the language of the city. When possible I have identified the source of the given dialect, but where this has not been done, it must be assumed that it was used either all across England (and possibly Scotland, Wales and Ireland too) or in too many and too disparate areas to list them all.

Sources

The nature of lexicography, there is little point in denying, bears within it a necessary strand of plagiarism. Like standard English, slang, however fecund and inventive, does not reinvent itself from the ground up each time a new lexicographer sets fingers to database. While there have appeared, naturally, a wide range of glossaries, usually pertaining to criminal language, the hard core of slang dictionaries runs to perhaps twenty-five major titles, starting with the 16th-century glossarist Robert Copland, and moving on to this book. And like mainstream English, there are certain way-stations, after which one sees effective repetition until the next major dictionary appears. And while standard English can call on a wide range of literary productions from which to draw citations and usage guidance, slang has been relatively rarely recorded; not merely in the earliest days of collection, the mid-16th century, but right up until the last fifty years.

And when it did appear in these early days, typically in the early 17th-century plays of Thomas Dekker and Thomas Middleton, or their successors, authors of the Restoration comedies, it is too often in the form of a virtual glossary, a litany of cant or slang terms all in a single scene, rather than as a natural part of the dialogue. The material, fortunately, grows ever-more accessible, but it is not until the post-war era that slang has found a regular place in books, films, television programmes and the like. Thus, especially for the earliest material, one is thrown willy-nilly onto the mercies of such 16th-century glossarists as Robert Copland, Thomas Harman and Robert Greene. Indeed the list of canting, i.e. professional criminal, terms that they assembled remained pretty much unaltered until the efforts of the otherwise anonymous 'B.E., Gent.' in the *New Dictionary of the Canting Crew* (c.1698) brought a certain element of 'civilian', i.e. non-criminal, slang into his collection. B.E. dominated the 18th century, until in 1785 a new collector laid down his marker. *The Classical Dictionary of the Vulgar Tongue* by Captain Francis Grose, the slang equivalent of his near-contemporary Samuel Johnson, lasted unrivalled, and running to more than five expanded, re-edited or subsequently pirated editions, until his work was supplanted in turn by the publisher, bookseller and part-time pornographer John Camden Hotten, publishing his *Slang Dictionary* in 1859. Thirty years on, slang received not one but two multi-volumed dictionaries: first that of Barrère and Leland (1889) and then John Farmer's and W. E. Henley's seven-volume (eight if one adds Farmer's *Vocabularia Amatoria*) *Slang and Its Analogues*, which gave the world of slang lexicography what the magisterial *New* (later *Oxford*) *English Dictionary* did for the mainstream. And forty years later Farmer and Henley provided the backbone of Eric Partridge's own *Dictionary of Slang and Unconventional English* (1937).

Given the pre-eminence of America in today's slang vocabularies – Partridge may have been able to talk of unconventional English and mean that and only that; modern slang collectors have no such option – it may seem odd that there existed only one major 19th-century American slang dictionary: the *Vocabulum* (1859) by New York City's one-time police chief George Matsell; itself little more than yet another revision of Grose, or more properly the version of Grose edited in 1823 by the sporting journalist Pierce Egan. But slang is a city language and even at mid-century, America remained a primarily rural society. As that changed, and American cities became the world's greatest urban centres, so too did the generation of slang. The importance of that slang can be seen today in the on-going *Random House Historical Dictionary of American Slang*, edited by Jonathan Lighter. But Lighter's work, while undoubtedly the best, is only the latest. American slang has been collected by a wide variety of lexicographers, among them Hyman Goldin, David Maurer and Harold Wentworth and Stuart Berg Flexner, whose *Dictionary of American Slang* was for thirty years the standing authority.

As for other English-speaking countries, specific slang collections have been relatively rare. Australia's first dictionary of any sort was a slang one, the thrice-transported (and thrice-escaped) convict James Hardy

Vaux's *Vocabulary of the Flash Language* (1819), offered as an appendix to his memoirs. There have been a number of glossaries of criminal slang since then, but the main collector of Antipodean slang remains Sidney J. Baker, who wrote extensively on both Australian and New Zealand slang in the 1940s and produced a dictionary for each country. For the vocabularies of South Africa and the West Indies I have checked among other sources a number of general dictionaries, truffling out the slang from the wider lexicons there displayed.

Where I have benefited hugely is the ever-increasing presence of slang, right across the media, whether old – books and magazines – intermediate – film and television – or up-to-date – records, tapes and CDs, graphic novels or the Internet. My reading has been substantially augmented by all these sources, and the sources on which I have been able to draw are wide-ranging indeed. It is to my great regret that I can but list them in the Bibliography. Even more regrettable is the fact that I have been unable, despite my initial hopes, to offer citations for every term. But space has militated against such inclusion. There is no doubt that citations are vital in a properly historical dictionary and had it been possible it might, as seen superbly in Jonathan Lighter's effort, have put this dictionary on a par with any such work. But at the same time, as seen less satisfyingly in Lighter's work – only two volumes of which have appeared in the last four years – it would have undermined what I wish it most to be: an accessible, useable work of reference. I had no desire to see my efforts appearing over so long a period. Time and size both conspire against citations, at least for a one-volume work of the chronological spread that I have chosen, and I opted for immediacy and, as far as I can, linguistic comprehensiveness.

Insult and offence

The nature of slang is often, indeed almost invariably, rebarbative. Even its congratulations are mitigated by a certain edge. Its nature is to cause offence, to mock, to scorn, to savage, to dismay. It is no comforter. Whether geared for racial or national insult, describing human interactions, noting intelligence, or more usually lack of it, listing parts of the body, delineating the excesses of drink and drugs, or parading the vocabulary of a criminal underworld, it is often pertinent but rarely complimentary. Thus the nature of the beast. It would hardly be slang were it otherwise. And this, in itself, causes no problems. Those, as ever, emerge in the details.

Writing in 1937, and indeed in several subsequent editions, Partridge might have found himself unwilling to spell out such terms as fuck, cunt or shit, all proscribed by the current standards of 'taste' (and indeed by his own admitted squeamishness as

regarded such language), but when it came to insults, however vile, he had no problems: a nigger was a Black person, a kike, a Jew, a wog, a brown foreigner. The 'dirty words' might finally appear in full in the 1970 edition, but as for the insults, unmodified by any reference as to their possible offensiveness, they would remain part of his dictionary for the rest of his life. This is not, I stress, to impugn Partridge, or the ranks of his predecessors who similarly found themselves unphased by racism but aghast at 'obscenity', as a bigot. Such an attitude was a given of contemporary culture. One may deplore it, but the dictionary-maker's task is to display language, not moralize upon it. To describe, not proscribe. Sixty years on and the social background against which I operate has reversed the situation. I can and do spell out anything, but as for racial slurs, like the *OED*, which began inserting notes as to 'offensiveness' with its first post-war Supplement (1972), I prefer to offer some form of label, usually the phrase 'a derog.[atory] term for...'. The omission of such terms, as many US dictionaries are now considering, would be anathema, serving nothing but the diminution of the dictionary. I see no reason to leave them unadorned and unqualified, even if those who most need reminding of such qualifications are least likely to acknowledge them. So far, then, so good. But if race can be qualified, then why, it might be asked, should other groups – homosexuals, the disabled, the fat, the thin, the tall, the short, the stupid, the sexually active – all of whom get their fair share of invective, not claim equivalent status. Everyone's ass is up for grabs, remarked Lenny Bruce, but in the 'victim culture' of the 1990s everyone's 'ass' seems up for special treatment. I have chosen, and am quite satisfied with my choice, to resist such suggestions. Slang is as it is and what it is is largely cruel. So be it. It would be easier, were one to succumb to these politically correct sirens, to mark those terms that are not 'derog.' rather than those that are.

In conclusion

It is the duty of the lexicographer to amass the language and offer it for perusal. It is not a task that can be complete, nor ever completed. The idea of 'fixing' the language was abandoned by Dr Johnson in 1755, and his submission to the realities of an ever-expanding vocabulary has set the style for all major English dictionaries ever since. The same goes undoubtedly for slang, the creation of which is a non-stop process. The slang lexicographer can chase the booming vocabulary and even catch a good proportion, but it remains elusive. Any help would be cheerfully received. I remain open to suggestion.

Jonathon Green
August 1998
slang@crayford.demon.co.uk

How to use *Cassell's Dictionary of Slang*

The entry

Each entry in *Cassell's Dictionary of Slang* begins with the headword in bold type. This may include any variant spellings or alternative forms, which are indicated by one or more oblique slashes. The headword is immediately followed by the part of speech in italics, always includes the date of use in square brackets and may include a usage label in round brackets, followed by the definition itself. Etymologies are placed at the end of the entry in square brackets.

Organization of entries

Entries are arranged in alphabetical order on a letter-by-letter basis. Entries identical in spelling are ordered according to their part of speech, in the sequence noun, adjective, verb, adverb, phrase, exclamation. Where the noun or verb etc has more than one distinct meaning, these are divided up or homographed according to etymology. Within the parts of speech, each homograph is given a number in superscript, e.g. **dog** *n.*¹, **dog** *n.*², **dog** *n.*³ etc, followed by **dog** *v.*¹, **dog** *v.*². The sequence of all homographs is chronological, according to the first usage of each entry.

Where an entry or a distinct homograph has several different shades of meaning, these are given sense numbers in bold. The numbered senses may have their own dates and labels, or alternatively if either a label or a date, or both, applies to all senses of the entry, it will be placed before the first numbered sense. Sense numbers are also ordered according to chronological first appearance.

Dating

Where a date appears in the form [18C], [19C] or [20C] it indicates that the usage period of the term covers the whole century. The + sign indicates that a term is still in use, as does the label [1990s] which indicates a recent and current slang expression. Dating is based primarily on when a term, or the sense of a term, began to be used, but also takes into consideration the length of its usage, so for example the use might find **1** [18C] ...; **2** [mid-18C+] ...; **3** [late 18C-early 19C] ..., where the second entry is still in use and the third is not, but the second originated earlier than the third.

Labels

Usage labels are in round brackets, usually following the date label. These indicate either the geographical usage of a term, e.g. (W.I.) or the social/cultural usage e.g. (teen). A list of abbreviations used in the dictionary appears on p. x. The non-geographical usage labels should be self-explanatory, for instance the use of (juv.) as juvenile, to suggest pre-teenage children's usage, as distinct from (teen); however, some of the labels are included in the list of abbreviations with brief glossaries attached.

Cross-references

A word or expression which appears elsewhere in the dictionary is marked as a cross-reference, in small capital letters. Cross-references occur mainly in the etymologies, in cases where the origin of one slang expression resides wholly or partly in another slang term. For example, the entry **nabbing cheat** has the etymology [NAB *v.*¹ + CHEAT n.].

Cross-references also appear in round brackets following 'cf.', which refers the reader to other entries for comparison. Often where there is a cross-reference to one headword, that headword may contain a larger collection of comparative references. These larger lists comprise groups of related synonyms, collected only for the most commonly occurring types of expression.

Short forms of reference

Please refer to the Bibliography on p.1313, for further information.

AND	*The Australian National Dictionary* (*see* Ramson, W.S.)
B.E.	B. E., Gent.
B&L	Barrère and Leland
DARE	*Dictionary of American Regional English* (*see* Cassidy, F.G.)
DNZE	*The Dictionary of New Zealand English* (*see* Orsman, H.W.)
E.P.	Eric Partridge
F&H	Farmer and Henley
OED	*The Oxford English Dictionary*
RHDAS	*Random House Dictionary of American Slang* (*see* Lighter)

Chief Abbreviations

AAE	Afro-American English	Jap.	Japan/Japanese	S.Afr.Du.	South African Dutch
abbr.	abbreviation/ abbreviated	joc.	jocular	SAmE	Standard American English
Abor.	Aboriginal	journ.	journalistic	S&M	sado-masochistic
adj.	adjective	juv.	juvenile (pre-teenage)	SAusE	Standard Australian English
adv.	adverb	Lat.	Latin		
Afk.	Afrikaner/Afrikaans	Ling. Fr.	Lingua Franca	Scand.	Scandinavia/ Scandinavian
Antg.	Antigua/Antiguan	lit.	literally		
AS	Anglo-Saxon	ME	Middle English	Scot.	Scotland, Scottish
Aus.	Australian	Med.	Medieval	SE	Standard English
backform.	backformation	Mex.	Mexico/Mexican	SF	science fiction
backsl.	backslang	MHG	Middle High German	sfx.	suffix
Baha.	Bahamas/Bahamian	milit.	military	Skrt.	Sanskrit
Bdos.	Barbados/Barbadian	mispron.	mispronunciation	sing.	singular
C	century	mis-sp.	mis-spelling	sl.	slang
camp gay	stereotypically effeminate terms	MLG	Middle Low German	SNZE	Standard New Zealand English
		n.	noun		
Can.	Canada/Canadian	naut.	nautical	society	upper- and middle- class usage
Carib.E.	Caribbean English	neg.	negative		
colloq.	colloquial	Nor.	Norway/Norwegian	Sp.	Spanish
comb./	combination/	N.Z.	New Zealand	sp.	spelling
combs.	combinations	obs.	obsolete	spec.	specifically
Da.	Danish	occas.	occasionally	St Lu.	Saint Lucia
derog.	derogative	OE	Old English	subseq.	subsequent
dial.	dialect	OF	Old French	Sw.	Sweden/Swedish
dimin.	diminutive	OHG	Old High German	synon.	synonym/ synonymous
Dmnca	Dominica	ON	Old Norse		
Du.	Dutch	onomat.	onomatopoeia/ onomatopoeic	teen	teenage use
edn.	edition			Tob.	Tobago
esp.	especially	opp.	opposite	trad.	traditional/ traditionally
epon.	eponymous	Oxon.	Oxfordshire		
ety.	etymology	pej.	pejorative	Trin.	Trinidad
euph.	euphemism/ euphemistic	Pers.	Persian	Turk.	Turkish
		phr.	phrase	UK	United Kingdom
excl.	exclamation	pfx.	prefix	UKVI	United Kingdom Virgin Islands
f.	from	pl.	plural		
facet.	facetious	pos.	positive	ult.	ultimately
fig.	figurative	P.R.	Puerto Rico/ Puerto Rican	Und.	Underworld (criminal cant, *see* Introduction)
form.	formation				
Fr.	France/French	prep.	preposition		
Ger.	German	pron.	pronunciation	US	United States
Gk.	Greek	P.R.Sp.	Puerto Rican Spanish	USPR	United States Puerto Rican
Guyn.	Guyana/Guyanese	publ.	published		
Heb.	Hebrew	pvb.	proverb	USVI	United States Virgin Islands
Hind.	Hindustani	RAF	Royal Air Force		
Hisp.Am.	Hispanic American	redup.	reduplicated/ reduplication	usu.	usually
Icel.	Iceland/Icelandic			v.	verb
imper.	imperative	ref.	reference	W.I.	West Indies/ West Indian
interj.	interjection	rhy. sl.	rhyming slang		
Ind.	Indian	RN	Royal Navy	WW1	First World War
IVE	Indian Vernacular English	Rus.	Russian	WW2	Second World War
		S.Afr.	South Africa/African	Yid.	Yiddish
		S.Afr.E.	South African English	Yorks.	Yorkshire

A

a *n.*[1] **1** [20C] (W.I./Guyn.) a general term of dislike. **2** [1940s+] (US) used as euph. for ARSE, e.g. *haul a, bet your fat a.* [abbr. ARSE n.[1]]

a *n.*[2] [1960s+] (drugs) amphetamine (cf. AIMIES n.[1]; AMPHETS; A1 n.; BAM n.[3]; BEAUTY n.[3]; BENZ n.[1]; BILLY n.[6]; BILLY WHIZ; BLACK BEAUTY; BLACKBIRD n.[4]; BLACKBIRDS; BLACK BOMBER; BLACK CADILLAC; BLACKJACK n.[8]; BLACK MOLLY; BLACKS; BLACK WIDOW n.[1]; BLANCA; BLUE n.[8]; BLUE ANGEL; BLUE BOY n.[4]; BLUES n.[2]; BOMBIDO; BOMBITA; BOTTLES; BRAIN TICKLERS; BROWNIES; BUMBLEBEES; CHICKEN POWDER; CHOCOLATE n.[2]; CHRISTINA; COASTS TO COASTS; CO-PILOT; CRISSCROSS; CROSSROADS; CROSS TOPS; DIET PILLS; DOMINOES n.[2]; DOOB n.[2]; DOUBLECROSS; EYE-OPENER n.[2]; FAST n.; FOOTBALLS; FORWARDS; GLASS n.[3]; GO PILL; GREEN HORNET; GREENIES n.[4]; HALLOO-WACH; HEAD DRUGS; HEARTS; HELPERS; HORS D'OEUVRES; HORSE HEADS; ICE n.[5]; IN-BETWEENS; JAM n.[7]; JAM CECIL; JELLY BABY n.[2]; JOLLY BEANS; JUGS n.[2]; L.A. n.[2]; LID-PROPPERS; LIFT PILL; LOU REED; MACKA; MARATHONS; MEXICAN JUMPING BEAN; MINIBENNIE; MOLLIES; MONSTER n.; NUGGETS n.[2]; OLLY n.; ORANGES; PEP-EM-UPS; PEP PILL; P.H.; PIXIES; PULVER; PURPLE n.; PURPLE HEARTS; RHYTHM n.[1]; RIPPERS; ROAD DOPE; ROSA; ROSES n.[2]; ROUSER n.[3]; SNOW n.[2]; SNOW PALLETS; SPARKLE PLENTY; SPARKLER n.[3]; SPEED; SPEEDBALL n.[1]; SPLIVINS; STRAWBERRIES; SWEETS; THRUSTERS; TOFFY WHIZZ; TR-6; TRUCK-DRIVERS; TURKEY n.[4]; TURNABOUT n.[2]; UPPER n.[2]; WAKE-AMINE; WEST COAST TURNAROUNDS; WHITE n.[2]; WHITE CROSS; WHITES n.[4]). [abbr.]

a *n.*[3] [1970s+] (drugs) LSD, i.e. d-lycergic acid diethylamide-25 (cf. ACID n.[3]; ACID CAP; ALICE n.[3]; ANIMAL n.[4]; BARRELS; BATTERY ACID; BEAST n.[4]; BIG D; BLACK ACID; BLACK STAR; BLACK SUNSHINE; BLACK TABS; BLOTS; BLOTTER CUBE; BLUE ACID; BLUE BARRELS; BLUE CHAIRS; BLUE HEAVEN; BLUE MICRODOT; BLUE STAR; BLUE VIALS; BROWN BOMBER; BROWN DOTS; CALIFORNIA SUNSHINE; CAP n.[4]; CHOCOLATE CHIPS; 'CID; CONDUCTOR; CONTACT LENS; CRACKERS n.[5]; CRYSTAL TEA; 'CUBE n.[3]; D n.[4]; DEEDA; DOME n.[2]; DOSES; DOTS n.[2]; DOUBLE DOME n.[2]; FIELDS; FLASH n.[7]; FLAT BLUES; FRY n.[2]; GHOST n.[1]; GOLDEN DRAGON; GRAPE PARFAIT; GREEN WEDGE; GREY SHIELDS; HATS; HAWAIIAN SUNSHINE; HAWK n.[4]; HAZE; HEADLIGHTS; HITS; INSTANT ZEN; L n.[2]; LASON SA DAGA; L.B.J.; LENS n.; LIME ACID; LIQUID; LOGOR; LUCY IN THE SKY WITH DIAMONDS; ORANGE SUNSHINE; PURPLE HAZE; SACRAMENT; SANDOZ; SHEETS n.[1]; SMEARS; SMILEY n.[1]; STRAWBERRY FIELDS; SUGAR n.[6]; SUGAR CUBES; SUNSHINE n.[1]; SUPERMARIO; TWENTY-FIVE n.[1]). [abbr.; a powerful, synthetic hallucinogen, based on ergot and discovered in 1943 by Dr Albert Hofmann of Sandoz Laboratories, Basel, and massively popularized in 1960s by Dr Timothy Leary (1920–96), Ken Kesey (b.1935) and his Merry Pranksters, rock groups and the 'alternative society']

a! *excl.* [1940s+] (US Black) yes, absolutely, certainly (cf. FUCKING-A!).

-a *sfx.* [20C] used to denote a colloq. or slangy pron. of **1** have, e.g. *coulda, musta, shoulda.* **2** do, e.g. *whaddya, whodya.* **3** to, e.g. *gonna, gotta, oughta, wanna.* **4** of, e.g. *cuppa, kinda, lotsa, lotta.*

aachibombo *n.* [1940s+] (W.I.) codfish fritters. [W.I. *aachi*, codfish + BUMBO n.[1] (2), lit. 'codfish-arse']

aagey-wala *n.* [20C] (Anglo-Ind.) the penis. [Hind., the man in front]

aai-aai *see* AI-AI.

aap *n.* [1940s+] (S.Afr.) a cannabis cigarette (cf. ZOL). [Afk. *aap*, ape or monkey]

aardvark *n.* [1960s+] (US) a simpleton, a dullard, an oaf. [anthropomorphic use of SE; note the character *Aardvark* in Joseph Heller's *Catch-22* (1961), a cheery, bumbling oaf]

aardvark *v.* [1990s] (US campus) to engage in sex; thus *aardvarking*, sexual intercourse. [the animal's image ? + a pun on 'rooting about' in dark places]

aaron, the *n.* **1** [17C–19C] a criminal, esp. a gang leader (cf. COCK LOREL). **2** [19C] a cadger. [the biblical *Aaron*, Judaism's first high priest]

aaron's rod *n.* [19C] the penis. [punning on ROD, f. Num. 17:8: 'Behold, the rod of Aaron … was budded, and brought forth buds, and bloomed blossoms and yielded almonds']

aasbed *n.* [1950s] (W.I.) a rough bed. [? ARSE n.[1] + SE *bed*]

ab *n.*[1] [mid-19C] (US, South) a Northern soldier in the US Civil War. [abbr. SE *abolitionist*]

ab *n.*[2] [19C] (Aus.) Aborigine; the predecessor of the modern ABO. [abbr.]

abaa *adj.* [late 19C] **1** silly. **2** bad, e.g. *abaa cove*, a bad man. [ety. unknown; ? 'baaing' of a sheep]

abacter *n.* [18C] a dishonest drover or shepherd who connives at the stealing of cattle they are guarding. [Lat. *abigere*, to drive away]

abaddon *n.* [19C] a thief turned informer. [the punning *a bad 'un* + *Abaddon*, 'the angel of the bottomless pit', Rev. 9]

abaft the wheel-house *phr.* [late 19C] (US) just below the small of the back; thus euph. for the buttocks.

abandannad *n.* [mid–late 19C] a thief who specializes in stealing bandanna handkerchiefs. [SE *abandoned* (boy) + *bandanna*]

abandoned habits *n.* [late 19C] the riding dress of the up-market courtesans who frequented Rotten Row in London's Hyde Park. [pun on their SE *abandoned habits*, i.e. immorality + SE *riding habit*, their costume]

abareskin *adj.* [1960s] (US camp gay) embarrassing. [joc. mispron. and ref. to *bare skin*]

abbess/lady abbess *n.* [mid-18C–mid-19C] a brothel-keeper, a madame (cf. ABBOT; NUN; PRESBYTERESS; PROVINCIAL). [ironic use of SE]

abbey-lubber *n.* [16C] a lazy monk; a reproachful name in regular use after the Reformation. [SE *abbey* + *lubber*, f. OF *lobeor*, swindler, parasite; the word is the origin of the nautical use]

abbot *n.* [late 19C] a brothel-keeper's husband or lover (cf. ABBESS; ABBOT ON THE CROSS; CROZIERED ABBOT).

abbot on the cross n. [19C] a pimp (cf. ABBOT). [the male counterpart of the ABBESS]

Abbott's priory n. [19C] the King's Bench prison, also known as Abbott's Lodge; thus *Abbott's teeth*, the spikes that topped the prison wall. [Sir Charles *Abbott* (1762–1832), Lord Chief Justice (1818–32). The King's Bench prison was generically the Lodge or the *Priory*, and its 'given' name varied according to the current Lord Chief Justice; thus before 1818 'Abbott' had been 'Ellenborough', f. the previous office-holder]

a.b.c. n.¹ [19C] the vagina (cf. ALPHA AND OMEGA). [like *ABC*, it is the beginning, although of life rather than the alphabet]

ABC n.² [1920s] (Irish) scorch marks on one's legs. [? play on ABC bread company; i.e. one's legs have been toasted]

a.b.c. n.³ *see* ACE BOON COON.

abdabs/habdabs n. [1940s+] nervous anxiety (cf. COME THE ABDABS). [? echoic of the spluttering, hesitant speech of one who is thus afflicted]

abdar n. [19C] (Anglo-Ind.) a teetotaller. [Urdu *abdar*, the man in charge of the water, thus 'water-carrier'; in 19C Anglo-Ind. society the head servant]

abdicate v. [1960s+] (gay) to declare oneself openly as a homosexual (cf. COME OUT v.¹). [pun on SE]

abdicated adj. [1960s+] (gay) ordered out of the public lavatory where one is looking for sex (cf. THRONE). [play on QUEEN n.¹]

Abdul n. **1** [1910s–40s] (Aus.) a derog. term for a Turkish soldier. **2** [1920s] a derog. term for an Afghan. **3** [1980s+] (US) a derog. term for an Arab. [stereotypical 'Arab' name]

Abe n.¹ [19C+] a derog. term for a Jew (cf. ABIE KABIBBLE). [proper name, *Abraham*, the biblical patriarch]

Abe n.² **1** [1950s–60s] (US) a $5 bill (cf. BROWN ABE). **2** [1950s+] (US drugs) $5's worth of drugs. [ABRAHAM LINCOLN]

abear v. [late 19C; 1940s–70s] to abide, to tolerate. [OE *abearan*, to bear, to carry, thence to dial. 20C use is US Black]

Aberdeen cutlet n. [19C] a dried haddock (cf. ADIRONDACK STEAK; ALASKA TURKEY; ALBANY BEEF; BILLINGSGATE PHEASANT; BLOCK ISLAND TURKEY; CALIFORNIAN; CAPE ANN TURKEY; CAPE COD TURKEY; COLUMBIA RIVER TURKEY; CONNECTICUT RIVER PORK; CRAIL CAPON; DEEP-SEA TURKEY; DIGBY CHICKEN; DUNBAR WETHER; GLASGOW MAGISTRATE; GOUROCK HAM; HALIFAX MUTTON; IRISH GOOSE; NORFOLK CAPON; TAUNTON TURKEY; YARMOUTH CAPON). [the Aberdeen fishing trade]

abergavenny n. [19C] a penny. [rhy. sl.]

abe's cabe n. [1980s+] (drugs) a $5 bill. [ABE n.² + redup.]

a.b.f. n. [1910s+] the last drink of a session. [abbr. *a bloody final drink*]

abfab adj. [1960s+] (Aus. teen) a general term of approval; first-rate, very attractive. [abbr. of *absolutely fabulous*; the sl. predates the hit UK TV series of the 1990s]

Abie n. [1950s–60s] **1** a Jew. **2** (US Black) a tailor. [ABE n.¹ + trad. linking of Jews and tailoring]

Abie Kabibble n. [1920s–30s] (US) a Jew. [variation on US Yid. *ish kabibble*, who cares, don't worry; prob. ult. Yid. *nish gefidlt*. Adopted by the vaudeville star Fanny Brice (1891–1951), the term was picked up by America's 'dean of cartoonists' Harry Hershfield, who in 1917 launched a character called Abie the Agent, based on one *Abie Kabibble*. Highly successful, the strip lasted until 1932. The term was further popularized by a swing trumpeter, who adopted the name Ish Kabibble and started performing as a comic]

abigail n. **1** [18C–mid-19C] a lady's maid. **2** [1950s+] (camp gay) an ageing, conservative homosexual. [a character in Francis Beaumont and John Fletcher's play *The Scornful Lady* (c.1613), although she was possibly so named in allusion to the expression 'thine handmaid' used in the Bible by Abigail the Carmelitess, 1 Sam. 25:24–31]

abishag n. [19C] the bastard child of a woman who has been seduced and abandoned by a married man. [Heb. 'the mother's error']

able to crawl under a snake's belly, to be phr. [1910s+] (orig. Aus.) to act immorally and without the least ethics, sometimes extended as *able to crawl under a snake's belly with a top hat/with stilts on*.

able to kick the eye out of a mosquito, to be phr. [late 19C–1920s] (orig. US) to possess supreme competence.

abo n. [20C] (Aus.) an Aboriginal (cf. AB n.²). [? abbr. of the column 'Aboriginalities', launched in the Sydney *Bulletin*, 15 October 1887; *AND* suggests it was current orally somewhat earlier; the SE *aborigine* and *aboriginal* are found in 1829 citations; pl. *aborigines* is found in 1803]

aboard adv. [mid-19C–1940s] (US) in one's stomach, esp. of drink.

aboliar n. [1920s–30s] (Aus.) an expert on Aborigine customs and folktales. [ABO + SE *liar*]

a-bomb n. [1950s–70s] (US drugs) a combination of marijuana or hashish with opium or cannabis and cocaine (cf. ATOM BOMB; SPEEDBALL n.¹).

aboon v. [19C] (US) to think oneself superior. [northern dial. *aboon*, above, higher]

abort v. [1960s] (US gay) to defecate immediately following anal intercourse. [black humour]

abortion n. [1940s+] (Aus.) an all-purpose denigration of a person, an object or an enterprise.

about as high as six penn'orth of coppers *see* AS HIGH AS SIX PENN'ORTH OF COPPERS.

about east adv. [mid-19C] (US) properly, regularly, as it should be. [? sailing use]

about half adv. [1960s+] (US) **1** very, quite, exceptionally, much. **2** feeling well, healthy. [the positive synon. of NOT HALF]

about one's speed phr. [1920s+] (orig. US) suitable, to one's own taste.

about right adj.¹ [19C+] drunk; one of a number of terms implying the positive aspects of drinking (cf. AT REST; BANG-UP adj.; BRIGHT IN THE EYE; CHIRPING MERRY; ELECTRIFIED; FEELING FUNNY; FEELING GOOD; FEELING NO PAIN; FEELING RIGHT ROYAL; FETTLED; GAY adj.²; GEED-UP adj.²; GIFFED; GLAD adj.; GLORIOUS; GLOWING; GOLDED; HAPPY adj.; HEADY adj.¹; HEARTY adj.; IN A MERRY PIN; INSPIRED; JOLLY adj.¹; JUST NICELY; LOOKING LIVELY; MAXED; MAXED OUT; MELLOW adj.; MIRACULOUS; OFF NICELY; PRIMED; SALUBRIOUS; SNUG adj.; SPIFFED adj.¹; SPREEISH; STOKED; TAKING IT EASY; TEED UP; WELL AWAY).

about right adj.² [mid-19C+] correct (cf. ABOUT THE SIZE; BANG TO RIGHTS). [the implication is of a slightly grudging admission]

about the size/size of it phr. [mid-late 19C+] pretty much as required; usu. as *that's* ... (cf. ABOUT RIGHT adj.²). [ext. of SE use]

above board adj. [early 17C+] open, honest. [the image is of card-players keeping their hands in clear view above the table and thus resisting any temptation to cheat]

above one's bend phr. [mid-19C] (US) beyond one's abilities (cf. HUCKLEBERRY ABOVE ONE'S PERSIMMON). [the image is of an object beyond one's grasp or ? above, i.e. beyond, the bend of river on which one lives]

above oneself adj. [20C] over-confident, pushy, esp. of someone who is usually more self-effacing; usu. as *getting above ...* (cf. GET ABOVE ONESELF; GET PAST ONESELF v.¹).

above par adj. [19C] **1** in good spirits or health. **2** mildly drunk (cf. BELOW PAR). [Stock Exchange jargon *par*, face value]

above snakes adj. [19C] (US) **1** above the ground. **2** tall. ['a snake's eye-view' of life above ground]

A-box n. [1990s] (US campus) someone in an unpleasant mood. [ATTITUDE + SE *box*]

abrac n. [early–mid-19C] learning. [either SE *Arabic* or abbr. SE *abracadabra*]

abraham n. [19C] the penis (cf. CHARLEY n.[5]; JACK n.[8]; JACKIE ROBINSON; JACK ROBINSON; JACOB n.[1]; JIM JOHNSON; JOHN n.[9]; JOHN HENRY n.[2]; JOHNNIE n.[11]; JOHN THOMAS; JOHN WILLIE; JULIUS CAESAR n.[1]; OSCAR n.[3]; PERCY n.[3]; PETER n.[4]; ROGER n.[4]; TOM n.[3]; WILLIAM n.[2]). [*Abraham*, the biblical patriarch, i.e. the role of the penis in procreation]

abraham-cove n. [17C–early 19C] a wandering beggar, adopting tattered clothing and posing as a madman (cf. ABRAHAMER; ABRAHAM-MAN; ABRAM-COVE; ABRAM-MAN; BEDLAM BEGGAR). [ABRAM adj. (1) + COVE]

abrahamer n. [19C] a tramp (cf. ABRAHAM-COVE). [ABRAM adj.]

abraham grains n. [19C+] a publican who brews their own beer. [generic use of *Abraham* + SE *grains*]

Abraham Lincoln n. [1950s–60s] (US) a $5 bill (cf. ABE n.[2]; ALEXANDER HAMILTON n.[1]; BROWN ABE; DEAD PRESIDENT; DEAD WHITEBOY; GEORGE n.[3]; GEORGE WASHINGTON; GROVER; HAMILTON; LINCOLN; MARSHALL; OLD HICKORY; PICTURE OF ABE; PORTRAIT n.[1]; PORTRAIT OF MADISON). [the face of *Abraham Lincoln* (1809–65), 16th president of the US, is printed on $5 bills]

abraham-man n. [16C] a wandering beggar, adopting tattered clothing and posing as a madman (cf. ABRAHAM-COVE). [var. ABRAM-COVE]

Abraham Newland n. [early–mid-19C] a banknote. [proper name of *Abraham Newland*, chief cashier of the bank of England (1778–1807); thus the phr. *sham Abraham Newland*, to forge banknotes, and the rhy.: 'Sham Abraham you may/But you mustn't sham Abraham Newland']

abraham's balsam n. [18C] the gallows (cf. DEADLY NEVER-GREEN). [SE *Abraham's balm*, the chaste tree (*Vitex agnus-castus*), but presumably punning on *Abraham's bosom*, the abode of the dead]

abraham's bosom n. [19C] the vagina. [punning on the biblical use, e.g. at Luke 16:22: 'The beggar died, and was carried by the angels into Abraham's bosom.' In both SE and sl. defs. the implication is of 'lying on']

abraham sham *see* ABRAM SHAM.

abraham suit *see* ABRAM SUIT.

Abrahamstead n. [1970s+] Hampstead in north London (cf. CRICKLEWITCH; GOLDBERG'S GREEN; YIDSBURY). [play on the Jewish name *Abraham* + SE *Hampstead*, traditionally an area with a large Jewish population]

abraham's willing n. [19C] a shilling (5p) (cf. BARNEY DILLON; I'M WILLING; JOHN DILLON; THOMAS TILLING). [rhy. sl.]

abraham work *see* ABRAM WORK.

abram n. *see* ABRAM-COVE.

abram adj. 1 [mid-16C–mid-17C] insane, crazy (cf. MAUND ABRAM). 2 [17C–early 19C] naked. [ABRAM-MAN]

abram v. [19C] to malinger, to fake illness. [? naut. *abram*, a malingerer or rhy. sl. *abram* = sham]

abram-cove/abram n. [16C–early 19C] a wandering beggar, adopting tattered clothing and posing as a madman (cf. ABRAHAM-COVE).

abram-man n. [mid-16C–mid-19C] a wandering beggar, adopting tattered clothing and posing as a madman (cf. ABRAHAM-COVE). [? the Abraham Ward of the Hospital of St Mary of Bethlehem, London, in which the insane patients were housed. The hospital, known popularly as Bedlam, allowed certain inmates to go begging on a number of fixed days each year; the *abram-man* posed as one of these licensed beggars. Note the parable of the beggar in Luke 16:19–31]

abram/abraham sham v. [19C] of a beggar, to travel the country posing as a madman (cf. SHAM ABRAM).

abram/abraham suit n. [19C] the writing of spurious begging letters. [for ety. *see* ON THE ABRAM SUIT]

abram/abraham work n. [19C] any form of spurious occupation, esp. some form of confidence trick (cf. ABRAM SUIT). [ABRAM adj. + SE *work*]

abridgements n. [mid-19C] knee-breeches (cf. CONTINU-ATIONS).

abroad adj. [19C] 1 in error, confused; thus *all abroad*, wide of the mark. 2 of convicts, transported to a penal colony (cf. ABROADED).

abroaded adj. 1 [mid–late 19C] (society) living in exile somewhere other than in the UK. 2 [mid–late 19C] transported to a penal colony (cf. ABROAD). 3 [late 19C–1920s] imprisoned.

abscotchalater n. [19C] (US) one who runs away. [var. pron. of ABSQUATULATE]

absentee n. [19C] a convict. [? because they are absent from everyday life]

absent-minded beggar n. [late 19C–1900s] a soldier. [title of poem (1899) by Rudyard Kipling]

absent without leave phr. [mid-19C+] escaped from prison. [play on milit. use]

absoballylutely adv. [1910s–30s] extremely, very much indeed (cf. ABSOBLOODYLUTELY; ABSOFUCKINGLUTELY; ABSO-GODDAMLUTELY). [a more intense form of SE *absolutely*]

absobloodylutely adv. [1930s+] absolutely (cf. ABSO-BALLYLUTELY).

absofuckinglutely adv. [1910s+] very much so indeed, without the slightest doubt; also as excl. of affirmation (cf. ABSOBALLYLUTELY; FANFUCKINGTASTIC; GUARANFUCKINGTEE). [a more intense version of SE *absolutely*, coined by WW1 troops]

absogoddamlutely adv. [1960s] (US) absolutely (cf. ABSO-BALLYLUTELY).

absolutely! excl. [20C] yes!

absolutely not! excl. [20C] not a hope! not a chance!

absolutely true phr. [late 19C] (society) utterly false. [heavy-handed sarcasm]

absorb v. [late 19C+] (orig. US) to eat or, more often, drink (cf. SOAK v.[1]). [a slightly coy euph.]

absotively adv. [1920s+] (US) absolutely, positively. [comb. of the SE words]

absquattle v. [mid-19C] (orig. US) 1 of a person or animal, to leave, to run away, to abscond, sometimes abbr. to *absquat*. 2 of an object, to separate, to break away from. [var. on ABSQUATULATE]

absquatulate/obsquatulate v. [19C] (orig. US) 1 of people or animals, to leave, to run away, to abscond, sometimes abbr. to *absquat*. 2 of an object, to separate, to break away from. [cod Latin based on SE *abscond* + *squat* + sfx. *-ulate*]

abstain from beans, to phr. [1920s] to desist from politics. [? mid-19C *bean*, a benefactor, a philanthropist; the assumption being that politicians work to benefit their fellows]

abstropelous adj. [early 18C–mid-19C] aggressively resistant to control or restraint (cf. OBSTROPOLOUS; STROPPY). [corruption of SE *obstreperous*]

Abyssinia! excl. [1930s+] (orig. US) goodbye. [punning on 'I'll be seeing you']

Abyssinian polo n. [1940s+] (US) the game of craps (cf. AFRICAN BILLIARDS; AFRICAN DOMINOES; AFRICAN GOLF; AFRICAN PILLS; AFRICAN POOL; AMISH GOLF; INDOOR GOLF; NIGGER GOLF; ZULU GOLF). [stereotyping of craps as a Black person's favourite game]

ac n. [1990s] (US Black) the *Acura* Legend, a popular automobile. [abbr.]

a.c.a.b. phr. [1940s+] *all coppers are bastards*. [abbr.; a popular tattoo in the UK, esp. among Hell's Angels and other 'outlaw' groups]

academician n. [18C] a prostitute (cf. ACADEMY). [punning use of SE]

academy n. **1** [18C] a lunatic asylum. **2** [18C–early 19C] a brothel, one of a number of contemporary terms based on brothel = school (cf. CAVAULTING SCHOOL; DANCING ACADEMY; FINISHING ACADEMY; LADIES' COLLEGE; PUSHING SCHOOL; VAULTING HOUSE). **3** [19C] a billiard room. **4** [19C] used in combs. such as ADKINS'S ACADEMY; CAMPBELL'S ACADEMY; FLOATING ACADEMY. [joc. uses of SE]

Acapulco gold/Acapulco n. [1960s+] (orig. US drugs) a high-strength grade of marijuana (cf. ACAPULCO RED). [the drug derives in and around Acapulco de Juárez, in Guerrero state on the west coast of Mexico]

Acapulco red n. [1960s+] (drugs) marijuana. [a less potent form of ACAPULCO GOLD]

acca/acker n. [1970s+] (Aus.) **1** an academic, esp. one who trades on the proliferation of current, if ephemeral, intellectual fads. **2** quotidian, jargon-laden academic writing. [abbr. + a pun on OCKER]

acceleration n. [late 19C] (tramp) starvation; thus phr. *die of acceleration.* [? it speeds up the imminence of death]

accelerator n. [20C] (US Und.) an arsonist. [SE *accelerant,* a fire-lighter, fire-starter]

accident n.[1] [late 19C+] an illegitimate child (cf. AFTER-THOUGHT; MISTAKE). [euph.]

accident n.[2] [late 19C+] usu. of a child, the act of urinating or defecating in one's clothes. [ext. of SE use]

accidental daddy/a.d. n. [1970s+] a man who fathers a child by accident, usu. after a casual sexual encounter; esp. in abbr. phr. that precedes such intercourse, *b.c. or a.d.?,* 'Are you using *birth* control or do I risk becoming an *accidental daddy?*' [ironic use of SE]

accidentally on purpose phr. [mid-19C+] deliberately, used of a supposed accident that deliberately discomforts a disliked target.

accommodate v. [19C] to work as a prostitute. [back-form. of ACCOMMODATION HOUSE]

accommodation house n. [19C] a brothel (cf. BADGER HOUSE; BARRELHOUSE n.; BAT-HOUSE; BED-HOUSE; BENNY HOUSE; BOOGIE HOUSE; CALL HOUSE; CAN HOUSE; CASE HOUSE; CAT-HOUSE; CHIPPY HOUSE; CIRCUS HOUSE; COUPLING HOUSE; CREEP HOUSE; CRIB HOUSE; FANCY HOUSE; FAST HOUSE; FLASH HOUSE; FRANZY HOUSE; GARDEN HOUSE n.[1]; GAY HOUSE; GOAT HOUSE; GRINDING-HOUSE n.[2]; GRIND JOINT; HOOK HOUSE; HOUSE n.[1]; HOUSE OF CIVIL RECEPTION; HOUSE OF SALE; HUMP HOUSE; JAY HOUSE; JAZZ HOUSE; JOY HOUSE; JUKE HOUSE; KNOCKING-SHOP; LADIES' BOARDING HOUSE; LEANING HOUSE; LEAPING HOUSE; LONG HOUSE; MEAT HOUSE; MOLL HOUSE; MOT-HOUSE; NANNY HOUSE; NOOKIE HOUSE; NOTCH HOUSE; NUGGING HOUSE; OCCUPYING HOUSE; PANEL CRIB; PARLOR HOUSE; PEG HOUSE n.[2]; PUNCH HOUSE; SHOWHOUSE; SPORT-HOUSE; SPORTING HOUSE; TOMCAT HOUSE; TRICK HOUSE; TRUGGING HOUSE; VAULTING HOUSE. [SE *accommodation house,* a lodging house; such places, like their description, may have begun as respectable buildings, but soon changed their use]

according/that's according phr. [mid-19C+] that depends, it all depends. [abbr. SE phr. *according to circumstances*]

according to Cocker phr. [early 19C+] properly, correctly, as laid down by the rules (cf. ACCORDING TO GUNTER; ACCORDING TO HOYLE). [Edward *Cocker* (1631–76), an engraver and teacher, the writer of *Cocker's Arithmetic* (published posthumously in 1678); he is also credited with an *English Dictionary* (published 1704), although it was more likely compiled by his son, which dealt specifically in commercial questions. Its pre-eminence in its field lasted for at least a century, thus engendering the phrase]

according to Gunter phr. [late 19C+] (US) properly, correctly, as laid down by the rules (cf. ACCORDING TO COCKER).

[Edmund *Gunter* (1581–1626), a leading contemporary mathematician, inventor of the sector and author of *Gunter's Rules of Proportion* (1623); this work was especially popular at the time of the Puritan emigration to America. He is said to have invented the terms 'sine' and 'cosine']

according to Hoyle phr. [20C] properly, correctly, as laid down by the rules (cf. ACCORDING TO COCKER). [Edmund *Hoyle* (1672–1769), editor in 1752 of *The Polite Gamester,* soon retitled *Mr Hoyle's Games of Whist* (1760), then *Hoyle's Games Improved* (1786); editions continue to appear]

accost the Oscar Meyer, to phr. [1980s+] to masturbate (cf. BEAT ONE'S MEAT; BEAT THE BOLOGNA; BEEF-STROKE-IT-OFF; BLUDGEON THE BEEFSTEAK; BOB ONE'S BALONEY; BOP ONE'S BALONEY; COME ONE'S MUTTON; COME ONE'S TURKEY; CUDDLE THE KIELBASA; DO THE PORK SWORD JIGGLE; FIGHT ONE'S TURKEY; FLOG ONE'S MUTTON; HAVE A HAM SHANK; HOLD THE SAUSAGE HOSTAGE; JERK ONE'S JELLY; KNEAD ONE'S KNOCKWURST; MASSAGE THE FRANK-FURTER; OSCILLATE THE OSCAR MEYER; PLAY A SOLO ON ONE'S MEAT WHISTLE; POUND ONE'S MEAT; POUND ONE'S PORK; PULL ONE'S JOINT; RAM THE HAM; SLAKE THE BACON; SLAM THE HAM; SLAM THE HAMMER; SLAP THE SALAMI; TAME THE BEEF WEASEL; TEASE THE WEENIE; TOSS THE HAM JAVELIN; WASH THE MEAT; WHIP THE BALONY PONY). [SE *accost* + brandname *Oscar Meyer,* a popular US wiener]

account of/on account of phr. [1930s+] because, on account of the fact that.

accoutrements n. [19C+] the male genitals (cf. EQUIPMENT; GEAR n.[2]; KIT n.[3]; TACKLE n.[1]; WEDDING KIT). [SE *accoutrements,* apparel, outfit, equipment]

AC/DC adj. [1940s+] **1** bisexual (cf. AM/FM). **2** (gay) ambivalent as to taking an active or passive role in a relationship. [the opposite varieties (alternating and direct) of electrical current]

ace n.[1] **1** [mid-19C+] (orig. US) something or someone of high quality or held in high esteem. **2** [late 19C+] (orig. US) an expert. **3** [late 19C–1940s] (US) an important, influential person. **4** [1910s+] (orig. US) an outstanding person, whether in character or qualifications. **5** [1940s+] (US) a friend, a hero. **6** (US Black) a very close friend (cf. ACE BOON COON). [all uses of ACE adj.]

ace n.[2] (US) **1** [late 19C+] $1, $1's worth. **2** [1970s+] (gambling) $100. [SE *ace,* one (at dice, in cards)]

ace n.[3] (drugs) **1** [1930s+] one single pill of amphetamine, barbiturate or tranquillizer. **2** [1970s+] marijuana. **3** [1970s+] phencyclidine (PCP), a dangerous hallucinogen based on animal (pig) tranquilliser (cf. A.D. n.[4]; ALIAMBA; AMOEBA; ANGEL n.[4]; ANGEL DUST; ANGEL HAIR; ANGEL MIST; ANIMAL TRANQ; AURORA BOREALIS; BELLADONNA; BLACK WHACK; BLUE MADMAN; BOAT n.[4]; BOHD; BOLT n.[3]; BUSY BEE; BUTT NAKED; CADILLAC; CIGAROOE CRISTAL; C.J.; CLICKER n.[6]; CLIFFHANGER n.[2]; COLUMBO; COZMO'S; CRAZY COKE; CRAZY EDDIE; CRYSTAL JOINT; CRYSTAL T; CYCLINE; CYCLONES; D n.[6]; DEATH WISH; DETROIT PINK; DEVIL'S DUST n.[2]; DIPPER n.[3]; D.O.A. n.; DO-IT-JACK; DOMEX; DRINK n.[4]; DUMMY DUST; DUST n.[6]; DUSTED PARSLEY; DUST JOINT; DUST OF ANGELS; ELEPHANT n.[4]; ELEPHANT TRANQUILLIZER; EMBALMING FLUID; ENERGIZER; ERTH n.[2]; FAIRY DUST; FLAKES; FRESH n.; FUEL n.[2]; GOOD n.; GOOFY'S GOON; GOON n.[2]; GORILLA BISCUITS; GREEN n.[3]; GREEN LEAVES; GREEN TEA; HEAVEN AND HELL n.[2]; HERMS; HOG n.[8]; HOMEBAKE n.[1]; HORSE TRACKS; HORSE TRANQUILLIZER; JET FUEL; K n.[4]; KAPS; K-BLAST; KI n.[3]; KILLER n.[3]; KILLER JOINT; KILLER WEED; K.J.; KOOLS; KRYSTAL; L.B.J.; LEAKY HOLLA; LEMON 714; LEÑOS; LETHAL WEAPON; LITTLE ONES; LIVE ONES; LOG n.[2]; LOVE BOAT; MAD DOG n.[1]; MADMAN; MAGIC n.; MEAN GREEN; MISSILE; MIST; MONKEY DUST; MONKEY TRANQUILLIZER; MORE; NEW ACID; NEW MAGIC; NIEBLA; OIL n.[2]; O.P.P. n.; ORANGE CRYSTAL; OZONE n.[2]; P n.[3]; PARSLEY n.[3]; PAZ; PCP; PEACE n.; PEACE PILLS; PEACE WEED; PEEP n.[2]; PEP n.[2]; PETER PAN n.[2]; PIG KILLER; PIT n.[4]; POLVO; POLVO DE ANGEL;

POLVO DE ESTRELLAS; PUFFY n.; PURPLE RAIN; RED DEVIL; ROCKET FUEL; SCAFFLE; SCUFFLE n.²; SERNYL; SHEETS n.¹; SHERM; SKUFFLE; SMOKING n.²; SNORTS; SOMA; SPEED BOAT; SPORES; SQUEEZE n.⁶; STARDUST; STEAM n.¹; S.T.P.; SUPER n.⁴; SUPERGRASS n.¹; SUPER JOINT; SUPER KOOLS; SURFER; T n.²; TAC; T-BUZZ; TEA n.²; TIC; TIC-TAC n.²; TISH n.; TRANK; T-TAB; WATER n.²; WHITE DUST; WHITE HORIZON; WOBBLE n.²; WOLF n.³; WORM n.²; YELLOW FEVER n.²; ZOMBIE n.²; ZOOM n.²]. [SE *ace*, one (at dice, in cards)]

ace *n.*⁴ [1940s–50s] (US) a detective. [ACE adj.]

ace *n.*⁵ [1960s+] (US campus) the grade A. [ACE adj. + the initial letter]

ace *adj.* [1930s+] (orig. US) the best, excellent, expert.

ace *v.*¹ (US) **1** [1920s+] to manipulate someone, esp. through flattery or deception. **2** [1950s+] (orig. campus) to do well, to succeed, e.g. in an examination. **3** [1960s+] to outwit (cf. ACE OUT).

ace *v.*² [1990s] (US) to hold in high esteem. [ACE adj.]

ace! *excl.* (US) **1** [1920s+] used ironically to address a clumsy or incompetent person. **2** [1960s+] a term of endearment between any two males; the implication is of fondness and respect.

ace boon coon/a.b.c./ace boom boom/ace coon poon/ace spoon coon *n.* [1960s+] (orig. US Black) one's best and most trustworthy friend. [ACE adj. + BOON COON + joc. vars.]

ace buddy *n.* [1970s+] (US campus) a best friend. [ACE adj. + BUDDY n.]

ace cool *n.* [1980s+] (US Black) a very close friend. [var. of ACE BOON COON]

ace coon *n.* [1960s+] (US Black) **1** a best friend (cf. ACE BOON COON). **2** an important person. [ACE + COON]

ace coon poon see ACE BOON COON.

ace-deuce *n.*¹ [20C] (US/W.I.) a best friend (cf. ACE BOON COON). [lit. 'one-two']

ace-deuce/acey-deucey *n.*² [1920s+] (US) a panic attack, a fit of nerves, a sudden fit of temper. [ACE n.² + DEUCE n.², lit. 'one-two'; in craps 'ace-deuce', i.e. a point of three, means one 'craps out' and loses one's money]

ace-deuce/acey-deucey *adj.*¹ [1920s+] (US) excellent, first-rate. [both first, *acey*, and second, *deucey*, best; note ACE adj.]

ace-deuce *adj.*² [1970s] (US) bisexual (cf. ACEY-DEUCEY adj.⁴). [AC/DC]

ace-flat *adj.* [1940s] (US) excellent, first-rate (cf. ACE-HIGH). [ACE adj. + SE *flat*, absolute, downright, unqualified]

ace gear *n.* [1960s+] (US gay) a sexually talented homosexual, capable of both active and passive roles. [ACE adj. + GEAR n.³]

ace-/aces-high *adj.* [late 19C+] (US) valued or esteemed highly. [poker imagery]

ace in the hole *n.* [20C] (orig. US) a hidden asset. [poker use, the 'hole card' is that which is kept face-down on the table]

ace it *v.* [1950s+] (US) to make a perfect score on a school or college test. [ACE v.¹ (2)]

ace kool *n.* [1980s+] (US Black) a very close friend. [ACE (BOON COON) + COOL adj.³]

ace-lover *n.* [1940s] (US Black, mainly South/Midwest) one's most important lover, the most important member of the opposite sex one knows, e.g. a husband, a pimp, a boyfriend. [ACE adj. + SE *lover*]

aceman *n.* [1950s] (US teen) the leader of a teen street gang. [ACE adj. + SE *man*]

ace-note *n.* [1920s–60s] (US) a $1 bill (cf. ACE-SPOT). [ACE n.² + SE *note*]

ace of spades *n.* [20C] (US Black) the pudendum (cf. RED ACE; WANTON ACE). [supposed resemblance to the shape of pubic hair]

ace out *v.* [20C] to defeat, to take something away. [poker jargon *ace*, the highest card, which beats any others]

aces *adj.* [20C] (US) of both people and objects, wonderful, marvellous, excellent; thus *you're aces!* [ACE n.¹ (1), (2)]

aces and eights *phr.*¹ [20C] (US) **1** a poker hand of mixed aces and eights. **2** bad luck (cf. DEAD MAN'S HAND). [Wild Bill Hickok was allegedly holding such a hand when he was gunned down on 2 August 1876]

aces and eights *phr.*² [1920s] wonderful, marvellous, excellent. [var. on ACES adj.; the idea of bad luck has been ignored]

aces high *n.* [1970s+] (orig. US prison) an inmate popular among their peers (cf. ACES).

aces-high see ACE-HIGH.

ace spoon coon see ACE BOON COON.

ace-spot *n.* [1910s–20s] (US) a $1 bill (cf. ACE-NOTE). [ACE n.² + -SPOT]

aces-up *adj.* [1900s–30s] (US) esteemed, well-respected, favoured. [poker imagery + ACES]

ace up one's sleeve *n.* [1920s+] (orig. US) a hidden advantage, not to be revealed until a suitable moment (cf. ACE IN THE HOLE). [poker use, but with suggestions of underhand methods, rather than careful, but still legal, planning]

acey-deucey *n.* see ACE-DEUCE n.².

acey-deucey *adj.*¹ [20C] of a friend, close, intimate. [ACE-DEUCE n.¹]

acey-deucey *adj.*² see ACE-DEUCE adj.¹.

acey-deucey *adj.*³ see ACE-DEUCE adj.¹.

acey-deucey *adj.*⁴ [1970s+] **1** (US Black) complex, unstable, neither one thing nor the other. **2** (gay) bisexual (cf. AC/DC; ACE-DEUCE adj.²). [the difference between the *ace* and the *deuce* in cards]

acher see ACRE n.¹, n.².

aching for a side of beef *phr.* [1970s+] (US Black) of a woman, eager to have sex (cf. BEEF BAYONET; BEEF INJECTION; DO A BIT OF BEEF; GIVE MUTTON FOR BEEF; HAVE A BIT OF BEEF; HOT BEEF; IN A WOMAN'S BEEF; SERVICE OF BEEF; TAKE IN BEEF). [SE *ache* + (*side of*) BEEF]

acid *n.*¹ [20C] (W.I.) rum; thus *fire the acid*, to drink rum. [joc. allusion to its strength]

acid *n.*² [1920s+] cheek (cf. COME THE ACID).

acid *n.*³ [1960s+] (drugs) LSD (cf. A n.³). [abbr. SE *lycergic acid*]

acid *n.*⁴ [1980s+] (drugs) MDMA (cf. ECSTASY). [originally used for LSD (see A n.³), acid re-emerged as a nickname for another hallucinogen (albeit with a very different chemistry) in the late 1980s]

acid *n.*⁵ [1990s] (W.I./UK Black teen) a special unit of the Jamaican police force, especially feared because of their severe tactics. [COME THE ACID]

acid cap *n.* [1990s] one tablet or capsule of LSD (cf. A n.³). [ACID n.³ + CAP n.⁴]

acid casualty *n.* [1960s+] one whose brain is deemed to have suffered from an excess of hallucinogens. [ACID n.³ + SE *casualty*]

acid freak *n.* [1960s–70s] (drugs) a regular user of LSD. [ACID n.³ + sfx. -FREAK]

acid-head *n.* [1960s+] (drugs) a regular user of LSD (cf. A-HEAD; BASE-HEAD; BLOCKHEAD n.²; C-HEAD; CLUCKHEAD n.²; COKEHEAD; CRACKHEAD; HIT-HEAD; PILL-HEAD; POTHEAD n.²; SMACK-HEAD). [ACID n.³ + sfx. -HEAD (2)]

acid house party *n.* [1980s] an illegal party, often held in a large building, such as a warehouse, and often outside the big cities, where thousands of young people pay for their entertainment and, allegedly, consume MDMA and other illegal drugs. [ACID n.⁴ + HOUSE n.³ + SE *party*]

acid pad *n.* [1960s] (US drugs) a place where LSD is consumed. [ACID n.³ + PAD n.² (2)]

acid rapper *n.* [20C] one who takes extra-large doses of LSD. [ACID n.³ + RAP v.⁶]

acid rock *n.* [1960s+] a musical style allegedly influenced by, and purporting to recreate the sensations of, LSD and similar psychedelics; orig. in 1960s but underwent a minor revival in 1980s. [ACID n.³, n.⁴ + SE *rock*]

acid test *n.* [1960s] a party. [ACID n.³ + SE *test*; a pun on SE, accentuated by the contemporary slogan *Can you pass the acid test?* as a form of initiatory challenge. The party, orig. held in a San Francisco dance-hall, was arranged by Ken Kesey's Merry Pranksters group, and the participants took LSD, many for the first time]

acid trip *n.* [1960s+] the experience, often characterized as a 'journey', of taking a hallucinogenic drug, esp. LSD. [ACID n.³ + TRIP n.³ (1)]

ackamaraka/ackamaracker *n.* [1920s+] tea. [? an exaggerated, intensified play on CHA n.¹]

ackamarackus/ackamaraka/ackamaracker *n.* [1930s–50s] a fraudulent tale, a tall story, nonsense, usu. in phr. *old ackamarakus* (cf. ARKYMALARKEY). [cod Latin]

acker/akka *n.*¹ [1930s+] (orig. milit.) money, whether change or notes, often found in pl. *ackers*. [Arab. *akka*, one piastre; imported by returning British soldiers post-WW1]

acker *n.*² see ACCA.

acker/ackie fortis see AGGIE FORTIS.

ackman see ARK-MAN.

acknickelous *adj.* [1980s+] (US Black/teen) wonderful, marvellous. [? SE *acknowledged* + *ridiculous* + *marvellous*]

acknowledge the corn, to *phr.* [early 19C–1940s] (orig. US) to admit an error. [? in a horse-stealing case in a western state, the defendant, accused of stealing 4 horses and 4 feeds of corn, declared *I acknowledge the corn* but denied the actual horse-stealing. 'Legend says he was lynched in spite of the admission' (Ware)]

acknowledge the malt, to *phr.* [19C] (US) to admit an error. [var. on ACKNOWLEDGE THE CORN]

ack-ruff *n.* [18C] a river thief (cf. ARK-MAN). [var. on ARK-RUFF]

acky *adj.* [20C] (usu. juv.) dirty, disgusting (cf. ICKY; UCKY; YUCKY). [? CACKY adj.]

acorn *n.* [1900s] (US) the head. [supposed resemblance]

acorn calf *n.* [19C] (US) of humans and animals, a runt, a weakling. [western US belief that a cow that ate too many acorns produced weak offspring]

acorn-cracker *n.* [1900s] (US) an uncouth rural person. [SE *acorn* + CRACKER n.⁴ (1); such individuals allegedly eat acorns]

acorns *n.* [1970s] (US) the testicles (cf. BALLS n.¹).

acquire *v.* [20C] to steal (cf. ATTRACT; BORROW; CONVEY; FIND; FREE v.; LIBERATE; ORGANIZE; SALVAGE; SCAVENGE; SOUVENIR; WIN v.). [ironic use of SE]

acre/acher *n.*¹ [20C] (Aus.) the buttocks. [SE *acre*, a large area]

acre/acher *n.*² [20C] the testicles. [? physical proximity to n.¹]

acre/acre of corn *n.*³ [1940s+] (Aus.) a lengthy prison sentence, cited variously as one month, 12 months or simply 'plenty'; thus phr. used of a recidivist, *there's corn growing for some.* [the use of corn is a ref. to hominy, a staple of Aus. prison food; one will eat that much corn during the sentence]

acre-foot *adj.* [19C] (US) large-footed. [joc. exaggeration]

acre of corn see ACRE n.³.

acres *n.* [18C–mid-19C] a coward. [the character of Bob *Acres*, in R.B. Sheridan's *The Rivals* (1775), whose 'courage always oozed out of his finger ends']

acrobat *n.* [1950s] (W.I.) a fool. [? they 'fall over' themselves]

across lots *phr.* [mid-19C+] (US) via a short cut; thus the curse, *go to hell across lots!* [SE *lot*, a piece of land set aside for building or for cultivation or pasturage]

across the pavement *phr.* [1960s+] (Und.) phr. used of any crime committed in the street.

across the track *phr.* [20C] inferior, second-rate (cf. WRONG SIDE OF THE TRACKS). [the area of a town in which the poor supposedly live; f. an era when many US towns were literally divided, socially as well as physically, by the railroad tracks]

act *n.* **1** [1940s–50s] (Aus.) pretended illness or ill-temper. **2** [1970s+] (orig. US) a routine, a way of behaving, a performance (cf. SCHTICK).

act as if one's knickers were on fire, to *phr.* [1960s+] to panic, to behave hysterically (cf. GET ONE'S KNICKERS IN A TWIST).

act-ass *n.* [20C] (US) one who sees themself as cleverer than they really are (cf. SMART-ARSE). [SE *act* + ARSE n.¹]

action *n.* **1** [1920s+] (orig. US Black) what is going on; thus a situation or state of affairs, anything exciting, current, interesting, depending on the context, e.g. the chance for sex, a musical performance, a night's gambling, often used in the greeting, *Where's/what's the action?* (cf. WHAT'S HAPPENING?). **2** [1920s+] (US) sexual ability, lit. the erotic 'action' of the hips or pelvis. **3** [1950s+] (US) money (cf. PIECE OF THE ACTION). **4** [1960s+] (US) a revolver (cf. ACTION PIECE). **5** [1960s+] (US) financial transactions, esp. bets and wagers. **6** [1960s+] (US) one's choice, one's preference. **7** [1960s+] (drugs) the current availability of drugs and the best place to obtain them. **8** [1960s+] (US Black) a woman. [all fig. uses of SE]

-action *sfx.* [1980s+] (US campus) combining form denoting activity, e.g. *dope action, babe action.*

action on a/the solid half traction *phr.* [1940s–70s] (US Black, mainly Harlem) ready for anything.

action piece *n.*¹ [1960s] (US Black) a woman. [ACTION + PIECE n.¹ (1)]

action piece *n.*² [1960s] (US Black) a pistol, a revolver, a shotgun. [ACTION + PIECE n.⁴ (1)]

active citizens *n.* [18C] lice, fleas.

act like dead lice are falling off, to *phr.* [19C+] (US) to act lethargically or lazily. [the image of dead lice falling from one's body]

act like one's shit don't smell/stink, to *phr.* [20C] (orig. US) to behave affectedly and in an arrogant manner; also as *act like shit wouldn't melt in one's mouth.*

actor *n.* **1** [20C] (US Black) anyone out to deceive or project a phoney image (cf. PLAYER). **2** [1940s–50s] a con-man or liar.

actorine *n.* [late 19C–1930s] (US) an actress. [SE *actor* + fem. sfx. *-ine*]

act possum *v.* [mid-19C+] to play dead (cf. COME POSSUM OVER). [var. on PLAY POSSUM]

actress *n.* [1950s–60s] (US camp gay) an egocentric show-off, but amusing and witty nonetheless. [camp feminization]

act the angora, to *phr.* [20C] (Aus.) to play the fool (cf. ACT THE GOAT; ACT THE HOG; ACT THE JINNIT; PLAY THE GIDDY GOAT). [the SE *angora* goat, thus a laboured pun]

act the gig, to *phr.* [1940s+] to pretend to be a fool when caught in a criminal act. [SE *act* + GIG n.¹²]

act the goat, to *phr.* [late 19C] to behave foolishly (cf. ACT THE ANGORA). [the assumption is that the animal is naturally foolish]

act the hog/monkey, to *phr.* [20C] to play the fool (cf. ACT THE ANGORA). [the assumption is that animals are naturally foolish]

act the jinnit, to *phr.* [20C] (Irish) to play the fool, to act irrationally (cf. ACT THE ANGORA). [SE *act* + JINNIT n.²]

act the linnet, to *phr.* [20C] (Irish) to flirt.

act the maggot, to *phr.* [1950s+] (Irish) to play the fool, to clown.

act the mohawk, to *phr.* [1960s] (Irish) to misbehave.

act the nigger, to phr. [mid-19C+] **1** (US) a derog. term meaning to play the fool (cf. LET OFF A LITTLE NIGGER). **2** (US Black) to act in a manner White racists expect of Black people, i.e. foolish, subservient, clownish. [NIGGER]

actual, the n. [20C] money. [as in SE, where 'the actual' is opposed to 'the idea', the sense here is of concrete, hard cash]

act up v. [20C] to make a fuss in order to attract attention to oneself.

act your age! excl. [1930s+] (orig. US) a term of contempt, based in the condemnation of one who the speaker considers is acting childishly; also ext. as act your age, not your shoe size! (cf. BE YOUR AGE!).

a.d. n.[1] [late 19C–1900s] (society) a drink. [used on dance cards to disguise a preference for alcohol over dancing; partners' names were also abbreviated]

a.d. n.[2] see ACCIDENTAL DADDY.

a.d. n.[3] [1930s–70s] (US drugs) a drug addict. [reversed to avoid confusion with the law's DA, a district attorney]

a.d. n.[4] [1980s+] phencyclidine (cf. ACE n.[3]). [ety. unknown]

a.d. v. [1990s] (US campus) to leave. [AUDI 5000]

ad n. **1** [mid-19C+] an advertisement. **2** (US gay) a graffito, offering sexual services, found on a public lavatory wall. [abbr.]

adad! excl. [mid-17C–mid-18C] God! (cf. ADOD!; AGAD!; BEDAD!; BEDIDE!; BEGAD!; BEGAR!; COCK n.[1]; COSH!; DOG! excl.[1]; EGAD!; GED!; GOLES!; GOLLY!; GORRY!; GOSH!; GOSSE!; OD!; ODSO!). [DAD n.[1] or DOD, two of the many euph. expressions for God]

ada from Decatur / eighter Decatur / eighter from Decatur n. [20C] (US gambling) the point of 8 in craps dice (cf. ADA ROSS; BIG DICK FROM BOSTON). [pun on eighter + proper name Decatur, Alabama or Texas]

adam n.[1] **1** [late 16C–early 17C] a bailiff, a sergeant. **2** [late 17C–19C] a fence, a criminal receiver (cf. ADAM TILER). **3** [late 19C] a foreman. [the biblical Adam, the first man]

adam n.[2] [mid-19C+] used in a variety of phr. indicating a very long time ago, e.g. SINCE ADAM NAMED THE ANIMALS; WHEN ADAM WAS AN OAKUM BOY IN BROOKLYN NAVY YARD. [use of the first man, Adam, as a generic for a very long time ago]

adam n.[3] [1950s–60s] (camp gay) one's first (paid) sexual partner (cf. TRICK n.[4]). [biblical]

adam n.[4] [1960s+] MDMA (cf. ECSTASY; EVE n.[2]). [the initial letters + ref. to the primal intensity of the drug experience]

adam v.[1] [late 18C] to marry. [the biblical 'first couple']

adam v.[2] **1** [late 19C+] to leave. **2** [1920s+] to believe, often in the interrog. phr. would you Adam and Eve it? [rhy. sl. Adam and Eve]

adam and eve n. [20C] (orig. US short-order jargon) two poached or fried eggs; thus adam and eve on a raft, two poached eggs on toast; thus adam and eve on a raft and wreck 'em, scrambled eggs on toast (cf. BRIDE AND GROOM). [note army use adam and eve wrecked, scrambled eggs]

adam and eve, to phr. [18C] to have sexual intercourse (cf. ADAMIZE). [the first act thereof in the biblical Garden of Eden]

adam and eve ball n. [1920s+] an early dancing party to which the guests are invited until 12 o'clock only (cf. CINDERELLA). [when they are, as it were, ejected from (social) Eden]

adam and eve's p.j.s/togs n. [late 19C+] nudity; the terms are US and UK respectively (cf. ADAM'S P.J.S). [SE Adam and Eve + P.J.S/TOGS their initial nakedness in Eden]

adamitical adj. [20C] nude, naked. [the pre-lapsarian biblical Adam was naked]

adamize v. [19C] to have sexual intercourse (cf. ADAM AND EVE phr.).

adam's ale n. [mid-17C+] water; found in Scot. as adam's wine. [the biblical Adam to whom alcohol was unknown; 'the only drink of our first parents' (OED)]

adam's arm n. [1940s] (US) a shovel, a spade.

adam's arsenal n. [19C] the penis (cf. ADAM'S DAGGER; ADAM'S WHIP; OLD ADAM). [SE Adam, generic for man + arsenal; it is 'loaded' with semen]

adam's dagger n. [late 18C] the penis (cf. ADAM'S ARSENAL). [lit. euph.]

adam's off-ox n. [late 19C+] a headstrong person (cf. BELTESHAZZAR'S OFF-OX; GABE'S OFF-OX; GOD'S OFF-OX). [SE Adam, generic for man + OFF-OX]

adam's own altar n. [19C] the vagina (cf. ALTAR OF HYMEN; ALTAR OF PLEASURE; MARBLE ARCH).

adam's p.j.s n. [1960s] (US gay) nudity (cf. ADAM AND EVE'S P.J.S). [SE Adam + P.J.S]

adam's whip n. [1950s] (US) the penis (cf. ADAM'S ARSENAL).

adam tiler/tyler n. [18C–early 19C] **1** a fence or criminal receiver. **2** a pickpocket's assistant. [? SE Adam, generic for man + Ger. Teile, a share or slice; note 20C US Und. adam, a pickpocket's assistant]

ada ross/ada ross the stable boss n. [1940s+] (US) the 8 point in craps dice. [var. on ADA FROM DECATUR]

à d'autres! excl. [late 17C] a general excl. of dismissal or disbelief (cf. TELL IT TO THE MARINES!). [Fr. à d'autres, (tell it) to the others]

add v. [mid-19C] to work out as required (cf. ADD UP).

add/drive a peg/nail into one's coffin, to phr. [late 19C+] to drink heavily. [pun on the sealing of a coffin + the pegs that once marked off alcoholic measures in a tankard]

added to the list phr. [19C] castrated. [turf jargon; the list was of geldings in training]

addict n. [1960s+] (US Und.) one who seemingly cannot resist the blandishments of confidence tricksters and falls for every variety of trick.

addition n. [late 17C–early 18C] make-up, cosmetics. [an addition to one's natural complexion]

addle v. [19C] (US) to earn by one's labour. [13C northern dial. addle, to acquire or gain as one's own]

addle-cove n. [18C–mid-19C] a fool. [SE addle, to confuse + COVE; the sl. synon. of addle-pate or addle-head. Note mid-19C use is US and f. Matsell (1859), thus poss. merely reproduced f. Grose]

addled adj. [18C+] drunk; one of a number of synonyms meaning defective and thus ill or denoting the drunkard's confusion (cf. AFFLICTED; BEMUSED; BLEARY; CONCERNED; DIZZY adj.[1]; FAR GONE; FLAWED; FLUFFED; FLUFFY; FLUMMOXED adj.[1]; FLUSTERED; FOG-BOUND; FOGGED; FOGGY; FOXED; FRUSTRATED; FUDDLED; FUZZY adj.[1]; GOOFY; MIXED; MOONY adj.[1]; MUCKIBUS; MUDDLED; MUGGY; MUZZY; NON COMPOS; OBFUSCATED; ODDISH; OFF ONE'S NUT; PALATIC; PARALYSED; PARALYTIC; PETRIFIED; POLLUTED; PUTRID adj.[2]; REEKING; RIPE adj.[1]; ROTTEN; SCHIZZED; STINKING adj.[1]; STINKO adj.; TANGLED; WOOZY). [SE addle-pated, stupid]

addle-plot n. [18C–early 19C] a spoil-sport who 'addles' the 'plots' or plans of others.

address congress v. [1990s] (US) to masturbate (cf. CONVERSE WITH HARRY PALM; SHAKE HANDS WITH ABRAHAM LINCOLN). [a slur on political speechifying]

add up v. [1930s+] to make sense, to work out as expected, esp. in phr. it all adds up, it doesn't add up; also as add up to, to amount to, to signify.

adept n. **1** [17C] an alchemist. **2** [18C] a conjuror. [Lat. adeptus, skilled in; a Med. alchemist who had attained 'the great secret' was entitled adeptus, completely skilled (in all the secrets of his art)]

adidas phr. [1990s] all day I dream about sex. [abbr.; pun on brandname of sports shoes]

adios v. [19C] to leave (cf. VAMOOSE). [Sp. adios, goodbye, lit. 'to God']

adios amoebas n. [1980s] (US campus) a farewell. [a pun on the more common adios amigos, popularized by the 1950s TV series The Cisco Kid]

Adirondack steak n. [20C] (US) salt pork (cf. ABERDEEN CUTLET; ARKANSAS CHICKEN; ARKANSAS T-BONE; BOSTON WOODCOCK; BUSH BACON; CHICAGO CHICKEN; CHUCK WAGON CHICKEN; CINCINNATI CHICKEN; CINCINNATI OYSTERS; CINCINNATI QUAIL; FLORIDA CHICKEN; GEORGIA BACON; GEORGIA CHICKEN; IRISH CHICKEN; IRISH HORSE; IRISH TURKEY; MOUNTAIN LAMB). [SE Adirondack + steak; the Adirondacks area is generally regarded as impoverished]

adjust one's set, to phr. [1980s+] to masturbate (cf. APPLY THE HAND BRAKE; CHECK ONE'S OIL). [THREE-PIECE SET + pun on TV-related SE]

adjust the bowl of fruit, to phr. [1980s+] to masturbate (cf. DO A FRUIT SALAD; JUICE ONE'S FRUIT; JUICE THE PLUM; PEEL THE BANANA).

adkins's academy n. [early–mid-19C] a London house of correction, named for its governor (cf. CAMPBELL'S ACADEMY; FLOATING ACADEMY). [Adkins + ACADEMY (4)]

ad lib n. [1920s+] (orig. US) a pointed, provocative or sarcastic comment. [SE adlib, to extemporize; ult. Lat. ad libitum, as much as one desires]

Admiral Browning n. [20C] (orig. naut.) human excrement (cf. BROWNING FAMILY). [facet. use of SE admiral + BROWN n.³ (2)]

admiral of the blue n. [early 18C–mid-19C] a publican, an innkeeper (cf. ADMIRAL OF THE NARROW SEAS; ADMIRAL OF THE RED; HOIST THE BLUE FLAG). [? his blue apron]

admiral of the narrow seas n. [early 17C–mid-19C] a drunkard who vomits over their neighbour at table (cf. ADMIRAL OF THE BLUE). [facet. use of SE admiral + narrow seas, the British Channel/the Irish Sea]

admiral of the red n. [19C] one whose favourite drink is wine (cf. ADMIRAL OF THE BLUE). [as well as the colour of wine, the term may also refer to the drunkard's red nose]

admiral of the white n. [mid-19C–1900s] a coward. [white is the colour of cowardice]

admirals of the red, white and blue n. [19C] over-dressed, flashy beadles or other minor, uniformed officials. [their over-elaborate uniforms]

adobe adj. [19C] (US) generic, and in sl. use derog., term meaning Mexican, hence generic for second-rate, inferior (cf. DOBE). [Sp. adobe, sun-dried mud or clay, widely used as a building material in Mexico]

adobe dollar n. [20C] (US) a Mexican peso (cf. ADOBE). [Sp. adobe + SE dollar]

adobe maker n. [20C] (US) a derog. term for a Mexican or Mexican-American (cf. ADOBE).

adod! excl. [18C] God! (cf. ADAD).

adonee n. [mid-16C–late 19C] (Und.) God. [Heb. adonai, the Lord, God]

adonis adj. [late 18C+] a very attractive male. [Greek god Adonis, known for his outstanding beauty]

adonize v. [17C–19C] of a man, to adorn oneself. [ADONIS]

Adrian/Adrian Quist adj. [1970s+] (Aus.) drunk. [rhy. sl. Adrian Quist = PISSED; ult. the tennis player Adrian Quist (b.1913)]

adrift adj. **1** [17C] harmless. **2** [18C] missing. **3** [20C] confused. [all from the SE naut. term and orig. in navy use]

'ads n. [late 17C–mid-19C] God; thus adsbleed, adsbud, God's blood, adsflesh, God's flesh, adsheart, God's heart, adsheart's wounds, God's heart's wounds, adsooks, God's 'hooks' (hands) (cf. COCK n.¹; 's abbr.¹).

advertise v. [1930s+] (orig. US) to show off, to act in an exhibitionist manner.

advertisement conveyancer n. [late 19C] a sandwich-man. [the euph. term (PC long before its time) was coined by

W.E. Gladstone (1809–98) and duly mocked by London society]

advertising adj.¹ [20C] self-aggrandizing, self-promoting.

advertising adj.² [1960s+] (gay) **1** dressing in a sexually provocative manner. **2** (camp) plucking and then painting the eyebrows.

advertising bar n. [1960s] (US gay) a bar frequented by male prostitutes and their clients. [ADVERTISING adj.² + SE bar]

advertising pilgrim see PILGRIM n.².

adzooks! excl. [mid-18C–mid-19C] a mildly blasphemous oath (cf. CUTZOOKS!; GADZOOKS!). [SE God's hooks]

aerated/aeriated adj. [1930s+] over-excited, angry (cf. UP IN THE AIR).

aerial pingpong n. [1950s+] (Aus.) Australian Rules football. [mainly used in New South Wales to tease the fans, who centre on Victoria]

aeriated see AERATED.

aeroplane n. [1930s+] (Aus.) a bow tie. [? resemblance to a propeller]

af/aff n.¹ [1960s+] (drugs) Afghani hashish (cf. AFGHAN n.²). [abbr.]

af/aff n.² [1960s+] (S.Afr.) a derog. term for an African; thus aftax, a Black-owned taxi (usu. an old, American-made car) (cf. KAFFIR n.; MUNT). [abbr.]

affair n.¹ [mid-19C] **1** the penis (cf. CONCERN). **2** the vagina. [SE affair, a thing]

affair n.² [1970s] (gay) one's current lover. [SE affair, a sexual relationship]

affair of honour n. [early–mid-19C] a duel that results in the death of an innocent man. [ironic reversal of the SE meaning]

affidavit men n. [late 17C–late 18C] professional witnesses who, with pay, will swear to anything. [SE affidavit, a sworn statement that can be used in evidence]

affigraphy see AFFYGRAPHY.

afflicke n. [early 17C] a thief (cf. FLICK n.¹). [the word has always been assumed, by the OED and others, to have been a misprint of a flick. That said, it has no proven ety. and may indeed be one, equally incomprehensible word]

afflicted adj. [early 18C+] drunk (cf. ADDLED).

afflictions n. [mid-19C–1900s] (orig. drapers) mourning clothes; thus mitigated afflictions, half-mourning.

affygraphy/affigraphy n. [19C] an exact match, usu. as to an affygraphy. [SE autograph, poss. + affidavit]

afgay adj. [20C] homosexual (cf. FAG n.⁵; FAGGAMUFFIN; FAGGOT n.³; FAGOLA; FAYGELE). [pig Latin afgay = FAG]

afghan n.¹ [1960s] (US gay) a middle-aged gay man, who sometimes cross-dresses. [afghan, a coarse-woven afghan shawl]

Afghan/Afghani n.² [1960s+] Afghan hashish (cf. ACAPULCO GOLD; AF n.¹; BLACK PAK; MEXICAN GREEN; RED LEB).

afkop n. [20C] (S.Afr.) an ageing prostitute (cf. GOFFEL). [Afk. afkop, no head; such women supposedly hide their unalluring faces beneath the bedclothes]

afloat adj. [early 19C+] drunk (cf. ALL AT SEA phr.²; AWASH; BUOYANT; CARRYING A LOAD; DECKS-AWASH; HALF SEAS OVER; HALF THE BAY OVER; HAVE ONE'S BACK TEETH AFLOAT; HAVE ONE'S BACK TEETH AWASH; NEEDING A REEF TAKEN IN; OVERSEAS; OVER THE BAY; THREE SHEETS IN THE WIND).

a.f.o. phr. [20C] exhausted by sexual excess. [abbr. all fucked out]

a-forty n. [1960s+] (US Black/Bronx) a 40-ounce (1.2l) bottle of Old English 800 Malt Liquor.

Africa/African n. [early 17C–1900s] (US) bad temper, anger; thus get one's African up, to lose one's temper (cf. DUTCH n.³; INDIAN n.¹; IRISH n.; ITALIAN). [neg. stereotyping]

African n. [1940s+] (Aus.) a 'tailor-made', rather than hand-rolled, cigarette (cf. AFRICAN WOODBINE).

African *adj.* [20C] a derog. generic word, used in several combs. below to mean stupid, slow, unskilled and a number of similar pej. stereotypes attached to Black people, whether Africans or Afro-Americans.

African ape *n.* [19C+] (US) a derog. term for a Black person (cf. APE n.; BLACK APE; ORANGUTAN).

African billiards *n.* [1910s–60s] (US) the game of craps (cf. ABYSSINIAN POLO).

African black *n.* [1970s+] (drugs) marijuana. [SE *African* + *black*]

African bush *n.* [1960s+] (drugs) cannabis (cf. BOBO BUSH; CONGO BUSH). [SE *African* + BUSH n.⁶]

African dominoes *n.* [1910s–60s] (US) craps dice (cf. ABYSSINIAN POLO).

African dust *n.* [1950s] (US) gold. [the gold-mines of South Africa; the equation of gold with money = DUST n.¹ is presumably coincidental]

African engineering *n.* [20C] shoddy, second-rate workmanship (cf. MEXICAN adj.; NIGGER RIGGED).

African golf *n.* [20C] (US) the game of craps (cf. ABYSSINIAN POLO).

African golf ball *n.* **1** [1920s–70s] (US) a die, usu. in pl. **2** [1970s+] (US Black) a watermelon (cf. AFRICAN GRAPE; AFRICAN PLUM; CULTURAL FRUIT).

African grape *n.* [1970s+] (US Black) a watermelon (cf. AFRICAN GOLF BALL).

African lager *n.* [20C] Guinness stout (cf. NIGERIAN LAGER). [apart from its creamy head, the drink is virtually black]

African people's time *n.* [1920s–60s] unpunctuality, flexible time, a general disregard for punctuality (cf. AFRICAN TIME; ALASKA TIME; BLACK PEOPLE'S TIME; BLACKTIME; B.M.T. n.; B.P.T.; BRAZILIAN TIME; COLORED PEOPLE'S TIME; C.P.T.; FARMER'S TIME; HAWAIIAN TIME; INDIAN TIME; JEWISH TIME; J.S.T.; KAFFIR APPOINTMENT; MEXICAN TIME; NAVAJO TIME; PORTUGUESE TIME; SPANISH TIME; TINKER'S TIME). [racial stereotyping]

African pills *n.* [1910s] (US) craps dice (cf. ABYSSINIAN POLO).

African plum *n.* [1960s–70s] (US Black) a watermelon (cf. AFRICAN GOLF BALL).

African pool *n.* [1910s] (US) the game of craps (cf. ABYSSINIAN POLO).

African queen *n.* [1950s+] (gay) **1** a Black homosexual male. **2** a White homosexual who prefers Black partners. [SE *African* + QUEEN n.¹]

African skyscraper *n.* [1950s+] (US) a giraffe.

African time *n.* [1960s+] (S.Afr.) unpunctuality (cf. AFRICAN PEOPLE'S TIME).

African woodbine *n.* [1970s+] (drugs) marijuana cigarette cf. AFRICAN n.²). [Wills' *Woodbines*, popular, cheap UK cigarettes]

Africa speaks *n.* [1940s–50s] (Aus./N.Z.) strong liquor imported f. South Africa.

Africky *adj.* [early 17C–1900s] African. [the term is descriptive and, unlike AFRICAN adj., there is no specific pej. other than that inevitably pertaining to anything Black]

Afriks/Afrix *n.* [1970s+] (S.Afr.) English-speaking children's use for Afrikaans as a school lesson.

afro *n.*¹ [1930s–70s] an English or American person of African descent, a Black. [abbr.]

afro/'fro *n.*² [1960s+] (US Black/campus) a Black (and White) hairstyle in which normally short, curly black hair is allowed to grow out in a bush around the head, supposedly in the style of one's African forebears; thus *afroed*, wearing an Afro hairstyle (cf. BUSH n.⁴). [abbr.]

afromobile *n.* (US Black) **1** [late 19C] a three-wheeled vehicle used to convey tourists in Palm Beach, Florida; the drivers are invariably Black. **2** [1970s+] any fashionable automobile, e.g. a BMW, Lexus, Mercedes. [SE *Afro*, AFRICAN adj. + *automobile*; (1) implies subservience, (2) success]

afro set *n.* [1970s] (US Black) anywhere that Blacks use for talking or acting in furtherance of their own social and political betterment. [AFRO n.¹ + SET n.³]

aft *n.* [1910s+] *aft*ernoon. [abbr.]

after *n.* [20C] (Aus./US) *aft*ernoon. [abbr.]

after davy *n.* [mid-19C] an affidavit (cf. ALFRED DAVID; ALFRED DAVY). [mispron.]

after-dinner man *n.* [19C+] an afternoon drinker (cf. AFTERNOON MAN).

after hair *phr.* [late 19C+] in pursuit of a woman for sexual purposes. [SE *after* + HAIR]

afternoon *n.* [20C] (W.I./Bdos., Guyn.) the buttocks, esp. when large and female. [? naut. *aft*, the 'behind' of a boat + play on SE *afternoon*]

afternoon delight *n.* [1960s+] sex in the afternoon (cf. MORNING GLORY; NOONER).

afternoon farmer *n.* [mid–late 19C] one who wastes time rather than busying themselves with proper work. [thus they get down to work only in the afternoon]

afternoonified *adj.* [late 19C–1900s] smart, chic. [the regular afternoon calls made on each other by society ladies]

afternoon man *n.* [early 17C+] a tippler, a drunkard (cf. AFTER-DINNER MAN). [note the use as Anthony Powell book title, *Afternoon Men* (1931)]

after one's greens *phr.* [late 19C+] of a man, sexually eager. [GREENS n.²]

afters *n.* [1940s+] (orig. milit.) pudding, dessert (cf. STARTER n.⁵).

afterthought *n.* [1910s+] the youngest child of a family, conceived long after its siblings (cf. ACCIDENT n.¹).

after you is manners *phr.* [late 17C–1900s] phr. used to express the speaker's awareness of their own social inferiority.

after you with the po, Jane *phr.* [late 19C–1920s] a ref. to the need to take turns in using an outdoor privy; transferred in joc. usage to indoor facilities. [PO]

after you with the push! *phr.* [late 19C–1900s] phr. used as a reproof to someone who has pushed roughly past the speaker.

afto/arfto *n.* [1930s+] (Aus./N.Z.) afternoon (cf. ARVIE; ARVO). [abbr.]

ag! *excl.* [1950s+] (S.Afr.) a general excl., esp. of pleasure, irritation or exasperation; usu. with *man* or *sis*; also used to preface a reply to a question one finds hard to answer, e.g. *Ag, I don't really know*, or to denote a sense of resignation, *Ag, I'll have some more pap then*. [Afk. *ach*, a general interj.]

ag/ag coll/aggie *n.* [1910s+] (US) an *ag*ricultural *coll*ege. [abbr.]

agad! *excl.* [mid-18C] euph. excl. meaning God! (cf. ADAD).

against *prep.* [late 19C–1930s] (drugs) addicted to or under the influence of, usu. opium or heroin. [note that *RHDAS* offers one 1960s citation referring to cocaine]

against the collar *phr.* [mid–late 19C] in difficulties. [? the discomfort of one's neck rubbing against a tight collar]

against the pluck *phr.* [mid-18C–early 19C] reluctantly, 'against the grain'. [SE *against* + PLUCK n.¹]

agate *n.* [late 16C–early 17C] a very small person. [the carving of tiny figures into agate]

agates *n.* [1940s+] (US) the testicles; thus *agate-cracker*, a demanding task, *get one's agates cracked*, of a man, to have sexual intercourse (cf. BALLS n.¹; STONE n.¹). [SE *agate*, a semi-precious stone]

ag coll *see* AG.

-age *sfx.* [1960s+] (mainly US campus) a sfx. forming an abstract noun, e.g. *rainage*, a situation in which it is raining; *babage*, attractive young women. [adoption of SE use as sfx. for abstract nouns, names of persons or verbs expressing action]

agent *n.* [1960s–70s] (US Black) any policeman or police-woman. [an agent properly works only for the FBI and is not, as such, a police officer]

age stratify! *excl.* [1990s] (US campus) a synon. for 'grow up', esp. when used as an imper. [pun on sociological jargon]

agfay *n.* [1940s–70s] a male homosexual (cf. AFGAY). [pig Latin *agfay* = FAG]

agg *n.* [1990s] problems, trouble, annoyance (cf. AGGRO n.). [abbr. SE *aggravation*]

aggerawator/haggerawator *n.* [mid-19C–1900s] a favoured costermongers' hairstyle, consisting of a well-greased lock of hair twisted and pointing either at the corner of an eye or at an ear (cf. BEAU-CATCHER; BELL ROPE n.[1]; COBBLER'S KNOT; HEARTBREAKER; KNOCKERS n.[1]; MEAT-HOOK; NEWGATE KNOCKER). [? its 'aggravation' of admiring glances]

aggie *see* AG.

aggie fortis/acker fortis/ackie fortis/agur forty *n.* [19C] (US) very strong drink, usu. alcoholic but sometimes coffee (cf. FORTY-AX). [Lat. *aqua fortis*, strong water, an alternative name for nitric acid]

aggranoy/agronoy *v.* [late 19C+] to irritate, to annoy (cf. AGGROVOKE). [SE *aggravate* + *annoy*]

aggravation *n.* [1960s+] (orig. police/Und.) the difficulties that both sides of the professional law make for each other (cf. AGGRO n.).

aggravation *n.* [1920s] a station. [rhy. sl.]

aggro *n.* **1** [1960s+] problems, trouble. **2** [1960s+] violence, typically as enjoyed by skinheads, esp. at football matches, beating up Asians etc (cf. AGG). **3** [1960s+] any form of problems, difficulties, harassment. **4** [1990s] (Aus.) an aggressive person. [abbr. SE *aggravation*]

aggro *adj.* [1990s] (US campus) hot-headed, wild, un-predictable. [SE *aggravating*]

aggrovoke/agrovoke *v.* [1920s+] (Aus.) to annoy, to irritate (cf. AGGRANOY). [SE *aggravate* + *provoke*]

agility *n.* [19C] a euph. for the vagina; thus *show one's agility*, for a woman inadvertently to reveal her vagina (cf. FLASH ONE'S GASH).

aginner *n.* [20C] (Irish) one who automatically takes an oppositional stance usu. out of envy or spite. [dial. *agin*, against]

agitator *n.* [mid–late 19C] a bell-pull, a door-knocker.

agnes *n.* [1960s+] (US gay) a term of address used to one who is presumed to be a fellow homosexual (cf. ANGIE n.[1]; ANNIE; BELLE; BETTY n.[2]; BRUCE; DAISY n.[2]; ETHEL; JESSIE n.[1]; LILY n.[5]; MARGERY; MARY n.[2]; MARY ANN n.[1]; MAUD; MOLLY n.[1]; NANCY n.[2]; NELLIE n.[1]; NOLA). [use of female proper name]

agonies *n.* [1950s+] (drugs) withdrawal symptoms.

agonizer *n.* [late 19C] (society) one who makes intense efforts to gain a specific effect.

agony *n.* **1** [1930s+] problems, difficulties; thus *put on the agony*, to complain, to moan (the implication is that the problems are not wholly genuine) and thus to exaggerate. **2** [1980s+] (W.I./UK Black teen) the sensations felt during sex, notably popularized by the reggae singer Pinchers in a dance-hall song of the same name.

agony aunt *n.* [1970s+] a problem-solving (usu. woman) columnist of newspapers and magazines to whom the love-lorn and generally wretched can write; their letters will be answered in print or privately; thus the male equivalent, *agony uncle*. [the first *OED* citation is 1975, but it refers, in a biog. of the prototype Evelyn Home, to the "agony aunties" [of] the 'thirties'; note AGONY COLUMN n. (2) dates from 1950s]

agony box *n.* (US) **1** [1900s] a piano. **2** [1920s] a record player, a phonograph. **3** [1940s–60s] a radio. [the effect these objects supposedly have on hearers]

agony column *n.* **1** [late 19C] the section of a newspaper dedicated to special advertisements, particularly those for missing relatives or friends, and thus filled with personal agony. **2** [1950s+] a regular newspaper or magazine feature containing readers' questions about personal problems with replies from a (usu. woman) columnist (cf. AGONY AUNT).

agony in red *n.* [late 19C] a vermilion costume. [a satire on the aesthetic movement of the early 1880s when paintings were described in musical terms, e.g. 'a symphony in amber', 'a nocturne in silver-grey']

agreeable rattle *n.* [early 19C] a chattering, but not unpleasant, young man. [he 'rattles along']

agreeable ruts of life *n.* [18C] the vagina (cf. ARBOUR; AXIS; CENTRAL CUT; CLEFT n.[2]; CLOVEN SPOT; FURROW; GROOVE n.[1]; ONE-ENDED FURROW; RIGOL). [pun on SE *rut*, meaning both to have sexual intercourse and a cleft or furrow]

agree like cat and dog, to *phr.* [late 17C] of a married couple, to fight continually (cf. LEAD A CAT AND DOG LIFE). [a play on SE phr. *fight like cats and dogs*]

agree like the clocks of London, to *phr.* [late 16C–early 18C] to disagree on everything. [note SE pvb. *agree like bells, they want nothing but hanging*]

agricultural studies *n.* [1990s] (US campus) the cultivation of home-grown marijuana.

agronoy *see* AGGRANOY.

aground *adj.* [late 18C–late 19C] ruined, at a loss. [nautical imagery]

agrovoke *see* AGGROVOKE.

agteros *n.* [late 19C+] (S.Afr.) a plodder, a dawdler, one who lags behind. [Du. *achter*, behind + *os*, ox]

ague-faced *adj.* [20C] (US) twitchy. [SE *ague*, a malarial fever usu. intensified by severe chills; the sufferer is likely to shake in its throes + SE *faced*]

agur forty *see* AGGIE FORTIS.

a.h. *n.* [1930s–60s] (US) euph. abbr. of ASSHOLE; thus *in the pig's a.h.*, in very great trouble.

ah-ah *n.* [1970s+] (US Black) a fool. [onomat. grunting noise]

a-head *n.* [1960s+] **1** a regular or excessive amphetamine user (cf. ACID-HEAD). **2** a regular or excessive user of LSD. [A n.[3] + sfx. -HEAD (2)]

a-hole *n.* [1940s+] (US) euph. abbr. of ASSHOLE (cf. A.H.); thus *a-hole buddy* (cf. ASSHOLE BUDDY).

-aholic *sfx.* [1980s+] suffix indicating one who indulges excessively. [on pattern of SE *alcoholic*]

ah-pen-yen *n.* [late 19C–1930s] (drugs) opium. [? Mandarin/Cantonese]

ah que je can be bête! *phr.* [late 19C] what a fool I am! (cf. TWIGGY-VOUS THE CHOSE?). ['half-society' (Ware); a 'macaronic' or mixed-language phr.]

ah seh one *phr.* [1980s+] (W.I./UK Black teen) that's really something outstanding, important, meaningful. [pron. of SE *I say one*]

ai-ai/aai-aai *n.* [1960s+] (S.Afr.) methylated spirits or absolute alcohol, as drunk by alcoholics. [Zulu *hhayi*, no, or pron. of A.A., *absolute alcohol*]

AIDS for grades *n.* [20C] (US campus) the course Biology 40, 'AIDS and Other Sexually Transmitted Diseases' (cf. BLABS IN LABS; GODS FOR CLODS; SHOCKS FOR JOCKS).

a.i.f. *adj.* [1960s+] deaf. [rhy. sl. *A.I.F.* = Australian *I*mperial *F*orces]

aikies! *excl.* [20C] (US) that's mine! I want to do that! I want a share! a child's term used to claim the whole or an equal part of an object; the negative response to the cry is *no aikies*, no shares (cf. BAGS !; BALLOW; BONERS!; CHIPS!; DIBS!; DIVVIES!; SHACKIES!). [dial. pron. of SE *equal* or the 18C Yorks. dial. *hake*, to hanker or gape after]

aikona! *excl.* [1960s+] (S.Afr.) never! absolutely not! [Nguni *hayikhona*, no]

aimie *see* AMY.

aimies *n.*[1] [1970s+] (drugs) amphetamine (cf. A n.[2]). [abbr.]

aimies *n.*[2] [1970s+] (drugs) amyl nitrite (cf. AMES; AMIES; AMY; AMYL; AMYS; AROMA; BANANAS n.[3]; BANANA SPLITS; BOPPERS n.[2]; CRACKERS n.[6]; JOY JUICE; OZ n.[2]; PEARLS; POPPER n.[3]; RICE CRISPIES; SNAP n.[3]; SNAPPERS n.[2]; SNIFF n.; TOILET WATER). [pron. 'ay-mill' nitrite]

ainoch *n.* [late 19C] (tinker) a thing. [Shelta]

ain't down with *phr.* [1980s+] (US Black/campus) used when referring to a situation one does not particularly like, e.g. *I ain't down with this idea!* [DOWN adj.[2]]

ain't holding no air *phr.* [1960s+] (US Black) unimpressive, lacking credibility, lacking the basic knowledge required to take care of oneself within the ghetto. [one's ego/image is deflated]

ain'ting *see* HAINT'ING.

ain't it *phr.* [1940s–60s] (US Black) expression of affirmation. [abbr. *ain't it the truth*]

ain't it a treat *phr.* [late 19C+] a street. [rhy. sl.]

ain't long enough *phr.* [1970s+] (US Black) of money, not enough, insufficient. [fig. use of SE + ref. to LONG GREEN]

ain't love grand *phr.* [1930s+] phr. delivered, usu. ironically, on seeing two lovers embracing in public.

ain't nature grand *phr.* [late 19C+] phr. used on encountering a variety of 'natural' situations, usu. those otherwise seen as neg.

ain't nothing to it *phr.* [1960s–70s] (US Black) everything is simple, there are no problems; usu. in answer to question 'How are you doing?'

a into g *phr.* [1970s+] (N.Z.) abbr. of *arse into* gear, usu. in phr *get one's a into g*, to get on with things, hurry up. [ARSE n.[1]]

ain't shit *phr.* [1950s+] (US Black) useless, worthless, of absolutely no value. [SHIT n.[3]]

ain't today story *phr.* [20C] (W.I.) said of a woman whose age is greater than she looks. [lit. 'she's not today's (i.e. a new) story']

a.i.p. *n.* [1980s+] (drugs) heroin from *A*fghanistan, *I*ran and *P*akistan. [abbr.]

air *n.* [1920s–50s] (US) nonsense, rubbish, empty chatter. [abbr. HOT AIR]

air *v.* [1910s–40s] (US) to dismiss, to jilt. [GIVE THE AIR]

air bags *n.* [1940s+] (US Black/Harlem) the lungs.

airball *n.* [1980s+] (US) an idiot, a fool, someone who has nothing but air, and no brains, in their head (cf. AIRHEAD).

air blast *n.* [1980s+] (drugs) an inhalant when used for 'recreational' drug use. [SE *air* + BLAST n.[2]]

air-condition *v.* [1930s+] (orig. US) to fill full of holes, often by shooting; thus *air-conditioned*, full of holes, e.g. *air-conditioned socks*. [pun on SE]

air dance *n.* [1920s+] (US prison) a hanging (cf. DANCE ON AIR). [ironic use of SE]

airedale *n.* (US) **1** [1920s–40s] a fool, a worthless person. **2** [1950s] an unattractive woman (cf. DOG n.[4]). **3** [1960s+] a drifter, a tramp. [horse-racing jargon *airedale*, a worthless racehorse]

air guitar *n.* [1980s+] the non-existent (or at best cardboard cut-out) 'guitar' that is 'played' at concerts by fans of heavy metal rock bands.

airhead *n.* [1970s+] (US) **1** (orig. teen) an idiot, a fool, someone who has nothing but air, and no brains, in their head (cf. AIRBALL; BUBBLEHEAD; HELIUM-BRAIN). **2** (drugs) a marijuana user. [AIR n. + sfx. -HEAD (1)]

air Hebrews *n.* [1990s] (US campus) sandals (cf. AIRS). [? a pun on the popular make of athletic shoes, Air Jordans, and ref. to the biblical Hebrews crossing the River Jordan]

airhole *n.*[1] [late 19C–1900s] a small public garden, usu. on the site of a former church graveyard; the gravestones were re-sited against the garden walls. [cf. Lord Chatham's 18C coinage of the SE phr. 'lungs of London', the parks]

airhole *n.*[2] [1920s+] (US) euph. for ASSHOLE.

air hook *n.* [20C] (US) the nose. [its shape]

air hose *n.* [1980s] (US preppie) loafers worn, as is preppie style, without socks. [pun]

airified *adj.* [19C] (US) haughty, affected. [SE *to put on airs*]

airish *adj.*[1] [20C] (orig. US Black) **1** affected, inclined to put on airs. **2** effeminate. [SE *to put on airs*]

airish *adj.*[2] [20C] (orig. US Black) chilly, windy. [SE (*cold*) *air*]

airlock *v.* [20C] (Ulster) to stop in one's tracks.

airlocked *adj.* [20C] (Ulster) drunk. [AIRLOCK v.]

airmail *n.* [1950s+] **1** (US prison) garbage that is thrown out of cell windows instead of being taken to dustbins, loaded into disposal chutes etc. **2** (prison) anything that is thrown out of a cell window; esp. when the lack of flush lavatories means that prisoners parcel up their faeces and toss the resulting parcel from the window. [pun]

air-man-chair *n.* [late 19C–1900s] (music-hall) the chairman or master of ceremonies. [jumbled SE]

air off oneself *v.* [20C] (W.I.) to show off one's own superior status at others' expense. [SE *to put on airs*]

air one's dirty linen, to *phr.* [late 19C+] to discuss otherwise private matters (often pertaining to one's private life) in public (cf. PUT ON THE CLOTHES-LINE; WASH ONE'S DIRTY LINEN).

air one's heels, to *phr.* [mid-19C–1900s] to loiter about, to dawdle. [SE *air*, to take the air]

air one's lungs, to *phr.* **1** [1910s] (US) to complain, to curse. **2** [20C] to swear. **3** [20C] to argue or talk at length. [SE *air*, to expose the air + *air*, to give expression to]

air one's paunch, to *phr.* (US, mainly West.) **1** [1920s] to boast, to brag. **2** [1930s–40s] to vomit. [SE *air*, to give expression to]

air one's pores, to *phr.* [1900s–30s] to be naked. [SE *air*, to expose to the air]

air one's tonsils, to *phr.* [1960s] (US) to talk emptily. [SE *air*, to give expression to]

air one's vocabulary, to *phr.* [early 19C–1920s] to talk for the sake of talking or hearing one's own voice. [SE *air*, to give expression to]

air out *v.* [20C] (US, orig. Black) **1** to go for a walk. **2** to leave (cf. TAKE THE AIR). [SE *air*, to take the air]

air out one's mouth on, to *phr.* [20C] (W.I.) to speak aggressively or abusively. [SE *air*, to expose to the air + *air*, to give expression to]

air pie and a walk around *n.* [late 19C–1930s] a clerk's lunch (cf. AIR PUDDING; BARBER'S BREAKFAST; BUSHMAN'S BREAKFAST; DINGO'S BREAKFAST; DROVER'S BREAKFAST; MEXICAN BREAKFAST; POMMY'S BREAKFAST; SOLDIER'S SUPPER; SPITALFIELDS' BREAKFAST). [i.e. no food]

airplane *n.* [1960s–70s] (US drugs) **1** marijuana. **2** a relit marijuana cigarette stub. [it gets one 'high']

air pudding *n.* [mid-19C–1920s] (US) **1** nothing to eat. **2** nothing (cf. AIR PIE AND A WALK AROUND).

airs *n.* [1990s] (US teen) state-of-the-art, high-priced trainers (cf. AIR HEBREWS). [Nike *Air Jordan* trainer, particularly prized *c.*1990]

airs and graces *n.* [20C] **1** faces. **2** braces. **3** horse-races. [rhy. sl.]

air the dairy, to *phr.* [18C–19C] of a woman, to reveal her naked breasts (cf. DAIRY; DUGS; SPORT THE DAIRY). [SE *air*, to expose to the air + DAIRY]

airy *n.*[1] [19C] the 'area' of a house, adjacent to the basement steps. [pron.]

airy n.[2] [1960s+] a ventilator in a prison cell. [SE *air*]

airy adj.[1] [mid-19C+] (Irish) mentally unbalanced, fey.

airy adj.[2] [1960s] (US) inclined to pretentiousness, to putting on airs; thus **airily**, pretentiously (cf. AIRISH adj.[1]). [SE *to put on airs*]

airy-fairies n. [1930s] large feet. [joc. reverse of AIRY-FAIRY]

airy-fairy adj. [1920s+] insubstantial, trivial, of minimal importance.

ajax n. [late 16C] a lavatory (cf. JACK n.[6]; JACQUE'S; JAKEHOUSE; JAKES; JOHN n.[10]). [a pun on 'a jakes', a lavatory appears in Shakespeare's *King Lear* (1605–6), and in *The Metamorphosis of Ajax* (1596) by Sir John Harington (c.1561–1612), a plea for the introduction of the water-closet, the supposed coarseness of which so displeased Queen Elizabeth I that its author was temporarily banned from Court]

a.k. n.[1] [1920s–60s] (US) an old fogey. [abbr. Yid. *alter kocker*, old shit]

a.k. n.[2] [1930s–70s] (US) a toady. [abbr. ASS-KISSER]

a.k. n.[3] [1980s+] (US Black) the AK–47 automatic or semi-automatic assault weapon. [the Chinese-made AK–47 was the preferred weapon of the world's guerrilla fighters and has found its way to America's urban battlefields via mail-order purchases and illicit gun supplies]

a.k. v. [1930s–70s] (US) to curry favour with, to toady to. [A.K. n.[2]]

a.k.a. phr. [1950s+] (orig. Und.) an alias, a false name. [abbr. *also known as*]

akerman's hotel n. [late 18C–mid-19C] a prison (cf. BOARDING HOUSE; BOARDING SCHOOL; BURDON'S HOTEL; CAMPBELL'S ACADEMY; CASTIEAU'S HOTEL; CITY COLLEGE; COUNTY HOTEL; CROSS-BAR HOTEL; CROWBAR HOTEL; FAMILY HOTEL; FARRINGDON HOTEL; FLOATING ACADEMY; FREE HOTEL; GAMMONING ACADEMY; GRAYBAR HOTEL; GREEN LIGHT HOTEL; HARD-ROCK HOTEL; HOTEL; HOTEL CROWBAR; MACGORREY'S HOTEL; MALABAR HILTON; NEWMAN'S COLLEGE; NEWMAN'S HOTEL; SHERIFF'S HOTEL; SPIKE PARK). [the name of a celebrated gaoler, c.1787]

akimbo adj. [1940s] (society) arrogant, stand-offish. [SE arms *akimbo*, standing with one's hands on hips, elbows pointed outwards]

akimbo v. [late 19C–1940s] (US Black/Southern) to saunter, esp. with one's hands in pockets or on the hips (cf. CATTING n.[3]; DIDDY-BOP; GANGSTA LIMP; KIMIBLE; PIMP STRIDE; SLIDEWALK). [for ety. *see* AKIMBO adj.]

akka *see* ACKER n.[1].

Alabama n. [20C] (US Black) **1** a native of that US state. **2** a generic term for poverty, rural backwardness, based on the neg. image of the state and used in combs. below.

Alabama kleenex n. [1960s] (US) toilet paper or absorbent kitchen paper. [ALABAMA (2) + proprietary name, *Kleenex* tissues]

Alabama marbles n. [1910s–20s] (US) dice.

Alabama wool n. [1940s+] (US) cotton clothing.

alacompain/allacompain n. [mid-19C] rain (cf. ANDY CAIN; FRANCE AND SPAIN). [perversion of rhy. sl. 'all complain']

alans n. [1960s+] knickers. [abbr. ALAN WHICKERS]

Alan Whickers n. [1960s] knickers. [rhy. sl.; ult. *Alan Whicker* (b.1925), BBC TV personality]

alarm clock n. **1** [1920s] a worrier, a nag. **2** [1920s] (US campus) a chaperon. **3** [1940s] (US Black) a college professor. [one who keeps one, in real or fig. uses, from 'falling asleep']

Alaska time n. [20C] (US) unpunctuality (cf. AFRICAN PEOPLE'S TIME). [neg. image of the natives of the state]

Alaska turkey n. [19C] (US) a salmon (cf. ABERDEEN CUTLET). [the local salmon trade]

Albany beef n. [late 18C–1900s] (US) Hudson River sturgeon (cf. ABERDEEN CUTLET). [the one-time easy availability of sturgeon in the Hudson River near Albany, NY]

albertine n. [late 19C–1900s] an adroit, calculating, business-like mistress. [the character Albertine in Alexander Dumas fils' novel *Un Père prodigue* (1859)]

Albertopolis n. [mid-19C] Kensington Gore, London, site of the Royal Albert Hall and the Albert Memorial. [proper name of Queen Victoria's husband, Prince *Albert* of Saxe-Coburg-Gotha (1819–61) + sfx. *-opolis*]

alberts/prince alberts/prince alfreds n. [mid-late 19C] (Aus.) **1** strips of cloth, usu. calico, and rubbed with suet to cut down chafing, used as a substitute for socks, usu. by tramps. **2** rough, lace-up boots. [proper name *Prince Albert* (1819–61), consort of Queen Victoria. The use came from the myth that Albert, before his marriage, was so poor that he was forced to use foot-bindings (cf. TOERAG n.[1]) instead of proper socks]

Al Capone n. [1930s] (Aus.) 'phone, the telephone. [rhy. sl.; ult. the Chicago gang-boss Alphonse '*Al*' Capone (1899–1947)]

Al Capone ride n. [1970s+] (US Black) **1** any old car, both the original Capone-era models and more recent ones that lack the most up-to-date gimmicks and accessories and are thus *de facto* 'old fashioned'. **2** any broken-down, dilapidated car. [for ety. *see* AL CAPONE]

alderman n.[1] **1** [18C] a turkey, esp. one roasted and served with sausages (cf. ALDERMAN DOUBLE-SLANG'D; ALDERMAN IN CHAINS). **2** [early-mid-19C] a long pipe. **3** [mid-19C] half-a-crown, 2s 6d (12½p). **4** [late 19C–1940s] a paunch. [the image of a paunchy, pipe-smoking, wealthy administrator of the City of London]

alderman n.[2] [late 19C] a crowbar. [on pattern of CITIZEN n.[2], LORD MAYOR n., smaller and larger versions of the tool]

alderman double-slang'd n. [18C] a turkey garlanded with sausages. [ALDERMAN n.[1] + SLANGS]

alderman in chains n. [18C–19C] a turkey garlanded with sausages. [ALDERMAN n.[1], 'from the appearance of the City fathers, generally portly – becoming more so when carrying their chains of office over their powerful bust' (Ware)]

alderman lushington n. [early 19C] a drunkard (cf. LUSH n.[1]; VOTE FOR THE ALDERMAN). [joc. use of a proper name as an embellishment of LUSHINGTON]

alderman's nail n. [19C] an animal's tail. [rhy. sl.]

alderman's pace n. [late 16C–late 19C] a steady, careful pace, as befits an official with a fine sense of his own importance.

Aldershot ladies n. [20C] **1** (darts) double 4. **2** (bingo or lotto) 44. [pun on 'two fours' = two whores; Aldershot is an 'army town' in the UK]

Aldgate *see* BILL ON THE PUMP AT ALDGATE.

alec/aleck n. [1910s+] (Aus.) a fool or simpleton, a confidence man's victim. [SMART ALEC]

alecan n. [late 19C–1910s] a heavy drinker (cf. BEER BARREL; BUMPER n.[1]; CUPMAN; PISSPOT; RUM-BUMPER; RUMPOT; WHISKY-BOTTLE; WINEBAG).

alecie/alecy n. [late 16C] mental aberration, due to ale-drinking; intoxication. [lit. *ale-cy*, on pattern of luna-cy]

aleck n.[1] [1900s–30s] (orig. US) an unpleasant, conceited, smug person (cf. CLEVER DICK). [abbr. SMART ALEC]

aleck n.[2] *see* ALEC.

alecy *see* ALECIE.

ale-draper n. [late 16C–mid-18C] an alehouse-keeper. [SE *ale* + *draper*, seller]

aled up adj. [20C] drunk on beer (cf. BEERED UP; BEERY; CHATEAUED; CORNED; GINNED UP adj.[1]; GROGGY adj.[1]; LACED adj.[1]; LUBRICATED; MALTED; MALTY; MULLED; PICKLED adj.[1]; SALTED adj.[1]; SOUSED; STEWED adj.[1]; SWIPEY; WINEY).

ale-knight n. [late 16C–17C] a drunkard, a drinking companion. [SE *ale* + KNIGHT]

alemnoch n. [18C–late 19C] (tinker) milk. [Shelta]

ale-spinner n. [19C] a brewer, a publican (cf. GIN-SPINNER). [SE *ale* + *spinner*, in sense of a general manufacturer]

alexander v. [late 17C–early 18C] (Anglo-Irish) to hang someone. [proper name Sir Jerome *Alexander*, a hanging judge, active in Ireland 1660–74]

Alexander Hamilton n.[1] [20C] (US) a $10 bill (cf. ABRAHAM LINCOLN). [the picture of the US politician, *Alexander Hamilton* (1757–1804), is printed on the note]

Alexander Hamilton n.[2] [20C] (US) one's signature. [for ety. see ALEXANDER HAMILTON n.[1]; a confusion with JOHN HANCOCK n.]

Alexandra limp n. [late 19C] (society) a manner of walking taken up by fashionable society as a deliberate tribute to the way in which Princess Alexandra (1844–1925), then Princess of Wales, walked *c.*1870 (cf. BUXTON LIMP; GRECIAN BEND; KANGAROO DROOP; ROMAN FALL). ['The name given an erstwhile fit of semi-imbecility on the part of ... a crowd of limping, petticoated toadies' (F&H)]

alf n. [1960s+] (Aus.) an unsophisticated, nationalistic, basic Aus. male; recently overtaken by OCKER (cf. ROY). [SE name *Alfred*]

alfalfa n. (US) **1** [late 19C–1920s] a beard. **2** [20C] the countryside (as opposed to the town/city). **3** [1910s] a bed (f. the mattress). **4** [1910s+] money (cf. CABBAGE n.[8]; CABBAGE LEAF n.[2]; GREEN n.[2]; KALE; LEAF n.[1]; LETTUCE n.[1]; LONG GREEN; PLANTAIN LEAF; SPINACH n.[1]). **5** [1920s–50s] dried spinach or other dehydrated vegetables. **6** [1930s–40s] tobacco. **7** [1930s–60s] (US) nonsense, rubbish (cf. GAMMON AND PICKLES; PARSLEY n.[2]; SPINACH n.[2]). [SE *alfalfa*, a form of Lucerne grass, used for fodder]

alfalfa adj. [1910s–60s] (US) rustic, slow, peasant-like. [ALFALFA n. (2)]

alf/arf a mo n. [1910s] a cigarette, esp. when it proves hard to keep alight. [Cockney pron. of SE *half a moment*]

'alfpenny bumper n. [late 19C–1900s] a halfpenny omnibus fare. [the passengers are bumped up and down]

'alfpenny dip n. [mid-19C+] a ship. [rhy. sl.]

alfred david n. [mid–late 19C] an affidavit (cf. AFTER DAVY).

alfred davy n. [mid-19C] an affidavit (cf. AFTER DAVY).

Algie/Algy n. [late 19C] a generic name for any young male aristocrat (cf. ARCHIE; RUPERT). [proper name *Algernon*, seen as typically upper-class]

Ali n. [20C] a nickname for any man surnamed Barber. [story of 'Ali Baba and the 40 Thieves']

aliamba n. [1980s+] phencyclidine (cf. ACE n.[3]). [ety. unknown; ? Sp.]

alias adj. [1950s+] (W.I.) dangerous, violent. [ALIAS MAN]

alias man n. [1960s+] (orig. W.I., Und.) a cheat, a hypocrite, anyone unethical. [SE *alias*, another name, an assumed name]

alibi n. [1910s+] an excuse. [weakened form of SE]

alibi v. [20C] to provide an excuse for.

alibi ike n. [1910s+] (US) one who never takes the blame and invariably has a quick excuse for their faults and failings. ['Alibi Ike' (1915), the title of a short story by Ring Lardner (1885–1933), featuring a fictional baseball player]

Alice, The n.[1] [late 19C+] (Aus.) the town of Alice Springs.

alice n.[2] [1970s] (camp gay) the police. [song 'My Sweet Little Alice Blue Gown' by McCarthy & Tierney (1918); thus the ref. is to the uniform]

alice n.[3] [1970s] (drugs) LSD (cf. A n.[3]). [L.S. – i.e. LSD – but note Jefferson Airplane song 'White Rabbit' (1967), with its drug-orientated lyrics esp. line 'Go ask Alice, when she's ten feet tall'; both refs. go back to Lewis Carroll's *Alice's Adventures in Wonderland* (1866), which was seized on by the hippies for drug refs.]

Alice Blue gown/Alice Blue n. [1970s] the police (cf. ALICE n.[2]). [the blue uniform]

Alice B. Toklas n. [1960s] (drugs) a marijuana brownie (cf. BROWNIE n.[6]). [proper name *Alice B. Toklas* (1877–1967), lifetime companion to Gertrude Stein, who in her eponymous cookbook gave a receipe for this drug-based sweetmeat]

a-licker n. [1990s] (US) a toady, a sycophant (cf. A-WIPER). [abbr. ARSE-LICKER].

ali shuffle n. [1970s] (US Black) fancy footwork, orig. in the boxing, ring, latterly on the dance-floor, also fig. [the trademark move created by boxing superstar Muhammad *Ali* (b.1942)]

alive adj. [mid-18C+] knowledgeable, aware, esp. of a criminal scheme (cf. FLY adj.[1]).

alive and kicking phr. [early 19C+] absolutely alert and lively; often as a response to a speaker who assumes the opposite of an (absent) person, 'No, he's still alive ...'.

alive and well and living in ... phr. [1960s+] used to denote that, despite rumours to the contrary, someone or something is flourishing; esp. used of faded celebrities or once popular inventions, fads etc.

aliveo adj. [late 19C] alert, active. [abbr. ALL ALIVO]

alive or dead n. [late 19C+] the head. [rhy. sl.]

alkalied adj. [19C] (US) experienced at living in the West. [the alkali-dense streams from which humans and cattle were forced to drink]

alkied adj. [1940s+] drunk (cf. ALKY). [SE *alcohol*]

alkie's itch n. [1940s–50s] (Aus./US) the twitching and nervousness that are seen in an advanced alcoholic. [ALKY + SE *itch*]

alko n. [20C] an alcoholic (cf. ALKY). [SE *alco(holic)*]

alky n. **1** [mid-19C+] (US) alcohol. **2** [1950s+] an alcoholic, a drunk (cf. ALKIED; ALKO).

alky-cooker n.[1] [1930s+] (US) one who is employed in the illegal distillation of 'moonshine' whisky. [ALKY n. (1) + SE *cooker*, a cook]

alky-cooker n.[2] [1930s+] (US) an illegal still. [ALKYN. (1) + SE *cooker*, a stove]

alky joint n. [late 19C+] (US) a bar or saloon (cf. BEER JOINT; JUICE JOINT n.[1]; SKEE JOINT). [ALKY (1) + JOINT n.[3] (3)]

alky stiff n. [1910s] (US) an alcoholic tramp. [ALKY n. (2) + STIFF n.[3] (3)]

all adv. [1920s+] used to intensify an oath or obscenity, e.g. *damn all*, *fuck all*, *sod all*.

allacompain see ALACOMPAIN.

all a-cock adj. [late 19C] defeated, overthrown. [? KNOCK INTO A COCKED HAT or f. cockfighting jargon *all a-kick*, defeated (the cock's legs kick in its death-agony)]

all afloat n. [mid-19C] a coat. [rhy. sl.]

all airts/arts and parts phr. [1930s+] (Irish) **1** everywhere. **2** anything.

all/still alive and kissing phr. [20C] phr. applied to a pretty young woman. [a play on ALIVE AND KICKING]

all alivo adj. [mid-19C+] alert, active. [SE + sfx. -O]

all-American drug n. [1980s+] (US drugs) cocaine. [its popularity in the US + its source in South America and consumption (mainly) in North America]

all-and-all n.[1] [20C] (US) one's wife. [SE *and all*, and everything else and everything connected to; ? Scot. phr. 'wooed and married and all'].

all-and-all n.[2] [20C] (US) one's best suit of clothes. [? 'all (dressed up) and all']

all anymore adj. [19C] (US) used up, finished, gone. [Ger. *alle*, all gone]

all around my hat phr. [late 19C–1920s] all over, completely.

all arts and parts see ALL AIRTS AND PARTS.

all a-treat adj. [1900s] excellent, wonderful, sometimes used ironically to mean a mild disaster. [SE *a-* + *treat*, something highly enjoyable]

all at sea phr.[1] [late 19C+] confused. [losing one's bearings]

all at sea phr.[2] [late 19C+] drunk (cf. AFLOAT). [bobbing up and down and possibly vomiting]

all balls/all balls and bang-me-arse n. [20C] nonsense. [the ext. is post-1940s]

all beer and skittles n. [mid-19C+] pleasure, enjoyment, hedonism; also as neg., i.e. *not all …* .

all behind in Melbourne phr. [20C] (Aus.) fat, heavy-buttocked. [pun on BEHIND/SE *behind*]

all behind like a fat woman phr. [20C] tardy, dawdling, slow. [pun on BEHIND/SE *behind*]

all behind like barney's bull phr. [20C] (Aus./N.Z.) late, delayed, overweight (cf. BARNEY'S BULL). [pun]

all behind like the cow's tail phr. [20C] (Irish) late. [pun]

all bets are off phr. [20C] (gambling) **1** all deals are cancelled, all agreements are forgotten. **2** in fig. use to refer to one who is dead and thus beyond gaming or anything else. [no money can be won or lost]

all brandy adj. [mid-19C–1910s] of an object, excellent, admirable, as desired (cf. DOUBLE-DISTILLED). [brandy as a luxury drink]

all buck-up goes phr. [20C] (W.I.) all ethical standards are abandoned, 'anything goes'. [SE *buck (oneself) up*, to make an effort]

all bum adj. [mid-late 19C] of a woman, wearing a noticeably large bustle (a stuffed pad that emphasized the rear of the dress). [SE *all* + BUM n.[2]]

all chiefs and no Indians/too many chiefs and not enough Indians phr. [1940s+] (orig. Aus. milit.) all officers and no 'other ranks'; also, for a situation in which no one in a group of people wants to be anything but the boss. [Wild West imagery]

all cock and ribs like a musterer's dog phr. [1980s+] (N.Z.) said of a very thin person (cf. ALL PRICK AND RIBS LIKE A DROVER'S DOG). [COCK n.[2] (1) + N.Z.E. *barber*, a shearer]

all day n. [20C] (US Und.) a life sentence (cf. FROM NOW ON).

all day from a quarter phr. [20C] (US Und.) a sentence of 25 years to life (cf. PHONEY BALONEY LIFE). [ALL DAY + QUARTER n.[1]]

all day/yes, all day phr. [20C] slightly jeering phr., used in answer to the question, 'Is today …?'

all dicky/dickey with phr. [late 18C–early 19C] all over, ruined, finished, 'all up with'. [SE *all* + DICKY adj.[1]]

all dolled up like a barber's cat phr. [mid-late 19C] (Can.) dressed in the height of fashion.

all done by mirrors phr. [1920s+] any event that seems remarkable but that obviously hides tricks beneath the surface. [? an off-stage phr. used by professional magicians facetiously 'explaining' their tricks]

all down the line phr. [1940s+] in every way, to the furthest or fullest extent. [? railway imagery]

all dressed up and no place/nowhere to go phr. [1910s+] (orig. US) both a literal description and one implying anti-climax or disappointment. [the lyrics of a song by US comedian Raymond Hitchcock (1865–1929)]

allee-samee phr. [mid-late 19C] all the same, notwithstanding. [pidgin]

alleluia lass n. [late 19C–1900s] a young Salvation Army woman. [SE *alleluia*, praise the Lord + *lass*]

all ends up phr. [1920s+] easily, utterly, without difficulty.

allergic adj. [1930s+] (orig. US) sensitive to, usu. with hostile overtones, e.g. *Sorry, but I'm absolutely allergic to Tories.*

allerickstix adv. [19C] (US) all right, satisfactorily. [Ger. *alles richtig*, all right]

alleviator n. [mid-19C–1940s] a drink, esp. in a 'medicinal' context (cf. ANTIFOGMATIC; BRACER; CHEERER; CORPSE-REVIVER; EYE-OPENER n.[2]; HEART-STARTER; INVIGORATOR; LIVENER; PICK-ME-UP; PHLEGM-CUTTER; QUENCHER; REFRESHER; REVIVER; ROUSER n.[2];

SOOTHER; WARM-MOUTH). [ext. use of SE; i.e. it 'alleviates' one's feelings; 20C use is Aus. only]

alley n.[1] [19C] the vagina; one of a number terms equating the vagina with a road or path (cf. BLIND ALLEY; COCK ALLEY; COCK LANE; COVERED WAY; CROOKED WAY; CUPID'S ALLEY; DEAD-END STREET; HIGHWAY; JOY TRAIL; LEATHER LANE n.; LOVE LANE; MAIN AVENUE; PIPE n.[8]; RED LANE; ROAD; ROAD TO A CHRISTENING; SHOOTER'S H!LL; SMOCK ALLEY; SPEW ALLEY; TUNNEL n.; TURNPIKE).

alley n.[2] [late 19C–1900s] a go-between. [? Fr. *aller*, to go]

alley n.[3] [20C] (US Und.) the open area outside a row of cells (cf. RANGE n.). [ext. of SE use]

alley n.[4] [1980s] (US Black) a hospital corridor. [northeastern urban use; the image is of poor people crowding the hospitals as they do their own slums]

alley apple/lily/rifle n.[1] [1920s+] (US) a brick or stone when used as a missile (cf. GROUND APPLE; GROUND BISCUIT; IRISH CONFETTI; MEADOW MUFFIN; NIGGER PANCAKE). [generic use of SE *alley*, the unsavoury area of a town or city + pun on SE *apple*; *lily*, 1920s, *rifle*, 1940s]

alley apple n.[2] [1950s–60s] (US) excrement (cf. APPLE n.[1]; ROAD APPLE). [SE *alley* + supposed resemblance]

alley bat n. [20C] (US) **1** a promiscuous woman. **2** a prostitute (cf. ALLEY CAT n.). [SE *alley*, the unsavoury area of a town + BAT]

alley cat n. [1920s+] (US) **1** a promiscuous woman. **2** a prostitute. **3** an illegitimate child. **4** a street urchin.

alley cat v. [1920s+] (US) of a woman, to act in an overtly promiscuous manner. [ALLEY CAT n.]

alley-cleaner n. [1950s] (US) a riot gun, usu. a shotgun with a wide blast and thus used to disperse a mob. [the breadth of the shot 'cleans out' those standing across a narrow alley]

alley lily see ALLEY APPLE n.[1].

alley rat n. (US) **1** [1910s+] a particularly unpleasant, villainous and impoverished person. **2** [1930s] a pimp, esp. one involved in cheating a prostitute's clients (cf. MURPHY n.[3]). [SE *alley*, the unsavoury area of a town + RAT n.[3] (1)]

alley rifle see ALLEY APPLE n.[1].

alley up v. [20C] (Aus.) to pay one's share. [SE *alley*, a marble; lit. to hand over one's marble]

alley-waiter n. [late 19C] (US) an elevator or lift. [play on the SE, with added overtones of the narrowness of an alley and the elevator car, and of dumb waiter]

alley-whipped adj. [20C] (US) unpaid despite one's having done the work required. [image of the hapless worker being taken out into an alley and beaten when money is requested]

allez-oop! excl. [late 19C+] phr. used when boosting someone over a fence or onto a wall etc. [orig. circus use, excl. used by acrobats when one is thrown into the air, a mix of Fr. imper. *allez!* go! + Frenchified pron. of SE *up*]

all fine and dandy see FINE AND DANDY phr.

all-fire/-fired adv. [mid-19C+] (US) extremely, very much so; thus *all-firedly*, particularly, excessively. [euph. for HELL-FIRED]

all for it phr. [1920s+] (orig. RN) very keen (cf. UP FOR).

all fruits ripe phr. [1980s+] (W.I./UK Black teen) everything is fine, OK, all right, fit, all systems are go; popularized by reggae singer Junior Reid in a song of the same name. [image of a bumper harvest]

all fuss and feathers phr. [late 19C] (US) nonsense, pretence.

all gab and guts/guts like a young crow phr. [20C] (Ulster) used of a raucous, noisy chatterer. [GAB n. (2) + SE *guts*]

all gas and gaiters phr. [late 19C+] nonsense, rubbish, pomposity, bombast (cf. GAS). [GAS n.[1] (1) + SE *gaiters*; image of a pompous, sermonizing bishop]

all gay/all so gay/that's all gay phr. [1900s–10s] that's fine, everything's all right. [SE *gay*, light-hearted, cheerful, merry]

all get out *phr.* [mid-19C+] (US) very much, to a great extent; usu. prefixed by *as* or *like*.

all get outdoors *phr.* [20C] (US) very much, to a great extent, usu. prefixed by *as …* or *like …* . [ext. of ALL GET OUT]

all girls together *see* GIRLS TOGETHER.

all gong and no dinner *phr.* [1970s+] all talk but no action. [in an era when a gong was rung to announce the imminence of dinner]

all good *adv.* [1990s] (US Black teen) everything is fine. [ext. of SE use]

all hair by the nose *phr.* [20C] (US) very angry, in a rage (cf. GET A HAIR UP ONE'S ASS; HAVE A HAIR CROSSED).

All Hallows *n.* [16C] (Und.) the tolling place, presumably the place where the theft actually takes place, as described by those working as horse-stealers. [poss. an ironic reflection on orig. meaning of *All Hallows*, all holy men or all martyrs; the martyrs in question being those who are duped]

all hands *n.* [early 18C+] all concerned, the entire group or team. [orig. naut. use; SE *hand*, a crew member]

all hands to the pump *phr.* [18C+] *phr.* used to call all concerned to join in a group effort. [orig. naut. use; for ety. *see* ALL HANDS]

all holiday at Peckham *phr.* [late 18C–mid-19C] all over, finished, hopeless. [SE *holiday*, i.e. no work + pun on PECK n.[1] + *ham*, eat(ing) ham]

all honey or all turd with them *phr.* [17C–19C] said of those whose relationship fluctuates violently, they are either the closest of friends or the deepest of enemies. [antithesis of SE *honey* + TURD]

all-hot *n.* [mid-19C] a baked potato, as sold in the street. [the street cry]

all hot and bothered *phr.* [1920s+] flustered, maniacally nervous, sometimes through the suppression of lust (cf. BOTHERED UP). [ext. of SE use]

all hunk *adv.* [mid-19C–1900s] (US) satisfactory, fine (cf. HUNK adj.). [fig. use of Du. *hunk*, home, e.g. a place of safety or security, as used in juv. games]

allicholy *adj.* [late 16C] maudlin, esp. through drink. [SE *ale* + *melancholy*; used by Shakespeare in *Two Gentlemen of Verona* (1591)]

Allied Irish *n.* [1990s] (Irish) an act of masturbation. [rhy. sl. *Allied Irish Bank* = WANK n.]

alligator/alligator horse *n.*[1] (US) **1** [19C] a notably tough man (cf. HALF-HORSE, HALF-ALLIGATOR). **2** [mid-19C–1940s] a worthless, unpleasant person. [the animals' characteristics, and usu. used of a Kentucky frontiersman]

alligator *n.*[2] **1** [early–mid-19C] a singer who opens their mouth wide. **2** [mid–late 19C] a herring. **3** [late 19C] a shoe of which the upper and the sole have become separated. **4** [1920s+] (Aus.) a horse. **5** [1970s] (US) a chatterbox, a 'big mouth'. [the amphibian's gaping jaw]

alligator *n.*[3] [late 19C+] (US) a native of Florida. [the state's indigenous animal]

alligator *n.*[4] (US Black) **1** [20C] any sexually aggressive male. **2** [1930s–50s] anyone, usu. non-Black, who listens to and appreciates jazz, but does not play. **3** [1930s–50s] a White jazz musician. [the jazz musicians' ref. to someone who 'swallowed up' everything on offer, ? coined by Louis Armstrong (1901–71) to describe White musicians who pirated the original ideas created by their Black peers]

alligator! *excl.* [1950s] later (cf. SEE YA LATER ALLIGATOR). [rhy. sl.]

alligator bait *n.*[1] [late 19C–1960s] (US) **1** a derog. term for a Black native of Florida. **2** a Black child. [image of racist Whites lynching Blacks and tossing them to the alligators and f. the practice of Southern Whites, who found it amusing to threaten such children with 'throwing them to the alligators']

alligator bait *n.*[2] [1920s–30s] (US) any inedible food, esp. liver. [the practice in early 20C US construction camps of letting bull's liver rot before cooking it; the meat was thus tenderized, but simultaneously rendered too foul for any human to eat]

alligator bait *n.*[3] [1950s] (US) a worthless, unpleasant person, of any race.

alligator bull *n.* [20C] (Aus.) nonsense, rubbish. [SE *alligator* (of which there are none in Aus.) + BULLSHIT n.]

alligator horse *see* ALLIGATOR n.[1].

alligator mouth *n.* [1960s+] (US) a boaster, a braggart, someone with an inclination to boast or brag but insufficient courage to back up their words; such a person is usu. described in the extended phr. (*he's got*) *an alligator mouth and a hummingbird/canary ass.* [like the amphibian, the mouth is always yawning open]

all in *adj.* **1** [late 19C+] exhausted, utterly tired (cf. ALL OUT). **2** [20C] drunk. **3** [20C] of an object, run-down, dilapidated. [SE *all in*, everyone (thus every thing/faculty/emotion) included]

all in a bust *phr.* [1910s–20s] very excited. [BUST n.[3]]

all in a twitter *phr.* [late 18C+] nervous, worried. [SE *twittering birds*; but note WW2 RAF sl. *twittering ringpiece*: a state of extreme nervousness]

all in but one's shoestrings/bootstraps/shoelaces *phr.* [20C] (US) utterly exhausted. [ALL IN]

all in one *n.* [1970s] an orgy. ['person' or 'orifice' is unstated + ? ref. to carnival jargon *ten in one*, a sideshow that offers 10 performers, often freaks]

all in the eye *phr.* [mid–late 19C] nonsense, humbug. [ALL MY EYE]

all in the Kool-Aid/Kool-Aid and don't even know the flavor *phr.* [1990s] (US Black teen) a nosy, inquisitive person. [*Kool-Aid*, a popular US soft drink]

all is gas and gaiters *phr.* [early 19C+] all is satisfactory. [but note ALL GAS AND GAITERS]

all is same khaki pants *see* ALL SAME KHAKI PANTS.

all jake *adv.* [1910s+] (US) right, OK, satisfactory. [JAKE adj.]

all jaw/all jaw like a sheep's head *adv.* [late 19C–1910s] overly talkative, a chatterbox. [pun on JAW n. and SE *jaw*]

all jemmy!/jimmy! *excl.* [19C] all nonsense! [JEMMY adj.[2]]

all keyhole *n.* [mid-19C+] alcohol, a drink; thus *to be all keyhole*, to be drunk. [pun]

all kinds of *phr.* [late 19C+] (US) extremely, a great deal of. [ext. of SE use]

all know *adj.* [late 19C] bookish, like a bookworm. [KNOW-IT-ALL]

all laired up *phr.* [late 19C+] (Aus.) flashily dressed. [LAIR n.]

all languages *n.* [early–mid-19C] (euph.) bad language, obscenity. [? euph. phr. *he was using all sorts of language*]

all leather *adj.* [19C+] **1** of an object, excellent, first-rate. **2** of a person, dependable, trustworthy (cf. ALL WOOL AND A YARD WIDE; ALL OAK AND IRON BOUND). [the toughness and durability of leather]

all lit up *phr.* [1960s+] (drugs) under the influence of drugs. [LIT adj.[1] (2)]

all mockered up *phr.* [1940s+] (Aus. use) flashily dressed (cf. ALL LAIRED UP). [MOCKER]

all mops and brooms *see* MOPS AND BROOMS.

all mouth *adj.* [20C] (W.I./Bdos., Guyn.) talkative and unreliable. [ALL MOUTH AND TROUSERS]

all mouth and trousers *phr.* [late 19C+] all talk and no action, a braggart, a fake (cf. ALL PISS AND WIND; ALL PRICK AND BREECHES; ALL WIND AND PISS; COCK-AND-BREECHES). [MOUTH n.[1] (3) + SE *trousers*; i.e. a pushy sexual bravado]

all my eye *phr.* [mid-18C+] utter, absolute nonsense (cf. ALL MY EYE AND BETTY MARTIN).

all my eye and Betty Martin/that's my eye *phr.* [late 18C+] utter, absolute nonsense (cf. ALL MY EYE AND ELBOW; ALL MY EYE AND MY GRANDMOTHER; ALL MY EYE AND TOMMY; ALL MY WHISKERS). [while the first part of the phr. was in general, abbreviated use in the mid-19C, *Betty Martin* herself continues to be a source of controversy. E.P. suspects that she was a late 18C London character and that no record of her exists other than this catchphrase. Jon Bee (1823) and Hotten (1860) refer to the alleged Latin prayer, *Ora pro mihi, beate Martine* ('Pray for me blessed Martin'), i.e. St Martin of Tours, the patron saint of publicans and reformed drunkards. It has yet to be found in any version of the liturgy. Writing in 1914, Dr L.A. Waddell suggests another Latinism, *O mihi Britomartis* ('O bring help to me, Britomartis'), referring to the tutelery goddess of Crete. More likely is the idea, proposed in Charles Lee's *Memoirs* (1805), that there had once been 'an abandoned woman called Grace', who, in the late 18C, married a Mr Martin. She became notorious as *Betty Martin*, and *all my eye* was apparently among her favourite phrases. A northern version of the phr. has *Peggy Martin*, while London usages include *... and my elbow* or *... and my grandmother*]

all my eye and elbow/and my elbow *phr.* [late 19C–1900s] nonsense (cf. ALL MY EYE AND BETTY MARTIN). [ALL MY EYE + SE *elbow*]

all my eye and my grandmother *phr.* [late 19C] nonsense (cf. ALL MY EYE AND BETTY MARTIN). [ALL MY EYE + SE *grandmother*]

all my eye and Tommy *phr.* [late 19C] nonsense (cf. ALL MY EYE AND BETTY MARTIN). [ALL MY EYE + TOMMY (ROT)]

all my whiskers *phr.* [1930s] nonsense, rubbish (cf. ALL MY EYE AND BETTY MARTIN).

all nations *n.* **1** [late 18C–early 19C] a mixture of drinks assembled from the dregs of bottles and glasses (cf. ALLS; ALL SORTS; LOVEAGE). **2** [19C] a coat of many colours or covered in patches. [SE phr. *flags of all nations*]

all-nighter *n.* **1** [late 19C+] a prostitute's client who pays for a whole night's sex (cf. SHORT-TIMER). **2** [1930s+] anything that lasts all night, whether work or entertainment. **3** [1930s+] an all-night concert or dance. **4** [1960s+] (orig. US campus) working all night before an examination (cf. PULL AN ALL-NIGHTER).

all-night man *n.* [early–mid-19C] a body-snatcher, a 'resurrectionist'. [ext. use of SE; i.e. he is working all night]

allo *adj.* [mid-19C+] all. [pidgin; the *-o* sfx. makes up for the lack of a final 'l' in Chinese speech]

all oak and iron bound *phr.* [19C+] dependable (cf. ALL LEATHER). [the ref. is to the RN's 'wooden walls', its men o'war]

all of a dither *phr.* [early 19C+] in a state of nervousness, trembling with fear or apprehension. [SE *dither*, a state of nervous excitement or apprehension]

all of a doodah *phr.* [1910s+] in a fluster, in a state, very agitated. [DOODAH n.¹]

all of a flare *phr.* [mid–late 19C] in a clumsy, incompetent manner. [FLARE n.]

all of a glow *phr.* [mid-19C] feeling pleasantly warm. [ext. of SE; note phr. 'horses sweat, men perspire, ladies glow']

all of a heap *phr.* [18C+] prostrate, collapsed; thus *chuck all of a heap, strike all of a heap, knock all of a heap*, to shock, to paralyse mentally, to astonish.

all of a hough/hugh/huh *phr.* [early–mid-19C] lopsided, askew, falling with a thump. [Somerset dial. *ahuh, huh,* askew, ult. OE *awoh*, aslant; note tailors' jargon *all of a hough*, poor, clumsy work]

all of a jump *phr.* [late 19C] (US) nervous, on edge.

all of a/in a muck *phr.* [mid-18C–mid-19C] in a dirty, filthy state. [SE *muck*]

all of a piece *phr.* [late 19C–1900s] awkward. ['without proper distribution or relation of parts' (Ware)]

all of a screw *phr.* [late 19C] very twisted, very crooked. [the screw's shape]

all of a sweat *phr.* [late 19C] of urban pavements, slushy, wet, muddy. [SE *sweat*, to exude moisture]

all of a tiswas/tizwas *phr.* [1940s+] (orig. RAF) utterly confused, very excited. [? SE 'it is, it was', the image is of confusion or TIZZY n.²; note *Tiswas*, Central TV's children's light entertainment programme, 1970s]

all of a tizzy *phr.* [1930s+] confused (cf. ALL OF A TISWAS).

all of a tremble *phr.* [mid-18C–mid-19C] very nervous, agitated.

all of a wonk *phr.* [1910s+] jumpy, nervous, tense. [WONKY adj.¹ (1)]

all one's born days *phr.* [mid-18C+] ever, at any time at all. [dial.]

all one's nat *phr.* [1900s–10s] for ever, always. [abbr. SE phr. *all one's natural life*]

all one's natural *phr.* [late 19C+] all one's life. [abbr. SE phr. *all one's natural born days*]

all one's puff *phr.* [1920s+] all one's life. [PUFF n.²; breath, i.e. life]

all on one side like Lord Thomond's cocks *phr.* [late 18C–early 19C] used of a group of people who appear to be united but are, in fact, more likely to quarrel. [18C anecdote of *Lord Thomond*'s (1769–1855) Irish cock-feeder, who foolishly confined a number of his lordship's cocks, due to fight the next day for a considerable sum, all in the same room. Stereotyped for the story as a stupid Irishman, he supposedly believed that since they were all 'on the same side', they would not squabble. He was wrong, and the valuable cocks destroyed each other]

all on top *phr.* [1920s+] that's a lie, that is not so. [the statement is 'on top' of the facts]

all-originals *adj.* [1920s–70s] (US Black) Black people only; thus *all-originals scene*, a Blacks-only party etc. [ext. of SE use]

all out *adj.* [20C] exhausted (cf. ALL IN).

all out *phr.* [19C+] in error. [? 'all inside out']

all outdoors *phr.* [mid-19C+] (US) a general intensifier, as in *big as all outdoors, tall as all outdoors.* [the 'big skies' and wide prairies of the US West]

all-over *n.* **1** [mid-19C] a feeling of unease or illness that extends throughout one's body. **2** [1910s] (US) a thorough inspection, a lengthy visual assessment (cf. ONCE-OVER). **3** [20C] (US) a generalized intensive for either best or worst, as in *all-over wonderful, all-over crazy.* [16C SE *all over*, complete, to the full extent]

all over *adj.*¹ [late 19C] dead. [SE *all over*, finished]

all over *adj.*² [1920s+] absorbed in, obsessed by; thus *all over oneself*, extremely self-satisfied.

all over *adj.*³ [1980s+] making physical advances, often when not desired. [SE *all over*, to display great affection]

all over bar the shouting *phr.* [mid-19C+] a foregone conclusion; often preceded by *it's ....* [the 'shouting' being applause]

all over grumble *phr.* [late 19C] unsatisfactory, second-rate. [SE *all over*, complete, all-encompassing + *grumble*]

all-overish *adj.* [mid-19C+] feeling slightly unwell, usu. as a preliminary to a full-blown attack of some illness; thus *all-overishness*, the sensation of feeling unwell. [ALL OVER adj.¹ + sfx. *-ish*]

all over oneself *phr.* [1920s+] (orig. milit.) absorbed in oneself (cf. ALL OVER adj.²).

all-overs *n.* [late 19C+] **1** nervous or apprehensive feelings. **2** feelings of irritation. **3** feelings of ill-health. [ALL-OVER n. (1)]

all over the auction *phr.* [1930s–50s] (Aus.) everywhere, all over the place (cf. ALL OVER THE SHOP).

all over the board *phr.* [1960s–70s] eccentric, unstable.

all over the place *phr.* [1920s+] in a great mess, utterly disorganized.

all over the place like a mad woman's shit/knitting/lunchbox *phr.* [1950s+] (Aus.) confused, extremely messy.

all over the shop *phr.* **1** [mid–late 19C] in chaos, in a mess. **2** [mid-19C+] everywhere, esp. in phr. *knock all over the shop*, to beat severely. [(1) is SE in 20C]

all pills! *excl.* [late 19C+] rubbish! nonsense! (cf. BALLS!). [PILLS n.³]

all piss and wind *phr.* [20C] all talk and no action (cf. ALL MOUTH AND TROUSERS; ALL WIND AND PISS). [fig. use of PISS n. + SE *wind*]

all piss and wind like the barber's dog *phr.* [1980s+] (N.Z.) said of a very thin person (cf. ALL PRICK AND RIBS LIKE A DROVER'S DOG).

all pissed-up and nothing to show *phr.* [1910s–60s] a general phr. of discontent, one has drunk away one's wages and there's nothing left to show for a week's work. [PISSED adj.²; lower class variation on usual 'all dressed up …']

all-points *n.* [1970s] a general alert, a search for a missing person. [fig. use of police jargon, *all points bulletin*]

all points bulletin *n.* [1960s+] (US campus) a plea for help, with work, emotions and so on. [fig. use of A.P.B.]

all poshed up *phr.* [late 19C+] dressed up (cf. DOLLED OUT). [POSH n.¹]

all prick and breeches *phr.* [1920s+] all talk and no action, a braggart, a fake (cf. ALL MOUTH AND TROUSERS). [joc. use of sl.]

all prick and ribs like a drover's/shearer's/swaggie's dog *phr.* [1960s+] (Aus.) lean and eager (cf. ALL COCK AND RIBS LIKE A MUSTERER'S DOG; ALL PISS AND WIND LIKE A BARBER'S DOG; ALL RIBS AND DICK LIKE A ROBBER'S DOG).

all revved up *phr.* [1960s+] tense, nervous, excited, ready to be off. [SE *rev up*, to speed up]

all ribs and dick like a robber's dog *phr.* [1990s] (Aus.) very thin (cf. ALL PRICK AND RIBS LIKE A DROVER'S DOG).

all-right *adj.* [1950s+] an equivocal term of measured praise, acceptable, passing muster.

all right *adv.* [mid–late 19C] safely, securely. [SE in 20C]

all right *phr.* [20C] a general phr. of greeting; a question mark is assumed; the answer is often 'all right' or 'not so bad'.

all right! *excl.* [mid–late 19C] yes indeed! I agree! [SE in 20C]

all right for some *phr.* [1940s+] phr. of jealousy or envy, directed at another whose fortune seems better than one's own. [ext. of SE use]

allrightnik *n.* [late 19C+] (US) one who has succeeded, one who has raised themself from immigrant poverty to material success, esp. of New York Jews; thus *Allrightnik's Row*, Riverside Drive, home at one time of many successful Jews. [SE *all right* + sfx. *-nik* but the proper ety. is in Yid. *olraytnik*, an upstart, a parvenu]

all right up to now *phr.* [late 19C] smiling, serene (cf. ALL VERY FINE AND LARGE). [a pregnant woman's response to the question, 'How are you?'; coined by Herbert Campbell (1846–1904) in the Covent Garden Theatre, London, pantomime of 1878]

all-rounder *n.* [mid-19C] a collar that meets at the front, a style fashionable during the mid-19C.

all round the option *phr.* [1950s+] everywhere.

all rug *phr.* [late 17C–18C] (Und.) everything is secure. [? the comfort and security provided by a *rug*, or corruption of SE *right*]

alls *n.* [mid-19C–1910s] a drink, consisting of the dregs collected from the overflow from the pouring taps, the ends of spirit bottles and similar leavings, which was sold cheap in gin shops, especially to women (cf. ALL NATIONS). [? SE *all the dregs/leftovers*]

all same/all is same khaki pants *phr.* [20C] (W.I.) it's all the same, it makes no difference, they're all alike. [*khaki pants* are the most common of trousers]

allsbay *n.* [1940s+] nonsense, rubbish. [pig Latin = BALLS!]

all serene/sereno *adj.* [mid-19C+] all in order, satisfactory. [Sp. *sereno*, the 'equivalent to the *English* "all's well", a counter-sign of sentinels, supposed to have been acquired by some filibusters (pirates) who were imprisoned in Cuba, and liberated by the intercession of the British ambassador' (Hotten, 1867); E.P. prefers Gibraltar to Cuba as the passage through which the term entered English]

all set *adj.* **1** [late 17C–early 19C] of a villain, ready for any criminal undertaking. **2** [mid-19C+] ready, prepared. [ext. of SE use]

all seven *adv.* [1990s] (US Black) everything, all that is required; thus *six out seven*, nearly everything. [? dice playing, in which 7 is a winning throw]

all-shot *adj.* [late 19C+] (orig. milit.) exhausted, worn out, finished. [*all shot to pieces*]

all sigarno/sigarneo *see* ALL SIR GARNET.

all-singing, all-dancing *adj.* [1970s+] highly embellished, heavily ornamented, very fashionable. [fig. use of ad. copy used in the promotion of musical shows, music-hall programmes etc]

all Sir Garnet/sigarno/sigarneo *phr.* [late 19C+] all in order, everything as it should be (cf. SIR GARNET). [a ref. to the military successes of *Sir Garnet* (later Lord) Wolseley (1833–1923), whose reputation was further enhanced by his efforts to improve the lot of the private soldier]

all skin and whipcord *phr.* [late 19C–1930s] (US/British colonial) in top physical condition, very fit.

allslops *n.* [late 19C–1900s] Alsopp's ale. [the poor opinion drinkers had of it, by mid-20C abbr. to 'slops', though the origin was long lost]

all so gay *see* ALL GAY.

all sorts *n.* [early 19C] a drink consisting of the dregs collected from the overflow from the pouring taps, the ends of spirit bottles and similar leavings; it was sold cheaply in gin-shops, particularly to women (cf. ALL NATIONS). [ext. of SE use]

allspice *n.* [mid-19C–1900s] a grocer. [as, *inter alia*, a purveyor of SE *allspice*, the aromatic spice]

all squeegee *adj.* [mid-19C–1900s] all askew, out of kilter. [joc. mispron. of 'askew']

all's snug *adv.* [early 18C–early 19C] all is quiet. [SE *snug*, comfortable]

all star *n.* [1980s+] (drugs) a user of multiple drugs. [? SE *all-star*, extra-special, celebrity-packed or SE *all*, i.e. all drugs + STAR n.¹ (1)]

all stations *n.* [20C] (Aus.) an Alsatian dog. [rhy. sl. or joc. mispron.]

all talk and no cider *phr.* [19C] (US) all theory and no practice, all proposals and no concrete results. [supposedly orig. at a party in Buck County, PA, which had been arranged to enjoy a particularly good barrel of cider; a political argument began and emotions became so heated that half the guests left, claiming that the 'party' had been merely an excuse to wrangle, rather than drink]

all that *n.¹* [1920s+] a euph. for physical sex in its various aspects (cf. IT n.¹).

all that *n.²* [1990s] (US teen) a very important, influential person; thus *one thinks one is all that*, to overestimate oneself.

all that *adj.* [1960s+] **1** of an object, excellent, wonderful. **2** of a person, in possession of all good qualities. [SE phr. *and all that*, and all the rest of it]

all that and a bag of chips *phr.* [1990s] (US teen) something or someone considered absolutely excellent. [note that *chips* in the US are crisps in the UK]

all that and then some *phr.* [1980s+] (US Black) the extended, intensified form of ALL THAT adj.

all that jazz *phr.* [1950s+] (orig. US) that sort of thing, usu. following a list of proper nouns *... and all that jazz.* [SE *jazz*, meaningless or empty talk, nonsense]

all the beans *n.* [20C] (bingo) the number 57. [Heinz *57* Varieties, of which baked beans are the best known]

all the best *phr.* [20C] goodbye, farewell. [SE *all the best*, luck, wishes etc]

all the fat is in the fire *see* FAT IS IN THE FIRE.

all the go *phr.* [late 18C+] fashionable. [GO n.[1] (1)]

all there *adj.* **1** [mid–late 19C] honest, reliable. **2** [late 19C+] as desired, satisfactory. **3** [late 19C+] smart, aware. **4** [late 19C+] sane, in one's right mind.

all there and a ha'porth over *phr.* **1** [mid–late 19C] honest, reliable. **2** [late 19C] as desired, satisfactory. **3** [late 19C+] smart, aware. **4** [late 19C+] sane, in one's right mind. [ext. of ALL THERE adj.]

all there but the most of you *phr.* [mid-19C–1940s] having sexual intercourse. [*all* is the genitals, the *most* is the rest of the body]

all the steps *n.* [20C] (bingo) the number 39. [the WW1 thriller *The Thirty Nine Steps* (1915) by John Buchan]

all the twos *n.* [20C] (bingo) the number 22; thus *all the threes*, 33, *all the fours*, 44, up to *all the nines*, 99.

all the way *phr.*[1] [1950s+] (US) of a hamburger, with a full complement of condiments and garnishes.

all the way *phr.*[2] [1960s+] (orig. US Black) a general term of agreement, of encouragement and support. [abbr. *let's go all the way*]

all the way down *phr.* [mid-19C–1910s] absolutely right, completely suited. [ALL THE WAY phr.[2] + DOWN adj.[2] (1)]

all the way live *phr.* [1980s+] (US Black) anyone or anything considered exceptionally lively, exciting, desirable. [ALL THE WAY phr.[2] + LIVE adj. (2)]

all the way there *phr.* [mid–late 19C] honest, reliable. [ext. of ALL THERE adj.]

all the world and his wife/his dog *phr.* [early 18C+] absolutely everyone. [the 'dog' usage is mainly Aus.]

all the world is oatmeal *phr.* [mid-16C–late 17C] everything is fine. [pvb. 'all the world is (not) oatmeal', synon. 'all that glisters is not gold']

all the world to a china orange *phr.* [late 19C] the longest possible odds, an absolute certainty (cf. APPLES TO ASHES; BET A MILLION TO A PIECE OF DIRT; BET A POUND TO A PINCH OF SHIT; BET LONDON TO A BRICK; CHELSEA COLLEGE TO A SENTRY-BOX; DOLLARS TO BUTTONS; DOLLARS TO DOUGHNUTS; LOMBARD STREET TO A BRUMMAGEM SIXPENCE; LOMBARD STREET TO A CHINA ORANGE; LOMBARD STREET TO AN EGGSHELL; LOMBARD STREET TO NINEPENCE; LONDON TO A BRICK; ONE'S HEAD TO A TURNIP; POMPEY'S PILLAR TO A STICK OF SEALING WAX; POUND TO AN OLIVE; ROSEMARY LANE TO A RAG SHOP).

all the year round *n.* [1920s+] (Aus.) a 12-month prison sentence.

all-time *adj.* [1940s+] (US) the very best, the most memorable on record. [abbr. SE *in all of time*]

all-timer *n.* [1970s] the supreme example of, an 'all-time' version. [ALL-TIME]

all tits and teeth *phr.* [20C] used of a woman who capitalizes on her physical charms, esp. her smile and (presumably) large breasts, to make up for the lack of more subtle attractions; sometimes expanded by *... like a third-row chorus-girl.*

all to bits *phr.* [early 18C+] shattered, broken. [*to* substituted for SE *in*]

all to buggery *phr.* [20C] unsatisfactory, mixed up, useless (cf. ALL TO COCK; ALL TO PIECES; ALL TO SMASH). [SE *buggery* + BUGGER UP]

all to cock *phr.* [20C] unsatisfactory, mixed up, useless (cf. ALL A-COCK; ALL TO BUGGERY). [COCK n.[4] (2)]

all together like Brown's cows *phr.* **1** [late 19C+] (Anglo-Irish) alone. **2** [1920s+] (Aus.) in single file. [an anecdote in which the otherwise unidentified *Brown* possessed only one cow]

all/gone to hell *phr.* [19C+] financially ruined (cf. ALL TO COCK).

all to pieces *phr.*[1] [late 16C–19C] exhausted, collapsed, bankrupt. [fig. use of SE; *to* substituted for SE *in*]

all to pieces *phr.*[2] [19C] completely, utterly, to the furthest extent (cf. ALL TO COCK). [for ety. *see* ALL TO PIECES phr.[1]]

all to smash *phr.* [mid-19C+] bankrupted, utterly destroyed; usu. in phr. *go all to smash* (cf. ALL TO COCK; SMASH v.[1]).

all to the mustard *phr.* [1900s–20s] (US) keen, sharp, excellent. [the 'sharpness' of mustard]

all up *adj.* **1** [late 18C+] ruined, finished, defeated. **2** [early 19C+] dead, esp. in phr. *it's all up with ...* (cf. DONE FOR). [*up* as synon. with SE *over/finished*]

all up the country with, to be *phr.* [late 19C–1930s] to be the ruin of, to be death for. [ext. of ALL UP WITH]

all up with *phr.* [late 18C+] **1** of an object or plan, ruined, pointless, destroyed, finished. **2** of a person, doomed, bankrupt, hopeless. [ext. of SE *up*, used to indicate completion]

all very fine and large *phr.* [late 19C] (usu. ironic) very good, very satisfactory (cf. ALL RIGHT UP TO NOW; FINE AND DANDY). [the refrain of a popular song sung by Herbert Campbell (1846–1904)]

all washed up *see* WASHED UP adj.[1].

all wet *adj.* **1** [early 18C+] drunk. **2** [1920s+] (Aus.) silly, foolish. [WET adj.[1] (1)]

all white and spiteful *phr.* [20C] **1** applied to a menstruating woman. **2** applied to a child that, long past its bedtime, has become irritatingly fractious. **3** applied to anyone whose emotional state has rendered them annoying to their companions. [their complexion and their character]

all wind and piss *phr.* [late 19C+] a loudmouth, a braggart, all talk and no action (cf. ALL MOUTH AND TROUSERS; ALL PISS AND WIND). [SE *wind* + PISS n.]

all wool *adj.* [mid-19C] (US) excellent, first-class. [? ALL WOOL AND A YARD WIDE]

all wool and a yard wide *phr.* [late 19C+] of people, excellent, dependable. [advertising copy for clothing trade promotions, but note WOOL n.[1]]

all wool and no shoddy *phr.* [late 19C+] of people, excellent, dependable (cf. ALL WOOL AND A YARD WIDE). [SE *shoddy*, second-rate woollen yarn made from a mix of recycled old rags and a small proportion of new wool]

ally-beg *n.* [18C–19C] a comfortable bed. [? according to B&L Gaelic *aille*, pleasant + *beg*, little (place); thus a pleasant little place]

alma gray *n.* [20C] (Aus.) a threepenny piece (cf. DOLLY GRAY; DORA). [rhy. sl. *alma gray* = TRAY n.[1]]

almanack *n.* [late 19C–1900s] the vagina (cf. AMULET). [? it brings one good fortune]

almighty *adj.* [early 19C] mighty, great, exceedingly.

almond *n.* [late 19C+] the penis. [rhy. sl. *almond rock* = COCK n.[2]]

almond rocks/almonds *n.* [late 19C+] socks (cf. ARMY ROCKS; BOBBY ROCKS). [rhy. sl.]

aloft *adj.* [late 18C+] dead; thus *go aloft*, to die. [i.e. gone up to heaven]

alone on a raft *n.* [20C] (US short-order) a single poached egg on toast (cf. ADAM AND EVE n.).

-alorum/-alorium sfx. [late 19C+] a fake Latin sfx. used to create joc. emphasis from a noun, e.g. *scorchalorum*, *crapalorium*. [? on pattern of SE *cockalorum*]

alpha and omega n. [19C] the vagina (cf. A.B.C. n.[1]). [SE *alpha and omega*, 'the beginning and the end ... of the divine being' (*OED*)]

Alphabet City n. [1980s+] (US) Avenues A, B, C and D (and the relevant cross-streets) on New York's Lower East Side. [the initial letters]

alphabet-slinger n. [20C] (US) a school teacher (cf. INK-SLINGER). [on model of HASH-SLINGER; they *sling* the alphabet to the pupils]

alpha-chimp v. [1990s] (US teen) to establish dominance. [biological jargon *alpha*-, dominant, most successful, e.g. *alpha-male*]

alpha-ET n. [1980s] (drugs) *alpha-et*hyltyptamine. [abbr.]

alphonse n.[1] [late 19C] a gigolo. [the character in the play *Monsieur Alphonse* (1873) by Alexander Dumas fils]

alphonse n.[2] [1950s+] (Und.) a ponce (cf. CHARLIE RONCE; JOE BONCE; JOE RONCE). [rhy. sl.]

already adv. [19C] **1** as used by Pennsylvania Germans, previously, before, ago. **2** as used by Yid. speakers and those wishing to indicate Yid. speech rhythms, an intensifier indicating immediacy, even exasperation, e.g. *So tell me, already*. [both terms are ult. rooted in the Ger. *schon*, already, yet, so far; in these uses (1) is f. Penn. Ger. *schun* and (2) f. Yid. *shoyn*]

Alsatia n. [late 16C–mid-19C] the criminal 'no-man's-land' of 16C London; divided into Higher Alsatia (Whitefriars in the City) and Lower Alsatia (around the Mint in Southwark) (cf. BERMUDAS; CARIBEE ISLANDS; CLINK n.[1]; CRIBBEYS ISLANDS; SQUIRE OF ALSATIA). [named for *Alsace-Lorraine*, the marginal, disputed border area between France and Germany. Higher Alsatia, its earlier manifestation, was once the lands of the Whitefriars Monastery, extending from The Temple to Whitefriars Street and from Fleet Street to the Thames. After the Dissolution of the Monasteries (1536–9) the area went downhill, and, as allowed by Elizabeth I (r.1558–1603) and James I (r.1603–25), its inhabitants claimed exemption from jurisdiction of City of London. As such, the area became a centre of corruption, a refuge for villains and a no-man's-land for the law. The privileges were abolished in 1697, but it was decades before the old habits died out]

alsatian adj. [late 17C–18C] criminal, roguish. [ALSATIA]

alsatians n. [18C–19C] members of London's criminal underworld. [ALSATIA]

alsatia phrase n. [early–mid-17C] terms from slang or criminal jargon. [ALSATIA + SE *phrase*]

also-ran n. [late 19C+] (orig. Aus.) a useless person, a failure. [horse-racing use]

altamel n. [late 18C] a financial summary or account produced without detail and demanded as a lump sum (cf. DUTCH RECKONING. [18C Du. *altemal*, wholly, all at once]

altar n. [20C] the lavatory (cf. TEMPLE; THRONE).

altar of hymen/love n. [19C] the vagina (cf. ADAM'S OWN ALTAR). [SE *altar* + *Hymen*, the Greek god of marriage/*hymen*, the virginal membrane]

altar of pleasure n. [19C] the vagina (cf. ADAM'S OWN ALTAR). [a lit. euph.]

alter ego n. [1990s] (US campus) a form of identification, like a driver's licence. [Lat. *alter ego*, a second self]

alter kacker/kocker n. [20C] (US) old fool, old fogey (cf. A.K. n.[1]. [Yid. *alter kocker*, old shit. A facetious 'bilingual' version is *alter coyote*]

alter one's dial-plate, to phr. [early 19C] to disfigure one's face. [SE *alter* + DIAL-PLATE]

alter the property, to phr. [late 17C–early 18C] to disguise oneself.

altham n. [16C] (Und.) the wife or female companion of a mendicant villain. [E.P. sees this as ? root of AUTEM; if so, such a link would require a pun of the ALTAR OF HYMEN type]

altitudes see IN ONE'S ALTITUDES.

altogether, the n. [late 19C+] nudity, esp. in phr. *in the altogether*, naked. ['altogether naked/nude'; coined by George Du Maurier in his novel *Trilby* (1894): 'I have sat for the "altogether" to several other people.']

altogethery adj. [early 19C–1930s] (society) tipsy, drunk. [SE *altogether*, completely, utterly (drunk) + sfx. -y]

altumal n. [early–mid-18C] sailor's slang, nautical jargon. [Lat. *altum mare*, the deep sea]

alum, the n. [late 19C] (US) the ideal, exactly what one desires. [? phr. *à la mode*]

alvin n. [1940s+] (US) a yokel, an unsophisticated dweller in a small-town or rural settlement (cf. APPLE-KNOCKER n.[2]; BOBO JOHNNY; CLEM n.; CLYDE n.[1]; CORNCRACKER n.[1]; ELMER; JAKE n.[1]; JOSH n.[2]; JOSKIN; REUBEN; RUBE n.[1]). [a 'typically' rural name]

always in trouble like a Drury Lane whore phr. [late 19C+] a phr. used to condemn one who is frequently in trouble, esp. a woman who is seen as promiscuous. [*Drury Lane*, near Covent Garden, London, was a contemporary centre of prostitution]

a.m. n. [late 19C+] the morning (cf. P.M.). [colloq. version of SE *a.m.*, ante meridiem, used in chronological notation]

amateur/enthusiastic amateur n. [1910s+] a promiscuous young woman; thus [1920s+] (orig. US) *lose one's amateur standing/status*, to move into the world of professional, full-time prostitution. [the term depends on the assumption that for women any sex before marriage is tantamount to unpaid prostitution]

amateur night/hour n. [1930s+] (orig. US) an exhibition of more than usual ineptitude, esp. by one who is supposedly more competent. [orig. theatrical use, when on special nights amateur hopefuls were encouraged to 'try their stuff' on a real stage]

ambassador n. [1920s] (US) the penis. [it 'presents its credentials' to the vagina]

ambassador of Morocco n. [early 19C] a shoemaker. [pun on Morocco leather]

amber fluid/liquid n. [20C] (Aus.) beer; thus *amber transfusion*, a drink of beer. [its colour]

ambidexter n. **1** [16C–18C] (gambling) a house player (cf. SHILL n.[2]). **2** [17C–late 18C] a corrupt lawyer who takes fees from both plaintiff and defendant. [SE *ambidextrous*, in both cases the subject is seen as 'playing with both hands']

ambidextrous adj. [1930s+] (euph.) bisexual (cf. AC/DC). [SE *ambidextrous*, capable of using both hands equally well]

ambisextrous adj. [1920s+] (US) bisexual. [pun on AMBIDEXTROUS + SE *sex*]

ambo n. [1990s] (Aus.) **1** an ambulance. **2** an ambulance officer. [abbr. SE *ambulance* + sfx. -O]

ambs-ace n. **1** [13C–19C] bad luck, misfortune, worthlessness. **2** [17C–18C] nothing, next to nothing; [early 18C–late 19C] *within ambs-ace of*, within an ace of. [SE *ambs-ace*, double ace or both aces; thus the lowest possible throw in dice]

ambulance-chaser n. [late 19C+] a lawyer who specializes in representing the victims of street and other accidents, to whom they offer their services, often appearing at the victim's hospital bed to promise a substantial claim, which is accepted while the victim is still too shocked to make proper and rational arrangements (cf. FEE-CHASER).

ameche n. [1930s–50s] (Can./US) a telephone. [proper name of actor Don *Ameche* (1908–93), who portrayed the telephone's inventor, Alexander Graham Bell, in a 1939 biopic]

amen-bawler n. [19C] a parson, a preacher (cf. AMEN-CURLER; AUTEM-BAWLER). [SE *amen*, as a generic for prayers + SE *bawler*, one who shouts]

amen bench/corner n. [late 19C–1940s] (US Black) the front seats in a church, on either side of the pulpit (cf. MOANER'S BENCH). [the seats of the most enthusiastic congregants, who punctuate the prayer and sermon with cries of *Amen!*]

amen-curler n. [18C–early 19C] a parish clerk. [? SE *amen* + *curler*, one who writhes about; thus the clerk, wishing to demonstrate his piety]

amener n. [late 19C–1900s] a devout Anglican. [in allusion to their frequent use of *amen*]

amen-preacher n. [early 19C+] (W.I.) the carrion crow. [its black plumage, and the dislike felt by many West Indians for the White missionaries who preached at them]

amen-snorter n. [late 19C] (mainly Aus.) a parson.

amen theatre royal n. [late 19C] a church. [? the innate theatricality of religious services]

amen-wallah n. [19C+] the chaplain's clerk. [SE *amen* + WALLAH n. (1)]

American business college n. [1940s] (US Black) a liquor store (cf. AUNT BETSY'S COOKIE STORE). [initials A.B.C., which are also those of the Alcoholic Beverage Commission]

American culture n. [1960s+] sexual intercourse in the face-to-face 'missionary position' (cf. CHINESE FASHION; ENGLISH CULTURE; FRENCH CULTURE; GREEK CULTURE; ROMAN CULTURE; SWEDISH CULTURE). [the supposed blandness of Middle American lifestyles]

American lad n. [20C] (Irish) unpopular fatty bacon, imported from the US. [SE *American* + LAD n.² (1)]

American workhouse n. [1910s–30s] Park Lane Hotel, London. [its many American guests; it is, of course, far from a 'workhouse']

Amerika/Amerikkka n. [1960s–70s] (orig. US) America, viewed as the embodiment and headquarters of a right-wing, establishment-controlled, quasi-fascist conspiracy by the revolutionaries of the period. [the initials of the Ku Klux Klan, although note standard Ger. *Amerika*, America; an identification with Germany, however, still implied fascism/or Nazism]

ames n. [1970s+] (drugs) amyl nitrite (cf. AIMIES n.²). [abbr. SE; pron. *ay-mill*]

a.m.f. phr. [1960s+] a euph. abbr., goodbye, that's it, it's all over. [abbr. *adios motherfucker*]

AM/FM adj. [1980s+] bisexual (cf. AC/DC). [the two varieties of radio frequency]

amidships adv. [1930s+] in the stomach, in the solar plexus, usu. relating to a blow. [naut.]

amies n. [1970s+] amyl nitrite (cf. AIMIES n.²). [abbr.]

amigo n. [19C] (US) an affectionate term of address. [Sp. *amigo*, friend]

Aminadab/Aminidab n. [early 18C–early 19C] a Quaker. [a 'typical' Quaker name; 'from old comedies' (Hotten, 1867)]

Amish golf n. [20C] (US) croquet (cf. ABYSSINIAN POLO). [SE *Amish*, a strict sect of the Mennonite church in the US + SE *golf*; the theory is that the Amish are especial fans of the game]

ammunition n. **1** [19C+] lavatory paper. **2** [1920s–40s] (US) food, esp. as given out by the Salvation Army and similar institutions. **3** [1940s+] a tampon or sanitary towel.

ammunition leg n. [19C] a wooden leg. [SE *ammunition*, as supplied to soldiers]

ammunition wife n. [early–mid-19C] a prostitute. [such a woman, like fired ammunition, was 'hot']

amoeba n. [1980s+] (drugs) phencyclidine (cf. ACE n.³). [? the state to which it reduces its users]

amoeba-brained adj. [1960s+] (US) very stupid (cf. B.B.-BRAINED; CLAY-BRAINED; CORK-BRAINED; DOSS-BRAINED; FUZZ-BRAINED; JINGLE-BRAINED). [the tiny size]

among the missing phr. [mid-19C+] (US) absent; thus *be among the missing*, to absent oneself.

amorosa n. [early 17C–early 18C] a promiscuous woman, a courtesan. [Sp./Ital. *amorosa*, a female lover]

amoroso n. [early 17C–late 18C] a male lover. [Sp./Ital. *amoroso*, a lover]

amos and andy n. [1940s–50s] brandy. [rhy. sl.; the *Amos and Andy* radio show was highly popular in the US in the 1930s–40s; it featured two White actors, Freeman Gosden (1899–1982) and Charles Correll (1890–1972), faking it as 'dumb but happy darkies', and as such was one of the last interpretations of the old 'minstrel show']

amourette n. [mid-19C–1910s] a trifling, short-lived love affair. [Fr. *amourette*, little love affair]

amp n. **1** [1950s+] (drugs) an *amp*oule. **2** [1960s+] an *ampl*ifier. [abbr.]

amp adj. [1990s] (US Black) stirred up, very emotional. [SE *amplified*]

amped adv. [1970s+] (US) **1** high on drugs or caffeine. **2** ready, enthusiastic. [SE *amplified*; there may also be a subtler link to an AMP n.¹ (1) of methedrine]

amped-out adj. [1970s+] (drugs) fatigued after using amphetamines (cf. CRACKED-OUT; SMACKED-OUT; WEED OUT). [AMPED + abbr. of amphetamine]

ampersand n. [19C] the buttocks. [the fact that in late 19C nursery alphabets the symbol was usually printed after ('behind') the 26 letters + the suitably curving shape of the &]

amphets n. [1980s+] amphetamines (cf. A n.²). [abbr.]

amping n. [1970s+] (drugs) experiencing the accelerated heartbeat that is one of the effects of taking amphetamines. [AMPED]

amp joint n. [1980s+] (drugs) a marijuana cigarette laced with some form of narcotic. [AMP n. (1) + JOINT n.⁴ (2)]

ampster see AMSTER.

amputate one's mahogany/timber, to phr. [mid-19C+] to run away (cf. CUT QUICK STICKS; SAW YOUR TIMBER!; UP STICKS). [synon. for CUT ONE'S STICK]

amscray v. [1930s+] (orig. US) to leave quickly, to run off. [pig Latin, *scram*]

amster/ampster n. [1940s+] (Aus.) one who works outside a carnival, sideshow, strip club etc, touting the pleasures inside and pulling in the customers (GEE n.³). [rhy. sl. *Amsterdam* = *ram* = RAMP n.² (3)]

amulet n. [19C] the vagina (cf. ALMANACK). [SE *amulet*, a charm against evil]

amuse v. [late 18C–early 19C] (Und.) to fool shopkeepers and other tradesmen in order to cheat or rob them. [for ety. see AMUSER]

amuser n. [late 18C] (Und.) one who throws dust in a victim's eyes and then runs off; a companion then appears and, while ostensibly offering sympathy, picks the victim's pockets. [pun on SE *amuse*, to beguile with entertaining tales or to 'throw dust in one's eyes']

amy/aimie n. [1960s–70s] (drugs) amyl nitrite (cf. AIMIES n.²). [abbr.]

amy-john n. [20C] a lesbian. [play on SE *Amazon* + the comb. of male and female names]

amyl n. [1960s+] (drugs) amyl nitrite (cf. AIMIES n.²). [abbr.]

amyl queen n. [1960s+] (US gay) a gay man who enjoys sniffing amyl nitrite, which is supposed to enhance orgasm (whether hetero- or homosexual). [AMYL + QUEEN n.¹]

amys n. [1970s+] (drugs) amyl nitrite (cf. AIMIES n.²). [abbr.]

anabaptist *n.* [late 18C] a pickpocket who had been caught in the act and 'baptized' by being dumped into a pond. [pun on SE *Anabaptist*, an early 16C German Protestant sect, typified by the re-baptism of all members; ult. f. Gk. *anabaptismos*, baptize over again]

anaconda *n.* [1990s] a mixture of strong beer and rough cider or scrumpy.

anal astronaut *n.* [1990s] a male homosexual (cf. CACKPIPE COSMONAUT).

analken *v.* [late 19C] (tinker) to wash. [Shelta]

analt *v.* [late 19C] (tinker) to sweep. [Shelta]

anarchists *n.* [20C] (Aus.) non-safety matches. [they are 'likely to explode']

anatomy *n.* [late 19C–1900s] a very thin, emaciated person. [SE *anatomy*, a skeleton; used by Shakespeare in *Comedy of Errors* (1590)]

anca *n.* [19C] a man. [Gk. *aner*, a man]

anchor *n.*[1] [mid-19C–1930s] (US) a pick-axe. [resemblance]

anchor/anchor and chain *n.*[2] [20C] (US) one's wife (cf. ASS-BREAKER; BALL AND CHAIN; BITTER HALF; EVIL *n.*[2]; TROUBLE AND STRIFE). [derog. stereotype of a wife as the restraint on male freedoms]

anchor *v.* [1900s–60s] (US) to stop for a while, to settle. [naut. imagery]

anchored *adj.* [20C] (US) married (cf. ANCHOR *n.*[2]).

anchors *n.* [1930s+] brakes; thus *drop the anchors*, *slam on the anchors*, put on the brakes. [nautical]

ancient and modern *n.* [20C] a hymnbook. [the best known British hymnbook is *Hymns Ancient and Modern*]

ancient Chinese secret *n.* [1990s] (US Black teen) a non-committal response when one is asked how one managed a task.

and a bit in *phr.* [1920s] with a little extra added, with a tip.

and a half *phr.* [early 19C+] a general intensifier, e.g. *a cunt and a half*, a very unpleasant person indeed, *a party and a half*, a really good party (cf. AND THEN SOME!).

and a merry Christmas to you too! *excl.* [1920s] a dismissive, disparaging excl. that implies quite the opposite of its SE meaning.

and, and, and ... *phr.* [1970s+] used as synon. for 'and so on' to end an otherwise unfinished list.

and co *phr.* [mid-19C+] and all concerned, and their group or gang. [the commercial use *and co.*, and company]

and did he marry poor blind Nell? *phr.* **1** [mid-18C–mid-19C] a phr. used to imply one's disbelief in the previous statement. **2** [1910s+] (Aus.) an excl. of disbelief (cf. DID I BUGGERY!; LIKE FUCK!). [play on the clichéd conventions of popular fiction]

and don't you forget it! *excl.* [late 19C+] (orig. US) an excl. used to emphasize a critical or admonitory statement.

and how! *excl.* [1920s+] (orig. US) a general excl. of agreement or approval, placed at the end of a sentence. [synon. Ger. *und wie!*; RHDAS offers single mid-19C citation, a direct translation of the Ger., then notes that there is nothing until 1926]

and I don't mean maybe *phr.* [1920s+] a phr. used to affirm one's absolute faith in a sentiment, statement etc, i.e. there are no half-measures.

and like it! *excl.* [1940s+] (orig. naut.) an excl. used as part of an order or command, esp. when the recipient is definitely going to complain at having to carry it out, e.g. *You'll eat that semolina, and like it!*

and no error *see* AND NO MISTAKE.

and no flies *phr.* [mid-19C] a general intensifier, and no doubt about it. [the image is of flies settling on something that is fig. 'off']

and no messing about *phr.* [1930s+] a general intensifier, no doubt whatsoever.

and no mistake/error *phr.* [early 19C+] a general intensifier, certainly, without any doubt.

andramartins/andremartins *n.* [20C] (Irish) horseplay, fooling around (cf. STOP YOUR ANDREW MAKINS). [? anecdotal]

andrew *n.*[1] [late 17C–early 18C] a servant, a lazy fellow. [? SE merry-*Andrew*, a buffoon, an entertainer]

andrew *n.*[2] [mid-19C+] **1** the Royal Navy. **2** a government department or authority. [proper name of Lieutenant ANDREW MILLAR/MILLER, which gave orig. naut. jargon *Andrew Millar's lugger*, a ship of war]

andrew millar/miller *n.* [19C] a man o'war; thus also *Andrew Millar's lugger* (cf. ANDREW *n.*[2]). [? the name of a (then) well-known member of a press gang]

Andrex fart *n.* [1990s] a silent, smelly breaking of wind that lasts for quite some time. [the *Andrex* advertising slogan 'soft, strong and very long']

and shit *phr.* [1980s+] (US Black) a general abstract term, usu. thrown into the end of a sentence, similar to YOU KNOW (cf. AND STUFF). [SHIT *n.*[3]]

and stuff *phr.* [late 17C+] a meaningless addition to the end of a sentence, the implication is that the 'stuff' is essentially meaningless, irrelevant (cf. AND SHIT).

and that's flat *phr.* [late 16C+] without a doubt, absolutely, either of a statement or as an expression of one's determination (to perform or usu. not perform a task). [SE *flat*, absolute, downright, unqualified, peremptory]

and that's no lie *phr.* [1920s+] a phr. used to emphasize a previous statement esp. when the speaker fears they are being implausible.

and that's that *phr.* [early 19C+] a statement of finality; when modified as *well, that's that/that then* it implies an air of regret.

and the best of British luck *phr.* [1940s+] (orig. milit.) a slightly ironic way of wishing good luck; the implication is that with or without luck, the problem is still unlikely to be solved.

and the horse you rode in on *phr.* [20C] (US) a dismissive, antagonistic phr.; the pfx. FUCK YOU! is unspoken. [Wild West imagery]

and then some! *excl.* [20C] (orig. US) a rejoinder to the last speaker, that's not all of it, either! (cf. AND A HALF). [E.P. suggests an origin in 18C Scot. 'and some']

and things *phr.* [late 16C–1920s] synon. for SE *etcetera*.

and very nice too *phr.* [late 19C+] a phr. of appreciation used between men about a passing attractive woman.

and whose little girl are you? *phr.* [20C] used by a leering, older male as a means of introducing himself to an attractive woman.

andy cain *n.* [late 19C+] rain (cf. ALACOMPAIN). [rhy. sl.]

andy capp *n.* [1960s+] (Aus.) a crap, a defecation. [rhy. sl.; *Andy Capp* is a well-known strip cartoon character, created in 1956 by Reg Smythe for the *Daily Mirror*]

andy gump *n.* [1920s+] (US) **1** a conspicuously receding chin. **2** a notably prominent chin. [the eponymous cartoon character created by Sidney Smith in 1917; he was virtually chinless; in southwest US the banded sand snake, with its deeply countersunk jaw, is an *andy gump* snake]

Andy McGinn *n.* [1930s–50s] the chin. [rhy. sl.]

Andy Maguire *n.* [20C] (Aus.) a fire. [rhy. sl.]

Andy McNish *n.* [20C] fish. [rhy. sl.]

and you!/and you too! *phr.* [1910s+] a dismissive, antagonistic phr., a general admonition to anyone listening after one has made a pronouncement to someone. [i.e. 'and that means you (too)']

angel *n.*[1] [19C] **1** a prostitute (cf. SLUKER). **2** a young woman, esp. a pretty one. **3** an older homosexual man (cf. ANGELINA n.²). **4** (US tramp) a young homosexual companion. [the original, specific coinage applied only to those prostitutes whose beat ran near the Angel public house in Islington, north London]

angel *n.²* **1** [19C] (US Und.) the prospective victim of a swindle or confidence trick. **2** [late 19C+] the financial backer of an enterprise or scheme, esp. one who puts up money for a theatrical production. [the positive characteristics, including innocence, attributed to an SE *angel*]

angel/angelina *n.³* [1930s–60s] a passive homosexual. [SE *angel* + fem. sfx. *-ina*]

angel *n.⁴* [1980s] (drugs) phencyclidine (cf. ACE n.³). [? it takes one to heaven]

angel *v.* [1920s–40s] to use one's money to back an enterprise, esp. a theatrical production. [ANGEL n.² (2)]

angel cake and wine *n.* [20C] (US Und.) bread and water (cf. PISS AND PUNK).

angel drink *n.* [1980s+] a wine made from marijuana. [it sends the drinker 'to heaven']

angel dust *n.* (drugs) **1** [1960s+] phencyclidine (cf. ACE n.³). **2** [1970s] a mixture of cocaine, heroin and morphine, which can be smoked or injected. **3** [1970s+] anything smokeable, e.g. tobacco, marijuana, parsley, mixed with phencyclidine. **4** [1970s+] finely chopped marijuana.

angel dust hero *n.* [1980s+] (US) a regular user of cocaine. [ANGEL DUST n. (2) + SE *hero*]

angel factory *n.* [1920s+] (US) a seminary. [the assumption being that its products, priests, are guaranteed entry to heaven]

angel food *n.¹* [1920s–30s] (US tramp) preaching as experienced in a mission. [the sermon is the 'price' of the free meal]

angel food *n.²* [1950s–60s] (US gay) an air force serviceman. [as a flier he reaches heaven, as a potential conquest he is someone one can EAT v.³]

angel hair *n.* [1970s+] (drugs) phencyclidine (cf. ACE n.³). [var. on ANGEL DUST n. (1)]

angelic/angelica *n.* [early–mid-19C] an unmarried young woman. [SE *angel* + proper name]

angelina *n.¹* see ANGEL n.³.

angelina *n.²* [1950s+] (camp gay) a young man, the partner of an older one. [ANGEL n.¹ (4) + sfx. *-ina*]

angelina sorority *n.* [1950s+] (camp gay) the world of young gay men. [ANGEL n.¹ (4) + sfx. *-ina* + camp use of the usu. all-woman SE *sorority*]

angel kisses *n.* [20C] freckles. [the myth that freckles are a sign of angelic affection]

angel liquor *n.* [1940s] (US Black) a sweet, fortified wine. [California use; a pun on SE *angelica*; angelica liquor (angelica mixed with water) was orig. seen as a preventative against poison and the plague]

angel-maker *n.¹* **1** [19C+] an abortionist. **2** [1930s+] anything, usu. a weapon or a defective piece of military hardware (ship, plane), that causes death. [euph. phr. 'join the angels']

angel-maker *n.²* [late 19C–1900s] a baby-farmer, a woman who takes in (usu. illegitimate) babies on the pretext of bringing them up in return for a fee. [the frequency of infant mortality among 'farmed' babies]

angel mist/poke *n.* [1970s+] (drugs) phencyclidine (cf. ACE n.³).

angel puss *n.* [1940s+] (US) a pretty young woman, often used as an affectionate term of address. [SE *angel* + PUSS n.¹]

angels *n.* [1970s+] (drugs) **1** amytal. **2** sodium crystals. **3** alkyl nitrates. [initial 'a' + concept of getting HIGH adj.¹]

angel's food *n.* [late 16C–early 17C] strong ale. [i.e. nectar]

angel's kiss *n.* [20C] (Aus.) a piss. [rhy. sl.]

angel's tit *n.* [1980s+] (US) a cocktail made by pouring heavy cream onto dark crème de cacao and floating a cherry (the nipple) on top of that (cf. ANGEL TEAT). [SE *angel* + TIT n.¹]

angel suit *n.* [late 19C] a 'combination' suit, offering a coat and waistcoat made in one, with the trousers buttoned onto it. [? similar to a one-piece burial shroud in which one 'ascends to heaven']

angel/angel's teat *n.* [1940s] (US) notably mellow whisky (cf. ANGEL'S TIT). [stillers' jargon, a mellowed whisky with a rich bouquet]

angel together *n.* [late 19C–1910s] (mainly W.I.) a drunkard. [ety. unknown]

angel with a dirty face *n.* [1960s] a covert, undeclared male homosexual. [ANGEL n.³ + joc. use of SE; note film *Angels with Dirty Faces* (1938)]

angie *n.¹* [1960s] (US gay) a general form of address (cf. AGNES). [? ANGEL n.³]

angie *n.²* [1980s+] (drugs) cocaine. [? ANGEL DUST n. (2)]

angle *n.* [1940s+] (orig. US) any plan that should benefit its maker, an exploitable gimmick, an ulterior motive; thus *get an angle on*, to work out the optimum way of doing something; *shoot an angle/the angles*, to scheme, to plot. [? the calculation of angles necessary to play a winning game of pool, snooker or billiards]

angle *v.* [1920s+] (US) to scheme.

angled up *adj.* [1900s–70s] (US Black, South) confused, mixed up. [SE *angled*, skewiff, out of kilter]

angle for farthings, to *phr.* [late 18C] to dangle a cap, box or other makeshift container from a prison window into the street below in the hope of picking up alms from kind-hearted passers-by.

angler *n.* (Und.) **1** [16C–early 19C] a thief who uses a pole with a hook at one end to 'fish' items from open windows, unguarded market stalls, passing carts etc (cf. CANTING CREW; HOOKER n.¹). **2** [1900s] (US) a petty thief, working in the street and always on the lookout for opportunities to commit small larcenies. [fishing imagery]

angle-shooter *n.* [1940s+] (US) a schemer, a plotter. [ANGLE n. + SE *shooter*]

Anglican inch *n.* [late 19C] the short, square whiskers affected by members of the Broad Church or liberal wing of the Church of England. [coined by the High Church ritualists]

angling-cove *n.* [18C] a receiver of stolen goods. [ANGLER + COVE; i.e. 'one who fishes in troubled waters']

anglo *n.* [19C] anyone of ostensibly Anglo-Saxon appearance; i.e. a White person. [SE *Anglo-*, English]

Angola *n.* [1970s+] (drugs) marijuana. [its origin]

angry boy *n.* [late 16C–early 17C] a rake, a young man about town, a 'blood'. [SE *angry*, troublesome, vexatious, annoying + *boy*]

anguagela *n.* [late 19C–1900s] language. [transposition]

anguish *adj.* [1940s–50s] (middle-class) of a disliked person, unpopular, disliked, extremely boring, esp. in phrs., e.g. *she's total anguish*. [PAIN n.²]

animal *n.¹* **1** [18C+] a general derog. description of a man, esp. a braggart. **2** [1910s+] a policeman (cf. PIG n.³). **3** [1920s+] (orig. US) a physically strong man, a 'tough guy', a hired thug. **4** [1950s+] a wild, crazy person. **5** [1950s+] (Aus.) an unpleasant person. **6** [1960s+] (orig. US) a passionate sexual partner. **7** [1970s] (US campus) an athlete.

animal *n.²* [late 19C–1900s] a public house whose sign shows a lion, bull, bear or other creature (cf. JUMBO n.²). [the original animal was the Elephant and Castle in south London]

animal *n.³* [1900s] (US) a word-for-word translation used by US students studying foreign languages (cf. BICYCLE; CRIB n.⁴; TROT n.³). [var. on HORSE n.⁷ or PONY n.³]

animal n.⁴ [1980s+] (drugs) LSD (cf. A n.³). [? it makes some users behave wildly]

-animal sfx. [1980s+] (US campus) a combining form indicating one who does something excessively, e.g. *party animal*. [ANIMAL n.¹]

animal cracker n. [1920s+] (US) an eccentric. [pun on CRACKERS adj. + ref. to Nabisco's Barnum's Animals, biscuits first marketed in 1904]

animal house/farm/zoo n. [1960s+] (US campus) a fraternity house that is generally rated the least efficient, the most degenerate and, overall, the one to avoid. [the phr. *animal house* gained international popularity with the release of the film *Animal House* (1978), starring John Belushi]

animal tranq n. [1970s+] (drugs) phencyclidine (cf. ACE n.³). [in non-recreational use, an animal tranquillizer]

animal zoo see ANIMAL HOUSE.

ankle n. [1940s] (US) a young woman (cf. LEG n.⁵). [metonymy]

ankle/ankle about v. [1920s+] (orig. US) to walk (cf. ANKLE EXPRESS).

ankle-beater n. [19C] a boy who drives cattle from the market to the slaughterer. [to avoid damaging the flesh, he would hit only the animals' ankles]

ankle-biter n.¹ [1920s] in pl., tight trousers, as worn by hussars.

ankle-biter n.² [1950s+] (orig. US) a small child (cf. RUG RAT). [its crawling around at ankle-height]

ankle express n. [1910s+] (US) transportation by foot, walking (cf. ANKLE v.; FOOTBACK; FOOTMOBILE; SHANKS'S PONY). [ironic use of SE]

ankle-spring warehouse n. [late 18C–mid-19C] (Anglo-Irish) the stocks. [var. on SPRING ANKLE WAREHOUSE]

ann n. [1990s] a derog. term for a White woman (cf. MR CHARLIE). [abbr. MISS ANN]

anna maria n. [late 19C+] a domestic fire (cf. AUNT MARIA n.²; JEREMIAH n.). [rhy. sl.]

Anna May Wong n. [1920s+] a stink, a smell. [rhy. sl. *Anna May Wong* = PONG; ult. f. film star *Anna May Wong* (1907–61)]

anne's fan see QUEEN ANNE'S FAN.

annie n. [1950s] an effeminate male homosexual (cf. AGNES). [use of female proper name]

Annie Laurie n. [1940s] a bus conductress. [*Annie Laurie* (1682–1764); her grandson Alexander Fergusson of Craigdarroch was the hero of Robert Burns's poem 'The Whistle'; thus *whistler*, another WW2 synon. for a conductress]

annie louise n. [20C] (Aus.) cheese. [rhy. sl.]

annie no-rattle n. [20C] (Ulster) one who waits until a conversation is over to put in their own opinion. [proper name *Annie* + SE *no* + RATTLE v.²]

Annie Oakley n. [1910s+] (US) a free pass, orig. to a circus, but latterly to the theatre. [the markswoman *Annie Oakley* (Phoebe Ann Mozee Butler, 1860–1926); the holes punched in such tickets supposedly resembled the aces out of which Ms Oakley would shoot the pips]

annie's room phr. [1910s+] (Aus.) a phr. used in answer to the question 'Where is ...?' when the speaker does not actually know. [orig. milit.]

annihilated adj. [1970s+] (orig. US campus) extremely drunk or intoxicated by some drug.

anno domini n. [late 19C+] old age and its deleterious effects, esp. on physical prowess (cf. A.D.; B.C.). [Lat. *anno domini*, in the year of Our Lord]

annual n. **1** [late 19C–1900s] an annual holiday. **2** [20C] (Aus.) a bath.

anodyne necklace n. [late 18C] the hangman's noose (cf. CAUDLE OF HEMPSEED). [ironic use of SE, such a necklace was originally a form of medicinal amulet and based on the original definition of *anodyne* as soothing pain, in this

context that of a misspent life; thus the phrase is a pun on 'painkiller']

anoint/anoint with birchen salve v. [16C–early 19C] to beat, to thrash (cf. BASTE). [ironic use of SE]

anoint a/the palm, to phr. [16C–18C] to bribe (cf. GREASE SOMEONE'S PALM).

anointed adj. [mid-19C] used to intensify a noun, e.g. *an anointed rascal*, a very definite rascal. [ext. of SE *anointed*, consecrated king or queen]

anoint the palm see ANOINT A PALM.

anoint with birchen salve see ANOINT.

anonyma n. [mid-late 19C] a courtesan, a high-class prostitute (cf. INCOGNITA). [Lat. *anonyma*, an unknown woman]

anorak n. [1980s+] **1** anyone outside a peer group who thus fails to fit in with 'the gang', esp. a studious individual who eschews drink, drugs and similar teen pleasures. **2** an obsessive, typically as regards computing (in an earlier age their interest would have been trainspotting) (cf. NERD). [SE *anorak*, a style of short coat, orig. worn by Greenland Inuits, that is seen as typifying such figures]

another clean shirt ought to see you out phr. [1930s+] (N.Z.) you look very ill; i.e. you look as if you'll soon be dead.

another county heard from phr. [1930s+] (Can.) a remark made when one of a group breaks wind. [joc. use of SE phr. usually used of election results]

another day, another dollar phr. [1910s+] (orig. US) **1** a phr. of relief used at the end of the working day. **2** a phr. used to point up the tedium of quotidian existence.

another good man gone phr. [19C+] a phr. used by male friends on the announcement of a man's engagement to be married. [sexist stereotyping]

another one for the van phr. [1920s+] another person's gone mad. [the 'van' being that which conveys the sufferer to a psychiatric institution]

another push and you'd have been a chink/nigger phr. [20C] a general insult; the implication (in this context a slur) is that one's mother was happy to have sex with all races.

answer is a lemon, the phr. [1920s+] (orig. US) a generally neg. reply to a fellow speaker. [LEMON n.¹ (3) + the fact that the fruit, like this phr., is sour]

answer Scotch fashion, to phr. [mid-19C–1920s] to answer one question by posing another. [a supposed Scot. characteristic]

answer the last muster, to phr. [20C] to die. [milit. imagery]

answer the last roll-call, to phr. [20C] to die. [milit. imagery]

answer the last round-up, to phr. [20C] to die. [Western cowboy imagery]

ante n. [late 19C+] (orig. US) money in hand, cash (cf. ANTE v.; ANTE-UP). [Lat. *ante*, before, in this case, before one plays or bets]

ante/ante up v. [mid-19C+] to pay out money in advance; the variants *andy up* and *annie up* are simply folk misprons. [poker use, each player must *ante up* (f. Lat. *ante*, before) a specified sum in order to enter each successive hand dealt during the game]

ante-up n. [late 19C–1950s] (Aus.) the game of poker. [the necessity to *ante up* (place a preliminary bet) to indicate one's playing a round]

anthony/tantony n. [late 18C] the runt of the litter (cf. FOLLOW LIKE A TANTONY PIG). [SE *St Anthony's pig*; St Anthony is the patron of swine-herds, and is always represented as accompanied by a pig; and Berkshire dial. *t'anthony*, the smallest pig in a litter]

anthony cuffin n. [19C] a knock-kneed man. [CUFF ANTHONY]

anti n. [late 19C] an objector, a rebel, a dissenter, one who rejects the social status quo. [Lat. *anti*, against; 20C use is SE]

antidote n. [late 17C–early 18C] a very plain woman. [ext. of SE use, i.e. an 'antidote against attraction']

antifogmatic n. [late 18C–late 19C] an alcoholic drink taken (ostensibly) to counteract the effects of cold and damp (cf. ALLEVIATOR; FOGMATIC n.). [ANTI + *fog* + sfx. *-matic*, sfx. used to indicate a mechanical device]

antifreeze n. **1** [1940s+] whisky. **2** [1980s+] (drugs) heroin. [ext. of SE use, i.e. both refer to their supposed prophylactic powers against cold]

anti-lunch n. [19C] an appetizer, a drink taken before lunch. [either the drink is seen as counteracting one's appetite or the sp. should be *ante-*]

antipodean adj. [mid–late 19C] in a mess, chaotic. [the Antipodes are 'the world turned upside down']

antipodes n. [mid-19C–1920s] **1** the vagina (cf. BOTANY BAY n.[2]; CAPE HORN; CAPE OF GOOD HOPE n.[1]; GEOGRAPHY n.[1]; GREAT DIVIDE; SOUTH POLE). **2** the posterior. [SE *Antipodes*, Australia and thus, f. UK perspective, 'the bottom of the world']

ant-killer/-masher n. [mid-19C] (US) **1** a large foot, a large, heavy shoe (cf. ANT-STOMPER; BEETLE-CRUSHER). **2** by metonymy, a man who has or wears one.

an't please the pigs phr. [late 17C–late 19C] (? orig. Irish) if circumstances permit. [? SE *pixies*; *Ware* prefers *pyx*, the vessel in which the host or consecrated bread of the sacrament is reserved, thus making it a synon. for 'God willing', or 'please God']

ants n. (US) **1** [1930s] restlessness. **2** [1940s–60s] sexual enthusiasm. [HAVE ANTS IN ONE'S PANTS]

ant's pants n. [1990s] (Aus.) the height of fashion (cf. BAT'S BALLS; BEE'S KNEES; CAT'S; CAT'S ARSE; CAT'S ASS n.[1]; CAT'S BALLS; CAT'S KITTENS; CAT'S MEOW; CAT'S MITTS; CAT'S NUTS; CAT'S PYJAMAS; CAT'S WHISKERS; DUCK'S QUACK).

ant-stomper n. [1970s] (US) **1** a large foot, a large, heavy shoe (cf. ANT-KILLER). **2** by metonymy, a man who has or wears one.

antsy adj. [mid-19C+] twitchy, nervous. [ANTS + sfx. *-y*]

A-number-one n. [1920s–30s] (US) oneself (cf. A1 adj.; NUMBER ONE n.[2]). [both parts indicate 'the first']

anvil chorus n. [late 19C+] (orig. US) carping, neg. criticism. [the 'Anvil Chorus', featured in Verdi's opera *Il Trovatore* (1853)]

anxious adj. [1940s–70s] (US Black) good, enjoyable, admirable, pleasant. [on bad = good model]

anxious meeting n. [late 19C–1910s] (orig. US) the gathering, after a revivalist meeting, of those earnest souls who are 'anxious for salvation'.

anxious seater n. [20C] (US) a nervous person. [ON THE ANXIOUS BENCH]

any n. [1950s+] sexual pleasures (cf. GETTING ANY?). [CUNT n.[1]; PUSSY n.[1] etc are assumed]

anybody's guess phr. [1930s+] (orig. US) used of a situation the outcome of which has yet to be determined or of a question to which no one has yet provided an answer.

any dog's bottom? phr. [1930s+] (Aus.) a phr. used to enquire if someone is any use. [ety. unknown; ? canine habit of sniffing at their fellows]

any God's quantity n. [late 19C–1930s] many, a good number.

any good/no good/some good adj. [mid-19C+] of use, of no use at all or of some use.

anyhow adv. **1** [mid-19C] indifferently, carelessly. **2** [mid-19C+] disorganized, messy.

any joy? phr. [1940s+] (orig. US) a question asking 'did you have any luck?' (with your search, enquiry etc) (cf. NO JOY!).

any more for any more? phr. [late 19C+] (orig. milit.) does anyone want anything more? (usu. of food).

any more for the Skylark? phr. [20C] will anyone else be

joining the group, journey etc. [the supposed enquiry of a generic seaside pleasure-boat operator]

any old adj. [late 19C+] (orig. US) anything, whatever, a general term of vagueness, e.g. *any old way, any old job.*

any old how phr. **1** [1920s+] in any case, no matter what. **2** [1930s+] in any way or manner whatever or however imperfect, in random fashion, unmethodically. [ANY OLD + SE *how*]

any old thing n. [1900s–10s] (US) any thing whatever. [ANY OLD + SE *thing*]

any racket n. [mid-19C–1900s] a penny faggot. [rhy. sl.]

anything for a laugh phr. [1950s+] a slightly regretful, ironic phr., usu. justifying something one does through necessity or desperation rather than choice. [the laugh may well be a rueful one]

anything goes phr. [late 19C+] anything is acceptable, permissible.

anything in trousers n. [late 19C+] a man, esp. in phr. *she'll go for/fuck/have anything in trousers*, said of a woman who is considered to be completely indiscriminate in her amours (cf. ANYTHING ON TWO LEGS).

anything on two legs n. [late 19C] a woman, in the context of her sexual availability (cf. ANYTHING IN TROUSERS; HE'LL FUCK ANYTHING ON TWO LEGS).

any Wee Georgie? phr. [1930s+] any good? [rhy. sl. *Wee Georgie* Wood = good; Wood was a popular music-hall entertainer in 1920s–30s]

anywhere adv. [1950s+] (drugs) possessing drugs, as in question *are you anywhere?* (cf. HOLDING).

Anzac Day dinner n. [1930s] (N.Z.) a meal, usu. lunch, that is mainly (if not entirely) composed of alcohol. [Anzac Day, a public holiday held on 25 April (the anniversary of the Gallipoli landing in 1915) in Australia and New Zealand in memory of the nations' war dead]

A-OK phr. [20C] intensifier of OK, all's well, everything's absolutely fine. [A1 adj. + OK!; originated in spaceflight jargon and spread to the wider public after the broadcast of the Mercury flight of Commander Alan Shepard (1923–98) on 5 May 1961]

A1 n. [1980s+] (drugs) amphetamine (cf. A n.[2]). [abbr. + comment on its supposed quality]

A1 adj. [mid-19C+] excellent, perfect, first-class, in prime condition; alternatives are *A1 copper-bottomed* and (US) *A1 and no mistake, letter A, number 1* (cf. A-NUMBER-ONE) [insurance jargon *A1*, the top rating given to a ship at the insurers Lloyds of London]

a. over t. adv. [20C] head-over-heels, usu. as *go a. over t.* (cf. ARSE OVER APEX; ARSE OVER TIT). [abbr.]

apache n.[1] [20C] (gay) a man who uses cosmetics (cf. WARPAINT). [the wearing of 'warpaint' by Apaches and other Native Americans]

apache n.[2] [1980s+] (drugs) fentanyl, a synthetic opiate (cf. CHINA GIRL; CHINA WHITE; DANCE FEVER; FRIEND n.[3]; GOODFELLAS; GREAT BEAR; HE-MAN; JACKPOT n.[2]; KING IVORY; MURDER 8; POISON n.[3]; TANGO & CASH; T.N.T. n.[3]). [? its effect]

apartment/house/tenements to let n. [18C–19C] **1** a widow's weeds (cf. SIGN OF A HOUSE TO LET). **2** the widow herself. [a widow becomes 'vacant' for new (male) 'occupation']

apartments to let phr. [mid-19C+] unhinged, insane, crazy. [the image is of a certain emptiness in the 'upper storey']

a.p.b. n. [20C] (US police) a general alert, a search for a missing person. [abbr. *all points bulletin*, a general alert broadcast to all officers and vehicles]

apcray n. [1930s+] (US) nonsense, rubbish. [pig Latin *apcray*, CRAP n.[3] (2)]

ape n. **1** [19C+] (US) a derog. term for a Black person (cf. AFRICAN APE). **2** [20C] a thug, a hoodlum (cf. BABOON).

ape *adj.* [19C+] a generic term meaning aggressive and danger-ous. [SE *ape*]

ape *v.* [1910s+] (US) to lose control, to act in a wild manner.

apehangers *n.* [1960s+] (orig. US) high, extra-long motorcycle handlebars, favoured by outlaw riders such as Hell's Angels. [APE adj.; when riding with such equipment one's arms dangle forward like those of an ape]

apehead *n.* [1920s] (US) a fool, an idiot. [APE adj. + sfx. -HEAD (1)]

ape oil *n.* [20C] (US) liquor. [? it makes the drinker GO APE]

ape out *v.* [1960s] (US) to lose control, to act in a wild manner. [ext. of APE v.]

apeshit *adj.* [1950s+] (orig. US Black) berserk, crazy, extremely upset (cf. GO APE; RATSHIT). [APE adj. + SHIT n.[1]]

apey *adj.* [1950s+] (US) crazy, unstable. [APE adj. + sfx. -y]

aphrodisiacal tennis court *n.* [17C] the vagina (cf. GYMNASIUM). [euph. coined by Britain's first translator of Rabelais, the Scot Sir Thomas Urquhart (1611–60)]

apollo play *n.* [1940s–70s] (US Black) the planet Earth. [ety. unknown]

Apostle's Grove *n.* [mid-19C–1910s] St John's Wood, London NW8 (cf. GROVE OF THE EVANGELIST). [pun. The area was well known for its up-market courtesans and 'kept women']

apostle's pinch *n.* [20C] a pinch on the buttocks. [? fig. link to APOSTLE'S GROVE]

apothecaries' Latin *n.* [mid-18C+] the mangled Latin used by apothecaries (cf. BOG LATIN; GARDEN LATIN; KITCHEN LATIN; LATIN MYSTERY).

apothecary's bill *n.* [late 18C] a substantial bill. [stereotyping of an apothecary as grasping]

applause *n.* [1990s] (US Black) gonorrhoea. [pun on CLAP n.]

apple *n.[1]* [early 19C–1920s] (US) a piece of horse manure. [abbr. ROAD-APPLE]

apple *n.[2]* [late 19C+] a person. [the image of apple in 'one rotten apple']

apple *n.[3]* [late 19C+] a foolish person, a 'sucker'. [? the innocent wholesomeness of the fruit]

apple *n.[4]* [20C] the head. [supposed resemblance]

Apple *n.[5]* [1930s+] (orig. US jazz) New York City. [abbr. BIG APPLE]

apple *n.[6]* [1960s–70s] (US Black) money.

apple *n.[7]* [1960s+] (drugs) any pill capsule coloured red (cf. REDS). [resemblance to the fruit]

apple *n.[8]* [1960s+] (drugs) anyone who does not use drugs. [? the sort of person who would bring an apple for teacher]

apple *n.[9]* [1960s+] (orig. US Black) a large-brimmed, oversized hat, in 1930s–40s style. [? APPLE-KNOCKER n.[2]; such a hat being similar to those worn by a farm-worker to keep off the sun or f. the size, fig. resembling that of the BIG APPLE]

apple *n.[10]* [1970s+] (US Black) the vagina (cf. BANANA n.[2]; BIT OF JAM; BONNE-BOUCHE; BREAD n.[3]; BUTTER n.[3]; CAKES n.[1]; CHERRY PIE; DOUGHNUT n.[3]; FLY n.[3]; FLITTER n.[1]; GOLDEN DOUGHNUT; GROCERIES n.[1]; HO CAKE; HOLY DORITO; HONEY ALTAR; HONEYPOT n.[1]; JAM n.[3]; JAMPOT n.[2]; JELLY n.[1]; JELLY BAG; JELLY BOX; JELLY ROLL; LEMON n.[3]; LOLLIPOP n.[1]; MEDLAR; MOSSY DOUGHNUT; MUFFIN n.[4]; ORANGE n.[1]; PANCAKE n.[1]; PIE n.[3]; PINEAPPLE n.[1]; PLUM-TREE; SPLIT APRICOT; SPLIT FIG; SUGAR BASIN). [back-form. f. 16C APPLE SQUIRE, although that *apple* orig. meant breast; it also can be some-thing to EAT v.[3]]

apple *n.[11]* [1980s+] a derog. term for a Native American who is condemned as insufficiently nationalistic (cf. BANANA n.[2]; BOUNTY BAR; COCONUT n.[3]; OREO; UNCLE TOMAHAWK). [such a person is 'red on the outside but white within']

apple and pip, to *phr.* [late 19C+] **1** to sip. **2** to urinate. [rhy. sl. *apple and pip* = backsl. *sip* = PISS]

apple-blossom two-step *n.* [20C] diarrhoea, often contracted on a foreign holiday (cf. AZTEC HOP; AZTEC REVENGE; AZTEC TWO-STEP; CAIRO CRUD; CRAB-APPLE TWO-STEP; DELHI BELLY; GIS; GREEN-APPLE QUICKSTEP; GYPPY TUMMY; HONG KONG DOG; KING TUT'S REVENGE; MEXICALI REVENGE; MEXICAN FOXTROT; MEXICAN TOOTHACHE; MEXICAN TWO-STEP; MONTEZUMA'S REVENGE; PATA-GONIAN PASODOBLE; RANGOON RUNS; SINGAPORE TUMMY; SPANISH TUMMY; TOURISTAS; WOG GUT). [? play on SOUR-APPLE QUICKSTEP]

apple-cart *n.* [18C+] the human body. [pun on the SE, a *cart* for carrying *apples*, with a poss. link to APPLE n.[4]; there is no connection, despite appearances, to the phr. *upset the apple-cart*, which refers directly to the SE. However, the phr. *down with his apple-cart!*, knock or throw him down! (Hotten, 1867), seems to suggest a human rather than a vegetable image]

apple-catchers *n.* [1990s] outsized knickers. [one could use them for harvesting apples]

apple core *n.* [1950s] £20. [rhy. sl. *apple core* = SCORE n.[1]]

apple-dumpling shop *n.* [late 18C] the female breasts (cf. APPLES n.[1]).

apple fritter *n.* [20C] bitter beer. [rhy. sl.]

applehead *n.* [1950s+] (US) a fool. [APPLE n.[3] + sfx. -HEAD (1)]

apple in the white folks' yard *phr.* [1900s–20s] (US Black/South) a Black person who is very well thought of by Whites. [? f. SE phr. *apple of one's eye*]

applejack *n.[1]* [1950s–60s] (US Black) a generic name for a dance, esp. the current vogue step.

applejack *n.[2]* [1970s] (US Black) a large-brimmed, oversized hat in 1930s–40s style. [ext. of APPLE n.[9]]

applejack *n.[3]* [1980s+] (drugs) cocaine. [rhy. sl. CRACK n.[17]]

apple-john *n.* [17C] a foolish old man. [SE *apple-john*, a kind of apple said to keep for two years and to have reached perfection when shrivelled and withered]

apple knock *v.* [20C] to act the yokel, to behave in an unsophisticated manner. [APPLE-KNOCKER n.[2]]

apple-knocker *n.[1]* [20C] (US) a privy. [such a privy is situated beneath an apple tree and the user can hear apples knocking on its roof]

apple-knocker *n.[2]* [1910s+] (US) **1** a rural, unsophisticated person (cf. ALVIN; APPLE-PICKER; CLOD n.1; CLOD-BUSTER; CLOD-HOPPER; CLOD-JUMPER; CLOD-KNOCKER; CLOD-MASHER; CLOVER-KICKER; CORNCRACKER n.[1]; CORNTHRASHER; COUNTRY BOOKIE; CRACKER n.[4]; GULLY-JUMPER; HAYMAKER n.[2]; HAY-PITCHER; HAY-POUNDER; HAYSEED; HAY-TOSSER; MOSS-JUMPER; PECKERWOOD; RIDGERUNNER; STOMP-JUMPER; STUBBLE-JUMPER; STUMP-JUMPER; WHITE TRASH). **2** a fool. [APPLE n.[3] + SE *knocker*, one who hits. The image is of the fool or unsophisticate knuckling his forehead in wonder or incomprehension; ult. origin may be in New York City, referring to the up-state, rural areas with their many apple orchards]

apple-monger *n.* [18C] a pimp (cf. APPLE SQUIRE; APRON KNIGHT; APRON SQUIRE; SMOCK MERCHANT; SMOCK PENSIONER; SMOCK PIECE; SMOCKSTER; SQUIRE OF THE BODY; SQUIRE OF THE PLACKET). [APPLE n.[1] + SE *monger*, dealer or trafficker]

apple-peeler *n.* [mid-19C; 1970s] a knife. [the term was revived by Citizens' Band radio users]

apple-picker *n.* [1910s] (US) a fool, an unsophisticated person, a country person. [var. on APPLE-KNOCKER n.[2]; their stereotyped occupation]

apple pie *n.* [20C] the sky. [rhy. sl.]

apple pie *adj.* [20C] (US) neat, tidy. [abbr. APPLE-PIE ORDER]

apple-pie order *adj.* [18C+] neat, tidy. [ety. unknown. Such suggestions that exist include a corruption of *cap à pie* (Fr. head to foot), the arrangement of the ingredients of an apple pie as they are laid neatly in a dish, and a corruption of *alpha-beta*, esp. as in the nursery rhyme that runs 'A ate it, B bit it, C cut it, D divided it …'. Perhaps the most acceptable is that proposed in *Brewer* (1995): f. Fr. *nappe plié*, folded linen, which may also give the practical joker's 'apple-pie bed']

apple-pips *n.* [1900s–20s] the lips. [rhy. sl.]

apple polish *v.* [1920s+] to curry favour, to toady (cf. APPLE UP). [back-form. f. APPLE-POLISHER]

apple-polisher *n.* [1920s+] a toady, a sycophant; alternative US versions incl. *apple-pusher, apple-shiner, apple-washer.* [APPLE POLISH; the image suggests that the apple being polished is that presented to the teacher by the class goody-goody]

apples *n.*[1] [16C+] **1** the female breasts (cf. APPLE-DUMPLING SHOP; AVOCADOS; BAPS; CAKES; CASABA; CATHEADS; CHESTNUTS; COCONUTS n.[1]; CUPCAKE; DANGLEBERRIES; DINGLEBERRIES; DOO-BERRY; DUMPLINGS; GOODIES; GRAPEFRUIT; GRAPES n.[1]; JUJUBES; LEMONS n.; LOLLIES; MANGOES; MELONS; WATERMELONS). **2** [19C+] the testicles (cf. APRICOTS). [the rounded shape; in (1) the term has survived but became more a euph. than sl. by 20C]

apples *n.*[2] [mid-19C+] stairs (cf. APPLES AND PEARS). [rhy. sl.]

apples *n.*[3] [1990s] (drugs) MDMA (cf. ECSTASY). [the vague similarity of the pill to the fruit]

apples *adj.* [1940s+] (Aus./N.Z.) satisfactory, as required, esp. in phr. *she'll be apples,* it will be fine. [APPLE-PIE ORDER or rhy. sl. APPLES AND SPICE; although primarily assoc. with Aus., apples is used by the residents of Brooklyn, New York, to mean the same thing]

apples and pears *n.* [19C+] stairs; in mid-19C *apple and pears.* [rhy. sl.]

apples and rice *phr.* [20C] nice, usu. ironic (cf. APPLES adj.). [rhy. sl.]

apples and spice *adj.* [1940s+] (Aus.) satisfactory. [rhy. sl. apples and spice = SE *nice;* note APPLES adj.]

apple sauce *n.*[1] [20C] (Aus.) a horse. [rhy. sl.]

apple sauce *n.*[2] [1920s+] (US) nonsense, balderdash (cf. BALONEY n.[1]; BANANA OIL; GAMMON n.[1]; MACARONI n.[5]; RHUBARB n.[3]). [orig. 1920s journalese]

apple sauce *n.*[3] [1920s+] (orig. US) flattery, insincere talk, impudence. [the old boarding-house trick of serving an excess of cheaply produced apple sauce to mask the deficiencies in the portions and quality of other food]

apple sauce *n.*[4] [1920s+] (US) anything easy (cf. CAKEWALK n.; DUCK SOUP; EASY AS CAKE AND ICE-CREAM; PIECE OF CAKE;). [APPLE SAUCE n.[2]]

apple sauce *v.* [1920s+] (US) to take advantage of, to flatter. [APPLE SAUCE n.[3]]

applesauce! *excl.* [late 19C] (US) rubbish! piffle! [APPLE SAUCE n.[2]]

apple-shaker *n.* [mid–late 19C] (US) a rural, unsophisticated person (cf. APPLE-KNOCKER n.[2]).

apple shine *v.* [20C] to toady, to curry favour (cf. APPLE POLISH; APPLE UP).

apple-squeezer *n.* [1930s] (US) a rural, unsophisticated person (cf. APPLE-KNOCKER n.[2]).

apple squire *n.* [16C–18C] a pimp (cf. APPLE-MONGER; SQUIRE n.[1]). [poss. f. APPLES n.[1] (1) + SE *squire,* mocking the esquire or the 'country squire'; cf. KNIGHT OF THE ... and its combs.]

apples to ashes *phr.* [late 19C–1900s] (US) an absolute certainty (cf. ALL THE WORLD TO A CHINA ORANGE). [the odds are absurd]

apple tart *n.* [20C] (Aus.) a breaking of wind; thus used as v., e.g. *he apple tarted.* [rhy. sl. SE *fart*]

Appleton/Fernandez talking *phr.* [20C] (W.I.) used of one who is drunk and talking nonsensically or aggressively (cf. IT'S THE BEER TALKING; LIQUOR'S TALKING; RUM TALKING). [the brandnames of two popular rums, distilled in, respectively, Jam. and Trin.]

apple up *v.* [20C] (US) to toady, to curry favour (cf. APPLE POLISH; GRAPE UP; WAX UP). [the image of giving an apple to teacher]

apply a crimp, to *phr.* [late 19C] (US) to thwart, to impair, to interfere with (cf. PUT A CRIMP INTO). [SE *apply + crimp* v. to compress, to crumple]

apply lawyer foot, to *phr.* [1950s] (W.I.) to run away. [the image is of a foot that, like a lawyer, helps one 'get away']

apply lip gloss, to *phr.* [1980s+] of a woman, to masturbate. [the image of vaginal secretions coating the labia]

apply the hand brake, to *phr.* [1980s+] to masturbate (cf. ADJUST ONE'S SET).

apply the oil, to *phr.* [19C+] to flatter, to curry favour. [SE *apply* + BANANA OIL]

appropriate the means, to *phr.* [1980s+] to masturbate. [pun. on the language of revolutionary manifestos, 'appropriate the means of production']

appy *n.* [1980s+] (S.Afr.) an apprentice. [abbr.]

apricock water *n.* **1** [early 18C] apricot ale. **2** [early–mid-18C] gin. [16C–18C sp. of SE *apricot*]

apricots *n.* [1990s] (Aus.) the testicles (cf. APPLES n.[1]; BERRIES n.[1]; CHRIST-APPLES; CONKERS; DINGLEBERRY; GOOSEBERRIES; JINGLE-BERRY; LOVE APPLES; PLUMS). [shape]

April fools *n.* [20C] **1** stools (for sitting). **2** tools. **3** football pools. [rhy. sl.]

April gentleman *n.* [late 16C] a newly married man. [the popularity of spring weddings]

April showers *n.* [20C] flowers. [rhy. sl.]

apron *n.*[1] [17C+] a wife, a woman, esp. when used generically (cf. CRINOLINE; PETTICOAT; SKIRT; SMOCK). [20C use is mainly US Black]

apron *n.*[2] [20C] a bartender. [metonymy; i.e. the garment they wear]

apron and gaiters *n.* [late 19C–1910s] a bishop, a dean. [metonymy; i.e. their vestments]

aproneer *n.* **1** [mid-17C] a Roundhead. **2** [mid-17C–early 18C] a shopkeeper. [the aristocratic Cavaliers made this contemptuous link between 'trade' (symbolized by a worker's apron) and their parliamentary rivals]

aproner *n.* [early–mid-17C] a bartender. [APRON n.[2]]

apron husband *n.* [17C] a man who is seen as involving himself excessively in his wife's business (cf. APRON-STRING HOLD). [APRON n.[1] + SE *husband*]

apron knight *n.* [16C] a pimp (cf. APPLE-MONGER).

apron-rogue *n.* [17C] a labourer, an artisan. [a play on SE synon. *apron-man*]

apron squire *n.* [16C] a pimp (cf. APPLE-MONGER).

apron-string hold/tenure *n.* [mid-17C–early 19C] an estate that a man holds only during the lifetime of his wife (cf. APRON HUSBAND; PETTICOAT HOLD).

apron-up *adj.* [19C+] pregnant. [the use of an apron to hide a pregnancy, also f. the inevitable raising of the apron's profile as the foetus grows]

apron-washings *n.* [late 19C–1900s] porter. [image of a brewery worker wringing out their beer-soaked apron]

apsay *n.* [19C+] (US) a fool. [pig Latin, SAP n.[2]]

aqua *n.* [19C] water. [Ital. *acqua,* Ling. Fr. *akwa*]

aqua lung *n.* [1980s+] (US drugs) a long pipe, which is placed in a bucket of water to cool the smoke (cf. AUTO). [SE 'a portable diving apparatus consisting of containers of compressed air ... which feed air automatically through a valve and mouthpiece to the diver as he requires it' (*OED*)]

arab *n.*[1] [19C] **1** a street urchin. **2** (US) any wild or excitable looking person. **3** (US) a street pedlar. [orig. 'Arab of the streets', 'city Arab' f. the traditionally nomadic and derog. stereotype of Middle Eastern Arabs]

arab *n.*[2] [20C] (US) a derog. term for a Jew. [ARAB n.[1] (3) + a ref. to Jewish and Arabic Semitic origins; coined by *Variety* magazine writer Jack Conway *c.*1925]

arab *n.*[3] [20C] (US) a street bookmaker, an illicit bookmaker. [ARAB n.[1]]

arab v.[1] [20C] (US) to sell or peddle on the streets. [ARAB n.[1] + negative racial stereotype]

arab v.[2] [20C] to work as a street bookmaker. [ARAB n.[3]]

arabber n. [20C] a street urchin (cf. AYRABA). [ARAB n.[1]]

arbor vitae n. [18C] the penis. [Lat. *arbor vitae*, the tree of life; the SE use to refers to various evergreen trees; thus ? pun on GREENS n.[2]]

arbour n. [19C] the vagina (cf. AGREEABLE RUTS OF LIFE; AXIS; BREACH; CANYON; CAVE OF HARMONY n.[1]; CHASM; CHINK n.[2]; CRACK n.[1]; CRANNY n.[1]; CREVICE; CRINKUM-CRANKUM; CUPID'S ARBOUR; CYPRIAN ARBOUR; CYPRIAN CAVE; DITCH n.[1]; GAP n.[1]; GAPE n.[1]; GASH n.[1]; GROTTO; GULF; GUTTER n.[1]; HARBOUR; LOVE'S HARBOUR; NEST n.[1]; NICK n.[3]; NICK IN THE NOTCH; NOTCH n.[1]; PLACKET; PLACKET-BOX; PRIME CUT; SLASH n.[2]; SLICE OF LIFE; SLIT n.[1]; SLOT n.[2]; TRENCH). [SE *arbour*, a shady retreat]

Archbishop Laud n. [1950s] fraud. [rhy. sl.; the term (used in Cook, *The Crust on its Uppers* (1962)) may, like a number of similar citations, be a nonce-word; ult. William *Laud* (1573–1645), Archbishop of Canterbury]

Archbishop of Cant n. [1930s+] any Anglican archbishop. [the obvious abbr. is f. Archbishop of Canterbury, but note SE *cant*: 'affected or unreal use of religious or pietistic phraseology. Language (or action) implying the pretended assumption of goodness or piety' (*OED*)]

arch-cove n. [17C–19C] (Und.) the leader of a gang of thieves (cf. ARCH-ROGUE). [SE *arch*, principal + COVE]

arch-dell n. [17C–late 18C] (Und.) the woman accomplice of a criminal gang-leader (cf. ARCH-DOXY; ARCH-ROGUE). [SE *arch*, principal + DELL n.]

arch-doxy n. [17C–18C] (Und.) the woman accomplice of a gang-leader (cf. ARCH-DELL). [SE pfx. *arch-* + DOXY]

arch-duke n. [late 17C–late 18C] a comical or eccentric person. [? a specific archduke. E.P. suggests the Duke in Shakespeare's *Measure for Measure* (1604), who is 'certainly eccentric enough to serve as an archetype']

archer n. [20C] £2000 (cf. BERNIE n.[2]; BRADBURY; BRADS; FISHER n.[2]; FISHER'S FLIMSIES; SCROPE). [a sum of £2000, the disputed payment of which formed the basis of the libel case brought in 1987 against the *Daily Star* newspaper by the writer Jeffrey *Archer* (now Lord Archer, b.1940)]

archer up n. [late 19C] a certainty. [the champion jockey Fred *Archer* (1857–86) and thus phr. 'Archer is up in the saddle', which, to betting men, more than likely meant a winning horse]

arch-gonnof n. [19C] (Und.) the leader of a gang of thieves (cf. ARCH-ROGUE). [SE *arch*, principal + Yid. *gonnif*, a thief]

archie/archy n. [20C] (Aus.) a young station-hand, prob. a well-connected young man out from the UK (cf. ALGIE). [proper name, seen as upper class]

architorture n. [1990s] (US campus) a course in architecture. [perversion of SE]

archives n. [1980s+] (US campus) a thing of the past, used in phr. *I'm archives*, 'goodbye, I'm leaving' (cf. ART).

arch-rogue n. **1** [early 17C–late 18C] the leader of a gang of thieves (cf. ARCH-COVE). **2** [mid-17C–late 19C] a confirmed villain. [SE *arch*, chief, principal + ROGUE n.[1]]

archy see ARCHIE.

arctic adj. [20C] (US campus) of a person, emotionally chilly, very distant (cf. CHILLY adj.; COOL adj.[2]). [SE *arctic* conditions, extremely cold]

ard adj. [17C–19C] hot. [Fr. *ardent*, passionate, eager]

ardent n. [mid–late 19C] (orig. US) spirits. [SE *ardent* spirits]

ards n. [17C] (Und.) the foot. [? related to the Nordic *ard*, plough, a term used in archaeology to describe the style of plough in use during the Bronze Age]

area n. **1** [19C] the pubic hair. **2** [1970s+] (US campus) the genitals. [euph. abbr. SE *pubic area*, genital area]

area-sneak n. [19C] a thief who specializes in robbing basements. [SE *area*, the small sunken court adjacent to the basement of a house + *sneak* (thief), a small-time thief]

aren't you the one! excl. [1940s+] an excl. expressing one's grudging admiration (cf. YOU ARE A ONE!). [ONE n.[4] (1)]

arer adv. [late 19C] more so, to any greater extent. [a fake 'comparative' of SE *are*, e.g. 'We *are*, and what's more, we can't be any arer' (Ware)]

are you kidding? phr. [1940s+] you can't be serious, surely you're joking. [KID v.]

are you prepared?/ready? excl. [1960s+] (gay) implying amazement or shock, both approving and disapproving.

are your boots laced? phr. [1930s–40s] (US Black) a general query as to the state of affairs; is everything in order? are you ready? do you understand?

are you saving it for the worms? phr. [1940s+] (orig. US) addressed to a supposed virgin, this phr. is intended to shame or bluster her into intercourse. [SE *worm's meat*, a corpse]

arf a mo see ALF A MO.

arfto see AFTO.

arfy-darfy see ON THE ARFY-DARFY.

arge n. [1940s–50s] silver. [SE *argent*, silver]

argee/r.g. n. [mid-19C] (US) inferior whisky. [abbr. ROTGUT]

Argie n. [1980s+] an Argentinian. [coined 1982 by Britain's *Sun* newspaper, as part of its jingoistic approach to the Falklands War (1982)]

argle-bargle/argol-bargol v. [late 19C] to have an argument (cf. ARGY-BARGY). [? SE *argue* + *haggle*; note *argle*, 16C, to dispute, 19C to bandy words]

argue/talk the leg off an iron pot/the hind leg off a donkey, to phr. [late 19C+] to be extremely contentious or argumentative. [iron pots are inanimate; donkeys are very stubborn]

argue the toss, to phr. [late 19C–1920s] to argue long and loud. [the tossing of a coin; later use is SE]

argufy v. [18C–1940s] (US Black/South) to argue. [Gullah, the dial. spoken by Black people living on the sea islands and tide-water coastline of South Carolina and Georgia]

argy-bargy n. [19C] argument, confusion, confrontation (cf. ARGLE-BARGLE). [SE *argument*, abbr. to 'argy', then re-duplicated]

ari see ARRIS.

aries n. [1980s+] (drugs) heroin. [ety. unknown; the obvious link is to the astrological sign, but why?]

aristippus n. [early 17C–late 18C] **1** Canary wine. **2** a diet drink, made of sarsaparilla, cinchona bark and other in-gredients, available at certain coffee houses. [proper name *Aristippus* (c.435–366BC), Greek philosopher and founder of the rigorously hedonistic Cyreneiac school of philo-sophy]

aristotle n. [late 19C+] **1** the buttocks, the behind (cf. ARRIS). **2** a bottle. [rhy. sl.]

arithmetic bug n. [1910s+] (US) a louse. [so-called because 'they added to our troubles, subtracted from our pleasures, divided our attention and multiplied like -ll' (W. Carter, *Devil Dog*, 1920)]

arithmetic midget n. [1990s] (US teen) an individual lack-ing maths skills. [note US Army *double-digit midget*, one whose 365 days' service in Vietnam has fallen to 99 days or less]

Arizona n. [20C] in short-order use, buttermilk. [the belief that anyone who orders buttermilk (rather than liquor) ought to be in Arizona for their health]

Arizona adj. [20C] (US) a generic derog. term, usu. found in a variety of combs. (cf. ALABAMA; ARKANSAS). [the stereotyping of the state and its natives as poor and backward]

Arizona cloudburst n. [20C] (US) a sandstorm (cf. IDAHO RAINSTORM; MORMON RAIN; OKLAHOMA RAIN). [ARIZONA adj. + SE *cloudburst*]

Arizona nightingale n. [20C] a donkey or mule (cf. COLORADO MOCKINGBIRD; DESERT CANARY; MEXICAN CARRIAGE; MEXICAN JEEP; MEXICAN QUARTER-HORSE; MOUNTAIN NIGHTINGALE; ROCKY MOUNTAIN CANARY). [ARIZONA adj. + SE *nightingale*; its bray is quite the opposite of that of the mellifluous bird]

Arizona paint job n. [20C] (US) no paint at all. [ARIZONA adj. + SE *paint job*]

Arizona tenor n. [20C] (US) a victim of tuberculosis who coughs deeply and often. [ARIZONA adj. + SE *tenor*]

ark n. [1920s+] (US) a low bar-room, a 'dive'. [? fig. use of Noah's *Ark*, i.e. a refuge from the hostile world]

ark and wins/winns n. [late 18C–mid-19C] a sculler, a rowing boat. [SE *ark* ? + WIN n., i.e. the cost of its hire]

Arkansas/arkansaw adj. [20C] (US) a generic derog. term, usu. found in a variety of combs. (cf. ALABAMA; ARIZONA). [the stereotyping of the state and its natives as poor, dishonest and backward]

Arkansas asphalt n. [20C] (US) logs laid side by side to form a 'corduroy' road. [orig. logging jargon]

Arkansas chicken n. [20C] (US) salt pork (cf. ADIRONDACK STEAK). [ARKANSAS + SE *chicken*]

Arkansas credit card n. [1970s] (US) a piece of hose used to syphon petrol from another car into the tank of one's own (cf. HARLEM CREDIT CARD; OKLAHOMA CREDIT CARD). [ironic use of SE]

Arkansas fire extinguisher n. [20C] (US) a chamberpot. [ARKANSAS + SE *fire extinguisher*]

Arkansas lizard n. [20C] (US) a flea, a louse. [ARKANSAS + SE *lizard*]

Arkansas special/traveller n. [20C] (US) a little-used railway branchline. [ARKANSAS + SE *special/traveller*]

Arkansas T-bone n. [20C] (US) bacon (cf. ADIRONDACK STEAK). [ARKANSAS + SE *T-bone* (steak)]

Arkansas toothpick n. [19C] (US) a large knife, similar to a Bowie knife (cf. CALIFORNIA TOOTHPICK; HARLEM TOOTHPICK; KANSAS NECK-BLISTER; TOOTHPICK n.[1]). [ARKANSAS + SE *toothpick*]

Arkansas traveller see ARKANSAS SPECIAL.

Arkansas wedding cake n. [20C] (US) corn bread. [ARKANSAS + SE *wedding cake*; plain corn bread is the antithesis of a rich wedding cake]

arkansaw adj. see ARKANSAS.

arkansaw v. [20C] (US) **1** to cheat, to take advantage of. **2** to shoot in an unsportsmanlike manner, whether targeting animals or humans. **3** to share expenses, esp. of a meal (cf. GO DUTCH). [ARKANSAS]

ark-floater n. [19C] a veteran actor. [Noah's *Ark* (synon. for antiquity) + theatre jargon *floats*, footlights]

Arkie see ARKY n.

ark-man/ackman n. [18C] (Und.) a river thief, who specializes in robbing river traffic (cf. ACK-RUFF; ARK-PIRATE; ARK-RUFF). [SE *ark*, a ship or boat]

ark-pirate n. [18C–19C] (Und.) a river thief. [var. on ARK-MAN]

ark-ruff/-ruffian n. [18C–19C] (Und.) a river thief. [var. on ARK-MAN]

Arky/Arkie n. [1920s+] (US) a (usu. White, usu. poor) native of Arkansas (cf. OKIE n.[1]). [abbr.]

arky adj. [late 19C] (US) old-fashioned, out-of-date. [SE Noah's *Ark*, back to which the things in question may supposedly date, although there may also be a link to *archaic*]

arkymalarkey n. [1930s] (US) nonsense. [ACKAMARACKUS (2)]

arm/arm of the law n.[1] [19C+] a policeman, often as *long arm …* (cf. LIMB OF THE LAW). [such an 'arm' reaches out towards the criminal]

arm n.[2] **1** [1960s] influence, power (cf. PUT THE ARM ON). **2** [1990s] (Black) an armed robbery.

arm n.[3] [1960s+] (S.Afr. drugs) a measure of cannabis, approx. the size of a maize cob and weighing about 2kg (4¼lb) (cf. HAND n.[3]).

arm n.[4] [1970s+] the penis (cf. SHORT ARM). [it, too, sticks out from the body]

arm aerobics see DO THE ARM AEROBICS.

arm candy n. [1990s] a pretty girl whose role is merely to adorn the arm of her male companion (cf. EAR CANDY; EYE CANDY).

armed for bear, to be phr. [20C] to be very heavily armed. [hunting jargon, the killing of bears requires a large weapon]

arming the cannon n. [1990s] masturbation. [CANNON n.[1] (2)]

arm of the law see ARM n.[1].

armour see IN ONE'S ARMOUR.

armpit n. [1960s+] (orig. US) the least appetizing, poorest, most rundown and possibly dangerous area of a city or town; often as *armpit of the nation/universe* (cf. ARSEHOLE n.). [the link of the SE *armpit* with dirt and smell]

arm-props n. [19C] crutches.

arms and legs n. [19C+] weak beer or tea, i.e. a drink that has 'no body'.

armstrong adj. [20C] used to describe anything that is operated by hand rather than by machinery. [SE *arm* + *strong*]

armstrong heater n. [20C] (US) one's arms, when embracing a loved one. [a pun on SE *strong arm*]

army and navy n. [20C] gravy. [rhy. sl.]

army brat n. [1930s+] (orig. US) the son, or more usually daughter, of a commissioned officer.

army game n. [late 19C+] (US) **1** poker, chuck-a-luck, FIND THE LADY or any other gambling game played outside the casino in army camps and similar establishments. **2** trickery, deceit, passing responsibility onto others. [the popularity of chuck-a-luck among US Civil War soldiers. The hit 1950s British Army-based sitcom, *The Army Game*, may have reflected (2), but more likely refers to 17C SE *game*, dodges, tricks + an ironic use of *game* as 'life, way of doing things']

army Latin n. [mid-19C] (US) obscene language. [typically that used by irascible drill sergeants]

army rocks n. [late 19C+] socks (cf. ALMOND ROCKS). [rhy. sl.]

army style n. [1960s+] (US gay) oral sex followed by beating up the fellator, presumably to prove one's 'masculinity'. [ironic use of SE]

arnchy n. [20C] (US Black) one who puts on airs. [? corruption of SE *aren't you*, e.g. 'aren't you the one', 'aren't you the big shot' etc]

arnold/Mr Arnold n. [1970s+] (W.I.) pork. [ety. unknown]

aroma n. [1970s+] (drugs) amyl nitrite (cf. AIMIES n.[2]). [amyl nitrite, used in medicine to stimulate the heart and recreationally to enhance the moment of orgasm, has a strong 'rotten banana' smell]

aroma of men n. [1970s+] (drugs) isobutyl nitrite. [a substitute for amyl nitrite popular in gay clubs]

-aroonie see -EROONIE.

around adj. [18C] at a loss, ruined.

around the bend phr. [20C] mad, insane (cf. AROUND THE TWIST; HARPIC). [old naut. jargon *round the bend*, mad; the image is one of one who is 'not straight']

around the horn phr. [1940s+] (US) having experienced unpleasant treatment. [? ref. to a voyage 'around Cape Horn', a notably rough journey]

around the twist phr. [20C] mad, insane (cf. AROUND THE BEND).

around the way phr. [1980s+] (W.I./UK Black teen) from the neighbourhood.

around-the-way girl n. [1990s] (US Black) a young woman from the neighbourhood or ghetto (cf. HOMEGIRL). [AROUND THE WAY + SE *girl*]

around the world/tongue bath *phr.* [1960s+] licking and sucking the partner's body, incl. the genitals and sometimes the anus. [the tongue 'travels' around the body; usu. used by a prostitute as part of the 'menu' of paid services she can offer]

array *v.* [late 14C–mid-16C] to discomfit, to thrash, to drub. [SE *array*, to dress, thus to 'dress down']

arrest *v.* [20C] (US campus) to accuse another of dressing unfashionably, usu. behind their back (cf. FASHION ARREST). [SE *arrest*; note 'fashion police', journalists and other 'style makers' who determine what is and is not fashionable]

arrested by the bailiff of marshland *phr.* [late 16C–19C] stricken with ague. [ague, a malarial fever, can be caused by damp conditions]

arrested by the white serjeant *phr.* [late 18C–late 19C] said of a man who has been fetched out of the tavern by his wife.

'arrico veins *n.* [late 19C–1900s] varicose veins. [mispron. + ? a pun on Fr. *haricot verts*, green beans]

'arriet *see* 'ARRY.

arris/ari/arry *n.* [20C] the buttocks, the behind. [rhy. sl. *Aristotle* = BOTTLE = BOTTLE AND GLASS = ARSE n.[1]]

arrive at the end of the sentimental journey, to *phr.* [late 19C–1910s] of a man, to have sexual intercourse. [literary euph.; the conclusion of Laurence Sterne's *Sentimental Journey* (1768), in which the narrator obviously retires to bed with a chambermaid]

arrow *n.* [late 19C+] a dart; thus the *arrows game*, darts (cf. IN GOOD ARROW).

arry *see* ARRIS.

'arry/'arriet *n.* [late 19C–1900s] the typical Cockney man or woman; thus *'arryish*, typical of a coster (cf. LIZE; MOSE n.[1]; 'RIA). [popular proper name]

'arrydom *n.* [late 19C–1900s] the world of the typical Cockney costermonger. ['ARRY + sfx. *-dom*, position, condition]

arry's gators *phr.* [1940s+] (Aus.) thank you. [Jap. *arigato*, thank you]

'arry's worrier *n.* [late 19C–1900s] a concertina. ['ARRY + SE *worrier*]

arse/ass *n.*[1] **1** [17C+] the buttocks. **2** [19C+] (in a sexual context) the vagina (cf. ARSE-OPENER) **3** [20C] one's person, one's body (cf. BOHUNKUS). **4** [20C] an unpleasant person, esp. a fool, idiot (cf. ARSEHOLE). **5** [1940s+] (orig. US/Aus.) sexual conquests; thus generic for a woman when viewed purely as a sex object, often as *a bit of arse/ass* (cf. PIECE OF ARSE/ASS). [note: the spellings ARSE and ASS (respectively UK and US) are often interchangeable and in that case have been included at the same headword, e.g. ARSEHOLE/ASSHOLE. Where usage is nation-specific, the relevant sp. has been used. SE to *c.*1660, then sl. Its sources include a variety of words found in several Teutonic and Scandinavian languages. The nearest relation is the German *arsch*, and there are definite links back to the Greek *orros* and *orsos*. In English it dates at least to 1000, when it is spelt *ars*, *ears* or *ars*. The modern sp. appears *c.*1300. Britain's a-r-s-e and America's a-s-s are synonymous, but it should be noted that Shakespeare opts for *ass*, often in a punning context, on several occasions. Once rendered taboo, *arse* was to be resisted in polite conversation and printed only after the exclusion of crucial consonants, typically by Grose, who prefers *a–e* to the full-blown word. It remained off-limits, at least in print, until 1930, when Frederic Manning used it in full in his memoir of World War I, *Her Privates We* (itself a slightly bawdy pun). Since then the word has become relatively acceptable, and such phr. as ARSE ABOUT or NOT KNOW ONE'S ARSE FROM ONE'S ELBOW, while not yet SE, are as much colloq. as sl. That said, *arse/ass*, remains one of those 'filthy words' cited in 1978 by the US Federal Communications Commission as indecent, if not actually obscene]

arse *n.*[2] [20C] (W.I.) **1** an intensifier, used when referring to a person as 'self', e.g. *he pays their arse to do nothing*. **2** a comparative intensifier, e.g. *cold as arse*. [fig. use of ARSE n.[1]]

arse *n.*[3] [1940s+] (Aus.) cheek, effrontery. [fig. use of ARSE n.[1]]

arse *n.*[4] [1950s+] (Aus.) dismissal from a job; thus *get/give the arse*, to be dismissed, to dismiss. [fig. use of ARSE n.[1]]

arse/ass, the *n.*[5] [1960s+] (orig. US) a bad temper (cf. RED ARSE). [fig. use of ARSE n.[1]]

arse/ass *v.*[1] [17C+] to act, to behave, usu. in a comb. and usu. in a manner that is disapproved or incompetent (cf. ARSE ABOUT; ARSE AROUND; ARSE UP). [SE *ass*, to act the ass, to behave like a donkey. The orig. ety. undoubtedly refers to the animal, but the sense, as born out by the sp. of the combs., refers to ARSE n.[1] (4), since in all cases the behaviour is related to an ARSE, a fool. That said, US sp. uses *ass around* etc, thus further confusing the issue]

arse/ass *v.*[2] [late 19C+] to leave, to exit, usu. in combs. e.g. ARSE OFF; ARSE OUT. [ARSE n.[1] (1)]

arse *v.*[3] [1950s+] to reverse a vehicle. [ARSE n.[1] (1)]

arse about *v.* [1920s+] **1** to fool around. **2** to waste time (cf. BUGGER ABOUT; FUCK ABOUT; PISS ABOUT; SOD ABOUT). [ARSE/ASS v.[1] + SE *about*; note the *OED* does offer one 17C citation – from Charles Cotton's *Scarronides* (1664) – but none after that until James Joyce's *Ulysses* (1922)]

arse about face *phr.* [late 19C+] back-to-front, in confusion (cf. ARSE BACKWARDS; ARSE ON BACKWARDS; ARSEY-VARSEY; ASS-BACKWARDS; ASS-END-BACKWARDS; ASS-END-TO; ASS-FRONTWARDS; ASS-SIDE-BEFORE; ASSWAYS; ASSY-FUSSY; BACK-ASSWARD; BACK-ENDED; BACK-END-TO; BASS-ACKWARDS; HALF-ASSED-BACKWARDS). [ARSE/ASS n.[1] (1) + SE *about face*]

arse/ass around *v.* [20C] to mess about, to play the fool, waste time (cf. ARSE ABOUT). [fig. use of ARSE/ASS v.[1] + SE *around*]

arse/ass backwards *adv.* [20C] out of order, back-to-front (cf. ARSE ABOUT FACE; BASS-ACKWARDS). [ARSE n.[1] (1) + SE *backwards*]

arse/ass bandit/brigand/king *n.* [20C] a homosexual male; thus *arse-banditry*, homosexuality (cf. ARSE PIRATE; ASS BURGLAR; BALLOON-KNOT BANDIT; BLUE-ARSED BANDIT; BOMB BANDIT; BOOTY BANDIT; BUM BANDIT; BUTT PIRATE). [ARSE n.[1] (1) + ironic use of SE *bandit*]

arse-cabbage *n.* [1990s] haemorrhoids (cf. ARSE-GRAPES). [ARSE n.[1] (1) + SE *cabbage*; f. the site and the physical appearance]

arse-cooler *n.* [mid–late 19C] a bustle on a woman's dress. [ARSE n.[1] (1) + SE *cooler*]

arse crawl *v.* [late 19C+] to toady to, to act as a sycophant; thus *arse-crawler*, a sycophant (cf. ARSE-LICK; ARSE-LICKER). [ARSE n.[1] (1) + SE *crawl*]

arsed/assed *adj.* [1980s+] bothered, concerned, e.g. *I can't be arsed to do it*. [ARSE n.[5]]

-arsed *sfx.* [16C+] having an ARSE, often describing shape or size, e.g. *bare-arsed*, *big-arsed*, *broad-arsed*. [ARSE n.[1] (1); the initial citation, before any use of arse became sl., is in Abbot Aelfric's *Glossary*, *c.*1000, as trans. of the Latin *tergosus*]

arsed/assed up *adj.* [20C] confused, mixed up; the mildest of such synons. as BUGGERED UP. [ARSE v.[1] (1) + SE *up*]

arse-/ass-end *n.* **1** [1930s+] the end, the rear end. **2** [1940s+] the least desirable piece of. **3** [1940s+] a very unappealing place, esp. in phr. *the arse-end of the universe*. [ARSE n.[1] (1) + SE *end*]

arse-grapes *n.* [1990s] haemorrhoids, piles (cf. ARSE-CABBAGE). [ARSE n.[1] (1) + SE *grapes*]

arsehole/asshole *n.* **1** [19C+] the anus. **2** [19C+] a general derog. term (cf. ARSEPIECE; CUNT n.[2]; PRICK; SHIT n.[2]). **3** [mid-19C+] (orig. US) the least appetizing, poorest, most rundown and possibly dangerous area of a city or town (cf. ARMPIT; ARSEHOLE OF THE UNIVERSE). [ARSE n.[1] (1) + SE *hole*]

arsehole v. [1950s+] (Aus.) to dismiss, to get rid of (cf. ARSE n.[1]). [ARSEHOLE n.]

arsehole bandit n. [1960s+] a homosexual male. [ext. of ARSE BANDIT]

arsehole crawl v. [1940s+] to grovel unashamedly, to play the sycophant. [ext. of ARSE CRAWL]

arsehole-crawler/-creeper n. [late 19C+] a sycophant (cf. ARSE-CRAWL; ARSE-LICKER). [ARSEHOLE n. + SE *crawler/creeper*]

arseholed/assholed adj. [20C] very drunk. [PISSED AS ARSEHOLES]

arsehole lucky adj. [1950s+] extremely fortunate.

arsehole/asshole of the universe/the world phr. [20C] applied to anywhere considered especially unpleasant, usu. hot and in the Third World by a Western expatriate. [note Primo Levi's ref. to Auschwitz as *anus mundi*, a Latin synon.]

arsehole-perisher n. [19C] a short jacket (cf. ARSEHOLE-SHAVER; BUM-FREEZER; BUM-BANGER; BUM-COOLER; BUM-CURTAIN; BUM-FREEZER; BUM-PERISHER; PERISHER n.[1]; SHAVER n.[3]). [ARSEHOLE n. + SE *perish*, to suffer the cold]

arseholes! excl. [20C] rubbish! nonsense! [ARSEHOLE]

arsehole-shaver n. [19C] a short jacket (cf. ARSEHOLE-PERISHER). [ARSEHOLE n. + SE *shave*, to touch lightly, to graze]

arseholes to breakfast time phr. [late 19C+] very unsatisfactory, totally confused, very chaotic (cf. BACKBONE TO BREAKFAST TIME).

arseholey adj. [20C] sycophantic. [ARSEHOLE CRAWLER]

arse king see ARSE BANDIT.

arse-/ass-kissing n. [1940s+] sycophancy. [ARSE n.[1] (1) + SE *kissing*]

arse/ass lick n. [1930s+] (orig. US) a toady, a sycophant, a groveller. [ARSE n.[1] (1) + SE *lick*]

arse-/ass-licker n. [1930s+] a toady, a sycophant (cf. A-LICKER; ARSE-WIPER; ASS-KISSER; ASS-SUCKER; ASS-WIPER; A-WIPER; BROWN-NOSER; BUM-CREEPER; BUM-SUCKER; FOOT-KISSER; HEEL-LICKER). [ARSE LICK]

arse-/ass-licking n. [1910s+] sycophancy, grovelling. [ARSE-LICKER]

arse-/ass-licking adj. [1930s+] extremely servile, grovelling. [ARSE n.[1] (1) + SE *licking*]

arselins coup n. [19C] sexual intercourse. [ARSE n.[1] (1) + sfx. *-ling*, implying direction + SE *coup*, fall; thus lit. 'falling backwards']

arse/ass man n. [1950s+] a man who finds a woman's buttocks her most alluring feature (cf. LEG MAN n.[2]; TIT MAN). [ARSE n.[1] (1) + SE *man* meaning an expert or specialist in or one who favours a specified product]

arsenal n. [1990s] the genitals (cf. ADAM'S ARSENAL).

arseness n. [20C] (W.I./Trin., Tob.) wilful stupidity. [ARSE n.[1] (4) + sfx. *-ness*, state or condition]

arse off v. [late 19C+] to leave quickly. [ARSE n.[2] + SE *off*]

arse/ass on backwards adj. [20C] back-to-front, confused (cf. ARSE ABOUT FACE). [ARSE n.[1] (1) + SE *backwards*]

arse-opener n. [19C+] the penis; one of a number of words that equate the penis with a weapon (cf. ARSE WEDGE; AX n.[2]; BACON BAZOOKA; BATTERING PIECE; BAYONET; BEARD-SPLITTER; BEAVER CLEAVER; BELLY RUFFIAN; BOW; BUSH-BEATER; CHERRY-SPLITTER; CHOPPER n.[1]; CLEAT; COCK-OPENER; CROWBAR; DING-DONG n.[4]; DONG n.[2]; GUN n.[2]; HAIR-DIVIDER; INSTRUMENT; MARROWBONE AND CLEAVER; MEAT AXE; MEAT-CLEAVER; PILE-DRIVER; PLUG-TAIL; POLL AXE; QUIMSTAKE; RUMP-SPLITTER; SHIT-STABBER; SHIT-STICK; SWACK n.[2]; SWIPE n.[2]; WEAPON; WEDGE n.[3]; WHAMMER). [ARSE n.[1] (1) + SE *opener*]

arse out v.[1] [late 19C+] to leave quickly. [ARSE v.[2] + SE *out*]

arse out v.[2] [1900s–10s] to dismiss from a job. [ARSE n.[4] + SE *out*]

arse/ass over apex phr. [1920s+] head-over-heels (cf. A. OVER T.; ARSE OVER APPETITE; ARSE OVER KETTLE; ARSE OVER TIT; ARSE OVER TURKEY).

arse/ass over appetite phr. [1930s+] head-over-heels (cf. ARSE OVER APEX). [ARSE n.[1] (1) + SE *appetite*]

arse over header n. [20C] (Aus.) the varsovienne, a dance, ? French origin, resembling some of the Polish national dances. [rhy. sl.; lit. Fr. *Varsovien*, f. *Varsovie*, Warsaw]

arse/ass over kettle/teakettle phr. [1940s+] head-over-heels (cf. ARSE OVER APEX; ARSE OVER KITE; ARSE UP-TO-TEACUP). [ARSE n.[1] (1) + SE *tea-kettle*]

arse over kite phr. [1960s+] (N.Z.) head-over-heels (cf. ARSE OVER KETTLE). [ARSE n.[1] (1) + northern UK dial. *kite*, the stomach]

arse/ass over tit phr. [1930s+] head-over-heels (cf. A. OVER T.; ARSE OVER APEX). [ARSE n.[1] (1) + TIT]

arse over turkey phr. [late 19C–1920s] head-over-heels (cf. ARSE OVER APEX). [ARSE n.[1] (1) + SE *turkey*]

arse-paper n. [1930s+] (N.Z.) lavatory paper. [ARSE n.[1] (1) + SE *paper*]

arsepiece n. [1990s] a general term of derision (cf. ARSEHOLE). [ARSE n.[1] (1) + SE *piece*]

arse pirate n. [1990s] a male homosexual man. [var. on ARSE BANDIT]

arse-piss n. [1990s] diarrhoea. [ARSE n.[1] (1) + PISS]

arser n. [20C] (orig. hunting/riding) a fall on one's behind. [ARSE n.[1] (1)]

arse rugs n. [19C] trousers. [ARSE n.[1] (1) + SE *rug*, a coarse material used as a cloak]

arse-stabber n. [1990s] a sodomite. [ARSE n.[1] (1) + SE *stabber*]

arse up v. [20C] to ruin, to make a mess of; thus intensified as *arse up with care* (cf. BUGGER UP; COCK UP v.[3]; FUCK UP v.[2]; SCREW UP v.[3]). [ARSE v.[1] (1) + SE *up*]

arse-/ass-up-to-teacup phr. [20C] head-over-heels (cf. ARSE OVER KETTLE).

arse upwards phr. [17C+] lucky, fortunate; thus [19C] pun *Mr R. Suppards*, a very lucky man. [ARSE n.[1] (1) + SE *upwards*]

arse wedge n. [19C] the penis (cf. ARSE-OPENER). [ARSE n.[1] (1) + SE *wedge*]

arsewipe n. [1950s+] lavatory paper (cf. ASSWIPE). [ARSE n.[1] (1) + SE *wipe*]

arse-wiper n. [20C] a sycophant (cf. ARSE-LICKER; ASS-WIPER). [ARSEWIPE]

arse-wise adj. [20C] absurd, ludicrous. [ARSE n.[2] (1) + SE *wise*; used as a generic neg.]

arse-worm n. [late 17C–early 18C] a diminutive person. [ARSE n.[1] (1) + SE *worm*]

arsey/arsie/arsy adj. [1950s+] (Aus.) lucky, occas. as *arsey*, lucky person. [TIN-ARSED]

arsey-turvey adj. [mid-19C–1930s] (US) upside down (cf. ARSEY-VARSEY).

arsey-varsey/arsey-versey/arsy-versy adv. [late 18C+] **1** upside down, topsy-turvey, back-to-front (cf. ARSE ABOUT FACE). **2** contrary, perverse, preposterous. **3** head-over-heels, usu. in phr. *fall arsey-varsey*, fall head-over-heels. [ARSE n.[1] (1) + sfx. *-y* + redup.; on model of SE *vice-versa*. Prior use from mid-16C was SE]

arsie see ARSEY.

arsle/assle n. [20C] the rectum, the anus. [pron. of ARSEHOLE; ASSHOLE]

ars musica n. [late 18C–19C] the anus, esp. when it breaks wind (cf. BACK-DOOR TRUMPET). [pun on Lat. *ars musica*, the musical art + a second pun on BUM-FIDDLE]

arsy see ARSEY.

arsy-versy see ARSEY-VARSEY.

art *n.* [1980s] (US campus) a thing of the past, used in phr. *I'm art*, goodbye, I'm leaving (cf. ARCHIVES). [the image is of an 'old master']

artesian *n.* [late 19C–1910s] (Aus.) beer brewed in Australia. [orig. a very popular beer brewed with water from a well-known artesian well at Sale, Gippsland, Victoria]

art fag *n.* [20C] (US campus) one who is overly affected, pretentious or 'arty'. [SE *art* + FAG n.⁵; however there is no need for the target actually to be gay, the term merely reflects the time-honoured, philistine association of the arts with effeminacy]

artful as a wagon-load of monkeys *see* CUNNING AS A WAGON-LOAD OF MONKEYS.

artful dodger *n.* [mid-19C+] a lodger. [rhy. sl.; the original *Artful Dodger* appears in Charles Dickens's *Oliver Twist* (1838); the 'artful' here implies the lodger's traditional interest in his landlady]

artful fox *n.* [late 19C–1900s] a box in the theatre. [rhy. sl.]

arthur *n.* [20C] a bank (cf. J. ARTHUR). [rhy. sl. *J. Arthur Rank*; ult. f. J. Arthur, later Lord Rank (1888–1972), the British flour producer turned film magnate who dominated the British film business during the 1930s–40s]

artical *adj.* [1950s+] (W.I./UK Black teen) bona fide, genuine, sincere, respected. [var. on HORTICAL]

artichoke *n.* [19C] a debauched old woman. [like the vegetable, such a woman is supposedly spiky on the outside but still tasty within]

artichoke ripe *v.* [mid–late 19C] to smoke a pipe. [rhy. sl.]

article *n.* **1** [early 19C] a woman (cf. PIECE n.¹). **2** [early 19C+] a general pej. description of any person, often as sarcastic 'pretty article' (cf. PIECE n.⁷). **3** [1920s–50s] (euph.) a chamber-pot.

article nine *n.* [20C] (US Und./drugs) one who is due for drug rehabilitation. [SE *Article 9*, a Federal legal provision that states that anyone considered to be acting under the influence of drugs, esp. an addict, cannot be responsible for committing a crime. They must, however, be confined in the Federal Narcotics Farm at Lexington, Kentucky, where they must undertake a cure]

article of virtue *n.* [mid-19C–1910s] a virgin. [pun on Fr. *objet de vertu*, a curio, an antique]

articles *n.* [late 18C–early 19C] breeches, trousers (cf. DON'T-NAME-'EMS). [euph.]

artillery *n.*¹ (US) **1** [19C+] personal weaponry. **2** [1930s] (drugs) equipment for injecting drugs.

artillery *n.*² [20C] (US) beans. [beans, traditionally and physiologically, are equated with the breaking of wind and are thus empowered with 'shooting' ability]

artillery/field artillery *n.*³ [1920s+] (US) **1** the attractive female figure. **2** the female breasts (cf. BAZOOKAS n.; BOMBERS; BOMBS; GUNS; ROCKETS). [image of a woman as a rival in 'the sex war']

artilleryman *n.* [late 19C–1910s] a drunkard. [the 'explosiveness' of his talk and actions]

artist *n.*¹ **1** [mid-19C+] (US Und./Irish) an adroit rogue, usu. a pickpocket, sneak thief or confidence trickster. **2** [late 19C] (US Und.) a skilful card-sharp (cf. MECHANIC).

artist *n.*² [late 19C+] (orig. US/Aus./N.Z.) a generic term for a person, esp. when cited as an expert or devotee of an activity; usu. in such combs. as BACK-DOOR ARTIST; BEAT ARTIST; BIG-NOTE ARTIST; BILGE ARTIST; BOOZE ARTIST; BROWN ARTIST; BULLSHIT ARTIST; BUNCO ARTIST; BURN ARTIST; CON-ARTIST; FACE ARTIST; FANG ARTIST; FAST-BUCK ARTIST; FINGER ARTIST; GUMSHOE ARTIST; GUN ARTIST; HOLD-OUT ARTIST; LEGSHAKE ARTIST; MAKE-OUT ARTIST; NECKLACE ARTIST; NEEDLE ARTIST; PIGSKIN ARTIST; PISS ARTIST; PUFF ARTIST; PUNCH-OUT ARTIST; PUT-ON ARTIST; RIP-OFF ARTIST; SACK ARTIST; SHAG ARTIST; SKID ARTIST; STICK-UP ARTIST; TAKE-OFF ARTIST; TRAPEZE ARTIST; WIND-UP ARTIST (cf. BANDIT; CUSTOMER; MERCHANT). [note the mid-19C US Und. use, a skilful pickpocket or thief]

artiste *n.* [1980s+] (US gay) an especially competent fellator. [the final 'e' reflects both theatrical use and feminization]

artsy-craftsy *adj.* [20C] pretentious, humourless, self-opinionated (cf. ARTSY-FARTSY; ARTY; ARTY-CRAFTY; ARTY-FARTY). [the Arts and Crafts Exhibition Society, founded in London in 1888, but more generally an attack on the perceived failings of those condemned as 'artistic']

artsy-fartsy *adj.* [1960s+] pretentious (cf. ARTSY-CRAFTSY). [var. on ARTY-FARTY]

arty *adj.* [20C] pretentious (cf. ARTSY-CRAFTSY).

arty-crafty/arty-and-crafty *adj.* [20C] pretentious, humourless. [for ety. *see* ARTSY-CRAFTSY]

arty-farty *adj.* [20C] pretentious, overly intellectual or artistic, exhibiting superficial form and little positive content etc (cf. ARTSY-CRAFTSY). [SE *art* + FART]

arty roller *n.* [1910s+] (Aus.) a collar. [rhy. sl.]

arvie *n.* [1960s+] (S.Afr.) the afternoon, often in comb. *this arvie*, this afternoon (cf. AFTO). [abbr.]

arvo *n.* [1930s+] (Aus.) **1** afternoon (cf. AFTO). **2** afternoon tea. [abbr. SE + sfx -O]

as a bastard *phr.* [1920s+] (orig. US) a general intensifier.

as a bean *phr.* [20C] (Aus.) a general intensifier, e.g. *as keen as a bean*.

a.s.a.f.p. *phr.* [1980s+] (US campus) very quickly indeed, immediately (cf. A.S.A.P.). [abbr. *as soon as fucking possible*]

a.s.a.p. *phr.* [1950s+] *as soon as possible* (cf. A.S.A.F.P.). [abbr.]

as all get-out *phr.* [late 19C+] (orig. US) very much so, to a very great extent. [SE *get out*, to transpire]

as and when *phr.* [1960s+] eventually, if ever possible. [SE phr. 'as it happens and when it happens']

as anything *phr.* [16C+] very much so (cf. LIKE ANYTHING; LIKE BILLY-O).

as arse *phr.* [20C] (W.I.) a general intensifier, e.g. *cold as arse* (cf. AS BUGGERY). [ARSE n.² (2)]

as a starter *phr.* [late 19C+] to begin with (cf. FOR STARTERS).

as buggery *phr.* [20C] a general intensifier, e.g. *hot as buggery*. [SE *buggery*]

Ascot races *n.* [20C] the horse-races. [rhy. sl.; usu. as 'ascots']

asexual *adj.* [1980s+] (US campus) uninterested in sex. [variation on SE *asexual*, sexless]

as good a scholar as my horse Ball *phr.* [mid-17C] no scholar at all, an ignoramus. [? anecdotal]

as good as ever twanged *phr.* [early 17C] as good as possible. [TWANG v.]

as good as you would desire to piss on/upon *phr.* [late 17C–early 19C] excellent, first-rate.

ash *n.* [1990s] (Black) hashish. [London pron. of HASH]

ash beans and long oats *n.* [mid-19C] a beating, a flogging. [SE *ash(plant)*, a walking-stick + GIVE BEANS]

ashcan *n.*¹ [1930s] (US) **1** an unpleasant person. **2** the buttocks. [SE *ashcan*; (2) note CAN n.⁴]

ashcan *n.*² [1950s+] (US) a small but powerful firecracker, its explosive effects intensified by the layer of tinfoil in which it is wrapped. [US Navy *ashcan*, a depth charge]

ashcan *v.* [1930s+] (US) to discard, to throw away. [ASHCAN n.²]

ash-cat *n.*¹ [19C] (US) a dirty, dishevelled child. [UK dial. *ashcat*, anyone, usu. a child, who sits near the fire, poking at the ashes]

ash-cat *n.*² [20C] (US) a thin, wasted, ragged Black person. [the tendency of Black flesh tones, when unhealthy, to seem grey]

ash-cat sam *n.* [mid-19C–1900s] a sooty, dirty individual, esp. a child. [ASH-CAT n.¹ + generic use of proper name *Sam*]

ash cookie *n.* [1910s] (S.Afr.) a ne'er-do-well. [Afk. *askoek*, a dough cake baked in hot embers; ? those who eat such food are considered untrustworthy]

ashes *n.* [1980s+] (drugs) marijuana (cf. ASH).

ash-faced *adj.* [19C] (US) having a light complexion, applied to light-skinned Blacks (cf. ASH-CAT n.²). [the 'grey' skin tone]

as high/about as high as six penn'orth of coppers *phr.* [19C] used of a very short person.

ash-spots *n.* [20C] **1** goose pimples. **2** (US Black) lighter spots that appear on one's arms and legs when one gets cold.

ashy *adj.* [20C] (US Black) pale, ashen-faced (cf. ASH-SPOTS).

Asia Minor *n.¹* [mid-19C] Belgravia, London (cf. MESOPOTAMIA, NEW JERUSALEM). [ext. of SE; i.e. the wealthy Jews who bought houses there]

Asia Minor *n.²* [late 19C–1910s] Kensington and Bayswater, London. [the large population of retired Indian civil servants]

asiatic *adj.* [late 19C+] (US) insane, crazy (cf. BAMBOO adj.; DOOLALLY; TROPPO). [coined by the US Marines whose experiences beneath the Asian sun had driven some of them mad]

as if! *excl.* [1980s+] (US campus) an excl. of disbelief, you must be joking. [SE phr. 'as if I would do/say/think such a thing']

as I live by bread *phr.* [late 19C–1910s] a general phr. of emphasis, underlining the probity of one's statements and actions. [since bread is 'the stuff of life', a synon. for 'on my life']

asinico/asinego *n.* [early 17C–early 18C] a fool, a simpleton. [Sp. *asnico*, a small donkey]

as Irish as Paddy's/Patrick Murphy's pig *phr.* [late 19C+] quintessentially Irish (cf. PADDY n.¹).

ask bogy!/bogey! *excl.* [late 18C+] go to hell! (cf. ASK MY ARSE!; GOOSEBERRY GRINDER). [SE *bogy*, a goblin, but ? link to BOG]

ask cheeks near Cunnyborough *phr.* [mid-18C–mid-19C] a woman-only phr., equivalent to ASK MY ARSE! [CUNNY + SE -*borough*]

asker *n.* [mid-19C] a beggar. [SE *ask*]

askew *n.* [mid-16C–mid-17C] a cup. [? Fr. *escuelle*, a cup]

ask for a piece of wife, to *phr.* [20C] (W.I.) to ask a woman to whom one is not married for sex; thus *give wife*, to permit such an adulterous affair.

ask for it *v.* [20C] to act in such a manner that unpleasant consequences will (almost) inevitably follow, to 'ask for trouble'. ['it' being trouble]

ask for one's cards, to *phr.* [1940s+] to resign from a job. [SE *cards*, various documents pertaining to employment, e.g. one's P45]

ask for the ring, to *phr.* [1950s+] to perform anal intercourse. [RING n.¹ (2)]

ask another!/ask me another! *excl.* [late 19C+] a riposte to one who has just recited a riddle or a dated or unfunny joke.

ask me one on sport *phr.* [1990s] used to deflect a question to which the speaker does not know the answer. [a knowledge of sport being seen as the least 'intellectual' of attainments]

ask mine/my arse/ass *phr.* [mid-18C+] a coarse and evasive response (cf. ASK BOGY!; ASK CHEEKS NEAR CUNNYBOROUGH). [ARSE n.¹ (1)]

ask my arse! *excl.* [19C+] in response to what is considered an irrelevant or over-familiar question, 'go to hell!' (cf. ASK MY AUNT!; ASK MY NANCY!; AX MY ARSE).

ask my aunt! *excl.* [late 19C] go to hell! (cf. ASK MY ARSE!). [euph.]

ask my nancy! *excl.* [early 19C–1900s] go to hell! (cf. ASK MY ARSE!). [euph.]

asleep at the switch, to be *phr.* [late 19C+] (US) to be inattentive, not concentrating on a task (cf. ASLEEP AT THE WHEEL). [railroad jargon 'switch', the points lever]

asleep at the wheel, to be *phr.* [20C] to be inattentive, not concentrating on a task (cf. ASLEEP AT THE SWITCH). [motoring imagery]

as long as one's arm *phr.* [late 19C+] extensive, substantial.

as many faces as a churchyard clock *phr.* [20C] used of anyone seen as duplicitous or unreliable. [church clocks can have faces on all 4 sides of a rectangular tower]

as melancholy as … *phr.* a variety of phrs. implying unhappiness; [late 16C–mid-19C] *as melancholy as a cat/gib cat*, [mid-17C–mid-18C] *as melancholy as a collier's horse*, [mid-17C–mid-18C] *as melancholy as a sick parrot*, [mid-19C] *as melancholy as a sick monkey*.

as mim as old Betty Martin at a funeral, to be *phr.* [early 19C] to walk in a prim, orderly manner. [dial. *mim*, affectedly modest, demure, primly silent or quiet; the term is imitative of pursed lips (cf. MUM n.¹). Whether this is the same *Betty Martin* as ALL MY EYE AND BETTY MARTIN is unknown]

as much … as a … *phr.* a variety of similes, all meaning no use whatsoever; [late 19C+] *as much use as my arse*, [20C] *as much use as a headache/sick headache*, [1970s+] *as much use as a chocolate teapot*.

as muck *phr.* [late 19C+] extremely, utterly; either succeeding a pej., e.g. *as sick as muck*, or implying one, e.g. *as rich as muck*.

asoc/asocial *n.* [20C] (US Und.) a child molester. [sociological jargon 'antagonistic to society or social order' + SE *asocial*, inconsiderate of or hostile to other people]

as often as not/more often than not *phr.* [1910s+] usually, most likely.

asparagus *n.* [1910s+] (orig. US) mispron. of SE *aspersion*; thus usu. in phr. *cast asparagus* (cf. CAST NASTURTIUMS).

aspect *n.* [late 19C–1900s] an amorous glance. [Ital. *aspetto!* look!]

as per usual/per usual *phr.* [late 19C+] as usual. [ext. of SE]

asphalt arab *n.* [20C] (US) a city person, as nicknamed by a country dweller. [SE *asphalt* + ARAB n.¹]

aspinall *n.* [late 19C–1900s] enamel. [*Aspinall*, the inventor and manufacturer of a variety of oxidized enamel paint]

as popular as a pork chop at a Jewish wedding *phr.* [20C] extremely unpopular. [the Jewish religious prohibition of pork]

aspro *see* ASS PRO.

ass for all uses other than those included below *see* note under ARSE n.¹.

ass *conj.* [1990s] (US campus) synon. for SE *but*.

-ass *sfx.* [20C] **1** a person, a character (cf. BAD-ASS; HARD-ASS; SLOW-ASS). **2** (US Black) used to form generally neg. adjs., e.g. BITCH-ASS; CANDY-ASS n.¹; DOG-ASS; DRAG-ASS. [ARSE n.¹ (3)]

ass about *v.* [late 19C–1930s] to play the fool. [SE *ass*, donkey; note ARSE ABOUT, although the homonymity with US *ass* and *arse* is coincidental]

assassin *n.* [1900s–10s] an ornamental bow worn at a woman's breast. [it 'kills' her admirers]

ass-backwards *adj.* [late 19C+] (US) back-to-front, thus fig. in a mess, chaotic (cf. ARSE ABOUT FACE). [ARES n.¹ (1) + SE *backwards*]

ass-belly *n.* [1970s+] (US) a grotesquely fat person. [ARSE n.¹ (1) + SE *belly*; the similarity of the two fleshy protuberances]

ass-bite *n.* [1970s] (US) a very unpopular person (cf. ASSWIPE). [ARSE n.¹ (1) + SE *bite*]

ass bite *v.* [1970s] (US) usu. of an employer/employee relationship, to harass, to nag.

ass blow *v.* [1980s+] (US gay) to lick or suck the anus (cf. BLOW JOB). [ARSE/ASS n.¹ (1) + BLOW v.⁶ (1)]

assbone *n.* [1970s] (US) the buttocks. [ARSE n.¹ (1) + SE *bone*]

ass boy *n.* [1990s] (US) a male homosexual (cf. ARSE MAN). [ARSE n.¹ (1) + SE *boy*]

ass-breaker *n.* (US) **1** [20C] a dive in which the diver lands stomach down on the water, rather than cutting through it (cf. BELLYFLOP). **2** [1950s] a difficult, boring or exasperating job, problem or situation. **3** [1960s] a nag, a dominating woman, one who destroys the self-confidence of a man (cf. ANCHOR n.[2]; BALL-BREAKER; BALL-BUSTER; BALL-CRUSHER; BALL-CUTTER; BALL-TEARER). [fig. use of ASS + SE *breaker*]

ass-bucket *n.* [1950s] (US) an unpopular or unimportant person. [ARSE n.[1] (1) + SE *bucket*]

ass burglar *n.* [1970s+] a male homosexual (cf. ARSE BANDIT). [ARSE n.[1] (1) + SE *burglar*)

ass-buster *n.* **1** [20C] (US) a dive in which a swimmer jumps, holds their nose and hits the water buttocks-first, the aim, and the result, being to make a big splash (cf. ASS-RIPPER). **2** [1970s] an outstanding person. [ARSE n.[1] (1) + BUSTER n.[5]]

ass-busting *adj.* [1970s] (US) exhausting, tiring. [BUST ONE'S ASS]

ass-chewing *n.* [1950s+] (orig. US milit.) a scolding, a serious reprimand. [ARSE n.[1] (1) + SE *chew*]

ass-deep *adj.* [1950s+] (US) **1** very deep, usu. in such phrs. as ASS DEEP TO A TALL MOOSE. **2** totally involved with, with an excessive amount of. [ARSE n.[1] (1) + SE *deep*; lit. 'deep enough to reach one's buttocks']

ass deep to a tall moose *phr.* [20C] very deep, often used of water or snow. [fig. use of ASS-DEEP + SE *tall moose*]

-assed *sfx.* [1960s+] (orig. US) a general intensifier, e.g. TIGHT-ASSED. [ARSE n.[1] (3)]

assed-out *adj.* [1980s+] (US Black) dead, killed. [ARSE n.[1] (3)]

ass-end-backwards *phr.* [20C] in confusion (cf. ARSE ABOUT FACE). [ARSE n.[1] (1) + SE *end* + *backwards*]

ass-end of nowhere *n.* [1960s+] (US) nowhere, a very out-of-the-way place (cf. BACKSIDE OF NOWHERE). [ARSE n.[1] (1) + SE *end* + *nowhere*]

ass-end-to *phr.* [20C] in confusion (cf. ARSE ABOUT FACE).

assface *n.* [20C] (US campus) an unpleasant, stupid person. [ARSE n.[1] (1) + SE *face*]

ass-fault *n.* [1990s] (US campus) **1** the crease between one's buttocks. **2** extreme stupidity. [ARSE n.[1] (1) + SE *fault*, a crevice]

ass-frontwards *adj.* [20C] head-over-heels (cf. ARSE ABOUT FACE). [ARSE n.[1] (1) + SE *frontwards*]

assfuck *n.* (orig. US) **1** [1940s+] an act of anal intercourse. **2** [1970s] an instance of cruel victimization. **3** [1990s] (orig. US) an all-purpose derog. term of address (cf. ASSHOLE n.; SHITHEAD). [ARSE n.[1] (1) + FUCK v.[1]]

assfuck *v.* [1940s+] (orig. US) to have anal intercourse. [ASSFUCK]

assfucking *n.* [1950s+] anal intercourse. [ASSFUCK v.]

ass gasket *n.* [1990s] (US campus) the paper protector that is placed over a lavatory seat to indicate its sanitized state. [ARSE n.[1] (1) + SE *gasket*, a thin, flat ring used as a seal between two surfaces]

ass-grabbing *adj.* [1960s] (US) irritating. [ARSE n.[1] (1) + SE *grabbing*]

ass hammer *n.* [1960s+] (US campus) a motorcycle. [ARSE n.[1] (1) + SE *hammer*; the battering one receives from its seat on one's own]

asshead *n.* [1960s] (US) a fool. [ARSE n.[1] (1) + sfx. -HEAD (1)]

ass-/hip-/knee-high to a tall Indian *phr.* [late 19C+] (US) an unspecified measure of height. [ARSE n.[1] (1)]

asshole for combs. *see also* ARSEHOLE.

asshole *n.* **1** [1930s+] the anus; thus a derog. description of a subject. **2** [1960s+] the anus as a sexual object (cf. ARSE n.[1]). [(1) note Wright, *Vol. Vocabs.*, 1857, citing 14C AS/Lat. vocab., *Arce-hoole, podex*]

asshole *adj.* [1930s+] (US) a general, neg. description, unpleasant, worthless, obnoxious etc (cf. ARSEHOLE).

asshole *v.* [1940s] to grovel, to beg, to toady. [ASSHOLE n. (1)]

asshole around *v.* [1950s+] (US) to idle, to loiter, to waste time. [ASSHOLE n. (1)]

asshole buddy *n.* **1** [1940s+] an extremely close friend. **2** [1950s+] (US gay) a normally heterosexual man who, deprived for whatever reason of women, enjoys anal intercourse, both as an active or passive partner.

asshole-deep *adj.* [1960s+] (US) extremely deep. [ext. of ASS-DEEP]

assholingest *adj.* [1970s] (US) the notional superlative of ASSHOLE adj.

ass-hound *n.* [1940s] (US) a womanizer, a 'skirt chaser' (cf. PUSSY HOUND). [ARSE n.[1] (5) + sfx. -HOUND]

assig *n.* [late 17C–early 19C] an *assig*nation. [abbr.]

ass-kick *n.* [1970s] (US) a very demanding task. [fig. use of KICK ASS]

ass-kicker *n.[1]* [20C] (US) a shoe, esp. a pointed man's shoe. [for ety. *see* ASS-KICK]

ass-kicker *n.[2]* (orig. US) **1** [1960s+] an aggressive, domineering person, a bully. **2** [1970s+] an amusing, successful, exciting person. [ARSE n.[1] (1) + SE *kicker*]

ass-kicking *adj.* [1970s+] (US) a general intensifier, extremely, very much, powerfully.

ass kiss *v.* [1940s+] (US) to toady (cf. ASS LICK; ASS UP TO). [backform. f. ASS-KISSER]

ass-kisser *n.* [20C] (US) a sycophant, a toady, one who curries favour (cf. ARSE-LICKER; ASS UP TO; KISS ASS). [ARSE n.[1] (1) + SE *kisser*]

assle *see* ARSLE.

ass-lick *n.* [1960s+] a sycophant, a toady. [ARSE n.[1] (1) + SE *lick*]

ass lick *v.* [1960s+] to behave sycophantically (cf. ASS KISS).

ass-licker *see* ARSE-LICKER.

assload *n.* [1950s+] an excess (cf. SHITLOAD). [ARSE n.[1] (1) + SE *load*]

associates *n.* [1990s] (US Black) friends.

ass off *phr.* [1940s+] a general intensifier (cf. EAT SOMEONE'S ARSE OFF; FUCK THE ARSE OFF; WORK ONE'S ARSE OFF). [ARSE n.[1] (1), (3) and (5)]

ass on backwards *phr.* [20C] drunk (cf. CAN'T FIND ONE'S ARSE WITH BOTH HANDS).

ass pack *n.* [1980s+] (US) a small pouch-like bag strapped around the wearer's waist (cf. BUM BAG; FANNY PACK). [ARSE n.[1] (1) + SE *pack*]

ass paper *n.* [1930s+] (US) lavatory paper (cf. ASSWIPE). [ARSE n.[1] (1) + SE *paper*]

ass peddler *n.* [1940s+] (US) anyone who sells their body as a prostitute, male or female (cf. ASS PRO; BUSINESS BOY; CAREER BOY; CHARITY; C.O.D.; COIN COLLECTOR; COMMERCIAL n.[2]; COMMERCIAL QUEER; CRACK SALESMAN; DICK PEDDLER; PEDDLER; TRADE n.[1]; WORKING GIRL). [ARSE n.[1] (1), (5) + SE *peddler*]

ass-poots *n.* [20C] (US) beans. [ARSE n.[1] (1) + POOT, the propensity of beans to cause an excess of breaking wind]

ass pro/aspro/asspro *n.* [1920s+] (Aus./US) a male homosexual prostitute (cf. ASS PEDDLER). [ARSE n.[1] (5) + SE *prostitute/professional*; despite the apparent simplicity of the ety., Hancock (1984) suggests Ling. Fr. *aspro*, money]

ass-ripper *n.* [1950s+] (US) a dive in which a swimmer jumps, holds their nose and hits the water buttocks-first; the aim, and the result, is to make a big splash (cf. ASS-BUSTER).

ass-scratcher *n.* [1930s] (US) a loafer, an idler. [ARSE n.[1] (1) + SE *scratcher*; one who simply sits around, scratching their buttocks]

ass-side-before *phr.* [20C] head-over-heels, in confusion (cf. ARSE ABOUT FACE).

ass-sucker *n.* [1940s+] (US) a sycophant, a toady (cf. ARSE-LICKER). [ARSE n.[1] (1) + SE *sucker*]

ass-tickler *n.* [1970s] (US) something amusing. [ARSE n.[1] (1) + SE *tickler*]

ass-tight adj. [1960s] (US) **1** of things, very tight. **2** of friends, very intimate. [ARSE n.[1] (1) + SE tight]

ass up to v. [20C] (US) to toady to, to curry favour (cf. ASS KISS). [ARSE n.[1] (1)]

ass watcher n. [1950s–60s] (gay) one who walks the streets looking for a potential sexual partner. [ARSE n.[1] (1) + SE watcher]

ass-waxing n. [1960s] (US) a thrashing, a beating. [ARSE n.[1] (1) + WAX SOMEONE'S ASS]

assways adv. [1930s+] (US) skew-whiff, back-to-front (cf. ARSE ABOUT FACE).

ass-whipped adj. [1970s] (US) utterly exhausted. [ARSE n.[1] (1), (3) + SE whipped]

ass-whipping n. [1950s] (US) a particularly savage beating. [ARSE n.[1] (2) + SE whipping]

asswipe n. [1950s+] **1** lavatory paper (cf. ARSEWIPE). **2** a general term of abuse. **3** any worthless piece of paper, like a parking ticket. [ARSE n.[1] (1) + SE wipe]

ass-wiper n. **1** [1950s] a sycophant, a toady (cf. ARSE-WIPER; ASS-KISSER). **2** [1960s+] something extremely difficult, demanding. [for ety. see ASSWIPE]

assy-fussy adj. [20C] (US) back-to-front (cf. ARSE ABOUT FACE).

astard-ba n. [1930s] a bastard. [semi-backsl.]

aste n. [early 17C] (Und.) money. [? Ital. asta, auction]

astern the lighter phr. [19C] (US) late, behind (cf. BEHIND THE LIGHTER). [nautical jargon astern, behind + SE lighter, a flat-bottomed boat used for the transportation of people and cargoes between the shore and larger boats anchored in the harbour. The lighters were de facto slow; thus for a boat to be 'astern' of the lighter implied even greater sloth. A linked ety. suggests that a slow passenger who was 'astern of the lighter' had, literally, 'missed the boat' that connected with their ocean-going vessel]

as the actress said to the bishop phr. [20C] turning what may have been a perfectly innocent phr. into a sexual innuendo, e.g. 'Pull it out and we'll see how long it is,' as the actress said . . . .

as the devil loves holy water phr. [late 18C–19C] not at all. [holy water is supposedly a preventive against the Devil]

Astorbilt/Mr Astorbilt n. [20C] (US) **1** a member of high society. **2** one who considers themself a cut above their peers (cf. ASTORPERIOUS; ASTOR'S PET HORSE; MISS ASTOR). [names Astor + Vanderbilt, two of America's wealthiest families]

astorperious adj. [20C] (US) arrogant, haughty (cf. ASTORBILT). [Astor + SE imperious]

astor's pet horse n. [20C] (US) **1** an over-made-up or over-dressed woman (cf. HORSED UP). **2** an arrogant, haughty person (cf. ASTORPERIOUS). [joc. use of proper name Astor + SE pet horse]

astronomer n. [19C] a horse that holds its head high (cf. STAR-GAZER). [it is always staring at the sky]

as you were! excl. **1** [mid-19C+] calm down, slow down, restrain yourself. **2** [1920s+] a phr. used to withdraw the previous statement, my mistake, forget what I just said. [milit. jargon as you were, return to the position specified in the previous order. 'A military phrase in drilling, used in a slang sense to one who is going on too fast in his assertions and wants recalling to moderation' (Hotten, 1864)]

at a good ready phr. [late 19C–1900s] absolutely certain, totally alert.

at a loose end phr. [mid-19C+] not regularly occupied, having no settled employment, not knowing what to do. [a person thus situated figuratively resembles a loose bit of rope or string]

at a rate of knots adv. [late 19C+] very fast. [naut. use]

at/upon a squeeze phr. [late 19C] in extreme circumstances, if absolutely necessary.

at bat adv. [late 19C+] (orig. US) **1** involved in, occupied by. **2** taking one's turn. [baseball use; the UK use reflects cricket]

at/in bushey park/the park phr. [early 19C] poor, impoverished (cf. AT STAINES; AT THE BUSH). [BUSHED adj.[1]]

atch v. [1920s] (tramp) to arrest (cf. ATCHKER). [SE catch]

atchker v. [1910s–20s] to arrest (cf. ATCH). [pig Latin for SE catch]

ate-the-bolts n. [20C] (Ulster) one who is a glutton for work.

ate-your-bun n. [1990s] (Irish) a general term of abuse.

at full belt phr. [1960s+] at top speed. [BELT v.]

at full bottle phr. [1950s+] at the maximum, usu. of noise or speed. [fig. use of BOTTLE n.[3]]

at full/great lick phr. [late 19C+] (US) at full speed, at high speed. [SE full + LICK n.]

at full split phr. [mid-19C+] (orig. US) at top speed; thus go like split, to go very fast.

at great lick see AT FULL LICK.

at gut level phr. [1960s+] (US) instinctively, in one's deepest feelings.

at half-mast phr. [late 19C+] (US) in a partially lowered position, used esp. of trousers or a partial erection of the penis.

athanasian wench n. [late 18C] a promiscuous young woman, a prostitute. [a pun on the Athanasian Creed, which begins with the words QUICUMQUE VULT]

atheneum n. [late 19C–1900s] the penis. [? the Athenaeum Club, London, which might be seen as the fount of all wisdom]

Athenian n. [1950s–60s] (gay) a pederast (cf. GREEK CULTURE). [stereotyped link between homosexuality and Greece]

at her last prayers phr. [late 17C–mid-19C] a phr. used to typify an old maid.

at/in full blast phr. [mid-19C] very busy, doing very well. [the imagery of an industrial revolutionary blast furnace]

at it adv. **1** [late 19C+] indulging in sexual intercourse (cf. ON THE JOB). **2** [1950s+] involved in something illegal. [SE at + IT n.[1]/SE it, i.e. crime]

atkins n. [late 19C] a generic term for a typical private solider in the British army. [abbr. TOMMY ATKINS]

Atlantic ranger n. [late 19C] a herring (cf. BILLINGSGATE PHEASANT). [its breeding grounds]

atlas n. [1930s+] (US prison) **1** a very strong prisoner. **2** a prisoner who attempts to carry out everything unaided. [both ult. f. the mythical Atlas who held up the earth in his hands, though note 20C US strong man Charles Atlas (1894–1972)]

atmos n. [1990s] (US teen) atmosphere or ambience, used in a positive fashion. [abbr.]

at number one London phr. [19C] of a woman, to be menstruating. [ety. unknown; 'Number One London' is traditionally Apsley House, former home of the Duke of Wellington, at Hyde Park Corner]

at nurse phr. [late 18C–early 19C] of a person, to be in the hands of dishonest trustees.

atom bomb n. [1960s+] (US drugs) a combination of marijuana or hashish with opium or cannabis and cocaine (cf. A-BOMB). [play on SE atomic bomb, intensified by BOMB n.[3]]

atom-bombo n. [1940s+] (Aus.) strong, cheap wine. [SE atomic bomb]

atomic atmosphere n. [1980s+] (US campus) the stink created by someone's having recently broken wind.

atomy n. [late 16C–mid-19C] a small, thin or deformed person (cf. OTTOMY). [SE anatomy]

at one/the first go-off phr. [mid-19C] at the very beginning. [SE go-off, a starting, commencement]

at one's high jinks phr. [mid-19C] taking an arrogant, overbearing position.

at one smack phr. [late 19C–1920s] at the first try, all at once. [SMACK n.[2] (2)]

at one's very nose phr. [mid-16C–early 18C] extremely close. [SE phr. 'plain as the nose on one's face']

atop of the house phr. [late 17C] in a state of excitement. [fig. image of one who is HIGH adj.[1]]

at par adj. [19C] first-rate, excellent. [Stock Exchange jargon *at par*, at the face value]

at rest adj. [19C] tipsy, drunk (cf. ABOUT RIGHT adj.[1]).

at rug adj. [early–mid-19C] asleep, in bed. [SE *rug*]

atshitshi n. [1980s+] (drugs) marijuana. [ety. unknown]

at sixes and sevens adv. [late 19C] (US) badly. [dicing use; 'set on six and seven', to create chaos and disorder]

at sparrow crow n. [20C] (Aus.) dawn. [euph. for AT SPARROW'S FART]

at sparrow's fart n. [late 19C+] (orig. Aus.) dawn, early in the morning; usu. *up at …* . [the dawn chorus; note synon. use by British Army in North Africa during WW2, *crow-pee*]

at Staines phr. [early 19C] in financial difficulties (cf. AT BUSHEY PARK). [the Bush Inn at *Staines*, ? a popular refuge for London debtors]

attaboy!/attagirl!/attababy! excl. [20C] (orig. US) a general excl. of admiration and encouragement. [? phr. 'that's the boy' etc or 'at her, boy' (E.P.), where 'her' is neuter. Note US milit./police jargon *attaboy*, a commendation]

attack v. [mid-19C] to begin, to address oneself to, e.g. *attack that beef*.

attack of the week's/month's end phr. [late 19C–1910s] the poverty that comes after one's weekly or monthly wages have run out.

attagirl! see ATTABOY!

attend to v. [late 19C+] to thrash, to flog (cf. SEEING-TO). [ironic use of SE]

at the best phr. [early 19C] by criminal or fraudulent means. [*the best* ways are those that involve no work]

at the Bush phr. [early 19C] in financial difficulties (cf. AT BUSHEY PARK). [the *Bush* Inn at Staines, ? a popular refuge for London debtors]

at the death phr. [20C] in the end, in conclusion. [SE *death*, termination, finality]

at the drop of a hat phr. [mid-19C+] (orig. US) promptly, immediately.

at the heel of the hunt/reel phr. [1930s+] (Irish) eventually, in due course. [hunting imagery]

at/in/up the house-roof phr. [16C] very angry (cf. AT THE HOUSETOP; HIT THE ROOF).

at/in/up the housetop/top of the house phr. [mid-17C–mid-19C] to be very angry (cf. AT THE HOUSE-ROOF; HIT THE ROOF].

at the mark-up phr. [1960s+] (Und.) taking an unfairly large proportion of the loot or proceeds from a swindle, robbery, pay-off etc. [SE *mark up*, to increase the price]

at the micks phr. [1960s+] causing trouble (cf. MIX IT). [pun on micks/MIX v.[1] ? + ref. to MICK n.[1], a (rowdy) Irishman]

at the outs phr. [early 19C] arguing or angry with someone (cf. ON THE OUTS).

at the pinch phr. [late 18C–early 19C] working as a thief, esp. petty theft from shops, carried out during a purchase, giving short change or passing counterfeit money in exchange for good (cf. PINCHER n.[1]; PINCHING LAY). [PINCH v.[1]]

at the races, to be phr. [20C] to work as a street-walker. [? her euph. to prying acquaintances]

at the school of placebo, to be phr. [mid-14C–late 17C] to be a toady or sycophant (cf. GO TO THE SCHOOL OF PLACEBO; HUNT A PLACEBO; MAKE PLACEBO; PLACEBO; PLAY A PLACEBO; SING PLACEBO). [SE *placebo*, the Vespers for the Dead, ult. Lat. *placebo*, I shall please]

at the sign of the horn phr. [19C] suffering cuckoldry. [HORN n.[4] + image of a fake tavern sign]

at the sit phr. [1900s] (Und.) working as a pickpocket on public transport. [one *sits* next to one's victim]

at the switch phr. [1960s+] (Und.) stealing property from a shop and then taking it back and demanding a cash refund. [SE *switch*]

at the wash phr. [1960s+] (police/Und.) stealing from coats and jackets left hanging in a washroom or public lavatory. [SE *wash(room)*]

attic n. [early 19C+] (orig. boxing) the head (cf. BELFRY; COCKLOFT; CUPOLA; DOME n.[1]; GABLE; GARRET; HAVE A GUEST IN THE ATTIC; HAVE BATS IN THE BELFRY; QUEER IN THE ATTIC; RATS IN THE ATTIC; TOP END; TOP FLAT; TOP KNOT; TOP PIECE; UPPER APARTMENT; UPPER CRUST n.; UPPER STOREY; WEATHERCOCK; WIG n.[1]).

attitude/'tude n. [1960s+] one's whole posture towards society, its rules and one's own place among them. [the assumption is that an attitude is hostile to the prevailing establishment status quo, although it may well fit happily into the complementary rebellious teenage standpoint. Thus the GANGSTA RAP band NWA, Niggers With Attitude, meaning shifted slightly f. 1970–80s, negative, antisocial, to 1990s, haughty, pretentious]

attitude! excl. [1960s+] a comment made to a person who is seen as displaying ATTITUDE. [ATTITUDE]

Attleborough n. [mid–late 19C] (US) cheap or sham jewellery (cf. BRUMMAGEM n.). [? the town of its manufacture]

attorney n. [early 19C] a grilled and devilled goose or turkey drumstick. [legal jargon *devil*, a lawyer working free for another lawyer]

attract v. [late 19C–1930s] to steal, to pilfer (cf. ACQUIRE). [ironic euph.]

Auckland Park n. [1980s+] (S.Afr.) the South African Broadcasting Corporation (SABC). [by metonymy, *Auckland Park* is the Johannesburg suburb where the SABC headquarters is situated]

auctioneer n. [mid-19C–1900s] (orig. boxing) the fist. [it 'knocks things down'; the orig. auctioneer was that of prizefighter Tom Sayers (*fl.*1845–60)]

Audi/Audi 5000 v. [1990s] (US teen) to rush away, to run off, to escape. [pron. of *Audi*, an upscale automobile (the Audi 5000 is a favoured model), as 'out of (here)']

Audi! excl. [1990s] (US Black/teen) a general excl. of farewell, good bye, see you etc. [pron. of *Audi* as 'outi', i.e. '(I'm) out (of here)']

Audi 5000 see AUDI.

audition the finger puppets, to phr. [1980s+] to masturbate.

auger n. [1900s–10s] the penis. [SE *auger*, a tool for boring]

augur n. [19C] (US) a bore, an excessive talker. [a pun on SE *auger*, a bore; note SE *augur*, a prophet]

August ham n. [20C] (US Black) a watermelon (cf. GEORGIA HAM). [the month of ripening + the pinkness of both foodstuffs]

aunt n.[1] **1** [early 17C+] a procuress, a madame. **2** [18C+] an old Black woman, used by both Blacks and Whites. [note synon. Yid. *mume*, lit. 'aunt']

aunt, the n.[2] [mid-19C–1920s+] (society) the lavatory; thus *go to see one's/the aunt/auntie*. [euph.]

aunt n.[3] [20C] (US) menstruation. usu. in such phrs. *as Aunt Flo is visiting*, *my redheaded aunt has arrived*, *Aunt Jody's come with her suitcase* etc (cf. AUNT FLO; AUNTIE n.[2]; AUNT JODY). [euph.]

Aunt Betsy's cookie store n. [1990s] (US campus) Alcoholic Beverage Control store (cf. AMERICAN BUSINESS COLLEGE). [initial letters]

Aunt Fanny n. [1940s+] used to express negation or disbelief, e.g. *tell that to my Aunt Fanny*, *Agree? My Aunt Fanny*. [joc. use of proper name + an added emphasis from FANNY n.[1]]

Aunt Flo/Flo *n.* [1950s+] (US) menstruation (cf. AUNT n.³). [euph.; AUNT n.² + pun on SE *flow*]

Aunt Hagar/Aunt Hagar's children *n.* [1900s–40s] (US Black) the Black race. [Gen. 21:9, *Hagar* the Egyptian, the wife of Abraham and the mother of Ishmael]

Aunt Hazel *n.* [1980s+] (drugs) heroin. [the shared initial *H* + the hazel-brown colour of some heroin]

auntie *n.*¹ [mid-19C+] the lavatory (cf. AUNT n.²). [euph.]

auntie *n.*² [20C] (W.I.) menstruation (cf. AUNT n.³); thus phr. *auntie coming to town*, menstruation is starting.

auntie *n.*³ [1930s+] (US gay) an ageing male homosexual (cf. AUNTIE-MAN).

auntie *n.*⁴ **1** [1940s+] the British Broadcasting Corporation, orig. use by independent TV companies, but now general. **2** [1950s+] (Aus.) the Australian Broadcasting Commission (ABC). [in both cases the implication is of prissiness, paternalism, reticence and traditional conservatism]

auntie *n.*⁵ [1980s+] (drugs) opium. [abbr. AUNTIE EMMA]

Auntie Ella *n.* [1940s+] an umbrella. [rhy. sl.]

Auntie Emma *n.* (drugs) **1** [1970s] morphine. **2** [1980s+] opium (cf. AUNTIE n.⁵). [initial *M*]

Auntie Flora *n.* [20C] (W.I./Antg., St Lucia) the floor; *knock/take Auntie Flora*, to sleep on the floor. [partial rhy. sl.]

auntie-man *n.* [1940s+] (W.I.) an effeminate man (cf. KITCHEN-BITCH; MAMA-MAN). [AUNTIE n.³ + SE *man*]

Auntie Meg *n.* [20C] (Aus.) a keg (of beer). [rhy. sl.]

Auntie Nelly *n.* [20C] the belly. [rhy. sl.]

auntie's ruin *n.* [1900s–60s] a disreputable, untrustworthy, seedy man (cf. MOTHER'S RUIN). [the type of Lothario who might charm a spinster aunt]

Aunt Jane *n.*¹ [1920s] (US) the town of Tijuana, Mexico. [lit. trans. of Sp. *tía*, aunt + *juana*, Jane]

Aunt Jane *n.*² [1960s] (US Black) **1** a subservient, obsequious Black woman (cf. AUNT JEMIMA; AUNT MARY n.¹; AUNT SALLY; AUNT THOMASINA; UNCLE TOM n.). **2** a Black woman whose world is defined by spiritual rather than secular values; a regular church-goer and religious believer. [generic use of proper name]

Aunt Jemima *n.* [1960s+] (US Black) a subservient, obsequious Black woman, the female version of UNCLE TOM n.; an early fast-food chain, Aunt Jemima's Kitchen, featuring pictures of a stereotype 'Black Mammy' existed in the 1960s (cf. AUNT JANE n.²). [generic use of proper name]

Aunt Jody *n.* [20C] (US) euph. menstruation (cf. AUNT n.³). [AUNT n.² + name *Jody*]

Aunt Maria *n.*¹ [late 19C–1900s] the female genitals. [? AUNT MARIA n.², i.e. they get 'hot']

Aunt Maria *n.*² [late 19C+] a fire (cf. ANNA MARIA). [rhy. sl.; note pron. Mar-eye-a]

Aunt Mary *n.*¹ [1960s] **1** a downtrodden, subservient Black woman (cf. AUNT JANE n.²). **2** a Black woman who is a regular church-goer and religious believer. [generic use of proper name]

Aunt Mary *n.*² [1980s+] (drugs) marijuana (cf. MARY n.⁴; MARY ANN n.³; MARY JANE; MARY WARNER; MARY WEAVER).

Aunt Minnie is visiting *phr.* [20C] a euph. phr. used by a woman who is menstruating (cf. GEORGE CALLED). [AUNT n.³]

Aunt Nell *v.* [1980s+] (Ling. Fr./Polari) to listen.

Aunt Nora *n.* [1980s+] (drugs) cocaine. [ety. unknown, ? N of Nora and *ne* of cocaine]

Aunt Sally *n.* **1** [late 19C+] a scapegoat, often unfairly so. **2** [1960s] (US Black) a subservient Black woman, happy to curry favour with Whites at the price of her autonomy (cf. AUNT JANE n.²). [SE *Aunt Sally*, 'a game much in vogue at fairs and races, in which the figure of a woman's head with a pipe in its mouth is set up, and the player, throwing sticks from a certain distance, aims at breaking the pipe' (*OED*). The

original Aunt Sally was a black-faced doll, popular in early 19C London; its face also served as the shop-sign for a second-hand clothiers. The doll, in turn, came from Black Sal, a character created by Pierce Egan in *Life in London* (1821–8)]

Aunt Thomasina *n.* [1960s] (US Black) a subservient, obsequious Black woman (cf. AUNT JANE n.²). [female var. on UNCLE TOM n.]

aunt tillies *n.* [1940s] (US) an old-fashioned woman's nightgown. [the image of *Tillie* as an old-fashioned name, accentuated by pfx. *Aunt*]

au reservoir! *excl.* [mid-19C–1920s] (orig. US) goodbye (cf. OLIVE OIL!; SEAFOOD PLATE; SILVER PLATE). [play on Fr. *au revoir*, goodbye]

aurev! *excl.* [1920s] goodbye. [abbr. Fr. *au revoir*]

aurium *n.* [16C] (Und.) a wandering beggar posing as some type of priest (cf. CLEWNER; PARDONER; ROGER n.²; SAPIENT). [? Lat. *aurius*, an ear, i.e. that which hears confession]

aurora borealis *n.* [1990s] phencyclidine (cf. ACE n.³). [SE *aurora borealis*, the 'northern lights', lit. northern dawn, but note NORTHERN LIGHTS]

Aussie *n.* [late 19C+] **1** Australia. **2** an Australian. [abbr.]

Australian *n.* [1950s–70s] (gay) an anilinguist. [punning on SE come/COME v.¹ from SE *down under*]

Australian cigs *n.* [1940s] cigarettes sold surreptitiously and illicitly during wartime rationing. [kept beneath the shop counter, such cigarettes, like Australia, were DOWN UNDER]

Australian flag *n.* [late 19C–1910s] a shirt tail, protruding between the trousers and waistcoat. [like Australia, it is DOWN UNDER]

Australian salute *n.* [1970s+] (Aus.) a characteristic gesture in Australia of brushing away flies from one's face (cf. BARCOO SALUTE).

autem *n.* [16C–early 19C] (Und.) a church. [possibly f. SE *anthem*, or poss. f. Yid. *a'tume*, a forbidden church, although the Yid. may be a later coinage. E.P. opts for ALTHAM and a further theory suggests Fr. *autel*, an altar (note Fr. Und. *entonne*, church) and the SE *altar* may indeed be the actual root]

autem-bawler *n.* [late 18C] a parson. [AUTEM + SE *bawler*, shouter]

autem-cackler *n.* [17C–early 19C] a dissenter, spec. a Puritan (cf. AUTEM PRICKEAR). [AUTEM + SE *cackle*, to talk]

autem cackle tub *n.* [late 18C] a conventicle or dissenters' meeting house (cf. TUB n.¹; TUB-MAN). [AUTEM CACKLER + CACKLE TUB]

autem-dipper *n.* [17C–early 19C] **1** an Anabaptist. **2** a Baptist meeting house. [AUTEM + the *dipping* of baptism]

autem-diver *n.* [17C] **1** a pickpocket specializing in the robbery of church congregations (cf. KIRK-BUZZER). **2** a church-warden or other petty official charged with responsibility for distributing alms to the poor; their charges regarded them as little more than licensed robbers. [AUTEM + DIVER]

autem-gogler/-goggler *n.* [late 18C] (Und.) a fortune-teller, a conjuror. [AUTEM + GOGGLER]

autem jet *n.* [17C–18C] a parson. [AUTEM + SE *jet*, black, i.e. the black clerical gown]

autem-mort *n.* [16C–late 18C] (Und.) lit. a married woman, the companion of one of the higher ranks of mendicant villains (cf. CANTING CREW). [AUTEM + MORT, lit a 'married woman', although there may never have been a ceremony. 'Shee is a wyfe married at the church and they be as chaste as a cowe, [which] gooeth to bull every month, with what bull she careth not' (Harman)]

autem prickear *n.* [17C–early 19C] a dissenter, spec. a Puritan (cf. AUTEM CACKLER). [SE *prick-ear*, skullcap]

autem quaver *n.* [17C–early 19C] a Quaker; thus *autem quaver tub*, a Quaker meeting house. [AUTEM + SE *quaver*, to shiver or tremble. Quakers 'tremble' at the word of the Lord]

auto *n.* [1980s+] (US drugs) a device consisting of an aquarium pump and an oxygen mask used to smoke cannabis (cf. AQUA LUNG). [SE *automatic*]

autumn *n.* [mid-19C] death by hanging. [play on GO OFF WITH THE FALL OF THE LEAF]

automobubble *n.* [1900s] (US) an automobile. [joc. mispron.]

avast! *excl.* [mid-19C+] stop (what one is doing). [naut. jargon *avast*, stop; ult. f. Du. *hou'vast, houd vast*, hold fast]

'ave a Jew boy's *n.* [1910s+] weight. [Cockney mispron. of SE *avoirdupois*]

Avenoodles/Fifth Avenoodles *n.* [mid-late 19C] (US) the élite residents of New York City. [proper name Fifth Avenue, pron. 'avenoo' + SE *noodle*, a fool]

avenue-tank *n.* [1940s] (US Black/Harlem) the double-decker buses on New York's Fifth Avenue route.

average bear, the *phr.* [1980s+] (US) an average person. [the TV cartoon *Yogi Bear*, whose catchphrase was 'smarter than the average bear']

avo *n.* [1980s+] (Aus./S.Afr.) an avocado pear. [abbr.]

avocados *n.* [1930s] (US) the female breasts (cf. APPLES *n.*¹). [their shape]

avoirdupois-man *n.* [late 18C] a thief of brass weights from shop counters; his profession was known as the *avoirdupois lay*. [*avoirdupois*, the standard system of weights used in the UK before metrication; it covered all goods except precious metals, precious stones and medicines]

awake, to be *v.* [early 19C] to see through or understand a (criminal) scheme.

awash *adj.* [20C] drunk (cf. AFLOAT).

away *adj.* [late 19C+] **1** in prison; (London) any prison outside London (cf. DOWN *adj.*³; UP THE RIVER). **2** (prison/police) escaped, from prison or police cells. **3** dead.

away *adv.* [mid-19C+] straightaway, forthwith, directly, without hesitation or delay, esp. in imper., e.g. FIRE AWAY!, SAY AWAY!, start talking, 'say your piece'; *right away*, at once, immediately.

away and claw mould on yourself! *excl.* [20C] (Ulster) a general excl. of dismissal.

away for slates *phr.* [20C] (Irish) on the way to success. [ety. unknown; ? success brings a house with a slate roof]

away on a hack *phr.* [20C] (Irish) lucky, successful. [SE *hack*, a horse]

away the trip *phr.* [20C] (Scot.) pregnant. [ety. unknown]

away to fuck! *excl.* [20C] a general dismissive phr., usu. Scot. (cf. FUCK OFF!).

away to scrapings, to be *phr.* [1900s–10s] to be doomed, to have no hope. [SE *scrapings*, useless, rejected material + ? phr. 'scrape the barrel']

away to the hills *phr.* [20C] (Irish) mentally unbalanced.

away with the band *phr.* [20C] (Ulster) drunk.

away with the fairies *phr.* [20C] (Irish) **1** out of this world. **2** mentally unbalanced. [fig. uses of SE]

awerdenty *n.* [19C] (US) strong drink, often whisky, brandy. [Sp. *aguardiente*, strong water, thus brandy]

awesome *adj.* [1970s+] (orig. US teen) wonderful, excellent, the best. [the term gained a new currency, especial among the pre-teens, with the popularity *c.*1990 of the cartoon/film heroes Teenage Mutant Ninja Turtles, in whose dialogue it featured heavily]

awful *n.* [mid-late 19C] (Can.) a 'blood-and-thunder' romance, a 'penny dreadful'.

awful *adj.* [1930s+] (US) excellent, first-rate. [a 1930s version

of the bad = good equation that underpins such latterday sl. terms as BAD *adj.* and WICKED (cf. DANK *adj.*; EVIL *adj.*; ILL *adj.*; MEAN; NASTY *adj.*; ROUGH *adj.*²; TERRIBLE; TREACH; VICIOUS)]

awful *adj., adv.* [19C] **1** a general neg. intensifier, orig. frightful, very ugly, monstrous. **2** awfully, very, extremely. [SE by late 19C]

awful people *n.* [1940s–60s] (society) the police.

a-wiper *n.* [20C] a sycophant, a toady (cf. A-LICKER; ARSE-LICKER). [abbr. ASS-WIPER]

'awkins *see* HAWKINS *n.*¹.

awkward *adj.* [late 19C–1910s] pregnant.

awkward as a Chow on a bike *phr.* [1920s+] extremely clumsy, uncoordinated. [CHOW *n.*²; the apparently unlikely pairing of Chinese immigrants and bicycles]

awkward squad *n.* [late 19C+] (orig. milit.) a bunch of new recruits, employees or schoolchildren who prove less than tractable when it comes to training or obeying rules.

awning over the toy shop *n.* [1990s] (Aus.) a male beer belly. [the *toy shop* is the genitals]

a.w.o.l. *phr.* **1** [1910s+] (orig. milit.) *absent without leave.* **2** [1980s] *amour without love*, used by habituees of singles bars to denote their brief (strictly sexual) entanglements. [abbr.]

awright! *excl.* [1960s+] that's good, I feel great etc. [phonetic trans. of US pron. of *all right* as a greeting or excl.]

awse *adj.* [1980s] (US) wonderful, perfect, first-rate. [abbr. AWESOME]

ax *n.*¹ [late 19C+] (US Black) a knife, esp. a switchblade.

ax *n.*² [1910s–60s] (US) the penis (cf. ARSE-OPENER).

ax *n.*³ [1930s–60s] (US Black) any musical instrument, esp. guitar. [orig. Black jazz use, when instrument more likely saxophone or trumpet]

ax/axe *v.* [1920s+] to close down, to terminate, esp. of businesses, jobs.

axman/axe-man *n.* (US Black) **1** [late 19C+] one who carries or wields a knife. **2** [1970s] a musician, esp. a guitarist. [AX *n.*¹/*n.*³ + SE *man*]

axe wound *n.* [1990s] the vagina (cf. EVERLASTING WOUND). [AX *n.*² + SE *wound*]

axholder *n.* [late 19C] (US) the hand.

axis *n.* [19C] the vagina, one of several terms noting the organ's bodily centrality (cf. AGREEABLE RUTS OF LIFE; ARBOUR; CENTRAL CUT; CENTRE OF ATTRACTION; CENTRE OF BLISS; CENTRIQUE PART; MIDDLE CUT; MIDDLE KINGDOM; MIDLANDS).

axle *n.* [1930s–50s] the buttocks. [play on ARSEHOLE *n.*]

axle grease *n.* **1** [1910s+] (orig. Aus.) butter. **2** [1920s+] (Aus.) money. **3** [1930s+] a thick application used for one's hair. **4** [20C] semen.

ax/axe my arse *phr.* [mid18C+] a harshly neg. response to what is considered an irrelevant or over-familiar question, i.e. go to hell!, fuck off! [var. on ASK MY ARSE]

Ayrab *n.* [1960s+] (US) a derog. term for an Arab. [deliberate mispron. and popularized in song 'Ahab the Ayrab' (1962) by Ray Stevens. While usually used of Arabs or Muslim believers, occas. used by European Jews (Ashkenazis) of Eastern and North African Jews (Sephardis)]

ayraba *n.* [20C] a street urchin. [accentuated pron. of ARABBER]

ayrton *n.* [1990s] £10, a £10 note. [rhy. sl. *Ayrton Senna* = TENNER *n.* (1); ult. champion racing driver Ayrton Senna (1960–94)]

Aztec hop *n.* [1960s+] diarrhoea (cf. APPLE-BLOSSOM TWO-STEP). [var. on AZTEC TWO-STEP]

Aztec revenge *n.* [1950s+] diarrhoea (cf. APPLE-BLOSSOM TWO-STEP). [var. on AZTEC TWO-STEP]

Aztec two-step *n.* [1950s+] diarrhoea (cf. APPLE-BLOSSOM TWO-STEP). [the 'dance' is towards the bathroom]

B

b *n.*[1] [mid-19C+] a policeman. [abbr. BLUE n.[3]]

b *n.*[2] [late 19C–1900s] a bug. [abbr. B FLAT]

b *n.*[3] [1920s+] a bastard. [abbr.]

B *n.*[4] [1950s] (drugs) enough marijuana to fill a matchbox. [abbr. SE *box*]

B *n.*[5] [1950s+] (drugs) Benzedrine; thus *B-head*, a user of Benzedrine (cf. BEAN n.[6]; BENNY n.[4]; BENZ n.[1]). [abbr.]

B *n.*[6] [1990s] (US Black) a form of address for either sex. [abbr. BLOOD n.[5]]

B *n.*[7] [1990s] (US Black) a woman. [abbr. BITCH n.[1]]

b *n.*[8] [1990s] (US) a person. [? abbr. BUGGER n.[1] (1)]

b *adj.* [1920s+] euph. for BLOODY adj.; thus also *bee aitch*, bloody hell, *bee eff*, bloody fool (cf. B.F.). [abbr.]

b.a. *n.* [20C] (W.I./Guyn.) a general term of great dislike. [abbr. SE *big* + ARSE n.[1] (4)]

b.a. *adj.* [1930s+] (US) naked. [abbr. BARE-ASS]

b.a. *v.* [1980s+] (US campus) to expose one's buttocks for the purpose of evoking shock and/or amusement; also *hang a b.a.* (cf. MOON n.[1]). [abbr. BARE-ASS]

b.a. *phr.* [1950s+] absolutely nothing (cf. SWEET B.A.). [abbr. BUGGER ALL]

baa cheat *n.* [18C] a sheep. [SE *baa* + CHEAT n. (1)]

baa-lamb *n.*[1] [20C] anyone mild, pleasing, amicable; often used by women of malleable men. [nursery use *baa-lamb*, a lamb]

baa-lamb *n.*[2] [20C] euph. for BASTARD. [assonance]

baam!/baam on your monkey ass/azz! *excl.* [1990s] (US Black teen) excl. used to emphasize the act of handing something to someone else; the ext. is optional.

baana *n.* [20C] (W.I./USVI) the buttocks (cf. BAM-BAM). [echoic of the 'bang' as one sits down]

baarie, baarie *n.* [1990s] (S.Afr.) a fool. [Zulu sl. *ubari*, a bumpkin, an unsophisticated person]

b.a.b. *n.* [1980s+] (US) a nude bathing beach. [abbr. *bare ass beach*]

bab *n.*[1] [1920s–60s] **1** a cook. **2** a crook. [BABBLER; rhy. sl. *babbling brook*]

bab *n.*[2] [1970s+] (W.I.) a policeman. [BABYLON n.[1] (1)]

baba *v.* [20C] (W.I.) to dribble. [Sp. *baba*, spittle, slaver]

babalaas/babalazi/babelaas/bubblejas *n.* [1940s+] (S.Afr.) a hangover; thus *babalaas/babalaased*, suffering from a hangover, *babalaasdop*, a drink taken to alleviate the hangover, the 'hair of the dog'. [Zulu *i-babalazi*, the after-effects of a drinking-bout]

babaton/babarton *see* BARBERTON.

babbie-shop *n.* [1970s+] (S.Afr.) an Indian-owned store. [Hind. *babu*, a gentleman, Mr; used derog. in Raj period for an Indian clerk + SE *shop*]

babbitt *n.* [1920s+] (US) a self-opinionated, self-satisfied small-town bourgeois, with all the prejudices of such a figure. [George F. *Babbitt*, the hero of Sinclair Lewis's novel *Babbitt* (1922); *babbitt* appears itself to be a symbolic

concoction of *babble* and *rabbit*, summarizing its bearer's qualities]

-babble *sfx.* [1980s+] used to denote a variety of pretentious or incomprehensible jargon, e.g. *ecobabble*, *technobabble*. [on model of the slightly earlier PSYCHOBABBLE]

babbler/babbling brook *n.* (Aus./N.Z.) **1** [1910s+] a cook, esp. in an institution, mining camp or farm. **2** [1920s–60s] a criminal, a villain. [rhy. sl. *babbling brook* = cook, crook]

babe *n.*[1] (orig. US) **1** [1910s+] a girl, girlfriend or young woman, esp. if attractive. **2** [1910s+] a form of address, irrespective of sex, e.g. *Where you goin', babe?* **3** [1980s+] used congratulatorily, a person of either sex (though still usu. female); thus *babe alert*, a warning to other men to note the approach of an attractive woman (cf. BABE-A-LONIAN; BABE LAIR; BABELICIOUS; BABE MAGNET; BABYLEGS; BABYLON n.[2]; REAL BABE). [the term entered sl. *c.*1915, waned somewhat after 1950 but gained a new lease of life, and referring to either sex in late 1980s; Thompson (1967) has it in use (2) in a 1920s context]

babe *n.*[2] [1980s+] (drugs) a drug used for detoxification. [? abbr. of brandname]

babe-a-lonian *n.* [1990s] (US campus) a good-looking woman (cf. BABE n.[1]). [BABYLON n.[2] + pun]

babe in the wood *n.* [late 17C–early 19C] one who is imprisoned in the stocks or pillory. [SE *babe* + the wooden construction of the stocks/pillory + pun on the title of the folktale]

babe lair *n.* [1980s+] (US) an apartment used by a man for the seduction of women (cf. BABE n.[1]; FUCK PAD). [BABE n.[1] (3) + SE *lair*; coined in the skit (and later film) 'Wayne's World' on US TV *Saturday Night Live*, the major contemporary popularizer of the word *babe*]

babelaas *see* BABALAAS.

babelicious *adj.* [1990s] of a woman, very beautiful, very sexy (cf. BABE n.[1]; BODELICIOUS). [BABE n.[1] (3) + SE *delicious*]

babe magnet *n.* [1990s] a man who is irresistibly alluring to a woman (cf. BABE n.[1]; MAGNET). [BABE n.[1] (3) + SE *magnet*]

babe of grace *n.* [early–mid-19C] one who looks 'holier-than-thou' but is not. [lit. 'child of grace']

baberton *see* BARBERTON.

babes *n.* [1960s+] a term of affection or simply of address between either sex. [BABE n.[1] (2)]

babe's good to go *phr.* [1990s] (US Black teen) said by males when referring to a woman they presume to be sexually available. [BABE n.[1] (1)]

baboon *n.* [early 16C+] a thug, a ruffian (cf. APE n.). [SE; like APE, the *baboon* is stereotyped as an aggressive, thuggish creature]

baboon-faced *adj.* [1940s+] very ugly. [BABOON]

babu/babu-man *n.* [20C] (W.I.) **1** an old East Indian man, usu. bearded and poor. **2** an ugly old man. **3** an imaginary figure, ugly and old, conjured up to frighten children. [Hind. *babu*, a term of respect (Mr, Esquire) or an educated man]

baby n.[1] [mid-19C+] **1** a bottle or glass of liquor; thus *kiss the baby*, to take a drink, *the baby is born*, there is enough money to buy a bottle. **2** a small or half-sized bottle, whether of spirits or a non-alcoholic drink, orig. soda water; thus *baby and nurse*, a small bottle of soda water with twopennyworth of spirits.

baby n.[2] (orig. US) **1** [late 19C+] a person, often a woman (cf. BABE n.[1]). **2** [late 19C+] a person, often self-referential as in *this baby*. **3** [late 19C–1900s] an object of excellence. **4** [20C] an otherwise unnamed item or object, esp. used of automobiles, weapons and machinery. **5** [1920s+] one's special interest or responsibility, usu. with the possessive pronoun, e.g. *it's my baby*. **6** [1960s+] (US Black) a term of affection or general address between men and women or men and men.

baby n.[3] [1980s+] (drugs) marijuana. [BABY n.[2]; as a term of affection for the drug]

baby adj. [late 19C–1940s] small.

baby benz n. [1980s+] (US Black) the Mercedes Benz model 190E, which is small and sporty. [BABY adj. + BENZ n.[2]]

baby bhang n. [1980s] (drugs) marijuana. [BABY adj. + BANG n.[10]; the implication is of inferior potency]

baby-blues n. [1970s] (orig. US) human eyes, irrespective of their actual colour. [SE *baby-blue*, a light shade of blue, often associated with a baby's eyes; the implication is of candour and innocence]

baby bonus n. [1940s+] (Can.) a family allowance.

baby bumpers n. [1960s+] the female breasts. [SE *baby* + *bumper*, a railway buffer]

baby buster n. [1980s+] one who was born in the period after the *baby boom* that followed WW2. [on analogy of the *boom* and *bust* of economic jargon]

baby butch n. [1980s+] (US gay) a young, boyish lesbian (cf. DINKY DYKE; GAYCHICK). [BABY adj. + DYKE n.]

baby button n. [1960s+] the navel (cf. BELLY BUTTON). [the umbilical cord, connecting baby to mother]

babycakes n. [1960s+] (US) a term of affection between friends. [SE *baby* + *cake*; so intimate a friend is 'good enough to eat']

baby-catcher n. **1** [1930s+] (US) a midwife. **2** [1960s+] a doctor (cf. BABY-SNATCHER).

baby child n. [1970s] (US Black) **1** a younger, less respected or less experienced individual. **2** an immature person. **3** a child.

baby chute n. [1990s] the vagina (cf. BRAT-GETTING PLACE; CERTIFICATE OF BIRTH; GENERATING PLACE; NURSERY).

baby crew n. [1980s+] the junior member of a hooligan gang. [BABY adj. + CREW]

baby crockett n. [1970s] (camp gay) a fake cowboy (cf. CLONE). [proper name of *Davy Crockett* (1786–1836), the 19C Western hero, whose adventures were fictionalized in the 1950s US TV series]

baby-daddy n. [1990s] (UK/US Black) a boyfriend, esp. the father of one's child although not one's legal husband (cf. BABY-FATHER; BABY-MOTHER).

baby-doll n. [20C] (US) **1** a girl, a woman, esp. when attractive. **2** a direct term of address. [SE *baby* + DOLL n.[1]]

baby-dreads n. [1990s] (US Black) a short version of the braided hair worn by Rastafarians. [BABY adj. + DREAD(LOCKS)]

baby factory n. [1990s] (US Black) a woman who has had a large number of children.

baby-farmer n. [20C] an older person, usu. a woman, who prefers affairs with people much younger than themselves (cf. CRADLE-SNATCHER). [play on SE *baby-farmer*, one who reared orphan children, often in atrocious conditions]

baby-father n. [1980s+] (W.I.) a boyfriend, esp. the father of one's child although not one's legal husband (cf. BABY-DADDY).

baby gravy n. [1990s] semen (cf. BEEF GRAVY; BOLLOCK YOGHURT; BUTTER n.[2]; COCOA n.[4]; CREAM n.[1]; CREAMED BEEF; CUSTARD; FRENCH DRESSING; FRENCH-FRIED ICE-CREAM; GRAVY n.[1]; HONEY n.[2]; ICE-CREAM n.[2]; JAM n.[8]; JELLY n.[1]; LIVING SAUCE; LOVE CUSTARD; MELTED BUTTER n.[1]; WHIPPED CREAM). [SE *baby* + GRAVY n.[1] (1)]

baby habit n. [1950s+] (drugs) the occasional use of drugs. [BABY adj. + HABIT]

baby in the boat n. [1930s] the clitoris (cf. BALD MAN IN A BOAT; BOY IN THE BOAT; KISS THE BABY; LITTLE BOY IN THE BOAT; LITTLE MAN; LITTLE OLD MAN IN THE BOAT; LITTLE PLOUGHMAN; MAN IN THE BOAT).

baby in the bushes n. [1970s+] (US) an illegitimate child (cf. BUSH BABY; WOODS COLT). [such a baby is traditionally conceived and/or delivered in the bushes]

baby-kisser n. [1960s+] (US Black) a politician. [the campaigning politician's propensity to believe that the babies encountered enjoy being kissed by a total stranger]

babylegs n. [1980s+] a teenage girl, usually pretty and sexually alluring (cf. BABE n.[1]).

baby life n. [1950s+] (US prison) the maximum sentence that prisoners must serve (6 years, 4 months) before a parole board is bound to consider their case for the first time. [BABY adj. + LIFE n.[2]]

Babylon n.[1] (orig. W.I., then UK/US Black) **1** [1940s+] the police. **2** [1950s+] a generic term for White Western society. **3** [1970s+] any oppression or the forces that oppress the Black (esp. Rastafarian) man. **4** [1970s+] anyone perceived as putting material gains before spiritual ones. [*Babylon*, the ancient capital of Mesopotamia and used fig. to imply sinful luxury, esp. the Church of Rome. In Rastafarian iconography Babylon is opposed to Zion – the promised land of Africa, esp. Ethiopia]

Babylon n.[2] [1980s+] anywhere that attractive women are supposed to congregate or, mythically, are supposed to have their origin (cf. BABE n.[1]). [pron. *Baby-lon*]

Babylon-land n. [1970s+] (W.I.) any country, typically a materialist Western state, seen by Rastafarians as corrupt and materialistic. [BABYLON n.[1] + SE *land*]

baby-maker n. [late 19C–1900s] the penis (cf. BRAT-GETTER; CHILD-GETTER). [the procreative function of the organ]

baby-mother n. [1980s+] (Black) a girlfriend, spec. the woman who has one's baby but with whom one may not actually live (cf. BABY-DADDY).

baby/baby's pap n. [mid-19C] a cap. [rhy. sl.]

baby pro n. [1970s+] (US) **1** a prostitute under the age of legal consent. **2** the profession of child prostitution. [SE *baby* + *pro(stitute)*]

baby-rape n. [1970s+] (US) statutory rape. [SE *baby-rape*, paedophilia]

baby-raper n. [1960s+] **1** a man who commits statutory rape. **2** a general derog. term of abuse; thus *baby-raping*, of a person, despicable, disgusting. [BABY-RAPE]

baby's cries n. [1920s+] the eyes. [rhy. sl.]

baby's done it phr. [1940s+] (bingo) the number two. [a pun on NUMBER TWO n.[1]]

baby's head n. [1910s–60s] steak and kidney pudding (cf. BABY-SKULL; BABY'S LEG; LILIAN BAYLIS'S LEG). [the supposed resemblance; presumably that of the smooth suet cover rather than the meat and gravy it contains]

babysit v. **1** [1960s+] (drugs) to take care of someone either under the influence of a drug (esp. the hallucinogenic LSD) or, more often, recovering from an unpleasant, drug-induced experience. **2** [1970s+] to monitor progress, to take care of.

babysitter n. [20C] (Can.) a prison officer. [ironic use of SE]

baby-skull n. [20C] (US campus) an apple dumpling (cf. BABY'S HEAD). [the supposed resemblance]

baby's leg n. [late 19C+] meat loaf, jam-roly-poly (cf. BABY'S HEAD). [the supposed resemblance]

baby-snatcher n. [1960s+] (US) an obstetrician (cf. BABY-CATCHER). [ironic use of SE *baby-snatcher*, a kidnapper]

baby-snatching n. [1920s+] of either sex, marrying or having an affair with someone much younger than oneself; thus *baby-snatcher*, one who marries a noticeably younger partner.

baby's-pap see BABY PAP.

baby's pram n. [20C] jam. [rhy. sl.]

baby's public house n. [late 19C] the female breasts.

baby T n. [1980s+] (drugs) crack cocaine. [SE *baby* + T n.² (1)]

bacca/baccy n. [early 19C+] to*bacco*. [abbr.]

bacca-/baccy-box n. [1900s–20s] **1** the mouth. **2** the nose. [BACCA + SE *box*]

bacca-pipes n. [mid–late 19C] whiskers curled in small, close ringlets. [the similarity to a type of *tobacco-pipe*]

bacchus marsh v. [1990s] (Aus.) to have a semi-erect penis (cf. BALLARAT; BUNGAREE v.; G.P.O.; LAKE WENDOUREE). [*Bacchus Marsh*, a town half-way between Melbourne and Ballarat]

bacco n. [late 18C] to*bacco*. [abbr.]

baccy see BACCA.

baccy-box see BACCA-BOX.

baccy stick n. [late 19C] (US) the human leg. [tobacco was orig. sold in short twists a few inches long]

bach/bache n. [mid-19C–1940s] (US) a *bach*elor; thus *old bach*, a confirmed bachelor (cf. BACHIE; BATCHER). [abbr.]

bach v. [late 19C+] (orig. US) to live by oneself (cf. BATCH; KEEP BACHELOR'S HALL). [BACH n.]

bache see BACH n.

bachelor's baby n. [mid-19C+] an illegitimate child (cf. BACHELOR'S SON; TRICK BABY).

bachelor's buttons n. [20C] buttons that have a small ring on the back and can therefore be attached to a garment with a safety pin or other fastening. [a pun on SE *bachelor's button*, the double yellow buttercup (*Ranunculus acris* 'Flore Pleno'). The point is that a bachelor supposedly cannot sew]

bachelor's fare n. [late 18C] bread and cheese and kisses.

bachelor's son n. [late 18C] an illegitimate child (cf. BACHELOR'S BABY). [euph.]

bachelor's wife n. [1950s+] (US) a metal plunger with a long wooden handle, used for washing clothes in a tub. [the implement performs the stereotypically wifely chore]

bachie n. [20C] (W.I.) a room or any small place kept by a man for solo living or for conducting love affairs away from the family home; thus *live bachie*, to live alone (cf. BACH n.). [abbr. SE *bachelor*]

back n.¹ [mid-19C+] (US) a privy, an outside lavatory (cf. BACKHOUSE; BACKY; BACKYARD TELEPHONE BOOTH; REAR n.²). [the privy is usu. situated on land at the back of the house]

back n.² **1** [20C] a painful or 'bad' back (cf. HEAD n.⁴; LIVER; MOUTH n.²). **2** [1990s] (US Black teen) the posterior, the buttocks; thus *baby's got back*, used to remark favourably on a woman's posterior.

back n.³ [1960s] a dollar bill. [abbr. GREENBACK n.²]

back adj.¹ [1930s–50s] (US Black) well-established, traditional, tried and tested. [abbr. WAY BACK]

back adj.² [1940s+] (US) served and drunk alongside or together with an alcoholic drink, usu. as an order to the barman, e.g. *Scotch with soda back*.

back adv. [1940s+] (US Black) really, very much, completely.

back-a-bush adj. [20C] (W.I./Jam.) far away, deep in the countryside, in the 'back of beyond'.

back-ah-yard n. [1960s+] (W.I.) **1** the Caribbean. **2** home. [SE *back* + SE *yard*, garden]

back alley n. [late 19C+] (US Black) the main street of an otherwise run-down or 'red-light' area. [a term of approval, *back alley* is another variety of the Black reversal of White values, cf. AWFUL adj.]

back-alley deal n. [late 19C+] (US Black) a deal between one unsuspecting victim and the person who intends to and succeeds in cheating them.

back-and-belly n.¹ [1950s] (W.I.) a very thin person (cf. BACK-AND-NECK). [for ety. *see* BACK-AND-BELLY n.²]

back-and-belly n.² [1950s] (W.I.) a hypocrite, an untrustworthy person (cf. BACK-AND-FRONT; BADGER-BILL; CHEMIST BILL; SPANISH MACHETE; TWIN-MOUTH; TWO-MOUTH). [dial. *back and belly*, a two-edged machete, which can cut with either edge and is thus 'two-faced']

back and belly phr. [18C–19C] all over.

back and fill, to phr. [20C] to charm a potential victim before subjecting them to a confidence trick. [SE *back and fill*, to go backwards and forwards; thus the trickster bemuses the victim with a lengthy, convoluted patter]

back-and-front n. [1950s] (W.I.) a hypocrite. [var. on BACK-AND-BELLY n.²]

back-and-neck n. [20C] (W.I./St Kitts) a very thin person (cf. BACK-AND-BELLY n.¹). [the back and neck of a chicken, the cheapest portion available and one that is almost devoid of meat]

back-assward/-asswards adj. [1940s+] (US) confused, muddled, backwards (cf. ARSE ABOUT FACE).

back a tail, to phr. [1960s+] (Aus.) to sodomize. [SE *back*, to mount from behind + TAIL n.¹]

backbeat n. [1970s] (US Black) **1** an underlying theme or quality. **2** one's heartbeat. [jazz use *backbeat*, a secondary beat that underlies the main theme]

backbeat of the trey thirty phr. [1940s] (US Black/Harlem) the third day of the month.

backbone to breakfast time phr. [1900s] (US) very unsatisfactory, totally confused, chaotic. [var. on ARSEHOLES TO BREAKFAST TIME]

backbreaker/back-breaker n.¹ [18C+] an exhausting, demanding, usu. physical, task.

backbreaker n.² [1980s+] (drugs) LSD cut with strychnine. [the spine-wrenching contortions that accompany poisoning by strychnine]

back-buster n. [1960s+] (US) a dive in which one lands flat on the water (cf. BELLY-BUSTER; BELLYFLOP).

backcap n. [1930s–50s] (US Black) **1** an insult based on attacking the subject's family (cf. DOZENS). **2** a sharp or witty reply, as offered in the ritual name-calling known as dozens. [it 'caps' the previous statement]

backcap v. [late 19C+] (US Black) to insult someone by disparaging their family (cf. CAP v.⁵; DOZENS). **2** [late 19C–1900s] to speak evil of someone, so as to spoil their game. [BACKCAP n.]

backchat n. [20C] (orig. S.Afr.) cheek, impudence (cf. BACK JAW; BACK SASS; BACK TALK). [SE *back* + *chat*; ? orig. milit. use]

back-cheat n. [early 18C–early 19C] (Und.) a cloak. [SE *back* + CHEAT n. (1), lit. 'back thing']

backclap v. [late 19C] to insult someone (cf. BACKCAP v.). [SE *back* + 14C SE *clap*, to talk loudly, chatter]

back door n.¹ [mid-18C+] the anus (cf. BACK-DOOR COMMANDO; BACK-DOOR TRUMPET; BACKSLICE; BACKSLIT; GENTLEMAN OF THE BACK DOOR). [pun on SE]

back door n.² [1980s+] (drugs) the residue left in a pipe.

back-door adj. [20C] (US Black) devious, cunning, untrustworthy, usu. in combs., e.g. BACK-DOOR ARTIST. [*back door*, while often referring to the anus in White use (cf. GENTLEMAN OF THE BACK DOOR), almost always means underhand or secretive for Blacks]

back-door action n. [1970s+] (US) adultery (cf. BACK-DOORING; BACK-DOOR MAN n.[1]). [the adulterer metaphorically comes in 'through the back door']

back-door artist n. [1970s] (US Black) a drug addict who preys on fellow addicts for money or drugs. [BACK-DOOR adj. + ARTIST n.[2]]

back-door commando n. [1990s] a male homosexual (cf. BACK-DOOR KICKER). [BACK DOOR n.[1] + SE commando]

back-dooring n. [1980s] (US) adultery. [BACK-DOOR ACTION]

back-door kicker n. [1990s] a male homosexual (cf. BACK-DOOR COMMANDO). [BACK DOOR n.[1] + SE kicker]

back-door man n.[1] [late 19C+] (orig. US Black) an adulterer (cf. BACK-DOOR ACTION). [he comes in 'through the back door']

back-door man n.[2] [1960s+] one who practises anal intercourse (cf. BACKGAMMONER; BACKGAMMON PLAYER; GENTLEMAN OF THE BACK DOOR; USHER OF THE BACK DOOR). [BACK DOOR n.[1] + SE man]

back-door parole n. [1920s+] (US prison) **1** dying in prison before one's sentence is over (cf. BACK-GATE EXIT; BACK-GATE PAROLE; PINE-BOX PAROLE). **2** parole. [SE back-door, clandestine + parole. The remains of those who die in prison are taken out surreptitiously and buried in the prison cemetery]

back-door trot/trots n. [late 18C+] **1** diarrhoea (cf. RUNS; TROTS n.[1]). **2** over-frequent urination (cf. BACKYARD TROTS; B.D.T.). [BACK DOOR n.[1] + SE trot]

back-door trumpet n. [mid-19C+] the anus (cf. ARS MUSICA; BACK DOOR n.[1]). [BACK DOOR n.[1] + SE trumpet; the 'tune' it plays is, of course, a FART n.1]

back-door work n. [late 19C+] anal intercourse, sodomy (cf. BACK EYE; BACK-JUMP n.[2]; BACKSCUTTLE n.; BACKSHOT). [BACK DOOR n.[1] + SE work]

back double n. [late 19C+] a back street. [SE back + double, a twist or turn]

backed adv. [late 17C–early 19C] dead. [either f. lying on one's back, or, according to B.E. and then Grose, f. being supported on the backs of those who carry one's coffin; SE backed, supported at the back, underpins the latter ety.]

backed-up adj. [late 19C+] (US) constipated (cf. BALLED-UP adj.[1]). [SE backed up (usu. of water or of traffic), to have met an obstruction in the flow]

back-ended adj. [20C] **1** back-to-front. **2** of a person, perverse, eccentric (cf. ARSE ABOUT FACE).

back-end-to adj. [20C] (US) in confusion (cf. ARSE ABOUT FACE).

back eye n. [1950s+] **1** the anus (cf. BACKSLICE; BACKSLIT). **2** anal intercourse (cf. BACK-DOOR WORK). [SE back + (ROUND)EYE n. (1)]

backfire v. [1950s+] to break wind. [SE backfire, for an internal-combustion engine to ignite prematurely; such ignition causes a loud explosion]

back forty n. [1950s+] (US) an out-of-the-way, usu. barren piece of land (cf. PLOW THE BACK FORTY phr.). [SE back, out of the way + forty, a plot of 40 acres (16 hectares)]

backgammoner n. [early–mid-19C] a sodomite, one who practises anal intercourse (cf. BACK-DOOR MAN n.[2]). [pun on SE]

backgammon player n. [mid-18C–19C] a sodomite (cf. BACK-DOOR MAN n.[2]). [pun on SE]

back-gate exit n. [1920s+] (US prison) an inmate's death in prison (cf. BACK-DOOR PAROLE). [dead prisoners are taken out through the back gate of the prison and buried without ceremony]

back-gate parole n. [1920s+] an inmate's death in prison (cf. BACK-DOOR PAROLE). [for ety. see BACK-GATE EXIT]

back-hairing n. [1900s] fighting among women. [such fights often involve the pulling of the long hair at the back of a woman's head]

back-hand v. [mid-19C–1900s] to drink more than one's share. [BACK-HANDER (2)]

back-hander n. **1** [early 19C+] a slap in the face. **2** [mid-late 19C] a drink taken out of turn or an extra drink taken while the decanter circulates (cf. BACK-HAND). **3** [1910s+] a bribe (cf. KICKBACK n.). [all are given with or out of the back of the hand]

backhouse/back-house n. [late 19C+] a privy (cf. BACK n.[1]). [its position behind the house]

backhouse flush n. [1950s+] (Can. gambling) a poor hand. [fit only to be thrown down the BACKHOUSE]

back in the day/days phr. [1980s+] (orig. US Black teen) synon. for 'once upon a time'.

back in the saddle/saddle again phr. [1950s+] (US) menstruating. [SE back in the saddle, getting back to a regular routine; ? milit. or cowboy use]

back in the woods phr. [1960s+] (US) unsophisticated, gauche. [the stereotype of those who live there]

backjack n. [1980s+] (drugs) injecting a solution of opium. [SE back + JACK UP v.[8]]

back-jaw n. [1950s+] (US Black) an insolent reply (cf. BACKCHAT). [SE back + JAW v.[1]]

back jaw v. [1920s+] (US Black) to answer back rudely. [SE back + JAW v.[1]]

back-jump n.[1] [early 19C+] a back window, spec. a prison window (cf. BACKSLANG IT). [SE back + JUMP n.[1]; presumably from the robber or villain's jumping out through the entry]

back-jump n.[2] [1950s+] (US Black) anal intercourse, either hetero- or homosexual (cf. BACK-DOOR WORK). [SE back + JUMP n.[2]]

back jump v. [mid-19C+] to enter a house by a back entrance, either a door or window. [BACK-JUMP n.[1]]

back-jumper n. [mid-19C+] a thief who enters houses via a back door or window (cf. JUMP n.[1]; PARLOUR-JUMPER). [BACK JUMP]

back-land n. [late 17C–mid-19C] (W.I.) the buttocks. [pun on SE]

backlands bree n. [1930s–40s] (Glasgow) gas bubbled through milk (cf. CORPORATION COCKTAIL). [Scot. backlands, the back portion of a building or a tenement built behind another + bree, broth]

backlip v. [1950s] (US) to cheek, to speak insolently to. [SE back + LIP n.[1] (1)]

backlog n. [1960s] (US) a wife. [17C SE backlog, a large log that rests at the back of the fire and provides steady heat as its burns. As she lies in bed, a wife provides a similar function]

backmark n. [1950s+] (US Black) **1** an undesirable characteristic. **2** an informer, esp. in prison. [SE back + mark; in both senses the image is of secrecy and deliberate concealment]

backnail n. [1980s+] (Aus.) a cigarette (cf. COFFIN NAIL n.[2]). [resemblance to SE backnail, a nail made with flat shanks so that it does not split the grain of the wood

back number n. [late 19C+] an irrelevant person, a 'has-been', used esp. of a former lover, now discarded, a person or a thing that is behind the times, out of date or useless. [the previous and thus 'dead' editions of newspapers]

back of beyond n. [early 19C+] anywhere considered by the speaker as inaccessible, outside the purlieus of acceptable life. ['civilization' is implied]

back of Bourke n. [1910s–30s] (Aus.) the wilds, the back of beyond, the edge of 'civilization' (cf. BEYOND THE RABBIT-PROOF FENCE). [proper name Bourke, a town in the extreme west of New South Wales]

back off! excl. [1950s+] (orig. US Black) go away! stop bothering me!

back off Jackson! excl. [1990s] (US teen) calm down. [BACK OFF! + JACKSON]

back off the boards/earth, to phr. [late 19C+] (US) to surpass. [SE back, to push away, to cause to retreat]

back of/behind of God speed n. [20C] (Irish) very far away. [SE *God speed*, farewell]

back of my hand/back of my hand and the sole of my foot phr. [19C] (Irish/Scot.) phr. implying contempt and rejection. [the object of the rejection will get a slap or a kick]

back of the hand down phr. [late 19C] bribery. [BACK-HANDER]

back of the net! excl. [1980s] wonderful, perfect. [football jargon, meaning the ball has entered the net and a goal has been scored]

back-out n.[1] [early 19C–mid-19C] (US) cowardice (cf. BACK ONE OUT).

back-out n.[2] [1970s] (W.I.) a woman's dress cut very low in the back.

back out v. [early–mid-19C] to retreat. [horse-racing jargon *back out*, to bring a horse backwards out of a stall]

back-pedal! excl. [1910s–20s] an excl. calling for restraint, steady on! hold it!

back-porch n. [1950+] (US) the buttocks.

back someone out v. [mid-19C+] (US) to challenge, to face down. [SE *back*, to cause to retreat]

back someone's play, to phr. [20C] (US) to support one's own statement or action or back up those of another person. [gambling jargon]

backra/buckra n. (W.I./US Black) **1** [late 18C+] a master, a boss. **2** [19C+] a White man; thus *buckra-nigger*, a 'White man's negro' or subservient Black, *buckra-bittle*, buckra victuals or White man's food. **3** [19C+] white as a colour, e.g. *buckra yam*, a white yam. **4** [mid-19C+] one who, while Black, moves in White society and sees themself as the White man's equal. [Black patois of Surinam *bakra*, master. This in turn was based on Efik (the language of the Calabar coast) *mba*, all + *kara* to encompass, get round, to master (a subject); thus *mbakara*, *makara*, a White man, a European, with a parallel meaning of a demon, a powerful and superior being (cf. OFAY n.). Note the popular (if erroneous) ety. *back raw*; the White man was known for his beatings]

back-racket n. [early–mid-17C] a sharp response. [SE *back-racket*, the return of a ball in tennis]

backra fire n. [20C] (W.I.) electricity. [BACKRA n. (2) + SE *fire*]

backra johnny n. [19C+] (W.I.) **1** a poor White. **2** a light-skinned Black person (cf. BACKRA NIGGER). [BACKRA + JOHNNIE n.[2] (1) = generic for man]]

backraman n. [late 18C+] a master, a boss (cf. BACKRA). [BACKRA n. (1) + SE *man*]

backra nigger n. [19C+] (W.I.) a light-skinned person and, as such, one who is despised (cf. BACKRA JOHNNY). [BACKRA n. (1) + NIGGER n.]

backra pickney n. [19C+] (W.I.) **1** a White child. **2** a light-skinned mixed-race child. [BACKRA n. + W.I. pron. of PICCANINNY]

back roll v. [1980s+] (drugs) to roll a joint so that only one layer of paper surrounds the mix.

backroom boys n. [1940s+] unsung, anonymous but vital experts, inventors, scientists, theorists etc, who provide much of the muscle behind a business, factory or other organization (cf. BOYS n.[2]). [coined by Lord Beaverbrook (1879–1964) in March 1941: 'Now who is responsible for this work of development on which so much depends? To whom must the praise be given? To the boys in the back rooms. They do not sit in the limelight. But they are the men who do the work']

back-row hopper n. [late 19C–1900s] a scrounger who frequents taverns in the hope of finding someone willing to buy them a drink. [theatrical imagery]

back sass v. [1950s+] (US) to answer back rudely; thus *back-sasser*, a cheeky person (cf. BACKCHAT). [SE *back* + SASS n.]

back-scratcher n. [1940s+] (US) a sycophant, a toady.

backscull v. [19C] to enter a house from the back way (cf. BACKSCUTTLE v.).

backscuttle n. **1** [19C] heterosexual anal intercourse (cf. BACK-DOOR WORK). **2** [late 19C+] sodomy performed by homosexuals; thus *do a back scuttle*, to have sex from the rear, to sodomize. [for ety. see BACKSCUTTLE v.[1]]

backscuttle v.[1] [late 19C+] (Und.) to enter a house from the back way. [SE *back* + *scuttle*, to bore a hole (in order to sink a ship)]

backscuttle v.[2] [late 19C+] to have homosexual or heterosexual anal intercourse. [for ety. see BACKSCUTTLE v.[1]]

backscuttler n. [1920s+] (Aus.) a sodomite. [BACKSCUTTLE n.; although v.[2] works for both hetero-and homosexual intercourse, the n., apparently found only in Aus., refers only to homosexuals]

back-seat driver n. [1920s+] (orig. US) anyone who offers unwanted advice to the person who is actually in charge of, or at least performing, the task for which the advice is given (cf. KIBITZER).

backshot n. [1950s+] (Black) anal intercourse (cf. BACK-DOOR WORK).

backside n. [late 18C+] the posterior, the buttocks, esp. as synon. with ARSE n.[1] (1), as in *kiss one's backside, kick one's backside* etc. [*backside* has been SE in the UK since 1500 but is still considered improper in the W.I.]

backside of nowhere n. [1960s+] (US) nowhere, a very out-of-the-way place (cf. ASS-END OF NOWHERE).

backslack n. [1900s] (US) cheek, insolence. [SE *back* + SLACK n. (1)]

backslang it v. **1** [early 19C–1900s] to leave by the back door. **2** [19C] to leave surreptitiously, quietly (cf. BACK JUMP). **3** [19C] to make a deliberate detour to avoid meeting a certain person or persons. **4** [19C] (Aus.) to request lodgings from strangers as one travels through the back country. **5** [late 19C+] to enter a house from the back way (cf. BACKSCUTTLE v.[1]). [? link to BACK SLUM; the term predates the linguistic variety of backsl., while there seems to be no link to SLANG n.[1] itself; ? link to SLING ONE'S HOOK phr.[1]]

backslice n. [mid-19C] of a man or woman, the anus (cf. BACK DOOR n.[1]). [SE *back* + SLICE n.[1] (1)]

backslit n. [mid-19C] the anus (cf. BACK DOOR n.[1]). [SE *back* + SLIT n.[1] (1)]

back slum n. [19C] the back entrance to a building, the back door or window (cf. BACK JUMP; BACKSLANG IT). [SE *back* + SLUM n.[2] (1)]

back slums n. [19C] areas or streets known for a high proportion of criminal residents. [later SE for very poor slums]

back-staircase n. [mid–late 19C] a bustle on a dress.

backstall n. (Und.) **1** [19C] a member of a garrotting gang who keeps watch and provides physical assistance to the actual garrotter if necessary (cf. NASTYMAN; UGLYMAN). **2** [19C–1900s] a thief's accomplice. [SE *back* + STALL n.[1]]

backstop n. [1950s+] **1** (US Und.) in a pickpocket team, the one who works directly behind the victim. **2** (Aus.) a supporter, accomplice, one on whom one can rely. [(1) baseball jargon *backstop*, the catcher; (2) cricket jargon *backstop*, a fielder who stands behind the wicket-keeper to stop any balls the keeper may have missed]

back-street wife n. [20C] (US) a mistress.

back swap v. [late 19C] to renege on a bargain.

back-talk n. [mid-19C+] cheek, impertinence; thus imper. *no back-talk*, that's it, there's no more to be said (cf. BACK-CHAT; BACK-TALKING). [Ulster dial. *backtalk*, to answer back rudely]

back-talking n. [1960s+] (US) gossip (cf. BACK-TALK). [SE *talk behind one's back*]

back the breeze, to phr. [20C] (US) to chatter, to gossip (cf. BAT THE BREEZE; BEAT THE BREEZE; BREEZE n.²; FAN THE BREEZE phr.²; FAN THE FIRE; SHOOT THE BREEZE phr.¹).

back-timber n. [mid-17C] clothing.

back time n. [1950s+] (US Und.) time spent in prison awaiting sentencing (cf. JAWBONE TIME).

back to back n. [1980s+] (drugs) smoking crack cocaine after injecting heroin or using heroin after smoking crack cocaine.

back-to-back adj. [1980s+] (US Black) affectionate, friendly, intimate.

back to the drawing board phr. [1930s+] (orig. US) start again with new plans, when one plan or idea has come to nothing. [a cartoon in the New Yorker by Peter Arno (Curtis Arnoux Peters, 1904–68); in the background an aircraft explodes in flames while in the foreground a group of designers intone: 'Ah well, back to the old drawing board']

back to the salt mines! phr. [1930s+] (orig. US) let's get back to work.

back up n.¹ [20C] (Aus.) a second helping of food.

back up n.² [1980s+] (N.Z.) retaliation, revenge. [BACK UP v.⁴]

back up v.¹ [20C] (Aus./US) to have serial sex with a woman. [SE back up, to form a queue]

back up v.² [1950s+] (drugs) to distend the vein during drug taking, thus making it easier to insert the needle. [? SE put one's back up; the distension of the vein raises it above the surrounding flesh]

back up v.³ [1950s+] (drugs) 1 to pump the hypodermic so that blood comes into the tube, mixing with the drug/water solution before shooting it back into the vein. 2 to refuse to sell drugs on the premise that the purchaser might be an informer or undercover policeman. [SE back up, to reverse (either the movement of the plunger or the decision to sell drugs)]

back up v.⁴ [1980s+] (N.Z.) to gang up on, esp. to take revenge. [SE back up, to support]

back up off my tip for the simple fact you on it like a gnat on a dog's dick phr. [1990s] (US Black teen) don't annoy me.

back-up pills n. [20C] aphrodisiacs. [they supposedly SE back up one's potency or make seduction easier]

backwards n. [1990s] (drugs) 1 an unpleasant experience while using LSD. 2 a depressant.

backward thinking n. [1950s+] (US Black) confused, muddled thinking.

backwash n.¹ [1900s–20s] (US) 1 insolent talk, cheek. 2 non-sensical talk.

backwash n.² [1970s+] liquid that flows back into a bottle, possibly after being in one's mouth when one drinks straight from it.

back water v. [1950s+] (US) to retract a statement, to back down from a position; thus take back water, to back down, to accept defeat. [nautical jargon back water, to reverse a boat]

back wheels n. [1990s] testicles. [the penis is presumably the vehicle]

backy n. [late 19C+] (US) a privy (cf. BACK n.¹). [abbr. BACK-HOUSE]

back yard n. [20C] (US) that area of a town where the poorer citizens live (cf. BACK-AH-YARD; FRONT YARD).

backyard adj. [1920s+] (orig. Aus.) small, trivial, insignificant, esp. of business conducted from one's own home.

backyard cousin/relation n. [20C] (US) a relation, possibly an illegitimate child, of whom the speaker is not proud. [BACKYARD + SE cousin]

backyard telephone booth n. [20C] (US) a privy (cf. BACK n.¹). [its position and size]

backyard trots n. [20C] (US) 1 diarrhoea. 2 over-frequent urination (cf. BACK-DOOR TROT). [one 'trots' through the back door on the way to the privy]

bacon n.¹ 1 [late 16C–17C] human flesh, a human being (cf. PULL BACON; SAVE ONE'S BACON). 2 [late 16C–17C] a rustic, a clown. 3 [1910s–20s] the penis (cf. BACON BAZOOKA; BALONEY n.²; BANGER n.⁴; BEEF n.¹; BUTCHER n.¹; CANADIAN BACON; CHITTERLINGS n.¹; CRIMSON CHITTERLING; GOOSER n.²; GOOSE'S NECK n.¹; HAIRY SAUSAGE; HAMBONE n.³; HORSEMEAT; HOT DOG n.¹; KIELBASA; KNOCKWURST; LIVE SAUSAGE; LOVESTEAK; MEAT; MUTTON n.¹; SAUSAGE n.¹; SCHNITZEL; SMALL MEAT; SNORKER; SPLIT MUTTON; TADDLER; TUBESTEAK; TUBESTEAK OF LOVE; TURKEY NECK; WEENIE n.¹; WHITE MEAT). [SE bacon; the role of bacon as the staple meat of peasant England]

bacon n.² 1 [1920s] money (cf. BRING HOME THE BACON). 2 [1950s–60s] (US Black) the good life, material success. [SE bacon; the rich fattiness of the meat as a metaphor for wealth]

bacon n.³ [1970s+] the police (cf. ROBIN HOG). [ext. of PIG n.³]

bacon adj. [1990s] (US campus) good-looking, sexy. [BACON n.¹ (1)]

bacon and eggs n. [1950s+] (orig. Aus.) legs (cf. HAM AND EGGS; SCOTCH PEGS; SCRAMBLED EGGS n.¹). [rhy. sl.]

bacon bazooka n. [1990s] the penis (cf. BACON n.¹; BAYONET; BAZOOKA; BEEF BAYONET; HAM HOWITZER; LAMB CANNON; MEAT AXE; MEAT-CLEAVER; MEAT LANCE; MUTTON BAYONET; MUTTON-DAGGER; MUTTON GUN; MUTTON MUSKET; PORK SWORD; SPAM JAVELIN; TROUSER MAUSER).

bacon-bonce n. [20C] 1 a dullard, a simpleton, a yokel. 2 one who is partially bald. [SE bacon + BONCE; lit. 'pig-head']

bacon-faced adj. [late 17C–early 19C] fat-faced, heavily jowled. [SE bacon + faced]

bacon fed adj. [late 17C–early 19C] fat, greasy. [the qualities of the cooked pig]

bacon hole n. [1940s+] the mouth (cf. BUN-TRAP; CAKEHOLE; FAG-HOLE; HOLE n.¹; PORRIDGE HOLE).

bacon sandwich n. [20C] the vagina; one of a number of terms that equate the vagina with raw meat (cf. BEEF n.¹; BIT OF MEAT; BIT OF PORK; BIT ON A FORK; BRASOLE; BUTCHER'S SHOP n.¹; BUTCHER'S WINDOW; CHOPPED LIVER n.¹; MEAT; MEAT CURTAINS; MUTTON n.¹; PRIME CUT; SPLIT MUTTON). [coarse fig. use of SE]

bacon-slicer n. [mid-17C] a rustic, a yokel. [the occupation]

bad n.¹ [1980s+] (US campus) fault, as in my bad.

bad n.² [1980s+] (drugs) crack cocaine. [BAD adj.]

bad adj. [1920s+] (orig. US Black) good, exciting; the implication being that the individual/object so defined as bad in establishment eyes and thus good in those of any outlaw/criminal, drug or other minority culture, esp. in Black use; thus comparative, badder, superlative baddest (cf. AWFUL adj.). [note Ger. schlecht, bad, orig. meant good; also 19C Aus. convict jargon bad fellow, a convict who cooperates with the authorities; good fellow, one who maintains intra-convict solidarity; Smitherman (1994) suggests Mandingo a ka nyi ko-jugu, it is good, badly, i.e. so good that it is bad]

bad actor n. [20C] 1 an unpleasant individual, an aggressive trouble-maker. 2 a vicious or unbroken horse.

bad-ass/badass n. [1950s+] (US) an unpleasant, aggressive individual. [SE bad + sfx. -ASS]

bad-ass/badass adj. [1910s+] (orig. US Black) 1 tough, aggressive, frightening. 2 formidable, admirable, first-rate. [BAD-ASS n.; given the use of bad, the term is as much congratulatory as not]

bad ass v. [1970s+] (US) to bully, to behave like a thug. [BAD-ASS n.]

bad-ass nigger n. [20C] (US Black) an aggressive, tough Black man who rejects the constraints and humiliation of the role the White authorities have selected for him. [BAD-ASS adj. + NIGGER n.]

bad bongos n. [1970s] (US campus) a situation in which things do not go well (cf. TOUGH TITTY). [? assonance]

bad boy *n.* **1** [1950s+] (W.I./Guyn.) a tearaway, a young criminal (cf. BAD-HEAD; BAD-JOHN). **2** [1970s+] (US Black) a general term of approval, referring both to individuals and to objects. **3** [1970s+] (US Black) a Black who rejects the second-class role offered by the dominant White society (cf. BAD NIGGER). **4** [1980s+] (US) anything considered impressive. [BAD adj. + SE *boy*]

bad break *n.* [1950s+] (orig. US) a stroke of bad luck. [SE *bad* + BREAK n.² (1)]

bad bundle *n.* [1980s+] (drugs) inferior quality heroin. [SE *bad* + BUNDLE n.⁴]

bad bwoy *n.* [1970s+] (W.I./UK Black teen) a villain, a criminal, a rebellious young male. [W.I. pron. of BAD BOY; given the bad = good pattern it is not necessarily pej.]

bad/good cess to you! *excl.* [mid-19C] (orig. Irish) bad/good luck to you! [? abbr. SE *success* (*OED*); Ware suggests dial. *cess*, a piece of turf; thus 'may you live in a good/bad place'; E.P. prefers *cess*, assessment; thus 'may you suffer a good/bad (tax) assessment']

bad clothes *n.* [1960s] (US Black) one's best, most fashionable clothes (cf. BAD RAGS). [BAD adj. + SE *clothes*]

bad count *n.* [20C] (US) **1** an unfair decision. **2** a short measure of drugs. [boxing jargon *bad count*, a count that is too long or too short]

bad crowd *n.* [late 19C–1900s] (US) an unpleasant, untrustworthy person (cf. BADDIE; BAD EGG; BAD HALFPENNY; BAD HAT; BAD LOT; BAD PENNY).

baddest *adj.* [mid-19C+] (US Black) the very best, supreme. [the superlative of BAD adj.]

baddie/baddy *n.* [1930s+] **1** an unpleasant person (cf. BAD CROWD). **2** in film or TV melodramas, the stereotyped villain who must, and will, be vanquished (cf. BAD GUY; GOODIE). [nursery use of SE *bad*]

baddiwad *n.* [1990s] (US teen) something that is bad. [BADDIE + sfx. -WAD]

bad dog *n.* [1940s+] (Aus.) a bad debt. [unpaid, it won't 'lie down']

bad-doing *adj.* [1950s+] (US Black) first-rate, excellent superior (cf. BAD-ASS adj.). [BAD adj. + SE *doing*]

baddy *see* BADDIE.

bad egg *n.* [mid-19C+] (orig. US) **1** a rogue, a villain (cf. BAD CROWD; GOOD EGG). **2** a worthless speculation. [SE *bad* + EGG n.¹ (1)]

Baden-Powell *n.* [late 19C+] a trowel. [rhy. sl.; ult. Robert Baden-Powell (1857–1941), the founder of the Boy Scouts]

baderbus *n.* [1990s] a wheelchair (cf. BADERED). [Douglas *Bader* + SE *bus*]

badered *adj.* [1980s] drunk (cf. BREAKYLEG n.¹; LEGLESS). [the RAF's 'legless ace' Sir Douglas *Bader* (1910–82), immortalized in the film *Reach for the Sky* (1956)]

bad-eye *n.¹* [late 17C+] (orig. US Black) a threatening glance, a threat, the evil eye (cf. BADMOUTH n.). [? Mandingo *nyejugu*; unlike many Black uses of *bad*, this uses the SE *bad*, evil, rather than bad adj., good]

bad-eye *n.²* [late 19C] (US) cheap, home-distilled whisky. [? var. on RED-EYE n.¹]

bad eye *v.* [1960s+] (US Black) to stare down (cf. MAD DOG v.).

bad fall *n.* [1950s+] (US Und.) an arrest and charge from which one cannot escape, despite attempting to intimidate or bribe the plaintiff or a prosecution witness. [SE *bad* + FALL n.]

bad-food *n.* [20C] (W.I.) food that supposedly contains 'magic' ingredients, which will influence a man to choose a particular woman.

bad form *n.* [late 19C+] (society) anything socially unacceptable (cf. GOOD FORM; NOT DONE; NOT ON). [horse-racing use *form*, the state of a horse's health etc]

badge *n.¹* [late 18C] **1** (Und.) one who has been branded as a judicial punishment. **2** the brand itself.

badge *n.²* [1920s+] **1** (US prison) a warder, a guard, anyone in authority. **2** (US) a policeman (cf. SHIELD). [the wearer's badge of office]

badge-cove *n.* [early 18C–early 19C] (Und.) one who draws a pension from the parish. [SE *badge* + COVE, badge in this case meaning an official document or licence; an Und. version of SE *badge-man*, a licensed beggar or almsman]

badger *n.¹* (Und.) **1** [late 18C–mid-19C] a thief who specializes in robbery on the riverbank, after which he murders the victim and disposes of the corpse in the water. **2** [late 19C–1920s] a thief who rifles the pockets of a man who is currently engaged with his accomplice, a prostitute (cf. PANEL THIEF). [? the badger's worrying of its prey]

badger *n.²* [19C] (US) a chamberpot; thus *the badger fight*, *pulling the badger*, a practical joke whereby an innocent is lured into a hoax fight between a dog and a badger but ends up being splashed by the contents of a chamberpot.

badger *n.³* [early 19C+] (US) an old man. [? the ill-temper of the animal]

badger *n.⁴* [mid–late 19C] (US) a rogue who specializes in robbing clients who are visiting a brothel (cf. BADGER n.⁶; BADGER-CRIB; BADGER GAME; BADGER HOUSE; BADGER MOLL; BADGER WORKER; CLIP-JOINT; CLIPPING n.; CROCODILE SCAM; CROSSBITE; MURPHY n.³; PANEL CRIB; PANEL GAME; PANEL THIEF).

badger *n.⁵* [mid-19C+] (US) the nickname of the natives or inhabitants of Wisconsin. [the early Wisconsin lead-miners (*badgers*) who lived in subterranean diggings alongside the seams of lead they were mining]

badger *n.⁶* [late 19C–1920s] (US) a prostitute, esp. one who participates in a scheme to rob her clients (cf. BADGER n.⁴). [SE *badger*, an animal which is both nocturnal and carnivorous; the prostitute too 'devours' her victims after dark]

badger *n.⁷* **1** [1990s] (US) an unattractive woman; thus *badger set*, anywhere that such women can take advantage of a young man. **2** [1990s] (orig. US) the female genital area (cf. BEARSKIN; BEAVER n.⁴; CHINCHILLA; CIVET; FEATHER n.¹; FLUFF n.¹; FUR; MINK; MUFF n.¹; PUSSY n.¹; SCUT n.¹; STOAT; TAIL n.¹). **3** [1990s] (US) a male homosexual. **4** [1990s+] (US) an attractive woman or generic for attractive women as a class. [less 'aggressive' versions of BADGER n.⁶]

badger-bill *n.* [1940s+] (W.I.) a hypocrite, a 'two-faced', untrustworthy person (cf. BACK-AND-BELLY n.²). [dial. *badger-bill*, a two-edged machete]

badger-crib *n.* [19C–1900s] a brothel that specializes in robbing its clients (cf. BADGER n.⁴). [BADGER GAME + CRIB n.³ (2)]

badger game *n.* [mid-19C+] (orig. US) the ensnaring of a client by a woman, often a prostitute, and his subsequent robbery, either by the woman herself or more often by her pimp, posing as an 'outraged boyfriend'; the man often emerged, while the pair were *in flagrante*, from a hidden door or panel in the bedroom wall (cf. BADGER n.⁴). [BADGER n.⁶ + SE *game*, scheme, intrigue]

badger house *n.* [mid-19C–1900s] (US) an establishment, often a brothel, where the client is robbed (cf. ACCOMMODATION HOUSE; BADGER n.⁴). [BADGER n.⁶ + HOUSE n.¹ (1)]

badger-legged *adj.* [mid-17C–early 18C] used of a person with one leg shorter than the other. [the erroneous belief that badgers are similarly equipped]

badger man *n.* [1910s+] (Aus.) the accomplice of a prostitute who tricks her clients (cf. BADGER n.⁴). [BADGER n.⁶ + SE *man*]

badger moll *n.* [1900s] (US) the woman, often a prostitute, who tricks her client (cf. BADGER n.⁴). [BADGER n.⁶ + MOLL n.]

badger worker *n.* [late 19C–1940s] (US) the accomplice of a prostitute who tricks her clients (cf. BADGER n.⁴). [BADGER n.⁶ + SE *worker*]

bad go n. [1980s+] (drugs) a bad reaction to a drug. [SE *bad* + GO n.[6]]

bad guy n. [1930s+] (orig. US) in film or TV melodramas, the stereotyped villain (cf. BADDIE). [SE *bad* + *guy*]

bad hair n. [1950s+] (US Black/W.I.) a Black person's naturally kinky hair (cf. GOOD HAIR; HARD HAIR). [BAD adj. + SE *hair*]

bad hair day n. [1980s+] a 'difficult' or demanding day. [the image of one's hair being a mess, thus rendering any social interaction impossible]

bad halfpenny n. **1** [early 19C] any errand or task that proves pointless. **2** [mid-19C] an unpleasant, untrustworthy person (cf. BAD CROWD).

bad hat n. [early 19C–1950s] a rogue, an untrustworthy person (cf. BAD CROWD). [according to Charles Mackay's *Memoirs of Extraordinary Popular Delusions* (1841) f. a London election in the borough of Southwark, c.1838, in which one of the candidates was well known as a hat-maker. As he campaigned he would single out any voter whose hat fell beneath the highest standards and declare: 'What a shocking bad hat you have got, call at my warehouse and you shall have a new one.' On the day of the election, as he gave his final speech, his opponents urged a hostile crowd to drown him out by chanting: 'What a shocking bad hat!' The phr. caught on and first in its entirety, and subsequently in its abbr. form entered popular sl. It survived through the 19C and gradually declined through the first half of the 20C. An alternative ety. attributes the phr. to the Duke of Wellington, who on his first visit to the Peer's Gallery of the House of Commons remarked, on looking down on the members of the Reform Parliament: 'I never saw so many shocking bad hats in my life']

bad-head n. [20C] (W.I./Belz.) a tearaway, a young criminal (cf. BAD BOY).

bad in the head phr. [1980s+] (US Black) **1** eccentric, out of control. **2** unhappy.

bad iron n. [mid-19C–1910s] bad luck, a failure, a disaster. [ety. unknown]

bad-john n. [1960s–70s] (W.I.) a tearaway, a young criminal; thus *play bad-john*, to act like a hooligan (although not actually to be one) (cf. BAD BOY). [SE *bad* + JOHN n.[1]]

bad lands n. [late 19C+] (US) **1** the slum area of a city (orig. coined for that in Chicago). **2** any dangerous area. [ironic use of SE *badlands*, arid, barren areas of the western US]

bad lot n. [mid-19C+] an unpleasant, untrustworthy person (cf. BAD CROWD). [auction house jargon *bad lot*, one that will not sell]

badly done adj. [20C] (Ulster) embarrassed. [SE *badly* + DO v.[4] (1)]

Bad Man n. [18C+] (US Black) the Devil.

bad medicine n. [mid-19C+] (orig. US) something or someone sinister or ill-fated (cf. MEDICINE MAN). [the SE use of *medicine* to translate terms used in a variety of native American languages meaning a fetish, spell or charm; note use of 'bad juju' and 'juju-man' in the spy novels of John le Carré (b.1931)]

bad-mind n. [20C] (W.I.) malice, spite, animosity (cf. PLAY BAD-MIND).

badminton n. [mid-19C] claret cup. [the iced cup, made of claret, sugar, spice and cucumber peel, was invented at Badminton, the country seat of the Duke of Beaufort; the term was extended to boxing jargon where it meant blood, as does CLARET]

badmouth n. (orig. US Black/W.I.) **1** [late 17C+] a curse, a spell (cf. BAD-EYE n.[1]). **2** [1970s+] malicious gossip. [Mandingo *dajugu*, bad mouth]

badmouth v. [1940s+] **1** to attack verbally, to slander, often in phr. *put the bad mouth on one*. **2** to best someone in an argument or verbal contest. [BADMOUTH n.]

badness n. [1980s+] (W.I./UK Black teen) delinquency or unruly behaviour, often just for the sake of it (cf. SLACKNESS).

bad news n. (orig. US) **1** [1920s+] an unattractive, unpleasant person or thing (cf. BAD CROWD; BADDIE). **2** [1920s+] an unpleasant situation, difficulty, trouble (cf. BAD MEDICINE; BAD SCENE). **3** [1920s] (US) a shotgun. **4** [1920s–30s] (US) the bill in a café or restaurant.

bad nigger n. **1** [early 18C+] (US Black) a Black who rejects the second-class role offered by the dominant White society (cf. BAD-ASS NIGGER; DOG NIGGER). **2** [1910s+] (Aus.) an Aborigine who refuses to cooperate with the authorities. [BAD adj. + NIGGER n.]

bad paper n. [20C] **1** any form of fraudulent documents, counterfeit money or similar written or printed frauds or forgeries (cf. PAPER n.[1]). **2** (US prison) a negative report on a prisoner. [SE *bad* + PAPER n.[1]]

bad patter n. [1940s+] a bad situation. [SE *bad* + PATTER n., lit. 'bad speech']

bad-pay adj. [20C] (W.I.) extremely slow to pay debts or any money that is owed and expected.

bad penny n. [early 19C+] an unpleasant, untrustworthy person (cf. BAD CROWD).

bad place/spot in the road n. [1950s–60s] (US) an out-of-the-way, unimportant place or settlement.

bad rags n. [1960s–70s] (US Black) one's best, most fashionable clothes (cf. BAD CLOTHES). [BAD adj. + RAGS n.[2]]

bad rap n. [1960s+] (US) **1** a serious criminal charge. **2** an unfair criminal charge. **3** a sentence of 20 years or more. [SE *bad* + RAP n.[3]]

bad rap v. [1960s–70s] (orig. US) to malign, to criticize unfairly (cf. BADMOUTH v.; BUM-RAP). [SE *bad* + RAP v.[2]]

bad scene n. [1950s+] an unpleasant situation; on the bad = good theory, 'it's a really bad scene' could be a term of approval (cf. BAD NEWS). [BAD adj. + SCENE]

bad scran phr. [mid-19C] (orig. Anglo-Irish) bad luck, usu. as phr. *bad scran to*. [SE *bad* + SCRAN n.]

bad seed n. [1980s+] (drugs) **1** peyote. **2** heroin. **3** marijuana. [BAD adj. + SE *seed*]

bad shag n. [late 18C–early 19C] an unsatisfactory lover, usu. in phr. *he is but bad shag*. [SHAG n.[1]; note later 20C 'a good shag', 'a bad shag']

bad shilling n. **1** [late 19C] one's last shilling. **2** [late 19C–1930s] (Aus.) a remittance man (cf. BAD PENNY).

bad shit n.[1] [1960s+] better than average marijuana. [BAD adj. + SHIT n.[5]]

bad shit n.[2] [1960s+] worse than average problems. [SE *bad* + SHIT n.[3]]

bad shot n. [mid-19C+] a poor guess. [SE *bad* + SHOT n.[2] (2)]

bad show! excl. [20C] a general excl. of disappointment or disapproval.

bad siddown n. [20C] (W.I./Jam.) poor behaviour in public, disregard of other people's feelings. [SE *bad sit-down*; the image is of a prostitute lazing around on a street corner; also note Krio (Sierra Leone Creole) *bad sidom*, a woman sitting so as to expose her genitals]

bad smash n. [20C] counterfeit coins. [SE *bad* + SMASH n.[3]]

bad spot in the road see BAD PLACE IN THE ROAD.

badster n. [1920s+] (Aus.) a villain, a morally bad person. [SE *bad* + sfx. *-ster*]

bad talk n. [1960s–70s] (US Black) **1** conversation or writing that considers and/or urges revolutionary attitudes and actions; such talk is *bad* both in White eyes and as the prerogative of Blacks (cf. BAD NIGGER). **2** a form of ritual name-calling, based on insulting one's target's family (cf. DOZENS). [BAD adj. + SE *talk*]

bad trip *n.* [1960s+] **1** a bad or frightening experience while taking psychedelic drugs (cf. BUMMER n.³; BUM TRIP; DOWNER n.⁵; DOWN TRIP). **2** any sort of unpleasant or unnerving experience. [SE *bad* + TRIP n.³]

bad trot *n.* (Aus.) **1** [20C] an unfair situation or result. **2** [1920s+] a run of bad luck. [SE *bad* + TROT n.² (5)]

bad 'un *n.* [early–mid-19C+] a rogue, an untrustworthy person (cf. BAD CROWD). [lit. 'a bad one']

bad weave *n.* [20C] (US Black) one's best clothes (cf. BAD RAGS). [BAD adj. + WEAVE]

bafan *adj.* [1950s+] (W.I. Rasta) clumsy, awkward; thus *bafang*, a child who has not learned to walk for its first 2–7 years. [synon. Twi *bafan*]

bafber *n.* [20C] a thief who specializes in robbing bedrooms while their occupant is asleep. [ety. unknown]

bafflegab *n.* [1950s+] (US) (deliberately) unintelligible jargon, esp. as used for the purposes of obfuscation by politicians, civil servants, bureaucrats, businessmen etc. [SE *baffle* + GAB n.; coined by the asst. general counsel of the US Chamber of Commerce, Milton Smith: 'I decided we needed a new and catchy word to describe the utter incomprehensibility, ambiguity, verbosity and complexity of government regulations']

bafoon/puffoon *n.* [1940s] (W.I.) a stench, esp. a fart. [echoic]

bag *n.*¹ [late 19C–1930s] **1** the womb. **2** the scrotum. **3** the vagina.

bag *n.*² [late 19C–1950s] (US) an informer. [they place their victims IN THE BAG phr.² (2)]

bag *n.*³ **1** [late 19C+] (US) a promiscuous woman, a prostitute (cf. HAG n.). **2** [1920s+] (orig. US) an unattractive woman, esp. as *old bag*. **3** [1920s+] a homosexual man, esp. an unattractive and/or passive one.

bag, the *n.*⁴ [late 19C+] (Glasgow) money.

bag *n.*⁵ [1920s+] (US) a contraceptive sheath (cf. JIZZBAG; SCUMBAG). [SE *bag*, a receptacle]

bag *n.*⁶ [1930s+] (orig. US Black) taste, disposition, attitude, occupation, preference, way of life. [used in 1930s to refer to an actual *bag* used to hold bootleg liquor and in 1940s–50s to that which held narcotics, bag took on its abstract (and still current) meaning in the 1960s]

bag *n.*⁷ [1940s+] (US campus) a despised person, an outsider. [the sort of person who 'brings their lunch in a bag']

bag *n.*⁸ (US drugs) **1** [1950s+] a measure of narcotics, typically sold as a *nickel bag*, $5 worth or a *dime bag*, $10 worth. **2** [1980s+] a quarter-ounce (7g) measure of a drug, usu. marijuana (cf. BAGMAN n.³). [the glassine bags into which the drugs are divided]

bag *n.*⁹ [1960s+] (US) a bed, esp. in phr. *bag it*, *hit the bag*, go to bed, go to sleep (cf. HIT THE SACK; SACK n.²).

bag *n.*¹⁰ [1960s+] (US/Aus.) a suit of clothes. [rhy. sl. *bag of fruit* = suit]

bag *v.*¹ **1** [early 19C+] to seize, to catch, to arrest, to steal. **2** [1910s+] to claim (cf. BAGS I!). **3** [1910s+] to gain, to secure possession of, to win for oneself (esp. after repeated efforts). **4** [1960s+] to get something non-material (cf. BAG SOME RAYS; BAG ZS). **5** [20C] (Irish) to poach fish. [ext. uses of SE *bag*, to place in a bag]

bag *v.*² [mid-19C+] to shoot (to kill).

bag *v.*³ [mid–late 19C] to dismiss (cf. SACK v.²).

bag/bag school *v.*⁴ [1930s–40s] (US) to play truant; often as *bag it*. [BAG v.¹²]

bag *v.*⁵ [1950s+] (US Black) to swallow semen or vaginal fluid during oral intercourse. [SE *bag*, a receptacle, in this case the mouth]

bag *v.*⁶ [1950s+] (Aus./US) to denigrate, to criticize. [dial. *bag*, to dismiss, to jilt/ext. BAG v.³]

bag/bag up *v.*⁷ [1950s+] (drugs) to divide bulk purchases of drugs into smaller quantities for dealing. [BAG n.⁸]

bag *v.*⁸ [1960s+] (US) to make a mess of, to fail at, to botch.

bag *v.*⁹ [1960s+] (US) to classify, to put into categories. [BAG n.⁶]

bag *v.*¹⁰ [1960s+] (US drugs) to inhale glue or a similarly intoxicating substance. [the glue is poured into a paper or polythene *bag*, from which the fumes are sucked into one's mouth]

bag *v.*¹¹ [1970s] (US) to wear. [the image of 'getting into a bag']

bag *v.*¹² [1970s] (US campus) to neglect, to stop, to disregard. [one tosses things into 'a bag']

bag/bag it *v.*¹³ [1970s+] (US campus/teen) to bring one's lunch in a paper bag. [Yorkshire dial. *bag out*, for a farm-worker to bring their packed lunch to the fields]

bag *v.*¹⁴ [1970s+] (US campus/teen) of a man, to seduce, to have sexual intercourse with. [BAG n.⁹]

bag *v.*¹⁵ [1980s+] **1** (US) to hide something unpleasant from the speaker's sight (cf. BAG YOUR FACE!). **2** (US campus) to kidnap, esp. as part of a fraternity prank. [SE *bag*, a receptacle, in which the distasteful matter or the victim of the kidnapping is hidden]

bag *v.*¹⁶ [1980s+] (US campus) to break a date, to 'stand someone up'. [ext. BAG v.¹³]

bagadga/bagaga *n.* [mid-19C+] (Ling. Fr./Polari) the penis (cf. CATSO; GADSO; PACKET n.⁴). [Ital. *baggagio*, baggage]

bagaga *v.* [1960s] (US) of a man, to have sexual intercourse. [BAGADGA]

bag and bottle *n.* [mid–late 17C] food and drink.

bag-blind *adj.* [20C] (W.I.) socially contemptible, very low class, slum-dwelling. [Bdos. *bag-blind*, a rudimentary window blind made of a jute sack used for sugar, flour etc]

bag bride *n.* [1990s] (drugs) a prostitute who is addicted to crack cocaine. [BAG n.⁸ + ironic use of SE *bride*]

bagel *n.*¹ **1** [1950s+] (US) a Jew. **2** [1970s+] (S.Afr.) a spoilt, wealthy, upper-class (Jewish) young man (cf. KUGEL). [Yid. *bagel*, a style of doughnut-shaped bread roll popular among Jews]

bagel *n.*² [1970s] (US) in sporting use, a score of zero; thus *bagel job*, a defeat in which the losers fail to score. [the circular shape of the *bagel* with its O-shaped hole]

bagel baby *n.* [1950s+] (US) a young middle-class Jewish woman, active in liberal causes (cf. BAGEL BENDER). [SE *bagel* + BABY n.² (1)]

bagel bender *n.* [1970s+] (US) a Jew (cf. BANANA BENDER). [SE *bagel* + *bender*]

bagels *n.* [1950s] (US) bulges of fat that accumulate around the hips and thighs, usu. used of women despite their universality among the overweight of either sex (cf. LOVE HANDLES; SPARE TYRE). [the curved shape of the SE *bagel*]

baggage *n.*¹ [16C–17C] **1** a worthless man. **2** [16C–17C] rubbish, nonsense.

baggage *n.*² [16C+] a woman, esp. one considered immoral or sexually autonomous. [the image of woman as a man's burden or encumbrance; the initial use is often synon. with camp-follower (a woman who follows the military) but by 17C is more commonly found as a comb, e.g. *a saucy baggage, a sly baggage* and as such is relatively affectionate; however, there may also be links to Fr. *bagasse*, a prostitute, a wanton]

baggage *n.*³ [20C] (US) one who watches a gambling game and advises the players but does not participate (cf. KIBITZER). [they are 'carried' by the actual players]

baggage *n.*⁴ [1900s–10s] a woman due to be sent to South America in the White slave trade. [ext. of SE]

baggage bouncer *see* BAGGAGE SMASHER.

baggage-box/-boy *n.* [1960s+] (US) a homosexual prostitute who offers active sex to clients, i.e. as well as the usual passive participation in sodomy, he will play the active sodomizer and also offer fellatio. [? BAGGAGE n.² + SE *box/ boy*]

baggage-man *n.* [18C] (Und.) that member of a pickpocketing team who is handed the booty and then runs off with it. [pun on SE]

baggage-room *n.* [mid-19C] (US) the stomach.

baggage smasher/bouncer *n.* [mid-19C+] (US) **1** a railway porter. **2** one who steals unguarded luggage from railway stations. **3** a clumsy person. **4** a coarse, brutal person.

bagged *adj.*¹ [19C+] drunk. [printers' jargon *bag*, a pot of beer and the phr. *put one's head in a bag*, to be drunk]

bagged *adj.*² (orig. US) **1** [mid-19C+] arrested, caught (cf. IN THE BAG phr.¹). **2** [1970s+] bagged up, in one's cell (cf. BANGED UP adj.¹). [BAG v.¹ (1) + SE *bag*, a game-bag, in which dead and thus captive birds are placed]

bagged *adj.*³ [20C] easy, simple, no problem. [IN THE BAG phr.¹]

bagged *adj.*⁴ (US) **1** [1940s+] of sporting contests, when the outcome has been rendered certain by underhand or illicit means. **2** [1970s+] made amenable by a bribe. [IN THE BAG phr.¹ (2)]

bagged out *adj.* [1980s+] (US) style-less, shabby, run-down. [a supposed resemblance to a BAG LADY n.²]

bagger/bag-thief *n.*¹ [late 19C–1900s] a thief who specializes in stealing rings. [? Fr. *bague*, a ring]

bagger *n.*² [1980s+] a clumsy person (cf. DOUBLE-BAGGER; ONE-BAGGER). [one who should be put in a bag or have a bag placed over their head]

baggie *n.* [1970s+] (US) a contraceptive sheath. [BAG n.⁵]

baggie bags *n.* [1970s+] (drugs) plastic food bags used for holding small amounts of marijuana. [ext. of BAGGIES n.²]

baggies *n.*¹ [1960s+] (orig. surfing) loose-fitting 'boxer short' style of swimming trunks. [SE *baggy*; note W.I. use *baggie*, underpants for a baby or small girl]

baggies *n.*² [1970s+] (drugs) plastic bags used popularly for holding small amounts of marijuana (cf. BAG n.⁷; BAGGIE BAGS; DIME BAG; NICKEL BAG). [SE *bag*, a receptacle + trademark *Baggies*, a branded form of plastic sandwich bag]

bagging *n.* [1960s+] (drugs) using inhalant. [BAG v.¹⁰ + sfx. -*ing*; the pouring of the inhalant into a bag before use]

baggodbajee!/bagodbajees!/bagodbajingoes! *excl.* [19C+] (US) euph. excl. *by God*, *by Jesus* (cf. BEJABERS!). [pron.]

bag it *v.*¹ [late 19C+] (US) **1** to play truant. **2** to fake illness to get out of work. **3** to disregard, to give up; thus imper. *bag it*, go away! [SE *bag*, a satchel or BAG v.³; NB milit. jargon *bag it*, to malinger]

bag it *v.*² *see* BAG v.¹³.

bag job/black bag job *n.* [1970s+] (US) 'an illegal search of a suspect's property by agents of the Federal Bureau of Investigation, esp. for the purpose of copying or stealing incriminating documents etc' (*OED*).

bag lady *n.*¹ [1960s+] a woman who acts as a go-between, carrying money, esp. in the form of bribes or illicit pay-offs, between two parties (cf. BAGMAN n.²; BAG WOMAN).

bag lady *n.*² [1970s+] (orig. US) a female derelict, usu. sleeping rough or in shelters, often an alcoholic or meths drinker, whose most cherished possessions are the numbers of (to an outsider) junk-filled shopping bags, which festoon her as she walks and which never leave her side. [abbr. shopping *bag lady*. Coined for such women living on the streets of New York City]

bagman/bag man *n.*¹ **1** [mid-late 19C] a commercial traveller. **2** [1930s+] (Aus.) a tramp who travels on horseback; thus *bagman's leg*, the loss of a leg through falling under rolling stock, *bagman's union*, the brotherhood of travellers (cf. BAGMAN'S GAZETTE; SWAGMAN n.²). [SE *bag*, whether of samples or possessions]

bagman/bag man *n.*² **1** [20C] (orig. US) a messenger, a go-between, esp. one who conveys a bribe from the one who offers it to the one who accepts. **2** [20C] (orig. US) an employee, a menial, esp. one who takes the blame for the decisions and activities of their employer (cf. GOFER). **3** [1920s+] (Aus.) one who collects or administers the collection of money obtained by various criminal activities. [SE *bag* + *man*, lit. one who carries a bag; Funk's *Standard Dict.* (1928) suggests 'one to whom graft is paid', but this is not sustained elsewhere]

bagman/bag man *n.*³ [1950s+] a drug dealer. [BAG n.⁸ + SE *man*]]

bagman's gazette, the *n.* [1920s+] (Aus.) gossip and rumour, reified as an imaginary 'newspaper' (cf. BUSH TELEGRAPH). [BAGMAN n.¹ (2)+ SE *gazette*]

bag o' beer *see* BAG OF BEER.

bagodbajees!/bagodbajingoes! *see* BAGGODBAJEE!

bag of/o' beer *n.* [late 19C–1900s] a quart pot of beer. [? joc. use of SE]

bag of bones *n.*¹ [early 19C+] a noticeably thin person.

bag of bones *n.*² [1950s+] (US Black) marijuana cigarettes. [SE *bag* + BONES n.³]

bag of coke *n.*¹ [1940s+] (Aus.) a man, a fellow. [rhy. sl. *bag of coke* = BLOKE]

bag of coke *n.*² [20C] sexual intercourse. [rhy. sl. *bag of coke* = POKE n.¹ (2)]

bag off *v.* [1980s+] to pair off. [? SE *put in a bag*, lumped together]

bag of flour *n.* [1970s+] a (bathroom) shower. [rhy. sl.]

bag/box of fruit *n.* [1920s+] (Aus./N.Z./S.Afr.) a suit. [rhy. sl.]

bag of guts *n.* [late 19C+] (US) a fat person.

bag of nails *n.* [mid-late 19C] (Aus./US) chaos, disorder. [the disorder of such a bagful]

bag of shells *n.* [1950s+] (Aus.) a trifle, an unimportant object.

bag of shit tied up with string *phr.* [1950s+] a derog. personal description; usu. as *he looks like a ...* .

bag of smacked twats *phr.* [1990s] a general derog. description of an unattractive woman. [TWAT]

bag of snakes *n.*¹ [1910s–50s] (Aus.) a drooping female breast. [such a bag is misshapen, lumpy, soft]

bag of snakes *n.*² [1950s+] (Can.) a lively, sexy young woman. [the liveliness of such a bag]

bag of tricks *n.* [mid-19C+] whatever one needs (cf. BOX OF TRICKS; WHOLE BAG OF TRICKS). [SE *bag of tricks*, a clever or dextrous device]

bag of tripe *n.* [mid-19C+] an unpleasant person. [SE *bag* + TRIPE n.¹]

bag of wind *n.* [19C+] a talkative person (cf. BLOWHARD; GASBAG; GASSER n.¹; WINDBAG).

bag on *v.* [1980s+] (US campus) to criticize, usu. wittily. [BAG v.⁶]

bag one's bowline, to *phr.* [20C] to perform a job badly or incorrectly. [naut. jargon; if a reef knot (required to tie the *bowline*) is tied wrongly and thus becomes a granny knot, the sail to which the bowline is attached will *bag*, causing the boat to sail badly]

bag one's head, to *phr.* [mid-late 19C+] (US) to give in, to back off, to admit defeat (cf. BAG YOUR FACE!; GO BAG YOUR HEAD!). [lit. 'put one's head in a bag']

bag onto *v.* [1940s] (US) to notice, to pay attention to, often as imper. *bag onto ...* , take a look at ... , do you see. [fig. use of BAG v.¹ (1)]

bag o' wank *n.* [1990s] a general term of abuse (cf. SCUMBAG). [SE *bag* + WANK n.]

bag-o-wire *n.* [1950s+] (W.I. Rasta) a betrayer. [i.e. if one grasps a bag of (barbed) wire one will get hurt]

bagpipe *n.* **1** [19C] a long-winded, monotonous speaker. **2** [1940s] (US Black) a vacuum cleaner.

bagpipe it *v.* [1980s+] (US) forget it. [expansion of BAG v.¹²]

bagpipes *n.* [early–mid-19C] (US) the lungs.

bagpiping *n.* [late 19C+] intercourse under the armpit, generally a homosexual practice (cf. HUFFLE). [the required posture may be seen as resembling a piper at work]

bags *n.*¹ [mid-19C+] trousers. [? BUMBAGS]

bags/bags of *n.*² [1910s+] many. [sporting jargon *bag*, the day's kill; the sl. use emerged in WW1]

bags *n.*³ **1** [1930s+] (US) the female breasts. **2** [1960s] (US gay) the testicles.

bag school *see* BAG v.⁴.

bags I!/bagsy! *excl.* [mid-19C+] (juv.) that's mine, I want to do that!; an allied formula, mainly in preparatory schools, is *quis?* (Lat. who?) to offer an object, to which the responses are *ego!* (Lat. I) if one wishes to make a claim, or *baggy/bags I no par* (no part) if one wishes to be excluded (cf. AIKIES!).

bag-slinger *n.* [1930s] (US) a street-walker (cf. BAG-SWINGER). [the trad. street prostitute carried a large bag]

bags of *see* BAGS n.².

bags of mystery/mysteries *n.* [mid-19C–mid-20C] sausages or saveloys. [their dubious constituents; note RN use *mystery torpedoes*, *links of love*; British Army use *spotted mystery*]

bag some rays, to *phr.* [1950s+] (US) to sunbathe, to get a suntan. [BAG v.¹ + RAYS]

bag-swinger *n.* (Aus.) **1** [1930s+] a bookmaker. **2** [1960s] a street-walker, a prostitute (cf. SWING A BAG). [their essential equipment]

bagsy *adj.* [1920s–30s] (Glasgow) shapeless, lumpy. [ext. of SE *baggy*]

bagsy! *see* BAGS I!

bag that! *excl.* [1980s+] (US) forget it! [SE *bag*, to put in a bag]

bag-thief *see* BAGGER n.¹.

bag up *v.*¹ *see* BAG v.⁷.

bag up *v.*² [1980s] (UK/US Black/W.I. teen) to laugh very hard at something. [BAG v.³]

bag up *v.*³ [1980s] (UK/US Black/W.I. teen) to be caught or arrested by the police. [BAG v.¹ (1)]

bag woman *n.* [1960s+] (US) a female go-between, taking money (usu. bribes or other illicit pay-offs) between two parties (cf. BAG LADY n.¹). [the female version of BAGMAN n.²]

bag your face! *excl.* [1980s+] a general term of abuse (cf. BAG ONE'S HEAD; PUT YOUR HEAD IN A BAG!). [BAG v.¹⁵; basically requesting a person to put their face into a rubbish bag and throw it away]

bag Zs *v.* [1980s+] (US campus) to nap, to sleep (cf. BLOW ZS; CATCH SOME ZS; COP ZS; PILE UP SOME ZS; SEND UP ZS; STACK ZS; Z v.). [BAG v.¹ + Z n.¹]

bah! *excl.* [early 19C+] an excl. of contempt. [somewhat defunct in general use, but taken up in 1990s by US teenagers]

bahakas *n.* [1950s+] (US) buttocks, behind. [ety. unknown]

bahama mama *n.* [1980s+] (US Black) a fat, unattractive 'Black Mammy' stereotype, supposedly typical of the West Indies. [proper name *Bahamas* + SE *Mama*]

bah-fungoo!/fungoo! *excl.* [1950s+] (US) an excl. of contempt or dismissal, e.g. go fuck yourself! [Ital. *va t f'an culo*, go fuck yourself in the ass]

bail *v.* [1970s+] (US Black/teen) **1** to leave, to play truant. **2** to terminate a relationship, to break up. [SE *bail out*, to escape from an airplane cockpit]

Bailey, the *n.* [mid-19C+] the Central Criminal Court, London; generally known as the Old *Bailey*. [abbr.]

bailiff of marsham *n.* [17C] the ague or malarial fever; thus *arrested by the bailiff of marsham*, stricken with the fever. [such a fever sprang from the mosquitoes and poisoned air of the damp and stagnant marshlands]

bail/bale on *v.* [1960s+] (US teen) **1** to oppress, to give a hard time to, to trouble. **2** to break a date. [? SE *bale*, torment, sorrow, misery, or dial. *baleise*, to beat, to thrash, to flog]

bail out *v.* (US) **1** [1940s+] to leave in a hurry, to run off, to escape from a difficult situation. **2** [1970s] to go mad. [orig. milit. use]

bail/bale up *v.* **1** [mid-19C–late 19C] (Aus.) to trap, to corner; the orig. use was to describe the 'stand and deliver' tactics of late 19C bushrangers. **2** [1990s] (Aus.) to stop someone in the street for a chat. [SE *bail*, a bar or frame used to confine an animal, esp. a cow when milking; the term flourished during the bushrangers' heyday, although it is still occasionally used, either of animals or of the victims of criminals]

bail/bale up! *excl.* [mid–late 19C] stop! [adopted in UK from BAIL UP v.]

bain *n.* [1910s] (W.I.) the buttocks, esp. in dismissive excl. *yo' bain!* (cf. BAM-BAM).

baister *see* BASTER n.².

bait *n.*¹ **1** [mid–late 19C] (US) one's intended prey or victim. **2** [20C] an attractive man or woman used to lure a victim into a con-game or a mugging. [SE *bait*, a lure]

bait/bate *n.*² [mid-19C–1950s] a temper, a tantrum. [16C *bait*, to be snarling and snapping, like a dog endeavouring to break its chain and attack a persecutor; orig. juv. use, esp. in preparatory and public schools and carried over by former pupils into their adult lives]

bait *n.*³ [1940s+] an individual who is likely to get into trouble or face unwanted attention, esp. as sfx. *-bait*, e.g. JAILBAIT n.¹. [SE *bait*, a lure]

bait *n.*⁴ [1980s+] (US Black) a woman with noticeable body odour. [the rotting meat or fish that is often used as a hunter's bait]

Bajan spree *n.* [20C] (W.I./Trin.) a small, spontaneous party. [SE *Bajan*, a native of Barbados + SPREE n.¹]

baje/bajee/bajie *n.* [20C] (W.I.) a Bajan, a native of Barbados (cf. BIM n.¹).

bake *n. see* HOMEBAKE n.².

bake *v.*¹ [1950s+] (US prison) to execute in the electric chair (cf. BARBECUE n.²; BURN v.³; COOK v.²; FRY v.²). [blackly humorous use of SE]

bake *v.*² *see* HOMEBAKE v.

bakebrain *n.* [1940s] (US) a fool, an idiot (cf. BALLOON-BRAIN; BATBRAIN; BEANBRAIN; BEEF-BRAIN; BEETLE-BRAIN; BIRDBRAIN; BOLLOCKBRAIN; BUTTERBRAIN; CHICKENBRAIN; DICKBRAIN; DORKBRAIN; DOUGH-BRAIN; FUCKBRAIN; GOOBERBRAIN; GUMBRAIN; HELIUM-BRAIN; JINGLE-BRAINS; LAMEBRAIN; MEATBRAIN; MOUSE-BRAIN; MUSHBRAIN; PEABRAIN; SPARROW-BRAIN; SQUAREBRAIN). [SE *bake* + sfx. *-brain*, the image is of hardness]

bake break *n.* [1980s+] (US drugs) a break from work during which one smokes a pipe of cocaine. [one 'bakes' the ROCK n.⁴ in order to smoke it]

baked *adj.* **1** [late 18C–1900s] exhausted. **2** [1930s+] sun-burned or very tanned. **3** [1970s+] (US) under the influence of marijuana. **4** [1970s+] (US campus) drunk.

baked dinner *n.* [late 19C–1900s] (Und.) bread. [used to fool new arrivals at a prison who assume such a dinner will be somewhat more extensive]

baked wind *n.* [1900s–20s] (US) nonsense, rubbish. [var. on HOT AIR]

bake it *v.* [late 19C+] to refrain from visiting the lavatory, however desperate the need to defecate. [the excreta remain in the 'oven' of one's intestines]

baker *n.* [mid–late 19C] (US Und.) a loafer, an idler. [? SE *baker*, who must wait for bread to rise]

baker flying *n.* [20C] menstruation (cf. FLYING BAKER). [naut. jargon *baker* = B; the flag signifying the second letter of the alphabet is red]

baker-kneed *adj.*[1] [17C–18C] effeminate. [in folk myth knock-knees are one of the 'proofs' of effeminacy]

baker-kneed *adj.*[2] [18C–19C] knock-kneed. [a physical problem that supposedly results from a baker's job]

baker-legged *adj.*[1] [17C–18C] effeminate. [var. on BAKER-KNEED adj.[1]]

baker-legged *adj.*[2] [18C–19C] knock-kneed. [var. on BAKER-KNEED adj.[2]]

bakers *n.* [19C] large or clumsy boots or shoes. [as worn by bakers]

baker's dozen *n.*[1] [16C–late 18C] 13 or occas. 14. [SE post-1800; according to Ware, the term refers to laws of Edward I (r.1272–1307) controlling the sale of bread; so frightened were bakers of being accused of giving short measure that they added one, sometimes two, extra loaves to the dozen ordered]

baker's dozen *n.*[2] [late 19C+] a cousin. [rhy. sl.]

bake sale *n.* [1980s+] (US drugs) a session of smoking crack cocaine. [play on SAmE phr.]

bake someone's bread, to *phr.* [14C] to kill, to 'do for'.

bakey *see* BAKIE.

bakgat *adj.* [1960s+] (S.Afr.) splendid, first-rate, 'posh'; thus also as excl. [? Afk. *bak*, fine + *gat*, hole (anus)]

bakie/bakey *n.* [late 19C+] a *bake*d potato. [abbr.]

baking-spittle *n.* [late 19C] (Lancashire/Yorks.) the human tongue. [dial. *baking-spittle*, 'a thin, spade-shaped board, with a handle, used in baking cakes' (*EDD*)]

bakkie *n.* [1960s+] (S.Afr.) a light truck, a pick-up, a 4×4 vehicle. [Afk. *bak*, a container + dimin. sfx. *-ie*]

bakore *n.* [1970s+] (S.Afr.) large, protruding ears. [Afk. *bak*, a bowl + *ore*, ears]

backshee *adj.* [mid-18C+] free (cf. BUCKSHEE adj.). [BAKSHEESH n.]

baksheesh/backshee/buckshee/buckshish *n.* [mid-18C+] a gratuity, a tip. [Pers. *bakhshish*, present, ult. f. *bakhshi-dan*, to give. Given the stereotyping of the 'Oriental merchant' or the Third World beggar, the implication tends to be slightly pej.]

baksheesh/buckshish *v.* [mid-18C+] to give a tip. [BAKSHEESH n.]

bala *n.* [early–mid-19C] coarse or senseless talk. [Cornish *bal*, loud talking]

balaclava *n.* [mid-19C] a full beard. [the beards worn by many soldiers who had returned from the rigours of the Crimean War of 1854–6]

balaclava *v.* [20C] to have sexual intercourse. [rhy. sl. *bala-clava* = CHARVER v. (1)]

balahack/ballyhack/ballywack/ballywrack *n.* [late 19C+] euph. for *Hell*; thus combs. *all to ballyhack*, *go to ballyhack*. [? Irish *baile*, a town + HECK!]

balahack *v.* (US) **1** [late 19C+] to confuse, to blunder. **2** [1930s+] to impose upon. **3** [1930s+] to beat severely. [BALAHACK n.]

balahu *n.* [1940s+] (W.I.) a noisy, boisterous person. [BALLY-HOO n.]

balangas *n.* [1980s+] (US) the female breasts. [P.R. Sp.]

balcony *n.* [1940s+] (Aus.) the female breasts, esp. as thrust up and forward in the brassieres of the 1940s–50s.

bald as a bandicoot *phr.* [1910s+] (Aus.) totally bald; the bandicoot has been adapted to a variety of Aus. phr., *bandy as a …*, *barmy as a …*, *miserable as a …*, *not the brains of a …*. [SE *bald* + *bandicoot*, a destructive insectivorous Australian marsupial resembling a large rat the size of a cat]

bald-coot *n.* [early–mid-19C] an old man who has lost all his money gambling. [SE *bald*, i.e. one who has been 'plucked' + COOT n.[1]; SE phr. *bald as a coot*]

balderdash *n.* **1** [16C–17C] any adulterated or mixed drink, typically milk and beer, beer and wine, brandy and mineral water, which, while duly consumed, was generally considered unpleasant. **2** [17C–18C] a jumble of nonsensical words (cf. BALDUCTUM n.). **3** [18C] obscenity. [both (1) and (2) and the SE meaning of 'nonsense', which is the sole 20C survivor, come f. 16C *balderdash*, frothy water. The origin appears to be Scand., whether in Da. *balder*, noise or clatter, Nor. *bjaldra*, to speak indistinctly or Icel. *baldras*, to make a clatter. *Dash* comes f. Da. *daske*, to slap or flap; thus *dask*, a slap. The Welsh *baldorddus*, noisy, f. *baldordd*, idle, noisy talk, chatter, may also play a role. An alternative ety. has been suggested (and backed up by a 16C ref. to 'barbers balderdash') as coming from the froth and foam made by barbers in *dashing* their *balls* (spherical pieces of soap) backwards and forwards in hot water]

baldface dish *n.* [19C] (US) a plain white china plate (cf. BALDFACED SHIRT). [its lack of ornamentation]

baldfaced shirt *n.* [mid-19C+] (US) a dress shirt with a starched front. [SE *baldfaced cattle*, Herefords, which have white faces; the bald element, pointing up the lack of pattern, may be the root of the boiled shirt, another term for a dress shirt, although such starched, formal shirts were literally boiled to achieve the rigid front]

baldfaced stag *n.* [mid-19C] a bald man. [play on SE]

baldface/ballface whisky *n.* [early 19C+] (US) cheap, potent whisky. [? the *baldfaced hornet*, which has a notable sting + SE *whisky*]

baldhead *n.* **1** [early 19C–1900s] (orig. US) an old man. **2** [20C] (W.I.) a member of the Rastafarian cult who does not, however, sport the characteristic beard and dreadlocks (cf. CLEAN-FACED MAN). **3** [1950s+] (W.I.) a White person (cf. BALLHEAD).

bald-headed *adj.*[1] [late 19C+] (US) bare, hairless, shining white.

bald-headed *adj.*[2] [late 19C+] (US Black) deliberately deceptive, underhand, e.g. *a bald-headed lie*. [one who makes no effort to mask their bald head]

bald-headed *adj.*[3] [late 19C+] (US Black) stupid, foolish. [such a person has nothing 'on top']

bald-headed *adj.*[4] [late 19C+] totally unprepared, utterly spontaneous. [the image of one who rushes out without pausing even to put on a hat]

bald headed *adv.* [late 19C+] precipitately. [BALD-HEADED adj.[4]]

bald-headed bandit *n.* [1960s+] the penis.

bald-headed butter *n.* [late 19C–1900s] a portion of butter in which there are no hairs. [the pre-industrial era of butter manufacture]

bald-headed hermit/champ/friar/sailor *n.* [late 19C+] the penis, esp. an uncircumcised penis. [the *glans penis* which, in uncircumcised men, 'hides away' beneath the foreskin; the sense appears in late 17C, as 'a friar with a bald head' (D'Urfey)]

baldie/baldy *n.* [mid-19C+] (orig. US) a *bald* man. [abbr.]

bald man in a boat *n.* [20C] the clitoris (cf. BABY IN THE BOAT).

baldober/baldover/baldower *n.* [late 19C–1900s] (Und.) a boss, a leader, a spokesman. [Ger. Und., ult. Heb. *baal*, master + *dovor*, a word]

bald-rib *n.* [early 17C] a thin, bony person. [SE *bald-rib*. 'A joint of pork cut from nearer the rump than the spare-rib, so called "because the bones thereof are made bald and bare of flesh"' (Minsheu)' (*OED*)]

bald-tyre bandit *n.* [1960s+] (Und.) a traffic police officer (cf. GAS-METER BANDIT; KNICKERS BANDIT). [SE *gas-meter* + BANDIT n.;

such police are considered less competent or important than their criminal-catching peers]

balductum n. [late 16C–early 17C] nonsense, rubbish. [SE *balductum*, a posset, hot milk curdled with ale or wine]

balductum adj. [late 16C–early 17C] nonsensical, rubbish. [BALDUCTUM n.]

baldwin n. [18C] a donkey (cf. DICKY n.[3]; EDWARD; ISSACHAR; JENNY n.[1]; NEDDY n.[1]; TOM n.[2]). [proper name *Baldwin I* (c.1058–1118), first Christian king of Jerusalem; thus linked to the arrival in Jerusalem of Christ, the 'King of the Jews', on a donkey]

baldy see BALDIE.

bale n. [1980s+] (drugs) marijuana. [SE *bale*, a (wrapped) bundle]

bale of hay/straw n. [1920s+] (orig. US theatre) a White woman, esp. a blonde. [SE *bale* + *hay*/STRAW n.[2]]

bale on see BAIL ON.

bales of briquettes n. [1970s+] (Irish) platform-soled shoes. [resemblance]

bale up see BAIL UP.

Balkan tap n. [20C] madness (cf. DOOLALLY). [proper name *Balkans* + *tap*, sunstroke; the term evolved to characterize the growing, happy indolence that took over men involved in the Macedonian campaign in WW1]

ball n.[1] [19C] (US) a shot of liquor, esp. in phr. *a beer and a ball*, a beer and a shot of whisky. [BALL OF FIRE n.[1]]

ball n.[2] [mid-19C] (Und.) a prison ration, 170g (6oz) of meat. [? the resemblance of the lump of meat]

ball n.[3] [late 19C–1920s] (US) a silver dollar. [? its circularity]

ball n.[4] [20C] **1** a walk. **2** a talk. [rhy. sl. *ball of chalk*]

ball n.[5] [1910s] a small package of a narcotic (cf. BAG n.[8]). [the drug package is rolled into a ball]

ball n.[6] [1920s+] (orig. US Black) **1** a party, a celebration. **2** a riotously, extravagantly good time.

ball n.[7] [1950s+] (orig. US) sexual intercourse. [BALLS n.[1] (1), but note SE *ball*, a dance (cf. combs. at DANCE v.[1])]

ball n.[8] [1980s+] (drugs) crack cocaine. [? the approx. shape of a ROCK n.[4] (2)]

ball n.[9] [1980s+] (US Black) basket*ball*. [abbr.]

ball n.[10] [1990s] (US) a stupid or silly person; used in response to an unintelligent action, as a sarcastic response to a foolish remark or as an observation of another's character (or lack thereof). [BALLS n.[1] (3)]

ball v.[1] [20C] **1** to walk. **2** to talk. [rhy. sl. *ball of chalk*]

ball v.[2] [1930s+] to travel at high speed. [abbr. BALL THE JACK]

ball v.[3] [1940s+] (orig. US Black). to have a good time, to enjoy oneself (cf. BALL n.[6]).

ball v.[4] [1950s+] to have sexual intercourse. [BALLS n.[1] (1)]

ball v.[5] [1980s+] (drugs) to secrete a pack of drugs in the vagina. [BALL n.[5]]

ball v.[6] [1980s+] (US Black) to play basketball. [BALL n.[9]]

balla see BALLER.

ballad-basket n. [19C] a street-singer.

ballahoo adj. [20C] (W.I.) noisy, boisterous, obstreperous. [BALLYHOO]

ball and bat n. [1900s–10s] a hat. [rhy. sl.]

ball and chain n. [1920s+] (orig. US Black) one's wife or regular girlfriend; thus *ball-and-chained*, married (cf. ANCHOR n.[2]). [SE *ball and chain*, a device that secured convicts during 19C]

ball and chalk see BALL OF CHALK n.

ballarag see BALLYRAG.

ballarat v. [1990s] (Aus.) to have an erection (cf. BACCHUS MARSH). [joc. us of proper name *Ballarat*, the last stop on the railway line from Melbourne]

ballarat lantern n. [late 19C–1900s] (Aus.) a candle stuck in the neck of a bottle, the bottom of which has been knocked off. [proper name *Ballarat* + SE *lantern*; a necessity in pre-electrified days]

ballast n.[1] [mid-19C–mid-20C] money. [SE *ballast*; it helps one stay 'afloat' and 'on an even keel']

ballast n.[2] [mid-19C–mid-20C] heavy food. [SE *ballast*, seen as 'stuffing' a ship and thus a stomach]

ball-bag n. **1** [19C+] the scrotum (cf. LAST SHAKE OF THE BAG). **2** [1960s+] (US) a jockstrap. [BALLS n.[1] (1) + BAG n.[1] (2)]

ballbasket n. [1960s+] the scrotum (cf. BALL-BAG). [BALLS n.[1] (1) + SE *basket*]

ball-breaker n. (orig. US) **1** [1950s+] a difficult, boring or exasperating job, problem or situation. **2** [1970s+] a person who sets difficult work or problems, a hard taskmaster. **3** [1970s+] a dominating woman, one who destroys the self-confidence of a man (cf. ASS-BREAKER). [BALLS n.[1] (1) + SE *breaker*]

ball-breaking/-busting n. [1940s+] (orig. US) harassment. [BALL-BREAKER/BALL-BUSTER in all senses]

ball-breaking/-busting adj. [1940s+] (orig. US) acting as a hard taskmaster or dominating woman. [BALL-BREAKER]

ball-buster n. **1** [20C] (US Und.) a thief who grabs his victim by the testicles while his accomplice takes his wallet. **2** [1950s+] (orig. US) a nagging woman (cf. ASS-BREAKER). **3** [1950s+] any overbearingly unpleasant person or circumstances. **4** [1950s+] any thing or person seen as extraordinary or outstanding. **5** [1970s+] a tease. [BALLS n.[1] (1) + SE *buster*; but note Yid. *baleboosteh*, a bossy woman, lit. 'mistress of the house']

ball-busting see BALL-BREAKING.

ball-clanker n. [1960s] (US) a man who boasts, probably groundlessly, of his sexual prowess (cf. WAVE ONE'S WILLY). [BALLS n.[1] + SE *clanker*]

ball-crusher n. **1** [1970s+] a dominating woman who 'emasculates' her partner, usu. a husband (cf. ASS-BREAKER). **2** [1980s+] a sexually voracious woman who exhausts her partner's virility. [fig. use of BALLS n.[1] (1) + SE *crush*]

ball-cutter n. [1960s+] (US) a nagging, domineering or demanding woman (cf. ASS-BREAKER). [BALLS n.[1] (1) + SE *cutter*]

balled-up adj.[1] [late 19C+] constipated (cf. BACKED-UP). [SE *balled*, clenched in a tight knot or lump]

balled-up adj.[2] [late 19C+] (US) confused, mixed up, in a mess. [BALLS v.]

baller/balla/bawla n. [1980s+] (US Black) one who is extremely rich, esp. from the profits of criminality (cf. BALLING n.; HIGH ROLLER; PLAYER). [? HAVE A BALL; the term is used esp. by the Los Angeles gang the Bloods; *balla*/*bawla* are consciously 'wrong' spellings, designed to emphasize the 'outlaw' status of such individuals]

ballface n. [mid–late 19C] (US Black) a White person (cf. BALLHEAD).

ballface whisky see BALDFACE WHISKY.

ballgame/ball game/ball-game n. [1960s+] a state of affairs, a situation, esp. in phr. *different*/*whole new ball game*, a radically new situation (to which one will be forced to adapt). [SE *ball-game*, a sporting event, esp. a baseball game]

ball-gusted adj. [mid-19C] (US) disgusted, appalled. [BALLY adj. + SE *disgusted*]

ballhead n. **1** [1950s+] (Black) a White person. **2** [1980s+] (N.Z./Maori) an outsider. [SE *ball-head*, a head shaped like a ball; thus the person who has one. In Rastafarian use most Whites, however hirsute, may be considered to be *ballheads*, in comparison with the Rastaman and his flowing dreadlocks]

ballhop n. [20C] (Irish) a rumour, an unsupported theory, a lie; thus *ballhopper*, a rumour-monger. [Gaelic sport]

balling n. **1** [1930s+] (orig. US Black) having fun. **2** [1930s+]

(orig. US Black) having sexual intercourse. **3** [1980s+] (US Black) enriching oneself by selling drugs (usu. crack cocaine) (cf. BALLER). **4** [1980s+] (US Black) excelling in the playing of basketball. [BALL v.³]

balling adj. [1950s+] (US) excellent, wonderful, first-rate. [BALLING n]

ballinocack n. [late 18C–early 19C] the anus (cf. STREAM'S TOWN; TIPPERARY FORTUNE). [? Irish baile, a town + CACK n.¹; thus lit. 'shit-town']

ball is in someone's court/with you phr. [1950s+] one has the responsibility, it is one's turn to answer or act. [tennis imagery]

ballistics n. [1990s] (US Black) the facts, information. [SE ballistics + implication of statistics]

ball is with you see BALL IS IN SOMEONE'S COURT.

ball it off v. [mid-19C] (US) to travel at speed (cf. BALL THE JACK). [the rolling of a ball]

ball it up v. [1950s–60s] (US) to celebrate in an uproarious manner (cf. BALL v.³).

ball-less adj. [1950s+] weak, emasculated; thus ball-less wonder, an especially weak individual. [BALLS n.¹ (1) + sfx. -less]

ball naked adj. [20C] (US) utterly naked (cf. BALLOCK NAKED; BOLLOCK NAKED).

ballock n. [early 18C+] a testicle (cf. BALLOCKS n.²; BOLLOCK n.).

ballock/bollock v. [mid–late 18C] (US) to grab by the genitals when fighting. [OE beallucas, itself Teut. root ball-, thus more immediately ext. of BALLS n.¹ (1)]

ballocking n. [1930s+] a severe telling off, a scolding (cf. BOLLOCKING). [BALLOCKS v.²]

ballock/ballocky naked/bare-assed/arsed adj. [1960s+] utterly naked (cf. BALL NAKED).

ballocks/bollocks n.¹ **1** [18C–early 19C] a parson. **2** [late 19C+] rubbish, nonsense (cf. BALLS n.¹). **3** [1910s–20s] a person in a state of confusion, who is talking BALLOCKS n.². [? (2) developed f. (1) on the premise that sermonizing is, de facto, nonsense]

ballocks/bollocks/bollox n.² [late 18C+] **1** the testicles. **2** a mess. [ballock(s) meant testicle(s) f. 11C but remained SE until late 18C; it appears in Nathaniel Bailey's Universal Etymological English Dictionary in all editions f. 1721–1800 but was not included in Samuel Johnson's Dictionary, which drew heavily on Bailey's word-list, in 1755; one must thus assume that the word was passing then from polite use; it was definitely slang by 1800 and appears as such in Grose (1796) though, oddly, in neither Grose (1785), Hotten nor F&H]

ballocks/bollocks/bollux v.¹ [20C] (Aus.) to ruin, to make a mess of, also as ballocks up, make a ballocks of (cf. BALLS UP).

ballocks v.² [1930s+] to reprimand, to scold (cf. BALLOCKING).

ballocks! excl. [late 19C+] rubbish! nonsense! (cf. BOLLOCKS!). [BALLOCKS n.² (2)]

ballocks about/around v. [20C] **1** to mess about, to play the fool. **2** to infuriate, to waste someone's time. [BALLOCKS v.¹]

ballocksed adj. [20C] ruined, messed up, thwarted. [BALLOCKS v.¹]

ballocks in brackets n. [20C] a bow-legged man.

ballocks worker n. [1950s] any overbearingly unpleasant person or circumstance (cf. BALL-BUSTER). [BALLOCKS n.¹ + SE worker]

ballocky naked see BALLOCK NAKED.

ball of/and chalk n. [20C] a walk. [rhy. sl.]

ball of chalk v. [20C] to talk. [rhy. sl.]

ball of dirt n. [late 19C] (US) the earth. [fig. use of SE; ? + rhy. sl.]

ball off v.¹ [late 19C] (US) to treat to a drink. [BALL n.¹ (1)]

ball off v.² [20C] to masturbate (cf. BEAT OFF). [BALLS n.¹ (1)]

ball of fire n.¹ [18C–late 19C] a glass of brandy (cf. FIRE A SLUG). [the effect of the liquor]

ball of fire n.² **1** [20C] an individual known for their energy, resourcefulness or drive. **2** [1940s–50s] (US) a fast vehicle.

ball of lead n. [1900s–10s] the head. [rhy. sl.]

ball of muscle n. [1930s+] (Aus.) an energetic, lively person.

ball of twine n. [20C] (Aus.) a railway line. [rhy. sl.]

ball of wax n. [19C] a shoemaker. [the wax used in shoe-making]

ball of yarn n. [1940s–60s] (US) the female genitals (cf. WIND ONE'S BALL OF YARN). [19C Anglo-Irish bawdy folk-song, e.g. the lyric 'Keep both hands on your little ball of yarn']

balloon n.¹ (US) **1** [late 18C] a security certificate issued by the Confederation (the original 13 colonies that seceded from Britain). **2** [1970s+] $1. **3** [1970s+] (gambling) $100.

balloon n.² [20C] the saloon bar of a public house. [rhy. sl. balloon car = bar]

balloon n.³ [20C] (Ulster) a garrulous person. [they are 'full of hot air']

balloon n.⁴ [1910s–30s] (US) a bedroll. [the supposed resemblance]

balloon n.⁵ [1950s+] **1** a condom. **2** (drugs) a condom that is used to carry heroin, cocaine or any other powdered narcotic drug. **3** (drugs) a heroin supplier. [portions of heroin are often sold in a contraceptive, tied off at the end]

balloon v.¹ [1950s+] to package narcotic drugs for distribution and sale. [BALLOON n.⁵ (2)]

balloon v.² [1950s+] to try out a new idea or concept, on the same lines as 'let's run it up the flagpole and see if anyone salutes'. [the image of flying a balloon]

balloon-brain n. [1940s–60s] (US) a fool, a simpleton (cf. BAKEBRAIN; BALLOON-HEAD). [SE balloon + sfx. -brain; the image is of emptiness or hot air]

balloon-head n. [1930s+] (US) a fool, a simpleton (cf. BALLOON-BRAIN). [SE balloon + sfx. -HEAD (1)]

balloon it v. [1910s–30s] (US) to pack up one's bedroll and set off travelling. [BALLOON n.⁴]

balloon-juice n.¹ [late 19C+] **1** soda-water; thus balloon juice lowerer, a teetotaller, who only drinks or 'lowers' soda-water. **2** (W.I./Bdos., Guyn.) any form of sweet, colourful fizzy drink. [? gaseous nature of soda-water; contemp. use is W.I. only]

balloon juice n.² [20C] (US) nonsense, rubbish, empty chatter (cf. HOT AIR). [SE balloon + JUICE n.⁶ (2)]

balloon-knot bandit n. [1990s] a male homosexual (cf. ARSE BANDIT). [BALLOON n.⁵ (1) + BANDIT n.¹; the knotted condom that signifies intercourse]

balloon room n. [1950s–70s] (US Black) a place where people gather to smoke marijuana. [like the SE balloon, marijuana smokers get HIGH adj.¹ (2)]

balloon room without a parachute phr. [1950s–70s] (US Black) a disappointment, a let-down, esp. a place where one has been promised a smoke of marijuana but which, in fact, offers no supply. [BALLOON ROOM]

balloons n. [1950s+] conspicuously large female breasts.

balloon soup n. [1920s–30s] (US) nonsense, empty chatter (cf. HOT AIR).

ballow v. [19C+] (US) to lay claim to (cf. AIKIES!). [Lancashire dial. ballow, balla, I claim]

ball-park figure n. [1950s+] (orig. US) a round figure for general estimation, assessment. [SE ball-park, a baseball stadium + figure; thus the rough estimate of fans watching a sporting event]

balls n.¹ **1** [mid-18C+] the testicles (cf. AGATES; BALLOCKS n.¹; BUM-BALLS; CANNONBALLS). **2** [mid-19C+] a blunder, an error (cf. BALLS-UP). **3** [late 19C+] courage, bravery; supposedly quintessential male qualities, but now as often applied to women. **4** [1950s+] substance, power, strength. **5** [1960s+] effrontery, gall, audacity. [the shape]

balls n.[2] [late 19C+] rubbish, nonsense.

balls n.[3] [1930s–40s] (orig. US) nothing, e.g. 'What kind of a tip do I get?' 'Balls.'

balls, the n.[4] [1930s+] (US) a superlative, either good or bad according to context. [BALLS n.[4]; their importance to a man]

balls n.[5] [1950s–60s] (US) the female breasts (cf. BALLOONS). [the shape]

balls n.[6] [1960s+] synon. with ARSE n.[1], e.g. *work one's balls off*, *put one's balls on the line*.

balls adj. [1980s+] (US) tough, masculine, courageous (cf. BALLSY). [BALLS n.[1] (2)]

balls v. [1910s+] to make a mess of (cf. BALLS UP v.).

balls! excl. [late 19C+] rubbish! nonsense! (cf. BALLOCKS!). [BALLS n.[1] (1)]

balls-ache v. [late 19C+] to nag, to whinge; thus adj. *[20C] balls-aching* nagging, complaining (cf. BALL-BUSTER; BELLYACHE). [BALLS n.[1] (1) + SE *ache*]

balls and all phr. [1950s+] (orig. US) everything. [BALLS n.[1] (1)]

balls-ass adj. [1960s+] (US) tough, masculine, courageous (cf. BALLSY). [BALLS n.[1] (2) + ARSE n.[1] (1)]

balls-ass naked see BALLS NAKED.

balls, bees and buggery! excl. [late 19C+] a general excl. [assonance]

ballsed-up adj. [1940s+] in chaos, in a mess, ruined (cf. COCK UP v.[3]). [BALLS v.]

ball slap v. [1990s] of a man, to have sexual intercourse. [BALLS n.[1] (1) + SE *slap*]

balls/balls-ass naked adj. [1950s+] (US) stark naked (cf. BALLOCK NAKED).

balls out adv. [1940s+] at full tilt, absolutely committed, all out. [BALLS n.[1] (1); the implication is that one is willing to risk injuring the genitals]

balls, picnics and parties! excl. [1920s+] a general excl. [euph. + punning]

balls to phr. [1930s+] a dismissive phr. aimed at people, objects or circumstance; thus *balls to you! balls to that!* [BALLS n.[1] (1)]

balls-to-the-wall adj. [1980s+] **1** desperate. **2** all-out, at maximum speed, with one's greatest effort. [BALLS n.[1] (1) + SE *wall*; a coarse version of SE *back(s) to the wall*]

balls to the walls phr. [1970s] (US campus) a tense or frantic time or situation that requires the ability to fight back.

balls-to-the-wind adv. [1980s+] (US) at top speed. [BALLS n.[1] (1) + SE *wind*]

balls-up n. [1910s+] (orig. milit.) a blunder, an error (cf. BALLOCKS n.[2] (2); COCK-UP; MAKE A BALLS-UP). [BALLS n.[1] (2)]

balls up v. [1910s+] to make a mess of, to ruin, to blunder, to make a mistake (cf. BALLOCKS v; COCK UP v.[3]). [BALLS-UP n.]

ballsy adj. [1930s+] **1** absurd, ridiculous. **2** tough, masculine, courageous. [BALLS n.[1] (1) + sfx. *-y*]

ball-tearer n. **1** [1950s+] (orig. US) usu. of a woman, esp. a wife, a nag (cf. ASS-BREAKER). **2** [1960s+] (Aus.) a physically demanding task. **3** [1970s+] (Aus.) a violent person. **4** anything spectacular or notably impressive. **5** [1970s+] (Aus.) a major problem, an exasperation. [BALLS n.[1] (1) + SE *tearer*]

ball the jack, to phr. [1920s+] (US) **1** to drive very fast, to work very hard (cf. HIGHBALL v.[1]). **2** (Black) to perform an energetic dance to a backing of hand claps. **3** to move in a noticeable manner. **4** to enjoy a riotous party. **5** to risk everything on a single throw. **6** to be the last straw. [SAmE phrase *high-ball*, the railway man's hand signal to set a train in motion + (orig. US Black) *jack*, a locomotive, abbr. of SE *jackass*, a donkey that, like the locomotive, works very hard; used first in the lumberjack jargon *ball the jack*, of a logging

train, to go very fast; thence to general railroad jargon and after that mainstream sl.]

ballum/balum rancum n. [late 17C–late 19C] an orgy, lit. a dance at which all concerned 'dance in their *birthday* suits' (Grose, 1785). [BALLS n.[1] (1) + pun on SE *ball*, a dance + *rank*, rancid]

ball-up n. [20C] (US) a mess, a confusion (cf. BALLOCKS n.[1] (2)). [var. on BALLS-UP]

ball up v. (US) **1** [mid-19C+] to become confused, muddled. **2** [late 19C+] to muddle, to err, to blunder, to make a mistake, to entangle oneself with; thus *balled up*, confused, eccentric. **3** [1910s+] to ruin, to make a mess of, to clog up, to confuse, to botch. [BALL-UP n.]

bally adj. [mid-19C–1940s] a general neg. intensifier, very, exceedingly; euph. for BLOODY; thus *bally heck*, bloody hell.

bally v. [late 19C–1900s] to leave, to depart (cf. WALTZ v.[1]). [SE *ballet*]

Ballygobackwards n. [1990s] (Irish) urban nickname for what is seen as a typical rural town. [Irish *baile*, a town + SE *go backwards*]

ballyhack see BALAHACK n.

ballyhoo n. [20C] rubbish, nonsense, empty praise. [carnival and fairground jargon *ballyhoo*, a barker's speech or a performance given outside the actual attraction, both aimed at touting the attraction itself. The ety. remains obscure; these are some of the theories, as cited in Mencken, f. Gaelic *bailinghadh*, collect (pron. *ballyhoo*); the predominantly Irish fairground touts of the mid-19C shouted 'Bailinghadh anois!' ('Collection now!') when they passed the hat for payment; f. the cod Arabic cry *b'Allah hoo*, 'through God it is', used by the 'dervishes' in the Oriental Village sited at the Chicago World's Fair of 1893; a comb. of SE *ballet* + *whoop*. Note 19C naut. jargon *ballyhoo of blazes*, a term of contempt for an unpopular vessel]

ballyhoo v. [20C] (orig. US) to publicize to excess, often when the product cannot live up to the manufactured image (cf. HYPE v.[1]). [BALLYHOO n.]

ballyhooly n. **1** [late 19C+] (Irish) bad trouble. **2** [1910s–20s] rubbish, nonsense (cf. BALLYHOO n.). [note music-hall use *Ballyhooly truth*, a lie; the Cork village of *Ballyhooly*, near Fermoy, notable for its faction fights + BALLYHOO n.]

ballyrag/ballarag v. [late 18C–mid-19C] (Irish) to bully, to pressurize, to scold. [var. on BULLYRAG]

ballywack/ballywrack see BALAHACK n.

balmedest balm n. [late 19C–1900s] the ultimate in soothing.

balm of Gilead n. [late 19C] (US) **1** money (cf. BALSAM; CALABASH n.[2]; PLASTER n.[1]; SHINPLASTER). **2** illicitly distilled whisky. [the phrase 'Is there no balm in Gilead?' Jer. 8:22, meaning 'is there no remedy or consolation?'; both money and whisky provide a much-needed consolation for life's problems]

balmy, the n. [mid-19C] sleep. [cf. *balmy slumbers* (Shakespeare, *Othello* II.ii)]

balmy adj. **1** [mid–late 19C] drunk. **2** [mid-19C+] insane, eccentric (cf. BARMY). [SE *balm*, soothing]

balmy breeze n. [20C] cheese. [rhy. sl.]

baloney/boloney n.[1] [1920s+] (orig. US) **1** nonsense, rubbish, humbug; thus *baloney-bender*, one who talks nonsense (cf. APPLE SAUCE n.[2]). **2** a worthless, stupid person. [? *Bologna* sausage; the *OED* rejects the connection as 'conjectural', but note Adams (*Western Words*, 1968): 'Bologna bulls, animals of inferior quality whose meat is used to make Bologna sausage'. E.P. offers Rom. *peloné*, testicles; thus BALLS n.[1] (1) or BALLOCKS n.[1] (1)]

baloney/boloney n.[2] [20C] (orig. US) the penis (cf. BACON n.[1]). [the *Bologna* sausage, transformed in US to *baloney*]

balooey *n.* [20C] (orig. US) **1** nonsense, rubbish, humbug. **2** a worthless, stupid person. [BALONEY n.¹ + SE excl. *pooh*!]

balot *n.* [1970s] (US drugs) **1** opium. **2** heroin. [Sp. *balota*, a small ball (usu. used in voting, thus a 'ballot'); presumably the shape of pellets of opium]

balsam *n.* [late 17C–19C] money (cf. BALM OF GILEAD). [SE *balsam*, a soothing, healing unguent; it 'heals' financial pains]

Balt *n.* [1940s–50s] (Aus.) any European refugee or immigrant. [the mistaken belief that all such people came from the Baltic states]

baltic *adj.* [1990s] (US) cold, usu. in phr. *it's bloody baltic*. [the low temperatures of the Baltic Sea]

Balto *n.* [mid-19C+] (US) *Balt*imore, Maryland. [abbr.]

baluba *n.* [1960s+] (Irish) a general term of abuse. [the *Baluba* tribe in Katanga, the former Belgian Congo; coined by Irish soldiers serving with the UN who stereotyped the Baluba as notably savage]

balum rancum *see* BALLUM RANCUM.

bam *n.*¹ [late 18C–late 19C] a hoax. [BAMBOOZLE]

bam *n.*² [20C] a violent person. [onomat.]

bam *n.*³ (drugs) **1** [1950s+] low-grade marijuana. **2** [1970s+] amphetamine (cf. A n.²). **3** [1970s+] a barbiturate/amphetamine mix. [Mex. *bombita*, a little bomb + SE *bam!* echoic of an explosion]

bam *v.*¹ [late 18C–late 19C] to hoax. [BAM n.¹]

bam *v.*² [20C] to hit. [BAM n.²]

Bama *n.* [1940s+] **1** Ala*bama*. **2** (US Black) a generic term for the south and things southern (cf. BAMA CHUKKER; BAMMER). [abbr. *Alabama*, the archetypal southern state]

bama chukker *n.* [1940s+] (US Black) a poor southern rural White (cf. PECKERWOOD). [BAMA + SAmE *chucker*, one who husks corncobs]

bambache *n.* [late 19C–1920s] (US Black) a riotous, wild party. [Sp.]

bambalacha *n.* [1930s–40s] (drugs) marijuana; thus *bambalacha rancher*, a marijuana smoker. [Sp.]

bam-bam *n.* [20C] (W.I.) the buttocks, the posterior. [echoic of the buttocks' slap onto a solid surface]

bamber *n.* [1980s+] (US drugs) second-rate marijuana. [? BAMBALACHA]

bambi *v.* [mid-17C–1950s] (US Black) to lie down, esp. to lie down in the grass. [Bantu *mubambi*, to hide in the grass]

Bambi effect *n.* [1950s–60s] (gay) the turning of a young (otherwise homosexual) man's fancy to (heterosexual) love. [the parting of the youthful Bambi and his erstwhile pal Thumper in the Disney film *Bambi* (1942)]

bamblusterate *v.* [19C] to hoax or confuse in a noisy manner. [BAM n.¹ + SE *bluster*]

bamboo *n.* [1970s] (W.I.) the penis (cf. BOG BAMBOO).

bamboo *adj.* **1** [1930s–60s] used of a Westerner who has 'gone native' while stationed in the Far East. **2** [1950s–60s] eccentric, mad (cf. ASIATIC). [a very common plant in the area]

bamboo baksheesh *n.* [mid-19C] a tip that is accompanied by a blow (cf. BAMBOO CHOW-CHOW). [SE *bamboo* + BAKSHEESH n.; the demands for baksheesh were seen as so irritating by White people in the East that the overly importuning natives, while receiving their money, were made to pay for it]

bamboo chow-chow *n.* [mid–late 19C] a thrashing (cf. BAMBOO BACKSHEESH). [pidgin use]

bambooing *n.* [mid-19C] a thrashing, a whipping. [the *bamboo* cane employed]

bamboo-wedding *n.* [20C] (W.I.) a wedding according to Hindu rites; thus *marry under bamboo*. [the *bamboo* tent set up for the ceremony]

bamboozlable *adj.* [late 19C+] gullible. [BAMBOOZLE v.]

bamboozle/bumfoozle *v.* [early 18C+] to hoax, to trick, to confuse. [prob. Und. origin, although no proof exists; the term appears in the *Tatler* no. 230, as an illustration of 'the continual Corruption of our English Tongue' along with such new sl. terms as BANTER (cited by E.P. as a poss. root); BUBBLE v.¹; BULLY n.¹; *kidney*; MOB n.¹; PUT n.1 (1); SHAM. Hotten (1860) suggests that it might have emerged in late 17C (Jonathan Swift thought so) and that it was ult. 'a term derived from the *Gipsies*']

bamboozled *adj.* [early 18C+] confused. [BAMBOOZLE]

bamboozler *n.* [early 18C+] a trickster. [BAMBOOZLE]

bambosh *n.* [mid-19C] deceptive humbug. [BAMBOOZLE + BOSH n.¹]

bambs *n.* [1980s+] (drugs) depressants. [ety. unknown; BAM n.³ (3)]

bamfoozle *v.* [19C] (US) **1** to trick, to hoax (cf. BAMBOOZLE). **2** euph. to damn, e.g. *I'll be bamfoozled.*

bam, in yo face! *excl.* [1990s] (US teen) an excl. of triumph, of victory in an argument.

bamma *n.* [1980s+] (US Black) an unsophisticated person, esp. one lacking in dress sense (cf. BAMA; BAMA CHUKKER). [Alabama]

bammer *n.* [1990s] an unsophisticated person (cf. BAMA).

bammer *adj.* [1990s] (US Black teen) bad, fake (cf. BAMA).

bammer-boat *n.* [20C] (W.I./Guyn.) a small boat used by smugglers; thus *bammer-boy*, one who uses such a boat for smuggling. [SE *bum-boat*, a small boat used to ferry provisions out to moored ships]

bammy *n.* [1950s+] (US drugs) marijuana. [BAM n.³ (1)]

bamo! *excl.* [1940s+] (W.I.) let's go! [Sp. *vamos!* let's go!]

bamsie/bamsee/bamsey *n.* [20C] (W.I.) the buttocks, the posterior (cf. BAM-BAM). [BUM n.²]

bamsie-fly *n.* [20C] (W.I.) a persistent nuisance. [BAMSIE + SE *fly*]

bamsie-man *n.* [20C] (W.I.) an effeminate man (cf. AUNTIE-MAN). [BAMSIE + SE *man*]

bamsquabbled *see* BUMSQUABBLED.

ban *n.* [19C] (Anglo-Irish) a Lord Lieutenant of Ireland. [? pun on SE *ban*, a curse, or *ban*, a proclamation; note Slav. *ban*, lord, master]

banana *n.*¹ [1910s+] (US) a stupid or worthless person, a simpleton. [? the fruit is SOFT adj. + YELLOW adj.²]

banana *n.*² **1** [1910s+] the penis (cf. TUMMY BANANA). **2** [1940s+] (US Black) a light-skinned Black person, esp. an attractive woman; one of the many terms that equate women with food (cf. APPLE n.¹⁰; BISCUIT n.²; BIT OF CRUMB; BIT OF JAM; BIT OF RASPBERRY; BUTTER BABY; CAKE n.³; CANDY n.¹; CHEESECAKE n.¹; COOKIE n.²; CREAMIE n.²; CRUMB n.²; CRUMPET n.⁴; CUPCAKE; DISH n.²; FILET; FINE BANANA; GOOD EATING; GREEN BANANA; HONEY n.⁴; JAM n.³; KUMQUAT; PANCAKE n.¹; PASTRY; PEACH n.¹; PIE n.³; POUNDCAKE; SWEET POTATO PIE; TART; TOMATO; TOOTSIE ROLL n.²; YUMMY n.). **3** [1960s+] a derog. term for an Asian who has chosen to adopt White, Western values (cf. APPLE n.¹¹). [the colour and/or shape of the fruit; in (3) the person is 'yellow outside but white inside']

banana *n.*³ [1930s] (US Und.) a homosexual. [like the SE *banana* he is BENT + note FRUIT n.² (2)]

banana *n.*⁴ [1950s+] (Aus.) a fool, an idiot, an incompetent. [backform. of NANA n.]

banana *n.*⁵ [1950s] (Aus.) a £1 note. [it is 'sweet and acceptable']

Banana/banana *adj.* [1970s+] (S.Afr.) referring to the province of Natal, now KwaZulu-Natal; thus *Banana Republic, banana country, Bananaland, Bananalander* etc. [the province's main crop]

banana bender *n.* [1960s+] (Aus.) a Queenslander (cf. BAGEL BENDER; BANANALAND; BANANASKIN). [the state's major crop]

banana boy *n.*¹ [20C] a member of one of Dr Barnardo's homes for orphaned and deprived children. [joc. mispron. of *Barnardo*]

banana boy *n.*[2] [1950s+] (S.Afr.) a resident or native of Natal. [BANANA adj.]

banana cake *n.* [1970s+] (US) an eccentric. [var. on FRUITCAKE n.[2]]

Banana City *n.* **1** [late 19C+] (Aus.) Brisbane, Queensland. **2** [1960s+] (S.Afr.) Durban. [on model of BANANALAND]

banana factory *n.* [1980s+] (US campus) a hectic, horrible or futile situation. [? BANANAS adj. + SE *factory*]

banana-farm *n.* [1960s+] a psychiatric institution in a tropical or semi-tropical country. [BANANAS adj. + FUNNY FARM]

bananahead *n.* [1940s+] (US) a simpleton, a fool. [BANANA n.[1] + sfx. -HEAD (1)]

banana-jockey *n.* [20C] (W.I./Gren.) one who gets a free ride from the country by climbing onto a banana lorry heading for town. [SE *banana* + JOCKEY n.[2]]

Bananaland *n.* [late 19C+] (Aus.) Queensland; thus *Bananalander*, a native of Queensland. [the banana crop produced there]

banana man *n.* [mid-19C+] (Aus.) an inhabitant of Queensland. [BANANALAND]

banana-nose *n.* [1920s+] (US) a long or hooked nose; thus used as a nickname or epithet. [resemblance]

banana oil *n.* [1920s+] (US) nonsense, insincere or hypocritical talk (cf. APPLE SAUCE n.[2]; BANANAS n.[1]). [the supposed smoothness of the fig. oil]

banana peddler/pusher *n.* [1920s–40s] (US) an Italian immigrant. [the trade in which some immigrants worked]

bananas *n.*[1] [1920s+] (US) nonsense. [abbr. BANANA OIL]

bananas *n.*[2] [1970s+] corrupt policemen. [coined during the 1970s investigation of London's Special Patrol Group, declared to be 'yellow, bent and hanging around in bunches]

bananas *n.*[3] [1980s+] (drugs) amyl nitrite (cf. AIMIES n.[2]). [the smell, reminiscent of over-ripe bananas]

bananas *adj.* [1930s+] **1** crazy, eccentric (cf. DRIVE BANANAS; GO BANANAS). **2** sexually perverse. [? one's mind is 'bent out of shape']

bananas! *excl.* [1940s] (US) goodbye, see you tomorrow (cf. HASTY BANANA!). [play on Sp. *manañas*]

Bananaskin *n.* [late 19C] (Aus.) a native of Queensland. [BANANA BENDER]. [BANANALAND]

banana split *n.* [1990s] (US Black teen) a sexy Asian woman. [BANANA n.[2] (2) + SPLIT n.[7]]

banana splits *n.* [1960s+] (drugs) amyl nitrite (cf. AIMIES n.[2]). [the drug's odour of 'rotten bananas']

banbury *n.* [late 19C–1910s] a promiscuous woman. [the supposed link between *Banbury* cakes and (jam-)TART(s)]

banbury-blood *n.* [17C] a Puritan. [SE *Banbury*, the Oxfordshire town, once a centre of highly enthusiastic Puritanism + BLOOD]

banbury story/story of a cock and a bull *n.* [late 18C–early 19C] nonsense, foolish chatter. [nursery rhyme 'Ride a cock-horse to Banbury Cross'; the sl. ref. is presumably punning on 'cock' (as in 'cock and bull'), since the rhyme itself refers either to the destruction of Banbury Cross by Puritan zealots, a ride taken by Queen Elizabeth I or the need for an extra 'coach' horse to ascend the steep hills on the London-Banbury journey, rather than any particular garrulousness on behalf of the natives of the town]

banchoot/beteechoot *n.* [late 18C–1930s] (Anglo-Ind.) a coarse insult, which carries far greater weight in India than in the UK. [Hind. *ban*, sister or *betee*, daughter + *choad*, a male copulator; thus lit. 'sister-/daughter-fucker']

band *n.* **1** [1920s–30s] (US Black) a woman (cf. BANTAM; CHICK n.[4]; HEN n.). **2** [20C] (Aus.) a prostitute. [? SE *bantam* (*hen*)]

banda *n.* [1990s] (US Black) a poor, ghetto child. [? SE *abandoned*]

Band-Aid *n.* [1980s+] (orig. US milit.) a doctor. [brandname *Band-Aid*; the US equivalent of the UK Elastoplast]

Band-Aid liberal *n.* [1980s] a half-hearted liberal, whose beliefs can be easily compromised; such an individual would rather place a Band-Aid on an issue and cover it up than dig into the roots and deal with it. [proprietary name *Band-Aid* + SE *liberal*. Note the Band-Aid rock concerts of 1982, which themselves punned on the name *Band-Aid* + SE *band* + *aid*]

bandalu *adj.* [20C] (W.I.) crooked, illicit; thus a *bandulu bizness*, a racket, a swindle. [ety. unknown]

bandbox *n.* [20C] (US Und.) country workhouse or local prison. [SE *bandbox*, a fragile structure or one in which space is restricted]

b & d *n.* [1960s+] bondage and discipline, a sexual 'speciality' (cf. ENGLISH CULTURE; FLADGE). [abbr.]

b and e *n.* [1950s+] (orig. police jargon) breaking and entry. [abbr.]

banded *adj.* [19C] hungry. [? the tightening of the band or belt around one's diminishing waist]

bander *n.* [20C] (Aus.) soap. [pron. of rhy. sl. BAND OF HOPE (1)]

bandicoot *v.* [late 19C+] (Aus.) to steal potatoes from the fields by removing the potatoes from the soil and carefully replacing the plant on which they grow; thus *bandicooter*. [SE *bandicoot*, a small marsupial known for its burrowing]

band in the box *n.* [1960s+] venereal disease (cf. CARDBOARD BOX; COACHMAN ON THE BOX; JACK IN THE BOX n.[3]; NERVO AND KNOX; REVEREND RONALD KNOX). [rhy. sl. *band in the box* = POX n.[1]]

bandit *n.*[1] [1950s+] (police) a villain, often used in combs. as generic for a criminal practising a speciality (cf. ARTIST n.[2]; BALD-TYRE BANDITS; GAS-METER BANDIT; KNICKERS BANDIT; PARKING-METER BANDIT; PISSHOLE BANDIT; PUSSY BANDIT). [ironic use of SE]

bandit *n.*[2] [1960s+] (US) a coin-operated gaming machine, a fruit machine. [abbr. ONE-ARMED BANDIT]

band moll *n.* [1960s] (Aus.) a woman who associates herself with rock or jazz bands, offering her body for a share in their celebrity (cf. GROUPIE n.[1]). [SE *band* + MOLL n.]

band of hope *n.* [late 19C+] soap (cf. BANDER). [rhy. sl.; the *Band of Hope*, formed 1847, was a temperance society]

bandog *n.* **1** [15C–late 18C] a bailiff or a bailiff's assistant (cf. LURCHER OF THE LAW). **2** [late 18C] a bandbox. **3** [19C] a policeman. [SE *band*, chain + *dog*. Orig. a large guard-dog, the term re-entered SE in the 1980s to describe a cross-breed of Neapolitan mastiffs and US pit bull terriers]

bandog and Bedlam *see* SPEAK BANDOG AND BEDLAM.

bandook/bundook *n.* [18C+] (orig. Anglo-Ind.) a musket, a rifle, a crossbow. ['*Bunduk* was a name applied by the Arabs to filberts (as some allege) because they came from Venice (*Banadik*, ? f. Ger. *Venedig*). The name was transferred to the nut-like pellets shot from crossbows and thence the crossbows or arblasts were called bundooks, f. *kaus al-bundook*, pellet bow. From crossbows the name was transferred again to fire arms' [Yule & Burnell]

bandore *n.* [late 17C–late 18C] a widow's head-dress, worn to signify her mourning state. [Fr. *bandeau*]

bandowzer *n.* [early–mid-19C] a heavy blow. [ety. unknown; ? var. on FERRICADOUZER]

b & p *n.* [late 19C–1900s] an effeminate young man (cf. BEANPEA). [a case involving two such youths, known only, so taboo was the thought of homosexuality, by their initials *B* and *P*]

band rat *n.* [1940s–50s] a woman who associates herself with musicians, usu. offering sex in return for proxy celebrity (cf. GROUPIE).

b and s *n.* [mid-19C+] brandy *and* soda; occas. reversed as [late 19C] *s and b* (cf. G AND T; V.A.T.). [abbr.]

bandulu *n.* [20C] (W.I. Rasta) a bandit, a criminal, one who lives by guile. [ety. unknown; ? link to Fr. *bandeau*, a headscarf, i.e. worn here as a mask]

bandy *n.*[1] [mid-19C–1900s] a silver sixpence (cf. BENDER n.[2]; CRIPPLE n.[1]; CROOKBACK). [SE *bandy*; the easy bending of the thin silver]

bandy *n.*[2] [1990s] (US teen/campus) a dedicated member of a marching band whose social life is limited to fellow musicians.

bandy chair *n.* [late 19C] a *Banbury* chair, i.e. a chair formed by two people crossing their hands.

bane, the *n.* [late 19C–1910s] brandy. [SE *bane*, that which causes ruin; on model of MOTHER'S RUIN]

bang *n.*[1] [16C+] a blow, a hit, as aimed at and received by a person. [ON *banga*, to hammer]

bang *n.*[2] **1** [late 17C–late 18C] a pelvic thrust during intercourse. **2** [1920s+] (Aus.) a brothel. **3** [1930s+] an act of sexual intercourse, used in both hetero- and homosexual contexts. **4** [1960s+] a man or woman as a sexual performer, e.g. *he's/she's a great bang.* **5** [1980s+] (US Black gang) a multiple rape, an orgy (cf. GANGBANG n.). [(2) thus according to Baker (1941) but note Simes (1993): 'the sense is not recorded by other writers or dictionaries']

bang *n.*[3] [mid–late 19C] a lie; thus *bang word*, a curse word, an oath.

bang *n.*[4] [20C] (US) a crowd of people. [ext. of SHEBANG]

bang *n.*[5] [1920s+] (orig. US) a thrill (cf. GET A BANG OUT OF). [SE *bang*, a hit, a knock; thus a stimulus]

bang *n.*[6] [1920s+] (drugs) a single injection of a narcotic drug, e.g. *a bang of cocaine* (cf. HIT n.[4]). [the force used to push the needle into one's flesh + the instantly pleasurable sensation (cf. BANG n.[5]) that the drug creates. Note the erroneous sp. *bhang*, which is cited in the *OED* (1922) and leads that dictionary to assume it is a 'revived' version of the proper use, as a synonym for Indian cannabis]

bang *n.*[7] [1930s–40s] (US) luck, fortune, situation; thus a *bad bang*, bad luck, an unfortunate situation.

bang *n.*[8] [1940s+] (US) a try, an attempt, usu. in phr. *take a bang/bang at*, to have a try, to make an attempt.

bang *n.*[9] [1960s] (US campus) a grade of B; thus *bang and a half*, a grade of B+. [initial letter]

bang *n.*[10] [1960s+] cannabis, esp. in the form of hashish. [Urdu *bhang*, Indian hemp (*Cannabis indica*); the term appears in Eng. in mid-16C but its use (through to mid-20C) is simply as an exotic foreign word; only with the spread of the Hippie Trail of the 1960s was it incorporated, slightly mis-spelt, into popular slang; *bhang* itself remains a technical term, used to describe cannabis as produced and consumed in India and Pakistan]

bang *n.*[11] [1980s+] (US) a murder. [BANG v.[3]]

bang *adj.*[1] [early–mid-19C] smart, alert. [abbr. BANG-UP adj.]

bang *adj.*[2] [mid-19C+] (S.Afr.) scared; thus *bangbroek*, a coward (cf. FRAIDY-CAT). [Afk. *bang*, scared + *broek*, trousers]

bang *v.*[1] **1** [16C+] to hit, to thump. **2** [late 17C+] to copulate; like many sl. terms involving sex, this implies an aggression irrespective of any affection (cf. BASH n.[2]; BATTER v.; BIFF v.[1]; BOINK; BONK v.; BORE v.[2]; BOUNCE v.[1]; BUST SOME BOOTY; CLUB v.[1]; CUT A SIDE; DRILL v.[2]; FLIMP; FOIN v.; GO THROUGH v.[2]; GRIND v.[2]; HUMP v.[1]; HUSTLE v.; IMPALE; JOUNCE; KNOB v.; KNOCK v.[1]; MUDDLE v.; MUSS v.; NAIL v.; NUDGE v.; PEG v.[3]; PERFORATE; PLANK v.[1]; PLONK v.; PLUG v.[1]; POKE v.; POUND v.[2]; PROD v.; PUNCH v.; RAKE v.; RASP v.; ROOT v.[3]; RUMMAGE; SCOUR v.[2]; SCREW v.[1]; SERVE v.[1]; SHAFT v.; SHAG v.[1]; SHAKE v.[1]; SHOOT v.[3]; SNABBLE; SPEAR THE BEARDED CLAM; SPIT v.[1]; SPLIT v.[2]; SPREAD v.[1]; STAB v.; STAB IN THE THIGH; STICK v.[2]; STUFF v.[3]; SWINGE; SWITCH v.; THRUM; TONK v.; TOUZLE; TOWZE;

TROUNCE; TUMBLE v.[1]; WAP). **3** [1940s+] to impress. **4** [1960s+] to thrill. **5** [1970s+] (US) to inflict, to 'hit with'.

bang *v.*[2] [19C] to surpass, esp. as phr. *bang bob-tail, bang everything* etc. [Cumbrian dial.]

bang *v.*[3] [1920s+] (US) to kill by shooting. [noise of the weapon]

bang *v.*[4] [1920s+] (drugs) to use heroin (cf. HIT v.[2]; SLAM v.[3]). [BANG n.[6]]

bang *v.*[5] [1960s+] (US) to make a turn while driving, usu. as *bang a U-ie*, to make a U-turn etc.

bang *v.*[6] [1980s+] (orig. US Black) to fight, to kill. [abbr. GANGBANG v. (2), (3)]

bang *adv.* [early 19C+] extremely, very, e.g. *bang in trouble, bang up to date.* [SE *bang*, meaning a sudden action or shock]

bang a hanger, to *phr.* [20C] to steal a purse. [BANG n.[1] (1) + HANGER]

bang and biff *n.* [20C] syphilis. [rhy. sl. *bang and biff = the siff* = syphilis]

bang a pitcher, to *phr.* [late 19C–1900s] to empty a pot of beer. [BANG n.[1] (1) + SE *pitcher*]

bangarang *n.* [20C] hubbub, uproar, disorder. [BANG n.[1] + echoic redup.]

bang around *v.* [20C] to make one's presence felt, with little practical result. [SE *bang around*, to make noise]

bang-beggar *n.* [mid–late 19C] (mainly Scot.) a constable. [BANG v.[1] (1) + SE *beggar*; their ill-treatment of tramps]

bang-bellied *adj.* [1940s+] (W.I.) having a large paunch. [dial. *bang-belly*, a swollen abdomen, whether of a malnourished child or a pregnant woman]

bang-belly *n.* [20C] (W.I.) a starving child (cf. RICE-BELLY n.[1]). [BANG v.[1] (1) + SE *belly*; the child hits its stomach to indicate its hunger]

bange *n.* [mid-19C+] (Aus.) a rest, a sleep. [dial. *benge*, to lounge, to laze about; note New Eng. dial. *bange*, to idle about, to take advantage of another's hospitality]

banged-up *adj.*[1] [20C] (Und.) locked up in one's cell; thus, generically, in prison. [SE *bang*; the cell door is literally banged shut]

banged-up *adj.*[2] [20C] **1** of people, beaten up, injured. **2** of objects, broken, battered esp. of a car with notable damage to the panel-work (cf. BANGER n.[7]). [BANG v.[1] (1)]

banged-up *adj.*[3] [1920s+] (drugs) under the influence of a drug. [BANG n.[6]]

banged up to the eyes *phr.* [mid-19C–1920s] very drunk. [fig. use of BANGED-UP adj.[3]]

banger *n.*[1] **1** [mid-17C–late 19C] a notable lie (cf. LICKER n.[1]; THUMPER n.[3]; WHOPPER). **2** [mid-17C–late 19C] a person who lies. **3** [mid-19C] something excellent. [BANG v.[1] (1)]

banger *n.*[2] [late 19C–1950s] a kiss (cf. SMACKER n.[1]). [the slap of lips on lips]

banger *n.*[3] [late 19C+] (Aus.) a morning coat (cf. STEEL-PEN). [play on CLAW-HAMMER]

banger *n.*[4] [20C] the penis (cf. BACON n.[1]). [BANG v.[1] (2); but note BANGER n.[5]; like a sausage it 'spits' when it gets put in the OVEN]

banger *n.*[5] [1910s+] (orig. Aus.) a sausage. [? its propensity to explode if cooked without initial pricking of the skin]

banger *n.*[6] [1930s–40s] (US) $1 (cf. SMACKERS). [one 'bangs it down' on a counter or table]

banger *n.*[7] [1960s+] **1** a dilapidated motorcar. **2** a cylinder, usu. in combs. *four-banger, six-banger.* **3** an automobile engine. [the sound of an ill-tuned, ageing engine]

banger *n.*[8] [1980s+] a fan of 'heavy metal' rock. [abbr. HEAD-BANGER (1)]

banger *n.*[9] [1980s+] (US Black) a gang member (cf. BANGING n.). [abbr. GANGBANGER]

banger *n.*[10] [1980s+] (drugs) a hypodermic syringe. [BANG n.[6]]

bangers *n.* [1980s+] (Irish) the testicles. [BANG v.[1] (2)]

bangers and red lead *n.* [20C] tinned sausages and tomato sauce. [BANGER n.[5] + naut. sl. *red lead*, tomato ketchup or tinned tomatoes]

banging *n.*[1] [1980s+] (US Black) **1** indulging in multiple rape or, if the woman is willing, in an orgy. **2** fighting. [abbr. GANGBANG v.]

banging *n.*[2] [1980s+] (drugs) the state of being under the influence of drugs. [BANG v.[4]]

banging *adj.* [late 18C] big, great in size. [BANG adv.]

banging-shop *n.* [1960s–70s] (US) a brothel (cf. BANG n.[2]; BLACKSMITH'S SHOP; BUMSHOP; BUTTOCKING SHOP; CUNT-SHOP; FISH MARKET; FLESH MARKET; FUCKERY n.; GIRLERY; GIRL-SHOP; GREENGROCERY n.[1]; GRINDING-HOUSE n.[2]; GRIND JOINT n.[2]; HOOK SHOP; KNOCKING-SHOP; MOLL SHOP; NANNY SHOP; WARM SHOP; WHORE SHOP). [BANG n.[2] (3) + SE *shop*; note synon. US milit. jargon *bang house*]

bang like a hammer/rattlesnake on a nail, to *phr.* [1950s+] (orig. Aus.) to rate as an enthusiastic sexual performer (cf. BANG LIKE A SHITHOUSE DOOR).

bang like a shithouse/dunny door/door in a gale, to *phr.* [1950s+] (orig. Aus.) to rate as an enthusiastic sexual performer; usu. said by men of women. [BANG v.[1] (2) + SHITHOUSE n. (1) + SE *door*]

bang mary *n.* [late 19C–1900s] a *bain-marie* or double-boiler. [mispron.]

bang of the latch *n.* [20C] (Irish) one final drink after 'time' has been called. [i.e. before the pub door is latched for the night]

bang on *v.* [1940s+] to talk repetitiously and tediously. [SE *bang*; the noise of one's monologue]

bang on *adv.* [1930s+] exactly right, extremely apposite, excellent. [RAF jargon *bang on the target*]

bangotcher *n.* [1940s+] (Aus.) a Western film. [shouts of *Bang! I've got you!*]

bang out *v.* [19C+] to rush away, to leave quickly. [SE *bang*, make a noise]

bang-pitcher *n.* [mid–late 17C] a drunkard. [BANG v.[1] (1) + SE *pitcher*; the thumping of a tankard on the table]

bang shoot *see* WHOLE BANG SHOOT.

bang someone's ear, to *phr.* [1960s+] (US) to talk incessantly (and tediously) (cf. BANG ON v.).

bangster *n.*[1] [mid-16C–late 18C] **1** a boaster, a braggart. **2** a bully. [BANG v.[1] (1)]

bangster *n.*[2] [1920s] (US drugs) a narcotics addict. [BANG v.[4]]

bang-stick *n.* [1960s+] any form of firearm.

bang-straw *n.* [late 18C] a farm-worker, esp. a thresher. [metonymy]

bang-tail/bangtail *n.*[1] [early 18C+] a prostitute (cf. BOBTAIL n.[1]; COCK-TAIL n.[1]; FLASHTAIL; TICKLE-TAIL; WAGTAIL). [BANG v.[1] (2) + TAIL n.[1] (2); a 19C term in the UK, it has been sustained through 20C US Black use]

bang-tail *n.*[2] [late 19C–1920s] (Aus./US) a horse, spec. any animal which has its tail cropped square; thus (Aus.) *bang-tail muster*, a round-up of cattle during which the tuft at the end of the tail is cut straight across as the cattle are counted. [SE *bang*, to cut (the front hair) square across, so that it ends abruptly]

bangtail *v.* [1940s+] (US) to hurry. [SE *bang* + TAIL n.[1] (3)]

bang/flog/murder the bishop, to *phr.* [late 19C+] to masturbate (cf. BASH THE BISHOP; BASH THE PRIEST; BATTER THE BISHOP; BEAT THE BISHOP; BOX THE JESUIT AND GET COCKROACHES; BUFF THE BISHOP; CAPTURE THE BISHOP; CONK THE CARDINAL; DISOBEY THE POPE; FLIP THE BISHOP; MASSAGE THE ONE-EYED MONK; PLEASE THE POPE; PUMMEL THE PRIEST; PUNISH THE POPE; ROPE THE POPE). [ety. unknown, although E.P. suggests a resemblance of the penis to a bishop's mitre or to the *bishop* in a traditionally

designed 'Staunton' chess set; however, simple assonance is equally likely]

bang the bush, to *phr.* [mid-19C] (US) to surpass everything (cf. BEAT BANAGHAN). [BANG v.[2] + SE *bush*]

bang the gong, to *phr.* [late 19C–1940s] (US drugs) to smoke opium. [BANG v.[1] (1) + GONG n.[2] (1) + pun]

bang/beat the hoof, to *phr.* [late 17C–early 19C] to walk (cf. BEAT FEET; PAD THE HOOF). [BANG v.[1] (1) + HOOF n.]

bang the plank, to *phr.* [1990s] to masturbate. [rhy. sl. *bang the plank* = WANK v., but note other terms for masturbation based on beating or slapping]

bang through the elephant, to *phr.* [19C] to plumb the depths of dissipation. [BANG adv. + ? ELEPHANT'S TRUNK but cf. BANG UP TO THE ELEPHANT]

bang to rights *adj.* [1920s+] (orig. US) caught in the act, caught red-handed, esp. in Und. use (cf. ABOUT RIGHT adj.[2]; DEAD-BANG; DEAD TO RIGHTS). [BANG adv. + SE *to rights*, fairly, according to the law]

bang-up *n.* **1** [19C] a dandy, a fashionable man. **2** [late 19C–1910s] (Anglo-Irish) an overcoat with a cape and high collar. [BANG-UP adj. (1)]

bang-up *adj.* **1** [early 19C+] first-rate, excellent, fashionable, stylish; often as *bang up to the mark* (cf. SLAP UP). **2** [19C] drunk (cf. ABOUT RIGHT adj.[1]). **3** [mid-19C] (US) impoverished, penniless. **4** [mid-19C] (US) finished. [onomat., but note Fr. *bien*, well or good as excl.]

bang up *v.*[1] [1920s+] to inject a narcotic drug (cf. HIT v.[2]; SHOOT UP v.[2]). [BANG v.[4] + SE *up*]

bang up *v.*[2] [20C] (prison) to imprison, spec. to lock a prisoner in a cell. [the banging of the cell door]

bang up *adv.* [1920s+] (US) completely, very much so, directly. [ext. BANG adv.]

bang/bung up/up against *adv.* [19C+] very close. [BANG adv. + SE *up against*]

bang-up prime *adj.* [19C] absolutely excellent. [BANG-UP adj. (1) + SE *prime*]

bang up to the elephant *phr.* [late 19C–1900s] perfect, beyond comparison, ideal. [BANG adj.[1] + the *Elephant and Castle*, South London's best known public house, a by-word of excellence of its type]

bang wagon *n.* [1960s] (US) an ambulance. [it carries those who have 'had a bang']

bang water *n.* [1920s+] (Can.) petrol. [the sound of a car's engine]

bang-word *n.* [late 19C–1900s] a highly expressive word, a 'swear-word'.

banjax *v.* [1930s+] to batter, to destroy, to ruin, to get in the way of. [usu. in Irish use; f. ? Dublin sl.]

banjaxed *adj.* [1930s+] broken, ruined, smashed up. [BANJAX]

banjo *n.*[1] **1** [late 19C+] (orig. Aus.) a shoulder of mutton. **2** [1910s+] (orig. Aus.) a shovel; thus *banjo and anchor*, a shovel and pick (cf. IDIOT STICK; IRISH BANJO). **3** [mid-19C–1900s] a bedpan. **4** [late 19C+] (Aus.) a frying pan. [the shape]

banjo *n.*[2] [1920s] (US) an eye. [back-form. f. BANJO-EYES]

banjo/banjo string *n.*[3] [1990s] the ridge of skin connecting the foreskin to the base of the 'bell end' of the penis. [? resemblance]

banjo *v.* [1970s+] **1** to force a door or window. **2** (orig. milit.) to hit, to beat up. [BANJO n.[1] (2)]

banjoey *n.* [late 19C–1900s] a banjo player. [SE *banjo* + *joey*, a clown, supposedly coined by the banjo-playing Prince of Wales, later King Edward VII (r.1901–10)]

banjo-eyes *n.* [1920s–70s] (US) one who has large, wide-open eyes; thus *banjo-eyed*. [SE *banjo*; the round, white drumskin on the instrument]

banjo string *see* BANJO n.[3].

banjy boy *n.* [1990s] (US Black) a gay male who dresses as if he were part of the heterosexual hip-hop culture. [? BUM-BOY/BATTIE-BOY]

bank *n.*[1] [19C] the vagina, esp. when seen as a means of making money; one of a number of terms pointing up the commercial potential of the vagina (cf. BAZAAR n.[1]; BOODLE n.[3]; BREADWINNER; BUDGET; COMMODITY; EXCHEQUER; MONEY n.[1]; MONEYBOX; MONEY MACHINE; MONEY-MAKER; MONEY-SPINNER; PURSE n.; TILL n.; WARE).

bank *n.*[2] [20C] (US prison) a shot of a narcotic. [BANG n.[6]]

bank *n.*[3] [20C] (Aus./US Black/campus) money, one's fortune (cf. BANK ON).

bank *n.*[4] [1930s–40s] (US Black) the lavatory, esp. *visit the bank, take a trip to the bank.* [euph.]

bank *v.*[1] [19C+] (Und.) **1** to steal. **2** to hide away in a safe place. **3** to go fair shares.

bank *v.*[2] [20C] to fail in a task, esp. when it is beyond one's abilities. [? SE *bank*, to save up; the image is of saving one's abilities for a task to which one is better suited]

bank *v.*[3] [20C] (US Und.) to prove someone guilty in court (cf. MAKE v.[4]). [? SE *bank*, to put on deposit; thus cf. PUT AWAY v.[2]]

bank bandit pills *n.* [1990s] (drugs) depressants. [their calming effect, suitable for use during a robbery]

banker *n.* [20C] (orig. gambling) a sure thing, something on which one can depend, a safe bet (fig. and lit.). [SE *banker*, one who runs a bank; such figures are supposedly dependable and trustworthy]

banker chapel ho *n.* [late 19C–1900s] Whitechapel in east London. [cod Ital. *bianca capella*, white chapel + excl. *ho!*]

bank of Dunlop *n.* [1990s] a fig. 'bank' on which 'rubber' cheques are drawn. [brandname *Dunlop*, manufacturer of rubber tyres]

bank off *v.* [mid–late 20C] (US prison) to place an inmate in the punishment cells. [similarity of the punishment block to a bank vault]

bank on *v.* [late 19C+] to take for granted, to assume as a certainty; thus phr. *(you can) take that to the bank*, that's a promise, you can be sure. [gambling jargon *bet the bank*, to commit oneself completely]

bankroll *v.* [1920s+] (orig. US) to provide financial backing for a project, legal or otherwise. [SE *bankroll*, a roll of bank notes]

bankrupt cart *n.* [late 18C] a one-horse chaise. ['said to be so called by a Lord Chief Justice, from their being so frequently used on Sunday jaunts by extravagant shopkeepers and tradesmen' (Grose)]

Bankside lady *n.* [17C] a prostitute (cf. CITY ROAD AFRICAN; COVENT GARDEN NUN; DRURY LANE VESTAL; FLEET STREET DOVE; FLEET STREET HOURI; FULHAM VIRGIN; HAYMARKET WARE; PICKETHATCH VESTAL; ST JOHN'S WOOD VESTAL; WHETSTONE PARK DEER). [*Bankside*, the centre of London prostitution during the 17C]

banna *n.* [20C] (W.I. teen/Guyn.) a young man or woman. [? BANGER n.[9]]

banneger *n.* [1950s] (US) a hard blow (with the fist). [? link to BEAT BANAGHAN]

banner *n.*[1] [19C] the pubic hair. [? SE *banner*, a flag; in this context the 'flag' displayed by the genitals]

banner *n.*[2] [1920s–30s] (US tramp) a bedroll. [one unfurls it]

bannocks *n.* [1990s] (Scot.) the testicles. [SE *bannock*, a round, flat loaf + ref. to BALLOCK n.]

bans *n.* [20C] (W.I. Rasta) a whole lot, a great deal. [? SE a *bunch of*]

bant *v.* [mid–late 19C] to diet. [proper name William *Banting* (1797–1878), a fashionable undertaker who reduced his own weight through dieting and a tight-laced corset]

bantam *n.* [1940s–50s] (US Black) a young woman (cf. BAND).

[SE *bantam*, a small variety of domestic fowl; note WW2 US Black milit. jargon *banta issue*, a Black female soldier]

banter *n.* [late 17C–late 18C] good-humoured nonsense or teasing. [cited by B.E. *c.*1700, the term was one of those, along with *bamboozle*, *mob*, *kidney* and *country put*, attacked by Swift in 1710 and inspired his proposals to reform the language; despite his condemnation of the term as 'first borrowed from the bullies in White Friars, then fell among the footmen' and as an 'Alsatia phrase' it had joined SE by 1800]

bantling *n.* [late 18C–mid-19C] **1** a child. **2** an illegitimate child. [Ger. *Bänkling*, bastard, ult. SE *bank*, bench; thus 'a child begotten on a bench, and not in the marriage-bed' (Webster, 1864)]

Bantu beer *n.* [1960s+] (S.Afr.) a drink made from fermented prickly pears and honey. [SE *Bantu*, derog. generic for a Black African + *beer*]

banty *adj.* [mid-19C–mid-20C] saucy, impudent. [northern dial. *banty*, a small conceited person]

banzai! *excl.* [1940s+] a general excl. of exultation, excitement. [Jap. *banzai*, hurrah!, lit. 'let him (the Emperor), live ten thousand years!']

b.a.p. *n.* [1980s+] (US) an upwardly mobile Black achiever, usu. from the Black middle class (cf. J.A.P.). [abbr. *Black American prince/princess*]

bapper *n.* [mid-19C–1920s] (Scot.) a baker. [*bap*, a small (soft) bread roll]

bappo *n.* [1920s+] (Aus.) a Baptist (cf. CONGO n.[3]; METHO n.[2]; PRESBO). [SE *Bap(tist)* + sfx. *-o*]

baps *n.* [1990s] (orig. Ulster) the female breasts (cf. APPLES n.[1]). [SE *bap*, a small (soft) bread roll]

bapsouse *v.* [early 19C] (US) to baptize. [SE *baptize* + *souse*, immerse]

baptist *n.* [early–mid-19C] a pickpocket who has been caught and ducked or 'baptized'. [pun on SE *Baptist*, who immerse new converts in water]

baptize *v.* [17C+] to dilute wine or alcohol. [i.e. to 'immerse in water']

baptized *adj.* **1** [17C–early 19C] of alcohol, usu. spirits, watered down (cf. CHRISTENED). **2** [early 19C] (Aus.) drowned. [the immersion in water of religious baptism]

bar *n.*[1] [16C] (Und.) a kind of false die, on which certain numbers are prevented from turning up (cf. BARRED; DEMI-BAR). [SE *bar*, a solid object of which one pair of sides is longer than the other]

bar *n.*[2] **1** [late 19C+] £1 sterling. **2** [1900s–60s] (Irish) a shilling (5p). [SE *bar*, a standard of weight or a denomination of currency, esp. as used by 18C merchants in trading with Africans who exchanged their goods for a set number of iron bars; or ? Rom. *bauro*, heavy, big]

bar *n.*[3] [1970s] (US gay) any public area, such as a park or beach, that is frequented by gay men looking for sex (cf. OFFICE n.[1]). [? on the basis of a SE *bar* being a popular site for such activities]

bar *n.*[4] [1980s+] (drugs) hashish. [the shape of a typical lump of the drug]

bar *n.*[5] [1980s+] an erection. [its rigidity]

bar *v.* [1930s+] (Aus.) **1** of people, to dislike intensely. **2** of actions, to reject unequivocally. [? 17C law, to take exception to + dicing and two-up jargon *bar*, to declare a throw void]

Bara *n.* [1970s+] (S.Afr.) *Bara*gwanath Hospital, Soweto. [abbr.]

barb *n.*[1] [late 19C] (US campus) a student who is not a member of a Greek-letter fraternity. [play on SE *barbarian*, to ancient Greeks, one who is not a Greek]

barb/barbie *n.*[2] [1960s+] (drugs) any of the hypnotic drugs derived from *barb*ituric acid. [abbr.]

barb v.[1] [early 17C] (Und.) to clip gold. [abbr. SE *barber*]

barb v.[2] [late 19C] (US) to *barb*er, to cut hair. [abbr.]

barbadoes v. [mid-17C] (Irish) to transport to the West Indies. [proper name *Barbados*; after the Drogheda massacre of 1655, Oliver Cromwell transported many Irish people as an added punishment]

Barbary Coast n. [mid-19C–1940s] the 'red-light' area of a city, esp. as frequented by sailors on leave. [16C proper name *Barbary Coast*, the countries of the northern coast of Africa; as a sl. term the phr. has applied specifically to the San Francisco waterfront before the 1906 earthquake, Water Street, New York City, and part of Elizabeth Street, Sydney (from Campbell Street to Devonshire Street) during WW2; E.P. cites late 17C–early 19C *Little Barbary*, Wapping, home of the Ratcliff Highway, once London's tough port area]

barbecue n.[1] [20C] (US prison) the murder of a fellow-inmate by tossing a Molotov cocktail or petrol bomb into their cell. [SE *barbecue*, the roasting of a whole animal over an open fire]

barbecue/barbecue stool n.[2] [20C] (US prison) the electric chair (cf. BAKE v.[1]; HOT SEAT). [ironic use of SE *barbecue* + *stool*]

barbecue n.[3] [1930s–40s] (US Black) an attractive woman, esp. one who enjoys or offers oral sex (cf. CHICK n.[4]). [? such a woman is a 'hot piece of meat']

barbecue stool *see* BARBECUE n.[2].

barbed wire/barbwire n. [late 19C–1920s] (US) strong whisky or brandy. [it 'tears you up']

barber n.[1] [early 19C+] (Can./US) a bitterly cold wind. [it appears to 'cut' one's exposed face]

barber n.[2] [late 19C–1930s] (Aus.) a shearer; thus *barber's delight*, a silk shirt. [they 'shave' sheep]

barber n.[3] [1920s+] (Aus.) a hotel manager or owner. [he 'trims' the customers]

barber n.[4] [1920s+] (US) a tediously talkative person, esp. in sports use. [the trad. loquacious *barber*, underpinned by US commentator Walter 'Red' Barber (1908–92)]

barber n.[5] [1930s+] a tramp. [? BARBER'S CAT n.[1] (1); i.e. he is undernourished and thin]

barber v.[1] [1910s+] (orig. Aus.) to rob, to steal; thus *hotel barber*, a thief who specializes in robbing hotel guests. [a pun on SE *barber*, who gives customers a 'trim']

barber v.[2] [1930s+] (US) to gossip, to chatter. [the supposed predilection of *barbers* for chattering on at their captive customers]

barber a joint, to phr. [20C] to rob a bedroom while its occupant is sleeping. [BARBER v.[1] + JOINT n.[3] (2)]

barbered broads n. [1950s] (Aus.) cards that have been shaved down one side to facilitate cheating. [SE *barber*, who gives customers a 'trim']

barber's block n. **1** [early 19C+] the head. **2** [late 19C–1920s] an overdressed man (cf. BLACKFORD-BLOCK). [ext. of SE *barber's block*, the wooden 'head' on which a barber placed a wig]

barber's breakfast n. [1960s+] (N.Z.) a cough or dry retch, a glass of water and a cigarette (cf. AIR PIE AND A WALK AROUND). [N.Z.E. *barber*, a shearer]

barber's cat n.[1] **1** [mid–late 19C] a sickly, malnourished person. **2** [1930s] (drugs) an emaciated opium addict. [the lack of edible scraps at a barber's shop. 'An expression too coarse to print' (Hotten, 1867)]

barber's cat n.[2] [mid–late 19C] a gossip, a chatterer. [phr. *like the barber's cat – all wind and piss*]

barber's chair n. [18C] a promiscuous woman (cf. BARRACK HACK; TOWN PUMP). [abbr. of phr. *common as a barber's chair*, which can be read by all-comers]

barber's clerk n. [mid–late 19C] an overdressed man (cf. DONE UP LIKE A POX DOCTOR'S CLERK).

barber's knock n. [early–mid-19C] a double-knock, the first hard, the second far softer (cf. SHAVE-AND-A-HAIRCUT).

barber's sign n. [late 18C–early 19C] the penis and testicles. [the red-and-white striped pole that signified *barber*; 'a standing pole and two wash-balls' (Grose, 1796). Note SE *wash-ball*, a ball of soap, often used for shaving]

barberton/babaton/babarton/baberton n. [1940s–60s] (S.Afr.) an illicit liquor (Blacks were not allowed to buy 'Whiteman's liquor' before 1962) composed of bread, malt, sugar, yeast and warm water. [proper name *Barberton*, a town in the East Transvaal]

barbie n.[1] *see* BARB n.[2].

barbie n.[2] [1970s+] (orig. Aus.) a *barb*ecue. [abbr.]

Barbie/Barbie Doll n.[3] [1970s+] (orig. US) a super-conformist, conventionally attractive woman (cf. KEN n.[2]). [the name of a blue-eyed, blonde-haired designer-labelled plastic doll, created for little girls and apparently a role-model for some of their elder sisters]

barbs n. (drugs) **1** [1960s+] barbiturates. **2** [1980s+] cocaine. [(2) is a mis-reading of (1)]

barbwire *see* BARBED WIRE.

barb wire deal n. [1960s] (US) a difficult situation. [SE *barbed wire* + *deal*]

barclay perkins/barclay and perkins n. [mid-19C–1900s] beer, stout. [the London brewers Barclay, Perkins & Co.]

barclay's n. [1930s+] masturbation (cf. HAM SHANK; J. ARTHUR; JODRELL; LEVY v.; MERCHANT BANKER; PIGGY BANK; SHERMAN; YORKSHIRE PENNY BANK). [rhy. sl. *Barclay's Bank* = WANK n.]

barcoo n.[1] [late 19C] (Aus.) language heavily peppered with obscenities. [proper name *Barcoo*, a region of Queensland where, presumably, such speech was frequent]

barcoo n.[2] [late 19C] (Aus.) bouts of vomiting caused by the ingestion of fly-polluted food. [abbr. *Barcoo sickness*]

barcoo rot n. [late 19C+] (Aus.) a form of scurvy. [*Barcoo* + SE *rot*, a putrescent, wasting disease]

barcoo/Queensland salute n. [late 19C+] (Aus.) a characteristic gesture in Aus. of brushing away flies from one's face (cf. AUSTRALIAN SALUTE). [*Barcoo* + SE *salute*]

barcoo sandwich n. [1960s+] (Aus.) **1** a curlew between two sheets of bark. **2** a goanna between two sheets of bark. **3** a double rum between two beers. [*Barcoo* + SE *sandwich*]

barcoo shout n. [1910s] (Aus.) three drinks for half-a-crown (12.5p); a bargain at a time when drinks were usually a shilling (5p) each. [*Barcoo* + SHOUT n.[1]]

barcoo spew/vomit n. [1910s+] (Aus.) severe vomiting brought on by drinking bad water and often accompanied by attacks of dysentery. [*Barcoo* + SE *spew/vomit*]

bardache n. [mid-16C–early 18C] a male homosexual. [SE *bardash*, a catamite, ult. ? f. Arabic *bardaj*, a slave]

bardacious adj. [1920s] excellent, wonderful, the very best. [var. on BODACIOUS]

bar-dog n. [1940s] (US West) a bartender; thus *bardogging*, tending bar. [SE *bar* + *dog*(sbody), a worker, a drudge; note SE *sea-dog* for model]

bardolph n. [1990s] a red nose, the result of excessive drinking. [*Bardolph*, a character in Shakespeare's *Henry V* (1598–9)]

bare-arsed adj. [mid-16C+] naked (cf. BARE-ASS).

bare-ass/assed adj. [late 19C+] naked (cf. BOLLOCK NAKED). [SE *bare* + ARSE n.[1] (1)]

bareback adv. [1950s+] used to describe having sexual intercourse without using a contraceptive sheath; thus *bareback riding*, having unprotected sex (cf. RAW adj.[1]). [the nakedness of the penis; note RIDE v.[1]]

bare-balls adj. [1960s] (US) completely naked (cf. BARE-ASS). [SE *bare* + BALLS n.[1] (1)]

barebones n. [late 16C–early 19C] a thin person.

bare-brisket *n.* [19C–1900s] a thin person (cf. BAREBONES). [SE *bare* + BRISKET]

bare-bum *n.* [20C] (Aus.) a dinner jacket (cf. BUM-FREEZER). [SE *bare* + BUM n.²; the jacket is short, as opposed to a tailcoat]

bared *adj.* [mid-19C–1900s] shaved. [SE *bare*, to denude]

barefoot/barefooted *adj.* [mid-19C+] (US) **1** of an alcoholic drink, undiluted, 'straight'. **2** of tea or coffee, without milk/cream or sugar.

barelegged *adj.* [early 18C] (US) of an alcoholic drink, undiluted (cf. BAREFOOT).

bares *n.* [1960s] (US) the *bare* hands. [abbr.]

barf *n.* [1960s+] (US) **1** vomit. **2** any form of repulsive food. [BARF v.]

barf *v.* [1940s+] (mainly US campus) to vomit (cf. HUGHIE; RALPH v.). [echoic]

barf!/barfaroo! *excl.* [1970s+] (US) that's disgusting! don't make me sick! (cf. BARF CITY; BARF ME OUT!). [BARF v.]

barfbag *n.* [1960s+] (US) an air-sickness bag, as provided on air flights. [BARF n. + SE *bag*]

barf city *n.* [1960s+] (US teen) anything particularly unpleasant. [BARF n. + sfx. -CITY]

barfer *n.* [1940s] (US) a disgusting, worthless person. [BARF v.]

barfly *n.* [20C] (orig. US) the habitual occupier of a bar, day in, day out. [ext. of SE use, one who 'buzzes around' a bar]

barf me out! *excl.* [1980s+] (US) an excl. indicating absolute disapproval (cf. BARF CITY). [BARF!]

barf on a board *phr.* [1960s+] (US) chipped creamed beef on toast. [BARF n. Note synon. US milit. jargon 'shit on a shingle']

barf someone out *v.* [1980s+] (US) to disgust, to revolt; thus *barfed out*, disgusted. [BARF v.]

barfulous *adj.* [1980s+] (US campus) repellent, disgusting. [BARF n.]

barfy *adj.* [1950s+] (US campus) nauseating, repulsive. [BARF n.]

bargain basement *n.* [1960s] anywhere sex partners can be found easily. [joc. use of SE *bargain basement*, the bargain dept. of a large store]

bargain bucket *n.* [1990s] **1** a fat woman. **2** her vagina (cf. BARGE n.³). [SE *bargain* + BUCKET n.⁴; n.¹ (3)]

barge *n.¹* [late 19C–1900s] an imitation (padded) breast. ['from their likeness to the wide prow of canal-barges' (Ware)]

barge *n.²* **1** [late 19C–1940s] an argument, a dispute. **2** [20C] (Irish) a cantankerous, argumentative woman. [BARGE v.]

barge *n.³* [1970s+] (US) **1** a large foot (cf. CANAL BOAT n.²). **2** a particularly large vagina (cf. BARGAIN BUCKET). **3** (US Black) a large car, esp. a Cadillac. [SE *barge*; barges are generally large and unwieldy vessels]

barge *v.* [mid-19C–1920s] to abuse, to attack verbally, to 'slang'; thus *barge the point*, to argue, to dispute. [? SE *bargee*, a bargeman, an occupation known for its 'colourful' language, or Scot. *bargle*, to squabble; 20C use mainly Irish]

barge-arse *n.* [mid-19C–1900s] one who has fat buttocks. [SE *barge* + ARSE n.¹ (1)]

barge at *v.* [late 19C+] to argue aggressively. [BARGE v.]

barge in *v.* [late 19C+] to interrupt rudely, to push one's way in. [SE *barge*, a flat-bottomed canal- or river-boat, esp. its clumsy motions]

bar golf *n.* [1980s+] (US campus) the practice of going from bar to bar drinking. [play on a round of golf/a round of drinks]

bar handles *n.* [1960+] an excess of fat around one's stomach, a 'spare tyre' (cf. LOVE HANDLES). [SE *bar* + *handle*; the fat has developed after too many trips to the bar]

bar-hog *n.¹* [1930s] (US) a heavy drinker who spends most of their time in the bar. [SE *bar* + joc. use of *hog*]

bar-hog *n.²* [1960s] (US) a part-time prostitute, who frequents bars and uses them as a base for soliciting (cf. B-GIRL). [SE *bar* + HOG n.⁷]

bar-hop *n.* [1900s–30s] (US) a bartender. [they 'hop' around the bar]

bar hop *v.* [1980s+] (US campus) to go from bar to bar, drinking and investigating the social possibilities.

barhound *n.* [1920s+] the habitual occupier of a bar (cf. BARFLY). [SE *bar* + sfx. -HOUND]

bari *n.* [1960s+] (S.Afr. township) a newly arrived and thus unsophisticated country dweller, as yet unversed in township ways. [? SE *barbarian*, but note S.Afr.E. *baar*, a novice]

bark *n.¹* [mid-18C–1940s] the human skin; thus *take the bark off*, to beat, to thrash. [SE *bark*, the outer surface of a tree; coined *c*.1750 but all 20C use is US Black]

bark *n.²* [19C] an Irish person; thus *Barkshire*, Ireland. [various northern dials.; ? f. image of a noisy Irish person shouting or 'barking']

bark *v.* **1** [early 19C+] to tout a shop or attraction. **2** [mid-19C+] to cough. **3** [mid-19C+] to make a loud, sudden noise, esp. that of firing a handgun. **4** [late 19C+] (US) to boast, to brag. [all fig. uses of SE]

bark and growl *n.* [mid-19C+] a trowel. [rhy. sl.]

barked *adj.* [20C] (US) bald. [trapper jargon *bark*, to scalp; lit. to remove bark from a tree]

barker *n.¹* **1** [late 15C–late 17C; 19C] a thug, esp. one who offers verbal, but perhaps not physical, aggression. **2** [early 19C+] a pistol (cf. BARKING IRON). **3** [late 17C+] a shop tout, esp. the tout who stands outside a second-hand clothes shop attempting to lure customers within (cf. BOW-WOW SHOP). **4** [mid-19C–1900s] (US) an employee of a saloon or similar place of recreational entertainment who lures in passers-by from the street (cf. PULLER-IN). **5** [late 19C+] one who coughs. **6** [1900s–20s] (US) an auctioneer. [SE *bark*, to shout loudly; (1) 19C use is US; (2) 20C use is mainly US]

barker *n.²* [20C] a sausage (cf. HOT DOG n.¹). [a ref. to the once popular song 'Oh vare and oh vare is my leedle vee dog/Oh vare, oh vare is he gone?']

barker's *adj.* [20C] naked, nude. [rhy. sl. *Barker's* = STARKERS; ult. Barker's, a large department store in High Street Kensington, London]

barkers *n.* [1940s–50s] (US Black) tight, painful shoes (cf. BARKING DOGS). [tight shoes hurt one's feet (cf. DOGS n.³), which therefore 'bark' with pain]

barker's egg *n.* [1990s] (Aus.) dog excrement. [SE *barker*, a dog + *egg*]

barkey *n.* [19C] (Ling. Fr./Polari) a sailor. [Ital. *barca*, a boat]

barking *adj.* [1960s+] absolutely crazy, highly eccentric; usu. as *barking mad*. [? the image of a rabid dog]

barking dogs *n.* [1920s–40s] (US) aching or sore feet (cf. BARKERS). [a pun on SE; note DOGS n.³]

barking iron *n.* [late 18C–mid-19C] a pistol, usu. in pl. (cf. BARKER n.¹). [the noise]

barking spider *n.* [1980s+] the anus. [the resemblance + the noise of defection or farting]

barking spiders *n.* [1980s+] (US campus) the audible breaking of wind.

Barkis is willing *phr.* [late 19C] a phr. indicating that a man is willing to marry. [the phr. coined in Charles Dickens's novel *David Copperfield* (1850)]

bark up the wrong creek, to *phr.* [20C] to make a mistake (cf. BARK UP THE WRONG TREE).

bark up the wrong tree, to *phr.* [early 19C+] (orig. US) to make a mistake, to misdirect one's efforts. [the image of a dog chasing a racoon into a tree]

barkwell and holdfast *n.* [mid-19C] (US) someone who will back their words with deeds; a tough fighter. [pvb. 'Brag's a good dog, but Holdfast is better']

Bar L *n.* [20C] (Scot.) Barlinnie Prison, Glasgow (cf. BARLINNIE

DRUMSTICK). [abbr. of proper name, but note the poss. pun on use of *Bar* in many brands used by US ranchers to distinguish their cattle, e.g. Bar X, Bar Y (in which the bar is a horizontal line drawn beneath the letter); Bar L thus offers a suggestion of the Wild West, in this case of Scotland]

barley/barley pop/water *n.*[1] [early 19C+] beer (cf. BARLEYBREE; BARLEYBROTH). [SE *barley* + *pop*, a fizzy drink; late 19C+ is US Midwest/Black/campus use]

barley *n.*[2] [1990s] cocaine (cf. OATS *n.*[2]). [rhy. sl. *oats and barley* = CHARLIE *n.*[7] (1)]

barleybree *n.* [late 18C] (Scot.) strong ale (cf. BARLEY *n.*[1]). [SE *barley* + 15C *bree*, broth or juice in which anything has been boiled or marinated]

barleybroth *n.* [late 16C–late 19C] strong ale (cf. BARLEY *n.*[1]).

barleybun gentleman *n.* [17C] a rich gentleman who prefers to live poorly. [SE *barleybun*, a plain bun made with barley + *gentleman*]

barley pop/water *see* BARLEY *n.*[1].

Barlinnie drumstick *n.* [1930s+] (Glasgow) a lead pipe studded with nails (cf. BAR L). [Scotland's high-security *Barlinnie* prison, where the carrier of such a weapon might end up]

barmaid's blush *n.*[1] [20C] (Aus.) **1** ginger beer and raspberry cordial. **2** port and lemon (cf. MAIDEN'S BLUSH).

barmaid's blush *n.*[2] [20C] (Aus.) a flush, as in poker. [rhy. sl.]

barmpot *n.* [1950s+] an eccentric (cf. CRANKPOT; FUSSPOT). [BARMY + sfx. -POT]

barmy *adj.* [mid-19C+] insane, eccentric; thus *put on the barmy/balmy stick*, to feign insanity; (Und.) *barmies*, those categorized as weak-minded in prison (cf. BALMY). [dial. *barm*, yeast; thus frothing like fermenting yeast; note also the lunatic asylum in Barming, Kent]

barmy as a bandicoot *phr.* [1950s+] (N.Z.) highly eccentric, deranged. [BARMY + SE *bandicoot*]

barn *n.*[1] [late 19C–1900s] a public ballroom (cf. BARNER). [Highbury *Barn*, north London, site of one of the last such venues]

barn/barn door *n.*[2] [1930s+; 1950s+] (US) the trouser fly (cf. LOCK ONE'S BARN DOOR).

Barnaby Rudge *n.* [20C] a judge. [rhy. sl.; ult. the proper name coined by Charles Dickens as the title of his novel, 1841]

barnacle *n.*[1] (Und.) **1** [16C] that member of a team of swindlers who poses as an independent individual, ostensibly having no knowledge of their new companions but keenly ready to befriend the victim, often pretending to be drunk (cf. BARNARD). **2** [mid-16C–mid-17C] one who speaks through their nose. **3** [17C] one who pays too close an attendance, a hanger-on. **4** [late 17C–18C] a decoy swindler, a swindler's assistant. [all f. 14C SE *barnacle*, a type of pincer used to restrain recalcitrant horses; thus an instrument of torture for humans, which in turn must come from the shellfish that clings to ships' bottoms. The image in all cases is of clinging tight]

barnacle *n.*[2] [late 17C–18C] **1** a good job or quick profit easily obtained. **2** a tip given to a groom at a horse sale. [the recipient 'sticks onto' both]

barnacled *adj.* [late 17C–18C] wearing spectacles. [BARNACLES]

barnacles *n.* [mid-16C–early 19C] spectacles, eye-glasses. [like the SE *barnacle*, a horse's bit, they pinch the nose]

barnard *n.* [early 16C–mid-17C] (Und.) that member of a team of swindlers who poses as an independent individual, ostensibly having no knowledge of their new companions but keenly ready to befriend the victim and often pretending to be drunk (cf. BARNACLE *n.*[1]; CONY-CATCHING; POT-HUNTER *n.*[1]; SETTER *n.*[1]; VERSER). [SE *berner*, one who waits with a relay of hounds to intercept a hunted animal]

barnard's law *n.* [early 16C–mid-17C] (Und.) a form of card-sharping in which a team of 4 con-men fleece a victim (cf. BARNARD; RUBBER *n.*[1]; SETTER *n.*[1]; VERSER). [BARNARD + LAW *n.*[1]]

barnburner *n.* [1930s+] **1** a huge and resounding success. **2** a very stylish, classy woman. [(1) ? f. a party so riotously enjoyable that one ends up by burning down the barn in which it is held]

barnburners *n.* [1970s+] (Can.) the Royal Canadian Mounted Police. [the burning down by the RCMP, in 1976, of a barn in rural Quebec which was being used as a meeting place for French-Canadian separatists]

barn dance *n.* [1950s+] (Aus./N.Z.) pedestrians rushing across a 'buzz crossing', in which one 'buzzes' a button to change the traffic light (cf. SCRAMBLE *n.*[2]). [SE + ref. to Traffic Commissioner *Barnes*, inventor of the buzz crossing, first seen in New York City]

barn door *see* BARN *n.*[1].

barn door/gate is open, the *phr.* [1950s+] (US) a phr. used to warn a man that his trouser-fly is undone.

barndoor savage *n.* [late 19C–1900s] a rustic, a yokel (cf. BARNYARD SAVAGE).

barner *n.* [late 19C–1900s] a fashionable young working-class man of north London. [BARN]

barneries *n.* [late 19C–1900s] the Adelphi Stores, in the Strand, London. [Miss *Barnes*, the proprietress]

barnet *n.* [mid-19C+] hair. [rhy. sl. *Barnet Fair* = hair]

barnet cut *n.* [1940s–50s] a haircut, esp. in prison; those who received this cut were presumed to be serving a short sentence. [BARNET + SE *cut*]

barnet fair *n.* [mid-19C+] the hair (cf. BONNY FAIR; FANNY BLAIR). [rhy. sl.; the actual Barnet Fair *fl.* 16C–18C as the country's major horse fair; so important was the town's position on a main northbound thoroughfare that it became known as 'the town of inns']

barney *n.*[1] [mid-19C+] **1** a rowdy party. **2** a fight; also as *bit of/bit of a barney*. **3** a crowd of people. [proper name *Barney*, assoc. with the Irish and their stereotyped aggression (cf. DONNYBROOK *n.*; PADDY *n.*[1]). Poss. orig. Aus. use. *OED*'s first citation is 1864 (from a vol. entitled *The Colonial Songster*), that of *AND* is 1958]

barney *n.*[2] **1** [late 19C+] humbug, cheating, fraud, esp. of a 'fixed' sporting event. **2** [late 19C+] (US) a hoax. [? the holding of dubious sporting events, e.g. bare-knuckle boxing, in or behind the *barn*, and thus a fig. use of BARNEY *n.*[1]. However E.P., quoting Apperson, refers to the phr. *come, come, that's Barney Castle*, a response to anyone making a particularly specious excuse. This in turn, it is claimed, refers to the Catholic earls' Northern Rising of 1569, when Barnard Castle was held by Sir George Bowes who refused, despite many challenges, to leave his fortifications and engage in battle. The 'Rising in the North' certainly created the Durham dial. *Barnard Castle*, a coward, taken from the jibe 'A coward, a coward, o' Barney castle/Dare na come out to fight a battle']

barney *n.*[3] [20C] (Aus.) the 'inevitable' name of anyone surnamed Allen. [the celebrated Aus. bookmaker *Barney Allen*]

barney *n.*[4] [20C] (Irish) one's head, mind; usu. in phr. *don't bother your barney*. [? BARNET]

barney *n.*[5] **1** [1970s] (US Black) the penis; thus *put barney in the VCR*, to have sexual intercourse (cf. DINOSAUR *n.*[2]). **2** [1980s] (US campus) an unsophisticated person, one who is not part of currently approved fashions or attitudes (cf. BETTY *n.*[4]; FRED *n.*[2]; WILMA). [plays on the proper name *Barney Rubble*, a character in the TV cartoon (and latterly the film) *The Flintstones*, and thus believed by college students; note however *RHDAS* has a 1929 citation – and then nothing until 1989]

barney *adj.* [late 19C] unfair, crooked (esp. by pre-arrangement). [BARNEY n.²]

barney *v.* **1** [late 19C] (Aus./N.Z.) to fight, to argue; also *barney over*. **2** [20C] to cheat, to act unfairly. [BARNEY n.¹]

barney dillon *n.* [1930s] (Scot.) a shilling (5p) (cf. ABRAHAM'S WILLING). [rhy. sl.]

barney maguire *n.* [20C] (Aus.) a fire. [rhy. sl.]

barney moke *n.* [1930s–50s] a pocket. [rhy. sl. *Barney moke* = SE *poke*, a bag a pocket]

barney's bull *n.* [20C] (Aus./N.Z.) **1** a worthless person or thing. **2** nonsense, rubbish (cf. LIKE BARNEY'S BRIG). [BULLSHIT n.; *Barney* may simply add assonance]

barney's bull *adj.* [20C] (Aus./N.Z.) exhausted, tired out (cf. ALL BEHIND LIKE BARNEY'S BULL).

barn gate is open *see* BARN DOOR IS OPEN.

barnstormers *n.* **1** [mid–late 19C] groups of actors who tour the country specializing in plays that will appeal to their rustic audiences; their improvised stages are often set up in barns. **2** [1920s–30s] (US) itinerant flyers who travel the country putting on flying and aerobatic displays. [SE *barn* + *storm*, to attack]

Barnwell ague *n.* [mid-17C–mid-19C] gonorrhoea (cf. COVENT GARDEN AGUE; FRENCH CROWN). [proper name *Barnwell*, ? a brothel quarter or f. joc. 'burn well' + SE *ague*]

Barnyard *n.* [1960s+] (US campus) Barnard College.

barnyard golf *n.* [1930s–40s] (US) pitching horseshoes.

barnyard pimp *n.* [mid–late 20C] (US prison) fried chicken. [the role of the cockerel]

barnyard preacher *n.* [early 19C+] (US) an unprofessional or part-time lay preacher (cf. HEDGE-PRIEST).

barnyard savage *n.* [1900s–50s] (US) a loutish country yokel (cf. BARNDOOR SAVAGE).

bar of soap *n.* [1970s+] drugs. [rhy. sl. *bar of soap* = DOPE n.¹ (7)]

baron/tobacco baron *n.* [1930s+] (Und.) **1** an influential convict within a prison, esp. one who trades in tobacco or drugs (cf. CARVIE; DADDY n.¹ (9)). **2** [1950s] anyone who has money.

baron *v.* [1930s+] (prison) to control the traffic in tobacco or drugs, the primary prison commodities. [BARON n.]

baronet *n.* [mid-18C] a sirloin of beef [play on SE *baron of beef*]

Baron George *n.* [late 19C] a fat man. [South London use; f. George Parkes, a portly theatrical landlord, nicknamed *Baron George*]

barossa *n.* [1980s+] (Aus.) a woman. [*Barossa Pearl*, a sweet white wine]

barouche *n.* [1980s+] a car, a taxi. [SE *barouche*, a 4-wheeled carriage]

barprop *n.* [1980s] (US) the habitual occupier of a bar (cf. BARFLY). [SE *bar* + *prop*, support]

barrack *v.* [late 19C+] (Aus.) to support a team or individual in a sporting context; thus *barracker*, a supporter. [Northern Ireland dial. *barrack*, to brag, to be boastful of one's fighting powers; unlike SE use, no antagonism is implied, other than the usual partisanship; E.P., via a correspondent in 1944, offers an alternative ety., 'from the rough teams that used to play football on the vacant land near the Victoria barracks (in Melbourne)'; such players were known as *barrackers*]

barrack hack *n.* [mid-19C] **1** a prostitute (cf. BARBER'S CHAIR; BIKE; FERRY; OMNIBUS; TOWN BICYCLE; TOWN BIKE; WAGON n.²). **2** a woman who regularly attends military balls. [SE *barrack hack*, a horse available to any soldier in a barracks; like the animal, the human is available to anyone who wishes to 'ride']

barrack-room/barrack lawyer *n.* [1940s+] any amateur, esp. in the services or in prison, who considers themself more expert in the law, esp. Queen's Regulations or prison rules, than any professional and who will offer services, often to their detriment, to others (cf. BUSH LAWYER; GAOLHOUSE LAWYER; HAPAS CAPUS; JAILHOUSE LAWYER; WRIT BUG; YARDBIRD LAWYER).

barracuda *n.* (US) **1** [1930s+] a violent, aggressive criminal. **2** [1950s+] a domineering, argumentative person. **3** [1960s] a predatory homosexual, desperate to obtain a desired partner no matter what it takes. **4** [1970s+] a sexual enthusiast, esp. female. [SE *barracuda*, a large and voracious fish (*Sphyraena barracuda*) of the perch family]

barrakin *n.* [late 19C–1900s] nonsense, gibberish, double-Dutch (cf. BARRIKIN).

barred *adj.* [mid-16C–mid-18C; 1950s] (Und.) referring to a type of false or 'barred' dice, with one of the sides fractionally longer than the others so that they will not easily lie on certain sides; such dice might be *barred sice-aces* (six-aces), *barred cater-treys* (four-threes) etc (cf. BAR n.¹; FLAT n.¹). [SE *bar*, a piece of material that is long in proportion to its thickness; although the last *OED* citation is in 1753, when the term has been trimmed to *barr dice*, and E.P. dates it 16C–17C; Aus. use, with the same meaning, persists into mid-20C]

barrel *n.¹* [late 19C–1900s] (US) a political 'slush' fund. [PORK BARREL]

barrel *n.²* [late 19C–1900s] (US) a large amount, usu. of money. [SE *barrel of money*]

barrel *n.³* [20C] a fat person. [resemblance]

barrel *v.* **1** [1930s+] (orig. US) to charge along, to move swiftly. **2** [1950s+] (Aus.) to knock down, to hit, esp. as a result of a tackle in football. **3** (Aus.) to kill. [SE *barrel into*, to crash into at speed, like a barrel rolling downhill]

barrel-ass *n.* [1940s] (US) a fat person. [SE *barrel* + ARSE n.¹ (1)]

barrel-ass *v.* [1930s+] (US) to rush headlong, to charge at. [SE *barrel into* + ARSE n.¹ (1)]

barrel-boarder *n.* [mid–late 19C] (US) one who frequents low drinking saloons (cf. BARRELHOUSE n.). [SE *barrel* + *boarder*]

barrel fever *n.* [late 18C+] drunkenness; thus delirium tremens.

barrelhouse/barrel-house *n.* [late 19C–1940s] (US) a brothel or cheap saloon (cf. ACCOMMODATION HOUSE; BARREL-BOARDER). [the barrels of beer available in such places]

barrelhouse/barrel-house *adj.* [1910s–40s] (US, orig. jazz) of both music and places, rough, tough, unpretentious music that started off in the repertoire of the musicians who played for cheap saloons. [BARRELHOUSE n.]

barrelhouse/barrel-house *v.* (US) **1** [1910s–40s] to frequent a cheap saloon or brothel. **2** [1950s] to drive very fast. [BARRELHOUSE n.]

barrelled *adj.* [1910s+] (US) drunk (cf. BASTED).

barrel-/wagon-load of monkeys *phr.* [late 19C+] a type that is very cunning, mischievous, jolly or disorderly, usu. in phr. *artful as a wagon-load of monkeys*.

barrel of fat *n.* [20C] (Aus.) a hat. [rhy. sl.]

barrel of treacle *n.* [late 19C–1900s] love, esp. the outward signs of being in love. [the fig. sticky sweetness thereof]

barrels *n.* [1980s+] (drugs) LSD (cf. A n.³). [the shape of some LSD capsules]

barren Joey *n.* [1940s] (Aus.) a prostitute. [SE *barren* + ? SAusE *joey*, a young kangaroo; she 'jumps around' but has no children]

barres *n.* [17C–early 19C] in gambling, money that has been lost but is still owed to the winner. [? SE *barrace*, hostility, contention, strife]

barrikin *n.* [mid-19C] **1** unintelligible language (cf. BARRAKIN; GREEK n.²; HEBREW). **2** a hawker's sales patter. [Fr. *baragouin*, an incomprehensible or alien language, itself f. Breton *bara*, bread + *gwîn*, wine or *gwenn*, white, referring to the astonishment of Breton soldiers at the sight of white bread (Roulin in *Littré Supp.*) and thus transferred to describe bizarre, unintelligible speech]

barrister's *n.* [late 19C–1900s] (Und.) nickname of a thieves' coffeehouse, popular at the time. [the host's name]

barrow *n.* **1** [20C] (Aus.) a police van. **2** [1950s+] a secondhand motorcar.

barrow *v.* [mid-19C–1910s] to take home a drunkard who is reclining or passed out in a wheel-barrow.

barrow-bunter *n.* [mid-18C–19C] a female costermonger. [SE *barrow* + BUNTER n. (1)]

barrowed *adv.* [late 19C] taken away in a barrow, esp. of a drunkard (cf. SHUTTERED adj.[2]) [BARROW v.].

barrow-man *n.*[1] [17C] a costermonger. [SE from 18C]

barrow-man *n.*[2] [early–mid 19C] a man under sentence of transportation. [the employment of such convicts, awaiting their ship in prison, in wheeling around barrows full of earth]

barrow-tram *n.* [19C] a clumsy, ungainly person. [SE *barrow-tram*, the shaft of a barrow]

barry *adj.* [20C] lovely, sweet. [? dial.]

barry johnson *n.* [1990s] fellatio. [initial letters of BLOW JOB n. (1)]

barse *n.* [1990s] the portion of flesh between the underside of the testes and the anus. [BALLS n.[1] (1) + ARSE n.[1] (1)]

bar steward *n.* [1920s+] euph. for bastard (cf. BASKET n.[2]). [joc. pron. of SE]

barstool jockey *n.* [1980s] (US) the habitual occupier of a bar (cf. BARFLY). [SE *barstool* + JOCKEY n.[2] (2)]

bart *n.* [late 19C–1910s] (Aus.) a woman. [TART n. (1)]

bar the bubble, to *phr.* [late 18C] to make an exception against the general rule. [SE *bar*, except + play on BUBBLE n.[1] (1)]

bartholomew baby *n.* [late–mid-19C] one who is dressed in tawdry finery (cf. BARTHOLOMEW DOLL; BARTHOLOMEW PIG). [the dolls sold at the annual Bartholemew Fair, which flourished 1133–1855, when it was suppressed and its grounds replaced by the Smithfield Meat Market]

bartholomew doll *n.* [late 18C–early 19C] an overdressed, vulgar woman (cf. BARTHOLOMEW BABY). [the bright, tawdry dolls sold at Bartholomew Fair]

bartholomew pig/boar pig *n.* [16C–17C] a fat man (cf. BARTHOLOMEW BABY). [SE *Bartholomew-pig*, roast pork sold at Bartholomew Fair]

bas *n.* [1970s] *bas*tard. [abbr.]

bascomb mule out of the stable *phr.* [20C] (W.I.) things have got out of control. [presumably based on an anecdote concerning an actual animal]

base *n.* **1** [1970s+] cocaine. **2** [1970s+] coca paste, from which cocaine is processed. **3** [1980s+] a synonym for crack cocaine. [abbr. FREEBASE n. (1), although this itself refers not to crack, but to base cocaine, the enjoyment of which predated crack and appealed, through its high price and complex paraphernalia, to a higher social group than the often impoverished crack-users]

base *v.*[1] [20C] (orig. US Black) **1** to disparage, criticize or humiliate another person. **2** to argue. [SE *debase*]

base *v.*[2] [1980s+] (drugs) to smoke cocaine. [abbr. FREEBASE v.]

base! *excl.* [1980s+] (US) excl. of approval at another person's cruel but accurate attack on a third (absent) party. [SE *base*, low]

baseball *n.* [1980s+] (drugs) **1** coca paste (cf. BASE n.). **2** crack cocaine. [pun on *base(ball)*/ BASE n.]

baseball *adj.* [late 19C–1900s] (US) small, insignificant. [the small size of the baseball]

baseburner *n.* [late 19C] (US) the buttocks.

base cranes *n.* [1980s+] (drugs) the act of searching on hands

and knees for dropped flakes of crack cocaine. [BASE n. (3) + SE *crane*]

base crazies *n.* [1980s+] the psychosis that can overtake regular consumers of crack cocaine, typically manifested in a feverish desire to find and consume every last granule of the drug. [BASE n. (3) + SE *crazy*]

base gallery *n.* [1980s+] a place where users of crack cocaine gather to consume their drug (cf. BASING GALLERY). [BASE n. (3) + SE *gallery*; on model of SHOOTING GALLERY]

base-head *n.* **1** [1970s+] one who smokes cocaine (cf. FREEBASE v.]. **2** [1980s+] a regular consumer of crack cocaine (cf. ACID-HEAD). [BASE n. (3) + sfx. -HEAD (2)]

basehouse *n.* [1980s+] a place where users gather to consume crack cocaine (cf. BASING GALLERY). [BASE n. (3) + SE *house*]

basement *n.* [20C] (Aus. Und.) **1** the punishment cells, situated usually below ground level. **2** solitary confinement.

basengro *n.* [1900s–10s] (tramp) a shepherd. [Rom.]

base on *v.* [1980s+] (US campus) to criticize. [SE *debase*]

base out *v.* [20C] (W.I.) to sit around, to hang about with friends or family, watching the passing world and occasionally commenting upon it (cf. LIME v.). [SE *base*, i.e. the posterior]

base over apex *phr.* [1920s+] head-over-heels.

bash *n.*[1] [late 19C–1930s] a judicial flogging; thus *9 months and a bash*, a sentence of 9 months' prison and a flogging. **2** [1920s+] (Aus.) brutality, harsh treatment.

bash *n.*[2] **1** [20C] sexual intercourse (cf. BANG v.[1]; BIFF n.[3]; BONK n.; DO n.[7]; GRIND n.[3]; KNOCK n.; POKE n.[1]; PROD n.[2]; ROOT n.[1]; SCREW n.[1]; TUMBLE n.[1]). **2** [20C] a party. **3** [1920s+] an attempt, a try, esp. as phr. *give it/have a bash/bash at.* **4** [1960s+] a thrill of pleasure (cf. KICK n.[5]). [SE *bash*, a heavy blow]

bash *n.*[3] [1990s] (drugs) marijuana. [? misprint for BUSH n.]

bash *v.*[1] [late 18C+] to hit, to batter (with the fist). [Sw. *basa*, to baste, whip, flog, lash, or Da. *baske*, to beat, strike, cudgel; but possibly onomat.]

bash *v.*[2] **1** [1930s+] to work as a prostitute (cf. BATTER v.). **2** [1930s+] (Aus.) to drink heavily; also *bash it, give it a bash.* **3** [1960s+] (US) to berate, to criticize, to abuse, esp. in sfx. form -*bashing*, e.g. *gay-bashing*, attacking homosexuals, *Paki-bashing*, attacking Asian immigrants.

bashed *adj.* [1980s] (US campus) drunk (cf. BASTED). [BASH v.[2] (2)]

basher *n.*[1] **1** [mid-19C+] a thug. **2** [mid-19C+] a professional fighter (and as such used as a professional nickname). **3** [1940s+] (orig. milit.) generic for fellow, chap, person (cf. BIBLE-BASHER; SWEDE-BASHER). [BASH v.[1]]

basher *n.*[2] [1900s–30s] a straw hat, a boater. [ety. unknown; ? link to BASHER n.[3], i.e. the attap could be seen as straw]

basher *n.*[3] [1980s+] a makeshift shelter. [milit. jargon *basha*, a shelter made of bamboo and attap (a type of palm frond used for thatching), which was common in Southeast Asia. More recently it has been found among the homeless denizens of London's CARDBOARD CITY or the protesters at the women's camp at Greenham Common, Berkshire]

bashi-bazouk *n.* [mid-19C+] a ruffian, a hooligan, a thug. [Turk. *Bashi-Bazouk*, lit. 'one whose head is turned'; in 19C mercenary soldier, fighting for the Turks and known for his blood-thirsty excesses]

bashing *n.*[1] [late 19C+] masturbation. [BASH THE BISHOP]

bashing *n.*[2] [late 19C+] a beating. [BASH v.[1]]

bashing *n.*[3] [1930s+] prostitution. [BASH v.[2]]

bashing-in/-out *n.* [late 19C] the flogging administered to prisoners on their arrival in prison and immediately before their release. [BASH v.[1]]

bash into *v.* [1920s+] to meet by chance (cf. BUMP INTO). [BASH v.[1]]

bash it up you! *phr.* [1940s+] (Aus.) go away, leave me in peace! [BASH v.¹]

bash on *v.* [1940s+] (orig. milit.) to persist, to keep making an effort. [BASH v.¹]

bash out *v.* [1960s+] to produce with only minimal care, esp. of writing (cf. KNOCK OUT v.¹). [BASH v.¹]

bash the bishop, to *phr.* [late 19C+] to masturbate. [for ety. see BANG THE BISHOP]

bash the candle, to *phr.* [1990s] to masturbate.

bash the priest, to *phr.* [1990s] to masturbate. [var. on BANG THE BISHOP]

bash the spine, to *phr.* [1940s+] (Aus.) to idle, to waste time, to loaf around (cf. SPINEBASHER). [BASH v.¹ + SE *spine*]

bash the stick, to *phr.* [1950s+] (Aus.) to masturbate. [BASH v.¹ + STICK n.]

bash up *v.* [1940s–50s] (mainly juv.) to beat up, to thrash. [ext. of BASH v.¹]

basic *adj.* [1960s+] unexciting, unexceptional, uneventful.

basically *adv.* [1990s] (US Black teen) used to show one's agreement with any truism that is mentioned.

basil *n.* [late 16C–mid-18C] an iron fetter worn on one leg only. [? SE *basilisk*, a large cannon, generally made of brass, and throwing a shot weighing about 90kg (200lb)]

basinful *n.* [1930s+] an excessive amount, more than enough, usu. as phr. *I've had a basinful of.* [SE *basinful*, the contents of a basin]

basing *n.* [1980s+] driving up and down playing music loudly through one's car windows. [? the throbbing bass]

basing *adj.* [1980s+] using crack cocaine. [BASE n.³ (3)]

basing gallery *n.* [1980s+] a place where crack cocaine users gather to consume their drug (cf. BASE GALLERY; BASEHOUSE; CRACK GALLERY; CRACK HOUSE; LAUNCHING PAD; RIFLE RANGE; SHOOTING GALLERY). [BASING adj. + SE *gallery*, on the model of the heroin-users' SHOOTING GALLERY]

basin of gravy *n.* [20C] a baby. [rhy. sl.]

baskerville *n.* [1970s+] (Aus.) an informer (cf. DOG n.⁸). [ult. a pun on Arthur Conan Doyle, *The Hound of the Baskervilles*, 1902]

basket *n.*¹ **1** [late 19C+] the stomach (cf. BREADBASKET). **2** [1940s+] (gay) the male genitals (cf. BASKETEER; TAKE ONE'S MEAT OUT OF THE BASKET).

basket *n.*² [1930s+] euph. for bastard (cf. BAR STEWARD).

basket *n.*³ [1930s+] an interfering, nosy old woman. [? BASKET n.² but note SE *basket*, seen as part of such a woman's 'uniform']

basket! *excl.* [late 18C] an exclamation directed at those who are unable or unwilling to pay their gambling debts. [from the practice at 18C cockpits whereby such debtors were placed in a *basket*, suspended above the pit until the fights ended]

basket case *n.* **1** [1910s+] a cripple, either mentally or physically. **2** [1950s+] one who is incapable of tackling a situation. **3** [1970s+] one who behaves in a notably eccentric manner. [orig. WW1 milit. use, a quadriplegic, who, bereft of all four limbs, is carried around in a basket]

basket days *n.* [1960s–70s] (US gay) a spell of fine weather, permitting one to wear light clothes that reveal one's genitals. [BASKET n.¹ (2) + SE *days*]

basketed *adj.* [late 18C–19C] abandoned, ignored, misunderstood, confused. [BASKET!]

basketeer *v.* [1940s–50s] (gay) to wander the streets gazing at male genitals; this can provide some men with adequate satisfaction, others may be simply sizing up the available talent for later developments. [BASKET n.¹ (2); coined by the homosexual community, like a number of others, e.g. CRUISE v., the term is now occasionally applied to women]

basket job *n.* [1950s+] (mainly gay) fellatio (cf. BLOW JOB). [BASKET n.¹ (2) + JOB n.⁵]

basket lunch *n.* [1950s+] (mainly gay) fellatio. [BASKET n.¹ (2) + SE *lunch*]

basket-maker *n.* [18C] the vagina. [BASKET-MAKING]

basket-making *n.* [early 18C–early 19C] sexual intercourse. ['making feet for children's stockings' (Grose, 1785)]

basket of oranges *n.* [late 19C–1900s] (orig. Aus.) an attractive woman. [fig. use of mining jargon *basket of oranges*, nuggets of gold, as discovered in the gold fields]

basket picnic *n.* [1940s–70s] (gay) staring at other men's genitals while wandering the streets (cf. BASKETEER). [BASKET n.¹ (2) + SE *picnic*]

basket-scrambler *n.* [mid-17C] one who subsists on charity. [they *scramble* for goods or money in an *alms-basket*]

basket-watch *v.* [1940s–70s] (gay) to wander the streets gazing at male genitals (cf. BASKETEER). [BASKET n.¹ (2) + SE *watch*]

bass *n.* [1970s] US campus a large glass of liquor (cf. BREAM; PERCH n.³). [the use of sizes of fish to define sizes of glass]

bassa-bassa *n.* [20C] (W.I.) trouble, a fuss, a noisy argument. [Yoruba *basa-basa*, nonsense]

bass-ackwards *adj.* [1930s+] back-to-front, thus fig. a mess, chaos (cf. ARSE ABOUT FACE). [a joc. rearrangement of ARSE BACKWARDS, which emphasizes the overall meaning]

bastard *n.* **1** [late 16C+] a contemptible, objectionable person. **2** [late 19C+] (orig. Aus.) a general term for a man, a person; not esp. derog. **3** [1910s+] (orig. Aus.) a situation, a circumstance, usu. a problematic one.

bastardly *adj.* [1910s+] a neg. intensifier.

bastardly gullion *n.* [late 18C–early 19C] a bastard's bastard. [SE *bastardly* + Lancashire dial. *gullion*, a mean worthless wretch]

bastard well *adv.* [1920s–50s] extremely, very much.

baste *v.* [1950s+] (US Black) to attack or ridicule someone behind their back. [SE *baste*, to beat, to thrash]

basted *adj.* [20C] drunk; one of a number of terms that equate drunkenness with suffering violence; many of the terms can also apply to the effects of drugs (cf. BARRELLED; BASHED; BELTED; BIFFED; BLASTED adj.²; BLIGHTED; BLITZED; BOILED; BOMBED; BUCKLED; BUFFED; BUMMED adj.²; CHUCKED adj.²; CLINCHED; CLOBBERED; CROAKED; CROCKED; CROCKO; CROOKED adj.¹; CUPSHOT; DAMAGED; DEADO adj.; DESTROYED; DONE-OVER adj.²; DOZED; EMBALMED; FLOORED; FRACTURED; FRIED; GASSED adj.¹; HAMMERED; HIT ON THE HEAD BY THE TAVERN BITCH; JUG-BITTEN; LAID OUT adj.¹; MAULED; OBLITERATED; OVERSHOT; PLASTERED; POT-SHOT; SCAMMERED adj.¹; SCRATCHED; SCRAUNCHED; SCROOCHED; SEWED UP; SHATTERED; SHAVED; SHELLACKED; SHICKERED; SHIP-WRECKED; SHOT adj.; SHOT FULL OF HOLES; SHOT IN THE NECK; SHREDDED; SKUNKED adj.¹; SLAMMED; SLAUGHTERED; SLOSHED; SLUGGED; SMASHED; SMUCKERED; SNOCKERED; SOZZLED; SPIFLICATED; SQUASHED; STITCHED adj.¹; STONKERED; STUNNED; SWACKED; SWACKO; SWATTLED; SWIZZLED; TOTALLED; TRASHED; TWISTED adj.²; WASTED adj.; WAZZOCKED; WHAZOOD; WRECKED]

baster *n.*¹ [mid-19C+] (Aus./US) a house thief (cf. BUSTER n.¹).

baster/baister *n.*² [late 19C+] (US) something notably large of its type, often as *old baster*. [? BASTARD or (less likely) f. the large roast that needs substantial *basting* in the oven]

baste someone's coat, to *phr.* [16C–early 18C] to thrash, to beat severely (cf. COIL SOMEONE'S COAT; PAY SOMEONE'S COAT). [ext. of SE *baste*, to beat]

baste the tuna, to *phr.* [1980s+] of a woman, to masturbate. [SE *baste* + TUNA n. (2)]

basticles *n.* [1990s] a general term of annoyance, abuse etc. [SE *bastard* + *testicles*]

bastille *n.* **1** [late 18C–early 19C] a prison, spec. Coldbath Fields in London. **2** [mid-19C–1900s] a workhouse. **3** [late 19C+] (US) any prison. [Fr. *bastille*, a fortified tower, and esp. the main Paris prison, built in 14C, the destruction of which in 1789 triggered the French Revolution]

basuco/bazuko *n.* [1980s+] (drugs) coca paste, part of the process that produces cocaine, mixed with a variety of impure and possibly toxic substances, e.g. leaded gasoline, kerosene, sulphuric acid and potassium permanganate; smoking *basuco* as a 'cigarette' (mixing basuco either with tobacco or marijuana) is common in cocaine-producing countries. [Colombian Sp., + ? links to Sp. *bazucar*, to shake violently or *basura*, waste, rubbish; a parallel ety. suggests the SE *bazooka*, with a ref. to the drug's 'explosive' effect]

bat *n.*[1] [early 17C–early 19C] a prostitute or promiscuous woman (cf. ON THE BAT phr.[2]). [like the creatures, they appear at night]

bat *n.*[2] **1** [early 19C+] a pace, a speed, a stroke. **2** [mid-19C+] (orig. US) a spree, a binge; thus *go on a bat*, to go out on a spree (cf. BATTER n.[3]). **3** [1940s–60s] (US Black) a job. [dial. *bat*, a stroke, a pace]

bat *n.*[3] **1** [late 19C+] (orig. US) a foolish, worthless person. **2** [1920s+] an unattractive woman, often old (cf. BUZZARD; COW n.[1]; CULL BIRD; DOG n.[4]; HEDGEHOG n.[1]; HEIFER n. (2); HOG n.[4]; MULE n.[5]; OLD BAT). **3** [20C] a quarrelsome, unpleasant woman. [SE *bat*, the animal]

bat *n.*[4] [20C] insanity, esp. manifested in a drinker's delirium tremens. [BATTY adj., although it could be a result of a BAT n.[2] (2)]

bat *n.*[5] (US) **1** [20C] (US) a hard blow. **2** [1920s–50s] a complaint. [SE *bat*, to hit]

bat *n.*[6] [1930s+] (Aus.) a riding-whip. [SE *bat*, a stick, used as a weapon]

bat *n.*[7] [1940s+] (US/Aus.) the penis; thus (Aus.) *go off the bat*, to masturbate, *bat and balls*, the penis and testicles; one of number of terms equating the penis with a stick or rod (cf. BILLY n.[2]; BLOW STICK; BLUDGEON; BROOM-HANDLE; CLAW-BUTTOCK; CLOTHES-PROP; CLUB n.[1]; COPPER-STICK; DIBBLE n.[2]; DRUMSTICK; FUCKSTICK; GULLEY-RAKER; GUTSTICK; HAMMER n.[1]; HANDSTAFF; KENNEL RAKER; LIFE PRESERVER n.[1]; NIGHT STICK n.[1]; PESTLE n.; PILE-DRIVER; PILGRIM'S STAFF; PIPE n.[8]; PLOUGHSHARE; POLE; PROD n.[2]; PRONG n.[2]; RAMROD; REAMER; ROD n.[1]; ROLLING-PIN; ROLY-POLY n.[2]; SCEPTRE; SENSITIVE TRUNCHEON; SHIT STICK; SHOVE-STRAIGHT; SPIKE-FAGGOT; SPINDLE; STAFF OF LIFE; STICK n.[1]; TENT PEG n.[1]; TRUNCHEON; TUBE n.[2]; WAND; WOOD n.[2]; YARD n.[1]). [SE *bat*, a stick, a stout piece of wood]

bat *n.*[8] [1980s+] a marijuana or hashish cigarette. [pun on STICK n.[14]]

bat *adj.* [20C] (US campus) good, attractive. [BAD adj.]

bat *v.* (US) **1** [late 19C+] to hit. **2** [late 19C+] to wander (aimlessly) around. **3** [1920s+] to complain. **4** [1930s] (campus) to earn a grade. **5** [1930s] to substitute. [(1) is SE to mid-19C]

bat and ball *n.* [20C] (Aus.) a wall. [rhy. sl.]

bat and bowl, to *phr.* [1950s+] to be bisexual (cf. AMBIDEXTROUS; BOWL FROM THE PAVILION END; SWITCH-HITTER). [cricket imagery, *batting* and *bowling* are the two antithetical positions in the game]

bat and wicket *n.* [20C] a ticket. [rhy. sl.]

bat around *v.* [1910s–40s] to waste one's time. [ext. of BAT v. (2)]

bat-ass *v.* [1980s+] (US) to move at top speed. [(*like a*) *bat* (*out of hell*) + ARSE n.[1] (1)]

bat a thousand, to *phr.* [1920s–50s] (US) to succeed absolutely; thus *bat zero*, to fail completely; *bat five hundred*, to be reasonably successful. [all f. baseball imagery]

bat-bat *n.* [20C] (W.I. juv.) the buttocks, the posterior. [SE *butt(ocks)*]

batbrain *n.* [1940s–60s] (US) a fool; thus *batbrained*, stupid (cf. BAKEBRAIN). [SE *bat*, a piece of wood + sfx. *-brain*]

batcave *n.* [1970s–80s] (gay) the anus. [the *Batman* comics and films, in which the *batcave*, dark, subterranean and mysterious, is the headquarters where Batman (and Robin) keep their car, their hi-tech weapons and other crime-fighting materiel; also note BAT n.[6], although this is a primarily heterosexual term]

batcave *v.* [1980s+] (US campus) to sleep. [see BATCAVE n.; Batman's HQ as a place of rest from crime-fighting]

batch *n.* [late 18C–early 19C] a quantity of liquor; thus a heavy night's drinking. [SE *batch*, a quantity, a number; in this case of bottles or glassfuls]

batch *v.* [late 19C+] (Aus.) to live as a bachelor (cf. BACH v.). [SE *bachelor*]

batcher *n.* [20C] (Aus.) one who lives alone (cf. BACH n.). [BATCH v.]

batch up *v.* [1950s] (US) for a man and woman, to cohabit. [i.e. the couple make themselves into a SE *batch*, a quantity]

batchy *adj.* [late 19C+] silly, stupid. [? BATTY adj.]

bate *see* BAIT n.[2].

Bate's Farm/Garden *n.* [mid–late 19C] Cold Bath Fields Prison, in Farringdon, London, *fl.* 1794–1877, and known for its severity, often as *Charley Bate's farm*; thus *feed the chickens on Charley Bate's farm*, to be sentenced to the treadmill. [the name of a well-known warder]

bate up *n.* [20C] an act of sexual intercourse. [? 16C SE *bate*, an argument]

bat for the other side, to *phr.* [1990s] to be a homosexual. [cricket/baseball imagery]

bat-fowl *v.* [late 16C] to swindle, to hoax. [BAT-FOWLER]

bat-fowler *n.* [late 16C–early 17C] a swindler, a sharper; thus *bat-fowling*, swindling, hoaxing. [SE *bat-fowl*, to catch birds at night by dazzling them with a light and knocking them down or netting them]

bat-fowling *n.* [16C] (Und.) swindling, hoaxing (cf. CONY-CATCHING). [BAT-FOWLER]

bath bun *n.* **1** [late 19C+] a son. **2** [1970s+] the sun. [rhy. sl.]

bathers *n.* [20C] (orig. Aus.) a bathing costume. [abbr. SE]

bat hide/batwing *n.* [late 19C–1920s] (US) paper money, esp. a $1 bill. [? thinness of the paper money]

bath of birth *n.* [19C] the vagina. [lit. euph. coined by US writer Walt Whitman (1819–92)]

bat-house *n.* [20C] (Aus.) a brothel (cf. ACCOMMODATION HOUSE). [BAT n.[1] + HOUSE n.[1]]

bat-house *adj.* [20C] mad, crazy, insane (cf. ATTIC; BATS adj.; BATSHIT; BATTY adj.; HAVE BATS IN THE BELFRY; RATS IN THE ATTIC). [BATS adj. + SE *house*]

bathsheba *n.* [1980s+] (US gay) one who frequents gay bath-houses. [SE *baths* + pun on Biblical name *Bathsheba*]

bathtub scum *n.* [1980s+] (US campus) an unpleasant person (cf. SHOWER SCUM).

bathtub speed *n.* [1960s+] (drugs) methcathinone, a form of amphetamine that produces a more intense and longer lasting 'high' than does cocaine (cf. C n.[2]; CADILLAC EXPRESS; CAT n.[14]; GAGERS n.[2]; GO-FAST; GOOB n.[2]; SLICK n.[2]; STAR n.[5]; STAT n.[2]; TWEEK; WILDCAT n.[2]; WONDER STAR). [artificial amphetamine, on pattern of *bathtub gin/whisky* etc., i.e. home-produced liquor]

bati/batti/batty *n.* [1910s+] (W.I.) the buttocks (cf. BATTYMAN). [abbr./pron. of SE]

batner/battener/battner *n.* [18C] an ox. [16C SE *batten*, for an animal to put on weight]

bato *n.* [20C] **1** (US Black) any Mexican, Puerto Rican or other Latin person. **2** (Sp.) a general term of address (cf. DUDE). [Sp. *bato*, a guy, a bloke, a dude]

bato loco *n.* [20C] (US-Sp.) an affectionate nickname for a fellow Spanish-American. [Sp. *bato loco*, crazy dude]

bat on a sticky wicket, to *phr.* [1940s+] to be facing

problems. [cricket imagery; a *sticky wicket* makes for unpredictable and thus hard to play bowling]

bat oneself out *v.* [1940s] (US) to work oneself to exhaustion. [BAT v.[1] (1)]

bats *n.* [mid-19C–1920s] a pair of bad boots. [? they are no more comfortable than walking on a pair of flat *bats*]

bats *adj.* [20C] crazy, insane, eccentric. (cf. BAT-HOUSE). [HAVE BATS IN THE BELFRY]

bat's balls *n.* [1960s] (US) the very best, the ultimate (cf. ANT'S PANTS).

batshit/bat crap *n.* (US) **1** [1940s+] lies, nonsense, rubbish. **2** [1960s–70s] an insane person. [BATS adj. + APESHIT]

batshit *adj.* [1960s+] insane, crazy; often in phr. *go batshit*, to become insane, to act crazily (cf. BAT-HOUSE adj.). [BATSHIT n. (2)]

batshit *v.* [1960s–70s] (US) **1** to tell lies, to tease, to confuse with false information. **2** to gossip, to chatter inconsequentially (cf. BULLSHIT v.). [BATSHIT n. (1)]

batso *adj.* [1970s] (US) crazy, eccentric. [BATS adj. + sfx. -O]

batt *n.*[1] [mid-19C] a shoe. [Polari]

batt *n.*[2] [1990s] (drugs) an intravenous needle. [? resemblance to SE *bat*]

batt *v.* [mid-19C] to dance or shuffle around on stage. [BATT n.[1]]

battalion *n.* [18C] a criminal gang.

battener *see* BATNER.

batter *n.*[1] **1** [early 19C+] flattery (cf. BUTTER n.[1]). **2** [1990s] semen (cf. BELT ONE'S BATTER; FANNY BATTER; SPLATTER ONE'S BATTER).

batter *n.*[2] [mid-19C] wear and tear, stress and strain; thus *can't stand the batter*, not up to the stress. [SE *batter*, to hit]

batter *n.*[3] [mid-19C+] a drinking spree (cf. ON THE BAT phr.[1]). [BAT v.[1] (1)]

batter *n.*[4] [late 19C] (US) money. [pun on DOUGH]

batter *v.* [1920s+] of a man, to have sexual intercourse. [fig. use of BAT v.[1] (1); for synon. terms equating sex with aggression *see* BANG v.[1]]

battered *adj.* [late 19C+] **1** drunk. **2** debauched. [ON THE BAT phr.[1]]

battered bully *n.* [late 17C–early 18C] 'an old well-cudgell'd and bruis'd huffing fellow' (B.E.). [SE *battered* + BULLY n.[1] (3)]

batter-fang *n.* [mid-19C] a violent person (cf. BATTY-FANG).

battering piece *n.* [19C] the penis (cf. ARSE-OPENER). [SE *battering piece*, a heavy cannon specially designed for besieging and destroying fortifications]

battering ram *n.* [1920s–30s] a formidable (older) woman (cf. BATTLE-AX).

Battersea'd *adj.* [18C] to have one's penis treated for venereal disease (cf. CUT FOR THE SIMPLES). [the curative herbs that grew in the market-gardens of Battersea]

batter the bishop, to *phr.* [1990s] to masturbate (cf. BANG THE BISHOP).

batter through *v.* [late 19C+] to struggle on.

battery *v.* [mid–late 19C] (Ling. Fr./Polari) to knock, to strike; thus *battery carsey*, to knock on a door. [Ital. *battere*, to hit]

battery acid *n.* [1970s+] (drugs) LSD (cf. A n.[3]). [pun on ACID n.[3]; note milit. jargon *battery acid*, bad coffee or lemonade/ grapefruit juice]

battery girl *n.* [1960s–70s] a prostitute who works as one of a group and who is paid in food and drugs and 'pocket-money' (cf. STABLE). [SE *battery*, a collection of similar objects grouped together + SE *girl*]

bat the breeze, to *phr.* [1940s+] (orig. Aus./US milit.) to chatter, to gossip (cf. BACK THE BREEZE). [BAT v. (1) + SE *breeze*]

bat them out *v.* [1920s] (US) to gossip, to chatter. [BAT THE BREEZE]

batti *see* BATI.

battie-boy *n.* [20C] (orig. W.I.) a male homosexual. [BATI + SE *boy*]

batting practice *n.* [1990s] (US campus) the custom of going from bar to bar drinking until drunk. [joc. use of baseball jargon]

battle *n.* [1940s] (US Black/Harlem) a very unattractive woman. [abbr. BATTLE-AX]

battle *v.* **1** [late 19C+] (Aus.) to struggle for a livelihood, to work in a low-paid job; both senses imply some self-congratulation. **2** [late 19C+] (Aus.) of a tramp, to subsist between periods of employment. **3** [late 19C+] (Aus.) to subsist by making small bets at the racetrack. **4** [late 19C+] (Aus.) to work as a prostitute (cf. BAT n.[1]; ON THE BAT phr.[1]). **5** [1980s+] (W.I./UK Black teen) to compete, usually in freestyle rapping, sometimes in breakdancing. [SE *battle*, to struggle]

battle and cruiser *see* BATTLE-CRUISER n.[2].

battle-ax/axe *n.* **1** [late 19C+] (orig. US) a formidable (older) woman (cf. BATTLE n.; BATTLE-CRUISER n.[1]; BATTLER; BATTLESHIP). **2** [1980s+] (US campus) an ex-girlfriend, usu. as *old battle-ax*.

battle-cruiser *n.*[1] [1910s+] a tough and aggressive (older) woman (cf. BATTLESHIP).

battle-cruiser/battle/battleship and cruiser *n.*[2] [1940s+] a public house. [rhy. sl. *battle cruiser* = BOOZER]

battle-hammed *adj.* [early 18C+] (US Black) misshapen about the hips. [SE *hams*, thighs, which 'battle' against each other as one walks]

battle of the Nile *n.* [mid-19C–1900s] a hat. [rhy. sl. *battle of the Nile* = TILE; in the Battle of the Nile (1 August 1798) Nelson defeated Napoleon's fleet, thus wrecking the French expedition to Egypt]

battle of Waterloo *n.* [mid-19C+] a stew. [rhy. sl.; the actual battle, between Britain and France, took place on 18 June 1815]

battler *n.* [late 19C+] (Aus.) **1** one who uses natural, rather than social or economic, advantages to pursue the struggle for existence and is seen as brave in doing so. **2** a small-time racecourse bettor. **3** a prostitute. **4** a formidable or domineering woman (cf. BATTLE-AX). **5** (Glasgow) a thug, a violent gangster. [BATTLE v.]

battle-royal *n.* [late 16C–late 18C] a serious quarrel, an impassioned argument. [SE *battle-royal*, any battle in which a king leads his forces; also f. cockpit jargon, a cockfight in which a number of cocks fight until only one remains alive]

battleship *n.* (US) **1** [1910s–40s] a large, heavy shoe. **2** [late 19C+] (Black) a formidable or domineering woman (cf. BATTLE-AX). **3** [1910s+] a tough, physically large and aggressive (older) woman. **4** [1940s+] a shapely young woman; thus *built like a brick battleship*, having a very shapely figure.

battleship and cruiser *see* BATTLE-CRUISER n.[2].

battle the bones, to *phr.* [mid-19C] to play at dice. [SE *battle*, to fight + BONES n.[1] (1)]

battle the purple-helmeted warrior, to *phr.* [1980s+] to masturbate.

battle the rattler, to *phr.* [1920s+] (Aus.) to travel on the railways without paying (cf. JUMP THE RATTLER). [BATTLE v. (1) + RATTLER n.[1] (2)]

battle the subs, to *phr.* [1920s+] (Aus.) to sell goods door-to-door in the suburbs. [BATTLE v. (1) + SE sub(urb)s]

battling-stick *n.* [mid-19C] (US Black) **1** a stick used to beat slaves. **2** a stick used for stirring clothes as they boiled in the laundry. [SE *batter*, to beat + *stick*]

battner *see* BATNER.

batty *n.*[1] [mid-19C] wages, tips. [Anglo-Ind. *batta*, an extra allowance given to troops or public servants while serving in the field or on a variety of special postings; also subsistence money given to prisoners, witnesses etc. The payment to soldiers, originally restricted to field service, became recognized as a regular perk of Indian service, irrespective of the posting; the word comes from Hind. *bhata*, ult. f. *bhat*, an advance without interest made to a ploughman or *bat*, a pack-saddle (as used in the field)]

batty *n.*[2] *see* BATI.

batty *adj.* [20C] insane, crazy, eccentric (cf. BAT-HOUSE adj.; CARLO). [either HAVE BATS IN THE BELFRY or (although the chronology militates against it) f. the proper name Fitzherbert *Batty*, a 19C barrister whose certification as mad in 1839 caused much interest]

batty bwoy *n.* [1960s+] (W.I./UK Black teen) a homosexual; a gay person (usually a man). [BATI + Carib. pron. of SE *boy*]

batty-fang *v.* [mid-19C] to beat; thus *batty-fanging*, *batty-fagging*, a beating. [SE *batter* + *fang*, to seize, to attack]

batty-hole *n.* [20C] (W.I.) the anus. [BATI + SE *hole*]

battyman *n.* [1950s+] (W.I.) a homosexual. [BATI + SE *man*]

batty paper *n.* [20C] (W.I.) lavatory paper. [BATI + SE *paper*]

batty rider *n.* [20C] (W.I./UK Black teen) a type of skimpy, cut-off shorts worn so tight that they 'ride' up and expose the sides of the wearer's bottom. [BATI + SE *rider*]

batty-wax *n.* [20C] (W.I.) a stupid, gullible person. [BATI + SE *wax*, i.e. excrement]

batu *n.* [1980s+] (drugs) smokeable methamphetamine. [? Sp.]

batwing *n.*[1] *see* BAT HIDE.

batwing *n.*[2] (US) **1** [1940s] a swinging door, e.g. in a saloon; thus usu. in pl. **2** [1980s] a bow-tie. **3** [1970s] a half-pint flask of liquor, esp. bootleg liquor. [resemblance]

baubee/bawbee *n.* **1** [late 17C–19C] a halfpenny. **2** [19C+] money in general. [Scot. *bawbee*, a coin equivalent in value to an Eng. halfpenny; despite the useful similarity to SE *bauble*, a trinket and Fr. *bas billon*, mixed metal, the term appears to come f. the proper name of a 16C mint-master, the laird of *Sillebawby*.]

baubles/bawbles *n.* [late 18C–19C] the testicles (cf. BOBBIES; BOBBLES; CROWN JEWELS; DIAMONDS; FAMILY JEWELS). [SE *bauble*, a showy trinket]

baudrons *n.* [mid-17C–early 19C] a pet name for a cat. [? Scot. Gaelic *beadrach*, a playful girl]

b.a.v. *phr.* [1980s+] (US campus) one has not had sexual intercourse for a long time. [abbr. *born again virgin*]

bawbee *see* BAUBEE.

bawbles *see* BAUBLES.

bawcock *n.* [late 16C–early 17C] a fine fellow. [Fr. *beau coq*, lit. 'a fine cock'; the term was briefly resuscitated by the 19C historical novelist Harrison Ainsworth in *Constable of the Tower* (1862)]

bawd-/bawdy-physic *n.* [mid-late 16C] a 'saucy fellow' (Awdeley). [lit. a lewd, vulgar doctor]

bawdy bachelor *n.* [late 17C–19C] a bachelor who has no intention of altering his status.

bawdy banquet *n.* [mid-16C] whoremongering.

bawdy-basket *n.* [mid-16C–late 18C] (Und.) a female beggar who sells obscene literature, as well as pins, ballads and other goods (cf. CANTING CREW). [one of the 23 ranks of professional mendicant villains, as listed in a number of contemporary glossaries]

bawdy house bottle *n.* [late 17C–late 18C] **1** a particularly small bottle. **2** the very last bottle of a drinking session. [such bottles were designed to be sold at *bawdy houses* (brothels), where they offered the owner yet another means of fleecing clients. Grose notes that of these frauds this 'is one of the least reprehensible; the less they give a man of their infernal beverages, the kinder they behave']

bawdy-ken *n.* [19C] a brothel. [SE *bawdy* + KEN n.[1]]

bawdy-physic *see* BAWD-PHYSIC.

bawker *n.* [late 16C] one who cheats at bowls. [SE *balker*, one who hinders deliberately]

bawla *see* BALLER.

bawl off *v.* [1960s+] (Irish) to attack verbally, to scold severely. [for ety. *see* BAWL OUT]

bawl out *v.* (orig. US) **1** late 19C+] to scold, to reprimand, to criticize; all such attacks are delivered in a loud voice. **2** [20C] to announce oneself. [SE *bawl*, to shout at the top of one's voice, orig. to howl like a dog]

bawly-ike *n.* [1910s+] (US) a complainer, a whinger. [SE *bawl* + IKE]

Bay, the *n.* **1** [early 19C+] (S.Afr.) Port Elizabeth. **2** [early–mid-19C] (Aus.) Botany *Bay*. **3** [mid-19C+] (Can.) the Hudson's *Bay* Company or one of its stores. **4** [1910s+] (Aus.) the State Penitentiary, Long Bay, New South Wales. [abbr.]

Bay City *n.* [20C] (US) the city of San Francisco, California. [the San Francisco Bay on which the city stands; however the fictitious (and massively corrupt) *Bay City* created by Raymond Chandler (1888–1959), is generally seen to be Oakland, California]

bay fever *n.* [early–mid-19C] the shamming of illness by convicts, in an attempt to avoid transportation to Botany Bay, New South Wales.

bay horse *n.* [1950s–60s] (US tramp) bay rum, a hair tonic; thus *bay horse jockey*, a drinker of bay rum.

bayonet *n.* [19C] the penis; one of a number of terms equating the penis with a cutting or stabbing weapon (cf. ARSE-OPENER; BEEF BAYONET; BLADE n.[2]; BODKIN n.[1]; BRACMARD; BUTCHER KNIFE; BUTTER-KNIFE; CULTY-GUN; CUTLASS; CUTTY GUN; DAGGER n.[1]; DARD; DIRK n.[1]; FIXED BAYONET; HARPOON n.; LANCE n.; LANCE IN REST; LANCE OF LOVE; LOVE DART; LOVE TORPEDO; MUTTON-DAGGER; PIKE n.[2]; PORK SWORD; PRICK; SAMURAI SWORD; STRIKER n.[1]; SWORD).

bayoo *n.* [mid-late 19C] (US Black) an unpopular, unappealing person, 'a man of whom Quashie thinks very little, "a low down mean cuss"' (*Farmer*). [? BOYO]

Bays, the *n.* [1940s–50s] Bayswater Road, London W2 (cf. BAZE).

Bay Street boys *n.* [20C] (W.I./Baha.) the White mercantile élite who control the Bahamas. [the business centre of Bay Street, Nassau]

Bayswater captain *n.* [late 19C] a layabout, a sponger (cf. DRY-LAND SAILOR). [so many of them choosing Bayswater, London, as a residence. It was cheap but within reasonable distance of the West End and Mayfair]

bay window *n.* **1** [mid–late 19C] the stomach of a pregnant woman. **2** [mid-19C+] a man's fat stomach.

bay-window *adj.* [1910s–40s] smart, fashionable. [lower-middle-class use, a house boasting such a window was sought after]

bazaar *n.*[1] [19C] the vagina, considered as an economic adjunct (cf. BANK n.[1]).

bazaar *n.*[2] [mid-19C] a shop, a shop counter. [Pers. *b(z(r*, a market; thence to Hind.]

bazaar *n.*[3] [late 19C+] a bar in a public house. [rhy. sl.]

bazaar *v.* [late 19C–1910s] (society) to rob, whether lit. or fig. ['the extortion practised by remorseless, smiling English ladies at bazaars' (*Ware*)]

bazaared *adj.* [late 19C–1900s] (society) cheated, robbed, over-charged. [BAZAAR n.[2]]

Baze, the *n.* [1940s–50s] Bayswater Road, London W2 (cf. DILLY n.[3]; PIC n.[2]). [before the Street Offences Act 1959, Bayswater Road was one of London's centres of street prostitution, seen as slightly less classy than its rivals Piccadilly and, even smarter, Mayfair]

bazongas/bazoongas/bazonkas *n.* [1970s+] the female breasts (cf. BAZOOM; GAZONGAS; GAZONKAS). [SE *bosom*]

bazonkas *adj.* [1970s] (US) crazy. [SE *berserk* + BONKERS; BANANAS adj. (1)]

bazoo *n.*[1] [late 19C–1940s] mouth. [Du. *bazu(in)*, a trumpet]

bazoo/bazzonus *n.*[2] [1900s–20s] (US) a lout. [? BAZOO n.[1], i.e. the unchecked noisiness]

bazooka *n.* **1** [1950s+] the penis (cf. BACON BAZOOKA; CANNON n.[1]; GUN n.[2]). **2** [1950s+] the buttocks. **3** [1950s+] (US Black) an especially large and potent marijuana cigarette, laced with cocaine. **4** [1950s+] petting (cf. BAZOOKAS). **5** [1980s+] (drugs) cocaine, crack cocaine. [all f. the anti-tank rocket launcher, first used in WW2; like BAZOO n.[1]; the term may stem f. the Du. *bazu(in)*, a trumpet, in this case f. the shape, but for (5) note BASUCO]

bazookas *n.* [1960s+] the female breasts; thus *bit of bazooka*, petting, i.e. touching the breasts (and perhaps other parts of the body), but stopping short of penetration (cf. ARTILLERY n.[3]). [play on SE *bosom*]

bazookas *adj.* [1970s] (US) crazy. [SE *berserk*]

bazoom *n.* [1950s+] the female breasts. [joc. pron. of SE *bosom*]

bazoombas *n.* [1980s+] (US) the female breasts (cf. BAZOOM).

bazoongas *see* BAZONGAS.

bazuca *n.* [1950s+] (US Black) a large and potent marijuana cigarette, laced with cocaine (cf. BAZOOKA).

bazuco *n.* [1980s+] the oily substance in freebase cocaine. [Sp. *base*]

bazuko *see* BASUCO.

bazulco *n.* [1980s+] (drugs) cocaine. [BASUCO]

bazzonus *see* BAZOO n.[2].

b.b. *n.*[1] [20C] bloody *b*astard. [abbr.]

b.b. *n.*[2] [20C] a male homosexual. [abbr. BUM-BOY]

b.b. *n.*[3] [1910s–40s] (US) a *b*ed*b*ug. [abbr.]

b-ball *n.* [1990s] (US Black) *b*asket*ball*. [abbr.]

b-ball *v.* [1990s] (US Black) to play basketball. [B-BALL n.]

b.b.-brained *adj.* [1968] (US) stupid (cf. AMOEBA-BRAINED). [the minuscule size of *B.B.* shot]

b.b. head *n.* [20C] (US Black) **1** a boy with a tight-curled, 'knotty' head. **2** an unattractive woman, esp. one with short, fuzzy, nappy hair (cf. NAILHEAD n.[1]; TACKHEAD n.[1]). [the supposed resemblance to *b.b.* shot]

B-boy *n.* [1970s–80s] (orig. US Black) a Black male teenager, focused on RAP n.[5] music and the ghetto street lifestyle (cf. FLY-GIRL n.[2]). [abbr. *beat-boy*; coined in 1975 to describe those who followed DJ Kool Herc of the Hevalo Club in New York]

b.c. *n.* [1960s–80s] (US Black) contraception, usu. contraceptive pills. [abbr. *b*irth *c*ontrol]

b.c. *adj.* [late 19C–1900s] extremely old (cf. ANNO DOMINI). [chronological notation *BC*, before Christ]

b-drink *n.* [1930s] (US) a drink that resembles whisky (and charged as such) but is in fact cold tea; served to the female companion of a man who has entered a club in the hope of sex; thus *b-drinker*, the woman who consumes such drinks. [B-GIRL; i.e. the sort of drink she consumes]

b.d.t. *n.* [20C] (US) **1** diarrhoea. **2** over-frequent urination. [abbr. BACK-DOOR TROT]

b.d.v. *n.* [1920s+] (tramp) a cigarette stub, picked up in the street (cf. STOOPER n.[2]). [abbr. *b*end *d*own *V*irginia]

beach bitch *n.* [1980s+] (US gay) one who frequents holiday resorts and beaches looking for sex. [SE *beach* + BITCH n.[1]]

beach bum *n.* [1960s+] (Aus./US) a person, usu. a teenager, who hangs around the beach all day and surfs. [SE *beach* + BUM n.[3] (6)]

beach bunny *n.* [1960s+] a young woman who frequents the world of surfing, but does not herself surf (cf. SNOW BUNNY). [SE *beach* + BUNNY n.[2]]

beach-cadger *n.* [mid-19C–1910s] a beggar who favours seaside resorts. [SE *beach* + CADGER n.]

beachcomber *n.*[1] **1** [1910s–50s] (Can.) a White man living with an Inuit woman. **2** [1950s] (Aus.) one who walks the streets in the hope of picking up a woman; thus *beach-combing, combing.* [SE *beachcomber*, a settler in the Pacific islands, living by pearl-fishing and other means]

beachcomber *n.*[2] [1990s] a male homosexual. [pun on *log*/LOG n.[4]; the beachcomber pushes logs; the homosexual is a LOG-PUSHER]

beached *adj.*[1] [late 19C+] (N.Z) unemployed, impoverished (cf. ON THE BEACH). [ext. of SE; one is living as an impoverished beachcomber]

beached *adj.*[2] [1990s] (US teen) absolutely exhausted. [the imagery of a beached whale]

beacon *n.* [late 19C] a red nose.

bead *n.* [19C] a glass of spirits. [SE *bead*, a bubble found in spirits or wine]

bead-counter *n.* [19C] a clergyman; an overtly religious person; a recluse (cf. BEAD-JIGGLER; BEAD-PULLER; STATUE-LOVER). [the rosary beads of Roman Catholics]

be a devil! *excl.* [20C] take a risk! I dare you!; usu. used facetiously to someone for whom the tiniest breach of 'normality' is a major event.

beadie *v.* [1990s] to look at. [SE cliché 'a beady eye', coined early 19C]

bead-jiggler/-mumbler *n.* [1960s] (US) a Roman Catholic (cf. BEAD-COUNTER). [the use of a rosary]

beadle *n.* [early 19C] anyone who wears a long, blue overcoat (the uniform of a parish *beadle*).

beadles *n.* [late 19C–1900s] (US) inhabitants of the state of Virginia. [? their serious, beadle-like demeanour]

bead-mumbler *see* BEAD-JIGGLER.

bead-puller *n.* [20C] (US) a Roman Catholic (cf. BEAD-COUNTER). [SE *rosary beads*]

beady *n.* [1970s] (US) an eye. [SE phr. *beady (little) eye*]

beagle *n.*[1] [mid-19C] a native of Virginia. [the popularity of fox-hunting in the state]

beagle *n.*[2] (US) [1920s–30s] a nose. [the dog's sniffing abilities]

beagle *n.*[3] (US) [1920s–30s] a sausage, esp. a 'hot dog'. [pun]

beagle *n.*[4] (US) [1940s–50s] an unattractive young woman. [DOG n.[4] (6)]

beagle *v.* [1960s–70s] to pick pockets. [the dog's 'sniffing-out' qualities]

beak *n.*[1] **1** [mid-16C+] a judge, a magistrate. **2** [late 19C+] a schoolmaster. [Hotten/Ware suggest OE *beag*, a necklace worn as a badge of office, but (1) more likely f. HARMAN (-BECK)]

beak *n.*[2] [early 18C+] the nose.

beak *v.*[1] [late 16C–early 17C] to beg. [like a bird, the beggar 'pecks around']

beak *v.*[2] [late 19C] to bring an offender before a magistrate. [BEAK n.[1]]

beaker *n.* [19C] a fowl, a chicken.

beaker-hauler *n.* [19C] a poultry thief, who hawks booty from door to door (cf. BEAK-HUNTER). [SE *beak*, generic for poultry + *haul*]

beak-gander *n.* [late 19C] a senior judge. [BEAK n.[1] (1) + SE *gander*, a foolish (old) man]

beak-hunter *n.* [late 19C–1900s] a poultry-thief; thus *beak-hunting*, poultry-stealing (cf. BEAKER-HAULER). [SE *beak* + *hunter*]

beak off *v.* [20C] (Ulster) to truant. [[synon. Scot. *bake*]

beaksman *n.* [18C–19C] a policeman. [BEAK n.[1] (1) + SE *man*]

beaky lady/man *n.* [20C] (Ulster) a truancy officer. [BEAK OFF]

be all *v.* [20C] to take an attitude, to adopt a pose; the phr. is often used with an accompanying gesture, *He was all … .*

beam *n.* [20C] (US Black) the sun. [abbr. SE *sunbeam*]

beam v. [20C] (US Black) to look at, to stare. [obs. SE *beam*, to shed light upon]

beamer n.[1] [1950s+] a blush. [SE *beam*, to smile broadly]

beamer n.[2] [1980s+] (drugs) a user of crack cocaine (cf. BEAMING; BEEMERS). [? the triple-beam scales used in weighing drugs and/or spurious *Star Trek* line, BEAM ME UP, SCOTTY!, i.e. get me HIGH adj.[1]]

beamer/bimmer n.[3] [1990s] (orig. US) a BMW motorcar (cf. BEEZA). [more elliptical refs. are found on a variety of RAP songs to specific BMW models, e.g. 325i, 735i, 740i, 750iL, 850i]

beaming n. [1980s+] (US Black) using drugs, esp. crack cocaine. [BEAMER n.[2]]

beam me up, Scotty n. [1980s+] (drugs) a mixture of phencyclidine and cocaine (cf. BEAMER n.[2]; BEAMING). [*see* BEAM ME UP, SCOTTY!]

beam me up, Scotty! excl. [1970s] **1** (US campus) an expression of the desire to be elsewhere. **2** (drugs) give me some drugs! usu. crack cocaine (cf. KLINGON; MISSION; SCOTTY n.[2]). [the TV series *Star Trek* (from 1966), in which Captain's Kirk's injunction to the chief engineer, *Scotty*, became a trademark catchphrase]

beam on v. [1990s] (US Black) to stare at. [BEAM v.]

beam out v. [1980s+] (US campus) to daydream. [BEAM v.]

beam up v. [1980s+] (US Black/teen) to become intoxicated through drug-taking. [sl. use of the *Star Trek* catchphrase BEAM ME UP, SCOTTY!]

beamy adj.[1] (US) [20C] of a person, broad, wide, overweight; thus *broad in the beam*. [naut. jargon *beam*, the width of a ship]

beamy adj.[2] (US) [1960s] eccentric, crazy. [OFF BEAM]

bean n.[1] **1** [19C] a sovereign, a guinea. **2** [19C] money, irrespective of the coin; *not a bean*, absolutely nothing. **3** [late 19C–1950s] a poker chip. **4** [1960s] (US) $100.

bean n.[2] [late 19C] (US) a foolish, silly notion. [? corruption of 'bee in one's bonnet']

bean n.[3] **1** [late 19C–1900s] the penis (cf. STRING BEAN). **2** [1940s] (US) the hymen; thus *cop a bean*, to deflower, to have sexual intercourse. **3** [1990s] the clitoris.

bean n.[4] [20C] the head (cf. COCONUT n.[1]; COSTARD; NUT n.[3]; ONION n.[1]; PUMPKIN n.[2]; SWEDE n.[2]).

bean n.[5] [1910s+] (US) a foolish or unpleasant person (cf. OLD BEAN). [abbr. *beanstalk* or *beanpole* or f. BEAN-TOSSER]

bean n.[6] (US Black/drugs) **1** [1920s] a package of a drug. **2** [1960s+] any form of tablet, esp. Benzedrine; thus *beaned up*, under the influence of Benzedrine (cf. B n.[1]). [resemblance]

bean n.[7] [1940s+] (US) a Mexican, any Spanish-American (cf. BEAN-EATER). [stereotyping of the Mexican diet]

bean v. [1910s+] (orig. US) to hit on the head. [BEAN n.[4]]

beanbag n. [1970s] (US) a Mexican (cf. BEANER n.[3]). [for ety. *see* BEAN n.[7]]

beanbag v. [1980s] to have sexual intercourse. [BEAN n.[3] + SE *beanbag*, a possible site for the sex]

bean bandit n. [1950s–70s] (US) a Mexican (cf. BEANER n.[3]). [BEAN n.[7] + SE *bandit*]

beanbelly/bean-belly n.[1] [mid-17C–19C] a native of Leicestershire. [that county's production of beans]

beanbelly/bean-belly n.[2] [1960s] (US) a pot belly. [the general 'inflationary' effect of eating lentils etc]

beanbrain n. [1950s+] (US) a fool (cf. BAKEBRAIN; BEAN-HEAD). [the implication is of minimal size]

bean-choker n. [1980s+] (US) a Spanish-American (cf. BEAN n.[7]; BEAN-EATER; CHILE-CHOKER). [SE *bean*, the stereotypical Hispanic food + *choker*]

bean counter n. [1970s+] (US) anyone who deals with financial matters, esp. an accountant or statistician.

bean-date *see* JELLY-DATE.

bean-eater n. (US) **1** [late 19C–1940s] an inhabitant of Boston, Massachusetts; thus *bean-eating*, Bostonian in manner (cf. BEAN TOWN n.[1]). **2** [1910s+] a Mexican (cf. BEAN-CHOKER; BEANER n.[3]; BEANO; CHILE-CHOKER; CHILE-EATER; FRIJOLE-EATER; TACO-BENDER; TACO-EATER; TACO-HEAD). [the supposed preference of Bostonians and Mexicans for beans]

beaner n.[1] [late 19C–1920s] a scolding, a telling-off. [GIVE SOMEONE BEANS]

beaner n.[2] [1910s–40s] (US) something excellent. [? Fr. *bien*]

beaner n.[3] [1960s+] (US) **1** a Mexican; thus *beaner shoes*, huaraches (leather-thonged sandals, orig. worn by Mexican Indians), *beaner wagon*, an old, dilapidated car typically driven by Mexican immigrants (cf. BEAN-EATER). **2** a Cuban or other Latin-American. [stereotyping; beans are seen as a staple of the Hispanic immigrant diet]

beanery n. [late 19C+] (US) **1** a cheap restaurant, orig. one that specialized in beans. **2** a boarding house. [SE *beans*, seen as part of the staple menu]

beanfeast n. [late 19C+] any form of festivity or celebration. [SE *beanfeast*, an annual dinner given by employers to their workers; in its original form beans were a featured dish]

bean flicker n. [1990s] a lesbian. [BEAN n.[3] (3) + SE *flicker*]

bean foundry n. [1900s] (US) a cheap restaurant (cf. BEANERY).

bean-head n. [1910s+] (US) a fool (cf. BEANBRAIN). [SE *bean* + sfx. -HEAD (1)]

bean house n. [1970s] (US) a cheap restaurant; thus *bean house bull*, extravagant stories, 'tall tales' (cf. BEANERY).

beanie n.[1] [1940s+] (US) **1** a small, tight-fitting cap, similar to a large skull-cap; thus *propeller-beanie*, such a cap with a small propeller affixed to its top. **2** a blackjack, a cosh. [BEAN n.[4] + dimin. sfx. -ie]

beanie n.[2] [20C] (US) a pot belly (cf. BEANBELLY n.[2]). [it is filled with/created by beans]

bean-jacks n. [1930s+] (Irish) a female public convenience. [Irish *bean*, a woman + JAKES]

beano n.[1] [late 19C–1920s] a Mexican (cf. BEANER n.[3]). [BEAN n.[7]]

beano n.[2] [late 19C+] a party, a celebration. [BEANFEAST; the abbr. originally used by printers, who usu. called it a *goose* or *wayzgoose*]

beanpea n. [late 19C–1900s] an effeminate young man. [a case involving two such youths, known only, so taboo was the thought of homosexuality, by their initials *B* and *P*]

beanpole n. [mid-19C+] a tall, thin person (cf. STRING BEAN).

bean queen n. [1980s+] (US gay) a non-Hispanic person who prefers Hispanic partners for sex (cf. CHACHA QUEEN; SENOR-EATER). [BEANER n.[3] + QUEEN n.[1]]

beans n.[1] **1** [early–mid-19C] a guinea. **2** [late 19C] a sovereign. **3** [mid-19C+] money. [Fr. *biens*, property; but note BEAN n.[1]]

beans/bean time n.[2] [1940s+] (US) **1** food. **2** a mealtime.

beans! excl. **1** [1910s–20s] (US) a mild excl. of surprise, annoyance, disbelief etc. **2** [1950s+] (US, usu. juv.) a claim, esp. a claim of first rights to something (cf. BENCHES!; KEEPSIES).

bean-shooter n. (US) **1** [19C] a catapult or slingshot. **2** [19C–1940s] a gun.

bean time *see* BEANS n.[2].

bean-tosser n. [19C] the penis. [? shape]

Bean Town n.[1] [20C] (US) Boston, Massachusetts. [the supposed local staple]

bean town n.[2] [20C] (US) that part of a town in which the poor or the immigrants live, such immigrants are stereotypically, but not invariably, Hispanics (cf. BLACK TOWN; CABBAGE TOWN; COON BOTTOM; DAGO TOWN; DUTCH TOWN; JEW TOWN; JIG TOWN; JIM TOWN; NIGGER HILL; PIGTAIL ALLEY; POLACK TOWN; TACO TOWN; WOP TOWN). [the equation of a mainly bean diet with poverty]

bean wagon *n.* [1940s–50s] (US) a cheap restaurant, esp. one that has been converted from a disused railway car.

beany *n.* [20C] (US) a gun, a pistol. [BEAN-SHOOTER n. (2)]

beany *adj.*[1] [mid-19C] fresh, spirited, in good condition. [FULL OF BEANS (2)]

beany *adj.*[2] [1910s] (US) eccentric. [OFF ONE'S BEAN]

bear *n.*[1] **1** [18C+] a gruff, irritable person, amplified in phr. *a bear with a sore head*. **2** [1910s+] (US) someone who overworks their employees or students, a hard taskmaster/ mistress. **3** [1950s+] (US Black) a particularly ugly person, man or woman (cf. BOOGER BEAR). **4** [1990s] (US) a hairy, beefy gay male.

bear *n.*[2] [mid-18C+] the pupil of a private tutor (cf. BEAR-LEADER). [the tutor is seen as 'leading' a pupil, esp. on the 'Grand Tour' of cultural/social Europe, like a keeper with a tame bear]

bear *n.*[3] [early 19C+] a Russian, also as *the Bear*. [the Russian 'national animal']

bear *n.*[4] [1910s–40s] (US) **1** an exciting or otherwise exceptional example. **2** an attractive (young) woman. **3** an expert, an adept. [the strength and power of the animal]

bear, the *n.*[5] [1930s] (US Black) poverty, misery. [BEAR n.[1]]

bear *n.*[6] [1940s+] **1** (US Black) a misfortune, an unfortunate situation, a feeling of depression. **2** (US Black) an unpleasant lifestyle. **3** (US campus) any difficult course {cf. GUT n.[2]}. **4** [20C] sunstroke. [the animal's neg. characteristics]

bear *n.*[7] [1960s] (US) the vulva (cf. BEAR-TRAPPER'S HAT; SNAPPING TURTLE). [it is furry and it 'bites']

bear *n.*[8] [1970s] (US) a policeman; thus *bear in the air*, a police helicopter (cf. SMOKY n.[2]). [US Forest Service's mascot *Smokey the Bear*]

bear a bob, to *phr.* [19C] to lend a hand. [SE *bear a bob*, join in a chorus]

bear a hand, to *phr.* [early 18C+] to hurry up, to make haste.

bear cat *n.* [1910s–30s] (US) **1** something excellent, first-rate. **2** an aggressive or forceful person; one of great energy or ability. [BEAR n.[4]/SE *bearcat*]

beard *n.*[1] **1** [early 18C; late 19C+] female pubic hair (cf. SILENT BEARD). **2** [1920s+] a bearded man; thus, by stereotyping, a beatnik, an intellectual (cf. HIPPIE n.[2]; LONGHAIR n.).

beard *n.*[2] **1** [1950s–60s] a male friend who acts as a 'cover', usually for extramarital affairs. **2** [1970s+] (US gay/lesbian) a male used as an ostensible lover or even husband, as a disguise for one's real preference. [gambling jargon *beard*, a go-between who places bets for another person; thus protecting their identity]

bearded clam *n.* [1960s+] the vagina; one of several terms linking the organ to fish (cf. BEARDED LADY; BEARDED OYSTER; BIT OF FISH; BIT OF SKATE; BUMBO n.[1]; CLAM n.[1]; COD TRENCH; FISH n.[4]; FISH MARKET; FISH MITTEN; FISH-TANK; FREE-FISHERY; FUZZY LAP FLOUNDER; HADDOCK PASTIE; HIRSUTE OYSTER; HUNT THE ANCHOVY; KIPPER n.[4]; KIPPER BOX; LING; LOBSTER-POT; OYSTER n.[1]; OYSTER-CATCHER; PERIWINKLE; RED SNAPPER; SALMON CANYON; SEAFOOD n.[2]; SEAFOOD BLANCMANGE; SHELL; SNAPPER n.[7]; SNAPPING TURTLE; SPLIT KIPPER; STINKPOT; TENCH n.[2]; TROUT n.[2]; TUNA; WHELK). [BEARD n.[1] (1)]

bearded lady/taco *n.* [1960s+] the vagina (cf. BEARDED CLAM). [BEARD n.[1] (1) + joc. use of SE]

bearded oyster *n.* [1910s+] the vagina (cf. BEARDED CLAM). [BEARD n.[1] (1) + joc. use of SE]

bearded taco *see* BEARDED LADY.

beardie *n.* [late 19C+] **1** a bearded person. **2** (Aus.) a member of a body of Southcottians (believers in the teaching of Joanna Southcott (1750–1814), who announced herself as the woman spoken of in Rev. 12), followers of the local prophet John Wroe (1782–1863), who called themselves Christian Israelites.

beard-jammer *n.* [1920s+] (US) **1** a promiscuous man, a successful womanizer (cf. BEARD-SPLITTER; JUMBLER; KNOCKER n.[1]; QUIM-STICKER; RUMP-SPLITTER). **2** a pimp. [BEARD n.[1] (1) + SE *jammer*]

beard-man *n.* [1960s+] (W.I.) a Rastafarian (cf. DREAD n.; LOCKSMAN). [his appearance]

beard ride *n.* [1980s] (US) cunnilingus. [BEARD n.[1] (1) + RIDE n.[3]]

beard-splitter *n.* **1** [late 17C–early 18C] a seducer, a sexual athlete (cf. BEARD-JAMMER). **2** [18C] the penis (cf. ARSE-OPENER; HAIR-DIVIDER). [BEARD n.[1] (1) + SE *splitter*]

bearer-up *n.* [mid–late 19C] a thief who robs men who have been decoyed by a female accomplice (cf. BADGER n.[1]; MURPHY n.[3]). [BEAR UP]

bear fight *n.* [late 19C] (society) a play fight, a bit of 'rough-and-tumble'.

bear-garden discourse *n.* [late 17C–early 19C] coarse language, vulgarity; sometimes as abbr. *bear-garden*. [SE *bear garden*, orig. a venue for bear-baiting, latterly any scene of rowdy behaviour]

bear-garden jaw *n.* [late 17C–early 19C] coarse language (cf. BEAR-GARDEN DISCOURSE). [SE *bear garden* + JAW n.]

be-argued *adj.* [mid-19C–1900s] drunk. [SE *argumentative*]

bearings *n.* [20C] (Aus.) the stomach. [SE *bearing*, that part of a machine that supports a shaft or axle]

bearing up *phr.* [1950s+] response to the greeting 'how are you?'; similar is *mustn't grumble*.

bear-leader *n.* [mid-18C+] an expert who teaches by example (cf. BEAR n.[2]). [the nickname for the tutors of the 18C who ferried their aristocratic pupils around the 'Grand Tour' of Europe]

bear meat *n.* [1970s] (US) an easy target. [the size of a bear]

bear party *n.* [mid-19C] an all-male party, esp. on the night preceding the wedding of one of the men (cf. STAG PARTY).

bear's ass *n.* [1990s] (US) a harsh taskmaster. [BEAR n.[3] (2) + ARSE n.[1] (1)]

bear sign *n.* [19C] (US) a doughnut. [cowboy/trapper jargon *bear sign*, bear droppings; a doughnut has a similar shape]

bearskin *n.* [19C] the pubic hair (cf. BADGER n.[7]). [resemblance]

bear's paw *n.* [20C] a saw. [rhy. sl.]

bear story *n.* [19C] (US) a 'tall story', an exaggerated story. [the wildly overblown stories told by bear-trappers and other woodsmen to credulous listeners]

bear-tracker *n.* [20C] a detective.

bear trap *n.* [19C] (US) a difficult situation.

bear-trapper's hat *n.* [1990s] a large, hairy vagina, esp. one that is dark in colour (cf. BEAR n.[7]).

bear-up *n.* [late 19C–1900s] (Aus.) the pursuit of a woman. [SE *bear-up*, a hold-up]

bear up *v.* [early 19C] to help in the commission of a swindle or fraud. [SE *bear up*, to support]

beast *n.*[1] [late 19C–1900s] a bicycle. [synon. with SE *beast*, a horse]

beast *n.*[2] [1940s+] **1** (US, mainly campus) a young woman, esp. an unattractive but sexually voracious one. **2** (US/W.I.) a girlfriend viewed in a sexual context, esp. when she has another established relationship already.

beast *n.*[3] (drugs) **1** [1950s] heroin; thus heroin addiction (cf. MONKEY n.[14]). **2** [1980s+] LSD (cf. A n.[3]). [? their unpredictable effects]

beast *n.*[4] [1960s+] (US Black) a White person. [coined by Black Nationalists in the 1960s; it lapsed thereafter but reappeared among rebellious youths in the 1990s]

beast *n.*[5] [1980s+] (prison) a child molester, a sexual offender (cf. NONCE; SHORT EYES; SHUT EYES). [SE *beast*, a brutal, very unpleasant person]

beast, the n.[6] [1980s+] (W.I./UK Black teen) the police, authoritarian figure or anyone who represents the real or perceived oppressors (cf. BABYLON n.[1]).

beast adj. [20C] (W.I.) a general intensifier, very good, excellent. [survival of schoolboy intensifier *beastly*, very good, very bad]

beast v. [1980s+] to molest a child. [BEAST n.[5]]

beast-boy n. [1990s] (Black) a policeman. [BEAST n.[6] + SE *boy*]

beastie n. [1980s] (US teen) anyone considered outside the group talking, esp. if unattractive, empty-headed etc. [juv. use of SE *beast*]

beast-lick n. [1940s+] (W.I.) a harsh, heavy blow, such as might be given to an animal. [SE *beast* + *lick*, a blow]

beastly adv. [19C+] (society) exceedingly, excessively, very.

beastmaster n. [1980s+] (US campus) a man who consistently dates unattractive women. [BEAST n.[2] (1) + SE *master*; note the similarly titled 'sword and sorcery' film of the period]

beastness n. [20C] (W.I.) male promiscuity. [SE *beastliness*]

beast of a phr. [late 19C+] applied to anything seen as unpleasant.

beasty n. see BHEESTIE.

beasty adj. [1980s+] (US campus) disgusting, repellent, unattractive. [BEAST n.[2] (1)]

beat n.[1] 1 [mid-19C+] (orig. Und.) one's own area of activity, operation (cf. MANOR; TURF n.[1]). 2 [1940s+] (Aus.) the area patrolled by a sheep or cattle musterer. [SE *beat the bounds*]

beat n.[2] (US) 1 [mid-19C–1930s] an unreliable person, esp. one who fails to pay their debts (cf. BEAT FOR v.[2]). 2 [mid-19C–1930s] a loafer, a layabout, a sponger. 3 [late 19C–1900s] a swindler, a confidence trickster (cf. ON THE BEAT). [i.e. they 'beat' the rules of society]

beat n.[3] [mid-19C–1950s] (US) an escape, usu. from prison. [BEAT IT]

beat n.[4] [late 19C] (US) an outstanding person, one who defeats all rivals. [SE *beat*, to overcome]

beat n.[5] [1970s] a prostitute's client who likes to be beaten, often bringing his own equipment with him. [SE *beat*, to hit]

beat n.[6] [1980s+] (US drugs) a pipeful of marijuana that has been reduced to ashes. [BEAT adj.[1] (1)]

beat adj.[1] 1 [early 19C+] exhausted, tired out. 2 [mid-19C–1930s] (US) amazed, astonished, at a loss. [SE *beaten*]

beat adj.[2] [1930s+] 1 (orig. US Black) of people, out of funds. 2 of objects, shabby, battered, worn-out. [SE *beaten*]

beat adj.[3] 1 [1940s+] (US) useless, worthless; boring. 2 [1940s+] (orig. US) disillusioned, sad, world-weary. 3 [1980s+] (US campus) very ugly. 4 [1980s+] (US campus) stupid, weak, ineffectual. [SE *beaten*]

beat v. (US) 1 [mid-19C+] to steal from, to defraud; often as *beat one for*. 2 [1910s+] to escape punishment. 3 [20C] to escape from prison. 4 [1950s+] to leave quickly.

beat about/around the bush, to phr. [early 18C+] to avoid a topic, to fail deliberately to come to the point. [hunting imagery]

beat a djé, to phr. [20C] (W.I./Gren.) to be in the mood for a physical fight or verbal confrontation, esp. one that will last for several days. [SE *beat* + Fr. *guerre*, war]

beat akeybo, to phr. [mid-19C] to be confusing; thus *he beats akeybo, akeybo, he acts in an extreme manner, akeybo beats the devil*, to be extremely confusing. [ety. unknown; note Norfolk dial. *acabo, akeybo*, used in phr. *that would puzzle acabo*]

beat all v. [late 19C+] to surpass in every way, often in phr. *don't that beat all* (cf. BEAT BOBTAIL; BEAT THE BAND).

beat all cockfight, to phr. [20C] (W.I.) to be unbelievable, unheard of, utterly ridiculous.

beat/knock all to sticks, to phr. [mid-19C] to thrash, to beat severely. [SE *to knock to pieces*]

beat a rap, to phr. [1920s+] to be found not guilty in a court. [SE *beat* + RAP n.[3] (4)]

beat around the bush see BEAT ABOUT THE BUSH.

beat artist n. [1980s+] (US Black) one who sells poor quality or fake drugs. [DEADBEAT n. + ARTIST n.[2]; note BEAT FOR v.[1]]

beat ass, to phr. [1970s+] (US) to leave, to depart (cf. BEAT FEET). [BEAT v. (4) + ARSE n.[1] (1)]

beat a trick, to phr. [1970s+] (sex industry) to rob a client. [BEAT v. (1) + TRICK n.[4] (2)]

beat Banaghan/Banagher v. [late 18C–1920s] to tell fabulous, fantastic tales, often with addition *and Banagher beat the Devil* (cf. BEAT THE BAND). [? name of a real story-teller who is surpassed by the current talker f. the town of Banagher, a notorious 'rotten borough'. To 'beat it' would be to surpass any extreme]

beat bobtail, to phr. [19C] (US) to surpass in every way (cf. BEAT ALL; BEAT THE BAND). [? euph. for *beat the devil*, but also ? link to the 'bob-tailed nag' of Stephen Foster's song 'Camptown Races' (1850)]

beatbox n. [1980s+] 1 an electronic drum machine. 2 a large, portable tape deck (cf. GHETTOBLASTER). [SE *beat*, rhythm + BOX n.[4]]

beat buck v. [late 19C] to do something outstanding (cf. BEAT THE CATS; BEAT THE DUTCH). [? poker imagery; cf. PASS THE BUCK]

beat-down n. [1980s+] (US Black) a fight, a beating.

beat down v. [1980s+] (US Black) to fight, to beat up. [BEAT-DOWN n.]

beaten-out adv. [mid-19C] impoverished. [BEAT adj.[2] (1)]

beater n.[1] [16C] (Und.) one who lures a victim into a crooked game of cards or dice. [SE *beater*, one who drives game towards the guns]

beater n.[2] [mid–late 19C] (US) a person or thing that beats or excels others.

beater n.[3] [1940s] (US Black) one who refuses to pay their debts. [DEADBEAT n.]

beater-cases n. [18C–mid-19C] shoes (cf. TROTTER-BOXES). [DEW-BEATERS + SE *case*].

beaters n. [mid–late 19C] (US) shoes, boots (cf. BEATER-CASES). [DEW-BEATERS]

beat feet, to phr. [1940s+] (US campus) to leave, to depart (cf. HIT THE ROAD).

beat for v.[1] [mid-19C+] to take a person's money, whether it is offered or not. [BEAT v. 1]

beat for v.[2] [1930s+] to be short of, usu. money. [BEAT adj.[2] (1)]

beat for the yolk phr. [1940s] (US Black/Harlem) short of cash, temporarily impoverished. [BEAT adj.[2] + SE *yolk*]

beat/blast/kick/punch/thump hell/the hell out of, to phr. [mid-19C+] (orig. US) to beat severely (cf. KNOCK HELL OUT OF).

beat hens a-pacing, to phr. [20C] (US) to be highly unusual, to be noteworthy, to be very annoying.

beat into fits, to phr. [mid-19C+] to defeat or surpass completely.

beat it v. [19C+] (US) to go away in a hurry; usu. as excl. *beat it!*; also ext. as *beat it while the beating's/going's good*. [SE *beat a path*]

beat it on the hoof, to phr. [late 17C–early 18C] to walk on foot. [BEAT IT + HOOF n.]

beat it up v. [1930s–50s] to have a good time, to go on a spree, to 'whoop it up'.

beat liquor, to phr. [20C] (W.I.) to drink heavily. [SE *beat*, to hit]

beat-nuts n. [1970s] (US) an obsessive masturbator. [BEAT ONE'S MEAT + NUTS n.[2] (1)]

beat-off n. [1970s] 1 (US) an act of masturbation. 2 (US campus) an unpleasant person (cf. JERK-OFF n.[2]). [back-form. of BEAT OFF v.]

beat off v. [1960s+] (US) **1** to masturbate (cf. BALL OFF v.[2]; BIFF OFF; BRING ONESELF OFF; DO ONESELF OFF; DUB OFF; FLIP OFF v.[1]; FLIP ONESELF OFF; FREAK OFF; FRIG OFF; GET OFF v.[6]; GET ONE'S NUTS OFF; HAVE IT OFF v.[2]; JACK OFF v.[1]; JAG OFF; JERK OFF v.[1]; PULL OFF v.[3]; PUMP OFF; RUB OFF v.; SCREW OFF; SMACK OFF; SPUFF OFF; TOSS v.[1]; TOSS OFF v.[1]; WHACK OFF; WHIP OFF v.[2]; WORK OFF v.[1]; YANK OFF). **2** to waste time, to loaf around. [BEAT ONE'S MEAT + COME OFF v.[1]]

beat/beat up one's chops/choppers/gums, to phr. [1930s+] (US) to chatter, to talk, esp. in an irritating manner (cf. GUM-BEATING). [SE beat + CHOPS n. (1)/CHOPPERS/SE gums]

beat/cuff/flog/whip one's dummy, to phr. [1970s+] to masturbate. [BEAT OFF + DUMMY]

beat one's hog, to phr. [1970s+] to masturbate. [BEAT OFF + HOG n.[4]]

beat one's little brother, to phr. [1960s+] to masturbate. [BEAT OFF + LITTLE BROTHER]

beat one's meat, to phr. (orig. US) **1** [late 19C+] to masturbate (cf. ACCOST THE OSCAR MEYER). **2** [1940s+] to brag, to boast. [BEAT OFF + MEAT n. (2)]

beat one's nut/nuts see BUST ONE'S NUT.

beat one's skin see BEAT SKIN.

beat one's way, to phr. [late 19C–1910s] (US) to make one's way by employing illegal means, e.g. cheating, swindling, sponging. [SE beat one's way, to cut a path]

beat-out adj. [mid-19C] exhausted. [BEAT adj.[1]]

beat out v. [late 19C+] (US) to overcome, to beat a rival.

beat out adv. [18C] (US) exhaustedly. [BEAT adj.[1]]

beat pad n. [1950s] (US drugs) a place where drugs are consumed. [SE beat(nik) + PAD n.[2] (2)]

beat pete v. [1980s+] to masturbate. [BEAT OFF + PETER n.[4]]

beat-pounder n. [20C] a policeman.

beat skin/one's skin v. [1940s] (US Black/Harlem) to applaud, to clap.

beats me! excl. [mid-19C+] a general excl. of incomprehension, 'I just can't understand it'. [? poker imagery, the loser, on viewing a better hand, declares '(That) beats me']

beat someone out of v. [mid-19C+] (orig. US) to cheat, to steal from, to defraud. [BEAT v. (1)]

beat someone's jock off see KNOCK SOMEONE'S JOCK OFF.

beat someone's time, to phr. **1** [mid-late 19C] (US) to confuse, to confound. **2** [1940s–50s] (US Black) to cheat or be cheated in a love affair. [BEAT v.[1] (1) + SE time]

beat someone to the punch, to phr. [1960s+] **1** (US Black) to arrive at a destination sooner than another person. **2** to appreciate or understand something faster than another person. [boxing imagery]

beat/slap tar v. [20C] (W.I./Bdos.) to walk around (cf. SLAP THE PAVEMENT). [SE beat + tar, by metonymy the pavement]

beat the bags off, to phr. [1920s–40s] to overcome totally (cf. KNOCK THE SOCKS OFF). [SE beat + BAGS n.[1]]

beat the bald-headed bandit, to phr. [1960s+] to masturbate. [BEAT OFF + BALD-HEADED BANDIT]

beat the band, to phr. [late 19C+] (orig. US) to surpass comprehensively, esp. in excl. that beats the band! that's beyond rival/compare (cf. BEAT ALL; BEAT BOBTAIL; BEAT THE DUTCH).

beat the beaver, to phr. [1970s+] of a woman, to masturbate. [BEAT OFF + BEAVER n.[4] (1)]

beat the bishop, to phr. [1960s+] (orig. US) to masturbate. [var. on BANG THE BISHOP]

beat the bologna, to phr. [20C] to masturbate (cf. ACCOST THE OSCAR MEYER). [BEAT OFF + BALONEY n.[2]]

beat the booby, to phr. [late 18C–early 19C] to beat one's

hands against one's sides to get warm on a cold day (cf. BEAT THE GOOSE; CUFF ANTHONY; CUFF JONAS; TWO THIEVES BEATING A ROGUE). [pun on SE booby, a large, slow-flying bird/booby, a fool]

beat the books, to phr. [1940s+] (US/W.I.) to work very hard (cf. HIT THE BOOKS).

beat the breeze/bull, to phr. [1940s+] (US) to chatter, to gossip (cf. BACK THE BREEZE). [SE beat + BREEZE n./BULL n.[12] (1)]

beat the bricks, to phr. [1920s+] (US) to walk the streets in search of work (cf. BEAT THE ROCKS; HIT THE BRICKS; PRESS THE BRICKS).

beat the bugs, to phr. [mid-19C–1910s] to surpass any contender (cf. BEAT THE DUTCH; BEAT THE JEWS).

beat the bull see BEAT THE BREEZE.

beat the bush, to phr. [16C] (Und.) to ensnare a victim. [hunting jargon beat the bush, to beat the undergrowth to drive out game]

beat the butter, to phr. [1990s] to masturbate. [BEAT OFF + BUTTER n.[2] (1)]

beat the cars, to phr. [19C] (US) to surpass in every way (cf. BEAT ALL). [SE beat + street cars]

beat the cats, to phr. [1900s] to do something outstanding (cf. BEAT BUCK).

beat/flog the daisy, to phr. [1950s+] to masturbate.

beat/scare/thrash the daylights/living daylights out of, to phr. [mid-18C+] to beat severely. [DAYLIGHTS]

beat the dog, to phr. [1930s+] to masturbate (cf. FLOG THE DOG). [SE beat + DOG n.[12]]

beat the Dutch, to phr. [18C] to do something outstanding; thus that beats the Dutch, describing something that is otherwise barely credible.

beat the gong, to phr. [1930s] (drugs) to smoke opium (cf. BANG THE GONG; BOOT THE GONG; KICK THE GONG AROUND phr.[1]). [SE beat + GONG n.[2] (2)]

beat the goose, to phr. [late 19C] to strike one's hands under the armpits to warm them (cf. BEAT THE BOOBY). [the movement supposedly resembles a goose in flight]

beat the gun, to phr. [1940s+] (Aus.) for an engaged woman to have sex with her fiancé and to get pregnant thereby (cf. BEAT THE STARTER). [sporting imagery]

beat the hell out of see BEAT HELL OUT OF.

beat the hoof see BEAT THE HOOF.

beat the hound out of, to phr. [20C] (US) to thrash severely. [SE beat, hit + SE hound, cussedness, stubbornness]

beat the Jews, to phr. [mid-19C–1960s] to surpass any contender (cf. BEAT THE BUGS; BEAT THE DUTCH). [SE beat, surpass + Jews; i.e. the stereotype of Jewish ambition/ deviousness]

beat the lard out of, to phr. [1950s] (Irish) to beat, to thrash.

beat the little/wee wheel, to phr. [1920s–40s] (Irish) to surpass everything (cf. BEAT BANAGHER).

beat the priest, to phr. [20C] (W.I./Gren.) to commit a major crime and act brazenly in acknowledging it without any form of shame or sorrow. [SE beat, defeat + neg. image of clerical hypocrisy]

beat the pup, to phr. [1950s] (US) to masturbate (cf. BEAT ONE'S MEAT). [BEAT OFF + PUPPY n.[2] (2)]

beat the rap, to phr. [1920s+] (US) to be found innocent of a charge in court. [SE beat + RAP n.[3]]

beat the road, to phr. [late 19C] (US) to travel by train without paying. [BEAT v.[1] (1) + (rail)road]

beat the rocks, to phr. [1930s+] (US Black) to walk the streets (cf. BEAT THE BRICKS). [esp. used in the context of walking the streets in search of employment]

beat the sheets, to phr. [1950s] to sleep deeply.

beat the shit out of, to phr. [1950s+] (orig. US) **1** to beat severely (cf. BEAT THE STUFFING OUT OF; BEAT THE TAR OUT OF;

KICK THE SHIT OUT OF). **2** to improve upon, to be superior to. [SE *beat*, hit + SHIT n.¹ (1)]

beat/cheat the starter, to *phr.* [1910s+] to have a child out of wedlock; to become pregnant before the wedding (cf. BEAT THE GUN). [sporting imagery]

beat the stick, to *phr.* [1990s] to masturbate. [BEAT OFF + STICK n.¹]

beat the streets, to *phr.* [19C] to walk around. [20C is SE]

beat the stuffing out of, to *phr.* [late 19C] to beat someone up very badly (cf. BEAT THE SHIT OUT OF; KNOCK THE STUFFING OUT OF).

beat/knock the tar out of, to *phr.* [late 19C+] (US) to beat someone up very badly (cf. BEAT THE SHIT OUT OF; WHALE THE TAR OUT OF).

beat the tracks, to *phr.* [20C] (Aus.) to walk a long way, usu. over rough country. [SE *beat*, hit + *tracks*]

beat the wee wheel *see* BEAT THE LITTLE WHEEL.

beattie and babs *n.* [1930s+] body lice. [rhy. sl. *beattie and bab*(s) = CRAB n.²]

beat to snuff, to *phr.* [early 19C–1900s] to defeat comprehensively. [SE *beat*, defeat + *snuff*, powdered tobacco; thus lit. 'to reduce to powder']

beat to the socks *adv.* [1930s–40s] (US Black) tired out, utterly exhausted. [the image is of a long, fruitless trudge that has worn out one's shoes]

beat-up *adj.* **1** [mid-19C+] (US) exhausted. **2** [1930s+] (US/ W.I.) dilapidated, run down, ageing.

beat up *v.* [20C] (orig. US) to nag, harass.

beat up one's chops/choppers/gums *see* BEAT ONE'S CHOPS.

beat up/beat up the quarters of, to *phr.* [late 19C] (society) to call upon unceremoniously (cf. STIR UP). [BEAT UP + SE *quarters*, dwelling-place, home; SE use is to arouse, disturb]

beat vials *n.* [1980s+] (drugs) vials containing sham crack cocaine to cheat buyers. [BEAT adj.³ + SE *vials*]

beat with an ugly stick *phr.*¹ [1960s–70s] (US) to be unattractive; often as a supposed reason for one's lack of good looks, *he was beat with an ugly stick* (cf. SLAPPED WITH AN UGLY STICK).

beat with an ugly stick, to *phr.*² [1980s+] (US campus) of a man, to have sexual intercourse with.

beau *n.* [1980s+] (US campus) **1** a stupid or clumsy person. **2** a boyfriend (cf. BEAUHUNK). [SE *beau*, a suitor, a sweetheart]

beau-catcher *n.* [mid-19C–1920s] a lock of hair equivalent to the modern *kiss-curl* (cf. AGGERAWATOR). [SE *beau* + *catcher*; such a lock was calculated to ensnare young men. The term did not survive the 19C in the UK but lasted until the 1920s or beyond in the US. 'In olden times this was called a *lovelock*, when it was the mark at which all the Puritan and ranting preachers levelled their pulpit pop-guns, loaded with sharp and virulent abuse' (Hotten, 1867)]

beaucoup/beaucoups *n.* [1910s+] (US) a large quantity of; very much. [Fr. *beaucoup*, many]

beaucoup/beaucoups *adj.* [1920s] (US) excellent, first-rate. [BEAUCOUP n.]

beaucoup *adv.* [1910s+] (US) very (much). [despite this early origin, the term was properly popularized during the Vietnam War, when it was picked up by GIs as part of the recently used French/Vietnamese pidgin and usu. pron. 'boo-coo']

beau-dollar *n.* [20C] (US Black) a silver dollar. [SE *beau*, a dandy, the presumption being that the dandy carried a good supply of such coins. Other suggestions incl. abbr. HOBO n.¹ or SE *boat* or *boar* (the hog seen as desirable commodity), corruption of SE *Boer* (a supposed lucky piece carried by British soldiers during the Boer Wars (1880–1, 1899–1902)]

beauhunk *n.* [1980s+] (US campus) **1** a boyfriend (cf. BEAU). **2** a sexy-looking boy. [BEAU + HUNK n.¹ (5) + pun on derog. BOHUNK]

beau-nasty *n.* [late 18C] a well-dressed, but ill-kempt and grubby dandy (cf. DIRTY BEAU). [SE *beau* + *nasty*]

beaut *n.* (orig. US) **1** [mid-19C+] a beautiful person or thing. **2** [late 19C+] a splendid example of a type (human or not). **3** [mid-19C+] ironic uses of **1** and **2**. [abbr. SE; coined in US, but most common use is Aus.]

beaut! *excl.* [late 19C+] (Aus./N.Z.) all-purpose Aus. term of approbation, can equally well be used as adj.; also as *beauty!* (pron. bewdy), *you beaut!* [abbr.]

beautiful *adj.* [mid-19C+] (orig. US) **1** clever, shrewd. **2** pleasing, admirable. **3** happy, satisfied.

beautiful boulders *n.* [1980s+] (drugs) crack cocaine. [ROCKS n.⁴]

beautiful pair of brown eyes *n.* [1940s–60s] attractive female breasts. [heavy-handed euph.]

beau-trap *n.* [17C–early 19C] **1** a confidence trickster, esp. a card-sharp. **2** a badly laid paving stone that traps water beneath it and, when it is stepped on, squirts that water onto the dandy's finery.

beauty *n.*¹ [early 19C+] an admirable person.

beauty *n.*² [19C] the vagina (cf. BEAUTY SPOT n.¹). [one of the relatively congratulatory terms]

beauty *n.*³ [1960s] Biphetamine, a strong amphetamine (cf. A n.²). [abbr. BLACK BEAUTY]

beauty! *excl.* [1940s+] (Aus.) thank-you. [abbr. SE *that's beautiful*]

beauty mark/spot *n.* [mid-19C] (US) one's face.

beauty spot *n.*¹ [19C] the vagina, one of a number of terms linking the female genital area with nature (cf. BEAUTY n.²; BELLE-CHOSE; BELLY DALE; BOSKAGE OF VENUS; BOWER OF BLISS; BUSHY PARK n.¹; DAISY n.¹; EVERGREENS; FLOWER OF CHIVALRY; FLOWERPOT; FRUITFUL VINE; GARDEN n.¹; GARDEN OF EDEN; GARDEN OF PLEASURE; GENTLEMAN'S PLEASURE-GARDEN; GOOSEBERRY BUSH n.¹; MIRACULOUS CAIRN; MOSS ROSE; MOUNT PLEASANT; NATURE'S TREASURY; NATURE'S TUFTED TREASURE; NETTLE BED; PARSLEY BED; ROSE n.¹; SHADY SPRING; TEAZLE]

beauty spot *n.*² *see* BEAUTY MARK.

beav *n.* [1980s+] (US campus) name that indicates that the referent is acting like a little brother. [US TV show *Leave It To Beaver*]

beaver *n.*¹ [19C] (US) money. [use of beaver pelts as a mode of exchange]

beaver *n.*² [late 19C+] **1** a beard. **2** a bearded man. [SE; thus the early 20C street game in which children would compete to be the first to spot a bearded man and signify their success by shouting *Beaver!*]

beaver *n.*³ [late 19C] a hat of any sort. [abbr. SE *beaver hat*]

beaver *n.*⁴ (orig. US) **1** [1920s+] the female pubic hair, the vagina, esp. in commercial pornography use; thus *beaver book*, a pornographic book, *beaver film*, a pornographic film etc. (cf. BADGER n.⁷). **2** [1960s+] a woman. [the supposed similarity between the beaver's coat and the pubic hair]

beaver cleaver *n.* [1990s] the penis (cf. ARSE-OPENER). [BEAVER n.⁴ + SE *cleaver*]

beaver patrol *n.*¹ [1960s+] a group of young men looking for suitable female company. [BEAVER n.⁴ + SE *patrol*]

beaver patrol *n.*² [1970s] a group or team of enthusiastic (young) workers. [EAGER BEAVER]

beaver shot *n.* [1960s+] **1** a close-up photograph of, or camera-angle on, the female genitals; used in commercial pornography. **2** a chance glimpse (by a man) of the same area (cf. SHOOT THE BEAVER). [BEAVER n.⁴ + SE *shot*]

beaver-tail *n.* [mid-19C] a hairstyle, popular *c.*1860–70, whereby middle-class women wore their hair in a net, which then fell onto their shoulders. [the similarity of 'the shape of the netted hair to a beaver's flat and comparatively shapeless tail']

beavertail *n.* [1970s+] (US) a cosh, a sap. [the similarity in shape]

be a wall-prop *see* MAKE WALLPAPER.

beazel *n.* [1930s+] a young woman. [? SE *besom*]

beazle *n.* [1930s] (US campus) an unappealing person. [? 16C SE *beazler*, a drunkard, a sot]

bebe *n.* [1980s+] (drugs) crack cocaine. [ety. unknown]

bebee/beebee *n.* **1** [mid-19C] a woman, a lady. **2** [late 19C] a female bed-mate. [Hind. *bibi*, a lady]

be-blowed! *excl.* [mid-19C] a general excl. of surprise, annoyance etc, i.e. I'll be damned. [euph.]

bebop *v.* **1** [1960s] to fight, esp. as one of a street gang; thus *bebopping*, a juvenile delinquent. **2** [1970s+] to walk in an arrogant, 'cocky' manner. [BOP v. (3), (4)]

bebop glasses *n.* [1940s] (US Black) a then fashionable style of dark glasses, with notably thick frames as well as blackened lenses. [SE *bebop*, the style of jazz played in 1940s by such musicians as Charlie Parker, Kenny Clarke and Bud Powell, as well as Dizzy Gillespie; the glasses were popularized by the jazz stars of the 1940s, esp. Gillespie]

bebopper *n.* **1** [1960s] (US) a juvenile delinquent. **2** [1980s+] (US Black) an inexperienced, naïve and on those grounds unpopular person. [the SE *bebop* jazz craze, new and sophisticated in 1940s, but archaic by 1980s]

becall *v.* [late 19C] to reprimand, to scold, to slander. [13C–14C SE *becall*, to accuse, to challenge]

beck *n.* [mid-16C] a constable (cf. HARMAN). [abbr. HARMAN-BECK]

becket *n.* [19C] (US) pocket. [naut. jargon *becket*, a loop of rope with a knot on one end and eye at the other, used to secure various pieces of tackle]

becks *n.* [1980s+] well-off, middle-class Jewish teenagers and young people, usu. from North London (cf. BEXANDERS). [*Becks* beer, their supposedly favoured drink]

becky *n.* [19C] (US) a firearm, esp. a shotgun (cf. BETSY). [joc. abbr. of proper name *Rebecca*]

bed *n.* [1940s+] sexual intercourse (cf. SLEEP WITH). [metonymy]

bed *v.* [1940s+] to seduce, to have sexual intercourse with. [abbr. SE *take to bed*]

bedad! *excl.* [early 18C+] (Irish) by God! (cf. ADAD!; BY GOLLY!; BY GORRAM!; BY GORRY!; BY GOSH!; BY GRABS!; BY GRAVY!; BY GUM!). [SE *by* + DAD n.¹]

bed and breakfast *n.* [20C] (bingo) the number 26 [2s 6d (12½p), at one time the going rate for a B & B establishment]

bed/bedroom athlete *n.* [1940s+] (orig. US) a promiscuous person.

bedbait *n.* [1930s+] (US) an underage sexual partner, who can be of either sex although most often a teenage girl (cf. JAILBAIT n.¹).

bedbug *n.*¹ [1920s–30s] (US Black) a Black Pullman porter. [SE *bedbug*; among their other duties the porters turned back beds for their (mainly White) passengers]

bedbug *n.*² [1920s–30s] (US Black) an unpleasant person. [identification]

bedbug alley/row *n.* [20C] (US) the poorest area of a town. [the supposed infestation of *bedbugs*]

bedbugs *n.* [1920s+] (drugs) fellow addicts. [BEDBUG n.²]

bedder *n.* [late 19C–1900s] a bedroom. [SE *bed* + 'Oxford' sfx. *-er*]

beddy *n.* [1980s+] (US campus) an attractive, sexually available young woman. [SE *bed* + sfx. *-y*; but cf. BETTY n.⁴]

bed-faggot/-fagot *n.* [mid-19C] a prostitute. [SE *bed* + FAGGOT n.² (1)]

bed-fellow *n.* [19C] the vagina. [pun]

Bedfordshire *n.* [late 18C+] bed; thus *go up the wooden hill to Bedfordshire*, to go to bed.

bedhop *v.* [1960s+] to live a sexually promiscuous life.

bed-house *n.* **1** [19C] (US) a 'short-time' hotel. **2** [1920s–30s] (US Black) a brothel (cf. ACCOMMODATION HOUSE). [SE *bed* + HOUSE n.¹]

bedide! *excl.* [19C] euph. by God (cf. ADAD!; BEDAD!).

Bedlam beggar *n.* [16C–early 19C] a genuine beggar (cf. ABRAHAM-COVE; TOM OF BEDLAM).

bedonderd/bedonnerd *adj.* [1960s+] (S.Afr.) crazy. [Du. *bedonderd*, mad]

bedoozle *v.* [mid–late 19C] (US) to confuse; thus *bedoozling*, astounding, amazing. [? SE *bedazzle* + BAMBOOZLE]

bed-presser *n.* [19C] **1** a prostitute. **2** a dull and heavy man.

bedroom athlete *see* BED ATHLETE.

bedroom eyes *n.* [1950s+] a look in the eyes that invites the person on whom it is focused towards seduction.

bed-sit/-sitter *n.* [late 19C+] a *bed-sitting* room. [abbr.]

bedstead relation *n.* [20C] (US) in-laws, relations by marriage. [SE *bedstead*, occupied by the married couple]

bed-worthy *adj.* [1930s+] sexually alluring, attractive; thus *bed-worthiness*, the quality of being sexually attractive.

bee *n.*¹ **1** [1900s–20s] (US) ambition. **2** [1950s–60s] drug addiction. **3** [1950s–60s] (US Black) an idea. [the image is of 'stinging', in (2) with pain, in (1) and (3) as a jolt of inspiration; but for (3) note phr. *bee in one's bonnet*]

bee *n.*² [1980s+] (US) a frisbee. [abbr.]

Beeb *n.* [1960s+] the British Broadcasting Corporation (BBC). [pron. of BB(C)]

Beecham's *n.* [late 19C+] the testicles. [*Beecham's* PILLS n.³, the popular UK medicine]

Beecham's pill *n.* **1** [1920s+] a bill. **2** [1930s] in pl. any form of sign (i.e. a handbill) denoting one's qualifications for begging ('blind', 'ex-soldier' etc). **3** [1950s+] a still (photograph). **4** [1950s+] (Aus.) a fool, a simpleton. [rhy. sl.; (4) *Beecham's Pill* = DILL]

beef *n.*¹ **1** [late 18C+] human flesh. **2** [late 18C+] the vagina (cf. BACON SANDWICH). **3** [early 19C+] (mainly US Black in 20C) the penis (cf. BACON n.¹). **4** [mid-19C+] (orig. US) physical strength, power, muscles. **5** [late 19C] used in Clare Market to describe cat's meat. **6** [20C] (W.I./Jam.) a sexually appealing woman. **7** [1990s] (US) a well-built male; used by both heterosexuals and homosexuals (cf. BEEFCAKE).

beef *n.*² **1** [late 19C+] (US) a complaint, a problem, an altercation; thus *what's one's/the beef*, what's one's/the problem? **2** [late 19C–1910s] (US campus) a mistake; thus *make a beef*, to err, to blunder. **3** [1920s+] (US) a criminal charge, a court case, usu. as defendant. **4** [1930s] (US) a (hotel or restaurant) bill. [BEEF v.¹]

beef *n.*³ [1940s–50s] (US) liquor. [? BEEF n.¹ (4)]

beef *v.*¹ **1** [early–mid-19C] to raise a hue and cry. **2** [mid-19C+] (US) to talk loudly (esp. to no real purpose), to complain. **3** [late 19C] (orig. theatrical) to shout. **4** [1900s] (US) to bully. **5** [1900s] (US) to waste time. **6** [1900s] (US) to blunder, to make a mistake. **7** [1950s] (US) to argue. [CRY BEEF]

beef *v.*² **1** [late 19C+] to engage in sexual intercourse. **2** [1900s–50s] (orig. US) to knock (someone) down. [agricultural jargon *beef*, to slaughter an ox]

beef-a-roni *n.* [1990s] (US campus) a sexy male. [play on BEEFCAKE + popular US fast-food]

beef-bag *n.* [mid-19C–1930s] (Aus.) a shirt. [BEEF n.¹ (1) + SE *bag*]

beef bayonet *n.* [1960s+] the penis (cf. BACON BAZOOKA; BAYONET). [play on SE, but note BEEF n.¹ (3)]

beef-brain *n.* [18C] a fool; thus *beef-brained*, foolish, stupid (cf. BAKEBRAIN; BEEF-HEAD; MEATBRAIN; MEATHEAD; MUTTON-HEAD; SHEEP'S HEAD). [SE *beef* + sfx. *-brain*]

beefcake *n.* (orig. US) **1** [1940s+] a male pin-up. **2** [1980s+] any attractive, muscular man. [on model of CHEESECAKE n.¹]

beef curtains n. [1990s] (US) an offensive term for the female genitals. [BEEF n.[1] (2) + SE *curtains*]

beefeater n.[1] [20C] (US) an Englishman or woman. [SE *beefeater*, a Yeoman of the Guard, one of London's tourist icons]

beefeater n.[2] [20C] (US) a cattle rustler or poacher. [his 'appetite' for cattle]

beefer n.[1] [late 19C–1930s] (US) a whinger, a complainer. [BEEF v.[1] (2)]

beefer/beef eye n.[2] [20C] a black eye (cf. BEEFSTEAK EYE). [the placing of raw beef on the wounded eye]

beef gravy n. [1980s+] (US gay) semen (cf. BABY GRAVY). [BEEF n.[1] + GRAVY n.[1]]

beef-head n. 1 [late 18C–early 19C; mid-19C+ in US] a fool, a simpleton; thus *beef-headed*, stupid, foolish (cf. BEEF-BRAIN). 2 [19C] (US) a Texan, a cowboy. [BEEF n.[2] (2) + sfx. -HEAD (1)]

beef-heart n. [late 19C] 1 a bean. 2 a fart. [loose rhy. sl.; (1) presumes the effect; the true rhy. is (2)]

beef injection/hot beef injection n. [1980s+] (US campus) sexual intercourse, sometimes *hot beef incision*; thus *slip one the hot beef*, to have sexual intercourse from the male point of view (cf. ACHING FOR A SIDE OF BEEF; HOT MEAT INJECTION). [BEEF n.[1]]

beef it v. [19C] to eat heartily. [SE *beef*, as symbol of the ultimate in consumption]

beef it out v. [1900s–10s] (Aus.) to sing loudly and enthusiastically (cf. BELT v.[2]). [BEEF v.[2] (2)]

beefsteak eye n. [20C] (US) a black eye (cf. BEEFER n.[2]). [the practice of putting raw steak on a black eye]

beef-stroke-it-off, to phr. [1990s] to masturbate (cf. ACCOST THE OSCAR MEYER). [BEEF n.[1] + pun on SE *beef Stroganoff*]

beef to the heel/heels phr. [mid-19C+] 1 bulky, brawny, stocky, esp. of thick, strong legs. 2 of a woman's ankles, thick, inelegant. [BEEF n.[1] (1)]

beef trust n. [1940s+] (US) an obese person, a group of obese people. [ironic use of SE *beef trust*, a conglomerate of beef producers/processors; orig. late 19C carnival use, created by showman W.B. 'Billy' Watson, who thus named his sideshow of grotesquely overweight women]

beef-tugging n. [late 19C–1900s] (city) eating at City cafés and restaurants. [SE; the indigestibility of the tough meat served there]

beef up v. [1940s+] to strengthen, to improve. [i.e. to add SE *beef* or BEEF n.[1] (4)]

beef-witted adj. [early 17C] stupid, simple. [BEEF n.[1] (1) + sfx. -witted; used by Shakespeare in 1606, the term resurfaced briefly in late 19C, describing 'this British bull-neckedness, this British beef-wittedness']

beefy adj.[1] [mid-19C+] 1 well-built, muscled, stolid. 2 thick, usu. of a woman's ankles or wrists. 3 fleshy, overweight. 4 lucky. [BEEF n.[1] (1) + sfx. -y]

beefy adj.[2] [1990s] used to describe somebody with an obvious under-arm odorous problem. [BEEF n.[1] (1); the implication of 'animal' odours]

bee-gum n. [19C] (US) 1 a top hat (cf. BEAVER n.[3]). 2 a hairstyle in which a woman piles her hair on the top of her head. [Southern dial. *bee-gum*, a hollow tree or log used as a beehive]

bee-gum hat n. [late 19C] (US) a tall hat. [for ety. see BEE-GUM]

beehive n.[1] [19C] the vagina (cf. HIVE; HONEYPOT n.[1]). [the implication is of honey rather than stings]

beehive n.[2] [1920s+] the number 5. [rhy. sl.]

beek n. [1990s] cocaine. [BEAK n. (2)]

beel n. [1950s+] (W.I./USVI) a motorcar. [abbr. SE *automobile*]

bee-luther-hatchee n. [1920s–40s] (US Black) the ultimate in far-away, unpleasant places (cf. B. LUTHER HATCHETT; BELUTHAHATCHIE; DOO-WAH-DIDDY; GINNY GALL; NAR NAR GOON; WEST HELL; ZAR].

beemer n. [1980s+] a BMW motorcar (cf. BEAMER n.[3]).

beemers n. [1980s+] (drugs) crack cocaine (cf. BEAMER n.[2]).

been and gone and done it phr. [late 19C+] mocking response to a confession of some minor error or peccadillo; usu. as *now you've been and gone ... .*

been in the sun phr. [late 18C–late 19C] drunk. [? the red face of drunkenness and sunburn]

been there phr. 1 [mid-19C+] (orig. US) dismissive phr. used to imply that one has already experienced the so-called 'novelty' of which another person is speaking (cf. BEEN THERE, DONE THAT). 2 [late 19C+] a remark passed by a man on seeing a passing woman with whom (he claims) he has slept.

been there before phr. [late 19C+] to have had previous experience of an activity.

been there, done that phr. [1990s] used to summarize the assumed youthful ennui of the 1990s; voiced when offered some new stimulus and often appended by the phr. *got the T-shirt*. [the phr. was adopted in soft-drink advertising of the mid-1990s; the ref. to *T-shirt* underpins the marketing that accompanies any new cultural phenomenon, especially mass popular films]

been to see Captain Bates? phr. [late 19C] a greeting to a person one knows or suspects to have been in prison. [proper name of *Captain Bates*, a well-known London prison governor]

been to three county fairs and a goat-fucking/-roping phr. [1970s+] (US, mainly South) phr. implying one's astonishment (one has had many, varied experiences, but never one such as this) (cf. GOAT-FUCK).

beer v. 1 [late 18C+] to get drunk on beer. 2 [1980s+] to give someone a beer, usu. in imper. *beer me!* [mid-19C+ use is Aus.]

beerage n. [late 19C+] 1 the great brewing families of Britain, esp. those, e.g. Guinnesses, Youngers, who have been ennobled (cf. BEEROCRACY). 2 (on a ship) steerage (the lowest class). [SE *beer* + *peerage/steerage*. (2) implies the staple drink of the poor traveller]

beer barn see BOOZE BARN.

beer barrel n. 1 [19C] the stomach. 2 [19C] the body as a whole. 3 [1930s] (orig. US) a (beer-drinker's) paunch (cf. BEER GUT; BEER MUSCLE; BOOZE BALLOON; BOOZE BELLY). 4 [1940s] a beer drunkard (cf. ALECAN).

beer bong n. [1990s] (US campus) a device consisting of a funnel attached to a tube, which facilitates the speedier drinking of beer; thus *do a beer bong*, drink beer through such a device. [SE *beer* + BONG n. (2)]

beer-boep see BOEP.

beer-bottle n. [late 19C–1900s] a stout, red-faced man. [metonymy]

beer bottle beat n. [1970s] (US) a client who likes to be beaten by a prostitute who is wielding a beer bottle.

beer bust n. [1960s] (US) a drinking party that concentrates on beer. [SE *beer* + BUST n.[3]]

beer-buzzer n. [late 19C] (US) one who frequents saloons in the hope of cadging free beer. [SE *beer* + BUZZ v.[1]]

beer-chewer n. [late 19C+] (Aus.) a heavy drinker of beer; also *beer-guzzler*, *beer-sparrer*, *beersucker*.

Beer City/Town n. [1970s] (US) Milwaukee, Wisconsin. [famous for its breweries]

beer-crawl n. [1900s] a leisurely progress from public house to public house, drinking one or more beers in each (cf. GIN-CRAWL; PUB-CRAWL).

beer-eater n. [late 19C–1900s] a heavy drinker. [note P.G. Wodehouse: 'It was my uncle George who discovered that alcohol was a food well in advance of modern medical thought' (*The Inimitable Jeeves*, 1923)]

beered up *adj.* [1930s+] (US) drunk on beer (cf. ALED UP).

beer goggle *v.* [1980s+] (US campus) to find someone attractive because of the influence of alcohol. [SE *beer* + GOGGLE v.]

beer goggles *n.* [1980s+] (US campus) blurred vision that follows an excess of (beer) drinking; such vision has the added effect of making hitherto unexciting individuals appear sexually alluring.

beer gut *n.* [1950s+] a paunch, a beer belly (cf. BEER BARREL).

beerhead *n.* (US) **1** [1940s] a German. **2** [1970s] a beer drunkard. [SE *beer* + sfx. -HEAD (2)]

beer-jerker *n.*[1] [mid–late 19C] (US) a drunkard.

beer-jerker/-slinger/-yanker *n.*[2] [late 19C] a bartender who draws beer in a saloon. [SE *beer* + *jerk*/SLING v.[3]/YANK v.[1]]

beer joint *n.* [mid-19C+] (US) a saloon or bar serving primarily beer (cf. ALKY JOINT). [SE *beer* + JOINT n.[3] (3)]

beer-jugger *n.* [late 19C–1900s] (US) a barmaid.

beer keg *see* KEG n.[1].

beer mill *n.* [late 19C] a saloon that sells beer. [on pattern of GIN-MILL]

beer muscle *n.* [1930s–40s] (US) a pot belly, engendered by excessive beer-drinking (cf. BEER BARREL). [the 'muscle' is in fact fat]

beer-o! *excl.* [mid–late 19C] a cry raised by workers when one of their number commits a blunder that has to be paid for by buying their fellows a round of drink. [SE *beer* + sfx. -O]

beerocracy *n.* [late 19C] the world of brewers and publicans (cf. BEERAGE). [SE *beer* + *aristocracy*]

beer-off *n.* [1930s–50s] an off-licence, a liquor store.

beer pot *n.* [1980s+] a fat stomach caused by a steady intake of beer (cf. BEER GUT). [SE *beer* + POT n.[7]]

beerskin *n.* [1990s] (Aus.) a drunkard. [? pun on *bearskin*/HAVE A SKINFUL]

beer-slinger *n.*[1] [mid–late 19C] a regular beer-drinker. [they 'sling it down']

beer-slinger *n.*[2] *see* BEER JERKER n.[2].

beer's talking *phr.* [20C] a phr. used to excuse a belch or a social error committed through drunkenness (cf. IT'S THE BEER TALKING).

beer street *n.* [mid-19C] the mouth or throat (cf. GIN LANE). [fig. street name; note William Hogarth's celebrated engraving of 1751]

Beer Town *see* BEER CITY.

beer-trap *n.* [late 19C–1930s] the mouth. [SE *beer* + TRAP n.[3]]

beer-up *n.* [1910s+] (Aus.) a riotous, drunken party. [on model of PISS-UP]

beery *adj.* [mid-19C+] drunk, tipsy (cf. ALED UP).

beer-yanker *n. see* BEER JERKER n.[2].

beery buff *n.* [20C] a fool. [rhy. sl. *beery buff* = MUFF n.[2] (1)]

bees *n.* [late 19C+] money. [rhy. sl. BEES AND HONEY]

bees and honey *n.* [late 19C+] money (cf. POT OF HONEY). [rhy. sl.]

bee's knees/nuts *n.* [1920s+; 1970s] (orig. US) **1** the best. **2** a superior person, or someone who poses as such (cf. ANT'S PANTS). [created by the US columnist T.A. 'Tad' Dorgan (1877–1929)]

bees swarm *phr.* [20C] (US) a child is born. [this runs counter to the usual superstition that swarming bees symbolize an imminent death]

bee-stings *n.* [1950s+] (orig. US) small female breasts. [supposedly comparable size]

beeswax *n.* [mid-19C] **1** second-rate, soft cheese. **2** a bore, usu. as *old beeswax*. [(1) is 'full of holes'; (2) puns on SE *bore*, a hole]

bees wingers *n.* [1960s+] the fingers. [rhy. sl.]

beetle *n.*[1] [1910s–60s] (US) an eccentric, a madman, an obsessive fan. [BUG n.[4]]

beetle *n.*[2] [1930s–60s] a young woman, esp. one who dresses in flashy clothes. [ety. unknown; ? she 'beetles' around]

beetle bonnet *n.* [1990s] the female pubic mound, especially when shaven. [supposed resemblance to a beetle's smooth back]

beetle-brain *n.* [17C] a fool (cf. BAKEBRAIN; BEETLE-HEAD). [SE *beetle*, an instrument used in various industrial applications to drive, wedge, flatten or ram, used in combs. to imply dullness, heaviness or stupidity + sfx. -*brain*]

beetle-case *n.* [mid–late 19C] a large boot or shoe (cf. BEETLE-CRUSHER).

beetle-crusher *n.* [mid-19C+] **1** the foot. **2** a shoe, esp. a large, heavy boot, often as worn by policemen, labourers or the army (cf. ANT-KILLER; BEETLE-SQUASHER).

beetle-head *n.* [16C–late 18C; 1940s–50s] a fool; *beetle-headed*, stupid (cf. BEETLE-BRAIN). [SE *beetle* + sfx. -HEAD (1); 20C use is US]

beetle off *v.* [1920s+] (orig. RAF) to leave, to wander off. [the orig. image was of flying directly (as a beetle flies) back to base]

beetle's blood *n.* [1920s–30s] (Anglo-Irish) stout beer. [the *beetle*, like the beer, is black]

beetle's bonnet *see* HERBIE'S BONNET.

beetle-squasher *n.* [mid-19C] **1** the foot. **2** a shoe (cf. BEETLE-CRUSHER).

beetle-sticker *n.* [mid-19C] an entomologist. [the mounting of specimens]

beetroot mug *n.* [late 19C–1910s] a red face. [? coined by Charles Ross, creator, *c.*1867, of the comic character Ally Sloper, a dissipated looking old man with a red and swollen nose. Possibly the orig. of SE phr. *red as a beetroot*]

beevos *n.* [1970s] (US campus) beer. [BEVVY n.]

beeza/beezer *n.* [1920s+] a Birmingham Small Arms (BSA) motorcycle (cf. BEAMER n.[3]). [pron.]

beeze *n.* [1940s] the penis. [ety. unknown; ? obs. SE *bezel*, a cutting tool]]

beezer *n.*[1] (orig. US) **1** [20C] (orig. boxing) the nose. **2** [1910s+] the head.

beezer *n.*[2] *see* BEEZA.

beezer *n.*[3] [1920s–40s] (mainly juv.) a 'fellow', a 'chap'. [? BUGGER n.[1] + GEEZER n.[1]]

beezer *adj.* [1930s] very attractive, excellent. [? PIZZAZZ]

bef *adj.* [1940s+] (W.I.) stupid, useless. [? Scot. *beff*, a fool, a stupid person]

befok *adj.* [1970s+] (S.Afr.) **1** of people, unhappy, lacking in good sense, crazy, exhausted. **2** of objects, ruined, spoiled, out of order. [Afk. *befok*, FUCKED]

before Abe *n.* [1940s] (US Black/Harlem) the era of slavery; the period before Emancipation. [for Afro-Americans any time before 1 January 1863, when President *Abraham Lincoln* signed the Emancipation Proclamation]

before Abe jive *n.* [1940s] (US Black/Harlem) hard, thankless work. [BEFORE ABE + JIVE n.[1] (1)]

before day creep *n.* [1920s–40s] (US Black) a surreptitious late-night or early morning visit to one's lover. [SE *before day*(*break*) + CREEP v. (4)]

beforehand with the world *phr.* [mid-16C–18C] having money in reserve. [SE *beforehand*, anticipating paying in advance]

before one can/could say Jack Robinson *phr.* [19C] instantly, at once, very quickly. [there is no specific *Jack Robinson*; perhaps it was a minor tongue-twister]

before/while one can/would say knife *phr.* [late 19C+] very quickly, suddenly. [*knife* being a very short word]

before this/my spit dry *phr.* [20C] (W.I./Guyn.) very quickly, as soon as possible; other forms include *before fowl-cock put on his trousers/pants*, *before bird-wife wake*, *before the cat (can) lick its ear*.

before you can say parsnips *phr.* [early 19C] very fast.

begad! *excl.* [mid-18C–mid-19C] a mild, if once blasphemous oath, by God! (cf. ADAD!).

begar! *excl.* [mid-18C] a mild oath (cf. ADAD!).

begarra! see BEGORRA!

Begats, the *n.* [mid-19C+] the Book of Genesis. [the constant use of the phr. *X begat Y*]

beg/chase/get/look for a piece, to *phr.* [20C] (W.I.) to pursue a woman for sex. [SE *beg* etc + PIECE *n.*[1]]

beggar *n.*[1] [mid-19C] a man, a person, used both neg., *a nasty-looking beggar*, and pos. or affectionately, *you're a funny beggar*.

beggar/beggar for *n.*[2] [mid-19C+] an enthusiast, one who is keen on, e.g. *a beggar for work*, *a beggar to argue*. [they lit. *beg for* the subject]

beggar boy's *n.* [late 19C–1930s] a bottle of Bass ale. [rhy. sl. BEGGAR BOY'S ASS = Bass]

beggar boy's ass *n.* [late 19C–1930s] Bass ale. [note this is the UK SE *ass*, donkey, not the US sl. ASS; *see* ARSE *n.*[1]]

beggared *adj.* [late 19C+] euph. for BUGGERED; thus *I'll be beggared if ...* .

beggar for see BEGGAR *n.*[2].

beggar-maker *n.* [late 18C] a publican. [their depriving people of money]

beggar my neighbour *phr.* [1920s+] visiting the labour exchange/unemployment office to draw unemployment benefit. [rhy. sl. *beggar my neighbour* = *on the labour*]

beggars *n.* [19C–1900s] in card-playing, the lower cards, marked 2–10. [they are inferior to the 'court' cards]

beggar's benison *n.* [late 18C] a popular toast, 'may your prick and your purse never fail you' (Grose, 1796) (cf. CABMAN'S FAREWELL; SAILOR'S FAREWELL; SOLDIER'S FAREWELL). [SE *beggar* + *benison*, blessing]

beggar's bolts *n.* [late 16C] stones (cf. BEGGAR'S BULLETS). [SE *beggar* + *bolt*, an arrow; thus a projectile]

beggar's bullets *n.* [late 18C] stones (cf. BEGGAR'S BOLTS). [poverty deprives the beggar of an actual weapon]

beggar's lagging *n.* [1940s–50s] (prison) a sentence of 90 days imprisonment, commonly that meted out for vagrancy (cf. TRAMP'S LAGGING). [SE *beggar* + LAGGING]

beggar's plush *n.* [late 17C–early 18C] corduroy, cotton velvet. [SE *beggar* + *plush*, a kind of cloth having a nap longer and softer than that of velvet; used for rich garments, e.g. footmen's liveries]

beggar's velvet *n.* [mid-19C] particles of lint and similar household dirt that gather behind or beneath sofas, tables or beds (often following the shaking of an eiderdown).

beggar-trash *n.* [20C] (US) of people, worthless, low-class, inferior. [SE *beggar* + TRASH *n.*[2]]

begging for it *adv.* [1950s+] a male comment on a woman who, supposedly if not actually, is inflamed with lust (cf. GAGGING FOR IT). [SE *beg* + *it*, but note IT *n.*[1]]

begin on/upon *v.* [early–mid-19C] (orig. US) to attack verbally (cf. START ON).

be good!/if you can't be good, be careful! *phr.* [20C] joc. phr. used on parting; sometimes ext. by *if you can't be careful, buy a pram.*

begorra!/begarra! *excl.* [early 19C+] by God! the clichéd expletive of each and every stage Irishman yet created (cf. BEJABERS!).

begum *n.* [mid-19C–1900s] (Anglo-Ind.) a rich widow. [Urdu *begam*, a queen, princess, or lady of high rank]

beg your pardon *n.* [late 19C] a garden. [rhy. sl.]

behani ghani see BHANI GHANI.

behave local *v.* [20C] (W.I.) to act in a crude, unsophisticated manner. [SE *behave* + *local*, rough, of inferior quality]

behavish *adj.* [1980s+] (US Black) badly behaved. [SE *behave* + sfx. *-ish*, of the nature or character of]

beheaventers!/be hivinders!/be hivins! *excl.* [1920s+] (Irish) a mild oath, lit. 'by heaven!'

behind *n.*[1] [late 18C+] the buttocks, the posterior.

behind *n.*[2] [1950s+] (Black) the cause of something.

behind *adv.* (orig. US) **1** [1960s+] involved with, concerned about, believing in. **2** [1960s+] in full understanding of (cf. HIP *adj.*). **3** [1960s+] (Black) as a result of, as a consequence of, in reference to. **4** [1970s] excited by, obsessed with.

behind a dime *phr.* [1980s+] (US) to any extent, under any circumstances, usu. in phr. *I wouldn't trust (one) behind a dime.* [SAmE *dime*, the tiny 10-cent coin; i.e. there is no way such a person can 'hide']

behindativeness *n.* [late 19C] a large dress-pannier, fashionably affixed to a lady's dress *c.*1888. [SE *behind*/BEHIND *n.*[1] + sfx. *-ative*, tending to point out]

behind God's back *phr.* [1960s+] (W.I.) in a very far-off, inaccessible rural area, very far away (cf. BEHIND THE BANANAS; BEYOND THE RABBIT-PROOF FENCE).

behind like a slave-driver/tak-tak, to be *phr.* [20C] (W.I.) to beg, to harass, to pressurize. [the *tak-tak* or *acoushi* ant, a fierce pest]

behind of God Speed see BACK OF GOD SPEED.

behind one's door *adv.* [1950s+] (prison) locked up in solitary confinement.

behind oneself *adv.* [late 19C] out of date, out of fashion, not up with the latest situation. [SE *behind*, backward]

behind the bananas *phr.* [20C] (W.I.) very far away, deep in the countryside (cf. BEHIND GOD'S BACK). [note Trin. use *behind the bridge*, in the back streets or slums; the ref. is to the slum area of Port-of-Spain at the back of the East Dry River]

behind the behind *n.* [1930s] sodomy. [SE *behind* + BEHIND *n.*[1]]

behind/not behind the door when ... *phr.* [19C] a phr. implying that one is (or is not) endowed with a given characteristic, often a physical attribute, e.g. *you weren't behind the door when noses were handed out*, you have a big nose.

behind the eight ball *phr.* [1930s+] (orig. US) in trouble, in a difficult situation (cf. SNOOKERED). [pool imagery]

behind the lighter *phr.* [19C] late, behind (cf. ASTERN THE LIGHTER).

behind the scales *phr.* [1980s+] (US Black) a drug seller's place of business. [drugs are bought in bulk then weighed out in smaller measures for sale; the image is of a small shopkeeper behind the counter]

behind the walls *adj.* [20C] in prison (cf. OVER THE WALL).

be hivinders!/hivins! see BEHEAVENTERS!

beige *n.* [1930s–40s] (US Black) a light-skinned Black person (cf. YELLOW *adj.*[3]). [SE *beige*, yellowish-grey]

beige *adj.* [1980s+] (US) deeply tedious, very bland. [BEIGE *n.*]

beiging *n.* [1980s+] (drugs) a process that alters the colour of cocaine to light brown, thus making it appear purer than it actually is. [SE *beige* + sfx. *-ing*]

be-in *n.* [1960s] (orig. US) a gathering of young people, usu. hippies, for mutual admiration, smoking cannabis and listening to music. [play on SE *be in (touch)/being*; taken from the original *Human Be-in* at Golden Gate Park, San Francisco, 1967; the *-in* sfx. extended to incl. *fuck-in*, *smoke-in*, *love-in* etc]

be in a great way about *phr.* [20C] (Ulster) infatuated by someone.

bejabers! *excl.* [early 19C+] a mild excl. *by Jesus!* (cf. BAGGODBAJEE!; BEJAMINTY!; BEJAZUS!; BUDDHIST PRIEST!; BY GIGS!; BY GINGER!; BY JACKS!; BY JIGGERS!; BY JIMMINY!; BY JING!; BY JINGO!; BY JOCKIES!; CRACKY!; GEE!; GEE WHIZ!; GEE WILLIKINS!; GEMINI!; JANEY MACK!; JAPERS!; JEEMS!; JEEPERS! JEEPERS CREEPERS!; JEEZ!; JEHOSHAPHAT!; JEMINY-O!; JERUSALEM!; JERUSALEM CRICKET!; JESUS H CHRIST!; JESUS KATE!; JESUS WEPT!; JIGGER! excl.¹; JIMINETTY!; JIMINY CRICKET!; JINGS!; JIS; JOCKS n.¹; JUDAS PRIEST!; JUMPING JEHOSHAPHAT!; JUMPING MOSES!). [those stage Irishmen who do not say *begorra!* will certainly say *bejabers!* Many manage both]

bejaminty! *excl.* [1920s] (Ulster) a mild oath, lit. 'by Jesus!' (cf. BEJABERS!).

bejazus!/bejasus!/bejesus! *excl.* [mid-19C+] a mild excl. *by Jesus!*; esp. in phr. *knock the bejazus out of* (cf. BEJABERS!)

bejesus *adj.* [late 19C+] (US) a general intensifier, esp. with implications of assurance, arrogance. [euph. for blasphemous SE *by Jesus!*]

belagot *n.* [1940s+] (W.I.) a large iron pot, used for cooking cow-tripes after butchering (cf. BIG DADDY POT). [dial *belagot*, tripes; lit. *belly-gut*]

belch *n.*¹ **1** [early 18C–mid-19C] second-rate beer (cf. BELLY VENGEANCE). **2** [1930s] (US) a drunken vagrant. [the effects of the beer]

belch *n.*² [late 19C–1940s] (US) a noisy complaint. [SE *belch*, an eructation]

belch *v.* [20C] (US) to complain; thus *belcher*, a whinger. [BELCH n.²]

belcher *n.*¹ **1** [early–mid-19C] a costermonger's handkerchief, blue with white or occasionally yellow spots (cf. BILLY n.⁴; BIRD'S EYE FOGLE; BIRD'S EYE WIPE; BLOOD-RED FANCY; BLUE BILLY; CREAM FANCY; KINGSMAN; RANDAL'S MAN; WATER'S MAN; YELLOW FANCY; YELLOW MAN). **2** [mid-19C] a thick ring. [the boxer Jim *Belcher* (d.1811), whose preferred adornments these were; since the 19C a *belcher* can be any spotted handkerchief]

belcher *n.*² [mid–late 19C] (orig. showmen's) a dedicated beer-drinker. [BELCH n.¹]

belcher *n.*³ [20C] (US Und.) an informer. [ironic use of SE *belch*]

be left *see* GET LEFT.

belfa *n.* [early 18C] a prostitute. [? Fr. *belle*, beautiful]

belfry *n.* [1900s–10s] the head (cf. ATTIC). [HAVE BATS IN THE BELFRY]

Belgie *n.* [20C] a Belgian (cf. BLACKIE). [note a single early 17C SE use]

believer *n.* [1960s+] (orig. US campus) a gullible person, who will believe whatever they are told; thus *make a believer (out of)*, to convince.

be like that/be like that see if I care *phr.* [1960s+] a dismissive, if petulant (and not wholly sincere) phr. denoting one's refusal to care about another's (injurious) actions (cf. DON'T BE LIKE THAT).

bell *n.*¹ [19C] a song.

bell *n.*² [20C] o'clock, usu. in pl. e.g. *eight bells*, eight o'clock. [naut. use; a bell was struck to indicate the change in the day's watches]

bell *n.*³ [1950s+] (US Black) personal notoriety, reputation. [the image of a bell around a cat's neck, announcing its imminent arrival]

bell *n.*⁴ [1970s] a hotel doorman (cf. BELLHOP). [? abbr. *bell captain*]

bell *n.*⁵ [1970s+] (orig. US) a call on the telephone, usu. in phr. *give one a bell* (cf. BUZZ n.²).

bell *v.* [1970s+] to call on the telephone. [BELL n.⁵]

belladonna *n.* [1980s+] (drugs) phencyclidine (cf. ACE n.³). [SE *belladonna*, deadly nightshade (*Atropa belladonna*)]

bell-bastard *n.* [19C] the bastard child of a bastard mother. [? pfx. *bel*, indicating relationship, as used in SE *belfader*, *beldame*, grandfather, grandmother]

bell cow *n.* [19C] (US) a leader, a boss. [rural *bell cow*, the lead cow or ox, which wears a bell and is the herd leader]

belle *n.* [1940s+] (gay) a good-looking, young homosexual (cf. AGNES). [Fr. *belle*, a beautiful woman]

belle-chose *n.* [14C] a literary euphemism for the vagina (cf. BEAUTY n.²; BEAUTY SPOT n.¹). [Fr. *belle chose*, a beautiful thing; coined by Geoffrey Chaucer (*c.*1345–1400)]

bell end *n.* [1990s] the tip of the penis. [the shape]

beller-croaker *adj.* [late 19C] noticeably beautiful, outstandingly attractive. [Fr. *belle à croquer*, beautiful enough to command desire]

bellers *n.* [18C–1920s] the lungs (cf. BELLOWS). [Cockney pron.]

bellhop/bellhopper *n.* [20C] (US) a hotel doorman, a bell-boy (cf. BELL n.⁴). [they 'hop to it' when the desk clerk rings the bell]

bellibone *n.* [1910s–20s] a well-dressed young woman. [Fr. *belle et bonne*, beautiful and good]

bellier *n.* [early 19C] a punch to the belly (cf. BELLOWSER n.¹). [lit. 'belly-er']

bellower *n.* [late 18C–early 19C] a town crier. [SE *bellow*, to shout loudly]

bellows *n.* [18C–1920s] the lungs (cf. BELLERS; BELLOWSER n.¹; BELLOWS TO MEND). [SE, 'an instrument or machine constructed to furnish a strong blast of air' (*OED*); 20C use mainly US]

bellowsed *adv.* [18C] transported as a convict (cf. GIVE BELLOWS). [? 'blown away' (across the sea)]

bellowser *n.*¹ [early 19C] a punch in the stomach, a 'blow in the wind'. [BELLOWS]

bellowser *n.*² [early–mid-19C] (Aus.) a sentence of lifetime transportation. [such a sentence 'takes one's breath away']

bellows to mend *phr.* [late 18C–1900s] used to describe a broken-winded horse or human. [BELLOWS]

bell-ringer *n.* [1940s–60s] (US) a great success. [the fairground attraction in which one proves one's strength by hammering on a spring and, if successful, ringing a bell]

bell ringers *n.* [20C] the fingers. [rhy. sl.]

bell rope *n.*¹ [mid-19C] a fashionable hairstyle in which men wore their hair twisted into two ropes, on each side of the face (cf. AGGERAWATOR). [pun, such a hairstyle is designed to 'draw the belles']

bell rope *n.*² [1960s–70s] (US) the penis. [it gets 'pulled']

bells *n.*¹ [1940s+] *bell*-bottomed trousers. [abbr.]

bells *n.*² [1960s+] (US Black) an expression of approval, in phr. *that rings my bells, I hear bells*. [? abbr. *wedding bells*, or phr. *you ring my bell*]

bells! *excl.* [1920s+] a general excl. of alarm, anger, surprise. [abbr. HELL'S BELLS!]

bells and whistles *n.* [1960s+] (orig. US) embellishments, gimmicks, esp. used in advertising copy to 'talk up' a product that, bereft of such add-ons, would have little to offer over its peers (cf. WITH BELLS ON).

bell shiner *n.* [1990s] homosexual anal intercourse. [BELL END + SE *shine*]

bell-swagged *adj.* [late 19C+] describing a penis that is larger at the top than it is at the base (cf. BELL-TOPPED). [BELL END + SE *swag*, to sway heavily]

bellswagger/belswagger *n.* **1** [late 16C–early 19C] a noisy braggart, a bully. **2** [18C] a womanizer, a pimp. [one who 'swaggers his belly']

bell the cat, to *phr.* [18C] to undertake something dangerous. [the nursery tale; SE f. 1800+]

bell-topped *adj.* [late 19C+] describing a penis that is larger at the top than it is at the base (cf. BELL-SWAGGED). [BELL END + SE *topped*]

bell-topper *n.* [mid-19C–1940s] (Aus./N.Z.) a top hat. [SE *bell* + TOPPER n.[1] (4)]

bell-wether *n.* **1** [mid-15C–mid-18C] the leader of a mob. **2** [late 17C–early 19C] a very noisy man. [SE *bell-wether*, the leading sheep of a flock, on whose neck a bell is hung]

belly *n.* [1940s–60s] (US) bravery, courage (cf. GUTS n.[2]).

belly-ache *n.* [mid-19C+] a stomach-ache. [SE 16C–early 19C]

bellyache *v.* [late 19C+] to complain, to moan; thus *belly-acher*, a whinger, a moaner; *bellyaching*, moaning. [BELLY-ACHE]

belly and back *adv.* [20C] (W.I./Guyn.) utterly, completely, ruthlessly. [lit. 'on both sides']

belly-bachelor *n.* [20C] (Irish) a man whose amorous pursuits are determined by the income of potential female. [a rich wife will help pay the food bills]

belly-band *n.* [late 19C–1920s] a wide belt, a corset. [SE *belly-band*, the strap that passes round the belly of a horse in harness]

belly-bomber *n.* [1980s+] (US) a hamburger, esp. when particularly greasy.

belly-bottom concrete *n.* [1950s+] (W.I.) a very large, round boiled dumpling (cf. CONCRETE). [its weight and consistency]

belly-bound *adj.* [17C+] (usu. of horses) constipated. [SE *belly* + *bound*, constipated]

belly bristles *n.* [19C] pubic hair.

belly bump *v.* [19C] **1** to have sexual intercourse. **2** (US) to slide downhill, face-down on a sledge.

belly bumper *n.* [19C] a womanizer, a promiscuous man (cf. BUMP n.2). [BELLY BUMP v. (1)]

belly burglar/robber *n.* [20C] (US) a cook or steward (cf. BELLY CHEATER). [orig. milit. jargon, the trad. meanness of cooks]

belly-buster *n.* [1940s+] (Aus.) a dive that knocks the wind from the diver (cf. BACK-BUSTER). [SE *belly* + BURSTER n.[2] (2)]

belly button *n.* [mid-19C+] (US) the navel, esp. in juv. use; thus *my belly button is playing hell with my backbone*, I am very hungry.

belly cheat *n.* **1** [16C–early 19C] an apron. **2** [17C] food. **3** [early 19C] padding worn by a woman in the hope of counterfeiting pregnancy. [SE *belly* + CHEAT n.; lit. 'stomach thing']

belly cheater *n.* [1910s+] (US) a cook (cf. BELLY BURGLAR).

belly chere/cheer *n.* [17C–mid-19C] food; thus *belly-cheering*, eating and drinking (cf. BELLY FURNITURE; BELLY TIMBER).

belly dale *n.* [19C] the vagina (cf. BEAUTY SPOT n.[1]; BELLY DINGLE; BELLY ENTRANCE; ENTRANCE; FRONT GARDEN; GUT ENTRANCE; IVORY GATE; MARBLE ARCH; WAY-IN). [SE *belly* + *dale*, a (river) valley]

belly dingle *n.* [19C] the vagina (cf. BELLY DALE). [SE *belly* + *dingle*, a wooded hollow, a deep narrow cleft between hills]

belly entrance *n.* [19C] the vagina (cf. BELLY DALE).

belly fiddle *n.* [1900s–40s] (US Black) a guitar. [the normal fiddle or violin is held beneath the chin, while the guitar is strapped across the stomach]

bellyflop *n.* **1** [19C+] (US) the act of throwing oneself face-down onto a sledge before coasting downhill, also (US) *belly-bumper*, *belly-bumbo*, *belly-guts*, *belly-flounders*, *belly-flumps*, *belly plumper*. **2** [1930s+] a dive in which one lands flat on the belly (and, in extreme circumstances, winds oneself), rather than cutting through the water (cf. BACK-BUSTER; BELLY-WASHER n.[2]).

bellyful *n.*[1] [late 16C–19C] a thrashing. [one has *a bellyful* of pain]

bellyful *n.*[2] [mid-19C+] a sufficiency. [ext. of SE use; rendered colloq. only because *belly* itself is considered coarse]

belly full and behind drunk *phr.* [20C] (W.I.) immobile, incapable of movement after a large meal and a good deal to drink. [BEHIND n.[1]]

belly furniture *n.* [17C] food (cf. BELLY CHERE). [SE *belly* + *furniture*; that with which something is stocked or filled; contents]

belly grease *n.* [1930s] (US) hard liquor. [lit. 'stomach-fat']

belly-grunting *n.* [1920s+] (Aus.) a bad stomach-ache. [one 'grunts' with pain]

belly gun *n.* [1920s+] (orig. US) a small gun that is most effective when fired at short range, esp. when aimed at a victim's abdomen.

belly-gut *n.* [mid-16C–mid-18C] a greedy, lazy person. [the greediness is implied in the redup., lit. 'stomach-stomach']

belly habit *n.* [1970s+] (drugs) pains in the stomach that may accompany withdrawal from continued heroin use. [SE *belly* + HABIT]

belly is a burying ground *phr.* [20C] (W.I.) describing a woman who has had a number of abortions.

belly laugh *n.* [1920s+] a deep, sonorous laugh. [it appears to come from deep in the stomach]

belly-paunch *n.* [mid-16C–17C] a glutton. [BELLY-GUT]

belly-piece *n.*[1] [17C] a prostitute, a mistress. [SE *belly* + *piece*; but note PIECE n.[1] (1)]]

belly-piece *n.*[2] [17C–18C] an apron. [SE *belly* + *piece*]

belly-plea *n.* [late 18C] a plea, offered by a female criminal facing the death sentence, that since she is pregnant, the law should spare her unborn child's life; thus *plead one's belly*, to make such an entreaty.

belly queen *n.* [1960s+] (US gay) **1** a gay man who enjoys face-to-face intercourse. **2** one who rubs his penis on his partner's stomach to produce ejaculation. **3** one who only likes partners with flat, hard stomachs. [SE *belly* + QUEEN n.1]

belly robber *see* BELLY BURGLAR.

belly rub *n.* [1920s+] (US) a dance (cf. RUB n.[3]; RUB JOINT). [BELLY RUB v.]

belly rub *v.* [1920s+] (US) to dance close to one's partner.

belly ruffian *n.* [late 17C–18C] the penis (cf. ARSE-OPENER). [affectionate play on that]

belly timber *n.* [early 17C–late 19C] food (cf. BELLY CHERE). [SE *belly* + *timber*, the 'stuff' of which a person is made; note that *RHDAS* adds a single 1970s citation, from *American Speech*]

belly-up *adj.*[1] [17C–1900s] of a woman, pregnant. [the shape of her stomach]

belly up *adj.*[2] **1** [1970s+] dead. **2** [1920s+] failed, finished, esp. bankrupt; usu. prefaced by *go.* **3** drunk. [resembling a dead fish]

belly up!/belly up to the bar, boys! *excl.* [20C] (Can.) the drinks are on the house! [BELLY UP TO]

belly up to *v.* [20C] to move straight towards, to approach directly. [the pushing forward of one's stomach]

belly up to the bar, boys! *see* BELLY UP!

belly vengeance *n.* [mid-19C] **1** weak, sour beer, often the cause of stomach upsets. **2** the stomach upset itself. [East Anglian dial. *bellywengins*]

belly wash *n.*[1] [late 19C+] (US) **1** a soft drink. **2** a weak or bad alcoholic drink. [SE *belly* + *wash*, kitchen swill, liquid food for animals]

belly wash *n.*[2] [late 19C+] (US) nonsense (cf. BOLLYWASH; HOGWASH). [fig. use of BELLY WASH n.[1]]

belly-washer *n.*[1] [20C] (US) **1** a soft drink (cf. BELLY WASH n.[1]). **2** wine.

belly-washer *n.*[2] [1930s+] (US) a dive in which one lands flat on the belly (and, in extreme circumstances, winds oneself), rather than cutting through the water (cf. BELLYFLOP).

belly whiskers *n.* [late 19C] the female pubic hair.

belly-woman n. [1950s+] (W.I.) **1** an unmarried pregnant woman. **2** a cutlass with a rounded blade.

belong to Greater London, to phr. [late 19C] to be well known in the metropolis. [a play on SE *Greater London*, the suburbs immediately surrounding the capital and included with the central districts when assessing its population]

below Nathaniel adv. [late 19C–1910s] even further down than hell. [*Nathaniel*, Satan (Ware) or f. rhy. sl. *Nathaniel* = hell (E.P.)]

below par adj. [19C+] unwell, emotionally low (cf. ABOVE PAR). [Stock Exchange jargon *below par*, at a discount]

belows n. [1990s] (US) intestines, bowels. [SE *below*; they are 'below the belt']

below the belt adv. [late 19C] underhand, illegal, cheating. [boxing use, which declares such blows as foul; 20C use is SE]

below the mahogany adj. [20C] drunk. [the *mahogany* is the bar, beneath which the drinker has slipped]

Belsen n. [1940s+] a very unpleasant place. [proper name of *Bergen-Belsen*, a major Nazi extermination camp and the most notorious after Auschwitz, which was not dedicated to death]

bel-shangle n. [late 16C–early 17C] a fool. [? SE *bell-jangler*; a fool capering with cap and bells]

belt n.[1] **1** [late 19C+] a blow, a hit, a punch. **2** [late 19C+] an act of sexual intercourse. **3** [1920s+] (Aus.) a prostitute. **4** [1920s+] a sexually appealing woman (cf. FUCK n.[4]; SHAG n.[1]). **5** [1950s] (US) a try, an attempt. **6** [1960s+] (drugs) the immediate effect of a drug, usu. one that has been injected (cf. RUSH).

belt n.[2] [1920s+] (orig. US) **1** a measure of spirits. **2** a drink of, e.g. *a belt of coffee*. [BELT n.[1], BELT v.[1] (3)]

belt v.[1] **1** [early 19C+] to hit (with a fist), to flog, to thrash. **2** [mid-19C] to trounce, to defeat soundly. **3** [mid-19C+] to drink heavily, straight from the bottle (cf. BELT THE BOTTLE). **4** [late 19C+] to rush, to hurry. **5** [1940s] of a man, to have sexual intercourse. [(1) lit. to hit with a belt; (2-5) fig. uses of (1)]

belt/belt along v.[2] **1** [late 19C] to hustle about. **2** [late 19C+] to run fast, to hurry. [BELT v. (4)]

belt/belt it out v.[3] [1950s+] to sing loudly and enthusiastically (cf. BELT OUT). [BELT v.[1] (1); 'it' is the song]

belt along see BELT v.[2].

belt-and-braces adj. [1920s+] cautious, extremely careful, taking no risks. [usu. only one of the items is required to hold up one's trousers]

belt down v. [20C] to rain very hard. [BELT v.[1] (1)]

belted adj. [1930s+] (US) drunk (cf. BASTED). [BELT v.[1] (3)]

belter n.[1] [18C] a prostitute. [BELT n.[1] (3)]

belter n.[2] [20C] an admirable, exciting, thrilling etc event or circumstance. [northern dial. *belter*, a heavy blow or series of blows]

Belteshazzar's off-ox n. [late 19C+] a headstrong person (cf. ADAM'S OFF-OX). [also see Dan. 4:8–27, in which Daniel, also known as Belteshazzar, foretells Nebuchadnezzar's decline into a state of ox-like stupidity]

beltinker n. [late 19C] a beating, a thrashing. [? BELT v.[1] (1); i.e. a *belting*]

belt it v. [1970s] **1** to drive exceptionally fast. **2** to masturbate (cf. BELT ONE'S BATTER). [BELT v. (1)]

belt it out see BELT v.[3].

belt of the crozier n. [1990s] a reprimand from the Church, spec. from a bishop. [belt n.1 (1) + SE *crozier*]

belt one's batter, to phr. [1900s–40s] **1** to copulate with a woman. **2** to masturbate (cf. PULL ONE'S PUD). [BELT v. (1) + BATTER n.[1] (2)]

belt one's hog, to phr. [20C] (US) to masturbate. [BELT v. (1) + HOG]

belt out v. (orig. US) **1** [1940s+] to knock down, to destroy. **2** [1950s+] to sing lustily. **3** [1960s+] to murder. **4** [1960s+] to eat heartily. [BELT v.[1] (1)]

belt the bottle, to phr. [1930s+] (orig. US) to drink heavily. [fig. use of BELT v.[1] (3) + SE *bottle*]

belt the grape, to phr. [1930s+] to drink heavily (cf. BELT THE BOTTLE). [BELT v.[1] (3) + SE *grape*]

belt up v. [1930s+] (orig. RAF) to be quiet, esp. in excl. *belt up!* shut up! [BELT v.[1] (1)]

be lucky phr. [1930s+] (mainly London) goodbye.

belushi n. [1980s+] (drugs) a mixture of cocaine and heroin (cf. SPEEDBALL n.[1]). [the fatal overdose taken by film star John *Belushi* (1949–82)]

beluthahatchie n. [1920s–40s] the ultimate in far-away, unpleasant places (cf. BEE-LUTHER-HATCHEE). [elision of B. LUTHER HATCHETT]

belvedere n. [late 19C–1900s] a good-looking man. [the statue of the *Apollo Belvedere*]

belyando spew n. [late 19C–1900s] (Aus.) a rural sickness, mainly in Queensland (cf. BARCOO SPEW). [*Belyando* River, in central Queensland + SE *spew*, vomit]

belyando spruce n. [1980s+] (Aus. drugs) marijuana. [a popular 'home-grown' crop in the *Belyando* River area of Queensland]

b.e.m. n. [1950s+] (orig. US) *bug-eyed monster/monsters*; a popular category of SF writing and described as such by fans. [abbr.]

bembe n. [20C] (W.I.) a bully, a large, strong person of either sex. [? *bam-boy* or Sp. *bemba*, a Black person's thick lips or *Bemba*, a Central African people]

be missing! excl. [1920s+] (US) go away! [a phr. first used by Chicago mobster Spike O'Donnell in rejecting the overtures/threats of Al Capone (1899–1947)]

bemused/bemused with beer phr. [mid-19C] drunk (cf. ADDLED).

be my guest/be my Georgie Best phr. [1950s+] (orig. US) phr. of encouragement (esp. in response to a request to borrow something), go ahead, 'feel free', 'help yourself', 'make yourself at home' etc. [the rhy. sl. version hymns the celebrated footballer, *George Best* (b.1946)]

ben n.[1] [18C] a simpleton, a fool (cf. BENNISH; BENNY n.[3]). [? link to BENE; thus 'good fellow'; if so cf. GOOD OLD BOY]

ben n.[2] [19C] a coat (cf. BENJIE; BENJY; BENNY n.[1]; JOSEPH n.; UPPER BENJAMIN). [abbr. BENJAMIN]

ben n.[3] [late 19C] (society) a lie. [Ital. proverb *se non e vero, e ben trovato*, even if it is not true, it is a happy invention; this was anglicized as *benjamin trovato*, a lie, then shorted to *ben trovato*, *ben tro* and finally *ben*]

benbouse n. [16C] the best beer (cf. BENE BOUSE). [BENE + BOUSE n.]

bencher n. [late 19C+] (US) any idle or ineffectual person (cf. CHAIR-WARMER). [BENCH-WARMER n.[1]]

benches! excl. [1950s+] (US, usu. juv.) a claim, esp. of first rights to something (cf. KEEPSIES). [ety. unknown; ? link to marbles use *benching!* used to restrain a player from moving their hand when tossing the marble, thus, loosely, 'play fair']

bench-legged adj. [19C] (US) of people, but more usu. of dogs, bowlegged. [legs that could straddle a bench]

bench-man n. [20C] (US Und.) a judge. [the SE *bench* on which they sit + *man*]

bench-points n. [late 19C–1900s] physical advantages. [used of people but f. dog and cat shows where the animals are placed on a bench for judging]

bench-warmer n.[1] [late 19C+] (US) **1** any idle or ineffectual person (cf. BENCHER). **2** a substitute in a sports team.

bench-warmer *n.*[2] (US) [20C] a tramp, a vagrant. [the proliferation of tramps sleeping on the benches of city streets and parks]

ben cove *n.* [17C–18C] a good fellow, a friend (cf. BENE COVE; BENE CULL). [BENE + COVE]

bend *n.*[1] [mid-late 19C] a waistcoat. [? it 'bends' around the stomach]

bend *n.*[2] [late 19C+] a drunken spree. [abbr. BENDER *n.*[1]]

bend *n.*[3] [20C] (Anglo-Irish) an appointment, a rendezvous. [? SE *bond*/*bind*]

bend *n.*[4] [1960s] an experience created by a hallucinogenic drug. [BENT OUT OF SHAPE]

bend *n.*[5] [1990s] (rap music) a prostitute. [BEND OVER]

bend *v.*[1] [mid-18C] to drink hard (cf. BEND ONE'S ELBOW). [? SE *bend*, to apply oneself, to pull or strain]

bend *v.*[2] [19C+] **1** to pervert, to corrupt, to commit some form of fraudulent manoeuvre, esp. as in losing a race deliberately, bribing a policeman or a sporting competitor. **2** to allow oneself to be corrupted. [ext. of SE; i.e. to *bend* the rules]

bend down for *v.* [late 19C+] to consent to buggery.

bend-down plaza *n.* [20C] (W.I./Jam.) a row of roadside pedlars, specializing in items that are hard to get in shops, because of import restrictions. [the customers have to *bend down* + sarcastic use of *Plaza*, often used as the name of a shopping mall]

bended knees *n.* [20C] a cheese. [rhy. sl.]

bender *n.*[1] **1** [19C+] a bout of riotous drinking, often lasting several days and including random acts of excess, violence etc; thus *on a bender*. **2** [mid-19C] (US) a rampage. **3** [mid-19C–1910s] anything exceptional, astounding (cf. CORKER *n.*[2]; HUMDINGER). **4** [1960s+] (drugs) a drug party. [the image of a drunkard as unsteady on their feet, or ? f. an image of bending a bow or elbow. Note naut. jargon *benjo*, a spree, f. Ital./Lingua Fr. *buen giorno*, a good day]

bender *n.*[2] **1** [mid-late 19C] a sixpence (2½p). **2** [mid-19C] a shilling (5p). [the ease with which the thin metal could be bent]

bender *n.*[3] [mid-19C+] **1** the leg. **2** the knee. **3** the arm. **4** the elbow. [lapsed in mainstream sl. by 1900 but adopted US Blacks *c.*1940; f. its physical function as a joint]

bender *n.*[4] [1930s+] a male homosexual (cf. BENT *n.*).

bender! *excl.* [19C] nonsense! humbug! rubbish! (cf. WALKER!). [ety. unknown]

bendigo *n.* [mid-19C] a rough fur cap (cf. HARD-HITTER; HARD-PUNCHER). [the professional name of William Thompson (1811–89), the Nottingham prize-fighter who fought as *Bendigo* and ended his days as an evangelical preacher]

bend of the filbert *n.* [18C] a bow of the head, a nod (cf. NUT *n.*[3]). [SE *bend* + pun on SE *filbert*, a nut]

bend one's back, to *phr.* [1920s–30s] (Aus.) to work hard.

bend one's elbow, to *phr.* [20C] to have a drink (cf. BEND *v.*[1]). [the physical action of tipping up a glass]

bend over/over for/b.o. *v.* [1960s+] **1** to submit to; the image is of submitting to buggery, but the popular use is less specific. **2** to get into difficulties, to be put at a disadvantage; also as excl. *bend over!* you're bothering me!

bend over backwards *v.* [1940s+] to go out of one's way to do something, usu. altruistically (cf. FALL OVER BACKWARDS).

bend someone's ear, to *phr.* [1940s+] (orig. US) **1** to chatter on interminably and probably tediously. **2** to speak privately, to whisper. [the speaker forces the listener to bend their ear towards their mouth. Note mid-17C SE use by John Milton]

bendy *adj.* [1990s] (US teen) extremely fashionable, smart, 'cool'. [? spod = bad model, is not STRAIGHT *adj.*[1] (5)]

bene/ben/bien *n.* [16C] good; it can be conjugated as *benar*, better and *benat*, best. [Lat. *bonus* and Fr. *bon*, good]

bene bouse/bowse *n.* [mid-16C–late 18C] drink, lit. good

liquor; thus *bene-bowsy*, tipsy (with good drink) (cf. BENBOUSE). [BENE + BOUSE *n.*]

bene cove *n.* [17C–early 19C] a friend, lit. 'a good fellow' (cf. BENE CULL). [BENE + COVE *n.*[1] (5)]

bene/ben cull *n.* [19C] a good fellow, a friend (cf. BENE COVE). [BENE + CULL *n.*[1]]

bene darkmans! *excl.* [mid-16C–18C] good night. [BENE + DARKMANS]

benedict/benedick *n.* [early–mid 19C] a married man, esp. a newly married man or a formerly confirmed bachelor who changes his mind. [Shakespeare's character *Benedict* in *Much Ado About Nothing* (1599)]

beneek/bneekte *see* BENEUKT.

bene-faker *n.* [17C] a counterfeiter, initially of documents, later of money (cf. BENE-GYBE). [BENE + FAKE *v.*[3], lit. 'well make']

bene feaker/benfeaker *n.* [17C] a counterfeiter of bills. [BENE + FAKER *n.*[1]]

bene-feaker of gybes *n.* [late 17C–early 18C] a forger of passes and similar documents. [BENE FEAKER + GYBE]

benfeaker *see* BENE FEAKER.

bene-gybe *n.* [17C] counterfeiter (cf. BENE-FAKER). [BENE + GYBE]

bene mort *n.* [mid-16C–late 18C] a pretty woman. [BENE + MORT]

bene peck *n.* [mid-16C–17C] good food. [BENE + PECK *n.*[1] (1)]

beneship/benship *n.* [mid-16C–18C] something that is very good. [BENE; the term moved into SE by 18C, when Bailey's *Universal Etymological English Dictionary* defined *beenship*, worship, goodness. Note Carew, who defines 'beenship rat' as 'goodnight' in his list of Scot. gypsy terms]

beneshiply *adv.* [17C–18C] worshipfully. [BENESHIP + sfx. *-ly*]

beneukt/beneek/beneekte *adj.* [1960s+] (S.Afr.) **1** contrary, impossible. **2** bad-tempered, insane. [Du. *neuk*, to deceive, to push]

benevolence *n.* [early 19C] (society) doing good for others in the hope that one will receive equal good in return. ['Ostentation and fear united, with hopes of retaliation in kind hereafter' (Jon Bee)]

ben-flake *n.* [mid-19C–1900s] a steak. [rhy. sl.]

Bengal blanket *n.* [19C] (Anglo-Ind.) the sun, a blue sky. [the good weather that 'blankets' Bengal]

bengal lancers *n.* [1930s–40s] (Aus.) razor gangs. [pun on SE *Bengal Lancers*, an Indian Army regiment]

benies *n.* [1940s+] (US campus) *benefits*, spec. those of the GI Bill that puts US service veterans through college for free. [abbr.]

benjamin *n.* [early–mid 19C] a coat (cf. BEN *n.*[2]; UPPER BENJAMIN). [? the name of a tailor; according to Hotten (1874), an acknowledgemenet of the many (Jewish) tailors thus named]

benji *n.* [1980s+] a $100 bill (cf. ABE *n.*[2]; PORTRAIT OF MADISON). [the picture of *Benjamin* Franklin (1706–90) printed on the bill]

benjie *n.* [19C] a coat (cf. BEN *n.*[2]). [abbr. BENJAMIN]

benjy *n.* [early–mid 19C] a coat (cf. BEN *n.*[2]). [abbr. BENJAMIN]

bennie/bennies *see* BENNY *n.*[2].

bennish *adj.* [17C–18C] foolish. [BEN *n.*[1]]

benny *n.*[1] (US) **1** [1900s–50s] an overcoat (cf. BEN *n.*[2]). **2** [mid-19C–1940s] (orig. naut.) a straw hat. [Black jazz musicians adopted *benny*, which entered mainstream Black sl. as BENJAMIN *c.*1940]

benny *n.*[2] [20C] (US) a Jew. [popular Jewish name]

benny *n.*[3] [1920s+] (US) a person, a fellow; thus [1970s] (US gay) *steam bath benny*, a male homosexual who frequents steam baths. [? generic use of proper name]

benny/bennie/bennies *n.*[4] [1940s+] (orig. US drugs) *Benzedrine*; thus *benny-head*, a Benzedrine user (cf. B *n.*[5]). [abbr.]

benny *n.*[5] [1980s] as used by the British Army, an inhabitant of the Falkland Islands. [a derog. ref. derived from an intellectually deficient rural character in the UK TV soap opera *Crossroads*]

benny house *n.* [20C] a brothel that essentially caters for heterosexuals but that will obtain male prostitutes on request (cf. ACCOMMODATION HOUSE). [BENNY n.[3]; note US milit. *benny*, a young male Filipino transvestite]

benny mason *n.* [1990s] (US campus) particularly strong marijuana. [? a proper name or f. *best* marijuana]

beno *n.* [1950s+] the period of menstruation and thus, for many couples, no sex. ['there'll *be no* fun']

benship *see* BENESHIP.

bent *n.* [1950s+] a homosexual (cf. BENDER n.[4]).

bent *adj.* **1** [mid-19C+] intoxicated by liquor or [1960s+] drugs (cf. BENT OUT OF SHAPE). **2** [20C] impoverished, penniless. **3** [1910s+] corrupt (cf. BENT COPPER). **4** [1930s+] illegal, stolen. **5** [1930s] spoiled, ruined. **6** [1940s+] eccentric. **7** [1950s+] sexually eccentric, esp. homosexual. **8** [1940s+] (orig. US) acting oddly, behaving in a strange manner (cf. BENT OUT OF SHAPE). **9** [1960s+] (US) angry, excited, usu. in phr. BENT OUT OF SHAPE. **10** [1980s+] addicted to drugs. [all fig. uses of SE + (2) pun on BROKE]

bent as a butcher's hook *phr.* [1970s] extremely corrupt, highly criminal. [an intensified form of BENT adj. (3)]

bent as a nine-bob note *phr.* [1950s+] **1** of a person, dishonest. **2** of an object, stolen. [BENT adj. (3); the UK's pre-decimal currency included a '10-bob', i.e. 10-shilling note, but not a 'nine-bob' one]

bent copper *n.* [1910s+] a corrupt policeman. [BENT adj. (3) + COPPER n.[3] (1); pun on SE]

benton's mint-drops *n.* [mid-19C] (US) gold coins. [proper name Thomas Hart *Benton* (1792–1858), campaigner for a gold currency in US + MINT DROPS]

bent out of shape *phr.* [1960s+] **1** intoxicated by a drug, esp. cannabis or LSD, or extremely drunk. **2** very angry. **3** socially inept, embarrassing. [ext. of BENT adj. (1), (8) + pun on SE]

bent screw *n.* [1940s+] (prison) a corrupt prison warder. [BENT adj. (3) + SCREW n.[2] (2) + pun on SE]

bent up *adj.* [late 19C] (US) infatuated, obsessively in love. [pun on MASHED adj.[1]]

benz/benzie *n.*[1] [1940s+] (drugs) amphetamine (cf. A n.[2]; B n.[3]). [*Benzedrine* + ref. to a Mercedes Benz, which also 'makes one go fast']

benz/benzie *n.*[2] [1940s+] a Mercedes *Benz* automobile. [abbr.]

benzine *n.* **1** [mid-19C–1900s] (US) cheap 'rotgut' whisky; thus *hit the benzine can, maul the benzine,* to drink whisky to excess; *benzinery,* a saloon. **2** [20C] (W.I./Guyn., Trin.) a form of unlicensed and very potent rum distilled secretly in the countryside (cf. BUSHIE). [SE *benzine,* petroleum ether]

benzine buggy *n.* [1900s] (US) an automobile. [SE *benzine* + BUGGY n. (1)]

benzo *n.*[1] [1990s] (US Black) a Mercedes *Benz* automobile. [abbr.]

benzo *n.*[2] [1990s] (drugs) *Benzodiopate.* [abbr.]

be off!/be off with you! *excl.* [late 19C+] go away!

be off the handle *see* GO OFF THE HANDLE.

be off with you! *see* BE OFF!

beong *n.* [mid-19C] one shilling (5p) (cf. SALTEE). [Polari *bianco,* white; the shilling is a 'silver' coin]

be on the jack *see* LAY ON THE JACK.

be/fall on the wrong side of the hedge, to *phr.* [19C] to be thrown from a coach. [one lands off the road and in a field]

be out! *excl.* [1990s] (US Black) a general excl. of encouragement, enjoy yourself, have fun, GO FOR IT!

bequeath one's genes, to *phr.* [1990s] to masturbate (cf. KEEP DOWN THE CENSUS; KILL SOME BABIES). [pun on SE]

Berdoo *n.* [20C] (US) San *Bernardino,* California. [abbr.]

bereavement lurk *n.* [mid–late 19C] a form of begging that depends on attracting sympathy for the fact that one's wife has supposedly just died. [SE *bereavement* + LURK n.]

bergie *n.* [1970s] (S.Afr.) a vagrant living on the slopes of Table Mountain, Cape Town (cf. OUTIE n.[1]). [Afk. *berg,* mountain]

berick *v.* [1980s+] (US drugs) to smoke an outsized marijuana pipe (2m (6ft) or longer). [ety. unknown]

berk *n.* [1930s+] a fool, an incompetent. [rhy. sl. *Berkeley hunt* or *Berkshire hunt* = CUNT]

Berkeley/Berkshire/Burlington hunt *n.* [1930s+] **1** the vagina (cf. BIRCHINGTON HUNT; GASP AND GRUNT; GRUMBLE AND GRUNT; LADY BERKELEY; MICHAEL n.[2]; SHARP AND BLUNT; SIR BERKELEY). **2** a fool, an incompetent (cf. BERK). [rhy. sl. *Berkeley/Berkshire/Burlington hunt* = CUNT]

berkeleys *n.* [late 19C] the female breasts. [Rom. *berk,* breast]

berko *adv.* [1980s+] (Aus.) berserk. [abbr. SE + sfx. -o]

Berkshire hog *n.* [1950s+] (W.I.) **1** an ugly person. **2** a very dark-complexioned Black man. [SE *Berkshire hog,* a large, dark-skinned pig]

Berkshire hunt *see* BERKELEY HUNT.

berley/burley *n.* [1940s+] (Aus.) nonsense, humbug. [? SE *berley,* ground bait]

Bermondsey banger *n.* [late 19C–1900s] 'a society leader among the South London tanneries. He must frequent "the star", be prepared to hold his own and fight at all times for his social belt' (Ware). [*Bermondsey,* an area of south London + *banger,* one who both 'bangs' his fellows physically, and makes a 'bang' in society]

Bermudas *n.* [late 18C] certain areas of London that were considered safe havens for criminals and debtors (cf. ALSATIA). [proper name *Bermuda Islands,* where certain well-connected debtors fled to avoid their creditors. London's *Bermudas* were either the alleys and passageways running near Drury Lane, Covent Garden, and/or the Mint in Southwark]

bernice *n.* [late 19C+] (US drugs) cocaine. [BURNIE]

bernie *n.*[1] [late 19C+] (US drugs) cocaine. [BURNIE]

bernie *n.*[2] [1990s] the sum of £1 million (cf. ARCHER). [*Bernie* Ecclestone, the Formula One motor-racing chief, whose gift of this amount to the Labour Party caused a short-lived scandal in 1997]

bernie's flakes *n.* [1980s+] (drugs) cocaine. [BERNIE n.[1] + FLAKE]

bernie's gold dust *n.* [1980s+] (drugs) cocaine. [BERNIE n.[1]; the price of the drug]

berries *n.*[1] **1** [20C] the testicles (cf. APRICOTS). **2** [1970s+] (US Black) a woman's nipples. [resemblance]

berries, the *n.*[2] [20C] (US) **1** the best, the superlative. **2** the ultimate, the last straw. [fig. use of SE; but note Scot. *to be no the berry,* to be a bad character]

berries *n.*[3] [1910s–40s] dollars, money.

berries *n.*[4] [1970s+] (US Black) wine. [its basic component]

berry *n.*[1] **1** [late 19C] (US) an easy opponent, anyone seen as 'soft'. **2** [1910s–40s] (US) $1 (cf. BERRIES n.[3]). **3** [1920s+] (US) a testicle, usu. in pl. **4** [1920s] (US drugs) a small package of narcotics (cf. BINDLE). **5** [1930s] (US) a person (cf. HUCKLEBERRY n.[3]). **6** [1930s] a £1 note.

berry *n.*[2] [1990s] **1** one who is into bizarre, 'kinky' sex. **2** one who cannot get a partner. [? STRAWBERRY n.[2] (2)]

berry picker *n.* [20C] (US) a rural person, a country dweller.

bertha *see* BIG BERTHA.

bertiss *n.* [1940s+] (W.I.) the buttocks. [BATI]

be said and led *phr.* [20C] (Irish) take my advice.

beserko *n.* [1980s] (US) an unstable, eccentric person. [SE *beserk* + sfx. -o]

beside the book *phr.* [late 17C] utterly mistaken (f. BESIDE THE CUSHION; BESIDE THE LIGHTER). [SE *beside*, in addition, over and above + *book*, in the sense of an authority, a book of rules; 18C+ use is SE]

beside the bridge *phr.* [17C–18C] out of line, astray. [the 'proper' line crosses the bridge]

beside the cushion *phr.* [17C] in error (cf. BESIDE THE BOOK). [billiards jargon *beside the cushion*, wide of the mark]

beside the lighter *phr.* [17C–18C] in a poor condition (cf. BESIDE THE BOOK). [? SE *lighter*, a boat used to transport goods/passengers to and from a vessel that has to be moored in deeper water]

besognio *n.* [early 17C] a greedy beggar, a worthless person. [It. *bisogno*, need, want; also a newly levied, untrained and unblooded soldier]

bespattered *adj.* [1910s–20s] euph. for BLOODY *adj.*

bess *n.*[1] [17C–19C] a short iron bar, used to break open doors, force locks etc (cf. BILLY *n.*[1]; JEMMY *n.*[4]). [BETTY *n.*[1]]

bess *n.*[2] [early 18C–mid-19C] a firelock or musket. [abbr. BROWN BESS]

bessie *n.* [19C] (US) a firearm, esp. a shotgun (cf. BETSY).

Bess of Bedlam *n.* [mid-19C] a lunatic vagrant (cf. TOM OF BEDLAM). [SE *Bess*, generic female name + *Bedlam*]

bessy *n.* [19C+] (W.I.) a busybody, a gossip. [dial. *bessy*, an ill-mannered woman or girl]

best *n.* [late 18C] a popular toast, abbr. of *to the best cunt in Christendom* (cf. BEST IN CHRISTENDOM).

best *v.* [mid-19C+] **1** to get the better of (cf. BESTED; BESTER). **2** to cheat. [orig. dial.]

best bib and tucker *adv.* [late 18C+] (orig. US) in one's best clothes. [SE *bib*, top part of an apron + *tucker*, a piece of lace or similar material worn by women around the top of the bodice or the neck]

best-boy *n.* [1990s] (US Black) a bodyguard. [? film jargon *best boy*, an assistant to the key grip and as such one who does heavy work on the set or on pattern of MAIN MAN *n.*[1] (4)]

best-built *adj.* [1970s] describing a woman with a voluptuous figure. [SE; lit. built in the best way possible]

bested *adv.* [mid-19C+] defeated, defrauded. [BEST *v.*]

bester *n.* **1** [mid-19C] a villain who is equally happy to use physical force or verbal deceits to extract money from victims. **2** [1940s+] (Aus.) a fraudulent bookmaker. [phr. *get the best of*]

best girl *n.* [late 19C] (orig. US) a sweetheart, a girlfriend, a wife.

best in Christendom *n.* [late 17C] the vagina (cf. BEST *n.*). [coined by John Wilmot, Earl of Rochester (1647–80), who was also responsible for the synon. BULL'S EYE *n.*[2]; CROWN OF SENSE; KENNEL; TARGET *n.*[1])]

best leg of three *n.* [late 19C–1900s] the penis (cf. MIDDLE LEG; SHORT ARM; THIRD LEG).

best of a charley *n.* [early 19C] upsetting a watchman in his box. [BEST *v.* + CHARLEY *n.*[1]

bestow the order of the sack, to *phr.* [late 19C+] to dismiss from employment. [SACK *n.*[3]]

best part *n.* [late 16C–early 17C] the vagina (cf. WORST PART). [coined by John Donne (1572–1631)]

best/greatest thing since sliced bread *phr.* [1960s+] the best thing ever. [the implication is of convenience rather than quality]

bet! *excl.* **1** [mid-19C+] (US) a general excl. of affirmation or agreement (cf. YOU BET!). **2** [1980s+] (US campus) a response to an event that is totally unexpected but greatly appreciated, e.g. *Class is cancelled today? Bet!*

bet a fat man, to *phr.* (US Black) **1** [1950s–60s] a general oath (cf. BET ONE'S BOOTS; BET ONE'S BOTTOM DOLLAR). **2** [1950s+] to

assure or to believe with absolute confidence. [? the fig. size of one's wager]

bet a million to a piece of dirt *phr.* [late 19C–1910s] phr. denoting the bettor's unassailable confidence (cf. ALL THE WORLD TO A CHINA ORANGE). [the disparity underlines one's certainty]

bet a pound to a pinch of shit/poop, to *phr.* [1940s+] statement denoting speaker's absolute confidence, whether in a real bet or merely a point of view (cf. ALL THE WORLD TO A CHINA ORANGE).

betcha! *excl.* [1920s+] (orig. US) a general excl. of affirmation or agreement (cf. YOU BET!). [elision of SE *bet you*]

beteechoot *see* BANCHOOT.

be/by the hokey! *excl.* [1920s+] (Irish) a mild oath. [var. on BY THE HOLY POKER!]

be/by the holies! *excl.* [20C] (Irish) a mild oath.

bethel the city, to *phr.* [early 18C] **1** to be a poor host. **2** to eat in chop-houses. [proper name of Slingsby *Bethel* (1617–97) who, with Henry Cornish, was elected Sheriff of London in 1680; according to the historian Roger North, Bethel 'used to walk about more like a corncutter than sheriff of London. He kept no house, but lived upon chops, whence it is proverbial for not feasting "to Bethel the city"' (*Examen*, 1740)]

be there *v.* **1** [late 19C] to be in one's element. **2** [1980s+] (US) to make a definite plan, usu. in form of a statement, *I'm there*, I'm definitely doing that.

bethlehemites *n.* [late 18C] (Und.) carol-singers. [the staple topic of most carols]

Bethlehem steel *n.* [1970s] (US Black) a boastful description of the rigidity of one's erect penis. [play on name of the US steel manufacturer]

bet like the Watsons, to *phr.* [1940s–70s (Aus.) to bet heavily. [the *Watson Brothers* (*fl.*1880s–1910s). They were legendary punters but their background is unknown; possibly b. in Bendigo, Victoria they have been variously cited as Sydney hoteliers and outback shearers in New South Wales]

bet London to a brick, to *phr.* [1940s+] (Aus.) to lay long odds (cf. ALL THE WORLD TO A CHINA ORANGE).

betoger *n.* [1970s+] (S.Afr.) a political demonstrator. [Afk. *betoog*, demonstrate]

bet one's boots, to *phr.* [late 19C+] (orig. US) to be certain, to wager everything in total confidence (cf. BET A FAT MAN). [betting one's boots in a US frontier state would be a very serious bet]

bet one's bottom dollar, to *phr.* [mid-19C+] to be absolutely certain (cf. BET A FAT MAN). [SE *bottom dollar*, one's very last one; such certainty encourages a wager of one's complete assets]

bet one's buttons/hat/neck/shirt, to *phr.* [late 19C] to bet all one's money, to go the limit.

bet one's kettle, to *phr.* [20C] to be drunk. [? a degree of drunkenness that has one betting one's valued possessions, e.g. a SE *kettle* or KETTLE *n.*[2] (2)]

bet on the blue, to *phr.* [1920s+] (Aus.) to bet on credit. [? BLUE *v.*[2]]

bet on the Mary Lou, to *phr.* [1920s+] (Aus.) to be on credit (cf. BET ON THE BLUE). [rhy. sl. *Mary Lou* = blue]

bet on the wrong side of the post, to *phr.* [early 19C] to make a losing bet. [SE *winning post*]

betsy *n.* [mid-19C] (US) a gun, thence a pistol. [abbr. BROWN BESS]

better *v.* [early–mid-19C] (Und.) to relock a door. [BETTY *n.*[1]]

better fraction *n.* [late 16C+] one's wife. [play on BETTER HALF]

better half *n.* [late 16C+] one's wife, usu. joking use (cf. BITTER HALF).

better than a dig/poke in the eye with a blunt/burnt stick *phr.* [mid-19C+] a situation that might be worse than it actually is (cf. BETTER THAN A KICK IN THE ASS; BETTER THAN A KICK IN THE ASS WITH A FROZEN FOOT; BETTER THAN A SLAP IN THE BELLY WITH A WET FISH; BETTER THAN A SMACK IN THE EYE; BETTER THAN A THUMP ON THE BACK WITH A STONE).

better than a drowned policeman *phr.* [1900s–10s] attractive, pleasant, expert, competent.

better than a kick in the ass/a kick in the ass with a frozen foot *phr.* [20C] (Can.) a situation that might certainly be worse (cf. BETTER THAN A DIG IN THE EYE WITH A BLUNT STICK).

better than a poke in the eye with a blunt stick *see* BETTER THAN A DIG IN THE EYE WITH A BLUNT STICK.

better than a slap in the belly with a wet fish *phr.* [late 19C+] a situation that certainly might be worse (cf. BETTER THAN A DIG IN THE EYE WITH A BLUNT STICK).

better than a smack in the eye *phr.* [20C] a situation that certainly might be worse (cf. BETTER THAN A DIG IN THE EYE WITH A BLUNT STICK).

better than a thump on the back with a stone *phr.* [18C] a phr. implying that bad though they are, things could be worse.

betty *n.*[1] [late 17C–mid-18C] **1** a short iron bar, used to break open doors, force locks etc; the predecessor of the 19C JENNY *n.*[2] and JEMMY *n.*[4] (cf. BESS *n.*[1]) **2** a skeleton key, a picklock. [fig. use of proper name]

betty *n.*[2] [19C] **1** a man who takes on a woman's household duties. **2** a homosexual man (cf. AGNES). **3** (S.Afr. gay) a light-skinned Black man (cf. COLORA; ZELDA *n.*[2]). [fig. use of proper name; note Scot./US dial. *jenny*(-*woman*) a man who meddles in or assists in a woman's housework]

betty *n.*[3] **1** [mid-19C] (South US) a cowhide whip. **2** [20C] a chamberpot. **3** [20C] a schoolteacher. [dimin. of SE *Elizabeth*; the implication, in all cases, is of domesticity]

betty *n.*[4] [1980s+] (US campus) a pretty young woman (cf. BARNEY *n.*[5]). [the character *Betty* in the *Flintstones* TV cartoon]

betty *v.*[1] [early 19C] to pick a lock or to relock a lock after committing a robbery so as to avoid detection (cf. UNBETTY). [BETTY *n.*[1]]

betty *v.*[2] [mid-19C–1900s] to potter about, to fuss, esp. of a man who supposedly ought to eschew such 'feminine' pursuits. [BETTY *n.*[2] (1)]

betty coed *n.* [1950s+] (US) a generic for a wholesome, middle-class sorority girl. [song 'Betty Coed' (Paul Fogarty and Rudy Vallee, 1930) and film *Betty Co-Ed* (1947)]

Betty Grable *n.* [1950s+] (Aus.) a table. [rhy. sl., ult. film star and WW2 pin-up *Betty Grable* (1916–73)]

betty lea/lee *n.* [20C] tea (cf. ROSIE LEA). [rhy. sl.]

betty rub! *n.* [1980s+] (US campus) phr. used by one male to another, meaning 'you're going to get lucky with her' (cf. IN THERE adj.[2]). [BETTY *n.*[4]]

betty swallocks *n.* [1990s] itching, uncomfortable testicles, lit. 'sweaty bollocks'.

betwattled *adj.* [late 18C] bewildered, confused. [orig. dial.]

between hell and high water *phr.* [1910s+] caught between two extremes, neither of which is particularly palatable (cf. BETWEEN THE DEVIL AND THE DEEP BLUE SEA; BETWEEN THE ROCK AND THE HARD PLACE).

between jobs *n.* [20C] (US) a small cigar. [? analogous with brandname small cigar, Between the Acts (launched 1948); travelling salesmen could smoke them between their calls]

between melts and rounds *phr.* [20C] (Irish) between one thing and another (cf. BETWEEN THE JIGS AND THE REELS). [SE *melt and rounds*, the milt and roe of a herring]

between the devil and the deep blue sea *phr.* [mid-17C+] caught between two equally unappealing extremes. [the orig. phr. lacked the 'deep', which was added in the 20C]

between the horns *phr.* [1930s+] (US) in the centre of the forehead. [the supposed devil's horns]

between the jigs and the reels *phr.* [20C] (Irish) between one thing and another (cf. BETWEEN MELTS AND ROUNDS).

between the rock and the hard place *phr.* [1920s+] (mainly US) **1** without a satisfactory alternative, in difficulty. **2** bankrupt (cf. BETWEEN HELL AND HIGH WATER).

between the sheets *phr.* [mid-19C+] in bed. [esp. with sexual overtones]

between the two Ws *phr.* [mid-19C] infected with venereal disease. [SHOT BETWEEN WIND AND WATER]

between you and me and the bedpost *phr.* [mid-19C+] in the strictest confidence; variations include [mid-19C+] ... *the doorpost*, [20C] ... *the gatepost*, [late 19C] ... *the lamp-post*.

betwixt and between *adv.* [early 19C+] undecided, uncertain, 'neither one thing nor the other'.

bet your ass/buns/katookus, to *phr.* [1950s+] to bet heavily on an apparent 'sure thing'. [SE *bet* + ARSE *n.*[1]/BUNS *n.*[3]/TOCHES]

bet your ass!/buns!/katookus! *excl.* [1950s+] an excl. of dismissal or disbelief, i.e. 'you must be joking!' [BET YOUR ASS]

bet your life!/sweet life! *excl.* [mid-19C+] (orig. US) an excl., i.e. 'you must be joking'; also found in print as *betcha*, *betcher*, emphasizing the 'slanginess' (cf. BET YOUR ASS!).

bev *n.* [mid-19C+] alcohol, especially beer. [abbr. SE *beverage* or BEVVY *n.*]

beverage *n.* [late 18C–early 19C] money for drink, demanded of anyone wearing a new suit of clothes; thus in general use to mean a tip. [SE, though similar to Fr. *pourboire*, a tip, lit. 'in order to drink']

bevvied *adj.* [1930s+] drunk. [BEVVY v.]

bevvy *n.* [mid-19C+] alcohol, esp. beer; thus *bevvy-casey*, a beer-house, a public house; *bevvy-homey*, a drunkard (lit. 'beer-man') (cf. BEEVOS). [Lat. *bibere*, to drink. Note East Anglia dial. *bever*, a four o'clock halt on the road for drink; Eton/Winchester *bevers*, afternoon tea, Charterhouse *bevor*, a wedge of bread eaten between dinner and supper]

bevvy *v.* [late 19C+] to drink. [BEVVY *n.*]

bevvy omee *n.* [mid-19C] (Ling. Fr./Polari) a drunkard. [BEVVY *n.* + OMEE]

bevvy up *v.* [1940s+] to drink heavily. [BEVVY v.]

beware *n.* [mid-19C] anything one can drink (cf. BEVVY *n.*). [Polari]

bewattled *adj.* [late 18C–early 19C] bewildered, confused (cf. BETWATTLED).

bewer *see* BUER.

be with *v.* [20C] to understand a person's line of thought, to follow their reasoning, e.g. *I'm definitely with you on that* (cf. BEHIND adv.; DOWN WITH).

bex *adj.* [20C] (W.I. Rasta) angry. [SE *vex*, *vexed*]

bexandebs *n.* [18C–late 19C] young Jewish women from the ghetto area of Wentworth Street, London (cf. BECKS). [common Jewish names, *becks*, Rebeccas, *debs*, Deborahs]

Bexley Heath *n.* [late 19C+] the teeth. [rhy. sl.]

beyond the beyonds *n.* [1910s+] (Anglo-Irish) the furthest, absolute limit.

beyond the beyonds *phr.* [1960s] (Irish) excessive, beyond reason.

beyond the rabbit-proof fence *phr.* [late 19C+] (Aus.) the wilds, the back of beyond, the edge of 'civilization'; also in fig. use (cf. BACK OF BOURKE; BEHIND GOD'S BACK). [the rabbit-proof fencing erected in Aus. to protect crops]

be your age! *excl.* [1920s+] (orig. US) a term of contempt, based in the condemnation of one whom the speaker considers is acting childishly (cf. ACT YOUR AGE!).

bezabor n. [1930s–40s] (US) a strange, eccentric person. [SE *bizarre* + SAmE *neighbor*]

bezark n. [1920s–40s] (US) an eccentric or unpleasant person. [? SE *berserk*]

bezazz n. [1970s] style, glamour. [var. on PIZZAZZ]

bezoomy adj. [1990s] (US teen) angry. [SE *berserk* + *zoom*]

bezzler n. [19C] (US) a self-important person. [Lancashire dial. *bezzler*, something large]

b.f.a. see B.F.E.

b.f. n. [late 19C+] (orig. US) a *bloody fool*. [abbr.]

b.f.d. phr. [1970s+] (US) so what! I should care less! [abbr. *big fucking deal*]

b.f.e./b.f.a. n. [1980s+] (US campus) somewhere very far way. [abbr. *butt fucking Egypt*, *butt fucking Africa*; orig. US jargon *bumfuck, Egypt*, a very distant and remote place]

b flat n. [mid-19C] a bedbug (cf. F SHARP). [B n.[2] + MAHOGANY FLAT n.[1]]

b.f.n. phr. [1940s] *bye for now* (cf. T.T.F.N.). [abbr.]

B-40 n. [1980s+] (drugs) a cigar laced with marijuana and dipped in malt liquor. [ety. unknown]

b.g. n. [1980s+] (orig. US Black teen) *baby gangster*, one who is a member of a gang, but has yet to shoot or kill anyone (cf. G n.[7]; O.G. n.[2]). [abbr.]

b-girl n. [1930s–60s] **1** (US) a dance-hall hostess whose primary job is not to dance but to promote liquor sales to the clientele. **2** (orig. US) a part-time prostitute, who frequents bars and uses them as a base for soliciting. [abbr. *bar-girl*; RHDAS suggests ult. ety. in *beading-oil* and/or PUT THE BEE ON phr.[3]]

b.h. n. [late 19C–1930s] a *bank holiday*. [abbr.]

b.h.! excl. [1920s+] *bloody hell*. [abbr.]

bhani/behani ghani! excl. [1960s–70s] (US Black) a form of greeting (cf. WHAT'S HAPPENING?). [? Swahili *abari gani*, what's news?]

bheestie/beasty n. [late 18C–mid-19C] (Anglo-Ind.) a water carrier. [Persian *bihishti*, water-carrier (lit. 'person of paradise)]

bhowji n. [20C] (W.I.) an elderly East Indian woman. [Hind. *bhaabii*, one's elder brother's wife]

b'hoy n. [mid-19C+] (orig. US) a 'lad', a young rowdy (cf. G'HAL; LIZE; MOSE n.[1]). [Irish pron. of SE *boy*]

bhuttu/buhtuh n. [20C] (W.I. Rasta) an uncouth, out of fashion, uncultured person. [ety. unknown]

bi adj. [1950s+] *bi*sexual (cf. AMBIDEXTROUS). [abbr.]

bianc/bionc n. [mid–late 19C] a shilling (5p). [Ital. *bianco*, white = silver]

bianca capellas n. [late 19C–1900s] White Chapel cigars. [a heavy-handed Ital. pun]

biatch n. [1990s] (US Black/teen) variant of *bitch*; can be used to refer to a male or a female, a friend or an enemy. [deliberately exaggerated pron.]

bib v. [late 18C–early 19C] to weep. [one uses a *bib* to wipe one's tears]

bib-all-night n. [early 17C] a heavy drinker. [SE *bib*, to drink + *all night*]

bib and bub n. [20C] (Aus.) a tub; thus *have a bib and bub*, take a bath. [rhy. sl.]

bibble n. [early 18C] beer. [dial.]

bibble chunks n. [1990s] the female breasts. [ety. unknown]

bibbling adj. [1900s] (Irish) drunken. [SE *bib*, to drink]

bibe n. [1930s] (Anglo-Irish) a bringer of bad luck. [? Irish word]

bible n.[1] [19C+] absolute authority, the truth.

bible n.[2] [mid-19C+] a pedlar's box of pins, needles and other items of haberdashery. [Und. *bible*, lead that is stolen from roofs and then wrapped around one's body for ease

of transportation; that which is placed in the pockets is *testament*]

bible n.[3] [mid–late 19C+] (US) a book of cigarette papers (cf. PRAYER BOOK).

bibleback n. [mid-19C–1930s] **1** a sanctimonious, 'holier-than-thou' person. **2** a missionary, a 'preachy' Christian.

bible-backed adj. (US) **1** [19C] of a person, round-shouldered and hump-backed. **2** [20C] sanctimonious, oppressively pious; esp. a Protestant who is conspicuously anti-Catholic. [BIBLEBACK; the image in (1) is that the self-proclaimedly pious have such a bearing]

bible-banger n. **1** [19C] a clergyman, a preacher; similarly *Bible-ranter*/*-reader*/*-spouter*/*-toter* (cf. AUTEM BAWLER). **2** [1940s+] (Aus./N.Z./US campus) a religious fanatic (cf. BIBLE-BASHER; BIBLE-BEATER; BIBLE-POUNDER; BIBLE-PUNCHER; BIBLE-THUMPER).

bible-basher n. [1950s+] (Aus.) **1** a clergyman. **2** a religious fanatic; thus *bible-bash*, to act in an overly pious fashion (cf. BIBLE-BANGER).

bible-beater n. [1970s] (US campus) an evangelizing, fundamentalist Christian (cf. BIBLE-BANGER).

bible-belter n. [20C] a native of those (mainly southern) US states where fundamentalist Christianity dominates social mores. [SE *Bible Belt*]

bible-carrier n. [mid-19C] a streetseller of songs who offers the sheet-music but does not give a performance to encourage sales.

bible mill n. [late 19C–1900s] a public house. [SE *bible* + *mill*, the noise there, reminiscent of a church full of praying congregants]

bible-pounder n. [late 19C+] a clergyman, a preacher (cf. BIBLE-BANGER).

bible-puncher n. [1930s+] (orig. milit.) a religious person, usu. one who wishes to thrust their beliefs on any who will listen and many who would rather not; thus *bible-punching*, giving a sermon (cf. BIBLE-BANGER).

bible-thumper n. [19C] a notably religious person; esp. a clergyman (cf. BIBLE-BANGER). [one who thumps the Bible in order to underline the points they are expounding, often in a sermon]

biblical neckline n. [1940s–60s] a low neckline. [pun on the biblical phr. 'lo and behold']

bicarb n. [late 19C+] *bicarb*onate of soda. [abbr.]

biccies see BIKKIES.

bice/byce n. [20C] £2, £20. [Fr. *bis*, twice]

bicho n. [1960s+] (US, orig. Hispanic) the penis. [synon. Sp. sl.]

bickies see BIKKIES n.[1].

bicycle n. **1** [1900s] (US campus) a lit. trans. of a classical text, a 'crib' (cf. ANIMAL n.[3]). **2** [1940s+] a prostitute, a promiscuous woman. **3** [1970s+] a bisexual. [all pun on SE *ride*/ RIDE n.[3]]

bicycle bum n. [1920s+] a seasonal worker, cycling between jobs. [SE *bicycle* + BUM n.[3]]

bid n.[1] [late 18C+] a young girl. [abbr. BIDDY n.[2] (1)]

bid n.[2] [1950s+] (US Black) a prison sentence (cf. BIT n.[7]).

biddie n. [1940s] (US Black) a young girl; thus *little biddie*/ *biddie baby*, a small girl, a small woman. [BIDDY n.[2]]

bid-dims n. [20C] (W.I.) a young man's trousers that are too short and narrow (cf. GUN-MOUTH). [onomat. *bid-dim*, the sound of a rifle shot; such trousers supposedly resemble a rifle barrel]

biddy n.[1] [17C] a chicken (cf. CHICKABIDDY). [dial.]

biddy n.[2] **1** [late 18C+] a young girl. **2** [19C+] any woman, esp. an Irish female servant. **3** [1940s] (US Black) a teenage girl. **4** [1980s+] (US campus) an irritating, interfering old woman (cf. OLD BIDDY). [Irish popular name *Bridget*]

biddy-peck v. [20C] (US) to nag mildly. [BIDDY n.[1] + SE *peck*]

bidgee n. [1920s+] (Aus.) an alcoholic's drink, consisting primarily of methylated spirits. [*Murrumbidgee River*, Australia]

bid stand/bid-stand/bidstand n. [late 16C–late 17C] a highwayman. [he 'bids' victims 'stand and deliver']

bienly adv. [late 18C] very well, excellently. [Fr. *bien*, well]

biff n.[1] (orig. US) **1** [late 19C+] a blow, a slap, a punch. **2** [1910s] energy, spirit, 'zip'. [Scot. *beff*, a blow, a buffet; *RHDAS* has one mid-19C cit., but it appears echoic rather than a noun use]

biff n.[2] [1920s+] (US campus) an unattractive, stupid and/or promiscuous woman. [? BIFFER]

biff n.[3] [1990s] euph. for FUCK in all uses (cf. BASH n.[2]).

biff v.[1] (orig. US) **1** [late 19C+] to hit. **2** [mid-19C+] to kill, to murder. **3** [late 19C–1910s] to rebuff, to reject, to leave without an answer. **4** [20C] (orig. US) to have sexual intercourse (cf. BANG v.[1]). **5** [1940s+] (Aus.) to throw. **6** [1980s+] (US campus) to fail (an examination). [BIFF n.[1]]

biff v.[2] [1920s] to go, to move, to proceed. [ext. use of BIFF v.[1]; ? only thus used by P.G. Wodehouse]

biff adv. [mid-19C+] (orig. US) used adverbially with *go*, in the sense of 'with a violent blow', e.g. *the brick went biff through the plate-glass window*. [echoic]

biffed adj. [1920s] (US) drunk (cf. BASTED). [fig. use of BIFF v.[1] (1)]

biffer n. [1920s+] (US Black) an unpleasant, unattractive and/or promiscuous woman. [cf. BIFF n.[2]]

biffin n.[1] [mid-19C] an intimate friend. [dial. *biffin*, a variety of cooking apple, cultivated especially in Norfolk]

biffin/biffon n.[2] [1990s] **1** the perineum, that area between the scrotum and anus or the vagina and anus. **2** sweat secreted in this area during intercourse. [fig. use of BIFF v.[1] (1), i.e. one is *biffing* against it]

biffo n. [1990s] (Aus.) a fight. [BIFF v.[1] (1)]

biff off v. [1990s] to masturbate (cf. BEAT OFF). [BIFF v.[1] (1)]

biffon see BIFFIN n.[2].

biffs n. [1920s+] (Aus. school) a beating, a caning. [BIFF n.[1] (1)]

biffy n. [1930s+] (US) **1** a privy, an outdoor lavatory. **2** an indoor lavatory. [? milit. jargon *bivvy*, a small shelter, ult. SE *bivouac*]

biffy adj. [20C] drunk. [? BEVVY n. or a play on SQUIFFY]

biftah n. [1980s+] (drugs) cannabis or a cannabis cigarette. [ety. unknown; ? link to BIFF n.[1] (1), i.e. one 'takes' a hit]

big n. [1940s+] (US) **1** a superior person or one who claims to be so (cf. BIG SHOT). **2** in sporting use, the Big League(s).

big adj.[1] [late 19C+] (US) used of large amounts of money; thus in gambling use multiples of 10,000; high stakes used in poker games where (as in drug) the convention talks of nickels ($500) and dimes ($1000); thus *big nickel* ($5000), *big dime* ($10,000).

big adj.[2] [1930s+] (orig. US) generous, magnanimous, usu. in phr. *that's big of you*. **2** [late 19C] (US) excellent, wonderful. **3** [1960s–70s] (US) well known, understood.

big v.[1] [1950s] (US/W.I.) to make pregnant; thus *big, bigged*, pregnant. [biblical *big with child*]

big/big it up v.[2] [1980s+] (W.I./UK Black teen) to aggrandize, to embellish, to praise, to extol (cf. BIG UP v.). [fig. use of BIG v.[1]]

big adv. [mid-19C+] (orig. US) **1** to a great extent. **2** notably, conspicuously, e.g. *win big, go over big*.

big a n.[1] [20C] (Aus.) brush-off, rejection, dismissal (cf. BIG E). [the *big arse* (cf. ARSE n.[1])]

Big A n.[2] **1** [1970s+] (US) Amarillo, Texas. **2** [1970s+] (US) Atlanta, Georgia. **3** [1980s+] (US) New York. **4** [1980s+] (Aus.) Australia. [abbr.; (3) BIG APPLE]

big A n.[3] [1980s+] (US) Acquired Immuno-Deficiency Syndrome (AIDS). [on model of BIG C; BIG H n. (2)]

big-able adj. [20C] (W.I.) massive, frighteningly huge.

big alley n. [20C] (orig. US tramp) the main street (cf. MAIN ALLEY).

big and bulky n. [late 19C] (Aus.) a sulky (a horse-drawn carriage). [rhy. sl.]

big-and-plenty/big-and-so-so adj. [20C] (W.I./Gren.) fat and clumsy, and of low quality (used of people and things, e.g. vegetables).

Big Apple n. [1920s+] New York City (cf. APPLE n.[5]). [in the *New Yorker* of 6 August 1984 Charles Gillett, the president of the New York Convention & Visitors Bureau, Inc., spoke on the value of the image of New York as the 'Big Apple'. It was his organization that plucked the term from the jazz lingo of the 1920s. The phrase in the jazz world, he said, had been playing 'the Big Stem in the Big Apple, the Big Stem being Broadway. For an exhaustive study of 'big apple' *see* Cohen (1993, 1995)]

big ass n. [1960s] (US) a superior person or one who claims to be so (cf. BIG SHOT). [SE *big* + ARSE n.[1] 1]

big ass adj. (US) **1** [1940s+] big. **2** [1960s] large, powerful, self-opinionated. [BIG ASS n.; the supposed crushing power of such massive buttocks]

big-ass v. [1980s+] (US southwest) to make a fool of. [BIG ASS n.]

big auger n. [mid-19C+] (US, mainly west) an important person, a boss (cf. BIG BUG; BIG BUTT; BIG CASINO; BIG CHEESE; BIG COG; BIG DEALER; BIG DOG; BIG DUDE; BIG ENCHILADA; BIG GEORGE; BIG GUN; BIG HAT n.[1]; BIG HERB; BIG IKE; BIG I, LITTLE YOU; BIG INJUN; BIG NOISE; BIG POTATO n.[1]; BIG ROD; BIG SCREECH; BIG SHOT; BIG SHOW; BIG SPENDER; BIG SQUEEZE; BIG STICK; BIG STUFF n.[2]; BIG TIMER; BIG WHEEL). [SE *big* + *auger*, a tool that bores holes; thus one who makes 'a big impression']

Big B n. [1970s] (US) Baltimore, Maryland. [abbr.]

big bag n. [1980s+] (drugs) heroin. [SE *big*, important + BAG n.[8]]

big ballocks n. [1950s] an important man. [SE *big* + BALLOCKS n.[1]]

big banana n. [1980s+] (US) **1** the most important thing, the crux of a matter. **2** a superior person or one who claims to be so (cf. BIG SHOT). [on model of BIG CHEESE + showbiz *top banana*, the star comedian]

big-belly adj. [1920s+] (W.I.) greedy.

big ben n.[1] [20C] **1** the number ten. **2** £10. [rhy. sl.; *Big Ben* is the clock in the tower of the Houses of Parliament]

big ben n.[2] [1960s] (US gambling) the point of 10 in craps dice. [var. on BIG DICK n.[1]]

big bertha/bertha n. [1920s–40s; 1980s+] (US) a fat person. [WW1 Ger. gun, *Big Bertha*, a 42cm (16½in) mortar; ult. the proper name Frau *Bertha* Krupp von Bohlen und Halbach (1886–1957), the owner of the Krupp steelworks in Germany]

big bird n. [1960s+] a large penis. [SE *big* + BIRD n.[6]; ? mockery of the child-friendly character *Big Bird*, on TV's *Sesame Street*]

big bit n. [1930s–50s] (US Und.) a long prison sentence (cf. LONG BIT). [SE *big* + BIT n.[7]]

big blink n. [1970s–80s] death. [variation on BIG SLEEP]

big bloke n.[1] [late 19C–1910s] (Aus.) a boss, a superior. [SE *big* + BLOKE]

big bloke n.[2] [1980s+] (drugs) cocaine. [? rhy. sl.]

big blow n. [20C] (Aus./US) a hurricane. [SE *big* + SAusE *blow*, a storm]

big board n. [1920s+] the New York Stock Exchange. [SE *board*, a board at the Stock Exchange on which share prices are displayed]

big boat *n.* [1970s] a large, traditional American car, esp. a large station wagon. [SE *big* + BOAT n.¹]

big bopper *n.* [1960s+] (US) a superior person or one who claims to be (cf. BIG SHOT). [SE *big* + BOPPER n.¹, a gang member, lit. 'big hitter'; note *The Big Bopper*, the nickname of DJ and rock singer J.P. Richardson (1930–59)]

big boss, the *n.* [1920s] (US) God (cf. BIG BOY n.¹; BIG GUY). [joc. cod-intimacy]

big boy *n.¹* **1** [1910s+] (US) a general term of address, sometimes sincere, often ironic. **2** [1920s+] (US) a superior person or one who claims to be so (cf. BIG SHOT). **3** [mid-19C–1940s] (US Black) a foolish, reckless, devil-may-care young man. **4** [1960s] (US) God (cf. BIG BOSS).

big boy *n.²* [20C] (US) a shotgun (cf. BIG TOTER). [? an affectionate nickname]

big brown ones *n.* [1980s+] (drugs) MDMA (cf. ECSTASY). [the capsules in which the drug is sold]

big-buck *adj.* [1990s] (US Black) expensive. [BIG BUCKS]

big bucks *n.* [1970s+] large sums of money, esp. those earned by performers or stolen by criminals, or as a large, but non-specific price. [SE *big* + BUCK n.² (1)]

big bug *n.* [19C] (US) an important person, an aristocrat; esp. one who considers themself to be one and acts accordingly (cf. BIG AUGER). [SE *big* + 18C *bug*, someone who sets themselves up as important; ult. f. *bug*, an object of fear, a hobgoblin]

big bull *n.* [20C] (US prison) the senior guard on a shift. [SE *big* + BULL n.¹⁰]

big bull with the brass collar *see* BIG DOG WITH THE BRASS COLLAR.

big burg *n.* [1910s–40s] (US) New York City. [SE *big* + BURG n.¹]

big butt *n.* [1910s–40s] (US) an important person (cf. BIG AUGER). [SE *big* + BUTT n.¹]

big C *n.* **1** [1960s+] *cancer*; the horror disease (*pace* AIDS) of the 20th century which, as the supreme threat to life, cannot be named in full without a shudder (cf. BIG A; BIG H). **2** [1950s+] (drugs) *cocaine*. [abbr.]

big casino *n.* (US) **1** [late 19C+] an important person (cf. BIG AUGER). **2** [1950s+] anything terminal, fatal, esp. a disease, e.g. cancer. **3** [1980s+] the best, the ultimate, the most important. [the big wins and big losses involved]

big cheese *n.* [1910s+] (orig. US) an important person, an influential figure, a boss in a situation or job (cf. BIG AUGER; CHEESE n.¹).

big chief *n.* [1930s+] an important or the most important man (cf. BIG WHITE CHIEF).

big chill *n.* [1980s+] death (cf. BIG SLEEP; COLD STORAGE). [coined in the synon. film (1983)]

big-cock *adj.* [1960s–70s] (US) enormous, outsized. [SE *big* + COCK n.² (1)]

big cog *n.* [20C] an important or self-important person (cf. BIG AUGER). [play on BIG WHEEL]

big coin *n.* [1990s] (US teen) a large amount of money. [SE *big* + COIN]

Big D *n.* (US) **1** [1960s+] the nickname of a variety of suitably initialled US cities, i.e. *D*allas, Texas; *D*etroit, Michigan; *D*enver, Colorado (cf. D n.⁴). **2** [1970s+] death. **3** [1980s+] (drugs) LS*D* (cf. A n.³). [abbr.]

big daddy/papa *n.* (US) **1** [20C] an important person (cf. BIG SHOT). **2** [1940s–50s] (US Black) any influential Black man, a power in his own community, aged 30 and more (cf. MACK DADDY). **3** [1950s–60s] (mainly Black) one's grandfather (cf. BIG MAMA). **4** [1950s–70s] a male lover, a sweetheart. **5** [1960s] a pimp. **6** [1960s+] the most important of its kind (not necessarily a human being). [fig. uses of SE]

big daddy pot *n.* [1950s+] (W.I.) a large iron pot, used for cooking cow-tripes after butchering (cf. BELAGOT). [BIG DADDY n. (1) + SE *pot*]

big deal *n.* [1940s+] (orig. US) **1** an important person. **2** anything that is considered important to the speaker; often ironic. [SE *big* + DEAL n.²]

big deal *adj.* [1960s+] important, urgent, impressive etc. [BIG DEAL n.]

big deal *v.* (US) **1** [1940s] to get what one wants by clever, forceful negotiation. **2** [1960s] to aggrandize, to magnify the importance of. [BIG DEAL n.]

big deal! *excl.* [1940s+] (orig. US) a dismissive, sarcastic phr., 'what's important about that?' 'why bother me?' (cf. BIG WHOOP!). [BIG DEAL n.]

big dealer *n.* [20C] (US) an important person (cf. BIG AUGER). [BIG DEAL n.]

big deuce *n.* [1950s] (US teen) the Second World War. [SE *big* + *deuce*, two]

big dick *n.* [late 19C+] **1** (US gambling) the point of 10 in craps dice, usu. ext. as *big Dick from Boston* (cf. BIG BEN n.²). **2** an important person (cf. BIG SHOT). [SE *big* + generic use of proper name]

big dish *n.* [1940s] (Aus.) a big win; thus *go for the big dish*, to place a large bet, to gamble heavily.

big ditch *n.* (US) **1** [19C] the Erie Canal. **2** [mid-19C+] the Atlantic Ocean (cf. DITCH n.²). [joc. deliberate understatement]

big do *n.* [1900s–20s] (US Black) any notable event. [var. on BIG DOING]

big dog *n.* [19C] **1** a thug (cf. BOUNCER n.¹). **2** (US) an important person (cf. BIG AUGER).

big dog/bull/man with the brass collar *n.* [mid-19C+] an important person, esp. in a business context (cf. BIG DOG OF THE TANYARD).

big dog of the tanyard *n.* [mid-late 19C] an important or the most important person (cf. BIG DOG WITH THE BRASS COLLAR; BIGGEST TOAD IN THE PUDDLE). [fig. use of SE ? a fierce dog kept in a tanyard]

big doing/doings *n.* [1900s–20s] (US Black) **1** any notable event, esp. a party or celebration. **2** a boaster, a braggart. [SE *big* + *doing*, what is being done]

big doing *adj.* [20C] (US) conceited, self-opinionated, snobbish. [SE *big* (*things*) + *doing*, performing.]

big drink *n.* [mid-19C+] (US) **1** (west) the Mississippi River. **2** the ocean, esp. the Atlantic Ocean (cf. BIG DITCH). [joc. deliberate understatement]

big-dubs *n.* [20C] (W.I.) a large and good-humoured man. [Carib.E. *big-dubs*, a large, polished marble]

big dude *n.* [20C] (US) an important person (cf. BIG AUGER). [SE *big* + DUDE n. (1)]

big Dutchman *n.* [late 19C+] (US) a general term of disparagement. [SE *big* + DUTCHMAN n.¹, lit. 'German'/'foreigner', here used as a general pej.]

big E *n.* [1980s+] a brush-off, a rejection. [ELBOW v.²]

Big Easy, the *n.* [1970s+] (US) New Orleans, Louisiana. [? coined by Conaway as the title of his novel *The Big Easy* (1970), later a popular film (1986); presumably f. the stereotype of its free-and-easy lifestyle]

big eight *n.* [1980s+] (drugs) one-eighth of a kilogram of crack cocaine.

big enchilada *n.* [1970s+] (US) an important person (cf. BIG AUGER). [very popular during the Watergate Scandal (1973–4) when the White House tapes used it variously to describe corrupt personnel.

big end of *n.* [late 19C–1900s] (orig. US) the majority; thus *big end of a month*, three weeks.

big enough to choke a cow/an elephant/a horse/an ox *phr.* [late 19C+] (US) of a bankroll, extremely big.

big eye *n.* (US) **1** [19C+] avarice, greed; thus *have the big* *eye/eye for*, to covet. **2** [1950s] a stare, esp. when hostile or curious; thus *big eye*, to stare at. **3** [1960s–70s] a television.

big eye *v.* **1** [20C] to act greedily. **2** [1920s] (US) to stare at amorously. [BIG EYE n.]

big eyes *n.* [20C] (US) police officers engaged in surveillance duties. [BIG EYE n. (2)]

big-feeler *n.* [20C] (US) an arrogant, self-important person (cf. BIG AUGER). [BIG-FEELING]

big-feeling *adj.* [19C] haughty, conceited (cf. BIGGITY). [one who feels themself *big*]

big ferry *n.* [mid-19C] (US) the Atlantic Ocean (cf. BIG DITCH).

big figure *n.* [mid-19C] (US) large scale; thus *do something on the big figure, go the big figure*, to do something on a large scale. [SE *big* + *figure*; a number, a sum]

big fish *n.* (US) **1** [early 19C+] an important, powerful person. **2** [mid-19C–1950s] an important event, undertaking etc. [SE *big* + FISH n.[1]]

big flake *n.* [1980s+] (drugs) cocaine. [SE *big* + FLAKE n.[3]]

big foe *see* BIG FOUR.

big foot country *n.* [1940s–60s] (US Black) the southern United States. [? the population 'walks tall']

big foot Joe *n.* [20C] the penis. [? nickname]

big four/foe *n.* [1980s+] (US Black) tough, élite (often physically large) detectives, dealing with organized crime and similar areas; such police officers match their wide powers with indiscriminate physical violence and the general belief that all members of the Black community are *de facto* criminals. [the old practice of manning all police vehicles with four officers]

big gates *n.* [late 19C+] (Und.) a prison. [metonymy]

big george *n.* [1940s] (US) an important person (cf. BIG AUGER). [SE *big* + generic use of proper name]

bigger thomas *n.* [1960s] (US Black) a rebellious Black man, who refuses to abide by White society's rules and struggles against them (cf. BAD NIGGER). [proper name of *Bigger Thomas*, the hero of Richard Wright's novel *Native Son* (1940)]

biggerty *see* BIGGITIVE.

biggest toad in the puddle *n.* [mid–late 19C] (US) a leader, a chief, the most important person in a situation. [fig.]

biggie/biggy *n.* **1** [1920s+] (orig. US) anything or anyone large, important, successful, esp. used in entertainment industries (cf. GORILLA n.[1]). **2** [1950s+] (W.I.) a 750ml (26fl oz) bottle of rum. [SE *big* + sfx. *-ie/-y*]

big girl's blouse/girl's blouse *n.* [1960s+] a weakling, an ineffectual person; usually found as a direct statement, *You big girl's blouse!* [the phrase, now widespread, originated like the similarly deracinated GOBSMACKED in the north of the UK]

biggitive/biggerty *adj.* [20C] (W.I.) bumptious, pushy, showing off; thus *biggitive with yourself*, self-satisfied. [SE *big*]

biggity *adj.* [mid-19C–1900s] (orig. US Black) haughty, conceited (cf. BIG-FEELING). [SE *big*]

Big Green *n.*[1] [1930s+] (US campus) nickname for Dartmouth College. [the college colour]

Big Green *n.*[2] [1990s] California's Environmental Protection Act (1990). [SE *big* on pattern of SAmE *big steel* etc., a generic word for a whole industry + *green*, relevant to ecology/conservationism]

big gun *n.* [mid-19C+] (orig. US) an important person (cf. BIG AUGER).

big guy *n.* (US) **1** [1920s+] God (cf. BIG BOSS). **2** [1980s] a joc. form of address (cf. BIG BOY n.[1]).

biggy *n.*[1] *see* BIGGIE.

biggy *n.*[2] [1950s+] (W.I.) a man who is both tall and lazy. [SE *big*]

big H *n.* **1** [1950s+] (drugs) heroin. **2** [1980s+] a *h*eart attack (cf. BIG A; BIG C). [initial letters]

big hair *n.* [1980s+] (orig. US) teased hair, typically as worn by the heroines of such TV soap operas as *Dallas*, but also seen on men.

big Harry *n.* [1980s+] (drugs) heroin (cf. BIG H; HENRY n.[2]). [initial letters]

big hat *n.*[1] (US) **1** [1960s+] a policeman or state trooper. **2** [1950s+] an important person (cf. BIG AUGER). [the headgear worn as part of many US police uniforms]

big hat *n.*[2] (US) a Mexican. [the clichéd large Mexican hat]

big head *n.*[1] [mid-19C+] a conceited or arrogant person; thus *big-headed*, conceited, arrogant.

big head *n.*[2] [late 19C] a hangover. [SE *big* + HEAD n.[4]]

big Herb *n.* [19C+] (US) an important person (cf. BIG AUGER). [either SE *herb*, and thus the size to which it can grow, or the slightly foolish proper name *Herbert*]

big hit *n.*[1] [1920s+] (Aus.) excrement or an act of defecation. [rhy. sl. *big hit* = SHIT n.[1]]

big hit *n.*[2] [1970s+] (US prison) a long term of imprisonment, usu. 3 years or more (cf. BIG TIME n.[2]). [ironic use of SE *big* + *hit*, a success]

big house *n.* **1** [mid-19C] the workhouse (cf. LARGE HOUSE). **2** [1910s+] (US Und.) prison, esp. (S.Afr. Und.) Pretoria Central prison. **3** [1950s+] any large, forbidding institution, esp. a psychiatric institution.

big house nigger *n.* [20C] (US Black) any proud, arrogant person. [SE *big* + HOUSE NIGGER]

bigified *adj.* [20C] (US) haughty, conceited (cf. BIGGITY). [SE *big* + sfx. *-ified*]

big Ike *n.* [20C] (US) an important person (cf. BIG AUGER). [SE *big* + IKE n. (2)]

big I, little you *n.* [20C] (US) an important person (cf. BIG AUGER).

big Injun *n.* [20C] (US) an important person (cf. BIG AUGER). [SE *big* + INJUN, lit. 'big Indian'; thus, note BIG WHITE CHIEF]

big it up *see* BIG v.[2].

big job *n.* [mid-19C] (US) murder, assassination; thus *do the big job*, to kill. [euph.]

big jobs *n.* [20C] (juv.) excreta; thus *do big jobs*, to defecate (cf. JOB n.[4]). [euph.]

big john *n.* [1950s+] (US Black) the police. [SE *big* + JOHN n.[3]]

big juice *n.* [1960s–70s] (US Black) a White gang-boss. [SE *big* + JUICE n.[1]]

big jump *n.* [20C] (US) death.

big juta, little juta, all same price *phr.* [20C] (W.I.) anything goes, irrespective of size or quality; usu. used of a country person who lacks the city dweller's standards of choice. [Hind. *juutaa*, a shoe, and orig. used of shoes]

big L *n.* [1980s] *l*ove. [abbr. on pattern of BIG C]

big-league *adj.* [1910s+] (US) important, substantial, powerful. [sporting imagery]

big-leaguer *n.* [1950s–60s] a resourceful person who can handle any situation. [BIG-LEAGUE]

big legs *n.* [1970s–80s] a big spender. [? who has trousers with big pockets]

big licks *n.* [mid–late 19C] (US/Aus.) hard work. [SE *big* + *lick*, a blow]

big M *n.* **1** [1950s+] £1 *m*illion. **2** [1950s+] (drugs) *m*orphine. **3** [1960s] *m*arriage. **4** [1970s] *M*emphis, Tennessee. [initial letters]

big mama *n.*[1] [1920s–60s] (US Black) one's grandmother. [BIG DADDY]

big mama *n.*[2] [1970s+] anything notably large, substantial. [euph. for SE *big* + MOTHERFUCKER n. (6)]

big man *n.* **1** [20C] (US) a gallon of wine. **2** [1980s+] (drugs) a dealer, esp. a major dealer, selling bulk quantities of drugs (cf. MAN n.[3]).

big man – big prick; little man – all prick *phr.* [20C] a phr. that both lauds virility but at the same time brands any size of man as a fool. [PRICK]

big man with the brass collar *see* BIG DOG WITH THE BRASS COLLAR.

big medicine *n.* [late 19C; 1980s] (US) an important or influential person or thing. [BAD MEDICINE]

big mitt *n.* [1900s] (US) a form of swindling involving the use of a stacked hand while playing poker. [SE *big* + MITT n.]

big moment *n.* [1920s–40s] (Irish/US) the person with whom one is infatuated.

bigmouth *n.* 1 [1930s+] a braggart, a boaster. 2 [1940s+] (orig. US) an informer, a tell-tale. 3 (W.I.) empty boasting, showing off.

bigmouth *v.* [1960s+] (US) to brag (about). [BIGMOUTH n. (1)]

big mover *n.* [1940s+] (Aus.) one who is a consistent success, e.g. as a womanizer. [SE *big* + MOVER]

bignaduo *n.* [1910s+] (W.I.) a boaster, a bumptious person, a show-off, one who puts on airs. [lit. 'big as a door']

big nickel *n.* [1920s+] (US) a sum of $5000 (cf. SMALL NICKEL).

big nigger *n.* [20C] (US) in poker, a game in which the high spade splits the pot (cf. LITTLE NIGGER). [the blackness of the spade suit]

big nigger in charge *see* HEAD NIGGER IN CHARGE.

big noise *n.* 1 [mid-19C] (US) trouble, disturbance. 2 [20C] (orig. US) an important, powerful person (cf. BIG AUGER).

big-noise *adj.* [1990s] important. [BIG NOISE n.]

big nose – big cock/cunt *phr.* [late 19C+] a phr. underpinning the popular theory that those with large noses have correspondingly large genitals.

big-note *v.* [1940s+] (Aus.) to boast, usu. as *big-note oneself*, to inflate one's achievements. [SE *big* + *note*, paper money, currency]

big-note artist *n.* [1940s+] (Aus.) a show-off, a braggart, esp. concerning alleged sums of money owned. [BIG-NOTE + ARTIST n.²]

big noter *n.* [1940s+] (Aus.) a show-off, a braggart. [BIG-NOTE ARTIST]

big number *n.*¹ [mid-19C–1900s] a brothel. [the outsize numbers painted on brothel doors in Paris]

big number *n.*² [1940s–50s] (US) an important person (cf. BIG SHOT). [SE *big* + NUMBER n.³ (4)]

big O *n.* 1 [1950s+] (drugs) *opium*. 2 [1960s+] an *orgasm*. [initial letter]

big—o, the *phr.* [1980s+] (orig. US) used of landmark birthdays, e.g. those that mark another decade, *three-o*, *four-o* etc.

big on *adv.* [mid-19C+] (orig. US) keen on, enthusiastic about. [the size of one's enthusiasms]

big one *n.*¹ 1 [early–mid-19C] an important person. 2 [20C] (orig. US) a tall story, an exaggerated tale. 3 [1990s] the penis (cf. BITE THE BIG ONE).

big one *n.*² 1 [mid-19C+] £100, $100. 2 [mid-19C+] (US) $1000. 3 [1960s+] (US) $1 million. 4 [1970s+] $1.

big one, the *n.*³ 1 [1930s] (US) death. 2 [1960s+] (orig. US) a major disaster, esp. California's long-awaited major earthquake or a nuclear war.

Big Orange *n.* [1980s+] (US) Los Angeles, California. [on model of BIG APPLE; the ref. is to the state's orange groves]

big papa *see* BIG DADDY.

big/tall paper *n.* [20C] (US Black) a great deal of money. [SE *big/tall* + PAPER n.¹ (5)]

big parade, the *n.* [1920s–50s] (US) the First World War (cf. BIG SNARL; BIG STUNT). [the title of the film *The Big Parade* (1925), screenplay by Laurence Stallings, although the phr. is never used in the film itself]

big pasture *n.* [20C] (US) a prison (cf. BIG HOUSE). [as used by cowboys and other Westerners]

big people *n.* [mid-19C+] important, influential people.

big pond *n.* [late 19C+] (orig. US) the Atlantic Ocean (cf. BIG DITCH; BIG DRINK; POND). [deliberate understatement]

big poppa *n.* [1990s] (US Black teen) any influential Black man, a power in his own community, aged 30 and over (cf. BIG DADDY).

big pot *n.* [mid-19C+] a leader, an important person. [? SE *potentate*; which was also Oxford jargon in 1850s to mean a don or a prominent undergraduate]

big potato *n.*¹ [late 19C+] an important person (cf. BIG AUGER).

big potato *n.*² [1980s+] Moscow. [on model of BIG APPLE; BIG ORANGE; potatoes are the main constituent of vodka]

big razzoo *n.* [1930s+] a gesture of extreme contempt or scorn (cf. RASPBERRY n.¹). [SE *big* + RAZZ n.]

Big Red *n.* [20C] (US campus) Cornell University. [the college colour]

Big Red with the long green stem *n.* [1940s–50s] (US Black) Seventh Avenue, between the 130s and 140s, the centre of Harlem nightlife. [BIG APPLE + LONG GREEN + MAIN STEM]

big rock *n.* [20C] (US) a prison (cf. BIG HOUSE). [SE *big* + ROCK n.³]

big rod *n.* [1920s+] (US) an important person (cf. BIG AUGER).

big rush *n.* [1980s+] (drugs) cocaine. [SE *big* + RUSH n.²]

big screech *n.* [1910s+] (US) an important person (cf. BIG AUGER; BIG NOISE).

big shit *n.* [1930s+] an important person or one who claims to be so (cf. BIG SHOT).

bigshit *adj.* [1960s] (US) self-important. [BIG SHIT n.]

big shit! *excl.* 1 [1910s+] a response to the indicating of someone as a BIG SHOT, *big shot – big shit!* 2 [1980s+] (US campus) a dismissive, sarcastic phr. (cf. BIG DEAL!). [BIG SHIT n.]

big shot *n.* [1920s+] (orig. US) a superior person or one who claims to be (cf. BIG ASS; BIG AUGER; BIG BANANA; BIG BOPPER; BIG BOY; BIG DADDY; BIG DICK; BIG NUMBER n.²; BIG SHIT; BIG SMOKE n.²; BIG SQUASH; CANNONBALL; GREAT SHOT; HIGH SHOT). [the term began as a positive ref. to a major criminal, but by 1930s it was mainly used ironically and implied that the individual in question was rather too pleased with themself. Note dial. *queer shot*, an odd fellow, a strange 'customer', *great shot* [mid-19C], an important person]

big shot/bigshot *v.* [1950s+] (US) to show off, to act like an important person. [BIG SHOT n.]

big show *n.* [20C] (US) an important person (cf. BIG AUGER). [SE *big* + *show*(-*off*).

big six *n.* [1950s+] (US prison) the prison riot squad. [? their are 6 officers]

big sleep *n.* [1930s+] (orig. US) death. [coined by Raymond Chandler as title of his book *The Big Sleep* (1939), although *RHDAS* suggests (without confirmatory citations) that he 'gave currency' to the term]

Big Smoke *n.*¹ 1 [mid-19C+] any town. 2 [mid-19C+] London (cf. SMOKE n.²). 3 [late 19C+] (Aus.) Sydney. 4 [late 19C+] (Aus.) Melbourne. 5 [1930s+] Pittsburgh, Pennsylvania. [the pollution and general dirt associated with a major city. *OED* suggests orig. Aus. trans. of Aboriginal *toom-virran*, big-smoke]

big smoke *n.*² [1900s–30s] (US) an important person (cf. BIG SHOT).

big snarl/stoush *n.* [1910s+] (Aus. ex-soldiers) the First World War (cf. BIG PARADE). [SE *big* + *snarl*; STOUSH n.]

big spender *n.* [1940s+] a spendthrift, one who flashes their money around, esp. in phr. *last of the big spenders*, used ironically to mock a cheapskate or someone who is spending a great deal of money that they patently cannot afford. [usu. slightly derog., the implication being that any such 'spender' will also be a SUCKER n.¹]

big/long spit *n.* [1960s+] (Aus.) the act of vomiting.

big squash n. [1910s–60s] an important person or someone who think they are so (cf. BIG SHOT). [BIG SQUEEZE, ? on pattern of BIG CHEESE, SE *squash*, the vegetable]

big squeeze n. [20C] (US) an important person (cf. BIG AUGER; MAIN SQUEEZE). [SQUEEZE n.⁶]

big stick n. [20C] (US) **1** an important person (cf. BIG AUGER). **2** a figure of authority, esp. a policeman or foreman. [? their real or fig. truncheon or similar badge of office/chastisement. Note Theodore Roosevelt's dictum: 'Speak softly and carry a big stick']

big stiff n. [late 19C+] (US) a general term of abuse. [SE *big* + STIFF n.³]

big stoush see BIG SNARL.

big stuff, a n.¹ [late 19C] (US) a general term of abuse (cf. BIG STIFF).

big stuff n.² **1** [1910s+] (orig. US) an important or self-important person (cf. BIG AUGER). **2** [20C] (US) a term of address, usu. slightly derog. **3** [1920+] (US) a major criminal (cf. MR BIG). [WW1 milit. jargon *big stuff*, heavy artillery shells]

big stunt n. [1910s] the First World War (cf. BIG PARADE).

big swing n. [1960s] (US) the prison gallows. [SE *big* + SWING v.¹]

Big T n. [1970s] (US trucker) **1** Tucson, Arizona. **2** Tampa, Florida. [abbr.]

big talk n. [mid-19C+] boasting, braggartry, verbal self-aggrandizement.

big talk v. [1950s] (US) to show off, to try to impress. [BIG TALK n.]

big thing n.¹ [mid-19C+] anything important, noteworthy; often as a neg. phr. (*that's*) *no big thing*.

big thing, the n.² [20C] a generous, magnanimous act, often as *do the big thing*, make a generous gesture.

big thing on ice, a phr. [mid-19C] an amazing thing. [ext. of BIG THING n.¹]

big ticket/ticket item n. [1940s+] (US) something that is expensive, requiring a considerable financial outlay. [the high-priced ticket placed on expensive retail goods in a shop]

big time n.¹ **1** [mid-19C–1950s] (US) an exciting, enjoyable time. **2** [20C] success, fame, power; thus *get big time*, to put on airs and graces (cf. SMALL TIME). **3** [1960s] an important person, esp. in ironic use. [theatrical use, vaudeville theatres with top-line acts and thus only two (long) shows per day, the opposite of 'small time', which featured shorter acts]

big time n.² [1930s+] (US prison) a lengthy sentence, three years plus (cf. BIG BIT). [SE *big* + TIME n.¹]

big-time adj. [1910s+] (orig. US) important, successful, powerful. [BIG TIME n.¹]

big time v. [1940s+] **1** (US) to act in a self-important manner. **2** (US Black) to live well. [BIG TIME n.¹]

big-time adv. [1950s+] (US Black) very much, completely, absolutely, e.g. *she really loves him big time*. [BIG TIME n.¹]

big timer n. [1920s+] (orig. US) an important person (cf. BIG AUGER). [BIG-TIME adj.]

big toter n. [20C] (US) a shotgun (cf. BIG BOY n.²). [SE *big* + *tote*, to carry]

big town n. [20C] (US) New York City, occas. Chicago.

big-tree adj. [1940s+] violent, bullying, gangsterish. [BIG-TREE BOY]

big-tree boy/man n. [1910s+] (W.I.) an idler, a semi-gangster, esp. if idling near a large banyan tree in Victoria Park, Kingston, Jamaica.

big twist n. [1940s+] (Aus.) a cause for celebration, a great success. [SE *big* + 'twist of fate']

big up v. [1990s] **1** (Black) to act in a proud, self-confident matter. **2** (Black) to promote, to boost, to praise. **3** (W.I./UK Black teen) to greet friends, to pay tribute to something or someone big or important. e.g. *Big up the dancehall crew dem, seen, come again.*

big up adj. [20C] (W.I.) important, socially or otherwise powerful. [BIG UP v.]

Big V n. [1970s] (US) Las Vegas, Nevada. [abbr. on model of BIG A]

big vegetable n. [1970s] (orig. US) an important person, an influential figure, the boss (cf. BIG POTATO).

big wheel n. [1930s+] an important, influential person, esp. in business (cf. BIG AUGER). [the image of a smooth-running, powerful machine]

big white chief n. [1930s+] (orig. US) an important or the most important man (cf. BIG CHIEF). [cod Native American]

big whoop! excl. [1980s+] (US) a dismissive, sarcastic phr., 'why bother me?' (cf. BIG DEAL!). [SE *whoop*, a cry (of exultation, triumph)]

big wig n. [early 18C+] a powerful, important person, often a politician or bureaucrat. [SE *big* + *wig*]

big willie n. [1990s] (US Black) a sophisticated, successful urban Black male (cf. MACK n.¹). [SE *big* + generic use of proper name; ? + WILLIE n.¹; 'the Big Willie ... is ... the strong, silent type ... an old-school romantic (and) a savvy business-man ... a free thinker, fluent with modern technology. He is fearless, vigilant and innovative.' *Vibe* magazine, September 1996]

big willie adj. [1990s] (US Black) important, influential, powerful. [SE *big* + name *Willie*, but note WILLIE n.¹]

big Wind/Windy n. [1940s+] (US) Chicago, Illinois. [var. on WINDY CITY]

big X n. [1980s+] (US campus) one's menstrual period. [marked on a calendar with an X]

big yard n. [1940s+] (W.I.) a prison (cf. BIG HOUSE). [SE *big* + *yard*, the exercise area of a prison]

bijou adj. [late 19C+] small and pretty, usu. in combs. with nouns + the sfx. *-ette*, e.g. *I'll have just a bijou drinkette*, 'just a little' drink. [Fr.]

bijoux n. [1980s+] jewels. [synon. Fr.]

bike n. [1940s+] a promiscuous woman (cf. BARRACK HACK). [she is available for 'riding']

biker n. [1950s+] (orig. US) a motorcycle rider, usu. a member of an outlaw motorcycle gang. [SE (*motor*)*bike*]

bikie/bikey n. [1960s+] (Aus./N.Z.) an 'outlaw' motorcyclist, e.g. a Hell's Angel. [var. on BIKER]

bikini burger n. [1990s] wisps of pubic hair protruding from a bikini. [SE *bikini* + FURBURGER]

bikkies/biccies/bickies n.¹ [1960s+] (Aus.) money; thus *big bikkies*, a large amount of money. [dimin. of SE *biscuits* and thus the roundness of coins]

bikkies/biccies n.² [1980s+] (Aus. drugs) biscuits cooked with a dose of hashish (cf. BROWNIE n.⁶). [dimin. of SE *biscuits*]

bil n. [late 17C–mid-18C] a sword. [abbr. of BILBO]

bilayutee pawnee n. [late 19C] (Anglo-Ind.) soda water. [Arab. *wildayat*, kingdom, province, then Hind. *bilayuti*, Europe + *panee*/*pawnee*, water]

bilbo/bilboa n. [late 17C–mid-19C] a ruffian's sword; thus *bilbo's the word*, it's time for swords, i.e. fighting (cf. TOL n.¹). [SE *bilbo, bilboa*, a high-quality sword, imported from Bilboa in Spain]

bilge n. [1900s–50s] nonsense, rubbish. [abbr. BILGEWATER]

bilge artist n. [1920s+] (Aus.) a braggart, one given to boasting (cf. BULL ARTIST). [BILGE + ARTIST n.²]

bilgewater n. [late 19C+] **1** (mainly juv.) nonsense, rubbish, piffle (cf. BILGE). **2** thin beer; thus any thin, tasteless drink, alcoholic or otherwise. [SE *bilgewater*, the foul water that collects in a vessel's bilges]

bilingual adj. [1980s+] (US gay) referring to one who licks and sucks both the anus and penis of his partner. [pun on SE]

biljim see BILLJIM.

bilk n. **1** [late 17C–mid-18C] an empty, meaningless statement. **2** [late 17C–mid-18C] a hoax. **3** [mid-19C+] a swindler or cheat. [cribbage jargon *balk*, to spoil an adversary's score in their crib. (2) orig. SE late 18C–mid-19C]

bilk adj. [mid-18C] wrong, misleading, meaningless. [BILK n. (1)]

bilk v. [mid-18C+] **1** to cheat, to swindle. **2** to evade payments, esp. of a prostitute's client. [BILK n.]

bilker n. [early 18C–1910s] one who habitually cheats, esp. in refusing to pay a cabman's fare. [BILK n.]

bilk the blues, to phr. [mid-19C] to evade capture by the police. [BILK v. + BLUE n.[3]]

bilk the schoolmaster, to phr. [early 19C] to get knowledge without paying for it, e.g. the experience that comes with living one's life. [BILK v. + SE *schoolmaster*]

bill n.[1] [19C] (US) a divorce. [abbr. SE *bill of divorce*]

bill n.[2] [early–mid-19C+] (US) the nose.

Bill n.[3] [20C] the 'inevitable' nickname of those surnamed Sykes or Bailey. [the character in Dickens's *Oliver Twist*; the song 'Won't You Come Home Bill Bailey']

bill, the n.[4] [1920s+] the 'short-change' swindle (cf. HYPE n.[1]). [SE *bill*, a bird's beak, i.e. one 'dips' into the victim's money]

bill n.[5] **1** [1940s+] $1 bill (cf. BILLIES). **2** $100. [abbr. SE *dollar bill*]

bill n.[6] [1950s+] (camp gay) a macho homosexual, whether in fact or in pose. [? stereotyped 'macho' name]

Bill, the n.[7] [1960s+] the police. [ety. unknown; ? abbr. OLD BILL. There is a poss. semantic link to BEAK n., but in reality it is unlikely]

bill v. [19C] (US) to divorce. [BILL n.[1]]

billabonger n. [late 19C–1950s] (Aus.) a vagrant (cf. SWAGMAN n.[2]). [SE *billabong*, a dry watercourse, in which such men took shelter and slept]

bill-be-damned/billy bedam n. [20C] (US) a comparative phr. used to indicate absoluteness, e.g. *dead as ...*, *cold as ...* (cf. BILLY HELL). [euph. for BLOODY adj.]

bill blass n. [1980s+] (drugs) crack cocaine. [*Bill Blass*, a top couturier]

billet n. [late 19C+] an appointment, a job; thus (Aus.) *billet-hunter*, a job-seeker. [SE *billet*, a place in which a soldier is billeted; a soldier's lodging or quarters]

billiard ball n. [19C] the head (presumably of a bald person).

billie hoke n. [1980s+] (drugs) cocaine. [rhy. sl. *billy hoke* = COKE n.[1] (1)]

billies/billys n. [1980s] (US teen) money. [dimin. of BILL n.[5]]

billing n. [1980s+] rolling a cannabis cigarette. [? SE *building*]

Billingsgate pheasant n. [19C] a red herring (the fish) (cf. ABERDEEN CUTLET; ATLANTIC RANGER). [*Billingsgate*, London's wholesale fish market]

billjim/biljim n. [late 19C+] (Aus.) **1** the typical Aus. male. **2** the typical Aus. soldier in WW1 (cf. TOMMY ATKINS); a synthetic variation, *billzac* (SE *bill* + ANZAC) was created by the Aus. press during WW1, but never spread beyond their own columns. [the proper names *Bill* + *Jim*]

bill-o! excl. [20C] (London school) a cry of warning. [SE (*watch out*) *below!* or the BILL n.[7]]

bill of goods n. [1920s+] (orig. US) false promises, a hoax, theories that are not followed up by practice; thus *sell one a bill of goods*, to persuade (someone) to accept something undesirable, swindle someone. [SE *bill of goods*, a consignment of merchandise]

bill of sale n. **1** [17C] a widow's peak. **2** [18C–mid-19C] a widow's weeds (cf. APARTMENT TO LET). [? a widow is 'back on the (marriage) market']

bill on the pump at Aldgate/Aldgate n. [late 18C–19C] a bad bill of exchange. [proper name *Aldgate Pump*, near junction of Fenchurch Street and Leadenhall Street in London; the pump was a City institution, but hardly a safe financial one]

bill shop n. [1960s+] a police station (cf. COP SHOP). [BILL n.[7] + SE *shop*]

bill up v. [1980s+] (drugs) to roll up a cannabis cigarette. [ety. unknown; ? SE *build*]

billy n.[1] **1** [19C] stolen metal (cf. BILLY-FENCING SHOP; BILLY-HUNTING). **2** [mid-19C–1930s] (orig. US) a policeman's wooden club (orig. untanned cowhide, covered in wool), now SE (cf. MR WOOD). **3** [19C] a short iron crowbar, used by criminals (cf. BESS n.[1]).

billy n.[2] [19C] the penis (cf. BAT n.[6]). [either f. BILLY n.[1] (2) or a pun on the *billycock* hat (see BILLY n.[3])]

billy n.[3] [mid-19C] (Aus.) a billycock hat. [SE *billycock*, a low crowned felt hat; ult. f. *bully-cocked*, used 1721, prob. meaning 'cocked after the fashion of the bullies' or street thugs of the period]

billy n.[4] [mid-19C] a silk handkerchief, worn by London costermongers (cf. BELCHER n.1; BIRD'S EYE FOGLE; BIRD'S EYE WIPE; BLOOD-RED FANCY; BLUE BILLY n.[1]; CREAM FANCY; KINGSMAN; RANDAL'S MAN; WATER'S MAN; YELLOW FANCY; YELLOW MAN). [? King *William* IV, in whose reign (1830–37) the practice began. The silk handkerchief was a central part of costermonger fashion, often apeing that of the prize-ring, where fancy handkerchiefs were an essential trademark of certain fighters. As Mayhew notes: 'The costermonger ... prides himself most of all upon his neckerchief and boots. Men, women, boys and girls all have a passion for these articles. The man who does not wear his silk neckerchief/his "King's-man" as it is called – is known to be in desperate circumstances, the implication being that it has gone to supply the morning's stock money']

billy n.[5] [20C] a policeman. [BILL n.[7]]

billy n.[6] [1980s+] (drugs) amphetamine (cf. A n.[2]). [abbr. BILLY WHIZ]

billy/billy-joe bad-ass n. [1970s+] (orig. US) usu. in ironic use, anyone who sets themselves up as tough, aggressive. [generic name *Billy-Joe* + BAD-ASS n.]

billy barlow n.[1] [19C] a fool (cf. JIM CROW n.[2]). [*Billy Barlow*, a real-life street clown, *fl.*1840 around the East End of London. 'Billy was a real person, semi-idiotic, and, though in dirt and rags, fancied himself a swell of the first water. Occasionally he came out with real witticisms' (Hotten, 1867)]

billy barlow n.[2] [20C] (US) a large pocket knife with folding blades. [? brand name]

billy-be-damned n. [mid-19C+] (US) euph. for hell, usu. in phr., e.g. *dead as billy-be-damned, blacker than billy-be-damned* (cf. BILLY HELL). [? orig. euph. for the Devil or euph. for BLOODY adj.]

billy bluegum n. [20C] (Aus.) a koala bear. [generic use of proper name + SE *bluegum*, the koala's habitat]

billy born drunk n. [late 19C–1900s] a drunkard all one's life. [proper name *Billy* + quasi-nickname *Born-Drunk*]

billy-boy n. [20C] (US) a policeman (cf. BILLY n.[5]).

billy button n.[1] [mid-19C] mutton. [rhy. sl.]

billy button n.[2] [20C] (W.I.) a gullible fool, esp. one who performs a job of work without first making sure that they will be paid. [joc. use of 'proper name' + rhy. sl. *billy button* = (gets) nothing]

billy buzman n. [19C] a pickpocket who specializes in stealing silk handkerchiefs. [BILLY n.[4] + BUZMAN]

billy call father n. [19C] weak tea. [Oxford dial.; ? the child has made the tea too weak and is due for punishment]

billy-cart n. [1990s] (Aus./N.Z.) a child's homemade 'go-kart'. [abbr. SE *billy-goat cart*]

billycock *n.* [early 18C–late 19C] a hat with a low crown; primarily worn by carters, it was also popular among the clergy; thus *billycock gang*, the clergy as a group. [? *bully-cocked*, 'cocked after the fashion of the bullies' (the sp. of the orig. 1721 citation)]

billy d. juice *n.* [1990s] (US Black/teen) Colt .45 malt liquor. [proper name *Billy D* + JUICE n.[3]]

billy fencer *n.* [mid-19C] a marine store owner. [BILLY n.[1] (1) + FENCER]

billy-fencing shop *n.* [18C] a shop that specializes in buying stolen precious metals. [BILLY FENCER + SE *shop*]

billy-goat *n.*[1] [19C] a bearded man. [the goat's 'beard'; thus SE *goatee*]

billy-goat *n.*[2] **1** [mid-19C–1930s] (US) a lecher. **2** [1920s] (US) a bad-tempered man. [the goat's supposed characteristics]

billy goat *v.* [1930s–60s] to philander (cf. TOM CAT). [the image of the goat as the epitome of lechery]

billy-goat alley/hill *n.* [20C] (US) the poorest section of a town (cf. GOAT HILL). [? the denizens keeping goats or, since such areas are associated with various social excesses, f. their 'goatishness']

Billy Harran's dog *n.* [20C] (Irish) a time-server, one who befriends whoever they happen to be with (cf. LANTY MACREE'S DOG; O'BRIEN'S DOG). [anecdotal]

billy hell *n.* (US) **1** [19C] a fantasy place that epitomizes the ultimate in bleakness and desolation, usu. in comparative phr. for intensification, e.g. *meaner than ...*, *hot as ...* (cf. BILLY-BE-DAMNED). **2** [late 19C+] used in phr. as synonym for SHIT n.[1], STUFFING n.[1] etc, e.g. *knock the billy hell out of*.

billy-hunting *n.* [mid-19C] **1** trading in old (poss. stolen) metal. **2** stealing handkerchiefs. [BILLY n.[1] (1) + SE *hunting*]

billy-jack *adj.* [1970s] (US Black) unsophisticated, from the back woods. [the title of a film featuring a raw country-boy]

billy-joe bad-ass *see* BILLY BAD-ASS.

billy knife *n.* [20C] (US) a large pocket knife. [abbr. BILLY BARLOW n.[2]]

billy man *n.* [20C] a policeman. [ext. of BILLY n.[5]]

billy muggins *n.* [20C] (Aus.) a fool (cf. JUGGINS). [ext. of MUGGINS n.[1] (2)]

billy-noodle *n.* [19C+] (US/Aus.) a man who firmly believes, all evidence to the contrary notwithstanding, that no woman can resist his charms. [SE *billy*, generic for a man + *noodle*, a fool; US use is 19C; Aus. is 20C]

billy of the wash-house, the *n.* [20C] an argumentative, 'difficult' person, a 'dog in the manger'. [Scot. *billy*, a young man, a companion, a friend or *billy*, goat; thus kin to *bull in a china shop*; the wash-house is presumably occupied primarily by women]

billy turniptop *n.* [late 19C–1900s] an agricultural labourer. [generic use of proper name + joc. use of SE; Ware suggests that it is 'probably an outgrowth of TOMMY ATKINS']

billy whiz/whizz *n.* [1980s+] (drugs) **1** amphetamine (cf. A n.[2]; TOFFY WHIZZ). **2** a mixture of heroin and cocaine (cf. SPEEDBALL n.[1]). [*Billy Whizz*, a character in a children's comic; as his name suggests, he moves fast]

biltong curtain *n.* [1970s–80s] (S.Afr.) a joc. name for the borders of pre-independence South Africa. [SE *biltong*, salted, wind-dried meat, a S.Afr. national foodstuff + a pun on SE *iron curtain*]

bim *n.*[1] [mid-19C+] a Bajan, a native of Barbados; thus *Bimshire*, Barbados.

bim *n.*[2] [1920s+] (US) a person, usu. male. [abbr. BIMBO]

bim *n.*[3] [1930s–40s] the bottom, the buttocks. [var. on BUM n.[2]]

bim *n.*[4] [1950s] (US Black) a policeman. [ety. unknown; ? abbr. BIMBO n.]

bimbette *n.* [1980s+] a junior or aspirant 'good-time girl' (cf. CHUBETTE). [BIMBO + fem. dimin. sfx *-ette*]

bimbo *n.* **1** [1910s–40s] a young man. **2** [1920s+] a woman. **3** [1920s+] (Ling. Fr./Polari) a dupe. [the earliest use of bimbo is found *c.*1900 in America, where it was synonymous with 'bozo' to mean a tough guy. A parallel use was that to mean 'baby', abbr. from the Italian *bambino*. By the 1920s the word meant young woman, often a prostitute; simultaneously it meant a tramp's companion (cf. GUNSEL) possibly gay. The writer Jack Conway (of *Variety* magazine) used it specifically to mean a 'dumb girl'. *Bimbo* gained a new currency during the 1980s when it came to describe a young woman, usually something of a gold-digger and indulged as such by rich and/or powerful older men and the media to whom they tell or sell their tales. The original 1980s bimbo was a 'model', Fiona Wright, who delighted the press with revelations of her relationship with Sir Ralph Halpern, a millionaire businessman]

bimi *n.* [1970s] a West Indian. [BIM n.[1]]

bimmer *see* BEAMER n.[3].

bimp *n.* [20C] (tramp) a shilling (5p). [BEONG]

bimp *v.* [1960s+] to spy, esp. as a sexual voyeur. [ety. unknown]

bimphead *n.* [1990s] (US teen) a person who interacts better with a computer than with people (cf. NERD). [? pun on BIMPS, French fries, i.e. chips, the essential motive power of a computer]

bimps *n.* [1970s] (US campus) French fried potatoes. [ety. unknown]

bin *n.* **1** [1920s+] a pocket. **2** [1930s+] a psychiatric institution (cf. LOONY BIN). **3** a police or prison cell. **4** (US) a safe.

bin *v.* **1** [1940s+] to throw away. **2** [1960s] to commit to a psychiatric institution (cf. LOONY BIN). [abbr. SE *throws in the bin*]

binco *n.* [mid-19C] (Ling. Fr./Polari) a kerosene flare. [Ital. *bianco*, white]

bind *n.* **1** [mid-19C+] a difficult situation, a predicament. **2** [1930s+] a bore, nuisance. [such problems 'tie one up']

bind *v.* **1** [1920s–40s] to bore intensely. **2** [1940s–50s] to complain, to scold. [orig. RAF use, and poss. the most commonly used of all RAF sl.; thus the celebrated BBC radio comedy programme of the late 1940s, *Much Binding in the Marsh*]

binder *n.*[1] **1** [late 19C–1900s] an egg. **2** [20C] (N.Z.) a good, filling meal; thus *go a binder*, to eat a meal. **3** a piece of bread and cheese (cf. TITLEY n.). [all f. their 'binding' or costive properties]

binder *n.*[2] [late 19C–1950s] **1** a last drink (cf. ONE FOR THE ROAD; OTHER HALF; SWING OF THE DOOR). **2** one who orders a drink in a public house after 'last orders'. [? it 'binds' its predecessors together]

binder *n.*[3] [1930s–40s] **1** a bore. **2** an habitual complainer. [BIND v. (1)]

binders *n.* [1940s–60s] brakes; thus *jump on the binders*, to put on the brakes, excl. *hit the binders! brake!* [their tightening on a moving wheel]

bindle *n.* [late 19C+] (US) **1** a bundle containing clothes and possessions, esp. a bedding-roll carried by a tramp. **2** (drugs) a small measure of narcotics, wrapped in a folded square of paper. [Ger. *Büntel*, a package]

bindle bo/bum *see* BINDLE STIFF.

bindle-man *n.* [late 19C+] (US) a tramp (cf. BINDLE STIFF). [BINDLE + SE *man*]

bindle punk *n.* [late 19C+] (US) a tramp (cf. BINDLE STIFF). [BINDLE + PUNK n.]

bindle stiff/bo/bum *n.* (US) **1** [late 19C+] a tramp, spec. one carrying a bedroll; formerly a migrant worker (cf. BLANKET STIFF; MISSION STIFF). **2** [1920s–60s] an unimportant man. [BINDLE + STIFF n.[3]/BO n.[1]/BUM n.[3]]

bines *n.* [1950s] spectacles. [BINNS]

bing *n.*[1] [20C] (US Und.) solitary confinement. [ety. unknown; image of one being thrown into a cell and landing 'bing!']

bing *n.*[2] [1980s+] (drugs) enough of a drug for one injection. [BING v.[2]]

bing *v.*[1] [mid-16C] to go (cf. BING A WASTE). [? Rom.; Walter Scott resurrected it for his literary romances of the period in early 19C]

bing *v.*[2] [20C] to hit (cf. BIP v.; BOP). [echoic]

bing a waste, to *phr.* [16C–late 18C] (Und.) to go away, to depart. [the *OED* suggests a poss. Gypsy root but offers no elaboration + SE *waste*, wasteland, desert or f. 16C SE *aways*, away; Carew has *bing feck you*, devil take you, and *bing lee ma*, devil miss me as 'gypsy language']

bing-bang *n.* [1910s–20s] a repeated heavy thump or a continued banging noise. [echoic]

binge *n.* [mid-19C+] excessive consumption, usu. of drink and (latterly) drugs. [dial. *binge*, to soak (a wooden vessel)]

binge *v.* **1** [mid-19C+] to drink heavily. **2** [1990s] (drugs) to indulge in a continuous period of crack cocaine use; thus *binging*, using crack cocaine for long periods. [BINGE n.]

binged/binged up *adj.* [20C] drunk. [BINGE v.]

bingee *see* BINGY.

bingers *n.* [1980s+] (drugs) addicts of crack cocaine. [BINGE v. (2)]

binge up *v.* [1910s] to cheer someone up, to enliven. [ext. of BINGE v. (1)]

bingey *n.*[1] *see* BINGY.

bingey *n.*[2] [late 19C] (Anglo-Irish) the penis. [? dial. *bing* n., a heap, a pile or *bing* v., to hit]

binghi/Binghi *n.* [1930s] (Aus./N.Z.) an aboriginal or Native Australian. [Dharuk *binghi*, a brother]

bingie *see* BINGY.

bingle *n.* [1940s+] (Aus.) **1** a fight. **2** a collision, a crash. [? echoic *bing*, the sound of a collision]

bingo *n.*[1] [17C–late 19C] brandy or any hard liquor (cf. BINGO-BOY; BINGO-CLUB). [? *B* for brandy + Yorkshire dial. *stingo*, strong ale (*OED*) or SE *binge* (E.P.)]

bingo *n.*[2] **1** [17C–late 19C] a drinking-bout. **2** [1950s+] (Can. prison) a riot (cf. KICK-UP; ROCKIN' n.). [ext. of BINGO n.[1]]

bingo *n.*[3] [1900s–20s] a hard blow. [? misuse of baseball jargon *bingle*, a hit for a single]

bingo *v.* [1980s+] (drugs) to inject a drug. [BINGO n.[3]]

bingo! *excl.* [1920s+] used to imply a moment's surprise, excitement, suddenness etc, e.g. *There I was, walking along, then bingo! a cat fell on my head*. [echoic of SE *bing!* a thump; in a flash]

bingo-boy *n.* [17C–late 19C] a male lover of brandy (cf. BINGO-MORT). [BINGO n.[1] + SE *boy*]

bingo-club *n.* [17C–late 19C] a set of rakes whose favourite tipple is brandy. [BINGO n.[1]]

bingoed *adj.* [1920s+] (society) drunk. [BINGO n.[1]]

bingo-mort *n.* [17C–late 19C] a female lover of brandy (cf. BINGO-BOY). [BINGO n.[1] + MORT]

bings *n.* [1980s+] (drugs) crack cocaine. [BING n.[2]]

bingy/bingee/bingey/bingie/binjy *n.* [mid-19C+] (Aus./N.Z.) the stomach. [Dharuk *bingy*, the stomach]

binky *n.*[1] [20C] (US) the buttocks. [? Scot. *bink*, a bench]

binky *n.*[2] [20C] (drugs) a needle used for injecting narcotic drugs, most often a disposable needle that is prescribed to a diabetic (cf. BIZ n.[2]). [BING v.[2]]

binlid *n.* [20C] (Ulster) a fool. [fig. use of abbr. SE *dustbin lid*]

binned *adj.* [late 19C] hanged. [proper name Bartholomew Binns, the London hangman in 1883]

binns *see* BINS n.[1].

binocs *n.* [1940s+] *binoc*ulars. [abbr.]

bins/binns *n.*[1] [1930s+] **1** glasses, spectacles. **2** binoculars. **3** the eyes. [abbr. SE *binoculars*]

bins *n.*[2] [1930s+] a pair of trousers. [BIN n. (1), i.e. the pockets that they contain]

bint *n.* [mid-19C+] a young woman; thus *lush bint*, a very good-looking woman. [Arabic *bint*, daughter; thus a woman who has yet to bear a child; noted in 1855 by the explorer Richard Burton (1821–90), the term gained fuller currency during WW1 and WW2, when it was adopted by Allied servicemen]

bio *n.*[1] [1910s+] (S.Afr.) the cinema. [Afk. *bioscope*, a cinema; obs. elsewhere, the term remains current in South Africa]

bio *n.*[2] [1930s+] a *bio*graphy. [abbr.]

biockey *n.* [mid–late 19C] (Anglo-Ital.) money. [Ital. *baiocchi*, lit. 'browns', thus cf. BROWN n.[2]]

biog *n.* [1940s+] (orig. US) a *biog*raphy. [abbr.]

bionc *see* BIANC.

bionic *adj.* [1970s+] exceptional, outstandingly gifted. [SE *bionic*, 'having or being an artificial, esp. electromechanical, device that replaces part of the body; having ordinary human capabilities increased (as if) by the aid of such devices' (*OED*); coined 1963 but popularized by the 1970s TV series *Six-Million Dollar Man*, starring actor Lee Majors]

bioscope *n.* [1910s] a drink of brandy. [SE *bioscope*, a cinema; the more one drinks the more 'moving pictures' one sees]

bip, the *n.*[1] [1920s+] (society) the *bi*shop. [abbr.]

bip *n.*[2] [1990s] (Can.) semen. [? supposed echoic of the 'sound' of ejaculation]

bip/bip into *v.* [19C] to hit (cf. BING; BOP). [echoic]

bip-bam-thank-you-ma'am *n.* [20C] quick, spontaneous intercourse, with the implication that only the man will achieve pleasure (cf. WHAM-BAM-THANK-YOU-MA'AM).

bipe *n.* [1960s+] (US) a bisexual. [? joc. use of SE *bipolar*]

bippy *n.* [1960s+] (orig. US) a synon. for ASS (cf. ARSE n.[1]), esp. in phr. *you can bet your (sweet) bippy*. [coined on NBC-TV's *Rowan and Martin's Laugh-In*, c.1967]

birch broom *n.* [mid-19C] a room. [rhy. sl.]

Birchen/Birchin/Birching Lane *see* SEND TO BIRCHEN LANE.

Birchington hunt *n.* [1930s+] the vagina. [rhy. sl.; var. on BERKELEY HUNT + ? overtones of sado-masochism]

bird *n.*[1] [16C] (Und.) **1** a confidence trickster's victim. **2** a prisoner; thus *a bird has flown*, a prisoner has escaped. [the imagery reflects the world of hunting (cf. BEATER n.[1]; BUSH n.[1]; VERSER)]

bird *n.*[2] **1** [17C+] a person, a man, a 'bloke' (cf. NEWGATE BIRD; QUEER BIRD). **2** [mid–late 19C] (US) a dissolute or degenerate person. **3** [mid-19C–1910s; 1970s] (US) an exceptionally clever or accomplished person, esp. when used ironically. **4** [mid-19C+] (US) anything first rate. **5** [1920s+] (US) an eccentric.

bird *n.*[3] [early 19C] a Black slave. [abbr. BLACKBIRD]

bird *n.*[4] [mid–late 19C] (US) $1 (cf. YELLOW BIRD). [the American eagle engraved upon it]

bird *n.*[5] **1** [mid-19C+] a young woman, a girlfriend (cf. DOLLY-BIRD). **2** [1950s–70s] (US Black) an experienced, tough female prostitute. [note first use of sense (1) c.1300, meaning a maiden or girl and not sl. until 1900 when it meant a sweetheart or a prostitute]

bird *n.*[6] **1** [late 19C+] (mainly US) the penis; thus *beat/jerk one's bird*, to masturbate, *get one's bird in a splint*, to get into (painful) difficulties; *eat/gobble/swallow one's bird*, to fellate, *how's your bird?* a phrase of greeting, *not on your bird!* in no way! impossible (cf. HOW ARE THEY HANGING?). **2** [1960s–70s] (US) the vagina; thus *bird-washing*, mutual cunnilingus.

bird *n.*[7] **1** [1920s+] a prison sentence; thus *birded (up)*, imprisoned, *in bird*, in prison, *do bird*, serve a sentence.

2 [1920s–30s] previous convictions. [rhy. sl. BIRDLIME = TIME n.¹]

bird n.⁸ [1920s+] (US) **1** a loud, derisive noise, imitative of a fart, esp. in phr. *give one the bird* (cf. BRONX CHEER, RASPBERRY n.¹). **2** any form of ridicule or derision. [echoic of a harsh bird-call]

bird n.⁹ [1930s+] (mainly US) an aircraft, esp. a helicopter, spacecraft, missile etc.

bird n.¹⁰ [1960s–70s] the Thunder*bird*, a motorcar. [abbr.]

bird n.¹¹ [1960s+] (US) an obscene gesture of dismissal, mockery (cf. FINGER n.³; FLIP THE BIRD; GIVE THE BIRD). [ext. of BIRD n.⁸]

bird n.¹² [1970s+] the mind, sanity; thus *lose one's bird*, to go mad, *out of one's bird*, crazy, mad. [ety. unknown]

bird n.¹³ [1990s] (drugs) 1kg (2.2lb) weight. [ety. unknown]

bird v.¹ [late 16C–early 17C] to rob, to steal, to search for plunder. [BIRD n.¹]

bird v.² [1940s–60s] (US) to talk nonsense, usu. in phr. *not just birding* (cf. BIRD TURD). [one is as incomprehensible as a bird]

birdbrain n. [1930s+] a fool; thus *bird-brained*, stupid (cf. BAKEBRAIN). [SE *bird* + sfx. *-brain*]

birdcage n. **1** [mid–late 19C] a bustle on a woman's dress. **2** [mid-19C–1900s] a four-wheeled cab. **3** [late 19C–1950s] (US) a prison cell. **4** [1920s] (US) a brothel. **5** [1930s–60s] (US) an elevator with an openwork sliding metal gate. **6** [1940s–50s] a sleeping cubicle in a flophouse, separated from its neighbours by a 'wall' of chicken wire. [resemblance]

birdcage hype n. [1930s–50s] (US drugs) the lowest class of heroin addict. [? BIRDCAGE (6) + HYPE n.²]

birdcages, the n. [mid-19C] (Can.) the first ever legislative buildings erected in Victoria, British Columbia. [? resemblance]

bird colonel n. [1940s+] (US) a full colonel in the US marines; thus *make bird*, to gain this promotion (cf. CHICKEN COLONEL). [the silver eagles affixed to the uniform's shoulders denote the rank]

birdcrap n. [1970s] (US) nonsense, rubbish (cf. BIRDSHIT). [SE *bird* + CRAP n.]

bird dog n.¹ **1** [20C] a receiver of stolen goods. **2** [1940s+] a watcher, an observer. **3** [1940s+] (US Und.) a contact man for stock and bond thieves. **4** [1940s+] (US campus/teen) a young man, bereft of a partner of his own, who attempts to steal a woman from someone else. **5** [1940s] a persistent, tenacious person. [SE *bird dog*, a retriever, which fetches things]

bird dog n.² [20C] (US) the buttocks. [? SE *buttock*]

bird dog v.¹ [1950s+] **1** (US teen) to steal another person's girlfriend, to break up a school or college romance. **2** to pimp for, to solicit for another person. **3** to hang around in the hope of making a pick-up. **4** to spend more time away from home than staying in with one's family. [BIRD DOG n.¹ (4)]

bird dog v.² [1950s+] to observe, to lie in wait. [BIRD-DOG n.¹ (2)]

bird dogger n. [20C] (US) one who tries overly hard to gain acceptance or approval. [SE *bird dog*, a retriever, which is seen as especially keen to please]

bird eater n. [20C] (US) a finicky eater. [SE phr. *eat like a bird*]

birder n. [19C] (Aus.) a slave-trader. [abbr. SE *blackbirder*, a slaver]

birdhouse n. [1940s] (US) a prison. [BIRD n.⁷ + SE *house*]

birdie n.¹ [20C] the penis. [ext. of BIRD n.⁷]

birdie n.² [1960s+] an effeminate male. [BIRD n.² (2), BIRD n.⁵; note 14C–16C SE *bird*, a young man]

birdie powder n. [1980s+] (drugs) **1** heroin. **2** cocaine. [? BIRDSEYE or joc. use of SE *birdseed*]

bird-lime n. [18C] a thief. [SE *bird-lime*, a sticky substance spread on twigs so that birds may be caught; the ref. is to the thief's 'sticky fingers']

birdlime/bird's-lime n. [mid-19C+] a prison sentence (cf. BIRD n.⁷).

bird-mouthed adj. [16C] said of one who minces matters. [the tiny bites of a bird's beak]

bird never flew on one wing, a phr. [20C] used as a formula for accepting a second drink (and pretending that one is doing so more from duty than pleasure).

bird of passage n. [mid-19C+] a tramp, a vagrant.

bird of the game n. **1** [17C] a prostitute. **2** [19C] a womanizer (cf. COCK OF THE GAME). [BIRD n.⁵ + GAME n.¹]

birds n. [1980s+] (drugs) amobarbitol, Amytal. [they make one 'fly']

birdseed n. (US) **1** [20C] rubbish, nonsense. **2** [1910s–60s] any breakfast cereal seen as resembling birdseed.

birdseye n. [1960s+] (drugs) a small amount of narcotics. [resemblance]

bird's eye fogle n. [mid-19C] a silk handkerchief with a 'bird's-eye' pattern (cf. BILLY n.⁴; BIRD'S EYE WIPE). [FOGLE]

bird's eye wipe n. [mid-19C] any spotted silk handkerchief, as sported by fashionable costermongers (cf. BILLY n.⁴). [BIRD'S EYE FOGLE + WIPE n.²]

birdshit n. [1950s–70s] (US) nonsense, rubbish (cf. BIRDCRAP; BULLSHIT). [SE *bird* + SHIT n.¹]

bird's nest n. **1** [20C] the vagina (cf. CUCKOO'S NEST n.¹; GOLDFINCH'S NEST; PHOENIX NEST). **2** [1970s] (gay) a hairy chest.

bird's-nester n. [19C] a promiscuous man, a womanizer. [puns on BIRD n.⁵ (1) + NEST n.¹]

birds of a feather n. [17C–18C] members of the same gang. [pvb. *birds of a feather flock together*]

bird taker n. [1950s] the vagina. [BIRD n.⁶ (1) + SE *taker*]

bird turd n. [1950s–70s] (US) **1** nothing, an insignificant amount. **2** an insignificant, worthless person.

bird turd v. [1940s+] (US) to talk nonsense, esp. in phr. *you ain't just (a-)bird-turding* (cf. WHISTLE DIXIE). [BIRD TURD n.]

bird-witted adj. [17C–late 18C] foolish, scatter-brained, gullible.

birdwood n. [1940s] (US) **1** a cigarette. **2** (drugs) marijuana, a marijuana cigarette. [ety. unknown]

birk n. [mid-19C] a house. [backsl. = CRIB n.³ (1)]

Birkenstock buddy n. [1990s] (US campus) an environmentalist. [the *Birkenstock* shoe, popular among such individuals + BUDDY]

birl n. [19C] (Scot.) a twist or turn; thus (Aus.) phr. *give it a birl*, to give it a try, to make an attempt. [dial. *birl*, a rapid twist or turn]

Birmingham/Brummagem screwdriver n. [20C] a hammer (cf. CHINESE SCREWDRIVER; FRENCH SCREWDRIVER; IRISH SCREWDRIVER; JEWISH SCREWDRIVER). [the supposed oafishness of the Birmingham worker who would rather hammer in a screw than use the correct tool; despite normal racial stereotypes (and their supposed jobs) a US usage *yiddish screwdriver* has been noted c.1939]

birthday suit n. [mid-18C+] the naked body. [the state in which one emerges from the womb]

bis n. [1990s] (US) a pistol, a handgun. [abbr. BISCUIT n.⁶]

biscuit n.¹ **1** [19C] the face, the head (cf. CRUMPET n.¹; CRUST n.²; LOAF n.²; SCONE n.²; TWOPENNY n.¹). **2** [late 19C–1900s] (US) a watch. **3** [1980s] a record. [the resemblance of these round objects]

biscuit n.² [mid-19C+] a young woman; thus *reel in the biscuit*, to seduce a woman (cf. BANANA n.²). [her being 'sweet' and/or 'good enough to eat']

biscuit n.³ [20C] (US) a woman's hairstyle in which the hair is done up in a small knot, usu. favoured by elderly women with thinning hair. [a pun on SE *biscuit*, a small bun]

biscuit n.⁴ [20C] (US) euph. for BITCH, as in SON OF A BITCH (cf. BISCUIT-EATER).

biscuit *n.*[5] [1930s–40s] (US Black) a pillow. [resemblance]

biscuit *n.*[6] [1940s+] (US) a pistol, a handgun. [? one 'snaps' it]

biscuit *n.*[7] (drugs) **1** [1970s] a tablet of methadone. **2** [1980s+] 50 rocks of crack cocaine. **3** [1990s] a tablet of MDMA (cf. DISCO BISCUIT; ECSTASY; GREY BISCUIT). [the shape]

biscuit *n.*[8] [1980s+] (US Black) a type of shoe worn for comfort rather than style and favoured by older people.

biscuit and beer *v.* [late 19C–1900s] to swindle a gullible dupe by betting them a biscuit against a glass of beer; one will, of course, win.

biscuit-arsed *adj.* [20C] (Scot.) dirty, grubby. [? the image of a badly cleaned anus with traces of dried faeces]

biscuit beggar *n.* [20C] (US) a Native American. [? their poverty]

biscuit-eater/-hound *n.* [20C] (US) **1** a worthless dog. **2** a worthless person. [such a dog will eat biscuits provided by its owner but will not forage for its own food]

biscuit factory *n.* [1900s–50s] Reading gaol. [it was sited next to the Huntley & Palmer's biscuit factory; thus the *Biscuit Men*, the Reading football team]

biscuit-headed *adj.* [mid-19C] (US) foolish.

biscuit hooks *n.* [1930s] (US) the hands (cf. BREAD HOOKS; FLESH HOOKS; LUNCH HOOKS). [SE *biscuit* + HOOKS *n.*[2]]

biscuit-hound *see* BISCUIT-EATER.

biscuit-roller *n.* [1930s–40s] (US Black) a (usu. female) lover. [BISCUITS]

biscuits *n.* [1930s+] (orig. US Black) the buttocks (cf. BISCUIT-ROLLER). [the roundness]

biscuits and cheese *n.* [1940s+] the knees. [rhy. sl.]

biscuit shooter *n.* [19C] (US) **1** a cook. **2** a waiter or waitress (cf. COOKIE-PUSHER). [SE *biscuit* + *shoot*, the throw violently]

bish *n.* [1990s] an effeminate man, a weakling. [? SE *bishop*]

bish *v.* [1940s] (Aus./N.Z.) to throw. [var. on BIFF *v.*[1] (6)]

bishop *n.*[1] [late 16C–mid-17C] a fly that is burnt in a candle flame. [BISHOP *v.*[1]]

bishop *n.*[2] [late 18C] a mixture of wine and water, topped off by a roasted orange. [a clergyman's favourite]

bishop *n.*[3] **1** [late 18C] a large condom. **2** [19C–1900s] a chamberpot. [the size/rotundity]

bishop *n.*[4] [mid–late 19C] a broken signpost, which 'neither points the way nor travels it' (Grose) (cf. PARSON). [mild anti-clericalism]

bishop *n.*[5] [1950s–70s] a private detective. [he 'searches out sin']

bishop *v.*[1] [18C–19C] to burn, to let burn. [proverbial saying 'the bishop hath played the cook' or 'the bishop has put his foot into the pot']

bishop *v.*[2] [early 18C–late 19C] to use any form of trickery, esp. the burning of marks into the teeth, in order to reduce the appearance of a horse's age. [a man called *Bishop* who specialized in such frauds]

bishop *v.*[3] [early 19C] (Und.) to change the markings on a stolen watch to facilitate its resale (cf. CHRISTEN). [pun on SE *bishop*, to administer the rite of confirmation]

bishop *v.*[4] [mid–late 19C] to murder by drowning. [the murderer *Bishop*, who in Bethnal Green in 1831 drowned a boy in order to sell the body for dissection]

Bishop Barker *n.* [late 19C–1910s] a drinking glass of the largest size (cf. DEEP SINKER). [Frederick *Barker* (1808–82), Anglican Bishop of Sydney; the bishop was a teetotaller, but he was extremely tall]

bishop's finger *n.* [mid-19C] a signpost (cf. PARSON). [BISHOP *n.*[4] + SE *finger*(-*post*)]

bishop's nose *n.* [1960s] (US) the rump of a chicken, duck, goose or other poultry. [var. on PARSON'S NOSE]

bismarcker/bismarquer *n.* [mid–late 19C] a cheat, esp. at cards or billiards. [the foreign policy of the German

Chancellor Otto von *Bismarck* (1815–98), which, while it benefited Germany, was seen elsewhere as duplicitous; Ware cites *Bismarck* as 'a term of contempt' and labels it 'political; South German and French']

bisom *n.* [20C] (Aus.) an undisciplined child. [SE *besom*, a witch]

bison *v.* [1980s+] (US campus) to vomit (cf. WATER BUFFALO; YAK *v.*[2]). [echoic]

bit *n.*[1] **1** [16C–19C] money (cf. BITE *n.*[2]). **2** [18C–19C] the silver coin of the lowest denomination. **3** [19C+] any low-denomination coin, e.g. *threepenny bit, fourpenny bit*. **4** [early 19C+] (US) 12.5 cents, but usu. in phr. *two bits*, 25 cents, *six bits*, 75 cents, *long bit*, 15 cents, *short bit*, 10 cents.

bit *n.*[2] [mid-17C+] a short time, a brief period, usu. as *for a bit*.

bit *n.*[3] [late 19C+] sexual intercourse (cf. BIT OF BRAILLE; BIT OF BRUSH; BIT OF BUM; BIT OF CUFF; BIT OF HOW'S YER FATHER; BIT OF KEG; BIT OF MEAT; BIT OF MUTTON; BIT OF SLAP AND TICKLE; BIT OF SNUG; BIT OF TAIL; BIT OF TICKLE; BIT OF TIT; BIT OF UNDER; BREAK A BIT OFF; DO A BIT phr.[1]; DO A BIT OF BEEF; DO A BIT OF BUSINESS; DO A BIT OF CAULIFLOWER; DO A BIT OF COCK-FIGHTING; DO A BIT OF DANCING; DO A BIT OF FLAT; DO A BIT OF FRONT-DOOR WORK; DO A BIT OF GIBLET PIE; DO A BIT OF LADIES' TAILORING; DO A BIT OF SKIRT; DO A BIT OF STUFF phr.[2]; HAVE A BIT OF BEEF; HAVE A BIT OF BUM; HAVE A BIT OF CAULIFLOWER; HAVE A BIT OF COCK; HAVE A BIT OF CREAMSTICK; HAVE A BIT OF CUNT; HAVE A BIT OF CURLY GREENS; HAVE A BIT OF FISH; HAVE A BIT OF FUN; HAVE A BIT OF GUT STICK; HAVE A BIT OF JAM; HAVE A BIT OF KEIFER; HAVE A BIT OF MEAT; HAVE A BIT OF MUTTON; HAVE A BIT OF PORK; HAVE A BIT OF QUIMSY; HAVE A BIT OF ROUGH; HAVE A BIT OF SKIRT; HAVE A BIT OF SPLIT MUTTON; HAVE A BIT OF SUGAR STICK; HAVE A BIT OF SUMMER CABBAGE).

bit *n.*[4] [20C] (Aus.) a jemmy, a crowbar. [SE *bit*, a biting or cutting tool]

bit *n.*[5] [1920s–50s] a young woman (cf. BIT OF CRACKLING; BIT OF CRUMB; BIT OF JAM; BIT OF MUSLIN; BIT OF SKIRT; BIT OF SOAP; BIT OF SPARE; BIT OF STUFF).

bit *n.*[6] [1930s+] (Ulster) a worker's or schoolchild's packed lunch. [abbr. SE *a bit to eat*]

bit *n.*[7] [1930s+] a prison sentence of any length; thus *one-year bit, two-year bit* etc (cf. BIG BIT).

bit *n.*[8] [1950s+] (orig. US jazz) **1** any well-defined action, plan, series of events, or attitudes, usu. but not necessarily, of short duration. **2** one's attitude, personality, or way of life. **3** the role that one assumes in a situation or in life, e.g. *the college-boy bit, the hippie bit*.

bit, the *n.*[9] [1990s] (Irish) sexual intercourse. [euph.]

bit *adj.* [late 17C–early 18C] robbed, cheated, outwitted. [BITE *v.*[1]]

bit *v.* [1950s–60s] (US Black) to be cheated or otherwise treated badly. [bite *v.*[1]]

bit above one's weight, a *phr.* [1910s+] somewhat beyond one's abilities, bank-balance, social standing etc. [boxing imagery]

bitch *n.*[1] **1** [15C+] a derog. term for a woman, usu. judged an unpleasant one. **2** [17C+] a derog. term for a weak or sub-servient man. **3** [late 18C–mid-19C] a prostitute. **4** [mid-19C+] the queen in playing cards. **5** [1920s+] anything unpleasant, difficult, problematic, 'the devil', e.g. *that's the bitch of it*. **6** [1930s+] (gay) an effeminate male, supposedly the 'passive' partner in a homosexual couple; a male prostitute. **7** [1940s+] (orig. US) an exceptionally skilled person. **8** [1940s+] (orig. US) something or some one considered extraordinary or surprising. **9** [1950s+] (Can. prison) an habitual criminal. **10** [1950s+] (US prison) a homosexual. **11** [1990s] (W.I./UK/US Black teen) a person, neither necessarily negative nor aimed solely at women, nor used solely by men. [*bitch* as derog. sl. dates to early 17C, before which it had been SE. By 18C it was seen, according to Grose, as 'the most offensive appellation that can be given to an English woman, even more provoking than that of whore', and he cites the 'Billingsgate' rejoinder: 'I may be a whore, but can't be a bitch.' The original use implied disapproval of the woman's sexuality, e.g. *bitch in heat*; today's use focuses on her personality]

bitch *n.*[2] [late 19C–1930s] (US West) an improvised lamp made of a twist of rag in a container of grease. [ety. unknown]

bitch *n.*[3] [1930s+] (orig. US) a complaint. [BITCH v.[2] (2)]

bitch *n.*[4] [1980s+] (US drugs) one who knowingly dispenses unpleasantly adulterated varieties of marijuana (cf. BITCHWEED). [BITCH n.[1] (2)]

bitch *v.*[1] [late 17C+] to go whoring. [BITCH n.[1] (3)]

bitch *v.*[2] **1** [early 19C+] to spoil, to ruin. **2** [1910s+] (orig. US) to complain. **3** [1920s–60s] (US) to cheat, to swindle. **4** [1950s+] (orig. US) to criticize, to attack verbally, to nag. [all imply that the subject is acting like a BITCH n.[1]]

bitch-ass *adj.* [1980s+] (US Black) a general pej. [BITCH n.[1] (1), (5) + sfx. -ASS]

bitch-ass nigga *n.* [1990s] (US Black teen) a general term of Black-on-Black abuse, lit. a Black person who complains. [BITCH-ASS + NIGGA]

bitch bath *n.* [1940s–50s] (US) a 'bath' in which the usual water is replaced by an application of cosmetics, masking the dirt rather than removing it. [BITCH n.[1] (1) + SE *bath*]

bitch booby *n.* [late 18C] a rough, unsophisticated country woman (cf. DOG BOOBY). [BITCH n.[1] (1) + BOOBY n.[1]]

bitch box *n.* [1960s+] (US) a small box into which employees of a business can put their complaints/suggestions. [BITCH v.[2] (2) + SE *box*]

bitch butter *n.* [1970s] (US Black) vaginal secretions. [BITCH n.[1] (1) + BUTTER n.[2] (1)]

bitched/bitched up *adj.* **1** [early 19C+] ruined, spoilt. **2** [1960s–70s] (US) angry. [BITCH v.[2]]

bitchen *adj.* [1950s+] excellent, wonderful (cf. BITCHIN!). [lit. BITCHING]

bitcher *n.* [20C] a complainer, a whinger. [BITCH v.[2] (2)]

bitch-fou *adj.* [17C+] (Scot.) very drunk (cf. FOU adj.[1]; GREETIN' FOU; PIPER FOU; PISSING FOU; ROARING FOU). [lit. 'full as a bitch']

bitchin!/bitching! *excl.* [1950s+] (US) wonderful, great, esp. in surfer use, subsequently adopted by teen girls of 1980s Calif. [pos. use of BITCH n.[1] (3) on bad = good model, or BITCH n.[1] (8)]

bitching *adv.* **1** [mid-19C+] (orig. Aus.) an intense pej., euph. for BLOODY. **2** [1950s+] (orig. US Black) a general intensifier, e.g. *a bitching snowstorm, a bitching big knife* (cf. BITCHIN!).

bitching session *see* BITCH SESSION.

bitchin twitchin *adj.* [1960s+] superlative form of BITCHIN! [redup./assonance]

bitch-kitty *n.* [1940s+] (US) something extraordinary, esp. extraordinarily hard to achieve. [BITCH n.[1] (5)]

bitch off *v.* [1970s] (US campus) to annoy, to irritate. [BITCH v.[2] (2)]

bitch party *n.* [late 19C+] a party composed solely of women guests (cf. CAT PARTY; HEN PARTY; STAG PARTY; TABBY PARTY). [BITCH n.[1] (1) + SE *party*]

bitch's bastard *n.* [1950s+] (prison) a severe, possibly violent warder.

bitch/bitching session *n.* [1940s+] (orig. US army) a conversation in which one airs one's complaints. [BITCH v.[2] (2) + SE *session*]

bitch slap *v.* [1990s] (US Black) for a woman to hit, occas. to harangue, her male partner. [BITCH n.[1] (1) + SE *slap*]

bitch's wine *n.* [mid–late 19C] champagne. [BITCH n.[1] (1) + SE *wine*; ? supposedly preferred by women drinkers]

bitch up *v.* [late 19C+] to make a mess of things, to make a mistake. [BITCH v.[2] (1)]

bitch water *n.* [1940s] (US) cologne. [BITCH n.[1] (1) + SE *water*]

bitchweed *n.* [1980s+] (US drugs) adulterated, contaminated, inferior or otherwise 'bad' marijuana. [BITCH n.[1] (4) + WEED n.[1] (4)]

bitch wheel *n.* [1950s] (W.I.) a large, round boiled dumpling. [? BITCH n.[1] (1) or W.I. pron. of SE *big* + shape (of a wheel)]

bitchy *adj.* **1** [1920s+] malicious, sarcastic. **2** [1930s+] (orig. US) sexually provocative. **3** [1940s+] (US) difficult. [BITCH n.[1] (1)]

bite *n.*[1] [16C–18C; 20C] the vagina, 'secreta ( ) mulierum' (cf. SNAPPER n.[7]; SNATCH n.[3]). [SE *bite* or Anglo-Saxon *byht*, the fork of the legs; 20C use mainly US Black]

bite *n.*[2] **1** [16C–early 19C] a sum of money. **2** [18C–1900s] a cheat, a confidence trickster. **3** [early 18C–1900s] (Und.) that which is cadged; thus *a good bite*, a complaisant victim, *on the bite*, cadging, begging. **4** [early 18C–mid-19C] a hoax, a confidence trick, a fraud. **5** [20C] (orig. Aus.) an attempt to obtain a loan (cf. PUT THE BITE ON). **6** [1920s–60s] (US) a share of profits (cf. CUT n.[4]). **7** [1940s+] (Aus.) a cadger (cf. PUT THE BITE ON). **8** [1940s–50s] (US) the price, the cost, esp. when the item is expensive. **9** [1950s+] (US) an unpleasant surprise or experience, abbr. of *bite in the ass*.

bite *n.*[3] [late 19C] a Yorkshireman. [abbr. YORKSHIRE BITE]

bite *v.*[1] **1** [17C+] to 'fall for', to 'take the bait'. **2** [late 17C–early 19C] to rob, to steal. **3** [early 18C–mid-19C] to cheat, to deceive; thus *bitten*, deceived, hoaxed. **4** [late 18C] to overreach, to impose. **5** [1910s+] (Aus.) to cadge or borrow, usu. money. **6** [late 19C+] (US) to worry, to annoy, to irritate, often ext. as *bite one's ass, bite one's britches*; thus *what's biting you?* **7** [1960s+] (US) to ask for money, esp. when one has no real intention of repaying it. **8** [1970s+] to be objectionable, distasteful, unpleasant (cf. SUCK v.[2]). **9** [1970s+] to take adverse effect. **10** [1970s+] (rap music) to plagiarize lyrics from other people; thus *biting*, copying another artist.

bite *v.*[2] [1960s+] (US) to die. [abbr. BITE THE DUST]

bite! *excl.* [early–mid-18C] tricked you! caught you! (cf. GOTCHA!). [BITE v.[1] (3)]

bite a blow, to *phr.* [late 17C–early 18C] to accomplish a major theft. [BITE v.[1] + SE *blow*, a hit]

bite-and-blow *n.* [1900s+] (W.I.) successful deceit, emollient hypocrisy (cf. WHITE-BELLY RAT). [dial. *bite-and-blow*, to blow a cool breath on a place before biting it and thus (theoretically) minimizing the pain]

bite-etite/bitytite *n.* [late 19C–1900s] hunger, appetite (cf. DRINKITITE). [SE *bite* + *appetite*]

bite it! *excl.* [1940s+] (US) phr. of aggressive dismissal (cf. GO TO HELL!; GO FUCK YOURSELF!). [SE *bite*, 'it' is the penis or posterior]

bit it off *see* BITE OFF.

bite me! *excl.* [1980s+] (US campus) a general derog. excl. (cf. FUCK OFF!; KISS MY ASS!; SCREW YOU!; UP YOURS!). [BITE MY ASS!]

bite my ass!/arse! *excl.* [1950s+] (orig. US) a general excl. of contempt or dismissal (cf. BITE ME!; BITE THIS!).

bite off/bite it off *phr.* [mid-19C–1910s] (US) to restrain oneself, to stop talking. [lit. *bite one's tongue off*]

bite off more than one can chew, to *phr.* [late 19C+] (orig. US) to undertake something that is beyond one's capabilities. [an image of taking too large a 'chaw' of tobacco]

bite on *v.* [1980s+] (US campus) to imitate. [BITE v.[1] (10)]

bite one off *v.* [1910s+] to take a drink of spirits (cf. CHEW ONE'S EAR phr.[2]).

bite one's bait, to *phr.* [20C] (US) to pause before making too precipitate a decision (cf. CHEW OVER). [SE *bite* + 16C *bait*, food; the image is of 'chewing over' the topic]

bite one's grannam, to *phr.* [17C] to become very drunk (cf. BITE ONE'S NAME IN). [SE *bite* + *grannam*, corn, the basic constituent of some spirits]

bite one's lips, to phr. [1980s+] (drugs) to smoke marijuana. [? one's intoxicated state leads to such injury]

bite one's name in, to phr. [19C] to drink heavily (cf. BITE ONE'S GRANNAM).

bite one's thumb at/to, to phr. [late 16C–late 17C] to make a gesture of contempt or of threat. [the gesturer extends the thumb and clicks its nail forward on the front teeth]

bite on the bridle see BITE THE BRIDLE.

bite on the nail, to phr. [1940s] (US) to suffer in silence (cf. BITE THE BULLET).

bite someone's crank, to phr. [1960s+] to fellate. [SE bite + CRANK n.⁵]

bite someone's ear, to phr.¹ [mid-19C+] to borrow money. [BITE v.¹ (5), (7)]

bite someone's ear, to phr.² [mid-19C+] to nag, to importune. [BITE v.¹ (5)]

bite someone's head off, to phr. [20C] to attack verbally, esp. in response to an ostensibly mild statement.

bite someone's name, to phr. [1920s+] (Aus.) to eat a meal for which someone else has paid. [the payer has fig. 'signed' for the food]

bite someone's nose off, to phr. [20C] to attack verbally (cf. BITE SOMEONE'S HEAD OFF).

biter n.¹ **1** [late 17C–early 18C] a card-sharp. **2** [late 17C–mid-19C] a confidence trickster. **3** [1950s+] (Aus.) a cadger. **4** [1980s+] (US) an unpleasant, contemptible person. [BITE v.¹]

biter n.² [late 18C] a lascivious woman. [BITE n.¹]

biter of peters n. [late 18C–early 19C] (Und.) one who specializes in stealing trunks and boxes from the back of stage-coaches or carts (cf. PETER LAY; VAN DRAGGER). [BITE v.¹ (2) + PETER n.³ (1)]

bite the bag, to phr. [1960s+] (US) to be very unsatisfactory; esp. in imper. bite/go bite the bag, an excl. of dismissal, disapproval or contempt.

bite the big one, to phr. [1970s+] (US) **1** to be distasteful, unpleasant, second-rate (cf. BITE IT!; SUCK v.²). **2** to die, to suffer harm. [SE bite + 'the big one', (1) = the penis; (2) = any serious injury or harm]

bite the bone, to phr. [1970s] (US teen) to be disgusting, unpleasant. [SE bite + ? BONE n.¹ (1)]

bite/bite on the bridle, to phr. [14C–19C] to be in reduced circumstances, to be impoverished. [SE bite on the bridle, to champ at the bit, like a restless horse]

bite the bullet, to phr. [late 19C+] to suffer in silence. [the placing of a bullet between the teeth of wounded soldiers or sailors when undergoing surgery in pre-anaesthesia days]

bite the dust, to phr. **1** [mid-19C+] to die. **2** [1980s+] (US campus) to be defeated, prevailed over. [US Wild West cliché]

bite the hand that feeds one, to phr. [mid-19C+] to injure a benefactor, to act ungratefully. [the image is of an ungrateful horse or dog]

bite the ice! excl. [1980s] (US teen) an excl. of dismissal, 'go to hell!' [the pain of chewing ice]

bite the peter, to phr. [late 17C–19C] to steal suitcases or portmanteaux (cf. BITER OF PETERS). [BITE v.¹ (2) + PETER n.³ (1)]

bite the roger, to phr. [18C] to steal a portmanteau. [BITE v.¹ (2) + ROGER n.³]

bite this! excl. [1980s+] (US) a general derog. excl. (cf. BITE ME!).

bite your bum!/back! excl. [1950s+] (N.Z.) an excl. of contemptuous dismissal.

bit faker n. [19C] (Und.) a coiner, a counterfeiter; thus bit-faking, counterfeiting, coining (cf. BIT TURNER-OUT). [BIT n.¹ + FAKER]

bit for the finger phr. [19C] **1** sexual fondling (cf. FINGER PIE). **2** a woman.

bities n. [1990s] (Aus.) a general term for biting insects. [SE bite]

bit lit adv. [1920s+] tipsy, slightly drunk. [SE bit + LIT adj.¹]

bit-maker n. [early–mid-19C] (Und.) a coiner, a counterfeiter (cf. QUEER BIT-MAKER). [BIT n.¹ + SE maker]

bit more like it, a phr. [late 19C+] phr. indicating that after one or more attempts, what is being done or said is finally approaching satisfaction, accuracy, the truth.

bit much, a n. [1930s+] a little too much (to have to endure), a euph. disguise for something considered excessive or annoying.

bit of/of a n. [early 19C+] a good example of, a specimen of, e.g. bit of a lad, bit of a horseman.

bit of a brothel n. [1990s] (Aus.) a mess. [the (erroneous) assumption that immorality equals untidiness]

bit of a lad n. [1910s+] a cheeky, self-possessed youth who 'fancies himself' (cf. JACK THE LAD). [BIT OF + SE lad]

bit/little bit of all right, a n. **1** [late 19C+] an attractive woman, usu. young. **2** [20C] anything good and advantageous, esp. a pleasant surprise.

bit of bazooka n. [1950s–60s] sexual petting. [BAZOOKA (4)]

bit of beef n. [late 19C–1900s] a quid of tobacco, less than a pipeful. [? tobacco's use as an appetite suppressant]

bit of blink n. [late 19C–1900s] drink. [rhy. sl.]

bit of blood n. [19C] a spirited, mettlesome horse. [SE bit + blood, pedigree]

bit of braille n. (Aus.) **1** [1930s+] a racing tip. **2** [1940s+] a tip-off. **3** [1940s+] sexual groping (cf. BIT n.³). [SE bit + Braille, the alphabet for the blind; the image of 'feeling something out']

bit of brown n. [mid-19C+] sodomy (cf. BRONZE n.; BROWNING FAMILY). [SE bit + BROWN n.³]

bit of brush n. [1950s] **1** sexual intercourse. **2** a young woman, viewed purely sexually (cf. BIT n.³). [SE bit + BRUSH n.³ (2)]

bit of bull n. [19C] beef.

bit of bum n. [late 19C+] sexual gratification, whether homo- or heterosexual (cf. BIT n.³; PIECE OF ARSE). [SE bit + BUM n.²]

bit of calico n. [19C] sexual groping (cf. BIT OF SKIRT). [SE bit + CALICO n.]

bit of cavalry n. [early 19C–1910s] a horse. [SE bit + cavalry, horses]

bit of crackling n. [1940s+] an attractive woman. [SE bit + CRACKLING]

bit of crumb n. [late 19C] a plump, attractive woman (cf. BANANA n.²). [SE bit + CRUMB n.² (1)]

bit of cuff n. [late 19C] **1** a young woman, regarded as a sex object. **2** sexual intercourse (cf. BIT n.³). [SE bit + (off the) cuff, i.e. spontaneous sex, or SE cuff, a blow; thus one of the wide range of terms that equate sex with violence]

bit of ebony n. [mid-19C+] a Black woman, viewed as a sex object. [SE bit + EBONY n.]

bit off adj. **1** [20C] eccentric. **2** [1950s+] socially unacceptable, 'not the done thing', usu. in phr. that's a bit off. [SE bit + OFF adv.]

bit of fat n. [19C+] an unexpected advantage. [SE fat, of a profitable occupation]

bit of fish n. [mid-19C–1900s] **1** the vagina (cf. BEARDED CLAM). **2** sexual intercourse. [SE bit + FISH n.⁴ (1)]

bit of fluff n. **1** [20C] an attractive, but otherwise unexceptional woman (cf. AIRHEAD; BIMBO). **2** [1980s] any thing or person considered insignificant, ineffectual. [SE bit + FLUFF n.¹ (2)]

bit of gig n. [early 19C] a spree, a bit of fun. [SE bit + gig, merriment, fun]

bit of goods n. [mid-19C+] a young woman (cf. LOOSE BIT OF GOODS; STRAIGHT BIT OF GOODS).

bit of grease *n.* [late 19C–1900s] (Anglo-Ind.) a stout, smiling Hindu woman. [E.P. stresses 'non-derogatory', although that assessment may vary as to one's viewpoint]

bit of grey *n.* [late 19C] an elderly person who is recruited to attend weddings or funerals and by their presence add a degree of solemnity to the proceedings. [SE *bit* + *grey* (hair; note 1990s business jargon *grey matter*, an older person recruited to a young firm to give it some gravitas]

bit of hair *n.* [late 19C+] sexual intercourse; thus *get/have a bit of hair*. [SE *bit* + HAIR n.³ (2)]

bit of hard/stiff *n.* [19C] an erection. [SE *bit* + HARD n.³/STIFF n.¹]

bit of haw-haw *n.* [late 19C–1900s] a fop, a dandy. [SE *bit* + *haw-haw*, echoic of an aristocratic drawl]

bit of how's yer father *n.* [1940s+] sexual intercourse (cf. BIT n.³; HOW'S-YER-FATHER). [orig. music-hall use as a 'nudging' euph.]

bit of jam *n.* [late 19C] **1** the vagina (cf. APPLE n.¹⁰). **2** an attractive woman (cf. BANANA n.²; BIT OF CRUMB). [SE *bit* + JAM n.³]

bit of keg *n.* [late 19C] sexual intercourse (cf. BIT n.³; BIT OF MEAT; BIT OF MUTTON; CARVE A SLICE). [abbr. SE *kegmeg* or *cagmag*, rotten meat or a tough old goose]

bit of leaf *n.* [mid-19C–1920s] tobacco. [SE *bit* + (tobacco) *leaf*]

bit of meat *n.* [early 18C+] **1** the vagina (cf. BACON SANDWICH). **2** sexual intercourse (cf. BIT n.³; BIT OF KEG). **3** a woman considered as nothing more than a sex object. [SE *bit* + MEAT]

bit of mess *n.* [1950s+] (Und.) a prostitute's male lover, who is neither ponce nor client. [? affectionate nickname]

bit of muslin *n.* [mid–late 19C] a young woman (cf. PIECE OF MUSLIN; PIECE OF SKIRT). [SE *bit* + *muslin*, a cloth used for dress-making]

bit of mutton *n.* [19C] **1** a woman, esp. a prostitute. **2** sexual intercourse (cf. BIT n.³; BIT OF KEG; PIECE OF MUTTON). [SE *bit* + MUTTON n.²]

bit of nifty *see* NIFTY n.¹.

bit of no good *phr.* [1950s+] a good deal of harm, usu. in phr. *do oneself a bit of no good.*

bit of nonsense *n.* **1** [20C] (society) a mistress. **2** [1950s+] any form of villainy, esp. when easily accomplished.

bit of pooh *n.* [late 19C–1900s] flattery, esp. in the context of courtship. [SE *bit* + excl. *pooh!* nonsense!]

bit of pork *n.* [18C–1900s] the vagina (cf. BACON SANDWICH). [SE *bit* + PORK n.¹]

bit of prairie *n.* [late 19C–1900s] a momentary lull in the flow of traffic down the Strand, then London's busiest street. [SE *bit* + *prairie*, an open space]

bit of raspberry *n.* [20C] an attractive woman (cf. BANANA n.²).

bit of red *n.* [18C–19C] a soldier. [his uniform]

bit of ring *n.* [1970s+] anal intercourse. [SE *bit* + RING n.¹ (2)]

bit of rough *n.¹* [mid-19C+] the vagina. [its rubbing against the penis]

bit of rough *n.²* [20C] a lover, orig. female but from mid-20C+ male, from a lower class and tougher background than their partner (cf. ROUGH TRADE). [ext. of ROUGH n.¹ + SE *rough*]

bit of skate *n.* [late 19C+] the vagina (cf. BEARDED CLAM).

bit of skirt *n.* [20C] a woman (cf. BIT OF MUSLIN). [SE *bit* + SKIRT]

bit of slap and tickle *n.* **1** [1910s+] sexual by-play, necking. **2** [1950s+] sexual intercourse; thus *have a bit of slap and tickle*, to have sexual intercourse (cf. BIT n.³). [in trad. stereotyping, he tickles, she slaps]

bit of snug *n.* [late 19C] **1** sexual intercourse (cf. BIT n.³). **2** the penis. [SE *bit* + SNUG v.¹]

bit of soap *n.* [late 19C–1900s] a woman (cf. LUMP OF SOAP). [SE *bit* + SOAP n.⁴]

bit of Spanish *n.* [18C] (Und.) a natural wig, made from human rather than animal hair. [? use of long, dark Spanish tresses in wigs]

bit of spare *n.* **1** [1930s] a married man's mistress, a wife's lover. **2** [1960s+] an unattached woman, usu. at a party or club; thus *have a bit of spare*, to commit adultery. [SE *bit* + SPARE n.²]

bit of stiff *n.¹* *see* BIT OF HARD.

bit of stiff *n.²* [mid-19C+] money as notes or bills of exchange; thus *do a bit of stiff*, to accept a post-dated cheque. [SE *bit* + STIFF n.⁵]

bit of stuff *n.* **1** [19C] an overdressed man; an over-confident man. **2** [late 19C+] a young woman, usually attractive and often out, enjoying herself (cf. BIT OF MUSLIN; BIT OF SKIRT; STUFF n.⁴). [SE *bit* + *stuff*, material]

bit of sugar for the bird *phr.* [late 19C] an unexpected bonus or surprise, esp. monetary. [a treat for a (caged) bird]

bit of tail *n.* [1950s+] sexual intercourse (cf. BIT n.³). [SE *bit* + TAIL n.¹ (6)]

bit of tape *n.* [18C] gin (cf. BLUE TAPE; HOLLAND TAPE; RED TAPE; WHITE TAPE). [SE *bit* + BLUE TAPE; its being 'measured out']

bit of tickle *n.* [1920s+] **1** a woman, regarded as a sex object. **2** sexual intercourse (cf. BIT n.³). [abbr. BIT OF SLAP AND TICKLE]

bit of tit *n.* [1920s+] **1** a woman regarded as a sex object. **2** sexual intercourse (cf. BIT n.³). [SE *bit* + TIT n.³]

bit of tripe *n.* [late 19C] one's wife. [? rhy. sl.]

bit of under *n.* [19C] sexual intercourse (cf. BIT n.³). [SE *bit* + UNDER]

bit of window *n.* [late 19C] a monocle. [SE *bit* + WINDOW]

bit on a fork *n.* [mid-19C] the vagina (cf. BACON SANDWICH). [pun on SE phr. + BIT n.³; SE *fork*, crotch]

bit on the cuff *phr.* [1930s+] (Aus./N.Z.) excessive, severe, 'over the top'. [rhy. sl. *bit on the cuff* = a bit rough]

bit on the side *n.* [1920s+] an affair; a lover other than one's regular partner (married or otherwise). [the side of the marital 'straight and narrow']

bit previous *adv.* [1970s+] in poor taste, uncalled for (cf. GET PREVIOUS; OUT OF ORDER). [SE *bit* + PREVIOUS adj. (3)]

bit rough, a *phr.* [1940s+] (Aus.) unreasonable, unfair.

bits and bats *n.* [20C] **1** knick-knacks. **2** (Und.) small pieces of jewellery. [Yorks. dial. *bits and bats*, bits and pieces]

bits and bobs *n.* [20C] bits and pieces. [Midlands dial.]

bitser *see* BITZA.

bit slow upstairs *phr.* [1950s+] dull-witted, stupid. [SE *bit, slow* + UPSTAIRS n.² (1)]

bit swift, a *n.* [1970s+] (criminal/police) the taking of unfair advantage, usu. the complaint is made by the villain against the arresting officer. [SE *bit* adj. + SWIFT adj.³]

bitten by a barn-mouse *phr.* [late 18C–early 19C] drunk. [? the barn-mouse consumes barley, from which beer is brewed]

bitten by the tavern bitch *phr.* [17C–18C] drunk.

bitter-ender *n.* [mid-19C+] a diehard, one who does not give up until the bitter end.

bitter-gatter *n.* [late 19C] a mixed drink of beer and gin. [SE *bitter* (ale) + GATTER]

bitter half *n.* [20C] one's wife, occas. one's husband (cf. ANCHOR n.²). [ironic pun on BETTER HALF]

bitter mouth *n.* [1930s–40s] (US Black) cynical, negative talk (cf. BADMOUTH n.). [mainly southern; talk that 'leaves a bad taste in one's mouth']

bitter oath *n.* [19C] an emphatic intensification of any oath (cf. BLOOD OATH!).

bit to go with *n.* [late 19C–1900s] (orig. US) generosity. [? parting comment, 'Here's a bit to go with']

bit turner-out *n.* [early–mid-19C] a counterfeiter (cf. BIT FAKER). [BIT n.¹ (1) + SE *turn-out*, to make]

bitty n.[1] [late 19C–1900s] a skeleton key. [SE *bit*, a small piece (of something mechanical)]

bitty n.[2] [1990s] (US Black) a young woman. var. on BIDDY n.[2]]

bitty adj. [20C] tiny, small, insignificant, often preceded by 'little'. [dimin. of SE *bit*]

bitumen blonde n. [1930s+] (Aus.) a derog. name for an Aborigine woman (cf. COAL-SCUTTLE BLONDE; DARWIN BLONDE; SKILLET BLONDE). [SE *bitumen*, black asphalt + *blonde*]

bitytite see BITE-ETITE.

bitza/bitser n. (Aus.) **1** [1920s+] a contraption made of a selection of disparate bits and pieces. **2** [1930s+] a mongrel dog. [SE *bits and pieces*]

bivvy n. [mid–late 19C] alcohol, esp. beer. [var. on BEVVY n.]

biyeghin n. [late 19C] (tinker) stealing, theft. [Shelta]

biz n.[1] **1** [mid–late 19C] (orig. US) business. **2** [20C] as *the biz*, the real thing (and to be respected as such). [abbr.]

biz n.[2] [1980s+] (drugs) **1** the kit (eye-dropper, needle, spoon etc) used by a narcotic addict for injections (cf. BINKY n.[2]; FIT n.[1]; GIMMICKS; MACHINERY; OUTFIT n.[2]; RIG n.[5]; TOYS n.[1]; WORKS n.[3]). **2** a bag or portion of drugs. [BUSINESS n.[5]]

bizarro n. [1980s] a strange, eccentric person. [SE *bizarre* + sfx. -O, but note *Bizarro*, a character in *Superman* comics]

bizzaz n. [1970s+] (US) style, glamour. [PIZZAZZ + ? BUSINESS n.[4]]

bizzo n. [1950s+] (Aus.) business. [abbr. SE *business* + sfx. -O]

b.j. n. [1940s+] (US) fellatio. [abbr. BLOW JOB]

b-joint n. [1960s+] (US) a bar that employs women whose primary job is not to dance but to promote liquor sales to the clientele (cf. B-GIRL). [B-GIRL + JOINT n.[3] (3)]

b.j.s n. [1980s+] (drugs) crack cocaine. [? pun on BLOW n.[7] (2)/BLOW JOB]

B.K. n. [1990s] (US Black) *B*urger *K*ing. [abbr.]

blab n. [early 17C+] **1** a tell-tale. **2** the mouth. [*Blab* and its verb forms *blab* and, apparently, *blabber* are the first slang terms relating to speech and can be found as such in the 17C. Their history, however, is somewhat older. There is even, according to the *OED*, a question whether what appears to be an obvious link even exists. *Blab*, then spelt *blabbe* and meaning a 'chatterer', occurs in Chaucer *c.*1374; *blab*, meaning simply 'chatter' or 'loose talk', can be found in *The Tale of Beryn* (*c.*1400), but then promptly vanishes until the 16C, when it is augmented by a verb form, *blab*, to chatter (1535). This, in turn, creates a noun, *blabber*, a chatterer. However the verb *blabber* predates all these; it occurs in *Piers Ploughman* (1362) and, with its noun *blabberer*, is common in the works of John Wyclif (1330–84). Thus, however tempting it may seem, one cannot simply assume that *blab* is a 14C abbr. of *blabber*. Instead, the *OED* suggests, it is related to the noun *labbe*, a revealer of secrets, in Chaucer, and the verb *labbe* in *Piers Ploughman* and to *labbyng*, open-mouthed. It can also be linked to the Old Dutch *labben*, to chatter. Thus *blab/blabbe* might be a mixture of *labbe* and *blabber*; but might also be simply onomat.]

blab v. [early 17C+] **1** to talk. **2** to inform. **3** to confess. [BLAB n.]

blabber n. [16C] the mouth. [BLAB n.]

blabberer n. [mid-18C+]a talker. [BLAB n.; orig. 14C–18C SE]

blabberguts n. [1910s] (US) a gossip (cf. BLABBERMOUTH). [BLABBER + SE *guts*]

blabbermouth n. [1930s+] a gossip, an indiscreet talker. [BLABBER + SE *mouth*]

blabberskite n. [16C+] a voluble, boastful speaker (cf. BLATHERSKITE). [BLAB n. + BLATHERSKITE]

blab-blab n. [20C] (US) a gossip. [BLAB n.]

blabfest/talkfest n. [20C] (US) a gathering where those involved devote themselves to talking, esp. unashamed gossip (cf. BREAST-FEST; BULLFEST; BUMFEST; CHINFEST; HEN-FEST; SCHMOOZEFEST). [BLAB n. + -FEST]

blabs in labs n. [1970s+] (US campus) a course in linguistics, the 'labs' are language laboratories (cf. AIDS FOR GRADES). [BLAB n. + SE *lab*(oratory)]

black n.[1] **1** [early–mid-19C] a blackguard. **2** [1920s+] a blackmailer; thus blackmail. **3** [1940s] the black market; thus *on the black*, engaged in the black market. **4** [1940s+] (drugs) opium. **5** [1960s+] (drugs) a generic term for hashish, esp. varieties that are very dark khaki (cf. BLACK GOLD; BLACK MO; BLACK PAK).

black n.[2] [1930s+] (orig. milit.) a mistake, a serious error. [SE *black mark*]

black n.[3] [1980s+] (US Black) a form of address, e.g. *Whassup, Black?* [abbr. SE *black man*]

black adj. [19C+] depressed, sullen, irritable. [SE in 18C; a *black mood*]

black v. [1920s+] to blackmail; thus *put the black on*, to blackmail. [abbr.]

black ace n. [mid-17C] the female pudendum (cf. ACE OF SPADES; RED ACE; WANTON ACE). [? the colour and shape of the pubic hair]

black acid n. [1980s+] (drugs) **1** LSD (cf. A n.[3]). **2** LSD and phencyclidine. [? packaging, ? its negative image]

black act n. [mid–late 19C] (US) the profession of undertaking. [var. on BLACK ART n.[2]]

black-and-tan n.[1] **1** [mid-19C] (US Black) the southern states. **2** [mid–late 19C] (US) a mulatto, a person of mixed race. [the violence (cf. TAN v.) meted out to the *Black* population]

black-and-tan n.[2] [late 19C+] a drink composed of porter or stout and ale. [the respective colours of the stout (*black*) and ale (*tan*)]

black and tan club/joint/resort n. [late 19C+] (US) **1** referring to a place where both Blacks and Whites can meet and mingle. **2** a place patronized by African Americans. [Smitherman suggests (2) on the basis of African American skin tones rather than the greater division between the two races]

black and tans n. [1970s] (drugs) capsules of the amphetamine Durophet (cf. BLACK AND WHITE n.[3]). [the colours of the capsule]

black and white n.[1] [late 19C–1900s] (Und.) night. [rhy. sl.]

black and white n.[2] **1** [1950s+] (US) a police car painted black and white (cf. BLUE-AND-WHITE). **2** [1960s–70s] (US) a policeman. **3** [1970s+] (US drugs) a black and white capsule, esp. Biphetamine, Dilantin/Phenobarbitol mix.

black and white n.[3] [1970s] (drugs) a 12.5mg capsule of the amphetamine Durophet (cf. BLACK AND TANS). [the colours of the capsule]

black ankle n. [late 19C–1930s] (US) a person of mixed race; usu. Black, Indian and White (cf. BRASS ANKLE). [for ety. see DOMINICKER n.]

black annie n. **1** [mid-19C+] a police or prison van (cf. BLACK BETSEY; BLACK BETTY; BLACK MARIA n.[1]; BLUEBIRD n.[2]; BLUE BOY n.[4]; BOOGER WAGON; SABLE MARIA; SALAD BASKET; SARDINE BOX n.[1]). **2** [1930s–60s] (US prison) a whip, used for punishments. [the colour + generic use of proper name]

black ape n. [19C+] (US) a derog. term for a Black person (cf. APE n.).

black army n. [1920s] the female underworld. [? their chosen clothing, their sinister image]

black arse n. [late 17C–early 19C] a kettle, esp. in phr. *the pot calls the kettle black arse*. [SE *black* + ARSE n.[1]; both utensils have been discoloured by the flame; this is the same phr. as the modern one; but the final vulgarism has been quietly dropped]

black art n.[1] [16C–early 19C] (Und.) lock-picking. [SE *black art*, magic or necromancy; thus extended to a criminal activity that required 'devilish ability']

black art n.[2] [mid-19C+] the profession of undertaking. [the role of black in a funeral]

black as a bull's backside phr. [1980s+] (N.Z.) extremely black, usu. of darkness.

black as a musterer's billy phr. [1980s+] (N.Z.) extremely black, usu. of darkness.

black as a sweep's arse phr. [20C] extremely black. [chimney sweeps are, *de facto*, filthy]

black as B-flat phr. [1960s+] (N.Z.) of colour, very dark skinned. [a black note on the piano]

black/dark as Newgate phr. [19C] **1** of an expression, frowning, glowering. **2** of a garment, dirty. **3** of a night, very dark. [*Newgate*, 19C London's main convict prison and the site of many executions; its reputation was fig. *black*]

black as Newgate's knocker phr. [19C+] very dirty.

black ass n. [1940s–60s] (US) a state of depression or disgust; thus *black-assed*, depressed, disgusted. [SE *black* + ARSE n.[1] (3)]

black-assed peas n. [1940s+] (US Black) soul food, esp. black-eyed peas. [the colouring of the legume]

black as the ace of spades phr. [late 19C+] very black, usu. of people rather than objects.

black as the devil's arse phr. [late 18C] extremely dark. [the devil is trad. seen as pitch-black]

black as Toby's arse phr. [1910s+] (Can.) of the night, extremely dark, pitch-dark. [? *Dog Toby* in Punch and Judy shows]

black backra n. [1950s+] (W.I.) a respected Black man (cf. SAMBO BACKRA). [SE *black* + BACKRA]

black bagging n. [20C] (US) the genitals of Black women, seen collectively, i.e. for sexual exploitation. [SE *black* + BAG n.[1] (3)]

black-bagging n. [late 19C–1900s] setting off dynamite bombs. [dynamite was carried in *black bags* and deposited at railway stations and other targets]

black bag job see BAG JOB.

blackball v. [mid-18C–early 19C] to exclude a person, esp. from a club or other closed group. [SE f. 1830s; the placing of black balls in a ballot box; depending on the rules, a majority or even one black ball rendered a candidate ineligible for membership]

black bart n. [1980s+] (drugs) marijuana. [BLACK n.[1] (5) ? + ref. to US outlaw Black *Bart* (d.1883)]

black bass n. [1990s] excrement; thus *setting a black bass free*, *letting go of a black bass*, defecating. [pun on SE *black bass*, a fish of the perch family (*Perca huro*) found in Lake Huron]

black beauty n. [1960s+] (US drugs) **1** Biphetamine, a strong amphetamine (cf. A n.[2]). **2** a depressant. [the colour of the capsules]

black beetle n. [mid–late 19C] a constable in the Thames River police (cf. WATER RAT n.[1]). [? his uniform]

black beetles n. [early–mid-19C] the proletariat. [a derog. view of the scurrying, indistinguishable masses]

black beezer n. [20C] a Black person's face. [SE *black* + BEEZER n.[1] (2)]

black belt n. [1930s+] that part of a larger urban area in which the Black community lives, the Black ghetto (cf. BLACK BOTTOM; BLACK TOWN; BORSCHT BELT). [SE *black* + *belt*, a zone or district]

blackberry n. [mid-19C; 1980s+] (US) a Black person. [pun on the SE fruit]

blackberry swagger n. [mid-19C–1900s] a hawker of shoelaces, tapes and similar small items. [? the black colour of the laces + *swagger*, one who carries a 'swag' or pack]

black bess n. [early 18C–mid-19C] a firelock or musket (cf. BROWN BESS n.) [SE *black* + generic use of proper name]

black betsey n. [mid-19C+] a police van. [var. on BLACK ANNIE]

black betty n. **1** [mid-18C–late 19C] (US) liquor, esp. a bottle that is circulated among the guests at a wedding party; tradition demands that everyone, irrespective of age, must *kiss black betty*, take a swig from the bottle. **2** [1960s+] a police van (cf. BLACK ANNIE). [SE *black* + *betty*, a pear-shaped bottle, covered with straw and often used to contain olive oil; properly known as a *Florence flask*]

black bird n.[1] [19C] one whose family/friends disapprove of their activities. [? SE *black sheep*]

blackbird n.[2] [mid–late 19C] **1** a slave *en route* from the place of capture to their destination; thus *blackbirder*, a slave-trader, *blackbird-catcher*, a slaver or slave ship (cf. BLACK-BIRDING). **2** (Aus.) an Aborigine; thus *blackbird shooting*, the killing for 'sport' of Aborigines by White settlers. **3** a Melanesian.

black bird n.[3] **1** [late 19C+] a derog. term for a Black person. **2** [1960s–70s] (US Black) a particularly dark-skinned Black person. [SE *black* + BIRD n.[2] (1)]

blackbird n.[4] [1970s+] (drugs) strong (20mg) capsules of amphetamine (cf. A n.[2]). [the colour of the capsules]

blackbird and thrush v. [late 19C] to clean one's boots or shoes. [rhy. sl. *blackbird and thrush* = brush]

blackbirding n. [mid–late 19C] the slave trade, esp. between the Pacific Islands and the Queensland sugar plantations in Australia. [BLACKBIRD n.[2]]

black bomber n. [1960s+] (drugs) strong (20mg) capsules of amphetamine, coloured black (cf. A n.[2]). [packaging + BOMBER n.[1] (1)]

black boogaloo n. [1960s] (US Black) a feeling of blackness. [name of a dance popular in 1960s]

black bottle n. [20C] (US) any poisonous drink, esp. knock-out drops. [SE, the use of *black* carries overtones of death, but presumably the term is also a descendant of 19C 'black drop', a dark-coloured medicine, mainly composed of opium, plus vinegar and spices. It was widely believed by 20C tramps that such a drink was administered to men in charity wards whose resulting death saved the administration the trouble of caring for them]

black bottom n. [1900s–30s] that part of a larger urban area in which the Black community lives (cf. BLACK BELT). [SE *black* + BOTTOM n.[3]]

black box n. [18C–19C] a lawyer. [the *black*-painted deed boxes]

black boy n. [17C–mid-19C] a parson, a clergyman (cf. BLACK CATTLE; BLACK COAT; BLACK FLY; BLACK GOWN; CHIMNEY SWEEP n.[2]; CROW n.[1]; ROOK n.[3]. [his vestments]

black buggy n. [mid-19C+] a hearse (cf. BLACK MARIA n.[1]). [SE *black* + *buggy*]

black cadillac n. [1970s+] (US drugs) amphetamine (cf. A n.[2]). [fig. ref. to the quality of the car]

black cattle n. **1** [late 18C] lice (cf. CHATS n.[2]; GOLD-BACKED ONES; GREYBACKS; HAMPSTEAD DONKEYS; LIVESTOCK; SADDLEBACK). **2** [mid-18C–1900s] clergymen as a group; thus *black cattle show*, a gathering of clergymen (cf. BLACK BOY). [the colour, either of the insect or the vestments]

black cat with its throat cut n. [1950s+] the female pubic hair and vagina. [CAT n.[4] (2)]

black cloud n. [1930s] (US) a group of Black people.

black coat n. **1** [mid-17C–early 19C] a clergyman, a parson (cf. BLACK BOY). **2** [1920s+] (Aus.) a waiter. [the traditional clothing]

black cow n. [1910s–50s] (US teen/campus) chocolate milk. [SE *black* + COW n.⁴]

black diamond n. [mid-19C] a person whose tough exterior hides a 'heart of gold'.

black diamonds n. [mid-19C] coal. [the value of the mineral, if only to the mine-owners]

black dog n.¹ [early 18C] a counterfeit silver coin, e.g. a shilling (cf. CHANGE BLACK DOG FOR MONKEY). [use of SE *black* as generic negative, evil, sinister, illicit etc + DOG n.¹]

black dog n.² [early 19C+] a fit of depression or ill humour (cf. BLACK ROT; RED DOG). [the most celebrated of such depressions was that suffered by the former prime minister Sir Winston Churchill]

black-dogged adj. [20C] (US) euph. for *darned*, *damned*.

black duck n. [18C] a Native American Indian. [SE *black duck*, any dark duck, e.g. mallard, redleg; like the birds, the Native Americans were considered prey by the 18C colonists]

black dust n. [1970s] (US Black) an extremely dark-skinned person.

black-eyed susan n. [mid–late 19C] (US, Texas) a revolver. [? the black 'eye' of the barrel]

black fay n. [1960s] (US Black) a Black person considered subservient to Whites. [SE *black* + FAY]

blackfellows'/dog act n. [1920s+] (Aus.) a government order than can be used by publicans to discipline or bar drunkards. [SAusE *blackfellow* (now derog.), a Native Australian]

blackfellow's game n. [1940s] (Aus.) the game of euchre. [see BLACKFELLOWS' ACT; its popularity among Native Australians]

black fly n. [18C] a parson (cf. BLACK BOY). ['the greatest drawback on the farmer is the black fly, i.e. the parson who takes a tithe of the harvest' (Grose)]

blackford-block/-swell/-toff n. [late 19C–1900s] a sporadically well-dressed man. [the London clothes-hire firm of *Blackford's* + SE *block*, the wooden head on which wigs were displayed; SWELL n.; TOFF]

blackfriars! excl. [mid–late 19C] (US Und.) a shout of warning, 'someone's coming, let's run for it!' [? the black uniform of various authorities, reminiscent of the black-garbed Dominicans]

black gang n. [1910s–30s] villains who prey upon other villains, esp. on racecourse confidence tricksters, 'find-the-lady' men, fairground showmen and the like. [BLACK n.¹ (2) + SE *gang*; such villains blackmail their peers for a share of their profits]

black ganja n. [1970s+] (drugs) dark-coloured marijuana. [SE *black* + GANJA]

black gentleman see BLACK MAN.

black gold n. [1970s+] (drugs) high potency marijuana. [BLACK n.¹ (5) + ACAPULCO GOLD]

black gown n. [early–mid-18C] a clergyman (cf. BLACK BOY). [his customary garb]

blackguard n.¹ [18C] a shabby dirty fellow. ['a term said to be derived from a number of dirty tattered and roguish boys, who attended at the horse guards [in] St James's Park, to black the boots and shoes of the soldiers, or to do any other dirty offices, these were nick-named the black guards' (Grose, 1785)]

blackguard n.² [19C] (US) a foul-mouthed person, a slanderer; thus *blackguarding*, talking obscenely. [ext. of BLACKGUARD n.¹]

black gungeon n. [1930s+] (drugs) an especially potent form of marijuana. [SE *black* + GANJA]

black gungi n. [1970s+] (drugs) marijuana from India. [SE *black* + GANJA]

black gunion n. [1960s+] (drugs) marijuana (cf. BLACK GUNGEON). [SE *black* + GANJA]

black hash n. [1970s+] (drugs) hashish that has been mixed with opium during its manufacture. [SE *black* + HASH n.². Opium is black; thus darkening the usually khaki-coloured hashish]

black hat n.¹ [mid–late 19C] (Aus.) a newly arrived immigrant. [he would still wear his black, citified hat in the bush]

black hat n.² [1970s+] a villain, a 'baddie'. [the traditional means of identifying a villain in films]

black hole n.¹ [19C] the vagina; one of a number of terms that equate the vagina with hell or any similar dark, threatening place (cf. BLACK RING; BOB AND HIT; BORE n.²; BOTTOMLESS PIT; CAVE OF HARMONY n.¹; CELLAR n.¹; DARK n.¹; DRAIN n.¹; FURRY HOOP; GLORY HOLE n.²; GOLDEN DOUGHNUT; GRUMMET; GULLY n.¹; HOLE n.¹; HOLE OF CONTENT; HOLE OF HOLES; HOLLOWAY; HOOP n.³; INKWELL; JOY HOLE; LOVE HOLE; MAW; MOLLY'S HOLE; MOUSEHOLE; PASSION PIT n.¹; PIGEONHOLE; PIT n.²; QUARRY; QUEEN OF HOLES; RING n.¹; SEAR; SECOND HOLE FROM THE BACK OF THE NECK; SOCKET; SPORTSMAN'S GAP; TOUCH-HOLE; UPPER HOLLOWAY).

Black Hole n.² [late 19C–1930s] Cheltenham. [the large number of ex-Indian Army or Indian Civil Service officers who retired there; the ref. is to the *Black Hole* of Calcutta (1756)]

black house n. [mid-19C] **1** a prison. **2** any place of business where the employees are exploited by long hours and low wages. [SE *black*, evil + *house*]

blackie/blacky n. [early 19C+] a Black person. [SE *black* + sfx. -*ie*, -*y*; the sfx. ensures the term's negative, patronizing implication (cf. BELGIE; CHINK adj.)]

blackie-/blacky-white n. [1930s–40s] (Anglo-Ind.) a half-caste (cf. CHILLICRACKER). [BLACKIE + SE *white*]

Black Indies n. [late 17C–19C] Newcastle upon Tyne, where the coals come from. [the Indies, whether East or West, were the sources of great mercantile wealth; *black* implies the area's mines]

black Irish n. [20C] (US) **1** a person with a terrible temper. **2** a lower-class Irish person, typically an unsophisticated new immigrant (cf. SHANTY IRISH). **3** an Irish Protestant. **4** a former slave, who took their surname from an Irish owner. [SE *black Irish*, an Irish person with notably Mediterranean features – dark hair and eyes – but with no overtones of ill temper. One theory suggests that the original 'black Irish' were the descendants of mixed marriages between the Irish and the shipwrecked sailors of the Spanish Armada, cast ashore in 1588]

black-is-white adv. [20C] (W.I.) thoroughly, comprehensively, without restraint. [i.e. one will argue that 'black is white']

black ivory n. [late 19C] Black slaves. [their value]

black jack n.¹ **1** [late 16C+] a leather jug used for drinking, coated with tar on its exterior. **2** [late 19C] a type of suitcase or portmanteau. **3** [late 19C–1900s] (Aus.) a tin pot used for boiling tea. [SE *black* + *jack*, a vessel for liquor (either for holding it or from drinking from); orig. and usually of waxed leather coated outside with tar or pitch]

black jack n.² [early 19C] the Recorder of London. [? specifically nicknamed Recorder]

blackjack n.³ **1** [mid–late 19C] (US) rum sweetened with molasses. **2** [late 19C+] (US) very strong black coffee, usu. sweetened with molasses. **3** [20C] (Aus.) treacle. **4** [20C] (US) illegally distilled whisky. [SE *black*, the colour of the drinks/treacle + JACK n.²¹; note BLACK JACK n.¹ (1), (3)]

black jack n.⁴ [mid-19C+] the ace of spades. [SE *black* + generic use of proper name]

blackjack n.⁵ [1920s] (US) a thug. [his weapon]

black jack n.⁶ [1950s+] a Black woman's genitals (cf. BLACK

JOKE; BLACK MARIA n.^{2}; BLACK MEAT; BLACK MOUTH n.^{2}; COAL-BLACK JOKE; DARK MEAT). [ext. of BLACK JACK n.^{5}]

black jack n.^{7} [1950s+] (gay) a Black man's penis (cf. LIQUORICE STICK). [SE *black* + JACK n.^{8}]

blackjack n.^{8} [1960s] (US drugs) amphetamine (cf. A n.^{2}).

blackjack n.^{9} [1970s+] (S.Afr.) a Black municipal policeman. [his uniform colour ? + his weaponry]

black job n. [mid–late 19C] a funeral (cf. BLACK ART n.^{2}).

black jock n. [late 18C] the pubic hair (cf. ACE OF SPADES). [SE *black* + JOCK n.^{1} (1)]

black joint n. [1920s] (US Black/Harlem) any Black nightclub catering specifically to White 'tourists'. [SE *black* + JOINT n.^{3} (3)]

black joke n. [late 18C+] the female genitals (cf. BLACK JACK n.^{6}). [contemporary popular song, *The Harlot Unmasked* (*c*.1735) the chorus of which ran, 'Her black joke and belly so white']

black justice n. [1960s+] (US Black) Black self-determination as opposed to White justice, which Black radicals experience only as a prejudiced farce.

blackleg n.^{1} **1** [late 18C–1910s] a racecourse swindler (cf. LEG n.^{1}). **2** [late 18C–1910s] any swindler; thus *blacklegging, black-leggery*, swindling. **3** [late 19C] (US) a fashionable dandy. [? SE *game-cocks*, which have black legs, or f. the black boots such swindlers always wore; another suggestion notes a pun on ROOK n.^{1}, a bird that also has black legs]

blackleg n.^{2} [mid-19C+] a strike-breaker (cf. SCAB n.). [ety unknown; ? link to Scot. *blackleg*, a go-between (usu. in love-affairs, but fig. between bosses and workers]

blackleg n.^{3} [20C] a Black man's penis. [SE *black* + THIRD LEG]

black lock/lockup n. [20C] (US Und.) solitary confinement for disciplinary reasons. [the blackness of 'the hole']

black man/gentleman n. [17C] the Devil. [the Devil, personifying evil, is naturally black]

black man kissed her n. [20C] a sister. [rhy. sl.]

black maria n.^{1} **1** [mid-19C+] (orig. US) a prison van for conveying prisoners (cf. BLACK ANNIE). **2** [20C] (US) a hearse. **3** [20C] (US) an ambulance. [SE *black*, the colour of the van, but the ety. of *Maria* is unknown; suggestions include an abbr. of *married*, two or more prisoners chained together; a play on the *-ria* of Queen Victoria's name (which fails in the face of its origins in the US, although *V.R.* was inscribed on the British vans) and Brewer's suggestion of a derivation f. one Maria Lee, a Black madam of Boston, Massachusetts. So large and fearsome was Ms Lee that she was regularly called upon by the local police to help them first arrest and then take criminals to prison. According to F&H, themselves citing 'a writer on slang', the term was coined *c*.1838 in Philadelphia, although the *OED* first use is 1847 (usefully for Brewer from a Boston newspaper) and E.P. notes Joseph Neal's story *The Prison Van, or, The Black Maria* (1844)]

black maria n.^{2} [20C] **1** a Black woman's genitals (cf. BLACK JACK n.^{6}). **2** a Black prostitute. [SE *black* + generic use of proper name]

black meat n. [20C] **1** a Black woman's genitals (cf. BLACK JACK n.^{6}). **2** Black women considered collectively. [SE *black* + MEAT n. (7)]

black mo/moat/mote n. [1960s+] (drugs) **1** a particularly potent variety of marijuana, with notably dark colouring. **2** marijuana mixed with honey. [SE *black* + MO n.^{5}/MOTA]

black molly n. [1970s] (US drugs) amphetamine (cf. A n.^{2}). [SE *black* + MOLLIES]

black Monday n. **1** [mid-18C–early 19C] the first day back at school after the holidays (cf. BLOODY MONDAY). **2** [mid-19C] the day on which a death sentence is carried out. [SE *black* as generic for bad, evil, depressing]

black mote *see* BLACK MO.

black mouth n.^{1} [17C–19C] a slanderer. [SE *black*, malicious, evil + *mouth*]

black mouth n.^{2} [20C] a Black woman's genitals (cf. BLACK JACK n.^{6}).

blackmouth n.^{3} [20C] (Ulster) a Presbyterian (cf. BLACK NEB).

black mouth adj. [17C–19C] slanderous, malicious. [BLACK MOUTH n.^{1}]

blackmun n. [1970s] the anus. [in his novel *Myron* (1974), Gore Vidal responded to a US Supreme Court decision whereby any local authority can censor any book, play, film etc by replacing the 'bad' or 'dirty' words by the surnames of the current Supreme Court Justices; thus *Blackmun*; 'Whizzer' White, CUNT n.^{1}; Powell, BALLS n.^{1} (1); Rehnquist, COCK n.^{2} (1); *Father Hill* (a 'warrior against smut'), a TIT n.^{1} (1); *Burger* (the chief justice), FUCK v.^{1}]

black muns n. [17C–18C] hoods and scarves made of lutestring (a glossy silk fabric) or alamode (a thin, light, glossy black silk). [SE *black* + MUNS]

black-'n'-deckering *see* BOSCHING.

black neb n. [20C] (Ulster) a Presbyterian (cf. BLACKMOUTH n.^{3}). [SE *black* + NEB n.^{1} (3)]

black nigger n. [19C–1950s] (US Black) a derog. term of address used by one Black man to another. [SE *black* + NIGGER n.]

black nigger in charge n. [1930s+] (US Black) a sarcastic reference to any Black authority figure (cf. B.N.I.C.; HEAD NIGGER IN CHARGE).

black nob n. [mid–late 19C] a racecourse swindler (cf. BLACK-LEG n.^{1}). [SE *black* + NOB n.^{2}; presumably he poses as a gentleman]

black ointment n. [late 19C] a piece of raw meat. [its use as a cure for black eyes]

black-on-black n. [1940s+] (US Black) a car with black paintwork and all-black interior upholstery and fittings (cf. WHITE-ON-WHITE).

blackout/black-out n.^{1} **1** [1940s] (US Black) a very dark-skinned person. **2** [1940s] (S.Afr./US) black coffee. [pun on SE]

blackout/black-out n.^{2} [1990s] (US) a restaurant or store taken over and controlled by a group of (young) African-Americans (who then leave without paying for the food or goods). [the image of the young Blacks 'taking out' the goods]

black out with adj. [1930s+] (Irish) hostile towards.

black pak n. [1960s+] (drugs) a variety of hashish produced in Pakistan (cf. BLACK n.^{1}). [its dark colour]

black pearl n. [1970s+] (drugs) heroin. [? descendant of BLACK PILL]

black pencil n. [1970s] a Black man's penis. [SE *black* + PENCIL; play on SE]

black people's time n. [1990s] (Black) unpunctuality, lateness (cf. AFRICAN PEOPLE'S TIME). [joc. use of derog. racial stereotyping]

black-pepper brain/grains n. [1960s+] (W.I.) very short hair, growing close to the scalp in small balls of fluff (cf. PICKY-PICKY HEAD). [resemblance to black peppercorns]

black peter n. [late 19C+] (Aus.) a cell for solitary confinement. [SE *black* + PETER n.^{3} (5)]

black pill n. [20C] (drugs) an opium pill. [the colour of the drug; opium is rolled into *pills* for smoking]

black pimp n. [1930s–40s] (US Black/southern) a telephone that is hooked into a party line and thus offers its user free calls. [the image of a pimp endlessly making calls + the colour of early telephones]

blackplate n. [1960s] soul food. [a pun on the US restaurant dish, the 'blue plate special']

black pot n. [16C–18C] a drunkard. [SE *black pot*, a beer mug]

Black Power *n.* [1980s+] (US drugs) a variety of heroin. [SE *Black Power*, a political movement created *c.*1966 by Stokely Carmichael (b.1941) and H. Rap Brown. The spirit of Black Power lay behind the 1960s riots, when militant US Blacks looted in the big city ghettos. The ironic ref. is to the prominence in the ghetto]

Black Power dance/power dance *n.* [1960s] (US Black) **1** looting. **2** fighting back against White oppression. [SE *Black Power* + ironic use of *dance*]

black Protestant *n.* [20C] (US) **1** a derog. term used by Catholics to describe a violently anti-Catholic Protestant. **2** a non-practising Protestant. [SE *black* as generic for Protestant, on model of 'scarlet' for Catholicism]

black pudding *n.* [20C] a Black man's penis. [SE *black* + PUDDING *n.*¹ (2)]

black ring *n.* [19C] the vagina (cf. BLACK HOLE *n.*¹). [SE *black* + RING *n.*¹ (1)]

black rock *n.*¹ [1980s+] (drugs) **1** hashish, cannabis resin (cf. BLACK *n.*¹). **2** crack cocaine. [(1) the colour; (2) ext. of ROCK *n.*⁴]

black rock *n.*² [20C] (US) wind-dried pork, the porcine equivalent to beef jerky or biltong. [its colour and consistency]

black rot, the *n.* [mid-19C] (US) a fit of intense depression (cf. BLACK DOG). [it 'rots one's brain']

black Russian *n.* [1980s+] (drugs) cannabis resin, hashish, esp. when mixed with opium (cf. BLACK *n.*¹). [? ref. to the supposedly chic cigarette brand]

blacks *n.* [1960s+] (drugs) amphetamine (cf. A *n.*²). [the colour of the pills]

black sal/sukey *n.* [mid-19C–1900s] a kettle. [SE *black* + *sal*, abbr. Sarah/*sukey*, abbr. Susan; poss. ref. to the nursery rhyme 'Polly Put the Kettle On' ('Sukey take it off again'); but note E.P.'s suggestion Welsh Gipsy *sukar*, to hum, to whisper]

black sheep *n.* **1** [late 18C–late 19C] a 'bad lot', a badly behaved, disappointing or otherwise 'alien' individual, standing out from a crowd of conforming or well-behaved people. **2** [mid–late 19C] a strike-breaker (cf. BLACKLEG *n.*²).

black sheep *v.* [20C] (US) to take advantage of another person's temporary disability or absence to steal their job. [BLACK SHEEP *n.* (2)]

black-shoe *adj.* [1950s] (US campus) formal, sober (cf. WHITE-SHOE). [the formality of such footwear]

black-silk barges *n.* [late 19C–1900s] (society) stout women who ought to avoid dances. [their black silk clothes, chosen to minimize their bulk, fail to offset their barge-like proportions]

blacksmans *n.* [17C–18C] the night (cf. DARKMANS). [SE *black* + sfx. -MAN]

blacksmith's daughter *n.* [mid-19C] a key, a lock and key, a padlock (cf. LOCKSMITH'S DAUGHTER). [? ref. to a chastity belt]

blacksmith's shop *n.* [20C] a brothel run by a Black madam and presumably featuring a number of Black prostitutes. [play on SE, ? + HAMMA; HAMMER MAN *n.* (2)]

blacksnake *v.* [19C] (US) to whip, to punish. [SE *black snake*, a long braided whip, used by mule-drivers and teamsters]

black spy, the *n.* [18C] the devil.

black star *n.* [1980s+] (drugs) LSD (cf. A *n.*³). [? packaging]

black strap *n.* [late 18C] poor quality port wine. [SE *black strap*, molasses, and thus referring to its excessive sweetness]

black stuff *n.* [1950s+] (drugs) **1** opium. **2** heroin. [opium is black; the ref. to heroin, usu. brown or white, is based on its relation to opium]

black stump *n.* [1950s+] (Aus.) a symbolic marker that divides the known or 'civilized' world from the unknown wastelands beyond; usu. in phr. *this side of the black stump*, *beyond the black stump*. [SE *black* + *stump*, a free-standing post or pillar]

black sukey *see* BLACK SAL.

black sunshine *n.* [1980s+] (drugs) LSD (cf. A *n.*³; SUNSHINE *n.*¹). [its packaging]

black tabs *n.* [1980s+] (drugs) LSD (cf. A *n.*³). [SE *black* + TAB *n.*⁷]

black tar *n.* [1980s+] (drugs) heroin processed in Mexico. [SE *black* + TAR *n.*²]

black taxi *n.* [1980s] (Aus.) an official limousine that ferries government members etc to and from houses, appointments and the like (cf. Z CARS).

black teapot *n.* [19C] a Black footman. [? his duties include pouring tea]

black 360 degrees *phr.* [1960s+] (US Black) intensely and specifically Black in personality and consciousness. [360° describes a complete circle; thus totality]

blacktime *n.* [1900s] (Black) unpunctuality (cf. AFRICAN PEOPLE'S TIME). [neg. stereotyping]

blacktop *n.* [20C] (US) a minor road, a back road. [its black asphalt surface]

black town *n.* [late 19C–1970s] that part of a larger urban area in which the Black community lives (cf. BEAN TOWN *n.*²; BLACK BELT).

black-up *adj.* [1990s] (drugs) intoxicated by marijuana (cf. RED-UP). [ext. of BLACK UP]

black up *adv.* [1940s+] (W.I.) in a very drunken manner. [one is 'blind' drunk]

black velvet *n.* [19C+] **1** (Aus./N.Z.) any dark-skinned woman; thus *a bit of black velvet* (cf. BROWN VELVET). **2** a mixture of stout and champagne. [fig. use of SE, based on the smoothness, whether of skin or the drink]

black wagon *n.* [mid-19C+] a hearse (cf. BLACK BUGGY).

black wash *n.* [1940s+] (W.I.) coffee. [SE *black* + WASH *n.*² (1)]

black water *n.* [mid-19C–1920s] (US West) weak black coffee.

black whack *n.* [1980s+] (drugs) phencyclidine (cf. ACE *n.*³). [SE *black* + WHACK *n.*¹]

black widow *n.*¹ [1970s] (drugs) any black capsule that contains amphetamine (cf. A *n.*²). [the packaging]

black widow/widow *n.*² [1990s] Guinness, lager. [its colour]

black wings *n.* [1950s+] usu. of Hell's Angels for whom it is an alleged initiation rite, performing cunnilingus on a menstruating Black woman (cf. BROWN WINGS; RED WINGS). [the initiate is then given a patch of the appropriate colour and design]

black-work *n.* [mid-19C] funeral arrangements, undertaking (cf. BLACK ART *n.*²; BLACK JOB). [the pre-eminent role of black in funerary arrangements]

blacky *see* BLACKIE.

blacky-white *see* BLACKIE-WHITE.

bladder *n.*¹ [late 16C–late 18C] a talkative, long-winded and thus boring person. [SE *bladder of wind*]

bladder *n.*² [1930s+] (US) a newspaper. [Ger. *Blatt*, leaf and therefore newspaper]

bladder of fat *n.* [1900s–10s] a hat. [rhy. sl.]

bladder of lard *n.*¹ **1** [mid–late 19C] a bald-headed man. **2** [mid-19C+] a fat man. [derog. comparisons]

bladder of lard *n.*² **1** [20C] a playing card. **2** [1920s–50s] Scotland Yard, former headquarters of the Metropolitan Police. [rhy. sl.]

bladderscat *n.* [20C] (US) nonsense, rubbish, foolish talk. [var. on BLATHERSKITE]

bladdy/bleddy *adj.* [1960s+] (S.Afr.) a general expletive, the local pron. of the UK BLOODY *adj.* (cf. BLERRY).

blade *n.*¹ **1** [mid-18C–mid-19C] a 'sharp fellow'. **2** [19C] (US) one's wife, usu. *old blade*. **3** [mid-19C] a man. **4** [mid–late 19C] an expert, a connoisseur, a wise man or one posing as such. **5** [1960s+] (US Black) a Cadillac. [SHARP *adj.*]

blade *n.*² [late 19C] the penis (cf. BAYONET).

blade *n.*³ [late 19C+] (US) any knife, esp. a switchblade. [SE *sharp*, a sharp weapon]

blade *n.*⁴ [1980s+] (Ulster) **1** a showily or bizarrely dressed woman. **2** a cantankerous, verbally abusive woman. **3** a 'difficult' child. [they are all 'sharp']

blade *v.* [1980s+] (US campus) to get rid of. [? SE *blade*, a knife; thus the offending item is 'cut out' of one's life]

blades *n.* [1980s+] (US drugs) smoking hashish by placing a piece on a knife blade and then exposing it to a flame; e.g. *let's do some blades.*

bladhunk *n.* [18C–late 19C] (tinker) a prison. [Shelta]

blag *n.* **1** [late 19C+] robbery, often with violence. **2** [1920s+] bag-snatching, watch-stealing. **3** [1930s+] a wages' snatch. **4** [1940s+] (orig. Und.) a persuasive if lying story. **5** [1950s+] any form of robbery, esp. of a bank or post office. [? SE *blackguard*]

blag *v.* **1** [late 19C+] (orig. Und.) to steal. **2** [1940s+] to deceive, to hoax. **3** [1960s+] to persuade, esp. as in *blag in/in to*, to talk one's way in to a party, concert etc. [BLAG *n.*]

blagger *n.* [1930s+] **1** a thief, esp. a bank robber. **2** a smooth talker, a persuasive person. [BLAG *v.*]

blag-merchant *n.* [1950s+] a pay-roll robber. [BLAG *n.* (3) + -MERCHANT]

blah/blah-blah/blah-blah-blah *n.*¹ [1910s+] (orig. US) pompous, banal verbosity. [? BLAH *v.*, Ger. *Blech*, nonsense or onomat.]

blah *n.*² [1950s+] (S.Afr.) brother (cf. BRA *n.*²). [pron.]

blah *adj.* **1** [1920s+] (orig. US) insincere, verbose, pompous. **2** [1920s] (US) insane, crazy. **3** [1930s+] blind drunk. **4** [1960s+] blasé, uninterested, non-committal. [BLAH *v.*]

blah *v.* [1920s+] to speak in an insincere, pompous manner; thus intensified as *blah-blah-blah*. [onomat.]

blah, blah, blah *phr.* [1930s+] phr. used to imply that a statement is meaningless, hollow, nonsense, albeit delivered in the most serious of tones (cf. DI-DA, DI-DA, DI-DA). [BLAH *v.*]

blahs, the *n.* [1960s+] (Aus./US) depression, despondency, low condition (cf. BLUES *n.*¹).

blame/blamed *adj.* **1** [17C+] certain, sure, absolute, complete. **2** [mid-19C+] (US) euph. for DAMNED (cf. BLASTED *adj.*¹).

blame/blamed *adv.* [mid-19C–1900s] confoundedly, exceedingly. [BLAME *adj.*]

blame it! *excl.* [early 19C–1900s] euph. for DAMN IT! [BLAME *adj.*]

blamps *n.* [1990s] large breasts. [? SE *big* + HEADLAMPS *n.*²]

blanca *n.* [1950s–60s] (US drugs) amphetamines (cf. A *n.*²). [Sp. *blancas*, whites]

blanched/blanshed *adj.* [1990s] (US Black) ruined socially. [pun on SE *blanched*, whitened + *blanch*, to turn white with fear, embarrassment]

blanco *n.* [1980s+] **1** (US Black) a White person (cf. CHALK *n.*⁵; GRAY *adj.*; LILY *n.*⁶; PALEFACE; WHITEY). **2** (drugs) heroin. [Sp. *blanco*, white; some varieties of heroin are white, rather than the usual brown]

blandander *v.*¹ [late 19C] to cajole, to offer blandishments. [SE *blandish*]

blandander *v.*² [1930s+] to talk nonsense. [BLATHER and/or BLARNEY *n.*]

blank *n.* **1** [1950s+] (prison) a rejection, esp. of a parole application (cf. KNOCKBACK *n.*²). **2** [1960s+] (drugs) any powder sold as a narcotic but absolutely without effect.

blank *adj.* [18C+] euph. for DAMNED (cf. DASH!). [lit. the 'blank space' that replaces the unuttered oath]

blank *v.* [1930s+] to ignore, to wipe out, to reject. [SE *blank out*, to erase]

blankard *n.* [20C] (Aus.) a bastard. [BLANK *adj.* + SE (*bast*)*ard*]

blank blank *adj.* [late 19C+] a general term of condemnation (cf. BLANKETY-BLANK). [BLANK *adj.*]

blanket *n.*¹ [mid-19C+] (US) **1** money. **2** a $1 bill. [it offers its holder comfort]

blanket *n.*² **1** [late 19C+] (S.Afr.) a peasant, an unsophisticated African; thus in synon. combs. *blanket-boy, blanket-kaffir,* and *blanket-vote*, the collective Black vote. [the traditional blankets that such individuals wear]

blanket *n.*³ [1920s–30s] (US tramp) an overcoat, which regularly doubles as a blanket.

blanket *n.*⁴ **1** [1920s–40s] a cigarette paper; thus *tumblings and blankets*, tobacco and papers. **2** [1980s+] (drugs) a marijuana cigarette. [the shape]

blanket-ass/-head *n.* [1970s+] (US) a Native American (cf. BLANKET-BUCK). [SE *blanket*, used as adj. to denote Native American + sfx. -ASS/sfx. -HEAD (1) blankets are supposedly inseparable from Indians]

blanket-buck *n.* [20C] (US) a Native American. [SE *blanket* + BUCK *n.*¹ (6)]

blanket drill *n.* [1930s+] (orig. milit.) **1** sexual intercourse. **2** masturbation. [joc. use of milit. jargon]

blanket fair *n.* [19C] bed.

blanket fever *n.* [20C] the desire to lie in bed rather than get up and go to work.

blanket-head *see* BLANKET-ASS.

blanket hornpipe *n.* [19C] sexual intercourse (cf. DANCE *v.*¹).

blanket muster *see* TARPAULIN MUSTER.

blanket on the coals *n.* [1920s] (Aus.) a johnny-cake, i.e. a cake made of wheatmeal, baked on the ashes or fried in a pan. [abbr. HORSE BLANKET *n.*²]

blanket party *n.* [20C] (US prison) **1** the murder of a fellow prisoner by tossing a blanket over the head and then bludgeoning or stabbing them to death. **2** an initiation rite whereby a new prisoner is forcibly smothered in a blanket, then beaten up by their fellows. [ironic use of SE]

blanket stiff *n.* [late 19C+] (US) a tramp (cf. BINDLE STIFF). [SE *blanket*, a bedroll + STIFF *n.*³]

blankety *adj.* [mid-19C+] a general term of condemnation (cf. BLANKETY-BLANK). [BLANK *adj.*]

blankety-blank *phr.* [late 19C+] a general term of condemnation, which is found in all parts of speech, e.g. *you blankety-blank!* or *that blankety-blank, no-good* or *don't you blankety-blank me!* [a euph. in which the words indicate two blanks, for presumed obscenities, on the page]

blanks *n.*¹ [late 19C–1910s] (Anglo-Ind.) White people. [Fr. *blanc*, white]

blanks *n.*² [1980s+] (drugs) inferior, second-rate drugs. [they 'draw a blank' as regards their effects]

blanks! *excl.* [1990s] excl. of contempt, disdain, esp. when one has got the better of a rival. [? a euph. (like BLANKETY-BLANK and DASH!); in this case the most likely is BALLS!]

blank up *v.* [1980s+] (US Black) to trick, to murder. [to render one's victim 'blank']

blank your blinkers! *excl.* [late 19C–1900s] euph. for *damn your eyes!* [BLANK *adj.* + BLINKERS *n.*]

blanny *v.* [20C] to flatter. [BLARNEY]

blanshed *see* BLANCHED.

blaps *n.* [1960s+] (S.Afr.) a gaucherie, a blunder (cf. BLOOMER; BLOOP; BLOOPER). [Afk. *blaps*, a blunder, a howler, a 'blooper']

blared/blare-eyed *adj.* [20C] (US) having staring, wild eyes. [SE *blare*, to open wide]

blarey-eyed *adj.* [1970s] (US Black) a general insult, lit. wall-eyed. [? SE *bleary-eyed*]

blarge *v.* [20C] (Ulster) to do anything unceremoniously and loudly. [SE *blunder* + *barge*]

blarney *n.* [mid-18C+] nonsense, charming but empty chatter. [*Blarney*, a village near Cork in Ireland. Within the castle is an inscribed stone, which is hard to approach, and the popular belief is that any one who kisses this 'Blarney stone' will ever after be gifted with a persuasive, plausible tongue]

blarney v. **1** [late 18C+] to flatter, to talk nonsense; thus *blarneyed*, flattered, cajoled (cf. SCHMOOZE v.). **2** [mid–late 19C] (US) to pick locks. [BLARNEY n.]

blart n. [1990s] the vagina. [dial. *blart*, to howl]

blart v. [late 19C+] to talk wildly. [? SE *blurt* + BLAB]

blasé adj. [early–mid-19C] exhausted by enjoyment, weary and disgusted with it, used up. [SE f. 1860s; Fr. *blasé*, exhausted by pleasure; the word was popularized by a French farce *L'homme blasé*, which was staged (*c*.1840) in two versions. In the second of these a character was called Blasé; the modern use to mean 'supercilious' dates f. 1930s]

blast n.[1] [late 19C+] **1** a severe reprimand, a verbal attack. **2** a telephone call. [ext. use of SE]

blast n.[2] **1** [1950s+] (US) a drink of liquor. **2** [1950s+] (US) a puff of a marijuana cigarette. **3** [1960s+] a thrill, a very good time. **4** [1960s+] a wild, uproarious party. **5** [1970s+] (US Black) a song.

blast v.[1] (orig. US) **1** [1920s+] to shoot a gun. **2** [1960s–70s] to shoot or kill someone with a gun. **3** [1960s–70s] to defeat heavily. [SE *blast*, to blow violently]

blast v.[2] [1930s] to leave. [SE *blast off*]

blast v.[3] **1** [1940s+] to complain. **2** [1950s+] to scold, to criticize. [BLAST n.[1]]

blast v.[4] **1** [1940s+] to smoke marijuana or hashish cigarettes (cf. BLAST PARTY). **2** [1950s–60s] (US) to go completely mad (esp. under the influence of drugs). **3** [1980s+] to smoke crack cocaine. [the immediate effect of the drug on one's brain, but ult. early 16C Scot. *blast*, a smoke of tobacco]

blast v.[5] [1990s] (orig. US Black/teen) to play a record.

blast a joint, to phr. [1960s+] (drugs) to smoke marijuana. [BLAST v.[4] + JOINT n.[4] (2)]]

blast a pocket rocket, to phr. [1990s] to masturbate.

blast a roach, to phr. [1960s+] (drugs) to smoke marijuana. [BLAST v.[4] + ROACH n.[2]]

blast a stick, to phr. [1960s+] (drugs) to smoke marijuana. [BLAST v.[4] + STICK n.[14] (2)]

blasted adj.[1] [late 17C+] euph. for DAMNED. [abbr. SE *God blasted*]

blasted adj.[2] [1970s+] very drunk or heavily intoxicated by a drug (cf. BASTED).

blasted brimstone n. [late 18C] (Und.) a prostitute. [SE *blasted*, cursed + *brimstone*, a virago]

blasted fellow n. [mid-18C–early 19C] a complete villain. [SE *blasted*, cursed + *fellow*]

blaster n.[1] [1930s+] a pistol, a revolver. [BLAST v.[1] (1)]

blaster n.[2] [1980s+] a large, portable cassette recorder/player. [abbr. GHETTOBLASTER]

blast from the past phr. [1960s+] (orig. US) anything that, or anyone who, causes nostalgia, esp. a piece of music or a popular song.

blast hell out of see BEAT HELL OUT OF.

blast-off n. [1960s] (US) **1** an orgasm. **2** a thrill, a very good time (cf. BLAST n.[2]).

blast off v. (US) **1** [1950s+] to leave. **2** [1960s] (drugs) to experience a drug and thus get HIGH adj.[1]. **3** [1960s] to have an orgasm.

blast party n. [1940s–60s] (US Black) a gathering of marijuana smokers. [BLAST v.[4] (1) + SE *party*]

blast the hell out of see BEAT HELL OUT OF.

blat n. [1930s+] (US) a newspaper (cf. BLADDER n.[2]). [Ger. *Blatt*, leaf; thus newspaper]

blat v. **1** [18C–1910s] to talk wildly or loudly. **2** [late 19C–1920s] (US) to talk at length. [SE *blat*, bleating or shrill sound]

blatant adv. [1990s] (Black) a general intensifier, definitely, undoubtedly, very much so. [SE *blatant*, glaringly or defiantly conspicuous]

blate n. [1990s] the vagina (cf. BLART n.). [? BLOT n. but cf. dial. *blate*, shy, timid]

blater n. **1** [18C–mid-19C] a sheep. **2** [mid-18C–19C] a calf. [? SE *bleat*]

blather n. [early 19C+] nonsense (cf. BLETHER n.). [ME *blather*, nonsense; thus Scot. *blether*, Irish *bladar*, flattery]

blathergab n. [20C] (US) a gossip, a chatterer (cf. BLATHERSKITE). [BLATHER + GAB n.]

blatherskite/bletherskate/bletherskite n. **1** [16C+] a voluble, boastful speaker (cf. BLABBERSKITE). **2** [20C] nonsense, rubbish, foolish talk. [BLETHER v., to bluster and SE *skate*, to slide over]

blatherskite!/bletherskate!/bletherskite! excl. [20C] nonsense! [BLATHERSKITE]

-blatt sfx. [1980s+] (US campus) suffix of familiarity or endearment added to nouns.

blatter v. [20C] to hit, to attack. [Scot. *blatter*, to rush with clattering noise]

blaw n. [1980s+] (drugs) cannabis. [var. on BLOW n.[7]]

blaxploitation n. [1970s+] (orig. US) the use of Black actors in a (usually) low-budget film featuring a plot filled with sex and violence and peopled by stereotypes (pimps, prostitutes, drug dealers). [SE *Black* + *exploitation*]

blaze v. [1980s+] (US campus) to leave. [SE *blaze the trail*]

blaze away v. [mid-19C+] to work at anything with enthusiasm and energy. [SE *blaze*, to burn with the fervour of devotion, excitement, or passion + *blaze away*, to fire a weapon rapidly]

blazed adj. [20C] (drugs) intoxicated by a drug. [SE *blazed*, inflamed]

blaze on v. [1980s+] (US Black) to attack or knock down without warning. [? SE *blaze away/out*, to fire continuously]

blazer n. (US) **1** [mid–late 19C] someone or something exceptional of their type. **2** [1900s–30s] a hoax, a lie, a cheating trick. [SE *blazer*, anything that blazes or shines; thus in (2) dazzles the victim]

blazers n. [late 19C–1930s] spectacles. [the reflection of the sun in their lenses]

blazes n. [early 19C+] euph. for HELL in various phr., e.g. GO TO BLAZES!; HOW THE BLAZES etc. [the traditional fires of hell]

blazes, Kate! excl. [20C] (Irish) a general excl. of surprise, annoyance, etc. [BLAZES + generic use of proper name]

blazing adj., adv. [mid-19C+] **1** (orig. US) a general intensifier, esp. in *a blazing row*, a vicious argument (cf. FLAMING adj.[2]). **2** (US Black) very good, very well.

blazing adv. [1980s+] experiencing the extreme effects of a drug, esp. a hallucinogen. [? FIRED UP]

bleach v. [mid-19C] (US campus) to miss a class or other meeting. [? BLANK v.]

bleached mort n. [late 18C] a fair-haired woman. [SE *bleached* + MORT]

bleacher/bleecher n. **1** [late 18C–mid-19C] a woman, usu. pej. **2** [1930s] (Glasgow) a maidservant. [her job, bleaching clothes]

bleachification n. [1980s+] (US) the gentrification of former working-class blocks. [SE *bleach*, a whitening agent; such blocks were often Black or Puerto Rican; their new, richer owners will be White]

bleak adj. [mid–late 19C] (US) attractive, handsome; thus *bleak-mort*, a pretty young woman. [? SE *bleak*, pale, wan]

bleary adj. [20C] drunk (cf. ADDLED). [SE *bleary*, short-sighted]

bleat n. **1** [20C] a (feeble) complaint. **2** [1950s] (prison) a petition to the Home Secretary for reduction or repeal of one's sentence. [the weak chance this has of success is underlined by the allusion to the sound of a sheep]

bleat v. [mid-19C+] (orig. milit.) to complain, to whinge. [mid-16C–mid-19C use SE]

bleater n. [early 17C] (Und.) one who is tricked by a confidence trickster. [SE *bleater*, a lamb (to the slaughter)]

bleating cheat/chete n. [mid-16C–early 19C] a sheep. [SE *bleat* + CHEAT n.]

bleating cull n. [18C–early 19C] a sheep-stealer (cf. BLEATING RIG). [BLEATER + CULL n.[1] (3)]

bleating prig n. [18C–early 19C] sheep-stealing (cf. BLEATING CULL; BLEATING RIG). [BLEATER + PRIG n.[1]]

bleating rig n. [18C–early 19C] (Und.) sheep-stealing (cf. BLEATING CULL). [BLEATER + RIG n.[2] (2)]

bleddy see BLADDY.

bleecher see BLEACHER.

bleed n.[1] [late 19C–1900s] blood; usu. in phr. *she'll have his bleed*, and used of a woman's forthcoming attack on her husband.

bleed n.[2] [1980s+] (US Black) a Black person. [BLOOD n.[6]]

bleed v.[1] **1** [17C+] to extort money from. **2** [17C+] to part with one's money without complaint, to submit oneself to extortion. **3** [20C] (US) to take advantage of. [SE *bleed dry*]

bleed v.[2] [20C] (US) to sweat profusely.

bleeder n.[1] **1** [19C] a spur. **2** [mid-19C] (US) a knife, when used as a weapon. [SE *bleed*, to draw blood]

bleeder n.[2] [19C] a sovereign. [one 'bleeds' money to creditors]

bleeder n.[3] [late 19C+] a person, usu. but not invariably with derog. implications. [lit. one who draws blood]

bleeders n. [late 18C–1900s] spurs. [their effect on the horse; late 19C+ mainly Aus. use]

bleeding adj. [mid-19C+] exclamatory adjective, a euph. for BLOODY adj.; also as intensifier, *bleeding hell* etc.

bleeding cully n. [late 17C–early 19C] a gullible victim, who parts cheerfully with their money. [BLEED v.[1] (2) + CULLY n. (1)]

bleeding dirt n. [1970s] (gay) extorting money from homosexuals. [BLEED v.[1] (1) + DIRT n.[2]]

bleeding new adj. [late 18C] fresh, new. [the image of fish, which bleed only when they are fresh]

bleed like a pig/stuck pig, to phr. [17C+] to bleed heavily, to lose a good deal of blood.

bleed one's turkey, to phr. [1920s+] to urinate (cf. BLEED THE LIVER).

bleed the liver, to phr. [1920s+] to urinate (cf. BLEED ONE'S TURKEY).

bleed the lizard, to phr. [1990s] to masturbate. [SE *bleed* + LIZARD n.[3]]

bleed the weed, to phr. [1990s] to masturbate. [SE *bleed* + assonance]

bleed white v. [1930s+] to submit to excessive extortion, thus draining every drop of money/blood.

bleep n. [1970s+] euph. substitute for various taboo terms, e.g. SHIT in phr. *beat the bleep out of* or FUCK in phr. *bleeping around*. [the electronic 'bleeping' out of supposed obscenities on radio and TV]

bleeping adj. [1980s+] euph. for various taboo words, e.g. BLEEDING; FUCKING adj. [BLEEP n.]

bleet v. [19C] to roar or talk wildly. [? SE *bleat*]

blemm v. [1980s+] (Irish) to rush, to move at speed. [ety. unknown]

blend n. [1990s] (drugs) marijuana. [? a mixture of several varieties of the drug]

blend v. [20C] (US) to marry.

blender n. [1990s] anyone who interrupts one's conversation without being asked. [they attempt to *blend* into the conversation]

blenker v. [mid-19C] (US) to plunder. [Brigadier-General Louis *Blenker* (1812–63), whose troops, starving for lack of proper rations, plundered civilian homes near Warrenton, Virginia in April 1862]

blerry adj. [1920s+] (S.Afr.) a general expletive, the local pron. of the UK BLOODY adj. (cf. BLADDY). [Afk. pron.]

bleskop n. [1960s+] (S.Afr.) **1** a bald-headed person. **2** a bald head. [Afk. *bles*, bald + *kop*, head]

bless v. [early 19C] to curse someone, to reprimand, to scold. [ironic reversal of usual SE use]

blessing n. **1** [late 18C] a small quantity over and above the stated measure, given to a customer by a stall-holder or shopkeeper. **2** [late 19C] (Irish) a tip, a handout. [14C SE *blessing*, a present; note Devon dial. *blessing*, an extra handful of produce, thrown in as a bonus to an order, and also the belief, common to many religions, that those who give charity are blessed]

bless me! excl. [20C] a mild excl. [abbr. *Lord bless me!*, but note 17C *bless oneself*, to swear]

bless my heart! excl. [mid-18C+] a mild excl.

bless/'pon my soul! excl. [19C+] a mild oath. [SE before 19C]

bless oneself v. [early 17C–late 18C] to curse. [SE *bless oneself*, to say 'God bless me!']

bless one's gums! excl. [late 19C] a mild excl. [var. on BLESS MY SOUL!]

bless one's little cotton socks phr. [1910s+] a general expression of affection.

bless the world with one's heels, to phr. [mid-16C–mid-17C] to be hanged. [? the feet twitching in the air could be likened to making the sign of the cross]

blether n. [mid-19C+] nonsense (cf. BLATHERSKITE). [Scot.]

blether v. [mid-19C+] to talk nonsense, continually and at length. [Scot.]

blethering n. [1910s+] talking nonsense (cf. BLITHERING). [BLETHER v.]

bletherskate/bletherskite see BLATHERSKITE.

blew v.[1] [mid-19C+] to err, to blunder. [var. on BLUE v.[3]]

blew v.[2] [mid–late 19C] to inform on, to betray. [BLOW v.[1] (2)]

blew/blue in v. [mid-19C+] to waste, usu. money (cf. BLOW v.[3]); thus *blew one's screw*, to spend all one's wages at once. [? one 'explodes' or 'blows up' one's finances]

blew in one's red 'un, to phr. [late 19C] to pawn one's watch and spend the money thus realized on drink. [BLEW IN + RED 'UN n.[1] (2)]

blew it v. [mid-19C–1920s] to betray a fellow villain to the police. [BLEW v.[2]]

bliff v. [1990s] to masturbate; thus *bliff mag*, a pornographic magazine. [? dial. *bliffert*, a stroke, a blow]

bliggey/bliggey-de-bliggey n. [1960s] (US Black, mainly Calif.) a euph. oath, taking the place of an obscenity (cf. BLANK adj.; BLANKETY-BLANK; DASH!).

bligh n. [1980s+] (W.I./UK Black teen) a chance, an opportunity, an opening. [ety. unknown]

blighted adj. [1910s–40s] very drunk or heavily intoxicated by a drug (cf. BASTED).

blighter n. [late 19C+] a general derog. term. [lit. one who *blights* their surroundings but ? also a euph. for BUGGER n.[1]; later 20C use is usu. ironic, with images of such actors as Terry-Thomas (1911–90) or Leslie Phillips (b.1924)]

blighting adj. [1910s–30s] very drunk or heavily intoxicated by a drug (cf. BLIGHTED).

Blighty n. [1910s+] (orig. Ind. Army) England; thus *Blighty one*, a wound gained during WW1 that was sufficiently incapacitating to ensure one's being sent home to England from the front. [Hind. *bilyati* = *wilyati*, foreign, esp. European; ult. f. Arabic *wilayat*, an inhabited country, a foreign country;

bilyati was used in a variety of contexts, the best known being *bilyati panee*, 'European water', i.e. soda water]

blikkeys *n.* [1980s+] (drugs) fake crack cocaine that has been manufactured from flakes of soap powder. [ety. unknown]

Blikkiesdorp *n.* (S.Afr.) **1** [1950s+] a fictitious town, used to personify an insignificant, 'one-horse' town, also as *Blikkiesbaai, Blikkiesfontein, Overblikkiesberg*. **2** [1960s+] a slum, a shanty-town. [Afk. *blikkie*, little tin + *dorp*, town]

Blikoor *n.* [late 19C+] (S.Afr.) a derog. term for an inhabitant of the Orange Free State. [Afk. *blik*, tin + *oor*, an ear]

bliksem!/bliksom!/bluxom! *excl.* [1950s+] (S.Afr.) a general term of abuse, swine, bastard. [Afk. *bliksem*, lightning]

blikskottel *n.* [1950s+] (S.Afr.) a general term of abuse, less hostile than BLIKSEM. [Afk. *bliks*, tin + *skottel*, dish]

blim *n.* [1980s+] (drugs) **1** a small piece of hashish, not really sufficient to make a full-strength three-paper cigarette, but enough for perhaps a weak one or a single-skin effort. **2** the residue in a hash-pipe (cf. BONG *n.*). [ety. unknown]

blimey *n.* [1910s–30s] (US) a Briton (cf. LIMEY *n.*). [BLIMEY!]

blimey! *excl.* [late 19C+] denoting surprise or disbelief (cf. GORBLIMEY!; GORDON BENNETT). [oath 'God blind me!']

blimey Charlie!/Teddy! *excl.* [20C] (Aus./N.Z.) a general excl., used as sign of the relief of nervous tension. [BLIMEY! + generic use of proper names]

blimey O'Reilly! *excl.* [1920s+] a general excl., presumed to be an intensifier of BLIMEY (cf. BLIND O'REILLY). [ext. of BLIMEY!]

blimp *n.* **1** [1930s+] a backward-looking, ultra-conservative figure, orig. a military man, terrified of progress and determined to do anything to prevent it. **2** [1930s–40s] one who is 'full of hot air'. **3** [1930s–60s] a promiscuous young woman. **4** [1930s+] a very fat person. [the fictitious *Colonel Blimp*, the personification of such emotions, invented by the cartoonist and caricaturist David Low (1891–1963). Already widespread, the term and the image became even more popular with the Powell/Pressbuger film *The Life and Death of Col. Blimp* (1943)]

blimp boat *n.* [1980s+] (US campus) an obese person. [BLIMP + SE *boat*]

blimpo *n.* [1930s+] (US) a very fat person (cf. BLIMP). [BLIMP *n.* (4) + sfx. -o]

blimp out *v.* [1970s+] (US campus) **1** to eat voraciously. **2** to become grossly fat. [BLIMP *n.* (4)]

blind *n.*[1] [late 18C] an excuse, a pretence. [SE *blind*, any means or place of concealment.

blind *n.*[2] [19C] night-time; thus *do a blind*, to do a 'moonlight flit'.

blind *n.*[3] [late 19C–1920s] (US tramp) a baggage car; thus *beat the blind, jump the blind*, to ride in such a car. [SE *blind*, i.e. it has no windows]

blind *n.*[4] [1920s] (US campus) an evening out with someone whom one has never met (cf. BLIND DATE; DRAG A BLIND).

blind *adj.*[1] [early 17C+] (orig. Und.) extremely drunk (cf. BLIND DRUNK). [so drunk one cannot see]

blind *adj.*[2] **1** [late 19C+] complete, utter. **2** [1930s+] a neg. intensifier, e.g. *not a blind bit of use, not a blind word*. **3** [1940s+] (bingo) the round numbers, e.g. *blind 30, blind 20*.

blind *adj.*[3] [1920s+] (gay) uncircumcised (cf. NEAR-SIGHTED).

blind *v.*[1] **1** [early–mid-19C] to cheat. **2** [1900s] (US campus) to answer all the questions one is posed by an instructor, esp. when one has done no actual preparation. [SE *blind*, to conceal]

blind *v.*[2] [late 19C+] to swear (cf. EFF AND BLIND). [euph. for such words as BLOODY *adj.*; BLEEDING etc]

blind *v.*[3] [20C] (US) to expose another's ignorance. [? one 'blinds' them with one's own knowledge]

blind *v.*[4] [1920s–50s] to drive very fast and without noticing anyone else on the road.

blind *adv.* [1950s+] utterly, completely. [devoid of any external modification]

blind alley *n.* [late 19C+] an unlicensed drinking house (cf. BLIND PIG). **2** [late 19C] the vagina (cf. ALLEY *n.*[1]).

blind as Chloe *phr.* [late 18C–mid-19C. early 19C+] very drunk (cf. CAMP AS CHLOE; DO A CHLOE; DRUNK AS CHLOE). [mainly Aus. use from late 19C]

blind billy's bargain *n.* [late 19C+] a 'bargain' that is, in fact, no bargain at all, since one is unable to impose one's own conditions on the person with whom one is dealing. [*Blind Billy*, a former Limerick hangman; the soon-to-be-hanged person was in no position to bargain]

blind both eyes *phr.* [late 19C] of eggs, fried on both sides, 'turned over'.

blind charley *n.* [mid-19C] (US) a lamp-post. [SE *blind* + CHARLEY *n.*[1]]

blind cheeks *n.* [18C] the posteriors; thus *buss blind cheeks*, kiss my arse (cf. BLIND CUPID; TWO FAT CHEEKS). [the shape of the 'nether cheeks']

blind cobbler's thumb *phr.* [1990s] a derog. description of the face of an unattractive woman. [? covered in pockmarks, resembling needle-pricks]

blind cock *n.* [1980s+] (US gay) an uncircumcised penis. [BLIND *adj.*[3] + COCK *n.*[2] (1)]

blind Cupid *n.* [late 18C] **1** the buttocks. **2** an ugly blind man. [*Cupid*, the god of love, is often painted as blind]

blind date *n.* [1920s+] (orig. US) an evening out with someone whom one has never met but who will be introduced by a mutual friend. [SE *blind* + DATE *n.*[3]]

blind dragon *n.* [1920s–30s] (society) a chaperon(e). [SE *blind* + *dragon*, a fierce old woman; she casts a 'blind eye' on her charge's frolics]

blind drunk *adv.* [late 18C–late 19C] extremely drunk (cf. BLIND *adj.*[1]). [SE in 20C]

blinder *n.*[1] **1** [20C] a cheap, bad cigar. **2** [1930s] a Woodbine cigarette (the cheapest available brand). [ext. of SE use; ? the smoke or the smell gets in one's eyes]

blinder *n.*[2] [1930s+] a hard and exciting sporting encounter, esp. as *play a blinder*. [one is *blinded* by the quality of the game]

blind eye *n.* [late 18C–1900s] **1** the anus (cf. DEAD EYE *n.*[1]). **2** the buttocks (cf. BLIND CHEEKS; BLIND CUPID). [coarsely joc. use of SE]

blind fart *n.* [late 19C+] a noiseless, but very malodorous breaking of wind.

blindfolded lady with the scales *n.* [1940s–50s] (US Black) justice, as a concept rather than as a product of the legal system. [the traditional image of justice, seen in statues, illustrations etc]

blind Freddie *n.* [1940s+] (Aus.) an imaginary figure seen as representing the lowest denominator of incompetence; thus used in phr. such as *blind Freddie could see that, wouldn't fool blind Freddie*. [some commentators have posited a real-life 'blind Freddie' – a blind beggar in the streets of Sydney in the 1920s – but no one has yet properly identified him]

blind harper *n.* [late 17C–late 18C] a beggar who fakes blindness, distracting attention from the disguise by playing a harp or fiddle.

blind hookey *n.* [late 19C–1900s] madness, foolishness, a leap in the dark. [proper name *Blind Hookey*, a card-game in which 5 cards are dealt face down. The dealer takes the centre card and, if that is the highest, wins all the bets; if it is the lowest, the dealer pays all 4]

blind inches *n.* [late 19C] the measurement of the different lengths of one's penis when erect or flaccid. [one does not see the extra length when the penis is flaccid]

blinding adj. [1960s+] wonderful, terrific, perfect etc (cf. BLINDER n.²). [? so intense as to render one blind]

blindman's buff n. [1960s+] snuff. [rhy. sl.]

blind man's holiday n. 1 [late 16C–early 19C] night-time. 2 [late 17C–early 18C] nightfall, the dusk. [once night falls there is nothing – in a pre-street-light world – for a blind man to see]

blind meat n. [1920s+] (US gay) an uncircumcised penis. [SE blind + MEAT n. (2)]

blindo n.¹ [mid-19C–1900s] a drunken spree (cf. BLINDER n.²). [BLIND DRUNK + sfx. -O]

blindo n.² [20C] (tramp) sixpence (2½p).

blindo adj. [mid-19C–1900s] tipsy. [BLINDO n.¹]

blind O'Reilly! excl. [1940s] a general excl. of surprise, excitement etc (cf. BLIMEY O'REILLY!). [O'Reilly was apparently a real person, poss. a trade-unionist on the Liverpool docks]

blind pig n. (US) 1 [late 19C+] an unlicensed drinking house, a speakeasy, an 'after-hours' bar (cf. BLIND TIGER; HOLE IN THE WALL). 2 [late 19C+] the whisky served in such an establishment. 3 [1970s] a variety of cocktail. [? the typical architecture of the earliest of such bars, a blank facade bereft of windows and with only a small peep-hole in its door. Alternatively f. the practice of disguising the bar as an exhibition of natural freaks]

blind-pigger n. [late 19C+] (US) the proprietor of an illicit drinking establishment. [BLIND PIG]

blind robin n. [mid-19C+] (US) a smoked herring. [the red herring and the robin's red breast]

blindside v. [1960s+] (orig. US) 1 to take by surprise. 2 to take advantage of. [US football jargon blindside, to attack or strike (an opponent) on the side on which the view is obstructed]

blind staggers see STAGGERS.

blind tiger n. (US) 1 [late 19C+] an unlicensed drinking house (cf. BLIND PIG). 2 [1900s] illicit whisky. 3 [1920s] the owner of an illicit bar. [ety. unknown]

blind with science, to phr. [1930s+] to confuse with one's erudition or simple volume of (polysyllabic or abstruse) words.

blinger n. [1900s–40s] (US) the extreme example of a type or situation (cf. CORKER n.²). [SE blink or echoic bling, used for something that hits one with a sudden thump]

blink n.¹ 1 [early–mid-19C] a light. 2 [late 19C] (US) a look, a glance. 3 [1900s–30s] (US) an eye. 4 [1920s+] (US) a blind person.

blink n.² [late 19C–1900s] a drink (cf. BIT OF BLINK). [rhy. sl.]

blink n.³ [1910s+] (Aus.) a cigarette butt. [smoking it caused one to blink from the smoke entering the eyes]

blink v. [late 19C–1920s] (US) to see.

blinked out adj. [20C] malfunctioning, out of order. [ON THE BLINK]

blinker n. 1 [18C–1950s; mid-19C–20C use is US] the eye. 2 [19C] a hard blow in the eye. 3 [mid-19C] (orig. US) a black eye. 4 [late 19C] a man, a fellow (cf. BLEEDER n.²; BLIGHTER). 5 [1970s] a camera. 6 [1970s+] (US Und.) a police surveillance helicopter.

blinkers n. 1 [late 18C+] the eyes (cf. BLANK YOUR BLINKERS!). 2 [mid-19C–1930s] eyeglasses, spectacles (cf. BLINKS).

blink-fencer n. [mid–late 19C] a seller of spectacles. [BLINKERS + FENCER]

blinking adj. [1910s+] a mild pej. (cf. BLANKETY; BLINKERS). [euph.]

blinko n. [late 19C] an 'amateur night' at the local public house. [? one blinks at the mediocrity of it all]

blinko adj. [1950s] (US) very drunk (cf. BLOTTO). [one blinks to clear one's drunken vision]

blink-pickings n. [20C] (Aus.) cigarette stubs, picked up

from the gutter and either relit or recombined in a new 'roll-your-own'. [BLINK n.³]

blinks n. 1 [17C+] a nickname for one who blinks all the time. 2 [mid-19C] the eyes. 3 [mid-19C] a pair of spectacles (cf. BLINKERS).

blip n.¹ [late 19C. 1970s] a blow. [onomat. for a small, short, sharp sound, underpinned by milit. jargon blip, a small elongated mark projected on a radar screen, itself ref. to the 'bleeping' noise of radar]

blip n.² 1 [20C] a temporary hiatus. 2 [1940s+] (US Black) a surprise, a sudden disappointment. [for ety. see BLIP n.¹]

blip n.³ [1930s–40s] (US Black) a cent, a nickel. [ext. of BLIP n.¹; accentuating the smallness of the sound and the coin]

blip/blip off v.¹ (US) 1 [1920s] to hit hard, to shoot. 2 [1920s+] to kill, to murder. [BLIP n.¹]

blip v.² [1970s+] (orig. milit.) to open and close the throttle; thus reving an automobile engine while the clutch is disengaged. [milit. use orig. WW1 and applied. spec. to aeroplanes]

blip off see BLIP v.¹.

blipped n. [1980s+] (N.Z. drugs) intoxicated by a drug. [BLIP v.¹ (1)]

bliss out v. [1970s+] to experience a state of (usu. drug- or meditation-induced) ecstasy; thus blissout, a state of ecstasy. [according to RHDAS coined/introduced by followers of Maharaj Ji, c.1972]

blister n.¹ 1 [early 19C–1960s] an offensive or argumentative person, usu. old blister. 2 [1960s] an unattractive or promiscuous woman. [the unpleasantness of the physical blister]

blister n.² [20C] (Aus.) a mortgage. [? the cost of the mortgage 'scorches' one's pocket]

blister n.³ [1900s–40s] a legal summons. [the summons results from scorching, i.e. exceeding the speed limit (see SCORCH v.)]

blister v. 1 [late 19C–1900s] to punish, to fine, to hurt, esp. as excl. blister them! 2 [1900s–30s] for a policeman to take one's name in connection with an offence. 3 [1900s–30s] to be summoned or punished for an offence. [BLISTER n.³]

blistering adj. [1900s] a general expletive, used euph. for a variety of taboo synons. [the heat of one's language raises blisters]

blither v. [mid-19C+] to talk nonsense. [SE blether, to talk loudly and foolishly]

blithered adj. [1910s+] (Aus.) very drunk. [BLITHER v.]

blitherer n. [20C] a silly fool. [BLITHER v.]

blithering n. [late 19C+] talking nonsense, babbling on. [SE blither, to talk nonsense]

blithering adj. [19C+] absolute, complete, esp. in phr. blithering idiot, blithering fool etc. [BLITHERING n.]

blithero adv. [1950s] (Irish) extremely. [BLITHERING adj.]

blitter v. [20C] (Ulster) to break wind. [Scot. blitter, to rattle]

blitz, the n. [20C] (US) menstruation. [Ger. Blitzkrieg, lightning war; ? the suddenness of its onset]

blitz v. 1 [1940s+] (orig. US) to defeat comprehensively, to crush, to overcome. 2 [1940s+] to arrive or leave quickly. 3 [1970s+] (US campus) to perform well (in an examination). 4 [1960s+] to saturate with an advertising campaign or similar form of wide-spectrum information. [Ger. Blitzkrieg, lightning war]

blitzed adj. 1 [1960s+] drunk or experiencing the effects of a drug (cf. BASTED). 2 [1970s] absolutely exhausted, emotionally drained. [BLITZ v. (1)]

blitz it v. [1940s] (S.Afr. student) to hurry, to 'get a move on'. [BLITZ v. (2)]

blitzkrieged adj. [1970s+] (US campus) drunk or experiencing the effects of a drug (cf. BASTED; BLITZED adj.).

blivet/blivit n. [1940s+] (US, orig. Aus. milit.) 1 something useless, unnecessary, annoying (popularly defined as '10 pounds of shit in a 5-pound bag'). 2 a fat or unpleasant person or thing. **3** a distasteful job or situation (cf. TRIVET). ['the expression arose among American flyers in New Guinea and is of Australian origin' (*RHDAS*)]

blixen-bus *n.* [20C] (US) an automobile. [Ger. *Blitzen*, lightning + SE *bus*]

blizzard *n.*[1] (US) **1** [19C] a hard blow. **2** [19C] a stinging remark, esp. to end an argument or as a parting shot. **3** [mid–late 19C] a rifle shot. **4** [mid-19C] a large fire. **5** [late 19C] a drink of alcohol, a 'bracer'. [dial. *blizzer*, a heavy blow + SE *blizzard*]

blizzard *n.*[2] [1990s] (drugs) a cloudy white substance seen in a crack pipe.

blizzard *v.* [mid-19C] (US) to let off a volley of shots.

blizzard-dodger *n.* [1930s] (US) a tramp who travels south in the winter to avoid the cold weather.

bloak *n.* [mid-19C] a man. [var. BLOKE]

bloat *n.* [mid-19C–1910s] (US) **1** a worthless, conceited individual. **2** a drunkard.

bloater *n.* [late 19C–1900s] a fat person. [abbr. *Yarmouth bloater*; when the fish is first smoked it swells up conspicuously, although it then shrinks as it cools]

bloat the vein, to *phr.* [1990s] to masturbate.

blob *n.* [20C] (mainly Aus.) an insignificant person.

blob *v.*[1] [19C] (US) to make a mistake. [? a *blob* of ink that mars an otherwise faultless piece of handwriting]

blob *v.*[2] [18C–19C] to talk indiscreetly. [var. on BLAB *v.*]

blobbermouth *n.* [1930s+] an indiscreet talker (cf. BLABBERMOUTH). [BLOB *v.*[2] + SE *mouth*]

block *n.*[1] **1** [mid-16C–18C] a fool, an idiot (cf. BLOCKHEAD *n.*[1]). **2** [mid-17C+] the head, but nearly always in phr. *knock one's block off.*

block *n.*[2] [late 19C–1900s] (Scot.) a policeman. [? BLOCK *n.*[1] or a hard-hearted person]

block *n.*[3] [20C] (prison) the punishment cells. [abbr. SE *punishment block*]

block *n.*[4] [20C] a ban, a rejection.

block *n.*[5] [1980s+] (drugs) marijuana. [? packaging]

block *v.*[1] [late 19C] to have sexual intercourse. [abbr. PUT THE BLOCKS TO]

block *v.*[2] [mid-19C] to stand a drink. [SE phr. *put one on the block*]

block *v.*[3] **1** [late 19C–900s] to loiter, to 'hang around' (cf. BLOCK A PUB). **2** [1930s+] (Aus.) to deceive, to get the better of. **3** [1970s+] (N.Z.) to gang rape. **4** [1980s+] (US Black) to ruin another man's sexual activities by stealing his woman, interrupting his seduction etc (cf. COCK BLOCK). [SE *block*, to bar the way; (3) ? + implication of SE *block*, a group, a collection]

blockade *n.* [19C] (US) illicitly distilled whisky; thus *blockader*, a distiller. [the need to defeat the customs blockade to sell it]

blockade *v.* [19C] (US) to distil illicit liquor. [SE *blockade*, a barrier, in this case against whisky-runners]

block-and-block *adj.* [early–mid-18C] (US) very drunk. [Lincolnshire dial. *blocker*, extreme drunkenness]

block and fall joint *n.* [late 19C] (US) a tavern, catering mainly to Black people, in which one would most likely be given some form of knock-out drop in one's drink and then be robbed (cf. SHOCK HOUSE). [SE *block + fall + joint n.*[3] (3); 'you'd get a shock, walk a block and fall in the gutter' (Sante, 1991)]

block and tackle *n.*[1] [late 19C+] (orig. Aus.) a watch and chain.

block and tackle *n.*[2] [1970s] (US) a very strong drink. [the saying 'you have one, walk one block and you're ready to tackle anyone']

block a pub, to *phr.* [late 19C–1900s] to loiter in a public house. [BLOCK *v.*[3] (1)]

block boy *n.* [1990s] a gay male who dresses as if he were part of the heterosexual hip-hop culture (cf. BANJY BOY). [he looks as if he were someone 'off the block']

blockbuster *n.*[1] [1950s+] **1** a very hard blow. **2** anything enormous, gigantic; often used of a best-selling novel, film, TV series etc. [BLOCK *n.*[1] (2) + BUST *n.*[1] (1)]

blockbuster *n.*[2] **1** [1960s] the first Black family to move into a formerly all-White inner city area. **2** [1960s+] the first White family to move back into an inner city area, driving out the poor minority tenants and starting the process of gentrification. [SE *block* + BUSTER]

blockbusters *n.* [1950s+] (drugs) barbiturates (cf. BLOCKERS). [BLOCKBUSTER *n.*[1] (1) + BLOCKED]

blockbusting *n.* [1980s+] (US Black) an attack by one gang who move out of their own territory to invade that of another. [SE *block* + BUST *v.*[1] (1)]

blocked *adj.* [1950s+] drunk or intoxicated with a drug, usu. cannabis or barbiturates. [rational thought processes are impeded]

blocker *n.*[1] [20C] (US) a hanger-on. [SE *block*, a barrier; such a person will not 'get out of the way']

blocker *n.*[2] [1930s+] a bowler hat. [BLOCK *n.*[1] (2)]

blockers *n.* [1980s+] (drugs) barbiturates. [abbr. BLOCKBUSTERS]

blockhead *n.*[1] [16C] a fool, a simpleton, an idiot (cf. BLOCK *n.*[1]; BOOFHEAD; BUFFLE; BUFFLEHEAD; CABBAGE-HEAD; CARVED OUT OF WOOD; CHOWDER-HEAD; CHUCKLEHEAD; CHUGGERHEAD; CHUMP *n.*[2]; COD'S HEAD; PRAWNHEAD]. [SE *block*, a lump of wood + sfx. -HEAD (1)]

blockhead *n.*[2] [1980s+] (drugs) a dedicated user of cannabis (cf. ACID-HEAD). [BLOCK *n.*[4] + sfx. -HEAD (2); cannabis is manufactured and packaged in blocks]

blockhouse *n.* [late 18C] a prison. [SE *blockhouse*, a small fort or defensive wooden enclosure]

blockie/blocky *n.* [1940s+] (Aus.) a blocker, one who occupies a small block of rural or semi-rural land. [SAusE *block*, a parcel of land on which settlers could build or farm]

blocking *n.* [1970s+] (N.Z.) gang rape. [BLOCK *v.*[3]]

blockish *adj.* [16C–18C] stupid. [SE *block*, a barrier + sfx. -*ish*]

Block Island turkey *n.* [mid–late 19C] (US) salt cod (cf. ABERDEEN CUTLET). [proper name of *Block Island*, Connecticut]

block ornament *n.* [mid-19C] an eccentric-looking person. [SE *block ornament*, a small piece of meat displayed on a butcher's block]

block the mud slide, to *phr.* [1990s] to have anal intercourse. [coarse use of SE]

blocky see BLOCKIE.

bloke *n.* **1** [mid-19C+] a man; thus a *proper bloke*, a man who accords with the cultural standards of the speaker. **2** [mid-19C+] (Aus.) a person in authority or of superior status (cf. BIG BLOKE *n.*[1]). **3** [late 19C+] a lover, a boyfriend. **4** [late 19C+] (US) a fool. [either Shelta or Rom. In either case the term seems based in the Hind. *loke*, a man, although there is also a case for the Du. *blok*, a fool (thus BLOCKHEAD *n.*[1])]

blokie *n.* [late 19C–1920s] (US) a man (cf. BLOKE). [BLOKE *n.* (1)]

blonde *n.* [1980s+] (drugs) marijuana. [a light-coloured variety]

blonde and sweet *n.* [1940s+] (US) coffee with cream and sugar. [pun on SE]

blondie *n.* [20C] **1** a blonde person, usu. a woman. **2** (US Black) a White woman (irrespective of hair colour). [SE *blonde*]

blone *n.* [20C] (Irish) a woman. [BLOWEN]

blood *n.*[1] [mid-16C–late 19C] a rake, a roisterer, an aristocratic rowdy. [SE *blood*, either in the sense of the seat of the emotions or in that of breeding]

blood *n.*[2] [late 19C–1900s] a wallflower. [the colour]

blood *n.*[3] [late 19C+] a cheap 'blood-and-thunder' magazine, the precursor of 20C comics and even the bloodier examples of computer game.

blood *n.*[4] **1** [1930s–40s] (US) ketchup, tomato sauce. **2** [1950s–70s] (US Black) wine. [the colour]

blood *n.*[5] [1960s+] (US/UK Black) a term of address to a fellow Black; by extn. a general term of address (cf. BLEED *n.*[2]). [abbr. SE blood brother]

blood *n.*[6] [1960s+] (US Black) a young man. [racial kinship]

blood *v.* [mid-19C–1900s] to deprive of money. **2** [20C] (Aus.) to cause to bleed. [BLEED *v.*[1] (1)]

blood! *excl.* [mid-16C–mid-19C] a general intensifier, an oath, abbr. 'God's blood!' (cf. BLOODY).

blood alley *n.* [20C] (US) a place where a four-lane highway is narrowed down to a two-lane road. [the blood is that of the victims of the ensuing road accidents at such a narrowing]

blood and guts alderman *n.* [19C] a fat, pompous man.

blood and 'ounds!/'ounkers!/'ouns! *excl.* [late 19C–1900s] a mild oath, i.e. blood and wounds! (cf. ZOUNDS!).

blood and sand *n.* [20C] usu. male use, menstruation. [? ref. to the Rudolph Valentino silent classic *Blood and Sand* (1922)]

blood ball *n.* [late 19C–1900s] an annual butchers' ball. [the butchers' sanguineous trade]

blood blister *n.* [20C] (Aus.) a sister. [rhy. sl.]

blood box *n.* [20C] (US) an ambulance (cf. BUTCHER WAGON).

blood bucket *n.* [1960s] (US) a notably tough saloon or bar. [var. on BLOODY BUCKET]

blood claat/cloth *n.* [1950s+] (W.I.) a highly derog. description of another person (cf. BUMBO-CLOTH; PUSSYCLOT; RAASCLAT; SMEERLAP). [SE blood cloth, a sanitary towel]

bloodhound *n.* [early 19C+] a policeman. [reverse anthropomorphism]

blood house *n.* [1950s+] (Aus./N.Z.) a public house with a reputation for violence (cf. BLOODY BUCKET).

blood in, blood out *phr.* [20C] (US Und.) a ritual phr. meaning that to join a prison or street gang you must kill, and you may leave it (other than finishing your sentence) only by being killed yourself.

blood medicine *n.* [19C] (US) alcohol. ['a tonic']

blood/bloody oath! *excl.* [20C] (Aus.) a general expression of agreement.

blood or beer! *excl.* [late 19C–1900s] a street challenge, albeit usu. jocular, i.e. 'will you fight or buy a round?'.

blood-red fancy *n.* [mid-19C] a crimson handkerchief, as worn by costermongers (cf. BILLY *n.*[4]; CREAM FANCY; YELLOW FANCY). [SE blood-red + fancy handkerchief]

blood sports *n.* [1990s] performing cunnilingus on a menstruating woman.

blood tub *n.* [mid-late 19C] (US) **1** a thug, a tough, a street gangster. **2** a theatre presenting lurid melodrama. [the *Blood Tubs*, a Baltimore street gang, who allegedly earned their name from having 'on an election day, dipped an obnoxious German's head in a tub of warm blood, and then sent him running through the town' (Farmer, 1889)]

blood wagon *n.* [1920s+] an ambulance.

blood-worm *n.* [mid-19C–1900s] a sausage, esp. a black pudding. [its main ingredient and its appearance]

bloody *n.* [1980s+] (US preppie) a *bloody* Mary, a drink of which the chief constituents are vodka and tomato juice. [abbr.]

bloody *adj.* [late 17C+] a general neg. intensifier, very, exceedingly, abominably or desperately; esp. in the UK and Aus., where it is so widespread as to be termed 'the great Australian adjective'. Like FUCKING *adj.*, *bloody* is often inserted between the syllables of other words or phr., e.g. ABSOBLOODYLUTELY, *not bloody likely* etc. [SE *blood*. As E.P.

states: 'There is no need for ingenious etymologies, the idea of blood suffices.' There are also no links to theology, nor to the term *'sblood* (God's blood). In addition, declare F&H in their definition: 'In passing it may be mentioned that there is no ground for attributing its derivation to "By'r Our Lady".' Like other so-called 'obscenities' or 'Anglo-Saxon words', *bloody* has experienced a fluctuating position as regards usage. As *OED* put it in 1887, it has been 'in general colloquial use from the Restoration to *c.*1750. Now constantly in the mouths of the lowest classes, but by respectable people considered 'a horrid word', on a par with obscene or profane language, and usually printed in the newspapers [as] b——y.' The latter proscription has largely vanished. When *bloody* does crop up in the press it tends to be in direct, quoted speech and is printed in full, but the term, in the UK at least, has yet to enter 'polite' society. As to its etymology, the *OED* links it to the preoccupations of the 'bloods' or aristocratic rowdies of the end of the 17C and beginning of the 18C. Thus the phr. 'bloody drunk' meant 'as drunk as a blood'. Its associations with bloodshed and murder (typically a *bloody battle*) 'have recommended it to the rough classes as a word that appeals to their imagination' and the *OED* goes on to compare its late 19C popularity with other 'impressive or graphic intensives, seen in the use of jolly, awfully, terribly, devilish, deuced, damned, ripping, rattling, thumping, stunning, thundering etc'. Thus, *bloody* continues to exist on the margins (in the UK at least) between language that is acceptable if distasteful and that which is downright taboo. It is in Australia, however, that it has pride of place. Grose wrote in 1796 of how popular *bloody* was among the contemporary London underworld. There is no doubt that, along with the transported felons of the period, it made its way to the penal colonies of Botany Bay. Fifty years later it was well-established. In his book *Travels in New South Wales* (1847) Alexander Marjoribanks noted the prevalence of the word, claiming that he had heard a bullock-driver use it 27 times in 15 minutes, a rate of speech, he then calculated, that over a 50-year period would produce some 18,200,000 repetitions of the 'disgusting word'. The Sydney *Bulletin* called it 'the Australian adjective' in its edition of 18 August 1894, explaining that 'it is more used, and used more exclusively by Australians, than by any other allegedly civilized nation'. The term gained its final sanctification as the 'Great Australian Adjective' when W.T. Goodge used it as the title for one of the poems he included in his *Hits! Skits! and Jingles!* (1899)]

bloody back *n.* [late 18C] (US) a soldier (cf. LOBSTER *n.*[1]). [his scarlet jacket]

bloody bucket/bucket of blood/tub of blood *n.* (US) **1** [19C+] a notably tough saloon or bar (cf. BLOOD HOUSE). **2** [1920s] a speakeasy. **3** a tough area of a town or city, orig. that which surrounded a local rough tavern. **4** [1920s+] a cocktail made up of vodka and tomato juice, usu. a *bloody mary*. [the original 19C *Bucket of Blood*, Shorty Young's tavern in Havre, Montana; its reputation spread and the term became generic for similar establishments]

bloody flag is out/hang out the bloody flag *phr.* [late 17C–early 19C] drunk (cf. FLAG OF DEFIANCE IS OUT). [orig. in Shakespeare's *Henry V* (1598–9): 'Stand for your own; unwind yur bloody flag'; the aggressiveness that so often accompanies heavy drinking]

bloody jemmy/-jemmy *n.* [early 19C–1910s] an uncooked sheep's head (cf. SANGUINARY JAMES). [SE *bloody* + JEMMY *n.*[2]]

bloody mary *n.* [1960s+] (US) a menstruating woman, used by a woman of herself, e.g. *I'm bloody mary today*. [pun on Mary I of England (1516–58), known popularly as *Bloody Mary* for her vindictive attacks on Protestantism]

bloody Monday *n.* [late 17C–late 18C] the last day of the school term, on which holidays begin and on which punishments are traditionally given out. [thus the episode in Rudyard Kipling's *Stalky and Co.* (1899) when the headmaster canes the entire school before sending them home]

bloody monthlies *n.* [20C] usu. male use, menstruation. [masculine irritation puns BLOODY adj./SE *bloody*; thus the joc. def. 'a bloody waste of fucking time']

bloody oath! *see* BLOOD OATH!

bloody wounds! *excl.* [early 18C] a mild, blasphemous, oath, i.e. (God's) bloody wounds (cf. WOUNDS!).

blooie!/blooey! *excl.* [1910s+] (orig. US) used to mimic the sound of an explosion; thus *go blooey*, to explode suddenly, to go wrong, to fail, to break down. [echoic]

bloomer *n.* **1** [late 19C+] (orig. Aus.) an error, a slip; thus *make a bloomer* (cf. BLAPS). **2** [20C] a complete failure, a disaster. **3** [1910s] (US) a fraud. **4** [1910s] (US) a joke; thus *pull a bloomer*, make a joke. [BLOOMING + SE *error*]

blooming *adj.* [late 19C+] euph. for BLOODY adj., e.g. *blooming error*, a major mistake (cf. BLESSED). [popularized by the music-hall star Alfred 'The Great' Vance in the 1880s]

blooming shoot *n.* [late 19C] absolutely everything, 'the lot'. [BLOOMING + (WHOLE BANG) SHOOT]

blooming six foot of tripe *phr.* [late 19C] a large policeman (cf. SIX FOOT OF TRIPE).

bloop *n.* [1960s+] **1** (orig. US) an embarrassing verbal error, often delivered by a public figure or someone in authority to their own detriment (cf. BLAPS). **2** a euph. substitute for various taboo terms (cf. BLEEP).

blooper *n.* **1** [1940s] (US) a swinging blow. **2** [1940s+] (orig. US) an embarrassing verbal error, often delivered by a public or authority figure to their own detriment (cf. BLAPS). [? BLAB + *oops!*]

blooter *n.* [20C] (Ulster) a coarse, stupid peasant. [Scot. *bluiter*, a rough, clumsy fellow]

blootered *adj.* [1970s+] drunk (cf. PLOOTERED). [Scot. *blout*, of liquids, to boil over]

blooterer *n.* [20C] a scourge, a persecutor. [? BLOOTER or Scots *blouter*, a blast of wind]

blort *n.* [1980s+] (drugs) cocaine. [BLOW n.⁷ + SNORT n.(3)]

bloss *n.* [16C–18C] **1** a beggar's companion. **2** a woman (cf. BLOUSE). **3** a thief. **4** a prostitute. [BLOWSE]

blossom-top *n.* [mid–late 19C] (US) a red-headed or red-faced person. [SE *blossom*, presumably a red one + *top*]

blot *n.* [1940s+] (Aus.) the anus (cf. FRECKLE).

blotch *n.* [1950s+] (mainly school) blotting-paper.

blotch *v.* [1970s+] (US campus) to emit a small amount of liquid at the same time as breaking wind; thus *blotcher*, a liquid emitting FART that stains one's underwear. [echoic]

blot one's copybook, to *phr.* [1930s+] to make an error, practical or behavioural.

blots *n.* [1960s+] (drugs) LSD (cf. A n.³). [abbr. BLOTTER n.² (3)]

blotter *n.¹* [1930s–50s] (US) a drunkard with a seemingly infinite capacity for alcohol.

blotter *n.²* (drugs) **1** [1950s+] a small piece of cotton through which a drug solution is filtered as it is drawn into a needle. **2** [1950s+] any drugs that are retrieved by soaking or boiling such a cloth. **3** [1960s+] a dose of LSD carried on a small square of blotting-paper; the paper and the drug it has absorbed are consumed together.

blotter cube *n.* [1960s+] (drugs) LSD (cf. A n.³). [BLOTTER n.² (3) + CUBE n.³]

blot the scrip, to *phr.* [17C–18C] to put into writing; thus *blot the scrip and jark it*, to sign a contract (cf. JARK IT). [SE *blot* + *scrip*, a scrap of paper, a few lines of writing]

blotto *adj.* (orig. US) **1** [1910s+] very drunk. **2** [1920s+] of people, exhausted, dazed, mad. **3** [1920s+] of machines,

malfunctioning. **4** [1930s] absolutely forgotten. [? one's mind having *blotted out* reality, or one's body *blotted up* the alcohol]

blou, die *n.* [20C] (S.Afr.) methylated spirits, as used by alcoholics. [Afk. *blou*, blue, the colour of meths]

blou *adj.* [1940s+] (S.Afr. drugs) intoxicated by a drug, 'high'. [BLOU n.]

bloubaadjie *n.* [1970s] (S.Afr.) **1** an habitual criminal serving an indeterminate sentence (cf. BLUECOAT n.²). **2** an indeterminate prison sentence of 9–15 years. **3** a provincial traffic officer. [Afk. *blou*, blue + *baadjie*, badge]

blougat *n.* (S.Afr.) a national serviceman or woman who has completed half his training (cf. OUMAN; ROOFIE). [Afk. *blou*, blue + *gat*, anus (arse)]

bloupak *n.* [1980s+] (S.Afr.) an auxiliary police officer (used in those areas where the police wear blue uniforms). [Afk. *blou*, blue + *pakke*, suit]

blouperd *n.* (S.Afr.) methylated spirits (cf. BLOUTREIN). [Afk. *blou* + *perd*, horse; one who 'rides' it]

blouse *n.* [late 16C–early 18C] a slatternly woman, a prostitute. [BLOWSE]

blouser *v.* [late 19C–1900s] to cover up, to hide. [Fr. *blouse*, a jacket; thus to cover with one's jacket, to secrete. Ware suggests that the use is xenophobic, such a jacket would 'cover over an honest Englishman's waistcoat']

bloutrein/blue train *n.* [1980s+] (S.Afr.) methylated spirits (cf. BLOU; VLAM). [the *Blue Train*, a luxury passenger train running between Cape Town and Pretoria; those who drink meths take the 'fast train' to death]

blouzabella *n.* [late 18C–19C] a slattern (cf. BLOSS; BLOUZALINDA; BLOWSE). [BLOWZE + Ital. *bella*, a good-looking slattern]

blouzalinda *n.* [late 18C–19C] a slattern (cf. BLOUZABELLA). [BLOWSE + Sp. *linda*, beautiful]

bloviate *v.* [mid-19C] (US) to talk loudly or aggressively. [? SE *blow* + sfx. *-ate*, to 'blow off steam']

blow *n.¹* [19C] a shilling (5p). [ety. unknown]

blow *n.²* **1** [early 19C–1940s] (US) a celebration, a party, a spree. **2** [mid-19C] (US campus) a reveller, a party-goer. **3** [late 19C+] a breath of fresh air, esp. in phr. *get a blow*.

blow *n.³* [early 19C] **1** a prostitute. **2** sexual intercourse. [BLOWEN]

blow *n.⁴* [mid-19C] (US) a betrayal, the passing of information, esp. to the authorities.

blow *n.⁵* [mid-19C+] (Aus./US) a rest, a period of relaxation. [the image of stopping work for a cigarette]

blow *n.⁶* [1920s–30s] (US) a pistol. [SE *blow*, to explode]

blow *n.⁷* [1960s+] (drugs) a shot of heroin that misses the vein.

blow *n.⁸* [1960s+] (drugs) **1** cocaine. **2** a snort or sniff of cocaine. **3** marijuana/hashish. [BLOW v.²]

blow *v.¹* **1** [16C] to speak angrily. **2** [late 16C+] to inform on, to betray, to expose, to reveal (evidence of wrong-doing, espionage etc) (cf. BLOW THE GAB). **3** [mid-19C+] to inform, to confess. **4** [mid-19C+] to boast, to brag (cf. BLOWHARD). **5** [1910s–50s] (US) to become, e.g. *blow chilly*, to be standoffish. **6** [1960s+] (US Black) to talk (nonsense).

blow *v.²* **1** [late 18C+] to smoke, orig. a pipe, in [20C] marijuana; thus *blow dope*, *blow grass*. **2** [1910s+] (US drugs) to inhale a narcotic, usu. heroin or (more recently) cocaine.

blow *v.³* **1** [late 18C+] of money, to squander, to waste. **2** [late 19C+] to treat to a meal, to food and/or drink, usu. as *blow one to*.

blow *v.⁴* **1** [late 19C] (US) to go round with, to associate with. **2** [late 19C] (US) to depart at speed, to walk away quickly, usu. in phr., e.g. *blow the joint*, *blow the town*; thus imper. *go blow!* go away! *blow yourself!* go to hell! **3** [20C] (US prison) to escape from prison.

blow v.[5] **1** [late 19C+] to ruin, to upset, to destroy, to lose. **2** [20C] to botch, to bungle, to lose (a contest or game), esp. as *blow it*. **3** [20C] to crack under emotional or other pressure, to explode emotionally. **4** [1910s] (US) to fail. **5** [1910s+] (orig. US) to miss, e.g. a train, an appointment. **6** [1920s–60s] (US) to dismiss from a job, to break off a love affair.

blow v.[6] [1930s+] to fellate (cf. BLOW JOB). [the appearance of the physical act]

blow v.[7] **1** [1940s+] (orig. US Black) to play music. **2** [1950s+] (US Black) to talk enthusiastically and fluently. **3** [1950s+] (US Black) to perform on any 'instrument', e.g. a writer's word processor etc. **4** [1950s–60s] (US) to create, to 'whip up'. [the blowing and playing of various wind instruments]

blow v.[8] [1970s+] (orig. US) to reach orgasm. [SE *blow*, to explode]

blow! *excl.* [20C] go away! [BLOW v.[4]]

blow a cloud, to *phr.* [mid-19C] to smoke a pipe of tobacco.

blow a fix/shot/the vein, to *phr.* [1950s+] (drugs) to blunder when injecting oneself and miss the vein, wasting the narcotic in the skin. [BLOW v.[5] (2) + FIX n.[3]; SHOT n.[5] (2); SE *vein*]

blow a fuse, to *phr.* [1920s+] to explode with rage (cf. BLOW A GASKET; BLOW A VALVE).

blow a/one's gasket, to *phr.* [1940s+] to explode with rage (cf. BLOW A FUSE; BLOW ONE'S TOP).

blow a gut, to *phr.* [1950s–60s] (US Black) to explode with laughter. [var. on BUST A GUT]

blow a raspberry, to *phr.* [late 19C+] to make an obscene noise with one's lips, usu. intended to imply derision. [SE *blow* + RASPBERRY n.[1]]

blow a shot see BLOW A FIX.

blow ass, to *phr.* [1980s+] (US) to walk fast, to run off (cf. HAUL ASS). [BLOW v.[4] (2) + ARSE n.[1]]

blow a stick, to *phr.* [1950s+] (drugs) to smoke cannabis. [BLOW v.[7] (1) + STICK n.[14] (2)]

blow at v. [1980s+] (US campus) to became annoyed with, to attack verbally (cf. BLOW OFF STEAM; BLOW ONE'S TOP). [BLOW v.[1] (1)]

blow a valve/tube, to *phr.* [1950s+] (US) to explode with rage (cf. BLOW A FUSE).

blow a vein, to *phr.* [1980s] (US) to have an apoplectic fit (and die of it). [SE *blow*, to explode + *vein*]

blow away v. (orig. US Black) **1** [1910s+] to shoot dead (cf. BLOW DOWN). **2** [1960s+] to defeat decisively (cf. BLOW DOWN). **3** [1960s+] to make intoxicated with a drug or drink. **4** [1970s+] to impress, to bowl over. [ext. of SE use + southern dial. use or jazz use, for two bands to engage in an on-stage competition; the winner was deemed to have *blown away* its rival]

blowback n. [1980s+] (drugs) an exhalation of marijuana/hashish smoke into another's mouth (cf. SHOTGUN). [SE *blow back*]

blow back v. [20C] (US) to return, to pay back money. [BLOW v.[3] (2)]

blowbag n. [1920s+] (Aus.) a loud-mouthed braggart. [BLOW v.[1] (4) + WINDBAG]

blow black v. [1960s+] (US Black) to talk about and/or initiate Black activism, social change, revolution and any similar form of racial advancement (cf. BLOW GREAT GUNS phr.[2]). [BLOW v.[1] (1) + SE *black*]

blow blue v. [1980s+] (drugs) to inhale cocaine. [BLOW v.[2] (2)]

blow-boy n. [1930s+] (US) a male homosexual. [BLOW v.[6] (1) + SE *boy*]

blowcaine n. [1980s+] crack diluted with powdered cocaine. [BLOW n.[5] (2) + SE *cocaine* + play on SE *procaine, novocaine* etc]

blow change v. [20C] to squander one's money. [BLOW v.[3] (1) + SE *change*]

blow charlie v. [1960s–70s] (drugs) to take cocaine. [BLOW v.[2] (2) + CHARLIE n.[7]]

blow chow v. [1930s+] (US) to vomit. [BLOW ONE'S COOKIES + CHOW n.[1]]

blow chunks v. [1930s+] to vomit (cf. BLOW ONE'S COOKIES + SE *chunks* (of food)]

blow coke v. [1960s+] (drugs) to inhale cocaine. [BLOW v.[2] (2) + COKE n.+]

blow domes v. [20C] (US) to amaze, to astound (cf. BLOW ONE'S MIND). [SE *blow*, to explode + DOME n.[1]]

blow down v. (US) **1** [mid-19C+] to kill with a firearm, to shoot dead (cf. BLOW AWAY). **2** [1960s] to defeat comprehensively, to overwhelm (cf. BLOW AWAY). **3** [1980s+] to pass at high speed.

blow down someone's ear, to *phr.* [1930s+] to whisper, esp. to whisper information (accurate or otherwise) that is intended to persuade the hearer to do what one wishes.

blowed adj. [mid-19C+] used as euph. for *damned* in general mild oaths of surprise, shock, annoyance. [*damned*, basically SE, was seen as a profanity from the mid-19C+; today it is accepted and one of the mildest of imprecations]

blowed-in-the-glass/-bottle see BLOWN-IN-THE-GLASS.

blowen n. [late 17C–mid-19C] a woman, spec. a prostitute (cf. BLOWER n.[1]; BLOWING n.[1]). [according to George Borrow f. Rom. *beluñi*, 'a sister in debauchery'. Hotten (1867) notes Ger. *Bluhen*, bloom, and *Buhlen*, sweetheart, but adds 'the street term ... may mean one whose reputation has been BLOWN ON, or damaged']

blower n.[1] [18C–19C] a woman, spec. a prostitute (cf. BLOWEN; JOMER).

blower n.[2] [19C] a braggart (cf. BLOWHARD). [BLOW v.[1] (4)]

blower n.[3] [20C] (US) a shotgun (cf. BLOW n.[6]). [SE *blow*, to explode, underpinned by BLOW AWAY; BLOW DOWN]

blower n.[4] [1920s+] a telephone. [following on the earlier 'speaking tubes' down which one had to blow to alert the other person; note bookmaker jargon *blower*, the betting shop public address system that broadcasts races, odds and results]

blower n.[5] [1940s+] (W.I.) a spendthrift. [BLOW v.[3] (1)]

blower n.[6] [1940s–50s] (US Black) a handkerchief. [SE *blow* (one's nose)]

blow fire v. [1980s+] (US Black) to do anything well and keenly, esp. dancing, musicianship. [ext. of BLOW v.[7]]

blowfly n. **1** [late 19C+] (Aus.) an officious person; thus *blowflyism*, officiousness, 'red tape' (cf. JOBSWORTH). **2** [20C] (US) a braggart (cf. BLOWHARD). [BLOW v.[1] + SE *fly*]

blow foam v. [late 19C] (US) to drink beer.

blow gage/gauge v. [1950s–60s] (orig. US Black) to smoke marijuana. [BLOW v.[2] (1) + GAGE n.[2]]

blow great guns, to *phr.*[1] [early 19C+] to blow a violent storm.

blow great guns, to *phr.*[2] [early 19C+] (by extension) to make a great fuss about something. [BLOW v.[1] (1)]

blowgun n. [20C] (US) a braggart (cf. BLOWHARD). [BLOW GREAT GUNS phr.[2]]

blowhard/blow-hard n. [early 19C–1920s] (orig. US) a boaster, a loud and egocentric talker (cf. BAG OF WIND). [BLOW v.[1] (4) + SE *hard*; later 20C use is SE]

blow heavy v. [1980s+] (US Black) to talk seriously of a contextually vital matter. [BLOW v.[1] (1) + HEAVY adj.[1] (7); jazz imagery]

blowhole n. (US) **1** [1920s+] (Aus.) a talkative person. **2** [1940s+] the anus. **3** [1940s] the mouth. [pun on SE but for (1) and (3) note BLOW v.[1] (1) + CAKEHOLE]

blow hot and cold, to *phr.* [mid-16C–late 18C] to vacillate. [subseq. use is SE]

blowie/blowy n. [1910s+] (Aus.) a *blow*fly. [abbr.]

blow-in n. [1940s+] (Aus./Irish/US) a stranger, a newcomer, someone who has 'blown in', esp. one who is not yet accepted by the locals. [BLOW IN]

blow in v. **1** [1930s+] to arrive unexpectedly and casually; thus *what's this blown in*, who's this?, a usu. unfriendly reference to a new arrival. **2** [late 19C+] (US) to squander, to waste, usu. of money (cf. BLOW v.³; BLUE v.²). [image of being wafted by a chance breeze]

blow in a bowl, to phr. [16C] to be an habitual drunkard. [synon. with 20C HIT THE BOTTLE]

blowing n.¹ [19C] a woman, spec. a prostitute. [BLOWEN]

blowing n.² [mid-19C+] boasting. [BLOW v.¹ (4)]

blowing smoke n. [1980s+] (drugs) marijuana. [BLOW v.² (1) + SMOKE n.³ (2)]

blowing-up n. [early 19C+] a scolding. [BLOW v.¹ (1) + sfx. -ing]

blow in one's pipe, to phr. [mid-19C–1910s] to spend one's money. [BLOW v.³ (1)]

blow in someone's ear, to phr. [1970s] to whisper.

blow it! excl. [early 19C+] a mild of annoyance. euph. for a variety of 'stronger' synonyms, e.g. HELL WITH IT! (cf. BUGGER IT!; FUCK IT!; SOD IT!).

blow it out your ass! excl. [1940s+] (orig. US milit.) a general excl. of derision, contempt or dismissal of the previous speaker's statement. [SE *blow* + ARSE n.¹ (1)]

blow jaw v. [1980s+] (US) to smoke marijuana. [BLOW v.² (1) + stressed pron. of SE *(mari)jua(na)*.]

blow job n.¹ (orig. US) **1** [1940s+] fellatio (cf. BASKET JOB). **2** [1960s+] a fellator or fellatrix. [BLOW v.⁶ + SE *job*]

blow job n.² [1970s] (US campus) an unpleasant experience or situation. [SE *blow* + JOB n.⁵]

blow me! excl. [1950s+] an excl. of surprise (cf. BUST ME!). [abbr. BLOW ME TIGHT]

blow me down! excl. [19C+] a mild expletive.

blow me tight phr. [late 18C–1910s] a phr. expressive of surprise or denial, used as euph. for DAMNED in general mild oaths of surprise, shock, annoyance, usu. as *blow me tight if…*.

blow mud v. [1990s] to noisily expel a loose stool. [coarse use of SE]

blow-my-skull/-skull-off n. [mid-19C] (Aus.) an alcoholic drink that mixes wine, opium, cayenne pepper and rum, popular at the gold diggings; an alternative recipe mixes boiling water, sugar, lime or lemon juice, porter, rum and brandy. [SE *blow* + *skull*]

blow my wig! excl. [early–mid-19C] a mild excl. (cf. DASH MY WIG!).

blown/blown out adj.¹ **1** [mid-19C+] shocked, exhausted, overcome. **2** [1970s+] (US campus) drunk, under the influence of a drug. **3** [1980s+] (US campus) crazy, insane. [SE *blow*, to explode]

blown adj.² [1960s+] revealed. [abbr. SE *blown open*]

blown adv. [1980s+] (US) under the influence of either drink or drugs. [BLOWN UP]

blown/blowed-in-the-glass/-bottle adj. [late 19C+] (orig. US) **1** genuine, authentic. **2** trustworthy. [early glass-blowing often trapped bubbles in the finished object]

blown out see BLOWN adj.¹.

blown up adj. [1970s+] (US) drunk. [SE *blow*, to explode + ? image of a bloated drunkard]

blow off n.¹ **1** [mid-19C–1950s] (US) an emotional outburst, a sudden fight or argument. **2** [late 19C+] a party, a celebration. **3** [1960s+] a braggart (cf. BLOWHARD). [BLOW v.¹ (1), (4)]

blow off n.² **1** [1900s–10s] a decisive conclusion, an absolute end. **2** [1910s–50s] the very last tolerable happening in a series, 'the last straw'. [SE *blow*, to explode]

blow off n.³ **1** [1970s+] (US teen) anything considered exceptionally easy. **2** [1980s] (US campus) a lazy person, a 'layabout'. [SE *blow*, to blow something away with a puff of air]

blow off v.¹ (US) **1** [mid-19C] to stop, to cease. **2** [1910s] of events, to develop, to happen. **3** [1960s] to ignore, to get rid of. [SE *blow*, explode]

blow off/to v.² [late 19C+] (orig. US) to treat. [BLOW v.³ (2)]

blow off v.³ [20C] to release pent-up emotion. [BLOW OFF STEAM]

blow off v.⁴ [20C] (orig. naut.) to break wind. [SE *blow*, explode]

blow off v.⁵ [1980s+] (campus) to play truant. [BLOW v.⁴ (1)]

blow off v.⁶ [1990s] (US) to fellate (cf. BLOW). [BLOW v.⁶ (1)]

blow off at the mouth, to phr. to talk loudly or aggressively. to boast. [BLOW OFF v.³ + SE *mouth*]

blow off one's bazoo see BLOW ONE'S BAZOO.

blow off on the groundsills see BLOW THE GROUNDSILLS.

blow/let off steam, to phr. [mid-19C+] to release one's (pent-up) emotions, to become angry or noisy and excited (cf. BLOW ONE'S STACK).

blow off the loose corns, to phr. [late 17C–early 18C] to have sexual intercourse (cf. BLOW THE LOOSE CORN). [the image is of sex in a barn; one's panting blows away loose corn]

blow one out v. [1900s–30s] (orig. milit.) to make a rude noise in someone's direction. ['one' is a RASPBERRY n.¹]

blow one's bags, to phr. [1960s] (Aus.) to boast (cf. BLOW ONE'S OWN TRUMPET). [BLOW v.¹ (4)]

blow one's barrel, to phr. [1940s] (US) to lose control (cf. BLOW ONE'S TOP). [the barrel is that of a gun]

blow/blow off one's bazoo, to phr. [late 19C–1940s] (US) to boast. [BLOW OFF v.³ + BAZOO n.¹]

blow one's cookies, to phr. [1930s+] to vomit (cf. BLOW CHOW; BLOW CHUNKS; BLOW ONE'S DOUGHNUTS; BLOW ONE'S GROCERIES; BLOW ONE'S LUNCH; COOKIES n.²). [SE *blow* + *cookies* = food consumed]

blow one's cool, to phr. [1960s+] **1** to lose control, to become nervous or angry (cf. FREAK OUT). **2** to ruin someone's image, to discomfit, to make an exhibition of. [BLOW v.⁵ (1), (3) + COOL n.²]

blow one's copper, to phr. [1950s+] (US prison) to lose the reduction in sentence that would otherwise accrue for good conduct (cf. COPPER TIME). [BLOW v.⁵ (1) + COPPER n.³ (3)]

blow one's cork, to phr. [1930s+] (US) **1** to lose one's temper. **2** to go mad. **3** to become excited. **4** to achieve orgasm (cf. POP ONE'S CORK).

blow one's doughnuts, to phr. [1970s+] (US campus) to vomit (cf. BLOW ONE'S COOKIES).

blow one's dust, to phr. [1960s–70s] **1** to masturbate. **2** to ejaculate.

blow oneself out v. [early–mid-19C] to binge. [BLOW v.³ (2)]

blow one's gaff see BLOW ONE'S TOP.

blow one's gasket see BLOW A GASKET.

blow/flip/lose one's gourd, to phr. [1970s+] (orig. US) to lose emotional control. [SE *blow*/FLIP v.⁴/SE *lose* + GOURD n.² (1)]

blow one's groceries, to phr. [1970s+] (US campus) to vomit. [var. on BLOW ONE'S COOKIES]

blow one's head and horns off, to phr. [19C] (US) to talk too much. [BLOW v.¹ (4)]

blow one's head/skull, to phr. [1950s+] (US, orig. drugs) to become intoxicated by a drug (cf. BLOW ONE'S MIND). [SE *blow*, explode + *head/skull*]

blow one's hide out, to phr. [mid-19C–1920s] to overeat, to eat heartily. [SE *blow*, expand + HIDE n.¹ (1) + BLOW v.³ (2)]

blow one's horn, to phr.¹ [mid–late 19C] (US) to speak or sing out of turn.

blow one's horn, to phr.² [20C] (US) to break wind.

blow one's hump, to phr. [1950s+] (US) **1** to achieve orgasm. **2** (drugs) to become intoxicated on a drug, usu. marijuana. [HUMP n.⁴]

blow one's juice, to phr. [1990s] to reach orgasm. [SE blow + JUICE n.²]

blow one's/the lid, to phr. [1930s+] to go mad, to lose emotional control (cf. FLIP ONE'S LID). [SE blow, explode + LID n.³ (2)]

blow one's load, to phr. [1990s] usu. of a man, to ejaculate, to come to orgasm (cf. SHOOT ONE'S LOAD). [SE blow, explode + LOAD n.⁴ (2)]

blow one's lot, to phr. [1940s+] (Aus.) to come to orgasm, to ejaculate (cf. COME ONE'S LOT). [BLOW v.⁶ (2) + SE lot]

blow one's lunch, to phr. [1950s+] (US) to vomit (cf. BLOW ONE'S COOKIES).

blow one's/your mind, to phr. [1960s+] (orig. drugs) **1** to become intoxicated with a drug or drugs. **2** to shock, to surprise, to amaze. **3** to become mad. **4** to drive mad, to destroy one's powers of reasoning. [SE blow, explode + mind]

blow one's nose, to phr. [1950s] (US) to inform. [pun on SE blow/BLOW v.¹ (2), but note NOSE n.¹ (1)]

blow one's own horn, to phr. [1990s] to masturbate. [pun + HORN n.²]

blow one's own trumpet, to phr. [mid-19C+] to boast unashamedly.

blow one's pipes, to phr. [1970s+] (US teen) to make a loud noise through a car's exhaust pipe by suddenly pressing down on the accelerator.

blow one's roof, to phr.¹ [1950s] (US) to act hysterically, to act irrationally (cf. BLOW ONE'S STACK). [SE blow, explode + ROOF n.(2)]

blow one's roof, to phr.² [1980s+] (drugs) to smoke marijuana or cannabis. [BLOW v.² (1) + SE roof]

blow one's shoes, to phr. [20C] (US) to lose control, to lose one's composure. [BLOW v.⁵ (3)]

blow one's skull see BLOW ONE'S HEAD.

blow one's stack, to phr. [1940s+] (US) to lose control, to lose one's temper (cf. BLOW ONE'S TOP).

blow one's top/gaff, to phr. [1920s+] (orig. US) to lose one's temper, to lose one's sanity, to become violent. [SE blow, explode + top/GAFF n.² (4); the image is of a volcano]

blow one's tubes, to phr. [1990s] of a man, to achieve orgasm. [the image is of a submarine, but note BLOW v.⁶ (2) + TUBE n.² (2)]

blow one's wad, to phr.¹ [1990s] (US) **1** to ejaculate. **2** to indicate surprise or excitement. [SE blow; BLOW v.⁶ (2) + WAD n.³]

blow one's wad, to phr.² [1990s] (US) to spend all one's money. [BLOW v.³ (1) + WAD n.¹ (1)]

blow one's wig, to phr. [1930s–40s] (US Black) to feel excited, enthusiastic (cf. FLIP ONE'S WIG; WIG OUT). [SE blow, explode + WIG n.¹ (1)]

blow-out n.¹ **1** [early 19C+] a binge of eating, drinking and debauchery. **2** [early 19C+] (US) a brawl, a noisy argument. **3** [late 19C–1900s] an organized dance, held in a dance-hall and frequented by lower-class young people (cf. RACKET n.²).

blow-out n.² [1960s–80s] (US Black/campus) a hairstyle in which one's natural tight curls or kinks are blown out with a hairdryer (cf. BLOW-UP n.²).

blow-out n.³ [1980s+] a comprehensive defeat. [jazz use; when two bands staged a competition, the winner was to said to blow its rival out of the house; thus the defeat itself was a blow-out]

blow-out n.⁴ [1980s+] (drugs) crack cocaine. [BLOW n.⁷ (3)]

blow out v.¹ [mid-19C+] to eat and/or drink to excess. [SE blow out, to expand, but note BLOW v.³ (1)]

blow out v.² **1** [mid-19C+] (orig. US) to murder, to kill (cf. BLOW AWAY). **2** [1960s] (US) to die. **3** [1960s+] (orig. US) to reject, to break a promise, to neglect a rendezvous etc. **4** [1960s–70s] (US) to destroy, to spoil. **5** [1980s] (US) to collapse, to malfunction. **6** [1980s+] (drugs) to spoil an injection. [BLOW v.⁵ (1)]

blow out v.³ [late 19C–1900s] to steal.

blow out v.⁴ [1900s–20s] to arrive unexpectedly. [var. on BLOW IN]

blow out v.⁵ **1** [1970s+] (US campus) to shock, to embarrass. **2** [1970s] (orig. US) to astound, to amaze (cf. BLOW AWAY). [BLOW v.¹ (1), (2)]

blow out of v. [1910s+] to leave, to depart from a place. [BLOW v.⁴ (1)]

blow out someone's lamp/light, to phr. [20C] (US) to murder, to kill (cf. PUT OUT SOMEONE'S LIGHTS).

blow out the afterglow, to phr. [1930s–40s] (US Black) to turn out the lights. [many Blacks had moved from candles and oil lamps to electricity only in the 1930s–40s]

blow out the kite, to phr. [mid–late 19C] to have a full stomach. [the food makes one's stomach expand like the 'belly' of a kite in the wind]

blow past v. [1970s+] to deceive, to fool, to confuse.

blowpipe n. [20C] (US) a rifle.

blowse/blowze n. [late 16C–early 18C] a slatternly a woman, a prostitute (cf. BLOSS; BLOUSE; BLOUZABELLA; BLOUZALINDA; BLOWSER n.¹). [? link to Du. blos, blush. Bailey's Dictionary (1731) defines it as: 'a fat, red-faced, bloted wench, or one whose head is dressed like a slattern']

blowser n.¹ [1920s] a slatternly woman. [BLOWSE]

blowser n.² [1980s+] (drugs) a glue-sniffer; thus blowsing, glue-sniffing. [? Northumberland dial. blow, to breathe; but note BIG GIRL'S BLOUSE; the image is of the stupidity of this form of drug-taking]

blow sky high, to phr. [mid-19C+] (orig. US) to scold, to reprimand. [SE blow up]

blow smoke v.¹ [mid-19C+] to confuse, to mystify through speech. [SE blow + SMOKE n.¹]

blow smoke v.² [1980s+] (drugs) to inhale crack. [BLOW v.² (2)]

blow smoke up someone's ass, to phr. [1950s+] to confuse, to tell lies. [intensification of BLOW SMOKE v.¹]

blow snow v. [1960s] (drugs) to inhale cocaine. [BLOW v.² (2) + SNOW n.²]

blow someone away v. [1970s+] (orig. US teen) to astound, to amaze.

blow someone down v. [1930s–40s] to kill, to murder someone. [BLOW AWAY v.¹ (1)]

blow someone out v. [1960s+] **1** to exhaust. **2** to shock. **3** for one of a couple to abandon the relationship.

blow someone out of the water, to phr. [1950s+] (orig. US) to defeat comprehensively, to overwhelm.

blow someone's/the act, to phr. [1970s+] (US) to ruin, to spoil, to interfere (cf. CRAB SOMEONE'S ACT; QUEER SOMEONE'S ACT). [BLOW v.⁵ (1) + SE act]

blow someone's cookies, to phr. [1930s+] to fellate. [BLOW v.⁶ (1)]

blow someone's glass, to phr. [1970s+] to perform fellatio on a man (cf. BLOW THE GLASS). [BLOW v.⁶ (1)]

blow someone's/the pipe, to phr. [1910s] (US) to fellate. [SE blow, inflate; BLOW v.⁶ (1) + PIPE n.⁸ (1)]

blow some tunes, to phr. [1980s+] (US Black) to perform cunnilingus (cf. YODEL IN THE CANYON). [joc. use of BLOW v.⁷ (1) + SE tunes]

blow steam, to phr. [1950s] (US) to chatter aimlessly and pointlessly.

blow stick n. [1960s+] the penis (cf. BAT n.⁷). [BLOW v.⁶ (2) + STICK n.¹]

blow the act see BLOW SOMEONE'S ACT.

blow the coals, to phr. [late 17C–18C] to stir up trouble between two parties.

blow/tear the doors off, to phr. [1960s+] (orig. US) to drive at high speed past another car.

blow the duke, to phr. [1960s–70s] to make a complete mess of something. [BLOW v.⁵ (1), (2) + fig. use of DUKE n.³ (2)]

blow the froth/froth off, to phr. [1910s–30s] (Aus.) to drink beer.

blow the gab, to phr. [late 18C–early 19C] to betray a secret, to inform against (cf. BLOW THE GAFF). [BLOW v.¹ (2) + SE gab, speech, conversation]

blow the gaff, to phr. 1 [early 19C+] to reveal a secret, esp. a hoax or deception. 2 [late 19C+] (US) to make a mess of, to bungle. [? PENNY GAFF; thus fig. to give away the plot of a show]

blow the gap, to phr. [19C] to inform on, to betray. [var. on BLOW THE GAFF]

blow the gig, to phr. [1950s–60s] (orig. US Black) 1 to lose a job. 2 to resign from a job. [BLOW v.⁴ (1) + GIG n.⁸]

blow the glass, to phr. [1990s] (drugs) to smoke crack cocaine. [BLOW v.² (2) + the glass vial that contains the drug or the pipe through one smokes it]

blow/blow off on the groundsills/blow the groundsels, to phr. [18C] to have sexual intercourse while lying on the floor (cf. blow the loose corn). [SE blow + groundsills/groundsels, the foundation or lowest part of any structure, i.e. one's panting breath is exhaled at ground level]

blow the lid see BLOW ONE'S LID.

blow the lid off, to phr. [1930s+] to reveal, to uncover esp. a scandal involving those 'in high places'.

blow the loose corn, to phr. [18C] to have an intermittent sexual relationship with a woman (cf. BLOW THE GROUNDSILLS). [see BLOW OFF THE LOOSE CORNS for ety.]

blow the pipe see BLOW SOMEONE'S PIPE.

blow the show/scene, to phr. [1960s+] (orig. US) to ruin the entire situation, to miss an opportunity to do or gain something. [BLOW v.⁵ (1) + SHOW n.¹ (1)/SCENE n. (2)]

blow the skin flute, to phr. [20C] to fellate (cf. PLAY THE FLUTE phr.¹). [BLOW v.⁶ (1) + SKIN FLUTE]

blow the vein see BLOW A FIX.

blow the whistle on, to phr. [1950s+] 1 to inform against someone. 2 to bring to an end.

blow this popsicle stand, to phr. [1980s+] (US campus) to leave, esp. somewhere one dislikes or pretends to dislike. [BLOW v.⁴ (1) + generic use of SE popsicle stand]

blow through v. [1950s+] (Aus.) to leave, to run off, esp. as excl. blow through! go away! [BLOW v.⁴ (1) + SE through]

blow to see BLOW OFF v.².

blowtop n. [1930s+] (US Black) a violent, unstable person. [BLOW ONE'S TOP]

blow-up n.¹ 1 [late 18C–19C] a revelation, a discovery, esp. the embarrassment or confusion that follows such a revelation. 2 [19C] a financial collapse. 3 [mid-19C] a scolding, a telling off. 4 [late 19C+] a short-lived but emotional quarrel. [SE blow up, to explode]

blow-up n.² [1960s–70s] (US Black) a natural hairstyle, cut short (cf. BLOW-OUT n.²).

blow-up n.³ [1980s+] (drugs) crack cocaine cut with lidocaine to increase the size, weight and street value. [SE blow up, to inflate]

blow up v.¹ 1 [early 17C–1930s] to ruin, to thrash severely. 2 [early 18C+] to tell off, to reprimand. 3 [early 19C] (US) to make pregnant. 4 [20C] to lose control, to lose patience, to become enraged. 5 [20C] (US) to overpraise. 6 [1920s+] (US) to shoot. 7 [1930s+] to break down, of people (usu. athletes, animals (racehorses, greyhounds) and machinery.

blow up v.² [late 19C+] (orig. US) to sound a whistle as a signal, e.g. at the end of a working day.

blow up v.³ 1 [1980s] (US Black) to inherit a legacy. 2 [1980s+] (rap) to achieve great success, esp. after a time of struggle and obscurity.

blow upon v. 1 [15C–19C] to inform against, to betray (cf. BLOW THE GAB; BLOW THE GAFF). 2 [17C–19C] to discredit, to defame. [SE blow, to breathe; thus to use the breath in speaking + upon]

blow wise, to phr. [late 19C+] (US) to see one's own interest. [BLOW v.¹ (5) + WISE adj. (1)]

blow with a French faggot-stick phr. [late 17C–early 18C] the loss of one's nose through syphilis (cf. FRENCH CROWN; KNOCKED WITH A FRENCH FAGGOT).

blowy see BLOWIE.

blow-your-hat-off n. [mid-19C] an alcoholic drink (cf. BLOW-MY-SKULL).

blow your mind see BLOW ONE'S MIND.

blow your mind roulette n. [1960s] (US Black/drugs) a drug-based game whereby the participants toss a variety of unspecified pills onto a table and then take whatever they fancy and wait to discover what the effects will be. [BLOW ONE'S MIND + SE Russian roulette]

blowze see BLOWSE.

blow Zs v. [1960s+] (US) 1 to sleep (cf. BAG ZS). 2 to snore. [BLOW v.⁷ (3) + z n.¹]

blub v. [mid-19C+] (usu. juv.) to cry, to burst into tears. [abbr. SE blubber]

blubber n.¹ [late 18C] (Und.) the mouth. [BLAB n.]

blubber n.² 1 [late 18C] (Und.) the female breasts; thus sport the blubber, of a woman, to reveal her breasts. 2 [late 18C+] fatness, obesity. [SE blubber, fat]

blubberass n. [1950s] (US) a grossly fat person (cf. BLUBBER-BUTT; BLUBBER-GUT(S)). [SE blubber + ARSE n.¹]

blubberation n. [1910s] weeping. [BLUB + SE sfx. -eration]

blubber bags n. [late 18C–20C] the female breasts. [BLUBBER n.² (1) + SE bags]

blubber-belly n. [19C] a very fat person. [SE blubber + belly]

blubber-boiler/-bunter n. [mid–late 19C] (US) 1 a whaling ship. 2 a whaler's crew. [SE blubber, whale fat + boiler/hunter]

blubber-butt n. [1950s+] (orig. US) a grossly fat person (cf. BLUBBERASS). [SE blubber + BUTT n.¹ 1)]

blubber-gut/-guts n. [1940s+] (US) a grossly fat person (cf. BLUBBERASS). [SE blubber + guts]

blubber-head n. [early 19C–1940s] a fool. [SE blubber + sfx. -HEAD (1)]

blubber-mouth n. [1940s] (US) one whose face has heavy jowls. [SE blubber + mouth]

blucher n. [late 19C–1900s] an 'outsider' cab that is forbidden to enter the London railway termini. [proper name of Field-Marshal von Blücher (1742–1819). According to the Social Science Review (vol. I, 1864), the cabs were 'named after the Prussian Field Marshal who arrived on the field of Waterloo only to do the work that chanced to be undone']

bludge n. [1940s+] (Aus.) 1 a period of idleness, an undemanding job. 2 an imposition. [BLUDGE v.]

bludge v. (Aus.) 1 [late 19C+] to evade one's responsibilities. 2 [1900s–10s] to live on the earnings of a prostitute. 3 [1940s+] to loaf about, to idle. 4 [1950s+] to cadge, to scrounge. [back-form. of BLUDGER n.²]

bludgeon n. [19C] the penis (cf. BAT n.⁷).

bludgeon business n. [mid-19C] robbery with violence.

bludgeoner n. [mid-19C] 1 a pimp. 2 a tough man employed to keep order at a brothel (cf. BLUDGER n.¹).

bludgeon the beefsteak, to phr. [1980s+] to masturbate (cf. ACCOST THE OSCAR MEYER). [var. on BEAT ONE'S MEAT]

bludger *n.*[1] [mid-19C–1950s] a thief who is as willing to use violence as not. [? SE *bludgeoner*; thus ult. *bludgeon*]

bludger *n.*[2] (Aus.) **1** [late 19C+] a pimp. **2** [20C] a general term of abuse, usu. implying that the person in question lives off the efforts and money of others. **3** [1910s+] a white-collar worker (from the point of view of a manual labourer, who sees such work as idling). **4** [1940s] an idler, a lazy person. **5** [1950s+] one who does not contribute their fair share. **6** [1940s+] (Aus. Und.) a policeman. [SE *bludgeoner*]

bludget *n.* [1920s–30s] (Aus.) a female thief. [BLUDGER n.[1] + SE fem. sfx. -*et*(*te*)]

blue *n.*[1] **1** [18C] an intellectual woman. **2** [mid-19C] (US campus) a puritanical, strait-laced student. [abbr. SE *blue-stocking*, a term that originated *c.*1750 when a coterie of intellectual ladies – Mrs Montague, Mrs Vesey and Mrs Ord – set out to replace London society's traditional post-dinner pursuits – card-playing – with more cerebral amusements. Formal dress was no longer required and among those who attended their soirées was Benjamin Stillingfleet, who habitually wore grey or blue worsted, instead of black silk, stockings. Admiral Boscawen, a staunch traditionalist, labelled these events 'the Blue Stocking Society'; the ladies were called Blue Stockingers, then Blue Stocking Ladies and finally Blue Stockings]

blue *n.*[2] **1** [19C+] (US Black) a dark-complexioned Black person (cf. BLUESKIN n.[3]). **2** [20C] (S.Afr.) methylated spirits (cf. BLOU n.). **3** [1950s+] a £5 note. [note 18C–19C Louisiana dial. *blue*, a mix of Indian, Black and White]

blue *n.*[3] **1** [mid-19C+] (US) a policeman (cf. BLUEBELLY; BLUEBIRD n.[1]; BLUEBOTTLE; BLUE BOY n.[2]; BLUECOAT n.[1]; BLUE DANGERS; BLUE DEVILS n.[2]; BLUE HEELER; BLUEJACKET n.[1]; BLUE MEANIE; BLUE SPECIAL; BLUESUIT; GENTLEMAN IN BLUE; LITTLE BOY BLUE n.[2]; MAN IN BLUE; SKY n.[3]). **2** [mid-19C–1900s] a blue-uniformed soldier. [the colour of the uniform]

blue *n.*[4] **1** [mid-19C+] a 'smutty' anecdote, a piece of pornography. **2** [late 19C] an obscene or libidinous anecdote. [BLUE adj.[3]]

blue *n.*[5] [1900s–30s] a spree. [BLUE v.[2] (1)]

blue *n.*[6] [1930s+] (Aus./N.Z.) a summons (cf. BLUEY n.[1]). [the colour of the paper on which it is printed]

blue *n.*[7] [1940s+] (Aus./N.Z.) **1** a blunder, a mistake. **2** a brawl, a quarrel. [abbr. BLOOMER]

blue *n.*[8] (drugs) **1** [1960s+] usu. in pl., an amphetamine (cf. A n.[2]). **2** [1980s+] crack cocaine. [(1) the colour of the pills; (2) ? mis-reading]

blue *adj.*[1] **1** [late 18C–19C] confused, terrified, disappointed. **2** [late 18C+] miserable, depressed. **3** [early 19C+] (orig. US) a general intensifier, e.g. *blue murder, scared blue*. **4** [mid–late 19C] unpromising, discouraging. [Ware cites a ballad from the reign of George III entitled 'The All-devouring monster. or New Five per C—t', attacking a plan to levy a 5% tax on all imports: 'The effects of the Tax will soon make us look Blue']

blue *adj.*[2] **1** [early 19C+] (US/Aus.) drunk. **2** [1940s+] (S.Afr.) under the influence of marijuana. [? 'blue in the face'; (1) appears in the early 19C US, lasts until the mid-century then re-emerges in Australia by the early 20C]

blue *adj.*[3] [early 19C+] coarse, obscene, pornographic; thus *blue film, blue movie* (cf. BROWN adj.[2]). [? BLUEGOWN, the Fr. *Bibliothèque bleue*, 'a series of books of questionable character' (F&H) or as the opposite of BROWN adj.[2]]

blue *adj.*[4] [mid-19C] (US campus) excessively hard-working, overly dedicated. [BLUE n.[1] (2)]

blue *adj.*[5] [1910s–60s] euph. for BLOODY adj.

blue *v.*[1] [early 18C] to blush. [the colouring of one's complexion]

blue/blue in *v.*[2] [mid-19C+] **1** to waste money (cf. BLEW IN). **2** [mid-19C–1910s] to pawn.

blue *v.*[3] [late 19C] to make a blunder. [BLOW v.[5]]

blue *v.*[4] [1960s+] (Aus.) to argue, to fight. [BLUE n.[7] (2)]

blue/queer/yellow about/around the gills *adv.* [early 19C+] feeling and looking sick, esp. from an excess of alcohol (cf. GREEN ABOUT THE GILLS). [SE *blue* + *gills*, the flesh around the jaws]

blue acid *n.* [1980s+] (drugs) LSD (cf. A n.[3]). [SE *blue* + ACID n.[3]; ? the colour of a capsule]

blue-and-white *n.* [1970s+] (US) a police car, painted in those colours (e.g. in New York City) (cf. BLACK AND WHITE n.[2]).

blue angel *n.* [1960s+] (drugs) **1** amphetamine (cf. A n.[2]). **2** amytal barbiturate (cf. BLUE BANDS; BLUE BULLETS; BLUE DEVIL n.[2]; BLUE DOLLS; BLUE HEAVEN). [the drugs come in blue capsules]

blue-apron *n.* [early 18C] a tradesman. [his 'uniform']

blue-arsed bandit *n.* [1990s] a homosexual male. [ext. of ARSE BANDIT]

blue-backs/bluebacks *n.* [mid–late 19C] **1** (US) money issued by the Confederate States of America (cf. SHUCKS). **2** (S.Afr.) money issued briefly by the Orange Free State. [its colour]

blue balls *n.* **1** [20C] a venereal bubo (cf. BLUE BOAR). **2** [20C] a feeling of intense sexual frustration; thus *have blue balls*, of a man, to be very sexually frustrated. **3** [1930s+] (US) gonorrhoea. [SE *blue* + BALLS n.[1]]

blue bands *n.* [1960s+] (drugs) barbiturates (cf. BLUE ANGEL). [packaging]

blue barrels *n.* [1960s+] (drugs) LSD (cf. A n.[3]). [packaging]

blue-bellied *adj.* [mid-19C–1910s] (US) of a person, despicable, repellent. [BLUEBELLY (2)]

bluebelly *n.* (US) **1** [early 19C+] (US) a Northerner, a Yankee, esp. a Northern soldier during the Civil War (1861–5). **2** [19C] a pretentious, self-opinionated person. **3** [late 19C–1940s] a policeman (cf. BLUE n.[3]) [the uniforms of (1) the Northern troops, (2) the police]

blueberry pie *n.* [1980s+] (US gay) a sailor (cf. GOB-GOBBLER; GOB JOB; SEAFOOD n.[1]; SEA PUSSY; SHORE DINNER). [the blue uniform + something one can EAT v.[3]]

blue billy *n.*[1] [mid–late 19C] a blue handkerchief with white spots, worn and used a prize fights (cf. BELCHER n.[1]; BILLY n.[4]). ['Before a SET TO it is common to take it from the neck and tie it round the leg as a garter, or round the waist to "keep it in the wind"' (Hotten, 1867). The *blue billy* made its way to New York where it was defined in a detective manual (*c.*1870) as 'a strange handkerchief']

blue billy *n.*[2] [late 19C] refuse ammoniacal lime from gas factories.

bluebird *n.*[1] **1** [mid-19C] (US South) a Northern, Unionist soldier (cf. BLUEBELLY). **2** [1910s–60s] (US) a policeman (cf. BLUE n.[3]). [the colour of the uniform]

bluebird *n.*[2] [1930s–70s] (Aus./US) a police car, a police wagon (cf. BLACK ANNIE). [the colour of the Buicks and later Fords that fulfilled the role]

bluebird *n.*[3] **1** [1960s+] (drugs) a depressant. **2** [1950s–70s] (drugs) a capsule of sodium amytal. [packaging]

bluebird *n.*[4] [1990s] (US Black teen) something that is annoying, worrying or bothering the speaker, e.g. anything from the police to a nagging boy- or girlfriend. [BLUE adj.[1]]

blueblack *n.* [late 19C+] (US Black) a skin colour so dark it seems to have tints of blue (cf. BLUE n.[2]).

blue blanket *n.* **1** [late 18C–19C] the sky. **2** [mid-19C] a rough coat made of coarse pilot-cloth (an indigo cloth used for ships' officers' greatcoats).

blue-blasted *adj.* [mid-19C] (US) euph. for DAMNED.

blue blazes *n.* [19C+] euph. for *hell*, usu. in phr., e.g. *hot as blue blazes, go blue blazes*. [BLUE adj.[5] + BLAZES]

blue-blind/blue-blind paralytic *adj.* [1910s] (Aus.) extremely drunk. [BLUE adj.² + BLIND DRUNK]

blue boar *n.* [late 18C–mid-19C] a venereal bubo (cf. BLUE BOARD; BLUE BOY n.¹). [? the notorious *Blue Boar* tavern in London, sited on the corner of Oxford Street and Tottenham Court Road, next to the St Giles rookery, and thus a centre of lowlife]

blue board *n.* [20C] a venereal bubo. [ext. of BLUE BOAR]

blue bomber *n.* [1970s] (US drugs) valium (cf. BLACK BOMBER). [the colour of the pill or capsule]

bluebottle *n.* [mid-19C+] a policeman (cf. BLUE n.³). [Hotten notes a 'singular' pre-dating in Shakespeare's synon. use of *bluebottle* as a beadle in *King Henry IV* Pt. I (1597)]

blue boy *n.¹* [18C–19C] a venereal bubo. [var. on BLUE BOAR]

blue boy/blueboy *n.²* [late 19C+] a policeman (cf. BLUE n.³). [the uniform]

blue boy *n.³* [1950s] (US Black) a Black male. [? the blue-black tone of very dark skin + the emotional overtones of BLUE adj.¹]

blue boy *n.⁴* [1950s+] 1 (drugs) amphetamine (cf. A n.²). 2 a police car, a police wagon (cf. BLUEBIRD n.²). [the colour of the pill or the vehicle]

blue broadway *n.* [1940s] (US Black/Harlem) Heaven. [the *blue* sky + image of *Broadway*, New York, then in its prime, as an earthly version of paradise]

blue bullets *n.* [1960s+] barbiturates (cf. BLUE ANGEL). [PACKAGING]

blue butter *n.* [mid-19C–1900s] an ointment used for the treatment of venereal sores. [the mercury on which it was based]

blue cap *n.¹* [late 16C–late 18C] a Scotsman. [metonymy]

blue cap *n.²* [1960s+] (drugs) mescaline. [the colour of the capsule]

blue chairs *n.* [1980s+] (drugs) LSD (cf. A n.³). [ety. unknown]

blue cheer *n.* [1970s] (US drugs) a capsule of LSD cut with Methedrine or some other form of 'speed'. [the laundry detergent *Blue Cheer* and/or the rock band of the same name]

blue-chin *n.* [20C] (Aus.) an actor. [actors tend to shave for the evening performance rather than in the morning]

blue chips *n.* [20C] cast-iron, undeniable facts. [Stock Exchange use, ult. dependable securities]

bluecoat *n.¹* [16C] 1 one who wears a blue coat, spec. a beadle in the 16C and later a blue-coated soldier, sailor or policeman (cf. BLUE n.³). 2 a servant, who was similarly dressed. 3 [mid–late 19C] (US) a policeman. 4 [mid-19C] (US south) a Northern, Unionist soldier. 5 [mid-19C+] a blue-uniformed policeman.

bluecoat/bluejacket *n.²* [1940s+] (S.Afr.) 1 an habitual criminal serving an indeterminate sentence. 2 an indeterminate sentence of 9–15 years. [the colour of the uniform. Note the earlier UK use of BLUECOAT n.¹]

blued *adj.¹* [mid-19C] drunk. [BLUE adj.² (1)]

blued *adj.²* [mid–late 19C] depressed. [BLUE adj.¹ (2)]

blue damn *n.* [late 19C–1900s] an oath (cf. BLUE BLAZES). [BLUE adj.⁵]

blue dangers *n.* [1960s+] (US Und.) 1 marked police cars (when painted blue, as in New York). 2 blue-uniformed police officers (cf. BLUE n.³).

blue de hue *n.* [1970s] (drugs) marijuana from Vietnam. [internal rhy.; Hue ('Hoo-ay') is a major city in Vietnam]

blue devil *n.¹* [US] [mid-19C] a servant (cf. BLUECOAT n.¹). [the blue uniform]

blue devil *n.²* [1960s–70s] (drugs) a depressant, esp. Phenobarbitone (luminal), amobarbital (cf. BLUE ANGEL). [packaging]

blue devils *n.¹* 1 [18C] a fit of depression. 2 [19C] delirium tremens. [BLUE adj.¹]

blue devils *n.²* [19C] the police (cf. BLUE n.³). [the blue uniform + derog. use of SE]

blue dolls *n.* [1960s] (drugs) barbiturates (cf. BLUE ANGEL). [SE *blue* + DOLLS]

blue-domer *n.* [1920s+] one who does not go to church; thus *blue-domeist*, one who hold this attitude to religion; *blue-domeism*, the 'open-air' version of theology. [they prefer to pray beneath the 'blue dome' of the sky]

blue duck *n.* [late 19C+] (Aus.) a lost cause, a failure. [DEAD DUCK]

blue-eyed *adj.¹* [mid-19C] (US campus) drunk. [BLUE adj.² (1)]

blue-eyed *adj.²* [1930s–70s] (US) euph. for DAMNED. [note BLUE adj.⁵]

blue-eyed boy *n.* [1910s–20s] a special favourite. [SE f. 1930]

blue-eyed soul *n.* [1960s+] 1 a style of popular music in which White performers performed soul songs, usually the province of Black performers; most popular in 1960s. 2 (US Black) the characteristic of emotional sensitivity (i.e. 'soul') applied to White people. [SE *blue-eyed*, i.e. shorthand for White + *soul music*]

blue-eyed soul brother/sister *n.* [1960s+] (US Black) any White who is accepted as genuinely friendly towards Blacks. [SE *blue-eyed* + SOUL BROTHER/SOUL SISTER]

blue fear *n.* [late 19C] very great fear (cf. BLUE FUNK). [BLUE adj.¹ (3) = SE *fear*]

blue flag *n.* [mid-18C–early 19C] a publican; thus *hoist the blue flag*, to set oneself up as a publican. [their blue apron]

blue foot *n.* [1960s–70s] a prostitute. [? she is cold from standing in the street]

blue funk *n.* [mid-19C+] abject terror, utter cowardice, complete misery. [BLUE adj.¹ (3) + FUNK n.² ? + the colour of the terrified individual's skin, which turns a leaden blue-grey]

blue goose *n.* [20C] (US) 1 the general convict cage at a prison camp. 2 a small, run-down café or bar. 3 an establishment where liquor is sold illegally (cf. BLIND PIG; BLIND TIGER). [ety. unknown]

blue goose *v.* [20C] (US Black) to engage in sexual affairs. [GOOSE v.²]

bluegown *n.* [late 16C–early 16C] a prostitute. [metonymy; prostitutes confined in a house of correction wore a blue dress as their uniform]

bluegrass *v.* [1950s–60s] (US drugs) to commit a drug user to the Lexington Federal Narcotics Hospital in Lexington, Kentucky. [the *Bluegrass State*, the nickname of Kentucky]

blue gum *n.¹* [20C] (US) 1 a Black person, seen by the (White) speaker as especially malevolent; the belief was that their bite is supposedly poisonous. 2 a person of mixed Indian, White and Black ancestry. [the bluish gums that many Blacks have]

blue gum *n.²* [20C] (US) bootleg whisky.

bluehair *n.* [1980s+] (US campus) an old person, usu. female. [the bluish tint that old ladies sometimes have put into their otherwise grey hair]

bluehead *n.* [mid-19C] (US) strong and illicitly distilled whisky. [? it has a bluish tinge]

blue heaven *n.* (drugs) 1 [1950s+] amytal barbiturate (cf. BLUE ANGEL). 2 [1960s+] LSD (cf. A n.³). 3 [1980s+] alkyl nitrates. [colour of capsule/tablet + play on the popular song 'My Blue Heaven' (1927)]

blue heeler *n.* [1990s] (Aus.) a policeman (cf. BLUE n.³). [SAusE *blue heeler*, a cattle dog]

blue hen's chicken *n.¹* 1 [18C] (US) a spirited, plucky person, a good fighter. 2 [20C] a dominant, aggressive and esp. short-tempered person, esp. a woman. 3 [20C] an important person or one who poses as such. [SE *blue hen*, a hen supposed to breed first-rate fighting cocks]

blue hen's chicken *n.²* [late 18C+] a resident of the state of Delaware (cf. MUSK-RAT). [according to Niles' *National Register* (1840): 'In the revolutionary war Captain Caldwell [of Delaware] had a company called by the rest "Caldwell's game cocks", and the regiment after a time in Carolina was nicknamed from this, "the blue hen's chickens" and the "blue chickens." But after they had been distinguished in the south the name of the Blue Hen was applied to the state']

blue in v.[1] *see* BLEW IN.

blue in v.[2] *see* BLUE v.[2].

bluejacket n.[1] [mid-19C] **1** (US) a Northern, Unionist soldier (cf. BLUEBELLY). **2** a policeman (cf. BLUE n.[3]). [the uniform]

bluejacket n.[2] *see* BLUECOAT n.[2].

bluejay n. [1950s–70s] (US drugs) a capsule of sodium amytal (cf. BLUEBIRD n.[3]). [the capsule's colour]

blue john n. [19C] (US) **1** skim milk. **2** sour or nearly sour milk. [such milk has a slightly blue tinge]

blue johnny n. [mid-19C] (US) a Northern, Unionist soldier. [his uniform]

blue light n.[1] **1** [mid-19C] (US) a pious, sanctimonious individual. **2** [mid–late 19C] (US campus) a student who informs on other students to the authorities. [SE *blue laws*, severely puritanical laws enacted in New England; ? the blue light that signifies a police station]

blue light n.[2] [1940s+] (W.I.) an obscenity, a swearword, a coarse, vulgar expression. [? BLUE BLAZES + BLUE adj.[3]]

blue light n.[3] [1980s+] (US gang) a murder contract. [? blue lights of police cars, the implication is of 'legal' authorized killings done for specific reasons]

blue light v. [1980s+] (US Und.) to assassinate, to murder. [BLUE LIGHT n.[3]]

blue-light clinic n. [20C] (Aus.) a venereal disease clinic. [its 'signpost']

blue lightning n. [mid-19C] (US West.) a revolver, a 6-gun. [the flash when a bullet is fired]

blue lights n. [1980s+] (US Black) a police car. [the rotating/flashing blue lights on top of police cars]

blue-light special n.[1] [1990s] (US Black) a cheap, low-quality retail item. [play on SE *blueplate special* + ? implication of illegality; thus the BLUE LIGHTS might be interested]

blue-light special n.[2] *see* BLUE SPECIAL.

blue lips n. [20C] a Black person, seen by the (White) speaker as especially malevolent (cf. BLUE GUM). [metonymy]

blue madman n. [1980s+] (drugs) phencyclidine (cf. ACE n.[3]). [the colour of the capsule]

blue meanie n. [1960s–70s] **1** a policeman (cf. BLUE n.[3]; BROWN BOMBER n.[1]; GREY GHOST; MEANIE; STICKER-LICKER). **2** the establishment in general. [*Blue Meanies*, the 'villains' of the animated film *Yellow Submarine* (1968), featuring the Beatles]

blue-metal v. [late 19C–1940s] (Aus.) to throw pieces of stone, esp. in a street-fight. [SE *blue metal*, small pieces of stone, used in street-fights]

blue microdot/mist n. [1960s+] (drugs) LSD (cf. A n.[3]). [SE *blue* + MICRODOT; MIST]

blue Monday n. [late 19C–1920s] a Monday taken off work and dedicated to self-indulgence. [BLUE adj.[5] + SE *Monday*]

blue moon n.[1] [17C+] a moment in time that does not recur for a very long time. [abbr. ONCE IN A BLUE MOON]

blue moon n.[2] [late 19C] a spoon. [rhy. sl.]

blue moon n.[3] [1970s+] (Aus.) a pimp. [rhy. sl. *blue moon* = HOON n. (1)]

blue moon v. [late 19C–1930s] to romance, to 'chat up'. [rhy. sl. *blue moon* = SPOON v.[1]]

blue moons/sage n. [1960s+] (drugs) a variety of marijuana. [its bluish tinge]

blue murder n. [mid-19C] cries of terror, horror, alarm; usu. in phr. *cry blue murder, scream blue murder*. [BLUE adj.[1] (3) + SE *murder*]

bluenose n.[1] [late 18C+] (US) a Canadian, esp. a resident of

Nova Scotia. [SE *bluenose*, a variety of potato native to Nova Scotia, but note late 17C Scot. *bluenose*, a Scot. Presbyterian]

bluenose n.[2] [mid-19C] (US) a Northerner, esp. a New Englander (cf. BLUEBELLY). [joc. use of SE; the northern nose is *blue* with chilly disapproval]

bluenose n.[3] [1920s+] (US) a dedicated, fanatical puritan, almost invariably a teetotaller (cf. BLUESKIN n.[1]). [orig. an aristocrat (who had 'blue blood'), *bluenoses* passed the repressive 'blue laws' that restricted the morals of many states ? + the opposite of the drunk, who boasts a conspicuously red nose]

bluenose n.[4] [1920s+] (US) someone who sees themself as superior to their neighbours. [akin to BLUENOSE n.[2]; such people also tend to lay down the law]

bluenose n.[5] [1930s] (US) a sycophant, a toady. [analogous with BROWN NOSE n.]

blue-nosed adj. (US) **1** [early 19C+] pertaining to or being a Nova Scotian (cf. BLUENOSE n.[1]). **2** [late 19C–1940s] rigidly, repressively puritan. [BLUENOSE n.[3]]

bluenoser n. (US) **1** [mid-19C–1930s] a Canadian (cf. BLUENOSE n.[1]). **2** [1970s] a fanatical puritan. [BLUENOSE n.[3]]

blue ocean n. [1980s+] (S.Afr.) methylated spirits (cf. BLOUTREIN).

blue o'clock in the morning n. [late 19C–1900s] the last minutes of proper night-time, when darkness is gradually giving way to dawn. [rhy. sl. *two o'clock*]

blue pencil v. [late 19C+] to censor, to edit by cutting. [the trad. colour of the editor's pencil]

blue pig n. [late 19C+] (US) **1** an unlicensed drinking house, a speakeasy, an 'after-hours' bar. **2** the whisky served in such an establishment. [BLUE GOOSE + BLIND PIG]

blue pigeon n. [late 18C–late 19C] **1** a thief who specializes in stealing the lead from roofs (cf. BLUE PIGEON FLYER; BLUEY-HUNTER; FLY A BLUE PIGEON). **2** small off-cuts of lead or similar materials, taken from the job in hand and sold off as perks by plumbers (cf. BUNCE; CABBAGE n.[2]; JAM n.[2]; MANAVILINS; SKEWINGS). [like an avian pigeon, the thief 'perches' on a church roof]

blue pigeon flyer n. [mid-19C] a stealer of lead from the roofs of buildings; such a thief poses as a journeyman glazier, plumber or other workman who gets to the roof, strips off the lead and hides it (often by wrapping round the body) before leaving the house (cf. BLUEY-HUNTER). [ext. of BLUE PIGEON (1)]

blue pill n. [mid–late 19C] (US) a bullet (cf. BLUE PLUM; BLUE WHISTLER). [SE *blue*, lead + SE *pill*]

blue plum/plumb n. [late 18C–19C] a bullet; thus *give one a taste of plum*, to wound or kill with a bullet; thus *surfeited with a blue plumb*, wounded by gunfire (cf. BLUE PILL). [SE *blue* + *plumb*, a small piece of lead + pun on the fruit]

blue ribbon n. [mid-19C–20C] gin (cf. BIT OF TAPE; BLUE RUIN; BLUE TAPE; LIGHT BLUE; SKY BLUE n.[1]). [SE *blue ribbon*, a blue ribbon worn as a badge of honour; thus referring to the quality of the best gin]

blue ribboner/ribbonite n. [late 19C–1900s] a teetotaller, a total abstainer. [the *blue ribbons* such individuals wore to proclaim their drink-free status. A Blue Ribbon Army was instituted in 1882, but the Army and its ribbons had virtually vanished by 1896]

blue ribbon fakers n. [late 19C–1900s] a teetotaller, a total abstainer (cf. BLUE RIBBONER). [SE *blue ribbon* + FAKER n.[2] (2)]

blue ribbonite *see* BLUE RIBBONER.

blue room n. [20C] (US Und.) a punishment cell (cf. HOLE n.[2]). [its lack of light + once incarcerated there, one feels BLUE adj.[1]]

blue ruin n. **1** [early–late 19C] gin, esp. second-rate gin (cf. BLUE RIBBON; MOTHER'S RUIN; RED RUIN). **2** [mid-19C] (US) a strong kind of apple-jack, peach-brandy or whisky (cf. JERSEY LIGHTNING). [BLUE adj.[1] (3) + SE *ruin*; i.e. its effects]

blues *n.*[1] [mid-18C+] misery, depression, unhappiness. [orig. general, White use, despite assumption that the term was created/patented by US Blacks. The *OED*'s first citation is from a letter by the actor David Garrick (11 July 1741): 'I am far from being quite well, tho not troubled wth ye Blews as I have been']

blues *n.*[2] **1** [20C] (Aus.) the police (cf. BLUE n.[3]). **2** (US) [1960s+] amphetamines (cf. A n.[2]; PURPLE HEARTS; REDS n.3; WHITES n.[4]; YELLOWS). [the colour of the uniform or the pills]

blues *n.*[3] [1960s+] (W.I.) a shebeen, an illegal drinking club or a party where drink is sold without a licence. [BLUE n.[5]]

blues *n.*[4] [1970s] (US) blue eyes, esp. as *baby-blues*. [abbr.]

blue sage see BLUE MOONS.

blue shirt *n.*[1] [1920s+] (Aus.) **1** a farmer or estate owner. **2** a lazy worker, a slacker.

blueshirt *n.*[2] [1990s] (Irish) a member of the Fine Gael party, thus anyone espousing right-wing views. [the *Blueshirts*, a 1930s Irish fascist movement, named for their uniform]

blueskin *n.*[1] **1** [18C–early 19C]· a Presbyterian. **2** [late 18C–mid-19C] (US) a puritan, a repressive moralist (cf. BLUE STOCKING). [BLUE adj.[1] (2); i.e. their demeanour]

blueskin *n.*[2] **1** [late 18C] (US) a keen supporter of the American Revolution. **2** [mid-19C] (US) a Northern, Unionist soldier (cf. BLUEBELLY n.[1]). [uniforms]

blueskin *n.*[3] [late 18C–early 19C] **1** the offspring of a White man and a Black woman, a mulatto. **2** a Black person (cf. BLUE n.[2]). [skin tone]

blue sky *n.*[1] [1940s–80s] (S.Afr.) the Cinderella Prison in Boksberg. [? the view]

blue sky *n.*[2] [1980s+] (US drugs) heroin. [? BLUE SKY v.; i.e. the dreaminess produced by the drug]

blue sky *v.* [1950s+] (US) **1** to wonder about things in an unrestrained manner, preferring pleasurable fantasy to tedious fact. **2** to talk unrestrainedly, in a speculative manner; thus [1970s] *blue-skyer*, *blue-sky artist*, one who speculates freely, with little basis in fact. [one is day-dreaming, fig. gazing at the sky]

blue sky blond *n.* [1980s+] (drugs) high potency marijuana from Columbia. [the light colour of the leaves]

blue/blue-light special *n.* [1990s] (US Black) a policeman (cf. BLUE n.[3]). [SE *blue lights* on police cars + play on *blue-plate special*]

blue star *n.* [1980s+] (drugs) a variety of LSD, emblazoned with a blue star symbol (cf. A n.[3]).

blue-steel *n.* [1940s–60s] (US) a pistol. [its manufacture]

blue stocking *n.* [18C] (US) a puritan, esp. a Presbyterian (cf. BLUESKIN n.[1]). [17C *blue*, used after the Restoration of Charles II in 1660 to denote any diehard Puritan who disapproved of the new moral freedoms]

bluestone *n.* [late 19C] the very lowest quality of gin or whisky. [SE *bluestone*, copper sulphate or vitriol]

bluesuit *n.* [1970s+] (US) a uniformed policeman (cf. BLUE n.[3]). [the uniform]

blue tape *n.* [late 18C–mid-19C] gin, esp. second-rate gin (cf. BIT OF TAPE; BLUE RIBBON). [SE *blue* + TAPE]

blue tips *n.* [1980s+] (drugs) a depressant. [packaging of the capsule]

blue-tongue *n.* [late 19C+] (Aus.) a roustabout, an itinerant labourer. [SE *blue-tongue*, an Australian lizard of the genus *Tiliqua*, belonging to the family Scincidae; the ref. is to the sleepiness of such lizards]

blue train see BLOUTREIN.

Blue 'Un, the *n.* [late 19C–1900s] the *Winning Post*, a sporting newspaper. [so named to distinguish it from the PINK 'UN and the BROWN 'UN]

blue vein/veiner *n.* [late 19C+] an erection. [the vein that runs up the penis]

blue-veined custard chucker *n.* [1990s] the penis (cf. BLUE-VEINED HAVANA; BLUE-VEINED JUNKET PUMP; BLUE-VEINED PICCOLO; BLUE-VEINED STEAK; BLUE-VEINED TRUMPET). [BLUE VEIN + CUSTARD + SE *chucker*]

blue-veined havana *n.* [1990s] penis; thus *smoke the blue-veined havana*, to fellate someone (cf. BLUE-VEINED CUSTARD CHUCKER). [BLUE VEIN + SE *Havana* (cigar)]

blue-veined junket pump/porridge gun/yoghurt gun *n.* [1990s] the penis (cf. BLUE-VEINED CUSTARD CHUCKER). [BLUE VEIN + SE *junket* + *pump*; *porridge/yoghurt* + *gun*]

blue-veined piccolo *n.* [1980s+] the penis (cf. BLUE-VEINED CUSTARD CHUCKER). [BLUE VEIN + SE *piccolo*]

blue-veined porridge gun see BLUE-VEINED JUNKET PUMP.

blue-veined root-on *n.* [1990s] an erection. [BLUE VEIN + ROOT n.[1] (2)]

blue-veined steak *n.* [1980s+] the penis (cf. BLUE-VEINED CUSTARD CHUCKER). [BLUE VEIN + SE *steak*]

blue-veined trumpet *n.* [1980s+] the penis (cf. BLUE-VEINED CUSTARD CHUCKER). [BLUE VEIN + SE *trumpet*]

blue-veined yoghurt gun see BLUE-VEINED JUNKET PUMP.

blue veiner see BLUE VEIN.

blue velvet *n.* [1970s] (drugs) a mixture of an antihistamine and paregoric. [the 'smoothness' of its effects]

blue vials *n.* [1980s+] (drugs) LSD (cf. A n.[3]). [packaging]

blue whistler *n.* [mid-19C] (US) a bullet (cf. BLUE PILL). [the *blue* lead in the bullet and the noise it makes]

bluey *n.*[1] **1** [mid–late 19C] (Und.) lead. **2** [20C] (Aus./N.Z.) a summons, a traffic ticket. **3** [20C] (orig. Aus.) a red-headed person. **4** [1930s+] a blue heeler, an Australian cattle dog. **5** [1970s+] a £5 note (cf. GREENIE n.[2]). [all SE *blue* + sfx. -*y*]

bluey *n.*[2] (Aus.) **1** [late 19C+] a pack. **2** [1950s+] any form of luggage. [the traditional blue blanket that covered a pack]

bluey *n.*[3] [20C] a drinker of methylated spirits. [SE *blue*, the colour of meths + sfx. -*y*]

bluey-cracking *n.* [mid-19C] stealing lead from the roofs of buildings (cf. BLUE PIGEON FLYING; BLUEY-HUNTER). [BLUEY n.[1] (1) + CRACK v.[5] (1)]

bluey-hunter *n.* [mid-19C] a thief who specializes in stealing lead from the roofs of houses and other buildings. [BLUEY n.[1] (1) + SE *hunter*]

bluff *n.*[1] **1** [mid-19C–1910s] an excuse. **2** [late 19C–1930s] (US) an impostor, a deceiver, one who bluffs. [BLUFF v.]

bluff *n.*[2] [1950s+] a female homosexual who can alternate between active/passive roles. [BUTCH n.[3] (2) + FLUFF n.[1] (3)]

bluff *v.* [early 18C–late 19C] to confuse, to mislead or deter by a show of confidence or superiority. [20C use is SE poker jargon: 'To impose upon (an opponent) as to the value of one's hand of cards, by betting heavily upon it, speaking or gesticulating or otherwise acting in such a way as to make believe that it is stronger than it is, so as to induce him to "throw up" his cards and lose his stake, rather than run the risk of betting against the bluffer' (*OED*); ult. a late 17C Und. term (cf. BAM v.[1]; BAMBOOZLE) + ? link to SE *bluff*, a blinker for a horse]

bluff cuffs with the solid senders *n.* [1940s] (US Black) trousers with large, ballooning turn-ups.

bluffer *n.*[1] (Und.) **1** [18C] an innkeeper. **2** [mid–late 19C] (US) the landlord of a hotel. [? their 'bluff' manners, whether using *bluff* as hearty or as in setting out to deceive]

bluffer *n.*[2] [late 19C+] one who relies on an assumed manner to get away with lies. [BLUFF v.]

bluff the rats, to *phr.* [1910s–20s] to spread panic. [BLUFF v. + SE *rats*]

bluggy *adj.* [mid–late 19C] (US) a deliberate mispron. (as if one were drunk or otherwise verbally impaired) of BLOODY adj.

blunderbus *n.* [20C] an automobile (cf. BLIXEN-BUS). [pun]

blunderbuss n.[1] [17C–late 18C; 1960s] a fool, a clumsy, noisy fellow. [20C use is US. SE *blunderbuss*, a short gun with a large bore; its unwieldy clumsiness and inaccuracy are transferred to the human version]

blunderbuss n.[2] [1940s+] any large motor vehicle that handles badly. [pun on SE *blunder bus*]

Blundstones n. [20C] (Aus.) elastic-sided boots. [the proprietary name]

blunjie/blunjy adj. [1950s] yielding, squeezable. [? onomat.]

blunk adj. [1960s–70s] (drugs) intoxicated. [? BLOTTO + SE *drunk*]

blunt n.[1] [mid-18C–late 19C] money, esp. cash in hand. [? Fr. *blond*, yellow, using as in other sl. terms the colour of the coin to denote its name; or f. SE *blunt*, referring to the edge of unmilled coins, or, least feasibly, from Mr John *Blunt*, chief architect of the South Sea Bubble financial scandal of 1720]

blunt n.[2] [1980s+] (drugs) a marijuana cigarette made of buds rolled in a tobacco leaf, taken from the wrapper of a Phillies Blunt cigar (cf. EL PEE; HAMPS n.[2]). [note the cigar can be of any brand, and can contain crack cocaine as well as marijuana; one version of the *blunt* is also sealed with a layer of honey]

blunt n.[3] [1980s+] (drugs) any drug available in a blunt-ended capsule.

blunted adj. [1980s+] (drugs) under the influence of a marijuana/cannabis cigarette. [BLUNT n.[2]]

blunt magazine n. [early–mid-19C] a bank. [BLUNT n.[1] + SE *magazine*, a warehouse]

blurb n. [1910s+] (orig. US) a brief piece of promotional material, typically as printed on the back of books. [coined 1907 by the US humorist Gelett Burgess (1866–1951), after designing a humorous bookplate (to be given away at a booksellers' dinner), which featured an attractive young women (lifted from an advertisement for tooth powder or health tonic and suitably embellished by Burgess) whom he christened 'Miss Belinda Blurb']

blurry adj. [1910s+] slurred mispron. of BLOODY adj. (cf. BLUGGY).

blurt n. [1990s] the vagina (cf. BLART). [? an anatomic variation on BLOT]

blurt! excl. [late 16C–early 17C] a general excl. of disdain. [SE *blurt*, to make a contemptuous puffing gesture with the lips, to puff in scorn]

blushing adj. [20C] euph. for BLOODY adj.

blush like a blue dog, to phr. [late 18C] not to blush at all. [a blue dog will not turn pink]

blut n. [1990s] the vagina. [BLART]

B. Luther Hatchett n. [1920s–40s] (US Black) the ultimate in far-away, unpleasant places, the 'back of beyond' (cf. BEE-LUTHER-HATCHEE). [nonsense words]

bluxom! see BLIKSEM!

bly n. [1950s+] (W.I. Rasta) a chance. [? SE (*proba*)*bly*, (*possi*)*bly*]

bly!/bly me! excl. [late 19C–1900s] a general excl. of surprise, alarm. [abbr. BLIMEY!]

bly-hunka/bly-hunker n. [early–mid-19C] (tramp) a horse. [? Shelta]

b.m. n.[1] [1950s–60s] (S.Afr. gay) a heterosexual person. [abbr. *baby maker*]

b.m. n.[2] [1960s+] **1** a visit to the lavatory. **2** a piece of excrement. [abbr. *bowel movement*]

b.m.o.c./b.w.o.c. n. [1930s–70s] (US college) a socially prominent, important person in the context of student life. [abbr. *big man/woman on campus*]

b.m.t. n. [1990s] unpunctuality (cf. AFRICAN PEOPLE'S TIME). [abbr. *Black Man's Time*]

b.m.t. phr. [1990s] (US Black) a phr. designed to affirm one's authority, masculinity etc and thus reinforce one's argument. [abbr. *Black man talking*]

b.m.w. n. **1** [1980s+] the BMW motorcar, esp. popular as a status symbol and as a target for theft. **2** [1990s] (US Black) *Black man working*. [abbr. There are various 'translations' of *BMW*, 'Black man's wheels', 'Black man's wagon', 'Bob Marley and the Wailers', 'break my windows'. The actual name comes from that of the German manufacturer, *Bayerische Motor Werke*]

b.n.! excl. [1900s–30s] a bloody nuisance. [abbr.]

b.n.i.c. phr. [1930s+] (US Black) a sarcastic reference to any Black authority-figure (cf. BLACK NIGGER IN CHARGE). [abbr. *Black Nigger in charge; head nigger in charge*]

b.o. n. [1930s+] (orig. US) body odour; thus *B.O. juice* (US campus) deodorant. [abbr.; invented and widely popularized by the Lifebuoy soap advertising campaign *c.*1930]

b.o. v. see BEND OVER.

b.o. phr. [1950s+] go way, leave me alone. [abbr. BUGGER OFF]

bo n.[1] [early 18C+] **1** a fellow, a man, a friend, often as form of address, e.g. *Hey, bo.* **2** [late 19C+] (US) a vagrant, a tramp (cf. HOBO n.[1]). [SE *boy*, or abbr. HOBO n.[1]]

bo n.[2] [1950s] (US campus) a bohemian (cf. BOHO n.[2]).

bo n.[3] [1970s+] (US drugs) Colombian marijuana. [abbr. Colom*bo*]

bo v. [1910s–20s] (US) to live as a tramp. [HOBO v.]

boag v. [1980s+] (US campus) to vomit. [BOGUE n.[2]]

boang see BOONG.

boar n. [1950s+] (W.I.) a straight cutlass with a hooked end. [? resemblance to a boar's tusks]

board n.[1] [early 17C] one shilling (5p). [var. on BORD]

board n.[2] [20C] (tramp) a picture sold in the street. [it is painted on a *board*]

board n.[3] [1960s] (US) the human leg. [? it gives one support]

board v. [1930s–40s] (US Black) to eat. [SE *board*, a table, esp. one spread with food]

boarding house n. [late 17C+] a prison (cf. AKERMAN'S HOTEL). [note *the boarding house*, the old nickname for New York City's Tombs prison]

boarding-house reach n. [1900s–30s] (US) reaching rudely across the table to grab what one wants, rather than asking for it to be passed. [the presumed selfishness of boarding-house guests, each of whom attempts to corral the most food for themself]

boarding school n. [late 17C– mid-19C] a prison (cf. AKERMAN'S HOTEL). [ironic use of SE]

boardman n. [mid-19C] 'men who take a stand on the curb of a public thoroughfare, and deliver prepared speeches to effect a sale of any articles they have to vend' (Hotten, 1859) (cf. STANDING PATTERER). [he augmented his pitch by displaying a board to which were affixed coloured pictures]

board of green cloth n. **1** [late 18C+] a billiard table. **2** [mid-19C+] a card-table. [the green baize that covers it]

board out v. [19C] (US) to spend time in prison. [BOARDING SCHOOL]

boards n. [1920s] playing cards. [the material of which they are made]

boar pig see BARTHOLOMEW PIG.

boar pussy n. [1980s+] (US prison) homosexual anal intercourse. [SE *boar*, generic for a male animal + PUSSY n.[1] (1)]

boar's nest n. [late 19C+] (US) **1** anywhere, orig. a logging or mining camp, where only men live or only men are admitted. **2** an untidy room or house. [SE *boar* + *nest*; note the bar in the TV series *The Dukes of Hazzard*, set in America's bootlegging country, which was named the Boar's Nest, although it appeared to entertain women customers]

boasie/boasy n. [1950s+] (W.I.) **1** a show-off, a boaster. **2** a flashily dressed person. [BOASIE adj.]

boasie/boasy/bosy adj. [1930s+] (W.I.) proud, boastful, showy. [SE *boastful* and/or Yoruba *bosi*, proud and ostentatious]

boasy-naked n. [1950s+] (W.I.) a shameless show-off. [BOASIE adj.]

b.o.a.t. n. [1980s] a semi-professional prostitute whose clients tend to be wealthy and whose payments are often less obvious than mere cash. [abbr. *bordering on a tart*]

boat n.[1] **1** [20C] a Cadillac or any other large car (cf. BARGE n.[3]). **2** [1950s] (US Black) the vagina (cf. BARGE n.[3]). **3** [1950s+] (US) a large foot. **4** [1950s+] (US) a large shoe or boot. [the size and supposed resemblance]

boat n.[2] [20C] (US Und.) transportation from one prison to another; the mode of transport is irrelevant (cf. BOAT v.; DRAFT; TRAIN n.[1]).

boat n.[3] [1940s+] the face. [rhy. sl. BOAT-RACE n.[1]]

boat n.[4] [1980s+] (drugs) phencyclidine (cf. ACE n.[3]). [? one 'sails away']

boat v. (Und.) **1** [early–mid-19C] to transport a convict. **2** [mid-19C–1900s] to sentence to penal servitude; thus *get the boat*, to receive a harsh or lengthy sentence, *in the boat*, sentenced to penal servitude. [the ships that transported the convicts to Australia]

boat and oar n. [1950s] a prostitute. [rhy. sl. *boat and oar = whore*]

boated adj. [mid–late 19C] sentenced to a long term in prison. [BOAT v.]

boat-jumper n. [1980s+] (US) a recently arrived immigrant. [the pej. image of immigrants as stowaways who have to avoid immigration procedures by jumping from boat to dock]

boatrace n.[1] [1940s+] the face (cf. BOAT n.[3]). [rhy. sl.]

boatrace n.[2] [1960s+] (US) any form of 'fixed' sporting contest. [orig. horse-racing jargon only; the winner 'sails in']

boat ride n. [1960s] (US) a pleasant, undemanding task. [one 'sails' through it]

boats, the n. [early 19C] the penal hulks, moored on the Thames (cf. FLOATING ACADEMIES).

b.o.b. n. [1990s] (US) an extremely obese woman. [abbr. *big old bitch*]

bob n.[1] [18C] gin. [BOBSTICK, i.e. a shilling's worth of gin]

bob n.[2] **1** [18C] a generic term for a man, on the lines of such equally common names as Jack, Tom etc. **2** a shoplifter's assistant, to whom the stolen goods are quickly passed by the actual lifter.

bob n.[3] **1** [late 18C+] a shilling (5p). **2** [1930s+] (US) $1. [BOBSTICK]

Bob n.[4] [19C+] euph. for God, esp. in phrs. *s'elp me Bob!*, *no sirree, Bob!* (cf. COCK n.[1]).

bob n.[5] [mid-19C] (Aus.) 50 strokes of the lash (cf. BULL n.[4]; CANARY n.[3]; TESTER). [ety. unknown]

bob n.[6] [1980s+] (drugs) crack cocaine. [abbr. BOBO n.[2] (2)]

bob adj. **1** [16C+] (Und.) pleasant, satisfactory, usu. in phr. *all is bob*. **2** [early 18C–mid-19C] lively, cheery. [abbr. BOBBISH]

bob v. [17C–19C] to cheat, to deceive; thus *bobbed*, cheated. [OF *bober*, to deceive. SE to late 17C and found as such in Shakespeare]

bob! excl. [late 19C] (society) stop! enough! esp. as response to the drink pourer's request 'Say when?'

bob and dick n. [1970s] the penis. [rhy. sl. *bob and dick = PRICK* n. (2)]

bob and dick adj. [1960s+] sick, esp. after drinking (cf. BOB, HARRY AND DICK). [rhy. sl.]

bob and hit n. **1** [19C] the vagina (cf. BLACK HOLE n.[1]). **2** 1990s excrement. [rhy. sl. *bob and hit* = (1) PIT n.[2] (2); (2) SHIT n.[1]]

bob and weave, to phr. [1920s+] to avoid direct action, either confrontation, explanation, aggression etc. [boxing imagery]

bob a nob phr. [early 19C] one shilling each person, used when estimating the cost of meals, outings, tickets etc. [BOB n.[3] (1) + NOB n.[1] (1)]

bob around v. [mid-19C+] to move quickly from place to place (cf. SHIFT ONE'S BOB).

bobbasheely n. [19C] (US) a friend. [Choctaw *itibapishili*, my brother]

bobbasheely v. [19C] (US) to saunter, to move in a friendly fashion, to mix with. [BOBBASHEELY n.]

bobbe mayse *see* BUBBE MAYSE.

bobber n. [mid–late 19C] a friend, a chum, a fellow worker. [Salop. dial. *bobber*, a term of friendly greeting, e.g. 'Hellow bobber']

bobbers n. [1940s+] (Aus.) the corks that are worn around the rim of a hat to keep away the flies. [SE *bob* v.; their movement]

bobbery n. [19C] an argument, a disturbance (cf. CON-BOBBERATION). [Hind. *Bap re!* O father!, a common exclamation of surprise or grief. A popular term, apparently coined *c.*1816 in the Raj, it had spread to such widely separated areas as East Anglia and Australia by the mid-century. Note Anglo-Ind. hunting use *bobbery pack*, a mongrel, mixed pack of hounds]

bobbies n. [19C] the testicles (cf. BAUBLES). [SE *bauble*, a trinket]

bobbish adj. [late 18C+] healthy, in good spirits, cheery. [SE *bob* v. + sfx. -*ish*; one 'bobs up and down' with good humour and energy]

bobble v.[1] [mid-17C–early 18C] to swindle, to cheat. [? misprint or mis-reading for BUBBLE v.[1]. E.P. cites a correspondent who found 'an "indignant gentleman captain" writing to the Navy Board' *c.*1688 and using the word, but BOBBLE v.[2] has not been found until 1812]

bobble v.[2] [early 19C+] to bob up and down. [ext. of SE *bob*]

bobbles n. **1** [late 19C–1920s] the testicles (cf. BAUBLES). **2** [20C] (US Black) gaudy, flashy, ostentatious jewellery. [SE *baubles*]

bobbly adj. [1900s] jerky, jumpy. [BOBBLE v.[2]]

bobby n. **1** [mid-19C+] a British policeman (cf. PEELER n.[1]). **2** [20C] (US) an Englishman. [Sir Robert Peel (1788–1850), who established the force in 19C. 'The term is, however, older. The official square-keeper, who is always armed with a cane to drive away idle and disorderly urchins, has, time out of mind, been called by said urchins *Bobby the Beadle*. BOBBY is also an old English word for striking, or hitting, a quality not unknown to policemen' (Hotten, 1867)]

bobby atkins n. [1900s–10s] a private soldier. [var. on TOMMY ATKINS]

bobby-dangler n. [1930s+] (Can.) the penis. [play on BOBBY-DAZZLER + SE *dangle*]

bobby-dazzler n. [late 19C+] anything or person seen as exceptional, wonderful (cf. RUBY-DAZZLER). [dial. ? f. intensification of dial. *bobby*, smartly dressed, in high spirits (cf. BOBBISH) + SE *dazzler*]

bobby martin n. [20C] (Aus.) a carton. [rhy. sl.]

bobby peeler n. [mid–late 19C] a policeman (cf. BOBBY; PEELER n.[1]). [Sir *Robert Peel*]

bobby rocks n. [20C] (Aus.) a pair of socks (cf. ALMOND ROCKS). [rhy. sl.]

bobby's helmet/hat n. [1930s+] the glans penis (cf. GERMAN HELMET). [BOBBY n. (1) + SE *helmet/hat*; the shape of the 'bell end']

bobby's labourers n. [late 19C] volunteers who joined up as special constables during the Fenian scares of the 1860s. [BOBBY n. (1) + SE *labourer*]

bobby soxer *n.* [1940s+] (US) a teenage girl wearing bobby-socks (cf. SOCKER n.²). [orig. describing the fans of Frank Sinatra in 1940s and thus teenage girls of the late 1940s–50s who enjoyed pop music and its ancillary pleasures]

bobby-twister *n.* [19C] a thug who will stop at nothing, even killing a policeman. [BOBBY n. (1) + SE *twist*]

bob cull *n.* [late 17C–late 18C] a pleasant, good-natured person. [BOBBISH + CULL n.¹ (4)]

bob, harry and dick *adj.* [late 19C–1900s] sick, usu. from drinking (cf. TOM AND DICK). [rhy. sl.]

Bob Hope *n.* [1960s] **1** (drugs) cannabis. **2** (Aus.) soap. [rhy. sl.; (1) *Bob Hope* = DOPE n.¹ (7); ult. f. the US comedian Bob Hope (b.1903)]

bob in *n.* (Aus./N.Z.) **1** [late 19C+] a dicing game in which all players contribute a shilling (5p). The winner then buys the round of drinks. **2** [1960s] the payment of a shilling into a common pot, esp. as used for buying drinks. [BOB n.³ + SE *in*]

bob ken *n.* [18C] (Und.) a house considered worth robbing. [BOB adj. (1) + KEN n.¹]

bobkhes/bubbkis/bubkhes/bubkis *n.* [20C] an absurd idea, an insulting sum, price or proposition; nothing (in sense of a return, a reward) esp. in show business use. [Yid. *bobkhes*, goat droppings]

bob, line and sinker *phr.* [mid-19C+] completely, wholly. [pieces of fishing tackle; cf. SE *hook, line and sinker*; *lock, stock and barrel*]]

bob-my-nag *n.* [17C] the penis. [the image of 'riding' a NAG n.¹ (2)]

bob my pal *n.* [mid-19C+] a girl (cf. ROB MY PAL). [rhy. sl. *Bob, my pal* = gal]

bobo *n.¹* [1940s] (W.I.) **1** a fool. **2** an ugly, fat oaf. [? Sp. *bobón*, a clumsy simpleton]

bobo *n.²* [1980s+] (drugs) **1** (drugs) marijuana. **2** crack cocaine. [BOBO adj.; ? BOO n.³]

bobo *adj.* [1980s+] (US campus) drunk or intoxicated with a drug. [? proper name, *Bobo* the Clown]

bobo bush *n.* [1980s+] (drugs) marijuana (cf. AFRICAN BUSH). [BOBO n.² + BUSH n.⁶]

bo-bo jockey *n.* [1940s] (US drugs) a cannabis smoker (cf. BOO). [BOBO n.² + JOCKEY n.² (3)]

bobo-johnny *n.* [20C] (W.I.) **1** a bogeyman, an imaginary monster conjured up to frighten naughty children. **2** a peasant, an unsophisticated country person (cf. ALVIN). [? Yoruba *buburu*, bad, evil + JOHNNIE n.² (1)]

bobol *n.* [1920s+] (W.I.) fraud and corruption, practised by senior figures in government, business or any position of power; thus *make/run a bobol*, to organize a fraud, *bobol(ize)*, to steal a company's or the public's funds, *bobolism*, large-scale corruption, *bobolist*, a fraudster. [? Fr. Creole *Vaval*, a masque king of the St Lucia carnival, symbolically thrown into the sea on Ash Wednesday. Orig. 1920s, the term became associated with corrupt 'speculators' trading between Martinique and St Lucia and thence to the larger world of fraud]

bob on *v.* [1920s–30s] (orig. milit.) to await anxiously. [SE *bob* v.; the image of a cork bobbing on choppy water]

bob one's baloney, to *phr.* [1990s] to masturbate (cf. ACCOST THE OSCAR MEYER). [SE *bob*, move up and down + BALONEY n.²]

bob powell *n.* [20C] (Aus.) a towel (cf. BADEN-POWELL). [rhy. sl.]

bobsey twins *n.* [1950s–60s] (US camp gay) the police, when working as a pair. [the children's adventure story characters + ref. to UK BOBBY]

bob squash *n.* [20C] **1** a wash. **2** a public convenience; thus *work the bob*, for a pickpocket to rob jackets and coats that have been hung up while people wash their hands. [rhy. sl.]

bobstain *n.* [1990s] faecal stains in one's underwear. [BOB (AND HIT) n. (2) + SE *stains*]

bobstay *n.* [late 18C+] the frenum or ligament of the penis. [naut. jargon *bobstay*, a rope that holds down the bowsprit of a ship, counteracting the upward force of the fore-mast stays]

bobstick *n.* [late 18C–mid-19C] **1** a shilling (5p). **2** a shilling's worth. [ety. unknown; ? link to BOB n.³]

bob's your rudd *phr.* [20C] (Irish) everything will be all right. [var. on BOB'S YOUR UNCLE + Irish *rud*, a thing]

bob's your uncle *phr.* [20C] everything will be absolutely fine, there'll be no worries; sometimes prefixed by *and*. [according to A.J. Langguth, *Saki* (1981), f. the apparently nepotistic choice by Tory leader Robert Cecil of his nephew Arthur Balfour as Chief Secretary for Ireland in 1900, a decision that was both surprising and unpopular]

bobtail/bob-tail/bob tail *n.¹* **1** [17C] an unpleasant person. **2** [17C+] a prostitute (cf. BANG-TAIL n.¹). [pun on SE *bobtail*, a horse or dog with its tail cut short; thus in (1) a *cur*, but in (2) cf. SE *bob*, go up and down + TAIL n.¹ (6); a horse is also good for a RIDE n.³ (1)]

bobtail *n.²* [early 19C] a dandy. [the wide skirts of his coat]

bobtail/bobtail car *n.³* [late 19C] (US) 'a small tram-car horsed by a single animal, and on which the only official is a driver, whose office it is to collect fares and generally perform the duties of conductor in addition to his own' (Farmer, *Americanisms*, 1888). [SE *bobtail*, a horse's tail that has been docked or cut short]

bobtail *adj.* [19C] (US) worthless. [poker jargon *bobtail flush*, *bobtail straight*, hands that have only 3 of the 5 cards required to make them bettable]

bobtail car see BOBTAIL n.³.

bob up *v.* [20C] to appear (unexpectedly).

bob-wire *n.* [1910s–30s] (US) barbed wire. [pron.]

Boche *n.* [20C] **1** a German, esp. a German soldier. **2** the German language. [post-WW1 use is historical, f. Fr. *caboche*, head, or *Alboche*, a modification of *Allemand*, German]

bock *n.* [20C] (US) a Bohemian, a Czech (cf. BOHUNK). [Ger. *Bock*, he-goat, or SE *bock*, a sweetish dark beer, originating in Germany (as *Eimbockbier*), brewed in winter to be drunk in spring]

boco *n.* [mid-19C+] the head. [var. on BOKO]

bocoo see BOOCOO.

bod *n.* **1** [late 18C+] a person, a 'body'. **2** [1930s+] the human body. **3** [1930s+] a corpse. **4** [1960s] (US campus) a physically attractive person of the opposite sex. **5** [1970s] the body as an object for sexual intercourse, e.g. *give out bod*, make oneself available for sex. [SE *body*]

bod *adj.* [1960s+] (US campus) outstanding, exceptional. [abbr. BODACIOUS]

bodacious/bowdacious *adj.* **1** [mid-19C+] (US) excellent, wonderful (cf. BARDACIOUS). **2** [1960s+] (US) audacious, unceremonious, insolent. **3** [1970s+] (US) exciting, impressive. **4** [1980s+] (US campus) of a young woman, attractive, esp. possessed of large breasts. [SE *bold* + *audacious*. Coined in the 19C, the term was 'relaunched' on 1970s Citizen's Band radio and with the release of the hit teen film *Bill and Ted's Excellent Adventure* (1989). Major (1994) suggests earlier US Black use, and root in Bantu *botesha*, grand, big]

bodaciously *adv.* (US) **1** [early 19C+] impressively, entirely. **2** [1930s+] extremely, very. [BODACIOUS]

bodacious tatas *n.* [1980s+] (US campus) large breasts. [BODACIOUS + TATAS]

bodaggle *n.* [1970s] (US) a masculine lesbian. [BULL-DAGGER]

bodastop *adj.* [1990s] (US teen) wonderful, excellent, but also in ironic use. [BODACIOUS + SE *fantastic*]

bodelicious *adj.* [1980s+] (US) excellent, first rate (cf. BABELICIOUS). [BODACIOUS + SE *delicious*]

bodger *n.* [1940s+] (Aus.) anything or anyone second-rate, fake or otherwise worthless. [SE *bodge*, to mend badly, to patch up]

bodger *adj.* [1940s+] (Aus.) **1** fraudulent, second-rate, worthless. **2** of names, assumed, false (cf. BODGIE). [BODGER n.]

bodgie *n.* [1950s+] (Aus.) **1** anything worthless; thus *pull a bodgie*, to pose as something one is not. **2** a misfit, a person who does not 'fit in'. **3** the equivalent of a teddy boy (cf. WIDGIE). [BODGER n.; f. the post-war black market in American-made cloth and attempts by crooked salesmen to pass off inferior cloth as this; when young men started using US accents in order to aggrandize themselves they were termed *bodgies*, a fig. ref. to the cloth]

bodice-ripper *n.* [1980s+] a historical novel (or film), with a greater than usual emphasis on sex, esp. the seduction or even rape of the heroine. [the period costumes and their fate]

bo-dick *see* BO-JACK.

bodini/budini *n.* [1960s+] (US) the penis. [Ital. *bodino*, blood sausage]

bodkin *n.*[1] [19C] the penis (cf. BAYONET). [SE *bodkin*, a large needle or small dagger, esp. a large needle-shaped instrument with a blunt, knobbed point]

bodkin *n.*[2] [19C] a person who is wedged between two others, esp. when there is room for only the original couple; thus *ride bodkin*, for a coach passenger to ride wedged between two fellows when there is insufficient room for three abreast. [SE *bodkin*; the earliest cognate use is in John Ford's *The Fancies* (1638) when it refers to the person squashed between two others in the same bed]

body *n.* **1** [1910s–60s] (US) generic for women, esp. as sex objects. **2** [1960s] (US) sexual intercourse. **3** [1950s+] (Und.) a person, esp. a suspect or wanted criminal, or one who is to be 'framed' for a crime.

body *v.* [early 19C] to hit someone in the body; thus *bodier*, a body-blow.

body bag *n.* (US) **1** [early–mid-19C] an undershirt, a (UK) vest. **2** [mid-19C] a shirt. **3** [1990s] a condom (cf. BODY-COVER).

body-basher/panel-beater *n.* [1930s+] (Aus.) a garage owner. [SE *body* (of a car) + BASH v.; i.e. panel-beating]

body-binder *n.* [early 19C] (orig. boxing) a waistcoat or a broad belt.

body companion *n.* [mid-19C] (US) a louse (cf. BODY GUARD).

body count *n.* [1970s+] (US) those people who are present. [Vietnam war jargon *body count*, the number of dead enemy bodies counted after a battle/operation]

body-cover *n.* [19C] an overcoat (cf. BODY BAG).

body exchange *n.* [1960s–70s] anywhere that people can meet in the hope of meeting a new sexual partner, e.g. a singles bar, a party (cf. BODY SHOP n.[1]).

body guard *n.* [mid-19C] (US) a louse (cf. BODY COMPANION).

body lover *n.* [1950s–60s] a homosexual who prefers rubbing and fondling a body to anal penetration or fellatio.

body of divinity bound in black calf *phr.* [mid-18C–early 19C] a parson. [a description usu. attached to a Bible]

body-packer *n.* [1990s] (drugs) a person who ingests cocaine, either in powder form or as crack in order to transport it (cf. BODY-STUFFER). [the drug is 'packed' into their body]

body queen *n.* [1960s+] (gay) one who looks primarily for partners who specialize in body-building. [SE *body* + QUEEN n.[1]]

body shop *n.*[1] [1970s+] (US) anywhere that people can meet in the hope of meeting a new sexual partner (cf. BODY EXCHANGE). [the implication is that one can 'buy' a new partner]

body shop *n.*[2] [1970s+] (US) a morgue, a cemetery. **2** [1990s] (US Black) a hospital. [a play on the SE, which, as used in (2), refers to the 'mending' of automobiles]

body-slangs *n.* [early 19C] body irons. [SE *body* + SLANG n.[2] (2)]

body-snatcher *n.* (US) **1** [late 18C–mid-19C] a bailiff. **2** [late 18C–mid-19C] a cat-stealer. **3** [late 18C–mid-19C] a cabman. **4** [early–mid-19C] a resurrectionist. **5** [early 19C–1930s] a policeman. **6** [late 19C+] an undertaker. **7** [late 19C–1930s] a promiscuous, 'forward' woman, esp. a prostitute. [ext. use of SE; (4) SE after mid-19C]

body-stuffer *n.* [1990s] (drugs) a person who ingests crack cocaine vials to avoid prosecution (cf. BODY-PACKER).

body wax *n.* [20C] human excrement. [? play on SE *ear wax*]

boep/beer-boep *n.* [1970s+] (S.Afr.) a paunch, a beer belly. [Afk. *boepens*, a paunch]

boer *n.* [1960s+] (S.Afr. Und.) any member of the S.Afr. security forces, whether in the services, the police force or the prison department. [Du. *boer*, a farmer, and among various fig. uses a pej. name for an Afrikaner]

boer baroque *n.* [1980s] (S.Afr.) vulgar, if expensive, interior decoration (cf. JEWY LOUIS). [SE *Boer* + *baroque*, 'a florid style of architectural decoration, which arose in Italy in the late Renaissance and became prevalent in Europe during the 18th century' (*OED*)]

boeretroos *n.* [20C] (S.Afr.) strong, flavoursome black coffee (cf. BULLOCKY'S DELIGHT; COCKY'S DELIGHT). [Afk., lit. 'Boer's solace']

boers *n.* [late 19C] (S.Afr.) S.Afr. whisky or brandy, distilled in the colony (cf. CAPE SMOKE). [Du. *boer*, a farmer and thus an Afrikaner]

boesman *n.* [1950s+] (S.Afr.) a derog. term of address to an Indian or Coloured person. [Afk. *boesman*, bushman]

boet/boetie/boeta *n.* (S.Afr.) **1** [mid-19C+] a brother, usu. the eldest/favourite. **2** [20C] a friendly mode of address between Whites. **3** [1970s] a pej. nickname for a Black male employee. **4** [1970s] a political fellow-traveller. **4** [1970s] an Afrikaner or any overly aggressive, macho male. [Afk. *boet*, brother]

boetie-boetie *adv.* [1950s–70s] (S.Afr.) overly friendly, using flattery with an ulterior motive, sycophantic. [BOET]

b.o.f. *n.* [1970s+] a tedious, conventional, killjoy older person. [abbr. *boring old fart*]

boff *n.*[1] (US) **1** [1920s–40s] a strong blow. **2** [1930s+] an act of sexual intercourse (cf. BANG n.[2]). [SE *buff*, a blow, stroke, buffet]

boff *n.*[2] [1940s+] (orig. entertainment) a laugh, a joke. [BOFFO n.[2]]

boff *v.* (orig. US) **1** [1920s+] to hit, to assault. **2** [1930s+] to copulate. **3** [1930s+] to masturbate. [BOFF n.[1]]

boffer *n.* [1930s+] one who engages in masturbation. [BOFF v. (3)]

boffer's bridge *n.* [1990s] the anus. [BOFF v. (3) + SE *bridge*]

boffin *n.* [1940s+] any form of scientific expert, orig. those RAF scientists who were working on radar. [ety. unknown, although according to Robert Watson-Watt (1892–1973), the inventor of radar, the term 'has something to do with an obsolete type of aircraft called the Baffin, something to do with that odd bird, the Puffin' (*Three Steps to Victory*, 1957]

boffo *n.*[1] (US) [1920s+] $1. [ety. unknown]

boffo *n.*[2] [1960s+] a big laugh, a very funny joke. [BOFFO adj.]

boffo *adj.* [1940s+] (US) superb, magnificent, excellent, usu. show business use (cf. SOCKO). [fig. use of BOFF v. (1) + sfx. -O]

boffo! *excl.* [1940s] (US) an excl. indicating suddenness, abruptness. [BOFFO adj.]

boffola *n.* [1910s+] (orig. US) a laugh, esp. a loud 'belly laugh', usu. show business use (cf. BOFF n.[2]). [BOFFO adj. + sfx. -OLA]

boff one's boner, to *phr.* [1990s] to masturbate. [BOFF v. (3) + BONER n.[3]]

bog *n.* [late 18C+] a lavatory (cf. BOGGARD; BOG-SHOP, DIKE n.²). [BOGHOUSE; 'a low word, scarcely found in literature, however common in coarse colloquial language' *OED*]

bog *v.*¹ **1** [26C] to defecate. **2** [16C] to defile with excrement. **3** [1960s+] to make a mess of. [SE *bog*, to be enmired in a bog]

bog *v.*² [1960s+] to wet the end of a cigarette while smoking it. [SE *bog*, a marsh]

bogan *n.* [1980s+] (Aus./N.Z.) **1** an uncouth person. **2** one who is mindlessly conventional. **3** a social misfit, a 'nerd'. [ety. unknown; ? link to BODGIE]

bogard *v.* [1960s+] (drugs) to monopolize or smoke too much of a cannabis cigarette. [var. on BOGART v. (2)]

bogart *n.* [1950s–70s] (US Black) a bully; thus *pull a bogart*, to act tough, *jump bogart*, to become aggressive. [Humphrey *Bogart* (1899–1957), whose roles often portrayed a gangster or tough-guy]

bogart *v.* **1** [1950s+] (orig. US Black) to act aggressively, in a bullying manner. **2** [1960s–70s] to retain something selfishly, esp. to hold on to a marijuana cigarette for longer than one's companions feel is fair. [BOGART n.]

bogart a joint, to *phr.* **1** [1960s+] to salivate on a marijuana cigarette. **2** [1960s+] (drugs) to take more than one's fair share of a cigarette. **3** [1970s+] (US campus) to steal, to take an unfair share. [BOGART v. + JOINT n.⁴ (2); the legendary fact of Humphrey *Bogart*'s alleged greediness in this area and the sl. it generated was popularized in the film *Easy Rider* (1969)]

bog bamboo *n.* [1970s+] the penis.

bogblocker *n.* [1980s+] a general term to denote anything particularly unpleasant. [BOG n. + SE *blocker*; the image is of some obstruction, probably faecal, blocking a lavatory]

bogbrush *n.* [1960s+] **1** a lavatory brush. **2** a cropped, spiky haircut, supposedly resembling a lavatory brush. [BOG n. + SE *brush*]

bog bumf *n.* [20C] lavatory paper. [BOG n. + BUMF]

bogel *v.* [1990s] (US campus) to do nothing. [? BOGLE]

bogey/bogy *n.*¹ [early–mid-19C] the devil (cf. OLD BOGEY). [? 16C SE *bog/bogle/boggard*, a goblin, a terrifying creature, source of dread]

bogey/bogy *n.*² **1** [mid-19C+] a landlord. **2** [1920s+] a policeman, a detective. [BOGEY n.¹; play on this devilishness]

bogey *n.*³ [mid-19C+] (Aus.) **1** a bathe. **2** a bathing-place, a bath. [? Abor.]

bogey/bogy *n.*⁴ [1900s–30s] a heating stove. [? the blackness of the metal/the 'hellish' fire inside]

bogey/bogy *n.*⁵ [1930s+] **1** a piece of dried mucus. **2** a nickname given to a man with prominent, wide nostrils. [? SE *boggy*, soft, spongy; thus the consistency of such pieces of mucus]

bogey *n.*⁶ [1940s–50s] (US) a Black person. [BOOGIE n.²]

bogey *v.*¹ [mid-19C+] to bathe; thus *bogying*, bathing. [BOGEY n.¹]

bogey *v.*² [1980s+] (US) to act greedily, esp. in consumption of drugs. [BOGART v.]

bog-eyed *adj.* [1940s+] having tired eyes, the result of too little sleep or too much alcohol. [one's eye seem 'muddy']

boggard *n.* [16C] a privy (cf. BOG n.; BOG-SHOP). [var. on BOGHOUSE]

bogger *n.* [20C] a derog. term for an Irish person (cf. BOGTROTTER). [SE *bog*, the supposed orig. dwelling-place of many immigrants]

boggeral/boggerall/bokkerol *n.* [1960s+] (S.Afr.) nothing at all. [pron. of BUGGER ALL]

boggin' *adj.* [1950s+] of a film, X-rated. [ety. unknown]

bogging *n.* [20C] getting oneself filthy. [BOG n.]

boggins *n.* [mid-19C–1920s] (Aus.) plenty, a great deal. [*AND* states 'ety. unknown', but ? BOG IN v.]

boggle *n.* [mid-19C] a mess, a mistake, an error. [BOGGLE v.]

boggle *v.* [19C] (US) to blunder, to do something very badly (cf. BOG v.¹). [SE *boggle*, to fumble]

boggle-de-botch/boggledybotch *n.* [early–mid-19C] a mess, a blunder, a bungling. [BOGGLE n. + SE *botch*, a mess, an error]

boggling *n.* [19C] (US) **1** hesitating unnecessarily. **2** delaying, finding something difficult. [? BOGGLE v.]

boghopper *n.* [20C] **1** a derog. term for an Irish person (cf. BOGTROTTER). **2** (US) a peasant, an unsophisticated rural person. [SE *bog* + *hopper*]

boghouse *n.* [late 17C+] a lavatory, a privy. [BOG n. + SE *house*]

bogie *n.* [mid-19C+] the devil (cf. BOGEY n.¹).

bogie house *n.* [late 19C+] (Aus.) a bathroom. [BOGEY n.³ + SE *house*]

bog-in *n.* [1910s+] (Aus.) a heavy meal. [BOG IN v.]

bog in/into *v.* (orig. Aus.) **1** [late 19C+] to eat heartily. **2** [late 19C+] to work hard. **3** [1910s+] to get started. **4** [1910s+] not to stand on any ceremony. [? SE *bog* n., the image is of 'getting stuck in']

bogish/boguish *adj.* [1930s–40s] (US Black) bogus. [var. on SE]

boglander *n.* [17C+] an Irishman (cf. BOGHOPPER; BOGTROTTER). [SE *bog* + *land*]

bog Latin *n.* [late 18C–1900s] fake Latin (cf. APOTHECARIES' LATIN). [the term is found as synon. with SE *shelta*, a form of jargon used by tinkers, which is based on Gaelic and rendered further incomprehensible to non-adepts by the inversion or arbitrary alteration of initial consonants]

bogle *n.* [1990s+] (W.I./UK Black teen) a dance originated by Jamaican Gerald Levy in 1991 and popularized in song by artists such as Buju Banton. [named a Jamaican national hero; its main characteristic is the bending backwards of one's body]

bogman/bog person *n.* [1980s+] (Irish) a general term of abuse, presuming rural origins and general backwardness (cf. BOGTROTTER).

bog off *v.* [1950s+] (orig. RAF) to go away, usually as a dismissive excl. *bog off!* [BOG n.; euph. for FUCK OFF!]

bog-oranges *n.* [19C] potatoes. [racial stereotyping, the main constituent of the Irish diet is supposedly potatoes (cf. BOGTROTTER)]

bog person see BOGMAN.

bog queen *n.* [1960s+] (gay) a gay man who frequents public toilets for sex. [BOG n. + QUEEN n.¹]

bog-rat *n.* [20C] an Irish person. [BOGTROTTER + SE *rat*]

bogroll *n.* [20C] lavatory paper. [BOG n. + SE *roll*]

bog-shop *n.* [mid-19C–1900s] an outside lavatory (cf. BOGHOUSE). [BOG n. + SE *shop*]

bog standard *n.* [1980s+] average. [BOG n. + SE *standard*]

bogtrotter *n.* [late 17C+] a derog. term for an Irish person (cf. BOGHOPPER). [lit. 'one who runs through the bogs'; thus those who live among the peat bogs of Ireland. B.E. states that the orig. use was 'Scotch or North Country Moss-trooopers or High-Way Men'. Camden (1605) used the term to describe the inhabitants of the 'debtatable' borders between Scotland and England]

bogue *n.*¹ [19C] (US) a native of Florida (cf. ROSIN-HEEL). [Choctaw *bog*, a stream or creek; thus the swamps that typify the topography of southern Florida]

bogue *n.*² [1960s+] (US drugs) the sickness that follows an addict's withdrawal from regular narcotic use. [ety. unknown; ? BOGUS n.; Smitherson suggests Hausa *boko*, bad, fake]

bogue *n.*³ [1970s] (US) a stupid, unpleasant person. [BOGUS adj.]

bogue *adj.* **1** [1950s+] (US teen) fake, unsophisticated, naïve. **2** [1960s+] (US campus/teen) disgusting, unappealing. **3** [1960s–70s] (US drugs) suffering from narcotic withdrawal symptoms. [BOGUE n.²]

boguish *see* BOGISH.

bogus *n.* **1** [late 18C+] counterfeit money. **2** [early–mid-19C] (US) a machine used to produce counterfeit money. **3** [mid-19C+] (US) a fake, a spurious imitation. [note *OED*: 'Dr S. Willard, of Chicago ... quotes from the Painesville (Ohio) *Telegraph* of July 6 and Nov. 2, 1827, the word bogus as a n. applied to an apparatus for coining false money. Mr Eber D. Howe, who was then editor of that paper, describes in his *Autobiography* (1878) the discovery of such a piece of mechanism in the hands of a gang of coiners at Painesville, in May 1827; it was a mysterious-looking object, and some one in the crowd styled it a "bogus", a designation adopted in the succeeding numbers of the paper. Dr Willard considers this to have been short for "tantrabogus", a word familiar to him from his childhood, and which in his father's time was commonly applied in Vermont to any ill-looking object. He points out that "tantarabobs" is given in Halliwell as a Devonshire word for the devil; bogus seems thus to be related to bogy etc.' Farmer (1889), posits an Italian swindler called Borghese, working across the southwest US distributing fictitious notes, cheques etc, *c*.1837; this surname was gradually changed to Borges and thence bogus. The writer J.R. Lowell, also cited by Farmer, opted for Fr. *bagasse*, the refuse of sugar cane after the juice was extracted]

bogus *adj.* [1930s+] a general term of disapproval, unpleasant, undesirable, untrustworthy, unfair. [BOGUS n.]

bogus beef *n.* [1930s+] (US Black) a groundless complaint. [BOGUS adj. + BEEF n.²]

bogy *n. see* BOGEY n.¹, n.², n.⁴, n.⁵.

bohak/bohawk *see* BOHUNK.

bohd *n.* [1980s+] (drugs) **1** marijuana. **2** phencyclidine (cf. ACE n.³). [ety. unknown]

boheme/bohemian *n.* [1980s+] (US campus) one who identifies with the 1960s. [SE *Bohemian*, an artist, literary man or actor, who leads a free, vagabond or irregular life, despising accepted conventions]

Bohemie *n.* [20C] (US) a Czech or Slavic immigrant (cf. BOHUNK). [SE *Bohemian*, i.e. Czechoslovak]

boho *n.*¹ [1920s–30s] (US) a Czech immigrant (cf. BOHUNK; BOOTCHKEY). [abbr. SE *Bohemian*, a Czechoslovak]

boho *n.*² [1950s+] (US campus) one who identifies with the 1960s (cf. BOHEME). [abbr. SE *Bohemian*, a literary/social 'vagabond']

bohunk/bohak/bohawk *n.* (US) **1** [late 19C+] a Slav immigrant f. Eastern Europe. **2** [1910s+] an oafish, dull, if muscular person (cf. HONKIE). **3** [1930s+] an East European language. [SE *Bohemian* + *Hungarian*]

bohunkus/bohunky *n.* [1940s+] (US) the buttocks, thus fig. oneself, e.g. in phr. *get your bohunkus out of here!* [BOHUNK (2) + ? echoic of buttocks slapping onto a hard seat]

boil *v.* **1** [late 16C–early 17C] (Und.) to find out, to unmask, to betray (cf. HOT WATER; SMOKE v.¹). **2** [mid-19C–1930s] (US) to rush along. **3** [1950s] (US) to annoy, to infuriate.

boil down *v.* [late 19C] (US Black) to correct or rebuke.

boiled *n.* [early–mid-19C] *boiled* beef or *boiled* mutton. [abbr.]

boiled *adj.* **1** [late 19C+] drunk (cf. BASTED). **2** [1920s+] angry, furious. [fig. uses of SE]

boiled dog *n.* [1910s+] (Aus./N.Z.) snobbery, stand-offishness, 'side'. [? SE *boiled shirt* + PUT ON DOG]

boiled lobster *n.* [early 19C] a soldier (cf. UNBOILED LOBSTER). [LOBSTER n.¹ (1); cooked lobsters turn red/pink]

boiled-owlish *adj.* [late 19C] having a washed-out complexion with staring, sleepy eyes, the result of working all night.

boiled rag *n.* [1910s+] (Aus.) a starched dress shirt. [joc. var. on BOILED SHIRT]

boiled shirt *n.* [mid-19C+] a starched dress shirt (cf. FRIED SHIRT). [such shirts were literally boiled in the wash to remove the starch]

boiled stuff *n.* [late 16C–early 17C] prostitutes, viewed collectively. [used by Shakespeare in *Cymbeline* (1610); the ref. is to the sweating tubs, used to treat venereal diseases]

boiler *n.*¹ (US) **1** [20C] a tobacco pipe. **2** [1910s–50s] an automobile. [the steam or smoke that pours from both]

boiler *n.*² [1920s–60s] (US) the stomach. [play on SE]

boiler *n.*³ [1920s+] **1** an old woman, without any remaining sexual appeal (cf. OLD BOILER). **2** an unattractive woman (cf. CHICK n.⁴). **3** (US) a quarrelsome, irascible person. [the old, tough birds used for boiling chickens]

boiler acid/compound *n.* [1940s–60s] (US) extremely unpleasant tasting coffee.

boilermaker *n.* **1** [1920s+] a 50/50 mix of mild and brown ale. **2** [1940s–50s] (US) beer with a whisky chaser, the US working man's traditional drink. [? the preferred drink of a SE *boiler-maker*, or strong enough to clean a boiler. Subseq. use of **2** is SE]

boilerplate *n.* [20C] (US) clichéd writing. [legal and journalistic jargon *boilerplate*, standard practice used by lawyers (the regular clauses in any contract) or the media (the basic syndicated wire-service stories used throughout the US newspaper system)]

boiler-plated *adj.* [20C] absolutely dependable and consistent (cf. BOILERPLATE). [SE *boiler-plate*, the iron used in the manufacture of boilers]

boiler-room *n.* [1930s+] (US) any room full of noisy, energetic activity, e.g. a political campaign headquarters, a newspaper cityroom, a room used by illegal bookmakers, stock swindlers or confidence tricksters.

boilers/Brompton boilers, the *n.* [mid–late 19C] the buildings of the Victoria and Albert Museum (orig. the Kensington Museum and School of Art) in Brompton Road, London. [their supposed resemblance to a large boiler, and their being covered in sheet iron]

boiling *n.*¹ [early–mid-17C] a betrayal, an unmasking. [BOIL v. (1)]

boiling *n.*² [1930s+] absolutely everything. [abbr. WHOLE BOILING LOT]

boiling *adj.* [late 19C] (US) drunk (cf. BOILED adj.).

boiling-out *n.* [20C] (US) a scolding, a telling-off.

boilo *n.* [1930s] (US) hot, illicit whisky. [SE *boil* + sfx. -o]

boil off the stomach, to *phr.* [20C] (US) to vomit copiously.

boil/chew one's cabbage twice, to *phr.* [late 19C+] (US) to repeat oneself.

boil one's lobster, to *phr.* [late 18C–early 19C] for a clergyman to become a soldier (cf. BOILED LOBSTER; LOBSTER n.¹; RAW LOBSTER). [the unboiled lobster is blue-black, thus resembling a clergyman's black garb; the boiled lobster turns red, recalling the soldier's scarlet uniform]

boilover *n.* [late 19C+] (Aus.) in sport, spec. horse-racing, an upset, the failure of a favourite to win.

boil over *v.* [mid–late 19C] to lose one's temper; thus *at/at the boiling point*, on the verge of losing one's temper. [SE in 20C]

boil-pricker *n.* [20C] (US) a pointed shoe (cf. WINKLEPICKERS). [SE *boil*, a pustule + *pricker*]

boil the billy, to *phr.* [1950s+] (Aus.) to make a cup of tea. [an actual 'billy' (traditionally associated with cooking in the open) need not be used; the term can be applied to a kettle]

boil-up n. [1940s] (Aus.) an argument. [one's temper *boils up* (and over)]

boil water v. [20C] (US) to waste time on trifles. [the 'watched pot never boils']

boing-boing n. [1960s] (US) a tourist (cf. RUBBERNECK n.). [SE *boing*, the sound of elastic snapping back; the image is of the head twanging backwards and forwards as its owner gazes at the big city sights]

boink v. [1980+] (US) to have intercourse with (cf. BANG v.¹). [BONK v.]

bo-ink-um n. [19C] guts, stamina, endurance (cf. SPIZZERINK-TUM). [ety. unknown]

boja n. [1950s] (W.I.) an untrustworthy person. [? BUDGE (as sneak thief) or BODGER/SE *botcher*]

bo-jack/-dick n. [1990s] (US Black) **1** a form of address to a male. **2** the scrotum, the penis (cf. BOZACK). [BO n.¹ + JACK n.⁸ (2)/DICK n.⁵ (1)]

bok n. (S.Afr.) **1** [1950s] a young woman, a girlfriend. **2** [1970s+] an enthusiast; thus *bok for*, 'up for', game for. **3** [1970s+] a hero, a masculine or athletic male. [Afk. *bok*, a 'flame', a beau]

bokbaard n. [1910s+] (S.Afr.) a goatee baard. [Afk. *bok*, a goat + *baard*, a beard]

bokbaardjie n. [1960s+] (S.Afr.) a goatee beard (cf. BOK-BAARD).

bokdrol n. [1970s+] (S.Afr.) **1** a chocolate-covered peanut. **2** anything, e.g. a hairstyle, that resembles a pile of goat droppings. [Afk. *bok*, goat + *drol*, dropping]

boke n. [mid-19C] (US) the nose. [BOKO]

bokin-a-smowl n. [1980s+] (US drugs) smoking a pipe or other container filled with cannabis (cf. SMOKE A BOWL). [joc. reversal]

bokkerol see BOGGERAL.

bokkie n. [1950s+] (S.Afr.) **1** an affectionate form of address, esp. to woman. **2** a girlfriend. [Afk. *bok*, a kid (antelope, goat etc) + dimin. sfx. -*ie*]

boko/koboko n. [mid-19C+] **1** the nose. **2** (Aus.) a person or animal blind in one eye. [(1) ? BEAK n. (2) and/or COCONUT n.¹. Ware suggests an alternative ety.: the clown Joseph Grimaldi's (1779–1837) trademark tapping of his nose with the comment, *C'est beaucoup*, that's plenty]

boko-smasher n. [late 19C–1900s] a thug. [BOKO + SE *smasher*, lit. 'nose-smasher']

boldacious adj. (US Black) excessive behaviour (over-aggressive, arrogant, unrestrained etc) that is inappropriate for a situation. [BODACIOUS]

bold as a miller's shirt phr. [late 18C] very bold. [pvb. 'bold as a miller's shirt, which every days takes a rogue by the collar']

bold as brass adj. [late 18C+] arrogant, impudent, outspoken, shameless. [var. on SE *brazen*]

bold thing, the n. [1980s+] (Irish) sexual intercourse (cf. WILD THING).

boldrumptious adj. [late 19C–1900s] presumptuous. [SE *bold* + *rumpus*]

Bolivian marching powder n. [1970s+] (drugs) cocaine (cf. BOUNCING POWDER; GERMAN MARCHING PILLS). [Bolivia, like Colombia, is a major source of cocaine]

bollemakiesie adv. [1920s+] (S.Afr.) head-over-heels. [Afk. *bollemakiesie*, a somersault]

bollicking adj. [1920s] (US) a general intensifier, e.g. *bollicking great*, *bollicking awful* (cf. BLOODY adj.; BLOOMING). [BALLOCKS n.²]

bollicky adj. [20C] naked (cf. BOLLICKY BARE-ASS; STARK BALLOCK NAKED). [BALLOCKS n.²]

bollicky bare-ass phr. [20C] absolutely naked (cf. STARK BALLOCK NAKED). [BALLOCKS n.² + BARE-ASS]

bollicky bill adj. [late 19C+] naked. [*Bollicky Bill (the Sailor)*, a character in a coarse late 19C song]

bollicky naked see BOLLOCKY NAKED.

bollinger bolshevik n. [1980s+] one who preaches socialism but espouses a capitalist lifestyle (cf. CADILLAC COMMMIE; CHAMPAGNE SOCIALIST; LIMOUSINE LIBERAL; PARLOUR PINK; PINK n.⁴). [*Bollinger* champagne]

bollix n. [1930s+] (Irish) an unpleasant person, esp. as (*right*) *old bollix*. [fig. use of BALLOCKS n.¹]

bollix v. [1930s+] (US) to make a mess of, to do badly. [var. on BALLOCKS v.¹]

bollixed/bollixed up adj. [20C] (US) **1** ruined, messed up, performed very badly. **2** drunk. [BALLOCKS v.¹]

bollock n. **1** [mid-18C+] a testicle, usu. pl. (cf. BALLOCK n.). **2** [1970s+] (society) a ball (hunt, charity etc). [BALLOCK n.; (2) is pun on (1)]

bollock v.¹ see BALLOCK v.

bollock v.² [1930s+] to reprimand, to tell off. [var. on BALLOCKS v.²]

bollockbag n. [1990s] the scrotum, container of testicles. [BALLOCK n. + SE *bag*]

bollockbrain n. [1960s+] a general term of abuse (cf. BAKE-BRAIN; DICKHEAD). [BALLOCK n. (1) + sfx. -*brain*]

bollocking n. [1910s+] a severe telling off (cf. BALLOCKING). [BALLOCK v.]

bollock naked adj. [1950s+] totally naked, and thus revealing one's genitals (cf. BALL NAKED; STARK BALLOCK). [BALLOCKS n.² + SE *naked*]

bollocko adj. [1950s+] naked (cf. BOLLOCKY). [BOLLOCK (NAKED) + sfx. -O]

bollocks n. see BALLOCKS n.

bollocks v. see BALLOCKS v.¹.

bollocks! excl. [20C] rubbish, nonsense! (cf. BALLS!; BAL-LOCKS!). [BALLOCK n. (1)]

bollocksed/bollixed up adj. [1910s+] (UK/US) in a mess, in a muddle. [BALLOCKS v.¹]

bollocky/bollicky naked adj. [1950s+] (Aus./US) stark naked (cf. BOLLOCKO). [BALLOCKS n.² + SE *naked*]

bollock yoghurt n. [1990s] semen (cf. BABY GRAVY). [BOLLOCK n. + SE *yoghurt*]

bollox see BALLOCKS n.².

bollux see BALLOCKS v.¹.

Bolly n. [1980s+] *Boll*inger champagne. [abbr.]

bolly dog n. [17C] a bailiff; thus a prototype policeman. [? *bolly*, hobgoblin, itself based in Lancashire dial. *bogle*]

bollywash/bollywog n. [late 19C+] nonsense (cf. BOTTLE WASH). [? var. on BELLY WASH n.²]

boloney see BALONEY.

bolshie/bolshy n. **1** [1910s+] a Bolshevik. **2** [1920s+] a left-winger, a socialist. **3** [1920s+] an unconventional person (judged by a conservative), an opponent of the status quo. [abbr. Rus. *Bolshevik*, the majority; 'a member of that part of the Russian Social-Democratic Party which took Lenin's side in the split that followed the second Congress of the party in 1903, seized power in the 'October' Revolution of 1917, and was subsequently renamed the (Russian) Communist Party' (*OED*)]

bolshie adj. [1920s+] uncooperative, obstructive, subversive, left-wing. [BOLSHIE n.]

bolshy see BOLSHIE n.

bolster-pudding n. [late 19C+] roly-poly pudding. [its supposed resemblance to a *bolster*]

bolt n.¹ [mid-19C] the throat. [? SE *bolt*, to swallow hastily, to gulp down whole]

bolt n.² [mid–late 19C] (US campus) **1** the act of deliberately missing a class or meeting. **2** the cancellation of a class or meeting.

bolt *n.*[3] [1980s+] (drugs) **1** phencyclidine (cf. ACE n.[3]). **2** isobutyl nitrite. [tradename for amyl nitrite]

bolt *v.* **1** [early 19C+] to leave. **2** [mid–late 19C] (US campus) to cut a class. [(1) 20C use SE; use of SE *bolt*, a missile, as an image of moving at speed]

bolter/bolter of Whitefriars/the Mint *n.*[1] [17C–early 19C] (Und.) 'one that doth but peep out of Whitefriars, and retire again like a rabbit out of his hole' (Shadwell, *The Squire of Alsatia*) (cf. ALSATIA). [SE *bolter*, a fugitive from justice. *Whitefriars*, near St Paul's Cathedral, and the *Mint*, near Southwark, were both well-known refuges for 17C–18C villains]

bolter *n.*[2] [early 19C+] one who flees their obligations and responsibilities; thus esp. a woman who runs away from her husband, home and family. [SE *bolt*, to run off, esp. used of horses and, as such, suitable for the upper/upper-middle class milieu in which BOLTER is used. The *locus classicus* is in Nancy Mitford's novel *The Pursuit of Love* (1945), where an errant figure is known simply as 'The Bolter']

bolter's chance *n.* [1940s+] (Aus.) an outside chance; thus *not have a bolter's chance*, to have no chance at all. [SAusE *bolter*, a fugitive convict, an absconder]

bolt from the blue *n.* [late 19C] anything wholly unexpected. usu. unpleasant. [the image is of a thunderbolt; 20C use SE]

bolt-in-tun *v.* [early 19C] to run off, to escape; found in such deliberately oblique phrases as *he's gone to bolt-in-tun* or *the bolt-in-tun is concerned*. [var. on BOLT v. (1); *Bolt-in-Tun*, a well-known London inn]

boltop *phr.* [1940s+] *better on lips than on paper*, written over an 'X' (signifying a kiss) (cf. BURMA; EGYPT phr.; I.L.U.V.M.; ITALY; L.Y.K.A.H.; NORWICH; SWALK). [abbr.]

boltsprit *n.* [17C–18C] the nose; thus *break one's boltsprit*, to lose one's nose as a result of syphilis. [SE *bowsprit*, a large spar extending from the stem of a vessel, to which the foremast stays are fastened]

bolt street *n.* [early 19C] an escape (cf. BOLT-IN-TUN). [play on BOLT v. (1)]

bolt the moon *see* SHOOT THE MOON.

bolus *n.* [late 18C–late 19C] an apothecary. [SE *bolus*, a large pill, part of their stock-in-trade]

boman *n.* [17C–18C] a gallant, a bold fellow. [? Fr. *beau*, good-looking + SE *man*]

bomb *n.*[1] **1** [1910s+] (US) a surprise event, a sensational development. **2** [1950s+] a large sum of money. **3** [1950s] (US) a very sexy woman (cf. BOMBSHELL). **4** [1960s+] (orig. theatrical) a major success. **5** [1960s+] (US, orig. theatrical) a disaster, a flop. **6** [1970s+] (US) a hard blow (with a fist).

bomb *n.*[2] **1** [1950s+] (orig. Aus./N.Z./US) a dilapidated, run-down old car. **2** [1950s–70s] (US) a fast car.

bomb *n.*[3] (drugs) **1** [1950s+] a very large and potent cannabis cigarette. **2** [1960s+] any form of pill containing sleep-inducing or depressant drugs. **3** [1960s–70s] heroin of well-above-average purity. **4** [1980s+] crack cocaine. **5** [1990s] (US) a package of drugs.

bomb, the *n.*[4] [1990s] (US Black) the best. [BOMB n.[1]]

bomb *v.*[1] **1** [1940s+] (Aus.) to dope a horse. **2** [1960s+] (US) to hit hard. **3** [1970s] (US) to criticize harshly. **4** [1980s+] (US Black) to spray-paint a subway car, a building or similar space with graffiti.

bomb *v.*[2] [1950s+] to move, esp. to drive fast, usu. as *bomb along, bomb down* (the road), *bomb off, bomb around*, to rush around (aimlessly).

bomb *v.*[3] **1** [1960s+] (US) to fail, to do badly. **2** [1970s] (US) of machinery or other equipment, to break down, to malfunction.

Bombay fornicator *n.* [20C] (Anglo-Ind.) a wickerwork chair with arms and an extended footrest. [presumably long enough to double as a bed]

bombazine *see* BUMBAZINE.

bomb bandit *n.* [1990s] a homosexual (cf. ARSE BANDIT). [BUM BANDIT]

bombed *adj.* **1** [1950s+] (orig. US) drunk (cf. BASTED). **2** [1960s+] (orig. US) intoxicated by a drug. **3** [1980s+] (US) absolutely exhausted.

bombed out *adj.*[1] [20C] (Irish) **1** jilted. **2** sent on one's way, rejected.

bombed out *adj.*[2] [1950s+] overcome by an excess of drugs. [BOMBED adj. (2)]

bomber *n.*[1] (drugs) **1** [1950s+] a barbiturate or an amphetamine drug (cf. BLACK BOMBER; BLUE BOMBER). **2** [1950s+] a very large and potent cannabis cigarette. **3** [1960s+] any form of pill. [resemblance]

bomber *n.*[2] [1980s+] (US teen) a loud breaking of wind.

bombers *n.* [1970s] (US) the female breasts (cf. ARTILLERY n.[3]).

bombhead *n.*[1] [1950s–60s] a happy-go-lucky, eccentric person. [BOMB v.[2] + sfx. -HEAD (1)]

bombhead *n.*[2] [1990s] the head of the penis. [? resemblance to the shape of the explosive]

bombido *n.* [1960s+] (drugs) **1** injectable amphetamine (cf. A n.[2]; BAM n.[3]; BOMBITA). **2** heroin, esp. when mixed with cocaine. **3** a form of depressant. [Sp. *bombido*, a little bomb]

bombita *n.* [1980s+] (drugs) **1** amphetamine (cf. A n.[2]). **2** methamphetamine, a compound 'designer drug' made from ingredients easily extracted from over-the-counter drugs (cf. BUSINESSMAN'S TRIP; CHALK n.[6]; CHRIS; CHRISTY; GLASS n.[3]; ICE n.[5]; ICING). **3** a mix of heroin and cocaine. [Sp. *bombita*, a little bomb]

bombo *n.* [1940s+] (Aus.) cheap wine, methylated spirits or a combination of the two. [SE *bomb* + sfx. -O (4); it 'knocks one out'. Note SE *bumbo*, 'A liquor composed of rum, sugar, water and nutmeg' (*OED*)]

bombo-claat/-cloth *see* BUMBO-CLAAT.

bomb off *v.* [1970s+] of machinery, to break down. [ext. of BOMB v.[3]]

bombosity *n.* [20C] (US) the buttocks. [BUM n.[2]]

bomb out *v.* [1970s] **1** (US) to fail to make an expected appearance. **2** (US campus) to perform poorly (in an examination). [BOMB v.[3]]

bomb-proof *adj.* [mid-19C+] (orig. US milit.) untouchable, absolutely secure and safe.

bombs *n.* [1960s–70s] (US) the female breasts (cf. ARTILLERY n.[3]; BOMBERS).

bombs away *n.* [1980s+] (drugs) heroin. [orig. milit.; its effect on one's brain/central nervous system]

bombshell *n.* **1** [1930s+] (orig. US) a very sexy woman, esp. as *blonde bombshell*. **2** [1960s+] a shock, a surprise, usu. unpleasant; thus *drop a bombshell*, to deliver such a shock. [fig. uses of SE]

bomb squad *n.* [1980s+] (drugs) a group of crack cocaine dealers. [BOMB n.[3] (4) + SE *squad*]

bombsville *n.* [1950s–60s] any kind of failure in life. [BOMB n.[1] (5) + sfx. -VILLE]

bomb the German helmet, to *phr.* [1990s] to masturbate. [BOMB v.[1] (2) + GERMAN HELMET]

bommy-knocker *see* DONGER-KNOCKER.

bona *n.* [late 19C–1930s] a woman. [Ital. *buona*, a good woman]

bona *adj.* [mid-19C+] (Ling. Fr./Polari) good, pleasant, agreeable. [Ital. *buono*, good]

bona *adv.* [mid-19C+] (Ling. Fr./Polari) very. [Ital. *buono*, good]

bona fide *n.* [1910s–50s] (Irish) **1** a genuine traveller, as defined by the WW1 Defence of the Realm Act, which allowed anyone who had genuinely travelled 3 miles to be served drink at any hour of the day or night; thus *phr. do the bona* *fide*, to travel the requisite distance in order to indulge in after-hours drinking. **2** one who was enjoying such extending drinking time. **3** the premises that provide the drink. [Lat. *bona fide*, in good faith; the act was amended to restrict the drinking to 2 hours after closing time (10 p.m.) and 3 miles beyond the city limits; it was abolished on 4 July 1960]

bona fide *adj.* [20C] (Aus.) terrified. [rhy. sl.]

bonanza *n.* [mid-19C+] (orig. US) good luck, esp. in quantity and unexpected. [Sp. *bonanza*, good weather, prosperity. orig. applied to wealth taken from the silver mines of the Comstock lode in US]

bona roba *n.* [17C] a prostitute. [Ital. *bona roba*, a fine dress]

bonaroo/bonneroo/bonny-roo *adj.* [1920s+] (US prison) excellent, first-rate; thus *bonaroos*, special items of clothing, laundered clothing. [Cajun; thus Fr. *bon*, good]

bonce *n.* **1** [late 19C+] the head. **2** [20C] a hat. [SE *bonce*, a large marble]

bondage *n.* [1940s] (US Black/Harlem) debts.

bonds *n.* [1960s+] (US) the clothes with which a pimp bedecks his working women. [since his money has paid for them, this 'binds' the women to him]

bone *n.*[1] (US) **1** [mid-19C] a gambling chip. **2** [1960s] a (loaded) die, usu. in pl.; thus phr. *roll the bones*, to play dice. **3** [1970s] a domino, usu. in pl. [the use of ivory in the manufacture]

bone *n.*[2] [mid–late 19C] a subscriber's ticket for the opera. [Fr. *abonnement*, a subscription. Note the small ivory disc, also called a *bone*, issued by theatre managers to favoured friends and acquaintances]

bone *n.*[3] [late 19C] (US campus) a very hard-working student. [BONE v.[3] + ref. to *Bohn's Classical Library*]

bone *n.*[4] **1** [late 19C+] (US) $1. **2** [late 19C] a bribe. [SE *throw one a bone*]

bone *n.*[5] [1910s] (US) a fool, a dullard, an idiot (cf. BONEHEAD). [the hardness of a *bone*]

bone *n.*[6] **1** [1910s+] the erect penis, also as *bone-on* (cf. BONE PHONE; HARD-ON; JIGGLING BONE). **2** [late 19C] a thin man.

bone *n.*[7] [1910s+] (US Black) a woman.

bone *n.*[8] [1940s] a person of mixed race, esp. Anglo-Irish-Black. [BONES *n.*[1]; they are also 'black and white']

bone *n.*[9] [1940s] (US) something annoying or irritating. [SE *bone in one's throat*]

bone *n.*[10] **1** [1970s+] (US drugs) a cannabis cigarette. **2** [1980s+] (Black) a cigarette that mixes tobacco and crack cocaine. **3** [1990s] a $50 piece of crack. [the whiteness of the cigarette/crack]

bone *n.*[11] [1980s+] (W.I./UK/US Black teen) one's core, one's soul.

bone *v.*[1] **1** [17C+] (Und.) to arrest, to seize; thus *boned*, arrested, captured. **2** [17C+] to rob, to steal; thus *bone the fence*, to find out where goods have been hidden by a receiver (cf. FENCE *n.*[1]) and then steal them. **3** [19C+] (Und.) to interrogate. **4** [mid-19C] (US) to betray, to inform against. **5** [mid-19C+] (US) to beg for (cf. JAWBONE v.). **6** [mid-19C+] to nag, to pester. **7** [1900s] (US) to annoy, to infuriate (cf. BONE *n.*[9]). **8** [1900s] (US) to look for and find. **9** [1980s] (US teen) to victimize, to treat unfairly. [? the image of a dog finding and/or worrying a bone]

bone *v.*[2] [mid-19C+] (US, orig. milit.) to work hard, also extended as *bone down, bone in, bone through* etc. [? the use of a flat bone surface to polish one's boots to a shine]

bone/bone up on *v.*[3] [mid-19C+] (orig. US) to learn, to revise, to study hard. [? SE *bone*, to polish or *Bohn* translations of the classics, the latter underpinned by alt. sp. *bohn* in US college *c.*1900]

bone *v.*[4] [20C] (Aus.) to jinx, to bring bad luck to. [SAusE *point a bone*, an Aborigine practice]

bone *v.*[5] [1970s+] to have sexual intercourse. [BONE *n.*[6] (1)]

bone *v.*[6] [1980s+] to drive fast. [bone adj.]

bone *adj.* [mid-19C–20C] good (cf. BONA adj.). [Ital. *buono*, Fr. *bon*, good]

bone *adv.* [1980s+] (US Black) thoroughly, completely. [SE *bone*; i.e. to one's very depths]

bone-ache *n.* [late 16C–early 17C] venereal disease. [the side-effects of syphilis]

bone-baster *n.* [late 16C–mid-17C] a cudgel. [SE *bone* + BASTE v. (1)]

bone-bender/-butcher/-carpenter/-chiseller *n.* [late 19C+] (US) a surgeon.

bone box *n.*[1] [late 18C–mid-19C] the mouth.

bone box *n.*[2] [1970s+] **1** (US prison) a hearse. **2** (US) an ambulance.

bone-breaker *n.* [late 19C–1910s] fever, ague. [the aches it induces in the bones]

bone-butcher/-carpenter *see* BONE-BENDER.

bone carrier *n.* [20C] (US) a gossip, a rumour-monger. [CARRY A BONE]

bone-chiseller *see* BONE-BENDER.

bone-cleaner *n.* [late 19C–1900s] a domestic servant. [SE *bones*, objects made of ivory + *cleaner*]

bonecrusher *n.*[1] [late 19C] (sporting) a large-calibre sporting rifle, used on large game. [its effects]

bonecrusher *n.*[2] [1990s] (US drugs) **1** a near-overdose in which the user feels as if the injection they have just taken is crushing their bones. **2** crack cocaine.

boned *adj.*[1] [20C] tipsy (cf. LEGLESS). [the image of a *boned* carcass, reduced to flabby, floppy meat]

boned *adj.*[2] [1960s–70s] hit hard on the head. [the *bone* is that of the battered skull]

bone dance *n.* [1980s+] (US campus) sexual intercourse; thus *do the bone dance*, to have sexual intercourse (cf. BONE *n.*[6]; BONER *n.*[3]; DANCE *v.*[1] + combs).

bone-dome *n.* [1930s+] a protective helmet, initially for fliers, latterly [1950s] motorcyclists and [1980s+] cyclists.

boned out *adj.*[1] [1990s] (US Black) exhausted, esp. of a man who has just had sex (cf. FUCKED OUT). [BONE *n.*[6] (1)]

boned out *adj.*[2] [1990s] (US Black) out of money. [BONE *n.*[4] (1)]

bone down *v.* [20C] (US) to have sexual intercourse. [BONE *n.*[6] (1)]

bone-gobbler *n.* [20C] (US) one who performs oral sex, whether hetero- or homosexual. [BONE *n.*[6] (1) + SE *gobbler*]

bone-grubber *n.* [mid-19C] a scavenger who specializes in collecting old bones and selling them to rag-shops or to the bone-grinders. [SE *bone* + *grubber*]

bonehead *n.*[1] [20C] (orig. US) **1** a stubborn person. **2** a fool, a dullard, a idiot; thus *boneheaded*, stupid (cf. HULVERHEAD; LOGGERHEAD; LUNKHEAD). **3** a stupid error (cf. BONEHEAD PLAY). [SE *bone* + sfx. -HEAD (1); the image is of the hardness of bone]

bonehead *n.*[2] [1950s+] a bald person (cf. SKINHEAD). [the head is shaved to the bone]

bonehead English *n.* [1920s+] (US campus) a remedial course in elementary English composition. [BONEHEAD *n.*[1] + SE *English*]

bonehead play *n.* [1910s+] (US) an elementary, obvious error or mistake; thus *pull a bonehead play*, to make an elementary error. [BONEHEAD *n.*[1] + PLAY *n.*[1]]

bone-house *n.* **1** [late 18C–late 19C] a coffin. **2** [early–mid-19C] a house or vault in which the bones of the dead are piled up, a charnel-house. **3** [19C] the human body (cf. SOUL-CASE). [SE *bone* + *house*]

bone-in-a-valley *n.* [1950s+] (W.I.) a thin person. [BONE *n.*[6] (2)]

bone in the throat *n.* [early 17C–late 18C] a spurious excuse, usu. in phr. *have a bone in one's throat*; vars. include a *bone in the arm*, a *bone in the leg*.

bone it off *v.* [1990s] to masturbate. [BONE n.⁶ (1)]

bone-lazy *adj.* [late 19C] very lazy. [lit. lazy 'to the bone' (cf. TO THE BONE), on pattern of SE *bone-idle*]

bone orchard *n.* [early 19C+] (US) a cemetery (cf. MARBLE ORCHARD).

bone out *v.* [1990s] (US Black) to run away, to leave fast. [? BONE v.⁶ + ? *move one's bones*]

bone phone *n.* [20C] (US) the penis (cf. BONE n.⁶). [BONE n.⁶ (1) + SE *phone*]

bone-picker *n.*¹ [late 18C–mid-19C] a footman. [the poor standard of the meals, often based on leftovers, given to servants]

bone-picker *n.*² [mid-19C–1900s] a scavenger, a rag and bone man.

bone-polisher *n.*¹ [early–mid-19C] a footman. [ext. of SE use; the *bones* used for cleaning]

bone-polisher *n.*² [mid-19C] the cat-o'-nine-tails. [the 'polishing' of the malefactor's bones]

boner *n.*¹ [20C] the last straw. [SE *bone*, the last thing to be eaten]

boner *n.*² **1** [1910s+] (US) a serious mistake (cf. BONEHEAD PLAY; PULL A BONER). **2** [19C] a hard blow. [BONEHEAD n.¹ (3)]

boner *n.*³ [1960s+] an erection (cf. HARD-ON). [BONE n.⁶ (1)]

boner nochy! *phr.* [late 19C] (Ling. Fr./Polari) good night! [Ital. *buona notte*, good night]

boners!/boney!/bonny! *excl.* [20C] (US teen) that's mine! (cf. AIKIES!). [? pidgin *bon eye*, good eye]

bones *n.*¹ **1** [14C+] dice, esp. in exhortation *roll them bones!* **2** [19C] the human teeth. **3** [19C] a surgeon. [ext. of SE use; dice were originally made of bone]

bones *n.*² [20C] (US) a Black person. [? old vaudeville crosstalk act in which one speaker was Mr *Bones*]

bones *n.*³ (drugs) **1** [1970s+] marijuana cigarettes. **2** [1980s+] crack cocaine. [the cigarette and crack are both white]

bone-setter *n.*¹ [mid-18C–early 19C] a horse that gives its rider an uncomfortable journey (cf. BONE-SHAKER). [SE *bone-setter*, a surgeon]

bone-setter *n.*² [early 19C] (US) a surprise, i.e. a jolt. [it shakes one's bones]

bone-shaker *n.* **1** [late 19C] an early model of bicycle, with solid rather than rubber tyres. **2** [1920s+] a decrepit vehicle with, *inter alia*, inadequate springs, thus jolting its passengers.

boneshop *n.* [late 19C–1900s] the workhouse. [the paucity of the provisions]

bone smuggler *n.* [1990s] a male homosexual. [BONE n.⁶ (1); the 'smuggling' is into the anus]

bone-sore/-tired *adj.* [late 19C] very lazy (cf. BONE-LAZY). [SE *sore/tired* + *to the bone*]

bone-stroker *n.* [1990s] **1** a masturbator. **2** a male homosexual. [BONE n.⁶ (1) + SE *stroker*]

bone-tired *see* BONE-SORE.

bonetop *n.* [1910s] (US) a fool, a dullard (cf. BONEHEAD n.¹). [SE *bone* + TOP n.]

bone up on *see* BONE v.³.

boney *n.*¹ [20C] (Ulster) a bonfire, esp. one lit on 12 July, Orangeman's Day. [abbr. SE, ult. *bone-fire*]

boney/bonie *n.*² [1970s+] (S.Afr.) **1** a bicycle. **2** a motorcycle. [BONE-SHAKER]

boney! *see* BONERS!

boneyard *n.* **1** [19C] a very thin or emaciated person or animal (cf. BONE n.⁶). **2** [mid-19C+] a cemetery (cf. BONE ORCHARD).

bonfire *n.* [1940s] (US Black) a cigarette, a cigarette stub.

bong *n.* [1980s+] **1** (US drugs) a kind of bowl-shaped waterpipe used for smoking marijuana; thus (Aus.) *bongineering*, *bongology*, the construction of such pipes. **2** (US campus) a device that helps someone drink quickly, usu. a tube attached to a funnel (cf. BEER BONG). [Thai *baung*, lit. 'cylindrical wooden tube']

bong *adj.* [1940s+] (Aus.) dead. [? SE *bong*, echoic of the noise of a body hitting the ground]

bong *v.* [1990s] (US campus) to engage in sex. [var. on BONK v. (2)]

bong! *excl.* [1970s+] term used to suggest the sound of a blow or a sudden noise. [onomat.]

bongo *n.* [1980s+] (Aus. drugs) a kind of bowl-shaped waterpipe used for smoking marijuana. [BONG n.]

bongo *adj.* [1950s–70s] (US) crazy, eccentric. [BONKERS]

bongo lips *n.* [20C] (US) a derog. term for a Black person. [*Bongo*, seen as a stereotypically 'African' name + the image of thick lips]

bongos *n.* [1980s+] (US) the female breasts. [they 'bong' up and down]

bong swat *n.* [1980s+] (US drugs) an inhalation of a pipeful of marijuana (cf. BONG n.). [BONG n. (1) + SE *swat*, a hit]

bong tong *n.* [late 19C–1900s] (Aus.) the social élite and their lifestyle and manners, used ironically. [a deliberate deflatory mispron. of Fr. *bon ton*, good taste, good breeding]

bonie *see* BONEY n.².

boniface *n.* [early 18C–mid-19C] a public house landlord. [*Boniface*, the jovial innkeeper in George Farquhar's *The Beaux' Stratagem* (1707)]

bonified *adv.* [20C] (US Black) competent, qualified, the right man for job. [? Fr. *bon*, good + sfx. *-ified* or pron. of Lat. *bona fide*, genuine, lit. 'in good faith']

boning *n.* [1960s+] (US campus) sexual intercourse. [BONE n.⁵]

bonita *n.* [1980s+] (drugs) heroin. [Sp., lit. 'good little girl']

bonk *n.* **1** [1930s+] an abrupt, heavy sound, a thump. **2** [1970s+] sexual intercourse (cf. BASH n.²). **3** [1970s+] a blow, esp. on top of the head. [echoic]

bonk *v.* **1** [1930s+] to hit (on the head). **2** [1970s+] to have sexual intercourse (cf. BANG v.¹). [echoic + note WW1 milit. use *bonk*, to shell]

bonk! *excl.* [1990s] (US teen) used after a statement to emphasize one's feeling that it is unbelievable, fantastic.

bonkers *adj.* [1940s+] (orig. RN) **1** stupid, insane, eccentric. **2** mildly drunk. [BONK n.(1)]

bonne-bouche *n.* [19C] the vagina (cf. APPLE n.¹⁰; BIT n.³; P.E.E.P.; YUM-YUM n.). [Fr. *bonne bouche*, a 'pleasant taste', anglicized as a 'tasty morsel']

bonneroo *see* BONAROO.

bonnet *n.*¹ **1** [early 19C] a pretext or pretence, esp. as the legitimate job behind which a thief hides their true occupation, e.g. a newspaper seller or porter. **2** [mid-19C] a gambling cheat, who poses as a normal player, thus luring the victim to join the game, but who, as the play proceeds, begins cheating in favour of the bank or house (cf. BONNETER). **3** [mid-19C] a sham bidder at auctions who works to drive up the price. [fig. use of BONNET v. (2)]

bonnet/cap *n.*² [late 19C] a woman (cf. PETTICOAT; SKIRT). [metonymy]

bonnet *v.* [mid-19C] **1** to pull or crush a person's hat over their eyes, thus temporarily blinding them. **2** to cheat (cf. BONNET n.¹)

bonnet-builder *n.* [early 19C–1920s] a milliner.

bonneter *n.* **1** [mid-19C–1900s] a smashing blow on one's hat. **2** [mid-19C] a cheat's accomplice, who lures victims into the game (cf. BONNET n.¹). [BONNET v.]

bonnet for *v.* [early 19C] to back up someone in their claims, to provide an alibi for someone. [BONNET v. (2)]

bonnets so blue n. [mid-19C+] (Irish) stew. [rhy. sl.]

bonnie Brillo n. [1980s+] (US campus) one who is obsessively neat and tidy. [proper name *Bonnie*, with implications of domestic cheeriness + *Brillo*, the scouring pad]

bonny! see BONERS!

bonny fair n. [20C] (US) the hair (cf. BARNET FAIR). [rhy. sl.]

bonny-roo see BONAROO.

bono adj. [mid–late 19C] good. [Polari]

bono Johnny n. [late 19C–1900s] an Englishman. [Chinese pidgin, 'a good John Bull']

bono omee n. [mid-19C–1950s] a husband. [BONO + OMEE n. (1)]

bonsai n. [1990s] a small child. [SE *bonsai*, a miniature tree]

bonsella n. [1940s+] (S.Afr.) a present, a gratuity, a 'perk'. [Zulu *ibhanselo*, a small present or *bansela*, thanks in a tangible form]

bont adj. [1970s+] (S.Afr.) gaudy, lurid, colourful. [Du. *bonte*, gaudy]

bontoger/bontogeriro/bontoser/bonziorie/bonzrino adj. [20C] (Aus.) good, extremely, very (cf. BONZER). [var. on BONTOSHER]

bontosher n. [20C] (Aus.) a term of the highest praise (cf. BONZER). [Fr. *bon toujours*, good all the time]

bonus! excl. [1980s+] (US campus) excellent! wonderful! first-class! [SE *bonus*, something extra, but cf. BONA adj.]

bonz! excl. [20C] good! excellent! [abbr. BONZER]

bonzarina n. [1900s–50s] (Aus.) a notably beautiful woman. [BONZER + fem. sfx. *-arina*]

bonzer adj. [20C] (Aus./N.Z.) good; thus extremely, very (cf. BOSHTA; BOSKER). [mongrel mixture of Fr. *bon*, good + SE *bonanza* + BONTOGER]

bonziorie see BONTOGER.

bonzo adj. [1970s+] eccentric. [? the UK 1920s cartoon puppy *Bonzo* or 1951 film *Bedtime for Bonzo* (a chimp)]

bonzrino see BONTOGER.

boo n.[1] [late 19C] (US) money. [BOODLE n.[1]]

boo n.[2] **1** [1930s–50s] (US Black) a bad scare, a serious fright. **2** [1970s] a ghostwriter. [(1) ? JABOOBY (marijuana), among the effects of which can be temporary paranoia; (2) pun on SE *boo!* + *ghost*(-writer)]

boo/bu n.[3] [1950s+] (drugs) marijuana. [abbr. JABOOBY]

boo n.[4] [1990s] (US Black) a sweetheart, a loved one. [? BABY n.[2] (6)]

boo n.[5] [1990s] (US) nasal mucus. [BOOGER n.[1]]

booai/booay n. [20C] (N.Z.) the backwoods, remote rural areas; thus *up the booai*, totally confused, absolutely wrong. [? Maori *puhoi*, dull, slow or *Puhoi*, a failed mid-19C utopian settlement]

boob n.[1] **1** [late 19C+] (orig. Aus.) orig. milit. use, a prison; thus (all Aus./N.Z.) *boob blue*, illicitly manufactured prison alcohol, *boob dot*, a small blue dot tattooed beneath the eye, indicating a spell in borstal or prison, *boob happy*, mentally unstable as a result of imprisonment, *boob heads*, influential, powerful prisoners, *boob rat*, a recidivist, *boob talk*, prison jargon, *boob tat*, a prison tattoo, *boob tea*, weak, prison-brewed tea, *boob weed*, prison-issue tobacco, *do boob*, to serve time in prison. **2** [1900s–50s] (US) a police station, esp. the police cells, a local or city prison. [BOOBY-HATCH n. (1); note WW1 milit. use for detention cells]

boob n.[2] **1** [20C] (orig. US) a fool, an idiot. **2** [1900s–40s] (US) an inmate of a psychiatric institution (cf. BOOBY-HATCH).

boob n.[3] [1940s+] (orig. US) the female breast, usu. in pl. [BUB n.[4]; since 1970s one of the terms esp. favoured by women]

boob adj. [late 19C+] (Aus.) inferior, second-rate. [BOOB n.[2]]

boob v. [1910s+] to make a mistake, to blunder. [BOOB n.[2]]

boobatch n. [1930s–40s] (US) an old Polish immigrant (cf. BOOTCHKEY). [? Polish = grandfather]

booberkin n. [early 17C+] a fool, a simpleton. [BOOBY n.[1] + dimin. sfx. *-kin*]

boobies n. [1930s+] (orig. US) the female breasts (cf. BOOB n.[3]). [BUB n.[4]]

boob job n. [1980s+] cosmetic/plastic surgery on the breast, usu. for enlarging with some form of implant. [BOOB n.[3] + JOB n.[5]]

Boob McNutt n. [1940s–60s] (US) a fool, a simpleton. [BOOB n.[2] (1) + NUTCASE; ult. f. *Boob McNutt*, a strip cartoon character (running 1915–34) created by Rube Goldberg]

booboisie n. [1920s+] (US) respectable fools, considered as a class in their own right; a synonym for the modern 'Middle America'. [BOOB n.[2] (1) + *bourgeoisie*. Coined by H.L. Mencken as part of a list of words describing 'the victims of the Depression, then current' and published in the Baltimore *Evening Sun* on 15 February 1922 in a list of 50 similar terms, incl. *boobariat*, *booberati*, *boobarian*]

boo-boo n.[1] [1900s] (US) a joke. [ety,. unknown]

boo-boo n.[2] [1900s–20s] (US) $1. [abbr./redup. BOODLE n.[1]]

boo-boo n.[3] [1950s] (US) usu. in pl., the testicles. [? Yid. *bulba*, potato. Major (1994) suggests link to Bantu *mbubu*]

boo-boo n.[4] [1950s+] (orig. US) a blunder, usu. embarrassing. [BOOB n.[2]]

boo-boo n.[5] [1950s+] (US) a minor scar or bruise, an acne spot etc. [BOOB v. + redup.]

boo-boo v. [1950s+] (orig. US) to blunder, to make a mistake. [BOOB v. + redup.]

booboos n. [20C] (US) a Black person. [? BOOB n.[2] (1)]

boob play n. [1930s+] a foolish action, an error, a blunder. [BOOB n.[2] (1) + PLAY n.[1]]

boob trap n. [1920s–50s] (US) a nightclub or similar place of entertainment where gullible customers are defrauded of their cash (cf. CLIP-JOINT). [BOOB n.[2] (1) + SE *trap*]

boob-tube n.[1] [1950s+] (orig. US) television. [BOOB n.[2] (1) + TUBE n.[3] (2)]

boob-tube n.[2] [1970s+] a woman's tight, strapless top, usu. of knitted or elasticated fabric. [BOOB n.[3] + SE *tube*]

boobus n. [1990s] (US Black/Los Angeles) small breasts. [BOOB n.[3]]

booby n.[1] [early 17C+] a fool, an idiot, a peasant. [? Sp. *bobo*, a fool]

booby n.[2] [1910s–30s] (US) a cell, a lock-up (cf. BOOB n.[1]). [BOOBY-HUTCH n.[2] (1)]

booby n.[3] [1910s+] (orig. US) the female breast (cf. BUBBY n.). [BOOB n.[3]]

booby-box n. [late 19C+] a lunatic asylum (cf. BOOBY-HATCH; BOOBY-HOUSE; BOOBY-HUTCH n.[2]). [BOOBY n.[1] + SE *box*]

booby-hatch n. **1** [mid-19C–1960s] (orig. US) a prison, a police station. **2** [late 19C+] a lunatic asylum. [BOOBY n.[1] + SE *hatch*, hutch, underpinned by the well-known asylum at Colney Hatch near London]

booby-house n. [late 19C–1910s] (US) a lunatic asylum (cf. BOOBY-BOX).

booby-hutch n.[1] [18C] **1** a one-horse chaise, thus any clumsy carriage. **2** a leather bottle. [BOOBY n.[1] + SE *hutch*; (2) plays on the idea of the bottle, full of liquor, 'ensnaring' the fool]

booby-hutch n.[2] [late 19C–1930s] **1** a lunatic asylum (cf. BOOBY-BOX). **2** (US) a police station (cf. BOOBY-HATCH). [BOOBY n.[1] + SE *hutch*. Note milit. use *boobies' hutch*, a tolerated if unofficial bar in a barracks, which is open after the canteen shuts]

booby-wagon n. [1960s] (US) the vehicle in which arrested people are transported to the local police station or prison (cf. PADDY WAGON). [BOOBY n.[2] + SE *wagon*]

booch/boogh v. [20C] (Ulster) to slap. [echoic]

boocoo/bocoo/boo-koos *adv.* [1960s+] very much, extremely, used as a general intensifier. [Fr. *beaucoup*, very much; used f. 1920s by Blacks in some southern states (Louisiana, Florida, Georgia) but popularized in 1960s–70s by returning US soldiers, who picked it up from the Francophone Vietnamese]

boocoodles/bookoodles *n.* [20C] (US) many, a good deal. [Fr. *beaucoup*, many. ? imported to US by Vietnam veterans who picked up BOOCOO; however WW1 and WW2 veterans had had similar opportunities and the term predates Vietnam]

booda *n.* [1990s] (US Black gang) a large, cannabis-impregnated cookie or biscuit. [pun on BUDDHA n.]

boodgeree! *excl.* [1910s+] (Aus. pidgin) a general excl. of approval, pleasure. [Dharuk *bujari*, good]

boodle *n.*[1] **1** [19C] (orig. US) a crowd or collection of people or things (cf. CABOODLE). **2** [mid-19C+] booty, money, esp. money that has been acquired illegally or through corruption. **3** [mid-19C+] a large amount of money. **4** [mid–late 19C] (US) counterfeit money. **5** [late 19C–1960s] a roll of banknotes. **6** [20C] (US Und.) anything sent to a prisoner from the outside world, not necessarily money (cf. RELIEF; SCORE n.[3]). **7** [1900s–70s] (US campus) a parcel of food, usu. sweets or snacks, sent to a student. **8** [1950s] (US Black) a fake bankroll, i.e. a bill of large denomination wrapped around a roll of smaller bills (or even paper) (cf. CALIFORNIA BANKROLL). [either Du. *boedel*, household effects, and thus one's personal estate, or Scot. *bodle*, a small coin worth two Scot. pence (or one-sixth of an English one) and as such usually glossed as 'worthless'. It is in the US that the modern meaning, whether of criminal or political graft, has developed]

boodle *n.*[2] [mid-19C] a fool. [? link to NOODLE n.[1]; ? Devon dial. *buddled*, drunk]

boodle *n.*[3] [1980s] (US) the vagina (cf. BANK n.[1]). [BOOTY n., but note image of the vagina as a commercially useful commodity]

boodle *v.*[1] [late 19C] (US) to engage in corruption, in graft (cf. BOODLER). [BOODLE n.[1] (2)]

boodle *v.*[2] [1940s–70s] (campus) to pet, to neck. [SE *bundle*, of an engaged couple, to sleep together, but fully clothed]

boodle bag *n.* [1920s–50s] (US) a purse, a small money-pouch, usu. worn around the neck. [BOODLE n.[1] + SE *bag*]

boodler *n.* [late 19C+] (Aus./US) **1** a swindler, specializing in passing counterfeit notes. **2** a corrupt politician. [BOODLE n.[1]. US use late 19C; Aus. use 1920s+]

boody *see* BOOTY n.

boody call *n.* [1990s] (US Black) a late-night telephone call, esp. a call from a man looking for an invitation to join his girlfriend for sex. [BOOTY n. (1) + SE *call*]

boodylicious *adj.* [1990s] (US Black) a general term of approval/disapproval, wonderful, marvellous, stunning, mildly unpleasant. [BOOTY adj.[1] + BODACIOUS + SE *delicious*]

booed and hissed *adj.* [1980s] drunk. [rhy. sl. *booed and hissed* = PISSED adj.[1]]

boof *v.* [1960s+] (Aus.) to top up a container. [? SE *buff up*, lit. to polish]

boofa *n.* [1980s+] (US campus) a fool, an incompetent. [BOOFHEAD n. (1)]

boofed/boofed out *adj.* [1980s+] (US campus) puffed out, usu. of hair. [SE *bouffant*]

booferbox *n.* [1980s+] a large radio/tape recorder/stereo particularly popular among ghetto youths (cf. GHETTO-BLASTER). [*boof*, echoic of the heavy bass notes emerging from the machine + SE *box*]

boofhead *n.* [1940s+] (orig. Aus.) **1** a fool, an idiot, a simpleton (cf. BLOCKHEAD n.[1]). **2** a person or animal having a large head. [Lincolnshire dial.]

boog *n.* [1930s+] **1** (US) a Black person. **2** (Aus.) an Aborigine. [BOOGIE n.[2]]

boog *adj.* [1930s+] Black, Negro (cf. BOOGERLEE). [BOOG n.]

boog *v.*[1] [1930s] (US Black) to irritate, to annoy. [BUG v.[2] (2)]

boog *v.*[2] [1930s–70s] (US Black) to enjoy oneself, to 'party'. [BOOGIE v.]

boogaloo *n.* [1970s–80s] (US) a Black person. [BOOGIE n.[2] + SE *boogaloo*]

boogaloo *v.* [1960s+] (orig. US Black) **1** to dance. **2** to fool around. [SE *boogaloo*, a dance step of the 1960s]

booge *v.* [1970s] (US campus) to move, to dance, to perform. [BOOGALOO v. (1)]

booger *n.*[1] [late 19C+] (US) a piece of nasal mucus. [BOGEY n.[3] (1)]

booger *n.*[2] **1** [1940s+] (US Black) anything unpleasant, burdensome, difficult. **2** [1950s+] (US south) sexual intercourse with a woman. **3** [1980s+] (US campus) an extremely unattractive woman. [BUGGER n.[1]]

booger *v.*[1] [late 19C+] (US West) to shy, to panic, usu. of an animal; thus *boogery*, jumpy. [BUGGER ABOUT]

booger *v.*[2] [20C] (US) to sodomize. [SE *bugger*]

booger bear *n.* [late 19C–1960s] (US Black) **1** a notably ugly person. **2** any difficult situation or unpleasant thing. [BOOGER n.[2] + BEAR n.[1]]

boogerboo *n.* [1940s–60s] (US Black) an unpleasant situation or person. [BOOGER BEAR]

boogering/booging *adj.* [1960s] (US) damned, in the sense of irritating, infuriating (cf. FUCKING adj.). [BUGGERING]

boogerlee *n.* [20C] (US) **1** a Cajun (a person of French descent in Louisiana). **2** a Frenchman. **3** a person of mixed Black and White ancestry. [? BOOGIE n.[2] + proper name *Stagolee*]

boogerman *n.* [20C] (US) a policeman (cf. BOGEY n.[3]). [SE *bogeyman*]

booger wagon *n.* [20C] a prison van (cf. BLACK ANNIE). [BOOGERMAN + SE *wagon*]

boogery/buggery *adj.* [20C] (US) frightened, frightening; thus *boogery-eyed*, wide-eyed. [dial. *booger*, of a horse, to be frightened, to shy]

booget *n.* [mid-16C–mid-17C] (Und.) an itinerant tinker's basket. [SE *budget*, a pouch, bag, wallet, usually of leather]

boogh *see* BOOCH.

boogie *n.*[1] [late 19C+] (US) a piece of nasal mucus. [BOOGER n.[1]]

boogie *n.*[2] [1920s+] a Black person. [SE *bogey* or US dial. *boogerman*, *bogeyman*]

boogie *n.*[3] (US Black) **1** [1940s–60s] sexual intercourse. **2** [1950s] a sexually promiscuous person. **3** [1960s+] the vagina. **4** [1980s] energy. **5** [1990s] (drugs) marijuana, esp. when more than usually strong. [BOOGIE v.]

boogie *v.* (orig. US Black) **1** [1940s+] to dance (cf. BOOGALOO v.). **2** [1940s+] to go, to move, to do something quickly. **3** [1940s+] to enjoy oneself, to have a party, a good time, extended in excl. *boogie down!* let's have fun! **4** [1960s+] to have sexual intercourse. [SE *boogie-woogie*, a form of jazz-based dance, or PITCH A BOOGIE-WOOGIE]

boogie board *n.* [1980s+] (orig. Aus.) a cut-down, half-sized surfboard. [BOOGIE v.[3] + SE *board*]

boogie box *n.* [1980s] a large, portable cassette/tape player (cf. GHETTOBLASTER). [BOOGIE v. + SE *box*]

boogie house/joint *n.* [1930s–70s] (US Black) a brothel (cf. ACCOMMODATION HOUSE). [BOOGIE v.[4] + HOUSE n.[1] (1)/JOINT n.[3] (3)]

boogie-joogie/-joogy *n.* (US Black) **1** [1950s] boogie-woogie music. **2** [1970s] trickery, deceit. [BOOGIE v. (1) + redup. or JUKE n. (2)/JUKE v.[1]]

boogie-joogie/-joogy *v.* [1950s] (US Black) to deceive, esp. sexually. [BOOGIE-JOOGIE n.]

boogie-woogie *v.* [1930s+] (US Black) to leave, to depart. [BOOGIE v. (2) + redup.]

booging see BOOGERING.

boogler *n.* [1960s] (US Black) a regular party-goer. [BOOGIE v. (3)]

boohonged *adj.* [1980s+] (US campus) drunk. [? BEER BONG]

boohoo *v.* [mid-19C+] (orig. US) to cry, to weep, to burst into tears. [echoic]

booie/bovey *n.* [1920s+] (Aus.) nasal mucus. [? Fr. *boue*, mud or BOGEY n.⁵ (1)]

booitjie see BOYKIE.

boojee/boojie/boojum/boojy/bourgie *n.* [1950s+] (orig. US Black) a bourgeois, middle-class, thus law-abiding Black (equally applicable to Whites). [SE *bourgeois*, middle class]

boojie *n.*¹ [1930s] (drugs) a marijuana cigarette (cf. BOOGIE n.³). [? BOO n.³]

boojie *n.*² see BOOJEE.

boojum/boojy see BOOJEE.

book *n.*¹ **1** [late 19C+] a magazine, a periodical; mainly illiterate use. **2** [1950s+] (Black pimp) a supply of names and addresses of clients (cf. WORK FROM A BOOK).

book *n.*² **1** [late 19C+] (Aus./US) a *book*maker. **2** [1910+] a *book*maker's business. [abbr.]

book *n.*³ [20C] (Irish) a class in primary school. [the role of reading]

Book, the *n.*⁴ **1** [1920s–40s] (US Und.) a maximum sentence (cf. THROW THE BOOK AT). **2** [1920s+] (US Black) the oral tradition that forms the basis of Black pimping.

book *n.*⁵ [1990s] (Irish) a single parent's allowance. [? the book in which payments are registered]

book *v.*¹ [late 19C+] to work as a bookmaker. [BOOK n.²]

book *v.*² [1930s+] **1** to arrest, to write down in a police charge book. **2** to note, to understand.

book/book it *v.*³ (US campus) **1** [1960s+] to look at, to examine. **2** [1970s+] to study assiduously. [SE *book*]

book *v.*⁴ [1970s+] (US campus) to leave, to go fast. [BOOGIE v.]

book/book it *v.*⁵ [1980s+] (US Black) to run away, to move fast. [BOOGIE v. (2)]

bookbinder's wife *n.* [late 19C] the vagina. [play on 'her' occupation: 'manufacturing in sheets']

booked *adj.*¹ **1** [19C] (orig. boxing) destined, fated, caught, disposed of. **2** [20C] (US) fatally ill; thus *booked for kingdom come*. [? having *booked* one's space in the graveyard or 'set down in the book of history' (Jon Bee)]

booked *adj.*² [1990s] (US campus) ugly. [? BOOG n. (1)]

bookful *n.* [20C] (US Und.) a life sentence (cf. DO THE BOOK; DO THE BOOK AND COVER). [BOOK n.⁴ (2)]

bookie *n.* [late 19C+] a *book*maker. [abbr.]

bookie mill *n.* [1950s+] (US) a bookmaker's office. [BOOKIE + SE *mill*, used to mean a place of work/activity]

book it see BOOK v.³, v.⁵.

bookity-book *v.* [late 19C] (US Black) to run fast, to move quickly. [echoic of the sound of shoes slapping on the ground]

book-keeper *n.* [late 18C–early 19C] one who fails to return borrowed books. [pun]

book/history of the four kings, the *n.* [late 18C–19C] a pack of cards; thus *study the history of the four kings*, to play cards.

book of words *n.* [late 19C+] a catalogue, a manual, any form of printed instructions.

bookoo *v.* [1920s–60s] (US Black) to talk loudly and aggressively. [Fr. *beaucoup*, very much, thus very much noise]

bookoodles see BOOCOODLES.

boo-koos see BOOCOO.

book-pad *v.* [late 17C–mid-18C] to plagiarize. [SE *book* + model of FOOTPAD]

bookra/bukra *n.* [1900s–10s] (N.Z.) tomorrow. [Arabic]

book rat *n.* [late 19C] (US) an obsessive reader, a bookworm. [they 'chew up' books]

books *n.* [early 18C–mid-19C] a pack of playing cards (cf. KING'S BOOKS). [abbr. DEVIL'S BOOKS; i.e. the pious identification of gambling with sin]

Booksellers' Row *n.* [mid-19C] Holywell Street, London, WC2. [a deliberate euph. since the 'books' sold in Holywell Street, before it was knocked down for the Aldwych development, were strictly pornographic]

book-sharp *n.* [late 19C] (US west) an intellectual. [SE *book* + SHARP n.¹ (2)]

book smart *adj.* [1980s+] (US campus) academically high-flying, but low on common sense and social skills (cf. SCHOOLBOOK CHUMP).

book the joint, to *phr.* [1970s+] (US teen) to look over a place, to check its amenities. [BOOK v.³ + JOINT n.³ (3)]

book up *v.* [1960s+] (US) to study assiduously (cf. BOOK v.³).

booky *n.*¹ [late 19C] a bouquet. [mispron.]

booky *n.*² [late 19C+] a *book*maker, also as *bookie/booky-boy*. [abbr.]

boola-boola *n.* [1960s+] (US campus) college chauvinism. [college sports cheer *boola-boola*]

boolhipper *n.* [1970s+] (US Black) a leather coat. [ety. unknown; ? link to BULLY n.]

boom *n.*¹ [late 19C–1900s] (US) a positive endorsement, a 'plug'. [BOOM v.¹ (2)]

boom *n.*² [1940s+] (S.Afr., drugs) marijuana; thus *boom-boy*, a marijuana smoker, *boom-skuif*, *boomstop*, a marijuana cigarette. [Afk. *boom*, a tree]

boom *n.*³ [1950s+] (drugs) cannabis, marijuana. [BOO n.³]

boom *adj.* [1990s] the very best. [BOOM v.¹ (2)]

boom *v.*¹ (US) **1** [early 19C] to hurry. **2** [late 19C+] to promote, to extol. **3** [20C] to live as a transient worker (cf. BOOMER n.²). [naut. jargon *boom*, for a sailing ship to reach top speed (the wind-filled sails 'boom' with the movement). (2) is SE since 1960s]

boom *v.*² [1990s] (drugs) to experience waves of elation while under the influence of LSD. [the *boom* of a soundwave]

boom! *excl.* **1** [1950s+] suddenly, all at once, also as *boom-boom*. **2** [1980s+] (US Black) a general excl. of agreement. [onomat. sound of an explosion]

boom-boom *n.*¹ **1** [1910s+] (juv.) a soldier. **2** [1940s+] (US Black) a pistol or shotgun. [the sound of a shot]

boom-boom *n.*² [1960s+] (US juv.) excrement. [? echoic of defecation]

boombox *n.* [1980s+] a large, portable cassette player (cf. GHETTOBLASTER). [ext. of SE; i.e. its reverberating bass]

boomer *n.*¹ [late 19C] (US) **1** an enthusiast, esp. one who promotes or pushes a new enterprise. **2** a boom town. [BOOM v.¹ (2)]

boomer *n.*² [late 19C+] (US) a transient worker, a migrant; thus *boomer reporter*, a journalist who works on papers all over the country, never keeping one job for too long (cf. BUMMER n.¹; HOME GUARD). [SE *boom*, an economic upswing; the US *boomers* moved from one boom oil camp to the next during the 1920s–30s]

boomer *n.*³ [late 19C+] (Aus./US) anything considered exceptionally large or strong. [SAusE *boomah*, a large kangaroo]

boomer *n.*⁴ [1970s+] (US) a thunderstorm, a thunder-cloud. [the noise of thunder]

boomer *n.*⁵ [1980s+] (orig. US) a member of the 'baby-boom' generation (born in the late 1940s).

boomerang *n.* [1930s+] (Aus.) something, esp. a book, that one wishes to have returned. [SE *boomerang*, which comes back to its thrower]

boomerang *v.* [20C] (US Und.) to return to prison almost immediately on finishing the last sentence (cf. COME BACK FOR SECONDS). [SE *boomerang* which, after one has thrown it, returns]

boomerang cheque *n.* [1950s–60s] (Aus.) a 'bouncing' cheque, which is not honoured and is 'returned to drawer'. [SE *boomerang* + *cheque*]

boomers *n.* [1980s+] (drugs) psilocybin, psilocin. [they make one 'high'] [SE *boom*, echoic of an explosion; i.e. they 'blow' one up]

booming *adj.* **1** [mid-19C+] (Aus.) large (cf. BOOMER n.³). **2** [late 19C+] successful, flourishing. **3** [late 19C] grand. **4** [1990s] (US Black) good-looking. **5** [1990s] (US campus) excellent, worthy of approval. [SE *boom*, to advance keenly, to prosper]

boom! pow! bam! *excl.* [1990s] (US Black teen) an excl. used to place emphasis in one's conversation. [orig. in comic books]

boomster *n.* [late 19C] (US) a speculator. [SE *boom*, an economic upturn]

boon *n.¹* [1950s] (US Black) $1. [? BONE n.⁴ (1)]

boon *n.²* [1960s+] **1** (US Black) a close friend (cf. ACE BOON COON). **2** a Black person. [? SE *boon companion* or Fr. *bon*, good + poss. link to BONE n.⁷ (2)]

boon coon *n.* [1950s–70s] (US Black) a close companion (cf. ACE BOON COON). [SE *boon (companion)* + COON n.³]

boondock *v.* [20C] (US campus) to neck, to pet or make love in an automobile. [BOONDOCKS, a secluded rural spot suitable for love-making]

boondocker *n.* [1960s+] (US campus) a picnic held in the woods where students can drink, play around, neck etc. [BOONDOCKS]

boondockers *n.* [1950s+] (US) a pair of strong shoes suitable for rough use. [BOONDOCKS]

boondocks *n.* [1940s+] (US) rough country, jungle, an isolated or wild region. [Tagalog *bundock*, a mountain; orig. used by US milit. (esp. US Marine Corps) to mean the field, the bush, the jungle, anywhere the troops operate that is not designated a firebase, a basecamp or occupied by civilians]

boondoggle *n.* [1930s+] (US) a waste, of time, of money, of energy. esp. used by US govt. for a project that is considered to waste tax dollars; thus *moondoggle*, any form of lunar exploration judged to be a waste of public money. [according to the term's coiner, Robert Marshall: '"Boon doggles" is simply a term applied back in the pioneer days to what we call gadgets today.' The term also referred to the braided leather lanyard worn by scouts (a *woggle* in the UK) and earlier still to the cowboy term for making saddle trappings out of odds and ends of available leather, something they did when there was no proper work. The 1940s edn. of Brewer notes the Scot. *boondoggle*, a marble given as gift and for which one has not had to make any effort – that ety. has been dropped from the 1995 edn.]

booner *n.* [1970s+] (US) a Black person. [BOON COON ? + overtones of BOONDOCKS, i.e. rural stupidity]

boong/boang *n.* [1940s+] (Aus.) **1** a derog. term for an Aborigine. **2** a native of Papua New Guinea. **3** any non-White person. [Wemba *boong*, a human being, a man]

boong-moll *n.* [1930s+] (Aus.) **1** a passive male homosexual. **2** a prostitute who prefers Aborigine clients. [BOONG + MOLL n.; ? (1) refers to sexual exploitation of female Aborigines]

boongy bungee *see* BOUNGI BUNGEE.

boonie *n.¹* **1** [1950s+] a peasant, a country person. **2** [1950s+] an outdoor lavatory. **3** [1960s–70s] a picnic held in the woods (cf. BOONDOCKER). [BOONDOCKS]

boonie *n.²* [1970s+] a Black person. [BOONER]

boonies *n.* [1960s+] (US campus) rural areas, the country-side (not necessarily rough or unpleasant) (cf. STICKS n.³). [abbr. BOONDOCKS]

boon lip *n.* [1990s] the labia. [BOON n.² (2) + SE *lip*; link to HOTTENTOT APRON]

boopety *adj.* [20C] (US) arrogant, self-important. [UPPITY]

boops *n.* [1970s+] (W.I./Jam.) a wealthy lover (cf. SUGAR DADDY). [? POPS n.⁸]

boopsie *n.* [1970s+] (W.I.) a woman who enjoys the favours (material and otherwise) of her wealthy lover. [BOOPS + sfx. -*ie*; note POPSIE]

boose *n.* [20C] (US) the mouth. [Scot. *buss*, mouth]

booshwa/booshwah *see* BUSHWA.

boost *v.¹* [early 19C+] (US) to praise, to extol, esp. one's own town or city; thus *booster*, one who makes such promotions.

boost *v.²* **1** [1950s+] (US) to steal, esp. to shoplift. **2** [1980s+] (US drugs) to inject a drug. [SE *boost*, to lift, to push, to hoist]

boost *v.³* [1980s+] (US campus) to seduce, to have sexual intercourse with. [ext. of BOOST v.²]

boost and shoot, to *phr.* [1960s+] (drugs) to steal to support a drug habit. [BOOST v.² + SHOOT v.⁶, lit. to steal and inject]

booster *n.¹* [20C] (US) something exceptional of its type (cf. BUSTER). [BOOST v.¹]

booster *n.²* [20C] (US) **1** a shoplifter on a large and professional scale. **2** a thief. [BOOST v.² (1)]

booster *n.³* [20C] (US) a house player in a casino who entices genuine players to bet (and usu. lose) their money (cf. SHILL n.²). [BOOST v.² (1)]

booster *v.* [1970s+] (drugs) to inhale cocaine. [ext. of SE *boost*, to raise; i.e. one 'raises' the drug up one's nose]

boost up *v.* [1990s] (US) to increase the volume.

boot *n.¹* **1** [late 19C+] as *the boot*, ejection, dismissal, defeat in all cases, esp. when sudden and ruthless; thus *get the boot*, to be dismissed (cf. FOOT n.). **2** [1920s+] (US) a thrill; *boot in the ass*, a thrill, a jolt of pleasure. [fig. uses of SE *boot*, a kick]

boot *n.²* [1900s–10s] (US campus) a toady, a sycophant. [abbr. BOOTLICKER]

boot *n.³* **1** [1910s+] (US milit.) any new recruit in the US armed forces; thus *boot camp*, basic training camp, *boot second lieutenant*, a newly commissioned second lieutenant. **2** [1950s+] (US/UK Black) a fellow Black (usu. derog.). **3** [1950s+] (orig. US) an automobile tyre. **4** [1950s+] a woman, the implication is an unattractive one; thus often as *old boot*. [SE *boot*, the orig. ref. was to the leggings worn by recruits to the US Navy during training]

boot *n.⁴* [1920s–40s] (US) a *boot*legger. [abbr.]

boot *n.⁵* [1970s+] (US) a condom.

boot *v.¹* [20C] (US) to walk or run away.

boot *v.²* [1900s–10s] (US campus) to toady to. [BOOT n.²]

boot *v.³* [1920s–30s] (US) to bootleg. [BOOT n.³]

boot *v.⁴* [1920s–50s] (US Black) to give, to hand over. [SE *boot*, to share (booty)]

boot *v.⁵* **1** [1940s] (US Black) to introduce. **2** [1940s–50s] (US Black) to become aware.

boot *v.⁶* [1950s+] (drugs) to inject a drug. [the user inserts the needle, draws up a little blood into the syringe, then injects it; this can be repeated several times and this 'pumping' supposedly intensifies the RUSH n.² that accompanies the injection; ? thus it 'gives one a kick']

boot *v.⁷* [1970s+] (US campus) to vomit. [? echoic]

boot around *v.* [20C] to kick, usu. in a fight.

boot-catcher *n.* [late 18C–early 19C] the servant whose task it is to help guests off with and to clean their boots on arrival at an inn.

bootchkey/butchski *n.* [20C] (US) a Czech immigrant (cf. CHESKY). [Czech *pockej*, wait, used by Czech youngsters while playing games and thus adopted as generic by early Eastern European immigrants to US]

boot-eater *n.* [late 19C] a juror who would rather 'eat their boots' than find anyone guilty.

booted *adj.*[1] [mid-19C+] (US campus) expelled. [SE *boot*, to eject]

booted/booted on *adj.*[2] [1900s–40s] (US Black) aware, knowledgeable, smart (cf. HAVE ONE'S BOOTS ON). [BOOT v.[5] (2)]

booted *adj.*[3] [1950s+] (drugs) under the influence of (narcotic) drugs. [BOOT v.[6]]

booter *n.*[1] (US) [1920s–40s] a bootlegger. [BOOT n.[4]]

booter *n.*[2] [1940s] (US campus) a toady, a sycophant. [BOOT n.[2]]

bootfaced *adj.* [1940s+] gloomy, miserable-looking. [naut. jargon *have a sea-boot face*, to look unhappy]

booth *n.* [mid-16C–19C] (Und.) a house; thus *heave a booth*, to rob a house. [SE *booth*, a dwelling, a stall]

boot-haler *n.* [16C] a highwayman. [SE *booty* + *hale*, haul]

boot hill *n.* (US) **1** [19C] a cemetery. **2** [20C] a prison cemetery. [orig. Western *Boot Hill*, in Dodge City, the cemetery set aside for those who died 'with their boots on', i.e. in a gunfight]

boot-hill two-step *n.* [20C] (US) diarrhoea. [SE *boot-heel* + *two-step*]

bootie *n.* [1920s–30s] (US) a *boot*legger. [abbr.]

booting *n.*[1] [1920s–30s] (US Black) having sexual intercourse. [BOOTY n.[1]]

booting *n.*[2] [1960s] (drugs) enjoying the immediate effects of a narcotic injection (cf. RUSH n.[2]). [BOOT v.[6]]

bootkisser *n.* [19C] a sycophant, a toady (cf. ASS-KISSER; BOOTLICK; BOOTLICKER; SUCK-UP).

bootlace *n.* [20C] thin twist tobacco. [resemblance]

bootleg *n.* **1** [late 19C+] (orig. US) illicit liquor, usu. whisky (other than during US Prohibition). **2** [1900s–20s] (US) adulterated coffee, usu. mixed with chicory. **3** [1920s–30s] (US Black) a bootlegger. **4** [1950s+] (orig. US) a bootleg or pirated record or tape. **5** [1990s] (US teen) anything or anyone considered pitiful, embarrassing, second-rate etc. [the orig. practice of carrying the illicit liquor hidden in one's bootlegs]

bootleg *adj.* (orig. US) **1** [late 19C+] transported illegally, smuggled. **2** [late 19C–1900s] fake, counterfeit. [BOOTLEG v.]

bootleg *v.* **1** [late 19C+] to smuggle, to transport illegally (generally, but not invariably of liquor). **2** [1920s–30s] to manufacture illegal liquor. [BOOTLEG n.; later 20C use of (2) is SE]

bootlegger *n.* [late 19C–1930s] (orig. US) a smuggler or manufacturer of illicit liquor; thus *bootlegger turn*, a hand-brake turn (performed to avoid an on-coming car full of revenue officers or police). [BOOTLEG v.; 1940s+ use is SE and covers the pirating of records, tapes, computer games etc]

bootlick *n.* [mid–late 19C] (orig. US) a cowardly, obsequious person, a toady, one who curries favour (cf. BOOTKISSER; SUCK-UP).

bootlick *v.* [mid-19C+] (orig. US) to toady, to curry favour. [BOOTLICK n.]

bootlicker *n.* [mid–19C+] (orig. US) a cowardly, obsequious person, a toady, one who curries favour (cf. BOOTKISSER). [ext. of BOOTLICK n.]

boot lip *n.* [20C] (US) a Black person (cf. BONGO LIP; BOOON LIP). [BOOT n.[2] (2) + SE *lip*]

boots *n.*[1] [early 17C+] a fellow, a person, usu. in combs. e.g. CLEVER-BOOTS; SMARTY-BOOTS.

boots *n.*[2] [late 18C–mid-19C] the servant assigned to the cleaning of boots and other odd jobs. [late 19C+ use SE]

boots *n.*[3] [early 19C] the youngest member, i.e. of a regiment, a club etc. [BOOTS n.[2]]

boots *n.*[4] [1960s] (US Black) a fellow Black person, sometimes derog. [BOOT n.[3] (2)]

boots and all *phr.* [1940s+] (Aus./N.Z.) absolutely, completely, with no reservations.

boots and socks *n.* [20C] (Aus.) venereal disease. [rhy. sl. *boots and socks* = POX n.[1]]

bootsie/bootsy *adj.* [1990s] (US Black teen) bad, phoney, inferior, second-rate. [? BOOTLEG adj. or BOOT n.[1] (1)]

boot-snitch *n.* [1900s–40s] (US Black/Harlem) an informer, a tell-tale. [BOOT n.[2] + SNITCH n.[2]]

bootstrap *v.* [1950s+] (orig. US) to improve one's lot in life by one's own efforts. [phr. *pull oneself up by one's bootstraps*. Note computer jargon *boot(strap)*, to start the machine]

bootsy *see* BOOTSIE.

boot the gong, to *phr.*[1] [1940s+] (US) **1** to fool around. **2** to gossip, to chat.

boot the gong, to *phr.*[2] [1980s+] (drugs) to smoke marijuana. [marijuana-based development of KICK THE GONG AROUND phr.[1]]

boot-trees *n.* [19C] feet.

boot up *v.*[1] **1** [1950s–60s] (US drugs) to use a drink or drug to improve one's feelings, e.g. inject heroin, drink wine. **2** [1970s+] (US Black) to get ready for a fight. [BOOT v.[6]]

boot up *v.*[2] [1970s+] (US Black) to put on a condom. [BOOT n.[5]]

booty/boody *n.* [1920s+] (US Black) **1** a woman, esp. as a sex-object. **2** the vagina. **3** the buttocks; thus *booty-bandit*, a sodomist, a homosexual rapist; *booty-struck*, obsessively lecherous (cf. CUNT-STRUCK). [SE *body*; note BUTT n.[1] (1)]

booty *adj.*[1] [1990s] (US teen) excellent, first-rate, wonderful. [? BEAUTY! or BOOTY adj.[2] (2) on good = bad model]

booty *adj.*[2] [1990s] (US Black/W.I./UK Black teen) **1** weak. **2** second-rate, inferior (cf. BOOTSIE). **3** gullible. [? fig. use of BOOTY n. (3) as a neg. in the same way as ARSE is used]

booty *v.* [17C–18C] to cheat, to play falsely. [PLAY BOOTY]

booty bandit *n.* [20C] (US) a homosexual male. [BOOTY n. (3) + ARSE BANDIT]

booty-buffer *n.* [1990s] **1** a male homosexual. **2** a sodomite. [BOOTY n. (3) + SE *buffer*, one who polishes]

booty call *n.* [1990s] (US Black teen) a late-night rendezvous. [BOOTY n. (1) + SE *call*]

booty drought *n.* [1980s+] (US Black/campus) a lack of sex. [BOOTY (1) + DROUGHT]

booty-fellow *n.* [late 17C–early 19C] one who takes a share of the booty. [SE *booty* + *fellow*]

boo-ya *adj.* [1990s] (W.I./UK/US Black teen) totally wonderful, incredibly fine. [? hip-hop group the *Boo-Ya Tribe*]

booya!/booyah! *excl.* [1980s+] **1** (US campus) a term used to indicate suddenness or surprise (cf. BANG; WHAM!). **2** (US Black gang) an echoic term used to imitate the sound of a shotgun being fired (cf. BOOYAKA!). [SE *excl. boo!* + *yah*]

booyaka! *excl.* [1980s+] (W.I./UK Black teen) an excl. of delight, pleasure, made by using the mouth to simulate gun shots fired in celebration or appreciation of something (cf. BOOYA!; PRAM! PRAM!).

booze *n.* **1** [mid-16C+] alcohol, a drink. **2** [late 18C–late 19C] a drinking spree. [BOUSE n.; the orig. spelling is *bouse*, but it has been superseded by *booze* since the mid-16C]

booze *v.* [mid-16C+] to drink. [BOUSE v.]

booze artist *n.* [1920s+] (orig. Aus.) a drunkard. [BOOZE n. (1) + ARTIST n.[2]]

booze balloon *n.* [1970s+] (N.Z.) a fat stomach that has resulted from sustained heavy drinking (cf. BEER BARREL). [BOOZE n. (1) + SE *balloon*]

booze/beer barn *n.* [1980s+] (N.Z.) anywhere dedicated to the large-scale and rapid service of alcohol. [BOOZE n. (1) + SE *barn*]

booze belly *n.* [20C] (US) a fat stomach that has resulted from excessive drinking (cf. BEER BARREL). [BOOZE n. (1) + SE *belly*]

booze bus *n.* [1990s] (Aus.) a police van used for random breath tests (for excess alcohol). [BOOZE n. (1) + SE *bus*]

booze-capper *n.* [1900s–10s] a woman who works in a bar to persuade customers to drink more than they wish or should (cf. B-GIRL). [BOOZE n. (1) + CAPPER n.¹]

booze clerk *n.* [late 19C–1910s] (US) a bartender. [BOOZE n. (1) + SE *clerk*]

booze crib/joint/mill *n.* [mid-19C–1930s] (US) a bar, a tavern, any drinking establishment. [BOOZE n. (1) + CRIB n.³ (1)/JOINT n.³ (3)/SE *mill*, a place of activity, work]

boozed *adj.* [mid-19C+] drunk. [BOOZE n. (1)]

boozed up *adj.* [late 19C+] drunk. [BOOZED adj.]

booze-fencer *n.* [late 19C] a licensed victualler. [BOOZE n. (1) + FENCER]

boozefest *n.* [1920s–60s] (US) a drunken party. [BOOZE n. (1) + FEST]

booze-fighter *n.* [1910s+] (Aus./US) a drunkard; thus *booze-fighting*, rowdy, regular drinking. [BOOZE n. + SE *fighter*]

booze-head *n.* [1960s–70s] (US) a drunkard. [BOOZE n. (1) + sfx. -HEAD (2)]

booze-hoister *n.* [1910s–20s] (US) a prodigious drinker. [BOOZE n. + SE *hoister*]

booze hound *n.* [1920s+] (US) a dedicated drinker (cf. BOOZE ARTIST; LUSH HOUND; SAUCE HOUND). [BOOZE n. (1) + sfx. -HOUND]

booze joint/mill *see* BOOZE CRIB.

booze-pusher *n.* [late 19C] a licensed victualler (cf. BOOZE-FENCER). [BOOZE n. (1) + SE *pusher*]

boozer *n.* [late 19C+] **1** a public house (cf. BOUSING-KEN). **2** a drunkard. [BOOZE n. (1)]

boozeroo *n.* [1940s+] (N.Z.) a drinking spree. [BOOZE n. (1) + sfx. -EROO]

booze-rooster *n.* [1960s] (N.Z.) a heavy drinker. [play on BOOZEROO]

boozery *n.* [1910s–50s] (US) a drinking place. [BOOZER n. (1) + sfx. -y]

booze-shunter *n.* [late 19C–1900s] a beer drinker. [BOOZE n. (1) + SE *shunter*; coined by railwaymen working for the Southern Region]

booze-up *n.* [late 19C+] a drinking party. [BOOZE n. (2)]

booze up *v.* [1960s] **1** to drink, to get drunk. **2** to make someone else drink or drunk. [BOOZE v.]

boozician *n.* [late 19C–1930s] (Aus.) a drunkard (cf. BOOZINGTON). [BOOZE n. (1)+ sfx. -ician, on pattern of physician, mortician]

boozing-ken *see* BOUSING-KEN.

boozington/Mr Boozington *n.* [mid-19C–1910s] (Aus.) a drunkard (cf. LUSHINGTON). [BOOZE n. + sfx. -ington]

boozle *n.* [1940s–60s] sexual intercourse. [? fig. use of BAMBOOZLE, i.e. a confusion of bodies]

boozle *v.* [late 18C] to confuse, to outwit. [abbr. BAMBOOZLE]

boozorium *n.* [1960s+] (Can.) a bar-room, esp. in a hotel. [BOOZE n. + sfx. -orium]

boozy *n.* [1920s+] (Anglo-Irish) a drunkard. [BOOZE n. (1) + sfx. -y]

boozy *adj.* [late 18C+] drunk. [BOOZE n. (1) + sfx. -y]

bop *n.*¹ **1** [1940s+] a blow. **2** [1950s+] a dance. **3** [1950s–60s] (US) a member of a teen street gang. **4** [1950s–60s] (US) a fight between teen street gangs (cf. BOPPING CLUB). **5** [1970s+] (drugs) an injection of a narcotic drug, the immediate effect of any drug, e.g. a puff on a cannabis cigarette (cf. HIT n.⁴)

bop *n.*² [1970s+] (US Black) foolish talk, prattle, nonsense. [abbr. REBOP]

bop *n.*³ [1980s+] (S.Afr.) the former Republic of Bophuthatswana, one of the Black 'homelands' with its territory surrounded by the Transvaal and Orange Free State. [lit. 'gathering of the Tswana']

bop *v.* **1** [1920s+] (orig. US) to hit. **2** [1930s+] to kill. **3** [1930s+] to walk in a carefree, bouncy way. **4** [1950s] [(US) to fight (with a weapon). **5** [1970s] (US) to have sexual intercourse.

6 [1980s] to be exciting (cf. JUMP v.). [Kentish dial. *bop*, to throw anything down with a resounding noise; ult. onomat.]

bop around *v.* [20C] to keep moving, to wander about rather than stay put. [BOP v. (3)]

bo-peep *n.* [late 19C+] sleep (cf. LITTLE BO-PEEP). [rhy. sl.]

bop one's baloney, to *phr.* [1970s+] to masturbate (cf. ACCOST THE OSCAR MEYER). [BOP v. (1) + BALONEY n.²]

bop one's richard, to *phr.* [1990s] to masturbate. [BOP v. (1) + SE *Richard*, i.e. DICK n.⁵ (1)]

bop out *v.* [20C] (US) to faint. [BOP v. (1); the image is of being knocked over]

bopper *n.*¹ [1950s–60s] (US) a gang fighter. [BOP v. (4)]

bopper *n.*² [1970s] a young girl, usu. in very early teens, with a predilection for rock music and the boys who play it. [abbr. TEENYBOPPER]

boppers *n.*¹ [1960s–70s] (US campus) boots, shoes. [echoic of the noise of one's footsteps]

boppers *n.*² [1980s+] (drugs) amyl nitrite (cf. AIMIES n.²). [var. POPPERS n.³]

bopping club *n.* [1950s] (US) a street gang that has regular fights with opponents. [BOP v. (4)]

bopping gang *n.* [1950s] (US) a street gang with active fighters (cf. BOPPING CLUB). [BOP v. (4)]

boppy *adj.* [1940s+] jolly, cheery, upbeat. [jazz use, *bop* music]

bora *n.* [1990s] (Black) a knife. [? SE *borer*]

borachio/borarco *n.* [late 17C–early 19C] a drunkard. [synon. Ital./Sp.]

boracic/brassic/brassick *adj.* [1950s+] out of funds, impoverished, pron. 'brassic' [rhy. sl. *boracic lint* = SKINT]

borak/borack/borax *n.* [mid-19C+] (Aus./N.Z.) nonsense, humbug, chaff, banter (cf. MULLOCK; POKE THE BORAK). [Wathawurung *burag*, no, not, via. Aus. pidgin *borak*, used to express negation]

borarco *see* BORACHIO.

borass/boress *n.* [1950s] (US campus) a trick, a prank, a hoax. [? fig. use of BORAX or *bore ass*]

borass/boress *v.* [1950s] (US campus) to hoax, to play tricks. [BORASS n.]

borax *n.*¹ *see* BORAK.

borax *n.*² [1920s+] (US) rubbish, lies, exaggeration. [SE *borax*, cheap and shoddy material, esp. as peddled by immigrant Jews; supposedly orig. in the practice of a maker of borax (acid borate of sodium) soap offering coupons for cheap furniture]

bord/borde *n.* [16C–late 18C] a shilling (5p). [SE *bord*, shield]

bordeaux *n.* [mid-19C–1900s] blood (cf. CLARET). [SE *bordeaux*, a variety of red wine]

bordello *n.* [late 16C–18C] a brothel. [SE *bordel*, a brothel; ult. OF *bordel*, cabin, hut, brothel. Post-18C use is SE, if (consciously) archaic]

bordens *n.* [1940s–70s] (US) the female breasts; also ext. as *borden's and elsie's*, *bordens and bowman* (cf. CREAM JUGS; NORKS). [the firm *Borden's*, producers of milk and dairy products; *elsie* presumably refers to a 'typical' name for a cow]

borders/border reds *n.* [1980s+] (drugs) non-proprietary capsules of barbiturate powder sold on the black market and with implication of having been made up on the US/Mexico border. [their container, a capsule with a red border]

bore *n.*¹ [18C] the vagina (cf. BLACK HOLE n.¹). [SE *bore*, a hole, a chink, crevice, or cranny]

bore *n.*² **1** [mid-18C] the equivalent of Fr. *ennui*, a feeling of world-weariness, the equivalent of Eng. *spleen*; thus *French bore*, one who feels or at least affects indifference to all things and people. **2** [late 18C–early 19C] a tedious person or thing, a nuisance. **3** [early 19C] (US) a trick, a hoax. [*OED* states ety. unknown. ? f. SE *bore*, to drill into, but this fails to account for sense (1), from which (2) and (3) presumably stem. E.P. suggests poss. link to *boar*, an uncouth, ignorant person, but this still ignores (1), which lasted as sl. no later than the 1760s. Grose notes that (2) and (3) were very fashionable *c*.1780 and then vanished. 'Not so, burly Grose,' says Hotten in 1867, 'the term is still in favour and as piquant and expressive as ever.' However, although Hotten includes it the word was by then virtually, if not actually SE]

bore v.[1] [early 17C–early 19C] (US) to tease, to mock, to humiliate. [SE *bore*, to drill a hole; 19C use US only]

bore v.[2] [18C] to have sexual intercourse (cf. BANG v.[1]). [SE *bore*, to drill a hole]

bore v.[3] [mid-18C+] to impose ones views, opinions or simply presence upon those who find them tedious and irritating. [BORE n.[1]; SE in 20C]

bore v.[4] [late 18C–mid-19C] to irritate, to annoy. [SE from mid-19C]

bore v.[5] [mid-19C–1950s] (US) to shoot a hole in (cf. DRILL v.[3]). [note 17C SE *bore*, to run through with a sword]

bore a hole in, to phr. [mid-19C] (US) to shoot.

bore for the simples phr. [19C] (US) a phr. used with ref. to a simpleton, e.g. *he ought to be bored for the simples*, he is a fool. [SE *bore*, to make a hole + dial. *simples*, simple-mindedness; ? a ref. to trepanning]

bore it up v. [1940s+] (Aus.) to attack viciously or energetically. [SE *bore*, to pierce, stab, run through with a weapon; to wound]

bore someone a new one, to phr. [1950s] (US) to attack savagely, either physically or verbally (cf. TEAR SOMEONE A NEW ASS).

bore someone rigid, to phr. [1970s+] to bore very much. [fig. use of BORE v.[1] + SE *rigid*]

bore someone's ear, to phr. [late 18C–late 19C] to bore (as a talker). [BORE v.[1] + pun]

boress see BORASS.

bore stiff v. [20C] (orig. US) to bore completely. [BORE v.[3] + SE *stiff*, corpse-like; one is rendered virtually dead by tedium]

bore the pants off, to phr. [1930s+] to bore completely and totally.

boretto-man n. [early 18C] a male homosexual. [SE *bore* + Ital. dimin. sfx. *-etto*; i.e. 'a little borer']

bore up v. [1990s] (Black) to fight, to assault (cf. BORE IT UP). [SE *bore*, to drill a hole]

boris n. [1990s] the vagina. [? somewhat far-fetched resemblance; note the song 'Boris the Spider', by the Who (1967)]

born-again n. [1990s] (US campus) a fundamentalist Christian. [SE *born* + *again*, after John 3:3: 'Except a man be born again, he cannot see the kingdom of God']

born at Hogs Norton/Hogs Norton where the pigs play upon the organs phr. [mid-16C–19C] used of one who is boorish, uncouth. [according to Apperson (1929), the village of Hock Norton, Leicestershire, did once have an organist named Piggs]

born in a mill phr. [late 16C–late 17C] deaf. [mills are noisy]

born near the plantain root phr. [mid-19C] (W.I.) used of a dyed-in-the-wool country person. [SE *plantain*, a typical W.I. crop]

born on Wednesday looking both ways for Sunday phr. [19C] (US) cross-eyed; also *born in the middle of the week, looking...*

born under a threepenny halfpenny planet/planet, never to be worth a groat phr. [17C–19C] a complete failure.

born with burned feet phr. [20C] (US) illegitimate (cf. BRED IN THE DITCH; HAVE CALLUSES ON ONE'S FEET).

boro-onions n. [early–mid-19C] (Cockney) inhabitants of Southwark. [*Boro(ugh)nians*]

borrachio/borracho n. [17C–19C, UK; 20C, US] **1** a drunkard. **2** a skin for holding wine. [Sp. *borracho*, a drunkard, drunk]

borrow v. [late 19C+] (US Und.) to steal (cf. ACQUIRE). [ironic use of SE]

borrow and beg n. [late 19C+] an egg. [rhy. sl.]

borscht belt/circuit n. [1930s+] (show business) a circuit of predominantly Jewish hotels in the Catskill Mountains, New York State (cf. BLACK BELT). [Rus. *borshch(t)*, a soup made predominantly of beetroot and cabbage and highly popular among Middle-European Jews + SE *belt*, a zone, an area]

borstal mark/spot n. [1990s] a blue dot tattooed on the face, the mark of a spell in borstal.

b.o.s. phr. [1990s] (US P.R. gangs) a beating on sight (cf. T.O.S. n.[2]). [abbr.]

bosbefok see BOSSIE.

bosca/boscar see BOSKER.

bosching/black-'n'-deckering. n. [1990s] drilling a hole between cubicles in a public lavatory with the intent of spying on one's neighbour. [*Bosch, Black and Decker*, two popular proprietary brands of electric drill]

bosco n. [1920s–70s] a foolish, unimportant person. [? BOSKY]

bosh n.[1] [mid-18C+] nonsense, rubbish. [Turk. *bosh*, empty, worthless. The term gained enormous popularity from the success of James Morier's novel *Ayesha* (1834), a bestseller, especially in the Standard Novels' edition of 1846]

bosh n.[2] [19C] a fiddle; *bosh-faker, bosh-killer, boshman*, a fiddle player. [Rom. *bosh*, to fiddle, to crow]

bosh n.[3] [late 19C–1900s] margarine or any other substitute (e.g. the short-lived *butterine*) for butter. [abbr. *bosch butter*, artificial butter manufactured at 'Hertogenbosch' or 'Bosch' (Bois-le-duc) in Holland; but note BOSH n.[1]]

bosh v. [late 19C] **1** to spoil, to render useless. **2** to apply liberally (used of paint, plaster etc). [BOSH n.[1]]

bosher n. [1910s–30s] one who talks nonsense. [BOSH n.[1]]

bosh-shot n. [1930s–50s] a bad shot, an unsuccessful attempt (cf. BOSS-SHOT). [BOSH v. + SE *shot*]

boshta/boshter adj. [1900s–20s] (Aus.) good (cf. BONZER). [? SE *bonanza*]

bosh up v. [20C] to go bankrupt. [BOSH v. (1)]

boshy adj. [mid-18C+] foolish, nonsensical. [BOSH n.[1]]

bosie v. [1970s+] (W.I./Trin.) to beat extremely hard, so as to bend the victim double. [W.I. *bosie*, a hunchback; ? link to Aus. cricket jargon *bosie*, a googly or 'wrong 'un'; it 'bends' across the pitch]

boskage of Venus n. [19C] the vagina (cf. BEAUTY SPOT n.[1]). [SE *boskage*, a thicket, grove, woody undergrowth]

bos-ken/bosken n. [19C] a farm house. [Lat. *bos*, ox + KEN n.[1]]

bosker/bosca/boscar adj. [20C] (Aus./N.Z.) good. [var. on BONZER]

boskiness n. [late 19C] drunkenness. [BOSKY + sfx. *-ness*]

bosky adj. [early 18C–mid-19C] drunk. [? SE *bosky*, wooded, bushy; thus one's vision is obscured and one's feet may stumble]

bos-man/bosman n. [18C] a farmer (cf. BOS-KEN). [Lat. *bos*, ox]

bosom friend n. **1** [18C+] a louse (cf. FAMILIARS; FRIEND IN NEED; GENTLEMAN IN BROWN; GENTLEMAN'S COMPANION). **2** [19C] alcoholic drink. **3** [20C] (US) a pack of money kept for security inside her brassiere by a woman while she is travelling. [play on SE *bosom friend*, an especially intimate friend]

boss n.[1] [late 16C–mid-17C] a fat woman. [SE *boss*, a swelling or protuberance]

boss n.[2] [mid-17C+] the master, the manager, the 'guvnor'. [Du. *baas*, master, in which form it first appeared in the American colonies in mid-17C. The term did not arrive in the UK until the mid-19C and has always been sl. or colloq.]

Boss, the n.³ [20C] (orig. US) God. [the use of sl. to 'humanize' the Deity]

boss adj. [mid-19C+] (US) **1** the best. **2** excellent, wonderful; also intensified as *boss like hot sauce*. [BOSS n.²]

boss v. [late 19C–1900s] **1** to domineer, to order about. **2** to make a mess of, to spoil. [BOSS n.²; (1) is SE in 20C]

boss adv. [1980s+] (US) splendidly, excellently, perfectly. [BOSS adj.]

boss! excl. [mid-19C–1910s] (orig. US) a term of address to a man whose name one does not know. [BOSS n.²]

boss-boy n. [20C] (S.Afr.) a Black foreman or overseer in charge of subordinate Black workers. [BOSS n.² + S.Afr. derog. *boy*, an African, usu. a servant or labourer]

boss charlie/charley n. [20C] (US Black) a White man, esp. in authority (cf. MR CHARLIE). [BOSS n.² + generic use of proper name *Charlie*]

boss cocky n. [late 19C+] **1** (Aus.) a farmer who employs labour and still works. **2** (Aus.) a person in authority. **3** (Aus./N.Z.) the overseer of a shearing-shed. [BOSS n.² + COCKY n.²]

boss dog n. [20C] (US) an important person or one who poses as such (cf. BIG DOG). [BOSS n.² + SE *dog*]

bossers n. [late 19C–1900s] spectacles. [? BOSS-EYED]

boss-eye n. [late 19C+] one who squints or has an injured eye. [BOSS v. (2) + SE *eye*]

boss-eyed adj. [mid-19C+] squinting. [BOSS-EYE]

bossie/bosbefok adj. [1970s+] (S.Afr.) used orig. in army to indicate one has gone mad through exposure to tropical heat and life in the bush, lit. 'bush-fucked'. [Afk. *bos*, bush + *befok*, FUCKED]

boss-lady/-woman n. [20C] (US) a wife who dominates her husband. [fem. version of BOSS-MAN]

boss-man n. [19C] (US) the overseer, foreman, employer, chief prison guard, anyone in authority. [BOSS n.² + SE *man*]

boss nigger in charge n. [1930s+] (US Black) a sarcastic reference to any Black authority-figure (cf. HEAD NIGGER IN CHARGE). [BOSS n.² + NIGGER n.]

bosso n. [1930s] a glance. [BOSS-EYED + sfx. -O, on model of DEKKO]

boss one's own shoes, to phr. [late 19C+] (US) to take care of one's business. [lit. 'to manage one's own shoes']

boss player n. [1960s] (US Black) a thoroughly experienced, professional, worldly wise pimp who may even transcend pimping for superior occupations; the term can be applied to any admirable figure outside the pimp milieu. [BOSS adj. + PLAYER]

boss-shot n. [late 19C–1910s] (orig. US) a bad shot, an unsuccessful attempt. [BOSS v. (2) + SE *shot*]

boss the show, to phr. [late 19C] to take charge of events (cf. RUN THE SHOW). [BOSS v. (1) + SHOW n.¹ (1)]

boss trick n. [1960s+] a good customer. [BOSS adj. + TRICK n.⁴ (2)]

boss up v. [20C] (S.Afr.) **1** to manage a house, to organize the servants. **2** to work hard. [BOSS v. (1)]

boss up! excl. [late 19C+] (S.Afr.) take care! look out! [calque f. Cape Du. *pas op! look out!*]

boss-woman see BOSS-LADY.

bossy adj. [late 19C+] (orig. US) officious, domineering. [BOSS n.² + sfx. -y]

bossy-barefoot n. [20C] (US) one who is dedicated to telling others what to do. [BOSSY + SE *barefoot*, unadorned; thus unrestrained]

bossy-boots n. [20C] (usu. children) an officious, domineering person. [BOSSY + BOOTS n.¹, on model of SMARTIEPANTS; note

the nickname given to essayist and critic Cyril Connolly (1903–74): Smartyboots]

bosta n. (W.I.) **1** [1940s+] a tough, chewy sweet (cf. BUSTA BACKBONE). **2** [1950s] a sandal made from recycled tyres (cf. DONE PROMOTE). [proper name of the populist politician Sir Alexander *Bustamente* (1884–1977), seen as tough]

Boston strawberries n. [late 19C] (US) baked beans. [the city's stereotyped dish. The other stereotype is meanness; thus railroad use *Boston quarter*, a nickel or dime tip]

Boston woodcock n. [20C] (US) pork and beans (cf. ADIRONDACK STEAK). [analogous with SE *Scotch woodcock*, hardboiled eggs chopped up, mixed with anchovy sauce, and then laid on slices of hot buttered toast. The foodstuffs here are staples of the Boston area]

bosy see BOASIE adj.

bot n.¹ [19C] a *bottle*. [abbr.]

bot n.² **1** [late 19C] (Aus.) a scheme, a plot, a plan. **2** [1910s] (Aus./N.Z.) a cadger, a scrounger, a hanger-on. [for ety. see BOTFLY]

bot v. [1920s+] (Aus./N.Z.) to scrounge; thus *on the bot*, scrounging, *cold botting*, knocking on a stranger's front door and asking for food. [BOT n.²; note salesman's jargon *cold call*, to arrive without a prior appointment in the hope of making a sale]

bot about v. [1920s+] (Aus./N.Z.) to wander around. [BOT v.]

botanical excursion n. [mid-19C] transportation to New South Wales. [a pun on the penal colony at *Botany Bay*]

Botany Bay n.¹ [late 18C–late 19C] penal servitude. [Australia's earliest convict settlement was at *Botany Bay*, New South Wales]

Botany Bay n.² [19C] the vagina (cf. ANTIPODES). [the penal colony of *Botany Bay* was 'down under']

Botany Bay v. [1940s+] (Aus.) to run away. [rhy. sl.]

Botany Bay coat-of-arms n. [early–mid-19C] (Aus.) a broken nose and black eyes (cf. COLONIAL LIVERY). [the violence that was prevalent at the convict settlement]

Botany Bay fever n. [early–mid-19C] transportation to New South Wales.

Botany beer party n. [late 19C] a party at which there is no form of intoxicating liquor. [brandname of *Botany beer*, which was declared after a court case in 1883 not to be real beer]

bot/bott n. [1920s+] the posterior. [abbr. SE *bottom*]

botch n.¹ [late 18C] a tailor. [abbr. SE *botcher*, one who repairs or patches; also note SE *bodger* and dial. *botch*, a cobbler]

botch n.² [1960s] (US) gonorrhoea. [SE *botch*, an eruptive sore, an ulcer, a plague-spot]

bote n. [20C] (US prison/Hisp.Am.) a county prison. [Sp.; pron. bo-tay]

botfly n. (Aus.) **1** [20C] an unpleasant, troublesome, interfering person. **2** [1940s+] a scrounger. [SE *botfly*, an insect of the genus *Oestrus*; its eggs produce the parasitical worm or maggot, the bot]

botha's babes n. [1970s+] (S.Afr.) members of the South African Army Women's College at George, Cape Province; also known as Afk. *soldoedie*, 'soldier lass'. [name of President P.W. *Botha* (b.1916), who established the corps in 1971]

both ends of the busk phr. [late 18C–early 19C] a toast. [SE *busk*, a corset, spec. its stiffening/supporting whalebone or other agent; the top would support the breasts, the bottom be near the vagina, the parts of the body that are being celebrated]

bother n. [mid-19C+] trouble, difficulties; thus *in bother*, in trouble.

bother! excl. [mid-19C+] euph. for BUGGER! [Anglo-Irish but no spec. root found. ? corruption of *pother*, disturbance]

botherate v. [1960s] (US Black) to annoy, to menace, to threaten. [SE *bother*, to annoy + sfx. *-ate*]

botheration n. [late 18C–1960s] annoyance, irritation. [SE *bother*, late 19C+ use is mainly US Black]

botheration! excl. [mid-19C+] euph. for BUGGERATION!; a mild excl. of annoyance that precludes anything more lurid and thus taboo.

bothered up adj. [1920s+] flustered, maniacally nervous, sometimes through the suppression of lust (cf. ALL HOT AND BOTHERED).

botherment n. [mid-19C] annoyance, irritation (cf. BOTHERA-TION). [SE *bother* + sfx. *-ment*]

bother one's soul-case see BURST OUT ONE'S SOUL-CASE.

both-side adj. [20C] (W.I./Trin.) deceitful, hypocritical (cf. TWO-MOUTH). [one who speaks out of 'both sides' of their mouth]

both ways from the ace phr. [1910s] (US) in every way, completely. [playing card imagery]

botray n. [1980s+] (drugs) crack cocaine. [? Sp.]

bots n. [19C] a general sense of physical unease (cf. MULLI-GRUBS). [SE *bots*, a disease of horses caused by infestation of botfly larvae in the digestive tract]

botsie n. [20C] (W.I.) the posterior, the buttocks. [SE *bottom*]

bott n. see BOT.

bott v. [1990s] to sodomize. [abbr. SE *bottom*]

bottie/botty n. [mid-19C+] (juv.) a baby's or small child's buttocks. [abbr. SE *bottom*]

bottle n.[1] [late 19C–1930s] a share of money. [BOTTLE v.[1]]

bottle/bottle and stopper n.[2] [1950s–70s] a policeman. [rhy. sl. *bottle and stopper* = COPPER n.[3] (1)]

bottle n.[3] [1950s+] courage, bravery. [rhy. sl. *bottle and glass* = ARSE n.[1], which, in turn, plays on 18C SE *bottom*, character]

bottle v.[1] [late 19C+] to collect money from a busker's audience; thus *bottling*, collecting money from the audience, 'passing round the hat'. [ext. use of SE *bottle* as a general container]

bottle v.[2] [20C] 1 to sodomize. 2 of a man, to have sexual intercourse. 3 (gay) to lick the anus. [rhy. sl. *bottle and glass* = ARSE n.[1] (1)]

bottle v.[3] [20C] to stink, to smell badly. [? rhy. sl. *bottle of drink* = stink]

bottle v.[4] [20C] to hit someone (in the face) with a broken bottle (cf. GLASS v.).

bottle-ache n. [mid-19C–1900s] delirium tremens.

bottle and stopper see BOTTLE n.[2].

bottle and glass n. 1 [20C] (Aus.) the posterior. 2 [1950s+] courage, bravery 'spirit' (cf. BOTTLE n.[3]). [rhy. sl. *bottle and glass* = ARSE n.[1]; for semantics see BOTTLE n.[3]]

bottle-arse n. [late 19C–1910s] a person with notably broad buttocks; thus *bottle-arsed*. [SE *bottle* + ARSE n.[1]; resemblance]

bottle baby n.[1] [1920s+] (orig. US) an alcoholic tramp who has become insane and whose mental age is that of an infant. [pun on SE *bottle baby*, an infant fed by bottle rather than by breast]

bottle baby n.[2] [1940s+] a woman with dyed blonde hair (cf. BOTTLE BLONDE; BUSHFIRE BLONDE; SUICIDE BLONDE). [SE *bottle*, i.e. the hair colour 'comes out of a bottle + BABY n.[2] (1)]

bottle blonde n. [1940s+] a woman with dyed hair (cf. BOTTLE BABY n.[2]).

bottle-boy n. [1930s–40s] (US) a drunkard, an alcoholic.

bottled adj.[1] [late 19C] 1 stuck in one place, halted. 2 arrested. [BOTTLE UP. Note Ware's suggestion that it refers to the trapping by the US Navy of the Spanish fleet in Santiago in 1898]

bottled adj.[2] [1920s–40s] drunk.

bottled bellyache n. [20C] (tramp) cheap beer. [its effects]

bottled earthquake n. [mid-19C] a very powerful fighter.

bottled in a pepper-patch phr. [20C] (US) of whisky, extremely potent. [the chilli-pepper as emblematic of 'heat', thus strength]

bottled in the barn n. [20C] (US) illicitly distilled whisky (cf. MOONSHINE n.). [pun on SE *bottled in bond*, bottled and then held in a Customs' warehouse until the appropriate duty is paid]

bottled up adj. [late 19C] fully occupied, unable to take on any new commitments. [SE *bottled up*, contained in a bottle]

bottlegreen and lousy adj. [1940s–50s] (Aus.) utterly down-and-out. [one's complexion and the state of one's body]

bottlehead n. [mid-17C–late 18C] 1 a fool; thus *bottle-headed*, foolish. 2 a drunkard. [SE *bottle* + sfx. -HEAD (1); their brains are fuddled by alcohol, whether actually or figuratively]

bottle-holder n. [19C] a supporter, an assistant. [boxing use, where the fighter's 'second' holds a bottle of water]

bottle it phr.[1] [late 19C+] (US) be quiet, shut up. [SE *bottle it up*]

bottle it phr.[2] [1950s+] to back down, to act in a cowardly manner (cf. BOTTLE OUT). [BOTTLE n.[2]]

bottle legs n. [20C] crooked legs. [their shape]

bottleneck n. [1970s+] (S.Afr. drugs) a mixture of tobacco and marijuana (sometimes with other forms of drugs) packed into the neck of a broken bottle, which serves as a pipe and through which it is smoked.

bottle-nose n. [late 19C–1900s] one who has a large, prominent nose. [its shape + the implication of drunkenness]

bottle-o n. [late 19C+] (Aus./N.Z.) a collector and seller of used bottles. [SE *bottle* + sfx. -O (4)]

bottle of beer n. [20C] the ear. [rhy. sl.]

bottle of cola n. [1940s–50s] a bowler hat. [rhy. sl.]

bottle of fizz n. [20C] pickpocketing. [rhy. sl. *bottle of fizz* = WHIZ n.[4]]

bottle of sauce n. [late 19C+] a horse. [rhy. sl.]

bottle of scotch n. [late 19C] a watch, spec. one of the cheap Waterbury watches, produced since 1884 in Waterbury, Connecticut (cf. GORDON AND GOTCH; WATERBURY WATCH). [rhy. sl.]

bottle of spruce n.[1] [19C] zero, nothing; thus *I don't care a bottle of spruce*. [proper name of *Spruce* Beer, a weak, cheap and thus essentially valueless commodity; its price was 2d.]

bottle of spruce n.[2] [mid-19C] twopence. [rhy. sl. *bottle of spruce* = DEUCE n.[2] (1)]

bottle of water n. [1920s–30s] a daughter. [rhy. sl.]

bottle out v. [1970s+] to be a coward, to run away, to back down from a challenge (cf. LOSE ONE'S BOTTLE). [BOTTLE n.[3]]

bottler n. 1 [mid-19C+] (Aus./N.Z.) anyone outstanding, either in a positive or negative manner, usu. congratulatory, e.g. *you little bottler*. 2 [1930s+] a sodomite. 3 [1940s+] a coward, someone who 'bottles out'. 4 [1940s+] (N.Z.) a 'hard case', a thug, usu. as *bloody bottler*. [BOTTLE v.; the pos./neg. division is between one who has 'bottle' and one who 'bottles out']

bottles n. [1980s+] (drugs) 1 crack cocaine vials. 2 amphetamine (cf. A n.[2]). [the containers in which the drug is sold]

bottlescrews n. [early–mid-19C] stiff, formal curls, shaped like a corkscrew.

bottle tokes n. [1980s+] (US drugs) a method of smoking hashish where a small hole is made in a bottle (usually a beer bottle), then a cigarette with a small chunk of hashish on the tip is inserted in the hole. [SE *bottle* + TOKE n.[3]]

bottletop n.[1] [20C] a gain, a benefit, something good. [rhy. sl. *bottletop* = COP v.[1] (1)]

bottletop n.[2] [1950s] (N.Z.) a policeman's helmet. [resemblance + ref. to BLUEBOTTLE]

bottletop v. [20C] to catch, to take in. [rhy. sl. *bottletop* = COP v.[1] (1)]

bottle up v. **1** [17C–19C] to hold back, to keep. **2** [19C] to restrain, to exercise control, esp. of one's emotions. **3** [late 19C–1940s] to abandon an argument, to 'call it quits'. [SE post-1900]

bottle up and go, to phr. [1930s–40s] (US Black) to leave, esp. after an unpleasant disagreement. [? BOTTLE IT]

bottle wash n. [late 19C+] nonsense, rubbish (cf. BELLY WASH n.[2]; BOLLYWASH). [i.e. the dregs washed out of a bottle]

bottling adj. [late 19C+] (Aus.) excellent, first-class; also note approving/congratulatory phr. *your blood's worth bottling*. [BOTTLER n. (2)]

bottom n.[1] [late 18C–mid-19C] stamina, endurance, 'grit'; note 17C–18C phr. *stand on one's own bottom*, to act independently, to act for oneself. [sporting jargon]

bottom n.[2] [mid-19C] a measure of spirits poured into a glass before adding water. [it is the *bottom* of the mixture]

bottom n.[3] [mid-19C–1930s] (US Black) the Black area of a town (cf. COON BOTTOM). [such areas were often on low-lying land, near a river]

bottom n.[4] [1960s+] in sado-masochistic sex, a passive or masochistic person.

bottom v. [1980s+] (US campus) to finish off a drink, to empty a glass. [one reaches the *bottom*]

bottom burp n. [1980s+] a fart; generally a children's usage, but popularized on BBC TV's 1980s comedy *The Young Ones*.

bottom drawer n. [1910s+] wherever an engaged woman starts collecting the necessities of her trousseau.

bottomer n. [late 19C] a draught that empties the glass or tankard. [SE *bottom*]

bottom feeder n. [1970s+] (US teen) **1** a despicable, unpleasant person. **2** one who has yet to make their mark, a 'wannabe'. **3** a social outcast. **4** a gossip, esp. a trader in malevolent and harmful stories. [SE *bottom-feeder*, a fish that feeds off the sea- or riverbed]

bottom hole working phr. [20C] having sexual intercourse.

bottomless pit n. [late 18C–early 19C] the vagina (cf. BLACK HOLE n.[1]).

bottom line n. [1970s+] the end result, the final assessment. [Yid. *di untershte sture*, the bottom line, in the context of denoting the final profit/loss figure on an account]

bottom line v. [1980s+] (orig. US business) to sum up, to speak succinctly. [BOTTOM LINE n.]

bottom man n. [1950s+] the submissive partner in a homosexual S&M couple (cf. TOP MAN). [metaphorically rather than always physically 'on the bottom']

bottom of a woman's tu quoque n. [late 18C–early 19C] the crown of a woman's head (cf. TU QUOQUE).

bottom road n. [1930s] (tramp) a road leading from London to the South Coast. [the 'bottom' of the UK]

bottoms n. [20C] (US Black) the least pleasant, the poorest part of a ghetto or inner-city area (cf. COON BOTTOM). [lit. the physically low-lying areas of a town]

bottoms up! excl. [20C] (orig. RN) a popular toast before drinking. [the *bottoms* are those of the glasses as the drinks are emptied into the drinkers' mouths]

bottom-wetter n. [late 19C+] sexual intercourse, from the point of view of a woman. [vaginal secretions and semen]

bottom woman n. [1950s–60s] (US Black) the most reliable and experienced of a pimp's stable of prostitutes. [SE *bottom*, a foundation]

botty see BOTTIE.

boubou n. [1980s+] (drugs) crack cocaine. [ety. unknown]

boudoir bandicoot n. [1980s] (Aus.) a promiscuous male. [var. on LOUNGE LIZARD]

bought it adv. [1940s+] killed, esp. in battle. [BUY THE FARM phr.[1]]

bougie adj. [1960s+] taking on the attitudes and lifestyle of the middle classes (cf. BOOJEE). [SE *bourgeois*]

boulder n. [1980s+] (drugs) **1** generic for crack cocaine. **2** $20 worth of crack cocaine. [play on ROCK n.[3]; (2) is a 'large' rock]

bouldered adj. [1980s+] (Aus. drugs) very heavily intoxicated by a drug, usu. cannabis. [pun on STONED]

boulder-holder/over-the-shoulder-boulder-holder n. [1950s+] (Aus./US) a brassiere.

boulevard boy n. [1970s+] a Los Angeles male homosexual prostitute who works Sunset or Hollywood Boulevards.

boulevard cowboy n. [1940s] (US) a reckless cab-driver whose driving style is uninhibited by the presence of other drivers, let alone pedestrians.

boulevard westerner n. [1940s+] (US) a reckless cab-driver (cf. BOULEVARD COWBOY).

boulya n. [1980s+] (drugs) crack cocaine. [ety. unknown; ? link to BOOYA]

bouman n. [1910s+] (Irish) a friend, a 'pal'. [ety. unknown]

bounce n.[1] **1** [early 18C–mid-19C] impudence. **2** [late 18C] boast, a self-aggrandizing lie. **3** [early 19C] a well-dressed braggart and/or swindler.

bounce n.[2] [late 19C] cherry brandy. [? its effects]

bounce n.[3] [late 19C] (US) a trip, a journey.

bounce, the n.[4] [late 19C+] (US) ejection, esp. from a saloon or bar; usu. as *the grand bounce* (cf. BOUNCER n.[1]; BUM's RUSH; HEAVE-HO).

bounce n.[5] [20C] **1** (US Und.) arrest and subsequent trial. **2** (Und.) fiddling and dishonest practice (adjusting invoices, stealing stock etc) by retail shop employees.

bounce v.[1] **1** [late 18C] to boast, to brag, to bully, to scold, to intimidate (cf. CAPTAIN BOUNCE). **2** [late 18C] to escape arrest/prosecution through posing as a respectable person. **3** [19C+] of a man, to have sexual intercourse (cf. BANG v.[1]). **4** [mid-19C+] (US) to attack, esp. from an ambush. **5** [mid-19C–1920s] (US) to persuade, to influence by flattery. **6** [late 19C] (US) to kill. **7** [late 19C+] to throw out of a party, a place of entertainment etc. **8** [late 19C+] to dismiss from a job. **9** [late 19C] (US) to reject, esp. of a proposal of marriage. **10** [1930s+] (US) to treat, to pay for (cf. SPRING v.[3]). **11** [1940s] (US) as *bounce for*, to agree. **12** [1940s] (US) to rob. **13** [1970s+] to work as a strong-arm man in a bar etc (cf. BOUNCER n.[1]). **14** [1990s] (US Black/teen) to leave.

bounce v.[2] [1930s–50s] **1** to pay a cheque, knowing that one has insufficient funds in one's bank account. **2** of a bank, to refuse to honour a cheque, marking it 'return to drawer'. [SE since 1960s]

bounceable/bouncible adj. [mid-19C] prone to boasting or showing off. [BOUNCE n.[1] (1) + sfx. *-able*]

bounceful adj. [mid–late 19C] arrogant, domineering. [BOUNCE n.[1] (2) + sfx. *-ful*]

bounceful cut-up adv. [mid-19C] depressed, miserable, 'out of sorts'. [ext. of sl.; i.e. the BOUNCEFUL person has been fig. 'cut up']

bounce it off v. [mid-17C–mid-18C] to drink heartily.

bounce one's boner, to phr. [1990s] to masturbate. [SE *bounce* + BONER n.[3]]

bouncer n.[1] **1** [17C+] a liar. **2** [late 17C–19C] a swaggerer, a blusterer. **3** [18C] a braggart. **4** [late 18C–late 19C] an unashamed lie (cf. WHOPPER). **5** [late 18C–19C] (Und.) a thief who steals from shops while distracting the merchant's attention with argumentative bargaining (cf. SHOP-BOUNCER). **6** [mid-19C] (Und.) a sharp, a cheat. **7** [mid-19C+] (orig. US) a large, tough man employed to keep order in premises, often a pub, club, concert hall etc (cf. CHUCKER-OUT; PULLER-IN). **8** [19C] a pimp. [BOUNCE v.[1]]

bouncer *n.*[2] [19C] (US) something exceptionally large of its kind.

bouncer *n.*[3] [mid–late 19C] (US) a social climber. [SE *bounce*, to rebound. The social climber rebounds from any number of rebuffs, secure in the overwhelming power of money]

bounce refrigerators *v.* [1980s+] (US campus) to have sexual intercourse.

bouncers *n.* [1950s–70s] female breasts.

bounce-up *n.* [1990s] an argument, an altercation. [BOUNCE v.[1] (1)]

bouncible *see* BOUNCEABLE.

bouncing *n.* [late 19C] a severe scolding. [BOUNCE v.[1] (1)]

bouncing *adj.* [late 16C–17C] big, lusty, energetic. [SE f. 1700]

bouncing ben *n.* [mid-19C–1920s] an intellectual, a learned person. [? a sceptical view of learning, i.e. a BEN n.[1], who 'bounces' with their own self-importance]

bouncing buffer *n.* [early–mid-19C] a beggar. [London dial. *bouncer*, professional beggar + BUFFER n.[4]]

bouncing cheat *n.* [18C] (Und.) a bottle. [SE *bounce* + CHEAT n. (1); the bottle 'bounces' as the cork is drawn]

bouncing powder *n.* [1980s+] (drugs) cocaine (cf. BOLIVIAN MARCHING POWDER). [the effect it has on its temporarily enlivened users]

bouncy in one's deuce of benders *phr.* [1900s–40s] (US Black) subservient to White people (cf. UNCLE TOM n.). [lit. *bouncing* up and down on one's legs, 'bowing and scraping']

bounder *n.*[1] [mid-19C] a 4-wheeled cab (cf. RUMBLER). [the 'bounding' motion as the cab runs along uneven roads]

bounder *n.*[2] [late 19C+] one who is considered socially unacceptable or ill-mannered (cf. CAD n.[1]). [orig. university use, one who 'bounds' about; but note B&L: '[one] who is beyond the boundary of good fellowship.' The individual so branded may not be intrinsically ill-mannered, but has been declared so by the prevailing standards of his fellows; post-1930s use usu. ironic or historic]

bounder *n.*[3] [20C] (US) a severe blow. [SE *bound*, to leap]

bounder *v.* [19C] (US) to scrub or wash thoroughly. [SE *bound*, to jump; i.e. the energy expended]

bounetter *n.* [mid-19C] a confidence trickster who makes a living telling fortunes. [? BONNETER n. (2)]

boung for this and all combs. with *boung*, e.g. *boung-nipper*, *see* BUNG.

boungie/boongy bungee *n.* [20C] (W.I.) the buttocks, the posterior (cf. BAM-BAM; BUNGHOLE n.[1]). [var. on BUM n.[2]]

bounty bar *n.* [1980s+] (Black) a Black man or woman who is 'black on the outside but white inside' (cf. APPLE n.[11]). [the *Bounty Bar*, a popular sweet, made of chocolate-covered flaked coconut]

bourbon *adj.* [1980s] (US teen) hazy, unable to focus mentally. [? SE *bourbon* whisky, and thus its effects]

bourgie *see* BOOJEE.

bourke-street *adj.* [1940s] (Aus.) citified (cf. PITT STREET FARMER). [the financial centre of *Bourke Street*, Sydney]

Bourneville boulevard *n.* [1990s] the anus (cf. BOVRIL BYPASS; CADBURY ALLEY; CHOCCY; CHOCOLATE HIGHWAY; HERSHEY HIGHWAY). [*Bourneville* chocolate, a popular dark chocolate]

bouse *n.* [mid-16C+] (Und.) drink; thus *ben bouse*, good drink (cf. BOOZE n.). [Du. *buizen* or Ger. *bausen*, to drink to excess. The *OED*'s first use is *c*.1300, but this may be only the drinking vessel not its contents; the Du. term too is rooted in *buise*, a large drinking vessel. Although *bouse* can be found in ME, its popularity came with its Und. usage]

bouse *v.* [mid-16C] to drink (cf. BOOZE v.). [BOUSE n.]

boushwa/boushwah *see* BUSHWA.

bousing-/boozing-ken *n.* [16C–mid-19C] (Und.) an ale-house. [BOUSE n. + KEN n.[1]]

bousy *adj.* [16C] (Und.) drunken (cf. BOUSE n.). [BOUSE n. + sfx. *-y*]

bovey *see* BOOIE.

Bovril *n.* [1930s] (Aus.) a general term of dismissal, abuse, rubbish, nonsense, anything unimpressive. [? a play on BULLSHIT n.; in Aus./UK Bovril is a beef extract-based spread, often taken as a hot drink]

Bovril bypass *n.* [1990s] the anus (cf. BOURNEVILLE BOULEVARD). [for ety. *see* BOVRIL]

Bovril hornpipe *n.* [1990s] the anus. [for ety. *see* BOVRIL]

bovver *n.* [1960s+] fighting, disturbance, esp. that caused by skinhead youths (cf. AGGRO n.). [Cockney pron. of SE *bother*]

bovver boots *n.* [1960s+] high-laced boots preferred as footwear by skinhead youths, usu. merchandised under the brandname Dr Martins. [BOVVER + SE *boots*]

bovver boy *n.* [1960s–70s] a hooligan, usually a SKINHEAD, and quite likely a football fan and member of the right-wing National Front; his female equivalent was a *bovver bird*. [BOVVER + SE *boy*]

bow *n.* [17C] the penis (cf. ARSE-OPENER). [it shoots 'arrows', presumably of desire]

bow and arrow *n.*[1] [20C] a sparrow. [rhy. sl. + ref. to poem 'Who Killed Cock Robin?']

bow and arrow *n.*[2] [20C] (US) a Native American. [the stereotypical weaponry]

bow and quiver *n.* [20C] the liver, as a human organ rather than as edible offal (cf. CHEERFUL GIVER). [rhy. sl.]

bow-catcher *n.* [19C] a lock of hair equivalent to the modern kiss-curl. [var. on BEAU-CATCHER]

bowdacious *see* BODACIOUS.

bowel off *v.* [20C] (US) to have an attack of diarrhoea.

bower *n.* [20C] (Aus.) a prison. [ironic use of SE *bower*, a shady grove]

bower-bird *n.* [1920s+] (Aus.) **1** a petty thief. **2** a scavenger of waste and similar trifles. [SE *bower-bird*, one of several Aus. birds of the starling family, which build bowers or 'runs' and adorn them with feathers, bones, shells etc]

bower bird *v.* [1920s+] (Aus.) to hang around, to scavenge. [BOWER-BIRD]

bower of bliss *n.* [17C–19C] the vagina (cf. BEAUTY SPOT n.[1]). [SE *bower of bliss*, 'a vague poetic word for an idealized abode, not realized in any actual dwelling' (*OED*)]

bowhead *n.* [1980s+] (US campus) a young woman who pays a good deal of attention to her looks, dress and general image; she is assumed to be foolish, at best. [SE *bow* + sfx. -HEAD (1); lit. a woman with bows in her hair. The image is of a 'nice little girl']

bow-jawed *adj.* [20C] (US) having a prominent jaw. [SE *bow-window*, a curved window that protrudes into the street]

bowl *n.* [1970s+] (drugs) **1** a pipeful of marijuana. **2** a pipe used for smoking marijuana. [cf. BONG n.).

bowlas *n.* [mid–late 19C] round tarts made of sugar, apple and bread, sold in the streets. [Anglo-Ind. *bowla*, a portmanteau; ult. f. Hind. *baola*]

bowlegged *adj.* [20C] (US Und.) concurrent, referring to a prison sentence (cf. WILD adj.).

bowler *n.* [20C] (Irish) a dog, usu. a mongrel. [SE *bawl*, i.e. bark]

bowler-hatted *adj.* [1920s+] dismissed, retired. [milit. use *bowler-hatted*, retired from active service (and thus from wearing a uniform) and given a desk job in Whitehall]

bowles *n.* [mid-19C–1900s] shoes. [? the shape]

bowl from the pavilion end, to *phr.* [1990s] to be a male homosexual (cf. BAT AND BOWL). [cricket imagery; no especial gay relevance to *the pavilion end*, other than (prob. coincidentally) that the pavilion is likely to contain the lavatories]

bowl me the time *phr.* [1950s–80s] (S.Afr.) what's the time? [SE *bowl*, to deliver (a ball); orig. milit. use]

bowl off *v.* [mid-19C] to die. [SE *bowl*, to ride along on wheels]

bowl of jelly *n.* [1960s+] (US) a notably fat person (cf. JELLY-BELLY).

bowl-out *n.* [19C] a discovery, an unmasking. [cricket imagery]

bowl out *v.* **1** [early–mid-19C] to kill. **2** [mid-19C+] to defeat, to overcome, to get the better of. [cricket imagery]

bowl-over *n.* [20C] (Aus.) a fight, a brawl. [BOWL SOMEONE OVER]

bowl someone over *v.* [mid-19C+] **1** to astonish, to surprise. **2** to defeat. [cricket imagery]

bowl the hoop *n.* [mid-19C] soup. [rhy. sl.]

bowman *n.* [early 18C] a thief. [abbr. BOWMAN-PRIG]

bowman *adj.* [early 18C] excellent, first-rate; thus *all's bowman*, all's safe, everything is in order. [? Fr. *beau*, good-looking]

bowman ken *n.* [late 17C–early 19C] (Und.) a house considered worth robbing (cf. BOB KEN). [BOWMAN adj. + KEN n.[1]]

bowman-prig *n.* [early 18C] a first-rate thief. [BOWMAN adj. + PRIG n.]

bow out *v.* [1940s+] to retreat or withdraw, to resign.

bowse-/bowsing-ken *n.* [16C–mid-19C] a public house, a tavern, an inn (cf. BOUSING-KEN). [BOUSE v. + KEN n.[1]]

bowser *n.* **1** [1960s+] generic for any species of dog. **2** [1980s] (US campus) an ugly woman (cf. DOG n.[4]). [the once-common dog name]

bowser bag *n.* [1960s+] (US) a bag provided by some restaurants for customers to take home left-overs, ostensibly for later consumption by a pet dog (cf. DOGGY BAG). [BOWSER n. (1) + SE *bag*]

bowsered *adj.* drunk. [BOUSE v.]

bowsie/bowsy *n.* **1** [20C] a street urchin, a lout. **2** a general term of abuse. [Share suggests Ger. *böse*, evil]

bowsing-ken *see* BOWSE-KEN.

bowsprit *n.* **1** [late 17C–19C] the nose (cf. BOLTSPRIT). **2** [mid-18C+] the penis. [SE *bowsprit*, 'a large spar or boom running out from the stem of a vessel, to which (and the jib-boom and flying jib-boom, which extend beyond it) the foremast stays are fastened' (*OED*)]

bowsprit in parenthesis *n.* [mid-19C] (US) a nose that has been pulled, presumably during a fight or argument. [BOWSPRIT n. (1) + SE *in parenthesis*, a digression, an interlude]

bowsy *n.* see BOWSIE.

bowsy *adj.* [late 17C] drunk. [var. on BOOZY adj.]

bow the crumpet, to *phr.* [1930s+] (Aus.) to plead guilty (cf. DUCK THE SCONE; NOD THE NUT). [SE *bow* + CRUMPET n.[1]]

bow-tie *n.* [1940s] (N.Z.) a married woman's lover, a 'fancy-man'. [the image of the smooth, *bow-tied* lothario]

bow to the porcelain god/goddess *see* KISS THE PORCELAIN GOD.

bow up *v.* [19C] (US) to stand firm to improve. [the opposite of SE *bow down*]

bow-window *n.* [early 19C+] a large, protruding stomach.

bow-wow *n.[1]* **1** [late 18C+] (juv. or facetious) a dog. **2** [19C] (US) a native of Boston, Massachusetts. **3** [1900s–30s] (US) a sausage (cf. DOG n.[6]). **4** [1960s+] an ugly woman (cf. DOG n.[4]). **5** [1990s] (Aus.) an unattractive person (cf. DOG n.[4]). [(2)–(5) play on (1)]

bow-wow *n.[2]* **1** [mid–late 19C] (mainly Ind.) a lover. **2** [1930s–70s] (US Black) a gun (cf. BARKER n.[1]; BOOM-BOOM n.[1]; DOG n.[3]). [the noises, the pistol 'barks', the lover 'yaps']

bow-wow mutton *n.* [late 18C–late 19C] dog's flesh. [BOW-WOW n.[1] (1) + SE *mutton*]

bow-wow shop *n.* [18C] a second-hand clothes shop in London's Monmouth Street, the city's old-clothes centre through to 19C (cf. BARKER n.[1]). [BOW-WOW n.[1] (1) + SE *shop*; 'so called because the servant barks and the master bites' (Grose)]

bowyer *n.* [late 18C] one who exaggerates, who tells implausible, if grandiose tales. [SE phr. *draw the long bow*, to exaggerate]

box *n.[1]* [17C–18C] a small drinking house or tavern. [Fr. *boîte*, lodging house or restaurant]

box *n.[2]* **1** [19C] a prison cell. **2** [late 19C+] a coffin. **3** [late 19C+] a safe (esp. an old-fashioned model); thus *boxman*, a safe-cracker. **4** [1950s+] the witness box; thus Aus. *jump in the box*, to turn Queen's evidence.

box *n.[3]* [20C] (US prison) a carton of cigarettes, the equivalent of $15 in a barter economy.

box *n.[4]* **1** [20C] a piano; thus *bang the box*, play the piano. **2** [1910s+] (orig. US Black) a guitar, a fiddle, a banjo. **3** [1920s+] a radio, a record-player. **4** [1950s+] television; thus *on the box*, on television. **5** [1960s+] a tape-recorder, stereo system, cassette tape deck (cf. GHETTOBLASTER). **6** [1970s+] (US) a jukebox. **7** [1980s] (US) an accordion.

box *n.[5]* [1920s+] (Aus.) a blunder, a mix-up, a mess. [BOX v.[2]]

box *n.[6]* **1** [1930s–50s] (US) the mouth. **2** [1940s+] the vagina; thus generic for a woman. **3** [1940s+] (US gay) the male genitals. **4** [1960s] (US Black) sexual intercourse. **5** [1960s] (US Black) the buttocks.

box *n.[7]* [1970s] (US) a refrigerator. [abbr. SE *icebox*]

box *v.[1]* [mid-19C] to overturn someone in a sentry or similar box (cf. BOX THE WATCH).

box *v.[2]* [1920s+] (Aus./N.Z.) to make a blunder, to mix something up. [farming jargon *box*, to mix up two herds or flocks by mistake]

box-about *n.* [1950s] (W.I.) **1** a man who is an idler, a loafer. **2** a trollop, a promiscuous woman, esp. when she has a number of children, each by a different father. [SE *box about*, to sail up and down, often changing the direction, ult. ? f. *boxing the compass*]

box/box it about *v.[1]* [late 17C–early 18C] to drink briskly. [SE *box*, to fight with the fists; thus to 'hit (the drink) hard'; 19C use is SE]

box about *v.[2]* [20C] to move from place to place without any steady job. [to carry one's *boxes*, i.e. possessions, around; but see BOX-ABOUT]]

box a charley, to *phr.* [early–mid-19C] to turn over a watchman in his box. [BOX v.[1] + CHARLEY n.[1] (1)]

box along with *v.* [1960s+] to get along with someone, however 'difficult' and awkward they may be. [? SE *box*, to fight, or to fit into the same fig. *box*]

box-ankled *adj.* [20C] (US) having legs so made that the ankle-bones knock together.

box around *v.* [1950s] (W.I.) to move from place to place without any steady job. [BOX ABOUT v.[2]]

box-beater *n.* [1910s–40s] (US) a piano-player. [BOX n.[4] (1) + SE *beater*]

boxcar *n.* [1950s–70s] (US) **1** usu. in pl., a large foot or shoe. **2** a large, clumsy person. **3** (Und.) a prison cell. [SE *boxcar*, a large closed-in railway goods wagon]

boxcars *n.* [20C] (gambling) the point of 12 in craps dice. [the resemblance of the two 'sixes', side-by-side to a railway wagon]

box city *adj.* [1980s+] (US) dead. [BOX n.[2] (2) + sfx. -CITY]

box clever *v.* [1930s+] to carry out any enterprise smartly and efficiently. [boxing imagery]

boxed *adj.* **1** [1930s+] (US) drunk or overcome by drugs. **2** [1980s+] in prison. **3** [1960s+] (US) dead (cf. BOX CITY). [OUT OF ONE'S BOX or BOX n.[2]; one is effectively 'dead', i.e. ready for one's coffin]

boxed-up *adj.* **1** [20C] (N.Z.) imprisoned. **2** [1930s+] (Aus.) confused, muddled. [BOX n.²]

box egg *n.* [1930s+] an unpleasant person, a 'bad egg'. [mass-produced eggs, sold in boxes, were still more likely to prove bad than those laid by one's own hens]

boxer *n.*¹ **1** [late 19C] (Aus.) a low-crowned felt hat (cf. HARD-HITTER). **2** [late 19C–1900s] a tall hat, a top-hat (cf. BOX-HAT). [the shape]

boxer *n.*² [1910s+] (Aus.) in the game of two-up the person who takes charge of the apparatus and of the money staked by the main bettors. [SE *box*]

box fire *n.* [1940s] (US Black/Harlem) a cigarette.

box-getter *n.* [20C] one who steals from tills. [BOX n.² (3) + SE *getter*]

box Harry *v.* [early 19C–1900s] **1** to take lunch and tea at the same time. **2** to go without a meal. **3** to take things as they are. [northern dial.; thus Lancashire *Boxharry week*, 'the blank week between payweeks when the workmen lived on credit or starved' (*EDD*). Jon Bee suggests that 'confined truants, at school, without fire, fought or boxed an old figure nicknamed 'Harry', which hung up in their prison/to keep heat'. B&L suggest that it means 'box or fight the devil' (cf. OLD HARRY)]

box-hat *n.* [late 19C] a silk top-hat (cf. BOXER n.¹). [orig. dial.]

boxhead *n.* **1** [1920s–40s] (US) a Scandinavian (cf. SQUAREHEAD n.²). **2** [1920s+] a fool, a simpleton; thus *box-headed*, stupid. [SE *box* + sfx. -HEAD (1)]

box-irons *n.* [late 18C–mid-19C] shoes. [SE *box-iron*, a smoothing iron with a cavity to contain some form of heating]

box-it *n.* [1980s] a drink composed of wine and cider, consumed by alcoholics. [? the use of cheap boxed rather than bottled wine]

box it about *see* BOX ABOUT v.¹.

box job *n.* [1930s+] (US) breaking open a safe. [BOX n.² (3) + SE *job*]

box-lobby puppy *n.* [late 18C] a would-be man of fashion, with ambition, but lacking income; thus the *box-lobby loung-er*, one who frequents this area (cf. UPPER-BOX JACKADANDY). [SE *box lobby*, the area outside a theatre's boxes, patronized by the fashionable and would-be fashionable + SE *puppy*]

box lunch *n.* [1960s+] cunnilingus. [BOX n.⁶ (2) + SE *lunch*]

box of assorted creams *n.* [1990s] (Aus.) a woman known to have had sex with a large number of men. [BOX n.⁶ (2) + CREAM v.²]

box of birds/fluffy ducks, to be a *phr.* [1940s+] (N.Z.) to be very cheerful.

box of dominoes *n.* **1** [mid-19C] the mouth. **2** [late 19C–1920s] a piano.

box of fluffy ducks *see* BOX OF BIRDS.

box of fruit *see* BAG OF FRUIT.

box of glue *n.* [1950s] (US) a Jew (cf. BUCKLE MY SHOE; FIFTEEN AND TWO; FIVE BY TWO; FIVE TO TWO; FOUR BY TWO; HALF PAST TWO; KANGAROO n.³; POT OF GLUE; QUARTER TO TWO; SARAH SOO; TEN TO TWO). [rhy. sl.]

box of ivories *n.* [mid-19C] the mouth (cf. BOX OF DOMINOES).

box of minutes *n.* [mid-19C] **1** a watch. **2** a watch-maker's shop.

box of sharks *n.* [1950s+] (Can.) used when one wishes to express surprise, shock, e.g. *she nearly had a box of sharks* (cf. HAVE KITTENS).

box of toys *n.* [late 19C–1930s] noise. [rhy. sl.]

box of tricks *n.* [mid-19C+] **1** whatever one needs (cf. BAG OF TRICKS). **2** [1910s+] a tool-box.

box of worries *n.* [19C] the teeth (cf. BONE BOX n.¹; BOX OF DOMINOES; BOX OF IVORIES; IVORY BOX; SPOKE-BOX). [? 'worries' is mispron. of 'ivories']

box on *v.* [1910s+] (Aus.) to keep going, to persevere; thus *box on with*, to fight with, to punch. [the boxing referee's command *Box on!* after a brief stoppage in the fight]

box out of the ring, to *phr.* [1970s+ (Aus./N.Z.) to have an affair, to have extra-marital sex.

box rustler *n.* [late 19C] (US west) a chorus-girl who followed her performance by mixing with the patrons in their boxes, promoting the sale of drinks (and, when desired, offering herself as a part-time prostitute). [SE *box* + *rustler*, a cattle-thief]

box the bald champ, to *phr.* [1990s] to masturbate. [SE *box* + *bald champ*]

box the bozack, to *phr.* [1990s] to masturbate. [SE *box* + BOZAK]

box the clown, to *phr.* [1990s] to masturbate. [SE *box* + *clown*]

box the compass, to *phr.* [mid-18C+] to answer all possible questions, to adapt oneself to a wide variety of circumstances. [naut. jargon *box the compass*, to name the points of the compass, either backwards or in random order]

box the fox, to *phr.* [20C] (Irish) to rob fruit from an orchard. [ety. unknown]

box the Jesuit and get cockroaches, to *phr.* [late 16C–early 19C] to masturbate (cf. BANG THE BISHOP). [pun on SE *cock-roaches* + the stereotyping of Jesuits as alien and repellent beings. Like many terms for masturbate this one relies on an image of using violence against the penis, e.g. *box*, to hit]

box the watch, to *phr.* [mid-19C] to over-turn a watchman's box, a practice popular among young hooligans (cf. BOX A CHARLEY). [BOX v.¹ + SE *watch*]

box the wine bin, to *phr.* [early–mid-19C] to leave the table after drinking only moderately. [SE *box*, to put in a box]

box-up *n.* [1940s+] (N.Z.) a quandary, a state of confusion. [farming jargon *box*, the mixing up of different flocks of sheep]

box with *v.* [1940s+] to get along with someone, however 'difficult' and awkward they may be (cf. BOX ALONG WITH).

box with five nails *n.* [19C] (US) the fist, esp. when giving a blow. [pun on SE *box*, a bow and *nails*, fingernails]

box with richard, to *phr.* [1990s] to masturbate (cf. BOP ONE'S RICHARD). [SE *box* + *Richard*; i.e. DICK n.⁵ (1)]

box with two handles *n.* [19C] a fist (cf. BOX WITH FIVE NAILS). [pun on hand/handles]

boy *n.*¹ [late 18C+] a sovereign, thus latterly £1 sterling. [abbr. JINGLEBOY; YELLOW BOY]

boy *n.*² [19C] a hump on a person's back; thus *him and his boy*, a hunchback. [the hunchback is seen as carrying a small child]

boy, the *n.*³ [late 19C+] the penis (cf. BOYO n.¹). [its innate masculinity]

boy *n.*⁴ [1900s] champagne. [allegedly f. Edward VII's habit of merely saying 'Boy!' to an attendant page who automatically brought him a glass of that wine]

boy *n.*⁵ [1920–40s] (drugs) heroin (cf. GIRL n.³). [the image of heroin as a 'masculine' drug, i.e. one that 'knocks you down', rather than cocaine or girl, the injecting of which gives a sexual thrill (although heroin, too, has that effect on some users)]

boy *n.*⁶ [1960s+] (gay) a male prostitute.

boy *n.*⁷ [1990s] (US Black) a friend or neighbour, one of one's group or gang (cf. HOMEBOY).

boy! *excl.* [late 19C+] (US) a general excl. of excitement, surprise, amazement. [abbr. OH BOY!]

boy-ass *n.* [1960s+] a boy who exists simply as a sex object for his homosexual partners. [SE *boy* + ARSE n.¹ (1)]

boy-buster *n.* [1940s–50s] (Aus.) a man, esp. a prisoner, who specializes in seducing young men (cf. CHERRY-BUSTER). [SE *boy* + BUST v.¹]

boychick/boychik *n.* [1960s+] a general term of affection between males. [SE *boy* + Yid. dimin. sfx. *-tschik*]

boy-farm *n.* late 19C a school; thus *boy-farmer*, a schoolteacher.

boy-girl *n.*[1] [1950s–70s] a homosexual (cf. OMEE-POLONE).

boy-girl *n.*[2] [1980s+] (US drugs) a mixture of heroin and cocaine, usu. as an injection but sometimes inhaled (cf. SPEEDBALL *n.*[1]). [BOY *n.*[3] (2) + GIRL *n.*[3]]

boygul *n.* [1980s+] (US gay) an effeminate youth. [Yid. *bagel*, a soft, circular doughnut-like bread + BOY-GIRL *n.*[1]]

boy in the boat *n.* [late 19C+] the clitoris (cf. BABY IN THE BOAT).

boy jones, the *n.* [mid 19C–1900s] a teller of secrets. [one *Jones*, a chimney-sweep, who, *c.*1840, was cleaning the chimneys at Buckingham Palace, fell into an empty hearth and supposedly overheard Queen Victoria and Prince Albert talking of state secrets]

boykie /booitjie/boytjie *n.* (S.Afr.) **1** [1970s+] a generally affectionate term for a male, a fellow, a chap, a bloke. **2** [1970s+] a whizz-kid, an exceptional person. **3** [1970s–80s] a male African servant. [SE *boy* + Afk. sfx. *-kie*]

boy-meets-girl *adj.* [1940s+] stereotypically romantic, esp. as in the plots of popular films or books.

boyo *n.*[1] [late 19C+] the penis. [ext. of BOY *n.*[3]]

boyo *n.*[2] [late 19C+] a term of address, usu. Irish or clichéd. [SE *boy*]

boy of the Holy Ground *n.* [early 19C] a prize-fighter. [? a then well-known prize-fight arena]

boy of the slang *see* SLANG-BOY.

boy racer *n.* **1** [1940s+] a Model 7R AJS racing motorcycle, manufactured for the mass market in 1948. **2** [1990s] a daredevil young car-driver; the term implies disdain for such puerile antics.

boys, the *n.*[1] **1** [early-19C] (orig. US) a criminal or violent gang, esp. the hangers-on of a corrupt politician. **2** [mid-19C] (US) the police. **3** [mid-19C+] one's (male) social circle. **4** [mid-19C+] criminals in general, esp. the thieves and swindlers who frequented race-courses in the 1920s–50s. **5** [1920s+] (Irish) Republican revolutionaries, esp. when fleeing capture.

boys *n.*[2] [1940s+] individuals conforming to a specific job description, e.g. the *software boys*, the *public relations boys* (cf. BACKROOM BOYS).

boys-a-boys!/boys-o-boys! *excl.* [20C] (Irish) a general excl. of amazement, disbelief.

boys and girls *n.* [1920s–40s] a general term of address, in fact the audience may be all male.

boy's favourite *n.* [1950s+] (bingo) the number 16. [16 is the age of consent in the UK]

boysie *n.* [1920s+] a general term of address to a male. [SE *boy* + dimin. sfx. *-sie*]

boy's/maid's/servant's meat *n.* [1930s+] (S.Afr.) cheap cuts of meat that are cooked for the servants' meals. [S.Afr. English *boy*, *maid*, the male and female servant]

boys-o-boys! *see* BOYS-A-BOYS!

boys on ice *n.* [late 19C+] lice. [rhy. sl.]

boytjie *see* BOYKIE.

Boystown *n.* [1940s–60s] (gay) the predominantly gay neighbourhood in West Hollywood (cf. SWISH ALPS). [pun on *Boys Town*, a celebrated home for delinquent boys]

boystown sound *n.* [1970s] music popular in gay discos. [BOYSTOWN + SE *sound* + play on popular musical descriptions, e.g. the Liverpool sound, the Motown sound]

boy with the boots *n.* [late 19C+] (Anglo-Irish) the knave or jack in a pack of cards (cf. NAILER *n.*[3]). [the use of the card as a trump, 'booting' other cards]

bozack/'zack *n.* [1990s] (rap music) the scrotum, the penis. [ety. unknown; ? Black pron. of BALLS *n.*[1] (1) + sfx. *-ack*]

bozo *n.*[1] [1910s+] (orig. US) **1** a person, a fellow, a man; there is a slight overtone of clownishness. **2** a fool, an idiot. **3** a tough, a thug. [? Sp. term meaning the light beard of adolescence or Sp. *bozal*, simple, stupid, or US fairground use BO *n.*[1] (2), or Ital. *bozzo*, a cuckold, a bastard]

bozo *n.*[2] [1980s+] (drugs) heroin. [BOZO *n.*[1] (2)]

bozo *adj.* [1980s+] (US) crazy, eccentric. [BOZO *n.*[1] (2)]

b.p. *n.* [1970s] (US) a child prostitute. [abbr. BABY PRO]

b.p.n. *n.* [1900s–40s] a bloody public nuisance. [abbr.]

b.p.o.m. *n.* [1950s–70s] (gay) a big piece of meat. [abbr.]

b.p.t. *n.* [1990s] unpunctuality (cf. AFRICAN PEOPLE'S TIME) [abbr. Black people's time]

b.r. *n.* [1910s–60s] (US) a bank roll. [abbr.]

bra/bras *n.*[1] [1910s+] a brassiere. [abbr.; both pron. 'brah']

bra *n.*[2] (S.Afr.) **1** [1950s+] brother, esp. as pfx. to a given name, e.g. *Bra Victor*. **2** [1970s+] an informal term of address, mate, buddy, pal. **3** [1970s+] an important, influential person, 'one of the boys'. **4** [1980s] 'a Black man who is acknowledged to be particularly STREETWISE and adept at making the most of urban life, while remaining part of working-class Black society' (*DSAE*). [abbr. SE *brother*]

braa *n.* [1950s+] (W.I. Rasta) brother. [pron.]

braata *n.* [1910s+] (W.I.) a little extra, like the 13th biscuit in a baker's dozen, or an extra helping of food; in musical shows it has come to be the encore. [Mex. Sp. *barata*, cheap]

brace *n.*[1] [late 18C] a room in the King's Bench prison, London (cf. BRACE TAVERN).

brace *n.*[2] [late 19C] a drink taken as a pick-me-up, a 'bracer'. [SE *bracer*, a nerve tonic]

brace *n.*[3] [late 19C] (US) any form of gambling game in which there is concealed cheating (cf. BRACE GAME). [SE *brace*, to bluster, to domineer]

brace *v.* [late 19C+] (US) **1** to demand, esp. money. **2** to face up to, to shake up, to grab. **3** to accost, to solicit. [? 15C SE *brace*, to bluster, to domineer; in phr. *face and brace*]

brace and bits *n.* [20C] (US) female breasts. [rhy. sl. + pun on SE *brace*, a pair]

brace game *n.* [late 19C–1910s] (US) any form of gambling game in which there is concealed cheating. [SE *brace*, to bluster, to domineer]

bracelets *n.* [18C+] (Und.) handcuffs, also as *black bracelets*.

brace of broads *n.* [late 19C–1940s] (US Black) one's shoulders (cf. BRACE OF HOOKERS; BRACE OF HORNED COWS). [SE *brace*, a pair + *broad* shoulders]

brace of hookers *n.* [late 19C–1940s] (US Black) one's arms (cf. BRACE OF BROADS). [SE *brace* + ext. of HOOK *n.*[2]]

brace of horned cows *n.* [late 19C–1940s] (US Black) a pair of aching feet (cf. BRACE OF BROADS).

brace/couple of shakes *adv.* [mid-19C+] at once, immediately, often as *in a brace of …* (cf. TWO SHAKES OF A LAMB'S TAIL). [SE *brace*, pair + *shakes*]

bracer *n.* [late 19C+] (orig. US) an alcoholic drink, esp. as a 'pick-me-up' (cf. ALLEVIATOR). [SE *bracer*, a nerve tonic]

brace tavern *n.* [late 18C–early 19C] a room in the southeast corner of the King's Bench prison, London, where prisoners can buy beer (cf. BRACE *n.*[1]). [its 'barmen', a pair or *brace* of brothers surnamed Partridge]

brace up *v.* [mid–late 19C] to pawn stolen goods. [? Fr. argot *braser des faffes*, to forge documents]

brace-up-'tomach *n.* [1970s] (W.I.) a woman with larger-than-average breasts (cf. PIGEON-'TOMACH). [SE *brace up*, to firm up + *stomach*]

brackers *adj.* [1950s+] impoverished. [BORACIC]

bracket *n.* [1950s+] an unspecified part of the body, presumably the nose; thus usu. in phr. *a punch up the bracket*. [the resemblance]

bracket-face *n.* [17C–late 18C] an ugly person (cf. BRACKET).

bracket-mug n. [19C] an ugly face. [SE *bracket* + MUG n.[1] (1)]

bracmard n. [17C] the penis (cf. BAYONET). [Fr. *braquemard*, a short broad sword]

brad n. [1950s+] **1** excrement. **2** an act of defecation. [rhy. sl. *brad pitt* = SHIT n.[1]; ult. US film star Brad Pitt (b.1964)]

bradarax! / bragadap! / bram! / braps! / brudum! / brugadum! *excl.* [20C] (W.I.) echoic, onomat. words representing the sound of an object or objects crashing to the floor (cf. BUDUP!).

bradbury n. [1910s] a banknote (cf. ARCHER). [proper name of Sir John *Bradbury*, secretary to the Treasury c.1915]

brad-faking n. [mid-19C] playing cards (cf. BROAD-FAKING). [BRADS + FAKE]

Bradford cities n. [1990s] breasts (cf. BRISTOL BITS; BRISTOL CITY; BRISTOLS; JERSEY CITY; JERSEYS; MANCHESTER CITIES; TOWNS AND CITIES). [rhy. sl. = *titties* (*see* TITTY n.[2])]

bradleys n. [1990s] the female breasts. [rhy. sl. *brad(ley) pitts* = TITS; ult. Hollywood film star Brad Pitt (b.1964)]

brads n. [early 19C+] cash money; thus *tip the brads*, to be generous with one's cash (cf. ARCHER). [? f. SE *brad*, a shoemaker's rivet]

bradshaw n. [late 19C–1900s] a precise person, one who is good at figures. [*Bradshaw's Railway Guide*, the comprehensive Victorian timetable, founded by George Bradshaw (1801–53) and published 1839–61]

bradys n. [1990s] (US Black) young, middle-class, suburban Whites. [the type of character portrayed in the 1960s TV series *The Brady Bunch*]

brag n. [late 17C–late 18C] a swaggering braggart. [abbr. SE; 19C+ use is SE]

brag adj. [19C] (US) first-rate, out of the ordinary, notable. [SE *brag*, to boast; thus worth boasting about]

bragadap! *see* BRADARAX!

brag as a body louse *phr.* [late 16C–17C] very busy (cf. BRISK AS A BODY LOUSE; BUSY AS A BODY LOUSE). [SE *brag*, spirited/ brisk/busy]

braggadocio n. [mid-19C] a sentence of three months' imprisonment given to a known thief or regular offender (cf. DOLLOP n.[2]; DOSE n.[2]). [SE *braggadocio*, an empty, idle boast; thus the professional thief's boast that they will never be caught]

brag/face it out with a card of ten, to *phr.* [mid-16C–late 17C] to brazen out a situation. [the image of bluffing in a card game, in which 10 is only an average card]

brag the potatoes, to *phr.* [20C] (US) to say grace before a meal (cf. TALK TO ONE'S PLATE). [SE *brag*, to boast about, to talk up]

brahma n. [late 19C+] a pretty woman. [BRAHMA adj.]

brahma adj. [late 19C+] anything good, enjoyable, attractive. [Skrt. *Brahma*, the supreme God of post-Vedic Hindu mythology]

brahms and liszt/mozart and liszt adj. [1920s+] drunk. [rhy. sl. *Brahms and Liszt* = PISSED adj.[1]]

brain n. **1** [mid-19C–1940s] (orig. US) a planner, an 'ideas man', a mastermind, often in criminal context, i.e. planning a bank aid but not participating in the actual action; often found in fiction as *The Brain* or *Brains* (cf. BRAINS). **2** [1910s+] an intellectual, an intelligent person, esp. as one who is unpleasantly, anti-socially intellectual.

brain v. [1930s+] to hit on the head (and knock out); thus *brained*, hit very hard on the head. [note 14C–19C SE *brain*, to kill by dashing out the brains of]

brainbox n. **1** [late 18C+] the head, the skull (cf. BRAIN BUCKET; BRAIN-CANISTER; CANISTER n.[1]). **2** [early 19C+] the mind. **3** [1950s] (US) a crash helmet.

brain bucket n. [mid-19C] (US) the head, the skull (cf. BRAINBOX).

brain burp n. [1990s] (US campus) a random thought (cf. BRAINFART!). [the spontaneity of an explosion of wind]

brain-canister n. [mid–late 19C] the head (cf. BRAINBOX).

brain capsule n. [1900s] (US) a cigarette. [the supposedly stimulating properties of nicotine]

brainchild n. **1** [late 19C+] an idea, an inspiration. **2** [1960s] (US) a very intelligent person.

brain college n. [late 19C] (US) a lunatic asylum. [ironic use]

brain damage n. [1980s+] (drugs) heroin. [its supposed effects]

brain-dead adj. [1980s+] utterly stupid, completely inept. [SE *brain-dead*, used of one who, while still technically alive, is in a persistent vegetative state]

brain drain n. [1960s+] the emigration of highly qualified people, generally scientists and academics, from Britain in search of more prestigious jobs, better facilities for research and higher salaries.

brain fart n. [1980s+] (orig. US campus) a nonsensical idea.

brainfart! *excl.* [1990s] (orig. US campus) a general excl. implying that the speaker has lost the thread, forgotten what they were talking about, made a major mental error and all in all lost the power of rational speech and thought (cf. BRAIN BURP). [BRAIN FART]

brainless wonder n. [1920s] (US) a fool, a scatter-brained person. [SE *brainless* + *wonder*, an outstanding specimen of something + ? play on a carnival attraction, the 'Boneless Wonder']

braino n. [1980s+] (US) a very clever person. [SE *brain* + sfx. *-o*]

brainpan n. [mid-17C–mid-19C+] **1** the human head. **2** the mind. [mid-19C+ use is US]

brains n. [1900s–30s] (orig. US) the head of a criminal gang, often as *the brains*. [note police jargon *the brains*, the CID or plain-clothes detective department, usu. ironic]

brain-smasher n. [1910s] a difficult puzzle, a 'brain-teaser'.

brainstem n. [1980s] (US campus) an eccentric. [SE *brainstem*, 'the central trunk of the brain upon which the cerebrum and cerebellum are set, and which continues downwards to form the spinal cord' (*OED*)]

brainstorm n. [20C] (orig. US) a sudden inspiration or bright idea (cf. BRAINWAVE). [ext. of SE use; popularized by the murder trial of society architect Harry Thaw in 1907–8, during which his lawyer claimed he had suffered a 'brain storm']

brain tablet n. [1930s] (US) a cigarette (cf. BRAIN CAPSULE).

brain ticklers n. [1980s+] (drugs) amphetamine (cf. A n.[2]). [amphetamine accelerates the activity of the central nervous system and thence the brain]

brainwave n. [late 19C+] a sudden inspiration or bright idea (cf. BRAINSTORM).

bram! *see* BRADARAX!

brama n. [1920s+] a pretty woman (cf. BRAHMA n.).

bran n. [mid-19C] a loaf. [one of its constituents]

Branch, the n. [1970s+] (UK/S.Afr.) the Special Branch, that department of the national police force that deals with 'subversion'.

branch out v. [1920s+] (Aus.) to become very fat. [SE *branch out*, to expand]

brand-fire new adj. [19C] (US) absolutely new.

brand X n. [1970s+] (US Black) marijuana. [joc. play on the drug's illegality]

brandy/brandy-coatee/coortee n. [19C] (Anglo-Ind.) a coat, a raincoat. [Hind. *barani*, a cloak + SE *coat* + Hind. *kurta*, a form of knee-length shirt, worn outside the trousers]

brandy and fashoda n. [late 19C–1900s] (society) brandy and soda. [play on SE based on the *Fashoda Incident* of 1898, when French and British forces clashed in the Sudan following the battle of Omdurman]

brandy blossom *n.* [late 19C] a red-pimpled nose, the result of excessive drinking of brandy (cf. GIN BLOSSOM; GIN-BUD; GROG BLOSSOM).

brandy coatee/-coortee *see* BRANDY.

brandy-face *n.* [late 17C–early 19C] a drunkard; thus *brandy-faced*, red-faced. [the effects of consistent over-drinking]

brandy is Latin for pig and goose *phr.* [late 18C–late 19C] used to apologize for drinking brandy after eating either goose or pig (cf. TACE IS LATIN FOR A CANDLE).

brandy-pawnee *n.* [mid-19C–mid-20C] (Anglo-Ind.) brandy and water. [SE *brandy* + Hind. *pani*, water]

brandy-shunter *n.* [late 19C–1900s] a heavy drinker of brandy. [SE *brandy* + *shunter*, a mover]

brandy-snap *n.* [1920s+] (Aus.) a scab on one's face. [its resemblance to SE *brandy-snap*, a very thin gingerbread biscuit]

bran-faced *adj.* [late 18C–early 19C] freckled (cf. CHRISTENED BY A BAKER). [SE *bran*, the husk of a cereal after grinding + sfx. *–faced*]

brangle *v.* [early–mid-17C] to have sexual intercourse. [SE *brangle*, shake, dance]

brannigan *n.* (US) **1** [late 19C+] a drunken spree. **2** [1940s+] a fight, a violent argument (cf. DONNYBROOK n.). **3** [1970s] a farce, a fiasco. [? proper name, but more likely f. stereotype of the fighting Irish drunk]

bran up *v.* [20C] (US) to eat. [SE *bran*]

braps! *see* BRADARAX!

brary *n.* [1980s] (US campus) the library; thus *brary dog*, someone who studies in the library. [abbr. *brary dog*]

bras *see* BRA n.¹.

brasole *n.* [1990s] (US) the vagina (cf. BACON SANDWICH). [? Ital. *bresaola*, cured, wind-dried beef, from which one 'cuts a slice']

brass *n.*¹ **1** [late 16C+] money; esp. as in northern phr. *where there's muck there's brass* and similar homilies. **2** [1940s+] (W.I.) a penny.

brass *n.*² [mid-19C+] audacity, gall, cheek. [BRASS NECK]

brass *n.*³ [late 19C+] a senior officer in the police or armed services (cf. BRASS-HAT).

brass *n.*⁴ [1930s+] a prostitute. [rhy. sl. *brass nail* = TAIL n.¹ (4)]

brass *n.*⁵ [1980s+] (drugs) cannabis. [ety. unknown]

brass *adj.*¹ [1950s+] fashionable, chic. [as preferred by the BRASS n.³ or those of similar social status]

brass *adj.*² [1950s+] out of cash, impoverished. [abbr. BORACIC, pron. 'brassic']

brass *v.* [1920s+] (Aus.) to defraud, to trick. [Und. *brass*, a fraudulent betting 'system', ult. BRASS n.¹]

brass along *v.* [1910s+] to go through life cheerfully, without much regard for the feelings of others. [BRASS n.²]

brass ankle *n.* [late 19C–1960s] a person of mixed race (cf. BLACK ANKLE). [1930s+ is US]

brass ass *n.* [1970s+] (US) insolence; thus *brass-assed*, insolent (cf. BRASS NECK). [SE *brass* + ARSE n.¹; cf. SE *brazen*]

brass balls *n.* [1960s+] **1** anything severely challenging, esp. in a 'masculine' context. **2** courage, 'guts'; thus *brass-balled*, courageous, tough. **3** cheek, effrontery. [SE *brass* + BALLS n.¹]

brass band *n.* [20C] the hand (cf. GERMAN BANDS). [rhy. sl.]

brass button *n.* [mid-19C–1930s] (US) a soldier, esp. an officer. [metonymy]

brass buttons *n.* [19C] a policeman. [metonymy]

brassco *n.* [1960s+] (Aus.) a lavatory. ['where the brass knobs go']

brassed/brassed off *adj.* [1940s+] irritated, fed up, annoyed (cf. BROWNED OFF; CHEESED OFF). [BRASS OFF]

brasser *n.* [1930s+] (Irish) a slut, a prostitute. [ext. of BRASS n.⁴]

brassey *n.* [19C] a policeman (cf. BRASS BUTTONS; BUTTONS n.²). [metonymy]

brass-face *n.* [mid-19C] an impudent person. [BRASS n.² + SE *face*]

brass fart/farthing *n.* [mid-17C–mid-19C] something of the utmost insignificance, usu. in phr. *I don't give a brass farthing*. [mid-19C+ use of *brass farthing* is SE]

brass guts *n.* [1940s+] **1** cheek, insolence. **2** courage, nerve (cf. BRASS BALLS). [SE *brass* + *guts*]

brass hat *n.* [late 19C+] a senior officer in the police or services. [the gold braid or similar adornment on their caps, itself known as SCRAMBLED EGG n.² (1)]

brass-head *n.* **1** [1950s] (US) a fool. **2** [20C] (W.I.) a Black person who has a reddish tint to their hair, the result of a diet lacking sufficient protein. [SE *brass* + (1) the hardness; (2) the colour]

brassic/brassick *see* BORACIC adj.

brass it out *see* BRASS OUT.

brass-knocker *n.* [late 19C–1900s] (vagrants) left-over food, scraps. [if a house boasts a brass knocker it is likely that the owners are wealthy enough to give away their leftovers. Note Hobson-Jobson *brass-knocker*: 'a term applied to a *rechauffé* or serving up again of yesterday's dinner or supper; a piece of Anglo-Ind. slang it is supposed to be a corruption of (Hind.) *basi khana*, stale food']

brass man *n.* [1930s+] (Aus.) a confidence trickster. [BRASS n.² + SE *man*]

brass monkey *n.* [1990s] (US) an alcoholic concoction available in liquor stores. [? brandname]

brass monkey weather *n.* [mid-19C+] (orig. US) extremely cold temperature. [phr. *cold enough to freeze the balls off a brass monkey*; thus army var. 'cold enough to make a Jew drop his bundle']

brass-mounted *adj.* [mid–late 19C] (US) a general intensifier, e.g. *I don't give a brass-mounted cuss*.

brass-nail *n.* [20C] a prostitute. [rhy. sl. *brass-nail* = TAIL n.¹ (4)]

brass neck *n.* [20C] impudence, audacity. [orig. northern dial.; the toughness of SE *brass* + NECK n.¹, but note BRASS n.²]

brass-neck *adj.* [20C] (orig. milit.) shameless, impudent. [BRASS NECK]

brass off *v.* [1920s+] (orig. naut. jargon) to tell off, to scold, to grumble. [? the primary activity of the BRASS n.³]

brass out/brass it out *v.* [1950s+] to bluff, bluster or brazen one's way out of a situation. [BRASS n.¹]

brass-plater *n.* [1920s] a professional person. [one who advertises their place of work by the *brass plate* placed at its doorway, e.g. a consultant, a lawyer. Note mid-19C coal trade jargon *brass-plate merchant*, a second-rate coal retailer]

brass tacks *n.* [20C] (orig. US) the facts, as in the central issues or heart of a matter, usu. in *let's get down to brass tacks* (or *nails*) and as such almost SE (cf. COME DOWN TO BRASS TACKS). [rhy. sl.]

brass up *v.* [late 19C+] to hand over money. [BRASS n.¹]

brass wig *n.* [1940s] (US Black) a senior officer of the police or armed services (cf. BRASS HAT).

brassy *adj.* **1** [mid-16C–late 18C] impudent, shameless. **2** [20C] of a woman, showy, flashy, ostentatious; implies a superficial bright hardness, but also possible prostitution (cf. BRASS n.³). [BRASS n.² + sfx. *-y*]

brat-getter *n.* [19C] the penis (cf. BABY-MAKER). [SE *brat* + *get*, to procreate]

brat-getting place *n.* [19C] the vagina (cf. BABY CHUTE).

brat pack *n.* [1980s+] any selection of successful young hopefuls, novelists, chefs, Black success stories (*Black pack*) whatever. [on pattern of the Hollywood's *Holmby Hills Rat Pack*, a coterie of film stars and singers led by Humphrey

Bogart in the 1950s and boosted by the mid-1980s *brat pack* of youthful Hollywood up-and-comers]

brattery *n.* [late 18C–mid-19C] a nursery. [SE *brat*]

bratty *n.* [1990s] (US teen) brother. [SE *brat*]

brave *n.* [late 16C–late 17C] a thug, a hired assassin. [BRAVO]

brave and bold *adj.* [late 19C–1920s] cold. [rhy. sl.]

bravo *n.* [late 16C–mid-18C] a hired killer (cf. BRAVE). [Ital. *bravo*, brave]

brawl *n.* [1920s–50s] a riotous, noisy party.

brawny-buttock *n.* [early 18C] a general epithet of abuse, presumably aimed at a large or fat person.

Brazilian time *n.* [1960s+] unpunctuality (cf. AFRICAN PEOPLE'S TIME). [derog. stereotyping]

breach *n.* [19C] the vagina (cf. ARBOUR).

bread *n.*[1] **1** [late 18C] employment; thus *out of bread*, unemployed (cf. BREAD AND BUTTER *n.*[1]). **2** [1930s+] money (cf. CAKE *n.*[2]; DOUGH; MOTSER). [(1) Yid. *broyt*, money, but note E.P. suggestion rhy. sl. BREAD AND HONEY. (2) something one might eat but also basic to life, as is bread]

bread *n.*[2] [20C] (US) a Black person. [? the centrality of the foodstuff]

bread *n.*[3] [1950s–60s] (orig. US Black) the vagina (cf. APPLE *n.*[10]). [? the 'staff of life' or, if seen as a generator of money, BREAD *n.*[1] (2)]

bread and bread *phr.* [1960s+] a homosexual couple; thus *bread and bread don't make a sandwich*, the reply given by one effeminate gay man when partnered with another, a parallel phrase is 'I'm a pouf, not a lesbian.'.

bread and butter *n.*[1] [mid-19C+] one's basic income and the work that provides it (cf. NO BREAD AND BUTTER OF MINE; QUARREL WITH ONE'S BREAD AND BUTTER). [the foodstuffs as staples]

bread and butter *n.*[2] [20C] the gutter. [rhy. sl.]

bread and butter *adj.* [mid–late 19C] childish, juvenile, esp. schoolgirlish. [the blandness of the food]

bread and butter fashion *n.* [late 18C–19C] sexual intercourse. [the proximity of the *bread* and *butter*, which 'lie on' each other]

bread and butter letter *n.* [20C] a letter of thanks sent to one's host shortly after having enjoyed the hospitality. [note journalistic jargon *bread and butter column*, a column fuelled in the main by press agent handouts and similar varieties of free publicity for those who send it to the writer; such a column harms no one, 'butters up' a variety of individuals and keeps the writer off the breadline]

bread-and-butter teeth *n.* [20C] buck teeth (cf. BUTTER TEETH). [large and white, they resemble slices of bread and butter]

bread and butter warehouse *n.* [18C–19C] Ranelagh Gardens in Chelsea, London, which was built as a pleasure garden in 1741, but gradually fell into disrepute and was shut down in 1803; it is now part of the gardens of the Chelsea Hospital. [? the teas served in its tea rooms or BREAD AND BUTTER FASHION]

bread and cheese *n.* [late 19C+] a sneeze. [rhy. sl.]

bread and cheese *adj.* [17C–18C] ordinary, run-of-the-mill, unexceptional. [the quotidian edibles]

bread and cheese, to *phr.* [late 19C+] to sneeze. [BREAD AND CHEESE *n.*]

bread and honey *n.* [20C] money (cf. BEES AND HONEY). [rhy. sl.]

bread and jam *n.* [20C] a tram. [rhy. sl.]

bread and lard *adj.* [20C] hard. [rhy. sl.]

bread and pullet *n.* [1900s–10s] bread with no butter, jam or other additive. [SE *bread* + pun on SE *pull it*]

bread and scrape *n.* [mid-19C+] a piece of bread barely covered in a thin layer of *scrape* of butter.

bread and skip *n.* [20C] (US) an inadequate meal (cf. BREAD AND WITH IT). [e.g. 'bread and molasses, and skip the molasses']

bread and with it *n.* [20C] a light meal, e.g. *a loaf of bread and* (*something else*) *with it* (cf. BREAD AND SKIP).

bread-bag *n.* [mid-19C] the stomach (cf. BREADBASKET).

breadbasket *n.* [early 19C+] the stomach (cf. BREAD-BAG; BREAD BOX; BREAD ROOM; DUMPLING DEPOT; VICTUALLING OFFICE). [boxing jargon]

bread box *n.* [1910s] (US) the stomach (cf. BREADBASKET).

bread-cutter/-grinder *n.* [20C] (US) a tooth.

breadearner *n.* [early 19C] (Irish) a knife, as used by a shoe-black.

bread-grinder *see* BREAD-CUTTER.

breadfruit swapper *n.* [20C] (W.I./Bdos.) a very poor person. [such a person is forced to barter rather than pay for goods]

breadhead *n.* [1960s+] an individual who is interested primarily in acquiring money. [BREAD *n.*[1] (2) + sfx. -HEAD (2); coined during the anti-money 1960s]

bread hooks *n.* [20C] (US) the hands (cf. BISCUIT HOOKS).

bread room *n.* [mid-18C–mid 19C] the stomach (cf. BREADBASKET).

breadsnapper *n.*[1] [late 19C+] (Scot./Glasgow) a child (cf. SNAPPER *n.*[8]).

breadsnapper *n.*[2] [20C] (Ulster) a baby, lit. 'a child who can eat their weight in groceries' (cf. SNAPPER *n.*[8]).

breadsnatchers *n.* [1960s] (US) the hands.

bread trap *n.* [mid-19C] (US) the mouth.

breadwinner *n.* [19C] the vagina (cf. BANK *n.*[1]). [the vagina viewed as a commercial commodity]

break *n.*[1] [mid-19C+] (Und.) a collection taken to give money to a prisoner either awaiting trial or recently discharged.

break *n.*[2] **1** [mid-19C+] (orig. US) a piece of luck, usually good, but note BAD BREAK. **2** [late 19C+] (US) an error, a mistake. **3** [20C] (orig. US) a piece of special treatment, kindness, fair treatment.

break *n.*[3] [20C] (orig. US) an escape from prison.

break *v.*[1] (US) **1** [mid-19C+] of people, to rush off, to leave suddenly. **2** [20C] of things, events, to turn out, to transpire, to develop. [SE *break away/break down*]

break *v.*[2] [late 19C–1900s] to cut, to ignore deliberately, to snub. [SE *break away (from)*]

break *v.*[3] [20C] (Ulster) to embarrass. [? to make blood 'break out' in a blush]

break *v.*[4] [1920s+] to give change for a note or large-denomination coin.

break *v.*[5] [1940s+] (Aus.) to cost, e.g. *that'll break for five dollars*.

break a bit off, to *phr.* [20C] to have sexual intercourse (cf. BREAK IT OFF). [? the equation of sex and violence or the 'breaking' of the erect penis following orgasm]

break a bottle in an empty sack, to *phr.* [late 18C–mid-19C] to make a cheating bet. [a sack that is empty cannot contain a bottle]

break a gut *see* BUST A GUT.

break a leg, to *phr.* **1** [1900s–30s] (US) to be arrested. **2** [1910s–40s] (orig. US) to hurry.

break a leg! *excl.* [1960s+] to an actor, good luck! [theatrical superstition outlaws the actual phr. 'good luck']

break an ankle, to *phr.* [late 18C+] to become pregnant out of wedlock (cf. BREAK ONE'S LEG *phr.*[1]; MAKE A TRIP). [euph.; orig. 18C–19C UK, now survives mainly in US]

break an egg, to *phr.* [1980s+] (US) to kill, to murder. [? phr. 'you can't make an omelette without breaking eggs']

break a pudding, to *phr.* [20C] (Irish) to belch. [the result of one's eating]

break-ass *adv.* [1960s] (US) at top speed. [SE *break* + ARSE n.[1] (1)]

break a trace-chain, to *phr.* [19C] (US) to make a supreme effort. [SE *break* + *trace-chain*, the long chain by which a team is yoked to the plough]

break-away/-in/-out *n.*[1] [late 19C–1900s] (Aus./N.Z.) a drinking bout, a spree.

break-away *n.*[2] [1910s+] (Aus.) a person who has been 'broken', whether mentally or physically.

break bad *v.* [1970s+] (US Black) to become angry or aggressive. [BREAK v.[2] (2) + SE *bad*]

break-down *n.*[1] [mid-19C–1900s] (Aus.) a measure of liquor. [a bottle 'breaks down' into several such measures]

break-down *n.*[2] [1990s] (US Black) a shotgun. [such weapons can be 'broken' between the barrel and the stock]

break down *v.*[1] [20C] (N.Z.) to make lighter. [SE *breakdown*, to dismantle]

break down *v.*[2] [1960s+] (US Black) to explain, to tell.

breakdowns *n.* [1990s] (drugs) a $40 piece of crack cocaine sold for $20. [the dealer 'breaks down' the price]

break 'em off a lil' sum, to *phr.* [1990s] (US Black teen) to hand out or show off something that you have.

breaker *n.*[1] [19C] a burglar. [SE *break in*]

breaker *n.*[2] [1970s] a Citizen's Band radio enthusiast. [the code-word *breaker*, signifying one's desire to join a conversation]

breakfast of champions *n.* [1990s] **1** the labia. **2** mutual oral-genital stimulation. [pun on the slogan for US breakfast cereal, Wheaties, long celebrated as the *breakfast of champions*]

breakfast pipe *n.* [mid-19C] (US) the gullet.

break ill *v.* [1990s] (US Black) to make a mistake, to take the wrong course of action. [BREAK v.[1] (2) + ILL adj. (1)]

break-in *n.*[1] *see* BREAK-AWAY n.[1].

break-in *n.*[2] [1980s] (US teen) someone who is leaving. [the exit 'breaks in' to the social occasion]

breaking *n.*[1] [1950s+] *breaking* and entering (cf. B AND E). [abbr.]

breaking *n.*[2] [1980s+] (US) a dance style perfected in New York's South Bronx, in which dancers spin, whirl and twist, pivoting on heads, elbows, knees etc, performed to HIP-HOP or RAP music. [abbr. SE *break dancing*]

breaking *n.*[3] [1990s] (US Black) becoming obsessive, going to extremes. [one 'breaks out' of the status quo]

breaking up of the spell *n.* [19C] the end of the nightly performance at the Theatres-Royal, London; as the crowds disperse pickpockets move among them looking for valuables. [SPELLKEN]

break it big, to *phr.* [20C] (Aus.) to win heavily, esp. when gambling.

break it down *v.*[1] [1930s+] (US Black) to get excited, to become emotional. [ext. of SE *break down*, to become distraught[

break it down *v.*[2] [1930s+] (Aus.) to give in, to desist. [SE *break down*, to dismantle]

break it down *v.*[3] [1930s+] (US Black) to explain, to put the listener right. [ext. of BREAK DOWN v.[2]]

break it off *v.* **1** [19C] (US) to wound or hurt verbally. **2** [1990s] (US Black) to have sexual intercourse (cf. BREAK A BIT OFF).

break it off in *v.* [late 19C+] (US) to treat or hurt badly. [the image is of some form of knife]

break it up! *excl.* [1930s+] a general admonition to stop what one is doing, e.g. to move on, to break up a meeting, of several people or a couple.

break me off a piece *phr.* [1980s+] (orig. US Black) I want some, give me some.

break night *v.* [1980s+] (US) to stay up all night partying. [one 'breaks through' the night + ref. to the SE *break of day*]

break-o'-day drum *n.* [late 19C] an all-night tavern. [SE *break-o'-day*, dawn + DRUM n.[2] (1)]

break off *v.* [1990s] to share, esp. to share one's pleasures. [i.e. *breaking off* a small piece of hashish and offering it as a gift]

break on *v.* [1990s] (US Black) **1** to denigrate someone behind their back. **2** to humiliate someone in public. [one 'breaks' their image]

break one's arm, to *phr.* [20C] (US) to boast. [the idea of breaking one's arm while patting oneself on the back]

break one's arse/ass *see* BUST ONE'S ARSE.

break one's back, to *phr.* [mid-19C+] to stretch beyond one's limits, esp. financially, to become bankrupt.

break/bust one's balls, to *phr.* (orig. US) **1** [1950s+] to complain, to nag. **2** [1950s+] to attack, to persecute, to harass (cf. BALL-BREAKER). **3** [1930s+] to work very hard, esp. at a physically demanding task. **4** [1930s+] to force someone else to work hard. **5** [1950s+] to meet with disaster. [SE *break/bust* + BALLS n.[1] (1)]

break one's chops, to *phr.* [1930s+] **1** to talk incessantly. **2** to make a great fuss about something (cf. BEAT ONE'S CHOPS). [SE *break* + CHOPS n.[1] (1)]

break one's gall, to *phr.* [late 18C] to cheer up, esp. of one who has just arrived in prison and is still suitably dejected. [SE *break* + *gall*, bitterness]

break one's leg/leg above the knee/one's toe, to *phr.*[1] [17C–18C] **1** to become pregnant out of wedlock (cf. BREAK ONE'S ANKLE). **2** of a young woman, to lose one's virginity, to be seduced.

break one's leg, to *phr.*[2] [17C–18C] of a womanizing man, to become father to a child, whether one wishes to or not. [ext. of BREAK ONE'S LEG phr.[1]]

break one's luck, to *phr.* [1930s–60s] of a prostitute, to encounter the first customer of the day.

break one's neck, to *phr.* [1910s+] to need to urinate urgently.

break one's neck for, to *phr.* [late 19C+] to yearn for, to be desperate for.

break one's own neck, to *phr.* [20C] (US) to get married. [? the weight of matrimonial responsibilities that form a yoke across one's neck]

break one's shins against Covent Garden rails, to *phr.* [late 18C–early 19C] to catch venereal disease (cf. COVENT GARDEN AGUE; COVENT GARDEN GOUT). [Covent Garden, London, being a centre of prostitution]

break one's toe *see* BREAK ONE'S LEG.

break out *n.* *see* BREAK-AWAY n.[1].

break out *v.*[1] [mid-19C+] to break open a package and remove its contents, to get articles from a place of storage.

break out *v.*[2] **1** [mid–late 19C] (US) to appear. **2** [1990s] (US Black) to leave.

break out into assholes, to *phr.* [1970s+] (US) to become terrified. [SE *break out* + ARSEHOLE n. (2); a play on SE *break out into a rash* etc]

break/bust out with *v.* [1940s+] (US Black/campus) **1** to do, say or wear something surprising or exciting. **2** to produce something unexpected and/or suddenly.

break-pulpit *n.* [late 16C–17C] a noisy, melodramatic preacher. [their excess energy]

breaks *n.* [mid-19C+] (orig. US) luck, chance, opportunities, either *good breaks* or *bad breaks*. [SE *break* (*in the road*)]

break shins *v.* [late 17C–late 19C] to borrow money, esp. during an emergency, when one is forced to run from person to person in the hope of a loan (cf. SHIN v.). [Rus. tradition of beating the shins of those who refuse to pay their debts]

break shit *v.* [1980s+] **1** to sell drugs. **2** to do something, to act. [SE *break* + SHIT n.⁵, n.³]

break someone in two, to *phr.* [20C] to beat up someone badly, to break their bones.

break someone off some, to *phr.* [1990s] (US Black) to give, esp. to hand over drugs.

break someone's arse/ass *see* BUST SOMEONE'S ARSE.

break someone's ear, to *phr.* [1970s] to interrupt, to chatter continually.

break/change someone's face *phr.*¹ [late 19C+] (US) to beat someone up.

break someone's face, to *phr.*² [1990s] (US Black) to hurt someone's feelings.

break-teeth words *n.* [late 18C–early 19C] words considered hard to pronounce, long and incomprehensible words (cf. JAWBREAKER).

break the neck of, to *phr.* [19C] to commence, to set events in motions. [synon. of SE *break the back of*]

break the needle, to *phr.* [1940s] (US drugs) to use up all the available drugs. [the *needle* being a hypodermic syringe]

break the sound barrier, to *phr.* [1960s+] (Can.) to break wind. [a pun on SE]

break to *v.* [1990s] (US Black) to transport oneself to, often quickly. [BREAK v.¹ (1)]

break to the set, to *phr.* [1970s+] (US Black) to move to or arrive at a gathering. [BREAK v.¹ (1) + SET]

break-up *n.* [1920s+] (Aus.) anyone or anything considered highly amusing or risible. [BREAK UP v. (3)]

break up *v.* **1** [early 19C–1930s] (US) to make someone very upset, to make one ill with tension, to cause someone to cry. **2** [late 19C+] to collapse in laughter. **3** [late 19C+] (orig. US) to cause someone to laugh heartily. **4** [1940s+] (US) to act hysterically, to act irrationally.

break weak *v.* [20C] (US) to act in a cowardly manner. [BREAK v.² (2) + SE *weak*]

break wide *v.* [20C] (US Black) **1** to lose interest. **2** to leave in a hurry. [BREAK v.¹ + SE *wide*]

breakyleg *n.*¹ [mid-19C] strong drink, esp. whisky; thus *break one's leg*, to become badly drunk (cf. BADERED). [the concept is an old one. Hotten (1867) notes that 'in the ancient Egyptian language the determinative character in the hieroglyphic verb 'to be drunk' has the significant form of the leg of man being amputated']

breakyleg *n.*² [mid-19C] a shilling (5p). [ety. unknown; ? the price of BREAKYLEG n.¹]

break yourself! *excl.* [1990s] (US Und.) a command used by a mugger who wishes their victim to turn out their pockets or hand over their purse. [lit. make yourself BROKE]

bream *n.* [1970s] (US) a half-pint (300ml) of liquor (cf. BASS). [the use of fish to denote varying sizes, as are the fish themselves, of glass; note a similar form of ranking used by British Rail freight wagons, which were labelled *trout, perch, whale* etc]

breast/breast up to *v.* [1910s+] (Aus.) to accost; thus *breast the bar*, to walk up to a bar to order a drink.

breast-fest *n.* [1990s] the opportunity for men to enjoy the sight of women's breasts, thanks to the lighter clothes, swimming costumes and so on worn in summer. [SE *breast* + -FEST]

breast fleet *n.* [late 18C] Roman Catholics, seen as a group (cf. BRISKET-BEATER; CHEST-POUNDER; CRAW-THUMPER). [the beating of their breasts during certain prayers]

breast up *see* BREAST v.

breastworks *n.* [early 19C+] the female breasts. [pun on SE]

breath-and-britches *n.* [1920s–30s] (US Black) a ne'er-do-well, an untrustworthy, disreputable man (cf. ALL MOUTH AND TROUSERS). [breath that smells of liquor and britches that are constantly being dropped at another woman's bedside]

breathe *v.* [19C] to permit one's horse or horses to have a rest.

breathe down someone's neck, to *phr.* **1** [1930s+] to be physically close. **2** [1940s+] to be in hot pursuit or in competition.

breather *n.*¹ [mid-19C] (US) something superlative. [? it makes one draw a breath in awe]

breather *n.*² [1910s] a lung.

breathe someone's air, to *phr.* [20C] (US prison) to get on someone's nerves, to invade someone's privacy.

bred in the ditch *phr.* [20C] (US) illegitimate (cf. BORN WITH BURNED FEET).

bredren/bredrin *n.* [1950s] (W.I./UK Black) a friend. [SE *brethren* + biblical overtones of Rastafarian *bredren*]

bree *n.* [1930s] (US Black/Harlem) a young woman. [ety. unknown]

breeched *adj.* [early 19C–mid 20C] (Und.) well-off. [having money in one's breeches]

breechloader *n.* [1910s] one who is sodomized, usu. a male homosexual. [pun on SE *breechloader*, a firearm loaded at the back of the bore + *breech*, the anus]

breechy *adj.* [20C] (US) of a woman, immoral. [dial. *breachy*, of cattle, liable to break through the pasture fence]

breed *n.* [late 19C+] (orig. US) a half-*breed*, a derog. term for a Native American. [abbr.]

breed a black eye/black eye for oneself, to *phr.* [20C] (US) to stir up trouble for oneself (cf. BREED A SCAB).

breed a scab/scab on one's nose, to *phr.* [20C] (US) to stir up trouble for oneself. [someone is likely to punch your nose]

breeder *n.* [1970s+] (gay) **1** a heterosexual. **2** a married homosexual who produces children.

breeding-cage *n.* [late 19C] a matrimonial bed.

breefs *n.* [mid-19C] a pack of cards used by cheats, the edges have been minutely trimmed to indicate the high cards (cf. BRIEF n.¹).

breeker *see* BREKER.

breeze *n.*¹ [late 18C] an argument, a disturbance, a quarrel; thus *have a breeze in one's breech*, to be disturbed, confused. [dial. *breeze*, a gadfly]

breeze *n.*² **1** [late 19C] a rumour, a scandal. **2** [1910s] (US) empty chatter (cf. BACK THE BREEZE).

breeze *n.*³ **1** [1920s+] (US Black) a relaxed person. **2** [1990s] a smart, fashionable person. [the positive image of SE *breeze*]

breeze *n.*⁴ [1920s+] anything easy, simple, no problems, usu. as *phr. it's a breeze*. [one simply 'blows' through it]

breeze *n.*⁵ [1940s+] (W.I.) freedom; thus *give me breeze*, leave me in peace, give me some room (cf. BREEZE v.¹). [like the wind, it cannot be controlled]

breeze *n.*⁶ [1950s+] (W.I.) small change, anything less than a shilling. [ety. unknown; ? it is as insubstantial as a SE *breeze*]

breeze *n.*⁷ [1960s+] (US Black) a person, esp. as a greeting, 'Breeze!' [COOL BREEZE!]

breeze *v.*¹ [1920s–60s] (US/W.I.) to leave, to go away; thus (US) *breeze off*, go away, leave me alone, (W.I.) *breeze me a bit*, go away, leave me in peace, (W.I.) *breeze me ase* (ears), shut up, be quiet (cf. BREEZE ALONG).

breeze/breeze it/through *v.*² [1940s+] (Aus.) to do something easily. [BREEZE n.⁴]

breeze along *v.* [1920s+] to visit, with an implication of casual, unplanned dropping in.

breeze in *v.* [1920s+] to arrive unexpectedly (cf. BLOW IN; BREEZE ALONG).

breeze it *see* BREEZE v.².

breeze puncher *n.* [1910s] (US) an excessive talker. [BAT THE BREEZE]

breezer *n.*¹ [1920s] (US) an open-topped car.

breezer *n.*² [1960s+] (Aus.) a fart. [like the breeze it is 'wind']

breezer to sneezer/sneezer to breezer *phr.* [late 19C] (Aus.) from nose to tail. [SE *breezer* + SNEEZER n.¹ (3)]

breeze through *see* BREEZE v.².

breezing *n.* [mid-19C] (US) a scolding, a telling-off. [BACK THE BREEZE]

breezy *adj.*¹ [1910s+] frightened, fearful. [SE *get the wind up*]

breezy *adj.*² [1920s+] (Aus.) short-tempered. [SE *blow up*, lose one's temper]

breezy *adj.*³ [1920s+] bright and cheery.

breezy bertie *n.* [1920s] a brash, self-confident, insensitive young man. [BREEZY adj.³]

breker/breeker *n.* [1970s+] (S.Afr.) **1** a tough, macho man, a fighter. **2** a motorbike rider dressed in the classic 'leathers', jeans, boots etc (cf. BIKIE; ROCKERS n.¹). [Afk. *breek*, to break]

brekker *n.* [late 19C+] breakfast. [SE *break(fast)* + 'Oxford' sfx. -*er*]

brekkie/brekky *n.* [20C] breakfast.

brekky bong *v.* [1980s+] (Aus. drugs) to smoke cannabis as soon as one wakes up. [BREKKIE + BONG n.]

brenda *n.*¹ [1940s+] (US) a journalist. [the strip cartoon journalist *Brenda* Starr, created by Dale Messick]

brenda/brenda bracelets *n.*² [1980s+] (camp gay) a policeman (cf. HILDA HANDCUFFS; TERESA TRUNCHEON). [joc. assonance, but note BRENDA n.¹]

brer *n.* [1990s] (Black) a fellow Black. [SE *brother*]

br'er nancy *n.* [20C] (W.I.) an untrustworthy, cunning person (cf. NANCY TALES). [*Br'er*, brother + *Anansie*, the folk-tale hero, who escapes trouble through lying]

brevet wife *n.* [late 19C] a woman with whom a man cohabits, but to whom he is not legally married. [SE *brevet*, a nominal rank that confers extra authority but no extra pay]

brew *n.*¹ **1** [late 19C+] a pot of tea. **2** [1910s+] (US) a pot or cup of coffee; thus *cup of brew*, one's preference (cf. CUP OF TEA n.²). **3** [1940s+] (US) beer, ale, esp. in the UK Carlsberg Special Brew, poss. the strongest canned beer on sale in the UK. **4** [1980s+] (N.Z. prison) illicitly brewed alcohol.

brew *n.*² *see* BUROO.

brew *v.* [1950s+] (drugs) to prepare heroin for injection by heating with water in a spoon or bottle cap (cf. COOK v.³).

brew dog *n.* [1980s+] (US campus) beer. [BREW n.¹ (3) + DOG n.¹⁰]

brewer's asthma *n.* [1920s+] (Aus.) **1** shortness of breath. **2** a very bad hangover.

brewer's droop *n.* [1970s+] (orig. Aus.) temporary impotence due to the effects of alcohol on the erectile tissue.

brewer's fizzle *n.* [18C] beer, ale.

brewer's goitre *n.* [1950s+] (Aus.) a beer belly. [SE *goitre*, a swelling on the neck]

brewer's horse *n.* [late 16C+] a drunkard. [i.e. one who has fig. been 'bitten by the brewer's horse']

brewery *n.* [1950s+] (drugs) a place where drugs are manufactured. [BREW v.]

brewha/brewhaha *n.* [1980s+] (US campus) a can of beer. [puns on BREW n.¹ (3) + SE *brouhaha*]

brewhound *n.* [1980s+] (US campus) a regular drunkard. [BREW n.¹ (3) + sfx. -HOUND]

brew house *n.* [1990s] (US Black) a liquor store. [BREW n.¹ (3) + SE *house*]

brewising/bruising the bed *n.* [late 18C] fouling one's bed. [supposed similarity of the mess to SE *brewis*, a broth made from beef and vegetables or the fat scum from the pot in which salt beef has been boiled]

brewski/brewsky *n.* [1960s+] (US campus) beer (cf. BREWHA). [BREW n.¹ (3) + 'Russian' sfx. -*ski*]

brew-up *n.* [1940s+] **1** the making of tea. **2** a pause in one's activities to allow tea to be made. **3** a meal, including tea.

brew up *v.* [1910s+] to make tea. [BREW-UP n. (1)]

Brian O'Flynn *n.* [20C] gin. [rhy. sl.]

Brian O'Linn/O'Lynn *n.* [mid-19C+] gin. [rhy. sl.]

briar-/brier-breaker/-hopper *n.* [1930s+] (US, mainly Midland) a rustic, a peasant, an unsophisticated person (cf. CLODHOPPER).

briar-root *n.* [late 19C] an ill-shaped, battered nose. [resemblance to a SE *briar-root pipe*]

brick *n.*¹ [mid-19C] (Aus.) a gang member; thus *brickism*, the philosophy of joining and acting in a gang. [? ironic use of BRICK n.³]

brick *n.*² [mid-19C] (US) a punishment, performed by bringing someone's knees close up to the chin and lashing the arms tightly to the knees. [the body becomes 'brick-shaped']

brick *n.*³ [mid-19C+] a reliable, kind, selfless person (cf. BRICKY adj.¹). [the solidity of the object]

brick *n.*⁴ [1910s+] (Aus.) **1** a £10 note (cf. LONDON TO A BRICK). **2** a 10-year prison sentence. [the colour (red) of the Aus. note]

brick *n.*⁵ **1** [1950s] (US prison) a carton of cigarettes (cf. BOX n.³). **2** [1960s+] (drugs) 1kg (2.2lb) of marijuana (cf. KEY n.⁴). **3** [1980s+] (US) a brick-shaped package. **4** [1990s] (US Black) an attractive, well-built woman (cf. BRICKHOUSE). [the shape]

brick *n.*⁶ [1980s+] (US campus) a mess, a failure. [BRICK v.³ (1)]

brick *v.*¹ [1960s] (US) to throw bricks at the police, the national guard or any other form of authority against whom one is demonstrating.

brick/bricker *v.*² [1960s–70s] to steal, to filch. [note bus-drivers' jargon *make a brick*, to defraud London transport]

brick *v.*³ [1980s+] (US campus) **1** to fail, to receive a failing grade. **2** to perform badly in one's work. [DROP A BRICK]

bricked *adj.* [late 16C–mid-17C] smartly dressed. [? SE *breeched*]

bricker *see* BRICK v.².

brickfielder *n.* [mid-19C+] (Aus.) **1** a hot, dusty wind that blows over parts of northern Australia. **2** a nuisance. [orig. a thick cloud of dust brought over Sydney, New South Wales, by a south wind from neighbouring sandhills (called the 'brickfields')]

brick gum *n.* **1** [1930s–50s] a block of unprocessed opium. **2** [1980s+] (drugs) heroin. [SE *brick* + GUM n.³]

brickhouse *n.* [1970s+] (US campus) **1** a woman with a large chest. **2** an attractive woman (cf. BRICK n.⁵). [BUILT LIKE A BRICK SHITHOUSE]

brickie *n.* [late 19C+] (orig. Aus.) a *brick*layer. [abbr.]

brickish *adj.* [mid-19C] a general term of approbation. [BRICK n.³]

brick it *v.* [1950s+] to be terrified, to be very nervous. [SHIT A BRICK]

bricklayer *n.* [late 19C] a clergyman. [? SE *rubrick layer*; but F&H note, first, the medieval church official the *operarius*, the workman 'on whom devolved the charge of repairing and maintaining the sacred fabric' of a church or cathedral; and, second, the line in Ephesians that compares such early Christians as St Paul to 'master-builders' whose greatest 'building' is the Church]

brick-presser *n.* [1920s–30s] (US Black) a tramp, a vagrant. [HIT THE BRICKS]

bricks *n.* [20C] **1** the city streets, esp. seen f. a prison cell. **2** the urban environment in general. **3** a street prostitute's beat. [metonymy]

bricks and mortar *n.*¹ [late 19C+] a house, a building, property in general, esp. as an image of secure investment. [metonymy]

bricks and mortar *n.*² [20C] a daughter. [rhy. sl.]

bricktop *n.* [19C] (US) a redhead (cf. BRICKYARD BLONDE). [the redness of 'typical' bricks]

brick wall *phr.* [1990s] (US teen) phr. of dismissal, i.e. 'I'm ignoring you now. I don't care about what you're saying'.

bricky *adj.*[1] [mid–late 19C] plucky, courageous. [BRICK n.[1] (2)]
bricky *adj.*[2] [mid–late 19C] tipsy. [HAVE A BRICK IN ONE'S HAT]
brickyard blonde *n.* [20C] (US) a redhead (cf. BRICKTOP).
bridal suite *n.* [1970s+] (N.Z. prison) a two-man cell. [it is seen as encouraging prison homosexuality]
briddy *n.* [1990s] (US Black) a woman (cf. BRIDY). [? proper name *Bridy*, i.e. Bridget, or SE *bride*]
bride *n.* **1** [late 19C+] a prostitute. **2** [1930s+] a woman, esp. a girlfriend.
bride and groom *n.*[1] [late 19C–1950s] **1** a broom. **2** a room. [rhy. sl.]
bride and groom *n.*[2] [20C] (orig. US short-order jargon) two poached or fried eggs (cf. ADAM AND EVE n.).
bride's biscuit *n.* [20C] (US) a badly made biscuit, tough and heavy. [a new bride is traditionally unable to cook properly]
bridge *n.* **1** [1920s+] (N.Z.) a glance, a look. **2** [1920s+] (Aus.) an introduction. **3** [1930s+] (Aus.) a plausible excuse. [differing senses of SE *bridge a gap*]
bridge *v.*[1] [19C] (Und.) **1** to double-cross, to betray (a confidence). **2** in gambling, to deceive one's backer by deliberately losing the game. [the image is of two confederates getting together to throw a third party from a (metaphorical) bridge]
bridge/bring up *v.*[2] [1950s+] (drugs) to ready a vein for injection, by making it swell out of the surrounding flesh.
bridge and tunnel/bridge and tunnel people *n.* [1980s+] (US) used by Manhattanites to describe those who live in the outer boroughs (Queens, Brooklyn, Long Island) or New Jersey and travel to Manhattan via the Holland Tunnel (New Jersey) or over the East Side bridges.
bridget *n.*[1] [17C] a chicken. [BIDDY n.[1], the popular abbr. of the name *Bridget*]
bridget *n.*[2] [mid–late 19C] (US) a servant girl. [proper name *Bridget*, a popular Irish name and thus common among the Irish maids of New York]
bridget *v.* [late 19C–1900s] (orig. US) to obtain money from servant girls by false pretences. [BRIDGET n.[2]; Ware notes that the late 19C Fenians commonly used such servants to 'launder' their otherwise illicit funds]
bridle-cull *n.* [mid-18C] (Und.) a highwayman. [SE *bridle* + CULL n.[1] (4)]
bridle-string *n.* [late 19C] the frenum or ligament of the penis. [it is attached to the 'head' of the penis]
brief *n.*[1] [late 17C–mid-19C] a pack of doctored playing cards; the edges have been carefully trimmed to indicate, to the cheat, which cards are high (cf. BREEFS). [Ger. *Briefe*, a playing card]
brief *n.*[2] **1** [mid-19C] a pawnbroker's ticket. **2** [mid-19C] a raffle ticket. **3** [mid-19C+] a ticket in general (bus, tube etc). **4** [mid-19C+] (Und.) a note or letter. **5** [late 19C+] any form of false document, typically a reference or recommendation. **6** [20C] (Anglo-Irish) a banknote. **7** [1930s] a cheque. **8** [1930s+] a barrister, whose legal commissions are their briefs. **9** [late 19C+] (Aus.) a letter on official paper. **10.** [1960s+] (police) a warrant to arrest or search. [Lat. *breve*, a letter or note; ult. f. *brevis*, short]
brief *adj.* [19C] (US Black) elegant, well-dressed, smart. [i.e. 'no frills']
brief-snatcher *n.* [19C] a pickpocket who specializes in stealing from members of a racecourse crowd. [BRIEF n.[1] + SE *snatcher*]
brier-breaker/-hopper *see* BRIAR-BREAKER.
brierpatch child *n.* [20C] (US) an illegitimate child. [note US dial. *lap child*, the youngest child, still confined to their mother's lap, a spoiled child; *yard child*, a child old enough to play in the yard]
briffen *n.* [1920s+] a woman (cf. CRUMPET n.[4]). [? Liverpool tramps' use *briffen*, bread and dripping]

brig *n.* [mid-19C+] (orig. US naut.) a prison. [orig. sited between the two forward guns on the starboard side of the gun-deck]
brigade *n.* [20C] any collection of supposedly like-minded individuals, e.g. the *dirty mac brigade*, middle-aged men with a taste for pornography.
briggity *adj.* [20C] (US) arrogant, self-opinionated. [BIGGITY, but ? link to SE *brag*, to boast]
briggle *v.* [19C] (US) to act ineffectively, to move from one task to another without completing any one successfully. [? Scot. *breeghle*, to fiddle about; or a corruption of SE *wriggle*]
brigg's rest *n.* [20C] a vest. [rhy. sl.]
brigh *n.* [mid-late 19C] (Und.) a trouser pocket; thus *brighful*, a pocketful.
bright *n.*[1] [1920s–50s] (US Black) a day, daylight, morning (cf. BRIGHTENING). [note poetic use of 13C–19C SE *bright*, brightness, light]
bright *n.*[2] [1940s–50s] (US Black) a light-skinned Black person (cf. BRIGHT-SKIN).
bright as a button/new pin *phr.* [20C] clever, aware, sophisticated.
bright bastard *n.* [1910s+] (Aus.) a general term of ironic disparagement. [SE *bright* + BASTARD n. (2)]
bright boy *n.* [1920s–30s] (US) often used ironically, a clever person, a 'know-it-all'.
brightening *n.* [1940s] (US Black) dawn. [BRIGHT n.[1]]
bright-eyed and bushy-tailed *phr.* [1950s+] alert, lively. [the stereotyped image of a squirrel]
bright in the eye *phr.* [late 19C–1920s] tipsy, drunk (cf. ABOUT RIGHT adj.[1]).
Brighton pier *adj.* **1** [mid-19C+] peculiar, strange. **2** [1950s+] homosexual. [rhy. sl. *Brighton pier* = queer/QUEER adj.[1] (2)]
Brighton pier *v.* [1990s] to leave, to run off. [rhy. sl. *Brighton pier* = *disappear*]
brights *n.* [1970s] (US Black) the eyes.
bright-skin *n.* [mid-19C–1950s] (US Black) a light-skinned person (cf. BRIGHT n.[2]).
bright spark *n.* [20C] a lively, energetic person, but often used ironically as a derog. (cf. BRIGHT SPECIMEN).
bright specimen *n.* [late 19C] a term, based on irony, for a lively, energetic person (cf. BRIGHT SPARK).
brill! *excl.* [1980s+] wonderful! excellent! [SE *brilliant!*]
brilliant/brilliant stark-naked *n.*[1] [early 19C] raw, un-diluted gin. [it shines in the glass]
brilliant *n.*[2] [20C] (gay) an obviously, exaggeratedly homosexual man. [SE *brilliant*, having showy good qualities]
brilliant *adj.* [1990s] (US campus) excellent, worthy of admiration.
brilliant stark-naked *see* BRILLIANT n.[1].
brillo! *excl.* [1990s] (Irish) wonderful! excellent! [BRILL! + sfx. *-o*]
brillohead *n.* [1980s+] (US campus) a person with very coarse hair. [brandname of *Brillo*, a pan scourer]
brim *n.*[1] **1** [late 17C–mid-19C] an abandoned or promiscuous woman. **2** [late 18C–mid-19C] a termagant. [abbr. SE *brimstone*. In both cases she is 'hot']
brim *n.*[2] [1950s] (US Black) a hat (cf. BRIMMER).
brim *v.* [17C–18C] of a man, to have sexual intercourse. [dial. *brim*, of a boar, to have intercourse with a sow]
brimmer *n.* [mid-17C–early 18C] a broad-brimmed hat (cf. BRIM n.[2]).
brimstone *n.* [17C–early 18C] a prostitute. [SE *brimstone*, sulphur; this brimstone is 'hot stuff']
brimstone buster *n.* [19C] (US) a ranting preacher (cf. AUTEM BAWLER; BIBLE-BANGER; TUB-THUMPER). [SE *brimstone*, hellfire + *buster*, a breaker or smasher]

brindle n. [20C] (Aus.) a half-caste. [SE brindled, usu. of an animal, streaked]

brindle v. [1950s+] (W.I. Rasta) to be angry. [? SE bridle, to draw back resentfully, to exhibit an offended air]

briney see BRINY.

bring v. [early 19C] to steal. [euph.]

bring an old house on one's head, to phr. [19C] to get oneself into trouble (cf. PULL AN OLD HOUSE ON ONE'S HEAD).

bring-and-carry see CARRY-GO-BRING-COME.

bring a noble to ninepence, to phr. [mid-16C–early 19C] to throw away money, to dissipate a fortune. [SE noble, a gold coin valued at 6s 8d (34p)]

bring ass to get ass, to phr. [1950s+] (US) to take a risk in order to make a gain. [ARSE n.1]

bringdown n. [1930s+] (orig. US) anything depressing, either a person or a circumstance. [SE bring + DOWN adj.¹; but note US Black phr. bring down my love on me, make me happy]

bring down v. [1930s+] (orig. US Black) to depress. [SE bring + DOWN adj.]

bring-go-bring-come see CARRY-GO-BRING-COME.

bring home the bacon, to phr. [1920s+] to deliver whatever is requested and required.

bring it all back home, to phr. [1980s+] (US campus) to have a good time.

bring it away v. [20C] to effect an abortion. ['it' being the foetus]

bring mud v. [1920s] (US Black) to let down, to disappoint.

bring off v. [20C] to bring to orgasm. [E.P. suggests 'probably since 16C' (as he does for BRING ON) but offers no citation or further proof; nor is there any ref. in a dictionary (slang or standard) before his own]

bring off by hand, to phr. [early 19C+] to masturbate (someone else). [BRING OFF + SE hand]

bring on v. [20C] to excite sexually. [see comment at BRING OFF]

bring one's arse to an anchor see BRING ONE TO AN ANCHOR.

bring oneself off v. [1960s+] to masturbate (cf. BEAT OFF).

bring/have one's heart up, to phr. [late 19C] to be sick; thus enough to have one's heart up, enough to make one sick.

bring one's hogs to a fair/fine market, to phr. [18C] to be particularly successful in one's business (cf. DRIVE ONE'S DUCKS TO A POOR MARKET).

bring one's Jonah on, to phr. [20C] (W.I.) to attack verbally, to vilify. [naut. sl. Jonah, a person who personifies bad luck; such individuals were sometimes tossed overboard, esp. in a storm, to placate the elements. The term in itself goes back to the biblical prophet Jonah, who, while supposedly 'fleeing the Lord', was similarly tossed overboard and swallowed by 'a great fish', presumably a whale]

bring one's ring up, to phr. [1970s] to vomit violently (cf. SPEW ONE'S RING).

bring one/one's arse to an anchor, to phr. [mid-19C+] to sit down. [naut. imagery]

bring on the china, to phr. [1900s–30s] to bring to orgasm (cf. BRING OFF). [BRING ON + ? rhy. sl. but with what or ? pun on SE China root, a once-popular medicinal plant]

bring on your bears phr. [late 19C] (US) a challenge, 'do your worst'. [SE bear, a rough, uncouth person]

bring out v. 1 [1940s–50s] (US Black) to introduce a hitherto ignorant or naïve person to a faster, more sophisticated lifestyle (cf. TURN ON). 2 [1960s+] (gay) to recruit a male prostitute.

bring owls to Athens, to phr. [late 16C–late 18C] to perform a superfluous and futile task (cf. CARRY COALS TO NEWCASTLE). [the owl was the pet of the Greek goddess Athena, and thus symbolic of her city, Athens]

bring pinnock to pannock, to phr. [16C–early 17C] to bring to grief, to cause to be ruined, bring something to nothing.

[? dial. but none of the extant dial. meanings of pinnock – a small bridge or a drain or culvert, the hedge-sparrow or the blue titmouse, a sticky red clay, mixed with small stones – is relevant (pannock seems to be redup.); the change from 'i' to 'a' could be said to 'ruin' the word, but seems insufficient]

bring someone up v. [1970s+] (US Black) to criticize, to tell off. [SE bring up short + mid-19C SE bring up, to bring into the presence of authority or for examination]

bring the house down, to phr. [mid-18C+] to delight, to gain overall approval. [theatrical imagery]

bring the noise! excl. (US Black) 1 [1970s+] play music. 2 [1990s] turn up the volume.

bring to light, to phr. [early 19C] of a thief, to produce stolen property in order to claim a reward or quash a prosecution.

bring to someone's milk, to phr. [late 19C] (US) to subdue someone. [? image of a baby quietening when given its milk]

bring up v.¹ [early 18C+] to vomit. [the contents of one's stomach]

bring up v.² see BRIDGE v.².

bring up by hand, to phr. [19C] to achieve an erection (cf. HAND-REARED; TAKE ONESELF IN HAND). [pun]

brinjer n. [19C] (US) something exceptional. [? Scot. breenger, a formidable foe, ult. f. breenge, to rush forward recklessly]

brinks n. [1960s+] (W.I. Rasta) title given to a man who is supplying a woman with money. [SE brings (the money) or ? the firm of Brinksmat Security, used to transport large sums of cash]

briny/briney n. [mid-19C+] the sea. [SE brine + sfx. -y; its saltiness]

Bris/Brissie n. [20C] (Aus.) Brisbane, the capital of Queensland. [abbr.]

brisby n. [1910s–20s] a net or lace curtain used to cover the lower part of a (sash) window. [SE brise-bise, f. Fr. brise-bise, windbreaker]

brisk about/up v. [mid-19C] to enliven, to animate.

brisk as a bee/bee in a tarpot phr. [18C–late 19C] very busy (cf. BRAG AS A BODY LOUSE).

brisk as a body louse phr. [mid-17C–late 19C] very busy (cf. BRAG AS A BODY LOUSE).

brisket n. [20C] the human chest. [SE brisket, the breast of an animal]

brisket-beater n. [late 18C–mid-19C] a Roman Catholic (cf. BREAST FLEET).

brisket-cut n. [early 19C] a blow to the chest. [BRISKET + SE cut, a blow]

briskets n. [20C] the female breasts. [BRISKET]

brisk up see BRISK ABOUT.

Brissie see BRIS.

bristles n. [16C] (Und.) dice whose weight has been altered by having bristles forced into them.

Bristol n. [late 19C–1900s] a visiting card. [SE Bristol-board, a type of pasteboard with a smooth surface, popular for printing such cards]

Bristol bits n. [1960s] the female breasts (cf. BRADFORD CITIES). [rhy. sl. Bristol bits = TITS n.²]

Bristol City n. [1960s+] a female breast (cf. BRADFORD CITIES). [rhy. sl. Bristol City = TITTY n.²]

Bristol hog n. [late 18C–mid-19C] a native of Bristol.

Bristol man n. [early–mid-19C] a villain, a rogue. [such figures would often drift towards Bristol, presumably, as a major port, conducive to villainy]

Bristol milk n. [17C–18C] sherry, esp. rich, sweet sherry. [now a trademark of Harvey's, the Bristol sherry importers]

Bristols n. [1960s+] the female breasts (cf. BRADFORD CITIES). [rhy. sl. Bristol bits = TITS n.²]

Bristol stone n. [16C–18C] sham diamonds. [SE Bristol stone, Bristol diamonds, Bristol gems, a kind of transparent rock-crystal found in the Clifton limestone near Bristol, Avon, resembling the diamond in brilliancy]

Brit n. [20C] a *Brito*n. [abbr.]

britannia n. [1950s] (Aus.) a double-headed penny used in two-up. [the engraving of Britannia on the reverse of pre-decimalization pennies]

britannia metal n. [19C] **1** the erect penis (cf. ENGLISH SENTRY). **2** something fake, sham. [SE *britannia metal*, an alloy of tin and regulus of antimony, resembling silver in appearance; users of (1) ignored the underlying negative implications]

britch n. [late 19C+] (US) the inside jacket-pocket. [var. on BRIGH]

British champagne/champaigne n. [early 19C] porter, dark ale. [a tribute to the quality of the beer or a sneer at the lack of homegrown wines]

British roarer n. [late 19C–1900s] the lion that appears alongside the unicorn on the British national coat of arms.

brits/britts n. [1940s+] (Aus.) terror; thus *have the Brits up*, to be terrified (cf. SHITS). [JIMMY BRITTS]

britton n. [1960s+] (drugs) peyote. [ety. unknown]

britts see BRITS.

bro n. [1940s+] (orig. US Black) brother, i.e. a fellow Black (cf. BRA n.[2]). [note public school use]

broad n.[1] [17C–19C] a sovereign, a 20-shilling coin. [? its size]

broad n.[2] [1910s+] (US) **1** a prostitute. **2** a woman. **3** a male homosexual prostitute. [early Black use, *c.*1930s, added to (2) an implication of a shapely, well-built woman (cf. BRACE OF BROADS), although this may have been a pun on the mainstream use)]

broad adj. [late 19C–1900s] knowing, alert, 'on the ball'; if not actually criminal then willing and able to bend any rule. [var. on WIDE adj.]

broad and shallow n. [mid-19C] the 'Broad Church' (cf. HIGH AND DRY; LOW AND SLOW). [*Broad Church* members of the Church of England, 'who take its formularies and doctrines in a broad or liberal sense and hold that the church should be comprehensive and tolerant' (*OED*)]

broad-arsed adj. [late 19C+] having wide hips. [SE *broad* + ARSE n.[1] (1)]

broad boy n. [20C] a male homosexual. [BROAD n.[2] (3) + SE *boy*]

broadbrim n. **1** [early 18C] a Quaker; thus *broad-brimmed*, sedate. **2** [mid–late 19C] a quiet, sedate old man, irrespective of religion. [the broad-brimmed hats adopted by many members of the Society of Friends]

broadbrow n. [1920s] a person of wide tastes and interests (cf. HIGHBROW; LOWBROW n.; MIDDLEBROW).

broadcast v. [1920s+] to talk loudly and aggressively.

broad cove n. [early 19C–1910s] a card-sharp. [BROADS n. (1) + COVE n. (1)]

broad faker n. [late 19C–1900s] a card-player, usu. a cheat. [BROADS n. (1) + FAKER n. (1)]

broad-faking n. [mid-19C] **1** card-playing, esp. with a tinge of illegality/cheating. **2** the three-card trick. [BROAD FAKER + sfx. *-ing*]

broad-fencer n. [mid-19C] (Und.) a peddler of lists of racing tips (known as 'correct cards') at horse-races. [BROADS + FENCER]

broad-gauge lady n. [late 19C] a woman with wide hips. [a pun on her breadth, and a ref. to the *broad-gauge* railway tracks, 7ft (2.1m) wide, which were abandoned when British railways were standardized at 4ft 8½in (1.44m) in the 1890s]

broadie n. [1930s+] (US) **1** a prostitute. **2** a woman. [BROAD n.[2] (1), (2)]

broad in the beam phr. [1940s+] fat, overweight, esp. around the hips and buttocks (cf. DRAG WATER AFT). [naut. jargon]

broadman/broadsman n. [1930s] a card-sharp. [BROADS n. (1) + SE *man*]

broad mob n. [late 19C+] a gang of card-sharpers. [BROADS n. (1) + MOB n.[1]]

broad-pitcher n. [mid–late 19C] (Und.) a street criminal one who works the three-card trick. [BROADS n. (1) + PITCHER n.[3] (2)]

broad-player n. **1** [early–mid-19C] an expert card-player. **2** [late 19C+] a card-sharp. [BROADS + SE *player*]

broads n. **1** [late 18C+] playing cards. **2** [late 19C+] the three-card trick. **3** [1920s] money. **4** [1940s+] any form of documentation, e.g. identification papers, rations book, driving licence. **5** [1970s+] credit and similar cards. [? the 'breadth' of the piece of card; but note G. Parker (1789), 'who are continually looking out for flats in order to do upon them the broads,' implying a play on FLAT n.[2], although note also FLAT n.[1], i.e. dice]

broadsman see BROADMAN.

broad tosser n. [1920s+] (US) a card-sharp. [BROADS n. (1) + SE *tosser*]

Broadway joe n. [late 19C–mid-20C] (US) a well-dressed idler, living off his wits and, when possible, gullible women (cf. CHIPPY-CHASER; DUDE; HOG IN TOGS; MASHER; PLEASURE HOUND). [*Broadway*, New York City's entertainment centre + JOE n.[7]]

broady n. [mid-19C] **1** cloth. **2** anything considered worth stealing. [SE *broadcloth*, 'fine, plain-wove, dressed, double width, black cloth, used chiefly for men's garments' (*OED*)]

broady-worker n. [mid-19C–1910s] (Und.) a criminal who sells third-rate cloth as the finest material or stolen goods as legitimate. [BROADY (2) + SE *worker*]

broccoli n. **1** [1980s+] (drugs) marijuana (cf. GREENS n.[5]; LEAF n.[2]). **2** [1990s] (US) pubic hair (cf. MUSTARD-AND-CRESS; PARSLEY n.[1]). [supposed similarity to the green vegetable]

brodie n. (US) **1** [late 19C+] a jump, a leap, a dive. **2** [1910s+] long odds. **3** [1950s+] a spin made by a skidding vehicle. [for ety. *see* TAKE A BRODIE]

broer n. [1970s+] (S.Afr.) **1** brother. **2** one's best friend (cf. MAIN MAN n.[1]). [abbr. Afk. *broeder*, brother]

brogan n. [19C] (US) a shoe, esp. a stout, coarse shoe. [Irish and Gaelic *brògan*, dimin. of *bròg*, shoe (cf. SE *brogue*)]

broganeer/broganier n. [late 18C–early 19C] one who has a noticeable Irish accent. [SE *brogue*, the Irish accent]

brogue v. [19C] (US) to walk around, esp. to walk heavily (cf. BROGAN). [SE *brogue*, a stout walking shoe]

broiler n.[1] [19C] a very hot day (cf. SCORCHER). [ext. of SE *broil*, to grill; SE in 20C]

broiler n.[2] [1900s–10s] (US) a small chorus-girl (cf. CHICKEN n.[6]). [pun on SE *broiler* (chicken)]

broke adj. [mid-17C+] out of funds, impoverished, poor (cf. SKINT). [orig. image was of creditors physically 'breaking' a debtor]

broke arm n. [1920s–30s] (US Black) leftovers. [for ety. *see* BROKEN ARMS]

broke-dick adj. [1960s+] (US) worthless, useless. [SE *broke* + DICK n.[5] (1), i.e. impotent]

broke for adv. [20C] (Aus.) in great need of, desperate for, esp. in phr. *broke for a feed*, very hungry. [fig. use of BROKE]

broken arms n. [20C] (US) leftover food (cf. BROKE ARM). [? pun on SE *broken victuals*, when *victuals*, usu. food, takes its secondary 17C meaning of weapons or military 'arms']

broken arrow n. [1960s] (US) **1** a malfunctioning penis. **2** an impotent male.

broken arse n. [1980s+] (N.Z. prison) a prisoner who sides with the authorities and thus ranks lowest in the prisoners' hierarchy. [SE *broken* + ARSE n.[1]]

broken brigade n. [late 19C–1900s] (society) aristocratic younger sons, impoverished through the inequalities of primogeniture, who are forced to live on their wits. [BROKE + BRIGADE]

broken hill *n.* [1920s+] (Aus.) any silver coin. [proper name *Broken Hill*, a major Aus. silver mining area]

broken-kneed *adj.* [18C–19C] seduced, deflowered. [var. on BROKEN-LEGGED]

broken-legged *adj.* [17C–1910s] seduced, deflowered (cf. BROKEN-KNEED). [BREAK ONE'S LEG phr.[1]]

broken packet of biscuits, to be a *phr.* [1990s] (Aus.) to live a life that looks good to outsiders but is really filled with problems. [the crumbs are invisible through the outer wrapping]

broken stick *n.* [20C] (US) an unreliable person.

broken wrist *n.* [1960s–70s] a male homosexual (cf. LIMP WRIST). [the stereotypical gay gesture]

broker *n.*[1] [late 19C+] (orig. Aus.) someone who is usually having financial problems, a poor person (cf. BROKIE; DEAD-BROKER). [BROKE ? + pun on SE]

broker *n.*[2] [1980s+] (drugs) a go-between in a drug deal.

brokered *adj.* [late 19C] having had one's possessions removed by law. [SE phr. *have the brokers in* ? + pun on BROKE]

broke to the wide/world *phr.* [1910s+] absolutely penniless. [BROKE]

broke up *adj.* [20C] (US) **1** injured, hurt. **2** depressed, badly upset. [suffering from a 'broken heart']

brokie *n.* [1950s] (Aus.) one who has no money (cf. BROKER n.[1]; DEAD-BROKER). [BROKE + sfx. *-ie*]

brolly *n.* **1** [mid-19C+] (orig. school/university) an umbrella. **2** [1930s–40s] a parachute; thus *brolly-hop*, a parachute jump. [abbr.]

brom *v.* [1970s+] (S.Afr.) to complain. [Afk. *brom*, growl]

bromide *n.* [1900s–60s] (US) **1** a person whose thoughts and conversation are conventional and commonplace. **2** a commonplace saying, a trite remark. A soothing statement; thus *bromidic*, commonplace, conventional. [SE *bromide*, a dose of potassium bromide taken as a sedative]

Bromigham *see* BRUMMAGEM.

Brompton boilers *see* BOILERS.

Brompton cocktail *n.* [1960s+] a drug 'cocktail' of a variety of strong painkillers mixed with alcohol, supposedly created for terminally ill patients at the Brompton Hospital, London.

bronco *n.* [1950s+] a young man, a novice in the gay world and thus somewhat rough. [SE *bronco*, an unbroken horse]

bronco/broncho *adj.* [late 19C+] (US) wild, untameable. [Sp. *bronco*, rough, esp. as applied to an untamed or half-tamed horse]

bronski *n.* [1990s] (Can.) the perineum, the area between the testicles and the anus (cf. JIMBROWSKI). [ety. unknown]

Bronx cheer *n.* [1920s+] (orig. US) a loud, derisive noise, imitative of a fart (cf. RASPBERRY n.). [the uncouth manners of the Bronx, New York]

Bronx Indian *n.* [1940s] (US) a Jew (cf. BROOKLYN INDIAN). [the once-large Jewish population of the Bronx; the area, like the rest of the US, was orig. populated by Native Americans]

bronza/bronzer/bronzo *n.* [1950s+] (Aus.) the anus, the posterior (cf. BRONZE n.).

bronze *n.* [1920s+] (Aus.) the anus, the posterior. [its colour]

bronze *v.* [early 19C] to impose upon, to cheat. [play on DO UP BROWN]

bronze eye *n.* [1990s] the anus. [ext. of BRONZE]

bronze eye optician *n.* [1990s] a homosexual. [BRONZE EYE + facet. use of SE *optician*]

bronze john *n.* [mid-19C] (US) yellow fever. [play on YELLOW JACK]

bronzer *see* BRONZA.

bronzewing *n.* [20C] a member of the lower classes. **2** a half-caste Native Australian. [the colour of the *bronzewing* pigeon]

bronzo *see* BRONZA.

broodish *adj.* [19C] (US) contemplative, (sullenly) meditative, feeling depressed or moody. [BROODY]

broody *adj.* [19C] **1** contemplative, (sullenly) meditative, feeling depressed or moody. **2** of a woman, feeling a maternal desire to have a(nother) baby. [SE *broody*, of a hen, sitting on her eggs]

Brooklyn butterflies *n.* [1980s+] cockroaches. [their frequency in Brooklyn, New York (and the other four boroughs)]

Brooklyn Indian *n.* [20C] (US) a Jew (cf. BRONX INDIAN). [Brooklyn, New York, home to many Jews + *Indian*, a Native American]

brooks *n.*[1] [1900s–10s] (S.Afr.) trousers. [Du. *broeks*, breeches]

brooks *n.*[2] [1950s] (US Black) an expensive, esp. silk shirt. [New York's up-market clothiers *Brooks* Brothers]

Brooks of Sheffield *n.* [mid–late 19C] nobody, a nameless person. [Charles Dickens's *David Copperfield* (1850) in which the villainous Mr Murdstone initially uses the name instead of David's own]

broom *n.*[1] [19C] **1** the pubic hair. **2** the female genitals (cf. BROOMSTICK n.[1]). [synon. with BRUSH n.[5]. Note early 17C *broom*, a horse's tail]

broom *n.*[2] [late 19C–1900s] a would-be dandy, who fails in his ambitions. [mispron. of *brum*, abbr. BRUMMAGEM adj.]

broom *n.*[3] [1940s] (US Black) a cigar. [SE *broomstick*]

broom *v.* [late 18C–early 19C; 1940s] to disappear quickly. [the image of sweeping away. Orig. UK use faded but was revived by US Blacks, esp. in Harlem]

broom-handle *n.* [19C] the erect penis (cf. BAT n.[7]; CLOTHES-PROP).

broomhilda *n.* [1980s+] (US campus) a short, unattractive woman. [a US comic strip character, itself a pun on the Wagnerian heroine *Brünhilde*]

broomie/broom-tail *n.* [1920s] (orig. US) a mustang (esp. a mare) with a short bushy tail. [SE *broom*, a horse's tail]

broomstick *n.*[1] [19C] the penis (cf. BAT n.[7]).

broomstick *n.*[2] [late 19C–1900s] (Can.) a gun or rifle. [it 'cleans up']

broomstick marriage *n.* [19C] a common-law marriage, in which the partners have never actually gone through with a civil or religious ceremony. [JUMP THE BROOMSTICK]

broomsticks *n.* [early 19C] fraudulent bail (cf. QUEER BAIL). [play on legal jargon *straw bail*, insufficient bail. Broomsticks were often made with straw brushes]

broom-tail *see* BROOMIE.

broom to the slammer that fronts the drape crib, to *phr.* [1940s] (US Black) to walk over to the clothes closet. [BROOM v. + SLAMMER n.[2] (2) + SE *front* + DRAPE n. + CRIB n.[3] (4)]

brooze *see* BROWSE.

brophys, the *n.* [1950s+] (Irish) venereal disease. [joc. nickname for the supposed insects, relations of body lice or crabs, which allegedly carried the disease]

broseley *n.* [19C] a pipe, esp. in phr. *cock a broseley*, to smoke a pipe. [proper name *Broseley*, Salop, famous for its 'churchwarden' pipes]

broth *n.*[1] [19C] breath. [mispron.]

broth *n.*[2] [1970s] (US campus) *brother*. [abbr.]

brothel creepers *n.* [1950s+] suede shoes, often in lurid colours, with extra thick rubber soles, esp. popular among rock 'n' roll fans of the 1950s (and in 1980s revival) (cf. CAD'S CRAWLERS). [orig. 1940s service use, referring, first, to officers' suede shoes and then to a form of 'desert boot' issued during WW2]

brothel stompers *n.* [1970s+] (US campus) suede shoes. [var.

on BROTHEL CREEPERS, although these 'respectable' versions have no great thickness of sole]

brother *n.* [1940s–50s] (orig. US Black) a form of address to fellow Black male (cf. BRO).

brother *adj.* [20C] (US Black) Black, Afro-American. [BROTHER n.]

brother blade *see* BROTHER OF THE BLADE.

brother bung *see* BROTHER OF THE BUNG.

brother chip *n.* [mid–late 19C] **1** a carpenter (cf. CHIPS n.¹). **2** a fellow professional of any sort.

brother hod *see* HOD.

brother in blackness *n.* [19C+] (US Black) a form of address from one Black man to another (cf. BRO; BROTHER n.).

brother-in-law *v.* [1920s] (US) to pursue clandestinely the wife or girlfriend of another man.

brotherman *n.* [1960s+] (US Black) form of address from one Black man to another (cf. BRO; BROTHER n.).

brother of … *phr.* [mid-17C–late 19C] phr. used of members of various professions, a member of, a practitioner of; always constructed with a noun denoting, lit. or fig., the occupation, e.g. BROTHER OF THE BLADE; BROTHER OF THE BOLUS; BROTHER OF THE BRUSH; BROTHER OF THE BUNG; BROTHER OF THE BUSKIN; BROTHER OF THE COIF; BROTHER OF THE GUSSET; BROTHER OF THE QUILL; BROTHER OF THE STRING; BROTHER OF THE WHIP.

brother of the blade/brother blade *n.* [late 17C–19C] **1** a swordsman, a fellow soldier. **2** a fellow member of the same profession or occupation (cf. BROTHER OF …).

brother of the bolus *n.* [mid-19C] (US) a physician. [BROTHER OF … + SE *bolus*, a large pill]

brother of the brush *n.* **1** [late 17C+] an artist. **2** [19C+] a house painter. [BROTHER OF + SE *brush*]

brother of the bung/brother bung *n.* [mid-18C–1900s] a publican, an inn-keeper (cf. BROTHER OF …; BUNG n.²).

brother of the buskin *n.* [late 18C] a musician (cf. BROTHER OF …).

brother of the coif *n.* [late 18C] a barrister. [BROTHER OF … + SE *coif*, a coiffed wig, part of his 'uniform']

brother of the gusset *n.* [late 17C–19C. 19C. 19C] a pimp, a procurer (cf. KNIGHT OF THE GUSSET). [BROTHER OF … + GUSSET]

brother of the quill *n.* [late 17C–20C] a writer, an author. [BROTHER OF … + SE *quill*]

brother of the string *n.* [late 17C–20C] a musician. [BROTHER OF … + SE *string*]

brother of the whip *n.* [late 18C] a coachman. [BROTHER OF … + SE *whip*]

brother round mouth *n.* [early 19C] the anus. [its 'speech' is a fart]

brothers, the *n.* [1960s+] (US) Black people, orig. in 1960s Black radical use, now used by both Black and White speakers with only residual political overtones.

brother smut *see* DITTO BROTHER SMUT.

brother starling *n.* [17C–19C] one who shares a friend's mistress (cf. BROTHER CHIP; BROTHER OF THE BLADE; BROTHER OF THE BUNG). [SE *brother* + *starling*; ? the characteristics of the bird]

brother-where-are-you? *n.* [1920s] a drunkard. [his being 'blind' drunk]

broth of a boy *n.* [early 19C+] (orig. Irish) the essence of what a boy should be, a downright good fellow. [the image of broth being the distilled essence and 'goodness' of the meat]

brougham *n.* [1980s+] (US Black) an elegant, expensive and prized motorcar. [the smart 19C carriages named for Lord Henry *Brougham* (1778–1868)]

brought down *adv.* [1950s+] (orig. drugs) depressed, esp. after a period of elation. [BRING DOWN v.]

broughtonian *n.* [late 18C–early 19C] a boxer; thus *Broughton's mark*, the pit of the stomach. [proper name Jack

Broughton, 'Captain of the Boxers', inventor of the first prototype 'muffler' or boxing glove, writer of 'Broughton's Rules' (which lasted 1743–1838) and champion of England 1730–5]

brought out *v.* [1950s+] (gay) initiated into the homosexual life (cf. COME OUT v.³). [BRING OUT]

brought/go to the basket *phr.* [early 17C–early 18C] sent to prison. [the *alms-basket* on which poor prisoners in the public prisons were mainly dependent for food]

brow *n.¹* [mid-17C–early 18C] cheek, effrontery (cf. NECK n.¹). [abbr. SE an *unabashed brow*]

Brow/Brow, the *n.²* [1970s+] (S.Afr.) Hillbrow, a densely populated, tough, high-rise suburb of Johannesburg. [abbr.]

brown *n.¹* **1** [19C] porter, stout. **2** [late 19C–1910s] two pennyworth of whisky, esp. as sold in Mooney's Tavern in the Strand, London. [the colour]

brown *n.²* **1** [19C] a halfpenny (cf. TOWN). **2** [20C] (US) a 'penny' (a cent). [the colour of the 'copper' coin]

brown *n.³* [mid-19C+] **1** the anus. **2** sodomy (cf. BIT OF BROWN). [the colour]

brown *n.⁴* [1910s–50s] (US Black) a young, brown-skinned person, esp. as a boy- or girlfriend.

brown *n.⁵* [1960s+] (drugs) **1** heroin. **2** hashish. **3** (US) a Mexican. [the colour of hashish and of, *inter alia*, Mexican heroin]

brown *n.⁶* [1960s+] (gay) the dominant partner in anal sex (cf. BROWNIE n.⁵). [BROWN n.³]

brown *v.¹* [19C] (US) to understand. [DO BROWN]

brown *v.²* [mid-19C–1920s] **1** to do perfectly. **2** to get the better of, to surpass (cf. DO BROWN).

brown *v.³* [20C] to act the toady, to be a sycophant. [abbr. BROWN NOSE v.]

brown *v.⁴* [1920s] (US) used in a number of semi-euph. excl. e.g. *I'll be browned!, brown me!* [? BROWN n.³]

brown/do a brown *v.⁵* [1920s+] (orig. US) to perform anal intercourse, to sodomize (cf. brown family). [BROWN n.³]

brown *adj.¹* [early 19C] alert, aware, *au fait*. [BROWN v.² (2)]

brown *adj.²* [mid-19C] worthy, earnest, totally devoid of any *double entendre* or 'smut' (cf. BLUE adj.³). [the brown clothes popular among the sedulously pure Quakers]

brown abe *n.* [1930s+] (US Black) a cent; thus *brown Abes and buffalo heads*, small change, cents and nickels (cf. ABRAHAM LINCOLN). [President *Abraham* Lincoln's head is on the cent, a *buffalo head* is on the nickel]

brown ankle *n.* [1970s+] (N.Z. prison) a sycophant, a toady. [he has crawled so far 'up the arse' of the authorities that only his ankles are visible]

brown artist *n.* [1950s+] a male homosexual (cf. BROWN-HATTER; BROWNING FAMILY; BROWNING SISTERS). [BROWN v.⁵ + ARTIST n.²]

brown-back *n.* [1910s–70s] a 10-shilling note (cf. GREENBACK n.²). [its colour; the notes were issued in 1914 and superseded by the 50p piece after decimalization in 1971. From 1940 until 1948 the notes were mauve rather than brown]

brownbag *v.* [1960s+] (US) **1** to drink liquor from a bottle 'hidden' in the (brown-paper) bag in which it is bought from the liquor store and which is necessary in US states where drinking in the street is illegal. **2** to take a packed lunch to work.

brownbagger *n.* [1950s+] (US) **1** an office worker (cf. DINNER PAILER; NINE-TO-FIVER). **2** an excessively hard-working student. [BROWNBAG (2)]

brown bess/bessie *n.* [early 18C–mid-19C] a firelock or musket, otherwise known as the 'soldier's best friend'; thus *hug brown bess*, to carry a firelock, to serve as a private soldier (cf. BLACK BESS). [the brown walnut stock, although there may be links to Du. *bus* or Ger. *Busche*, a gun barrel]

brown bess *adv.* [mid-19C] yes (cf. BROWN JOE adv.). [rhy. sl.]

brown bessie *n.*[1] [17C] a prostitute.

brown bessie *n.*[2] *see* BROWN BESS n.

brown bessie *adv.* [19C] yes (cf. BROWN BESS adv.).

brown bomber *n.*[1] [1980s] **1** (Aus., Sydney) a parking policeman (cf. BLUE MEANIE). **2** a laxative pill. **3** (drugs) LSD (cf. A n.[3]). [the colour of the uniform, pill or capsule]

brown bomber *n.*[2] [1960s+] (N.Z.) DB (Dominion Breweries) brown ale.

brown bread *adj.* [1990s] dead. [rhy. sl.]

brown bullethole *n.* [1990s] the anus. [joc. use of SE + ext. of BROWN n.[3]]

brown cow *n.* [18C–early 19C] a barrel of beer. [presumably f. shape]

brown creatures *n.* [1910s–20s] bronchitis. [joc. mispron.; note milit. use *Bill Harris*, bilharzia, *Corporal Forbes*, cholera morbus]

brown crystal *n.* [1980s+] (drugs) heroin. [its colour]

brown dirt cowboy *n.* [1990s] a male homosexual. [BROWN v.[5] + SE *dirt, cowboy*]

brown dots *n.* [1960s+] (drugs) LSD (cf. A n.[3]). [its packaging]

browned off *adj.* [1930s+] (orig. milit.) irritated, annoyed (cf. BRASSED OFF; CHEESED OFF). [accumulation of brown rust on fatigued or worn out metal; but note the various uses of BROWN in the context of sodomy]

browned up *adj.* [1930s] irritated, annoyed. [var. on BROWNED OFF]

brown eye *n.*[1] [1930s+] the female breast. [the colour of a nipple]

brown eye *n.*[2] [1970s+] **1** the anus. **2** anal intercourse (cf. BROWN n.[3], v.[5], BROWNIE n.[4]). [play on SE]

brown-eye *v.* [1990s] (Aus.) to drop one's trousers and underwear and reveal one's naked buttocks to anyone who is watching, a mainly juv. prank (cf. MOON v.[2]). [BROWN-EYE n.[2] (1)]

brown family *n.* [20C] a generally obsolete generic term for homosexuals, referring to the predilection for anal intercourse (cf. BROWN n.[3]; BROWN ARTIST; BROWN EYE n.[2]; BROWNING FAMILY; BROWN-HATTER; BROWNIE n.[4]; BROWNING SISTERS). [BROWN v.[5] + SE *family*]

brown flight *n.* [1980s+] (N.Z.) the removal from predominantly Maori schools of the children of Pacific islanders, fearful of supposedly low standards (cf. WHITE FLIGHT).

brown gal *n.* [1980s+] (Black) a Black woman. [ironic use of US original]

brown gargle *n.* [1950s+] (Irish) stout. [SE *brown* + GARGLE n.]

brown george *n.* **1** [17C–early 19C] bread (cf. TOMMY n.[1]). **2** [late 18C–19C] a hard, coarse biscuit. **3** [late 18C–mid-19C] a brown wig. **4** [mid-19C] an earthenware jug. [ety. unknown; cf. naut. jargon *negroes' heads*, brown loaves eaten on board ship]

brown hat *n.* [late 19C–1920s] a cat. [rhy. sl.]

brown-hatter *n.* [1910s+] (orig. naval) a homosexual. [? a jibe at a long-dead gay fashion or the coarse image of an excrement-coated meatus]

brownie *n.*[1] **1** [mid-19C+] (US) a brown-skinned person, an Asian. **2** [late 19C+] (Aus.) a cake made of flour, fat and sugar, and filled with raisons or currants. **3** [20C] (US) a mulatto. **4** [1940s–50s] (US Black) a young, brown-skinned person (cf. BROWN n.[4]). **5** [1980s+] a shot of whisky.

brownie *n.*[2] [late 19C] small, cheap cigarettes. [the maker's name *Brown's*]

brownie *n.*[3] [late 19C–1950s] (Aus.) a penny (cf. BROWN n.[2]).

brownie *n.*[4] [1910s+] a homosexual. [abbr. BROWN-HATTER]

brownie *n.*[5] (US) **1** [1920s+] the anus. **2** [1960s] (gay) the passive partner during anal sex. **3** [1970s] the buttocks. **4** [1970s]

the vagina; thus *hawk one's brownie*, to work as a prostitute (cf. BROWN MADAM; MISS BROWN). [BROWN n.[3]]

brownie *n.*[6] [1960s+] (US) a small (usu. chocolate) cake impregnated with hashish or marijuana (cf. ALICE B. TOKLAS; BIKKIES n.[2]). [*brownie*, a traditional US biscuit]

brownie *v.* [20C] to curry favour (cf. BROWN NOSE v.).

brownie arcade *n.* [1940s] (US Black/Harlem) an amusement arcade. [the slot-machines that take 1 cent or a BROWN ABE]

brownie point *n.* [1960s+] a commendation awarded to the Girl Guides' junior branch and thus usu. a sarcastic and backhanded form of compliment when handed out by adults.

brownie/browning queen *n.* [1940s+] (US gay) a gay man who takes the passive role in anal intercourse. [BROWNIE n.[5]/BROWNING FAMILY + QUEEN]

brownies *n.* [1980s+] (US drugs) amphetamine (cf. A n.[2]). [the colour of the pill or capsule]

browning *n.* [late 19C] anal intercourse. [BROWN v.[5]]

browning family *n.* [20C] the world of homosexuals (cf. BROWN FAMILY). [BROWN v.[5] + SE *family*]

browning queen *see* BROWNIE QUEEN.

browning sisters *n.* [20C] homosexuals in general (cf. BROWNING FAMILY). [BROWN v.[5] + SE *sisters*]

brown job *n.*[1] [1960s+] flattery, empty praise. [BROWN NOSE v.]

brown job *n.*[2] [1960s+] (gay) anilingus. [BROWN v.[5]]

brown joe *v.* [1930s–40s] (Aus.) to know; thus *brown joe*, in the know. [rhy. sl.]

brown joe *adv.* [mid-19C] no (cf. BROWN BESS adv.).

brown madam *n.* [late 18C] the vagina (cf. MISS BROWN).

brown man *n.* [1950s+] (W.I.) **1** a light-skinned Black man. **2** a prosperous Black man. [the belief that light skin is best]

brown nose *n.* [1930s+] (orig. US milit. jargon) a toady, a sycophant (cf. BROWN-NOSER). [BROWN NOSE v.]

brown nose *v.* [1930s+] (orig. US milit. jargon) to play the sycophant, to curry favour, to toady. [SE *brown* + SE *nose*, one achieves this coloration by 'kissing arse']

brown-noser *n.* [1930s+] (orig. US milit. jargon) anyone who pays excessive court to authority, at school, in work etc (cf. ARSE-LICKER). [BROWN NOSE n.]

brown out *v.* [1980s+] (US gay) to lick or suck the anus. [BROWN v.[5]]

brown paper *n.* [1970s] a trick, a pursuit, a profession, a 'game' [rhy. sl. *brown paper* = caper]

brown paper men *n.* [mid-19C] the poorest class of gamblers. [their wagering in pence (cf. BROWN n.[2])]

brown pipe *n.* [1990s] the anus; thus *brown pipe engineer*, a male homosexual, a sodomite.

brown polish *n.* [late 19C–1900s] (orig. US) **1** a Black person. **2** a mulatto (cf. SHINE n.[5]).

brown powder *n.* [1950s–60s] (drugs) heroin. [Mexican heroin, and some other varieties, is brown rather than the usual white]

brown rhine *n.* [1950s] (drugs) heroin. [BROWN POWDER + RHINE]

browns *n.* [early 19C] (Und.) counterfeit halfpennies (cf. WHISTLERS). [BROWN n.[2]]

brown salve! *excl.* [mid-19C] used as a rejoinder, meaning 'I understand'; the expression combines a degree of surprise at what has been said with, ultimately, comprehension of what it means. [ety. unknown]

brown shell *n.* [late 19C] an onion.

brownskin *adj.* [20C] (US Black) used of a light-skinned African American.

brown star/starfish *n.* [1990s] the anus. [resemblance]

brownstone front *n.* [mid-19C–1900s] (US) an aristocrat, a member of the upper classes. [their brownstone houses]

brownstoner *n.* [mid–late 19C] (US) a member of the upper-middle or mercantile class; thus *brownstone club*, a private club, *brownstone vote*, the political stance of the upper-middle class. [SE *brownstone*, a type of New York City house, built 1850–80, fronted with brownstone and favoured by this section of society]

brown stuff *n.* **1** [1930s–40s] (US drugs) opium. **2** [1940s] (US) whisky. **3** [1950s–60s] (US drugs) heroin. [the colour]

brown sugar *n.* **1** [20C] (orig. US Black) an attractive Black woman. **2** [1970s+] (drugs) heroin. **3** [1980s+] (S.Afr.) adulterated heroin. [all colour; the Black use of (1) crossed over into the White vocabulary with the success in 1971 of the Rolling Stones' song of the same name; the drug use was a spin-off from this]

brownsword *n.* [1990s] the male perineum. [? pun on SE *greensward*, turf on which grass is growing]

brown talk *n.* [early 18C+] earnest, serious talk, devoid of wit and the slightest implication of vulgarity. [BROWN adj.[2]]

brown tommy *n.* [late 18C–19C] brown bread (cf. BROWN GEORGE). [ext. of TOMMY n.[1]]

brown tongue *v.* [1930s+] to toady, to curry favour. [var. on BROWN NOSE v.]

brown-tonguer *n.* [20C] a toady, a sycophant (cf. BROWN-NOSER). [BROWN TONGUE v.]

brown trail *n.* [1950s+] the anus (cf. DIRT ROAD n.[2]; HERSHEY HIGHWAY). [BROWN n.[3] + SE *trail*]

brown trout *n.* [1990s] excrement. [it 'swims' in the lavatory bowl]

brown trout *v.* [20C] (US prison) to throw excrement or urine over another prisoner. [BROWN TROUT n.]

Brown 'Un, the *n.* [late 19C–1900s] the *Sportsman*, a sporting newspaper (cf. BLUE 'UN; PINK 'UN). [the colour of the newsprint]

brown velvet *n.* [1930s] (N.Z. a derog. term for a Maori woman, esp. when seen simply as a sex object (cf. BLACK VELVET).

brown wings *n.* [1950s+] (orig. Hell's Angels) anilingus or anal intercourse (cf. BLACK WINGS).

brown wink *v.* [1990s] to display one's anus. [BROWN n.[3] + SE *wink*]

browse/brooze/bruise/bruze *v.* [19C] (US) to loaf around, to wander idly, to dawdle. [SE *browse*, of cattle, to nibble on twigs or buds, ult. f. 16C *browse*, a bud, a young shoot]

browsing and sluicing *phr.* [1920s+] eating and drinking. [coined and most commonly used by P.G. Wodehouse (1881–1975), but echoed by many of his fans]

brr rabbit *v.* [1970s] (US campus) to complain about the cold. [SE *brr*, an echoic acknowledgement of cold weather + pun on the character *Br'er Rabbit*, the creation of Joel Chandler Harris (1848–1908)]

brr-y *adj.* [1970s] (US Black) chilly. [SE *brr* + sfx. *-y*]

bruce *n.* **1** [1940s–70s] (gay) a term of address among male homosexuals (cf. AGNES). **2** [1980s+] (US campus) a male who thinks he is suave and sophisticated but really is not. [*Bruce* is seen as a 'typical' gay name; ? its potential, in camp usage, for being lisped]

brudum! *see* BRADARAX!

bruffam *n.* [late 19C–1900s] a small, closed carriage, properly known as a *brougham*, pron. 'broom' and named for Lord Brougham. [deliberate mispron. of the SE, pretending that the 'gh', as in 'enough', is here pron. 'ff']

brugadum! *see* BRADARAX!

bruise/bruze *v. see* BROWSE.

bruise job *n.* [1990s] a beating. [SE *bruise* + JOB n.[5]]

bruiser *n.* **1** [late 16C+] a boxer, a prize-fighter. **2** [late 16C+] any form of thug who prefers to express himself with his fists. **3** [mid-19C] a pimp. **4** [1960s] (US) a black eye. [SE *bruise*]

bruising *n.* [late 18C–mid-19C] boxing; thus any form of fighting with the fists. [SE *bruise* + sfx. *-ing*]

bruising the bed *see* BREWISING THE BED.

brum *n.*[1] [18C+] something inferior (cf. BRUMMAGEM n.). [the reputation of Birmingham as a centre of cheap mass-production]

brum *n.*[2] [late 19C] a penny. [the copper coins struck in 19C by Boulton & Watt at their works in Birmingham]

brum *n.*[3] [1920s] (US) a prostitute. [? BRUM adj.; she is an 'inferior' form of woman]

brum *adj.* [late 19C+] fake, counterfeit, of inferior make. [BRUMMAGEM adj.]

brumbie/brumby/brum *adj.* [late 19C+] (Aus.) worn-out, ill-bred, uncouth. [SAusE *brumbie*, a wild or half-tamed horse]

brumby bull *n.* [late 19C+] (Aus.) a remittance man. [BRUMBIE + SE *bull*]

Brummagem/Bromigham *n.* **1** [late 17C–early 18C] counterfeit coins. **2** [18C+] anything fake or inferior in make (cf. ATTLEBOROUGH). **3** [mid-19C] a spur. **4** [mid-19C+] the city of Birmingham. [neg. stereotyping of Birmingham. Note late 17C citation of *Bromicham*: 'particularly noted a few years ago, for the counterfeit groats made here, and from hence dispersed all over the Kingdom' (G. Miege, *New State of England*, 1691)]

Brummagem *adj.* [17C+] cheap, second-rate, fake. [BRUMMAGEM n.]

Brummagem button *n.* **1** [early–mid-19C] one shilling, possibly a counterfeit one (cf. MANCHESTER SOVEREIGN). **2** [mid-19C+] a native of Birmingham. [BRUMMAGEM n. (1), (3) + SE *button*]

Brummagem conscience *n.* [17C] a very bad conscience. [BRUMMAGEM adj. + SE *conscience*]

Brummagem groats *n.* [17C] counterfeit coins manufactured in Birmingham. [BRUMMAGEM n. (1)]

Brummagem protestants *n.* [17C] Whigs or Dissenters. [BRUMMAGEM adj. + SE *protestant*]

Brummagem screwdriver *see* BIRMINGHAM SCREWDRIVER.

Brummagem wine *n.* [17C] any adulterated or mixed drink (cf. BALDERDASH n.). [BRUMMAGEM adj. + SE *wine*]

brummie *see* BRUMMY.

brummish *adj.* [19C] counterfeit, second-rate. [BRUMMAGEM adj.]

brummy/brummie *n.* **1** [1920s+] a counterfeit coin. **2** [1940s+] a native of Birmingham. [BRUMMAGEM (1), (3)]

brummy/brummie *adj.* [20C] second-rate, tawdry. [BRUMMAGEM adj.]

brums *n.* [1910s+] (Aus.) cheap, if showy clothes. [BRUM adj.]

brunette *n.* (US) **1** [late 19C–1903s] a Black person. **2** [1940s] a Native American.

Bruno *n.* [1970s+] (US campus) Brown University. [proper name *Bruno*, 'brown one']

brunser *n.* [1930s+] (US) **1** a homosexual, esp. a catamite (cf. BROWN FAMILY). **2** a general derog. term for an unappealing person. [? BRONZE n.]

brunswick *n.* [19C] (US) human excrement (cf. HEINIE n.[3]). [? BROWN n.[3]]

brush *n.*[1] [late 17C–18C] **1** a hasty exit. **2** one who rushes off. [BRUSH v.]

brush *n.*[2] [mid-18C–mid-19C] **1** the penis. **2** sexual intercourse. [the penis *brushes* against the vagina]

brush *n.*[3] [mid-19C–1900s] a house-painter (cf. BROTHER OF THE BRUSH). [his basic tool]

brush *n.*[4] [late 19C–1900s] **1** a small glass, made of an inverted cone fixed to a thick stem, which is used for drinking drams of whisky or other spirits (cf. BRUSH MOUTH). **2** a drink of whisky. [the supposed resemblance of the glass's shape to that of a house-painter's brush]

brush *n.*[5] **1** [1930s+] the pubic hair (cf. SCRUBBING BRUSH;

SHAVING BRUSH). **2** [1930s+] (Aus./N.Z.) a young woman, a generic term for women (cf. PUSSY n.¹). **3** [1940s] (US Black) a moustache. [SE *brush*, undergrowth]

brush v. [late 17C+] to rush off, to run away (cf. BUY A BRUSH). [SE *brush*, to rush into with force or collision; ult. Fr. *brosser*, to dash through dense underwood]

brush and lope, to phr. [late 18C–early 19C] to leave in a hurry. [BRUSH v. + SE *lope*]

brush ape n. [20C] (US) a hillbilly, a peasant. [SE *brush*, undergrowth, small branches + APE n. (2)]

brush colt n. [20C] (US) an illegitimate child (cf. CATCH COLT; COLT n.⁴; FIELD COLT; FILLY; WOODS COLT). [SE *brush colt*, a horse that has not been deliberately bred]

brusher n.¹ [late 17C–mid-19C] a very full glass. [? its contents brush against the rim or BRUSH n.⁴]

brusher n.² [18C] a schoolmaster. [abbr. BUM-BRUSHER]

brush mouth n. [mid-19C–1940s] (US Black) a sip of whisky. [BRUSH n.⁴ + SE *mouth*]

brush-off n. [mid-19C+] a snub, an act of rejection; thus *give the brush-off (to)*, to snub, to reject, to ignore. [SE *brush*, to sweep, as with a brush; the image of brushing specks of dirt from one's clothes]

brush off v. [mid-19C+] to ignore, to treat contemptuously, to dismiss. [BRUSH-OFF]

brush someone's coat, to phr. [mid-17C–early 19C] to thrash someone, to beat someone up.

brush someone's teeth, to phr.¹ [1970s] (US) to hit someone in the face. [pun on SE]

brush someone's teeth, to phr.² [1980s+] **1** (US gay) to perform fellatio. **2** (US Black) to perform cunnilingus. [pun on SE + BRUSH n.², n.⁵]

brush the beaver, to phr. [1990s] of a woman, to masturbate. [SE *brush* + BEAVER n.⁴]

brush-up n. [1940s] a scuffle, a skirmish. [SE *brush*, a collision]

brush up a flat, to phr. [19C+] to flatter a gullible person. [SE *brush*, to clean by brushing + FLAT n.²]

brush with a man, to phr. [18C] to have a fight. [SE *brush*, to rush (at), collide with]

brush with a woman, to phr. [late 18C] to have sexual intercourse (cf. BRUSH n.²). [SE *brush*, to rush (at), collide with]

Brussels n.¹ [1910s+] a Boy Scout. [abbr. BRUSSEL SPROUT]

Brussels n.² [1920–30s] a three-month prison sentence (cf. CARPET n.²). [SE *Brussels carpet*]

brussel sprout n. [1910s+] a Boy Scout. [rhy. sl.]

brutal adj. **1** [1960s+] (orig. US) very good, first-rate. **2** [1980s+] (Irish) terrible. [ext. of SE use; (1) on bad = good model]

brute n. [late 19C+] a general term used to imply the size or effect of the object and the distaste of the speaker, usu. in phr. *a brute of a …* (cf. BASTARD; SOD n.¹).

brutus n. [1980s+] (US campus) a mean, ugly person. [SE *brute* 'Latinized' by sfx. *-us*]

bruz n. [1950s+] (US Black) an affectionate term of address (cf. CUZ n.). [SE *brother*]

bruze see BROWSE.

bry n. [late 19C–1900s] gin. [BRIAN O'LINN]

Bryant and May n. [1920s+] a light ale. [pun on SE *lights*, i.e. the matches produced by the *Bryant and May* company]

bryant and mays n. [20C] stays (a form of light underbodice that preceded the corset). [rhy. sl.]

Bryant and May's chuckaway n. [late 19C–1900s] a woman working at Bryant and May's match factory. [pun on CHUCKAWAY, with a grim ref. to the disposability of those who worked at this dirty, dangerous task]

b.s. n. [late 19C+] (orig. US) rubbish, nonsense. [abbr. BULLSHIT n.]

b.s.h.s n. [1960s–70s] the female breasts. [abbr. the joc. notional administrative measure, *British Standard Handfuls*, a pun on the *BSI*, British Standards Institution]

b.t.m. n. [1910s+] the posterior. [euph. abbr. SE *bottom*]

b.t.o. n. [1940s+] (US campus) one who schemes successfully to get their own way. [abbr. *big time operator*]

b.u. n. [1930s] (US campus) sexual drive or desire. [abbr. *biological urge*]

bu see BOO n.³.

bub n.¹ [late 17C] the victim of a fraud or hoax. [BUBBLE n.¹]

bub n.² [late 17C–19C] drink, esp. strong beer. [Lat. *bibere*, to drink]

bub n.³ **1** [early 19C+] (US) a boy, esp. when used as derog. form of address, implying youth, insignificance etc (cf. BUBBA). **2** [1980s+] (US campus) a person devoid of redeeming qualities. [SE *bubby*, a little boy]

bub n.⁴ [mid-19C+] the female breast (cf. BOOB n.³). [BUBBY n.]

bub v.¹ [18C–early 19C] **1** to cheat. **2** bribe (cf. DRINK n.²) [BUB n.¹]

bub v.² [18C–19C] to drink. [BUB n.²]

bubba n. **1** [19C+] (US) a brother. **2** [19C+] (US) generic for an uneducated Southern male. **3** [20C] (Aus.) a young child. [? pron. by a (younger) sibling]

bubbed adj. [19C] drunk. [BUB v. (1)]

bubbelizer n. [20C] (Ulster) a stammerer. [their 'bu-bu-bu' stammering]

bubbe mayse/bobbe mayse n. [20C] an old wife's tale. [Yid. *Bovo Mayse*, the Story of Bovo (or Buovo), an early 16C narrative poem written in Italy and translated into Yid. by the scholar Elijah Bochur. Its unlikely tales, featuring the hero Bovo, were meant as satire. When rewritten in 19C prose it was corrupted as *bubbe mayse*, lit. 'a grandmother's story', since only a gullible old lady was presumed to believe the stories as they stood]

bubber n.¹ **1** [17C–18C] a heavy drinker. **2** [late 17C–early 19C] a drinking bowl. **3** [late 17C–early 19C] a thief who steals from taverns. [BUB v.²]

bubber n.² [19C] (US) an old woman with large, pendulous breasts. [BUB n.⁴]

bubbery n. [19C] noise, rowdiness. [BUB v.²; i.e. the behaviour of the drinkers]

bubbies n. [17C] the female breasts. [either f. Lat. *bibere*, to drink, or possibly – in the way that some claim that SE *pap* is onomat., stemming from the infant's sucking lips – from the hungry child's cries of 'Bub, bub!']

bubbing n. [late 17C] drinking. [BUB v.²]

bubbkis see BOBKHES.

bubble n.¹ **1** [late 17C–19C] a victim, one who is ripe for being fooled. **2** [mid-18C–mid-19C] a sham or otherwise dubious company. [the schemes so proposed are as insubstantial, if as superficially shiny, as a soap bubble; the (linguistic) archetype is the *South Sea Bubble* of 1721]

bubble n.² [20C] (US) the female breast. [BUB n.⁴]

bubble n.³ **1** [1910s+] (orig. US) any automobile. **2** [1960s] a small (three-wheeled) automobile, briefly popular in early 1960s. [abbr. AUTOMOBUBBLE]

bubble n.⁴ [1920s+] (Und.) information. [BUBBLE AND SQUEAK v.]

bubble/old bubble n.⁵ [1930s+] one's wife. [rhy. sl. *bubble* = TROUBLE AND STRIFE]

bubble n.⁶ [1950s+] a Greek (cf. BUBBLE AND SQUEAK n.³). [note the intensified *archbubble*, although this is poss. a nonce-coinage in Cook (1962)]

bubble n.⁷ [1960s] (drugs) a small, oval swelling on the skin caused by a careless injection of heroin.

bubble

bubble v.[1] [mid-17C–19C] to cheat, to hoax, to swindle; thus *bubbleable*, gullible. [the insubstantiality of a SE *bubble*]

bubble v.[2] [1900s–30s] (US) to drive a car. [SE *bubble car*]

bubble v.[3] [1920s] to inform, to betray. [abbr. BUBBLE AND SQUEAK v. or PUT THE BUBBLE IN].

bubble v.[4] [1990s] (US Black) to improve one's situation, to make money. [SE *bubble up*]

bubble and squeak/bubble-and-squeak n.[1] [late 18C–early 19C] (left-over) beef and cabbage and/or potatoes fried up together. [the noise of the cooking; subseq. use is SE]

bubble and squeak n.[2] [20C] (Aus.) an act of urination. [rhy. sl. *bubble and squeak* = LEAK n.[3]]

bubble and squeak n.[3] **1** [late 19C+] a schoolmaster (cf. BEAK n.). **2** [1950s+] a Greek. **3** [1970s] a week. [rhy. sl.]

bubble and squeak v. [mid-19C+] to speak, esp. to inform to the police. [rhy. sl.]

bubble and squeak adv. [early-mid-19C] vigorously. [the noise and action that gives the frying dish its name]

bubble around v. [late 19C] to make a harsh verbal attack on someone. [BUBBLE AND SQUEAK v.]

bubble-bow n. [early-mid-18C] a woman's tweezer-case. [BUBBLE v.[1] + SE *beau*]

bubblebrain see BUBBLEHEAD.

bubble buff n. [17C] a bailiff. [BUBBLE n.[1] + BUFF n.[1] (1)]

bubblebutt n. [1980s+] (US campus) **1** large, protruding, rounded buttocks. **2** the person who has such a physique. [SE *bubble* + BUTT n.[1] (1)]

bubbled adv. [mid-19C+] betrayed, informed against. [BUBBLE AND SQUEAK v.]

bubble dancing n. [1940s] (US Black) washing up. [SE *soap bubbles* + pun on SE *bubble-dancer*, a woman who dances, wearing nothing but strategically placed balloons]

bubble-duster n. [19C] a handkerchief. [SE *bubble* (of mucus) + *duster*]

bubble-gum n.[1] [1960s+] (orig. music business) catchy, simplistic pop music aimed specifically at the pre-pubescent and early teenage girl market, all, allegedly, prime consumers of bubble-gum.

bubble-gum n.[2] [1980s+] (drugs) **1** coca paste. **2** cocaine. **3** crack cocaine. [? one can chew it]

bubble-gum machine n. [1960s+] (US) **1** the flashing lights on top of a police car. **2** the vehicle itself. [resemblance]

bubble-gummer n. [1960s+] a girl aged 10–14. [BUBBLE-GUM n.[1]]

bubblehead/bubblebrain n. [1980s+] a foolish, careless person, with a brain full of air (cf. AIRHEAD). [SE *bubble* + sfx. -HEAD (1)]

bubblejas see BABALAAS.

bubbler n.[1] [late 17C–mid-19C] **1** a drinking bowl. **2** a heavy drinker. **3** a robber of plate from public houses. [BUB v.[2]]

bubbler n.[2] [18C] a swindler. [BUBBLE v.[1]]

bubbler n.[3] [1970s+] (Aus.) a school drinking fountain.

bubbles and squeaks n. [1950s] Greeks and Cypriots seen collectively. [BUBBLE n.[6] + pun on BUBBLE AND SQUEAK n.[1]]

bubble-top n. [1960s+] (US) a police car (cf. BUBBLE-GUM MACHINE). [the flashing lights on its roof, reminiscent of the sweet dispenser]

bubble water see BUBBLY WATER.

bubbling n. [early 18C] cheating, hoaxing, swindling. [BUBBLE v.[1]]

bubbling adj. [1990s] (US Black teen) rising up, coming up, emerging vigorously. [BUBBLE v.[4]]

bubbly jock n. [19C] **1** a turkey. **2** an excessive talker. **3** a foolish braggart. [rhy. sl. *bubbly jock* = turkey cock. (2) implies a turkey's characteristics, strutting and making too much noise. Note milit. jargon the *Bubbly Jocks*, the Royal Scots Greys, whose rival regiments equate them with the farmyard bird]

bubbly/bubble water n. [late 19C+] champagne (cf. CONVERSATION WATER; GIGGLE-WATER; KALI-WATER; LAUGHING SOUP).

bubby n.[1] [19C] a friendly term of address (cf. BUBBA). [BUDDY n. (1) + BABY n.[2]]

bubby n.[2] [20C] (W.I.) a woman's (large) breast or both breasts together. [late 17C–early 18C SE *bubby*, breast]

bube n. [late 18C] venereal disease, esp. syphilis. [SE *bubo*, an inflamed swelling or abscess, one of the possible signs of venereal disease]

bubele n. [20C] a general affectionate term of address. [Yid. *bubele*, little grandmother]

bubkhes/bubkis see BOBKHES.

bubonic adj. [20C] extreme, notably powerful. [SE *bubonic plague* which devastated Europe during the 14C Black Death]

bubs n. [1960s+] (Aus.) kindergarten. [SE *babies*]

bubu n. [1950s+] (W.I. Rasta) a fool. [? BOOB n.[2] (1)]

buck n.[1] **1** [18C] a bold, daring person of either sex. **2** [18C+] a bold, dashing man, a roisterer. **3** [mid-18C–early 19C] a cuckold. **4** [19C] a dandy. **5** [19C] (US) a peasant, a rural person (cf. BUCKWHEAT n.[1]). **6** [early 19C+] (US/Aus./N.Z.) a man, esp. Indian or Black, when it becomes derog. **7** [late 19C] a small dealer who works for a more powerful master. **8** [20C] (US prison) a priest. **9** [1900s–40s] (Aus.) a foreman. **10** [1920s+] (orig. Liverpool) a tearaway, a young, aggressive criminal. [all fig. uses of SE *buck*, a he-goat or male deer. The strength and sexuality of the male animal underpins (6) in particular, where buck is often an abbr. of the marginally more opprobrious *buck nigger*; the female equivalent is a *wench*. (5) is abbr. of BUCKWHEAT n.[1]. (1) is also abbr. of *buck-a-dandy*, a fop, but for (1) note Ware, who suggests a root in SE *buckram*, a stiffening fabric used by such dandies in the full-skirted coats of the 18C]

buck n.[2] **1** [mid-19C+] (US) $1, $100. **2** [19C+] sixpence, usu. preceded by a number of shillings, e.g. *six and a buck*, 6s 6d. **3** [1970s+] (S.Afr.) a rand. **4** [1980s+] (US) 100 of anything, not merely money. **5** [1980s] (US) $1000. [orig. abbr. SE *buckskin*, an item used as barter in 19C America]

buck n.[3] [late 19C] an unlicensed cab-driver. [cabman's jargon *buck*, a fraudulent passenger used by an unlicensed London cabbie, who could get near a theatre or restaurant in the Strand only if appearing to be bringing a fare; thus a reasonably respectable young man would be picked up, driven a few yards and then dropped]

buck n.[4] [late 19C–1930s] talk, conversation, esp. when garrulous or irritating. [Hind. *bak*, speech, talk]

buck n.[5] [1910s+] (Aus./N.Z.) a try, an attempt, esp. in phr. *give it a buck/have a buck at*. [SE *buck* v.]

buck n.[6] [1940s] (Irish) tuberculosis. [it was a 'galloping' disease]

buck n.[7] [1970s+] *buck*shot, used to load shotgun shells. [abbr.]

buck adj. **1** [mid-19C] (US campus) excellent, first-rate. **2** [1990s] (US Black) utterly, totally, completely. [BUCK n.[1] (1), (2)]

buck v.[1] [mid-16C+] to have sexual intercourse. [orig. used of rabbits; late 19C+ use is US]

buck v.[2] **1** [late 19C–1940s] to swagger, to talk big or bumptiously, to brag. **2** [late 19C] to talk, to chatter; thus *buck-stick*, a chatterer. [synon. Hind. *bakna, bukh*]

buck v.[3] [20C] to avoid, to resist, to oppose oneself to; thus *buck the system*, to fight against the status quo. **2** [20C] to protest, to object, to show irritation. **3** [1950s–60s] (US) to desire, to work towards, to aim for. **4** [1980s+] (drugs) to shoot someone (in the head). **5** [1980s+] (drugs) to steal someone's money. [SE *buck*, to oppose, to come up against]

buck a bull off the bridge, to phr. [19C] (US) to perform wonders, to achieve anything one wants.

buck against v. [late 19C–1900s] (orig. US) to oppose vehemently and determinedly. [the image of a bucking, uncontrolled horse]

buck-and-a-half n. [1960s+] (US) $150 (cf. YARD-AND-A-HALF). [BUCK n.² (1) + SE half]

buckaroo n. (US) **1** [17C+] (US Black) a poor person, of any race. **2** [early 19C+] a cowboy or cattle-driver. **3** [1930s+] a man, a fellow (cf. BUCKO n.¹). [Sp. vaquero, cowboy, cow hand]

buck bathing n. [20C] (US) nude bathing. [BUCK NAKED]

buck-buck! excl. [1980s+] (US Black teen) onomat. noise of a gun being fired.

bucked adj.¹ [20C] made to feel better, cheered, encouraged. [BUCK UP v.²]

bucked adj.² [1980s+] (Irish) finished, 'done for'. [? euph. for FUCKED]

bucked adj.³ [1990s] (US) shot, wounded. [SE buckshot]

buckeen n. [late 18C–early 19C] a bully. [Anglo-Irish buckeen, a younger son of the impoverished Anglo-Irish aristocracy. The term apes the better-known squireen, a petty landowner]

bucker n.¹ [19C] (US) a rebel, one who refuses to follow the party line. [SE buck, to go against, to oppose]

bucker n.² [mid-19C+] (US) a gambler. [gambling jargon buck the tiger, to play faro]

bucker n.³ [1970s+] (US) $1. [BUCK n.² (1)]

buckeroo n. [1940s+] (US) $1. [BUCK n.² (1) + sfx. -EROO]

bucket n.¹ **1** [20C] (US) buttocks (cf. CAN n.⁴). **2** [1930s+] (US) the anus. **3** [1990s] a large or loose vagina.

bucket n.² [1930s+] (US) an old car, any form of motor vehicle that has become run down and dilapidated. [RUST BUCKET n. (2) or BUCKET OF BOLTS]

bucket n.³ [1930s+] a county or local prison (cf. CAN). [rhy. sl. bucket and pail = gaol]

bucket n.⁴ [1950s–60s] (US) a plump woman, an unattractive woman. [resemblance]

bucket v.¹ **1** [early 19C] (Und.) to deceive, to cheat, to ruin, esp. to rob an accomplice of their share of a robbery. **2** [1970s+] (Aus.) to disdain, to denigrate, to despise (cf. DROP THE BUCKET ON). ['To bucket a person is synonymous with putting him in the well' (Vaux)]

bucket/bucket down v.² [1920s+] to rain very heavily. [as if poured from a bucket]

bucket v.³ [1980s+] (US drugs) to smoke marijuana through liquid. [BUCKET BONG]

bucket about v. [1920s] to move backwards/forwards/from side to side, to oscillate. [? image of a bucket floating on water]

bucket afloat/bucket and float n. [19C] a coat (cf. I'M AFLOAT). [rhy. sl.]

bucket and pail n. [1930s] prison (cf. BUCKET n.³). [rhy. sl.]

bucket bong n. [1980s+] (Aus. drugs) a form of gravity pipe for smoking marijuana, made with a 2-litre (3½-pint) plastic bottle and a bucket. [SE bucket + BONG n.]

bucket boy n. [1980s+] (US gay) a passive partner in anal intercourse. [BUCKET n.¹ (1) + SE boy]

bucket cunt n. [1990s] a large vagina (cf. BUCKET n.¹). [coarsely joc. use of sl.]

bucket down see BUCKET v.².

bucket-fed adj. [20C] (US) spoiled, over-indulged. [farming jargon bucket-fed, of a calf that has been fed by hand]

bucket gaff/job n. [1960s–70s] (Und.) a fraudulent company. [BUCKET v.¹ (1) + GAFF n.¹ (4); SE job]

buckethead n. [20C] (US) a fool, a simpleton; thus bucket-headed, stupid. [SE bucket + sfx. -HEAD (1)]

bucketing n. [1910s] a hard task, which one performs only when coerced. [the effort involved in a laborious task, e.g. filling a bath, using only a bucket]

bucket job see BUCKET GAFF.

bucketmouth n. [1970s] (US) **1** a chatterer. **2** one who habitually uses 'bad language'. [SE bucket + sfx. -mouth]

bucket of blood see BLOODY BUCKET.

bucket of blubber see BUCKET OF LARD.

bucket of bolts n. [1940s+] (US) a broken-down motor vehicle.

bucket of lard/blubber n. [20C] a very fat person (cf. LARDBUCKET; TUB OF LARD).

bucket of smashed crabs phr. [1990s] a general derog. description of an unattractive woman.

bucket of worms n. [1970s] (US) an unpleasant, complex and unappetizing situation (cf. CAN OF WORMS).

bucket shop n. [late 19C+] (orig. US) **1** an unauthorized office used orig. for smaller gambling transactions in grain, and subsequently extended to offices for other descriptions of gambling and betting on the markets, stocks etc. **2** a cut-price travel agent, specializing in long-haul air flights. **3** a gin-mill, a low-class liquor-shop. ['The market authority in Chicago, called the Board of Trade, would not allow a deal in "options" of less than 5,000 bushels of grain. In order to catch men of small means, what was called the "Open Board of Trade" commenced business in an alley under the regular Board of Trade Rooms. There was an elevator to carry the members of the board to their rooms, and occasionally a member, if trade was slack, would call out, "I'll send down and get a bucketful pretty soon," referring to the speculators in the "Open Board of Trade" below' (Leeds Mercury, December 1886)]

buckeye n.¹ (US) **1** [early 19C+] an inhabitant of Ohio. **2** [early 19C+] a rustic or country person. **3** [20C] an inferior person or thing, esp. one of no value, poor quality or cheap (but often showy). [(1) the buckeye tree (Aesculus glabra, the American horse chestnut), which flourishes in the state and is featured on its flag. (3) ? the poor reputation of Ohians]

buckeye n.² [late 19C– 1940s] (US) a small place of business, esp. one found in a slum area, esp. a cigar factory. [specific use of BUCKEYE n.¹ (3)]

buckeye n.³ [20C] rotgut whisky. [the addition of buckeye nuts to the liquor during its production]

buckeye n.⁴ [20C] a sheriff. [the practice of local Native Americans at Marietta, Ohio, who praised the fine figure of their local sheriff, calling him Hetuck, big buckeye]

buck-eyed adj. [20C] (US Black) having eyes considered out of the ordinary, cross-eyed, squinting, protruding etc (cf. BUGEYED). [SE buck, to project]

buck/buck's face n. [late 17C–early 19C] a cuckold. [SE buck, an animal that 'wears the horns']

buck fever n. [late 19C+] (S.Afr./US) nervousness in the face of an unknown or new situation that may render one incapable of action. [hunting jargon buck fever, the nerves felt by inexperienced hunters faced by the game they have been pursuing; they get so excited they fail to shoot]

buck-fitch n. [late 17C] an ageing lecher, an old roué. [SE buck-fitch, a male polecat]

buck for v. [1960s+] (orig. milit.) to struggle towards, to act energetically in one's own interest. [SE buck, to come up against]

buckhorse n. [mid-late 19C] a blow on the ear. [the pugilist Buckhorse (real name John Smith) who, for a small charge, allowed people to hit him hard on the side of the head]

Buck House n. [1930s+] Buckingham Palace, London home of the British royal family.

buckijit n. [20C] (Irish) a very great fool. [BUCK n.¹ (1) + EEJIT]

buckinger's boot n. [late 18C] the vagina. [proper name of Matthew *Buckinger* (*fl.*1750) who was born limbless 'notwithstanding which he drew coats of arms very neatly and could write the Lord's Prayer within the compass of one shilling, he was married to a tall handsome woman, and traversed the country, shewing himself for money' (Grose). For him, a boot could fit only his THIRD LEG]

buckingmatch n. [late 19C] (US Black) a fight in which each combatant uses only their head. [animal imagery]

buckish adj. [1900s–10s] in high spirits. [BUCK UP v.² + sfx. -*ish*]

buck-kneed adj. [20C] (US) having bent shin-bones. [horse-trading jargon]

buckle n.¹ [17C–early 18C] a fetter, usu. in pl. [ext. of SE use]

buckle n.² [mid-19C–1900s] (Aus.) a pos. or cheerful state, condition, mood. [SE *buckle*, to apply oneself vigorously]

buckle n.³ [20C] **1** a Jew (cf. BUCKLE MY SHOE). **2** (bingo) the number two (cf. BUCKLE MY SHOE).

buckle v. **1** [late 17C–early 19C] to be married. **2** [early 18C–early 19C] to marry. **3** [mid-19C+] to arrest; usu. as *buckled*. **4** [1970s+] (US) to argue, to fight. [SE *buckle*, to join. (2) E.P. suggests 20C Aus. use, but it is in neither *AND* nor *DNZE*]

buckle-beggar n. [early 18C–early 19C] a clergyman who performs irregular marriages (cf. COUPLE-BEGGAR; HEDGE-PRIEST). [BUCKLE v. (2) + SE *beggar*]

buckle-bosom n. [early 17C] a constable, a catchpoll. [SE *buckle*, to grapple, to engage + *bosom*]

bucklebury n. [1910s–20s] a euph. for SE *buggery*. [play on name of the Berkshire town]

buckled adj. [1980s+] (Irish) drunk (cf. BASTED).

buckle down v.¹ see BUCKLE TO.

buckle down v.² [mid-19C+] (orig. US) to set to work, to apply oneself vigorously. [SE *buckle*, to apply oneself vigorously]

buckle-hammed adj. [early 17C] having crooked legs. [SE *buckle*, to warp, to bend, to crumple + HAMS n. (1)]

buckle my shoe n. [late 19C+] **1** a Jew (cf. BOX OF GLUE). **2** (bingo) the number two. [rhy. sl.]

buckle to/down v. [early 18C+] (orig. US) to set to work, to apply oneself vigorously. [SE *buckle*, to apply oneself vigorously]

buckley's/buckley's chance n. [late 19C+] (Aus./N.Z.) no chance at all. [? proper name of *William Buckley*, an escaped convict who spent 32 years living with Aborigines in South Victoria; or pun on name of defunct firm of *Buckley and Nunn*, therefore one has two chances 'Buckley and Nunn', i.e. none]

buck-load n. [19C] (US) a large measure of liquor. [BUCK n.¹ (1) + SE *load* or play on SHOT n.⁵]

buck naked adj. [early 19C+] (orig. US) naked. [? corruption of BUTT n.¹ (1) + SE *naked*]

buck/buck's night n. [1910s+] (Aus.) a party for men only (cf. BUCK PARTY). [BUCK n.¹ (1) + SE *night*]

bucko n.¹ [late 19C+] **1** a bully, a blustering swaggerer. **2** a dandy. **3** a general term of address, e.g. *my bucko*. [BUCK n.¹ (2), thence naut. jargon *bucko*, an overbearing ship's officer, who enforces his will through (threats of) violence, usu. as *bucko mate*]

bucko n.² [1980s+] (US) $1. [BUCK n.² (1)]

bucko adj. [late 19C+] aggressive, overbearing, domineering. [BUCKO n.¹ (1)]

buck off v. [1990s+] (US Black) to murder, to kill. [BUCK v.³ (4)]

buck of the first head n. [late 18C] a celebrated debauchee, whose excesses outpace those of his peers. [BUCK n.¹ (2) + SE *first head*, primacy]

buck out v. [1920s–30s] (US West) to die. [equine imagery]

buck party n. [late 19C–1900s] (Aus.) a party for men only (cf. STAG PARTY). [BUCK n.¹ (2) + SE *party*]

buck private n. [1910s+] (US milit.) a private soldier who is 'bucking for' promotion; thus occas. other ranks in a similar position, e.g. *buck colonel*, who wishes to be a general. [BUCK FOR]

buckra see BACKRA.

buck's face see BUCK FACE.

buckshee n. see BAKSHEESH n.

buckshee adj. [1910s+] free, gratis. [Pers. *baksheesh*, a gift, a present; thus a tip; picked up by Middle East and Indian Imperial troops and thus brought to the West]

buckshine n. [mid-19C+] a native of Tennessee (cf. MUD-HEAD; WHELP n.). [ety. unknown]

buckshish see BAKSHEESH.

buck-sick adj. [20C] (W.I.) tired of a boring, but still vital task. [BUCK adj. (2) + SE *sick*]

buckskin n. [late 18C–early 19C] **1** an American soldier, fighting in the Revolutionary War. **2** a native of Virginia. [SE *buckskin*, leather (garments) made from the skin of a buck]

buck's night see BUCK NIGHT.

buck the bone, to phr. [1990s+] to masturbate. [SE *buck*, come up against + BONE n.⁶ (1)]

buck the horse, to phr. [20C] (Und.) to deliberately cause trouble in prison by refusing to accept discipline.

buck the saw, to phr. [1960s] (US Black) to overcome a challenge, to triumph despite heavy odds. [SE *buck* v. + pun on *bucksaw*, a heavy form of frame-saw used with a buck or sawing-frame]

buck the tiger, to phr. (US) [mid-19C+] to play the game of faro; thus *buck against the tiger*, to face overwhelming odds (cf. FIGHT THE TIGER; TIGER DEN). [SE *buck*, oppose + *tiger*]

bucktown n. [1990s] (US Black) Brooklyn, New York. [BUCK n.¹ (1), (6)]

buck-up n. [1950s+] (W.I.) a social gathering, for no specific purpose other than enjoyment. [BUCK UP v.² (1)]

buck up v.¹ [early–mid-19C] to dress oneself up. [BUCK n.¹ (1)]

buck up v.² [mid-19C+] to encourage, to cheer up. [orig. Winchester Coll. jargon; ult. SE *buck*]

buck up! excl. [mid-19C+] cheer up! [BUCK UP v.²]

buck up to v. [19C] **1** (US) to make advances, to court. **2** (US) to defy, to rebel against, to stand up to. **3** (Black) to challenge, to encounter. [BUCK v.³ (1), (2)]

buckwheat n.¹ [19C] (US) **1** a naïve peasant, a gullible country person. **2** a Black person. [SE *buckwheat*, the cereal grain *Fagopyrum esculentum*, used as cattle-feed in Europe, but cooked for humans in the US]

buckwheat n.² [19C+] (US Black) a light-complexioned Black person. [SE *buckwheat*, the foodstuff popularized by the Black child actor William 'Buckwheat' Thomas, who appeared in the 1930s *Our Gang* series of Saturday morning films]

buckwheat crop n. [20C] (US) a marriage that takes place when the bride is already pregnant. [*buckwheat* ripens faster than other grains]

buck-whyling n. [1990s] (US Black) chatting, engaging in general conversation. [BUCK n.¹ (1) + SE *while away* (time)]

buck-wild adj. [1980s+] (US Black) extreme, intense, desperate. [the state of a *buck* during the rutting season]

bucky n.¹ [mid-19C] (US) a general term of address to a male. [BUCK n.¹ (1) + sfx. -*y*]

bucky n.² [1950s+] (W.I. Rasta) a homemade gun. [SE *buck* v. + sfx. -*y*]

bucky adj. [20C] (US) out of order. [SE *buck the system*]

bud n.¹ **1** [late 19C] (US) a young, pubescent girl. **2** [1900s–10s] a debutante. [SE *bud*, a flower that is yet to be fully opened + phr. *bud of promise*]

bud *n.*[2] [20C] (US) a general nickname or term of address for a brother or eldest son, any boy or man, or a close friend. [BUDDY n.1]

bud *n.*[3] [1980s+] (US drugs) cannabis or the part of the cannabis that is smoked. [SE *bud*]

buda *see* BUDDHA n.

budd *n.* [1990s] **1** the clitoris. **2** a derog. description of a person. [SE *bud*]

buddha/buda *n.* [1990s] (drugs) **1** a potent form of marijuana (cf. THAI STICKS). **2** a mix of marijuana and crack cocaine. [its oriental origins]

buddha *adj.* [1990s] (US campus) excellent, worthy of admiration. [BUDDHA n. ult. the Buddha, *fl*.5C BC]

buddha belly *n.* [1970s+] (US) a very fat person. [the traditional statues of the *Buddha*, resplendent with a huge stomach]

buddhahead *n.* (US) **1** [20C] an Oriental or Asian person. **2** [1940s+] a Japanese-American born in Hawaii rather than in mainland US. [SE *Buddha* + sfx. -HEAD (3). (2) their less assimilated lifestyle, pidgin English and similarly 'unsophisticated' ways]

buddha sticks *n.* [1960s+] (drugs) marijuana grown in Thailand, which is sold wrapped around small, satay sticks (cf. THAI). [BUDDHA n. + SE *sticks*]

buddhist priest! *excl.* [1970s] (US) euph. for *Jesus Christ!* (cf. BEJABERS!).

buddley *n.* [20C] (Ulster) **1** a fat person. **2** a sausage. [Irish *bodalach*, a large, ungainly young person]

buddy *n.* **1** [mid-19C+] (orig. US) a friend, an acquaintance. **2** [1980s+] (US) the penis. **3** [1990s] (W.I./UK Black teen) the body. **4** [1990s] (W.I./UK Black teen) a sexual partner. [SE *brother* or dial. *butty*; itself ult. obs. SE *booty*, sharing]

buddy *adj.* [1990s] (rap music) referring to something that appears OK at first, but is actually a cheap imitation, a knock-off, rip-off or fake, e.g. *Get that buddy shit out of here.* [? *Buddies*, a brand of shoe that looks fashionable but is reputed to fall apart very quickly]

buddy/buddy up *v.* [1930s+] (orig. US) to become friendly, to travel as friends. [BUDDY n. (1)]

buddy-buddy *adj.* [20C] exceptionally and overtly friendly, prob. insincerely so. [US WW2 milit. jargon]

buddy-fuck *v.* [1960s+] (US) (mainly milit.) to impose on, betray or otherwise inconvenience a friend; thus *buddy-fucker*, *buddy-fucking* (cf. FUCK YOUR BUDDY WEEK). [BUDDY n. (1) + FUCK v.[2] (1)]

buddy-gee *n.* [1930s–40s] (US Black) a friend. [BUDDY n. (1) + GEE n.[4]]

buddyseat *n.* [190s+] the pillion seat on a motorcycle. [BUDDY n. (1) + SE *seat*]

buddy up *see* BUDDY v.

budge *n.*[1] [late 17C–late 18C] a sneak thief, esp. one who specializes in entering houses and taking furs, cloaks and coats (cf. BUDGE AND SNUDGE; RUNNER n.[1]; SNEAKING BUDGE). [SE *budge*, a kind of fur, consisting of lamb's skin with the wool dressed outwards]

budge *n.*[2] [18C–early 19C] liquor. [BUB n.[2]]

budge *v.*[1] [late 17C] to drink (cf. BUDGE KAIN). [BUB v. (1)]

budge *v.*[2] [mid-18C–19C] to leave. [SE *budge*, to move]

budge *v.*[3] [mid-19C–early 20C] to inform. [SE *budge*, to move against, act in hostility to]

budge a beak, to *phr.* [16C] to run away (from the law). [BUDGE v.[2] + BEAK]

budge kain *n.* [19C] (Scot.) a public house, a tavern. [BUDGE v.[1] + KEN n.[1]]

budge and snudge *n.* [late 17C–late 18C] (Und.) a housebreaker and their accomplice (cf. BUDGE n.[1]). [note the 1950s

British TV sit-com *Bootsie and Snudge*, based on the misadventures of two army friends]

budger *n.* [19C] a drunkard. [BUDGE v.[1]]

budget *n.* [19C] the vagina (cf. BANK n.[1]). [SE *budget*, a pouch, bag, wallet, usually of leather]

budgie *n.* **1** [late 19C+] a budgerigar. **2** [1960s+] (Und.) a talkative person, esp. in police use, a minor informer. [SE *budgerigar*, a popular cage bird, which can be taught to speak; thus RAF jargon (*paraffin*) *budgie*, a helicopter, presumably the source of the Duchess of York's storybook creation]

budging ken *n.* [mid-19C] a public house, a tavern; thus *cove of the budging-ken*, a landlord (cf. BUDGE KAIN). [BUDGE v.[1] + KEN n.[1]]

budgy *adj.* [mid-19C] drunk. [BUDGE v.[1]]

budhead *n.* [1970s+] (US Black) a beer drinker. [brandname *Budweiser* beer + sfx. -HEAD (2)]

budini *see* BODINI.

budion *n.* [20C] (Ulster) a small penis. [Irish *boidín*, the penis]

budiquette *n.* [1980s+] (US drugs) the etiquette the governs the smoking of marijuana. [BUD n.[3] + SE (*et*)*iquette*]

budli-budli *n.* [20C] **1** sodomy. **2** a male homosexual (cf. BUGGER n.[1]). [Urdu *badli*, change, used in late 19C as Raj sl. for a *locum tenens* and in 20C IVE as temporary employee]

budlies *n.* [1980s+] (drugs) cannabis or the part of the cannabis that is smoked (cf. BUDULARS). [BUD n.[3]]

budman *n.* [1980s+] (US campus) a marijuana dealer (cf. DOPEMAN). [BUD n.[3] + SE *man*]

budmash *n.* [late 19C+] (orig. Ind. army) a villain, a rascal. [Hind. *badmash*, a rascal]

buds *n.* [1980s+] (drugs) alkyl nitrates. [ety. unknown; ? link to BUD n.[3]]

bud-sack *n.* [1980s+] (US) a container for marijuana. [BUDDHA + SE *sack*]

bud sesh *n.* [1970s+] (US teen) getting together to smoke marijuana. [BUD n.[3] + SE *session* + pun on SE *bud*(*dy*) *session*, a friendly get-together]

budulars *n.* [1980s+] (drugs) cannabis or the part of the cannabis that is smoked (cf. BUDLIES). [BUD n.[3]]

budup!/budum!/bum! *excl.* [20C] (W.I.) echoic, onomat. words representing the sound of an object or objects crashing to the floor (cf. BRADARAX!).

buel *n.* [1980s+] (US campus) food. [SE *body* + *fuel*]

buel *v.* [1980s+] (US campus) to eat voraciously. [BUEL n.]

Buenos Aires *n.* [late 19C] Royal Crescent, Margate; thus *go/take the road to Buenos Aires*, to start working as a prostitute. [the numbers of street prostitutes in that part of Margate; Buenos Aires was seen as a centre of White slavery]

buer/bewer/buor/bure *n.* [early 19C+] (orig. tramp) a woman, esp. one seen as sexually appealing and/or of loose character (cf. BURICK). [? Shelta]

buf *n.* [1980s] (US teen) an attractive male. [? SE *beautiful/beautiful fellow* or one who is BUFFED adj.(2)]

bufe/bufa *n.* [16C–late 18C] (Und.) a dog (cf. BUFFER n.[1]). [echoic of a bark]

bufe nabber *n.* [16C–late 18C] a dog stealer. [BUFE + NABBER n. (3)]

buff *n.*[1] **1** [early 18C–mid-19C] a man, a person. **2** [20C] (Irish) a self-important person. **3** [20C] (Irish) a country-dweller. [SE *buff*, the bare skin]

buff *n.*[2] [1940s+] an enthusiast, a (knowledgeable) fan. [*The Buffs*, men or boys who follow firemen and the fires they fight; f. the buff uniforms worn by volunteer firemen in New York City. The term gradually expanded to take in any (amateur) enthusiast, e.g. *film buff*, *sports buff*]

buff *n.*[3] [1980s+] (drugs) money. [ety. unknown]

buff *adj.* **1** [17C+] naked, usu. as *in the buff*. **2** [1980s+] strong, muscular, healthy. [(2) f. SE *buffed up*, polished, in this case via workout sessions at a gymnasium]

buff *v.* [19C] to swear to, to testify. [BUFFER n.³]

buffalo *n.*¹ **1** [mid-19C] (US) a Southerner who does not support the Confederacy. **2** [mid-19C+; 1940s+] (orig. US use, then also W.I.) a large, stupid person. **3** [1960s] (US) a fat woman.

buffalo/buffalohead *n.*² [1920s–30s] (US) a nickel (5 cents). [the picture of a buffalo head on the reverse of the coin]

buffalo *v.* [19C+] (US) to overawe, to frighten, to confuse, to pressurize. [the size and strength of the animal]

buffaloed *adv.* [1900s–50s] (orig. US) coerced, crushed. [BUFFALO v.]

buffalohead *see* BUFFALO n.².

buffalo navigator *n.* [1930s–40s] (Aus.) a bullock-driver.

buffalo piss *n.* [1980s] (US) weak beer (cf. CAT'S PEE).

buffalo soldier *n.* [mid-19C+] (US) a Black soldier fighting in the US Army (cf. BUFFALO n.¹). [so called by the Native Americans who compared their hair to that of the matted hair between a buffalo's horns]

buffarilla *n.* [1960s–70s] (US campus) a plump, homely young woman (cf. BUFFALO n.¹). [SE *buffalo* + *gorilla*]

buff-ball *n.* [late 19C] a dance attended by prostitutes; thus, *de facto*, an orgy (cf. BUTTOCK-BALL). [guests are soon *in the buff*]

buff boy *n.* [20C] a male homosexual prostitute. [SE *buff* + *boy*]

buff-coat *n.* [mid–late 17C] a soldier. [the buff-coloured uniform; later use SE]

buffed *adj.* [19C] **1** drunk (cf. BASTED). **2** well muscled (cf. BUFF UP). [SE *buff*, to hit, to polish]

buffer *n.*¹ **1** [16C–late 18C] a dog (cf. BUFE). **2** [early 19C] a pistol. [i.e. 'it bites as well as barks']

buffer *n.*² [late 17C–18C] a villain who kills healthy horses and sells the skins. [SE *buff*, the skin]

buffer *n.*³ [18C] one who swears false oaths for a fee. [BUFF v.]

buffer *n.*⁴ **1** [mid-18C+] a fool, used with a degree of contempt. **2** [mid-18C+] a genial old fool, a description more affectionate than critical; thus often as *old buffer*. **3** [late 18C] an innkeeper (cf. BLUFFER). [Fr. *bouffard*, a fool or clown]

buffer *n.*⁵ [19C] a boxer. [SE *buff*, a blow]

buffer *n.*⁶ [1990s] (drugs) **1** a user of crack cocaine. **2** one who offers oral sex in return for cocaine. [SE *buffer*, a substance used in the manufacture of CRACK n.¹⁷]

buffer-/tike-lurking *n.* [mid-19C] (Und.) stealing dogs. [BUFE/TYKE n.¹ + LURKING n.]

buffer-nabber/-napper *n.* [18C] a dog stealer (cf. BUFF-KNAPPER; DOG-BUFFER). [BUFE + NAB v.¹ (1)/NAP v.¹ (1)]

buffers *n.* [late 19C+] the female breasts.

buffer's nab *n.* [late 17C–early 18C] (Und.) **1** a counterfeit seal, shaped like a dog's head, used to give spurious authenticity to counterfeit documents. **2** a fake pass. [BUFFER + NAB n.¹ (1)]

buffet *n.* [20C] (US) an establishment that sells illicitly distilled liquor, esp. a private house that does so; often as *buffet flat*. [Fr. *buffet*, a sideboard or corner cupboard; thus the food that is laid out upon it]

buffing the dog *n.* [late 18C–mid-19C] killing a stolen dog that has not been advertised for (and that can thus be sold back to its owner). The skin is sold and the flesh used for dog's-meat. [BUFF n.]

buffity *adj.* [1950s+] (W.I.) fat, clumsy and stupid. [dial. *buffo*, unwieldy; ult. Ewe *bofaa*, broad and thick]

buff-knapper *n.* [early–mid-18C] a dog stealer. [BUFE + NAPPER n.¹ (1)]

buffle *n.* [16C] a fool (cf. BLOCKHEAD n.¹). [Fr. *buffle*, a buffalo]

bufflehead *n.* [late 17C–mid-19C] a fool; thus *buffle-headed*,

stupid (cf. BLOCKHEAD n.¹). [BUFFLE + sfx. -HEAD (1). An alternative ety. suggests Du. *buffel*, blockhead]

buff the banana/happy lamp/one's helmet, to *phr.* [1980s+] to masturbate. [SE *buff*, to polish + BANANA n.² (1)/HAPPY LAMP/HELMET]

buff the bishop, to *phr.* [1980s+] to masturbate (cf. BANG THE BISHOP). [SE *buff*, to polish + *bishop*]

buff the wood, to *phr.* [1990s] to masturbate. [SE *buff*, to polish + WOOD n.² (1)]

buff to one's work, to *phr.* [early–mid-19C] to strip off preparatory to starting a fist-fight. [BUFF adj. (1)]

buff to the stuff, to *phr.* [19C] (Und.) to claim that stolen property is one's own. [BUFF v.]

buff up *v.* [1970s+] (orig. US) to work out in the gym to improve one's musculature (cf. BUFFED). [SE *buff*, to polish]

buffy *n.* [mid-19C] a genial old fool. [BUFFER n.⁴]

buffy *adj.* [mid-19C] drunk (cf. BUDGY). [? BEVVY n. or Fr. *bouffé*, bloated]

buft *n.* [late 16C] (Und.) **1** a decoy. **2** a bully. [SE *buff*, to puff out]

buftie/buftie-boy/bufty *n.* [20C] (Scot.) a male homosexual (cf. BATTIE-BOY). [? BUTTFUCKER]

bufu *n.* [1980s+] (orig. US) a male homosexual. [BUTTFUCKER]

bufu *v.* [1980s] to have anal intercourse. [BUTTFUCK v.]

bufu-bufu *adj.* [1940s+] (W.I.) fat, swollen, blubbery, too big, clumsy or lumbering. [Twi *bufoo*, swollen + Ewa *bofaa*, broad and thick]

bug *n.*¹ [18C] a person, esp. one who puts on airs (cf. BIG BUG).

bug *n.*² [late 18C] (Anglo-Irish) an Englishman. [the belief that English settlers imported insects to Ireland in mid-18C]

bug *n.*³ [late 18C] a man who incites homosexuals to join him in illegal pleasures. [? SE *bugger*]

bug *n.*⁴ **1** [mid-19C–1900s] a breast-pin. **2** [late 19C+] (US) a small object of any kind. **3** [1910s+] (US) a small car, esp. the Volkswagen Beetle. **4** [1910s–30s] (Can.) an old car rebuilt as a hot rod (cf. RACING-CAR). **5** [1920s–50s] (US) a makeshift lantern or flashlight. **6** [1920s+] (US Und.) a burglar alarm. **7** [1940s+] (orig. US) any form of electronic surveillance gadget. **8** [1960s+] (Can. prison) a homemade water heater for making coffee. [the size of a SE *bug*, an insect, usu. a beetle or similar]

bug *n.*⁵ **1** [mid-19C+] (orig. US) an enthusiast, a fan, a devotee. **2** [late 19C+] an insane, unstable person (cf. BUGSY). **3** [19C] (US) a fool. **4** [20C] an obsession, often in combs., e.g. *travel bug*, a desire to go travelling. **5** [20C] dishonesty, esp. in phrs. as *put the bug on*, to fool, to tease. **6** [20C] a cheat, an unreliable person. **7** [1940s+] an idea; thus *put a bug in one's ear*, to inspire. [all f. concept of an invasive insect]

bug *n.*⁶ [late 19C–1900s] a wallflower. [ety. unknown]

bug *n.*⁷ **1** [late 19C+] (orig. US) a defect, a problem in any form of machine (inc. computers and their software). **2** [1930s+] any form of error or delay.

bug *n.*⁸ (US) [20C] a nuisance. [SE *bugbear*]

bug *n.*⁹ (US) **1** [20C] a promiscuous woman. **2** [1980s] the vagina.

bug *n.*¹⁰ [1910s+] (orig. US) **1** a microbe, a germ. **2** an illness, a disease.

bug *n.*¹¹ [1990s] (Aus.) a Moreton Bay crab. [ext. of BUG n.⁴ (1)]

bug *v.*¹ **1** [late 18C–late 19C] to bribe (a policeman); thus *bugging*, the taking of bribes by the police. **2** [early 19C] to hand over, to give, often as *bug over*. **3** [20C] to obtain by underhand or illegal means. [(1) 19C use is mainly US]

bug *v.*² **1** [20C] (US Black) to fight. **2** [1940s+] to annoy, to irritate. [i.e. to act like a SE *bug*, an insect]

bug *v.*³ [20C] (US) to walk slowly, lethargically. [the pace of the insect]

bug v.[4] [1910s+] to tap a telephone or to install any form of electronic surveillance. [BUG n.[4] (7)]

bug v.[5] [1940s+] (orig. US) to be insane or to act as if one is. [BUG n.[5] (1)]

bug v.[6] [1980s+] (US) in rap music, to do something impressive in a performance. [ext. of BUG v.[5]]

bugaboo n.[1] [19C] a bailiff, a sheriff's officer. [SE bugaboo, a bogeyman, someone or something of whom one is scared]

bugaboo n.[2] [1910s+] (W.I.) nasal mucus, esp. when dry. [dial. boggle + bug, mucus. Note nursery synon. bogey]

bugbear n. [early 18C] the female pubic area. [the darkness, both lit. and fig., of the pubic hair]

bug bomb n. [1940s+] (US) an aerosol insecticide. [SE bug + bomb]

bug doctor n. [1930s+] any form of expert dealing with mental problems, a psychoanalyst, a psychologist etc (cf. LOONY DOCTOR). [BUG n.[5] (2) + SE doctor]

bug dust n. [20C] (US) something of little value or importance, esp. as that's a load of bug dust! [US coal-mining jargon bug dust, coal dust or small pellets of coal produced during the mining process]

bug-eater n. [19C] (US) 1 an inhabitant of Nebraska. 2 a unimportant or worthless person. [ext. uses of SE; the poverty-stricken appearance of the inhabitants; at some stage of the 19C the state was overrun by locusts (bugs) and a serious attempt was made to persuade the impoverished country-people to adopt them as a diet]

bug-eye n. [20C] one who has round or bulging eyes (cf. BUG-EYED). [SE bug, of eyes, to bulge]

bug-eyed adj. 1 [19C] cross-eyed (cf. BUCK-EYED). 2 [20C] drunk. [in (2) one's eyes are popping like those of some insects]

bugfucker n. [1970s] (US) a man with an extremely small penis. [SE bug + FUCKER n. (1)]

bugged adj.[1] [1970s+] (drugs) covered with sores and abscesses from repeated use of unsterile needles. [SE bug; the sores etc resemble small insects]

bugged adj.[2] [1980s+] crazy, insane, mentally unstable. [abbr. HAVE BUGS IN THE HEAD]

bugged on adj. [1940s–50s] (US Black) obsessed with, very enthusiastic about. [BUG n.[5] (1)]

bugged up adj. [19C] (US) dressed up. [BUG n.[1] ? + ref. to BUG n.[4] (1)]

bugger n.[1] 1 [early 18C+] a person, a man, a 'bloke', esp. as silly bugger, daft bugger etc, none of which is necessarily pej. 2 [1910s+] something unpleasant or undesirable, a great nuisance; thus a bugger to. 3 [1920s] a thing, with no special connotations. 4 [1980s+] (S.Afr.) a dedicatedly masculine male, whose lack of sensitivity is more than compensated in his enthusiasm for all forms of sport (cf. RUGGER-BUGGER). [SE bugger, a sodomite; a trans. of 14C Fr. bougre, ult. Lat. Bulgarus, a Bulgarian, a name given to a sect of heretics who came from Bulgaria in the 11C. The term was transferred to the Albigensian heretics, who it was believed were largely homosexual. Despite appearances, the term remains SE, although the OED, c.1900, states that 'in decent use only as a legal term'. Its verbal and comb. uses are, however, sl., as are the n. uses cited here]

bugger n.[2] [1980s+] (drugs) Mexican black tar heroin. [BOOGER n.[1]; i.e. its texture]

bugger v.[1] [late 18C+] synon. for damn; thus to curse.

bugger v.[2] [1910s+] to make a mess of. [BUGGER UP]

bugger! excl. [late 19C+] synon. for DAMN!, also in phr. give/not give a bugger, bugger that etc (cf. BOTHERATION!; BUGGERATION)

bugger about/around v. [1920s+] 1 to wander around. 2 to mess about with. 3 to waste time, to stall, to be unhelpful.

4 to make someone's life miserable or in some way difficult (cf. ARSE ABOUT). [BUGGER v.[2]]

bugger all n. [1930s+] absolutely nothing.

buggeranto n. [early 18C] a male homosexual. [SE bugger + 'Spanish' sfx. -anto]

bugger around see BUGGER ABOUT.

bugger around on v. [1970s+] (Can.) to commit adultery, to be unfaithful. [ext. of BUGGER ABOUT]

buggeration! excl. [20C] a general excl. of annoyance (cf. BOTHERATION!).

bugger-chick n. [1980s+] (S.Afr.) 'the compliant girlfriend of an aggressively masculine man' (DSAE). [BUGGER n.[1] (4) + CHICK n.[4]]

buggered adj. [mid-19C+] synon. for damned. [BUGGER!]

buggered if I know phr. [20C] phr. in answer to a question, stating one's absolute ignorance.

buggered up adj. [1910s+] 1 of people, physically beaten or hurt. 2 of objects, broken, out of order. 3 of plans, ideas, schemes, ruined, aborted (cf. ARSED UP). [BUGGER UP]

bugger for phr. [1950s+] phr. denoting an enthusiast, an obsessive, e.g. a bugger for work. [BUGGER n.[1] (1)]

buggering adj. [late 17C+] a general negative adj. (cf. COCKSUCKING; CUNTING; FUCKING; MOTHERFUCKING adj.; PISSING; SHITTING; SODDING). [BUGGER!]

bugger it! excl. [late 19C+] an excl. of annoyance, esp. when an inanimate object or a previously determined plan of action fails to function as required. [BUGGER! excl.]

buggerize about v. [1930s+] (Aus.) 1 to wander around. 2 to mess about with. 3 to waste time, to stall, to be unhelpful. 4 to make someone's life miserable or in some way difficult. [BUGGER ABOUT]

buggerlug v. [late 19C] to waste time on trivial activities (cf. BUGGER ABOUT).

buggerlugs n. [late 19C+] (orig. RN) 1 a general term of (affectionate) address, usu. among men (cf. FLABBY-KNACKERS; FUCK-KNUCKLE; HORROR-BOLLOCKS). 2 brushed back 'wings' of hair (cf. BUGGER'S GRIPS). [SE bugger + LUG n.[1]; lit. 'sodomite ears']

bugger me! excl. [late 19C+] a general excl. of surprise, annoyance, alarm.

bugger me dead! phr. [20C] (Aus.) a general excl. of surprise, annoyance, alarm. [ext. of BUGGER ME!]

bugger off v. [1920s+] to go away, esp. in imper. bugger off! go away (cf. FUCK OFF!).

bugger off! excl. [1920s+] a general excl. of disbelief in or dismissal of an idea or statement.

bugger one's hand, to phr. [1990s] to masturbate.

buggeroo n. [1940s+] an eccentric person, a 'character'. [BUGGER n.[1] (1) + sfx. -EROO + ? pun on BUCKEROO]

bugger's grips n. [20C] (orig. RN) the brushed back 'wings' of hair that adorn the temples of many upper class Englishmen. Coarse rumour imputes these as the handholds for those who are positioning such partners ready for anal penetration (cf. FAG TAG; FAIRY LOOP; FRUIT LOOP n.[1]). [SE bugger + grips. Note tailor's jargon bugger-bafflers, the side vents on a man's jacket]

bugger's woods n. [20C] an out of the way place, an unimportant place. [SAmE boogerman, bogeyman; he is supposed to live there]

bugger up v. [1920s+] 1 to make a mess of, to blunder. 2 to hurt, to injure (cf. ARSE UP). [note Papua New Guinea Tok Pisin bagarap, used as all-purpose neg., e.g. no good, broken]

buggery see BOOGERY.

buggery billet n. [1990s] a prison. [the prevalence of homosexuality in prison life]

bugger you! excl. [late 19C+] a vehement excl. expressing personal antagonism.

bugging n.[1] [late 17C] the taking of bribes by bailiffs and other court officials (cf. BUG THE WRIT). [BUG v.[1] (1)]

bugging n.[2] **1** [20C] (US) going crazy, suffering mental stress. **2** [1980s+] (US campus) acting in a foolish manner. **3** [1980s+] (US campus) asking someone to do something silly or foolish. **4** [1990s] (US teen) feeling stupid. [BUG v.[5]]

buggins' turn n. [20C] a sinecure that comes to all members of a committee, board of directors etc, as long as they remain members of that group and, in due course, inevitably take their turn at a task; the antithesis of promotion by merit. [proper name *Buggins*, used as a stereotype for a time-serving mediocrity]

buggy n. **1** [1920s+] (orig. US) a car. **2** [1930s] (US) a wheel-barrow. [the orig. SE *gasoline buggy*. The earlier *buggy* was a light one-horse (sometimes two-horse) vehicle, for one or two people]

buggy adj.[1] [19C] (US) unstable, insane. [BUGS]

buggy adj.[2] [19C] (US) infested with lice. [SE *bug*]

bughead n. [mid-19C+] a fool, a simpleton. [BUG n.[4] (1) + sfx. -HEAD (1)]

bugher n. [17C–early 19C] a little, yelping dog (cf. BUFE; BUFFER n.[1]). [echoic of its bark]

bughouse n. **1** [mid-19C+] (US) a vermin-infested lodging house (cf. CHINCH HOUSE; FLEABAG; FLEA BOX; FLEA TRAP; LOUSE CAGE; LOUSE TRAP n.[2]; SCRATCH HOUSE). **2** [late 19C+] (US) a prison. **3** [late 19C+] a hospital, esp. a lunatic asylum; thus *bughouse fable*, an exaggerated story. **4** [1960s+] (S.Afr.) a run-down, dirty, third-rate cinema (cf. FLEAPIT). [SE *bug + house*]

bughouse adj. [late 19C+] (US) insane, crazy. [BUGHOUSE n. (3)]

bughouse square n. [20C] (US) any centre of urban life, typically Union Square, New York City, or Washington Square, Chicago, where tramps, vagrants, the more or less deranged and any other eccentrics gather. [BUGHOUSE n. (1) + SE *square*]

bug-hunter n.[1] [late 18C–early 19C] an upholsterer. [SE *bug*; they dislodge the insects as they repair the furniture]

bug-hunter n.[2] [19C] a street thief who specializes in snatching (drunken) men's jewellery; thus *bug–hunting*, robbing or cheating drunks, esp. after dark. [BUG n.[4] (1)+ SE *hunter*; also a pun on schoolboy *bug-hunter*, a naturalist]

bug hut/hutch n. [1930s+] a tawdry, run-down cinema (cf. FLEAPIT).

bug in one's ear phr. [19C] (US) a friendly warning (cf. HAVE A FLEA IN ONE'S EAR). [SE *bug*]

bug juice/poison n. (US) **1** [late 19C+] illicitly distilled whisky; thus any form of alcohol, esp. cheap and appealing to alcoholics. **2** [1940s+] (prison) a depressant drug used for controlling violent or non-cooperative prisoners. **3** [1940s+] a soft drink. **4** [1940s+] petrol. **5** [1940s+] a mix of saliva and tobacco juice that forms the residue or 'dottle' in a pipe. **6** [1940s+] insecticide. [BUG n.[4] (1) + SE *juice*. Orig. the Schlechter whisky drunk by the Pennsylvania Dutch, cheap and second-rate. Subsequently generic for any bad whisky]

bugle n.[1] **1** [early 19C+] the nose; thus *blow one's bugle*, blow one's nose, *on the bugle*, smelly (cf. FOGHORN; HONKER n.[1]; HOOTER n.[3]; HORN n.[1]; PASTE-HORN; POST-HORN; TRUMPET). **2** [late 19C] a loud voice. **3** [1990s] (drugs) cocaine.

bugle n.[2] [1980s+] (Irish) an erection. [play on HORN n.[2]]

bugle duster n. [1960s+] a handkerchief. [BUGLE n.[1] (1) + SE *duster*]

bug off! excl. [20C] euph. for BUGGER OFF! [abbr.]

bugology n. [mid-19C–1920s] (US campus) biology, entomology. [SE *bug* + sfx. *-ology*]

bug on v. [1990s] (US teen) to aggravate. [BUG v.[2] (2)]

bug out v.[1] [1950s+] (US) to leave, to run away. [BUG v.[3]]

bug out v.[2] **1** [1970s+] to go insane. **2** [1970s+] to subject to psychotherapy. **3** [1990s] to lose one's temper. [BUG v.[5]]

bug over v. [19C] to hand over. [BUG v.[1] (2) + SE *over*]

bug pass n. [20C] (Can. prison) a prisoner so deranged as to be longer responsible for their actions. [BUG v.[5] + SE *pass*; i.e. he 'passes' the rules]

bug poison see BUG JUICE.

bug rake n. [1930s+] (juv.) a comb (cf. CRUMB-CATCHER n.[1]; RAKER n.[2]). [SE *bug + rake*]

bugs adj. [1920s+] (orig. US) crazy, eccentric. [HAVE BUGS IN THE HEAD]

bug's age n. [1930s] (US) a very long time (cf. IN A COON'S AGE). [SE *bug + age*]

Bugs Bunny n. [1950s+] (Aus.) money. [rhy. sl., ult. f. Warner Bros. character *Bugs Bunny*, created 1940, f. BUGS + SE *bunny*]

bugshit adj. [1970s+] (US) crazy, eccentric (cf. APESHIT). [BUGS + DIPSHIT]

bugsy adj. [1920s+] (orig. US) eccentric. [BUGS + sfx. *-y*; thus the nickname of gangster Benjamin 'Bugsy' Siegel (1906–47), New York hoodlum and the pioneer of Las Vegas]

bug the writ, to phr. [late 17C–19C] of a bailiff or other court officer, to postpone handing out a writ, having been given a suitable bribe. [BUG v.[1] + SE *writ*]

bug trap n. (US) **1** [1920s] a verminous lodging house. **2** [1960s] a bed. [SE (*bed*) *bug + trap*]

bug under the chip phr. [19C] (US) an ulterior motive, something underhand, done behind one's back. [SE *bug + chip*; the image of an insect hiding beneath a piece of wood]

bug up v.[1] [1940s] (US) to ruin, to spoil. [BUGGER UP]

bug up v.[1] [1950s+] to make nervous. [PUT THE BUG ON]

buguyaga n. [1950s+] (W.I. Rasta) a sloppy, dirty person, e.g. a vagrant. [SE *bugaboo*/Carib.E. *bugo-bugo*, rough and crusty + Ewe *yakayaka*, slovenly ? + Hausa *buguzunzumi*, a big, fat, sloppy person]

bug-walk n. **1** [mid-19C–early 20C] a bed. **2** [late 19C–1910s] the parting of the hair. [SE *bug + walk*. Note milit. jargon *bug-run*, a parting]

bug work n. [1930s+] clandestine surveillance operations. [BUG v.[4]]

buhtuh see BHUTTU.

buick v. [1960s+] (US) to vomit (cf. HUGHIE; RALPH v.; RIDE THE BUICK). [echoic]

build n. [mid–late 19C] the cut or style of one's clothes.

build v. [20C] (orig. Aus.) to prepare, food, drink, a marijuana cigarette etc.

build a log cabin, to phr. [1990s] (orig. US campus) to defecate. [LOG n.[4] + pun on SE]

build a sconce, to phr. [18C] to run up a large bill at a tavern or inn, esp. when one has no intention of paying it. [Oxford University jargon *sconce*, a fine of a tankard of ale imposed by undergraduates on each other for various small misdemeanours. Note the *OED* prefers to link the phr. to SE *sconce*, a small fort or earthwork, but this lacks any drinking ref.]

build a spliff, to phr. [1980s+] to roll a cannabis cigarette. [BUILD v. + SPLIFF]

builder's bum n. [1980s+] the crevice between a man's buttocks that is revealed when he bends forward and, if wearing low-cut trousers, the waist is forced downwards (cf. SMILE n.[2]; WORKING-MAN'S SMILE). [SE *builder* + BUM n.[2]; such a sight is traditionally allied to a builder's low-slung trousers]

builder-upper n. [1930s+] (orig. US) a promoter, a publicity man, a morale booster.

build pigpens v. [20C] (US) to deceive, esp. for a merchant to cheat a customer. [the practice of woodcutters who pile the wood on their carts in the shape of a pigpen; thus making the pile, which is hollow, appear larger than it is]

build the fence, to *phr.* [19C] (US) to marry, usu. after the bride is already pregnant. [*phr. plant the corn before you build the fence*, to act prematurely]

build-up *n.* [1920s+] (orig. US) preparation, esp. an accumulation of favourable publicity designed to popularize a person, product etc.

build up *v.* [late 19C] (Und.) to dress up in one's best clothes in order to present a respectable, if fraudulent, image.

built *adj.* [late 19C+] (US) **1** of a man, well muscled, poss. referring spec. to his penis. **2** of a woman, attractive and with a noticeably good figure.

built for comfort *phr.* [20C] **1** of a man, overweight, fat. **2** of a woman, agreeably plump.

built like a brick shithouse *phr.* [1920s+] (orig. US) describing a very strong, muscled man, who resembles a squat, four-square, solid edifice, often euphemized as 'schoolhouse', 'outhouse' etc. [SHITHOUSE n. (1)]

built like a tripod *phr.* [1990s] (US) having a large penis (cf. THIRD LEG).

buke *v.* [20C] (US) to sodomize. [abbr. SE *rebuke*, the image is one of punishment]

bukra *see* BOOKRA.

bulbs *n.* [1990s] the testicles. [resemblance]

bulchin/bulkin/bull chin *n.* [late 18C] a term of endearment to a child, usu. a chubby one, or as a term of contempt to any male. [SE *bulchin*, a bull-calf]

bulge *n.* [19C+] (US) an advantage, esp. as *get the bulge on*, to get an advantage over someone. [SE *bulge*, a protuberance]

bulge *v.* [mid-19C] (US) to make one rush off. [lit. to push one out]

bulger *n.* [mid-19C+] something very important of its type. [SE *bulge*, a protuberance]

bulger *adj.* [mid-19C+] large (cf. BUSTER n.²).

bulk/bulker *n.* [late 17C–mid-19C] (Und.) a thief's, esp. a pickpocket's accomplice who jostles the victim while their pocket is picked. [? SE *bulk*, a large lump; thus the image of this human 'lump' pushing one around]

bulk *adj.* [1970s+] (Aus.) many, lots. [? SE *bulk buying*]

bulk and file *n.* [late 17C–18C] (Und.) a pickpocket and their assistant; one jostles the victim, the other picks the pocket (cf. BULK n.; BUTTOCK AND FILE). [BULK n. + FILE n. (1)]

bulker *n.*¹ [late 17C] a poor prostitute who is forced to sleep in the streets. [SE *bulk*, a heap, on which she lies]

bulker *n.*² *see* BULK n.

bulkin *see* BULCHIN.

bulk-monger *n.* [18C] a prostitute who consorts with thieves, esp. pickpockets. [BULK n. + sfx. -*monger*]

bulky *n.* **1** [19C] (Scots) a policeman. **2** [1920s+] (Ulster) a member of the Royal Ulster Constabulary; thus the *bulkies*, the RUC. [SE *bulky*, sizeable, ? + 17C def. as pompous, self-important]

bull *n.*¹ [mid-17C–early 19C] a blunder, a self-contradictory proposition, esp. that which is made by an Irishman. [Grose (1785) posits an eponym, one Obadiah *Bull*, 'a blundering lawyer of London, who lived in the reign of Henry VII', but he appears to have no actual substance. The link to Ireland is simply another e.g. of derog. stereotyping; the term's uses predates any such link by many years]

bull *n.*² [late 17C–late 18C] false hair, worn by a woman (cf. BULL-HEAD n.²; BULL-TOUR). [? its resemblance to the hair between a bull's horns]

bull *n.*³ **1** [18C–early 19C] 5 shillings, a crown (25p). **2** [1910s–20s] a counterfeit coin. [BULL'S EYE]

bull *n.*⁴ [mid-19C] (Aus.) 75 strokes of the lash (cf. BOB n.⁵).

[BULL n.³; different numbers of lashes were named for different values of coin]

bull *n.*⁵ **1** [mid-19C] (US) an ox. **2** [1920s–30s] (US) a buffalo nickel (cf. BULL-HEAD n.³). [(2) the engraving on the coin]

bull *n.*⁶ [mid-19C–1920s] (US) an Englishman (cf. JUMBLE n.²). [JOHN BULL n.¹]

bull *n.*⁷ [mid-19C+] any form of prison meat. [orig. UK but by 20C mainly US]

bull *n.*⁸ [late 19C] (US) a railway locomotive (cf. BULLGINE). [i.e. its strength]

bull *n.*⁹ [late 19C–1900s] a second brew of tea, the once-used leaves are left in the pot and a new kettleful of boiling water poured over them (cf. BULL THE TEA). [SE *bull*, a drink made by putting water into an empty spirit cask, or over a sugar-mat, to catch some of the flavour]

bull *n.*¹⁰ **1** [late 19C+] (orig. US) a policeman. **2** [20C] (US Und.) a veteran, long-term convict. [Ger. sl. *Bulle*, policeman or poss. Sp. sl. *bul*, policeman; orig. US but Aus./UK Black use late 20C]

bull/buller/buller-man *n.*¹¹ [20C] (W.I.) a male homosexual. [SE *bull*]

bull *n.*¹² **1** [1910s+] (orig. US) lies, flattery, insincere talk of any kind. **2** [1940s+] (orig. milit.) unnecessary routine or discipline. [euph. for BULLSHIT n.]

bull *n.*¹³ [1930s+] (poker) an ace. [BULLET n.¹ (1)]

bull *n.*¹⁴ [1950s+] (Aus.) a casual wharf labourer who is given preferential treatment by the foreman; thus *bull system*, employment practices on the docks whereby the men line up for work every morning and the foremen pick them for a day's work.

bull *n.*¹⁵ **1** [1960s+] a womanizer, a successful philanderer (cf. STUD n.¹). **2** [1960s+] an aggressively masculine lesbian (cf. BULL-DYKE). **3** [1960s–70s] (US) a macho male homosexual. [the image of the animal]

bull *adj.* [late 19C–1940s] (US) large, powerful, authoritative. [the image of the animal]

bull *v.*¹ **1** [16C–17C] to mock, to tease. **2** [17C–18C] to cheat, to defraud. **3** [18C+] to have sexual intercourse. **4** [late 19C+] (US) to act violently, aggressively. [SE *bully*]

bull *v.*² [mid-19C–1930s] (US campus) to fail an examination. [BULL n.¹]

bull *v.*³ [late 19C+] (Aus.) to adulterate, to weaken; thus *bulled grog*, diluted liquor. [note RN jargon *bull the barrel/cask*, to pour water into an empty rum barrel; the resulting (weakly alcoholic) liquid can be drunk]

bull *v.*⁴ **1** [20C] (US) to chat, to gossip. **2** [1940s+] (Aus.) to brag, to boast. [abbr. BULLSHIT v.]

bull/bull something through *v.*⁵ [20C] (orig. US) to accomplish through brawn rather than brains.

bull *v.*⁶ [1980s+] (W.I.) to bugger, to pursue a gay sex-life. [the animal's image as a stud]

bullabananka *see* BULLAMAKANKA.

bulladen *n.* [1960s] (US Black) a policeman. [BULL n.¹⁰ (1)]

bullamakanka/bullabananka/bullamanka *n.* [1950s+] (Aus.) an imaginary place, supposedly far from any civilization (cf. OODNAGALAHBI; WOOP WOOP). [? Fiji *bullamacow*, bullybeef]

bull and cow *n.* [mid-19C+] a row, an argument. [rhy. sl.]

bull-ants *n.* [1920s–30s] (Aus.) trousers. [rhy. sl. *bull-ants* = pants]

bullaphants *adj.* [20C] (Irish) drunk. [rhy. sl. var. on ELEPHANT'S TRUNK]

bull artist *n.* [1960s+] a braggart, a boaster (cf. BULL MERCHANT; BULLSHIPPER; BULLSHIT ARTIST; BULLSHITTER; BULL SHOOTER; BULL SLINGER; BULL THROWER; SHITTER n.²). [BULL n.¹¹ + ARTIST n.¹]

bull-beef *n.* [16C+] meat, esp. beef.

bull-beef *adj.* [18C] fierce, intolerant, macho.

bull bitch n.[1] [1930s–50s] (US) something unimaginably bad. [BULL adj. + BITCH n.[1] (3)]

bull bitch n.[2] [1960s+] (US) a lesbian. [BULL adj. + BITCH n.[1] (10)]

bull-bucka/-bucker n. [1940s+] (W.I.) a thug, a bully, an aggressive man. [SE *bull* + 18C US dial. *buck*, to butt; thus one who thinks he is strong enough to butt a bull or ? BULL adj. + BACKRA]

bull butter n. [late 19C] (US) margarine. [its innate fakeness + coarse ref. to bull semen]

bull calf n. [late 16C–early 19C] a great, hulking, undisciplined oaf.

bull camp n. [1920s–30s] (US) a camp of outdoor workers. e.g. on an oil pipeline. [BULL adj.]

bull chin see BULCHIN.

bull come/gism n. [1940s+] cream gravy (cf. BULL FUCK). [SE *bull* + COME n.[1] (2)/JISM]

bull con n. [late 19C+] (US) specious, deceitful talk. [BULLSHIT n. + CON n.[3] (1)]

bullcorn n. [20C] (US) euph. for BULLSHIT n.

bullcrap n. [1950s+] any form of specious talk, nonsense, rubbish, lies, flattery. [BULLSHIT n. + CRAP n.[3] (2)]

bull-dag n. [1940s–60s] a masculine lesbian. [abbr. BULL-DAGGER]

bull-dagger/dagger n. [1940s–60s] a masculine lesbian; thus *bull-dagging*, engaging in lesbian love-making. [BULL-DYKE]

bull dicky/dinky n. [1940s+] (US) any form of specious talk, nonsense, rubbish, lies, flattery. [BULLSHIT n. + DICKY n.[7] (2)/DINGUS]

bull-dike see BULL-DYKE.

bull-diker see BULL-DYKER.

bull dinky see BULL DICKY.

bulldog n.[1] **1** [late 17C–early 19C] a sheriff's officer. **2** [early 19C] (US) a watchman. **3** [1940s] (US) a policeman. [Note Oxbridge jargon *bulldog*, an assistant to the Proctors, those dons charged with maintaining university discipline]

bulldog n.[2] [late 18C] a pistol (cf. BARKER n.[1]). [it 'growls']

bulldog n.[3] [early 19C] a sugar-loaf. [? both are squat, solid shapes]

bulldog v. [20C] (US prison) to harass, whether verbally or physically.

bulldogger n. [1980s+] (US Black) a violent person. [SE *bulldog*]

bulldose/bulldoze n. [mid–late 19C] (US) a severe flogging. [a *dose* of the *bull*-whip]

bulldose/bulldoze v. **1** [late 19C] to flog, to beat severely. **2** [late 19C+] to intimidate, to coerce, to force through violence. [BULLDOSE n.]

bulldoser/bulldozer n. **1** [19C] (US) a domineering woman. **2** [late 19C+] (US) a bully, a thug. [BULLDOSE/BULLDOZE]

bull-dragging adj. [20C] (Irish) tedious, laborious.

bull-driver n. [20C] (US) a peasant, a farmer.

bull durham! excl. [20C] (US) euph. for BULLSHIT n. [brand-name of rolling tobacco]

bulldust n. [1960s+] (Aus.) euph. for BULLSHIT n.; thus *bull-dust artist*, BULLSHIT ARTIST, *bullduster*, BULLSHITTER. [note DUST n.[3] (1)]

bull-dyke/-dike n. [1920s+] (orig. US) a masculine lesbian. usu. an unpleasant, excessively man-hating one (cf. BUMPER n.[6]). [SE *bull*; BULL adj. + DYKE]

bulldyke v. [1930s+] (orig. US) to engage in lesbian activities. [BULL-DYKE]

bull-dyker/-diker n. [1920s] (orig. US) a masculine lesbian (cf. BULL-DAGGER). [BULLDYKE]

buller n.[1] see BULL n.[11].

buller n.[2] [1980s+] (Black) a male homosexual. [BULL n.[15] (3)]

buller-man see BULL n.[11].

bullet n.[1] **1** [early 19C+] (poker) an ace, esp. in phr. *two bullets and a bragger*, a knave or a nine; thus (in brag) a winning hand. **2** [late 19C–1920s] (US) $1. **3** [1960s+] (US prison) a one-year sentence. **4** [1960s+] (drugs) a single capsule of a drug. **5** [1970s+] (N.Z. drugs) a portion of cannabis wrapped in silver foil. [the image is of a single bullet]

bullet n.[2] **1** [mid–19C+] a notice of dismissal; thus *get the bullet*, to be dismissed, *shake the bullet (at)*, to threaten with dismissal. **2** [1960s] (US) an ejaculation of semen (cf. SHOOT v.[3]).

bullet n.[3] [1970s+] (US campus) the grade of B. [initial letters]

bullet n.[4] [1980s+] **1** (drugs) isobutyl nitrite. **2** (N.Z. drugs) cooking foil, as used in heating and smoking heroin. [ety. unknown]

bullet bolt n. [1980s+] (drugs) isobutyl nitrite. [BULLET n.[4] (1) + BOLT n.[3]]

bullet-head n. [17C–18C] a fool, a dullard; thus *bullet-headed*, foolish. [SE *bullet* + sfx. -HEAD (1); the hardness of the projectile]

bullet/tinny house n. [1970s+] (N.Z. drugs) a house or flat used for cannabis dealing. [BULLET n.[1] (5)/TINNIE n.[2] + SE *house*]

bullet-proof adj. [1920s+] immune, irrefutable.

bullets n. **1** [19C] the testicles. **2** [1920s+] beans. **3** [1920s+] peas. [the shape]

bullets and blisters! excl. [mid–late 19C] (US) a mild oath.

bullfeathers n. [1920s+] (US) rubbish, nonsense (cf. HORSEFEATHERS). [BULLSHIT n. + SE *feathers*]

bullfest n. [1910s–40s] a group, usu. of men, sitting around gossiping (cf. BLABFEST; BULL SESSION). [BULLSHIT n. + sfx. -FEST]

bull fever n. [late 19C+] nervousness in the face of an unknown or new situation (cf. BUCK FEVER).

bull fiddle n. **1** [late 19C+] (US) the double-bass. **2** [20C] a stringed instrument made from a tin can; thus *bull-fiddle voice*, a deep bass voice. [BULL adj. + SE *fiddle*]

bullfinch n. [17C–18C] a fool, a simpleton. [? the bird's willingness to be trained to sing]

bull-flesh n. [19C] swagger, boastfulness, arrogance. [the innate bulkiness of the animal]

bull-fodder n. [1910s+] (orig. Aus.) rubbish, nonsense, lies. [euph. for BULLSHIT n.]

bull fuck n. [1940s+] (US) **1** cream gravy. **2** custard. **3** stew thickened with flour. [SE *bull* + FUCK n.[1], in fig. meaning of semen (cf. GRAVY n.[1])]

bull gang n. **1** [20C] (US) a team of manual labourers. **2** [1950s+] (W.I.) plantation labourers who perform odd jobs. [SE *bull*, generic for tough, masculine + *gang*]

bullgine n. [19C] a railway locomotive. [BULL n.[8] + SE (en)*gine*]

bull gism see BULL COME.

bull-goose n. [20C] (US) the leader, the boss. [SE *bull-goose*, the goose which maintains order among the rest of the flock]

bull gravy n. [1940s+] cream gravy. [pun on synon. BULL FUCK]

bull-head n.[1] [early 17C–mid-19C] a fool (cf. BUFFLEHEAD). [SE *bull* + sfx. -HEAD (1); the stolidity of a bull]

bull-head n.[2] [17C] a mass of curled or frizzled hair worn over the forehead by a woman (cf. BULL n.[2]; BULL-TOUR). [the resemblance of the style to a bull's matted 'forelocks']

bull-head n.[3] [1940s] (US) a 'buffalo' nickel (cf. BULL n.[5]; BULL MOOSE n.[2]). [it carried a bull's head on one face]

bullhead clap n. [1940s–50s] (US) extremely severe gonorrhoea. [SE *bullhead* used as an intensifier + CLAP n.]

bullhead luck n. [late 19C] very good luck. [SE *bullhead* used as an intensifier + SE *luck*]

bull hockey n. [1960s+] (US) any form of specious talk, lies, flattery, insincerity, nonsense etc (cf. BULLSHIT). [SE *bull* + HOCKIE]

bull horrors n.[1] [1920s–30s] (US, tramp) irrational fear of the police. [BULL n.[10] (1) + HORRORS n. (3)]

bull horrors n.[2] [1950s] (US) delirium tremens. [BULL adj. + HORRORS n. (3)]

bullia capital n. [1990s] (drugs) crack cocaine. [ety. unknown]

bullion n.[1] [19C] soup. [Fr. *bouillon*]

bullion/bullyon n.[2] [1980s+] (drugs) **1** marijuana. **2** crack cocaine. [? its value]

bullish adj. [late 19C+] enthusiastic, keen. [Stock Exchange jargon *bull*, one who trades on the premise of a rising market]

bullissimo adj. [mid-19C] (US) extremely good, absolutely excellent. [BULLY adj. + sfx. *-issimo*]

bullivant n. [late 19C–1930s] a large, clumsy person. [SE *bull* + *elephant*]

bull-jive v. [1970s+] (US Black) to tease, to hoax (cf. BULLSHIT v.). [BULLSHIT v. + JIVE v.[1] (3)]

bull luck n. [late 19C–1910s] (US) very good luck. [BULL adj. + SE *luck*]

bull merchant n. [1910s–50s] (US) one who speaks insincerely (cf. BULL ARTIST). [BULLSHIT n. + MERCHANT]

bull money n. [late 19C] money handed over to a potentially blackmailing discoverer by someone who has been caught *in flagrante delicto* in the open air. [BULL v.[1] (3) + SE *money*]

bull moose n.[1] [20C] the leader, the boss (cf. BULL-GOOSE).

bull moose n.[2] [20C] (US) 5 cents, a nickel (cf. BULL-HEAD n.[3]).

bull muffin n. [1980s] (US) specious talk, nonsense, rubbish, insincerity (cf. BULLSHIT n.). [SE *bull* + MEADOW MUFFIN]

bullo n. [1930s+] (Aus./US) nonsense, rubbish. [BULLSHIT n. + sfx. *-o*]

bullock n. [19C+] (Aus.) a countryman, a bushman.

bullock v. **1** [early 18C–1900s] to bully, to intimidate. **2** [late 19C+] (Aus.) to perform heavy manual labour. **3** [late 19C+] (Aus.) to push through.

bullock-and-file n. [17C–late 19C] a prostitute and pick-pocket team (cf. BUTTOCK AND FILE). [? BULK AND FILE + BUTTOCK AND FILE, but poss. no more than misreading]

bullocker n. [1920s+] (Aus.) **1** a bullock-driver. **2** a foreman, a boss.

bullock-puncher n. [mid-19C+] (Aus.) a bullock-driver. [on model of US *cow-puncher*]

bullock's blood n. [1920s–70s] a mixture of strong beer and rum.

bullock's eye n. [19C] port. [the colour]

bullock's heart n. [late 19C] the breaking of wind. [rhy. sl.]

bullock's horn n. [late 19C–1900s] pawn. [rhy. sl.]

bullock's liver n. [late 19C] a river. [rhy. sl.]

bullock wagon n. [1920s+] (Aus.) nonsense, rubbish. [BULLSHIT n.]

bullocky n. [mid-19C+] (Aus./N.Z.) **1** a bullock-driver. **2** the language or jargon of bullock-drivers.

bullocky's delight/joy n. [20C] (Aus.) treacle, golden syrup (cf. COCKY'S DELIGHT; KIDMAN'S BLOOD MIXTURE; SHEARER'S JOY; WHALER'S DELIGHT). [BULLOCKY n. (1) + SE *delight/joy*]

bull of the woods n. [19C] (US) the boss, the leader, or someone who poses as such. [logging jargon *bull of the woods*, the foreman]

bullox n. [1930s+] (US) an unpleasant person. [var. on BOLLIX n.]

bull party n. [19C–1900s] a men-only party (cf. STAG PARTY). [SE *bull* + *party*]

bullpen n. (US) **1** [early 19C+] (Und.) a holding cell surrounded by steel mesh or an open 'cage' made of steel bars (orig. of wooden bars). **2** [mid-19C–1930s] a small house or room used by a prostitute; thus a cheap brothel. **3** [late 19C+] (police) the holding cage in a precinct house. **4** [20C] any type of enclosed waiting area. **5** [1930s+] any enclosure (college

dormitory, factory changing room etc) where a group of men associate, gossip etc.

bull piss n. [20C] (US) very low quality, cheap liquor. [SE *bull* + PISS n. (1)]

bull point n. [mid-19C+] (US) a point of advantage or superiority. [the image of a bull's strength]

bull pucky/puckey n. [1970s+] (US) any form of specious talk, insincerity, flattery, lies (cf. BULLSHIT). [SE *bull* + PUCKEY]

bull-puncher n. [late 19C] (US) the driver of an ox-team (cf. BULL-PUSHER; COW-PUNCHER).

bull pup n. [mid-late 19C] (US) a pistol (cf. BARKER n.[1]; BULLDOG n.[2]). [it 'barks' or 'growls']

bull-pusher n. [late 19C] (US) the driver of an ox-team (cf. BULL-PUNCHER).

bull-ring n. [20C] a military training ground. [ext. of SE. use; orig. that sited at Étaples, northern France, the British Army training centre during WW1]

bull-roar n. [1960s+] (US) any form of specious talk, insincerity, flattery, lies. [euph. for BULLSHIT n.]

bulls n. [1940s+] (Aus.) (US) any form of specious talk, insincerity, flattery, lies (cf. BULL'S WOOL n.[2]). [euph. for BULLSHIT n.]

bull scare n. [1940s–50s] (US Black) an aggressive, menacing manner that is no more than a bluff. [BULLSHIT n. + SE *scare*]

bull session n. [1920s+] (US) usu. of men, a period of sitting around, gossiping. [BULLSHIT v. + SE *session*]

bull's eye n.[1] **1** [17C–early 19C] a crown or 5-shilling (25p) piece (cf. WORK THE BULLS). **2** [early–mid-19C] a large, round sweet. **3** [mid-19C] a bull's-eye lantern. **4** [late 19C] a thick, old-fashioned watch (cf. TURNIP n.[1]). [? the size and shape. (2) later use is SE]

bull's eye n.[2] [late 17C] the vagina (cf. BEST IN CHRISTENDOM). [joc. euph. coined by John Wilmot, Earl of Rochester (1647–80]

bull's eye n.[3] [20C] £50. [SE *bullseye*, the centre of the darts-board, worth 50 points]

bull's-eye day n. [1920s+] (Irish) Wednesday, the day on which British Army pensions are disbursed. [one scores a financial *bull's eye*]

bull-moose see MOOSE n.[2].

bullsh n. [1910s+] (Aus.) rubbish. [abbr. BULLSHIT n.]

bull-shiner n. [1920s] (US) a policeman's truncheon. [? the shininess of the wood or the BULL n.[10] (1), which gives one a SHINER]

bullshipper n. [1910s+] a braggart, a liar (cf. BULL ARTIST). [euph. for BULLSHITTER]

bullshit n. [1910s+] rubbish, nonsense, lies (cf. BULL n.[12]). [SE *bull* + SHIT n.[1]]

bullshit adj. [1980s+] (US campus) **1** very angry, furious. **2** drunk, intoxicated by a drug. [fig. uses of BULLSHIT n.]

bullshit v. [1920s+] **1** to tell lies, to tease, to confuse with false information. **2** to gossip, to chatter inconsequentially. [BULLSHIT n.]

bullshit! excl. [1910s+] (orig. US) rubbish! nonsense! [BULLSHIT n.]

bullshit artist n. [1960s+] anyone with a good line of persuasive, if insincere patter (cf. BULL ARTIST). [BULLSHIT + ARTIST n.[2]]

bullshitter n. [1910s+] (orig. Aus.) a braggart, a liar (cf. BULL ARTIST). [BULLSHIT n.]

bull shooter n. [1920s+] (US) a braggart, a liar (cf. BULL ARTIST). [BULLSHIT n. + SE *shooter*]

bull-shy adj. [20C] (US) timid, nervous. [agricultural jargon *bull-shy*, of a cow that is fearful of the bull]

bullskate v. [1940s] (US Black) to boast, to brag. [BULLSHIT v. + SKATE v. (2)]

bull slinger n. [1930s+] (US) a braggart, a liar (cf. BULL ARTIST). [BULLSHIT n. + SE *slinger*]

bull's look *n.* [1960s] (Irish) a hostile glare.

bull something through *see* BULL v.[5].

bull's wool *n.*[1] [1900s–40s] **1** second-hand, cheap or homemade clothes. **2** (US Black) stolen clothes. **3** (Aus.) a young man with a mop of bushy hair.

bull's wool *n.*[2] [1920s+] (Aus./N.Z.) any form of specious talk, lies, insincerity, rubbish. [euph. for BULLSHIT n.]

bull the tea, to *phr.* [20C] (N.Z.) to add soda to tea, which makes it more potent. [BULL n.[9] + SE *tea*]

bull thrower *n.* [1910s+] (US) a braggart, a liar (cf. BULL ARTIST). [BULLSHIT + SE *thrower*]

bull-tit *n.* [19C] (US) something superlatively good (cf. ROARER n.[3]). [? the idea of a bull that has added udders or tits (*see* TIT n.[1]), although note the neg. phr. *as much use as tits on a bull*]

bull-tour *n.* [early 18C] a mass of curled or frizzled hair worn over the forehead by a woman. [BULL-HEAD n.[2]]

bull trap *n.* [1930s+] (Aus.) a villain who impersonates a policeman and preys on couples in lover's lanes, extorting money from those who should not, for whatever reason, be there. [BULL n.[10] (1) + SE *trap*]

bullwash *n.* [1980s] (US) any form of specious talk, lies, nonsense, insincerity. [BULLSHIT n. ? + BUSHWA]

bull-week *see* CALF-WEEK.

bullwhack *v.* [mid–late 19C] (US) to drive an ox-team; thus *bull-whacker*, the driver. [SE *bull* + WHACK v.[1]]

bully *n.*[1] **1** [early 17C–1930s] a good fellow, a companion. **2** [late 17C–mid-18C] a pimp, a procurer. **3** [late 17C–mid-18C] a thug hired for purposes of violence or intimidation. **4** [late 17C–mid-18C] a braggart, a boaster. [? Du. *boel*, a lover of either sex. (1) post-18C use is mainly US]

bully *n.*[2] [19C] bully beef (pickled or tinned beef). [Fr. *boeuf boulli*, boiled beef]

bully *n.*[3] [20C] (Aus.) the *Sydney Bulletin*, a popular news magazine.

bully *adj.* [mid-19C+] (orig. UK but usu. US) excellent, first rate. [BULLY n. (2); the *locus classicus* is Theodore Roosevelt's remark, 'The White House is a bully pulpit' but the term, based in *bully*, a pimp, fits into the street-generated 'bad = good' category seen in BAD, WICKED etc. Note earlier use of *bully*, a good friend, fine fellow; thus Shakespeare *Midsummer Night's Dream* (1590), 'What saist thou, bully Bottom']

bully back *n.* [late 18C] a man hired by a brothel to act as a bouncer, strong-arm man, occasional lover or 'husband' of the madame or one of the prostitutes and a generally intimidating presence. [BULLY n.[1] (3) + SE *back*, to support, to back up]

bully back *v.* [late 18C] to be employed by a brothel as a bouncer or to be a generally intimidatory presence. [BULLY BACK n.]

bully beef *n.* [1950s+] (prison) a chief officer (cf. CORNED BEEF). [rhy. sl.]

bully-buck *n.* [18C] a thug who deliberately starts fights between others, so as to rob them in the confusion (cf. BULLY-COCK; VAMPER). [BULLY n.[1] (3) + BUCK n.[1] (1)]

bully-cock *n.* [late 18C] one who deliberately encourages quarrels so as to rob those who are engaged in the argument (cf. BULLY-BUCK). [BULLY n.[1] (3) + fig. use SE *cock*]

bully-fake *n.* [late 19C–1910s] a piece of luck. [BULLY adj. + FAKE n.[1] (1)]

bully-fake *adj.* [late 19C] lucky, advantageous. [BULLY-FAKE n.]

bully-fop *n.* [late 17C–18C] a brainless chatterer, a talkative bore. [BULLY n.[1] + *fop*]

bully for you! *excl.* [mid-19C+] (orig. US) well done! congratulations, usu. ironic/sarcastic use. [BULLY adj.]

bully huff/bully huff-cap *n.* [late 17C–late 18C] one who poses as a prostitute's husband then defrauds her client of his money by threats of violence or blackmail (cf. MURPHY n.[3]). [BULLY n.[1] (2) + HUFF n.[1] (1)]

bullyon *see* BULLION n.[2].

bullyrag *v.* [late 18C+] **1** to bully, to pressurize, to taunt (cf. BALLYRAG). **2** to cheat out of by intimidation. [BULLY n.[1] (3) + RAG v.[1] (1)]

bully-rock/-rook *n.* **1** [mid-17C–early 18C] a hired thug. **2** [late 17C–18C] a boon companion. [BULLY n.[1] (1), (3) + ROOK n.[1] (1)]

bully-ruffian *n.* [late 17C–18C] a highwayman who runs contrary to popular fantasies of gentlemanly robbers by shouting and swearing at his victims, in order to intimidate them further. [BULLY n.[1] (3) + SE *ruffian*]

bully-trap *n.* [late 17C–18C] **1** a card-sharp, a cheat. **2** a mild looking man, whose lack of overt aggression fools thugs into thinking that they can take advantage of him. [BULLY n.[1] (1) + SE *trap*]

bully-woolies *n.* [20C] (US) long underwear. [BULL'S WOOL n.[1]]

bum *n.*[1] [late 17C–early 18C] a bailiff. [? SE *bound*, bailiff (Blackstone, *Commentaries*, 1768) or physical proximity of the bailiff to those being arrested (Hotten, 1867); abbr. SE *bum-bailiff*, 'a bailliff of the meanest kind' (Johnson)]

bum *n.*[2] [late 18C+] the posterior, buttocks, anus, rectum. [ME than SE till late 18C; echoic of the smack of one's backside hitting a flat surface, and as such coined as early as 1387. The word is also allied to a variety of terms meaning protuberance or swelling, typically *bump*]

bum *n.*[3] **1** [mid-19C+] (US) a tramp, a vagrant. **2** [mid-19C+] (US) a term of abuse for anyone unpleasant. **3** [late 19C+] (boxing) a poor, incompetent fighter. **4** [1920s+] (US) a promiscuous woman. **5** [1930s+] (US) a fan or obsessive, usu. of a specified sport. **6** [1940s+] a semi-professional athlete who makes a living training others rather than entering high-grade competitions, e.g. *tennis bum, ski bum, surf bum*. [abbr. BUMMER n.[2]; (2), (3), (5,) (6) developments of (1). (4) pun on *bum*, tramp/TRAMP n.]

bum *n.*[4] [late 19C–1930s] a spree. [BUM v.[2]]

bum *n.*[5] [1980s+] (US drugs) the act of deliberately ruining, or attempting to ruin a drug experience via intimidation, ridicule etc. [abbr. BUMMER n.[3]]

bum *adj.* [late 19C+] **1** (orig. US) useless, second-rate, poor, inferior, dirty, ragged. **2** (orig. US) slightly ill, under the weather. **3** (US) depressed. [BUM n.[3] (2)]

bum *v.*[1] **1** [late 17C–18C] to arrest. **2** [19C] to serve with a summons. [BUM n.[1]]

bum *v.*[2] [mid-19C+] **1** to wander around. **2** to beg; thus *bum a fag*, ask for a cigarette. [BUM n.[3] (1)]

bum *v.*[3] [mid-19C+] (Irish/US) **1** to abuse. **2** to boast, to brag. [Irish *bommanach*, bragging, boastful]

bum *v.*[4] [1980s+] (US campus) to feel depressed. [BUM adj. (3)]

bum! *see* BUDUP!

bum a ride, to *phr.* [late 19C+] (US) to get a free ride. [BUM v.[2] (2)]

bumba/bumpa *n.* [20C] (US Black) the buttocks. [BUM n.[2]; but ? note BUMBO n.[1] (2)]

bum bacon *n.* [1990s] the labia (cf. KNICKER BACON). [BUM n.[2] + SE *bacon*]

bum bag *n.* [1950s+] (orig. skiing) a small bag or pouch, secured to a belt and worn around the waist (cf. ASS PACK). [BUM n.[2] + SE *bag*]

bumbags *n.* [mid-19C–1950s] trousers. [BUM n.[2] + SE *bags*]

bum-balls *n.* [19C] the testicles. [BUM n.[2] + SE *balls*]

bum bandit *n.* [1960s+] homosexual male; thus *bum-banditry*, homosexuality (cf. ARSE BANDIT). [BUM n.[2] + SE *bandit*]

bum-banger *n.* [1940s] (Aus.) a short jacket, just covering the buttocks (cf. ARSEHOLE-PERISHER). [BUM n.[2] + SE *banger*]

bum-bass n. [late 18C–19C] a 'cello.

bumbaste v. **1** [mid-16C–17C] to beat hard on the buttocks. **2** [18C–19C] to beat, to assault. [BUM n.² + SE *baste*, to thrash]

bumbazine/bombazine n. [mid-19C] (US) the buttocks. [? pun on BUM n.² + SE *bombasine*, 'a twilled or corded dress-material, composed of silk and worsted; sometimes also of cotton and worsted, or of worsted alone. In black the material is much used in mourning' (*OED*)]

bum-beating n. [early 17C] jostling. [BUM n.² + SE *beating*]

bum-beefed adj. [1960s] (US Und.) arrested on false charges, esp. after evidence (typically drugs) has been planted (see PLANT v.¹ (8)) on the defendant. [BUM adj. + BEEF n.² (3)]

bumbee work n. [20C] (Ulster) nonsense. [SE *bumble-bee* and its 'buzz']

bumbershoot/bumberella n. [19C+] (US) an umbrella. [joc. corruption]

bumble n. [mid-19C] a beadle; thus *bumble-crew*, a collective name for corporations, vestries and other official bodies. [*Mr Bumble* in Charles Dickens's *Oliver Twist* (1838)]

bumble v. [late 17C] to have sexual intercourse. [ext. of SE use ? + ref. to 'the birds and the bees']

bumblebee adj. [20C] (US) of a crop that has become dried up and stunted. [the crop has become so low that the saying has it that the bees can lie on their backs sucking the juice from the flowers or plants]

bumblebees n. [1970s+] (drugs) amphetamines (cf. A n.²). [? striped capsules of certain brands of the drug or f. their 'sting']

bumblebee whisky n. [mid-19C+] (US) especially potent whisky. [it 'stings']

bumblefuck n. [1980s+] (US campus) anywhere categorized as very far away (cf. B.F.E.). [var. on BUMFUCK, EGYPT]

bumble-puppy n. [mid-19C+] amateurish whist, and latterly bridge, the level typically played in family or friendly games. [SE *bumble-puppy*, an early form of bagatelle, usu. played in public houses, in which stone balls are rolled down a sloping board, which is pierced with numbered holes. This is based on an older 16C game, usu. played by women, *troule-in-madame* or *troll-madam*]

bumbo n.¹ [late 18C+] **1** the vagina (cf. BEARDED CLAM). **2** the buttocks, the anus. [BUM n.², but note Efik *mbumbu*, rotten, putrefied, decomposed; orig. W.I. use, where the term is also used to mean SE *alligator*; thus suggesting poss. *vagina dentata* imagery]

bumbo n.² **1** [late 18C+] a drink composed of brandy, sugar and water. **2** [1910s+] (Aus.) cheap (fortified) wine. [ety. unknown; ? (2) underpinned by BUM n.³ (1), its usual drinker]

bum-boat n. **1** [late 17C–early 18C] a scavenger's boat, used to pick up the debris of shipping disasters. **2** [mid-18C–mid-19C] a boat that brought provisions from land out to larger vessels anchored offshore. [BUM n.2 (1) + SE *boat*; the original role of such vessels was to collect human and other waste from boats at anchor; they also carried out vegetables etc to sell on board]

bumbo-/bombo-claat/-cloth n. [1950s+] (W.I.) **1** a sanitary towel. **2** a highly derog. term of abuse (cf. BLOOD CLAAT). [BUMBO n.¹ (1) + SE *cloth*]

bum-boozer n. [late 19C–1900s] a drunkard. [BUM n.³ (2) + BOOZER]

bumbosity n. [20C] (US) the buttocks (cf. BOMBOSITY). [artificially extended BUM n.²]

bum boy n. [19C+] a male homosexual (cf. BUMMER n.⁴; BUN BOY; BUTT BOY). **2** [20C] anyone regularly saddled with dirty jobs. **3** [20C] a toady, a sycophant (cf. ARSE-LICKER). [BUM n.² + SE *boy*]

bum-brusher n. [18C] a schoolmaster (cf. FLAYBOTTOMIST). [BUM n.² + SE *brush*, to thrash]

bumbud n. [1990s] (US Black teen) marijuana, a marijuana cigarette. [BUD n.³]

bum buddy n. [1990s] a homosexual (cf. BUM CHUM). [BUM n.² (1) + BUDDY n.]

bum card n. [mid-16C–early 17C] (gaming) a marked card. [fig. use of BUM n.² + SE *card*]

bum-charter n. [early 19C] (Und.) prison bread soaked in hot water. [ety. unknown]

bumchat v. [1950s+] (orig. W.I.) to make statements to a woman with the sole interest being in her seduction. [BUM n.² + SE *chat*]

bum chum n. **1** [1970s] (Aus.) an intimate friend. **2** [1990s] a male homosexual (cf. BUM BUDDY). [BUM n.² + CHUM n.¹]

bum clink n. [mid–late 19C] bad or second-rate beer (cf. CLINK n.³). [Midlands dial.]

bum-cooler n. [19C] a jacket (cf. ARSEHOLE-PERISHER). [BUM n.² + SE *cooler*]

Bum Court n. [mid–late 16C] the Ecclesiastical Court. [? BUM n.²; its members spent much time sitting down]

bum-creeper n. **1** [late 19C] one who walks with their back noticeably bent. **2** a sycophant, a creeper (cf. ARSE-LICKER). [BUM n.² + SE *creeper*]

bum-curtain n. [19C] a jacket (cf. ARSEHOLE-PERISHER). [BUM n.² + SE *curtain*]

bum deal n. [20C] (orig. US) a poor bargain, a mistaken agreement. [BUM adj. + SE *deal*]

bum-drops n. [1930s] hen's eggs (cf. HEN FRUIT). [BUM n.² + SE *drops*]

bumf n. [late 19C+] **1** paperwork. **2** lavatory paper. [abbr. BUMFODDER]

bumface n. [1960s+] a general term of disdain, usu. only used by children. [BUM n.² + SE *face*]

bum factory n. [1920s] (US) **1** a cheap hostel. **2** a mission. [BUM n.³ (1) + SE *factory*]

bum-faker n. [18C] a womanizer, a promiscuous man (cf. BUM-FIGHTER; BUM-RANGER; BUM-TICKLER; BUM-WORKER). [BUM n.² + FAKER n. (3)]

bum-feague/-feagle/-feg v. [late 16C–early 17C] to thrash, to beat severely. [BUM n.² + FEAGUE]

bumfest n. [1990s] a homosexual orgy (cf. BLABFEST). [BUM n.² + -FEST]

bum-fiddle n. [early 18C] the anus, esp. when it breaks wind (cf. ARS MUSICA). [BUM n.² + SE *fiddle*]

bum fiddle v. [17C–early 18C] to tickle. [BUM n.² + SE *fiddle*]

bum-fighter n. [early 18C] a womanizer, a whoremonger. [BUM n.² + SE *fighter*]

bum finger n. [20C] (US Und.) a false accusation or an unfair sentence (cf. BUM RAP). [BUM n.² + FINGER v.²]

bum-fluff n. **1** [late 19C+] the very light growth of hair on the face of a boy who is on the verge of needing to shave. **2** [1940s+] (Aus.) empty talk, nonsense. [BUM n.² + SE *fluff*]

bumflummux v. [early 19C] (US) to confound, to confuse. [BUM n.² + FLUMMOX v.¹]

bum-fodder n. [late 17C+] **1** lavatory paper (cf. BUM WAD; BUNG-FODDER). **2** [19C] trashy literature, only good for use as (1). **3** [1900s–10s] (US) tabloid newspapers. [BUM n.² + SE *fodder*]

bumfoozle see BAMBOOZLE.

bum-freezer n. [1930s+] a short jacket that stops short of covering the buttocks. orig. describing an Eton jacket, latterly the 'Italian' styles of 1950s and thence any short (men's) jacket (cf. ARSEHOLE-PERISHER; BARE-BUM). [BUM n.² + SE *freezer*]

bumfuck n. [1970s+] (US) an extremely unpleasant person. [BUMFUCK v.¹ (1)]

bumfuck adj. [1970s+] third-rate, nondescript. [BUMFUCK n.]

bumfuck v. (orig. US) **1** [mid-19C+] to sodomize. **2** [20C] to massage the prostate as a way of diagnosing and treating gonorrhoea. [BUM n.² + FUCK v.¹]

Bumfuck, Egypt *n.* [1970s+] (US milit./campus) a very distant place (cf. B.F.E.; BUMBLEFUCK). [BUMFUCK adj.]

bumfucker *n.* [20C] (orig. US) a sodomite, a pederast. [BUMFUCK n.]

bumfuddled *adj.* [20C] (US) confused, mixed up (cf. BAMBOOZLE). [BUM adj. + SE *fuddled*]

bumfuzzle *v.* [20C] (US) to hoax, to trick, to confuse (cf. BAMBOOZLE). [BUM adj. + SE *fuzzle*]

bumhole *n.* [mid-19C+] the anus (cf. ARSEHOLE n.). [BUM n.² + SE *hole*]

bumhole *adj.* [1950s+] second-rate, inferior (cf. PISSHOLE adj.). [BUMHOLE n.]

bum-jerker *n.* [early–mid-19C] a schoolmaster. [BUM n.² + SE *jerker*]

bum juice *n.* [1990s] sweat that gathers between the buttocks. [BUM n.² + SE *juice*]

bum kick *n.* [1940s–60s] (US) an unpleasant experience. [BUM adj. + KICK n.⁵]

bum kick *v.* [1960s+] (US) to depress, to annoy; thus *bumkicked*, depressed, irritated. [BUM KICK n.]

bumkin *n.* [late 18C] the buttocks. [BUM n.² + dimin. sfx. *-kin*]

bum-licker *n.* [1930s+] a toady, a sycophant (cf. ARSE-LICKER). [BUM n.² + SE *licker*]

bumly *adj.* [20C] (US) depressed. [BUM adj.]

bummaree *n.* [late 19C–1900s] a *bain-Marie* or double-boiler (cf. BANG MARY). [joc. mispron.]

bummed *adj.¹* [late 18C] arrested. [SE *bum-bailiff*]

bummed *adj.²* [20C] drunk or drugged (cf. BASTED). [? BUMMER]

bummed out *adj.* [1960s+] **1** suffering from an unpleasant drug experience. **2** drunk. **3** depressed, miserable. **4** disappointed, feeling 'put upon' by others. **5** angry. [ext. of BUMMED adj.²]

bummer/bummy *n.¹* [mid-17C–early 19C] a bum-bailiff.

bummer *n.²* [mid-19C] (US) a tramp, a vagrant (cf. BOOMER n.²). [the precursor of BUM n.³ (1)]

bummer *n.³* [1960s+] **1** (drugs) an unpleasant drug experience, esp. while using LSD or any other hallucinogenic (cf. BAD TRIP). **2** any unpleasant experience. [BUM TRIP, orig. Hell's Angels use for a bad crash; note 19C racing jargon *bummer*, a bad gambling loss]

bummer/bummer-boy *n.⁴* [1970s] a male homosexual. [ext. of BUM BOY]

bumming *n.* [mid–late 19C] (US) living as an idler or loafer (cf. ON THE BUM phr.¹). [BUM v.² (1)]

bummy *n. see* BUMMER n.¹.

bummy *adj.* [late 19C+] useless, second-rate, poor, inferior, ragged. [BUM adj.]

bum-numbing *adj.* [1970s+] infinitely tedious, usu. applied to work of some sort. [BUM n.² + SE *numbing*; the image is of sitting so long that one loses sensation in the buttocks]

bum out *v.* [1960s+] (US) to disappoint, to depress. [BUM adj.]

bump *n.¹* [1940s] dismissal, 'the sack'. [1940s–50s] (US) a raise, a promotion. [ext. use of SE *bump*, a blow]

bump *n.²* (US) **1** [1940s+] the action of thrusting forward the abdomen or hips, as in a dance. **2** [1970s+] spontaneous, cursory sexual intercourse.

bump *n.³* [1950s] the female breast, usu. in pl.

bump *n.⁴* (drugs) **1** [1980s] a draw on a cannabis cigarette (cf. TOKE n.). **2** [1990s] crack cocaine. **3** [1990s] fake crack cocaine. **4** [1990s] one dose ($20) of ketamine (cf. K n.⁴). [play on HIT n.⁴]

bump *v.¹* to murder (cf. BUMP OFF).

bump *v.²* (Aus.) **1** [1910s–50s] to get the better of, to outdo. **2** [1910s] to meet, to accost. **3** [1940s] to fight successfully.

bump *v.³* **1** [1940s+] to dismiss an employee. **2** [1940s+] to increase wages or, in gambling use, a bet. **3** [1960s+] in air travel, to move up one or more classes, while still travelling on one's original ticket, usu. in passive.

bump *v.⁴* [1950s–60s] (US Black) to steal. [synon. of CLOUT v.² (1)]

bump *v.⁵* [1980s+] **1** (US campus) to have sexual intercourse (cf. BUMP BELLIES; BUMP UGLIES). **2** (W.I./Baham.) to work as a prostitute.

bump *v.⁶* [1990s] to boost one's intoxication (by taking more drugs).

bumpa *see* BUMBA.

bump across *v.* [20C] (Aus.) to meet by accident. [a var. on SE *bump into*]

bump and grab, to *phr.* [1990s] (US Black) to drive deliberately into someone's car with the intention of stopping and then robbing them. [on model of SE *smash and grab*]

bump bellies *v.* [20C] (US campus) to have sexual intercourse (cf. BUMP UGLIES; HIT SKINS).

bumper *n.¹* **1** [late 17C–19C] a full glass, esp. when raised in a toast. **2** [mid-18C+] anything unusually large or plentiful (cf. LICKER n.¹; SPANKER n.²; THUMPER n.³; WHACKER n.¹; WHOPPER n.¹). **3** [1940s+] (W.I.) a drunkard, an habitual drinker, esp. of rum (cf. ALECAN; RUM-BUMPER). [the bumping of glasses in the toast or f. SE *bumping*, huge, great. Popular ety. suggests a supposed Fr. toast, *au bon père*, to the good pope]

bumper *n.²* [late 17C–mid-19C] (Und.) a pickpocket's assistant who bumps into the victim (cf. BULKER).

bumper *n.³* [late 19C+] (Aus./N.Z.) a cigarette butt; thus *bumper-dashing*, *bumper-shooting*, picking up cigarette butts from the street (cf. NOT WORTH A BUMPER). [BUTT n.² + SE *stump*]

bumper *n.⁴* [20C] (US) the buttocks. [ext. of BUM n.² + echoic of the buttocks hitting a hard surface]

bumper *n.⁵* [1930s–40s] (US) 5 cents, a nickel. [? ext. of BUMPER n.³; i.e. its relative worthlessness]

bumper *n.⁶* [1960s+] a masculine lesbian. [ext. of SE use; i.e. her aggressiveness]

bumper *n.⁷* [1980s+] (Irish) an amateur flat race. [? contestants may fall off with a *bump* or *bump* each other's horses]

bumper *adj.* [20C] especially large, especially abundant. [BUMPER n.¹ (2)]

bumper *v.* [1960s+] (Aus.) to construct a cigarette from cigarette ends. [BUMPER n.³]

bumper head *n.* [20C] (US) one who performs oral sex. [the head 'bumps' on the partner's body]

bum-perisher/-shaver/-starver *n.* [late 19C+] a short jacket (cf. ARSEHOLE-PERISHER). [BUM n.² + SE; the implication is of failing to warm, cover or reach the buttocks, but note PERISHER n.¹; SHAVER n.³]

bumper-jumper *n.* [1970s] (US) a driver who stays too close to the vehicle immediately in front, a 'tail-gater'.

bumper kit *n.* [1990s] (US Black) a woman's posterior or buttocks. [BUMPER n.⁴ + SE *kit*]

bumpers *n.* [1970s+] the female breasts (cf. BUMP n.³).

bumper-shooter *n.* [1940s+] (Aus.) a picker-up of discarded cigarette ends. [BUMPER n.³ + SE *shooter*; note Aus. army sl. *bumper-sniping*, a punishment that requires the defaulter to pick up cigarette-ends]

bumper-up *n.* **1** [20C] a dockyard labourer. **2** [1920s+] (Aus.) a pickpocket's assistant. **3** [1920s+] (Aus.) a handyman who works for a prostitute. **4** [1920s+] (Aus.) a general term for an absolute incompetent.

bumper-upper *n.* [1920s+] (Aus.) a handyman who works for a prostitute; thus derog. phr. *he couldn't get a job as a bumper-upper in a brothel*. [ext. of BUMPER-UP]

bump fuzz *v.* [1980s+] (US campus) to have sexual intercourse. [SE *bump* + FUZZIES]

bumpie *see* BUPPIE.

bumping n.[1] [1980s+] (US Black teen) the sound of a car stereo. [the 'bumps' come from the thud of the bass, which will be turned up high]

bumping n.[2] [1990s] (US Black) having an uproariously good time (cf. JUMPING adj.[2]).

bumping adj. **1** [mid–late 19C] large. **2** [1980s+] (US campus) exhilarating. [BUMPER adj.]

bump into v. [1950s+] to meet by accident.

bum plumber n. [1990s] a male homosexual, a sodomite. [BUM n.[2] + SE plumber]

bump off v. [1910s+] (orig. US) to murder; thus the bump, a murder, bump oneself off, to commit suicide. [SE bump, to push]

bump one's gums, to phr. [20C] (US) to argue.

bump pussies v. [1960s+] (gay) **1** of male homosexuals or lesbians, to have sexual intercourse. **2** of male homosexuals, to find themselves too sexually similar (both passive, both active) to have satisfactory sex. [SE bump n. + PUSSY n.[1]; the use of a 'vagina' word accentuates the effeminacy]

bumps n.[1] [20C] (US) an affectionate name for one's grandfather (cf. GRAMP). [? juv. mispron.]

bumps n.[2] [20C] **1** (US Black) a rash, esp. on the face. **2** hard treatment.

bumpsie/bumpsy adj. [early–mid-17C] drunk. [? liable to 'bump' into people or to fall over with a 'bump']

bump start n. [20C] a violent gesture or action (whether physical or metaphorical) (cf. KICK START).

bump start v. [20C] to make a violent gesture or action. [BUMP START n.]

bump-stick n. [late 19C–1910s] a police truncheon.

bumpsy see BUMPSIE.

bumptious adj. **1** [19C] offensively self-assertive. **2** [late 19C–1920s] (US Black) short-tempered. [SE bump + sfx. -ious on pattern of fractious, mendacious etc.]

bump titties v. [1990s] (US Black) to fight. [SE bump + TITTY n.[2]]

bump uglies v. [1970s+] (US Black/teen) to have sexual intercourse (cf. BUMP BELLIES). [SE bump + ugly (bodies)]

bum-puncher n. [1970s+] (Aus.) a homosexual (cf. BUM-ROBBER; DUNG-PUNCHER; PEANUT-PACKER; TURD-BURGLAR; TURD-PACKER; TURD-PUNCHER; TURD-ROBBER). [BUM n.[2] + SE puncher]

bumpy n. [20C] (US) the buttocks. [ext. of BUM n.[2] + the physical 'bump' of the buttocks]

bum-ranger n. [18C] a womanizer, a promiscuous man (cf. BUM-FAKER). [BUM n.[2] + RANGE v. (1)]

bum rap n. (US) **1** [1920s+] a false accusation or an unfair sentence (cf. BUM FINGER). **2** [1940s+] a misfortune, an unfair action. **3** [1950s+] harsh criticism. [BUM adj. + RAP n.[3]]

bum rap v. [1940s+] to slander, to attack verbally, to catcall. [BUM adj. + RAP v.[2]]

bum-robber n. [late 19C+] a male homosexual (cf. ARSE BANDIT; BUM BANDIT; BUMB-PUNCHER). [BUM n.[2] + SE robber]

bum-roll n. [17C] a bustle. [BUM n.[2] + SE roll; the shape]

bumrush n. [1980s+] (US Black) **1** a police raid. **2** a stampede, esp. of a crowd wanting to get into a rock concert or film show (usu. without tickets and dependent on force of numbers to overwhelm the security guards). [BUM n.[3] + SE rush]

bumrush v. [1980s+] (orig. US Black) **1** to attack, to destroy through violence. **2** (rap music) to get in (to a concert, a club) without having to pay. **3** to move as a crowd, using numbers to gain access. [BUMRUSH n.]

bum's comforter n. [20C] (US) the tabloid press (cf. CALIFORNIA BLANKET). [BUM n.[3] + SE comforter, a blanket; tramps use newspapers as substitute blankets]

bum-shaver n.[1] [18C] a womanizer, a promiscuous man (cf. BUM-FAKER). [BUM n.[2] + SHAVER n.[1]]

bum-shaver n.[2] see BUM-PERISHER.

bumshop n. [mid-19C–1900s] **1** a brothel. **2** the vagina. [BUM n.[2] + SE shop]

bumsky adj. [20C] (US) second-rate, inferior. [BUM adj. + 'Slavic' sfx. -sky]

bum soup n. [1990s] diarrhoea. [BUM n.[2] + SE soup]

bum spud n. [1990s] a lump of excrement. [BUM n.[2] + SPUD n.[1]]

bumsquabbled/bamsquabbled adj. [mid-19C] (US) **1** discomfited, defeated. **2** confused. [ety. unknown]

bum's rush n. [1920s+] (orig. US Und.) forcible ejection, esp. from a bar or club. [BUM n.[3] + SE rush]

bum-starver see BUM-PERISHER.

bum steer n. [1920s+] **1** a piece of bad advice or misinformation. **2** a mistake, the wrong direction. [BUM adj. + SE steer]

bumsuck v. [1930s+] to toady to, to act the sycophant. [BUM n.[2] + SE suck]

bum-sucker n. [1930s+] a sycophant, a crawler (cf. ARSE-LICKER). [BUMSUCK]

bumswiggled/bumwizzled adj. [19C+] confounded, ruined (cf. HORNSWOGGLED). [ety. unknown]

bum-tag n. [20C] deposits of faecal matter in the hairs around a badly cleaned anus (cf. CLINKERS n.[3]; DINGLEBERRIES n.[1]). [BUM n.[2] + SE tag]

bum-tickler n. [18C] a womanizer, a promiscuous man (cf. BUM-FAKER). [BUM n.[2] + SE tickler]

bum-trap n. [early 19C] a bailiff or bailiff's assistant. [BUM n.[2] + TRAP n.[2]]

bum trip n. [1960s–70s] an unpleasant experience while under the influence of drugs (cf. BAD TRIP). [BUM adj. + TRIP n.[3] (1)]

bum wad n. [20C] (US) lavatory paper (cf. BUM-FODDER). [BUM n.[2] + SE wad]

bum-worker n. [18C] a womanizer, a promiscuous man (cf. BUM-FAKER). [BUM n.[2] + SE worker]

bumzwizzled see BUMSWIGGLED.

bun n.[1] **1** [16C+] a squirrel. **2** [18C+] a rabbit (cf. BUNNY n.[1]). [dial.]

bun n.[2] **1** [17C] pubic hair. **2** [late 19C] a young woman (with no pej. links). **3** [1950s–70s] the buttocks (cf. BUNS n.[2]). [(1) also meaning squirrel and rabbit, which latter has strong sexual overtones. (3) ? 16C north. dial. bun, the tail of a hare]

bun n.[3] **1** [late 19C+] a state of drunkenness, esp. as get/have/tie a bun on. **2** [1910s] (US) a fit of laughter. [? links to Worcestershire dial. bun, a bung or cork or Angus dial. bun, a large cask]

bun n.[4] [20C] (N.Z.) a bowler hat. [resemblance]

bun n.[5] [1980s+] (drugs) a quantity of cannabis resin, either 1kg or 0.5kg.

bun v. [1990s] (US Black) to have sexual intercourse. [? the notoriously sex-driven SE bunny-rabbit]

bun beat n. [late 19C+] a party. [var. on BUNFIGHT]

bun boy n. [1950s–70s] a homosexual (cf. BUM BOY). [BUN n.[2] (2) + SE boy]

bunce/bunse/bunts n. [late 18C+] **1** extras, bonuses (cf. BLUE PIGEON). **2** money (esp. for nothing). [coster jargon bunts, second-rate apples, which were sold off cheap or even given away to market boys, who could in turn sell them at a small profit. Hotten (1867) adds 'money obtained by giving light weight, &c.'. Bunts were further divided into fair bunts and unfair bunts, depending on whether or not the coster was aware of his boy's tricks]

bunce v. [20C] (market) to overcharge. [BUNCE n.]

buncer n. **1** [mid-19C+] a salesperson who works for a commission. **2** [20C] (market) one who overcharges the customers. [BUNCE n.]

bunch n. [20C] a group, usu. in phr. *best of the bunch*, *best of a bad bunch*.

bunch v. [20C] (US) to leave a job, to leave something unfinished. [BUNK OFF]

bunch! *excl.* [late 19C] (US campus) nonsense! rubbish! [? abbr. *bunch of* BULLSHIT n.]

bunched adj. [1970s+] (Irish) exhausted.

bunch of charms n. [20C] a pretty young woman.

bunch of dog's meat n. [mid-19C] a squalling baby. [its fate if it does not stop whinging]

bunch of fives/five n. [early 19C+] the hand, usu. when clenched in a fist. [the five fingers]

bunch of sprouts n. [19C] the fingers (cf. BUNCH OF FIVES). [they 'sprout' from the palm]

bunch punch n. [1970s+] (orig. US campus) group sex in which a number of males have sex with one woman (cf. GANGBANG n.). [BUNCH n. + PUNCH v.]

bunch punch v. [1970s+] (orig. US campus) to have group sex, usu. a gang-rape (cf. GANGBANG v.). [BUNCH PUNCH n.]

bunchy n. [1940s+] (W.I.) the buttocks. [BUM n.² ? 14C SE *bunchy*, swelling]

bunchy adj. [20C] (US) chubby. [14C SE *bunchy*, swelling]

buncle/bunkle n. [late 19C] a car*buncle*. [abbr.]

bunco/bunko n. **1** [mid-19C+] (Und., esp. US) fraud, a dishonest gambling game. **2** [20C] a swindler (cf. BUNCO MAN). **3** [1910s–40s] deceit, flattery, empty nonsense. **4** [1940s+] a police squad devoted to combating confidence tricksters (cf. BUNCO SQUAD). [Sp. *banca*, a card-game similar to monte]

bunco adj. [20C] (US) deceptive, fraudulent. [BUNCO n.]

bunco v. [late 19C+] (US) to swindle, to defraud. [BUNCO n.]

bunco artist n. [20C] a confidence trickster. [BUNCO n. + ARTIST n.²]

bunco game n. [20C] (US) any form of 'fixed' gambling game. [BUNCO n. + SE *game*]

bunco man n. [late 19C+] (US) a swindler, a confidence trickster. [BUNCO n. + SE *man*]

buncombe n. [early 19C+] nonsense, rubbish, flattery. [var. on BUNKUM n.]

bunco squad n. [1940s+] (US police) a special squad devoted to combating confidence tricksters. [BUNCO n. + SE *squad*]

bunco-steerer n. [late 19C+] (US Und.) that member of a confidence trickster gang whose task is to entrap the victim into the current swindle. [BUNCO n. + STEERER n.¹]

bundabust/bundobust n. [late 19C–1950s] (orig. Ind. army) **1** discipline, regulations. **2** arrangements. **3** a revenue settlement. [Hind. *band-o-bast*, tying and binding]

bunder n. [late 19C–1930s] (Anglo-Chinese) any supposedly remarkable piece of information that turns out to be no more than a false rumour. [Hind. *band*, an artificial embankment or quay, esp. the Shangai *Bund*, the city's main (pre-revolutionary) commercial centre]

bundie n. [20C] (Irish) a child's buttocks. [BUNS n.²]

bundle n.¹ **1** [early 19C–1950s] a woman, esp. a fat one, or one's wife (cf. BAGGAGE). **3** [late 19C] (US) a girlfriend, a female companion (cf. RAG). [19C use of (2) is generally derog.; 20C use is neutral]

bundle n.² **1** [late 19C–1930s] (US) loot, plunder. **2** [late 19C+] a large amount of money; thus *go a bundle* (on), to bet heavily, to commit oneself unreservedly, to like a great deal (cf. PACKET n.³; PILE n.; WAD n.¹; WEDGE n.¹).

bundle n.³ [1930s+] **1** a fight. **2** sexual intercourse. [the participants have been 'bundled' together]

bundle n.⁴ (drugs) **1** [1950s] heroin. **2** [1990s] (US Black) a portion of crack cocaine or marijuana or any kind of drug available on sale. [BINDLE]

bundle v. [1930s+] **1** to fight. **2** to have sexual intercourse. **3** to pass something over. [BUNDLE n.³]

bundle off v. [early 19C] to send away in a hurry. [fig. use of SE; subseq. use is SE]

bundle of socks n. [late 19C+] (Aus.) the head. [rhy. sl. *bundle of socks* = THINKBOX]

bundle of ten n. [20C] a packet of 10 cigarettes.

bundletail n. [late 17C–early 18C] a short, fat, squat woman (cf. BUNDLE n.¹). [SE *bundle* + TAIL n.¹ (5)]

bundle up v. [19C] to attack. [BUNDLE v. (1)]

bundobust *see* BUNDABUST.

bundook *see* BANDOOK.

bundu-bashing n. [1970s+] (S.Afr.) travelling through wild or near-impenetrable rough country. [S.Afr.E. *bundu*, 'the back of beyond' + SE *bash*]

bun-duster n. [1920s] (US) an effete young man who attends smart tea parties and charms old ladies (cf. CAKE-EATER). [SE *bun* + *duster*, he 'dusts off', i.e. finishes, the buns]

bundy n. [1970s+] (Aus.) Bundaberg rum. [the proprietary name of a brand of rum, ult. f. the town in Queensland]

bun feast n. [late 19C–1900s] a third-rate feast, where even the buns are not enough to make one full. [ext. of SE use but ? ironic ref. to BEANFEAST]

bunfight n. [late 19C+] a tea party, esp. with image of children struggling for sticky buns (cf. CRUMPET-SCRAMBLE; FIGHT; MUFFIN-WORRY; TEA FIGHT). [SE *bun* + *fight*]

bung/boung n.¹ **1** [16C] a purse. **2** [16C] a pocket. **3** [16C] a cut-purse. **4** [1950s+] a bribe (cf. SLING n.¹). **5** [1950s+] a loan. [Frisian *pung*, purse]

bung n.² [late 18C–mid-19C] **1** a brewer. **2** an inn-keeper or publican; thus the *bung ball*, an annual publican's dance (cf. BLOOD BALL; BROTHER OF THE BUNG). [SE *bung*, the stopper of a barrel of beer]

bung n.³ **1** [late 18C] the anus. **2** [1960s] (US) the vagina. **3** [1960s+] (US) in fig. use, the buttocks (cf. ARSEHOLE n.). [SE *bung + hole*]

bung n.⁴ [late 19C+] **1** a blow, esp. in phr. *bung in the eye*, a blow in the eye. **2** a black eye. [dial., ult. echoic]

bung n.⁵ [late 19C–1910s] a lie. [ety. unknown; ? BUNG v.¹, i.e. it 'throws away' the truth]

bung n.⁶ [20C] (US) a lump, a swelling. [SE *bung up*, to bruise, to beat]

bung n.⁷ [1920s+] a *bung*alow. [abbr.]

bung n.⁸ [1980s+] (US drugs) a bowl-shaped water-pipe used for smoking marijuana. [var. on BONG n.]

bung adj. [18C–1900s] (Scot.) drunk. [BUNG n.²]

bung v.¹ **1** [early 19C+] to pass, to throw, usu. energetically or aggressively. **2** [late 19C+] to hand over, to give quickly, esp. in imper. e.g. *bung this round to Fred*. **3** [late 19C+] to place (inside). [echoic of tossing an article with some violence]

bung/bung out v.² [20C] (US) to protrude, to stick out. [fig. use of BUNG v.¹]

bung v.³ [1950s+] **1** to offer or give a bribe. esp. to the police. **2** to pay protection money (either to the police or to a criminal). [BUNG n.¹ (4)]

bung adv. [20C+] precisely, accurately, usu. as *bung in*, *bung on*. [BANG adv.]

bungalow bill n. [1980s] a man who is either not very intelligent ('nothing up top') or endowed with large genitals ('it's all down below'). [pun]

bungaree/bungary n. [late 19C–1900s] a public house. [BUNG n.²]

bungaree v. [1990s] (Aus.) to have an almost fully erect penis (cf. BACCHUS MARSH). [proper name *Bungaree*, the town just before Ballarat if travelling on the Melbourne–Ballarat railway]

bungary *see* BUNGAREE n.

Bungay-play n. [mid-19C] various styles of illicit or unskilful play in whist or billiards (cf. WHITECHAPEL PLAY). [? ref. to dial.

phr. 'been to Bungay fair and broken both his legs', he is drunk]

bungdung n. [1920s+] (Aus.) a large firecracker. [? BANDOOK]

bunged adj. [1930s+] (S.Afr.) tipsy. [BUNG-EYED]

bunged up adj.¹ [20C] in a prison cell. [var. on BANGED UP adj.¹]

bunged up adj.² [20C] **1** stuffy, blocked, esp. of one's nose during 'flu or a cold, or of constipation (cf. TIED UP adj.¹). **2** squashed, creased, pushed together uncomfortably. [SE bung]

bungee adj. [1990s] (US campus) extremely. [? SE bungee jumping, an 'extreme sport']

bunger n. [1900s–30s] (US) a black eye. [BUNG n.⁶]

bungery n. [late 19C–1900s] a tavern, a public house; thus Bohemian bungery, a public house frequented by (impecunious) writers and artists. [SE bung, the stopper of a beer-barrel]

bung-/bungy-eye n. [late 19C+] (Aus.) an eye infection caused by flies. [BUNGE UP] adj.² + SE eye]

bung-eyed adj. [mid-19C+] **1** drunk. **2** cross-eyed. [the volume of liquor 'bungs up' one's vision; but note SE bung, a stopper (for a cask)]

bung eyes n. [20C] (US) protruding eyes. [BUNG v.² + SE eyes]

bung-fodder n. [late 17C+] lavatory paper (cf. BUM-FODDER). [BUNGHOLE n.¹ (1) + SE fodder]

bung ho! excl. [1920s+] **1** a toast when drinking. **2** synonym for 'goodbye'. [SE bung or BUNG v.¹ (1); i.e. one 'throws' the drunk down]]

bunghole n.¹ **1** [17C; 1930s+] the anus, the rectum (cf. ARSEHOLE n.; BUNG n.³). **2** [1960s+] (US) the vagina. **3** [1960s+] (US) the buttocks. **4** [1990s] (Aus.) the mouth. [SE bung + hole]

bunghole n.² [1910s+] (orig. milit.) cheese. [? 'you bung it down your hole']

bunghole v. [1930s+] to sodomize. [BUNGHOLE n.¹ (1)]

bunghole buddy n. [1940s] (US) a very close friend (cf. ASSHOLE BUDDY). [BUNGHOLE n.¹ (1) + BUDDY]

bungi/bungie/bungy n. [1980s+] (S.Afr.) a 'drop-out', a hippie (cf. DOPER n.²). [Hind. bhang, cannabis or Ndebele im-banje, marijuana. Coined at Rhodes University, Grahamstown]

bungie/bungy n.¹ [1910s+] an eraser, a rubber. usu. school use. [echoic of the rubber's squashiness]

bungie n.² see BUNGI.

bungie-bird n. [late 16C] a Franciscan friar. [name Friar Bungay, as in Robert Greene's Friar Bacon and Friar Bongay (acted 1594)]

bung it/bung it in n. [1920s+] gin. [rhy. sl.]

bung it on v. [1940s+] (Aus.) to act affectedly, to assume an accent. [BUNG v.¹ (1)]

bung-juice n. [19C] beer, stout. [SE bung + juice]

bungle n. [1990s] (W.I.) someone who performs oral sex on a woman. [BUNGHOLE n.¹ (2), although the def. here is vagina rather than anus]

bungler n. [late 17C–18C] an impotent husband. [SE bungler, an unskilful worker]

bung-/boung-napper n. [late 17C] a cut-purse, a pickpocket (cf. BUNG NIPPER). [BUNG n.¹ (1) + NAPPER n.¹ (1)]

bung-/boung-nipper n. [mid-17C–mid-19C] (Und.) a cut-purse (cf. BUNG-NAPPER). [BUNG n.¹ (1) + SE nipper]

bungo n. [20C] (W.I./Jam.) a crude, boorish, ignorant Black person, a country bumpkin. [? Hausa bungu, a nincompoop, a country bumpkin]

bungo v. [1980s] (US campus) to mistreat severely, to inflict injury on. [BUNGO n. but ? BANJO v.]

bungo-bessy n. [1940s+] (W.I.) **1** an interfering busybody. **2** a boorish low-class woman. [BUNGO n. + BESSY]

bung off v. [20C] to leave. [BUNG v.¹ (1)]

bung on v. [20C] **1** to put on a garment, to get dressed, usu. in comb. with an article of clothing, e.g. bung on a jacket. **2** to organize, to arrange. [BUNG v.¹]

bung on a blue, to phr. [1950s+] (Aus.) to make a fuss, to create a disturbance. [BUNG v.¹ (1) + BLUE n.⁷ (2)]

bung on an act, to phr. [1920s+] (Aus.) to lose one's temper and deliver a stream of obscenities/oaths (cf. STACK ON AN ACT). [BUNG v.¹ (1) + SE act]

bung one on v. [1950s+] to hit (cf. PUT ONE ON). [BUNG v.¹ (1); 'one' is a blow or punch]

bung one's eye, to phr. [late 18C–19C] to drink a dram, to drink heartily, to get drunk. [lit. to drink until one's eyes are bunged, closed]

bung on side/swerve, to phr. [1910s+] (Aus.) to show off; thus more side than a billiard ball, very arrogant, snobbish. [BUNG v.¹ (1) + SIDE n.¹/SE swerve + pun on billiards/snooker use]

bung on the bull, to phr. [1940s+] (Aus.) to show off, to act in a pretentious manner. [BUNG v.¹ (1) + BULLSHIT n.]

bung out v.¹ see BUNG v.².

bung out v.² [1900s] (N.Z.) to die. [BUNG v.¹]

bungo-talk n. [1940s+] (W.I.) illiterate speech, the lowest level of uncultivated Jamaican speech. [BUNGO n. + SE talk]

bungo-toughy n. [1940s+] (W.I./Guyn.) a little child who eats or behaves like a hooligan. [BUNGO n. + TOUGHIE]

bung someone a toffee, to phr. [1940s+] to do someone a favour. [BUNG v.¹ (1) + SE toffee]

bung-starter n. [late 19C–1900s] (US) a bartender. [SE bung-starter, an implement used to remove the bungs from casks of beer]

bungs up adj. [20C] (US) very drunk, rolling drunk. [naut. jargon bungs up, a vessel that is rolling in a heavy sea to such an extent that the bungs in her planking are visible]

bung up v. [early 19C+] to close someone's eye with a punch. [SE bung; use before 19C use is SE]

bung up/up against adv. see BANG UP adv.

bung up and bilge free phr. [19C] (US) **1** in proper order. **2** referring to one whose behaviour, while utterly proper, errs towards the self-satisfied and sanctimonious. [New England naut. jargon bung up and bilge free, the correct storage of barrels in the hold of a whaler, with the bung upwards so that bilge water can not get in and dilute the contents]

bung upwards adv. [late 18C] lying on one's stomach. [BUNGHOLE n.¹ (1) + SE upwards]

bungwad n. [1920s] (US) lavatory paper (cf. BUM WAD). [BUNGHOLE n.¹ (1) + SE wad]

bungy n.¹ see BUNGIE n.¹.

bungy n.² see BUNGI.

bungy adj. [mid-18C] drunk. [BUNGED]

bungy-eye see BUNG-EYE n.

bun hat n. [20C] (N.Z.) a bowler hat. [its shape]

bunion derby n. [1920s] (US) a cross-country marathon. [SE bunion + The Derby, a well-known horse race in the UK and as the Kentucky Derby in the US]

bunji n. [1970s+] (Aus.) a White man, often old and impoverished, who pursues Aboriginal women for sex. [Goreng Goreng banji, friend + SE man]

bun joint n. [late 19C] (US) a coffeehouse. [SE bun + JOINT n.³ (3)]

bunk n.¹ [20C] (US) rubbish, nonsense; thus bunky, nonsensical. [BUNKUM n.]

bunk n.² **1** [20C] (US) a Slav immigrant f. Eastern Europe. **2** [1910s+] an oafish, dull, if muscular person (cf. BOHUNK).

bunk n.³ [1980s+] (drugs) fake cocaine. [BUNKUM n.]

bunk v.¹ **1** [18C+] to escape, to run off (cf. DO A BUNK). **2** [late 19C+] to leave, to be off. **3** [late 19C+] to be expelled from (public) school. [Lincolnshire dial. *bunk*, to run away, to make off.]

bunk/bunk down v.[2] [1930s+] (orig. US) to sleep. [SE *bunk* n.]

bunk v.[3] **1** [1950s] (Aus.) to carry someone on one's bicycle cross-bar. **2** [1990s] to travel without a fare, to get in (e.g. to a cinema) without a ticket. [BUNK UP v.]

bunk adj. [1970s+] **1** fake, counterfeit. **2** unsophisticated, unfashionable. **3** bad, second-rate, inferior. [BUNKUM n.]

bunk down v. see BUNK v.[2].

bunker n.[1] [mid-19C] beer. [? a fig. coal bunker at which one 'fuels up' or Ling. Fr. *bona acqua*, good water]

bunker n.[2] [20C] a sodomite. [euph. for SE *bugger*]

bunkered adj. [late 19C+] in difficulties (cf. STYMIED). [golfing imagery]

bunk habit n.[1] see BUNK YEN.

bunk habit n.[2] [1930s–60s] (US drugs) the desire to sleep excessively, resulting from one's addiction to narcotics. [SE *bunk* + HABIT]

bunkie n. (US) **1** [1910s] (campus) a room-mate. **2** [1970s+] a general term of address, usu. condescending. [US army use *bunkie*, a bunkmate; thus a friend]

bunk into v. [20C] (US) to meet by accident. [BUMP INTO]

bunk it v. [mid-19C+] (US) **1** to sleep in a bunk (rather than a proper bed). **2** to sleep in any rough, makeshift manner. [SE *bunk*]

bunkle see BUNCLE.

bunko see BUNCO n.

bunk off v. [1970s+] to play truant, usu. schoolchildren (cf. HOP THE WAG). [19C public school sl. BUNK v.[1] (3)]

bunk out v. [1970s+] (Irish) to play truant. [var. on BUNK OFF]

bunk over v. [20C] to go across. [BUNK v.[1] (2)]

bunks v. [1950s+] (W.I. Rasta) to knock or bump against; thus *bunks mi res*, catch my rest, take a nap. [SE *bounce*]

bunk sheet n. [1920s–30s] (US) a sensational newspaper. [BUNKUM n. + SE (*news*)*sheet*]

bunkum n. [19C] (orig. US) nonsense, rubbish, flattery. [proper name of *Buncombe County* in North Carolina. The word emerged during the debate on the 'Missouri Question' in 1821 when Felix Walker, the member from this district, rose to speak. Although the debate was due to end and members begged him to sit down, he refused, explaining that his constituents expected it, and that he was bound 'to make a speech for Buncombe'. The term stuck, first as *buncombe*, then *bunkum*, then, as abbr. by the satirist George Ade, *bunk*. An alternative ety. links it to the gambling dice game *banco* or *bunco* (cf. BUNCO n.), the cheating at which soon made it a synon. for fraud]

bunkum adj. [19C] (US) excellent, first-rate, esp. of food. [? link to Fr. *bon*, good]

bunkum town n. [20C] (US) that area of the town where the poor live. [BUNKUM n. + SE *town*]

bunk up n. [1930s+] (orig. services) sexual intercourse. [SE *bunk*]

bunk up v. [20C] to help, esp. in climbing up or over an obstacle, when one person either lets the other stand on their back or links their hands to make a 'stirrup' into which the climber can put one foot and boost themself upwards.

bunk yen/habit v. [late 19C–1930s] (US drugs) to frequent an opium den, too poor to buy one's own drugs but in the hope that someone else will offer a treat or simply to inhale the airborne fumes. [SE *bunk*, a rudimentary bed as used by a smoker + *yen*, desire/HABIT]

bunk you! excl. [1980s+] (US campus) euph. for FUCK YOU!

bunned adj. [1900s–20s] (US) drunk. [BUN n.[3]]

bunnick/bunnick up v. [late 19C–1910s] to beat, to ruin, to dispose of, to 'put paid' to. [? BUNKERED]

bunny n.[1] **1** [late 17C] a rabbit. **2** [20C] a poor player of a sport (cf. RABBIT n.[5]). **3** [1950s+] rabbit fur, as used for making garments; thus the garments themselves. [SE *bunny*, an affectionate name for both rabbits and squirrels; (1) subseq. use is SE]

bunny n.[2] **1** [18C+] the vagina. **2** [20C] (US Black) a promiscuous woman, whose habits emulate the preoccupations of rabbits. **3** [1920s+] a sanitary towel. **4** [1930s+] (US) the buttocks. [BUN n.[2]]

bunny n.[3] [1940s+] (orig. US/Aus.) a fool, a simpleton (cf. CONY n.[1]; DUMB BUNNY; RABBIT n.). [SE *bunny*; i.e. the supposed stupidity of a rabbit]

bunny n.[4] **1** [1950s+] a chat, a conversation. **2** [1950s–60s] a talkative person. [rhy. sl. *bunny* = rabbit and pork (cf. RABBIT v.[3])]

bunny boy n. [1940s+] (S.Afr.) a male homosexual (cf. HASIE). [SE *bunny* + *boy*]

bunny chow n. [1950s+] (S.Afr.) vegetarian curry sold as a take-away in a hollowed-out half-loaf of bread (cf. CURRY BUNNY; RABBIT FOOD). [Hind. *bania*, a caste of merchants, thus generic for a Gujerati businessman, who followed a vegetarian diet and for whom a café-owner originally created the dish]

buns n.[1] [20C] (Aus.) a tampon; thus *have the buns on*, to be menstruating (cf. BUNNY n.[2]; HAVE THE RAG ON). [coarse abbr. use of SE *jam buns* (cf. JAMRAG)]

buns n.[2] [1960s+] the buttocks. [joc. resemblance to the foodstuffs]

bunse see BUNCE n.

bunse up v. [20C] (Ulster) to pool resources. [BUNCE n.]

bun-struggle n. [late 19C–1900s] a tea party. [var. on BUN-WORRY]

bunt n. [late 17C–early 19C] an apron. [SE *bunt*, the part of a fishing net that forms a bag or pouch]

bunt v. [late 18C] to jostle against, to knock. [dial. *bunt*, to push, to butt]

bunter n. (Und.) **1** [early 18C] a woman who scavenges for rags in the street. **2** [early 18C–early 19C] a poor, possibly thieving prostitute. **3** [mid–late 19C] a prostitute who hires lodgings, uses them for a short time and then leaves without paying her rent. **4** [mid–late 19C] 'a woman thief of the lowest possible kind' (Ware). **5** [1950s–60s] a man who fails in almost everything he does. [ety. unknown; ? link to BUNT n.]

bunter's tea n. [early–mid-18C] strong liquor, usu. gin. [BUNTER n. (1) + SE *tea*]

bunting time n. [late 17C–18C] summer. [fig. use of BUNT v., to have sexual intercourse]

buntling/buntlings n. [late 17C–early 19C] a petticoat; thus *hale up the main-buntlings*, to pull up a woman's petticoats. [BUNT n., lit. 'a small apron']

bun-trap n. [20C] the mouth (cf. BACON HOLE).

bunts see BUNCE n.

bunty n. [19C] an affectionate term for a small, middle-aged woman. [Scot./Irish *bunty*, short and squat]

bununus n. [1940s] (W.I.) a term of endearment applied to a person or object. [? Sp. *bueno*, good; Fr. *bon à nous*, good to us]

bununus adj. [1940s] (W.I.) a general term of approval, pretty, wonderful, glorious, fantastic. [BUNUNUS n.]

bun-worry n. **1** [late 19C–1900s] (orig. milit.) a tea party. **2** [late 19C+] (Aus./N.Z.) a general jollification. [SE *bun* + *worry*, to bite at like a dog]

bunyip n. [mid-19C] (Aus./Sydney) an impostor, a pretender, humbug. [SE *bunyip*, 'the Aboriginal name of a fabulous monster inhabiting the rushy swamps and lagoons in the interior of Australia' (*OED*)]

buor see BUER.

buoyant adj. [20C] drunk (cf. AFLOAT). [play on SE; thus phr. 'my teeth are floating']

bup see BUPPER.

bupkes/bupkis n. [1940s+] nothing (whatsoever). [Yid. bupkes, beans]

bupper/bup/buppie/buppies/bups/bupsie n. [late 19C–1900s] (usu. children) bread and butter. [elision/ mispron.]

buppie/bumpie/buppy n. [1980+] (orig. US) a Black upwardly mobile young professional (cf. DINKY n.³; LOMBARD; YUMPIE; YUPPIE). [SE Black + YUPPIE]

buppies/bups/bupsie see BUPPER.

burbed-out adv. [1970s+] (US middle-class) conventional. [BURBS ? + ref. to that badge of conformity, the Burberry overcoat]

burble v. [mid-19C+] to chatter pleasantly. [? linked to Ital. borbogliare, to make a rumbling or grumbling noise, Port. borbulhar + Sp. borbollar but coined by Lewis Carroll in Through the Looking-Glass (1871) in which the Jabberwock 'came whiffling through the tulgey wood,/And burbled as it came!']

burbs n. [1970s+] (orig. US) the suburbs. [abbr.]

burdetts n. [1920s+] boots. [rhy. sl. Burdett Coutts, the bankers]

Burdon's hotel n. [19C] Whitecross Street prison, London (cf. AKERMAN'S HOTEL). [proper name of Mr Burdon, a one-time governor]

bure see BUER.

burerk see BURICK.

burg n.¹ [mid-19C+] (US) a town, a city. [Lat. burgus, thence Ger. Burg, a town (orig. a walled town)]

burg n.² [1980s] (S.Afr.) a fool, an idiot, an unpleasant person. [BERK]

burger/double burger/triple burger with cheese n. [1980s+] (US campus) a sexy/very sexy/very, very sexy woman. [she's 'very good to eat'; a savoury version of the usual identification of pretty women with sweetmeats or cakes]

burgers n. [1990s] (drugs) MDMA; usu. as brown burgers, white burgers (cf. DISCO BISCUIT; ECSTASY).

burglar n. 1 [1920s–40s] (US) a swindler, a bribe-taker. 2 [1960s+] a sodomite (cf. BUNKER). [play on SE; (2) euph. for SE bugger and implication of 'breaking in']

burglar hole n. [1970s+] (US) a peephole in a front door. [through which one can espy potential robbers]

burgle v. [1960s+] to sodomize. [BURGLAR n. (2)]

burgoo n. [20C] stew or porridge. [Arabic burgul, cooked, parched and cracked wheat. Orig. an 18C thick oatmeal gruel, consumed by seamen; also known as loblolly, a soup or stew made with a variety of meat and vegetables, often eaten at outdoor feasts in the US, esp. in Kentucky]

burick/burerk n. [mid-19C] 1 a wife. 2 a flashily-dressed woman. 3 a prostitute. [Rom. burk, breast or Scot. bure, a loose woman (cf. BUER)]

buried adv. [20C] (US Und.) 1 held incommunicado. 2 serving a life sentence.

buried in a napkin phr. [19C] asleep, stupid.

burk v.¹ [late 19C–1910s] (orig. N.Z.) to avoid work. [? rhy. sl. burk = SE shirk or f. SE burk, to smother, to 'hush up'. Both are ult. f. burke, to strangle (named f. the early 19C 'resurrectionists' or grave-robbers Burke and Hare; see BURKE)]

burk v.² [20C] (US) 1 to vomit. 2 to break wind. [? onomat.]

burke v. [early–mid-19C] 1 to hang. 2 to suppress, to cover up. [proper name of the Edinburgh criminal William Burke (1792–1829) who, along with his partner William Hare (1790–c.1860), murdered people in order to sell their corpses to the medical school for surgical dissection. Burke was hanged; Hare, who turned King's evidence, escaped the noose]

burker n. [early–mid-19C] a 'resurrectionist' or body-snatcher, esp. for the purpose of selling the corpse to a hospital's anatomy department (in an era when the dissection of human corpses was still illegal). [the proper name Burke; see BURKE]

Burketown mosquito net n. [1960s+] (Aus.) a bottle of rum and a cow-dung fire. [proper name of the outback town of Burketown, Queensland]

burley n.¹ [1930s–50s] (US) a burlesque show, a striptease show. [abbr.]

burley n.² see BERLEY.

burleycue/burley-que see BURLYCUE.

Burlington bertie n. [1900s–30s] a dandyish, over-dressed young man, very conscious of (and pleased with) his appearance. [the music-hall song 'Burlington Bertie from Bow', sung by Vesta Tilley c.1908]

Burlington hunt see BERKELEY HUNT.

burly adj. [1990s] (US teen) hard to achieve, challenging (physically or mentally). [SE burly, stout, sturdy]

burlycue/burleycue/burley-que n. [1920s–60s] (US) a burlesque show (cf. BURLEY). [abbr./pron.]

burma phr. [late 19C+] a lover's acronym, be undressed, ready, my angel, written on envelopes of love letters (cf. BOLTOP). [abbr.]

Burma Road n. [1940s–50s] a tough area of Sydney, running from King's Cross to the docks. [the Burma Road, built by China, 1937–9, between Kunming, China, and Lashio, Burma, plus its WW2 extension (under the Japanese occupation) to Ledo in India. Its construction was notoriously wasteful of life]

burn n.¹ 1 [late 19C+] (US) a joke, a prank. 2 [1960s+] (orig. US) a fraud, a confidence trick; thus the sale of bad or fake drugs. 3 [1960s+] (US) a major disappointment. [the victim 'gets their fingers burned']

burn n.² [20C] (US) a love-bite. [resemblance to a burn scar]

burn n.³ [1940s+] (orig. Und.) a smoke, a cigarette; thus (Aus.) twist a burn, roll a cigarette.

burn n.⁴ [1950s] (US) a permanent wave hairstyle. [it is 'burned' into the hair]

burn n.⁵ [1960s+] fast-driving in an automobile. [BURN-UP n.]

burn n.⁶ [1980s+] a hard stare.

burn v.¹ [16C; 20C] to infect with a venereal disease (cf. BURNED adj.¹; PASS THROUGH THE FIRE; SCALD v.¹). [20C use is US Black]

burn v.² (orig. US) 1 [20C] to fail, to go wrong (cf. CRASH AND BURN). 2 [1920s] to cheat (esp. at cards), to defraud. 3 [1920s+] to rob, to steal. 4 [1930s] to annoy, to infuriate, to embarrass (cf. BURN UP). 5 [1950s+] to fail to pay a debt. 6 [1950s+] (drugs) to sell cut or second-rate drugs, or simply to take a buyer's money and vanish without delivering the promised drugs. 7 [1960s–70s] to betray sexually. 8 [1960s+] to recognize. 9 [1960s+] to arrest. 10 [1970s] to dismiss an employee, to jilt a lover. 11. [1970s+] (campus) to grade harshly.

burn v.³ (orig. US) 1 [1920s+] to punish; ext. as burn one's ass. 2 [1920s+] to execute in the electric chair (cf. BAKE v.¹). 3 [1930s+] to shoot dead. 4 [1930s+] to kill, to murder. 5 [1960s+] to attack, verbally or physically.

burn v.⁴ [1940s+] (orig. US) 1 to go fast, to leave at high speed. 2 to drive a car or motorbike fast (cf. BURN UP v.²). [SE burn up the road]

burn v.⁵ [1960s+] (US Black) to prepare food, to cook, esp. to cook well.

burn v.⁶ 1 [1960s+] (drugs) to smoke a cannabis cigarette. 2 [1990s] (Black drugs) to smoke a cigarette laced with crack cocaine.

burn v.[7] [1970s+] (US) to photocopy. [the heating involved in the process]

burn! excl. [1980s+] (US campus) a triumphant or gloating excl. used after successfully insulting or verbally attacking someone (cf. GOTCHA!). [BURN v.[2] (4)]

burn artist n. [1960s+] a con-man, a cheat, esp. in the drug world where they will either sell second-rate drugs or take a buyer's money and vanish without delivering the goods. [BURN v.[2] (6) + ARTIST n.[2]]

burn bad powder, to phr. [1910s–20s] to break wind. [the stench]

burn bread on, to phr. [1950s+] (US prison) to make a verbal attack on a fellow prisoner. [BURN v.[2] (3)]

burn corncobs v. [1900s] (US) of a car, to give off a good deal of smoke through the exhaust. [the practice of burning waste corncobs in large fires, often smoky (because of the kerosene used to encourage the flames)]

burn-crust n. [mid-18C+] a baker.

burn down v. [20C] 1 to shoot, to kill. 2 to overdo, to use to excess. 3 to attack, verbally or physically. [BURN v.[3]]

burned/burnt adj.[1] [late 17C–19C] infected with venereal disease (cf. BURN ONE'S POKER; HOT adj.[3]). [BURN v.[1]; thus 18C naval joke, *to be sent out a sacrifice and come home a burnt offering*, to be sent off to fight for the Navy, but to return carrying venereal disease]

burned/burnt adj.[2] [1960s+] 1 (drugs) sold bad, adulterated or fake drugs (cf. RIPPED OFF). 2 cheated or robbed of any commodity or possession. [BURN v.[2] (5), (6)]

burned at adv. [1960s+] annoyed with. [BURN v.[2] (4)]

burned out adj. [20C] (Irish) annoyed, irritated. [var. on BURNED AT]

burned/burnt out adv. [1960s+] 1 having had too much drink and/or drugs, which have taken their toll both physically and esp. mentally (cf. CRISP adj.[2]). 2 (drugs) used of a vein that has collapsed due to an excess of injections. [SE *burned, burnt*, of a fire, out, extinct, used up]

burned out on adv. [1980s+] (US campus) tired of, exhausted by, infuriated by. [BURNED OUT]

burned to the socket phr. [late 17C] dying. [SE *burned + socket*, the part of the candlestick in which the candle is placed]

burned up adj. [1920s+] (US) 1 very excited. 2 extremely angry. [BURN v.[2] (4)]

burner n.[1] [18C] a card-sharp, a swindler. [BURN v.[2] (2)]

burner n.[2] 1 [mid-18C–19C] venereal disease. 2 [19C] a sharp blow or punch. 3 [1920s–60s; 1980s+] (US Black) a pistol. 4 [1940s] (US) a cheap cigar. 5 [1950s] an exceptional person. [all fig./ext. uses of SE *burn*]

burner n.[3] [1990s] (US Black/teen) a large piece of graffiti, usually involving many colours. [one 'burns' it onto the wall and/or it glows with colour]

burner n.[4] [1990s] (US Black/teen) a cellular telephone that is being used illegally. [BURN v.[2] (3)]

burners on high phr. [1990s] (US campus) being in a state of sexual excitement. [SE *(after)-burner*, an auxiliary burner fitted to the exhaust-pipe of a jet engine to increase its thrust]

burnese n. [1980s+] (drugs) cocaine. [BURNIE n.[1]]

burnie n.[1] [late 19C–1920s] (US drugs) cocaine. [BERNICE]

burnie n.[2] [1960s] (US drugs) a half-smoked marijuana cigarette. [SE *burn*]

burnie/burny blower n. [late 19C] (US drugs) a cocaine user. [BURNIE n.[1] + BLOW v.[2] (2)]

burning adj. [1920s] euph. for BLOODY adj.

burning-down habit n. [1950s+] an extremely heavy addiction to narcotics (cf. OIL-BURNER HABIT). [SE *burning down* + HABIT]

burning shame n. [late 18C] 1 a form of sexual 'game', whereby 'a lighted candle [is] stuck into the parts of a woman, certainly not intended by nature for a candlestick' (Grose, 1796). 2 a nightwatchman placed at the door of a brothel, holding a lantern, even in daylight, to deter people from wandering in and out. [puns]

burn it blue, to phr. [early 18C] to act outrageously, poss. by speaking very coarsely (cf. MAKE THE AIR BLUE). [SE *burn* + BLUE adj.[3]]

burn my breeches! excl. [early 19C] a general excl.

burn my skin! excl. [early–mid-19C] (US) a general oath.

burn off v. [1980s+] to accelerate past another driver. [BURN v.[4]]

burn on v. [1980s+] (US) to insult. [BURN v.[3] (5)]

burn one v. [1960s+] (drugs) to smoke marijuana. [BURN v.[6] (1)]

burn one on v. [1950s+] to become very drunk, to go on a drinking spree. [var. on TIE ONE ON]

burn one's collar, to phr. [1940s] (US) to get very angry. [GET HOT UNDER THE COLLAR]

burn one's foot, to phr. [20C] (US) to become pregnant (cf. BREAK ONE'S LEG phr.[1]; STUB ONE'S TOE).

burn one's poker, to phr. [19C–1900s] to catch a venereal disease. [fig. use of SE + BURN v.[1]]

burn one's shoulder, to phr. [20C] to be drunk. [the burn comes from a cigarette? by falling on the stove?]

burnout n. 1 [1960s+] (drugs) a heavy abuser of drugs. 2 [1980s+] one who has exhausted their capabilities, one who can no longer function efficiently at a job or discipline. [BURN OUT v. (3)]

burn out v. [1950s] 1 (US) to suffer a setback or failure. 2 (US Und.) to be arrested as a result of a tip-off or an informer. 3 [1960s+] to become mentally or physically exhausted.

burn powder v. [1930s+] (US) to fire a gun.

burn rubber v. [1970s+] to drive a car very fast (cf. BURN SMOKE; BURN THE EARTH). [the smoking tyres that accompany acceleration]

burn smoke v. [1970s] (US) to go very fast (cf. BURN RUBBER).

burn someone's ears, to phr. [1950s–60s] (US) to reprimand severely.

burn someone's goat, to phr. [1940s] (US) to infuriate, to annoy. [BURN v.[2] (4) + GET ONE'S GOAT]

burnt n. [1940s+] a window. [rhy. sl. *burnt cinder* = window (pron. winder)]

burnt adj.[1] see BURNED adj.[1].

burnt adj.[2] see BURNED adj.[2].

burnt adj.[3] [1970s+] (US campus) 1 disappointed, esp. sexually. 2 emotionally drained. 3 physically exhausted. [BURN OUT v. (3)]

burnt adj.[4] [1980s+] (US teen) terrible, hopeless. [BURNED OUT]

burnt out see BURNED OUT.

burn the breeze see BUST THE BREEZE.

burn the earth/ground/street, to phr. [late 19C+] (orig. US) to go very fast (cf. BURN RUBBER; BURN SMOKE). [one's acceleration causes the ground to catch fire]

burn the grass, to phr. [20C] (Aus.) to urinate in the open air. [the destructive effect of urine on grass]

burn the ground see BURN THE EARTH.

burn the ken, to phr. [early 18C–early 19C] to stay at an inn, then leave without paying one's bill. [BURN v.[2] (2) + KEN n.[1]]

burn the main line, to phr. [1980s+] (drugs) to inject a drug. [SE *burn* + MAINLINE n.]

burn the street see BURN THE EARTH.

burn the Thames, to phr. [late 18C] to accomplish a noteworthy feat (cf. SET THE THAMES ON FIRE).

burn the town, to phr. [late 17C–18C] of servicemen, to leave a town without paying for one's board and lodging. [BURN v.[2] (2) + SE *town*]

burn the water, to *phr.* [early–mid-19C] to spear salmon by torchlight. [late 19C+ use is SE]

burnt offering *n.* [late 19C+] a joking description of any food that has been burned on the stove.

burnt out *see* BURNED OUT.

burn-up *n.* [1950s+] fast riding of a motorcycle, esp. used by outlaw bike riders, Rockers etc (cf. BURN n.[4]). [BURN UP v.[2]]

burn up *v.*[1] (US) **1** [late 19C] to criticize severely. **2** [late 19C+] to annoy, to irritate (cf. BURNED AT). **3** [1980s+] to outdo, to surpass. [BURN v.[2] (4)]

burn up *v.*[2] [1950s+] to ride fast on a motorcycle.

burn up one's tail, to *phr.* [20C] (US) to work extremely hard. [SE *burn up* + TAIL n.[1]]

burn up the millpond, to *phr.* [19C] (US) to accomplish a noteworthy feat (cf. SET THE THAMES ON FIRE).

burn wheels, to *phr.* [1960s+] to drive a car very fast (cf. BURN RUBBER). [one's smoking wheels]

burn with a low blue flame, to *phr.* [1960s+] to be extremely drunk. [the image of lighting the alcohol fumes pouring from one's mouth]

burny blower *see* BURNIE BLOWER.

burn you! *excl.* [late 19C–1920s] go to hell! [earlier dial. use]

buroo/brew/buro *n.* [1930s+] (Ulster/Scot.) unemployment office, Labour exchange; thus *on the buroo*, unemployed and collecting benefits. [Scot. pron. of SE *bureau*]

burp *v.* **1** [1930s–70s] (US) to speak in a cheery or arrogant manner. **2** [1930s+] (orig. US) to belch. **2** [1960s+] (Aus.) to vomit, also as *burp a rainbow* (cf. TECHNICOLOUR YAWN). [echoic]

burp the baby, to *phr.* [1990s] to masturbate.

burp the worm, to *phr.* [1990s] to masturbate.

burr *n.* [16C–early 19C] a hanger-on, one who 'clings' (cf. BARNACLE n.[1]). [SE *burr*, a plant-head that clings to clothes etc]

burra *adj.* [19C–1950s] (Anglo-Ind.) great, large; thus *burra sahib*, a great man, *burra khana*, a banquet, *burra mem*, a great lady, *burra beebee*, a lady who claims precedence at social gatherings. [Hind. *burra*, great]

burrhead *n.*[1] [20C] (US) a Black person (cf. BURRHEADED adj.[2]). [SE *burr*, a rough file + *head*; the tightly curled Black hair]

burrhead *n.*[2] [1910s] (US) stupid. [SE *burr* + sfx. -HEAD (1)]

burrheaded *adj.*[1] [1940s] (US) stupid. [BURRHEAD n.[2]]

burrheaded *adj.*[2] [1950s+] (US) having the tight, curly hair typical of Black people. [BURRHEAD n.[1]]

burrito *n.* [1980s+] **1** (US campus) the penis. **2** (US) a derog. term for anyone of Latin or Spanish-American descent. [Mex. *burrito*, a maize-flour tortilla rolled round a savoury filling]

burrito on someone's nose, to *phr.* [1990s] (US Black) to interfere in another person's planned seduction (cf. SALT SOMEONE'S GAME). [for ety. *see* BURRITO]

burrito on your nose! *excl.* [1990s] (US Black teen) a general excl. of contempt, dismissal.

burrow *v.* [mid–late 18C] to live quietly or secretively. [later use is SE]

burry *n.* [1910s+] (Aus.) an Aborigine. [? pron. of A*borigine*]

burst *n.*[1] [mid-19C+] a burglary. [SE *burst*, the act of bursting, breaking open]

burst *n.*[2] [mid-19C+] a spree, a party with much eating and excessive drinking. [SE *burst*, a sudden flurry of activity; 20C use mainly Aus.]

burst *v.* **1** [late 19C–1900s] to spend one's money lavishly, to go out on a spree. **2** [late 19C+] to beat up, usu. as a threat *I'll burst him!*

burst/bust a blood-vessel, to *phr.* [20C] to lose one's temper, to lose emotional control (cf. HAVE A HAEMORRHAGE).

burst at the broadside, to *phr.* [late 17C–mid-19C] to break wind. [SE *burst* + joc. use of SE *broadside* as the buttocks]

burster *n.*[1] [mid-19C] a loaf of bread, also as *twopenny burster*, a twopenny loaf. [SE *burst*; it fills one's stomach]

burster *n.*[2] [mid-19C] **1** an exhausting physical effort. **2** anything of notable size or otherwise remarkable nature.

burster/buster *n.*[3] [mid–late 19C+] **1** a fall from a horse; thus *come a buster*, to fall from one's horse. **2** (Aus.) 'a cropper', in fig. uses. [one 'busts' oneself]

burst him!/burst her! *excl.* [late 19C] an excl. of annoyance, confound him! the hell with her! etc.

burst me bagpipes! *excl.* [1990s] (US Black teen) an excl. of surprise, astonishment, annoyance etc.

burst/bust one's boiler, to *phr.* [early–mid-19C] (orig. US) **1** to come to grief, to get into trouble. **2** to lose one's temper. **3** to cause trouble for. [fig. uses of SE]

burst/bust/cave in someone's crust, to *phr.* [mid-19C–1910s] (US) **1** to hit hard enough to break the skin. **2** to suffer a knock or injury that breaks the skin.

burst/bother/rack/wear out/work out one's soul-case, to *phr.* [late 19C+] (W.I.) to wear oneself out with hard work. [SE *burst/bother/rack/wear out/work out* + SOUL-CASE]

burst one's stay-lace, to *phr.* [late 19C] to become overexcited, over-emotional.

burst someone's bubble, to *phr.* [1970s+] (US campus) to humiliate, to deflate someone's ego.

burst up *v.* [late 19C–1920s] to become very angry or perturbed.

burton *n.* [1960s–70s] a male prostitute. [rhy. sl. *Burton-on-Trent* = RENT n.[2]]

Burton-on-Trent *n.* [late 19C+] the rent. [rhy. sl.; ult. the UK town]

bury *v.* (US) **1** [late 19C–1900s] to eat heartily. **2** [20C] to condemn to a long spell in prison. **3** [1930s+] to kill, to murder. [all fig. uses of SE]

bury a moll, to *phr.* [mid-19C] to run away from one's mistress. [SE *bury* + MOLL n. (3)]

bury a quaker, to *phr.* [18C–19C] to defecate (cf. MUFFIN BAKER). [SE *bury* + QUAKER]

bury Caesar *v.* [1920s] (US) of a man, to insert one's penis into a woman's vagina. [? pun on the speech that starts 'Friends, Romans, *count*rymen.']

bury ground *see* BURY PATCH.

burying face *n.* [late 19C–1900s] a miserable face. [an expression suitable for a funeral]

bury it *v.* [mid-19C+] of a man, to have sexual intercourse (cf. BURY CAESAR; BURY ONE'S BONE).

bury old fagin, to *phr.* [1950s] of a man, to have sexual intercourse (cf. BURY CAESAR; BURY ONE'S BONE; INTRODUCE HER TO FAGAN). [SE *bury* + FAGAN]

bury one's bone, to *phr.* [1980s+] (US Black teen) to have sexual intercourse. [SE *bury* + BONE n.]

bury one's bone in the back garden, to *phr.* [1990s] to sodomize. [BURY ONE'S BONE + pun on SE]

bury patch/ground *n.* [20C] (US) a cemetery. [dial. *bury*, to be buried]

bury the baldy fella/fellow, to *phr.* [1980s+] (Irish) to achieve vaginal penetration, thus to have sexual intercourse (cf. BALD-HEADED HERMIT).

bury the brisket, to *phr.* [1950s+] (US) to have sexual intercourse (cf. BURY ONE'S BONE; HIDE THE SALAMI).

bury the hatchet, to *phr.* [late 18C+] to make up one's differences; thus [late 19C] *dig up the hatchet*, to renew hostilities. [the *hatchet* as a symbol of hostility; 20C use is SE]

bury the knuckle, to *phr.* [1990s] of a woman, to masturbate.

bury the landlady, to *phr.* [late 19C] to leave one's lodgings without paying the rent.

bury the tomahawk, to *phr.* [20C] (US) to have sexual intercourse (cf. SHOOT v.[3] (1); STAB IN THE THIGH).

bus *n.*[1] [late 19C–1900s] a dowdy dress. [such a garment is only worth wearing for a trip on public transport]

bus *n.*[2] **1** [1910s–40s] an aeroplane. **2** [1920s] an automobile, esp. a large one (cf. BLIXEN-BUS; BLUNDERBUS). **3** [1920s] a motorcycle. **4** [1930s] (US) an elevator, a lift. [all exts. of SE (*omni*)*bus*]

bus/bus it *v.*[1] [mid-19C+] to travel by bus.

bus/bust *v.*[2] [1990s] (US Black) to have fun, to enjoy oneself. [abbr. BUST A GUT *phr.* (2)]

bus! *excl.* [mid–late 19C] enough! stop! [Hind. *bas*, stop!]

bus and tram *n.* [20C] jam. [rhy. sl.]

bus-bellied ben *n.* [late 19C–1900s] an alderman. [his stomach has the dimensions of an omnibus; hence the rhyme 'Bus-bellied Ben/Eats enough for ten']

busby *n.* [19C] the pubic hair. [SE *busby*, the tall fur cap as worn by various regiments of the British army]

bush *n.*[1] [16C] (Und.) the place where thieves defraud their victim (cf. CONY-CATCHER). [the imagery reflects the world of hunting; cf. BEATER n.[1]; BIRD n.[1]]

bush *n.*[2] [late 19C] the cat-o'-nine-tails. [resemblance]

bush *n.*[3] [20C] (US) an important person, or one who likes to pose as such (cf. BUSHWA; PUSH n.[2]). [? SE *bourgeois*]

bush *n.*[4] **1** [1920s+] the pubic hair of either sex (cf. DAMBER-BUSH; DILBERRY-BUSH; FOREST; FORT BUSHY; FURZE-BUSH; GARDEN n.[1]; GOOSEBERRY BUSH n.[1]; GRASS n.[3]; GREEN GROVE; GROVE OF EGLANTINE; LAWN n.[2]; MOSS n.[1]; MOSS ROSE; PARSLEY n.[1]; QUIM BUSH; SHRUBBERY; STUBBLE; SWEET BRIAR; WHIN-BUSH). **2** [1920s+] (Aus.) a young woman, seen in a purely sexual context. **3** [1920s+] (Aus.) a moustache. **4** [1960s+] a hairstyle in which normally short, curly black hair is allowed to grow out around the head (cf. AFRO n.[2]).

bush *n.*[5] [1930s+] (Aus.) the suburbs.

bush *n.*[6] (drugs) **1** [1960s+] marijuana (cf. AFRICAN BUSH). **2** [1980s+] cocaine. [both are plants]

bush/bush league *adj.*[1] [20C] (US) amateur, unprofessional, unsophisticated. [baseball jargon *bush leagues*, second-rate teams, leagues and thus players]

bush *adj.*[2] **1** [20C] (US) second-rate, unsophisticated, amateur (cf. BUSH adj.[1]). **2** [1970s+] (S.Afr.) uncivilized, inferior, rough-and-ready, esp. in combs., e.g. *bush justice*, *bush carpentry*, *bush education*. [SE *bush*, the rough, uncultivated country-side]

bush/bush it *v.*[1] [early–mid 19C] (Aus.) to live in the bush and survive the rigours of life there. [SE *bush*]

bush *v.*[2] [mid-19C+] (US) to exhaust, to tire out. [BUSHED adj.[2] (2)]

bush *v.*[3] [1940s+] (US) to ambush, to mug. [abbr. BUSH-WHACK]

bush *v.*[4] [1970s] to trick, to lie (to). [BUSHWA]

bush ape *n.* [1940s] **1** (US) a peasant (cf. BRUSH APE). **2** (Aus.) a rural worker. **3** (Aus.) an itinerant fruit-picker, usu. in Queensland.

bush around *v.* [20C] to consider, to ponder over. [BEAT ABOUT THE BUSH]

bush baby *n.* [20C] (US) an illegitimate baby (cf. BABY IN THE BUSHES; WOODS COLT). [SE *bush*, lightly forested land + *baby*; such a child is conceived or born there]

bush bacon *n.* [20C] (US) a rabbit (cf. ADIRONDACK STEAK).

bush baptist *n.* [late 19C] (mainly Aus./N.Z.) one who has either no religion or belongs to a dubious sub-cult. [BUSH adj.[2] + SE *baptist*]

bush-bashing *n.* [1960s+] (Aus.) driving around the bush in a 4-wheeled off-road vehicle.

bush-beater *n.* [19C] the penis (cf. ARSE-OPENER). [BUSH n.[4] (1) + SE *beater* + pun on SE *phr.* *beat around the bush*]

bushbitch *n.* [1980s+] (US) an ugly woman (cf. BUSHPIG). [SE *bush* + BITCH n.[1] (1)]

bush boogie *n.* [1990s] (US) a Black person. [SE *bush* + BOOGIE n.[2]]

bush bunny *n.* [1920s+] (Aus.) a gullible fool. [SE *bush* + BUNNY n.[3]]

bush carpenter *n.* [20C] (Aus.) a second-rate carpenter. [BUSH adj.[2] (1)]

bush college/university *n.* [1970s+] (S.Afr.) a derog. description (by Black students) of a segregated, Blacks-only college or university. [BUSH adj.[2] (2)]

bush-cove *n.* [19C] a gypsy. [SE *bush* + COVE n. (1); their sleeping under hedges]

bush dinner *n.*[1] [late 19C+] (Aus.) a damper (a form of unleavened cake, baked in the ashes), mutton and tea; thus *bushman's hot dinner*, a damper and mustard. [SE *bush* + *dinner*]

bush dinner *n.*[2] [1960s+] (US) cunnilingus. [BUSH n.[4] (1) + SE *dinner*]

bushed *adj.*[1] [early 19C] (Aus.) poor, impoverished. [SE *bush*]

bushed *adj.*[2] **1** [mid-19C+] (Aus.) disorientated, lost in the bush; thus fig. 'lost' (for ideas, words etc). **2** [late 19C+] (orig. US) exhausted, tired out, as if one had been wandering, lost, through the woods. [BUSH v.[1]]

bushed on *adj.* [19C] very pleased with.

bushel and peck *n.* [late 19C+] the neck (cf. GREGORY PECK). [rhy. sl.]

bushel bubby *n.* [late 18C] a woman with large breasts (cf. MISS VAN-NECK). [SE *bushel*, a dry measure + BUBBY n.]

bushel-cunted *adj.* [mid-19C+] having a large vagina (cf. COW-CUNTED; SLUICE-CUNTED). [SE *bushel*, a measure of volume; thus a large quantity + CUNT n.[1] (1)]

bushel of coke *n.* [20C] a man. [rhy. sl. *bushel of coke* = BLOKE]

busher *n.* [1920s+] (US) an amateur, an unsophisticated person. [BUSH adj.[1]]

bushey park *see* BUSHY PARK.

bushfire blonde *n.* [1940s+] (Aus.) a red-headed woman (cf. BOTTLE BABY n.[2]). [the flames of the bushfire]

bush-head *n.*[1] [1940s] a naïve, unsophisticated person, a peasant (cf. BUSHY). [BUSH adj.[2] + sfx. -HEAD (1)]

bush-head *n.*[2] [1980s] (US) a person with bushy hair.

bush hog *n.* [1980s] (US) a peasant (cf. BRUSH APE).

bushie *n.* [20C] (W.I.) a form of unlicensed and very potent rum distilled secretly in the countryside. [SE *bush*]

bush it *see* BUSH v.[1].

bush lawyer *n.* [early 19C+] (Aus.) one who claims to 'lay down the law', but has no real authority to do so (cf. BARRACK-ROOM LAWYER). [SE *bush* + *lawyer*]

bush league *see* BUSH adj.[1].

bushman's bible *n.* [late 19C+] (Aus.) the Sydney *Bulletin* (cf. BULLY n.[3]). [SE *bushman*, one who lives in the bush or outback + Bible. The magazine always backed the interest of those living outside the big cities]

bushman's breakfast *n.* [late 19C+] (Aus.) a look around and a cough (cf. AIR PIE AND A WALK AROUND). [the lack of 'civilized' amenities in the bush]

bushman's clock *n.* [late 19C+] (Aus.) a kookaburra or laughing jackass (cf. SHEPHERD'S CLOCK). [its sounds punctuate the day]

bushman's friend *n.* **1** [late 19C+] (S.Afr.) a large bush-cutting knife. **2** [1970s+] (N.Z.) any large-leafed plant that can be used as lavatory 'paper'.

bush parole *n.* [20C] (US prison) an escape (cf. JACKRABBIT PAROLE). [SE *bush* + *parole*]

bush patrol *n.* [1950s+] (US) **1** sexual fore-play. **2** sexual intercourse. [BUSH n.[4] (1) + SE *patrol*]

bushpig *n.* [1980s+] (US campus) an extremely ugly woman (cf. BUSHBITCH).

bush radio/wireless *n.* [1930s+] (Aus.) a network of gossip and rumour that brings news, often inaccurate, before the official sources (cf. BUSH TELEGRAPH).

bushranger *n.* (Aus.) **1** [20C] a petty swindler. **2** [1950s] a dubious business enterprise that exploits rather than serves its customers (cf. COWBOY n.[1]).

bush rat *n.* [1930s–40s] (US) a peasant, a hill-billy (cf. BRUSH APE).

bush-scrubber *n.*[1] [late 19C] (Aus.) a boor, a bumpkin. [SE *bush* + SAusE *scrubber*, one who lives in the scrub]

bush-scrubber *n.*[2] [20C] a rural prostitute. [SE *bush* + SCRUBBER n.[2]]

bush-tail *adj.* [20C] (Aus.) cunning, deceptive. [image of an animal vanishing into the bush]

bush telegraph *n.* (orig. Aus.) **1** [mid-19C–1900s] a member of a bushranging gang whose task is to keep colleagues informed of the whereabouts of potential victims or efforts to capture them. **2** [mid-19C+] a network of gossip and rumour that brings news, often inaccurate, before the official sources (cf. JUNGLE TELEGRAPH; MOCCASIN TELEGRAPH).

bush university *see* BUSH COLLEGE.

bush up *v.* [1970s+] (Aus.) to confuse, to baffle. [BUSH v.[4]]

bushwa / bushwah / booshwa / booshwah / boushwa / boushwah *n.* **1** [19C] a pretentious, arrogant person. **2** [20C] euph. for BULLSHIT n. [(1) f. Can. *bourgeois*, the head voyageur of a trading post or expedition. (2) f. BULLSHIT n., but ? link to Can. *bois de vache*, buffalo dung]

bush week *n.* [1940s+] (Aus.) a fig. 'week' when dubious deals may be proposed and confidence tricks carried out, usu. in phr. *What do you think of this? Bush Week?*, used to fend off what is considered a dubious suggestion. [the image of the rural 'bush' dwellers coming innocently to town]

bushwhack *v.* **1** [19C] (orig. US) to ambush, to attack without warning. **2** [19C] to borrow without permission; the theory is that such items will, eventually, be returned, but the term (and the action) is virtually synon. with stealing. **3** [1910s–40s] (US campus) to have sexual intercourse in a field or wood. **4** [1950s–70s] (US campus) to spy and sneak up on courting couples in automobiles. [SE *bushwhack*, to live in the backwoods. Those settlers who did so were doubtless versed in moving quietly through the woods in pursuit of prey]

bushwhacked *adj.* [1960s] (orig. US) very drunk. [BUSH-WHACK]

bushwhacker *n.* **1** [19C] (orig. US) an ambusher, an attacker. **2** [19C] (US) an illegitimate child (cf. BUSH BABY). **3** [20C] (Aus.) one who lives far from urban 'civilization'. [BUSH-WHACK]

bush whisky *n.* [20C] (US) illicitly distilled or contraband liquor (cf. MOONSHINE n.). [SE *bush* + *whisky*]

bush wireless *see* BUSH RADIO.

bushy *n.* **1** [mid-19C+] (Aus./W.I.) one who lives in the country. **2** [1980s+] (S.Afr.) a half-caste. [SE *bush*]

bushy *adj.* [mid-19C+] (Aus./W.I.) unsophisticated, countri-fied. [BUSHY n.]

bushy/bushey park *n.*[1] [mid-19C] female pubic hair; thus *take a turn at Bushy Park*, of a man, to have sexual inter-course (cf. BEAUTY SPOT n.[1]). [BUSH n.[4] (1) + pun on the proper name]

bushy/bushey park *n.*[2] [mid-19C–1900s] a lark, a joke. [rhy. sl.]

business *n.*[1] **1** [17C–18C] sexual intercourse. **2** [1900s–60s] (US) prostitution. **3** [1920s] (US) a woman. **4** [1940s+] (orig. US) the male or female genitals.

business *n.*[2] **1** [mid-17C–mid-19C] a vague description of un-specified mechanical/material objects. **2** [late 17C+] a matter in which one may interfere; thus *mind one's own business*, to keep out of other people's affairs. **3** [mid-19C+] a difficult situation.

business *n.*[3] [mid-19C+] a euph. term for faeces, esp. in phr. *do one's business*.

business, the *n.*[4] [late 19C+] the best, the peak of excellence, often found as *do the business* (although *do one's business* is a colloquial euph. for defecate).

business *n.*[5] [1930s+] (drugs) the equipment used to take opium and, latterly, heroin (cf. BIZ n.[2]).

business *n.*[6] [1940s] (US) intense interrogation, 'the third degree'.

business boy *n.* [20C] a homosexual male prostitute (cf. ASS PEDDLER). [BUSINESS n.[1] + SE *boy*]

business end *n.* [late 19C+] that part (practical or meta-phorical) that really matters; thus (US) *the business end of a tin tack*, the point. [BUSINESS n.[4]]

business girl *n.* [1920s+] a prostitute (cf. WORKING GIRL). [BUSINESS n.[1] + SE *girl*]

businessman's trip/special *n.* [1960s+] (drugs) methyl-amphetamine (cf. BOMBITA). [unlike the 8-hour duration of a 'normal' LSD TRIP n.[3], this vastly intensified experience lasts only a few minutes, leaving the user free to get on with other things]

busing *n.* [20C] (W.I.) verbal violence, using obscene and aggressive language. [SE *abuse*]

bus it *see* BUS v.[2]

busk *v.* **1** [mid-19C] to sell obscene songs and books in the streets and public houses. **2** [mid-19C+] to work as a street performer. [? naut. jargon *busk*, to cruise the seas, esp. as a pirate, ult. Ital. *buscare*, to filch, to prowl]

busker *n.* [mid-19C–1950s] one who sings, plays or otherwise entertains in public houses or, latterly, on the street, typically alongside a cinema queue. [BUSK v.; SE after mid-20C]

busman *see* BUSTMAN.

busnacking/buznacking *n.* [mid-19C–1900s] **1** prying, interfering, butting in. **2** acting in an excessively fussy, officious manner. [dial. *buzz*, to move around in an agitated manner + dial. *knack*, to talk in an affected manner. ? link to SE *nag*; note naut. jargon *busk*, to tack about]

bus-/buz-napper *n.* **1** [18C] a constable. **2** [20C] (Aus.) a policeman. [BUZZ n.[1] (2) + NAB v.[1] (2); lit. 'pickpocket-taker']

bus-/buz-nappers' academy *n.* [18C] a school for thieves. [BUS-NAPPER + SE *academy*]

bus-napper's kinchin *n.* [18C] a watchman. [BUS-NAPPER + KINCHIN]

buss *v.* [20C] (US) to court. [SE *buss*, a kiss]

buss a lime, to *phr.* [20C] (W.I.) to enjoy a spontaneous social gathering. [BUST v.[1] (1) + LIME n.]

buss arse *v.* [20C] (W.I.) to beat, to thrash. [BUST v.[1] (1) + ARSE n.1 (1)]

buss beggar *n.* **1** [17C–19C] an ageing prostitute. **2** [18C–early 19C] an aged roué whose enthusiasm for sexual encounters is matched only by the unwillingness of the young and pretty to offer them (cf. FUCK-BEGGAR; in both cases the subject is 'begging for a kiss']. [BUSS + SE *beggar*; in both cases the subject is 'begging for a kiss']

buss-belt *n.* [1960s+] (W.I.) a very fat man. [SE *burst belt*]

buss cunu *v.* [20C] (W.I.) to have sexual intercourse. [BUST v.[1] (1) + CUNNY]

buss dirt *v.* [20C] (W.I.) to make the fastest possible of exits. [BUST v.[4] (1) + SE *dirt*]

busser *n.*[1] [mid-19C] (US) the mouth (cf. KISSER n.[1]). [SE *buss*, to kiss]

busser *n.*[2] [late 19C] a bus horse.

bussie/bussy *n.* [1940s–50s] a bus worker.

buss me rass! *excl.* [late 18C+] (W.I.) kiss my arse! [SE *buss* + ARSE n.[1] (1)]

bussy *see* BUSSIE.

bust *n.*¹ **1** [mid-19C+] (orig. US) a financial collapse. **2** [mid-19C+] (US) an absolute failure, esp. an embarrassing one or a misjudgement. **3** [late 19C–1920s] (US campus) failure in one's examinations. **4** [1980s+] (US campus) fault, as in *my bust.* [dial. var. of SE *burst*]

bust *n.*² **1** [late 19C+] a burglary. **2** [late 19C only in UK but extended in Aus. use] breaking and entering. **3** [1950s+] (US Black) the police. **4** [1950s+] (orig. US) an arrest. **5** [1950s+] a police raid, esp. on drug-users or -dealers. [for ety. see BUST n.¹]

bust *n.*³ [late 19C+] (orig. US) a drinking party, a spree, a celebration; thus (Aus.) *on the bust*, on a spree (cf. BEER BUST; BURST n.). [SE *burst*, a frolic, a spree]

bust *n.*⁴ [1960s] (US Black) an orgasm. [BUST v.⁴]

bust *v.*¹ (orig. US) **1** [early 19C+] to smash, to break up. **2** [late 19C+] to hit (with the fist). **3** [late 19C+] to kill. **4** [late 19C+] to demote, often found as *bust down/down to.* **5** [1950s+] to arrest, to catch red-handed, esp. to catch in possession of drugs. **6** [1980s+] (US Black) to do, to perform, to act. [dial form of SE *burst*]

bust *v.*² **1** [early 19C+] (US) to cause to go bankrupt, to ruin. **2** [mid-19C+] (US) to get the better of, to 'put one over'. **3** [mid-19C+] (orig. US) to come to financial ruin, to go bankrupt; thus *go bust.* **4** [mid-19C+] to inform against (cf. SPLIT v.³). [for ety. see BUST v.¹]

bust *v.*³ (US campus) **1** [mid-19C–1970s] to fail an examination. **2** [1960s+] of a college professor, to fail a student. **3** [1980s+] to do well, esp. in a test, to receive a good grade, e.g. *he busted an A in Math.* [fig. use of BUST v.¹]

bust *v.*⁴ **1** [mid-19C+] (orig. US) to go very fast, also as *bust along, bust by* (cf. TEAR v.). **2** [late 19C+] to explode with rage and pent-up emotion. [var. on SE *burst*]

bust *v.*⁵ **1** [mid-19C+] (US) to defeat. **2** [late 19C+] to intrude, to break into. **3** [late 19C] to kill, to murder. **4** [1960s+] to rape, to deflower (forcibly). [ext. uses of BUST v.¹]

bust/bust up *v.*⁶ **1** [late 19C+] (Aus.) to waste money, usu. on drink. **2** [late 19C+] to have a major quarrel, to end a love-affair. **3** [1980s+] (US) to break down in laughter. **4** [1980s+] (US) to make someone else laugh (cf. BREAK UP). [fig use of BUST v.¹ (1) + SE *up*]

bust/busta joint *v.*⁷ [1950s–70s] (drugs) to smoke a cannabis cigarette. [fig. use of BUST v.¹ (6), although chronology as recorded is wrong]

bust *v.*⁸ [1980s+] (rap music) to pay attention, to notice. [fig. use of BUST v.¹ (1)]

bust *v.*⁹ *see* BUS v.

bust! *excl.* [1900s–30s] a mild excl., dash it!

busta *n.* [1990s] (rap music) **1** a fake person, a weak individual. **2** a snitch, a person who tattle-tales. [BUSTER n.² (5)]

busta backbone *n.* [1950s] (W.I.) a tough sugar candy, extremely hard to chew (cf. BOSTA; IRON CUNNY). [the effort of chewing it will *bust one's backbone*]

bust a blood-vessel *see* BURST A BLOOD-VESSEL.

busta brown *see* BUSTER n.¹¹.

bust a cap/caps, to *phr.* (drugs) **1** [1930s+] to fire a bullet. **2** [1950s] to inject a shot of heroin (which comes in capsule form). [BUST v.¹ (2) + CAP n.³, n.⁴]

bust a frog! *excl.* [mid-19C–1930s] (Cockney) a mild excl.

bust a grape, to *phr.* [1970s] (US Black) to engage in any form of hard, productive work. [? BUST v.¹ (1) + GRAPES n.²]

bust a gusset, to *phr.* [20C] (US) to break down with laughter, to lose control, to make a superlative effort. [BUST v.¹ (1) + SE *gusset*; the straining so hard that the seams of one's clothes split]

bust/break/rupture a gut, to *phr.* **1** [late 17C+] to work very hard. **2** [mid-18C+] to strain oneself by laughing (cf. BUST ONE'S FARTING STRINGS; BUST ONE'S NUT). **3** [1940s+] (US) to

explode with rage. [BUST v.¹ (1)/SE *break/rupture* + SE *gut*]

bust a ham string, to *phr.* [19C] (US) to work very hard (cf. BUST A GUT). [BUST v.¹ (1) + SE *hamstring*]

bust a joint *see* BUST v.⁷.

bust a move, to *phr.* [1980s+] (US Black) **1** to make a physical move. **2** to make a serious effort, to take action. [(1) BUST v.¹ (6) + SE *move*; (2) BUST v.¹ (6) + MOVE n. (1)]

bust a nut, to *phr.* [1990s] to masturbate. [BUST v.¹ (1) + NUT n.¹¹]

bust-ass *adj.* [1980s+] (US) a general derog. term. [BUST v.¹ (1) + ARSE n.1]

bust a sweat, to *phr.* [1980s+] (US Black) to be sexually excited. [BUST v.¹ (1) + SE *sweat*]

bust caps *see* BUST A CAP.

busted *adj.*¹ [mid-19C+] (orig. US) without money. [BUST v.¹ (5)]

busted *adj.*² [1950s] depressed, in pain. [BUST v.¹ (1)]

busted *adj.*³ [1950s+] arrested, esp. on drug charges. [BUST v.¹ (5)]

buster *n.*¹ **1** [mid-late 19C] a housebreaker. **2** [1950s+] (Can.) a shoplifter (cf. BOOSTER n.²). [BUST v.¹ (1)]

buster *n.*² **1** [mid-19C] a 'roistering blade'. **2** [mid-late 19C] a dandy. **3** [mid-19C+] something exceptional of its type (cf. BOOSTER n.¹). **4** [late 19C] the teenage Bavarian giantess, who appeared in London music-halls under the name 'Maid Marian' and after a brief but successful career died before she reached the age of 20. **5** [20C] a large or full-grown child. **6** [20C] (US Black gang) a loser, a failure, a coward, a general derog. term. [fig. uses of BUST v.¹ (1)]

buster *n.*³ [mid-late 19C] a spree; thus *in for a buster*, keen to go out on a spree. [BUST n.³]

buster *n.*⁴ *see* BURSTER n.³.

buster *n.*⁵ [late 19C+] (Aus.) an exhausting physical effort (cf. BURSTER n.²).

buster *n.*⁶ [20C] a person, often an old and cantankerous one; thus *old buster*, a general term of (affectionate) address.

buster *n.*⁷ *see* BALL-BUSTER.

buster *n.*⁸ [1920s+] (US) a general term of address to any otherwise unnamed male (cf. CHIEF n.¹; GUV; JOHN n.¹; MAC n.¹; MATE; SQUIRE n.²). [ext. of BUSTER n.⁶]

buster *n.*⁹ [1970s] (US) a motor vehicle that gives one a bumpy and painful ride. [abbr. *kidney-buster*; BUST v.¹ (1)]

buster *n.*¹⁰ [1990s] (US Black) an informer. [BUST v.² (4)]

buster/busta brown *n.* [1990s] (US Black) a hanger-on. [ext. of BUSTER n.¹⁰]

busters *n.*¹ [1960s–70s] (US Black) pleasure, enjoyment, 'kicks'. [fig. use of BUST v.¹ (1)]

busters *n.*² [1980s+] (drugs) depressant. [BUST v.¹ (1)]

busters *n.*³ [1990s] (US Black) the police. [BUST v.¹ (5)]

bust fresh *v.* [1980s+] (US teen) to look one's best, usu. coupled to a specific event, such as a party, an anniversary, a festival. [BUST v.¹ (6) + FRESH adj.³]

busthead *n.* [mid-19C+] (US) strong whisky, esp. when illegally distilled. [BUST v.¹ (1) + SE *head*]

bust him! *see* BUST ME!

busting *adj.*¹ [mid-19C–1920s] (US) very large; thus *busting big.* [BUSTER n.² (1)]

busting *adj.*² [1950s+] desperate. [SE *bursting*]

busting out *phr.* [1990s] (US Black) looking good, attractive, well-dressed, successful etc. [fig. use of BUST v.¹ (1)]

bust it! *excl.*¹ *see* BUST ME!

bust it! *excl.*² [1930s+] (N.Z.) an excl. of annoyance, frustration.

bustle *n.*¹ [early–mid-19C] money; thus *on the bustle*, cadging a loan (cf. SCRAMBLE; SCRATCH n.²). [SE *bustle*, stir, fuss, tumult]

bustle *n.*² [1920s–70s] (US) the buttocks, the posterior. [SE *bustle*, a 'dress-improver'; i.e. a small pad or wire framework that accentuates the back of the dress]

bustle *v.* [mid-19C+] to confuse, to perplex. [ext. use of SE *bustle*, to stir, to rouse]

bustle-punching *n.* [1960s+] (police) the action of the *frotteur*, using the anonymity of a dense crowd to rub one's penis against the nearby buttocks of defenceless women. [SE *bustle*, a 'dress-improver' and out of fashion in the 20C + *punching*]

bust loose *v.* [1940s+] (US) to break free of constraints. [BUST v.¹ (1) + SE *loose*]

bust-maker *n.* [19C] a seducer, a womanizer. [SE *bust*, the female breasts; i.e. the increased size of a pregnant woman's breasts]

bustman/busman *n.* [1940s+] (Aus.) a burglar, a housebreaker. [BUST n.² (1) + SE *man*]

bust me!/bust him!/bust it!/bust you! *excl.* [mid–late 19C] a mild oath (cf. BLOW ME!). [BUST v.¹ (1)]

bust my boiler! *excl.* [20C] an excl. of surprise or annoyance.

bust my gizzard! *excl.* [mid-19C] (US) a mild oath.

bust on *v.* [1990s] (US Black) to inform against someone. [BUST v.² (4)]

bust/break one's arse/ass, to *phr.* **1** [1930s+] (orig. US) to work exceptionally hard. **2** [1940s+] (orig. US) to get injured (esp. in a car or similar crash). [BUST v.¹ (1) + ARSE n.¹]

bust one's balls *see* BREAK ONE'S BALLS.

bust one's bananas, to *phr.* [1970s] (US) to work to the limits of one's ability and strength. [BUST v.¹ (1) + SE *bananas*]

bust one's boiler *see* BURST ONE'S BOILER.

bust one's buttons, to *phr.* [20C] (US) to strain oneself physically or emotionally. [BUST v.¹ (1) + SE *buttons*; the real or fig. bursting out of one's clothing]

bust one's chops, to *phr.* [1950s+] (US) **1** to talk incessantly. **2** to make a great fuss about something (cf. BEAT ONE'S CHOPS; BREAK ONE'S CHOPS). [BUST v.¹ (1) + CHOPS n.(3)]

bust one's conk, to *phr.* [1930s–40s] (US Black) **1** to work very hard. **2** to show one's happiness in an emotional outburst. [BUST v.¹ (1) + CONK n.¹ (6)]

bust one's farting strings, to *phr.* [1990s] to strain oneself through laughter or indignation (cf. BUST A GUT).

bust one's hump, to *phr.* [late 19C+] to work very hard (cf. GET A HUMP ON). [BUST v.¹ (1) + fig. use of SE *hump*, a humped back]

bust one's kicks off, to *phr.* [1920s+] (US) to reach orgasm. [fig. use of BUST v. (1) + KICK n.⁵ (3)]

bust/beat one's nut/nuts, to *phr.* **1** [1930s+] (US) to strain oneself, esp. by laughing (cf. BUST A GUT). **2** [1940s+] to have sexual intercourse, to come to orgasm. [BUST v.¹ (1) + NUTS n.² (1)]

bust open *v.* [1950s] (US) to distress, to make unhappy. [BUST v.¹ (1) + SE *open*]

bust-out *n.*¹ [20C] an enormous feast (cf. BLOW-OUT n.¹). [BUST v.¹ (1) + SE *out*]

bust-out *n.*² **1** [1930s+] (US) an escape, esp. f. prison. **2** [1960s+] (US) failure, ruin, a 'smash-up'. [BUST v.¹ (1) + SE *out*]

bust-out *adj.*¹ [1950s+] (US) an intensifying adj., extreme, tremendous, great, obvious, simple. [BUST v.¹ (1) + SE *out*]

bust-out *adj.*² **1** [1960s+] illegal. **2** [1970s+] (US) impoverished. [BUST v.¹ (1) + SE *out*]

bust out *v.* **1** [1930s+] (US campus) to expel a student. **2** [1960s+] (US) to ruin financially, esp. through gambling. [BUST v.¹ (1) + SE *out*]

bust out with *see* BREAK OUT WITH.

bust rhymes/rhythms, to *phr.* [1980s+] (rap music) to work as a rap music DJ or MC. [BUST v.¹ (6) + SE *rhymes*; *rhythms*]

bustskull *n.* [late 19C+] (US) strong whisky, esp. when illegally distilled (cf. BUSTHEAD). [BUST v.¹ (1) + SE *skull*]

bust slugs *v.* [1990s] to fire a gun (cf. BUST A CAP). [BUST v.¹ (1) + SE *slug*]

bust some booty, to *phr.* [1980s+] (US Black) **1** to perform sexual intercourse (cf. BANG v.¹). **2** to perform anal intercourse. [BUST v.¹ (1) + BOOTY n.]

bust someone out *v.* [1980s+] (US Black) of a man, to have sexual intercourse with someone, to bring to orgasm. [BUST n.⁴]

bust/break someone's arse/ass, to *phr.* **1** [1950s+] (orig. US) to beat up, to attack physically. **2** [1960s+] (US) to harass, to nag, to annoy. [BUST v.¹ (1) + ARSE n.¹]

bust someone's crust *see* BURST SOMEONE'S CRUST.

bust someone's horns, to *phr.* [1980s+] (US) to goad, to annoy someone.

bust someone's hump, to *phr.* [1920s+] (US) to harass, to annoy, to persecute someone.

bust someone up *v.* [mid-19C+] to beat someone up, to hurt someone in a fight. [BUST v.¹ (1) + SE *up*]

bust suds *v.* [1920s+] (US Black) to work as a washer-up. [BUST v.¹ (6) + SE *suds*]

bust/burn/fan the breeze, to *phr.* [late 19C+] (US) to go fast, orig. on horseback (cf. SPLIT THE BREEZE). [BUST v.¹ (1) + fig. uses of SE *burn/fan* + *breeze*]

bust this! *excl.* [1980s+] (US) (rap music) now look here! pay attention! (cf. BUST v.⁸). [BUST v.¹ (6)]

bust-up *n.* **1** [mid-19C+] (US) an explosion. **2** [late 19C+] a serious quarrel or argument.

bust up *v. see* BUST v.⁶.

busty *adj.* [1940s+] of a female, having large breasts, often in comb., e.g. *busty beauty*.

bust you! *see* BUST ME!

busy *n.* [20C] a CID officer, a detective (cf. FUZZ n.¹). [their rushing around, unlike a uniformed officer, who plods along a set beat]

busy as a body louse *phr.* [mid-17C–late 19C] very busy (cf. BRAG AS A BODY LOUSE).

busy as a hen with one chick *phr.* [17C+] very fussy, extremely punctilious. [a hen would not usually be able to concentrate all her attentions on but a single chick]

busy as a one-armed bill-poster/milker/milker with hives *phr.* [1950s+] (Aus.) extremely busy.

busy as a one-armed paper-hanger *phr.* [late 19C+] (Aus.) extremely busy.

busy as the devil in a gale/high wind *phr.* [18C] very busy.

busy bee *n.* [1970s+] (drugs) phencyclidine (cf. ACE n.³). [rhy. sl. *busy bee* = PCP]

busy-lickum *n.* [1940s+] **1** a gossip, a tattle-tale. **2** gossip (cf. CARRY-GO-BRING-COME). [fig. use of SE *busy* + *lick*, to hit]

busy-sack *n.* [mid-19C–1900s] a carpet-bag. [? SE *business*]

but *adv.* **1** [mid-19C+] (Aus.) used (mainly) at the end of sentences to give added emphasis, 'no doubt about it', 'absolutely'; e.g. *He's a nice bloke, but*. **2** [1930s+] (US) used as an intensifier, e.g. *but crazy, but cool*.

butch *n.*¹ [mid-19C] (US) a *butcher*'s knife. [abbr.]

butch *n.*² [1910s+] a vendor, a seller of sweets etc. [abbr. BUTCHER n.⁵]

butch *n.*³ (orig. US) **1** [1930s+] a nickname for a tough man, e.g. the hero of Damon Runyon's short story 'Butch Minds the Baby' (1930). **2** [1930s+] a masculine lesbian (cf. FEMME). **3** [1930s+] a masculine male homosexual. **4** [1940s+] a short, 'macho' haircut (used for either gender). [SE *butcher*, a 'man of blood', a violent person]

butch *adj.* (orig. US) **1** [1930s+] (orig. gay) studiously masculine, esp. when used of lesbians. **2** [1930s+] tough, manly. **3** [1940s+] heterosexual. **4** [1940s+] of a woman (irrespective of sexuality), masculine, aggressive. [BUTCH n.³]

butcha n. [mid-19C] (Anglo-Ind.) a child. [Hind. *butcha*, a child]

butch-broad n. [1930s+] a masculine lesbian (cf. BUTCH n.³). [BUTCH adj. (1) + BROAD n.²]

butcher n.¹ [19C] the penis (cf. BACON n.¹; BUTCHER'S SHOP).

butcher n.² 1 [mid-19C] (US) a butcher's knife. 2 [mid-19C+] (US) a surgeon, a doctor, esp. an inefficient surgeon. 3 [1940s+] (Aus.) a second-rate barber, who cuts people when shaving them. 4 [1950s–70s] (US) a bungler, an incompetent, irrespective of profession. 5 [1950s+] one who practises cosmetic work. [all SE *butcher*, the image is of hacking the meat to pieces]

butcher n.³ [mid-19C+] the king, in a pack of cards. [his warlike image or joc. ref. to the SE *occupation*]

butcher n.⁴ [late 19C–1900s] stout. [a pun on the SE description of the stereotypically rotund butcher]

butcher n.⁵ [late 19C–1920s] (US) a seller of sweets, fruit, soft drinks etc, working typically in a cinema or a railway train. [ety. unknown; ? *butcher* as generic for a salesman (cf. SE sfx. *-monger*)]

butcher n.⁶ [late 19C+] (Aus.) 1 a glass of beer, orig. two-thirds of a pint, later around half a pint. 2 a 6-ounce (170ml) glass. [? the popularity of beer among butchers, but note BUTCHER n.⁴; thus a pun]

butcher v. [1990s] to look at, to stare. [BUTCHER'S HOOK n.]

butchering adj. [late 19C+] euph. for BLOODY adj.

butcher knife n. [1980s+] (US gay) the penis (cf. BAYONET).

butchers n. [1930s+] (Aus.) a look. [abbr. BUTCHER'S HOOK n.]

butchers adj. [20C] 1 ill, sick. 2 [1940s+] angry, annoyed. [abbr. BUTCHER'S HOOK adj.]

butcher's n. [late 19C] noon. [Polari]

butcher's canary n. [1920s+] (Aus.) a blowfly. [such insects are often found in butcher's shops]

butcher's dog n. [late 18C–early 19C] a married man. [the *butcher's dog* can 'lie by the beef without touching it']

butcher's hook n. [1930s+] a look, a glance. [rhy. sl. *butcher's hook* = look]

butcher's hook adj. (Aus.) 1 [20C] ill, sick. 2 [1940s+] angry, annoyed; thus *go butcher's hook*, lose one's temper (with). [rhy. sl. *butcher's hook* = CROOK adj. (3)]

butcher's meat n. [late 18C–19C] meat bought on credit. [it remains the butcher's property, if only in theory, until fully paid for]

butcher's mourning n. [mid-19C] a white hat with a black band. [the normal mourning hat was black, but butchers apparently disliked the colour]

butcher's picnic n. [1960s+] (Aus.) a noisy party or other occasion that lacks decorum. [stereotype of the rumbustious butcher]

butcher's shop n.¹ [19C] the vagina (cf. BACON SANDWICH; BUTCHER n.¹). [the image of 'raw meat' + BUTCHER n.¹]

butcher's shop n.² [late 19C–1960s] the execution shed within a prison.

butcher's window n. [19C+] the vagina (cf. BACON SANDWICH). [the image of 'raw meat']

butcher wagon n. [20C] (US prison) an ambulance (cf. BLOOD BOX).

butch number n. [1930s+] (gay) a 'masculine' male homosexual, usu. in question, e.g. *who's that butch number over there?* [BUTCH adj. (2) + NUMBER n.¹]

butchy adj. [1950s+] (US) lesbian. [BUTCH n.³ (2)]

butchski see BOOTCHKEY.

but good phr. [1930s+] (orig. US) very much so, extremely. [BUT (2) + SE *good*]

but hey! excl. [1970s+] (US) used as an affectionate

acknowledgement or emphasis, esp. when the previous comments have been neg.; abbr. 'But hey, what does it really matter ...'.

butler's grace n. [17C] thanks, but no money.

butt n.¹ 1 [mid-19C+] the buttocks. 2 [20C] (US Und.) the final portion of one's sentence. 3 [1990s] (US) a fool, an unpleasant person (cf. ARSEHOLE n.; ASSHOLE n.). [note (1) is SE before 19C]

butt n.² [mid-19C+] a cigarette end. [ext. of BUTT n.¹ (3)]

butt adj. (US) 1 [1980s+] (campus) a general intensifier, very, truly, extremely, very much so, incredibly. 2 [1990s] (rap music) second-rate, inferior. [BUTT n.¹ (1) + BUT]

butt v. [1940s–50s] (US) 1 to pass someone a cigarette. 2 to crush out a cigarette. [BUTT n.²]

butta/buttah n. see BUTTER n.⁶.

butta/buttah adj. [1990s] (US teen) a general term of approval, the very best, the most fashionable, attractive etc. ['smooth as butter']

butt-ass adj. [1980s+] (US) very. [BUTT adj. (1) + ARSE n.¹]

butt bail v. [1990s] (US Black) to run off, to escape. [BUTT n.¹ (1) + BAIL, i.e. one 'shifts one's butt']

buttbeatle n. [1990s] a homosexual. [BUTT n.¹ (1) + SE *beetle*]

butt boy n. [1980s+] (US campus) 1 a homosexual male (cf. BUM BOY). 2 a stupid, inept youth. [BUTT n.¹ (1) + SE *boy*]

butt buddy n. [1990s] a very close friend (cf. ASSHOLE BUDDY). [BUTT n.¹ (1) + BUDDY n. (1)]

butt-chuckler n. [1990s] 1 a masturbator. 2 a general term of abusive address. [BUTT n.¹ (1) + pun on SE *chuck*, to toss]

butt down v. [20C] (W.I./Guyn.) to ignore, to cut dead, to pass by rudely. [SE *butt* v.]

butteker n. [late 18C–19C] a shop. [? Fr. *boutique*]

butter n.¹ [early 19C+] flattery, unctuousness (cf. BUTTER UP).

butter n.² 1 [late 19C+] semen (cf. BABY GRAVY; BEAT THE BUTTER). 2 [1920s] (US) nitroglycerine. [resemblance]

butter n.³ [1980s+] 1 (US Black) the vagina (cf. APPLE n.¹⁰). 2 a woman, esp. when sexually active. [SE *butter*, i.e. its smoothness]

butter n.⁴ [1980s+] (US Black) the buttocks. [BUTT n.¹ (1)]

butter n.⁵ [1980s+] (drugs) 1 marijuana. 2 crack cocaine. [(1) ? f. the resin; (2) ety. unknown]

butter/butta/buttah n.⁶ [1990s] (orig. US Black, US teen) a general term of approval, the best, the most fashionable, attractive etc; thus *like butter/butta*, well-executed or performed smoothly or well. ['smooth as butter']

butter adj. [1980s+] (orig. US campus) 1 of an object or person, unfashionable, unsophisticated. 2 of a woman, unattractive (cf. CHEESE n.³). [play on CHEESY adj.² (1)]

butter v. 1 [late 17C–mid-19C] of a gambler, to increase one's wager. 2 [early 19C–1920s] to whip, to thrash. 3 [mid-19C] to flatter.

butter a bun, to phr. [1950s+] (US) to have sexual intercourse (cf. BUTTERED BUN). [SE *butter* + BUN n.²]

butter-and-egg man n. [1920s–30s] (US) a prosperous farmer or small-town leading citizen who comes to the big city and poses embarrassingly as a playboy. [the dairy products such men often sold. The term was popularized by the nightclub owner Marie Louise 'Texas' Guinan (1884–1933), otherwise celebrated for her invariable greeting, 'Hello sucker!' Columnist Walter Winchell attributed the term to master of ceremonies Harry Richman, while the original 'butter-and-egg man' was supposedly 'Uncle Sam' Balcon, a New York provisioner. The term was further popularized first by Louis Armstrong's song 'The Butter-and-Egg Man' (1924) and George S. Kaufman's similarly named play of 1925]

butter-and-eggs trot n. [late 18C] a short jog-trot. [based on the way market women make their way, carrying butter and eggs, into the weekly market]

butter baby n. [1980s+] (US Black) 1 a woman, often a

mulatto, who is considered sexy (cf. YELLOW GIRL). **2** [1980s+] a woman with large breasts and buttocks. [SE *butter* + BABY n.² (6); one of a variety of sl. terms equating women with food; cf. BANANA n.²]

butterbag *n.* [mid-17C] a Dutchman (cf. BUTTERBOX n.¹). [stereotype of Dutch as butter-makers]

butterball *n.* [1960s+] an overweight young person. [SE *butter-ball*, a moulded ball of butter]

butter-basher *see* BUTTERBOY.

butter bean teeth *n.* [20C] buck teeth (cf. BUTTER TEETH). [resemblance to the large white beans]

butter beauty *n.* [late 19C–1900s] a yellow cab, running in London in 1890s (cf. MARGARINE MESS). [its colour]

butter-boat *n.* [19C] the vagina; one of many terms that refer to the vagina as no more than a receptacle for semen. [BUTTER n.² + SE *boat* + pun on SE *butter-boat*, a vessel in which one serves melted butter]

butterbox *n.¹* [early 17C–early 19C] a Dutchman (cf. BUTTERBAG). [Dutch butter production]

butterbox *n.²* **1** [early 18C] a fop. **2** [1960s+] an effeminate male. [the 'softness' of butter]

butterboy/butter-basher *n.* [1930s+] a novice, esp. a young policeman or a newly qualified taxi-driver. ['butter wouldn't melt in his mouth']

butterbrain *n.* [1970s] (US) a fool (cf. BAKEBRAIN). [BUTTER-FINGERS + sfx. *-brain*]

buttercup *n.* **1** [late 19C–1920s] a pet name for a child. **2** [20C] an effeminate male homosexual (cf. DAFFODIL; DAISY n.²; LILY n.⁵; PANSY).

buttered *adj.¹* [mid–late 19C] (US) whipped, flogged. [BUTTER v. (2)]

buttered *adj.²* [1940s+] (US Black) well-turned-out, elegant. [SE *butter* + sfx. *-ed*, i.e. smooth]

buttered bun *n.¹* [late 17C+] **1** a mistress, a prostitute. **2** a woman who has had intercourse with one man and is about to repeat this immediately with a new partner; thus [20C] (Aus.) *have the buttered bun/scone, go in on the buttered bun/scone*, of a man, to take second place in a bout of serial intercourse (cf. CRUMPET n.⁴). [note BUTTER n.²; BUN n.²]

buttered bun *n.²* [early 18C] a country fool, a rustic simpleton.

buttered scone *n.¹* [20C] a woman who has had intercourse with one man and is about to repeat this immediately with a new partner. [var. on BUTTERED BUN n.¹ (2)]

buttered scone *n.²* [1950s+] (bingo) the number one. [rhy. sl.]

butterfingers *n.* [mid-19C+] (mainly juv.) one who lets things slip through their fingers.

butter flap *n.* [mid-19C] **1** a trap or light carriage. **2** a cap. [rhy. sl.]

butterflies/butterflies in one's stomach *n.* [1940s] nerves, apprehension, tension. [the 'fluttering' sensation of adrenalin]

butter flower *n.* [1980s+] (drugs) marijuana. [? the smooth cannabis resin]

butterfly *n.¹* [1920s–30s] (US) a worthless cheque. [it flutters away]

butterfly *n.²* [1940s] **1** a male homosexual (cf. PRISSY n.; SWISH n.²). **2** (US Black) an over-dressed, flashy person. **3** (US Black) an attractive young woman. [SE ? + ref. to Black actress Thelma 'Butterfly' McQueen (b.1911) who played a weeping maid in *Gone With the Wind*]

butterfly *n.³* [1940s] (US Und.) a new, young and attractive prisoner, characterized as being potentially appealing to prison homosexuals. [? James M. Cain's novel *The Butterfly* (1947), which concerns a woman who is JAILBAIT n.¹]

butterfly kiss *v.* [late 19C+] (US) to caress one's partner's skin by fluttering one's eyelashes against it.

butterhead *n.* **1** [1940s] (US Black) a Black person who, for whatever reason, is considered an embarrassment to their race. **2** [1960s+] (US) a fool. [? BUTTHEAD]

butter-knife *n.* [19C] the penis (cf. BAYONET). [BUTTER n.² (1) + SE *knife*]

buttermilk bottom *n.* [1920s–40s] (US Black) the Black area of town (cf. BLACK BOTTOM; COON BOTTOM). [the stereotyped link between *buttermilk* and Black appetites; the term was coined for the Black section of Atlanta, Georgia, but spread to many towns and cities in the southern states]

butter money *see* EGG MONEY.

buttermouth *n.* [mid-16C–19C] a Dutchman (cf. BUTTERBOX n.¹).

butter mouth *v.* [1990s] (US Black) to flatter. [BUTTER UP]

butter one's bread on both sides, to *phr.* [mid-19C+] to act in a wasteful manner.

butter one's corn, to *phr.* [20C] to masturbate (cf. ADJUST ONE'S SET). [pun on SE + ? link to BUTTER n.² (1)]

butter-patter *n.* [1900s–40s] an assistant in a grocery shop. [SE *butter-pat*]

butter pecan *n.* [1990s] (US Black teen) an attractive Puerto Rican/Latino woman (cf. CARAMEL SUNDAE; CHOCOLATE DELUXE). [SE *butter pecan* ice-cream, which is light brown and sweet]

butter-print *n.* [17C–early 18C] a baby, a child, esp. when illegitimate.

butter-queen *n.* [17C] an ill-tempered butter-woman (cf. BUTTER-WHORE).

butter skin *n.* [1930s+] (US) money. [SE *butter* + SKIN n.⁷]

butter-snout *n.* [late 19C–1910s] an epithet aimed at anyone with a noticeably greasy complexion.

butter teeth *n.* [20C] (US) buck teeth. [var. on BREAD-AND-BUTTER TEETH or BUTTER BEAN TEETH]

butter the fish, to *phr.* [1920s] to win at cards. [ety. unknown; culinary imagery]

butter the muffin, to *phr.* [1990s] to masturbate. [MUFFIN n.⁴]

butter up *v.* [early 19C+] to flatter, to ingratiate oneself; thus *buttering up*, excessive flattery.

butter upon bacon *phr.* [late 19C] extravagance, excess. [an excess of fattiness]

butter-weight *n.* [early 18C] a good measure. [SE *butter-weight*, 18oz (510g) or more to the pound, when the normal equivalent is 16oz (450g)]

butter-whore *n.* [16C–18C] an ill-tempered butter-woman (cf. BUTTER-QUEEN).

buttery *adj.* [mid-19C] susceptible to flattery. [BUTTER UP]

buttface *n.* [1970s+] (US) a general term of contempt with the implication of unattractiveness. [BUTT n.¹ (1) + SE *face*]

butt fiend *n.* [20C] (US) a heavy smoker. [BUTT n.² + SE *fiend*]

buttfuck *n.¹* [1960s+] an act of anal intercourse. [BUTTFUCK v.]

buttfuck *n.²* [1980s+] a disaster, a piece of victimization. [BUTT n.¹ (1) + FUCK n.¹]

buttfuck *v.* [1960s+] (US) to subject to anal intercourse. [BUTT n.¹ (1) + FUCK v.¹]

buttfucker *n.* (US) **1** [1960s+] one who indulges in anal intercourse. **2** [1970s+] a bully. [BUTTFUCK n.¹]

butt-girl *n.* [1980s+] (US) a woman used to run errands, e.g. for a fashion photographer. [? fig. use of BUTT n.¹ (1), i.e. she has a menial status, or SE *butt*, a target (of derision)]

butthead *n.* [1980s+] (US) a stupid or obnoxious person. [BUTT n.¹ (1) + sfx. *-HEAD* (1); a term immortalized since the early 1990s in MTV's semi-animated series *Beavis and Butthead*]

butthole *n.* [1950s+] (US) **1** the anus. **2** a term of contempt (cf. ARSEHOLE n.; ASSHOLE n.). [BUTT n.¹ (1) + SE *hole*]

butthook *n.* [1980s] (US) a lout. [? play on SE *buttock*]

buttiken *n.* [mid–late 19C] a shop (cf. BUTTEKER). [? Fr. *boutique* + KEN n.¹]

butt-in *n.* [20C] (US) **1** concern, affair, usu. in neg. phr. *none of one's butt-in.* **2** a meddler, one who interferes. [BUTT IN v.]

butt in *v.* [late 19C+] (orig. US) **1** to interfere, to make a nuisance of oneself (cf. PRAT IN). **2** to arrive. [SE *butt*, to strike or push (with the head or horns)]

buttinski/buttinsky *n.* [1920s+] (orig. US) one who intrudes, interferes. [BUTT-IN + sfx. -SKI]

butt-kicker *n.* [1980s+] (US) an outstanding performer at a pursuit. [BUTT n.[1] (1) + SE *kicker*]

butt-kicking *adj.* [1980s+] (US) **1** outstanding. **2** strong, powerful, aggressive. [BUTT-KICKER]

buttlick *n.* [1980s+] (US campus) **1** a fool. **2** a toady (cf. ARSE-LICKER; ASS-KISSER; BROWN NOSE n.). [BUTT n.[1] (1) + SE *lick*]

buttloads *n.* [1980s+] (US campus) a large quantity. [BUTT n.[1] (1) + SE *load*]

buttly *adj.* [1980s+] (US) very ugly. [BUTT n.[1] (1) + SE *ugly*]

buttmunch *n.* [1990s] a fool. [BUTT n.[1] (1) + SE *munch*]

butt naked *n.* [1980s+] (drugs) phencyclidine (cf. ACE n.[3]). [ety. unknown]

buttock *n.* [late 17C–mid-18C] a prostitute, esp. one who dispenses her favours for free (cf. BUTTOCK AND FILE; BUTTOCK AND TONGUE; BUTTOCK AND TWANG; BUTTOCK BROKER).

buttock *v.* [early 18C] to have sexual intercourse; thus *buttocking*, whorish. [BUTTOCK n.]

buttock and file *n.* [17C–late 19C] a prostitute and pickpocket team. [BUTTOCK n. + FILE n. (1)]

buttock and tongue *n.* [17C–early 19C] a shrewish woman. [BUTTOCK n. + SE *tongue*]

buttock and trimmings *n.* [late 18C–early 19C] an Irish wager, a rump of beef and a dozen of claret (cf. RUMP AND A DOZEN).

buttock and twang *n.* [17C–early 19C] a prostitute and pickpocket team (cf. BUTTOCK AND FILE). [BUTTOCK n. + TWANG n.[1]]

buttock-ball *n.* [17C–19C] **1** a dance attended by prostitutes (cf. BALLUM RANCUM; BUFF-BALL). **2** sexual intercourse. [BUTTOCK n. + SE *ball*]

buttock-banqueting *n.* [17C–18C] working as a prostitute. [BUTTOCK n. + SE *banqueting*]

buttock broker *n.* [17C–early 19C] a brothel-keeper. [BUTTOCK n. + SE *broker*]

buttock jig *n.* [19C] sexual intercourse (cf. DANCE v.).

buttocking shop *n.* [19C] a brothel (cf. BUMSHOP; BUTTONHOLE-FACTORY; CUNT-SHOP; FISH MARKET; FLESH MARKET; GREENGROCERY n.[1]; GRINDING-HOUSE n.[2]; HOOK SHOP; KNOCKING-SHOP; MEAT FANCIER'S; MEAT HOUSE; MEAT MARKET; MOLL SHOP; NANNY SHOP; WHORE SHOP). [BUTTOCK v.]

buttock mail *n.* [16C–early 19C] a fine imposed for fornication. [BUTTOCK n. + SE *mail*, payment, tax]

button *n.[1]* **1** [19C] a shilling (5p). **2** [late 18C–19C] a counterfeit shilling (cf. BRUMMAGEM BUTTON).

button *n.[2]* [mid-19C] any form of illicit decoy. [? fig. use of SE *button*, something small and worthless]

button *n.[3]* **1** [19C+] a baby's penis. **2** [19C+] the clitoris. **3** [1920s+] the chin, esp. in phr. *on the button*, a blow square on the chin and thus in fig. use *on the button*, exactly, perfectly, quite correctly. **4** [1930s–40s] (US) the whole face. **5** [1960s] (US) a woman's nipple. [all f. shape and/or size of SE *button*]

button *n.[4]* [20C] a policeman; thus *buttons*, police in general. [the *buttons* on the uniforms]

button *n.[5]* [20C] (US Und.) a look-out. [? BUTTON MAN]

button *n.[6]* **1** [1960s] (drugs) a capsule containing heroin or opium. **2** [1970s+] (S.Afr. drugs) a Mandrax (methaqualone) tablet; thus *button-kop* (*button-head*), a regular Mandrax user (cf. WHITE PIPE).

button *v.* [mid-19C+] (Und.) to act as a confidence trickster's accomplice, a decoy. [BUTTON n.[5]; 20C use mainly Aus.]

button B *adj.* [1930s–50s] penniless. [the old payphones, where one could push *button B* in the hope of redeeming some other caller's forgotten change]

button-boy *n.* [late 19C+] a (hotel) page. [his button-adorned uniform]

button-bung *n.* [17C] a button thief. [SE *button* + BUNG n.[1] (3)]

button-down *adj.* [1960s+] (US) conforming, holding establishment, conservative values (cf. WHITE-SHOE n.). [the button-down collared shirts from Brooks Brothers (New York) that are the uniform of the US business establishment]

buttoned *adj.* [1940s] in order, sorted out, arranged successfully. [BUTTONED UP (1)]

buttoned up *adj.* **1** [1930s+] all prepared. **2** [1950s+] silent (cf. BUTTON ONE'S LIP). **3** [1980s+] emotionally balanced. **4** repressed (cf. BUTTON-DOWN). [all fig. uses of SE]

buttoner *n.* [mid-19C+] **1** a decoy. **2** (Aus./UK Und.) the member of a gang running a game of three-card monte who persuades passers by to bet on the inevitably fraudulent game. [BUTTON n.[5]]

button finger *n.* [1990s] the finger used by a woman to masturbate herself or her partner. [BUTTON n.[3] (2) + SE *finger*; pun on BUTTERFINGERS]

buttonhole *n.* [19C] the vagina (cf. BUTTON n.[3]).

buttonhole cousin *n.* [20C] (US) a distant relation (e.g. a third or fourth cousin), a family friend (cf. WOODPILE COUSIN). [ety. unknown; ? one SE *buttonholes* them and claims a relationship]

buttonhole factory *n.* [19C] a brothel (cf. BUTTOCKING SHOP). [BUTTONHOLE + SE *factory*]

buttonhole worker *n.* [19C] **1** the penis. **2** a womanizer, a promiscuous man; thus *buttonhole working*, sexual intercourse. [BUTTONHOLE + SE *worker*]

button jock *n.* [1980s+] anyone who operates a console. [SE *button* + JOCK n.[5]]

button lurk *n.* [1910s] (Aus.) a trick played on a naïve woman by a man, bent on intercourse, who removes a button from his coat and promises that it will serve adequately as a contraceptive pessary. [SE *button* + LURK n.]

button man *n.* [1960s+] (US) a lower echelon member of a Mafia family (cf. BUTTON n.[5]; SOLDIER n.[2]).

button one's lip/face, to *phr.* [mid-19C+] to be quiet, to stop talking; thus *keep one's lip buttoned*, to keep quiet.

button on to *v.* [1900s] to grab hold of someone before forcing oneself on their company, whether they like it or not. [the grabbing of the jacket buttons]

buttons *n.[1]* [mid-19C+] brains, native wit, esp. as phr. *doesn't have all his buttons*, *doesn't have a full row of buttons*, *has a few buttons missing*, *not to have/got all one's buttons on*, *to be a button short*, *has lost his buttons*, is not very intelligent; *have all one's buttons done up*, to be smart, to be aware, 'on the ball' (cf. LOST A BUTTON; NOT HAVE ALL ONE'S BUTTONS).

buttons *n.[2]* [mid-19C+] **1** a policeman. **2** a page-boy. [their uniforms]

buttons *n.[3]* [1960s+] (drugs) mescaline. [mescaline is synthesized from peyote SE *buttons*]

buttons *n.[4]* [1990s] (US teen) a television remote control.

buttons and bows *n.* [20C] (Aus.) toes. [rhy. sl.]

button short, a *phr.* [19C+] eccentric, one of many phr. implying the subject is 'not all there' (cf. BUTTONS n.[1]; NOT ALL THERE).

button up *v.* **1** [late 19C+] to be quiet (cf. BUTTON ONE'S LIP). **2** [late 19C+] to close, to shut down, to withhold information. **3** [1920s] (US) to quit work for the day, also as *button up the day*. [fig. uses of SE; orig. US stockbroker jargon]

butt out v. [20C] (W.I.) to emerge, to come out of a passage or hidden place. [SE *butt* v.]

butt out! *excl.* [1960s+] go away! leave me alone! [BUTT n.¹ (1) + SE *out*]

butt pirate n. [1980s+] (US) a homosexual male (cf. ARSE BANDIT). [BUTT n.¹ (1) + SE *pirate*]

butt plug n. (US) **1** [1970s+] a plug, usu. rubber, inserted in the anus during sexual 'games'. **2** [1990s] a fool. [BUTT n.¹ (1) + SE *plug*]

butt-plunger n. [1970s] (US) a man who inserts a dildo into his own anus then walks around naked while a prostitute looks on. [BUTT n.¹ (1) + SE *plunger*]

butt pussy n. [20C] (US) the anus, usu. in a gay context. [BUTT n.¹ (1) + PUSSY n.]

butt slut n. [20C] (orig. US) **1** a homosexual male, usu. taking a passive role (cf. SLUT-PUPPY). **2** a woman who prefers anal to vaginal intercourse. [BUTT n.¹ (1) + SE *slut*]

butt-sprung *adj.* [1930s–40s] (US Black) of a garment, ill-fitting, esp. around the buttocks. [BUTT n.¹ (1) + SE *slung*]

butt-suck v. [1970s+] (US) to toady (cf. ASS KISS). [BUTT n.¹ (1) + SE *suck*]

butt ugly *adj.* [1980s+] (US) very ugly. [BUTT n.¹ (1) + SE *ugly*]

buttwhip v. [1950s] (US Black) to spank, usu. a child; thus *buttwhipping*, a spanking. [BUTT n.¹ (1) + SE *whip*]

buttwipe n. [1970s+] (US) lavatory paper (cf. ARSEWIPE). [BUTT n.¹ (1) + SE *wipe*]

butty n.¹ [late 18C+] (mainly north) a friend, a 'mate' (cf. BUDDY n.). [orig. dial.]

butty n.² [late 18C+] (mainly north) a sandwich; thus *jam butty, chip butty* etc. [SE *butter(ed) bread*]

butu n. [1980s+] (drugs) heroin. [ety. unknown]

buvare n. [mid–late 19C] a drink. [Polari]

Buxton bloaters n. [late 19C–1900s] overweight invalids, wheeling around in bath chairs while they take the medicinal waters. [proper name *Buxton* + SE *bloat(ed)*]

Buxton limp n. [late 19C–1900s] the hobbling walk affected by invalids taking the waters (cf. ALEXANDRA LIMP). [the popular medicinal springs at *Buxton*, Derbyshire]

buy n. [1960s+] (drugs) **1** the purchase of a drug. **2** money required to purchase a quantity.

buy v. **1** [1920s+] to accept, to believe, often in interrog. phrs., e.g. *do you think he'll buy it?*, do you think he'll be persuaded? **2** [1930s+] (orig. US) to cause, to make happen, to bring upon oneself.

buy a brush, to phr. [late 17C–mid-19C] to run away. [SE *buy* + BRUSH n.¹]

buy a drink, to phr. [1930s–40s] (US) to pour a drink (cf. BUY ONE'S THIRST).

buyaka n. [1990s] (orig. Jam.) a gunfight, gunshots. [? echoic]

buy another man's boots, to phr. [late 18C–19C] to marry another man's ex-wife or to start keeping his former mistress.

buy a ticket, to phr. to call someone's bluff (cf. BUY A WOOF TICKET).

buy a woof/wolf ticket, to phr. [1960s+] (US Black) to call one's bluff (cf. SELL A WOOF TICKET). [WOOF v.¹]

buyer n. [20C] (criminal/police) a receiver of stolen goods.

buy into v. [1950s+] (Aus.) to involve oneself in.

buy it v. [1920s+] **1** to suffer a mishap, esp. to die or be badly hurt. **2** of an inanimate object, to be broken or destroyed (cf. BUY THE FARM phr.¹). [one prior citation exists for 1825, but nothing follows for a century]

buy one's boots in Crooked Lane and one's stockings in Bandylegged Walk, to phr. [18C] to have bandy legs.

buy on one's face, to phr. [19C] to obtain credit through verbal deceit (cf. RUN ONE'S FACE FOR). [one's supposedly trustworthy features]

buy on the never tick, to phr. [1920s] to buy on credit. [SE *buy* + NEVER-NEVER; TICK n.²]

buy someone a hat, to phr. [1970s+] (US) to bribe someone. [euph.]

buy someone's thirst, to phr. [late 19C] (orig. US) to pay for someone's drink (cf. BUY A DRINK).

buy the dick, to phr. [1960s–70s] (US) to get into trouble. [BUY THE FARM phr.¹ + fig. use of DICK n.⁵ (1)]

buy the farm, to phr.¹ [1940s+] to die (cf. BUY IT). [orig. US Air Force use: 'Jet pilots say that when a jet crashes on a farm the farmer usually sues the government for damage done to his farm by the crash, and the amount demanded is always more than enough to pay off the mortgage and then buy the farm outright. Since this type of crash (i.e. in a jet fighter) is nearly always fatal to the pilot, the pilot pays for the farm with his life' (Lighter). Note RAF sl. *bought it*, ult. f. WW1 *bought a packet*]

buy the farm, to phr.² [1980s+] (US) to accept whatever is offered without query, to be conned or hoaxed. [the image of a simple country person ensnared into a bad purchase by a smooth salesman]

buy the rabbit, to phr. [early 19C–1930s] (orig. US) to conclude a deal unfavourably, to do badly. [a rabbit is presumably the lesser bargain in this hypothetical deal. Note 16C proverb 'who will change a rabbit for a rat?']

buy the ring, to phr. [1960s+] to perform anal intercourse. [SE *buy* + BIT OF RING + pun on wedding preparations]

buy the sack, to phr. [early 18C–early 19C] to get drunk. [SE *sack*, a variety of white wine imported f. Spain and the Canaries]

buy the trunk, to phr. [1930s–40s] (US West) to leave (permanently). [SE *trunk*, a large case, purchased in readiness for departure]

buy the wad, to phr. [1960s] (US) to suffer whatever is worst. [SE *buy* + WAD n.¹ (2)]

buz/buzz n. [mid–late 19C] a game popular in inns and public houses in which the players count 1, 2, 3 etc with *buzz* substituted for 7 or its multiples. A forfeit is paid by those who fail to count properly.

buz/buzz v. [mid-19C] to share the last bottle of wine equally among all drinkers, when there is not enough for a whole glass each. [? BOOZE v.]

buz-faker n. [19C] a pickpocket, esp. one who makes the victims drunk before robbing them (cf. BUZMAN). [BUZ v. + FAKER; the buzzing of a fly, but also, given the victim is a drunkard; note BOOZE]

buz-/buzz-faking n. [19C] picking pockets. [BUZZ n.¹ (1) + FAKE v.]

buz-/buzz-knacker n. [mid-19C] a trainer of young pickpockets (cf. BUS-/BUZ-NAPPER). [BUZ + SE *knacker*, a harness maker and (?) a maker of small (harness-related) articles]

buzman n. [19C] a pickpocket (cf. BUZZER). [BUZZ n.¹ + SE *man*]

buznacking see BUSNACKING.

buz-napper see BUS-NAPPER.

buz-nappers' academy see BUS-NAPPERS' ACADEMY.

buzz n.¹ **1** [18C+] the picking of pockets. **2** [18C–early 19C] a pickpocket (cf. BUZ-FAKER; BUZMAN; BUZZER n.¹).

buzz n.² **1** [early 19C+] a rumour. **2** [1930s] (US) chatter, conversation. **3** [1930s+] a telephone call (cf. BELL n.⁵).

buzz n.³ *see* BUZ n.

buzz n.⁴ [mid-19C–1920s] the draining of a bottle or glass; thus *it's your buzz*, it's time you filled your glass. [BUZ n.]

buzz n.⁵ **1** [mid-19C+] (orig. US) a pleasant sensation from drinking. **2** [1930s+] (orig. US) a thrill. **3** [1940s+] the immediate response to taking a drug, esp. barbiturates or cannabis (cf. CALL n.). [ext. of SE; i.e. a sense of heightened emotion]

buzz *n*.[6] [1970s+] (US) a close haircut, given with clippers. [the noise of the clippers]

buzz *v*.[1] [early 18C–19C] to drain a glass or bottle. [? BOOZE v.]

buzz *v*.[2] [19C+] to pick pockets. [BUZZ n.[1] (1)]

buzz *v*.[3] *see* BUZ n.

buzz *v*.[4] **1** [mid-19C–1960s] (US) to question, to interview. **2** [mid-19C+] (US) to flirt with. **3** [late 19C] to talk. **4** [1910s–20s] to telephone. **5** [1910s–30s] (US tramp) to solicit handouts. **6** [1950s–60s] (US) to irritate. [subseq. use of (4) is SE]

buzz *v*.[5] [late 19C+] to throw (hard). [echoic]

buzz *v*.[6] [1960s+] **1** to experience a drug pleasurably. **2** (US teen) to drive around town in one's car, looking for amusement (cf. CRUISE v.[1]). [BUZZ n.[5]]

buzz *v*.[7] [1980s+] (US campus) to leave, to depart (cf. BUZZ OFF).

buzz *v*.[8] [1960s+] to become lively, energetic, esp. of the atmosphere at a party or the performance of a rock band.

buzza *v*. [late 18C] to challenge someone to empty what remains of a bottle into their glass and then to drink it all down (cf. BUZZ v.[1]). [? BOOZE v. + SE *all*]

buzzard *n*. **1** [late 14C–18C] a foolish person, a gullible dupe. **2** [late 18C+] an unattractive woman. **3** [19C+] an old and unattractive person, often as *old buzzard* (cf. BUFFER n.[4]). **4** [mid-19C+] (US) a native of the state of Georgia. **5** [1900s] (US) a worthless horse. [all fig. uses of SE]

buzzard-bait *n*. [mid-19C+] (US) **1** a corpse abandoned in the open. **2** a person fated for death or otherwise doomed (cf. BUZZARD-MEAT).

buzzard-meat *n*. [late 19C–1930s] (US) **1** a corpse abandoned in the open. **2** a person fated for death or otherwise doomed (cf. BUZZARD-BAIT).

buzzard/buzzard's roost *n*.[1] [late 19C–1940s] (US) a run-down or disreputable place, also as *Buzzard's Row*. [the slaughterhouse area, where buzzards gathered to eat the discarded entrails]

buzzard/buzzard's roost *n*.[2] [late 19C–1940s] (US South) the top gallery in a theatre, usu. reserved for Blacks (cf. ETHIOPIAN PARADISE; JIG GALLERY; NIGGER HEAVEN; PEANUT ALLEY; PEANUT GALLERY).

buzz around like a blue-arsed fly, to *phr*. [late 19C+] to be excessively busy, often to the detriment of others.

buzz bomb *n*. **1** [1940s] (US) any sort of strong cocktail. **2** [1980s+] (US drugs) nitrous oxide. [BUZZ n.[5] + BOMB + pun on SE *buzz-bomb*, a flying bomb]

buzz-box *n*. [1920s–30s] (US) an automobile (cf. BUZZ WAGON). [the sound of the engine]

buzz buggy *n*. [1900s–40s] (US) an automobile, esp. a cheap one (cf. BUZZ WAGON).

buzz-buzz *n*. [1900s–30s] (US) an automobile (cf. BUZZ-WAGON).

buzz crunchers *n*. [1980s] (US campus) anything that destroys a feeling of euphoria. [BUZZ n.[5] + SE *crunch*]

buzzed *adj*. [1960s+] **1** mildly drunk, tipsy. **2** mildly intoxicated by a drug. [BUZZ n.[5]]

buzzed off *adj*. [1980s+] (US drugs) **1** reacting negatively to the experience of a drug. **2** feeling hostile to the entire drug culture. [BUZZ n.[6]]

buzzed out *n*. [1980s+] (US drugs) taking so many drugs, or so much of one drug, that one falls asleep. [BUZZ n.[5]]

buzzer *n*.[1] [mid-19C+] a pickpocket. [BUZZ n.[1] (2)]

buzzer *n*.[2] [late 19C–1900s] any form of automobile (cf. BUZZ BUGGY; BUZZ WAGON). [the noise it makes]

buzzer *n*.[3] [20C] a male homosexual. [? he *buzzes* around]

buzzer *n*.[4] [1930s+] (US) a police badge. [the officer SE *buzzes* it in one's face]

buzz-faking *see* BUZ-FAKING.

buzz in *v*. [1930s] to arrive, to enter. [antonym of BUZZ OFF]

buzzing *n*. [mid–late 19C] stealing, esp. picking pockets. [BUZZ n.[1] (1)]

buzzkill/buzzstomp *n*. [1980s+] (US campus) **1** an unpleasant experience or event. **2** an unpleasant person, esp. one who ruins a hitherto enjoyable time. [BUZZ n.[5] + SE *kill/stomp*]

buzzkill!/buzzstomp! *excl*. [1980s+] (US campus) a general excl. of disappointment and irritation, e.g. too bad! that's awful! [BUZZKILL n.]

buzz-knacker *see* BUZ-KNACKER.

buzzman *n*. [20C] (US Und.) an informer. [BUZZ n.[1] (1) + sfx. -*man*]

buzz-nappers' academy *n*. [late 18C–mid-19C] a school for thieves (cf. BUS-NAPPERS' ACADEMY).

buzz off *v*. [20C] to leave, to depart. [ext. of SE; i.e. image of busy bees]

buzz off! *excl*. [20C] go away!

buzzstomp *n. see* BUZZKILL n.

buzzstomp! *see* BUZZKILL!

buzz the nab, to *phr*. [1980s] (US teen) to leave, to escape a situation. [BUZZ v.[7] + NABE n.[2]]

buzz wagon *n*. [1910s–20s] an automobile (cf. BUZZ-BOX). [the noise]

buzzy *adj*.[1] [mid-18C] tipsy. [BOUSY]

buzzy *adj*.[2] [late 19C–1910s] crazy, eccentric. [? 'bees in one's bonnet']

buzzy house *n*. [1900s] (US) a lunatic asylum. [BUZZY adj.[2] + SE *house*]

B-way/B'way *n*. [mid-19C+] (US) *Broadway*, New York City. [abbr.]

b.w.o.c. *see* B.M.O.C.

by *prep*. [1920s+] in one's opinion, as far as one is concerned, e.g. *by me, by you, by us.* [? Yid. form., e.g. *by me it's OK*]

by a jugful *phr*. [early 19C+] (US) by a great deal, 'by a long chalk', usu. in neg.

by all that's blue! *excl*. [mid-19C] a mild excl. or oath. [Fr. *parbleu!* lit. 'by (a) blue (thing)!']

by a long chalk *phr*. [mid-19C+] by a long way, often in neg. phr. *not by a long chalk, by long chalks*. [use of *chalk* in scoring points, e.g. in billiards, darts]

by a long shot *phr*. [mid-19C+] (orig. US) by a good distance, by a considerable amount; usu. as a neg., e.g. *too fast by a long shot*.

by a long sight *phr*. [early 19C+] (US) by a long way, by a good deal, usu. as a neg. and thus + pfx. *not ...*; also as *... damn sight, ... darned sight* etc.

by a street *phr*. [1960s+] by a long way.

by-blow *n*. [16C–early 19C] a bastard. [SE *by-blow*, anything that happens, usu. unfortunate, in parallel to the main thrust of one's life or intentions. Ware also suggests Fr. *bibelot*, a rare, precious small *objet d'art*. SE f. 1800]

by Cain! *excl*. [early–mid-19C] (US) a mild, euph. oath, *by hell!*

byce *see* BICE.

by chalks *phr*. [20C] (Aus.) by a long way. [abbr. BY A LONG CHALK]

by-chop *n*. [17C–18C] a bastard. [var. on BY-BLOW]

by Christchurch! *excl*. [1940s+] (N.Z./UK) a euph. oath. [using the towns of Christchurch, found in both countries]

by cob's body! *see* COB'S BODY!

by cock and pie!/cock and pie! *excl*. [mid-16C–mid-19C] a mild, euph. oath. [? COCK n.[1] + SE *pied friar*, a Carmelite or Cistercian]

by ding! *excl*. [1920s] (US) a euph. exclamation.

bye-bye/-byes *n*. [mid-19C+] sleep, unconsciousness. [earlier nursery use *bye-bye*, sleep]

bye-drink n. [mid-18C] an alcoholic drink, taken other than at mealtimes. [SE *bye and/the bye*]

by fits and starts as the hog pisseth phr. [18C] jerkily, unsteadily, inconsistently.

by gaineys! excl. [1940s–50s] a general excl. [JANEY MACK!]

by gigs! excl. [mid-16C–late 17C] a mild euph. for *by Jesus!* (cf. BEJABERS!).

by ginger! excl. [mid-19C] (US) a mild expletive, euph. for *by Jesus!* (cf. BEJABERS!).

by-god adj. [late 19C+] (US) a general intensifier, e.g. *the by-god worst thing ever.*

by god's dines! excl. [late 16C–early 17C] a mild oath. [? 14C SE *dignesse*, dignity]

by golly! excl. [late 18C+] a mild euph. for *by God!* (cf. BEDAD!; GOLLY!).

by good gravy! excl. [mid-9C+] (US) a mild oath (cf. BY GRAVY!).

by gorram! excl. [late 19C] (US) euph. for *by God!* (cf. BEDAD!)

by gorry! excl. [19C+] (orig. US) euph. for *by God!* (cf. BEDAD!; GORRY!).

by gosh! excl. [mid-18C+] a mild euph. for *by God!* (cf. BEDAD!; GOSH!)

by grabs! excl. [20C] (US) euph. for *by God* (cf. BEDAD!).

by gravy! excl. [mid-19C+] (US) a mild oath (cf. BY GOOD GRAVY!). [euph. for God]

by guess and by godfrey phr. [20C] taking a course of action or movement without any real plan. [naut. use; to steer 'at hazard without a set course or without the guidance of landmarks' (*OED*)]

by guess and by God phr. [1930s+] by sheer luck.

by guess and by golly/gosh phr. [19C] (US) haphazardly, without a planned direction, at random.

by gum! excl. [early 18C+] euph. excl. *by God!* (cf. BEDAD!).

by hedge or by stile phr. [late 17C–18C] by any means necessary, by hook or by crook. [SE *hedge* + *stile*, the image is of crossing a boundary, whether illicitly, through the hedge, or illicitly, over the stile]

by hokey! excl. [19C+] (US) a mild excl. [? euph. for *hell!* or f. SE *hocus-pocus*]

by/i jacks! excl. [late 19C+] used in mild oaths as a euph. for *by Jesus!* (cf. BEJABERS!).

by jiggers! excl. [late 19C] (US) a mild euph, euph. for *by Jesus!* (cf. BEJABERS!).

by jimminy! excl. [early 19C+] a mild oath, euph. for *by Jesus!* (cf. BEJABERS!),

by jing! excl. [1930s] euph. for *by Jesus!* (cf. BEJABERS!; BY JINGO!).

by jingo! excl. [mid-19C+] euph. for *by Jesus!* also intensified as *by the living jingo!* (cf. BEJABERS!). [presumably a euph. for JESUS!, but ? *St Gingoulph* (Hotten, 1867)]

by jings! see JINGS!

by jockies! excl. [late 19C] (US.) euph. for *by Jesus!* (cf. BEJABERS!).

by Joe! excl. [mid-19C–1940s] (US) a mild oath; euph. for *by Jesus!* but note BY JOVE!

by Jove! excl. [late 16C+] *by God!*

by my cadaver! excl. [late 19C] (Cockney) a mild oath.

by my hood! excl. [late 16C] a mild oath or excl.

by my 'sheath! excl. [mid-16C] a minor, mild oath.

by/upon my truly! excl. [late 16C–late 18C] a mild oath, used to underpin the veracity of one's statement.

b.y.o. phr. [1960s+] (US/Aus.) bring your own, refers to bringing drinks to a party or an unlicensed restaurant. [abbr.]

b.y.o.b. phr. [1920s+] (US/Aus.) bring your own bottle. [abbr.]

b.y.o.g. phr. [1920s+] (Aus.) bring your own grog. [abbr.]

b.y.o.l. phr. [1920s+] (US/Aus.) bring your own liquor. [abbr.]

by our lakin!/byr'lakin excl. [late 15C–mid-17C] a mild oath, euph. for *by our lady!* [lit. *by our little lady*]

by-scape n. [mid-17C] a bastard (cf. BY-BLOW). [SE *by-*, aside + abbr. *escape*]

b.y.t. phr. [1940s] bright young things. [abbr.]

by the balls phr. [1910s+] (orig. US) at one's mercy, usu. in phr. *have one by the balls.* [thus the celebrated Vietnam-era motto, 'if you have them by the balls, their hearts and minds will follow', which mocked the official instruction to win over the 'hearts and minds' of the Vietnamese]

by the clock phr. [1920s] (US) absolutely, definitely. [the regularity of time-keeping]

by the good Katty! excl. [19C] (northern) a mild oath, *by the good (St) Catherine!*

by the great horn spoon! excl. [mid-19C+] (US) a mild excl.

by the holy!/by the holy jumping mother of Moses! phr. [late 19C] a general excl. of surprise, excitement, alarm etc.

by the holy poker!/by the holy poker and the tumbling Tom! excl. [19C] a general oath. ['Irish' (Hotten, 1860)]

by the hokey! see BE THE HOKEY!

by the holies! see BY THE HOLIES!

by the jumping Judas!/great jumping Judas! excl. [20C] (US) a mild oath (cf. JUMPING JEHOSHAPHAT).

by the Lord Harry! excl. [17C–19C] a mild oath (cf. OLD HARRY).

by the mack! excl. [mid-16C–mid-17C] a general oath. [? SE *by the Mass!* or *by Mary!*]

by the mouse-foot! excl. [mid-16C–mid-17C] a mild excl.

by the new time adv. [1910s+] very quickly. [Irish *the new time*, popular name for daylight saving time]

by the piper!/piper that played before Moses! phr. [late 19C] a mild excl.

by the powers of Moll Doyle! excl. [mid-19C+] (Irish) a mild oath. [for ety. see GIVE SOMEONE MOLL DOYLE]

by the way of see BY WAY OF.

by this hat! excl. [late 16C] a general excl.

by way/the way of phr. [early 19C+] in the habit of, having a reputation for.

by way of Cheapside phr. [late 18C] on the cheap, at a bargain price; often as *come at it by way of Cheapside* or *come home by way of Cheapside.* [pun on proper name *Cheapside*, a well-known street in the City of London. This name comes from AS *chepe*, a market, a place of buying and selling; although directly linked, the adj. use, meaning low in price, does not emerge until the early 16C]

bywoner n. [late 19C+] (S.Afr.) a socially inferior person, one who has been dispossessed, a parasite. [Afk. *by*, with/at + *woon*, dwell + sfx. *-er*, in orig. S.Afr.E. a tenant-farmer or squatter, without land of their own]

C

C *n.*[1] (US) **1** [late 19C] cents. **2** [1930s+] $100 (cf. G *n.*[1]). [SE *century*]

C *n.*[2] (drugs) **1** [1950s+] cocaine (cf. C-GAME; C-JAM; H *n.*[2]). **2** [1990s] as *the* C, methcathinone (cf. BATHTUB SPEED). [abbr.]

ca- *see* KER-.

caad *v.* [20C] (W.I./UK Black teen) to jeer jokingly or mock someone about some event, their appearance or situation. [CARD *v.*[1]]

c.a.b. *phr.* [1990s] a general term of derision. [abbr. complete *arse bandit*]

cab *n.*[1] [mid-17C–early 18C] a Cavalier. [? Sp. *Caballero* or abbr. SE]

cab *n.*[2] [18C+] *cabbage*. [abbr.]

cab *n.*[3] [early–mid-19C] a brothel (cf. CAB MAT; CAB MOLL). [? SE *cabin* or *cabal*, a group that associates secretly and, by implication, for illegal or subversive activities]

cab *n.*[4] [late 19C] a cheat, a 'crib'. [abbr. CABBAGE *n.*[6]]

cab *v.*[1] [early 19C+] **1** to travel by cab; 20C use usu. *cab it*. **2** to drive a cab; thus *cabbing*, working as a cab-driver. [SE *cab*, which, despite Hotten (1860), may 'smack of slang' but is not]

cab *v.*[2] [late 19C] to cheat, to pilfer.

caballo/kabayo *n.* [1980s+] (drugs) heroin. [pun on Sp. *caballo*, a horseman/HORSE *n.*[12]]

cabbage *n.*[1] [late 17C–early 18C] a form of hairdressing resembling a chignon, popular at this time.

cabbage *n.*[2] **1** [late 17C–early 18C] a tailor. **2** [late 17C+] small off-cuts of material, taken from the job in hand and sold off as perks by tailors (cf. BLUE PIGEON). [? Corruption of 17C SE *garbage/carbage*, shreds and patches used as padding]

cabbage *n.*[3] [mid-18C] a person, a fellow, a chap. [Fr. *choux*, lit. 'cabbage', and used as a term of endearment]

cabbage *n.*[4] **1** [mid-19C] a cheap, inferior cigar. **2** [1980s+] (N.Z. drugs) low-grade marijuana. [its supposedly being made of *cabbage* rather than tobacco or marijuana leaves]

cabbage *n.*[5] [late 19C] a 'crib' or other form of cheat used by schoolchildren. [CABBAGE *n.*[2] (2), tailors' scraps, thus 'padding'; ? OF *cabuse*, imposture, trick; *cabuser*, to deceive, to cheat; also OF *cabas*, cheating, theft; Fr. *cabasser*, to pack up, to cheat, to steal; *cabasseur*, deceiver, thief; 'but evidence is wanting' (*OED*)]

Cabbage, the *n.*[6] [late 19C] the Savoy Theatre. [pun on SE *Savoy cabbage*]

cabbage *n.*[7] [late 19C] the vagina; one of a number of terms that equates the vagina with a vegetable (cf. CABBAGE PATCH; CAULIFLOWER *n.*[2]; GREEN MEADOW; GREENGROCERY *n.*[1]; GROCERIES *n.*[1]; LETTUCE *n.*[2]; MUSHROOM *n.*[2]; NETTLE BED; PARSLEY BED; SWEET POTATO PIE). [? a pun on GREENS *n.*[2]]

cabbage *n.*[8] **1** [1920s+] (orig. US) cash, banknotes (cf. ALFALFA *n.*). **2** [1980s+] (S.Afr.) money, esp. as a 10-rand banknote. [the colour of the notes]

cabbage *v.*[1] [18C–late 19C] to steal, to pilfer. [CABBAGE *n.*[2] (2)]

cabbage *v.*[2] [18C–late 19C] to use a 'crib' (cf. CABBAGE *n.*[5]). [CAB *n.*[4]]

cabbage-contractor *n.* [19C] a tailor. [CABBAGE *n.*[2] (1)]

cabbaged *adj.* [1990s] absolutely exhausted, metaphorically brain-dead from overwork (cf. VEG; VEG OUT). [one has become a 'vegetable']

cabbage-eater *n.* [19C] (US) **1** a German (cf. CABBAGETOWN). **2** a Russian. [racial stereotyping: both nationalities are allegedly devoted consumers of cabbage]

cabbage field/garden *see* CABBAGE PATCH *n.*[1].

cabbage garden/patch/state *n.* [late 19C+] (Aus.) Victoria; thus *cabbage gardener*, *cabbage patcher*, *cabbage stater*, a native of Victoria. [the state crop]

cabbage-gelder *n.* [late 19C–1900s] a gardener, a greengrocer. [joc. image of one who gelds or 'castrates', i.e. cuts, the stalks of cabbages]

cabbage-head *n.* [17C–late 19C] a fool, a stupid person (cf. BLOCKHEAD *n.*[1]). [SE *cabbage* + sfx. -HEAD (1); the shape and the supposed 'vegetable' matter of which the fool's brain is composed. Such a person is considered 'green']

cabbage leaf *n.*[1] [19C] (US) a poor-quality cigar; thus the joc. query *Who's smoking cabbage leaves?* [the quality of the tobacco]

cabbage leaf/leaves *n.*[2] [20C] (US) money, banknotes (cf. ALFALFA *n.*). [ext. of CABBAGE *n.*[8]]

cabbage leaves *n.* [20C] (US) large ears. [joc. resemblance]

cabbage patch/field/garden *n.*[1] [19C] the vagina (cf. CABBAGE *n.*[7]). [pun on GREENS *n.*[2]]

cabbage patch *n.*[2] [19C] (US) a thing or place of little importance. [the size of such a patch in one's garden and the commonness of the vegetable]

cabbage patch *n.*[3] *see* CABBAGE GARDEN.

cabbage plant *n.* [early 19C] an umbrella. [resemblance]

cabbager *n.*[1] [19C–1900s] a tailor. [CABBAGE *n.*[2] (1)]

cabbager *n.*[2] *see* CABBAGITE.

cabbage state *see* CABBAGE GARDEN.

cabbage stumps *n.* [19C] the legs. [supposedly reminiscent of cut-off cabbage stalks]

cabbage town *n.* [20C] (US) **1** the German immigrant section of a town (cf. BEAN TOWN *n.*[2]; CABBAGE-EATER; KRAUT). **2** the poor area of a town. [racial stereotyping: the Germans' taste for *Sauerkraut* or pickled cabbage]

cabbage-tree hat *n.* [20C] (Aus.) an informer. [rhy. sl. *cabbage-tree hat* = RAT]

cabbage-tree mob *n.* [mid-19C] (Aus.) a type of layabout, typified by the wearing of a *cabbage-tree hat* (a hat made of woven cabbage-tree or cabbage-palm leaves) (cf. LARRIKIN).

cabbagio perfumo *n.* [late 19C+] a cheap cigar (cf. CABBAGE LEAF). [cod Spanish meaning 'a perfumed cabbage'; mocking the Spanish/Cuban origin of the best cigars and their names]

cabbagite/cabbager *n.* [mid-19C] (Aus.) a layabout. [CABBAGE-TREE MOB]

cabber *n.* [20C] (Ulster) a ring of dirt around the neck, a 'tide-mark'. [dial. *cab*, to clog with dirt]

cabbie/cabby *n.* [mid-19C+] a cab-driver.

cabeza *n.* [mid-19C+] (US, Southwest) the head. [synon. Sp.]

cabin fever *n.* [1910s+] lassitude, restlessness or irritability as a result of being confined in too small a space, with no variety in companions or occupations. [coined for those suffering on long sea voyages]

cab joint *n.* [1930s+] (orig. US) **1** a nightclub to which patrons would be steered, were they to request such a place, by a complaisant cab-driver. **2** a brothel. [SE *cab* + JOINT, but cf. CAB n.³]

cabman's farewell *n.* [1940s–50s] any form of farewell that is essentially a curse (cf. BEGGAR'S BENISON).

cabman's rests *n.* [late 19C+] the female breasts. [rhy. sl.]

cab mat *n.* [19C] a prostitute. [CAB n.³]

cab moll *n.* [mid–late 19C] (orig. US) a prostitute who works either literally in cabs and trains or, possibly, from or at a brothel. [CAB n.³ + MOLL n.]

caboodle/calaboodle/kaboodle/kerboodle *n.* [19C+] a large mixed-up collection of objects or people. [? WHOLE KIT AND BOODLE or f. pfx. -KER + BOODLE]

caboose *n.¹* (US) **1** [19C] a cubby-hole, a small room. **2** [mid-19C+] a prison. [Du. *kabuis*, a cook's galley; briefly used in 18C UK naval jargon to mean a galley, but thereafter appears only in US]

caboose *n.²* [19C] (US) **1** the buttocks. **2** the last child in a family. **3** a person who continually follows along behind, a hanger-on. **4** a slow-witted person. [for ety. *see* CABOOSE n.¹; SAmE *caboose* as adopted in the American West to mean the cow-hide container stretched across the rear of the chuck wagon, which, when full, hangs down behind the wagon. Thence it was used by the railroads to mean a wagon (usu. attached to a freight train) in which the crew could eat, sleep and cook. (2) also puns on SE *papoose*]

caboose *v.* [late 19C–1930s] (US) to imprison. [CABOOSE n.¹ (2)]

cab-ranker *n.* [1920s] a cheap cigar. [punning on SE *cab*(*bage*) + *rank*, offensively smelly]

ca-ca/ka-ka/kaka *n.* **1** [18C+] excrement. **2** [1960s+] (US) nonsense, rubbish (cf. BULLSHIT n.). [Sp. *caca*, excrement]

caca *n.* [1950s+] (drugs) heroin. [pun on SHIT n.⁵]

cacada *n.* (W.I.) a little food or a very small amount of money, typically used to appease a beggar. [CA-CA + Fr. *dents*, teeth. Either no more food than would slightly dirty the teeth or bits of food that remain between the teeth after eating]

cacafuego *n.* [early 17C–late 18C] a braggart, a noisy bully (cf. SHITEFIRE). [Port. *cagar*, to excrete + Sp. *fuego*, fire, lit. *shit-fire*. Also the name of a Spanish galleon taken by Sir Francis Drake in 1577]

cacatorium *n.* [19C] a lavatory. [CA-CA + 'Latin' sfx. -*orium*]

cachero *n.* [20C] (US prison/Hisp.Am.) a prison homosexual. [? CATCHER]

cachunk! *excl.* [mid-19C] (US) onomat. term indicating the sound of a solid object hitting the ground (cf. KERCHUNK!).

cack *n.¹* **1** [late 19C+] excrement. **2** [late 19C+] nonsense, rubbish (cf. BULLSHIT n.). **3** [1970s+] (Irish) a general term of abuse (cf. SHIT n.²). [15C–16C SE *cack*, to void excrement, itself linked to synon. Lat. *cacare* and OE *cac-hús*, a latrine]

cack *n.²* [20C] (US) a small child (cf. BUGGER). [? CACK n.¹ (1) or SE *cackle*]

cack *n.³* [1900s–50s] (US Black) a respected person, an important figure in the community (cf. KACK). [CACK v.²]

cack *n.⁴* [1960s+] a left-handed person. [CACK-HANDED]

cack *n.⁵* [1990s] (Aus.) **1** a laugh. **2** someone who has a good sense of humour. [SE *cackle*]

cack *v.¹* [late 19C+] to make a mess. [16C–early 18C SE *cack*, to excrete]

cack *v.²* [1900s–40s] (US Black) **1** to boast, to brag, esp. of one's good fortune. **2** to kill. **3** to fall asleep. [mid-16C+ SE *cackle*, to brag about a petty achievement]

cack *v.³* [1990s] (Aus.) to joke, to (have a) laugh. [CACK n.⁵]

cack-broad *n.* [1940s] (US Black) one who flaunts their wealth, esp. a *nouveau riche* woman. [CACK v.² (1) + BROAD]

cacked *adj.* [1990s] (US teen) messed up. [CACK v.¹]

cacker *n.* [1990s] (US) a blunderer, one who makes a mess, lit. and fig. [CACK v.¹]

cack-handed *adj.* [mid-19C+] clumsy, awkward. [? CACK v.¹. Note Fr. *mains de merde*, awkward, butter-fingered, lit. 'shit-hands']

cackle *n.¹* [mid-19C+] empty chatter, foolish talk. [CACKLE v. (1)]

cackle *n.²* [20C] (US) an egg (cf. CACKLEBERRY; CACKLE FRUIT; CACKLING FART). [SE *cackle*, the sound made by a hen]

cackle *v.* **1** [mid-16C+] to talk, to chatter, to prattle. **2** [late 17C+] (Und.) to reveal secrets through indiscreet talk, to inform. [SE *cackle*, the sound made by a hen]

cackleberry *n.* [20C] (US) an egg (cf. CACKLE n.²).

cacklebird *n.* [20C] (US) a hen (cf. CACKLER n.¹; CACKLING-CHEAT).

cackle factory *n.* [1940s+] (US) a psychiatric institution. [SE *cackle*, to prattle + FACTORY]

cackle fruit *n.* [20C] an egg (cf. CACKLEBERRY). [CACKLE n.² + SE *fruit*]

cackle one's fat, to *phr.* [20C] to brag, to boast. [CACKLE + SE *fat*, abundance, wealth]

cackler *n.¹* [16C] a hen (cf. CACKLEBIRD). [the noise made by a hen]

cackler *n.²* **1** [18C–late 19C] a tale-teller, one who talks 'out of turn'. **2** [20C] (US) an office worker, a clerk. [the image, when in a group, of a flock of hens]

cacklers' ken *n.* [late 18C] (Und.) a hen roost. [CACKLER n.¹ + KEN n.¹]

cackle tub *n.* [mid-19C–1900s] a pulpit (cf. AUTEM CACKLE TUB). [SE *cackle* v. + TUB n.¹]

cackling-cheat/-chete *n.* [16C] (Und.) a cock, a capon (cf. CACKLEBIRD). [SE *cackle* + CHEAT]

cackling-cove *n.* [mid–late 19C] (tramp) an actor. [SE *cackle* + COVE. 'The cadger seeing no difference between observing Shakespeare and whining floridly for pence' (Ware)]

cackling fart *n.* [17C–late 18C] an egg (cf. CACKLE n.²; CACKLE-BERRY; CACKLE FRUIT). [CACKLER n.¹ + FART]

cacko *adj.* [1960s] (Aus.) extremely drunk (cf. SHIT-FACED). [CACK n.¹ + sfx. -o]

cackpipe *n.* [1990s] the anus, the rectum. [CACK n.¹]

cackpipe cosmonaut *n.* [1990s] a male homosexual (cf. ANAL ASTRONAUT). [CACKPIPE]

cacks *n.¹* [1920s] children's shoes. [Cumberland dial.]

cacks *n.²* [1980s] **1** knickers. **2** trousers. [var. on KECKS]

cacky *n.* [late 19C+] human excrement. [CACK n.¹]

cacky *adj.* [late 19C+] covered in excrement. [CACK n.¹]

cactus *n.* [1960s+] (drugs) mescaline. [its origin in the peyote cactus]

cactus *adj.* [1940s+] (Aus.) ruined, useless, finished, dead. [? pun on CACKED]

cactus buttons *n.* [1960s+] (drugs) mescaline. [CACTUS n.]

cactus head *n.* [1960s+] (drugs) mescaline. [CACTUS n.]

cactus juice *n.¹* [1960s–70s] tequila or mescal. [the origin of tequila/mescal in distilling the fermented sap of a maguey (*Agave tequilana*)]

cactus juice *n.²* [1970s] mescaline. [pun on *mescal/mescaline*, properly the alkaloid 3,4,5-trimethoxyphenethyl-amine, which is the active ingredient of mescal buttons]

cad *n.¹* **1** [late 18C–mid-19C] a passenger taken on board by a coachman for his own profit. **2** [early 19C+] a poorly behaved, ill-mannered lout; thus artists' jargon *cad-catcher*, pictures painted to attract the undiscriminating (cf. SNOB). **3** [mid-19C] an omnibus conductor. **4** [mid–late 19C] a lowly rated assistant. **5** [mid-19C–1910s] a messenger boy. **6** [late 19C–1900s] (US campus) an academy or prep school student. [SE *cadee, caddie*, a cadet; thence Eton and Oxford jargon *cad*, a townsman, the implication being that such a figure could not be 'a gentleman', and late 19C *cad-mad*, the excesses of a nouveau riche undergraduate; cf. the cognate, but somewhat later BOUNDER n.[2]]

cad *n.*[2] [1920s–60s] (orig. US) a *Cadi*llac (cf. CADDY). [abbr.]

cad *n.*[3] *n.* [1930s+] (drugs) 28g (1oz) of a narcotic. [abbr. CADILLAC n. (1)]

cadator *n.* [late 17C–early 18C] a confidence trickster, esp. one posing as a 'gentleman fallen on hard times'. [Lat. *cado*, I fall]

cadaver *n.* [late 19C–1900s] (orig. US) a bankrupt. [SE *cadaver*, a corpse]

cadaver cadet *n.* [1980s+] a necrophile. [SE *cadaver*, a corpse + *cadet*]

Cadbury alley *n.* [1990s] the rectal passage (cf. BOURNEVILLE BOULEVARD). [play on *Cadbury*, the major UK chocolate manufacturer/CHOCOLATE, used in combs. relating to homosexual anal intercourse]

Cadbury channel *n.* [1990s] the anus. [for ety. *see* CADBURY ALLEY]

Cadbury's canal boat cruiser *n.* [1990s] a male homosexual. [for ety. *see* CADBURY ALLEY + ref. to CRUISE v.[1]]

Cadbury's canal engineer *n.* [1990s] a male homosexual. [for ety. *see* CADBURY ALLEY]

caddee *n.* [mid-19C] **1** a thief's assistant. **2** a person who frequents tavern yards and persuades customers to patronize another inn, for which they are paid by its landlord. **3** a passer-on of counterfeit money. [CAD n.[1]]

caddie/caddy *n.* [late 19C] (Aus.) a slouch hat. [? CADY]

caddy *n.* [1940s+] (US) a *Cadi*llac (cf. CAD n.[2]). [abbr.]

cade *n.* [20C] (US) a spoilt child. [dial. *cade*, a lamb that has been rejected by its mother and reared as a pet]

cademy *n.* [late 19C–1910s] an a*cademy*. [abbr.]

cadet *n.*[1] **1** [late 17C–18C] 'a Gentleman that Bears Arms in hopes of a Commission' (B.E.). **2** [18C–19C] a street thug. **3** [mid-19C] (US) a pimp. [the essential image of a loafer and an idler persists as the meanings develop]

cadet *n.*[2] [1940s+] (drugs) a novice user of drugs.

cadet *n.*[3] [1970s+] **1** (drugs) any heavy user of drugs, esp. cannabis or hallucinogens, who is, thus, continually 'flying'. **2** an eccentric (drug use is not mandatory). [SPACE CADET]

cadge, the *n.* **1** [early–mid-19C] the profession or act of begging. **2** [1930s] (Glasgow) a message. [CADGE v.]

cadge *v.* [early 19C+] to wander the country as a beggar, to beg. [? SE *cadge*, a pannier, as used by beggars, ult. ? f. Fr. *cacher*, to hide away. By 20C use was more colloq. than sl.]

cadge-cloak/-gloak *n.* [18C–early 19C] (Und.) a beggar. [CADGE n. + GLOAK, lit. 'a wandering fellow']

cadger *n.* **1** [mid-19C] a beggar. **2** [late 19C–1900s] anyone in a service industry, e.g. a waiter, cab-driver, who solicits for tips. **3** [late 19C+] a genteel 'sponger'. **4** [1930s+] (Ulster) a hawker, esp. one who sells poteen or illicit whisky. **5** [1990s] a male homosexual. [CADGE v.]

cadging *n.* [19C+] begging; thus *cadging-bag*, a bag in which to put one's profits, *cadging-face*, an expression designed to elicit sympathy. [CADGE v.]

cadgy/cagy *adj.* [19C] (US) sexually adventurous. [18C Scot. *caigie* and Suffolk dial. *kedge*, cheerful, wanton, sportive]

cadillac *n.* (US drugs) **1** [1930s+] a 28g (1oz) packet of a powdered drug. **2** [1950s+] any powdered, thus usu. narcotic,

drug. **3** [1970s+] phencyclidine (cf. ACE n.[3]). [expensive drugs equated with an expensive car]

cadillac commie *n.* [1990s] (US) a liberal, the intensity of whose pronouncements on social problems is in direct proportion to their ability to escape their existence (cf. BOLLINGER BOLSHEVIK). [the cadillac car is trad. antipathetic to left-wing ideology]

cadillac express *n.* [1980s+] (drugs) methcathinone (cf. BATHTUB SPEED). [the drug's superiority to other forms of amphetamine]

cad's crawlers *n.* [1930s+] suede shoes (cf. BROTHEL-CREEPERS). [CAD n.[1] + SE *crawler*; such shoes were (? are) seen as somewhat raffish]

cads on castors *n.* [late 19C–1900s] bicyclists. [CAD n.[1] (1)]

cady *n.* **1** [mid-19C+] a hat (cf. CHARLEY BRADY; OFF ONE'S KADOOVA). **2** [1920s+] (N.Z.) a straw hat. [Scot. *cadie*, a cap]

caesaration! *excl.* [late 19C] (US) a mild oath (cf. GREAT CAESAR'S GHOST!). [proper name Julius *Caesar* + sfx. *-ation*, on pattern of BOTHERATION!; BUGGERATION!]

caf/caff *n.* [1930s+] corruption of café, usu. cheap and cheerful (cf. CAFE).

cafe/kayf *n.* [1960s+] a corruption of café, usu. cheap and cheerful (cf. CAF). [the Fr. é of the original has been dropped]

café au lait *n.* [1920s–30s] (US Black) a light-skinned woman. [the beverage; orig. coined to describe the women chosen for the chorus line of Harlem's Cotton Club; thus ? pun on *café*]

café de move-on *n.* [1920s–50s] (S.Afr.) a small mobile canteen catering for workers at their place of work. [S.Afr.E. *café*, a convenience store + the need for the canteen to 'move on' when the authorities arrive. The whole phr. is a play on a notional upmarket *Café de …*]

cafeteria *n.* [1980s+] (US gay) anywhere that plays host to repeated oral sex, e.g. a public lavatory or bath-house. [one goes there to EAT]

caff *see* CAF.

cafishio/cafinflero *n.* [1920s] an Argentine white slaver who doubles as a pimp. [ety. unknown; ? Sp.]

caflugalty/cafugelty *n.* [20C] (US) a row, an argument. [? KERFUFFLE]

caf up *v.* [1980s] (US campus) to drink coffee or eat something containing caffeine for energy. [SE *caffeine*]

cag/kagg *n.* [late 18C–19C] an argument, a dispute. [dial. *cag*, an argument]

cag/keg *v.* [mid-19C] to irritate, to annoy; thus *caggy*, ill-natured; *cagged*, irritated, angry. [dial. *cag*, tainted, 'off' meat]

cage *n.* **1** [17C+] a prison (cf. COOP). **2** [mid-19C] a dress-improver or bustle (cf. BIRD-CAGE). **3** [late 19C] a bed (cf. BREEDING-CAGE). **4** [1930s+] (US) an elevator, a lift. **5** [20C] (US Und.) a holding cell (cf. BULLPEN). [all fig. uses of SE; (1) SE in earlier use]

cage and key man *n.* [20C] (US prison) a prison guard responsible for a particular row of cells.

cage of ivories *n.* [late 18C] a set of good teeth. [SE *cage* + IVORIES]

cagey *adj.* [20C] **1** non-committal, reticent, wary. **2** cunning, crafty. [SE *cage*; the image of a caged animal, gazing suspiciously at human onlookers]

caggie *n.* [1970s+] a *cag*oule or hooded anorak (cf. HOODIE). [abbr.]

cagmag *n.* **1** [late 18C–mid-19C] refuse, rubbish, odds and ends. **2** [late 18C–mid-19C] a plain or slovenly woman. **3** [late 19C–1920s] gossip, tittle-tattle. [dial. *cag-mag*, an old goose, not fit for eating (according to Grose (1796), such geese were dumped on the undiscriminating London market), an inferior breed of sheep, a disreputable old woman, anything valueless or second-rate. Hotten's (1864) suggestion – a corruption of the Gk. *kakos mageiros*, a bad cook, and used as such in university sl. – must be rejected]

cag out v. [20C] (US) to break down, to stop working. [Midlands dial. *cag*, to crawl, to move slowly]

cagy see CADGY.

cahoot v. [19C] (US) to act in partnership. [backform. f. IN CAHOOTS]

cain and abel n. [mid-19C+] a table. [rhy. sl.]

caine n. [1980s+] (drugs) **1** co*caine*. **2** crack co*caine*. [abbr.]

cainsham smoke n. [late 17C–early 18C] the tears of a man who is beaten by his wife. [? a lost story pertaining to *Keynsham*, nr. Bristol]

Cairo crud n. [1940s+] diarrhoea (cf. APPLE-BLOSSOM TWO-STEP). [proper name *Cairo* + CRUD]

caj see CAS adj.[1].

cajita n. [20C] (US prison/Hisp.Am.) a bag of marijuana. [Sp. *cajita*, a little cage]

cajunk! see KERCHUNK!

cake/cakey n.[1] **1** [late 18C–late 19C] a fool. **2** [early 19C] (US) a dandy, a fop. **3** [1920s] (US) as *the cake*, a (self-appointedly) wonderful person. [the 'softness' of the unintelligent head, or the 'tastiness' of the person]

cake n.[2] **1** [20C] (a pile of) money. **2** [20C] (Aus.) a gold nugget. **3** [1960s] (US Black) money. [ext. of BREAD n.[1] (2)]

cake n.[3] **1** [1910s+] (Aus.) a prostitute (cf. CAKE SHOP; TART). **2** [1940s–60s] (US Black) an attractive woman (cf. BANANA n.[2]). [one of a number of words that equate attractive young women with sweetmeats]

cake/cakes n.[4] [1960s+] (US) a term of affection between friends (cf. BABYCAKES).

cake n.[5] [1980s+] (US campus) anything easy, simple (cf. EASY AS PIE). [PIECE OF CAKE]

caked adj.[1] [1940s+] well-off. [CAKE n.[2]]

caked adj.[2] [1990s] (US campus) drunk. [? CACK v.[1]]

cake-date see JELLY-DATE.

cake-eater n. [1910s+] (US) **1** a self-indulgent or effeminate young man. **2** an effete young man who attends smart tea parties and charms old ladies (cf. COOKIE-PUSHER). **3** any wealthy young man, a playboy.

cakehole n. [1940s+] the mouth (cf. BACON-HOLE).

cake is dough phr. [mid-16C+] one's project has failed, one's plans have not worked out. [the image is of a cake mixture failing to rise in the oven]

cake is getting thin phr. [20C] one's money is running low. [CAKE n.[2]]

cakes n.[1] **1** [1960s] (US) the buttocks (cf. BUNS). **2** [1960s+] (US Black) the vagina (cf. APPLE n.[10]). **3** [1970s+] (orig. US) the female breasts (cf. APPLES n.[1]). **4** [1990s] (drugs) round discs of crack cocaine. [all fig. use of the size and shape of a SE *cake*]

cakes n.[2] see CAKE n.[4].

cake shop n. [1910s+] (Aus.) a brothel. [CAKE n.[3] (1)]

cakewalk n. [20C] **1** anything considered very easy (cf. APPLE SAUCE n.[4]). **2** money that has been obtained without effort. [SE *cakewalk*, a dance in which the contestants (usu. US Black) promenade around a cake placed in the centre of the dance-floor; those who perform the fanciest steps literally 'take the cake'. Orig. as WW1 milit. jargon, an attack or raid that met with little or no opposition]

cakewalk v. [1930s] (US) to succeed without problems. [CAKEWALK n.]

cakey n. see CAKE n.[1].

cakey adj. **1** [late 19C] stupid, foolish, 'soft'. **2** [1930s] (US) a fop, a dandy. [CAKE n.[1]]

cakey-pannum fencer n. [mid-19C] a street-seller of pastries. [SE *cake* + PANNUM + FENCER]

cal n.[1] [mid-19C] a hangman (cf. DERRICK; GREGORIAN TREE;

JACK KETCH). [abbr. of proper name Thomas *Cal*craft (*fl.*1860), a hangman]

Cal n.[2] **1** [mid-19C+] (US) *Cal*ifornia. **2** [late 19C] (Anglo-Ind.) *Cal*cutta. [abbr.]

calabash n.[1] [mid-19C] the human head (cf. GOURD; PUMPKIN). [Persian *kharbuz*, or *kharbuza*, meaning melon, or watermelon; ult. Arabic *khirbiz*, melon or *kirbiz*, pumpkin or gourd]

calabash n.[2] [mid–late 19C] (Aus.) a promissory note or IOU (cf. BALM OF GILEAD). [the image is of the essential worthlessness of such notes, which were no more valid as money than had they been written on a *calabash* or gourd-shell]

calabash cover n. [late 19C] (US) a hat. [CALABASH n.[1]]

calaboodle see CABOODLE.

calaboose n. [mid-19C+] (orig. US) a prison. [Sp. *calabozo*, gaol]

calaboose v. [mid-19C] (US) to imprison. [CALABOOSE n.]

calamity-howler/-shouter n. [late 19C] (US) a prophet of doom.

calamity jane n. [20C] (US) a nagging woman, a pessimist, a worrier. [the markswoman Martha Jane Canary Burke (1852–1903) known as *Calamity Jane* for the effect her 6-guns had on those who opposed her]

calamity-shouter see CALAMITY-HOWLER.

calathumpian n. [1920s+] one who claims an imaginary religion. [ety. unknown; ? SE *calamity* + *thump*]

calculate v. [mid-19C] (US) to think, to opine.

caldee/chaldee v. [mid-17C–early 18C] to trick, to swindle. [? SE *Chaldee*, an astrologer]

caldron n. [19C] the vagina (cf. MORTAR). [SE *cauldron*]

caleb quotum n. [mid–late 19C] **1** a parish clerk. **2** a jack of all trades. [proper name of a character in the play *The Wags of Windsor*]

caledonia n. [1920s–50s] (US Black) a Black woman who refuses to accept the traditional role into which her birth is supposed to have thrust her. [? a book ? play ? song ?]

caleery/kileery n. [20C] a mischievous, scatterbrained, overexcitable person; thus *caleeried*, scatterbrained, *caleeriness*, mischief. [dial. *caleer*, to caper]

calendar n. [1920s+] (US) a year spent in prison. [abbr. SE *calendar year*]

calf n.[1] **1** [mid-16C–mid-19C] a fool, a simpleton. **2** [20C] (US) a coward (cf. HAVE A CALF). [dial. Note the UK comedian Steve Coogan's 1990s character Paul *Calf*, a loutish, stupid, hedonistic Mancunian]

calf n.[2] [late 19C] a native of Essex, as used by those of Suffolk who look down on their southern neighbours. [abbr. ESSEX CALF]

calf n.[3] [1940s+] 50p. [rhy. sl. *cow and calf* = half = half a pound, orig. 10 shillings, now 50p]

calf n.[4] [1940s] (US Black) a Cadillac.

calf v. [20C] (US) to vomit (cf. BARF; HUGHIE; RALPH). [? onomat.]

calf-clingers n. [early 19C–1910s] very tight-fitting trousers.

calf-lolly n. [17C–early 18C] an idle simpleton. [CALF n.[1] + dial. *lolly*, a fool, an idler]

calf's head n. **1** [late 16C–early 19C] a fool. **2** [late 19C] a white-faced man with a large head. [CALF n.[1]]

calfskin fiddle n. [late 18C–early 19C] a drum. [its calfskin head]

calf-slobber n. (US) [1920s+] a meringue topping for pastry; thus fig. [1980s+] nothing whatsoever, e.g. *that's just calf-slobber to me*. [dial. *calf-slobber*, the saliva that forms around a calf's mouth]

calf-sticking n. [mid-19C–1910s] (Und.) pretending that perfectly normal goods have supposedly been stolen; a greater price can thus be asked, since some customers like the idea of obtaining stolen goods. [CALF n.[1] + STICK v.]

calf-/cow-/bull-week *n*. [mid-19C] the three weeks immediately before Christmas, characterized in shops and factories by an increasingly heavy workload. [the cattle names imply stolid labouring]

Cali *n*. [1980s+] the state of *Cali*fornia. [abbr.]

calico *n*. [19C] (US) a woman; thus *calico fever*, the desire to pursue women. [SE *calico*, a cloth, somewhat coarser than muslin, from which women's dresses were often made. There may also be links to Scot. *cailliach*, an old woman, *calik*, a gossip and *callack*, a young woman]

calico *adj*. [early 18C–mid-19C] thin, wasted. [the thinness of the cotton cloth]

calico *v*. [19C] (US) to court women, to associate with women. [CALICO *n*.]

calico ball/hop *n*. [mid-19C–1910s] (US) a cheap, popular public dance. [the *calico* (rather than silk or satin) dresses worn by the women]

calico muster *see* TARPAULIN MUSTER.

calicot *n*. [late 19C–1900s] a 'counter-jumper' (cf. CAD *n*.[1]). [Fr. *calicot*, a draper's assistant, though sl. use is the same]

California *n*. [mid-19C] money, esp. a gold piece. [the *California* Gold Rush of the 1840s]

California banknote/shinplaster *n*. [early–mid-19C] (US) an animal hide used as money in early 19C California. [replaced by coins and notes subsequent to the 1849 Gold Rush]

California/Kansas City/Philadelphia bankroll/roll *n*. [1970s+] (US Black/gambling) a show bankroll in which one large-denomination note is exhibited on the outside, concealing a quantity of small bills (cf. CHICAGO BANKROLL; FLASH ROLL; GANGSTA ROLL; GLORY ROLL; MEXICAN BANKROLL; MICHIGAN ROLL; MISSOURI BANKROLL; NIGGER'S BANKROLL; TOPS AND BOTTOMS). [a general slur, to which states and countries are variously subject, depending on a speaker's prejudice]

California bible/prayerbook *n*. [mid-19C+] (US) a deck of cards. [the stereotyped sinfulness of California]

California/Tucson blanket *n*. [1920s–30s] (US) newspapers, when used by tramps as a substitute for blankets (cf. BUM'S COMFORTER). [SE *California/Tuscon* + BLANKET]

California collar *n*. [19C] (US) a noose, used for hangings (cf. HEMPEN COLLAR). [the numbers of vigilantes to be found in California, most of whom favoured hanging first and ascertaining guilt later]

California cornflakes *n*. [1970s+] (drugs) cocaine. [joc. play on the breakfast cereal's slogan: it's 'good for you each morning']

California house *n*. [20C] (US) an outside privy. [? the good weather in California, which permits an outdoor lifestyle]

California moccasins *n*. [1920s–30s] (US) makeshift 'socks' made from sacks or similar rags (cf. CALIFORNIA OVERSHOES; CALIFORNIA SOCKS). [as worn by impoverished tramps who travelled to and then in California]

Californian *n*. [mid–late 19C] a dried red herring (cf. ABERDEEN CUTLET). [the association of the red i.e. gold colour, with the Californian Gold Rush]

California overshoes *n*. [19C] (US) makeshift 'socks' made by wrapping the feet in sacks, often flour sacks, over which boots can then be put on (cf. CALIFORNIA MOCCASINS). [as used by hoboes and/or unsuccessful gold prospectors]

California prayerbook *see* CALIFORNIA BIBLE.

California roll *see* CALIFORNIA BANKROLL.

California shinplaster *see* CALIFORNIA BANKNOTE.

California socks *n*. [1950s–60s] (US) makeshift 'sock's made from sacks or other rags (cf. CALIFORNIA MOCCASINS).

California/Hollywood stop *n*. [1970s+] (US) the running of a stop sign by a motorist. [stereotyped Californians are seen as contemptuous of the law]

California sunshine *n*. [1960s+] (drugs) LSD (cf. A *n*.[3]). [*California* + SUNSHINE *n*.[1]]

California toothpick *n*. [mid-19C] (US) a large knife (cf. ARKANSAS TOOTHPICK).

caliwampus *see* CATAWAMPUS *adj*.

call *n*. [1960s–70s] **1** the first feelings that follow the taking of an alcoholic drink. **2** (drugs) the immediate response to an injection of a drug (cf. BUZZ *n*.[4]; RUSH). [a pun on the religious use of *call*, a summons to a higher spirituality]

call *v*.[1] **1** [mid-18C+] to beg. **2** [late 19C+] to blame. [fig. uses of SE]

call *v*.[2] [1990s+] (Aus.) to vomit. [abbr. CALL FOR HUGHIE; CALL FOR RALPH]

call a go, to *phr*. [mid-19C] **1** to move on. **2** to give up (cf. CALL IT A DAY).

callan park *n*. [20C] (Aus.) a psychiatric institution (cf. DOOLALLY; GONE TO HASLAR; GO YARMOUTH; WINNICK; YARRA). [the name of a psychiatric hospital in Sydney, used to represent any such hospital]

call a spade a shovel/bloody shovel, to *phr*. [1910s+] to speak aggressively or vehemently. [a play on the usu. phr. *call a spade a spade*]

callawampus *adj*. [1940s+] (W.I.) big, fine, stout, grand (cf. CATWAMPUS *n*.[2]).

call-boy *n*. [1970s+] a male prostitute who can be hired on the phone. [a male version of a CALL-GIRL]

call copper *v*. [1930s–40s] (Und.) to inform the police. [SE *call* + COPPER *n*.[3]]

call-dog *n*. [1940s+] (W.I.) a fish too small for human consumption. [one *calls the dog* to eat it]

calldown *n*. [late 19C–1900s] (US) a telling-off, a scolding.

call down *v*. [late 19C+] to scold, to reprimand.

calle *n*. [late 17C–early 19C] (Und.) a cloak. [SE *caul*, a (net) bag, usu. for the hair]

call flat *n*. [1910s–20s] (US) a brothel. [var. on CALL HOUSE]

call for bill *see* CALL FOR HUGHIE.

call for herb, to *phr*. [1960s+] (Aus.) to vomit (cf. CALL FOR HUGHIE; CALL FOR RALPH; CRY HUGHIE; CRY RALPH). [echoic; *herb* can be seen as echoing the sound of vomiting]

call for hughie/bill, to *phr*. [1960s+] (society) to vomit (cf. CALL FOR HERB). [onomat.]

call for ralph, to *phr*. [1960s+] to vomit (cf. CALL FOR HERB). [onomat.]

call full-mouth/raw *v*. (W.I.) to address an elder or senior person without using Mr, Mrs or Miss. [FULLMOUTH/SE *raw*; i.e. 'uncooked' by good manners]

call-girl *n*. **1** [late 19C+] a woman who works in a brothel (cf. CALL HOUSE). **2** [1930s+] (orig. US) a prostitute who advertises her services through an agency, through the (print) media, in telephone kiosks etc and visits a client in his own home or hotel room (cf. CALL-BOY). [SE *call*, to make a telephone call + GIRL *n*.[1] (2)]

call hogs *v*. [1910s–60s] (US) to snore (cf. DRIVE PIGS). [the noise]

call house *n*. [late 19C+] **1** a brothel to which men can come without making any prior appointment. **2** a hetero- or homosexual brothel to which women or men are summoned by telephone after they have been selected, via some form of visual 'menu', by the male clientele (cf. ACCOMMODATION HOUSE; CALL FLAT; CALL JOINT). [SE *call* (on), to visit + HOUSE *n*.[1] (1)]

callibisters *n*. [16C] the testicles. [*callistris*, the penis]

callibogus *n*. [late 18C–late 19C] (US) a mixture of rum and spruce beer. [ety. unknown]

callie *see* CALLY.

callinado *v*. [20C] (US prison/Hisp.Am.) to act coolly, calmly (cf. CHILL *v*.[3]). [Sp.]

call in someone's chips, to phr. [late 19C] (US) to challenge, to call someone's bluff. [poker imagery]

call in someone's marker, to phr. (US) **1** [20C] to call in a gambling debt. **2** [1980s+] to demand repayment of a favour. [MARKER n.²; (2) is fig. use of (1)]

call it a day, to phr. [20C] **1** to stop, to go no further, to express satisfaction with progress or acceptance that one cannot improve a position; also as *call it a night, call it a go*. **2** to die. [? cribbage jargon *call a go*, to change one's tactics, to give in]

call it george/wally, to phr. [20C] (W.I.) to agree that a matter is concluded, bring to an end, e.g. a day's work. [joc. generic use of proper names]

callithumpian n. [mid-19C+] (US) a band or member of a band that makes discordant so-called 'music' by playing a number of instruments, either in an unlikely combination or conjured up from unlikely objects, such as washboards, tin kettles etc. [ety. unknown, ? link to SE *thump*]

call it 'it', to phr. [1950s+] to come to a conclusion, to abandon further effort, to be satisfied (cf. CALL IT A DAY).

call it quits, to phr. [20C] to die (cf. CALL IT A DAY).

call it wally see CALL IT GEORGE.

call joint n. [1930s–40s] (US) a brothel (cf. CALL HOUSE). [SE *call* (on) + JOINT n.³ (3)]

call off all bets, to phr. [1930s–40s] (US Black) to die (cf. CASH IN ONE'S CHECKS). [poker imagery]

call on the carpet, to phr. [20C] **1** (US prison) to challenge another speaker to justify their remarks, whether hostile, gossiping or whatever. **2** (US) to reprimand, to scold (cf. CARPET v.).

call out v. [late 19C+] to challenge to a fight. [early 19C SE *call out*, challenge to a duel]

call over the coals, to phr. [19C+] to scold, to tell off. [var. on HAUL OVER THE COALS]

call raw see CALL FULL-MOUTH.

call sir and something else, to phr. [mid-17C–late 18C] to abuse, to address contemptuously. [the use of the derog. *sirrah*, which is made up of 'sir' and 'something else'; cited by Minsheu as the interj. *ah* or *ha*]

call someone for everything under the sun, to phr. [late 19C+] to abuse severely. [Midlands dial. *call*, to abuse, to scold]

call someone out of their name, to phr. [1930s+] (US Black) to insult through name-calling.

call someone's card, to phr. [1970s–80s] (US) to call someone's bluff. [poker imagery]

call someone's game, to phr. [1980s+] (US) to call someone's bluff, to challenge. [poker imagery]

call someone's hand, to phr. [mid-19C–1950s] (US) to issue a challenge, to call someone's bluff. [poker imagery]

call the coin, to phr. [1950s] (US) to call 'heads or tails' when a coin is tossed.

call the dogs, to phr. [1990s] (US campus) to vomit. [one's 'barking' noises]

call the game in, to phr. [1910s+] (Aus./N.Z.) to abandon one's efforts, to admit defeat. [lit. to bring a game, e.g. of rugby, to an end]

call the punches/shots, to phr. [1960s+] to dictate a course of action, to say what should happen. [dice gambling]

call the turn, to phr. [late 19C+] (US) to predict accurately. [gambling use: calling the next turn of the wheel in the game of faro]

Cally, the n.¹ [late 19C+] (London) **1** the *Cale*donian Market. **2** the *Cale*donian Road. [abbr.]

cally/callie n.² [1910s–20s] (US tramp) a prison. [abbr. CALABOOSE]

Cally n.³ [1930s+] (US) *Cali*fornia (cf. CAL; CALI). [abbr.]

caló n. [1940s+] (US) Chicano street slang, linked to Mexican and gypsy patois.

calonkus n. [late 19C+] (Aus.) a fool. [? echoic of the 'kalonk' of hitting one's head with a palm or fist]

caloop v. [20C] (US) to go courting, to kiss and cuddle. [? pfx. KER- + SE *loop*, to encircle (with one's arms)]

calp see KELP n.¹.

calve v. [mid-19C] (US) to vomit. [echoic]

calves gone to grass phr. [late 18C–19C] denoting someone who has noticeably thin legs; thus joc. remark: 'veal will be cheap, calves fall' on noticing a man whose calves fall away. [a pun]

calves' heads are best hot phr. [19C] a derog. remark aimed at a person who sits down to eat with their hat on. [CALF n.¹]

cam/cami/cammy n.¹ [20C] a *cami*sole or underbodice. [abbr.]

Cam n.² [1970s+] *Cam*bodian marijuana, usu. very strong (cf. CAMBODIAN RED). [abbr.]

camac n. [19C] (Irish) anything that is over-complex or over-expensive to achieve its essentially simple purpose. [two clergymen, named Ryan and *Camac*, hanged for counterfeiting at Wexford in the early 19C]

camarada de aquella n. [1960s+] (US) a general term of high praise, 'a number one guy', 'a real down dude'. [Sp.]

Camberwell death trap, the n. [late 19C–1900s] the Surrey Canal. [the drownings that occurred there]

Cambodian red n. (drugs) [1960s+] a slightly reddish variety of marijuana grown in Cambodia (cf. CAM n.²).

Cambodian trip see CAM TRIP.

cambra/komra n. [18C+] a dog. [Shelta]

Cambridge fortune n. [late 17C–late 18C] a woman who has no fortune of her own and must rely for attraction on her personal charms alone (cf. TIPPERARY FORTUNE; WHITECHAPEL FORTUNE). [punning on two staples of the Cambridgeshire countryside, the term is defined by Grose as 'a wind-mill and a water-mill', i.e. she can talk and urinate but that is all]

Cambridge/Cambridgeshire nightingale n. [late 18C] a frog (cf. CAPE NIGHTINGALE; FEN NIGHTINGALE; IRISH NIGHTINGALE). [the large numbers of croaking frogs found in the marshy fens]

Cambridge/Cambridgeshire oak n. [late 18C] a willow. [the frequency of willows in that county]

Cambridgeshire camel n. [late 17C–early 19C] a native or established resident of Cambridgeshire. [the stilt-walkers once found in the fens]

Camden Town n. [19C] a halfpenny. [rhy. sl. *Camden Town* = BROWN]

camel n.¹ [mid-19C–1910s] (S.Afr.) a giraffe. [joc. substitution; both have prominent necks]

camel n.² [late 19C] (US) a bustle or 'dress-improver'. [the camel's and the bustle's 'hump']

camel chaser/jockey/jock n. [1960s+] (US) a derog. term for a Syrian or an Indian (from India) or any form of Arabic Middle Easterner (cf. SAND SCRATCHER). [SE *camel* + *chaser/jockey/jock* n.⁴ (1)]

camel's complaint n. [late 19C–1920s] depression. [pun on the HUMP n.¹]

camel toe/toes n. [1990s] (orig. US) the vulva as seen through a tight pair of jeans or trousers. [supposed resemblance]

cameo cut n. [1990s] (US Black) short-cropped Black hair, pioneered by the hip-hop culture (cf. FADE n.).

camera obscura n. [late 19C–1900s] (US) the buttocks, the anus. [pun on Lat. *camera obscura*, a dark place]

camerer cuss n. [1920s–30s] a London bus. [rhy. sl.; the clockmakers *Camerer Cuss* was founded in 1788]

camesa/kemesa n. [mid-17C–late 19C] a shirt (cf. COMMISSION; COMISH n.¹; MISH; SHIMMY; SMISH). [Ital. *camisa*, a shirt]

cami *see* CAM n.[1].

cami-knicks *n.* [1930s+] an undergarment that combines camisole and knickers. [abbr. SE *cami-knickers*]

camister *n.* [mid-19C] (Und.) a clergyman (cf. CANISTER n.[2]; COMMISTER). [SE *camis*, a surplice + CAMESA]

cammie/camo *n.* [1970s+] (orig. US milit.) *camo*uflage (uniforms). [abbr.]

cammy *see* CAM n.[1].

camo *see* CAMMIE.

Camp, the *n.[1]* **1** [late 18C–early 19C] (Aus.) Sydney. **2** [mid-19C] (Aus.) Hobart. **3** [20C] the area outside Port Stanley in the Falkland Islands.

camp *n.[2]* [mid-19C+] (Aus.) a short rest, a lie-down; thus *have a camp, go to camp*, to take a rest.

camp *n.[3]* **1** [1930s] (orig. US) a male homosexual. **2** [1930s–40s] a gathering place for male homosexuals. **3** [1930s+] flamboyance, overt exhibitionism. [CAMP adj.]

camp *adj.* [late 19C+] effeminate, affected, exaggerated; the general image is that of limp-wristed homosexuality. ['Actions and gestures of exaggerated emphasis. Probably from the French. Used chiefly by persons of exceptional want of character. "How very camp he is."' (Ware). Anthony Burgess suggests a link to SE *camp*, a military base, mining or railroad camp, in which, as in a prison, a lack of women might lead to homosexuality and where effeminate men would act deliberately in this manner to attract admirers. He also notes the availability, in London, of soldiers from the city barracks, willing to indulge gay men-about-town]

camp *v.[1]* (Aus.) **1** [mid-19C+] to rest, to lie down. **2** [late 19C] to die. [CAMP n.[2]]

camp *v.[2]* [1930s+] to act ostentatiously and outrageously in a homosexual manner, although by no means restricted, verbally or physically, to the gay world; thus *campy*. [CAMP adj.]

camp about/around/it up *v.* [1930s+] of a man, to act in a deliberate and exaggeratedly effeminate manner; used of effeminate male homosexuals and those who, maliciously or otherwise, are attempting to mimic them. [ext. of CAMP v.[2]]

campaign coat *n.* [mid-17C–early 18C] a tattered old coat, worn by beggars specifically to excite sympathy in passers-by. [orig. a military uniform, then in civilian tailoring a style of coat that resembled military uniform; as worn by a beggar such a coat was supposed to present the image of an old soldier]

camp around *see* CAMP ABOUT.

camp as a row of tents/pink chiffon tents *phr.* [1950s+] of a male homosexual, extremely, ostentatiously effeminate. [pun on SE *camp*/CAMP adj.]

camp as Chloe *phr.* [1950s–60s] of a man or a male homosexual, extremely affected, effeminate. [? the same portrait of Chloe as inspired BLIND AS CHLOE]

campbell's academy *n.* [late 18C–early 19C] the hulks, or floating prisons, sited in ships moored in the Thames Estuary (cf. ADKINS'S ACADEMY). [*Campbell*, the name of the first director of such prisons + ACADEMY]

camp candlestick *n.* [late 18C] an empty bottle (cf. DEAD MARINE; DEAD SOLDIER). [the use of such an empty bottle as a candlestick in army camps etc]

camp down *v.* [late 19C+] (Aus.) to go to bed. [CAMP v.[1]]

camper *n.* [1980s+] (US) a person, an individual; usu. in (ironic) phr. *happy camper*. [the studied jollity of a holiday camp]

campery *n.* [1970s+] the exhibition of those qualities that make one appear CAMP adj.

camp it up *see* CAMP ABOUT.

camp meat *n.* [20C] (US) deer that has been illegally shot by poachers (cf. COUNTY BEEF; FARMER'S BEEF; GOVERNMENT BEEF;

HEMLOCK STEAK; SIDE-HILL HALIBUT; UNCLE SAM'S SHEEP; WHITE-FACED CALF). [i.e. *meat* obtained by those in a *camp*, rather than on a farm]

campy *adj.* **1** [1950s–60s] ostentatious, affected, effeminate. **2** [1970s] (US Black) extremely close-knit, happy, gay and free-spirited to the point of sickening others around one. [CAMP adj.]

cam/Cambodian trip *n.* [1960s+] (drugs) a very potent, almost hallucinogenic variety of marijuana. [abbr. *Cambodian* + TRIP n.[3]]

can *n.[1]* **1** [19C] (US) a water closet, a lavatory. **2** [late 19C+] a prison, a police station lock-up. **3** (US Und.) a safe. [SE *can*, a container]

can *n.[2]* [mid-19C] (US) $1. [ety. unknown]

can *n.[3]* [late 19C] a barman. [he fills the beer cans for his customers]

can *n.[4]* (US) **1** [late 19C+] the buttocks. **2** [1930s+] (US) used as a euph. for ASS in various senses, e.g. *pain in the can, flatter the can off* etc. **3** [late 19C+] (US) the human head. [SE *can*, a container]

can *n.[5]* [1910s+] a pocket (cf. BIN; TOUCH THE CAN).

can *n.[6]* [1920s] (US) a bomb; thus *can-maker*, a bomb-maker.

can *n.[7]* [1920s+] (US) a dilapidated, run-down, malfunctioning vehicle (cf. BUCKET; PISS-CAN). [SE *tin-can*]

can *n.[8]* [1960s] (drugs) approx. 1oz (28g) of marijuana (cf. LID). [a (notional) can into which marijuana is measured out]

can *v.[1]* [20C] to stop doing something, esp. in imper., e.g. *can that noise!* [fig. place it in a can]

can *v.[2]* [20C] (orig. US) to reject, to abandon, to discard, to dismiss, to throw out, to ignore (cf. BIN). [toss out on one's CAN n.[4]]

can *v.[3]* [1920s+] (US) to put in prison. [CAN n.[1]]

can *v.[4]* [1940s–70s] (US) to have anal sex with. [CAN n.[4] (1)]

Canadian bacon *n.* [1960s+] (gay) an uncircumcised penis. [play on foodstuff + BACON n.[1] (3)]

Canadian black *n.* [1960s+] (drugs) marijuana. [the country of origin + the dark green colouring]

canadoe *n.* [early 17C] a drink. [? SE *can* + Fr. *d'eau*, of water]

can a duck swim? *phr.* [late 19C+] used to emphasize one's absolute agreement (cf. CAN NIGGERS DANCE?).

canal boat *n.[1]* [20C] the Tote (the Totalizator). [rhy. sl.]

canal boat *n.[2]* [20C] (US) a large foot or shoe. [supposed resemblance]

canaller *n.* [late 19C] (orig. US) **1** a canal boat. **2** one who lives on a canal boat.

cañamo *n.* [1960s+] (US drugs) marijuana. [Sp. *cañamo*, a reed]

canappa *n.* [1930s] (drugs) marijuana. [Sp. ?]

canaries *n.[1]* [late 17C–mid-19C] guineas, gold coins (cf. CANARY-BIRD n.[3]).

canaries *n.[2]* [1930s+] bananas. [SE *canary* yellow]

canary *n.[1]* **1** [mid-17C] a prisoner. **2** [19C] (Aus.) a convict. [the yellow uniforms that they wore and their being 'caged']

canary/canary-bird *n.[2]* **1** [18C–early 19C] a mistress. **2** [18C–early 19C] a prostitute (cf. CHICKEN n.[6]; GAME PULLET; NIGHT-INGALE; PARTRIDGE; PHEASANT; PLOVER; QUAIL). **3** [mid-19C] a thief's female accomplice. [? the gaudy colouring of her clothes]

canary *n.[3]* [mid-19C] (US) a mule, usu. in comb. with a geographical name, e.g. ROCKY MOUNTAIN CANARY, *Indiana canary* etc. [its 'hee-hawing']

canary *n.[4]* [mid-19C–1900s] a sovereign (cf. CANARY-BIRD n.[3]; GOLDFINCH; MARIGOLD n.; YELLOW n.; YELLOW BOY; YELLOW GEORGE; YELLOWHAMMER). [the colour of the gold coin]

canary *n.[5]* [mid-19C] (Aus.) 100 strokes of the lash (cf. BOB; BULL n.[4]; TESTER). [CANARY n.[4]; the term plays on the monetary value signifying the number of strokes]

canary n.[6] [late 19C–1900s] a form on which one signs a promise to make a donation to the Salvation Army, a charity subscription. [the yellow paper used by the Salvationists, whose colours were red and yellow. The nickname came from William Booth (1829–1912) himself. Ware notes that red paper was more expensive]

canary n.[7] [late 19C–1900s] an ornament worn at the hip. ['in true descent from the cod-piece, though not so glaring in its declaration' (Ware)]

canary n.[8] **1** [late 19C+] a chorus-singer placed in the gallery from where they urge on the rest of the audience. **2** (US) [1920s–50s] (show business) a female singer, usu. fronting a band. **3** [1930s+] (UK/US/S.Afr. Und.) an informer (cf. NIGHTINGALE; SING LIKE A CANARY). [SE canary, a popular song-bird]

canary n.[9] [late 19C+] (Aus./N.Z.) a Chinese immigrant. [the yellow stereotype]

canary n.[10] [1900s] (US campus) a cigarette. [? a specific brand with yellow packaging]

canary v. **1** [1930s+] of a criminal, to confess (cf. SING LIKE A CANARY). **2** [1940s] (US) to work as a band vocalist. [CANARY n.[8]]

canary-bird n.[1] [late 17C–mid-19C] **1** a prisoner. **2** a young villain. [the cage in which the prisoner is kept, or the young villain will end up in; (2) has an added inference of his smartness of dress]

canary-bird n.[2] [late 17C–mid-19C] a guinea or gold coin. [ext. of CANARY n.[4]]

canary-bird n.[3] see CANARY n.[2].

canary hatch n. [1960s] (US) a psychiatric institution. [var. on BOOBY HATCH]

canasta n. [1960s–70s] the male genitals. [the card-game, ult. f. Sp. canasta, a basket; thus pun on BASKET]

canat see KINAT.

cancelled stick n. [1960s+] (drugs) marijuana cigarette. [pun on CANCER STICK]

cancel someone's ticket, to phr. [1960s+] to murder, to assassinate.

cancer n. [1970s+] (US) rusting on an automobile.

cancer alley n. [1980s+] (US) the industrial area of a city. [the polluting factories may well issue carcinogens into the atmosphere]

cancer stick n. [1950s+] a cigarette. [the proven link between tobacco and lung cancer]

C&A adj. [1950s–70s] homosexual. [rhy. sl. C&A = GAY adj.[1] (3); C&A is the name of a chain of clothing stores in the UK]

C and E man n. [20C] (US) someone who attends church only rarely. [Christmas and Easter; the two festivals that attract the irregular attender]

C and H n. [1960s+] (US Black) a mixture of cocaine and heroin (cf. SPEEDBALL). [C n.[2] (1) + H n.[2]; also pun on brand-name of C & H cane sugar]

candle/candle-sconce n. [1920s+] a pimp, a ponce (cf. CHARLIE RONCE). [rhy. sl.]

candle v. [late 19C] to check carefully. [SE candle, to test an egg's freshness by holding it to a candle flame]

candle-basher n. [late 19C–1950s] a spinster. [the candle's use as a dildo]

candlelight n. [1970s] (US Black) the last vestiges of twilight; thus early candlelight, the earliest signs of nightfall.

candle shop n. [late 19C] a Roman Catholic church. [the many candles that burn in one]

candlesperm n. [1970s] (US Black) melted wax from a candle, which drips down into globular beadlets. [resemblance to drops of semen/sperm]

candlestick n. **1** [mid-19C] one of the fountains in Trafalgar Square, London. **2** [20C] (Irish) a drop of mucus running from the nose.

candlesticks n. [late 18C–early 19C] small, bad or untunable bells. [? the impossibility of getting a clear note when striking a candlestick]

candle-waster n. [late 16C] someone who stays up late at night, either studying or enjoying themself.

C and M n. [1960s+] (drugs) cocaine and morphine mixture. [C n.[2] + M n.[2] (1)]

can-do adj. [20C] (orig. US) positive, enthusiastic, aggressive. [affirmative phr. I can do it]

can do phr. [mid-19C] it is possible, it is within my power; thus no can do, it is impossible.

candy n.[1] **1** [mid-19C+] (US Black) sex as an abstract; thus sexual intercourse. **2** [20C] a sexually desirable person of either sex (cf. BANANA n.[2]). **3** [1960s+] (gay) the passive partner in anal intercourse.

candy n.[2] (drugs) **1** [1930s+] (US Black) heroin (cf. NOSE-CANDY). **2** [1960s+] any drug in capsule form. **3** [1970s+] cocaine. [SAmE candy, sweets; i.e. an adult 'sweet']

candy adj.[1] [mid-18C–early 19C] (mainly Anglo-Irish) drunk. [ety. unknown; ? link to SE can, a container for liquids]

candy adj.[2] (US) [1910s+] of a person, soft, weak, effeminate. [abbr. CANDY-ASS adj.]

candy adj.[3] (US) **1** [1930s+] of a job, easy, undemanding, 'soft'. **2** [1990s] (campus) excellent, worthy of admiration. [SAmE candy, sweets]

candy-ankle n. [1930s+] (US) a coward, a weakling, an oversensitive person. [euph. for CANDY-ASS n.[1]]

candy-ass n.[1] [1930s+] a coward, a weakling, an oversensitive person (cf. MARD-ARSE). [SAmE candy + sfx. -ASS]

candy-ass n.[2] [1960s+] (US) **1** (camp gay) an attractive young man. **2** a sweet, sexy young woman. [SAmE candy + -ASS]

candy-ass adj. [1950s+] (US) **1** of a person, weak, ineffectual. **2** of a job, examination etc, insufficiently challenging, too easy. [CANDY-ASS n.[1]]

candy-bag/-boy n. [1920s+] (Aus.) a handyman who works for a prostitute (cf. BUMPER-UP). [CANDY n.[1] + BAG(MAN) n.[2]]

candy-bar punk n. [1960s] (US prison) a prisoner who has become a passive homosexual while in prison. [the gifts or payments of candy bars that he receives for his services]

candy-boy see CANDY-BAG.

candy-butt n. [1970s+] (US Black) a young, inexperienced male (cf. CANDY-ASS n.[1]). [SAmE candy + BUTT n.[1]]

candy C n. [1950s–70s] (drugs) cocaine. [SAmE candy + C n.[2] (1)]

candy cane n.[1] [late 19C–1960s] (US) the penis (cf. VARNISH THE CANE). [like the synon. sweet, it can be sucked]

candy cane n.[2] [1980s+] (US Black) cocaine, whether as powder or crack (cf. CANDY C). [SAmE candy + (co)caine + play on SE]

candy cock n. [1920s] (US) a well-behaved, pleasant person (cf. CANDY KID).

candy kid n. **1** [1900s–50s] (US) a well-behaved, pleasant person. **2** [1900s–50s] (US) a weakling, a mother's boy. **3** [1900s–40s] (US) a successful womanizer. **4** [1910s–40s] (US) a dandy, a fashionably dressed person. **5** [1940s–50s] (Aus.) a jack-of-all-trades employed by a brothel (cf. CONDY BOY). [SAmE candy + KID n.[1]]

candy-leg n. [1920s–40s] (US campus) a rich student who is also attractive to women.

candyman n.[1] **1** [late 19C+] (US Black) a pimp. **2** [late 19C+] (US Black) a woman's male partner or (illicit) lover. **3** [1950s+] (drugs) a drug dealer (cf. CANDY n.[2]; NOSE-CANDY). [the 'sweetness' of SAmE candy]

candyman n.[2] [1910s–30s] (US) a dandy. [var. on CANDY KID (4)]

candystriper *n.* [1960s+] (US) a volunteer nurse's aide; thus *candystripe*, to work as such an aide. [the usu. red and white striped uniform]

candy team *n.* [1930s] (US) a docile team of mules.

candy wagon *n.* (US) **1** [1930s] a buggy. **2** [1940s+] a light truck (cf. PUDDLE JUMPER).

cane *n.*[1] [late 19C+] (Und.) a short house-breaker's crowbar (cf. JEMMY n.[4]). [resemblance]

cane *n.*[2] [1980s+] (US Black) cocaine, whether as powder or crack. [abbr. CANDY CANE]

cane *v.* [20C] **1** to defeat, to treat harshly. **2** to have sexual intercourse. [fig. uses of SE]

caned *adj.* [1980s+] (drugs) extremely intoxicated by a drug, usu. cannabis. [the equation of the effects of drink/drugs with suffering violence]

cane nigger *n.* [late 19C] a cheerful person. {SE (*sugar*)cane + NIGGER; i.e. stereotyped image of a cane field worker]

cane oil *n.* [1970s] (W.I.) rum. [SE *cane oil*, liquor of the sugarcane]

cane toad *n.* [1990s] (Aus.) a rich old man. [SE *cane toad*, the large toad, *bufo marinus*]

can house *n.* [20C] (US, mainly Chicago) a brothel (cf. ACCOMMODATION HOUSE). [CAN n.[4] (2) + HOUSE n.[1] (1)]

can I help you with that? *phr.* [late 19C–1900s] a phr. used to mean 'I'd like some of that too'. When used to a man it refers either to money or food and drink; when used to a woman it can become a suggestion of sex. [euph.]

can I speak to you? *phr.* [1960s+] (Und.) acknowledged code between a newly arrested criminal and his arresting officer; the topic of their conversation would be the possibility and quantity of a bribe, which would secure the villain's freedom or at least a reduction in the charges (cf. DO YOU DRINK?).

canister *n.*[1] **1** [late 18C] the vagina. **2** [mid-19C] the head (cf. BRAINBOX). **3** [late 19C] a hat. **4** [1900s] (US) a watch. **5** [1910s–30s] (US) a pistol. **6** [1930s] (US) a safe or bank vault. [all fig. uses of SE *canister*, a container]

canister *n.*[2] [late 19C–1900s] a clergyman (cf. CAMISTER). [SE *camis*, a surplice + CAMESA]

canister-cap *n.* [mid-19C] a hat. [CANISTER n.[1]]

can it *v.* [20C] (orig. US) to stop, esp. to stop talking; usu. in excl. *can it!*, shut up! [CAN v.[1]]

cank *n.* [mid-17C–early 19C] (Und.) a dumb person. [? ironic reverse of dial. *cank*, a gossip, a chatterer]

cank *adj.* [mid-17C–early 19C] (Und.) dumb. [CANK n.]

canker *see* KANKER.

cankywampus *see* CATAWAMPUS adj.

cannakin *see* CANNIKEN n.[1].

canned *adj.*[1] [late 19C+] arrested. [CAN n.[1] (2)]

canned *adj.*[2] [1910s–40s] drunk. [SE *can*, a container for liquids]

canned goods *n.* [1910s–30s] a virgin of either sex (cf. DAMAGED GOODS). [pun on *can*/CAN n.[4] (2) + the image of a sealed tin]

canned heat *n.* [1920s–60s] (US) a form of crude alcohol, intended for heating purposes but drunk, as is methylated spirits, by down-and-out alcoholics who can afford nothing better.

canned sativa *n.* [1980s+] (drugs) cannabis. [pun on Lat. *Cannabis sativa* + ? drug use of CANNED adj.[1]]

canner *n.* [1930s] (US) a scraggy cow or other animal fit only for the lower end of the canned meat market (cf. HAT RACK; NELLIE].

cannibal *n.*[1] [late 17C–18C] a notably harsh bargainer or grasping tradesman (cf. SHARK). [a pun on SE *cannibal*, one who 'eats' his fellow human beings]

cannibal *n.*[2] [1960s+] (US Black) one who indulges in oral sex (cf. MEATHOUND). [pun on EAT v.[3]]

cannibal *v.* [1960s+] to indulge in mutual and simultaneous fellatio and cunnilingus. [CANNIBAL n.[2]]

can niggers dance? *phr.* [20C] a general phr. of affirmation, the unspoken reply is 'Of course they can' (cf. CAN A DUCK SWIM?; DO BEARS SHIT IN THE WOODS?; IS THE POPE A CATHOLIC?). [NIGGER; i.e. derog. stereotyping]

canniken/cannikin/cannakin *n.*[1] [16C–18C] (Und.) the plague. [? SE *canker*]

canniken/cannikin *n.*[2] [late 18C] a small can. [SE *can* + diminutive sfx. *kin*]

cannister *n.* [20C] (US Und.) a safe (cf. CAN n.[1].).

cannock *see* CANUCK.

cannon *n.*[1] (US) **1** [1900s–20s] a large gun; thus [1910s+] a hired gunman. **2** [1960s–70s] the penis (cf. BAZOOKA). **3** [1970s] a gun barrel.

cannon *n.*[2] [1910s+] a pickpocket (cf. CANNON MOB; ON THE CANNON). [? they 'cannon into' or fig. 'shoot at' a victim]

cannon *adj.* [mid-19C] drunk (cf. CUPSHOT). [SE *cannon*; i.e. one has been knocked down]

cannonball *n.* [1960s] (US) a superior person or one who claims to be so (cf. BIG SHOT).

cannonballs *n.* [19C] the testicles. [the shape]

cannon mob *n.* [1910s+] a pickpocketing gang. [CANNON n.[2] + MOB n.[1] (2)]

cannot look at *phr.* [late 19C+] bears no comparison, cannot equal, has no chance of competing with.

cannot tie bundle *phr.* [20C] (W.I.) not in agreement, divided.

canoe *n.* [1930s+] (US) a large car (cf. JEW CANOE).

canoe *v.*[1] [1920s–50s] to cuddle, to caress sexually. [CANOODLE]

canoe *v.*[2] [1980s+] of a cigarette or cannabis cigarette, to burn down one side rather than evenly. [the burned side presumably resembles the hollowed portion of a canoe]

canoevre *n.* [early–mid-19C] an attempt at swindling or a similarly dubious enterprise. [? link to SE *manoeuvre*]

can of oil/canov *n.* [late 19C+] a boil. [rhy. sl.]

can of worms *n.* [1950s+] (orig. US) an unpleasant, complex and unappetizing situation (cf. OPEN A CAN OF WORMS).

canoneer *n.* [mid-17C] an interpreter of ecclesiastical canons, a canonist.

canoodle *v.* [mid-19C+] (orig. US) to cuddle, to caress sexually; thus *canoodler*, one who is devoted to giving or getting such caresses. [ety. unknown but presumably linked to SE *cuddle*]

can opener *n.*[1] [1910s–30s] (US Und.) any tool used for the breaking open of a safe, when explosives would lead to discovery. [CAN n.[1] (3)]

can opener *n.*[2] [1910s–40s] (US) a cook.

canov *see* CAN OF OIL.

can racket *n.* [late 19C] (US) a party devoted to drinking beer. [SE *can* + RACKET]

cans *n.* [1950s–60s] (US) the female breasts. [? cans of milk or just resemblance]

cant *n.*[1] [16C+] the language of the world of professional thieves and itinerant criminal beggars; the term echoes the whining tones in which they 'chant' for alms (cf. CANTING CREW). [Lat. *cantare*, to sing. The term originates in conventional 12C society as a pej. description of church services that were condemned as substituting rote mouthings for real devotion. It was this use that led to the application of the term to, and adoption by, criminal beggars. SE *cant*, while obviously linked, is generally seen as relating to a pair of 17C Presbyterian ministers, Andrew Cant and his son Alexander]

cant *n.*[2] [late 18C–mid-19C] (tramp) food. [SE *cant*, to toss or throw; thus that which one 'cants' down one's throat]

cant *n.*[3] [mid-19C] **1** a blow. **2** a gift. [SE *cant*, a throw: (1) which knocks someone down. (2) the gift is 'thrown' to the recipient]

cant v. [mid-16C–19C] (Und.) **1** to speak, to talk. **2** to beg for alms. [CANT n.[1]]

cantankerous adj. [late 18C+] irritable, ill-tempered, quick to become angry. [SE in 20C. ? f. ME contak, quarrelling, argument. Grose derives it f. Wilts dial. and spells it contankerous]

can't beat time on a big drum/with a drumstick/to a slow band phr. [1950s] (Aus.) a phr. used of a weakling or coward.

can't be bad phr. [1960s+] a general phr. of approval.

can't do it for toffee phr. [1910s+] said of a particularly incompetent person; 'it' varies as to context.

canteen n. [early 19C+] (S.Afr.) a public house, a tavern; thus canteen-keeper, a publican. [? orig. milit. use]

canter n. [mid-16C–19C] a professional thief or criminal mendicant (cf. CANTING CREW).

canterbury n. [late 17C] a pace between a trot and gallop. [abbr. SE Canterbury trot; the pace, which is the root of SE canter, is supposedly that adopted by the Canterbury pilgrims as they rode on their way to the cathedral]

Canterbury story/tale n. [mid-16C–late 18C] a long, elaborate and ultimately tedious story. [the tales told by pilgrims on the way to Canterbury, and esp. f. the title of Chaucer's Canterbury Tales (c.1387)]

can't find one's arse/ass with both/two hands phr. [20C] very drunk (cf. ASS ON BACKWARDS). [ARSE n.[1]]

can't go no further, just like a bear's brother phr. [20C] (US Black) miserable, out of sorts, dejected (cf. JUST LIKE A BEAR).

can't hit a lick phr. [1920s–30s] (US Black) used of an inability to succeed in a given aim, esp. that of making money either legally or otherwise. [SE hit + LICK; musical imagery]

canticle n. [late 18C–early 19C] a parish clerk. [SE canticle, a hymn used during church services. The clerk traditionally led the congregation in singing]

cantilever bust n. [1950s+] (Aus.) notably large female breasts, apparently (thanks to a foundation garment) defying the laws of gravity.

canting n. [mid-16C–early 18C] thieves' jargon (cf. CANTING CREW). [CANT n.[1]]

canting crew n. [mid-16C–19C] the world of professional thieves and criminal mendicants. [CANT v. + CREW. The 'official' canting crew, as delineated by Grose, encompassed 23 orders. Men (in descending order of status): RUFFLER; UPRIGHT MAN; HOOKER n.[1] or ANGLER; ROGUE n.[1]; WILD ROGUE; PRIGGER OF PRANCERS; PALLIARD; FRATER; JARKMAN or PATRICO; FRESHWATER MARINER or WHIP-JACK; DOMMERER; DRUNKEN TINKER; SWADDER; ABRAM. Women: DEMANDER FOR GLIMMER; BAWDY-BASKET; MORT; AUTEM-MORT; WALKING MORT; DOXY; DELL; KINCHIN MORT; KINCHIN CO]

can't-keep-still n. [mid–late 19C] a prison treadmill. [rhy. sl., accentuated by the endless movement of the machine]

can't mash ants phr. [1920s–50s] (W.I.) **1** weak or cowardly, devoid of spirit. **2** very gentle, kind (cf. WOULDN'T HURT A FLY).

cant of dobbin n. [early 19C] a roll of ribbon. [SE cant, a share, a portion + ? dial. dobbin, a form of weaving machine, or dobbie, worsted]

cant of togs n. [mid-19C] a gift of clothes. [CANT n.[3] (2) + TOGS]

canton n. [1950s+] (US/Hisp.Am) **1** one's house, one's home. **2** a prison cell. [Sp. cantón, a house]

can't say 'British constitution' phr. [late 19C] very drunk.

can't say 'naval intelligencer' phr. [20C] very drunk.

can't see a hole in a forty-foot ladder phr. [late 19C+] very drunk.

can't see it phr. [late 19C+] a phr. of rejection, usu. in response to a request, typically for a loan, that one does not wish to honour.

can't seem to phr. [late 19C+] a phr. meaning one finds oneself unable to (do something).

can't see someone's arse for dust phr. [late 19C+] a phr. used to describe a speedy departure. [ARSE n.[1] (1)]

can't/too drunk to see through a ladder phr. [mid-19C+] extremely drunk.

can't/don't shit a shitter phr. [1950s+] a phr. meaning one can't fool someone who deals in fooling others. [SHIT v.[3]]

can't show itself/oneself to phr. [late 19C] inferior to or not equal to.

can't speak threepenny bit phr. [late 19C] speechless, struck dumb. [? image of threepenny bit as an insignificant sum]

can't take a trick phr. [1940s+] (Aus.) consistently unlucky. [card-game imagery]

can't touch the sides phr. [1950s+] a coarse joke referring to a large, and thus loose, vagina or anus, used by both hetero- and homosexuals.

can't wait for phr. [1930s+] extremely eager, very anxious for (something to happen).

can't walk and chew gum at the same time phr. [1960s+] (US) exceptionally stupid.

can't win 'em all phr. [20C] a phr. expressing commiseration over a disaster or disappointment, sometimes, but not necessarily, involving actual competition.

canty adj. [1920s+] (Aus.) unpleasant, ill-tempered. [SE cantankerous]

can't you feel the shrimps? phr. [late 19C+] can't you smell the sea?; allied phrs. are can't you see the breeze?, can't you taste the sun?

canuck/canucker/cannock n. [19C] (US) a derog. term for a Canadian, esp. a French Canadian. [Can. Fr. canaque, f. Hawaiian kanaka, a man or simply Can(ada) + (chin)ook. The term supposedly orig. in the Maine lumber camps]

canvas n. [early 19C] the human skin.

canvasback n. [19C] (US) a peasant, a rustic who comes to town for work (cf. GREENHORN). [SE canvasback duck, a migratory duck + image of one who carries his possessions in a sack on his back]

canvas-climber n. [late 16C] a sailor. [SE canvas, the sails]

canvas muster see TARPAULIN MUSTER.

canyon n. [1970s+] the vagina (cf. ARBOUR; DIVE IN THE CANYON; GRIN IN THE CANYON; YODEL IN THE CANYON).

can you beat it/that? phr. [20C] (orig. US) a phr. used to express surprise or amazement.

can you imagine? phr. [1940s+] would you believe?

can you see green in my eyes? phr. [19C+] do you think I'm lying?

can you tie that? excl. [1910s+] (US) an excl. of surprise or amazement; would you believe it? [lit. 'can you equal that']

cap n.[1] see BONNET n.[2].

cap n.[2] [mid-19C+] (orig. mainly US) captain. [abbr.; Ware cites some UK use but cap'n is more common]

cap n.[3] [1920s+] (US) a bullet, a shot (cf. POP A CAP).

cap n.[4] (drugs) **1** [1940s+] a capsule containing a narcotic, usu. heroin. **2** [1960s+] a capsule of LSD (cf. A n.[3]). **3** [1980s+] crack cocaine. [abbr.]

cap n.[5] **1** [1960s] (US Black) the mind. **2** [1990s] (rap music) the top of the head, the cranium. [they 'cap' the body]

cap n.[6] [1960s–70s] (US Black) **1** the mouth. **2** oral-genital sex; thus in phr. give (someone) some cap, to fellate, to perform cunnilingus. [(2) strained parallel to HEAD n.[8]]

cap v.[1] [late 16C–early 17C] to be arrested (for debt). [abbr. SE capture]

cap v.[2] [late 17C–early 19C] to swear an oath. [Lat. capias, you may take, a term used in a variety of legal writs, e.g. capias ad respondendum, to enforce attendance at court, and capias ad *satisfaciendum*, after judgement, to imprison the defendant until the plaintiff's claim is satisfied]

cap *v.*[3] [early 19C+] to act as a confederate in a gambling game. [CAPPER n.[1] (1); 20C use mainly US]

cap *v.*[4] [late 19C+] (US Black) to insult someone by disparaging their family (cf. BACKCAP v.; CAP v.[5]; DOZENS).

cap/cap on *v.*[5] **1** [1940s–60s] (US Black) to surpass, to outdo. **2** [1940s+] (orig. US Black) to attack someone verbally, to discredit someone, to have the last word (cf. CAPPING). **3** [1960s] (US) to entice a victim into a swindle. [early 19C dial. *cap*, to surpass, to outdo; but note CAP n.[3]]

cap *v.*[6] [1960s] (drugs) to transfer bulk drugs (in powder form) into capsules for sale (cf. CAP UP).

cap *v.*[7] [1970s] to shoot a person in the knee or leg as a form of punishment. [abbr. SE *kneecap*]

cap *v.*[8] [1980s+] (US Black) **1** to fire a gun (cf. BUST A CAP). **2** to kill, to murder, to shoot dead. [CAP n.[3]]

cap *v.*[9] [1990s] (US campus) to punch someone in the face. [CAP n.[5]]

cap acquaintance *n.* [late 18C–early 19C] a slight or passing acquaintance. [a person one knows well enough to raise one's cap when one passes on the street, but not to speak to properly]

cape *n.* [1980s+] (US) a condom (cf. ONE-PIECE OVERCOAT). [SE *cape*, a form of cloak]

Cape Ann turkey *n.* [late 19C] (US) salt cod (cf. ABERDEEN CUTLET; CAPE COD TURKEY). [SE *Cape Ann*, a cape in northern Massachusetts]

Cape Cod turkey *n.* (US) **1** [mid-19C–1960s] salt cod (cf. ABERDEEN CUTLET; CAPE ANN TURKEY). **2** [mid-19C–1960s] a codfish dinner. **3** [20C] corned (salt) beef and cabbage (cf. IRISH TURKEY). [SE *Cape Cod* in Massachusetts]

capeesh! *excl.* [1970s+] (US) do you understand? [Ital. *capito*, I understand]

cape flyaway *n.* [20C] (US) a cloudbank on the horizon that gives the impression of being land. [SE *cape*, a promontory + *fly away*]

cape horn *n.* [19C] the vagina (cf. ANTIPODES). [pun on HORN]

cape kelly *n.* [1940s] (Aus.) the stomach (cf. NED KELLY n.[2]). [rhy. sl. *cape kelly* = belly]

capella *n.* [19C] an overcoat. [Lat. *cappella*, little cloak or cape, ult. f. *cappella* or cloak of St Martin, preserved by the Frankish kings as a sacred relic, carried into battle, and used to give sanctity to oaths. The name was then applied to the sanctuary in which the relic was preserved under the care of its *cappellani* (chaplains), and thence to any sanctuary containing holy relics and thus to any place used for worship, other than a church, the earlier name for which was *oratorium*, the oratory]

cape nightingale *n.* [late 19C+] (S.Afr.) a frog (cf. CAMBRIDGESHIRE NIGHTINGALE).

cape of good hope *n.*[1] [19C] the vagina (cf. ANTIPODES). [the pleasure it offers plus its position near the 'bottom' of the globe]

cape of good hope *n.*[2] [1900s–10s] soap (cf. LAND OF HOPE). [rhy. sl.]

caper *n.*[1] **1** [mid-19C+] a dodge, a trick. **3** [late 19C+] (mainly US) an occupation, a job. **2** [mid-19C] the proper course of action; esp. ext. as *the proper caper*, the right thing to do. **4** [1960s+] a large-scale crime, usu. involving a great deal of elaborate planning and aimed at very large sums of money, expensive pieces of jewellery etc. The supposed lack of violence in such enterprises lent them a somewhat jokey air. [SE *caper*, a frisky movement]

caper *n.*[2] [mid-19C] a chorister. [the SE *cape* that is part of their uniform]

caper *v.* [late 18C–mid-19C] to be hanged (cf. CUT A CAPER UPON

NOTHING; DANCE v.[2]). [SE *caper*, to dance or leap in a frolicsome manner]

caperdewsie *n.* [early–mid-17C] **1** stocks. **2** prison. [for ety. see CAPPADOCHIO]

caper juice *n.* [19C] whisky. [a sufficiency or an excess causes one to 'cut capers']

caper merchant *n.* [late 18C–mid-19C] a dancing master (cf. HOP MERCHANT). [SE *caper* + MERCHANT]

cape smoke *n.* [early 19C+] whisky or rough, strong brandy distilled in South Africa (cf. PICK-AXE). [Swahili *moshi*, banana liquor, lit. smoke, steam, soot, lamp-black]

capey/capie *n.* [1940s+] (S.Afr.) a Cape Coloured, a member of the Coloured population group of the Cape Province, especially of the Western Province of the Cape; thus *capeytaal*, 'capey language', the argot spoken by some Coloureds, a patois of Afrikaans, English and Xhosa.

capital H *n.* [1970s] (drugs) heroin. [initial letter]

capital K *n.* [1940s+] (W.I.) knock-knees (cf. K-FOOT). [the approximate shape]

capitation drugget *n.* [late 17C–18C] cheap, second-rate fabric. [SE *drugget*, a coarse woollen material used mainly for floor-coverings or tablecloths + SE *capitation*, a tax that was levied on the fabric]

cap'n *n.* [mid-19C+] captain (cf. CAP n.[2]). [abbr.]

cap'n oates *n.* [1990s] sexual intercourse. [OATS + pun on the Antarctic explorer, Captain Lawrence *Oates* (1880–1912), famed for his last words]

cap'n toke *n.* [1980s+] (US campus) a marijuana smoker. [TOKE + honorary rank of Captain, a hippie term used *inter alia* for Jerry Garcia (1942–95) of the Grateful Dead, known as 'Captain Trips']

cap on see CAP v.[5].

capon *n.*[1] [18C] **1** a red herring. **2** a bloater (cf. ABERDEEN CUTLET). [the cheap herring as a substitute for the more expensive SE *capon*]

capon *n.*[2] [late 18C] a eunuch. [SE *capon*, a castrated cock]

capon *n.*[3] [1930s–40s] a young gay man, sometimes but not invariably a prostitute (cf. CHICKEN). [SE *capon*, a castrated cock; the reference is to CHICKEN rather than to any sexual malfunction]

cap one's lucky, to *phr.* [20C] (Aus.) to run off, to leave at speed. [SE *cap*, to protect + *lucky*; i.e. to take advantage of one's opportunity to run away]

capot me! *excl.* [mid-18C] a general excl. (cf. SWIPE ME!). [piquet jargon, *capot*, to score a capot against, to win all the tricks from. In this context 'to score off']

cappadochio *n.* [early 17C] **1** the stocks. **2** prison. [? the country of Cappadocia, the ruler of which, according to Horace (65–8BC), was rich in slaves but lacked cash. That ety. dismissed as 'far-fetched' by the *OED*]

capped *adj.* [1970s+] (US) shot dead. [CAP n.[3]]

capper *n.*[1] **1** [18C+] a confederate in a gambling game who poses as another gambler but actually works to swindle the genuine participants (cf. DICE CAPPER; SHILL). **2** [1950s+] (US) an employee of a casino, brothel, strip-club etc, who points a potential client towards the variety of self-indulgence they seek (cf. STEERER). [(1) such a confederate is always able to CAP v.[5] or surpass everyone else's bet. (2) is ext. use of (1)]

capper *n.*[2] [20C] an anecdote that steals the limelight from a previous anecdote, a punchline. [CAP v.[5]]

capperclaw see CLAPPERCLAW.

cappie *n.* [mid-19C] whisky. [orig. 'a kind of beer between table-beer and ale, formerly drunk by the middling classes' (Jamieson quoted in *OED*), ult. Scot. *cappie*, a small drinking-vessel]

capping *n.* [1940s–50s] (US Black) the ritual exchange of verbal insults (cf. DOZENS). [CAP v.[5]]

capricornified adj. [late 18C] cuckolded. [proper name of the astrological constellation of *Capricorn*, the He-Goat; thus one who has been made to 'wear the horns']

capron hardy n. [mid-15C–early 17C] an impudent fellow. [Fr. *capron hardi*, lit. 'bold hood']

caps n. (drugs) **1** [1960s+] heroin. **2** [1960s+] psilocybin/psilocin. **3** [1980s+] crack cocaine. [CAP n.⁴]

cap-sick adj. [early 17C] drunk. [SE *cap*, i.e. the head or brain + *sick*]

capsize v. [late 18C] **1** to overturn. **2** to fall over when drunk.

captain n.¹ [17C–mid-19C] a general term of address, e.g. Shakespeare *Timon of Athens* (1602): 'Why how now Captaine? what do you in this wise Company?'

captain n.² [18C–early 19C] money; thus *the captain is not at home*, I have no money. [a reference to money's importance]

captain n.³ **1** [late 18C] a successful highwayman. **2** [late 18C] a pimp (cf. LED CAPTAIN). **3** [early 19C–1900s] the leader of a gang of tramps. **4** [20C] (S.Afr.) the third most important member of a prison gang (cf. GENERAL).

captain n.⁴ [1960s+] (Aus.) someone who has money to spend, and uses it on the assembled company (cf. CAPTAIN CASH).

Captain Armstrong n. [18C] a corrupt jockey (cf. CAPTAIN BLUFF; CAPTAIN CHEAT; CAPTAIN SHARP; CAPTAIN STANDISH). [CAPTAIN n.¹ + SE *armstrong*, he uses his 'strong arms' to rein in his horse]

captain bloods n. [20C] (Aus.) spuds, potatoes. [rhy. sl.]

Captain Bluff n. [18C] a bully, a braggart (cf. CAPTAIN BOUNCE; CAPTAIN GRAND; CAPTAIN HACKUM). [CAPTAIN n.¹ + SE *bluff*, big, surly, blustering]

Captain Bounce n. [18C] a bully, a braggart (cf. CAPTAIN BLUFF). [CAPTAIN n.¹ + SE *bounce*]

Captain Cash n. [1950s+] (Aus.) that member of a group who, recently or temporarily well-off, is expected to buy drinks for the rest. [CAPTAIN n.¹ +SE *cash*]

Captain Cheat n. [early 17C–19C] a card-sharp, a cheat (cf. CAPTAIN ARMSTRONG; CAPTAIN SHARP).

Captain Cheddar n. [1980s+] (US campus) an unattractive, 'cheesy' male. [CAPTAIN n.¹ + SE *cheddar(cheese)*]

Captain Cook n.¹ [late 19C] (N.Z.) a pig, esp. one which is run-down or ill-kempt. [proper name of *Captain* James *Cook* (1728–79), the explorer who introduced pigs to New Zealand]

Captain Cook n.² [1930s+] (Aus.) **1** a look. **2** a book. [rhy. sl.; ult. navigator and explorer *Captain* James *Cook* (1728–79)]

Captain Cook adj. [1950s] (Aus.) ill, sick. [rhy. sl. *Captain Cook* = CROOK; ult. *Captain* James *Cook* (1728–79)]

Captain Copperthorne's crew n. [late 18C] (orig. naut.) a group or team without a stated hierarchy, where everyone concerned wishes to lead. [? the inadequacies of some long-vanished officer]

Captain Crank n. [18C–early 19C] the leader of a band of highwaymen. [CAPTAIN n.¹ + ? pun SE *crank*, that which is crooked]

Captain Grand n. [18C–19C] a haughty, blustering man (cf. CAPTAIN BLUFF). [CAPTAIN n.¹ + SE *grand*]

Captain Grimes n. [1980s] *The Times* newspaper (cf. CURRANT BUN). [rhy. sl. + ? ref. to Evelyn Waugh's Captain Grimes, the raffish schoolmaster of *Decline and Fall* (1928)]

Captain Hackum n. [late 17C–early 19C] a bully, a braggart (cf. CAPTAIN BLUFF). [CAPTAIN n.¹ + SE *hack them*]

Captain Hicks n. [1930s–40s] in craps dice, the point of 6 made with a pair of threes. [rhy. sl.]

Captain Huff n. [late 17C–18C] a braggart, a bully, a thug (cf. CAPTAIN HACKUM). [CAPTAIN n.¹ + HUFF v.¹]

captain is at home/come phr. [late 18C–mid-19C] a euph. phr. used to indicate that a woman is menstruating (cf.

CARDINAL IS COME). [play on Gk. *catamenia*, monthly + elision of SE *captain*+ *home/come*]

captain kettle v. [late 19C–1940s] to settle (after some energetic dispute). [rhy. sl. The character *Captain Kettle*, created by Cutliffe Hyne, appeared in stories published 1893–1938]

captain lieutenant n. [late 18C] the flesh of an old calf. [thus meat that is neither quite veal nor yet proper beef. In milit. jargon a *captain lieutenant* has the rank of the former but remains on the pay of the latter]

Captain Podd n. [late 18C] a puppeteer. [the proper name of *Captain Podd*, a celebrated puppeteer of the period]

Captain Queer-nabs n. [late 17C–early 19C] a shabby, ill-dressed person. [CAPTAIN n.¹ + QUEER NAB]

Captain Quiz n. [18C] a mocker. [CAPTAIN n.¹ + SE *quiz*, to mock, to make fun of]

Captain Save-a-ho n. [1990s] (US Black teen) a man who lavishes attentions and gifts on a woman; his aim is seduction, but despite his expensive efforts he is rarely successful. [CAPTAIN n.¹ + SE *save a* + HO]

Captain Sharp n. [early 17C–19C] **1** a card-sharp, a cheat. **2** a hired thug used to police corrupt gambling games. [CAPTAIN n.¹ + SHARP n.¹]

Captain Standish n. [18C] the penis. [he 'stands erect']

Captain Tom n. [late 17C–early 19C] **1** the leader of a mob. **2** the mob itself. [CAPTAIN n.¹ + TOM]

capture n. [1940s+] (Und.) an arrest and conviction for a crime.

capture the bishop, to phr. [1990s] to masturbate. [var. on BANG THE BISHOP]

capture the pickled biscuit, to phr. [late 19C–1940s] (Aus.) to beat all rivals, esp. with the implication that the person, announcement, event etc is even more startling or appalling than might have been expected (cf. TAKE THE BISCUIT).

capun n. [20C] (US prison) one who has been sentenced to death. [abbr. *capital punishment*]

cap up v. [1960s] (drugs) to transfer bulk drugs (in powder form) into capsules for sale. [ext. of CAP n.⁶]

capurtle n. [1950s+] a woman seen as a sex object. [? *capital*, excellent, first-class]

caput adj. [1910s+] finished, over, ruined etc. [Ger. *kaputt*, done for; also milit. use as 'stolen' during WW1]

car n. [20C] (US drugs) in a prison, a group of friends who associate to share their marijuana supplies (cf. DRIVE THE CAR). [the image of the prisoners driving/sitting in the same car]

caramel sundae n. [1990s] (US Black teen) an attractive, sexy, medium- to light-complexioned Afro-American woman (cf. BUTTER PECAN).

caravan n. **1** [late 17C] a coach travelling from the provinces to London. **2** [late 17C–late 18C] a large sum of money, esp. when seen by thieves as potential booty. **3** [late 17C–late 18C] the victim of financial fraud. **4** [mid-19C] a railway 'special' taking London boxing fans to a fight held outside the capital. [SE *caravan*, a procession of merchants, travelling together for mutual safety, usu. as found in the Middle or Far East]

caravan v.¹ [1910s–1920s] to have a picnic. [the SE *caravan* or procession of vehicles that convey the picnickers]

caravan v.² [1980s+] (US teen) to drive (stolen) cars in groups and to perform a variety of elaborate manoeuvres on the street. [for ety. *see* CARAVAN n.]

caravansera n. [mid-19C] a railway station (cf. CARAVAN n.). [*caravanserai*, a form of Oriental coaching inn where the merchant caravans could find food and shelter; ult. Per. *karwan*, caravan + *sara*, palace]

carb n. [1930s+] (orig. US) a *carb*urettor. [abbr.]

carbie n. [1920s+] (Aus.) a *carb*urettor. [abbr.]

carbine v. [late 19C] (US West.) to cheat, to victimize. [SE *carbine*, a short musket, presumably used by the villain]

carbo *n.* [1970s+] (orig. US) *carbo*hydrates, or a meal or food that contains a high percentage of carbohydrate. [abbr.]

carbolic naked *adj.* [1950s+] completely naked. [var. on STARK BOLLOCK NAKED + ref. to SE *carbolic (soap)*]

carbo-load *v.* [1990s] (US campus) to drink beer. [SE *carbo-load*, to ingest carbohydrates (of which beer contains many)]

carbonado *v.* [late 16C–early 19C] to cut, to slash, to hack. [Sp. *carbonado*, to score meat before grilling or broiling it]

carbon copy *n.* [1980s+] (US Black) **1** an imitator, someone who seems to emulate their hero or heroine (cf. WANNABE). **2** someone who resembles their parents.

carbuncle face *n.* [late 17C–late 18C] a face covered in boils and pimples. [SE *carbuncle*, an inflamed abscess + *face*]

carburettor *n.* **1** [1920s] the heart. **2** [1980s+] (drugs) a water pipe, used for smoking cannabis or crack cocaine. [fig. uses of SE]

carby *n.* [1950s+] (Aus.) a *carb*urettor. [abbr.]

card *n.*[1] [early 18C–late 19C] a device, an expedient; thus *one's best card*, the best plan, the ideal way of acting. [SURE CARD]

card, the *n.*[2] [mid-19C] the correct thing (cf. TICKET *n.*[1]). [abbr. SE *invitation card / card of admission*]

card *n.*[3] **1** [mid-19C+] a character, a noticeable person, a likeable eccentric. **2** [late 19C–1930s] an attraction, a 'drawing card'. **3** [20C] a joker, a clown. **4** [1920s] an amusing thing or circumstance. [? one who stands out from the 'pack']

card *v.*[1] [20C] (W.I./UK Black teen) to jeer jokingly or mock someone about some event, their appearance or situation. [Scots *card*, to scold, to tell off]

card *v.*[2] [1950s+] (W.I. Rasta) to fool someone. [CARD *n.*[1]]

card *v.*[3] [1970s+] (US campus) to request proof of age (in a bar) by producing an identification card.

cardboard box *n.* [1970s+] venereal disease (cf. BAND IN THE BOX). [rhy. sl. = POX *n.*[1]]

cardboard city *n.* [1980s+] the cardboard box 'homes' that are used as shelter by the homeless. [the original *Cardboard City* was situated on the London's South Bank, but increasing homelessness has meant that the term now applies to any such gathering]

card-carrying *adj.* [1960s+] (US) genuine, dependable, the 'real thing'. [the application of the phr. to Communists, who carried their Party card]

card-cony-/coney-catching *n.* [mid-16C–late 18C] trickery, cheating (cf. CONEY-CATCHER).

cardinal *n.*[1] [mid-19C] a lady's cloak. [resemblance to a cardinal's cloak]

cardinal *n.*[2] [mid-19C+] mulled red wine. [it is red, as are a cardinal's outer vestments]

cardinal is come *phr.* [late 18C–mid-19C] a euph. phr. used to indicate that a woman is menstruating (cf. CAPTAIN IS AT HOME). [the red of the cardinal's hat and that of menstrual blood]

cardinals *n.* [late 19C–1910s] a shoeblack. [ety. unknown; ? the use of a red cloth]

card mechanic *n.* [1900s] (US) **1** a professional card or dice cheat. **2** any notably successful player (cf. MECHANIC). [play on SE]

career boy *n.* [20C] a male homosexual prostitute (cf. ASS PEDDLER). [play on SE *career girl*]

care factor zero *phr.* [1990s] (US teen) a phr. indicating indifference; 'I really couldn't care less'. [the use of SE *factor* as a measure of sunblock strength]

careful *adj.* [late 19C+] miserly. [joc. understatement]

careless talk *n.* [1940s] a stick of chalk, usu. as used by darts players for scoring. [rhy. sl.; the ref. is to the WW2 posters with the legend 'Careless talk costs lives']

care package *n.* [1960s+] (US campus/teen) a package of 'supplies' sent to a student or solo teenager by a parent.

[SE *care package*, a package of goods distributed by the Co-operative for American Relief Everywhere to the poor citizens of foreign countries]

carga *n.* [1960s+] (US prison/Hisp.Am.) heroin (cf. ? CHARGE). [Sp.]

cargo *n.*[1] [early 17C] a person. [ety. unknown. Despite the apparent logic of relating CARGO *n.*[1] to CARGO *n.*[2], i.e. a person as a fig. burden or load, this use precedes the adoption of the Sp. word into SE, and there is no evidence of Sp. *cargo* being used in this way]

cargo *n.*[2] **1** [late 17C–18C] a large sum of money. **2** [1980s+] (W.I./UK Black teen) a heavy gold chain and medallion sported as an outward (sometimes pretentious) show of wealth. [SE *cargo*, freight carried on a ship; ult. Sp. *cargo*, loading, *carga*, freight]

cargo! *excl.* [20C] a general excl. [? euph. for CHRIST!]

carhop *n.* [1930s+] (US) **1** a waiter or waitress who serves customers in their parked cars. **2** a street prostitute who has sex in clients' cars. [i.e. one who *hops* between cars]

carhop *v.* [1930s+] (US) **1** to work as a waiter or waitress, serving customers in their parked cars. **2** to work as a street prostitute, having sex with clients who drive up in their cars. [CARHOP *n.*]

Caribee Islands *n.* [late 18C] certain areas of London that were considered safe havens for criminals and debtors (cf. ALSATIA). [SE *Caribbean Islands*, symbolizing far distance from any authority]

car-jockey *n.* [1950s+] (US) a carpark or garage attendant. [SE *car* + JOCKEY *n.*[2] (2)]

cark *n.* [1970s] (US) the penis. [COCK *n.*[2] (1)]

cark/kark *v.* [1970s] (Aus.) to die; often as *cark it*. [dial. *cark* or *kark*, to caw like a crow; thus the association is with a carrion bird]

carked *adj.* [1970s] (Aus.) ruined, destroyed, exhausted. [dial. *cark*, care, sorrow, anxiety]

carl comedian *n.* [1960s+] (US campus) a dismissive term for a raconteur whose jokes and stories fail to make the desired impact. [ironic use of SE *comedian* + assonant 'proper' name]

carleycue/carlique/curlicue *n.* [late 19C–1910s] (Irish) anything small or of little value. [ext. of SE *curlicue*]

carlo *adj.* [1900s–30s] eccentric, mad. [rhy. sl. *Carlo Gatti* = BATTY *adj.*; ult. the firm of *Carlo* Gatti, suppliers of ice to London restaurants pre-refrigeration]

carlotta *n.* [1950s–70s] (camp gay) a heterosexual who interferes in the gay world, either as a homophobe or as a 'tourist' (cf. MR CHARLIE). [the effeminization used by the camp gay world]

carl rosa *n.* [1960s+] a poser, anyone pretending to be something that they are not; thus the *old carl rosa*, a fraud. [rhy. sl. The ref. is to the popular *Carl Rosa* Operatic Society, founded in London in 1875]

carmes/carnes *n.* [mid-19C–1900s] flattery. [Rom.]

carmine *n.* [early–mid-19C] blood (cf. CLARET; RUBY). [SE *carmine*, red or crimson pigment obtained from cochineal]

carn *n.* [20C] money. [? COIN]

carnal/carnales *n.* [20C] (US Spanish) someone from one's own social group, a friend from the same neighbourhood (cf. HOMEBOY; HOMEGIRL; HOMEY *n.*[2]). [Sp. *carnal*, flesh]

carnal-trap *n.* [16C] the vagina. [coined by Sir Thomas Urquhart (1611–60) for his translation of Rabelais]

carnapper *n.* [1950s+] (orig. US) one who steals a car for joyriding (rather than for resale), and then dumps it or returns it to the place from where it was taken (cf. TWOCKER). [play on SE *kidnapper*]

carne *n.* [1980s+] (drugs) heroin. [Sp. *carne*, meat; the image is of the drug's strength]

carnes *see* CARMES.

carney *n.*[1] [early 19C–1920s] **1** soft, hypocritical talk. **2** a smooth talker; thus *come the old carney*, to flatter, *carneying*, smooth talking, flattery. [Yorkshire dial. *carney*, cajolery, flattery. Despite the poss. link to CARNEY *n.*[2], this use precedes it by a century; ult. ety. unknown]

carney/carny *n.*[2] [1930s+] (US) a carnival worker.

carney *n.*[3] [20C] (Aus.) a lizard. [Wemba *gaani*, any of the lizards used in the Aboriginal diet, e.g. the Jew lizard, lace lizard etc]

carney/carny *adj.* [late 19C–1950s] sly, artful.

carney/carny *v.* [early 19C+] to wheedle, to flatter. [CARNEY *n.*[1]; there is, alas, no link to later US CARNEY *n.*[2], for all that the carney is likely to employ wheedling tones to encourage patrons to spend their money]

carnie *n.*[1] (Aus.) a *carn*ation (cf. DAFF *n.*[2]; GLAD *n.*; GLADDIE; GLADS). [abbr.]

carnie/carny *n.*[2] (N.Z.) **1** [1960s+] an under-age girl seen as a sex object. **2** [1980s+] a young person living on the streets. [SE *carnal knowledge*]

carnish *n.* [mid-19C] (Und.) meat; thus (northern Und.) *carnish-ken*, a thieves' eating-house, *cove of the carnish-ken*, the owner of such a place. [Ital. *carne*, meat. Imported via Ling. Fr.]

carny *n.*[1] *see* CARNEY *n.*[2].

carny *n.*[2] *see* CARNIE *n.*[2].

carny *adj. see* CARNEY *adj.*

carny *v. see* CARNEY *v.*

carob *v.* [18C+] (tramp) to cut. [Shelta]

Carolina racehorse *n.* [mid-19C] (US) a razorback hog. [joc. ref. to the prevalence of the animal in North and South Carolina]

caroline *n.* [late 19C] (Irish) a style of tall hat. [? anecdotal]

carol singer *n.* [1930s+] (Aus./Brisbane) a police car with a loud-speaker.

caroon *n.* [mid–late 19C] a crown or 5 shillings (25p) (cf. MADZA CAROON). [Ital. *corona*, a crown]

carp *n.* [1900s–30s] (US) a whinger, a complainer. [SE *carp*, to find fault with, reprehend, take exception to]

carpark *n.* [1960s+] an informer. [rhy. sl. *carpark* = NARK]

carpenter's dream *n.* [1970s+] an available woman. ['flat as a board and easy to screw']

carpet *n.*[1] [late 19C+] the ground, the grass.

carpet *n.*[2] [late 19C+] (prison) a three-month sentence. [rhy. sl. *carpet-bag* = DRAG *n.*[3], or f. the earlier assumption that prison workshops took just 90 days to produce a particular type of regulation size carpet. But note No. 77 *Mark of Broad Arrow* (1903): 'Your "Auto-leyne" cares little about a "drag" (three months), a sixer (a "carpet" it is generally called), or a "stretch"']

carpet *n.*[3] [1920s+] (Aus.) £1. [ety. unknown; ? misprint of CARPET *n.*[4]]

carpet *n.*[4] [1940s–50s] (Aus.) £3. [CARPET *n.*[2]; thus giving various jargon terms, e.g. bookmakers' odds of 3 to 1, car dealers' £300]

carpet, the *n.*[5] [1960s] (US Black) a confidence trick practised by a street criminal.

carpet *n.*[6] [1980s+] (US campus) the female pubic hair.

carpet *v.* [mid-19C+] to reprimand, esp. in the context of a superior telling off an employee; thus *carpeting*, a telling-off. [the miscreant is standing on his or her superior's office carpet while receiving a reprimand]

carpet-bag *n.* [1930s] (prison) a three-month sentence. [ext. of CARPET *n.*[2]]

carpetbag *v.* [20C] **1** (US campus) to attempt to make a good impression, usu. on one's teachers, by pretending to have an all-consuming interest in a given subject. **2** to deceive. [SE *carpetbagger*, a derog. description applied, after the

American Civil War (1861–5), to immigrants from the northern into the southern states, whose 'property qualification' consisted merely of the contents of the carpet-bag they had brought with them. Hence, applied to all northerners who went south and tried, by a variety of deceitful tricks, to obtain political influence, esp. by claiming an interest in local areas of which, in fact, they had no real knowledge]

carpet-biter *n.* [1940s+] someone who becomes so enraged that they start chewing the carpet. [? the myth that Adolf Hitler was prone to such hysterical rages]

carpet-cleaning *n.* [1990s] cunnilingus (cf. CARPET-MUNCHER *n.*[2]). [CARPET *n.*[6]]

carpet dance *n.* [late 19C–1900s] (society) a dance for close friends, held in one's drawing room. [unlike a larger dance, held in a ballroom with a properly sprung floor, the boards are kept covered]

carpet knight *n.* **1** [late 16C–late 18C] a man whose 'knightly exploits' concentrate on the boudoir rather than the battle-field. **2** [early–mid-19C] a man who frequents drawing rooms rather than places of work. [orig. a soldier who was dubbed knight at court (thus kneeling on a carpet) rather than in the chaos of a battlefield]

carpet-man/-monger *n.* [late 16C] a man whose activities are concentrated on the boudoir (cf. CARPET KNIGHT).

carpet-muncher *n.*[1] [1940s+] someone who becomes so enraged that they start chewing the carpet (cf. CARPET-BITER).

carpet-muncher/rug-muncher *n.*[2] [1980s+] (US campus) **1** a lesbian. **2** a person who performs cunnilingus. [CARPET *n.*[6] + MUNCH *v.*[1]]

carpet-munching *n.* [1980s+] cunnilingus. [CARPET *n.*[6] + MUNCH *v.*[1]]

carpet patrol *n.* [1980s+] (drugs) smokers of crack cocaine who search the floor for any grains of the drug they may have dropped.

carpet rat *n.* [1970s+] (US) a small child (cf. RUG RAT).

carpet road *n.* [late 17C–early 18C] a smooth, well-maintained road.

carpet-swab *n.* [mid-19C] a carpet-bag.

carpet trade *n.* [late 16C] sexual dalliance. [i.e. 'the occupations and amusements of the chamber or boudoir' (*OED*); such rooms would be carpeted]

carpy *adj.* [1940s–1950s] (prison) locked away in one's cell at night. [Lat. *carpe diem*, 'make the most of the day']

carra/carrer *n.* [1920s+] (Aus.) a *car*avan. [abbr.]

carriage trade *n.* [20C] the upper classes, usu. used ironically. [a hangover f. earlier divisions of transport. Note mid-19C SE *carriage company*, those who own their own carriage(s); thus the wealthy or upper classes]

carrie/carrie nation *n.* [1980s+] (drugs) cocaine (cf. CHARLIE). [proper name *Carrie Nation* (1847–1911), the US temperance campaigner]

carried *adj.* [late 19C+] married (cf. CASH AND CARRY). [rhy. sl.]

carried story *n.* [20C] (Ulster) a piece of gossip, a rumour. [it is *carried* from person to person]

carrier *n.* [17C–late 18C] that member of a criminal gang who either carries information between gang members or carries away the proceeds of a robbery, of pickpocketing etc (cf. DEUSEAVILLE STAMPERS).

carrier-pigeon *n.* [18C–mid-19C] one who specializes in swindling lottery office-keepers.

car-ringing *n.* [1950s+] the practice of altering a car for the purposes of using it as a getaway vehicle, hold-up van etc or for reselling it to an unsuspecting customer. [SE *car* + RING *v.*[1]]

carrion *n.* [late 18C] **1** the human body. **2** a prostitute. [SE *carrion*, used derog. to denote the body and thus a human being]

carrion-case *n.* [19C] a shirt (cf. FLESHBAG). [the shirt's enclosing of the CARRION (1)]

carrion-crow man *n.* [20C] (W.I./Guyn.) a man who canvasses business for an undertaker following a death. [SE *carrion-crow*, a species of crow that feeds on dead flesh]

carrion-hunter *n.* [late 18C–mid-19C] **1** a promiscuous woman. **2** an undertaker. [both supposedly search for bodies, whether warm or cold]

carrion-row *n.* [18C] a place where one buys second-rate meat. [SE *carrion* + *row*, a street + pun on SE *carrion-crow*]

carriwitchet *n.* [mid-19C] a hoaxing, puzzling question. [ety. unknown; ?link to SE *witch*]

carrot *n.*[1] **1** [mid-18C–19C] a large bundle of tobacco. **2** [1980s+] (drugs) a very large cannabis cigarette packed to the brim and generally the size of an average garden carrot. [note the *Camberwell carrot*, an extra-large cannabis cigarette, coined in the film *Withnail & I* (1987)]

carrot *n.*[2] [19C] the penis. [its shape, also f. the consumption of carrots by rabbits or coneys (cf. CUNNY; CUNNY WARREN)]

carrot cruncher *n.* [1960s+] a visitor to London from the provinces and the countryside (cf. SWEDE). [the equation of root vegetables and country-dwellers]

carrothead/-top *n.* [mid-19C–1930s] (US) a red-head person (cf. CARROT-PATED; CARROTS; CAROTTY).

carrot-pated *adj.* [late 17C–early 18C] having red hair (cf. CARROTHEAD).

carrots *n.* [late 17C+] a red-headed person (cf. CARROTHEAD). [the colour of the vegetable. Ware declares that 'it has not in origin anything to do with "carrots"', preferring an association with Judas *Iscariot*, traditionally seen as a red-head]

carrotty *adj.* [mid-18C–mid-19C] having red hair (cf. CARROTHEAD).

carrucha *n.* [1960s+] (US) a broken-down old car. [Sp.]

carry *n.* [1970s] (drugs) the amount of drugs one is carrying at any given moment (cf. HOLDING).

carry *v.* (US) **1** [1930s+] to carry money. **2** [1940s+] to carry drugs. **3** [1950s+] to carry arms. [ext. uses of SE]

carry a bone, to *phr.* [20C] (US) to gossip, to spread rumours. [proverb: a dog that will bring you a bone will carry one away]

carry a broom at the masthead, to *phr.* [19C] to work as a prostitute. [the naval tradition of hoisting a broom to signify that a ship has been sold]

carry a case, to *phr.* [20C] (US Und.) to be out on bail. [pun on SE *case*, bag/*case*, impending trial]

carry/have a chip on one's shoulder, to *phr.* [late 19C+] (orig. US) to bear a grudge against the world at large; thus *a chip on one's shoulder*, a grudge or display of defiance or ill-humour, a sense of inferiority characterized by a quickness to take offence. [the traditional 19C US way of offering a challenge to fight was to place a chip of wood on one's shoulder - most US homes had a pile of wood for fuel – and challenge someone to knock it off; thus to go around with such a chip meant one challenged the whole world]

carry/have an M under the girdle, to *phr.* [mid-16C–early 19C] to be polite and courteous in one's speech. [M *n.*[1]; i.e. one speaks like a gentleman/lady]

carry a torch, to *phr.* [1940s+] (orig. US) to mourn a dead love affair, to feel love without its being returned. [the 'light of love' is still burning, albeit unreciprocated]

carry a turkey on one's back, to *phr.* [19C] to be drunk. [DRIVE TURKEYS TO MARKET]

carry ballast *v.* [20C] to hold one's liquor (cf. HAVE BALLAST ON BOARD).

carry both ends of the log, to *phr.* [1920s+] (Aus.) to take all the work on oneself (despite there being others equally qualified in attendance).

carry/take coals to Newcastle, to *phr.* [17C–early 19C] to perform a superfluous and futile task. [the indigenous Newcastle coalfield; the phr. began life as sl., becoming SE during 19C]

carry-come-and-bring-come *n.* [1940s+] (W.I.) a gossip (cf. CARRY-GO-BRING-COME).

carry corn *v.* [mid-19C] to behave well when successful; i.e. to be a modest winner, to restrain oneself despite gaining power on money. [Yorks. dial.]

carry dog *v.* [mid-19C+] to put on airs. [var. on PUT ON DOG]

carry-go-bring-come/bring-and-carry/bring-go-bring-come *n.* [1940s+] (W.I.) **1** a gossip, a tattle-tale. **2** gossip. [the sequence of events]

carry/pack guts to a barrel/bear, to *phr.* [19C] to perform an extremely distasteful or absolutely basic task, usu. implying inadequacy or stupidity; thus *he's not fit to ...* , *he hasn't enough/the brains to ...* .

carry heavy rakes, to *phr.* [17C] to act in an arrogant manner, to 'put on side'. [SE *rake*, a load, something carried from A to B]

carrying *adj.* [1960s+] in possession of illicit drugs (cf. HOLDING). [CARRY *v.* (2)]

carrying a load *phr.* [20C] drunk (cf. AFLOAT).

carrying-/carryings-on *n.* [mid-19C+] any form of conspicuous behaviour, e.g. making a fuss, flirting ostentatiously. [SE *carry on*, to do, to act]

carry in one's heart, to *phr.* [1940s–50s] (S.Afr.) to bear a grudge in the hope of getting eventual revenge.

carry-knave *n.* [17C–18C] a cheap prostitute.

carry matilda *v.* [late 19C+] (Aus.) to go on the tramp, carrying one's pack (cf. WALTZ MATILDA). [SE *carry* + MATILDA]

carry me out!/carry me out and bury me decently! *excl.* [late 18C+] a general excl. of disbelief and displeasure. [play on Lat. *nunc dimittis*, 'Now let thy servant depart ...', the first words of the Song of Simeon in Luke 2:29]

carry milk-pails, to *phr.* [mid-19C] of a man, to walk with a woman on each arm. [the image of a milkmaid with her yoke and two pails]

carry no coals, to *phr.* [late 17C–18C] to show oneself proof against swindling or insults. [reverse of SE phr. *carry coals*, to do dirty or degrading work, thus to accept insults]

carry-on *n.* [late 19C+] a commotion, an exciting event, a disturbance, fuss, excitement; usu. as phr. *what a carry-on! a right/real carry-on.* (cf. CARRYING-ON).

carry on *v.* **1** [early 19C+] to make a fuss. **2** [mid-19C] (orig. US) to flirt. **3** [1930s+] to have an adulterous relationship, usu. as *carry on with*.

carry one's arse/ass, to *phr.* [20C] (W.I./Bdos./Trin.) to leave, to run off (cf. HAUL ASS). [SE *carry* + ARSE *n.*[1] (1)]

carry one's bat, to *phr.* [late 19C+] to outlast one's rivals. [cricketing imagery; a player who 'carries his bat' remains undefeated until all his partners have been dismissed and the innings is over]

carry one's tail, to *phr.* [20C] (W.I.) to leave, to run off (cf. HAUL ASS). [SE *carry* + TAIL *n.*[1]]

carry on proper, to *phr.* [late 19C+] to behave properly.

carry-over *n.* [1940s] a hangover that lingers on. [SE *carry-over*, something remaining or transferred from one period to the next]

carry the ball, to *phr.* [1930s+] (orig. US) to take responsibility. [US football imagery, but the same meaning could come from rugby]

carry/pack the banner, to *phr.* [late 19C–1900s] (US) **1** to walk the streets as a tramp. **2** to sleep rough, esp. of the thousands of homeless children who are forced to sleep in the New York streets. [? the carrying of banners at left-wing protest marches, many of which focused on the plight of the poor or homeless]

carry the cag, to *phr.* [early 19C] to be easily irritated, to lack a sense of humour, esp. as regards jokes against oneself (cf. CARRY THE KEG). [SE *carry* + CAG]

carry the can for/back, to *phr.* [1920s+] (orig. naut.) to take the blame that should be another's, to do the 'dirty work', esp. in *phr. left carrying the can* (cf. HOLD THE CAN).

carry the keg, to *phr.* [early 19C] to be easily annoyed, to be unable to take a joke (cf. WALKING DISTILLER). [pun on SE *keg*/CAG]

carry the mail, to *phr.*[1] [20C] (Aus.) to stand a round of drinks. [the 'delivery' of the drinks]

carry the mail, to *phr.*[2] [1950s–70s] (US) to take responsibility for a difficult task. [the reputation of the US postal service for overcoming any object in order to deliver the mail]

carry the stockwhip, to *phr.* [1930s+] (Aus./Northern Terr.) of a wife, to dominate one's husband.

carry the war into Africa, to *phr.* [early 19C–1930s] (US) to act aggressively, to go over to the attack. [? some lost political promise]

carry weight, to *phr.* [1950s–60s] to be depressed. [one is bowed beneath one's cares]

carry your hip! *excl.* (W.I.) get out! go away! [euph. *hip*, the buttocks, the backside]

carsey/carsy/causey/cawsey *n.* [late 19C+] **1** a house. **2** a brothel. **3** a thieves' den. **4** a privy (cf. KARSY). **5** any messy or otherwise unappealing place that resembles a lavatory. **6** a public house. [Ital. *casa*, a house]

cart *n.*[1] [mid–late 19C] the carapace of a crab. [resemblance; orig. Norfolk dial.]

cart *n.*[2] [late 19C–1900s] the gallows. [the *cart* that takes the prisoner from prison to the gallows, esp. from Newgate to Tyburn]

cart *v.* [mid-19C+] to carry, to drag; thus *cart away, cart out* etc.

cart-grease *n.* **1** [mid-19C] orig. rancid butter and then any butter (cf. COW GREASE). **2** [20C] margarine.

cart-loads *n.* [late 16C–late 18C] many, a great quantity, esp. of a desirable commodity (cf. LOADS).

cartocracy *n.* [late 19C–1900s] (society) those rich enough to afford a dog-cart (cf. CARRIAGE TRADE). [SE *cart* + (*aris*)*tocracy*]

cartoon *n.* [1920s+] a fool, an absurd person. [metonymy]

cart out with *v.* [late 19C+] to court, to 'go out with'.

car trick *n.* [1960s+] **1** an act of prostitution carried out in an automobile. **2** the client who participates in such an act. [SE *car* + TRICK n.]

car trick *v.* [1960s+] to perform paid sex in an automobile. [CAR TRICK n.]

carts *n.*[1] [mid-19C] a pair of shoes (cf. CRAB-SHELLS). [? echoic of the sound of a labourer's heavy, boot-clad step, or CART n.[1]]

carts *n.*[2] [1980s+] (Polari) the male genitals.

cartucho *n.* [1980s+] (drugs) a package of marijuana cigarettes. [? Sp. *cartucho*, a small box]

cartwheel *n.*[1] [19C] a broad hint. [a cartwheel is too large to be ignored]

cartwheel *n.*[2] **1** [mid–late 19C] a crown or 5 shilling (25p) piece (cf. HIND COACH-WHEEL; WHEEL). **2** [late 19C+] (Can./US) a silver dollar. **3** [1960s–70s] (drugs) a drug in pill form, usu. amphetamine or Benzedrine. [the shape]

cartwheel *n.*[3] [1900s–40s] (Aus.) a round damper marked with a cross. [the resemblance to spokes on a wheel]

cartwheel *n.*[4] [1930s] (US drugs) a fake heroin withdrawal spasm.

carty *adj.* [mid–late 19C] of a horse, like a carthorse, whether in build or breed.

cartzo *see* CATSO.

carve *v.* (US) **1** [late 19C–1940s] to destroy, to annihilate completely, esp. in a financial or business context (cf. CARVE UP). **2** [late 19C+] to attack (and cut) with a bladed weapon (cf. CARVE UP). **3** [1940s] to thrill, to excite.

carve a slice, to *phr.* [20C] **1** to have sexual intercourse (cf. BIT OF KEG; CUT A SLICE; TAKE A SLICE OFF THE JOINT). **2** to take a portion of the profits.

carved out of wood *phr.* [1950s] stupid (cf. BLOCKHEAD n.[1]).

carver *n.* [1900s] (US) a knife when used as a weapon. [CARVE v. (2) + SE *carver*, a carving knife]

carver and gilder *n.* [early 19C] a match-maker. [ironic use of SE; the elite professions are reduced to sl. in the lowly context of match-making]

carve-up *n.* [1930s+] **1** any situation in which one feels oneself unfairly deprived of a desired aim or object. **2** (Und.) a share-out of loot, profits etc (cf. CARVE A SLICE). **3** a legacy, i.e. one's share of a will. [fig. uses of SE]

carve up *v.* **1** [late 19C+] (orig. US) to destroy, to annihilate completely, esp. in a financial or business context. **2** [20C] to swindle, to cheat. **3** [1920s+] to attack (and cut) with a razor, a knife or other bladed weapon. **4** [1930s+] (Und.) to share out booty, profits etc. **5** [1970s+] of a driver, to force another out of the way through aggressive (and potentially dangerous) driving. [fig. uses of SE]

carve up scores, to *phr.* [1930s] (US) to reminisce with an old friend (cf. CHEW UP OLD TOUCHES; CHOP IT UP; CUT UP v.[5]; CUT UP TOUCHES). [SE *carve up*/CARVE UP v. (4) + SCORE n.[2] (2)]

carvie *n.* [1940s–50s] (prison) one who helps share or divide up a ration of tobacco; a prisoner may take on a regular 'carvie' for periods of their sentence. [CARVE UP v. (4)]

carving knife *n.* [20C] wife. [rhy. sl.]

cas/caj/cazh/kasj *adj.* [1970s+] a term of general approval for anything favoured, e.g. a close friend, an item of clothing, a rock band. [pron. 'cazz'; abbr. SE *casual*. Note 19C use *casual*, not to be depended on, uncertain, 'happy-go-lucky'; thus another e.g. of the bad = good pattern]

ca-sa/ca.sa. *n.* [late 18C–late 19C] a writ of *capias ad satisfaciendum*, after judgement, to imprison the defendant until the plaintiff's claim is satisfied (cf. CAP v.[1]). [abbr.]

casa *n.* [late 18C–1900s] a house, a brothel (cf. CASE n.[2]). [Ital./Sp. *casa*, a house]

casaba *n.* (US) **1** [1950s+] the head. **2** [1970s+] in pl., the female breasts (cf. APPLES n.[1]). [SE *casaba*, a large fruit]

casanova's rubber sock *n.* [1990s] a condom. [the great lover, Giovanni Giacomo *Casanova* (1725–98)]

cascade *n.* [late 19C] (Aus.) beer. [orig. Tasmanian use. f. the *Cascade Brewing Company* of Hobart; ult. f. the *cascade* of water that was used for brewing]

cascade *v.* [17C–mid-19C] euph. for to vomit. [from the visual imagery]

case/kaze *n.*[1] [17C] the vagina. [SE *case*, a container (for the penis)]

case *n.*[2] [late 18C–1900s] **1** a house. **2** a shop, a warehouse. **3** a brothel, esp. those sited in the Haymarket, London, in mid–late 19C. **4** a lavatory. [Ital. *casa*, house]

case *n.*[3] **1** [19C] (US) $1. **2** [mid-19C] a counterfeit crown (5s, 25p); thus *half-a-case*, a counterfeit half-crown (2s 6d (12½p). [? Fr. *caisse*, cash or CASER n.[1]]

case *n.*[4] [19C] a ne'er-do-well, a dubious character. [abbr. SE *dubious case, hard case*]

case *n.*[5] (orig. US) **1** [mid-19C+] an infatuation, a love affair. **2** [mid-19C+] an adulterous affair. **3** [1970s] a pair of lovers (cf. GO CASE). [SE *case*, a circumstance, a happening, an event; thus essentially a euph.]

case *n.*[6] [mid-19C+] (orig. US) an eccentric person, esp. as *rum case, you are a case*. [? a suitable *case* for the police courts]

case *n.*[7] [20C] (US Und.) the charge or crime for which one is tried and possibly convicted. [ext. of SE *case*, the actual judicial proceedings]

case *n.*[8] [1920s+] (US) a situation, usu. in phr. e.g. *have a bad case of the brokes*, to be poor; *get off my case*, leave me alone.

case *adj.* [1900s–50s] (US) usu. of money, the last available. [? it has been kept in a case or similar receptacle]

case *v.*[1] (orig. US) **1** [1910s+] to look over, to appraise, esp. before a robbery (cf. CASE THE JOINT). **2** [20C] (prison) to discipline, to put on report. [orig. faro jargon *case*, to watch carefully]

case *v.*[2] [1920s–30s] (Und.) to delay, to put off, to postpone. [? to put aside in a fig. *case*]

case *v.*[3] [1970s] (US Black) **1** to joke about. **2** to tell off, to scold. [ext. of CASE v.[1] (2)]

cased *adj.*[1] [1940s–50s] (Und.) charged with an offence. [CASE n.[7]]

cased *adj.*[2] [1950s+] (S.Afr.) infatuated with, having a relationship with. [CASE n.[5] (1)]

case dough/dollar *n.* [1900s–50s] (US prison/gambling) limited money, one's last available funds. [CASE adj. + DOUGH/ dollar]

cased-up *adj.*[1] [1930s] living together. [CASE n.[5] (1)]

cased-up *adj.*[2] [1930s] visiting a brothel. [CASE n.[2] (3)]

case-fro/-vrow *n.* [late 17C–18C] a prostitute, esp. one who works in a brothel. [CASE n.[2] (3) + Ger. *Frau*/Du. *vrow*, a woman]

case house *n.* [1910s–20s] a brothel (cf. ACCOMMODATION HOUSE). [CASE n.[2] (3) + HOUSE n.[1] (1)]

case it around *v.* [1980s] (US teen) **1** to check a place or situation. **2** to move on to a new activity. [CASE v.[1] (1)]

case-keeper *n.* [19C] a brothel-owner. [CASE n.[2] (3)]

caseo *n.* [1930s+] **1** a brothel. **2** the hiring of a prostitute for a whole night (cf. GO CASE). [CASE n.[2] (3)]

case of crabs *n.* [late 19C] a failure. [? rowing jargon *catch a crab*]

case of pickles *n.* [19C–1910s] a serious problem. [IN A PICKLE]

case o' pistles *n.* [20C] (Ulster) the buttocks. [lit. a *case of pistols*; ? ref. to SE *pizzle*, a bull's penis]

case of stump *n.* [late 19C] poverty, pennilessness. [STUMPED]

case of the reds *phr.* [1990s] (US teen) to be irritated at the world. [RED ARSE]

case out *v.* [1950s–60s] (US) to join forces for any undertaking. [ext. of CASE v.[1] (1)]

case out! *excl.* [1950s–60s] (US) go away! [CASE OUT v.]

case over *v.* [1910s+] to assess. to judge the quality. to look at. [CASE v.[1] (1)]

caser *n.*[1] [mid-19C–1950s] **1** (orig. Aus.) 5 shillings. **2** (US) $1. **3.**(Aus.) a 5-year prison sentence. [Yid. *kesef*, silver; thus the silver 5-shilling piece, and the dollar, then worth 5 shillings (25p)]

caser *n.*[2] [1940s+] (prison) a prison officer notorious for excessive discipline. [CASE v.[3] (2)]

caser *n.*[3] [1950s+] a brothel. [CASE n.[2] (3)]

caser *n.*[4] [1950s+] one who inspects a property before burglary. (cf. CASE THE JOINT). [CASE v.[1] (1)]

case-ranging *n.* [1920s] the inspection of a property with the intention of robbing it (cf. CASE THE JOINT). [CASE v.[1] (1) + SE *range*, to look over, to survey]

cases *n.* [early-mid-19C] shoes. [abbr. TROTTER-CASES]

case the joint/gaff/job, to *phr.* [1910s+] to survey a house, shop etc. with a view to subsequently robbing it. [CASE v.[1] (1) + JOINT n.[3] (2)/GAFF n.[1] (4)/JOB n.[3]]

case-vrow *see* CASE-FRO.

casey/cassey *n.*[1] [19C+] cheese. [CASSAN]

casey/cassey *n.*[2] [late 19C+] a house (cf. CARSEY). [Ital. *casa*]

casey/k.c. brown *n.* [late 19C–1940s] (US Black) a mythical figure endowed with the ability to fight for Black rights and against racism. [an artificial proper name *Casey* or *K.C. Brown*]

casey jones *n.*[1] (US) **1** [1920s+] a train-driver, a locomotive engineer. **2** [1940s+] a railway train. [the legendary John Luther Jones (1864–1900)]

casey jones *n.*[2] [1960s+] a lavatory. [play on MRS JONES HOUSE + CARSEY]

cash *n.* [late 17C–early 19C] cheese. [CASSAN]

cash *v.* [1900s] (US) to quit, to give up one's efforts. [abbr. CASH IN ONE'S CHIPS]

cash and carry, to *phr.* [late 19C+] to marry; thus *cash and carried*, married (cf. CUT AND CARRIED). [rhy. sl.]

cash-ass *n.* [1960s+] (gay) a male prostitute who pretends innocence until promised cash. [SE *cash* + sfx. -ASS; a pun on SE *cautious*]

cash carrier *n.* [mid-late 19C] a pimp.

cashed *adj.* [1980s+] **1** (US campus) physically, mentally or economically exhausted. **2** (drugs) used of a marijuana bowl or pipe that contains nothing but ash. [? CASH IN ONE'S CHIPS]

cashed up *adj.* [1930s+] (Aus./N.Z.) wealthy, well-off, albeit temporarily (cf. CHEQUED UP).

cashie *adj.* [1980s+] (US campus) acceptable, satisfactory. [var. on CAS]

cash-in *n.* [1920s] (US) the end, i.e. death. [CASH IN v. (2)]

cash in *v.* **1** [late 19C+] (orig. US) to settle up one's accounts or debts, esp. in card-playing. **2** [late 19C+] to die (cf. CASH IN ONE'S CHIPS). **3** [late 19C+] to give up. **4** [1920s+] to make a profit, often as *cash in on*.

cash in one's checks, to *phr.* [late 19C+] (orig. US) to die (cf. CALL OFF ALL BETS; CASH IN ONE'S CHIPS; CRAP OUT; GET ONE'S CHECKS; HAND IN ONE'S CHECKS; HAND IN ONE'S CHIPS; HAVE ONE'S CHIPS; HAVE ONE'S NUMBER COME UP; PASS IN ONE'S CHECKS; PASS IN ONE'S CHIPS; PUT ONE'S CHECKS IN THE RACK; SEND IN ONE'S CHECKS; THROW A SEVEN phr.[1]; THROW IN ONE'S CARDS; THROW IN ONE'S HAND). [CASH IN v. (1) + SE *checks*, gambling chips]

cash/throw in one's chips, to *phr.* (orig. US) **1** [late 19C] to change one's way of life. **2** [late 19C+] to die (cf. CASH IN v.; CASH IN ONE'S CHECKS). **3** [1960s+] to commit suicide. **4** [1980s+] to kill. [gambling jargon; the action one takes on leaving a game, assuming one still has some chips in hand]

cash in the food stamps of love, to *phr.* [1970s] (US Black) to accept a less than ideal sexual partner through one's needs or frustration.

cashmere *n.* [1940s–50s] (US Black) a sweater, irrespective of the material.

cashola *n.* [1970s] (US) cash. [SE *cash* + sfx. -OLA; on the pattern of PAYOLA]

cash one's last check, to *phr.* [20C] euph. for to die (cf. SIGN ONE'S LAST CHECK).

cash one's pistol, to *phr.* [late 19C] (US, West.) to rob a bank at gunpoint. [joc. image of presenting a pistol at the counter rather than a cheque]

cash out *v.* [1960s+] **1** to die. **2** to kill oneself. **3** to murder, to kill.

cashunk! *see* KERCHUNK!

cash up *v.* **1** [early 19C+] to pay up, to pay over; thus to pay one's debts. **2** [1950s+] (Aus.) to earn money.

casian *n.* [1990s] (Black) a policeman. [? pron. of SE *catch* + *man*]

casing *n.* [1920s+] (orig. US) the assessment of a place or person to calculate how vulnerable it is or they are to robbery. [CASE v.[1] (1)]

cask *n.* [mid-19C] 'fashionable Slang for a brougham, or other private carriage' (Hotten 1860). [SE *cask*, 'a wooden vessel of cylindrical form' (*OED*)]

casket nail/tack n. [1960s] (US) a cigarette. [var. on COFFIN NAIL n.[2]]

casmash! see KERSMASH!

caspar milquetoast/casper milktoast/milquetoast/Mr Milquetoast n. [1930s+] a cowardly, weak person. [the central character in the cartoon 'The Timid Soul' created by H.T. Webster, first pub. in New York World, May 1924]

casper n. [1950s] (US Black) a particularly light-skinned Black person. [1950s cartoon character Casper the Friendly Ghost, who is white]

casper milktoast see CASPAR MILQUETOAST.

casper the ghost n. [1980s+] (drugs) crack cocaine. [for ety. see CASPER]

casplash! excl. [mid-19C] onomat. term indicating a fall into liquid (cf. KERSPLASH!).

cass see CASSAN.

cassa n. [1940s+] (Aus.) a ladies' man. [abbr. proper name Giovanni Casanova (1725–98), the eponym for a sexually successful man]

cassan/cass/cassam/cassom/casson/casun/caz n. [16C–mid-19C] cheese. [Rom. cas, cheese; cf. SE casein, the milk ingredient that is basis of cheese]

cassava n. [1980s+] (UK Black) a woman. [SE cassava, a fleshy tuber, the basis of tapioca]

cass-cass adj. [20C] (W.I.) untidy, disreputable, inferior, low-class. [Twi kasakasa, very thin, akasakasa, a dispute]

cassey see CASEY n.[1].

cassom/casson see CASSAN.

casspir n. [1980s+] (S.Afr.) an armoured vehicle used by the South African police and army, usu. in the context of keeping order in the townships. [anagram of CSIR, Council for Scientific & Industrial Research + SAP, South African Police]

cast adj. [1930s+] (Irish/N.Z.) drunk. [? pun on SE cast down]

cast a net, to phr. [20C] (Aus.) to have a bet. [rhy. sl.]

cast an optic, to phr. [late 19C+] to look at. [SE cast + OPTICS]

castell v. [late 16C–early 17C] to look, to see. [? SE castle, from the battlements of which one can get a long-range view]

caster n.[1] [16C–late 18C] (Und.) a cloak. [ety. unknown, but F&H suggest a link to CASTOR n.]

caster n.[2] [mid-19C+] anything or anyone that has been rejected or cast aside. [SE cast off. Note milit. jargon caster, a horse considered no longer fit for the cavalry or horse artillery and sold at public auction]

caster n.[3] [late 19C] (US) a testicle. [? SE castor, a small, round wheel used to make furniture mobile]

castieau's hotel n. [mid-19C] (Aus.) a prison (cf. AKERMAN'S HOTEL). [the name of its one-time governor]

casting n. [mid-19C] (US) a coin; thus castings, cash. [SE cast, to form molten metal into a shape with a mould]

cast in someone's dish see LAY IN SOMEONE'S DISH.

cast-iron and double-bolted adj. [late 19C+] extremely strong. [fig. use of engineering terminology]

cast-iron horrors n. [20C] (Anglo-Irish) delirium tremens (cf. STONEWALL HORRORS). [SE cast-iron, 'hard-and-fast', unyielding + HORRORS]

castle n. [1930s–40s] (US Black) one's house, one's home. [the cliché, an Englishman's home is his castle]

castle v. [16C] to see or look (cf. TOUR). [? f. the idea of standing on a high castle battlement and surveying the surrounding area]

castle Catholics n. [early 19C–1920s] Irish Catholics who rejected nationalism, preferring to curry favour with and ape the lifestyle of the ruling British. [Dublin Castle, the seat of British rule]

castle hack n. [1900s–10s] (Irish) an informer. [Dublin Castle (see CASTLE CATHOLICS) + HACK n.[1]]

castle rag n. [19C] (Und.) fourpence. [rhy. sl. castle rag = FLAG]

cast nasturtiums v. [20C] a joking mispron. of SE cast aspersions (cf. ASPARAGUS).

cast one's cap, to phr. [late 16C–17C] to be indifferent, to abandon as lost. [proverb, cast one's cap at the wind]

cast one's skin, to phr. [late 19C] 1 (society) to rejuvenate oneself. 2 to strip oneself naked. [animal imagery]

castor n. [late 17C–19C] a hat. [14C castor, a beaver. Such hats were made of beaver fur or, if as was increasingly the case, of rabbit, disguised to look as if they were]

castor adj. [1940s+] (Aus.) excellent, admirable, first-rate; thus be on the castor with, to be popular with. [? SE castor sugar; thus parallel to SWEET adj.[3]. Simes prefers the old criminal sign of tugging one's hat or CASTOR n., to indicate 'all clear', used fig. in the non-criminal world]

castro n. [1970s+] (gay) a popular variety of post-gay liberation stereotype (cf. CLONE), the castro poses as a lumberjack type with checked flannel shirt, Levis, heavy boots etc. [Castro Street, San Francisco, the centre of the gay community]

cast/slip the calf, to phr. [mid-17C–mid-19C] of a woman, to suffer an abortion. [ext. of SE use about cows]

cast the house out of the windows, to phr. [16C–17C] to make a great deal of noise or disturbance in one's house.

cast the net, to phr. [1970s] (US) of a pimp, to employ an experienced prostitute to lure a new woman into joining his team.

cast up v. [20C] (Ulster) to bear a grudge, to remind someone of their failings. [abbr./play on SE cast up accounts, to make a reckoning]

cast up one's accounts/reckoning, to phr. [late 18C–19C] to vomit. [play on SE cast up accounts, to make a reckoning]

casual n.[1] 1 [early 19C+] a part-time labourer or other employee (cf. OCCASIONAL). 2 [mid-19C+] the casual ward in a hospital. 3 [mid-late 19C] a casual pauper. [SE casual, non-essential or, in the case of paupers, only temporarily needy]

casual n.[2] [1980s] 1 a working-class youth who dresses in the designer-labelled clothing of their society peers but whose accent and lifestyle remains resolutely proletarian. 2 a football hooligan who adopts such a style. [SE casual clothing]

casual adj. [1970s+] (US campus) 1 acceptable, satisfactory. 2 not worth becoming upset about. 3 clever, witty. [for ety. see CAS]

casualty n. [late 19C–1900s] a black eye.

casualty adj. [mid-late 19C] casual; thus casualty-boy, a boy who hires himself out to a costermonger or market greengrocer.

casun see CASSAN.

caswash! excl. [mid-19C] an onomat. term indicating a collision or crash, esp. of one object falling on top of another. [pfx. KER- + SE wash]

cat n.[1] 1 [16C–18C] a prostitute. 2 [18C+] a gossip. 3 [late 18C+] a woman, esp. a spiteful and malicious one; thus old cat, an unpleasant, gossiping old woman. 4 [late 19C] a drunken, violent prostitute. 5 [1920s–30s] (US) an itinerant worker (cf. GEYCAT n.). 6 [1920s–30s] (US prison) an informer. [a variety of supposedly feline qualities]

cat n.[2] [late 18C–early 19C] the cat-o'-nine-tails; thus get the cat, to be given a judicial whipping, and the right-wingers' litany of bring back the cat (cf. NINE-TAIL BRUISER; PUSSY n.[2]). [later use is SE]

cat n.[3] [early 19C] a quart pot. [a double-KITTEN]

cat n.[4] [mid-19C] 1 a ladies' muff; thus free a cat, to steal a muff. 2 the female pubic hair and genitals (cf. BADGER n.[7]). [(2) fig. use of (1)]

cat n.[5] [mid-late 19C] a person, as needed in a given situation, e.g. she's never going to be their kind of cat.

cat *n.*[6] [late 19C] a native of Cheshire. [phr., immortalized in Lewis Carroll's *Alice in Wonderland* (1866), to 'grin like a Cheshire cat']

cat *n.*[7] [20C] (US) illicitly distilled whisky (cf. MOONSHINE). [abbr. WILDCAT *n.*[2]]

cat *n.*[8] [1910s+] (orig. US) *Cat*erpillar tractor; thus a tractor of any make. [abbr.]

cat *n.*[9] (orig. US Black) **1** [1920s–40s] a jazz musician. **2** [1950s] a jazz fan. **3** [1950s+] a person, usu. male (like so many initially Black terms, adopted by beatniks and then hippies). [jazz use *c.*1950s poss. f. ALLIGATOR *n.*[4], early Black use for worldly, smart, sophisticated male, abbr. to gator, gate, *cat* (?)]

cat *n.*[10] [1950s+] the vagina; thus *cat-lapper*, one who performs cunnilingus (cf. CATSMENAT; CATTY-CAT; CHAT *n.*[2]; KITTY *n.*[2]; MALKIN; POOZLE; PUSS *n.*[1]; PUSSY *n.*[1]; ROUGH MALKIN). [var. on CHAT *n.*[2]]

cat *n.*[11] (Aus.) **1** [1950s+] a passive male homosexual. **2** [1970s+] (prison) a weakling; thus *cats' yard*, an area where gay or otherwise vulnerable prisoners can be segregated. **3** [1970s+] (sporting) a player who cannot take the rough-and-tumble of the game. [(1) ? f. SE *catamite*, a boy kept for homosexual purposes; but note PUSSY]

cat *n.*[12] [1960s] (US campus) the grade C (cf. HOOK *n.*[7]).

cat *n.*[13] [1980s] (US) a *cat*burglar. [abbr.]

cat *n.*[14] [1990s] (drugs) meth*cathinone (cf. BATHTUB SPEED). [abbr.]

cat *adj.* [20C] (Irish) terrible, shocking, unpleasant, rough. [Irish *cat marbh*, mischief, calamity or abbr. of SE *catastrophe*]

cat/cat up *v.*[1] [late 18C+] to vomit; thus fig. *cat with laughter*, to laugh 'until one is sick'. [20C use mainly US. ? f. abbr. SE *cataract* (cf. CASCADE) but cf. SHOOT THE CAT]

cat *v.*[2] [1940s+] of either sex, to be sexually unfaithful; thus (US Black) *cat out*, to wander the streets aimlessly, to stay out all night. [abbr. TOMCAT *v.*]

catacoined *adj.* [1990s] (US teen) suffering a swindle or theft. [? SE *catty-corner*, diagonally opposite]

catalogue queen *n.* [1960s+] (US gay) a gay man who uses physique and body-building magazines as masturbatory pornography. [SE *catalogue* + QUEEN]

catamaran *n.* [late 18C–19C] an old scraggy woman, a disagreeable harridan. [pun on CAT *n.*[1] + poss. pun on orig. SE *catamaran*, a fireship. But note poss. pun on CAT O'MOUNTAIN]

cat and dog life *phr.* [mid-16C+] an unhappy marriage, in which the partners fight like cat and dog (cf. PARROT AND MONKEY).

cat and kitten hunting/sneaking *n.* [mid-19C] (Und.) the stealing of pint and quart pots from public houses. [CAT *n.*[3] + KITTEN *n.*[1]]

cat and kitten rig *n.* [early 19C] (Und.) the stealing of pint and quart pots from public houses (cf. CAT AND KITTEN HUNTING). [CAT *n.*[3] + KITTEN *n.*[1] + RIG *n.*[2] (2)]

cat and kitten sneaking *see* CAT AND KITTEN HUNTING.

cat and mouse *n.* [mid-19C] a house. [rhy. sl.]

Cat-and-Mouse Act *n.* [1910s] the nickname for the Prisoners (Temporary Discharge for Ill-health) Act of 1913 to enable (suffragette) hunger-strikers to be released temporarily (and thus defuse public outrage at their treatment and their own desire for well-publicized martyrdom).

cataract *n.* [mid-19C] a large, many-layered black cravat, used to show off one's stick-pin and similar jewellery; such an item was especially favoured by 19C commercial travellers. [SE *cataract*, a waterfall; it 'flows' down the wearer's chest]

cat around *v.* [1940s+] (orig. US) **1** to wander purposelessly

about. **2** to search for a sexual partner (cf. ALLEY CAT). [TOM-CAT *v.*]

catarumpus *n.* [mid-19C] (US) a riot, a commotion, a rumpus. [? CATAWAMPUS *adj.*[2] (1)]

catawampus *n.*[1] [mid–late 19C] a biting, stinging insect. [CATAWUMPUS *adj.*[1]]

catawampus *n.*[2] [mid-19C–1930s] (US) a peculiar or remarkable thing or person.

catawampus / caliwampus / cankywampus / cattywampus *adj.*[1] (US) **1** [mid-19C] fierce, pitiless. **2** [1930s] ill-tempered, crotchety. [ety. unknown]

catawampus / caliwampus / cankywampus / cattywampus *adj.*[2] [19C] (US) **1** askew; thus *catawampously*, *catawamptiously* (cf. KITTYWAMPUS). **2** out of order. [ety. unknown. ? SE *cater-/catty-cornered*, diagonal]

catawampus *v.* (US) **1** [mid-19C–1900s] to confuse, to confound. **2** [mid-19C–1900s] to injure, to harm. **3** [1900s] to move in a diagonal line. [CATAWAMPUS *adj.*[2]]

catawampus! *excl.* [19C] (US) a general excl., often as *Great catawampus!* (cf. KITTYWAMPUS). [SE *catawampus*, a hobgoblin or imaginary demon; in turn ? f. 17C *catamount*, a panther]

cat bar *see* CAT'S BAR.

catbird *n.* [20C] (US) **1** a mischievous or cunning person. **2** a person of authority or power (cf. TOP DOG). [the SE *catbird* (*Dumatella carolinensis*) is so-called f. its habit of harassing cats; thus trans. to the human *catbird*'s dealings with fellow humans]

catbird *adj.* [mid-19C] (US) perfect, ideal. [CATBIRD *n.* (2)]

catbird seat *n.* [1940s+] a privileged or advantageous position. [SE *catbird* (*Dumatella carolinensis*) + *seat*. The catbird takes up a high, exposed position to deliver its song. The image is of a cat looking down on a targeted bird. Orig. a term used by a poker opponent of the sportscaster Red Barber (1908–92) and popularized first by him and latterly by a James Thurber story, 'The Catbird Seat']

catch *n.* **1** [mid-18C+] one who is seen as matrimonially desirable, often in phrs. *a good catch*, *no catch*. **2** [1960s] (US Black) a woman, esp. a woman recruited into prostitution; thus *catching*, seducing a woman into prostitution (cf. CATCH ACTION). **3** [1960s] (US Black) the number of clients a prostitute has serviced within a given time.

catch *v.*[1] **1** [late 19C+] to grasp the meaning, often in neg., e.g. *I didn't quite catch ...*. **2** [late 19C+] to find out, to discover. **3** [1920s–50s] to listen to, to watch. **4** [1960s+] to notice, to appreciate.

catch *v.*[2] [late 19C+] **1** to ensnare a victim in a confidence trick or crooked gambling game. **2** to seduce. **3** to come into possession of a given item.

catch *v.*[3] [late 19C+] to become pregnant (cf. GET CATCH).

catch *v.*[4] [1950s] (orig. US) to have a casual social encounter with (cf. CATCH YOU LATER).

catch *v.*[5] [1960s+] **1** to attend, esp. a show or other type of entertainment. **2** to obtain, to get (cf. CATCH SOME RAYS).

catch *v.*[6] [1960s+] to take the passive role in sexual intercourse (cf. PITCH *v.*[3]). [baseball imagery]

catch a buzz, to *phr.* [1970s+] **1** to start experiencing the (pleasurable) effects of alcohol or a given drug. **2** (lesbian) to masturbate with an electric vibrator. [CATCH *v.*[5] + BUZZ *n.*[4]; (2) puns on (1)]

catch a cold, to *phr.* [late 18C+] **1** to get into trouble, poss. through impetuousness. **2** to lose out financially, poss. after purchasing a supposed 'bargain', which proves to be otherwise (cf. CATCH COLD; COLD *adj.*[4]; HAVE A BAD COLD).

catch action *n.* [1960s] (US Black) young women, typically runaways who have just arrived in the big city and are vulnerable to being recruited as prostitutes. [CATCH n. (2) + ACTION]

catch a duck asleep *see* CATCH A WEASEL ASLEEP.

catch a face *see* THROW ON A FACE.

catch a fox, to *phr.* [late 17C–18C] to be very drunk. [FOX v.[1]]

catch a glad, to *phr.* [20C] (W.I.) to experience an outburst of spontaneous joy. [CATCH v.[5] (2)]

catch a horse, to *phr.* [20C] (Aus.) to urinate. [euph.]

catch air *v.* [1920s–70s] (US Black) to leave quickly, to rush off. [CATCH v.[5] (2)]

catch and kill one's own, to *phr.* [1970s] (Aus.) to look after oneself, to sort out one's own problems without outside aid. [the image of the self-sufficient dweller in the outback]

catch an oyster, to *phr.* [19C] of a woman, to have sexual intercourse. [play on SE *oyster*]

catchar *n.* (W.I.) **1** one who attempts to interfere maliciously in a couple's love affair. **2** one who talks out of turn, who does not 'mind their own business'. [Bhojpuri *khachchar*, lit. mule, and used as a term of abuse]

catch arse *v.* [20C] (W.I.) to find it hard to make enough money to live (cf. CATCH HELL; CATCH FRANCE; CATCH NENNEN). [SE *catch* + fig. use of ARSE n.[1] (1)]

catch a tartar, to *phr.* [18C] to encounter an apparent victim or weakling who turns out to be much stronger than suspected. [TARTAR n. (3)]

catch a vap/vapse, to *phr.* [20C] (W.I.) to be suddenly inspired to do something, to do something on the spur of the moment. [VAP (2)]

catch a weasel/duck asleep, to *phr.* [19C] (US) to catch a shrewd person off guard.

catch-bet *n.* [mid-19C] a bet made with the intention of ensnaring a gullible punter.

catch cold *v.* [mid–late 18C] to suffer punishment, to regret (cf. CATCH A COLD).

catch colt *n.* [20C] (US) an illegitimate child (cf. BRUSH COLT) [dial. *catch colt*, a colt that was bred unintentionally]

catch copper *v.* [16C] to come to harm, to suffer grief. [ety. unknown]

catch 'em-alive *n.* [mid-19C] **1** a trap. **2** a tooth-comb (cf. CATCH 'EM ALIVE-O; LOUSE TRAP n.[1]).

catch 'em alive-o/all alive-o *n.* **1** [mid-19C] the vagina; one of a number of terms equating it with a threat to the penis (cf. EEL POT; EEL-SKINNER; MANGLE n.[1]; MANHOLE n.[1]; MAN-TRAP n.[1]; NUMBER NIP; PRICK-HOLDER; RASP; RATTLE BOLLOCKS; ROB THE RUFFIAN; ROUGH AND READY; ROUGH-O; SKIN-THE-PIZZLE; SUCK AND SWALLOW). **2** [mid-19C] a fly-paper. **3** [mid-19C–1900s] a small comb (cf. CATCH 'EM-ALIVE).

catcher *n.*[1] [mid-19C] (US) a watchman, a policeman.

catcher *n.*[2] [1950s+] one who plays the passive role during sexual intercourse; this can relate to homosexual, sado-masochistic or 'straight' heterosexual intercourse (cf. PITCHER n.[5]). [baseball imagery]

catcher's mitt *n.* [1980s+] (US) a contraceptive diaphragm. [CATCHER n.[2] + baseball imagery]

catch-fart *n.* [late 18C] a footman. [var. on FART-CATCHER]

catch/get flack *v.* [1940s+] (US) to receive criticism, to face verbal attacks. [SE *catch*/*get* + FLAK]

catch fleas for someone, to *phr.* [19C–1910s] **1** to be extremely intimate with someone. **2** to have sexual intercourse with someone. [the image of monkeys removing each other's fleas]

catch France *v.* [20C] (W.I.) to find it hard to make enough money to live (cf. CATCH HELL; CATCH NENNEN; MEET HELL; SEE FRANCE; SEE HELL). [SE *catch* + FRANCE]

catch/get on the hop/h.o.p., to *phr.* [mid-19C+] to catch unawares. [SE *catch* + ON THE HOP]

catch/get the flavour, to *phr.* [19C] to get drunk.

catch/get hell *v.* **1** [mid-19C+] (orig. US) to get into trouble, to suffer a telling-off. **2** [20C] (W.I.) to find it hard to make enough money to live, to subsist, to suffer great hardship (cf. CATCH FRANCE).

catching flies *phr.* [late 19C+] standing with one's mouth gaping open as sign of incomprehension, surprise or stupidity.

catching harvest *n.* [late 17C–mid-19C] (Und.) a bad time for highway robbery since heavy traffic is likely to impede a safe getaway. [SE *catching harvest*, unpredictable, unsettled weather + a pun on SE *catch*, implying that the highwayman may get caught]

catching the bird *phr.* [1930s+] (Aus.) picking up a woman while driving one's car and then persuading her to agree to sex. [SE *catch* + BIRD n.[4]]

catch in hock/the hock, to *phr.* [mid–late 19C] (US) to catch in the act of cheating. [HOCK v.[1]]

catch it/catch it hot *v.* [mid-19C+] to be severely reprimanded, punished or beaten (cf. GET IT; GET IT HOT; GET IT IN THE NECK). [euph. for CATCH HELL]

catch me!/catch me at it! *excl.* [mid-19C–1930s] a defiant excl. implying that one will never be caught.

catch nennen/royal/skin/tail *v.* [20C] (W.I./Trin.) to find it hard to make enough money to live (cf. CATCH FRANCE). [SE *catch* + fig. uses of NENNEN/ROYAL n.[3]/SKIN n.[2]/TAIL n.[1]]

catch on/catch on to *v.* [late 19C+] (orig. US) **1** to attach or fix oneself to, to join on, to catch hold of. **2** to understand. **3** to become popular or fashionable.

catch one's balls/tit in a wringer, to *phr.* [1970s+] to find oneself in trouble, in an unpleasant situation. [the most famous use was during the Watergate Affair (1972) when US Attorney General John Mitchell suggested that if Katherine Graham, proprietor of the *Washington Post*, were to permit the printing of revelations on White House involvement, she would 'catch her big fat tit in a wringer']

catch one's death/death of cold, to *phr.* [early 18C+] to catch a (bad) cold.

catch oneself on *v.* [1980s+] (Irish) to come to one's senses. [CATCH ON v. (2)]

catch one's finger, to *phr.* [1930s–40s] (US) to be arrested.

catch one's length, to *phr.* [20C] (W.I.) to settle down, to understand what must be done. [lit. to estimate the size of the problem]

catch one's lunch, to *phr.* [1960s+] (US) to be defeated so comprehensively as to feel physically sick.

catch one's tit in a wringer *see* CATCH ONE'S BALLS IN A WRINGER.

catch on fire, to *phr.* [late 19C] to lose one's temper, to become excessively emotional.

catch on the fly, to *phr.* [1920s–30s] (US hobo) to board a moving (freight) train. [SE *catch* + ON THE FLY]

catch on the non-plus, to *phr.* [late 19C] to catch unawares.

catch on to *see* CATCH ON.

catch out *v.* [1970s+] (US tramp) to leave by train. [i.e. to *catch* a railroad *out* of town]

catchpenny *n.* [early 19C–1900s] **1** a pamphlet or broadsheet sold in the streets and detailing a lurid, if imaginary, murder. **2** a cheap theatre or music-hall (cf. PENNY GAFF). [SE *catchpenny* adj., designed for sales rather than quality]

catchpole *n.* [late 17C–late 18C] a sergeant or bailiff, esp. one who arrests for debt (cf. BUM n.[1]). [Lat. *cacepollus*, chicken catcher, dating from a period when debts were paid in kind as well as cash]

catchpole rapparee *n.* [early 18C] a constable. [CATCHPOLE + SE *rapparee*, a bandit, a robber]

catch rapid *v.* [1980s+] (Irish) to catch in the act.

catch royal *see* CATCH NENNEN.

catch shit, to *phr.* [1980s+] (orig. US) to be scolded or told off, to get into trouble (cf. CATCH FLACK). [SE *catch* + SHIT n.[4] (2)]

catch skin *see* CATCH NENNEN.

catch someone bending, to *phr.* [20C] to catch someone at a disadvantage.

catch someone napping, to *phr.* [19C+] to take someone by surprise, to catch someone off their guard. [20C use is SE]

catch some rays, to *phr.* [1980s] **1** to sunbathe. **2** (US teen) goodbye, a feasible alternative farewell in sun-drenched California. [CATCH v.[5] (2) + RAYS]

catch some Zs, to *phr.* [1960s+] (US) to have a nap (cf. BAG ZS). [CATCH v.[5] (2) + z n.[1]]

catch tail *see* CATCH NENNEN.

catch the chain, to *phr.* [20C] (US Und.) to move from a local jail to a proper prison (cf. RIDE; SHIP). [the chain that links the prisoners together during their journey]

catch the owl, to *phr.* [late 18C–early 19C] to play a trick on an innocent countryman, who is decoyed into a barn under the pretext of catching an owl; when he enters, a bucket of water is poured upon his head.

catch the stifles, to *phr.* [17C] to be hanged (cf. NAB THE STIFLES). [SE *catch* + *stifle*]

catch under the pinny, to *phr.* [1900s–30s] of a man, to have sexual intercourse with a woman, to seduce. [SE *catch* + abbr. *pinafore*]

catch up *v.* [1980s+] (drugs) to withdraw from drug addiction. [one 'catches up' with life. The image of addiction is one of suspended animation]

catch wise *v.* [1930s–70s] (US) to understand, to grasp. [CATCH (ON) + WISE (UP)]

catchy *adj.* **1** [early 19C] attractive, esp. when seen as 'cheaply' so. **2** [mid-19C] tending to take an undue advantage.

catch you later *phr.* [1970s+] (orig. US Black) goodbye. [CATCH v.[4]]

catch you on the flip flop *phr.* [1970s] (US campus) goodbye. [CATCH v.[4] + SE *flip-flop*, a reversal, lit. a somersault]

cat eat one's dinner/supper *phr.* [20C] (W.I.) in a hopeless situation (cf. CRAPAUD SMOKE YOUR PIPE). [the image is of having a regular pleasure taken away]

caterpillar *n.*[1] **1** [16C–17C] a ne'er-do-well, one who lives on their wits and others' gullibility. **2** [mid-18C–early 19C] a soldier. [SE *caterpillar*, a rapacious person]

caterpillar *n.*[2] [late 19C] a girls' school. [? the girls will emerge as adult 'butterflies']

caterpillar *n.*[3] [20C] (Aus.) a drunkard. [the drunkard crawls, caterpillar-like, from pub to pub or along the floor]

caterpillar *v.* [1900s] (US) to leave quietly. [SE *caterpillar*, the larva of a butterfly or moth, it moves slowly]

cater-trey *n.* [early 16C–early 18C] (Und.) dice or crooked dice. [*cater*, four + *trey*, three. ult. f. Fr. *quatre* + *trois*]

caterwaul *v.* [late 16C–late 19C] **1** to indulge in sexual foreplay. **2** to have sexual intercourse. **3** to wander the streets at night, looking for excitement, esp. sexual conquests. [SE *caterwaul*, to make a noise like rutting cats]

catever/kerterver *n.* [mid-19C] **1** a strange affair. **2** an eccentric person. [Ital. *cattivo*, bad]

cat-eye *n.* [20C] (W.I.) a Black (or other non-European) person with cat-like grey-green irises in their eyes.

catface *n.* [1930s–50s] (US) a wrinkle in one's clothing. [fanciful resemblance. Note timber jargon *catface*, a mark in a piece of lumber-wood]

cat-fart about/around *v.* [1950s–60s] to act in a fussy manner. [SE *cat* + FART ABOUT/AROUND]

catfish *n.* (US) **1** [mid-19C] an unpleasant person. **2** [1940s–50s] a mild oath, e.g. *suffering catfish!* [the unattractiveness of the SE *catfish*]

catfish row *n.* [20C] (US) an area of a town in which the Black population live (cf. CODFISH ROW). [SE *catfish*, supposedly a staple of a Black person's diet]

cat-fit *n.* [1900s–30s] (US) a tantrum. [reverse anthropomorphism]

catflap *n.* [1990s] the anus.

cat food *n.* [1970s] (US Black) sexual intercourse. [CAT n.[4] (2) + SE *food*]

cat-foot *v.* [1910s+] (US) to move stealthily. [var. on PUSSYFOOT]

cat got your tongue? *phr.* [mid-19C+] used to someone who fails to answer a question, or, having been very talkative and opinionated, suddenly falls silent.

catgut *n.* [20C] (US) cheap whisky. [var. on ROTGUT]

catgut-scraper *n.* [late 17C–1900s] a fiddler or violinist (cf. GUT-SCRAPER). [the *catgut* violin strings]

catharpin fashion *n.* [late 17C–18C] 'When People in Company Drink cross, and not round about from the Right to the Left' (B.E.). [? Gk. *kata*, across + *pinein*, to drink; or naut. jargon *cat-harpings*, 'the ropes or (now more generally) iron cramps that serve to brace in the shrouds of the lower-masts behind their respective yards, so as to tighten the shrouds and also give more room to draw the yards in when the ship is close-hauled' (*OED*)]

cathead *n.* [1950s] (US) a fool. [SE *cathead*, a large biscuit eaten in the US; he or she has no more brains than a biscuit]

catheads *n.* [18C] the female breasts (cf. APPLES n.[1]). [SE *cathead*, a large biscuit eaten in the US; thus the breast's roundness reflects that of the foodstuff; however, the term predates US use. E.P. cites 18C naut. jargon *cathead*, 'a beam projecting almost horizontally at each side of the bows of a ship, for raising the anchor from the surface of the water to the deck without touching the bows, and for carrying the anchor on its stock-end when suspended outside the ship's side' (*OED*). But other than there being a pair of *catheads*, it is hard to see any more concrete a link]

cathedral *adj.* [late 17C–late 18C] antique, ancient, out-of-date. [the antiquity of the great *cathedrals*]

catherine hayes *n.* [mid–late 19C] (Aus.) a drink made of claret, sugar and nutmeg. [proper name *Catherine Hayes*. E.P. suggests an 'Irish singer so popular in Australia', but given slang's love of crime, note Catherine Hayes (1690–1725), who murdered her lover following a drinking bout]

catherine wheel *n.* [20C] the vagina.

cat-house *n.* [1930s+] (US) a brothel (cf. ACCOMMODATION HOUSE). [CAT n.[4] (2) + HOUSE n.[1] (1)]

cat in a sack *n.* [20C] (US) something to suspect or be wary of; thus *buy a cat in a sack*, to buy something that one has not actually inspected.

cat in the pan *n.* **1** [16C] a traitor, one who changes sides to advance their self-interest. **2** [mid-19C] a traitor; thus *turn cat in the pan*, to inform, to betray, to change sides. [phr. *turn the cat in the pan*, 'to reverse the order of things so dextrously as to make them appear the very opposite of what they really are' (*OED*) and/or ? *cake in the pan*, a pancake, which must be turned if it is to be cooked]

catish *adj.* [19C] (US) elegant, stylish. [the popular idea of the sinuously elegant feline]

cat-lap *n.* **1** [late 18C–19C] tea or coffee. **2** [19C] any form of weak drink, incl. watered-down alcohol (cf. CAT'S PEE). [SE *cat* + LAP]

cat-lick *n.* [mid-19C] a casual, perfunctory wash. [the phr. is supposedly reminiscent of a cat, although, in fact, cats are punctilious in their self-cleansing]

cat-licker *n.* [20C] (US) a Roman Catholic. [mispron. of SE *Catholic*]

cat-meat pusher *n.* [late 19C–1900s] a street-seller of cooked horsemeat, presumably as petfood.

cat melodeon/melodium *adj.* [20C] appalling, disastrous. [? CAT adj. + the supposed tendency of accordion (*melodeon*) players to fluff their notes]

catnip *n.* [1960s+] (drugs) inferior or fake marijuana. [the US name for UK *catmint*; gullible buyers might well be sold bags of catnip (*Nepeta cataria*) or 50% catnip and 50% marijuana]

catolla *n.* [early 19C] a noisy, foolish person, esp. one who makes foolish bets. [ety. unknown; ? Ital./Sp.]

cat o'mountain *n.* [mid–late 19C] (US) a shrew (cf. CATAMARAN). [SE *catamount*, a cougar or panther]

cat o'nine *n.* [1950s+] (W.I.) severe punishment, a beating (cf. CAT n.[2]). [SE *cat o'nine tails*]

cat on testy dodge *n.* [late 19C] a genteel female beggar who asks for money at people's houses, often backing her request with a (fake) testimonial from a charity. [CAT n.[1] (2) + TESTER + DODGE]

cat on the peek port *n.* [1940s] (US Black) a lookout man. [CAT n.[9] (3)]

cat party/cats' party *n.* [late 19C+] a party consisting of women only (cf. BITCH PARTY). [CAT n.[1] (2)]

cat road *n.* [1930s] (US) a back road. [a cat's nocturnal wanderings]

cat's *n.* [1920s] 1 anything exceptional, superlative. 2 a superior person, or someone who poses as such (cf. ANT'S PANTS). [abbr. CAT'S PYJAMAS]

cats and kitties *n.* [1930s–50s] the female breasts (cf. BRISTOLS; KITTEN HAMMOCK; TALE OF TWO CITIES). [rhy. sl. *cats and kitties* = TITTIES]

cats and mice *n.* [20C] (Aus.) dice. [rhy. sl.]

cat's ass/arse/meow/miaou/miaow *n.*[1] [20C] (US/Can.) 1 anything exceptional or superlative. 2 a superior person or someone who poses as such (cf. ANT'S PANTS; CAT'S BALLS; CAT'S KITTENS; CAT'S MITTS; CAT'S NUTS; CAT'S PYJAMAS; CAT'S WHISKERS). [SE *cat* + ARSE n.[1] (1)]

cat's ass *n.*[2] [1940s+] (US campus) a love bite, usu. on the neck (cf. HICKEY n.[2]). [SE *cat* +ARSE n.[1]]

cat's ass *adj.* [1970s+] (US) excellent, first-rate (cf. CAT'S PYJAMAS). [CAT'S ASS n.[1]]

cat's balls *n.* [1960s] (US) 1 anything exceptional, superlative. 2 a superior person, or someone who poses as such (cf. ANT'S PANTS; CAT'S ASS n.[1]). [SE *cats* + BALLS n.[1] (1)]

cat's bar/cat bar *n.* [1950s–70s] (N.Z.) a bar set aside for women and their escorts (cf. MARE'S NEST). [CAT n.[1] (1) + SE *bar*]

cat's breakfast *n.* [1920s+] (Scot./northern) a distasteful mess (cf. DOG'S DINNER).

cat sense *n.* [1930s–40s] (US Black) common sense, intelligence.

cat's face *n.*[1] [1940s+] in cards, the ace. [rhy. sl.]

cat's face *n.*[2] [1990s] the female genitals (cf. CAT'S HEAD CUT OPEN). [supposed resemblance]

cat's foot *n.* [18C] a dupe (cf. CAT'S PAW). [the fable of a monkey (or a fox) using the foot or paw of a cat to rake roasted chestnuts out of the burning coals]

cat-shag *v.* [1970s] (Aus.) to fool around. [SE *cat* + SHAG v.[1]]

cat's head cut open *n.* [19C] the labia minora (cf. CAT'S FACE n.[2]). [supposed resemblance]

cat-shop *n.* [1930s–50s] (US) a brothel (cf. CAT-HOUSE). [CAT n.[1] (1) + SHOP n.[1] (2)]

catskin *n.* [17C–mid-19C] a second-rate silk hat.

cat's kittens *n.* [1920s] (US) 1 anything exceptional, superlative (cf. ANT'S PANTS; CAT'S ASS n.[1]). 2 a superior person or someone who poses as such. [var. on CAT'S PYJAMAS]

cat's meat *n.* [early–19C+] the human lungs. [the lungs and similar animal intestines are used for cat's and dog's meat]

catsmeat *n.*[1] [19C] the vagina (cf. CAT n.[10]).

catsmeat *n.*[2] [1960s] (N.Z) something easy to achieve.

cat-smellers *n.* [mid-19C] (US) facial hair, whiskers. [a cat uses its whiskers as an extra sense]

cat's meow/miaou/miaow *see* CAT'S ASS n.[1].

cat's mitts *n.* [1910s] (US) 1 anything exceptional, superlative. 2 a superior person, or someone who poses as such (cf. ANT'S PANTS; CAT'S ASS n.[1]). [abbr. SE *cat's mittens*; var. on CAT'S PYJAMAS]

cat's mother, the *n.* [1950s+] a response to the question 'Who are you?' when that question is considered impertinent or over-intrusive. [? the (middle-class) admonition to a child talking of 'she', when describing a woman, who ought to be 'Mrs X' or 'Miss Y': *'She' is the cat's mother*]

cat-sneaking *n.* [late 19C] the stealing of pewter tankards from public houses (cf. CAT AND KITTEN HUNTING). [CAT n.[3]]

cat's nouns!/nouns! *excl.* [early 18C] a mild, blasphemous oath, *God's wounds*.

cat's nuts *n.* [1920s+] (US) 1 anything exceptional, superlative. 2 a superior person, or someone who poses as such (cf. ANT'S PANTS; CAT'S ASS n.[1]). [SE *cat's* + NUTS n.[2] (1); var. on CAT'S PYJAMAS]

catso/cartzo *n.* [17C–early 18C] 1 a rogue or rascal. 2 the penis (cf. GADSO). [Ital. *cazzo*, the penis, lit. 'thrust']

catso! *excl.* [17C–early 18C] a general excl. of annoyance, surprise etc. [CATSO n.]

cats' party *see* CAT-PARTY.

cat's paw *n.* [late 18C–19C] a dupe (cf. CAT'S FOOT). [the softness of the animal's paw + the fable of the monkey and the cat, latterly of the fox and the cat. The pair were cooking potatoes in hot ashes and when they were cooked the fox grabbed the cat's paw and used it to extract the hot potatoes, thus the implication is of using another to perform one's own work. The term became SE in 20C]

cat's pee/piss *n.* [20C] any form of weak alcoholic drink (cf. BUFFALO PISS; CAT-LAP; CAT'S WATER). [SE *cat* + PEE n.[1]/PISS n. (1)]

cat spraddle *v.* [20C] (W.I.) 1 to fall spreadeagled on the ground. 2 to beat severely. [dial. *spraddle*, to sprawl + ? SE *spreadeagle*; the image is of a falling cat]

cat's pyjamas *n.* [1920s+] 1 anything exceptional, superlative. 2 a superior person, or someone who poses as such (cf. ANT'S PANTS; CAT'S ASS n.[1]). [coined, like many other similar terms, by the US sportwriter T.A. 'Tad' Dorgan (1877–1929)]

cat sticks *n.* [late 18C–19C] very thin legs.

cat's water *n.* [19C] gin (cf. CAT'S PEE; JACKEY; OLD TOM).

cat's whiskers *n.* [1920s+] 1 anything exceptional, superlative. 2 a superior person, or someone who poses as such (cf. ANT'S PANTS; CAT'S ASS n.[1]). [var. on CAT'S PYJAMAS. Later use is mainly Aus.]

cattie/catty *n.* [late 19C+] (juv.) a *cata*pult. [abbr.]

catting *n.*[1] [late 17C+] looking for female company and/or conquests. [TOM-CAT; obs. in the UK by the early 19C; 20C use is US Black]

catting *n.*[2] [late 18C+] vomiting. [abbr. SHOOT THE CAT]

catting *n.*[3] [1980s+] (US Black) a style of walking, characterized by a slight dip in the stride, adopted by young urban Black men (cf. AKIMBO v.). [CAT n.[9] (3)]

cattle *n.* 1 [late 16C–18C] a collective noun for prostitutes (cf. SAD CATTLE). 2 [late 17C–mid-19C] people.

cattle *v.* [20C] to copulate. [abbr. CATTLE TRUCK]

cattle-banger *see* COW-BANGER.

cattle dog *n.*[1] [20C] (Aus.) a catalogue. [rhy. sl.]

cattle dog *n.*[2] [20C] (N.Z., mainly juv.) a derog. name for a Roman Catholic.

cattle-duffer *n.* [mid-19C+] (Aus.) a cattle thief. [SE *cattle* + DUFFER]

cattle racket *n.* [mid–late 19C] (Aus.) any form of organized swindle. [originating in a large-scale cattle-rustling racket in New South Wales during the 1840s]

cattle stiff n. [1910s] (US tramp) a cowboy. [SE *cattle* + STIFF]

cattle ticks n. [20C] (Aus.) Catholics. [rhy. sl.]

cattle train n. [1940s–50s] (US Black) a Cadillac. [the name + the size of the car]

cattle truck v. [20C] to copulate, also fig.; thus *cattled*, ruined, hurt, destroyed, beaten etc (cf. FUCKED). [rhy. sl. *cattle truck* = FUCK]

catty n.[1] see CATTIE.

catty n.[2] [1950s+] (Irish) a *Cat*holic. [abbr.]

catty adj. [20C] (Can.) agile, smart. [qualities of a SE *cat*]

catty-cat n. [1970s+] (US Black) the vagina (cf. CAT n.[10]).

catty-cornered adj. [19C] (US) ill-tempered, tetchy. [SE *catty-cornered*, askew, diagonally opposite]

cattywampus see CATAWAMPUS adj.

cat up v.[1] see CAT v.[1].

cat up v.[2] [1920s–30s] (US) to hold up at gunpoint. [? GAT]

cat up v.[3] [1950s] (US) to hide away, esp. from the police. [the elusiveness of a cat]

cat valium n. [1990s] (drugs) ketamine (cf. K n.[4]).

cat wagon n. (US) **1** [19C–1960s] a travelling brothel. **2** [1970s] a van used to take prostitutes to prison. [CAT n.[1] (1). Found in many US rural areas before the anti-'white slavery' legislation of 1913. The women travelled and worked from a horse-drawn covered wagon, following the cattle trails or visiting cowboys out on the range]

cat walk n. [1960s+] (US Black) a strutting style of walking, intended to emphasize one's pride, independence and masculinity (cf. GANGSTA LIMP; PIMP WALK). [CAT n.[9] (3)]

catwanker n. [1990s] a general term of derision. [SE *cat* + WANKER]

cat-whipper n. [20C] (Aus.) one who whinges over their misfortunes. [WHIP THE CAT v. (7)]

cat-witted adj. [mid-17C–1920s] obstinate and spiteful. [the cat's supposed characteristics]

caudge-pawed adj. [late 17C–late 18C] left-handed (cf. CAW-HANDED). [var. on CAW-PAWED]

caudle of hempseed n. [18C] the hangman's noose (cf. ANODYNE NECKLACE). [pun on SE *caudle*, a gruel spiced with wine or ale and given to the sick, and especially to women in labour; thus the noose is ironically also a form of 'painkiller']

caught a rat phr. [1990s] a menstruating woman may be said to have 'caught a rat'. [ref. to the tampon string]

caught holding one's dick phr. [20C] (US) to be caught in an embarrassing or generally disadvantageous situation (cf. CAUGHT WITH ONE'S PANTS DOWN). [SE *caught holding* + DICK n.]

caught in a snowstorm adj. [1930s–40s] (US) under the influence of cocaine (cf. SNOW; WIRED FOR SOUND).

caught/caught out adj. [mid-19C+] pregnant.

caught short adj. **1** [20C] (US) a euph. phr. meaning expecting a child out of wedlock. **2** [1930s+] desperate to visit a lavatory as soon as possible. **3** [1930s+] of a woman, surprised by menstruation starting, beyond reach of tampons, sanitary towels etc.

caught with one's breeches/britches down phr. [mid-19C+] to be caught unprepared (cf. CAUGHT WITH ONE'S PANTS DOWN).

caught with one's pants down phr. [1930s+] (orig. US) caught in a state of embarrassing unpreparedness, caught 'red-handed'.

caught with one's trousers down phr. [1960s+] surprised in an embarrassing position or, on a metaphorical level, caught without adequate defences or preparation (cf. CAUGHT WITH ONE'S PANTS DOWN).

caught with rem-in-re phr. [mid-19C] caught having sexual intercourse. [fake legalese, lit. 'caught with thing in thing']

cauli n. [late 19C+] a *cauli*flower. [abbr.]

cauliflower n.[1] [late 18C] a large white wig 'such as is commonly worn by the dignified clergy, and was formerly by physicians' (Grose 1785).

cauliflower n.[2] [late 18C–19C] the vagina (cf. CABBAGE n.[7]; HAVE A BIT OF CAULIFLOWER). ['A woman, who was giving evidence in a case wherein it was necessary to express those parts, made use of the term cauliflower. for which the judge on the bench, a peevish old fellow, reproved her, saying she might as well call it an artichoke. Not so, my lord, replied she, for an artichoke has a bottom, but a **** and a cauliflower have none' (Grose 1785)]

cauliflower n.[3] [mid-19C] (US) a person, a fellow. [? Fr. *choux*, cabbage, used as a term of affection]

cauliflower n.[4] [late 19C+] the foaming top of a newly-poured glass of beer. [its whiteness]

cauliflower n.[5] [1940s+] a 'cauliflower ear', the sign of a boxer whose ears have taken too many punches to retain their original shape.

cauliflower n.[6] [1970s] (US) cowardice, fear. [? its white 'heart']

caulk v. **1** [19C] to have sexual intercourse. **2** [1970s] as *caulk off*, to idle, to waste time on the job. [either SE *caulk*, to fill, to stuff, or ME *cauk*, for a male bird to tread the female]

caulked adj. [19C] (US) exhausted. [naut. jargon *caulk*, to lie down on a soft plank, to sleep with one's clothes on; thus the sailor, rather than the usual pitch or oakum, was fig. 'stopping up the cracks' in the deck]

caulker n. **1** [19C] the last drink of an evening. **2** [19C+] an exceptionally amusing story, which 'cannot be topped', usu. as *corker* in 20C (cf. CHOKER). **3** a lie (cf. CRACKER n.[1]; WHACKER n.[1]; WHOPPER). [either f. mis-sp. of CORKER, that which 'puts the cork on' or f. naut. jargon *caulk*, to stop up the seams of a ship to 'keep out the wet']

cause it v. [1940s+] to cause trouble, to damage, esp. in phr. *that's caused it*.

cause whore n. [1990s] a voluble female proselytizer for modish, leftish causes.

causey/cawsey see CARSEY.

caution n. [mid-19C+] **1** a 'character', an eccentric, a 'difficult' person, sometimes extended as *a caution to snakes*. **2** anything staggering or alarming. [i.e. one with whom caution must be exercised]

caution sign n. [1970s+] (US Black) anyone who dresses in an excessively gaudy and vulgar manner, with many clashing bright colours (cf. SANTA CLAUS). [image of bright red 'Stop' signs etc]

cavalier n. [20C] (orig. RN, usu. juv.) **1** an uncircumcised penis. **2** the boy who has one. [the antonym of ROUNDHEAD n.[2]]

cavalry curate n. [late 19C–1910s] a curate who rides rather than walks round his parish.

cavault v. [late 17C–early 19C] to have sexual intercourse; one of a number of words equating sex with horse-riding (cf. CAVAULTING SCHOOL; CHIVALRY; HORSE v.[1]; PRIGGING; RANTIPOLE; RIDE v.[1]). [Ling. Fr. *cavolta*, riding]

cavaulting school n. [late 17C–early 19C] a brothel (cf. ACADEMY). [CAVAULT]

cave n.[1] [1930s] (US Black) one's room, one's home, one's dwelling place.

cave n.[2] [1990s] (US Black) a White person (cf. CAVEBOY).

cave v. [mid-19C+] (mainly US) **1** to give in, to yield to pressure from above, to break down, give way, collapse (cf. CAVE IN). **2** to die.

cave! excl. [mid-18C+] (schoolboy) (pron. kay-vee) look out! (cf. KEEP CAVE). [Lat. *cave*, beware]

caveboy n. [1990s] (US Black) a White person. [the belief that the early cave-dwellers were all White, as Black Africans lived on the plains]

cave-dweller *n.* [late 19C] (US) a member of the old New York aristocracy (cf. CLIFF-DWELLER). [such aristocrats still lived in the dark, old mansions their families had built earlier in the century]

cave in *v.* [early 19C+] (orig. US) to give in, to yield to pressure from above, to break down, to give way, to collapse.

cave in one's crust *see* BURST IN ONE'S CRUST.

cave-man *n.* [late 19C+] an ostentatiously macho male, a 'he-man'; thus *cave-man stuff*, a rough form of wooing or love-making, reminiscent of the clichéd cave-man who (at least in cartoons) drags his woman around by her hair.

cave of harmony *n.*[1] [mid-19C] the vagina (cf. BLACK HOLE *n.*[1]).

cave of harmony *n.*[2] [mid-19C] the Cider Cellars or Evans's singing saloon in London.

cave out *v.* [late 19C] (orig. US) to come to an end. [mining jargon *cave out*, the metal casing at the end of a tunnel]

cavey *see* CAVY.

caviar/caviare *n.*[1] [late 19C–1920s] a passage of printed text that has been erased by a (Russian) censor. [the criss-cross pattern of white lines and black diamonds which was stamped over the offending material, and which, given its Russian provenance, could be seen as resembling caviar]

caviar *n.*[2] [1980s+] (drugs) crack cocaine. [? the resemblance of small ROCKS *n.*[4] of crack cocaine to grains of caviar]

cavite all star *n.* [1970s] (drugs) marijuana. [*Cavite*, a US marshal port in Manila Bay]

cavvy *n.* [1980s+] marijuana. [? SE *caviar*, the reference is presumably to its cost and quality rather than to its fishiness]

cavy/cavey *n.* [mid-17C] a Cavalier. [abbr.]

cawallux!/cawhalux! *excl.* [mid-19C] (US) onomat. term indicating the sound of a slap or a box on the ear. [pfx. KER- + SE *wallop*]

caw-handed *adj.* [late 17C–18C] clumsy, awkward (cf. CAUDGE-PAWED). [Oxon. dial. *caw*, a fool and *cawing*, awkward]

cawhop! *see* KERWHOP!

caw-pawed *adj.* [18C–20C] clumsy, awkward (cf. CAUDGE-PAWED). [*see* CAW-HANDED for ety.]

cayac *n.* [20C] (W.I./Gren.) a country bumpkin. [generic use of *Cayac*, a native of the island of Carriacou]

cayuse *n.* (US) **1** [mid-19C+] an Indian pony. **2** [mid-19C+] any (inferior) horse. **3** [1900s–20s] a worthless person. ['The wild horse of Oregon, named for the Cayuse Indians, an equestrian people ... . The name is now commonly used by the northern cowboy to refer to any horse. At first the term was used for the western horse, to set it apart from a horse brought overland from the East. In later years the name came to be applied as a term of contempt to any scrubby, undersized horse.' Francis Haines, *Western Horseman*, vol. II no. 2 (March–April 1937)]

caz *see* CASSAN.

cazh *see* CAS.

caze *n.* [late 19C–1910s] the female genitals. [? misreading of Ital. *cazzo*, the penis]

c.b. *v. see* COCK BLOCK.

c.b. *phr.* [1970s+] cock and *b*alls. [abbr. used in S&M contact advertisements to advertise 'cock and balls torture']

c.c. *n.* [20C] (US prison) the condemned cells (cf. D.C.; DEATH ROW; X-ROW). [abbr. condemned to capital punishment]

c.c.c. *phr.* [1990s] red female pubic hair. [abbr. copper coloured cunt]

c.c.m. *phr.* [1990s] (US Black) cold cash money. [abbr.]

c.c.w. *phr.* (US police/Und.) carrying a concealed weapon. [abbr.]

C-dust *n.* [1970s] (US drugs) cocaine.

cease *v.* [1920s–50s] (US Black) to die. [abbr. SE *decease*]

cecil *n.* [1980s+] (US prison) cocaine (cf. C *n.*[2]; CARRIE; CHARLIE *n.*[7]). [note US pron. *seesul*]

cedar *n.*[1] [19C] (US Und.) a pencil. [the cedar wood of which it is made; such pencils are usu. unpainted and cheap to purchase]

cedar *n.*[2] [1930s+] (Aus.) a fool (cf. HULVERHEAD; KNOTHEAD). [SE *cedar*, i.e. a 'wooden' head]

celeb *n.* [1910s+] (orig. US) a *celeb*rity. [abbr.]

celebrity fucker *n.* [1970s+] (orig. US) anyone who courts the famous with the hope of enjoying some proxy fame (cf. GROUPIE; STAR-FUCKER). [SE *celebrity* + FUCKER]

celestial *adj.* [mid–late 19C] used of a turned-up nose. [SE *celestial*, heavenly, such a nose 'points to the heavens']

celestial poultry *n.* [late 19C–1920s] angels.

cell *v.* [20C] (Und.) to share a cell with (cf. JAIL). [the *OED* cites two 16C uses, but they apply to a monk's not a prisoner's cell]

cellar/cellarage/cellar-door *n.*[1] [19C] the vagina (cf. BLACK HOLE *n.*[1]).

cellar *n.*[2] [19C] a shoe, a boot, usu. in pl. (cf. GARRET).

cellarage/cellar-door *see* CELLAR *n.*[1].

cellar-flap *n.* [late 19C] a tap-dance. [rhy. sl.; the image is of a dance performed on a space no larger than the trap-door leading to a cellar]

cellar-flap *v.* [20C] to borrow. [rhy. sl. *cellar-flap* = SE *tap*, i.e. on the shoulder, preparatory to asking for money]

cellier *n.* [late 17C–early 18C] an outright lie. [proper name Elizabeth *Cellier*, implicated, with her partner Thomas Dangerfield, in the Meal Tub Plot of 1679. This plot, which accused various prominent Roman Catholics of treason, hinged on papers supposedly hidden beneath Mrs Cellier's meal tub. It collapsed when Dangerfield was imprisoned for perjury and Cellier was sent to the pillory]

cells *n.* [1910s+] a (brief) term of imprisonment. [SE phr. *night(s) in the cells*]

cell task *n.* [1940s+] (prison) a pin-up picture. [ironic reference to the official *cell tasks* set prisoners. The pin-up's real-life incarnation would obviously make a preferable 'task' to that set by the authorities]

cement *n.* [1970s+] (Aus.) any form of diarrhoea cure, such as kaolin (and morphine), which depends for its efficacy on 'hardening' the contents of the stomach.

cement city *n.* [1970s] (US) a cemetery.

cement-head *n.* [1940s+] (US teen) a gullible, conventional person. [SE *cement* + sfx. -HEAD (1)]

cement kimono/overcoat/overshoes *n.* [1960s+] (US gangster) a method of disposing of a corpse by placing it inside a barrel filled with wet cement and tossing the resultant lump into a river (cf. CHICAGO OVERCOAT; CONCRETE OVERCOAT; WOODEN KIMONO; WOODEN OVERCOAT).

cement-mixer *n.*[1] (US) **1** [1910s+] a rickety, broken-down vehicle. **2** [1930s–40s] a dance. [its movement + (2) ? its being a *mixer* that *cements* relationships]

cement-mixer *n.*[2] [1960s] an overweight, aggressive woman. [resemblance]

cement overcoat/overshoes *see* CEMENT KIMONO.

cent *n.* [1960s–70s] (US Black) $1.

centerfield on *v.* [1930s] (US) to perform cunnilingus on (cf. AXIS). [the 'centrality' of the vagina to the female body]

centerman *n.* [20C] (Can./US prison) a prisoner who toadies to the guards. [prison use *center*, the guards' 'office' in a prison wing]

centipees *n.* [late 18C–early 19C] a tailor of soldiers' clothing. [synon. milit. use *sancipees*, ult. *sank*, to work as a menial servant in a dining room]

cent per cent *n.* [late 18C] a usurer. [their graspingness; they take back 100% interest for every £100 loaned]

central cut/furrow/office *n.* [19C] the vagina (cf. AGREEABLE RUTS OF LIFE; AXIS).

centre of attraction *n.* [19C] the vagina (cf. AXIS).

centre of bliss *n.* [late 18C] the vagina (cf. AXIS).

centrique part *n.* [17C] the vagina (cf. AXIS). [coined by John Donne]

century *n.* [19C+] $100 or £100 (cf. C n.¹). [16C SE *century*, a group of 100 things]

century note *n.* [1900s–40s] (US) a $100 bill. [CENTURY]

cereb *n.* [1970s+] (US campus) one who works exceptionally hard (cf. CONCH n.²; CONSHY; GRUB n.²; PENCIL GEEK). [SE *cerebral*]

cert *n.* [late 19C+] a definite winner, usu. in a sporting context (cf. DEAD CERT). [SE *certainty*]

certificate of birth *n.* [19C] the vagina, one of the few terms that deal with the vagina in its procreative rather than sexual role (cf. BABY CHUTE).

cess *n.* [1980s+] (US drugs) third-rate marijuana. [SE *cesspit*]

cess! *see* SIS!

c.f.m. *phr.* [1980s+] (US) sexually suggestive; thus *c.f.m. shoes*, *c.f.m. dress* etc (cf. FUCK-ME SHOES). [abbr. come fuck me]

c.g. *adj.* [1970s+] used in S&M contact advertisements for cross-gender. [abbr.]

C-game *n.* [1960s] (drugs) cocaine (cf. C n.²).

c.h. *n.* [late 19C] conquering *hero*, usu. used ironically. [abbr. The frequent playing, subsequent to the Egyptian War (1882), of the tune 'See the Conquering Hero Comes']

cha/chah/char *n.¹* [20C] tea. [Mandarin *ch'a*, tea]

cha *n.²* [1980s+] (drugs) cocaine.

cha!/cho! *excl.* [1950s+] (W.I. Rasta) a disdainful expletive, a very common, mild excl. of impatience, vexation or disappointment. [onomat.]

chaar/char ou *n.* [1970s+] (S.Afr.) an Indian. [? Hind. *chaar admi*, people in general + Afk. *ou*, a person]

chabbies/chabs *n.* [1990s] the female breasts. [SE *chubby*]

chabby/chabs *n.* [1990s] a very fat person. [SE *chubby*]

chaben/chabin/shabeen *n.* [20C] (W.I.) a person of mixed African/European descent; such people have pale brown skin, coarse reddish hair and, sometimes, freckles and greyish eyes. [Fr. *chabins*, sheep bred in Bery, with thick, long hair. Such sheep were once seen as a sheep/goat cross, and the term, exported to Dominica, was used as a synon. for 'half-breed']

chabobs *n.* [1960s] (US) the female breasts. [? BOOB n.³; note CHORB, a spot or pimple f. Bantu *chubaba*, a skin blemish]

cha-cha *n.* [1950s+] (US Black) sexual intercourse. [SE *cha-cha*, a popular ballroom dance]

cha-cha *adj.* [1960s–70s] (US) fashionable, smart. [var. on CHI-CHI adj.]

cha-cha *v.* [1950s+] (US Black) to have sexual intercourse. [CHA-CHA n.]

chacha queen *n.* [1980s+] (US gay) a Hispanic male homosexual. [*chacha*, generic for Spanish-American + QUEEN n.¹]

cha-ching! *excl.* [1990s] (US teen) an excl. phr. used to signify that something or someone has made one happy. [echoic of the sound of a cash register and popularized by the film *Wayne's World* (1992); it can still be used in the context of money, but refers more commonly to general pleasures, esp. a passing pretty woman]

chachundar *n.* [20C] (W.I.) used by those of Indian descent to describe an East Indian woman who has a close friendship or even a child with a Black man. [Hind. *chhachuudar*, a mole or shrew]

chad/Mr Chad *n.* [1940s+] a chalked-up, cartoon-style picture of a rudimentary human head 'looking over' an equally basic brick wall plus the slogan *Wot, no … . [ety. unknown]

chafe *v.* [late 17C] to beat, to thrash; thus *chafed*, beaten. [SE *chafe*, to warm, to heat]

chafe at the bit, to *phr.* [1990s] to masturbate.

chafe-litter *n.* [mid-16C–early 17C] (Und.) an impudent, cheeky person.

chafer *v.* [late 19C–1910s] to have sexual intercourse. [var. on CHARVER v.]

chaff *n.* [1930s+] (Aus.) money (cf. DUST n.¹; MUCK n.¹). [SE *chaff*, husks of corn after threshing]

chaff *v.* **1** [early 19C+] to banter, to tease, usu. gently; thus *chaff down a peeler*, to tease a policeman, (university) *chaff a cad*, for an undergraduate to insult a townsman. **2** [1960s+] (S.Afr.) to give someone something, to tell someone something. **3** [1970s+] (S.Afr.) to flirt, to approach sexually, to 'get fresh'. [SE *chafe*, to rub]

chaff-cutter *n.¹* [mid-19C] a malicious talker, a slanderer. [CHAFF v. (1)]

chaff-cutter *n.²* [1920s+] (Aus.) a typewriter. [SE *chaff-cutter*, a machine that cuts chaff for fodder; i.e. the noise of the keys]

chaffer *n.* **1** [19C] the throat. **2** [early–mid-19C] one who banters or teases, a teaser. [CHAFF v. (1)]

chaffing-crib *n.* [19C] a man's private room, where he receives and entertains his friends. [CHAFF v. (1) + CRIB n.³]

chaffy *adj.* [19C] jolly, bantering, light-hearted. [CHAFF v. (1)]

chah *see* CHA n.¹.

chai/chy *n.* [mid-19C+] (tramp) a woman (cf. CHAL). [Rom.]

chain and crank *n.* [20C] a bank. [rhy. sl.]

chain and locket *n.* [20C] a pocket. [rhy. sl.]

chain gang *n.¹* [late 19C+] **1** the Lord Mayor and Lady Mayoress of London. **2** married men. [actual and metaphorical 'chains of office']

chain gang *n.²* [1960s+] (US gay) a circle of three or more people, hetero- or homosexual, all linked physically in mutual sex acts (cf. DAISY CHAIN). [pun on SE]

chain jerk *n.* [1930s+] (US) joint masturbation, often in competition, by a group of boys, poss. sitting in a circle (cf. CIRCLE JERK). [SE *chain* + JERK (OFF)]

chain lightning *n.¹* [19C–1930s] **1** potato spirit. **2** (orig. US) strong, if cheap, whisky (cf. RED-EYE n.¹; WHITE LIGHTNING). [SE *chain lightning*, lightning that moves rapidly in a forked or zigzag course. The image is of immediacy and strength of the whisky's effect. 'Potato spirit, import from Germany. Filthy mess – poisonous to a degree. Smuggled mainly' (Ware)]

chain lightning *n.²* [mid-19C] (US) misery, punishment, hell. [the fiery torments of hell]

chain lightning *n.³* [late 19C–1920s] an exceptionally able person.

chains, the *n.* [late 19C–1900s] (S.Afr.) the Johannesburg Stock Exchange. [the chains that closed off a portion of Simmonds Street so that dealers could conduct their business. 'The Chains' lasted from 1887–1902, being replaced by a new Stock Exchange building in 1903]

chain up! *excl.* [1920s] shut up! be quiet! [fig. use of phr. *chain up that dog*]

chain up a pup, to *phr.* [1900s–20s] (Aus.) to get drinks on credit (cf. TIE UP A DOG). [DOG n.⁹ (2)]

chair, the *n.* [20C] (orig. US) the electric chair.

chairbacker *n.* [20C] (US) an unprofessional, part-time lay preacher (cf. CHICKEN-EATER; CHICKEN-PREACHER; FRY-MEAT PREACHER; GOSPEL BIRD; STUMP-KNOCKER; TABLE-TAPPER). [the chair that such a preacher carries for use as an impromptu pulpit]

chair days *n.* [late 19C–1900s] (society) old age. [when one is confined to a chair]

chair-pounder *n.* [1910s] (US) an office worker. [they spend the day sitting down]

chair-warmer *n.* [20C] a supernumerary, one who is there but does nothing, an observer (cf. BENCHER). [theatrical jargon *chair-warmer*, 'a lady whose talent is comprised in her physical charms, and who can neither sing, dance, nor act' (Ware)]

chaka-chaka *adj.* **1** [1950s+] (W.I. Rasta) messy, disorderly, untidy. **2** [1980s+] (W.I./UK Black teen) untidy or unkempt. [Ewe *tsáka*, to mix, be mixed]

chal *n.* [19C+] a man (cf. CHAI). [Rom.]

chaldee *see* CALDEE.

chal droch *n.* [18C–19C] (tinker) a knife. [Shelta]

chale! *excl.* [1950s+] (US) no. [Sp.]

chalewa *see* CHALICE.

chalfonts *n.* [1970s+] haemorrhoids (cf. FARMER GILES; SEVEN DIALS). [rhy. sl. *Chalfont St Giles* = piles]

chalice/chalewa *n.* [1950s+] a pipe used for smoking marijuana, which, when used by Rastafarians, takes on a sacred and ritualistic role; thus the 'religious' name (cf. CHILLAM).

chalk *n.*[1] [late 18C–early 19C] (US) a quarter dollar, 25 cents.

chalk *n.*[2] [mid-19C] a scar or scratch. [CHALK V.[1]]

chalk, the *n.*[3] [mid–late 19C] (US) **1** the fashion. **2** the absolute truth. [? the use of *chalk* by a teacher]

chalk *n.*[4] *see* CHALK FARM.

chalk *n.*[5] **1** [1930s+] (US) milk or cream. **2** [1970s–80s] (US Black) a White person (cf. BLANCO). [the colour]

chalk *n.*[6] (US drugs) **1** [1960s–70s] methylamphetamine, Methedrine. **2** [1960s+] cocaine. **3** [1970s] Methadone. [the white colour; (3) may be an error, confusing the abbr. 'meth' used for (1)]

chalk *adj.* [late 19C+] **1** spurious, unknown. **2** incompetent. [the use of chalk to mark up the names of new jockeys on the telegraph board at a racetrack; those of established riders are painted]

chalk *v.*[1] [18C–19C] (Und.) to slash or cut someone's face. [resemblance to a chalk mark]

chalk *v.*[2] [1980s+] (drugs) to lighten the colour of cocaine in order to make it appear more pure; thus *chalking*, chemically altering the colour of cocaine so it looks white (cf. BEIGING).

chalk against *v.* [late 19C] to bear a grudge against. [the chalking up of one's debts on a piece of wood by shopkeepers, publicans etc]

chalk and talk/chalk-and-talker *n.* [1920s+] (Aus.) a schoolteacher, esp. an old-fashioned, traditional teacher (cf. CHALKIE).

chalked up *adj.* [1950s+] (drugs) under the influence of cocaine (cf. CHALK N.[6]). [the whiteness of cocaine]

chalker *n.* [mid-19C] a London milkman. [his supposed watering down of milk with chalky water]

chalkers *n.* [late 18C] Irish thugs, the equivalent of London's mohocks, who specialize in roaming the streets and slashing the face of any unfortunate victim; thus *chalking*, carrying out this species of urban terrorism or 'amusement' as Grose (1785) grimly notes it. [CHALK V.[1] + ironic use of SE *chalk*, to draw a line]

chalk farm/chalk *n.* [mid-19C–1910s] an arm. [rhy. sl.; ult. Chalk Farm, London NW1]

chalk head *n.* [mid-19C] **1** one who is good at calculating figures. **2** a waiter. [calculation with chalk on a slate; (2) is specific ext. of (1)]

chalkie *n.* [1940s+] (Aus.) a schoolteacher. [who wields chalk]

chalkies *n.* [mid-19C] (US) the teeth. [the whiteness]

chalk it up! *excl.* [1910s–20s] look at that! [fig. use of *chalk it up*, make a note]

chalk marquis *n.* [late 19C–1900s] a spurious marquis. [CHALK adj. (1) + SE *marquis*]

chalk off *v.*[1] [mid-19C] (US) to leave. [WALK ONE'S CHALKS]

chalk off *v.*[2] [mid-19C–1910s] to look at closely (cf. CHALK IT UP!). [one stares at a metaphorical chalk mark]

chalk off *v.*[3] [1930s] (Glasgow) to tell off, to scold. [SE *chalk up against*]

chalk one's hat, to *phr.* [19C] to travel for free, orig. and esp. in railroad use. [the custom of the conductor placing a white mark or ticket on the headgear of the passenger]

chalk out *v.* **1** [late 19C] to describe clearly, to give directions. **2** [1940s] (US) to murder, to kill. [the drawing of a line with chalk; in (2) that drawn around the corpse]

chalks *n.* [mid-19C] the legs. [abbr. WALK ONE'S CHALKS]

Chalk Sunday *n.* [20C] (Irish) the first Sunday in Lent. [the backs of those still unmarried on that day were marked with chalk]

chalubbies *n.* [1970s] (US) the female breasts (cf. CHABOBS). [JABONGOES + BUBBIES]

cham/chammy *n.* [mid–late 19C] *cham*pagne (cf. SHAM N.[2]). [abbr.]

cham *v.* [mid–late 19C] to drink *cham*pagne. [abbr.]

chamber *n.* [20C] (US prison) the gas chamber.

chamber lye *n.* [late 18C–early 19C] urine standing in a chamberpot. [play on SE *chamber(pot)* + *lye/lie*; note late 19C–early 20C Southern US Black use *chamber lye*, urine sprinkled around a garden to keep wandering deer away]

chamber music *n.* [late 19C+] the sound of a chamberpot being used. [pun]

chamber of commerce *n.* [1940s] (US Black) a lavatory. [SE *chamber*, a lavatory + pun on DO ONE'S BUSINESS]

chamber of horrors *n.*[1] [19C] sausages. [the supposedly dubious contents]

chamber of horrors *n.*[2] [late 19C] the Peeresses' gallery at the House of Lords. ['its being railed round as if it contained objectionable or repulsive inmates' (B&L)]

chameleon diet *n.* [late 17C–early 18C] a poor diet. [? SE *chameleon*, an inconstant or variable person]

chamming *n.* [mid–late 19C] drinking champagne (to excess). [CHAM V.]

chammy *see* CHAM N.

champ *n.*[1] [19C] appetite. [SE *champ*, to eat, to chew]

champ *n.*[2] [1950s+] (drugs) a drug user who refuses to reveal their sources to the police. [CHAMPION]

champ/champed *adj.* [1990s] (US teen) much favoured or much used, excellent, fine, beyond the average. [CHAMPION]

champ! *excl.* [1980s+] (US campus) calm down, wait a minute. [SE *champ (at the bit)*, to gnash one's teeth]

champagne charlie *n.* [mid-19C+] **1** a devotee of champagne. **2** a debauchee, a dissipated man (cf. GOOD-TIME CHARLIE). [the song 'Champagne Charlie is My Name' by H.J. Whymark and Alfred Lee was written in 1867 and was a hit on both sides of the Atlantic. The original *Champagne Charlie* was a wine-merchant who was very free with gifts of his stock]

champagne country *n.* [early–mid-19C] self-indulgence in eating and drinking. [SE *champagne* as a metaphor for luxury]

champagner *n.* [late 19C–1900s] a fashionable prostitute. [her consumption of this expensive drink]

champagne shoulders *n.* [late 19C] (society) sloping shoulders. [resembling a champagne bottle]

champagne socialist *n.* [1980s+] one who preaches socialism but espouses a capitalist lifestyle (cf. BOLLINGER BOLSHEVIK).

champagne trick *n.* a particularly wealthy or generous client for a prostitute. [fig. use of *champagne* + TRICK N.[4] (2)]

champagne weather *n.* [late 19C] (society) bad weather. [ironic or ? one needs a glass of *champagne* to cheer oneself up]

champers n. [1950s+] champagne. [abbr. SE champagne + 'Oxford' sfx. -ers]

champion adj. [late 19C+] (usu. north) first-rate, excellent.

champion adv. [late 19C+] (usu. north) excellently, perfectly.

champion slump of 1897 n. [late 19C] the motorcar. [London's motor manufacturers staged a great procession of their products on Lord Mayor's Day, 1896. The aim was to launch the new mode of transport with a great fanfare, as the term implies, it failed – at least initially]

champy n. [late 19C] (US) champagne. [abbr.]

chance blow n. [19C] (US) an illegitimate child (cf. CHANCE CHILD). [SE chance + BY-BLOW]

chance child n. [mid–late 19C] an illegitimate child (cf. CHANCE BLOW).

chance it v. [mid-19C+] to take risks, to gamble. [abbr. CHANCE ONE'S ARM]

chance one's arm, to phr. [late 19C+] to take risks. [? orig. tailor's jargon, but according to Share, the ref. is to a 1492 feud between the Ormondes and Kildares. The earl of Kildare cut a hole in the door of St Patrick's Cathedral in Dublin and thrust in his arm, hoping that it would be grabbed rather than simply cut off. Thus it was, and the feud ended]

chance one's mitt, to phr. [1910s] to take risks (cf. CHANCE ONE'S ARM). [SE chance + MITT n.]

chancer n. [late 19C+] **1** anyone who risks their luck, usu. foolishly, although the over-riding image is of their 'getting away with it'. **2** a bet, a wager.

chance the ducks phr. [mid-19C–1920s] come what may, anyhow, anyway. [hunting imagery; i.e. whether or not there are ducks to shoot]

chance would be a fine thing phr. [20C] phr. used of anything that seems absolutely unlikely.

chancy adj. **1** [18C] lucky. **2** [19C+] untrustworthy, undependable. [SE chance, which can be fortunate or otherwise]

chandler-ken n. [19C] a chandler's shop, selling general provisions, groceries etc. [SE chandler + KEN n.[1]]

chaney-eyed adj. [17C] **1** small-eyed; thus like a China doll. **2** glass-eyed. [? chaney = China, as in china-ware or porcelain; china being the original material used for 'glass' eyes]

chang-chang v. [20C] (W.I./Gren.) to cut a man or boy's hair in an amateurish, raggedy manner (cf. ZUG UP). [? echoic of the sound of the barber's scissors]

change, the n.[1] [early 19C+] the menopause. [euph. SE the change of life]

change n.[2] [mid-19C+] something given or taken in return, usu. in phr., e.g. give someone change, to do them a service, to pay back (for a verbal or physical attack); to take one's change out of, to take one's revenge on (a person) or for (a thing); take your change out of that! used when giving an opponent a return on either a rude comment or a blow; not to get any (or much) change out of, to get no return, result or satisfaction from (a person), to fail to get the better of (a person).

change n.[3] [1920s+] (US Black) money, whether in notes or coins (cf. COINS); thus fig. [1970s+] any insignificant, unquantifiable amount, not necessarily monetary.

change black dog for monkey, to phr. [1920s+] (W.I.) to get nothing from a deal, to remain as poor as one already was (cf. BLACK DOG n.[1]). [one is still left with a useless animal]

change channels/the channel, to phr. [1950s+] (US) to change the subject of conversation. [TV imagery]

change foot v. [early 17C–mid-18C] to change sides, to become a traitor.

change one's breath, to phr. [mid-19C+] (US) to drink alcohol.

change one's note, to phr. [early 18C+] to alter one's opinions or statements, esp. to go back on what one has previously said (cf. CHANGE ONE'S SONG; CHANGE ONE'S TUNE; PLAY ANOTHER TUNE). [musical imagery]

change one's song, to phr. [late 18C–early 19C] to alter one's opinions or statements (cf. CHANGE ONE'S NOTE). [musical imagery]

change one's tune, to phr. [late 16C+] to alter one's opinions or statements, esp. to go back on what one has previously said (cf. CHANGE ONE'S NOTE). [musical imagery]

changes n. [1960s+] (orig. US Black) any alteration in one's mental or emotional state; thus go through changes, put through changes.

change someone's face see BREAK SOMEONE'S FACE phr.[1].

chank v. [19C] (US) to eat noisily, to chew loudly. [? SE champ or echoic]

channel n. [1950s+] (drugs) the vein into which a drug is injected.

channel fleet n. [20C] (Irish) a street. [rhy. sl.]

channel swimmer n. [1930s–70s] (drugs) one who injects heroin. [CHANNEL + pun]

chant n. [19C] **1** (Und.) a song; thus throw off a rum chant, to sing a good song. **2** one's name (and address); thus (Und.) tip one a queer chant, to give a false name, esp. to a tradesman one wishes to defraud. **3** any form of marking, on silver, linen etc; thus chanted, marked. **4** a newspaper advertisement. **5** a piece in a newspaper describing a thief or a robbery and advertising a reward for the arrest of the thief or the return of the goods, such a thief or item was chanted. [all fig. uses of SE chant, to sing]

chant/chaunt v. **1** [early–mid-19C] to sell a horse fraudulently. **2** [mid-19C] to sing, esp. to sing for money in the street. **3** [mid-19C] to mark one's personal possessions with an identifying name. **4** [mid-19C] (US) to talk (about). **5** [late 19C–1900s] to swear. **6** [1930s] (tramp) to sing for alms. [CHANT n.]

chanted/chaunted adj. [early 19C] famous, celebrated, lit. 'sung'. [CHANT v. (2)]

chanter/chaunter n. [mid-19C] **1** a crooked horse dealer. **2** a seller and singer of street ballads. [CHANT v. (1), (2)]

chanticleer n. [mid–late 19C] the penis. [a pun on COCK n.[2] (1)]

chanting/chaunting n. [19C] **1** the selling of a poor horse by concealing its defects and 'crying up' its good ones. **2** street-singing. [CHANT v.]

chanting ken n. [late 19C–1900s] a music-hall. [CHANT v. (2) + KEN n.[1]]

chanting slum n. [mid-19C] a music-hall (cf. CHANTING KEN). [CHANT v. (2) + SLUM n.[2] (1)]

chant the poker, to phr. [19C] to exaggerate; thus don't chant the poker, don't exaggerate (cf. DON'T SING IT). [CHANT v. + POKER TALK]

chap n. **1** [early 18C+] a man, esp. in sense of 'one of us'; thus (Und.) one of the chaps, a member of one's own gang or group (cf. CUSTOMER). **2** [late 19C] a male sweetheart. **3** [late 19C] a sailor. [abbr. of late 16C SE chapman, a customer, and as such relates to COVE. An alternative ety., however, links it to the Romany chavo or chavi, a child, and thus places it as the antecedent of the 19C use. Todd (revised edn. of Johnson's Dictionary, 1818) notes 'it usually designates a person of whom a contemptuous opinion is entertained', but the OED adds 'it is now merely familiar and non-dignified, being chiefly applied to a young man']

chap v. [1920s–30s] to chaperon. [abbr.]

chapel n.[1] see CHAPEL OF EASE.

chapel, the n.[2] [mid-19C+] Whitechapel, London. [abbr.]

chapel hat pegs n. [20C] erect female nipples; usu. in phr. stand/standing up like chapel hat pegs]

chapel of ease/chapel n. [17C–mid-19C] a privy, a lavatory (cf. CLOSET OF EASE; HOUSE OF EASEMENT; STOOL OF EASE). [play on SE]

chapel of little ease n. [mid-19C] a police station. [SE little-ease, 'a place in which there is little ease for him who occupies it. A narrow place of confinement; spec. the name of a dungeon in the Tower of London, and of an ancient place of punishment for unruly apprentices at the Guildhall, London. Also, the pillory or stocks.' (OED) + play on CHAPEL OF EASE]

chapped/chapt adj. [late 17C–1900s] thirsty. [SE chapped, cracked, dried out]

chapper n.[1] [late 19C] the mouth. [? SE chaps, the mouth]

chapper n.[2] [20C] (Und.) a policeman. [? Yid.]

chapper v. [late 19C–1900s] to drink. [CHAPPER n.[1]]

chappie/chappy n. 1 [early 19C+] a person, esp. a close friend (cf. JOHNNIE n.[2]). 2 [late 19C] a man about town. [CHAP n. (1)]

chappy adj. [late 17C–mid-18C] talkative. [SE chaps, the mouth, the jaws]

chap someone's ass, to phr. [1960s] (US) to annoy, to irritate. [SE chap, to crack the skin + ARSE n.[1] (3)]

chapt see CHAPPED.

char n.[1] [20C] a charwoman. [note orig. [18C] char, to do odd jobs. The modern synon. charlady began as late 19C joc. but now, like tea-lady, cleaning-lady etc is almost SE]

char n.[2] see CHA n.[1].

char v. [20C] to work as a cleaner, usu. in a private house. [CHAR n.[1]]

chara/sharry n. [1920s–60s] a charabanc, a coach. [abbr.]

character n. 1 [mid-18C+] an eccentric or otherwise distinctive person. 2 [1930s+] (orig. US) a person. [(1) abbr. SE odd character]

character academy n. [mid-19C] (Und.) a place where unemployed (and possibly previously dismissed) servants concoct spurious references or 'characters'.

charactered adj. [early 18C–early 19C] (Und.) branded on the hand (cf. LETTERED). [SE character, a brand, a stamp]

charas/churus n. [1960s+] (drugs) hashish. [Hind. charas, hashish]

charcoal n. [19C] (US) a derog. term for a Black person; thus charcoal blossom, a young Black woman; charcoal lily, a very dark Black boy (cf. CHEESE n.[6]; COAL n.[2]).

charcoal tart n. [1900s+] (Aus.) a thin, unleavened loaf baked in the embers.

charge n.[1] [20C] (Irish) 1 a loud-mouthed woman. 2 a lazy, loutish person. [Anglo-Norman kark, a burden]

charge n.[2] 1 [1920s+] drugs in general, spec. marijuana. 2 [1920s+] the effect of a given drug. 3 [1920s+] an injection of a narcotic drug. 4 [1950s+] a thrill, a feeling of excitement or satisfaction; thus get a charge out of. 5 [1960s+] (Aus.) a glass of liquor, esp. spirits. [SE charge, an accumulation of electricity]

charge v. (US) 1 [late 19C] to have a riotously good time. 2 [1930s+] to hold up (a bank) at gunpoint. 3 [1960s] to arouse sexually. [SE charge, to attack]

charged/charged up adj. 1 [19C+] intoxicated by alcohol. 2 [20C] intoxicated by drugs. [CHARGE n.[2]]

charge it to the dust and let the rain settle it phr. [20C] (US) a phr. by which the speaker rejects all responsibility for a given action; actual cash debt may or may not be involved.

charge someone off v. [20C] (US) 1 to end a relationship. 2 to ignore someone one knows well. [SE charge at, i.e. to push someone away]

charge the rod, to phr. [1990s] to masturbate. [the rubbing of a rod to produce an electrical charge]

charging n. [1960s+] (US Black) an instance of outwitting,

insult or verbal humiliation. [SE charge, to command, to exhort authoritatively]

Charing Cross n. [mid-19C] a horse. [rhy. sl.; note Cockney pron. 'crorss']

chariot n. 1 [mid–late 19C] an omnibus. 2 [1940s–50s] a motorcar.

chariot-buzzer n. [mid-19C] a pickpocket who specializes in the passengers of an omnibus. [CHARIOT n. (1) + BUZZER n.[1]]

charity n. [1960s+] (Aus. gay) a promiscuous man, who 'gives it away for free' (cf. ASS PEDDLER).

charity ass n. [1920s–50s] a woman who 'gives it away'; thus sexual intercourse for which no payment is expected. [SE charity + ARSE n.[1] (2)]

charity bob n. [late 19C–1900s] a form of quick curtsy peculiar to charity-school girls.

charity case n. [1960s+] an older sexual partner whose needs are gratified by a young boy or girl out of kindness rather than desire.

charity chippy n. [1930s+] an amateur prostitute or a professional who undercuts her peers. [SE charity + CHIPPIE n.[2]]

charity cunt n. [1940s+] (US) a promiscuous woman who 'gives it away for free' (cf. CHARITY DAME; CHARITY GIRL; CHARITY WORKER). [SE charity + CUNT n.[1] (1)]

charity dame n. [1930s+] (Aus.) a promiscuous woman who 'gives it away for free' (cf. CHARITY CUNT). [SE charity + DAME]

charity fuck n. [1960s+] an act of sexual intercourse engaged in out of pity (cf. MERCY FUCK). [SE charity + FUCK n.[1] (1)]

charity girl n. [20C] (US) a promiscuous woman who 'gives it away for free' (cf. CHARITY CUNT).

charity moll n. [1940s+] (Aus.) an amateur prostitute, or a professional who undercuts her peers (cf. CHARITY CHIPPY). [SE charity + MOLL n. (1)]

charity worker n. [1940s+] (US) a promiscuous woman who 'gives it away for free' (cf. CHARITY CUNT).

charles n.[1] [mid-19C+] (US Black) a derog. term for a White man (cf. MR CHARLIE). [BOSS CHARLEY]

charles n.[2] [1960s+] (drugs) cocaine (cf. C n.[2]; CHARLIE n.[7]). [initial letter]

charles james n. [late 19C–1930s] 1 a theatrical box. 2 (hunting) a fox. [rhy. sl. The ref. is to the politician Charles James Fox (1749–1806)]

charley/charlie n.[1] 1 [late 17C–mid-19C] a watchman, a beadle. 2 [mid-19C] a gold watch. [punning cant]

charley/charlie n.[2] [1920s–60s] (US Black) $1.

charley n.[3] see CHARLIE n.[7].

Charley n.[4] [1950s–60s] a general term for anyone whose name has been forgotten (cf. SAM n.[3]). [generic]

charley/charlie n.[5] [1960s] (US) the penis (cf. ABRAHAM).

charley/charlie n.[6] [1960s+] (US Black) a derog. term for a White man (cf. BOSS CHARLEY; MR CHARLIE). [CHARLES n.[1]]

Charley Bates's farm/garden n. [late 19C] Coldbath Fields Prison, in Clerkenwell, London; thus feed the chickens on Charley Bates's farm, to be placed on the treadmill. [the name of a notorious warder]

charley brady n. [late 19C–1940s] a hat. [rhy. sl. charley brady = CADY]

Charley Dilke n. [late 19C–1930s] milk. [rhy. sl. The ref. is to the radical politician Sir Charles Dilke (1843–1911)]

charley frisky n. [mid-19C–1900s] whisky. [rhy. sl.]

charley horse n. [late 19C+] (orig. US) a cramp or sudden stiffness in the leg. [orig. baseball use c.1887]

charley howard n. [1930s] a coward. [rhy. sl.]

charley-ken n. [early 19C] (cant) a watchman's box. [CHARLEY n.[1] (1) + KEN n.[1]]

charley lancaster n. [mid-19C] a handkerchief. [rhy. sl. charley lancaster = 'handkercher']

charley-man *n.* [late 17C–mid-19C] a watchman, a beadle (cf. CHARLEY n.[1]).

charley mason *n.* [late 19C+] a basin. [rhy. sl.]

charley-/charlie-pitcher *n.* [mid-19C] **1** a gambler. **2** one who runs a FIND THE LADY or THREE-CARD MONTE card-game. [? OE *ceorl* or SE *churl*, a peasant; however, *charley* may simply be a generic term for the peasant to whom he 'pitches the tale', or a euph. for the derisive *churl*]

charley pope *n.* [1910s] soap. [rhy. sl.]

charley randy *n.* [mid-19C–1900s] brandy. [rhy. sl.]

charley's fiddle *n.* [early–mid-19C] a watchman's rattle. [CHARLEY n.[1] (1)]

charley sheard *n.* [1970s+] a beard. [rhy. sl.]

charley skinner *n.* [mid-19C–1900s] dinner (cf. JIMMY SKINNER; LILLEY AND SKINNER; NED SKINNER). [rhy. sl.]

charley wiggins *n.* [late 19C+] (orig. theatrical) lodgings. [rhy. sl. *charley wiggins* = DIGGINGS]

charlie *n.*[1] *see* CHARLEY n.[1].

charlie *n.*[2] [mid-19C] a small, pointed beard. [that worn by King *Charles I* (r.1625–49)]

charlie *n.*[3] [mid–late 19C] a fox. [CHARLES JAMES n. (2)]

charlie *n.*[4] [mid-19C+] a hunchback. [who supposedly carried his 'little brother Charlie' on his back. Note army jargon *charlie*, a pack]

charlie *n.*[5] [20C] a chamberpot.

charlie *n.*[6] [20C] (US) a generic term for a person, usu. a man (cf. JOHN n.[1]; MAC n.[1]).

charlie/charley *n.*[7] [1920s+] (drugs) **1** cocaine; thus *charlie coke*, *charlie girl* (cf. GIRL n.[3]; HENRY n.[3]). **2** a heavy user of cocaine. [the same initial letter but note US Black use MR CHARLIE, a White man; cocaine, too, is white]

charlie *n.*[8] *see* CHARLEY n.[2].

charlie *n.*[9] [1930s+] a ponce. [abbr. CHARLIE RONCE]

charlie *n.*[10] [1940s+] a fool, esp. in phr. *proper charlie*, *right charlie*. [rhy. sl. *charlie hunt* = CUNT n.[1] (1). Given the popularity of the term among otherwise 'clean' radio and TV comedians, one must assume their (and their audiences') ignorance of the ety.]

charlie *n.*[11] [1940s+] **1** (Aus.) a woman. **2** (Aus.) a prostitute. **3** (Aus.) a lesbian. **4** a male homosexual. [CHARLIE WHEELER, but Simes adds: '"Charlie" was an old Eng. name for nightwatchman: this may be the origin']

charlie *n.*[12] *see* CHARLEY n.[5].

charlie *n.*[13] *see* CHARLEY n.[6].

charlie *adj.*[1] **1** [early 19C+] wary. **2** [1930s+] cowardly; thus *turn charlie*, to become frightened. [CHARLEY n.[1] (1)]

charlie *adj.*[2] [1980s+] (society) flashy, ostentatious, not socially acceptable. [? image of *Charlie* as a working-class name, except that *Charles* is stereotypically upper-class]

charlie blow *n.* [1970s] (US drugs) cocaine. [CHARLIE n.[7] + BLOW n.[7] (2)]

charlie-boy *n.* [late 19C–1910s] (US) an effeminate young man. [CHARLIE n.[10]]

charlie britt *n.* [20C] (Aus.) a fit; thus *throw a Charlie*, have a fit. [rhy. sl.]

charlie chan *n.* [1930s] (US) an Asian man. [the fictional Chinese detective *Charlie Chan*, created in 1925 by Earl Derr Biggers]

charlie chase *n.* [20C] (Aus.) a race; thus *not in the charlie*, not worthy of consideration. [rhy. sl.]

charlie freer *n.* [late 19C–1900s] beer. [rhy. sl.]

charlie goon/goons *n.* [1930s+] (US Black) a policeman, the police. [MR CHARLIE + GOON n.[1]]

charlie nebs *n.* [1960s] (US Black) the police (cf. HARMAN). [MR CHARLIE + SE *neb*, a beak, although *neb* may be mispron. for NAB n.[2]]

charlie-on-the-spot *n.* [late 19C+] (US) a reliable or punctual person. [var. on JOHNNY-ON-THE-SPOT]

charlie-pitcher *see* CHARLEY-PITCHER.

charlie/colonel prescott/prescott *n.* [mid–late 19C] a waistcoat (cf. JIMMY PRESCOTT). [rhy. sl.]

charlie ronce *n.* [1930s+] a ponce (cf. ALPHONSE n.[2]; JOE RONCE). [rhy. sl.]

charlies *n.* [mid-19C+] the female breasts. [? Aus. rhy. sl. CHARLIE WHEELER = SHEILA = a woman, and thus her distinguishing characteristics. Ware attributes the term to the predilection of King Charles II (r.1660–85) for décolletage, which would seem fanciful but for the date, which well precedes Aus. use. E.P. suggests Rom. *chara*, to touch, to meddle with]

charlie's dead! *excl.* [1950s+] (school) your slip is showing! (cf. DADDY LOVES YOU BEST; JOHN IS DEAD; MONDAY COMES BEFORE SUNDAY; MRS WHITE IS OUT OF JAIL; YOUR BOYFRIEND'S THINKING OF YOU).

Charlie Smirke *n.* [1970s+] a fool. [rhy. sl. *Charlie Smirke* = BERK. Smirke was a jockey in 1922–53, claiming three Derbies and the St Leger among other successes]

charlie taylor *n.* [1930s–50s] (US, Southwest) syrup or molasses into which bacon or ham fat has been poured. [? anecdotal]

charlie wheeler *n.* [1940s+] (Aus.) **1** a woman. **2** in pl. *charlie wheelers*, the female breasts (cf. CHARLIES). [rhy. sl.; ult. proper name *Charles Wheeler* (1881–1977), a painter specializing in nudes]

charlie whitehouse *n.* [20C] (US) a chamberpot (cf. CHARLIE n.[5]). [the whiteness of the porcelain utensil]

charlotte *n.* [1970s] (US drugs) cocaine. ['feminized' version of CHARLIE n.[7]]

charm *n.* [16C–late 18C] a pick-lock. [it 'charms' locks open]

charmer *n.* [late 19C+] an attractive young woman.

charming! *excl.* [1960s+] an excl. used as a response to a statement that the speaker feels to be rude, crude or otherwise unacceptable, sometimes as *charming, I'm sure.*

charming mottle *n.* [late 19C–1900s] (Aus.) a bottle. [rhy. sl.]

charming wife *n.* [20C] a knife. [rhy. sl.]

charms *n.*[1] [19C] (US) money. [the effect of money on otherwise intractable situations]

charms *n.*[2] [mid-19C+] the female breasts, esp. in phr. *flash one's charms*, to reveal one's breasts. [euph.; prior 18C–early 19C use is SE]

charm the serpent/snake, to *phr.* [1990s] to masturbate. [a snake-charmer traditionally makes the snake rise into the air]

char ou *see* CHAAR OU.

charper *v.* [mid-19C+] (Ling. Fr./Polari) to search; thus *charpering omi*, a policeman, *charpering carsey*, a police station. [Ital. *cercare*, to seek]

charra *n.* [1970s+] (S.Afr.) a derog. mode of address to an Indian. [CHAAR]

charrshom/chershom *n.* [18C+] (tinker) a crown, a 5-shilling (25p) coin. [Shelta]

charter the bar, to *phr.* [20C] to buy drinks for everyone in a bar or public house. [SE *charter*, to hire]

charver/charva *n.* [late 19C+] sexual intercourse; thus *bona palone for a charver*, an 'easy lay', a 'good-time girl' (lit. 'a good girl for a fuck'). [Polari *chauvering*, sexual intercourse itself; ? linked to SE *chafe*/Fr. *chauffer*, to heat up (cf. HOT adj.[1]) or Sp. *chava*/Polari, a girl]

charver/charva *v.* [late 19C+] **1** to have sexual intercourse. **2** (market) to ruin, to spoil or interfere in another's business (cf. FUCK UP v.[1]). [CHARVER n.]

charvered *adj.* [late 19C+] ruined, wrecked, exhausted (cf. FUCKED). [fig. use of CHARVER v.]

charvering/chauvering donna/dona/doner *n.* [mid–late 19C] (Ling. Fr./Polari) a prostitute. [CHARVER v. + DONA]

chase *v.*[1] (US) **1** [late 19C–1900s] to run off, to leave. **2** [1970s+] to pursue women, esp. as an adulterer.

chase *v.*[2] [1970s+] (drugs) **1** to smoke cocaine. **2** to smoke marijuana. [? misuse of CHASE THE DRAGON which strictly refers to heroin]

chase a piece *see* BEG A PIECE.

chase a rabbit, to *phr.* [20C] (US) euph. for to go to the lavatory.

chase cheers *v.* [1930s+] (Aus.) to curry favour with the masses; thus *cheer-chaser*, a toady to popular opinion, *cheer-chasing*, taking a deliberately populist stand.

chaser *n.*[1] [late 19C+] (orig. US) a glass of water or beer taken after a shot of spirits. [1940s+ use is SE]

chaser *n.*[2] **1** [late 19C+] (mainly US) a womanizer. **2** [1900s] one who runs errands (cf. GOFER). [note SE *woman-chaser* for (1)]

chaser *n.*[3] [1990s] (drugs) a frequent user of crack cocaine. [CHASE v.[2] (2)]

chase the bag, to *phr.* [1960s+] (drugs) to seek out supplies and/or to be addicted to heroin. [SE *chase* + BAG]

chase/rush the can, to *phr.* [1910s–40s] to drink freely at a bar (cf. RUSH THE GROWLER).

chase the dragon, to *phr.* [1960s+] (drugs) to smoke heroin, sucking up the smoke of the drug, which is burned on a piece of kitchen foil. The heated heroin liquefies and flows across the paper, gradually giving off smoke, which is sucked into the smoker's lungs by a tube, also usually made of kitchen foil. [the 'dragon' underlines the Oriental origin of much of the heroin found in the UK]

chase the hares, to *phr.* [20C] to chase women. [a pun on HAIR]

chase the sun, to *phr.* [1940s] (Aus.) to live as a tramp (cf. SUNDOWNER).

chase the sunset, to *phr.* [1910s] (Aus.) to live as a vagrant (cf. SUNDOWNER).

chase the weight/penny weight, to *phr.* [1930s–40s] (Aus.) to prospect for gold.

chase up *v.* [1950s+] **1** to pursue (a matter or person) vigorously with a specific intent, esp. after an earlier unsatisfactory response. **2** to make efforts to find or obtain quickly.

chase-up *n.* [1940s–60s] a car chase.

chase/hunt up a cow, to *phr.* [1950s] (Aus.) of an amorous couple, to search out a secluded spot in the bush in order to have sexual intercourse. [the ideal patch would have been literally used by a sleeping cow, and would thus be pre-warmed]

chasing *n.* [1980s+] (drugs) the smoking of heroin. [CHASE THE DRAGON]

chase the tiger, to *phr.* [1980s+] (drugs) to smoke heroin. [var. on CHASE THE DRAGON]

chasm *n.* [19C] the vagina (cf. ARBOUR).

chasse *n.* [mid-19C–1910s] **1** a cup of coffee that accompanies a shot of spirits, usu. whisky. **2** a liqueur taken after or with coffee. [CHASER n.[1]]

chassé *v.* [mid-19C] (society) to dismiss, to send away. [SE *chassé*, a gliding step, in a quadrille and other dances; it gives the illusion of walking]

chassis *n.*[1] [1920s+] a chaotic, unpleasant, confused state; thus (Irish phr.) *in a terrible state of chassis*, extremely drunk. [a (deliberate) mispron. of SE *chaos* with the final 's' sounded]

chassis *n.*[2] [1930s+] the female figure; thus *classy chassis*, an attractive figure, and thus an attractive woman. [automobile imagery]

chat *n.*[1] **1** [late 17C–late 19C] a louse. **2** [1960s+] (Aus.) a general insult, usu. aimed at an old man, esp. an alcoholic. [19C use mainly Aus.]

chat *n.*[2] **1** [18C] a cat. **2** [19C+] the vagina (cf. CAT n.[10]). [Fr. *chat*, cat]

chat *n.*[3] [early–mid-19C] the truth, the apposite thing, the subject under discussion. [SE *chat*, a conversation, a discussion]

chat *n.*[4] **1** [mid-19C] a house (cf. CHEAT). **2** [mid-16C–18C] the gallows. **3** [mid–late 19C] a thing, an object. **4** [late 19C] a criminal 'job' or undertaking. [CHEAT]

chat *n.*[5] **1** [late 19C] cheek, impudence. **2** [1940s+] verbal skills, fluency, articulacy, the ability to charm a victim with words alone. **3** [1950s+] terminology, a special language, jargon.

chat *n.*[6] [1930s] (Irish) methylated spirits, as drunk by alcoholics. [its effects, but note CHAT n.[1] (2)]

chat *n.*[7] [1950s] (W.I.) a male gossip. [CHAT-CHAT]

chat *v.*[1] [late 17C–19C] to search for lice. [CHAT n.[1] (1)]

chat/chat up *v.*[2] **1** [late 19C+] to attempt the first, verbal stages of seduction (cf. CHAT DOWN). **2** [20C] (W.I.) to gossip, to talk familiarly. **3** [20C] (W.I.) to trick verbally, to 'con'. **4** [1970s+] to interview. [fig. uses of SE]

chat-chat *v.* [1950s+] (W.I.) to gossip (cf. MISS LASHEY). [SE *chat* + redup.]

chat down *v.* [1950s+] (W.I.) to make one's first advances to a young woman or man in the hope of eventual sexual conquest (cf. CHAT v.[2]).

chateau cardboard *n.* [1980s+] (S.Afr.) wine sold in 2.5 or 5 litre (4½–9 pint) containers, placed in a cardboard box. [play on Fr. *chateau*; the labels on bottles of Bordeaux wine always indicate the *chateau* at which they are produced]

chateaued *adj.* [1980s+] (society) very drunk on wine (cf. ALED UP). [puns on SE *shattered* and Fr. *chateau*]

chates *see* CHATS n.[1].

chatham and dover, to *phr.* [late 19C] to stop, to cease. [rhy. sl. *chatham and dover* = (give) over]

chat someone's name, to *phr.* [1950s+] (W.I./Jam.) to gossip maliciously about an absent third party (cf. POUND SOMEONE'S NAME). [CHAT v.[2] (2)]

chats/chates/chattes/cheats *n.*[1] [16C–early 19C] (Und.) the gallows (cf. TREYNING CHEAT). [AS *cheat*, a thing; the gallows, signifying death, is in this usage taboo]

chats/chatts *n.*[2] [late 17C–early 19C] lice (cf. BLACK CATTLE). [SE *chattels*, moveable property, typically livestock, 'lice being the chief livestock of beggars, gypsies, and the rest of the canting crew' (Grose, 1785)]

chatta *n.* [late 18C–1930s] an umbrella. [Skrt. *chhatra*, an umbrella]

chatter-basket *n.* [mid-19C] a small, noisy child; synons. incl. *chatter-bladder*, *chatter-cart* and (US) *chatter-bones*.

chatterbox *n.* [1930s–40s] (US) **1** a record player. **2** a telephone. **3** a car radio; thus *chatterbox and fish pole*, a radio and aerial.

chatter-broth *n.* [late 18C–early 19C] tea (cf. PRATTLE-BROTH). [the stereotypical chattering women supposed to gather around the tea-table]

chatterer/chattering *n.* [19C] a blow to the mouth that makes the recipient's teeth chatter. [fig. use of SE and pun on *shattering*]

chatterers *n.* [early 19C–1900s] the teeth.

chattergun *n.* [1930s+] a machinegun or sub-machinegun. [its noise]

chattermag *n.* **1** [late 19C] chatter, gossip. **2** [20C] a gossip, a chatterbox. [SE *chatter* + MAG n.[2]]

chattermag *v.* [1900s] to chatter. [CHATTERMAG n.]

chattery *n.* [early 19C] (Und.) one or more linen articles. [? they are easily infested by lice (cf. CHATS n.²)]

chattes *see* CHATS n.¹.

chatts *n.*¹ *see* CHATS n.².

chatts *n.*² [mid-19C] dice. [they 'chatter' as they hit the table]

chatty *n.*¹ [mid-18C–1950s] a pot. [Tamil *shatti*, Telegu *chatti*, a pot; orig. Anglo-Ind. but spread across the British Empire]

chatty *n.*² [19C] a spoon. [Millbank Prison use *chattry feeder*]

chatty *n.*³ [19C] a filthy man. [CHATTY adj.; abbr. of *chatty dosser*, a louse-ridden tramp]

chatty *adj.* [early 19C–1900s] lousy, infested; thus *chatty doss*, a louse-infested bed. [CHATS/CHATTS n.²]

chatty-chatty *n.* [1950s+] (W.I.) a habitual gossip. [SE *chatty*, talkative + redup.]

chat up *see* CHAT v.².

chauki *see* CHOKEY.

chaunt *v. see* CHANT v.

chaunted *see* CHANTED.

chaunter *see* CHANTER.

chaunter cove *n.* [mid–late 19C] a journalist, a reporter. [CHANT n. (5) + COVE]

chaunter cull *n.* [mid-18C–late 19C] a composer of ballads, broadsides and similar productions for the use of street singers and versifiers. [CHANTER n. (2) + CULL n.¹ (4)]

chaunter upon the leer *n.* [mid-19C] an advertiser. [CHANT n. (4) + LEER]

chaunting *see* CHANTING.

chaunting-cove *n.* [19C] a dishonest horse-dealer. [CHANTER n. (1) + COVE]

chaunting-lay *n.* [mid–late 19C] street-singing. [CHANT v.(2) + LAY n.⁴ (1)]

chaunt the play, to *phr.* [mid–late 19C] (Und.) to explain the criminal lifestyle and methods. [fig. use of CHANT v. (2)]

chauverer-/chauvering-cove *n.* [mid-19C] a womanizer, a promiscuous man. [CHARVER v. + COVE]

chauvering donna *see* CHARVERING DONNA.

chauvering moll *n.* [mid–late 19C] a prostitute. [CHARVER v. + MOLL]

chavalas *n.* [1960s+] (US) **1** women. **2** men, used in a derog. way. [Sp. *chava*, a girl]

chavy/chavvy *n.* **1** [mid–late 19C] (Polari) a child. **2** [late 19C+] a form of address to a man, e.g. *wotcher chavvy*. [Rom. *chavi*, a child]

chaw *n.*¹ **1** [mid–late 19C] a yokel. **2** [19C–1930s] (US) an Irish immigrant (cf. CHAW-BACON). [? dial. *chaw*, chew, as in chewing tobacco]

chaw *n.*² **1** [mid–late 19C] (US campus) a trick, a prank. **2** [late 19C–1920s] a conversation (cf. JAW n.]. [fig. uses of dial. *chaw*, to chew]

chaw *v.* (US) **1** [mid–late 19C] to mangle, to defeat, to kill. **2** [mid-19C–1900s] (campus) to trick, to hoax. **3** [late 19C–1900s] used in oaths, e.g. *chaw me up if...* . [fig. uses of dial. *chaw*, to chew]

chaw-bacon *n.* [early 19C+] a rustic, a peasant. [SE *chew bacon*]

chawed *adj.* (US) **1** [mid-19C+] completely overcome by emotion, e.g. embarrassment, surprise, exhaustion. **2** [1940s–50s] angry. [CHAW v.]

chaw-mouth *n.* [late 19C+] (US) **1** a talkative person (cf. FLANNEL MOUTH). **2** a derog. term for an Irishman. [*chaw* = SE *chew* + *mouth*, the noisy talker 'chews on' his words; (2) f. alleged talkativeness of the Irish]

chaws *n.* [mid-19C] sexual intercourse. [? CHARVER]

chaw up *v.* [mid-19C] (US) to get the better of, to surpass, to destroy; thus *chawed up*, totally defeated. [ext. of CHAW v.(1)]

chay *n.* [mid-18C–mid-19C] a chaise or light carriage. [pron. 'shay']

chazerai *n.* [20C] a 'pigsty', a mess. [Yid./Heb. *chazer*, a pig]

chazerai *adj.* [20C] cheap, worthless, rubbish. [CHAZERAI n.]

chbye! *excl.* [1980s+] (US campus) goodbye (cf. CHELLO!). [joc. mispron.]

C-head *n.* [1980s+] (drugs) a cocaine user (cf. ACID-HEAD). [C n.² + sfx. -HEAD (2)]

cheap *adj.* [late 19C–1920s] **1** out of sorts, feeling ill. **2** mean, miserly, grasping.

cheap and cheerful *phr.* [1950s+] a phr. used either to deprecate one's own lapses in taste or to criticize the taste of others.

cheap and nasty *n.* [20C] (Aus.) a meat pasty. [rhy. sl.]

cheap as dirt *phr.* [early 19C+] extremely cheap.

cheap basing *n.* [1980s+] (drugs) crack cocaine. [SE *cheap* + FREEBASE v.]

cheap charlie *n.* **1** [late 19C–1900s] (US) a candy store. **2** [20C] a mean person. [SE *cheap* + CHARLIE n.⁶]

cheapie *n.* **1** [late 19C+] anything of little value or poor quality. **2** [1940s+] anything, e.g. a film or play, produced on a low budget. **3** [1970s+] (orig. US) a mean person. [SE *cheap* + sfx. -ie]

cheap john *n.*¹ **1** [mid-19C+] (US) a pawnbroker. **2** [mid-19C+] a pawnshop. **3** [mid-19C+] a shop selling cheap goods. **4** [mid-19C+] cheap goods, items considered poor taste. [SE *cheap* + JOHN n.¹ (1)]

cheap john *n.*² [20C] a mean, miserly person (cf. CHEAP CHARLIE). [CHEAP adj. (2) + JOHN n.¹ (1)]

cheap johnny *n.* [mid-19C] (US) a seller of cheap goods (cf. CHEAP CHARLIE). [SE *cheap* + JOHNNIE n.²]

cheapness *n.* [late 19C–1920s] a hangover (cf. FEEL CHEAP).

cheapo *n.* [1970s+] **1** a mean person. **2** something that is produced cheaply (cf. CHEAPIE). [SE *cheap* + sfx. -o]

cheapo/cheapo-cheapo *adj.* [1960s+] cheap, produced cheaply; thus often also of inferior quality. [CHEAPO n. (2) + redup.]

cheap shot *n.* [1970s+] (US) a wounding, sneering remark; thus *cheap-shot artist*, one who habitually makes such remarks. [SE *cheap*, in sense of (1) costing little effort, (2) being vulgar, in poor taste + fig. use of *shot*]

cheap shotter *n.* [1970s+] (US) one who makes wounding, cruel remarks. [CHEAP SHOT]

cheapskate *n.* (orig. US) **1** [late 19C+] an unpleasant person. **2** [20C] a mean, ungenerous person. [SE *cheap* + SKATE n.² (2); orig. 'cheap skate', later use is one word]

cheapskate *adj.* [1920s–30s] (orig. US) mean, stingy. [CHEAPSKATE n.]

cheapwad *n.* [1970s] (US) a mean, ungenerous person (cf. CHEAPSKATE n.). [SE *cheap* + (TIGHT)WAD]

cheat/chete *n.* [mid-16C–mid-18C] **1** a thing, usu. in combs. (cf. BELLY CHEAT; GRUNTING-CHEAT; PRATTLING-CHEAT; QUACKING CHEAT; SMELLING-CHEAT). **2** [16C–19C] the gallows (cf. HANGING CHEAT; TREYNING CHEAT). **3** [late 16C] a stolen thing. [AS *chete*, a thing]

cheat/cheat on *v.* [1930s+] (orig. US) to betray one's partner or spouse; thus to commit adultery.

cheater *n.* (US) **1** [1920s] an act of adultery. **2** [1920s+] an adulterer. **3** [1940s] a condom. **4** [1940s+] anything that makes a task simpler, provides safety, gives one advantage etc. [fig. uses of SE]

cheaters *n.*¹ [16C] crooked dice.

cheaters *n.*² **1** [1910s+] close-fitting men's underpants, usu. with elastic legbands. **2** [1920s+] (orig. US) glasses, spectacles, esp. dark glasses. **3** [1920s+] (orig. US) false teeth. **4** [1940s+] pads which are placed in a brassiere (cf. FALSIES). [they help the male genitals, eyes, teeth or female breasts *cheat* their own inadequacies]

cheating law n. [16C] (Und.) crooked dice play or card-sharping (cf. FIGGING LAW; HIGH LAW; SACKING LAW). [SE *cheating* + LAW]

cheat on see CHEAT v.

cheators n. [16C] (Und.) those who play crooked dice (cf. CHEATING LAW). [SE *cheat*]

cheats n.[1] [16C] money won by dice cheats (cf. CHEATING LAW).

cheats n.[2] see CHATS n.[1].

cheats n.[3] **1** [late 17C] an ostentatious, fur-backed waistcoat. **2** [late 17C–early 19C] sham cuffs or wristbands.

cheat sheet n. [1950s+] (US campus) notes smuggled into an examination.

cheat-/cheating-stick n. [1930s–50s] (US campus) a slide-rule.

cheat the worms, to phr. [late 19C] to recover from a serious illness. [the worms are those encountered in the grave]

cheba see CHEEB.

chebs n. [1990s] the female breasts. [CHABOBS]

checaco/chechaco see CHEECHAKO.

che-che n. [20C] (W.I.) **1** a poor White (cf. BACKRA JOHNNY). **2** a person with a light complexion and freckles. **3** a cowardly, ugly boy. [FRENCHIE n.[2] (4) OR RED CHENKE]

check n.[1] (US) **1** [late 19C] money. **2** [1920s–60s] $1. [SE *check*, a counter]

check n.[2] (drugs) **1** [1920s–40s] a measure of a drug, usu. 28g (1oz) in a folded packet (cf. BINDLE). **2** [1980s+] one's personal supply of drugs. [SE *check*, a token, a ticket]

check v.[1] (orig. US) **1** [1940s+] to look over, to inspect (cf. CHECK OUT v.[1]). **2** [1940s+] to criticize, to attack verbally.

check/check to v.[2] **1** [1960s+] (orig. US) to meet, to chat with, esp. in phr. *check you later*, see you later. **2** [1980s+] (W.I./UK Black teen) to see someone, to have a (usu. sexual) relationship with someone; thus *checking*, having a relationship. **3** [1980s+] (W.I./UK Black teen) to visit or call on someone.

check! excl. [1920s+] (orig. US) general term of affirmation, OK, that's right, everything's in order.

check a/one's trap, to phr. [1990s] (US Black) **1** to monitor a given situation, to oversee one's business, esp. when it is illicit. **2** to spend time with a lover, esp. one with whom one is having an affair. [play on SE *check one's trap*, but note CHECK v.[1]]

checkerboard n. [20C] (US) a work crew or work gang composed of Black and White people.

checker, the n. [mid-19C–1910s] (US) the ideal, the very thing (cf. CHEESE n.[1]). [that which *checks* everything else]

check for v. [1990s] (W.I./UK Black teen) to hate or dislike someone or something, to avoid, to resist becoming involved with. [CHECK v.[1] (2)]

check in v. (US) **1** [20C] to die (cf. CASH IN ONE'S CHECKS; CHECK OUT v.[2]). **2** [20C] to go to bed. **3** [20C] (Und.) to move from the general prison population into protective solitary confinement (cf. GET ONESELF A BANNER). **4** [1970s] (campus) to say hello. [SE *check in*, to register (i.e. at a hotel)]

check it in phr. [1990s] (US Black) imper. used by a mugger to his or her victim, when demanding that they hand over his money, valuables etc. [the idea of checking possessions into a left-luggage locker]

check it out, to phr. [1980s+] (US campus) to look for a partner for romance or sex. [CHECK OUT v.[1]]

check one's nerves, to phr. [1940s] (US Black) to take a grip on oneself, to control one's emotions. [SE *check*, to stop + *nerves*]

check one's oil, to phr. **1** [1930s+] (US) to have sexual intercourse. **2** [1990s] to masturbate (cf. ADJUST ONE'S SET).

check one's trap see CHECK A TRAP.

check out v.[1] [1950s+] **1** (orig. US) to look over, to sum up,

esp. as excl. *check this out!* **4** (W.I.) of a young man, to date a woman regularly and/or visit her home.

check out v.[2] **1** [1950s+] (orig. US) to die. **2** [1950s+] (orig. US) to leave. **3** [1970s] to kill. [SE *check out*, to sign out of a hotel, office etc]

checks! excl. [1950s+] (US, usu. juv.) a claim, esp. a claim of first rights to something (cf. DUCKS!; KEEPSIES; KINGS!).

check someone's chin, to phr. [1990s] (US Black teen) to hit on the jaw; such a blow is a *chin-check*. [CHECK v.[1] (2)]

check the war! excl. [1940s] (US Black) stop fighting! [SE *check*, to stop, to cease + *war*]

check up on v. [1930s+] to eye in a sexual manner (cf. CHECK OUT v.[1]).

check you later phr. [1980s+] see you later, goodbye. [CHECK v.[2] (1)]

check you on the flip side phr. [1970s] (US campus) goodbye. [CHECK v.[2] (1)]

check you/check you out phr. (orig. US Black) goodbye, see you later.

check yourself! excl. [1960s] (US Black) do what you're told! [SE *check*, to stop + *yourself*]

cheddar n. [1990s] (US campus) someone who is socially unacceptable, who does not fit in (cf. CAPTAIN CHEDDAR; CHEESEBALL; CHEESEMAN; CHEESE WHIZ; FROMAGE; GOUDA, GOUDA, GOUDA; VELVEETA). [CHEESY adj.]

cheder n. [20C] a prison cell. [Yid. *cheder*, a small room, a study; usu. used as a schoolroom for the teaching of religion]

cheeb/cheeba/cheba n. [1970s+] (US drugs) marijuana (cf. SHEEBA). [Mex. Sp.]

cheechako/checaco/chechaco/cheechaker n. [late 19C+] a newcomer, a novice, esp. a newly arrived immigrant in the mining districts of northwestern North America. [Chinook jargon *chee*, new + *chako*, to come; thus 'newcomer']

chee-chee/chi-chi n. [mid-19C+] a derog. term for a half-caste or Eurasian (the child of an English father and Indian mother). [south Indian excl. *chi!*, fie! or nonsense! or as onomat. representation of the accent. Yule & Burnell note, however: 'there are many well-educated East Indians who are quite free from this mincing accent.' Ironically, the accent appears to have been that expressly taught at the convents and Christian Brothers' schools set up by the Raj to educate the children of such unions. Note Du. *lip-lap*, the equivalent term for Dutch-Javans]

chee-chee/chi-chi adj. [mid-19C+] having the characteristics of the Eurasian stereotype, esp. the supposed mincing pronunciation. [CHEE-CHEE n.]

cheek n. [early 19C+] **1** verbal insolence. **2** audacity, impudence, esp. in phr. *have the cheek* (to), to dare, to have the nerve (to do something). [the movement of the *cheeks* when speaking]

cheek v.[1] [early 19C+] to address in an impudent or insolent manner. [CHEEK n.]

cheek v.[2] [1980s+] (drugs) to smuggle drugs by placing them in the rectum or mouth. [SE *cheek*, either of the face, or synon. with buttocks]

cheeker n. [mid-19C] an impudent, shameless person. [CHEEK v.]

cheekiness n. [mid-19C+] audacity, effrontery, impudence.

cheekish adj. [mid-19C] impudent.

cheek it/cheek it out v. [mid–late 19C] to face down, to brazen out. [CHEEK v.]

cheeks n.[1] [early 17C, 1920s+] the posterior, the buttocks (cf. BLIND CHEEKS; CHEEKS NEAR CUNNYBOROUGH; TWO FAT CHEEKS AND NE'ER A NOSE). [the *OED* cites a one-off use in 1660, the term is then lost (at least from print) until James Joyce's *Ulysses* (1922)]

cheeks n.[2] [late 18C–late 19C] an imaginary person, usu. used in a rude reply to an irritating question. [note synon. 19C naut. jargon *Cheeks the Marine*. In both cases the phr. refers to the buttocks and equates with ASK MY ARSE!]

cheeks! *excl.* [mid–late 19C] a coarse and insulting excl. (cf. ASK MY ARSE!; CHEEKS NEAR CUNNYBOROUGH).

cheeks and ears *n.* [early 17C] a form of head-dress, briefly in fashion. [? it covered them all]

cheeks near cunnyborough *phr.* [mid-18C–early 19C] a coarse rejoinder to what the speaker (invariably a woman) categorizes as a stupid question (cf. ASK MY ARSE!). [CHEEKS n.[1] + CUNNY]

cheeky *adj.* [mid-19C+] impudent, esp. in the context of a younger person failing to respect their elder. [CHEEK n. (2)]

cheeky-arsed *adj.* [20C] rude, impudent. [CHEEKY + ARSE n.[3]]

cheeky possum *n.* [1930s+] (Aus.) an impudent (young) person. [CHEEKY + POSSUM n. (3)]

cheena *n.* [1990s] (US teen) a woman. [? Sp.]

cheeo *n.* [1970s+] (drugs) marijuana seeds, which are chewed. [SE *chew*]

cheep *n.* [1960s+] a sound, a noise, esp. of complaint, usu. in phr. *not a cheep out of*, not a sound from. [SE *cheep*, a faint, shrill sound, esp. of a young bird]

cheerer *n.* [19C] a revivifying glass of alcohol (cf. ALLEVIATOR). [late 18C Scot. use]

cheerful earful *n.* [1940s+] (US) unpleasant news. [ironic]

cheerful giver *n.* [20C] the human liver (cf. BOW AND QUIVER). [rhy. sl.]

cheeri! *excl.* [1930s+] (N.Z.) goodbye. [CHEERIO!]

cheeribye! *excl.* [1940s+] goodbye. [CHEERIO!]

cheerio *n.* [1960s] (N.Z.) a small sausage, like a frankfurter. [? *cheers*, a toast. These sausages are the sort that would be served as a snack with drinks]

cheerio *adj.* **1** [1910s–30s] cheerful, merry. **2** [1930s+] (S.Afr.) tipsy, slightly drunk. [CHEERS!, the toast that precedes that drunkenness]

cheerio!/cheeri-ho! *excl.* [1910s+] **1** goodbye. **2** a toast (cf. CHEERS!).

cheerioski! *excl.* [1920s–30s] goodbye. [CHEERIO! + 'Russian' sfx. *-ski*]

cheers! *excl.* **1** [1910s+] one of the most common toasts before drinking. **2** [1960s+] goodbye (cf. CHEERIO!). **3** [1970s+] thank-you.

cheery *adj.* [17C] excellent, first-rate.

cheese, the *n.*[1] **1** [early-19C+] the best (of a given type or style), the superlative (cf. BIG CHEESE; CHESHIRE; STILTON). **2** [mid-19C+] just what is wanted. **3** [1900s–20s] an admirable person, esp. as *the real cheese*. **4** [1900s+] an important or influential person, the boss. [Persian and Urdu *chiz*, thing. 'The expression used to be common among Anglo-Indians, e.g. "My new Arab is the real *chiz*", i.e. the real thing.' *Yule and Burnell*. Note Charles Kingsley's punning nonce-word *casein*, the real thing, f. SE *casein*, the basic ingredient of cheese]

cheese *n.*[2] [mid-19C+] **1** the smegma that accumulates around the uncircumcised penis (cf. COCK CHEESE; FUMUNDA CHEESE; HEADCHEESE n.[1]; MONTEREY JACK; PECKER CHEESE). **2** [1920s+] (US) secretions found between the toes. [resemblance and smell of over-ripe cheese]

cheese *n.*[3] **1** [late 19C+] an unpleasant, incompetent, stupid person, usu. ext. as *big cheese, old cheese, piece of cheese, plate of cheese, poor cheese* etc. **2** [1950s] (US) nonsense. **3** [1980s+] (US campus) something out-of-date (cf. BUTTER adj.). **4** [1980s+] (US campus) someone or something unattractive, unappealing, undesirable. [CHEESY adj.[3]]

cheese *n.*[4] [late 19C] (US) one's affair, one's concern. [ety. unknown]

cheese *n.*[5] [1950s+] (Aus.) **1** one's girlfriend. **2** (US campus) a

young woman; thus *check the cheese*, watch women pass by. [CHEESE AND KISSES]

cheese *n.*[6] [1970s] (US) a light-skinned Black person (cf. CHARCOAL). [the yellowish colour of many cheeses]

cheese *n.*[7] [1990s] (drugs) crack cocaine. [? the colour]

cheese *n.*[8] [1990s] (US teen) money. [? play on BREAD n.[1] (2)]

cheese *v.*[1] **1** [early 19C–1930s] to stop, to leave off (cf. CHEESE IT!). **2** [late 19C] (US) to disregard, to ignore. [SE *cease*]

cheese *v.*[2] [20C] (US) to play up to, to toady to (cf. EAT CHEESE v.[1]). [CHEESE-EATER]

cheese *v.*[3] [1930s–40s] to smile. [the photographer's demand that one 'say cheese' to produce a smile]

cheese *v.*[4] **1** [1950s+] to break wind (cf. WHO CUT THE CHEESE?). **2** [1950s+] to ejaculate. **3** [1980s+] (US campus) to vomit (cf. CHEW THE CHEESE). [(1) the smell; (2), (3) ext. uses]

cheese! *excl.* [1910s+] (US) euph. for *Jesus!*

cheese and crackers! *excl.* [20C] (US) euph. for *Jesus Christ!*

cheese and crust! *excl.* [late 19C–1920s] euph. for *Jesus Christ!* (cf. CORKSCREW!).

cheese and kisses *n.* [late 19C+] one's wife. [rhy. sl. *cheese and kisses* = MISSUS. Now mainly Aus. and usu. abbr. to *cheese*]

cheeseball *n.* [1990s] (US campus) someone or something unattractive, unappealing, undesirable or not attuned to group standards (cf. CHEDDAR). [CHEES(Y) adj.[3] + (*sleaze*)*ball* see SLEAZEBAG]

cheesebox *n.* [1930s] (US) a run-down, dilapidated vehicle.

cheesecake *n.*[1] [1930s+] (orig. US) **1** a pin-up girl (cf. BEEFCAKE). **2** [1930s+] pin-up pictures; thus [1950s] *cheesecaker*, a photographer who specializes in pin-up shots. [? the photographer's call for the woman to 'Say cheese' (cf. CHEESE v.[3]) or f. common equation of foods with attractive women; cf. BANANA n.[2]]

cheesecake *n.*[2] [1930s+] something which is easy or simple, with no problems (cf. DUCK SOUP). [var. on PIECE OF CAKE]

cheese-cutter *n.* **1** [mid-19C] an aquiline nose. **2** [mid–late 19C] a large, square peak on a cap; thus [1990s] a flat cloth cap. [resemblance to a cheese knife]

cheese-cutters *n.* [mid-19C] bandy legs.

cheese dagger/slicer *n.* [1900s–50s] (US) a knife. [note US milit. use *cheese-knife*, a sword]

cheesedick *n.* [1980s+] (US) an obnoxious person. [CHEESE n.[3]/CHEESY adj.[2] + DICK(HEAD)]

cheesed off *adj.* [1940s+] miserable, annoyed, fed up (cf. BRASSED). [? euph. for PISSED OFF; earlier Liverpool excl. *cheese off!*, run away, stop irritating me]

cheese dong *n.* [1980s+] (US campus) a stupid, unpleasant person. [CHEESE n.[2]/CHEESY + DONG n.[2]]

cheese-eater *n.* (US) **1** [late 19C+] a toady, a sycophant. **2** [1950s–60s] an informer (cf. CHEESY RIDER; EAT CHEESE v.[1]). [equation of *cheese* with RAT]

cheesehead *n.* **1** [1910s+] (US) an idiot, a fool. **2** [1960s+] (US teen) a general pej. term, esp. directed at an overly emotional or dramatic person.

cheese it! *excl.* **1** [early-19C+] stop it! **2** [early 19C] (Und.) be off! run away! **3** [mid-19C+] be quiet! [? SE *cease* or f. proverb, *after cheese* (*at the end of a meal*) *comes nothing*. Orig. 19C UK, then Aus. Und. but latterly in general use, esp. juv.]

cheesekop *n.* [1970s+] (S.Afr. Black) a shaven head, lit. 'cheese head' (cf. CHEESEHEAD; KAASKOP). [SE *cheese* + Afk. *kop*, head]

cheeseman *n.* [1980s] (US campus) a socially inept person (cf. CHEDDAR). [CHEESE n.[3] (4)]

cheese off *v.*[1] [1980s+] (US campus) to beg from (cf. CHEESER n.[2]).

cheese off *v.*[2] [1990s] to masturbate. [CHEESE n.[2] (1)]

cheese-on!/cheese on bread!/cheese and bread! *excl.* [20C] (W.I./Bdos.) euph. for *Jesus!*

cheeser *n.*[1] **1** [19C] a burp. **2** [early 19C+] a strong-smelling fart. **3** [late 19C] a chestnut. **4** [1960s–70s] one who has smelly feet. [all supposedly smell like a ripe cheese]

cheeser *n.*[2] [1990s] (US campus) **1** one who is not attuned to the prevailing group standards. **2** one who is constantly asking to borrow things, usually without having much to offer in return (cf. MOOCHER). [CHEESE n.[3] (4)]

cheese ridge *n.* [1990s] the part of the penis between the glans and the shaft. [CHEESE n.[2] (1)]

cheeses, the *n.* [1940s] the 'utility' mark, made of two capital Cs, meaning 'civilian clothing' plus the date of manufacture. [resemblance to wedges of cheese]

cheese slicer *see* CHEESE DAGGER.

cheese-toaster *n.* [late 18C–1910s] **1** a sword. **2** a bayonet. [in an era before grills, one skewered the lump of cheese and held it to the fire]

cheese tube *n.* [1990s] the urethra. [CHEESE n.[2] (1)]

cheese/cheez whiz *n.* [1980s+] (US campus) someone who mistakenly thinks that they are impressive (cf. CHEDDAR). [CHEESE n.[3] (4) + WHIZ n. A pun on the name of a proprietary US cheese spread]

cheese/cheez whiz! *excl.* [1980s+] (US campus) a mild oath, synon. of GEE WHIZ!

cheesy/cheezy *adj.*[1] [mid-19C] fine or showy. [CHEESE n.[1]]

cheesy/cheezy *adj.*[2] **1** [mid-19C+] outdated, unfashionable, cheap and nasty (cf. CHEESE n.[3]). **2** [late 19C+] unwell, peaky. **3** [late 19C+] smelly, esp. in [1930s+] gay use where it refers to a smegma-coated foreskin. **4** [1950s] (US teen) disloyal. [all f. actual or fig. smell given off by ripe cheese]

cheesy/cheezy *adj.*[3] [late 19C+] false, hypocritical. [the 'say cheese' ritual for the summoning up of instant false smiles for the camera]

cheesy-feet *n.* [1960s–70s] a general term of abuse, the implication is that the person addressed suffers from smelly feet.

cheesy head *n.* [1990s] a penis that has not been cleansed of smegma. [CHEESE n.[2] (1)]

cheesy kiss *n.* [20C] (Aus.) a miss, esp. a missed catch at cricket. [rhy. sl.]

cheesy rider *n.* [1960s–70s] a sycophant (cf. CHEESE-EATER). [pun on film title *Easy Rider* (1969)]

cheesy, sleazy, greasy *phr.* [1980s+] (US campus) used of a woman of questionable reputation. [CHEESY adj.[2] + SLEAZY + SE *greasy*]

cheever *n.* [1990s] marijuana. [CHEEB]

cheez whiz *see* CHEESE.

cheezy *see* CHEESY.

chef *n.* [1910s–20s] (drugs) one who prepares the pipes in an opium den.

chefeneer *n.* [20C] (Irish) a small cupboard-cum-sideboard, often used to hold one's best plates, etc. [Fr. *chiffonier*, 'a piece of furniture with drawers in which women put away their needlework, cuttings of cloth, etc' (Littré, *Dictionnaire* (1863–72)]

chello! *excl.* [1980s+] (US campus) a greeting (cf. CHBYE!). [joc. mispron. or ? link to Ital. *ciao*, hello/goodbye]

Chelsea college to a sentry-box *phr.* [late 19C+] the longest possible odds (cf. ALL THE WORLD TO A CHINA ORANGE). [Chelsea College, the second London Polytechnic, was founded in 1891. It originally contained the Chelsea Art School]

Chelsea smile *n.* [1970s+] a knife slash that runs from the corner of the mouth up and across the cheek (cf. GLASGOW KISS; GORBALS KISS). [such cuts are inflicted on rival supporters by knives wielded by the more violent section of the fans of Chelsea Football Club]

Cheltenham *adj.* [late 19C+] cold. [rhy. sl. *Cheltenham Gold* (*Cup*)]

chemical *n.* [1980s+] (drugs) crack cocaine (cf. CHEMICALS). [its manufacture]

chemical head *n.* [1930s+] (US Black) hair that has been straightened through the application of a special mixture (cf. CONK n.[3]).

chemicals *n.* [1970s] (drugs) any of a number of 'recreational' drugs, usu. in phr. *got any chemicals?*

chemise-lifter *n.* [1960s+] a male homosexual (cf. SHIRTLIFTER). [? a nonce-coinage by the Australian writer and comedian Barry Humphries (b.1934), playing on the widely used synon.]

chemisery *n.* [1980s+] (US campus) chemistry.

chemist *n.* [20C] (W.I.) **1** one who runs an illicit still. **2** an abortionist.

chemist bill *n.* [mid-19C+] (W.I.) a deceitful, hypocritical person (cf. BACK-AND-BELLY n.[2]). [dial. *chemist's bill*, a two-edged machete, ult. f. an apothecary's knife, which 'cuts on both sides']

chemistry *n.* [1990s] (US drugs) the manufacture of drugs, e.g. LSD, crack cocaine, PCP (phencyclidine), with common household items and chemicals often stolen from the local hospital or pharmacy.

chemmy *n.* [1920s+] the card-game *chemin-de-fer*. [abbr.]

chemozzle *see* SHEMOZZLE.

chepemans *n.* [16C] (Und.) Cheapside Market. [*Chepe*, Cheapside + sfx. -MAN. Cheapside, ult. f. OE *ceap* or *chepe*, market, was medieval London's main market, flourishing until Henry III (r.1216–72) decided to diversify food-selling into other areas]

chepooka *n.* [1990s] (US teen) nonsense. [ety. unknown; ? a nonsense word in itself]

cheque-book farmer *n.* [1920s+] (S.Afr.) a farmer who is not primarily dependent on agriculture for income (cf. PITT STREET FARMER; STOEP-SITTER). [they pay the farm's expenses from other income, rather than from the produce of the farm itself]

cheque-busting/-bursting *n.* [20C] (Aus.) going on a spending spree; thus *cheque-buster/burster*, one who does this. [SE *cheque*, the lump-sum payment given to a rural worker at the end of his season-long contract]

chequd up *adj.* [20C] (Aus.) one who is well-supplied with money (cf. CASHED UP). [for ety. *see* CHEQUE-BUSTING]

cheque-man *n.* [20C] (Aus.) a spendthrift, one who spends his season's wages in a single glorious spree. [for ety. *see* CHEQUE-BUSTING]

cheque-proud *adj.* [1930s] (N.Z.) recently paid, and keen to start spending. [for ety. *see* CHEQUE-BUSTING]

Chequer Inn in Newgate Street *see* KING'S HEAD INN IN NEWGATE STREET.

cher *adj.* [1960s] (US campus) attractive. [CHERRY adj. (1)]

cheri *n.* [mid-19C] a charming woman. [Madame Montigny, an actress at the Gymnase in Paris who appeared under the stage name of Rose *Cheri*. 'A singularly pure woman and an angelic actress. Used by upper-class gentlemen to describe their mistresses' (Ware)]

cherrie *n.* [1960s+] (S.Afr.) a woman, a girlfriend. [var. on CHERRY n.[1] (7)]

cherries *n.*[1] [20C] (US) the female nipples. [resemblance]

cherries *n.*[2] [1970s] greyhound racing tracks. [rhy. sl. *cherry hogs* = DOGS n.[2]]

cherry *n.*[1] **1** [1920s+] (orig. US) a female virgin; thus *bust a cherry*, to deflower. **2** [1920s+] (gay) an anal virgin. **3** a male virgin; thus *harvest the cherries*, to take a youth and deprive him of his virginity. **4** [1930s+] (orig. US) the hymen; thus *lose one's cherry*, to lose one's virginity. **5** [1950s+] (US) an old car in near-mint condition. **6** [1960s+] (orig. US milit.) a novice, e.g. a fresh troop, one who has yet to be 'blooded' in combat. **7** [1960s+] (S.Afr.) a woman, a girlfriend (cf. CHERRIE; FLOSSIE). [SE *cherry*, the image is of ripeness]

cherry *n.*[2] [1930s+] a love bite, usu. on the neck (cf. HICKEY n.[2]). [resemblance]

cherry *n.*[3] [1970s+] (US) the red revolving light on top of a police car; thus *cherrytop*, a police car.

cherry *n.*[4] [1990s] an annoying individual. [ext. of CHERRY n.[1](6)]

cherry *adj.* (US) **1** [1920s+] virgin, virginal. **2** [1950s+] of goods etc., in mint condition, brand-new. **3** [1960s+] (orig. milit.) inexperienced, new, untested. **4** [1960s+] of a given experience or action, the very first, initiating; thus *cherry kicks*, the first injection after a former drugs user is freed from prison. **5** [1980s+] innocent, naïve. **6** [1980s+] (campus) very attractive. [CHERRY n.[1]]

cherry ace *n.* [1940s–50s] the face. [rhy. sl.]

cherry blossom kiss *n.* [1990s] the act of performing oral sex with a woman during her menstrual period. [the colour of blood]

cherry-bounce *n.*[1] **1** [late 17C–mid-19C] cherry brandy. **2** [mid-18C] brandy mixed with sugar. [its effects]

cherry-bounce *n.*[2] [late 19C+] a charabanc. [mispron. + ref. to the bouncy ride]

cherry-boy *n.* [1970s] (US) a male virgin. [CHERRY adj. (1)]

cherry-buster *n.* [1950s+] (US) a (young) man who specializes in deflowering virgins (cf. BOY-BUSTER). [CHERRY n.[1](1) + BUST v.]

cherry-colour *adj.* [mid-19C] red or black. [the term is most used in a cheating trick with cards, in which the trickster bets an innocent victim that he can accurately predict the colour of the next card to appear. Since cherries are both red and black, as are cards, he cannot lose]

cherry-coloured *adj.* [late 18C+] coloured black or red. [the usual assumption is red, but black cherries are equally common; thus a *cherry-coloured cat*, a black cat (Grose 1785)]

cherry farm *n.* [1960s–70s] (US) a prison that houses first-offenders. [CHERRY adj. + SE *farm*, a prison]

cherry hog *n.* [mid-19C+] a dog. [rhy. sl.]

cherry-merry *n.* [mid-19C] a present of money. [CHERRY-MERRY adj.]

cherry-merry *adj.* [late 18C] cheerful, merry, esp. after drinking. [? the *cherry-red* colour of wine + SE *merry*]

cherry-merry bamboo *n.* [mid-19C] (Anglo-Ind.) a beating. [ironic use of CHERRY-MERRY, in this case as an unwanted gift + SE *bamboo* (*cane*)]

cherry-nose *n.* [1940s] (S.Afr.) sherry. [SE *sherry* + the effect of excess sherry consumption on the complexion]

cherry oggs *n.* [1920s+] greyhound racing (cf. CHERRY HOG). [rhy. sl. *cherry oggs* = DOGS n.[2]]

cherry out *v.* [1980s+] (US) to make as good as new. [CHERRY n.[1]]

cherry-picker *n.*[1] [20C] (US) a large, hooked nose. [such a nose is supposedly big enough to hang over a branch as a hook while one picks cherries from the tree]

cherry-picker *n.*[2] [20C] (US) a pointed shoe.

cherry-picker *n.*[3] [1920s–70s] a yokel, a peasant (cf. APPLE KNOCKER n.[2]). [a typical rural occupation]

cherry-picker *n.*[4] [1950s+] a seducer of virgins. [CHERRY n.[1]]

cherry-picker *n.*[5] [1970s] £1. [rhy. sl. *cherry-picker* = NICKER]

cherry pie *n.* [late 19C+] **1** a virgin. **2** a woman. **3** the vagina, esp. if the woman is menstruating (cf. APPLE n.[10]; FINGER PIE). [CHERRY n.[1] + SE *pie*]

cherry-pipe *n.* [late 19C] a woman. [rhy. sl. *cherry-pipe* = CHERRY-RIPE n.[3]]

cherrypop *v.* [1950s+] (orig. US) to seduce and deflower virgins, usu. women. [CHERRY n.[1] + POP v.[1]]

cherry prick *n.* [20C] a male virgin. [CHERRY adj. (1) + PRICK n. (2)]

cherry reds *n.* [1960s+] Doc Martens boots, as worn as part of the skinhead uniform. [the colour of a particular style]

cherry-ripe *n.*[1] [late 18C–early 19C] a Bow Street Runner. **2** [mid–late 19C] a footman dressed in red plush. [their uniforms]

cherry-ripe *n.*[2] **1** [mid-19C] a pipe. **2** [20C] nonsense. [rhy. sl. (2) *cherry-ripe* = TRIPE n.[2]]

cherry-ripe *n.*[3] [mid–late 19C] (Und.) a woman. [CHERRY n.[1] + SE *ripe*, the implication is of virginity, albeit temporary]

cherry-splitter *n.* [19C] the penis (cf. ARSE-OPENER). [CHERRY n.[1] + SE *splitter*]

cherry-top *n.* [1970s+] (US) **1** a police car with a red light on its roof. **2** a policeman. [CHERRY n.[3]]

chershom see CHARRSHOM.

cherubim *n.*[1] [late 18C] a whinging child. [joc. ref. to the line 'To Thee cherubim and seraphim continually do cry' in the *Te Deum*]

cherubim *n.*[2] [mid-19C+] a choirboy. [his supposedly angelic persona]

Cheshire, the *n.* [late 19C–1900s] the best, the ideal (cf. STILTON). [brand-specific var. on CHEESE n.[1](1)]

chesky *n.* [20C] (US) a derog. term for a Czech immigrant (cf. BOOTCHKEY).

chester *n.* [1990s] (US campus) a socially inept person. [? CHESTER MOLESTER]

chester molester/the molester *n.* [20C] (US campus/Und.) a child abuser, a sex criminal.

chest flesh *n.* [1990s] the female breasts.

chestnut *n.* [late 19C+] (orig. US) an old, much-repeated joke that has long-since lost any real humour. [the term emerged c.1880 but appears to have originated in the play *Broken Sword* (1816) by W. Dimond. The relevant passage reads: 'Zavior: When suddenly from the thick boughs of a cork tree. Pablo: (Jumping up.) A chestnut, Captain, a chestnut. Captain, this is the twenty-seventh time I have heard you relate this story, and you invariably said, a chestnut, till now']

chestnuts *n.* [1950s–60s] the female breasts (cf. APPLES n.[1]). [pun on SE *chest* + *nuts*/NUTS n.[2]]

chest-plaster *n.* [late 19C] a flat cravat that covers the shirt front between the coat and the throat (cf. SEPULCHRE). [it 'bandages' the sometimes less than spotless shirt front]

chest-pounder *n.* [20C] (US) a Roman Catholic (cf. BREAST FLEET). [the ritual tapping of the chest that accompanies statements of *Mea culpa*]

chest puppy *n.* [1990s] (Aus.) the female breast. [? 1960s description of film star Elizabeth Taylor (b.1932) as 'two small dogs fighting under a mink rug']

chesty *adj.* **1** [19C+] (US) arrogant, conceited. **2** [1930s+] prone to suffer from infections of the chest; thus *chestily, chestiness*. **3** [1950s+] of a woman, having prominent breasts (cf. BUSTY). [all SE *chest*; note US military hero 'Chesty' Pullar]

chete see CHEAT n.

chev see CHIV v.

chevalier Atkins *n.* [late 19C–1900s] a generic term for the typical private soldier in the British army (cf. TOMMY ATKINS). [SE *chevalier*, a Knight + (TOMMY) ATKINS]

chevvy *n.* [1920s+] (orig. US) a *Chevrolet* automobile. [abbr.]

chevy chase *n.* [mid-19C–1950s] the face (cf. JEM MACE; ROACH AND DACE). [rhy. sl., ult. the proper name *Chevy Chase*, the site of a celebrated 17C border skirmish and thus the subject and title of a popular ballad]

chew n. **1** [19C] a quid of chewing tobacco. **2** [20C] (S.Afr.) food.

chew v. **1** [mid-19C–1930s] (US) to eat. **2** [20C] (US) to talk. **3** [20C] (US) to embarrass. **4** [20C] (US) to argue, to protest. **5** [1940s+] (US Black) to abuse, to attack verbally or physically (cf. CHEW OUT).

chewallop n. [mid-19C+] to hit hard and suddenly, to smack. [var. on KERWHALLOP v.]

chew arse/ass v. [1910s+] (orig. US milit.) to tell off, to berate, to criticize severely. [SE chew + ARSE n.¹]

chew down v. [1930s–60s] (US) to cheat financially. [joc. use of SE + ref. to jew down at JEW v.]

chewed adj. [19C] (US) **1** embarrassed. **2** angry, annoyed, defeated.

chewed to loon shit phr. [1930s+] ground up, ruined, e.g. of a road. [SE chewed + fig. use of loon, an aquatic diving bird + SHIT n.¹]

chewed-up adj. **1** [1910s+] suffering from a telling-off. **2** [1920s+] nervous, out of sorts.

chewers n. [1940s] teeth, real or false.

chew face v. [1970s+] (US campus) to kiss.

chew fish see EAT FISH.

chewie/chewy n. [1920s+] (orig. Aus.) chewing gum; thus chewie on your boot, phr. used by barrackers at football matches in an attempt to put off a place-kicker by suggesting that they have chewing gum on their boot. [abbr.]

chewies n. [1980s+] (drugs) Tuinals. [one can chew up the tablets]

chewing/chewings n. [20C] (US) **1** food. **2** a telling-off, a scolding (cf. CHEW OUT). [that which is actually or fig. chewed]

chewing gum n. [1920s] (US) empty, meaningless chatter. [CHEW n. (2)]

chewing match n. [20C] (US) an argument. [CHEW v. (3)]

chew into dishcloths, to phr. [late 19C–1900s] (US) to destroy completely, to annihilate.

chew it over see CHEW OVER.

chew lead v. [19C] (US) to be shot to death. [SE chew + LEAD n.]

chew on v. [1980s+] (US) to nag, to pester (cf. CHEW OUT).

chew one's/the balls/ballocks off, to phr. [20C] to reprimand severely (cf. CHEW OUT). [SE chew + BALLS n.¹ (1); BALLOCKS n.¹ (1)]

chew one's bit, to phr. [20C] (US) **1** to be anxious or upset. **2** to argue or talk loudly. [SE champ at the bit, (of horses) to be restive]

chew one's cabbage twice see BOIL ONE'S CABBAGE TWICE.

chew one's ear/lug, to phr. [1900s–10s] to drink, esp. beer (cf. BEER-CHEWER). [rhy. sl. ear = beer; LUG n.¹ (1) is synon.]

chew one's own tobacco/meat, to phr. [19C] (US) **1** to rely on oneself. **2** to ponder an action or opinion before committing oneself.

chew one's tobacco twice, to phr. [20C] to be mean, to be tight-fisted.

chew on this/it phr. [1970s+] an obscene retort. [this/it is the penis]

chew out v. [1940s+] (orig. US) to tell off, to harangue (cf. CHEW ON). [ext. of CHEW ARSE]

chew over/it over v. [20C] to discuss, to consider, to ponder (cf. BITE ONE'S BAIT; CHEW THE FAT).

chew someone's ear/lug, to phr.¹ [late 19C] (Aus.) to cadge, to beg. [SE chew + ear/LUG n.¹ (1)]

chew someone's ear off/out, to phr.² [1910s–50s] (US) to talk at someone in a tedious manner (cf. BITE SOMEONE'S EAR phr.²).

chew someone's lug see CHEW SOMEONE'S EAR phr.¹.

chew the boot, to phr. [1950s] (US) to converse, to talk something over (cf. CHEW THE FAT).

chew the carpet, to phr.¹ [1950s+] (US) to lose emotional control, to suffer a temper tantrum (cf. CARPET-BITER).

chew the carpet, to phr.² see MUNCH THE CARPET.

chew the cheese, to phr. [1980s+] (US campus) to vomit (cf. CHEESE v.⁴).

chew the cud, to phr. **1** [mid-19C] to chew tobacco. **2** [mid-19C+] to ponder, to think something over.

chew the fat, to phr. [late 19C+] to converse, to talk something over (cf. CHEW OVER). [rhy. sl. chew the fat = have a chat]

chew the grease, to phr. [1910s–20s] to talk something over (cf. CHEW THE FAT).

chew the rag, to phr. [late 19C+] (US) **1** to gossip, to chatter. **2** to grumble, to complain. **3** to argue, to speak irresponsibly. [RAG n.⁴; orig. use held overtones of grumbling and complaining, but this vanished by the 1920s]

chew the rug, to phr. **1** [late 19C+] to gossip, to chatter (cf. CHEW THE RAG). **2** [1970s+] (US) to lose emotional control, to suffer a temper tantrum (cf. CHEW THE CARPET phr.¹).

chewtobaccy n. [1900s–40s] (US Black) chewing tobacco. [cf. synon. Bahamas dial. chewbaca]

chew up v. (US) **1** [mid-19C–1900s] to defeat, to overcome; ext. as [1940s+] chew up and spit out. **2** [1910s+] to scold harshly, to reprimand severely.

chew up old touches, to phr. [1950s] (US) to reminisce (cf. CARVE UP SCORES). [SE chew + TOUCH n.¹ (3)]

chew-water n. [1940s+] (W.I.) thin, tasteless soup. [dial. chew-water, left-over cooking water, thrown out for the pigs]

chewy n.¹ see CHEWIE.

chewy n.² [1990s] (US Black/drugs) a cigar or marijuana-filled cigar, rolled with cocaine powder (rather than crack) (cf. BLUNT n.²). [? one chews at it as one smokes]

Chi n.¹ [late 19C+] (US) Chicago. [abbr.]

chi n.² [1980s+] (drugs) heroin (cf. CHICLE; CHINA CAT; CHINA WHITE; CHINESE BROWN; CHINESE H; CHINESE NO. 3; CHINESE RED; CHINESE ROCKS). [abbr. CHINESE H or CHINA WHITE]

chiack n. see CHI-IKE n.

chiack v. see CHI-IKE v.¹.

chian see CHRISTACRUTCHIAN.

chib n. **1** [late 19C] the face. **2** [1930s+] a knife or razor (cf. CHIV n.¹).

chib v. see CHIV v.

chiba/chiba-chiba n. [1970s+] (drugs) high potency marijuana; spec. from Colombia but used for any powerful marijuana. [var. on CHEEB]

chibe see CHIV v.

Chicago bankroll n. [1970s+] (US Black/gambling) a show bankroll (cf. CALIFORNIA BANKROLL).

Chicago black/green n. [1980s+] (drugs) varieties of marijuana, characterized by the colour, popular (and presumably grown) in and around Chicago.

Chicago chicken n. [1940s] (US, West.) salt pork or bacon (cf. ADIRONDACK STEAK). [the meat-packing industry of the city]

Chicago lightning n. [1920s–30s] gunfire. [the city's reputation as a centre of gangland warfare]

Chicago overcoat n. [1930s–40s] (US) death, murder (cf. CEMENT KIMONO). [the practice of sealing corpses in cement prior to disposing of them at sea]

Chicago piano n. [1920s+] a Thompson sub-machinegun, which achieved notoriety as the preferred weapon of Chicago gangsters in the 1920s and later (cf. CHICAGO TYPEWRITER; CHOPPER n.⁴). [note WW2 RN jargon Chicago piano, a multiple pom-pom]

Chicago typewriter n. [1920s+] a Thompson sub-machinegun.

chicalean adj. [1990s] (US campus) excellent, stylish, worthy of admiration. [ety. unknown. ? SE chic]

chice/chice-am-a/a-trice n. [early 19C] (tramp) nothing, no good (cf. SHICER). [? SHIT n.¹ (1)]

chicharra see CHIRA.

chi-chi n.¹ see CHEE-CHEE n.

chi-chi n.² [20C] (US) the female breast; usu. in pl. [Jap. *chi-chi*, milk, the breast]

chi-chi adj. see CHEE-CHEE adj.

chichi/shishi adj. [1960s+] **1** affected, pretentious, 'pretty-pretty'. **2** homosexual. [Fr. *chi-chi*]

chichibangas n. [1960s+] (US) the female breasts. [CHI-CHI + BONGOS]

chick n.¹ [mid-19C] (Anglo-Ind.) a coin worth 4 rupees. [SE *chequeen*, (Ital. *zecchino*) a Venetian coin, also known as a *sequin* and worth at various times from 7 shillings (35p) to 9 shillings 6 pence (47½p) in pre-decimalized money]

chick n.² [mid–late 19C] (US) a man. [SE *chicken*, lively, perky and 'good enough to eat'; the opposite of CAT n.⁹ (3). Although *chick* has become sl. only in the 20C, it has been used as a general term of affection since 16C]

chick/chickie n.³ [20C] (US) a warning of the impending approach of authority – whether policeman, parent or teacher – and thus a command to stop whatever one is doing that might cause that authority to act against one (cf. KEEP CHICK). [CHICKEN n.²]

chick n.⁴ **1** [1920s+] a young woman (cf. BARBECUE n.³; CHICKABIDDY; CHUCK n.¹; CHUCKABOO; CHUCKABY; CHUCKY n.¹; HEN; PHEASANT; PLOVER; QUAIL). **2** [1940s+] a male prostitute. [ext. of CHICK n.²]

chick adj. [1960s+] (orig. US) of interest to girls or women, e.g. *a chick movie*. [CHICK n.⁴]

chickabiddy n. **1** [late 18C+] a chicken. **2** [19C] a young woman (cf. CHICK n.⁴). [nursery use, ult. rural dial. Note BIDDY n.¹ + n.²]

chickadee n. [1930s–70s] (US) a young woman. [ext. of CHICK n.⁴]

chickaleary cove n. [mid-19C] an artful, knowing, 'clever' fellow. [popularized by the song 'The Chickaleery cove' by the music-hall star Alfred 'The Great' Vance (1839–88). ? f. CHEEKY + LEARY]

chicken n.¹ [17C] a pint pot. [? on pattern of KITTEN n.¹, although no *hen* = quart]

chicken n.² **1** [early 17C+] a timid creature, a coward; thus *chicken-hearted*, cowardly. **2** [late 19C+] a weak or naïve person. **3** [1950s+] (orig. US teen) a contest of nerve in which two cars drive either at each other, the loser being the driver who is seen to turn aside first, or towards an obstacle, cliff edge etc; thus any form of foolish dare-devilry (cf. PLAY CHICKEN v.²). **4** [1960s+] (US Black) a sheepish, foolish grin. [SE *chicken*, a stereotypically 'cowardly' creature]

chicken n.³ **1** [late 17C+] used as a direct address to a child or young woman. **2** [mid–late 19C] a young man, often as a direct address. [for ety. see CHICK n.²]

chicken n.⁴ **1** [late 18C+] a young woman, esp. [late 18C–mid-19C] a prostitute (cf. CANARY n.²). **2** [mid-19C+] (US) young women considered collectively; thus sexual intercourse with one. **3** [1960s+] (US Black) an unattractive old woman. **4** [1960s+] (US Black) an aggressive woman. [note (3) and (4), on the bad = good pattern, are the direct reverse of usual White equivalents]

chicken n.⁵ **1** [mid-19C] anything young, small or insignificant. **2** [1940s+] (gay) an underage boy, or such boys considered collectively (cf. MYSTERY n.²). **3** [1940s+] a young man used as a lure (usu. to blackmail or pressurize gay men) by swindlers. **4** [1960s+] a child who is used for paedophiliac sexual exploitation (cf. CHICKEN-HAWK). [(2)

note 19C US milit. jargon *chicken*, a close friend or young 'buddy']

chicken n.⁶ [mid-19C] (US) a thing, a phenomenon.

chicken n.⁷ [1900s–40s] (US) bacon, sausages (cf. CHICAGO CHICKEN).

chicken adj.¹ [1910s+] (orig. US) petty, insignificant. [CHICKEN n.⁵ (1)]

chicken adj.² [1940s+] cowardly. [CHICKEN n.² (1)]

chicken! excl. [1950s+] (orig. US) a derisive cry, coward! [CHICKEN n.²]

chickenbone special n. [1950s] (US Black) anything second-rate, inferior, cheap and unattractive. [the bags of homemade fried chicken taken by Southern Blacks on railroad trips. Segregation kept them from using the Whites-only dining cars]

chickenbrain n. [1920s] (US) a fool (cf. BAKEBRAIN). [SE *chicken*/CHICKEN n.² (1) + sfx. -*brain*]

chicken-butcher n.¹ [late 18C+] **1** a poulterer. **2** one who shoots very young game.

chicken-butcher n.² [1930s–40s] (US campus) a womanizer. [CHICKEN n.⁴ (1)]

chicken butt phr. [1960s] (US Black) nothing, no matter, forget it; used in response to the query *what's up?* [SE *chicken* + BUTT n.¹ (2); its innate insignificance]

chicken colonel n. [1940s+] (US) a full colonel in the US Air Force (cf. BIRD COLONEL). [the silver eagles affixed to the uniform's shoulders that denote rank]

chicken coop n. [20C] (US) **1** a police car or patrol wagon. **2** an outside lavatory.

chicken dinner n. [1940s] (US Black) an attractive young woman. [CHICKEN n.⁴ (1)]

chicken-eater n. [20C] (US) **1** an unprofessional, part-time lay preacher (cf. CHAIRBACKER). **2** a Methodist. [members of the congregation would give the preacher roast chicken for their Sunday lunch]

chicken-feed n. [mid-19C+] **1** small change. **2** derisorily small amounts of money or anything else (cf. CHICKEN MONEY).

chicken fight n. [1930s] (US) a contest of nerves. [CHICKEN OUT]

chicken fixings/fixins n. [mid-19C] (US) trifles, small possessions. [SE *fixings*, the trimmings that accompany a roast chicken]

chicken-fucker n. [1950s+] (US) a general derog. term, often intensified by ext. *bald-headed chicken-fucker*.

chicken gizzard n. [mid-19C] (US) a coward. [CHICKEN n.² (1) + SE *gizzard*]

chicken-gutted adj. [1950s+] (US) cowardly. [CHICKEN n.² (1) + SE *gutted*]

chicken-hammed adj. [18C] bandy-legged. [SE *chicken* + *ham*, a thigh]

chicken-hawk n. (orig. US) **1** [1960s+] an older male homosexual with a preference for young boys (cf. CHICKEN QUEEN; HAWK n.⁵). **2** [1980s] an older man who prefers teenage girls for sex. [CHICKEN n.⁵ (2), n.⁴ (3) + SE *hawk*]

chickenhead n.¹ [1960s+] (US Black) **1** an aggressive, unpleasant woman. **2** a stupid, immature girl. **3** a fellatrix. **4** a promiscuous woman. [CHICKEN n.⁴]

chickenhead n.² [1990s] (US teen) one who talks a lot. [the chicken's bobbing head and constant squawking]

chicken-hearted adj. [late 18C+] cowardly. [CHICKEN n.² (1) + SE *hearted*]

chicken hockey n. [1970s] (US) one's fig. intestines, innards, i.e. the 'stuffing', the 'daylights'; usu. in phr. *kick/knock the chicken-hockey out of* (cf. CHICKENSHIT n.). [SE *chicken* + HOCKIE n.]

chicken inspector n. [1920s+] (US) a womanizer, a lady-killer. [CHICKEN n.⁴ (1) + SE *inspector*]

chicken-lifter n. [late 19C–1900s] (US) a chicken thief; thus any form of petty thief. [SE *chicken* + LIFT v.[1] (1)]

chicken-liver n. [1930s] a coward. [CHICKEN n.[2] (1) + SE *liver*; note SE *lily-liver(ed)*]

chicken money n. [19C] (US) spending money, small change. [var. on CHICKEN-FEED]

chicken nabob n. [late 18C–early 19C] a merchant who has returned from India with a moderate rather than a magnificent fortune. [SE *chicken*, diminutive ('borrowed from the chicken turtle' notes Grose (1796), who defines 'moderate' as £50,000–60,000) + *nabob*, one who has returned from India with great wealth, ult. f. Urdu *nawab*, deputy governor]

chicken out v. [1930s+] (orig. US) to be scared, to be too frightened to act, to back out. [CHICKEN n.[2] (1)]

chicken-perch n. [late 19C+] a church. [rhy. sl.]

chicken-picker n. [1930s+] (Aus.) a one-finger typist. [image of a chicken pecking at corn]

chicken-plucking adj. [1960s] (US) a general term of abuse, second-rate, vulgar, insignificant (cf. COTTON-PICKING). [euph.]

chicken powder n. [1980s+] (drugs) amphetamine (cf. A n.[2]). [? it makes the user 'run around like a headless chicken' or it makes the user brave, i.e. no longer CHICKEN adj.[2]]

chicken pox n. [1960s+] (US gay) the urge to have sex with underage boys. [CHICKEN n.[5] (2) + pun on SE; there is no apparent link to the POX n.[1]]

chicken-preacher n. [20C] (US) an unprofessional, part-time lay preacher (cf. CHAIRBACKER; CHICKEN-EATER). [abbr. *chicken-eating preacher*]

chicken queen n. [1980s+] (US gay) an older homosexual male who prefers sex with teenage boys (cf. CHICKEN-HAWK). [CHICKEN n.[5] (2) + QUEEN n.[1]]

chicken ranch n. [1960s+] a brothel (cf. HOG RANCH). [the original mid-19C *Chicken Ranch* was at Gilbert, Texas. One ety. suggests that the clients, mainly local farmers, paid for their pleasures with chickens, but more likely is a use of CHICKEN n.[4] (2)]

chicken run n.[1] [1950s+] a teenage virility ritual involving the driving of two cars at high speed towards each other, or towards a dangerous obstacle; the first one to turn aside or brake is 'chicken'. [CHICKEN n.[2] (3)]

chicken run n.[2] **1** [1970s+] (S.Afr.) the flight from South Africa of (White) people, fearing for their future in a non-apartheid world. **2** [1990s] the attempt by Conservative MPs in marginal seats to find safer ones, in the knowledge that governmental unpopularity would condemn them to defeat in the UK General Election.

chicken rustler n. [1960s+] (US gay) a male homosexual who has been placed in charge of underage boys, e.g. a scoutmaster or choirmaster. [CHICKEN n.[5] (2) + *rustler*]

chicken scratch n.[1] **1** [19C] (US) illegible handwriting (cf. CHICKEN TRACKS; CROW'S FEET; CROW TRACKS; HEN TRACKS). **2** [1950s] (US Black) short, tightly curled hair. [resemblance]

chicken scratch n.[2] [1940s–50s] (US Black) a very small amount of money (cf. CHICKEN-FEED). [? the small impression it makes on one's expenses; or CHICKEN adj.[1] + SCRATCH n.[2]]

chicken scratch n.[3] [1980s+] (drugs) the searching on hands and knees for grains of crack cocaine that have dropped to the floor.

chicken scratching n. [1940s–50s] (US Black) an inadequate effort, a poorly done job, a lack of real commitment to a task. [the lack of real impression a chicken's scratching makes on the ground]

chickenshit n. [1940s+] (orig. US) **1** a coward. **2** a contemptible, disgusting person. [CHICKEN n.[2] (1)/SE *chicken*

+ SHIT n.[1] (1); the cowardice of the person/the essential insignificance of the substance]

chickenshit adj. [1940s+] (orig. US) **1** weak. **2** insufficient, inadequate, of poor quality. **3** cowardly, fearful. [CHICKENSHIT n.]

chickenshits, the n. [1950s] diarrhoea. [SE *chicken* + SHITS]

chicken's neck n. [20C] a cheque. [rhy. sl.]

chicken thief n. [mid-late 19C; 1940s] (Aus./US) a petty thief. [CHICKEN adj.[1]; 20C use is Aus. only]

chicken tracks n. [late 19C+] (US) illegible handwriting (cf. CHICKEN SCRATCH n.[1]).

chicken wings n. [1990s] the labia.

chickie n. [1940s+] (orig. Aus.) a young woman. [CHICK n.[4] (1)]

chickle-a-leary chap n. [early–mid-19C] an artful, knowing fellow (cf. CHICKALEARY COVE).

chicklet n. [1920s+] (orig. US) a young woman. [CHICK n.[4] (1) + dimin. *-let*]

chickster see SHICKSA.

chicle n. [1980s+] (drugs) heroin (cf. CHI n.[2]). [SE *chicle-gum*, chewing gum; thus a pun on GUM n.[3]]

chiclets n. [1950s+] (US) the teeth. [trademark *Chiclets*, a popular chewing gum; the pieces of gum resemble teeth]

chico n. [1960s+] a Mexican, esp. one considered lower class or of mixed blood (cf. CHOLO). [*Chico*, a popular Mexican name, esp. during ascendancy of baseball stars Chico Cardenas, Chico Fernandez, Chico Salmon and Chico Ruiz]

chic sale n. [1940s+] (US) a privy, an outside lavatory. [proper name *Chic Sale*, 'the champion privy builder of Sangamon Co., Ill.' and best known for his book *The Specialist* (1929)]

chief n.[1] **1** [late 19C+] a general term of address to an unknown person (cf. GUV; JOHN n.[1]; MAC n.[1]; MATE). **2** [1940s+] (W.I.) a potential victim of a confidence trickster, a credulous person. The term, common as a form of address, is used ironically by the con-man when he approaches the dupe. **3** [1970s+] (S.Afr.) a form of address, either between those of the same race or by Whites to a Black whose name they do not know.

chief n.[2] [1980s+] (drugs) a hallucinogenic drug, esp. LSD or mescaline. [? the association of such drugs with Mexican Indians and Native Americans]

chief n.[3] [1990s] (US) a stupid person. [SE *chief*, the head of a tribe; thus the stereotyping of Native Americans as stupid]

chief/head cook and bottle-washer n. [mid-19C+] **1** a foreman, a person in authority. **2** a general factotum who may, in fact, carry out neither of these duties.

chief muck of the crib n. [early 19C] an important person, but within only a small field of activity. [*muck* is synon. with both HIGH MUCKY-MUCK and LORD MUCK but predates both and must thus be a fig. use of colloq. *muck*, anything filthy, disgusting or abhorrent + CRIB n.[3]]

chief of the dishrag n. [mid-late 19C] (US) a cook.

chieva n. [1980s+] (drugs) heroin. [ety. unknown; CHEEB etc. usu. refer to marijuana]

chiff see CHIV n.[1].

chiggers n. [1930s–40s] (US) a neighbourhood policeman. [CHIGGERS!]

chiggers! excl. [1930s–40s] (US) a cry of warning, alerting others to the approach of authority. [var. on JIGGER! excl.[2]]

chi-ike/chiack/chi-hike/chyack n. [mid-19C+] a hearty greeting. [CHI-IKE v.[1]; orig. costermonger use]

chi-ike/chiack/chi-hike/chyack v.[1] [mid-19C+] to shout *chi-ike* as a hearty greeting or salutation. [echoic]

chi-ike/chyack v.[2] [mid-19C] (mainly Aus./N.Z.) to tease, to fool, to deceive. [echoic]

chikwa see CHINKER.

child n. [mid-19C–1930s] (US) a person, usu. as *this child*, me, myself.

child-getter n. [19C] the penis (cf. BABY-MAKER).

child of darkness *n.* [late 17C–early 18C] (Und.) a bellman or nightwatchman who walked the streets at night calling out the hours.

child of the horn-thumb *n.* [17C] a cut-purse. [SE *child* + HORN-THUMB]

children in the wood *n.* [mid–late 19C] dice in a box.

child's best guide to the gallows *n.* [late 18C–19C] a pack of playing cards. [the association by the pious of gambling with 'a bad end'. The use, like the phr. itself, is presumably ironic]

chile/chili *n.* [1930s] (US) a derog. name for a Mexican; thus *chile-/chili-* as prefix to anything supposedly Mexican (cf. PEPPER GUT). [the SE *chile-/chili-pepper*, a stereotypically popular Mex. food]

chile/chili bean *n.* [1960s+] a Mexican. [CHILE + BEAN n.[7]]

chile-/chili-belly/gut *n.* [1960s+] (US) a Mexican. [CHILE + SE *belly/gut*]

chile-/chili-head *n.* [1970s+] (US) a Mexican. [CHILE + sfx. -HEAD (3)]

chile-/chili-chaser *n.* [1950s+] (US) a US border patrolman, employed to prevent Mexicans from entering the country illegally. [CHILE + SE *chaser*]

chile-choker/chili-choker *n.* [1950s+] (US) a Mexican (cf. CHILI-EATER).

chile-chomper *see* CHILE-EATER.

chile/chili chump *n.* [1940s+] (US Black) a pimp who has only one woman working for him, an inexperienced pimp. [CHILE + CHUMP n.[2]; the ref. is to the incompetence of small-time Mexican pimps]

chile-/chili-eater/-chomper/-picker *n.* [20C] (US) a Mexican (cf. CHILE).

chile/chili pimp *n.* [1970s+] (US Black) a pimp who has only one woman working for him (cf. CHILE CHUMP; CIGARETTE PIMP; COFFEE-AND PIMP].

chili *n. see* CHILE.

chili *v.* [1940s–50s] (US Black) to ignore, to brush off. [? CHILL n.[1]]

chili-eater/-chomper/-picker *see* CHILE-EATER.

chill *n.[1]* [20C] (US) rejection, 'the cold shoulder'; thus *play the chill (for)*, to ignore, to snub.

chill *n.[2]* [1930s+] murder, death, assassination; thus *put the chill on*, to murder. [the cold corpse]

chill *n.[3]* [1970s] (US campus) beer. [it has been chilled]

chill *adj.* [1980s+] (US Black) fashionable, chic, 'with it' (cf. COOL adj.[3]).

chill *v.[1]* [mid-19C] to heat up. [abbr. SE *take the chill off*]

chill *v.[2]* [1940s+] to murder, to assassinate. [CHILL n.[2]]

chill/chill out *v.[3]* (orig. US Black) 1 [1970s+] to calm down, to control one's emotions, to relax, to act 'cool'. 2 [1970s+] to calm someone down. 3 [1980s+] to pass the time of day, to 'hang out'. [originated by US Black teenagers, the term has now spread to the UK, and is used by both Blacks and Whites]

chill *adv.* [1900s–10s] (US campus) totally, completely. [var. on COLD adv.]

chillam/chillum *n.* 1 [late 18C+] (Anglo-Ind.) a pipeful of tobacco. 2 [1950s+] (orig. W.I.) a pipe used for smoking marijuana (cf. CHALICE). [Hind. *chilam*, the bowl of a *hugga* pipe or *hookah*]

chilled-off *adj.* [1930s+] (US) killed, murdered. [CHILL v.[2]]

chillers *n.* [20C] (Irish) 1 jowls. 2 a double chin. [OE *ceolor*, the throat]

chillicracker *n.* [1930s+] (Anglo-Ind.) a derog. term for a person of mixed racial descent (esp. Eurasian) (cf. BLACKIE-WHITE).

chilling *n.* [1980s+] relaxing; acting in a cool manner. [CHILL v.[3] (1)]

chill out *see* CHILL v.[3].

chill-out *adj.* [1980s+] designed to create a relaxed atmosphere; thus *chill-out room*, that part of a nightclub where people can relax and chat rather than dance. [CHILL v.[3] (1)]

chill pad *n.* [1990s] (US Black) one's home (cf. CRIB n.[3]). [CHILL v.[3] (1) + PAD n.[2] (2)]

chillum *see* CHILLAM.

chilly *n.* [1980s+] (US campus) a cold beer (cf. CHILL n.[3]).

chilly *adj.* [20C] 1 emotionless, detached (cf. ARCTIC; COOL adj.[3]); thus *play it chilly*, to act in a cool, controlled manner. 2 cold-blooded. 3 acceptable. 4 skilful, competent at a given task or profession. [CHILL v.[3] (1)]

chilly dog *n.* [1980s+] (US campus) beer (cf. CHILL n.[3] + pun on US fast food *chili dog*).

chilly down *v.* [1980s+] to pass the time of day, to 'hang out' (cf. CHILL v.[3]).

chilly mitt, the *n.* [1900s] (US) a rejection, a snub, usu. in phr. *get/give the chilly mitt*. [SE *chilly* + MITT n.]

chilly most *n.* [1990s] (US Black) a relaxed, composed person. [CHILLY adj. + MOST]

chilly most *adj.* [1990s] (US Black/teen) wonderful, perfect, excellent. [CHILLY MOST n.]

chime *n.* 1 [mid-19C] (US) false praise, empty flattery, esp. when aimed at tricking or defrauding its object. 2 [1940s] (US Black) one hour. 3 [1940s] (US Black) the beating of one's heart (cf. CHIMER). [note 17C–18C *chime*, a mere empty 'jingle' of words]

chimer *n.* [1940s] (US Black) 1 a clock or watch. 2 the heart, which also 'ticks'. [17C SE *chimer*, one who rings bells]

chimes *n.* [1960s] (US) the testicles (cf. CLAPPERS n.[2]). [the facet. resemblance to a pair of hanging bells]

chimleyco *n.* [early–mid-19C] Pimlico, London SW1. [the ranks of chimneys or 'chimleys' that can be seen in this stucco-laden London 'village']

chimmy *n.[1] see* SHIMMY n.[2].

chimmy *n.[2]* [20C] (W.I.) a woman's undergarment, essentially synon. with a petticoat (cf. SHIMMY n.[1]). [SE *chemise*]

chimmy *n.[3]* [1950s+] (W.I.) a chamberpot.

chimney *n.* 1 [late 19C] a heavy smoker (cf. SE *smoke like a chimney*). 2 [1920s–40s] (US Black) a hat (cf. CHIMNEY-POT). [(2) the chimney's position on top of the house and (1) the smoke issuing from it]

chimney chops *n.* [late 18C] a derog. term for a Black person. [the blackness of a *chimney* + CHOPS n. (3); given the continuing arguments vis-a-vis the inclusion of racial abuse in dictionaries, it is interesting, perhaps, to note that Grose (1785), in a relatively rare acknowledgement of such a problem, defines this term as 'an abusive appellation']

chimney-corner *adj.* [20C] (US) unofficial, not genuine, on the basis of popular acceptance; thus *chimney-corner law*, popular opinion, saloon-bar opinion. [the image of people chatting in a chimney corner]

chimney-pot *n.* [mid–late 19C] a cylindrical black silk hat, fashionable during the latter half of the 19C (cf. CHIMNEY). [resemblance]

chimney sweep *n.[1]* [mid-19C] an aperient medicine otherwise known as the 'black drop'. [its colour + the fact that it 'cleans one out']

chimney sweep *n.[2]* [late 19C] a clergyman. [his black clothing]

chimney-sweeper *n.* [mid-19C] nickname for an aperient, known as 'the black dose' or 'black drop', composed mainly of opium, mixed with vinegar and spices.

chimpung *n.* [1940s+] (W.I.) a derog. name for a Chinese person. [supposed imitation of Chinese speech]

chin/chin-chin *n.[1]* 1 [19C] talk, chatter, conversation (cf. CHIN MUSIC; CHINWAG). 2 [mid-19C–1900s] (US) cheek, impudence.

chin *n.*[2] [1960s–70s] (S.Afr. township) money. [ety. unknown; ? a local language]

chin *v.*[1] [late 19C] (US) to chatter; thus *chinning*, idle conversation, chatter. [CHIN n.[1] (1)]

chin *v.*[2] [1910s+] (orig. Glasgow) to hit someone (on the chin).

china *n.*[1] [late 19C+] (Cockney) anywhere other than England (possibly even other than London) or the place rich people go for their holidays.

china/china plate *n.*[2] [late 19C+] one's (best) friend. [rhy. sl. *china plate* = MATE]

china *n.*[3] [1940s] (US) money.

china *n.*[4] (US) **1** [1940s+] teeth. **2** [1960s] tea, as served at a lunch counter. [SE *china*, crockery]

China boy *n.* [mid-19C+] a derog. term for a Chinese man.

China cat *n.* [1960s+] (drugs) high potency heroin (cf. CHI n.[2]). [the trad. link of heroin and the Orient; note Grateful Dead song title c.1969, 'China Cat Sunflower']

china clippers *n.* [1950s+] (US) false teeth. [CHINA n.[4] (1); pun on Pan-American Airlines 'China Clipper' flying-boat service to the Far East]

China girl/town *n.* [1980s+] (drugs) fentanyl (cf. APACHE n.[2]). [a powerful synthetic opiate; ? the trad. link of opium (thus opiates) to China]

Chinaman *n.*[1] [late 19C] (US) a cup of tea. [SE *Chinese tea*]

Chinaman *n.*[2] [late 19C+] an Irishman. [fig. use that implies the alienation of an immigrant]

Chinaman *n.*[3] [1940s+] (US drugs) withdrawal from a narcotic, usu. heroin; thus *a Chinaman on one's back*, the pain of withdrawal.

Chinaman *n.*[4] [1940s–50s] (W.I.) a farthing. [like the stereotyped Chinese, the coin is small]

Chinaman *n.*[5] [1970s] (US) one who has political influence; thus *have a Chinaman*, to have political influence. [the image of the 'wily Oriental', now derog.]

Chinaman's/Chinese chance *n.* [1910s+] no chance whatsoever, no luck. [orig. gold rush use, when the Chinese worked otherwise abandoned claims]

Chinaman's nightmare *n.* [1980s] (US) bedlam, chaos (cf. CHINESE FIRE DRILL). [racial stereotyping]

Chinaman's shout *n.* [20C] (Aus.) a supposed 'treat' for which everyone involved must pay (cf. DUTCH TREAT). [the presumed miserliness of the Chinese]

Chinaman's trot *n.* [late 19C–1900s] (Aus.) a slow and steady jog.

Chinamat *n.* [1930s–50s] (US) a cheap Chinese restaurant. [SE *China* + (auto)mat]

china plate *see* CHINA n.[2].

China Street *n.* [early–mid-19C] Bow Street, London. [its proximity to Covent Garden, then a market, and thus to 'China oranges']

China Street pig *n.* [early 19C] a Bow Street officer; thus *floor the pig and bolt*, knock down the policeman and run off. [CHINA STREET + PIG n.[3]]

China town *see* CHINA GIRL.

China/Chinese white *n.* [1970s+] (drugs) **1** heroin (cf. CHI n.[2]). **2** fentanyl, a powerful synthetic narcotic (cf. APACHE n.[2]).

chin-/ear-biter *n.* [1990s] a general derog. term. [the image is of an uncoordinated person, unable to control their physical actions]

chinch *n.*[1] [mid-19C–1950s] a bedbug. [Sp. *chinche*, a bedbug]

chinch *n.*[2] [1940s+] (US) a miser. [ME + OF *chiche*, parsimonious, mean, early 14C–late 16C SE]

chinch house *n.* [late 19C+] a cheap hotel or lodging house (cf. CHINCH PAD; BUGHOUSE). [CHINCH n.[1] + SE *house*]

chinchilla *n.* [20C] (US) the vagina (cf. BADGER n.[7]).

chin-chin *n. see* CHIN n.[1].

chin-chin! *excl.* [mid-19C+] a popular toast when drinking,

synon. with 'Good health!' or 'Cheers!'. [Chinese *ts'ing ts'ing*, a general salutation, and as such picked up by sailors on Far East tours. A response, which has not entered the vocab., is *pa pa*]

chinch pad *n.* [late 19C–1950s] (US Black hobo) a very low standard of rooming house or hotel (cf. BUGHOUSE; CHINCH HOUSE). [CHINCH n.[1] + PAD n.[2]]

chinchy *adj.* [mid-17C–1950s] (US) miserly, mean, stingy. [CHINCH n.[2]; 14C–late 17C SE]

chincough *n.* [20C] (Irish) **1** whooping cough. **2** a spasm of laughter or tears. [OE *cincian*, to gasp and cough]

'chine *n.* [1950s–60s] (US Black) ma*chine*, either a car or a motorcycle (cf. SHEEN n.[2]). [abbr.]

chinee *n.*[1] [19C] a derog. term for a Chinese person (cf. HEATHEN CHINEE). [abbr. SE *Chinese*]

chinee *n.*[2] [19C] (US) a complementary ticket. [abbr. CHINESE DUCKET]

Chinese *n.* [20C] a Chinese meal (cf. INDIAN n.[3]).

Chinese *adj.* [20C] one of the racial stereotypes used in many contexts; the Chinese eye-shape, plus the supposed cunning of the 'wily Orientals' always has 'Chinese' implying something slightly out of true, physically, ethically or otherwise; thus used in the following combs. and phr. (cf. FRENCH adj.; IRISH adj.; JEW adj.; MEXICAN adj.).

Chinese angle *n.* [1930s–40s] (US) a strange twist. [the stereotype of *Chinese* as crooked, off-angle]

Chinese B *n.* [1950s+] (US) a grade that is marked higher than the student's work really deserved. [the preferential treatment given to supposedly disadvantaged Oriental students in an early form of affirmative action]

Chinese brown *n.* [1970s+] (drugs) a form of heroin (cf. CHI n.[2]).

Chinese/Indian burn *n.* [1930s+] a schoolyard torture whereby one child twists the skin on another's arm or wrist. [the stereotyped 'fiendish cruelties' of the Chinese or 'Red' Indians; note Chinese is UK, Indian is US]

Chinese chance *see* CHINAMAN'S CHANCE.

Chinese consumption *n.* [1930s+] (Aus.) a smoker's cough. [pun on 'wun bung lung', a 'Chinese' name]

Chinese copy *n.* [1940s+] (US) any copy that faithfully reproduces not just the accurate work but the mistakes, too. [? the stereotype (usually ascribed to Japan) of Oriental workmen as taking Western inventions and faithfully copying them in order to sell the cheaper reproductions back to the West]

Chinese deal *n.* [1930s+] a deal that fails to materialize. [negative stereotype of a Chinese businessman as one who enjoys the minutiae of bargaining but cannot be trusted to deliver the goods]

Chinese ducket *n.* [19C] (US) a complimentary ticket to a theatrical or sporting event (cf. CHINEE n.[2]). [the punch-holes in such tickets supposedly resembled Chinese money]

Chinese fashion *adv.* [1960s+] used to describe having sexual intercourse with the couple lying on their sides (cf. AMERICAN CULTURE; DOGFUCK n.[1]; DOGGY FASHION; GREEK WAY). [the implication is that such a position accommodates the supposedly transverse Chinese vagina]

Chinese fire drill *n.* [20C] **1** bedlam, chaos (cf. CHINAMAN'S NIGHTMARE). **2** (US campus) a student game whereby a car stops at the traffic lights and all those inside jump out, run round and round the car and then jump in again before driving away.

Chinese flush/straight *n.* [1930s+] in poker, a worthless hand, i.e. four cards of a flush or a straight. A proper hand requires five. [neg. stereotyping]

Chinese H *n.* [1980s+] (drugs) heroin (cf. CHI n.[2]). [SE *Chinese* + H n.[2]]

Chinese molasses *n.* [20C] (drugs) opium (cf. GUM n.[3]). [the origin and consistency of opium]

Chinese needlework *n.* [1940s] (US drugs) **1** the world of drug-dealing. **2** the injection of narcotics (cf. CHINESE TOBACCO). [the hypodermic *needle* used for injecting heroin and the stereotyped linking of the East to narcotics, orig. opium, subseq. heroin]

Chinese No. 3 *n.* [1970s+] (drugs) a variety of heroin, processed in Hong Kong and imported by Chinese smugglers (cf. CHI n.[2]).

Chinese red *n.* [1970s+] (drugs) heroin (cf. CHI n.[2]).

Chinese rocks *n.* [1970s+] (drugs) heroin (cf. CHI n.[2]).

Chinese rot *n.* [1940s–60s] (US) **1** venereal disease. **2** any form of unspecified 'mystery' disease. [the 'inscrutable' East]

Chinese screwdriver *n.* [1950s+] (Aus.) a hammer (cf. BIRMINGHAM SCREWDRIVER). [the supposed inability of the Chinese to perform simple physical tasks]

Chinese smoking *n.* [1960s] (N.Z.) sucking tobacco smoke through the mouth and exhaling through the nostrils. [? the smoke is reminiscent of the typical long 'Chinese' whiskers]

Chinese straight *see* CHINESE FLUSH.

Chinese take-away *n.* [1970s+] (gay) a bar where Oriental boys or young men are available for picking up by Western men. [pun on SE]

Chinese tobacco *n.* [1950s] opium. [despite the fact that Britain introduced China to opium *c.*1840, the drug and the nation have been inextricably linked ever since]

Chinese white *see* CHINA WHITE.

chinfest *n.* [20C] (US) any meeting at which there is a good deal of talking and gossip (cf. BLABFEST). [CHIN n.[1] + sfx. -FEST]

ching/ching-ching *n.*[1] [late 19C–1900s] (US) a derog. term for a Chinese person (cf. CHINK n.[3]; GINK n.[1]; GOOK n.[3]). [common Chinese name]

ching *n.*[2] [1970s–80s] (S.Afr.) money (cf. CHINK n.[1]; CHINKERS; CLINK n.[2]; JINGLE-BOYS; JINK]. [echoic]

chingao! *excl.* [1960s+] (US) what the FUCK! [imper. of Sp. sl. *chingar*, FUCK v.[1]]

chingazo *n.* [1970s+] sexual intercourse. [Sp. sl. *chingar*, FUCK v.[1]]

ching-ching *see* CHING n.[1].

chinger *v.* [20C] (market traders) to whinge, to complain, to scold; thus *chingerer*, one who complains, whinges. [? CHIN n.[1] + SE *whinge*]

chingo *n.* [1960s+] (US) a great deal. [Sp. sl., lit. 'a fuck of a lot']

chingus *n.* (US) **1** [1950s–60s] the penis. **2** [1980s+] any unnamed object (cf. THINGUMABOB). [DINGUS but in (1) note Sp. sl. *chingar*, FUCK v.[1]]

'chining *n.* [1950s–60s] (US Black) driving an automobile. ['CHINE]

chin-jaw *n.* [1940s] (US) idle chatter (cf. CHINWAG n.). [CHIN n.[1] + JAW n.]

chink *n.*[1] [late 16C–late 19C] money; often in pl. as *chinks* (cf. CHING n.[2]). [echoic]

chink *n.*[2] [18C] the vagina (cf. ARBOUR).

chink *n.*[3] **1** [late 19C+] (orig. Aus.) a derog. term for a Chinese person. **2** [1930s] (US) the Chinese language. **3** [1940s+] (orig. US) a derog. term for any Oriental or Asian person (cf. CHING n.[1]). **4** [1970s+] a Chinese meal (cf. INDIAN n.[5]; WOG n.[1]). [SE *China* or f. Chinese *ching-ching*, a courteous excl. (*DARE*)]

chink/chinkie/chinky *adj.* [late 19C+] Chinese; thus a derog. term for Oriental in general.

chink chow *n.* [20C] a derog. term for Chinese food. [CHINK adj. + CHOW n.[1] + ? pun on CHOW n.[2]]

chinker/chikwa/cinqua *n.* [mid-19C+] (Ling. Fr./Polari) the number five. [Ital. *cinque*, 5]

chinkers *n.* [mid–late 19C] money, esp. as coins (cf. CHING n.[2]). [CHINK n.[1]]

chinki-/chinky-chonks *n.* [1970s+] a derog. term for Asians in general (cf. NIGNOG). [CHINK n.[3] (3) + redup.]

chinkie *see* CHINK adj.

chinkie-jog *n.* [1930s] (Aus.) a slow and steady jog (cf. CHINAMAN'S TROT).

chink joint *n.* [1920s+] a derog. term for a cheap Chinese restaurant. [CHINK adj. + JOINT n.[3] (3)]

chinko *n.* [late 19C] (N.Z.) a derog. term for a Chinese person. [CHINK + sfx. -O]

chinks *n.*[1] [1930s+] (Irish) the 'creeps', the 'shivers', esp. in phr. *give one the chinks*. [dial. *chink*, a coughing fit]

chinks *n.*[2] [1940s–70s] (US) a derog. term for Chinese food (cf. CHINESE n.; CHINK CHOW).

chink-stick *n.* [1950s+] (W.I.) a rough board bed. [CHINCH n.[1], a bedbug, with which such beds are often infested + SE *stick*, a plank of wood]

chink-stopper *n.* [19C] the penis. [CHINK n.[2] + SE *stopper*, a plug]

chinky *n.* [1970s+] a derog. term for a Chinese restaurant.

chinky *adj.*[1] *see* CHINK adj.

chinky *adj.*[2] [20C] (US campus) stingy, mean. [CHINCHY + ref. to a SE *chink*, i.e. the tightness of one's wallet and pockets]

chinky-chonks *see* CHINKI-CHONKS.

chinless wonder *n.* [1960s+] a male scion of the British upper classes. Probably wealthy, certainly well-connected, but essentially devoid of intelligence or 'character'. [his stereotyped receding chin; a firm chin supposedly indicates a 'firm' personality]

chin music *n.* [early 19C+] conversation, chatter, talk, esp. defiant, aggressive, cheeky talk (cf. PEDAL MUSIC). [CHIN n.[1] + SE *music*]

chinny *adj.* [late 19C] (US) talkative, garrulous. [CHIN n.[1]]

chin-prop *n.* [19C] a brooch. [SE *chin* + PROP n.[3] (2); it sits at the top of a blouse]

chin rest *n.* [1990s] the female perineum, considered in the context of giving a woman oral sex.

chin-splitter *n.* [1900s] (US) a narrow goatee beard.

chinstrap *n.*[1] [20C] (Ulster) a dirty ring around an unwashed neck, a 'tide-mark'.

chinstrap *n.*[2] [1910s+] the buttocks. [thus note army jargon *on one's chinstraps*, absolutely exhausted]

chintz *n.* [late 19C] a bedbug. [CHINCH n.[1]]

chintzy *adj.* (US) **1** [20C] stingy, mean (cf. CHINCHY). **2** [1950s+] second-rate. [dial. *chincy*, mean, niggardly, ult. the *chinch* or *chintz*, an insect that attacks corn or grain and when squashed has an unpleasant smell]

chinwag *n.* [mid-19C+] a chat, a conversation (cf. CHIN MUSIC). [CHINWAG v.]

chinwag *v.* [mid-19C+] to chat, to converse (cf. CHIN n.[1]).

chinwork *n.* [1970s] (US) a chat, a conversation (cf. CHINWAG n.).

chip *n.*[1] [late 17C–early 19C] a child. [CHIP OF THE OLD BLOCK]

chip *n.*[2] [mid-19C+] £1, a sovereign (cf. CHIPS n.[2]). [? gambling *chips*. Note racing jargon *chip*, one shilling; Indian army jargon *chip*, a rupee]

chip *n.*[3] [late 19C–1950s] (US) **1** a woman (cf. CHIPPIE n.[2]). **2** a promiscuous woman, esp. a prostitute (cf. CHIPPIE n.[2]).

chip *n.*[4] [20C] (Aus.) a quarrel, an argument. [CHIP v.[1]]

chip *n.*[5] [1940s] (US Black) a sip (of liquor). [SE *chip*, a small amount]

chip *n.*[6] [1980s+] (drugs) heroin, esp. that has been diluted or 'cut'. [CHIP v.[2] (3)]

chip *n.*[7] [1990s] (US Black teen) a cellular/portable phone that is stolen and therefore used to make illegal and free phone calls. [the SE *microchip* that powers it]

chip v.[1] [late 19C+] (Aus./N.Z.) **1** to interrupt, to speak impudently. **2** to tease, to banter with. [dial. *chip*, a tiff, a quarrel]

chip v.[2] **1** [20C] (US Und.) to carry out a small crime with only minimal profits. **2** [1950s+] (drugs) to dabble in narcotic drug use. **3** [1950s+] to dilute drugs. [SE *chip*, a small amount]

chip v.[3] [1940s] (US Black) to sip one's drink.

chip v.[4] [1980s+] (orig. Black) to leave, to depart, to go somewhere. [ety. unknown; ? link to UK dial. *chip*, to step down]

chip at v. [late 19C+] to quarrel with, to criticize. [ext. of CHIP v.[1]]

chiphead n. [1980s+] a computer enthusiast. [SE (*silicon*) *chip* + sfx. -HEAD (2)]

chip in v. [mid-19C+] (orig. US) **1** to join in, to contribute. **2** to butt in, to interrupt. [poker jargon *chip in*, to put one's gambling chips on the table to signify one's joining in the round of betting]

chip in broth n. [17C–early 19C] a thing or matter of no importance, an addition that does neither good nor harm (cf. CHIP IN PORRIDGE; CHIP IN POTTAGE). [SE *chip*, anything unimportant, without flavour or nutrition]

chip in porridge n. [mid-17C+] a thing or matter of no importance (cf. CHIP IN BROTH).

chip in pottage n. [late 17C–18C] a thing or matter of no importance (cf. CHIP IN BROTH).

chip of/off the old block n. [mid-17C+] **1** someone that resembles their father, or reproduces the family characteristics. **2** something which resembles an original or source object. [*off* version has been preferred in the 20C]

chip of the same block n. [early–mid-17C] a person or thing derived from the same source or parentage (cf. CHIP OF THE OLD BLOCK).

chip one's teeth, to phr. [1940s+] (US, orig. milit.) to talk, esp. to excess or angrily. [one's fury fig. damages one's teeth]

chippens n. [20C] (Irish) money. [? SE *chippings*]

chipper n.[1] [early–mid-19C] a cheerful, lively young man.

chipper n.[2] [1910s+] (Irish) a fish and chip shop (cf. CHIPPIE n.[4]).

chipper n.[3] [1980s+] (drugs) an occasional user of narcotics (cf. CHIPPY n.[4]). [CHIP v.[2] (2)]

chipper adj. [late 19C+] (orig. US) cheerful, lively, perhaps slightly drunk. [dial. *chipper*, a cheery song, amiable chatter]

chippery n. [1900s–10s] a verbal exchange, an argument. [SE *chipper*, to twitter, to babble]

chippie n.[1] **1** [late 19C–1970s] (US) a beginner, an innocent. **2** [late 19C–1930s] (US) a young person. [CHIP OF THE OLD BLOCK or they have only just *chipped in*]

chippie/chippy n.[2] **1** [late 19C+] (orig. US) a promiscuous young woman, a prostitute (often a part-timer or 'amateur') (cf. CHIPPY-CHASER). **2** [1930s–40s] (US Black) a slim, attractive 'glamour girl'. [? CHEAPIE or Fr. *chipie*, a shrewish woman]

chippie/chippy n.[3] [20C] **1** a carpenter, esp. theatrical, film use. **2** the 'traditional' nickname of men called Carpenter or Wood. [SE *chips* of wood. orig. RN jargon *chippy*, the ship's carpenter, *chippy chap*, a carpenter's mate]

chippie/chippy n.[4] [1910s+] a fish and chip shop (cf. CHIPPER n.[2]). [abbr.]

chippie/chippy v.[1] **1** [1930s+] to be sexually unfaithful. **2** [1990s] to act as a prostitute. [CHIPPIE n.[2]]

chippie/chippy v.[2] [1950s+] (drugs) to use narcotics, esp. heroin, only on an irregular basis rather than to be a habitual addict (cf. CHIPPER n.[3]). [? CHEAPIE or CHIP v.[3]]

chippie/chippy v.[3] [1970s] to work half-heartedly (cf. CHIP v.[2]). [? SE *chip away at*]

chipping n.[1] [late 19C+] (Aus.) the act of being cheeky, impudent. [CHIPPY adj.[1]]

chipping n.[2] [1920s] the act of tipping. [CHIP IN]

chipping n.[3] [1950s+] (drugs) the occasional use of drugs. [CHIPPIE v.[2]]

chippy n.[1] *see* CHIPPIE n.[2].

chippy n.[2] *see* CHIPPIE n.[3].

chippy n.[3] *see* CHIPPIE n.[4].

chippy n.[4] [1970s+] (drugs) cocaine.

chippy adj.[1] **1** [late 19C+] cheeky, impudent. **2** [late 19C–1940s] angry, irritated. **3** [1970s+] resentful, jealous. [*have a chip on one's shoulder*. usu. in middle-class use and often as a means of dismissing genuine complaints, the implication is that such 'chippiness' has no real justification other than class-based resentment]

chippy adj.[2] [late 19C] feeling hungover. [FEEL CHEAP]

chippy adj.[3] [1940s+] (US) cheap.

chippy v. *see* CHIPPIE v.

chippy-chaser n. [early 19C+] **1** a well-dressed loafer who specifically pursues young shopgirls and even schoolgirls. **2** a devotee of prostitutes (cf. CUNT-HOUND; PLEASURE HOUND). [CHIPPIE n.[2] + SE *chaser*]

chippy habit n. [late 19C–1930s] the occasional use of opium, rather than the regular use necessitated by addiction (cf. ICE-CREAM EATER). [CHIPPIE v.[2] + HABIT]

chippy house/joint n. [1920s–30s] (US) a brothel (cf. ACCOMMODATION HOUSE). [CHIPPIE n.[2] + HOUSE n.[1] (1)/JOINT n.[3] (3)]

chippy on v. [1950s+] (US) to cheat on one's wife or husband with a new sexual partner. [CHIPPIE v.[1] (1)]

chips n.[1] [late 18C+] a carpenter; hence the 'inevitable' nickname *Chippy Wood*.

chips n.[2] [mid-19C+] (mainly US) money, orig. a sovereign; thus *in the chips*, well-off (albeit temporarily), *when the chips are down*, in the final assessment, when it comes to the point (cf. CHIP n.[2]). [SE *chip*, a counter used in a game of chance]

chips n.[3] [1950s+] (US) the buttocks. [? SE *chip*, buffalo dung]

chips n.[4] [1950s–60s] *chip*olata sausages. [abbr.]

chips! excl. [20C] (US) that's mine! I want to do that! I want a share! a child's term used to claim the whole or an equal part of a given object; the negative response to the cry is *no chips*, no shares (cf. AIKIES). [SE *chip*, a small piece]

chipsy adj. [1980s+] (US campus) arrogant and superficial (cf. CHIPPY adj.[1]). [one who has a 'chip on their shoulder']

chip together v. [mid-19C] (orig. US) to join in, to contribute (cf. CHIP IN).

chira/chicharra n. [1960s+] (drugs) marijuana. [Sp. *chicharra*, a cicada; thus ? play on ROACH]

chirk/chirky adj. [18C] (US) cheerful, happy (cf. CHIRPY). [SE *chirk*, chirrup]

chirk v. [mid-19C–1930s] (US) to make cheerful. [CHIRK adj.]

chirk up v. [19C] (US) to cheer up. [CHIRK adj.]

chirp/chirper n. [1940s–50s] (US) a female vocalist.

chirp v. **1** [mid-19C+] to inform (cf. SING). **2** [late 19C–1930s] (US) to talk loudly, to interrupt. **3** [1980s+] (US campus) to vomit. **4** [1990s] (S.Afr.) to tease, to taunt, to complain.

chirper n.[1] **1** [19C] a singer. **2** [19C+] the mouth.

chirper n.[2] [mid-19C] a glass or tankard. [CHIRPING MERRY]

chirpiness n. [mid-19C+] happiness, cheerfulness. [one *chirps* with pleasure]

chirping merry adj. [late 17C–early 19C] cheerfully drunk; thus *chirping glass*, 'a cheerful glass, that makes the company chirp like birds in spring' (Grose 1785) (cf. ABOUT RIGHT adj.[1]).

chirp out/pull a chirper, to phr. [1970s] (US) to accelerate one's car from a standstill so as to make the tyres screech. [SE *chirp*]

chirpy adj. [19C] happy, gay, cheerful (cf. CHIRK adj.). [SE *chirrup*]

chirrup v. [late 19C] to cheer or boo a music-hall turn. [the response varies as to whether or not the singer has tipped the gallery]

chirruper *n.* [19C] an extra glass of alcohol (cf. CHIRPER n.²). [its effect will make the drinker CHIRPY]

chirrupy *adj.* [late 19C] (orig. US) cheerful. [var. on CHIRPY]

chis/chise *n.*¹ [early 19C] a knife. [var. on CHIV n.¹]

chis/chise *n.*² [early 19C] (tramp) nothing, no good. [var. on CHICE; SHICER]

chisel/chizzel/chizzle *v.*¹ **1** [early 19C+] to cheat; thus *chisel out of*, to defraud. **2** [1940s] (US) to be unfaithful. [SE *chisel*, to cut or pare down; thus 'to take a slice off' (Hotten, 1867). (2) fig. use of (1)]

chisel *v.*² **1** [1920s–40s] to butt in, to intrude, to insinuate oneself. **2** [1920s–60s] (US) to beg.

chisel-chin *n.* [20C] (US) one whose lower jaw protrudes. [supposed resemblance]

chiseler/chiseller *n.* [mid-19C+] (orig. US) a cheat, a swindler. [CHISEL v.¹ (1)]

chisel in *v.* [1920s–50s] (US) to butt in, to intrude, to insinuate oneself. [ext. of CHISEL v.²]

chiseller *n.*¹ *see* CHISELER.

chiseller/chisler/chissler *n.*² [20C] (Irish) a child. [var. on dial. *childer*, a child]

chiser/chiver *n.* [early–mid-19C] a knife. [var. on CHIV n.¹]

chisler *see* CHISELLER n.².

chism *see* JISM.

chissler *see* CHISELLER n.².

chit *n.* [late 18C+] a letter, a note. [CHITTY]

chitari *n.* [1960s+] (drugs) a variety of cannabis. [? Hind.]

chitchat *n.*¹ [18C] banter, light talk. [SE *chat* + redup.; SE f. 1800]

chitchat *n.*² [19C] a measure of alcohol. [? enough to foster a pleasant CHITCHAT n.¹]

chitlins *n.* [mid-19C+] (US, South) the bowels. [Black/South. pron. of SE *chitterlings*, the intestines, usu. of pigs]

chitlins 101 *n.* [1960s–70s] (US Black college) any form of Black Studies course. [self-mockery; the stereotyped Black love of soul food, the recipes of which often feature offal or CHITLINS]

Chi town *n.* [1920s+] (US) *Chi*cago, Illinois. [abbr.]

chitral/citrol *n.* [1960s+] (drugs) high potency hashish, from Nepal. [the local name]

chits *n.*¹ [19C] bugs, lice. [var. on CHATS n.²]

chits *n.*² [1940s–50s] (US Black) pig intestines. [abbr. CHITLINS]

chitterling/chitterlin *n.* [19C] the penis (cf. BACON n.¹; CRIMSON CHITTERLING). [SE *chitterlings*, the small intestines of animals, especially pigs]

chitterlings/chitterlins *n.*¹ [late 18C–19C] the bowels. [for ety. *see* CHITTERLING]

chitterlings/chitterlins *n.*² [mid-19C] shirt frills affected by ageing dandies. [orig. late 16C. the term ? f. butchers' jargon *frill*, the mesentry veins, suspending the viscera from the backbone]

chitty *n.* [late 18C+] (orig. Anglo-Ind.) a letter, a note, any small piece of paper inscribed with writing, usu. instructions. [Hind. *chitthi*, 'a letter or note. Also, a certificate given to a servant or the like, a pass' (Y&B); ult. Skrt. *chitra*, a spot or mark]

chitty-face *n.* [early 17C–late 18C] a child with a pinched face or a baby-face. [dial. *chitty*, thin, baby-faced]

chiv/chive/chiff *n.*¹ [17C+] a knife. [Rom. *chiv, chive*, a knife]

chiv *n.*² [mid–late 19C] (US, west) a White Southerner. [SE *chivalry*; f. the South's obsession with 'honour' and 'chivalry']

chiv *n.*³ [1910s] (Aus.) the face (cf. SHIF n.²). [CHEVY CHASE]

chiv *adj.* [1990s] (US teen) gentlemanly. [SE *chivalrous*]

chiv/chev/chib/chibe *v.* [mid-19C+] **1** to stab. **2** to cut off. **3** to saw or file. **4** to smash a glass in someone's face and slash them with the shards. [Rom. *chiv*, to stab]

chiva *n.* [1960s+] (US drugs) heroin. [Sp. + ? CHEEB or CHIBA, although this is usu. marijuana]

chivalry *n.* [mid-19C] sexual intercourse (cf. CAVAULT).

chiv artist *n.* [1930s] (US) an expert in using a knife. [CHIV n.¹ + ARTIST n.²]

chive *see* CHIV n.¹.

chive-fencer *n.* [mid-19C] **1** a street-seller of knives and cutlery (cf. HAND-SAW). **2** one who harbours murderers. [CHIV n.¹ + FENCER]

chiver *see* CHISER.

chivey *n.* **1** [late 18C–mid-19C] a scolding, a telling off. **2** [mid-19C] a shout. [dial. *chevy*, to pursue, to hunt, to tease; ? ult. proper name *Chevy Chase*, the site of a celebrated border skirmish, soon memorialized in a popular 17C ballad. Also note the game *Chevy Chase*, which depends on the shouting of the word 'chive']

chivey *adj.* [mid-19C] noisy. [CHIVEY n.]

chivey *v.* [mid-19C] to chase around, to hunt about. [CHIVEY n.]

chiving lay *n.* [late 18C] (Und.) **1** cutting open the back of a coach to steal the large wigs worn by the passengers. **2** cutting the braces of a coach (the strong leather straps that suspend the body of a coach from the springs), the coachman dismounts and, while his attention is distracted by one robber, an accomplice plunders the boot of its contents. [CHIV v. + LAY n.⁴ (2)]

chivver/chiv-man *n.* [1920s+] an expert in using a knife (cf. CHIV ARTIST). [CHIV n.¹ + sfx. -MAN]

chivy/chivvy *n.* [late 19C–1950s] the face. [CHEVY CHASE]

chivvy *n.* **1** [1920s] a general term of address, 'old chap'. **2** [1940s–50s] a moustache. [CHEVY CHASE]

chivvy *v.*¹ **1** [mid–late 19C] to tease, to mock, to make fun of. **2** [19C+] to scold, to tell off. [CHIVEY n. (1)]

chivvy *v.*² [20C] to slash with a knife. [CHIV n.¹]

chivy *adj.* [late 19C] relating to the use of knives; thus *chivy duel*, a knife fight. [CHIV n.¹]

chizz *v.* [late 19C–1950s] (juv.) to cheat, to swindle. [CHISEL v.¹]

chizzel *see* CHISEL v.¹.

chizzer *n.* [1930s] a cheat, a swindler. [CHIZZ]

chizzle *see* CHISEL v.¹.

cho! *see* CHA!

choad *n.* **1** [1960s+] (orig. US high school) the penis; thus *choadsmoker*, a fellator or fellatrix (cf. CHODE). **2** [1980s+] a piece of excrement. [? Navajo *chodis*, penis]

choak pear *see* CHOKE PEAR.

choan/chrome *n.* [1960s] (US campus) sexual intercourse. [ety. unknown; ? abbr. ACTION n.² (2)]

choc *n.* [20C] (US) second-rate beer. [CHOCTAW n.²]

choccy *n.* [1990s] the anus (cf. BOURNEVILLE BOULEVARD). [abbr. CHOCOLATE EYE]

chocha *n.* [1960s+] (US) **1** the vagina. **2** sexual intercourse. [Sp. *chocha*, a doddering woman]

choc-ice *n.* [1990s] (US Black) a derog. term for a Black person whose colour may be Black, but whose opinions, attitudes, lifestyle and goals are all taken from White society and standards (cf. OREO). [the SE *choc-ice* is black outside but white within]

chockablock *adj.* [mid-19C+] crammed full, crammed together; thus *chockablock full*. [naut. jargon *chockablock*, 'said of a tackle with the two blocks run close together so that they touch each other—the limit of hoistingg' (*OED*); transferred to people this became naut. sl. and thence sl.]

chock and log *n.* [20C] (Aus.) a dog. [rhy. sl.]

chocker *adj.* [1940s+] (orig. naut.) fed up, disgruntled. [SE *chockablock*]

chocker *n.* [1940s] (US Black) a tie. [SE *choker*]

chockers *n.* [late 19C+] (market traders) the feet. [ety. unknown; ? *chalk* = walk]

chocko see CHOCO n.[1].

chocks away! excl. [1930s+] (orig. RAF) let's go! let's be off! [the chocks, orig. wood, that were positioned as 'brakes' next to aircraft wheels]

chocky jockey n. [1990s] a male homosexual. [CHOCCY + JOCKEY n.[1]]

choco/chocko n.[1] [1930s+] (Aus.) **1** a militiaman or conscripted soldier, esp. one who was drafted into the WW2 militia but never left Australia. **2** a conscientious objector. [CHOCOLATE SOLDIER]

choco n.[2] [1970s+] (usu. middle/upper class) a derog. term for a Black person. [abbr. CHOCOLATE n.[1]]

chocolate n.[1] [20C] a derog. term for a Black person; thus extended to chocolate to the bone, referring to a very dark skin. [colour or ? f. rhy. sl. chocolate frog = WOG. According to Maledicta II 'especially a woman or homosexual']

chocolate/chocolate stuff n.[2] (drugs) **1** [1950s] opium. **2** [1950s+] (Mexican) heroin (cf. TOOTSIE ROLL n.[1]). **3** [1960s+] hashish. [the colour of the drugs]

chocolate n.[3] [1980s+] (S.Afr. Black) a 20-rand note (cf. CLIPPER n.[3]; TIGER n.[12]). [its colour]

chocolate adj. [20C] **1** used derog. in ref. to a Black person. **2** pertaining to the anus, to defecation and, by ext. to homosexuality. [in both cases, ext. in a variety of combs. below, the brownness of the chocolate is equated with the sl. use]

chocolate baby n. [1900s] (US) a derog. term for a Black person (cf. CHOCOLATE n.[1]). [CHOCOLATE adj. (1)]

chocolate bar n. [20C] (US) a derog. term for a Black person (cf. CHOCOLATE n.[1]). [CHOCOLATE adj. (1)]

chocolate bunny n. [1980s] (US) a derog. term for a Black person (cf. CHOCOLATE n.[1]). [CHOCOLATE adj. (1)]

chocolate cha-cha v. [1990s] (US) to have anal intercourse. [CHOCOLATE adj. (2)]

chocolate chips n. [1970s+] (drugs) LSD (cf. A n.[3]). [a variety of LSD packaged in brown capsules/pills]

chocolate chutney n. [1990s] diarrhoea. [CHOCOLATE adj. (2) + CHUTNEY n.]

chocolate city n. [1970s+] a Black ghetto, any concentration of Blacks (cf. VANILLA SUBURB). [coined by George Clinton, founder of the funk band Parliament-Funkadelic]

chocolate deluxe n. [1990s] (US Black teen) an attractive, sexy, dark-complexioned Afro-American woman (cf. BUTTER PECAN). [a popular brand of ice-cream]

chocolate drop n. [late 19C+] a derog. term for a Black person (cf. CHOCOLATE n.[1]). [CHOCOLATE adj. (1)]

chocolate ecstasy n. [1980s+] (drugs) crack cocaine made brown by adding chocolate milk powder during production (cf. COCOA ROCKS).

chocolate eye n. [1990s] the anus.

chocolate freeway see CHOCOLATE HIGHWAY.

chocolate frog n. [1970s+] **1** (Aus.) an informer. **2** influenza. [rhy. sl. chocolate frog = (1) DOG n.[7]; (2) WOG n.[1] (4)]

chocolate highway/freeway/speedway/tunnel n. [1970s+] (US) the rectum (cf. BOURNEVILLE BOULEVARD).

chocolate lover n. [1960s+] (US) one who prefers Black sexual partners, whether hetero- or homosexual. [CHOCOLATE n.[1]]

chocolate rock n. [1990s] (drugs) a dark substance that is produced in the pipe during the smoking of crack cocaine. [SE chocolate, brown + ROCK n.[4]]

chocolate runway n. [1990s] the anus.

chocolate runway pilot n. [1990s] a male homosexual. [CHOCOLATE RUNWAY + SE pilot]

chocolate soldier n. [20C] (Aus.) **1** a member of the 8th Infantry Brigade of the Australian Imperial Forces (A.I.F.) who arrived in Egypt too late to join in the Gallipoli campaign. **2** a soldier who was drafted into the WW2 militia but never left Australia. [SE chocolate solider, a soldier who will not fight]

chocolate speedway see CHOCOLATE HIGHWAY.

chocolate speedway rider n. [1990s] a male homosexual. [CHOCOLATE adj. (2)]

chocolate starfish n. [1990s] the anus. [CHOCOLATE adj. (2)]

chocolate tea-towel holder n. [1990s] the anus. [CHOCOLATE adj. (2)]

chocolate thunder n. [1980s+] (US Black) any Black basketball player. [CHOCOLATE n.[1] + SE thunder]

chocolate tunnel see CHOCOLATE HIGHWAY.

chocolate whizzway n. [1990s] the anus.

choctaw n.[1] [mid-19C–1930s] (orig. US) an unknown, foreign or otherwise incomprehensible language (cf. GREEK n.[2]; HEBREW; ST GILES'S GREEK). [SE choctaw, the language of the Choctaw, a Muskogean North American Indian people, originally inhabiting Mississippi and Alabama]

choctaw n.[2] [20C] (US) second-rate beer (cf. CHOC). [? proper name Choctaw; the stereotypical Native American being satisfied with inferior products]

chode n. [1990s] (US) used to indicate a fool. It can be used alone, e.g. You're a chode! or as a pfx. or sfx., e.g. Shut up, chodelick! Piss off, dickchode! [CHOAD, the difference may only be in sp.]

choff n. [1950s–60s] food. [CHOW n.[1]+ SCOFF n.; Cape Du. (and orig. European Du.) term meaning a quarter of a day, and thus one of the four meals eaten in a day]

choice adj. [1970s+] excellent, first-rate.

choice riot n. [late 19C–1900s] an unpleasant noise.

choice spirit n. [late 18C] a devil-may-care, selfish, drunken person. [SE choice spirit, a spirit of special excellence, worthy of being chosen; SE was coined by Shakespeare in Henry VI Pt 1 (1599)]

choir bird n. [late 18C–early 19C] (Und.) a mendicant villain who, recently released from prison, returns to robbery. [var. on QUEER BIRD n. (1)]

choirboy n. [1970s+] (US) **1** a innocently honest person. **2** a naïve person, a fool.

choke n.[1] **1** [late 19C] prison bread, which is hard to swallow and indigestible. **2** [1920s+] (Aus.) an act of garrotting. **3** [1940s+] a shock to the nerves.

choke n.[2] [20C] (US) a derog. term for a Mexican. [abbr. CHILE-CHOKER]

choke v.[1] [1910s–40s] (US) to stop talking, esp. as imper. Choke it!, shut up!

choke v.[2] [1930s+] to surprise, to shock, to disgust (cf. ENOUGH TO MAKE A BLACK MAN CHOKE).

choke v.[3] [1980s+] **1** (US campus) to do badly in work that one should have found easy. **2** (US Black) to lose one's nerve when faced by pressure. [sports jargon choke up, to become tense and thus ineffective under pressure]

choke a darkie, to phr. [1960s+] (Aus.) to excrete. [coarse pun]

choke and chew/puke n. [1970s+] (US) a roadside café, a truckstop. [SE choke, chew + puke; the poor quality of the food]

chokebored adj. [20C] (US) (of a person) thin; thus chokebore pants, trousers that narrow towards the bottom, esp. riding breeches. [SE chokebore, a shotgun of which the bore narrows towards the muzzle, keeping the shot together and increasing the effective range]

choked adj.[1] [1940s+] upset, annoyed, depressed, having 'a lump in one's throat'. [CHOKE v.[2]]

choked adj.[2] [1990s] (US campus) drunk. [one's inability to speak coherently]

choked by a hempen quinsey phr. [late 18C–early 19C]

hanged. [SE *quinsey*, inflammation of the throat, tonsillitis; *hempen* refers to the hangman's noose]

choked down *adj.* [1970s+] (US Black) well dressed (cf. CHOKE-RAG). [? CHOKER n.[1] (4), a cravat; thus one who wears one must look smart]

choke dog *n.* **1** [early 19C–1910s] cheese (cf. CHOKE'EM ARSE). **2** [early 19C] rum, grog. [joc. ref. to the effects]

choked up/up tight *adj.* [1960s] (US Black) formally and thus uncomfortably dressed. [the tight collar and tie to which the wearer is unaccustomed]

choke'em arse *n.* [1900s] (Can.) cheese (cf. CHOKE DOG). [SE *choke* + ARSE n.[1]; its constipatory effects]

choke Kojak *v.* [1990s] to masturbate (cf. GIVE YUL BRYNNER A HIGH FIVE; SLAP HIGH FIVES WITH YUL BRYNNER). [SE *choke* + proper name *Kojak*, a bald-headed TV detective (cf. BALD-HEADED HERMIT)]

choke-me *n.* [1950s] (W.I.) foofoo, a mixture of yams, plantains and cassava boiled and then pounded into a thick mass. [its heavy, cloying consistency]

choke off *v.* **1** [19C] to get rid of someone. **2** [19C] to halt a person's activities. **3** [mid-19C+] to upbraid, to reprimand. **4** [mid-19C+] to silence (in mid-flow). [SE *choke* v. + the use of a *choke* to force a bulldog to relinquish its grip]

choke/choak pear *n.* [late 18C] an unanswerable objection. [SE *choke pear*, an instrument of torture, similar in shape to the rubber gags favoured by today's S&M adepts, made of an iron 'pear', which is forced into the victim's mouth, a key is turned and spikes protrude from the metal into the mouth, rendering it impossible to remove unless the mouth is cut or another key obtained. This object was itself derived f. 16C *choke pear*, an inedible, hard pear, suitable for making the drink *perry*, but rejected as a dessert]

choker *n.*[1] **1** [18C–19C] the hangman's noose. **2** [mid-19C] a garrotter (cf. WIND-STOPPER). **3** [mid-19C] a large neckerchief, which is worn high round the throat. **4** [mid-19C] a cravat; thus *white-choker*, the white cravat worn by tavern waiters or mutes at a funeral and thus the waiter himself. **5** [mid-19C] a clergyman. **6** [late 19C] a high collar. [fig. uses of SE *choker*, that which chokes]

choker *n.*[2] **1** [early 19C] a rebuff. **2** [mid-19C] an especially amusing story or anecdote, a lie (cf. CAULKER). **3** [late 19C–1910s] an embarrassing question. **4** [1950s+] a disappointment, an annoyance (cf. SICKENER). **5** [1950s+] (Irish) a person who fails to come up to expectations. [CHOKE v.[1]]

choker *n.*[3] [mid-19C+] a prison (cf. CHOKEY).

choke-rag/-strap *n.* [20C] (US) a necktie (cf. CHOKER n.[1]). [SE and its supposed effect on the (reluctant) wearer]

choker-hole *n.* [1920s–30s] (US) a doughnut. [the fat-saturated dough is likely to choke the eater]

chokes *n.* [1980s+] (US drugs) an extreme response to taking an extra-large puff on a marijuana cigarette or a pipe.

chokes and croaks *n.* [1960s+] (US campus) a course in first aid and safety education.

choke-strap *see* CHOKE-RAG.

choke/milk the chicken/chook, to *phr.* [20C] to masturbate (cf. ACCOST THE OSCAR MEYER; CHOKE THE GOPHER).

choke the gopher, to *phr.* [1970s+] (US) to masturbate (cf. CHOKE THE CHICKEN).

choke up *v.* [20C] (US) to give unwillingly, esp. to pay a long-standing debt (cf. COUGH UP).

chokey/chauki *n.* [mid-19C+] **1** a prison. **2** (Und.) the punishment cells. **3** imprisonment. **4** the prison punishment diet of bread and water. [Hind. *chauki*, a 4-sided building or a shed, esp. a custom's house or police station and thus a lock-up]

choking/cold pie *n.* [mid-17C–mid-19C] a heavy-handed practical joke played on someone who falls asleep in

company; cotton is wrapped up in a tube of paper, this is then set on fire and the smoke is directed up the sleeper's nostrils.

choking/stopping oyster *n.* [mid–late 16C] a reply that silences one's opponent.

chokka/chokker *adj.* **1** [1920s+] full to the brim. **2** [1940s+] extremely dissatisfied, unhappy, 'fed up'. [SE *choc full* or CHOCKABLOCK]

choky *adj.* [mid-19C+] having a tendency to make one feel as if one were choking.

chola/cholillo *see* CHOLO.

cholly *n.*[1] [1940s] (US Black) a $1 bill. [? MR CHARLIE, the source of employment and thus money]

cholly *n.*[2] [1980s+] (drugs) cocaine. [CHARLIE n.[7] (1)]

cholo/chola/cholillo *n.* **1** [19C+] (US) a derog. term for a Mexican, esp. one considered lower class or of mixed blood (cf. BATO; CHICO). **2** [1960s+] (US) a teenage gang member. [*Chololán*, now *Cholula*, a district of Mexico]

chome *see* CHOAN.

chommie/tjommie *n.* [1940s+] (S.Afr.) a friend, a pal, a mate, also as a form of address. [SE *chum*]

cho-mo *n.* [20C] (US Und.) child molester. [abbr.]

chomp *v.* [1980s+] (US campus) to be disgusting, unappealing, second-rate (cf. SUCK v.[2]).

chompers *n.*[1] [20C] (US) teeth, either genuine or false.

chompers *n.*[2] [1980s+] (US campus) anyone or anything inferior, second-rate, unappealing. [CHOMP + 'Oxford' sfx. *-ers*]

chomus/chom *n.* [1930s+] (US) a (private) detective. [var. on SHAMUS]

chong your schlong, to *phr.* [1990s] to masturbate. [*chong*, echoic of a hit + SCHLONG]

chonkeys *n.* [mid-19C] a form of meat pasty, sold in the streets. [ety. unknown. E.P. suggests the proper name of a long-forgotten pieman, but note Fr. sl. *chancre*, a paunch (lit. 'ulcer') and *manger comme un chancre*, to eat heartily]

chooch *n.*[1] [1970s+] (US) a fool. [southern Ital. *ciuccio*, lit. a donkey; thus a fool]

chooch *n.*[2] [1980s+] (US drugs) a stingy dealer. [? CHINCH n.[2]]

choof *n.* [1980s+] (Aus. drugs) cannabis. [? SE *chuff*, to puff]

choof/choof off *v.* [1940s+] (Aus.) to go, to move, to leave. [SE *chuff*, to go, usu. of a locomotive]

choogle *v.* [1960s+] (US) to drive around. [? *choo-choo* + *chug*]

chook *n.* [late 19C+] (Aus.) **1** a chicken. **2** a woman (cf. CHICK n.[4]). **3** a punning nickname of anyone called Fowler. [SE *chicken*]

chookie/chooky *n.* [1990s] (Aus.) a general term of affection. [CHOOK]

choom *n.* [1910s+] (Aus./N.Z.) an Englishman. [northern pron. of *chum*]

choops! *excl.* [mid-19C–1900s] (orig. Anglo-Ind.) be quiet! shut up! [Hind. *chuprao*, keep quiet]

choose *v.* [1950s–60s] (US Black) for a prostitute to select the pimp for whom she will work; thus *choosing money*, the voluntary donation of her earnings by the prostitute to signify to her new pimp that she has chosen him.

choose off *v.* [1970s+] (US Black) to challenge to a fight; thus imper. *choose off!*

choose out *v.* [1930s+] (US) to challenge to a fight (cf. CHOOSE OFF).

chooser *n.* [19C] a plagiarist. [ironic use of SE *choose*, the plagiarist decides what he will steal]

choose up *v.* [1960s+] (US prison) for an experienced inmate to select a newcomer as a homosexual partner, whether or not the latter agrees to act as one.

chootah *adj.* [mid-19C–1930s] (orig. Anglo-Ind.) small, insignificant. [Urdu *chota*, small]

choozies *n.* [1990s] (Aus.) the female breasts. [? corruption of SE *bosom* or abbr. *buzzies*]

chop n.[1] [early 19C+] food; thus *small chop*, small items of food. [orig. W.Afr. pidgin, where colonists and Africans alike used it to describe indigenous food. It was further suggested that orig. chop had meant only one dish, *long pig*, human flesh]

chop n.[2] **1** [early 19C] a blow with the fist, esp. to the face (cf. CHOPPER n.[2]). **2** [1960s+] a blow in martial arts, using the side of the hand.

chop n.[3] **1** [19C+] (Aus.) a share, portion. **2** [19C] (Aus.) something to be valued or prized (cf. FIRST CHOP).

chop n.[4] [1920s+] (Aus./N.Z.) a wood-chopping contest.

chop n.[5] [1940s+] (orig. US) a cut, usu. in a salary or in a price.

chop n.[6] [1950s–70s] (US juv.) an insult, a cruel remark. [CHOP v.[4] (2)]

chop n.[7] [1980s+] (UK Black) gold, as in chains, rings and similar jewellery. [? SE *chop*, goods bearing a mark that determines their quality]

chop/chop up v.[1] (Und.) **1** [17C–18C] to do something quickly. **2** [18C–19C] to speak; thus *chop the whiners*, to say one's prayers. [SE *chop*, to thrust or move with force or suddenness]

chop v.[2] [mid–late 19C] to eat a chop.

chop v.[3] **1** [late 19C–1900s] (US) to stop what one is doing. **2** [1950s–1960s] (US Black) to attack someone verbally, to discredit someone, to have the last word (cf. CAP ON). **3** [1980s+] to dismiss from a job. [ext. of SE *chop*, to cut (off)]

chop v.[4] [1920s+] (US) to shoot, esp. with an automatic weapon. [CHOPPER n.[4]]

chop v.[5] [1940s–50s] to hang someone. [? the 'chopping off' of the victim's breath]

chop v.[6] [1950s+] (orig. US) to customize a car. [one 'chops' it down in size]

chop v.[7] [1960s+] (drugs) to adulterate, usu. a drug in powder form. [SE *chop*, to cut; one chops up the drug with whatever adulterant one is using]

chop v.[8] [1960s+] to eat. [CHOP n.[1]]

chop by chance n. [late 17C–early 18C] a very rare or extra-ordinary event.

chop-chop v. [mid-19C+] to hurry, esp. as imper. *chop-chop!* hurry up!

chop-chop adv. [mid-19C+] quickly, fast. [Chinese pidgin, orig. Chinese *k'wâi-k'wâi*]

chop-church/church-chopper n. [late 18C] a corrupt dealer in benefices, the choicest of which could be sold off to the highest bidder. [SE *chop*, to barter + *church*]

chop cotton v. [20C] (US) to work hard.

chop it up v. [1950s–60s] (US) to discuss, to talk about (cf. CARVE UP SCORES).

chop-logs n. [16C–17C] a contentious, sophistical arguer. [SE *chop-logic*]

chop off v. [late 19C–1930s] (US) to finish, to bring to a conclusion. [SE *chop*, to cut]

chopped hay n. [1910s–20s] imperfectly assimilated knowledge.

chopped liver n.[1] [20C] the vagina (cf. BACON SANDWICH).

chopped liver n.[2] [1950s+] (US) anything seen as trivial, esp. in phr. *now that ain't chopped liver*, that is important.

chopper n.[1] **1** [early 19C] a blow to the face. **2** [1910s+] (Aus.) a blow to the back of the neck, given with the side of the hand. **3** [20C] the penis (cf. ARSE-OPENER). [SE *chop*, to cut]

chopper n.[2] [late 19C–1900s] (US) a ticket-taker. [they *chop* or tear in half the tickets]

chopper n.[3] [late 19C+] a tail.

chopper n.[4] [1920s+] a Thompson sub-machinegun, usu. gangster use; thus *chopper squad*, a group of men carrying such guns (cf. CHICAGO PIANO). [it 'chops down' its targets]

chopper n.[5] [1940s–50s] (Aus.) a Roman Catholic. [abbr. ROCK-CHOPPER]

chopper n.[6] [1950s+] a helicopter. [the rotor blades resemble those of a food processor, i.e. they 'chop']

chopper n.[7] [1960s+] a cut-down, 'chopped' motorbike, spec. a Harley-Davidson, preferred for speed and style by outlaw motorcycle gangs, e.g. Hell's Angels. [CHOP v.[5] (1)]

chopper n.[8] [1980s] (N.Z. campus) a derog. term for a Malaysian.

chopper v. [late 19C] to drink. [echoic of gulping liquid]

choppers n. [1940s+] the teeth; thus *china choppers*, false teeth.

chopping adj.[1] [late 18C–19C] lusty, sexually forward. [SE *chopping*, vigorous, large, strapping]

chopping adj.[2] [late 19C+] of a woman, sexually voracious. [SE phr. *chopping and changing* (her lovers)]

chopping high adj. [1950s] (US Black) living well (cf. HIGH ON THE HOG). [CHOP v.[7]]

chopping sticks n. [late 19C+] (bingo) the number six (cf. CHOPSTICKS). [rhy. sl.]

chops n. **1** [18C+] the jaws, the mouth, the lips. **2** [1940s+] (orig. US Black) ability, skill, competence. **3** [1960s+] synon. for ARSE n.[1], esp. in phr. *freeze/sweat/work one's chops off*. [16C SE; (2) f. jazz musicians fig. ref. to the use of one's mouth and lips in playing a wind instrument]

chop-shop n. [1960s+] a garage where cars or motorbikes can be customized (cf. CHOPPER n.[7]). [CHOP v.[5] (1) + *shop*]

chopstick n. [1960s+] (US Black) a derog. term for an Asian or Oriental person, esp. Chinese. [the use of chopsticks in eating Oriental food]

chopsticks n. [1960s+] (bingo) the number six (cf. CHOPPING STICKS). [rhy. sl.]

chop suey n. [20C] (US) a person of mixed ancestry. [SE *chopped up* + *chop suey*, a dish of stir-fried meat and vegetables, created by Chinese chefs for their Western customers. Not part of Oriental cuisine, it was seen as adequate for the Western palate. The orig. Chinese is *shap sui*, mixed bits]

chop ten v. [20C] (W.I.) to sit around while others are working (cf. COCK OFF ONESELF; COCK TEN).

chop-up n. [20C] (Aus. Und.) a division of plunder. [CHOP n.[3] (1)]

chop up v. *see* CHOP v.[1].

chop up prayers, to phr. [late 17C–18C] to mumble one's prayers speedily and with no interest in their meaning (cf. PATTER v.). [CHOP v.[1] (2)]

chop wood v. [20C] (US) to snore (cf. SAW WOOD v.[2]).

chorals n. [20C] (drugs) a depressant. [? brandname *chloral*]

chorb n. [1970s+] (S.Afr. teen) acne, a spot, a pimple. [? Bantu *chubaba*, a skin blemish]

chore/chorie v. [19C+] (Scot.) to steal (cf. CORING). [Rom *cor*, to steal; thus link to market traders' *chordy gear*, stolen goods]

chorister n. [late 19C] a chorus girl. [play on SE]

chorrie/tjorie/tjorrie n. [1960s+] (S.Afr.) a broken-down old car. [Afk. *tjor*, a crock]

chosen adj. [1960s+] (US prison) selected, like it or not, as the homosexual lover of an older, tougher inmate. [CHOOSE UP]

chosen pals/pels n. [late 18C] (Und.) highwaymen who go out robbing in pairs. [SE *choose* + Gypsy *pal*, an accomplice in crime]

chossel n. [20C] (W.I.) a girlfriend. [CHOSSEL v.]

chossel v. [20C] (W.I.) to start a romantic or sexual relationship (cf. CHAT v.[2]; CHAT DOWN). [? SE *choose* + HUSTLE]

chota n. [1960s+] (US) the police. [Sp.]

chote n. [20C] (W.I.) flattery of another person or boasting about oneself; thus *give one (a lot of) chote*, to attempt to persuade someone through such talk. [CHOTE v.]

chote *v.* [20C] (W.I.) to flatter, to persuade through compliments. [Sp. *chotear*, to joke, to banter]

chounter *v.* [late 17C–18C] to talk sharply and sometimes aggressively. [either earlier form of *chunter* (as suggested by *OED*) or f. Devon dial. *chounting*, taunting, jeering, grumbling]

chouse/chowse *n.* **1** [mid-17C] a cheat, a swindler (cf. CHOUSER). **2** [mid-17C–mid-18C] a dupe, a gullible victim. **3** [early–mid-18C] a swindle, a confidence trick. [Turkish *chiaus*, *chaus*, an official messenger. The link here comes either from the fleecing in 1609 of some Turkish and Persian merchants by an agent or *chiaus* of Sir Robert Shirley, or by the philologist Thomas Henshaw's remark that a Turkish messenger 'is little better than a fool', a dictum that he claimed was sufficient proof of an ety.]

chouse/chowse *v.* [mid-17C–late 19C] to trick, to defraud, often as *chouse one out of*. [CHOUSE n.]

chouser *n.* [early 18C–late 19C] a swindler, a confidence trickster (cf. CHOOSER). [CHOUSE n. (1)]

chout *n.* [mid-19C] (East London) a show, an entertainment. [? SE *shout* or f. East Anglian dial. *chout*, merry-making, a frolic]

chovey *n.* [19C] (costermonger) a shop; thus *ann-chovey* and *man-chovey*, the female and male shop assistant. [ety. unknown]

chow *n.*[1] **1** [late 19C+] food, esp. in an institutional setting, i.e. an army mess-hall, prison etc. **2** [1920s+] (Aus.) cabbage. [Anglo-Chinese pidgin *chow*, a mixture (of any kind) thus food. (2) ? Fr. *choux*, cabbage]

chow *n.*[2] [late 19C+] (Aus.) a derog. term for a Chinese person, esp. an immigrant or descendant of one (cf. AWKWARD AS A CHOW ON A BIKE). [abbr. pidgin *chow-chow*, food; ult. ? the *chow* dog, eaten in China]

chow *n.*[3] [late 19C–1910s] talk; thus *have plenty of chow*, to be highly loquacious. [orig. theatrical use; ult. ety. unknown; ? JAW n.]

chow *v.*[1] [late 19C+] to eat, often as *chow down*. [CHOW n.[1] (1)]

chow *v.*[2] [19C] to chatter, to prattle. [CHOW n.[3]; mainly theatrical use]

chow! *excl.* [1980s+] (US campus) goodbye. [Ital. *ciao* (pron. 'chow'), goodbye]

chow box *v.* [1990s] (US) to perform cunnilingus. [CHOW v.[1] + BOX n.[6] (2)]

chow-chow *n.* [mid-19C–1930s] **1** (orig. Anglo-Chinese, latterly Aus./N.Z.) food (cf. CHOW n.[1]). **2** (Aus.) a derog. term for a Chinese person (cf. CHOW n.[2]). [pidgin *chow-chow*, an edible mixture, typically of pickles or preserves, also a mixed cargo]

chowdar *n.* [mid-19C] a fool. [? Anglo-Chinese, but note CHOWDER-HEAD]

chowder-head *n.* [19C] (US) a fool, a stupid person (cf. BLOCKHEAD n.[1]). [SE *chowder*, a fish stew + sfx. -HEAD (1)]

chow down *v.* **1** [1940s+] (US) to eat voraciously. **2** [1950s+] (US) to perform oral sex. [CHOW v.[1]]

chow for now *phr.* [1990s] (US campus) goodbye. [Ital. *ciao* (pron. 'chow'), goodbye]

chow hound *n.* [1910s+] a glutton. [CHOW n.[1] (1) + sfx. -HOUND]

chow miaow *n.* [1940s+] (Aus.) Chinese food. [CHOW n.[2]; but note the pej. suggestion that Chinese restaurants serve up domestic pets – a slur usu. linked to Indian ones]

chow out *v.* [1970s+] (US campus) to overeat. [CHOW v.[1]]

chowse *see* CHOUSE.

chriggie *n.* [1970s] Christmas (cf. CHRISSIE n.[2]).

chris *n.* [1980s+] (drugs) methylamphetamine (cf. BOMBITA). [abbr. CHRISTMAS TREE n.[2]]

chrissie *n.*[1] [1950s+] (Irish) a working-class person with

delusions of grandeur, esp. as shown in their dress sense. [*Chrissie*, a character in the play *Liffey Lane* (1951) by Maura Laverty]

chrissie/chrissy *n.*[2] [1970s+] Christmas (cf. CHRIGGIE). [abbr.]

Christ! *excl.* [mid-18C+] the main blasphemous oath, which carried a good deal more resonance when religion (and thus potential blasphemy) had greater power.

christacrutchian/chian *adj.* [1990s] (US) a Bible-thumping, back-sliding hypocrite. [CHRIST ON A CRUTCH!]

Christ almighty!/allbloodymighty! *excl.* [20C] a common blasphemous excl.

Christ almighty wonder *n.* [late 19C+] a remarkable person, an expert, an egomaniac. [CHRIST ALMIGHTY! + SE *wonder*, an outstanding specimen]

Christ-apples *n.* [20C] (US) the testicles (cf. APRICOTS).

Christ-awful *adj.* [1940s+] (orig. US) especially appalling. [var. on GOD-AWFUL]

Christ-bitten *adj.* [1930s–50s] (US) a general derog. description e.g. *these Christ-bitten idiots*. [lit. *bitten by Christ*, i.e. fanatically religious]

christen *v.* **1** [late 18C–mid-19C] (Und.) to change the markings on a stolen watch to facilitate its resale (cf. BISHOP v.[3]). **2** [19C] to water down wine or spirits. **3** [late 19C+] to carry out a practical joke in which a chamberpot is emptied over someone's head. **4** [late 19C+] to mark or otherwise damage, esp. of a dog that reveals its lack of house-training. **5** [late 19C+] to use for the first time.

christened *adj.* [18C–early 19C] of alcohol, usu. spirits, watered down (cf. BAPTIZED). [CHRISTEN v. (2)]

christened by a/the baker *phr.* [late 18C–early 19C] freckle-faced (cf. BRAN-FACED). [freckles are reminiscent of spots of brown flour]

christened in pump-water *phr.* [late 18C–early 19C] said of a red-faced man. [image of the drunkard attempting to regain sobriety under a pump]

christener *n.* [late 18C–late 19C] a criminal who fakes the identity marks – the 'christening' – on cheap gold and silver watches. [CHRISTEN v. (1)]

christer *n.* [1920s+] (US) a derog. term for an overly religious person, esp. a proselytizing teetotaller. [SE *Christ*; orig. referring to those who belonged to US college Christian Associations of the 1920s]

Christian *n.*[1] [17C+] **1** of things, 'decent', 'respectable' or 'presentable'. **2** an overly religious person (cf. CHRISTER).

Christian *n.*[2] [early–mid-19C] a tradesman who is willing to give credit. [? as opposed to a Jew]

Christian pony *n.* **1** [late 18C] a sedan chair man. **2** [late 18C] a chairman of a meeting. **3** [mid–late 19C] (Can.) a handcart man. [SE *Christian*, a human being + *pony*, generic for a beast of burden]

christina/cristina *n.* [1960s+] (drugs) amphetamine (cf. A n.[2]). [Sp. *cristal*, crystal]

Christ-killer *n.*[1] [mid-19C+] (US) a derog. term for a Jew. [the teaching by traditional Christianity that the Jews killed Christ and should be punished accordingly]

Christ-killer *n.*[2] [1930s] (US) a noisy political orator. [the majority of such orators were self-proclaimed atheists]

Christless/Christly *adj.* [1910s+] (US) god-damned.

Christmas *v.* [late 19C+] (society) to spend Christmas with, to enjoy the Christmas festivities (cf. SUNDAY).

Christmas! *excl.* [20C] euph. for CHRIST! (cf. CRACKY!).

Christmas card *n.* [20C] a train guard. [rhy. sl.]

Christmas compliments *n.* [late 18C–early 19C] a cough, 'kibed' (chillblained) heels and a snotty nose. [the effects of winter weather. Grose (1796) includes the synon. *Christian compliments* but it is a misprint, as can be seen by his cross-ref. to 'Christmas' at 'compliment']

Christmas crackers *n.* [1970s+] the testicles; thus *Christmas crackered*, utterly exhausted. [rhy. sl. *Christmas crackers* = KNACKERS. *Christmas crackered* = KNACKERED]

Christmas hold *n.* [1950s+] (Aus.) a squeeze of one's opponent's testicles. [pun on 'hand full of nuts (testicles)', in SE a popular Yuletide pleasure]

Christmas log *n.* [1970s] a dog (cf. YULETIDE LOG). [rhy. sl.]

Christmas rolls *n.* [1960s–70s] (drugs) a mixture of different coloured depressant pills.

Christmas tree *n.*[1] [20C] (US) a heavily over-made-up or over-dressed woman. [abbr. phr. *lit up like a Christmas tree*]

Christmas tree *n.*[2] [1960s+] (drugs) **1** a stimulant (deximal spansules). **2** a depressant (butabarbital, Tuinal) (cf. CHRIS). [the multi-coloured pills that are reminiscent of a Christmas-tree's lights]

Christ on a bike! *excl.* [1990s] a mild excl. (cf. CHRIST ON A CRUTCH!; CHRIST ON A FIRE ENGINE!; JESUS CHRIST ON A RAFT!).

Christ on a crutch! *excl.* [1960s+] a mild excl. (cf. CHRIST ON A BIKE!).

Christ on a fire engine! *excl.* [1990s] a general expression of surprise (cf. CHRIST ON A BIKE!).

Christopher Columbus! *excl.* [19C] euph. for CHRIST! (cf. CRACKY!).

christy *n.* [1980s] (drugs) methylamphetamine (cf. BOMBITA). [abbr. CHRISTMAS TREE *n.*[2]]

chro *see* CHROMO *n.*

chrome *n.* **1** [1970s+] (US Black) a gun. **2** [1990s] (US Black) loose change, esp. dimes, quarters and half-dollars. [(1) the *chrome* finish applied to many models of pistol/revolver. (2) its silvery colour]

chrome dome *n.* [20C] (orig. US) **1** a bald head. **2** a bald-headed person. [SE *chrome* + DOME]

chromo/chro *n.* [late 19C+] (Aus.) **1** (Aus.) a prostitute. **2** an ugly, distasteful person. [SE *chromolithograph*, a picture printed in colours from stone. Although the term is uniquely Aus., it originates in the comparison by US writer Francis Brett Harte (1836–1902) of an over-dressed, over-made-up prostitute with a chromolithograph – both are colourful and flashy, but neither resembles natural beauty]

chromo *adj.* [late 19C+] (US) spurious, fake, counterfeit. [abbr. SE *chromolithographic*]

chronic *n.* [1980s+] (drugs) **1** extra-strong marijuana, marijuana mixed with crack cocaine. **2** a person who smokes cannabis every day. [SE *chronic*, severe, extreme; thus the drug's effects. In both cases an example of the bad = good mode ? + CHRONIC adj.]

chronic *adj.* [19C] extreme, usu. in a neg. sense and often as phr. *something chronic.*

chrysanth *n.* [1910s+] a *chrysanth*emum (cf. CHRYSSIE; GLADDIE; RHODO). [abbr.]

chryssie *n.* [1920s+] (Aus.) a *chrys*anthemum. [abbr.]

chub *n.*[1] **1** [mid-16C–late 18C] an inexperienced, naïve person, a fool. **2** [mid-16C–late 18C] a rustic simpleton. **3** [20C] a fat person. [SE *chub*, a short, squat fish; thus a pun on 'thick' or 'dense'; (1), (2) the fish is 'easily taken' notes Grose (1785)]

chub *n.*[2] [19C] a Texan. [ety. unknown]

chubb/chubb up *v.* [1940s–50s] (prison) to lock up a cell for the night (cf. MILN UP). [the proprietary name of *Chubb* locks]

chubbingly *adj.* [late 17C–early 18C] chubby.

chubbly *n.* [1990s] a fat woman's breast. [SE *chubby*]

chubbo/chub-chub *n.* [1970s+] (US) a fat person. [CHUB *n.*[1] (3)]

chubbs *n.* [1990s] (US Black) a fat person. [CHUB *n.*[1] (4)]

chubby *n.*[1] [1920s] a short, squat umbrella.

chubby *n.*[2] [1990s] an erection. [play on CRACK A FAT]

chubby-chaser *n.* [1970s+] a man who prefers (unfashionably) plump or fat women or, if gay, men.

chubbyfat *adj.* [1940s–50s] (US Black) very fat, obese.

chub-chub *see* CHUBBO.

chubette *n.* [1970s+] a fat person, usu. a young woman, but in camp gay use a boy (cf. BIMBETTE). [CHUB *n.*[1] (4) + fem. sfx. -ette]

chuc/chuco *n.* [1940s+] **1** a Mexican-American, esp. a member of a street gang (cf. BATO; CHOLO). **2** a pointed shoe, associated with Mexican youths. [abbr. PACHUCO]

chuck *n.*[1] [16C+] a term of endearment (cf. CHICK *n.*[4]). [dial. The term also meant a call to fowls (or pigs). It persists in 20C northern dial., typified by its use in the TV soap opera *Coronation Street*]

chuck *n.*[2] [late 17C–early 19C] a parish clerk. [abbr. for CHUCK-FARTHING. An early form of 'pitch and toss' in which 'coins were pitched at a mark, and then chucked or tossed at a hole by the player who came nearest the mark, and who won all that alighted in the hole' (*OED*)]

chuck *n.*[3] [mid-19C+] a verdict of not guilty. [CHUCK OUT]

chuck *n.*[4] **1** [mid-19C+] a toss, a throw. **2** [20C] vomit, an act of vomiting. **3** [1920s+] the act of rejection, usu. as *the chuck* and usu. in the context of terminating a relationship; thus *get the chuck*, to be rejected by a lover or partner. [CHUCK *v.*[2]]

chuck *n.*[5] **1** [mid-19C–1900s] the act of eating, a mealtime. **2** [mid-19C+] food. [orig. referring to bread or ship-biscuit only, ult. ? f. *chuck*, a lump or hunk (of food)]

chuck *n.*[6] [1960s–70s] (US Black) a White man (cf. MR CHARLIE). [colloq. *Chuck*, the nickname derived from Charles]

chuck *v.*[1] **1** [18C] to have sexual intercourse. **2** [late 18C–19C; 1990s] to make sexual advances. [1990s use of (2) is Black. Grose (1796) suggests that the term applies to women only]

chuck *v.*[2] **1** [mid-19C+] to throw away/down/into/over/up. **2** [late 19C+] to end an affair, to reject a lover. **3** [late 19C+] to give up, to abandon. **4** [late 19C] to spend extravagantly. **5** [late 19C+] (orig. US/Aus.) to vomit. **6** [late 19C+] to have a fit (cf. CHUCK A/THE DUMMY) **7** [1930s–40s] (US) to throw a party.

chuck *v.*[3] [mid-19C] (US) to hit (with the fist).

chuck *v.*[4] [20C] (US prison) to eat prison food (cf. GRAZE *v.*; JUMP UP *v.*; SCOFF *v.*). [CHUCK *n.*[5] (2)]

chuck *v.*[5] [1930s] to put on, to assume, to act, to perform, usu. in phr. *chuck a ....* [ext. of SE *chuck*]

chuckaboo *n.* [late 19C–1900s] a general endearment (cf. CHUCK *n.*[1]).

chuck a bridge, to *phr.* [1970s+] (Aus.) of a woman, to reveal one's underwear (inadvertently or otherwise). [SE *chuck* + *bridge*; i.e. the crotch of her knickers]

chuck/kick a brown dog, to *phr.* [1990s] (Aus.) to let off steam, to get rid of tension.

chuckaby *n.* [17C] a general term of endearment (cf. CHUCK *n.*[1]).

chuck a charley, to *phr.* [1940s+] (Aus.) to throw a fit. [CHUCK *v.*[5] + CHARLIE *n.*[10]]

chuck a cheesy, to *phr.* (Aus.) to grin. [SE *chuck* + CHEESE *v.*[3]]

chuck a/the dummy, to *phr.* [late 19C] **1** to vomit. **2** to have a fit. [CHUCK *v.*[5] + SE *dummy*, a fake; (2) orig. milit., to pretend to faint on parade in order to escape duties]

chuck a fit, to *phr.* [mid–late 19C] to fake a fit. [CHUCK *v.*[5] + SE *fit*]

chuck a heartie, to *phr.* [1980s+] (Aus.) to have a heart attack. [CHUCK *v.*[5] + SE *heart* + sfx. -ie]

chuck a jolly, to *phr.* [mid-19C] to praise enthusiastically, to 'talk up' inferior goods. [CHUCK *v.*[5] + SE *jolly*; orig. used by costermongers to describe their habit of boosting the dubious virtues of some otherwise unappealing item offered on a friend's stall]

chuck a mental, to *phr.* [1980s+] (Aus.) to lose one's temper. [cf. GO MENTAL]. [CHUCK *v.*[5] + MENTAL *n.*]

chuck a mickey, to phr. [1950s+] (Aus.) to lose one's temper, to have a tantrum (cf. THROW A MICKEY). [CHUCK v.[5] + ? MICKEY n.[2]]

chuck a seven/seven, to phr. (Aus.) **1** [late 19C+] to die. **2** [1970s+] to vomit. **3** [1970s+] to lose control in some way; also as *do a/the seven, throw a seven*. [craps dice, when a throw of 7, other than on one's first throw, 'craps out' and one loses the stake]

chuck a shoulder, to phr. [late 19C–1900s] to ignore, to 'cut'. [CHUCK v.[5] + SE *cold shoulder*]

chuck a sixer, to phr. [1940s+] (Aus.) to become hysterical, to lose one's temper. [CHUCK v.[5] + fig. use of Aus. rules *sixer*, a scoring kick]

chuck a spas/spaz, to phr. [1990s] (Aus.) to lose one's temper. [CHUCK v.[2] (6) + SPAS]

chuck a stall, to phr. [mid-19C] (Und.) to perform a pickpocketing technique, where one member of the team walks in front of the victim, slowing them down while another picks the pocket. [CHUCK v.[2] + STALL n.[1]]

chuck a tread, to phr. [late 19C–1900s] of a man, to have sexual intercourse. [CHUCK v.[1] + SE *tread*, for a cock to have intercourse with a hen]

chuck a turd, to phr. [19C+] to excrete. [CHUCK v.[2] + TURD n. (1)]

chuckaway n. [late 19C–1900s] a lucifer or non-safety match (cf. BRYANT AND MAY'S CHUCKAWAY). [CHUCK v.[2] + SE *away*]

chuck a willie/willy, to phr. [1940s+] (Aus.) to throw a fit (cf. CHUCK A CHARLEY). [CHUCK v.[5] + ? abbr. SAusE *willy*, a whirlwind or link to SE *willy-nilly*]

chuck-bread n. [late 19C–1900s] (tramp) waste bread that would be thrown away were it not offered to tramps.

chuck-chuck n. [19C] a chicken. [echoic]

chucked adj.[1] [early 19C] (Und.) amorous. [CHUCK v.[1]]

chucked adj.[2] **1** [mid–late 19C] disappointed, tricked. **2** [late 19C] slightly drunk, tipsy. **3** [late 19C+] thrown out. **4** [late 19C+] rejected by a lover. [CHUCK v.[2]]

chucker-out n. [late 19C+] a staff member at pubs, dancehalls, concert- halls and similar places of public entertainment who ejects, by force if necessary, rowdy and undesirable people (cf. BOUNCER n.[1]). [CHUCK OUT]

chuck-farthing n. [late 17C–18C] a parish clerk. [SE *chuck-farthing*, a precursor of 20C pitch and toss, in which coins are first pitched at a mark, and then tossed at a hole by the player who came nearest the mark, and who wins everything that landed in the hole; used as the proper name of a character in the *Satire against Hypocrites*, cited by B.E.]

chuck horrors n. [1940s+] (drugs) the craving for food or, paradoxically, the obsessive loathing of food that accompanies one's withdrawal from heroin (cf. CHUCKS n.[1]). [CHUCK n.[5] (2) + HORRORS]

chuckie n. **1** [20C] a delusion (cf. CHOOK). **2** [1990s] (US teen) something or someone highly admirable, first-rate.

Chuckie Armani n. [1980s+] (Ulster) the Sinn Fein leader Gerry Adams (b.1949). [the IRA slogan *tiocfaidh ár lá*, our day will come + Adams's well-known taste in upmarket tailoring]

chuckies n. [1990s] testicles. [pun on BALLS n.[1] (1), which one can 'chuck']

chuck-in n. [late 19C+] (Aus.) a voluntary subscription. [CHUCK v.[1] (1)]

chuck in v. [late 19C+] to add as a bonus, to throw in. [CHUCK v.[2] (1)]

chucking-out time phr. [late 19C+] closing time at a public house; this was originally 12.30 am, before the WWI legislation limiting open hours, which made it, according to the time of day, 2.30 pm (3.00 in London) and 10.30 pm (11.00 in London). The afternoon closing time has since been abandoned.

chuck in the towel, to phr. [20C] to give in, to surrender (cf. CHUCK UP THE SPONGE; THROW IN THE TOWEL). [boxing imagery]

chuck it/it in v. [mid-19C+] to give up, esp. of a job. [CHUCK v.[2] (1)]

chuck it in! excl. [mid-19C+] stop it! [CHUCK v.[2] (1)]

chuck it out v. [20C] to speak without restraint. [CHUCK v.[2] (1)]

chuckle v. [1960s+] (Aus./Queensland) to vomit.

chucklehead n. [early 18C–late 19C] a dolt, a simpleton, a fool (cf. BLOCKHEAD n.[1]). [18C SE *chuckle*, a clumsy or stupid fellow + sfx. -HEAD (1)]

chuck me in the gutter n. [20C] (Aus.) butter. [rhy. sl.]

chuck off/off at v. [1910s+] (Aus./N.Z.) to sneer at, to speak sarcastically; the addition of *at* implies bantering, teasing. [CHUCK v.[2] (1)]

chuck one's biscuits, to phr. [1990s] to vomit. [CHUCK v.[2] (5)]

chuck oneself into v. [mid–late 19C] to involve oneself enthusiastically, to commit oneself fully. [CHUCK v.[2] (1); synon. for SE *throw oneself into*]

chuck one's fat around, to phr. [late 19C] to talk loudly and stupidly.

chuck one's hand in, to phr. [late 19C+] to die. [card-playing imagery]

chuck one's load, to phr. [1990s] to ejaculate (cf. CHUCK ONE'S MUCK). [CHUCK v.[2] + LOAD n.[4] (2)]

chuck one's muck, to phr. [1990s] to ejaculate (cf. TIP ONE'S DIRT). [CHUCK v.[2] (1) + MUCK n.[6]]

chuck one's weight around, to phr. [1910s+] to act in an arrogant, aggressive manner (cf. THROW ONE'S WEIGHT ABOUT).

chuck-out n. **1** [late 19C+] (N.Z.) a dismissal (from a job). **2** [1920s+] the end of drinking time in a public house, when customers are asked to drink up and leave (cf. CHUCKING-OUT TIME). [CHUCK OUT v.]

chuck out v. [late 19C+] **1** of people, to throw out, to expel physically. **2** of objects, to get rid of, to throw away. [CHUCK v.[2] (1)]

chuck out one's chest/throw a chest, to phr. [mid-19C+] to play the man, to act in an aggressive 'manly' way.

chuck over v. [late 19C+] to abandon, to dismiss, to throw over, to jilt. [CHUCK v.[2] (1)]

chucks n.[1] [1940s+] (drugs) the craving for food that affects a heroin addict once they have withdrawn from using the drug, which, on the whole, destroys the appetite during its regular use. [abbr. CHUCK HORRORS]

chucks n.[2] [1960s+] Converse All-Star baseball boots, signed by designer *Chuck* Taylor.

chucks n.[3] [1970s+] the *nunchuku*, a martial arts weapon modelled on a Chinese rice flail and made of two hardwood sticks linked by a chain.

chucks! excl. [mid-late 19C] (juv.) look out! (cf. CAVE!).

chuck seven see CHUCK A SEVEN.

chuck the gab, to phr. [1930s] **1** to 'tell the tale' for the purposes of begging or confidence trickery. **2** to talk eloquently and articulately. [CHUCK v.[2] (1) + GAB n.]

chuck/throw a wobbly/wobbler, to phr.[1] [1960s+] to exhibit signs of mental stress, to have a (minor) breakdown. [CHUCK v.[5] + WOBBLY n.[1]]

chuck a wobbly/wobbler, to phr.[2] [1960s+ (Aus.) to tell a dubious story. [CHUCK v.[2] (1) + WOBBLY n.[2]]

chuck-up n. [1910s–40s] a cheer, encouragement. [CHUCK v.[2] (1); i.e. one 'throws up' the cheer]

chuck-up adj. [1940s+] (W.I.) short and stout; thus *chuck-up man*, a short, stout person. [CHUCK n.[5]]

chuck up v.[1] [mid-19C+] to surrender. [abbr. CHUCK UP THE SPONGE]

chuck up v.[2] [late 19C+] to abandon, to dismiss, to throw over, to jilt. [CHUCK v.[2] (3)]

chuck up the sponge, to phr. [mid-19C+] to give in, to

surrender (cf. CHUCK IN THE TOWEL; THROW IN THE TOWEL). [boxing imagery]

chuck wagon n. [20C] (US) **1** a small restaurant or café. **2** a buffet. [cowboy jargon *chuck wagon*, the wagon that carried the provisions and cooking equipment for a ranch; ult. CHUCK n.[5] + SE *wagon*]

chuck wagon chicken n. [20C] (US) bacon (cf. ADIRONDACK STEAK). [CHUCK WAGON]

chucky n.[1] [18C] a term of endearment (cf. CHICK n.[4]). [CHUCK n.[1]]

chucky n.[2] [late 18C+] a chicken, a fowl (cf. CHOOK).

chuck you, Farley! excl. [20C] joking euph. expletive, reversing *fuck you, Charley!*

chuco see CHUC.

chud adj. [1980s+] (US campus) disgusting, repellent. [film title *Chud*, cannibalistic humanoid underground dwellers]

chuddy see CHUTTY.

chuff n.[1] **1** [mid-15C–early 17C] a generally derisive name for anyone seen as boorish, unsophisticated or rude. **2** [16C–mid-19C] a miser. [dial. *chuff*, surly, ill-tempered]

chuff n.[2] **1** [1940s+] the buttocks, the anus. **2** [1940s+] (mainly Aus./northern UK) the vagina. **3** [1970s] (gay) pubic hair. [dial. *chuff*, fat, plump; (2), (3) are ext. of (1)]

chuff adj. [1900s] rude, impudent. [CHUFF n.[1] (1)]

chuff v.[1] [20C] euph. synon. for FUCK, mainly used in the north of England.

chuff v.[2] [1940s+] (Aus.) to go, to move, to leave. [var. on CHOOF]

chuff v.[3] [1940s+] to break wind. [echoic]

chuff adder n. [1960s] a male homosexual. [CHUFF n.[2] (1) + pun on *puff*/POOF n. *adder*]

chuff-box n. [20C] the vagina (cf. CHUFF n.[2]). [CHUFF v.[1] + BOX n.[6] (2) or dial *chuff*, to cuff, to hit. The penis 'hits' the vagina during intercourse]

chuff chum n. [1990s] a male homosexual. [CHUFF n.[2] (1) + CHUM n.[1]]

chuffed adj. [1950s+] (orig. milit.) **1** very pleased, delighted, happy; often extended to *chuffed to fuck*, *chuffed to arseholes*, *chuffed to buggery* etc. **2** annoyed, disgruntled. [16C SE *chuff*, swollen out or puffed as fat, or the muzzle of an animal]

chuff it! excl.[1] [mid-19C] go away! take it away! get rid of yourself!/it! [CHUFF v.[2]]

chuff it! excl.[2] [20C] as euph. for FUCK IT! [CHUFF v.[1]]

chuffy adj.[1] [18C] chubby, round-faced. [dial. *chuffy*, chubby-cheeked, healthy]

chuffy adj.[2] [late 19C] surly. [CHUFF n.[1]]

chuftie n. [1990s] the vagina; thus *chuftie-plug*, a tampon. [CHUFF n.[2] (2)]

chug/chug-a-lug v. [20C] to drink down in a single draught, to drink quickly; thus (US campus) *chugging contest*, a drinking competition in which each contestant has to down a succession of drinks in a single swallow. [an Australian toast of the 1950s]

chugarrow! excl. [20C] shut up! [milit. *chubarrow*, itself adopted f. Hind. *chuprao*, be quiet!]

chuggerhead n. [1970s] (US) a dolt, a simpleton, a fool (cf. BLOCKHEAD n.[1]).

chugs n. [1960s–70s] (US) the female breasts. [var. on JUGS n.[1]]

chugwagon n. [1920s] (US) a motorcar. [SE *chug* (*along*) + pun on cowboy jargon *chuck wagon*]

chul v. [mid–late 19C] to succeed. [? Hind. *chul*, go along, hurry]

chularka/chulahka n. [1940s+] (orig. milit.) a minor gangster, a 'wide boy'. [Hind.]

chullo! excl. [mid-19C] (orig. Anglo-Ind.) hurry up! move along! (cf. JILDI). [Hind. *chello*, move along]

chulo n. [1990s] (US) a Mexican-American teenage gangster (cf. CHOLO; VATO). [Sp. *chulo*, pimp]

chum n.[1] [late 17C–mid-19C] a close friend, a room-mate. [mid-19C+ use is SE, although Hotten (1859) includes it since it is 'in such frequent use with the lower orders that it demanded a place in this glossary']

chum n.[2] [19C] (Aus.) a new immigrant, a newcomer. [abbr. NEW CHUM]

chum n.[3] [late 19C] the vagina. [CHUM n.[1], i.e. the 'friend' of the penis]

chum v. [18C] to live with, to befriend. [coined by John Wesley (1703–91) in 1730, drawing on 17C SE *chum*, one who lodges in the same college rooms. Presumably f. *chamber*, poss. abbr. *chamber-fellow* or *chamber-mate*, although no proof has been discovered]

chum along/in/up with v. [late 19C+] to become friendly with. [CHUM v.]

chummage n. [late 18C–mid-19C] **1** a sum of money paid by a rich prisoner to a poorer one, for which payment the latter forfeits their part of a shared cell, leaving it all to the rich prisoner and taking up a position in some communal area of the prison. **2** a monetary forfeit, usually 2s 6d (12½p), paid over by a new prisoner to those who have already established themselves in the prison. [SE *chummage*, the sharing of rooms by a number of people. The rich-to-poor bribe has also been recorded as taking place at mid-19C universities]

chummery n. [mid-19C] **1** friendship, friendliness. **2** the sharing of rooms with a friend. [CHUM n.[1]]

chummo n. [1940s] (US) a friend. [CHUM]

chummy n.[1] [19C] a low-crowned hat. [it was notably comfortable and as such seen as *chummy*, or friendly, to the wearer]

chummy n.[2] [mid-19C+] a chimney sweep or his assistant. [SE *chimney* or his preferred hat, a CHUMMY n.[1]. Note police use [1940s+] *chummy*, a form of address from anyone to whom the policeman is talking, a suspect]

chummy adj. [late 19C+] friendly. [CHUM n.[1]]

chummy v. [1980s+] (US campus) to vomit. [CHUM THE FISH]

chump n.[1] [19C+] the head, the face. [ext. of 18C SE *chump*, a short thick lump of wood chopped or sawn from timber]

chump n.[2] **1** [late 19C+] anyone gullible, easily taken in (cf. BLOCKHEAD n.[1]). **2** [20C] a regular working man; thus, in sl. terms, a fool (cf. WORKING STIFF). [SE *chump*, a short, thick lump, usu. of wood]

chump v. [1920s] to trick, to deceive, to make a fool of someone. [CHUMP n.[2]]

chump change n. [1950s+] (US Black) small change, esp. a sum of money that is too small to buy anything worthwhile. [CHUMP n.[2] (1) + SE *change*]

chump-change adj. [1970s+] second-rate, inferior, good only for fools. [CHUMP CHANGE n.]

chumpie n. [1980s+] (US campus) something that causes happiness, joy or excitement (cf. DECENT n.). [SE *champion*]

chump job n. [1930s+] (US) respectable, low-paying, regular work (cf. NINE-TO-FIVE). [CHUMP n.[2] (2)]

chump off v. (US Black) **1** [1930s+] to act like a fool. **2** [1950s] to lose money irresponsibly. **3** [1970s+] to look down on, to disdain. **4** [1970s+] to dupe, to get the better of. [CHUMP v.]

chump of wood phr. [mid-19C] no good. [rhy. sl.]

chumps elizas n. [mid-19C+] the Champs Élysées, Paris. ['Five Pounder Tourists' (Ware)]

chump squeeze n. [1950s–60s] (US Black) a punch on the arm or shoulder, its meaning varying according to context. [CHUMP n.[2] (1) + SE *squeeze*]

chumpy adj. [1960s] **1** naïve, stupid, gullible. **2** eccentric, odd (cf. OFF ONE'S CHUMP) [CHUMP n.[2] (1)]

chum the fish, to *phr.* [1980s+] (US campus) to vomit (cf. CHUMMY v.). [SE *chum*, to throw ground-bait into the water to attract fish]

chum up with *see* CHUM ALONG WITH.

chunder *n.* [1960s+] (Aus.) an act of vomiting; thus *chunderous, chundersome*, fit to make one vomit. [CHUNDER v.]

chunder *v.* [1950s+] (Aus.) to vomit. [according to Barry Humphries (b.1934), the great popularizer of the word in his 'Barry Mackenzie' strip in *Private Eye* and on film, f. naut. shout of warning 'watch under!' He also offers rhy. sl. f. *Chunder Loo of Akim Foo* = SPEW = vomit. Chunder Loo featured in a long-running series of advertisements for Cobra boot polish (*c.*1910–29), drawn by Norman Lindsay (1879–1969) and featured in the Sydney *Bulletin*. Thence it moved from public school slang to surf jargon to popular use]

chunder bunny *n.* [1980s+] (N.Z.) one who cannot hold their liquor. [CHUNDER v. + BUNNY n.³]

chungo bunny *n.* [1950s+] a derog. term for a Black person. [mispron. of JUNGLE BUNNY]

chunk *n.*¹ [late 19C+] (orig. US) a large amount, a good deal of. [dial. *chuck*, a lump, a large, awkwardly shaped piece]

chunk *n.*² [20C] (Can. Und.) a handgun. [? its shape, size and weight]

chunk *v.*¹ [late 19C–1930s] (US Black) to discard, to throw away. [CHUCK v.² (1)]

chunk *v.*² [1980s+] (US campus) to do badly. [echoic of one's 'hitting the bottom']

chunk *v.*³ [1980s+] (US campus) to vomit. [BLOW CHUNKS]

chunka/chunker *n.* [20C] (Aus.) the chief. [abbr. CHUNK OF BEEF]

chunk of/chunka beef *n.* [20C] (Aus.) the chief, the boss. [rhy. sl.]

chunk of wood *phr.* [mid-19C] no good (cf. CHUMP OF WOOD). [rhy. sl.]

chúpame! *excl.* [1960s+] (US) a general term of dismissal, rudeness (cf. BITE THIS!). [Sp., lit. 'suck me']

chupidee/chupidie/chupidy/chupiddy *n.* [20C] (W.I.) a gullible, ignorant fool; thus *chupidness* stupidity, *talk chupidness*, to talk silly nonsense. [*chupid*, local pron. of stupid]

church *n.*¹ [late 19C–1900s] a general term of endearment, e.g. *my church*, my dear.

church *n.*² [1970s] (US) the end (cf. CURTAINS n.¹). [in the context of a funeral]

church a jack, to *phr.* [late 19C] (Und.) to take the works of one watch and place them in the case of another with the aim of disguising its origins. [play on CHRISTEN v.]

church a yack, to *phr.* [mid-19C] (Und.) to take the works of a watch from one case and put them into another one. [play on CHRISTEN v. + YACK n.¹]

church-bell *n.* [late 19C–1900s] (rural) a talkative woman.

church-called *adj.* [1920s–50s] (US Black) drawn to the vocation of preaching (cf. COLLEGE-CALLED).

church-chopper *see* CHOP-CHURCH.

churcher *n.* [late 19C] a threepenny piece. [the Cockney version of society's CHURCH-PIECE]

church is out *phr.* [20C] (US) everything is finished, no alternative is available (cf. CHURCH n.²). [i.e. the service is over; one has no further chance to pray]

church key *n.* [1950s+] (US) a can-opener. [the similarity in shape of the WW2 US forces GI can-opener and an old-fashioned key]

church mouse *n.* **1** [late 19C+] a regular attender at church. **2** [1960s] (gay) a male homosexual who frequents crowded churches in order to fondle any potential sex partners.

church parade *n.* [late 19C–1900s] (society) the regular post-Sunday matins promenading of fashionable people.

church-piece *n.* [late 19C–1900s] (society) a threepenny piece. [it was the smallest silver coin and thus the least one could decently place in the collection plate]

churchwarden *n.* [mid-19C+] a clay pipe with a very long stem. [the supposed predilection of churchwardens for such pipes]

church work *n.* [late 18C] any work that proceeds slowly. [? the time taken to build the great cathedrals or the tedium of religious services]

churchyard cough *n.* [late 17C+] a particularly bad cough, that is likely to lead to the sufferer's death. [both the likelihood of death and burial and the reputation of churchyards as centres of disease]

churchyard luck *n.* [late 19C–1900s] the death of one child in a large, but impoverished family. [cruel but pragmatic, the loss of one extra mouth to feed is 'lucky' for the penniless parents]

churn *n.* [19C] the vagina. [it makes BUTTER n.² (1)]

churn butter *v.* [20C] to masturbate. [SE *churn* + BUTTER n.² (1)]

churn man cream, to *phr.* [20C] to masturbate.

churus *see* CHARAS.

chury *n.* [early 19C] a knife. [Welsh Rom. *chury*, a knife, ult. f. Hind. *chhuri*]

chute *n.*¹ [late 19C] (US) a cheap eating place. [the serving and quality of food in such places is compared with the tossing of rubbish down the garbage chute of a tenement block]

chute *n.*² [1970s+] (US) the rectum.

chutney *n.* [1970s+] sodomy. [like CHOCOLATE adj. (2), *chutney* is brown and thus generic for matters referring to defecation and sodomy]

chutney farmer *n.* [1990s] a male homosexual. [CHUTNEY + fig. use SE *farmer*]

chutney ferret *n.* [1970s+] the penis. [CHUTNEY + SE *ferret*]

chutney locker *n.* [1990s] the rectal passage. [CHUTNEY + SE *locker*]

chutty/chuddy *n.* [1940s+] (orig. Aus./N.Z.) chewing gum.

chutzpah *n.* [late 19C+] gall, cheek, outrageousness, audacity, bravado, nerve, courage. [Heb. *chutzpah*, insolence, audacity]

chuzzle *v.* [early 19C+] to cheat, to defraud (cf. CHISEL v.¹).

chy *see* CHAI.

chyack *see* CHI-IKE.

ciao! *excl.* [1960s+] goodbye. [Ital.]

cicisbeo *n.* [mid–late 18C] a knot of ribbon fastened to a sword-hilt, walking-stick etc. [Ital. *cicisbeo*, the recognized gallant or *cavalier servente* of a married woman; such a man might well wear this knot]

'cid *n.* (drugs) [1970s+] LSD (cf. A n.³). [abbr. ACID n.³]

cider-and *n.* [18C] any form of mixed drink in which the basic constituent is cider (cf. COFFEE-AND n.).

cig *n.* [late 19C+] a *cig*arette, a *cig*ar (cf. CIGGY). [abbr.]

cigar box *n.* [19C] **1** a violin. **2** (US) a cheaply built house; thus *cigar box row*, the area of town in which the poor live. [the flimsiness of the cigar-box construction]

cigar burn *n.* [1990s] the anus. [resemblance]

cigarette paper *n.* [1930s–40s] (drugs) a packet of heroin. [a WRAP n.² or BINDLE of heroin (or cocaine) is approx. the size of a cigarette paper]

cigarette pimp *n.* [1950s–60s] (US Black) a second-rate pimp, esp. a pimp who solicits for his women (cf. CHILE PIMP). [his women make no more than cigarette money]

cigarette swag *n.* [1940s–60s] (Aus.) a very thin pack or swag, implying poverty. [resemblance]

cigarrode cristal *n.* [1980s+] (drugs) phencyclidine (cf. ACE n.³). [ety. unknown]

cigga n. [1950s+] (Aus.) a *ciga*rette. [abbr.]

cigger n. [1920s+] (Aus.) a cigarette (cf. CIGGIE). [abbr.]

ciggie/ciggy n. [20C] a *ciga*rette (cf. CIG). [abbr.]

ciggy-boo/-poo n. [1940s+] (Aus./US) a cigarette. [abbr. + sfx. *-boo/-poo*]

cinch n.[1] **1** [late 19C+] (orig. US) a simple, easily attained thing, a certainty; thus *cinchy*, easy, easily attained or attainable. **2** [1940s+] (US) an easily seduced woman. [SE *cinch*, grip tightly; thus something one can grasp easily. Orig. f. Sp. *cincha*, a saddle girth or bellyband, adopted in US West]

cinch/cinch-notice n.[2] [20C] (US campus) a note sent to a student warning them to work hard and generally 'get a grip'. [SE *cinch*]

cinch v. **1** [late 19C] (US) to impose upon. **2** [late 19C–1910s] (US) to defeat, to overcome, to trounce. **3** [20C] (orig. US) to guarantee, to make certain, to make conclusive. [fig. use of SE; underpinned by CINCH n.[1]]

Cinci/Cincy n. [late 19C–1960s] (US) *Cinci*nnati, Ohio. [abbr.]

Cincinnati chicken/turkey n. [mid–late 19C] salt pork (cf. ADIRONDACK STEAK). [contemporary identification of *Cincinnati* with pig products]

Cincinnati doubloon n. [mid-19C] (US) a penny, a cent. [proper name *Cincinnati* + SE *doubloon*, a coin worth 36/-; the ref. is to the reputation of Cincinnati businessmen as cheats]

Cincinnati oysters n. [late 19C] (US) pickled pigs' feet (cf. ADIRONDACK STEAK). [for ety. *see* CINCINNATI CHICKEN]

Cincinnati quail n. [late 19C] (US) pork or bacon (cf. ADIRONDACK STEAK). [for ety. *see* CINCINNATI CHICKEN]

Cincinnati turkey see CINCINNATI CHICKEN.

Cincy see CINCI.

cinder n. [mid-19C] any form of spirit (brandy, whisky etc), taken in tea, soda water or other drink; thus *put a cinder in*, to add liquor to an otherwise non-alcoholic drink. [SE *cinder*, an ember or piece of glowing coal; thus it makes the basic drink 'hot']

cinder bull n. [1930s+] (US tramp) a railroad detective. [the *cinders* that lie on the tracks + BULL n.[8]]

cinder dick n. [1920s+] a railroad detective (cf. CINDER BULL). [f. the *cinders* that lie on the tracks + DICK n.[6]]

cinderella n. [late 19C] (society) a dance that ends at midnight (cf. ADAM AND EVE BALL). [the fairy-tale of *Cinderella*]

cinder-garbler n. [late 18C–early 19C] a servant girl. [SE *cinder* + *garbler*, a sifter; the servant's morning duty of cleaning out last night's dead fires]

cinder-grifter n. [1920s+] (US) a tramp, a hobo. [the *cinders* that lie on the tracks + GRIFTER]

cinder-shifter n. [1920s+] (Aus.) a dirt-track motorcycle racer. [such tracks are covered with dead cinders]

cinder-sifter n. [late 19C] a hat with an open-work brim, which supposedly resembles the household tool (cf. COALSCUTTLE). [SE *cinder-sifter*, a contrivance for sifting dust or ashes from cinders]

cinnamon stick n. [1950s+] (gay) the faeces-stained penis after anal intercourse. [resemblance; SE *cinnamon sticks* are brown]

cinqua see CHINKER.

cinquanter n.[1] [early–mid-17C] an old stager. [Fr. *cinquante*, 50; i.e. years of age]

cinquanter n.[2] [early–mid-17C] a gambler. [Fr. *cinque*, the number 5, marked on a die]

cinqua soldi n. [mid-19C] 5 pence (cf. DACHA SALTEE; MADZA SALTEE). [Ital. *cinque*, 5 + *soldi*, pl. of *soldo*: one-twentieth of a lira]

cipher n. [1990s] (US Black/teen) a circle of Black friends. [ety. unknown]

cipher v. [mid-19C] to calculate, to think out. [SE *cipher*, to work out arithmetically]

circle jerk n. **1** [1950s+] (orig. US) joint masturbation, often in competition, by a group of boys, poss. sitting in a circle (cf. CHAIN JERK). **2** [1970s] (orig. US) a pointless or inconclusive discussion by a number of people. **3** [1970s+] (US) chaos, a mess. [SE *circle* + JERK (OFF); (2) and (3) are fig. uses of (1)]

circler n. [1950s] (W.I.) a small, round, boiled dumpling (cf. CONCRETE). [its shape]

circling boy n. [early 17C] (Und.) a thug who works in a criminal gang and helps lure victims into a position where they might be robbed, with or without violence. [SE *circling*, moving around]

circs n. [late 19C+] *circ*umstances (cf. PROB). [abbr.]

circular file n. [1940s+] (orig. US) a waste-paper basket.

circumbendibus n. [late 18C–late 19C] **1** a long and winding route. **2** a long and winding story. [17C cod Latin *circum* + *bend*, bend around + Lat. ablative pl. *-ibus*]

circumference n. [20C] a fat person's waist.

circus n. (US) **1** [mid-19C+] a commotion, an adventure. **2** [late 19C–1960s] a live sex show. **3** [1950s+] an orgy. **4** [1950s+] a company, group or set of people acting or performing together, esp. in sport or entertainment, e.g. the *Grand Prix circus*. [fig. uses of SE]

circus cowboys n. [1960s+] young male gay prostitutes who congregate in and around Piccadilly Circus, London.

circus house n. [1900s–1930s] (US Black) a brothel, esp. one featuring sex shows (cf. ACCOMMODATION HOUSE). [CIRCUS n. (2) + HOUSE n.[1] (1); such establishments originated in New Orleans and also saw the birth of jazz]

circus love n. [1950s+] sex shows (cf. CIRCUS n.).

circus try n. [1940s] (US) a determined effort, a good try (cf. COLLEGE TRY). [the supposed pluckiness of circus performers]

cissie/cissy see SISSIE.

cit/citt n. [mid-17C–late 19C] a citizen, spec. of London. [the implication is of an urban dweller as opposed to a countryman or of a tradesman or shopkeeper as opposed to a gentleman. 'A pert low tradesman, a pragmatical trader.' (Johnson)]

citizen n.[1] [19C+] (US) **1** a person, the implication is of a respectable individual as opposed to a criminal. **2** a rough, possibly criminal person. [SE; note *citizen*, a civilian as opposed to a soldier, used by Shakespeare in *Coriolanus* (1607)]

citizen n.[2] [mid–late 19C] (Und.) a wedge used for opening safes; thus *citizen's friend*, a smaller form of wedge. [play on ALDERMAN n.[2]]

citrol see CHITRAL.

citt see CIT.

-city sfx. [1960s+] (orig. US) a general sfx. meaning place or situation, whether concrete or abstract (cf. ALPHABET CITY; BARF CITY; BAY CITY; EDGE CITY; FAT CITY n.[1]; FIST CITY; NOWHERE CITY etc). [SE *city*]

city bug n. [20C] (US) a city person, as seen from a farmer's point of view. [SE *city* + BUG n.[1]]

city bulldog n. [early 18C] a constable. [SE *city* + BULLDOG n.[1] (3)]

city clag blues n. [1980s+] (Aus. drugs) the unpleasant sensation in one's mouth following excessive smoking of cannabis. [proprietary name, *Clag* glue]

city college n. **1** [late 18C] Newgate prison (cf. AKERMAN'S HOTEL; COLLEGE n.[1]; COLLEGE CHUM; KING'S COLLEGE; NEWMAN'S COLLEGE; WHITTINGTON COLLEGE). **2** [1930s] (US) the Tombs Prison, New York City. [ironic uses]

city gent n. [late 18C+] a businessman working in the City of London.

city light horse n. [1930s] a secretary who has become her employer's mistress. [such a 'light horse' is 'easy to mount']

city road African *n.* [late 19C–1900s] a prostitute (cf. BANK-SIDE LADY). [? the relative exoticism of the City Road for those who normally looked for prostitutes in the West End]

city sherry *n.* [late 19C] bitter beer.

city slicker *n.* [20C] a city person. [SE *city* + SLICKER]

city stage *n.* [18C–early 19C] the (Newgate) gallows. [the position of Newgate in the City of London; also the condemned villains' 'dance' for their audience]

civet *n.* [18C–19C] the vagina (cf. BADGER n.[7]). [the musky odour of *civet*, used in perfumes and viewed as overtly erotic; thus *civet-cat*, a general term of abuse for a women seen as too (threateningly) sexy, e.g. as used by Virginia Woolf (1882–1941) of Katherine Mansfield (1888–1923)]

civilian *n.* [1940s+] (US) an outsider, one who is not a part of a given group.

civility money *n.* [late 18C–early 19C] a cash payment claimed by bailiffs for discharging their duty in a courteous manner.

civvie/civvy *n.* [early 19C+] a civilian; thus termed by members of the forces, the prison service, police etc; thus [1910s+] *civvies*, civilian clothing, i.e. not a uniform.

civvy street *n.* [1910s+] the world of civilian life, usu. service use.

c.j. *n.* [1970s] (drugs) phencyclidine (cf. ACE n.[3]). [abbr. CRYSTAL JOINT]

C-jam/C-jame *n.* [1960s] (drugs) cocaine (cf. C n.[2]).

C-joint *n.* [1940s] (drugs) a place where cocaine is sold. [C n.[2] + JOINT n.[3] (3)]

clack *n.* **1** [late 16C–mid-19C] the tongue. **2** [19C] a noisy conversation. [SE *clack*, idle gossip. Grose (1785) links it to the clapper that regulates a water-mill and claims that the term is 'chiefly applied to women']

clack-box *n.* [19C] **1** the mouth (cf. CLACKER). **2** a garrulous person. [CLACK n. (1)]

clacker *n.* **1** [19C] the mouth. **2** [19C] the teeth. [CLACK n. (1); the noise of the teeth rattling together]

clackers *n.* [1930s+] false teeth. [CLACKER]

clack-loft *n.* [late 18C] a pulpit. [CLACK n. (2) + SE *loft*, a church gallery]

clad in Stafford blue *phr.* [late 14C–early 15C] bruised from a beating. [SE *clad*, dressed + *Stafford blue*, a type of blue cloth; pun on SE *staff*]

claggy *adj.* [1950s+] unpleasantly tight, e.g. of trousers. [dial. *claggy*, forming sticky lumps, tenaciously adhesive]

clagnut *n.* [1990s] a small piece of excrement clinging to the anal hairs (cf. CLINKER n.[3]; CLINKERS n.[4]). [northern dial. *clag*, a sticky mass entangled in hair]

claim *n.* [20C] (Irish) a woman who is picked up at a dance.

claim *v.*[1] [late 19C] **1** to steal. **2** (Und.) to arrest; thus *claimed*, under arrest (cf. BORROW).

claim *v.*[2] [1990s] (US Black gang) to claim membership in a gang.

clam *n.*[1] **1** [early 19C–1950s] the mouth (cf. CLAMSHELL n.[1]). **2** [mid-19C+] a tight-lipped person. **3** [mid-19C+] (US) a mean person; thus *tight as a clamshell*, very close-fisted. **4** [20C] (US) the vagina, the hymen (cf. BEARDED CLAM). [fig. uses of SE; all open and/or shut like the bivalve]

clam *n.*[2] [mid-19C+] (US) a fool, a worthless individual. [its unmoving stolidity + ? phr. HAPPY AS A CLAM]

clam *n.*[3] [late 19C+] (US) $1, usu. in pl. [ety. unknown; ? link to WAMPUM, another shell = money term]

clam *n.*[4] [1970s+] a lump of phlegm. [punning var. on OYSTER n.[1] (4)]

clam/clam up *v.* [1910s+] to stop talking, to become deliberately secretive. [the strength with which the bivalve shuts itself tight]

clambake *n.* (US) **1** [1930s+] an event, esp. one that fails to

live up to the obvious efforts that have been put into its preparation. **2** [1950s–60s] a party or get-together. **3** [1990s] a smelly vagina. [plays on SE]

clambake *v.* [1980s+] (US drugs) to smoke marijuana in a car with the windows up.

clam-basket *n.* [early 19C] (US) the stomach.

clam-catcher *n.* [mid-19C–1900s] (US) a native or inhabitant of New Jersey. [the prevalence of clams off the state's shores]

clam-diggers *n.* [20C] (US) **1** the hands. **2** the nickname of the inhabitants of various towns in northeast US.

clamjam *n.* [1990s] vaginal secretions. [BEARDED CLAM + JAM n.[8]]

clammed *adj.* [1930s+] silent, discreet, refusing to talk. [CLAM v.]

clamp *v.* [mid-19C–1920s] (US) to arrest, to seize.

clampers/clamps *n.* [late 19C+] (US) the hands (cf. CLAMS).

clamp the pipe, to *phr.* [1990s] to masturbate. [pun]

clams *n.* [1960s] (US) the hands. [CLAM-DIGGERS (1)]

clamshell *n.*[1] [early–mid-19C] (US) the mouth. [ext. of CLAM n.[1] (1)]

clamshell *n.*[2] [1920s] (US) $1. [CLAM n.[3]]

clamshells *n.* [mid-19C] (US) the lips. [ext. of CLAM n.[1] (1)]

clam smacker *n.* [1990s] (US) a lesbian. [BEARDED CLAM + SMACKER n.[1]]

clamtrap *n.* [early 19C–1940s] (US) the mouth. [play on SE, but note CLAM n.[1] (1)]

clandy *adj.* [1980s+] *cland*estine. [abbr.]

clang *v.* [1940+] to make a social gaff. [CLANGER]

clanger *n.* [1940s+] **1** a mistake, esp. a social solecism; thus intensified as *clangeroo*. **2** (Aus.) a lie, a shock. [the 'noise' of its 'hitting the ground']

clank *n.* **1** [late 17C–late 18C] a silver tankard; thus *rum clank*, a double tankard. **2** [late 17C–early 19C] (Und.) a silver plate. **3** [19C] (Und.) a pewter tankard. **4** [1920s] (US) a silver dollar. [echoic; i.e. the tankard, plate or dollar hitting a table]

clanker *n.* [late 17C–late 18C] a gross, deliberate lie (cf. CLINKER n.[1]). [? the fig. 'thump' of the lie as it falls from one's mouth]

clanker-napper *n.* [late 17C–early 19C] a thief who specializes in stealing silver plate. [CLANK n.[1] (2) + NAPPER n.[1]]

clank-napper *n.* [17C–late 18C] one who steals tankards from public houses. [CLANK n.[1] (1) + NAPPER n.[1]]

clanks *n.* [1980s+] (US) delirium tremens. [? aural hallucinations]

clap *n.* [late 16C+] venereal disease, esp. gonorrhoea (cf. APPLAUSE). [OF *clapoir*, bubo; thus *clapoire* or *clapier*, a place of debauchery and the illness one can contract there. The term appears as SE in late 16C and is only relegated to sl. with the onset of Victorian verbal prudery *c.*1850]

clap *v.*[1] [late 16C+] to infect with venereal disease. [CLAP n.]

clap *v.*[2] [mid-19C] to seize, to arrest. [SE *clap one's hands on*]

clap *v.*[3] [1950s+] (W.I. Rasta) **1** to hit, to break. **2** to stride. [SE *clap*, to strike a hard surface]

clap eyes on, to *phr.* [19C] to catch sight of.

clapier/clapoire *n.* [16C] **1** a place of debauchery. **2** the venereal disease one can contract there. [for ety. *see* CLAP n.]

clap in *v.* [early 17C–late 18C] to rush in vigorously, to push oneself forward, to arrive or leave in a decisive manner. [SE *clap (of thunder)*; i.e. the energy of one's arrival/departure]

clap of thunder *n.* [early–mid-19C] a glass of gin. [play on FLASH OF LIGHTNING]

clapoire *see* CLAPIER.

clap on *v.* [mid-19C] to commit oneself, to make a determined effort. [ext. SE *clap on*, to place with promptness and effect]

clap one's clit, to *phr.* [1970s+] of a woman, to masturbate. [SE *clap*, to hit + CLIT]

clap on one's rags, to *phr.* [early–mid-19C] to get dressed. [SE *clap on* + RAGS n.²]

clap on the shoulder *n.* [17C–early 19C] an arrest for debt; thus *clap-shoulder*, a bailiff.

clapped *adj.* [1960s+] **1** exhausted. **2** worn out, useless. [abbr. CLAPPED-OUT]

clapped-out *adj.* [1940s+] worn out, useless, esp. of machinery, cars etc. [CLAP n. and its deleterious effects, even on things that could not possibly contract it]

clapper *n.*¹ **1** [mid-17C–mid-19C] the tongue, esp. of a talkative person. **2** [1930s+] the mouth. [SE *clapper*, tongue of a bell]

clapper *n.*² [mid-18C+] **1** gonorrhoea. **2** (US) one who has contracted it. [CLAP n.]

clapper *n.*³ [1910s–30s] **1** a sandwich-man. **2** the boards carried by a sandwich-man. [the fig. clapping together of the boards]

clapperclaw/capperclaw *v.* [late 16C–early 19C] **1** to claw or scratch with the open hand and nails, to beat, to thrash, to drub. **2** to abuse verbally, to revile. [SE *clapper*, tongue + *claw*. The term vanished in the UK but has survived in parts of the US, where both senses are usu. applied to women]

clapperdudgeon/clapperdogeon *n.* [16C–early 18C] (Und.) a beggar who worked with a female companion, posing as man and wife and complete with counterfeit marriage licence; he might deliberately poison himself with ratsbane or spearwort (arsenic) to raise impressive sores (cf. PALLIARD; STAFF STRIKER). [SE *clapper*, hitter + *dudgeon*, the hilt of a dagger. Its origins remain a mystery, but it has been suggested that it comes from the beggar hitting his clapdish (a wooden dish with a lid, carried by lepers, beggars and mendicants generally, to give warning of their approach and to receive alms) with a dudgeon. *Clapdish* is, in turn, behind the phr. *your tongue goes like a baker's clap-dish*]

clappers *n.*¹ [1920s–40s] (US Black) an evangelical church, typified by a high degree of participation by the congregation, typically singing, hand-clapping, responding to the prayers and sermon (cf. HAPPY-CLAPPIES).

clappers *n.*² [1930s+] (orig. milit.) the testicles (cf. CHIMES). [their 'clapping together']

clapping for credit *n.* [1970s+] (US campus) a music appreciation course. [one claps in time to the music]

clapping the dog *n.* [1990s] stimulating a woman's genitals with one's fingers. [SE *clap* v. + DOG n.¹⁵]

clappy *adj.* [1960s+] suffering from venereal disease. [CLAP n.]

clap-shoulder *n.* [17C–early 19C] a bailiff or watchman. [he *claps a hand on one's shoulder*]

clapster *n.* [19C+] **1** one who suffers regularly and often from venereal disease. **2** a promiscuous man. [CLAP n.]

clap-trap *n.*¹ **1** [20C] idle chatter, meaningless, often positively incorrect or misinformed talk. **2** [1960s–70s] (US Black) the mouth (cf. TRAP n.³). [CLAPPER n.¹ (1)]

clap-trap *n.*² [20C] **1** the vagina. **2** a brothel where one might contract venereal disease. [CLAP n. + pun on CLAP-TRAP n.¹ (1)]

Clare Market cleavers *n.* [late 19C–1900s] butchers working in and around Clare Market, London WC2; thus butchers' jargon *cleavin*, boastful. [Clare Market was established in 17C, but vanished beneath the Kingsway/Aldwych developments (1900–5)]

Clare Market duck *n.* [late 19C–1900s] a bullock's heart stuffed with sage and onions (cf. COLONIAL DUCK; FIELD LANE DUCK; MOCK-DUCK; SNOB'S DUCK). [for ety. *see* CLARE MARKET CLEAVERS]

claret *n.* [early 17C+] blood; thus [1920s] (boxing jargon) *claret*, to draw blood from an opponent, *claret-christening*, the first blow to draw blood. [OF *claret*, clear, bright, light. orig. used to describe yellowish or light red wines from plain red or white wines. Used in UK *c.*1600 to describe red wines of the Bordeaux vineyards only]

claret-jug *n.* [mid-19C] the nose. [CLARET + pun]

clarinet-player *n.* [1950s] (Aus.) a fellator or fellatrix (cf. BLOW THE SKIN FLUTE; PICCOLO PLAYER). [pun on SE, the key image is that of *blowing*]

clarity *n.* [1980s+] (drugs) MDMA (cf. ECSTASY). [its effects]

clart *n.* [1970s+] **1** sticky excrement (orig. coined 1808 as sticky mud; often used as *in the clarts*, suffering from diarrhoea). **2** (Ulster) an untidy woman. [(2) is fig. use of (1)]

clashbag/clashbeg *n.* [20C] (Ulster) a gossip, a tattle-tale. [dial. *clash*, to gossip]

clashy *n.* [mid-19C] (orig. Anglo-Ind.) a labourer; thus any 'low fellow'. [Urdu *khlasy*, a tent-pitcher, a surveyor's chainman, a native sailor]

class *n.* [mid-19C+] distinction, quality, orig. used of athletes.

class act *n.* [1970s+] (orig. US) an impressive performance, example or instance, both literally and metaphorically, used of things or individuals. [CLASS + SE *act*]

classic *n.* [1980s+] (orig. US campus) anyone or anything that is regarded as out of the ordinary, eccentric; the implication is one of ironic appraisal.

classic *adj.* [1960s+] general adj. of supreme approval, wonderful, admirable, incomparable, the best. [ext. of SE use, but perhaps, given its use in sl., with a slight ref. to the *classic* horse-races]

class up *v.* [1980s+] (US) to make classy, esp. in phr. *class up one's act*, to start living in a more classy manner.

classy *adj.* [late 19C+] of high or superior class, stylish, smart.

classy chassis *n.* [1950s–60s] (US) the body of a good-looking, well-built woman.

clatter *n.*¹ [20C] (orig. Irish) a blow, a beating, esp. given by a parent to a child. [CLATTER v.¹]

clatter *n.*² [20C] (Irish) a large number. [they knock together]

clatter *n.*³ [1910s+] (US) a time, each (cf. POP n.⁵). [the fig. 'explosion' that punctuates each instance of an act]

clatter *v.*¹ [20C] to hit, to beat up; thus *clatters*, a smacking. [orig. UK northern dial.]

clatter *v.*² [20C] (Irish) to gossip.

clatterbrain/clatterbox *n.* [19C] a gossip. [US dial. *clatter*, idle gossip, and earlier UK dial. *clatterbrains*, an idle, lazy gossip]

claven *n.* [1990s] (US campus) a know-it-all. [ety. unknown]

claw *n.* [mid-18C+] a hand, a finger (cf. CLAWS).

claw *v.* [19C] to masturbate.

claw-back *n.* [16C–17C] a sycophant, a toady (cf. CLAW-POLL). [he or she metaphorically 'claws' at one's back. Note obs. SE *claw*, to flatter, to wheedle, to cajole]

claw-buttock *n.* [19C] the penis (cf. BAT n.⁷).

clawed off *adj.* [late 17C–late 18C] severely beaten or thrashed; thus also suffering a severe dose of venereal disease. [CLAW OFF]

claw-hammer *n.* **1** [19C] a tailcoat, as worn with full evening dress (cf. BANGER n.³). **2** [20C] (Ulster) a pig's foot. [supposed resemblance of the divided tail or foot to the tool]

claw me and I'll claw you *phr.* [early 19C] an early version of 20C *scratch my back and I'll scratch yours*.

claw off *v.* [late 17C–early 19C] to thrash, to beat severely. [SE *claw*, to scratch; but note ? pun on naut. *claw off*, to keep far away enough from the shore to avoid shipwreck]

claw one's toes, to *phr.* [mid-15C] to indulge oneself. [the pleasure of scratching one's feet]

claw-poll *n.* [16C–17C] a sycophant, a toady (cf. CLAW-BACK). [he or she metaphorically 'claws' at one's SE *poll*, hair. Note obs. SE *claw*, to flatter, to wheedle, to cajole]

claws *n.* [17C+] the fingers (cf. CLAW n.).

claw-thumper *n.* [mid–late 19C] (US) a Roman Catholic (cf.

BREAST FLEET). [the chest-thumping that accompanies certain Roman Catholic prayers]

clay *n.* [mid–late 19C] a clay pipe.

clay-brained *adj.* [late 16C–late 17C] stupid (cf. AMOEBA-BRAINED). [SE *clay*, i.e. its density + sfx. *-brained*]

clay-eater *n.* [19C] (US) a poor White, esp. a native of North or South Carolina or Georgia (cf. CLOVER-EATER; GRIT-SUCKER). [the literal eating of clay by such people in order to supplement their otherwise meagre diet]

clayton's *n.* [1980s+] (Aus.) a myth, an illusion, a fantasy. [the advertising line for *Clayton's* non-alcoholic drink (made from African kola nuts and citrus essences): 'It's the drink I have when I'm not having a drink', written by Noel Delbridge, creative director of ad agency D'Arcy, McManus & Masius]

clean *adj.*[1] **1** [late 19C–1960s] (US) penniless, without money. **2** [1920s+] (Und.) without any form of incriminating identification, not carrying a gun. **3** [1930s+] not using any form of drug, not currently addicted (cf. COOL *adj.*[4]). **4** [1960s+] beyond any possible suspicion, guiltless. [neg. uses of SE *clean*, i.e. not dirty]

clean *adj.*[2] **1** [1930s+] (US Black/prison) dressed in the height of current male fashion, perfectly groomed (cf. CLEAN TO THE BONE). **2** [1960s] (US) first-class, excellent. [poss. uses of SE *clean*]

clean *v.* **1** [late 19C+] to tell off severely. **2** [1910s+] (orig. gambling) to take all of an opponent's money (cf. CLEAN OUT).

clean *adv.* [mid-19C+] entirely, completely; thus *clean away*, escaped completely, *clean forget*, completely forget.

clean around the bend *phr.* [1920s+] utterly insane (cf. HARPIC). [CLEAN *adv.* + AROUND THE BEND + pun on advertising slogan use for the lavatory cleaner *Harpic*]

clean as a penny *phr.* [early 19C–1900s] extremely clean. [SE in 18C]

clean broke *adj.* [mid-19C+] absolutely penniless. [CLEAN *adv.* + BROKE]

cleaned out *adj.* [early 19C+] bereft of money, either through gambling or some form of confidence trick or hoax. [CLEAN OUT *v.*[3]]

cleaner than the board of health *phr.* [1960s–70s] (US Black) extremely well turned-out, dressed in the height of fashion (cf. CLEAN *adj.*[2]). [play on SE *clean*/CLEAN *adj.*[2]]

clean-faced man *n.* [1960s+] (W.I.) a Rastafarian who does not, however, sport the characteristic beard and dreadlocks (cf. BALDHEAD).

clean gone *adj.* [1920s] utterly insane (cf. CLEAN AROUND THE BEND). [CLEAN *adv.* + GONE *adj.*[3] (2)]

clean house *v.* [1910s+] (US) to sort things out once and for all, to punish, to beat.

clean one's fur coat, to *phr.* [1990s] of a woman, to masturbate. [SE *fur coat*, the pubic hair]

clean one's rifle, to *phr.* [20C] to masturbate (cf. GREASE ONE'S PIPE; SHINE ONE'S POLE; UNCLOG THE DRAIN; VARNISH ONE'S POLE).

clean out *v.* **1** [early 19C+] to thrash. **2** [early–19C+] to ruin financially. **3** [early 19C+] (gambling) to take all of an opponent's money (cf. FLAY; TAKE SOMEONE TO THE CLEANERS). **4** [mid-19C+] (US) to defeat heavily, to trounce, to 'make short work of'. **5** [1910s–30s] to do well financially.

clean potato, the *n.*[1] [19C] the right thing, the apposite thing (cf. POTATO *n.*[2]).

clean potato *n.*[2] [19C+] (Aus.) anyone who is not a convict.

clean queen *n.* [1960s+] (US gay) a gay man who combines trips to the launderette with the opportunity to look for partners. [SE *clean* + QUEEN *n.*[1]]

clean-shirt day *n.* [19C] Sunday. [the one day of the week on which even the poorest wore a clean shirt]

clean shot *n.* [1920s+] a piece of good luck, a favourable opportunity. [SE *clean* + SHOT *n.*[2]; fig. use of hunting jargon]

cleanskin/clearskin *n.* [1940s+] (Aus./N.Z.) **1** a person without a criminal record (cf. RAWSKIN). **2** an honest person, esp. in politics. [SE *cleanskin/clearskin*, an unbranded cow]

clean sneak *n.* [1930s–40s] (US) a getaway (from a robbery, killing or other crime) without leaving incriminating clues. [SE *clean* + SNEAK *n.*[1]]

clean someone's clock, to *phr.* [1940s+] (orig. US) **1** to beat up severely. **2** to take all someone's money, esp. during gambling (cf. CLEAN OUT). [fig. use of SE; ? link to US railroad jargon *clean the clock*, to apply the airbrakes and thus bring the train to a sudden stop. The 'clock' in question is the air gauge, which on halting, immediately registers zero and is thus 'clean']

clean someone's greens, to *phr.* [1960s–70s] (US) to beat up severely (cf. CLEAN (SOMEONE'S) CLOCK).

clean someone's/the pipe *n.* [20C] (US) to perform oral sex on a man. [SE *clean* + PIPE *n.*[8] (1)]

clean someone's plow, to *phr.* [20C] (US) to thrash, to beat severely; thus *clean someone's plow off*, to reach the limit of one's patience (cf. CLEAN SOMEONE'S CLOCK).

clean the board, to *phr.* [late 19C] to eat everything that is put in front of one; thus fig. use, to finish completely, to empty. [SE *clean* + *board*, a table]

clean the slate, to *phr.* [mid-19C+] to pay off one's outstanding debts.

clean/ragged to the bone *phr.* [1930s+] (US Black) **1** exceptionally well dressed (cf. MOD TO THE BONE; SILKED TO THE BONE; TABBED TO THE BONE; TO THE BONE). **2** handsome (cf. FONKY TO THE BONE). [CLEAN *adj.*[2] (1)/RAGGED (DOWN) + TO THE BONE]

clean-up *n.* [late 19C+] (orig. US) **1** a profit, an exceptional financial success. **2** a robbery or its proceeds. [CLEAN UP *v.*[1] (1)]

clean up/clear up *v.*[1] **1** [mid-19C+] to do very well out of a project, esp. in gambling use (cf. TAKE SOMEONE TO THE CLEANERS). **2** [late 19C+] to beat, to overcome. **3** [20C] to get rid of (hostile or alien elements). **4** [1910s+] to empty, to empty of its contents. **5** [1920s+] to make a large profit. **6** [1950s] (US) to kill for revenge. **7** [1960s] (US Black) to make excuses, to create an alibi. **8** [1960s] (US Black) to confess, esp. to telling lies or to failure. [fig. uses of SE]

clean up/it up *v.*[2] [20C] (US Und.) to explain.

clean up on *v.* [mid-19C+] to deal with successfully. [CLEAN UP *v.*[1] (1)]

clean up one's act, to *phr.* [1970s+] (orig. US) to modify or improve one's behaviour. [CLEAN UP *v.*[1] (3) + ACT *n.* (2)]

clean up/scrub the kitchen, to *phr.* [1930s+] (US) to perform anilingus or cunnilingus. [SE *clean up* + KITCHEN]

clean up the walls, to *phr.* [1950s+] (US Black) to chatter, to gossip, to talk nonsense.

clean wheat *n.* [mid-19C–1900s] the best, the supreme exemplar of a type. [? wheat that has been threshed and thus free of all impurities]

clear *adj.*[1] [late 17C–late 18C] very drunk. [? an ironic use of SE *clear*, the drunkard's head is of course far from clear]

clear *adj.*[2] [mid–late 19C] (US) pure, unadulterated (cf. CLEAR GRIT; PURE QUILL).

clear *adv.* [17C+] completely, totally.

clear as mud *phr.* [mid-19C+] completely unclear.

clear crystal *n.* [mid-19C–1920s] any clear spirit, e.g. gin, but also extended to brandy or rum.

clear cut *n.* [1950s+] (US Black) **1** stylish clothes. **2** pure drugs. [var. on SE *clean cut*]

clear field *n.* [1960s–70s] (US) an unimpeded opportunity, esp. for making contact with or pursuing a member of the opposite sex. [sporting imagery]

clear grit *n.* [mid–late 19C] the real thing, the genuine article; thus *be the clear grit*, to have genuine spirit or pluck. [CLEAR *adj.*[2] + GRIT *n.*[1]]

clearly *adj.* [1980s] (US teen) totally, maximally, perfectly etc.

clear off *v.* [early 19C+] to leave, to depart, esp. as excl. *clear off!*

clear one's coppers, to *phr.* [mid-19C] to clear one's throat. [SE *clear* + (HOT) COPPERS n.[1]]

clear out *v.* **1** [19C] to leave, to run away. **2** [mid-late 19C] to take all an opponent's money, to ruin financially (cf. CLEAN OUT). [(1) to 'clear away' one's presence; (2) fig. use of SE]

clear quill *see* PURE QUILL.

clearskin *see* CLEANSKIN.

clear the coop, to *phr.* [mid-19C] (US) to rush off, to vacate. [CLEAR OUT v. (1) + SE *coop*]

clear the custard, to *phr.* [1990s] to masturbate, after a long period of continence. [SE *clear* + CUSTARD]

clear up *see* CLEAN UP.

cleat *n.* [late 19C] the penis (cf. ARSE-OPENER). [SE *cleat*, a wedge]

cleatis *n.* [1990s] a general term of derision, abuse. [ety. unknown, ? SE *clitoris*]

cleave *n. see* CLOVEN.

cleave *v.* [18C–early 19C] **1** of a woman, usu. a prostitute, to pose as a virgin while not being one (cf. CLOVEN). **2** of a woman, to behave promiscuously. [SE *cleave*, to split; i.e. her legs or her supposed hymen]

cleaver *n.*[1] [18C–19C] a butcher. [his job and his tools]

cleaver *n.*[2] [late 18C–early 19C] a promiscuous woman (cf. CLOVEN). [CLEAVE v. (2)]

cleek *n.* [1950s] (orig. US) one who spoils a party (cf. PARTY POOPER). [jazz use *cleek*, a sad, melancholy person]

cleety *see* CLUTEY.

cleft *n.*[1] *see* CLOVEN.

cleft/cleft of flesh *n.*[2] [19C] the vagina (cf. AGREEABLE RUTS OF LIFE).

cleft *n.*[3] *see* CLIFT n.

cleft *adj.* [18C–early 19C] of a woman, posing as a prostitute while not being one (cf. CLOVEN). [CLEAVE v. (1)]

cleft of flesh *see* CLEFT n.[2].

clefty *see* CLIFTIE.

cleg *n.* [20C] (Ulster) a parasite, a hanger-on. [lit. 'a horsefly']

clem *n.* [20C] (US) a farmer, a peasant (cf. ALVIN). [proper name *Clarence* and considered a stereotypical 'country' name]

clem *adj.* [1970s] (US campus) well-dressed. [? CLEAN adj.[2]]

clem *v.* [20C] (tramp) to go hungry, to starve. [16C+ dial. *clem*, to starve, to waste from hunger; ult. f. various Teut. roots meaning 'pinch' or 'squeeze']

clenchpoop *see* CLINCHPOOP.

clergyman *n.* [late 18C–19C] a chimney sweep. [the colour of both professions' clothes]

clericals *n.* [mid-19C] clerical garments (i.e. those worn by clergymen).

clerked *adj.* [18C] soothed, gulled, imposed upon. [SE *clerk*, such 'learned' figures were automatically distrusted by the illiterate masses]

clerk of the kitchen *n.* [mid–late 17C] one who goes to the tavern for food as well as drink.

clerk of the works *n.* [early–mid-19C] a minor functionary.

clerk to the teethward/teeth-ward *n.* [late 16C–early 17C] one who parades learning that they do not fully or properly possess. [SE phr. *from the teeth forwards, teeth outwards*, used of one who pretends to emotions, learning etc that they do not possess]

clever/u-clever *n.* [1960s+] (S.Afr.) a gangster, a streetwise individual (cf. GHETTO STAR). [SE + Isicamtho *uclever*]

clever *adj.* **1** [19C+] (orig. Aus./N.Z.) in good health, in order, working well etc; thus *not too clever*, generally neg. response to 'how are you?', 'how is it?' etc. **2** [19C] (US) good-natured, well-disposed, amiable (often too well-disposed for one's

own good and thus applied to those whose intelligence is considered somewhat deficient). **3** [late 19C+] skilful, adroit (cf. BOX CLEVER). **4** [20C] (Ulster) of a garment, roomy. [18C SE *clever*, 'active' rather than 'infirm', healthy]

clever boots *n.* [20C] a clever person, esp. one who is 'too clever for their own good' (cf. CLEVER CLOGS; SMARTIE-PANTS).

clever clogs *n.* [mid-19C+] a slightly derogatory description (usu. used by children) of anyone considered notably clever (often 'too clever for their own good') (cf. CLEVER BOOTS).

clever dick / clever dog / cleverguts / cleverpot / clever shins / cleversides / cleversticks *n.* [19C+] a clever person, esp. when considered suspiciously so (cf. CLEVER BOOTS; CLEVER CLOGS; SMART ALEC).

clever Mike *n.* [20C] a bicycle. [rhy. sl. *clever Mike* = bike]

cleverpot / clever shins / cleversides / cleversticks *see* CLEVER DICK.

clewner *n.* [16C] a senior rank of villain: 'Sir, yet there is another company/Of the same sect, that live more subtly,/ And be in manner as master wardens,/To whom these rogers obey as captains/And be named clewners, as I hear say' Copland (cf. AURIUM). [ety. unknown]

cleyme/clyme *n.* [late 16C–late 18C] (Und.) an artificial sore or wound, as placed on the body by a variety of mendicant villains. [ety. unknown, the *cleyme* is created by 'bruising Crowsfoot, Speerwort, and Salt together, and clapping them on the Place, which frest the Skin, then with a Linnen rag, which sticks close to it, they tear off the Skin, and strew on it a little Powder'd Arsenick, which makes it look angrily ...' B.E.]

clica *n.* [1960s+] (US) a gang. [Sp. *clica*, a clique]

click *n.*[1] [late 18C–mid-19C] (Und.) a blow (cf. CLICKER n.[4]). [dial.]

click *n.*[2] [late 19C] a robbery, a theft. [? the SE *click* of a lock]

click *n.*[3] [1910s+] a clique, a gang; thus *click up*, to form or join a gang. [SE *clique*, orig. Aus. but still popular in late 20C with US Black teens]

click *v.*[1] [late 17C–19C] (Und.) to snatch, to rob. [northern dial. *cleek*, to snatch, to clutch eagerly]

click *v.*[2] [mid-18C–early 19C] to stand at one's shop doorway and inveigle customers in. [CLICKER n.[1]]

click *v.*[3] **1** [1910s+] to get on with, to strike up a friendship with. **2** [1920s+] to become proficient or successful at. **3** [1930s+] to work out exactly as planned. **4** [1930s+] for something to become clear or comprehensible, esp. after a period of puzzlement, to 'ring a bell'. **5** [1940s+] (Irish) to pick up a member of the opposite sex. [the image of a lock or similar form of machinery working as planned]

click *v.*[4] [1930s+] to become pregnant. [also used in rural Aus. of a cow]

clicker *n.*[1] [late 17C–late 19C] a shopkeeper's (orig. a shoe-mender's) tout (cf. CLICK v.[2]). [shoemaker's jargon *clicker*, a foreman shoemaker who cuts out the leather for boots and shoes, and gives it out to the workmen, or a workman who works at cutting the uppers of boots and shoes]

clicker *n.*[2] [18C] the gang member deputed to divide up the spoils fairly. [CLICK v.[1]]

clicker *n.*[3] [18C] (prison) a warder. [one who 'clicks the key']

clicker *n.*[4] **1** [late 18C–mid-19C] (orig. boxing jargon) a knock-out blow. **2** [1940s] (US) a photographer. [the noise of the blow or the camera shutter]

clicker *n.*[5] [1910s–30s] one who makes new friends or contacts. [CLICK v.[3] (1)]

clicker *n.*[6] [1980s+] (drugs) **1** crack cocaine. **2** phencyclidine (cf. ACE n.[3]).

clickers *n.* [20C] false teeth (cf. CLACKERS). [the sound they make]

clicket *v.* [17C–early 19C] to copulate; thus *at the clicket*, having intercourse. [SE *clicket*, of the fox, to be in heat, to copulate]

clicketty-clicks *n.* [20C] women's underpants. [rhy. sl. *clicketty-clicks* = KNICKS]

clickety-click *n.* [20C] **1** (bingo) the number 66. **2** (Aus.) a stick. [rhy. sl.]

clicking/clicking with *n.* [1910s+] making a successful contact, usu. with a member of the opposite sex (albeit not necessarily sexual). [CLICK v.³ (1)]

clickman toad *n.* **1** [late 18C–early 19C] a watch. **2** [late 18C–mid-19C] a West Countryman. ['A West-country man, who had never seen a watch, found one on a heath near Pool, which, by the motion of the hand, and the noise of the wheels, he concluded to be a living creature of the toad kind, and, from its clicking, he named it a clickman toad.' (Grose)]

click with *v.* [1910s+] to get on with, to strike up a friendship with (cf. CLICK v.³).

cliff ape *n.* [1910s+] (US) a rough, thuggish man. [SE *cliff* + APE]

cliff-dweller *n.* [late 19C–1900s] (US) one who lives in a skyscraper apartment block, esp. in New York City (cf. CAVE-DWELLER). [SE *cliff dwellers*, a tribe of Native Americans living literally in cliffs in the Southwest]

cliffhanger *n.*¹ [1930s+] any suspenseful, threatening situation, although usu. one from which one is eventually delivered. [orig. the film description of such silent-era serials as 'The Perils of Pauline' (starring Pearl White) in which the heroine, at an episode's end, was often literally hanging from a cliff]

cliffhanger *n.*² [1980s+] (drugs) phencyclidine (cf. ACE n.³). [? its effects]

clift/cleft *n.* [late 19C+] (orig. Irish) a fool; thus the levels of stupidity, *quarter clift*, *three-quarter clift*, *the two ends of a clift*, an utter fool. [? SE *cleave*, i.e. their brain has been cut in several pieces]

clift *v.* [mid-19C–1900s] to steal. [? SE *cleave*, adhere to or *clift*, to split, to divide (in this case possessions from their owner)]

cliftie/clifty/clefty *v.* [20C] (Aus.) to steal. [CLIFT v., but note Gk. *klephtys*, a thief]

cligh *v.* [late 17C–18C] (Und.) to steal. [var. on CLOY]

climax *n.* (drugs) [1980s+] **1** crack cocaine. **2** isobutyl nitrite. **3** heroin. [the quasi-orgasmic effects]

climb *n.*¹ [1930s+] (Und.) cat burglary; thus *at the climb*, *climbing*, working as a cat burglar.

climb *n.*² [1980s+] (drugs) a marijuana cigarette. [ety. unknown; ? it makes one CLIMB THE WALLS]

climb *v.* [1920s+] (US) from male view, to have sexual intercourse (cf. CLIMB ALL OVER).

climb all over *v.* [1960s+] **1** to attack verbally, to reprimand. **2** to maul sexually, usu. spoken by a woman of a man.

climb-a-pole *n.* [mid-19C] (US) an arrogant, 'stuck-up' person.

climb-a-pole *adj.* [mid-19C] (US) arrogant. [CLIMB-A-POLE n.]

climb-down *n.* [late 19C+] a humiliating surrender in an argument, esp. after one has doggedly held one's own position for some time.

climber *n.* [20C] (Und.) a cat burglar. [CLIMB n.¹]

climbing Mary *n.* [1940s] a female window-cleaner.

climbing trees to get away from it *phr.* [1940s+] (Aus. male) in answer to query 'getting any?' Allied phrs. are *got to swim underwater to get away from it*, *so busy I've had to put a man on to help*.

climb in on *v.* [late 19C] (US) to overcome easily, to get the better of, esp. by trickery.

climb mount baldy, to *phr.* [1990s] to masturbate.

climb someone's frame, to *phr.* [1930s–60s] (US) to assault physically.

climb the golden staircase, to *phr.* [late 19C] (US) **1** to die. **2** to fail badly.

climb the leafless tree, to *phr.* [early–mid-19C] to be hanged (cf. CLIMB THE STALK; CLIMB THE TRIPLE TREE; CLIMB THREE TREES WITH A LADDER; MOUNT THE LADDER; WALK UP LADDER LANE AND DOWN HEMP STREET). [SE *climb* + LEAFLESS TREE]

climb the mountain of piety, to *phr.* [late 19C–1900s] to take possessions to the pawnshop. [the world's first government-authorized pawnbrokers, which were established in Rome and sited on the Monte di Pietà ('the mountain of piety')]

climb the rigging, to *phr.* [1910s+] (orig. naut.) to lose one's temper (cf. CLIMB THE WALLS).

climb the stalk, to *phr.* [18C] to be hanged (cf. CLIMB THE LEAFLESS TREE). [SE *climb* + STALK n.²]

climb the tree, to *phr.* [20C] to masturbate.

climb the triple tree, to *phr.* [18C] to be hanged (cf. CLIMB THE LEAFLESS TREE). [SE *climb* + TRIPLE TREE]

climb/run up the walls, to *phr.* [1950s+] **1** to lose one's temper, to run out of patience. **2** to approach insanity through nerves, irritation, tension etc.

climb three trees with a ladder, to *phr.* [mid-16C–19C] to be hanged (cf. CLIMB THE LEAFLESS TREE; THREE TREES). [the framework of the wooden gallows]

clinah *see* CLINER.

clinch *n.* **1** [mid-19C] a prison cell; thus *get the clinch*, to be locked up, *clinched*, imprisoned. **2** [late 19C+] a sexual embrace.

clinched *adj.* [20C] drunk. ['in the grip' of alcohol]

clincher *n.* [mid-18C+] **1** the ultimate solution, the culmination. **2** an irrefutable lie.

clinchpoop/clenchpoop *n.* [late 16C] an ill-mannered lout, one who lacks gentlemanly breeding. [? *clincher*, the workman who clinched the bolts in ship-building, in this case of the poop. E.P. notes its nonce re-emergence in the early 1960s, used in court by a Mod or a Rocker]

cliner/clinah *n.* [late 19C–1940s] (Aus.) a woman, a girlfriend. [ety. unknown, ? Ger. *Kleine*, little one]

clinger *n.* [late 19C] a woman who holds tightly to her partner during a dance.

clingy *adj.* [20C] over-dependent, esp. emotionally (cf. CLINGER).

clinic *n.* [1950s] a public house. [one visits for 'a bit of what the doctor ordered']

clink *n.*¹ [early 16C+] **1** prison. **2** a sanctuary for criminals in Southwark; the villains who frequented this area were known as *clinkers* (cf. ALSATIA). [either SE *clink*, to secure, to fasten securely, or onomat. noise of clinking chains]

clink *n.*² **1** [early 18C+] money (cf. CHING n.²). **2** [late 19C] a coin. [echoic]

clink *n.*³ [mid–late 19C] bad or second-rate beer (cf. BUM CLINK).

clink *n.*⁴ [1930s–40s] (US Black) a Black man. [? CLINK n.¹, so many Blacks being imprisoned, or f. *clinker*, a grey-black ash that remains after a fire]

clinker *n.*¹ [late 17C–mid-18C] a crafty person. [? CLINKERS n.¹ (2)]

clinker *n.*² [late 17C–mid-18C] fetters or any other form of chain.

clinker *n.*³ [mid-19C+] a piece of excrement adhering to the anus; thus *have clinkers in one's bum*, to act nervously or restlessly (cf. CLAGNUT). [? SE *cling*]

clinker *n.*⁴ [mid-19C–1930s] anything considered excellent, first-rate. [orig. sporting use. f. something that 'rings a (celebratory) bell']

clinker *n.*⁵ [mid–late 19C] a sharp blow. [it 'clinks' on its target]

clinker n.[6] [1900s–30s] (US) a hard biscuit. [SE *clinker*, a very hard brick, ? since its ult. ety. is Du., imported by Dutch immigrants]

clinker n.[7] **1** [1930s–50s] (US) a musical discord, a fluffed note. **2** [1960s] (US) a problem, a difficulty. **3** [1960s+] something second-rate, inferior, esp. a performance. [orig. baseball use]

clinkers n.[1] [late 17C–18C] **1** chains and fetters worn by imprisoned felons. **2** those villains who inhabited the early 16C criminal sanctuary of the CLINK n.[1] in Southwark. [the sound of the fetters on stone floors]

clinkers n.[2] [20C] (Ulster) the testicles. [they 'clink' together]

clinkers n.[3] [1970s+] bedbugs.

clinkers n.[4] [1990s] (Aus.) lumps of excrement adhering to the rectum (cf. CLAGNUT). [SE *clinker*, a hardened mass]

clinkerum n. [19C] a prison. [CLINK n.[1] (1)]

clinking adj. [mid–late 19C] excellent, admirable, first-rate, esp. of racehorses (cf. CLINKER n.[4]; CLIPPING adj.[1]; WHACKING adj.).

clink rig n. [mid-19C] (Und.) the stealing of tankards from taverns (cf. CAT-SNEAKING). [backform. f. CLINK RIGGER]

clink rig v. [mid-19C] (Und.) to steal tankards from taverns. [CLINK RIG n.]

clink rigger n. [late 18C–late 19C] one who steals silver tankards from public houses (cf. CLANK-NAPPER). [SE *clink*, the noise of tankards hit together + RIG v.[1]]

clip n.[1] **1** [mid-19C+] a rate of movement, a pace; thus *fair/good clip*, a (reasonably) high speed. **2** [1900s–30s] (US) a lively young woman. [CLIP v.[1]; note (2) is fig. use of (1)]

clip n.[2] [1940s] (US) a theft. [CLIP v.[2] (3)]

clip n.[3] [1940s] a male Jew (cf. CLIPDICK). [CLIP v.[2] (4)]

clip n.[4] [1990s] (drugs) a bundle of the bottles in which crack is distributed, tied with a rubber band to facilitate carriage.

clip v.[1] **1** [mid-19C+] to move quickly, to run. [SE *clip*, of a bird, to fly fast]

clip v.[2] **1** [mid-19C+] to hit, to tap sharply. **2** [1920s+] (US) to shoot dead. **3** [1920s+] (orig. US) to defraud, to steal from, to rob. **4** [1940s+] (US) to circumcise. **5** [1940s–60s] (US) to place under arrest. **6** [1980s+] to kill, to murder. [SE *clip*, to cut or snip]

clip artist n. [1940s–60s] (US) a petty thief. [CLIP v.[2] (3) + ARTIST n.[1]]

clipdick n. [1940s+] a derog. term for a male Jew. [CLIP v.[2] (4) + DICK n.[5]; his circumcision]

clip-joint n. [1930s+] a club or similar place of entertainment where the customers are deliberately and systematically defrauded under the guise of charging them for their pleasure (cf. BADGER n.[4]). [CLIP v.[2] (3) + JOINT n.[3] (3)]

clip-nit n. [early 18C] a dirty ruffian. [SE *clip*, to grasp + *nit*, a louse egg]

clipped adj.[1] [1930s+] (US) shot. [CLIP v.[2] (2)]

clipped adj.[2] [1940s+] (US) circumcised. [CLIP v.[2] (4)]

clipped within the ring phr. [late 16C–early 17C] deflowered. [SE *clip* + RING n.[1]]

clipper n.[1] (Und.) **1** [early 18C] a cut-purse. **2** [1940s] a philanderer, a womanizer. **3** [1960s+] a professional store thief. [(2) CLIP v.[2] (3), but despite the obvious synonymy, chronology makes (1) and (3) fig. uses of SE]

clipper n.[2] [mid-19C] **1** an excellent thing. **2** an attractive person, esp. a woman. [SE *clipper*, a fast-sailing vessel, esp. the raked schooners of America and subseq. the Aus. passenger ships]

clipper n.[3] [1980s+] (S.Afr.) a 100-rand note (cf. CHOCOLATE n.[2]). [? Afk. *klippe*, diamonds or the need for a *paper-clip* to keep 100 rand's worth of 10-rand notes together]

clippie n. [1940s–50s] a bus conductress, who then *clipped* tickets.

clipping n. [1970s+] (Und.) posing as a prostitute, obtaining the money, but absconding before intercourse takes place (cf. BADGER n.[4]). [CLIP v.[2] (3)]

clipping adj.[1] [mid-19C] excellent, first-rate. [CLIPPER n.[2] (1)]

clipping adj.[2] [mid–late 19C] of a pace, fast. [CLIP v.[1]]

clippings of tin n. [1940s] (Irish) a trifling, worthless quantity.

clip queen n. [1940s] (US gay) a male prostitute who specializes in robbing clients. [CLIP v.[2] (3)]

clip side of big moist phr. [1940s] (US Black/Harlem) Europe. [at that time the western battleground of WW2]

clipster n. [1940s–60s] (US) a swindler. [CLIP v.[2] (3)]

clip the King's English, to phr. [late 17C–late 18C] to slur one's words when drunk. [SE *clip*, to mutilate]

clit n. [1950s+] the *clit*oris. [abbr.]

clit fight n. [1990s] (US) a sexual game between two women (cf. SEX FIGHT). [CLIT + SE *fight*]

clithopper n. [1960s+] (lesbian) a promiscuous lesbian. [CLIT; on pattern of BEDHOP, lit. to move or 'hop' from clitoris to clitoris]

clitty n. [1950s+] the *clit*oris. [abbr.]

clitty adj. see CLUTEY.

cloak n. [mid–late 19C] a watch-case.

cloak-twitcher n. [early 18C–early 19C] (Und.) a thief specializing in the theft of cloaks.

clobber/klobber n. [late 19C+] clothes, esp. good quality or conspicuous clothes; thus *clobbered*, well-dressed. [ety. unknown. ? Yid., so claimed by Ware who suggests 'Hebrew KLBR' (the Hebrew has been anglicized without vowels)]

clobber v. [1940s+] **1** to hit, to beat up, to kill (cf. SCHMEER v.). **2** to defeat heavily. **3** to criticize, to treat harshly. [ety. unknown, ? echoic of the sound of the blow]

clobbered adj. [1940s+] **1** hit. **2** drunk. [CLOBBER v.]

clobbering machine/great Kiwi clobbering machine n. [1970s+] (N.Z.) a strain of innate conservatism found in local or national bureaucracy or government that invariably opposes change. [CLOBBER v. + SE *machine*]

clobber someone with v. [1940s+] to force an unpleasant or unwanted task or duty on someone. [CLOBBER v.]

clobber the kleenex, to phr. [1990s] to masturbate. [CLOBBER v. + *Kleenex*, proprietary brand of paper tissues]

clobber up v. **1** [mid-19C] to mend or patch clothes. **2** [mid–late 19C] to dress smartly. [tailor's jargon *clobber*, to renovate old garments, ? ult. cobblers' jargon *clobber*, a black paste used by cobblers to fill up and conceal cracks in the leather of boots and shoes]

clock n.[1] **1** [mid-19C+] the face (cf. DIAL). **2** [1920s+] a speedometer or similar dial that has a 'face'. **3** [1940s+] (US Black) the heart (cf. CHIMER). **4** [1950s+] a blow, esp. to the face. [fig. uses of SE]

clock n.[2] [late 19C] a bomb; thus *got a clock*, carrying a handbag (in which the bomb is hidden). [a bomb-carrier who, when stopped during the dynamite scare of the 1880s by an alert policeman, on being asked what was in his bag, replied 'A clock']

clock n.[3] [1950s–60s] (Aus.) a prison sentence of 12 months; thus synon. phr. *round the clock*. [the 12 hours of the clock face]

clock/clock up v.[1] [late 19C+] to attain or record a given time or number in a race or similarly measured distance or quantity. [the clock used to measure such times]

clock v.[2] [1920s+] (orig. Aus./N.Z.) to hit in the face. [CLOCCK n.[1] (1)]

clock v.[3] **1** [1930s+] to see, to recognize, to watch, to understand, to work something out. **2** [1970s] (US) to reconnoitre, usu. of a possible crime site. **3** [1980s+] (US) of a prostitute, to pick up a customer. [the image of checking the time on a clock]

clock v.[4] [1990s] (US Black) **1** to achieve, to accomplish, to succeed. **2** to earn money. [CLOCK v.[1]]

clock v.[5] [1990s] (US Black) to sell drugs. [CLOCKER, but note CLOCK v.[4] (2)]

clock a daffy, to phr. [20C] (S.Afr.) to tell a deceitful story with the intention of tricking the hearer. [CLOCK v.[3] (2) + DAFFY adj.]

clock a grip, to phr. [1990s] (US Black) to make a sudden windfall of money, esp. through drug sales or some other illegal scheme. [CLOCK v.[4] (2)]

clocker n. [1980s] (drugs) a dealer of crack cocaine; thus *clocking*, working as a crack dealer. [SE *clock*, a time piece. The need for the drug and the appearances of the dealer both seem to occur at regular intervals, these dealers are on call 'around the clock', but note CLOCK v.[3]/v.[5]]

clock in v. [1910s] to arrive. [SE *clock in/on/off/out*, to register one's arrival at and departure from work on a time-clock]

clocking n.[1] [1980s] (US Black) saying inappropriate, tactless things, acting insanely. [CLOCK v.[3]]

clocking n.[2] [1980s] (US Black) working as a drug seller. [CLOCK v.[5]]

clocking adj. [1990s] (rap music) worried, disturbed. [CLOCK v.[3] (1)]

clocking paper n. [1980s] (drugs) profits from selling drugs. [CLOCKING n.[2] + PAPER n.[1] (8)]

clock on to v. [1930s] to recognize. [CLOCK v.[2]]

clock-weights n. [19C] the testicles. [resemblance]

clockwork n. [1940s] (US Black) the human brain, the mind.

clocky n. [early–mid-19C] a watchman. [the regularity of his rounds]

clod n.[1] [17C] **1** a stupid person, esp. a dull-witted peasant (cf. APPLE-KNOCKER n.[2]; CLODPATE; CLODPOLL). **2** a rude, awkward person. [SE *clod*, a lump of earth or mud]

clod n.[2] [1930s] (tramp) a penny or any copper coin, usu. in plural. [rhy. sl. *clodhopper* = copper]

clod-buster n. [1950s] (US) a rustic, a farmer (cf. APPLE-KNOCKER n.[2]). [CLOD n.[1] + BUST v.[1]]

clod-crusher n. [late 19C] (US) a rustic, a farmer (cf. APPLE-KNOCKER n.[2]). [note also: 'an epithet used by Americans to describe the large feet which they believe to be the characteristics of English women as compared with those of their own country' (B&L)]

cloddy adj. [late 19C] aristocratic-looking. [dog-fanciers' jargon *cloddy*, low to the ground, short in the back and thickset (the characteristics of the ideal bulldog)]

clodhopper n. **1** [18C] a clumsy oaf, a boor, a dull-witted peasant. **2** [19C] (US) a rustic, a farmer (cf. APPLE-KNOCKER n.[2]). **3** [mid-19C] a heavy work shoe. **4** [mid-19C] a large and clumsy foot. [SE *clod* + *hopper* lit. one who hops over the clods of earth; note SE *clod-hopper*, a ploughman]

clod-jumper n. [1910s] (US) a rustic, a farmer (cf. APPLE-KNOCKER n.[2]). [CLOD n.[1] + SE *jumper*]

clod-knocker n. [20C] (US) a rustic, a farmer (cf. APPLE-KNOCKER n.[2]). [CLOD n.[1] + SE *knocker*]

clod-masher n. [1960s–70s] (US) **1** a clumsy oaf. **2** a rustic (cf. APPLE-KNOCKER n.[2]). **3** a heavy shoe (cf. CLODHOPPER). [CLOD n.[1] + SE *masher*]

clodpate n. [late 17C–mid-18C] a fool, a dullard. [CLOD n.[1] + SE *pate*, the head]

clodpoll/clodpole n. [late 17C] a fool, an incompetent. [CLOD n.[1] + SE *poll*, the head]

clods and stickings n. [mid-19C–1910s] gruel with dumplings (cf. SKILLY n.).

clod-skulled adj. [17C–early 18C] stupid. [CLOD n.[1] + SE *skulled*]

clomp n. **1** [20C] (US) a heavy boot or shoe. **2** [1910s] the sound of something heavy or solid hitting the ground. **3** [1960s] (US) a blow. [echoic]

clompers n. [20C] (US) false teeth (cf. CHOMPERS n.[1]). [SE *clomp*, to make the sound of clogs hitting the ground]

clone n. **1** [1970s] anyone who imitates another person to a slavish extent. **2** [1970s] (gay) a general description of a gay man who poses as one of a variety of super-masculine stereotypes, e.g. truck-driver, military man, cowboy etc, a style epitomized by the members of the 1970s disco group Village People. **3** [1980s] (US campus) a tedious, unimportant person. [SE *clone*, a thing produced in imitation of, or closely resembling, another]

clonk n. [20C] **1** a blow, a hit. **2** the noise of one hard object striking another (cf. CLUNK n.[1]). [echoic]

clonk v. [20C] to hit (cf. CLUNK v.). [CLONK n.]

clonker see CLUNKER n.[1].

clootie see CLUTEY.

clop n. [1940s] (orig. US) a blow. [echoic]

clop v. [1950s] (orig. US) to hit hard. [CLOP n.]

close as God's curse to a whore's arse phr. [18C] very close (cf. CLOSE AS SHIRT AND SHITTEN ARSE).

close as ninety-nine is to one hundred phr. [1930s–40s] (US Black) extremely close, as close as possible.

close as shirt and shitten arse phr. [18C] extremely close (cf. CLOSE AS GOD'S CURSE TO A WHORE'S ARSE).

close, but no cigar phr. [20C] (orig. US/carnival) used when commiserating with a 'near-miss' or a good try. [the proprietor of the 'Highball' (the player thumps a platform with a hammer in the hope of ringing a bell) awarded successful competitors a cigar]

close call n. [late 19C] (orig. US) a very near thing (cf. CLOSE SHAVE). [sporting imagery]

closed swinging n. [1970s] swapping parties in which only husband-and-wife partnerships take part, no singles are allowed to unbalance the situation (cf. OPEN SWINGING). [SE *closed* + SWINGING]

close file n. [early–mid-19C] a secretive or uncommunicative person. [SE *close* + FILE n. (3)]

close shave n. [late 19C] (orig. US) a very near thing (cf. CLOSE CALL).

closet n. [1950s] (orig. gay) a metaphorical 'cupboard' in which a homosexual who is unwilling to reveal their sexuality is said to live.

closet adj. [1960s] secretive, clandestine, hidden. [CLOSET n.]

closet baser n. [1990s] (drugs) one who uses crack cocaine in secret. [CLOSET adj. + BASE v.[2]]

closet case n. **1** [1950s] (US campus) a socially inept, unattractive person. **2** [1960s] (gay) a homosexual who finds it difficult or impossible to admit their sexuality in public. [CLOSET adj. + CASE n.[6]]

close the deal, to phr. [1990s] to masturbate.

closet-man n. [1950s] (W.I.) a sanitary inspector. [SE *water closet*]

closet of ease n. [late 17C] a lavatory or water closet (cf. CHAPEL OF EASE). [euph.]

close to the blanket phr. [1900s] (US, West) almost totally impoverished, very poor. [gambling use, when a poker game would be played on a spread blanket; thus when one's pile of money gets smaller and smaller and 'close to the blanket']

closet queen n. [1960s] (gay) a homosexual man who finds it difficult to admit his sexuality (cf. CLOSET CASE). [CLOSET adj. + QUEEN n.[1]]

close-up n. (US) **1** [1920s] a close look. **2** [1990s] a frighteningly sudden, unexpected and sometimes unwanted, kiss (cf. ZOOM-IN). [ext. of film use]

close your head! excl. [1930s–40s] shut up! be quiet!

closh *n.* [late 18C] a Dutch seaman. [common Du. proper name *Klaas*, itself abbr. of *Nicolaas*]

closhy *adj.* [1910s] stupid. [? CLOSH; thus the derog. stereotype of a slow, stolid Dutchman]

clot *n.*[1] [1940s+] a fool, often used affectionately, e.g. *you silly clot.* [CLOD *n.*[1]]

clot *n.*[2] [1950s+] (W.I.) a highly derog. description of another person. [abbr. BLOOD CLAAT]

cloth, the *n.*[1] [early 18C+] generic term for the clergy, the world of clergymen. [their vestments]

cloth *n.*[2] [19C] the vagina (cf. CLOUT *n.*[1]). [? play on theatre use *cloth*, the curtain which stands between the audience and the stage]

cloth-ears *n.* [20C] a general term of mild abuse, esp. to someone who at first seems to not have heard one's comment. [abbr. of phr. *have cloth-ears*, to be stupid, lit. to be unable to hear due to a flap-eared cap]

clothes *n.* [1960s+] (US) a detective. [abbr. SE *plain clothes*]

clotheshorse *n.* **1** [1930s+] a fashion model. **2** [1940s+] an over-dressed woman. **3** [1940s+] an exquisitely well-dressed, fashionable person, although the implication is that beyond such perfection lies little else.

clothes-peg *n.* [20C] an egg. [rhy. sl.]

clothes-pegs *n.* [20C] the legs. [rhy. sl.]

clothes-prop *n.* [19C] the erect penis (cf. BAT *n.*[7]).

cloth-head *n.* [1920s+] a fool. [SE *cloth* + sfx. -HEAD (1)]

cloth market *n.* [late 17C–early 19C] bed. [its linen covers]

clotty *n.* [1960s+] (Irish) a general term of abuse. [ety. unknown; ? link to Yorks. dial. *cloddy*, an awkward, ill-dressed person]

cloud *n.*[1] **1** [late 17C–18C] tobacco, tobacco smoke. **2** [1990s] (drugs) the stimulating effect that follows smoking crack cocaine. **3** [1990s] crack cocaine. **4** [1990s] the smoke that one inhales from a pipe of crack cocaine.

cloud *n.*[2] [20C] a derog. term for a Black person, esp. a crowd of Black people. [play on SMOKE *n.*[4]]

cloud nine *n.* **1** [1960s+] a state of bliss, often drug-induced. **2** [1980s+] (drugs) crack cocaine. [according to Brewer (1995) the term stems from the classification of clouds by the US Weather Bureau. There are 9 divisions, and number 9 is cumulonimbus, a cumulus cloud of great vertical extent, topped with shapes that resemble mountains or towers]

cloud seven *n.* [1960s+] a state of bliss, often drug-induced. [var. on CLOUD NINE; presumably less blissful, but 7 is trad. a 'lucky' number]

cloudy *adj.* [late 19C] in disgrace, in trouble, disreputable. [UNDER A CLOUD]

clout *n.*[1] **1** [17C–19C] a cotton handkerchief (cf. CONCH-CLOUT). **2** [17C–19C] a sanitary towel. **3** [1990s] the vagina (cf. CLOTH *n.*[2]). [14C SE *clout*, handkerchief]

clout *n.*[2] [late 18C+] a heavy blow. [ety. unknown; ? link to SE *clout*, a cloth, thus a 'lump' of material, thus any sort of lump; or link to SE *clod*. Earlier use was SE]

clout *n.*[3] [20C] a stupid, oafish person (cf. CLOD *n.*[1]). [SE *clout*, a lump of earth; thus a synon. ety. with CLOD *n.*[1]]

clout *n.*[4] **1** [20C] a philanderer. **2** [1940s+] (US) a pickpocket. [fig. use of CLOUT *v.*[1] (1)]

clout *n.*[5] [1930s+] (orig. US) influence, esp. in politics (cf. PULL *n.*[1]). [coined *c.*1937 in Chicago and quickly disseminated across the US and thence the English-speaking world. According to William Safire either f. baseball jargon *clout*, a big hit; thus one who 'packs a punch' in government, or CLOUT *v.*[2], to steal (itself orig. f. CLOUTER, a petty thief, lit. a handkerchief thief); thus a thief. In the cynical world of US politics all politicians tend to larceny]

clout *v.*[1] [late 18C+] to hit, to give heavy blow to. [CLOUT *n.*[2]; earlier use was SE]

clout *v.*[2] [20C] **1** (US) to steal. **2** (Aus.) to cheat by palming a card or cards. **3** (Aus.) to short change. [orig. 18C Und. to steal handkerchiefs, i.e. *clouts*]

clouted-/clout-shoe *n.* [late 18C] a yokel, an unsophisticated peasant (cf. HIGH-SHOE; HOBNAIL). [SE *clouted shoe*, a shoe tipped with iron and secured with iron nails, the footwear of such individuals]

clouter *n.* [mid-19C] a pickpocket whose speciality is stealing silk handkerchiefs. [CLOUT *n.*[4] (2) + *v.*[2]]

clouting *n.* [early 19C] the stealing of handkerchiefs (cf. CLOUTING LAY). [CLOUT *n.*[1]]

clouting lay *n.* [late 18C–19C] (Und.) the stealing of handkerchiefs. [CLOUT *n.*[1] (1) + LAY *n.*[4] (2)]

clout one's cookie, to *phr.* [1970s] (US) of a woman, to masturbate. [SE *clout* + COOCHIE]

clout-shoe *see* CLOUTED-SHOE.

clove-hunter *n.* [late 19C] (US) a theatre patron who drinks (from a flask) during a play and then chews cloves in an attempt to disguise the smell of the liquor on their breath.

cloven/cleave/cleft *n.* [late 18C] a woman, usu. a prostitute, who poses as a virgin but, in reality, is not (cf. CLEAVER *n.*[2]). [SE *cloven*, split]

cloven hoofter *n.* [20C] (Aus.) a male homosexual. [rhy. sl. *cloven hoofter* = POOFTER]

cloven spot *n.* [mid-18C] the vagina (cf. AGREEABLE RUTS OF LIFE). [one of a number of synons. coined by John Cleland for his 1749 novel *Memoirs of a Woman of Pleasure* ('Fanny Hill'), a pornographic work, paradoxically without obscenities]

clover-eater *n.* [19C] (US) an inhabitant of Virginia (cf. CLAY-EATER). [the diet of the very poor]

clover-kicker *n.* [1910s+] (US) **1** a clumsy oaf, a boor, a dull-witted peasant. **2** a rustic, a farmer (cf. APPLE-KNOCKER *n.*[2]). [play on SE]

clowes/clows *n.* [late 18C] a rogue, a villain. [CLOY *n.*]

clown *n.* **1** [1940s+] a general term of abuse, esp. as a fool, an idiot. **2** [1990s] (US Black) a state of having fun, one's frivolous, self-indulgent, partying side; thus *get one's clown down*, to indulge that aspect of one's character.

clown *v.* [1990s] (US Black) to ridicule, to humiliate. [i.e. to make into a fig. clown]

clown around *v.* [late 19C+] to play the fool. [ext. of SE *clown*, to act like a clown]

clows *see* CLOWES.

cloy/cloye *n.* [late 17C–18C] (Und.) a thief, a pickpocket (cf. CLOWES; CLOYER).

cloy/cloye *v.* [late 17C–18C] (Und.) to steal. [CLY *v.*]

cloyer *n.* [17C] a pickpocket or cut-purse, spec. an experienced one who demand a share of their younger peers' profits (cf. SNAP *n.*[1]). [poss. CLY *n.*, or SE *cloyne*, to act deceitfully or fraudulently, to cheat]

club *n.* **1** [18C] a thick pigtail, shaped like a club and worn by men and subseq. women, which was fashionable in 1750–1800 in the UK; the term has survived in US dials. meaning *bun*. **2** [19C] the penis (cf. BAT *n.*[7]).

club *v.*[1] [19C] to have sexual intercourse, one of a number of terms equating sex with aggression (cf. BANG *v.*[1]).

club *v.*[2] [1980s+] to go to nightclubs; thus *clubber*, one who makes regular visits to nightclubs.

club and stick *n.* [20C] a policeman. [rhy. sl. *club and stick* = DICK *n.*[6] (2), the implements are, of course, apposite]

club Fed *n.* [1990s] (US) a Federal penitentiary. [pun on *Club Med*, the holiday firm]

club-first *n.* [late 16C–early 17C] a thug.

club-foot *n.* [20C] (US) a large, clumsy foot. [SE *clubfoot*, a deformed foot]

clubhouse *n.* [1900s] a police station (cf. IRISH CLUBHOUSE).

clubs are trumps *phr.* [19C+] a phr. denoting that force, rather than argument, rules. [pun on the weapon and the card suit]

club the clam, to phr. [1960s+] of a woman, to masturbate. [SE club + CLAM n.[1] (4)]

cluck n.[1] **1** [1900s] (orig. US) a counterfeit coin. **2** [1970s] (US) a tedious situation. [fig. use of cluck as a dud, a second-rate object; ? (2) the 'clucking' noise one makes when irritated or bored]

cluck n.[2] **1** [1920s] (orig. US) a dull, stupid person (with the brains of a chicken). **2** [1940s+] (US) an egg.

cluck n.[3] [1940s] (US) a derog. term for a person with notably dark skin. [ety. unknown]

cluck/clucker n.[4] [1990s] (drugs) a user of crack cocaine. [ety. unknown; ? link to CLUCK v., i.e. the loquacity engendered by the drug]

cluck v. [late 19C] (US) to speak.

cluckhead n.[1] [1940s+] a fool. [CLUCK n.[2] + sfx. -HEAD (1)]

cluckhead n.[2] [1990s] (US Black gang) a regular user of crack cocaine (cf. ACID-HEAD). [CLUCK n.[4] + sfx. -HEAD (2)]

clucky adj. [1940s+] (Aus./N.Z.) pregnant. [dial. clucky, used of a broody hen]

cludgie n. [1990s] a lavatory. [dial. cludgy, sticky, wet and heavy]

clue n.[1] [1920s+] knowledge in general, or a specific piece of information, esp. in phr. doesn't have a clue.

clue n.[2] [1930s+] (Aus.) a woman. [? Abor. language]

clued in adj. [1940s+] aware. [CLUE SOMEONE IN]

clue in! excl. [1980s+] (US campus) pay attention! [CLUE SOMEONE IN]

clueless adj. [1940s+] stupid, ignorant, incompetent. [CLUE n.[1] + sfx. -less]

clue someone in v. [1940s] (orig. US) to explain, to inform, to make aware. [CLUE n.[1]]

clue up v. [1940s+] to explain; thus clued up, well aware, properly informed (cf. CLUE SOMEONE IN).

cluey adj. [1940s+] (Aus.) properly informed (cf. CLUE UP).

clump n. [late 19C+] a blow, a heavy hit. [CLUMP v.]

clump v. [mid-19C+] to hit heavily, to thump. [SE clump, a lump, then a heavy stick]

clumper n. **1** [19C+] one who hits hard. **2** [mid–late 19C] a heavy-soled walking boot. [CLUMP v.]

clumperton n. [mid-16C–early 18C] a fool, a yokel. [fig. use of CLUMP v. on pattern of SE simpleton]

clumping adj. [20C] unwieldly, heavy, clumsy. [CLUMP n.]

clumsy as a cub-bear handling his prick phr. [20C] (Can.) very clumsy.

clumsy dick n. [late 19C–1920s] a very clumsy person. [SE clumsy + generic DICK n.[5]]

clunge n. [1990s] the anus, esp. in abusive, dismissive phr. up your clunge! [dial. clung, tight shrivelled, ult. SE cling]

clunk n.[1] [early 19C+] **1** a noise, typically of a door shutting, one hard object hitting another etc (cf. CLONK). **2** a blow. [echoic]

clunk n.[2] (Aus./US) **1** [20C] a man. **2** [1940s+] a fool. [LUNK n.; LUNKHEAD]

clunk v. **1** [late 18C–mid-19C] to make the sound of a cork being withdrawn from a bottle or of liquid pouring through a narrow-necked vessel or being shaken around in a half-empty vessel. **2** [1940s+] to hit, to strike (cf. CLONK v.).

clunker/clonker n.[1] [1940s] a worn-out, useless car. [? the noise it makes]

clunker n.[2] **1** [1950s+] a fool, a dolt, an incompetent (cf. CLUNK n.[2]). **2** [1970s+] (US) a blunder, a mistake (cf. CLINKER n.[7]). [CLUNK n.[2] (2)]

clunkhead n. [1950s+] (US) a fool (cf. LUNKHEAD). [CLUNK n.[2] (2) + sfx. -HEAD (1)]

clunky adj. [1950s+] (Can.) ill-bred, stupid. [CLUNK n.[2] (2)]

clush adj. [mid-19C] easy, simple (cf. CUSHY). [ety. unknown]

clusterfuck n. **1** [1960s+] (orig. US) an orgy, irrespective of sexual preference. **2** [1960s+] (orig. US) gang rape (cf. GANG-BANG v.). **3** [1980s+] a group of indecisive people, unable to decide what to do next.

cluster-screw n. [1970s] (US) an orgy. [SE cluster + SCREW n.[1] (2); a semi-bowdlerized version of CLUSTERFUCK]

clutch n.[1] **1** [late 18C] the hand. **2** [late 19C] (society) a dance (the activity, not the event). [(1) its action; (2) the physical proximity of the dancers]

clutch n.[2] [1970s] (US) a clumsy person. [KLUTZ]

clutch-butt n. [1960s] (US) sexual intercourse. [SE clutch + BUTT n.[1]]

clutched/clutched up adj. [1950s+] (US) frightened, nervous, tense. [the physical effects of such emotions]

clutch-fisted adj. [early–late 18C] mean, miserly; thus clutch-fist, a miser.

clutey/cleety/clitty/clootie adj. [late 19C+] (Irish) awkward. [dial. clootie, a left-handed person]

cly/clie n. [late 17C–mid-19C] **1** money (cf. CLY-FAKER). **2** a pocket. [? CLY v.]

cly v. **1** [16C] to seize, to get, to take. **2** [17C] to steal. [poss. f. Ger. kleien and Du. kleyen, to scratch (with the nails), to claw the head]

clyde n.[1] [1940s+] (orig. US Black) an unsophisticated person, a provincial, a yokel (cf. ALVIN). [a stereotypical 'peasant' name]

clyde n.[2] [1950s–60s] (US) an all-purpose word used to cover a multitude of personal observations, e.g. I don't like her clyde, 'I don't like her voice.' [ety. unknown]

clyde n.[3] [1970s] (US) a wide-brimmed hat, a fedora. [a style worn by 'Clyde Barrow' (Warren Beatty) in the film Bonnie & Clyde (1968)]

clydesdale n. [20C] (US) an attractive male. [? the solid dependability of the Clydesdale horse or the attractiveness of the Clydesdale terrier]

cly-faker n. [early–mid-19C] a pickpocket. [CLY n. (2) + FAKER]

clyme see CLEYME.

clyster-pipe n. [early 17C–late 18C] a doctor, an apothecary. [SE clyster-pipe, a pipe used to administer clysters, or enemas]

cly the jerk/gerke, to phr. [16C–17C] (Und.) to be whipped. [CLY v. (1) + SE jerk, a stroke of the whip]

C-note n. [20C] a $100 bill. [C n.[1] (2)]

c.n.r. strawberries n. [1960s+] (Can. prison) prunes.

co n.[1] [mid-16C] a man (cf. COE; COFE; COFFIN n.[1]; COVE; COVESS; CUFFIN; KIVEY). [abbr. COVE]

co n.[2] [1900s–20s] (society) a co-respondent (in a divorce case). [abbr.]

co n.[3] [1990s] (drugs) marijuana. [ety. unknown]

coach/coach it v. [17C+] to travel by coach. [the original was extended to motor vehicles in the 20C]

coachee/coachie see COACHY.

coachman on the box n. [20C] venereal disease (cf. BAND IN THE BOX). [rhy. sl. coachman on the box = POX n.[1]]

coach-wheel n. **1** [late 18C–1960s] a 5-shilling (25p) piece, a crown (cf. FORE COACH-WHEEL; HIND COACH-WHEEL). **2** [mid-19C] (US) a silver dollar. [like the SE coach-wheel, the crown piece was, by numismatic standards, large and round]

coachy/coachee/coachie n. [late 18C–mid-19C] a coachman. [on the model of cabbie, bargee, but note synon. Magyar kocsi, Bohemian koèi, Ger. kutsche]

coal n.[1] [late 17C–late 18C] money (cf. COLE). [SE coal, the staple, as a source of heat, of everyday life, as is money]

coal n.[2] **1** [1940s] a derog. term for a dark-skinned Black person (cf. CHARCOAL). **2** [1990s] (Aus.) dark 'bags' under the eyes.

coal *adj. see* COLD adj.[1] for US Black usages.

coal/coals and coke *adj.* [late 19C+] penniless, impoverished. [rhy. sl. *coals and coke* = BROKE]

coal-black joke *n.* [late 18C+] the female genitals (cf. BLACK JACK n.[6]). [ext. of BLACK JOKE]

coalbox *n.* [20C] (Aus.) the chorus (of a song).

coal burner *n.* [1970s+] a White man or woman who enjoys sexual relations with a Black man or woman. [COAL n.[2] + SE *burner*, pun on SE]

coalie/coaley *n.* **1** [early 19C+] a coal-heaver. **2** [mid-19C+] a wharf labourer who loads ships with coal. [SE; post-1840s use is Aus.]

coal juice *n.* [20C] (US) illicitly distilled whisky. [the use of charcoal in distilling]

coalopolis *n.* [late 19C+] (Aus.) Newcastle, New South Wales (cf. COTTONOPOLIS). [its coal mines]

coal sack *n.* [late 19C] a blind alley. [mispron. of *cul-de-sac*]

coal-scuttle *n.* [late 19C] a poke bonnet, which it supposedly resembled (cf. CINDER-SIFTER). [its chief characteristic was the sides, which projected well beyond those of the face; fashionable *c.*1850]

coal-scuttle blonde *n.* [1930s–50s] (US) a Black woman with a blonde wig.

coarse Christian *n.* [20C] (Ulster) a person of innate worth but poor manners, a 'rough diamond'.

Coast, the *n.* [1960s+] the West Coast of America, esp. Los Angeles. [the Pacific Coast has been thus known since the mid-19C, but the current use refers spec. to Los Angeles, the home of the film and rock industries]

coast/coast about *v.* **1** [late 19C–1940s] (Aus.) to live as a tramp or vagrant. **2** [1960s+] (drugs) to be (pleasurably) under the influence of drugs (cf. NOD n.). [SE *coast*, to wander]

coaster *n.* [late 19C–1950s+] **1** (Aus.) a tramp. **2** (Aus.) a loafer, an idler (cf. SCOWBANKER). **3** (N.Z.) one who is a native of, or was born in, the west coast of the South Island. [COAST v.]

coast home *v.* [1930s+] (orig. US) to win easily, usu. in a sporting context.

coasts to coasts *n.* [1960s+] (US drugs) amphetamine (cf. A n.[2]). [? their use by long-distance truck-drivers]

coat *v.* **1** [20C] to reprimand, to scold. **2** [1910s+] to arrest. **3** [1930s+] to beat up, to hit. **4** [1940s+] (Aus.) to ostracize. [the image of grabbing a lapel (cf. SE *buttonhole*, PULL SOMEONE'S COAT). In Aus. prison the person thus victimized is indicated by a tug on their lapel]

coat and badge *v.* [mid-19C+] to cadge (cf. ON THE C AND B). [rhy. sl. *Doggett's Coat and Badge*, awarded to Thames watermen who, with this prize, had the right to charge higher fares in their mid-19C heyday]

coathanger *n.* [1930s] (Aus.) the Sydney Harbour bridge. [the shape]

coats an''ats *n.* [1950s+] the Dutch-owned department store, C&A.

coax *v.* [late 18C] to pull down the soiled or holed part of one's stocking so that it is hidden by the heel of one's shoe. [orig. use of SE *coax*, to fool, to take in, this use is apparently linked to 16C *cokes*, a simpleton, a gullible fool]

coaxyorum *n.* [1990s] (Irish) **1** an opportunist. **2** a cake prepared by a putative mother-in-law to show respect to her daughter's boyfriend. [SE *coax* + 'Lat.' sfx.]

cob *n.*[1] [19C] (US) a farmer, a rustic. [SE *corncob*. ? + derog. ref. to supposed use of corncobs in the privy as a substitute for lavatory paper]

cob *n.*[2] [mid-19C–1910s] a chignon. [Cornwall dial. *cob*, a bunch of hair on the forehead; often applied to the top locks of a horse's mane.]

cob *n.*[3] [1920s–60s] (US) the penis. [orig. dial.]

cob *n.*[4] [1940s–50s] (Und.) prison bread. [orig. dial. *cob*, a small roundish loaf]

cob *n.*[5] [1950s–70s] (N.Z.) a friend, a mate. [abbr. COBBER n.[2]]

cob *n.*[6] [1970s+] (S.Afr. drugs) a quantity of marijuana, about the size of a corncob and sometimes packaged in maize leaves.

cob *v.* [20C] (US) to take, to steal. [var. on COP v.[1]]

Cobar shower *n.* [1950s] (Aus.) **1** a flower. **2** a shower of rain. [rhy. sl.; Cobar is a copper-mining town in New South Wales. In the case of (2) other Aus. names can be substituted according to local geography]

cobber *n.*[1] [19C–1910s] a great lie (cf. THUMPER n.[3]). [naut. jargon *cob*, to hit on the buttocks with something flat]

cobber *n.*[2] [late 19C+] (Aus.) friend, mate. [? dial *cob*, to take a liking to someone or Heb./Yid. *chaver*, a 'pal', a 'chum'. Like the other great clichéd Aus. word BONZER, *cobber* is now nearly defunct]

cobber-dobber *n.* [1960s–70s] (Aus.) one who informs on a friend. [COBBER n.[2] + DOB IN]

cobber/cobber up *v.* [1940s–60s] (Aus./N.Z.) to befriend. [COBBER n.[2]]

cobble-colter *n.* [late 17C–mid-19C] (Und.) a turkey. [*cobble* = gobble]

cobbler *n.*[1] [late 19C–1940s] (Aus./N.Z.) the last and least willing sheep to be sheared (cf. SNOB). [based on an old joke, quoted in *OED*: 'In the harvest field English rustics used to say, when picking up the last sheaf, "This is what the cobbler threw at his wife." "What?" "The last."']

cobbler *n.*[2] [20C] (US Und.) a forger, esp. of passports, currency and stocks and bonds. [? SE *cobble*, to put together or join roughly or clumsily]

cobblers *n.* [late 19C] the past. [rhy. sl. *cobbler's last* = past]

cobbler's/cobblers' awls/stalls/cobblers *n.* [1930s+] **1** the testicles. **2** rubbish, nonsense, esp. as excl. *cobblers!* [rhy. sl. *cobbler's awls* = BALLS n.[1]]

cobbler's knot *n.* [mid-19C] a lock of hair shaped like the figure 6 and twisted from the temple back towards the ear (cf. AGGERAWATOR).

cobbler's punch *n.*[1] [late 18C] a mixture consisting of treacle, vinegar, gin and water. [pun on the cobbler's *punch*, a fool]

cobbler's punch *n.*[2] [early–mid-19C] urine with a cinder in it. [COBS, testicles]

cobbler's stalls *see* COBBLER'S AWLS.

cobbo *n.* [1920s+] (Aus.) a close friend. [COBBER n.[2] + sfx. -O]

co-bim! *excl.* [mid-19C] an onomat. term indicating a sudden blow (cf. KERBIM!). [pfx. KER- + *bim*]

cobitis *n.* [1940s–50s] (Und.) a loathing of invariably unpleasant prison food. [COB n.[4] + sfx. *-itis*, usu. used in diseases]

cob o' coal *n.* [1920s–50s] unemployment benefit. [rhy. sl. *cob o'coal* = dole]

cobs *n.* [19C] testicles (cf. COBBLER'S AWLS; CODS n.[1]). [dial.]

cob's body!/by cob's body! *excl.* [early 18C] a euph. oath, properly *God's body!* (cf. COCK n.[1]).

cobweb-cheat *n.* [late 17C–18C] a swindler who can be easily found out. [SE *cobweb* + *cheat*, his swindles have no more substance than a cobweb]

cobweb-pretence *n.* [late 17C–18C] an inadequate ruse, a plot that can be detected simply. [*cobweb* + *pretence*, such ruses are utterly insubstantial]

cobweb rig *n.* [late 18C–early 19C] a form of swindle or confidence trick. [despite COBWEB-CHEAT and COBWEB-PRETENCE, which imply incompetence; ? SE *cobweb*, a subtly woven snare + RIG n.[2]]

cocabola *n.* [1940s–50s] (US) a Black person. [? play on Coca-Cola, which is black in colour]

Coca-Cola *n.* [1950s+] (Aus.) a bowler, in cricket. [rhy. sl.]

cocaine blues *n.* [1970s+] (drugs) the depression that may follow extended cocaine use.

cochore *v.* [20C] (W.I./Guyn.) **1** to tell tales of others in order to curry favour with a superior. **2** to persuade, to charm, to lull into false confidence (cf. SWEET-TALK). [? SE *cajole*]

cochornis *n.* [1980s+] (drugs) marijuana. [? Sp.]

cochunk! *excl.* [mid-19C] (US) an onomat. term indicating the sound of two solid objects colliding (cf. KERCHUNK!).

cock *n.*[1] [late 14C–mid-19C] euph. for God (cf. ADAD!; BOB n.[4]; DAD n.[1]; DAG n.[1]; DOD; ECOD; GAD n.[1]; GAR n.[1]; GOG; GOM n.[1]; GOSH n.; GUD; GUM n.[2]). [mispron.]

cock *n.*[2] [early 17C+] (UK/US North) the penis. **2** [20C] (US South/US Black) the vagina (cf. NUTS n.[2]). **3** [20C] (US Black) sexual intercourse. **4** [1960s+] (US South campus) a woman, viewed solely as a sexual object; thus *a piece of cock*. [(1) Lat. *cuccus*, the male domestic fowl; thus the term has been used for any object that resembles a cock's head. As far as its use as a sexual term is concerned, *cock* here mixes the basic image of the cock as rooster (itself a 19C US euph.) and the cock's head seen as a tap-like shape, this secondary aspect emphasized by its function in 'pouring' semen. It remained in perfectly standard use until Queen Victoria's coronation, shortly after which it joined the ranks of the taboo. It has yet to return to the mainstream. Note that E.P. claims 'always SE but since 1830 a vulgarism' and *OED* (in late 19C) notes 'the current name among the people, but, *pudoris causa*, not admissible in polite speech or literature']

cock *n.*[3] [mid-17C–late 18C] a man, spec. a plucky fighter. [characteristics of the bird]

cock *n.*[4] **1** [mid-19C] a broadsheet or pamphlet, sold in the streets and relating some form of lurid and sensational incident, typically a fire, a murder or an accident. **2** [mid-19C+] nonsense, rubbish, also in phr. (*load of*) *old cock*. [SE *cock and bull story* but note COOK UP v.[1] + the *Cock Lane ghost*, 'which had a great run, and was a rich harvest to the running stationers' (Hotten, 1867) (cf. RUNNING PATTERER)]

cock *n.*[5] [mid-19C+] general term of address, esp. Cockney use. [abbr. SE *Cockney*]

cock *n.*[6] [1970s] a man who is easy to sponge on, spec. one who buys more than his necessary share in a pub. [SE *cock*, i.e. like the bird, he enjoys showing off]

cock *adj.*[1] [mid-17C+] chief, top, most important.

cock *adj.*[2] [1960s+] (US) pornographic. [COCK n.[2]]

cock *v.*[1] [19C] to smoke. [17C SE *cock*, to place a match in the cock of a matchlock gun]

cock *v.*[2] [19C+] to have sexual intercourse; thus *cocking*, sexual intercourse, *cock in one's eye*, amorous. [COCK n.[2]]

cock *v.*[3] [20C] (US) to knock out. [abbr. COLD-COCK v.]

cock a deaf 'un, to *phr.* [1920s+] to pretend to be deaf, or at least to ignore by 'not hearing' the speaker (cf. COP A DEAF 'UN). [SE *cock*, to turn up + *deaf one*, i.e. an ear]

cockadoodle *n.* [1920s+] (Aus.) nonsense, rubbish. [COCK n.[4] (2) + SE *cock-a-doodle*, the noise of a cockerel]

cock-a-double *n.* [mid-19C] a very strengthening form of broth made with beaten eggs in brandy and water. [? play on SE *cock-a-doodle*, the noise of a cockerel]

cock-a-hoop/-whoop *adv.* [17C–early 19C] in high spirits, transported with joy. [ety. unknown. The *OED* cites it as a 'phrase of doubtful origin, the history of which has been further obscured by subsequent attempts, explicit or implicit to analyse it', but offers a number of such attempts, the most interesting being that cited in Thomas Blount's *Glossographia* (1670): 'Cock-on-Hoop, our Ancestors call'd that the Cock which we call a Spigget, or perhaps they used such Cocks in their vessels, as are still retained in water-pipes. The Cock being taken out, and laid on the hoop of the vessel, they used to drink up the ale as it ran out without intermission ... and

then they were Cock-on-Hoop, i.e. at the height of mirth and jollity. A saying still retained'. SE *c.*1830]

cock-ale *n.* [mid-17C–mid-19C] a variety of beer that supposedly has aphrodisiac properties. [SE *cock-ale*, ale mixed with the jelly or minced meat of a boiled cock, besides other ingredients + a pun on COCK n.[2] (1)]

cockalize *v.* **1** [1930s+] (US juv.) to humiliate/initiate a boy by smearing his penis with some substance, urinating on him, hitting his penis with a knotted handkerchief etc. **2** [1960s] (US) to beat, to defeat heavily. [COCK n.[2] (1)]

cock alley *n.* [18C–20C] the female genitals (cf. ALLEY n.[1]; COCKCHAFER; COCK HALL; COCK-HOLDER; COCK INN; COCK LANE; COCK-LOCKER; COCK PIT; COCKSHIRE; COCKSHY; NICHE COCK; PRICK-HOLDER). [COCK n.[2] (1)]

cock-a-loft *adj.* [late 19C] affected, pompous (cf. WILLIE-WAVING). [SE *cock* v. to swagger, to boast + ? fig. brandishing of the erect penis]

cockalorum *n.* [early 18C–late 19C] a self-important little man. [joc. nonce-word, but note Du. *kockeloeren*, to crow. The first *OED* citation specifies cockalorum as 'the Marquis of Huntly, whose father, the Duke of Gordon, was called "Cock of the North"']

cockalorum *adj.* [early 18C–late 19C] swaggering, boastful, self-important. [COCKALORUM n.]

cockamamie *n.* (US) **1** [1930s+] an absurd, eccentric person. **2** [1960s] an absurd situation, a 'nonsense'. [COCKAMAMIE adj.]

cockamamie/cockamamy *adj.* [1940s+] confused, ludicrous, fake, fraudulent, absurd. [? *decalcomania*, a picture or design left on the skin as a 'transfer', from specially prepared paper, which is wetted and rubbed (popular *c.*1862–4). Rosten (1968) suggests that the shift came because 'on the Lower East Side ... no one knew how to spell "decalcomania"']

cock-and-breeches *n.* [mid-19C] a small, sturdy boy (cf. ALL MOUTH AND TROUSERS).

cock and hen *n.* **1** [mid-19C+] £10 (cf. COCKLE). **2** [20C] (bingo/gambling) the number 10 (cf. DOWNING STREET). **3** [20C] a pen. [rhy. sl.]

cock and hen club *n.* [19C] a club that admits both men and women.

cock and pie *see* BY COCK AND PIE!

cock and pinch *n.* [mid-19C] an old-fashioned hat, favoured by early 19C dandies (cf. BEAVER n.[3]). [the hat was *cocked* back and front and *pinched* at the sides, it was made of beaver fur]

cock a snoot/a snoot at, to *phr.* [late 19C+] to disdain, to ignore, to turn up one's nose. [SE *cock*, to turn up + SNOOT n. (1)]

cockatoo *n.*[1] (Aus.) **1** [mid-19C+] a lookout for those engaged in some form of illegality. **2** [mid–late 19C] a convict serving time on Cockatoo Island. [the noted wariness of the bird or *Cockatoo* Island, Sydney, where criminals were held *c.*1870]

cockatoo *n.*[2] [mid-19C+] (Aus./N.Z.) a small farmer; thus *cockatoo fence*, a fence erected by such a farmer, *cockatoo's weather*, fine by day, wet at night or fine in the week, wet on Sunday (cf. COCKY n.[2]). [ult. COCKATOO v.[1]; the originals of such farmers had come from Sydney to the Port Fairy area]

cockatoo *v.*[1] [mid–late 19C] (Aus.) to serve a sentence on Cockatoo Island, in Sydney Harbour.

cockatoo *v.*[2] [late 19C] (Aus.) to farm on a small scale. [COCKATOO n.[2]]

cockatrice *n.* **1** [late 16C–mid-18C] a prostitute. **2** [18C–19C] a baby. [SE *cockatrice*, a hybrid monster with head, wings and feet of a cock, terminating in a serpent with a barbed tail. (1) such a monster can kill with a mere glance + pun on COCK n.[2] (1) + fem. sfx. *-trix*. (2) the monster is born from an egg]

cock-a-wax/cockawax/cockowax *n.* **1** [early–mid-19C] a cobbler, who uses wax in his work. **2** [late 19C] a familiar term of address, esp. as *my old ...* (cf. COCK n.⁵).

cock-bawd *n.* [17C–early 19C] a pimp. [COCK n.² (1) + SE *bawd*, lit. as male whore]

cockbite *n.* [1960s+] (US) a repellent, unpopular person. [? a person who, if permitted, would bite one's penis]

cock block/c.b. *v.* [1980s+] (US Black) to ruin another man's sexual activities by stealing his woman, interrupting his seduction etc; thus *cock-blocker*, one who does this.

cock book *n.* [1960s+] (US) pornography (cf. FUCK BOOK). [COCK n.² (1) + SE *book*]

cock-brain *n.* [late 16C–late 17C; 20C] a foolish young man. [SE *cock* + sfx. -*brain*; ? + a young man's traditional obsession with sex. 20C use is US only]

cock-broth *n.* [20C] (tramp) any form of strong, satisfying soup.

cock-catch *v.* [late 19C–1900s] to obtain money on false pretences. [orig. milit. use]

cockchafer *n.* **1** [mid–late 19C] a prison treadmill. **2** [late 19C] a woman who permits or encourages a good deal of sexual intimacy but not intercourse (cf. COCKTEASER; DICK-TEASER; PRICKTEASER; TEASER n.⁴). **3** [late 19C] the vagina. [COCK n.² (1) + SE *chafer*, that which chafes or rubs painfully]

cock/knob cheese *n.* [mid-19C+] smegma. [COCK n.² (1)/KNOB n.¹ (1) + CHEESE n.²]

cock collar *n.* [1960s] (US Black) the head of the penis, esp. its base, where it joins the main shaft. [COCK n.² (1) + SE *collar*]

cock-diesel/strong *n.* [1990s] (US Black/campus) a strong, muscular, attractive man. [COCK n.² (1) + DIESEL n.¹ (2)]

cock doctor *n.* [20C] a venerealogist. [COCK n.² (1) + SE *doctor*]

cocked *adj.* [20C] (US) drunk (cf. HALF-COCKED adj.²). [SE *cock*, to pull back the hammer of a gun]

cocked and ready to rock *phr.* [1970s] (US Black) completely prepared. [firearms imagery]

cocker *n.¹* [late 19C+] a general term of address, usu. to a man (cf. COCKY n.¹; OLD COCK). [COCK n.⁵]

cocker *n.²* [late 19C+] (orig. Aus.) a cockroach.

cockerel *n.* [mid–late 17C] the penis. [COCK n.² (1) + pun on the bird]

cockers-p *n.* [1980s] (society) a cocktail party. [elision of SE and + 'Oxford' sfx. -*er*]

cock-eye *n.* [mid-19C] a squinting eye. [SE *cock*, to bend (a joint or limb) at an angle + *eye*]

cock-eye *adj.* [late 19C] messy, topsy-turvey (cf. COCK-EYED adj.¹). [fig. use of COCK-EYE n.]

cock-eye/cock-eyed Bob *n.* [1920s+] (W. Aus.) a cyclone or thunderstorm. [COCK-EYED adj.¹ (2) + generic use of *Bob*]

cock-eyed *adj.¹* **1** [early 19C+] squinting. **2** [late 19C+] topsy-turvy, ludicrous, absurd (cf. COCK-EYE adj.). **3** [1910s+] crazy, irrational, eccentric, odd. **4** [1910s+] out of true, at an angle. **5** [1920s+] very drunk. [all fig. uses of COCK-EYE n.]

cock-eyed *adj.²* [1910s+] used in excl. as a synon. for *confounded*.

cockface *n.* [1960s+] (US) a general term of abuse. [COCK n.² (1) + SE *face*]

cockfighter *n.* [19C] a womanizer, a philanderer. [the 'manly' sport of cockfighting, but also a pun on COCK n.² (1)]

cock hall *n.* [late 18C–20C] the vagina (cf. COCK ALLEY). [COCK n.² (1) + SE *hall*]

cockhead *n.* [1970s] (US) a general term of abuse. [COCK n.² (1) + sfx. -HEAD (1)]

cock-holder *n.* [19C] the vagina (cf. COCK ALLEY; NEEDLECASE; PIN-CASE; PIN-CUSHION; PINTLE-CASE; POLE HOLE; SERPENT SOCKET; TOOLBOX; TOOL CHEST). [COCK n.² (1) + SE *holder*]

cock-horse *adj.* [mid-18C–mid-19C] excited, elated. [the pleasure of a child riding 'a-cockhorse']

cock-hound *n.* [1960s+] (US Black) a man devoted to sex before all things (cf. PUSSY HOUND). [COCK n.² (2) + sfx. -HOUND; f. the Southern use of *cock* as vagina rather than penis]

cockie *see* COCKY n.².

cockies' clip *n.* [late 19C+] (Aus.) **1** a pickpocket. **2** a swim. [rhy. sl. *cockies' clip* = DIP n.³ + SE *dip*]

cocking *adj.* [mid-17C–early 19C] impudent, cheeky.

cock inn *n.* [19C–20C] the vagina (cf. COCK ALLEY; CUPID'S ARMS; HOTEL). [COCK n.² (1) + SE *inn*, a pun on the fictitious public house]

cockish *adj.* [late 17C–early 19C] esp. of a woman, wanton, sexually forward. [SE *cock*, a cockerel + sfx. -*ish*]

cock it! *excl.* [1920s+] a mild excl. of annoyance, that's it! that's all over! [euph. for the 'harder' FUCK IT!]

cock it over *v.* [1920s] to dominate, to lord it over. [SE *cock*, to behave boastfully or defiantly, to swagger]

cock it up *v.¹* [1940s+] to blunder, to make a mistake. [COCK UP v.³]

cock it up *v.²* [1960s+] (Aus.) for a woman to offer herself sexually in an obvious manner. [COCK n.² (1)]

cock-knocker *n.* [1950s+] (US) an unpleasant, worthless person (cf. COCKBITE). [COCK n.² (1) + SE *knocker*; lit. 'penis-hitter']

cock-knocking *adj.* [1980s+] (US) synon. for DAMNED. [COCK-KNOCKER]

cock lane *n.* [19C] the vagina (cf. ALLEY n.¹; COCK ALLEY). [COCK n.² (1) + SE *lane*. The term was reinforced by the real-life *Cock Lane* (in the City), which in the 14C was the only street on which London's prostitutes were licensed to ply their trade in public. The Great Fire was supposed to have stopped at its junction with Giltspur Street, while in February 1762 thousands of the curious (including Dr Johnson, the Duke of York and other grandees) flocked to number 33 Cock Lane to hear the scratchings and knockings of the alleged 'Cock Lane Ghost']

cockle/cockle and hen *n.* [mid-19C+] 10, usu. £10 (cf. COCK AND HEN). [rhy. sl.]

cockles *n.* [18C+] the labia minora (cf. PLAY AT HOT COCKLES).

cock linnet *n.¹* [late 19C] a small but dapper East End youth.

cock linnet *n.²* [late 19C+] a minute. [rhy. sl.]

cockloche *n.* [early 17C–mid-19C] a term of reproach or contempt. [? Fr. *coqueluche*]

cock-locker *n.* [1980s] the vagina (cf. COCK ALLEY). [COCK n.² (1) + SE *locker*]

cockloft *n.* [mid-17C–18C] the head (cf. ATTIC). [SE *cockloft*, the room over the garret]

cock lorel *n.* [16C] (Und.) the chief rogue or rascal. [COCK adj.¹ + *losel*, a worthless rogue, a profligate. Usu. as the proper name Cock Lorel, who may possibly have been a genuine person and who features largely in the literature of Elizabethan villainy, orig. as the eponymous anti-hero of *Cock Lorel's Bote* (c.1500), a ship-master (Rowlands claims 'a tinker', whose 'crew' is a group of rogues drawn from the workshops and gutters of the London. Together they 'sail' the country, engaging in a variety of villainies. He appears in a number of works, as well as in the glossaries compiled by Awdeley (whose *Fraternity of Vagabonds* (1561) was 'confirmed by Cock Lorel') and Rowlands. In all he remains at the head of his marauding beggars, sometimes plotting against the State, on one occasion even entertaining the Devil to dinner. According to Rowlands' generally fictitious 'history' of the canting crew, Cock Lorel's rule supposedly lasted c.1511–33]

cock movie *n.* [1960s+] a pornographic film. [COCK adj.² + SAmE *movie*]

cockmunch *n.* [1990s] a general term of abuse, a very unpleasant person (cf. COCKBITE).

cock-my-cap *n.* [early–mid-18C] gin.

cockney *n.* **1** [early 16C–early 19C] a townee. **2** [early 17C+] a Londoner, esp. one 'born within the sound of Bow Bells'; thus an East Ender. **3** [early 17C] an overly squeamish or wanton woman. [14C SE *cockney*, a mother's darling, a spoilt child; thus a weak, effeminate adult. This was adopted in rural dial. to describe the supposedly 'soft' inhabitants of cities and large towns, who compounded their unpopularity by their ignorance of country ways and words. The link to 'Bow bells' is first cited in 1600 and appears for the first time as a dictionary definition in Minsheu's *Ductor in Linguas* (1617). The SE itself seems to be rooted in *cocken ay*, a cock's egg, or a small or malformed egg. E.P. also suggests, on the basis of a rhyme attributed to Hugh Bigot, Earl of Norfolk (d. *c.*1177) that a parallel root of *cockney* lies in the fabulous land of *Cockaigne*, and as such a synon. for London. *OED*, however, notes that the ref. is probably to the traditional 'King of Cockneys', a kind of Master of the Revels chosen by the students at Lincoln's Inn on Childermas Day (28 December). Note S.Afr. use *cockney*, a member of the Muslim Indian community who comes from Kokan, near Bombay]

cockney-shire *n.* [19C–1910s] London.

cockney's luxury *n.* [late 19C–1950s] breakfast in bed and using the pot for defecation, rather than leaving the warm house for a trip to the outdoor privy.

cocko *n.* [1920s–40s] a general term of address (cf. COCKER; OLD COCK). [COCK n.[5]]

cock of a different hackle *n.* [mid-19C] an opponent of a different character. [COCK n.[3] or SE *cock*, the bird + *hackle*, plumage]

cock off *see* COCK UP v.[3].

cock off oneself *v.* [20C] (W.I.) to sit around looking important, esp. with one's feet up (cf. CHOP TEN). [SE *cock*, to boast, to swagger]

cock of the game *n.* [19C] a promiscuous man. [SE *cock of the game*, a champion; the 'game' in this case is not a sport, but that 'of love']

cock of the walk *n.* [mid-19C+] an important man. [SE *cock* + *walk*, a place or enclosure where poultry can exercise]

cock on/cock it on *v.* [1910s+] **1** to overcharge. **2** to exaggerate. [SE *cock*, to boast, strut]

cock one's beaver, to *phr.* [17C] to assume an affected, swaggering air. [SE *cock*, to turn up + BEAVER (*hat*)]

cock one's eye, to *phr.* [mid–late 18C] to wink. [thereafter SE, but cf. *have a cocky eye*, to glance sideways]

cock one's pistol, to *phr.* [20C] (US) to surprise, to astonish, esp. in phr. *that cocks my/his pistol.*

cock one's shotgun, to *phr.* [1990s] to masturbate.

cock/cock up one's toes, to *phr.* [mid-19C] to die (cf. TURN UP ONE'S TOES).

cock-opener *n.* [1920s–40s] (US Black) the penis (cf. ARSE-OPENER; EYE-OPENER n.[1]; LEG-OPENER; THIGH-OPENER). [COCK n.[2] (2) + SE *opener*]

cockowax *see* COCK-A-WAX.

cock-pimp *n.* [late 17C–late 18C] a pimp who poses as his prostitute's husband. [SE *cock*, the male bird + PIMP n.[1] (1)]

cock pit *n.* [late 18C–20C] the vagina (cf. COCK ALLEY). [COCK n.[2] (1) + SE *pit* + a pun on SE *cockpit*]

cockpit *n.* [late 18C] a Dissenters' meeting-house. [i.e. they are 'fighting' established religion]

cock pluck *v.* [1970s+] (US Black) to stimulate a woman's genitals manually. [COCK n.[2] (2) + SE *pluck*]

cock puke *n.* [1990s] semen. [COCK n.[2] (1) + SE *puke*, vomit]

cockquean *n.* [mid-19C] an effeminate man, who is seen as dealing too keenly with domestic duties that are properly those of his wife. [var. on COTQUEAN]

cockrag *n.* [1960s+] (Aus.) a loincloth, as worn by Aborigines. [COCK n.[2] (1) + SE *rag*]

cockroach *n.[1]* [20C] **1** (US) a despicable person. **2** (Aus.) a native or inhabitant of New South Wales. [the cockroach is especially loathed in New York's steam-heated apartments, where it thrives]

cockroach *n.[2]* [1940s+] a motor (rather than railway) coach. [rhy. sl.]

cockroach business *n.* [20C] (US) a small, mean enterprise. [the implication is of the insignificant size of the insect rather than the dirt that attracts it]

cockroach joint *n.* [20C] (US) the lowest, filthiest possible café or restaurant. [SE *cockroach* + JOINT n.[3] (3); the infestation of cockroaches in such places]

cockroach killers *n.* [20C] (US) pointed boots or shoes (cf. ROACH KILLERS; WINKLEPICKERS).

cock robin *n.[1]* [late 17C–late 18C] a complaisant, weak person. [nursery rhyme, in which the hapless *Cock Robin* is killed. The original rhyme, first noted *c.*1744, may have concerned the fall in 1742 of Prime Minister Robert Walpole's ministry. It may, on the other hand, have its roots in much earlier events, notably the mythical death of the Norse hero Balder]

cock-robin *n.[2]* [1970s] the penis. [a pun]

cock rock *n.* [1970s+] heavy metal music with even more than the usual macho strutting and posturing. [COCK n.[2] (1) + SE *rock*('*n'roll*)]

cock-rot *n.* [1980s+] (US) a venereal disease. [COCK n.[2] (1) + SE *rot*]

cocks *n.* [1930s] (W.I.) slight of hand used by a dice cheat to defraud his fellow players. [COG v.[1]]

cock's hair *n.* [20C] (US) an infinitely tiny measure (cf. GNAT'S EYEBROW).

cockshire *n.* [late 18C–20C] the vagina (cf. COCK ALLEY). [COCK n.[2] (1) + sfx. *-shire*]

cockshy *n.* [19C] the vagina (cf. COCK ALLEY). [COCK n.[2] (1) + SE *shy*; a pun on SE *cockshy*, a fairground game that involved throwing broomsticks at a cock. If the thrower could knock over the cock and grab it before it regained its feet, they would win the bird]

cocksman *n.* [late 19C+] **1** an exceptionally virile man (cf. COCK-HOUND). **2** (US Black) a male prostitute (cf. COCK-TAIL n.[1]). [COCK n.[2] (1) + sfx. *-MAN*]

cocksmith *n.* [1950s–60s] (US) a womanizer, a philanderer (cf. COCKSMAN). [COCK n.[2] (1) + sfx. *-smith*]

cock-smitten *adj.* [19C] (of a woman) keen on sex. [COCK n.[2] (1) + SE *smitten*]

cocksmoker *n.* [1990s] (Can.) **1** a fellator; a semi-euph. for COCKSUCKER. **2** any male person.

cock snot *n.* [1990s] semen (cf. FLAP SNOT; KNOB SNOT; PECKER SNOT). [COCK n.[2] (1) + SNOT n.]

cock sparrow *n.* [late 19C+] an arrow. [rhy. sl.]

cock-sparrow *adj.* [1960s+] (Aus.) mad, insane. [rhy. sl. *cock-sparrow* (pron. 'sparra') = YARRA]

cockstand *n.* [mid-19C+] an erection; thus [1910s–40s] *this will give you the cockstand* (cf. STAND n.[2]; PUT LEAD IN ONE'S PENCIL). [COCK n.[2] (1) + SE *stand*]

cock strong *see* COCK-DIESEL.

cocksuck *n.* (orig. US) **1** [1940s+] the act of fellatio. **2** [1960s+] a general term of abuse. [backform. of COCKSUCKER]

cocksucker *n.* (orig. US) **1** [late 19C] a sycophant, a toady. **2** [late 19C+] a fellator or fellatrix. **3** [1910s+] an abusive term, generally considered to be one of the worst (cf. MOTHERFUCKER). **4** [1940s+] a male homosexual. **5** [1940s+]

(US Black/South) one who performs cunnilingus. [COCK n.[2] (1) + SE *sucker*]

cocksucking *adj.* [20C] (orig. US) **1** performing oral sex. **2** vile, repellent, disgusting; one of the most taboo adj. of abuse (cf. FUCKING adj.; MOTHERFUCKING adj.). [COCKSUCKER]

cocksy/coxy fuss *n.* [early–mid-19C] amatory play, 'billing and cooing'. [COCK n.[2] (1)]

cock-tail *n.*[1] [19C] a prostitute (cf. BANG-TAIL n.[1]). [COCK n.[2] (1) + TAIL n.[1] (2)]

cock-tail *n.*[2] [mid–late 19C] an efficient, energetic, but not quite socially acceptable, person. [racing use, a horse that tries but is still no thoroughbred]

cock-tail *n.*[3] [mid–late 19C] a coward. [SE *cock*, to life up + *tail*]

cocktail *n.*[4] (drugs) **1** [1960s+] (US) the very last portion of a cannabis cigarette placed on the end of a cigarette. **2** [1980s+] a cigarette laced with cocaine or crack.

cocktail *v.* [1950s–60s] (drugs) to place the last unsmoked portion of a cannabis cigarette into the end of a regular cigarette so as to make it more easily smokeable. A folded matchbook can be used for the same effect (cf. ROACH n.[2]; ROACH CLIP). [COCKTAIL n.[4] (1)]

cocktails *n.* [1920s+] (Aus.) diarrhoea.

cock-tax *n.* [1950s] (Aus.) alimony. [COCK n.[2] (1) + SE *tax*]

cocktease *v.* [late 19C+] to lead on in a sexual manner but never to permit actual intercourse (cf. DICKTEASE; PRICKTEASE v.). [COCKTEASER]

cockteaser/c.t. *n.* [late 19C+] a woman who permits or encourages a good deal of sexual intimacy but not intercourse (cf. COCKCHAFER). [COCK n.[2] (1)]

cock/cut ten *v.* [20C] (W.I.) to sit around while others are working (cf. CHOP TEN; SIT DOWN LIKE MISS PRISS). [SE *cock/cut + ten* (minutes); i.e. to take 10 minutes off the working day]

cock-up *n.* [1920s+] (orig. milit.) an error, a blunder. [SE *cock*, to bend at an angle, but with undertones of COCK n.[2] (1), on the pattern of FUCK-UP, BALLS-UP]

cock up/cock up one's foot/feet *v.*[1] [20C] (W.I.) to sit around looking important while others work (cf. COCK OFF ONESELF). [ext. of SE use; synon with SE *put up one's feet*]

cock up/cock up one's foot/feet *v.*[2] [20C] (W.I.) of a woman, to sit with one's legs sprawled in what is considered an indecent manner. [SE *cock*, to bend at an angle]

cock up/off *v.*[3] [1920s+] (orig. milit.) to blunder, to make a mess of (cf. ARSE UP; BALLSED-UP; BALLS UP). [COCK-UP n.]

cock wagon *n.* [1970s] (US) a car, usu. flashy, new and expensive, that is owned specifically to attract easily impressed young women (cf. PASSION WAGON). [COCK n.[2] (1) + SE *wagon*]

cocky *n.*[1] [late 17C+] general term of address to a man. [COCK n.[5]]

cocky/cockie *n.*[2] [mid-19C+] (Aus.) **1** a small farmer. **2** the rural interest, whether small farmers or large landowners, with the main crop often indicated; thus *cane cocky, wheat cocky* etc (cf. GROUND-PARROT). [COCKATOO n.[2]]

cocky *adj.* [mid-18C+] bumptious, self-satisfied, arrogant. [SE *cock*, the characteristics of the bird; the assumption is that such posturing is unjustified]

cocky *v.* [late 19C+] (Aus.) to work as a small farmer. [COCKY n.[2]]

cockydom *n.* [20C] (Aus.) the world of small farmers. [COCKY n.[2] + sfx. *-dom*]

cocky's clip *n.* [1920s+] (Aus.) sheep dip. [rhy. sl.]

cocky's coal *n.* [1900s–40s] (Aus.) dry corncobs used as fuel. [COCKY n.[2] + SE *coal*]

cocky's crow *n.* [20C] (Aus.) dawn. [COCKY n.[2] + pun on SE *cock's crow*]

cocky's delight *n.* [20C] (Aus.) molasses, treacle or golden syrup (cf. BULLOCKY'S DELIGHT). [COCKY n.[2] + SE *delight*]

cocky's friend *n.* [1930s] (Aus.) fencing wire. [COCKY n.[2] + SE *friend*]

cocky's hours *n.* [late 19C–1930s] (Aus.) dawn to dusk. [COCKY n.[2] + SE *hours*, the time in which farming can be pursued]

cocky's string *n.* [20C] (Aus.) fencing wire, which has a variety of everyday uses in addition to marking boundaries. [COCKY n.[2] + play on SE *string*]

coco/cocoa/koko *n.*[1] [early 19C+] (orig. US) **1** the head. **2** (W.I.) a bump on the head. [abbr. *coconut*]

coco *n.*[2] [1990s] an uncleansed anus. [SE *cocoa*; i.e. the colour]

cocoa *n.*[1] see COCO n.[1].

cocoa *n.*[2] [late 19C] (Aus.) praise, esp. if 'laid on with a trowel' (cf. TOKO n.[2]). [the drink is 'sweet']

cocoa *n.*[3] [20C] (US) a derog. term for a Black person, esp. light-skinned. [the colour]

cocoa *n.*[4] [1970s+] semen (cf. BABY GRAVY; COME ONE'S COCOA).

cocoa *v.* [1930s+] to speak. [rhy. sl. *cocoa* = say so]

cocoa payol/pagnol *n.* [20C] (W.I./Trin.) a mixed-race person who retains traces of Spanish ancestry and culture. [SE *cocoa* + PAYOL. The payol was mainly employed on cocoa and coffee plantations]

cocoa press *n.* [1900s–30s] newspapers, e.g. *The Daily News*, owned by the chocolate-making Cadbury family.

cocoa puff *v.* [1980s+] (drugs) to smoke cocaine mixed with marijuana. [abbr./redup. *cocaine* + PUFF v.[2] + play on *Cocoa Puffs*, the popular breakfast cereal]

cocoa rocks *n.* [1980s] (drugs) crack cocaine made brown by adding chocolate milk powder during production (cf. CHOCOLATE ECSTASY).

cocoa-shunter *n.* [1990s] a male homosexual. [the link of anything 'chocolate' to sodomy/the anus]

cocobay *adj.* [20C] (W.I.) having a skin covered in repulsive sores; thus *have cocobay on top of yaws*, to add new troubles to a situation that seemed bad enough already. [Twi *kokobé*, leprosy]

cocobola *n.* [1990s] (US) a police nightstick. [Arawak *kakabali*, thence Sp. *cocobolo/cocobola*, the timber from any one of several species of tree of the Central American genus *Dalbergia*, or the tree itself. Nightsticks are made from this timber]

cocola *n.* [1990s] (US prison) a Black person. [? var. on COCABOLA]

coconut *n.*[1] [mid-19C+] the head (cf. BEAN n.[4]; COCO n.[1]). [resemblance]

coconut *n.*[2] [1920s–40s] (US) $1; thus *coconuts*, money. [? barter imagery]

coconut *n.*[3] [1980s+] **1** (W.I./UK Black teen) a Black person who has 'sold out' to White values (cf. APPLE n.[11]). **2** (US) a Hispanic person trying to be White. ['brown on the outside but white within']

coconut-dodger *n.* [1920s] (US Black) a South American or African Black. [the image of coconut palms shedding their fruit]

coconut head *n.*[1] [20C] (US) a fool. [the hardness of the coconut + sfx. -HEAD (1)]

coconut head *n.*[2] [20C] (US) a derog. term for a Black person. [the jungle associations]

coconuts *n.*[1] [late 19C–1900s] large female breasts (cf. APPLES n.[1]). [resemblance]

coconuts *n.*[2] [1930s] (US) intelligence. [COCONUT n.[1]]

coconuts *n.*[3] [1970s+] (drugs) cocaine. [the use of pfx. *coc-*]

cocooning *n.* [1970s+] (US) staying at home with one's family.

coco snow *n.* [1980s+] (drugs) benzocaine used as cutting agent for crack. [SE *cocaine* + SNOW n.]

cocum *n.* [mid-19C+] **1** advantage, luck, resource. **2** knowledge; thus [mid–late 19C] *fight cocum*, being cunning, artful, usu. in illegal contexts. [Heb. and thence Yid. *kochum*, wisdom]

c.o.d. *n.* [1960s+] a male prostitute (cf. ASS PEDDLER). [abbr. cock *on* delivery + a pun on SE *c.o.d.*, cash on delivery]

cod *n.*[1] [late 18C+] the penis. [SE *cod*, a bag; thus early 16C SE *cod*, the scrotum; only pl. CODS *n.*[1], testicles, is sl.]

cod *n.*[2] [mid-16C–19C] euph. for God.

cod *n.*[3] [late 17C–18C] **1** a fellow. **2** a fool (cf. COD *v.*). **3** a friend; thus *honest cod*, a good friend. [(2) ? f. COD'S HEAD. (3) in this context *cod* has been linked to SE *codger*, and it is found as an abbr., but *cod* is a much earlier word]

cod *n.*[4] **1** [late 17C–late 18C] a purse. **2** [late 17C–18C] money; thus *rum cod*, *jolly cod*, *lusty cod*, a good sum of money. **3** [1980s+] (drugs) a large amount of money. [SE *cod*, a bag]

cod *n.*[5] [late 19C–1900s] a drunkard. [? COD *n.*[3] (2) or ? like the fish he 'swims' in alcohol]

cod *n.*[6] **1** [1900s–50s] a joke, a leg-pull, a parody. **2** [20C] (Irish) deception, deceit, a lie; thus *cod-acting*, foolish behaviour. [COD *v.*]

cod *adj.*[1] [1950s+] fake, parodic; usu. in combs., e.g. *cod-Russian*, *cod-typewriter* etc. [? *cod* = FISHY *adj.*[1], note theatrical jargon *cod version*, a burlesque of a well-known play]

cod/codalina/codette/codettareenarone *adj.*[2] [1980s+] (Polari) a general neg. (cf. NAFF *adj.*[1]).

cod *v.* **1** [18C] to cheat, to defraud. **2** [mid-19C+] to tease, to hoax. [? COD *n.*[3] (2)]

codalina *see* COD *adj.*[2].

coddam/coddem/coddom *n.* [mid-19C] a public house game played with a button or coin. [COD *v.* (2); lit. *cod 'em*, hoax them, fool them. 'The game is "simplicity itself" but requires a great amount of low cunning' (Hotten, 1867)]

codder *n.* [mid-19C] a teaser, a hoaxer. [COD *v.* (2)]

codding *n.* [late 19C+] teasing, chaffing, hoaxing. [COD *v.* (2)]

coddom *see* CODDAM.

codesa-desa *v.* [1990s] (S.Afr.) to negotiate (something). [CODESA, the Convention for a Democratic South Africa, held 1991–3 to prepare guidelines for a new constitution and for multi-party democracy]

codette/codettareenarone *see* COD *adj.*[2].

codfish *n.* (US) **1** [late 18C–mid-19C] a fool. **2** [19C] one who thinks himself superior to their peers. [COD *n.*[3] (2). Note *codfish aristocracy*, a mocking New England term for those 19C *nouveaux riches* whose fortunes sprang from the Massachusetts cod industry]

codfish flats *n.* [20C] (US) the poor area of town (cf. CATFISH ROW).

codge *n.* [19C] (US) a vagrant, a tramp. [Yorks. dial. *cadger*, a beggar, a petty thief]

codge/codge up *v.* [19C] to repair, usu. badly or clumsily; thus (US) *codge-job*, a second-rate piece of work. [Yorks. dial. *codge*, to patch up, to mend badly. ? link to SE *bodge*, to patch or mend clumsily, ult. f. *botch*]

codger *n.* [18C+] **1** a fellow, a man; usu. in *old codger*, with the implication of crotchety old age. **2** a 'roystering, ageing boon companion' (Ware). [? 15C SE *cadger*, although its derog. use, as a whining beggar rather than the earlier, unqualified, itinerant hawker, is 19C and *codger*, by definition derog., predates this]

cod-heads *n.* [1930s] (Glasgow) shoes that have worn out at the toe.

codling *n.* **1** [early 17C–mid-18C] an innocent, naïve young man. **2** [late 18C–early 19C] an affectionate term of address. [SE; either *codling*, a young codfish, or *codling*, a variety of apple, somewhat hard and raw (thus 'immature') and best eaten cooked. SE *coddle*, while otherwise feasible, post-dates *codling*]

cod ogles *n.* [1980s+] (Polari) contact lenses. [COD *adj.*[1] + OGLES]

codology *n.* [1910s+] (orig. Anglo-Irish) the practice of teasing (cf. KIDOLOGY). [COD *v.* (2)]

cod-on *n.* [20C] (Irish) a practical joke. [COD *v.* (2)]

cod-riah *n.* [1980s+] (Polari) a wig. [COD *adj.*[1] + RIAH]

cods *n.*[1] [19C+] **1** the testicles. **2** a curate. **3** courage (cf. BALLS *n.*[1]). [(1) SE *cod*, a bag, thus the scrotum. The term was SE until 19C, when Victorian language prudery rendered it taboo. (2) teases the curate for his sermonizing (with a ? ref. to his hopes of a good marriage), i.e. he is talking BALLS *n.*[2]; (3) fig. equation of the testicles with manliness]

cods *n.*[2] [20C] a mess (cf. BALLS *n.*[1]; BALLS-UP; COCK-UP *n.*). [OED suggests abbr. CODSWALLOP but given syns. ? f. CODS *n.*[1]]

cod's head *n.* [mid-16C–mid-19C] a dupe, a fool; also found in 19C as *cod's head and shoulders* (cf. BLOCKHEAD *n.*[1]; CHUB *n.*[1]; COD *n.*[3]). [dial. ? the 'thickness' of the cod's head, note slightly later COD *n.*[3] (2)]

cod's roe *n.* [20C] money. [rhy. sl. *cod's roe* = DOUGH]

codswallop *n.* [1960s+] nonsense, rubbish, drivel. [ety. unknown; there is an implication of CODS *n.*[1] (1), but no proven link. Linguistically COD *n.*[3] (2) + dial. *wallop*, to chatter, to scold is feasible, but the chronology may militate against it]

cod trench *n.* [1990s] the vagina (cf. BEARDED CLAM). [COD *n.*[1] + SE *trench*]

coe *n.* [16C+] (Und.) a man (cf. CO *n.*[1]). [COVE *n.* (1)]

cofe *n.* [16C] a man (cf. CO *n.*[1]). [contemporary Scot. *cofe*, a chapman or pedlar, or, like a number of 16C cant terms, f. Rom. *cova* or *covo*, man]

coffee-and *n.* [20C] **1** coffee and cakes or coffee and doughnuts, i.e. the cheapest meal available in a café or diner. **2** just enough money to buy coffee and doughnuts.

coffee-and *adj.* [20C] in context, referring to anything seen as cheap, minimal, second-rate, e.g. (theatre) *coffee-and role*, a small part that will pay for little more than snacks (cf. COFFEE-AND HABIT; COFFEE-AND PIMP). [fig. use of COFFEE-AND *n.*]

coffee-and-B *n.* [late 19C–1900s] a coffee and brandy.

coffee and cakes *n.* [1920s] (US) a very small salary (cf. COFFEE-AND *n.*). [it provides just about enough to buy coffee and cakes]

coffee and cocoa *phr.* [20C] say so; thus *I should cocoa* (esp. in *The Billy Cotton Band Show* BBC radio in the 1950s). [rhy. sl.]

coffee-and doughnut gun *n.* [20C] (Und.) a small, relatively powerless gun. [COFFEE-AND *adj.*]

coffee-and habit *n.* [1950s+] (US drugs) a small-time heroin habit, adopted either through grim self-control or simple poverty. [COFFEE-AND *adj.* + HABIT]

coffee-and pimp *n.* [1950s–70s] a small-time pimp, whose women barely make him a living, let alone provide the high style to which he would aspire (cf. CHILE PIMP). [COFFEE-AND *adj.* + PIMP *n.*[1]]

coffee-bag *n.* [1920s] (US Black/tramp) a coat pocket.

coffee-break parole *n.* [1960s+] (US prison) nickname for a Special Circumstances release. [so called because it is granted very quickly]

coffee coke *n.* [1980s+] (drugs) **1** cocaine. **2** crack cocaine.

coffee cooler *n.* [19C] an idler, a shirker. [milit. jargon *coffee cooler*, 'one who blows his coffee while the brigade is going by', i.e. a soldier who is constantly searching for a soft job]

coffee coolers *n.* [1950s] (US Black) the lips, esp. when large and protuberant. [used to blow on hot coffee]

coffee grinder *n.* [1910s+] (orig. US) any old and unstable machine, typically a veteran propeller-driven aeroplane. [its noise, which resembles that of the SE *coffee grinder*; orig. milit. use for a Gatling machine gun]

coffee-house *n*. [late 18C] a privy (cf. COFFEE-SHOP). [the colour of coffee and of urine and faeces]

coffee-house *v*. **1** [mid-19C+] to chatter, to gossip. **2** [20C] (poker) to bluff a rival verbally rather than by betting. [orig. fox-hunting use, the image is of habitués of an 18C coffee-house]

coffee-mill *n*. **1** [early–mid-19C] the mouth. **2** [19C] an early form of machine gun, used in the US Civil War (1861–5). [fig. uses of SE *coffee-mill*, a coffee grinder that was worked by turning a handle]

coffee-milling *n*. [mid-19C] working very hard. [one 'grinds it out']

coffee-pot *n*.[1] [19C] (US) any small-scale operation, esp. a small lumber mill. [railroad jargon *coffee-pot*, a small steam engine]

coffee-pot *n*.[2] [1920s+] (US) a small lunch-room. [the coffee that is the mainstay of the menu]

coffee-pot canyon *n*. [1920s–50s] Broadway, New York City. [coined by columnist Walter Winchell (1897–1972)]

coffee-shop *n*. [late 18C–mid-19C] a privy (cf. COFFEE-HOUSE *n*.). [the colour of its contents]

coffee stalls *n*. [20C] the testicles (cf. ORCHESTRA STALLS). [rhy. sl. *coffee stalls* = BALLS *n*.[1]]

coffee-strainer *n*. [20C] (US) a bushy moustache.

coffee up *v*. [1960s+] (US) to drink a large quantity of coffee.

coffin *n*.[1] [mid-16C–early 19C] a man, a fellow (cf. CO *n*.[1]). [var. on CUFFIN]

coffin *n*.[2] **1** [mid–late 19C] (US) a clumsy, heavy boot or shoe. **2** [20C] (US Und.) a prison cell.

coffin-dodger *n*. **1** [20C] an old person, probably ill. **2** [1900s] (US campus) a heavy smoker (cf. COFFIN NAIL *n*.[2]). [the image is of being 'one step ahead' of death or, in the case of smokers, mocking death]

coffin meat *n*. [mid-19C] (US) a corpse.

coffin nail *n*.[1] [19C] a drink; thus the invitation to drink, *let's put another nail in our coffins*, *let's drive another nail ...* . [the assumption that drink, esp. in the outposts of the Empire, was a killer. Folk etymology erroneously links this nail with PEG]

coffin nail/tack *n*.[2] [mid-19C+] a cigarette (cf. BACKNAIL; CASKET NAIL). [? no more than the resemblance of the cigarette to the nail; nicotine's cancerous potential is very much a phenomenon of 1960s+]

coffin varnish *n*. [20C] (US) liquor, esp. that which was sold during the Prohibition era (1920–33) (cf. VARNISH). [joc. use of SE + ref. to its dubious, even fatal, quality]

coffs harbour *n*. [20C] (Aus.) a barber. [rhy. sl.]

coflumpux! *excl.* [mid-19C] (US) onomat. term indicating the sound of a body falling to the ground with a thump. [pfx. KER- + FLUMMOX *v*.[1] + THUMP *v*.]

cog *n*.[1] [late 16C–18C] (Und.) **1** money. **2** a lure, esp. in the form of money, designed to entice a gambler into a game, before cheating them of their own funds. [COG *v*.[1]]

cog *n*.[2] [late 19C] (US) a name. [abbr. SE *cognomen*]

cog *v*.[1] [early 16C–mid-19C] **1** (Und.) to use any form of illicit sleight of hand, spec. to make a surreptitious change of a crooked dice for a legitimate one (or vice versa) during a game (cf. FOIST *v*.[1]; QUOIT *v*.; SLIDE *v*.[1]). **2** to cheat at cards, or in any other manner. **3** to deceive, to cheat out of; thus *cog a dinner*, to cheat one out of a dinner. [ety. unknown; note that while acknowledging it as a 'ruffian's term', the *OED* categorizes the word as SE]

cog *v*.[2] [early 16C–mid-19C] to agree with. [the action of one cog wheel linking smoothly with another. Note 19C UK and

late 20C W.I. use: 'to copy work surreptitiously from another student' (Allsopp)]

cog *v*.[3] **1** [late 16C–early 18C] to flatter, to wheedle, to wheedle someone out of (something). **2** [mid-16C–mid-18C] to palm off fraudulently, to put out or utter falsely. [fig. uses of COG *v*.[1]]

cog a/the dice, to *phr*. [mid-16C–mid-19C] to control the fall of dice by sleight of hand. [COG *v*.[1] (1)]

coge it *v*. [19C] (US) to drink heavily. [Scot. *cogue*, a small drinking vessel]

cog-foist *n*. [early 17C] (Und.) a cheat. [COG *v*.[1] (1) + FOIST *n*.[1]]

cog forth-in, to *phr*. [early–mid-17C] to control the fall of dice by sleight of hand. [COG *v*.[1] (1)]

cogger *n*. [16C] a card-sharp. [COG *v*.[1]]

cogie *n*. [19C] the vagina. [Scot. *cogue*, [16C] a small pail used for milking cows, or [17C] a drinking vessel]

cognoscenti *n*. [1950s+] (gay) the world of homosexuals, its style, language, ethos etc. [Ital. *cognescenti*, the knowing ones, i.e. the cultured élite]

cogs *n*. [1940s] (US Black/Harlem) sunglasses. [such glasses can be seen as 'fooling' other people; ? link to COG *v*.[1] (1)]

cog-shoulder *n*. [early 16C] an arrest. [SE *cog*, to place an impediment in front of + *shoulder*]

coguey *adj.* [19C] drunk (cf. COGE IT). [Scot. *cogue*, to drink drams]

coil *n*. [1950s+] (W.I. Rasta) money. [? the circular shape of coins, a roll of banknotes; or fig. ref. to the *mortal coil*, i.e. life and thus money as a basic necessity for life]

coiler *n*. [20C] (Aus.) a vagrant who sleeps in the open air. [he simply 'coils up' and falls asleep]

coil one's ropes, to *phr*. [20C] (US) to die (cf. GIVE UP THE SHIP; KEEL OVER; LOSE THE NUMBER OF ONE'S MESS; SLING ONE'S HOOK *phr*.[1]; SLIP ONE'S BREATH; SLIP ONE'S CABLE; SLIP ONE'S WIND). [naut. imagery: a good sailor always coiled his ropes properly at the end of his work]

coil someone's coat, to *phr*. [16C] to thrash, to beat severely (cf. BASTE SOMEONE'S COAT). [ext. of SE *baste*, to beat]

coin *n*. [mid-19C] money.

coin/coin it *v*. [mid-19C+] to make a great deal of money. [COIN *n*.]

coin collector *n*. [20C] a male homosexual prostitute (cf. ASS PEDDLER). [play on SE]

coin it see COIN *v*.

coinkidink *n*. [1980s+] (US campus) coincidence (cf. QUINKYDINK). [deliberately 'jokey' mispron.]

coins *n*. [1900s–50s] (US Black) money, whether actual coins or notes (cf. CHANGE *n*.[3]).

coiny *adj.* [late 19C] rich. [COIN *n*.]

coiny cove *n*. [1920s+] (Aus.) a rich man. [COINY + COVE]

coiny-moneyed *adj.* [1920s] rich. [ext. of COINY]

cojones *n*. [1920s+] testicles, used both to mean the physical organ and metaphorical courage (cf. BALLS *n*.[1]). [synon. Sp. Popularized first by the works of Ernest Hemingway (1899–1961) and latterly by Puerto Rican immigrants to US]

coke *n*.[1] **1** [20C] (drugs) cocaine; thus *coked*, *coked up*, under the influence of cocaine. **2** [1920s] any injectable opiate drug, usu. morphine or heroin.

coke *n*.[2] [1920s] (US) the head. [COCONUT *n*.[1]]

coke bar/joint *n*. [1980s+] (US Black) any bar or club where the patrons openly use crack cocaine. [COKE *n*.[1] (1)]

coke-blower *n*. [1920s] (drugs) a cocaine user. [COKE *n*.[1] (1) + BLOW *v*.[7] (2)]

coke-blunt *n*. [1980s+] a mixture of hashish/marijuana and cocaine, made into a cigarette when rolled in a tobacco leaf, taken from the wrapper of a Phillies Blunt cigar. [COKE *n*.[1] + BLUNT *n*.[2]]

coke bottle eyes *n*. [1980s+] (US campus) a state achieved by the drunkard to whom all members of the opposite sex seem far more attractive than they might be when viewed in sobriety (cf. BEER GOGGLES). [used with COKE BOTTLE GLASSES]

coke bottle glasses *n.* [1950s+] (orig. US) spectacles with very thick lenses, used by those with seriously short sight (cf. COKE BOTTLE EYES). [such glasses supposedly resemble the glass in a trad. Coca-Cola bottle]

coke-date *see* JELLY-DATE.

coke fiend *n.* [1910s+] (drugs) a cocaine user. [COKE n.[1] (1) + SE *fiend*; later use tends to be ironic]

coke frame *n.* [1940s] (US Black) a curvaceous figure; thus *banter play built on a coke frame*, an attractive woman with a good figure. [brandname *Coke*, Coca-Cola + FRAME n.[2] (1), i.e. a body curved like the traditional Coca-Cola bottle; *banter* = BANTAM]

cokehead *n.* [1920s+] (drugs) a regular cocaine user (cf. ACID-HEAD). [COKE n.[1] (1) + sfx. -HEAD (2)]

cokehound *n.* [1930s] (drugs) a cocaine user. [COKE n.[1] (1) + sfx. -HOUND]

coke joint *see* COKE BAR.

coke party *n.* [1960s] (drugs) a party at which the principle aim is to consume cocaine. [COKE n.[1] (1)]

coker *n.* [late 17C–mid-19C] a lie (cf. CAULKER).

cokes *n.* [mid-16C–late 17C] a fool. [? SE *cockney*]

coke stare *n.* [1970s+] (US Black) the 'evil eye', a deliberately aggressive and unpleasant look. [COKE n.[1] (1); the rigid gaze that may overtake the more paranoid cocaine user]

coke-upon-littleton *n.* [mid-18C] a form of mixed drink, brandy and tent (*vino tinto*). [a famous legal textbook, the commentary upon *Littleton* by Sir Edward *Coke* (1628)]

cokey *n.*[1] *see* COKIE.

cokey *n.*[2] *see* KOKI.

cokey *adj.* [1920s–50s] (US) foolish, silly (cf. DOPEY adj.[2]). [? COKE n.[1] (1); although cocaine tends to excite rather than dull the senses]

cokey-eye *n.* [20C] (W.I.) a squint; thus derog. nickname *cokey*, a squinter. [SE *cock-eye*]

cokie/cokey *n.* [1910s+] (drugs) a habitual user of cocaine; thus [1930s–50s] *Cokie Joe*, a personification of a regular cocaine user. [COKE n.[1] (1), on pattern of JUNKIE]

cokk *n.* [14C] a euph. for God and as such used in mild (but then blasphemous) oaths (cf. COCK n.[1]; GOG].

col *n.* [16C] the neck. [Fr. *col*, the neck, or abbr. SE *column*]

colcher/colsher *n.* [late 19C] a heavy fall, esp. in phr. *come a colcher*, to fall heavily. [dial. *colch*, a heavy fall, the sound of a blow]

cold *n.* [1980s+] (US Black) a cigarette end. [? it is no longer alight]

cold *adj.*[1] **1** [late 19C] (US campus) perfect, complete. **2** [1930s+] (US Black/teen) unpleasant, difficult, unnecessary. **3** [1930s+] (gambling) unlucky, unfavourable. **4** [1940s+] (US Black/teen) by bad = good, excellent, first-rate, superb. **5** [1960s+] (orig. US) heartless, ruthless, cruel. **6** [1960s+] (US Black) emotionless, unfeeling, callous, uncaring. [all uses, pos. or neg., stem from the unadorned 'iciness' of SE *cold*]

cold *adj.*[2] [20C] dead. [the chilliness of a corpse]

cold *adj.*[3] [1910s] (US) of money, the actual sum, i.e. abbr. *cold cash*. [SE *cold* meaning unadorned]

cold *adj.*[4] [1920s+] (US) of a cheque, fraudulent, worthless (cf. CATCH A COLD; HAVE A BAD COLD). [fig. use of SE; i.e. it has lost its 'life']

cold *adv.* **1** [late 19C] (US) absolutely, completely, utterly. **2** [1980s+] (orig. rap music) definitely, indeed, just (cf. STONE adv.[1]).

cold as a cocksucker's knees *phr.* [1950s+] (Aus.) of temperature, extremely cold. Other Aus. similes include *cold enough to freeze the balls off a billiard table, as cold as a polar bear's bum.*

cold as a mother-in-law's breath/kiss *phr.* [1950s+] (Aus.) of the climate or of a person's emotions, very cold, also found as *step-mother's ... .*

cold as Kelsey's ass *phr.* [20C] extremely cold (cf. COLDER THAN KELSEY'S NUTS). [for ety. *see* TIGHT AS KELSEY'S NUTS]

cold-bite *n.* [1920s+] (Aus./N.Z.) one who will lend money, a 'soft touch'. [COLD-BITE v.]

cold-bite *v.* [1920s+] (Aus./N.Z.) to ask a stranger for money. [SE *cold* + BITE v.[1] (5); note commercial jargon *cold-call*, for a salesman to approach a potential client without making a prior appointment]

cold blood *n.* [mid-19C] a liquor store or 'off licence' that can sell beer but cannot have it drunk on the premises.

cold-blooded *adj.*[1] [late 19C] said of one who has poor circulation.

cold-blooded *adj.*[2] [1990s] (US Black/campus) **1** honest, open, candid. **2** harshly critical, extremely judgmental, used of actions that are done or people who act without heart.

cold busted *adj.* [1980s+] (US campus) caught in the act. [COLD adv. (1) + BUSTED adj.[3]]

cold case *n.* [1980s+] (US Black/Los Angeles) a very bad situation. [COLD adj.[1] (2)]

cold chill *v.* [1980s+] (US) to relax. [COLD adv. (2) + CHILL v.[3] (1)]

cold-choke *n.* [mid-19C+] (W.I.) cold food, which is hard to swallow (cf. CHOKE-ME). [SE *cold* + *choke*; but note CHOKE n.[1] (1)]

cold cock *n.* [1940s+] (orig. US) a knock-out blow. [COLD-COCK v.]

cold-cock *v.* [1920s+] to knock unconscious (cf. COLD-DECK v.[2]). [SE (*out*) *cold*, unconscious/(KNOCK) COLD + COCK v.[3]]

coldcock *adv.* [1980s+] (US) completely, utterly (cf. COLD adv.). [COLD-COCK v.]

cold coffee *n.*[1] [mid-19C] **1** bad luck. **2** a snub. [SE *cold coffee*, which, other than in hot weather, is usu. considered an un-appetizing drink]

cold coffee *n.*[2] [late 19C–1910s] beer. [the colour ? + euph.]

coldconk *v.* [1960s–70s] (US) to knock unconscious (cf. COLD-COCK v.). [SE (*out*) *cold*, unconscious/(KNOCK) COLD + CONK v.[1] (1)]

cold cook *n.* [early 18C–late 19C] an undertaker; thus *cold cook shop*, an undertaker's shop (cf. COLD MEAT). [both are puns]

cold cream *n.* [mid–late 19C] gin (cf. CREAM OF THE VALLEY).

cold-creams *n.* [late 19C–1900s] the Coldstream Guards. [pun on the SE, but also ref. to the noted dandyism of the regiment]

cold-cunt *v.* [1970s+] (lesbian) to ignore, to brush off. [pun on COLD SHOULDER v.; SE *cold* + CUNT n.[1] (1)]

cold cut *n.* [1940s–50s] (US) an unfriendly, reserved person.

cold day *n.* [late 19C+] (US) bad luck, an unfortunate situation.

cold-deck *v.*[1] [19C] (US) to cheat, to deceive. [gambling jargon *cold deck*, for a card-sharp to introduce a prepared deck of cards into the game; thus guaranteeing his success]

cold-deck *v.*[2] [20C] to knock unconscious (cf. COLD-COCK v.; COLDCONK). [SE (*out cold*), unconscious/(KNOCK) COLD + DECK v.[2]]

colder than a wedge *phr.* [late 19C] (US) very cold. [the chilliness of an iron *wedge*, used to split timber]

colder than a witch's tit *phr.* [1960s+] **1** of weather, very cold. **2** of emotions, very unfriendly.

colder than Kelsey's nuts *phr.* [20C] extremely cold. [for ety. *see* TIGHT AS KELSEY'S NUTS]

cold-fang *v.* [1920s+] (Aus.) to ask a stranger for money (cf. COLD-BITE). [SE *cold* + *fang*]

cold fish *n.* [1940s+] an unemotional person. [SE *fish*/FISH n.[1]]

cold-footer *n.* [1910s–20s] (orig. Aus.) a timid, nervous person; thus *cold-footed*, timid, cowardly. [GET COLD FEET]

cold four *n.* [late 19C–1900s] the cheapest variety of beer (cf. FANCY FOUR). [SE *four-ale*, beer sold at fourpence a quart]

cold gold *n.* [1980s+] (Aus.) a can of beer (cf. COLD ONE n.²). [advertising slogan for Toohey's KB lager: 'Shake hands with a cold gold']

cold gruel *n.* [mid-19C] **1** bad luck. **2** a snub (cf. COLD COFFEE n.¹).

coldie *n.* [1950s–60s] (Aus.) a can or bottle of cold beer (cf. COLD GOLD). [abbr. COLD ONE n.²]

cold in hand/cold hand *adj.* [1940s] (US Black) without money, penniless (cf. COLD adj.⁴; CATCH A COLD; HAVE A BAD COLD). [gambling jargon, to be *cold* is to have poor cards, unlucky dice etc; however, in poker jargon a *cold deck* for an honest player is a good hand, requiring no change of cards, while for a sharp it is one that has been stacked, guaranteeing a win for the cheat]

cold iron *n.* [mid-17C–late 18C] a sword.

cold lamping *n.* [1990s] (US Black) explaining hitherto complex, impenetrable matters. [COLD adv. + LAMP v.² (1)]

cold meat *n.* [late 18C+] a corpse; thus *cold meat box*, a coffin, *cold meat train*, a funeral procession or a train that serves a cemetery, *cold meat job* (police jargon), any case that involves a corpse (cf. COLD COOK). [the first use of the term appears to be that of Grose himself, used as its definition: 'A dead wife is the best *cold meat* in a man's house.' (1785) Mainly obs. although *cold meat* as a n. is still used and COLD MEAT PARTY survives into 20C US Black use]

cold meat cart *n.* [early 19C+] (US) a hearse (cf. LIVE MEAT WAGON). [COLD MEAT + SE *cart*]

cold meat party *n.* [1940s+] (US Black) a funeral, a wake. [COLD MEAT + SE *party*]

cold mitt *n.* [1920s] (US) a snub, a rejection (cf. COLD SHOULDER n.). [SE *cold* + MITT n.]

cold muffin *n.* [late 19C–1900s] anything mediocre, second-rate.

cold nantz *n.* [late 17C–early 19C] cognac (cf. COOL NANTZ). [SE *cold* + NANTZ]

cold one *n.*¹ [1900s] (US) $1. [COLD CASH]

cold one *n.*² [1920s+] (orig. US) a bottle of beer. [orig. a conscious euph. for a cold beer, used during Prohibition (1920–33) when it was better not to mention alcohol in any form]

cold pie *n. see* CHOKING PIE.

cold pie *v.* [17C–late 19C] to pour cold water onto a sleeping person in order to wake them up.

cold pig *v.* [mid-19C] to pour cold water over a sleeper. [for ety. *see* GIVE COLD PIG]

cold-pigging *n.* [20C] (Aus./N.Z.) hawking goods from door to door.

cold potato *n.*¹ [20C] a waiter. [rhy. sl.; note Cockney pron. 'pertater']

cold potato *n.*² [20C] (US) someone or something judged to be worthless, insignificant or boring.

cold quack *n.* [1960s] (drugs) sudden and total withdrawal from heroin addiction without tapering off or using any assistance from medication. [punning var. on COLD TURKEY n.]

coldrifed *adj.* [1940s+] nervous, hesitant, unwilling to take a risk. [dial. *coldrife*, indifferent, spiritless; ult. SE *cold*]

cold shake *n.* [late 19C] (US) rejection, dismissal, betrayal. [abbr. SE *cold handshake*]

cold shot *n.* [1970s+] (US Black) **1** unnecessary and aggressive behaviour. **2** cruel, emotionless behaviour. [COLD adj.¹ (6) + SHOT]

cold shoulder *n.* [early 19C+] rejection, dismissal, usu. as phr. *get/give the cold shoulder* (cf. CHILL n.¹; MARBLE HEART). [Ware roots it in 'the Italian of Dante's time', but the earliest

use appears to have been in Scotland, and is found as such in Sir Walter Scott's *Antiquary* (1816) where it is explained in the book's Glossary. 19C use occas. added 'of mutton']

cold shoulder *v.* [early 19C+] **1** to act in a reserved manner. **2** to ignore, to snub deliberately. [COLD SHOULDER n.]

cold slaw *n.* [late 19C] (US) small off-cuts of material, taken from the job in hand and sold off as perks by tailors. [play on CABBAGE n.² (2)]

cold storage *n.* [20C] **1** death. **2** a prison.

cold tea *n.* [late 17C–1900s] brandy. [the colour]

cold turkey *n.* [1920s+] **1** (orig. US drugs) sudden and total withdrawal from heroin addiction without tapering off or using any assistance from medication. **2** the fundamental level, the basic situation. **3** an easy target, a vulnerable person. [COLD TURKEY adv. (1), boosted by the image of the pallid flesh of a cold, dead, plucked turkey, and a withdrawing addict]

cold turkey *adj.* [1930s–60s] (US) **1** dead. **2** emotionless.

cold turkey *v.* [1920s+] to subject oneself or another heroin user to COLD TURKEY n.

cold turkey *adv.* (US) **1** [1910s+] directly, openly, candidly, without any warning. **2** [1950s+] with total conviction (cf. COLD adv.).

cold water army *n.* [late 19C] the teetotal, total abstinence movement. [their favourite drink + ? ref. to Salvation Army]

cold wire *n.* [1940s] (US) an unsuccessful person. [opposite of LIVE WIRE]

cold without *n.* [early–mid-19C] spirits and water mixed, no sugar is added. [abbr. SE *a cold drink without sugar*]

cole *n.* [late 17C–late 18C] money; thus [mid-19C] *post the cole*, pay down money; [late 17C–early 19C] *tip the cole*, to pay out money. [SE *coal*, the staple, as a heat-provider, of everyday life, is as money. *Cole* had faded by 19C but *post the cole* lasted, increasingly in metaphorical use, until late 19C. Also ? link to SE *cole*, brassica (cf. CABBAGE n.⁸)]

colfabias *n.* [mid-19C] a privy. [fake Latin; coined at Trinity College, Dublin]

coli *n.* [1980s+] (drugs) marijuana. [abbr. COLIFLOR TOSTAO]

coliander/coliander-seed *n.* [mid-17C–18C] money (cf. ACTUAL; BALLAST n.¹; BREAD n.¹; COLE; CORKS n.¹; FEATHERS n.¹). [SE *coliander*, the earliest sp. (*c.*1000) of coriander, which is found as a seed. Seeds provide a form of growth, necessary for life; thus fig. synon. with money]

colies *n.* [1950s–60s] (US drugs) barbiturates, sleeping pills (cf. REDS n.³). [Sp. *colorados*, reds]

coliflor tostao *n.* [1980s+] (drugs) marijuana. [Sp. sl.]

colinderies *n.* [late 19C] (society) the *Col*onial and *Ind*ian Exhibition, South Kensington, London, held in 1886 and visited by more than 81,000 people (cf. FREAKERIES; HEALTHERIES; MUCKERIES; SODGERIES; SPOOFERIES; TOOLERIES; WHISKERIES; YANKEERIES). [abbr.]

coll *n.*¹ [early 18C] **1** a dupe, a silly fellow. **2** a man, a fellow, a chap. [CULL n.¹]

coll *n.*² [mid-18C+] a *coll*ege, esp. of schools with *College* in their name. [abbr.]

collar *n.*¹ [late 18C–early 19C] the hangman's noose (cf. COLLAR DAY; HEMPEN COLLAR; NEWGATE COLLAR). [play on SE]

collar *n.*² (US) **1** [late 19C+] an arrest; thus [1970s+] the person who has been arrested. **2** [late 19C–1900s] a policeman. [COLLAR v.]

collar *n.*³ **1** [late 19C+] the foam on a glass of beer. **2** [20C] (drugs) in a makeshift syringe, the strip of paper wrapped around a dropper to ensure a tight fit with the needle.

collar *v.* **1** [early 17C+] to arrest (cf. FEEL ONE'S COLLAR). **2** [early 18C+] to grab, to appropriate. **3** [mid-19C–1940s] (US) to master, to deal with. **4** [late 19C] (US) to catch out. **5** [1930s–40s] (US Black) to understand, to work out (cf. COLLAR THE JIVE;

COLLY). **6** [1930s+] (orig. US Black) to get hold of, to obtain. [SE *collar*, to get hold of]

collar/cop a broom, to *phr.* [1930s–40s] (US Black) to leave quickly, to rush away. [COLLAR v.[1] (2)/COP v.[1] + SE *broom*, the image of a witch flying off on her broomstick]

collar a duster up the ladder, to *phr.* [1930s–40s] (US Black) to climb the stairs.

collar a hot, to *phr.* [1940s] (US Black) to eat a meal (cf. COLLAR A NOD). [COLLAR v. (2) or (6) + SE *hot* (*meal*)]

collar and cuff *n.* [20C] a homosexual. [rhy. sl. *collar and cuff* = PUFF n.[3]]

collar and elbow/shoulder *adj.* [20C] (US) family style, informal, esp. of a restaurant or café. [orig. hobo jargon *collar and shoulder style*, a meal where the food is placed on the table and everyone, sitting shoulder to shoulder, grabs what they can from the platters. The idea of struggling for one's share may link the phr. to *collar and elbow*, a style of wrestling practised in Devon and Cornwall]

collar and tie *n.*[1] [20C] a lie. [rhy. sl.]

collar and tie *n.*[2] [1950s+] a masculine lesbian. [her adoption of men's clothing]

collar a nod, to *phr.* [1940s] (US Black) to sleep, to take a nap (cf. COLLAR A HOT). [COLLAR v. (2) + NOD n.]

collar-band pint *n.* [20C] a short-measure pint of beer (cf. COLLAR n.[3]). [SE *collar-band*, the band to which the collar is attached (slightly lower than the collar itself). Note synon. RAF jargon *cap-tally drink*]

collar day *n.* [late 18C–early 19C] the day of execution. [COLLAR n.[1]]

collared on *adj.* [mid-19C–1910s] (Aus.) obsessively in love with. [COLLAR v. (2)]

collared up *adj.* [mid-19C] kept hard at work, closely involved with one's business. [one is unable to remove one's collar, a sign of relaxation]

collar the jive, to *phr.* [1930s–40s] (US Black) to understand every aspect of a situation. [COLLAR v.[1] (5) + JIVE n.]

collar-work *n.* [late 19C] hard, strenuous work. [the image of a horse pulling against its collar]

collect *v.* [1940s+] (Aus.) to be hit by, to collide with, usu. of a car.

collector *n.* [late 18C–early 19C] a highwayman.

collect rent *v.* [late 18C–mid-19C] to practise highway robbery.

colleen bawn *n.* [19C] an erection (cf. MARQUIS OF LORNE). [rhy. sl. *Colleen Bawn* = HORN n.[2] (2); ult. the anglicized version of Irish *cailín bán*, the white or fair woman]

college *n.*[1] **1** [17C] Newgate prison (cf. CITY COLLEGE). **2** [early 18C+] any prison; thus [early 18C–mid-19C] *go to college*, to go to prison. **3** [19C+] (US) a state prison, a penitentiary. **4** [late 19C] the workhouse. [ironic uses of SE, the overall ref. is to prison as a 'university of crime'; note [mid-17C] Oxbridge use *college*, a public house or tavern with a sign of a green garland or painted hoop]

college *n.*[2] [19C] (US) a privy. [euph./derog. pun on SE]

college-called *adj.* [1950s–60s] (US Black) experiencing the wish to attend a college (cf. CHURCH-CALLED). [college attendance was still a relative rarity for young Blacks at this time]

college chum *n.* **1** [late 17C–early 19C] a shopkeeper who trades with prisoners. **2** [19C] a prisoner (cf. COLLEGIAN; COLLEGIATE). [COLLEGE n.[1] (2) + CHUM n.]

college-cove *n.* [early 19C] a turnkey. [COLLEGE n.[1] (2) + COVE]

college hill *n.* [20C] (US) that part of a town or city where the rich live. [the habit of building colleges or universities in the better-off areas of a town]

colleger *n.* [late 19C–1950s] a mortar-board.

College Street solicitor *n.* [1940s–60s] (Aus.) a male prostitute. [College Street, Sydney, a gay centre since the mid-19C. The street runs into Queen's Square, itself frequented by lawyers visiting the nearby law courts; thus giving puns on QUEEN n.[1] and SE *solicitor*]

college try *n.* [1920s+] (US) a plucky effort, esp. against heavy odds, usu. in phr. (*let's*) *give it the old college try* (cf. CIRCUS TRY). [the myth of 'college spirit']

college widow *n.* [late 19C] (US) an unmarried woman, in some way associated with a given college, whose advancing age does not deter her from associating with successive generations of students.

collegian *n.* [19C] a prisoner (cf. COLLEGE CHUM).

collegiate *n.* [mid-17C–early 19C] a prisoner (cf. COLLEGE CHUM). [COLLEGE n.[1] (2); ironic use of SE]

collegiate fucking *n.* [20C] (gay) body-to-body rubbing (cf. PRINCETON RUB). [SE *collegiate* + FUCKING n.[1]]

colley thumper *n.* [late 19C] a very good hand at cards. [Gen. Sir George Pomeroy Colley (1835–81), defeated and killed by the Boers at the Battle of Majuba Hill, 27 February 1881; but ? note CALLITHUMPIAN]

collie/colly/colly-weed *n.* [1950s+] (W.I./Jam.) marijuana; thus *collie-man*, a marijuana seller. [? joc. abbr. SE *broccoli*]

collie knox *n.* [1960s+] venereal disease (cf. NERVO AND KNOX; REVEREND RONALD KNOX). [rhy. sl. = POX n.[1]]

collies *n.* [20C] (drugs) heroin. [abbr. COLLYWOBBLES; i.e. the effects of the drug on one's stomach, or those that accompany withdrawal sickness]

colli-mollie *see* COLLY-MOLLY.

collins *n.* [19C] a 'thank-you letter' (cf. ROOFER n.[2]). [fictional character William *Collins*, a foolish sycophant in Jane Austen's *Pride & Prejudice* (1813)]

Collins Street farmer/grazier *n.* [1970s+] (Aus.) a businessman who owns or shares a farm from which he takes annual profits but rarely visits (cf. PITT STREET FARMER). [*Collins Street*, the financial and social centre of Melbourne]

Collins Street squatter *n.* [1960s] (Aus.) a man, usu. a youth, who frequents bars, cafés etc for no other reason than meeting his friends, gossiping and wasting time (cf. DRUGSTORE COWBOY). [*Collins Street*, the centre of Melbourne + SAusE *squatter*, a grazier]

collogue *n.* [early–mid-19C] a private talk, a secret plan or scheme. [? Fr. *colloque*, conference, communication, consultation]

collogue *v.* [early–mid-19C] to confer privately and confidentially, to confabulate. [COLLOGUE n.]

colloquials *n.* [late 19C–1900s] (society) informal conversation. [play on SE *colloquial*]

colly *n. see* COLLIE.

colly *v.* [1920s–40s] (US Black) to understand, to comprehend. [? COLLAR v.[1] (5) or Fr. *comprendre*, to understand]

colly-molly/colli-mollie *n.* [17C] melancholy. [play on SE]

colly-weed *see* COLLIE.

collywobbles *n.* **1** [mid-19C] the stomach. **2** [mid-19C+] feelings of tension, fear or sickness, usu. seen as stemming from the stomach. **3** [20C] diarrhoea. **4** [20C] (US) euph. for menstruation. [SE *colic* + *wobble*]

colney *n.* [1930s] a match. [rhy. sl. *Colney Hatch* = match]

colom *n.* [1990s] (drugs) marijuana from *Colom*bia. [abbr.]

Colombian/Columbian *n.* [1960s+] (drugs) marijuana from Colombia. [the mis-sp. is almost as common as the correct one]

Colombian necktie *n.* [1980s+] a method of killing whereby the throat is cut and the tongue pulled through the resulting wound; such embellishment is usually meted out to one who has betrayed the killer or the killer's boss. [orig. in the drug wars of Colombia]

colon choker/commando n. [1990s] a male homosexual. [SE *colon*, the large intestine, which ends in the rectum + *choker*, *commando*]

colonel n. [1940s+] (Aus.) a general, joc. form of address.

colonel of the regiment n. [mid-17C] one who 'drinks in his boots and gingling spurs'. [not necessarily a soldier]

colonel prescott *see* CHARLIE PRESCOTT.

Colonel Sanders n. [1960s+] (gay) an older male homosexual with a preference for young boys (cf. CHICKEN-HAWK). [the name, quite possibly libellous, puns on the Colonel's internationally franchised product]

colonel's cure n. [late 19C–1900s] any form of medicine swallowed at a single gulp. [the image is of a colonel making a toast after a regimental dinner]

colonial adjective n. [1900s] (N.Z.) euph. for BLOODY adj.

colonial duck/goose n. [late 19C+] (Aus.) a boned roast shoulder of mutton stuffed with sage and onions (cf. CLARE MARKET DUCK). [fig. use of *colonial* to mean second-rate, substitute]

colonial livery n. [19C] (Aus.) a bloody nose and a black eye (cf. BOTANY BAY COAT-OF-ARMS). [the image of Aus. as a violent country]

colonial Robert n. [late 19C–1910s] (Aus./N.Z.) one shilling. [SE *colonial* + BOB n.³ (1)]

colonist n. [early–mid-19C] a louse. [it 'colonizes' one's body]

color v. [1960s+] (US) to see as, to present as. [imagery of a children's colouring book]

colora n. [1960s+] (S.Afr. gay) a mixed-race gay man (cf. BETTY n.²). [SE *coloured* + fem. sfx. -*a*]

Colorado cocktail n. [1980s+] (drugs) marijuana.

Colorado Kool-Aid n. [1970s+] (US) Coors beer. [Coors is brewed in Colorado + the soft-drink mix Kool-Aid]

Colorado mockingbird n. [20C] (US) a donkey, an ass (cf. ARIZONA NIGHTINGALE). [the noise of its braying, the antithesis of that of a mellifluous bird]

color-blind adj. [1940s–60s] (US) larcenous. [the inability to distinguish between colours is substituted by the inability to tell the difference between one's own possessions and those of another]

colored people's time n. [1920s–60s] (US Black) unpunctuality (cf. AFRICAN PEOPLE'S TIME). [racist stereotyping]

color-struck adj. [1920s–30s] (US Black) **1** conceited on the grounds of one's light skin colour. **2** of a Black person, preferring light-skinned to dark-skinned Black people.

colossal adj. [late 19C+] immense, tremendous, magnificent, stupendous.

colouring n. [20C] (Irish) milk as poured into tea.

colour of Paddy Brophy, the phr. [1950s+] pallid, unhealthy looking. [? anecdotal]

colours n. [1950s+] of 'outlaw' motorcyclists, one's club emblem. Orig. used for the first such outlaws, the Hell's Angels, consisting of an embroidered patch of a winged skull wearing a motorcycle helmet, the name Hell's Angels, the name of the chapter (town etc) and the letters MC (motorcycle club); thus (N.Z.) *run for one's colours*, to serve as a probationary member of the club (cf. RAGS n.²).

colour the meerschaum, to phr. [late 19C] to get a red nose through excessive drinking. [the gradual darkening of the white-clay bowl of a *meerschaum* pipe over years of use]

colquarron n. [late 17C–mid-19C] the neck. [? Fr. *col*, neck + QUARROM]

colsher *see* COLCHER.

colshie v. [1990s] of a man, to follow one's stimulation of a woman's vagina by placing one's fingers in the woman's mouth. [dial. ? *colsie*, snug or *colch*, to fall]

colt n.¹ [16C] (Und.) anyone, usu. an inn-keeper, who provides and stables horses for a highwayman.

colt n.² **1** [late 17C–early 19C] a young man who has just been initiated into crime. **2** [mid-19C] one who serves on a jury for the first time (cf. COLT v.).

colt n.³ [late 18C–late 19C] a piece of rope with something heavy fastened to the end, used as a weapon. [naut. jargon *colt*, a piece of knotted rope, used as a weapon]

colt n.⁴ [20C] (US) an illegitimate child. [abbr. BRUSH COLT]

colt v. [mid-19C] to 'fine' a first-time server on a jury a sum which is spent on drink for his colleagues. [COLT n.² (2)]

colting n. [19C] a thrashing. [COLT n.³]

colt over the fence n. [20C] (US) an illegitimate child (cf. COLT n.⁴; FENCE-CORNER).

colt party n. [late 19C] (US society) a party for young people only.

colt veal n. [late 18C] very red veal. ['more like the flesh of a colt than that of a calf' (Grose 1785)]

columbered adj. [early 17C] drunk. [ety. unknown. ? fig. use of LUMBER v.]

Columbian *see* COLOMBIAN.

Columbia River turkey n. [20C] (US) a salmon (cf. CAPE COD TURKEY). [the Chinook salmon is abundant in the Columbia River]

Columbine n. [19C] a prostitute. [literary euph. *Columbine*, a character in Italian Comedy, thence trad. pantomime, the mistress of Harlequin]

Columbo n. [1970s+] (drugs) phencyclidine (cf. ACE n.³). [ref. to the 1970s TV detective series *Columbo*, starring Peter Falk as the bumbling hero]

Columbus black n. [1970s+] (drugs) marijuana. [marijuana supposedly grown in Columbus, Ohio]

columns of venus n. [18C] the labia. [literary euph.; the image is of a temple portico, flanked by a pair of pillars]

com n. **1** [mid-19C+] a *com*mission (in a non-pecuniary sense). **2** [late 19C+] a *com*mission (in a pecuniary sense). **3** [late 19C–1900s] a *com*mercial traveller. **4** [1920s+] (orig. Aus.) a *com*munist (cf. COMMIE; COMMO). [abbr.]

coma'd adj. [1990s] passed out from an excess of alcohol.

comanche n. [1960s–70s] (gay) a man who uses cosmetics (cf. INDIAN n.⁴; WARPAINT). [proper name *Comanche*; thus Native American use of warpaint]

comanche pill n. [20C] (US) a laxative. [? 19C Mexican use of *Comanche*, the lowest of the low]

comatose adj. [1980s+] (US campus) drunk.

comb and brush n. [late 19C] a drink. [rhy. sl. *comb and brush* = LUSH n.¹]

comb and brush, to phr. [late 19C] to treat to a drink. [COMB AND BRUSH n.]

combat zone n. [1970s+] (US) that part of the inner city where racial, social, economic and other tensions are at their height (cf. FRONT LINE).

comb-brush n. [mid-18C–early 19C] a lady's maid. [her primary task was brushing her mistress's hair]

comb-cut adj. [mid-19C] disgraced, socially or professionally embarrassed. [SE *have one's comb cut*, to be humiliated]

comb down v. [mid-19C+] (Aus.) to thrash, to beat (cf. COMB SOMEONE'S HAIR phr.¹).

combie n. [late 19C–1950s] the all-in-one underwear known as *combi*nations. [abbr.]

combo/kombo n.¹ [late 19C+] (Aus.) a White man who cohabits with or marries an Aborigine woman; thus *go combo*, to live with an Aborigine woman. [abbr. SE *combination* + -*o*]

combo n.² **1** [1920s+] a partnership, esp. a group of musicians. **2** [1920s+] (Und.) a combination lock (on a safe). **3** [1920s+] (US) any form of combination, whether of people, things, sandwich ingredients, wagers etc. **4** [1980s+] (US campus) a bisexual person. [abbr. SE *combination* + sfx. -*o*]

combolo n. (W.I.) **1** [1940s+] an old, trusted machete. **2** [1950s+] a sexual partner. [dial. *combolo*, a companion, ult. Sp. *compañero*, friend or ? *combolo*, an African song-dance]

comboman n. [1920s–30s] (Aus.) a White man who cohabits with or marries an Aboriginal woman. [COMBO n.[1] + sfx. *-man*]

comb someone's hair/head, to phr.[1] **1** [16C+] to thrash, to beat severely; sometimes extended by 'with a joint/three-legged stool' (cf. COMB DOWN). **2** [18C+] to tell off, to scold, to reprimand.

comb someone's hair, to phr.[2] (US) [19C+] to pistol-whip.

comb someone's noddle/comb someone's noddle with a three-legged stool, to phr. [late 16C–18C] to beat severely (cf. COMB SOMEONE'S HAIR phr.[1]).

comboozelated adj. [1970s+] (US campus) drunk. [DISCOM-BOBULATE + BOUSE + sfx. *-ated*]

comb out v. [1960s+] to sort out, to put in order.

combs n. [late 19C+] *combinations*, i.e. a woman's or child's garment consisting of combined chemise or undershirt and drawers (cf. COMBIE). [abbr.]

comb the kinks out of, to phr. [20C] (US) to correct errors in another's views or actions, to 'set straight'.

come n.[1] **1** [mid-17C+] an orgasm. **2** [1920s+] semen (cf. CUM n.). **3** [1940s+] vaginal secretions. [COME v.[1]]

come n.[2] [1980s+] energy, spirit, esp. in phr. *young, dumb and full of come*. [fig. use of COME n.[1]]

come v.[1] [mid-17C+] to achieve orgasm; thus [20C] *come a river*, for a woman, to have multiple orgasms. [abbr. SE *come to a climax*]

come v.[2] [late 17C–18C] (Und.) to lend (money) (cf. COME ACROSS). [one 'comes' forth with the loan]

come v.[3] [late 18C+] to practise some form of dodge, to act in a certain way, e.g. *come the Yorkshire, come the religious dodge*. [abbr. SE *come over*, to become]

come/come right out with v.[4] [late 19C+] (orig. US) to speak openly, candidly, tactlessly.

come about v. [19C] to have sexual intercourse.

come a clover, to phr. [1910s–20s] to fall or trip over. [rhy. sl.]

come/go a cropper, to phr. [mid-19C+] to suffer an accident, usu. a fall (cf. COME A PURLER; PURLER). [? SE *neck and crop*]

come across v. [1910s+] **1** to pay up money, esp. reluctantly (cf. COME THROUGH). **2** to deliver, to surrender, esp. sexually.

come after with salt and spoons, to phr. [late 17C–early 18C] to be slow, to waste time. [image of a person who is eating with their hands being pursued by a servant carrying utensils and salt]

come again! excl. **1** [late 19C+] a general phr. indicating either that one has failed to hear a speaker or finds it hard to believe the statement, 'please repeat yourself', 'could you say that again?', 'you must be joking'. **2** [1980s+] (W.I./UK Black teen) a call to the disc jockey to replay a piece of music.

come all over v. [20C] **1** (Aus.) to thrash, to defeat completely. **2** to experience certain emotions, usu. with various modifiers, e.g. *come all over queer*, suddenly to feel physically unwell.

come aloft v. [mid-16C–mid-19C] to have an erection.

come aloft! excl. [17C] let's have fun, let's enjoy ourselves.

come and get it! excl. [late 19C+] general cry indicating that a meal is forthcoming (cf. COMING UP). [orig. milit. mess-hall use]

come and go phr. [20C] (US) easy-going; thus *come and go party*, an informal party, 'open house'.

come and have a pickle phr. [late 19C] an invitation to join the speaker in a meal.

come and have one! excl. [late 19C–1900s] an invitation to join the speaker for a drink.

come and see your pa! excl. [mid-19C–1900s] an invitation to join the speaker for a drink.

come and see your pal phr. [late 19C] come and have a drink. [note naut. use, *come and wash your neck*]

come/fall apart at the seams, to phr. [1940s+] **1** of people, to lose emotional control. **2** of objects, ideas, plans, to collapse.

come a purler, to phr. [mid-19C+] to fall down, to trip over an obstacle, usu. sustaining some form of injury (cf. COME A CROPPER). [SE *come* + PURLER]

come around n. [20C] (US) menstruation. [euph. The cyclical occurrence of menstruation]

come around v. [20C] (US) to menstruate. [COME AROUND n.]

come a stumer, to phr. [1910s] (Aus.) to be financially ruined. [STUMER n.[1] (2)]

come at v. [1910s+] (Aus./N.Z.) to undertake, to take on, to get up to, to 'try on'.

comeback n.[1] [late 19C+] (orig. US) **1** a verbal rejoinder. **2** repercussions, results.

comeback n.[2] [1980s+] (drugs) benzocaine and mannitol, chemicals used in the manufacture of crack cocaine.

come back for seconds, to phr. [20C] (US Und.) to be a recidivist (cf. BOOMERANG v.).

come back to the field, to phr. [1910s+] (Aus.) to come down to earth, to abandon one's fantasies and dreams.

come-/cum-bucket n. [1970s+] (US) a repellent person. [COME n.[1] + SE *bucket*; lit. 'a bucket of ejaculate']

come-by-chance n. [18C+] an illegitimate child (cf. COME-TOO-SOON).

come clean v. **1** [1910s+] (orig. US) to confess, to make an admission (cf. MAKE A CLEAN BREAST OF). **2** [1910s–20s] (US) to pay one's debts in full.

come copper v. [1930s+] to become an informer (cf. TURN COPPER). [SE *come* + COPPER]

come correct v. [1990s] (rap music) to do something the way it should be done.

come countryman over, to phr. [early 19C] to wheedle, to cajole, to trick. [the gullibility of the country-dweller]

come crook v. [1950s] (Aus.) to menstruate. [SE *come* + CROOK adj. (3)]

come-down n. **1** [mid–late 19C] a fall from grace, a humiliating decline in one's material circumstances. **2** [1950s–70s] (US Black) a bad situation, esp. an embarrassing one. **3** [1960s+] (drugs) the after-effects of drug use. **4** [1960s+] (drugs) the withdrawal from drug use. [(1) SE in 20C; (3) is not necessarily unpleasant and not specifically applied to addictive drugs; (4) is unpleasant and refers to addiction]

come down v.[1] [early 17C–mid-19C] to give or lend money, usu. in phr. *come down with*.

come down v.[2] [1930s+] **1** to become permanent or established. **2** (orig. US Black) to occur, to turn out, to develop, to transpire, to happen.

come down v.[3] [1960s+] for the effect, good or bad, of a given drug to end. [one has been HIGH]

come down v.[4] [1970s+] (US) to talk or behave; usu. in comb. e.g. *she comes down all crazy*. [ext. of COME DOWN v.[2] (2)]

come down curtain-rods see COME DOWN STAIR-RODS.

come down fonky, to phr. [1950s+] to belittle, to insult, to talk to severely, to criticize harshly. [COME DOWN v.[4] + FONKY]

come down front, to phr. [1950s–60s] (US Black) to confess, to tell the truth, to speak openly, usu. as imper. *come down front!* [image of a congregant approaching the front of the church to confess their sins]

come down hard, to phr. [1930s+] (orig. US Black) to attack, whether physically or verbally (cf. COME DOWN ON).

come down in a pile, to phr. [20C] (US) to die. [the image of physical collapse]

come down on v. **1** [1930s+] (orig. US Black) to belittle, to insult, to talk to severely, to criticize harshly. **2** [1930s+] (orig. US Black) to assault. **3** [1950s+] (drugs) for the pains of withdrawal symptoms, and thus the demands of drug-need, to intensify.

come down on someone like a ton of bricks, to phr. [1910s+] to unleash the full force of one's anger or aggression on someone.

come down/rain stair-/curtain-rods, to phr. [20C] to rain very heavily.

come down the pike, to phr. [1950s+] (US) to appear, to arrive, to happen.

come/get down to brass tacks, to phr. [20C] to get down to basics, to deal with the essentials. [BRASS TACKS]

come down with v. [early 18C–late 19C] to hand over money; usu. extended as *come down with the needful/dust/pelf* etc.

come down with the derbies, to phr. [late 18C] pay money (cf. COME v.[2]). [DARBY n.]

comedy n. [1910s–30s] (US) irrelevant, impertinent, cheeky talk.

come flat out with, to phr. [late 19C+] (orig. US) to state unequivocally, to make one's point without hesitation (cf. COME OUT STRONG).

come for horse and harness, to phr. [15C–16C] to do something for one's interests. [the contemporary importance of such items]

come-freak n. [1950s+] anyone who is obsessed with physical sex and the delights thereof (cf. CUM-FREAK). [COME n.[1] (2) + FREAK n.]

come-from n. [1920s–30s] one's birthplace. [where one *comes from*]

come from Bangkok see GO TO BANGKOK.

come from Liquorpond Street, to phr. [early 19C–1900s] to be drunk.

come from Tripoli, to phr. [mid–late 19C] to be a lively, energetic performer, esp. acrobatically. [? the troupes of North African dancers who were then popular in London or f. a play on SE *trip*, to tumble]

come good v. [1930s+] (orig. Aus./N.Z.) **1** (of things) to turn out well. **2** (of people) to prove themselves (especially after an unpromising start), to 'come up trumps'. [COME DOWN v.[2]]

come grass v. [20C] to turn informer. [SE *come* + GRASS n.[5]]

come half larks with, to phr. [1910s–20s] to deceive, to fool. [SE *come* + LARK n.[1]]

come handsomely over, to phr. [late 18C–early 19C] to persuade, to win over.

come/have her country cousins/relations, to phr. [mid-19C–1910s] used of a woman who is menstruating. [euph. ? + pun on CUNT n.[1] (1)]

come home v. [1960s+] (drugs) to reach the end of an LSD experience. [play on SE *trip*/TRIP n.[3]]

come home by rail, to phr. [1930s+] (Aus.) to be so drunk that one can only proceed by hanging onto things (cf. TRAVEL BY RAIL).

come home by Spillsbury, to phr. [late 17C–early 18C] to tumble, to fall over, to have a 'spill'.

come home by weeping cross, to phr. [late 18C] to regret one's actions, to fail badly.

come home short, to phr. [17C–18C] to be imprisoned.

come home with the milk, to phr. [late 19C+] to come home in the very early morning. [one supposedly meets the milkman on his morning rounds]

come home with your knickers torn and say you found the money, to phr. [20C] a phr. used to indicate the speaker's inability to believe an extremely unlikely story.

come-home Yankee n. [1930s] (Irish) a returned immigrant.

come in Berlin phr. [1970s] (US campus) an exhortation to pay attention, a greeting. [? a radio call-sign]

come in for it v. [mid-19C+] to face trouble, to expect future difficulties. [IN FOR]

come in on a sparrow's ticket, to phr. [20C] (Aus.) to gain admission to a sporting event or other entertainment without paying. [one has 'flown over the wall']

come in one's pants, to phr. [1960s+] to behave in an exaggerated, over-excited manner; the image is of extremely premature ejaculation (cf. CREAM ONE'S JEANS). [COME v.[1]]

come in pudding-time, to phr. [late 17C–late 19C] to happen in good time. [? the slow cooking of a pudding]

come into one's own, to phr. [1980s+] to masturbate. [pun]

come it v.[1] [late 17C–early 19C] to lend money. [ext. of COME v.[2]]

come it v.[2] [19C] to attain, to reach, to achieve.

come it v.[3] **1** [early 19C+] to divulge a secret, to confess. **2** [20C] (Aus.) to betray, to inform against.

come it v.[4] **1** [mid-19C+] to act aggressively, often with no grounds for so doing. **2** [mid-19C+] to show off. **3** [late 19C+] to act, to perform, to behave in a certain manner, usu. constr. with an adv., e.g. *come it strong*. **4** [late 19C+] to deceive another for one's own benefit, esp. to avoid an unpleasant task (cf. COME THE OLD SOLDIER).

come it as strong as a horse, to phr. [early–mid-19C] (Und.) to turn King's/Queen's evidence. [ext. of COME IT v.[3]]

come it on v. [mid-19C] (US) to treat roughly, to manhandle. [abbr. COME IT STRONG]

come it over v. [19C+] **1** to compel, to intimidate. **2** (US) to trick, to deceive. [abbr. COME IT STRONG]

come-it-over man n. [20C] a domineering, intimidating person. [COME IT OVER v. (1)]

come it strong, to phr. **1** [19C] to act, to practise, to perform one's part. **2** [mid-19C] to act in a challenging, aggressive manner; sometimes intensified by 'as mustard' (cf. COME ON STRONG). **3** [mid-19C] to tell lies.

come it with v. [late 19C+] to act in a certain way in order to take advantage of (someone). [abbr. COME IT STRONG]

come-juice n. [20C] semen. [COME v.[1] + JUICE n.[1] (2)]

come lickety-split see GO LICKETY-SPLIT.

come like a parolee at the ho shack, to phr. [1970s] (US Black) to move very fast. [pun on SE *come*/COME v.[1]; the image is of a long-term prisoner having the first sex of his freedom]

come-love tea n. [1930s+] (Aus.) weak tea. [the phr. *come, love* seen as a mild suggestion]

come-loving adj. [1950s–70s] (US Black) obsessed with sex (cf. COME-FREAK). [COME n.[1]]

come-off n. [late 19C+] (US) a result. [earlier use is SE]

come off v.[1] [17C+] to experience orgasm (cf. CUM v.). [ext. of COME v.[1] (1)]

come off v.[2] **1** [late 19C] (US) to stop, to refrain from a course of action (cf. COME OFF IT!). **2** [1960s] (US) to hand over reluctantly.

come off v.[3] [1930s+] (drugs) to stop using a given (addictive) drug. [one has been 'on' heroin, 'on' cocaine etc]

come off v.[4] [1980s+] (US Black) to profit. [abbr. SE *come off best*]

come off! excl. [late 19C] (US) stop it! don't keep trying that line! (cf. COME OFF IT!). [COME OFF v.[2]]

come off bluely, to phr. [mid-17C–mid-19C] to have bad luck, to fail. [BLUE adj.[1]]

come off crabs, to phr. [mid-18C–mid-19C] to turn out a failure or disappointment (cf. CRAP OUT). [gambling jargon *crabs*, two aces, the lowest throw at hazard]

come off it! excl. [late 19C+] stop it! don't keep trying that line! [ext. COME OFF!]

come off one's perch, to *phr.* [late 19C+] to climb down, to adopt a less arrogant posture.

come off the bird-lime! *phr.* [1910s–20s] a general phr. of disbelief, 'you must be joking', 'you don't fool me'. [COME OFF v.² + the use of SE *bird-lime* as a snare or trap]

come off the grass! *excl.* [late 19C+] (orig. US) stop telling lies, stop exaggerating.

come off the roof! *excl.* [late 19C–1930s] used to a peer who is considered to be 'getting above themself', 'stop acting so superior'.

come-on *n.* (orig. US) **1** [19C+] (Und.) a con-man, a swindler. **2** [19C+] (Und.) a dupe, a victim of a confidence trickster. **3** [19C+] a snare, an inducement, a lure. **4** [19C+] patter, sales or seduction talk, a line. **5** [1910s+] a sexual invitation, either through a look or through words. **6** [1950s] a dare. [SE excl. *come on!*]

come on *v.*¹ [mid-19C+] to seem, to appear, always modified by an adj., e.g. *come on tough, come on nasty* etc.

come on *v.*² [mid-19C+] esp. of women, to become sophisticated and worldly. [SE *come on,* to progress, to get on]

come on *v.*³ **1** [20C] of a woman, to start menstruation. **2** [1940s+] (drugs) for a drug to begin affecting its user, esp. of a hallucinogen (which takes a short time to enter the bloodstream and hit the brain) (cf. COME UP). [SE *come on,* to begin]

come on *v.*⁴ **1** [1940s+] (US) to speak aggressively, forcefully; ext. as COME ON STRONG. **2** [1950s] (US) to joke.

come on! *excl.* [1940s+] a general excl. of disbelief, disapproval, irritation (cf. COME OFF IT!).

come on bad, to *phr.* [1960s–70s] (US Black) **1** to act aggressively, to threaten. **2** to defeat someone in a contest of words. [COME ON v.¹ + BAD adj.]

come-on boy *n.* [1910s+] a male prostitute who entices a client and then, instead of sex, has him beaten and robbed by a confederate. [COME-ON n. (3) + SE *boy*]

come one's cocoa, to *phr.* [1970s+] **1** to ejaculate. **2** (police/Und.) to inform or to confess one's crimes (cf. COME ONE'S FAT; COME ONE'S GUTS; COME ONE'S LOT). [COME v.¹ + COCOA n.⁴]

come one's fat, to *phr.* [1970s+] **1** to ejaculate. **2** of a suspect, to confess (cf. COME ONE'S COCOA). [COME v.¹ + SE *fat*]

come/give one's guts, to *phr.* [1950s–60s] (Aus.) to give information to the police (cf. COME ONE'S COCOA). [COME v.¹ + GUTS n.³ (2)]

come one's lot, to *phr.* [1970s+] **1** to ejaculate. **2** of a suspect, to confess (cf. COME ONE'S COCOA). [COME v.¹ + SE *lot*]

come one's mutton, to *phr.* [late 19C+] to masturbate (cf. ACCOST THE OSCAR MEYER). [COME v.¹ + MUTTON n.¹ (2)]

come one's turkey, to *phr.* [late 19C+] to masturbate (cf. ACCOST THE OSCAR MEYER). [COME v.¹ + TURKEY(-NECK)]

come-on girl *n.* [20C] (US) an immoral woman. [COME-ON n. (5) + SE *girl*]

come-on guy *n.* [1930s] (US) the member of a confidence trickster team who lures the victim into the circle. [COME-ON n. (3) + SE *guy*]

come on like a test pilot, to *phr.* [1940s] (US Black/Harlem) to act in a speedy, efficient manner. [COME ON v.¹. The test pilot, as a figure of technologically sophisticated derring-do, had a higher profile then than now]

come on like gangbusters, to *phr.* [1940s+] to act aggressively, to commit oneself wholeheartedly (cf. COME ON STRONG). [COME ON v.¹ + *Gangbusters,* the US radio serial of 1940s, which featured hard-hitting, intrepid crimefighters]

come on, Steve! *excl.* [1920s–30s] a general phr. of encouragement, urging one to hurry up (cf. UP THERE CAZALY!). [proper name of jockey *Steve* Donaghue]

come on one's/slip on one's guava, to *phr.* [1970s] (S.Afr.) to make a fool of oneself. [Afk. *koejawel,* backside]

come on strong, to *phr.* [mid-19C+] to make one's presence and opinions felt; used both positively and negatively, the latter often as *come on too strong* (cf. COME ON LIKE GANGBUSTERS). [COME ON v.⁴ (1) + SE *strong*]

come on the piper's invitation, to *phr.* [19C+] (Irish) to come uninvited. [a piper always receives a welcome]

come on to *v.* [1960s+] (orig. US) **1** to approach reasonably aggressively, to solicit. **2** to make sexual advances towards. [orig. jazz use]

come-out *adj.* [early 19C] disgusting, appalling.

come out *v.*¹ [mid–late 19C] (US Black) to declare one's faith in religion, to join the church.

come out *v.*² [20C] (W.I.) to be born in poverty or in some unknown place. esp. in question 'where you come out?' [i.e. 'come out from']

come out *v.*³ [1960s+] (gay) to declare oneself openly as a homosexual. [abbr. COME OUT OF THE CLOSET; note COME OUT v.¹]

come out *v.*⁴ [1970s+] (US Black) to abandon the respectable nine-to-five world for a more sophisticated lifestyle. [abbr. COME OUT OF THE HOUSE]

come out/up moldy, to *phr.* [1980s+] (US campus) to be humiliated.

come out of a bag, to *phr.* **1** [1930s] (US Black) to act in an obnoxious manner. **2** [1990s] to act contrary to expectations, to behave illogically in a given situation. [SE *come out* + BAG n.⁶]

come out of that hat – I can't see your feet! *phr.* [late 19C] a mocking phr. used by street-boys to a man wearing a top hat.

come out of the closet, to *phr.* [1960s+] (orig. US) to reveal one's gay sexuality in public; thus *out of the closet,* acknowledging one's homosexuality. [SE *come out* + CLOSET n.]

come out of the cupboard, to *phr.* [late 19C–1900s] to start work on one's first ever job.

come out of the house, to *phr.* [1950s+] (US) to grow up, lit. to leave one's home life for that of the streets and the larger world.

come/crawl/creep out of the woodwork, to *phr.* [1970s+] to emerge, to appear, always of someone/something unpleasant. [the normal woodwork dweller being a beetle, cockroach etc]

come out strong, to *phr.* **1** [mid-19C+] to speak emphatically and frankly (cf. COME ON STRONG). **2** [late 19C] to act generously.

come over *v.*¹ **1** [mid-18C+] to trick, to cheat. **2** [19C] to get the better of. [ext. use of SE *come over,* to prevail]

come over *v.*² [mid-19C+] to experience a sudden (unpleasant or disorientating) feeling, e.g. *come over queer, come over strange.* [reverse of SE; i.e. the feeling 'comes over' the subject]

come over *v.*³ [mid-19C+] as *come the ... over,* to act in a given manner, defined by a missing noun. [var. of COME ON v.¹]

come over/go all unnecessary, to *phr.* [1930s+] to become sexually excited. [COME OVER v.²]

come over at *v.* [1910s–20s] (orig. US) to excite passion in someone.

come over on a whelk-stall, to *phr.* [late 19C–1900s] (coster) to be very flashily dressed. [? the flashy dress preferred by whelk-sellers]

come possum over, to *phr.* [mid-19C+] **1** to pretend to be ill or even dead. **2** to dissemble (cf. ACT POSSUM; PLAY POSSUM). [image of the cowardly, dissembling *possum*]

comer *n.* [19C+] an ambitious, go-ahead person, 'the coming man'. [SE *come (on),* to advance (in one's aims, development)]

come right out with *see* COME v.⁴.

come round v. [mid-19C] **1** to get the better of by cunning or artifice. **2** to persuade, to influence strongly, to make a serious impression.

come sick v. [20C] (US) euph. to menstruate (cf. COME ON v.[3]).

come/cum stain n. [1990s] (US) a general derog. term. [lit. COME n.[1] (2) + SE *stain*, a semen stain]

comet n. [1920s–30s] (US tramp) the aristocrat of tramps, travelling only on express trains and only for lengthy journeys.

come the .../come the old ..., to phr. [19C+] in a wide variety of combs. this means to act, to pose as, to attempt to be; it is always constrained by a noun, e.g. *come the artful*, *come the paddy* etc. The word 'old' is often inserted between the phr. and the defining noun, e.g. COME THE ACID WITH (cf. COME OVER v.[3]). [var. on COME ONE v.[1]]

come/give the abdabs/old abdabs, to phr. [1940s] to hoax, to fool, to 'tell the tale', often as phr. *don't come/give me the (old) abdabs*, don't try to fool me. [COME THE ...; but *abdabs*, i.e. delirium tremens, seems to be unrelated]

come the acid/old acid with, to phr. [1920s+] **1** to act contrarily, aggressively, to argue. **2** to be unpleasant or offensive, to speak in a caustic or sarcastic manner. [COME THE ... + ACID n.[2]]

come the after game phr. [1920s+] (Aus.) synon. for 'I told you so'. [image of those who analyse a sporting fixture *after the game*, when they naturally know better than those who actually had to play it]

come the artful, to phr. [19C+] to hoax, to deceive. [COME THE ... + SE *artful*]

come the bag/old bag, to phr. [1920s] (orig. milit.) to bluff, to 'try it on'. [COME THE ... + SE *bag*]

come/go the big figure, to phr. [mid-19C] (US) to do or provide what is required. [COME THE ... + BIG FIGURE]

come the big note, to phr. [1940s+] (Aus.) to boast, to set oneself as a richer or more important person than is true. [COME THE ... + BIG-NOTE (ARTIST)]

come the blarney/blarney over, to phr. [19C+] to flatter. [COME THE ... + BLARNEY n.]

come the bludge on, to phr. [20C] (Aus.) to sponge on. [COME THE ... + BLUDGER n.[2] (5)]

come the bounce/bouncer, to phr. [mid-late 19C] (Aus.) to threaten, to intimidate, to suggest blackmail; thus *common bounce(r)*, a man who uses a boy to claim that he has been abused so as to threaten a homosexual with a charge of 'unnatural intercourse'. [COME THE ... + BOUNCE n.[1] (2)]

come the carney/old carney, to phr. [early 19C–1920s] to flatter. [COME THE ... + CARNEY n.[1]]

come the cunt/old cunt, to phr. [20C] to act in an obnoxious or obstreperous manner, esp. in phr. *don't come the old cunt with me*. [COME THE ... + CUNT n.[2]]

come the don, to phr. [mid-19C–1910s] to put on airs. [COME THE ... + SE *don*, a university teacher]

come the drunkard, to phr. [mid-19C] to pose as a drunkard. [COME THE ... + SE *drunkard*]

come the fob on, to phr. [mid-19C] (US) to cheat, to trick (cf. FOB n.).

come the gammon, to phr. [19C] to wheedle. [COME THE ... + GAMMON n.[1]]

come/go the grope, to phr. [1960s+] (Aus.) to fondle someone sexually.

come the gum over, to phr. [early–mid-19C] (US) to hoodwink, to trick. [COME THE ... + GUM n.[1]]

come the gypsy, to phr. [mid-19C] to cheat, to defraud. [COME THE ... + SE *gypsy*; stereotyping]

come the heavy, to phr. [mid-late 19C] to pose as a member of a superior class to that to which one actually belongs. [COME THE ... + HEAVY n.[2] (6)]

come the heavy father, to phr. [mid-19C+] to moralize to one's errant child (cf. HEAVY STUFF). [COME THE ... + SE *heavy father*, an overbearing 'Victorian' father]

come the lardy-dardy, to phr. [mid-late 19C] to dress in a showy manner. [COME THE ... + LARDY-DARDY adj.]

come the nob, to phr. [early 19C+] to give oneself airs (cf. COME THE DON). [COME THE ... + NOB n.[3]]

come the old man, to phr. [late 19C] to act in a lazy manner, to shirk one's duties. [to pretend to infirm old age, or naut. use of *old man*, the captain]

come the old/tin soldier, to phr. [mid-19C+] to deceive another for one's own benefit, esp. to avoid an unpleasant task. [COME THE ... + *old soldier*, the skills of a veteran who, supposedly, knows every trick when it comes to avoiding onerous duties. Ware also cites the rash of beggars who proliferated in London after Waterloo (1815), all claiming to have taken part in the battle. Note naut. jargon *soldier*, a poor or lazy seaman, a shirker]

come the paddy/paddy over, to phr. [early 19C] to bamboozle, to confuse, to 'blarney'. [COME THE ... + PADDY n.[1] (1); thus negative racial stereotyping]

come the raw prawn, to phr. [1960s+] (Aus.) to act resentfully or unpleasantly, to be rude. [COME THE ... + SE *raw prawn*]

come the Rothschild, to phr. [late 19C–1910s] to pretend to great wealth. [COEM THE ... + the proper name *Rothschild*, the epitome of the fabulously wealthy banker, esp. during the reign of the magnate-loving Edward VII]

come the rubber pig, to phr. [1970s] (Irish) to act in a recalcitrant manner. [COME THE ...]

come the sergeant, to phr. [mid-late 19C] to act in an unpleasantly authoritarian manner. [COME THE ... + SE *sergeant*]

come the smart-arse, to phr. [1930s+] to pose as being cleverer than one actually is. [COME THE ... + SMART-ARSE]

come the spoon, to phr. [mid-late 19C] to court, to make love. [COME THE ... + SPOON n.[1] (4)]

come the tin man, to phr. [20C] **1** to deceive, to bluff. **2** to make oneself a nuisance. [SE *tin*, petty, worthless, counterfeit (as opposed to precious metal) + *man*]

come the tin soldier see COME THE OLD SOLDIER.

come the touch on, to phr. [20C] (Aus.) to adopt a manner or attitude.

come the Traviata, to phr. [mid-late 19C] of a prostitute, to pretend to be suffering from phthisis or pulmonary consumption. [COME THE ... + the Verdi opera *La Traviata* (1853), which was based on Dumas' *fils La Dame aux Camélias*, in which the heroine dies of that disease]

come the ugly over/with, to phr. [mid-late 19C] to make threats, to menace. [COME THE ... + SE *ugly*, unpleasant]

come through v. **1** [19C+] (US) to pay one's debts (cf. COME ACROSS). **2** [1900s–30s] (US) to confess. **3** [1910s+] to act as desired, to do what is wanted. **4** [1940s+] to take over in an emergency, to carry out requirements. [fig. uses of SE]

come through a side door, to phr. [mid-late 19C] to be born out of wedlock.

come to a sticky end, to phr. [1910s+] **1** to meet great misfortune, esp. a violent death or a prison sentence, usu. said of a person already condemned as 'a bad lot'. **2** to die.

come/go to bat, to phr. [1900s–60s] (US) to take one's turn. [baseball/cricket imagery]

come-to-bed eyes n. [1960s+] eyes (of either sex) that convey infinite, if not always delivered, sexual promise.

come to grief, to phr. [19C+] to fall into difficulties, to fail. [orig. a sporting phr. meaning to fall from one's horse]

come to grips with oneself, to phr. [1990s] to masturbate. [pun on SE]

come-to-heaven collar n. [20C] (US) a wing collar (cf.

COME-TO-JESUS COLLAR). [the wings of the collar presumably resemble those of an angel]

come-to-Jesus coat n. [1930s–40s] (US) a frock coat. [as worn by, *inter alia*, ministers and preachers]

come-to-Jesus collar n. [20C] (Can.) a stiff dress collar (cf. COME-TO-HEAVEN COLLAR). [the preference for such collars among revivalist preachers]

come to light/light with, to phr. [1910s–40s] (Aus.) to produce, to deliver, esp. money.

come-too-soon n. [20C] (US) an illegitimate child (cf. COME-BY-CHANCE; SOONER n.[3]). [? *too soon* for the parents to get married]

come to someone's milk, to phr. [20C] (US) to yield to authority, to accept orders when facing no alternative. [? a stubborn calf that refuses to drink but gives in when overwhelmed by hunger]

come to stay, to phr. [mid-19C–1900s] to become permanent or established (cf. HERE TO STAY).

come to that! phr. [1920s+] now you mention it.

come to the goat's house for wool, to phr. [20C] (US) to ask someone for something that it is presumed they would not possess. [sheep have wool, goats (other than Angoras) do not]

come to the heath, to phr. [early 19C] to pay out or give money. [? pun on Tiptree Heath, in Essex]

come to the mark, to phr. [early 19C] (Und.) to fulfil a contract, to keep a promise. [thus SE *come up to the mark*]

come/go to the wrong shop, to phr. [late 19C+] to make a mistake, esp. in the context of asking the wrong person or going to the wrong place to get one's desires.

come town/towny/towney over, to phr. [early 19C] to dupe, to hoax, to 'con'. [COME THE ... + TOWN(IE), as in the fooling of a countryman by a street-smart town-dweller]

come undone/unstuck v. [1940s+] to find oneself in difficulties.

come unglued v. [1940s+] to become mentally and emotionally unstable.

come unstuck see COME UNDONE.

come up v. 1 [1930s+] (US Black) to turn out, to happen (cf. COME DOWN v.[2]). 2 [1930s+] (US Black) to grow up. 3 [1980s+] (drugs) for a drug to start taking effect (cf. COME ON v.[3]).

come up for air, to phr. 1 [1930s+] to come to the end of a lengthy kiss. 2 [1940s+] (Aus.) to take a rest. [diving imagery]

come up lovely, to phr. [20C] to turn out well (esp. when it appeared that no such positive outcome was feasible). [ext. of COME UP v. (1)]

come up moldy see COME OUT MOLDY.

come up on v. [1950s+] to succeed at or with.

come up on the last load/up the river on a bike, to phr. [20C] (Irish) to be naïve, gullible, usu. in phr. *do you think I came up ... /I didn't come up ...* .

come up smelling of violets, to phr. [20C] to survive an unpleasant experience not only unscathed, but actually better placed; thus *so lucky that if he fell in shit he'd come up ...* .

come up smiling, to phr. [mid-19C+] (orig. boxing) to face a difficult circumstance without showing fear or complaining. [i.e. when knocked to the canvas one comes up with a (false but brave) smile]

come up the Foyle in a bubble, to phr. [20C] (Ulster) to be naïve, gullible; usu. in phr. *do you think I came up ... /I didn't come up ...* .

come up the river on a bike see COME UP ON THE LAST LOAD.

come up to the chalk, to phr. [mid-19C] (US) to perform as expected, to meet expectations. [the chalk mark that indicates the start of a race]

come up to the rack or jump the fence, to phr. [late 19C] (US) to make a decision to do one thing or another, to stop dithering (cf. SHIT OR GET OFF THE POT!). [SE *rack*, racket, i.e. the

noise and bustle of a city; thus the image is of entering the urban hustle-bustle, or jumping the fence and heading off for the quiet open spaces of the country]

come up trumps, to phr. [mid-19C+] to turn out satisfactorily, esp. when a bad result seems more likely (cf. TURN UP TRUMPS). [card-playing imagery]

come up weak, to phr. [1960s] (US Black) to disappoint, to fail to reach expectations (whether one's own or those of others). [COME UP v. (1) + SE *weak*]

come up with v. [1930s+] (orig. US) to produce, to provide, to present.

come up with the rations, to phr. [1920s+] (orig. milit.) to be worthless, to be gained without effort. [the image of supplies being sent 'up the line' to the front-line trenches; the orig. WW1 use was to disparage a variety of medals and decorations, handed out for no real achievement]

come with one's horns down, to phr. [19C+] (US) to be spoiling for a fight. [the image of a bull charging with his horns down]

come/play Yankee over/with, to phr. [mid-19C] (US) to cheat, to defraud. [COME OVER v.[3]/SE *play* + SE *Yankee*, i.e. the poor reputation of New England businessmen and lawyers]

come Yorkshire over/put Yorkshire on, to phr. [18C+] to cheat. [local stereotyping]

come-you-all n. [20C] (US) a ruckus, a large-scale fist-fight, a brawl. [phr. *come one, come all*, used as a challenge, or punning on hymn title 'O come all ye faithful']

comflogsticate v. [late 19C] to astound, to puzzle. [ety. unknown, a nonsense word orig. used in the RN]

comfoozled adj. [mid–late 19C] exhausted, overcome. [used and probably coined by Charles Dickens (1812–70)]

comfort n. [early–mid-18C] gin (cf. CONSOLATION). [its soothing effects; E.P. also notes the US liquor, *Southern Comfort*]

comfortable as a pig/pigs in shit see HAPPY AS A PIG IN SHIT.

comfortable importance n. [late 17C–1910s] one's wife (cf. COMFORTABLE IMPUDENCE). [play on SE]

comfortable impudence n. [18C–19C] a mistress, esp. when posing as one's wife (cf. COMFORTABLE IMPORTANCE). [play on SE and parody of COMFORTABLE IMPORTANCE]

comical n. [late 19C–1910s] a table-napkin. [? users seemed amusing to those who usually did not bother with such items]

comical chris n. [1970s–80s] an act of urination. [rhy. sl. *comical Chris* = PISS n.]

comical farce n. [late 19C–1910s] a glass. [rhy. sl.]

comic cuts/comics n. [1940s+] (Aus.) the stomach. [rhy. sl. *comic cuts* = GUTS n.[1] (1)]

coming adj. [late 17C–19C] 1 of a woman, wanton, promiscuous. 2 pregnant. [sense is fig. 'coming forward']

coming! excl. [early 18C+] 'I'll be with you at once', 'I won't be long'; thus derisive phr., aimed at a slow person, *coming? so is Christmas*.

coming out of one's ears phr. [1960s+] (US) in great abundance, very plentiful.

coming-out pants n. [20C] (US) torn trousers, revealing one's flesh. [pun on SE *come out*, to make one's social debut]

comings n. [mid-19C+] semen. [COME n.[1] (2)]

coming up phr. [1940s+] a phr. used in restaurants, bars etc to indicate that one's ordered food or drink is on its way (cf. COME AND GET IT!). [SE phr. *coming up (from the kitchen)*]

commercial n.[1] [1930s] (Aus./N.Z.) an itinerant worker, who travels with his pack on his back while looking for employment (cf. SWAGMAN). [an ironic use of SE *commercial traveller*. Note Und. *commercial*, a thief who travels to pursue his profession]

commercial n.[2] [1960s+] (Aus. gay) a male prostitute (cf. ASS-PEDDLER).

commercial n.[3] [1960s+] (orig. US) any form of praise, a good reference. [SE *commercial*, a paid advertisement, on radio or TV]

commercial n.[4] [1980s+] (US drugs) **1** marijuana buds that come in a brick. **2** Colombian marijuana (which is packaged in this manner).

commercial queer n. [20C] a homosexual male prostitute (cf. ASS PEDDLER). [SE *commercial* + QUEER n.[1]]

commercial traveller n. [1930s] a person with bags under their eyes. [like the traveller they carry 'bags']

commersh n. [1990s] (drugs) average, unexceptional quality marijuana or hashish. [SE *commercial* (*grade*)]

commie n. [1940s+] a *comm*unist (cf. COM). [abbr.]

commish/commister n.[1] [mid–late 19C] a shirt. [abbr. COMMISSION]

commish n.[2] [20C] a *commis*sion (on a financial or other transaction). [abbr.]

commissariat n. [1910s–30s] the pantry. [SE *commissariat*, that department of the military service that is charged with the duty of providing food and other supplies for the army; popularized by veterans of WW1]

commissary department n. [late 19C–1900s] (US) the stomach. [SE *commissary department*, in milit. use that department that deals with the buying, preparing and distribution of food]

commission n. [mid-16C–mid-19C] a shirt (cf. CAMESA). [Ital. *camisa*, shirt]

commissioner n. [mid-19C] a book-maker. [? ironic use of next, given the role of Newmarket in racing and the bookmaker's extraction of money from his clients]

commissioner of Newmarket Heath n. [late 16C] a footpad. [the site of many highway robberies]

commister n.[1] [mid-19C] (orig. Und.) a clergyman (cf. CAMISTER). [his *chemise* or surplice]

commister n.[2] *see* COMMISH n.[1].

commit oneself v. [20C] (Ulster) usu. of children, to dirty oneself with excrement. [euph. use of SE]

commit the seventh, to phr. [late 19C] to commit adultery. [the *Seventh Commandment*: 'Thou shalt not commit adultery']

commo n. [1940s+] (Aus.) a *comm*unist (cf. COM). [abbr. + sfx. -O; note Aus. *commie* does not have the same political use as UK/US, but refers to those who live in rural communes]

commode-hugging drunk adj. [1970s+] (US campus) extremely drunk, to the point of hugging the lavatory bowl and vomiting within (cf. DRIVE THE PORCELAIN BUS; TALK TO THE BIG WHITE TELEPHONE).

commodity n. **1** [16C] a prostitute (cf. ARTICLE; CONVENIENT). **2** [late 16C–19C] the female genitals (BANK n.[1]). [SE *commodity*, something available for sale or trade; in both senses the woman and/or her body are seen as no more than pieces of merchandise]

common n. [20C] common sense. [abbr. SE; note RN jargon *common dog*, common sense]

common as the hedge/highway phr. [late 17C–early 18C] very common, usu. applied to a 'loose woman'.

common garden gout *see* COVENT GARDEN GOUT.

common law n. [late 18C] sexual intercourse. [? coined by Robert Burns]

commons n. [late 18C–mid-19C] a privy, a lavatory (cf. HOUSE OF COMMONS).

commonsensible adj. [late 19C] (society) being possessed of common sense.

common sewer n. **1** [17C] a prostitute. **2** [19C] the throat (cf. DRAIN n.[1]). **3** [19C] a drunkard (cf. DRAIN n.[2]). [all plays on SE *common sewer*, into which everything is poured]

communists n. [1930s] (US) menstruation. [pun on 'the reds']

comp n. (US) **1** [mid-19C+] a *comp*liment. **2** [late 19C+] a *comp*limentary pass or ticket. **3** [late 19C+] a *comp*limentary gift, e.g. as given to 'high-rolling' gamblers by a resort hotel. **4** [1940s+] (campus) a course in English *comp*osition. [abbr.]

comp v. [late 19C+] to give free tickets, free board and lodging etc, usu. in the context of show business or casino hotels. [COMP n.(3)]

compa n. [1960s+] (US) a friend, a fellow gang member. [abbr. Sp. *compadre*, a companion]

compadre/companero n. [mid-19C+] (US) a close male friend. [Sp.]

Company, the n. [1960s+] (US) the Central Intelligence Agency (CIA). [Sp. *Cia*, abbr. for Company (equivalent of SE *Co.*)]

company man/stiff n. [1940s–50s] (US) a worker who is seen by his peers as loyal to the employers rather than the union. [SE *company* + *man*/STIFF n.[4]]

compellance weed n. [1940s+] (W.I.) marijuana. [under its influence one is supposedly 'compelled' to do something. This hardly fits, however, with the normal image of the marijuana user as a rather comatose figure. Note *compelling oil/powder*, a sweet-smelling oil or powder prepared by an obeahman and used in the hope of winning over or controlling a lover or defeating an evil spirit]

complete and utter n. [1940s+] (Aus.) an absolutely unpleasant person. [abbr. SE *complete and utter bastard*]

completely adj., adv. [1980s] (US teen) an all-purpose term of approval (cf. CLEARLY).

compo n. [1940s+] (Aus./N.Z.) workers' *comp*ensation, payment for time lost after an injury at work. [abbr. + sfx. -O]

compo artist/king n. [1940s+] (Aus./N.Z.) one who is a specialist in the extraction of monetary compensation by faking or exaggerating their supposedly work-related injuries. [COMPO + ARTIST n.[2]/SE *king*]

compo-itis n. [1940s+] (Aus./N.Z.) the feigning of disability to gain compensation. [COMPO + sfx. -*itis*]

compo king *see* COMPO ARTIST.

compoodle n. [19C] (US) a large, mixed-up collection of objects or people. [var. on CABOODLE]

compost hole n. [19C] a lavatory.

comprador n. **1** [early 17C–early 19C] (Anglo-Ind.) a house steward. **2** [mid-19C] (Anglo-Chinese) a butler. [Port. *comprador*, a purchaser, in this case of household supplies]

comprendo? excl. [1980s+] (orig. US) you understand? [Sp. Note WW2 *compree*, understand, f. Fr. *compris*]

compress v. [19C] of a man, to have sexual intercourse. [the effect of his weight when adopting the SE *missionary position*]

compute v. [1960s+] (orig. US) to work out, usu. in neg. phr. *that doesn't compute*. [lit. 'add up'. Popularized in 1964 CBS TV series *My Living Doll*. Note mid-17C–late 18C SE *compute*, to estimate, to reckon, to take account of, to take into consideration]

compy v. [1940s] (US Black) to understand, often as interrog. *compy?* you understand? (cf. COMPRENDRO?). [SE *comprehend* or f. Fr. *comprenez*? do you understand?, imported by GIs returning from WW2. Note WW1 equivalent *compris*]

comrade wobbly n. [1990s] (mainly upper-middle class) the penis; thus *play comrade wobbly hides his helmet*, to have sexual intercourse.

con n.[1] **1** [early 19C] a *con*fidant. **2** [mid-19C] a *con*undrum. **3** [late 19C] a *con*formist. **4** [late 19C] a *con*tract. **5** [late 19C+] a *con*fidence man, *con*fidence trick or game. **6** [late 19C+] a *con*vict; thus *ex-con*, a former prisoner. [abbr.]

con n.[2] [late 19C] a male homosexual. [? Fr. *con*, the vagina. The ref. is to the effeminacy of some homosexuals]

con n.[3] [20C] (US) tuberculosis. [abbr. SE *consumption*]

con v. [late 19C+] (orig. US) **1** to fool a victim in one or another form of confidence trick. **2** to persuade, to coax (without criminal intent), usu. as *con ... into*. [abbr. SE *confidence trick*]

con along v. [20C] to subject to a confidence trick, esp. the early stage when the victim is being gradually drawn into the hoax. [CON v. (1)]

con and coal n. [20C] the dole. [rhy. sl.]

conan doyle n. [late 19C+] a boil (on the neck). [rhy. sl.; ult. f. Sir Arthur *Conan Doyle* (1859–1930), novelist and creator of Sherlock Holmes]

conan doyle v. [late 19C+] to boil (a kettle). [rhy. sl.; for ety. see CONAN DOYLE n.]

con-artist n. [20C] a confidence trickster, a fraud. [CON n.¹ (5) + ARTIST n.²]

conbobberate v. [19C] (US) to upset, to disconcert, to disturb (cf. DISCOMBOBULATE). [CONBOBBERATION]

conbobberation n. [19C] (US) a disturbance, an argument (cf. CONBOBBERATE). [SE *con*, with + BOBBERY]

conbobbolate v. [mid-19C] (US) to think, to ponder, to 'calculate'. [CONBOBBERATE + SE *calculate*]

concaves and convexes n. [mid-19C] 'a pack of cards contrived for cheating, by cutting all the cards from the two to the seven concave, and all from the eight to the king convex. Then by cutting the pack breadthwise a convex card is cut, and by cutting it lengthwise a concave is secured' (Hotten, 1864).

concern n. [19C] the penis (cf. AFFAIR n.¹).

concerned adj. [late 18C–mid-19C] euph. term meaning drunk; thus *concerned with drink, concerned in drink* (cf. ADDLED).

concertina n. [late 19C+] (Aus.) **1** a wrinkly sheep. **2** a side of lamb or mutton. **3** a style of leggings with wrinkles in them. [resemblance]

conch n.¹ [19C+] **1** (W.I.) a native of the Bahamas (cf. CONCHY JOE). **2** (US) a poor White native of the Florida Keys. **3** a native of South Carolina (cf. CORNCRACKER n.¹). [SE *conch*, a variety of shellfish for which such people fish]

conch n.² [20C] (US campus) a devotedly hard worker (cf. CEREB). [abbr. SE *conscientious*]

conch-clout n. [19C] a cotton handkerchief (cf. CLOUT n.¹). [CONK n.² (1) and SE *clout*, cloth]

conchers n. [mid-19C–1900s] (Aus.) tame or placid cattle.

conchie/conchy n.¹ [1910s+] a *consci*entious objector. [abbr.]

conchie n.² see CONSHY.

concho n. [1960s] (US) a conscientious objector (cf. CONCHIE n.¹).

conchy Joe n. (W.I./Baham.) **1** a creole White or Caribbean person who has, to all appearances, no Black ancestry (although there will be a distant relation). **2** a poor White. **3** a mixed-race Bahamian, who sees themself as socially superior to Blacks. [CONCH n.¹ (1) + generic *Joe*]

con-con n. [1980s+] (drugs) a dark, oily substance that remains in a pipe after crack or FREEBASE cocaine has been smoked.

concrete n. [1940s+] (W.I.) any starchy, indigestible foods, e.g. dumplings, fufu, usu. with peas (legumes) or beans mixed in (cf. CIRCLER).

concrete overcoat/overshoes/slippers n. [1970s+] a supposed gangland method of murder; the victim's feet are dunked in quick-drying concrete and they are then dumped into a river or overboard from a boat, the irremovable weight ensuring that they drown (cf. CEMENT KIMONO).

condemned adj. [late 19C–1920s] euph. synon. for *damned*; thus *condemnation*, damnation.

condo n. [1960s+] (US) a *condo*minium, i.e. an apartment house in which the units are owned individually, not by a company or co-operative. [abbr.]

condog v. [late 16C–late 17C] to concur, to agree. [*condog* is the source of a long-lived lexicographical 'chestnut'. While assembling his dictionary, the lexicographer Adam Littleton (1627–94) gave the Latin word *concurro* (to meet, to assemble) to his assistant. The assistant, assuming, from the similarity of sounds, that the English followed the Latin, asked Littleton: 'Concur, I suppose, Sir.' Littleton replied tetchily, 'Concur! condog!' Fearing to argue, the assistant listed 'condog' in the manuscript as one of the meanings of *concurro*. It duly appeared in the first edition. Unfortunately the story is marred by chronology, the *OED*'s first citation predates Littleton's work by 75 years]

conductor n. [1970s] (drugs) one who guides a person who is taking LSD. [plays on the LSD TRIP n.³ (1) + SE *bus conductor*]

condy n. [mid–late 19C] *Condy*'s fluid, a strong solution of sodium manganate or permanganate, used as a disinfectant. [abbr.; proper name of Henry Bollmann *Condy*, 19C English manufacturer of chemicals; thus WW2 milit. phr. used by troops serving in the Middle East *maleesh condy's*, lit. never mind the condy's, i.e. forget the preliminaries, let's get on with it]

condy boy n. [1940s–50s] (Aus.) a jack-of-all-trades employed by a brothel. [the use of diluted *Condy's fluid* as a post-intercourse disinfectant]

condy's, the n. [1920s–40s] (Aus.) advice. [*Condy's fluid*, which, as a disinfectant, presumably 'deals with any problem']

cone n.¹ [late 19C] (US) the head. [resemblance]

cone n.² [1980s+] **1** (Aus. drugs) a metal cone with a hole in the centre, usu. made of aluminium or brass and used for smoking cannabis. **2** (US drugs) a conical cannabis cigarette, which is tapered by rolling with two or more papers glued at an angle.

conehead n. [1980s+] (orig. US) a strange and foolish person. [the *Coneheads*, a bizarre space-dwelling 'family', were created for the TV show *Saturday Night Live* in 1976]

coner n. [1950s+] a pickpocket who makes contact with a prospective victim by dropping an ice-cream cone at his or her feet.

coneroo/conneroo n. [1930s–40s] (US) a confidence trickster. [abbr. SE + sfx. -EROO]

coney n. [mid-19C+] (US Und.) counterfeit banknotes.

Coney Island n. [late 19C+] **1** a snack consisting of fried clams. **2** a hot dog, esp. when served in a bun with fried onions, chili sauce and mustard. **3** a long bun filled with meat, cheese and various relishes (cf. SUBMARINE n.²). [the *Coney Island* resort in Brooklyn, New York, where such foodstuffs were the staple of visitors. (1) popular 1870–80 gave way to (2) and (3)]

Coney Island chicken n. [20C] a spiced, heated sausage or frankfurter, esp. when served in a bun with fried onions, chili sauce and mustard (cf. HOT DOG n.¹). [CONEY ISLAND n. (2) + SE *chicken*]

Coney Island head n. [20C] (US) a beer that has more frothy head than actual beer. [the way visitors were defrauded by the bartenders of Coney Island, New York's leisure centre]

Coney Island red hot n. [20C] a spiced, heated sausage or frankfurter, esp. when served in a bun with fried onion, chili sauce and mustard (cf. HOT DOG n.¹). [CONEY ISLAND n. (2) + RED HOT n.¹]

Coney Island whitefish n. [1960s+] (US) a used contraceptive floating at the edge of the beach. [the popularity with lovers of the beaches of New York's Coney Island]

confab n. [18C+] a conversation, an argument (cf. CONFLAB). [SE *confabulation*, a chat, a conversation]

confeck adj. [late 17C–18C] (Und.) counterfeit, fake. [SE *confect*, to prepare or mix up ingredients]

confectionary *n.* [1920s–30s] (US) an illegal drinking establishment (cf. DELICATESSEN; GREENGROCERY n.²; GROCERY n.³; SPEAKEASY). [the term had been used as a euph. for a legal liquor store or small bar in the 19C]

confer the order of the sack *see* GIVE THE ORDER OF THE SACK.

confessional *n.* [19C] the vagina. [where a FATHER CONFESSOR appears]

confess the corn, to *phr.* [early 19C–1940s] (orig. US) to admit an error. [for ety. *see* ACKNOWLEDGE THE CORN]

confidence *v.* [late 19C] (US) to defraud, to swindle. [abbr. SE *confidence trick*]

confidence buck *n.* [late 19C] a confidence trick. [SE *confidence* + BUCK v.²]

confidence-queen *n.* [late 19C] (US) a female detective. [? in plain-clothes she 'cons' her criminal victims]

confiscate the macaroon, to *phr.* [20C] to surpass, to outdo, esp. in excessive or extreme behaviour or of a near-intolerable situation or happening. [ponderously joc. synon. or TAKE THE CAKE]

conflab *n.* [mid-19C–1940s] (US) a conversation, an argument. [var. on CONFAB]

conflabberate *v.* [mid-19C–1910s] to upset, to perturb, to unnerve. [ety. unknown, a nonsense word]

conflabberation *n.* [mid-19C–1920s] a confused wrangle. [CONFLABBERATE]

confloption *n.* [late 19C] an unshapely, grotesquely twisted thing. [nonsense word, ? formed f. SE pfx. *con-*, together + *flop* v., collapse]

conflummox *v.* [19C+] to fool, to confuse, to overcome by trickery. [ext. of FLUMMOX v.¹]

confo *n.* [1930s–50s] (Aus.) a conference. [abbr. SE + sfx. -O]

confound! *excl.* [early 14C+] an all-purpose euph., used as a mild oath, esp. as adj. *confounded*, and excl. *confound it!* (orig. *God confound it!* or *Mahound confound it!*). [a special use of SE *confound* to mean 'bring to perdition']

confusion *n.* (W.I.) **1** [late 19C+] an argument leading to a fight. **2** [1970s] a street fight, a riot.

confusticate *v.* [late 19C–1930s] (US) to confuse. [SE *confound* or *confuse*]

con-game *n.* [late 19C+] (orig. US) a piece of confidence trickery (cf. CON-MAN). [CON v. + GAME n.⁴]

conger *n.* [late 17C–18C] 'A Set or Knot of Topping Booksellers of London, who agree that whoever of them Buys a good Copy, the rest are to take off such a particular number in Quires, on easy Terms' (B.E.). [? SE *conger*, a large species of saltwater eel, or f. Fr. *congrès*, a congress or SE *congeries*, a pile, a heap, a mass. B.E.'s 'knot' became known as the 'Old Conger' and was succeeded *c*.1700 by their rivals, the 'New Conger', publishers, *inter alia*, of Bailey's and Cocker's Dictionaries]

congo/congou/kongo *n.*¹ [18C] tea. [Chinese *kung-fu*, work, and workman; thus *kung-fu-ch'a*, tea on which work or labour is expended; *congou*, *congo* or *kongo* was a type of black tea, imported to England during 18C]

congo *n.*² [19C+] a derog. term for a Black person, esp. one with a notably dark complexion. [US slave trade jargon *Congo*, a slave brought from the Congo nation. The term is also used in the W.I. with an additional element of poverty and a rough appearance]

congo *n.*³ [20C] (Aus./US) a *Cong*regationalist (cf. BAPPO). [abbr. + sfx. -O]

Congo bush *n.* [1960s+] (drugs) marijuana from the Congo area of Africa (cf. AFRICAN BUSH). [SE *Congo* + BUSH n.⁶]

congo patois *n.* [late 19C] (US) slang, usu. Black slang. [CONGO n.² + SE *patois*, a local dialect]

congou *see* CONGO n.¹.

congrats! *excl.* [late 19C+] *congrat*ulations; thus synon.

[1930s] *congraggers*, [20C] *congratters*. [abbr. + sfx. 'Oxford' -*ers*]

coniacker *see* KONIACKER.

conish *adj.* [early–mid-19C] fashionable, smart, genteel; thus (Scot.) *conish cove*, a fashionable gentleman. [? CONY n.¹ on the theory that such a figure may well fall prey to a clever con-man]

coniwobble *n.* [early 18C] a dupe, a fool. [ext. of CONY n.¹]

con job *n.* [20C] (US) a confidence trick. [CON n. + JOB n.³]

conjobble *v.* **1** [late 16C–late 17C] to settle, to discuss. **2** [early 18C] to have sexual intercourse. [SE pfx. *con-*, together + JOB, but note *jabber*]

conjugals *n.* [20C] sexual intercourse, esp. in a marital context.

conjuror *n.* [late 17C–18C] (Und.) a trial judge; *go before the conjuror*, to be tried at the assize (cf. FORTUNE-TELLER). [what he 'pulls out of his hat' is a sentence]

conk *n.*¹ **1** [early–mid-19C] (Und.) an informer, a thief who betrays their accomplices. **2** [early 19C–1900s] a policeman. [CONK n.²; i.e. one who 'sniffs things out']

conk/konk *n.*² **1** [early 19C+] the nose; thus a nickname for one who has a large nose. **2** [late 19C+] a punch on the nose. **3** [late 19C+] the head; thus *off one's conk*, crazy, eccentric. [? f. Lat. *concha*, a shell, and Gk. *kogcha*, anything hollow]

conk *n.*³ [1930s+] (US Black) hair that has been straightened through the application of a special mixture (cf. CHEMICAL HEAD; PROCESS). [*Congolene*, a fiery liquid, combining lye, eggs, potatoes and other ingredients, used in the artificial straightening of naturally kinky Black (Negro) hair]

conk *v.*¹ **1** [early 19C+] to hit, esp. on the nose, to knock out. **2** [1910s–20s] (US) to kill. **3** [1940s] (US) to die. [CONK n.² (3) + echoic]

conk/konk *v.*² [1930s+] (US Black) to straighten hair with a mixture based on Congolene. [CONK n.³]

conk-/konk-buster *n.* [1930s–50s] (US Black) **1** a difficult problem. **2** an intellectual. **3** cheap liquor. [CONK n.² (3) + BUST v.¹; all three meanings imply the straining of one's brain]

conked *adj.*¹ [20C] (US Black) having hair that has been straightened. [CONK n.³]

conked/conked out *adj.*² [1910s+] usu. of a machine or engine, broken, no longer working. [CONK v.¹]

conked *adj.*³ [1950s] (US) drunk. [CONK v.¹]

conked out *see* CONKED adj.²

conked up *adj.* [1970s] (US) injured, hurt. [CONK v.¹]

conker *n.*¹ [19C+] a very hard blow. [CONK v.¹]

conker *n.*² **1** [20C] (US) an old, unreliable car, prone to breaking down. **2** [1970s] a slow driver whose dawdling speed creates a tailback of many others (cf. CLUNKER n.¹). [CONK OUT v. (1)]

conkers *n.* [1990s] bollocks, testicles (cf. APRICOTS). [resemblance to SE *conker*, a horse chestnut]

conkhouse *n.* [20C] (US Black) the head (cf. CONKPIECE). [CONK n.² (3)]

conk off *v.* (US) **1** [1940s] to kill. **2** [1940s] to malfunction, to fail. **3** [1940s+] to fall asleep. **5** [1960s+] to die. [CONK v.¹ (2)]

conk out *v.* [1940s+] **1** usu. of machinery, to collapse, to break down, to malfunction (cf. CRUMP). **2** to die; thus *conked*, dead. **3** to fall asleep. **4** to knock someone out. [CONK v.¹ (1)]

conkpiece *n.* [1940s] (US Black) the head (cf. CONKHOUSE). [CONK n.² (3)]

conk the cardinal, to *v.* [late 19C+] to masturbate (cf. BANG THE BISHOP).

conky/konky *n.* [mid-19C+] a nickname given to anyone with an especially prominent nose. [CONK n.² (1); the best known such figure was the Duke of Wellington, widely known as 'Old Conky']

con-man *n.* **1** [late 19C–1920s] (orig. US) a confidence trickster; thus *con-woman*. **2** [late 19C] (US) a flatterer. **3** [1930s] (US) a former convict. [CON v.; (1) later use is SE]

con-merchant *n.* [1960s+] (US) a confidence trickster (cf. CON-ARTIST). [CON n.^{1} (5) + MERCHANT]

connaught rangers *n.* [1940s–1950s] (bingo) the number 88. [the *Connaught Rangers* (disbanded 1922) were also the 88th Regiment of Foot; their army nickname was The Devil's Own]

connect *v.* **1** [20C] (US) to meet, usu. as *connect with*. **2** [1920s–30s] (US) to succeed in obtaining something, e.g. the spoils of a burglary. **3** [1930s+] (drugs) to obtain drugs, usu. by keeping a specific appointment with the dealer (cf. CONNECTION). **4** [1980s] to achieve sexual fulfilment. [fig. uses of SE]

connected *adj.* [1970s+] **1** (US) being a member of an organized crime syndicate. **2** (orig. US) having links to someone influential, whether legitimate or otherwise.

connected dirty *adj.* [1980s+] (US) having links to a powerful or criminal person, usu. through the payment of bribes. [CONNECTED + DIRTY adj.]

Connecticut River pork *n.* [19C] (US) shad (cf. ABERDEEN CUTLET). [the plentiful supplies of shad in the Connecticut River]

connection *n.* [1930s+] (orig. US) **1** a supplier of drugs. **2** the person with whom one achieves sexual fulfilment. [CONNECT]

connie/conny *n.*^{1} [1930s–40s] (Aus.) a tram or bus *con*ductor. [abbr.]

connie *n.*^{2} [1950s] **1** a Lincoln *Con*tinental. **2** a *Con*stellation airliner. [abbr.]

conniver about *v.* [1930s+] (Aus.) to wander aimlessly. [dial. *conniver*, to stare or gape]

conny *see* CONNIE n.^{1}.

conny wobble *n.* [late 18C–early 19C] a drink made of eggs and brandy beaten up together (cf. CONIWOBBLE). [? CONY n.^{1} + SE *wobble* or cf. COLLYWOBBLES]

cono *n.* [1940s+] (US) the vagina; thus, women in the context of potential seduction. [Sp. sl. *coño*, CUNT n.^{1}]

con out of *v.* [1940s+] to trick someone into handing over or giving up something they would prefer to hold on to. [CON v.]

cons *n.* [1960s+] *Con*verse All-Star basketball boots (cf. CHUCKS n.^{2}). [abbr. tradename]

con safos *phr.* [1960s+] (US) **1** 'nobody can mess with this', a slogan used by the Mexican gangs of Los Angeles, often abbr. as *c/s* and written, as a graffito, after the gang's name. **2** a general term of approval (and latterly used as a magazine title). [Sp.]

consarn *v.* [19C] (US) euph. for to damn; thus used as a substitute for *damn* in mild oaths, e.g. *consarn it!* (cf. CONFOUND!). [SE *concern*]

consarned *adj.* [19C] (US) euph. for damned. [CONSARN]

conscience-keeper *n.* [late 18C] 'a superior, who by his influence makes his dependants act as he pleases' (Grose, 1788).

conshun's price *n.* [mid-19C] (Anglo-Chinese) a fair price. [mispron. of *conscience's price*]

conshy/conchie *n.* [1960s+] (Aus.) a hard worker (cf. CEREB). [SE *conscientious*]

considerable *adj.* [mid–late 19C] (US) a large amount (of), a good deal.

considering *adv.* [mid-18C+] usu. at the end of sentences to mean considering the circumstances, taking everything into account.

consolation *n.* [mid-19C] (US) alcohol, usu. whisky (cf. COMFORT).

consonant-choker *n.* [late 19C–1900s] someone who slurs their 'r's and drops their 'g's.

constab *n.* [20C] (W.I.) a policeman, a constable. [note dial.

constab tick, a cattle tick – its stripes resemble those on the constable's trousers]

constant *n.* [1990s] (US Black) a regular member of a given social scene. [? abbr. SE *constant attender*]

constant screamer *n.* [late 19C–1910s] a concertina. [joc. mispron.]

consti *adj.* [1980s] *consti*pated. [abbr.]

constipated *adj.* [1920s–1930s] reluctant to part with money.

constitutional *n.* **1** [early 19C+] a walk taken for health's sake. **2** [1930s+] (Aus.) gin and bitters. [SE *constitution*, one's physical and mental state]

consult Dr Jerkoff, to *phr.* [20C] (US) to masturbate. [SE *consult* + JERK OFF v.^{1}]

consumah/consumer *n.* [17C–19C] (Anglo-Ind.) a butler. [Persian *khansamah*, house-steward]

consume *v.* [1980s+] (US campus) to drink alcohol. [euph.]

consumedly *adv.* [early 18C] extremely, very much so. [coined as sl., the term was taken up by 18C dramatists and absorbed into literary SE]

consumer *see* CONSUMAH.

consumption stick *n.* [1910s] (Aus.) a cigarette (cf. CANCER STICK). [SE *consumption*, tuberculosis, a disease of the lungs]

contact habit *n.* [1950s–60s] (drugs) the drug-like sensations a non-user, usu. a dealer, gains from constant association with users (cf. CONTACT HIGH). [SE *contact* + HABIT]

contact high *n.* [1960s+] (drugs) the marijuana world's equivalent of passive smoking; the sensations that a non-smoker can achieve through the simple act of being in the same room as those who smoke; thus inhaling the drug willy-nilly, as well as picking up on the particular atmosphere generated by a roomful of smokers. [SE *contact* + HIGH n.]

contact lens *n.* [1980s+] (drugs) LSD (cf. A n.^{3}). [its hallucinatory effects ? + ref. to 'making contact' with one's inner self]

con talk *n.* [late 19C–1900s] (US) insincerity, lies. [CON n.^{1} (5) or CON v. + SE *talk*]

content *adj.* [18C–early 19C] dead. [ironic use of the SE; a euph. that compares with such as 'gone to his heavenly rest' etc]

continent *n.* [late 19C] (US) euph. for hell, e.g. *what the continent do you mean by that?* [? link to CONTINENTAL]

continental *n.* [19C+] (orig. US) something worthless; usu. used as an adj. in combs., e.g. *a continental cuss, a continental copper, a continental damn*, and phr. *not worth a continental* (cf. TINKER'S CUSS). [SE *continental*, a coin issued by the Continental Congress during the American War of Independence (1775–83); the coins lost all value with the ending of the war]

continuando *n.* [late 17C–early 18C] a very long time, usu. in phr. WITH A CONTINUANDO. [Sp.]

continuations *n.* [mid-19C] trousers. [orig. gaiters; trousers 'continue' the waistcoat]

contract *n.* [1940s+] a paid assignment to murder someone; thus phr. *put/take out a contract on*, to arrange to have someone killed, *contract killer*, a killer for hire (cf. HIT MAN).

contrapunctum *n.* [17C] the vagina. [Lat. *contrapunctum*, lit. 'counter-point'. The penis is the 'point' in this context]

contraries *n.* [16C] any form of false or legitimate dice, to be brought into and withdrawn from a game as the cheater desires. [such dice are 'contrary' to those currently in play]

contrary *adj.* [mid-19C+] antagonistic, perverse, obstinately self-willed.

control *v.* [1950s+] (W.I. Rasta) to be in charge of, responsible for, to own, to take.

control freak *n.* [1960s+] (orig. US) a person who is never satisfied unless he or she is in absolute control of a situation. [SE *control* + FREAK n.]

contwisted *adj.* [mid-19C] (US) confused. [SE pfx. *con-*, together + *twisted*]

conundrum *n.* [mid-17C–early 19C] the vagina. [SE *conundrum*, 'a whim, crotchet, maggot, conceit'. ? intensified by 19C 'a thing that one is puzzled to name, a "what-d'ye-call-it"' (*OED*)]

convenience *n.* [19C] euph. use for a privy, a chamberpot.

conveniency *n.* [late 17C–18C] **1** a wife, **2** a mistress (cf. CONVENIENT). [ironic use of SE]

convenient *n.* [late 17C–early 18C] **1** a prostitute (cf. COMMODITY; CONVENIENCY). **2** a mistress.

convent *n.* [mid-18C] a brothel (cf. NUNNERY). [ironic use of SE]

conversate *v.* [1980s+] (US Black) to talk, usu. in a lively, demonstrative manner. [abbr. SE *conversation*]

conversation *n.* [1990s] (US Black) a romantic 'line', used for the purposes of seduction. [CONVERSATE]

conversation fluid *n.* [20C] (US) illicitly distilled whisky (cf. CONVERSATION WATER; EMBALMING FLUID). [it 'lubricates' conversation]

conversation water *n.* [1900s–20s] (US) champagne (cf. CONVERSATION FLUID). [it 'lubricates' conversation]

converse with harry palm, to *phr.* [1990s] to masturbate (cf. ADDRESS CONGRESS; DATE ROSY PALM AND HER SISTER; FUCK MRS PALMER; FUCK PAMELA; GO ON A DATE WITH HANDREA AND PALMELA; GO ON A DATE WITH ROSY PALM AND HER FIVE DAUGHTERS; HAVE A BIG DATE WITH ROSY PALM; HAVE A DATE WITH FISTY PALMER; HIT ON ROSY PALM; MAKE A RENDEZVOUS WITH MRS HAND; MEET MARY PALM AND HER FIVE SISTER; MEET ROSIE HANCOCK; MEET WITH MOTHER THUMB AND HER FOUR DAUGHTERS; MISS FIST; SING WITH ROSIE; TAKE AN OUTING WITH TOM THUMB AND HIS FOUR BROTHERS; VISIT ROSY PALM AND HER DAUGHTERS). [? pun. on the 'hairs that will grow on a masturbator's palm'; ? ref. to Len Deighton's anonymous intelligence agent anti-hero, named Harry Palmer for the films (1960s) starring Michael Caine]

conversion job *n.* [1940s+] a severe beating, with or without some form of weapon. [a healthy body is 'converted' into a seriously injured, even dead one]

convey *v.* [mid-15C+] to steal (cf. ACQUIRE; CONVEYANCING).

conveyance/conveyancer *n.* **1** [mid-18C] a thief. **2** [mid-19C] a pickpocket. [CONVEY + pun on SE]

conveyancing *n.* [mid-18C] theft, stealing (cf. CONVEY). [the sense is intensified by the pun on SE *conveyancer*, a lawyer who investigates titles to property]

convictitis *n.* [1940s–50s] (prison) the illusion, fostered by too long a career in the prison service, that every prisoner is about to attack one for no other reason than that one is a warder (cf. COBITIS). [SE *convict* + sfx. *-itis*, usu. used of a disease]

convincer *n.* [20C] a weapon (cf. EQUALIZER; KEEPER; PERSUADER). [SE *convincer*, that which convinces]

convincing ground *n.* [mid-19C] (Aus.) a place at which prize or grudge fights are held. [the fighters attempt to 'convince' each other of the error of their ways]

convoy *n.* [1930s] (Irish) a party or gathering to say goodbye to a departing emigrant.

conwise *adj.* [20C] (US Und.) well-adjusted to prison life, capable of sustaining one's existence in prison (cf. STREETWISE). [CON n.¹ (6) + sfx. -WISE]

con work *n.* [1910s] (US) insincerity, lies (cf. CON TALK). [CON n.¹ (5) or v. + SE *work*]

cony *n.¹* [late 16C–early 18C] a dupe, the victim of a confidence trick, of card-sharping etc (cf. CONY-CATCHER; GULL). [SE *cony*, a rabbit]

cony *n.²* [early 17C+] the vagina (cf. CUNNY). [SE *cony*, rabbit; the stereotyped sexuality of rabbits + the pubic hair is supposedly reminiscent of the rabbit's tail]

cony-catcher *n.* [late 16C–mid-17C] a confidence trickster. [CONY n.¹ + SE *catcher*]

cony-catching *n.* [16C–late 17C] any form of confidence tricking, spec. card-sharping. [CONY-CATCHER]

cony-dog *n.* [late 17C] one who assists a confidence trickster in CONY-CATCHING. [CONY n.¹ + SE *dog*; lit. a dog that catches rabbits]

cony-fumble *n.* [early 18C] a constable. [mispron.]

coo/cou/cu *n.* [late 19C+] **1** the vagina (cf. COOCH n.¹). **2** a woman regarded as a sex object (cf. COOCH; COOCHIE; COOZE). [abbr./euph. for CUNT n.¹]

coo *adj.* [1990s] (US teen) a general term of approbation. [abbr. COOL adj.³]

coo!/coo-er! *excl.* [late 19C+] an excl. expressing surprise or incredulity.

cooch *n.¹* **1** [20C] (US) the vagina (cf. COOT n.³; COOZE; COO n.; CUZZY). **2** [1910s+] (US) a 'hootchy-kootchy' dance, i.e. belly-dancing; thus [1920s–60s] *coocher*, a belly dancer. [abbr./euph. for CUNT n.¹]

cooch *n.²* [1960s] (US) liquor. [? var. on HOOCH n.¹]

coochie/cookie *n.* [1990s] (US Black) the female genitalia. [COOCH n.¹ (1)]

cook *n.¹* [1930s+] (orig. US drugs) **1** an expert who prepares an opium pipe. **2** a manufacturer of illicit drugs. [COOK v.³]

cook *n.²* [1940s+] (Aus.) a look, a glance (cf. CAPTAIN COOK n.²). [rhy. sl. but note Yid. *guck*, a look, a glance, usu. in phr. 'geb a guck', have look]

cook *v.¹* **1** [mid-17C+] to tamper with, to falsify; thus *cook the books*, *cook the accounts*. **2** [mid–late 19C] to ruin, to spoil. **3** [mid-19C] to bribe, to arrange illicitly. **4** [mid-19C+] (US) to kill, to murder. **5** [mid-19C+] to give someone their due deserts (cf. COOK SOMEONE'S GOOSE).

cook *v.²* **1** [mid-19C+] to suffer from the heat. **2** [1930s+] (US) to die in the electric chair.

cook *v.³* (drugs) **1** [late 19C–1950s] to heat opium before smoking it. **2** [1950s+] to prepare a narcotic (esp. heroin) for injection by heating a solution of powder and water for use in a syringe. **3** [1980s+] to heat cocaine until it hardens (cf. FREEBASE v.).

cook *v.⁴* [1940s+] (orig. US Black) **1** of a musician or group of musicians, to be playing in harmony and particularly creatively. **2** used fig. to cover any activity; thus [1980s] business phr. *we're cooking with gas* ....

cook cucumbers *v.* [1960s+] of a woman, to masturbate. [the presumed use of a cucumber as a dildo]

cook-down *n.* [1970s+] (drugs) the process whereby users liquefy heroin in order to inhale it.

cooked *adj.* **1** [early 19C+] exhausted, finished, destroyed, in serious trouble. **2** [1930s] (US) drunk. [fig. uses of SE + COOK SOMEONE'S GOOSE]

cookee *n.* [19C+] (US) **1** the head cook. **2** a cook's assistant.

cooker *n.¹* **1** [mid-19C] that which settles a situation, a clincher, a finisher. **2** [1940s+] anything exciting e.g. a sexy person, an emotive piece of music. **3** [1950s] (US Black) a sophisticated, worldly person.

cooker *n.²* [late 19C] (N.Z.) a pig. [CAPTAIN COOK n.¹]

cooker *n.³* [1910s+] (drugs) a container, usu. a bottle cap, in which the mixture of heroin and water can be heated before drawing it into a syringe and thence injecting it into one's arm. [COOK v.³ (2)]

cookie *n.¹* **1** [1920s+] an attractive woman. **2** [1920s+] (Glasgow) a prostitute. **3** [1970s] a lesbian who plays the passive 'feminine' role in sex. [SE *cookie*, biscuit, a common example of the equation of sex and food in sl.; cf. BANANA n.²]

cookie *n.²* [1920s+] a man, often with a qualifying adj., e.g. *smart cookie, tough cookie*.

cookie *n.³* [1950s+] (US Black) a derog. term for a Black person who is seen as espousing White values to the detriment of their own background (cf. OREO).

cookie n.⁴ **1** [1950s] (US) $1. **2** [1970s] (US) a cigarette. **3** [1990s] (drugs) crack cocaine in its solid, rock form.

cookie n.⁵ see COOCHIE.

cookie-dipper see COOKIE-PUSHER.

cookie-duster n. [1930s+] (US) a moustache.

cookie-pusher/-dipper n. [1930s+] (US) **1** a young man who errs to the 'feminine side of life', tea parties, conversation, the niceties of dress and of gossip, art, rather than sport etc. **2** a waitress. [*cookie + pusher*; the cakes that such men are continually passing around such tea parties or that waitresses serve in cafés]

cookies n.¹ [20C] **1** any form of desired object, esp. sex or money. **2** emotions, feelings.

cookies n.² [1920s+] the contents of one's stomach, lit. things that have been cooked, usu. in phr. meaning to vomit, e.g. *chuck one's cookies, heave one's cookies, lose one's cookies, throw one's cookies, toss one's cookies, woof one's cookies* (cf. BLOW ONE'S COOKIES phr.¹; SHOOT ONE'S COOKIES).

cookies n.³ [1980s+] (drugs) crack cocaine.

cookie-shine n. [mid-late 19C] (US) a tea-party (cf. COOKIE-PUSHER).

cookie-truck n. [1970s+] (US) the van that transports patients to a psychiatric institution. [KOOK + SE *truck*]

cookie-wagon n. [1920s] (US) a police van, a 'black maria'. [see COOKIE-TRUCK]

cooking adj. [1940s+] (orig. US Black) responsive, appreciative, esp. of an audience. [COOK v.⁴]

cooking adv. [1990s] working or acting with absolute commitment. [COOK v.⁴]

cook on all four, to phr. [1940s+] (Can./US) to be very busy, to be working very well (cf. COOK WITH GAS). [the 4 burners of a typical stove]

cook on the front burner, to phr. [1940s+] (US) to do something very well, to act or think correctly (cf. COOK WITH GAS).

cook-ruffian n. [late 17C–early 19C] (Und.) a bad or bad-tempered cook.

cook someone's bacon, to phr. [late 19C+] (US) to ruin (cf. FRY SOMEONE'S BACON). [var. on COOK SOMEONE'S GOOSE]

cook someone's goose, to phr. [mid-19C+] **1** to kill. **2** to give someone their due deserts.

cook's own, the n. [mid-late 19C] the police force. [a play on regimental nicknames + the force's supposed affection for the cooks working in the great London mansions]

cook up v.¹ [late 19C+] to tamper with, to falsify. [ext. of COOK v.¹]

cook up v.² [1930s–50s] (US Black) to enjoy oneself, to have a good time. [COOK v.⁴ (2)]

cook up v.³ (drugs) **1** [1950s+] to prepare an injection of a narcotic drug, usu. heroin, by heating a measure of the powdered drug plus some water in a teaspoon or bottle cap. **2** [1980s+] to make crack cocaine from cocaine hydrochloride base. [COOK v.³]

cook up a pill, to phr. [20C] (drugs) to prepare a pipe of opium. [COOK UP v.³ + SE *pill*, a ball of opium]

cook up with v. [1980s+] (US campus) to 'neck' with, to pet. [? GET HOT]

cook with gas/electricity/radar, to phr. [1940s+] (orig. US Black) to succeed, to do very well, to tackle a project in the right way, esp. after misdirected efforts have failed, and thus usu. in phr. *now we're cooking with gas*.

cool n.¹ [late 16C] (Und.) a cut-purse. [ety. unknown]

cool n.² [1950s+] (US teen) **1** a temporary armistice between opposing street gangs. **2** temper, poise, composure, attitude to life and ability to deal with it.

cool adj.¹ [early 18C–late 19C] used to describe a large sum of money, e.g. *a cool thousand, a cool hundred*. [? the image of a calm and deliberate counting of that money, esp. since the usu. context is of gambling in some form]

cool adj.² [early 19C+] insolent, arrogant, impudent (cf. ARCTIC). [orig. Eton College jargon *cool fish*, a cocky, self-possessed schoolboy]

cool/kool adj.³ **1** [late 19C+] (orig. US Black) good, fine, pleasing. **2** [20C] (orig. US Black) calm, self-possessed, aware, sophisticated. **3** [1940s+] (orig. US) fashionable, chic, 'with it'. [*cool* is usu. associated with the cool jazz movement of the 1940s, esp. Charlie Parker's record *Cool Blues* of 1947, but a single citation in *DARE* sets (1) at least as early as 1884. Given that the SE 19C use of *cool* meant dispassionate, emotionally withdrawn, and as such a negative, its use as a term of approbation gives it some claim to be the first example of Black bad = good sl. forms, e.g. BAD adj.; WICKED]

cool adj.⁴ [1940s+] (drugs) not carrying or owning drugs, or believing that one has hidden them well enough to defy any search of one's body or premises (cf. CLEAN adj.¹).

cool v.¹ [mid–late 19C] to look at, esp. in *cool esclop!*, look, the police! [backsl.; thus *cool him*, look at him, 'a phrase frequently used when one costermonger warns another of the approach of a policeman' (Hotten, 1867)]

cool v.² (US) **1** [1930s+] to kill, to murder, to assassinate. **2** [1960s+] to die. [the chilliness of the corpse]

cool v.³ **1** [1950s+] (orig. US) to calm down, to deal with a problem (cf. COOL IT). **2** [1950s+] to calm someone or some situation down. **3** [1950s+] to knock out. **4** [1960s] (US) to postpone, to put off. **5** [1980s+] (US Black/teen) to lounge around, to 'hang out' (cf. CHILL v.¹).

cool v.⁴ [1970s] (drugs) **1** to sell heroin. **2** to inject oneself with heroin. [the calming effects of the drug, either as ending withdrawal symptoms or simply removing oneself from 'reality']

cool as a cucumber phr. [early 18C+] unemotional, in total control of oneself. [f. earlier 17C *cold as cucumbers*. Note milit. uses *cool as lambs, cool as a virgin*]

cool as a moose/cool as a moose and twice as hairy phr. [1960s+] (US campus) **1** very fashionable, of both persons and things. **2** handsome. [COOL adj.³]

cool beans! excl. [1980s+] (US teen) excellent! wonderful! [COOL adj.³]

cool breeze n. (US Black/campus) **1** [1980s] a person who is sharp-witted, athletic, well liked. **2** [1990s] a person who thinks themself to be sophisticated but is not. [joc. use of SE + COOL adj.³]

cool-breeze adj. [1960s+] (orig. US) **1** cool, calm. **2** first-rate, wonderful. [COOL adj.³ + fig. use of SE]

cool breeze! excl. [1960s+] excellent, wonderful, first-rate. [COOL-BREEZE adj.]

cool cat n. [1950s+] a sophisticated, competent, unruffled, able person. [COOL adj.³ + CAT n.⁹]

cool-cock v. [1950s] (US) to knock unconscious. [var. on COLD-COCK v.]

cool-crack v. [1940s] (US Black) to knock unconscious. [var. on COLD-COCK v.]

cool crape n. [late 18C] a shroud; thus *be put into one's cool crape*, to die. ['*Cool-crape*, a slight Chequer'd Stuff made in imitation of Scotch Plad' (B.E.)]

cool deal! excl. [1990s] (US campus) exclamation of approval, admiration. [COOL adj.³ + DEAL n.²]

cooled out adj. [1970s+] (orig. US Black) calm, unperturbed, in control. [COOL v.³]

cooler n.¹ **1** [late 17C–18C] a woman, esp. a wife (who 'cools one's passions') as opposed to a mistress or lover (who 'heats them up'). **2** [mid-19C] a glass of beer taken after drinking spirits and water. **3** [late 19C+] (orig. US) a prison. **4** [late

19C+] (orig. US) a punishment or solitary confinement cell (cf. HOLE n.[2]). **5** [20C] (Aus.) a chilly glance. **6** [1930s+] (US Black) a funeral home (cf. CHILL n.[2]; COLD MEAT). [fig. uses of SE]

cooler n.[2] [19C] a 'finisher', a 'clincher', e.g. a knock-out punch, a crushing statement. [COOL v.[2]]

cooler n.[3] [1980s+] (drugs) a cigarette laced with a drug, usu. crack cocaine. [COOL v.[4]]

cool hand n. [mid-19C+] (US) a cool, calm, controlled and competent individual. [note *locus classicus*, the book title *Cool Hand Luke* (1965) by Donn Pearce]

cool-head n. [20C] **1** (US campus) a calm, unflappable person. **2** a pleasant person. [COOL adj.[3] + HEAD (2)]

coolie/koelie n.[1] **1** [mid-19C+] (S.Afr.) a derog. term for an Indian; thus *coolie Christmas*, the Islamic festival of Moharram or the Hindu festival of Diwali, *coolie creeper*, in cricket, a ball that stays low without bouncing, *coolie pink*, shocking pink, seen as vulgar and 'typically Indian', *coolie shop/store*, a shop owned or managed by an Indian. **2** [mid-19C+] (S.Afr.) a derog. term for a Black person, esp. as *coolie-boy*, *coolie-girl*. **3** [mid-19C-1900s] (US) any East Asian. **4** [20C] (W.I.) the traditional Jamaican epithet for East Indians, usu. in the form *coolie-man* or *coolie-oman*. [a variety of Indian languages in all of which the term means lit. a man for hire and thus a (menial) labourer; note Zulu *amakula*, a person of Indian origin]

coolie n.[2] [mid-late 19C] a private soldier. [fig. use of COOLIE n.[1]]

coolie n.[3] [1950s-60s] (US teen) any youth unaffiliated to a street gang. [SE *cool*; he remains *cool* towards their approaches]

coolie n.[4] [1970s+] (US) the anus. [Sp. sl. *culo*, the anus]

coolie n.[5] [1980s+] a cigarette laced with a drug (cf. COOLER n.[3]).

cooling n. [1980s+] (US) relaxing (cf. CHILLING). [COOL v.[3]]

cooling card n. [17C] something that defuses one's enthusiasm or deflates one's passion. [card-playing jargon; in a now lost card-game the *cooling card* was apparently played to quash an opponent's hitherto winning card]

cool it v. **1** (orig. US Black) [1950s+] to calm down, to relax, often as imper. *cool it!* **2** (orig. US Black) [1950s+] to stop, to cease from an action. **3** [1960s] (US) to die. **4** [1960s] (orig. US) to leave. [COOL v.[3]]

cool-lady n. [late 17C-late 18C] a female camp follower, specializing in selling brandy to the troops. [COOL (NANTZ) + SE *lady*]

cool nantz n. [late 17C-early 19C] cognac (cf. COLD NANTZ; NANTZ).

cool off v.[1] **1** [mid-19C+] to kill, to murder. **2** [1930s-60s] to knock out, to subdue with physical force. [COOL v.[2]]

cool off v.[2] (orig. US) **1** [mid-19C+] to become bored. **2** [mid-19C+] to calm down. **3** [1930s] of a criminal, to lie low until the hue and cry has passed. [COOL v.[3]]

cool one n. [1950s+] (orig. US) a bottle of beer (cf. COLD ONE n.[2]).

cool one's copper/coppers, to phr. [19C] to take a drink to ease the parched throat caused by excessive drinking. [SE *cool* + HOT COPPERS]

cool one's cubes, to phr. [1950s+] to calm down, to relax (cf. COOL IT). [COOL v.[3] + assonance or ? *cubes*, fig. use for buttocks]

cool one's jets, to phr. [1970s] (US campus) to calm down, to relax.

cool one's toes, to phr. [mid-late 16C] to be kept waiting (cf. KICK ONE'S HEELS).

cool out v.[1] [mid-19C+] (orig. US) to subdue physically, to kill. [COOL v.[2]]

cool out v.[2] **1** [1950s+] to calm down, often as imper. *cool out!*

also to pacify another. **2** [1950s+] (W.I.) to take a rest from work by lying in the shade of a tree. **3** [1960s-70s] to make manageable. [COOL v.[3]]

cool out v.[3] [1970s] to become chic, smart, 'cool'. [COOL adj.[3] (3)]

cool papa n. [1940s] (US Black) a self-possessed, sophisticated and, as such, alluring male (cf. SWEET DADDY). [COOL adj.[3] + SE *papa*]

cool runnings n. [1980s+] (W.I./UK Black teen) everything is fine, all is going smoothly. [COOL adj.[3] (1) + ext. use of SE *run*]

cool smoke n. [1980s+] (drugs) a smoke of methylamphetamine.

cool tankard n. [late 17C-18C] a cool drink, made of wine and water with lemon, sugar and nutmeg.

cool the beef, to phr. [1950s+] to deal with a problem or a complaint. [COOL v.[3] (1) + BEEF n.[2]]

cool the rock, to phr. [1980s] (US teen) to calm down, to restrain one's excessive behaviour. [COOL v.[3] (1) + SE *rock 'n' roll*]

cool whip n. [1980s+] (US campus) something very new and appealing. [COOL adj.[3] (3) + pun on brandname of the US sweet]

cooly see KALI.

coon n. **1** [mid-19C] (US) a person, esp. a rustic, a peasant. **2** [mid-19C] (US) a sly person, a cunning fellow. **3** [mid-19C+] (orig. US) a derog. term for a Black person (cf. EGG AND SPOON n.[1]; HARVEST MOON; SILVERY MOON). **4** [late 19C-1930s] (US) a petty thief. [fig. uses of SE *racoon*, typified as a cunning creature. Unlike many other overtly racist terms *coon* had a non-racial meaning before its derog. one. Slightly earlier (c.1832) it described any man, especially a sly and shrewd one. A further meaning (c.1840) was of a member of the old US Whig party, which for a while had the racoon as its emblem. By the late 19C the meaning was unequivocally racist, and used as such in Aus. too, where it described not Blacks but Aborigines; in S.Afr., despite its overt racism, the term describes only the music-hall's 'black and white minstrel' or 'chocolate coloured coon', both of whom are white actors 'blacked up' for their performance, à la Al Jolson (1886-1950)]

coon adj. [mid-19C] (US) sly, cunning. [COON n. (2)]

coon v. (US) **1** [mid-19C-1950s] to crawl stealthily (like a racoon). **2** [late 19C+] to pilfer, esp. fruit or other objects of little value. [COON n. (2)]

coon-ass n. [19C+] a Cajun (a person of French descent in Louisiana) (cf. BOOGERLEE). [Fr. *conasse*, the female genitals; thus *conassière*, sl. for Fr. *femelots*, the gudgeon. The Cajuns known as *coon-asses* were fishers of gudgeon]

coon bottom/town n. [mid-19C-1930s] within a larger urban area, that part recognized as reserved for the Black community (cf. BEAN TOWN n.[2]; BUTTERMILK BOTTOM; DARKTOWN; NIGGER ROW; NIGGERTOWN). [COON n. (3) + BOTTOM n.[3]]

coon dick n. [1920s-30s] (US) illicitly distilled whisky (cf. COON JUICE). [COON n. (3) + DICK n.[5] (1), compounded of 'grapefruit juice, cornmeal mash, beef bones and a few mo' things' (Zora Neale Hurston, *Mules & Men*, 1935)]

coonie/coondie/cundy n. [1940s+] (Aus.) a small stone suitable for a missile. [Abor.]

coon jigger n. [mid-19C-1920s] (US) a derog. term for a Black child. [COON n. (3) + JIGGER n.[1]]

coonjine n. [19C+] (US) **1** the rhythmic swaying gait used when loading and unloading freight. **2** a song used by the Black dockhands to set the rhythm for loading and unloading freight. **3** sexual intercourse. [COONJINE v.]

coonjine v. [19C+] (US) **1** to move with a special rhythmic swaying gait, adapted from the shuffling step used by Black dockhands as they walked up and down the gangplanks of

Mississippi steamers carrying heavy bundles and packages. **2** to have sexual intercourse. [? SE *racoon*, it has a notably waddling step or COON n. (3) + SE *engine*]

coon juice *n*. [1920s–30s] (US) illicitly distilled whisky. [COON n. (3) + SE *juice*]

coon-lover *n*. [mid-19C+] (orig. US) a derog. term, as used by racists, for those who are seen as insufficiently hostile to Blacks (cf. NIGGER-LOVER). [COON n. (3) + SE *lover*]

coon out *v*. [1960s] (US) to leave surreptitiously. [COON v.]

coon's age *n*. [mid-19C+] (US) a very long time (cf. DOG'S AGE; IN A COON'S AGE). [the life-span of a SE *racoon* although the phr. is inevitably seen as linked to COON n. (3)]

coonshine *n*. [late 19C] (US) an all-night party. [COON n. (3) i.e. racial stereotyping + MOONSHINE/SE *moonshine*]

coonskin *n*. [20C] (US) a $1 bill (cf. FROG n.⁵). [? as used in the fur trade, when furs were the barterers' equivalent of cash]

coon squall *n*. [late 19C] (US) empty chatter. [COON n. (3) i.e. racial stereotyping + SE *squall*]

coon town *n*. [20C] a derog. term for the Black section of a town or city. [COON n. (3) + SE *town*]

coony *adj*. [late 19C+] (US) sly, cunning. [COON n. (2)]

coop *n*.¹ **1** [16C+] a prison. **2** [20C] (US Und.) a solitary confinement cell. **3** [20C] (US Und.) a hideout.

Co-op, the *n*.² [mid-19C+] the Co-operative Store. [the first such store was opened in the UK in 1856]

coop *n*.³ [1900s–20s] (US) the head, the mind (cf. BELFRY). [? SE *pigeon coop*, on top of a house; note synon. Ger./Yid. *kopf*]

coop *n*.⁴ [1940s] a *coup*on. [abbr.]

coop *v*. [late 19C] (US) to stay, to hide. [note New York City police jargon *coop*, to sleep while on duty in a motel room or similar hideaway]

cooped up *adj*. [late 17C–early 18C] (Und.) imprisoned. [COOP n.¹]

cooper *n*. [19C] a mixture composed of equal parts of stout and porter. [the allowance of as much stout and porter as they liked, which was permitted to coopers (barrel-makers) at London breweries]

cooper *v*.¹ **1** [early–mid-19C] to make presentable, to 'rig up'. **2** [mid-19C] to forge, to counterfeit. **3** [mid-19C] to spoil, to ruin. [fig. uses of SE *cooper*, to make casks or barrels; the journeymen coopers or barrel-makers employed on Thames vessels were meant to mend cargo containers; in fact, they often pillaged them and deliberately broke open hogsheads and barrels]

cooper *v*.² [late 19C] (US) to understand. [? SE *comprehend*]

coopered *adj*. **1** [mid-19C] spoilt, adulterated, worn out. **2** [late 19C] drunk. [COOPER v.¹ (3)]

coopy *n*. [late 19C–1940s] a hen. [it lives in a *coop*]

coosh *adj*. [1910s+] (Aus.) comfortable. [CUSHY]

coot *n*.¹ **1** [late 18C+] a fool, a simpleton, usu. as *old coot*, *silly old coot* etc. **2** [1900s–10s] (Aus.) a general derog. description. [pvb. phr. *stupid as a coot*, ? play on Lat. *Fulica*, the species/ SE *foolish*. The popular link with the undoubtedly eccentric Sir Eyre *Coote* (1762–1823) is specious]

coot *n*.² [1910s+] a body louse. [abbr. COOTIE n.²]

coot *n*.³ (US campus) **1** [1980s+] the vagina (cf. COOCH n.¹). **2** a woman considered solely as a sexual object. [abbr. COOTER n.²]

cooter *n*.¹ *see* COUTER.

cooter *n*.² [1980s+] (US campus) the vagina (cf. SNAPPING TURTLE). [US dial. *cooter*, a freshwater turtle]

cootie/cutie/cutey *n*.¹ [20C] (US Black) an inexperienced, naïve young person, keen to improve his or her status. [fig. use of COOTIE n.² (1)]

cootie *n*.² (US) **1** [1910s+] a body louse, a bedbug. **2** [1970s+] (US juv.) an imaginary germ or 'bug'. **3** [1970s+] a fig. repellent quality that can be picked up from those one dislikes. **4** [1970s] (US juv.) a piece of nasal mucus. [?

Malayan *kutu*, a dog tick; Lighter (1994) rejects this for lack of any real link]

cootie drapes *n*. [1940s] (US Black) a style of trousers, wide and draped and thus a possible home for lice. [COOTIE n.² (1) + DRAPES]

cootie garage *n*. [1920s] (US) the hair, esp. when styled elaborately (cf. LOUSE BAG; LOUSE LADDER; LOUSE TRAP n.¹; LOUSE WALK). [COOTIE n.² (1) + SE *garage*, such a hairstyle may, supposedly, provide a welcome to insect infestation]

cooty *adj*. [1930s+] suffering an infestation of body lice or similar vermin. [COOTIE n.² (1)]

cooze/coozie/coozy *n*. [1920s+] (US) **1** the vagina (cf. COOCH n.¹). **2** a woman (usu. promiscuous or unattractive). **3** sexual intercourse with a woman. [var. on CUNT n.¹/COO n.]

cop *n*.¹ [mid-19C+] **1** (orig. US) a policeman (cf. COPPER n.³). **2** an arrest, esp. in the old (and prob. fictional) cliché, *It's a fair cop, guv, slap the bracelets on*. [note Cumbrian dial. *cop*, a prison]

cop *n*.² **1** [1940s+] (Aus./N.Z.) a good job obtained by shrewdness or luck, an agreeable proposition, a bit of luck or a trick that leads to large profits, often ext. to *soft cop*, *sweet cop*. **2** [1960s] (US) an acquisition. [COP v.¹ (1)]

cop *v*.¹ **1** [early 18C+] to capture, to catch. **2** [mid-19C+] (US) to obtain, to purchase, to get; 20C use esp. refers to drugs. **3** [late 19C+] to steal. **4** [20C] (US) to grab for oneself, esp. unfairly. **5** [1910s–20s] (US) to kill, to shoot dead. **6** [1940s+] usu. of a prostitute, to fellate (cf. COP A BIRD). **7** [1960s+] to acquire, spec. to buy drugs (cf. SCORE v.²). **8** [1960s+] (UK Und.) to receive bribes, esp. of a policeman. **9** [1950s–60s] (US Black) of a pimp, to seduce a girl, spec. with the intention of making her into a prostitute. **10** [1960s+] (orig. US Black) to seduce; thus, of a man, to have sexual intercourse. [OF *caper*, to seize]

cop *v*.² [mid-19C] (Anglo-Ind.) to beware, to take care; thus excl. *cop!*, look out! [Port. *coprador*]

cop *v*.³ **1** [mid-19C+] to experience, to undergo, e.g. *cop a beating* (cf. CATCH v.⁵; COP IT v.¹). **2** [1930s+] (orig. Aus.) to notice, to look at, esp. in phr. used by one young man to another, indicating an attractive woman, *cop a load of that…* or *cop that lot!*, look at them. **3** [1960s+] (US Black) to affect a manner, to pose, esp. in phr. *cop an attitude*. [ext. COP v.¹]

cop a bird, to *phr*. [1940s] (US) usu. of a prostitute, to fellate. [COP v.¹ (6) + BIRD n.²]

cop a broom *see* COLLAR A BROOM.

cop a bundle, to *phr*. [late 19C+] to earn a good deal of money, to prosper. [COP v.¹ (2) + BUNDLE n.¹]

cop a buzz, to *phr*. [1970s+] (US) to get drunk, to get 'high' on a drug. [COP v.¹ (2) + BUZZ n.⁵ (3)]

copacetic/copasetic *adj*. (US) **1** [1910s+] excellent, first-rate (cf. COPASETTY). **2** [1950s+] confidential, secret. [? Chinook jargon *copasenee*, everything is satisfactory, esp. as originally used on the waterways of Washington state. Other etys. include the painfully contrived phr. *the cop is on the settee*, i.e. the cop is not paying attention, which elided into *copacetic* and was supposedly used as such by US hoodlums. A word presumed to be Ital. but otherwise unknown. Fr. *coupersetique*, f. *couper*, to strike; thus striking or worth a strike; the Yid. phr. *hakol b'seder*, all is in order or, earlier, *kol b'tzedek*, all with justice. Note that Lighter (1994) dismisses all these and states 'ety. unknown']

cop a cherry, to *phr*. [1940s+] to take a woman's virginity (cf. CRACK A CHERRY; CRACK A PIPKIN; POP A CHERRY). [COP v.¹ (1) + CHERRY n.¹ (1)]

cop a deaf 'un, to *phr*. [1920s+] to pretend to be deaf or at least not to hear the last statement. [COP v.³ (3) + *deaf one*, i.e. a deaf ear]

cop a deuceways, to *phr.* [20C] (US Black) to obtain $2-worth of something. [COP v.¹ (2) + DEUCEWAYS]

cop a dose, to *phr.* [1940s+] to catch venereal disease. [COP v.¹ (2) + DOSE n.⁴]

cop a drill, to *phr.* [1940s] (US Black) to move off at a steady, regular pace. [COP v.¹ (2) + SE *drill*; the orderly pace of military drill]

cop a drop, to *phr.* (Und.) of police, to accept a bribe. [COP v.¹ (8) + DROP n.⁵]

cop a feel, to *phr.* [20C] (US) to indulge in some form of petting, but not intercourse. [COP v.¹ (2) + FEEL n.]

cop a final, to *phr.* [1940s] (US Black/Harlem) **1** to leave. **2** to get rid of someone who has been used temporarily to help work a confidence trick on a victim. [COP v.¹ (2) + SE *final*]

cop a flower-pot, to *phr.* [1930s] to be severely reprimanded, punished or beaten (cf. COP IT HOT). [rhy. sl.]

cop a/and heel, to *phr.* [20C] **1** (US Und.) to run off, to escape (cf. COP A MOKE; COP A MOPE). **2** (US prison) to attack from behind (cf. YOKE v.). [COP v.¹ (2) + HEEL ON]

cop a/one's joint, to *phr.* [1960s+] (US) to perform fellatio. [COP v.¹ (6) + JOINT n.⁵ (1)]

cop a moke, to *phr.* [20C] (US Und.) to escape (cf. COP A HEEL). [COP v.¹ (2) + MOKE n.² (1), lit. 'grab a donkey']

cop/take a mope, to *phr.* [1920s+] (US) to escape, esp. from a prison (cf. COP A HEEL). [COP v.¹ (2) + MOPE n.²]

cop a mouse, to *phr.* [late 19C] to get a black eye. [COP v.¹ (2) + MOUSE n.⁴]

cop an attitude, to *phr.* [1960s+] (orig. US Black) to take a negative stance on a given topic, to make one's own position adamant despite prevailing opinions and pressures. [COP v.³ (3)]

cop and blow, to *phr.* **1** [1950s–60s] (Black pimp) to exploit an unsatisfactory prostitute for as much money as possible before discarding her. **2** [1970s+] (US teen) to make a purchase (of fast food, drugs, prostitutes etc) and then leave. [COP v.¹ (2) + BLOW v.⁴]

cop and heel *see* COP A HEEL.

cop a nod, to *phr.* [1940s–50s] (US) to have a nap, to go to sleep. [COP v.¹ (2) + NOD n.]

cop/get/have a packet, to *phr.* [1930s+] **1** to be killed or wounded, to get into trouble. **2** to suffer a dose of venereal disease. **3** to gain a great deal, poss. more than one bargained for; this can either be good (more money than expected) or bad (a longer prison sentence than feared). [COP v.¹ (2) + fig. uses of SE *packet*]

cop a plea *n.* [1930s+] (US Und.) a lawyer. [COP A PLEA phr.]

cop a plea, to *phr.* [1930s+] (orig. US) **1** to plead guilty to a lesser charge in return for the dropping of a greater one (cf. COP OUT v.³). **2** to give in, to surrender, to compromise. [COP v.¹ (2) + *plea*]

cop a reeler, to *phr.* [1930s] to get drunk. [COP v.¹ (2) + SE *reel*]

copasetic *see* COPACETIC.

copasetty *adj.* [1920s–30s] (US) excellent, first-rate. [var. on COPACETIC]

cop a/the slave, to *phr.* [20C] (US Black) to work, to go out and find work. [COP v.¹ (2) + SLAVE]

cop a squat, to *phr.* [1940s] (US Black) to sit down; also as imper. *cop a squat!* take a seat, make yourself at home. [COP v.¹ (2) + SE *squat*]

cop a steal, to *phr.* [20C] (US) to steal. [COP v.¹ (2) + SE *steal*]

cop a Sunday, to *phr.* [1930s+] (US prison) to attack suddenly, by surprise. [COP v.¹ (2) + SUNDAY PUNCH]

cop a tude, to *phr.* [1980s+] (US campus) to act in an uncooperative or angry manner. [COP v.³ (3) + (ATTI)TUDE]

cop a walk, to *phr.* [1950s–70s] (US) to leave, usu. as imper. *cop a walk!* go away. [COP v.¹ (2) + SE *walk*]

cop bung! *excl.* [late 19C] (Und.) look out! the police are coming! [COP n.¹ + fig. use of BUNG v.¹]

copbusy *v.* [mid-19C–1930s] (Aus. Und.) to hand whatever one has just stolen to a confederate or a girlfriend. [COP n.¹ + SE *busy*, to busy oneself; i.e. to act fast to elude possible police interference]

cop deuces *v.* [20C] (US prison) to make excuses. [rhy. sl. + COP v.¹ (2) + DEUCE n.² (2); ? ref. to the losing roll of 2 in craps dice]

cope *n.* [mid-19C] a deal, a bargain. [16C SE]

cope *v.* [20C] (Ulster) to defecate. [dial. *cope*, a pile]

Copenhagen capon *n.* [1960s+] (gay) a transsexual. [the reference is to the pioneering operation undergone in Denmark by Christine Jorgensen]

copess *n.* [1950s+] a policewoman. [COP n.¹ (1) + fem. sfx. *-ess*]

cop for *v.¹* [20C] to confess, to own up to, to admit (cf. COP A PLEA phr.). [COP v.¹ (2)]

cop for *v.²* [1950s+] **1** to have a relationship with. **2** (US) of a pimp, to entice a prostitute to join the group of women under his protection. [COP v.¹ (2)]

cop house *n.* [1920s+] (US) a police station. [COP n.¹ (1) + SE *house*]

co-pilot *n.* [1960s+] (drugs) an amphetamine (cf. A n.²). [it helps you 'fly']

co-pilots *n.* [1980s+] (drugs) two or more people taking LSD together. [they are 'flying']

cop it *v.¹* **1** [late 19C+] to get into trouble, to receive a severe reprimand. **2** [1910s+] to be hit, to suffer in a given way, to die. [COP v.¹ (2) + SE *it*; 'it' being trouble]

cop it *v.²* [1960s] to surpass, to outdo.

cop it hot, to *phr.* **1** [late 19C+] to get into trouble, to receive a severe reprimand (cf. CATCH IT). **2** [1910s+] to be hit, to suffer, to die. [COP IT v.¹ (1) + HOT adv.]

cop it sweet, to *phr.* [1960s+] (Aus.) **1** to accept problems without complaining, to get one's due desserts. **2** to have a stroke of luck. [COP IT v.¹ (2) + SWEET adj.²]

cop-killer *n.* [1980s+] (US) a Teflon-coated bullet capable of penetrating the body armour worn by policemen; such bullets are outlawed.

copman *n.* **1** [late 19C] (Aus.) a policeman. **2** [1980s+] (drugs) a drug runner. [COP n.¹ (1) + SE *man*]

cop off *v.¹* (US) **1** [late 19C] to die. **2** [1920s] to meet someone later. **3** [1940s+] to make an excuse. **4** [1940s+] to inform someone of something (cf. COP A PLEA phr.; COP DEUCES). [var. on COP OUT v.³]

cop off *v.²* [20C] to embrace sexually, to indulge in petting; usu. *cop off with*. [orig. northern dial. *cop*, to act saucily or to catch (hold of)]

cop off *v.³* [1920s] to steal from. [COP v.¹ (2) + SE *off*]

cop on *v.* [late 19C+] (Ulster) to seduce, to pick up and, poss., to go to bed with (cf. COP OFF v.²; GET OFF WITH).

cop one *v.* [late 19C–1930s] to hit someone. [COP v.¹ (5)]

cop one's drawers, to *phr.* [1960s+] (US) of a man, to seduce a woman. [COP v.¹ (2) + SE *drawers*]

cop one's joint *see* COP A JOINT.

cop on the cross, to *phr.* [late 19C] (Und.) to discover that someone is cheating, usu. by using cunning or deception oneself. [COP v.¹ (1) + ON THE CROSS]

cop-out *n.¹* [1900s] (US) a chance or spontaneous meeting, esp. a pick-up by a street prostitute.

cop-out *n.²* [1940s+] **1** a flight, an escape, a cowardly compromise or evasion, a retreat from reality. **2** a person who drops out from society. **3** a coward, someone who runs away from problems, a weakling. [COP OUT v.³]

cop out *v.¹* [mid–late 19C] to get into trouble.

cop out *v.²* (US) **1** [late 19C–1900s] (US) to obtain or to take for oneself. **2** [1900s] to steal. **3** [1900s–40s] to arrest. [COP v.¹ (2)]

cop out *v.*[3] [1940s+] **1** to avoid a problem or a difficult situation, to run away, to give up trying. **2** (US Und.) to use legal plea-bargaining to plead guilty to a lesser charge in return for having one dropped. **3** (US Und.) to confess. [COP A PLEA phr.]

cop out on *v.* [1950s–60s] to inform against. [COP OUT v.[3] (3)]

copped *adj.* [1930s+] arrested. [COP v.[1] (1)]

copper/copperhide/copperskin *n.*[1] [late 18C–late 19C] (US) a Native American. [the skin colour]

copper *n.*[2] [mid-19C] a halfpenny; thus *coppers*, mixed pennies and halfpennies. [the colour]

copper *n.*[3] [mid-19C+] **1** a policeman. **2** (US prison) good conduct marks. **3** a prisoner who gains such marks (and who is thus considered to resemble a policeman) (cf. BLOW ONE'S COPPER; COPPER TIME). **4** an informer, whether in or out of prison. [the SE *copper* badges carried by New York City's first police sergeants; patrolmen had brass badges, lieutenants and captains silver ones. Also one who COPS v.[1] (1) or seizes]

copper *n.*[4] [20C] (US) illegally distilled whisky. [SE *copper*, the copper tubes used in an illegal still]

copper *v.*[1] [late 19C–1920s] **1** to arrest. **2** to inform. [COPPER n.[3] (1)]

copper *v.*[2] (US) **1** [late 19C] to steal, to embezzle. **2** [1900s–30s] to obtain, to make sure of getting. [COP v.[1] (2)]

copper-belly *n.* [late 19C+] a fat man. [SE *copper*, a large pot + *belly*]

copper bolts *n.* [20C] human excrement. [colour + shape]

copper captain *n.* [late 19C] a fraudulent, 'self-promoted' officer. [his 'brass' or cheek in posing in this way]

copper-clawing *n.* [late 19C] a fight between two women. [? *cap-a-clawing*, the clawing off of each other's cap]

copper crack *n.* [1990s] ginger female pubic hair. [SE *copper* + CRACK n.[1] (1)]

copperhead *n.* (US) **1** [late 18C–late 19C] a Native American (cf. COPPER n.[1]). **2** [early–mid-19C] an unpleasant person. **3** [mid-19C] a Northerner who backed the Confederacy. [SE *copperhead*, a venomous snake (*Agkistrodon contortrix*) common in the United States]

copper-hearted *adj.* [20C] (US prison) an informer by nature. [COPPER n.[3] (1) + SE *hearted*]

copperhide see COPPER n.[1].

copper house *n.* [1930s] a police station (cf. COP SHOP). [COPPER n.[3] (1) + SE *house*]

copper jitters *n.* [20C] (drugs/Und.) excessive fear of the police, verging on obsession. [COPPER n.[3] (1) + SE *jitters*]

copper-knob see COPPER-NOB.

copper magnet *n.* [1990s] anything or anyone that attracts the unwelcome interest of the police (cf. BABE MAGNET). [COPPER n.[3] (1) + SE *magnet*]

copper nickel see WOODEN NICKEL.

copper-nob/-knob *n.* [mid-19C+] a red-headed person. [SE *copper* + NOB n.[1] (1)]

copper-nosed *adj.* [late 17C–18C] red-nosed (from drinking). [SE *copper* + sfx. *-nosed*, faded in mainstream use by 19C but was revived *c.*1940 by US Black users; albeit their pigmentation cannot turn lit. red]

copper-plated *adj.* [late 19C–1920s] (US) absolute, certain, definite. [var. on SE *gold-plated*]

copper pox *n.* [1920s–1930s] syphilis. [SE *copper* + POX n.[1] (1); f. the folk belief that were one to hold two copper coins beneath one's tongue during intercourse, one's partner would be infected with syphilis]

copper shop *n.* [1910s+] a police station (cf. COP SHOP). [COPPER n.[3] (1) + SHOP n.[1] (2)]

copper show *n.* [1900s–10s] (Aus.) a copper mine.

coppers in disguise *n.* [20C] the C.I.D., i.e. their 'plain clothes'. [COPPER n.[3] (1) + SE *disguise* and/or acronym of *C.I.D.*]

copperskin see COPPER n.[1].

copper-slosher *n.* [late 19C] one who picks fights with the police. [COPPER n.[3] (1) + SLOSH n.[2]]

copper's nark *n.* [late 19C+] a police informer. [COPPER n.[3] (1) + NARK n. (1)]

copper's shanty *n.* [late 19C] a police station. [COPPER n.[3] (1) + SE *shanty*]

copper-stick *n.* [19C] **1** a policeman's truncheon. **2** the penis (cf. BAT n.[7]). [COPPER n.[3] (1) + SE *stick*; (2) is fig. use of (1)]

coppertail/coppertop *n.* [late 19C–1950s] (Aus.) an unimportant person, a person of little social standing (cf. SILVERTAIL). [the inferiority of *copper* compared with silver]

copper time *n.* [20C] (US Und.) time off for good behaviour in prison (cf. COPPER n.[3]; BLOW ONE'S COPPER; GOOD TIME n.[1]). [COPPER n.[3] (2) + TIME n.[1]]

coppertop *n.*[1] [late 19C–1910s] a red-headed person (cf. COPPER-NOB).

coppertop *n.*[2] see COPPERTAIL.

copping *n.* [1960s+] (Und.) the practice by corrupt policemen of taking bribes from criminals, to turn a blind eye when necessary, to drop charges, to lose evidence etc. [COP v.[1] (8)]

copping clothes *n.* [1960s+] (US) of a pimp, a particularly smart, legitimate suit of clothes, worn specifically to entice and seduce potential prostitutes. [COP v.[1] (9) + SE *clothes*]

copping corner *n.* [1980s+] (US drugs) a street corner on which drug dealers collect to sell their wares. [COP v.[1] (7) + SE *corner*]

copping zone *n.* [1980s+] (drugs) that area of a town or city where users will find the main drug market. [COP v.[1] (7) + SE *zone*]

cop shop *n.* [1940s+] (orig. Aus.) a police station (cf. BILL SHOP). [COP n.[1] (1) + SHOP n.[1] (2)]

cop some Zs see COP ZS.

cop the brewery, to *phr.* [mid-19C–1900s] to get drunk. [COP v.[1] (2) + SE *brewery*]

cop the bullet, to *phr.* [mid-19C+] to be dismissed from a job. [COP v.[1] (2) + BULLET n.[2]]

cop the currant, to *phr.* [late 19C+] **1** to surpass, to outdo, esp. in excessive or extreme behaviour or in a near intolerable situation or circumstances. **2** to be highly improbable. [var. on TAKE THE CAKE]

cop the drop, to *phr.* [1910s+] (Und.) of a policeman, to take bribes. [COP v.[1] (8) + DROP(SY) n.[2] (2)]

cop the lot, to *phr.* [1940s+] to gain everything. [COP v.[1] (2) + SE *lot*]

cop the needle, to *phr.* [mid-19C+] to be extremely annoyed (cf. GET THE NEEDLE phr.[1]). [COP v.[1] (2) + NEEDLE n.[3]]

cop the tale, to *phr.* [1910s+] to be fooled by a confidence trickster. [COP v.[1] (2) + TALE]

cop up *v.* [1960s+] (drugs) to buy drugs. [COP v.[1] (5)]

copycat *n.* [late 19C+] **1** a cheat at school. **2** one who mimics another, whether in their work, mannerisms, speech or other faculty. [SE *copy* + *cat*, an unpleasant person]

copyhold *n.* [17C] the vagina. [heavily joc. use of the legal terminology *copyhold*, 'the tenure of lands being parcel of a manor, at the will of the lord according to the custom of the manor' in law of King Richard III, 1483]

copyholder *n.* [mid–late 17C] a drinker who argues about the bill with the landlord. [for ety. see COPYHOLD]

cop Zs/some Zs *v.* [1950s+] (US) to sleep, to have a nap (cf. BAG ZS). [COP v.[1] (2) + Z n.[1]]

cor!/gor! *excl.* [1920s+] euph. for God (cf. COR BLIMEY!; GORBLIMEY!).

coral *n.*[1] [mid-19C] money (cf. CLAM n.[3]; WAMPUM). [? its one-time role as an object of barter]

coral *n.*[2] [1970s+] (drugs) chloral hydrate. [mispron.]

coral branch *n.* [19C] the penis. [literary euph.]

corbie *n.* [20C] a miser, a mean person. [OF *corb*, a crow]

cor blimey! *excl.* [late 19C+] a mild, euph. oath, lit. 'God blind me!' (cf. GORBLIMEY!). [COR! + pron. of SE *blind me*]

cor! chase me round the gasworks! *excl.* [20C] a general excl. of astonishment or incredulity.

cord *n.* [mid-19C] (US) a great deal, a large amount. [SE *cord*, a measure of cut wood, usu. 8ft long, 4ft broad and 4ft high (2.4 x 1.2 x 1.2m)]

corduroy voice *n.* [1950s–60s] (US) a voice that continually fluctuates between high and low. [the up-and-down ridges in corduroy]

cordwood *n.*[1] [20C] (US) a rustic, a farmer. [SE *cordwood*, lengths of wood cut and stacked for fuel]

cordwood *n.*[2] [20C] (US) **1** a kitchen match. **2** a toothpick. [a joking comment on the respective sizes of 'timber' involved]

co-re *n.* [1920s–40s] a *co-res*pondent in a divorce case (cf. CO n.[2]). [abbr.]

core *v.* [early–mid-19C] to steal small articles from shops. [? Rom. *cor*, to steal]

corie/corey *n.* [20C] the penis (cf. PRICK n.). [Rom. *kori*, a thorn]

coring *n.* [19C] petty shoplifting. [CORE]

coring mush *n.* [1930s] a boxer. [Rom. *koor*, to fight + MUSH n.[4]]

corinne *n.* [1980s+] (drugs) cocaine. [initial letters + play on female name (cf. GIRL n.[3])]

corinth *n.* [early 17C–mid-19C] a brothel. [SE *Corinthian*, a wealthy, dissolute man about town; thus a woman who indulges his pleasures. The Greek city of Corinth, home to the temple of Aphrodite, goddess of love, was renowned for its depraved and licentious lifestyle. The term died out in the UK by the 19C but was perpetuated until the mid-century in the US]

corinthian *n.* [late 16C–early 19C] **1** a dandy, a rake (cf. SWELL n.). **2** a regular frequenter of a brothel (cf. CORINTH). [note ancient Gk. sl. *corinthianize*, to associate with courtesans. As 19C SE the term came to mean an idealized form of sportsman, this time in the field rather than the bed-room. It was widely popularized with the publication in 1821 of Pierce Egan's *Life in London, The Day and Night Scenes of Jerry Hawthorne and his Elegant Friend, Corinthian Tom*, the original Tom and Jerry and thus fathers to the eponymous Warner Bros. cartoon and the male leads of the 1970s BBC TV series *The Good Life*]

corinthian *adj.* [late 16C–early 19C] possessing the qualities of a dandy or rake. [CORINTHIAN n.]

cork *n.*[1] [mid–late 19C] a bankrupt. [he bobs up and down like a cork, for lack of pecuniary 'ballast']

cork *n.*[2] [19C+] (US campus) the absolute inability to answer a question in class or to recite a passage from memory (cf. CURL v.). [one's mouth is stopped with a *cork*]

cork *n.*[3] [20C] (US) an Irish person; thus *corktown, cork hill*, the Irish part of a town or city (cf. NIGGERTOWN). [proper name *Cork*, a city from whence many immigrants arrived in the US]

cork *n.*[4] [1930s+] (US) the penis. [ext. of SE use; i.e. as a 'stopper']

cork *v.*[1] **1** [19C+] (US campus) to baffle, to stun into silence. **2** [late 19C+] to hit hard. **3** [late 19C+] to get the better of; thus *wouldn't that cork you?*, doesn't that infuriate or amaze you? **4** [late 19C+] to be quiet, to stop talking. [fig. uses of SE *cork*; (1) pun on SE *cork*, a 'stopper']

cork *v.*[2] **1** [1970s+] of a man, to have sexual intercourse. **2** [1980s] to idle, to waste time. [CAULK + CORK n.[4]]

cork-/corky-brained *adj.* [late 17C–early 19C] foolish, stupid (cf. AMOEBA-BRAINED). [SE *cork*, which is notably light; thus lit. 'light-headed']

corked *adj.* [late 19C+] **1** drunk. **2** constipated. **3** exhausted. [fig. uses of SE *cork*]

corker *n.*[1] [19C] **1** a stiff drink. **2** (W.I.) alcohol, typically strong rum punch (cf. CAULKER). [SE *caulk*, to fill up cracks; as a fig. sealant, rum can keep out the cold]

corker *n.*[2] **1** [19C] the last word in an argument (cf. CAULKER). **2** [mid-19C+] a knock-out punch. **3** [late 19C+] anything or anyone excellent, superlative, first-rate; sometimes used ironically (cf. CAULKER). **4** [late 19C+] an attractive young woman. [SE *cork*, a stopper; the cork fits the top of the bottle and thus 'tops' or 'corks up' all else]

corkhead *n.* [1940s] (US) a fool. [SE *cork* + sfx. -HEAD (1)]

corking *adj.* [late 19C] excellent, wonderful. [CORKER n.[2] (3)]

cork off *v.* (US) **1** [20C] to fall asleep. **2** [1940s] to go mad. **3** [1960s] to produce quickly, easily, to 'knock off'. [SE *cork off*, to stop up with a cork]

cork out *v.* (US) **1** [1950s] to collapse exhausted. **2** [1960s] to fall asleep (cf. CONK OUT v.). [var. on CORK OFF v. (1)]

corks *n.*[1] [mid-19C] (orig. milit.) money. [a cork is something that 'keeps one afloat']

corks *n.*[2] [mid-19C] a butler. [among his jobs is drawing the corks from bottles]

corks! *excl.* [1920s] a mild oath. [? COCK n.[1], God or var. on LAWKS!]

corksacking *adj.* [1970s+] euph. for COCKSUCKING. [coined by Anthony Burgess in *New York Times*, 1972 (cf. FUG n.[2]; FUGH; MOTHER-FOULER etc)]

corkscrew! *excl.* [late 19C] a mild oath, God's truth! (cf. CHEESE AND CRUST!). [mispron.]

corkscrewed *adj.* [1910s] drunk (cf. TWISTED adj.[2]). [fig. use of SE, esp. as a synon. for DUTCH COURAGE]

corkscrews *n.* [mid-19C] corkscrew curls or ringlets.

cork the air, to *phr.* [1980s+] (drugs) to inhale cocaine.

cork up *adj.* [1950s+] (W.I. Rasta) jammed, filled, crowded. [SE *corked up*]

cork up *v.* (US) **1** [mid-19C–1950s] to be quiet, to stop talking. **2** [late 19C] to make someone be quiet. **3** [1960s] to get drunk. [fig. uses of SE *cork* + CORK v.[1]]

corky *adj.* [17C–19C] **1** drunk, tipsy. **2** skittish, restless, frivolous, lively. [CORKED]

corky-brained *see* CORK-BRAINED.

cor love-a-duck! *see* GAWD LOVE-A-DUCK!

cor lumme! *excl.* [mid-19C+] a mild euph. oath, lit. 'God love me!' (cf. GORBLIMEY!). [COR! + pron. SE *love me*]

corn *n.*[1] **1** [19C+] (US) corn whisky (cf. CORNED; CORN JUICE). **2** [20C] (W.I.) rum. **3** [mid-19C+] (US) a drunkard. [SE *corn*, its main constituent]

corn *n.*[2] [mid-19C+] money; thus *earn one's corn, worth one's corn*, to deserve one's wages (cf. BREAD n.[1]; CORN IN EGYPT). [the roles of corn and money as staples of existence]

corn *n.*[3] [late 19C] (US Black) insincere chatter, flattery, deceit. [CON v.]

corn *n.*[4] [1930s+] (orig. US) anything unsophisticated, irritatingly or foolishly old-fashioned or sentimental, hackneyed, trite, inferior (cf. CORNY). [such things supposedly appeal to country people, i.e. growers of *corn*]

corn *n.*[5] [1950s+] (W.I. Rasta) marijuana (cf. HAY n.[3]). [euph.]

corn *n.*[6] [1950s+] (W.I. Rasta) a bullet. [? it resembles a small ear of corn]

cornball *adj.* [1940s+] (US) naïve, unsophisticated. [CORNY]

cornbread *n.* [1950s+] **1** (US Black) a naïve, unsophisticated Southern person. **2** (US) anything old-fashioned, sentimental, hackneyed (cf. CORN n.[4]). [SE *cornbread*, a rural staple in southern US]

cornbread *adj.* **1** [20C] (US) plain, simple, down-to-earth. **2** [1950s] (US Black) conventional, 'square'. [CORNBREAD n.]

corncake *n.* [1960s] (US) $1. [SAmE *corncake*, a cake made of Indian cornmeal, but why?]

corncob/corncob oil *n.* [mid-19C] (US) corn whisky.

corncob v. [1970s+] (US) **1** to have anal intercourse with someone (cf. CORNHOLE v.). **2** to attack, to punish. [the image of forcing a corncob in someone's anus]

corncobber n. [1970s] (US) a countryman, a rustic. [his growing and eating of *corncobs*]

corncracker n.[1] [mid-19C+] (US) **1** a poor White farmer, a rustic (cf. ALVIN; APPLE-KNOCKER n.[2]; COUNTRY BOOKIE). **2** natives of Florida, Georgia, Kentucky or Tennessee. [? their subsisting on *corn* or maize]

corncracker n.[2] [mid-19C+] (US) a good thing. [elaboration on CRACKER n.[6]]

corndog n. [1980s+] (US campus) someone who is socially inept or acts bizarrely. [CORNDOG v.; fig. one who has either suffered or enjoys this; thus essentially a homophobic term]

corndog v. [1980s+] (US) to sodomize (cf. CORNHOLE v.).

corned adj. [late 18C–19C] drunk (cf. ALED UP). [the use of SE *corn* in the distillation of spirits]

corned beef n. **1** [20C] a thief. **2** [1950s+] (prison) chief officer (cf. BULLY BEEF). [rhy. sl.]

corned beef island n. [1920s–30s] a council estate. [a form of architecture that is reminiscent of tins of corned beef]

cornelian tub n. [late 18C] a sweating tub, used in the cure of venereal diseases. [? a pun on Lat. *cornu*, a horn; one's current incapacity is the result of one's HORN n.[2] (3)]

cornel wilder n. [1950s] (Aus.) a hairstyle once popular among Aus. youth. [the film star *Cornel Wilde* (1915–89)]

corner n.[1] [late 19C+] (US Und.) a share, usu. in the spoils of a robbery.

corner, the n.[2] [20C] (Aus.) the junction of the states of Queensland, South Australia and New South Wales.

corner n.[3] [1920s+] (Und.) confidence trickery; thus *at the corner*, working as a confidence trickster. [the image of standing on the corner, waiting for a victim to appear + SE *corner*, to 'put into a tight place']

corner n.[4] [1970s] (Und.) **1** a confidence trick whereby shoddy goods are sold by pretending they are high-grade stolen property and playing on the 'thrill' some people derive from such a purchase. **2** arranging to sell stolen goods and then having fake 'policemen' break in, confiscate the goods and threaten the victim with charges of receiving; the charges can, naturally, be dropped in return for a bribe, which is arranged by a fake 'solicitor', who makes sure there is no real police involvement by assuring the victim that they have no rights in law and that paying and shutting up is the best thing to do. [ext. of CORNER n.[1]]

corner v. [early 19C+] (orig. US) to put into a position of difficulty or embarrassment. [ext. of SE]

corner boy n. [late 19C+] (orig. US) an idler who whiles away the time hanging around on street corners (cf. CORNER COVE; CORNER COWBOY; CORNER MAN; DRUGSTORE COWBOY; LOUNGE LIZARD; SALOON-BAR COWBOY).

corner cove n. [mid-19C] (orig. US) an idler who hangs around on street corners (cf. CORNER BOY). [SE *corner* + COVE]

corner cowboy n. [20C] (orig. US) a youth given to standing around on street corners with his peers, gossiping, fooling around and ogling passing women (cf. CORNER BOY). [SE (*street*) *corner* + *cowboy*]

corner creeper n. [mid–late 16C] a furtive person. [early 18C use is SE]

corner cupboard n. [19C] the vagina. [the 'corner' being the fork of the legs]

corner-ender n. [1920s+] an unemployed loafer. [such people congregate on street corners]

cornerer n. [late 19C] a difficult question. [SE *corner*, to drive into a (fig.) corner]

corner man n. [late 19C] an idler who hangs around on street corners (cf. CORNER BOY).

corney-faced/corny-faced adj. [late 17C–early 19C] **1** acned, heavily pimpled. **2** red in the face (with drink). [SE *corn*, a horny lump that appears on the feet]

cornfed n.[1] [mid-19C] (US) **1** a Confederate soldier. **2** money issued by the Confederacy. [pun on SE *Confed(erate)*]

cornfed n.[2] [1910s] (US) a country person. [their supposed diet]

cornfed adj. **1** [late 18C+] plump, chunkily built. **2** [1920s+] (orig. US) banal, provincial, naïve (cf. CORNY).

cornflake n. [1970s+] an eccentric (cf. TWINKIE n.[1]). [CORNY + FLAKE n.[2] (2)]

cornflakes in a can phr. [1990s] (US campus) beer. [use of corn in brewing]

corn-grinders n. [mid-19C] (US) the teeth.

cornhole n. **1** [1910s+] (orig. US) the anus, the rectum. **2** [1910s+] (orig. US) anal intercourse; thus *cornhole cowboy*, one who enjoys anal intercourse. **3** [1970s] (US) an aggressor, a victimizer.

cornhole v. [1930s+] (US) to have anal intercourse; thus *cornholer*, a sodomite of men or women (cf. CORNCOB v.). [CORNHOLE n.]

cornhusker n. [19C] (US) a farmer, a peasant. [SE *cornhusker*, one who strips the husks from the ears of Indian corn]

cornichon n. [late 19C] (society) a poor shot. [Fr. *cornichon*, lit. a gherkin, and used in Fr. argot to mean a novice or greenhorn]

corn in Egypt n. [19C] money. [phr. *corn in Egypt*, a plentiful supply, f. Gen. 42:2]

Cornish duck n. [late 19C] a pilchard. [the local fishing trade]

corn juice n. [19C+] (US) whisky, whether legally or illicitly distilled.

corn mule n. [1920s–40s] (US) illicitly distilled corn whisky.

corn off the cob n. [1940s+] (Aus./US) banality (cf. CORNY). [play on CORNY]

corn on the cob n.[1] [1970s+] (US Black) sexual intercourse in which the partners are partially clad.

corn on the cob n.[2] [1990s] smegma.

cornpone n. [19C+] (US Black) a rustic, a peasant, esp. a person obviously from the southern US. [SE *cornpone*, a cornmeal cake or bread made of maize, milk and eggs, formed into ovals and baked or fried]

cornpopper n. (US) **1** [1940s] a large truck. **2** [1970s] a cheap car. [? the noise of the exhaust]

corns and bunions n. [late 19C+] onions. [rhy. sl.]

cornshucking adj. [mid–late 19C] (US, South) euph. for DAMNED (cf. COTTON-PICKING).

corn squeezings n. [20C] (US) illicitly distilled whisky. [its main ingredient]

cornstalk n. **1** [early 19C] (US) a tall, thin person. **2** [late 19C–1940s] (Aus.) a European native of New South Wales (cf. GUM-SUCKER). **3** [mid-19C–1940s] (N.Z.) an Australian. [their characteristic tall slimness. Like corn, they 'shoot up']

cornstealer n. [mid-19C] the human hand.

cornswoggled see HORNSWOGGLED.

cornthrasher n. [19C] (US derog.) a farmer, a rustic (cf. APPLE-KNOCKER n.[2]).

cornucopia n. **1** [19C] the vagina. **2** [late 19C] (US) a rich person. [Lat. *cornucopia*, the horn of plenty + ? pun on HORN n.]

corn up v. [late 19C] (US) to get drunk. [CORN n.[1] (1)]

cornuted adj. [late 17C–early 18C] cuckolded. [lit. 'horned']

corny adj. [1930s+] sentimental, naïve, unsophisticated. [such characteristics are attributed to country folk, surrounded by cornfields]

corny-faced see CORNEY-FACED.

coroner n. [mid–late 19C] a heavy fall. [i.e. one that may prove fatal and lead to the coroner's court]

corp *n.*[1] [20C] (orig. milit.) *corp*oral. [abbr.]

corp *n.*[2] [20C] (Ulster) a useless person. [SE *corpse*]

corpie *n.* [1940s+] (W.I.) a policeman. [SE *corporal*]

corporal/corporal love *n.* [20C] (US) the penis. [pun on SE; it 'stands to attention']

corporate *adj.* [1980s+] (US campus) appearing sophisticated, business-like. [ext. of SE use]

corporation *n.* [18C–late 19C] the body or stomach, esp. when fat. [play on ALDERMAN *n.*[1] (4)]

corporation cocktail *n.* [1970s] coal gas bubbled through milk, a down-and-out alcoholic's tipple (cf. BACKLANDS BREE). [although in an age of natural gas this drink is redundant]

corporation hair oil *n.* [1980s+] (Irish) water, as used in smoothing down the hair.

corporosity *n.* [mid-19C+] (US) one's self, one's being, one's body, esp. in phr. *how does your corporosity sagaciate?*, how do you feel? [Lat. *corpus*, the body]

corpse *v.* [late 19C] to kill, to murder. [abbr. SE *to make a corpse of*; note theatrical use *corpse*, to cause (intentionally or not) a fellow performer to forget their lines and/or laugh on stage; thus to make him or her 'die']

corpse-provider *n.* [mid-19C–1920s] a doctor. [cynical assessment of their role]

corpse-reviver *n.* [mid-19C+] (orig. US) a kind of mixed drink, now esp. a pick-me-up for a hangover (cf. ALLEVIATOR).

corral *n.* [1960s–70s] a group of prostitutes working for a single pimp (cf. STABLE). [ext. of SE use]

corral *v.* [mid-19C+] (orig. US) to secure, to lay hold of, to seize, to capture, to 'collar'. [orig. Sp. *corral*, an enclosed place, yard, courtyard, pen, poultry-yard etc]

corral the tadpoles, to *phr.* [1990s] to masturbate. [SE *corral* + the *tadpole*-like shape of sperm under a microscope]

correct card *n.* [mid–late 19C] the 'done thing', the fashionable object or style. [racing use]

correct tittup, the *phr.* [late 19C–1900s] the right thing. [SE *correct* + *tittup*, 'get-up', style of dress, ult. dial. *tittup*, an impudent or forward woman, a hussy]

corroboree *n.* [20C] (Aus.) a social gathering, a noisy party, a disturbance. [a word in the extinct language of Port Jackson, New South Wales; *corroboree*, an Aborigine dance held at night by moonlight or a bush fire, either of a festive or warlike character]

corroboree water *n.* [1920s+] (Aus.) cheap wine. [CORROBOREE + SE *water*]

corrode *v.* [1970s+] (US campus) to be overcome with disgust or repulsion. [SE *corrode*, to eat away at, to wear away, esp. through the action of chemicals on metal]

corroded *adj.* [1970s+] **1** (US Black) unappealing, unattractive (cf. CORRODE). **2** (US) very drunk.

corybungo/corybungus *n.* [early 19C] (orig. boxing) the posterior, the buttocks. [ety. unknown; ? link to SE *bung*, a stopper]

'cos *conj.* [early 19C+] because.

cosa *n.* [1980s+] (drugs) marijuana. [? Sp. *cosa*, a thing; thus euph.]

cosey *n.* [late 19C–1900s] **1** a love affair (cf. CASE *n.*[5]). **2** 'a small, hilarious public-house, where singing, dancing, drinking etc goes on at all hours' (Ware). [SE *cosy*]

cosh *n.* [mid-19C+] a stout stick, bludgeon or truncheon, a 'life-preserver'; thus *cosh-bandit*, *cosh-boy*, *cosh-man*, *the cosh*, one who uses a cosh. [echoic. Note dial. *cosh*, stick (of any kind), but it may not predate sl.]

cosh *v.* [mid-19C+] to hit (with a bludgeon or 'life-preserver'). [COSH *n.*]

cosh! *excl.* [19C] an extra-mild euph. for God! (cf. ADAD!) [var. of GOSH!]

cosh-carrier *n.* [late 19C] one who works with and acts as bodyguard for a prostitute. [COSH *n.* + SE *carrier*]

cosher *v.* [mid-19C–1920s] to talk amicably and in a relaxed manner. [dial. *cosh*, comfortable, snug; ult. SE *cosy*]

coslush! *see* KERSLOSH!

cosmic *adj.* [1970s+] excellent, first-rate, perfect. [SE *cosmic*, i.e. the contemporary interest in psychedelic drugs]

cosmo *adj.* [1980s+] (US campus) fashionable, trendy. [fig. use of abbr. SE *cosmopolitan*]

cossack *n.* [mid-19C+] a policeman, esp. one used to break a strike. [proper name *Cossack*, the Turkish tribe living to the north of the Black Sea, who were organized into cavalry and fought for the Polish, then the Russian army; ult. Turki *quzzaq*, adventurer, guerilla]

cossie/cozzie *n.* [1920s+] (orig. Aus./S.Afr.) a swimming costume. [abbr.]

cost *v.* [late 19C+] to prove expensive, to cost a great deal.

cost a bomb, to *phr.* [1960s+] to cost a great deal. [ext. of COST]

costa del crime *n.* [1980s+] that part of southeastern Spain which a large number of British criminals have chosen to make their homes. [coined by tabloid press on model of tourist brochure SE *Costa del Sol*]

cost a packet, to *phr.* [1960s+] to cost a great deal. [SE *cost* + PACKET *n.*[3]]

costard *n.* [16C–late 18C] the human head (cf. BEAN *n.*[4]). [SE *costard*, a large apple]

coster *n.* [mid–late 19C] *n.* costermonger. [abbr.; orig. *costard-monger*, apple seller, a street seller of fruit or vegetables, poultry or fish. 'A great being in low life, generally a sort of prince ... . To be really royal he must make money, but save nothing, dress beautifully ... , be handsome in a rough way, be always flush of cash and liberal with it, possess a handsome girl or wife ... and above all, fight well, and be always to fight. Reign generally extends five years (nineteen to twenty-four), when he either takes a shop and does well, takes to drink and does worse, or growing ancient, grizzly, or broken with disease, loses a fight, abdicates and sinks into the ranks' (Ware). Hotten (1860) echoes this picture, noting their use of 'a Cant or so-called *back Slang* language']

coster *v.* [mid–late 19C] to work as a costermonger or to act in a way expected of a coster. [COSTER *n.*]

cost ya!/it'll cost ya! *excl.* [1960s+] it will *cost you* something, i.e. don't ask for favours, but most things can be done – for a price. [abbr.]

cosy *v.* [1930s+] (orig. US) to comfort, to reassure, to delude. [ext. of SE use]

cosy up to *v.* [1930s+] (orig. US) to become intimate with, to ingratiate oneself with.

cot *n.* [late 17C–late 18C] a man who meddles in 'women's work' around the house (cf. COTBETTY; COCKQUEAN). [abbr. COTQUEAN]

cotbetty *n.* [19C+] a man who meddles in 'women's work' around the house (cf. COCKQUEAN). [orig. Lincolnshire dial. The term survived up to mid-20C in areas of the US]

cot-case *n.* [1930s+] (Aus./N.Z.) **1** an invalid (cf. BASKET CASE). **2** a drunkard. [(1) one who is confined to their bed. (2) fig. use of (1)]

cotch *n.* [1970s+] (S.Afr.) sickness, vomit. [COTCH *v.*[3]]

cotch *adj.* [1970s+] (S.Afr.) unpleasant, disgusting. [COTCH *v.*[3]]

cotch *v.*[1] [20C] (W.I.) to shirk work, to behave lazily. [*cotch*, to lean on, ult. f. SE *scotch*, to wedge or block]

cotch/cotch up *v.*[2] [1950s+] (W.I. Rasta) to support something else, as with a forked stick, to balance something or place it temporarily; thus *beg someone a cotch*, to find a place on a crowded bus seat or bench, *cotch a while*, to stay somewhere temporarily. [UK dial. *scotch*, to squeeze or wedge in]

cotch/kotch v.[3] [1970s+] (S.Afr.) to vomit. [Afk. *kots*, to vomit]

coté-si-coté-la/koté-si-koté-la n. [20C] (W.I.) amusing (rather than pointedly malicious) gossip. [Fr. 'on this side and on the other']

cot house *see* RAG HOUSE.

'cotics n. [1980s+] (drugs) nar*cotics*. [abbr.]

cotquean n. [late 16C–early 19C] an effeminate man, who is seen as dealing too keenly with domestic duties that are properly those of his wife (cf. COTBETTY; COCKQUEAN). [SE *cotquean*, a peasant housewife]

cotso! excl.[1] [18C] euph. for God's oath!

cotso! excl.[2] [mid-18C] a general excl. of annoyance, surprise etc. [var. on CATSO!]

Cotswold lion n. [15C–late 18C] a sheep (cf. LAMMERMOOR LION).

cott *see* ENDACOTT.

cottage n. **1** [late 19C+] a public convenience. **2** [1950s+] (gay) anywhere male homosexuals gather for sex, often a public lavatory (cf. GLORY HOLE n.[2]). [categorized by Ware as a usage of 'fast youths' and attributed to 'the published particulars of an eccentrically worded will in which the testator left a large fortune to be laid out in building "cottages of convenience"']

cottage/cottage crawl v. [1950s+] (gay) to frequent public lavatories for sex. [COTTAGE n. + SE *crawl*]

cotterell's salad n. [late 18C] hemp (cf. SIR JAMES COTTER'S SALAD). [a pun on proper name Sir James *Cotterell*, an Anglo-Irish nobleman, hanged for rape, itself both a crime and a plant, *Brassica napus*]

cotton n.[1] [1930s+] (drugs) a small piece of material through which heroin has been sucked up into a syringe and which can be boiled, when no better supplies exist, to extract one final measure of heroin.

cotton n.[2] [1930s+] money. [its role as a commodity; it 'sews' life together]

cotton n.[3] [1970s+] (US Black) the female pubic hair. [resemblance + abbr. COTTON AND WOOL]

cotton and wool n. [19C] the pubic hair. [resemblance]

cotton brothers n. (drugs) cocaine, heroin and morphine. [all of which are filtered through a COTTON n.[1] before injection]

cotton-chopper n. [1970s] (US) a derog. term for a Southerner. [play on SE; the one-time importance of cotton in the economy of the Southern states]

cotton curtain n. [1950s] (US Black) the Southern states, esp. as seen by those Blacks who had moved north during the previous decade. [for ety. *see* COTTON-CHOPPER + a play on SE phr. the *iron curtain*]

cottonhead n. [1930s+] (US) a fool. [SE *cotton* + sfx. -HEAD (1)]

cotton is low phr. [20C] (US) a warning to a woman that her slip is showing, also as *cotton is going down, cotton is hanging (below the market), cotton is pretty*.

cotton lord n. [mid-19C] a wealthy Manchester cotton manufacturer (cf. COTTONOPOLIS).

cottonmouth n. [1960s+] **1** the dry mouth that comes with a hangover. **2** (drugs) a mouth that has become dry through smoking marijuana.

cottonocracy n. [mid-19C] cotton magnates viewed as a group. [SE *cotton* + (arist)*ocracy*]

cotton/cotton on to v. **1** [late 17C+] to agree, to get on with. **2** [1920s+] to understand, to get to know about. [SE *cotton*, to succeed, to prosper. Hotten (1859) suggests to adhere to, like cotton threads sticking to a rough or napped material]

cottonopolis n. [mid-19C] Manchester (cf. COALOPOLIS; COTTON CORD; COTTTONOCRACY). [its world-dominating 19C cotton industry]

cotton picker n. (US) **1** [1910s+] an unpleasant, unpopular person. **2** [1930s+] a derog. term for a Black person. [COTTON-PICKING]

cotton-pickers n. [1960s+] (US) the hands. [their function]

cotton-picking adj. [1900s+] (US) **1** a general term of abuse, second-rate, vulgar, insignificant (cf. CHICKEN-PLUCKING; CORN-SHUCKING). **2** a euph. for DAMNED. [the role of the slaves who picked cotton in the American South and as such an implicitly racist term]

cottontail n. [1960s+] (US) an attractive young woman (cf. BUNNY n.[2]). [the common rabbit of the United States (*Lepus sylvaticus*), which has a white fluffy tail + the trad. sexuality of rabbits]

cottontop n.[1] [mid-late 19C] a 'loose' woman who keeps up quasi-respectable appearances. [a style of stockings of which the lower, visible portion was silk and the remainder cotton]

cottontop n.[2] [20C] (US) **1** a person with light-coloured hair, a white blond(e). **2** a Swede. [equation of white cotton buds with hair; (2) stereotypically blond Swedes]

cotton up/up to v. [mid-late 19C] to make friendly overtures towards (cf. COTTON WITH).

cotton/cotton together with v. [17C] **1** of people, to get on with. **2** of things, to suit, to agree. [the way in which cotton stitches two pieces of material into one garment]

cotzooks! excl. [early 18C] a general oath, lit. 'God's hooks' (cf. GADZOOKS!).

cou *see* COO n.

couch v. [1980s+] (US) to lounge around on the couch (watching television). [COUCH POTATO]

couch a hogshead/cod's head, to phr. [early 16C–early 19C] (Und.) to lie down and sleep. [SE *couch*, to lie down + SE *hogshead*, comparing the sleeper to a recumbent pig or COD'S HEAD]

couch a porker, to phr. [18C] to lie down and sleep. [var. on COUCH A HOGSHEAD]

couch case n. [1960s+] an eccentric, a mad person, one in need of psychiatric help. [the traditional analyst's *couch* + CASE n.[6]]

couch checkers n. [1960s] (US) love-making on a couch. [SE *couch* + *checkers* (UK draughts)]

couch commander n. [1980s+] (US campus) **1** a TV remote control unit. **2** the person operating the controller (cf. COUCH POTATO).

couch cootie n. [1910s–20s] (US) a poor or miserly man who prefers to court a woman in her own house than take her out on the town (cf. LOUNGE LIZARD). [SE *couch* + COOTIE n.[2] (1)]

couch hockey n. [1990s] sexual intercourse (on a couch). [the penis is presumably the 'stick', the vagina the 'goal']

couch hockey for one n. [1990s] masturbation. [COUCH HOCKEY]

couch potato n. [1980s+] (orig. US) one who is addicted to watching TV and who does this while lying on the couch, as inert and brain-dead as a potato (cf. COUCH COMMANDER).

cougar juice/milk n. [20C] (US) rough, illicit whisky, esp. that sold during the Prohibition (1920s).

cough n. [1920s+] a confession (esp. one that is presumed to be sincere and factual). [COUGH v.]

cough/cough it v. [late 19C+] **1** (orig. US) to confess, to inform. **2** to vomit (cf. COUGH UP).

cough and sneeze n. [late 19C+] cheese. [rhy. sl.]

cough and stutter n. [20C] butter. [rhy. sl.]

cough drop n. **1** [late 19C+] poison, or anything disagreeable. **2** [late 19C+] a disagreeable person. **3** [late 19C+] a 'character', a 'card'. **4** [1940s+] (S.Afr.) a pretty woman. [fig. uses of SE; (1) the slogan of a popular cough lozenge, 'cough no more']

cough it *see* COUGH v.

cough medicine/syrup n. [1910s] (US) whisky (cf. COMFORT; CONSOLATION).

cough up v. [late 19C+] **1** to reveal, to hand over (objects or information) (cf. CHOKE UP). **2** to vomit, ext. as *cough up one's guts* (cf. COUGH). [ext. of COUGH + SE]

could/would fuck up a wet dream phr. [1960s+] referring to one who is exceptionally incompetent, stupid or clumsy.

could it be ... Satan? phr. [1980s+] (US campus) a reaction to something seen as naughty. [the catchphrase of the Church Lady, in the TV show *Saturday Night Live*]

couldn't beat a carpet phr. [late 19C+] a phr. used to indicate weakness.

couldn't blow the froth off a glass of beer phr. [1980s] (Aus.) a phr. used in contemptuous dismissal of a weakling, an incompetent or other inadequate, also as *couldn't find a grand piano in a one-roomed house, ... knock the dags off a sick canary, ... knock the skin off a rice-pudding, ... pick a seat at the pictures, ... tell the time if the town-hall clock fell on top of him/her, ... train a choko vine over a country dunny.*

couldn't fight a bag of shit phr. [20C] (Aus.) a phr. used of a poor fighter.

couldn't fight one's way out of a paper bag phr. [20C] (orig. Aus.) a phr. used to imply physical weakness on the part of the subject.

couldn't get pussy in a cathouse phr. [1970s] (US Black) phr. used of someone who is utterly incompetent. [play on PUSSY n.[1] (1)]

couldn't hit him/her in the behind with a red apple phr. [1990s] (US Black) a phr. used of a conceited or arrogant person, a headstrong person or one who believes themselves intellectually superior.

couldn't knock/pull a sick moll off a pisspot phr. [1950s+] (Aus.) a phr. used of a weakling or coward. [play on sl.]

couldn't organize a fuck in a brothel phr. [1950s+] a phr. used to indicate that the subject is utterly incompetent.

couldn't organize/run a piss-up in a brewery phr. [1930s+] a phr. used of an individual with such minimal competence that even provided with everything necessary to achieve a given aim, that aim remains beyond them.

couldn't pull a sick moll off a pisspot see COULDN'T KNOCK A SICK MOLL OFF A PISSPOT.

couldn't pull the tail out of a peewee phr. [1980s+] (Aus.) said of a weakling.

couldn't run a piss-up in a brewery see COULDN'T ORGANIZE A PISS-UP IN A BREWERY.

council gritter n. [1990s] the anus. [rhy. sl. *council gritter* = SHITTER n.[1] (1)]

council houses n. [1920s+] trousers. [rhy. sl.]

councillor of the piepowder court n. [mid-18C–mid-19C] a pettifogging lawyer. [SE *Court of Piepowders*, the court of wayfarers or travelling traders; ult. Fr. *pieds poudreux*, dusty feet]

council-of-ten n. [mid-19C] the toes of a man whose feet turn inwards when he walks. [proper name *Council of Ten*, a secret tribunal of the Venetian Republic (1310–1797)]

count n. [mid-19C] a dandy, a swell. [play on SE]

count v. [mid-19C] to reckon, to consider, to believe. [SE *count*, account regard, hold that]

counter-caterpillar n. [early 18C] a constable. [SE *counter*, a prison attached to a city court or a mayor's office + CATERPILLAR n. (1), (2)]

counterfeit crank n. [16C–early 19C] (Und.) a mendicant villain who specializes in faking sickness, esp. epilepsy; he would often display convincingly horrific sores and wounds, created by the application of various herbs. [SE *counterfeit* + Du. or Ger. *krenk*, sickness]

counter-hopper n. [mid-19C] a store clerk, a male shop assistant. [var. on COUNTER-JUMPER]

counter-jumper n. [mid-19C–1900s] **1** a store clerk, a male shop assistant. **2** one who has 'ideas above his or her station' and who wishes, as it were, to 'jump the counter' to the customers' side. [play on SE]

counter-rat n. [17C–early 18C] **1** an inferior officer of a counter. **2** a criminal inmate of a counter. [SE *counter*, a (debtor's) prison + SE *rat*]

countess/duchess of puddle-dock n. [mid-17C–mid-19C] a self-appointed but spurious aristocrat. [*Puddle Dock* in London, now the site of the Mermaid Theatre, but orig. a large stagnant pool off the River Thames]

count in v. [mid-19C+] (orig. US) to include in a reckoning, esp. in phr. *count me in*, include me, don't forget me; thus the reverse, *count out, count me out.*

counting-house n. [late 19C] the human face. [mispron. SE *countenance*]

count lasher n. [1950s] (W.I.) a womanizer, a Don Juan. [SE *count* + LASHER n.[2]]

count no-account n. [late 19C–1910s] (Can.) one who poses fraudulently as an aristocrat. [SE *count* + *no-account*]

country adj. [19C+] (US) all-purpose ref. to a lack of sophistication, naïveté, and similar rustic stereotypes; usu. in combs., e.g. *country boob, country gook, country hink, country ike, country jig, country joker, country peck, country punk, country pumpkin, country rube, country slicker, country squash.* See also combs. below.

country bookie/boo-boo/buck n. [20C] (W.I.) an unsophisticated country person (cf. APPLE-KNOCKER n.[2]; BOBO-JOHNNY; CORNCRACKER n.[1]; COUNTRY COKES; COUNTRY CRACKER; COUNTRY GAWK; COUNTRY HICK; COUNTRY JAY; COUNTRY JERK; COUNTRY JOHNNY; COUNTRY PUT). [SE *country* + ? BUCK n.[1] (5)]

country-captain n. [late 18C–mid-19C] (orig. Anglo-Ind.) a very dry curry, usu. with a spatchcocked chicken. [the dish was esp. popular among *country captains*, masters of *country ships*, vessels that traded between the ports of the East Indies]

country chub n. [early 18C] a fool, a dupe. [SE *country* + CHUB n.[1] (2)]

country cokes n. [early 18C] a country fool, a rustic simpleton (cf. COUNTRY BOOKIE). [SE *country* + COKES]

country cousin n.[1] [19C+] (US) euph. for menstruation. [such relations make regular, if unwanted, visits]

country cousin n.[2] [late 19C+] a dozen. [rhy. sl.]

country cracker/gawk n. [19C] (US) an unsophisticated, backward country-dweller (cf. COUNTRY BOOKIE). [SE *country* + CRACKER n.[4]/GAWK]

country harry n. [late 18C] a waggoner. [SE *country* + proper name *Harry* as generic]

country hick n. [early 18C] a country person, a rustic (cf. COUNTRY BOOKIE). [SE *country* + *hick*]

country jack see JACK n.[20].

country jake see JAKE n.[1].

country jay n. [late 19C–1910s] a country person, a rustic (cf. COUNTRY BOOKIE). [SE *country* + JAY]

country jerk n. [20C] (US) a country person, a rustic (cf. COUNTRY BOOKIE). [SE *country* + JERK (OFF) n.]

country johnny n. [19C] an unsophisticated country person (cf. COUNTRY BOOKIE). [SE *country* + JOHNNIE n.[2]]

country put n. [late 17C–late 18C] a country person, a rustic (cf. COUNTRY BOOKIE). [SE *country* + PUT n.[1] (1)]

country work n. [19C] work that progresses very slowly. [supposed tardiness of rural workers]

count the railings, to phr. [mid-19C–1910s] to be hungry. [SE *count* + RAILINGS n. (1)]

count worms/the worms, to phr. [20C] to be dead.

county *n.* [1950s–60s] (US) trousers that resemble those worn in county prisons.

county beef *n.* [20C] (US) deer that has been illegally shot by poachers (cf. CAMP MEAT). [note synon. US regional (Maine) *orchard beef*]

county crop *n.* [mid-19C] a rough haircut, shorn to equal length all round the scalp. [SE *county* (*prison*) + *crop*; i.e. the sort of crop given to inmates of such institutions]

county down *n.* [19C] the female pubic hair (cf. DOWNSHIRE). [pun on *county*/CUNT(Y) + SE *down*, any substance of a feathery or fluffy nature]

county hotel *n.* [1960s+] (US) a county prison (cf. AKERMAN'S HOTEL). [SE *county* + HOTEL]

county mountie *n.* [1970s+] (US) a local (rather than state) policeman. [SE *county* + *mountie*, a member of the Royal Canadian Mounted Police]

Coupar justice see CUPAR JUSTICE.

couple, a *n.* [late 19C+] several drinks; at least, but not restricted to, two.

couple-beggar *n.* [mid-19C] a complaisant clergyman who specializes in solemnizing marriages among the inmates of London's Fleet Prison (cf. BUCKLE-BEGGAR).

couple freak *n.* [1970s+] in sex contact advertisements, a couple who seek a man to join them in sex. [SE *couple* + FREAK *n.* (4)]

couple of bob *n.* [1960s+] a reasonably large sum of money, usu. in phr., e.g. *that must have cost a couple ...* . [deliberate understatement, lit. two shillings]

couple of cents *n.* [1960s] (US Black) $2. [CENT]

couple of chips short of a fish dinner *phr.* [20C] not very intelligent (cf. NOT ALL THERE).

couple of ducks *n.* [1950s+] (bingo) the number twenty-two.

couple of shakes see BRACE OF SHAKES.

couple of ticks *phr.* [20C] a very short time. [SE *couple* + TICK *n.*³ (2)]

couple of tinnies short of a slab *phr.* [1980s+] (Aus.) eccentric, foolish, simple-minded (cf. NOT ALL THERE). [TINNIE *n.*¹ (1) + SLAB *n.*¹ (4)]

coupler *n.* [19C] a woman when viewed as nothing more than a sex object. [SE *coupling*, sexual intercourse]

coupling bat *n.* [20C] the penis (cf. SHUNTER'S POLE). [railway imagery]

coupling house *n.* [18C–19C] a brothel (cf. ACCOMMODATION HOUSE). [SE *coupling* + HOUSE *n.*¹ (1)]

coupling pin *n.* [1910s] (US) the penis. [pun on SE]

coupon *n.* [20C] (Scot.) the face; thus *fill in* (*someone's*) *coupon*, to hit in the face, esp. with a weapon.

courage bump *n.* [20C] (US) acne. [dial. *courage*, sexual desire; the assumption is that the emergent sexuality of the adolescent male manifests itself in infected pimples]

courage pills *n.* [1980s+] (drugs) 1 heroin. 2 any form of anti-depressant. [heroin, which is based on the Gk. root meaning *hero*, works to counteract one's fears]

course *conj.* [late 19C+] abbr. of SE *of course*.

court card *n.* [late 17C–late 18C] a dandy, a 'gay, fluttering coxcomb' (Grose 1796). [note Lincolnshire dial. 'one who has risen very much in social position']

court cream *n.* [17C–18C] empty speeches, filled only with fake sincerity (cf. COURT ELEMENT). [the mannered speech of a royal court]

court element/holy bread/holy water/water *n.* [16C–18C] empty speeches, filled only with fake sincerity (cf. COURT CREAM). [the mannered speech of a royal court]

courtesy-man *n.* [16C] (Und.) a confidence trickster, well-dressed and spoken, and without any visible weapon, who poses as a gentleman down on his luck and tells his 'tale' to the passing victim whom he picks up in the street. They also stay in hostels from which they leave early, paying no bill but taking the bedlinen with them. [SE *courtesy*]

court holy bread/water see COURT ELEMENT.

court in *v.* [1980s+] (US gang) to subject to a ritual initiation, usu. involving a mild beating from fellow gang members, followed by some form of blooding, typically an armed attack on members of a rival gang (cf. JUMP IN; VEE-IN). [the other members fig. 'hold court']

court noll *n.* [mid-16C–mid-17C] a courtier. [SE *court* + *noll*, a dull, drunken person]

court of assistants *n.* [late 18C] the young men with whom young wives, unhappy in their marriages to older men, are likely to seek solace. [pun on SE *court of assistants*, senior members of city companies, responsible for managing their affairs]

court water see COURT ELEMENT.

cous-cous *n.* [1950s+] (W.I.) old, ragged work clothes. [SE *cous-cous*, granulated flour; this can be seen fig. as grains of dirt or specks of dust, and thus stretched further to encompass the sl. meaning]

cousin *n.*¹ [16C] (Und.) the victim, usually a rural visitor to London, of a confidence trickster who uses counterfeit gold. [SE. The implication is of 'country cousin'; ? + pun on SE *cozen*, to cheat, to defraud]

cousin *n.*² 1 [17C] a prostitute. 2 [late 19C+] (US) a friend, usu. a term of address. 3 [1950s+] (gay) an older man's younger lover. [in (1), (3) the euph. is used when introducing the young man or woman to an acquaintance who might otherwise frown on the relationship]

cousin *n.*³ [20C] (US) a mosquito. [mosquitoes 'stick so close']

cousin betty *n.* 1 [18C–mid-19C] a prostitute. 2 [19C] a foolish woman (cf. COUSIN TOM).

cousin jack/jacky/jan *n.* [mid-19C+] a Cornishman. [note dial. *cousin jack/jacky*, a fool, a coward]

cousin sally ann/sal/sally *n.* [mid–late 19C] (US) the Confederacy. [Confederate States of America]

cousin sis *n.* [20C] urination. [rhy. sl. *cousin sis* = PISS *n.*]

cousin tom *n.* [mid-19C] a madman, a beggar, tramp or similar person (cf. COUSIN BETTY). [SE *cousin* + TOM OF BEDLAM]

cousin up *v.* [20C] (US) to curry favour, to toady. [the supposed intimacy of cousins]

couter/couta/cooter *n.* [mid-19C] a sovereign; thus *half-a-couter*, a half sovereign. [Rom. *kotor*, guinea or Danubian-Gipsy *cuta*, gold coin]

couthed up *adj.* [1960s+] (US campus) neat, tidy, well-behaved. [back-form. of SE *uncouth*]

cove *n.* 1 [16C+] (Und.) a man (cf. CO *n.*¹). 2 [19C–1910s] (Aus.) the owner or manager of an establishment, esp. of a sheep station. [either 16C Scot. *cofe*, a chapman or pedlar or, like a number of 16C cant terms, Rom., in this case *cova* or *covo*, man]

covee *n.* [early 19C] a landlord. [COVE *n.* (2)]

cove-juice *n.* [20C] (US) illicitly distilled whisky. [dial. *cove*, a valley enclosed by mountains + SE *juice*; such valleys provide suitable hideouts for clandestine distilling]

Covent Garden *n.* [mid-19C] a farthing. [rhy. sl.; pron. of *farthing* as 'farden']

Covent Garden abbess *n.* [18C–early 19C] a procuress. [*Covent Garden*, the site of prostitution + ABBESS]

Covent Garden ague *n.* [17C–late 18C] venereal disease, esp. gonorrhoea (cf. BARNWELL AGUE). [SE *Covent Garden*, centre of 17C–18C prostitution in London + SE *ague*]

Covent Garden/common garden gout *n.* [late 17C] venereal disease (cf. BARNWELL AGUE). [for ety. see COVENT GARDEN AGUE]

Covent Garden nun/lady *n.* [18C] a prostitute (cf. BANKSIDE

LADY). [SE *Covent Garden*, centre of 17C–18C prostitution in London + NUN n. (1)]

Covent Garden nunnery n. [18C] a brothel (cf. COVENT GARDEN ABBESS; COVENT GARDEN NUN). [SE *Covent Garden*, centre of 17C–18C prostitution in London + NUNNERY]

coventry n. [mid-19C] a three-cornered puff with jam inside. [? its being first manufactured in the Warwickshire town]

cove of the dossing-ken n. [19C] the landlord of a lodging house. [COVE + DOSS-KEN]

cove of the ken n. [early–mid-19C] the master of the house. [COVE + KEN n.¹]

cover/coverer n. [early–mid-19C] (Und.) a confederate who screens the operations of a thief or pickpocket.

cover-down n. [mid-19C] a coin that has a false cover, which can be used or removed as required and which is used by cheats in games of coin tossing.

covered way n. [19C] the vagina (cf. ALLEY n.¹).

coverer *see* COVER n.

cover for v. [1940s+] **1** to protect a confederate. **2** to conceal wrong-doing. **3** to substitute for, to take over someone else's duties.

cover-me-decent/-decently n. [early–mid-19C] a greatcoat, an overcoat.

cover-me-properly n. [mid-19C] fashionable, smart clothing.

cover-me-queerly n. [mid-19C] ragged clothing.

cover one's/someone's ass v. [1950s+] to look after oneself or someone else. [SE *cover* + ARSE n.¹ (1)]

cover-slut n. [17C] an apron. [SE *cover* v. + *slut*, a kitchen-maid]

cover the waterfront, to phr. [20C] (US) **1** a euph. for to menstruate. **2** a euph. for to change a baby's nappy or diaper. [pun on SE phr., itself a journalistic cliché]

cover-up n. [1940s+] an alibi, concealment, usu. illegal or at least unethical.

covess n. [18C–early 19C] a woman. [COVE + fem. sfx. *-ess*]

covess dinge n. [mid-19C] (US) a Black woman. [COVESS + DINGE n.]

covey/covey of partridge n.¹ [late 17C–late 18C] a group or collection of prostitutes, usu. as found in a brothel. [joc. use of SE collective phr.]

covey n.² **1** [19C] a child (cf. COVE; KIVEY). **2** [early 19C–1910s] a fellow, a man (cf. COVE).

cow n.¹ **1** [late 17C+] a woman, esp. an obese or unattractive one. **2** [late 19C] a prostitute. **3** [1930s] a tramp's female companion. [on model of BITCH n.¹; SOW n.¹]

cow n.² [19C+] (Aus./N.Z.) an objectionable person or thing, a distasteful situation. [ext. of COW n.¹]

cow n.³ [mid-19C] £1000 sterling (cf. MONKEY n.⁴; PONY n.²). [ety. unknown]

cow n.⁴ (US) **1** [late 19C+] milk, cream. **2** [1910s–40s] beef.

cow n.⁵ [1940s] (W.I.) a man who is seduced by a woman and abandoned when the money runs out. [SE *milch-cow*, one who can be easily and continually used as a source of money]

cow v. [1970s] (US drugs) to put together one's resources to buy drugs. [ety. unknown; ? link to SE *collect*]

cow! excl. [mid-19C–1930s] (US) a mild excl. euph. for God! (cf. HOLY COW!).

cowabunga! excl. [1950s+] (orig. surf) excl. of pleasure, victory (over the waves) etc. [the term gained a whole new currency, especial among the pre-teens, with the popularity (c.1990) of the TV programme *The Teenage Mutant Ninja Turtles*, where it featured heavily. Its ultimate origin seems to have been in *Howdy Doody*, a US children's TV programme of the 1950s, in which *Cowabunga!* was the greeting exchanged by Buffalo Bob and Chief Thunderthud]

cowan n. [mid-19C] a sneak, an eavesdropper. [ety. unknown. Hotten (1860) offers Gk. *kuon*, a dog (as general pej.) or Scot.

cowan or *kirwan*, a man who builds dry-stone walls without mortar, and thus one who builds but is not a fully qualified mason. Note freemasons' jargon *cowan*, one who has not been initiated into the craft]

cow and calf n. [20C] (orig. sporting) a half. [rhy. sl.]

cow and calf v. [mid-19C] to laugh. [rhy. sl.]

cow-and-kisses n. [mid-19C] one's wife. [rhy. sl. *cow-and-kisses* = MISSUS]

coward's castle/corner n. [19C–1910s] a pulpit. [the occupier is 'above' argument]

cow-baby n. [late 16C–18C] a coward (CALF n.¹).

cow-/cattle-banger n. [20C] (Aus./N.Z.) a dairy farmer or any employee of a dairy farm (cf. COW-COCKY; COW-SPANKER). [SE *cow* + SE *bang* or BANG v.¹ (2)]

cow barn is open, the phr. [1960s+] a warning to a man that his trouser-fly is undone (cf. YOUR BARN DOOR IS OPEN).

cowbay n. [mid–late 19C] a cheap brothel, a prostitute's room. [New York City's 'red light area' was known as *Cow Bay*]

cowboy n.¹ **1** [20C] (orig. US) a reckless driver. **2** [1920s+] (US) a man, usu. a youth, who frequents drugstores for no other reason than to meet his friends, to gossip and to waste time (cf. DRUGSTORE COWBOY). **3** [1920s+] (US) a ruthless, un-restrained criminal. **4** [1930s+] (orig. US) a reckless man. **5** [1950s+] (US, poker) a king. **6** [1960s+] (US Black) an aggressive, tough Black man whose role has been selected for him by the White authorities (cf. BAD-ASS NIGGER). **7** [1960s+] a tradesman (esp. of the building and allied trades), who ignores the basic ethics and business standards of his peers and aims only for money; thus *cowboy builder*, *cowboy plumber* etc (cf. BUSHRANGER). [fig. uses of SE; note the earliest *cowboy* (18C–early 19C) was always a Black man; his White peers were *cattlemen*]

cowboy n.² [1950s+] a bow-legged man. [the stereotype of one whose legs are bowed from riding horses]

cowboy n.³ [1960s+] (US) a Marlboro cigarette. [the cigarette's advertising features 'the Marlboro *cowboy*']

cowboy v. [1960s+] (US Black) to rob in a reckless manner. [the style (or certainly as enshrined by Hollywood) of a classic Wild West hold-up]

cowboy Bible n. [1970s+] (US, West.) a pack of cigarette papers.

cowboy cadillac n. [1970s+] (US, southwest) any form of open-topped vehicle, e.g. a pick-up truck.

cowboy city n. [1970s] (US trucker) Cheyenne, Wyoming.

cowboy cocktail n. [20C] (US) straight whisky (cf. COWBOY COFFEE).

cowboy coffee n. [20C] (US) black coffee (cf. COWBOY COCK-TAIL).

cowboy question n. [1980s+] (US campus) a dare. [the stereotypical devil-may-care *cowboy*]

cowboys n. [1950s+] the police.

cowboy up v. [1990s] (US) to control one's emotions, to put on a brave, tough face. [the supposed stoicism of cowboys]

cowcatcher n. (US) **1** [mid-19C] a full moustache. **2** [1940s–60s] a large bosom. [SE *cowcatcher*, an apparatus fixed in front of a locomotive engine, to remove straying cattle and other obstructions from the rails in front of a train]

cowclap n. [1940s] (Irish) cow dung. [? rhy. sl. *cowclap* = CRAP n.³ (1)]

cow-cocky n. [20C] (Aus./N.Z.) a dairy farmer or any employee of a dairy farm (cf. COW-BANGER). [SE *cow* + COCKY n.²]

cow college n. [1930s+] (US) an agricultural college (cf. AG n.).

cow conductor n. [20C] (Aus.) a bullock-driver.

cow confetti n. [1930s+] nonsense, rubbish (cf. COWYARD CONFETTI; FARMYARD CONFETTI). [euph. for BULLSHIT n.]

cow-cow v. [mid-19C] (Anglo-Chinese) to scold, to reprimand severely. [? pidgin]

cow-crazy adj. [1920s] (US) foolishly obsessed with a woman or with women in general. [COW n.¹ (1) + SE crazy]

cow-cunted adj. [mid-19C+] having a large vagina (cf. BUSHEL-CUNTED). [SE cow + CUNT n.¹]

cowes coat n. [late 19C] a dinner jacket. [? as worn at the yachting centre Cowes]

cow express n. [1940s] (US Black) shoe leather. [the cowhide provides leather]

cow grease n. [20C] (US) butter (cf. COW n.⁴; COW JUICE).

cowgut n. [1940s] (W.I.) a tin lamp. [? some resemblance]

cow-handed adj. [late 18C] clumsy, awkward.

cow-hearted adj. [late 17C–late 19C] cowardly (cf. CHICKEN-HEARTED).

cowhide adj. [20C] (Irish) aware, knowledgeable. [rhy. sl. cowhide = WIDE]

cow-hocked adj. [mid–late 19C] having thick ankles or clumsy feet.

cowing adj. [1950s+] (orig. milit.) euph. for FUCKING adj.

cow-jerker n. [20C] (N.Z.) a cow hand, a milker.

cow jockey n. [20C] (US) a farmer, a rustic. [SE cow + JOCKEY n.² (2)]

cow juice n. [17C+] milk (cf. COW n.⁴; COW GREASE).

cow-killer n. [late 19C] (US) a quack, a poor doctor. [he is barely safe with animals, let alone humans]

cowlick n. [mid-19C+] a hairstyle, smoothed down over the forehead, which looks as if a cow had licked it into place (cf. DUCK'S ARSE; D.A.; NEWGATE KNOCKER).

cow-neck n. [1940s+] (W.I.) newly distilled white proof rum. [ety. unknown; ? play on the horse's neck, a mixed drink]

cow-oil n. [20C] (US) butter (cf. COW GREASE).

cow pie n. [1970s+] (US) a piece of cow dung.

cowpoke n. [late 19C+] (US) a cowboy (cf. COW-PUNCHER). [SE cow + poke; orig. referred specifically to those men who used long sticks to push cows aboard cattle-trains, bound for the slaughterhouses]

cow-prod/-prodder n. [1930s+] (US) a cowboy (cf. COWPOKE).

cow-puncher n. [late 19C+] a cowboy (cf. BULL-PUNCHER; COW-POKE).

cow-quake n. [19C] (Irish) a bull's roar.

cow's n. [20C] 10 shillings (50p). [rhy. sl. cow's calf = half (a pound)]

cow salve n. [1940s+] (US) butter (cf. COW GREASE).

cows and kisses n. [mid-19C] women. [rhy. sl. cows and kisses = misses or mistress]

cow's baby n. **1** [late 18C–20C] a calf (cf. COW'S SPOUSE). **2** [mid-19C] an awkward, loutish person (cf. COW-BABY). [lit./fig. ext. of SE]

cow's breakfast n. [20C] (Can.) a large straw hat.

cowscape n. [late 19C–1930s] a painting of a country scene that includes cows. [SE cow + landscape]

cow's courant n. [late 18C] diarrhoea (cf. RUNS; TROTS n.¹). [SE cow + SE courant, coranto, a dance characterized by a running or gliding step]

cow's grease n. [mid-19C] butter (cf. COW SALVE).

cowsh n. [1910s] (Aus./N.Z.) nonsense, rubbish (cf. BULLSHIT n.). [abbr. COWSHIT n. (2)]

cowshit n. (US, West.) **1** [1960s] an unpopular person. **2** [1960s+] nonsense, rubbish (cf. BULLSHIT n.).

cow-simple adj. [1920s–50s] (US) foolishly obsessed with a woman or with women in general (cf. COW-CRAZY). [COW n.¹ (1) + SE simple]

cowskin n. [mid-19C] (US) a whip; thus cowskin, to whip.

cowskin hero n. [late 18C] (W.I.) a plantation overseer. [their use of the cowskin, a rawhide whip]

cow's lick n. [1960s] prison. [rhy. sl. cow's lick = NICK n.⁶ (1)]

cow's licker n. [1930s+] £1. [rhy. sl. cow's licker = NICKER]

cowson n. [1930s] a general pej. description of a person (cf. SON OF A BITCH). [on pattern of SE whoreson]

cow-spanker n. [20C] (Aus./N.Z.) a dairy farmer or any employee of a dairy farm (cf. COW-BANGER).

cow's spouse n. [late 18C] a bull (cf. COW'S BABY). [facet. use of SE]

cow town n. [1970s+] (US) Fort Worth, Texas. [its former principle industry]

cow-turd n. [mid–late 18C] a cheap cigar. [SE cow + TURD; i.e. a derog. comparison]

cow-waddie n. [19C] (US) a cowboy, esp. a temporary cowhand. [SE cow + WADDIE]

cow-week see CALF-WEEK.

cow with the iron tail n. [mid-19C] a water pump. [the ref. is to the milkmen's habit, before legislation passed in 1865, of watering the milk]

cowyard n. [late 19C–1910s] (US) a cheap brothel (cf. COWBAY). [COW n.¹ (2) + pun on SE]

cowyard cake n. [1920s–50s] (Aus.) a type of cake or bun that contains sultanas. [it is supposedly reminiscent of a cowpat + attendant flies]

cowyard confetti n. [1940s+] (Aus.) nonsense, rubbish (cf. COW CONFETTI). [euph. for BULLSHIT n.]

coxcomb n. [late 16C–early 18C] the head. [SE coxcomb, a cock's head]

coxy fuss see COCKSY FUSS.

coynte n. [19C] the vagina (cf. QUAINT). [euph. for CUNT n.¹]

coyote n. (US) **1** [19C] a half-breed. **2** [19C] the vagina. **3** [late 19C–1900s] a very unpleasant person. **4** [1920s+] a smuggler of illegal immigrants from Mexico into the US. **5** [1980s+] an ugly woman; thus (US campus) coyote date 'a woman who is so ugly that when her companion for the night wakes up the next morning and she is asleep on his arm, he would rather chew off his arm than wake her up'. [all fig. uses of SE coyote, a prairie dog, generally considered as a 'negative' animal]

coyote v. (US, West.) **1** [mid-19C+] to run off, esp. in a clandestine manner. **2** [late 19C] to hoax, to deceive. **3** [1920s+] to wander about. [for ety. see COYOTE n.]

coyote getaway n. [1990s] sneaking out of a woman's room after a one-night stand without waking her. [the supposed willingness of a coyote to gnaw its own leg off in order to escape a trap]

coyote ugly adj. [1980s+] (US campus) extremely ugly. [COYOTE n. (5)]

cozmos/cosmos n. [1970s] (drugs) phencyclidine (cf. ACE n.³). [it gets on HIGH adj.¹ (2)]

cozy adj. [1950s+] (US) sly, cunning; thus play it cozy, to act in a cautious or secretive manner, cozy up (to), to ingratiate oneself with, to toady to.

cozza n. [mid–late 19C] pork. [Yid./Heb. chazer, a pig]

cozzer n. [early 19C+] a policeman (cf. PIG n.³). [Yid./Heb. chazer, a pig]

cozzie see COSSIE.

cozzpot n. [1960s] a policeman. [COZZER + sfx. -pot on model of tosspot]

c.p. n. [1920s] **1** a kept man. **2** a pimp (cf. PENSIONER; PETTICOAT PENSIONER). [abbr. CUNT-PENSIONER]

c.p.s.i. phr. [1990s] usu. in phr. more c.p.s.i. in ... than ... , and defining anywhere that there is a good chance of picking up women. [abbr. cunt per square inch]

c.p.t./c.p. time phr. [20C] an hour or two later than the prescribed time, sooner or later (cf. AFRICAN PEOPLE'S TIME). [abbr. coloured people's time; the stereotype is that Blacks have a less immediate sense of time than their White peers]

crab *n.*[1] **1** [late 16C–early 17C; late 19C+] a sour, ill-tempered person. **2** [late 19C+] an ill-tempered, thus unpopular child, esp. as *old crab*. [SE *crab-apple*; later use is US]

crab *n.*[2] [late 19C+] a pubic louse. [supposed resemblance]

crab *v.*[1] **1** [early 19C+] to spoil, to upset, to ruin; thus (Aus.) phr. *he'd crab on a marble shit house, he'd bring crabs on blue ointment*. **2** [early 19C+] to use offensive language so as deliberately to annoy someone. **3** [early 19C+] to tear at, to find fault, to criticize heavily; thus [early–mid-19C] *throw a crab*, to criticize harshly. **4** [early 19C+] (mainly US) to steal. **5** [mid-19C+] to back down, to surrender in a humiliating manner, to run away, esp. as *crab off* (cf. CRAWFISH v.). [all uses of SE with emphasis on the crab's snapping pincers]

crab *v.*[2] [1950s+] (W.I. Rasta) to scratch or claw. [the crustacean's movement]

crab-apple *n.* [mid-19C–1920s] (US) a sour, ill-tempered person (cf. CRAB n.[1]). [SE *crab-apple*, a very sour fruit]

crab-apple two-step *n.* [20C] (US) diarrhoea (cf. APPLE-BLOSSOM TWO-STEP). [the result of eating sour fruit]

crab-ass *n.* [1930s] (US) an unpleasant person. [CRAB n.[1] + ARSE n.[1] (4)]

crabbed *adj.* [late 18C–19C] sour, ill-tempered, difficult. [CRAB n.[1]]

crabber *n.* [1930s] a fault-finder, a nag. [CRAB v.[1] (3)]

crabby *adj.*[1] [late 19C+] infected with pubic lice. [CRAB n.[2]]

crabby *adj.*[2] [20C] nagging, cantankerous. [CRAB n.[1]]

crab ladder *n.* [1990s] the penis. [CRAB n.[2] + SE *ladder*]

crab lanthorn *n.* [late 18C] a peevish, surly person. [CRAB n.[1] + SE *lanthorn*; *crab* in SE can mean a small machine or a trivet, which would make the fig. use more logical, but there is no record of a *crab lanthorn*]

crab on the rocks *n.* [late 19C] itching testicles. [pun on SE *crab*/CRAB n.[2], SE *rocks*/ROCKS n.[3](1)]

crabs *n.*[1] [18C–19C] in the game of hazard, the lowest throw, a pair of aces; thus *come off crabs, turn out crabs*, to prove disappointing. [? the precursor of SE *craps* dice]

crabs *n.*[2] [late 18C–1910s] **1** the feet. **2** boots, shoes; thus *move one's crabs*, to run off. [abbr. CRAB-SHELLS]

crab-shells *n.* [late 18C–mid-19C] a pair of shoes (cf. CARTS n.[1]; TROTTING-CASES). [a play on Norfolk dial. *cart*, the carapace or shell of a crab]

crab someone's/the act, to *phr.* [1900s–40s] (US) to spoil someone's plans, to interfere. [CRAB v.[1] (1)]

crabtree comb *n.* [late 16C–19C] a cudgel (cf. LEAD TOWEL; OAKEN CUDGEL). [SE *crabtree*, a wild-apple tree + *comb*]

crabwalk *n.* [1970s] (US) the perineum. [CRAB n.[2] + SE *walk*]

crack *n.*[1] **1** [16C+] the vagina (cf. ARBOUR). **2** [late 17C–18C] a generic term for women. **3** [late 17C–18C] a prostitute. **4** [1960s] sexual intercourse with a woman (cf. ARSE n.[1]; CUNT n.[1]; PUSSY n.[1]). **5** [1960s+] (gay) the anus.

crack *n.*[2] [early 17C–early 19C] a lie. [SE *crack*, bragging, exaggeration]

crack *n.*[3] **1** [mid-17C+] any person or thing that approaches perfection. **2** [early 18C] a fop, a dandy. **3** [late 18C+] the current fashion. **4** [early 19C] the fashionable world, the social and sporting élite. [late 16C SE *crack*, a 'lively lad', a wag]

crack *n.*[4] [18C] a fool. [CRACKBRAIN]

crack *n.*[5] [18C] a jolly, high-spirited party. [the *cracking* or opening of bottles]

crack *n.*[6] [early 18C+] an instant, a very brief moment. [SE *crack*, the noise of a gunshot or a whip; the time it takes to make this noise]

crack *n.*[7] [mid-18C–mid-19C] a burglar. [abbr. CRACKSMAN n.[1]]

crack, the *n.*[8] [late 18C–mid-19C] (Und.) housebreaking (cf. CRACK LAY). [CRACK v.[5]]

crack *n.*[9] [19C] a crown. [? perversion of SE *crown*]

crack *n.*[10] [mid–late 19C] dry wood (cf. CRACKMANS). [the noise it makes when snapped or burned]

crack *n.*[11] [mid-19C+] a heavy blow, e.g. *a crack over the head*.

crack *n.*[12] **1** [late 19C] (London) a narrow passage of houses. **2** [20C] the divide between the buttocks.

crack *n.*[13] **1** [late 19C+] (orig. US) a telling, sharp remark. **2** [1920s+] (orig. US) a joke. **3** [1970s] (US campus) a funny or witty person. [WISECRACK n.]

crack *n.*[14] **1** [late 19C+] an opportunity, a try, a chance, esp. in phr. *have a crack/crack at* (cf. FIRST CRACK OUT OF THE BOX; GET A CRACK AT). **2** [1930s+] (US) a go, a time (cf. POP n.[5]). [SE *crack*, the act of snapping]

crack, the *n.*[15] [1920s+] **1** (orig. Irish) conversation, chatter, gossip. **2** (Irish) fun, amusement, informal entertainment; thus *cracksome*, jolly, amusing. [Irish *craic*; ult. OE *cracian*, a crack]

crack *n.*[16] [1980s+] (Black) a thrill, excitement. [SE *crack* of thunder, i.e. a sudden excitement]

crack *n.*[17] [1980s+] a purified and potent form of cocaine; a mixture of cocaine, baking powder and water, which is smoked rather than snorted; crack is heated and the resultant pellets are smoked through a small glass pipe. [SE by late 1990s. Its strength, alleged addictiveness and destructive popularity have made it a source of social disruption. Unlike its powdered form, known as 'the rich man's drug', *crack*, for all that it has many middle-class devotees, is very much a drug of the ghetto and the housing estate, bringing the effects of cocaine to an underclass market]

crack *adj.* [late 18C–1910s] excellent, first-class; thus *the crack*, the fashionable, smart world. [CRACK n.[3] (1)]

crack *v.*[1] [15C+] to boast or brag; thus *cracking*, boasting. [SE *crack*, to make a loud or sudden noise]

crack *v.*[2] [mid-16C] to move suddenly, to move with a jerk.

crack *v.*[3] [early 17C+] to work something out, to find a solution. [abbr. of fig. phr. *crack a nut*]

crack *v.*[4] **1** [17C–19C] to fall into disrepair. **2** [late 19C+] to collapse, to break down (emotionally). **3** [20C] to change money, to break a note into change.

crack *v.*[5] **1** [early 18C–mid-19C] to break open, to break into; thus *crack a crib*, to break into a house, *cracking*, robbery. **2** [early 18C–1930s] to deflower. **3** [late 18C+] to escape from prison. [later use of (2) is US]

crack *v.*[6] **1** [mid-19C] to let off a firearm. **2** [late 19C+] to hit (with a loud noise), to slap, esp. in threat *I'll crack you one*. **3** [late 19C+] to talk; thus *crack on*, to talk at length. **4** [late 19C+] (US) to break wind. **5** [1920s+] to open a bottle, can etc. **6** [1950s+] to break a record, to surpass. [fig. uses of *crack*, a sharp noise; note (4) late 14C–early 17C SE *crack*, the breaking of wind; (5) previous use, in phr. *crack a bottle*]

crack/crack on *v.*[7] **1** [mid-19C–1900s] to inform (against). **2** [late 19C+] to tell tales, to boast. **3** [late 19C+] to pretend. **4** [1990s] (US Black) to disparage, to attach verbally. [15C *crack*, to brag, to boast]

crack *v.*[8] **1** [late 19C–1940s] (US Black) to tease, to insult, to make jokes at another's expense. **2** [1980s+] (US campus) to be very funny, to make people laugh (cf. CRACK UP v.[4]). [CRACK n.[13]]

crack *v.*[9] **1** [20C] (orig. Aus.) to act in a given manner, defined by some form of comb., e.g. *crack hardy*. **2** [1900s–10s] (Aus.) to pretend, to sham; thus *crack a deaf 'un*, to pretend to be deaf, or not to hear.

crack *v.*[10] [1920s+] (US) to pass on a secret, to give information. [SE *crack open* or *crack under pressure*]

crack *v.*[11] (Und.) **1** [1920s+] to ask for, to demand, ext. as *crack on*. **2** [1950s+] to arrest. [SE *crack open*]

crack *v.*[12] [1930s–70s] (US) to open a book (for the purpose of study). [CRACK THE BOOKS]

crack a bell, to phr. [late 19C] to tell a secret, to betray a confidence. [the belief that it is necessary to remain silent while casting a spell; the slightest sound may produce a flaw]

crack a boo, to phr. [1900s–10s] (Aus.) to betray a secret, to display one's emotions. [? CRACK A BELL]

crack a bottle, to phr. [late 16C+] to have a drink (cf. CRACK A TUBE).

crack a brew, to phr. [1990s] to open a beer. [CRACK v.⁶ (5) + BREW n.¹ (3)]

crack a case, to phr. [mid–late 19C] (Und.) to break into a house. [CRACK v.⁵ (1) + CASE n.² (1)]

crack a cherry, to phr. [20C] to take a woman's virginity (cf. COP A CHERRY). [SE crack + CHERRY n.¹ (1)]

crack a crib, to phr. [19C] (Und.) to break into a house or shop. [CRACK v.⁵ (1) + CRIB n.³ (1)]

crack a crust, to phr. [mid-19C] to earn a living; ext. as crack a tidy crust, to make a very good living.

crack a fart, to phr. [1980s+] (US campus) to break wind. [SE crack + FART; but note CRACK v.⁶ (4)]

crack a fat, to phr. [1940s+] (Aus.) to achieve erection (cf. CHUBBY n.²).

crackajack see CRACKERJACK adj.¹.

crack a Judy/Judy's tea-cup, to phr. [early 19C+] to deflower a woman. [SE crack + JUDY n.¹]

crack a ken/swag, to phr. [18C] to break into and rob a house. [CRACK v.⁵ (1) + KEN n.¹]

crack a kirk, to phr. [mid-19C] 1 (Und.) to break into a church (cf. DEAD LURK; KIRKING). 2 to break into a house while its owners are at church. [CRACK v.⁵ (1) + Scot. kirk, a church]

crack a lay, to phr. [1940s+] (Aus.) to betray, to gossip about, to 'spill the beans'. [CRACK v.⁶ (3) + ? LAY n.⁴ (2)]

crack along/on v. [mid-16C+] to move along at speed, to bustle about. [CRACK v.² + SE along/on]

crack a/one's pipkin/pitcher, to phr. [late 18C–early 19C] 1 to take a woman's virginity (cf. COP A CHERRY). 2 to lose one's virginity. [SE crack + pipkin, a small earthenware cookpot or pan]

crack a quart, to phr. [late 16C] to have a drink. [var. on CRACK A BOTTLE]

crack a short, to phr. [1930s–50s] (US Und.) to break into a car. [CRACK v.⁵ (1) + SHORT n.²]

crack a smile see CRACK ONE'S FACE.

crack a stiffie, to phr. [1940s+] to get an erection. [CRACK A FAT + STIFFIE n.²]

crack a swag see CRACK A KEN.

crack attack n. [1980s+] (drugs) a sudden craving for crack cocaine. [CRACK n.¹⁷ + SE attack; play on McDonald's hamburger's coinage Mac attack, a sudden craving for a hamburger]

crack a tube, to phr. [1960s+] (Aus.) to open a can of beer (cf. CRACK A BOTTLE). [CRACK v.⁶ (5) + TUBE n.² (6)]

crack a whid, to phr. [early 19C] to speak; thus crack some queer whids, to speak badly, to use coarse expressions (cf. CUT BENE WHIDS; CUT QUEER WHIDS).

crack baby n. [1980s+] the child of an addict of crack cocaine; thus a general pej. [CRACK n.¹⁷ + SE baby]

crack back n. [1980s] (drugs) a cigarette made with crack and marijuana. [CRACK n.¹⁷ + ? play on BACK adj.², i.e. marijuana 'on the side']

crack bitch n. [1990s] (Black) a female crack addict (cf. CRACK HO). [CRACK n.¹⁷ + BITCH n.¹]

crackbrain n. [18C] a fool (cf. CRACK n.⁴). [SE crack + sfx. -brain]

crack cooler n. [1980s+] (drugs) crack cocaine soaked in a wine cooler. [CRACK n.¹⁷ + SE cooler]

crack-corn n. [19C+] (US) White people, esp. and orig. the White natives of Kentucky. [var. on CORNCRACKER n.¹]

crack diet n. [1990s] (drugs) a few sweets and a soft drink. [CRACK n.¹⁷ + SE diet; a minimal diet, high on sugar, that is preferred by regular crack users]

crack down v. 1 [1930s–40s] to let off a firearm. 2 [1940s+] to repress, to take harsh measures against, esp. used of a campaign against vice or crime. [CRACK v.⁶]

crack down on v. [20C] (Aus.) to grab and make off with something.

cracked adj.¹ 1 [17C+] insane, crazy, eccentric; thus cracked about/on, obsessed with, infatuated with. 2 [18C–19C] bankrupt, financially ruined. [fig. uses of SE cracked, broken]

cracked adj.² [1980s+] under the influence of crack. [CRACK n.¹⁷]

cracked/slit groat n. [early 17C] something absolutely worthless. [SE cracked, broken/slit + groat, a coin worth fourpence; thus of very low value]

cracked ice n. [1940s] (US Black) diamonds. [SE cracked + ICE n.² + joc. use of SE phr.]

cracked in the filbert phr. [late 19C–1920s] eccentric, slightly crazy. [SE cracked + FILBERT n.¹]

cracked in the ring phr. [late 16C–late 19C] deflowered. [CRACK v.⁵ (2) + RING n.¹ (1)]

cracked-out adj. [1980s+] (drugs) wholly addicted to crack cocaine (cf. AMPED-OUT). [CRACK n.¹⁷]

cracked pitcher n. [mid-18C–mid-19C] 1 a woman living between respectability and prostitution. 2 a recently lost virginity (cf. CRACK A PIPKIN).

cracked up adj. [mid-19C] impoverished, destitute.

cracker n.¹ [early 17C–1900s] a lie (cf. CAULKER). [CRACK n.²]

cracker n.² 1 [late 17C–18C] the backside. 2 [early 19C] (S.Afr.) sheep-skin trousers. [CRACK n.¹² (2)]

cracker n.³ 1 [mid-18C] a pistol. 2 [19C] the penis. 3 [1910s+] (N.Z.) a cartridge. [SE crack, to make a sharp noise; they all 'go off']

cracker n.⁴ 1 [mid-18C+] (US) a poor Southern US White farmer (cf. APPLE-KNOCKER n.²). 2 [1920s+] (orig. US Black) a White racist. [CRACK v.¹. 'I should explain to your Lordship what is meant by crackers, a name they have got from being great boasters, they are a lawless set of rascalls on the frontiers of Virginia, Maryland, the Carolinas and Georgia, who often change their places of abode' G. Cochrane, letter, 27 June 1766]

cracker n.⁵ [mid-19C] 1 a heavy blow. 2 a fall. [CRACK n.¹¹]

cracker n.⁶ [mid-19C+] someone or something notable, e.g. a fast pace, a dandy, a large sum of money, an exceptional individual. [CRACK adj.]

cracker n.⁷ [1920s] (US Black) a very light-coloured person. [? SE cracker, a biscuit; thus biscuit-coloured, or ref. to their similarity to CRACKER n.⁴]

cracker n.⁸ 1 [1930s] (US) $1. 2 [1930s+] (Aus./N.Z.) the smallest feasible amount of money. 3 [1930s+] (Aus./N.Z.) anything worthless, valueless; thus not have a cracker, to be penniless. [Baker (1966) adds cracker, a £1 note, and this has been taken up by the OED, but Wilkes (1985) rejects it: 'No evidence has been found ...']

cracker n.⁹ [1940s+] a worn-out sheep, horse or bullock. [CRACKED UP]

cracker n.¹⁰ 1 [1950s+] an attractive young woman, usu. as in a little cracker. 2 [1960s] (Aus.) a brothel. 3 [1960s] (Aus.) a prostitute. [CRACK n.¹; but for (1) note CRACK adj.]

cracker-ass n.¹ [20C] (US) a skinny person. [SE cracker, a thin biscuit + sfx. -ASS]

cracker-ass n.² [20C] (US Black) a White person. [CRACKER n.⁴ + sfx. -ASS]

crackerbox n. [1980s+] (US) an eccentric, a madman. [CRACKERS adj. + SE box; pun on SE]

cracker factory n. [1980s+] (US) a psychiatric institution. [CRACKERS adj. + SE *factory*; pun on SE]

crackerjack n. 1 [late 19C+] (orig. US) someone or something exceptional. 2 [1910s] (US) an arrogant, 'cocky' person. 3 [1970s] (US campus) a fool, an oaf. [ext. of CRACKER n.⁶]

crackerjack/crackajack adj.¹ [19C+] excellent, first-class, superlative. [CRACKERJACK n. (1)]

crackerjack adj.² [20C] fake, make-believe. [? US sweet *Crackerjack*, which contained toy police badges]

crackerjacks n. [1980s+] (drugs) smokers of crack cocaine. [play on CRACKERJACK n. + ? ref. to CRACK n.¹⁷ + JACK n.⁵]

crackers n.¹ [20C] hair curlers. [the shape, similar to that of trad. nut-crackers; ? + pun on NUT n.³]

crackers n.² [20C] (orig. US) euph. for *Christ*, usu. as used in mild oaths (cf. CRACKY!).

crackers n.³ [1900s–10s] (US) beans. [CRACK v.⁶ (4)]

crackers n.⁴ [1930s+] the teeth. [SE *crack*]

crackers n.⁵ [1960s] (drugs) LSD (cf. A n.³). [? CRACKERS adj., but Spears (1986) suggests 'an animal cracker containing a drop of hallucinogen']

crackers n.⁶ [1970s] (drugs) amyl nitrite (cf. AIMIES n.²). [SE *crack*, to break open; i.e. one snaps open the vial that contains the drug]

crackers adj. [1920s+] mad, crazy. [SE *cracked* (in the head)]

cracker state n. [early 19C+] (US) Georgia. [CRACKER n.⁴ + SE *state*]

crack-fencer n. [mid-19C] a street-seller of nuts. [SE *crack* to mean a nut + FENCER]

crack gallery n. [1980s+] (drugs) a place where users of crack congregate to buy and smoke the drug (cf. BASING GALLERY). [CRACK n.¹⁷ + (SHOOTING) GALLERY]

crack halter/hemp n. [16C–17C] a rogue, a villain (cf. CRACK-ROPE). [the *halter* is the hangman's noose/*hemp* refers to the hempen noose]

crack hand n. [19C] an able, competent person. [CRACK adj. + SE *hand*, a person, esp. a regards their working at a job]

crack hardy v. [20C] (Aus.) 1 to put up with discomfort, to 'grin and bear it'. 2 to keep a secret. [CRACK v.⁹]

crackhead n. [1980s+] a smoker of crack cocaine (cf. ACID-HEAD). [CRACK n.¹⁷ + sfx. -HEAD (2)]

crack hemp see CRACK HALTER.

crack ho n. [20C] (US Black) a woman who will offer sex in return for crack cocaine (cf. CRACK BITCH). [CRACK n.¹⁷ + HO]

crack house n. [1980s+] a room or whole house in which users gather to take crack (cf. BASING GALLERY; CRACK GALLERY; SHOOTING GALLERY). [CRACK n.¹⁷ + SE *house*]

crack-hunter/-haunter n. [19C] the penis. [CRACK n.¹ + SE *hunter/haunter*]

crackiness n. [mid–late 19C] eccentricity. [CRACKED adj.¹; CRACKERS adj.]

cracking adj. [early 19C+] (orig. US) 1 vigorous. 2 excellent, first-rate. [CRACK adj.]

cracking but facking phr. [1930s–40s] (US Black) conveying hard factual information in the guise of jokes and humour. [CRACK v.⁸ + SE *fact*]

crack into fame/reputation/repute, to phr. [late 19C–1920s] to make famous by constant praise. [CRACK v.⁷ + SE *fame*]

crackish adj. [late 17C–19C] of a woman, wanton, promiscuous. [CRACK n.¹ (3)]

crack it v. [1930s+] (orig. Aus./N.Z.) to succeed, to overcome obstacles, esp. to achieve a successful (from the male point of view) seduction. [CRACK v.⁵ (2)]

crack it for a quid, to phr. [1960s+] (Aus.) to work as a prostitute. [SE *crack*, to open, in this case her legs]

crack lay n. [late 18C–late 19C] (Und.) house-breaking. [CRACK n.⁸ + LAY n.]

crackle n. [19C–1950s] (Und.) banknotes, usu. of £5 and up. [the noise of the paper]

crackling n. [late 19C+] attractive women, used as a generic (cf. CRACKER n.¹⁰). [SE *crackling*, tasty roast pork fat]

crack loose v. [19C+] (US) to threaten, verbally or physically (cf. CRACK WISE; CUT LOOSE). [CRACK v.⁶ + SE *loose*]

crackmans n. [16C–late 18C] (Und.) a hedge (cf. RUFFMANS). [CRACK n.¹⁰ + sfx. -MANS]

crack mugs v. [1910s+] (Aus.) to sell racing tips. [CRACK v.⁷ + MUG n.⁵; the implication is of their worthlessness and the gullibility of the purchasers]

cracko n. [20C] a madman, a lunatic (cf. CRACKPOT). [CRACKED adj.¹]

cracko adj. [20C] eccentric, insane. [CRACKO n.]

crack of dawn/day n. [late 19C+] (orig. US) daybreak.

crack off v. [1980s+] (US) to make jokes, to make 'smart' comments (cf. CRACK WISE). [CRACK v.⁸ (2)]

crack off/off a batch, to phr. [1990s] to masturbate. [CRACK v.⁶ (2) + SE *batch* (of semen)]

crackola n. [1990s] (US Black/drugs) crack cocaine. [CRACK n.¹⁷ + sfx. -OLA]

crack on v.¹ 1 [mid-19C] to load up, to 'clap on'. 2 [mid-19C+] to travel at full speed (cf. CRACK v.²).

crack on v.² see CRACK v.⁷.

crack on v.³ [1980s+] (US campus) of a man, to strike up a friendship with a woman in the hope of moving onto a deeper relationship; the alluring factor is not her status or possessions but her personality. [ext. of CRACK v.⁸]

crack one's face/a smile, to phr. [1940s+] to laugh, to smile.

crack one's jaw, to phr. [1930s–40s] (US Black) to boast, to brag. [CRACK v.¹]

crack one's marbles, to phr. [1930s] (US) 1 of a man, to achieve orgasm or to induce it in a woman. 2 to delight, to please. [SE *crack* + MARBLES n.³ + pun]

crack one's nuts, to phr. [1940s–60s] (US) of a man, to achieve orgasm. [NUTS n.² + pun]

crack one's pipkin/pitcher see CRACK A PIPKIN.

crack one's ribs, to phr. [mid-19C+] to laugh uproariously, until one feels actual pain.

crack one's side, to phr. [1930s–50s] (US Black) to laugh uproariously, until one feels actual pain (cf. CRACK ONE'S RIBS).

crack one's whip, to phr. [1950s–70s] (N.Z.) to take one's share or turn, esp. in buying a round of drinks.

crack onto v. [1950s+] (Aus.) to pursue sexually (cf. CRACK ON v.³). [CRACK v.⁹ (1)]

crackpot n. [late 19C+] an eccentric, a madman. [SE *crack* + *pot* (of the head), the skull, the cranium]

crackpot adj. [late 19C+] (usu. of ideas) absurd, bizarre, unworkable. [CRACKPOT n.]

crack-rope n. [16C–early 17C] a rogue, a villain. [SE *crack* + *rope*; thus one who might stretch the hangman's rope]

crack salesman n. [1960s+] a gay prostitute (cf. ASS PEDDLER). [CRACK n.¹ (5)]

crackskull n. [mid-19C+] (US) whisky. [a melodramatic version of its effects]

cracksman n.¹ [18C–19C] a burglar. [CRACK n.⁷ + sfx. -*man*; the *locus classicus* is in the title of E.W. Hornung's *The Amateur Cracksman* (1899), featuring the exploits of the gentleman-thief A.J. Raffles]

cracksman n.² [19C] the penis. [CRACK n.¹ (1) + sfx. -*man*]

crack someone up v.¹ [20C] to praise, to eulogize. [CRACK v.¹]

crack someone up v.² [20C] to make someone laugh. [SE *crack*, to break]

crack spot n. [1980s+] (drugs) an area where people can purchase crack. [CRACK n.¹⁷ + SE *spot*, a place]

crack the bat, to phr. [1990s] to masturbate. [cricket/baseball imagery]

crack the bell, to *phr.* [late 19C–1900s] to muddle, to ruin, to blunder. [a *cracked* bell is useless as it cannot ring]

crack the books, to *phr.* [1930s+] (orig. US) to open books; thus to read, to study.

crack the jackpot, to *phr.* [1930s+] (Aus./N.Z.) to win, to get absolutely right, to succeed. [var. on HIT THE JACKPOT]

crack up *v.*[1] [early 19C+] to boast or praise; esp. in phr. NOT ALL IT'S CRACKED UP TO BE. [CRACK v.[1]]

crack up *v.*[2] [mid-19C+] (orig. US) to have a nervous breakdown.

crack up *v.*[3] [1920s+] to crash some form of vehicle or conveyance, e.g. a car, an aeroplane. [SE *crack*]

crack up *v.*[4] [1940s+] to laugh uproariously. [CRACK v.[8]]

crack-up *n.*[1] [mid-19C+] (orig. US) a nervous breakdown, a mental collapse. [CRACK UP v.[2]]

crack-up *n.*[2] [1990s] (Black) anything considered hilariously funny. [CRACK v.[8]]

crackwise *n.* [1940s–50s] (US Black) one who pretends to a greater sophistication and knowledge of 'the scene' than he or she actually possesses, a poseur. [CRACK WISE v.]

crack wise *v.* [1940s+] (orig. US Black) to make a 'clever' comment that impresses no one, to pose as more sophisticated than one actually is (cf. CRACK LOOSE; WISE GUY). [CRACK v.[8] (1) + WISE adj.]

cracky *adj.* [mid-19C+] eccentric, mentally unstable. [CRACKERS adj.]

cracky! *excl.* [20C] euph. for CHRIST!, usu. in mild oaths (cf. BEJABERS!; CHRISTMAS!; CHRISTOPHER COLUMBUS!; CRACKERS n.[2]; CRAMP!; CREATION; CREEPERS!; CRIKEY!; CRIMAST!; CRIMES!; CRIMINY!; CRIMPS!; CRIPES!; CRUMBS!; CRUMMY!).

cradle *n.* [19C] the vagina.

cradle-robber *n.* **1** [1920s+] (orig. US) one who pursues lovers who are younger than themself (cf. CRADLE-SNATCHER). **2** [1940s] (US) a child-molester.

cradle-snatcher *n.* [20C] (orig. US) an older person, usu. a woman, who prefers affairs with people substantially younger than they are.

craft *n.* [late 19C–1900s] a bicycle. [SE *craft*, a ship]

crag *n.* [1970s+] (US campus) an irritable, nagging woman. [CRAB n.[1] + NAG n.[1] (2)]

cragmans *n.* [17C] a hedge. [var. on CRACKMANS]

craik/crake *v.* [20C] (Ulster) to nag, to grumble, to talk without stopping. [dial. *crake*, an ill-natured gossip; ult. SE *crake*, the cry of the corncrake]

Crail capon *n.* [mid-19C] a salt herring (cf. ABERDEEN CUTLET). [the local fishery trade]

crake *see* CRAIK.

cram *n.*[1] [late 18C–mid-19C] a lie; thus *crammer*, a liar. [SE *cram*, to fill up, the liar's victim is 'filled up' with untruths]

cram/cram-coach *n.*[2] [early–mid-19C+] (orig. Oxon. university) a tutor; thus *cram-book*, a book used for intensive learning; *cram-paper*, a prepared list of examination answers, to be learned parrot-fashion; *cram-shop*, a school run by a crammer; *crammable*, work that can be learned by rote; *crammed*, tutored for examinations rather than actual knowledge; (US) *cram session*, a burst of study immediately before an examination.

cram *n.*[3] [mid-19C] a jam, a crush of people.

cram *v.*[1] [late 18C–mid-19C] to lie, to deceive, to make a person believe false or exaggerated statements. [CRAM n.[1]; the gullible victim 'swallows' the misinformation]

cram *v.*[2] **1** [mid-19C] to urge a horse on by force. **2** [mid-late 19C] of a man, to have sexual intercourse.

cram *v.*[3] [mid-19C+] (US campus) to study hard at the last minute. [CRAM n.[2]]

cramber *v.* [20C] to defecate. [ety. unknown]

cram it! *excl.* [1950s+] (US) a general excl. of dismissal, rejection, *the hell with it! shove it!* etc.

crammer *n.*[1] **1** [mid-late 19C] a lie. **2** [mid-19C] the stomach. [CRAM n.[1]; SE *cram*, to fill up]

crammer *n.*[2] [late 19C+] a tutor; thus [late 19C–1920s] *crammer's pup*, a pupil of such a high-pressure tutor. [CRAM n.[2]]

cramming *n.* [early 19C+] intensive learning aimed purely at passing necessary examinations. [CRAM n.[2]]

cram-o-matic *v.* [1980s+] (US campus) to study hard at the last minute. [CRAM n.[2] + 'technological' sfx. *-omatic*]

cramp *n.* [1990s] (US Black) an unpleasant, unpopular woman. [? image of one suffering badly from menstrual cramps]

cramp *v.* (US) **1** [mid-19C] to execute, to kill (cf. CRAMPING CULL). **2** [late 19C] to annoy. [fig. uses of SE *cramp*, to compress, to restrict, to limit]

cramp! *excl.* [20C] euph. for CHRIST!, usu. as in mild oaths (cf. CRACKY!).

cramped *adj.* [18C] **1** hanged. **2** killed. [SE *cramp*, to torture by compressing or 'cramping' the body]

cramping-cull *n.* [18C–early 19C] the hangman. [CRAMP v. (1) + CULL n.[1] (4)]

cramp in the hand *n.* [19C] meanness.

cramp someone's style, to *phr.* [1910s+] to handicap, to hinder, to hold back, to get in someone's way, both fig. and lit.

cramp-ring/queer cramp-ring *n.* [16C–late 17C] (Und.) shackles or fetters. [SE *cramp*: a small iron bar with its ends bent into hooks ? + pun on the orig. 15C SE *cramp-ring*, a ring worn on the finger to ward of cramp, epilepsy etc + QUEER adj.[1] (1)]

cramp words *n.* [late 18C] (Und.) a sentence of death. [CRAMP v. (1) + SE *words*; note SE *cramp word*, a long, difficult or unusual word]

cranberry eye *n.* [late 19C] (US) a bloodshot eye (from excessive drinking). [the colour]

crane *v.* [mid-late 19C] to hesitate or balk before an obstacle. [SE *crane one's neck*, to stretch the neck to look around + hunting jargon *crane*, to pull up at a hedge or other obstacle and look over before leaping]

crank *n.*[1] **1** [late 16C–early 17C] a mendicant villain who specializes in faking sickness, esp. epilepsy, and who often displays convincingly horrific sores and wounds, created by the application of various herbs (cf. COUNTERFEIT CRANK). **2** [late 18C] the 'falling sickness', epilepsy. [Ger. *krenk*, sick]

crank *n.*[2] [late 18C] gin and water. [SE *crank*, lively]

crank *n.*[3] **1** [early 19C+] an eccentric. **2** [early 19C+] an obsessive, a monomaniac. **3** [early 19C+] a bad-tempered person, a 'grouch'. **4** [late 19C] (US) a baseball fan. **5** [late 19C] (US) a craze, a fad, an obsession. **6** [1950s+] (US prison) a veteran warder or inmate who finds it amusing to persecute younger and/or newer prisoners. [? back-form. of SE *cranky*, of capricious or wayward temper, difficult to please or *crank*, an eccentric notion or action, fig. a mental twist]

crank *n.*[4] **1** [1960s+] (drugs) any form of amphetamine drug. **2** [1970s+] a thrill of excitement, esp. when drug-generated. **3** [1980s+] (drugs) crack cocaine. [SE *crank* (up), i.e. such drugs *crank up* one's bodily 'motor']

crank *n.*[5] [1960s+] (orig. US) the penis (cf. DANGLE n.; DERRICK n.; DINGLE-DANGLE; PENDULUM). [resemblance to SE *crank*, a handle]

crank *adj.* [mid-19C] (US) proud. [SE *crank*, exultant, 'cocky']

crank/crank up *v.*[1] **1** [1930s+] to start up a mechanical device, esp. a car engine (but not with an actual crank handle). **2** [1960s+] (US) to get, to prepare (oneself). **3** [1960s+] to intensify, to do something more energetically.

4 [1960s+] to turn up the volume of a radio, etc. **5** [1980s] (US teen) an all-purpose word of movement, e.g., *crank oneself together, crank to school ...* . [SE *crank* v.]

crank/crank up v.[2] (drugs) **1** [1960s+] to inject narcotics with a hypodermic syringe. **2** [1980s+] to become intoxicated by amphetamine. [fig. uses of CRANK v.[1]]

crank cuffin n. [18C] (Und.) a tramp who poses as a sufferer from a sympathy-inducing illness. [CRANK n.[1] + CUFFIN]

cranked adj.[1] [late 19C] (US) mentally unbalanced. [CRANK n.[3] (1)]

cranked adj.[2] [1980s+] under the influence of amphetamine. [CRANK n.[4] (1)]

cranked up adj. [1950s+] (US) excited, 'revved up'. [CRANKED adj.[2]]

cranker n.[1] [1940s] (US) a doctor. [Ger. *krenk*, sick]

cranker n.[2] [1970s] (drugs) a heavy user of amphetamines. [CRANK n.[4] (1)]

cranking adj. [1980s+] (US campus) enjoyable, exciting. [? CRANKED UP]

cranking up n. [1970s+] (drugs) injecting a narcotic drug. [CRANK v.[2]]

crank it out v. [1970s+] to write (usu. rubbish) more from duty than pleasure or interest, to be a hack writer. [SE *crank*, to turn a handle]

crank it up v. [1980s+] to intensify, esp. to make louder, to turn up the volume. [CRANK v.[1] (4)]

crank off v. [1960s+] (US) to fire a round from a weapon.

crank on v. [1980s+] (US campus) to work hard and efficiently. [CRANK v.[1] (3)]

crank one's/the shank, to phr. [20C] to masturbate (cf. YANK ONE'S CRANK). [SE *crank*, to wind up, to twist + *shank*, a shaft, stem or 'neck']

crank out v. [1970s] (US campus) to produce large amounts of work, energy, sound etc. [CRANK v.[1] (3)]

crankpot n. [20C] (US) a mean, ill-tempered individual (cf. BARMPOT; CRACKPOT n.). [CRANK n.[3] (1) + *pot* (*of the head*), the skull, the cranium]

crankster n. [1980s+] (drugs) a user of amphetamine (cf. CRANKER n.[2]). [CRANK n.[4] (1)]

crank the monkey, to phr. [1990s] to masturbate. [var. on SPANK ONE'S MONKEY]

crank up *see* CRANK v.[1], v.[2].

cranky adj. **1** [mid-19C–late 19C] eccentric, foolish, rickety, capricious (cf. COUNTERFEIT CRANK). **2** [late 19C+] irritable, tetchy. [CRANK n.[3] (1); SE from 1900]

cranky hatch n. [20C] (US Und.) a psychiatric institution. [CRANKY + (BOOBY) HATCH]

cranky hutch n. [mid-19C] (US) a lunatic asylum (cf. CRANKY HATCH).

cranny n.[1] [19C] the vagina (cf. ARBOUR).

cranny n.[2] [mid-19C] (Anglo-Ind.) a (Bengali) clerk who writes in English. [Hind. *karani*, lit. 'a doer'. The Karana caste (Sudra mother and Vaisya father) specializes in accountancy and writing]

cranny-hunter/-haunter n. [19C] the penis. [CRANNY n.[1] + SE *hunter*]

crap n.[1] [late 17C–18C] money (cf. DUST n.[1]; MUCK n.[1]). [SE *crap*, waste, chaff]

crap n.[2] [late 18C–mid-19C] the gallows; thus *knock down/up for the crap*, to sentence to be hanged. [Du. *krap*, cramp or clasp]

crap n.[3] **1** [late 19C+] excrement. **2** [late 19C+] rubbish, nonsense, anything useless. **3** [late 19C+] an act of defecation. **4** [1920s+] (orig. US) the guts, the stuffing, esp. in phr. *beat/clean/kick/knock/whale the crap out of*, to give a thrashing to, *scare the crap out of*, to terrify. [mix of Du. *krappen*, to pluck off, cut off or separate + OF *crappe*, waste or rejected matter,

siftings, particularly 'the grain trodden under feet in the barn, and mingled with the straw and dust', ult. Med. Latin *crappa, crapinum*, the smaller chaff]

crap n.[4] [1910s+] (US) insolence, cheek, e.g. *don't give me that crap!* [but note CRAP n.[3] (2)]

crap, the n.[5] [1940s+] (US) used in excl., e.g. *what the crap do you want?* (cf. FUCK n.[3]).

crap n.[6] (US) **1** [1940s+] nothing at all. **2** [1950s+] trouble, problems (cf. SHIT n.[4]). [fig. uses of CRAP n.[3] (2)]

crap n.[7] [1950s+] a damn, esp. in phr. *give/not give a crap* (cf. GIVE A FUCK). [orig. UK dial., then US *c*.1920s, then back to UK in the 1950s]

crap/crop n.[8] [1980s+] (drugs) low quality heroin. [CRAP n.[3] (2)]

crap adj. [1950s] a general neg. description; unpleasant, disgusting, repellent, worthless etc. [CRAP n.[3] (2)]

crap/crop v.[1] [late 18C–mid-19C] to hang. [CRAP n.[2]]

crap v.[2] [late 19C+] to go to the lavatory, to defecate. [CRAP n.[3] (1)]

crap v.[3] **1** [late 19C+] to annoy, to irritate, to tell deliberate lies (to) (cf. CRAP AROUND). **3** [1930s+] to chatter (cf. CRAP ON). [CRAP n.[1] (2)]

crap around v. [1930s+] **1** to fool about. **2** to tell deliberate lies. **3** to annoy, to irritate. [ext. of CRAP v.[3] (1)]

crap artist n. [1930s+] (US) a liar, an exaggerator, a deceiver. [CRAP n.[3] (2) + ARTIST n.[2]]

crap a smoke, to phr. [1940s] (US) to smoke surreptitiously in a lavatory. [CRAP v.[2] +SE *smoke*]

crap-ass n. [1970s+] (US) a despicable, unpleasant person. [CRAP n.[3] (1) + ARSE n.[1] (4)]

crapaud smoke your pipe phr. [20C] (W.I.) a phr. meaning in a hopeless situation, in irretrievable difficulties (cf. GONE THROUGH THE EDDOES; IN DUCK'S GUTS). [Fr. *crapaud*, a toad]

crapbrain n. [1950s+] a general term of abuse, based on alleged stupidity of the recipient. [CRAP n.[3] (2) + sfx. -*brain*]

crap/crapping can n. [1930s+] (US) a lavatory. [CRAP n.[3] (3) + SE *can*, but note CAN n.[1] (1)]

crap course n. [1950s+] (US campus) an easy course. [CRAP adj. + SE *course*]

crap creek n. [1970s] (US) a troublesome, threatening situation (cf. SHIT CREEK). [fig. use of sl. phr.]

crape-/crêpe-hanger n. [1920s–40s] a pessimist, a kill-joy. [the hanging of black crape to signify mourning]

craperoo n. [1940s+] (US) absolute rubbish, nonsense. [CRAP n.[3] (2) + sfx. -*eroo*]

crap-happy adj. [1960s+] (US) foolishly happy. [play on SLAP-HAPPY adj.]

craphead n. [1950s+] (orig. US) a fool, an unpleasant person (cf. CRAPBRAIN; SHITHEAD). [CRAP n.[3] (2) + sfx. -*HEAD* (1)]

craphole n. [1930s+] a filthy, disgusting place (cf. SHITHOLE). [CRAP n.[3] (1) + SE *hole*]

craphouse n. [1930s+] (orig. US) **1** a lavatory (cf. CRAPPER n.[3]; CRAPPING CASTLE; CRAPPING KEN). **2** any unpleasant, dirty place. **3** (show business) a small, unfashionable venue. [CRAP n.[3] (1) + SE *house*]

craphouse luck n. [1960s] (US) unexpectedly good luck. [CRAPHOUSE + SE *luck*]

craphouse rat n. [1940s+] (US) an image of unpleasantness, in phr. *as cunning as a craphouse rat, as dirty as a craphouse rat*. [CRAPHOUSE + SE *rat*]

crapless adj. [1970s+] (US) terrified. [CRAP n.[3] (1) + sfx. -*less*; var. on SCARED SHITLESS]

crapola n. [1960s+] (US) nonsense, rubbish. [CRAP n.[3] (2) + sfx. -OLA]

crap on v.[1] [1940s+] (orig. US) **1** to treat contemptuously, to victimize. **2** as imper. to hell with, e.g. *crap on this job*. [fig. use of CRAP v.[2]]

crap on/on about v.[2] [1940s+] (orig. US) **1** to talk lengthily, if irrelevantly (about). **2** to complain (about). [CRAP n.[3] (2)]

crap-out n. [1960s+] (US) defeatist, a quitter. [CRAP OUT]

crap out v. (US) **1** [20C] to fail, to go wrong, to blunder. **2** [1920s+] to kill. **3** [1920s+] to back down, to give up, esp. in humiliating circumstances. **4** [1940s+] of people, to collapse, to become exhausted, to fall asleep. **5** [1940s+] to die (cf. CASH IN ONE'S CHECKS). **6** [1950s+] of machinery, to break down. [SE *crap out*, to make a losing throw in the game *craps*. Note COME CRABS, taken f. the losing cards, two aces, in the game of hazard; in the dice game *craps* a pair of ones, known as *snake-eyes*, is similarly a losing throw]

crapped/cropped adj. [late 18C–mid-19C] hanged. [CRAP n.[2]]

crapped out adj. [1930s+] (US) **1** to have been defeated in any challenge. **2** to have hit rock bottom. [CRAP OUT v.]

crapper n.[1] [late 19C+] (US) a liar, a very unpleasant person. [CRAP n.[3] (2)]

crapper n.[2] [20C] (Irish) a half-glass of whisky. [? dial. *crap*, settlings of bear at the bottom of a barrel]

crapper n.[3] [1920s+] (US) **1** a lavatory. **2** the anus, the buttocks. [CRAP n.[3] (3)]

crapper dick n. [20C] (US) a policeman who specializes in hanging around public lavatories in the hope of entrapping gay men having sex (cf. PRETTY POLICE). [CRAPPER n.[3] + DICK n.[6] (2)]

crapping adj. [1950s+] general pej. description, useless, second-rate, disgusting. [CRAP adj.]

crapping casa/case n. [mid-19C] a privy or water-closet (cf. CRAPPING CASTLE; CRAPPING KEN). [CRAP v.[2] + CASA/CASE n.[2]]

crapping castle n. [mid-19C] a privy. [var. on CRAPPING CASA]

crapping/cropping ken n. [late 18C–mid-19C] a privy (cf. CRAPPING CASA). [CRAP v.[2] + KEN n.[1]]

crappo n. [19C] a Frenchman (cf. FROG n.[1]). [Fr. *crapaud*, toad]

crappo adj. [20C] disgusting, appalling (cf. CRAPPY). [CRAP adj. + sfx. -o]

crappy adj. **1** [mid-19C+] fouled with excrement. **2** [1920s+] unpleasant, distasteful. **3** [1930s] (Glasgow) terrified. **4** [1940s+] second-rate. [CRAP n.[3] (2) + sfx. -y]

craps n. [1940s+] dice (cf. COME OFF CRABS; CRAP OUT). [the dice game SE *craps*]

craps! see CRIPES!

crap-shoot n. [1960s+] any situation in which luck, not judgement, is of paramount importance. [SE *shoot craps*; thus an image of random luck]

crap-slinger n. [1930s] (US) one who talks nonsense, whether for personal advantage or simply through lack of intelligence (cf. CRAP ARTIST). [CRAP n.[3] (2) + SE *slinger*]

crap up v. (orig. US) **1** [1940s+] to ruin by adding unnecessary or distasteful accessories. **2** [1950s+] to make a mess of (cf. FOUL UP). [fig. use of CRAP v.[2]]

crap work n. [1970s+] (orig. US) unpleasant, exhausting, dirty, menial or repetitive work. [CRAP adj. + SE *work*]

crash n.[1] **1** [late 19C–1910s] (US) an outstanding success. **2** [1900s] (US campus) a crush, an infatuation. [SE *crash*]

crash n.[2] [20C] (Aus.) an act of defecation. [? the noise]

crash n.[3] [1900s] (US campus) a complete failure in an examination. [SE *crash*]

crash n.[4] **1** [1940s+] a nap, a sleep. **2** [1960s+] (drugs) the return to 'normality' that follows drug-taking. [CRASH v.[4]]

crash v.[1] **1** [late 17C–19C] to kill. **2** [1940s+] (US) to hit someone hard. [dial. *crash*, to break violently into pieces]

crash/crash out v.[2] [20C] (US prison) to escape.

crash v.[3] [1920s+] (orig. US) to appear uninvited at a given party or other function. [abbr. GATECRASH]

crash v.[4] **1** [1940s+] (orig. Aus.) to sleep, to collapse exhausted, ext. as *crash out*. **2** [1960s+] to stay, to lodge, to board; thus *crash at*, stay at; *crash with*, stay with. **3** [1960s+]

(drugs) to collapse, esp. after a bout of heavy drug (esp. amphetamine) use. [orig. from RN sl. *crash the swede*, to sleep; as such it migrated first to Aus. then to US and finally back to UK]

crash a bottle, to phr. [16C] to be drunk. [lit. to 'crush a bottle']

crash and burn v. **1** [1970s+] to collapse emotionally (and sometimes physically too). **2** [1980s+] (US campus) to sleep. **3** [1980s+] (US campus) to have a disastrous social experience.

crasher n.[1] **1** [late 19C] a lie. **2** [1910s+] usu. of people, a (very great) bore. **3** [1980s+] (US campus) one who cannot tolerate alcohol.

crasher n.[2] [1920s+] an uninvited guest at a party. [CRASH v.[3]]

crasher n.[3] [1940s+] someone who collapses from fatigue. [CRASH v.[4]]

crash-hot adj. [1950s+] (Aus.) first-rate, excellent (cf. SHIT-HOT). [fig. use of CRASH n.[1] + SE *hot*]

crashing adj. [1930s+] overwhelming, extreme, esp. in phr. *crashing bore*, an extremely boring person. [SE *crash* + sfx. -*ing*]

crashing-/crassing-cheats n. [mid-16C–mid-19C] (Und.) **1** the teeth. **2** apples, pears or any other fruit. [SE *crash* + CHEAT n., lit. 'crushing or crunching things'; thus, for (2), things that may be crunched]

crash-o! excl. [1910s+] excl. of wonder or surprise, or regret at having to face unpleasant circumstances.

crash out see CRASH v.[2].

crash-pad n. [1960s–70s] a flat or house in which any passing friends or strangers can find a bed at short notice. [CRASH v.[4] (2) + PAD n.[2] (2)]

crash the gate, to phr. [1920s–50s] (US) to enter uninvited. [abbr. GATECRASH]

crassing-cheats see CRASHING-CHEATS.

crate n.[1] **1** [mid–late 19C] (US) an old or worthless horse. **2** [1920s+] an aeroplane. **3** [1920s+] an automobile. [SE *crate*, a container; all descriptions carry a taint of inferiority and/or the possibility of a physical or mechanical breakdown]

crate n.[2] [1920s] (US) a coffin. [ext. of SE use]

crater/cratur/crathur n.[1] [mid-17C+] (Irish) whisky, esp. Irish whisky. [Irish pron. of CREATURE n.[1]]

crater n.[2] (US) **1** [1960s+] (drugs) an abscess that is caused by the long-term injection of narcotics. **2** [1980s+] (campus/teen) an acne scar; thus *craterface*, a term of abuse used to mock an acne sufferer.

cratur/crathur see CRATER n.[1].

crave n. [1980s+] (US campus) the object of one's infatuation.

craven/cravicious adj. [1950s+] (W.I. Rasta) greedy, gluttonous (cf. LICKERISH). [ext. of SE *crave*, to desire intensely]

craw n. **1** [late 16C–early 19C] the stomach, the guts. **2** [late 18C–mid-19C] a cravat that falls over the chest and stomach. **3** [20C] (W.I.) cheek, audacity, nerve. [SE *craw*, the crop of a bird or insect]

crawfish n. **1** [mid-19C+] (orig. US) a coward, a groveller, one who backs down from a challenge, esp. a physical one (cf. CRAB n.[1]). **2** [mid-19C+] (orig. US) a political turncoat or rebel. **3** [1960s] (US) a French person. **4** [1970s+] (US campus) a stingy, mean person. [CRAWFISH v.]

crawfish v. **1** [19C] to grovel, to abase oneself before another. **2** [mid-19C+] to back down, to renege on a previous statement or commitment. **3** [mid-19C] to move backwards, to retreat, to run away. [SE *crawfish*, the US synon. for *crayfish*, a lobster-like crustacean. The term echoes the characteristic backwards movement of the fish]

crawl n. (US) **1** [mid-19C] a promenade, a street used for parading and socializing by the local youth (cf. STROLL). **2** [1920s] a dance.

crawl v.[1] [early 19C+] to be (over-)abundantly supplied (cf. CRAWLING adj.).

crawl v.[2] **1** [late 19C] (US) to leave quietly or stealthily. **2** [late 19C–1930s] (US) to mount a horse. **3** [late 19C+] to assault. **4** [late 19C+] to spend a night moving from one nightclub, bar or public house to the next; thus *beer crawl, gin crawl, pub crawl*. **5** [1940s+] (US) to have sexual intercourse.

crawl/crawl to v.[3] [1940s+] to behave sycophantically; thus *do a crawl*, to grovel, to act the toady.

crawler n.[1] **1** [18C] an insect, spec. a louse. **2** [early 19C+] a lazy person, a loiterer; thus ext. as *old crawler*. **3** [mid–late 19C] a cab moving slowly along the streets in search of a fare. **4** [mid-19C+] (Aus.) a slow-moving, unexcitable domestic animal, esp. a sheep. **5** [late 19C] (Aus.) a shepherd, a musterer; one who mends boundary fences (cf. LIZARD n.[2]). **6** [1920s] (US) a legless beggar, usu. moving with the aid of a small wheeled platform.

crawler n.[2] [mid-19C+] (orig. Aus.) one who acts in a mean or servile way. [CRAWL v.[3]]

crawling/crawling with adj. **1** [mid-19C+] infested with insects or vermin and by extension with a crowd of (unappealing) people. **2** [1910s+] very rich (cf. LOUSY WITH). [CRAWL v.[1]]

crawling dandruff see GALLOPING DANDRUFF.

crawl-out n. [1900s] (US) an excuse, an evasion.

crawl out of the woodwork see COME OUT OF THE WOODWORK.

crawl someone's frame, to phr. [1900s–40s] (US) to give someone a beating or thrashing. [dial. *crawl*, to reprimand, to tell off, to attack physically; ? ult. 16C SE *crawl*, to entangle + SE *frame*]

crawl someone's hump, to phr. [19C+] (US) to attack, to assault. [for ety. see CRAWL ONE'S FRAME + SE *hump*]

crawl to see CRAWL v.[3].

crawl up the wall, to phr. [late 18C–mid-19C] to run up credit at a public house (cf. WALK UP THE WALL). [the inscribing of one's debts on a slate mounted on the wall]

crawly-mawly adj. [mid-19C] ill, sickly, ailing. [Norfolk dial.; cf. synon. Sussex dial: *frobly-mobly*]

crawsick adj. [1920s+] (Irish) suffering from a hangover. [SE *craw* + *sick*]

craw-thumper n. [late 18C+] **1** a Roman Catholic (cf. BREAST FLEET). **2** (US) a native of Maryland. **3** (Irish) an overtly pious individual. [CRAW n. (1) + SE *thumper*, lit. breast-beater; Catholics were heavily represented amongst the founders of the colony that became the state of Maryland]

cray n. [20C] (Aus.) a crayfish. [abbr.]

crayfish n. [late 19C–1930s] (Aus./N.Z.) a coward, a groveller, one who backs down from a challenge, esp. a physical one. [var. on CRAWFISH n.]

crazo n. [1970s+] (orig. US) a mad person, an eccentric. [CRAZY n. + sfx. -O]

crazy n. [19C+] (orig. US) a mad person.

crazy adj.[1] **1** [late 19C+] keen on, enthusiastic, esp. as *crazy for*. **2** [1940s–50s] (US Black/beatnik) a general intensifier, wonderful, amazing, weird, according to context (cf. MAD adj.[2]; MENTAL adj.).

crazy adj.[2] [1990s] (US Black) a lot, very much, a great deal.

crazy adv. [1990s] (US Black) extremely, very.

crazy alley n. [20C] (US Und.) a special part of a prison used for insane prisoners.

crazy-arse see CRAZY-ASS.

crazy as a bedbug phr. [1920s+] (orig. US) extremely eccentric. [such bugs make one 'itch']

crazy as/like a fox phr. [1930s+] (US) cunning, shrewd. [the *locus classicus* is its use as a book title by the US humorist S.J. Perelman in 1944]

crazy-ass/-arse adj. [1930s+] (US) insane, utterly eccentric. [SE *crazy* + sfx. -ASS]

crazy-back n. [late 19C] a foolish young woman.

crazy brim see CRAZY RIM.

crazy coke n. [1970s+] (drugs) phencyclidine (cf. ACE n.[3]). [SE *crazy* + COKE n.[1] (1)]

crazy eddie n. [1970s] (drugs) phencyclidine (cf. ACE n.[3]).

crazy farm/house n. [1960s] (US) a psychiatric institution (cf. CUCKOO FARM; FARM n.[4]; FOOL FARM; FRUIT FARM; FUNNY FARM; LOONY FARM; NUT FARM).

crazy for adj. extremely enthusiastic, obsessed by.

crazyhead n. [1970s] (US) a mad person. [SE *crazy* + sfx. -HEAD (1)]

crazyhead whisky n. [late 19C] (US) very strong whisky. [CRAZYHEAD + SE *whisky*; the effect it has on one's head]

crazy house see CRAZY FARM.

crazy jack n. [late 19C] an affected young man. [SE *crazy* + JACK n.[5]/generic use of proper name]

crazy, mixed-up kid n. [1950s] (orig. US) one (esp. a young person) who is seen as emotionally unbalanced due to a variety of social and personal circumstances; esp. as used of teenagers by conventional speakers who, ultimately, could not understand what they saw as mad behaviour.

crazy rim/brim n. [1960s] (US Black) a desirable style of hat. [CRAZY adj.[1] (2) + SE *rim/brim*]

crazy water n. [1930s–50s] (Can./US) whisky. [its effects]

crazy weed n. [1920s+] (orig. US, drugs) marijuana (cf. LOCOWEED). [its supposed effects]

creaker n. [1900s–40s] (US Black) an old person. [SE *creak*; the ref. is to one's joints]

c.r.e.a.m. n. [1990s] (US Black) money. [abbr. *cash rules everything around me*]

cream n.[1] **1** [late 19C+] semen (cf. BABY GRAVY). **2** [late 19C+] vaginal secretions. **3** [1920s+] (Aus.) whisky.

cream n.[2] [1990s] anything simple or very easy.

cream v.[1] **1** [1920s+] (orig. US) to destroy, to beat up comprehensively, to overcome easily (cf. SCHMEER v.). **2** [1930s+] to win a sporting competition, to pass an examination easily or decisively. [the perceived superiority of cream to milk]

cream v.[2] [1950s+] **1** of a man, to ejaculate. **2** of a woman, for the vagina to become wet. [CREAM n.[1] (1), (2)]

cream billy see CREAM FANCY.

cream crackered adj. [1990s] exhausted, tired out. [rhy. sl. *cream crackered* = KNACKERED]

cream crackers n. [1990s] the testicles. [rhy. sl. *cream crackers* = KNACKERS]

creamed adj. **1** [1920s+] utterly defeated. **2** [1960s+] (US) very drunk. [CREAM v.[1] (1)]

creamed beef n. [1990s] semen; thus *cream one's beef*, to masturbate (cf. BABY GRAVY). [CREAM n.[1] (1) + BEEF n.[1] (3)]

creamer n. **1** [1950s+] (Aus.) one who lacks control of their emotions. **2** [1990s] a chronic premature ejaculator. [CREAM v.[2]]

cream fancy/billy n. [19C] a decorated handkerchief prized by London costermongers; the *cream fancy* had a white or cream background with a variety of patterns. [SE *cream* + *fancy* (*handkerchief*)/BILLY n.[4]]

cream-ice jack n. [late 19C–1900s] a street-seller of ice-cream.

creamie n.[1] [20C] (Aus.) a derog. term for the offspring of White and Aborigine parents. [their complexion]

creamie n.[2] [1970s] an attractive and sexually malleable woman (cf. BANANA n.[2]). [SE *creamy*, smooth; ? she makes the onlooker 'cream his jeans']

creamie/creamy piece n. [1970s] (Aus.) a half-Aboriginal woman. [CREAMIE n.[1] + PIECE n.[1]]

creaming n. [1960s+] (Und.) stealing from one's employer, usu. on a small, but protracted scale (cf. SKIMMING). [fig. 'skimming the cream' from the firm's income]

cream in one's jeans *see* CREAM ONE'S JEANS.

cream jugs *n.* [20C] the female breasts (cf. BORDENS; DUGS; FEEDING BOTTLES; JUGS n.¹; JUJUBES; MILK BAR n.²; MILK-BOTTLES; MILKERS; MILK FACTORIES; MILK SHAKES; MILK-SHOP; MILKY WAY; NINNY JUGS; NORKS; UDDERS).

cream of the valley *n.* [19C] **1** whisky. **2** gin (cf. COLD CREAM; MOUNTAIN DEW).

cream one's cock, to *phr.* [1990s] to masturbate. [CREAM v.² + COCK n.² (1)]

cream one's corn, to *phr.* [1990s] to masturbate. [CREAM v.2 + pun on SE *cream corn*]

cream/cream in one's jeans, to *phr.* [1960s+] to become very excited, lit. to ejaculate while still fully dressed (cf. COME IN ONE'S PANTS). [CREAM v.² + SE *jeans*]

cream-pot love *n.* [late 18C] false protestations of love, esp. as offered dairymaids by amorous young men.

cream puff *n.* **1** [late 19C–1900s] (US) an excellent person or object. **2** [20C] (orig. US) a weakling. **3** [1960s+] a male homosexual. [fig. uses of SE; (3) pun on PUFF n.³]

cream puff freak *n.* [1960s+] (US) a prostitute's client who achieves sexual arousal by throwing gooey cakes at the woman. [SE *cream puff* + FREAK n. (4)]

creams *n.* [late 19C–1900s] the Coldstream Guards (cf. COLD-CREAMS).

creamstick *n.* [19C+] the penis; thus *have a go at the cream-stick*, of a woman, to have sexual intercourse. [CREAM n.¹ (1) + SE *stick*; 20C use mainly US Black]

cream the cheese, to *phr.* [1990s] to masturbate. [CREAM v.² + (COCK) CHEESE]

cream the pie, to *phr.* [1990s] to masturbate. [CREAM v.²]

creamy *n.* [1990s] (US Black/drugs) premium grade crack cocaine. [CREAMY adj.]

creamy *adj.* [late 19C+] **1** excellent, first-rate. **2** of women, very attractive.

creamy do *n.* [1950s+] a piece of exceptionally fortunate luck. [CREAMY adj. + DO n.²]

creamy love bullets *n.* [1990s] ejaculation. [CREAM n.¹ (1)]

creamy piece *see* CREAMIE PIECE.

crease *v.* [20C] **1** to harm, to spoil. **2** to beat severely.

creased *adj.* [1940s+] **1** collapsing in laughter. **2** exhausted, tired out. [CREASE v.; underpinned by the image of one's body bent double with laughter or tiredness; thus 'creasing' at the waist]

crease up *v.* [1940s+] **1** to collapse with laughter. **2** to cause someone to collapse with laughter. [for ety. *see* CREASED]

create *v.* [1910s+] to make a fuss, to 'go on about'. [abbr. SE *create a fuss*]

create an arch, to *phr.* [1990s] to masturbate (cf. PAINT THE CEILING). [? the ejaculation's curve through the air]

create fuck, to *phr.* [1920s+] to display anger or annoyance. [SE *create* + FUCK n.²]

creation *n.* [19C+] euph. for *Christ*, usu. as used in mild oaths (cf. CRACKY!).

creature, the *n.¹* [mid-17C+] **1** wine. **2** whisky, esp. Irish whisky.

creature *n.²* [20C] (W.I.) an ugly person. [? the 'creatures' that populate horror films]

cred *n.* [1970s+] lit. *credibility*. The term, as used mainly in the 1970s–80s by young people (and those who purvey their material wants), was used to indicate that something had a populist, anti-establishment, 'street' level of acceptability (cf. CRED adj.; STREET CRED). [abbr.]

cred *adj.* [1970s+] lit. *credible*. The term, as used mainly in the 1970s–80s by young people (and those who purvey their material wants), meant acceptable on a populist, anti-establishment, 'street' level, unaffected by puffery, artistic pretentiousness and similar negative trappings (cf. CRED n.; STREET CRED). [abbr.]

credentials *n.* **1** [late 19C+] the male genitals. **2** [1960s+] (US) the female breasts (cf. PARTICULARS).

credit card *n.* [1980s+] (drugs) a crack cocaine pipe. [ety. unknown]

creeme *v.* [late 17C–18C] (Und.) to slip something unobtrusively into another person's hand. [? slippery smoothness of SE *cream*]

creep *n.* **1** [mid-19C+] an unpleasant person, with poss. implication of some physical peculiarity or of criminality. **2** [1910s+] a stealthy robber, a sneak thief, esp. one who works in a brothel. **3** [1920s–50s] the profession of sneak-thieving, esp. when pursued in a brothel. [fig. uses of SE; (1) orig. dial.]

creep *v.* **1** [mid-19C+] to forgo one's pride and beg unashamedly, to curry favour, to 'suck up to' (cf. CRAWL v.³). **2** [1910s+] to rob stealthily, to work as a sneak-thief. **3** [1910s+] (US) for a prostitute to distract her customer while an accomplice slips into the room and rifles his wallet; since he always has to pay in advance, he won't check his money till they have parted. **4** [1920s+] (US Black) to flirt, to make sexual advances, to have a clandestine meeting, usu. that between two adulterous or cheating lovers. **5** [1920s+] (US Black) to sneak up on, to stalk someone with malice aforethought. **6** [1940s+] to inform. **7** [1980s+] (US Black teen) to go about one's business surreptitiously and quietly. **8** [1980s+] (US campus) to go out on the town. **9** [1990s] (US Black) to ride slowly in a car.

creep! *excl.* [1950s] go away!

creep away and die! *excl.* [1920s] a cruel dismissal.

creepazoid *n.* [1980s+] (US) an unpleasant person. [CREEP n. (1) + quasi SF sfx. *-azoid*]

creeper *n.¹* [17C+] a toady, a sycophant (cf. ARSE-CRAWLER; CRAWLER n.²). [CREEP n.¹ (1)]

creeper *n.²* **1** [17C+] a louse. **2** [early 19C] a penny-a-line hack. **3** [19C] a foot. **4** [19C+] (Und./police) a sneak-thief, esp. when also a prostitute. **5** [1920s–40s] (US Black) an adulterous or cheating lover. **6** [1940s] (US Black) a policeman. [fig. uses of SE, they all *creep around*]

creeper joint *n.* [1930s] (US) an opium den where the semi-conscious sleepers are robbed of their possessions. [CREEPER n.² (4) + JOINT n.³ (1)]

creepers *n.* **1** [19C+] the feet. **2** [late 19C+] (US) soft shoes worn by burglars, sneak-thieves and prison guards. **3** [1950s+] suede shoes, often dyed in lurid colours, with thick rubber soles (cf. BROTHEL CREEPERS).

creepers! *excl.* [1940s] (US) euph. for CHRIST!, usu. as a mild oath (cf. CRACKY!; JEEPERS CREEPERS!).

creep house *n.* [1910s+] (US) a brothel or unwholesome apartment house, esp. one where patrons are robbed (cf. ACCOMMODATION HOUSE; CREEP JOINT). [CREEP v. (3) + HOUSE n.¹ (1)]

creepie-crawlies *n.* [late 19C+] a feeling of dread, of foreboding. [ext. of CREEPS n.¹]

creeping *n.* [late 16C–early 17C] (Und.) men and women robbing together (cf. CREEPING AND TILLING). [CREEP v. (3)]

creeping and tilling *n.* [1910s+] (US Black) diverting a store cashier's attention while a confederate opens and robs the till. [CREEP v. (2) + LAW n.¹]

creeping Jesus *n.* [early 19C+] a whining, sneaking person (cf. HOPPING JESUS; SLEEPING JESUS). [CREEP v. (1) + SE *Jesus* as a timid, weak person]

creeping law *n.* [late 16C–early 17C] (Und.) robbery carried out by minor thieves, concentrating on suburban homes. [CREEP v. (2) + LAW n.¹]

creep joint *n.* [1920s+] **1** a brothel or unwholesome apartment house, esp. one where patrons are robbed (cf. CREEP PAD). **2** a gambling game operating in a different location each night. **3** anywhere run by unpleasant or unpopular people. [CREEP v. (3) + JOINT n.³]

creepo n. [1950s+] an unpleasant person. [CREEP n. (1) + sfx. -O]

creepola n. [1980s] (US) anything or anyone unpleasant. [CREEP n. (1) + sfx. -OLA]

creep on v. (US Black) **1** [1920s–40s] to cheat, esp. sexually. **2** [1990s] to sneak up on someone, with the intention of attacking them physically. **3** [1990s] to follow. [CREEP v. (2)]

creep out of the woodwork see COME OUT OF THE WOODWORK.

creep pad n. [1940s] (US) a brothel or unwholesome apartment house, esp. where patrons are robbed (cf. CREEP JOINT). [CREEP v.² (3) + PAD n.² (2)]

creep someone out, to phr. [1980s+] (US) to terrify, to unnerve, to 'give the creeps'. [CREEPS n.¹]

creeps, the n.¹ [mid-19C+] a feeling of dread, of foreboding; thus *give one the creeps*, to worry, to perturb, to disgust. [the image of something creeping on one's body]

creeps n.² [20C] (US Black) the feet.

creepshow adj. [1980s+] awful, disgusting. [the horror film title]

creepsville n. [1980s+] any unappealing place. [CREEP n. (1) + sfx. -VILLE]

creep up someone's arse/ass, to phr. [late 17C+] to toady, to 'suck up' to. [CREEP v. (1) + ARSE n.¹]

creepy-crawly n. [19C+] an insect, usu. juv. use. [its movements]

creepy pete n. [1950s] (US) cheap, rotgut wine. [SE *creepy* + (SNEAKY) PETE; i.e. its effects 'creep up' on the drinker]

crem n. [1940s+] a *crem*atorium. [abbr.]

cremmie n. [1960s+] (Aus.) a *crem*atorium (cf. CREM). [abbr.]

cremorne n. [19C] the penis. [pun on CREAM n.¹ (1) + HORN n.² (1) but note *Cremorne* Gardens, Chelsea, the increasingly notorious 'pleasure gardens']

crêpe-hanger see CRAPE-HANGER.

crepe sole n. [1940s] (W.I.) a large, solid cake (cf. JOE LOUIS). [resemblance, texture]

cretin n. [1970s] an obnoxious person.

crevice n. [19C] the vagina (cf. ARBOUR).

crew n. **1** [1960s+] a gang, usu. football supporters, who engage in fights with rivals. **2** [1980s+] (US) orig. used in US by young Blacks to denote a teen gang, spec. of rap singers, break dancers or graffiti, the term has crossed the Atlantic and now, in UK use, both Black and White means simply a gang (cf. MASSIVE n.; POSSE n.). [note *crew*, meaning a villainous gang, dates back at least to late 17C (B.E., 1690); 'a crew of rogues' + note 16C CANTING CREW]

Cri, the n. [late 19C+] the *Cri*terion (bar, restaurant) at Piccadilly Circus, London, which was ultra-fashionable in the late 19C and revamped in the 1990s. [abbr.]

crib n.¹ **1** [mid-17C–early 18C] provisions. **2** [late 19C+] (Aus.) a snack, a light meal, a piece of bread, cake etc. [SE *crib*, a container for animal fodder]

crib n.² [late 17C+] *crib*bage. [abbr.]

crib n.³ **1** [19C] (Und.) a dwelling house, a shop, a public house, an apartment (cf. CRACK A CRIB). **2** [19C] a small, cheap brothel or 'low' saloon. **3** [19C] a berth, a situation, e.g. a *snug crib*, a safe. **4** [19C+] (US Black) a house or other living place. **5** [early 19C+] a bed. **6** [20C] (US) a prison cell. **7** [1980s+] (US Black/campus) one's home. [16C SE *crib*, a small house or narrow room; the term evolved into 19C cant, and has survived in 20C US Black use]

crib n.⁴ **1** [early 19C+] a translation of a classic or other work in a foreign language, for the illegitimate use of students (cf.

ANIMAL n.³). **2** [1980s+] (US campus) an easy course. [CRIB v.¹ (1)]

crib n.⁵ [1940s] a grumble, a complaint. [CRIB v.⁴]

crib n.⁶ [1980s+] (drugs) crack cocaine.

crib v.¹ [mid-18C–19C] **1** to steal, to take surreptitiously. **2** 'to withhold, keep back, pinch, or thieve a part out of money given to lay out for necessaries' (Dyche, 1748). [? SE *crib*, a small wickerwork container, poss. used by a poacher]

crib v.² [late 18C+] (student) to cheat, to take or copy (a passage, a piece of translation etc) without acknowledgement, to plagiarize. [ext. of CRIB v.¹ (1)]

crib v.³ [early–mid-19C] to fight, using the fists and in an honourable manner. [the prize-fighter Tom *Cribb*]

crib v.⁴ [1920s–40s] to complain, to grumble. [SE *crib-biting*, of a horse, to bite the crib or fodder container]

crib v.⁵ [1960s+] (US Black) **1** to live one's uneventful, daily life. **2** to live at home. **3** to sleep. **4** to stay in a place. [CRIB n.³ (4)]

cribbage-faced adj. [late 18C–mid-19C] a face marked with small-pox scars. [the supposed resemblance of such scars to the small holes found in a cribbage board]

cribbage-peg n. [1920s] a leg. [rhy. sl.]

cribber n.¹ [late 19C] one who uses some form of illicit aid when taking examinations or similar tests. [CRIB v.²]

cribber n.² [late 19C+] a horse that bites parts of its stall, sucking air into its lungs. [SE *crib-biter*, a horse that bites the metal crib in which its fodder is placed]

Cribbeys/Cribbey Islands n. [late 18C–early 19C] back alleys, narrow courts and by-ways (cf. ALSATIA). [derived f. older nicknames BERMUDAS and thence CARIBEE ISLANDS, both of which had been applied to the alleyways of 16C–18C Covent Garden, then a centre of vice and criminality. Grose (1785) offers an alternative ety.: 'perhaps from the houses built there being cribbed (stolen) out of the common way or passage']

cribbing n. [mid-17C] (Und.) provisions. [CRIB n.¹]

crib-biter n. [mid-19C] a grumbler. [SE *crib-biter*, a horse that bites the metal crib in which its fodder is placed]

crib course n. [1960s+] (US campus) a very easy course. [CRIB v.²]

crib-cracker n. [mid-19C–1900s] a house-breaker. [CRIB n.² + CRACK v.⁵ (1)]

crib-crust Monday n. [mid-19C] (juv.) the Monday before Advent (cf. PAY-OFF WEDNESDAY; STIR-UP SUNDAY; TUG-BUTTON TUESDAY). [? CRIB v.¹ (1) + SE *crust*; one has no money for food and must scrounge crusts]

crib house n. [1910s–40s] a brothel, esp. a small and dirty one (cf. ACCOMMODATION HOUSE; CRIB JOINT). [CRIB n.³ (2) + HOUSE n.¹ (1)]

crib joint n. [1920s–40s] a brothel, esp. a small and dirty one (cf. CRIB HOUSE). [CRIB n.³ (2) + JOINT n.³ (3)]

crib man n. [1920s–40s] (US Und.) one who specializes in breaking into houses and apartments. [CRIB n.³ + sfx. -*man*]

cribsheet n. [1950s+] a translation of a classic or other work in a foreign language, for the illegitimate use of students. [CRIB n.⁴ + SE *sheet*]

cricket bats n. [20C] (Aus.) the teeth. [rhy. sl. *cricket bats* = TATS n.¹]

crickets adj. [1990s] (US teen) quiet, silent. [phr. *It's so quiet one could hear the crickets chirping*]

cricket team n. [1940s–50s] (Aus.) a small, sparse moustache. [it only has 11 (hairs) each side]

crickey! see CRIKEY!

Cricklewitch n. [1970s+] (derog.) the London suburb of Cricklewood (cf. ABRAHAMSTEAD). [*Cricklewood* + 'Jewish' sfx. -*witch* (*vich*); there is a large Jewish population in the district]

cries and screeches n. [20C] (Aus.) leeches. [rhy. sl.]

crig *n.* [1940s+] (Irish) a testicle. [? Irish *creag/creig*, a rock, thus pun on ROCKS n.³ (1)]

crikey!/crickey! *excl.* [mid-19C+] euph. for CHRIST! (cf. CRACKY!).

crim *n.* [1950s+] (US/Aus./N.Z.) a *crim*inal. [abbr.; one of the three classes in Aus. prison: *screws* (warders and other prison employees), *gigs* (visitors and casual workers) and *crims*]

crimast! *excl.* [20C] (orig. US) euph. for CHRIST!, usu. in mild oaths (cf. CRACKY!).

crim. con. *n.* [late 18C–19C] adultery; thus *crim. con. money*, the damages that a jury directs to be paid by a convicted adulterer as compensation to the husband whose wife has allegedly been seduced. [abbr. legal jargon *criminal conversation*, 'the trespass against the husband at common law' (the concept was abandoned in 1857). *Conversation* in this context means sexual intercourse]

crime *v.* [1980s+] to commit crimes (cf. JAIL v.).

crimea *n.¹* [mid-19C] a full beard. [the troops serving in the Crimean War (1854–6) grew their beards long in a small attempt to alleviate the cold]

crimea *n.²* [late 19C+] beer. [rhy. sl.]

crime-buster *n.* [1950s+] a detective, a policeman, a melodramatic image esp. popular in tabloid press. [SE *crime* + BUST v.¹]

crimes! *excl.* [mid-19C+] euph. for CHRIST!, usu. in mild oaths (cf. CRACKY!).

crimey *n.* [1980s+] (US Und.) a partner in crime, an accomplice, a friend (cf. HOMIE). [note the association is usu. but need not invariably be criminal]

criminy!/criminey! *excl.* [17C+] (orig. US) euph. for CHRIST!, usu. in mild oaths (cf. CRACKY!; JIMINY). [the euph. interpretation is the most likely, but the *OED* also suggests ? Ital. *crimine*, a crime, used as a 17C ejaculation]

crimmie *n.* [1980s+] (drugs) a cigarette laced with crack cocaine. [? SE *crime*; i.e. the CRACK n.¹⁷ renders the cigarette illegal]

crimmo *n.* [1950s+] (Aus./N.Z.) a *crim*inal. [abbr. + sfx. -O]

crimp *n.* [20C] (Aus.) a swindler, a cheat.

crimp *v. see* PLAY CRIMP.

crimper *n.* [1960s] a hairdresser. [SE *crimp*, to curl]

crimping fellow *n.* [late 17C–early 18C] a blackguard, an untrustworthy villain. [SE *crimp*, one who 'presses' men into the RN against their will]

crimps! *excl.* [20C] (orig. US) euph. for CHRIST!, usu. in mild oaths (cf. CRACKY!).

crimp the wire, to *phr.* [1990s] to masturbate. [SE *crimp*, to pinch + WIRE n.³]

crimson *n.* [late 19C+] (US campus) Harvard University. [the university colours]

crimson chitterling *n.* [19C] the penis (cf. BACON n.¹; CHITTERLINGS n.¹).

crimson dawn *n.* [1930s] (Glasgow) cheap red wine (cf. RED BIDDY).

crimson rambler *n.* [19C+] (US) a bedbug. [SE *crimson rambler*, a variety of climbing rose]

crinched *adj.* [1970s+] (US campus) bent, dented. [SE *crimped*, pinched]

cringe, cringe, grovel, grovel *phr.* [1950s+] a phr. used after one has committed some form of embarrassing solecism and wish to leave the error with humour.

crink *n.* [1980s+] (drugs) methamphetamine. [? CRANK n.⁴ (1)]

crinkle *n.* [1940s+] paper money (cf. CRINKLER).

crinklepouch *n.* [late 16C] a sixpence. [it makes barely any impact on the shape of one's purse]

crinkler *n.* [20C] (Irish) a currency note (cf. CRINKLE; FOLDING).

crinkle top *n.* [1970s] (US Black) a woman with hair that

remains in an unstraightened or otherwise 'Whitened' style (cf. AFRO n.²; NATURAL n.⁶).

crinkly *adj.* [1980s+] (drugs) used to describe the user's mind after substantial and continuous use of nitrous oxide.

crinkum/crinkums *n.* [early 17C–late18C] venereal disease (cf. CRINKUM-CRANKUM; GRINCOMBE). [for ety. *see* CRINKUM-CRANKUM; i.e. the pain that accompanies the disease]

crinkum-crankum *n.* [late 18C–early 19C] the vagina (cf. ARBOUR; CRINKUM). [SE *crinkum-crankum*, a narrow, twisting passage]

crinkums *see* CRINKUM.

crinoline *n.* [mid–late 19C] a woman (cf. APRON n.¹). [metonymy]

crip *n.¹* [1910s+] **1** a handicapped person. **2** a wounded animal. [abbr. SE *cripple*. Note hobo jargon *straight crip*, a genuinely handicapped person, *phoney crip*, one who poses as handicapped for begging purposes]

crip *n.²* [1920s+] (US campus) anything easy, esp. of a given college course. [fig. use of CRIP n.¹]

crip course *n.* [1920s+] (US campus) an easy course. [CRIP n.²+ SE *course*]

cripes!/craps! *excl.* [20C] euph. for CHRIST! (cf. CRACKY!).

cripple *n.¹* [late 18C–late 19C] a sixpence (cf. BENDER n.²). [its thin metal being susceptible to bending or distortion]

cripple *n.²* [1980s+] (drugs) a marijuana cigarette. [its effect on one's mind]

cripple-cock *n.* [1960s+] a general pej. (cf. BREWER'S DROOP). [SE *cripple* v. + COCK n.² (1). Note Dorset use *cripple-cock*, cider]

cris/cristina *n.* [1980s+] (drugs) methamphetamine. [SE *crystal*]

cris'/kris' *adj.* [1980s+] (W.I./UK Black teen) used of anything rated as new, fashionable, attractive etc. [CRISP adj.¹]

crisco frisco *n.* [1950s–60s] (gay) the gay community in San Francisco. [proper name *Crisco*, a cooking oil + abbr. 'Frisco']

crisp *n.* [mid–late 19C] paper money (cf. SOFT MONEY).

crisp *adj.¹* **1** [1920s–30s] new, interesting. **2** [1980s+] excellent, first-rate, attractive. [the crispness of new money]

crisp *adj.²* [1980s+] of people, suffering from an excess of drugs, drink, fast living. [play on BURNED OUT]

crispin *n.* [mid-17C–mid-18C] a shoemaker; thus *St Crispin's lance*, an awl; *St Crispin's holiday*, each successive Monday, and especially 25 October (St Crispin's Day) 'whereon the whole Fraternity fail not to lay their Hearts in Soak' (B.E.). [proper name *St Crispin* whose non-theological profession this was]

crispy/crispy critter *n.¹* [1960s+] (US, orig. milit./medical) anyone who has suffered burns or actually burned to death. [lit. 'crispy creature' + play on popular breakfast cereal]

crispy *n.²* [1980s+] (US teen) anyone whose faculties are impaired (either in the short or long term) by an excess – of drugs, drink etc – and is thus 'burnt out'. [CRISP adj.²]

crispy *adj.* [1980s+] (US drugs) to be very inspired by consumption of marijuana. [CRISP adj.²]

crissars *adj.* [1950s+] (W.I. Rasta) crisp, brand-new, slick-looking. [CRISP adj.¹]

crisscross *n.* [1960s+] (drugs) amphetamine (cf. A n.²). [a cross is cut in the pill]

criss cross *v.* [1950s+] (US Black) to deceive or cheat. [SE *double-cross*]

crisscross! *excl.* [late 19C] euph. for *Christ's Cross*, e.g. *so help me crisscross!*

criss-miss *n.* [1950s+] (W.I.) a pretentious woman who overestimates her abilities, charms and allure. [dial. *kris*, proud, aware (rightly or not) of one's beauty (ult. SE *crisp*) + SE *miss*]

cristina *n.¹ see* CHRISTINA.

cristina n.[2] see CRIS.

cristy n. [1980s+] (drugs) smokeable methamphetamine. [CRIS]

critical adj. [1990s] (US campus) excellent, worthy of admiration.

critter n.[1] [19C+] **1** a bull, thence any farm animal, incl. a horse. **2** a person. [SE creature, the use for bull is in fact a euph. 19C US rural speech is full of such often ludicrous euphs., e.g. brute, cow critter, gentleman cow, male-cow]

critter n.[2] [19C] (US) whisky. [regional US pron. of CREATURE n.[1]]

crivens! excl. [1910s–1930s] an excl. of astonishment or horror. [? Christ + heavens]

cro/cros n.[1] [early–mid-19C] a professional gambler. [Fr. escroc, a card-sharp. The 's' in cros is silent]

cro n.[2] [1950s+] (Aus.) a prostitute. [CROW n.[8]]

croak n.[1] **1** [mid-late 19C] a dying speech (cf. TOP n.[1]). **2** [1910s] (US) a boring complainer, a whinger. [CROAK v.[1]]

croak n.[2] [1980s+] (drugs) crack and methamphetamine. [CRACK n.[17] + CRANK n.[4] (1); or ? CROAK v.[1] (1) i.e. its potentially fatal effect]

croak v.[1] **1** [early 19C+] to die. **2** [early 19C+] to kill, to murder. **3** [1900s] (US campus) to fail an examination or a course. [(1) the death-rattle; (3) is fig. use of (1)]

croak v.[2] [19C] (society) to act in a hypocritical manner.

croaked adj. [20C] **1** very drunk (cf. BASTED). **2** dead. [CROAK v.[1] (1)]

croaker n.[1] **1** [17C+] a congenital pessimist. **2** [late 18C–19C] a whiner or whinger. **3** [mid-late 19C] a beggar. **4** [20C] (US) one who talks too lengthily and too loudly. **5** [20C] (US) one who backs out of undertakings they have promised to perform. [? the harsh, miserable croaking of ravens, supposedly ominous birds]

croaker n.[2] [19C] a silver sixpence. [? play on CRIPPLE n.[1]]

croaker n.[3] **1** [mid-19C+] (US) a doctor, esp. in drug use; thus croaker joint, a hospital (cf. CROCUS). **2** [mid-late 19C] a dying person, beyond hope of recovery, a corpse. [CROAK v.[1] (1)]

croaker n.[4] [1910s+] (Aus.) a newspaper. [? CROAKER n.[2] i.e. the price; or CROAKER n.[1] (2)]

croaker n.[5] [1920s] (Anglo-Irish) a potato (cf. CROKER).

croaker sacks n. [1970s+] (US) shoes made of burlap sacks. [CROAKER n.[5] + SE sacks]

croaker's chovey n. [19C] a pharmacy (cf. CROCUS-CHOVEY). [CROAKER n.[3] + CHOVEY]

croaks n. [mid-19C] final speeches from the gallows and murderers' confessions, as peddled by street-sellers. [SE croak + CROAK v. (1)]

croakumshire n. [late 18C] Northumberland. [the guttural, rolled 'r' that typifies Northumberland speech]

croakus n. [19C] a doctor, a quack (cf. CROAKER n.[3]). [var. sp. of CROCUS]

croc/crock n. [late 19C+] **1** (Aus.) a horse, esp. a broken-down, old horse (cf. CROCODILE). **2** a crocodile. **3** a line of schoolchildren, walking in pairs.

crock n.[1] [19C] a fool.

crock n.[2] **1** [late 19C–1900s] an old or broken-down horse. **2** [late 19C+] a broken-down or physically debilitated person. **3** [late 19C+] an invalid, a hypochondriac. **4** [late 19C–1900s] a bicycle. **5** [20C] a broken-down or mechanically unreliable car, aeroplane or any other vehicle (cf. JUNKER n.[2]). [SE crack, to break (down); all often with pfx. old; note medical jargon crock, a patient whose complaints far outweigh the seriousness of their illness]

crock n.[3] [20C] a drunkard. [SE crock, a jug]

crock n.[4] **1** [1920s+] (US) the head, esp. in phr. off one's crock, out of one's mind, crazy. **2** [1930s+] (US) a bottle of (illicitly distilled) whisky. [fig. and lit. uses of SE crock, a pot]

crock n.[5] [1920s–30s] (US) an injury, a blow. [CROCK v.[1] (1)]

crock n.[6] [1940s+] (orig. US) a useless, unpleasant event or experience. [abbr. CROCK OF SHIT]

crock v.[1] **1** [mid-19C+] to become feeble, to collapse, to give way, to break down; thus crocked, injured. **2** [1910s+] (US) to hit on the head, to injure. [dial]

crock/crock up v.[2] [late 19C–1960s] to break down, (of a person) to become disabled, to fall ill. [CROCK n.[2] (2)]

crocked adj. [1920s+] **1** drunk. **2** hurt, damaged, disabled, esp. through a sporting accident. [CROCK v.[2]]

crockery n. **1** [1910s–40s] (US) teeth. **2** [1940s–60s] (Aus.) false teeth.

crockful n. [1980s+] (US) anything unpleasant, disgusting, repellent (cf. CROCK OF SHIT).

crocko adj. [1920s+] drunk. [CROCKED adj. (1) + sfx. -o]

crock of shit n. [1940s+] a useless, unpleasant event or experience (cf. CROCK n.[6]). [SE crock, a pot + SHIT n.[1] (1)]

crocks n. [20C] crockery, esp. in context of washing it up. [abbr.]

crocky n. [20C] (Aus.) a crocodile. [abbr.]

crocky adj. **1** [late 19C+] (Aus.) unwell, shaky, 'under the weather' (cf. CROOK adj.). **2** [1920s+] (US) infirm, shaky. [CROCKED]

crocodile n. **1** [late 19C+] (Aus.) a horse, esp. a broken-down, old horse (cf. ALLIGATOR n.[2]). **2** [1900s] (Aus.) a roustabout (cf. ALLIGATOR n.[1]).

crocodile scam n. [1980s+] (US) the ensnaring of a client by a girl, often a prostitute, and his subsequent robbery, either by the girl herself or, more often, by her pimp, posing as an 'outraged boyfriend', who emerges, while the pair are in flagrante, from a hidden door or panel in the bedroom wall (cf. BADGER GAME). [SE crocodile + SCAM n.; the amphibian opens its jaws to embrace its victims]

crocs n. [1980s+] shoes made of crocodile skin.

crocus/crocus metallorum n. [late 18C] (orig. milit.) a doctor, a surgeon, esp. a quack (cf. CROAKER n.[3]). [? pun on croak us (though croak, to die or kill is first recorded slightly later), but OED suggests 'the Latinized surname of Dr Helkiah Crooke, author of a Description of the Body of Man, 1615, Instruments of Chirurgery, 1631, etc ...'. The quack implication suggests a further pun on hocus-pocus. Note fairground use, crocus, a doctor, a herbalist, a miracle-worker; market use, a fair-weather trader who only works during the spring or summer (f. the flower). Metallorum, lit. 'of metals' plays on crocus metallorum or crocus antimonii, which are more or less impure oxysulphides of antimony, obtained by calcination]

crocus-chovey n. [mid-19C–1920s] **1** a doctor's consulting room, a surgery. **2** a chemist's shop. [CROCUS + CHOVEY]

crocus metallorum see CROCUS.

crocus-pitcher n. [mid-19C+] an itinerant quack doctor. [CROCUS + PITCHER n.[3](1)]

crocussing n. [mid-19C–20C] working as a travelling quack doctor or surgeon. [CROCUS]

crocussing rig n. [mid-19C–1920s] the profession of working as a wandering quack doctor. [CROCUSSING + RIG n.[2] (2)]

crocus-worker n. [late 19C+] a seller of patent medicines. [CROCUS + SE worker]

croker n. [late 18C] **1** a potato (cf. CROAKER n.[5]). **2** a groat, fourpence.

crombie n. [1960s+] an overcoat. [the tradename of a particular coat, particularly beloved by SKINHEADS in the late 1960s]

cronk/kronk n. [late 19C–1910s] (Aus.) a criminal. [CRONK adj.]

cronk adj. [late 19C+] (Aus.) dishonest, illegal, untrustworthy. [? dial. cronk, weak, infirm]

cronkite n. [1990s] news, information. [the newsreader Walter Cronkite (b.1916)]

cronky *adj.* **1** [1920s+] unsound, second-rate. **2** [1960s+] (Aus.) corrupt, dishonest, lying. [CRONK adj. + sfx. *-y*; orig. racing use]

crony *n.*[1] [late 17C–early 18C] a tough old hen, a boiling chicken. [SE *crone*, a gnarled old woman + sfx. *-y*]

crony *n.*[2] [late 17C–mid-19C] an intimate friend or associate. [ety. unknown; the earliest citation has sp. *chrony*, which might suggest a root in SE *chronology/chronological*, i.e. a friend of long standing. 20C SE use replaced 'straight' friendship with implications of (political) corruption]

cronz *n.* [1990s] (US Black) a gun. [ety. unknown]

crook *n.*[1] [19C] a silver sixpence. [CROAKER n.[2]]

crook *n.*[2] [mid–late 19C] a professional criminal. [SE *crooked*; SE since 20C]

crook *adj.* (Aus./N.Z.) **1** [late 19C+] dishonest, illegal. **2** [20C] of people and objects, defective, useless, unpleasant. **3** [20C] ill, out of sorts; thus *go crook*, to lose one's temper. [SE *crooked*]

crook *v.* [19C] (US) to steal. [CROOK n.[2]]

crookback *n.* [late 18C] a sixpence (cf. BENDER n.[2]; CRIPPLE n.[1]). [the thin silver sixpence was easily bent or distorted]

crooked *adj.*[1] [19C+] drunk.

crooked *adj.*[2] [mid-19C+] used to describe anything that has been obtained dishonestly or done in a dishonest manner, e.g. *crooked whisky*, illicitly distilled whisky. [orig. sporting jargon]

crooked *adj.*[3] **1** [20C] ill, sick, 'under the weather'. **2** [1940s+] (Aus.) annoyed; thus *crooked on*, infuriated by.

crooked as a dog's hind leg *phr.* [late 19C+] very dishonest, devious, deceptive.

crooked as George Street West *phr.* [late 19C–1950s] (Aus.) extremely corrupt. [a street in Sydney, latterly renamed Broadway]

crooked as the letter zed *phr.* [late 18C–mid-19C] very corrupt.

crooked on *adj.* [1940s+] (Aus./N.Z.) averse to, hostile to, angry with. [CROOK adj. (3)]

crooked rib *n.* [late 18C–early 19C] an ill-tempered wife. [SE *crooked* + (*Adam's*) *rib*, a wife]

crooked stick *n.* [19C] (US) a dishonest person, an untrustworthy person.

crooked way *n.* [19C] the vagina (cf. ALLEY n.[1]).

crooklyn *n.* [1990s] (US Black) Brooklyn, New York. [SE *Brooklyn* + *crook*; the borough's associations with (organized) crime]

crookshanks *n.* [late 18C–19C] a bandy-legged person. [SE *crooked* + *shanks*, legs]

crook the elbow, to *phr.* [late 19C+] to drink (cf. BEND ONE'S ELBOW; CROOK THE LITTLE FINGER).

crook the little finger, to *phr.* [19C] (US) to drink (cf. CROOK THE ELBOW). [the 'elegant' manner of drinking]

crook up *v.* [1910s+] (Aus.) to fall ill. [CROOK adj. (3)]

crooky *v.* [mid-19C] **1** to walk arm in arm. **2** to court a woman. [the bending of the couple's arms]

croop *n.* [mid-19C–1910s] the stomach. [SE *crop*]

crop *n.*[1] [late 17C–18C] money (cf. CRAP n.[1]; DUST n.[1]; MUCK n.[1]). [SE *crap*, waste, chaff]

crop *n.*[2] **1** [late 17C–early 18C] a person with very short hair. **2** [late 18C] a Presbyterian. [(2) the severely cropped haircut favoured by the sect]

crop *n.*[3] [1970s] (US campus) one-fifth of a gallon of wine. [? SE *crop*, the throat or *grape crop*]

crop *n.*[4] *see* CRAP n.[8]

crop *v. see* CRAP v.[1]

crop and mat *n.* [mid-19C] a fashionable style in which the hair and beard were both cut short.

crople on *v.* [1920s] (Aus.) to grab, to seize. [? dial. *criple*, to cripple or SE *grapple*]

cropoh *n.* [19C] a Frenchman (cf. FROG n.[1]). [var. on CRAPPO n.]

cropped *see* CRAPPED.

croppen/croppin *n.* [late 18C–early 19C] the tail of both an animal and a vehicle. [dial. *croppen, croppin(g)*, the tail; ult. f. SE *crop*, to cut off the extremity of the ears, tail etc]

cropper *n.* [mid-19C+] a fall. [orig. hunting jargon; one falls over the horse's crop or phr. *neck and crop*]

croppie/croppy *n.* [mid-19C] **1** anyone who has suffered a prison haircut. **2** a Puritan or Roundhead (both of whom might have not their hair, but their nose and/or ears cropped in a judicial punishment). [note the *croppies* or *croppy-boys*, the Irish rebels of 1798, who wore their hair cut very short as a sign of sympathy with the French Revolution]

croppin *see* CROPPEN.

cropping ken *see* CRAPPING KEN.

croppy *n.*[1] *see* CROPPIE.

croppy *n.*[2] [1920s] a corpse. [CROPPY v.]

croppy *v.* [1910s] (US) to kill. [SE *crop*, to cut off, to harvest]

cropsick *adj.* **1** [mid–late 18C] drunk. **2** [late 18C] feeling sick after a drinking bout. [SE *crop*, the throat + *sick*]

crop the conjuror *n.* [late 18C] a nickname for one who has noticeably short hair (cf. CROP n.[2]).

cros *see* CRO n.[1]

Cross, the *n.* [1940s+] (Aus.) King's Cross, Sydney, the 'bohemian' area of the town; thus *crossite*, one who lives there.

cross/crosso, the *n.* [early 19C+] anything deceitful or dishonest (cf. ON THE CROSS). [the opposite of SQUARE n.[1]]

cross *adj.* **1** [mid-17C+] ill-tempered, peevish. **2** [19C] dishonest, dishonestly come by (cf. SQUARE adj.; STRAIGHT adj.[1]). **3** [mid–late 19C] annoying, unkind. [fig. uses of SE *cross*, contrary, opposed]

cross *v.*[1] [mid-18C–mid-19C] **1** to sit astride a horse. **2** to have sexual intercourse (cf. GET ACROSS; RIDE v.[1]). [(2) is fig. use of (2)]

cross *v.*[2] [early 19C+] **1** to betray. **2** to let down. **3** to deceive or mislead. [abbr. SE *double-cross*]

cross *adv.* [early 17C–late 19C] unfavourably, in an unsatisfactory manner. [CROSS adj.]

cross as two sticks *phr.* [mid-19C] very angry. [punning on *cross*, irritable, peevish + *cross*, lying across each other]

cross-back *n.* [20C] (US) a Roman Catholic. [the Catholic habit of crossing oneself]

cross-bar hotel *n.* [20C] (US Und.) a prison (cf. AKERMAN'S HOTEL). [17C SE *cross-bar*, a horizontal bar, as of a window or cell + HOTEL n.[2] (2)]

crossbite *v.* [16C–late 18C] (Und.) **1** to cheat, usu. in cards or dice, esp. when the victim is another cheat. **2** to practise the 'crossbiting law' (the modern BADGER GAME or MURPHY), i.e. to beat up an unfortunate victim, previously ensnared by the prostitute with whom the trickster works. [CROSS v.[2] + BITE v.[1]. The image is of fleecing someone who had hoped in their turn to get 'something for nothing', although in the case of the crossbiting law, the client had merely hoped for some illicit, commercial sex]

crossbiter *n.* [mid–late 16C] a man who works with a prostitute to trap and then rob an unfortunate victim; his role was to rob the man and then beat him up, allegedly for his gall in attempting to seduce an innocent 'sister' or 'wife'. [CROSSBITE]

crossbiting cully *n.* [mid-17C–late 19C] a swindler, a cheat. [CROSSBITE + CULLY n.]

cross-boy *n.* [late 19C] (Aus.) a criminal (cf. CROSS-GIRL). [CROSS v.[2] + SE *boy*]

cross-built *adj.* [mid-19C] used of a person who moves or stands in an awkward manner. [SE *cross*, contrary, opposed + *built*]

cross-buttock *n.* [mid-19C–1900s] an unexpected rebuff. [wrestling jargon *cross-buttock*, a throw over the hip]

cross-chap *n.* [mid-19C] (coster) a thief. [CROSS adj. (2) + CHAP n.]

cross-chopping *n.* [mid-19C] arguing. [SE *cross* adj. + *chop*, to exchange or bandy words]

cross-cove *n.* [19C] a robber, anyone who lives by dishonesty or crime. [CROSS adj. (2) + COVE]

cross-cove and mollisher *n.* [mid-19C] a man and woman who work in tandem as thieves. [CROSS-COVE + MOLLISHER]

cross-crib *n.* [mid-19C] a house frequented by thieves (cf. SQUARE-CRIB). [CROSS adj. (2) + CRIB n.³]

cross-drum *n.* [mid-19C] a thieves' tavern. [CROSS adj. (2) + DRUM n.²(3)]

crosses *n.* [1950s+] (W.I. Rasta) problems, vexations, trials, bad luck, misfortunes. [SE phr. *a cross to bear*]

cross-eye *v.* [1930s–40s] (W.I.) **1** to look suspiciously, to look askance at. **2** to glance at, to look at furtively (cf. CUT ONE'S EYES).

cross-eyed *adj.* [20C] drunk.

cross-fam/-fan *v.* [early–mid-19C] (Und.) to pick a pocket by crossing one's arms in a particular position. [SE *cross*, opposed, contrary + FAM n.¹]

cross-girl *n.* [mid-19C] a prostitute who specializes in pro-positioning sailors, taking their money and then vanishing (cf. CROSS-BOY). [CROSS adj. (2) + SE *girl*]

cross I win, pile you lose *phr.* [17C] a phr. used, with or without actually coin-tossing, to indicate that the speaker is in an unassailable position (cf. HEADS I WIN, TAILS YOU LOSE). [*cross*, the 'head' of the coin + *pile*, 'the under iron of the minting apparatus with which money was struck ...' (*OED*); thus the reverse or 'tail' of the coin]

cross-kid *n.* [late 19C–1910] irony, teasing, deception. [CROSS-KID v.]

cross-kid/-kiddle *v.* [mid-19C] to interrogate, to cross-examine. [SE *cross* adj. + KID v.]

cross-lad/-man/-squire *n.* [mid-19C] (coster) a thief (cf. CROSS-CHAP).

cross-legged *adj.* [19C] knock-kneed.

cross-legs *n.* [19C–1900s] a tailor. [the traditional tailoring posture]

cross-life man *n.* [late 19C] (Und.) a professional thief. [CROSS adj. (2)]

crossman/cross-man *n.* **1** [mid-19C] a confidence trickster (cf. CROSS adj. (2); CROSS-COVE). **2** [1950s+] (US Black) anyone who manipulates others for his own advantage. [(double)-*cross* + *man*]

cross-mollisher *n.* [early 19C] a woman who works as a thief or lives in any way dishonestly. [CROSS adj. (2) + MOLLISHER]

crosso *see* CROSS n.

cross out *v.* [1980s+] (US Black) to perform a low-level form of gang warfare, the crossing out of a rival gang's graffiti.

cross over *v.* [19C+] to die, usu. in combs., e.g. *cross over the range*; *cross over jordan*; *cross over the river*; *cross the veil*.

cross-patch *n.* [late 18C+] a grumpy person, usu. a child, or someone acting in a childish manner. [SE *cross*, quarrelsome + *patch*, a fool or clown. The original Patch was, according to mid-16C refs., Cardinal Wolsey's personal jester, so-called either from his patched, parti-coloured fool's costume or f. Ital. *pazzo*, a fool. His real name was Sexton]

crossroader *n.* [20C] an itinerant card-sharp who travels in search of new victims for their cheating skills. [they stand at the crossroads or cross roads in search of victims]

crossroads *n.* [1960s+] (drugs) amphetamine (cf. A n.²; CROSS TOPS). [? the cross marked on some amphetamines]

cross-talk *v.* [20C] (US Black) to interrupt another speaker. [SE *talk across*]

cross the line, to *phr.* (US) of a light-coloured Black person, to attempt to pass for White (cf. TRY FOR WHITE).

cross the ruby, to *phr.* [late 19C] to take a decisive or final step. [abbr. SE phr. *cross the Rubicon*]

cross tops *n.* [1960s] (drugs) amphetamines (cf. A n.²; CROSS-ROADS). [the cross cut into the pill]

cross up *v.* [20C] to betray, to double-cross, to inform against. [SE *double-cross*]

crossways/crosswise *adv.* [20C] (US) **1** in a bad humour. **2** disagreeing with. [CROSS adj. (1) + play on SE]

crotch *n.* [1960s+] a woman, seen purely as an extension of her physical sexuality. [SE *crotch*, the fork or bifurcation of the legs; thus the genital area of either sex]

crotch *adj.* [1960s+] erotic, pornographic; thus *crotch novel*, a pornographic book.

crotchbuster *n.* [1980s+] (US campus) something extremely difficult and challenging. [SE *crotch* + *buster*; var. on BALL-BUSTER]

crotch cheese *n.* [1960s+] unwashed vaginal secretion (cf. HEADCHEESE n.¹).

crotch cricket/monkey/pheasant *n.* [1960s+] (US) a crab, a pubic louse.

crotch oil *n.* [1980s+] (US) vaginal secretions that result from sexual foreplay.

crotch rocket *n.* [1970s+] a motorbike, esp. a dirt bike.

crotch rot *n.* [1960s+] (Can./US) a fungal infection of the groin.

Croton cocktail *n.* [1900s–10s] (US, New York) water. [the *Croton Reservoir* + SE *cocktail*; the reservoir supplies the bulk of the city's drinking water]

crouton *n.* [1990s] an erection. [rhy. sl. *crouton* = BLUE-VEINED ROOT-ON]

crow *n.¹* **1** [late 18C–1900s] a clergyman. **2** [mid–late 19C] a doctor. [his black clothes or, for (2) SE *carrion/crow*, reflecting on his inadequacy as a healer]

crow *n.²* [19C+] a derog. term for a Black person. [JIM CROW n.¹ (3)]

crow *n.³* [mid-19C] a *crow*bar. [abbr.]

crow *n.⁴* [mid-19C] an unexpected or fluky piece of luck, usu. in phr. *regular crow*. [? one *crows* or exults over it]

crow *n.⁵* **1** [mid-19C+] a thief's lookout. **2** [20C] that member of a crooked dice or card-game who poses as a stranger, but affirms the supposed honesty of those who run the game. **3** [20C] a lookout in a game of three-card monte.

crow *n.⁶* [late 19C–1910s] a bar counter. [play on/abbr. SE *crowbar*]

crow *n.⁷* **1** [late 19C–1940s] (US) a young woman, esp. a sweetheart. **2** [1920s+] an unattractive (old) woman, esp. as *old crow*. **3** [1920s+] (US) an attractive woman. **4** [1920s–50s] (US) an unpleasant old man. **5** [1940s–70s] (N.Z. teen) a derog. male description of a young girl, from her black/navy school uniform.

crow *n.⁸* [1950s+] (Aus.) a prostitute; thus *charity crow*, a prostitute who does not charge, esp. to impecunious soldiers during WW2, *society crow*, an upmarket prostitute, a cour-tesan (cf. CRO n.²). [CHROMO n.; note Ital. *cornaccia*, a crow, a loose woman]

crow-bait *n.* **1** [mid–late 19C] (Aus.) a derog. term for an Aborigine. **2** [mid-19C+] (US) a corpse that has been exposed to the elements. **3** [late 19C] (orig. US) a scraggy old horse (cf. FOX BAIT). **4** [1940s–50s] (US) an unpleasant, despised person.

crowbar *n.* [1920s] (US) the penis (cf. ARSE-OPENER). [it 'prises open' the vagina]

crowbar brigade *n.* [mid–late 19C] (Irish) the police; thus *crowbar landlord*, a landlord who enforces his powers through heavy-handed policemen. [their breaking into houses with the help of a crowbar; the break-in was followed by the eviction of the tenants]

crowbar hotel *n.* [20C] a prison (cf. AKERMAN'S HOTEL). [var. on CROSS-BAR HOTEL ? + ref. to the need of a SE *crowbar* to escape]

crowd *n.* [mid-19C+] (orig. US) a group of people, a set, esp. a *bad crowd*, a group of (apparent) undesirables.

crowd *v.* [1940s+] (US) to be getting close to a stated age, e.g. *crowding fifty.*

crowded space *n.* [20C] a suitcase. [rhy. sl.]

crowder *n.* [18C–19C] a string. [Shelta *crowd*, a form of fiddle]

crowd pleaser *n.* [1980s+] (US police) the officer's gun. [ironic use]

crowd the mourners, to *phr.* [mid-19C–1920s] (US) **1** to intensify someone's embarrassment. **2** to act hastily, to act precipitately. **3** to add to someone's problems.

crowdy-headed jock *n.* [18C–19C] a Northcountry seaman, esp. a collier. [Scot./northern dial. *crowdy*, a gruel made from milk and meal; thus + JOCK n.¹]

crow-eater *n.* [late 19C+] **1** (Aus.) a white inhabitant of South Australia; thus *crowland*, South Australia. **2** (Aus./S.Afr.) a lazy person who will scrounge and otherwise live on their wits rather than do actual work. [(1) the canard that the original settlers of the state ate crow when nothing else was available]

crow fair *n.* [late 18C] a gathering of clergymen (cf. REVIEW OF THE BLACK CUIRASSIERS). [CROW n.¹ (1) + SE *fair*; their black garments]

crow jane *n.* [1900s–20s] (US Black) a very dark-skinned woman. [CROW n.² + generic proper name *Jane*]

crow jim *n.* [1950s+] (US) anti-White discrimination by Blacks; thus *crow jimism*, guilt-induced affection for and fascination with Blacks by White liberals. [the reverse of anti-Black discriminatory JIM CROW n.¹ (3) laws]

crow macgee *adj.* [20C] (US prison) no good, unreal, false. [ety. unknown]

crown *n.* [19C] the female genital area (cf. CROWN AND FEATHERS; CROWN JEWELS).

crown *adj.* [1920s+] (Aus.) very large. [? SE phr. *crowning glory*]

crown *v.* **1** [mid-18C+] to hit over the head. **2** [20C] (Aus. student) to empty a chamberpot over a victim's head.

crown and feathers *n.* [mid–late 19C] the pubic hair. [playing on a typical name for a public house]

crown crap *n.* [1980s+] (drugs) heroin. [CROWN adj. + CRAP n.⁸]

crowner *n.* [mid–late 19C] a fall (from horseback) onto the top of one's head (cf. CROWNING). [SE *crown*, the top of one's head]

crownie *n.* [1930s] (Aus.) a bus or tram inspector. [his rank is indicated by a crown on his uniform]

crowning *n.* [20C] a blow on the top of the head (cf. CROWNER). [SE *crown*, the top of one's head + sfx. *-ing*]

crown jewels *n.* [1960s+] the male genitals (cf. BAUBLES). [their importance to the possessor]

crown office *n.* [late 18C] the head. [a pun on legal SE]

crown of sense *n.* [late 17C] the vagina (cf. BEST IN CHRISTENDOM).

crown the king, to *phr.* [1990s] to masturbate.

crow's feet/marks *n.* [19C] (US) illegible handwriting (cf. CHICKEN SCRATCH n.¹).

crow's nest *n.* **1** [late 19C] (society) a small bedroom on the higher floors of country houses, reserved for the use of bachelor guests. **2** [20C] (US) a woman's hair when it has been pinned up in a bun. [naut. use *crow's nest*, the platform secured high on a mast that houses a look-out]

crow tracks *n.* [19C] (US) illegible handwriting (cf. CHICKEN SCRATCH n.¹).

croziered abbot *n.* [late 19C] a man who runs a brothel designed less for providing sex, and more for robbing or blackmailing the clients (cf. ABBESS). [pun SE *croziered*, bearing a crook + ABBOT]

c.r.s. *adj.* [1980s+] (US campus) forgetful. [abbr. *can't remember shit*]

crucial *adj.* [1980s+] (orig. W.I. Rasta) general term of praise, admiration; serious, important, excellent.

crud/krud *n.¹* **1** [early 16C+] any filthy and disgusting matter. **2** [1930s+] (orig. US milit.) any unidentified disease, often as *creeping crud, crawling crud* (cf. CAIRO CRUD). **3** [1950s+] dried semen, whether on the body, clothes or bedlinen. **4** [1950s+] dirt, in general. **5** [1950s+] (US) any venereal disease. **6** [1950s+] (orig. US milit.) diarrhoea. [Scot. *crud*, thickened or coagulated milk; note US regional *crud*, curdled milk]

crud *n.²* **1** [1940s+] anything or anyone worthless, repulsive. **2** [1940s+] (orig. US milit.) a slovenly, habitually dirty person. **3** [1950s+] (US) nonsense, rubbish (cf. CRAP n.³). [fig. uses of CRUD n.¹]

crud *n.³* [1950s–60s] daylights, guts, stuffing, e.g. *kick the crud out of* (cf. CRAP n.³). [fig. use of CRUD n.¹ (1)]

crudball *n.* [1960s+] (US) a filthy or disgusting person (cf. SLIMEBAG). [CRUD n.¹ (1) + sfx. *-ball*]

crudball *adj.* [1960s+] (US) filthy, disgusting. [CRUD n.¹ (1) + sfx. *-ball*]

cruddy *adj.* [1940s+] **1** useless, no good, second-rate. **2** dirty, unpleasant, unsavoury. [CRUD n.¹ (1) + sfx. *-y*]

crude *adj.* [1950s+] (US Black) worthless, excessive and as such useless.

crudget *n.* [1920s+] (Aus.) the human head (cf. CRUET).

crudhead *n.* [1980s+] a fool, an unpleasant person (cf. CRAP-HEAD). [CRUD n.¹ (1) + sfx. *-HEAD* (1)]

crud-sucking *adj.* [1960s] (US) a general term of abuse, revolting, disgusting etc (cf. SCUM-SUCKER). [CRUD n.¹ (1) + SE *sucking*]

crud up *v.* [1960s+] (orig. US) **1** to render disgusting, filthy. **2** to spoil. [CRUD n.¹ (1)]

crud work *n.* [1950s] (US) any menial, unpleasant or tedious work. [CRUD n.¹ (1) + SE *work*]

crudzoid *n.* [1980s+] (US) a repellent, disgusting person. [CRUD n.¹ (1) + sfx. *-ZOID*]

cruel *adj.* [19C] of conditions or circumstances, severe, hard. [ext. of SE use]

cruel/cruel the pitch *v.* [1910s+] (Aus.) to spoil, to ruin any chance of success with (cf. QUEER SOMEONE'S PITCH).

cruel *adv.* [19C] exceedingly, very. [ext. of SE use]

cruelty man *n.* [1920s+] an officer of the NSPCC or RSPCA. [both organizations deal with *cruelty*, to, respectively, children or animals]

cruelty-van *n.* [mid–late 19C] a 4-wheeled chaise (cf. BOOBY-HATCH). [? its discomfort]

cruet *n.* [1940s+] (Aus.) the human head.

cruff *n.* [1960s+] (W.I.) crude, coarse, uncouth manners. [? SE *scruffy*; note computer jargon *crufty*, disgusting, distasteful]

crug *n.* [mid-19C] food. [? SE *crust*; orig. used by boys at Christ's Hospital school to mean bread]

cruise *n.* [1960s+] (gay) a quick glance that assesses a passing individual in sexual terms. [CRUISE v.¹]

cruise *adj.* [1980s] (US teen) easy, simple, useful. [CRUISE v.²]

cruise *v.¹* **1** [20C] (orig. gay) to approach someone obviously with sexual intent, both for commercial or non-commercial purposes (cf. TROLL v.). **2** [1930s+] (US Black) to walk in a strutting manner. **3** [1940s+] to search for sexual contacts by walking specific streets, areas etc. **4** [1940s+] to drive around, often along a town's main street, surveying the situation, looking for friends, women to pick up etc. **5** [1960s] (US) of a mugger or thief, to search out a potential victim. [fig. uses of SE *cruise*, to sail to and fro with no particular destination]

cruise *v.*[2] [1960s+] to do something easily, effortlessly.

cruise for an oozing, to *phr.* [1990s] to masturbate. [pun on CRUISING FOR A BRUISING]

cruisemobile *n.* [1980s] (US teen) any favoured car. [CRUISE v.[1] + sfx. -*mobile*]

cruiser *n.* **1** [late 17C–18C] (Und.) a beggar. **2** [late 19C] a prostitute (cf. CURBSTONE SAILOR). **3** [1930s+] one who wanders the streets in searching for a casual pick-up (usu. assumed to be a male homosexual but of either gender in 1980s+ US campus use). [CRUISE v.[1]]

cruise the chocolate freeway, to *phr.* [1990s] (orig. US) of hetero- or homosexual anal intercourse, to sodomize. [SE *cruise* + CHOCOLATE HIGHWAY/FREEWAY]

cruising *n.* [1920s+] usu. of a male homosexual, walking or driving about the streets in search of a casual sexual partner. [CRUISE v.[1] + sfx. -*ing*]

cruising for a bruising *phr.* [1940s+] (orig. US) **1** looking deliberately to cause trouble. **2** acting in such a manner that will get one into trouble, usually of a physically harmful nature.

cruising with one's lights on *phr.* [20C] acting in a stupid manner (cf. LIGHTS ON BUT THERE'S NOBODY HOME).

cruisy *adj.* [1940s+] (gay) used of the sort of place in which one is likely to make a successful pick-up. [CRUISE v.[1]]

crum/crumb *n.*[1] **1** [mid-19C–1920s] a body louse, usu. in plural. **2** [1910s+] a filthy person, an objectionable, worthless or insignificant person. **3** [1970s+] a cruel, vicious person. [the diminutive size of the insects, the infestation of the human being]

Crum, the *n.*[2] [1970s+] (Ulster) the *Crum*lin Road prison in Belfast. [abbr.]

crumb *n.*[1] [mid-17C–18C] one's savings (cf. BREAD n.[1]).

crumb *n.*[2] [19C] **1** a pretty, plumpish woman (cf. BANANA n.[2]). **2** plumpness. [SE *crumb*, the soft heart of a risen loaf]

crumb *n.*[3] **1** [early–mid-19C] (US) the head. **2** [1920s] the penis. [? the shape]

crumb *n.*[4] *see* CRUM n.[1].

crumb *adj.* [20C] (US) filthy, dirty, disgusting. [abbr. CRUMMY adj.[2]]

crumb *v.* [1980s+] (US campus) to feel sad or depressed. [abbr. CRUMMY adj.[2]]

crumb! *excl.* [1950s–70s] (US) a mild excl. of annoyance. [abbr. CRUMMY adj.[2]]

crumb and crust man *n.* [mid-19C] a baker.

crumb boss *n.* [1920s+] (US, West./tramp) a janitor in a construction camp or mission. [CRUM n.[1] (1) + SE *boss*. Among their duties was delousing the beds]

crumb-catcher *n.*[1] [1930s–60s] (orig. US Black) a baby who is just beginning to eat solids (cf. CRUMB-CRUSHER).

crumb-catcher *n.*[2] [1940s] (US) a comb (cf. BUG RAKE). [CRUM n.[1] (1) + SE *catcher*]

crumb-cruncher *n.* [1930s–60s] (orig. US Black) a baby who is just learning to eat solids (cf. CRUMB-CRUSHER; CRUMB-GRABBER; CRUMB-SNATCHER; CRUST-BUSTER).

crumb-crusher *n.* **1** [1930s–60s] (US Black) a baby who is just learning to eat solids (cf. CRUMB-CRUNCHER). **2** [1940s–70s] (US Black) in pl., the teeth.

crumb-grabber *n.* [1930s–60s] (orig. US Black) a baby who is just beginning to eat solids (cf. CRUMB-CRUNCHER).

crumb-hall *n.* [1930s–40s] (US Black) a dining-room, esp. in an institution.

crumb-hunting *n.* [1940s] (Can.) housework.

crumb in *v.* [1960s] (US) to interfere, to butt in, esp. to interfere in (and possibly ruin) another confidence man's scheme. [CRUM n.[1] (2)]

crumb joint *n.* [1930s] (US) a filthy lodging house or hostel. [CRUMB adj. + JOINT n.[3]]

crumbly/crumblie *n.* [1970s+] (society) an older person, aged 50–70 (cf. DUSTY n.[2]; GRUNTER n.[6]; WRINKLY). [such people are fig. 'crumbling away']

crumbo *n.* [1930s+] (orig. US) a filthy, disgusting, despised person. [CRUM n.[1] (2) + -o]

crumbs *n.* **1** [19C] lice (cf. CRUM n.[1]). **2** [1950s] (US Black) very small sums of money (cf. BREAD n.[1]). **3** [1980s+] (drugs) tiny pieces of crack. [the diminutive sizes]

crumbs! *excl.* [1930s–60s] euph. for CHRIST! Usu. juv. use only, prob. the mildest of such euphs. (cf. CRACKY!).

crumb-snatcher *n.* [20C] **1** a baby who is just learning to eat solids (cf. CRUMB-CRUNCHER). **2** the hand.

crumb-stash *n.* [1930s–40s] (US Black/Harlem) a kitchen.

crumbum *n.* [1930s+] (orig. US) a filthy, disgusting, worthless person. [CRUM n.[1] (2) + BUM n.[3]]

crumbum *adj.* [1930s+] (orig. US) useless, awful, second-rate, inferior. [CRUMB adj. + BUM adj. (1)]

crumb up *v.* [1910s+] (US) to make filthy, disgusting. [CRUMB adj.]

crumby *see* CRUMMY adj.[1].

crummy *n.* [mid-19C] (US) a louse. [CRUM n.[1] (1) + sfx. -*y*]

crummy/crumby *adj.*[1] [18C–late 19C] **1** fat, fleshy. **2** attractive. **3** rich. [SE *crumb*, the soft inner part of a loaf, the antithesis of *crust*]

crummy *adj.*[2] [mid-19C+] **1** infested with lice. **2** generally filthy. **3** second-rate, inferior, unpleasant. [CRUM n.[1] + sfx. -*y*]

crummy! *excl.* [20C] a mild euph. for CHRIST! (cf. CRACKY!).

crummy-doss *n.* [mid-19C] a lousy or filthy bed. [CRUMMY adj.[2] + DOSS n.[1] (1)]

crump *n.* [late 17C–early 19C] a solicitor's assistant, who arranges for false witnesses to perjure themselves as required by a given case (cf. CRIMP). [? SE *crump*, crooked]

crump *v.* (US) **1** [1950s] (campus) to pass out through exhaustion or boredom. **2** [1960s] to kill. **3** [1980s] to destroy. **4** [1980s] of machinery, to break down (cf. CONK OUT). [SE *crump*, the noise of an object hitting the ground]

crump-backed *adj.* [late 18C] hump-backed. [SE *crump*, crooked + *backed*]

crumper *n.* [mid-late 19C] a hard hit, a blow. [dial. *crump*, a blow]

crumpet *n.*[1] [19C–1920s] the head; thus *barmy/balmy in/on the crumpet*, mad, eccentric (cf. SCONE n.[2]). [the supposedly similar shapes]

crumpet *n.*[2] [1900s–20s] a term of endearment, often as *old crumpet*. [note the P.G. Wodehouse title, combining three such terms, *Eggs, Beans and Crumpets* (1940)]

crumpet *n.*[3] [1920s+] (Aus.) a weakling, a fool. [the softness of the comestible]

crumpet *n.*[4] [1930s+] **1** a young woman, an example of sex = food equation (cf. BANANA n.[2]). **2** women viewed as no more than sources of sexual pleasure; thus *get a crumpet*, of a man, to have sexual intercourse.

crumpet-face *n.* [mid-late 19C] one whose face is covered with smallpox marks. [similarity to the pocked surface of a crumpet]

crumpet man *n.* [1960s+] a womanizer. [CRUMPET n.[4] + SE *man*]

crumpet-scramble *n.* [mid-late 19C] a tea party (cf. BUN-FIGHT).

crum/crumb up *v.* [20C] (US) to boil one's clothes to get rid of the lice. [CRUM n.[1] (1)]

crunch, the *n.*[1] [1930s+] the ultimate aspect of a given situation; often in phr. *when it comes to the crunch* ... .

crunch *n.*[2] [1970s] (US campus) a generic term for women. [? 'good enough to eat']

crunch *adj.* [1970s+] (orig. Aus.) critical, decisive, crucial, e.g. *a crunch situation*. [CRUNCH n.[1]]

crunch and munch *n.* [1980s+] (drugs) crack cocaine. [one grinds one's teeth after smoking]

cruncher *n.[1]* [1940s+] (Aus. prison) a small-time criminal. [play on PIE-EATER]

cruncher *n.[2]* [1940s] (US) the street, the pavement. [the sound of one's feet]

cruncher *n.[3]* [1980s] the ultimate aspect of a given situation. [CRUNCH n.[1]]

crunchers *n.* [1940s] (US) the feet. [the sound they make hitting the ground]

crunchie *n.* [1970s+] (S.Afr.) a derog. term for an Afrikaner. [? *mealie cruncher* or f. *krantzie*, abbr. of *krantz-athlete*, milit. sl. for an Afrikaner; the term also reflects their overall image of violence]

crunchy/crunchy granola *n.* [1980s+] (US campus) **1** a vegetarian. **2** a devotee of New Age philosophies. **3** someone who identifies with the styles and concerns of the 1960s. [the popular and supposedly healthy US cereal, *Crunchy Granola*; 'A hiking-boot-wearing, granola-eating, Grateful Dead/Blues Traveler-listening type of person.' (Shenk & Silberman)]

crunchy *adj.* [1990s] (US teen) embarrassed. [? the 'crunching up' of one's face/body in embarrassment]

crunchy granola *see* CRUNCHY n.

crunk *adj.* [1990s] (rap music) excellent, wonderful.

crunt *n.* [1950s–60s] (US Black) any form of dirt, esp. the (dried) residue of bodily fluids, e.g. blood, semen. [CRUD n.[1] (1)]

crupper *n.* [late 16C] the posterior, the buttocks; thus *ride below the crupper*, to have sexual intercourse. [SE *crupper*, the hind-quarters of a horse]

crusader *n.* [1990s] (US campus) an evangelistic, fundamentalist Christian.

crush *n.[1]* **1** [mid-19C] a crowded social occasion (cf. SQUEEZE n.[1]). **2** [1900s–30s] (US) a crowd, a gang.

crush *n.[2]* [late 19C+] **1** a romantic or sexual interest in someone. **2** (lesbian) the vagina. [one's emotions 'crush' their object]

crush *n.[3]* [1930s–40s] (US Black) a hat, esp. a soft, felt one. [note mid-19C UK SE *crush hat*, a soft hat that can be crushed flat, esp. a hat constructed with a spring so that it collapses and becomes flat]

crush *v.* [mid-19C] to run away, to escape. [? SE *crash*]

crush a bottle/pot of ale/cup of wine, to *phr.* [16C] to drink (cf. GIVE A BOTTLE A BLACK EYE).

crush a quart, to *phr.* [early 19C] to drink (cf. CRUSH A BOTTLE).

crushed on *adv.* [late 19C] (society) infatuated with. [CRUSH n.[2] (1)]

crusher *n.[1]* [early 19C+] a policeman. [the size of his feet; thus cf. BEETLE-CRUSHER. Note naut. use *crusher*, a ship's corporal]

crusher *n.[2]* [mid–late 19C] something that overwhelms or overpowers. [SE *crusher*, someone or something that crushes]

crusher *n.[3]* [20C] (US) a boor, an intruder. [GATE-CRASHER]

crusher *n.[4]* [20C] (US) one who persists in making unwanted advances to women. [CRASHER n.[2] and/or MASHER]

crushing *adj.* [mid-19C] excellent, first-rate. [SE *crushing*, bruising, overwhelming]

crush out *v.* [1920s+] (US Und.) **1** to escape from prison (cf. CRASH v.[2]). **2** to obliterate the body and the evidence of a murder by putting the corpse into a car and the car through a junkyard crushing machine.

crush the stir, to *phr.* [late 19C] (Und.) to break out of prison (cf. CRUSH OUT v.).

crust *n.[1]* [19C+] cheek, audacity, nerve. [SE *crust*, an outer covering or shell that is difficult to penetrate]

crust *n.[2]* [19C+] the head (cf. LOAF n.[2]). [it sits on top of the body]

crust *n.[3]* (orig. Aus./N.Z.) **1** [late 19C+] a living; thus *earn a crust*, work for a living. **2** [1910s–70s] a vagrancy charge, a vagrant. [both f. SE *crust of bread*. (2) implies that a vagrant has insufficient money to buy one]

crust *v.* [1910s–70s] (orig. Aus./N.Z.) to charge with vagrancy; thus *do the crust*, serve a sentence for vagrancy. [CRUST n.[3] (2)]

crust-buster *n.* [1950s+] (US Black) a baby who is just learning to eat solids (cf. CRUMB-CRUNCHER).

crust of bread *n.* [20C] the head (cf. CRUMPET n.[1]; LOAF n.[2]; SCONE n.[2]). [rhy. sl.]

crusty *n.* [1980s+] a member of the underclass of the 'punk' scene, who adopt deliberately filthy clothing (hence their 'crustiness'), live communally (often in squats) or on the streets, enjoy an excess of drink and drugs and generally set out to appal their less extreme peers. [note 1950s W.I. *crusty*, illiterate, backward, foolish]

crusty *adj.* [1980s+] (US juv.) unpleasant, nasty. [SE *crusty*, encrusted (with something unpleasant) + SE *crusty*, of a person, short-tempered, rebarbative]

crusty-beau *n.* [late 17C–late 18C] a dandy who takes especial care of his (? ageing) complexion, often with cosmetics. [SE *crusty*, encrusted + *beau*]

crusty gripes *n.* [late 19C] a grumbler. [SE *crusty*, short-tempered + *gripe*, a complaint]

crut *n.* [1920s–50s] unpleasant, disgusting matter. [CRUD n.[1] (1)]

crutch *n.[1]* [late 19C] a crutch-handled walking-stick, the badge of the late 19C man-about-town.

crutch *n.[2]* [20C] (bingo) the number 7; usu. as *one little crutch*; thus *all the crutches*, 77. [resemblance]

crutch *n.[3]* [1960s+] (drugs) a device (a thin piece of cardboard, usu. a matchbook cover, rolled into a cylindrical shape) used to hold the last portion of a marijuana cigarette that has become too hot to hold in the fingers (cf. ROACH CLIP).

crutch *n.[4]* [1970s] (US Black) a car; thus *fly crutch*, an expensive, fashionable car, *P-crutch*, a police car.

crutch and toothpick brigade *n.* [late 19C] a broad group of 'stage door johnnies' and men-about-town whose sartorial badges were a crutch-handled walking-stick and a toothpick (of the dental variety) (cf. CRUTCH n.[1]). [thus the music-hall rhymester's mock solicitous enquiry: 'What about that toothpick, and don't you like that crutch?/And are those trousers very tight, and do they hurt you much?']

crutch and toothpick parade *n.* [late 19C–1900s] generic term for old and decrepit males. [punning on CRUTCH AND TOOTHPICK BRIGADE]

cruz *n.* [1980s+] (drugs) opium from Veracruz, Mexico. [abbr. of *Veracruz*]

cry *n.[1]* [late 16C] a group of people. [the comparison is with a 'cry' or pack of hounds]

cry *n.[2]* [mid-19C+] a fit of weeping, usu. in phr. *a good cry*.

cry *n.[3]* [mid-19C+] (Aus.) one's turn to order a round of drinks (cf. SHOUT n.[1]).

cry a/cry crack, to *phr.* [20C] (Aus./Irish) to give in, to surrender, to cry 'quits'. [SE *cry* + CRACK v.[4] (2)]

cry a go, to *phr.* [late 19C] to give up, to surrender. [cribbage jargon *cry a go*, to pass]

cry and laugh *n.* [20C] (Aus.) a scarf. [rhy. sl.]

cry a rope, to *phr.* [late 16C] to shout a warning. [the hangman's rope that awaits those who pay no heed]

crybaby *v.* [20C] to collapse in the face of pressure and act like a weeping, pleading child.

cry/give beef/hot beef *v.* [late 18C–late 19C] to give the alarm, to call a hue and cry. [SE *cry* + HOT BEEF!]

cry bucket-a-drop, to *phr.* [20C] (W.I.) to make a good deal of fuss (and even cry) about an unimportant matter, to shed 'crocodile tears' (cf. CRY LONG WATER). [the image of filling a bucket with tears]

cry carrots and turnips, to *phr.* [18C] (Und.) to be whipped at the cart's tail. [? onomat. + ironic ref. to the carter's normal cries]

cry cockles *v.* [late 18C] to be hanged. [echoic; *cockles*, the sound made as one chokes]

cry copper *v.* [late 19C+] to raise the alarm (cf. HOLLER COPPER). [SE *cry* + COPPER n.³ (1)]

cry crack *see* CRY A CRACK.

cry-cry *adj.* [20C] (W.I.) of a child, continually or easily tearful, crybabyish.

cry cupboard, to *phr.* [late 17C] to complain of hunger.

cry halves *see* GO HALVES.

cry hughie/ralph/ruth *v.* [1960s+] to vomit. [echoic of the noise of vomiting]

crying *adj.* [late 19C+] a general intensifier, e.g. in *crying shame, crying dime, not a crying dollar.* [the use of *crying* as 'worthy of crying over', and referring to a variety of evils begins in early 17C with *crying sins* and has been used in *crying evil, crying injustice, crying grievance* etc, mainly in 18C–19C; 20C sees it as euph. for BLOODY or stronger terms]

crying buddy *n.* [1960s] (US Black) one's best friend. [? one on whose shoulder one may cry]

crying towel *n.* [1920s+] (US) a fig. *towel* used to mop the tears of self-pitying people.

crying weed *n.* [1950s] (drugs) marijuana. [SE *crying* + WEED n.¹ (4); ? its effects, although the tears are more likely to result from laughter than sorrow]

crying willie *n.* [20C] (US) a Baptist. [joc. use of SE + proper name; i.e. their religious lamentations]

cry long water/water out of your eye/eye-water/water to boil yams, to *phr.* [20C] (W.I.) to make a good deal of fuss (and even cry) about an unimportant matter, to cry 'crocodile tears'.

cry mapsticks! *excl.* [early–mid-18C] I beg for mercy! (cf. CRY UNCLE). [SE *cry* + play on *mopstick*, mop handle]

cryp *n.* [1980s+] (US drugs) a variety of marijuana that becomes hallucinogenic if smoked in large quantities. [it 'cripples' one's senses]

cry pork *v.* [late 18C–early 19C] to act as an undertaker's tout. ['a metaphor borrowed from the raven, whose note sounds like the word *pork*. Ravens are said to smell carrion at a distance' (Grose 1796)]

crypto *n.* [1980s+] (drugs) methamphetamine. [popular use of Greek pfx. *crypto*, hidden, secret, as extreme, ultimate]

cry ralph *see* CRY HUGHIE.

cry roast meat *v.* [late 17C–early 19C] to boast about one's good fortune (cf. ROAST-MEAT CLOTHES). [the assumed prosperity of those who eat roast meat. The *OED* suggests that such boasting is foolish]

cry ruth *see* CRY HUGHIE.

crystal/crystals *n.* [1960s+] (drugs) 1 a term covering a variety of drugs of the amphetamine type, e.g. amphetamine sulphate, powdered Methedrine, desoxyn. 2 uncut cocaine. [resemblance]

crystal bud *n.* [1980s+] (US drugs) a potent variety of marijuana in which the flowers are covered with tiny crystals. [SE *crystal* + BUD n.³]

crystal-gazer *n.* [20C] a person who manages to make successful predictions; thus an intelligent person.

crystal joint *n.* [1970s] (drugs) phencyclidine (cf. ACE n.³). [SE *crystal* + JOINT n.⁴]

crystal meth *n.* [1960s] (drugs) crystal Methedrine (cf. CRYSTAL). [it comes in a crystalline powder]

crystal T *n.* [1970s] (drugs) phencyclidine (cf. ACE n.³). [it comes in a crystalline powder]

crystal tea *n.* [1970s] (drugs) LSD (cf. A n.³). [it comes in a crystalline powder]

cry/holler/say uncle *v.* [1910s+] (US) to beg someone to stop an action, to surrender. ['"uncle" in this expression is surely a folk etymology, and the Irish original of the word is *anacol* (*anacal, anacul*) "act of protecting; deliverance; mercy, quarter, safety", a verbal noun from the Old Irish verb *aingid* "protects"' (*American Speech* LI, 1976)]

cry whore *v.* [mid-17C–late 18C] to put the blame on. [lit. to accuse someone of being a prostitute]

c.s. *n.* [1940s+] (orig. US) 1 a coward. 2 a contemptible, disgusting person. [abbr. CHICKENSHIT]

c.s.p. *n.* [1980s+] (US campus) a casual *sex* partner. [abbr.]

c.t. *see* COCKTEASER.

cu *n.¹* *see* COO n.

cu/cue/cuke *n.²* [1930s+] a *cuc*umber. [abbr.]

cub *n.¹* [late 17C–18C] a novice gambler, who is likely to be cheated of his cash. [*cub* meaning a child, a young person, a novice or a beginner was briefly sl. in early 17C but soon SE]

cub *n.²* [1920s+] (Aus.) a child's playhouse (cf. CUBBY n.).

Cubans/Cuban pumps *n.* [1970s+] (gay) heavy work-boots.

cubba *n.* [1940s+] (W.I.) 1 a promiscuous woman. 2 an effeminate man (cf. MISS CUBBA). [in W. African cultures *Cuba*, the day-name of a woman born on a Wednesday]

cubbitch *adj.* [1950s+] (W.I. Rasta) covetous, thus both mean and greedy. [SE *covetous*]

cubby *n.* 1 [1920s+] (Aus.) a child's playhouse, sited in the back garden. 2 [1930s–50s] (US Black) a small room. [abbr. SE *cubby-hole*]

cube *n.¹* [1950s–60s] an extreme conservative, an ultra-respectable person. [an intensified version or 'superlative' of SQUARE n.⁵ (3)]

cube/cubes *n.²* [1960s+] (drugs) morphine, esp. 1oz (28g) of morphine. [the shape of bulk supplies]

cube/cubes *n.³* [1960s+] (drugs) LSD (cf. A n.³). [early LSD doses were often dripped onto sugar cubes for easy ingestion]

cube *n.⁴* [1980s+] (US) a derog. term for a *Cub*an. [abbr.]

cubehead *n.* [1960s–70s] (drugs) an LSD user, esp. when dropped onto a sugar cube. [CUBE n.³ + -HEAD (2)]

cubes *see* CUBE n.², n.³.

cubesville *n.* [1950s–60s] the world of ultra-conservative, highly respectable people (cf. SQUARESVILLE). [CUBE n.¹ + sfx. -VILLE]

cubistic *adj.* [1960s] (US) extremely conventional. [CUBE n.¹ + sfx. -*istic*]

cubit, the *n.* [19C] the treadmill, as employed in prisons; thus *punishment by the cubit*, a spell on the treadmill. [William Cubitt (1785–1861) who invented the treadmill (albeit for grinding corn), which, from 1818, was introduced into British prisons as a form of punishment]

cubitopolis/cubittopolis *n.* [mid-19C] that area of London around Warwick and Eccleston Squares; thus Pimlico. [Thomas *Cubitt* (1788–1855), the greatest London builder of the early 19C, whose major creation, backed by his patron the Duke of Westminster, is Belgravia; ? + pun on the building measure, a *cubit*]

cubs *n.* [late 19C–1920s] (US Black) cards that have been fixed for use in crooked games.

cuckaboo *see* KOOKABOO.

cuckoldshire/cuckold's row *n.* [16C–17C] the fig. 'world' of cuckoldry.

cuckold the parson, to *phr.* [late 18C] to sleep with one's wife before one has been married.

cuckoo n.[1] [late 16C+] a fool, an eccentric, a silly person. [SE phr. *cuckoo in the nest*, denoting the oddness of such an individual]

cuckoo n.[2] [19C] the penis. [? COCK n.[1] (1)]

cuckoo adj. [1910s+] crazy, eccentric, insane. [CUCKOO n.[1]]

cuckoo academy n. [1960s] (US) a psychiatric institution (cf. CUCKOO FARM; CUCKOO HOUSE; CUCKOO'S NEST n.[2]). [CUCKOO n.[1] + SE *academy*]

cuckoo bird n. [1940s+] (US) an eccentric, a mad person. [CUCKOO n.[1] + BIRD n.[12]]

cuckoo farm n. [1960s] (US) a psychiatric institution (cf. CUCKOO ACADEMY; FUNNY FARM). [CUCKOO n.[1] + SE *farm*]

cuckoo house n. [1930s+] (US) a psychiatric institution (cf. CUCKOO ACADEMY). [CUCKOO n.[1] + SE *house*]

cuckoo juice n. [1960s–70s] (US) strong liquor. [CUCKOO n.[1] + SE *juice*; its potency sends one crazy]

cuckoos n. [17C] money. [ety. unknown; link to dial. *cuckoo-penny*, a penny that if turned in the pocket on hearing the first cuckoo, will guarantee cash for the next year]

cuckoo's nest n.[1] [mid-19C–1950s] the female genitals (cf. BIRD'S NEST). [CUCKOO n.[2] + SE *nest*]

cuckoo's nest n.[2] [1960s+] (US) a psychiatric institution (cf. CUCKOO ACADEMY).

cucumber n.[1] [late 17C–18C] a tailor; thus *cucumber season*, *cucumber time*, the summer time; thus a slack period in a job (cf. CABBAGE n.[2]). [in summer time, when cucumbers ripen, one's best customers, the gentry, are out of London, living on their country estates. Tailors traditionally took their holidays at this time]

cucumber n.[2] [late 19C+] (US) the penis. [resemblance]

cucumber n.[3] [20C] (Aus.) a number. [rhy. sl.]

cuddle and kiss n. [1930s+] a woman. [rhy. sl. *cuddle and kiss* = miss]

cuddle-bunny n. [1950s] (US) an affectionate, passionate or sexually alluring young woman. [SE *cuddle* + BUNNY]

cuddle-cook n. [1900s–10s] a policeman (cf. COOK'S OWN). [the popular reputation of contemporary policemen as pursuers of cooks]

cuddle the kielbasa, to phr. [1990s] to masturbate (cf. ACCOST THE OSCAR MEYER). [SE *cuddle* + *kielbasa*, a variety of Polish garlic sausage]

cuddy n. **1** [early 18C–mid-19C] a donkey. **2** [mid–late 19C] a fool (cf. ARSE n.[1]). [? dial. *cuddy*, a sucking lamb or kid]

cuddy-wifter n. [1960s+] a left-hander. [? link to dial. *cuddy-finger*, a little finger]

cuds n. [late 16C–mid-18C] used in oaths as a euph. for God's, e.g. *cud's bobs!* God's body!

cue n.[1] see CU n.[2].

cue n.[2] [1940s–50s] (US Black) a tip. [? mid-15C *cue* or *q* (Lat. *quadrans*), half a farthing]

cue v. [mid–late 19C] to swindle by abusing one's credit. [ety. unknown; ? Scots *cue*, to make drunk]

cue-ball n. [1940s] (US) a bald-headed person. [resemblance to a billiards/snooker ball]

cuete n. [1960s] (US) a gun. [Sp. *cuete*, a firecracker]

cuff n.[1] [early 17C–late 18C] a mean, surly old fellow, often as *old cuff*. [COVE; CUFFIN]

cuff n.[2] see CUFFY.

cuff n.[3] [late 19C+] (US) a subservient Black person, fitting willingly into the stereotyped image refined by generations of White supremacy (cf. UNCLE TOM). [*Cuffie*, a popular slave name]

cuff v.[1] **1** [1920s+] to place on credit. **2** [1930s] (US) to swindle. [ON THE CUFF phr.[1]]

cuff v.[2] [1930s+] (US Black) to hit, to fight. [SE *cuff*, to strike with the fist; note Rötwelsch (Ger. rogues' cant) *kuffen*, to thrash]

cuff v.[3] [1960s+] to hide a (marijuana) cigarette inside the cupped fingers. [one's cuffs help obscure the cigarette]

cuffa see CUFFER.

cuff/knock anthony v. [late 18C] **1** for one's knees to knock together (cf. ANTHONY CUFFIN). **2** to strike the hands under the armpits to warm them (cf. BEAT THE BOOBY). [SE *cuff*, to strike + generic use of *Anthony*, a person, oneself]

cuffee n. [1940s+] (W.I.) a fool, a gullible person (cf. CUFFY). [Twi *kofi*, a boy born on a Friday. Like other terms based on name-days, the underlying implication is always that of rural simplicity, even stupidity and backwardness]

cuffer/cuffa n. [late 19C–1920s] a tale or story. [dial. *cuff*, tell a tale]

cufferoo adj. [1940s] (US) free. [ON THE CUFF phr.[1] + sfx. *-eroo*]

cuffin n. [mid-16C–early 19C] a man, a fellow (cf. CO n.[1]). [? COVE]

cuffin-quire n. [17C] a magistrate. [var. on QUEER CUFFIN]

cuff it v. [20C] to extemporize, to respond to a situation spontaneously. [OFF THE CUFF]

cuff jonas v. [late 18C] to strike one's hands under one's armpits to warm them (cf. BEAT THE BOOBY). [SE *cuff*, to strike + generic use of *Jonas*, a person, oneself]

cuff link n. [20C] (Aus.) a drink. [rhy. sl.]

cuffo n. [1970s] (US) credit. [ON THE CUFF phr.[1] + sfx. -O]

cuffo adj. [1970s] (US) free. [CUFFO n.]

cuff one's dummy see BEAT ONE'S DUMMY.

cuffs n. [mid-19C+] (police/Und.) handcuffs. [abbr.]

cuffs and collars/cuffs n.[1] [late 19C] a nickname for the Duke of Clarence who introduced the high collar and the wide cuff to men's shirts.

cuffs and collars n.[2] [1950s] pubic hair that matches the colour of the visible hair; thus ostensibly proving that a woman is not dyeing her hair.

cuffs and collars adj. [late 19C+] (Aus.) middle-class, prissy, pernickety. [rather than more casual attire]

cuff-shooter n. [late 19C–1900s] a clerk. [his continual 'shooting' of his cuffs]

cuff the carrot, to phr. [1990s] to masturbate. [SE *cuff* + CARROT n.[2]]

cuff the dragon, to phr. [1990s] to masturbate.

cufuffle see KERFUFFLE.

cuffy/cuff n. (US) **1** [early 18C+] a Black person; thus patronizing phr. [19C] *proud as cuffy*, conceited, lit. proud as a Black man dressed up in his best clothes (cf. CUFFEE). **2** [19C] a bear. **3** [mid–late 19C] a young boy. [Twi *kofi*, the day-name for a male born on a Friday]

cuh see CUZ.

cuirass see CURE-ARSE.

cujo n. [1980s+] (US campus) a daredevil, one whose personal love for risk-taking tends to put others in danger. [title of *Cujo* (1983), a novel by horror writer Stephen King]

cuke see CU n.[2].

culch n. **1** [19C] second-rate (odds and ends of) meat. **2** [late 19C] (US) a derog. description of a person. [southern UK dial. *culch*, rubbish, refuse]

culchie n. [1940s+] (Irish) a derog. term for a country-dweller, as used by a townsperson. [coined at University College, Galway, to describe agricultural students; ? Irish *Coillte mach* (Kiltimagh) Co. Mayo; Irish *coillte*, woods; Irish *cúl a' tí*, the backdoor of the great house, to which peasants would be directed]

cule n. [mid-19C] a small bag, carried on a woman's arm (cf. CULING). [abbr. synon. SE *reticule*]

culican n. [1980s+] (drugs) high potency marijuana from Mexico. [proper name *Culican*, the area in which it grows]

culing/culling n. [mid-19C] (Und.) stealing (bags and purses) from carriage seats. [CULE + sfx. *-ing*]

cull *n.*[1] **1** [17C] a constable. **2** [late 17C–early 19C] a prostitute's customer. **3** [late 17C–mid-19C] a dupe, a silly fellow, a simpleton. **4** [late 17C–mid-19C] a man, a fellow, a chap. **5** [19C–1930s] a friend. [? CULLY n.; SE *cullion*, a contemptible person; fig. use of CULLS]

cull *n.*[2] [1980s+] (US campus) **1** a socially unacceptable person. **2** (spec. fraternity) anyone rejected for membership in a fraternity or sorority. [SE *cull*, to select weak animals for killing]

cull bird *n.* [1980s+] (US campus) any woman considered socially or physically unacceptable. [CULL n.[2] + SE *bird*, play on SE]

cullions *n.* [16C] the testicles. [Fr. *couillons*, testicles]

culls *n.* [16C–17C] the testicles. [abbr. CULLIONS]

cully *n.* **1** [mid-17C–late 19C] a simpleton, a victim. **2** [late 17C–late 19C] a man, a fellow, a companion (cf. CULL n.[1]). **3** [late 17C–late 19C] a fop, a dandy. **4** [early 18C] a prostitute's customer. [? as fool there may be links to Ital. *coglione*, a dolt, but as plain man it may well come from the Sp. Gypsy *chulai* or Turkish Gypsy *khulai*, both meaning man, or possibly fig. use of French *couillon*, testicles (cf. CULLS)]

cully *v.* [mid-17C–late 18C] to swindle, to cheat. [CULLY n. (1)]

cully-shangy *n.* [19C] sexual intercourse. [Scot. *collie-shangie*, a disturbance, a noisy argument, ult. ? f. the sound of *collie* dogs fighting or f. Gaelic *callaidh*, wrangling, outcry]

culo *n.* [20C] (US) the buttocks, behind. [Sp. sl. *culo*, the anus]

culp *n.* [late 17C–19C] a blow, a buffet. [Fr. *coup*, a blow, ult. Lat. *colaphus*, a box on the ear. though note SE *culp*, fault, blame]

cultural/culture fruit *n.* [1960s+] (US) a watermelon (cf. AFRICAN GOLF BALL). [neg. racial stereotyping; i.e. *Black* cultural fruit]

culture *adj.* [1950s+] (W.I. Rasta) reflecting or pertaining to the values and traditions respected by Rastafarians.

culture fruit *see* CULTURAL FRUIT.

culture-hound *n.* [1920s–30s] an intellectual, esp. one who is seen as too 'clever' for his or her own good.

culture-vulture *n.* [1940s+] **1** (orig. US) anyone who battens on to the prevailing cultural trends in order to debase and exploit them for economic gain, irrespective of the aesthetic loss involved. **2** (US campus) an over-zealous student. [derog. SE *culture-vulture*, one who is (affectedly) voracious for culture; thus an intellectual]

culty-gun *n.* [19C] the penis (cf. BAYONET). [Lat. *cultellus*, a knife + SE *gun*]

culver-headed *adj.* [mid-19C] foolish, weak-minded; thus *culver-head* a fool, a simpleton. [SE *culver*, a dove or young pigeon]

cum *n.* [1920s+] **1** semen. **2** an ejaculation. **3** an orgasm (for either sex). [often found, e.g. in written pornography, as an alternative to COME n.[1] + v.[1]; the sp. enhances the sexual aspect of the otherwise common word]

cum *v.* [1950s+] to achieve orgasm. [CUM n. (3)]

cum-bucket *see* COME-BUCKET.

cum chum *n.* [20C] (US) a homosexual male. [CUM n.(1) + CHUM n.[1]]

cum drum *n.* [1960s+] a condom with a reservoir for semen. [CUM n. (1) + SE *drum*]

cume *n.* [1960s+] (US campus) one's cumulative grade-point average. [SE *cumulative*]

cum-freak *n.* [1960s+] a promiscuous man or woman, obsessed with sexual gratification (cf. COCK-HOUND; COME-FREAK). [CUM n. + FREAK n.]

cummifo *adj.* [late 19C–1900s] as things should be, satisfactory. [mispron. of Fr. *comme il faut*]

cumshaw *n.* [mid-19C+] a bribe, a tip, a present. [Chinese *kam-sia*, the Amoy pronunciation of the Chinese words *kan*, to be grateful + *hsieh*, thanks; thus 'grateful thanks']

cum stain *see* COME STAIN.

cundum *n.* [late 18C] a false scabbard used to hide a sword. [SE *cundum* or *condom*, a contraceptive sheath]

cundy *n.*[1] *see* COONIE.

cundy *n.*[2] [1990s] a mix of semen and vaginal secretions, left after intercourse. [CUNT n.[1], but note CONDY]

cung *n.* [1980s+] (drugs) cannabis. [ety. unknown]

cunnel *n.* [18C–19C] (tinker) a potato. [Shelta]

cunnikin/cuntkin/cuntlet *n.* [18C] the vagina. [dimin. of *cunny*, ult. CUNT n.[1]]

cunning as a dead pig *phr.* [early–mid-18C] very stupid, i.e. not cunning at all.

cunning as a Maori dog *phr.* [1920s+] (N.Z.) very cunning (cf. LAZY AS A MAORI DOG). [racially derog. comparison]

cunning as a shithouse rat *phr.* [1960s+] (Aus.) very cunning; sometimes euph. as *...sewer rat*.

cunning/artful as a wagon-load/whole wagon-load of monkeys *phr.* [20C] very cunning.

cunningberry/cunningbury *n.* [early–mid-19C] a fool, a gullible person (cf. CUNNINGHAM). [ironic pun on SE *cunning* + SE *-berry/-bury*, a sfx. meaning 'place']

cunningham/mr cunningham *n.* [late 18C] a fool, a gullible person. [ironic pun on SE *cunning* + SE *-ham*, a sfx. meaning 'place']

cunning man *n.* [late 18C] a confidence trickster who used a (spurious) knowledge of astrology to help convince his or (more often) her victims; the preferred swindle was the 'miraculous' recovery of stolen goods. [SE; note dial. *cunning woman*, a witch]

cunning shaver *n.* [late 18C] a clever cheat. [a pun on SE *cunning* + SHAVER n.[1], but also one who 'shaves his victims close']

cunny *n.* [early 18C+] the vagina (cf. CUNT n.[1]; PUSSY n.[1]). [SE *coney*, rabbit]

cunny-burrow *n.* [17C] the vagina. [CUNNY + SE *burrow*]

cunny-catcher *n.* [17C] the penis. [CUNNY + SE *catcher*, a pun on CONY-CATCHER]

cunny-fingered *adj.* [19C] butter-fingered (cf. CUNNY-THUMBED). [CUNNY + SE *finger*]

cunny-haunted *adj.* [late 19C] of a male, obsessed with sex. [CUNNY + SE *haunted*]

cunnyskin *n.* [19C] the female pubic hair. [CUNNY + SE *skin*]

cunny-thumbed *adj.* [18C] 'to double one's fist, with the thumb inwards, like a woman' (Grose 1785). [CUNNY + SE *thumbed*]

cunny-thumper *n.* [1970s] (US) a villain, a rascal. [lit. 'vagina-hitter']

cunny warren *n.* **1** [18C] a brothel. **2** [18C] a girl's boarding school. **3** [19C] the vagina (cf. CUNNY-BURROW). [CUNNY + SE *warren*; the phr. puns on *bunny*, rabbit]

cunt *n.*[1] **1** [mid-15C+] the vagina. **2** [late 17C+] a woman considered purely as a sex object. **3** [late 17C+] copulation with a woman. [orig. ME but taboo since 15C. *Cunt* itself 'a nasty word for a nasty thing', as Grose (1796) dismisses it, appears as 'C—tt', although he offers roots in the Greek *konnos* and the Latin *cunnus*, and lists the French synonym *con*. This reticence was by no means limited to Grose (who, a single entry earlier, was perfectly happy to list CUNNY-THUMBED). Not until its supplement of 1972 did the *OED* (albeit unphased by PRICK since the late 19C) list the term, and other, lesser dictionaries, on both sides of the Atlantic, showed themselves equally coy. Many otherwise authoritative American tomes, hamstrung either by the religious right or the politically correct left, have yet to break the taboo. Yet as Eric

Partridge, writing in 1931 (six years before the term was included in the *DSUE*), put it: 'To ignore a very frequently used word – one indeed used by a large proportion, though not the majority, of the white population of the British Empire – is to ignore a basic part of the English language.' The first use the *OED* can find for the term appears *c*.1230, when *Gropecuntelane* is listed among the streets that made up the 'stews' (brothel area) of Southwark. Given the environment, it must be assumed that the term was already in general use. It would also appear from subsequent early citations that the term, while vulgar, was descriptive rather than obscene. Lanfranc, for instance, used it while writing on surgery around 1400. But by the end of the 15C cunt was unacceptable and two centuries later it was deemed legally obscene, and to print the word in full rendered one liable to prosecution. Its most notorious appearance in the dock came in 1960 in the trial of *Lady Chatterley's Lover*. It has yet, if ever, to return to grace. As Grose suggested, the word can be traced back to the Greek, although Partridge disputes whether *konnus* – a trinket, a beard, or the wearing of the hair in a tuft – is actually linked to the Latin *cunnus*, which meant both vagina and, like such English terms as CRACK n.[1], SLIT n.[1] and PUSSY n.[1], the woman (especially if seen as promiscuous) who possesses it. More likely Greek roots are *kusos* and *kusthos*, which are both related to the earlier Sanskrit *cushi*, meaning ditch. *Cunnus* itself, setting a pattern for its descendant, was already outlawed as obscene in Rome. Horace used it, Cicero did not. While the French, more heavily influenced by Latin, have *con* (and the Spanish *coño*), with its obvious links to *cunnus*, the English 'cunt' or *cunte*, as found in Middle English, takes its inspiration from a variety of German (*Kunte*) and Scandinavian (*kunta, kunte*) terms. It would appear, in this form, to be a combination of the ultimate root *cu* (which also lies at the basis of cow), which appears to imply quintessential femininity and the *nt* of the European synonyms. Note *val cava*, 'used by Boccaccio for a woman's private parts, a hollow cavity or valley' (Florio 1598)]

cunt n.[2] **1** [mid-19C+] a fool, a dolt, an unpleasant person of either sex (cf. ARSEHOLE n.). **2** [1920s+] a person. **3** [1930s+] an infuriating object, often mechanical. **4** [1960s+] something very difficult or unpleasant to do or achieve. [fig. uses of CUNT n.[1] (1). In some circumstances cunt, like the US Black use of MOTHERFUCKER, is so frequent and so repetitive as virtually to lose its shock or taboo value and become a neutral synonym for 'person']

cunt n.[3] [1970s] (drugs) the area of a vein into which one injects narcotics. [fig. use of CUNT n.[1] (1); it, too, is a hole]

cunt-collar n. [1960s] (US) the supposed entrapment of a man by a woman's sexuality (cf. PUSSY WHIP). [CUNT n.[1] (1) + SE *collar*]

cunt-curtain n. [19C] the female pubic hair. [CUNT n.[1] (1) + SE *curtain*]

cunted adj. [1990s] extremely drunk. [fig. use of CUNT n.[1] (1); ? one acts like a CUNT n.[2] (1)]

cunt-eyed adj. [1910s+] (US) used of a person with narrow, squinting eyes. [fig. use of CUNT n.[1] (1) as a 'slit' + sfx. -*eyed*]

cuntface n. [late 19C+] a term of address to an unattractive person. [CUNT n.[1] (1) + SE *face*]

cunt hair n. [1960s+] (US) an infinitesimally small amount. [CUNT n.[1] (1) + SE *hair*]

cunt-hat n. [1920s] a felt hat. [CUNT n.[1] (1) + SE *hat*; pun on 'felt', i.e. 'felt up']

cunthead n. [1970s+] (orig. US) a fool. [CUNT n.[1] (1) + sfx. -HEAD (1)]

cunt-/twat-hooks n. **1** [20C] the fingers (cf. DIVERS; FORK-HOOKS; FORKS; GRAPPLERS; GRAPPLING HOOKS; GRAPPLING IRONS n.[2]; HOOKS; LUNCH HOOKS; MEATHOOKS). **2** [1990s] a term of

endearment, may also be used as a casual greeting. [CUNT n.[1] (1) + SE *hooks*]

cunt-hound n. [1940s+] a man who is obsessed with sex and seduction (cf. CHIPPY-CHASER). [CUNT n.[1] (1) + sfx. -HOUND]

cunting adj. [late 19C] an intensive term of derision, dismissal etc (cf. BLOODY adj.; BUGGERING; FUCKING adj.). [CUNT n.[2] (4) + sfx. -*ing*]

cuntish adj. [1970s] **1** stupid, unpleasant. **2** effeminate. [CUNT n.[1] (1)/CUNT n.[2] (4) + sfx. -*ish*]

cunt-itch n. [18C–19C] sexual enthusiasm in a woman (cf. CUNT-STAND). [CUNT n.[1] (1) + SE *itch*]

cuntkin see CUNNIKIN.

cunt-lapper n. [1920s+] **1** a cunnilinguist. **2** a general term of abuse. [CUNT n.[1] (1) + SE *lapper*]

cunt-lapping/-licking adj. [1920s+] (US) of a person, despicable, repellent, disgusting. [CUNT-LAPPER]

cuntlet see CUNNIKIN.

cunt-licker n. [1940s+] (orig. US) **1** a cunnilinguist. **2** a general term of abuse (cf. CUNT-LAPPER). [CUNT n.[1] (1) + SE *licker*]

cuntock n. [1990s] a general term of abuse. [CUNT n.[1] (1) + COCK n.[1] (1)]

cuntocks n. [1990s] the labia. [CUNT n.[1] (1) + COCK n.[1] (1)]

cunt-pensioner n. [19C] a kept man, a pimp (cf. PENSIONER; PETTICOAT PENSIONER). [CUNT n.[1] (1) + Fr. *pensionaire*, a lodger]

cunt positive n. [1970s+] usu. in radical lesbian use, the concept of appreciating the vagina, despite its secondary image in a phallocentric world.

cunt's blood n. [1990s] an extremely unpleasant person. [CUNT n.[1] (1) + SE *blood*, i.e. menstrual blood]

cunt-shop n. [19C] a brothel (cf. BANGING-SHOP; BUTTOCKING SHOP). [CUNT n.[1] (1) + SHOP n.[1] (2)]

cunt-stand n. [19C+] sexual enthusiasm in a woman (cf. CUNT-ITCH). [CUNT n.[1] (1) + STAND n.[2]]

cunt-starver n. [1960s+] (Aus.) a man who defaults on his maintenance payments (cf. WIFE-STARVER). [CUNT n.[1] (1) + SE *starver*]

cunt-struck adj. [late 19C+] (of a man) obsessed with sex. [CUNT n.[1] (1) + SE *struck*]

cunt-sucker n. **1** [mid-19C] a cunnilinguist (cf. COCKSUCKER). **2** [1960s+] (orig. US) a repellent, loathed, unpleasant person. [CUNT n.[1] (1) + SE *sucker*]

cunt-teaser n. [20C] a man who excites a woman sexually but refuses to have intercourse (cf. PRICKTEASER). [CUNT n.[1] (1) + SE *teaser*]

cunt-tickler n. [1960s] (US) a moustache. [CUNT n.[1] (1) + SE *tickler*]

cunt wagon n. [1970s+] (US) a flashy car seen as an adjunct to the seduction of foolishly impressionable young women (cf. PASSION WAGON). [CUNT n.[1] (1) + SE *wagon*]

Cunty McCuntlips n. [1990s] an extremely unpleasant person. [CUNT n.[2] + pun on generic Scot. name]

cup and can phr. [mid-16C–mid-19C] great friends. [a cup is filled from a can; thus one friend nourishes the other]

Cupar/Coupar justice n. [18C–mid-19C] execution without trial, i.e. hanging first and asking questions afterwards (cf. JEDBURGH JUSTICE). [the alleged system in the Scottish town of *Cupar*]

cupboard n. [mid-19C] (US) the stomach (cf. BREADBASKET).

cupboard adj. [20C] (tramp/gypsy) mean, tight-fisted. [money and/or food is fig. locked away in one]

cupboard love n. [18C–early 19C] insincere love, however earnestly protested. [the orig. cupboard was open; thus such love is displayed rather than felt. SE after early 19C]

cupboardy adj. [late 19C] close, stuffy. [the claustrophobia of a closed cupboard]

cupcake *n.* (US) [1960s+] **1** a female breast (cf. APPLES n.¹). **2** an attractive young woman (cf. BANANA n.²). **3** (gay) a young homosexual man. [fig. uses of SE *cupcake*, a cake baked from ingredients measured by the cupful, or baked in a small cup]

cupcakes *n.* [1980s+] (US gay) tight, firm, small buttocks. [CUPCAKE]

cupid *n.*¹ [mid-18C–early 19C] a nickname for an ugly blind man. [*Cupid*, as the god of love, is trad. blind]

cupid *n.*² [19C] a pimp who lives with his prostitute. [ironic use; the relationship is rarely so affectionate]

cupid's alley *n.* [mid-19C] the vagina (cf. ALLEY n.¹; CUPID'S ARBOUR; CUPID'S ARMS; CUPID'S CAVE). [lit. euph., as are the synon. combs. that follow]

cupid's arbour *n.* [19C] the vagina (cf. ARBOUR; CUPID'S ALLEY).

cupid's arms *n.* [19C] the vagina (cf. CUPID'S ALLEY).

cupid's cave/cloister/furrow/hotel *n.* [19C] the vagina (cf. CUPID'S ALLEY).

cupid's itch *n.* [1930s+] (US) **1** gonorrhoea (cf. CUPID'S MEASLES). **2** crab lice. [SE *Cupid*, the god of love + SE *itch*]

cupid's kettledrums/kettldrums *n.* [late 18C–early 19C] the female breasts (cf. MARACAS). [SE *Cupid*, the god of love + SE *kettledrums*]

cupid's measles *n.* [1940s–50s] (US) secondary syphilis (cf. CUPID'S ITCH). [SE *Cupid*, the god of love + SE *measles*; the pustules that are a sign of the disease]

cupid's torch *n.* [19C] the penis. [SE *Cupid*, the god of love + SE *torch*]

cupman *n.* [mid–late 19C] a drunkard (cf. ALECAN).

cup of tea *n.*¹ [late 19C] **1** a comfort, a consolation, usu. of a person. **2** one's preference or taste, that which one chooses. [SE *cup of tea* as a restorative or a dependable pleasure]

cup of tea *n.*² [1920s+] a person, esp. in a teasing context, i.e. in phr. *you're a nice cup of tea, aren't you.* [SE *cup of tea* as a staple and thus here a generic]

cupola *n.* [late 19C–1950s] (US) the head (cf. ATTIC). [SE *cupola*, a rounded vault or dome forming the roof of any building or part of a building]

cuppa/cupper *n.* [1920s+] (orig. Aus.) a cup of tea.

cup rattler *n.* [late 19C] (US) a professional beggar.

cups *n.* [1940s–50s] (US Black) sleep (cf. IN ONE'S CUPS). [the implication being that the sleep is a drunken one]

cups *adj.* [1940s–50s] asleep, sleeping. [CUPS n.]

cup-shaken *adj.* [early–mid-17C] drunk.

cupshot *adj.* [late 16C–late 18C] drunk (cf. GRAPESHOT; OVERSHOT; POT-SHOT; SHOT adj.; SHOT IN THE NECK). [fig. *shot* by one's consumption of *cups*]

cup too low *n.* [late 17C–early 18C] one who remains silent in company. [they need another *cup* to become more loquacious]

cup-tosser *n.* **1** [19C] a juggler. **2** [mid–late 19C] a fortune-teller who uses tea leaves as a medium of prediction.

cura *n.* [1960s–70s] (US drugs) heroin, esp. when it is injected or smoked when one is suffering from withdrawal symptoms. [Sp. *cura*, a cure]

curate *n.* **1** [late 19C] a small poker, with an iron tip; such a poker is actually used, as opposed to the elaborate brass fire-irons, displayed only for show. **2** [late 19C] a handkerchief that is actually used, rather than one that is worn for fashionable display. **3** [late 19C] the top half of a sliced teacake, which receives less butter (cf. RECTOR). **4** [late 19C–1900s] (Irish) an assistant barman. **5** [late 19C–1900s] (Anglo-Irish) a grocer's assistant. [all play on the junior, and thus inferior, position of a curate in the local church hierarchy]

curate's delight *n.* [late 19C–1930s] a layered cakestand. [note CURATE n. (3)]

curb/kerb *n.* [late 16C] (Und.) the pole with a hook on one end that is used to steal items from stall or shop windows (cf. CURBING LAW). [SE *curb*, to bend]

curb/kerb *v.* [late 16C] to use a hook on a pole to steal from stalls, windows or open shop fronts. [CURB n.]

curber *n.* [16C] (Und.) a villain who steals by extracting goods from an open window; 'he that with a curb ... doth pull out of a window any loose linen, cloth, apparel, or else any other household stuff whatsoever ...' (Greene 1592) (cf. ANGLER; HOOKER n.¹). [CURB n.]

curbing law *n.* [16C–early 19C] (Und.) theft accomplished by 'fishing' for objects through open windows, using some form of hooked pole. [CURB n. or SE *curb*, the roadside, from which vantage point the criminal operates + LAW n.¹]

curbstone/kerbstone *n.* [late 19C] (US tramp) a cigarette made from the remains of extinguished cigarettes dropped in the gutter. [SE *curbstone/kerbstone*]

curbstone/kerbstone *adj.* [mid-19C+] a general term for informal, casual, often quasi-legal (cf. CURBSTONE BROKER n.¹; CURBSTONE JUSTICE; CURBSTONE PHILOSOPHER; CURBSTONE SAILOR). [SE *curbstone/kerbstone*; i.e. that which is delivered in the street]

curbstone/kerbstone broker *n.*¹ [mid-19C] anyone who operates an informal and possibly illicit business. [CURBSTONE adj. + SE *broker*. The original *kerbstone brokers* were those brokers of the New York Stock Exchange who were excluded from the reorganization of the institution in 1848 when it left the street, where it had operated, and moved indoors]

curbstone/kerbstone broker *n.*² [mid-19C–1900s] a street urchin. [SE *curbstone* + *broker*; i.e. they sell things in the street]

curbstone/kerbstone canary *n.* [1930s] (US tramp) a whinging beggar. [SE *curbstone* + ironic use of CANARY n.⁷]

curbstone/kerbstone justice *n.* [mid-19C] (US) rough justice, delivered impromptu and without benefit of official warnings of criminal proceedings, typically the policeman's 'clip around the ear' delivered to errant youngsters. [CURBSTONE adj. + SE *justice*]

curbstone/kerbstone mixture *n.* [20C] tobacco that is extracted from discarded 'fag-ends' and recycled in a pipe or 'roll-up' (cf. CURBSTONE n.). [SE *curbstone* + *mixture*]

curbstone/kerbstone philosopher *n.* [mid-19C+] anyone who appoints themselves a purveyor of knowledge and delivers that knowledge from a position on a street corner or outside a drugstore. [CURBSTONE adj. + SE *philosopher*]

curbstone/kerbstone sailor *n.* [early 19C+] a prostitute (cf. CRUISER). [CURBSTONE adj. + SE *sailor*; i.e. she 'sails' the streets]

curbstone/kerbstone setter *n.* [1930s+] (US) a mongrel. [SE *curbstone* + SE *setter*]

curby *n.* [1930s] (US) a waiter or waitress who serves customers in their parked car. [SE *curb* + sfx. *-y*]

curby hocks *n.* [mid-19C–1900s] clumsy feet. [SE *curby hocks*, the hock or other part of a horse's leg which is afflicted by a hard swelling]

curdler *n.* [late 19C] a blood-curdling story.

cure *n.* [mid–late 19C] an eccentric person. [SE *curiosity* or *curious person*]

cure *v.* (drugs) **1** [1960s+] to improve the quality of a batch of marijuana; methods include steeping it in rum or some other spirit, placing it in the deep freeze, mixing it with another variety of marijuana or some other drug and so on. **2** [1980s+] (US) to heat hashish so that it is easier to crumble and thus use in a cigarette or pipe. [SE *cure*, to improve, applied to a variety of substances including leather, rubber and plastic]

cure-arse/cuirass *n.* [late 18C] an absorbent plaster applied to buttocks and thighs that have been chafed by too much riding. [SE *cure* + ARSE n.¹ (1)]

cured of a tympany with two heels, to be *phr.* [late 16C–early 18C] to give birth. [SE *cured* + var. on TWO-LEGGED TYMPANY]

curflummux *see* KERFLUMMUX *v.*

curiosity *n.* [mid-19C] an eccentric. [ext. of CURE n.]

curious *adj.* [mid-19C] (US) excellent, first-rate. [obs. SE *curious*, of objects, carefully delicately or beautifully made; of people, exact, punctilious, expert]

curl *n.*[1] [1960s] (Aus.) a term of address. [SE *curly*, one who has curly hair]

curl, the *n.*[2] [1970s+] (US Black) a Jheri curl. [*Jheri* Redding, who in the 1970s invented this Black hairstyle, in which the normal tight curls of Black hair are replaced by straighter, softer curls, with a shiny wet look]

curl *n.*[3] [1990s] a piece of excrement. [resemblance]

curl *v.* [mid-19C+] (US campus) to do well in class, esp. to recite faultlessly; thus *curler*, a first-rate student. [? the curlicues and flourishes that adorn the handwriting of a good calligrapher. Good students would be assumed to write well as part of their overall excellence]

curle *n.* [late 17C–18C] clippings from money (cf. NIG n.[1]; PARINGS; SHAVINGS). [the slivers of metal curled as they were clipped]

curled darlings *n.* [mid-19C] (society) army officers, esp. those who had returned from fighting in the Crimean War (1854–6). [the long beards and curled moustaches such officers sported]

curlicue *see* CARLEYCUE.

curl one off *v.* [1990s] to defecate. [CURL n.[3]]

curl paper *n.* [late 19C] lavatory paper. [CURL n.[3] + SE *paper*]

curls *n.* [early 19C] human teeth, esp. as extracted by body-snatchers.

curl someone's hair, to *phr.* [late 19C+] (orig. US) **1** to scold severely. **2** to terrify.

curl/kurl the mo, to *phr.* [1940s+] (Aus.) to succeed brilliantly, to win. [the image of a man curling the tips of his moustache in a self-satisfied manner]

curl-/kurl-the-mo/curl-a-mo *adj.* [1940s+] (Aus.) excellent, first-rate, a good deal, e.g. *curl-the-mo mazuma*, a great deal of money. [CURL THE MO *phr.*]

curl up one's toes *see* TURN UP ONE'S TOES.

curly *n.* [1910s+] (Aus.) nickname for a bald person. [heavy-handed irony]

curly *adj.* [1930s+] (N.Z.) of a person, attractive; of an object or event, first-rate. [SE *curly* hair being seen as attractive]

curlyhead *n.* [early 19C] (US) a derog. term for a Black person.

curly locks *n.* [20C] (Aus.) socks. [rhy. sl.]

curly one *n.* [1950s+] (mainly Aus./N.Z.) a tricky problem, a challenge. [it is not 'straight']

curly water *n.* [20C] (Ulster) a mix of sugar and water that will, allegedly, help one's hair curl.

curly wolf *n.* [20C] a tough, tricky individual. [qualities of the animal, but note CURLY ONE]

curp/kcirp *n.* [1980s] the penis. [backsl. PRICK]

currant bun *n.* **1** [late 19C+] the sun. **2** [1980s+] *The Sun* newspaper (cf. CAPTAIN GRIMES). [rhy. sl.]

currant-cakey *adj.* [1900s–30s] shakey. [rhy. sl.]

currants and plums *n.* [mid-19C] threepence. [rhy. sl. *currants and plums* = THRUMS]

currency *n.* [19C] (Aus.) one born in Australia (cf. STERLING).

current *adj.* [late 19C–1900s] (Anglo-Irish) well, in good health. [i.e. *currently* healthy]

curry/curry-muncher *n.* [1970s+] (N.Z.) a derog. term for an Indian. [culinary stereotyping]

curry and rice *n.* [1950s+] (Aus.) the price. [rhy. sl.]

curry bunny *n.* [1950s+] (S.Afr.) vegetarian curry sold as a take-away in a hollowed-out half loaf of bread. [for ety. *see* BUNNY CHOW]

curry queen *n.* [1990s] (US) a gay man who is attracted to Indian homosexuals (cf. RICE QUEEN). [SE *curry* as a staple Indian food + QUEEN n.[1]]

curry someone's skin-coat, to *phr.* [18C–mid-19C] to thrash, to beat. [SE *curry*, to dress tanned leather]

curse, the *n.*[1] [20C] euph. for a menstrual period. [abbr. SE *the curse of Eve*]

curse/curse of Cain *n.*[2] [1920s–40s] (Aus.) the bundle or pack carried by an itinerant worker or tramp. [the suffering of the biblical villain *Cain*]

cursed-cull *n.* [late 17C–18C] an ill-natured person, esp. of women. [SE *cursed* + CULL n.[1]]

curse of God *n.*[1] [early 19C] a cockade. [the cockades worn by the atheistic French revolutionaries]

curse of God *n.*[2] [20C] a menstrual period (cf. CURSE n.[1]).

curse of God *n.*[3] [1920s–40s] (Aus.) the bundle or pack carried by an itinerant worker or tramp.

curse of Scotland *n.* **1** [18C–early 19C] the 9 of diamonds (cf. JUSTICE-CLERK). **2** [20C] whisky. [diamonds imply royalty, and according to legend every ninth king of Scotland was 'a tyrant and a curse to that country' (Grose 1785). A further suggestion is that the 9 of diamonds resembles the arms of Duke of Argyll, who was one of the leading proponents of union with England, a move that was not wholly welcomed by his compatriots. Hotten (1860) suggests that this card was that on which 'Butcher' Cumberland wrote the orders for the mopping up of rebels after Culloden (1746), that 9 lozenges are the arms of Dalrumple, Earl of Stair 'detested for his share in the Massacre of Glencoe', that the arrangement of diamonds resembles the St Andrew's Cross and adds 'the most probable explanation is, that in the game of Pope Joan the 9 of diamonds is the Pope, of whom the Scots have an especial horror']

curse out *v.* [mid-19C+] to become abusive.

cursetor/cursitor *n.*[1] [mid-16C–early 18C] a tramp, spec. one of the Forty-second Order of Vagabonds. [ext. of SE *cursitor*, a courier]

cursetor/cursitor *n.*[2] [late 18C] one of the 'broken, petti-fogging attornies or Newgate solicitors' (Grose, 1785). [Lat. *currere*, to run; (1) f. SE *cursitor*, a courier; (2) f. SE 'one of twenty-four officers or clerks of the Court of Chancery, whose office it was to make out all original writs de cursu, i.e. of common official course or routine, each for the particular shire or shires for which he was appointed' (*OED*)]

curtail *see* CURTAL.

curtain-climber *n.* [1960s] (US) a small child. [its habits]

curtain lecture/sermon *n.* [late 17C–18C] a telling-off from a wife to her husband, after they have gone to bed (cf. GIVE A CURTAIN LECTURE). [the curtains in question are those of the four-poster bed]

curtains *n.*[1] [1910s+] the end, finality (cf. CHURCH n.[2]). [theatrical imagery i.e. the curtain comes down to signal the end of the play]

curtains *n.*[2] [1980s+] (US gay) the foreskin; thus *draw the curtains*, to fellate an uncircumcised penis.

curtain sermon *see* CURTAIN LECTURE.

curtal/curtail/curtall *n.* (Und.) **1** [16C–late 18C] a mendicant villain, the 11th rank of the CANTING CREW and thus marginally less influential than the UPRIGHT MAN, distinguished by his short cloak, similar to that of the Grey Friars. **2** [18C] thieves who cut off pieces of silk, cloth, linen etc hanging from shop-windows. **3** [18C] a cut-purse. [SE *curtal*, anything docked or cut short (orig. a horse's tail)]

curve *n.* (US) **1** [late 19C–1910s] (US) a personal peculiarity. **2** [1920s–30s] an attractive young woman. **3** [1940s+] an occasion of unfair or surprising treatment, usu. in phr. *throw one a curve*, to surprise, to trick, to take advantage of.

curveball *n.* [1940s+] (US) a tricky or unexpected question or action. [baseball imagery]

curve-buster *n.* [1960s+] (US campus) a student whose grades exceed the average. [such grades are above the average curve plotted on a graph]

cus *see* CUZ.

cush *n.*[1] [1950s–60s] (US) money.

cush/kush *n.*[2] [1950s–60s] **1** sexual intercourse with a woman. **2** the vagina. **3** a woman seen strictly as a sex object. [Arabic *cush*, the vagina]

cush *adj.* [1920s+] (Aus.) fair, honourable. [? CUSHY]

cushat *n.* [19C] the vagina. [SE *cushat*, a wood pigeon or ring dove]

cushdi *see* CUSHTY.

cushion *n.* [1960s+] (drugs) a vein into which a drug is injected. [it is 'plumped up' for the injection]

cushion-cuffer *n.* [late 17C–mid-18C] a parson (cf. CUSHION-DUSTER; CUSHION-SMITER; CUSHION-THUMPER).

cushion-duster *n.* [early 18C–early 19C] a parson (cf. CUSHION-CUFFER). ['many of whom, in the fury of their eloquence, heartily belabour their cushions' (Grose 1796)]

cushions *n.* [20C] (US) the buttocks. [resemblance, they cushion one's body against the surfaces on which one sits]

cushion-smiter *n.* [mid–late 19C] a parson (cf. CUSHION-CUFFER).

cushion-thumper *n.* [mid-17C–late 19C] a parson (cf. CUSHION-CUFFER).

cushty/cushdi *adj.* [1910s+] (orig. market trader) first-rate, excellent, enjoyable (cf. CUSHY). [widely popularized by the 1980s BBC TV series *Only Fools and Horses*]

cushy *adj.* [20C] soft, comfortable, easy. [? Rom. *kushto*, good or Hind. *khush*, pleasure]

cuss *n.*[1] [late 18C+] **1** a curse. **2** obscenities, taboo language. [SE *curse*]

cuss *n.*[2] [late 18C+] (orig. US) a man, a fellow. [orig. US, either from SE *customer* or ? fig. use of CUSS n.[1]]

cuss/cuss down *v.* [1980s+] to abuse verbally, to insult (cf. CUSS OUT), [CUSS n.[1]]

cuss-cuss *n.* [1950s+] (W.I. Rasta) a quarrel or fracas, with lots of cursing. [CUSS n.[1] + redup.]

cussed *adj.* [late 19C+] cursed.

cussedness *n.* [mid-19C–1930s] (US) malignity, cantankerousness, contrariness.

cuss out *v.* [1960s+] to curse, to attack verbally, to criticize (cf. CUSS v.). [CUSS n.[1]]

cuss-word *n.* [late 19C] (US) an obscenity, an oath. [CUSS n.[1] + SE *word*]

custard *n.* [1950s] (Aus.) semen (cf. BABY GRAVY; LOVE CUSTARD). [resemblance]

custard and jelly *n.* [1960s+] television. [rhy. sl. *custard and jelly* = TELLY]

custards *n.* [1920s+] (Aus.) pimples, acne. [the yellow pus such eructations contain]

customer *n.* [mid-19C+] a person; usu. in combs, e.g. *tough customer*, *ugly customer* (cf. ARTIST n.[2]). [the image of humans as consumers]

custom house *n.* [late 18C] the vagina (cf. CUSTOM HOUSE GOODS; CUSTOMS OFFICER; EVE'S CUSTOM HOUSE; RECEIPT OF CUSTOM). [in which punning institution 'Adam made the first entry']

custom house goods *n.* [late 18C] the vagina (cf. CUSTOM HOUSE). ['the stock in trade of a prostitute, because fairly entered' (Grose 1796)]

custom house officer *n.* [mid-19C] a laxative pill. [pun on permitting goods to 'pass through']

customs officer *n.* [late 18C] the penis. [he 'works' in the CUSTOM HOUSE]

cut *n.*[1] **1** [late 18C+] an act of ignoring a friend or acquaintance both deliberately and pointedly. **2** [mid–late 19C] one who deliberately avoids another person. **3** [1980s+] (US) an insult.

cut *n.*[2] [early 19C] a degree (cf. CUT ABOVE).

cut *n.*[3] [mid-19C+] (US campus) **1** the failure of a class to meet. **2** absenting oneself from a class.

cut *n.*[4] [1910s+] a share, of profits, of loot, of the proceeds of a robbery etc.

cut *n.*[5] [1910s+] (Aus./N.Z.) corporal punishment, esp. of schoolchildren. [SE *cut*, a blow with a cane or stick]

cut *n.*[6] [1950s+] (orig. US sporting) a pre-arranged point at which a group of competitors or recruits to a team are reduced by those who fail to achieve a given standard; thus *make the cut*, to continue on the team, in the competition etc, also in fig. non-sporting use.

cut *n.*[7] [1970s] (US) a swing with the fist; thus *take a cut at*, to menace or hit with the fist. [SE *cut*, a blow]

cut *n.*[8] [1990s] a recently received haircut. [abbr.]

cut, the *n.*[9] [1990s] (US Black) the ghetto, the poor side of town. [SE *cut*, a passage; thus note *The Cut*, London SE1, one of 19C London's best known street markets; also (*Major*, 1994) f. the knives wielded in such a place]

cut *adj.*[1] [18C+] drunk. [abbr. CUT IN THE LEG phr. (1), a facet. euph. ref. to being staggering drunk]

cut *adj.*[2] [1980s+] (US gay) circumcised (cf. UNCUT).

cut/cut up *adj.*[3] [1980s+] (US) of a man, with well-defined or well-developed muscles (cf. RIPPED adj.[3]). [the muscles are 'cut out' and thus defined from the rest of the body]

cut *v.*[1] **1** [16C–early 19C] (Und.) to speak, to talk (cf. CUT BENE WHIDS). **2** [20C] (W.I.) to speak a language, esp. as *cut … good*. [E.P. suggests abbr. of the participle of Lat. *loquor, locutus*, spoken]

cut *v.*[2] **1** [mid-17C+] to ignore deliberately. **2** [1980s+] (US Black) to put someone in their place by a verbal attack, to reprimand, to scold.

cut *v.*[3] **1** [late 18C–late 19C] to absent oneself without good reason. **2** [mid-19C+] to leave, to desert, to run off, to escape (cf. CUT OUT v.[2]). [(1) 20C use is SE]

cut *v.*[4] [mid-19C+] to pose as, to act in the manner of. [abbr. SE *cut a figure*]

cut *v.*[5] [mid-19C] to stop doing something; thus *cut that*, be quiet, stop that.

cut *v.*[6] [20C] (orig. US) to understand, esp. as *cut it*.

cut *v.*[7] **1** [1900s–50s] to manage, to achieve, usu. as *cut it*. **2** [1930s+] (US Black) to surpass, to outdo. **3** [1970s] to be convincing, to be as one wishes.

cut *v.*[8] [1920s+] (US) of a man, to have sexual intercourse. [the image of the penis as a knife]

cut *v.*[9] **1** [1920s–30s] to divide, to receive or take a share, e.g. of a manager who takes a percentage of an artist's or sportsman's earnings or of criminals dividing up loot. **2** [1970s+] to give.

cut *v.*[10] [1930s+] (US) to stab.

cut *v.*[11] [1940s–50s] (Aus./N.Z.) to finish. [SE *cut off*]

cut *v.*[12] **1** [1950s+] (drugs) to dilute a drug with some adulterant. **2** [1980s+] (orig. US) to adulterate one's position, to sacrifice one's standards, to equivocate.

cut! *excl.* [mid-19C+] be quiet!

cut a block/blocks with a razor, to *phr.* [mid-18C–late 19C] to make a futile and absurd attempt.

cut a bosh, to *phr.* [mid-18C–mid-19C] to cut a figure. [ety. unknown; ? Fr. *ébauche*, outline, a rough-hewn figure]

cut above *n.* [early 19C+] a degree or stage above, esp. socially. [CUT n.[2] + SE *above*]

cut a bum card, to phr. [16C] (Und.) to cheat at cards by using one that has a slightly raised surface. [? f. 14C colloq. *bum*, the buttocks, which are 'raised' from the plane of the back; although the meaning is alluring, the use of BUM, bad is late 19C and US]

cut a cake see FROST A CAKE.

cut a caper upon nothing, to phr. [late 18C] to be hanged (cf. CAPER v.; CUT ONE'S LAST FLING; DANCE v.[2]; DANCE AT BEILBY'S BALL; DANCE AT THE SHERIFF'S BALL; DANCE AT TUCK 'EM FAIR; DANCE THE NEWGATE HORNPIPE; DO THE NEWGATE FRISK; DO THE PADDINGTON FRISK).

cut a deal, to phr. [1970s+] (orig. US) to compromise, to make an arrangement, to make a deal.

cut a finger, to phr. [late 19C–1900s] to break wind (cf. CUT THE CHEESE). [euph.]

cut a flash, to phr. [mid-19C+] to act in a vulgar manner. [CUT v.[4] + FLASH adj.[2]]

cut a gut, to phr. [1920s+] (US) to make a mistake, esp. an embarrassing one. [the butchering of an animal, when a slip of the knife, typically into the gall-bladder, can ruin the meat]

cut a hog, to phr. [1930s+] (US) **1** to make a mistake (cf. CUT A GUT). **2** to fail in a task, esp. when it is beyond one's abilities.

cut a joke, to phr. [19C] to talk, to tell a joke. [CUT v.[1]]

cut a long leash, to phr. [1970s+] to allow a good deal of freedom (cf. CUT SOME SLACK).

cut a melon, to phr. [20C] (US) to divide up, esp. the spoils of a large coup or a crime. [fig. use of SE + CUT v.[9]]

cut and carried phr. [20C] married (cf. CASH AND CARRY). [rhy. sl.]

cut and come again n. **1** [late 17C–19C] plenty, abundance. **2** [19C] the vagina. [fig. and punning use of 'Meat that cries come Eat me' (B.E.)]

cut and run, to phr. [mid-19C+] to run off, to escape. [naut. jargon *cut and run*, cut one's cable and run before the wind; note CUT v.[3]]

cut a/some rusty, to phr. [19C+] (US) to show off, to behave in a silly, unsophisticated manner. [CUT v.[4] + *rustic*, a peasant]

cut a sham, to phr. [late 17C–early 18C] to hoax, to trick. [CUT v.[4] + SHAM n.[1]]

cut a shine see CUT A SPLASH.

cut a side, to phr. [1980s+] (US Black) to have sexual intercourse (cf. BANG v.[1]). [CUT v.[8] + SIDE n.[4] + play on music use *cut a side*, to make a record]

cut a slice/slice off the joint, to phr. [late 18C+] of a man, to have sexual intercourse (cf. CARVE A SLICE). [esp. with a married woman, since proverbially 'a slice of a cut loaf is never missed']

cut/make a splash/shine, to phr. [19C] (orig. US) to be very well known or successful, to cut a 'fine figure'.

cut ass v. [1950s–60s] (US) to leave, to run off (cf. CUT TAIL). [CUT v.[3] (2) + ARSE n.[1] (1)]

cut a swathe/wide swathe, to phr. [mid-19C+] (orig. US) to swagger, to boast, to make a self-aggrandizing display.

cut a/do the swell, to phr. [early–mid-19C] to swagger. [CUT v.[4] + SWELL n.]

cut a tooth/one's eye-teeth, to phr. [19C] to become aware, knowing. [fig. use of SE, cutting teeth is a sign of growing older]

cut away/off v. [late 16C–19C] to leave, to run off. [CUT v.[3] (2)]

cut a wheedle, to phr. [late 18C–early 19C] to deceive by flattery. [CUT v.[4] + WHEADLE]

cut benely v. [16C] (Und.) to speak gently or kindly. [CUT v.[1] (1) + BENE]

cut bene whids, to phr. [16C–18C] **1** (Und.) to speak kindly. **2** to tell the truth (cf. CUT QUEER WHIDS). [CUT v.[1] (1) + BENE + WHID n.]

cut-buddy n. [20C] (US Black) a close friend. [CUT v.[9] + BUDDY n.]

cut caper-sauce, to phr. [late 18C] to be hanged (cf. CAPER v.).

cutcha/kutcha adj. [18C–19C] (Anglo-Ind.) makeshift, second-rate, fake, bad. [Hind. *kachcha*, raw]

cut cheese v. [late 19C–1920s] (US campus) to impress, to influence, to make a difference (cf. CUT ICE). [CUT v.[4] + CHEESE n.[1]]

cutchery n. [early 17C–19C] (Anglo-Ind.) a courthouse, a place of business. [Hind. *kacheri*, a hall or audience]

cutchie/kouchie n. [1950s+] (W.I./Jam.) a pipe used for smoking ganja, marijuana.

cut corners/the corners, to phr. [1950s+] to perform a job of work or a duty in a way that minimizes the effort but still capitalizes on the promised rewards.

cut-deck n. [1960s+] (drugs) heroin mixed with powdered milk. [CUT v.[12] + DECK n.[3]]

cut dicks v. [1950s+] (W.I.) to affect an English accent in the hope of impressing people. [? CUT v.[4] + SE *dignity*]

cut dirt v. [19C+] (US) to run away, to depart at speed. [the way a horse's hooves cut into the ground as it gallops at speed; note CUT v.[3] (2)]

cut-down adj. [late 19C] (US Black) dejected, miserable (cf. DOWN adj.[1]).

cut down v. [1960s+] (US campus) to insult. [CUT v.[2] (2)]

cut down to size, to phr. [1960s+] to reduce a person's (high) opinion of themself to a realistic estimate.

cute adj. **1** [mid-18C+] acute, clever, keen-witted, esp. in phr. [20C] *don't get cute with me*. **2** [early 19C+] attractive, charming. [SE *acute*; early 19C adoption in US developed and spread (1)]

cute chick n. [1950s+] an attractive young woman. [CUTE (2) + CHICK n.[3] (1)]

cuter/kyuter n. [1920s–50s] (US) 25 cents, a quarter. [note hotel jargon *cuter*, one who only tips a quarter]

cutes n. [20C] (orig. US) a pretty young woman, often as a term of address, e.g. *Hey cutes … .* [CUTE (2)]

cutesie/cutesy adj. [1910s–20s] (orig. US) excessively sweet, cloying, esp. in one's behaviour. [CUTE adj. (2) + sfx. -*sie*; later use is SE]

cutesie-/cutie-pie n. [20C] an attractive woman, usu. young, poss. a man's girlfriend. [CUTIE n.[1] (2) + SE *pie*]

cutesie-/cutie-pie adj. [1910s–20s] (orig. US) excessively sweet, cloying, esp. in one's behaviour.

cute suit with the loop droop n. [1940s] (US Black/Harlem) an ostentatious drape suit, popular at the time. [CUTE adj. (2)]

cutesy see CUTESIE.

cut eye v. [1920s+] (W.I./Jam.) to catch a person's eye then, with the intention of offering a deliberate insult, to turn away. [W.I. *cut*, to dance + *eye*]

cut for the simples phr. [late 17C–late 19C] cured of one's foolishness; esp. in phr. *go to Battersea to be cut for the simples.* [17C Battersea was best known for its market gardens and the medicinal herbs they grew, known as *simples*, basic herbs without any adulterants. The use of *simples* as a cure for physical ailments evolved into one for supposed mental problems once it was absorbed in sl.]

cut-glass accent n. [1950s+] the 'proper' accent of the British upper or upper-middle classes, esp. the women.

cut gravel v. [mid-19C] (US) to move very fast. [the image of a coach's wheels spinning up gravel]

cut Grecian v. [1940s] (W.I.) of a woman, to walk in a self-consciously 'stylish' manner, either arrogantly or proudly (cf. GRECIAN BEND). [CUT v.[4] + SE *Grecian*]

cuthbert n. [1910s–30s] **1** one who deliberately avoids military service, esp. by securing a post in a government office or the civil service. **2** a conscientious objector. [stereotype of *Cuthbert* as a slightly 'weak' or foolish name]

cut ice/cut ice with v. [late 19C+] (orig. US) to impress, to influence, to make a difference, usu. in neg. phr. *cut no ice/ice with*, to make no impression, to leave unmoved.

cutie/cutey n.[1] **1** [late 18C+] a superficially clever person. **2** [1920s+] (orig. US) a pretty young woman. **3** [1960s+] (US) someone who is extremely shrewd. [CUTE + sfx. -y]

cutie/cutey n.[2] *see* COOTIE n.[1].

cutie-pie *see* CUTESIE-PIE.

cut in v. [late 19C+] **1** to receive a share. **2** to give a share. [CUT v.[9]]

cut in the back phr. [mid-17C–mid-19C] **1** very drunk. **2** pregnant (cf. CUT IN THE LEG). [CUT adj.[1]]

cut in the leg phr. [late 17C–late 18C] **1** very drunk. **2** pregnant (cf. CUT IN THE BACK).

cut it/cut it down v.[1] [mid-19C–1940s] (US) to dance energetically (cf. CUT THE RUG).

cut it v.[2] [1970s+] (orig. US) to manage, to deal with (difficult) situations. [CUT v.[7] (1)]

cut it fat/too fat, to phr. [mid–late 19C] to show off, to make a vulgar display. [SE *cut (it) fat*, to leave too much fat on a slice of meat when carving]

cut/run it/something fine, to phr. [late 19C+] **1** to leave a very small margin of error; to leave something until the very last minute, usu. in the context of arriving at a meeting, catching a train etc. **2** to gamble that one will not be found out, nearly to break the law.

cut it out! excl. [20C] just stop that!

cut it up v. [20C] to have an uproarious good time. [CUT THE RUG]

cut joint n. [1970s+] (US gay) a circumcised penis. [CUT adj.[2] + JOINT n.[5] (1)]

cutlass n. [17C] the penis (cf. BAYONET).

cut lemons v. [late 19C] (US) to impress, to appear important. [? lemons are 'sharp']

cutlery n. [mid-19C–1900s] (US) any form of edged weapon, usu. a knife.

cut loose v. **1** [20C] (US prison) to release, to be released. **2** [1950s+] to terminate, to let go, to get rid of. **3** [1950s+] to abandon restraints, either in one's action or, in an argument, in one's language and abuse. **4** [1960s+] (US Black) to give up, to abandon. **5** [1960s+] (US Black) to jilt, to terminate a relationship.

cut loose one's dog *see* CUT ONE'S DOG LOOSE.

cut lunch n. [20C] (Aus.) a meal of sandwiches. [which are cut from a loaf]

cut mud v. [1930s–50s] (US) to move very fast (cf. CUT GRAVEL). [image of car wheels moving through mud]

cut mutton with v. [mid-19C–1900s] to share in someone's hospitality; thus *cut mutton*, to dine.

cut off at the pass, to phr. [20C] to intercept, to ambush: metaphorically as well as physically. [the cliché line of many Westerns: *We'll cut them off...*.]

cut off the joint n. [20C] sexual intercourse (cf. CUT A SLICE).

cut of one's jib n. [early 19C+] the way one behaves, one's character. [SE *cut*, style + *jib*, one of a variety of sails hoisted at the very front of the vessel]

cut old style *see* CUT STYLES.

cut one's cable, to phr. [19C] **1** to run away. **2** to die. [naut. imagery]

cut one's dog loose/cut loose one's dog, to phr. [19C+] (US) to act spontaneously, without restraint (cf. CUT LOOSE).

cut one's eyes/cut yai, to phr. [1930s–40s] **1** (W.I./US Black) to look suspiciously, to look askance at (cf. CUT EYE). **2** to glance at, to look at furtively (cf. CUTTY-EYE). [dial. *cut-eye*, a scornful gesture made with the eyes]

cut one's eye-teeth *see* CUT A TOOTH.

cut one's foot, to phr. [19C+] (US) a euph. for to step in excrement (cf. DUTCHMAN'S RAZOR).

cut one's horns *see* SCRAPE ONE'S HORNS.

cut one's last fling, to phr. [18C] to be hanged (cf. CUT A CAPER UPON NOTHING; DANCE v.[2]). [SE *cut a fling*, to dance, implying DANCE v.[2]]

cut one's leg, to phr. [late 17C–late 18C] to become pregnant (cf. CUT IN THE BACK).

cut/make one's lucky, to phr. [mid–late 19C] to run off. [? SE *lucky escape*]

cut one's own grass, to phr. [mid–late 19C] to earn one's own living.

cut one's own throat/one another's throats, to phr. [late 19C+] to ruin oneself or oneself and another through pure bloody-mindedness rather than any rational or commercial calculation.

cut one's stick/sticks, to phr. [early–mid-19C] **1** to leave quickly, to run off (cf. AMPUTATE ONE'S MAHOGANY). **2** to travel around looking for work. [(2) f. cutting a stick to help one as one walks along]

cut one's string, to phr. [19C+] (US) to abandon restraint, to let oneself go. [CUT LOOSE (3)]

cut one's wheels, to phr. [1950s] (US) to leave, to depart.

cut one's wolf loose, to phr. [19C+] to act spontaneously. [var. on CUT ONE'S DOG LOOSE]

'cutor n. [1920s–30s] (US) a prosecuting attorney. [abbr. SE *prosecutor*]

cut-out n. [1960s] a middleman, esp. in espionage.

cut out v.[1] [late 17C–19C] to find (work for someone).

cut out v.[2] [mid-19C] to rush away, to leave fast, to escape. [CUT v.[3] (2)]

cut out v.[3] [mid-19C] (US) to do better than, to surpass. [ext. of SE use]

cut out v.[4] [mid-19C–1930s] (US) to take over as someone's preferred love-object. [CUT OUT v.[3]]

cut out v.[5] [late 19C] (US) to recognize, to identify. [SE phr. *cut out from a crowd*]

cut out v.[6] [late 19C+] to stop, esp. in phr. *cut it out*. **2** [1940s+] (Aus.) to finish, to complete a job. **3** [1960s+] (US) to die. [ext. of CUT OUT v.[2]]

cut out a cheque, to phr. [20C] (Aus./N.Z.) to spend all one's earnings in one go.

cut out of v. **1** [late 17C+] to deprive of an opportunity. **2** [18C–19C] to cheat.

cut out of the whole cloth *see* OUT OF WHOLE CLOTH.

cut out to be a gentleman phr. [20C] circumcised. [pun + CUT adj.[2]]

cut over the head adj. [18C] drunk. [CUT adj.[1]]

cut-purse n. [17C–19C] a pickpocket. [the original *cut-purse* did just that: cut loose the bag or purse in which a person kept their money and which was attached to their belt]

cut puss n. [1950s] (W.I.) an effeminate, fat man. [SE *cut*, castrated + PUSS n.[5]]

cut queer whids, to phr. [16C–mid-19C] **1** (Und.) to speak unpleasantly or obscenely; thus [early 18C–mid-19C] *queer whidding*, telling off, reprimanding. **2** to tell lies (cf. CUT BENE WHIDS). [CUT v.[1] (1) + QUEER adj.[1] (1) + WHID n.]

cut quick sticks, to phr. [mid-19C] to be in a hurry (cf. AMPUTATE ONE'S MAHOGANY). [var. on CUT ONE'S STICKS]

cut-rate adj. [1960s+] cheap, unsatisfactory, limited. [SE *cut-rate*, economic, inexpensive]

cut round v. [mid–late 19C] (US) to show off, to make a display. [CUT v.[3] (2)]

cuts n. [late 17C–early 18C] in oaths, a euph. for God's, e.g. *Cuts plutteranails! Cuts bobs!*

cuts and scratches n. [late 19C+] matches. [rhy. sl.]

cut shit v. [1970s+] (orig. US) to impress, to influence, to make a difference (cf. CUT ICE). [SE *cut* + SHIT n.[1] (1)]

cut some rusty see CUT A RUSTY.

cut someone into v. (US) **1** [1930s+] to meet someone. **2** [1950s+] to introduce one person to another.

cut someone out of v. [mid-19C+] (US) to let go, to release someone (cf. CUT LOOSE).

cut someone's arse, to phr. [20C] (W.I./Guyn.) to thrash severely, to flog. [SE *cut* + ARSE]

cut someone's cart, to phr. [mid-19C–1920s] to expose someone's tricks.

cut some slack, to phr. [1960s+] (orig. US Black) to ease the pressure upon, to permit the subject to relax. [SE *cut* + SLACK n. (7)]

cut something fine see CUT IT FINE.

cut styles/old style v. [20C] (W.I.) to behave in an exhibitionist manner to attract attention. [CUT v.[4] + SE *style*]

cut tail v. [1950s–60s] (US) to run away (cf. CUT ASS). [CUT v.[3] + TAIL n.[1] (3)]

cut ten see COCK TEN.

cutter n.[1] **1** [mid-16C] a braggart, a boaster, a thug; thus *swear like a cutter*. **2** [1910s–60s] (US) an admirable or remarkable person. **3** [1960s–70s] (US) a remarkable occurrence or event. [someone or something who/that fig. 'cuts']

cutter n.[2] **1** [19C] a pickpocket, a cut-purse. **2** [1970s] (US) a knife.

cutter n.[3] [20C] (US) a revolver. [it 'cuts down' its targets]

cut that out! excl. [mid-19C+] stop doing that!

cut the buck, to phr. [20C] (US) to work hard. [dial. *cut the buck*, to dance vigorously; ult. f. *buck and wing*]

cut the cackle/cut the cackle and come to the horses, to phr. [late 19C+] to come to the point, usu. as imper. [CUT v.[5] + CACKLE n.[1]]

cut the cake, to phr. [20C] (US Black) **1** to get married. **2** to deflower a virgin. [fig. uses of SE]

cut the cheese, to phr. [1950s+] to break wind, esp. in phr. *who cut the cheese?* [the smelliness of certain cheeses]

cut the corners see CUT CORNERS.

cut the crap! excl. [1950s+] don't try to fool me! stop talking rubbish! etc. [CUT v.[5] + CRAP n.[3] (2)]

cut the flash, to phr. [20C] (Aus.) to show off, to be very well known or successful, to cut a 'fine figure' (cf. CUT A SPLASH). [CUT v.[4] + FLASH n.[6]]

cut the fool, to phr. [1930s–60s] (US Black) to act the fool, esp. when dealing with White people, to play tricks. [CUT v.[4] + SE *fool*]

cut the grass from under someone's feet, to phr. [late 16C] to foil, to thwart, to trip up.

cut the gutter n. [20C] (Ulster) an errand boy.

cut the line/rope/string, to phr. [19C] to cut a long story short.

cut the mustard, to phr. **1** [20C] (orig. US) to come up to a given standard, to prove satisfactory. **2** [20C] (W.I.) of a man, to satisfy a woman sexually. **3** [20C] to have sexual intercourse. **4** [1950s] (US) to show off. **5** [1980s+] (US) to impress, to influence (cf. CUT ICE). [the image of the condiment's piquancy. (3) is included by E.P. but his citation suggests a journalistic euph. rather than an established sl. phr.]

cut the painter, to phr. **1** [mid-17C–mid-19C] to dismiss or send away a person. **2** [mid-19C+] to slip away clandestinely. **3** [mid-19C+] to die. [all f. naut. use, the *painter* is the rope that secures a small boat to a larger ship]

cut the rope see CUT THE LINE.

cut the rug/rug cut v. [1920s–50s] to dance.

cut the string see CUT THE LINE.

cut-throat n.[1] **1** [late 18C–mid-19C] a dark lantern. **2** [19C] a butcher. **3** [late 19C+] an open-bladed, non-safety razor.

cut-throat n.[2] [1970s+] (US Black) a tough, aggressive or frightening Black man (cf. BAD-ASS NIGGER; BAD BOY). [his (potential) violence and aggressiveness]

cuttie n. [1950s+] (W.I.) **1** a 10-ounce beer bottle, known as a 'reputed half pint'. **2** a very short man. [SE *cut down*]

cutting-gloak n. [early–mid-19C] one who is known for using a knife to settle quarrels. [SE *cut* + GLOAK]

cutting ice n. [1960s–70s] (US Black) succeeding in a spectacular manner. [CUT ICE; there is no White use]

cutting man n. [1950s–60s] (US Black) one's best friend (cf. CRYING BUDDY). [jazz jargon *cutting*, competing musically]

cutting-shop n. [mid–late 19C] a shop selling cheap, badly made goods. [SE *undercut*]

cuttle n. [mid-16C–mid-17C] a knife. [obs. OF *coutel* (mod. Fr. *couteau*); ult. Lat. *cultellum*, a knife]

cuttle-bung n. [16C] (Und.) a knife used for cutting purses. [CUTTLE + BUNG n.[1] (1)]

cut to the chase, to phr. [1980s+] to get (immediately or quickly) to the point. [film imagery; the chase being generic for any dramatic/exciting sequence]

cut to waste, to phr. [mid-19C] to waste time. [tailors' jargon *cut to waste*, to cut cloth in a wasteful manner]

cutty n. [1970s+] (US Black) a friend, a close intimate (cf. CUTTING MAN). [? dial. *cutty*, small or diminutive; thus used as an affectionate term of address]

cutty-eye v. [late 18C] to gaze at in a suspicious manner, to look askance (cf. CUT EYE). [SE *cutty*, sharp + *eye*]

cutty-eyed adj. [19C] **1** suspicious (of someone). **2** suspicious-looking (cf. CUT ONE'S EYES). [SE *cutty*, sharp + *eyed*]

cutty gun n. [19C] the penis (cf. BAYONET). [image of the penis as a weapon]

cut under v. **1** [mid-19C] (US) to undersell. **2** [late 19C–1930s] (US Black) to insult.

cut-up n.[1] [late 19C+] an amusing person, a joker. [CUT UP v.[1] (3)]

cut-up n.[2] [1970s] (US prison) a knife-fight.

cut up adj. see CUT adj.[3].

cut up v.[1] **1** [mid–late 18C] to slander, to criticize, esp. behind the victim's back. **2** [late 18C+] to dance, to have a good time. **3** [late 18C+] to show off, to play the clown, to make people laugh. **4** [19C] to behave, to act. **5** [mid-19C+] (US) to complain, to make a lot of noise. **6** [1950s+] (US Black) to fight. **7** [1950s+] to act eccentrically. [fig. uses of SE; 1920s+ use of (2) is SE]

cut up v.[2] [late 18C– late 19C] used in the passive, to be in a difficult situation, esp. as regards money.

cut up v.[3] [late 18C–1900s] to become, to appear, to show up.

cut up v.[4] [late 18C+] **1** to divide, esp. money, loot. **2** to defraud, to deprive. **3** to leave a fortune, esp. in phr. *cut up big*, *cut up large*, to leave a good deal.

cut up v.[5] [1920s+] (US) to reminisce, to talk over. [abbr. CUT UP TOUCHES]

cut up v.[6] [1930s+] to overtake another vehicle by driving recklessly in front of it (and forcing it to take some form of evasive action).

cut up a curlicue, to phr. [19C] (US) to act in a deceitful manner, to play a trick. [CUT UP v.[1] (4) + SE *curlicue*, a twist or curl; note SE *cut up curlicues*, to cut capers]

cut up a dido/didoes, to phr. [early 19C–1920s] (orig. US) to play pranks, to act the fool. [SE *dido*, a prank, a disturbance]

cut up extras, to phr. [mid-19C] (US) to behave badly. [ext. of CUT UP v.[3] (3)]

cut up fat, to phr. [18C–19C] to leave a fortune after one's death. [butchers' jargon *cut up fat*, for an animal to be divided into profitably saleable pieces]

cut/kick/tear/turn up jack, to phr. [mid-19C+] (US) to cause a commotion. [ext. of CUT UP v.[3]]

cut up old scores, to *phr.* [1930s+] to reminisce over old success, major villainies etc (cf. CUT UP TOUCHES). [CUT UP v.⁵ + SCORE n.³ (1)]

cut up touches/old touches, to *phr.* [1920s+] (US Und.) **1** to reminisce over old successes, villainies etc (cf. CARVE UP SCORES). **2** to share out the spoils of criminal acts.

cut up rough, to *phr.* [mid-19C+] to react unpleasantly, to become annoyed, to make a fuss (cf. CUT UP RUSTY; CUT UP SAVAGE; CUT UP UGLY). [CUT UP v.³ (5) + SE *rough*]

cut up rusty, to *phr.* [early 19C+] to become annoyed (cf. CUT UP ROUGH).

cut up savage, to *phr.* [mid-19C] to become annoyed (cf. CUT UP ROUGH).

cut up shapes, to *phr.* [mid-19C] to play pranks, to act in a flighty manner. [CUT UP v.³ (3) + (SHOW) SHAPES]

cut up stiff, to *phr.* [19C] to leave a large estate. [SE *cut up*, divide + STIFF adj.²]

cut up ugly, to *phr.* [mid-19C+] to become annoyed (cf. CUT UP ROUGH).

cut up well *v.*¹ [18C–19C] to leave a fortune after one's death (cf. CUT UP FAT).

cut up well *v.*² [mid-late 19C] to display a well-shaped naked body (cf. CUT adj.³). [CUT UP v.² + SE *well*]

cutware bottoms up *phr.* [1940s] (US Black) holding one's glass upside down against one's lips so as to drain the last drops. [SE *cut glassware*]

cut yai *see* CUT ONE'S EYES.

cutzooks! *excl.* [early 18C] a general oath, one of many ways of euphemizing God; lit. 'God's hooks' (cf. ADZOOKS!).

cuz/cuh/cus *n.* [1960s+] (US Black) form of address between Black males (cf. BRUZ). [abbr. SE *cousin*, a development of mid-16C–mid-19C *coz*]

cuz john/cousin john *n.* [mid-18C–mid-19C] (US campus) a privy (cf. JOHN n.¹⁰)

cuzzy *n.* [20C] (US) the vagina (cf. COOCH n.¹). [? SE *cousin*]

cuzzy-bro *n.* [1990s] (N.Z.) a friend, a member of one's extended family. [SE *cousin* + *brother*; ? coined by Maori comedian Billy T. James (d.1992)]

c.y.a. *phr.* [1950s+] (orig. US milit.) look after yourself before worrying about anyone else, be it colleagues, customers, the larger world, whatever; the basic admonition to anyone, at any level, working in government or a large corporation. [abbr. *cover your ass*]

cyberpunk *n.* [1990s] (US teen) a computer obsessive who is still found socially acceptable. [popular def. of SE *cyber*, computer-related + PUNK n.¹ (6)]

cycline *n.* [1980s+] (drugs) phen*cyclidine* (cf. ACE n.³). [abbr.]

cyclones *n.* [1980s+] (drugs) phencyclidine (cf. ACE n.⁴). [CYCLINE + pun on SE *cyclone*]

cyclops *n.* [20C] (US Black) a television (cf. ONE-EYED MONSTER). [proper name *Cyclops*, a one-eyed giant who, in Greek mythology, forged thunderbolts for Zeus. A television, too, has 'one eye']

cymbal *n.* [mid-19C] a watch. [its ticking]

cynthia *n.* [1950s–60s] (camp gay) a 'synthetic', insincere person.

cypress hill *n.* [1990s] (US Black) gang rape. [? the rap band of this name]

cyprian *n.* [early 17C] a prostitute (cf. CYPRIAN ARBOUR). [coined by Thomas Carew (1594–1640). Lit. an inhabitant of Cyprus, an island that had once been celebrated for the worship of Aphrodite or Venus]

cyprian *adj.* [late 16C–19C] lewd, licentious; latterly used specifically of prostitutes. [CYPRIAN n.]

cyprian arbour *n.* [early 17C] **1** the vagina (cf. ARBOUR). **2** a brothel. [CYPRIAN n.]

cyprian cave/strait *n.* [early 17C] the vagina (cf. ARBOUR). [CYPRIAN n.]

c.y.t. *phr.* [1920s+] (US) an attractive young woman. [abbr. *cute young thing*]

D

d *n.*[1] [mid–late 19C] abbr. of DAMN!

d/dee *n.*[2] [mid-19C+] (Aus./N.Z.) a detective; thus (N.Z.) *the Dees*, the police as an organization (cf. DEMONS). [abbr.]

d *n.*[3] [1950s+] (drugs) heroin. [abbr. DUJI]

d *n.*[4] (drugs) **1** [1950s+] *d*ilaudid. **2** [1970s+] LS*D* (cf. A n.[3]). [abbr.]

D *n.*[5] [1970s+] (US) *D*etroit (cf. BIG D). [abbr.]

d *n.*[6] [1970s+] drugs phencyclidine (cf. ACE n.[3]). [abbr. (ANGEL) DUST]

d *n.*[7] [1990s] cannabis. [abbr. DOPE n.[1]]

d *n.*[8] [1990s] (US Black) the penis. [abbr. DICK n.[5] (1)]

d *n.*[9] [1990s] (US Black) looking after oneself, adopting a defensive posture to potential threats. [basketball use, *d*, defence]

d *adj.* [early 19C+] excellent, wonderful, first-rate (cf. JOLLY D!). [abbr. DANDY adj.]

d.a. *n.* **1** [1950s+] (orig. US) a *d*uck's *a*ss, a style of haircut popular in the 1950s but still found (cf. DUCK'S ARSE). **2** [1970s+] (US campus) *d*umb *a*ss, a fool, an idiot. [abbr.]

dab *n.*[1] [17C+] a skilful person (cf. DAB HAND). [gaming jargon *dab*, a top-flight gamester. ? orig. schoolboy slang, the obvious ety. is rooted in SE *adept* or *dapper*, but there is no positive proof of either]

dab *n.*[2] [early–mid-19C] a bed (cf. DAB IT UP; DEB n.[2]). [? backsl. Note SE *dab*, a flattish mass of a soft substance, typically butter]

dab *n.*[3] [19C] **1** a flat fish of any kind. **2** (Und.) the corpse of an impoverished, outcast woman. [SE *dab*, a small flat fish (*Pleuronectes limanda*), usu. the flounder]

dab *adj.*[1] [18C–19C] skilled, expert. [DAB n.[1]]

dab *adj.*[2] [mid–late 19C] bad. [backsl.]

dabble *n.* [late 19C+] stolen property. [ironic use of SE]

dabble *v.* [1950s+] (drugs) to use drugs, esp. narcotics, in moderation (cf. CHIPPIE v.[2]).

dabbler *n.* [late 19C–1910s] a farthing (cf. LITTLE DABBLER).

dab down *v.* [19C] to hand over, to pay out. [SE *dab*, to put down with a sharp, abrupt motion]

dab hand *n.* [early 19C+] an expert at an occupation, usu. as *dab hand at*. [DAB adj.[1] + SE *hand*, a person, with reference to their abilities or character]

dabheno/daheeno *n.* [mid-19C] among costermongers, something bad, usu. a poor market (cf. DOOG ENO). [DABHENO adj.]

dabheno *adj.* [mid–late 19C] among costermongers, bad. [backsl.; lit. 'one bad']

dab in the dook *n.* [1910s–20s] a tip. [SE *dab*, a pat + DUKE n.[3] (3)]

dab it up *v.* [early–mid-19C] to run up credit at a public house. [SE *dab*, the writing down of one's owings]

dab it up/up with *v.* [early 19C] of a man and woman, to cohabit. [DAB n.[2]]

dab out *v.* [mid–late 19C] to do the laundry. [SE *dab*, to strike or cause to strike (usually with something soft and of broadish surface); thus the slapping of clothes on a washboard etc]

dabs *n.*[1] [late 19C] an expert. [abbr. DABSTER]

dabs *n.*[2] [1920s+] fingerprints. [SE *dab*, to pat]

dabster *n.* [late 19C] an expert. [DAB n.[1] + sfx. -STER]

dabtros/dab tros *n.* [mid-19C] a bad sort, an unpleasant person. [backsl.]

dacca/dakker *n.* [1970s+] (Aus.) marijuana. [var. on DAGGA]

dace *n.* [late 17C–18C] twopence. [SE *deuce*, two]

dacey *adj.* [mid–late 19C] (Anglo-Ind.) Indian, native. [Hind. *desi*, country]

dacha/deger *n.* [mid-19C] (Ling. Fr./Polari) the number ten. [Ital. *deici*, 10]

dacha-saltee *n.* [mid-19C] (Ling. Fr./Polari) 10 pence. [Ital. *dieci soldi*]

dachs *n.* [late 19C+] a *dachs*hund (cf. DACHSIE; LAB; NEWF; POM n.[1]; ROTTIE; SAUSAGE DOG; YORKIE). [abbr.]

dachshund *n.* [1990s] an extremely large piece of human excrement. [resemblance + pun on dachshund's nickname, the SAUSAGE DOG]

dachsie/daxie *n.* [late 19C+] a *dachs*hund (cf. DACHS). [abbr.]

dack up *v.* [1990s] (N.Z.) to smoke marijuana. [DAGGA]

dad *n.*[1] [17C+] euph. for God in a variety of mild oaths, e.g. [early 19C] (US) *dad-fetched*, [early–mid-19C] (US) *dad-shimmed*, [early 19C+] (US) *dad-burned*, [mid-19C] (US) *dad-goned*, [mid-19C] (US) *dad-rotted*, [mid-19C] (US) *dad-shaved*, [mid-19C] (US) *dad-snatched*, [mid-19C] (US) *dad-swamped*, [mid-19C+] (US) *dad-blamed*, [mid-19C+] (US) *dad-blasted*, [late 19C–1910s] (US) *dad-gummed*, [late 19C–1940s] (US) *dad-gasted*, [late 19C+] (US) *dad-binged*, [1910s] (US) *dad-bloomed* (cf. COCK n.[1]). [the term flourished, like many similar euphemistic oaths, in the UK in the late 17C but re-emerged in the 19C in the US, where it remains in many combinations, a resurgence poss. helped by the similarity to another taboo word, DAMNED]

dad *n.*[2] [1920s–60s] (orig. US Black) a term of address by one male to another, esp. when slightly older (cf. POPS n.[3]). [mainly in Black/beatnik use; thus UK jazz-orientated film of 1960s, *It's Trad, Dad*]

dad *n.*[3] [1950s] (gay) an older male homosexual. [abbr. DADDY n. (8)]

dada *n.* [1950s+] (W.I. Rasta) father.

dad-dad/-mum *n.* [late 18C] a beginner's attempts at a drum-roll (cf. DADA-MAMA). [echoic]

dada-mama *n.* [1970s] (US Black) a drum roll (cf. DAD-DAD). [echoic]

dad and dave *n.* [1930s+] (Aus.) a peasant, an unsophisticated person. [DAD AND DAVE phr.]

dad and dave, to *phr.* [20C] (Aus.) to shave. [rhy. sl.; ult. f. the popular 1930s radio serial *Dad and Dave* concerning various aspects of rural Aus. life. The show was based 'somewhat remotely' (Wilkes, 1985) on characters in the novel *Our*

Selection by Steele Rudd (Arthur Hoey Davis, 1868–1935), itself taken from his columns in the *Bulletin*, starting in 1895]

dad and mum *n.* [20C] (Aus.) rum or the cordial Bonox and rum. [rhy. sl.]

daddle *n.* [late 18C–late 19C] the hand; thus *tip the daddle*, to shake hands. [dial.]

daddle *v.* [19C] to enjoy lesbian sex; the implication is of mutual masturbation. [DADDLE n.]

daddler *n.*[1] [late 19C] the hand. [DADDLE n.]

daddler/dadla/dadler *n.*[2] [1900s–10s] a farthing. [? SE *tiddler*, something very small]

daddy *n.* **1** [mid-19C] (Und.) 'At mock raffles, lotteries, &c., the Daddy is an accomplice, most commonly the getter up of the swindle, and in all cases the person that has been previously arranged to win the prize' (Hotten, 1867). **2** [mid-19C] the old man, generally an aged pauper, in charge at a tramp's lodging house or casual ward. **3** [mid–late 19C] the man who gives away the bride at a wedding, trad., but not invariably, her father. **4** [mid-19C+] the supreme example, the most important, powerful, best known etc, often as the *daddy of them/us all*. **5** [20C] (US) a pimp, a prostitute's boyfriend. **6** [1930s+] (orig. US) an older man who is willing to provide the various material desires of his younger mistress or, if gay, male lover (cf. SUGAR DADDY). **7** [1940s+] (US Black) a form of address to a Black male, esp. by a woman to her lover. **8** [1950s+] an older male homosexual. **9** [1950s+] a masculine lesbian (cf. PAPA). **10** [1960s+] (prison) a leader (through intimidation and other influence) of the inmates in a borstal (cf. BARON). **11** [1960s+] (US) a customer, a client.

daddy! *excl.* [20C] (W.I.) a general expression of surprise and approval (cf. PAPA!).

daddy-bag *n.* [1990s] (US Black) the testes and the scrotum. [their function in procreation]

daddy funk *n.* [19C] a form of stew. [ety. unknown; ? link to SE *funk*, a stench]

daddy loves you best *phr.* [20C] (US) a warning to a woman that her slip is showing (cf. CHARLIE'S DEAD). [ety. unknown; ? only a girl's father would mention it]

daddy-o *n.* **1** [1930s–60s] (orig. US Black) a term of address between males (cf. DAD n.[2]; POP n.[3]). **2** [1940s+] (orig. US) a boyfriend, male lover, husband. **3** [1960s] (US Black) a thing, an object. **4** [1960s] (US) one's father. [the jazz-based Black use transferred, as did many such terms, to White beatniks in the 1950s and thence hippie use, but is now obs.]

daddy one *n.* [20C] (US Black) a lover or any man who provides for a woman. [DADDY n. (7) + SE (*number*) *one*]

daddy tank *n.* [20C] (US Und.) an area set aside to provide protective custody for effeminate homosexuals. [DADDY n. (8) + TANK n.[2]]

daddy zoo *n.* [1990s] a prison. [DADDY n. (10) + SE *zoo*]

dadla/dadler *see* DADDLER n.[2].

dad-mum *see* DAD-DAD.

dads *n.* **1** [18C] an old man. **2** [20C] father (cf. POP n.[7]). **3** [1950s+] a term of address to anyone somewhat older than oneself (cf. DAD n.[2]).

Dad's Army *n.* **1** [1940s+] the Local Defence Volunteers, latterly the Home Guard. **2** [1980s+] (S.Afr.) compulsory military duty for older men, introduced in 1983; thus any one of the military units created under this scheme. [orig. in WW2, the term re-emerged as the title of the BBC-TV sitcom *Dad's Army* (1967–77)]

da-erb *n.* [mid-19C] bread. [backsl.]

daff *n.*[1] [19C] a simpleton, a fool. [SE *daft*; via. dial. *daff*, a fool]

daff *n.*[2] [1910s+] a *daff*odil, usu. in pl. (cf. CARNIE n.[1]). [abbr.]

daff *n.*[3] [1950s+] (Irish) excrement. [ety. unknown]

daffadown dilly/daffydown dilly/daffy-down-dilly *adj.*

[20C] foolish, simple (cf. DAFFY adj.). [rhy. sl. *daffadown dilly* = silly]

daffier *n.* [early 19C] a gin-drinker. [DAFFY n. (1)]

daffodil *n.* [1930s–70s] (gay) **1** an effeminate young man (cf. BUTTERCUP). **2** a young male prostitute. [the stereotyped linking of flowers to effeminacy]

daffy *n.*[1] **1** [early 18C–19C] gin. **2** [mid-19C] a small measure, usu. of spirits; thus synon. market traders' use *daffies*. **3** [mid-19C] tincture of senna. [proper name *Daffy's Elixir*, a proprietary remedy which was known as 'the soothing syrup']

daffy *n.*[2] [late 19C] (US) a promiscuous woman. [fig. use of DAFFY adj.]

daffy *adj.* [late 19C+] eccentric, foolish, esp. in *daffy about*, madly in love with. [SE *daft*]

daffydown dilly *see* DAFFADOWN DILLY.

daffy-down-dilly *n.* [mid–late 19C] a dandy (cf. DAFFODIL). [SE *daffydowndilly*, a daffodil]

daffy-down-dilly *adj. see* DAFFADOWN DILLY.

daffy-headed *adj.* [1960s+] foolish. [DAFFY adj. + SE -*headed*]

daffy house *n.* [1900s] (US) a psychiatric institution. [DAFFY adj. + SE *house*]

daffy/daffy it *v.* [early–mid-19C] to drink gin. [DAFFY n.[1] (1)]

daft and barmy *n.* [1960s+] the army. [rhy. sl.]

daft as a brush *phr.* [1940s+] very silly. [northern dial. The phr. was popularized by its use as a description of the footballer Paul Gascoigne (b.1967)]

daftie *n.* [late 19C+] a simpleton, a fool. [dial.; ult. SE *daft*]

dag *n.*[1] [19C] euph. for God (cf. COCK n.[1]).

dag *n.*[2] [late 19C–1900s] (Aus.) a feat of skill; thus [late 19C+] *be a dag at*, to be an expert at (cf. DAGS n.[1]). [dial. *dag*, a feat of daring]

dag *n.*[3] [1910s+] (Aus./N.Z.) **1** an unenterprising person, a coward. **2** in affectionate use, an appealingly eccentric person, a 'character', often ext. as *real dag*, *bit of a dag* (cf. CARD n.[3]). **3** a gauche, socially awkward adolescent. **4** an unfashionable dresser. [dial. *dag*, a piece of matted wool and excrement clinging to a sheep's tail. ? ult. f. SE *dangle*]

dag *adj.* [20C] (Aus.) first-rate, excellent. [DAG n.[2]]

dag! *excl.* [1910s] (N.Z.) a general excl. [euph. for DAMN!]

dagga *n.* [1940s+] (S.Afr. drugs) marijuana; thus *dagga-rooker*, a marijuana smoker (cf. DACCA). [Khoi, *daxab*, genus *Leonotis*. E.P. translates *dagga rooker* as 'a scoundrel, a wastrel', which may be his own moral viewpoint]

dagged *adj.* [mid-17C–18C] drunk. [Yorks. dial. *dagged*, damp]

dagger *n.*[1] [19C] the penis (cf. BAYONET).

dagger *n.*[2] *see* BULL-DAGGER.

dagger-ale *n.* [late 16C–17C] very cheap ale. [the *Dagger*, a low tavern sited in Holborn]

dagger-cheap *adj.* [late 16C–17C] very cheap. [DAGGER-ALE]

dagger-pointed goldies *n.* [1940s–70s] (US Black) yellow shoes with sharply pointed toes.

daggle-tail *n.* [mid–late 17C] a prostitute (cf. DRAGGLE-TAIL). [ext. of dial. *daggle-tail*, a woman whose skirts drag in the dirt; a slattern]

daggy *adj.* [1960s+] (Aus.) **1** messy, unkempt. **2** unfashionable, lacking grace. [DAG n.[3]]

dago *n.* **1** [mid-19C+] (orig. US) an Italian. **2** [mid-19C+] a South American. **3** [mid-19C+] (orig. US) a Mexican. **4** [late 19C–1920s] the Spanish or Italian language. **5** [1900s–50s] (N.Z.) a Maori. **6** [1930s+] (US) San Diego, California. [Sp. proper name *Diego*, James; all uses are derog.]

dago *adj.* [1940s+] (W.I.) bad. [non-specific use of DAGO n. as a derog. term]

dago bomb *n.* [20C] (US) a large firecracker (cf. GUINEA

FOOTBALL). [DAGO n. (1) + SE *bomb*; the popularity of fireworks in the US Italian community]

dagoland *n.* [1970s] (US) a derog. name for southern Europe, esp. Italy. [DAGO n. (1) + SE *land*]

dago red *n.* [20C] **1** the cheap, home-produced red wine made by Italian families and merchandised, during Prohibition, by Italian gangsters (cf. GUINEA RED; PURPLE DEATH; RED BIDDY; RED LIZZIE; RED NED). **2** cheap red wine, usu. drunk by alcoholics. [DAGO n. (1) + SE *red wine*]

dago's piano *n.* [20C] (US) an accordion. [DAGO n. (1) + SE *piano*; the popularity of the instrument among Italian immigrants]

dago town *n.* [1950s–60s] the Italian, Mexican or Puerto Rican area of a US town or city (cf. BEAN TOWN n.²). [DAGO n. + SE *town*]

dags *n.*¹ [mid-19C–1900s] a feat, an achievement, a performance; thus *do/set dags*, to do something that the other person cannot do, to show off (cf. DAG n.²). [? OE *daeg*, a task or Scot. *darg*, a job, lit. 'a day's work']

dags *n.*² [1950s+] (Aus.) pieces of excrement adhering to the anus. [dial. *dag*, *daglock*, a lock of wool matted with excrement on the tail parts of a sheep; ult. SE *dangle*]

dagwood *n.* [1940s+] (US) an extra-large sandwich. [the favoured food of the character *Dagwood Bumstead* in Chic Young's syndicated cartoon strip *Blondie*, launched in the US in 1930]

daily *n.*¹ **1** [mid-19C+] a *daily* newspaper. **2** [1920s+] a *daily* help, a charwoman. [abbr.]

daily *n.*² *see* DAILY MAIL.

daily body *n.* [1910s–30s] a charwoman. [ext. of DAILY n.¹ (2)]

daily bread/breader *n.* [late 19C; 1900s–40s] the head of the family. [rhy. sl. + the Lord's Prayer, 'Give us this day our daily bread …']

daily dozen *n.* [1920s+] regular physical exercises. [performed in sets of 12]

Daily Exaggerator/Suppress *n.* [1910s–30s] the *Daily Express*.

Daily Getsmuchworse *n.* [1970s+] the *Daily Express*.

Daily Levy *n.* [mid-late 19C] the *Daily Telegraph*. [its former owner, Joseph Moses *Levy* (1812–88) who took over the newly founded paper from its creator Colonel Sleigh in 1855. It was the first London paper to appear at 1d (½p) a copy]

Daily Liar *n.* [20C] the *Daily Mail* (cf. DAILY TELL-THE-TALE).

daily mail/daily *n.* [1930s+] **1** the buttocks; thus *up one's daily*, following close behind. **2** a tale; thus a lie. [rhy. sl. *daily mail* = TAIL n.¹ (3); TALE]

daily rags *n.* [late 19C] the tabloid press. [SE *daily* + RAG n.²]

Daily Suppress *see* DAILY EXAGGERATOR.

Daily Tell-the-Tale *n.* [1920s+] the *Daily Mail* (cf. DAILY LIAR).

Daily Wail/Whale *n.* [1910s+] the *Daily Mail*.

dairy/dairies *n.* [late 18C; 1970s+] the female breasts, esp. when lactating (cf. AIR THE DAIRY; CREAM JUGS). [20C use is US Black]

dairy arrangements *n.* [1910s–20s] the female breasts (cf. DAIRY).

dairy porn *n.* [1990s] (N.Z.) pornographic magazines sold at local dairies. [? + pun on DAIRY]

dairy queen *n.* [1960s+] (US gay) **1** a gay milkman. **2** a gay farmer. **3** a sexual encounter that takes place in the early morning. [SE *dairy* + QUEEN n.¹ + pun on *Dairy Queen* chain of restaurants]

daisy *n.*¹ [18C] the vagina (cf. BEAUTY SPOT n.¹).

daisy *n.*² **1** [mid-18C+] anything particularly appealing, excellent. **2** [late 19C–1940s] (US) a notably attractive young woman. **3** [1940s+] a male homosexual (cf. AGNES; BUTTERCUP). **4** [1970s+] (US Black) a housewife. [(1) moved to the US in the 19C, then returned to the UK at end of the century]

daisy *n.*³ [late 19C] (US) a mule. [? popular name given to mules, although in the UK this name is more often given to cows]

daisy beat *v.* [late 19C+] to cheat, to swindle. [rhy. sl.]

daisy-beaters *n.* **1** [late 19C+] feet (cf. DEW-BEATERS; DEW-DUSTERS; DEW-TREADERS). **2** [1940s+] shoes. [US Black/Harlem use post-1940s]

daisy chain *n.* **1** [1940s+] a spintry, i.e. a circle of three or more people, hetero- or homosexual, all linked physically in mutual sex acts; thus *daisy-chainer*, one who participates in such activities (cf. CHAIN GANG n.²). **2** [1990s] (US campus) the connection between people who have had sex with the same person at different times.

daisy-cutter *n.* [late 18C–mid-19C] a horse that refuses to raise its feet properly when moving (cf. DAISY-KICKER).

daisy dukes/dazzey duks *n.* [1990s] (US Black teen) very short shorts, 'hot pants'. [the minimal shorts worn by the character Daisy Duke in the 1970s TV series *The Dukes of Hazzard*]

daisy dumpling *n.* [1950s–60s] (camp gay) a middle-class, heterosexual housewife. [her 'common' name and her shape]

daisy-kicker *n.* [late 18C–early 19C] **1** a horse. **2** an ostler, working at a coaching inn (cf. DAISY-CUTTER).

daisy-picker *n.* [late 19C–1910s] (Anglo-Irish) one who accompanies an engaged couple on their walks, a chaperone; such an individual is invited and even paid (cf. GOOSEBERRY n.²). [ext. of SE use; i.e. she picks daisies while the couple attend to more pressing matters]

daisy roots/king canutes/recruits/recroots *n.* [mid-19C+] boots. [rhy. sl.]

daisyville *see* DEUSEAVILLE.

daiture *n.* [mid-19C+] (orig. Ling. Fr./Polari) the number ten. [Ital. *dieci*, 10]

dak *n.* [1980s+] (N.Z. drugs) marijuana. [DAGGA]

dakker *see* DACCA.

da kine *n.* [1960s] (US) **1** anything good, e.g. food, drugs, liquor. **2** marijuana (cf. KIND). [Hawaiian surf. sl. *da kine*, anything of which one forgets the precise name]

daks *n.* [1940s+] (Aus.) trousers. [the proprietary name for a make of clothes, especially men's trousers with a self-supporting waistband, patented by the London clothiers Simpson's in 1933; supposedly an elision of *dad's slacks*]

da land *n.* [1990s] (US Black/drugs) getting intoxicated on a drug while sitting in a car with the windows rolled up, thus intensifying the effects of the ambient smoke. [? *da* (i.e. the) *land* of NOD n.]

'dale *n.* [1990s] (US Black teen) Sunny*dale*, public housing in the southern part of San Francisco. [abbr.]

Dally/Dallie *n.* [1950s+] (N.Z.) a *Dal*matian (i.e. Balkan) immigrant. [abbr.]

dally plonk *n.* [1950s+] (N.Z.) cheap wine manufactured by Dalmatian settlers. [DALLY + PLONK n.]

dama blanca *n.* [1980s+] (drugs) cocaine. [Sp. *dama blanca*, white lady]

damage *n.* [mid-19C+] the cost; usu. in phr. *what's the damage?* how much is the bill?

damaged *adj.* [mid-19C+] (orig. US) drunk (cf. BASTED).

damaged goods *n.* [1950s+] one who is no longer a virgin, but may pose as one (cf. CANNED GOODS).

damager *n.* [late 19C+] a joc. corruption of SE *manager*, implying the alleged effect on those whose livelihoods are in their hands.

damask *v.* [late 17C–late 18C] to warm wine; thus '*Damask the Claret*, Put a roasted Orange flasht smoking hot in it' (B.E.). [SE *damask*, to weave with richly figured designs]

damber *n.* [late 17C] a rogue, a rascal (cf. DIMBER-DAMBER n.). [? DAMME-BOY)

damber-bush n. [19C] the pubic hair. [? SE *dame* + BUSH n.[4]]

damblack adj. [1930s–40s] (US Black) extremely dark-skinned. [DAMN! + SE *black*]

dambut adj. [20C] (Ulster) a general intensifying adj. [DAMN! + SE *but*]

dambut! excl. [20C] (Ulster) a general excl. [DAMBUT adj.]

dame n. [mid-19C+] (mainly US) a woman, often with the implication of promiscuity or unattractiveness.

damfino! excl. [late 19C] (orig. US) damned if I know. [pron.]

damme! excl. [17C+] euph. for DAMN!

damme-boy n. [17C–early 19C] a blustering, profane, aggressive thug (cf. DAMBER; ROARING BOY). [DAMME! + SE *boy*]

dammit!/damnit! excl. [20C] a mild excl., i.e. *damn it!*

dammit to hell!/hell and back! excl. [20C] a mild oath, based on *damn it!*

damn! excl. [late 16C+] an all-purpose profanity, used in a wide variety of contexts (cf. BUGGER!; FUCK!). [abbr. DAMNED; the term is not sl. *per se*, but as cited by the *OED* is 'used profanely' and (in late 19C and beyond, still often found as *d—nn* or even *d——*); thus it qualifies]

damnable/damnably adj. [late 19C+] a general term of dismissal and dislike. [prior use from 16C is SE]

damn all! excl. [1920s+] nothing, absolutely zero (cf. BUGGER ALL; FUCK-ALL n.; SOD-ALL).

damnation n. [17C+] euph. for SE *hell*.

damnation! excl. [17C+] an oath of annoyance (cf. DAMN!). [SE *damnation*, condemnation to eternal punishment]

damnation bow-wows n. [20C] euph. for SE *hell* (cf. DAMNATION).

damnation bow-wows! excl. [20C] euph. for DAMN! (cf. DAMNATION!).

damnation take it! excl. [19C+] a general curse.

damned adj. [late 17C+] **1** a strong expression of reprehension or dislike. **2** a general intensifier.

damned clever, these Chinese phr. [1940s+] remarking on some particularly ingenious invention. [racial stereotyping; the attribution is less to the skill of the Chinese than to their supposed wiliness]

damned good swine up n. [late 19C] a loud quarrel, a fierce argument, prob. leading to blows. [SE *swine*; i.e. the image of pigs fighting at the trough]

damned soul n. [late 18C] a customs house clerk. [who, according to Grose (1796), 'guards against the crime of perjury, by taking a previous oath, never to swear truly on these occasions']

damnit! see DAMMIT!

damn a horse/damn me for a horse if I do! excl. [early 19C] an excl. implying one's absolute refusal to do something.

damn-it-skin! excl. [20C] (Ulster) a mild excl.

damn me for a horse if I do! see DAMN A HORSE IF I DO!

damn my sakes! excl. [20C] (US) a mild oath.

damn my stars! excl. [20C] (US) a mild oath.

damn straight! excl. [1970s+] (US Black) a general excl. of enthusiastic affirmation, absolutely! undoubtedly! [DAMN + STRAIGHT adj.[2]]

damn tootin' adv. [1930s+] (US) absolutely, completely accurate, no doubt at all. [DAMN! + SE *toot*, to blow a wind instrument]

damn well adv. [late 19C+] certainly, definitely, very much.

damp n. **1** [mid-19C] a drink. **2** [1950s+] the vagina; one of a number of terms that equate the organ with wetness, whether that of urine, vaginal secretions or the use of the synon. FISH n.[4]; thus *a slice of damp* (cf. DUCKPOND; FOUNTAIN OF LOVE; LIVING FOUNTAIN; PUDDLE n.[1]; PUMP DALE; SHADY SPRING; SLUICE; STREAM'S TOWN; WATERBOX; WATERMILL; WAYSIDE DITCH). **3** [1970s] (US) sexual intercourse with a woman. [the wetness of the drink and of the stimulated vagina]

damp adj. **1** [early 19C] (US) tipsy, mildly drunk. **2** [late 19C–1910s] foolish, stupid (cf. DAGGED; WETBRAIN).

damp v. [mid-19C] to have a drink (cf. WET ONE'S WHISTLE). [DAMP n. (1)]

damp bourbon poultice n. [late 19C] (US) a shot of bourbon (cf. DAMP n.). [the image is of the restorative powers of the alcohol]

dampen the dust, to phr. [mid-19C] (US) to take a drink.

damper n.[1] **1** [late 18C] a snack, eaten between meals. **2** [late 19C] (society) the bill in a restaurant. [SE *damper*, that which damps down (the appetite) or depresses (the spirits)]

damper n.[2] **1** [mid-19C–1950s] a till, a cash drawer; thus *draw a damper, turn down the damper*, to rob a till. **2** [1940s–50s] (US) a small safe, a cashbox. **3** [1950s+] (US/Can. prison) solitary confinement, punishment cells (cf. HOLE n.[2]). [SE *damper*, that which calms or suppresses; in (1) and (2) the villain's hopes of an easy robbery, underpinned in (3) by a lit. interpretation, i.e. that which 'damps down; the spirits or emotions]

damp one's mug, to phr. [mid-19C] to take a drink. [SE *damp* + MUG n.[1] (2)]

damson-pie/-tart n. [late 19C] obscene language. [pun on DAMN!]

dan n. [1920s–60s] a man in charge of a public convenience. [the children's chant 'Dan Dan, dirty old man/Washed his face in the lavatory pan']

dance n.[1] [mid-19C] a flight of stairs. [abbr. DANCERS]

dance n.[2] [20C] (US prison) a hanging (cf. DANCE v.[2]).

dance v.[1] as a synon. for sexual intercourse, used in a variety of phr., e.g. [19C] *dance the buttock jig*, [19C] *dance the goat's jig*, [19C] *dance the kipples*, [19C] *dance the married man's cotillion*, [19C] *dance the matrimonial polka*, [19C] *dance the miller's reel*, [19C] *dance to the tune of shaking the sheets/sheets without music*, [19C] *dance with your arse to the ceiling*, [early 19C] *dance the blanket hornpipe*, [late 19C–1920s] *dance on the mattress*, [late 19C–1920s] *dance the mattress jig* (cf. DANCE SALLINGER'S ROUND; DANCE THE REELS O' BOGIE; DANCE THE REELS OF STUMPIE).

dance v.[2] as a synon. for being hanged, used in a variety of phr. (cf. DANCE AT BEILBY'S BALL; DANCE AT THE SHERIFF'S BALL; DANCE AT TUCK 'EM FAIR; DANCE ON AIR; DANCE ON NOTHING phr.[1]; DANCE ON NOTHING phr.[2]; DANCE THE NEWGATE HORNPIPE; DANCE THE PADDINGTON FRISK; DANCE THE TYBURN HORNPIPE ON NOTHING; DANCE THE TYBURN JIG; DO THE DANCE).

dance v.[3] [1970s] to steal from first or higher floors. [the light-footedness of the thief + ref. to US dancer Fred Astaire (1899–1987), up which he must climb; ult. rhy. sl. FRED ASTAIRES = stairs]

dance a haka, to phr. [1940s–50s] (N.Z.) to express one's pleasure. [SE *dance* + Maori *haka*, a posture dance, accompanied by chants; a war-dance]

dance at Beilby's ball, to phr. [late 18C] to be hanged; also with the sfx. ... *where the sheriff plays the music* or ... *where the sheriff pays the fiddlers* (cf. DANCE v.[2]; SHAKE ONE'S TROTTERS AT BEILBY'S BALL). [ety. unknown. As Grose put it in 1796, 'who Mr Beilby was, or why that ceremony was so called, remains with the quadrature of the circle, the discovery of the philosopher's stone and divers other desiderata as yet undiscovered', but there exist a number of suggestions. The most obvious is that *Beilby* was a well-known sheriff; a second is that *Beilby* is a mispronunciation of *Old Bailey*, the court in which so many villains were sentenced to death. The third, and that espoused by E.P., is that *Beilby* refers to the *bilbo*, a long iron bar, furnished with sliding shackles to confine the ankles of prisoners and a lock by which to fix one end of the bar to the floor or ground. *Bilbo* comes from the Spanish town of Bilbao, where these fetters were invented]

dance at the sheriff's ball/sheriff's ball and loll one's tongue out at the company, to *phr.* [late 18C–early 19C] to be hanged (cf. DANCE v.²; DANGLE IN THE SHERIFF'S PICTURE-FRAME; SHERIFF'S BALL). [ironic use of SE]

dance at Tuck 'em Fair, to *phr.* [18C] to be hanged (cf. DANCE v.²). [TUCK v.¹]

dance barefoot *v.* [late 16C–late 18C] for an older sister to remain single while a younger sister is married (cf. DANCE IN THE HOG TROUGH).

dance fever *n.* [1980s+] (drugs) fentanyl (cf. APACHE n.²). [its effect on one's stamina]

dancehall/dancehouse *n.* [1920s+] (US prison) 1 the cell in which a prisoner is placed before being executed. 2 the execution chamber. [DANCE v.²; thus ? only for those being hanged]

dance in the hog trough, to *phr.* [20C] (US) 1 for an older sister to be left unmarried when a younger sibling has found a husband; occas. also used of boys (cf. DANCE BAREFOOT). 2 to be the last child in a family to be married. [? to have no suitors and have, therefore, to dance with the swine]

dance in the sandbox, to *phr.* [1960s] (US Black) to scheme, to deceive. [var. on SE *throw sand in one's eyes*]

dance on air, to *phr.* [late 19C–1940s] (US) to be hanged (cf. AIR DANCE; DANCE v.²; DANCE ON NOTHING phr.¹; DANCE ON NOTHING phr.²).

dance on/upon nothing/nothing at the sheriff's door, to *phr.¹* [late 18C] to be hanged (cf. DANCE v.²).

dance on/upon nothing/nothing in a hempen cravat, to *phr.²* [late 18C–mid-19C] to be hanged (cf. CUT A CAPER UPON NOTHING; DANCE v.²). [SE *dance* + HEMPEN CRAVAT]

dance on someone's lips/face, to *phr.* [1980s+] (US Black) 1 to hit in the face. 2 to kick in the face.

dancer *n.* [mid-19C+] a cat burglar who 'dances' along the roof and in through a convenient window. The 20C use refers to those who steal from empty offices. [DANCE v.³]

dancers *n.* 1 [mid-17C–mid-19C] (orig. Und.) a flight of stairs. 2 [1940s+] the feet. [one *dances* down the stairs or on one's feet]

dance sallinger's round, to *phr.* [17C–early 18C] to have sexual intercourse. [DANCE v.¹ + *Sallinger's round* (see SALLENGER'S)]

dance the mill, to *phr.* [mid-19C] (W.I.) to walk on the prison treadmill.

dance the Newgate hornpipe, to *phr.* [late 18C–mid-19C] to be hanged (cf. DANCE v.²). [*Newgate*, the site of London's major prison and public executions]

dance the Paddington frisk, to *phr.* [late 17C–early 19C] to be hanged (cf. DANCE v.²; DO THE PADDINGTON FRISK; PADDINGTON FAIR). [Tyburn, the site of London's main 18C gallows, was in the then village of *Paddington*]

dance the reels o'bogie, to *phr.* [18C–19C] (Scot.) to have sexual intercourse. [DANCE v.¹ + joc. ref. to BOGEY n.³]

dance the reels of stumpie, to *phr.* [18C–19C] (Scot.) to have sexual intercourse. [DANCE v.¹ + dial. *stumpy*, something stump-like, i.e. the penis]

dance the Tyburn hornpipe on nothing, to *phr.* [late 18C–mid-19C] to be hanged (cf. DANCE v.²; DANGLE IN A TYBURN STRING). [the role of *Tyburn* as an execution ground]

dance/do the Tyburn jig, to *phr.* [late 17C–early 19C] to be hanged (cf. DANCE v.²; DANGLE IN A TYBURN STRING; TYBURN JIG). [*Tyburn*, the site of London's main 18C gallows, was in the then village of Paddington]

dance upon nothing see DANCE ON NOTHING.

dance with johnnie one-eye, to *phr.* [1980s+] to masturbate.

dancing academy *n.* [18C] a brothel (cf. ACADEMY). [DANCE v.¹ + ACADEMY]

dancing dog *n.* [late 19C–1900s] a man who enjoys dancing. [SE *dancing* + DOG n.⁸; the term was used in a period when dancing was no longer seen as fashionable]

dancing master *n.* 1 [17C] the hangman (cf. DANCE v.²). 2 [early 18C] an upper-class rowdy who found his amusement in making his victims 'dance' by stabbing at their legs with his sword. 3 a cat burglar (cf. DANCER). [SE *dance* v.]

d & d *adj.* [late 19C+] 1 drunk and disorderly. 2 deaf and dumb. [abbr.]

dand *n.* [late 19C] a dandy. [abbr.]

dander *n.* [mid-19C+] (orig. US) temper; thus *get one's dander up*, to get annoyed, to infuriate someone. [? SE *dander*, dandruff or *dander*, the fermentation of rum, but note various dial. uses as a commotion, a shivering fit]

dandery *adj.* [early 19C] (US) irritated, angry. [DANDER]

dandiprat/dandyprat *n.* [mid-16C–19C] an insignificant, contemptible person. [16–17C SE *dandiprat*, a small coin worth 1½ old pence. F&H says 'half a farthing' in late 15C]

dandisette/dandizette see DANDYSETTE.

d & m *n.* [1990s] (US teen) a deep and meaningful conversation. [abbr.]

dando *n.* [mid-19C–1910s] a glutton, a great eater, esp. one who runs up a large bill at a restaurant or hotel and then leaves without paying. [a proper name of such a man, according to Hotten (1864), although no specifics have been offered]

dandy *n.¹* 1 [late 17C–mid-19C] (Anglo-Ind.) a Ganges boatman. 2 [late 19C] 'a kind of vehicle used in the Himalaya, consisting of a strong cloth slung like a hammock to a bamboo staff, and carried by two (or more) men [dandy-wallahs]' (Y&B). [Hind. *dandi*, a staff or oar]

dandy *n.²* [mid-19C] (orig. Irish) 1 a small drink of whisky. 2 the glass in which it is served. [? fig. use of DANDY adj.]

dandy *n.³* [late 19C+] (US) an admirable person, a skilful person. [SE *dandy*]

dandy *adj.* [late 18C+] attractive, first-rate, excellent, a general term of approbation; thus [late 18C–mid-19C] *the dandy*, the correct thing, 'the ticket'. [SE *dandy*; i.e. something of which the fashionable dandy would approve]

dandy *adv.* [20C] finely, splendidly.

dandy-boy *n.* [1940s+] (W.I.) a well-dressed young man. [SE *dandy* + *boy*]

dandy-dude *n.* [1940s] (W.I.) a dandy. [SE *dandy* + DUDE n.]

dandyfunk/dunderfunk *n.* [mid-19C–1900s] (US) a mixture of powdered biscuit, molasses and fat. [? SE *dandy* + SE *funk*, a smell]

dandy grey russet *n.* [late 18C] a dirty brown. [dial. *dandy-go-russet*, worn out or rust-coloured clothing]

dandy horse *n.* [early–mid-19C] a velocipede, a cross between a child's hobby-horse and the most primitive of bicycles.

dandyprat see DANDIPRAT.

dandysette/dandisette/dandizette *n.* [early–mid-19C] a female dandy. [SE *dandy* + fem. sfx. -(s)*ette*]

dandy-trap *n.* [mid-19C] (US) a loose paving stone, over which an exquisite may trip.

dang *adj.* [mid-19C+] damned. [? euph.; DAMN! + SE *hang*]

dang! *excl.* [mid-19C+] euph. for DAMN! [DANG adj.]

danger light/signal *n.* [20C] a red nose.

dangerous *adj.* [late 19C] (US) serious, even terminally ill.

danger signal see DANGER LIGHT.

danger signal is up see FLAG IS UP.

dangle *n.* [1930s–50s] the penis (cf. CRANK n.⁵; DINGALING n.³; DINGLE-DANGLE). [metonymy]

dangle *v.* 1 [late 18C] to follow a woman, without actually addressing her. 2 [1930s] (US) to go away, esp. in imper. *dangle!* go away!

dangleberries *n.* **1** [1950s+] pieces of excreta clinging to the hairs around an inadequately cleansed anus (cf. DINGLE-BERRIES). **2** [1970s+] the female breasts (cf. APPLES n.¹). [ext. of SE *dangle*]

dangle from *v.* [1910s+] of a man, to have sexual intercourse. [though the physical logic would presume a female point-of-view]

dangle in a Tyburn string, to *phr.* [late 18C] to be hanged (cf. DANCE THE TYBURN JIG; DANCE THE TYBURN HORNPIPE ON NOTHING). [SE *dangle* + *Tyburn*, the site of the gallows]

dangle in the sheriff's picture-frame, to *phr.* [late 18C–early 19C] to be hanged (cf. DANCE AT THE SHERIFF'S BALL). [SE *dangle*]

dangle queen *n.* [1980s+] (US gay) one who wears clothes that deliberately emphasize the penis. [DANGLE n. + QUEEN n.¹]

dangler *n.*¹ **1** [late 18C–mid-19C] one who follows women in the street but does not actually speak to them. **2** [1920s+] (Aus./US) an exhibitionist. [DANGLE v. (1)]

dangler *n.*² [1990s] (US Black) a businessman, a thief. [? he keeps one *dangling* in expectation of money]

dangle roll *n.* [1990s] (US Black) a losing throw of the dice in craps. [it takes one's money and one must quite the game; i.e. DANGLE v. (2)]

danglers *n.* **1** [mid-19C] a bunch of seals (hanging from a watch chain). **2** [mid-19C+] the testicles.

dangling modifier *n.* [1980s+] (US campus) a single, long, flashy earring. [pun on the grammatical term]

daniel *n.* [1930s–40s] (US Black) the buttocks. [? corruption of SE *dangle*]

Danish pastry *n.* [1950s–60s] (gay) a transsexual. [the ref. is to the pioneering operation undergone in Denmark in 1952 by Christine (formerly George) Jorgensen]

dank *n.* [1980s+] (US Black/drugs) extremely strong marijuana. [DANK adj. (2)]

dank *adj.* [1980s+] (US campus) **1** bad, unpleasant. **2** excellent, first-rate. [(1) SE, which is always neg., usu. referring to swamps and marshes. (2) presumably the *bad = good* formula popular among the young (cf. AWFUL adj.)]

dank nugs/nuggets *n.* [1980s+] (US drugs) the very best marijuana. [DANK adj. (2) + SE *nuggets*]

danna *n.* [late 18C–mid-19C] **1** a privy (cf. DONAGHER; DONICKER; DONIGAN; DUNNAKEN; DUNNIGAN; DUNNY; DUNNYKEN). **2** human excrement; thus *danna drag*, a nightman's or dust-man's cart. [var. on DUNNAKEN]

dannie *n.* [20C] a drink of liquor. [ext. of DANDY n.²]

dant *n.* [early–mid-16C] a promiscuous woman. [synon. Du. *dante*]

dan tucker *n.* [mid-19C] butter. [rhy. sl.; ? anecdotal]

dao *n.* [late 19C–1930s] (US drugs) the knife used to cut up opium. [Chinese use]

dap *n.*¹ [1970s+] (US Black) a ritualistic handshake, differing from area to area, involving much slapping of palms, snapping of fingers etc (cf. GIVE ME FIVE; GIVE SOME SKIN). [SE *dab*, to strike]

dap *n.*² [1970s+] (US Black) credit, acknowledgement, respect, self-awareness (cf. PROPS n.²). [abbr. *dignity and pride*]

dap *adj.* [1950s+] (US Black) well-dressed; thus *dap daddy*, a well-dressed man, *dap to a tee* very well dressed. [SE *dapper*, spruce, neat]

dap *v.* [20C] to pick up or to steal, esp. luggage. [? SE *dab*, to touch lightly]

dapped down *adj.* [1950s+] (US Black) very well dressed. [DAP adj.]

dapped to a T *phr.* [1950s+] (US Black) very well dressed (cf. DAPPED DOWN). [DAP adj. + SE *to a T*]

dapper *n.* [1990s] (Black) a general term of congratulation, an admirable person. [SE *dapper* + DAP n.²]

daps *n.* **1** [1920s–30s] slippers. **2** [1940s+] gym shoes, tennis shoes. [? dial. *dap*, the bounce of ball, a hop; the image is of bouncing along in one's rubber-soled shoes]

darbies *n.* [late 17C–late 19C] shackles, fetters, handcuffs; thus *darbies and joans*, fetters linking a pair of prisoners. [16C SE *Father Darby's bands*, a moneylender's bond of particular severity, which effectively bound the borrower to the lender while the debt remained outstanding; for *darbies and joans* see DARBY AND JOAN n.]

darble *n.* [mid-19C] the devil. [mangled pron. of Fr. *diable*]

darbs *n.* [late 19C–1930s] playing cards. [? backsl., the pips on a card resembles the *brads* or shoemakers' rivets in the sole of a boot]

darby *n.*¹ **1** [late 17C–late 18C] money. **2** [mid-19C+] (Und.) a haul of stolen goods. [for ety. see DARBIES]

darby *n.*² [19C] (Irish) a glass of whisky, usu. as a *small darby*. [ety. unknown; ? anecdotal]

darby *adj.* [1910s–30s] (US) wonderful, excellent, first-rate. [? the pre-eminence of the Kentucky *Derby* as a horse-race]

darby and joan *n.* **1** [late 19C+] the telephone. **2** [1940s+] (Aus.) a loan. [rhy. sl.; the phr. *Darby and Joan*, a synon. for an elderly, possibly impoverished but long-married couple, first appeared in the *Gentleman's Magazine* (vol. V, 1735) in a verse titled 'The joys of love never forgot, a song'. The third verse runs: 'Old Darby, with Joan by his side,/You've often regarded with wonder,/He's dropsical, she is sore-eyed,/Yet they're never happy asunder.' Whether the names refer to real-life characters (*Darby* is not a common UK name) or are taken from some earlier fiction remains unknown]

darby and joan *phr.* [20C] alone; thus in phr. *on one's Darby*, by oneself. [rhy. sl.; *see* DARBY AND JOAN n.]

darby kelly *n.* [late 19C+] the stomach, esp. abbr. *darby kel* (cf. DERBY KELLY). [rhy. sl. *darby kelly* = belly]

darby-roll *n.* [19C] a style of walking that betrays an individual's experience of fetters and thus time spent in prison. [DARBIES + SE *roll*, to walk with a swinging gait]

darby's fair *n.* [19C] the day on which a prisoner is moved from one prison to another, and must thus be fettered. [DARBIES + ironic use of SE *fair*]

dard *n.* [17C–18C] the penis (cf. BAYONET). [Fr. *dard*, a dart]

dark/dark hole *n.*¹ [19C] the vagina (cf. BLACK HOLE n.¹).

dark *n.*² [mid-19C–1910s] (US) a derog. term for a Black person. [abbr. DARKIE]

dark *n.*³ **1** [mid-19C] (Aus.) Australian-distilled, dark, very strong brandy. **2** [1950s+] port. **3** [1950s+] any cheap wine, usu. muscatel. [the dark red colour]

dark *adj.*¹ **1** [mid-17C–early 18C; 1940s+] stupid, ignorant. **2** [1950s+] (Irish/W.I.) weak-sighted, nearly or actually blind. [SE *dark*, unenlightened, uninformed, as in *dark ages*. 20C use of (1) is W.I.]

dark *adj.*² [1990s] **1** (Black) aggressive, very serious. **2** (teen) a general neg., bad, unpleasant, second-rate etc.

dark and dim *n.* [20C] (Aus.) a swim. [rhy. sl.]

dark as a bag *phr.* [late 19C–1900s] used to describe sunless, lowering skies.

dark as Newgate *see* BLACK AS NEWGATE.

dark as the inside of a cow *phr.* [late 19C+] (Can./US) very dark. [UK use is naut. only]

dark brown shit *n.* [1950s–60s] (US Black) second-rate, inferior heroin. [SE *dark brown* + SHIT n.⁵; pure heroin is white, although the influx of equally pure heroin from Mexico and the Far and Middle East during the 1970s, all of which was brown, meant that the equation no longer held]

dark cell *n.* [20C] (US Und.) a prison punishment cell (cf. HOLE n.²). [its lack of amenities]

Dark City *n.* [1950s–60s] (S.Afr.) the township of Alexandra, near Johannesburg. [SE *dark*/DARK n.² + SE *city*]

dark cloud *n.* [1900s–30s] (Aus./US) a derog. term for a Black person, a Native Australian.

dark cull/cully *n.* [late 18C] one who keeps a mistress and only dares visit her surreptitiously at night. [SE *dark* + CULLY n. (2)]

dark engineer *n.* [early 18C] a villain. [SE *dark* + *engineer*, to manipulate, to perform]

darken someone's daylights, to *phr.* [late 18C] to black someone's eye (cf. SEW SOMEONE'S SEES). [SE *darken* + DAYLIGHTS]

darkers *n.* [1950s+] (W.I. Rasta) sunglasses. [SE *dark* (*glasses*)]

darkey/darky *n.* **1** [mid-18C–1930s] night time. **2** [early 19C–1900s] a dark, i.e. shuttered, lantern. [DARKMANS]

dark felt *n.* [20C] (Aus.) a belt. [rhy. sl.]

dark hole *see* DARK n.[1].

dark horse *n.* [mid-19C+] one of whom little is known, esp. one's opponent in a competition. [racing jargon *dark horse*, a horse about whose form little is known. The term appears to have been coined by Benjamin Disraeli in *The Young Duke* (1831), although his use appears to be purely descriptive]

dark house *n.* [early 17C–mid-19C] a room used to confine the insane.

darkie *n.* [late 18C+] a derog., patronizing description of a Black person (cf. DARKY n.[2]).

darkies *n.* [mid–late 19C] a variety of late-night music-halls and bars on or near the Strand, London, usu. situated below ground level, e.g. the Shades, the Cider Cellars and the Coal Hole (cf. DIVE n.[1]).

dark it *v.* [late 19C] to say nothing, esp. as imper. *dark it!*, be quiet! keep quiet!

dark lanthorn *n.* [late 17C–mid-18C] a servant or agent who takes and transmits a bribe offered to their master.

darkman *n.* [early–mid-18C] a nightwatchman.

darkmans *n.* [mid-16C–late-18C] (Und.) the night (cf. DARKS; LIGHTMANS). [SE *dark* + sfx. -MAN]

darkmans budge *n.* [mid-16C–late 18C] (Und.) a thief's accomplice, who climbs into a house through a window and opens a door to admit the rest of the gang (cf. FAGGER; STANDING BUDGE; TOOL n.). [DARKMANS + BUDGE n.[1]]

dark meat *n.* [late 19C+] Black people, esp. as sex objects (cf. BLACK JACK n.[6]; WHITE MEAT).

darkness at noon *n.* [1970s+] (US campus) the slide shows that form the basis of lectures in Art History. [pun on the novel *Darkness at Noon* (1940) by Arthur Koestler]

darks, the *n.* [late 18C] the night (cf. DARKMANS).

dark-sambo *n.* [1950s+] (W.I.) a person of mixed race, with one-quarter White to three-quarters Black. [SE *dark* + SAMBO n.[1] (2)]

darktown *n.* [late 19C–1970s] (US) the Black area of a town or city (cf. COON BOTTOM). [SE *dark*/DARK n.[2] + SE *town*]

dark 'un *n.* [mid-19C+] one of whom little is known (cf. DARK HORSE). [lit. 'dark one']

darkun/dark-'un *n.* [1930s–40s] (Aus.) a 24-hour shift, worked by a wharf labourer. [it involves working through the dark]

darky *n.[1] see* DARKEY.

darky *n.[2]* [late 18C+] a patronizing description of a Black person (cf. DARKIE). [coined in the UK, the term has spread to all English-language slangs, denoting Afro-Americans, Aborigines, Maoris and others]

darl *n.* [1930s+] (mainly Aus.) a general term of endearment. [abbr. SE *darling*]

darling it hurts *n.* [20C] (Aus.) Darlinghurst, a rough inner-city area of Sydney. [rhy. sl.]

Darlo *n.* [1930s+] (Aus.) *Darl*inghurst. [abbr. + sfx. -O]

darn *adj.* **1** [late 18C+] extremely, intensely, very much. **2** [mid-19C+] euph. for DAMNED.

darn!/dern! *excl.* [late 18C+] (US) damn; thus varieties incl. *goldarn*, *gosh darn* (both using euph. for God).

darnation! *excl.* [late 19C+] euph. for DAMN! (cf. DAMNATION!; DARN!; TARNATION!).

darry *n.* [1940s–50s] (prison) a look. [? DERREY]

dart *n.* [late 19C–1910s] (Aus.) **1** a plan, an aim, a scheme. **2** one's fancy or favourite. **3** an illicit activity, a 'racket'. [SE *dart* used fig. to describe the target as much as the missile]

dart accent/dortspeak/Roadwatch accent *n.* [1990s] (Irish) an affectedly quasi-British accent, adopted by the middle class in and around Dublin. [DART, *D*ublin *A*rea *R*apid *T*ransit, i.e. those areas served by the system. The accent was originally identified among radio/TV presenters (thus the ref. to the programme *Roadwatch*) and is typified by the use of the phoneme 'ou' in such words as 'cow']

Darth Vader's pencil box *n.* [1980s+] (N.Z.) the head office of the bank of New Zealand in Wellington. [its shape and the black, non-reflective material of its cladding are reminiscent of Darth Vader, the black-garbed villain of the *Star Wars* films 1977, 1980, 1983]

daru *n.* [20C] (W.I.) rum. [Bhojpuri *daaruu*, liquor]

Darwin blonde *n.* [1940s] (Aus.) a half-caste woman. [proper name *Darwin* + SE *blonde*; the ref. is to the Aborigine population of Northern Territory, of which Darwin is the capital]

Darwin stubby *n.* [1970s+] (Aus.) a 40-ounce bottle of beer. [proper name *Darwin* + STUBBIE]

d.a.s *n.* [mid-19C–1920s] the menstrual flow. [*d*omestic *a*fflictions]

dash *n.[1]* [late 17C–19C] a tavern waiter. [SE *dash*, to rush about or *dash*, style, flair]

dash *n.[2]* [19C] a drink. usu. as *a dash of* … . [SE *dash*, a small quantity]

dash *n.[3]* [early 19C] (US) an attractive young woman (cf. DASHER). [SE *dash*, style]

dash *n.[4]* [late 19C+] (Nigerian) a tip, bribery, the money paid as a bribe. [SE *dashee*, a gift, present, gratuity; a 'Negrish word' used on the Guinea Coast]

dash *n.[5]* [1920s+] an attempt, usu. in phr. *have a dash*.

dash *v.* [late 18C–early 19C] to make a display, to 'cut a dash'. [SE *dash*, style]

dash! *excl.* [early 19C+] a general euph. for FUCK!; DAMN! etc (cf. DASHED; DASH IT!; DASH MY BUTTONS!; DASH MY WIG!). [from the dash that replaces the 'am' in *damn!*; thus *d–n!* and subseq. in other 'obscenities']

dashed *adj.* [late 19C] a general adj. of annoyance or irritation; lit. the use of – as a euph. for DAMNED. [DASH!]

dasher *n.* **1** [late 18C–late 19C] a flashy prostitute. **2** [late 18C–late 19C] a 'fast' young woman. **3** [mid–late 19C] a smart young person, keen on parties and socializing. **4** [late 19C] a dashing attempt. **5** [late 19C+] (W.I.) a dandy. **6** [late 19C+] (W.I.) a womanizer. [ext. use of SE *cut a dash*]

dashes *n.* [20C] as used by market-traders, a smacking. [SE *dash*, a violent blow]

dashing *adj.* [19C] showy, given to excess, esp. in dress. [SE *cut a dash*]

dash in the bloomers *n.* [1960s+] sexual intercourse, usu. quick and adulterous. [SE *dash*, a rush + *bloomers*]

dash it!/dash it all! *excl.* [early 19C+] a general euph. excl.

dash my buttons! *excl.* [mid-19C–1910s] a mild oath. [ext. of DASH!]

dash my wig!/wigs! *excl.* [late 18C–mid-19C] a mild oath. [ext. of DASH!]

dash of the tarbrush *see* TOUCH OF THE TARBRUSH.

dash one's doodle, to *phr.* [19C] to masturbate. [SE *dash*, to hit (against) + DOODLE n.[2]]

dash on to *v.* [20C] (market-trader) to chastize, to scold. [SE *dash*, to abash, to embarrass]

dashy *adj.* [early–mid-19C] showy, ostentatiously fashionable, stylish. [SE *cut a dash*]

date *n.*[1] [1900s–50s] a foolish or comic person; thus school use *soppy date*, an affectionate term of abuse (cf. FRUITCAKE n.[2]; NUTCAKE; NUTCASE). [the common use of fruit to indicate stupidity]

date *n.*[2] [1910s+] (Aus./N.Z.) **1** the anus, the backside as a whole. **2** the vagina. [DOT n.[2]]

date *n.*[3] [1920s+] (orig. US) a person with whom one makes or has made an appointment or engagement, usu. for social/sexual purposes; thus *double date*, for two couples to join each other on the same engagement, *dated*, 'booked' for an engagement or meeting, *dating*, making dates.

date *n.*[4] [1950s+] (US Black) the arrangement a prostitute makes with her client (cf. WANNA GO OUT?). [ironic use of DATE n.[3]]

date *v.*[1] [20C] of an object or person, to bear evidence of its or their date or period, to be or become old fashioned or outdated (cf. DATED). [abbr. SE *show its/one's date*]

date *v.*[2] [20C] (orig. US) to have an affair with someone, to be going out together on a number of pre-arranged days (cf. DATE n.[3]).

date *v.*[3] [1910s+] (Aus./N.Z.) to caress the buttocks. [DATE n.[2]]

date bait *n.* [1940s+] (US campus) someone with whom one would like to form a relationship. [DATE n.[3] + SE *bait*]

dated *adj.* [20C] old-fashioned, out-of-date. [DATE v.[1]]

date rosy palm and her sisters/five sisters, to *phr.* [20C] to masturbate (cf. CONVERSE WITH HARRY PALM).

daub/dawb *n.*[1] [late 17C–18C] a bribe. [? SE *daub*, to lay on thick; cf. SE phr. *grease one's palm*, dial. *daub*, to flatter, to 'butter up']

daub *n.*[2] [mid-19C–1900s] an artist.

daub/dawb *v.* [late 17C–18C] to bribe. [DAUB n.[1]]

dauber/dobber *n.* [1910s+] (US) spirit, morale. [? link to dial. *dobber*, a 'wonder']

daughter *n.* [1960s+] **1** a male homosexual brought into the gay world by a homosexual friend. **2** (Black) any young woman, irrespective of relationship.

david *n.* [19C+] an affi*davit* (cf. ALFRED DAVID; DAVY; DICKY n.[5]). [abbr./pron.]

davy *n.* [late 18C–19C] an oath; thus *on my davy*, on my oath, on my honour (cf. AFFYGRAPHY; DICK n.[3]). [abbr. SE *affidavit*]

Davy Crockett *n.*[1] [1940s] (US Black/Harlem) a draft board official during WW2. [proper name *Davy Crockett* (1786–1836), frontiersman, US Congressman and one of those who died defending the Alamo]

Davy Crockett *n.*[2] [1950s] a pocket. [rhy. sl.]

Davy Crockett's hat *n.* [1990s] a vagina with red pubic hair. [the 'Davy Crockett hats' beloved of mid-1950s children and allegedly modelled on that worn by the frontiersman]

Davy Jones's locker/Davy's locker *n.* [mid-18C+] a watery grave. [at best *Davy Jones* represents the spirit of the sea, at worst he is the ocean's own devil; either way it is in his 'locker' that drowned seamen are stowed. The identification was first printed by Tobias Smollett in *Peregrine Pickle* (1751). The ety. remains obscure, but E.P. suggests that *Jones* refers to Jonah whose own 'locker' was the belly of the whale. *Davy*, it is proposed, may have been added by Welsh sailors]

davy large *n.* [late 19C] a barge. [rhy. sl.]

Davy's locker *see* DAVY JONES'S LOCKER.

dawamesk *n.* [1990s] (drugs) marijuana. [? Arabic]

dawb *n. see* DAUB n.[1].

dawb *v. see* DAUB v.

daw-daw *adj.* [1950s+] stupid, slow, dull (cf. DUH). [*duh*, the supposed sound of ignorance]

dawg! *excl.* [1990s] (US teen) an expression of approval. [joc. pron. of SE *dog*; thus cf. HOT DOG!]

dawn frazer *n.* [1960s+] (Aus.) a razor. [rhy. sl.; ult. the 1960s Aus. swimming star *Dawn Fraser* (b.1937)]

daxie *see* DACHSIE.

day and martin *n.* [19C] a derog. term for a Black person. [*Day and Martin's* shoe blacking]

day and night *n.* [late 19C–1900s] light ale. [rhy. sl.]

day-day *n.* [1900s–30s] (US Black) goodbye, farewell. [the daytime equivalent of *night-night*, goodnight, and similarly used to children or in a consciously joking manner]

day for/on a/the king/queen *phr.* [1940s+] (N.Z.) a day off, orig. when outdoor work was impossible, but used generally to cover any unofficial day off, e.g. one that follows a night of over-enthusiastic enjoyment. [SE phr. *a day (fit for) a king*, a very pleasant day + the idea of the king/queen, as ruler, paying for the day

day house *n.* [late 19C] (US) a cheap gambling house, which opened during the day (as opposed to the more sophisticated casinos, which serviced the evening and nighttime clientele) and took advantage of small-time gamblers, typically clerks on their lunch break or tourists from out of town.

daylight *n.*[1] [19C] **1** the space between the surface of the liquid and the top of a glass (cf. SKYLIGHT). **2** the space between a rider and the saddle.

daylight *n.*[2] [20C] (Ulster) the bare necessities of life.

daylight *v.* [1970s] (US Black) to enlighten, to explain. [SE *let in some daylight*]

daylights *n.* **1** [mid-18C+] the eyes (cf. DEADLIGHTS). **2** [mid-18C+] the space left in a glass between the top of the liquor and the rim; such a space is not allowed when drinking bumpers, thus the toast *no daylights or heeltaps!* **3** [mid-19C+] fig. ref. to one's innards, usu. in phr. *knock the daylights out of* (cf. CRAP n.[3]; GUTS n.[1]; SHIT n.[10]).

day on a king/queen *see* DAY FOR A KING.

day one *n.* [1980s+] (orig. US) **1** the beginning. **2** long ago. [lit. the first-ever day]

day on the king/queen *see* DAY FOR A KING.

day-opener *n.* [mid–late 19C] (orig. boxing) an eye.

day's dawning/a-dawning *n.* [20C] morning. [rhy. sl.]

daze *v.* [1970s] (US campus) to daydream.

dazzler *n.* [19C] **1** esp. of an ostentatious woman, one who dazzles. **2** [late 19C] a dazzling blow.

d-boy *n.* [1990s] (US Black teen) a drug dealer. [*d*, drugs + SE *boy*]

d.c. *n.* [20C] (US prison) the death cell (cf. C.C.). [abbr.]

d.d.f.m.g.! *excl.* [1990s] (US campus) an excl. on sighting a very attractive member of the opposite sex. [abbr. *drop dead fuck me gorgeous*]

d.d.t.! *excl.* [1940s–50s] (US campus) a general phr. of dismissal, contempt. [abbr. *drop dead twice*]

deacon *v.*[1] [19C] (US) **1** to pack (fruit etc) with the finest specimens on the top. **2** to deceive, esp. to make things appear better than they actually are. **3** to adulterate, to doctor, to get something for nothing, e.g. *deacon land*, to increase one's land by gradually extending one's fences or boundary lines into unclaimed or common property. [an old story; a farmer sold a barrel of apples to a minister, and when it was opened many of the apples that lay beneath the top layer were found to be bad. When the minister questioned the farmer he was informed: 'You must have opened them at the wrong end.' Henceforth the farmer took care to 'deacon' both ends of his apples]

deacon/deacon off *v.*[2] [mid-19C] (US) 'To read aloud (a hymn) one or two lines at a time, the congregation singing the lines as soon as read, according to the early practice of the Congregational Churches of New England' (*OED*). [as practised by church deacons]

dead *n.*[1] [19C] (US campus) a class recitation that is judged to be a total failure.

dead *n.*[2] [20C] (W.I./Bdos.) problems, trouble.

dead *adj.*[1] [19C] very drunk. [abbr. *dead drunk*]

dead *adj.*[2] **1** [early 19C+] of a bottle, finished, empty (cf. DEAD INDIAN; DEAD MAN *n.*[1]; DEAD MARINE; DEAD RECRUIT; DEAD SOLDIER; MARINE OFFICER). **2** [late 19C–1920s] of a house, uninhabited, empty, deserted. **3** [20C] (US Black) of people, forgotten; of things, ideas, unfashionable, out of style. **4** [1960s+] finished, lost, spec. arrested, captured. **5** [1980s+] (US campus) used of any event that was considered not worth attending.

dead *v.* **1** [19C] (US campus) of a student, to fail completely in one's recitation. **2** [19C] (US campus) of a teacher, to make a student botch the recitation. **3** [20C] (US) to loaf around, to idle.

dead *adv.* [mid-17C+] a general intensifier, very, extremely, absolutely, completely.

dead-alive/dead and alive *adj.* [mid-19C] dull, miserable, down in the mouth.

dead as a dodo *phr.* [20C] absolutely dead, utterly irrelevant (of information, news). [SE *dodo* (*Didus ineptus*), an extinct bird last seen alive in Mauritius in the 1680s]

dead as a doornail *phr.* [mid-14C–late 16C] absolutely dead. [SE *doornail*, the large-headed nails with which doors were studded for extra strength and protection; early 17C+ use is SE]

dead as a herring *phr.* [mid-17C+] completely dead, certainly dead.

dead as a maggot *phr.* [1940s+] (Aus.) unconscious, inert, dead.

dead as a tent-peg *phr.* [19C–1910s] completely dead, utterly dead.

dead as a wooden Indian *phr.* [20C] (US) dead. [the wooden Indians that stood outside US drugstores]

dead as dogshit *phr.* [1980s+] absolutely dead.

dead as Julius Caesar *phr.* [late 19C–1900s] absolutely dead, dead for some time.

dead as/deader than Kelsey's nuts *phr.* [1950s+] (US) very, definitely. [fig. use; death, as such, is irrelevant; for ety. *see* TIGHT AS KELSEY'S NUTS]

dead as mutton *phr.* [late 18C–1910s] completely dead, certainly dead.

dead ass *n.*[1] **1** [20C] an utterly boring, useless person. **2** [1950s+] (US) the seated rump. [SE *dead* + sfx. -ASS]

dead ass/butt *n.*[2] [1950s+] (US) an idler, a lazy person. [SE *dead* + sfx. -ASS/BUTT *n.*[1] (3)]

dead-ass/-butt *adj.* [1950s+] (US) lacking energy, listless, lifeless. [for ety. *see* DEAD ASS *n.*[2]]

dead-ass *adv.* [1970s+] (US) lifelessly, listlessly. [DEAD ASS *n.*[2]]

dead as small beer *phr.* [19C] absolutely dead. [the flatness of this weak form of beer]

dead-bang *adj.* [1930s+] (US) of a criminal prosecution, lacking any possibility of defence or argument because the case is watertight. [DEAD *adv.* + BANG TO RIGHTS]

deadbeat *n.* [mid-19C+] (orig. US) **1** of people, a failure, a down-and-out. **2** a malingerer, an idler, a wastrel. **3** of things, a failure, a deception. **4** a cadger, a sponge. [backform. DEADBEAT *adj.*]

deadbeat *adj.* **1** [early 19C+] absolutely defeated. **2** [mid-19C+] worn out, exhausted. [DEAD *adv.* + SE *beaten*]

deadbeat *v.* [late 19C+] (US) **1** to waste time, to idle around. **2** to sponge on. **3** to cheat. [DEADBEAT *n.*]

deadbeatism *n.* [mid-late 19C] worthlessness. [DEADBEAT *n.* + sfx. -*ism*]

deadbell *n.* [20C] (Ulster) a ringing in the ears.

dead bird *n.* [late 19C+] (Aus.) a certain bet, a sure thing. [like the bird, it cannot 'move']

dead broke *adj.* [mid-19C+] (orig. US) completely without funds. [DEAD *adv.* + BROKE]

dead-broker *n.* [late 19C+] (Aus.) a down-and-out (cf. BROKER *n.*[2]; BROKIE). [DEAD BROKE]

dead butt *n. see* DEAD ASS *n.*[2].

dead-butt *adj. see* DEAD-ASS *adj.*

dead card *n.* [late 19C–1900s] (US) something that is unfashionable or unpopular. [SE *dead card*, a card that has been discarded in a game and is no longer to be used by the players]

dead cargo *n.* [late 17C–19C] (Und.) the proceeds of a robbery that have turned out to be less valuable than hoped.

dead cat up the branch *phr.* [20C] a phr. used to suggest that something is suspicious, something is not as it should be, someone is attempting to deceive the speaker (cf. DEAD CAT UP THE LINE; DEAD DUCK UP THE STREAM; THERE'S A DEAD NIGGER IN THE WOODPILE). [SE *branch*, either that of a tree or a *branch line*, thus *see* DEAD CAT UP THE LINE]

dead cat up the line *phr.* [20C] (US Black) a phr. used when something seems suspicious (cf. DEAD CAT UP THE BRANCH). [a variety of etys. offer: (1) a dead catfish left too long on a fishing line, implying that something must have happened to the angler; (2) a woman who is obviously having an affair since she is utterly passive (i.e. SE *dead*) during sexual intercourse; (3) an actual dead cat that had climbed a telegraph pole and is now interrupting the telephone line]

dead centre *n.* [1940s+] a cemetery. [pun]

dead cert *n.* [late 19C+] (orig. racing) an absolute certainty, esp. in race-course betting. [DEAD *adv.* + CERT]

dead chicken *n.* [1960s+] (US) a doomed person, a lost soul.

dead chocker/chokka *adj.* [1950s] (orig. milit.) very bored. [DEAD *adv.* + CHOCKER *adj.*]

dead chuffed *adj.* [1950s+] (orig. milit.) extremely pleased. [DEAD *adv.* + CHUFFED]

dead-copper *n.* [1920s+] (Aus.) a police informer. [DEAD *adv.* + COPPER *n.*[3] (1)]

dead duck *n.* (orig. US) **1** [mid-19C+] a complete, irredeemable failure (cf. DEAD PIGEON; DEAD RABBIT *n.*[2]; DEAD TURKEY). **2** [1940s+] a hopeless person, one who has absolutely no chance, a 'goner'. [fig. use of SE + pvb. 'never waste powder on a dead duck']

dead duck up the stream *phr.* [20C] (US Black) something is suspicious. [var. on DEAD CAT UP THE BRANCH]

dead easy *adj.* [20C] **1** very easy. **2** said of any sexually available woman. [DEAD *adv.* + SE *easy*]

dead-end street *n.* [19C] the vagina (cf. ALLEY *n.*[1]). [synon. for cul-de-sac; there is in *dead* an extra implication of passivity on the woman's part]

deadener *n.*[1] [mid-late 19C] (US) a very attractive female (cf. KNOCKOUT *n.*; STUNNER). [SE *deaden*]

deadener *n.*[2] [1930s+] (Aus.) a bully, one who prefers to settle arguments through violence. [SE *deaden*]

deader *n.* [mid-late 19C] (orig. US) **1** an exhausted person. **2** a dead person, a corpse; thus *be a deader*, to be recently dead.

deaders *n.* [1980s+] (W.I./UK Black teen) animal flesh, meat by-products eaten as food. [SE *dead*; the implication is that such foods are unpalatable]

deader than kelsey's nuts *see* DEAD AS KELSEY'S NUTS.

deadeye *n.*[1] [late 18C–1900s] the anus (cf. BLIND EYE).

deadeye *n.*[2] *see* DEADY.

deadeye *v.* [1960s+] (US) to stare at in a chilly manner.

dead-eye dick *n.* [1950s+] (gay) one who performs anal intercourse. [nickname for a superlative marksman + puns on ROUNDEYE *n.* (1) + DICK *n.*[5] (1)]

deadfall *n.* [mid-19C–1950s] (US) a rough saloon. [the drunks 'fall down dead' ? + pun on SE *deadfall*, a trap for large game]

dead finish n. [late 19C+] (Aus.) the absolute, the complete. [DEAD adv. + SE *finish*]

dead fink n. [20C] (Irish) an attractive girl. [ety. unknown]

dead for phr. [late 19C] (US) desperate for, in great need of. [var. on SE *dying for*]

dead from the neck up phr. [1910s+] particularly stupid.

dead give-away n. [late 19C+] (orig. US) **1** a complete betrayal. **2** a swindle, a deception. [DEAD adv. + SE *give-away*]

dead gone adj. [late 19C+] utterly exhausted. [DEAD adv. + SE *gone*]

dead hand n. [mid-19C+] an expert. [DEAD adv. + SE *hand*, an expert + pun on SE; 20C use is Aus.]

deadhead n.[1] **1** [19C+] one who receives goods or services without paying. **2** [20C] a fool. **3** [20C] a lazy worthless person. **4** [20C] a non-participant, one who does not contribute. **5** [1930s+] a drunk. [orig. theatre jargon *deadhead*, one who does not pay for their ticket]

deadhead n.[2] [1970s+] **1** a fan and follower of the Grateful Dead, one of the earliest psychedelic bands, and still (late 1990s) one of the most popular in the US and the world. **2** a hippie, esp. a devotee of a 'back to nature' lifestyle. [proper name *Grateful Dead* + sfx. -HEAD (1); a development of the earlier synon. *Dead Freak*]

deadhead adj.[1] [mid-19C+] useless, spec. non-participant. [DEADHEAD n.[1] (3), (4)]

deadhead adj.[2] [late 19C+] (US) free of charge. [DEADHEAD n.[1] (1)]

deadhead v. (orig. US) **1** [mid-19C+] to obtain services without paying. **2** [1910s+] to ride for free, to drive a cab, aeroplane etc without its usual load, passengers. [DEADHEAD n.[1] (1)]

dead heart n. [20C] (Aus.) the uninhabited centre of Australia.

dead horse n.[1] **1** [late 17C+] work that has been already paid for but is yet to be done; thus *play a dead horse, pull a dead horse, work for a dead horse*, to perform such work. **2** [19C+] (US/Aus./N.Z.) a debt that has been incurred by accepting an advance on one's wages, it must now be worked off; thus *ride the dead horse, work off the dead horse, bury the dead horse*. **3** [19C+] any form of debt. **4** [19C+] any form of useless job, it doesn't bring in any profits but still must be done; thus *draw the dead horse*, to work at such a job.

dead horse n.[2] [20C] stew. [the disparaging comparison]

dead horse n.[3] [1940s+] (Aus.) tomato sauce. [rhy. sl.]

dead house n. **1** [mid-19C–1940s] (Aus.) a room in an outback public house set aside for those who are incapably drunk. **2** [late 19C] (US) a particularly unappealing bar or saloon (cf. MORGUE). [DEAD adj.[1] + SE *house*]

deadie n. [1970s] a dead person. [SE *dead* + sfx. -*ie*]

dead Indian n. [1960s] (US) an empty bottle (cf. DEAD adj.[2]). [the neg. stereotype of allegedly alcoholic Native Americans]

dead knowledge n. [late 19C] (Aus.) deceit, cunning.

deadleg n. [1970s] a down-and-out, a failure (cf. DEADBEAT n.).

dead-level best see LEVEL BEST.

deadlights n. [19C] the eyes. [var. on DAYLIGHTS]

dead line n. [1900s–10s] (US) the red light area of a town or city. [fig. use of US milit. jargon *dead line*, a line drawn around a military prison, beyond which a prisoner is liable to be shot down]

dead loads n. [19C+] (US) many, a great quantity. [DEAD adv. + LOADS (OF)]

dead lock n. [late 19C] a lock hospital, i.e. a hospital for venereal disease.

dead loss n. [1940s+] (orig. RAF) an absolutely useless person, idea or undertaking, a useless, unworkable object. [SE *dead loss*, of a charge or expense, totally unproductive, unprofitable]

dead lurk n. **1** [mid-19C] (Und.) breaking into houses while the occupiers are at church (cf. CRACK A KIRK; KIRKING). **2** [mid–late 19C] empty premises. [SE *dead*, abandoned, unused + LURK n.]

deadly adj.[1] [mid-17C+] very bad, utterly unpleasant.

deadly adj.[2] [1960s+] (US Black/campus) excellent, first-rate. [on *bad* = *good* principle]

deadly adv. [late 16C+] excessively, extremely.

deadly-lively adj. [19C] offering false joviality.

dead nail see NAIL n.[1].

deadly nevergreen n. [late 18C] the gallows (cf. ABRAHAM'S BALSAM; GREGORIAN TREE; LEAFLESS TREE; THREE-CORNERED TREE; THREE TREES; TREE THAT BEARS FRUIT ALL YEAR ROUND; TREE WITH THREE CORNERS; TRIPLE TREE; TYBURN TREE). [pun on SE *evergreen*]

deadly nightshade n. [mid-19C–1920s] the lowest grade of prostitute. [pun on the SE plant]

dead man n.[1] **1** [late 17C–late 19C] (orig. milit.) an empty bottle (cf. DEAD adj.[2]). **2** any large object (a baulk of timber, a steel stanchion, a lump of concrete etc) used as an anchor for hawsers, guy-ropes etc.

dead man n.[2] [mid-19C] 'Properly speaking, it is an extra loaf smuggled into the basket by the man who carries it out, to the loss of the master. Sometimes the dead man is charged to a customer, though never delivered' (Hotten, 1873). [? the role of a dead man as supernumerary to requirements]

dead man n.[3] [late 19C] a scarecrow, esp. when made in the traditional manner of old clothes stuffed with straw. [dial.]

dead man n.[4] [1930s] (Irish) a weekly insurance collector. [the insurance is paid off when one is dead]

deadman choppers/teeth n. [20C] (US Black) false teeth. [SE *dead man* + CHOPPERS]

dead man's arm n. [1980s+] (N.Z.) steamed (currant) roll pudding.

dead man's ears n. [1980s+] (N.Z.) stewed dried apricots.

dead man's hand n. [mid-19C+] **1** a poker hand of mixed aces and 8s (cf. ACES AND EIGHTS phr.[1]). **2** bad luck. [the lawman Wild Bill Hickok (1837–76) was allegedly holding such a hand when he was gunned down]

dead man's head n. [1980s+] (N.Z.) a round, steamed plum pudding, eaten hot or cold.

dead man's shoes n. [20C] (US Black) anything that one would rather not have to experience but that probably cannot be avoided. [note SE phr. [mid-16C+] *wait for dead man's shoes*, to wait for the death of a person with the expectancy of succeeding to his possessions or office]

deadman teeth see DEADMAN CHOPPERS.

dead marine n. [early 19C+] an empty bottle (cf. DEAD adj.[2]). [orig. naut. jargon, now mainly Aus. use]

dead meat n. **1** [mid-19C+] a corpse. **2** [mid-19C+] a stupid, dull person. **3** [mid-19C+] someone who is facing certain death. **4** [late 19C+] a prostitute. **5** [1920s] a horse that has no chance of winning a race. [lit. or fig. uses of SE]

dead-meat ticket n. [1910s+] (Aus.) an identity tag. [DEAD MEAT n. (1) + SE *ticket*; orig. milit. use, such tags identified the corpses of otherwise anonymous soldiers]

dead nap n. [19C] an absolute villain. [DEAD adv. + NAPPER n.[1]]

dead nark n. [20C] (Aus.) a spoil-sport. [DEAD adv. + NARK n. (3)]

deadneck n. [1930s] a very stupid person. [i.e. one who is DEAD FROM THE NECK UP]

dead nip n. [19C] an unimportant project that turns out to be a failure. [DEAD adv. + ? SE *nip*, a fragment a small portion]

dead number n. [late 19C] **1** the last house in a row or street. **2** the end of a street. [? link SE *dead end*]

dead-nuts adj. [late 19C+] (US) completely dead. [SE *dead* + NUTS n.[2] (1)]

deado *n.* [1910s+] a corpse.

deado/deadoh *adj.* [late 19C–1910s] **1** dead. **2** very drunk (cf. BASTED). [SE *dead drunk* + sfx. -O]

dead on *adj.*[1] [mid-19C+] very fond of (cf. DEATH ON adj.[1]). [DEAD adv. + SE *on*]

dead on *adj.*[2] [mid-19C+] (orig. US) **1** dealing very strictly and severely with a situation or person. **2** very good at dealing with (cf. DEATH ON adj.[2]). [fig. use of DEAD adv. + SE *on*]

dead on *adj.*[3] [late 19C+] (orig. US) absolutely right, utterly correct. [abbr. SE *dead on target*]

dead on arrival *n.* [1980s+] (drugs) heroin. [the frequency of fatal overdoses; the phr. is used of those who arrive at the hospital morgue]

dead one *n.* (US) **1** [late 19C–1910s] a horse that will not win, or has no chance of winning. **2** [late 19C+] one who is doomed, on the verge of death or actually dead (cf. GONER). **3** [late 19C–1930s] a useless, unsociable, impoverished person. **4** [1910s–30s] a fool.

dead on one's feet *phr.* [late 19C+] utterly drained, exhausted.

dead oodles *n.* [mid-19C+] (orig. US) a large quantity, many (cf. OODLES; SCADS). [ety. unknown, but Cohen (1985) suggests progression from *scadoodles* by mispron. of first syll.]

deadpan *v.* [1940s+] (orig. US) to speak without expression, esp. in a situation that would normally demand some emotion. [SE *dead pan*, an expressionless or impassive face; *deadpan* (as n., adj., adv.) is cited as SE in *OED*, though *pan* is acknowledged to be 'orig. US slang'; it would thus seem likely to have been sl. at its coinage]

deadpicker *n.* **1** [1930s] (US tramp) one who robs passed-out drunks. **2** [1930s–40s] (US) a general term of abuse.

dead pickles *see* PICKLES n.[2].

dead pigeon *n.* [1910s+] (US) a guaranteed and absolute failure, often in context of a forthcoming election (cf. DEAD DUCK).

dead president *n.* [20C] (US) a $1 bill (cf. ABRAHAM LINCOLN). [the pictures of US presidents that are printed on the various denominations]

dead rabbit *n.*[1] [mid-19C] (US) a street thug, a hoodlum. [the New York street gang, known as the Dead Rabbits, who would parade brandishing such a corpse, the symbol of their defeated rivals, as their standard]

dead rabbit *n.*[2] **1** [20C] an impotent penis, incapable of erection. **2** [1940s+] a hopeless person, one who has absolutely no chance (cf. DEAD DUCK).

dead rag *n.* [1980s+] (US Black gang) a dead gang member. [the RAG n.[5] or bandanna handkerchief, worn by gang members to indicate their affiliation]

dead recruit *n.* [20C] an empty bottle (cf. DEAD adj.[2]). [var. on DEAD SOLDIER]

dead ringer *n.* [late 19C+] (orig. US) usu. of people, an absolute replica (of); thus *to be a dead ringer/ringer for,* to resemble completely. [DEAD adv. + RINGER n.[2] (1)]

dead ring of *n.* [1910s+] (Aus./N.Z.) the absolute image of. [var. on DEAD RINGER]

dead set *n.* **1** [early 18C–mid-19C] a pointed attack on another person. **2** [late 18C–early 19C] (Und.) a scheme aimed at defrauding a victim through crooked gambling. [DEAD adv. + SE *set*, the act of a dog in setting game; orig. used by thief-catchers referring to their imminent arrest of a villain]

dead set *adj.* [1960s+] (Aus.) first-rate, excellent, very good. [DEAD adv. + SE *set*, positioned]

dead set against *adj.* [early 19C+] totally hostile towards. [DEAD SET n. (1)]

dead set on *adj.* [early 19C+] fascinated by, obsessed with, in love with. [DEAD SET n. (1)]

dead shot *n.*[1] [mid-19C] (US) very poor quality or adulterated whisky. [SE *dead*, worthless + SHOT n.[5]]

dead shot *n.*[2] [1970s+] (US Black) sexual intercourse, whether vaginal or anal. [SE *dead shot*, an expert marksman]

dead snooks on, to be *phr.* [1900s–30s] (Aus.) to be in love with. [DEAD adv. + affectionate nickname *Snooks/Snookums*]

dead soldier *n.* [1910s+] an empty bottle (cf. DEAD adj.[2]).

dead spit *n.* [20C] of another person (often a relative), the exact image (cf. VERY SPIT). [DEAD adv. + SE *spit(ting image)*]

dead spotted ling of *phr.* [1910s+] (Aus.) the absolute image of. [rhy. sl. *dead spotted ling* = DEAD RING OF]

dead thick *adj.* [late 19C+] (Glasgow) very clever. [ironic reversal of DEAD adv. + THICK adj.[1]]

dead time *n.* [20C] (US Und.) **1** any period of one's prison sentence when one is prohibited from associating with other prisoners. **2** any time spent in prison that does not actually diminish one's sentence.

dead to rights *adv.* [mid-19C+] **1** certain, sure. **2** caught in the act (cf. BANG TO RIGHTS). [DEAD adv. + TO RIGHTS]

dead to the wide/world *adj.* [late 19C+] (orig. US) **1** completely drunk. **2** utterly and completely exhausted, very deeply asleep.

dead turkey *n.* [1940s+] a hopeless person, one who has absolutely no chance (cf. DEAD DUCK).

dead 'un *n.*[1] [19C] a half-quartern loaf. [? DEAD MAN n.[2]]

dead 'un *n.*[2] **1** [19C] a bankrupt company (cf. CADAVER). **2** [late 19C+] in horse-racing, a mount that seems not to have been raced to its full capacity. [lit. a 'dead one'. (2) obs. in UK by 1900 but continued in Aus. use]

dead whiteboy *n.* [1990s] (US Black) a $ bill of any denomination (cf. ABRAHAM LINCOLN; DEAD PRESIDENT). [there have as yet been no Black presidents of the USA]

deadwood *n.* [mid-19C+] (US) a coffin. [pun]

deadwood *adj.*[1] [late 19C] (US) absolute, complete, unequivocal, e.g. *deadwood agreement.* [i.e. there is no possibility of further 'growth']

deadwood *adj.*[2] [20C] (US prison) caught in the act (cf. FOUR-CORNERED). [DEADWOOD adj.[1]]

dead wowsers *n.* [20C] (Aus.) trousers. [rhy. sl.]

deady/deadeye *n.* [early–mid-19C] gin, or a particular quality of gin. [name of the distiller D. *Deady,* listed in the London Directory (1812) as 'Distiller and Brandy-merchant, Sol's Row, Tottenham Court Rd']

deaf and dumb *n.* [1910s+] (Aus.) inside information, e.g. *I'll give you the deaf and dumb.* [rhy. sl. *deaf and dumb* = DRUM n.[4]]

deal, a *n.*[1] **1** [late 16C+] a large quantity. **2** [mid-18C–mid-19C] an undefined but considerable amount or extent. [SE *deal,* a portion, an amount]

deal *n.*[2] **1** [mid–late 19C] any form of financial or commercial transaction. **2** [late 19C+] (orig. US) an idea, a scheme, an arrangement, the current situation, esp. with implication of illegality, subterfuge. **3** [late 19C+] the treatment one has received, whether good or bad; thus a *square deal,* fair treatment. **4** [late 19C+] (orig. US) the situation, the state of affairs, e.g. *that's the deal.* **5** [1920s+] (US) a turn of events, a development. **6** [1940s+] (orig. US) an individual or thing. **7** [1950s] one's concern or business, e.g. *that's my deal,* that's my business. **8** [1960s+] (drugs) a purchase of drugs, esp. cannabis; thus *quid deal,* one pound's worth etc. [ult. SE *deal,* the act or system of dividing into parts for distribution; 20C use of (1) is SE]

deal *n.*[3] [1960s–70s] (US Black) a woman. [despite commercial overtones, not a prostitute]

deal *v.* **1** [1920s] (US) to give, to hand over. **2** [1920s+] to sell drugs, esp. marijuana (cf. CONNECT). **3** [1960s+] (US) to make a bargain, to conduct business. [DEAL n.[2]]

dealer *n.* [1920s+] (drugs) a drug seller. [a specific use of an 11C SE word meaning trafficker, in whatever he or she happened to deal]

deal from the bottom of the deck *see* DEAL OFF THE BOTTOM OF THE DECK.

deal in coal, to *phr.* **1** [1900s–40s] (US Black) to prefer darkskinned women. **2** [1940s] (US) of a White man, to have sex with a Black woman. [DEAL v. (1) + COAL n.² (1)]

deal in dirt, to *phr.* [1970s+] (US Black) to gossip (cf. DISH THE DIRT). [DEAL v. (1) + DIRT n.¹ (3)]

deal in zeroes, to *phr.* [1960s] (US Black) to achieve nothing, to fail completely, to draw a blank. [DEAL v. (1) + SE *zero*]

deal it out *v.* [20C] (Aus.) to attack, esp. verbally, to punish.

deal off/from the bottom of the deck, to *phr.* [1910s+] (orig. US) to cheat, to defraud, to swindle. [a classic method of cheating in cards]

deal someone a hand, to *phr.* [20C] to include, to involve. [card-playing imagery]

deal someone in *v.* [1940s+] (orig. US) to include in an undertaking, often a criminal one, to give one a share. [card-playing imagery]

deal suit *n.* [mid–late 19C] a coffin (cf. PINE DRAPE; WOODEN DOUBLET; WOODEN HABEAS; WOODEN KIMONO; WOODEN OVERCOAT; WOODEN SUIT; WOODEN SURTOUT; WOODEN ULSTER). [SE *deal*, a form of pine wood from which cheap coffins are constructed]

deal them off the arm, to *phr.* [1930s–40s] (US) to wait at tables. [the waiter's ability to carry a line of plates up the arm + ref. to gambling jargon *deal off the arm*, to cheat by sleight of hand; the implication is that the customer is being cheated on food quality]

deal someone one, to *phr.* [1980s+] (N.Z.) **1** to attack someone, to give someone a blow or a beating. **2** to pay someone back (for an injury or slight). [ext. DEAL TO]

deal to *v.* [1980s+] (N.Z.) **1** to beat up. **2** to treat roughly. [SE *deal*, to hand out]

deaner/dena/denar/dener *n.* [mid-19C–1960s] (Ling. Fr./Polari) a shilling (5p) (cf. DEENER; DINARLY). [Ital. *dinero*, ult. f. Lat. *denarius*. 20C use is Aus. before decimalization]

dean maitland *n.* [1940s+] (Aus.) a silent person, one who does not talk. [title *The Silence of Dean Maitland*, a film (1934) based on the novel (1914) by Maxwell Grey]

dearest bodily part *n.* [late 16C–early 17C] the vagina.

dearest member *n.* [mid-18C–late 19C] the penis (cf. FORNICATING ENGINE; FORNICATOR; HOT MEMBER; JOLLY MEMBER; MASTER MEMBER; MEMBER FOR COCKSHIRE; WARM MEMBER). [SE *dearest* + *member*, any organ of the body/MEMBER n.¹]

dear jane *n.* [1980s+] a letter concluding a relationship. [feminized version of DEAR JOHN]

dear john *n.* [1940s+] a letter concluding a relationship, usu. sent by the woman and received by the man, often in prison or serving in the forces. [its fig. salutation, *Dear John …*]

dear joy *n.* [late 17C–early 19C] an Irishman. [SE *dear joy!*, a supposedly favourite Irish expression]

dear me! *excl.* [late 18C+] a mild excl. [? Ital. *dio mio*, my God and poss. introduced to UK by Maria Beatrice of Modena (1658–1718), second wife of James II (r.1685–88)]

dear-stalker *n.* [1910s–30s] a wealthy idler who likes to follow and/or ogle attractive shopgirls or secretaries (cf. DEER-STALKING). [pun on SE *deer-stalker*, i.e. one who stalks deer, and on the 'little dears']

death *n.* **1** [mid-19C] the extreme of fashion; thus *dress to death*. **2** [1960s+] (US Black) something excellent, something outstanding (cf. DEF).

death! *excl.* [1960s+] (US juv.) an excl. of approval or admiration. [on *bad* = *good* model]

death adder *n.* (Aus.) **1** [1920s+] a solo prospector, living out in the desert and characterized by surliness, taciturnity and general misanthropy (cf. HAVE DEATH ADDERS IN ONE'S POCKET). **2** [1930s+] an ill-tempered gossip. [SE *death adder*, a venomous snake (genus *Acanthophis*) native to Australia and New Guinea]

death drop *n.* [20C] (drugs) butyl chloride. [SE *death* + *drop*, a medicinal preparation]

death-hunter *n.* **1** [18C] one who sells stories of interesting deaths to the press (cf. AMBULANCE-CHASER). **2** [late 18C–20C] an undertaker. **3** [early 19C] one who visits battlefields in order to scavenge for clothes and other saleable items. **4** [mid–late 19C] a seller of the printed versions of dying speeches, usu. of those made on the gallows (cf. RUNNING PATTERER).

deathing *n.* [1980s+] (drugs) smoking a pipe containing strong cannabis. [the intense inhalation of marijuana or hashish smoke has a concomitantly powerful effect on the user]

death loaf *n.* [20C] (US prison) meat loaf.

death on *adj.*¹ [mid-19C+] very fond of (cf. DEAD ON adj.¹). [fig. use of DEAD adv. + SE *on*]

death on *adj.*² [mid-19C+] (orig. US) **1** dealing very strictly and severely with a situation or person. **2** very good at dealing with (cf. DEAD ON adj.²). [fig. use of DEAD adv. + SE *on*]

death rain *n.* [1940s] (US Black) an extremely heavy downpour.

death row *n.* [20C] (US prison) the condemned cells (cf. C.C.).

death seat *n.* [1980s+] (Aus.) the passenger seat in a motorcar, shown statistically to be the seat most likely to bring death to its occupier when the car crashes. [trotting jargon *death seat*, the position outside the leader, from which it is difficult to win]

death's head upon a mopstick *n.* [late 18C–early 19C] a miserable, impoverished, emaciated person. [image of a skull mounted on a pole]

death trip *n.*¹ [1960s+] any situation considered potentially fatal or extremely life-threatening. [SE *death* + TRIP n.³ (2)]

death trip *n.*² [1960s+] a fantasy about death, often stimulated by (hallucinogenic) drugs. [SE *death* + TRIP n.³ (1)]

death wish *n.* [1970s–80s] (drugs) phencyclidine (cf. ACE n.³). [its potentially dangerous effects]

deathy *n.* [late 19C+] (Aus.) a death adder, a type of venomous snake.

deb *n.*¹ [early–mid-19C] a bed (cf. DAB n.²). [backsl.]

deb *n.*² [1950s] (US teen) a female member of a street gang. [SE *debutante*, itself commonly abbr. as *deb*]

de-bag *v.* [late 19C+] to remove someone's trousers, either as a joke or as a form of punishment. [*pfx. de-* + BAGS n.¹; now obs. except in some (public) school use]

de-ball *v.* [1950s+] to castrate (cf. DE-BOLLOCK). [SE pfx. *de-* + BALLS n.¹]

debbie *n.* [1920s] a *debutante*. [abbr.]

debblish *n.* [late 19C] (S.Afr.) a penny. [ety. unknown]

de-bollock *v.* [1960s+] to castrate, usu. in fig. sense of hurting or punishing severely (cf. DE-BALL). [SE pfx. *de-* + BOLLOCK n.]

deb's delight *n.* [1940s+] an eligible or attractive young man who frequents the season in which upper-class or rich young women 'come out' into society. [SE *debutante* + *delight*]

debug *v.* [1940s+] to remove faults from a machine, a system or, now most commonly, a computer or its software. [SE pfx. *de-* + BUG n.⁷ (1)]

debuggerable *adj.* [1930s] disreputable, unpleasant. [play on SE *disreputable* + BUGGER n.¹ (2)]

debut *n.* [1950s+] a first homosexual experience. [play on SE *debut*, pun on COME OUT v.³]

debutante *n.* [1950s+] someone new to the gay life.

decadence *n.* [1980s+] (drugs) MDMA (cf. ECSTASY). [its image]

dece/dees adj. [1970s+] (US) pleasant, amenable. [abbr. SE decent]

decent n. [1980s+] (US campus) something that causes happiness, joy or excitement (cf. CHUMPIE). [DECENT adj.¹ (3)]

decent adj.¹ **1** [18C] tolerable, fairly good, acceptable. **2** [mid-19C–1940s] kind, accommodating, likeable. **3** [1970s+] (US campus) very good, excellent. [(1) SE by 1800. (2) always mainly schoolboy use, e.g. jolly decent chaps, now only as a satirical/deeply ironic form]

decent adj.² [1940s+] (orig. theatrical) fully dressed, usu. in phr., e.g. Are you decent? or Wait a minute, I'm not decent. [SE decent, in accordance with or satisfying the general standard of propriety or good taste]

deck n.¹ [19C] Seven Dials, London, WC2; thus decker, an inhabitant of Seven Dials; on the deck, living in Seven Dials. [Seven Dials, near Covent Garden, was a criminal ROOKERY n. (2) of 19C London; Monmouth Street, one of the seven convergent streets that gave it its name, was a noted centre for second-hand clothes dealing]

deck n.² [mid-19C+] a look, a glance (cf. DEKKO). [Hind. dekha, sight]

deck n.³ [1910s+] (US drugs) a packet of heroin, cocaine or similar narcotic (cf. BAG n.⁸). [SAmE deck, a pack of cards; ult. 16C SE, then dial.]

deck n.⁴ [1940s+] (US) **1** the floor, the ground. **2** the roof of a building or its highest floor at a stage of building. [naut. use]

deck v.¹ [late 19C–1930s] (US tramp) to ride on the roof of a freight car. [DECK n.⁴ (2)]

deck v.² **1** [1940s+] to knock down. **2** [1960s] to press down the accelerator pedal of a car; thus to go fast. **3** [1960s] of a man, to have sexual intercourse. [DECK n.⁴ (1)]

decked/decked out adj. [1960s–70s] (US) intoxicated by drink or drugs. [fig. use of DECK v.² (1)]

decked-out chick n. [20C] (US Black) a woman or girl who uses an excess of cosmetics. [18C deck out, to decorate + CHICK n.³ (1)]

decker n.¹ **1** [early–mid-19C] a deckhand. **2** [mid-19C+] a deck passenger. **3** [1930s+] (Aus.) the top deck of a double-decker bus. [SE deck]

decker n.² **1** [20C] in a pickpocketing gang, the member who surveys the street for approaching policemen. **2** [1940s+] (Aus.) a glance. [DECK n.²]

decker n.³ [20C] (Aus.) a (peaked) cap or hat. [DECK n.⁴ (2)]

deckhand n. [1900s] (US) a menial labourer, a domestic servant.

deckie n. [1960s+] (Aus.) a deckhand. [abbr.]

decko see DEKKO.

decks-awash adj. [late 19C+] drunk (cf. AFLOAT).

deck up v. [1960s] (drugs) to portion out large measures of heroin into small portions. [DECK n.³]

declare off v. [mid-18C–late 19C] to withdraw from an undertaking, e.g. an engagement to be married. [horse-racing use]

decoct adj. [16C] bankrupt. [SE decoct, well cooked, i.e. 'done to a turn']

decoke v. [1940s+] to clean the spark plugs of an automobile of accumulated carbon; also in fig. use referring to human health.

Decomposition Row n. [mid-19C] Rotten Row, the track in Hyde Park frequented by fashionable horse-riders. [a pun on Rotten Row, itself ult. route du roi, the royal road, from Kensington Palace and St James's]

decongest the weasel, to phr. [1990s] to masturbate (cf. DRAIN THE MONSTER).

decorate v. [1910s–50s] (US) to injure, esp. to give a black eye.

decorate the mahogany, to phr. **1** [20C] (US) to lay down

money, whether for gambling or in payment of a bill. **2** [1930s+] of a man, to hand over one's housekeeping money to one's wife. [SE decorate + MAHOGANY n.²]

decoy n. [1990s] (drugs) fake drugs, esp. fake crack cocaine, which contains no cocaine but is composed of baby powder, quinine, baking soda etc. [SE decoy, a bait. a trap]

decoy dancer n. [mid-19C] (US) a dance-hall hostess whose primary job is not to dance but to promote liquor sales to the clientele (cf. B-GIRL).

decus n. [17C–early 19C] a crown piece, 5 shillings (25p). [from the Latin motto decus et tutamen, 'an ornament and a safeguard', from Virgil, Aeneid, Bk V, and originally describing a breast-plate. It was subsequently engraved on coins (where it referred both to the inscription and to its helping prevent their being clipped) and has reappeared on the English version of the modern £1 coin]

dedos n. [1960s+] (US) an informer (cf. FINGER n.²). [Sp. dedos, fingers]

deduction n. [1960s] (US) a small child. [the status in the tax laws]

dee n.¹ [mid-19C] a purse, a pocket-book. [orig. Rom.]

dee n.² see D n.².

dee n.³ [1980s+] (drugs) cannabis. [DRAW n.² (2)]

deeache n. [mid-19C+] head. [backsl.]

deece n. [1940s] (US Black/Harlem) a dime, 10 cents. [Fr. dix, 10]

deeda n. [1960s–70s] (US Black/Harlem/drugs) LSD (cf. A n.³).

dee-donk n. [mid-19C] a Frenchman. [Fr. dis donc, so tell me. Note antecedents in the synon. didones (used in Spain after the Peninsular War (1808–14), a century earlier), dido (as used in Ling. Fr.) as well as, somewhat later, the Javanese orang deedonc, 'the dis donc people']

deejay see DJ n.¹.

deek n. [1930s+] (US) a detective (cf. DICK n.⁶). [pron.]

deek v. [mid-19C+] (US) to look at. [DEKKO]

deelo/dillo adj. [mid-19C+] old. [backsl.]

deelo diam see DELO DIAM.

deelo/dillo namo n. [mid-19C] an old woman. [backsl.]

deelo nam of the barrack see DELO NAM OF THE BARRACK.

deemer n. (US) **1** [1920s–60s] a dime. **2** [1930s] the number ten. **3** [1930s–50s] one who tips a dime.

deenach n. [mid-19C+] a hand. [backsl.]

deener n. [late 19C+] (Aus./N.Z.) one shilling. [DEANER]

deep adj. [late 18C+] sly, artful. [ext. use of SE]

deep file n. [19C] an artful, cunning or shrewd person. [DEEP + FILE n. (3)]

deep freeze n. (US) **1** [1950s] a place of imprisonment, a prison. **2** [1960s+] ostracism.

deep-freezer n. [1960s] a prim, stand-offish, asexual woman. [SE deep freeze; one who 'gives you a chill']

deep grief n. [late 19C] a pair of blackened eyes (cf. FULL SUIT OF MOURNING). [the blackness of not one but both eyes]

deep hole n. [1970s+] a serious situation, a difficult problem (cf. DEEP SHIT).

deep noser n. [1940s–50s] (Aus.) a deep glass of beer (cf. DEEP SINKER). [one has to push one's nose deep into the glass]

deep pockets n. [1970s+] (US) a person who can always be counted on to provide cash.

deep-sea diver n. [1970s+] a £5 note. [rhy. sl. deep-sea diver = FIVER n. (1)]

deep-sea fisherman n. [1900s–50s] a confidence trickster working the transatlantic liners.

deep-sea turkey n. [20C] (US) **1** salt cod. **2** a codfish (dinner) (cf. ABERDEEN CUTLET).

deep shit n. [1970s+] a serious situation, a difficult problem, usu. as phr. in deep shit (cf. DEEP HOLE). [SE deep + SHIT n.³]

deep sinker n. [late 19C–1910s] (Aus.) **1** a drinking-glass of the largest size (cf. DEEP NOSER). **2** the drink served in such a glass. [supposed resemblance to a deep mine-shaft]

deep six *n.* [1920s–40s] a grave (cf. SIX n.²; SIX-FOOT BUNGALOW; SIX-FOOT SUBWAY). [it is 6 feet under]

deep six *v.* **1** [1940s+] (orig. US) to get rid of, to abandon. **2** [1950s+] (orig. US) to ruin, to destroy. **3** [1980s+] (US campus) to finish a 6-pack of beer. [naut. use *deep six*, to throw overboard; ult. phr. *6 feet under*, dead]

deep sugar *n.* [1940s] (US Black) a deep kiss (cf. FRENCH KISS; SUGAR n.³). [its 'sweetness']

deep throat *n.* [1970s+] deep fellatio, in which the penis is taken not simply into the mouth, but down the throat. [the term was popularized by the 'art porn' film *Deep Throat* (1973) starring Linda Lovelace. The term was also used as the nickname of the otherwise anonymous source who helped journalists investigate the Watergate Affair (1972–4)]

deep throat *v.* [1970s+] to take the entire length of the penis into one's mouth, and thus down one's throat, during fellatio. [DEEP THROAT n.]

deep yellow *see* HIGH YELLOW.

deer *n.* [mid-19C] a (promiscuous) young woman. [abbr. WHETSTONE PARK DEER]

deer-stalking *n.* [1920s] the practice of chasing women (cf. DEAR-STALKER). [pun on SE *deer/little dear* + *stalker*]

dees *see* DECE.

deevie/deevy *adj.* [1900s–40s] (society) wonderful, sweet, cute. [abbr. SE *divine*]

def *adj.* [1970s+] (orig. US Black) perfect, excellent, first-rate (cf. MONDO adv.; RAD adj.; SAFE!). [? Black pron. of SE *death* or abbr. SE *definitive*. Note 1907 citation in Cassidy & LePage, 'I never do him one def ting', where *def* means 'single']

de facto *n.* (Aus.) one of the two partners in an unmarried but steady relationship. [Lat. *de facto*, in fact, as opposed to *de jure*, in law]

defense plant on a square's dim *phr.* [1940s] (US Black/Harlem) amateur night at the Apollo Theatre, Harlem. [many performers were working in defence plants as a 'day' job]

deffo *adv.* [1950s+] (Irish) definitely.

deficient *n.* [20C] a derog. term for a mentally deficient person.

definitely! *excl.* [1920s+] yes.

def jam *n.* [1980s+] an outstanding record or track. [DEF + JAM n.⁶]

def O.J. *n.* [1990s] an extremely smart, fashionable automobile. ['In "Rapper's Delight" the term "Death OJ" is used. In current slang "death" means something good, while "OJ" is a ref. to a big car. Erstwhile football star and all-around adman O.J. Simpson does Hertz commercials featuring Ford and Lincoln Mercury cars. If we add "death" to Ford and Lincoln Mercury cars ... we come up with the "Rapper's Delight" character driving off in a Lincoln Continental' (Nelson George, 1992)]

defrost the fridge, to *phr.* [1990s] to masturbate.

defug *v.* [1970s+] (society) to open the doors or windows in order to get some fresh air into a musty or smoke-filled room. [SE pfx. *de-* + FUG n.¹]

dege/dege-dege *adj.* [1950s+] (W.I. Rasta) little, skimpy, e.g. a *two dege-dege banana* (cf. DOGI). [Ewe *deká*, single, solitary]

degen *n.* **1** [late 17C–early 19C] a sword. **2** [19C] an artful person. [Ger. *Degen*, a sword]

deger *see* DACHA.

dehorn *n.* [1920s–50s] (US) **1** denatured or adulterated alcohol, as drunk by alcoholics, tramps etc. **2** a person who becomes ill through drinking such liquor (cf. DERAIL).

dehorned *adj.* [20C] (US) demoted, deprived of a position of power or authority. [SE *dehorn*, to deprive an animal of its horns]

deke *n.* [late 19C+] (US campus) a member of the Delta Kappa Epsilon fraternity.

dekko/decko *n.* [late 19C+] a look, a view. [Hind. *dekho*, look!]

delf *n.* [1990s] oneself; thus *go for delf*, *release your delf*. [? SE *self*]

Delhi belly *n.* [1940s+] food poisoning, epitomized by diarrhoea, suffered by tourists in India (cf. APPLE-BLOSSOM TWO-STEP). [*Delhi*, capital of India + SE *belly*]

deli *n.* [1940s+] (orig. US) a *deli*catessen. [abbr.]

delicate *n.* [mid-19C] **1** a fake subscription list carried by one who poses as an alms collector. **2** a begging-letter. [? the need for *delicacy* in pursuing these tricks]

delicatessen *n.* [1920s–30s] (US) a euph. for an illicit saloon (cf. CONFECTIONARY).

delish *adj.* [1920s–60s] *delish*ious. [abbr./pron.]

deliver a baby, to *phr.* [1960s+] (US gay) to remove one's trousers in order to expose one's erect penis.

deliver the goods, to *phr.* [1940s+] (orig. US) to meet expectations, to fulfil one's promises.

dell *n.* [16C–early 19C] a young woman on the tramp, spec. a young or virgin prostitute; thus *wild dell*, such a young woman conceived or born under a hedge. [poss. SE name *Doll* (although *dell* may predate it, since *OED* first use is 1560) or, in the way that CUNT is linked to Welsh *cwm*, a valley, then a pun on SE *dell*, also meaning valley]

dell *v.* [20C] to beat, to hit with the fists. [? SE *deal a blow*]

delo/deelo diam *n.* [late 19C] an old maid. [backsl.]

delog/dilog/dlog *n.* [mid-19C] gold (cf. GELD; GELT; GILT n.³; GINGERBREAD n.²; GOLD n.¹; GOREE; OCHRE; OLD MR GORY; REDGE; RED 'UN n.¹; RIDGE). [backsl.]

delo/deelo nam of the barrack *n.* [late 19C] the master of the house. [backsl. 'old man' + SE *barrack*]

delonammon *n.* [mid-19C+] an old woman. [backsl.]

delouse *v.* [1940s] (US) to free from something unpleasant.

Delphi *n.* [late 19C] the A*delphi* Theatre, the Strand, London WC2. [abbr.]

del. trem. *n.* [mid–late 19C] *del*irium *trem*ens (cf. DTS). [abbr.]

deluge *n.* [1920s–40s] a Delage car.

deluxe *adj.* [1970s+] wonderful, perfect, extreme. [ext. of SE use]

deluxe *adv.* [1970s+] to a remarkable extent. [DELUXE adj.]

delve *v.* [mid–late 19C] (US) to work hard. [ext. of SE *delve*, to dig]

dem *see* DEMN.

demander for glimmer *n.* [16C] (Und.) a female beggar who poses as the victim of a fire (complete with fake documents to prove it) and begs alms on that basis. [SE *demand* + GLIMMER]

demento *n.* [1970s+] (US) a crazy, eccentric person. [? the 1970s US radio show *Dr Demento*]

demi-bar *n.* [16C] (Und.) a type of crooked dice (cf. DEMY). [BARRED]

demi-beau *n.* [late 17C–early 18C] a would-be dandy. [SE *demi*, half + *beau*, a dandy]

demi-doss *n.* [late 19C–1910s] (tramp) a penny bed. [SE *demi*, half + DOSS n.¹; ? one gets only half a bed or the comfort is substandard]

demi-rep/-rip *n.* [18C+] a relatively classy prostitute, and a figure defined by Henry Fielding in *Tom Jones* (1749) as one 'whom everybody knows to be what nobody calls her'. [SE *demi*, half + abbr. *reputation* or *reprobate*. Note synon. SE *demi-mondaine*]

demn/dem *adj.* [late 17C–mid-19C] var. on DAMN!

demnition *adj.* [mid-19C] damnation, esp. in Charles Dickens's coinage 'demnition bow-wows' (*Nicholas Nickleby*, 1839).

demo *n.*[1] [late 19C+] (orig. Aus.) *demo*nstration (of a political or pressure-group nature). [abbr.]

demo *n.*[2] [1920s+] (US) a dime. [pron.]

demo *n.*[3] [1940s+] *demo*lition. [abbr.]

demo *n.*[4] [1960s+] a demonstration record or tape, used to promote a band's or individual musician's work. [abbr. SE *demonstration disc/record/tape*]

demo *n.*[5] [1980s] (drugs) a pipe for smoking crack cocaine. [DEMOLISH]

demob *n.* [1920s+] demobilization from the armed forces; thus [1940s+] *demob suit*, the suit issued to discharged men on their quitting the services.

demob happy *adj.* [1940s+] excited at the prospect of being released from a long-term, usu. tedious job. [orig. milit. use, the sense of the nervous happiness that overtakes men nearing demobilization and whose military service is nearing its end. Note prison use *gate-happy*, the sense of nervous excitement that takes over those whose sentence is almost up]

demolish *n.* [1980s+] (drugs) crack cocaine. [the effect of the drug on one's life + pun on SE *demolish*, 'put cracks into a wall']

demolition party *n.* [1980s+] (N.Z.) a party held by tenants who are leaving a house or flat, in which the fixtures and fittings are deliberately destroyed (cf. HOUSE-TRASHING).

demon *n.*[1] [late 19C] (Aus.) a veteran bushranger. [proper name *Van Dieman's Land*, modern Tasmania where bushranging was supposed to have been inaugurated]

demon *n.*[2] [1940s] (US Black/Harlem) a dime. [pron.]

demon *adj.* [late 19C+] extremely skilful. [the *locus classicus* is the description of the cricketer F.J. Spofforth as 'the demon bowler']

demon from hell *n.* [1980s+] (US campus) a conniving, deceitful woman. [title of a song by Sam Kinison, but harking back to a long line of woman = devil sl. usage]

demons *n.* [mid-19C–1950s] (Aus./N.Z.) generic term for detectives. [D *n.*[2] + SE *men*]

demon vino *n.* [1940s] cheap Italian red wine (cf. DAGO RED). [a pun on SE *demon rum*]

dempstered *adj.* [mid-late 17C] hanged. [Scot. *dempster*, the official who had the duty of repeating the sentence in open court]

demure as a whore/an old whore at a christening *phr.* [early 18C+] extremely demure and well-behaved (cf. HOPPING AROUND LIKE A GIN AT A CHRISTENING).

demy *n.* [16C–17C] a type of crooked dice (cf. BARRED). [DEMIBAR]

Den, the *n.*[1] **1** [late 18C–19C] a public house frequented by a regular group of cronies and thus named by them. **2** [late 18C+] a small room, usu. occupied by a single male. **3** [early–mid-19C] the Stock Exchange. **4** [20C] New Cross, London, thence *The Den*, the nickname for the Millwall Football Club ground. [(3) SE f. 1900]

den *n.*[2] [20C] **1** [1940s+] (US Und.) one's home (cf. CRIB *n.*[3]; PAD *n.*[2]). **2** [1970s+] (US Und.) a single prison cell (cf. HOUSE *n.*[1]).

dena/denar/dener *see* DEANER.

dennis *n.* [early 19C] a small walking-stick. [? its manufacturer]

Dennis the Menace *n.* [1980s+] MDMA (cf. ECSTASY).

dennyaiser *n.* [20C] (Aus.) a knockout blow. [var. on DINNYHAZER]

denso *n.* [1980s+] (US) a very unintelligent person (cf. CRAZO; WEIRDO *n.*). [SE *dense* + sfx. *-o*]

dentals *n.* [20C] (US) teeth, false teeth.

de-nut/denut *v.* [1950s+] to castrate (cf. DE-BALL). [SE pfx. *de-* + NUTS *n.*[2]]

dep *n.* [mid-19C+] **1** a porter at a cheap lodging house. **2** a deputy, e.g. a prison's deputy governor.

dep *v.* [mid-19C+] to act as deputy. [DEP *n.*]

depresh *n.* [1930s] (orig. US) the *Depress*ion, the financial and industrial slump of 1929 and subsequent years. [abbr./pron.]

depressed area *n.* [1930s+] the stomach. [? esp. when hungry]

depresso *n.* [1970s+] (US) a deeply depressed individual. [SE *depressed* + sfx. *-o*]

depresso *adj.* [1970s+] (US teen) depressing. [DEPRESSO *n.*]

depth charge *n.* [1950s+] (orig. milit./prison) any form of stodgy food.

deputy do-right *n.* [1970s+] (US Black) the police.

derail *n.* [1920s–50s] (US/N.Z.) **1** denatured or adulterated alcohol, as drunk by alcoholics, tramps etc. **2** a person who becomes ill through drinking such liquor (cf. DEHORN).

derby *n.* **1** [1930s+] the head. **2** [1950s–70s] (US Black) an act of oral sex. **3** [1950s–70s] a (woman's) head while engaged in fellatio. [? the *Derby hat*, which sits on the HEAD *n.*[9]]

derby *v.* [late 19C] (orig. sporting) to pawn. [the popular excuse that a pawned watch or similar possession has been 'lost at the Derby']

derby kelly *n.* [late 19C+] belly (cf. DARBY KELLY). [rhy. sl.]

derby winner *n.* [20C] (Aus.) a dinner. [rhy. sl.]

deri/derry *n.* [1960s+] *der*elict house or other dwelling (cf. DERO). [abbr.]

derm *n.* [1970s+] (S.Afr.) courage, bravery, staying power (cf. GUTS *n.*[2]). [fig. use of Afk. *derm*, intestines]

dern! *see* DARN!

dero/derro *n.* [1970s+] (Aus./N.Z.) a *der*elict person, a down-and-out (cf. DERI). [abbr. + sfx. *-o*]

derrey *n.* [mid-19C–1920s] an eyeglass. [? play on SE *derry down*, one 'looks down']

derrick *n.* **1** [17C] the gallows, the hangman, the hanging (cf. GREGORY; JACK KETCH). **2** [19C] the penis (cf. CRANK *n.*[5]). **3** [1910s–40s] (US) a shoplifter, esp. a proficient one. [*Derrick*, a well-known hangman at Tyburn, *c*.1600; he appears, *inter alia*, in Thomas Dekker's *The Bellman of London* (1608)]

derrick *v.* (US) **1** [20C] to execute someone or to kill oneself. **2** [1930s] to shoplift. [DERRICK *n.*]

derro *see* DERO.

derry *n.*[1] [late 19C+] (Aus./N.Z.) **1** an aversion towards. **2** a feud (cf. HAVE A DERRY ON). [dial. *deray*, an uproar; ult. Fr. *derroi*, confusion]

derry *n.*[2] *see* DERI.

derwenter *n.* [late 19C] (Aus.) a released convict. [a veteran of the prison at the *River Derwent*, Tasmania]

desert *n.* [late 19C] (society) a ladies-only club. [i.e. the relative absence of members]

desert canary *n.* [20C] (US) a mule, a donkey (cf. ARIZONA NIGHTINGALE).

desert rat *n.* [19C+] (US) **1** one who lives in the desert, esp. a prospector working in the desert. **2** a native of the southwestern states. [SE *desert rat*, the jerboa]

deserve a/the cushion, to *phr.* [late 18C] of a man, to deserve one's rest, esp. after one's wife has given birth to a male child.

desiccate *v.* [late 19C] (US) to be quiet. [pun on SE *desiccate*, to dry up]

designer drugs *n.* [1980s+] (drugs) a variety of drugs, most obviously ECSTASY, which are prepared from chemical formulae and have pre-ordained effects that can be used to influence the user's mood in a (relatively) predictable way. [play on 1980s vogue use of SE *designer*]

designer reality *n.* [1990s] (US) a conscious life that is determined by the planned ingestion of a variety of drugs (cf. DESIGNER DRUGS). [ext. of SE use]

deskie/deskateer *n.* [1980s+] (US) a desk clerk. [SE *desk* +

sfx. -ie/-ateer, the latter hinting at the spurious romance of *musketeer*]

desk piano *n.* [1940s] (US Black/Harlem) a typewriter (cf. OFFICE PIANO).

despatch *see* DISPATCH.

despatcher *see* DISPATCHER.

despatchers *n.* [19C] a form of false dice, on which the pips are arranged in wrong numbers (cf. DISPATCHER). [such dice *despatch*, i.e. 'send away' the victims]

despatches *see* DISPATCHES.

despatch one's cargo, to *phr.* [1910s–20s] to defecate.

desperado *n.* [1960s+] a gambler who bets heavily but cannot pay off when he loses. [SE *desperado*, a despairing, reckless man]

desperate *adj.* [20C] (Ulster) very bad. [ext. of SE use]

desperate *adv.* [mid-17C–mid-19C] desperately, extremely, very much. [ext. of SE use]

de-stat *v.* [1950s–60s] of a landlord or owner, to evict sitting tenants so as to gain possession of a valuable property, which can then be sold for a high profit. [SE pfx. *de-* + *stat(utory tenant)*]

destroyed *adv.* [1960s+] (drugs) under the influence of either drugs or drink (cf. BASTED).

destroyer *n.* [1950s] (W.I.) a deceitful man.

d.e.t. *n.* [1980s+] (drugs) *d*im*e*thyl*t*ryptamine. [abbr.]

det/dett *adj.* [1990s] first-rate, excellent, wonderful. [var. on DEF]

detec *n.* [late 19C] a *detec*tive (cf. TEC). [abbr.]

dethroned *adj.* [1950s–60s] (gay) for a gay man to be ejected from the public lavatory where he is looking for sex (cf. ABDICATED; QUEEN n.¹). [punning use of SE]

detox *n.* [1970s+] *detox*ification after a period of drink or drug addiction; thus *Detox*, any hospital or similar establishment that specializes in detoxification of drink or drug addicts. [abbr.]

detrimental *n.* **1** [19C] (society) a younger brother of the heir to an estate. **2** [19C] (society) an ineligible suitor. **3** [19C] a male flirt. **4** [20C] a male homosexual. [note primogeniture rendered such younger sons ineligible to inherit]

Detrimental Club *n.* [late 19C] the Reform Club. [reform was *detrimental* to good order]

Detroit pink *n.* [1980s+] (drugs) phencyclidine (cf. ACE n.³).

dett *see* DET.

deuce *n.*¹ **1** [17C+] euph. for the devil, e.g. *the deuce! what the deuce! so/who/how/where/when the deuce? (the) deuce take it! the deuce is in it! to play the deuce* (with), [mid–late 18C] *the deuce and all/much*, [mid-19C+] *the deuce to pay, a deuce of a mess.* **2** [17C+] synon. for syphilis or the plague, e.g. *deuce on him, the deuce on it.* [? SE *deuce*, the lowest, and thus the least lucky throw in dice]

deuce *n.*² **1** [late 17C–mid-19C] twopence. **2** [mid-19C+] two, a pair. **3** [late 19C–1960s] a useless gambler, a worthless individual. **4** [1920s+] second in sequence, order or rank. **5** [1920s+] (US prison) a two-year sentences (cf. TWO SPACES; TWO-SPOTTER). **6** [1920s–40s] (US) $2. **7** [1930s] (drugs) two marijuana cigarettes, sold together. **8** [1960s–70s] (US drugs) a $2 package of heroin. **9** [1970s] (US drugs) two pills. [SE *deuce*, the two in dice or cards; note (3) the deuce is the lowest card in the deck]

deuce/deucer *n.*³ [20C] (Aus.) a champion shearer capable of shearing 200 sheep in a day (cf. DREADNOUGHT n.²). [DEUCE n.² (2)]

Deuce, the *n.*⁴ [1980s+] New York's 42nd Street, between 7th and 8th Avenues. [until the shutting down of many cinemas and bookstores specializing in pornography in the early 1990s, this was the centre of mid-town vice; now it is a shrine to anodyne 'family values']

deuce *v.* [20C] (Aus.) to shear approximately 200 sheep in one day. [DEUCE n.³]

deuce and ace *n.* [late 19C] the face. [rhy. sl.]

deuce and a quarter *see* DEUCE 25.

deuced *adj.* [late 18C–late 19C] euph. for DAMNED; thus [mid-19C] *deuced infernal*, very unpleasant. [DEUCE n.¹ (1)]

deuce-deuce *n.* [1980s+] a .22 revolver or pistol (cf. DEUCE-FIVE). [DEUCE n.² (2)]

deucedly *adv.* [early 19C+] synon./euph. for *damnably*. [DEUCED]

deuce-five *n.* [1980s+] a .25 pistol (cf. DEUCE-DEUCE). [DEUCE n.² (2) + SE *five*]

deuce of benders *n.* [1930s–40s] (US Black/Harlem) the knees. [DEUCE n.² (2) + BENDER n.³ (2)]

deuce of clubs *n.* [1940s] (US) the fists, used for violent assaults; thus *play the deuce of clubs*, to beat someone up. [pun]

deuce of deaners *n.* [late 19C] 2 shillings (10p). [DEUCE n.² (2) + DEANER]

deuce of haircuts *n.* [1940s] (US Black/Harlem) two weeks. [a fortnightly haircut]

deuce of nods on the backbeat *phr.* [1940s] (US Black/Harlem) two days ago. [DEUCE n.² (2) + NOD n. + SE *backbeat*]

deuce of peekers *n.* [1940s] (US Black/Harlem) a pair of eyes. [DEUCE n.² (3) + SE *peek* v.]

deuce of ruffs *n.* [1940s] (US Black/Harlem) 20 cents. [DEUCE n.² (2) + RUFF]

deuce of ticks *n.* [1940s] (US Black/Harlem) two minutes. [DEUCE n.² (2) + TICK n.³]

deuce out *v.* [1940s+] (US) to back down, to act the coward. [the weakness of the *deuce* in a pack of cards]

deucer *n.*¹ *see* DEUCE n.³.

deucer *n.*² [1930s] (US) a $2 bill. [DEUCE n.² (2)]

deuce 25/deuce and a quarter *n.* [1960s+] (US Black/teen) **1** a Buick Electra 225. **2** any car with a 225 h.p. engine (cf. SAGGING DEUCE). [DEUCE n.² (2)]

deuceways *n.* [1950s] (US Black) a pair. [DEUCE n.² (2)]

deuce/dews/deux wins *n.* [late 17C–late 18C] twopence. [DEUCE n.² (2) + WIN n.]

deuseaville/daisyville *n.* [19C] (US) the countryside (cf. DEUSEAVILLE STAMPERS; DEWSE-A-VILL; GRASSVILLE). [SE *daisy* + sfx. -VILLE]

deuseaville stampers *n.* [late 17C–18C] (Und.) members of a criminal gang who wander the country roads and frequent country inns in the hope of picking up information about possible robberies (cf. CARRIER). [DEUSEAVILLE + STAMPERS]

deux wins *see* DEUCE WINS.

devalve *v.* [1980s+] (Ulster) to stop talking. [automotive use]

devastating *adj.* [1920s+] (society) shocking, disturbing, distasteful etc, e.g. *too, too utterly devastating*.

devil *n.*¹ **1** [mid–late 18C] a firework. **2** [19C] a piece of firewood soaked in resin. [the association of the Devil and fire. Early 19C+ uses of (1) are SE]

devil *n.*² **1** [late 18C] a grilled chop or steak (Grose (1796) cites a broiled, seasoned turkey-gizzard). **2** [19C] gin seasoned with chillies. [its being hot in one's mouth; subseq. use is SE]

devil *n.*³ [late 18C–mid-19C] spirit, temper, energy.

devil *n.*⁴ [late 19C] one who performs odd tasks for others, esp. in the literary/dramatic world. [legal jargon *devil*, a junior counsel who works without fee to learn the profession; ult. the *printer's devil*, the errand boy in a printshop]

devil *n.*⁵ [1920s+] (US Black, esp. Black Muslim) a White person. [the role of the White race in Black Muslim iconography]

devil, the *n.*⁶ [1980s+] (drugs) crack cocaine (cf. DEVIL'S

DANDRUFF; DEVIL'S DICK; DEVIL SMOKE). [its effects on the individual and the community]

devil v.[1] [19C+] (US) to tease, to harass.

devil v.[2] [late 19C+] to perform odd jobs for others. [DEVIL n.[4]]

devil among the tailors n. [mid-19C] an argument, a row.

devil and tommy see HELL AND TOMMY.

devil and Tom Walker!, the excl. [1940s–60s] an expression of annoyance, euph. for *what the devil?* (cf. WHAT THE DICKENS?).

devil a, the phr. [mid-17C+] a neg. intensifier, e.g. *the devil a thing there was …* .

devil-catcher n. [late 18C] a parson (cf. DEVIL-DRIVER). [his continuing campaign against sin]

devil-chaser n. [20C] (US) a volunteer preacher, without proper qualifications but capable of earnestly quoting what they have read in the Bible.

devil-dodger n. [mid-19C] **1** a clergyman (cf. FIRE-ESCAPE). **2** one who sometimes attends an Anglican church and sometimes a Quaker meeting.

devil doubt you phr. [late 19C] I agree completely, usu. in phr. *the devil doubt you – I don't*.

devil-driver n. [late 18C–early 19C] a parson. [var. on DEVIL-CATCHER]

devil is beating his wife with a shoulder of mutton, the phr. [late 18C] a remark offered when it is both raining and the sun is shining (cf. DEVIL'S SMILE; MONKEY'S WEDDING).

devil may dance in his pocket, the phr. [late 18C] said of one who has no money. ['The cross on our ancient coins being jocularly supposed to prevent him from visiting that place' (Grose, 1785)]

devil me arse! excl. [20C] (Anglo-Irish) a general excl.

devil of a … phr. [mid-18C+] a general intensifier, e.g. *a/the devil of a row*.

devil-on-the-coals n. [mid-19C] (Aus.) a small unleavened loaf hastily baked in hot ashes.

devil-pitcher n. [late 18C–late 19C] a clergyman (cf. DEVIL-DODGER). [SE *devil* + *pitch*, to throw]

devil's adj. [early 17C+] used in a variety of combs. to denote bad luck, evil intent, sinfulness and other negative qualities.

devil's bedpost/bedposts n. [mid-19C] the 4 of clubs, considered to be unlucky. [note whist jargon *devil's bedstead*, the 13th card of whichever suit has been led]

devil's bones n. [mid–late 17C] dice (cf. BONES n.[1]). [the pious identification of gaming with sin]

devil's books n. [early 18C–mid-19C] a pack or deck of playing cards (cf. BOOKS; DEVIL'S PICTURE BOOKS; DEVIL'S PICTURE GALLERY; DEVIL'S PICTURES; DEVIL'S PLAYTHINGS; DEVIL'S PRAYER BOOKS; KING'S BOOKS). [the pious identification of gaming with sin]

devil's box n. [20C] (US) a violin. [the sinfulness of music]

devil's brew n. [1940s] (US) whisky (cf. DEVIL'S DYE). [the sinfulness of alcohol]

devil-scolder n. [mid-19C] a clergyman (cf. DEVIL-DODGER).

devil's colours/livery n. [mid-19C] black and yellow. [? black for 'the pit' and yellow for the flames]

devil's cure! excl. [1920s–50s] (Irish) a mild excl.

devil's dandruff n. [1980s+] (drugs) crack cocaine (cf. DEVIL n.[6]). [the innate evil of CRACK n.[17]; a late 20C version of the older characterization of drinking and gambling]

devil's daughter n. [late 18C–mid-19C] a shrewish woman.

devil's delight n. [mid-19C+] a row, a fuss; thus *kick up the devil's delight*, to have a rowdy argument or make a disturbance.

devil's dick n. [1980s+] (US Black) a pipe for smoking crack cocaine (cf. DEVIL n.[6]). [SE *devil* + DICK n.[5] (1)]

devil's dinner-hour n. [late 19C] midnight.

devil's dozen n. [early 17C–mid-19C] the number thirteen. [a supposedly unlucky number]

devil's dung n. [mid-19C] asafoetida (*Ferula assa-foetida*). [Pers. *aza*, mastic + Lat. *foetida*, stinking; the substance is used both in medicine and in cooking]

devil's dust n.[1] [mid-19C] shoddy, i.e. yarn made from reprocessed woollen rags. [SE *devil*, the machine that shreds the old rags + *dust*, refuse]

devil's dust n.[2] [1980s+] (drugs) phencyclidine (cf. ACE n.[3]). [SE *devil* + (ANGEL) DUST]

devil's dye n. [mid-19C] (US) whisky (cf. DEVIL'S BREW). [the sinfulness of alcohol]

devil's eyewater see EYEWATER.

devil's four-poster n. [mid-19C] the 4 of clubs (cf. DEVIL'S BEDPOST). [clubs, being black, are characterized as 'devilish']

devil's guts n. [mid-17C–early 19C] a surveyor's chain. ['so called by farmers, who do not like their land should be measured by their landlords' (Grose, 1785)]

devil's half-acre n. [20C] (US) **1** a rough or unworkable piece of land. **2** the rough area of a town.

devil's livery see DEVIL'S COLOURS.

devil's luck/luck and my own n. [late 19C+] extremely poor luck.

devil smoke n. [1980s+] (drugs) crack cocaine (cf. DEVIL n.[6]). [its deleterious effects]

devil's neckerchief/neckerchief on the way to Redriffe n. [18C] the hangman's noose.

devil's own …, the phr. [late 18C+] a phr. implying difficulty or problems, e.g. *I've had the devil's own business finding my way*.

devil's own boy n. [19C] a young villain.

devil's own luck n. [19C+] incredible luck, usu. very good, but occas. bad.

devil's own ship n. [19C] a pirate ship.

devil's picture books n. [late 18C–late 19C] a pack of playing cards (cf. DEVIL'S BOOKS). [the puritan's fear of gambling]

devil's picture gallery n. [1920s] a pack of playing cards (cf. DEVIL'S BOOKS). [the puritan's fear of gambling]

devil's pictures n. [1910s] a pack of playing cards (cf. DEVIL'S BOOKS). [the puritan's fear of gambling]

devil's playthings n. [19C] a pack of playing cards (cf. DEVIL'S BOOKS). [the puritan's fear of gambling]

devil's prayer books n. [mid-17C–early 18C] a pack of playing cards. [var. on DEVIL'S BOOKS]

devil's rattle-bag n. [early 18C–mid-19C] a bishop's summons. [insultingly joc. ref. to the clergy]

devil's regiment/regiment of the line n. [19C] prisoners. [coined by Thomas Carlyle (1795–1881)]

devil's rotgut n. [late 19C] particularly debilitating cheap spirits or wine. [DEVIL'S + ROTGUT]

devil's smiles n. [19C] spring weather, esp. the alternating sun and showers of a 'typical' April (cf. DEVIL IS BEATING HIS WIFE WITH A SHOULDER OF MUTTON).

devil's tattoo n. [late 18C–19C] the tapping of one's fingers or feet, often through boredom or irritation. [? pvb. 'The devil finds work for idle hands']

devil's teeth n. [mid-19C] dice. [the puritan's fear of gambling]

devil take … phr. [16C+] a phr. used with a suitable object to imply one's irritation with that object.

devil-teaser n. [1910s] (US) a clergyman.

devil thank you! excl. [1940s] (Irish) a mild excl.

devil to pay phr. [18C+] the promise of unspecified but definite problems in the future, which have been caused by an action in the present (cf. DEVIL TO PAY AND NO PITCH HOT). [supposed Faustian bargains made between mortals and the Devil, the 'live now and pay later' of the 18C]

devil to pay and no pitch hot *phr.* **1** [18C+] a mess, a chaotic situation. **2** [early 18C–mid-19C] trouble in prospect or coming as a consequence (cf. DEVIL TO PAY; HELL TO PAY AND NO PITCH HOT). [naut. jargon *pay*, to caulk + *devil*, a seam near the ship's keel]

devious *adj.* [1990s] (US teen) extreme. [ext. of SE use]

devirginize *v.* [1980s+] to relieve someone of their virginity, usu. in a sexual context, but equally applicable to any first experience or rite of teenage passage, e.g. smoking marijuana, taking LSD. [a nonce-word that is grammatically correct – *de* + *virgin* + *ize* – but linguistically atrocious]

devotional habits *n.* [mid-19C] used of a horse that persists in falling to its knees. [pun on SE]

dew *n.* **1** [mid-19C] (Anglo-Irish/US) whisky, usu. illicitly distilled (cf. MOUNTAIN DEW). **2** [1970s+] (US drugs) marijuana. [(2) depends on illegality rather than on any image of wetness]

dewbaby *n.* [1960s] (US Black) a very dark-skinned male child.

dew-beaters *n.* **1** [17C–early 19C] those who get up early, i.e. before the dew has evaporated. **2** [late 18C–late 19C] (Und.) the feet (cf. BEATER-CASES; DAISY-BEATERS; DEW-DUSTERS). [note Norfolk dial. *dew-beaters*, heavy, waterproof shoes]

dew-bit *n.* [mid-19C] a small meal or portion of food taken in the early morning, before the regular breakfast (cf. DEW-DRINK).

dew-drink *n.* [mid-19C] a drink served to farm labourers before they start work (cf. DEW-BIT).

dewdrop *n.* **1** [1900s–10s] the lock on a gas-meter. **2** [20C] a drop of mucus lodged at the opening of a nostril and hanging there before removal.

dewdrops in the nose *n.* [18C] a drop of mucus lodged at the opening of a nostril (cf. DEWDROP).

dew-dusters *n.* [19C] the feet (cf. DEW-BEATERS).

dewey *n.* [mid-19C+] (Polari) two. [Ital. *due*, two]

dew-flaps *n.* [1990s] the labia. [var. on PISS FLAPS]

dewitted *adj.* [late 17C–18C] murdered by a mob, lynched. [proper name of the brothers Jan and Cornelius *De Witt*, Dutch statesmen, who were cut to pieces by a mob in 1672. Compare the similarly eponymous SE *lynched*]

dew o' Ben Nevis *n.* [late 19C–1900s] whisky (cf. MOUNTAIN DEW).

dews *n.* [1970s+] (drugs) $10 worth of drugs. [DEUCE *n.*[2] (2); i.e. two $5 bags]

dews wins *see* DEUCE WINS.

dewse-a-vill *n.* [16C] (Und.) the country (cf. DEUSEAVILLE). [E.P. suggests a corruption of daisy-ville but *dewse* = deuce = the devil and thus a generic neg. If London, the big city is ROME-VILLE, lit. 'good town', might not the country, its opposite, be 'bad town'?]

dewskitch *n.* [mid-19C] a severe beating, a good thrashing. [? 'catch one's due']

dew-treaders *n.* [19C] the feet. [var. on DAISY-BEATERS]

dex *n.* [1950s+] *dex*edrine, a form of amphetamine (cf. DEXIES; DEXO). [abbr.]

dex *v.* [1950s+] (drugs) to take dexedrine. [DEX *n.*]

dexies/dexy *n.* [1950s+] (drugs) *dex*edrine (cf. DEX *n.*). [abbr.]

dexo *n.* [1940s+] (Aus. drugs) *dex*edrine (cf. DEX *n.*). [abbr. + sfx. -o]

dexter *n.* [late 18C–early 19C] the right hand. [Lat. *dexter*, right]

dexy *see* DEXIES.

d.f. *n.* [1910s–30s] (US) a *d*amned *f*ool (cf. B.F.). [abbr.]

d.f.f.l. *phr.* [1950s+] *d*ope *f*orever, *f*orever *l*oaded, a popular patch worn by Hell's Angels, hippies, and other 'outlaws'. [abbr.]

DFs *n.* [1970s+] (drugs) DF 118s, painkillers mainly made of synthetic codeine.

dhobi/dhoby/dobee *n.* [mid-19C+] (Anglo-Ind.) **1** a washer-woman. **2** the laundry. [Hind. *dhob*, washing]

diabolical *adj.* [1950s+] outrageous, disgraceful, disgracefully bad, esp. in phr. *diabolical liberty*. [the word remains essentially SE, but for whatever reason was plucked out for this definitely sl. usage]

Diagonal Street *n.* [1980s+] (S.Afr.) the Johannesburg Stock Exchange (cf. HOLLARD STREET). [its address]

dial *n.* [early 19C+] the human face. [SE *dial*, a clock-face]

dialogue *n.* [1980s] (US teen) a conversation. esp. one person's monologue.

dial-plate/-piece *n.* [early 19C] the human face (cf. DIAL). [SE *dial-plate*, the face plate of a clock]

Dials, the *n.* [early 19C+] Seven Dials, London WC2. [in its 18C–19C prime one of London's best known criminal enclaves]

diambista *n.* [1950s+] (drugs) marijuana. [Sp.]

diamond *adj.* [1990s] first-rate, excellent (cf. PEARL *adj.*). [the value of the precious stone]

diamond-cracking *n.* [late 19C–1910s] (Aus.) breaking rocks as part of one's prison sentence; thus *diamond-cracker*, one who is working off such a sentence.

diamonds *n.* [1960s] (US gay) the testicles (cf. BAUBLES). [play on CROWN JEWELS]

Diana Dors *n.* [1960s+] (bingo) the number 44, 'all the fours'. [rhy. sl.; ult. UK actress and personality *Diana Dors* (1931–84)]

diaper *n.* **1** [1930s–40s] clothes; thus *pin one's diapers on*, to get dressed. **2** [1970s+] (US Black) a sanitary towel; thus *diaper the baby*, to put on a sanitary towel. [16C SE, but now SAmE *diaper*, a nappy]

diarrhoea-mouth *n.* [1970s+] (US) a very talkative individual (cf. DIARRHOEA OF THE MOUTH).

diarrhoea of the mouth/jawbone *phr.* [1940s+] (US) excessive loquacity (cf. VERBAL DIARRHOEA).

diasticutis/diasticurious *n.* [1930s] (US Black) the buttocks, the posterior. [cod Latin formation based on ASS (*see* ARSE *n.*[1])]

dib *n.* [1930s+] a share. [DIBS!]

dibbi dibbi *n.* [1980s+] (W.I./UK Black teen) a small and insignificant thing or person. [DIBBI DIBBI *adj.*]

dibbi dibbi *adj.* [1980s+] (W.I./UK Black teen) stupid, useless, not resourceful, worthless. [? pron. of SE *little*]

dibble *n.*[1] [early 17C] a moustache. [ety. unknown]

dibble *n.*[2] [19C] the penis (cf. BAT *n.*[7]). [SE *dibbler*, a gardening implement with which one drills holes for planting]

dibble *n.*[3] [1990s] (drugs) a policeman. [proper name of *Officer Dibble*, a character in the TV cartoon series *Top Cat*]

dibble-dabble *n.* [mid-16C–late 18C] **1** noisy splashing. **2** rubbish, nonsense. [SE *dibble*, to fish by letting the bait (usually a natural insect) dip and bob lightly on the water + redup.]

dibbs/dibs *n.* **1** [early 19C+] money. **2** [1930s] $1. [*dibs* or *dibstones*, a children's game played with the knuckle-bones of sheep]

dib-dabs *n.* [1940s] delirium tremens (cf. COME THE ABDABS). [echoic of the babbling of the sufferer]

dibs *see* DIBBS.

dibs!/dibs on! *excl.* [1930s+] (US) that's mine! I want to do that, I want a share! A child's term used to claim the whole or an equal part of an object; the neg. response to the cry is *fen dibs* (cf. AIKIES!). [a corruption of SE, *division* or *divide*]

dibs and dabs *n.* [20C] (Aus.) crabs (body lice). [rhy. sl.]

dibs on! *see* DIBS!

dic/dick *n.* [mid-19C+] **1** a *dic*tionary. **2** 'jaw-breaking', pretentious language. [abbr.; (2) is fig. use of (1)]

dice *v.* [1940s–50s] (Aus.) to reject, to throw away, to leave alone. [an image of tossing a die and losing]

dice capper n. [18C+] one who makes and uses shaved or loaded dice. [CAPPER n.¹ (1)]

dice mechanic n. [20C] (orig. Aus./US) an expert dice cheat. [SE *dice* + MECHANIC]

dicer n. [early–mid-19C] a hat. [its resemblance to a dice-box]

dicey adj. [1950s+] (orig. RAF jargon) risky, dangerous, dubious. [gambling imagery]

dichty see DICTY.

dick n.¹ [mid-16C+] a man, a fellow. [generic use of proper name]

dick n.² [mid–late 19C] a riding whip. [? link to a celebrated contemporary coachman Walter Dickson, nicknamed Dickie the Driver]

dick n.³ [mid–late 19C] an oath, a statement, an affidavit; thus to *take one's dick*, to take one's declaration (cf. DAVY). [abbr. SE *declaration*]

dick n.⁴ see DIC.

dick n.⁵ **1** [late 19C+] the penis. **2** [1930s–40s; 1980s+] (US Black) a term of address between males. **3** [1950s] sexual intercourse (with a man). **4** [1960s+] (US teen) an unattractive male, esp. one who has an overly high self-image. **5** [1960s+] (US) a mean or offensive person. **6** [1960s+] a fool (cf. DICKHEAD). [all fig. uses of (1), itself based on DICK n.¹]

dick n.⁶ (US) **1** [late 19C+] a detective. **2** [20C] a policeman. [? gypsy use *dicked*, being watched (cf. DEKKO), DICK v.¹ or abbr. SE *detective*; the link to the fictional *Dick Tracy* (created 1931) is chronologically impossible]

dick n.⁷ [1910s] a perambulator. [? Sheffield dial. a leather apron worn by children + link to Du. *dek*, a cover]

dick n.⁸ [1910s+] nothing, e.g. *we ain't got dick*. [use of DICK n.⁵ (1) in synon. manner as FUCK n.²; SHIT n.⁴ (4)]

dick n.⁹ [1960s] (US) the clitoris. [COCK n.² (2). Note US Blacks have always preferred *dick* to *cock* for penis since coming from the south; *cock* means vagina]

dick v.¹ [mid-19C] to look at (cf. DEKKO). [northern dial.]

dick v.² **1** [20C] (mainly US Black) to have sexual intercourse. **2** [1950s+] (US) to ruin, to botch, to make a mess of. **3** [1960s+] (US) to trick or deceive, to be unfair to, to victimize (cf. FUCK AROUND v.¹; FUCK OVER). [DICK n.⁵ (1); (2) and (3) fig. uses]

dick around v. **1** [1940s+] to be sexually promiscuous, a womanizer. **2** [1960s+] to waste time, to dither. [DICKER v., but with overtones of acting like a DICK n.⁵ (1)]

dickbrain n. [1970s+] (US) a fool; thus a general derog. term (cf. BAKEBRAIN; DICKHEAD). [DICK n.⁵ (1) + sfx. -*brain*]

dick breath n. **1** [1970s+] (US) an unpleasant person. **2** [1990s] anyone, esp. a superior, who has foul breath. [DICK n.⁵ (1) + SE *breath*]

dick drink n. [1980s+] (US gay) semen. [DICK n.⁵ (1) + SE *drink*]

Dick Dunn n. [late 19C+] the sun. [rhy. sl. Richard 'Dick' Dunn (d.1905) was a well-known 'ready-money' bookmaker; there may have been an additional nod to the shine of the diamonds with which this 'Leviathan' of the turf adorned himself]

dicked adj.¹ [20C] euph. for DAMNED, e.g. *I'll be dicked!*

dicked adj.² (US) [1970s+] assured of success. [DICK n.⁵ (1); thus image of potency]

dicked in the nob phr. [early–mid-19C] insane. [ety. unknown; the sexual use of DICK v.², which would work in fig. use, is too late]

dicken! excl. [late 19C+] (Aus./N.Z.) a mild oath (cf. DICKENS), esp. in comb. *dicken on/to that!*, enough of that, the hell with that.

dickens n. [late 16C+] a euph. for the devil, most commonly in phr. *what the dickens?*; also as [17C–18C] *dickings*, [18C–19C] *dickons*, [19C] *dickins*. [all euph. for SE *devil*]

dicker n. [20C] a dictionary. [abbr. SE *dictionary* + 'Oxford' sfx. -*er*]

dicker/dicker around v. [20C] (US) to waste time, to dither (cf. DICK AROUND). [SE *dicker*, to bargain. ult. 13C *dicker* (Lat. *decuria*, a unit of 10 hides used in bartering)]

dickery n. [late 19C+] **1** a clock. **2** the penis (cf. DICKORY-DOCK). [rhy. sl. (2) *dickory dock* = COCK n.² (1)]

dickey (unless specified below) see DICKY for all uses of and combs.

dickey-dido n. **1** [mid-19C+] a complete fool. **2** [20C] the vagina and female pubic area.

dickface n. [1970s+] (orig. US campus) a general term of derision (cf. DICKNOSE). [DICK n.⁵ (1) + SE *face*]

dick-fingered adj. [1980s+] (US) maladroit. [DICK n.⁵ (1) + sfx. -*fingered*]

dickhead n. [1960s+] **1** a fool, an incompetent. **2** a general term of abuse (cf. DICK n.⁵; DICKBRAIN; DICKLICK; DILDO n.; DILL; DILLBRAIN; DILLYPOT; DINGALING n.²; DINGBAT n.⁹; DIPSHIT; DIPSTICK; DIPWAD; DOLLYPOT; DORK n.²; DORKBRAIN; DORKHEAD; DUMMY n.¹; GADSO n.; GOOBER n.¹; HORSE'S ASS; HORSE'S HANGDOWN; JACOB n.²; LOBCOCK; MOPSTICK; PANHANDLE n.²; PILLOCK n.²; PLONKER; PRICK; PUD n.²; PUTZ; SCHMUCK; TOM n.¹; TOOLHEAD; WEENIE n.¹; WOODEN SPOON n.¹; YOYO n.¹; YUTZ). [DICK n.⁵ (1) + sfx. -HEAD (1)]

dickhound n. [1980s+] (US Black) a promiscuous woman (cf. COCK-HOUND; PUSSY-HOUND). [DICK n.⁵ (1) + sfx. -HOUND]

dick in the green phr. [19C] inferior, second-rate (cf. DICKY adj.¹).

dickless adj. [1980s+] (orig. US) a general term of abuse. [DICK n.⁶ (1) + sfx. -*less*]

dickless tracy n. [1960s+] (US Und.) a woman police officer. [puns on DICK n.⁶ (1) + cartoon strip *Dick Tracy* + common female name *Tracey*]

dicklick n. [1980s+] **1** (US) a fool, an idiot, an unpleasant person (cf. DICKHEAD). **2** (US gay) fellatio. [backform. of DICKLICKER]

dicklicker n. [1960s+] **1** a fellator or fellatrix (cf. COCKSUCKER). **2** an unpleasant person; thus *dicklicking*. [DICK n.⁵ (1) + SE *licker*]

dick-nailer n. [19C+] (US) something outstanding, exceptional of its type. [NAIL v. (11)]

dicknose n. [1970s+] (orig. US) a general term of derision (cf. DICKFACE). [DICK n.⁵ (1) + SE *nose*]

dick off v. [1940s+] (US) to waste time, to shirk, to avoid work (cf. FUCK OFF v.). [DICK v.² (2) + SE *off*]

dickory dock n. **1** [late 19C+] a clock. **2** [20C] the penis (cf. DICK n.⁵). [rhy. sl. *dickory dock* = COCK n.² (1). The nursery rhyme from which this comes is itself a Romany creation. According to Gerald Denley: 'Hickory is derived from the Romany "Ek Ore" meaning one o'clock. The word for one in Romany varies according to the tribe, so it is either "ek", "yek" or "ik". The stress is on the first vowel, so that "ek ore" is pronounced as one word. Dickory Dock is often described as London rhyming slang. But it could mean the *dock* where the *dick* puts you when you are caught *choring* or stealing. The word for a Gypsyman is either a *rom* or a *mush*. This last word derives from the Sanskrit and means a mouse or a thief']

dick out v. [1970s+] (US) to persevere, to endure. [fig. use of DICK n.⁵ (1)]

dick/prick peddler n. [1960s+] a male prostitute who takes only active roles with his clients (cf. ASS PEDDLER). [DICK n.⁵ (1)/PRICK + SE *peddler*]

dick's hatband n. [late 18C+] anything makeshift (cf. QUEER AS DICK'S HATBAND; TIGHT AS DICK'S HATBAND). [the orig. hatband was a narrow strip of material wrapped around the hat, esp. as a badge of mourning. The identity of Dick is not known – 'some local character or half-wit' (*OED*) – but his hatband was presumably an improvised and absurd object]

dick shit *n.* [1980s+] (orig. US) absolutely nothing; always used with a qualifying neg. v., e.g. *you don't know dick shit about*... etc (cf. JACKSHIT n.). [DICK n.⁸ + SHIT n.⁴ (4)]

dick-shriveler *n.* [1980s+] (US) an unpleasant person. [fig. use of DICK n.⁵ (1) + SE *shriveller*]

dick smith *n.* [19C+] (US) **1** a solitary drinker (cf. JIMMY WOODSER). **2** a mean or reclusive person. [logger jargon; ult. *Richard Penn Smith* (1790–1854), a US playwright celebrated for his unsociability – and his plagiarism of others]

dick someone around *v.* [1980s+] (US) to harass, to impose on, to irritate, to 'mess someone about' (cf. FUCK ABOUT). [DICK v.² (2) + SE *around*]

dick spanner *n.* [1990s] a fool, an idiot. [DICK n.⁵ (6) + SE *spanner*; the innate absurdity of such a 'tool', thus ? + over-riding pun]

dicksplash *n.* [1990s] **1** a semen stain. **2** an unpleasant, unpopular person. [DICK n.⁵ (1) + SE *splash*]

dickstring *n.* [1960s+] (US Black) the notional governor of a man's ability to attain an erection. [DICK n.⁵ (1) + SE *string*]

dicksucker *n.* [1970s+] (US) **1** a fellator. **2** a general derog. term (cf. COCKSUCKER). [DICK n.⁵ (1) + SE *sucker*]

dicksucking *n.* [1970s+] fellatio. [DICKSUCKER]

dicksucking *adj.* [1970s+] unpleasant, disgusting, a general term of abuse. [fig. use of DICKSUCKING n.]

dicktease *v.* [1960s+] (orig. US) usu. of a woman, to appear to be offering unrestrained sexual favours but stopping short of intercourse, leaving the man frustrated (cf. COCKTEASE). [DICK n.⁵ (1) + SE *tease*]

dickteaser *n.* [1960s+] one who provokes their partner sexually but stops short of intercourse (cf. COCKTEASER). [DICKTEASE]

dick thang *n.* [1990s] (US campus) something charac-teristically associated with males. [DICK n.⁵ (1) + joc. pron. of SE *thing*; lit. 'a penis thing']

Dick Tracy *n.* [1930s–40s] a policeman, esp. a detective. [the cartoon strip created by Chester Gould in 1931 for the Chicago *Tribune*/New York *News* syndicate; ult. DICK n.⁶ (1) + SE *trace*]]

Dick Turpin *n.* [1930s] the number thirteen. [rhy. sl.; *Dick Turpin* (1705–39) was England's best known highwayman]

dickty *see* DICTY.

dickwad *n.* [1980s+] (US campus) a fool, an idiot, an un-pleasant person (cf. DICKHEAD; DICKWEED). [DICK n.⁵ (6) + WAD n.⁴]

dickweed *n.* (US) **1** [1980s+] a fool (cf. DICKWAD). **2** [1990s] the pubic hair. [DICK n.⁵ (1) + SE *weed*]

dick wheat *n.* [1990s] (US) the male pubic hair (cf. DICK n.⁵ (1) + SE *wheat*]

dick-whupped *adj.* [1990s] (US Black) describing a woman so besotted with her lover that she allows herself to be exploited and generally treated badly (cf. PUSSY-WHIPPED). [DICK n.⁵ (1) + SE *whipped*]

dick with *v.* [1970s+] (US) to mess someone around, to fool around with. [DICK v.² (3)]

dicky/dickey *n.*¹ **1** [late 18C] a worn-out shirt. **2** [early 19C] a woman's under-petticoat. **3** [early 19C+] a detachable shirt-front. **4** [mid–late 19C] a shirt-collar. **5** [late 19C] a detachable nameplate, used on a tradesman's van. [? link to dial. *dick*, a leather apron]

dicky/dickey *n.*² **1** [19C] the seat in a carriage on which the driver sits, often ext. as *dicky-box*. **2** [19C] a seat at the back of a carriage for servants etc, or of a mail-coach for the guard. **3** [1910s–20s] an extra seat at the back of a two-seater motor-car, which can be closed down when not in use. [? *Dicky*, used as a generic name for a coachman]

dicky/dickey *n.*³ [19C] a donkey (cf. BALDWIN). [East Anglian dial.; the habit of using proper names as sl. terms for donkeys]

dicky/dickey *n.*⁴ [19C+] a shirt. [rhy. sl. *dicky dirt* = shirt; despite obvious links to DICKY n.¹ (1), this appears to be a discreet coinage]

dicky *n.*⁵ [mid-19C–1920s] an affidavit (cf. DAVID). [SE *declaration*]

dicky/dickey *n.*⁶ [late 19C] a dandy, a 'swell'. [? his DICKY n.¹ (3) shirt-front; note naut. jargon *dickey*, an officer acting in commission]

dicky *n.*⁷ [late 19C+] **1** a dictionary. **2** any fine or long-winded vocabulary. [ext. of DICK n.²]

dicky *n.*⁸ [late 19C+] the penis. [ext. of DICK n.⁵ (1)]

dicky/dickey *adj.*¹ [late 18C+] **1** of things, second-rate, of poor quality, sub-standard, not working as they should. **2** of people or animals, sickly, unhealthy. **3** of plans, risky, ill-advised, overly complex. **4** (N.Z.) stupid. [dial.]

dicky/dickey *adj.*² [late 19C–1900s] smart, fashionable. [DICKY n.⁶]

dicky-/dickey-bird *n.*¹ **1** [mid-19C+] a small bird. **2** [mid-19C] a prostitute, esp. as *naughty dicky-bird*. **3** [mid-19C] a louse. **4** [late 19C] a professional singer (cf. CANARY n.⁸). **5** [1950s] the penis (cf. BIRD n.⁶).

dicky-/dickey-bird *n.*² [1930s+] a word; thus *not a dicky-bird*, lit. 'not a word', i.e. nothing at all. [rhy. sl.]

dicky-check *n.* [1980s+] (US Black) the inspection by police of one's genitals as a possible hiding-place for drugs. [DICKY n.⁸ (1) + SE *check*]

dicky diddle *n.* [20C] urine. [DICKY DIDDLE v.]

dicky diddle *v.* [20C] to urinate. [rhy. sl. *dicky diddle* = PIDDLE v.]

dicky dirt *n.* [late 19C+] a shirt (cf. DICKY n.⁴; DINKY DIRT). [rhy. sl.; note Dickie Dirts, a chain of cut-price shirt and jeans shops in late 1970s London]

dicky-/dickey-lagger *n.* [late 19C] a bird-catcher. [DICKY-BIRD n.¹ + LAG v.² (3)]

dicky lee *n.* [20C] (Aus.) tea (cf. ROSIE LEA). [rhy. sl.]

dicky-legged *adj.* [late 19C] a racehorse with unsound legs. [DICKY adj.¹ + SE *legged*]

dicky-licker *n.* [1930s+] (orig. US) **1** a homosexual. **2** a fellatrix. [var. on DICKLICKER]

dicky sam *n.* [mid-19C] a native of Liverpool. [Lancashire dial.]

dicky ticker *n.* [late 19C+] a weak heart. [DICKY adj.¹ + TICKER n.² (2)]

dicky up *v.* [20C] to adorn oneself, to dress up (cf. DIKE DOWN). [DICKY n.¹, esp. as a dress shirt]

dicky-waver *n.* [1970s+] (US) an exhibitionist. [DICKY n.⁸ + SE *waver*]

dicty/dichty/dickty/dictee *n.* [1920s+] (US Black) a stuck-up, conceited, snobbish person. [? SE *decked*, dressed (lit. covered)]

dicty/dichty/dickty/dictee *adj.* [1920s+] (US Black) **1** arrogant, snobbish, conceited. **2** elegant, high-class, sophist-icated. **3** of clothes, elegant, chic, smart. [? SE *decked*, dressed; lit. 'covered']

di-da, di-da, di-da *phr.* [1930s+] a phr. used to imply that the previous speaker's words have been overly tedious, drawn-out etc (cf. BLAH, BLAH, BLAH). [echoic]

diddicoi/diddiki/didekei/dideki *n.* [mid-19C+] a gypsy. [Rom.]

diddies/diddys *n.* [late 18C+] breasts. [dial. *diddy*, the female breast, usu. when feeding a baby; also used of animals. Note mispron. of TITTY n.²]

diddiki *see* DIDDICOI.

diddle *n.*¹ [late 17C–mid-19C] **1** gin; thus *diddle-cove*, a keeper of a gin or liquor tavern. **2** (US) liquor in general. [SE *diddle*, to walk unsteadily; i.e. the effects of the liquor]

diddle *n.*² [early 19C] the sound of a fiddle.

diddle *n.*³ [mid-19C+] **1** the penis. **2** sexual intercourse. **3** masturbation. [DIDDLE v.²]

diddle *n.*⁴ [late 19C+] a swindle. [DIDDLE v.¹ (2), (3)]

diddle *v.*¹ **1** [early 19C] to waste time; thus *diddle away*, to waste time. **2** [19C+] to cheat or swindle (cf. TARADIDDLE). **3** to victimize, to 'do'; thus *diddle out of*, to swindle out of. **4** [19C] to do for, to ruin, to kill. [(1) fig. use of SE *diddle*, to jerk from side to side, to quiver; (2) ? *diddler*, a swindler, fraud, itself f. Jeremy Diddler, the chief character in James Kenney's farce *Raising the Wind* (1803) and ult. f. DIDDLE v.¹ (1); or OE *didrian*, *dydrian*, to deceive, delude]

diddle *v.*² [mid-19C+] **1** to molest sexually. **2** to have sexual intercourse. **3** (orig. US) to masturbate. [SE *diddle*, to jerk from side to side + *didder*, to shake, to quiver]

diddle-daddle *n.* [19C] nonsense.

diddle daddle *v.* [19C] to dawdle, to waste time. [SE *diddle*, to dawdle]

diddle-diddle *n.* [early 18C] violin music. [DIDDLE n.² + redup.]

diddler/jeremy diddler *n.*¹ [early 19C] a cheat, a confidence trickster. [DIDDLE v.¹ (2)]

diddler *n.*² [19C] a small boy's penis (cf. TIDDLER). [DIDDLE n.³ (1)]

diddler *n.*³ [20C] (US Und.) child molester. [DIDDLE v.² (1)]

diddle the dinky, to *phr.* [1980s+] to masturbate. [DIDDLE v.¹ (3) + DINKY n.³]

diddleums *n.* [1920s+] (Aus.) delirium tremens.

diddley/diddly *n.* [1920s+] **1** (orig. US Black) anything unimportant or insignificant, usu. in phr. *not give a diddley*, couldn't care less. **2** (Irish) a small monetary payment; thus the *diddley club*, a savings club used by the poor, to which one could contribute as little as one halfpenny a week.

diddley/diddly *adj.* (US) **1** [1960s+] crazy, eccentric. **2** [1960s+] insignificant, unimportant, worthless. [DIDDLEY n.]

diddley-/diddly-/diddy-bop *adj.* [1960s+] (US Black) immature, unpleasant, stupid (cf. DIDDLY-SQUAT).

diddley-bop *v. see* DIDDY-BOP v.

diddley-bopper *n. see* DIDDLY-BOPPER.

diddley-/diddly-damn *adj.* [1920s–70s] (US) insignificant, irritating. [DIDDLEY adj. + DAMN]

diddley-/diddly-dick *n.* [1970s] (US) something of no value. [var. on DIDDLEY-SHIT + DICK n.⁸]

diddley-hop *n.* [1950s–60s] (US teen) a top gang fighter.

diddley-poo/diddly-poop *n.* [1950s+] (usu. juv.) excreta (cf. DIDDLY-SQUAT). [DIDDLEY n. (1) + POO n.¹]

diddley-pout *n.* [1950s+] the vagina. [? DIDDLE n.³ (1) for which, when stimulated, it 'pouts']

diddley-shit *adj.* [1950s+] (US) minimal, small, insignificant (cf. DIDDLY-SQUAT). [DIDDLEY adj. (2) + SHIT n.⁴ (4)]

diddling *n.* [early 19C+] petty criminality, cheating, constant borrowing. [DIDDLE v.¹ (2)]

diddlum *adj.* [1930s] illicit, crooked, swindling. [pron. of DIDDLE v.¹ (2) + SE *them*]

diddly *see* DIDDLEY.

diddly-bop *adj. see* DIDDLEY-BOP adj.

diddly-bop *v. see* DIDDY-BOP v.

diddly-bopper / diddley-bopper / diddy-bopper / ditty-bopper *n.* [1950s+] (US Black) a young street thug, a gang fighter (cf. DIDDY-BOP n.). [DIDDLY-BOP v.]

diddly-bopping *see* DIDDY-BOPPING.

diddly-damn *see* DIDDLEY-DAMN.

diddly-dick *see* DIDDLEY-DICK.

diddly-poop *see* DIDDLEY-POO.

diddly-squat *n.* [1950s+] (US) nothing, zero; thus *it don't mean diddly-squat*, it is totally irrelevant, unimportant. [euph. var. on DOODLEY-SQUAT]

diddlywhacker *n.* [1960s] (US) the penis (cf. DILLYWHACKER). [DIDDLE n.³ + SE *whacker*]

diddums *n.* [late 19C+] (nursery) term of soothing affection use by a parent to a small child; when used to older children or adults it is invariably mocking (cf. SNOOKUMS). [pron. of SE *did you/he?*]

diddy *n.*¹ [late 18C+] the female breast. [TITTY n.²]

diddy *n.*² [late 19C+] a gypsy. [dimin. of DIDDICOI]

diddy *n.*³ [1950s+] (Aus. juv.) a lavatory. [? DUNNY but see DIDDY adj., i.e. the 'little room']

diddy *adj.* [1930s+] small, diminutive. [nursery pron. of SE *little* + the popularity of the Diddy Men created by the UK comedian Ken Dodd (b.1927)]

diddy-/diddly-bop *n.* [1950s+] (US) **1** (Black) a pretentious Black person, pretending or trying to identify with Whites. **2** a worthless person. **3** a juvenile delinquent. **4** a style of walking typified by an exaggerated rolling gait and swinging arms, hips and shoulders, plus the locking of one knee (cf. AKIMBO v.).

diddy-bop *adj. see* DIDDLEY-BOP adj.

diddy-/diddly-/diddley-/ditty-bop *v.* [1950s+] (orig. US Black) to swagger, to saunter. **2** to be a street hoodlum. [? the *didd(l)y-bop, didd(l)y-bop* rhythm used in bebop jazz]

diddy-bopper *see* DIDDLY-BOPPER.

diddy-/diddly-bopping *n.* [1960s+] (orig. milit.) **1** walking carelessly. **2** walking in a swaggering or strutting manner. **3** living as a teen hoodlum. [DIDDY-BOP v.]

diddy-popper *n.* [1970s+] (US Black) a member of the Black bourgeoisie, one who does not live in a ghetto. [play on DIDDLY-BOPPER + SE *poppa/papa*; i.e. one's father or his chronological peers]

diddy ride *v.* [1990s] of a man, to masturbate oneself between a woman's breasts (cf. TITTY FUCK). [DIDDY n.¹ + RIDE v.¹]

diddys *see* DIDDIES.

diddywaddle *adj.* [1970s] (US) insignificant, unimportant. [ety. unknown; ? DIDDY-BOP v.; ext. of DIDDY adj.]

diddy-wah-diddy *see* DOO-WAH-DIDDY.

didekei/dideki *see* DIDDICOI.

did I buggery!/hell!/shit! *excl.* [late 19C+] an excl. of negation (cf. AND DID HE MARRY POOR BLIND NELL?; DID I FUCK!).

didies *n.* [1980s] underpants. [? SE *little*, i.e. a play on 'smalls']

did I ever! *excl.* [early 19C+] a general excl. of intensification, i.e. I certainly did! Usu. in answer to a question, also with other personal pronouns or 'anyone'.

did I fuck! *excl.* [20C] a general excl. of denial, rejection, e.g. *Did I steal that car, did I fuck!* Similarly *will I fuck!* = no, I certainly won't.

did I hell!/shit! *see* DID I BUGGERY!

didn't ought *n.* [late 19C–1940s] port (wine). [rhy. sl.]

didn't oughter *n.* **1** [late 19C–1910s] water. **2** [1970s+] a daughter. [rhy. sl.]

dido *n.*¹ [19C+] (US) **1** a caper, a prank. **2** an argument, a disturbance; thus *cut up didoes*, to cause or indulge in a row. **3** something fancy or frivolous. [ety. unknown; E.P. suggests the Greek *Dido*, 'the tragic queen', but why?]

dido *n.*² [1950s+] (Irish) **1** an overdressed female. **2** usu. in pl., tricks, antics.

dido *v.* [20C] (Aus.) to steal from carts in the street. [? DIDO n.¹ (1)]

did they forget to feed the dingoes? *phr.* [1960s] (Aus.) a joc. phr. used to greet an unexpected arrival.

did your mama have any sons that lived? *phr.* [1970s] (US Black) a phr. used by a woman to rebuff sexual cat-calling by men as she passes them.

did you tell your mother?/what will your mother say? *phr.* [late 19C+] a teasing comment implying that the subject, while perfectly entitled to do what they want, is in some way being 'naughty' (cf. DOES YOUR MOTHER KNOW YOU'RE OUT?).

die *n.* [mid-19C] **1** a last dying speech, usu. that delivered on the gallows, or the account of an especially gruesome trial. **2** a capital trial for which the condemned man may be executed.

die *v.* [20C] to fail utterly, to have a difficult time.

die dunghill *v.* [18C] to die in a cowardly manner, repenting or showing any act of contrition on the gallows, where a plucky villain was supposed to display bravado. [SE *die* + DUNGHILL]

die/go to rest in a horse's nightcap, to *phr.* [late 18C–mid-19C] to be hanged (cf. HORSE'S NIGHTCAP). [a *horse's nightcap* is a halter, thus a noose]

die in one's boots/with one's boots on, to *phr.* **1** [late 17C–1910s] to be hanged (cf. DIE IN ONE'S SHOES). **2** [mid-19C–1910s] (US) to die by violence, esp. in a gunfight.

die in one's shoes, to *phr.* [late 17C–mid-19C] to be hanged (cf. DIE IN ONE'S BOOTS).

die/fail in the furrow, to *phr.* [19C] of a man, to lose one's erection during intercourse. [SE *die* + FURROW]

die like a dog, to *phr.* [late 17C–18C] to be hanged (cf. DIE IN ONE'S SHOES; DIE ON A FISH DAY).

die like a hen, to *phr.* [18C–19C] (Scot.) to die unmarried. [a long-lost anecdote]

die like a rat, to *phr.* [late 17C–late 18C] to be killed with poison.

diener/diender *n.* [1940s+] (S.Afr.) a policeman. [Afk. *dienaaren*, lit. one who serves. [note Afk. sl. *dienaars*, prison warders known for their brutality]

die of a hempen fever, to *phr.* [18C–early 19C] to be hanged. [SE *die* + HEMPEN QUINSY]

die on a fish day, to *phr.* [late 17C–18C] to be hanged. [? hangings taking place on Catholic 'fish-days', i.e. Wednesdays and Fridays]

die on it *v.* [1910s+] (Aus.) to break one's promise, to fail to finish something one has undertaken to do.

die on the trigger, to *phr.* [1970s+] (US gang) to die in a gunfight.

diesel/dieseler *n.*[1] **1** [1950s+] (orig. US) an overtly masculine lesbian (cf. BUTCH n.). **2** [1990s] (US Black) one who has a muscular, well-developed physique. [SE *diesel*, a locomotive driven by a diesel engine]

diesel *n.*[2] [1970s+] (prison) prison tea. [its taste, supposedly reminiscent of diesel fuel]

diesel-dyke *n.* [1950s+] a conspicuously masculine lesbian (cf. BUTCH n.[3]). [DIESEL n.[1] + DYKE n.]

die the death of a trooper's horse, to *phr.* [late 18C–early 19C] to be hanged. [like the horse, the villain dies 'with his shoes on']

diet pills *n.* [1980s+] (drugs) amphetamines (cf. A n.[2]). [their appetite-reducing effects]

dieu et mon droit/dright *phr.* [1910s] a general phr. of self-satisfied dismissal, i.e. don't bother me, I don't care (cf. FUCK YOU, JACK, I'M ALL RIGHT). [rhy. sl. *dieu et mon dright* = I'm all right]

die with a hard-on, to *phr.* [1960s+] (US) to die violently, esp. by hanging. [HARD-ON; the victim's penis becomes erect during a hanging]

die with cotton in one's ears, to *phr.* [19C] to be hanged. [proper name *Cotton*, a 19C Newgate chaplain who would preach a last sermon to the condemned man]

dif/diff *n.* [late 19C+] difference, e.g. *that's the dif.* [? orig. Stock Exchange use]

diff *n.*[1] [19C] (US) a blow. [? Scot. *dowf*, a dull blow]

diff *n.*[2] *see* DIF.

diff *n.*[3] [1940s+] (Aus.) the *diff*erential gear on a motorcar. [abbr.]

differ *n.* [late 19C+] (Irish/N.Z.) *differ*ence. [abbr.]

difference, the *n.* [1900s–40s] (US) a telling advantage, e.g. a hidden weapon.

different *adj.* [1910s+] exceptional, out of the ordinary, unique; esp. used as a euph. when the speaker wishes in fact to express distaste.

different cup of tea *phr.* [1940s+] of people and things, very different. [SE *different* + CUP OF TEA n.[2]]

differs *n.* [1950s] (Anglo-Irish) *differ*ence. [abbr.]

diffs *n.* [late 19C] *diffi*culties, usu. financial ones. [abbr.]

diffy *adj.* [1940s–50s] (society) *diffi*cult. [abbr.]

dig *n.*[1] [early 19C–1900s] (US campus) a diligent or over-dedicated student, one who studies hard (cf. GRIND n.[2]). [they *dig* for knowledge. The term also flourished briefly in UK schools in the late 19C]

dig *n.*[2] [late 19C] dignity, also as phr. *otium dig.* [Lat. *otium cum dignitate*, the dignity of leisure, popularized in Cicero, *Ad Familiares*, I.xi.21]

dig *n.*[3] [20C] (Aus./N.Z.) **1** an Australian or New Zealander. **2** a friend. **3** a general form of address. [abbr. DIGGER n.[3]]

dig *n.*[4] [1970s] (US) a sex show. [DIG v.[5] (1), i.e. something one enjoys]

dig/dig it out *v.*[1] [19C+] (US) to leave quickly, to run off. [one *digs* oneself out of the current situation or one *digs* one's heels into the ground as one runs]

dig *v.*[2] [early 19C–1900s] (US campus) to work extremely hard.

dig *v.*[3] [1900s–50s] (US) to search in one's pockets for money.

dig *v.*[4] [1910s] to share lodgings or DIGGINGS with. [DIGS n.[1]]

dig *v.*[5] **1** [1930s+] (orig. US Black) to appreciate, to enjoy, to love. **2** [1930s+] (orig. US Black) to understand. **3** [1930s+] (orig. US Black) to pay close attention to, also ext. as *dig on*. **4** [1930s+] (orig. US Black) to get together, to meet (cf. DIG YOU LATER). **5** [1940s] (orig. US Black) to find out, to discover. **6** [1940s+] (orig. US Black) to imagine. **7** [1940s–60s] (US Black) to visit. **8** [1950s] (US Black) to discuss, to converse. [all orig. jazz musician use, thence adopted by the fans; ult. ? Wolof *dega*, to understand (Smitherman, although *DARE* remarks 'questionable' and Lighter 'not been substantiated'); SE *dig*, to excavate; TWIG v.[2] (4)]

dig a day under the skin, to *phr.* [late 19C] to shave on alternate days.

dig a grave, to *phr.* [20C] (Aus.) to have a shave (cf. DAD AND DAVE phr.; DIG IN THE GRAVE). [rhy. sl.]

Digby chicken *n.* [19C] a herring; when smoked it is known as a *Digby duck* (cf. ABERDEEN CUTLET). [the fishing trade of *Digby*, Nova Scotia]

dig down *v.* [1940s–50s] (US) to pay out of one's own pocket. [DIG v.[3]]

digester/jesta *n.* [1940s+] (W.I.) a large cast-iron pot, with a cover, used for cooking soup. [SE *digester*, 'an apparatus in which the carcases of beasts unfit for food are by the action of heat dissolved into their proximate elements, tallow, gelatine, earthy phosphates etc' *OED*]

dig foot *v.* [1930s+] (W.I.) to run away fast. [DIG v.[1]]

dig for change, to *phr.* [1900s] to masturbate (cf. POCKET POOL).

dig for gold, to *phr.* [1930s–60s] to sleep with or marry a man for his money (cf. GOLD-DIGGER).

digger *n.*[1] **1** [late 18C–late 19C] a spur. **2** [19C] a finger-nail. **3** [mid-19C+] a card of the spade suit; thus *big digger*, the ace of spades. [resemblance to a spade or shovel]

digger *n.*[2] [early 19C–1900s] a diligent student. [DIG n.[1]]

digger *n.*[3] [mid-19C+] **1** an Australian or New Zealander. [form of address used by miners in the 19C Aus./N.Z. gold-fields; it spread after Aus./N.Z. participation in WW1]

digger *n.*[4] [20C] (Can./US Und.) **1** a solitary confinement cell (cf. DIG-OUT; HOLE n.[2]). **2** a county or city prison (cf. JIGGER n.[9]).

[orig. late 19C UK army use *digger*, a guardroom, in which defaulters were 'buried']

digger *n.*[5] [1920s–40s] (US) a young woman, orig. typically from the chorus line, who swaps sexual favours for the monetary and material gifts of a (usually) older lover (cf. BIMBO; SACK-CHASER). [abbr. GOLD-DIGGER]

Diggerland *n.* [1910s] (N.Z.) New Zealand. [DIGGER n.[3] + SE *land*]

diggermania/diggerphobia *n.* [mid–late 19C] (Aus./N.Z.) an obsession with digging in the Antipodean goldfields, usu. fostered by one's failure to find anything. [SE *digger* + *-mania/-phobia*]

digger's delight *n.* [late 19C] (Aus.) a wide-brimmed felt hat. [DIGGER n.[3] + SE *delight*]

diggings *n.* [mid-19C] lodgings, temporary accommodation. [one *digs* oneself in]

diggish *adj.* [1960s] (school) excellent, first-class. [DIG v.[5] (1)]

dig gravel *see* SCRATCH GRAVEL.

diggums *n.* [19C] cards in the spade suit (cf. DIGGER n.[1]). [resemblance to a spade or shovel]

dig/get horrors *v.*[1] [1950s+] (W.I.) to be emotionally troubled. [DIG v.[5] (2)/SE *get* + HORRORS n. (1)]

dig/get horrors *v.*[2] [1950s+] (W.I.) to live in material squalor. [DIG v.[4] + HORRORS n. (1)]

dig in *v.* **1** [late 19C+] to set to work energetically. **2** [1910s+] to eat heartily, often as exhortation, *dig in!*

dig in one's feet/heels/toes, to *phr.* [1930s+] to maintain one's position stubbornly.

dig in the grave *n.* [1910s+] (orig. Aus.) a shave (cf. DIG A GRAVE). [rhy. sl.]

digital *n.* [mid-19C] a finger. [SE *digit*]

digitate *v.* [19C] of a woman, to masturbate; thus *digitating*, masturbation (cf. FINGER v.[1]; FINGER FUCK v.). [SE *digitate*, to point with the finger]

digithead *n.* [1980s+] (orig. US) an obsessive computer user. [SE *digits*, numbers]

dig it out *see* DIG v.[1].

digits *n.* [1990s] (US Black) **1** a telephone number (and address) (cf. SEVEN DIGITS). **2** the amount written on a cheque, usu. pay cheque.

digits dealer *n.* [1950s+] (US Und.) a numbers racketeer. [play on SE *digits*, numbers]

dignity *n.* [mid–late 19C] (W.I.) used by Europeans to describe a dance or ball given by the native West Indians. [the implication is of the Whites' mockery of the affected mannerliness of such gatherings]

dig on *v.* [1930s+] (US Black) to observe, to pay attention to, to watch. [ext. of DIG v.[5] (3)]

dig-out *n.* [1900s] (N.Z. Und.) **1** a pit into which recalcitrant prisoners are placed for punishment. **2** a solitary confinement cell (cf. DIGGER n.[4]).

dig out *v.* [late 19C] (US) to leave, to depart. [DIG v.[1]]

dig out after *v.* [1910s–20s] to attempt to get something one desires.

dig out someone's eye, to *phr.* [1950s+] (W.I.) to cheat in a business deal (cf. JOOK OUT SOMEONE'S EYE).

digs *n.*[1] [mid-19C+] (orig. Aus.) temporary rented accommodation. [SE *diggings*, the mining districts of Australia and California, first adopted in lodgings sense by UK actors]

digs *n.*[2] [1970s+] (US) the facts, information. [DIG v.[5] (5)]

dig someone out *v.* [mid-19C+] (society) to call for, to encourage one to take part in life outside one's home.

dig the dip on the four and two, to *phr.* [1940s] (US Black/ Harlem) to take a bath every Saturday night. [DIG v.[3] +SE *dip* + SE *four and two*, six, i.e. the sixth (day)]

dig up *v.*[1] [mid-19C+] **1** to discover, to unearth. **2** to look for.

dig up *v.*[2] [1910s–20s] to leave. [DIG v.[1]]

dig with both feet, to *phr.* [20C] (Ulster) to be duplicitous, cunning. [play on DIG WITH THE RIGHT FOOT]

dig with the right/left/other/wrong/same foot *phr.* [20C] (Ulster) used in various senses to denote one's religious persuasion; *dig with the right foot*, to be a Roman Catholic, *dig with the left foot*, to be a Protestant, *dig with the other/wrong foot*, to be of another religion, *dig with the same foot*, to share a religion. [in the Republic of Ireland (Catholic), people usu. press on the spade with the right foot; in Northern Ireland (largely Protestant), it is the reverse]

dig you later *phr.* [1940s+] see you later, goodbye. [DIG v.[5] (4)]

dik *n.* [1970s+] (S.Afr.) a fool. [fig. use of Afk. *dik*, dense, thick]

dik *adj.* [1970s+] (S.Afr.) **1** stupid. **2** sated, full. **3** fat. [fig. use of Afk. *dik*, dense, thick]

dikbek/diklip *n.* [1970s+] (S.Afr.) a sour-faced or sulky person. [Afk. *dik*, thick + or Afk. *bek*, mouth or SE *lip*]

dikbek/diklip *adj.* [1970s+] (S.Afr.) sulky, pouting. [DIKBEK n.]

dike *n.*[1] [19C+] (US) someone who is dressed up. [? SE *decked out*]

dike *n.*[2] [1920s+] (Aus.) a lavatory, esp. a communal urinal use by schoolboys, soldiers etc (cf. BOG n.). [SE *dike*, a pit]

dike *n.*[3] *see* DYKE.

dike *n.*[4] [1980s+] (drugs) Diconal. [abbr./pron.]

dike *v. see* DYKE v.

dike/dyke down *v.* [19C+] (US) to dress smartly; thus *diked/dyked down*, smartly dressed (cf. DICKY UP; DIKE n.[1]). [SE *decked out* ? + 13C SE *dight*, to put or place in order, to array, to arrange]

diked/dyked up *adj.*[1] [mid-19C+] (US) well-dressed. [DIKE DOWN]

diked/dyked up *adj.*[2] [1900s] drunk. [? SE *dike/dyke*, a water-course or channel, in this case for alcohol]

dike/dyke jumper *n.* [20C] (US) a person of Dutch origin. [the Netherlands is stereotypically identified with its system of dikes]

dikey *see* DYKEY.

dikk/dikk-dari *n.* [late 19C] (Anglo-Ind.) worry. [Hind. *dik*, vexed]

dikk/dikk-dari *adj.* [late 19C] (Anglo-Ind.) worried. [Hind. *dik*, vexed]

diklip *see* DIKBEK.

dilberry *n.* [mid-19C+] **1** a small piece of excrement clinging to the hairs around the anus or the female pubic hair, usu. in pl. **2** a stupid, dull or obnoxious person (cf. DINGLEBERRY).

dilberry bush *n.* [mid–late 19C] the pubic hair. [DILBERRY n. (1) + BUSH n.[4] (1)]

dilberry creek *n.* [mid–late 19C] the anus. [DILBERRY n. (1) + SE *creek*]

dilberry-maker *n.* [mid–late 19C] the anus. [DILBERRY n. (1) + SE *maker*]

dilbert dildo *n.* [1960s] (camp gay) a fool, a gullible person (cf. DILL). [*Dilbert*, a comic name + DILDO n. (1) or SE *dildo*]

dildo *n.* **1** [mid-17C+] a fool, an incompetent (cf. DICKHEAD), also ext. as *dildobrain*, *dildohead*. **2** [1990s] (Irish) a promiscuous woman. [SE *dildo*, an artificial penis; itself ? Ital. *diletto*, a (lady's) delight; thus fig. the lack of autonomous competence of the sexual aid so named]

dildo *v.* [mid-17C–mid-19C] to caress a woman sexually. [SE *dildo*]

dildock *n.* [1910s+] (US) a fool. [var. on DILDO n. (1)]

dill *n.* [1940s+] (Aus./N.Z.) a fool (cf. DICKHEAD). [DILLYPOT n. (2); the late 20C UK use may also be attributed to an abbr. of the comic name *Dilbert* (slightly transformed by the comedian Lenny Henry into his bumptious character Delbert Wilkins; also note DILDO n. (1)]

dillbrain *n.* [1950s+] (N.Z.) a fool (cf. DICKHEAD). [ext. of DILL *n.*]

diller *n.* [1960s] (US) the penis. [var. on DIDDLYWHACKER or DILLYWHACKER]

dillinger front *n.* [1970s+] (US Black) a double-breasted suit. [proper name of gangster John *Dillinger* (1903–34) + FRONT *n.*[1]]

dillo *see* DEELO.

dillo namo *see* DEELO NAMO.

dill pickle *n.* [1900s] (US) a fool (cf. DILL). [despite appearances, the ref. is to the apparent absurdity of a gherkin (? its phallic resemblance) thus cf. WALLY *n.*[2], and not to the later Aus./N.Z. DILL]

dilly *n.*[1] **1** [late 18C–early 19C] a coach. **2** [mid–late 19C] a night-soil cart. [SE *diligence*, a public stage-coach]

dilly *n.*[2] [mid-19C] a daffo*dil*. [abbr. + sfx. -*y*]

Dilly, the *n.*[3] **1** [mid-19C] the Piccadilly Saloon (cf. BAZE). **2** [1930s–50s] Piccadilly, esp. as a favoured area for prostitutes.

dilly *n.*[4] [20C] (Aus.) a fool. [ext. of DILL]

dilly *n.*[5] [1930s+] (US) anything outstanding or remarkable, often used ironically. [? SE *delightful* and/or *delicious*]

dilly *n.*[6] [1940s–60s] (US) a penis (cf. DILLER). [abbr. DILLY-WHACKER]

dilly *adj.*[1] [1900s–20s] *deli*ghtful. [abbr./pron. + sfx. -*y*]

dilly *adj.*[2] [20C] (orig. Aus.) foolish. [DILL + sfx. -*y*]

dilly-bag *n.* [1930s] (orig. Aus.) a small sack or similar container in which articles are carried; thus *dilly-bags of.* [synon. SE *ditty-bag*]

dilly boy *n.* [1950s+] (gay) a teenage male prostitute. [*Piccadilly* Circus, London, a long-time centre for gay prostitution]

dilly-dally *v.* [18C] to trifle, to waste time. [SE f. 1800]

dilly dude *n.* [1960s] (US Black) an eccentric, an outsider. [orig. Ohio use, f. Gloucestershire dial. *dilly*, cranky, odd + DUDE *n.*]

dillypot *n.* [1930s+] (Aus.) **1** the vagina. **2** a fool (cf. DICKHEAD). [rhy. sl. *dillypot* = TWAT]

dillywhacker *n.* [1920s] (US) a penis (cf. DIDDLYWHACKER).

dilog *see* DELOG.

dilsy *n.* [20C] (Ulster) **1** a foolish, usu. female, person. **2** an overdressed, showy female. **3** a social climber. [ety. unknown]

dim *n.* [1920s–40s] (US Black) the evening, the night. [note 15C SE *dim*, the dusk]

dim *adj.* [1920s+] **1** unsatisfactory, disappointing, dull. **2** unintelligent, undistinguished. [orig. Oxford Univ. use, with an implication of the 'subfusc' (i.e. black suit, white shirt and bow tie) formal university wear]

dim and bright *n.* [1970s] (US Black) a day. [the night and the day]

dimba *n.* [1980s+] (drugs) marijuana from West Africa (cf. DJAMBA). [used synon. in various West African languages]

dimber *adj.* **1** [17C–early 19C] (Und.) pretty; thus *dimber cove*, a handsome man, *dimber mort*, a pretty woman. **2** [late 19C] smart, active, adroit.

dimber-damber *n.* [17C–late 19C] a gang leader (cf. ARCH-ROGUE; COCK LOREL; UPRIGHT MAN). [DIMBER + DAMBER, lit. a 'handsome rascal']

dimber-damber *adj.* [17C–late 19C] smart, neat. [adj. use of the lit. meaning of DIMBER-DAMBER *n.*]

dimbo *n.*[1] [1970s+] a fool of either sex. [DIM *adj.* + sfx. -*bo*]

dimbo *n.*[2] [1970s+] a stupid woman. [DUMB *adj.* + BIMBO]

dim bulb *n.* [1910s+] (US/Can.) a fool, a dullard (cf. DIMWIT).

dime *n.*[1] **1** [1950s+] (in general US) the number 10, often as $10 (cf. NICKEL). **2** [1950s+] (gambling) $1000, $10,000.

3 [1960s+] (US prison) a 10-year prison sentence (cf. SAW-BUCK). [SAmE *dime*, 10 cents]

dime *n.*[2] (US drugs) **1** [1960s+] $10 worth of a drug (cf. DIME BAG). **2** [1980s+] crack cocaine. **3** [1980s+] $10 worth of crack cocaine, $10 worth of marijuana. [ext. use of DIME *n.*[1] (1)]

dime-a-dozen *adj.* [1930s+] (US) common, undistinguished. [ext. of SE use; i.e. the cheapness of such items]

dime bag *n.* [1960s–70s] (drugs) $10 worth of a drug (cf. NICKEL BAG). [DIME *n.*[2] + BAG *n.*[8]]

dime note *n.* [1930s–40s] (US Black) a $10 bill. [DIME *n.*[1] (1) + SE *note*]

dime piece *n.* [1990s] (US) an attractive woman. [fig. use of DIME *n.*[1] (1) + PIECE *n.*[1] (1)]

dimes, the *n.* [mid-19C] (US) money.

dime-store *adj.* [1940s+] (US) cheap, second-rate. [ext. of SE use; i.e. the poor quality of the goods sold in such stores]

Dimetown, USA *n.* [1990s] the world of street drug addicts. [DIME BAG; there is an added implication of the poverty of this figurative world (cf. DIME-STORE)]

dimey *n.* [1960s+] (US) a glass of beer costing 10 cents. [DIME *n.*[1] (1)]

dimmick *n.* [mid–late 19C] counterfeit coins. [var. on DIMMOCK *n.*[1]]

dimmo/dimo *n.*[1] [20C] a Greek. [mainly Cockney use, generic Greek name *Demosthenes*]

dimmo/dimo *n.*[2] [20C] (US) a dime, 10 cents. [SAmE *dime* + sfx. -*o*]

dimmo/dimo *n.*[3] [1970s+] a fool. [DIM *adj.* + sfx. -*o*]

dimmock *n.*[1] [early–mid-19C] money. [dial.; but note 14C *dime*, a tithe or tenth + US *dime*, 10 cents]

dimmock *n.*[2] [1990s] an unpleasant person. [SE *dim*; ? on pattern of DILDOCK]

dimmocking bag *n.* [mid–late 19C] a bag used to collect subscriptions, hold one's savings, set aside 'Christmas money' and similar tasks. [? DIMMOCK *n.*[1]]

dimmy *n.* [mid-19C] (US) money. [DIMMOCK *n.*[1]]

dimo *see* DIMMO.

dimp *n.* [1930s+] (orig. milit.) a cigarette end, esp. one that is large enough to be relit (cf. DINCH *n.*). [SE *dimple*, the indentation that is put in the cigarette when one pinches it out for further use]

dimple *n.* [19C] the vagina. [SE *dimple*, a depression in the flesh]

dims and brights *n.* [1920s–40s] (US Black) nights and days (cf. DIM AND BRIGHT). [DIM *n.* + BRIGHT *n.*[1]]

dim sim *n.* [1950s+] (Aus.) the victim of a confidence trickster. [DIM *adj.* + abbr. SE *simple*, but ? pun on Chinese *dim sum*, a lunchtime snack, i.e. 'I could eat him for lunch']

dimwit *n.* [1930s+] a fool.

din *n.* [19C] a Native Australian woman (cf. GIN *n.*[1]). [Dharuk *diyin*, woman]

dinah *n.*[1] [late 19C–1900s] one's favourite female companion. [? var. on DONAH]

dinah *n.*[2] [late 19C+] nitroglycerine. [abbr. SE *dynamite*]

dinarly/dinarla/dinaly *n.* [mid-19C] (Polari) a shilling (5p) (cf. DEANER). [Lat. *denarius*. The word is part of Ling. Fr. and cognate with Sp. *dinero*]

dinch/dincher *n.* [1920s–30s] (US Und.) a cigar or cigarette end. [DIMP + SE *pinch*]

dinch *v.* [1920s–30s] (US) to pinch out a cigarette for later use. [DINCH *n.*]

dincher *see* DINCH *n.*

din-din/din-dins *n.* [late 19C+] (juv.) dinner. [the pl. use is 1960s+]

dine *n.* [late 17C–early 19C] spite. [ety. unknown]

dine at the Y, to *phr.* [1940s+] (orig. US) to perform

cunnilingus. [the conjunction of the thighs, plus a pun on the YMCA/YWCA]

dine out v. [mid–late 19C] to go without a meal (cf. DINE WITH DUKE HUMPHREY; DINE WITH SIR THOMAS GRESHAM).

dinero n. [19C+] money. [Sp.]

dine with Duke Humphrey, to phr. [late 16C–mid-19C] to go without one's meal (cf. GUEST OF THE CROSS-LEGGED KNIGHTS). [Duke Humphrey's Walk at Old St Paul's Cathedral. The real Duke Humphrey of Gloucester was actually buried in St Albans, but a statue of Sir John Beauchamp, which stood in one of the cathedral aisles, was popularly supposed to be the duke; thus to *dine with Duke Humphrey* meant to frequent this aisle, in the hope, often vain, of being invited to dinner. The Scottish equivalent was to DINE WITH ST GILES AND THE EARL OF MURRAY; the earl was buried in St Giles' Church]

dine with St Giles and the Earl of Murray, to phr. [18C] to go without one's dinner. [for ety. *see* DINE WITH DUKE HUMPHREY]

dine/sup with Sir Thomas Gresham, to phr. [early–mid-17C] to go without one's dinner (cf. DINE WITH DUKE HUMPHREY). [*Sir Thomas Gresham* (1519–79) founder of the Royal Society and a well-known philanthropist; the image is of a poor person forced to appeal to Gresham for charity]

ding n.[1] **1** [1930s] a beggar, a tramp. **2** [1940s+] (Aus.) a derog. term for foreigners, esp. Italians and Greeks. **3** [1950s+] (US) a fool. [DINGBAT n.[9]]

ding n.[2] [1950s] (US drugs) marijuana. [ety. unknown; the *ding* of pleasure it creates]

ding n.[3] [1950s+] a notice of rejection, a negative assessment.

ding n.[4] **1** [1950s+] (Aus.) a party. **2** [1960s] (US) a drinking spree. **3** [1980s] a sudden feeling of pleasure, a thrill. [WINGDING]

ding n.[5] **1** [1950s+] (Aus.) a hole in the bottom of anything. **2** [1950s+] (Aus.) the anus. **3** [1960s+] a small knock or dent in an object. **4** [1960s+] (orig. US) a minor injury, a bruise. [DING v.[1] (1), (6)]

ding n.[6] [1960s–70s] the penis. [abbr. DINGUS]

ding v.[1] **1** [late 17C+] to knock down. **2** [late 18C–mid-19C] to throw away. **3** [early 19C] (Und.) to pass to a confederate. **4** [mid-19C+] to break off relations with, to abandon a person. **5** [1950s+] (US campus) to turn (someone) down, to blackball. **6** [1960s+] to dent, to scratch. [fig. uses of 14C SE *ding*, to beat heavily]

ding v.[2] **1** [1920s–50s] (US tramp) to beg money. **2** [1940s+] (US) to nag, to harass. **3** [1940s+] (US) in business, to come to a negative assessment. [SE *ding*, to nag, to bore with repetitious speech]

ding! excl. [19C+] euph. for DAMN!

dingable adj. [early 19C] worthless, to be discarded. [DING v.[1] (2)]

dingaling/ding-a-ling n.[1] [20C] (Aus.) the king. [rhy. sl.]

dingaling/ding-a-ling n.[2] (US) **1** [1930s+] (prison) a prisoner whose confinement has driven them mad (cf. STIR CRAZY). **2** [1930s+] a fool, an eccentric, a mad person (cf. DICKHEAD). **3** [1960s+] an effeminate man. [the ringing in the sufferer's head; (3) is seen as SE *queer*, i.e. eccentric]

dingaling/ding-a-ling n.[3] [1950s+] (orig. US Black) the penis (cf. DANGLE n.). [SE *dangle* + image of the testicles as bells (cf. DING-DONGS n.[2])]

dingaling/ding-a-ling n.[4] [1950s+] (Aus.) the buttocks, the backside. [DING n.[5] (2)]

dingbat n.[1] [mid-19C] (US) a strong drink. [? a specific bartender's name]

dingbat n.[2] [mid–late 19C] (US) a coin, a banknote; thus in pl. money. [DING v.[1]; i.e. the idea of smacking it down on a counter or table]

dingbat n.[3] **1** [mid–late 19C] balls of dung on buttocks of sheep or cattle (cf. DINGLEBERRIES). **2** [mid–late 19C] (US) a

cannon-ball, a bullet, a flying missile.

dingbat n.[4] [late 19C] a blow or slap on the buttocks. [DING v.[1]]

dingbat n.[5] [late 19C] (US) **1** verbal squabbling, physical pushing. **2** an affectionate embrace, esp. mothers hugging and kissing their children. [DING v.[1]]

dingbat n.[6] [late 19C] (US campus) various kinds of muffins or biscuit.

dingbat n.[7] [late 19C+] a term of admiration.

dingbat n.[8] [late 19C+] anything for which one cannot specify the proper name (cf. THINGUMABOB).

dingbat n.[9] **1** [late 19C+] (orig. US) a fool, an idiot (cf. DICKHEAD). **2** [20C] a tramp, a vagrant. [popularized by George Herriman's carton *The Dingbat Family*, created in 1909 and revived c.1971 in the TV sitcom *All in the Family*]

dingbat n.[10] [1910s–40s] the penis. [DING v.[1] (1); one of the many terms equating the penis with a weapon]

dingbatisis n. [1920s] (N.Z.) drunkenness, very heavy drinking. [DINGBATS n.]

dingbats n. [1910s+] (Aus./N.Z.) **1** madness. **2** delirium tremens; thus *give one the dingbats*, to drive one crazy, *be in/have the dingbats*, to be insane or suffering from delirium tremens. **3** an eccentric, a mad person. [DINGBAT n.[9]]

dingbats adj. [1940s+] (Aus.) eccentric, crazy. [DINGBAT n.[9]]

ding-boy n. [late 17C–18C] (Und.) a thug, esp. when he acts as a bodyguard or accomplice, providing the 'muscle' for a more skilful villain. [DING v.[1] (1) + SE *boy*]

dingbust/dingbusted adj. [late 19C+] (US) used in oaths or excl. [euph. for DAMNED]

ding-dong n.[1] **1** [late 19C+] a domestic sing-song. **2** [1920s–40s] (US) a bell, a gong. **3** [1920s+] a serious argument, a fight, esp. in phr. *a right old ding-dong*. **4** [1930s+] a noisy party or other gathering. [echoic]

ding-dong n.[2] [1920s] (US) the head.

ding-dong n.[3] [1920s+] (US) a stupid, dull person (cf. DINGALING n.[2]).

ding-dong n.[4] [1940s+] (US) the penis (cf. ARSE-OPENER; DINGALING n.[3]; DING-DONGS n.[2]; DONG n.[2]).

ding-dong adj.[1] (US) [late 19C–1920s] exciting, smart. [the ringing of bells in celebration]

ding-dong adj.[2] [20C] (US) euph. for DAMNED, e.g. *I feel like a ding-dong fool.*

ding-dong adj.[3] [1960s+] eccentric, insane (cf. DINGALING n.[2]; DINGBAT n.[9]). [DING-DONG n.[3]; the supposed ringing bells heard by the sufferer]

ding-dong v. [20C] (US) to annoy, to irritate. [SE *ding-dong*, the sound of a bell; thus its repetitiousness]

ding-dong bell n. [1940s+] a euph. for HELL. [rhy. sl.]

ding-dong pants n. [1960s] (US) bell-bottomed trousers (cf. DING-DONGS n.[1]). [pun]

ding-dongs n.[1] [1920s; 1960s] (US) bell-bottomed trousers (cf. DING-DONG PANTS). [pun]

ding-dongs n.[2] [1950s+] (US) the testicles. [DING-DONG n.[1] (3); i.e. they supposedly knock together, 'like bells']

ding-dust n. [20C] (Ulster) a noise. [ON *denja*, to thrash]

ding-dust adv. [20C] (Ulster) very fast. [ext. of DING v.[1]]

dinge n. [mid-19C+] a Black person. [SE *dingy*, grimy, shabby; ? Mandingo *den-ke*, black; now seen as pej.]

dinge adj. [mid-19C+] (US) Black. [DINGE n.]

dinge blowen n. [mid-19C+] (US) a Black woman (cf. COVESS DINGE). [DINGE adj. + BLOWEN]

dinged out adj. [1960s] (US) drunk. [fig. use of DING v.[1] (1)]

dinge kinch n. [19C] (US) a Black child. [DINGE adj. + KINCHIN]

dinge queen n. [1960s+] (US gay) a homosexual who prefers Black partners; used of both Whites and Blacks. [DINGE n. + QUEEN n.[1]]

dinger n.[1] [19C] a thief who throws away what they have stolen. [DING v.[1] (2)]

dinger *n.*[2] [mid-19C+] (Aus.) a *dingo*. [abbr.]

dinger *n.*[3] [late 19C+] (Aus./Irish/US) something exceptional, something striking (cf. HUMDINGER). [fig. use of DING v.[1] (1)]

dinger *n.*[4] [1920s] (US) a beggar or tramp, esp. one who pretends to have some sort of injury. [DING v.[2] (1)]

dinger *n.*[5] [1920s+] (Aus.) anything excellent. [DING n.[4]]

dinger *n.*[6] (US) **1** [1930s] an alarm bell. **2** [1930s+] a telephone. [echoic]

dinger *n.*[7] [1930s+] (Aus.) the anus or buttocks. [DING n.[5] (2)]

dinger *n.*[8] [1950s] (US) the penis (cf. DING n.[6]). [DINGUS]

dingey/dingy Christian *n.* [late 18C] a mulatto or anyone with a degree of mixed blood (cf. DINGE n.). ['anyone who has, as the West Indian term is, a lick of the tar-brush' (Grose, 1785); the presumption that a 'real' Christian is White]

dingle *n.*[1] [1910s+] (US) the penis (cf. BELLY DINGLE). [? DINGUS, SE *dangle*]

dingle *n.*[2] [1930s] (US campus) the regard of one's seniors; thus *get/have a dingle with*, to be in favour, *pluck a dingle*, to toady to. [? fig. use of SE *dingle*, to ring as a bell]

dingle *adj.* [late 18C] banal, clichéd, used up.

dingleberries *n.* **1** [1950s+] pieces of excreta clinging to the hairs around an inadequately cleansed anus (cf. DANGLE-BERRIES; DILBERRY; DILBERRY BUSH; DILBERRY CREEK). **2** [1970s+] the female breasts (cf. APPLES n.[1]). [SE *dangle*]

dingleberry *n.* **1** [1910s+] a testicle (cf. APRICOTS). **2** [1920s+] (US) someone stupid, dull, obnoxious. **3** [1930s+] a small piece of excrement clinging to the hairs around the anus (cf. DILBERRY). **4** [1970s] the vagina, the clitoris.

dinglebody *n.* [1950s] (US) someone stupid (cf. DINGLEBERRY).

dingle-dangle *n.* [late 19C+] the penis (cf. CRANK n.[5]; DANGLE n.; DINGLE n.[1]). [SE *dingle-dangle*, a dangling appendage]

dingo *n.*[1] **1** [1920s+] (Aus.) a cheat, a scoundrel, a traitor, a coward. **2** [1920s–30s] (US) a tramp, a minor confidence trickster. **3** [1950s+] (US) an eccentric. [SE *dingo*, Lat. *Canis dingo*, the wild, or semi-domesticated dog of Australia]

dingo *n.*[2] [1970s] (US) the penis. [DINGUS]

dingo *adj.* [1970s] (US) crazy, eccentric. [? Aus. *dingo dog* or DINGALING n.[2] (2)/DING(BATS) + sfx. -O]

dingo *v.* [1910s+] (Aus.) to act in a particularly cowardly and treacherous manner, to exhibit the mannerisms of the dingo, the native Aus. dog, a despised creature. [DINGO n.]

dingo's breakfast *n.* [1960s+] (Aus.) 'a piss and a look around' (cf. AIR PIE AND A WALK AROUND).

dingswizzled *adj.* [late 19C] (US) a general excl., e.g. *I'll be dingswizzled!*

ding the tot! *excl.* [late 19C] run off with the lot. [rhy. sl.]

dingus *n.* [19C+] **1** anything for which one cannot recall the proper name (cf. DINGBAT n.[8]; THINGUMMABOB; THINGUMMIJIG; WHATCHAMACALLIT). **2** euph. for the penis (cf. DING n.[6]; DINGALING n.[3]; DING-DONG n.[4]). [Du. *ding*, a thing; in S.Afr. (1) is extended to people as well as inanimate objects and usu. spelt *dinges*]

dingwallace *n.* [1920s] (US) the penis. [ety. unknown; ext. of DINGLE n.[1] but ? *wallace*]

dingy *adj.*[1] [mid-19C+] (US) pertaining to the Black community (cf. DINGE adj.).

dingy *adj.*[2] [1910s+] (US) silly, foolish, crazy (cf. DINGBAT n.[9]).

dingy *adj.*[3] [1960s] (US Black) impoverished, penniless. [DING v.[2]]

dingy Christian *see* DINGEY CHRISTIAN.

dining room *n.* [early 19C] the mouth.

dining room chairs *n.* [early 19C] the teeth (cf. DINING ROOM FURNITURE).

dining room furniture *n.* [early 19C] the teeth (cf. DINING ROOM CHAIRS).

dining room jump *n.* [late 18C–early 19C] (Und.) a species of robbery whereby one man poses as a lamplighter, leaning his ladder against the house that is to be robbed. The thief mounts it and makes an entry at a first-floor window. If the police appear and the 'lamplighter' runs, his partner has no means of leaving the house other than to jump (cf. DINING ROOM POST).

dining room post *n.* [late 18C] (Und.) a method of robbery in which the villain poses as a postman, sends up a sham letter to a resident of a lodging house and, while waiting for the postage to be brought down, robs the first open and empty room they encounter (cf. DINING ROOM JUMP).

dink/dinky *n.*[1] [late 19C–1920s] (US) a Black American. [? DINGE n.]

dink *n.*[2] (US) **1** [1900s] a flashy dresser. **2** [1910s] (campus) a small skullcap worn by freshmen. [? DINKY adj.[1]]

dink *n.*[3] **1** [20C] (US) the penis, esp. of a small boy or, if small, of an adult (cf. DINGUS; HORSEMEAT). **2** [20C] a person. **3** [1920s+] an Oriental, esp. Vietnamese. **4** [1920s+] any small person. **5** [1960s+] a fool, a laughable figure. [? SE *dinky*, small]

dink *n.*[4] [1930s–40s] (Aus.) a lift on the cross-bar of a bicycle (cf. DONK; PUG n.[7]). [ety. unknown]

dink *adj.* [1900s–30s] (Aus.) honest, genuine, trustworthy. [abbr. DINKUM adj.]

dink-do *n.* [1940s+] (bingo) the number 22. [rhy. sl.]

dinker *adj.* [1920s+] (Aus.) honest, genuine, trustworthy. [DINKUM adj.]

dinki-/dinky-di *adj.* [20C] (Aus.) real, genuine. [DINKUM adj.]

dinkie dow *n.* [1960s+] (drugs) marijuana. [imported by US troops in Vietnam (1964–75)]

dinkle farf *n.* [1990s] (US teen) a person who acts foolishly or stupidly. [nonsense words]

dinkum *n.* [late 19C+] (Aus.) **1** work, esp. hard work, a due share of work. **2** an Australian, spec. an Australian soldier in WW1. **3** the truth (cf. DINKUM OIL). [dial. *dinkum*, a fair share of work]

dinkum *adj.* [1910s+] (Aus.) honest, genuine, esp. as *fair dinkum*, fair play, on the level. [DINKUM n.]

dinkum *adv.* [1910s+] (Aus.) honestly, genuinely; thus *dinkum?* really? is that so? [DINKUM n.]

dinkum oil *n.* [1910s+] (Aus.) the honest truth, true facts (cf. GOOD OIL). [DINKUM n. + OIL]

dinky *n.*[1] [1940s] (Aus.) the truth. [abbr. DINKUM n.]

dinky *n.*[2] [1980s+] the penis. [DINK n.[3] (1) or DINGUS]

dinky *n.*[3] [1980s+] *dual income no kids yet*, a social acronym created to describe the ideal couple of the booming 1980s (cf. BUPPIE).

dinky *n.*[4] [1980s+] (society) a large car. [deliberate understatement + ref. to *Dinky Toys*, defunct brand of toy cars]

dinky *adj.*[1] [late 18C+] **1** neat, trim, dainty. **2** tiny, trifling. [Scot. *dink*, smartly dressed, neat and trim]

dinky *adj.*[2] [1950s–60s] (US Black) second-rate, poor quality. [RINKY-DINK adj.]

dinky-di *adj.*[1] *see* DINKI-DI.

dinky-di/-die *adj.*[2] [1910s+] (Aus./N.Z.) excellent, first-rate, the best of its type; also ext. to *dinky-di/die-do*. [DINKY adj.[1] + SE *di(amond)*]

dinky-di/-die *adv.* [1910s+] (Aus./N.Z.) truly, certainly. [DINKY-DI adj.[2]]

dinky dirt *n.* [20C] (Aus.) a shirt (cf. DICKY DIRT). [rhy. sl.]

dinky dyke *n.* [1980s+] (US gay) a feminine or boyish lesbian (cf. BABY BUTCH; GAYCHICK). [DINKY adj.[1] + DYKE n.]

dinky one's slinky, to *phr.* [1960s+] to masturbate. [assonance, but cf. DINK n.[3] (1)]

dinky up *v.* [1970s+] to smarten up. [DINKY adj.[1]]

dinner *n.* [1940s–60s] (US Black) an attractive young woman (cf. DISH). [she is 'good enough to eat']

dinner buckets *see* DINNERS.

dinner for tea, to be *phr.* [late 19C+] to be very easy and pleasant.

dinner masher *n.* [1990s] a male homosexual. [SE *dinner*, i.e. something to eat + MASHER]

dinner pailer *n.* [1940s–50s] (US) a regular working man or woman (cf. CHUMP n.^{2} (2); WORKING STIFF). [SE *dinner pail*; lit. one who carries a dinner pail]

dinners/dinner buckets *n.* [20C] (US) the female breasts. [their role as milk carriers]

dinner-set *n.* [late 19C] the teeth (cf. DINING ROOM CHAIRS; DINING ROOM FURNITURE).

dinnyhazer *n.* (Aus.) **1** [20C] a knockout blow (cf. DENNYAISER). **2** [1940s+] something large, outstanding, exceptional (depending on context). [E.P. suggests the Aus. boxer *Dinny Hayes*, but note that *AND* and *DNZE* claim 'of unknown origin']

dino *n.*^{1} [1910s] **1** (US) a tramp, a hobo, a layabout. **2** (US) an Italian or Hispanic labourer. [the 'typical' Mediterranean name, *Dino*]

dino *n.*^{2} [1930s+] (orig. US) a dinosaur. [abbr.]

dinosaur *n.*^{1} **1** [1970s+] anyone who refuses to move with the times, a conservative (cf. MOSS-BACK). **2** [1980s] a large, outmoded piece of equipment. **3** [1980s+] an ageing rock star, usually of the 1960s or early 1970s vintage. Such stars, and their bands, won't lie down and subsist gracefully on their royalties; instead they continue to stage concerts, make albums, tour the world and generally refuse to act their age.

dinosaur *n.*^{2} [1980s+] (US Black) the penis. [male bravado + supposed resemblance to a dinosaur's neck]

d.i.o. *phr.* [late 18C–mid-19C] *damn! I'm off* (cf. P.P.C.; P.P.M.). [abbr.; the phr. satirizes the various forms of polite initials left on visiting cards]

dip *n.*^{1} [18C–early 19C] a tallow-chandler. [abbr. SE *dip-candle*]

Dip, the *n.*^{2} **1** [late 18C–early 19C] a cookshop under Furnival's Inn, London, popular among legal clerks. **2** [20C] (gay) a stretch of Piccadilly adjoining St James's Park where gay prostitutes solicit for wealthy clients.

dip *n.*^{3} [19C+] a pickpocket. [DIP v.^{2}]

dip *n.*^{4} **1** [19C+] (US) a blow, a hit. **2** [1940s+] a bout of quick sexual intercourse. [ext. use of SE *dip*, to plunge in]

dip *n.*^{5} [mid-19C] (Aus.) a boiled flour dumpling (cf. DOUGHBOY n.^{1}).

dip *n.*^{6} [20C] (Ulster) **1** fried bread. **2** hot gravy or an egg to dip in.

dip *n.*^{7} [20C] (US) a hat. [one 'dips one's hat']

dip *n.*^{8} **1** [1920s+] (orig. Aus.) a fool (cf. DIPSHIT n.). **2** [1970s+] (US campus) a bore, a dullard. [? LOSE ONE'S DIP]

dip *n.*^{9} [1940s–60s] a drunkard. [SE *dip(somaniac)*]

dip *n.*^{10} [1940s+] a member of the *Diplomatic Service*. [abbr.]

dip *n.*^{11} (drugs) **1** [1950s] a dose or portion of a drug. **2** [1980s+] crack cocaine. [SE *dip*, a pinch of snuff]

dip *n.*^{12} [1960s] (US Black) a party, a get-together, esp. of those in their teens or twenties. [the *Beale Street Dip*, a popular jazz dance of early 20C]

dip *v.*^{1} [late 17C–late 19C] to pawn; thus *dipped*, in debt, mortgaged; *dip one's rigging*, to pawn one's clothes. [SE *dip*, to mortgage]

dip *v.*^{2} [19C+] to pick a pocket.

dip *v.*^{3} [20C] **1** to eavesdrop, to butt into another's conversation, to pay more attention to other people's business than to one's own. **2** (W.I.) to join a conversation, argument, quarrel etc without being asked to do so. [SE *dip in* or DIP ONE'S MOUTH IN SOMEONE'S BUSINESS]

dip *v.*^{4} [20C] (Irish) to work.

dip *v.*^{5} [1990s] (US Black teen) to drive. [ety. unknown]

dip and chuck it *n.* [20C] (Aus.) a bucket. [rhy. sl.]

diphead *n.* [1970s+] a fool, an unpleasant person (cf. DIPSHIT n.). [DIP n.^{8} + sfx. -HEAD (1)]

dip in the fudge pot, to *phr.* [1970s+] (US gay) to have anal intercourse.

dip into *v.* **1** [early 19C] to pick a pocket. **2** [mid-19C] (US) to attack physically.

dip it *v.* [20C] to have sexual intercourse (cf. DIP THE FLY). [abbr. DIP ONE'S WICK]

dip one's beak, to *phr.* [mid-19C+] to have a drink (cf. DIP ONE'S BILL).

dip one's/the bill, to *phr.* [17C] to be mildly tipsy, to be nearly drunk (cf. DIP ONE'S BEAK).

dip one's lid, to *phr.* [20C] (Aus.) to tip one's hat, esp. in fig. use, i.e. to acknowledge, to pay respect. [SE *dip* + LID n.^{1} (1)]

dip one's mouth/nose in someone's business, to *phr.* [20C] (W.I.) to interfere where one's interest is not required. [var. on SE *poke one's nose in*]

dip one's/the wick, to *phr.* [late 19C+] of a man, to have sexual intercourse (cf. DIP IT; DIP THE FLY). [SE *dip* + ? *Hampton Wick* (see HAMPTON)]

dip out on *v.* [1950s+] (Aus.) to fail, to miss an opportunity.

dipped in the Shannon *phr.* [late 18C–late 19C] shameless, devoid of shyness. [those who are dipped in the Irish River Shannon are supposedly rendered free of any self-effacement]

dipped in the wing *phr.* [late 19C] bested in a dispute, defeated. [a bird dips its wing as a sign of defeat]

dipper *n.*^{1} [late 17C+] (US) a Baptist. [SE *dip*, to plunge into water, thus the practice of baptism by total immersion]

dipper *n.*^{2} [19C+] a pickpocket (cf. DIPPING n.^{1}). [DIP n.^{3}]

dipper *n.*^{3} [1980s+] (drugs) phencyclidine (cf. ACE n.^{3}). [DIP n.^{11} (1)]

dipper *n.*^{4} [1990s] (US teen) a person who spends money just because he or she has it. [they keep dipping into their wallet or purse]

dipping *n.*^{1} [mid-19C+] the world and practice of pick-pocketing; thus *dipping-bloke*, a pickpocket. [DIP n.^{3} + sfx. -ing]

dipping/dipping in business *n.*^{2} [1970s] (US Black) interfering in affairs that are none of one's concern.

dipping in the bush *n.* [1970s+] cunnilingus. [SE *dip* + BUSH n.^{4} (1)]

dipping out *n.* [1980s+] (US drugs) of drug runners, the stealing of a portion of crack cocaine from the vials in which it is contained. [SE *dip into*]

dipping rather deep *n.* [19C] drinking heavily. [DIP ONE'S BEAK]

dippy *adj.* [20C] crazy, eccentric, mildly insane; thus *dippy about*, *dippy over*, obsessed with, usu. a person with whom one is in love. [? the image of a head that is 'not screwed on' and thus moves up and down like a bird dipping its beak or DIPSHIT adj.]

dips *n.* [19C] a grocer. [a period when the grocer dipped into various sacks or boxes of goods to measure out a customer's wants]

dipshit *n.* [1960s+] (orig. US) a fool (cf. DICKHEAD). [DIP n.^{8} (1) + SHIT n.^{2}]

dipshit *adj.* [1960s+] (orig. US) **1** stupid. **2** second-rate, inferior; thus *dipshitting*, horrible, vile. [DIPSHIT n.]

dipso *n.* [late 19C–1970s] an alcoholic. [abbr. SE *dipsomaniac*]

dip south *v.* [1940s+] (Aus./N.Z.) to put one's hand in one's pocket, esp. when one's funds are running low. [SE *dip* + SOUTH adj.]

dipstick *n.* [1960s+] **1** the penis (cf. DIP ONE'S WICK). **2** (orig. US) a fool, an incompetent (cf. DICKHEAD; MOPSTICK). [play on SE; widely popularized by the BBC TV series *Only Fools and Horses* (from 1981), whose star, David Jason, refused to use obscenities, but *dipstick* fits neatly in the range of words that mean both penis and fool, e.g. DICKHEAD, DORK.

dipsy *adj.*[1] [1970s] (US) drunk. [SE *dipsomaniac*]

dipsy *adj.*[2] [1980s] (US) eccentric. [DIPPY]

dipsy-doodle *n.* [1940s] (US) trickery, scheming. [baseball jargon *dipsy-do*, a deceptive sinking curveball, ult. SE *dip*]

dipsy-doodle *v.* (US) **1** [1940s–50s] to trick, to plot. **2** [1980s] to wander along. [DIPSY-DOODLE *n.*]

dip the bill *see* DIP ONE'S BILL.

dip the fly, to *phr.* [1980s+] (US Black) to have sexual intercourse (cf. DIP IT; DIP ONE'S WICK). [the dipping or lowering of the trouser fly before intercourse]

dip the schnitzel, to *phr.* [1950s+] (US) to have sexual intercourse. [SE *dip* + SCHNITZEL]

dipwad *n.* [1970s+] (US) a general term of abuse (cf. DICKHEAD). [DIPSHIT *adj.* + WAD *n.*[5]]

dire *adj.* [1920s+] dreadful, unpleasant, objectionable. [ext. of SE use]

directly minute *adv.* [late 19C] immediately, at once.

dirk *n.*[1] [18C; 1960s] the penis (cf. BAYONET).

dirk *n.*[2] [1960s+] a fool, an idiot, a failure. [var. on JERK *n.*[1] (2)]

dirt *n.*[1] **1** [19C+] (Aus./N.Z.) a bad or spiteful temper. **2** [mid-19C+] (Aus./N.Z./US) a mean action or a malicious remark. **3** [mid-19C+] (orig. US) gossip, malicious chatter. **4** [mid-19C+] (orig. US) information, not necessarily, but often scurrilous; often as [1930s+] *what's the dirt* (*on*) ... ? (cf. DISH THE DIRT). **5** [1920s+] (orig. US) an unpleasant individual. **6** [1980s+] (US) a male or female prostitute who steals from clients.

dirt *n.*[2] [late 19C] money (cf. CRAP *n.*[1]; DUST *n.*[1]). [the guilty image of money as filth]

dirt *n.*[3] [1940s+] in cards, a trump; thus *he's put a bit of dirt on it.*

dirt *n.*[4] [1980s+] (US drugs) **1** very poor quality drugs. **2** heroin.

dirtbag *n.* [1940s+] (orig. US) **1** a promiscuous woman. **2** a general term of abuse, irrespective of sex (cf. FUCKBAG; SCUMBAG). [SE *dirt* + SCUMBAG]

dirtball *n.* [1970s+] (US) a dirty or generally unpleasant person. [SE *dirt* + SLEAZEBALL (*see* SLEAZEBAG)]

dirt bird *n.* [1940s+] a general term of abuse (cf. DIRTBAG; DIRTBALL). [? dial. *dirt bird*, the skua but prob. SE *dirt* + BIRD *n.*[2] (1)]

dirt box *n.* [20C] the anus.

dirt-chute *n.* [1940s+] (US) the anus (cf. POOP-CHUTE; SHIT-CHUTE).

dirt-devil *n.* [1980s+] (US drugs) an individual who, on most occasions, has poor-grade marijuana. [DIRT *n.*[4] + SE *devil*]

dirt-dobber/-scratcher *n.* [1940s–60s] (US south/west) **1** a poor farmer. **2** a worthless person. [SE *dirt* + *dob*, to dab, to pat/*scratcher*]

dirt-eater *n.* [mid-19C–1940s] (US) a poor White. [for ety. *see* CLAY-EATER]

dirt farm *n.* [1970s+] (US Black) any centre for (malicious) gossip (cf. DISH THE DIRT). [DIRT *n.*[1] (3) + SE *farm* + pun on SE]

dirt grass *n.* [1980s+] (drugs) inferior quality marijuana. [DIRT *n.*[4] + GRASS *n.*[4]]

dirt, grime and dust *n.* [20C] (Aus.) a crust (on a pie). [rhy. sl.]

dirties *n.* [20C] (US) diarrhoea, sometimes modified as to source, e.g. *green-apple dirties.* [the possible effect on one's underwear]

dirt-nap *v.* [1990s] (US Black) to be dead. [SE *dirt* + *nap*]

dirt road *n.*[1] [late 19C+] (US) the road, the highway (as opposed to the railroad).

dirt road *n.*[2] [1910s+] the anus; thus *go up the dirt/old dirt road*, to sodomize. [fig. use of DIRT ROAD *n.*[1]]

dirts, the *n.* [1920s–30s] a mean trick (cf. DO THE DIRTY ON).

dirt sauce *n.* [1990s] a minor discharge of excrement following the breaking of wind.

dirt-surfer *n.* [1980s+] (US) one who has abandoned most if not all the normal standards of hygiene and cleanliness. [SE *dirt* + *surfer* used as explorer, e.g. *Net surfer*]

dirt-tamper *n.* [1970s] a male homosexual, a sodomite. [SE *dirt* + *tamp*, to ram down hard]

dirt track *n.* [1960s+] the anus; thus *dirt track specialist*, a sodomite (cf. DIRT ROAD *n.*[2]).

dirty *n.* [1980s+] (drugs) cannabis. [the brown colour of hashish]

dirty *adj.* **1** [1920s–50s] (US Black) bad, terrible, objectionable and similar negatives according to context. **2** [1920s–50s] (US Black) good, wonderful, excellent (on bad = good model). **3** [1950s+] (UK/US Und.) dubious, unsafe, to be avoided. **4** [1950s+] holding incriminating evidence. **5** [1950s+] (drugs) currently addicted to drugs (cf. CLEAN *adj.*[1]).

dirty *adv.*[1] [1920s+] a general intensifier, extremely, very, exceedingly, esp. in *dirty big, dirty great.*

dirty *adv.*[2] [1960s+] (Aus.) resentful (of).

dirty acres *n.* [late 17C–early 19C] a landed estate.

dirty a plate with, to *phr.* [late 18C–early 19C] to share a meal with (cf. FOUL A PLATE).

dirty basing *n.* [1980s+] (drugs) crack cocaine (cf. FREEBASING). [CRACK *n.*[17] is 'dirty', i.e. cheaper and less pure than freebase cocaine]

dirty beau *n.* [late 17C–18C] a slovenly man, who poses as a dandy despite his outward appearance (cf. BEAU-NASTY).

dirty bird *n.*[1] [1940s–50s] (US Black) Old Crow whisky. [the black bird on its label]

dirty bird *n.*[2] [1950s–70s] an unappealing individual, esp. in rhetorical phr. *I'll be a dirty bird!* [coined by comedian George Gobel on his 1954 TV show]

dirty bundle *n.* [1940s+] (W.I.) an untidy person.

dirty daughter *n.* [20C] water. [rhy. sl. Note lyrics of the once-popular song 'Wash me in the water/In which you wash your dirty daughter']

dirty dish *n.* [20C] (Aus.) fish. [rhy. sl.]

dirty dishes *n.*[1] [late 19C] poor relations. [they eat one's food]

dirty dishes *n.*[2] [1960s+] (Und.) planted incriminating evidence.

dirty dishes *v.* [1930s–40s] (US Black) to eat.

dirty dog *n.* **1** [late 19C+] a generally unpleasant person, with overtones of womanizing. **2** [1940s–50s] (US Black) a man who habitually mistreats women. [SE *dirty* + DOG *n.*[5] (6), (7)]

dirty dowager *n.* [1950s–60s] (gay) an unkempt, ill-preserved, older, gay man. [SE *dirty* + SE *dowager*, orig. the widow of a dead king, i.e. a QUEEN *n.*[1]]

dirty dozens *see* DOZENS.

dirty gertie *n.* [1920s–40s] (US) a promiscuous or sexually enthusiastic woman. [SE *dirty* + redup. Note that *Gertie* is a 'typically' vulgar name]

dirty great *adj.* [1920s+] to imply great size, the most common use of dirty as an intensifier. [DIRTY *adv.*[1] + SE *great*]

dirty half-mile, the *n.* (Aus.) **1** [1920s+] Kings Cross Road, Sydney. **2** [1930s+] William Street, Sydney. [both areas are/were known for roughness, decadence and excess]

dirty hearts *n.* [1960s–70s] (US Black) the card game Hearts.

dirty laundry/linen *n.* [1980s+] unpleasant, embarrassing or revelatory information; thus *air one's dirty laundry in public.*

dirty left/right *n.* [1910s+] (Aus.) a powerful fist, of the left or right hand.

dirty leg *n.* [1960s+] (US) a promiscuous woman (cf. DIRTY NECK; GRUBBER *n.*[1]; SCAB *n.*; SCUZZ *n.*; SLEAZE *n.*; SNOT *n.*; SWEAT HOG). [SE *dirty* + LEG *n.*]

dirty linen *see* DIRTY LAUNDRY.

dirty mac/macintosh brigade n. [1970s+] a generic term for those men who frequent sex shops and buy from the 'top shelves' of newsagents (cf. DIRTY OLD MAN). [such pilloried figures are invariably portrayed as skulking in a dirty raincoat]

dirty money n. [20C] **1** money that is considered not to have been earned honourably or respectably. **2** money from drug dealing.

dirty neck n. [1910s–60s] (US) a promiscuous woman (cf. DIRTY LEG). [coined by US troops in WW1 to describe French women]

dirty night at sea n. [20C] (Aus.) an all-night drinking session.

dirty old Jew n. [20C] (bingo) the number two (cf. ME AND YOU n.). [rhy. sl.]

dirty old man n. [1930s+] an older man whose sexual tastes (whether or not fulfilled) err towards much younger lovers, esp. when under the legal age of consent (cf. D.O.M.).

dirty pool n. [1940s+] (orig. US) unfair, duplicitous activity; thus *play dirty pool*, to behave in an underhand manner.

dirty puzzle n. [late 17C–early 19C] a slatternly woman. [SE *dirty* + dial. *puzzle*, a slut; ult. Fr. *pucelle*, a virgin]

dirty right see DIRTY LEFT.

dirty shirt n. [1940s+] (W.I.) a bulla cake (cf. DRAYMAN BIBLE). [a *bulla cake* is a flat cake, sometimes with a central hole, made of flour and brown sugar and cooked by country people and the urban poor (wearers of SE *dirty shirts*); also known as a *cartman's hymn-book*]

dirty shirt club n. [mid-19C] the Parthenon, a public house in Regent Street, London. [the 'great unwashed' who made up its clientele]

dirty shirt march n. [mid–late 19C] pre-Sunday lunch promenading by London slum-dwellers, before putting on clean clothes for the meal.

dirty spoon see GREASY SPOON.

dirty weekend n. [1930s+] a weekend spent either with one's lover (in the absence of one's spouse) or with one's spouse but without one's children. [the Puritan obsession that sex is 'dirty']

dirty whore n. [20C] (bingo) the number 34. [rhy. sl.]

dirty work at the crossroads n. [1910s+] **1** underhand, dishonourable actions. **2** sexual intercourse (cf. DO THE DIRTIES). [the image is of a highwayman or other robber lurking at a country crossroads]

dis/diss n. **1** [20C] a *dis*appointment. **2** [1980s+] (US Black) an act of *dis*paragement or of *dis*respect. [abbr.]

dis adj. [1920s+] eccentric, mentally unstable. [orig. naut. use; ult. telegraphist's jargon *dis*, disconnected]

dis/diss v. **1** [1920s] to disrespect. **2** [1920s] to disparage, to attack verbally. **3** [1980s+] (orig. US Black/campus) to denigrate someone in public to the extent that it makes that person feel bad. **4** [1980s+] (orig. US Black/campus) to deliberately break an appointment or date without consulting the second party. [the earlier UK use seems to have faded before its resurrection by US Blacks in 1980s]

disabilly see DISHABILLY.

disc n. [1910s] (US) a $1 coin. [the shape]

disco n. [1960s+] (orig. US) a discotheque. [Fr. *discothèque*, orig. a record library (on the model of *bibliothèque*, (book) library) and by mid-1950s a nightclub where a selection of records replaced the traditional live band]

disco biscuit n. [1990s] (drugs) MDMA (cf. BISCUIT n.[7]; ECSTASY). [DISCO + SE *biscuit*; its shape and the environment in which it is often consumed]

discombobberate v. [19C] (US) to discomfit, to perplex, to confuse (cf. DISCOMBOBULATE; DISCOMBOBBELATE; DISCONBOOBERATE).

discombobulate/discomboobble v. [early 19C+] to discomfit (cf. CONBOBBERATE; DISCOMBOBBERATE). [a nonsense word, playing on SE *discomfit* and/or *discompose*, ? + BOBBERY]

discomboobelate v. [1940s–60s] (US) to discomfit (cf. DISCOMBOBBERATE).

discomboobble see DISCOMBOBULATE.

disconbooberate v. [20C] to discomfit (cf. DISCOMBOBBERATE).

discount v. [late 19C–1920s] (US Black) to disparage, to hold in very low regard. [literal use, i.e. *dis-* + *count*; SE *discount*, to make a deduction in estimating the worth of]

discount justice n. [20C] (US Und.) the courtroom practice of letting small-time criminals plead guilty to the least of the charges levelled at them and thus receive the smallest feasible sentence. [SE *discount*, cut-price]

discover one's gender, to phr. [1950s+] (gay) to accept or acknowledge one's homosexuality.

discumnobulated/discumnockerated adj. [1990s] (US teen) broken (cf. DISCOMBOBULATE).

discuss v. [early 19C] to sample or enjoy one's food and drink; thus [mid-19C] *discussion*, the sampling of a commodity's quality.

dis di program, to phr. [1980s+] (W.I./UK Black teen) to put a planned thing on hold, to delay something, to disrupt a schedule. [DIS v./abbr. SE *dis(rupt)* + SAmE *program* (UK sp. would be *programme*)]

dise n. [1910s–20s] (US) goods, commodities. [abb. SE *(merchan)dise*]

disease n. [1980s+] (drugs) one's drug of choice (cf. POISON n.[1]).

disguise v. [mid-16C–mid-19C] to intoxicate, to make drunk. [DISGUISED]

disguised adj. [mid-16C–mid-19C] drunk (cf. DISGUISE ONESELF). [SE *disguised in liquor*]

disguise oneself v. [16C] to drink (cf. DISGUISED). [DISGUISE v.]

disgustingly adv. [1970s+] a general intensifier. [ironic use of SE]

dish n.[1] **1** [late 19C] the act of abusing, cheating. **2** [late 19C+] an embarrassing story about a subject's life; thus *know the dish*, to be aware of the embarrassing truth. [DISH v.]

dish n.[2] **1** [1910s+] something one likes, something suited to one's taste (cf. CUP OF TEA n.[1]). **2** [1930s+] (orig. US) an attractive female (cf. BANANA n.[2]). **3** [1950s+] an attractive person of either sex. **4** [1950s+] (gay) the buttocks. [SE *dish*, an item of food]

dish v. **1** [late 18C+] to hurt, to stop another's plans, to frustrate, to cheat (cf. DO BROWN). **2** [mid-19C] to stop, to suppress, to do away with. **3** [1950s+] (orig. US gay) to gossip maliciously, to tell tales (cf. DIS v.). [the image of food, which having been 'done' is 'dished up']

dishabells/dizybells n. [20C] (Irish) a state of undress (cf. DISHABILLY). [Fr. *déshabillé*, undressed]

dishabilly/disabilly n. [mid-19C+] a state of undress (cf. DISHYBILLY). [Fr. *déshabillé*, undressed]

dishclout n. [late 18C] a dirty, greasy woman. [metonymy; SE *dishclout*, a kitchen rag]

dish-down n. [1920s] a disappointment.

dished adv. [late 19C+] ruined (cf. DISHED UP). ['a correspondent suggests that meat is usually DONE BROWN before being *dished* and conceives that the latter term may have arisen as the natural sequence of the former' (Hotten, 1867)]

dished out adj. [late 16C–mid-17C] dressed up (flashily).

dished up adj. **1** [late 18C+] utterly ruined. **2** [1930s+] (Aus.) exhausted, tired out. [ext. of DISHED]

dish it out v. [20C] (orig. US) to hand out, usu. punishment, blows, abuse etc.

dish of chat n. [early 19C] (US) a talk, a conversation.

dish of rails *n.* [late 18C–early 19C] a scolding from a wife to her husband. [SE *rail*, an act of railing or reviling]

dish of red rag *n.* [early 19C–1910s] verbal abuse. [pun on SE *dish* + RED RAG *n.*[1], but note DISH *v.* (3)]

dishonourable discharge *n.* [1960s+] masturbation; thus (US gay) *have a dishonourable discharge*, to masturbate after failing to make a sexual connection.

dish out the gravy/porridge, to *phr.* [1940s–50s] of a judge, to hand out a heavy sentence.

dish queen *n.* [1950s+] a homosexual who enjoys slandering his peers (cf. DISH THE DIRT). [DISH *v.* (3) + QUEEN *n.*[1]]

dishrag *n.* [1970s] a person who is exploited, treated poorly (cf. DOORMAT).

dish ran away with the spoon *phr.* [1970s+] (Aus.) a pimp. [rhy. sl. *dish ran away with the spoon* = HOON]

dish the dirt, to *phr.* [1950s+] to gossip maliciously, to slander. [DISH *v.* (3)]

dishwater diarrhoea *n.* [19C+] (US) an imaginary disease, esp. one that appears when the 'sufferer' would otherwise face an unpleasant or tedious task.

dish-wrestler *n.* [1920s–30s] a restaurant dish-washer.

dishy *adj.* [1960s+] attractive, pretty. ['good enough to eat']

dishybilly *adj.* [20C] undressed, not fully dressed, dishevelled (cf. DISHABILLY). [Fr. *déshabillé*, undressed]

disinfectant *n.* [1960s+] any form of sauce or condiment.

dismal ditty *n.* [late 17C–early 19C] a psalm recited on the gallows by a criminal who is about to die. [SE *dismal*, dreary, cheerless + *ditty*]

dismal jimmy *n.* [1920s–40s] a miserable, gloomy person.

dismals *n.* [mid-18C–mid-19C] **1** low spirits, depression. **2** mourning wear. [later use is SE]

dismiss *v.* (US) **1** [mid-19C] to leave. **2** [1980s+] (campus) to end a relationship.

Disneyfied *adj.* [1970s] (US Black) sickeningly, sentimentally happy. [the 'family values' traditionally associated with and propagated by the Disney Company]

Disneyland *n.* [20C] (US Und.) a prison known for its liberal regime (cf. PLAYHOUSE *n.*). [note 1960s+ US milit. use *Disneyland East*, the Pentagon, the US Air Force Academy and similar headquarters]

disobey the pope, to *phr.* [1980s+] to masturbate (cf. BANG THE BISHOP). [the Catholic prohibition on 'self-abuse']

dispatch/despatch *v.* [early 18C+] to eat or drink up speedily.

dispatcher/despatcher *n.* [late 18C–late 19C] a form of false dice, on which the pips are arranged in wrong numbers; a *high dispatcher* cannot throw less than two, while a *low dispatcher* cannot throw higher than three (cf. DESPATCHERS; DOCTORS).

dispatches/despatches *n.* **1** [late 18C–early 19C] a justice of the peace's warrant for the commitment of a rogue. **2** [early-mid-19C] false dice.

disremember *v.* [mid-19C+] (Anglo-Irish) to forget.

diss *see* DIS.

distiller *n.* [19C] (Aus.) one who cannot take a joke (cf. CARRY THE KEG). [abbr. WALKING DISTILLER]

disturbance *n.* [late 19C] (US) alcohol. [its effects]

ditch *n.*[1] [19C] the vagina (cf. ARBOUR).

ditch *n.*[2] **1** [mid-19C–1900s] the Atlantic Ocean. **2** [late 19C+] (US) a canal, e.g. Panama, Suez, Erie. **3** [1920s+] the sea, esp. the English Channel or North Sea (cf. BIG DITCH).

Ditch, the *n.*[3] [late 19C] Calcutta; thus *ditcher*, an inhabitant of Calcutta. [the *Mahratta Ditch*, built by the East India Company in 1742 to protect Calcutta from the Mahratta tribesmen, it ran for 4.8km (3 miles) but the work was never finished]

ditch, the *n.*[4] [late 19C] an act of rejection. [DITCH *v.*[1] (1)]

Ditch, the *n.*[5] [late 19C+] **1** Shore*ditch*, East London; thus *Ditch and Chapel*, Shoreditch and Whitechapel. **2** Hounds-*ditch*. [abbr.]

ditch *n.*[6] [1960s] (drugs) the inside of the elbow, used for injections of narcotics.

ditch *n.*[7] [1980s+] (drugs) marijuana. [abbr. DITCHWEED]

ditch *v.*[1] **1** [late 19C+] of people and objects, to throw away, to dispense with, to abandon. **2** [late 19C–1910s] to ruin, to stand in the way of a plan. **3** [20C] (US) to leave in a hurry. **4** [1920s+] (US teen/campus) to play truant from school.

ditch *v.*[2] [1940s+] (orig. RAF) to land one's aircraft in the sea. [DITCH *n.*[2] (3)]

ditched *adj.*[1] [late 19C+] nonplussed, at a loss. [DITCH *v.*[1]]

ditched *adj.*[2] [late 19C+] (US) in difficulties, trouble. [? a hobo being tossed from a moving train]

ditch out *v.* [1920s+] (US) to leave quickly or clandestinely. [ext. of DITCH *v.*[1] (3)]

ditchweed *n.* [1980s+] (US drugs) **1** wild marijuana, which is usually less powerful than cultivated varieties. **2** any inferior quality marijuana, often from Mexico. [such plants grow lit. or fig. in the ditch]

dithered *adj.* [1920s+] (Aus.) mildly drunk, tipsy.

ditso *adj.* [1970s+] (US) useless, second-rate, no good. [DITZ *n.*[2]]

ditsy *adj.* [1970s+] (US) **1** wonderful, outstanding (cf. DITZY *adj.*[2]). **2** fussy, intricate. **3** esp. of women, scatterbrained (cf. DITZY *adj.*[1]).

ditties *n.* [1990s] female breasts (cf. TITTY *n.*[2]).

ditto/dittoes *n.* [late 18C–19C] a suit of clothes (jacket, waistcoat, breeches) all the same colour. [SE *ditto*, the same. The style is common today, but less so when the sl. was coined]

ditto brother/sister smut *phr.* [mid–late 19C] you too! the same to you! [phr. 'the pot calling the kettle black']

ditty *n.* [late 19C+] (Aus./N.Z.) **1** a lie. **2** a 'shaggy-dog story'.

ditty-bop *v. see* DIDDY-BOP *v.*

dittybopper *see* DIDDLY-BOPPER.

ditz *n.*[1] [1970s+] (US) a scatterbrained person, usu. a woman, a fool, an idiot (cf. DITZY *adj.*[1]). [SE *dizzy*]

ditz *n.*[2] [1970s+] (US) something excellent.

ditz *v.* [1970s+] (US) to treat like a fool.

ditzo *n.* [1970s+] (US) a scatterbrained person (cf. DITZ *n.*[1]).

ditzy *adj.*[1] (US) **1** [1970s+] eccentric. **2** [1980s+] nervous, edgy. [DITZ *n.*[1]]

ditzy *adj.*[2] [1970s+] (US) first-rate, excellent, exceptional. [DITZ *n.*[2]]

div *n.*[1] [late 19C] (Aus.) a sum of money, esp. money won from a bookmaker. [SE *dividend*]

div *n.*[2] [1970s+] a weakling, a fool. [ety. unknown; ? link to echoic DUH *n.*]

diva *n.* [1990s] (US Black) **1** a stately woman, not invariably beautiful, but always of a certain grandeur. **2** a highly talented female entertainer. **3** an accomplished woman in any occupation. [SE *diva*, a distinguished female singer; ult. Ital. *diva*, goddess]

diva *adj.* [1990s] (US campus) excellent, worthy of admiration. [DIVA *n.*]

dive *n.*[1] [mid-19C+] (orig. US) an illicit drinking establishment or any similarly down-market place of entertainment (cf. DARKIES; SHADES *n.*[1]). [SE *dive*. The implication is of both physical and social 'lowness'; such places were usually situated in a basement, cellar or other slightly clandestine place into which patrons could 'dive' without being noticed. *Dive* reached its heyday with US Prohibition (1920–33) but the phr. *dive bar* has persisted, lending an air of spurious romance to otherwise unexceptional drinking places]

dive/diver *n.*[2] [early 17C–late 19C] a pickpocket. [DIVE *v.*[1]]

dive v.[1] [early 17C–late 19C] to pick a pocket. [the plunging of one's hand into another's pocket or purse; thus the name of the celebrated pickpocket *Jenny Diver*]

dive v.[2] [1930s+] (orig. US) to perform cunnilingus (cf. DIVE IN THE BUSHES; GO DOWN v.[7]).

dive a muff, to phr. [1940s+] (orig. US) to perform cunnilingus (cf. MUFF-DIVE). [SE *dive* + MUFF n.[1] (2)]

divebombing n. [1970s+] picking up cigarette ends from the pavement.

dive for a meal, to phr. [late 18C–early 19C] to eat in a cellar (cf. DIVE n.[1]).

dive for pearls, to phr. [1940s+] (US) to work as a dishwasher (cf. PEARL DIVER).

dive in the bushes, to phr. [1960s+] (US) to perform cunnilingus. [DIVE v.[2] + BUSH n.[4] (1)]

dive in the canyon, to phr. [1960s+] to perform cunnilingus (cf. YODEL IN THE CANYON). [DIVE v.[2] + CANYON]

dive into one's sky, to phr. [late 19C] to put one's hand in one's pocket, esp. to remove money. [SE *dive* + SKY]

dive/do a dive into the dark, to phr. [late 19C+] to have sexual intercourse.

dive into the sack, to phr. [late 17C–early 19C] to pick a pocket.

dive into the sky, to phr. [1970s+] to penetrate the anus with one's penis.

diver n. **1** [16C–early 17C] a small boy who, like Oliver Twist in Charles Dickens's novel (1837–9), is put in through an otherwise impassably small window; once inside the house, he either lets in the gang or passes booty out to them. **2** [early 17C–19C] a pickpocket. **3** [early 17C–19C] one who lives in a cellar. **4** [1930s] (US) a beggar who forages in garbage cans for food.

divers n. [late 19C+] the fingers.

divi see DIVVY n.[1].

dividers n. [1910s–30s] a pair of divided knickers, the long legs resembling knickerbockers. [SE *divide*]

divide the house with one's wife, to phr. [late 18C] to throw one's wife onto the streets. ['to give her the outside, and to keep all the inside to one's self' (Grose, 1785)]

divine rights/right n. [1990s] (US Black) the police. [SE *Divine Right of Kings*, the concept that monarchs are answerable only to God for their actions]

diving-bell n. [late 19C] a basement tavern (cf. DIVE n.[1]).

diving-suit n. [1940s+] (Aus.) a condom (cf. DIVE INTO THE DARK]

divoon adj. [1940s–50s] (US) divine, wonderful. [joc. mispron.]

divorce mill n. [late 19C] (US) a divorce court that specializes in 'quickie' separations.

divot n. [1930s] a toupee. [resemblance]

divot-digger/divoteer n. [1920s–40s] (Aus.) a golfer, esp. an inexperienced one.

divvie n. [1920s+] one who can sense the right answer even when they have no facts or expertise on which to base their opinion. [? SE *diviner*]

divvies! excl. [20C] (US) that's mine! I want to do that! I want a share! a child's term used to claim the whole or an equal part of a given object (cf. AIKIES!). [SE *divide* or *division*]

divvy/divi n.[1] [late 19C+] *dividend*, the annual financial share-out by a cooperative society; thus *divvy-hunter*, one who joins the society purely to benefit from the dividend. [abbr.]

divvy n.[2] [20C] (Aus.) a very short time. [? SE a *division* of time]

divvy n.[3] [1970s+] a fool, a socially unacceptable person. [ext. of DIV n.[2]]

divvy adj. [1900s–20s] extremely pleasant, 'heavenly'. [SE *divine*]

divvy/divvy up v. **1** [late 19C+] **1** to divide up, usu. illicit profits. **2** [1930s] (US) to separate. [SE *divide*]

divvy van n. [1990s] (Aus.) a police divisional van.

Dixie n.[1] [mid–late 19C] (US) the American South, esp. those states that formed the Confederacy in the Civil War (1861–5). [20C use is SE. The song 'Dixie's Land' was written and first performed by the 'blackface minstrel' Daniel D Emmett (1815–1904) on 4 April 1859. The term 'Dixie Land' had appeared two months earlier in another Emmett song, 'Jonny Roach'. Of the various poss. etys. the preferred choice is an abbr. of the Mason–Dixon line (which divided the North and South in 1763–7). 'Dixie's land' was also a common term in 19C children's games of tag]

dixie n.[2] [1910s+] (Aus.) an ice-cream carton. [milit. jargon *dixie*, a small iron pot used for boiling tea, rice, stew etc; ult. Hind. *degchi*, a small iron pot]

dixie cup n.[1] [1970s+] an attractive Southern woman. [DIXIE n.[1] + CUPCAKE n. (2); but see DIXIE CUP n.[2]]

dixie cup n.[2] [1990s] (US) anyone seen as disposable (cf. KLEENEX n.[1]). [the brandname of America's best known disposable cup]

dizybells see DISHABELLS.

dizz n. [1960s+] (US) an eccentric (cf. DITZ n.[1]). [abbr. SE *dizzy*]

dizzie adj. [1990s] dyslexic.

dizzy n.[1] [mid-19C–1910s] a clever man, esp. in phr. *quite a dizzy*. [*Dizzy*, the popular nickname of British prime minister Benjamin *Disraeli*, Lord Beaconsfield (1804–81)]

dizzy n.[2] [1910s] (US) a madman. [DIZZY adj.[3]]

dizzy n.[3] [1910s–20s] (US) a cigarette. [its effect]

dizzy adj.[1] [18C] drunk (cf. ADDLED).

dizzy adj.[2] **1** [late 19C–1900s] (US) startling, astonishing, vivid. [it makes one SE *dizzy*]

dizzy adj.[3] [1930s+] **1** obsessed by; thus *dizzy with a dame, to* be obsessed with a woman. **2** eccentric, mad.

dizzy flat n. [late 19C] (US) a complete fool. [SE *dizzy* + FLAT n.[2] + the image of stupidity so great that it makes witnesses giddy]

dizzy limit n. [1930s+] (Aus.) the absolute limit (cf. FROZEN LIMIT).

dizzy-o adj. [1970s] (US) tipsy. [DIZZY adj.[1] + sfx. -o]

d.j. n. [1970s+] *d*inner *j*acket. [abbr.]

dj/deejay n. [1950s+] *d*isc *j*ockey. [abbr.]

dj v. [1980s+] (orig. US) to work as a disc jockey. [DJ n.]

djamba n. [1980s+] (drugs) marijuana (cf. DIMBA). [used synon. in various West African languages, e.g. Mende]

d.l. v. [1990s] (US teen) to keep secret or hidden. [abbr. DOWN LOW]

d.l. adv. [1990s] (US Black) in a clandestine, sneaky manner. [D.L. v.]

d.l.c. n. [1980s+] (US campus) a deep or heavy conversation. [abbr. *d*own *l*ow *c*onversation]

dlog see DELOG.

DMs n. [1980s+] a heavy boot favoured first by working men, then by skinheads and latterly by fashionable teenagers. [abbr. DOC MARTENS]

d.m.t. n. [1960s+] (drugs) *d*i*m*ethyl*t*ryptamine. [abbr.]

do n.[1] [17C+] a fraud, a swindle. [DO v.[4]]

do n.[2] [19C] a success, esp. in phr. *make a do/do of*.

do n.[3] [early 19C+] a party, a celebration, a dinner etc, often reasonably formal.

do n.[4] [late 19C+] a period of suffering, usu. physical, e.g. *I've had a rotten do today*.

do n.[5] [1900s–10s] a joke.

do n.[6] [1930s+] excrement, usu. animal (cf. DOGGY-DO; DO-DO). [euph. phr. 'do its business']

do n.[7] [1940s+] sexual intercourse (cf. BASH n.[2]). [DO v.[2] (4)]

do *n.*[8] [1940s+] murder. [DO v.[2] (3)]

do *n.*[9] [1940s+] (US Black) straightened hair (cf. CONK n.[3]).

do *n.*[10] [1940s+] (US Black/campus) a haircut. [hair that has been 'done']

do *n.*[11] [1950s] an attack, a gang fight. [note 1910s milit. jargon *do*, an offensive]

do *n.*[12] [1970s] (drugs) a shot of a narcotic drug. [DO v.[13]]

do.../have... *v.*[1] in addition to the many synonyms for sexual intercourse with individual entries are *do*/*have ... a ballocking, ... a beanfeast in bed, ... a bedward bit, ... a belly warmer, ... a bit of rabbit-pie, ... a blindfold bit, ... a bout, ... a lassie's by-job, ... a brush with the cue, ... a back scuttle, ... a buttered bun, ... a dash in the bloomers, ... a dash up the channel, ... a dog's marriage, ... a drop in, ... a double fight, ... a four-legged frolic, ... a fuck, ... a futter, ... a game in the cock loft, ... a goose and duck, ... a grind, ... a hoist-in, ... a jottle, ... an inside worry, ... a jumble giblets, ... a jumble up, ... a knee trembler, ... a leap/leap up the ladder, ... a little of one with the other, ... a mount, ... a mow, ... a plaster of warm guts, ... a poke, ... a put, ... a rasp, ... a ride, ... a roger, ... a rootle, ... a rush up the straight, ... a St George, ... a shag, ... a shot at the bull's eye, ... a slide up the board, ... a squirt and a squeeze, ... a touch off, ... a tumble in, ... a wet 'un, ... a wipe at the place, ... a wallop in, ... one's oats. See also* BIT n.[3].

do *v.*[2] **1** [16C+] to defeat. **2** [17C+] to assault, to beat up. **3** [early 19C+] to murder, to kill. **4** [late 19C+] of a man, to copulate with a woman. **5** [1950s+] (US gay) to perform fellatio. **6** [1950s+] to sodomize. [fig. uses of SE *do*, all implying a form of 'hitting']

do *v.*[3] [late 16C+] to act or behave in a manner characteristic of (a specified person etc), to mimic.

do *v.*[4] **1** [mid-17C+] to cheat, to defraud, to swindle (cf. DO BROWN; DO OVER v.[1]). **2** [late 19C+] to rob.

do *v.*[5] **1** [18C+] to sue, to take to court, to charge with a crime; thus *X was done for taking and driving away*. **2** [late 18C+] to arrest, to capture. **3** [20C] to prosecute, usu. *do for* burglary, rape etc.

do *v.*[6] [early 19C] (Und.) to counterfeit, to forge; thus *do a queer half-quid*, counterfeit a half-guinea coin, *do a queer screen*, counterfeit a banknote.

do *v.*[7] [early 19C+] **1** to inspect as a tourist, to visit, e.g. *do London*. **2** to attend an entertainment, e.g. *do a show*.

do *v.*[8] [mid-19C+] (orig. US) to suffice, e.g. *that will do fine*.

do *v.*[9] [mid-19C+] to work, to repair, to prepare, to clean, to keep in order. [all rooted in SE *do* (a job)]

do *v.*[10] **1** [mid-19C+] (Aus.) to eat or drink, usu. with the relevant food or drink attached, e.g. *do a couple of pints*, *do a burger*. **2** [1970s] to meet for a meal, esp. in a business context e.g. *do lunch*.

do *v.*[11] [mid-19C+] to serve a sentence in prison, usu. in phr. *do life*, *do five years* (cf. DO TIME).

do *v.*[12] [late 19C+] to squander one's money.

do *v.*[13] [1960s+] to consume a drug, e.g. *Do you do coke?*

d.o.a. *n.* (drugs) **1** [1970s+] phencyclidine (cf. ACE n.[3]). **2** [1980s+] crack cocaine. **3** [1980s+] a street name for a variety of heroin. [orig. police jargon *dead on arrival*]

d.o.a. *v.* [1970s+] to die before one arrives at a hospital. [orig. police jargon *dead on arrival*; i.e. its potentially fatal effects]

do a bathroom guitar solo, to *phr.* [1990s] to masturbate.

do a beer/drink/drop/meal, to *phr.* [mid-late 19C] to have a drink (cf. DO A WET). [ext. of DO v.[10]]

do a Bertie, to *phr.* [1970s] (Und.) to turn Crown's evidence against one's accomplices. [proper name *Bertie Smalls*, a well-known criminal turned confessor]

do a Bette Davis, to *phr.* [1950s–60s] (camp gay) to act in an ostentatious and overly effeminate manner. [the actress Bette Davis (1908–89), a by-word for melodramatic acting and, as such, a gay icon, esp. in the film *All About Eve* (1950)]

do a big, to *phr.* [1990s] (US Black) to commit a robbery.

do a bit, to *phr.*[1] [mid-late 19C] to have something to eat. [abbr. SE *bit to eat*]

do a bit, to *phr.*[2] [mid-19C+] to have sexual intercourse. [BIT n.[3]]

do a bit, to *phr.*[3] [mid-19C+] (US prison) to serve a prison sentence. [BIT n.[7]]

do a bit, to *phr.*[4] [late 19C+] (show business) to perform a routine on stage. [theatre use *bit*, a solo performance]

do a bit of beef, to *phr.* [19C+] to have sexual intercourse (cf. ACHING FOR A SIDE OF BEEF; BIT OF MEAT; BIT OF MUTTON; HAVE A BIT OF BEEF). [BEEF n.[1] (2, 3)]

do a bit of business, to *phr.* [mid 19C+] to have sexual intercourse. [euph.]

do a bit of cauliflower, to *phr.* [1990s] to have sexual intercourse (cf. HAVE A BIT OF CAULIFLOWER). [CAULIFLOWER n.[2]]

do a bit of cock-fighting, to *phr.* [19C+] to have sexual intercourse. [pun on SE *cock*/COCK n.[2] (1)]

do a bit of dancing, to *phr.* [mid–late 19C] to have sexual intercourse. [DANCE v.[1]]

do a bit of flat, to *phr.* [19C] esp. of a prostitute, to have sexual intercourse (cf. FLATBACKER). [SE *flat*; i.e. she is *flat* on her back]

do a bit of front-door work, to *phr.* [19C] to have sexual intercourse. [pun on SE *front door*/FRONT DOOR n.[1]]

do/have a bit of giblet pie, to *phr.* [19C] to have sexual intercourse (cf. CARVE A SLICE).

do a bit of good for oneself *see* DO ALL RIGHT FOR ONESELF.

do a bit of ladies' tailoring, to *phr.* [mid-19C–1920s] to have sexual intercourse (cf. NEEDLEWORK; SEW).

do a bit of skirt, to *phr.* [20C] to have sexual intercourse. [SKIRT]

do a/take the bit of stiff, to *phr.* [mid–late 19C] to accept a bill or promissory note. [BIT OF STIFF n.[2]]

do a bit of stuff, to *phr.* [late 19C+] to have sexual intercourse.

do a bit of tailoring, to *phr.* [mid-19C–1920s] to impregnate (cf. SEW UP).

do a bitter, to *phr.* [mid-19C] to drink beer. [older Oxford University use *do bitters*, to drink beer]

do/have/perform a bottom-wetter, to *phr.* [19C] of a woman, to have sexual intercourse (cf. DO A WET BOTTOM).

do a break, to *phr.* [1910s+] (Aus.) to run off, to depart (cf. MAKE A BREAK).

do a brodie, to *phr.* [late 19C+] to attempt a dangerous, foolhardy stunt, esp. a dive or leap and esp. one that ends in failure (cf. TAKE A BRODIE). [Steve *Brodie*, a 23-year-old New York saloon-keeper who on 23 July 1886 leaped some 41.5m (135ft) from the city's Brooklyn Bridge in order to win a $200 wager. He survived the fall and was scooped out of the East River by a friend in a small boat]

do a brown *see* BROWN v.[5].

do a bunk, to *phr.* [late 19C+] (orig. US) to run off, to escape, to go into hiding. [BUNK v.[1]]

do a burg, to *phr.* [1990s] (US Black gang) to commit a robbery. [abbr. SE *burglary*]

do a bust, to *phr.* [late 19C] (Und.) to break into a house. [BUST v.[5] (2)]

do a cadge, to *phr.* [19C] to exist by begging. [CADGE n.]

do a cat, to *phr.* [mid–late 19C] to vomit. [CAT v.[1]]

do a Chloe, to *phr.* [late 19C+] (Aus.) to appear in the nude (cf. BLIND AS CHLOE). [a nude portrait, entitled *Chloe*, rejected in 1883 by the Melbourne National Gallery and bought by a well-known local hotel; its popularity entered the national stock of idioms]

do a chuck, to phr. [mid–late 19C] **1** to throw (someone) out. **2** to leave. [CHUCK v.[1] (1)]

do a crawl, to phr. [late 19C+] to act subserviently, to grovel. [CRAWL v.[3]]

do a crib, to phr. [mid-19C+] (orig. US Und.) to break and enter premises for the purpose of robbery. [CRIB n.[3] (1)]

do/pull a croak, to phr. [1900s–20s] (US) to die. [SE *do*/PULL v.[2] (2) + CROAK v.]

do a dance on, to phr. [1970s+] (orig. US) to beat, esp. to kick, to stamp on.

do a/the disappearing act/trick, to phr. [1910s+] (orig. US) to vanish suddenly. [SE *disappear* + mock theatricality]

do a dive into the dark see DIVE INTO THE DARK.

do a doodle-dandler, to phr. [19C] to masturbate. [DOODLE-DANDLER]

do a doss, to phr. [mid-19C+] to go to sleep. [DOSS n.[1]]

do a drink/drop see DO A BEER.

do a dry waltz with oneself, to phr. [1940s+] to masturbate.

do a Dutch, to phr. [late 19C] (orig. US) **1** to leave without paying. **2** to remove one's possessions (and oneself) from a rented apartment or house without paying one's rent. [abbr. DO THE DUTCH ACT]

do/take a fade, to phr. [1940s+] to leave (cf. FADE v.[2]).

do a fade-out see PULL A FADE-OUT.

do a fair lick, to phr. [1950s+] to run fast. [LICK n.[1] (5)]

do a flop, to phr. [late 19C+] **1** to sit or fall down. **2** of a woman, to prostrate oneself for intercourse. **3** to faint.

do/have a flutter, to phr.[1] [mid–late 19C] to have sexual intercourse. [FLUTTER n.[1]]

do/have a flutter, to phr.[2] [late 19C+] to make a wager, to gamble (usu. for small stakes). [FLUTTER n.[2]]

do a foreigner, to phr. [1970s+] for a worker contracted to one job to take time off illegally to tackle another, more lucrative one. [SE *foreign*; i.e. somewhere 'away from home']

do a freeze, to phr. [1920s+] (Aus./N.Z.) to be ignored, to be overlooked. [FREEZE n.[2]]

do a fruit salad, to phr. [1980s+] (US campus) for a man to expose his genitals in public (cf. ADJUST THE BOWL OF FRUIT). [presumed resemblance to a banana and apples]

do a get, to phr. [1910s+] (Aus.) to leave quickly. [GET!]

do a ghost, to phr. [1990s] (US Black) to leave (cf. FADE v.[2]).

do a good turn to, to phr. [20C] to have sexual intercourse, usu. in the arrogant male phr. *I could do that a good turn.*

do a grand, to phr. [1950s–60s] (US Black) to do very well. [fig. use of GRAND n.]

do a grind, to phr. [mid-19C+] to have sexual intercourse. [GRIND n.[3]]

do a grouse, to phr.[1] [mid–late 19C] to search for sexually complaisant women. [Lancashire dial. *grouse*, to have sexual intercourse]

do a grouse, to phr.[2] [20C] to complain, to grumble. [orig. milit. use; ety. unknown but ? link to OF *groucier*, *groucher*, *grocier*, *grocher*, *grucer*, *gruchier*, to murmur, grumble]

do a gun croak, to phr. [1900s–20s] (US) to shoot oneself dead. [CROAK v.[1]]

do a guy, to phr. **1** [mid–late 19C] to leave stealthily or secretly. **2** [mid–late 19C] to escape. **3** [mid–late 19C] to absent oneself from work without asking permission. **4** [late 19C] to take a false name. [the early 17C anti-Parliament plotter *Guy Fawkes* (1570–1606)]

do a hand job, to phr. [1960s+] to masturbate.

do a Hank Snow see PULL A HANK SNOW.

do a Harvey Smith, to phr. [1970s+] to make the V-sign gesture. [the British show-jumper *Harvey Smith* (b.1938), who, on 15 August 1971, gave such a sign, outraging the staid world of show-jumping]

do a homo and blow, to phr. [1990s] (US Black) to leave, usu. as imper. [pun on BLOW v.[4] (1)/BLOW v.[6] (1)]

do a Houdini see PULL A HOUDINI.

do a job, to phr.[1] [late 19C+] (Und.) to commit a crime, esp. a robbery. [JOB n.[3]]

do a job/jobbie, to phr.[2] [late 19C+] to defecate. [JOB n.[4]]

do a job, to phr.[3] [20C] (Aus.) to make pregnant.

do a job for oneself, to phr. [20C] to defecate. [ext. of DO A JOB phr.[2]]

do a job on, to phr. [late 19C+] **1** to beat up, to murder. **2** to make someone the victim of a confidence trick or allied hoax or deception.

do a joint, to phr. [1960s+] (drugs) to smoke marijuana. [JOINT n.[4] (2)]

do a jottle/go jottling, to phr. [late 19C–1900s] to have sexual intercourse. [Lincolnshire dial. *jot*, to shake roughly, to jerk about + *jottle*, to busy oneself with trifles]

do a kindness, to phr. [late 19C–1920s] to have sexual intercourse.

do a kip, to phr. [late 19C+] to have a nap, a sleep. [SE *do* + KIP n.]

do a knock with, to phr. (Aus.) **1** [1920s+] to arrange a meeting with someone of the opposite sex. **2** [1930s+] to have sexual intercourse. [KNOCK n.[1] (4)]

do a lam, to phr. [late 19C] (US Und.) to escape from prison. [LAM n.[1]]

do a line, to phr. [1970s+] (drugs) to inhale cocaine. [LINE n.[4] (4)]

do/knock a line with, to phr. [1930s+] (Aus.) to talk amorously and seductively. [SE *do*/KNOCK v.[1] (1) + LINE n.[1] (3)]

do all right/a bit of/some good for oneself, to phr. [1930s+] (Aus.) **1** of a man, to seduce, to gain a woman's sexual favours. **2** of a prostitute, to get a client.

do all under one, to phr. [late 19C] to do everything at 'one fell swoop'.

do a meal see DO A BEER.

do a Melba, to phr. [1970s+] (Aus.) to announce, with great fanfare, one's imminent retirement, only to return, time and time again, for another 'farewell', a practice of Dame Nellie *Melba* (1861–1931) and many other 'showbiz greats'.

do a mick, to phr. [1930s–60s] to escape, to run away. [MIKE v. (1)]

do a mischief to, to phr. [20C] (orig. Und.) to harm, to beat up.

do a mount, to phr.[1] [19C+] to have sexual intercourse. [MOUNT v.[3]]

do a mount, to phr.[2] [20C] to give evidence. [one *mounts* the witness box]

do an agricultural, to phr. [20C] **1** to have sex in the open air. **2** to urinate or defecate in the open (cf. DO A RURAL).

do an ally slope, to phr. [1920s] to escape, to make off. [the comic character *Ally Sloper*, 'a seedy proletarian loafer', featured in *Alley Sloper's Half-Holiday*, pub. by Dalziel Bros., 1884–1923 and illus. (at first) by W.G. Baxter, an ex-patriate American. Note WW1 milit. use *Alley Sloper's cavalry*, Army Service Corps; ? underpinned by SE *slope off*]

do a Nelson, to phr. [late 19C–1940s] to show great bravery in the face of overwhelming difficulties. [the popular image of Admiral Lord Nelson (1758–1805), British hero]

do a nibble see NIBBLE v.[3].

do a nick, to phr. [20C] (Aus.) to run off. [NICK OFF n.]

do an inside worry, to phr. [mid–late 19C] to have sexual intercourse. [SE *inside* + *worry*, to gnaw, to shake]

do another proud see DO ONESELF PROUD.

do a number, to phr.[1] [1960s+] to make a fuss, to become emotional; thus *do a number on*, to subject someone to emotional blackmail or at least some form of moral, friendship or ethical pressure (cf. PLAY THE DOZENS). [NUMBER n.³ (2)]

do a number, to *phr.²* [1960s+] (drugs) to make and smoke a marijuana or hashish cigarette. [NUMBER n.⁵]

do a number, to *phr.³* [1970s+] (US) to have sexual intercourse. [NUMBER n.¹]

do a/one's oner, to *phr.* [1910s+] (Aus.) to die, to be killed. [it only happens once]

do a perish, to *phr.* [late 19C+] (Aus.) to suffer extreme privation, esp. for want of a drink. [SE *perish*]

do a perisher, to *phr.* [1900s–20s] (Aus.) to feel very cold. [PERISHER n.¹ (2)]

do a perpendicular, to *phr.* [1950s+] to have sexual intercourse while standing upright (cf. KNEE-TREMBLER).

do a piece of work, to *phr.* [20C] (US) to murder, to kill (cf. DO A JOB ON).

do a plaster of hot guts, to *phr.* [late 17C–18C] to have sexual intercourse, i.e. 'one warm Belly clapt to another' (B.E.). [PLAISTER OF WARM GUTS]

do a powder, to *phr.* [1940s–50s] **1** to escape, to run away. **2** to leave without paying one's rent (cf. TAKE A POWDER). [SE *powder*, a medicine or a dose of medicine, to be taken internally, in this case a 'moving' laxative]

do a push, to *phr.* **1** [mid-19C–1920s] to run away. **2** [late 19C+] of a man, to have sexual intercourse (cf. PUSH IN THE TRUCK; STAND THE PUSH). [PUSH IN THE BUSH]

do a put, to *phr.* [19C] to have sexual intercourse. [two-handed put]

do a rasp, to *phr.* [late 19C–1900s] to have sexual intercourse. [RASP v.]

do a rat, to *phr.* [mid-late 19C] to change one's tactics. [RAT v.¹]

do a ride, to *phr.* [mid-19C+] to have sexual intercourse. [RIDE n.³ (1)]

do a runner, to *phr.* [1970s+] (Und.) to abscond from the police or to be on the run, before possible capture by the police, or simply to run away. [RUNNER n.⁵]

do a rural, to *phr.* [20C] **1** to have sex in the open air. **2** to urinate or defecate in the open (cf. DO AN AGRICULTURAL). [SE *rural*]

do a scrap, to *phr.* [mid-late 19C] to have a fight. [SCRAP n.²]

doash *n.* [late 17C–early 19C] a cloak. [ety. unknown]

do a shift, to *phr.¹* [late 19C–1920s] to defecate. [euph. corruption of SHIT n.¹ (2); one also SE *shifts* or moves one's bowels]

do a shift, to *phr.²* [20C] (Aus.) to run off, to decamp. [SE *shift*]

do a shit, to *phr.¹* [mid-19C+] to leave fast or secretly. [LIKE SHIT]

do a shit, to *phr.²* [mid-19C+] to defecate. [SHIT n.¹ (2)]

do a shoot up the straight, to *phr.* [mid-late 19C] of a man, to have sexual intercourse. [SHOOT v.³ (1)]

do a shot, to *phr.* [late 19C] (S.Afr.) to cheat, to swindle. [? link to HAVE A SHOT AT]

do as I do *phr.* [mid-19C–1910s] an invitation to join the speaker in a drink.

do a sip, to *phr.* [mid-late 19C] to urinate. [backsl. sip = PISS n. (1)]

do a slide up the board/straight, to *phr.* [late 19C] of a man, to have sexual intercourse.

do a smile, to *phr.* [mid-19C+] to take a glass of whisky, or any other drink. [it promotes a smile or one's lips open in a 'smile' as one drinks]

do as my shirt does! *excl.* [18C–1940s] euph. but derisive excl. of abuse, rejection. [pun on KISS MY ARSE!]

do a snatch, to *phr.* [20C] to have quick, adulterous or paid-for sexual intercourse. [pun on SE *snatch*, to grab quickly/SNATCH n.¹]

do a solid, to *phr.* [1920s+] (US) to perform a great favour. [SOLID n.²]

do a solomon, to *phr.* [1900s–20s] to pretend to be wiser than one actually is. [the biblical king *Solomon*, supposedly of great wisdom]

do a spread, to *phr.* [mid-19C] of a woman, to offer oneself for sexual intercourse. [SPREAD v.]

do a stamp, to *phr.* [late 19C] (US) to go for a walk.

do a star pitch, to *phr.* [mid-late 19C] to sleep in the open air. [one 'pitches one's tent' under the stars]

do a starry, to *phr.* [20C] to sleep in the open air. [for ety. *see* DO A STAR PITCH]

do a starve, to *phr.* [1910s+] (Aus.) to go hungry. [SE *starve*]

do a swelter, to *phr.* [mid-late 19C] to sweat. [SE *swelter*]

do as you like *n.* [late 19C+] a bicycle. [rhy. sl. *do as you like* = bike]

do a thing, to *phr.* [1970s+] **1** (US) to have sexual intercourse. **2** (W.I./Jam.) to get married. **3** (drugs) to inject oneself with heroin. [euph. use of SE]

do a ton, to *phr.* [1960s+] to drive a motorcycle or car at 100 mph. [TON n. (3)]

do a Tower of Pisa, to *phr.* [1940s] (US Black) to lean over, usu. through drunkenness. [the Italian Torre Pendente di Pisa is famous for the settling of its foundation, causing it to lean 5.2m (17ft) from the perpendicular]

do a tread, to *phr.* [mid-19C+] to have sexual intercourse (cf. DO A RIDE). [SE *tread*, of the male bird, to copulate]

do a tumble, to *phr.* [1900s] of a woman, to have sexual intercourse with a man. [TUMBLE n.¹]

do a turn, to *phr.* [1930s+] of a woman, to make herself available for sexual intercourse. [for the woman to *turn* over onto her back + pun on theatrical use]

do a twos, to *phr.* [1980s+] (Black) to share a marijuana cigarette.

do a walk, to *phr.* [1930s–70s] (Aus.) to abandon a rural property when one's efforts have failed to make it pay.

do a wet, to *phr.* [mid-late 19C] to have a drink. [WET n.¹]

do/get a wet bottom, to *phr.* [19C] of a woman, to have sexual intercourse. [the result of male ejaculation and vaginal secretions]

do a wet 'un, to *phr.* [19C] of a woman, to have sexual intercourse. [for ety. *see* DO A WET BOTTOM]

do a zoo number, to *phr.* [1970s] to indulge in bestiality. [ext. of DO A NUMBER phr.³]

dob *n.¹* [20C] a small portion, a dab or pat or dollop. [dial.]

dob *n.²* [1970s] (US) the penis (cf. DOBBER n.²). [SE *dob*, a dab, i.e. the blow or thrust of penetration; also note Scot. *dob*, a prick]]

dob *v.* [20C] (Ulster) usu. of boys, to play truant. [ety. unknown]

do balloons *v.* [1980s+] to inhale nitrous oxide or 'laughing gas'. [a balloon is filled with the gas, which is then drawn into the mouth]

do bandies *v.* [20C] (US juv.) to perform feats of physical daring, esp. when one dares one's companions to follow suit. [? SE *bandy legs* or ? dial. *bandy*, to toss back and forth]

dobber *n.¹* *see* DAUBER.

dobber/dobber-in *n.²* [1950s+] (Aus./N.Z.) an informer, a tale-teller. [DOB IN]

dobber *n.³* [1970s] (US) the penis. [DOB n.²]

dobbin *n.¹* [16C] an ordinary farm horse, sometimes a broken-down or old one. [pet-name form of Robin/Robert]

dobbin *n.²* [mid-late 19C] a ribbon. [? link to weaving jargon *dobby*, an attachment to a loom for weaving small figures, though this presumably relates back to DOBBIN n.¹ or dial. *dobbin-wheels*, the large rear wheels of a cart, similar to spools on which ribbon was wound]

dobbin-rig *n.* [late 18C] (Und.) the stealing of ribbons from haberdashers. usu. performed by women. [DOBBIN n.² + RIG n.² (2)]

dobe *n.* [20C] (US) a cigarette or cigar butt. [ety. unknown]

dobee *see* DHOBI.

doberman *n.* [1960s] (US Black) a dishonest, cowardly or deceitful person. [? the character *Doberman*, in the US TV comedy *The Phil Silvers Show* (1955–9)]

dobie *adj.* [19C+] (US) inferior, second-rate. [ADOBE]

dob in *v.* [1950s+] (Aus./N.Z.) **1** to betray, to inform against. **2** to contribute (financially). **3** to impose a responsibility on. [dial. *dob*, to put down with a sharp, abrupt motion]

dob oneself in *v.* [1950s+] (Aus.) to let oneself in for problems. [DOB IN]

do brown *v.* [mid-19C+] to surpass, to defeat comprehensively (cf. BROWN v.¹). [cooking imagery]

doc *n.* [mid-19C+] (US) **1** an all-purpose form of address for a man whose real name is unknown (cf. JOHN n.¹; MAC n.¹). **2** abbr. of SE *doctor*.

do cap *n.* [1980s+] (US Black) a shower cap. [DO n.¹⁰ + SE *cap*]

doccy *n.* [mid-16C–18C] a beggar's female companion. [var. on DOXY]

dock *v.¹* [16C] (Und.) to have sexual intercourse; thus *dock the dell*, to deflower a young woman. [SE *dock*, to cut (esp. as in a TAIL n.¹ (2)) or Rom. *dukker*, to rape + DELL n.]

dock *v.²* [early 19C+] to cut, usu. in *dock one's pay*, (for one's employer) to retain a portion of one's wages. [SE *dock*, to cut off a dog's tail]

dock asthma *n.* [1970s+] (Und.) an ironic reference to the gasps of alleged 'surprise' from the accused when the police produce their evidence in court.

docker *n.¹* [20C] a half-smoked cigarette, put out for later re-ignition (cf. DIMP; DOG END). [SE *dock*, to cut the tail off]

docker *n.²* [1920s+] (Aus.) a large sum of money; thus *go a docker*, to spend extravagantly. [Scot. *docker*, to work (hard)]

docker's hook *n.* [20C] (Aus.) a book, i.e. *make a docker's hook*, to lay the odds or make a book. [rhy. sl.]

dockie *n.* [late 19C–1930s] a dock labourer.

docking *n.¹* [early 18C–mid-19C] 'A punishment inflicted by sailors on the prostitutes who have infected them with the venereal disease, it consists in cutting off all their clothes, petticoat, shift and all, close to their stays, and then turning them out into the street' (Grose, 1785).

docking *n.²* [1980s+] (US gay) a form of mutual masturbation, involving one partner with an exceptionally long foreskin, which is drawn over the glans of the other partner before commencing masturbation. [the image of docking spacecraft]

dock-shanker *n.* [late 18C–early 19C] a fellow sufferer in a venereal ward. [SE *dock*, in this case a hospital + shanker, mis-sp. of SE *chancre*, a venereal ulcer]

dock-walloper *n.¹* [mid-19C+] (US) **1** a dock-worker, a longshoreman. **2** an idler who frequents the waterfront.

dock-walloper *n.²* [20C] (Aus.) a policeman's truncheon. [presumably for use on sailors]

Doc Martens *n.* [20C] a variety of heavy, rubber-soled boots (cf. DMS). [brandname of *Doctor Martens*, patented in Germany in 1965 by Herbert Funck and Klaus Maertens. The original boots were for work only, but the firm diversified during the 1980s and their product, especially in the form of a Doc Martens sole attached to one of a variety of uppers, became a leading fashion staple for both sexes]

doco *n.* [1960s+] (Aus.) a do*co*mentary. [abbr. + sfx. -O]

do cold with *v.* [20C] (W.I.) to not be on speaking terms with (cf. PLAY THE CHILL).

doctor, the *n.¹* (Und.) **1** [16C] marked cards. **2** [late 17C–mid-18C] crooked dice; thus *put the doctor on*, to use crooked dice

to cheat a victim (cf. DISPATCHER). [either punning on SE *doctor*, who can cure one's (in this case financial) problems or SE *doctor*, to adulterate]

doctor *n.²* [mid-17C+] anything that is considered to have restorative or healthy properties, e.g. a drink on a cold morning or the [mid-18C+] 'Doctor Wind' of the West Indies, South Africa and Western Australia, a cool sea-breeze, which usually prevails during part of the day in summer.

doctor *n.³* **1** [18C] brown sherry. **2** [18C] milk and water with rum and nutmeg. **3** [1970s+] (US campus) any form of alcoholic drink. [SE *doctor*, to mix, to adulterate; brown sherry is a mix of sherry and wine, which gives it the darker 'brown' tint]

doctor *n.⁴* [19C+] (Aus.) the cook on a sheep station. [naut. use *doctor*, a shipboard cook or 19C N.Z. whalers' *doctor*, a Maori slave used as a cook]

doctor *n.⁵* [late 19C+] one who mends or repairs, usu. with a qualifying noun, e.g. a *play doctor*, one who fine-tunes dramatic scripts.

doctor *n.⁶* [1910s+] (bingo) the number 9 (cf. DOCTOR'S FAVOURITE; DOCTOR'S ORDERS). [milit. jargon *doctor*, pill number 9, the most frequently prescribed medicine in the Field Medical Chest + ref. to the 9 months of pregnancy, after which one 'calls for the doctor']

doctor *n.⁷* [1960s+] (S.Afr. Und.) a title given to a member of a prison gang, who, while probably not qualified, is responsible for checking fellow-inmates when they are sick.

doctor *n.⁸* [1980s+] (drugs) MDMA (cf. ECSTASY). [a pun on the degrees of MD and MA]

Dr Brighton *n.* [late 19C] (society) Brighton. [the supposedly restorative properties of the seaside resort; according to Ware, coined by King George IV and 'one of his few small witticisms']

Dr Cotton *adj.* [20C] rotten (cf. JOHNNY COTTON). [rhy. sl.]

Dr Crippen *n.* [1940s–50s] dripping, rendered fat. [rhy. sl., ult. Dr Hawley Harvey Crippen (1862–1910), a celebrated murderer]

Dr Curse *n.* [early 19C] a dose of calomel.

Dr Draw-fart *n.* [19C] an itinerant quack doctor.

Dr Feelgood *n.* [1960s+] a doctor who obliges patients, often showbusiness or entertainment celebrities, with amphetamines or narcotics, which, although the user has no real medical need for them, guarantee 'good feelings'. [the phr. was coined by the blues pianist Piano Red (William Perryman) in his record 'Dr Feelgood and the Interns' (1962); the drug ref. is a slightly later addition]

Dr Green *n.¹* [late 18C–19C] grass; thus *send to Dr Green*, to put a horse out to grass. ['a physician, or rather medicine, found very successful in curing most disorders to which horses are liable' (Grose, 1796)]

Dr Green *n.²* [mid-19C] (US) a naïve, gullible young person. [SE *green*, innocent; note 20C medical jargon *Dr Green*, a hospital tannoy announcement that will not alarm patients and visitors but that signifies the 'all clear' to staff after the termination of an emergency]

Dr Hall *n.* [1920s–30s] (US tramp) grain alcohol and water. [? a brand name]

Dr Jim/jimkwim/jimmunt *n.* [late 19C] a soft felt hat, with a wide brim. [Dr *Jameson*, whose Jameson Raid (1895) brought him much notoriety, sported one; the alt. uses mix DR (JIM) + QUIM n./CUNT n.¹ and are thus origins of CUNT-HAT]

Dr Johnson *n.* [19C] the penis. [JOHN THOMAS n. (2) or, E.P. suggests, because 'there was no one Dr Johnson was not prepared to stand up to']

doctors *n.* [1910s–20s] counterfeit coins. [SE *doctor*, to adulterate + DOCTOR n.¹]

doctor's favourite *n.* [20C] (bingo) the number 9 (cf. DOCTOR n.[6]). [the ubiquity, in the army, of the No. 9 pill as a general cure-all]

Dr Shop-knife n. [late 19C+] (W.I.) a deceitful, hypocritical person. [Carib.E. *doctor shop*, a chemist + SE *knife*; for semantics of ety. see CHEMIST BILL]

doctor's orders n. [20C] (bingo) the number 9 (cf. DOCTOR n.[6]). [the army's No. 9 pills, or the 9 months of pregnancy]

doctor/doctor's stuff n. [late 18C–mid-19C] medicine. [medicine that has been prescribed by a doctor, as opposed to folk medicines that are prepared in the home]

Dr Thomas n. [1970s+] (US Black) a middle-class Black aspiring to White status. [play on UNCLE TOM n. + ref. to the college degrees or qualifications that such figures gain]

do curious v. [mid–late 19C] to act in an eccentric manner.

dod n. [19C+] euph. for God (cf. COCK n.[1]).

do-dad n. [20C] any object or gadget without a specific name (cf. DOHICKEY).

dodder n. [mid–late 19C] burnt tobacco that is taken from a dead pipe and placed on a fresh plug in order to strengthen the flavour. [SE *dottle*, the residue of ash remaining in the bottom of a pipe after smoking]

doddies n. [late 19C] a selfish person. [the proletarian version of society's DO-UT-DES]

doddipool see DODDYPOLL.

doddle n. [1930s+] anything absolutely simple or easy to achieve. [? Scot. *doddle*, a small lump of homemade toffee, hence something attractive and easily obtained, or SE *dawdle/toddle*]

doddypoll/dodipol/doddipool n. [late 16C–mid-17C] a fool. [SE *dote* to be foolish or silly + SE *poll*, a head]

dode n. [1980s+] (US campus) an unappealing person, a fool. [? DORK n.[2] (2) + DUDE or SE *dodo*, a simpleton, a silly old man]

dodelheimer/dodenheimer n. [1910s+] any nameless small object, typically some form of gadget (cf. DOHICKEY). [? DO-DAD + 'German' sfx. *-enheimer*]

dodgast! excl. [early 19C+] (US) a general imprecation, curse, e.g. DAMN!; thus *dodgasted*, damned, cursed, confounded. [DOD + SE *gast*, to terrify]

dodge n. [mid-19C+] **1** a trick, a gimmick, a means of avoiding problems, esp. those encountered in work. **2** a job, an occupation, a profession. [other than in date, it is hard to differ between the orig. 16C SE *dodge*, a shifty trick, an artifice to elude or cheat' (*OED*) and this sl. 'a clever or adroit expedient or contrivance' (*OED*)]

dodge v.[1] [mid-19C] to follow someone surreptitiously.

dodge v.[2] [1910s+] (Aus.) to steal (cf. PODDY DODGER). [SE *dodge*, to act in a dubious, untrustworthy manner]

dodge and shirk n. [20C] (Aus.) work. [rhy. sl.]

dodge pompey v. [1930s] (Aus.) to steal grass, rather than to grow and harvest one's own crop. [naut. jargon *dodge pompey*, to skulk around, to avoid work by the use of any semi-legitimate excuse]

dodger n.[1] [mid-19C] one dram of spirits or the glass that holds it. [note Kent dial. *dodger*, a nightcap, the last drink of the day]

dodger n.[2] [mid–late 19C] a clergyman. [DEVIL-DODGER]

dodger n.[3] [late 19C+] (Aus./US) an advertising leaflet, a flyer. [SE *dodger*, a handbill]

dodger n.[4] [1910s+] (Aus.) bread, a sandwich, food in general; thus *hunk of dodger*, a slice of bread. [? Northumberland dial. *dodge*, a lump, a chunk]

dodger n.[5] [1990s] (US Black) a cockroach. [? the cockroach, like the clergyman, has a black 'coat' or the insect's dodging of its human enemies]

dodger adj. [1940s–50s] (Aus.) excellent, first-rate. [? DODGER n.[4]; i.e. the innate goodness of bread]

dodge the column, to phr. [1910s+] to shirk one's duty, to avoid work. [milit. imagery + orig. milit. use]

dodgy adj.[1] [mid-19C+] dubious, unreliable. [temporarily popularized as the catchphrase (cf. SWINGING!) of comedian Norman Vaughan, compere of UK TV's *Sunday Night at the London Palladium* during the 1960s]

dodgy adj.[2] **1** [mid-19C+] stolen, esp. in phr. *dodgy gear*. **2** [1950s+] in poor condition, out of sorts.

dodipol see DODDYPOLL.

do dirt to someone/do someone dirt, to phr. [late 19C+] **1** to harm, to injure deliberately. **2** to act in a deliberately immoral or unethical manner.

do dixie v. [20C] (W.I.) to make an exciting, successful show (of what is being done); to make events work out as one wishes. [*Dixieland* jazz and the energetic dancing it inspired]

do-do/doo-doo n. [1930s+] **1** excrement, usu. animal (cf. DOGGY-DO). **2** trouble, difficulties, esp. *deep doo-doo*, serious trouble (cf. IN THE SHIT). **3** (US Black) something utterly insignificant, usu. in phr. *don't mean do-do (to me)* (cf. SHIT n.[1]). [DO n.[6] + redup.]

dodo n. [late 19C+] **1** an idiot, a dullard, esp. an old one. **2** a conservative, one who refuses to change with the times. [DEAD AS A DODO]

do down v. [1910s+] to cause trouble for or take advantage of someone, esp. financially or by talking behind their back in a derog. way. [DO v.[4]]

dod rabbit it! excl. [mid–late 19C] (US) a mild oath, euph. of 16C *God rebate it!* [DOD]

dod rot it! excl. [late 17C–late 19C] a mild. oath. of exasperation. [lit. 'God rot it!']

dodrottest! excl. [late 19C] (US) euph. oath. [DOD ROT IT!]

dodsey n. [late 18C] (Und.) a woman. [? DOXY]

dodunk n. [19C+] (US) a fool, a simpleton. [? DODO + BOHUNK n. (2)]

doe n. **1** [late 17C–early 18C] a prostitute. **2** [1900s–60s] a woman. **3** [1950s–60s] (US Black) a sucker, a fool, a potential victim. [SE *doe*, a female deer]

doedie n. [1950s+] (S.Afr.) an attractive and sexually available woman. [Afk. sl. *doedie*, 'chick']

doee see DOOE.

doer n. **1** [mid-19C] a cheat, one who defrauds another. **2** [20C] (Aus.) a character, an eccentric, one who never gives up despite any circumstances, often intensified as *hard doer*. [DO v.[4]]

doer and gone phr. [1970s+] (S.Afr.) very far away, out of one's reach. [Afk. *doer*, far away]

does a bear shit in the woods? Is the pope a Catholic? phr. [1960s+] (orig. US) a rhetorical phr. of which the implication is, 'Don't ask me stupid questions. Of course … .' The phr. is also found reversed, 'Does the pope shit in the woods …?'

does a chicken have lips? phr. [1970s+] (US) a rhetorical phr. meaning 'obviously not'.

does it? phr. [late 19C+] a sarcastic retort, intended to nullify the preceding statement.

does it smell like cheese to anyone else? phr. [1990s] (US teen) does anyone else think this is totally disgusting, embarrassing, unfashionable etc. [ext. of CHEESY adj.[2] (1)]

doeskin n. [1960s] (US) money. [var. on FROGSKIN (see FROG n.[5])]

does she? phr. [late 19C+] a comment passed by men on an adjacent women, the implication being, *does she fuck?*

does your bunny like carrots? phr. [20C] a coarse comment made by a boy to a passing girl. [BUNNY n.[2] (1) + CARROT n.[2]]

does your mother know you're out? phr. [mid-19C+] a sarcastic comment to a person whom the speaker feels should be elsewhere, due to immaturity, foolishness, inexperience etc.

dof *adj.* [1970s+] (S.Afr.) stupid, simple, dim; thus *doffie*, a fool, a simpleton. [Afk. *dof*, stupid]

do for *v.*[1] **1** [mid-18C+] to beat up, to injure, to murder. **2** [early 19C+] to wear out completely. **3** [mid–late 19C] to convict. [abbr. SE phr. *do a bad turn for*]

do for *v.*[2] [mid-19C+] to take care of, to perform household chores for, esp. of a cleaning woman or char. [DO v.[9] + abbr. SE *do work for*]

do fries go with that shake? *phr.* [1970s] (US Black) a phr. called out by a man to a passing attractive woman (whose buttocks move as she walks). [burger bar imagery]

dog *n.*[1] [16C; 20C] (orig. UK, latterly US) euph. for God, used in a variety of mild, semi-blasphemous oaths (cf. ADAD!; DOG BITE 'EM!; DOG BLINE ME!; DOGGONE!). [var. on DAD n.[1]; DAG n.[1]; DOD; despite possibility, coinage is too early for backsl.]

dog/doggie *n.*[2] [late 18C] (W.I.) a small copper or silver coin. [ety. unknown]

dog *n.*[3] [early 19C+] (US) nothing, usu. in phr. *never say dog*, to stay silent. [? the animal's inability to speak]

dog *n.*[4] [mid-19C] (US) a pistol. [pun on BARKER n.[1] (2)]

dog *n.*[5] **1** [mid-19C+] a horse that is slow, difficult to handle etc. **2** [1930s+] (US) something poor or mediocre. **3** [1930s+] (US) a disappointment, a failure. **4** [1930s+] (US) in sports, a failure. **5** [1930s+] (commercial) anything that remains hard to sell in the antique trade, automobile business (esp. second-hand cars) etc. **6** [1930s+] an unattractive woman or man. **7** [1940s–50s] (US Black) an offensive or abusive man. **8** [1940s–50s] (US Black) a prostitute. **9** [1950s+] (US Black) a promiscuous man. **10** [1960s+] an untrustworthy, traitorous, completely venal man. **11** [1960s+] a general neg. description, something useless, worthless, broken down etc. **12** [1970s+] weakness, cowardice. [SE *dog*, a term of abuse, reproach or contempt; a worthless despicable, surly or cowardly person, a 'cur', all based on the image of a cringing, beaten dog (cf. BITCH n.[1])]

dog *n.*[6] [mid-19C+] ostentation, showiness, style, esp. if affected or pretentious (cf. PUT ON DOG). [congratulatory phr. *You old dog*, which has implications of the subject's swaggering around]

dog *n.*[7] [mid-19C+] a sausage (cf. HOT DOG n.[1]). [the belief that dog-meat was used to fill cheap sausages]

dog *n.*[8] **1** [mid-19C+] (US/Aus.) an informer, a 'stool pigeon', a traitor; esp. one who betrays fellow criminals. **2** [mid-19C+] meanness, treachery. **3** [1920s+] (Aus.) a plain-clothes detective working on the railways. **4** [1960s] (US Black) a notably brutal policeman. [the neg. connotations of the animal; *see* DOG n.[5]]

dog *n.*[9] **1** [late 19C] a clever, cheery, hearty person, esp. in affectionate phr. *You old dog*. **2** [1980s+] a good friend (cf. ROAD DOG). [the positive image of the animal as loyal, affectionate etc]

dog *n.*[10] **1** [20C] (Aus.) food. **2** [20C] (Aus.) a drinking debt. **3** [1920s] (US) a state of drunkenness. [ety. unknown]

dog *n.*[11] [20C] (US) a pint bottle (470ml) of liquor; thus *short dog*, a half pint bottle. [? Yorkshire dial. *dog*, a small pitcher]

dog *n.*[12] **1** [20C] a beggar who searches for cigarette ends (cf. DOG END). **2** [1960s] (drugs) the residue of poor-quality opium or heroin.

dog *n.*[13] **1** [20C] (US) the penis. **2** [1960s+] (US Black) lust, sexual desire.

dog *n.*[14] [1910s+] (US) a shoe. [DOGS n.[3] (1)]

dog *n.*[15] [1920s–30s] the female pubic area. [early 17C nonce-use *a dog with a hole in its head*]

dog *n.*[16] [1930s–70s] (US Black campus) a novice (cf. PUP n.[1]; PUPPY n.[3]). [the image of a 'young pup']

dog, the *n.*[17] [1940s] a venereal disease. [ext. of general neg. image attached to DOG n.[5]]

dog *n.*[18] [1940s+] the telephone. [rhy. sl.; abbr. DOG AND BONE]

dog *n.*[19] [1960s] (US) the hardest part of the job. [once done all that is left is the 'tail']

dog *n.*[20] [1960s] (US campus use) the grade D.

dog/doggie *n.*[21] [1960s+] euph. for dog excrement; thus *there's dog all over the pavement*. [abbr. *dog* SHIT n.[1] (1)]

dog *n.*[22] [1960s+] (US Black) anything exceptional.

dog, the *n.*[23] [1970s+] (US) a Greyhound bus. [play on proper name]

dog *n.*[24] [1980s+] (US Black use) a general term of address, usu. between males (cf. ROAD DOG). [US Black campus fraternity tradition of referring to members and pledges as *dogs*]

dog *v.*[1] **1** [late 19C+] (US) to nag, to criticize, to harass, to mistreat. **2** [late 19C] (US) to stare at, to glance unpleasantly at. **3** [late 19C+] (US Black) to abuse, to curse, to despise. **4** [20C] to pester. **5** [20C] (US Und.) to betray, to inform against. **6** [20C] (US) to cheat, to lie, to deceive. **7** [1970s] (US) to taunt, to tease, to be rude. **8** [1980s+] (US campus) to criticize unfairly. **9** [1990s] (US Black teen) to insult someone in front of their friends. [DOG n.[5], DOG n.[8]; all based on neg. images of the animal]

dog *v.*[2] **1** [late 19C+] to engage in sexual intercourse with the male using a rear entry position (cf. DOGGY FASHION). **2** [late 19C+] to pursue, to hunt down (usually with sexual intent). **3** [1980s+] to have sex with. **4** [1980s+] (US) to rape.

dog *v.*[3] **1** [20C] to act in a menial capacity. **2** [1930s–50s] to idle, to shirk work. [DOG n.[5]]

dog *v.*[4] [1980s+] to break an appointment, to stand someone up. [DOG n.[5] (11)]

dog *v.*[5] [1980s+] to filch, to steal. [abbr. BIRD DOG v.[1]]

dog *v.*[6] [1980s+] to break down under pressure, to act in a cowardly manner. [DOG n.[5] (13)]

dog *v.*[7] [1980s+] (US) to hold one's arm in a half-nelson. [? SE *dog-leg*]

dog *v.*[8] [1990s] (US campus) to get a grade D in an examination. [DOG n.[20]]

dog *v.*[9] [1990s] (US Black teen) to tear something up in the manner of a dog, to worry.

dog! *excl.* [20C] (US) euph. for DAMN!

dog act *see* BLACKFELLOWS' ACT.

dog along *v.* [20C] (Can.) to manage, to subsist. [? SE *dogged*]

dogan/dogun *n.* [mid-19C–1930s] an Irish Roman Catholic. [? Irish surname *Duggan* or f. TAIG]

dog and bone *n.* [1940s+] telephone (cf. DOG n.[18]). [rhy. sl.]

dog and goanna rules *n.* [1970s+] (Aus.) no rules at all (cf. RAFFERTY'S RULES). [the image of a fight between a dog and a goanna lizard]

dog and pony show *n.* [1950s+] (US) any elaborately formal occasion, used for official briefings, public relations etc. [the image of dressage and similar events, but also the pej. idea of the participants as performing animals]

dog around *v.*[1] [20C] to live a promiscuous life (cf. CAT v.[2]). [DOG v.[2]]

dog around *v.*[2] [20C] (US campus) to neglect one's academic work. [DOG v.[3]]

dog-ass/-arse *n.* [1950s+] (orig. US) an objectionable, unpleasant person. [DOG-ASS adj.]

dog-ass/-arse/-assed/-arsed *adj.* [1950s+] (orig. US) inferior, second-rate, unpleasant. [SE *dog* + ARSE n.[1] (4)]

dog away one's time, to *phr.* [late 19C] to waste time, to idle about. [DOG v.[3]]

dog back *v.* [20C] (W.I.) to swallow one's pride in the hope of regaining a formerly positive relationship. [DOG v.[6]]

dog behind *v.* [20C] (W.I.) to act in a servile manner, to toady to. [DOG v.[6]]

dog better than you/them *phr.* [20C] (W.I.) a general phr. of contempt, you/they are worthless or socially null.

dog bite 'em!/my ear! *excl.* [late 19C–1920s] (US) a mild oath. [DOG n.[1]]

dog bline me! *excl.* [1940s+] (W.I.) euph. for GORBLIMEY! [DOG n.[1]]

dog-bolt *n.* [mid-15C–late 17C] a term of contempt or reproach, a wretch, a contemptible fellow. [SE *dog-bolt*, a blunt-headed arrow or form of bolt, of no use other than to be aimed at a dog]

dog booby *n.* [late 18C] a country lout, a male peasant (cf. BITCH BOOBY). [SE *dog, male* + BOOBY n.[1]]

dog box *n.* **1** [20C] (Aus.) a railway compartment with no access to other compartments, usu. on a rural railway line. **2** [20C Aus.] a substandard railway carriage. **3** [1950s+] (N.A.) any small, cramped room or house.

dog-breath *n.* [1940s+] (orig. US) **1** bad breath. **2** one who has bad breath. **3** an offensive person.

dog buffer *n.* [18C] a dog stealer (cf. BUFFER-NABBER). [SE *dog* + BUFFER n.[2]]

dogcart *n.* [1920s+] (Aus.) a police car.

dog cheap *adj.* [late 16C–late 18C; 20C] extremely cheap. [backsl. *dog* = good (and) cheap; cf. SE *dirt cheap*. Modern use is W.I. only]

dog-collar *n.* **1** [mid-19C+] the reversed collar worn by clergymen. **2** [1910s+] a choker necklace.

dog-dancing *n.* [1960s+] (Can.) useless activity. [a dog leaping with glee at the return of its master]

dog-days *n.* [1950s+] (US) a menstrual period. [SE *dog-day*, an evil time, a period in which malignant influences prevail; lit. the rising of the Dog Star]

dog dead/dead with you/dead at your door *phr.* [1940s+] (W.I.) a phr. meaning one is in a hopeless situation, is in irretrievable difficulties (cf. CRAPAUD SMOKE YOUR PIPE; YOUR DOG'S DEAD).

dog dinger *n.* [1920s–70s] (US Black) the middle or index finger, depending on rival users; considered unlucky or taboo. [fig. uses of DOG n.[5], as a generic for bad luck + DING v.[1], to cause harm; if that finger is pointed at a person, they will have bad luck]

dog doctor *n.* [20C] (US) a second-rate or incompetent doctor. [ext. use of SE; i.e. one who is fit only to work with animals]

dog-drawn *adj.* [19C] of a woman, whose partner, in the act of intercourse, has been forcibly dragged away. [the image of two copulating dogs being drawn apart by their owners]

dog-driver *n.* [1910s+] (W.I.) a policeman. [the term sneers at the policeman, giving him the lowly task of driving off stray dogs]

dog-drunk *adj.* [early 17C; mid-19C+] very drunk. [SE *dog*, i.e. *as a dog*, symbolic of excess; i.e. thoroughly, utterly, extremely]

dog end *n.* [1930s+] the last fraction of a cigarette (cf. BUTT n.[2]; DIMP; DOCKER n.[1]). [? SE *docked end*]

dog-eye *n.* [1910s+] (US, mainly prison) a sidelong glance, usu. aggressive or unfriendly. [DOG v.[1] + SE *eye*]

dog-eye *v.* [1910s+] (US, mainly prison) to cast a sidelong glance at someone. [DOG-EYE n.]

dogface *n.* (US) **1** [mid-19C+] an unpleasant person. **2** [1930s+] a soldier, an infantryman. [coined as an insult by members of the US Marine Corps, who look down on infantrymen]

dog fever *n.* [1910s+] (Aus.) influenza. [var. on DOG'S DISEASE]

dogfight *n.* (US) **1** [late 19C] a fistfight, a brawl. **2** [1970s] any event considered coarse or vulgar.

dog food *n.*[1] [1940s–60s] (US) any form of canned meat.

dog food *n.*[2] [1960s] (US Black) a bribe paid to a corrupt policeman. [DOG n.[8] + ironic use of SE *food*]

dog food *n.*[3] [1980s+] (US gay) a soldier, viewed as a potential sexual partner (cf. SEAFOOD n.[2]). [DOGFACE (2) + SE *food*, i.e. something one can EAT v.[3]]

dog food *n.*[4] [1980s+] (drugs) heroin. [ext. of SE use; ? its colour (brown) or the low status of its users]

dog-foolish *adj.* [mid-19C] very stupid. [backsl. *dog* = good (and) foolish]

dogfuck *n.*[1] [1960s+] sexual intercourse in which entry is made from the rear (cf. CHINESE FASHION; DOG v.[2]; DOGGY FASHION; HORSE FUCK). [SE *dog* + FUCK n.[1]]

dogfuck *n.*[2] [1970s+] (US) trouble, usu. in phr. *in the dogfuck*. [fig. use of DOGFUCK n.[1]]

dog-/doggy-fuck *v.* [1960s+] to engage in sexual intercourse with the male using a rear entry position (cf. DOG v.[2]; DOGGY FASHION). [DOGFUCK n.[1]]

dogged *adj.* [19C] very, excessively. [dial., i.e. *as a dog*]

dogged out/up *adj.* [1910s+] (orig. US) dressed up. [PUT ON DOG phr. (2)]

dogger *n.*[1] [1910s+] (Aus.) **1** a hunter of dingoes; thus *dogging*, dingo-hunting (cf. DOG-STIFFENER). **2** one who slaughters horses for the pet-food market.

dogger *n.*[2] [1940s+] one who collects cigarette ends, cleans out the tobacco and resells it. [DOG END]

dogger out *n.* [1960s+] (Und.) a look-out man. [DOG v.[1] (5)]

doggers *n.* [1960s] (Aus./US) gaudily coloured swimming shorts. [? PUT ON DOG phr. (2)]

doggery *n.*[1] [mid-19C] **1** cheating (cf. DOG-TRICK). **2** nonsense. [SE *doggery*, dog-like behaviour or practice; mean and contemptible action]

doggery *n.*[2] [mid-19C] (US) a low drinking house. [neg. image of SE *dog*]

doggess *n.* [late 18C] euph. for bitch (cf. DOG'S LADY; DOG'S WIFE; PUPPY'S MAMMA).

doggie *n.*[1] *see* DOG n.[1].

doggie *n.*[2] [late 19C] an all-round stand-up collar. [SE *dog-collar*]

doggie *n.*[3] [20C] a beggar who searches for cigarette ends (cf. DOG n.[12]). [DOG END]

doggie *n.*[4] [1930s+] (US) a soldier, an infantryman. [abbr. DOGFACE]

doggie *n.*[5] *see* DOG n.[21].

doggin/doggins *n.* [1930s+] (N.Z.) a cigarette end. [DOG END]

dogging *n.*[1] [1980s+] **1** spying on others having sex in parked cars. **2** (US) offering sex in return for drugs. **3** (US campus) obtaining maximum sexual pleasure from a member of the opposite sex. [DOG v.[2]]

dogging *n.*[2] [1980s+] (US campus) student housing. [it resembles dog-kennels]

doggish *adj.* [20C] (US Black) obsessed with sex, lecherous (cf. DOGGY adj.[2]). [DOG n.[13]]

doggo *n.* [1920s] (US) a fellow, a man (cf. OLD DOG n.[1]). [DOG n.[9]]

doggone! *excl.* [early 19C+] (orig. US) a general intensifier (cf. DOG n.[1]). [SE *god-damned*]

doggy *n.* [1940s+] (Aus.) a hot *dog*. [abbr. + sfx. -*y*]

doggy *adj.*[1] [late 19C+] fashionable. [PUT ON DOG phr. (2)]

doggy *adj.*[2] **1** [20C] (US Black) hard, mean, thoughtless. **2** [20C] (US Black) obsessed with sex, lecherous. **3** lazy, sluggish. **4** [1930s] somewhat overly enthusiastic. [DOG n.[5]; i.e. all neg. images of the animal]

doggy bag *n.* **1** [1960s+] (orig. US) a bag provided by some restaurants for customers to take home left-overs, ostensibly for later consumption by a pet dog. **2** [1990s] a colostomy bag.

doggy-do *n.* [1960s+] euph. for canine excrement. [SE *doggy* + DO n.[6]]

doggy fashion *adv.* [1960s+] used to describe a way of having sexual intercourse in which entry is made from the rear (cf. DOGFUCK n.[1]).

doggy-fuck *see* DOG-FUCK v.

doggy paddle see DOG PADDLE.

dogheart *n.* [20C] (W.I. Rasta) a person who is especially cold and cruel. [neg. image of SE *dog* + *heart*]

doghouse *n.*[1] **1** [late 19C+] any small structure that seems to resemble a dog kennel. **2** [1940s+] (US Und.) a county prison. **3** [1940s+] (US Und.) the protective custody unit in a prison. **4** [1940s+] (US Und.) a solitary confinement cell.

doghouse *n.*[2] [1920s–50s] (orig. US) a double-bass. [its size would make it a good SAmE *doghouse* or kennel]

dogi *n.* [1940s+] (W.I.) a short, stocky person (cf. DEGE). [Bambara *dogo*, small, short]

dogie *see* DUJI.

dog in a blanket *n.* [mid–late 19C] a rolled currant dumpling ('roly-poly pudding') or jam pudding. [orig. naut. use]

dog in a doublet *n.* [late 18C] a daring, bold person; thus *proud as a dog in a doublet*, very proud, *a mere dog in a doublet*, a pitiful figure, one who shows off to no avail. [the custom in Germany and Flanders to dress the dogs used to hunt wild boar in a form of buff doublet]

dog it *v.*[1] (US) **1** [20C] to shirk, to waste time, to hang back. **2** [1920s+] to dawdle, to go slowly. **3** [1930s+] to run off. **4** [1930s+] to malinger, to act lazily (cf. DOG AROUND v.[2]). [DOG v.[3]]

dog it *v.*[2] **1** [20C] to dress up, to show off. **2** [1930s+] (N.Z.) to lord it over someone. [PUT ON DOG phr. (2)]

dog it *v.*[3] [20C] (gambling) to act weakly, to be a loser, to lack winning spirit (cf. POOCH n.[2]). [SE *underdog*]

dog it *v.*[4] **1** [1940s+] to have sexual intercourse from the rear (cf. DOG v.[2]; DOGGY FASHION). **2** [1980s+] (US campus) of a woman, to make oneself sexually available.

dog joint *n.* [1920s] (US) a cheap restaurant, a hot dog stand. [SE *hot dog* + JOINT n.[3] (3)]

dog juice *n.* [1970s+] (US Black) cheap liquor or wine. [only good enough for n animal or common *dog*]

dog-kickers *n.* [mid-19C] (US) the feet (cf. DOG n.[14]).

dog-killer *n.* [20C] (US) cheap or adulterated liquor. [its strength]

dog-knotted *adj.* [1950s+] of two lovers who are locked together during intercourse because of a vaginal muscle spasm brought on by a sudden shock.

dog-leech *n.* [16C–18C] a quack doctor. [SE *dog leech*, a veterinary surgeon]

dogleg *n.* [19C] (US) second-rate tobacco. [the twists in which the tobacco was sold, which resembled a dog's leg]

dog licence *n.* [1940s+] (Aus.) a certificate of exemption from the prohibition of alcohol to Native Australians that permits them to buy a drink in a hotel.

dogmeat *n.* [20C] (US) a worthless, despicable person.

dog my cats!/hide! *excl.* [19C+] (US) a general excl. of amazement, annoyance, surprise. [DOG n.[1]]

dognap *v.* [1940s+] (orig. US) to steal or kidnap a dog; thus *dognapper*, one who steals dogs. [play on SE *kidnapper*]

dog nigger *n.* [1970s] (US Black) a Black person who rejects the second-class role offered by the dominant White society (cf. BAD NIGGER). [DOG n.[5] + NIGGER n.]

dog-nose *n.* [late 19C–1900s] beer warmed nearly to boiling, mixed with gin or wormwood (the basis of absinthe), sugar and ginger; a later version substituted gin for the wormwood (cf. PURL n.[1]).

dog on *v.* [1980s+] (US campus) to criticize, usu. in the victim's absence. [DOG v.[1]]

dog on it! *excl.* [mid–late 19C] a mild expletive (cf. DOGGONE!). [DOG n.[1]]

do-gooder *n.* [late 19C+] a theoretically well-intentioned but often interfering and domineering figure, concerned with others' problems but lacking any real knowledge of how to alleviate them.

do gooseberry *v.* [mid–late 19C] (teen) to hang around a couple who would prefer to be left alone. [GOOSEBERRY n.[2]]

do gospel *v.* [mid-19C] to attend church.

dog out *v.* **1** [20C] (US prison) to intimidate (cf. PUT THE CHILL ON). **2** [20C] (US Black) to abuse, to attack. **3** [1940s+] to keep a look-out. **4** [1990s] (US campus) to betray, to neglect, to treat with disrespect. [DOG v.[1]]

dog/doggy paddle *v.* [20C] to swim like a dog, usu. the style of those who cannot perform a recognized stroke. [the term is modern, but note R. Thomas *Swimming* (1904): 'How did Beowulf swim? I should say the human stroke ... popularly but incorrectly known as dog paddle, which was the European stroke to about the year 1500']

dogpatch *n.* [1930s+] (US) a small town or hamlet (cf. DOGTOWN n.[1]). [*Dogpatch*, the hill-billy settlement in which the syndicated cartoon strip by Al Capp, *L'il Abner* (1934–77), takes place]

dogpile *v.* [1940s+] (US) for a group of people to leap on a single individual.

dog-poor *adj.* [19C+] (Aus./US) extremely poor.

dog-robber *n.*[1] [19C+] a subservient person, a menial (cf. DOG-ROBBER n.[2]). [milit. jargon *dog-robber*, an officer's servant, who gained his unflattering nickname from his post-mealtime habit of grabbing any edible left-overs from the mess tables before they could be tossed out to the dogs]

dog-robber *n.*[2] [20C] the tweed suit customarily worn by off-duty British officers. [milit. jargon *dog-robber*, an officer's servant, who would not wear a uniform]

dogs *n.*[1] [mid-19C+] **1** sausages. **2** hot dogs.

dogs, the *n.*[2] [1920s] the greyhound races, greyhound racing.

dogs *n.*[3] **1** [1910s+] shoes. **2** [1990s] (US Black) gym shoes, trainers. [coined by US sportswriter T.A. 'Tad' Dorgan (1877–1929) in the New York *Evening Journal*]

dogs *n.*[4] [1920s+] the feet. [rhy. sl *dog's meat* = feet]

dog's abuse *n.* [1920s+] (Irish) harsh verbal criticism.

dog's age *phr.* [19C+] (US) a very long time (cf. COON'S AGE).

dog-salmon aristocracy *n.* [19C] (US) one who thinks themself superior to their peers (cf. CODFISH).

dog's ballocks/bollocks *n.* [1920s+] **1** anything obvious. **2** anything excellent, admirable, first-rate. [orig. in phr. *sticks out like a dog's ballocks*]

dogsbody *n.*[1] [19C] a stew, esp. pease pudding.

dogsbody *n.*[2] [1920s+] any member of an organization who takes on all the menial and tedious tasks, often working for any senior person who gives out instructions. [naut. jargon *dogsbody*, a term for a midshipman or any junior officer, ult. ? f. 19C naut. jargon *dogsbody*, sea-biscuits soaked into a pulp with water and sugar]

dog's bollocks *see* DOG'S BALLOCKS.

dog's bottom *phr.* [1930s] a joc. form of address.

dog's breakfast *see* DOG'S DINNER.

dog's dick *v.* [1950s] (orig. US Black) to perform the lowest act of which one is capable (cf. SUCK A DOG'S DICK).

dog's dinner/breakfast/pig's breakfast *n.* [1930s+] a distasteful mess (but cf. DRESSED UP LIKE A DOG'S DINNER).

dog's disease *n.* (Aus.) **1** [1910s+] influenza (cf. DOG FEVER). **2** [1940s] malaria.

dog's dram *n.* [mid-18C–early 19C] the act of spitting in someone's mouth and hitting them on the back. [SE *dog*, an unpleasant person + *dram*, a measure of spirits]

dog's eye *n.* [1960s] (Aus.) a meat pie (cf. NELLY). [rhy. sl.]

dog's foot!, the *excl.* [20C] (US) a mild excl.

dogs have not dined, the *phr.* [late 18C] comment made to one whose shirt is hanging out. [the image of hungry dogs eating the shirt]

dog's head *n.* [late 19C] (US) a variety of beer.

dogshit *n.*[1] [1960s+] (orig. US) the essence, the spirit, as in phr. *kick/knock the dogshit out of* (cf. CRAP n.[3]; DAYLIGHTS).

dogshit *n.*[2] [1960s+] anything or anyone considered objectionable, unpleasant, disgusting.

dogs in the street *n.* [20C] (Irish) everyone, the whole world.

dog's lady *n.* [late 18C] euph. for BITCH n.[1] (cf. DOGGESS).

dog's licence *n.* [1930s+] the sum of 7 shillings and 6 pence. [a dog's licence cost 7s 6d (37½p)]

dog's match *n.* [19C+] sex in the open air, spec. by the wayside; thus to *make a dog's match of it*, to have sex in the open air, to have spontaneous sex. [the brevity of the intercourse and the lack of privacy of mating dogs]

dog's meat *n.*[1] [19C] anything considered worthless, e.g. a badly written book, a poorly executed painting etc.

dog's meat *n.*[2] [1960s+] (S.Afr.) cheap cuts of meat which are cooked for the servants' meals (cf. BOY'S MEAT). [otherwise good enough only for the dogs]

dog's nose/dogsnose *n.*[1] **1** [mid-19C] a mixture of gin and beer. **2** [mid–late 19C] an alcoholic whose preferred tipple is whisky. [like the animal's nose, alcohol is cold and wet]

dog's nose *n.*[2] [1960s] (US Und.) a paid informer. [DOG n.[8]]

dog's paste *n.* [mid–late 19C] sausagemeat or mincemeat. [HOT DOG n.[1]]

dog's portion *n.* [late 18C–late 19C] virtually nothing; esp. of a man who pursues a woman and gets only very little for his pains. [lit. 'a lick and a smell' (Grose, 1785)]

dog's rig *n.* [late 18C] sexual intercourse taken to exhaustion, followed by mutual disinterest. [SE *dog* + *rig*, a romp; i.e. the observation of dogs' mating]

dog's show *n.* [late 19C] (Aus.) a dog's chance, i.e. no chance at all.

dog's soup *n.* [late 18C+] rainwater. [post-19C use is US]

dog-stiffener *n.* [20C] (Aus.) a professional dingo-killer (cf. DOGGER n.[1]). [SE *dog* + STIFFEN v.[2]]

dog-stiffeners *n.* [20C] (Aus.) leather leggings. [DOGS n.[4]]

dog-style *adv.* [1950s+] having sexual intercourse in the rear-entry position (cf. DOGGY FASHION).

dog's wife *n.* [late 18C] euph. for BITCH n.[1] (cf. DOGGESS).

dogtag *n.* **1** [1910s+] (orig. US) an identification disk. **2** [1950s+] (US drugs) a legitimate prescription for otherwise illegal narcotics. [for a dog to be 'legal' (not a stray) in the US it must have a labelled collar]

dogtown *n.*[1] [late 19C+] (US) an out-of-the-way or small place, also as *dog holler*, *dog ridge*, *dogtail corners*, *dogtrot hollow*; thus *dogtowner*, a native of such a town (cf. DOG-PATCH). [orig. theatrical jargon *dogtown*, an out-of-town (i.e. out of New York City) theatre used to try out a new show before 'bringing it in']

dogtown *n.*[2] [1910s] (N.Z.) a derog. nickname for Port Chalmers. [? its fig. population of 'one man and a dog']

dog-trick *n.* [mid-16C–late 17C] a treacherous or spiteful act, an ill-turn, a mean, cruel trick (cf. DOGGERY n.[1]). [SE *dog* + *trick*; note DOG n.[5] (11)]

dog-tucker *n.* [1930s+] an old or unsaleable sheep killed for dog food. [SE *dog* + TUCKER n.]

dog-tucker *adj.* [1980s+] (N.Z.) **1** of a person or animal, useless, second-rate. **2** in serious difficulties. [DOG-TUCKER n.]

dog turd *n.* [20C] (US) a large cigar. [resemblance]

dogun *see* DOGAN.

dog wagon *n.*[1] [20C] (US) a small café or restaurant sited in a converted vehicle, a diner. [the quality of food is generally poor]

dog wagon *n.*[2] [20C] (US) a prison van for conveying prisoners. [play on SE *dog wagon*, used by the dog-catcher]

dog water *n.* [1960s+] (US) semen.

dogways *adv.* [late 19C] having sexual intercourse in the rear-entry position (cf. DOGGY FASHION).

dogwork *n.* [1980s+] (US) tedious, menial tasks.

do handiwork *v.* [1980s+] to masturbate. [pun]

do her job for her, to *phr.* [mid-19C+] of a man, to have sexual intercourse and give a woman an orgasm.

dohickey/doohickey *n.* [1910s+] (orig. US) **1** any nameless small object, typically some form of gadget (cf. DO-DAD; DODELHEIMER; DOJIGGER; DOOBOB; DOOBRIE; DOODACKIE; DOODAD; DOODAH n.[2]; DOODIBBIE; DOODINKUS; DOODLE n.[4]; DOODLEBUM; DOODLEFAGIT; DOODLEFLICKER; DOOFER; DOOFLICKER; DOOFLOP; DOOFUNNY; DOOLOLLY; DOOVER; DOOWHACKER; DOOWHANGER; DUMIFUTCHIT; GILHICKIE; JIGGER n.[3]; THINGUMABOB; THINGUMAJIG; THINGUMMY; THINGY). **2** something small, used for decoration. **3** a love-bite or a pimple. [ety. unknown; ? DO-DAD + HICKEY n.[1]]

do his job for him, to *phr.* [mid-19C–1920s] **1** to ruin. **2** to beat, to kill. [var. on DO A JOB ON]

do hooky *v.* [mid–late 19C] to make the coarse gesture of applying the thumb and fingers to one's nose. [? a *hook nose*]

do how? *excl.* [20C] (US) what did you say?, please repeat the question (cf. DO WHAT?).

do I ducks! *excl.* [20C] an excl. of absolute rebuttal, i.e. the hell I will! no I certainly won't/don't! [euph. for DO I FUCK!]

do I fuck! *excl.* [20C] an excl. of absolute rebuttal, i.e. the hell I will! no I certainly won't/don't! (cf. DO I DUCKS!).

do I have to spell it out for you? *phr.* [1950s+] a derog. remark indicating that one has made things clear enough for anyone with sufficient intelligence to have understood them already.

do ill to *v.* [19C] of a man, to have sexual intercourse (cf. DO OVER v.[2]; WALLOP IT IN; WHACK IT UP).

do in *v.* **1** [late 19C+] to kill, to beat; thus *do oneself in*, to commit suicide. **2** [late 19C+] (orig. Aus./N.Z.) to spend one's entire funds. **3** [late 19C–1900s] to steal. **4** [20C] (Aus.) to defeat. **5** [1910s+] to wear out, to exhaust; thus *done in*, exhausted, worn out, usu. of people. **6** [1950s+] to inject a narcotic drug (cf. DO UP v.[6]). **7** [1990s] (US Black/teen) to gang rape (cf. SEX IN). [all ext. uses of DO v.[2]]

doing *n.* **1** [early 17C+] sexual intercourse. **2** [late 19C+] a thrashing, a beating. [DO v.[2]]

doing a hundred *phr.* [1940s–50s] (US Black) in good shape, doing well. [ONE HUNDRED PER CENT]

doing bad *adj.* [1940s–50s] (US Black) unfortunate, impoverished.

doing dab *adj.* [mid-19C] doing badly (in business). [backsl.]

doings *n.*[1] **1** [mid-19C] (US) the trimming or ornaments that enhance a dress. **2** [1910s+] (orig. milit.) anything for which the precise name cannot be recalled at the moment of speaking. **3** [1910s+] the components, e.g. of a meal, of a piece of engineering. [ext. of SE *doing*, an act, a piece of business, a transaction]

doings *n.*[2] [1980s+] animal excrement (cf. DO n.[6]).

doing-up *n.* [1960s] the wilful destruction of property as part of a gang war. [DO UP v.[1]]

doink *n.* [1960s+] (US campus) **1** a clumsy, inept person. **2** an overly hard worker, a 'grind'. [echoic of their solidity/dullness]

do in/lose one's block, to *phr.* [1910s+] (Aus./N.Z.) to become angry, excited or anxious. [DO IN v. (1)/SE *lose* + BLOCK n.[1] (2)]

do in the eye, to *phr.* [19C+] to cheat. [DO v.[4] (1) + SE *eye*]

do I owe you anything?/do I owe you?/what do I owe you? *phr.* [late 19C+] phr. used to rebuff someone who appears to be staring at the speaker.

do it *v.* [18C+] to have sexual intercourse (cf. DO v.[2]). [euph.]

do it brown, to *phr.* [mid-19C] to take to the limit, esp. as in prolonging one's enjoyment to the point of excess. [cooking imagery]

do it fat, to *phr.* [1910s–20s] to pose as a gentleman. [SE *do*, perform + FAT adj.[1]]

do-it fluid *n.* [1970s+] (US Black) liquor, usu. gin, usu. as an enhancer of sexual potency. [DO IT + SE *fluid*]

do-it-jack *n.* [1980s+] (drugs) phencyclidine (cf. ACE n.[3]). [ety. unknown]

do it like mommy, to *phr.* [1980s+] to act in a domesticated manner, doing the housework, shopping etc.

do it one's own/own way, to *phr.* [1980s+] to masturbate. [? ref. to Frank Sinatra's 'theme-tune' 'My Way' (1968)]

do it on someone *v.* **1** [late 19C–1900s] to swindle, to defraud. **2** [20C] to get the better of, to surpass. [DO v.[4]]

do it standing on one's head, to *phr.* [late 19C+] to accomplish something with the minimum of effort (cf. DO IT WHILE ASLEEP; DO IT WITH ONE'S LEFT HAND; DO IT WITH ONE HAND TIED BEHIND ONE'S BACK).

do it up *v.* [early 19C+] to accomplish one's object, to have success; thus *do it up in good twig*, to live a constantly enjoyable (and ever-improving) life. [TWIG n.[1]]

do it up brown, to *phr.* [1950s+] (gay) to have anal intercourse. [pun. on DO UP BROWN/DO v.[2] (6) + BROWN n.[3]]

do it up right, to *phr.* [20C] to carry out fully and correctly, to achieve a set objective. [ext. of DO IT UP]

do it while asleep, to *phr.* [20C] to do something with ease (cf. DO IT STANDING ON ONE'S HEAD).

do it with one's left hand, to *phr.* [20C] to do something with ease (cf. DO IT STANDING ON ONE'S HEAD).

do it with one hand tied behind one's back *phr.* [20C] (orig. US) to do very easily, with minimal effort (cf. DO IT STANDING ON ONE'S HEAD).

do-it-yourself *n.* [1950s+] masturbation.

do it your way *see* DO IT ONE'S OWN WAY.

dojigger/doojigger *n.* **1** [1920s+] an indefinite expression used to describe a nameless object; also as *dojiggie, dojiggum, dojiggus, dojiggy, dojimmie, dojinnie, dojisser, dojohn, dojohnnie* (cf. DOHICKEY). **2** [1960s+] a euph. for the penis (cf. JIGGER n.[4]; JIGGLING BONE). [ety. unknown; ? link to SE *jiggle*]

do justice *v.* [late 17C–early 18C] to toast a person, to drink to a person.

do justice child, to *phr.* [late 17C–mid-18C] to act as an informer. [Sir Francis *Child* (1642–1715), banker and lord mayor of London]

dol/doll *n.* [mid-19C–1900s] $1. [abbr. SE *dollar*]

dolan's ass *n.* [20C] (Irish) a time-server (cf. BILLY HARRAN'S DOG). [proper name Dolan + SE *ass*; it goes 'a bit of the way with everyone'; ? anecdotal origins]

doldrum *n.* [early 19C] a dullard, a sluggish person. [? SE *dold*, inert, stupid]

dole-bludger *n.* [1970s+] (Aus.) one who claims unemployment benefit either when work is available or while actually employed in the Black Economy, the Aus. equivalent to a UK 'dole-scrounger'; thus *dole-bludgery, dole-bludging*. [SE *dole* + BLUDGER n.[2] (2)]

dolefuls *n.* [19C] a miserable, depressed state of mind.

do-less *adj.* [1950s] (US Black) lazy, lethargic, shiftless. [SE *do less* ? + Scot. *dowless*, feeble, weak]

dolie/doley *n.* [1950s+] (Aus.) anyone drawing unemployment benefit. [SE *dole*]

do-little *n.* [19C+] (US) an idler, a lazy person.

doll *n.*[1] **1** [late 16C–mid-18C] a prostitute. **2** [19C] a woman. **3** [mid-19C+] a conventionally attractive young woman. **4** [20C] (S.Afr.) a general term of affection. **5** [1970s+] (US campus) a conceited young woman.

doll *n.*[2] [19C] the penis. [abbr. DOLLY n.[2]]

doll *n.*[3] *see* DOL.

doll *n.*[4] [1960s–70s] (drugs) any drug in pill form, e.g. amphetamines, barbiturates. [popularized and apparently coined by the book/film *Valley of the Dolls* (1968) by Jacqueline Susann]

dollar *n.*[1] [20C] 5 shillings, and thus obsolete outside films, books etc; of a pre-metric era (cf. HALF-DOLLAR). [a time when exchange rate was US$4 to £1 sterling]

dollar *n.*[2] (drugs) **1** [1960s+] $100 worth of drugs. **2** [1990s] MDMA (cf. ECSTASY).

dollar-an-inch man *n.* [1960s+] (US gay) a male prostitute who claims that his penis is so large that even by charging fellators by the inch he could still get rich. [? play on SAmE *dollar-a-year man*, one who works for the government at a nominal salary]

dollar house *n.* [20C] (US) an outside lavatory (cf. DOLL HOUSE). [the timber required to build it costs no more than $1]

dollars *n.* [20C] money in general.

dollars to buttons/cobwebs *phr.* [mid-late 19C] (orig. US) a sure thing (cf. ALL THE WORLD TO A CHINA ORANGE). [the disparity of the wagers underlines the certainty of the bet]

dollars to doughnuts *phr.* [late 19C+] an absolute certainty (cf. ALL THE WORLD TO A CHINA ORANGE). [for ety. *see* DOLLARS TO BUTTONS]

dollar-woman *n.* [1930s–40s] (US) a cheap prostitute. [her price]

doll baby *n.* [19C+] (US) an attractive young woman. [DOLL n.[1] (3) + BABY n.[2]]

doll city *n.* [1980s+] (US teen) a conventionally pretty woman. [DOLL n.[1] (3) + -CITY]

dolled out *adj.* [1920s+] (US campus) dressed up, esp. for a night out (cf. ALL POSHED UP; DOLLED UP; DUDED UP; GUSSIED UP; TARTED UP; TOGGED DOWN; TOGGED OUT; TOGGED UP).

dolled up *adj.* [late 19C+] (orig. US) dressed up, esp. for a night out; thus ext. as *dolled up/all dolled up like a barber's cat* (cf. DOLLED OUT). [DOLL n.[1] (3); why the barber's cat should be especially decorated is unknown]

dolled up like a sore finger/thumb/toe *see* DRESSED UP LIKE A SORE FINGER.

dollface *n.* [20C] an attractive woman or boy; often used as form of address *Hey, dollface!* [DOLL n.[1] (3) + SE *face*]

doll house *n.* [20C] an outside lavatory. [abbr. of DOLLAR HOUSE]

dollies *n.*[1] [1950s+] (drugs) synthetic morphine (cf. DOLLS; DOLLY n.[6]). [brandname *Dolophine*]

dollies *n.*[2] [1960s+] (Irish) the female breasts (cf. LOLLIES). [one sucks them]

doll of a *phr.* [1950s–60s] phr. used of anything or anyone considered notably attractive. [DOLL n.[1] (3)]

dollop *n.*[1] [early 19C+] a lump; thus the *whole dollop*, the whole lot, *dollops of*, lots of. [note East Anglian dial. *dollop*, untidy woman, a slattern, a trollop]

dollop *n.*[2] [mid-19C] a three-month sentence (cf. BRAGGADOCIO; DOSE n.[2]). [fig. use of DOLLOP n.[1]]

dollop *v.* [mid-19C] to give up a share, lit. 'dole up'.

doll-rags *n.* [19C+] (US) small pieces. [SE *doll* + *rags*, clothes; thus pieces small enough to make a doll's wardrobe]

dolls *n.* [1960s+] (drugs) synthetic morphine (cf. DOLLIES n.[1]). [brandname *Dolophine*]

doll up *v.* [20C] to dress up a person or an object, esp. as *doll oneself up*, to smarten oneself up, put on one's best clothes. [DOLL n.[1] (3)]

dolly *n.*[1] **1** [17C] a female pet or favourite. **2** [17C–early 19C] a mistress, a prostitute. **3** [mid-17C–late 19C] a slattern, a dull, unattractive woman. **4** [late 19C–1900s] a servant girl. **5** [20C] any girl or woman, esp. when attractive. **6** [1960s+] a teenage girl or young woman, usu. associated with the 1960s and 'swinging London', usu. a young secretary or similar, dressed in the latest fashions, obsessed by the current 'in' rock group and other accoutrements of popular culture (cf. DOLLYBIRD). **7** [1960s+] (N.Z. prison) the younger lover of a 'butch' lesbian. [DOLL n.¹ (1), (3) + sfx. -*y*, but note Hancock, who suggests Ital. *dolce*, sweet and thus claims the word for Polari]

dolly *n.*² [19C] the penis (cf. DOLL n.²). [? it can be sucked]

dolly *n.*³ [mid-19C] anyone who has committed a *faux pas* or social solecism. [? they have as much sense as a child's doll]

dolly *n.*⁴ [late 19C] a binding of rag on a finger or toe. [Berks., dial. *dolly*, a wounded finger, bound up in a cloth]

dolly *n.*⁵ [20C] (tramp) a candle. [ety. unknown; ? link to SE *tallow*, of which candles were made; not school sl. *tolly*, a candle]

dolly *n.*⁶ [1960s+] (drugs) synthetic morphine (cf. DOLLIES n.¹). [brandname *Dolophine*]

dolly *adj.* (orig. Polari) **1** [mid-19C] silly, foolish. **2** [1960s] nice or pleasant. **3** [1960s] attractive, fashionable.

dolly *v.* [1930s+] (Aus.) **1** to treat harshly. **2** to interrogate. [fig. use of the v. form of gold-mining *dolly*, an implement for crushing quartz; ult. UK dial. *dolly*, a wooden implement for beating clothes in the wash]

dollybird *n.* [1960s] an attractive young woman, typically a secretary or shopgirl in her late teens or early twenties and found in such centres of 'swinging London' as Carnaby Street or the King's Road. [DOLLY n.¹ (6) + BIRD n.⁵; post-1960s use is only historical]

dolly boy *n.* [1970s+] (orig. gay) a young male prostitute (cf. RENT BOY). [var. on DOLLY n.¹ (6) + SE *boy*]

dolly cotten/cotton *n.* [20C] rotten (cf. DR COTTON). [rhy. sl.]

dolly gray *n.* [1910s+] (Aus.) a threepenny piece (cf. ALMA GRAY). [rhy. sl. *dolly gray* = TRAY n.¹]

dolly-/pitchy-man *n.* [late 19C] (Anglo-Irish) a Jew. [? DOLLY-SHOP, SE *trader's pitch*]

dollymop *n.* [mid–late 19C] **1** a part-time prostitute, often a shopgirl, esp. a milliner, who occasionally sold her body to supplement her otherwise meagre income. **2** (US) a prostitute specializing in sailors. **3** [mid-19C–1900s] a slovenly, ill-kempt servant girl. [DOLLY n.¹ (3) + the equation of women and fish (cf. FISH n.⁴), in this case the SE *mop*, a young whiting or gurnard, thus a young woman. Note obs. Ger. sl. *Backfisch*, a teenage girl, lit. a 'fish for baking']

dollymopper *n.* [mid–late 19C] a womanizer, esp. a soldier. [DOLLYMOP]

dollypot *n.* [1920s+] (Aus.) a fool (cf. DICKHEAD). [rhy. sl. *dollypot* = TWAT n. (2)]

dollyshop *n.* [mid-19C] a low or illegal pawnshop, whose owner may also act as a receiver. [orig. a marine store, signified by the black doll hanging outside as a sign]

dolly sisters *n.* [20C] (US) a pair of patrolmen. [the singers Janszieka (1893–1941) and Roszika (1893–1970) Deutsch, better known as Jenny and Rosie *Dolly*]

dolly up *v.* [20C] (tramp) to heat water or tea with a candle. [DOLLY n.⁵]

dolly varden *n.* [late 19C+] the garden. [rhy. sl.; ult. *Dolly Varden* from Charles Dickens's *Barnaby Rudge* (1841)]

dolly-worship *n.* [late 19C–1900s] a derog. term for Roman Catholicism. [the use of statues and religious images in Catholic churches]

dolo *adv.* [1990s] (US Black) on one's own, solo. [ety. unknown]

dolomite *n.* [1980s+] (US campus) cocaine. [SE *dolomite*, a form of rock, composed of lime and magnesia; thus a pun on ROCK n.⁴; ? + ref. to 1970s Black humorist *Dolomite*]

d.o.m. *n.* [1950s+] a dirty old man; poss. an actual or alleged child molester but usu. any older man who makes obvious

his preference for women younger than he might be expected to pursue. [abbr.]

dom *n.* [1960s+] a dominatrix. [abbr.]

domain cocktail *n.* [late 19C–1930s] (Aus.) 'a lethal concoction of petrol and pepper which reputedly once had a vogue among deadbeat drinkers in the Sydney Domain' (Baker); thus *domain dosser*, a loafer or down-and-out who frequents the Sydney Domain. [proper name of the *Domain*, a park in Sydney, Australia, popular for speech-making and frequented by the unemployed and the alcoholic]

domboek *n.* [1970s–80s] (S.Afr. Black) a pass book, i.e. the mandatory identity document formerly carried by all Blacks (cf. DOMPAS). [Afk. *dom*, stupid + *boek*, book]

dome *n.*¹ [mid-19C+] (orig. US) the head; thus [1950s] *dome-doctor*, a psychoanalyst, a psychotherapist (cf. ATTIC).

dome *n.*² [1980s+] (drugs) LSD (cf. A n.³). [? the shape of a capsule or the effect on one's head]

do me/us a favour *phr.* [1950s+] **1** phr. used to ask for something when the assumption is that the favour will be granted unwillingly or under duress. **2** synon. for 'you must be joking' or 'who do you think you're fooling?' **3** go away, be off. [all ironic uses of SE]

do-me-dags *n.* [late 19C+] cigarettes. [rhy. sl. *do-me-dags* = fags (see FAG n.⁴ (3)]

do me good *n.* [late 19C+] **1** a Woodbine cigarette. **2** wood. **3** (Aus.) firewood. [rhy. sl.]

doment *n.* [19C] a performance, a show. [DO n.³ + sfx. -*ment*]

dome piece *n.* [1970s] **1** (US) the head. **2** (US Black) a hat.

domestic *n.* **1** [mid-19C–1900s] (US) a brand of cigar manufactured in the US (as opposed to a Cuban-made Havana). **2** [1960s+] (drugs) locally grown marijuana.

domestic afflictions *n.* [mid–late 19C] the menstrual period. [euph.]

domex *n.* [1980s+] (drugs) **1** phencyclidine (cf. ACE n.³). **2** MDMA (cf. ecstasy). [ety. unknown; ? brandname]

domie/domi/dommy *n.* [1930s] (US Black) one's house, one's home. [Lat. *domus*, home]

domine/dominie/domini do-little *n.* [late 18C–early 19C] an impotent old man. [SE *dominie*, a schoolmaster + *do-little*]

dominicker/dommernecker *n.* [20C] **1** a coward (cf. CHICKEN n.²). **2** a person of mixed race, esp. of Black, Indian and White ancestry. [SE *dominicker*, the Dominique fowl or any other chicken with mottled or barred plumage. The dominicker rooster was believed always to back down when challenged by another rooster]

dominicker/dommernecker *v.* [20C] to back down, to act in a cowardly manner (cf. CHICKEN OUT). [DOMINICKER n.]

domini-/dominie-do-little *see* DOMINE DO-LITTLE.

domino *n.* **1** [early 19C–1910s] a tooth (cf. DOMINO-BOX). **2** [1920s] (US) a die, usu. in pl. **3** [1960s+] (drugs) a capsule containing a combination of an amphetamine and a sedative.

domino! *excl.* [mid–late 19C] a general excl. to signify the end of or last of a situation, that's it, that's done, all over etc; esp. among soldiers and sailors, to signify the last blow of a thrashing; thus [20C] *it is domino with ...* , it is finished, it is all over, it is hopeless. [the card-game *domino*, in which the winner is the player who gets rid of all their cards first]

domino-box *n.* [19C] the mouth (cf. BOX OF DOMINOES). [DOMINO n. (1)]

dominoes *n.*¹ [late 19C] **1** the teeth, esp. when yellow and rotten (cf. IVORIES). **2** piano keys.

dominoes *n.*² [1980s+] (drugs) amphetamines (cf. A n.²). [? the packaging]

domino-thumper *n.* [late 19C–1920s] a pianist. [DOMINOES n.¹ (2) + SE *thumper*]

domino-walloper *n.* [1930s] a pianist. [DOMINOES n.¹ (2) + SE *walloper*]

domkop *n.* [20C] (S.Afr.) a fool, also as derog. form of address. [Afk. *dom*, stupid + *kop*, head; note Ger. *Dummkopf*]

dommerer/dommerar *n.* [mid-16C–mid-18C] (Und.) a mendicant villain who feigned dumbness, often claiming to have suffered at the hands of the infidel Turk who, on capturing him during a sea voyage, had torn out his tongue for denying Muhammad (cf. CANTING CREW; DUMMERER). [SE *dumb*]

dommernecker *see* DOMINICKER.

dommy *see* DOMIE.

dommy-knocker *see* DONGER-KNOCKER.

dompas/dompass *n.* [1950s+] (S.Afr. Black) a pass book, i.e. the mandatory identity document formerly carried by all Blacks (cf. DOMBOEK). [Afk. *dom*, stupid + *pas*, pass]

doms *n.* [20C] **1** (Aus.) *Domi*nicans. **2** *domi*noes. [abbr.]

don *n.*[1] [mid-17C+] a clever or outstanding person, a distinguished individual, a leader. [the original use comes from the Sp. honorific *Don*. The term has been re-invented, with much the same meaning, in the late 20C (*see* DON n.[3]), mainly by teen gangs, with a ref. to the Italian Mafia's use of *Don* to refer to a senior Mafioso, a use that was spread through the popularity of the film *The Godfather* (1972), the story of the fictitious Don Corleone]

don *n.*[2] [19C] a Spaniard. [the common Sp. honorific *Don*]

don/donette/don man/donna *n.*[3] [1980s+] (W.I./UK Black teen) a respected boss or leader, the master or mistress of a situation.

dona/donna/doner *n.* [mid-19C+] (Ling. Fr./Polari) **1** a woman. **2** a landlady. [Ital. *donna*, woman]

donagher *n.* [early 19C–1920s] a privy. [DANNA; 20C use mainly US]

donah *n.* [19C+] **1** an attractive woman. **2** (Und.) the 'lady', the queen in a game of three-card monte. [Polari *donah*, ult. Ital. *donna*, a woman]

dona highland-flinger *n.* [late 19C–1900s] a music-hall singer. [rhy. sl.]

dona jack *n.* [late 19C–1900s] a pimp. [DONA + JACK n.[5]]

dona juanita *n.* [1970s+] (drugs) marijuana. [lit. *lady Jane*; play on Mex. *marijuana*, i.e. Mary Jane]

donaker *n.* [17C–early 18C] a cattle-stealer. [ety. unknown]

donald *n.*[1] [mid–late 19C] (Scot.) a glass of whisky. [? the name of a popular brand]

donald *n.*[2] [1960s+] (Aus.) sexual intercourse. [rhy. sl.; *Donald Duck* = FUCK n.[1]]

donald *n.*[3] (Aus.) **1** [1960s+] a truck. **2** [1970s+] luck. [rhy. sl.; abbr. *Donald Duck*]

Don Caesar spouting *n.* [late 19C] (society) haughty after-dinner speechifying. [the gravity of Spanish dons]

Doncaster-cut *n.* [16C] a horse. [the association of *Doncaster* with horses + SE *cut*, castrated]

Don Cypriano *n.* [17C] the penis. [play on Sp. honorific *Don* + CYPRIAN adj.; coined by Sir Thomas Urquhart for his translation of *Rabelais* (1653–93)]

don dada *n.* [1980s+] (W.I./UK Black teen) the highest ranking leader, Don of Dons. [DON n.[3] + SE *dada*; lit. 'don father']

donder *v.* [mid-19C+] (S.Afr.) to beat up, to thrash (cf. BLIKSEM!).

done *adj.*[1] **1** [17C+] cheated (cf. RIPPED OFF). **2** [1940s+] beaten up, assaulted. [DO v.[2] (2)]

done/done for *adj.*[2] [early 19C+] arrested, arrested on a charge of … . [DO v.[5]]

done brown *adj.* [mid-19C+] wholly taken in, utterly deceived, completely defeated (cf. DO BROWN). [cooking imagery]

done deal *n.* [20C] anything that has been brought to a satisfactory conclusion.

done fairly *adj.* [late 19C] cheated, defrauded. [DO v.[4]]

done for *adj.*[1] *see* DONE adj.[2].

done for *adj.*[2] [late 19C+] **1** finished, exhausted, used up (cf. DO FOR v.[1]; DONE IN). **2** dead (cf. DO FOR v.[1]; DO IN). **3** without a chance, hopeless, defeated, lost, abandoned. [DO v.[2]]

done for a ramp *adj.* [mid-19C] arrested for stealing. [DO v.[5] (2) + RAMP n.[2]]

donegan *see* DONIGAN.

done in *adj.* [1910s+] very tired, exhausted. [DO v.[2]]

done in a tick-tack *phr.* [late 19C] done very quickly. [SE *do* + TICK n.[3] (2)]

done like a dinner *adj.* [mid-19C+] (Aus.) 'done to a turn', i.e. utterly defeated (cf. DONE BROWN). [cooking imagery]

done like a dog's dinner *phr.* [1930s+] (N.Z.) trounced, utterly defeated (cf. DONE BROWN). [var. on DONE LIKE A DINNER]

done-over *adj.*[1] [18C–19C] of a woman, to have been used for sexual purposes. [DO v.[2] (4)]

done-over *adj.*[2] **1** [19C+] drunk (cf. BASTED). **2** [mid-19C] worsted, put at a disadvantage, forced to lose out in a disagreement or struggle. **3** [20C] beaten up. [DO v.[2] (1), (2) and (3)]

done promote *n.* [1940s+] (W.I.) sandals or shoes made from old automobile tyres. [? joking allusion, *I see you done promote* (have been promoted, i.e. from bare feet)]

doner *n.* [mid–late 19C] one who is ruined, on the verge of death or collapse. [DONE FOR adj.[2] + ? pun on GONER]

done thing *n.* [1920s+] whatever is currently accepted by a specific group of people, professional, social, economic etc.

done to a burn *see* DONE TO A TURN.

done to a frazzle *phr.* [late 19C+] (US) cooked perfectly. [? a variation of dial. *frizzle*, to fry (with a sizzle)]

done to a turn/burn *phr.* [early 19C+] **1** perfect. **2** worsted, beaten, at a disadvantage; the image of being spit-roasted and defenceless (cf. DONE UP LIKE A KIPPER). [pos. and neg. cookery images]

done to death *phr.* [late 19C–1900s] over-fashionable, clichéd. [later use is SE]

done to the wide/world *phr.* [1920s+] defeated, beaten utterly vanquished. [DO v.[2] (1)]

donette *see* DON n.[3].

done up *adj.*[1] **1** [late 18C–early 19C] (US) ruined (by gambling or other forms of speculation). **2** [19C] exhausted, worn out (cf. DONE IN). **3** [19C+] ill, whether mildly or extremely. **4** [late 19C+] (orig. US) beaten up. **5** [20C] very drunk. **6** [20C] out of order, not working. [DO v.[2] (2)]

done up *adj.*[2] [mid-19C+] worsted, put at a disadvantage, forced to lose out in a disagreement or struggle (cf. DONE-OVER adj.[2]). [DO v.[2] (1), (2)]

done up *adj.*[3] [20C] dressed up, esp. as *done up to the nines*. [DO v.[9]]

done up/dressed up/mockered up like a pox doctor's clerk *phr.* [1950s+] (Aus.) flashily dressed, overdressed (cf. BARBER'S CLERK). [DONE UP adj.[2] + stereotyping of these occupations as vulgarly dressed]

done up like a sore finger/thumb/toe *see* DRESSED UP LIKE A SORE FINGER.

done up like a kipper *phr.* [20C] **1** beaten up. **2** caught red-handed by the police, ambushed during a crime. [DONE UP adj.[1]]

doney *n.* [20C] (US) an attractive woman. [var. on DONAH]

dong *n.*[1] [late 19C+] a blow, esp. with the fist. [post-1930s use is mainly Aus.]

dong *n.*[2] [20C] (orig. US) the penis; thus (US gay) *dong and gongs*, the penis and testicles (cf. ARSE-OPENER). [? abbr. DING-DONG n.[4], which predates general sl. use in regional citations]

dong *v.* [late 19C+] to hit. [DONG n.[1]]

donger *n.*[1] [20C] (Aus./N.Z.) a blow. [ext. of DONG n.[1]]

donger n.[2] [20C] (Aus.) the penis. [ext. of DONG n.[2], but note *donger*, a fisherman's club]

donger-knocker/dongy-knocker/dommy-knocker/ bommy-knocker n. [1930s+] (N.Z., mainly juv.) a club, a bludgeon. [DONG v./SE *bomb* + *knocker*]

don gorgon n. [1980s+] (W.I. Rasta) outstanding dreadlocks; thus a person who is respected. [DON n.[3] + the mythical *Gorgon*, whose 'hair' was actually writhing snakes]

dongy-knocker *see* DONGER-KNOCKER.

donicker n. [18C–19C] a privy (cf. DANNA). [DUNNIKEN]

donigan/donegan n. [18C–19C] a privy (cf. DANNA). [DUNNIKEN]

don jem n. [1980s+] (drugs) marijuana. [var. on DJAMBA]

donk n. **1** [1910s+] a *donkey*. **2** [1910s+] (Aus.) a car or boat engine, a motorcycle. **3** [1940s+] (Aus.) a lift on the cross-bar of a bicycle (cf. DINK n.[4]; PUG n.[7]).

donkey n.[1] **1** [mid-19C+] a fool, a simpleton. **2** [mid-19C] (US campus) a notably religious student. **3** [1920s+] (US) a working-class Irish person. **4** [1930s+] a manual labourer.

donkey/donkey's n.[2] [20C] the penis. [rhy. sl. DONKEY DICK n.[2] = PRICK n. (2)]

donkey v. [1990s] (US teen) to do something really stupid, especially in a social situation.

donkey-deep in phr. [1910s–20s] (N.Z.) immersed in, up to one's neck. [lit. or fig.]

donkey dick n.[1] **1** [late 18C–early 19C] an ass (cf. DICKY n.[3]). **2** [1980s+] (US) a fool, a simpleton. [note late 18C–mid-19C *donkey* (? f. proper name *Duncan*) itself was orig. sl.]

donkey dick n.[2] [1970s+] a notably large penis, usu. in adj. *donkey-dicked*, having a large penis. [SE *donkey* + DICK n.[5] (1)]

donkey dust n. [20C] euph. for BULLSHIT n.. [SE *donkey* + *dust*, rubbish]

donkey lick n. [1940s] (Aus.) treacle or golden syrup. [? its appeal to the animal]

donkey lick v. [1920s–40s] (Aus./N.Z.) to defeat easily. [SE *donkey* + LICK v.]

donkey price n. [1950s+] (W.I.) an inflated price, one only a fool would pay. [DONKEY n.[1] (2) + SE *price*]

donkey-rigged adj. [19C+] in possession of a notably large penis (cf. DONKEY DICK n.[2]).

donkey roast n. [1960s] (US) a formal banquet.

donkey's n.[1] *see* DONKEY n.[2].

donkey's n.[2] *see* DONKEY'S YEARS.

donkey's ages n. [1940s–60s] a very long time (cf. DONKEY'S YEARS).

donkey's breakfast n. [late 19C–1910s] **1** a straw hat. **2** (Aus./US) a straw palliasse.

donkey's ears n. [mid–late 19C] a shirt-collar with long points.

donkey show n. [1990s] (US Black) a complete mess, a farcical situation. [? a sex show involving a donkey and a woman]

donkey's knob n. [1990s] **1** anything obvious. **2** anything excellent, admirable, first-rate (cf. DOG'S BALLOCKS).

donkey spanking n. [1980s+] masturbation. [SPANK v.[3]]

donkey's yawn n. [1990s] a large vagina (cf. HORSE-COLLAR).

donkey's years/donkey's n. [1910s+] a very long time. [the length of a donkey's ears and the addition of an extra *y*. Occas. as *donkey's ears*, a ref. to the beast's well-known feature + a pun on *years*]

donkey wallop v. [1920s–40s] (Aus.) to defeat easily. [var. on DONKEY LICK v.]

donkey work n. [1920s+] tedious, laborious, usu. heavy tasks.

donko n. [1970s+] (N.Z.) a room set aside in the workplace for smoking, relaxation etc. [? synon. N.Z.E. donkey room, orig.

(1920s) the enclosure on the Wellington docks where a donkey engine was kept and at the time was the only warm shelter available]

donks n. [20C] a very long time (cf. DONKEY'S YEARS; YONKS).

donette *see* DON n.[3].

donna n.[1] *see* DONA.

donna n.[2] *see* DON n.[3].

donna and feeles n. [mid-19C] a woman and children. [Ital. or Ling. Fr. *donna e figlie*, a woman and children]

donnelly n. [mid-19C] (US) a heavy blow or punch (cf. DINNYHAZER). [the prize-fighter Daniel *Donnelly* (1788–1820)]

donner v. (S.Afr.) **1** [mid-19C+] to beat up, to thrash. **2** [1960s+] to defeat, to overcome (cf. DONDER). [Afk. *donder*, to thrash]

donnie/donny n. [1950s–60s] (N.Z.) a fight, a disturbance. [abbr. DONNYBROOK]

donnybrook n. [19C+] a fight, a riot, a noisy brawl (cf. BRANNIGAN). [the notorious *Donnybrook* Fair in Eire, at which such events were a regular feature]

donnybrook v. [19C] to strike, to hit. [DONNYBROOK n.]

donor n. [1980s+] (US campus) one who makes themselves available for sexual intercourse.

do-nothing stool n. [1970s] (US Black) the buttocks, the posterior. [used when one is sitting down idly]

donovan n. [19C] (Anglo-Irish) a potato (cf. MURPHY n.[1]). [the commonness of the Irish surname and the stereotyping of the Irish appetite for potatoes]

don't all speak at once phr. [late 19C+] phr. used when one has called for volunteers (for something unpleasant or unappealing) and no one has spoken up.

don't ask me phr. [20C] a statement of ignorance or lack of interest in a previous query.

don't be auntie phr. [1920s+] (Aus.) don't be foolish (cf. UNCLE WILLIE). [the stereotyping of foolish (? maiden) aunts]

don't be funny n. [20C] (Aus.) a lavatory. [rhy. sl. *don't be funny* = DUNNY]

don't be funny phr. [1930s+] (orig. US) don't be stupid (cf. DON'T MAKE ME LAUGH).

don't be like that phr. [1940s+] don't be so bad-tempered, petulant, 'difficult' etc (cf. BE LIKE THAT).

don't call us, we'll call you phr. [1940s+] a semi-joking phr. of dismissal. [trad. theatrical use by producers/directors to auditioning actors whom, of course, they never do call]

don't-care-a-damnativeness n. [mid-19C] carelessness, unconcern. [phr. 'I don't care/give a damn']

don't-care-damn adj. [20C] (W.I.) absolutely indifferent, totally irresponsible.

don't-care-ish/-ishified adj. [1930s] (US Black) indifferent, uninterested.

don't do anything I wouldn't do! phr. [20C] exhortation to anyone who is leaving, esp. on holiday or in search of similar supposed pleasures; the implication is usu. sexual, and the point is to wish them as excessive a time as possible.

don't do anything you couldn't eat! phr. [1930s+] (Aus.) exhortation to anyone who is leaving, in search of supposed pleasures (cf. DON'T DO ANYTHING I WOULDN'T DO!).

don't dynamite phr. [late 19C] don't lose your temper, keep calm. [the Irish Republican dynamiting attacks of 1880s. 'Their chief result was to add a word to the army of phrases' (Ware)]

don't excite phr. [late 19C–1930s] don't get emotional, don't lose control.

don't fancy yours! [20C] phr. joking reflex comment when two young men see two women, irrespective of their real charms.

don't forget the diver phr. [1940s+] a joc. and generally meaningless phr. used as a synon. for 'good bye'. [the radio comedy show *It's That Man Again* (a great provider of catchphrases) and uttered by 'the Diver', played by Horace Perceval, who offered a secondary catchphrase: '(I'm) going down now, sir.' According to *ITMA* star Tommy Handley (1892–1949) it came from his recollections of a man who would dive from the New Brighton pier, *c*.1920; he was middle-aged, had one leg and dived from a great height as passengers left the ferry from Liverpool; he collected money for his 'act' in a fishing net]

don't fret/don't you fret *phr.* [late 19C+] a sarcastic phr. implying 'don't you worry, it may be your responsibility but I'll deal with it'.

don't get your bowels in an uproar *phr.* [20C] do not make so much (unnecessary) fuss.

don't get your shit hot *phr.* [20C] don't get over-excited.

don't give me that *phr.* [1920s+] you can't fool me (cf. TELL IT TO THE MARINES!).

don't hold no air *phr.* (US Black) a phr. meaning something has little impact or effect on either people or events.

don't hold your breath *phr.* [1970s+] (orig. US) a phr. used of an unreliable person or of a promise that may not be kept; i.e. don't expect anything to happen, don't expect promises to materialize.

don't I know it *phr.* [late 19C+] a phr. implying one's slightly regretful awareness of a (bad) situation, unpalatable truth etc.

don't just stand there – do something! *phr.* [1930s+] urging a quantity, if not a quality of action.

don't let your meat loaf *phr.* [1960s+] (US) a general phr. of encouragement, the implication being 'don't procrastinate'. [pun on SE *loaf*, the food/*loaf*, to loiter]

don't let your mouth/alligator mouth overload your ass/canary ass *phr.* [1960s+] (US) keep quiet, esp. in a difficult situation where words might complicate matters (cf. DON'T LET YOUR MOUTH BUY WHAT YOUR ASS CAN'T PAY FOR).

don't let your mouth buy what your ass can't pay for *phr.* [1980s+] (US) keep quiet, esp. when speaking might make matters worse (cf. DON'T LET YOUR MOUTH OVERLOAD YOUR ASS).

don't let your mouth write a check your ass can't cash *phr.* [1960s+] (orig. US Black) keep quiet, esp. when speaking might make matters worse (cf. DON'T LET YOUR MOUTH BUY WHAT YOUR ASS CAN'T PAY FOR).

don't lose your hair *phr.* [late 19C] calm down, keep cool (cf. KEEP YOUR HAIR ON!).

don't make a judy/judy fitzsimmons of yourself! *excl.* [1920s+] (Anglo-Irish) don't be a fool. [? a long-lost anecdote]

don't make a production out of it *phr.* [1960s+] 'don't make a mountain out of a molehill' (cf. MAKE A MEAL OF).

don't make me laugh *phr.* [1920s+] don't be stupid, ridiculous; thus [1920s–40s] ext. as *don't make me laugh I've got a split lip* (cf. DON'T BE FUNNY phr.).

don't — me/don't you — me *phr.* [late 19C+] a phr. used to deflect another person's attempt to make excuses, ameliorate a difficult situation, e.g. 'But ... .' 'Don't you "but" me!'

don't mention it *phr.* [mid-19C+] a phr. used to put off thanks or effusive acknowledgements of one's efforts; also used ironically as a counter to rudeness.

don't mention that *phr.* [late 19C] a phr. used to put off thanks or effusive acknowledgements of one's efforts. [this var. on the usual *don't mention it* was popularized during its use in a lengthy libel suit (Belt v. Lawes) in 1882]

don't mind/mine me I only live/work here *phr.* [mid-19C+] often ironical and slightly self-pitying, a resentful *cri-de-coeur* from a speaker who feels their territory is being taken over by strangers.

don't-name-'ems *n.* [mid-19C–1910s] trousers (cf. ARTICLES; DON'T-SPEAK-OF-'EMS; INDESCRIBABLES; INDISPENSIBLES; INEXPLICABLES; INEXPRESSIBLES; MUSTN'T-MENTION-'EMS; UNMENTIONABLES). [the image of trousers, so close to the genitals and legs, as taboo]

don't pay no rabbit foot *phr.* [1900s–40s] (US Black) an exhortation to ignore a person or situation. [? the use of a rabbit's foot as a totem]

don't pick me up before I fall *phr.* [late 18C+] a phr. used to admonish someone who wishes to correct someone before they have actually erred (cf. DON'T TAKE ME UP BEFORE I FALL). [*pick* is Anglo-Irish use]

don't play me *phr.* [1990s] (US teen) don't insult me. [PLAY v.²]

don't sell me a dog *phr.* [late 19C] (society) don't try to fool me (cf. SELL A PUP). [the perceived lack of ethics in such a transaction]

don't shit a shitter *see* CAN'T SHIT A SHITTER.

don't sing it *phr.* [late 19C–1900s] don't exaggerate (cf. CHANT THE POKER). [one 'sings' an exaggerated tale]

don't-speak-of-'ems *n.* [mid-19C] (US) trousers. [for ety. *see* DON'T-NAME-'EMS]

don't spend it all at once *phr.* [1960s+] joc. advice usu. offered on handing over a very small amount of money, in payment of a debt etc.

don't strain yourself *phr.* [20C] a phr. addressed to anyone deemed to be failing conspicuously at pulling their weight.

don't take any wooden money *phr.* [1920s] beware of being defrauded or hoaxed (cf. DON'T TAKE ANY WOODEN NICKELS).

don't take any wooden nickels *phr.* [1920s+] (orig. US) beware of being defrauded or hoaxed (cf. DON'T TAKE ANY WOODEN MONEY).

don't take me there *phr.* [1990s] (US teen) I am not interested, I don't want to hear it.

don't take me up before I fall *phr.* [late 19C+] a phr. used to admonish someone who wishes to correct someone before they have actually erred (cf. DON'T PICK ME UP BEFORE I FALL).

don't talk to me about — *phr.* [1950s+] a phr. that rejects the making of a remark that might rekindle memories of a bad experience; often used melodramatically or ironically.

don't tell me, let me guess *phr.* [1940s+] a joc. phr. used to cut off a revelation, esp. when the listener (i.e. the person speaking) probably knows what is about to come.

don't turn that side to London *phr.* [late 19C] a phr. used to condemn whatever object is under discussion. [the idea that only the best is good enough for display in the metropolis]

don't wake it up *phr.* [1920s+] (Aus.) don't talk about it. [cf. SE *let sleeping dogs lie*]

don't worry – it may never happen *phr.* [1910s+] usu. offered as advice to someone looking especially miserable or worried.

don't worry your fat *phr.* [1910s+] don't worry.

don't you be too sure *phr.* [mid-19C+] a phr. warning someone not to be absolutely certain of a particular statement or situation.

don't you fret! *see* DON'T FRET!

don't you — me *see* DON'T — ME.

don't *you* start *phr.* [1930s+] a phr. used to indicate that one is already sufficiently displeased or annoyed by statements that have been made and that one does not need the irritation that their repetition would cause; or, usu. to a child meaning, 'I'm annoyed already, don't start behaving badly and make things worse.'

don't you wish you may get it? *see* I WISH YOU MAY GET IT.

donut-bumper *n.* [20C] (US) a lesbian (cf. DONUT-PUNCHER). [SAmE *donut* (UK *doughnut*) + BUMPER n.⁶]

donut hole *n.* [1990s] (US campus) someone with no social skills. [the emptiness of the hole in a SAmE *donut*. Note US milit. use *donut hole*, a female volunteer worker with the US Red Cross]

donut-puncher *n.* [1990s] (US) a male homosexual (cf. DONUT-BUMPER; DUNG-PUNCHER).

doob *n.*[1] [1950s+] (Aus.) the penis. [ety. unknown]

doob *n.*[2] [1960s+] **1** (drugs) amphetamine (cf. A n.[2]). **2** (orig. US drugs) a cannabis cigarette. [ety. unknown; (1) originated with the UK Mods of the early 1960s and then spread among other users]

doobage *n.* [1980s+] (US campus) marijuana (cf. DOOBIE n.[1]). [DOOB n.[2] (2) + sfx. *-age*]

doober *n.*[1] *see* DOOBIE n.[1].

doober *n.*[2] [1970s+] (US) **1** a piece of excrement. **2** a foolish or unpleasant person. [ety. unknown; ? link to SE *daub*]

dooberry *n.* [1990s] a woman's breast, usu. in pl. *dooberries* (cf. APPLES n.[1]). [var. on DINGLEBERRIES (2)]

doobie/doober/dubee/duby *n.*[1] [1960s+] (drugs) **1** cannabis. **2** a cannabis cigarette. [ety. unknown; poss. same ety. as DOOBIE n.[2]]

doobie *n.*[2] [1980s+] (US) an unimportant, worthless or stupid person. [Scot. *dobie*, a dull, stupid fellow; ult. f. *Dobie, Robert*]

doobob *n.* [1910s+] (orig. US) any nameless small object, typically some form of gadget (cf. DOHICKEY). [ety. unknown]

doobrie/doobry/dubry *n.* [1950s+] (orig. milit.) anything for which one cannot recall the name (cf. DOHICKEY). [orig. in the army, the term gained a new lease of life thanks to the DJ and TV performer Kenny Everett, who used it frequently in 1970s–80s]

dooby *adj.* [1950s+] (Aus.) old-fashioned. [SE *dowdy* ? + BOOBY n.[1]]

dooce *n.* [late 18C–late 19C] euph. for damned (cf. DEUCED).

dood *n.*[1] [1910s+] (Aus.) a pipe. [Irish *dudeen*, a short clay pipe]

dood *n.*[2] [1920s–50s] (US) the penis. [for ety. *see* DOOD n.[1]]

doodackie *n.* [1940s+] (N.Z.) any nameless small object, typically some form of gadget; the *doodackied up*, dressed up (cf. DOHICKEY). [ety. unknown]

doodad *n.* [mid-19C+] (orig. US) **1** any nameless small object, typically some form of gadget (cf. DOHICKEY). **2** something small, used as a decoration. **3** nonsense, foolish chatter. [ety. unknown; the many synon. terms for the word may represent the stammering efforts of one who is struggling to recall the correct name]

doodads *n.*[1] [mid-19C+] (orig. US) morsels, pieces, odds and ends. [DOODAD]

doodads *n.*[2] [late 19C+] one's best clothes.

doodah *n.*[1] [1910s+] an emotional crisis, a nervous, tense state. [the refrain *doo-da(h)* of the plantation song 'Camptown Races' (1850)]

doodah *n.*[2] [1920s+] anything for which one cannot remember the name (cf. DOHICKEY). [DOODAD n.[1]]

doodgooi *n.* [1910s+] (S.Afr.) a lethal weapon. [Afk. *doodgooier*, a dumpling, lit. a 'dead-thrower', i.e. dough that has not risen]

doodibbie *n.* [1910s+] any nameless small object, typically some form of gadget (cf. DOHICKEY). [ety. unknown]

doodinkus *n.* [1910s+] any nameless small object, typically some form of gadget (cf. DOHICKEY). [ety. unknown]

doodlally *see* DOODLE-ALLY.

doodle *n.*[1] [early 17C–mid-19C] a fool, a dull person. [var. on SE *noodle*, a fool; ? link to Low Ger. *Dudeltopf*, a simpleton, lit. a 'nightcap']

doodle *n.*[2] [late 18C+] the penis, esp. a child's penis. [20C use is US]

doodle *n.*[3] [20C] (US) anything completely simple or easy to achieve. [var. on DODDLE]

doodle *n.*[4] [1910s] any nameless small object, typically some form of gadget (cf. DOHICKEY). [ety. unknown]

doodle *adj.* [early 18C] foolish. [DOODLE n.[1]]

doodle *v.*[1] [19C] to make a fool of, to cheat (cf. DIDDLE v.[1]). [DOODLE n.[1]]

doodle *v.*[2] [late 19C+] of a man, to have sexual intercourse. [DOODLE n.[2]]

doodle/doodle around *v.*[3] [1930s–50s] (US) to act idly, to laze around. [SE *doodle*, to draw idle patterns]

doodle-ally/doodlally *adj.* [1940s–50s] **1** mad, eccentric. **2** very drunk. [DOODLE n.[1] + DOOLALLY]

doodle-bug *n.* **1** [1930s+] a small cheap car or any small vehicle. **2** [1940s+] a German V-1 flying bomb. [? southeastern dial. *doodle-bug*, a booming cockchafer. Post-WW2 use of (2) is historical]

doodlebum *n.* [1910s] any nameless small object, typically some form of gadget (cf. DOHICKEY). [ext. of DOODLE n.[4]]

doodle-case *n.* [late 19C] the vagina (cf. DOODLE-SACK n.[1]). [DOODLE n.[2] + SE *case*]

doodle-dandler *n.* [19C] a masturbator (cf. DO A DOODLE-DANDLER). [DOODLE n.[2] + SE *dandle*, to fondle, to stroke]

doodle-dasher *n.* [19C] a masturbator (cf. DOODLE n.[2] + SE *dash*, to strike, to hit]

doodle-do *n.* [1960s+] (US) nothing at all, e.g. *I can't do doodle-do about it.* [the trad. phonetic version of the cock's crowing, *cock-a-doodle-do*]

doodlefagit *n.* [1910s] any nameless small object, typically some form of gadget (cf. DOHICKEY). [ext. of DOODLE n.[4]]

doodle-flap *n.* [late 19C] the flaccid penis. [DOODLE n.[2] + SE *flap*, to wave up and down]

doodleflicker/doodleflickus/doodlegadget *n.* [1910s] any nameless small object, typically some form of gadget (cf. DOHICKEY). [ext. of DOODLE n.[4]]

doodler *n.* [20C] a lazy person, an idler. [DOODLE v.[3]]

doodle-sack *n.*[1] [late 18C–early 19C] a pocket. **2** [19C] the vagina (cf. DOODLE-CASE). [DOODLE n.[2] + SE *sack*]

doodle-sack *n.*[2] [late 18C] (Scot.) a bagpipe. [Ger. *Dudelsack* bagpipes, ? ult. SE *tootle*]

doodley/doodly *n.* [1930s+] (US) nothing, with inference that the subject is additionally worthless. [abbr. DOODLEY-SQUAT]

doodley-/doodly-shit *n.* [1930s+] (orig. US) worthless rubbish, trash. [var. on DOODLEY-SQUAT]

doodley-/doodly-squat *n.* [1930s+] nothing, zero (cf. DIDDLEY-SQUAT).

doody-/doodey-squat *n.* [1950s+] nothing (cf. DIDDLEY-SQUAT; DOODLEY-SQUAT].

dooe/dooee/doee/duey *n.* [mid-19C+] (Ling. Fr./Polari) the number two. [Ital. *due*, two]

doof *n.* [1960s+] (US) a fool, a simpleton. [abbr. DOOFLUS, but note Scot. *doof*, a dull, stupid person; ? ult. Ger. *doof*, dense, stupid, dull-witted]

doofer *n.* [1970s+] (Irish) any otherwise unnamed object (cf. DOHICKEY). [? SE *do for*]

doofless *adj.* [1970s+] (US) idiotic, stupid, dull. [DOOFLUS]

dooflicker *n.* [1910s+] (orig. Can. milit.) any nameless small object, typically some form of gadget (cf. DOHICKEY). [ety. unknown]

dooflop *n.* [1950s+] any nameless small object, typically some form of gadget (cf. DOHICKEY). [ety. unknown]

dooflus *n.* [1930s+] (US Black) bizarre, eccentric (cf. DOOFUS adj.). [? Ger. *doof*, stupid]

doofunny *n.* [1910s+] any nameless small object, typically some form of gadget (cf. DOHICKEY). [ety. unknown]

doofus *n.* [1960s+] (orig. US Black) an odd person, an eccentric (cf. DOOFLUS; DUFUS). [DOOF]

doofus *adj.* [1960s+] odd, strange, eccentric. [DOOFUS n.]

doofy *adj.* [1970s] (US, usu. juv.) foolish, silly, eccentric. [DOOF + sfx. -y]

doog *adj.* [mid-19C+] good. [backsl.]

doog eno/doogheno *n.* [mid-19C+] good one. [backsl.]

doog gels *n.* [mid-19C+] of a passing woman, good legs. [backsl.]

doogheno hit *n.* [mid-19C] a good or profitable market. [DOOG ENO + SE *hit*]

doogie/doogy *see* DUJI.

doohickey *see* DOHICKEY.

dooie *n.* [1980s+] (US campus) an echoic equivalent of the sound of a punch or slap.

doojee *see* DUJI.

doojigger *see* DOJIGGER.

dook *n.*[1] [mid–late 19C] **1** a hand (cf. DUKE n.[3]). **2** a notably large nose. [mispron. of *duke* = Duke of Wellington (1769–1852), known for his large nose and thus nicknamed *Conky*]

dook *n.*[2] [1980s+] (US campus) something unpleasant, worthless. [DOOKEY n.[1]]

dook *v.* [1910s+] (Aus.) to give. [DUKE v.[1] (3)]

dookering *n.* [mid-19C+] (gypsy and tramp) fortune-telling (cf. DOOKIN-COVE). [Rom. *dukker*, to tell fortunes]

dookey/dookie/dooky/dukie *n.*[1] (US) **1** [1960s+] excrement (cf. DUKIE n.[3]). **2** [1960s+] rubbish, nonsense. **3** [1980s] the stuffing, the 'daylights'; thus *knock the dookey out of*. [? ext. of DO n.[6]]

dookey *n.*[2] *see* DUKIE n.[3].

dookin' *n.* [mid-19C] fortune-telling. [Rom. *dukker*, to tell fortunes]

dookin-cove *n.* [mid-19C] a fortune-teller. [DOOKIN' + COVE n. (1)]

dooks *n.* [mid-19C+] (US) the fists (cf. DUKES n.).

dooky *see* DOOKEY n.[1].

doola *n.* [1990s] (US Black) a son. [ety. unknown]

doolally *adj.* [late 19C+] (orig. milit.) **1** mad, eccentric (cf. ASIATIC; CALLAN PARK). **2** very drunk. [the Deolalie military sanatorium in Bombay, to which mentally ill troops were sent. However, according to the veteran Frank Richards, writing in his memoir *Old Soldier Sahib* (1936), the illness came not before one arrived at Deolalie but during one's stay there. Time-expired troops were sent to the sanatorium to await the next troop-ship home. It was during the long hot days of tedium that men, formerly first-class soldiers, might gradually go to pieces]

doolally tap *n.* [late 19C+] madness, eccentricity, orig. a form of madness that afflicted soldiers stationed in India, and spec. at Deolalie (cf. BALKAN TAP; TAPPED). [DOOLALLY + SE *tap*, malarial fever, ult. Skt. *tapa*, heat, pain, torment; for ety. *see* DOOLALLY]

doolally-trapped *adj.* [1910s–20s] knocked senseless. [pun on DOOLALLY TAP]

doolan *n.*[1] [20C] (Aus.) a policeman.

doolan/doolin *n.*[2] [1930s+] (N.Z) a Catholic, usu. an Irish Catholic (cf. DOOLIE n.[2]). [the common Irish surname]

dooley *n.* [1980s+] (drugs) heroin. [? DUJI]

doolie *n.*[1] [18C+] (Anglo-Ind.) an ambulance. [Hind. *doli*, a litter, a sedan for (lower-class) women; thus a rudimentary army ambulance]

doolie *n.*[2] [1930s+] (N.Z.) a Catholic, usu. an Irish Catholic. [abbr. DOOLAN n.[2]]

doolin *see* DOOLAN n.[2].

doololly *n.* [20C] any nameless small object, typically some form of gadget. [var. on DOHICKEY; DOJIGGER etc]

doomie *n.* [1950s] (Aus.) a teenage rebel with criminal tendencies (cf. BODGIE; WIDGIE). [? they are 'doomed']

doondoos *see* DUNDUS.

do one *v.* [1950s+] to run away.

do one a treat, to *phr.* [20C] to suit one absolutely. [SE *do* + TREAT adv.]

do one for me *phr.* [20C] phr. addressed by one male to another who is on his way to the lavatory and who may reply, 'Which side do you shake it?'

do one's balls on, to *phr.* [late 19C+] of a man, to fall obsessively in love with. [SE *do* + BALLS n.[1]]

do one's bit, to *phr.* [late 19C+] to make a contribution to the common good, esp. in joining the forces in a time of war.

do one's/the block, to *phr.* [1910s+] (Aus.) **1** to lose one's temper. **2** to fall in love. [DO v.[2] (2) + BLOCK n.[1] (2)]

do one's bun, to *phr.* [1940s+] (orig. N.Z. milit.) to lose emotional control. [var. on DO ONE'S SCONE]

do one's business, to *phr.* [mid-19C+] to visit the lavatory, used mainly to children. [SE *do* + BUSINESS n.[3]]

do one's cash, to *phr.* [20C] (Aus.) to spend all one's available funds. [DO IN v. (2) + SE *cash*]

do one's dash, to *phr.* [1910s+] (Aus.) to reach one's limit, to exhaust one's energies, to lose one's opportunity – and suffer accordingly. [DO IN v. (5) + SE *dash*]

do one's dirty, to *phr.* [1970s] (US) to defecate.

do one's do, to *phr.* [20C] (US) to do what is necessary, to do what one must do.

do one's dough, to *phr.* [1920s+] (orig. Aus.) to lose one's money, to spend up. [DO IN v. (3)]

do one's duty, to *phr.* [20C] to urinate, to defecate. [euph.]

do oneself *v.* [1980s+] (US) to make a fool of oneself, to embarrass oneself. [DO v.[2] (1)]

do oneself/another proud *v.* [early 19C+] to entertain, to provide food or other material comforts to one's own satisfaction (cf. DO ONESELF WELL).

do oneself in *v.* [1960s+] to commit suicide, to put oneself in a deliberately unpleasant situation or position. [DO IN v. (1)]

do oneself off *v.* [1960s+] to masturbate (cf. BEAT OFF). [DO v.[2] (4)]

do oneself well *v.* [late 19C+] to entertain, to provide food or other material comforts to one's own satisfaction.

do one's face, to *phr.* [1920s+] usu. of a woman, to apply make-up (cf. PUT ONE'S FACE ON).

do one's fruit, to *phr.* [1970s] to lose one's temper. [joc. var. on GO BANANAS]

do one's head, to *phr.* [1970s] (orig. US campus) **1** to take a preferred drug. **2** to annoy, to confuse. [DO v.[2] (2)]

do one's level, to *phr.* [late 19C+] to do one's very best. [abbr. SE *do one's level best*]

do one's luck, to *phr.* [1910s+] (Aus.) to use up or run out of luck. [DO IN v. (5)]

do one's nails, to *phr.* [1980s+] to masturbate.

do one's nana, to *phr.* [1940s+] to lose one's temper. [DO v.[2] (2) + BANANAS adj.]

do one's nut, to *phr.* [1910s+] to lose one's temper, to lose emotional control, to get worked up (cf. DO ONE'S BLOCK). [DO v.[2] (2) + NUT n.[3]]

do one's one-er, to *phr.* [20C] to die (cf. ONER n.[1]). [only one life to live]

do one's/one's own thing, to *phr.* [1950s+] **1** (orig. US Black) to behave as dictated by one's personal beliefs, wishes, idiosyncrasies etc. **2** (W.I.) to dance in an uninhibited manner, to enjoy oneself to the full. [? Mandingo *ka a fen ke*, to do one's thing. The term reached its peak in 1960s, as a hippie credo]

do one's own thing, to *phr.* [1980s+] to masturbate. [puns on popular hippie/New Age phr./DO v.[2] (4) + THING n.[4]]

do one's own time, to *phr.* [20C] (US Und.) to serve a prison sentence without becoming involved in any of the prison gangs, illicit business etc. [SE *do* + TIME n.[1]]

do one's pegs, to *phr.* [1940s] (Aus.) to become angry, excited or anxious (cf. DO ONE'S BLOCK).

do one's scone, to *phr.* [1940s+] (Aus./N.Z.) to lose one's temper (with someone) (cf. DO ONE'S BUN). [SCONE n.²]

do one's stuff, to *phr.* [mid-17C+] **1** to perform as one is expected. **2** to show off a speciality.

do one's top, to *phr.* [1910s+] to lose one's temper (cf. DO ONE'S NUT). [DO v.² (2) + SE *top*, i.e. the head/brain]

do on one's dick/prick, to *phr.* [1960s+] to do with ease, esp. to endure any challenging situation, e.g. a prison sentence, with no difficulty (cf. DO ON ONE'S HEAD). [SE *do* + DICK n.⁵]

do on one's ear, to *phr.* [1940s+] (Aus.) to accomplish something easily.

do on one's head, to *phr.* [19C+] to do with ease, esp. to endure any challenging situation, e.g. a prison sentence, with no difficulty (cf. DO IT STANDING ON ONE'S HEAD).

do on one's napper, to *phr.* [late 19C] to achieve something easily (cf. DO ON ONE'S HEAD). [SE *do* + NAPPER n.² (2)]

do on the rush, to *phr.* [mid-19C] to run away, to escape.

doonup/dunop *n.* [mid-19C] £1 sterling. [backsl.]

door *n.* [1920s+] (Aus.) a brothel. [euph.]

door and hinge *n.* [late 19C] the neck and breast of mutton. [the way in which the joint bends]

doorknob *n.¹* [late 19C–1900s] one shilling (5p). [rhy. sl. *doorknob* = BOB n.³ (1)]

doorknob *n.²* [20C] (US) **1** a doughnut. **2** the head. **3** the female breast. [resemblance]

doorknob *n.³* [1990s] a fool. [ext. var. on KNOB n.¹ (3)]

door-knock *n.* [1950s+] (Aus.) a door-to-door appeal for charity or similar collection.

door-knocker *n.* **1** [mid–late 19C] a beard that runs along and just beneath the jaw line; when linking up with a moustache it was seen as resembling a door-knocker (cf. DOORMAT). **2** [late 19C–1900s] a female hairstyle consisting of two plaits bunched on top of the head. [supposed similarities]

doormat/mat *n.* [mid–late 19C] **1** a short cropped beard. **2** a moustache (cf. DOOR-KNOCKER). [the heavy beards that veterans of the Crimean War (1854–6) wore against the Russian cold. These were cropped short when the soldiers returned to the UK]

doormat thief/grafter *n.* [mid-19C+] a petty or incompetent thief (cf. GAS-METER BANDIT; KNICKERS BANDIT).

door posts *n.* [early–mid-19C] the gallows. [the 'posts' were both those of the gallows and of the next world]

door shaker *n.* [1940s–60s] (US) **1** a policeman. **2** a security guard. [patrolling police or security guards shake doors to check that they are locked]

doorstep/flight of steps *n.* [late 19C+] a thickly cut slice of bread, sometimes extended to a *couple of doorsteps* (cf. DUCK-HOUSE DOOR; HEARTHSTONE; STEP n.¹; THICK 'UN).

doorstep child *n.* [20C] an illegitimate child. [such a child is traditionally abandoned on a, it is hoped, welcoming doorstep]

door-to-door *n.* [20C] (bingo) the number 4 or, if the context makes this obvious, any combination ending in 4.

doos *n.* [20C] (S.Afr.) a general term of strong abuse (cf. CUNT n.²; TWAT n.). [Afk. *doos*, box; thus used in sl. as CUNT n.¹ (1)]

dooteroomus/doot *n.* [mid–late 19C] (US) money. [? SE *duty* + *Deuteronomy*]. the book of the Pentateuch that dictates the rules of society]

dooty *n.* [1960s+] (US juv.) excrement. [? DOOKEY n.¹ or SE *dirty*]

do out *v.* [1950s+] (US prison) to behave; usu. in phr. *don't do out like that*, don't behave in a way likely to debase oneself in the eyes of one's fellow convicts.

doovah/doovah-dah *n.* [1930s] a cigarette end, preserved for later use. [var. on DOOVER]

do over *v.¹* **1** [late 18C–mid-19C] to disable, to wear out, to tire

out (cf. DO IN). **2** [late 18C+] to cheat, to defraud. **3** [mid-19C+] (orig. Aus./N.Z.) to beat up. **4** [mid-19C+] to ransack (a building). **5** [mid-19C+] to search thoroughly. [DO v.¹ (1), (2) + SE *over*]

do over *v.²* [mid-19C+] of a man, to seduce, to have intercourse with. [DO v.² (4)]

doover/dooverlackey *n.* [1930s+] **1** (Aus.) any nameless object or gadget (cf. DOHICKEY). **2** a cigarette end, preserved for later use. **3** (Aus.) a hospital urine bottle; thus *doover-joey*, a hospital orderly (among whose jobs is the emptying of such bottles). [? Heb. *davar*, a word or thing, but orig. use was as a shelter or rough dug-out]

doo-/diddy-wah-diddy *phr.* [1920s–60s] (US) **1** used as an all-purpose substitute for a word or phr. one does not wish to use properly. **2** an imaginary place, a very distant place, a place one dislikes (cf. BEE-LUTHER-HATCHEE). [nonsense word derived f. musical rhythms]

doowhacker *n.* [20C] any nameless small object, typically some form of gadget (cf. DOHICKEY). [ety. unknown]

doowhanger *n.* [1920s] (US) any nameless small object, typically some form of gadget (cf. DOHICKEY). [ety. unknown]

doowop *n.* [1970s] (US) a foolish, unimportant person. [SE *doowop*, a musical style esp. popular in the 1950s, featuring vocals sung against a 'backing track' of rhythmically chanted nonsense syllables]

dooze see DOOZIE n.

doozer *n.* [1950s+] (Can.) anything notably large or outstanding. [var. on DOOZIE]

doozie/doozy/dooze *n.* [1910s+] (US) a thing or person deemed to be extraordinary, remarkable or otherwise noteworthy. [DOOZIE adj.]

doozie/doozy *adj.* [1900s–20s] (US) splendid, wonderful. [? DAISY n.² + actress Eleanora *Duse* (1859–1924)]

doozy see DOOZIE.

dop *n.¹* (S.Afr.) **1** [late 19C+] brandy; thus *dop and dam*, brandy and water. **2** [1950s+] a drink, a tot; thus *doppie*, 'a little drink', 'just a small one'. [Afk. *dop*, brandy]

dop *n.²* [1970s] (S.Afr.) **1** one's head or brain. **2** a motorcycle crash helmet. [Du. *dop*, a husk, a shell, used generally for any bowl-shaped or spherical object]

dop *v.* [1950s+] (S.Afr.) to fail (an examination). [Afk. *dop*, fail]

dop down/down one's noddle *v.* [early 18C] to duck (one's head). [SE *dop*, to duck down suddenly]

dope *n.¹* **1** [early 19C+] (US) sauce, gravy. **2** [mid-19C] (US) an otherwise unspecified poison or adulterant. **3** [late 19C] any form of grease, lubricant, coolant etc. **4** [late 19C] (US) butter. **5** [late 19C–1910s] (US) alcohol, esp. whisky. **6** [late 19C–1920s] any preparation, mixture or drug that is not specifically named; thus [1920s] *dope finish*, make-up. **7** [late 19C–1940s] Coca-Cola or any other carbonated drink. **8** [late 19C–1940s] (US) coffee. **9** [late 19C–1950s] (orig. US) any form of medicine or medicinal preparation. **10** [late 19C–1960s] unspecified and wide-ranging 'stuff', varying as to context. **11** [late 19C+] a drug addict. **12** [late 19C+] (US drugs) any form of drug; orig. opium but taking in all popular 'recreational' drugs. **13** [20C] molasses, treacle. **14** [1900s–20s] (US) flattery, foolishness, nonsense. **15** [1910s–20s] (drugs) a state of drugged intoxication. **16** [1910s–20s] a cigarette. [? SE *daub*, the axle grease used on wagons or Du. *doop*, sauce]

dope *n.²* [mid-19C+] an ignoramus, a fool, a simpleton. [? Cumberland dial. + implication of DOPE n.¹ (11)]

dope *n.³* [20C] (orig. US) **1** fraudulent information. **2** any information. [fig use of DOPE n.¹ (3); i.e. the role of information in making people or events 'move']

dope *adj.* [1980s+] (rap music) very good, excellent. [DOPE n.¹ (12) + DOPE OUT]

dope *v.*[1] (US) **1** [mid-19C–1910s] to apply a lubricant or salve. **2** [mid-19C+] to administer drugs to a person, either to excite them or, usu., to knock them out. **3** [mid-19C+] to poison, to put drugs into food or drink. **4** [late 19C–1930s] to adulterate. **5** [late 19C+] to stimulate a racehorse through applying some form of drug, e.g. tobacco. **6** [20C] to drink to excess. **7** [20C] to use 'recreational' drugs. **8** [1900s] to give or take medicine. [DOPE n.[1]]

dope *v.*[2] **1** [late 19C+] to work (something) out (cf. DOPE OUT). **2** [1910s] to train, to study. **3** [1920s] to explain. [DOPE n.[3]]

dope *v.*[3] [20C] to idle, to loaf about. [DOPE n.[2]]

dope addict *n.* [late 19C+] (orig. US) a drug addict, orig. the drug was opium. [DOPE n.[1] (12) + SE *addict*]

dope-book/-sheet *n.* [late 19C+] (orig. US) a book of information on any subject, although mainly horse-racing. [DOPE n.[3] + SE *book/sheet*]

dope city *n.* [1950s–60s] (drugs) any area of a town known for its high level of drugs sales/consumption. [DOPE n.[1] (12) + sfx. -CITY]

dope crew *n.* [1980s+] (drugs) a group of drug dealers who divide up, package and then retail the bulk purchases of the drug (usu. crack cocaine). [DOPE n.[1] (12) + CREW n.]

doped *adj.* [20C] (US) drunk. [DOPE v.[1] (6)]

dope daddy *n.* [1930s–50s] (US drugs) a drug dealer. [DOPE n.[1] (12) + DADDY n. (6)]

dope fiend *n.* [1950s+] (drugs) a user of drugs, invariably used ironically; thus [1990s] (US Black) *dope fiend move*, a wild, bizarre move, an extreme action taken out of desperation. [DOPE n.[1] (12) + SE *fiend*; the original SE use, popularized in the US tabloid press of late 19C and referring to opium; the current incarnation refers to crack cocaine]

dopehead *n.*[1] [1900s–60s] (drugs) a drug user. [DOPE n.[1] (12) + sfx. -HEAD (2)]

dopehead *n.*[2] [1940s–60s] (US) a fool. [DOPE n.[2] + sfx. -HEAD (1)]

dope house *n.* [1960s+] (drugs) any room or apartment in which drugs are on sale (cf. SPOT). [DOPE n.[1] (12) + HOUSE n.[1]]

dope in *v.* [1960s] (US) to explain, to inform, to recount. [DOPE v.[2] (3)]

dopeman *n.* [1990s] a drug dealer (cf. BUDMAN). [DOPE n.[1] (12) + SE *man*, but note MAN n.[3] (3)]

dope off *v.* (US) **1** [1910s+] to fall asleep, to doze off; thus *doped off*, asleep. **2** [1920s+] (mainly milit.) to be inattentive, to malinger. [DOPE v.[1] (8)]

dope out *v.* [20C] (orig. US) to work out, esp. in working out possible winners in a horse-race. [DOPE n.[3], DOPE v.[2]]

doper *n.*[1] [16C] a female beggar, often a prostitute. [apparently a misprint in an unspecified play by Thomas Middleton (c.1570–1627), for DOPEY n.[1], although this use predates that *dopey* by at least a century]

doper *n.*[2] [1960s+] a drug user. [DOPE n.[1] (12)]

dope rope *n.* [1980s+] (US) the gold chains sported by well-off drug dealers. [DOPE n.[1] (12) + SE *rope*]

dope-sheet *see* DOPE-BOOK.

dope smoke *v.* [1980s+] (drugs) to smoke marijuana. [DOPE n.[1] (12) + SE *smoke*]

dopester *n.*[1] (orig. US) [20C] one who collects information on, and forecasts the result of, sporting events, elections etc. [DOPE OUT + sfx. -STER]

dopester *n.*[2] [1910s+] a poisoner. [DOPE n.[1] (2) + sfx. -STER]

dopester *n.*[3] [1930s] a drug user or seller. [DOPE n.[1] (12) + sfx. -STER]

dope stick *n.* [1920s+] a marijuana cigarette. [DOPE n.[1] (12) + STICK n.[14] (2)]

dope the ponies, to *phr.* [20C] (US) to work out possible winners among competing racehorses. [DOPE v.[2] (1) + PONY n.[5]]

dope trap *n.* [1960s] (drugs) any room or apartment in which drugs are on sale (cf. DOPE HOUSE). [DOPE n.[1] (12) + TRAP n.[5] (3)]

dopey *n.*[1] [late 18C] **1** a female beggar, often a prostitute. **2** the buttocks, the rump. [ety. unknown]

dopey *n.*[2] *see* DOPIE.

dopey *adj.*[1] [19C+] **1** mildly ill. **2** [20C] drunk. [DOPE n.[1] (2), (6) + sfx. -y]

dopey *adj.*[2] [late 19C+] dull, stupid, vapid. [DOPE n.[2] + sfx. -y]

dopie/dopey *n.* [1920s+] a drug user (cf. DOPER n.[2]). [DOPE n.[1] (12) + sfx. -ie/y]

dopium *n.* [1980s+] (drugs) opium. [DOPE n.[1] (12) + SE *opium*]

dopo *n.* [1940s–70s] a sycophant, a toady. [DOPE n.[2] + sfx. -o]

Dopper/Dorper *n.*[1] [mid-19C+] (S.Afr.) a member of the strictly Calvinist Dutch Reformed Church (Gereformeerde Kerk in Suid-Afrika). [? Du. *domper*, an extinguisher, implying the Church's desire to extinguish any form of what it saw as 'progressive' or 'liberal' thinking, theological or otherwise. Or f. *dorp*, a village, implying the rural backgrounds of most of its members. A final theory is f. *dop*, a shell, referring to the sect's haircuts, which resembled an inverted calabash]

dopper *n.*[2] [1990s] the penis. [? DOB n.[2]]

dopper *n.*[3] [1990s] (S.Afr.) a drinker. [DOP n.[1]]

dopress *n.* [20C] (US) **1** a blockhead, a slob. **2** an ineffectual observer who in a crisis offers no practical help, merely sympathetic banalities. [? Yid. *tipesh*, a fool, ult. f. Ger. *Täppisch*, fool. The term ult. is not European Yid. but an American word that merely seems Yid.]

doppie *n.* [1940s+] (S.Afr. Und.) a measure of tobacco, about one-40th of an ounce. [Du *dop*, a shell, thus a container]

doption *n.* [late 19C] an adopted child.

dora/dora gray *n.* [20C] (Aus.) a threepenny-bit (cf. ALMA GRAY; DOLLY GRAY). [rhy. sl. *dora gray* = TRAY n.[1]]

doradilla *n.* [1980s+] (drugs) marijuana. [Sp. term for a kind of fern, ? resembling marijuana]

do-rag *n.* [1940s–70s] (US Black) the scarf or similar cloth that is used to bind up one's newly straightened hair (cf. PROCESS). [DO n.[9] + SE *rag*]

do-ray-me *see* DO-RE-MI.

dorcas *n.* [late 19C] a seamstress, esp. one who works for a charity. [the sewing woman mentioned in the Bible, Acts 9:36; cf. Lincolnshire dial. *dorcas*, an overdressed woman]

do reason/right *v.* [19C] to honour a toast.

do-re-mi/do-ray-me *n.* [20C] money. [a pun on DOUGH/SE *do-re-mi* the first three notes of a musical scale]

dorf *n.* [1970s+] (US campus) a fool, an eccentric. [var. on DORK n.[2] (2), but note UK dial. *dorfer*, an impudent fellow]

dorian love *n.* [20C] (gay) homosexuality. [Oscar Wilde's novella *The Picture of Dorian Gray* (1891)]

do-right *n.* [1980s+] (US campus) a helpful deed. [DO-RIGHT adj.]

do-right *adj.* [1930s+] (US) law-abiding, honest, socially concerned.

do right *v. see* DO REASON.

do-right boys *n.* [1970s+] (US) the police, esp. the Highway Patrol.

do righteous *v.* [1950s+] (US) to do good (to).

do-right man *n.* [1930s+] (US) a conformist, esp. one who follows rules within an institution. [DO-RIGHT adj. + SE *man*]

do-right people *n.* **1** [1930s–40s] (US drugs) non-addicts. **2** [1930s+] (US) honest citizens.

dork *n.*[1] [late 19C–1930s] a thick slice of bread-and-butter.

dork *n.*[2] [1960s+] (orig. US) **1** the penis. **2** a fool (cf. DICKHEAD).

dork *v.* [1960s+] (orig. US) of a man, to have sexual intercourse. [DORK n.[2] (1)]

dork around *v.* [1980s+] (orig. US) to waste time, to play around, to mess about. [DORK n.[2] (2)]

dorkbrain n. [1970s+] (orig. US) a fool (cf. BAKEBRAIN; DICK-HEAD). [DORK n.² (2) + sfx. -*brain*]

dorkbreath n. [1970s+] an unpleasant person (cf. DORKFACE). [DORK n.² + sfx. -*breath*]

dorkface n. [1970s+] (US campus/teen) an unpleasant person; thus an insulting term of address. [DORK n.² + sfx. -*face*]

dorkhead n. [1970s+] (orig. US teen/campus) a fool (cf. DICK-HEAD).

dorkmunder n. [1980s+] (US campus) a fool, an idiot. [DORK n.² (2) but ? link to *Dortmünder Union Pils*, a beer; those who get drunk also get foolish]

dork off v. [1980s+] (US campus) **1** to fool around, to mess about. **2** to disobey orders. [DORK n.² (2)]

dorkum n. [1920s+] (Aus.) a damper. [? DORK n.¹]

dorkus/dorkus pretentious n. [1990s] (US campus) a pretentious fool. [DORK n.² (2)]

dorky adj. [1970s+] (US campus) odd, weird, bizarre. [DORK n.² + sfx. -*y*]

dorm n. [late 19C+] (school) a *dorm*itory. [abbr.]

dormie/dorm rat n. [1960s+] (US campus) a student living in a college dormitory. [DORM + sfx. -*ie*]

dormouse n. [19C] the female genitals. [? resemblance]

dorm rat see DORMIE.

dormy adj. [1930s] (US) quiescent, calm. [Fr. *dormir*, to sleep]

dornick n. [mid-19C] (US) a coin. [Irish *dornog*, a pebble, a stone]

dorothy n. [late 19C] simple, naïve love-making. [an opera, *Dorothy* (1886), by Alfred Cellier, which featured such activity]

Dorothy Dix n. [1970s+] (Aus. sporting) a six in cricket (cf. GEORGE MOORE). [proper name *Dorothy Dix* (pseudonym E.M. Gilmer; 1870–1951), a US journalist, who wrote a popular question-and-answer column]

dorothy's friend/friend of dorothy n. [1950s+] a homosexual. [Dorothy, the character played by Judy Garland (1922–69), still a deity to large parts of the gay world, in *The Wizard of Oz* (1939)]

Dorper see DOPPER.

dors and 4s n. [1980s+] (drugs) a combination of Doriden and Tylenol 4.

dorse n. [early 19C] a bed, a lodging. [var. on DOSS n.¹]

dortspeak see DART ACCENT.

dos a reno n. [mid-19C] a sod. [backsl.]

doscus/dosc n. [1970s] (US campus) a fool, an idiot. [ety. unknown; ? link to DOSS v., to sleep, thus one who is sleepy]

dose n.¹ [late 18C] (Und.) burglary.

dose n.² [mid-19C] a three-month sentence (cf. BRAGGADOCIO; DOLLOP n.²). [SE *dose*, a definite quantity, on the analogy of a medical prescription]

dose n.³ [mid-19C+] as much alcohol as one can hold (and probably more); thus *take a grown man's dose*, to drink very heavily.

dose n.⁴ [late 19C+] venereal disease. [abbr. *dose of the clap*]

dose n.⁵ [20C] (Ulster) a crowd of people. [SE *dose*, a quantity]

dose n.⁶ [20C] (Ulster) **1** a bad attack of an illness. **2** 'a sight'. [SE *dose*, an unpleasant experience]

dose v. [late 19C+] to infect with venereal disease; thus *dosed*, venereally infected. [DOSE n.⁴]

dosed adj. [20C] (Irish) impressed. [? one is responding as if energized by a SE *dose of salts*]

dosed up adj. [late 19C+] suffering from venereal disease. [DOSE n.⁴]

dose of locust n. [late 19C] (US/New York) a thrashing with the fists. [the *locust* or locust-wood club carried by New York policemen]

doses n. [1960s+] (drugs) LSD (cf. A n.³).

dosh n. [19C+] (orig. US) money. [? DOSS n.¹, a place to sleep (note in UK dial. *dosh* is synon for *doss*) thus, by extension, the money needed for accommodation; the term appeared in US *c*.1850, then vanished, to re-emerge in the UK in the 1950s]

dosh v. [1980s+] to pay. [DOSH n.]

dosh-burned adj. [late 19C] (US) euph. for God-damned (cf. GOSH-DARNED).

dosing n. [1900s–50s] (US Black) receiving medical attention. [SE *dose*, a quantity of medicine]

do skippers v. [1940s+] to sleep around on floors, sofas etc, to have no permanent home. [SE *do* + SKIPPER v.]

do social work, to phr. [1960s+] (US gay) to go out of one's way to have an inter-racial sexual partner; thus exhibiting one's liberal credentials. [cynical use of SE]

do someone a nasty, to phr. [1980s+] to do something unpleasant to someone, to cause someone trouble or problems.

do someone a thick 'un, to phr. [1920s+] to play a 'dirty trick' on someone. [SE *do* + thick 'un, something heavy, solid]

do someone blind, to phr. [late 19C+] to cheat, to deceive (cf. SELL SOMEONE BLIND). [DO v.⁴ + BLIND adj.²]

do someone dirt see DO DIRT TO SOMEONE.

do someone the dirty/the dirty on someone, to phr. [1910s+] to cheat, to inform against, to treat harshly.

do something at the slack of one's galluses, to phr. [20C] (Ulster) to do something with ease. [SE *gallus*, braces; coined in the UK or play on SE *gallows*; but 20C use only US/Ulster/Scot.]

do something for my chapped lips, to phr. [1980s+] of a woman, to masturbate.

do something/things for v. [1940s+] to enhance one's appearance or image, usu. of an article of clothing or some element of personal grooming, e.g. a hairstyle, *it really does something for me*.

doss n.¹ **1** [late 18C+] a place to sleep, a bed. **2** [late 19C+] a sleep. **3** [1920s] (US) a rest. [Lat. *dorsus*, the back, on which the sleeper lies]

doss n.² [19C+] something easy to accomplish. [ext. of DOSS n.¹, lit. something one can do 'with one's eyes closed']

doss adj. [1980s+] easy, simple, undemanding; thus a general pej. [DOSS n.²]

doss v. [late 18C+] to sleep. [DOSS n.¹]

doss-brained adj. [20C] stupid (cf. AMOEBA-BRAINED; DOSSHEAD). [DOSS n.¹ + sfx. -*brained*; lit. 'sleep(y)-headed']

doss down n. [late 19C] a cheap lodging-house. [DOSS DOWN v.]

doss down v. **1** [18C+] to fall asleep, usu. on a floor or similar temporary accommodation. **2** [1930s+] (drugs) to fall asleep after injecting heroin (cf. NOD v.). [DOSS v.]

dosser n. **1** [mid-19C+] a tramp, a vagrant, a homeless person. **2** [mid-19C+] someone who exists without working. **3** [late 19C] the head of a household. [DOSS n.¹; in (3) he is the person who pays for/provides the place to sleep]

dossers' hotel n. [20C] a workhouse or any form of lodging for homeless people (cf. DOSSHOUSE). [DOSSER n. (1) + SE *hotel*]

dosshead n. [20C] a fool, an idiot, a simpleton. [DOSS n.¹ + sfx. -HEAD (1); lit 'sleep head']

dosshouse/kiphouse n. [late 19C+] a lodging house, night shelter or similar refuge for homeless people. [DOSS v. + SE *house*]

dossie/dossy n. [late 19C–1920s] a tramp's female companion (cf. DOXY).

doss in the pure, to phr. [late 19C] (tramp) to sleep in the open air (cf. DOSS OUT v.¹). [DOSS v. + SE *pure*, i.e. unpolluted air]

doss-/dossing-ken n. [mid-19C] a lodging house (cf. DOSS-HOUSE). [DOSS n.¹ + KEN n.¹]

doss-man *n.* [19C] the keeper of a lodging house. [DOSS n.[1] + SE *man*]

doss-money *n.* [late 19C] the price of a night's lodging. [DOSS n.[1] + SE *money*]

doss out *v.*[1] [1910s–20s] to sleep in the open air (cf. DOSS IN THE PURE). [DOSS v.]

doss out *v.*[2] [1990s] (Black) to leave, to run off. [SE *dash*]

doss-ticket *n.* [late 19C] (tramp) a ticket giving one the right to a night's lodging. [DOSS n.[1] + SE *ticket*]

dossy *n. see* DOSSIE.

dossy *adj.*[1] [mid–late 19C] **1** excellent, first-rate. **2** smart, stylish. [the proletarian pron. of the *Count D'Orsay* (1805–52), a well-known dandy]

dossy *adj.*[2] [1940s–50s] ineffectual, weak, 'soft'. [? one who would DOSS DOWN rather than act]

dossy *adj.*[3] [1980s+] easy, effortless. [DOSS adj. + sfx. *-y*]

dot *n.*[1] [19C] a ribbon; thus *dot-drag*, a watch ribbon. [? Du. *dot*, a twirled knot of silk or thread]

dot *n.*[2] **1** [1950s+] (Aus.) the anus. **2** [1970s+] (lesbian) the clitoris. [resemblance]

dot *v.* [late 19C+] to hit (cf. DOT ONE ONE). [SE *dot*, a mark, a spot]

dot and carried *adj.* [late 19C–1910s] married. [rhy. sl.]

dot and carry/go one *n.* [late 19C+] a person with a wooden leg (cf. DOT AND GO ONE phr.). [the dot is the impression made by the bottom of the wooden leg, in an era before properly moulded 'feet' were available, while the good leg is 'carried']

dot and dash *n.* [1950s–60s] money. [rhy. sl. *dot and dash* = cash]

dot and go one *n. see* DOT AND CARRY ONE.

dot and go one, to *phr.* [late 18C+] to waddle or hobble, esp. of those who have lost a leg. [DOT AND CARRY ONE]

do tell! *excl.* [1950s+] **1** a sarcastic or ironic rejoinder to a piece of information in which one has no interest. **2** an exhortation to someone to impart a piece of juicy gossip.

dotey/doty *adj.* [1950s+] (Irish) cute, charming (cf. SE *darling* adj.). [dial. *doty*, a general term of affection, usu. of a child; ult., SE *dote* (*upon*)]

do/play/pull the ... act, to *phr.* [late 19C+] (US) to pretend to a particular (by context) style of behaviour, to assume (often deceitfully) specific characteristics.

do the ... thing *phr.* [19C+] to perform a particular action, as defined by the missing adj. and the word *thing*; thus *do the amiable* (thing), *do the charming* (thing), *do the civil* (thing) etc. [all such terms have a slight air of insincerity or at least of calculated performance, although they may equally well be quite genuine]

dothead *n.* [1980s+] (US) an Indian. [the Hindu *bindi* or caste mark worn by married women]

do the aqua, to *phr.* [mid-19C–1900s] to water down a drink. [Ital. *acqua*, water]

do the arm aerobics, to *phr.* [1960s+] to masturbate. [SE *aerobics*, a form of exercise based on the heart, lungs and respiratory system]

do the bachelor's shuffle, to *phr.* [1980s+] to masturbate (cf. DO THE KNUCKLE SHUFFLE).

do the backstroke roulette, to *phr.* [1980s+] to masturbate.

do the bear, to *phr.* [late 19C] (Mexican-US) a form of courtship that involves hugging. [Sp. *hacer el oso*, do the bear; such 'hands-on' courtship was sanctioned in Mexico]

do the big nasty *see* DO THE NASTY.

do the bird circuit, to *phr.* [1950s+] (US gay) to visit a succession of bars in order to ascertain the whereabouts of the most attractive men. [BIRD n.[6] (1) + SE *circuit*]

do the block, to *phr.* [mid-19C–1930s] (Aus.) to promenade along a variety of fashionable blocks or stretches of city street.

[the major blocks are Collins Street between Swanston and Elizabeth Streets in Melbourne, and George Street in Sydney]

do the book, to *phr.* [1920s+] (US Und.) to serve a life sentence (cf. BOOKFUL; DO THE BOOK AND COVER). [THROW THE BOOK AT]

do the book and cover, to *phr.* [1920s+] (US Und.) to be imprisoned for the rest of one's natural life (cf. BOOKFUL; DO THE BOOK). [THROW THE BOOK AT]

do the brown-eye express, to *phr.* [1980s+] (US) to sodomize. [BROWN EYE n.[2]]

do the business, to *phr.*[1] [20C] to settle a matter conclusively. [BUSINESS n.[4]]

do the business, to *phr.*[2] [1940s+] to have sexual intercourse. [BUSINESS n.[1] (1)]

do the civil, to *phr.* [mid-19C–1950s] to act in a civil manner, to do 'the right thing'.

do the dance, to *phr.* [1930s] (US) to be hanged (cf. DANCE v.[2]). [the twitching of the victim's feet]

do the deadly deed, to *phr.* [1980s+] (US campus) to have sexual intercourse without using a contraceptive (cf. DO THE DIRTIES). [ext. of do the deed]

do the decent thing, to *phr.* [1950s+] to act in a manner considered apposite by one's companions.

do the deed, to *phr.* [1960s+] (US campus) to have sexual intercourse (cf. DO THE BUSINESS phr.[2]).

do the dingo, to *phr.* [1990s] to have sexual intercourse. [DINGO n.[2]]

do the dirties/dirty deed, to *phr.* [1960s+] (orig. US teen/campus) to have sexual intercourse (cf. DO THE DEADLY DEED; DO THE NASTY).

do the dirty on someone *see* DO SOMEONE THE DIRTY.

do the disappearing act/trick *see* DO A DISAPPEARING ACT.

do the do, to *phr.* [1950s+] (US Black/campus) to have sexual intercourse.

do the ... dodge/dodge over, to *phr.* [1930s+] to take on a pose, e.g. a clergyman, an ex-soldier, for the purposes of fraud.

do the double act, to *phr.* [1910s–20s] to get married.

do the downy, to *phr.* [mid-19C] to lie in bed. [DOWNY n.[2]]

do the dutch, to *phr.* [1960s+] (Can. prison) to commit suicide. [DUTCH ACT]

do the dutch act, to *phr.* [20C] to run away, to escape. [DUTCH ACT]

do the fish, to *phr.* [1970s+] to suffer blackouts, seizures or convulsions following the inhalation of nitrous oxide (cf. FISHTAIL). [the image of a fish out of water, struggling for air]

do the five-knuckle shuffle on the old piss pump *see* DO THE KNUCKLE SHUFFLE.

do the full sesh, to *phr.* [1980s] (US teen) to indulge completely, to take to the limit. [abbr. SE *session*]

do the gentleman, to *phr.* [mid-19C] to urinate.

do the graceful, to *phr.* [late 19C] to fascinate, to charm.

do the grand, to *phr.* [late 19C] to make a great display, to put on airs.

do the hand jive/crazy hand jive, to *phr.* [1960s] to masturbate. [SE *hand jive*, a form of synchronized clapping popular in 1950s]

do the handsome/handsome thing, to *phr.* [mid-19C+] to behave in a decent, honourable way (cf. DO THE DECENT THING).

do the han solo, to *phr.* [1980s+] to masturbate (cf. HAND SOLO; IGNITE THE LIGHTSABER). [pun on *Han Solo*, the character from the film *Star Wars* (1974) and SE *hand* + SE *solo*]

do the heavy, to *phr.* [late 19C] to swagger, to show off. [HEAVY adj.[1]]

do the heisman, to *phr.* [1990s] (US campus) to leave, to spurn, to reject. [? football's *Heisman* Trophy, named for John William *Heisman* (1869–1936), a famous coach]

do the honours, to *phr.* [1950s+] to take on the role of host in pouring out alcoholic drinks (cf. BE MOTHER).

do the humpty-bump, to *phr.* [1990s] (US campus) to engage in sex (cf. RUMPY-PUMPY).

do the janitor thing, to *phr.* [1990s] to masturbate. [? image of a janitor mopping the floor]

do the job, to *phr.*[1] [mid-19C+] to harm, to ruin, to make uncomfortable.

do the job, to *phr.*[2] [1940s+] (US) to have sexual intercourse. [ext. of JOB v.[1] (1)]

do the job on, to *phr.* [mid-19C+] to murder, to kill.

do the knuckle/five-knuckle shuffle/shuffle on the old piss pump, to *phr.* [1970s+] to masturbate (cf. DO THE TWO-FINGERED SHUFFLE).

do/hit the lolly, to *phr.* [1940s+] (Aus.) to lose one's temper, to lose control of one's emotions or senses. [LOLLY n.[1]]

do the long trot, to *phr.* [mid–late 19C] to go home.

do the lot, to *phr.* [20C] to spend all one's available money. [DO v.[12]]

do the mean, to *phr.* [mid-19C] to act in an unpleasant manner. [SE *mean*, unpleasant]

do the milk route, to *phr.* [1970s+] of one who is searching for or selling sex, to tour bus stations or other such places very late at night or very early in the morning looking for trade. [the image of a milk roundsman]

do the nasty/big nasty, to *phr.* [1960s+] (orig. US) to have sexual intercourse (cf. DO THE DIRTIES). [NASTY n.[1] (2)]

do the natural thing, to *phr.* [1970s–80s] (US Black) to have sexual intercourse. ['just as nature intended']

do the/go naughty, to *phr.* [mid-19C] **1** to act the whore. **2** to have sexual intercourse. [NAUGHTY n. (2)]

do the Newgate frisk, to *phr.* [19C] to be hanged (cf. DANCE v.[2]; DANCE THE PADDINGTON FRISK). [*Newgate* prison, outside which public hangings were held + *frisk*, to twitch (in one's death agonies)]

do the overdo, to *phr.* [20C] (W.I./Guyn.) to take things too far. [SE *do*, anything done]

do the Paddington frisk, to *phr.* [late 17C–early 19C] to be hanged (cf. DANCE v.[2]; DANCE THE PADDINGTON FRISK). [the village of *Paddington* was the site of Tyburn, London's largest gallows]

do the polite, to *phr.* [mid-19C–1930s] to act courteously.

do the pork sword jiggle, to *phr.* [1990s] to masturbate (cf. ACCOST THE OSCAR MEYER). [PORK SWORD]

do the Portuguese pump, to *phr.* [1990s] to masturbate. [PORTUGUESE PUMP]

do the pretty, to *phr.* [late 19C] to speak in an affectionate, friendly manner (cf. SPEAK PRETTY).

do the push *see* STAND THE PUSH.

do the pussy, to *phr.* [1970s+] (US Black) to have sexual intercourse. [PUSSY n.[1] (1)]

do the rosary, to *phr.* [20C] (US Und.) to serve a sentence of imprisonment for the rest of one's natural life. [the SE *rosary* is made of decades of prayers]

do the rosy, to *phr.* [mid–late 19C] to enjoy oneself, to have a good time. [? ROSY n. or SE *rosy*, pleasant, enjoyable, positive]

do the soft/soft on, to *phr.* [1910s–20s] to flatter. [SOFT (SOAP) v.]

do the solitary rhumba, to *phr.* [1990s] of a man, to masturbate.

do the spin, to *phr.* [late 19C+] (Aus.) to toss the coins in a game of two-up.

do the story with, to *phr.* [18C] of a prostitute, to have sex with. [the basic falsehood underlying the exchange of counterfeit affection for money]

do the tightner/tightener, to *phr.* [mid-19C] (coster) to have dinner (cf. KAFFIR'S TIGHTENER). [it *tightens* one's belly]

do the trick, to *phr.* **1** [early–mid-19C] (orig. Und.) to get what one wants, to succeed. **2** [mid-19C+] of a man, to have sexual intercourse. **3** [mid-19C+] of a woman, to lose one's virginity, to be deflowered. **4** [mid-19C+] to impregnate a woman. [(1) is SE from mid-19C]

do the two-fingered shuffle, to *phr.* [1990s] of a woman, to masturbate (cf. DO THE KNUCKLE SHUFFLE).

do the two-finger slot rumba, to *phr.* [1990s] of a woman, to masturbate.

do the Tyburn jig *see* DANCE THE TYBURN JIG.

do the wash by hand, to *phr.* [1970s+] (US) to masturbate.

do the white knuckler, to *phr.* [1990s] to masturbate.

do the wild thing, to *phr.* [1990s] (US Black/campus) to engage in sex (cf. WILD v.).

do the zippy, to *phr.* [1990s] to caress the anus. [? ZIP n.[1] (4)]

do things by penny numbers, to *phr.* [mid-19C–1920s] to do things in instalments. [the stories serialized in weekly penny magazines]

do things for *phr.*[1] *see* DO THINGS TO.

do things for *phr.*[2] *see* DO SOMETHING FOR.

do things to/for, to *phr.* [1930s+] to excite sexually.

do time *v.* [19C+] to serve a prison sentence. [TIME n.[1]]

do to rights, to *phr.* [late 19C] to perform satisfactorily, to do properly (cf. DO TO WAINRIGHTS). [TO RIGHTS]

do/do you to wainrights, to *phr.* [late 19C] to perform satisfactorily; an intensification of DO TO RIGHTS. [pun on *rights* + ref. to Thomas *Wainewright* (1794–1852), an alleged murderer who was transported to Tasmania in 1826, but for forgery, not homicide]

dots *n.*[1] [late 19C+] money. [? shape of coins]

dots *n.*[2] [1960s+] (drugs) LSD (cf. A n.[3]). [abbr. MICRODOT]

dotted *adj.* [late 19C] having a black eye. [DOT SOMEONE ONE]

dotterel *n.* [17C] a dupe, a victim of a confidence trickster or fraudster (cf. PLOVER). [SE *dotterel*, a species of plover (*Eudromias morinellus*); the name comes f. SE *dote*, to be silly or foolish or to act foolishly, the *dotterel*, whether bird or human allows itself to be 'taken' easily]

do to def, to *phr.* [1980s+] (US) to do something as well as possible (cf. DO TO THE MAX). [SE *do it* + DEF]

do to the max, to *phr.* [1980s+] (orig. US Black) to do something as well as or as enthusiastically as possible. [SE *do it* + MAX n. (5)]

dot someone one, to *phr.* [late 19C+] to punch someone, esp. in the eye (cf. DOTTED). [? dial.; ult. SE *dot*, a mark or spot + *one*, a blow]

dotties man *n.* [late 19C] a greedy, grasping person. [DOTS n.[1]]

dotty *adj.* **1** [late 19C] unstable, unsteady on one's feet. **2** [late 19C+] eccentric, odd; thus *dottiness*, eccentricity. [orig. dial. phr. *dotty on one's pins*, unsteady on one's legs and thence in one's brain ? + link to DOT AND CARRY ONE]

do twelve-ounce curls, to *phr.* [1980s+] (US campus) to drink beer. [a play on weight-lifting jargon; the 'curling' of the hand around a 12oz beer can]

doty *adj.*[1] [20C] (US) senile, weak-minded (through old age) (cf. CRUMBLY n.). [dial. *doty*, old wood that is crumbling away, but ? abbr. SE *dotage*, feeble-minded old age; both terms have the same source, MDu. *doten*, to be crazy]

doty *adj.*[2] *see* DOTEY.

doub *n.* [1980s+] (drugs) a $20 rock of crack cocaine. [SE *double*, $10 being the basic unit of sale]

double *n.*[1] [18C–19C] a trick; thus [18C–19C] *tip the double*, to cheat, to hoax, [19C] *give the double*, to escape (from one's creditors), [late 19C] *put the double on*, to bypass, to circumvent (trouble). [abbr. SE *doublecross*]

double *n.*² [20C] (US) a $20 bill. [abbr. DOUBLE SAWBUCK]

double *n.*³ [1920s+] a pornographic picture that offers both the male and female genitals.

double *adj.* [mid-19C+] (? orig. US) qualifying adj. that intensifies another adj., e.g. *double-choked, double-good, double-quick.*

double *v.*¹ [early 19C] **1** to run off, to escape. **2** to avoid, to elude, to give the slip to. [SE *double*, to turn sharply and suddenly in running, to turn back on one's course]

double *v.*² (US) **1** [1930s+] to *double*-date, i.e. for two couples to go out together. **2** [1990s] to *double*-park. [abbr.]

double-arsed *adj.* [19C+] having very large buttocks. [SE *double* + ARSE n.¹ (1)]

double bag and stumper *n.* [1990s] a very unattractive young woman (cf. DOUBLE-BAGGER). [she is so ugly that one would have to place paper bags over both participants' heads in order to face up to intercourse, and one would, in any case, rather cut off all one's limbs than have sex with her]

double-/two-bagger *n.* [1980s+] (US) an intensely unappealing person, usu. used for an unattractive woman (cf. BAG YOUR FACE; DOUBLE BAG AND STUMPER; ONE-BAGGER). [either based on the need to place not just one but two bags over her before having sex or the need for each participant to be covered with a bag]

double-banger *n.* [1980s+] (N.Z.) a multi-orgasmic woman. [SE *double* + *bang*, i.e. the 'explosion' of the orgasm]

double-bank *v.* **1** [late 19C–1940s] (US) to trick, to doublecross. **2** [late 19C+] (US) to attack as a gang. **3** [late 19C+] (Aus./N.Z.) to carry two people on a single horse. **4** [1930s+] (Aus./N.Z.) to carry two people on one bicycle (cf. DINK n.⁴). [SAusE *double-bank*, to yoke together two oxen]

double-barrel *n.*¹ [late 19C] field-glasses, opera-glasses. [SE *double-barrel*, a double-barrelled gun]

double-barrel *n.*² [1990s] of a man, more than one orgasm in a single session of sex.

double-barrelled *adj.* **1** [mid-19C–1950s] (US) extreme, utter, complete. **2** [late 19C] used of a woman enjoying simultaneous vaginal and anal intercourse. **3** [late 19C+] used of a lesbian, e.g. *double-barrelled broad.*

double-barrelled ghee *n.* [1950s–60s] (gay) a male homosexual. [DOUBLE-BARRELLED adj. (2) + GHEE n.²; his mouth and anus]

double-barrelled gun *n.* [20C] a woman who is agreeable to group sex, involving vaginal and anal intercourse. [DOUBLE-BARRELLED adj. (2) + pun]

double-barrels *n.* [20C] (US) men's long underwear.

double black dog dare see DOUBLE DOG DARE.

double-bottomed *adj.* [late 19C–1900s] insincere, hypocritical. [? one 'bottom' is false]

double-breasted water-butt smasher *n.* [late 19C] a strong, athletically built man.

double-breasters *n.* [19C] the feet, esp. when one or both is a club foot.

double bubble *n.* [1980s+] (drugs) cocaine. [ety. unknown]

double bubblegum *n.* [1990s] (drugs) a variety of potent marijuana. [ety. unknown]

double-bunked *adj.* [20C] (US Und.) of two men sharing a cell (cf. TWOED-UP).

double burger see BURGER.

double Cape Horn, to *phr.* [19C] to be made a cuckold. [pun on the cuckold's HORNS + the naut. ref.]

double carpet *n.* [20C] (prison) 6 months' imprisonment. [SE *double* + CARPET n.²]

double-clutch *v.* [20C] (US drugs) to take more than one's share of a communally smoked marijuana cigarette. US smokers ritually take only one puff before passing on their cigarette (cf. BOGART v.). [trucker jargon *double-clutch*, to

change gears by changing first to neutral, then selecting the desired, usu. lower gear. The clutch is disengaged at each stage. The link to the drug use is the idea of doing something twice]

double-clutcher *n.* [1960s+] (US) euph. for MOTHERFUCKER n.

double-clutching *n.* [1960s+] (US) euph. for MOTHERFUCKING n.

doublecross *n.* [1980s+] (drugs) amphetamine (cf. A n.²). [the crosses stamped into the pill]

double-cunted *adj.* [mid-19C+] possessed of a large vagina (cf. COW-CUNTED). [SE *double* + CUNT n.¹ (1)]

double darse dare see DOUBLE DOG DARE.

double dash! *excl.* [late 19C] a more emphatic version of DASH!

double-decker *n.* [late 19C] (US) a double-strength cocktail, used as a pick-me-up.

double deuce *n.* [1990s] (US Black) a .22 calibre handgun. [SE *double* + DEUCE n.² (2)]

double-diddied *adj.* [19C+] having large breasts. [SE *double* + DIDDIES]

double dime *n.* [1960s–70s] (US) $20. [SE *double* + DIME n.¹]

double-distilled *adj.* [20C] (Aus.) excellent, the very best (cf. ALL BRANDY).

double dog/black dog/darse/nigger/niggle dare, to *phr.* [19C+] (US) to challenge defiantly.

double dome *n.*¹ [1940s+] an intellectual, a scholar, esp. one who seems to hold eccentric or impractical opinions. [SE *double* + DOME n.¹]

double dome *n.*² [1980s+] (drugs) LSD (cf. A n.³). [DOMES n.²]

double-doored *adj.* [20C] (Can. prison) from both ends.

double-dooring *n.* [20C] (US Und.) a method of defrauding hotels by which one arrives like a normal guest at the front-door but leaves by the backdoor; any form of illegal departure, leaving one's cases (filled with stones or telephone directories etc).

double dreads *n.* [1980s+] (drugs) a mixture of amphetamine and LSD (cf. DOUBLE TROUBLE; DOUBLE ZERO).

double-dugged *adj.* [19C+] having large breasts (cf. DOUBLE-DIDDIED). [SE *double* + DUGS]

double event *n.* **1** [late 19C] of a man, a simultaneous bout of syphilis and gonorrhoea. **2** [late 19C] of a woman, an act of intercourse that both deflowers the woman and leaves her pregnant. **3** [20C] (mainly Glasgow) an order of a shot of whisky alongside a pint of beer.

double fair! *excl.* [1950s+] the intensified version of FAIR ENOUGH! extremely satisfactory. [DOUBLE adj. + SE *fair*]

double fin/finnup *n.* **1** [late 19C] a British £10 note. **2** [1940s+] (US) a $10 bill. [SE *double* + FIN n.², n.⁴]

double-fisted *adj.* [19C+] (US) tough, strong, over-sized.

double-fuck! *excl.* [1960s+] (US) an intensified form of FUCK v.¹ when used as an excl. or curse. [note one-time use in 1910s, used by Robert Graves in *Goodbye to All That* (1929) in recounting a soldier's comments during WW1]

double-fucking *adj.* [1920s+] an intensified form of FUCKING adj.

double-gaited *adj.* [1920s–60s] (US) bisexual. [SE *gait*, a manner of walking]

double guts *n.* **1** [early 19C+] a very fat person. **2** [20C] (US) a large stomach, a pot belly. [SE *double* + GUTS n.¹ (1)]

double-gutted *adj.* [19C] very fat. [DOUBLE GUTS]

double happy *n.* [1980s+] (N.Z.) a nuclear explosion. [SNZE *double-happy*, a children's name for a large firecracker]

double harness *n.* [19C+] (US) marriage, usu. as *jump in a double harness, take on a double harness,* to get married (cf. DOUBLETREE UP WITH; DOUBLE UP v.¹). [coaching imagery]

double-headed *adj.* [20C] (US Black) very clever, exceptionally intelligent (cf. FOUR-HEADED; TWO-HEADED). [the idea of having two brains; the orig. use comes f. hoodoo, a variant form of voodoo]

double-header n. [late 19C–1940s] (Aus.) a double measure of a drink.

double-hocked adj. [mid–late 19C] having very thick ankles.

double in brass, to phr. [1950s+] (orig. US) to have a wide range of abilities. [circus/vaudeville jargon *double in brass*, to perform one's own speciality as well as play in the orchestra]

double jugg/juggs n. [late 17C–19C] the posterior.

double-life man n. [20C] a bisexual.

double-M n. [1980s+] (drugs) MDMA (cf. ECSTASY).

double master-blaster n. [1980s] (drugs) an orgasm reached through fellatio at the same time as one is smoking a pipe of crack cocaine.

double maw n. [1920s–60s] (US Black) a grandmother. [SE *double* + dial. pron. *maw*, ma, i.e. mother]

double-mouthed adj. [19C] having a notably large mouth.

double nickel n. [1970s+] (US) the 55mph (88.5kph) speed limit, introduced nationally in 1974. [SE *double* + *nickel*, 5 (cents)]

double nigger/niggle dare see DOUBLE DOG DARE.

double-O n.[1] [20C] (US prison) prison-issue bread (cf. DUMMY n.[5]; PUNK n.[2]).

double-O n.[2] [1910s–50s] a hard look. [the resemblance to a pair of eyes or glasses]

double-O v. 1 [1910s–50s] (US) to stare at. 2 [1920s] to doublecross. [DOUBLE-O n.[2]]

double one's milt, to phr. [19C] to ejaculate twice without withdrawing. [MILT]

double-Os n. [1950s+] (US prison) Kool brand cigarettes. [the 'double-o' of the spelling]

double pay n. [1980s] (Aus.) the upmarket Sydney suburb of Double Bay. [the area's inflated prices and the incomes of those who live there]

double-plated blowhard n. [late 19C] (US) a consummate braggart. [SE *double-plated* + BLOWHARD]

double-quick adj. [1960s+] extremely fast. [DOUBLE adj. + SE *quick*]

doubler n.[1] [early 19C] an extremely severe blow. [it causes the recipient to DOUBLE UP v.[2] (1)]

doubler n.[2] 1 [mid–19C] (N.Z.) a double portion of drink, two shots of spirits in the same glass. 2 [late 19C+] (Und.) a corrupt policeman who not only takes the offered bribe but still arrests one for the crime. 3 [1950s+] (Aus.) a lift on a bicycle crossbar (cf. DINK n.[4]).

double-ribbed adj. [19C] pregnant. [i.e. the mother's ribs plus those of her unborn child]

double rock n.[1] [1980s+] (drugs) crack cocaine diluted with procaine, a synthetic cocaine. [SE *double* + ROCK n.[4]]

double rock n.[2] [1990s] (US Black teen) a section of public housing across the street from Candlestick Park, San Francisco, notorious for its frequent (drug-related) killings. [SE *rock*, a hard place + ROCK n.[4]]

double sawbuck/sawski n. [20C] (US) 1 $20 (cf. DOUBLE n.[2]; DOUBLE-X n.[1]). 2 a 20-year prison sentence. [SE *double* + SAWBUCK]

double shot n. [1970s+] two ejaculations of semen.

double-shotted adj. [mid–late 19C] of a mixed drink, containing a double measure of alcohol. [milit. use *double-shotted*, loaded with two cannon balls]

double shuffle n. (US) 1 [late 19C–1950s] a doublecross. 2 [1930s] a quick get-away. [farming jargon *double shuffle*, a sudden shift of bucking style by a bronco, intended to throw an unwanted rider. Note also UK *double shuffle*, a shuffling, noisy dance, once popular among costermongers]

double slangs n. [early 19C] double irons. [SE *double* + SLANG n.[1] (5)]

double-sucker n. [late 19C] the *labia minora*, esp. when prominent.

double-take n. [1940s+] (orig. US) a second glance, esp. when one 'cannot believe one's eyes' after the first one. [film jargon]

double-team v. [mid–19C+] (US) 1 to gang up on, to use extra force against. 2 to work as a pair. [farming jargon *double-team*, to employ two teams of animals to haul heavy weights through difficult terrain; subseq. adopted in football use]

double-thumper n. [mid–late 19C] an especially audacious lie. [SE *double* + THUMPER n.[2] (3)]

double to v. [late 19C] to double one's effort or speed.

double-tongued squib n. [mid–19C] a double-barrelled shotgun. [SE *double-tongued* + SQUIB n.[1] (1)]

doubletree up with v. [20C] (US) to marry someone (cf. DOUBLE UP v.). [farming jargon *doubletree*, the draught-bar of a two-horse vehicle, to which the two animals are attached in tandem]

double trouble n. [1970s+] (drugs) Tuinal (cf. DOUBLE DREADS; DOUBLE ZERO). [Tuinal is a mixture of Seconal and Amytal]

double-U n. [late 19C–1910s] euph. for the lavatory (cf. W). [pron. of *W.C.*]

double up v.[1] 1 [late 18C+] to share quarters. 2 [19C+] (US) to get married, to become engaged, to live together (cf. DOUBLE HARNESS; DOUBLETREE UP WITH).

double up v.[2] [19C] 1 (orig. boxing) to cause to collapse. 2 to defeat, to someone stop in their tracks. [a blow that forces the recipient to bend double]

double-ups n. [1980s+] (drugs) a $20 piece of crack cocaine that can be broken into two piece, each of which is then sold for $20.

double whammy n. [1950s+] a double blow, an extreme problem; an intensifier of whammy. [best known as the title of US thriller-writer Carl Hiaasen's 1988 novel, the term (attempting to point up the Labour Party threats to the UK economy) was central to the Conservative Party's advertising campaign in the general election of 1992]

double-X n.[1] (US) 1 [mid-19C–1910s] $20, a $20 bill. 2 [1930s+] an act of doublecrossing. [*X* as (1) Roman numeral 10, (2) the mark of a cross]

double-X n.[2] [20C] (US) something superlative, outstanding. [racetrack jargon *double-X*, the horse most likely to win; thus the optimum bet]

double yoke n. [1980s+] (drugs) crack cocaine. [? pun on 'cracking an egg']

double zero n. [1990s] (drugs) prime grade hashish (cf. DOUBLE DREADS; DOUBLE TROUBLE).

doubloon n. [20C] money. [SE *doubloon*, a Spanish coin orig. worth a half-pistole, i.e. 33–36 shillings]

douchebag n. [1940s+] (US) 1 a term of general abuse, directed esp. at women. 2 a lesbian. [SE *douchebag*]

douche can alley n. [1910s–50s] (Aus.) Palmer Street, Sydney, the city's 'red-light' area. [the use of douches by the street's prostitutes + pun on music's *Tin Pan Alley*]

doudon n. [1910s–20s] a short, fat woman. [? SE *dowdy*]

dough n. [mid-19C+] (orig. US) money; thus *dough up*, to pay, *in the dough*, prospering, well-off (cf. BREAD n.[1]; CAKE n.[2]; COD n.[4]; DO-RE-MI; MOTSER). [the idea of bread as an essential constituent of life]

dough-baked adj. [late 16C–mid-19C] stupid, dull.

doughbanger n. [late 19C+] (Aus.) a cook.

doughbelly n. [1940s+] (US) a very fat person, a large stomach; thus *doughbellied*, fat.

doughboy n.[1] [mid-19C+] (US milit.) a US soldier, orig. those serving in the Mexican War *c.*1847; subseq. replaced by *boonierat*, *GI*, GRUNT n.[5] etc. [? the large round buttons worn by Civil War soldiers, reminiscent of doughnuts or the boiled dumplings, based on flour and rice and known as *doughboys* that were a military staple; or f. the *dough* or pipeclay used to clean US soldiers' belts in mid-19C]

doughboy *n.*[2] [1910s–30s] a punch in the face, usu. in phr. *give someone a doughboy*, to punch someone in the face.

dough-brain *n.* [1980s+] (US campus) someone who acts foolishly or as if they have not been thinking (cf. BAKEBRAIN).

doughface *n.* [20C] (US) a woman who wears an excess of cosmetics. [SE *doughface*, a whiteface mask made originally of flour and water and used for fancy dress; a *doughface* and a white sheet rendered the wearer a 'ghost']

dough-gods see DOUGH-JEHOVAHS.

doughguts *n.* [mid-19C] (US) an extremely fat person.

dough-head *n.* [19C+] (US) a very silly or stupid person. [SE *dough* + sfx. -HEAD (1)]

dough-Jehovahs/-gods *n.* [19C] a form of meat stew. [ety. unknown]

doughnut *n.*[1] [late 19C] (US) a baker. [one of his popular products]

doughnut *n.*[2] [1920s+] a rubber tyre. [resemblance]

doughnut *n.*[3] [1980s] of a woman, a state of sexual excitement, supposedly the vaginal equivalent of the penile erection (cf. APPLE n.[10]; HAIRY DOUGHNUT).

doughnut *v.* [1980s+] (US teen) to make an automobile spin by pulling on the hand-brake. The vehicle in question is usu. stolen (cf. HOTTING; TWOCKER).

doughnut foundry *n.* [1920s] (US) a very cheap restaurant or café.

doughnut-head *n.* [1970s] (US) a fool. [SE *doughnut* + sfx. -HEAD (1)]

dough-pop *v.* [1970s] **1** to hit hard. **2** to defeat completely. [SE *dough* + POP v.[1]; ? link to DOUGHBOY n.[2]]

dough roller *n.* [20C] (US) a cook; also *dough boxer, dough pounder, dough puncher*. [navy jargon *dough roller*, the ship's cook]

doughy *n.*[1] [mid-19C] a baker.

doughy *n.*[2] [1950s] (Aus.) the buttocks (cf. BUMPER n.[4]). [resemblance of plump, pale buttocks to dough]

doughy *adj.* [1950s] (Aus.) stupid; thus *doughy over*, in love with, 'mooning over'. [the 'thickness' of dough]

Douglas *n.* [late 19C+] an axe; thus *swing Douglas*, to swing an axe (cf. KELLY n.[1]). [brandname of the *Douglas* Axe Manufacturing Co., East Douglas, Massachusetts]

do under *v.* [1960s+] (US Black) to defeat, to ruin, to kill. [play on DO OVER v.[1] (3)]

do up *v.*[1] [mid-17C+] to rob, to cheat. [DO v.[4]]

do up *v.*[2] [mid-19C+] to deal with, esp. to beat up. [DO v.[2] (2)]

do up *v.*[3] [late 19C+] (Aus.) to squander all one's money. [DO v.[12]; DO IN v. (2)]

do up *v.*[4] [20C] to dress up, esp. as *done up*. [DO v.[9]]

do up *v.*[5] [1940s–50s] (US Black) to make something happen, to make things change. [SE *do*, to act, to perform]

do up *v.*[6] [1940s+] (drugs) to inject a narcotic.

do up brown, to *phr.* [19C+] **1** to beat up thoroughly. **2** (W.I.) to do thoroughly, to perform very successfully. **3** to deceive, to take in, to surprise. [pos. and neg. images DO UP v.[1] in overall sense of action + cooking imagery]

do-ups *n.* [1960s+] (drugs) the acting of injecting a narcotic drug. [DO UP v.[6]]

do us a favour see DO ME A FAVOUR.

douse *n. see* DOUSER.

douse *v.* [late 18C+] to take off; thus *douse the dog vane*, take the cockade out of one's hat. [SE *douse*, to turn off, to put out]

douser/douse/dowse/dowser *n.* [late 18C] a heavy blow. [SE *douse*, to strike, to punch; ult. Du. *doesen*, to beat with force and noise]

douse the edisons, to *phr.* [1970s+] (US teen) to turn off the lights. [SE *douse* + proper name Thomas Alva *Edison* (1847–1931), inventor of the electric lightbulb]

douse the glim, to *phr.* [mid-19C+] to turn off the light, usu. as imper. (cf. DOUSE THE EDISONS). [SE *douse* + GLIM n.[1]]

do-ut-des *n.* [late 19C] (society) a selfish person. [Lat. *do ut des*, I give in order that you may give back]

dove *n.* [1980s+] (drugs) **1** a variety of MDMA (cf. ECSTASY; LOVE DOVE; WHITE DOVE). **2** a $35 piece of crack cocaine.

dover *n.* [mid–late 19C] (Aus.) a clasp-knife; thus *flash your dover*, to use one's claspknife to cut up one's food. [proprietary name]

Dover Castle boarder *n.* [19C] a debtor. [a legally specified area around the Queen's Bench Prison in Southwark Bridge Road within which debtors, while not actually confined in the prison, were ordered to live during the period of their sentence. The nickname came from the prominent local landmark, the *Dover Castle* tavern]

dover's powder *n.* [20C] (drugs) opium. [proper name Thomas *Dover* (1660–1742), an English physician whose patented preparation of opium and ipecacuanha (*Pulvis doveri*) was used as a pain-killing medicine]

dove-tart *n.* [mid-19C] a pigeon pie (cf. SNAKE-TART).

dovey/dovy *adj.* [late 19C–1910s] of people or objects, delightful, attractive, sweet. [abbr. LOVEY-DOVEY adj.]

dowager *n.* [1950s+] (gay) an elegant, older, gay man. [SE *dowager*, orig. the widow of a dead king, i.e. a QUEEN n.[1]]

dowdy *v.* [late 18C] to play a practical joke based on one's pretending to be mad, esp. to have just escaped from one's keeper or from a psychiatric institution. [the sound *dow dow*, the basic lyric of a song chanted by one Pierce who, according to Grose (1785), was the first to play this 'joke']

do well *v.*[1] [late 19C+] to treat, to entertain; thus *do oneself well*, to indulge oneself. [DO v.[9]]

do well *v.*[2] [20C] (W.I.) to be inconsiderate of others or thoughtless of oneself, usu. in ironic phr. *you do well*.

do what? *excl.* [20C] (US) what did you say?, please repeat the question (cf. DO HOW?; DO WHICH?).

do which? *excl.* [20C] what did you say? (cf. DO WHAT?).

dowlas *n.* [late 18C–mid-19C] a linen-draper. [*Doulas*, near Brest, in Brittany, the eponymous name of a coarse kind of linen, much used in the 16C and 17C, and later a strong calico made in imitation of this; the sl. is more immediately linked to the character Daniel *Dowlas*, in George Colman's play *The Heir at Law* (1797)]

down *n.*[1] **1** [early–mid-19C] (Und.) a suspicion, a degree of illegality; thus *put down on*, to give information against, *take down off*, to render a (stolen) object less suspicious, *there is no down*, there is no risk. **2** [mid-19C+] (orig. Aus.) a prejudice against, a suspicion of (cf. HAVE A DOWN ON). **3** [late 19C] a tendency to be unkind towards. [DOWN adj.[2] (1)]

down *n.*[2] [late 19C–1920s] (US) a diluted or even alcohol-free drink, as consumed by a 'hostess' who is persuading her client to buy hugely overpriced 'champagne' etc. [SE *down*, under weight]

down *n.*[3] [1960s–70s] something depressing; thus [1960s] *the downs*, a fit of misery. [DOWN adj.[1]]

down *n.*[4] [1960s+] (drugs) barbiturates, heroin (cf. DOWNER n.[4]). [the calming, slowing down effect of the drugs]

down *adj.*[1] [17C+] depressed. [the lowering of one's spirits]

down *adj.*[2] [late 18C+] aware, conscious of, knowledgeable; thus *be down upon*, to be aware, to be knowledgeable (cf. DOWNY adj.[1]). **2** [late 18C+] suspicious. **3** [1940s+] first-rate, excellent. **4** [1940s+] (US Black) alert, keen to get on, tough, challenging in a fight. **5** [1950s+] (US Black) loyal, trustworthy. **6** [1960s+] (US Black) fashionably dressed, chic. **7** [1960s+] (US Black) feeling well, happy, at one with the world. **8** [1960s+] (US Black) interesting, current. [orig. Und. *down cove*, a potential victim of a robbery who is aware of being targeted. Originating among late 18C London criminals, the term survives mainly among US Blacks]

down *adj.*[3] [20C] (US Und.) serving time in prison (cf. AWAY adj.). [abbr. DOWN THE RIVER phr.[2]]

down *adj.*[4] [1970s+] (US Black) owing, deficient in (cf. LIGHT adj.). [SE *down*, under weight]

down *v.*[1] [1970s+] to denigrate. [abbr. PUT DOWN v.[2]]

down *v.*[2] [1980s+] (US campus) to beat up. [abbr. SE *knock down*]

down *adv.* **1** [late 19C–1940s] very much so, exceedingly. **2** [1920s+] (orig. US Black) to the limit. [DOWN adj.[2] (3)]

down a cuff/a lash in someone *see* DOWN BLOWS IN SOMEONE.

down among the dead men *phr.* [mid-19C] very drunk. [SE phr. + pun on DEAD MAN n.[1]]

down and dirty *phr.* [1980s+] (orig. US) **1** ethically unrestrained, ruthless. **2** earthily sexy.

down-and-out *n.* [19C+] (orig. US) a homeless or destitute person, a tramp. [*down* in the gutter and *out* of luck]

down and up *n.* [20C] (Aus.) a cup. [rhy. sl.]

down as a hammer/trippet *phr.* [early 19C] very well aware. [DOWN adj.[2] (1) + SE *hammer/trippet*, a trivet; such a person 'hits the nail on the head']

down-ass *adj.* [1980s+] (US Black) a general term of approval. [DOWN adj.[2] (3) + sfx. -ASS]

down at the club/club for members only *phr.* [1990s] masturbating. [pun on MEMBER n.[1]]

down below *n.* [20C] a coy reference to the vagina (cf. DOWN THERE; HOUSE UNDER THE HILL; INEFFABLE n.[1]; KNICK-KNACK n.[1]; NAME IT NOT; NICK-NACK n.[1]; PLACE n.[1]; THAT THERE; THAT THING; UNDENIABLE; UNDER-BELONGINGS; WHAT-DO-YOU-CALL-IT; YOU KNOW WHERE). [euph.]

down below nathaniel *phr.* [mid-19C–1910s] lower than hell. [*Nathaniel*, the devil]

downblow *n.* [1940s] (Irish) a disaster.

down blows/a cuff/a lash in someone, to *phr.* [20C] (W.I./Guyn.) to beat up severely.

down buttock and sham file *n.* [19C] a prostitute who does not resort to thieving. [DOWN adj.[2] (1) + BUTTOCK AND FILE, modified by SE *sham*, fake]

down by law *adj.* [1980s+] (orig. US Black) **1** expert, professional (within one's occupation). **2** used of the high status of a person or wholly admirable object or idea. [DOWN adj.[2] (1)]

down by the head *adj.* [19C] drunk. [naut. use *down by the head*, the ship's head is lower in the water than the stern]

downer *n.*[1] [mid-19C] **1** a sixpence (2½p). **2** (US) a nickel, 5 cents. [Rom. *tawno*, a little one]

downer *n.*[2] [1910s–30s] a grudge. [DOWN n.[1] (2)]

downer *n.*[3] [1920s–30s] (tramp) a bed (cf. DOWNY n.[2]). [on which one lies down]

downer *n.*[4] [1960s+] a barbiturate, a tranquillizer. [DOWN n.[4]]

downer *n.*[5] **1** [1970s+] a depressing, worrying situation (cf. BUMMER n.[3]). **2** [1970s+] a depressing person. [DOWN adj.[1]]

downey *see* DOWNY n.[2].

down for *adj.* [1950s] (US Black) loyal to, committed to, in favour of. [DOWN adj.[2] (5)]

down for mine *phr.* [1950s] (orig. US Black) able to look after oneself. [DOWN adj.[2] (5)]

down for the count *phr.* [1920s–30s] (orig. US) as good as defeated, virtually hopeless. [boxing imagery]

down for the last count *phr.* [20C] dead. [boxing imagery]

down-freak *n.* [1970s+] (drugs) a regular user of depressant drugs. [DOWN n.[4] + sfx. -FREAK]

down front *adj.* [1950s+] (US Black) open, honest, candid. [var. on UP FRONT v.]

down hand on someone, to *phr.* [20C] (W.I.) to seize firmly.

down-head *n.* [1960s+] (drugs) a regular user of depressant drugs (cf. DOWN-FREAK). [DOWN n.[3] + sfx. -HEAD (2)]

down-hills *n.* [late 17C–early 19C] doctored dice that will always show low numbers (cf. UP-HILLS).

down-home *adj.* [1930s+] (US Black) reminiscent or characteristic of one's home, esp. among Black speakers, of the South; thus to *talk down-home*, to speak Black English (cf. HOMEBOY). [however note [early 19C] *go down-home*, to visit one's home]

down-homer *n.* [1930s+] a friend from one's home town or village, usu. in the context of one's 'new' life in the city (cf. HOMEBOY). [DOWN-HOME]

downie *n.* [1970s+] (drugs) depressant. [DOWNER n.[4]]

down in *adv.* [mid–late 19C] lacking in, short of. [SE *down*, under weight]

Downing Street *n.* [20C] (bingo) the number ten. [the residence of UK prime ministers at 10 Downing Street, London SW1]

down in one's boots/the bushes/the cans *phr.* [20C] (US) miserable, unhappy, gloomy (cf. DOWN IN THE DUMPS). [DOWN adj.[1]]

down in the chops *phr.* [19C] depressed (cf. DOWN IN THE MOUTH). [DOWN adj.[1] + CHOPS n. (1)]

down in the dumps *phr.* [late 18C+] miserable, unhappy, gloomy (cf. IN THE PITS). [DOWN adj.[1]]

down in the kinks *phr.* [20C] (US) miserable, unhappy, gloomy (cf. DOWN IN THE DUMPS). [DOWN adj.[1] + SE *kink*, a state of madness]

down in the mouth *phr.* [20C] depressed, miserable (cf. DOWN IN THE CHOPS). [DOWN adj.[1]]

download one's floppy, to *phr.* [1990s] to masturbate. [punning on computer jargon]

down low *adj.* [1990s] (US Black) covert, secret (cf. D.L. adv.). [LOW PRO]

downmouth *v.* [1980s] (US) to attack verbally, to slander (cf. BADMOUTH v.). [DOWN n.[1] (2) + SE *mouth*]

down on *adj.* [1940s+] (orig. US Black) annoyed with, disappointed in, holding a negative opinion of. [DOWN n.[1] (2)]

down on one's luck *phr.* [mid-19C+] in difficulties, whether financial or otherwise.

down on the knuckle *phr.* [mid-19C–1930s] virtually penniless.

down on the knucklebone *phr.* [late 19C] in poverty, 'hard-up'. [ext. of DOWN ON THE KUCKLE]

down out *v.* [1970s+] (drugs) to become stupefied by consuming depressants. [DOWN n.[4]]

down pin *adj.* [late 19C–1900s] depressed, indisposed. [skittles imagery]

downpressor *n.* [1950s+] (W.I. Rasta) a preferred term for SE *oppressor*.

downright *n.* [1900s–30s] (tramp) begging, tramping, esp. in phr. *on the downright*, wandering the country as a beggar.

downright buttock and sham file *n.* [17C–early 19C] a prostitute and pickpocket team (cf. BUTTOCK AND TWANG). [BUTTOCK AND FILE]

downrighter *n.* [1930s] a beggar, a tramp. [DOWNRIGHT]

downs, the *n.* [mid-19C] Tothill Fields Prison (cf. TUTTLE NASK). [the site of the prison in the fields that surrounded and were geographically lower than Tothill]

downshire *n.* [19C] the female pubic hair (cf. COUNTY DOWN). [pun]

down six *adv.* [1990s] (US Black) properly, correctly. [? dice imagery]

downstairs *n.* **1** [19C] hell. **2** [20C] the female genital area.

down the banks *phr.* [late 19C] (Irish) a state of failure. [the steep banks found in peat bogs; those who fell off them rolled down into the deep, peaty water]

down the chute *phr.* [1920s+] (Aus.) in prison. [SE *chute*, a narrow passage through which animals are driven for branding, shearing etc]

down the drain/plug/plughole *phr.* [1930s+] lost, wasted, useless (cf. DOWN THE GURLER; DOWN THE PAN; DOWN THE SINK; GO DOWN THE PLUGHOLE).

down the gurgler *phr.* [1930s+] (Aus.) used of something that has not worked out (cf. DOWN THE DRAIN).

down the hatch! *excl.* [mid-19C+] (orig. naut.) popular toast before taking a drink.

down the pan *phr.* [1950s+] wasted, lost, abandoned (cf. DOWN THE DRAIN). [i.e. the lavatory *pan*]

down the plug/plughole *see* DOWN THE DRAIN.

down there *n.* [20C] a coy reference to the vagina (cf. DOWN BELOW). [euph.]

down the river *phr.*[1] [late 19C+] finished, over and done, used up. [a boat that has gone *down the river* has vanished from sight]

down the river *phr.*[2] [late 19C+] serving time in prison (cf. DOWN adj.[3]). [var. on UP THE RIVER]

down the road *phr.*[1] [mid–late 19C] **1** stylish, fashionable. **2** vulgar, showy. [Mile End *Road*, London, a favoured costermongers' market]

down the road *phr.*[2] [1960s+] (orig./mainly US) in the future.

down the sink *phr.* [1930s+] wasted, lost, abandoned (cf. DOWN THE DRAIN).

down to *adj.*[1] [19C] alert to, aware of, 'fly'. [DOWN adj.[2] (1)]

down to *adj.*[2] [1970s+] responsible for. [fig. use of abbr. of SE *written down to*]

down to dandy *phr.* [mid–late 19C] **1** clever, knowing, artful. **2** very good (cf. UP TO DICK). [DOWN TO adj.[1] + DANDY adj.]

down to larkin *phr.* [1960s–70s] free, esp. of a round of drinks that is 'on the house'. [? SE *larking*]

down to the ground *phr.* [mid-19C+] (US) perfectly, thoroughly, completely.

down to the short strokes *phr.* [1990s] approaching the end, very near a conclusion. [SE *short strokes*, i.e. the final thrusts of intercourse]

downtown *n.* [1920s+] the genital area.

downtown *v.* [1920s+] (US Black) to improve one's lot in society, to go 'up in the world'. [newly prosperous Harlemites signified their new status by leaving the ghetto and moving *downtown*, i.e. to more prosperous parts of New York]

down trip *n.* [1960s+] **1** (drugs) an unpleasant experience induced after taking LSD. **2** anything unpleasant, tedious, depressing (cf. BAD TRIP). [DOWN adj.[1] + TRIP n.]

down under *n.* [late 19C+] Australia; supposedly sited 'underneath' the UK on the globe.

down upon *adj.* [late 18C+] aware, knowledgeable. [DOWN adj.[2] (1)]

down upon oneself *phr.* [early–mid-19C] miserable, depressed. [DOWN adj.[1]]

down with *adj.*[1] [1930s+] (orig. US Black) **1** involved with. **2** enjoying, appreciating. **3** agreeing with, favouring, often in phr. *be down with*, *get down with*. [DOWN adj.[2] (1)]

down with *adj.*[2] [1940s+] empathetic, emotionally responsive. [DOWN adj.[2] (1)]

down with his apple-cart! *excl.* [mid-19C] knock him down! [northern dial.; SE phr. *down with* + APPLE-CART]

downy *n.*[1] [mid-19C] a knowledgeable, artful, aware person. [DOWN adj.[2] (1) + sfx. *-y*]

downy/downey *n.*[2] [mid–late 19C] a bed (cf. DO THE DOWNY). [SE *down* mattress + *lie down*]

downy *adj.*[1] [19C] aware, knowledgeable. [DOWN adj.[2] (1) + sfx. *-y*]

downy *adj.*[2] [19C] fashionable. [fig. use of DOWNY adj.[1]]

downy bird *n.* [19C] a knowledgeable, artful, aware person (cf. DOWNY n.[1]; DOWNY COVE). [DOWNY adj.[1] + BIRD n.[3]]

downy bit *n.* **1** [mid-19C] a young prostitute. **2** [late 19C] a young woman, esp. when attractive. **3** [late 19C] the vagina. [SE *down*, the first feathering of young birds + BIT n.[5]]

downy cove *n.* [early–mid-19C] a knowledgeable, artful, aware, 'fly' person (cf. DOWNY n.[1]; DOWNY BIRD). [DOWNY adj.[1] + COVE (n. (1)]

downy flea-pasture *n.* [mid-19C] a bed. [DOWNY n.[2]]

dowry *n.* [mid-19C] (Ling. Fr./Polari) a great deal, very much, plenty of. [SE *dowry*, money given with a bride, ult. Ital. *dare*, to give]

dowse *see* DOUSER.

dowse on the chops *n.* [late 18C] a blow on the jaw. [DOUSER + CHOPS n. (1)]

dowser *see* DOUSER.

dowsetts *n.* [17C] the testicles. [SE *dowset*, a deer's testicles, ult. Fr. *doucet*, a sweet]

doxey/doxie *see* DOXY.

doxology-works *n.* [late 19C] a place of Christian worship. [SE *doxology*, the praising of God]

doxy/doxey/doxie *n.* (Und.) **1** [mid-16C–18C] the female companion of a variety of mendicant villains (cf. CANTING CREW). **2** [16C+] a general term, usu. derog., for a woman or girl, esp. a mistress. [? Du. *docke*: a doll]

D'Oyly Carte *n.* [1970s–80s] a fart. [rhy. sl.; ult. proper name Sir Richard *D'Oyly Carte* (1844–1901), late 19C producer of many Gilbert and Sullivan operas]

do you drink? [1960s+] (Und.) a coded invitation by a criminal to a police officer whom they are hoping to bribe (cf. CAN I SPEAK TO YOU?). [DRINK v.]

do you feel a draft?/breeze? *phr.* [20C] a warning to a man that his trouser fly is open or that he has a rip in his trousers.

do you feel like that? *phr.* [late 19C] an ironic phr. addressed to someone who is doing what is considered an odd task, or to a normally lazy person who is, for a change, working.

do you know *phr.* [late 19C] a meaningless piece of conversational punctuation, e.g. *Do you know, I was on this bus the other day…* (cf. YOU KNOW). [coined by Max Beerbohm in *The Private Secretary* (1884)]

do you know any other funny stories? *phr.* [1930s+] a sarcastic phr. used to make it clear to a speaker that one is not as foolish or gullible as they seem to believe.

do you know something *phr.* [1950s+] an essentially meaningless phr. used to introduce a more meaningful statement, e.g. *Do you know something, I saw the strangest dog…*.

do you like hospital food? *phr.* [1980s+] a threatening phr. used immediately before administering a beating (cf. EVER BEEN TO FLIGHT SCHOOL, BOY?). [the potential assailant asks this of a victim, who probably replies 'No' and is told 'Well you'd better get used to it']

do you mind? *phr.* [1950s+] a phr. used to imply one's displeasure in another person's speech or actions; the implication is that whether or not they mind, you definitely do.

do you need a boy? *phr.* [1960s+] (drugs) a surreptitious request for heroin. [BOY n.[5]]

do you savvy? *phr.* [late 19C] (middle-class) do you understand?, do you know what I mean? [Fr. *savoir*, to know]

do you see any green in my eye? *phr.* [mid-19C+] a phr. meaning 'Do you think I'm a fool?' 'Do I look stupid?' [SE *green*, innocent, naïve]

do you see skid marks on my forehead? *phr.* [1990s] (US campus) do you think I'm a fool? [SKID MARK; thus synon. with 'do you think I'm talking out of my ass']

do you see what I see? *phr.* [1940s+] a phr. used to alert a companion to the appearance or activities of someone who does not know they are being observed, esp. when that person is an acquaintance.

do you spit much with that cough? *phr.* [1910s–20s] (Can.) a phr. used to acknowledge that one has heard a companion break wind.

do you think I'm made of money?/I'm not made of money! *phr.* [20C] a phr. admonishing someone, usu. a wife or child, who is spending the breadwinner's hard-earned cash with excessive abandon.

do you think you'll know me again?/you'll know me again, won't you? *phr.* [20C] a phr. used to embarrass someone the speaker feels is staring too hard.

do you want jam on it?/what do you want, jam on it? *phr.* [1910s+] a phr. used to deride someone seen as wanting everything to come without even the slightest problem.

dozed *adj.* [20C] (Ulster) very drunk (cf. BASTED). [fig. use of dial. *dozed*, of wood, rotten]

dozens/dirty dozens *n.* [20C] (US Black) a ritual game of testing a rival's emotional strength by insulting various relatives, especially their mother, in 12 'rounds' of attack and taking similar insults in return; the insults are usually sexual and/or scatological, hence the common addition of the adj. *dirty* (cf. BACKCAP n.; BAD TALK; DRAG n.[8]; PLAY THE DOZENS; SIGGING; SIGNIFY). [the throw of 12 in craps, the worst possible throw, or f. its folk origins as a set of ritualized verses, usu. in rhymed couplets, which ran through 12 specific sexual acts, each rhyming with the numbers 1 to 12]

dozing-crib *n.* [mid–late 19C] a bed. [SE *doze* + CRIB n.[3] (5)]]

dozy *adj.* [1950s+] (orig. milit.) mentally sluggish, stupid, lazy.

dozz *n.* [1990s] (US Black) a sleep, a nap. [var. on DOSS n.[1]]

d.p. *n.* [1960s+] (S.Afr. drugs) a highly regarded type of marijuana. [abbr. DURBAN POISON]

d.ph. *n.* [1910s+] (US) a damned fool. [pun on the degree of Ph.D.]

drab *n.[1]* [early 16C–19C] **1** a slattern, a dirty, untidy woman. **2** a prostitute. [Irish *drabog*, Gael. *drabag*, a dirty female, a slattern; presumably an early cant term]

drab *n.[2]* [mid-19C] poison. [Rom. *drab*, poison; thus *drabengro*, doctor, lit. 'poison-man']

drabbit! *excl.* [16C–17C] a mild excl., i.e. (Go)d rabbit!, (Go)d rat it! (cf. DRAT!).

drack/drac *n.[1]* (Aus.) [1930s+] rubbishy, worthless goods. [? Yiddish *dreck*, rubbish, dirt]

drack/drac *n.[2]* (Aus.) [1960s+] **1** an unattractive woman (cf. DRACK SORT). **2** a policeman. [proper name *Dracula* but *see* DRACK n.[1]]

drack *adj.* [1930s+] (Aus.) second-rate, inferior, unattractive. [DRACK n.[1]]

drack sort *n.* [1930s+] (Aus.) an unattractive person of either sex. [DRACK n.[2] + SE *sort*]

Dracula *n.* [1950s+] an unattractive woman (cf. DRACK n.[2]). [a cruel comparison to the well-known vampire]

draft *n.* [20C] (US Und.) the transportation of a convict from one prison to another (cf. BOAT n.[2]). [SAmE *draft*, the selecting of a smaller group from a larger body, usu. in milit. context]

draftnik *n.* [1950s–70s] (US campus) one who has avoided the military service conscription. [SAmE *draft* + sfx. -NIK]

draft/draught on the pump at Aldgate *n.* [late 18C–19C] a bad bill of exchange (cf. BILL ON THE PUMP AT ALDGATE). [SE *draft*, a written order for the payment of money]

draftpak *n.* [20C] (Scot.) an habitual drunkard. [Scot. *draftpak*, take-away packs of draft beer available over the bar in Scottish public houses]

drag *n.[1]* **1** [late 18C–mid-19C] a type of stage-coach, drawn by 4 horses, with seats on top. **2** [late 19C] a van. **3** [1930s–60s] a motorcar, thus vehicles in general. **4** [1930s–60s] a prison van. [in (1) it is 'dragged' by its team or horses; (2), (3) and (4) are subseq. developments]

drag *n.[2]* [late 18C+] the robbery of vehicles, initially horse-drawn, subseq. motorized; thus *go on the drag*, to pursue this as a profession. [DRAG n.[1]]

drag *n.[3]* [late 18C–1930s] a period of imprisonment lasting three months (cf. CARPET n.[2]; NAG-DRAG). [? DRAG n.[2]; i.e. the usual sentence for such a crime; 20C use mainly Aus.]

drag *n.[4]* [19C] a slow dance or the music that accompanies it.

drag *n.[5]* [19C–1950s] influence (cf. PULL n.[1]).

drag *n.[6]* **1** [mid-19C+] a street; thus *main drag*, the main street. **2** [1950s+] a long distance, which will make for tedious travelling. [its use by DRAG n.[1] (1)]

drag *n.[7]* **1** [mid-19C+] clothes. **2** [late 19C+] female dress as worn by men, but not in a homosexual context. **3** [1920s–70s] (US/Aus.) a party (with no specific gay overtones). **4** [1920s+] female dress as worn by homosexual males or female impersonators (cf. DRAG-QUEEN). **5** [1920s+] a party held *en travesti.* **6** [1930s] (US) a bar that caters primarily to a gay clientele. **7** [1950s+] a costume, a disguise. [orig. theatrical use, which stressed the *drag* of a long dress along the floor, as opposed to tight-fitting trousers; note [mid–late 19C] (Und.) *go on/flash the drag*, to wear female clothing for immoral purposes. First *OED* cits. (1870) imply fancy dress; gay refs. not overt until 1920s]

drag *n.[8]* [late 19C+] (US Black) a ritual game of testing a rival's emotional strength by insulting his various relatives (cf. DOZENS). [note this version of dozens is characterized by its extreme vulgarity and coarseness]

drag *n.[9]* [20C] (US) an unkempt or immoral woman, a slattern. [16C SE *draggle-tail*, an unkempt, slatternly woman, whose skirts drag along the ground]

drag *n.[10]* [1900s] (US campus) a joke. [ety. unknown]

drag *n.[11]* [1900s] (US campus) a toady, a parasite, a flatterer. [they are *dragged* along]

drag *n.[12]* [1910s] (US) wages. [what one can SE *drag* down or in]

drag *n.[13]* **1** [1920s+] (US) a young woman who is being taken to a party. **2** [1950s] (US) a girlfriend, a young woman. [SE *drag*, a heavy weight, an impediment]

drag *n.[14]* [1920s+] **1** a puff of a cigarette; thus the cigarette itself. **2** (W.I. drugs) a puff of a marijuana cigarette; thus *give a drag*, to pass a marijuana cigarette, *take a drag*, to take a puff on the cigarette. [SE *drag*, to draw, to pull]

drag *n.[15]* [1930s+] **1** a disappointment, a pity, a nuisance, a task that one has no desire to perform. **2** of a person, a disappointment, a hanger-on, a pest. [ext. use of SE *drag*, a bore; lit an obstruction to progress]

drag *adj.* [1920s+] relevant to the gay lifestyle. [DRAG n.[7] (4)]

drag *v.[1]* [early 19C–1930s] (Und.) to rob vehicles. [DRAG n.[2]]

drag *v.[2]* [late 19C] (US) to search for contraband.

drag *v.[3]* [late 19C+] (US campus) to escort to a dance. [SE *drag (along)*]

drag *v.[4]* **1** [20C] (US) to leave something unfinished (cf. BUNCH v.). **2** [20C] to leave quickly (cf. HAUL ASS). **3** [1920s+] (US) to resign from a job; also as *drag it.*

drag *v.[5]* [20C] to waste time, to idle, usu. as *drag around.*

drag *v.[6]* [1900s] (US campus) to toady to, to curry favour with a superior. [DRAG n.[11]]

drag *v.[7]* [1900s] (US campus) to joke, to jest. [DRAG n.[10]]

drag *v.[8]* [1900s] (US campus) to understand. [? SE *drag*, i.e. into one's brain]

drag *v.[9]* **1** [1920s+] to force someone to go to a place against their will, often as *drag along.* **2** [1950s+] (US Black/prison) to lead someone on, to persuade, to trick.

drag v.[10] [1940s–70s] (US) to irritate, to bore, to 'bring down'. [SE *drag*, a bore]

drag v.[11] [1960s+] to drive up and down, chatting to one's friends and displaying one's automobile. [DRAG n.[6]]

drag a blind, to phr. [1920s] (US) to go out with someone one has never met (cf. BLIND n.[4]). [DRAG v.[3] + BLIND DATE]

drag-ass adj. [20C] (US) **1** of a thing, tedious. **2** of a person, lazy, bedraggled. **3** annoying, irritating (cf. DAMNED). [DRAG n.[15] + sfx. -ASS]

drag-butch see DRAG-KING.

drag-cove n. [early 19C] a cart-driver. [SE *drag*, a cart, a wagon + COVE]

drag down v. [1920s+] (US) to earn a salary, wages (cf. PULL DOWN). [SE *drag*; note DRAG n.[12]]

drag-dyke n. [1960s+] a 'masculine' lesbian who chooses to dress in male clothing. [DRAG n.[7] + DYKE]

dragged/dragged out adj. [mid-19C+] (orig. US) exhausted, sickly.

dragged up adj. [late 17C+] educated or brought up 'any how'. [DRAG UP v.[1]]

dragger n. [late 18C] one who robs vehicles. [DRAG v.[1]]

dragging n.[1] [mid-19C+] stealing from carts and vans (cf. DRAG-LAY). [DRAG v.[1] + sfx. -ing]

dragging n.[2] [1980s+] (US campus) to feel ill or lethargic (cf. DRAGGED adj.). [abbr. *dragging one's ass*, feeling exhausted]

dragging lark n. [1910s–30s] stealing from automobiles (cf. DRAG-LAY). [DRAGGING n.[1] + SE *lark*]

dragging time n. [mid-19C] the evening of a country fair, when everyone has been drinking and the men begin to make robust physical advances towards the women.

draggin' wagon n. [1950s] (US teen) a fast car. [SE *drag racing*]

draggle-tail n. [late 18C] a prostitute (cf. DRAG n.[9]). [16C SE *draggle-tail*, an unkempt, slatternly woman, whose skirts drag along the ground]

draggy adj.[1] [1920s+] of people or events, boring. [DRAG n.[15]]

draggy adj.[2] [1920s+] unwell, sickly-looking. [DRAGGED OUT]

drag-king/-butch n. [1930s+] (gay) a woman who dresses as a man (cf. DRAG-QUEEN). [DRAG n.[4] + SE *king*/BUTCH n.[3] (2)]

drag-lay n. [late 18C–early 19C] the robbery of vehicles. [DRAG n.[1] + LAY n.[4] (2)]

dragon n.[1] **1** [17C–19C] a slattern, a promiscuous woman. **2** [1950s–60s] an old prostitute.

dragon n.[2] [early–mid-19C] a sovereign. [the image of St George and the dragon engraved on the coin]

dragon n.[3] [1980s+] (US campus) a person with particularly bad breath. [abbr. DRAGON BREATH; i.e. such a person 'breathes fire']

dragon n.[4] [1980s+] (drugs) heroin. [CHASE THE DRAGON]

dragon n.[5] [1980s+] (US) the penis (cf. DRAIN THE DRAGON).

drag on v. [1910s+] (Aus.) **1** to marry a woman. **2** to perform a task.

dragon breath n. [1970s+] (US) bad halitosis (cf. DRAGON n.[3]). [the image of one who 'breathes fire']

drag one's anchor, to phr. [1920s+] (US) to go slowly, to idle, to dawdle.

drag one's ass, to phr. (US) **1** [1920s+] to leave, to go, to move. **2** [1930s+] to be fatigued, to be run down, to be miserable. [SE *drag* + ARSE n.[1] (1)]

drag one's feet, to phr. [1950s+] (Aus.) to prove reluctant to pay one's share when drinking with friends.

drag one's hook, to phr. [1960s] (N.Z.) to leave. [SE *drag* + naut. *hook*, an anchor]

drag one's tail, to phr. [1920s+] (US) to mope around, to look miserable. [the image of a dog with its tail down, supposedly a sign of its unhappiness]

dragon lady n. [1950s+] (orig. US) a dominant, terror-inspiring woman. [a character, wicked and oriental, created for the cartoon strip *Terry and the Pirates* by Milton Caniff in 1934]

dragon upon St George n. [late 17C–18C] a position of sexual intercourse in which the woman is on top of the man (cf. RIDE A ST GEORGE). [the female *dragon* is on top of a male *St George*]

dragoon/dragoon it v. [late 18C–19C] to work at two jobs simultaneously. [SE *dragoon*, orig. a horse soldier, i.e. one who rode to battle on horseback but dismounted to fight like infantry]

drag-out n. [mid-19C] (US) **1** a rough party, a brawl (cf. KNOCK-DOWN n.[2]). **2** one who indulges in a fierce fight. [the loser, knocked unconscious, is *dragged out* of the way/room]

drag-queen n. [1930s+] a feminine homosexual who prefers to dress as a woman (cf. DRAG-KING). [DRAG n.[7] (4) + QUEEN n.[1]]

dragsman n. [19C] **1** a coachman. **2** a thief who robs goods or trunks from the back of vans or carts (cf. DRAG-SNEAK). [DRAG n.[1] + sfx. -MAN; 20C use of (1) is SE]

drag-sneak n. [mid-19C] a thief who specializes in the robbery of vehicles. [DRAG n.[1] + SNEAK n.]

drag the chain, to phr. [1930s+] (Aus./N.Z.) to be slow, to be inferior, to be last in any work or contest, to be the slowest drinker of a group (cf. SWING THE GATE). [sheep-shearing jargon]

drag the gut see SHOOT THE GUT.

drag the rag, to phr. [20C] (US) to hurry up. [SE *drag* + ? fig. use of RAGS n.[2] or simply assonance]

drag up v.[1] [late 17C+] to bring up or educate a child roughly, without controls, manners or discipline. [B.E. notes 'as the *Rakes* call it', i.e. upper-class society use; thus the irony is deliberate]

drag up v.[2] [1920s] (US) to leave one's job, to resign (cf. UP STICKS). [DRAG v.[4] (3)]

drag water aft, to phr. [20C] (US) to be fat, esp. around the hips and buttocks (cf. BROAD IN THE BEAM). [naut. jargon, a ship that is over-broad in the beam tends to *drag water*]

drag weed n. [1940s–50s] (US drugs) marijuana.

drain n.[1] [19C] **1** the throat. **2** the vagina (cf. BLACK HOLE n.[1]).

drain n.[2] [mid-19C] a drink; thus *do a drain*, to have a drink (with a friend), a *drain of pale*, a glass of brandy (cf. COMMON SEWER n.[2]). [SE *drain a glass*]

Drain, the n.[3] [1920s+] (London Transport) the Waterloo and City Line in London. [its subterranean route; it is not, however, part of the London Transport underground system, i.e. the TUBE n.[2] (1)]

drain Charles Dickens, to phr. [1990s] to masturbate (cf. CHOKE THE CHICKEN). [rhy. sl. *Dickens* = chickens, i.e. CHOOK n. (1)]

drain off v. [19C] to urinate (cf. RUN OFF v.[1]; TAP A KEG).

drain one's lizard, to phr. [20C] to urinate.

drain one's radiator, to phr. [1940s+] to urinate.

drainpipes n. **1** [late 19C] macaroni. **2** [1940s+] tight trousers (cf. GAS PIPES; STOVE-PIPE).

drain the dragon, to phr. [1980s+] to urinate (cf. DRAIN THE MAIN VEIN; WATER THE DRAGON). [DRAGON n.[5]]

drain the main vein, to phr. [1980s+] (US campus) to urinate (cf. DRAIN THE DRAGON).

drain the monster, to phr. [1980s+] to masturbate (cf. DECONGEST THE WEASEL).

drake n. [20C] (US) a cigar or cigarette end. [play on DUCK n.[6] + SE *drakes*; i.e. one 'ducks down' to pick them off the street]

drake v. [early 19C] to duck a thief in a pond. [pun on SE *duck*]

draked adj. [early 19C] ducked, a punishment sometimes meted out to pickpockets captured at fairs or races. [DRAKE v.]

Dralon n. [1990s] the anus. [brandname *Dralon*, a fabric esp. used for covering the seats of chairs]

drama queen n. [1960s+] (orig. gay) anyone considered to be making an excessive fuss or 'making a mountain out of a molehill'. [SE *drama* + QUEEN n.¹]

dram-a-tick n. [late 18C–early 19C] a shot of spirits obtained on credit. [SE *dram* + TICK n.²; a pun on SE *dramatic* (credit in a public house being hard to obtain)]

drap n. [late 18C] a low prostitute. [var. on DRAB n.¹ (2)]

drape n. [1930s–60s] (orig. US Black) a suit, typified by its generously cut, long, draped jacket with padded shoulders and high-waisted, tapering trousers (cf. ZOOT SUIT). [after its rejection by US Blacks, the *drape* suit was taken up by Teddy Boys in the UK in the 1950s]

drape v. [1940s+] to place oneself closely against someone (or something) else, especially when amorous and/or drunk.

draped adj.¹ [1940s] drunk. [? one is *draped* across the bar or around another's shoulders]

draped adj.² [1990s] (US Black) wearing large amounts of gold jewellery. [SE *draped (in)*, covered in]

drapery miss n. [19C] a woman who is considered sexually forward and who emphasizes her appeal by a flashy style of dress. [orig. cited by Lord Byron *c*.1811 as 'a pretty, a high-born, a fashionable young female, well-instructed by her friends, and furnished by her milliner with a wardrobe upon credit, to be repaid, when *married*, by her *husband*']

drapes n. [1940s+] (orig. US Black) clothes. [DRAPE n.]

drape shape n. [1940s–50s] a style of man's suit, typified by its generously cut, long, draped jacket with padded shoulders and high-waisted, tapering trousers (cf. ZOOT SUIT). [DRAPE n. + SE *shape*]

drat! excl. [19C+] a mild oath, euph. for *God rot it!*

dratsab n. [mid-19C+] bastard. [backsl.]

draughters n. [1920s] tight-fitting, undivided (i.e. legless) female knickers (cf. DIVIDERS). [i.e. they keep out the draught]

draught on the pump at Aldgate see DRAFT ON THE PUMP AT ALDGATE.

draw n.¹ [19C] **1** any device (or person) used to extract information from a third party. **2** the person from whom the information may be extracted.

draw n.² **1** [1950s+] (Aus.) a cigarette. **2** [1980s+] (drugs) cannabis, esp. as an ounce or multiples thereof, e.g. *five-draw, seven-draw* etc (cf. SKUIF). [one *draws* upon it]

draw v.¹ [mid–late 19C] to tease, to irritate, to exasperate, to induce (through teasing) to action.

draw v.² [mid-19C–1900s] to pick a pocket. [abbr. SE *withdraw*]

draw/draw out v.³ [mid-19C+] to elicit information from. [SE *draw out*, to extract, derive]

draw v.⁴ [20C] (W.I.) to be born with a skin-colour noticeably different from that of the rest of one's family. [SE *drawn*]

draw a cork, to phr. [19C] of a woman, to have sexual intercourse. [the image is of an exhausted, post-coital male]

draw a/the line, to phr. [mid-19C+] to set a limit, often moral, beyond which one will not go.

draw/pull a longbow, to phr. [late 17C–late 19C] to make exaggerated statements; thus [late 17C] *longbow man*, one whose words cannot be trusted. [20C use is SE]

drawback n.¹ [20C] a broken promise. [one *draws back* from one's initial suggestion]

drawback n.² [20C] (W.I.) a small bribe (cf. KICKBACK n.). [the recipient *draws back* some money for themself]

draw blanks v. [19C] to fail, to be disappointed, frustrated. [SE *draw a blank*, ult. drawing a blank ticket in a lottery]

draw bungy v. [1950s+] (W.I.) to snore. [? the sound of a bung being withdrawn from a cask]

draw caad/card, to phr. [1950s+] (W.I./UK Black teen) to trick or connive, to mislead, to 'pull a fast one' on someone. [SE *draw* + CAAD/CARD]

draw drapes n. [1950s–60s] (gay) a foreskin (cf. LACE CURTAINS).

drawer-on n. [17C–19C] an appetizer. [it draws the eater on to the rest of the meal]

drawers n. [16C] stockings. [? their being drawn on and off; the subseq. colloq. use to mean underpants does not materialize until 17C]

draw iron v. [mid–late 19C] (US) to draw a pistol. [SE *draw* + SHOOTING IRON n. (1)]

draw it easy! excl. [mid-19C] (US) a general excl. expressing incredulity or derision (cf. DRAW IT MILD!).

draw it mild! excl. [mid-19C] a general excl. expressing incredulity or derision, i.e. don't exaggerate! [public house imagery; i.e. the *drawing* of pints of beer]

draw it strong, to phr. [late-19C] to exaggerate.

draw-latch n. [late 17C–18C] a thief who enters a house by lifting the latch (cf. SNECK DRAWER). [SE *draw-latch*, a string hanging on the outside of a door by which a latch is drawn or raised]

draw mud from the well, to phr. [1990s] to expel a small amount of faeces when breaking wind.

draw off v.¹ [19C] of a woman, to calm a man's passion by consenting to sleep with him. [SE *draw off*, to divert one's attention]

draw off v.² [20C] of a man, to urinate. [SE *draw off*, to drain away]

draw/leave/put one's trademark on someone, to phr. [late 19C+] usu. of a woman, to scratch someone's face.

draw out see DRAW v.³.

draw someone for v. [19C] to borrow money from someone. [SE *draw*, to extract]

draw someone's fireworks, to phr. [19C] of a woman, to calm a man's passion by consenting to sleep with him (cf. DRAW A CORK; DRAW OFF v.¹).

draw/gather/pick straws v. [late 18C–mid-19C] to show signs of sleep, esp. as *one's eyes draw straws*. [pvb. *one eye draws straw, t'other serves the thatcher*; Grose (1796) has the single *straw*]

draw the blinds, to phr. [1980s+] (US gay) to fellate an uncircumcised penis. [the foreskin represents the *blinds* that cover the penis]

draw the crabs, to phr. [1950s+] (Aus.) to attract unwelcome attention, to draw enemy fire (actual or metaphorical).

draw the crow, to phr. [1940s+] (Aus.) to come off worst, usu. in a share-out or division of spoils, labour, prizes etc. [an anecdote in which a number of game birds and one crow were on offer and one hapless person *drew the crow*]

draw the king's/queen's picture, to phr. [late 18C–late 19C] to create counterfeit banknotes. [UK banknotes always carry the current monarch's head]

draw the line see DRAW A LINE.

draw the queen's picture see DRAW THE KING'S PICTURE.

draw the twine, to phr. [1990s] (Irish) to pursue a profitable activity. [? the twine used in bricklaying]

draw up v. [1950s+] (drugs) to inject a drug. [one draws blood into the syringe where it mixes with the narcotic/water mixture before being injected back into the vein]

draw water v.¹ [19C] to weep.

draw water v.² [20C] to have influence. [naut. jargon, a large ship draws more water than a smaller one]

drayman bible n. [1940s+] (W.I.) a bulla cake (cf. DIRTY SHIRT). [the *bulla cake* is a food of the poor; thus a drayman would rely on it for sustenance]

dread *n.* [1950s+] (W.I. Rasta) **1** a person with dreadlocks, thus a Rastafarian. **2** one who wears dreadlocks but follows no other Rastafarian teachings. **3** the beliefs, practice or expression of Rastafarianism. **4** a youngster, usu. a male teenager, who shows off by taking dangerous risks. [Exod 15:16: 'Fear and dread shall fall upon them; by the greatness of thy arm they shall be as still as a stone']

dread *adj.* [1960s+] (W.I./Rasta) of a situation, serious, important, whether positively or negatively. [DREAD n.]

dread! *excl.*[1] [late 19C] a mild oath (cf. DRAT!).

dread! *excl.*[2] [1950s+] (W.I./Rasta) **1** a form of address, e.g. *You looking good, dread!* (cf. MAN n.[1]). **2** a form of emphasis, underlining what has been said, e.g. *This herb is irey, dread!*

dreadful *n.* [late 19C] a sensationally written 'true crime' story, sold for one penny (cf. PENNY AWFUL; SHILLING SHOCKER; THREE AND SIXPENNY THOUGHTFUL). [abbr. PENNY DREADFUL]

dreadlocks *n.* [1960s+] (orig. W.I.) the long, braided hair worn by Rastafarians. [DREAD n. (1) + SE *locks*; Rastas have worn beards from the formation of the cult in the early 1950s, but *dreadlocks* were adopted later, in conscious imitation of Somali and Masai tribesmen, whose pictures were circulated in Jamaica]

dreadnought *n.*[1] **1** [1900s] a male pessary or suppository. **2** [1900s–10s] a high, stiff corset.

dreadnought *n.*[2] (Aus.) **1** [1910s–30s] a long, deep glass of beer. **2** [1980s+] a shearer who can shear 300 sheep in a day (cf. DEUCE n.[3]). [fig. uses of SE *dreadnought*, a large battleship, the first of which, HMS *Dreadnought*, was launched on 18 February 1906 and became the world's greatest armaments platform]

dreadnoughts *n.* [1900s–40s] tight-fitting flannel or woollen female drawers.

dready *n.* [1950s+] (W.I. Rasta) a friendly term for a fellow Rastafarian. [DREAD n. (1) + sfx. -*y*]

dream *n.*[1] **1** [20C] a very attractive, charming, personable individual. **2** [1910s] (US) an expert.

dream *n.*[2] [1920s] (US) a hand-rolled cigarette. [? a brandname]

dream *n.*[3] (drugs) **1** [1920s+] opium, morphine. **2** [1980s+] cocaine. [the effects on one's brain]

dream *n.*[4] [1920s+] (Aus.) a 6-month prison sentence. [? one can do it in one's sleep]

dreamboat *n.* [1940s+] **1** a particularly attractive man or woman, the fuel of one's fantasies (cf. DREAM n.[1]). **2** a general term of admiration or affection.

dreambox *n.* [1910s–40s] (US Black) the head (cf. THINKER).

dream dust *n.* [1950s+] (drugs) any narcotic in a powdered form (cf. DREAM n.[3]).

dreamer *n.* [1980s+] (drugs) morphine. [DREAM n.[3] (1)]

dreamers *n.* [1930s–40s] (US Black) sheets and blankets. [SE *dream*; one dreams between them]

dream girl/guy *n.* [1920s+; 1980s+] (orig. US) the ideal(ized) young woman or young man (cf. DREAM n.[1]).

dream gum *n.* [1900s–30s] (drugs) opium. [DREAM n.[3] (1) + GUM n.[3]]

dream guy *see* DREAM GIRL.

dreamland *n.* [20C] unconsciousness.

dream off *v.* [1930s–40s] (US) to fall asleep on the job, to drift off.

dream on! *excl.* [1980s+] a dismissive excl., i.e. 'don't you wish' (cf. IN YOUR DREAMS!). [your theory is, at best, a daydream]

dream puss *n.* [1940s] (US campus) the idealized young woman (cf. DREAM GIRL). [SE *dream* + PUSS n.[1]]

dreams *n.* [1900s–30s] (drugs) opium. [DREAM n.[3] (1)]

dream stick *n.* **1** [1920s+] (drugs) a pipe of opium. **2** [1940s]

(US) a (marijuana) cigarette. [DREAM n.[3]/SE *dream* + STICK n.[11]]

Dream Street *n.* [1930s+] 47th Street, New York City, between 6th and 7th Avenues. [the term was coined by the short story writer and chronicler of Broadway, Damon Runyon (1880–1946); the block was the site of the stage door to B.F. Keith's Palace Theater, 1913–32, the headquarters of American vaudeville]

dreamy *adj.* [1940s+] (orig. US teen) perfect, ideal, delightful, beautiful. [DREAM n.[1] (1)]

drear *n.* [1950s+] a depressing person. [abbr. SE *dreary*]

dreck/drek *n.* [1920s+] **1** excrement, filth. **2** anything worthless, second-rate, rubbishy. **3** (drugs) heroin (cf. SHIT n.[5]). [Yid. *drek*, thence Ger. *Dreck*, excrement, dung]

drecky *adj.* [1960s+] second-rate, trashy, rubbishy, dirty. [DRECK]

dredge-head *n.* [1970s+] an habitual drinker, who drinks up the dregs in each glass. [SE *dredge* + sfx -HEAD (2)]

dredgerman *n.* [mid-19C] a thief who poses as a dredgerman in order to get on board a boat and rob its passengers.

dregged *adj.* [1980s+] (Aus. drugs) tired and lethargic after smoking cannabis. [17C SE *dreg*, to render mentally confused, perplexed]

dreggy *n.* [1980s+] (Aus. drugs) cannabis that causes one to become tired and lethargic. [DREGGED]

drek *see* DRECK.

drenched *adj.* [1920s–60s] (US) very drunk.

drench one's gizzard, to *phr.* [20C] to drink heavily (cf. WET ONE'S WHISTLE).

dress *v.* [19C+] **1** to beat, to thrash. **2** to tell off, to reprimand, to criticize (cf. DRESS DOWN). [ironic use of SE *dress*, to treat a person properly]

dress a hat, to *phr.* [mid-19C] to carry out various methods of robbery contrived by two or more servants or shopmen, either exchanging their master's goods (e.g. shoes for a hat) or pooling them (the butcher's boy steals steaks, the potboy steals beer etc) and all is sold to a third party.

dress-and-breath *n.* [1920s–30s] (US Black) a very lazy woman. [the most effort she makes is to get dressed and breathe]

dress down *v.* [19C+] **1** to beat, to thrash. **2** to tell off, to reprimand, to criticize. [ext. of DRESS v.; but note SE *dress*, to treat leather; thus to 'tan a hide']

dressed *adj.* [1950s+] (US Black) a car filled with every conceivable decoration, gimmick and similar flashy adornment. [SE *dressed up*]

dressed in *n.* [20C] (US prison) a new inmate. [i.e. *dressed in* newly issued clothes]

dressed/dressed up like a deacon/preacher/nigger preacher *phr.* [20C] (US) dressed up, in one's best clothes. [a clergyman is presumed to dress properly in formal clothes]

dressed like Christmas beef *phr.* [mid-19C–1930s] wearing one's best clothes. [pun on SE *dressed*, clothed/*dressed*, of food, prepared]

dressed to kill *phr.* [early 19C+] dressed up in one's smartest clothes, with the intention of using one's appearance for (sexual) advantage.

dressed/dressed up to the nines *phr.* [mid-19C+] dressed up to the height of fashion; occas. variation as [1910s–20s] *dressed to the tens*.

dressed up like a dog's dinner *phr.* [1930s+] dressed in the height of chic and fashion (but cf. DOG'S DINNER).

dressed up like a pox doctor's clerk *see* DONE UP LIKE A POX DOCTOR'S CLERK.

dressed up like a preacher/nigger preacher *see* DRESSED LIKE A DEACON.

dressed up/dolled up/done up like a sore finger/thumb/ toe *phr.* [20C] (Aus./N.Z./US) overdressed, flashily dressed (cf. DONE UP LIKE A POX DOCTOR'S CLERK).

dressed up to the knocker *phr.* [19C] dressed in one's best clothes. [KNOCKER n.²]

dressed up to the nines *see* DRESSED TO THE NINES.

dresser *n.* [1990s] (gay) a transvestite. [abbr. SE *cross-dresser*]

dress flash *v.* [19C] to dress in a manner adopted by the fashionable or criminal classes. [FLASH adj.²]

dress for the part, to *phr.* [late 19C] (society) to act hypocritically. [theatrical imagery]

dress-lodger *n.* [mid-19C] a prostitute who is dressed in finery by her landlady and repays the favour by walking the streets and turning over her profits.

dress-puss *n.* [1940s+] (W.I.) an overdressed or fashionably dressed person, a provocatively dressed woman. [SE *dress* + PUSSY n.¹]

dress-up *n.* [1970s] a prostitute's client who enjoys dressing up, usu. in her clothes and make-up, although some prefer to provide their own wardrobe.

dress up drunk, to *phr.* [19C+] (US) to dress in an ostentatious manner. [the lack of discrimination in dressing supposed to be shown by a drunkard]

dreykop *n.* [1960s–70s] a trickster, a fraudsman. [Yid. *drey-kop*, lit. 'twisted head']

drib *v.* [late 17C] (Und.) to crop, to cut off. [SE *drib*, to fall drop by drop]

dribble *n.* [20C] meaningless chatter.

dribble *v.* [1940s] (US Black) to stutter.

dribble-lipped *adj.* [1980s+] (US Black) having a notably pendulous bottom lip.

dribble-puss *n.* [1940s+] a child. [SE *dribble* + PUSS n.³]

dribbler *n.* [19C] the mouth.

dribbling shits/dribbles *n.* [20C] incontinence, diarrhoea. [SE *dribble* + SHIT n.¹ (2)]

dribs and drabs *n.* [20C] (Aus.) the crabs, body lice. [rhy. sl.]

dried-barkers *n.* [1940s] (US Black) furs. [SE *dried* + *barker*, a dog, thus any furred animal]

drift *v.* [1950s] (US) to leave, to depart, esp. as imper. *drift!*, go away. [the overtone is of moving slowly and aimlessly, although the imper. dispenses with it]

drill *n.¹* [1910s–20s] (US) the penis (cf. AUGER).

drill, the *n.²* [1940s+] the proper way of doing things, the recognized procedure, esp. in phr. *what's the drill?* how are things done (round here). [ext. of milit. use]

drill *v.¹* **1** [late 17C–18C] to lure, to entice slowly. **2** [1960s] (US) to stare. [the slow progress of a *drill* as it penetrates wood]

drill *v.²* [18C+] of a male, to have sexual intercourse (cf. BANG v.¹).

drill *v.³* [early 19C+] (orig. US) to shoot (dead).

drill *v.⁴* [late 19C+] (US) to walk, esp. of a hobo who would normally ride in a boxcar. [SE *drill*, to perform military exercises on a parade ground]

drill for Marmite, to *phr.* [1990s] to sodomize (cf. MARMITE MOTORWAY). [*Marmite*, a spread made of yeast extract and, as such, brown]

drill for oil, to *phr.* [1940s] (orig. US Black) **1** of a man, to have sexual intercourse. **2** of a woman, to masturbate.

drink *n.¹* [late 19C+] one who is too tall for their age (cf. LONG DRINK OF WATER). [Scot. *drink*, a lanky, overgrown person]

drink *n.²* [1940s+] (orig. RAF) the ocean, the sea.

drink *n.³* [1950s+] **1** a bribe, a sum of money that would supposedly purchase 'a drink' but is usu. much larger. **2** in non-criminal use, a tip, a commission, a bonus.

drink *n.⁴* [1980s] (drugs) phencyclidine (cf. ACE n.³). [ety. unknown]

drink *v.* [1970s+] (Und.) to be susceptible to bribery; thus code between newly arrested criminal and policeman *Do you drink, officer?* (cf. CAN I SPEAK TO YOU?).

drinkage *n.* [1980s+] (US campus) beer. [SE *drink* + sfx. -AGE]

drink all out, to *phr.* [17C–19C] to empty one's glass.

drink/lush at Freeman's Quay, to *phr.* [19C] to drink at another's expense. [SE *drink*/LUSH v.¹; the free drinks distributed at this quay near London Bridge to porters and carmen in 1810–80; the RN amplified it to *Harry Freemans* (and used it for anything, not merely drink, that was free), while the British Army shortened it to *Freemans*]

drink at St Patrick's well, to *phr.* [mid-17C–mid-19C] to drink (Irish) whisky (cf. ST PATRICK). [*St Patrick*, patron saint of Ireland]

drink at the fuzzy cup, to *phr.* [1970s+] (US Black) to engage in cunnilingus.

drink by word of mouth, to *phr.* [late 18C–mid-19C] to drink straight from the bottle.

drink coffee *see* DRINK MUDDY WATER.

drinker *n.* [1950s+] an after-hours drinking club.

drinkery *n.* [mid-19C] (US) a liquor store, a bar, anywhere where alcohol is sold.

drink from both taps, to *phr.* [1990s] to be bisexual.

drink from the fountain of youth, to *phr.* [1990s] to fellate.

drink from the same quill, to *phr.* [20C] (US) to get along, to share the same opinions, activities. [SE *quill*, a tap, esp. of a container of wine]

drinkitite *n.* [late 19C] thirst; thus *on the drinkitite*, on a drunken spree (cf. BITE-ETITE). [pun on SE *appetite* + TIGHT adj.³]

drink like a fish, to *phr.* [17C–19C] to drink heavily. [SE in 20C]

drink more than one has bled, to *phr.* [19C] to drink heavily.

drink muddy water/coffee, to *phr.* [20C] (US) to be very thin. [one cannot see through muddy water; thus those who are so thin as to be virtually invisible have to drink muddy water to give themselves some substance]

drink of black coffee *n.* [20C] (US) a severe reprimand, a telling off. [like the coffee, the scolding is strong, HOT adj.¹ (2) and bitter]

drink of water *n.* [20C] (Ulster) **1** an irritating person. **2** a weakling.

drink/lick on the whip, to *phr.* [15C–16C] to receive a thrashing.

drink out of the island, to *phr.* [late 18C–19C] to drink to the bottom of a wine bottle. [the *island* is the inverted glass 'hillock' in the base of a wine bottle]

drink out of the same bottle, to *phr.* [1930s+] (US) to be close friends.

drink soup off/over someone's head, to *phr.* [20C] (W.I.) to be taller than someone.

drink the cross off an ass, to *phr.* [20C] (Irish) to have a substantial capacity for alcohol.

drink to one's oysters, to *phr.* [late 18C–late 19C] to take life (usu. as regards its neg. aspects) as it comes. [ety. unknown; image of opening oysters – some bad, some good – and drinking anyway]

drink with the flies, to *phr.* [1930s+] (Aus.) to drink by oneself. [a situation in which there are no companions other than the flies – whose presence is, of course, unwelcome]

drinky *adj.* [19C] (US) mildly drunk, tipsy.

drinky-poo *n.* [1980s+] a drink, rendered facetious by this arch baby-talk.

drip *n.¹* [1930s+] a weakling, a spineless person (cf. DRIPPY).

drip *n.*² **1** [1910s–40s] (US) nonsense, flattery, sentimental drivel. **2** [1940s+] complaints, grumbling. [the words drip from one's mouth; note RN *dripper*, an habitual whinger]

drip *n.*³ [1960s+] venereal disease, esp. gonorrhoea (cf. DRIPPER *n.*¹). [the discharge that oozes from the penis]

drip-dry lover *n.* [1960s+] (US gay) a gay man with a small penis. [the joke is that he has to let it drip dry – it's too short to shake]

drip it up *v.* [1960s+] to purchase on extended credit, to use hire purchase. [ON THE DRIP]

dripper *n.*¹ [late 17C–18C] **1** the discharge that accompanies venereal disease. **2** venereal disease, esp. gonorrhoea (cf. DRIP *n.*³). [SE *drip*, a falling drop; the pus-like discharge is a primary symptom of gonorrhoea]

dripper *n.*² [1930s+] an ageing prostitute. [? link to DRIPPER *n.*¹]

dripper *n.*³ [1980s+] (drugs) an eye-dropper, used to make a makeshift syringe or to drop LSD on to sugar-cubes, blotting-paper or some other medium of delivery.

dripping *n.* [mid-19C] a cook (cf. SLUSHY). [SE *dripping*, rendered animal fat]

dripping *adj.* [1970s+] (society) gutless, cowardly, weak (cf. DRIP *n.*¹). [such a person is *dripping* WET *adj.*³]

dripping for it/dripping for it like a butcher's daughter *phr.* [1910s+] (orig. Aus.) sexually voracious, sometimes abbr. to *like a butcher's daughter* (cf. DRIPPING PAN; DRIPPINGS; GAGGING FOR IT). [pun on *dripping*, fat/*dripping*, sexually excited; the image is of uncontrollable vaginal secretions]

dripping pan *n.* [18C] the vagina (cf. GRAVY-GIVER; GRAVY-MAKER). [DRIPPINGS + SE *pan*]

drippings *n.* [18C] vaginal secretions (cf. DRIPPING FOR IT; DRIPPING PAN).

dripping with *adj.* [1920s+] abundant with, overloaded with, usu. in context of jewels or money.

drippy *adj.* [1950s+] weak, ineffectual. [DRIP *n.*¹]

drippy tummy *n.* [1960s] (US) diarrhoea (cf. GYPPY TUMMY). [the watery stools thus engendered]

drive *n.*¹ [20C] (US Black) a highway.

drive *n.*² [1930s–40s] (US drugs) a thrill, a feeling of excitement, esp. after using narcotics (cf. RUSH *n.*²). [SE *drive*, energy, intensity]

drive *v.* [1950s+] (Aus.) to infuriate (cf. DRIVE BANANAS; DRIVE COCO). [abbr. SE *drive mad*, *drive crazy* etc]

drive at *v.* [mid-19C] to work hard at.

drive bananas *v.* [1970s+] (orig. US) to drive mad, to infuriate (cf. DRIVE V.; GO BANANAS). [SE *drive*, to impel, to push + BANANAS adj.]

drive coco *v.* [20C] to drive insane, to send mad, to infuriate (cf. DRIVE V.). [SE *drive*, to impel, to push + COCO *n.*¹; i.e. 'off one's head']

drive licks in someone's skin/tail, to *phr.* [20C] (W.I.) to beat severely. [SE *drive* + LICKS *n.* (1) + TAIL *n.*¹ (3)]

drive on *v.* [20C] (US Black) to hit hard and without warning.

drive one's ducks/geese to a poor market/puddle, to *phr.* [20C] (US) to marry unwisely, esp. to marry 'beneath oneself' (cf. BRING ONE'S HOGS TO A FAIR MARKET). [the *market* in question is the *marriage market*]

drive one's hogs/hogs to market, to *phr.* [early 18C–19C] to snore (cf. CALL HOGS; DRIVE ONE'S PIGS).

drive one's hos, to *phr.* [1960s+] (US Black) to keep one's group of prostitutes hard at work, observing one's rules and earning plenty of money. [SE *drive* + HO *n.*¹ (1)]

drive one's pigs/pigs to market, to *phr.* [19C+] (US) to snore (cf. CALL HOGS; DRIVE ONE'S HOGS).

drive on the other side of the road, to *phr.* [1990s] to be homosexual.

driver *n.* [mid-19C] a manager or foreman who forces employees to work much harder than their wages demand. [abbr. SE *slave-driver*]

drivers *n.* [1970s] (US campus) legs. [they 'drive one along']

drive/send someone up the wall, to *phr.* [1950s+] to infuriate, to annoy intensely, fig. to the point of insanity (cf. CLIMB THE WALLS; DRIVE V.; DRIVE COCO).

drive the brewer's horse, to *phr.* [19C] to be drunk.

drive the bus, to *phr.* [1970s+] to vomit. [abbr. DRIVE THE PORCELAIN BUS]

drive the car, to *phr.* [20C] (US drugs) in prison, for one prisoner to purchase the day's supply of marijuana for a small group of friends. Members of the group take it in turns to provide for their fellows. Those who are smoking the drugs but not purchasing that day are *hitch-hiking*. [SE *drive* + CAR]

drive the porcelain bus, to *phr.* [1970s+] (US campus) to vomit, spec. when hugging the circular (i.e. steering-wheel-shaped) lavatory bowl and vomiting therein (cf. DRIVE THE BUS; KISS THE PORCELAIN GOD; MAKE LOVE TO THE PORCELAIN GODDESS).

drive the skin bus, to *phr.* [1990s] to masturbate.

drive turkeys to market, to *phr.* [19C] to walk in a drunken, unsteady manner (cf. CARRY A TURKEY ON ONE'S BACK). [the turkey-driver is forced to follow the birds' meandering course along the road]

driving post *n.* [20C] the penis. [play on SE *driving stick*, a rod used to drive cattle]

driving stealth *n.* [1980s+] (US) driving a car without any bumper-stickers or similar advertisements of one's political affections, use of drugs or other beliefs that might antagonize the authorities. [milit. jargon *stealth*, a form of technology, best seen in the *stealth bomber* used in the second Gulf War (1991), in which all surfaces are made as radar-resistant as possible, thus helping the aircraft to operate largely unobserved by surveillance systems]

driz *n.* [early–mid-19C] lace; thus *driz fencer*, one who sells lace, *driz camesa/kemesa*, a lace-adorned shirt. [Rom. *doriez*, thread, lace]

drizzle *n.* **1** [1920s] (US) nonsense, empty chatter. **2** [1930s–40s] (US campus) a weakling, a whinger (cf. DRIP *n.*²).

drizzlepuss *n.* [1930s–40s] (US) a sour-faced person, a grumbler, a killjoy (cf. PICKLEPUSS; SOURPUSS).

drizzlies, the *n.* [1940s–70s] (US) diarrhoea.

drobe *n.* [20C] (US Black) clothes. [abbr. SE *wardrobe*]

droddum *n.* [mid–late 19C] the buttocks, the posterior. [synon. Scot.]

droid *n.* [1980s+] (orig. US) **1** a menial labourer. **2** a dull, uninspired, robotic person. [abbr. SE *android* but popularized in the *Star Wars* films of the 1970s]

drol *n.* [1960s+] (S.Afr.) a general term of abuse (cf. TURD). [Afk. *drol(letjies)*, animal droppings]

dromaky *n.* [19C] (mainly northern) a prostitute. [abbr. *Andromache*, wife of the Trojan hero Hector, referring to the poor reputation of the travelling actresses who played her in Euripedes' play (5C BC)]

drome/'drome *n.* [1900s–20s] an aero*drome*. [abbr.]

dromedary *n.* [late 17C–18C] a thief, esp. an incompetent one. [SE *dromedary*, a bungling fellow (although the dromedary or Arabian single-humped camel is, according to the *OED*, 'a light and fleet breed')]

dromomania *n.* [20C] (US) a tramp, a vagrant. [Gk. *dromos*, running + *mania*, madness; thus one who loves moving around]

drone *n.* [1940s+] (US campus) a tedious, unpleasant person. [SE *drone*, a parasite]

droned *adj.* [1980s+] (US drugs) both drunk and stoned.

drongo *n.* [1940s+] (Aus.) a simpleton, a stupid person. [orig. used of a recruit to the RAAF. Baker links the term to 'Drongo ... the name of a horse ... [which] won a certain claim to fame by consistently finishing last or near last'. The *OED* dismisses this as 'highly speculative', while the *AND* suggests that the horse's name might have 'influenced' the earlier use; thus ? f. *drongo cuckoo* the cuckoo genus *Surniculus*; this relates to CUCKOO n.[1], thus cf. BOOBY n.[1]]

drongo *adj.* [1940s+] silly, foolish. [DRONGO n.]

dronk *adj.* [1960s+] (S.Afr.) drunk. [synon. Afk.]

dronkie *n.* [1930s+] (S.Afr.) a drunkard, an alcoholic. [Afk. *dronk*, drunk]

dronklap *n.* [1950s+] (S.Afr.) a drunkard. [Afk. *dronk*, drunk + *lap*, clout]

droob/drube *n.* [1930s+] (Aus.) a useless, foolish, depressing person. [? link to RUBE n.[1] (2)]

droodle *v.* [20C] (US) to wander aimlessly, to laze around. [SE *drift* + *dawdle*]

droog *n.* [1990s] (US teen) a good friend. [coined by Anthony Burgess for *A Clockwork Orange* (1962); ult. Rus. *drug*, friend]

drool *n.* **1** [mid-19C–1940s] (US) spittle. **2** [20C] nonsense, rubbish. [SE *drivel*]

drool *v.*[1] (Aus.) to waste time, to idle around. [DROOL n. (2)]

drool *v.*[2] [1990s] to masturbate. [SE *drool*, to dribble]

drooly *n.* [mid-19C+] (US) a stupid, unpopular person. [DROOL n. (2) + sfx. *-y*]

droop/droops *n.*[1] [20C] a feeling of unhappiness, depression (cf. DOWN n.[3]).

droop *n.*[2] [1920s–60s] (US campus) an unpleasant, esp. boring person (cf. DRIP n.[1]).

droops *see* DROOP n.[1].

droopy *adj.* [20C] unpleasant, dull, weak (cf. DRIPPY). [DROOP n.[2]]

droopy-drawers *n.* [1930s+] an untidy, sloppy or depressing person.

drop *n.*[1] [early 19C] (Und.) a confidence trick, spec. ring-dropping (cf. DROP GAME).

drop/drop of the creature *n.*[2] [early 19C+] a drink. [SE *drop* + CREATURE n.[1]]

drop *n.*[3] [mid-19C+] an advantage; usu. in phr. *get the drop on*, to put at a disadvantage.

drop *n.*[4] [20C] **1** (US Black) an orphan, esp. one whose parents are unknown (cf. RUSTLE n.[3]). [farming jargon *drop*, an animal bred by accident]

drop *n.*[5] **1** [1910s+] a receiver of stolen goods (cf. FENCE n.[1]). **2** [1910s+] a delivery, usu. of stolen goods, contraband etc. **3** [1930s+] a hiding-place for stolen, smuggled, or illicit goods. **4** [1950s+] a place where letters, papers and similar material (usu. secret) can be left for subsequent collection by another person.

drop *n.*[6] [1930s] **1** a bribe. **2** the money used for a bribe. [one *drops* off the money]

drop *n.*[7] [1950s] (Aus.) the penis. [? DROPPING MEMBER]

drop *n.*[8] [1950s+] (W.I.) a free ride in a car or cart, at the end of which one is *dropped off*.

drop *v.*[1] [early 17C+] to abandon a friendship, to snub.

drop *v.*[2] [mid-17C+] to give birth. [SE *drop*, usu. of a sheep, to give birth]

drop *v.*[3] **1** [late 17C+] to lose money. **2** [late 18C–1930s] to pay over money, to spend money. **3** [1920s+] (orig. US) to pass dud cheques. **4** [1930s+] to pass counterfeit money. **5** [1960s] (US) to bet. [the money is *dropped* on the table]

drop *v.*[4] **1** [early 18C+] to shoot down, to kill. **2** [early 19C] to die. **3** [late 19C+] to knock down. [SE *drop*, to fall or make another fall to the ground]

drop *v.*[5] **1** [early 19C–1920s] to get to know about, to become aware of (cf. DROP TO). **2** [late 19C–1900s] to understand. **3** [1980s+] (rap music) to explain, to enlighten (cf. DROP KNOWLEDGE; DROP SCIENCE). [abbr. DROP TO; DROP ONTO]

drop *v.*[6] **1** [20C] to arrest, to be arrested. **2** [1970s+] (US) to be convicted of a crime (cf. FALL v.[1]).

drop *v.*[7] [1960s+] (drugs) to consume pills or any drug that can be taken orally. [one *drops* them down one's throat]

drop a banger *see* DROP A CLANGER.

drop a beast, to *phr.* [1970s+] (society) to break wind.

drop a brick, to *phr.* [1920s+] to make an error, a mistake, esp. verbally (cf. DROP A CLANGER).

drop a clanger/banger, to *phr.* [1940s+] to make a social error, the awfulness of which reverberates around the assembled gathering (cf. DROP A BRICK). [SE *clang*/*bang*]

drop a dime/dime on, to *phr.* [1970s+] to inform, to inform against. [the act of making a call from a public telephone, which in 1970s cost 10 cents. Note basketball jargon *drop a dime*, to shoot a three-point basket]

drop a frog, to *phr.* [1970s] (US) to give birth.

drop a hand in *see* DROP HAND IN.

drop a line, to *phr.* **1** [mid-18C+] to send a letter (cf. FLY A LINE). **2** [1990s] (US Black) to start a conversation with someone in the hope of establishing a longer relationship. **3** [1990s] (US Black) to ring on the telephone.

drop a lug on, to *phr.* [1960s+] (US Black) to confront someone either as to their character or actions, to criticize, both seriously and in fun. [SE *drop* + LUG n.[1] (2)]

drop a net on, to *phr.* [1940s–50s] (US) to commit to a psychiatric institution.

drop a pebble, to *phr.* [1990s] to excrete a small piece of excrement while in the process of breaking wind.

drop a thumper, to *phr.* [1960s+] to break wind. [SE *drop* + THUMPER n.[3]]

drop away *v.* [late 17C] to give, lose, or part with something, usu. money.

drop-case *n.* [1970s] (US) a fool.

drop-cove *n.* [early 19C+] (Und.) a confidence trickster. [DROP (GAME) + COVE]

drop dead! *excl.* [1930s+] (orig. US) a general excl. of dismissal (cf. GO TO HELL!).

drop-dead *adv.* [1970s+] (orig. US) extremely, esp. as in *drop-dead beautiful*. [so beautiful, striking etc as to cause the onlooker to *drop dead*]

drop-dead money *n.* [1980s+] money, the possession of which enables one to tell the world, *Drop dead!*, i.e. bestows freedom on its possessor (cf. FUCK-YOU MONEY).

drop down on oneself *v.* [early 19C] to feel depressed, esp. at the prospect of prison or judicially sanctioned death, to sink beneath one's problems.

drop down to *v.* [early 19C] to find out about one's character or plans. [var. on DROP v.[5] (1)]

drop 'em *v.* [20C] of a woman, to have sexual intercourse. ['em are her knickers]

drop foot *v.* [1950s+] (W.I./Jam.) to dance energetically.

drop game *n.* [early 19C+] (Und.) a confidence trick whereby the victim is persuaded to pay money for a wallet, ring or some valuable, supposedly found on the ground but actually planted by the con-man.

drop hairpins *v.* [1940s+] (gay) to reveal one's sexual preferences by dropping broad hints (cf. DROP ONE'S BEADS). [SE *hairpins* are seen as a quintessentially feminine possession]

drop hand/a hand in, to *phr.* [1950s+] (W.I.) to hit with the clenched fist.

drop-in *n.*[1] **1** [early 19C+] an unexpected or casual visit or visitor. **2** [1940s+] (orig. US) a place or function which one may visit without prior arrangement.

drop-in n.² [1930s–40s] (US) **1** something that is easy. **2** easy money. **3** a victim, a sucker. [the image of a gullible victim who may sometimes *drop in* to a confidence-game without having to be steered there first]

drop-in-his-eye adj. [late 17C–18C] almost drunk. [? SE *drop* of liquor, or one is on the verge of drunken tears]

drop in the bucket, to phr. [20C] (US Und.) to imprison.

drop into v. [mid-19C] to beat, to thrash. [the whip or fist is *dropped into* the victim]

drop it! excl. [mid-19C+] change the subject, stop talking that way, stop what you are doing.

drop knowledge v. [1980s+] (US Black) to demonstrate wisdom or skill (cf. DROP SCIENCE). [DROP v.⁵ + SE *knowledge*]

drop off v. [20C] to die. [abbr. DROP OFF THE TWIG]

drop off one's/the perch, to phr. [18C+] **1** to climb down, to adopt a less arrogant or condescending manner. **2** to die.

drop off the hook/hooks, to phr. [mid-19C–1920s] to die (cf. POP OFF THE HOOKS).

drop off the perch see DROP OFF ONE'S PERCH.

drop off the twig, to phr. [20C] to die, as if one were a bird (cf. HOP A TWIG).

drop of the creature see DROP n.².

drop one's bait-can, to phr. [19C] (US Black) to make a serious mistake (cf. DROP ONE'S CANDY). [the most serious mistake an angler can make is to drop their bait-can]

drop one's beads, to phr. [1950s+] (gay) accidentally to reveal one's homosexuality by a slip of the tongue or other blunder (cf. DROP HAIRPINS). [the stereotypical effeminacy of beads]

drop one's bundle, to phr. [late 19C+] (Aus./N.Z.) to panic, to lose (emotional) control, to give up hope.

drop one's candy/watermelon, to phr. [19C] to make a serious mistake.

drop one's/the gear, to phr. [1950s+] (Aus.) to undress (cf. GET ONE'S KIT OFF). [SE *drop* + GEAR n.¹ (5)]

drop one's guts, to phr. [1990s] to break wind.

drop one's leaf, to phr. [19C] to die. [autumnal imagery, but note GO OFF WITH THE FALL OF A LEAF]

drop one's load, to phr. [1970s+] (US Black) to reduce tension by having sexual intercourse (cf. EMPTY ONE'S TRASH). [SE *drop* + LOAD n.⁴ (2)]

drop one's watermelon see DROP ONE'S CANDY.

drop one's wing, to phr. [19C] (US Black) to flirt. [the way in which one bird drops a wing in order to attract the attention of another. Note UK dial. *wing down*, to court]

drop onto v. [mid-19C+] **1** to become aware of. **2** to accuse, to turn on someone suddenly. [the image of a bird of prey plummeting onto a victim]

dropout n. [20C] (orig. US) a dull, boring person. [SE *dropout*, one who abandons their education]

drop out v. [20C] to die.

dropped adj.¹ [mid-late 19C] of foodstuffs, coarse, stale, decaying (cf. ROUGH adj.¹).

dropped adj.² [1970s] (US campus) unofficially but dedicatedly engaged to be married. [the traditional gift by the man of a pendant or *drop*, bearing his initials]

dropped adj.³ [1980s+] arrested. [abbr. *dropped in (the) shit*]

dropper n.¹ see GOLD-DROPPER.

dropper n.² [late 17C–early 19C] a distiller (cf. RUM DROPPER). [the *drops* of alcohol created by the distillation process]

dropper n.³ (US) **1** [late 19C] a gun, a pistol. **2** [1920s+] a paid killer. [DROP v.⁴ (1)]

dropper n.⁴ [1930s–50s] one who passes counterfeit money, whether cheques or notes. [DROP v.⁵]

dropper n.⁵ (Aus./N.Z.) **1** [1910s+] one who delivers supplies of contraband liquor. **2** [1940s–50s] one who makes deliveries of goods to retailers (cf. SHODDY-DROPPER). [abbr. SHOP-DROPPER]

dropper n.⁶ [1950s+] (drugs) an eye-dropper used by narcotics addicts as a makeshift syringe when proper hypodermics are unavailable.

dropper v. [1950s] (drugs) to inject a drug. [DROPPER n.⁶]

dropping babies phr. [1990s] (US Black) giving birth to many children. [DROP v.²]

dropping member n. [19C] the flaccid penis, esp. when afflicted with (temporary) impotence or with venereal disease (cf. DROP n.⁷).

drop plates/plates on this mother, to phr. [1970s] (US Black) to lose one's temper, to get sufficiently annoyed to resort to physical violence. [fig. use of SE + abbr. MOTHER-FUCKER]

drops n. [1950s+] **1** money left in pre-arranged (secret) places for bribes, pay-offs, shares of a robbery etc. **2** the weekly housekeeping money for one's wife. [DROP n.⁵]

drop science v. [1990s] (US Black) to demonstrate wisdom or skill (cf. DROP KNOWLEDGE; SCIENCE n.²). [DROP v.⁶ + SCIENCE n.² (2); note W.I. dial. *science*, obeah, or ritual magic]

drop someone in it v. [1940s+] to put someone deliberately into difficulties. [*it* is trouble, but the implication is also of excrement]

drop sticks v. [1960s+] (UK/W.I. Und.) to work as a pickpocket.

dropsy n.¹ [20C] the habit of dropping things, usu. as *the dropsy*. [pun on SE *dropsy*, the falling sickness]

dropsy n.² [1930s+] **1** money. **2** a bribe. [SE *drop*/DROP n.⁵; the giver *drops* the money in someone's pocket or hand; a single nonce-use 'the silver dropsie' has been cited for 1616]

drop the apple, to phr. [1960s+] (US) to inform one in a way that is shocking or earth-shaking. [the role of the apple in the biblical Garden of Eden, or the story of Isaac Newton (1642–1727) discovering gravity through the fall of an apple]

drop the arm on, to phr. [1920+] (US) to arrest. [the physical action + the fig. SE *arm of the law*]

drop the ball, to phr. [1940s+] (orig. US) to make a mistake at a crucial moment. [sporting imagery]

drop the boom see LOWER THE BOOM.

drop the bucket, to phr. [1940s+] (Aus.) to 'leave in the lurch'.

drop/tip/turn the bucket on, to phr. [20C] (Aus.) to make damaging revelations about, esp. in political context.

drop the cue, to phr. [20C] to die (cf. TAKE THE LAST COUNT; STRIKE OUT). [billiards/snooker/pool imagery]

drop the duds, to phr. [20C] to get undressed. [SE *drop* + DUDS n.¹]

drop the gear see DROP ONE'S GEAR.

drop the hammer, to phr. [1970s+] (orig. US) to take decisive action.

drop the hook on, to phr. [20C] to make an arrest.

drop the lashes on, to phr. [20C] (W.I.) **1** to beat severely. **2** to make a surprising, shock decision.

drop the pill on, to phr. [20C] (US Und.) to execute in the gas chamber. [the gas is triggered by breaking open a pill of cyanide]

drop the rag, to phr. [late 19C+] (US) to give a signal, to set events in motion. [the dropping of a flag to signal the start]

drop the soap, to phr. [1950s+] to make oneself available for anal penetration. [orig. gay use, but also as a semi-jocular warning from one self-proclaimedly heterosexual young man to another, *I wouldn't drop the soap while he's around*]

drop to v. [early 19C+] to become aware of, to work out, to recognize. [DROP v.⁵ (1)]

drop-top n. [1990s] (US Black) a convertible, a soft-topped automobile.

drop trou v. [1950s] (US campus) to drop one's trousers (in public). [a classier version (supposedly) of MOON v.² (2)]

drop/throw words v. [20C] (W.I.) to utter veiled insults, to make sarcastic comments.

drought n. [1980s+] (orig. US campus) a period without sex or even dates.

drove adj. [20C] (US) very angry, infuriated. [SE *driven*]

drover's breakfast n. [1940s+] (Aus.) a look around and a cough (cf. AIR PIE AND A WALK AROUND). [SE *drover*, a shepherd; either the lack of 'civilized' amenities in the bush or his lack of desire for anything more]

drover's dog n. [1940s+] (Aus.) a useless or insignificant person, a drudge. [the *drover's dog* never stops working]

drover's guide, the n. [1920s+] (Aus.) gossip and rumour, reified as an imaginary newspaper (cf. BAGMAN'S GAZETTE).

drove up adj. [1970s] (US Black) excited. [DRIVE v.]

drown the brown turtle, to phr. [1990s] to defecate.

drown the miller, to phr. (orig. Scot.) **1** [19C] to go bankrupt. **2** [19C+] to put too much water in one's liquor or into one's dough mixture. [pvb. *too much water drowned the miller*, one can have too much of a good thing]

drown the shamrock, to phr. [20C] (Irish) to get very drunk on St Patrick's day. [the *shamrock* is the national plant of Ireland]

drowsy high n. [1980s+] (drugs) a depressant. [SE *drowsy* + HIGH n. (1); the effects]

drozel n. [early 18C] a young woman. [? archaic sp. *damozel*]

drube see DROOB.

drudge n. [late 19C] (US) whisky. [ety. unknown; ? link to SE *draught*]

drudge v. [1940s+] (W.I.) to wear boots regularly (rather than go bare-foot); shoes would normally have been worn only on special occasions. [SE *drudge*, a menial job; the implication is that the wearer has to wear shoes in their job]

drug adj. [1940s+] (US Black) exhausted, disinclined, bored; thus *I'm too drug to go out tonight.* [DRAG v.[10]]

drugged adj. [1960s] (US) annoyed, irritated. [DRAG v.[10]]

drugged cigarette n. [1980s+] (drugs) a cannabis cigarette; always used ironically. [ironic use of SE, coined by the tabloid press in the 1950s]

drugger n. [1940s+] a drug user (cf. DRUGGIE). [SE *drug*]

druggie/druggy n. **1** [20C] (US) a drugstore owner, a druggist. **2** [1960s+] a drug user; rarely used by anyone involved with drugs (cf. DRUGGER). [SE *drug*]

druggy adj. [1950s+] (orig. US) **1** of, pertaining to, or characteristic of recreational drugs or their users. **2** consisting of drug-takers.

drughead n. [1960s] (US) a consumer of illicit, recreational drugs. [SE *drug* + sfx. -HEAD (2)]

drugola n. [1970s+] (orig. US) bribery in which the pay-off comes not in money but in drugs. [SE *drug* + sfx. -OLA]

drugstore cowboy n. [1920s+] (US) a man, usu. a youth, who frequents drugstores for no other reason than meeting his friends, gossiping and wasting time (cf. CORNER COWBOY).

drugstore stuff n. [1960s+] (US drugs) painkillers, synthetic opiates, available from drugstores but less effective than heroin.

drukkie n. [20C] (S.Afr.) a hug, an affectionate squeeze. [Afk. *druk*, squeeze]

drum n.[1] [late 18C–late 19C] the road, the street. [Gk. *dromos*, thence Rom. *drom*]

drum n.[2] **1** [19C+] a house, a home. **2** [19C+] a prison cell. **3** [late 19C–1950s] (US) a saloon, a drinking house, a speak-easy. **4** [mid-19C] a brothel. [ety. unknown; ? the image of the hollow drum resembling a hollow house or room or the use of DRUM n.[1] as a fig. house for wandering gypsies and tinkers]

drum n.[3] [mid-19C+] (Aus.) a pack (cf. HUMP ONE'S DRUM; SWAG n.[1]). [the shape of the rolled pack]

drum n.[4] [1910s+] a tin or can in which tea etc is made. [shape]

drum n.[5] [1940s+] (Aus.) a warning, a piece of information, esp. a racing tip. [the image of drummers beating out information for transmission through jungles etc]

drum, the n.[6] [1940s+] (Aus.) the facts. true or reliable information. [DRUM n.[5]]

drum v.[1] [1910s+] (Aus.) to inform, to 'tip off'. [DRUM n.[5]]

drum v.[2] [1920s+] **1** to knock on a front door to ascertain whether or not the home owner is in; if they are not, the house is broken into and robbed. **2** to steal from an empty or unoccupied house. [DRUM n.[2] (1)]

drummed up adj. [late 19C+] artificially inflated, made to appear more important than reality allows. [SE *drum*, to obtain custom, draw attention, make an announcement, by beating a drum]

drummer n.[1] [mid-19C] a thug who robbed drunks, often after helping them to oblivion with a knock-out draught. [? the 'beating' he administered]

drummer n.[2] [mid-19C+] (US) a commercial traveller, a salesman. [SE *drum up trade* + DRUM n.[1]]

drummer n.[3] [late 19C] (Aus./N.Z.) an itinerant (cf. SWAGMAN n.[2]). [DRUM n.[1]]

drummer n.[4] (Aus./N.Z.) [late 19C+] the laziest and therefore the slowest shearer in a shed (cf. GUN n.[2]). [DRUMMER n.[2]; i.e. a commercial traveller is not a *real* workman]

drummer n.[5] [1960s+] a thief who specializes in robbing houses while their occupants are out, usu. for a short time. [DRUM v.[2]]

drumming n. [1920s+] (Und.) posing as a door-to-door sales-man to tour houses and thus identify empty ones, ripe for robbery. [DRUM v.[2]]

drumstick n. [19C–1900s] the penis (cf. BAT n.[7]).

drumstick case n. [1970s+] (US Black) rape. [DRUMSTICK (but note DRUMSTICKS n. (2)) + SE *case*, a legal proceeding]

drumstick cases n. [mid-19C] trousers. [DRUMSTICKS n. (1) + SE *cases*]

drumsticks n. **1** [mid-19C+] the legs. **2** [1970s+] (US Black) the well-rounded thighs of an attractive woman. [(2) ext. of (1) but ? reflects the shape of a chicken drumstick]

drum-up n. [1910s+] the preparation of a cup of tea (cf. BREW-UP n.). [DRUM n.[4]]

drum up v. [1920s+] **1** to make tea in a billy-can or similar container. **2** to prepare a meal under rough conditions (typically on a battlefield or out of doors). **3** to obtain or create anything despite a difficult situation. [DRUM n.[4]]

drunk n. [late 18C+] (orig. US) a bout of drinking, usu. to excess or oblivion.

drunk as a ... phr. the images of drunkenness are many and varied, for all that some comparisons seem somewhat far-fetched. All these nouns have been allied with the phr. *drunk as a ... bastard, bat, beggar, besom, big owl, boiled owl, bowdow, brewer's fart, cook, coon, coot, cooter, dog, fiddler, fiddler's bitch, fish, fly, fowl, Gosport fiddler, hog, king, little red wagon, log, lord, monkey, Perraner, pig, piper, poet, rolling fart, sailor, skunk in a trunk, sow, swine, tapster, tick, top, wheelbarrow* (cf. PISSED AS A ...).

drunk/full as a boiled-fresh/fresh-boiled owl phr. [late 19C+] (US) very drunk; intensified as *drunker than a boiled owl.*

drunk as a cootie phr. [20C] very drunk (cf. DRUNK AS COOTER BROWN). [COOTIE n.[2]]

drunk as a duck phr. [1910s+] drunk, often ext. by *and don't give a fuck/quack.*

drunk as a fresh-boiled owl see DRUNK AS A BOILED OWL.

drunk as an emperor phr. [late 18C] very drunk. ['ten times as drunk as a lord' (Grose, 1796)]

drunk as a polony *phr.* [late 19C] extremely drunk. [? Fr. phr *soul comme un Polonnais*, drunk as a Pole (supposedly mocking the Polish-French Maréchal de Saxe, a great tippler), although the phr. might simply mean drunk as a POLONY or sausage, which cannot stand upright]

drunk as a rat *phr.* [19C+] very drunk.

drunk as Chloe *phr.* [early 19C+] very drunk (cf. BLIND AS CHLOE). [20C use mainly Aus; orig. cited by Jon Bee (1823), who noted: 'she must have been an uproarious lass.' Possibly popularized in Aus. by the picture, *Chloe*, rejected in 1883 by the Melbourne National Gallery and bought by a well-known local hotel, where it became a point of attraction for many visitors]

drunk as cooter brown *phr.* [1900s–40s] (orig. US Black) very drunk (cf. DRUNK AS A COOTIE). [? anecdotal]

drunk as david's sow *phr.* [late 18C–mid-19C] very drunk. [according to Grose (1785), the phrase, which dates at least to Ray's *Proverbs* (1678), refers to one David Lloyd who had both a 6-legged sow and an alcoholic wife. On one occasion the wife, hoping to sleep off her excesses, threw out the sow and passed out in the stye. Unfortunately, Lloyd had chosen this time to exhibit his 6-legged freak to a group of friends. He escorted them to the stye, announcing: 'There's a sow for you, did you ever see another?' The friends saw only his wife and responded that it was indeed the drunkenest sow they had ever seen. The phrase stuck]

drunk as dogshit *phr.* [1980s+] very drunk.

drunk as floey *phr.* [late 19C–1900s] very drunk. [? misuse of DRUNK AS CHLOE]

drunked up/out *adj.* [1940s+] (US) drunk.

drunken piece *n.* [1910s–20s] a drunkard.

drunken tinker *n.* [16C–19C] a ne'er-do-well who, accompanied by his woman, wanders the country, mixing villainy and legitimate work, pursuing neither, it appears, with particular enthusiasm (cf. CANTING CREW; PRIG n.¹).

drunkery *n.* [19C] a cheap saloon (cf. GIN-MILL). [SE *drunk* + sfx. -*ery*]

drunkie/drunkman *n.* [1950s+] (W.I.) a drunkard.

drunkie/drunky *adj.* [mid-19C+] (US) drunken; esp. with a name, e.g. *drunkie John.*

drunkin/drunking *adj.* [1950s+] (W.I.) extremely drunk. [pron. of SE *drunken*]

drunkman *see* DRUNKIE n.

drunk-on *n.* [mid-19C–1920s] (US) the state of being drunk. [on pattern of HARD-ON]

drunk tank *n.* [1940s+] (US) short-term lock-up for a night's drunk arrests before sending them to court. [SE *drunk* n. + TANK n.²]

drunk to the pulp *phr.* [1970s] (US Black) drunk to the point of passing out.

drunky *see* DRUNKIE adj.

Druriolanus *n.* [late 19C] the Drury Lane Theatre, London. [its telegraphic address, a pun on Shakespeare's *Coriolanus*, coined by its celebrated manager Augustus Harris (1852–96), who (see the writings of J.B. Booth) was also called by the nickname]

Drury Lane ague *n.* [mid-18C–early 19C] venereal disease, esp. gonorrhoea (cf. BARNWELL AGUE). [the reputation of *Drury Lane* as a centre of prostitution]

Drury Lane vestal *n.* [mid-18C–early 19C] a prostitute (cf. PICKETHATCH VESTAL). [for ety. *see* DRURY LANE AGUE]

druthers *n.* [late 19C+] (orig. US) an alternative choice, a preference, esp. in phr. *have one's druthers*, to gain one's preference. [pron. of SE *I'd rather*]

dry, the *n.*¹ [mid-19C+] (Aus.) the dry season.

dry, the *n.*² [late 19C] champagne. [the English predilection for dry champagne rather than medium or sweet]

dry *n.*³ [late 19C+] (US) a Prohibitionist, dedicated to the cause of eradicating alcohol. [the term was picked up under Margaret Thatcher's rule of the UK Conservative party to define those who opposed policies dedicated to free-ranging, deregulated market forces and the resulting mass-unemployment, false economic booms etc]

dry *adj.* [20C] drunk. [play on SE *dry*, thirsty]

dry *v.* [1940s+] (W.I.) to deprive a person of everything they possess. [mainly in children's games]

dry as a... *phr.* (N.Z.) various phr. used to denote the intensity of one's thirst; [late 19C] *dry as a sack of gum-dust*, [1900s] *dry as a cocky's selection* [i.e. a small farm] *after a long drought*, [1910s] *dry as the rim of a lime-burner's hat*, [1950s+] *dry as a wooden god.*

dry as a dead dingo's donger *phr.* [1980s] (Aus.) of weather or one's throat, extremely dry (cf. DRY AS A POMMIE'S BATH-MAT).

dry as a Pommie's bath-mat/towel *phr.* [1980s] (Aus.) extremely dry. [the phr. is used of weather, but its ref. is to the belief that British immigrants (cf. POMMIE) don't wash]

dryball *n.* [1920s] (US campus) a student who does nothing but study. [they refuse to 'get wet', i.e. to drink and enjoy themselves]

dry balls *n.* [1930s–40s] (US) an impotent man. [SE *dry* + BALLS n.¹; i.e. they have 'dried up']

dry bath *n.* [1930s+] (Und.) the search of a prisoner who has been first stripped naked.

dry behind the ears *phr.* [1910s+] (US) experienced, sophisticated. [antonym of WET BEHIND THE EARS]

dry bob *n.*¹ [late 17C–18C] a smart response, sharp repartee.

dry bob/dry-bob *n.*² [late 17C+] sex without ejaculation by the man (cf. DRY FUCK n.). [SE *dry bob*, a blow that fails to break the skin]

dry-clean Methodist *n.* [20C] a Methodist (cf. WET-WASH BAPTIST). [Methodists baptize by sprinkling, rather than total immersion]

dry Dutch courage *n.* [1960s+] narcotics, esp. as a fig. 'killer of pain'. [a modern play on the traditionally wet dutch courage which refers to alcohol]

dry fuck *n.* (orig. US) **1** [1930s+] a simulated act of sexual intercourse, without penetration and usu. without removing the clothes. **2** [1930s+] an unsatisfactory act of intercourse, esp. one that does not result in ejaculation or orgasm. **3** [1940s] something tedious or disappointing. **4** [1950s+] (gay) anal intercourse without any form of lubricant. [SE *dry* + FUCK n.¹]

dry fuck *v.* [1920s+] to simulate intercourse by rubbing one's clothed body against that of one's partner. [DRY FUCK n.]

dryfucking *adj.* [1930s+] (orig. US) infuriating, disappointing and other negs., relevant to context. [fig. use of DRY FUCK n.]

dry gin *n.* [1930s] (W.I.) marijuana. [GANJA + pun on SE]

dry goods *n.*¹ [mid-late 19C] (US) a derog. term for a woman. [play on SE *dry/dry goods*]

dry goods *n.*² **1** [mid-19C–1960s] (US) clothing. **2** [1920s–40s] (US Black) a style of suit characterized by a long, draped jacket with padded shoulders and high-waisted, tapering trousers (cf. ZOOT SUIT). [retail jargon *dry goods*, items of drapery, haberdashery etc, as opposed to groceries]

dry gulch *v.* [1930s+] (US) to murder, to assault. [Western outlaws often ambushed and shot their victim as he passed through the narrow confines of a SE *dry gulch*, or f. the rustlers' killing of stolen animals by driving them over the edge of such a gulch]

dry head *n.* [1940s+] (W.I.) a bald person (cf. DRY SKULL).

dry-head/-headed *adj.* [1930s+] (W.I.) bald, when used of women it is an insult.

dry high *n.* [1980s+] (drugs) cannabis. [play on SE *sky high*]

dry horrors *n.* [1980s+] (Aus. drugs) a dry mouth and throat after smoking marijuana. [SE *dry* + HORRORS n. (4)]

dry hump *v.* [1920s+] to simulate intercourse (cf. DRY FUCK). [SE *dry* + HUMP v.[1]]

dry jag *n.* [1900s] (US) a sense of brief excitement similar to that produced by alcohol, but without any drinking. [SE *dry* + JAG n.[1]]

dry land *n.* [1970s] (US Black) a situation of safety; thus *dry land!* all clear. [one has fig. reached *dry land*]

dry land? *phr.* [mid-19C] you understand? [rhy. sl.]

dry-land sailor *n.* [19C] a criminal beggar who claims to have suffered shipwreck or piracy and requests alms to return home (cf. FRESHWATER MARINER).

dry money *n.* [1900s] (Irish) cash, ready money.

dry-mouthed widow *n.* [1960s+] of a man, masturbation (cf. FIVE-FINGERED WIDOW). [one's hand, rather than the vagina]

dry out *v.* [20C] (orig. US) to recover from alcoholism or from a bout of excessive drinking.

dry ride *n.* [1930s+] a simulated act of sexual intercourse, without penetration and usu. without removing the clothes (cf. DRY FUCK n.). [SE *dry* + RIDE n.[3] (1)]

dry room *n.* [19C] a damp prison cell. [irony]

dry run *n.* [1940s+] a test, a rehearsal.

dry screw *v.* [1920s] (US) to simulate intercourse. [var. on DRY FUCK v.]

dry shave *v.*[1] [17C–18C] to deceive, to defraud, to rob.

dry shave *v.*[2] [19C+] to rub one's knuckles hard across one's victim's skull (cf. DUTCH RUB; NOOGIE). [orig. a milit. punishment, men who had failed to shave adequately were roughly shaved on the parade-ground without benefit of soap or water]

dry skull *n.* [1950s] (W.I.) a completely bald person (cf. DRY HEAD).

dry snap *v.* [1940s+] to fire a gun that is either empty or does not have a round ready in the barrel.

dry snitch *v.* [1950s+] (US prison) to inform by innuendo, rather than by direct accusation. [SE *dry* + SNITCH v.]

dry stick *n.* [20C] an unpleasant, humourless person. [SE *dry* + STICK n.[7]]

dry straight *v.* [late 19C–1930s] to work out in time. [racing imagery]

dry up *v.* [mid-19C+] **1** to stop talking. **2** to refuse to give information (to the police).

dry up! *excl.* [mid-19C+] be quiet! [DRY UP v.]

dry whisky *n.* [19C+] peyote. [the mildly euphoric effect of chewing the 'buttons' of the cactus, *Lophophora williamsii*; presumably the quantities in question are small, since a full dosage of peyote can be highly hallucinogenic]

D.S., the *n.* [1960s+] *D*rug *S*quad. [abbr.]

d.t. *n.* [1920s+] (US) a *d*etective, in later 20C esp. a member of the drug squad. [abbr.]

d/t *n.* [1970s+] in sex contact advertisements, *d*irty *t*alk. [abbr.]

d.t. centre *n.* [late 19C–1900s] a small literary club. [DTS and thus a ref. to the enthusiastic drinking that takes place]

d.t.e. *n.* [1990s] a latterday hippie (cf. CRUNCHY). [abbr. *d*own *t*o *e*arth]

d.t.r. *phr.* [1990s] (US campus) *d*efining *t*he *r*elationship. [abbr.; used of a conversation, often between the partners]

DTs *n.* [mid-19C+] *d*elirium *t*remens (cf. SHAKES). [abbr.]

dub *n.*[1] [late 17C–mid-19C] a key, a pick-lock; thus *dubs*, a bunch of keys (cf. DUBBER n.[1]; DUBS n.[1]; DUBSMAN; DUB UP v.[2]). [DUB v.]

dub *n.*[2] (US campus) **1** [late 19C–1960s] a failure, an incompetent, a novice, an oaf. **2** [late 19C–1960s] something that fails, a disaster. [? SE *dubbed*, blunted, without a point]

dub *n.*[3] [1950s] (N.Z.) a *d*ouble-decker tram. [abbr./pron.]

dub *n.*[4] [1970s] a cigarette. [? link to DUB v. (2), i.e. it 'shuts up' one's mouth or northern dial. *tab*, a cigarette]

dub *n.*[5] [1940s+] (Aus./N.Z.) a lavatory. [abbr. of *double-you see*, i.e. W.C.]

dub *n.*[6] [1970s+] (W.I./UK Black) music with or without vocals invariably spiced up with snatches of echo and similar special effects, created by skilful, artistic re-engineering of recorded tracks.

dub *n.*[7] [1990s] a piece of graffito, painted on a wall or train. [SE *dub*, to smear, but given the lifestyle of the artists note DUB n.[6]]

dub *adj.* [mid-19C] bad. [backsl.]

dub *v.* **1** [late 17C] to open a door. **2** [mid-18C+] to lock up, to shut up, esp. in prison use. [dial. *dup*, to open; ult. SE *do up*]

dub along/around *v.* [late 19C–1960s] (US campus) to idle, to loaf, to fool about.

dubash *n.* [mid-19C–1900s] (Anglo-Ind.) **1** an agent. **2** an interpreter. **3** a commissionaire. [Hind. *dobashi*, a two-language man]

dubay *n.* [1990s] (Native Aus.) a woman. [? Aboriginal language]

dubbe *n.* [1990s] (drugs) cannabis. [DOOBIE n.[1]]

dubber *n.*[1] [late 17C–early 18C] a thief who specializes in picking locks. [DUB n.[1]]

dubber *n.*[2] [18C–19C] the mouth; thus imper. phr. *mum your dubber*, shut up. [DUB n.[1]; i.e. something that opens and shuts]

dubber *n.*[3] [1970s] (US campus) cigarette (cf. DUB n.[4]).

dubbies *n.* [1960s+] the female breasts. [var. on BUBBIES]

dubee *see* DOOBIE n.[1].

dub in *v.* [early 19C+] to pay a share of money, to contribute. [? DUB v. (1); thus 'open' one's pocket or purse]

Dublin *n.* [20C] (US) the Irish area of a town or city. [*Dublin*, the capital of the Republic of Ireland]

Dublin fair *n.* [20C] (Aus.) the hair. [rhy. sl.]

Dublin jackeen *see* JACKEEN.

Dublin University graduate *n.* [1950s+] a particularly stupid person. [an unexceptional example of the clichéd condemnation of the Irish as fools]

dub off *v.* [1910s] (US) to masturbate (cf. BEAT OFF). [? SE *dub*, to beat blunt]

dubry *see* DOOBRIE.

dubs *n.*[1] [18C–mid-19C] a bunch of keys. [DUB n.[1]]

dubs *n.*[2] [1930s+] (Aus.) marbles. [SE *doubles*]

dubsman *n.* [mid-19C] a prison warder or turnkey. [DUBS n.[1] + sfx. -MAN]

dub the gigger, to *phr.* [late 17C–18C] to open a door (cf. DUP THE JIGGER). [DUB v. (1) + GIGGER n.[1]]

dub up *v.*[1] [early 19C+] to pay over money, to pay on demand (cf. DUB IN). [ety. unknown; ? link to Essex dial. dubs, money, itself f. DIBBS]]

dub up *v.*[2] [early 19C+] to lock up in a cell. [DUB v. (2)]

duby *see* DOOBIE n.[1].

ducat *n.* **1** [late 18C–late 19C] usu. in pl., money, cash (cf. DUCKIES). **2** [mid-19C+] (US) $1. **3** [mid-19C+] a ticket, for the theatre, a sporting event etc (cf. DUCKET). [SE *ducat*. 'A gold coin of varying value, formerly in use in most European countries. That current in Holland, Russia, Austria and Sweden being equivalent to about 9s 4d. Also applied to a silver coin of Italy, value about 3s 6d' (*OED*). The UK use faded by 20C, but *ducat* reappeared in the US *c.*1950]

duce *n.* [mid–late 19C] twopence; thus *duce hog*, two shillings (10p). [DEUCE n.[2] (2)]

ducey *n.* [1920s–50s] (US) the penis. [ety. unknown; ? link to SE *juicy*]

duchess *n.*[1] **1** [late 17C–late 18C] a good-looking, even showy woman. **2** [19C+] a general term of address to a woman. **3** [late

19C+] a woman or girl. **4** [1920s+] a woman who is making money in films.

duchess n.² [late 18C] **1** a woman who has intercourse while still half-dressed. **2** a man who has intercourse without removing his boots; thus *make a duchess*, to have intercourse in this spontaneous manner. [? the diary of Sarah, *Duchess* of Marlborough (1660–1744), who, following the return of her husband, wrote: 'Today my Lord returned from the wars and pleasured me twice in his top-boots']

duchess/duchess of fife n.³ [mid-19C+] wife (cf. DUTCH n.⁵). [rhy. sl.]

duchess v. [1960s+] (Aus.) to treat extremely well, as it were, like a duchess.

duchess of puddle-dock see COUNTESS OF PUDDLE-DOCK.

duchill/ducle n. [20C] (Ulster) a general term of abuse. [? SE *dunghill* or Scot. *dochle*, an easy-going man]

duck n.¹ **1** [late 16C+] a lover, a sweetheart, a general term of affection. **2** [mid-19C–1900s] a fellow, a person, a CUSTOMER.

duck n.² [19C] (Anglo-Ind.) a nickname for soldiers of the Bombay Presidency. [the Bombay *duck*, the bummalo (*Harpodon nehereus*), a small local fish, usu. eaten dried as a relish]

duck n.³ [early 19C+] a fine example of. [ext. use of DUCK n.¹ (1)]

duck n.⁴ [mid-19C] a faggot, a parcel of meat scraps sold cheaply to the poor. [Yorkshire dial.]

duck n.⁵ [late 19C–1900s] an evasion; thus *do a duck*, to keep out of sight, to leave; *play the duck* [1930s+] (US) to evade notice, to keep out of sight. [SE *duck*, to bow the head suddenly]

duck n.⁶ [20C] (US) a cigarette or cigar end; thus *shoot ducks*, to relight a cigar or cigarette end (cf. DRAKE n.; DUCK BUDDY).

duck n.⁷ [20C] **1** (US Und.) a gullible fool. **2** (US campus) a misfit, an unappealing person. [? SE *lame duck*]

duck n.⁸ [1900s–10s] (US) a container used to bring back beer from the saloon; thus *chase the duck*, to bring home beer in a bucket or pail (cf. GROWLER n.³). [? its spout resembles a duck's neck]

duck n.⁹ [1910s+] (US) in gambling, two. [DEUCE n.² (2)]

duck n.¹⁰ [1940s–50s] (US) a ticket, e.g. for the theatre, a sporting event. [abbr. DUCAT n. (3)]

duck n.¹¹ [1950s–60s] (US) a type of hairstyle in which the back turns up. [DUCK'S ARSE]

duck n.¹² [1980s+] **1** (US campus) a snob, a conceited, stuck-up young woman. **2** an unpleasant person. [? SE *duchess*]

duck v.¹ [late 19C+] (orig. US) to avoid. [SE *duck*/DUCK n.⁵]

duck v.² [1960s+] to bend over in preparation for anal intercourse, usu. in phr. *fuck, suck and duck*.

duck buddy n. [1910s+] (US) one who, bereft of a cigarette themself, is given the last few puffs on a friend's. [DUCK n.⁶ + BUDDY n.]

duckbutt n. [1930s+] (US) a short person. [SE *duck* + BUTT n.¹]

duck butter n. [1930s+] (US) **1** semen. **2** smegma. [the smell, reminiscent of duck droppings + the colour of butter]

ducket n. [mid-late 19C] (US) a ticket. [var. on DUCAT n. (3)]

duckets/duckettes n. [1990s] (US Black/teen) money, cash (cf. DUCAT). [var. on DUCKET]

duckett n. [mid-late 19C] a hawker's license. [SE *ducket*, a ticket]

duckettes see DUCKETS.

duck fart n. [1940s–60s] (N.Z. juv.) the 'plop' of a stone falling into water.

duck fit n. [1900s–20s] (US) a temper tantrum. [one resembles an angry duck]

duck-fucker n. [1970s+] (US) an unpleasant, unpopular person. [SE *duck* + FUCKER; note Grose (1785): '*Duck f-ck-r*, The man who has care of the poultry on board a ship of war']

duckhead n. [1970s+] (US Black) a woman with short, nappy hair (cf. DUCK'S BUTT). [? resemblance]

duck-house door n. [20C] (Ulster) a very thick slice of bread (and butter) (cf. DOORSTEP).

duckies n. [1970s+] (US Black) money. [DUCAT]

duck of a phr. [early 19C+] a fine example of, e.g. a *duck of a bonnet*. [DUCK n.³]

duck out/duck out of v. [late 19C+] **1** to back out, to withdraw. **2** to make off, to abscond. **3** to default on, to avoid. [DUCK v.¹]

duckpond n. [19C] the vagina (cf. DAMP n.).

ducks n. [mid-17C+] a term of address, generally affectionate or friendly. [DUCK n.¹ (1)]

ducks! excl. [1950s+] (US, usu. juv.) a claim, esp. a claim of first rights to something (cf. CHECKS!).

ducks and drakes n. [1960s] (Aus.) delirium tremens. [rhy. sl. *ducks and drakes* = SHAKES]

ducks and geese n. [20C] (Aus.) the police. [rhy. sl.]

duck's arse/ass n. [1950s+] (orig. US) a type of hairstyle, esp. as adopted by teddyboys and rockers, in which the back of the hair is turned upwards in a manner similar to a duck's tail (cf. D.A.; DUCK n.¹¹; DUCKTAIL). [SE *duck* + ARSE n.¹ (1)]

duck's butt n. [1970s] (US Black) a woman with unkempt hair (cf. DUCKHEAD). [? resemblance; presumably it sticks up at the back]

duck's dinner n. [1990s] (Aus.) a drink of water, but no food to accompany it.

duck's disease n. [1920s] having short legs. [like a duck, one waddles around]

duck shoot n. [1940s+] (orig. milit.) a simple operation. ['like shooting ducks on a pond']

duck-shoving n. [1930s+] (Aus./N.Z.) fighting for status, rank, position, esp. in political terms; thus *duck-shover*, one who uses unfair business methods. [19C cabman's jargon *duck-shoving*, touting for passengers rather than waiting one's turn in line; ult. image is of the farmyard]

duck's neck n. [20C] (Aus.) a cheque. [rhy. sl.]

duck soup n. [1910s+] (US) **1** anything simple, easy (cf. APPLE SAUCE n.⁴). **2** a person who is easily persuaded or victimized. **3** a guaranteed success. **4** something that suits one perfectly.

duck's quack n. [1920s] (US) the very best (cf. ANT'S PANTS).

ducktail n. [1950s] **1** a type of hairstyle in which the back of the hair is turned upwards in a manner similar to a duck's tail (cf. DUCK'S ARSE). **2** (S.Afr.) a teddyboy. [the preferred hairstyle of the teen sub-culture]

duck the scone, to phr. [1930s+] (Aus.) to plead guilty in court (cf. BOW THE CRUMPET; NOD THE NUT). [SE *duck* + SCONE n.¹]

ducky n. [late 19C+] a term of address (cf. DUCKS n.).

ducky adj. [late 19C+] sweet, delightful, charming. [DUCK n.¹; an example of the apparent charm of farmyard animals (cf. CHICK n.³); late 20C use generally ironic]

ducle see DUCHILL.

duct n. [1980s+] (drugs) cocaine. [ety. unknown; ? link to SE *duct*, a pipe, i.e. the nasal passages or the crack pipe]

dud/dudde n.¹ [15C] an article of clothing, esp. a cloak made from rough, coarse cloth (cf. DUDS n.¹). [ety. unknown]

dud n.² **1** [early 19C+] one who is a failure, an incompetent, a weakling, a bore. **2** [late 19C+] anything that lit. or fig. 'does not work'. **3** [1920s–30s] a thing or event that is a failure, a disappointment, a 'flop'. [? DUDS n.¹ (1), clothes, thence rags and thus one who dresses in them, esp. a *dudman*, a scarecrow]

dud v. [20C] (US) to dress up, to dress smartly. [DUDS n.¹ (1)]

dudde *see* DUD n.[1].

dudder/whispering dudder *n.* [18C–mid-19C] a criminal beggar who wanders the country, selling goods that have supposedly been smuggled through the customs; thus capitalizing on the greed and gullibility of their provincial customers. The clandestine style of their encounter with a customer gives the synon. *whispering dudder* (cf. DUFFER n.[1]; SHAM-LEGGER). [DUDS n.[1]]

dud-dropper *n.* [1940s+] (Aus.) **1** a seller of stolen or inferior clothes. **2** a confidence trickster specializing in selling otherwise second-rate goods to those who believe that they have 'fallen off the back of a lorry'. [DUDS n.[1] + DROPPER n.[5]]

dude *n.* **1** [late 19C+] (orig. US) a man, a fellow. **2** [late 19C+] (orig. US) an overdressed, showy person, a fop or dandy. **3** [1960s–70s] (US campus) a fool. **4** [1960s+] (US) a thing. **5** [1970s+] (US campus) a person, irrespective of gender. [DUDS n.[1] or abbr. SE *attitude*. The term gained a whole new currency, especial among the pre-teens, with the popularity c.1990 of the cartoon characters Teenage Mutant Ninja Turtles, where it featured heavily]

dude! *excl.* [1990s] (US campus) a mild excl., synon. with SE *wow!* GEE! SHIT!, and generally implying agreement or approval.

duded up *adj.* [19C+] (US) dressed up, esp. for a party or night out (cf. DOLLED OUT). [DUDE UP]

dude man! *excl.* [1980s+] (US campus) what's happening? what's up?

dudester *n.* [1980s] (US) a person, irrespective of gender. [DUDE n. (5) + sfx. -STER]

dudette *n.* [1980s+] (US) a girl, a woman. [DUDE n. (5) + fem. sfx. -*ette*]

dude up *v.* [late 19C+] (US) to dress (oneself) up. [DUDE n. (2); ult. DUDS n.[1]]

dudhead *n.* [1960s] (US) an idiot. [DUD n.[2] + sfx. -HEAD (1)]

dudley *n.* [1980s] (US teen) a failure, a loser. [DUD n.[2] + play on proper name *Dudley*]

duds *n.*[1] **1** [mid-15C+] clothing. **2** [mid-17C+] one's possessions, one's things in general. [DUD n.[1]]

duds *n.*[2] [1960s] (N.Z.) the female breasts. [? BUB n.[4]]

dudsman *n.* [18C–mid-19C] a criminal beggar who wanders the country (cf. DUDDER).

dud up *v.* [1930s+] (Aus.) to misinform, to cheat, to swindle; thus *dudder*(-*upper*), one who fraudulently misrepresents the price and/or value of the goods they are selling, e.g. selling dyed aspirins as 'purple hearts', or claiming that perfectly legitimately purchased goods are actually 'off the back of a lorry' (and thus more glamorous) (cf. DUDDER). [DUD n.[2]]

'due *n.* [1980s+] (drugs) the resi*due* that remains in a pipe after smoking freebase cocaine. [abbr.]

due *adv.* [1950s+] (Und.) due to be arrested, as part of the everyday problems of a regular, known criminal, irrespective of whether the person in question had actually committed the crime of which he was suspected.

dues *n.* [19C] money.

duey *see* DOOE.

duff *n.*[1] **1** [late 18C] something useless or worthless. **2** [late 19C+] counterfeit money, smuggled goods. [? fig. use of dial. *duff*, a coward]

duff *n.*[2] [late 19C+] the buttocks. [west Yorkshire dial. *duff*, the posterior]

duff *n.*[3] [1950s] (US) a *duff*el bag. [abbr.]

duff *adj.* [late 19C+] useless, broken down. [DUFF n.[1]]

duff *v.*[1] [late 18C–19C] **1** to sell ordinary goods that are touted as smuggled contraband (cf. SHAM-LEGGER). **2** [19C] to make old goods look like new (cf. DUFFER n.[1]). **3** [mid–late 19C] (Aus.) to alter the brands on (stolen) cattle. **4** [mid–late 19C] (Aus.) to steal (cattle). [DUFF n.[1]]

duff *v.*[2] **1** [mid-19C] to cheat out of, to defraud. **2** [late 19C+] to blunder, to make a mess of. [DUFF n.[1]]

duff *v.*[3] [late 19C–1940s] to become foggy or hazy. [dial. *duff*, coal dust]

duff *v.*[4] [1960s] (US) to have sexual intercourse with. [DUFF n.[2] or fig. use of DUFF UP]

duff around *v.* [20C] to sit about, to act lazily. [DUFF n.[2]]

duffer *n.*[1] [mid-18C–19C] (Und.) **1** a hawker or pedlar. **2** a crooked salesman who pretends to deal in smuggled goods but whose stock is actually cheap, mass-produced items, sold at a substantial mark-up and who targets especially provincials up in London, mainly from a site at St Clement's Church in the Strand (cf. LUMPER n.[1]; SHAM-LEGGER). [DUFF v.[1]]

duffer *n.*[2] [19C+] **1** (prison) food, esp. pudding. **2** (US tramp/ prison) bread. [SE *dough*]

duffer *n.*[3] [mid–late 19C] a counterfeit coin or article; any spurious article. [DUFF n.[1] (2)]

duffer *n.*[4] [mid-19C+] **1** an incompetent, foolish person. **2** (Aus.) an unproductive mine or goldfield. [DUFF n.[1] (1); i.e. the item is 'no good' and so is the person. or Scot. *duffar*, a blunt, stupid person, or *dofart*, *doofart*, *dowfart*, a dull, heavy-headed, inactive fellow. Note angling jargon [1920s] *duffer's fortnight*, a fortnight of the angling season during which trout are supposed to be caught easily]

duffer *n.*[5] [late 19C] (Aus.) a cattle-stealer. [DUFF v.[1] (4)]

duffer *n.*[6] [1980s+] (drugs) a girl or woman who offers sex in return for drugs (cf. DOGGING n.[1]). [DUFF v.[4]]

duffer *v.*[1] [mid-19C+] (Aus.) **1** for a mine or goldfield to prove unproductive. **2** for a miner or prospector to fail in their searches. [DUFFER n.[4] (2)]

duffer *v.*[2] [late 19C] (Aus.) **1** to steal cattle. **2** to pasture one's stock illicitly on another person's land. [DUFF v.[1] (4)]

duffing *n.* [mid-19C] passing off of a worthless article as valuable. [DUFF v.[1] (1)]

duffing *adj.* **1** [mid-19C] worthless, false, esp. of goods sold as more valuable than they really are. **2** [late 19C] foolish, incompetent. [DUFF adj.]

duff up/over *v.* [1930s+] to beat up. [orig. RAF jargon; ? fig. use of DUFF v.[2] but more likely Scot. *duff*, to hit, to strike]

duffus *n.* [1940s] (US) the posterior, the buttocks. [var. on DUFF n.[2]]

duffy *n.*[1] [early 19C] a quarter-pint of gin. [? a brandname; var. on DAFFY n. (1)]

duffy *n.*[2] [1900s] (US) bread. [var. on DUFFER n.[2]]

duffy *n.*[3] [1920s–30s] (US) a derby hat. [? its popularity among Irish wearers; i.e. the common surname *Duffy*]

dufus *n.* [1960s+] **1** an eccentric, foolish or gauche person. **2** a thingummyjig. [var. on DOOFUS n.]

dugie *see* DUJI.

dug-in *adj.* [1910s+] safe, secure, entrenched, firmly established in a position. [imagery of 'digging in' for safety during a battle]

dug-out *n.* [1910s+] an old-fashioned person, either in ideas or appearance, esp. a retired officer etc, recalled for temporary military service. [SE *dugout*, a roofed shelter used in trench warfare]

dugs *n.* [19C] female breasts (cf. CREAM JUGS). [SE *dug*, the udder or teat of a female animal]

duh *n.* [1950s+] (S.Afr.) a fool. [echoic of a stupid person's uncomprehending grunt]

duh! *excl.* [1990s] a grunt of incomprehension. [echoic; popularized by the TV cartoon *The Simpsons*]

duji/dogie/doogie/doogy/doojee/dugie/dujie *n.* [1950s+] (drugs) heroin. [ety. unknown]

duke *n.*[1] [late 17C–early 18C; 1930s+] a showy, ostentatious man. [abbr. RUM DUKE; 20C use is US although its root may lie in the more recent DUDE n. (2)]

duke *n.*[2] [mid-19C] gin. [used by servants in upper-class houses]

duke *n.*[3] (US) **1** [mid-19C+] a hand, usu. in pl. **2** [1940s] a hand of cards. **3** [1950s] the bill, usu. in a restaurant. [? rhy. sl. *duke of yorks* = FORKS]

duke *n.*[4] [1930s+] a tough, dominant individual, a leader or boss, esp. in criminal world.

duke *v.*[1] **1** [mid-19C–1920s] to shake hands, to welcome. **2** [late 19C+] to fight with the fists (cf. DUKE IT OUT). **3** [1920s+] to give out, to hand over, to inform. **4** [1980s+] (US gay) to push one or more fingers or even the whole fist into one's partner's anus (cf. FIST FUCK). [DUKE *n.*[3] (1)]

duke *v.*[2] [1980s+] to get dressed. [ety. unknown; ? link to DUDE *n.* (2)]

duke in *v.* (US) **1** [20C] to fool, to trick. **2** [1930s+] to introduce, to bring in to a plan or group. [DUKE *v.*[1] (1); handshaking in both deceitful and sincere contexts]

duke it out *v.* [1930s+] (US) to fight with fists. [DUKE *n.*[3] (1)]

duke of Kent *n.* [20C] **1** the rent. **2** a homosexual. [rhy. sl.; (2) *duke of Kent* = BENT *n.*]

duke of limbs *n.* [mid-18C–mid-19C] an awkward, ungainly person.

duke of Seven Dials *n.* [late 19C] a conceited, self-opinionated (young) man. [*Seven Dials*, a well-known criminal enclave, and as such unlikely to boast many peers]

duke of york *n.* [19C+] a fork. [rhy. sl.]

duke of york, to *phr.* [19C+] **1** to talk. **2** to walk. [rhy. sl.]

duke-out *n.* [1970s+] (US) an argument, a fight. [DUKE *n.*[3] (1)]

duke out *v.* [1970s+] (US) to knock out. [DUKE-OUT]

dukes *n.*[1] [mid-19C+] the fists; thus *put up your dukes*, get ready to fight (cf. DOOKS). [DUKE *n.*[3] (1)]

Duke's, The *n.*[2] [late 19C] the Argyll Rooms, Windmill Street, London W1. [*fl.*1860–1900, and named, presumably, for the earlier, and more fashionable Argyll Rooms in Little Argyll Street, W1 (*fl.*1806–30). Liszt and Mendelssohn played there, and Byron versified upon its excesses]

dukey *n.* [mid–late 19C] a cheap theatre or music-hall (cf. PENNNY GAFF). [a particular theatre whose Jewish proprietor had a large nose, i.e. a DOOK *n.*[1] (2)]

dukey robe *n.* [1990s] (US Black/teen) a large, heavy gold chain, worn as jewellery.

dukie *n.*[1] [20C] (US) a light meal, esp. that carried to work by a labourer or factory worker. [DUKE *n.*[3] (1); thus something one can carry or ? dial. *docky*, a light meal taken in the fields]

dukie *n.*[2] see DOOKEY *n.*[1].

dukie/dookey/dookie *n.*[3] **1** [1970s+] (US Black) excretion; thus *dukie hole*, the anus. **2** [1990s] (US campus) an unpleasant, obnoxious person. [? Scot. *dook*, the bung of a cask]

dull as dog shit *phr.* [1970s+] utterly tedious.

dullhead *n.* [1970s] (US) a dullard. [SE *dull* + sfx. -HEAD (1)]

dull-pickle *n.* [late 17C–18C] a fool, a dullard. [SE *dull* + PICKLE *n.*[1]]

dullsville *n.* [1960s+] an imaginary town, characterized by extreme dullness or boredom; thus a state, environment or situation of extreme dullness (cf. SQUARESVILLE). [SE *dull* + sfx. -VILLE]

dull swift *n.* [late 18C] a stupid, sluggish person. [lit. a stupid messenger]

dumb *n.* [1920s+] (orig. US) a fool, a stupid person.

dumb *adj.* [1950s+] (orig. US) stupid.

dumb arm *n.* [late 18C–early 19C] a lame or maimed arm.

dumbarton/dumby *n.* [1910s] (W.I.) the buttocks. [joc. use of proper name, but note *dounby*, buttocks, used by Sir Thomas Urquhart (*c.*1611–60) in his translation of Rabelais]

dumb as four o 'clock *phr.* [20C] (US) very stupid. [ext. of DUMB *adj.*]

dumb-ass/-arse *n.* [1950s+] (orig. US) a fool. [DUMB *adj.* + sfx. -ASS/ARSE *n.*[1] (4)]

dumb-ass/-arse *adj.* [1950s+] (orig. US) stupid, unintelligent. [DUMB-ASS *n.*]

dumb-bell *n.* [1910s+] an idiot, a fool. [DUMB *adj.* + SE *bell*, i.e. lit. a bell that will not ring]

dumb bunny *n.* [1920s+] (US) a fool. [DUMB *adj.* + BUNNY *n.*[3]]

dumbbutt *n.* [1950s+] (US) a fool. [DUMB *adj.* + BUTT *n.*[1] (3)]

dumb cluck *n.* [1930s+] (orig. US) a fool. [DUMB *adj.* + CLUCK *n.*[2] (1)]

dumb dora *n.* [late 19C] **1** (US) a pretty but empty-headed woman, often a member of the chorus line (cf. BIMBO; O.M.D.). **2** (camp gay) a stupid person. [coined *c.*1890 by Anita Pines, the first female manager of a burlesque theatre]

dumb-dumb see DUM-DUM.

dumbed *adj.* [late 19C] (US) euph. for DAMNED.

dumbellina *n.* [1950s+] (camp gay) a fool. [DUMB-BELL + fem. sfx. *-ina* + pun on Disney character *Thumbellina*]

dumbfuck/dumb-fuck *n.* [1940s+] (orig. US) a fool, an idiot; thus *dumbfuckery*, behaviour typical of such an individual. [DUMB *adj.* + FUCK *n.*[5]]

dumb glutton *n.* [late 18C] the vagina (cf. DUMB ORACLE; DUMB SQUINT). [it 'eats' the penis]

dumbhead *n.* [late 19C+] a fool. [lit. translation of Ger. *Dummkopf*, a dumbhead]

dumb isaac *n.* [1900s–20s] (US) a fool. [play on SMART ALEC]

dumbness *n.* [mid-19C+] (orig. US) stupidity. [DUMB *adj.*]

dumbnuts *n.* [1970s+] (US) a fool. [play on NUMBNUTS]

dumbo *n.* (orig. US) **1** [1930s+] a fool, a dullard (cf. DUM-DUM; DUMB SOCK). **2** [1950s] a foolish blunder. [DUMB *n.* + sfx. -O. Note the Walt Disney cartoon *Dumbo* (1941), although the elephant in question was naïve rather than stupid and the chronology appears wrong]

dumb oracle *n.* [18C] the vagina (cf. DUMB GLUTTON; ORACLE *n.*[2]).

dumb ox *n.* [1940s+] a large, stupid man. [DUMB *adj.* + SE *ox*]

dumbshit *n.* [1960s+] (US) a fool. [DUMB *adj.* + SHIT *n.*[2]]

dumbshit/dumshit *adj.* [1960s+] (US) stupid. [DUMB *adj.* + SHIT *n.*]

dumbski *n.* [20C] (US) a fool. [DUMB *n.*/DUMBO + sfx. -SKI]

dumbsmack *n.* [1940s–50s] (US) a fool. [ext. of DUMB *n.*; ? smacking of the forehead in perplexity]

dumb sock *n.* [1930s+] (US) **1** a fool. **2** a Swede or any Scandinavian immigrant. [DUMB *adj.* ? + SOCK *n.*[3]]

dumbsquat *n.* [1980s+] (US) a fool. [? DUMBO + DIDDLY-SQUAT]

dumb squint *n.* [18C] the vagina (cf. DUMB GLUTTON).

dumbwad *n.* [1970s+] (US campus) a fool. [DUMB *adj.* + neg. sfx. -WAD]

dumb watch *n.* [late 18C] a venereal bubo in the groin. [SE *dumb* + ? *watch*, a sentinel; such a sentinel is looking out for any further sexual misadventures]

dumbwit *n.* [1930s] (US) a fool. [DUMB *adj.* + SE *wit*, on pattern of FUCKWIT]

dumby see DUMBARTON.

dum-dum/dumb-dumb *n.*[1] [1940s+] (orig. US) a deaf mute. [SE *dumb* + redup.]

dum-dum/dumb-dumb *n.*[2] [1960s+] (orig. US) **1** a fool, an idiot (cf. DUMBO; DUMMY). **2** a general term of abuse. [ext. of DUMB *n.*]

dumifutchit *n.* [20C] (US) any nameless small object, typically some form of gadget (cf. DOHICKEY). [ety. unknown]

dummacker *n.* [mid-19C–1900s] a knowing, aware person. [? devel. of DUNAKER]

dummerer *n.* [1930s] a beggar who fakes dumbness in order to gain alms. [DOMMERER]

dummo *n.* [1970s] (US) a fool (cf. DUMBO). [DUMB *n.* + sfx. -O]

dummock n. [19C] the buttocks. [Yorkshire dial. ? + Rom. *dummock*, back]

dummy n.[1] **1** [late 16C+] a dumb (i.e. mute) person. **2** [early 19C+] a fool, an idiot (cf. DICKHEAD). **3** [mid-19C+] a deaf mute, or a tramp or beggar who pretends to be deaf and dumb. [SE *dumb*; despite the use of DUMB adj. above, the chronology makes this SE, as does the UK rather than US use]

dummy n.[2] [late 18C+] a wallet (cf. DUMMY-HUNTER). [SE *dumb*; Hotten (1864) suggests that money in a pocket-book or wallet makes no noise, while coins in a purse chink together]

dummy n.[3] [mid-19C+] the penis. [its silence or its use for sucking on]

dummy n.[4] [late 19C+] (Und.) bread (cf. DOUBLE-O n.[1]; PUNK n.[2]). [? the softness of the crumb]

dummy n.[5] [20C] an empty bottle. [like a baby's *dummy* one can suck it, but nothing will come out]

dummy n.[6] [1930s–40s] (N.Z. Und.) the solitary confinement/ punishment cell in a prison. [SE *dumb*; the isolation renders the inmate silent]

dummy n.[7] [1980s+] (drugs) poor quality drugs. [they are effectively SE *dummy*, or fake]

dummy-chucker n. [1930s] (US) one who throws fake fits. [chuck a dummy]

dummy dust n. [1980s+] (drugs) phencyclidine (cf. ACE n.[3]). [a drug that appeals to or creates a DUMMY n.[1] (2)]

dummy-hunter n. [late 19C–1900s] a pickpocket specializing in stealing wallets. [DUMMY n.[2] + SE *hunter*]

dummy run n. [20C] (orig. naval jargon) a practice, a trial run.

dummy up v.[1] (orig. US) **1** [1920s+] to stop talking, to keep quiet. **2** [1960s] to keep something secret. [DUMMY n.[1]]

dummy up v.[2] [1960s+] (US) to concoct a fraud, to fake something up. [SE *dummy*, a sham]

dump n.[1] [19C] (Aus./US) **1** a small coin or small sum of money (cf. HOLY DOLLAR). **2** a button; thus *not care a dump*, not care at all. [SE *dump*, a coin worth 1s 3d (6½p), formerly current in Australia, made by punching a disk out of the middle of a Spanish dollar and milling the edge]

dump n.[2] [mid–late 19C] (US) a short, fat person. [? abbr. SE *dumpling*]

dump n.[3] [late 19C+] (orig. US) **1** an unpleasant, disgusting and unappealing place. **2** a place in general. **3** one's home, irrespective of its appearance. [SE *dump*, a pile or heap of refuse or other matter 'dumped' or thrown down]

dump n.[4] **1** [1940s+] (orig. US) an act of defecation. **2** [1940s+] (orig. US) a piece of excrement. **3** [1950s+] (drugs) the vomiting that may follow an injection of heroin (cf. LUNCH GUT). [SE *dump*, a heap]

dump v.[1] **1** [late 19C+] (US) to injure or kill by gunfire. **2** [late 19C+] (orig. US) to get rid of, to dispose of, to dismiss, to jilt. **3** [1930s+] to beat up. **4** [1940s+] to murder. **5** [1950s+] to knock down. **6** [1960s+] (US) to leave. **7** [1970s+] to defeat, to ruin. **8** [1970s+] to impose oneself or one's emotions on another person (cf. DUMP ON). [SE *dump*, to throw down in a lump or mass]

dump v.[2] **1** [1950s–60s] (drugs) to vomit through drug withdrawal sickness. **2** [1970s+] (US campus) to defecate. [for ety. see DUMP v.[1]]

dumper n.[1] [1960s+] (US) **1** a lavatory. **2** a sexual deviant (possibly with an obsession with excrement/defecation), as encountered by prostitutes. [DUMP v.[2] (2)]

dumper n.[2] [1960s+] (US) an ageing prostitute, i.e. over 40. [one who should be thrown into a DUMPER n.[1] (1) or SE *dumpster*, a large rubbish container or (UK) skip]

dumper n.[3] [1960s+] (N.Z. Und.) a racecourse detective. [ety. unknown]

dump-fencer n. [mid-19C] a button-seller. [SE *dump*, a lead counter, used for playing children's games + FENCER]

dumpie/dumpy n. [1960s+] (S.Afr.) a non-returnable 340ml (12fl oz) beer bottle. [cf. STUBBIE].

dumpish adj. [mid-19C] miserable, wretched, grumpy. [DUMPS n.[1]]

dumpling n. [late 19C] a native of Norfolk. [such individuals are supposed to be excessively fond of *dumplings*]

dumpling depot n. [mid-19C] the stomach (cf. BREAD BASKET; VICTUALLING DEPARTMENT). [boxing jargon]

dumplings n. [early 18C+] the female breasts; thus [20C] (Aus.) *her dumplings are boiling over*, her breasts are falling out of a low-cut dress (cf. APPLES n.[1]).

dump on/dump all over v. [1940s+] (orig. US) **1** to impose oneself or one's emotions on another person. **2** to criticize, to abuse. **3** to better in an argument; thus *dumped on*, abused, out-argued. [SE *dump*]

dump one's load, to phr. [1960s+] to vomit. [DUMP v.[2] (1) + SE *load*]

dumps, the n.[1] [late 17C+] a depression, esp. in phr. *down in the dumps*, miserable. [one's emotions have been 'dumped' in a heap]

dumps n.[2] [mid–late 19C] buttons and other small wares carried by a street-hawker (cf. SNELLS). [DUMP n.[1]]

dumptruck n.[1] [1930s+] (US Und.) a public defender (cf. MOUTHPIECE; TONGUE; WARBLER). [? one can DUMP v.[1] (8) all ones troubles on them]

dumptruck n.[2] [1960s+] a car full of lesbians. [the innate masculinity of the SAmE *dump truck*]

dumptruck v. [1960s+] (US prison) to fail through a lack of nerve and courage, rather than through actual physical inadequacy. [DUMP v.[2] (2); the image of losing control of one's bowels + pun]

dumptruck date n. [1980s+] (US campus) an overweight female. [SAmE *dumptruck* + DATE n.[3]]

dumpty/dumpty-doo/dumpy n. [1960s+] (Aus./M.Z.) an outside privy. [? DUNNY, but note DUMP v.[2]]

dumpy n.[1] [1920s] a short, squat umbrella (cf. CHUBBY n.).

dumpy n.[2] see DUMPIE.

dumpy adj. [19C+] (US) miserable, out of sorts. [DOWN IN THE DUMPS + 16C SE *dumpy*, melancholy, dejected]

dumshit see DUMBSHIT.

dun n. [mid-18C+] a demanding creditor or their agent. [? Fr. *donner*, to give, or eponymous *Joe Dun*, a notorious bailiff operating in Lincoln c.1500; SE f. 19C]

dun v. [mid-18C+] to demand one's debts. [DUN n.]

dunaker n. [late 17C–late 18C] a cow-stealer (cf. ABACTER). [DUNNOCK]

Dunbar wether n. [19C] a red herring (cf. ABERDEEN CUTLET). [the fishing trade of *Dunbar*, Scotland + SE *wether*, a castrated ram]

duncarring n. [late 17C–18C] the practice of male homosexuality. [? a proper name or corruption of DUNNAKEN]

dunced out adj. [1960s–70s] (US) dumbfounded, stupid. [SE *dunce*]

duncehead n. [1970s] (US) a fool, a simpleton. [SE *dunce* + sfx. -HEAD (1)]

dunderfunk see DANDYFUNK.

dunderhead n. [late 17C+] a fool, an idiot, an incompetent. [? Scot. *dunner*, to fall down with a loud noise, or *dunnered*, stunned, stupefied, stupid 'in a state of gross stupor'; both ult. Scot. *donner*, to stupefy as with a blow or a loud noise + sfx. -HEAD (1)]

Dundreary n. [mid-19C–1920s] one who poses as a dandy or swell; thus *Dundreary whiskers*, long side whiskers worn without a beard. [the name of Lord *Dundreary*, a character in Tom Taylor's comedy *Our American Cousin* (1858)]

dundus/doondoos n. [1940s+] (W.I.) **1** an albino. **2** a freak. [Kongo *ndundu*, an albino]

dune coon n. [1990s] an Arab. [SE (*sand-*)*dune* + COON n.]

dung n. **1** [mid-19C] a workman who accepts less than union wages. **2** a strike-breaker. [mid-18C tailors' jargon *dung*, a tailor who accepts the master's terms without argument, or who works when their fellows are striking; the *dung* is 'soft' (and disgusting), while the union man, the *flint*, is 'hard' (and admirable)]

dungaree adj. [mid-19C] (Anglo-Ind.) low, common, vulgar. [Hind. *dungri*, a coarse calico; also name of a disreputable Bombay suburb]

dunger n. [1970s+] (N.Z.) anything, usu. mechanical, that is worn out of malfunctioning, e.g. an old car. [echoic of the engine noises]

dunghill n. [late 18C] a coward. [cock-fighting jargon *dung-hill*, any cock but a fighting cock]

dung-puncher n. [1960s+] (Aus.) a derog. term for the homosexual (cf. BUM-PUNCHER). [SE *dung* + fig. use of *punch*]

dung-stabber n. [1990s] the penetrative partner in anal sex (cf. DUNG-PUNCHER). [SE *dung* + fig. use of *stabber*]

dunk v. [1990s] (US Black) to outwit, to overcome an opponent by an unorthodox move. [baseball use *dunk*, to push (the ball) down through the basket, esp. by jumping so that the hand is above the level of the ring]

dunking n. [1900s] having sexual intercourse. [the image is of *dunking* doughnuts or biscuits in coffee]

dunk sauce n. [1920s–40s] (US Black) left-over cooking liquid, into which bread can be dipped. [SE *dunk*, to dip; ult. Ger. *tunken*, to dip, via Pennsylvania Ger. *dunken*]

Dunlop cheque n. [20C] (Aus.) a cheque that has 'bounced', i.e. been marked 'return to drawer' by the bank (cf. RUBBER CHEQUE). [the *Dunlop* Rubber Company]

dunnage n. [mid–late 19C] baggage, esp. carried by a tramp or a sailor. [naut. use *dunnage*, material such as brushwood or mats, used to protect valuable or easily broken cargo; ult. Low Ger. *dün*, thin and *dünne Twige*, brushwood.]

dunnaken n. [17C] a lavatory (cf. DANNA). [DANNA + KEN n.¹]

dunnigan/dunnee n. [20C] (Aus.) a lavatory (cf. DANNA).

dunnigan worker n. [20C] a thief who hangs around public lavatories, hoping to steal from discarded coats or take parcels etc that have been put down. [DUNNIGAN + Und. use of SE *worker*, i.e. one who 'works' a racket]

dunnock n. [17C–19C] (Und.) a cow. [SE *dun*, brown, the colour of many cows]

dunny n. [1930s+] (Aus./N.Z.) **1** an outside lavatory or privy (cf. DANNA). **2** any lavatory; thus *dunny cart*, a vehicle used to remove excrement; *dunny man*, a night-soil cleaner. [DUNNAKEN]

dunny budgie n. [1990s] (Aus.) a fly. [DUNNEE + facet. use of BUDGIE n. (1); i.e. the size of noisiness of the flies is reminiscent of the bird]

dunnyken n. [18C–19C] a lavatory (cf. DANNA). [var. on DUNNAKEN]

dunop see DOONUP.

duns/dunsa n. [1950s+] (W.I. Rasta) money. [DUN v.]

dunsy adj. [20C] (Ulster) foolish, 'slow'. [SE *dunce*]

dunt n. [1980s+] (US campus) a person of ambivalent sexuality. [DICK n.⁵ (1) + CUNT n.¹ (1)]

d-up v. [1990s] (US Black) to protect oneself in those areas of one's life where one might be vulnerable. [D n.⁹]

dup v. [16C–18C] (Und.) to open (a door). [DUB v. (1) or SE *do up*, although this would imply closing, unless the image is of fastening the door]

dupa n. [20C] (US) the buttocks, the posterior, often used as an affectionate term, esp. among Polish speakers or the families of Polish immigrants. [Polish *dupa*, little ass]

dupe v. [1980s+] (US campus) to abuse, to do wrong to.

dupey-dupe n. [1970s+] a foolishly naïve (young) policeman (cf. CHOIRBOY).

dup the jigger, to phr. [16C–mid-19C] (Und.) to open a door (cf. DUB THE GIGGER). [DUP + JIGGER n.¹ (1)]

dup the ken, to phr. [late 17C–18C] to enter a house. [DUP + KEN n.¹]

Durban poison n. [1960s+] (S.Afr.) an exceptionally well-regarded variety of marijuana, grown near Durban, Natal.

Durbs n. [1970s+] (S.Afr.) *Durb*an. [abbr.]

Durham man n. [late 18C] one who's knees knock or rub together. [proper name *Durham*, home of high-quality mustard, which was ground between two stones]

durn n. [19C+] euph. for *damn*, usu. found in phr., e.g. *I don't give a durn*, I couldn't care less.

durog n. [1970s] (drugs) marijuana. [DUROS]

duros n. [1970s] (drugs) marijuana. [Sp. *duros*, hard, i.e. tough]

durry n. [1940s+] (Aus./N.Z.) **1** a cigarette butt. **2** a cigarette, esp. when hand-rolled. [? Ulster *durrie*, anything small]

durry v. [1960s+] (N.Z., usu. teen) to smoke illicitly. [DURRY n.]

durrynacker n. [mid-19C] a female lace-hawker, who may also tell fortunes to her customers. [Rom. *dukker*, to tell fortunes]

dust n.¹ [17C–19C] money, esp. as phr. *down with one's dust*, to lay down one's money (cf. CHAFF n.). [? SE *gold-dust*, but note the religious equation of money with dirt]

dust n.² [mid-18C–mid-19C] a fight, an argument, a disturbance; thus *kick up a dust* (cf. DUST-UP).

dust n.³ [19C] **1** excrement. **2** (fig.) nothing, a worthless object.

dust n.⁴ [19C–1950s] (US Black) a dark-skinned person.

dust n.⁵ **1** [mid–late 19C] (Aus.) gunpowder. **2** [late 19C–1930s] flour. **3** [1900s] (Aus.) tobacco. **4** [1930s+] (US) rolling tobacco. [the consistency of these substances]

dust n.⁶ (drugs) **1** [1910s+] heroin. **2** [1910s+] cocaine (cf. PIMP DUST). **3** [1970s+] phencyclidine (cf. ACE n.³; ANGEL DUST; DUSTED). **4** [1980s+] marijuana mixed with phencyclidine, cocaine or any other powdered drug. [all these drugs come in powdered form]

dust adj. [1980s+] (US campus) ruined, utterly exhausted. [SE *dust*, the condition of human decay]

dust v.¹ **1** [early 17C; 19C+] to thrash, to beat up, to hit hard esp. as phr. [late 17C–late 19C] *dust one's coat/jacket*; [20C] *dust the floor with*. **2** [19C+] to kill, to murder. **3** [1960s+] (US) to defeat. **4** [1970s+] (US) to destroy. **5** [1980s+] (US campus) to humiliate, to insult. [image of knocking the dust from someone's coat or jacket]

dust v.² **1** [mid-19C+] (orig. US) to rush off, to leave fast. **2** [late 19C+] (US) to overtake, to pass on the road. **3** [1940s+] (US) to leave, to abandon. **4** [1960s+] (US) to get rid of, to jilt. [all reflect an image of the dust raised by one's speedy movement]

dust v.³ **1** [early 19C] to deceive, to mislead. **2** [1950s] (US) to tease, to hoax. ['throw dust in someone's eyes']

dust v.⁴ [1990s] (drugs) to add phencyclidine or another other powdered drug to marijuana. [DUST n.⁶ (3)]

dustbin n. [1940s] (US Black) a grave. [note DUST v.¹]

dustbin lids n. [20C] children. [rhy. sl. *dustbin lids* = kids]

dust-cutter n. [1900s–50s] (US) a drink, esp. as a 'pick-me-up' or 'reviver' (cf. PHLEGM-CUTTER).

dusted adj.¹ [19C+] beaten, defeated, killed. [DUST v.¹]

dusted adj.² [20C] (drugs) having consumed and finished off a drug. [SE *dust*, to clean up]

dusted adj.³ [1970s+] (drugs) under the influence of phencyclidine (cf. ANGEL DUST). [DUST n.⁶ (3)]

dusted *adj.*[4] [1980s+] shamed, humiliated. [DUST v.[1] (5)]

dusted parsley *n.* [1980s+] (drugs) phencyclidine (cf. ACE n.[3]). [DUST n.[6] (3), which is often mixed with parsley]

duster *n.*[1] [1940s+] (US Black) the buttocks, the posterior. [RUSTY-DUSTY]

duster *n.*[2] **1** [1960s–70s] a cigarette laced with heroin. **2** [1970s+] (drugs) a user of phencyclidine. [DUST n.[6] (1), (3)]

dusters *n.* [1950s] (orig. milit.) the testicles. [? boastful image of testicles that hang so low as to 'dust' the floor]

dustie *n.* [1950s] (US drugs) a narcotics user. [DUST n.[6] + sfx. *-ie*]

dusting *n.*[1] [late 18C–late 19C] a beating or thrashing. [DUST v.[1] (1) + sfx. *-ing*]

dusting *n.*[2] [1970s+] (drugs) adding phencyclidine, heroin or another drug to marijuana. [DUST n.[6] + sfx. *-ing*]

dusting the duvet *n.* [1990s] masturbation. [euph.]

dust it *v.* [late 19C+] (US) to leave quickly, to run off. [DUST v.[2] (1); note a single 17C nonce-use]

dust joint *n.* [1980s+] (drugs) a cigarette made with phencyclidine (cf. ACE n.[3]). [DUST n.[6] + JOINT n.[4] (2)]

dustman *n.*[1] [late 18C] a corpse. [the line in the Church of England burial service: 'ashes to ashes and dust to dust']

dustman *n.*[2] [mid–late 19C] (nursery) sleep, personified; thus soothing phr. *the dustman's coming* (cf. DUSTMAN'S BELL). [he throws *sleep-dust* (or sand) into sleepy eyes]

dustman *n.*[3] [mid–late 19C] an energetic, fanatic preacher (cf. CUSHION-DUSTER). [DUST v.[1] (1); he thumps the pulpit as he preaches]

dustman's bell *n.* [mid–late 19C] (nursery) bedtime. [the DUSTMAN n.[2] who brings sleep]

dust of angels *n.* [1980s+] (drugs) phencyclidine (cf. ACE n.[3]). [ANGEL DUST]

dust off *v.* [1940s+] (US) **1** to reject, to snub. **2** to kill. **3** to finish off. [DUST v.[1]]

dust one's throat, to *phr.* [late 19C] (US) to take a drink.

dustoor/dustoorie *n.* [late 17C–19C] (Anglo-Ind.) a bribe, a sweetener, a commission. [Hind. *dastur*, custom, what is customary]

dust out *v.* [late 19C] (US) to overtake, to pass on the road. [DUST v.[2] (2)]

dust someone's jacket/coat, to *phr.* [late 17C–mid-19C] to thrash, to beat someone up (cf. TRIM SOMEONE'S JACKET).

dust the end-table, to *phr.* [1990s] to masturbate. [pun on END n.[3]]

dust the eyes/eyes of, to *phr.* [early–mid-19C] to befuddle, bamboozle. [abbr. phr. *throw dust in one's eyes*]

dust the family jewels, to *phr.* [1990s] to masturbate. [pun on SE *dust* + FAMILY JEWELS]

dust the sidewalk with, to *phr.* [late 19C] to beat up thoroughly, to defeat comprehensively. [DUST v.[1] + pun on SE]

dust-up *n.* [late 19C+] (orig. milit.) a fight. [DUST n.[2] + image of the dust generated by struggling men and horses]

dusty *n.*[1] [late 19C+] a *dust*man. [abbr. + sfx. *-y*]

dusty *n.*[2] [1980s+] (society) a very old person, 70 years old and onwards (cf. CRUMBLY). [one of a set of words implying the physical disintegration of the body as one ages]

dusty *adj.*[1] (US) **1** [mid-19C] tough, dangerous (cf. BAD adj.). **2** [1980s+] (US campus) tetchy, irritable, out of sorts. [DUST n.[2] + sfx. *-y*]

dusty *adj.*[2] [1970s] (US Black) unclear, unable to predict the future. [there is *dust* in one's eyes]

dusty behind *n.* [1980s+] (US Black) the buttocks, the posterior. [RUSTY-DUSTY + SE *behind*]

dusty bread *n.* [1970s] (US Black) a conventional, conservative woman. [? the poor quality of everyday bread]

dusty butt *n.* [1900s–40s] (US Black) **1** a low-grade,

unattractive prostitute. **2** a short person (cf. DRAG ONE'S ASS). [SE *dusty* + BUTT n.[1]]

dusty line *n.* [1980s+] (US Black) a piece of outmoded slang. [DUSTY adj.[2] + LINE n.[1] (3)]

Dutch *n.*[1] [mid-17C+] (US) nonsense, incomprehensible rubbish (cf. TALK DOUBLE DUTCH).

Dutch *n.*[2] [late 18C] beer (cf. ENGLISH n.[1]; LATIN n.; SPANISH n.[2]).

Dutch *n.*[3] [mid-19C+] (US) **1** bad temper, irascibility (cf. AFRICA). **2** a crewcut haircut. [(1) stereotyping; (2) confusion between Dutch and *Deutsch*, German]

Dutch/double-Dutch *n.*[4] [mid-19C] any foreign language (cf. GREEK n.[2]; HEBREW).

dutch *n.*[5] [late 19C+] a wife. [*Dutch* as a noun is best known as a Cockney term for wife. The precise origins of this remains debatable. Either, as is still the majority belief, the term is an abbreviation of the rhyming slang DUCHESS OF FIFE (*see* DUCHESS n.[3]), or, according to the 19C music-hall star Albert Chevalier (1861–1923), whose signature song was entitled 'My Old Dutch', the term was semantically linked to another piece of slang, DIAL n., face. In Chevalier's version, the original term was 'my old Dutch clock', whose face, i.e. dial, resembled that of his wife. Partridge, formerly a partisan of the Duchess, claimed to have changed his mind in the later editions of the *DSUE*. The *OED*, however, while citing Chevalier's song in 1893, has a previous citation, dated 4 years earlier, and states unequivocally that in this context *dutch* is 'an abbr. of duchess']

Dutch *n.*[6] [1960s–70s] a friend. [rhy. sl. *Dutch plate* = MATE]

Dutch *n.*[7] [1990s] (US) intercourse between the breasts (cf. DUTCH FUCK n.; TITTY FUCK).

Dutch *adj.*[1] **1** [17C+] a derog. racial stereotype, meaning stolid, miserly, dour and bad tempered, and used as such in the combs. below. [the mid-17C when the UK fought the Dutch as a national enemy]

Dutch *adj.*[2] [mid-19C] German (cf. DUTCH n.[3]). [the growth of German settlements in the USA, notably in Pennsylvania; *see* combs. below]

dutch *v.* [mid-19C+] (US) **1** to speak emphatically. **2** to ruin another's business, social standing, enjoyment etc with deliberate malice. **3** to bet in such a way that the bank is broken. [all racial stereotypes of Dutch]

Dutch act *n.* [20C] (US prison) suicide (cf. TAKE THE DUTCH ROUTE).

Dutch auction *n.* [19C+] a mock auction or sale in which the much-touted 'reductions' have no bearing in commercial fact.

Dutch bargain *n.* [17C] **1** a one-sided bargain. **2** a deal concluded over drinks (cf. WET BARGAIN).

Dutch bath *n.* [20C] (US) a very cursory wash.

Dutch brig *n.* [17C] the cells on board a ship. [SE *Dutch* + BRIG]

Dutch build *n.* [19C] a stocky, thickset individual.

Dutch built *adj.* [19C] stocky, thickset.

Dutch by injection *n.* [20C] any woman living with a foreigner (cf. FRENCH BY INJECTION; IRISH BY BIRTH BUT GREEK BY INJECTION).

Dutch caper *n.* [17C] a light privateering ship.

Dutch cheese *n.* [19C] a bald person. [the Dutch Edam cheese, which is round, red and shiny]

Dutch comfort *n.* [late 18C] a style of comforting in which the speaker intones 'Thank God it is no worse' (cf. DUTCH CONSOLATION).

Dutch concert/medley *n.* [18C–19C] any performance in which each musician plays a different tune; thus a general pej. for a bad performance, musical or metaphorical.

Dutch consolation *n.* [19C] a style of comforting in which the speaker intones 'Thank God it is no worse' (cf. DUTCH COMFORT).

Dutch courage *n.* [late 18C+] cowardice that, fortified by generous quantities of alcohol, becomes (temporary) bravery (cf. FEARNOUGHT). [coined as a propagandist measure during various Anglo-Dutch wars of 18C]

Dutch daub *n.* [late 19C] (US) a badly executed picture. [orig. the second-rate Dutch still-lifes that were imported in bulk into the US during the 1880s, an influx that was slowed only by the imposition of a 35% duty on such pictures]

Dutch distemper *n.* [early–mid-19C] (US) gaol fever. [the disproportionately large number of Dutch (or Germans) in the prison population]

Dutch doggery *n.* [mid-19C] a grog-shop. [SE *Dutch* + DOG-GERY n.², reinforced by the stereotypical surliness of the Dutch]

Dutch dumplings *n.* [1950s–70s] (gay) the buttocks.

Dutch feast *n.* [18C–19C] any meal where the host gets drunk before his friends. [the assumption is that he has mono-polized the supply of alcohol]

Dutch fit *n.* [mid-19C] (US) a fit of temper, an explosion of rage. [stereotype of the grumpy Dutch]

Dutch foil/gilding/gold/metal *n.* (US) an alloy of 11 parts copper and 2 parts zinc, used as a substitute for gold leaf, and presumably passed off as such to the unwary. [stereo-typically mean or duplicitous Dutch]

Dutch fuck *n.* **1** [1950s+] the lighting of one cigarette from another, thus saving matches. **2** [1990s] (US) intercourse between the breasts. [the implication in both is of mean-ness]

Dutch gilding see DUTCH FOIL.

Dutch girl *n.* [1930s+] a lesbian. [pun on SE *dike* (i.e. the dikes that form the basis of Holland's coast defences)/DYKE]

Dutch gleek *n.* [17C] any form of drinks. [? SE *gleek*, a trick or joke]

Dutch it *v.* [1910s+] to share expenses, usu. of a meal (cf. GO DUTCH). [stereotyping]

Dutch kiss *n.* [20C] (US) a kiss in which both participants grab the other's ears. [ety. unknown; ? a national peculiar-ity]

Dutch leave *n.* [late 19C] (US) taking time off without permission, absenting oneself illegally (cf. FRENCH LEAVE).

Dutch lunch see DUTCH TREAT.

Dutchman *n.*¹ **1** [19C+] (US) anyone of German origin. **2** [mid-19C–1920s] (orig. US) a foreigner, one who does not speak English well (cf. DUTCH n.¹). **3** a bar- or saloon-keeper. [Ger. *Deutsch*, German; (3) Germans were trad. linked to the brewing industry]

Dutchman, the *n.*² [late 19C] Deutz and Gelderman cham-pagne.

Dutchman's anchor *n.* [19C] anything that has been for-gotten or left behind. [? a possibly apocryphal Dutch skipper who claimed after suffering a shipwreck that while he had an excellent anchor, he had unfortunately left it at home]

Dutchman's breeches *n.* [19C] two streaks of blue in an otherwise cloudy sky. [the trad. Dutchman is pictured in blue pantaloons]

Dutchman's cape *n.* [20C] a cloudbank on the horizon that gives the impression of being land (cf. CAPE FLYAWAY). [SE *cape*, a promontory; the image is of the stupid Dutch sailor who confuses clouds with land]

Dutchman's drink *n.* [19C] a drink that empties the pot or drains some form of communal drinking vessel.

Dutchman's fart *n.* [20C] a sea urchin. [derog. joke]

Dutchman's headache *n.* [19C] a state of drunkenness (cf. IRISH TOOTHACHE).

Dutchman's razor *n.* [19C+] animal excrement, as found in fields or farmyards; thus *cut one's foot with a Dutchman's razor*, to step into excrement (cf. CUT ONE'S FOOT).

dutchmasta *n.* [1990s] a cigar, esp. when its tobacco is removed and replaced by marijuana (cf. BLUNT n.²). [brandname]

Dutch medley see DUTCH CONCERT.

Dutch metal see DUTCH FOIL.

Dutch nickel *n.* [20C] (US) a kiss (cf. YANKEE DIME). [in racial stereotyping *Dutch* = thief, therefore such a kiss has been 'stolen']

Dutch nightingale *n.* [late 18C] a frog. [the implied inability of the Dutch to sing]

Dutch oven *n.* **1** [1920s] the mouth. **2** [1920s] the smell of a bed in which someone has just farted. **3** [1980s+] (Aus. drugs) an enclosed area or room filled with cannabis smoke. [SE *Dutch oven*, a large pot that gains heat from coals placed around and on top of it; (3) is underpinned by Holland's liberal understanding of the harmless uses of cannabis]

Dutch palate *n.* [17C] a coarse palate, with no appreciation of the finer comestibles.

Dutch party see DUTCH TREAT.

Dutch pegs *n.* [20C] legs (cf. SCOTCH PEGS). [rhy. sl.]

Dutch pennants *n.* [19C] untidy ropes on board a ship.

Dutch pink *n.* [19C] blood. [SE *Dutch pink*, a yellow lake pigment]

Dutch reckoning *n.* **1** [17C] a bill presented as a lump sum, with no details attached. **2** [17C] a bill that, if disputed, only gets higher. **3** [19C] (naval) a bad day's work. [the poor image of Dutch businessmen]

Dutch red *n.* [19C–20C] a smoked Dutch herring.

Dutch row *n.* [late 19C] a spurious argument, generating far more sound than any real fury. [note Fr. synon *une querelle d'Allemand*, lit. a 'German argument']

Dutch rub *v.* [1930s+] to rub one's knuckles hard across one's victim's skull (cf. DRY SHAVE v.²).

Dutch supper see DUTCH TREAT.

Dutch town *n.* [20C] (US) that area of a town predominantly populated by German immigrants or their descendants (cf. BEAN TOWN n.²). [Ger. *Deutsch*, German + SE *town*]

Dutch treat/lunch/party/supper *n.* [20C] an outing, a visit to a restaurant etc in which costs are shared equally, i.e. there is no 'treat' at all in the sense of one party being entertained at the other's expense.

Dutch uncle/uncle *n.* [early 19C+] one who talks severely and critically, who lays down the law, usu. in phr. *talk like a Dutch uncle*.

Dutch widow *n.* [17C] a prostitute (cf. DUTCH WIFE).

Dutch wife *n.* [late 19C] a bolster, otherwise defined as a 'masturbation machine' (cf. DUTCH WIDOW).

dutchy *n.* [20C] (W.I. Rasta) **1** a Dutch cooking pot, a low, round-bottomed heavy pot. **2** a pipe or bowl used for smoking marijuana.

dutchy *adj.* [19C+] (US) **1** typically German, esp. recent immigrants who have yet to adapt to America and still retain their old-country crudities. **2** low-class, dowdy, slovenly. [DUTCH adj.² + sfx. -*y*]

duty *n.* [late 19C] pawnbrokers' interest. [pun on SE]

duty-frees *n.* [1950s+] goods bought by travellers in the duty-free shops that are found in airports, on boats etc, usu. alcohol or tobacco products.

d.v. *n.*¹ [late 19C] (society) divorce. [the initials, but also a cynical ref. to Lat. *deo volente*, God willing]

D.V. *n.*² [1970s+] (US Black) Cadillac Coupe *De Ville*. [abbr.]

dwaal *n.* [1960s–70s] (S.Afr.) a daze, a confusion, esp. in phr. *in a dwaal*, in a daze. [Afk. *dwaal*, to wander, to lose one's way]

dwaas *n.* [20C] (S.Afr.) a fool, an idiot. [Du. *dwaas*, a silly fellow]

dweeb/dweebie/tweeb *n.* [1980s+] (orig. US teen) an idiot, a fool. [ety. unknown; ? the name of a lost SF alien]

dweezle *n.* [1980s+] (US campus) a socially inept person. [ety. unknown; ? a devel. of DWEEB]

-dweller *sfx.* [1980s+] (US campus) combining form to indicate someone who frequents a particular place.

dwelling dancer *n.* [1940s] (Aus.) a thief. [SE *dwelling* + DANCER]

d-whupped *adj.* [1990s] (US Black) describing a woman who allows herself to be exploited and generally treated badly (cf. PUSSY-WHIPPED). [abbr. DICK-WHUPPED]

dyestuffs *n.* [mid–late 19C] (US) money. [a pun on SE + the metal *dies* used for printing notes]

dying *n.* [1980s+] (US campus) laughing hysterically.

dying *adv.* [1950s–60s] hyperbolic use of SE to mean emotionally disturbed, very worried, esp. in phr. *I'm dying*, I'm slightly upset.

dying duck in a thunderstorm *n.* [late 19C+] a lazy, weak, vapid person.

dyke/dike *n.* [1930s+] a lesbian. [ety. unknown. ? f. dyked down, dressed up; certainly some lesbians have always dressed as men. Another theory suggests the gradual corruption of SE *hermaphrodite* to *morphodite* to *dike* and *dyke* and thence, with the masc. generic *bull* to BULL-DYKE and BULL-DAGGER]

dyke/dike *v.* [1930s] to engage in lesbian sex.

dykey/dikey *adj.* [1930s+] having the appearance or characteristics of a lesbian. [DYKE + sfx. -y]

dyna *n.* [1960s] a male homosexual. [rhy. sl. *dynamite* = SE *catamite*]

dynamite *n.*[1] [late 19C] tea. [the use of 'tea' as a codeword for *dynamite* as revealed during a trial of 1888; but note SE *gunpowder*, a fine, green-leafed tea, popular in the UK from the 1770s]

dynamite *n.*[2] [late 19C+] (Aus.) baking powder. [it makes things 'blow up']

dynamite *n.*[3] (drugs) **1** [1920s+] heroin, morphine. **2** [1960s+] any pure, undiluted drugs. **3** [1960s+] a mixture of cocaine and morphine (cf. SPEEDBALL n.[1]). [the strength and effect]

dynamite/dynamo *adj.* [20C] excellent, wonderful, first-rate. often as *dynamite!* wonderful!

dynamite *v.* (US) **1** [1920s] to talk loudly, to complain, to make a fuss. **2** [1920s–50s] to talk in an aggressive manner, esp. when trying to sell something or seduce someone. **3** [1930s] to push something through, to make it happen fast. [i.e. to 'go off with a bang']

dynamiter *n.* (US) **1** [1910s] a whinger, a complainer. **2** [1910s–20s] a sponger, a cadger. **3** [1920s–40s] a very aggressive salesman. **4** [1930s–60s] a very ambitious person, a trouble-maker.

dynamo *adj.*[1] *see* DYNAMITE adj.

dyno *adj.*[1] [1960s+] (drugs) uncut, therefore stronger than usual heroin or any other drug. [DYNAMITE n.[3]]

dyno *adj.*[2] [1980s+] (US campus) a general term of approval or admiration, pretty, excellent, wonderful. [abbr. DYNAMITE adj.]

E

E *n.* [1980s+] the popular nickname of the hallucinogenic drug MDMA (methylene dioxymethamphetamine). [abbr. ECSTASY]

eager beaver *n.* [1940s+] (orig. US) an excessively earnest, keen person whose efforts are sometimes more notable for their sound and fury than their actual usefulness. [the ever-industrious beaver]

eagers, the *n.* [1920s–60s] (US) anxiety, apprehension or excessive keenness. [SE *eager*]

eager up *v.* [1960s] (US) to excite.

eagle *n.*[1] [early 16C–early 18C] (Und.) a gambler, presumably a crook, who wins. [the strength of the predatory bird?]

eagle *n.*[2] [1940s–50s] **1** a silver dollar. **2** a $10 bill. [the eagle that appears on the coin]

eagle *n.*[3] [1960s] (US campus) the grade of E. [the initial letter]

eagle beak *n.* [1920s+] (US) a derog. term for a Jew. [the stereotypically large-nosed Jew]

eagle day *n.* [1940s+] (US) payday. [WHEN THE EAGLE FLIES]

eagle eye *n.* [1910s–20s] (US Und.) a detective.

eagle eye *v.* [1960s] (US) to look closely, scrutinize. [the visual acuity of the bird]

eagle fly *v.* [1950s–60s] (US Black) to pay wages; thus *eagle fly on Friday*, Friday will be payday.

eagle-flying day *n.* [20C] (US Black) payday (cf. WHEN THE EAGLE FLIES). [the eagle on the US silver dollar.

ear *n.* [mid-19C] (US Black) a tuning peg on a guitar or fiddle. [resemblance]

earbash *v.* [1940s+] (orig. Aus./N.Z.) to talk incessantly; thus *ear-basher*, a garrulous talker, a bore. [SE *ear* + BASH v.[1];lit. to 'hit one's ear']

ear-basher *n.* [1940s+] (orig. Aus./N.Z.) a bore, a loudmouth who refuses to stop talking. [EARBASH + sfx. *-er*]

earbashing *n.* **1** [1940s+] (orig. Aus.) nagging, non-stop chatter. **2** [1990s] (Black) reprimands, scoldings. [EARBASH + sfx. *-ing*]

ear-bender *n.* [20C] (US) a chatterer, a bore. [BEND SOMEONE'S EAR]

ear between the legs *n.* [19C] the labia minora. [resemblance]

ear-biter *n.*[1] **1** [mid-19C] (US) a special agent of the US Post Office. **2** [1930s–50s] a cadger, one who seeks constantly to borrow money. [BITE SOMEONE'S EAR]

ear-biter *n.*[2] *see* CHIN-BITER.

ear candy *n.* [1980s+] (US) lightweight pop music (cf. ARM CANDY). [like SE *candy*, it is sweet but insubstantial and lacking in nourishment]

ear flap *n.* [mid-19C–1930s] (US) an ear.

earful *n.* [1910s+] (US) a forceful expression of opinion, esp. a complaint or rebuke.

earguard *n.* [1940s] (Aus.) short side-whiskers or sideboards. [SE *earguard*, a small flap, attached to the cap and covering the ear]

earhole *n.* [1920s+] the ear.

earhole *v.* [1920s+] to listen, to overhear.

ear-jerker *n.* (film) a film in which the main attraction is the volume and predominance of the music. [on the model of TEAR-JERKER]

ear job *n.* **1** [1960s] (US) a kissing and caressing of someone's ear with the tongue. **2** [1970s] a phone call to a sexual phone service, sexually stimulating talk on the phone (cf. EAR SEX). [SE *ear* + JOB n.[5]]

earl *v.* [1960s] (US) to vomit (cf. HURL); thus *call earl, go to see earl, earl's knocking at the door* (cf. HUGHIE; RALPH v.). [echoic]

earl of Cork *n.* [mid-19C] (Anglo-Irish) the ace of diamonds. ['the worst ace and the poorest card in the pack', so called from the contemporary earl, who was the poorest nobleman in Ireland]

ear-lugger *n.* [20C] (Aus.) a cadger, a scrounger (cf. EAR-BASHER). [SE *ear* + LUG v.]

early *adj.* [1980s+] (US Black) up-to-date.

early Battersea *n.* [1970s+] vulgar, tasteless decor (cf. EARLY ECLECTIC; EARLY HOMOSEXUAL). [the stereotyping of *Battersea* taste as vulgar]

early beam *n.* [1930s–40s] (US Black) dawn, the early morning (cf. EARLY BLACK). [the first sunbeams]

early bird *n.*[1] [19C+] one who habitually gets up early (cf. LATE BIRD).

early bird *n.*[2] [late 19C+] a word. [rhy. sl.]

early-bird *adj.* [20C] first of the day, e.g. *early-bird matinee*.

early black *n.* [1930s–40s] (US Black) dusk, nightfall (cf. EARLY BEAM). [the initial darkening of the sky]

early doors *n.* [1990s] something that happens prematurely.

early eclectic *n.* [1970s+] vulgar, tasteless decor.

early Halloween *n.* [1970s+] vulgar, tasteless decor.

early homosexual *n.* [1970s+] vulgar, tasteless decor.

early purl *n.* [19C] a drink made of hot beer and gin (cf. DOG'S NOSE n.[1]). [SE *early* + PURL n.[1]]

early riser *n.* [1960s+] (US prison) an inmate who is granted an early parole.

early variety *n.* [20C] (US) an illegitimate child. [horticultural jargon]

ear man *n.* [1970s] (US Black) an individual expressing a natural ability to excel at an endeavour, a virtuoso. [he picks it up *by ear*]

earmuffs *n.* [1940s+] (US) headphones.

ear music *n.* [1970s] (US Black) improvised music.

earn *v.* [1960s+] (Und.) to make a dishonest profit from a crime.

earner *n.* [1960s+] **1** (Und.) any job or plan that pays well, almost invariably criminal, often as *nice little earner*. **2** (police) a bribe, often paid as regularly as more legitimate wages.

earnest *n.* [late 17C–early 18C] (Und.) a share (of the booty); thus *tip one their earnest*, to hand out a share. [SE *earnest*, money, esp. as paid as a pledge for securing a contract]

earn/make one's tucker, to *phr.* [late 19C] to earn (at least enough for) one's bed and board. [SE *earn/make* + TUCKER]

ear of corn *n.* [1910s] (US) a country person.

ears *n.* **1** [1920s–30s] euph. for ARSE n.[1]. **2** [1970s] (orig. US) a citizens' band radio, its antenna or the vehicle carrying it; thus *have one's ears on*, to be tuned into one's CB transceiver.

ear sex *n.* [1980s+] (US) an instance of sexual talk on the phone (cf. EAR JOB).

earth *n.*[1] [mid-19C] three; thus *earth/erth sis noms*, a three-month prison term. [backsl.]

earth, the *n.*[2] [1920s+] everything, a large amount or quantity, e.g. *cost the earth*, *pay the earth*, *want the earth*.

earth *n.*[3] [1980s+] (drugs) a marijuana cigarette. [? its organic (rather than chemical) origins]

eartha *n.* [1950s+] **1** excrement. **2** an act of defecation. [rhy. sl. *Eartha Kitt* = SHIT n.[1]; ult. US singer Eartha Kitt (b.1928)]

earth biscuit *n.* [1990s] (US campus) someone who identifies with the styles and concerns of the 1960s (cf. EARTH CRACKER). [the *save the earth* attitudes of the period + the 'whole-grain' image of the *biscuit*]

earth cracker *n.* [1990s] (US campus) an environmentalist (cf. EARTH BISCUIT). [SE *save the earth* + *cracker*, a savoury biscuit with a 'whole-grain' image]

earth daddy *n.* [1980s+] (US campus) an older than average college male who professes the values of the 1960s. [play on a classic figure of the 1960s, the *earth mother*]

earth/erth gens *n.* [mid-19C] three shillings. [backsl.]

earth muffin *n.* [1990s] (US campus) an older than average college male (cf. EARTH DADDY). [SE *earth*, i.e. one who espouses the values of the sixties + (LOVE)MUFFIN]

earth pads *n.* [1940s] (US Black) **1** feet. **2** shoes.

earth-/erth-pu *n.* [mid-19C] three-up, a street gambling game based on coin-tossing. [backsl.]

earthquake *n.* [19C] (US) an alcoholic mixed drink. [its effects]

earth to … *phr.* [1970s+] (US) used to call someone's attention, also to tease. [the image is of their day-dreaming, 'out in space']

earthworm *n.* [1990s] the penis.

earth/erth yannops/yenneps *n.* [mid-19C] three pence. [backsl.]

earwig *n.* **1** [mid-17C–late 19C] a malicious gossip or flatterer. **2** [mid-19C] a clergyman. **3** [mid-19C] a close, intimate friend. **4** [late 19C] an inquisitive person. **5** [1940s+] an eavesdropper. **6** [1940s+] a lookout, one who listens for approaching steps, then checks the owner before admitting them. [play on SE *ear*]

earwig *v.*[1] **1** [19C] to gossip, esp. maliciously, to feed another with unpleasant rumours. **2** [1940s+] to eavesdrop. [EARWIG n. (1), (5)]

earwig *v.*[2] [20C] to understand. [rhy. sl. *earwig* = TWIG v.[2] (3)]

earwigging *n.* [mid-19C] a private rebuke (cf. WIGGING). [EARWIG v.[1]]

ease *v.*[1] [early 17C–late 19C] **1** to rob, to steal. **2** to have sexual intercourse, esp. to deflower. [SE *ease*, to deprive, to despoil]

ease *v.*[2] [1930s+] (orig. US Black) to leave, esp. quietly and discreetly; usu. in phr. *ease one out*.

easies *n.* [1950s+] (N.Z.) a woman's elasticated foundation garment.

ease it *v.* [1940s+] (prison) to relax, to let up on some form of crime or rule-breaking.

easeman *n.* [19C+] (US Black) a kept man (cf. EASTMAN).

ease off the salami *phr.* [1990s] (US teen) don't talk about that.

ease-up *n.* [20C] (W.I.) assistance, esp. in a difficult situation; thus *give one an ease-up*, to help. [orig. dial.]

ease up *v.* [20C] (W.I.) to forgive, to lighten up.

easily *adv.* [1940s+] at least, more than, e.g. *easily twenty*.

easing powder *n.* [late 19C] (drugs) opium. [SE *ease*, to relieve pain + *powder*]

east and south *n.* [mid-19C] the mouth (cf. NORTH AND SOUTH). [rhy. sl.]

east and west *n.* [20C] a vest. [rhy. sl.]

east and west/east, west and crooked *phr.* [20C] (US) disorderly, confused (cf. GALLEY-WEST; HIGH, WEST AND CROOKED).

easter bunny *n.* [1990s] (US campus) a benefactor, someone who does a favour. [the Easter bunny is a beneficent creature]

easter egg *n.* [20C] (US) a woman wearing too much make-up. [the traditional painted Easter eggs created annually in some cultures]

easter queen *n.* [1960s+] (US gay) one who ejaculates prematurely. [SE *easter (bunny)*, i.e. he 'comes quick as a rabbit' + QUEEN n.[1]]

east Jesus *n.* [20C] (gay) an out-of-the-way place, a small town.

eastman *n.* [19C+] (US Black) a kept man, one who lives on money earned by a woman; a pimp (cf. YEASTING). [Black pron. of *yeast* as *east*; thus the image of yeast as expanding and thus making a 'big man' or *yeast* = BREAD n.[1] (2) = DOUGH]

east of the Griffin *phr.* [late 19C] East London. [the statue of a griffin that in 1880 replaced the old east/west boundary of Temple Bar, removed because of traffic congestion in 1870]

Eastside O *n.* [1990s] (US Black teen) East Oakland.

eastside player *n.* [1990s] (drugs) crack cocaine. [the prevalence of the drug in east Los Angeles + PLAYER]

east, west and crooked *see* EAST AND WEST phr.

easy *n.* **1** [1910s] (US) a gullible person. **2** [1970s+] New Orleans, Louisiana (cf. BIG EASY).

easy *adj.*[1] **1** [late 17C; 20C] of a woman, sexually promiscuous. **2** [late 19C] (US campus) innocent, gullible. **3** [20C] (Can.) easily imposed upon.

easy *adj.*[2] [late 19C] (Und.) amenable to bribery.

easy *adj.*[3] [1980s+] (W.I./UK Black teen) an exhortation to relax, e.g. don't get flustered, stay cool, unhurried. [abbr. phr. *take it easy*]

easy *v.* [20C] of a woman, to lie back ready for intercourse. [EASY adj.[1] (1)]

easy a bit *phr.* [1920s] calm down.

easy as … *phr.* a variety of combs. all of which mean very simple indeed, sometimes almost criminally so, e.g. [18C] … *tilly*, [18C–1910s] … *pissing the bed*, [19C+] … *ABC*, [19C+] … *damn it*, [19C+] … *kiss my eye*, [19C+] … *shelling peas*, [late 19C+] … *kiss my arse*, [late 19C+] (orig. US) … *pie*, [late 19C+] … *winking*, [1920s+] (Aus.) … *apple pie*, [1950s+] … *taking candy from a baby/money from a child*.

easy as cake and ice-cream *phr.* [1930s+] very easy (cf. APPLE SAUCE n.[4]). [the ease and pleasure with which one consumes such foodstuffs]

easy as falling/rolling off a log *phr.* [late 19C+] very easy indeed.

easy as rolling off a log *see* EASY AS FALLING OFF A LOG.

easy digging *n.* [1930s] (US) granulated sugar. [ety. unknown; ? the ease with which one can spoon it into a cup]

easy does it *phr.* [late 19C+] a phr. used as a warning, go easy, take your time, careful (cf. EASY ON!).

easy game *n.* [late 19C+] a sexually available woman (cf. EASY RIDE).

easy lay *n.* [1930s+] usu. of a woman, one who can be easily seduced. [SE *easy* + LAY n.[2] (2)]

easy make *n.* [1940s+] (US) a promiscuous or easily seducible woman. [SE *easy* + MAKE n.[3] (1)]

easy mark/meat *n.* [late 19C+] someone or something overcome, mastered or persuaded without difficulty, anything achieved with ease. [SE *easy* + MARK n./*meat*]

easy mort *n.* [mid-17C–early 18C] a promiscuous woman. [SE *easy* + MORT]

easy on! *excl.* [1920s+] a general excl., go easy! stop it! be sensible! (cf. EASY DOES IT!).

easy on the eye *phr.* [1920s+] (orig. US) attractive, esp. of women or girls. [note 1900s synon. *easy to look at*]

easy-peasy *adj.* [20C] very simple; usu. juvenile use. [SE *easy* + redup.]

easy ride *n.* [1980s+] (US) a sexually available woman. [SE *easy* + RIDE n.³]

easy rider *n.*¹ [20C] (US Black) **1** a sexual athlete. **2** a pimp, a kept man. **3** a guitar. [SE *easy* + RIDE n.³; the term crossed briefly into White vocabulary with the release of the hit film *Easy Rider* (1969); thus *c.*1970 *easy rider*, a woman who agrees to sex on the first date]

easy rider *n.*² [1960s] any 'outlaw' motorcyclist. [film title (1969)]

easy rider *n.*³ [1970s] a calm, unruffled person.

easy score *n.* [1950s+] (drugs) obtaining drugs easily. [SE *easy* + SCORE n.³ (1)]

easy six *n.* [20C] (US gambling) the point of 6 in craps dice. [it is *easy* because of the number of combinations that equal 6]

easy street *n.* [20C] a secure, comfortable life; a situation free of problems, esp. material ones, usu. in phr. *on easy street* (cf. SITTING PRETTY).

easy stuff *n.* [1980s+] (US) a sexually available woman (cf. EASY RIDE). [SE *easy* + STUFF n.⁴]

easy time *n.* [20C] (US Und.) an uneventful time in prison (cf. LIGHT TIME). [SE *easy* + TIME n.¹]

easy touch *n.* [1950s+] one who can be easily solicited for money or favours (cf. SOFT TOUCH). [SE *easy* + TOUCH n.¹]

easy virgin *n.* [18C] a prostitute (cf. EASY VIRTUE). [SE *easy*, careless, unconcerned + *virgin*]

easy virtue *n.* [18C] a prostitute (cf. EASY VIRGIN). [SE *easy*, careless, unconcerned + *virtue*]

easy walkers *n.* [1920s–40s] (US Black) comfortable, well-fitting shoes.

eat *v.*¹ **1** [19C+] to defeat or destroy; thus *I'll eat him alive.* **2** [late 19C+] to annoy, bother; thus *What's eating you?* **3** [1970s+] to strike face-first or be hit by (e.g. a bullet). **4** [1980s+] (Irish) to abuse verbally, also ext. as *to eat the head off* (someone).

eat *v.*² [early 19C–1920s] (US) to provide with food.

eat *v.*³ [1920s+] to perform fellatio or, more usu. cunnilingus (cf. EAT OUT v.²; EAT PUSSY). [note RN synon. *chew*]

eat a child, to *phr.* [late 18C–19C] to share in a treat given to the parish officers (cf. GREASY CHIN). [the price for the commutation (registering as legitimate) of a bastard child was 'ten pounds and a greasy chin' (Grose 1785), i.e. a good meal]

eat acorns *v.* [1930s] (US Black) to suffer humiliation, to accept defeat (cf. EAT CROW; EAT DIRT; EAT DOG; EAT SHIT). [a peasant might eat acorns when deprived of a more nutritious source of food]

eat a dick *phr.* [1990s] (US Black teen) a general phr. of dislike or dismissal. [SE *eat* + DICK n.⁵ (1)]

eat a fig, to *phr.* [mid-19C] to commit burglary, to rob a house. [rhy. sl. *eat a fig* = CRACK A CRIB]

eat a furburger, to *phr.* [1980s+] (US) to perform cunnilingus. [EAT v.³ + FURBURGER]

eat an apple/a pumpkin through a knot hole, to be able to *phr.* [20C] (US) to have buck teeth.

eat at the Y/box lunch at the Y, to *phr.* [1950s+] (US) to perform cunnilingus. [EAT v.³ + SE *Y*, referring both to the spread legs and to the YMCA/YWCA]

eat boiled crow *see* EAT CROW.

eat box lunch at the Y *see* EAT AT THE Y.

eat bull beef, to *phr.* [late 16C–19C] to become strong, to become fierce. [the image of *bull beef* as tough meat]

eat cheese *v.*¹ [1940s+] (orig. US Black) to toady to, to ingratiate oneself with. [SE *eat* + CHEESY adj.³ ; i.e. the quality of one's smiles]

eat cheese *v.*² [1940s+] (orig. US Black) to have oral sex with a woman. [EAT v.³ + CHEESE n.⁵]

eat concrete *v.* [1970s] (US) to drive fast, esp. a truck, down a highway.

eat corn-on-the-cob through a picket fence, to be able to *phr.* [20C] (US) to have buck teeth.

eat crap *v.* [1930s+] (orig. US) to suffer and accept humiliation, to humble oneself, usu. in order to attain a desired goal (cf. EAT SHIT). [SE *eat* + CRAP n.³]

eat crow/boiled crow *v.* [19C+] to suffer humiliations and insults without responding in kind (cf. EAT DOG; EAT TURKEY). [the mid-19C story of a man who bet that he was able to eat a cooked crow, and duly did so, but remarked as he chewed the bird: 'Yes, I can eat a crow, but I'll be darned if I hanker after it!']

eat dirt *v.* **1** [19C+] to retract a previous statement, usu. incurring humiliation and embarrassment by so doing (cf. EAT CROW). **2** [1930s–70s] to be thrown or to fall on one's face. [pvb. 'Every man must *eat a peck of dirt* (i.e. retract a number of errors) before he dies']

eat dog *v.* [19C+] to suffer humiliation and insult with reciprocating (cf. EAT CROW).

eat dried apples/peaches/pumpkin seeds, to *phr.* [20C] (US) to become pregnant. [the way in which dried fruit swells up when placed in water]

eat dust *v.* [late 19C] (US) to be killed (cf. BITE THE DUST).

eater *n.* [1990s] a café, a restaurant.

eatery *n.* [20C] (US) a restaurant.

eat face *v.* [1960s+] (US campus) to kiss passionately on the mouth and face (cf. CHEW FACE; SUCK FACE).

eat fish/chew fish/the fish *v.* [1940s+] (US) to perform cunnilingus. [SE *eat/chew* + FISH n.⁴]

eat fist-meat *v.* [early 19C] to receive a punch in the mouth.

eat gravel *v.* [1930s–70s] (US) to be thrown or to fall on one's face (cf. EAT DIRT).

eat hair pie, to *phr.* [1960s+] to perform cunnilingus. [EAT v.³ + HAIR PIE]

eat in Dutch street, to *phr.* [1910s+] to share expenses (cf. GO DUTCH). [stereotyping]

eating *n.* [1980s+] (drugs) taking a drug orally.

eating irons *n.* [1900s–40s] utensils, knives and forks.

eating match *n.* [mid-19C] (W.I.) a feast.

eating midden *n.* [19C] (Scot.) a glutton. [SE *eating* + *midden*, a rubbish dump]

eatings *n.* [1920s–30s] (US Black) food.

eating tackle *n.* [20C] teeth.

eating tobacco *n.* [1900s–60s] (US) chewing tobacco.

eating tool *n.* [1920s–60s] (US) an eating utensil.

eat it *v.*¹ [1910s+] to perform oral sex. [EAT v.³]

eat it *v.*² **1** [1930s+] to suffer humiliation, esp. in attaining a desired goal (cf. EAT CRAP; EAT SHIT). **2** [1960s+] (US campus) to do poorly, to achieve low marks. **3** [1980s+] to die (cf. BITE THE DUST).

eat it!/this! *excl.* [1980s+] a general term of dismissal, disdain (cf. BITE THIS!). [*it/this* is the penis]

eat its head off *see* EAT ONE'S HEAD OFF.

eat jam *v.* [1940s+] (US gay) to lick the anus. [SE *eat* + JAM n.⁸ (3)]

eat lead *v.* [1920s+] (orig. US) to be shot. [note 16C SE *eat iron*, to be stabbed]

eat like a beggar man and wag one's under jaw, to phr. [late 18C] 'a jocular reproach to a proud man' (Grose 1785).

eat me! excl. [1980s+] (US) shut up! you make me sick! the hell with you! go away!

eat my shorts! excl. [1990s+] (US campus) a dismissive phr., drop dead! go to hell! etc. [SAmE shorts = SE underpants; the phrase moved into the mainstream with the success of television's cartoon family, The Simpsons, whose renegade son Bart took it as his personal catchphrase]

eat one's boots see EAT ONE'S HAT.

eat one's/the gun, to phr. [1970s+] (US) to commit suicide by shooting oneself in the mouth.

eat one's hat/boots, to phr. [20C] to go back on one's words, esp. to admit that a public statement was, in fact, wrong.

eat one's/its head off, to phr. [18C+] to cost more than a person/thing is worth.

eat one's heart out, to phr. [late 19C+] to be consumed by jealousy.

eat one's nails, to phr. [early 18C] to do something foolish. [ety. unknown]

eat one's tutu/toot, to phr. [mid–late 19C] (N.Z.) to become acclimatized, esp. to colonial life. [Maori tutu, a New Zealand shrub yielding shining black juicy berries which can be eaten, but also containing poisonous seeds]

eat out v.[1] [1940s] (US) to tell off, to reprimand. [var. on CHEW OUT]

eat out v.[2] [1960s+] (US) to perform cunnilingus. [EAT v.[3]]

eat parrot backside / bambam / bottom / parrot-head soup / bird-seed, to phr. [20C] (W.I.) to chatter on incessantly and irritatingly.

eat peaches see EAT DRIED APPLES.

eat pie v. [1980s+] to perform cunnilingus. [EAT v.[3] + HAIR PIE]

eat poundcake v. [1970s+] **1** (US Black) to have sexual intercourse. **2** (gay) to suck a partner's anus. [pun on SE + POUND v.[2] (2)]

eat pumpkin seeds see EAT DRIED APPLES.

eat pussy v. [1950s+] to perform cunnilingus. [SE eat/EAT v.[3] + PUSSY n.[1] (1)]

eat razor soup, to phr. [20C] (US) to say something cheeky or impertinent (cf. WHO SLEPT IN THE KNIFEBOX?).

eats n. [late 19C+] food. [orig. UK but in 20C US only]

eat sausage v. [1980s+] (N.Z.) of a woman, to fellate. [SE eat/EAT v.[3] + SAUSAGE n.[1]]

eat shit v. **1** [1930s+] to suffer and accept humiliation. **2** [1930s+] to humble oneself, usu. to attain a desired goal. **3** [1940s+] to be utterly contemptible. [SE eat + SHIT n.[1] (1)]

eat shit! excl. [1930s+] (US) a general dismissive, derog. expression; it has no specific meaning. [EAT SHIT v.]

eat someone's arse/ass off, to phr. [1950s+] (US) to criticize severely, to punish heavily (cf. CHEW OUT). [fig. use SE eat + ARSE n.[1]]

eat someone's cookies, to phr. [1970s] (US) to defeat someone.

eat someone's lunch, to phr. [1950s+] (US) to defeat, injure or outdo someone.

eat someone's meat, to phr. [1920s+] to fellate. [EAT v.[3] + MEAT n. (2)]

eat supper before you say grace, to phr. [20C] (US) to conceive a child before one gets married.

eat the big one! excl. [1980s+] (US) to hell with you! [var. on EAT ME!]

eat the cookie, to phr. [1970s] (US) to be defeated (cf. EAT SOMEONE'S COOKIES; EAT SHIT).

eat the greaser, to phr. [20C] (US) to swallow one's words, to recant (cf. EAT ONE'S HAT). [dial. greaser, a lump of salt pork used to grease the bars of a griddle]

eat the green weenie, to phr. [1940s+] (US) (orig. milit.) to get killed. [? the grass; thus cf. BITE THE DUST]

eat the gun see EAT ONE'S GUN.

eat the leek, to phr. [late 19C] to be forced to address unpleasant consequences. [the 'sharpness' of the SE leek]

eat this! see EAT IT!

eat turkey v. [mid-19C+] **1** to suffer humiliation and insult without reciprocating (cf. EAT CROW). **2** to take second best, to accept an inferior role. [SE eat + TURKEY n.[3]]

eat up adj. [1970s] (US campus) fatigued, exhausted. [SE eaten up]

eat up v. **1** [mid-19C+] to defeat or destroy. **2** [mid-19C–1950s] to scold or rebuke. **3** [20C] to believe unquestioningly. **4** [1910s+] (orig. theatre) to enjoy immensely, to acclaim. **5** [1940s+] to get the better of.

eat vinegar with a fork, to phr. [late 19C] to have a sharp tongue.

eau-de-Cologne n. [20C] (Aus.) the telephone. [rhy. sl.]

ebb-water n. [late 17C–18C] (Und.) a lack of money.

ebenezer n. [19C+] (US) temper, passion (cf. SET UP ONE'S EBENEZER). [Heb. eben ha-ezer, the stone of help, the memorial stone set up by Samuel after the victory of Mizpeh (1 Sam. 7:12); a misreading of Samuel's 'raising' of a memorial]

ebony n. **1** [early 19C+] (US) a Black person. **2** [20C] (US Black) the quintessence of Black sensibility.

ebony adj. [mid-19C+] a general reference to any Black person; thus ebony chick, ebony pidgeon, a Black girl; also as a bit of ebony.

E-boy n. [1980s+] a devotee of MDMA (cf. ECSTASY). [E + SE boy]

eccer/eccker/ecker/ekker n. [1970s+] (Irish) homework. [SE exercise]

eccy n. [1920s+] (US campus) economics. [abbr.]

ecker see ECCER.

eckied/eckied up adj. [1980s+] (drugs) under the influence of MDMA (cf. ECSTASY). [ECKY]

ecky n. [1980s+] (drugs) MDMA. [abbr. ECSTASY]

ecky-becky n. (W.I./Bdos.) a poor White. [? redup. of Ijo beke, a European or ironic use of Ijo ekee, God + beke]

ecky up v. [1980s+] (drugs) to take MDMA (cf. ECSTASY). [ECKY]

ecod n. [late 18C–mid-19C] God, as used in a variety of oaths (cf. COCK n.[1]).

ecofreak n. [1970s+] an extremist in the cause of environmentalism. [SE ecology + FREAK n. (6)]

econut n. [1970s+] (US) an extremist in the cause of environmentalism (cf. ECOFREAK). [SE ecology + NUT n.[8]]

ecstasy n. [1980s+] a sl. term for the drug known officially as methylene dioxymethamphetamine (MDMA) (cf. ACID n.[4]; ADAM n.[4]; APPLES n.[3]; BIG BROWN ONES; BISCUIT n.[7]; BURGERS; CLARITY; DECADENCE; DENNIS THE MENACE; DISCO BISCUIT; DOCTOR n.[8]; DOLLAR n.[2]; DOMEX; DOUBLE-M; DOVE; E; ECKY; EGGS n.[3]; ELKIES; ENERGIZER; ESSENCE n.[2]; EVE n.[2]; FANTASIA; GREY BISCUIT; HAMBURGER n.[3]; HAMMER AND SICKLES; HUG DRUG; KINDER EGGS; KLEENEX n.[2]; LOVE DOVE; LOVE DRUG; M n.[2]; MELLOW DRUG OF AMERICA; M25; NEW YORKERS; ORBIT n.; PINK FLAMINGOES; PINK STUDS; RHUBARB AND CUSTARDS; ROLLING n.[2]; RUNNING n.; SNOWBALLS; SPEED FOR LOVERS; SWANS; VITAMIN E; VITAMIN X; WHITE CALLIES; WHITE DOVE; WHIZZ BOMB; XTC). [ecstasy existed in the 1960s, as one of many synthetic hallucinogens (although it is more amphetamine than a 'real' hallucinogen) from a group known as 'Schulgin's Compounds' but only reached its apotheosis in the late 1980s. Its nickname comes from the indiscriminate affection that its ingestion promotes, and the earlier popular name of 'love-drug']

EC women n. [late 19C] (society) the wives of City businessmen. [the London postal code East Central; a snobbish usage by those who despise 'trade']

E'd *see* E-ED.

Eddie *n.*[1] [1920s] (US Black) a White male (cf. MR CHARLIE). [abbr. MR EDDIE]

eddie *n.*[2] [1980s+] (US campus) an ugly man. [ety. unknown; ? anecdotal or link to EDDIE n.[1]]

eddress *n.* [1990s] (US teen) an electronic-mail a*ddress.* [abbr. + pun on SE *address*]

edgabac/egabac *n.* [mid-19C] cabbage. [backsl.]

edgar britts *n.* [1960s+] (Aus.) diarrhoea (cf. JIMMY BRITTS). [rhy. sl. *edgar britts* = SHITS n. (1); ult. proper name of Aus. jockey *Edgar Britt* (b.1913)]

edgarism *n.* [late 19C] used by members of gentlemen's clubs, atheism. [*Edgar*, the hero of Alfred, Lord Tennyson's play *The Promise of May* (1882), an advocate of free love and a denier of the deity]

edge *n.*[1] [late 19C+] **1** tension, usu. creative. **2** concentration.

edge *n.*[2] [late 19C–1960s] a state of mild intoxication thus phr. *have an edge on*, to be slightly drunk.

edge *n.*[3] [1960s] (US Black) a knife (cf. BLADE n.[3]); thus phr. *pack an edge*, carry a knife.

edge *v.* [late 19C] (Und.) to escape, to run away, esp. as excl. *edge!*, run for it!, called out by a lookout.

edge city *n.* [1970s+] the extremes of experience, whether spiritual, physical, drug induced or whatever; usu. with overtones of fear and challenge. [EDGE n.[1] + sfx. -CITY]

edged *adj.*[1] (US) [late 19C–1930s] tipsy. [EDGE n.[2]]

edged *adj.*[2] (US) [1980s+] angry. [EDGE n.[1]]

edgenaro *n.* [mid-19C] an orange. [backsl.]

edge it! *excl.* [20C] (Aus.) be quiet! shut up!

edge-up *adj.* [20C] (W.I.) used of one who is trying excessively hard to become friends. [the image is of physically moving overly close]

edie *n.* [1940s–50s] a prostitute (working Piccadilly, Bayswater Road and other 'cheap' streets in London) (cf. TOM n.[9]). [the image of *Edie* as a poor person's name]

edison special *n.* [1970s] (US prison) death in the electric chair. [proper name Thomas Alva *Edison* (1847–1931), inventor of the electric light-bulb + SE *special*]

edmundo *n.* [1960s+] the leader, the most important person. [rhy. sl. *Edmundo Ros* = boss; ult. Edmundo Ros (b.1910), a popular Latin American band leader]

edna! *excl.* [20C] (Und.) a general excl. of dismissal, be off!, go away! [rhy. sl. *Edna May* = on your way!]

educated *adj.* **1** [20C] (US) fraudulent, esp. of a card deck that has been fixed. **2** [1940s+] clever but criminal. [ironic use of SE]

educated fool *n.* [1970s+] (US Black) one who is academic but not very sophisticated or worldly-wise (cf. EDUCATED IGNORANT; SCHOOLBOOK CHUMP).

educated ignorant *n.* [1950s+] (US Black) one who is academic but not very sophisticated or worldly-wise (cf. EDUCATED FOOL).

educated pussy *n.* [1950s–60s] (US Black) a weakling, an inadequate. [SE *educated* + PUSSY n.[1] (3); the image is of one who is 'not a real man']

edward *n.* [late 18C+] a donkey or ass (cf. BALDWIN).

E-ed/E'd *adj.* [20C] under the influence of MDMA; usu. as *E'd up* (cf. ECKIED; ECSTASY). [E]

eejit *n.* [20C] a fool. [mispron. of SE *idiot*]

eek *n.* [1950s+] the face. [Polari]

eekcher *n.* [late 19C–1900s] cheek, audacity. [pig Latin]

eeks *n.* [1950s+] the eyes. [Polari]

eel *n.*[1] **1** [19C+] (US West.) a native of New England. **2** [20C] (US) anyone who possesses the 'slippery' qualities of the fish, e.g. an accomplished escaper from prison, a spy, a confidence trickster. [SE *eel*, seen anthropomorphically as an untrustworthy creature]

eel *n.*[2] [1960s+] the penis. [resemblance]

eelerspee *n.* [1910s+] (Aus. Und.) a confidence trickster. [backsl. *eelerspee* = SPIELER]

eel juice *n.* [20C] liquor. [? it makes one wriggle like an eel]

eel out *v.* [20C] (US) to avoid a problem, esp. in a deceitful, self-serving way. [SE *eel*, thus its slippery qualities]

eel pot *n.* [late 18C–early 19C] the vagina (cf. CATCH 'EM ALIVE-O; EEL-SKINNER)

eel's ankle/hips *n.* [1920s] (US) something extraordinary or very special. [eels have neither ankles nor hips]

eel skin *n.*[1] [mid-19C] a banknote (cf. FROG n.[5]). [? its greenness]

eel skin *n.*[2] [mid-19C] a New Englander. [EEL n.[1] (1)]

eel skin *n.*[3] [late 19C] a tight skirt, fashionable *c.*1881 (cf. EEL SKINS). [it fits the wearer like an eel's skin]

eel skin *n.*[4] [late 19C] a cosh, made from a canvas tube filled with sand. [resemblance]

eel-skinner *n.* [late 18C–early 19C] the vagina (cf. CATCH 'EM ALIVE-O; EEL POT)

eel skins *n.* [mid-19C] extremely tight trousers (cf. EEL SKIN n.[3]).

eemosh *n.* [mid-19C+] home. [backsl.]

eenin *n.* [mid-19C+] the number 9 [backsl.]

eenque *n.* [late 19C] the queen. [backsl.]

eerquay *n.* [1930s–40s] (US) a male homosexual. [pig Latin, *eerquay* = QUEER n.[1]]

eeson *v.* [mid-19C+] to have a look. [backsl.]

eetswe *adj.* [late 19C] fond of. [backsl. *eetswe* = SWEET (ON)]

eevach a kool, to *phr.* [late 19C] to have a look. [backsl.]

eevige *v.* [late 19C] to give. [backsl.]

eff *v.* [1920s+] euph. for FUCK v. in various contexts.

eff and blind, to *phr.* [1940s+] to swear intensely. [*eff* = F = FUCK v.[1] + BLIND v.[2]]

effing *adj.* [1920s+] euph. for FUCKING adj.

effing and blinding *n.* [1920s+] using obscenities.

eff off! *excl.* [1950s+] euph. for FUCK OFF!

e-fink *n.* [mid-19C] a knife. [backsl.]

efter *n.* [mid-19C] a thief. [? SE *after*, he is *after the valuables* or backsl. *thief*]

egabac *see* EDGABAC.

egad! *excl.* [late 17C–late 19C] used in mild oaths as a euph. for *God* (cf. ADAD!). [? A God!]

egg *n.*[1] **1** [mid-19C+] a person, usu. qualified as *good egg, bad egg* etc. **2** [1910s–30s] a fool or obnoxious person.

egg *n.*[2] [20C] (US campus) a conspicuously studious and intellectual student. [abbr. EGGHEAD n.[2] (1)]

egg *n.*[3] [20C] (US) a henpecked husband. [pun on SE *egg*, thus *hen*]

egg *n.*[4] [1910s] (US) $1. [? abbr. SE *nest-egg*]

egg *n.*[5] **1** [1920s–30s] the head or skull. **2** [1970s+] (drugs) a capsule of a drug. [resemblance]

egg *n.*[6] [1980s+] (drugs) crack cocaine. [pun]

egg *v.*[1] [20C] (US) to move carefully, quietly. [phr. *walk on eggshells*, to tread delicately]

egg *v.*[2] [1930s–60s] to make fun of someone. [SE *egg on*]

egg-a-muffin! *excl.* [1980s+] (US campus) an enthusiastic response of agreement. [SE *egg on* + McDonald's egg *McMuffin*]

egg and spoon *n.*[1] [1960s+] a Black person. [rhy. sl. *egg and spoon* = COON n. (3)]

egg and spoon *n.*[2] [1970s+] (Aus.) **1** a fool, a silly person. **2** a pimp. [rhy. sl. (1) *egg and spoon* = GOON n.[1] (1); (2) *egg and spoon* = HOON n.[1] (1)]

eggbeater *n.* **1** [1930s+] (US) an autogiro or helicopter. **2** [1970s+] an old motorcar.

egg-boiler *n.* [1930s] (Aus.) a bowler hat. [in hot weather it 'boils' one's EGG n.[5] (1)]

egg crate n. [1920s–50s] (US) an old car or aeroplane. [resemblance]

egg flip n. [20C] (Aus.) a tip, in horse-racing. [rhy. sl.]

eggflipper n. [1960s] (Aus.) a horse-racing tipster. [rhy. sl. *eggflipper* = *tipper*]

egg-for-fuck n. [1990s] (US campus) a fool, a simpleton, an obnoxious person. [SE *egg* + FUCK v.; joc. var. on SHIT-FOR-BRAINS]

egghead n.[1] [20C] a bald person. [resemblance]

egghead n.[2] (orig. US) **1** [20C] an intellectual, anyone considered to work with brain rather than brawn. **2** [1940s–80s] an idiot. **3** [1950s+] a pretentiously intellectual type.

egg in your beer phr. [1930s–80s] (US) something for nothing, used as an ironical retort.

egg/butter money n. [19C+] (US) money earned by a farmer's wife through the sale of eggs, butter and other dairy products (cf. PIN MONEY).

eggnog n. [1920s] (US) a foolish or unpleasant person.

eggo n. [1980s+] (US campus) a fool, a misfit, a social anachronism. [? EGG n.[1] (2)]

eggplant n. [20C] (US) a Black person. [SE *eggplant* or aubergine, the vegetable has a shiny purple-black skin]

egg roll n.[1] [20C] (US) a derog. term for a Korean immigrant. [the foodstuff]

egg roll n.[2] [1980s+] (US gay) a Chinese man's penis (cf. SAMURAI SWORD). [the quintessential US Chinese restaurant dish]

eggs n.[1] **1** [1950s+] (US) the testicles. **2** [1950s–60s] courage, virility (cf. BALLS n.[1]).

eggs n.[2] [1980s+] (drugs) temazepam, a tranquillizer (cf. JELLIES). [the shape]

eggs n.[3] [1990s] (drugs) tablets of MDMA (cf. ECSTASY). [the shape]

eggs are cooked!, the excl. [1910s+] (N.Z.) that's it! that's all! it's over! etc.

eggs in the basket n. [1960s] (US gay) testicles. [EGGS n.[1] (1) + BASKET n.[1] (2)]

eggshell blonde n. [1940s+] (Aus./N.Z.) a bald person.

egg suck v. [1980s] (US) to curry favour. [SUCK UP v./obs. SE *suck-egg*, a foolish person]

egg-sucker n. **1** [19C+] (US) a worthless and unpleasant person. **2** [1950s+] (US gay) a description of an ageing or old homosexual. [dial. *egg-sucker*, a worthless animal, esp. a dog; in (2) the pun is on the *egg*, i.e. an unformed youth, who is the target of the older man's desires]

egg-sucking adj. [19C+] (US) worthless, contemptible, unpleasant. [EGG-SUCKER n. (1)]

ego! excl. [mid-19C+] (juv.) that's mine! I want to do that! (cf. BAGS I!).

ego trip n. [1960s+] (orig. US) self-aggrandizement, boastfulness, egocentricity. [SE *ego* + TRIP n.[3]]

ego trip v. [1960s+] (orig. US) to act in an egocentric, self-aggrandizing manner. [EGO-TRIP n.]

Egypt n.[1] [19C+] (US) an outside lavatory. [image of *Egypt* as a far distant place]

Egypt n.[2] [20C] (US) the Black section of a town or city. [the dark complexion of actual Egyptians and the exotic myths that, just as they do in regard to the Middle East, abound around Black culture]

egypt phr. [20C] *eager to grab your pretty tits*, written on envelopes of love letters (cf. BOLTOP). [abbr.]

Egyptian charger n. [early 19C] a donkey. [the association of the animal with the gypsies or *Egyptians*]

Egyptian flu n. [1960s] (US) a pregnancy. [i.e. one is going to be a mummy!]

Egyptian hall n. [mid-19C] a ball. [rhy. sl.; the *Egyptian Hall* was the popular name for the London Museum, established

at today's 170 Piccadilly *c.*1812, holding 'upwards of Fifteen Thousand Natural and Foreign Curiosities, Antiques and Productions of the Fine Arts'. It featured an 'Egyptian' façade, and among the many visitors was, in 1844, General Tom Thumb. The hall was demolished in 1905]

Egyptian queen n. [1960s+] (gay) a homosexual Black man, particularly if he is stately and proud. [the well-known picture of Queen Nefertiti]

eh? excl. [mid-19C+] used interrogatively, as a request for the repetition or explanation of something that has just been said, i.e. 'What did you say?'

eh, what! see WHAT! excl.[1].

eicespie n. [late 19C] money. [backsl. *eicespie* = pieces (of gold)]

Eiffel Tower n. [20C] (Aus.) a shower. [rhy. sl.]

eightball n.[1] [1930s+] (US) a derog. term for an Afro-American, a Black person. [the black 8 ball in the game of pool]

eightball n.[2] [1950s] **1** a fool. **2** a conventional, law-abiding person. [pool imagery; sinking the *eight ball* out of turn will lose the game]

eightball n.[3] (drugs) **1** [1970s+] a 'cocktail' of crack cocaine and heroin. **2** [1980s+] an eighth of an ounce (3.5g) of a drug.

eightball n.[4] [1990s] (US Black) Olde English 800, a popular beer in Black neighbourhoods.

eight ball v. [1940s+] (US) to ruin or frustrate, esp. by cheating (cf. BEHIND THE EIGHT BALL). [pool imagery]

eightballs n. [1980s+] (drugs) crack cocaine.

8–8–16 n. [20C] (US Und.) a prison cell. [the dimensions in inches of a single one of the concrete blocks that make up the cell walls]

eighteen n. [1910s+] (Aus.) an 18-gallon (82-litre) keg of beer (cf. NINE).

eighteen-carat adj. [late 19C–1910s] (US) first-class. [note in assessment of gold, the best is not 18 but 22 carat]

eighteen-carat lie n. [late 19C] (US) a downright, deliberate lie. [the measurement of gold]

eighteen pence n. [1950s+] **1** (Aus.) a garden fence. **2** (Aus.) a receiver of stolen goods. **3** sense. [rhy. sl.; *eighteen pence* = FENCE n.[1]]

eighter decatur/eighter from Decatur see ADA FROM DECATUR.

eighth n. [1950s+] (drugs) one-eighth of an ounce (3.5g) of a drug, usu. a narcotic.

808 n.[1] [1990s] (rap music) the bassdrum from a Roland TR-808 drum machine, which is now a popular make. [refers to the sound of bass from stereos]

808 n.[2] [1990s] (US) the police code for 'disturbing' the police.

eight-pager n. [1930s+] a small, illustrated 8-page pornographic booklet in which popular cartoon characters (Popeye, Mickey Mouse, Blondie etc) are crudely pastiched in erotic scenarios far removed from their everyday antics (cf. TIJUANA BIBLE).

eight rock n. [1930s–50s] (US Black) a very dark-skinned person. [? EIGHTBALL n.[1]]

eight track n. [1990s] (US Black) 2.5g of cocaine.

eighty days/miles n. [1900s–10s] (US) the point of 8 in craps.

eighty-eight n. [1940s] (US Black) a piano. [? number of keys or 8:8 time]

eighty-eighter n. [1940s+] (US) a pianist. [EIGHTY-EIGHT + sfx. -er]

eighty-eights n. [1930s–70s] (US) love and kisses. [orig. used by telegraph operators]

85% n. [1990s] (US Black) the great uneducated mass of (Black) people, who are destined to be taught and led by the knowledgeable 5 per cent. [for full ety. see 5% NATION]

eighty miles see EIGHTY DAYS.

80–90 *n.* [20C] a fool. [euph. among New York Hasidim for PUTZ n. (2); f. the numerical values *80 + 90*, which are ascribed to Hebrew letters *pay* and *tzadik*, which are in themselves a euph. for 'putz']

eighty-six/86 *adj.* [1960s] (US) unwelcome, esp. as at a bar. [EIGHTY-SIX v.]

eighty-six *v.* **1** [1960s+] (US) to throw out, to get rid of. **2** [1970s+] to kill, to murder. [rhy. sl. *eighty-six* = NIX v.; orig. restaurant and bar use, indicating that the supply of an item is exhausted or that a customer is not to be served]

eighty-six! *excl.* [1960s+] get out! go away! [EIGHTY-SIX v.]

eina! *excl.* [1910s+] (S. Afr.) an excl. of pain, i.e. *ouch!* [Khoi *é* + *ná*]

einstein *n.* [1980s+] (US campus) pubic hair. [the crinkly grey hair of the scientist Albert *Einstein* (1879–1955)]

ekame *n.* [mid-19C] a 'make', a swindle. [backsl.]

eke *n.* [1970s] (gay) make-up, cosmetics.

Ekka, the *n.* [1970s+] (Aus.) the annual Exhibition held at the Brisbane Exhibition Grounds.

ekker *see* ECCER.

ekom *n.* [mid-19C] a donkey. [backsl. *ekom* = MOKE n.²]

ek sê! *excl.* [1980s+] (S. Afr.) general intensifying excl.; 'I'm telling you', 'you know what I mean' etc. [Afk. phr. *ek sê vir jou*, I'm telling you]

elakazoo *n.* [1900s] (US) money. [ety. unknown]

elbow *n.*¹ [late 19C–1900s] (US) a policeman. [pun on the 'long arm of the law']

elbow *n.*² [1920s–30s] (Und.) a pickpocket's assistant. [he *elbow*s the victim to distract their attention from the pickpocketing]

elbow *n.*³ [1970s+] rejection, dismissal. [the image of an *elbow* pushed into someone's ribs]

elbow *v.*¹ [mid-19C–1930s] (US Und.) to warn an accomplice to get out of sight when police appear. [one nudges the person with an *elbow*]

elbow *v.*² [1970s+] to reject, to dismiss. [ELBOW n.³]

elbow bender *n.* [20C] a heavy drinker. [BEND ONE'S ELBOW]

elbow croooker. *n.* [mid-19C+] a heavy drinker. [BEND ONE'S ELBOW]

elbow grease *n.* **1** [late 17C–18C] sweat. **2** [late 17C+] physical effort. **3** [mid-19C] fiddle-playing. [the movement of one's *elbow*; B. E. defines *elbow-grease* as 'a derisory term for sweat' but his extra examples, e.g. *it will cost nothing but a little elbow-grease*, imply the later, colloq. use that still exists]

elbow jigger/scraper *n.* [mid-19C] a fiddle-player.

elbow shaker *n.*¹ [18C] a dice-player (cf. HAVE A SPRING AT ONE'S ELBOW; KNIGHT OF THE ELBOW). [the action of shaking the dice cup]

elbow shaker *n.*² [1950s+] (US Black) one who reminds others of a forgotten or overlooked fact or event by (fig.) digging them in the ribs.

el cheapo *adj.* [1960s+] (US) cheap. [cod Sp.]

el d/eldo *n.* [1970s–80s] (US) a Cadillac *El Do*rado. [abbr.]

elderberry *n.* [1950s–60s] (gay) an ageing or old homosexual. [pun on SE *elder* and FRUIT n.² (2)]

elderly jam *n.* [late 19C] an old woman. ['Elderly jam is – elderly jam, and heaven preserve it, for man turns from it' (Ware)]

elders *n.* [1960s+] (Irish) the female breasts. [SE *udders*]

el diablito *n.* [1980s+] (drugs) a mixture of marijuana, cocaine, heroin and PCP. [Sp. 'the little devil']

el diablo *n.* [1980s+] (drugs) a mixture of marijuana, cocaine and heroin. [Sp. 'the devil']

el dingo *adj.* [1980s] (US) dingy.

electric *adj.* [late 19C+] weird and wonderful, marvellous.

electric cure *n.* [20C] (US prison) the electric chair.

electric lettuce *n.* [1980s+] (drugs) very potent cannabis.

electric queen *n.* [1960s–70s] (US gay) a gay hippie. [fig. use of SE *electric*, to mean drugged + QUEEN n.¹]

electrified *adj.* [20C] drunk (cf. ABOUT RIGHT adj.¹).

elegant *adj.* [mid-18C+] excellent, first-rate.

element *n.* [mid-18C–mid-19C] (US) an alcoholic drink; thus *in one's element*, intoxicated.

element's embrocation *n.* [1920s–30s] windy weather that makes one's face red. [pun on *Elliman's Embrocation*]

elephant *n.*¹ [mid-19C+] an extraordinary sight or remarkable situation and the experience of such that leads to gaining knowledge or the loss of innocence; thus *see the elephant*, to see or experience a great deal, as much as one can manage. [the exoticism of the creature]

elephant *n.*² [late 19C+] abbr. of ELEPHANT AND CASTLE. [rhy. sl.]

elephant *n.*³ [20C] (US) a clumsy, awkward person. [reverse anthropomorphism]

elephant *n.*⁴ [1980s+] (drugs) **1** heroin. **2** phencyclidine (cf. ACE n.³). [such drugs could 'knock out an elephant']

elephant and castle *n.* [late 19C+] the anus. [rhy. sl. *Elephant and Castle* = ARSEHOLE n. (pron. 'arssle')]

elephant business *n.* [late 19C] (US) sightseeing. [SEE THE ELEPHANT]

elephant's trunk *adj.* [mid-19C+] drunk (cf. JUMBO'S TRUNK). [rhy. sl.]

elephant tranquillizer *n.* [1980s+] (drugs) phencyclidine (cf. ACE n.³).

elevate *v.*¹ (US) [late 19C] in poker, to raise an opponent.

elevate *v.*² (US) [1920s] (Und.) **1** to rob at gunpoint. **2** to put up one's hands in a hold up. [pun on HOLD UP v.¹]

elevated *adj.* [early 17C–late 19C] drunk, one of a number of words and phr. that equate drunkenness with 'getting high' (cf. EXALTED; FEELING HIGH; FIRED UP; FLYING HIGH; HIGH adj.¹; HIGH AS A KITE; IN ORBIT; IN ONE'S ALTITUDES). [pun on SE]

elevator *n.*¹ [late 19C] a crinolette or bustle used for distending the back of a woman's skirt. [it raises or 'elevates' the back of the skirt]

elevator *n.*² [1910s–20s] (Und.) a hold-up man, a robber. [pun on SE *hold up*/HOLD UP v.¹ (1)]

elevator jockey *n.* [1960s–70s] (US) a lift operator. [SE *elevator* + JOCKEY n.²]

elevenses *n.* [late 19C+] a mid-morning snack. [ext. of synon. dial. *elevens*]

eleven steps *n.* [1950s] (W.I.) an arrest, a trial (cf. FOUR-AND-TWENTY; UP THE STAIRS). [the 11 steps that led to the front door of a well-known court house]

eleventy-'leven/eleventeen *n.* [late 19C–1940s] (US Black) a very large or infinite number (cf. FIFTY-ELEVEN; FORTY-ELEVEN).

el foldo *n.* [1940s+] (US) a failure, esp. in sport or a feigned knockout in boxing. [FOLD v.² + cod Sp.]

Eli *n.* [19C+] (US campus) Yale University; thus *Elis*, alumni of Yale. [*Eli*hu Yale (1649–1721) founder of the original college at Saybrook before it moved to New Haven]

eligantifferously *adv.* [mid-19C] (US) outstandingly. [SE *elegant* + SPLENDIFEROUS]

e-light *n.* [1990s] (US Black) an elitist African American, with insufficient regard for their less well-off peers and their causes. [pron. of SE *élite*]

Elijah two *n.* [late 19C] (US) a false prophet. [Dr John Alexander Dowie (1847–1907), a US evangelist, who was thus satirically christened in memory of the original, biblical *Elijah*; his son, in time, became Elijah three]

elkies *n.* [1980s+] (drugs) MDMA (cf. ECSTASY).

el/L *n.* [late 19C+] (US) the *el*evated railway, usu. that of New York, but also in other cities, e.g. Chicago, where such transport systems existed. [abbr./pron.]

Ellenborough's lodge/park/spike *n.* [early–mid-19C] the

King's Bench prison. [Lord *Ellenborough* (1750–1818) Lord Chief Justice 1802–17]

Ellenborough's teeth *n.* [early–mid-19C] the spiked *cheveux-de-frise* that top the walls of the King's Bench prison. [Lord *Ellenborough* (*see* ELLENBOROUGH'S LODGE) + SE *teeth*]

ellersby *n.* [late 19C] the *London School Board*. [abbr. (LSB). Note printers' use *Ellessea*, London Society of Compositors (LSC)]

ellick *n.* [1900s–20s] (US) the penis. [ety. unknown; ? proper name *Alec*]

elly-bay *n.* [mid-19C+] the belly. [pig Latin]

elmer *n.* [1920s–60s] (US) a rural or unsophisticated man (cf. ALVIN). [the use of *Elmer* as a 'typical' country name]

el pee *n.* [1990s] (US Black) an El Producto cigar (cf. BLUNT n.²).

el primo *adj.* [1980s+] (US) first class. [Sp. *primo*, the best]

el ratto *n.* [1940s+] (US) a near-derelict, but just driveable, second-hand car (cf. JUNKER n.²). [such a car is RATTY adj.¹ in condition]

elrig *n.* [mid-19C+] a girl. [backsl.]

el ropo/el ropo stinkadoro/el stinko *n.* [20C] (US) a cheap, strong cigar. [cod Sp.; note Rudyard Kipling, *Stalky & Co.* (1899), 'pomposo stinkadoro', a large, malodorous cigar]

elsin *n.* [late 19C+] (Ulster) a 'sharp' individual. [dial. *elsin*, a shoemaker's awl; ult. MDu. *elssene* , an awl]

el stinko *see* EL ROPO.

elvis *v.* [1990s] (drugs) of a cannabis cigarette, to burn unevenly. [presumably the smoking habits of the singer *Elvis Presley* (1935–77)]

emag *n.* [late 19C+] a game, usu. as a term of disgust or disappointment meaning 'what's your game?' etc. [backsl.]

embalmed *adj.* [20C] very drunk. [EMBALMING FLUID n. (1)]

embalming fluid *n.* [20C] **1** whisky (cf. CONVERSATION FLUID). **2** (drugs) phencyclidine (cf. ACE n.³).

embarrassed *adj.* [1960s] (W.I.) of a woman, pregnant; of a man, castrated; thus as the major insult, *embarrassed sow*, *embarrassed hog*.

emboosticated *adj.* [1970s] (US campus) embarrassed.

embroidery *n.* [late 19C+] embellishments of the truth, fanciful tales, lies.

emcee *see* M.C.

em-eff/emm-eff *n.* [1960s+] (orig. US) euph. for MOTHERFUCKER. [pron. of initial letters]

em-eff/emm-eff *adj.* [1960s+] (orig. US) euph. for MOTHERFUCKING. [pron. of initial letters]

emergency gun *n.* [1930s] (drugs) any makeshift instrument used to inject when one does not have a syringe. [SE *emergency* + GUN n.² (3)]

emigrate *v.* [mid-19C] (US) to leave.

emmas *n.* [1990s] haemorrhoids (cf. SIGMUNDS). [rhy. sl. *emma freuds* = haemorrhoids; ult. *Emma Freud*, a UK TV presenter]

emm-eff *see* EM-EFF.

emok nye *phr.* [late 19C] come in. [backsl.]

empty *n.* [late 19C+] any container or vessel that has been emptied, esp. a bottle once containing alcohol.

empty *adj.* [1950s] (US) penniless, broke.

empty house is better than a bad tenant, an *phr.* [1930s+] (N.Z.) a phr. used after breaking wind in public.

empty one's trash, to *phr.* (US Black) to have sexual intercourse, usu. to ejaculate (cf. DROP ONE'S LOAD).

empty suit *n.* [1980s+] (US) a useless or insincere person.

empty the bag, to *phr.* [19C] to tell the whole story.

empty the butter-boat, to *phr.* [mid–late 19C] to flatter lavishly (and insincerely). [BUTTER UP]

empty the cannon, to *phr.* [1980s+] to masturbate (cf. SHOOT v.³).

emu *n.* [1960s+] (Aus.) a racecourse idler who picks up discarded tote tickets in the hope of finding one that has not been cashed. [the image of an *emu* pecking at the ground]

emu-bobber *n.* [1920s+] (Aus.) a man employed to pick up the remnants after clearing or burning off in the bush. [for ety. *see* EMU]

enamel *n.* [1940s] (US Black) skin.

enchilada *n.* [1970s] (US) the penis. [resemblance]

encore *adj.* (society) wonderful, very good. [Fr. *encore*, more, esp. in the context of an applauding audience]

encore! *excl.* [early 18C+] a general term of praise. [Fr. *encore*, more, orig. used as a call for the repetition of a song, piece of music etc]

end *n.¹* [late 19C–1960s] a share of profits or responsibility.

end *n.²* [20C] that area of a football stadium, behind the respective goals, traditionally reserved for the hard-core supporters of home and away teams and the scene of most fighting.

end *n.³* **1** [1910s+] the penis, esp. in phr. *get one's end away.* **2** [1990s] (US Black teen) the buttocks, the posterior. [euph. for ARSE n.¹ (1)]

end, the *n.⁴* **1** [1930s+] the absolute limit that the speaker will tolerate, 'the last straw'. **2** [1950s+] (orig. US Black) perfection, absolute excellence, the best possible (cf. DIE v.).

endacott/cott/endicott *v.* [late 19C] to arrest on false pretences, spec. those of being a prostitute. [one Constable *Endacott* who, in 1887, was tried and acquitted for the arrest on these grounds of a respectable dressmaker; the term, poss. coined by Annie Besant (1847–1933), was abbr. to *cott*]

end-around *n.* [20C] the result, the final assessment, the 'bottom line'.

endjie *see* ENTJIE.

endo *n.* [1980s+] (drugs) marijuana (cf. INDO).

end of the ball-game *n.* [20C] death; one of a number of games-playing/sporting metaphors for life's termination (cf. CASH IN ONE'S CHIPS; STRIKE OUT; THROW IN THE TOWEL).

end of the line *phr.* [1950s+] (orig. US) the very end, the ultimate. [railway imagery]

end-of-the-month *adj.* [late 19C+] impoverished. [one's wages are paid at the start of the month]

end over appetite *phr.* [20C] (US) head over heels (cf. ARSE OVER APPETITE). [END n.³ (2) + SE *appetite*]

ends *n.¹* [1950s–60s] (US Black) living expenses. [SE phr. *make ends meet*]

ends *n.²* [1960s] (US Black) shoes.

endsville *n.* [1950s+] (US) **1** the best, the ultimate. **2** the limit, the end, as far as one can go. **3** absolute, irretrievable failure (cf. BOMBSVILLE). [SE *end* + sfx. -VILLE]

end-to-end *v.* [1990s] to self-administer a suction enema.

end up *v.* [late 19C+] to result in, to come to a conclusion.

endways *adv.* [1900s–40s] (US Black) backwards, back-to-front. [SE *endways*, end on, with the end facing]

enemy *n.¹* [19C] the penis.

enemy *n.²* [mid-19C] time; thus *kill the enemy*, to pass time; *what says the enemy?*, what time is it?

energizer *n.* [1990s] (drugs) **1** phencyclidine (cf. ACE n.³). **2** MDMA (cf. ECSTASY).

enforcer *n.* [1930s+] **1** a thug used to enforce his (or another's) will through violence or threats of violence. **2** [1950s+] (gay) a lesbian who keeps the other women in line.

engabachado *n.* [1960s] (US) a Mexican who attempts to 'pass' as White. [Mex. Sp. *engabachado*, rendered white]

engage in three to one/three to one and bound to lose, to *phr.* [18C] to have sexual intercourse (cf. PLAY THREE TO ONE). [the image is of a conflict between the penis and two testicles and the vagina; the 'loss' is of semen]

engage in safe sex, to *phr.* [1980s+] to masturbate. [ironic]

engaging sixth gear *n.* [1990s] an act of mutual masturbation in the front seat of a parked car (cf. SHIFT GEARS).

engine *n.* [mid–late 18C] the penis (cf. FORNICATING ENGINE; GARDEN ENGINE).

English *n.*[1] [17C] ale (cf. LATIN; SPANISH *n.*[2]). [the national drink]

English *n.*[2] [20C] (orig. US) deceptiveness, duplicity, 'spin'. [billiards jargon *English*, spin imparted to one or other side of the ball]

English *n.*[3] [1990s] (US) Olde *English* Malt Liquor. [abbr.]

English *adj.* [1960s–70s] (US) sado-masochistic. [the national stereotype of the English as loving beatings]

English bearer *n.* [late 18C] a drunken man with a red face. [SE *bearer*, one who holds heraldic arms; the red is that of the English flag, St George's Cross]

English burgundy *n.* [mid-18C–mid-19C] porter (a type of dark beer brewed from malt) (cf. ENGLISH MANUFACTURE). [the real *Burgundy* is a variety of French wine]

English cane *n.* [late 17C–early 18C] a cudgel.

English channel *n.* [1950s–70s] the National Health Service. [rhy. sl. *English channel* = SE *panel* (of doctors)]

English cold/winter *n.* [20C] (US) iced tea. [tea is seen as a quintessential English pleasure]

English culture *n.* [1960s+] sex advertisements for bondage and discipline (cf. AMERICAN CULTURE; B & D). [ENGLISH *adj.* + ironic use of SE *culture*]

English disease *n.* **1** [18C–19C] melancholy, depression. **2** [mid–late 19C] rickets. **3** [1960s+] a propensity for industrial action and strikes. **4** [1960s+] erotic flagellation.

English guidance *n.* [1960s+] bondage and discipline. [the popular assumption that all Englishmen enjoy such activities]

Englishified *adj.* [20C] (W.I.) **1** said of one who has returned from a stay in England with an English accent and a generally more sophisticated persona. **2** of East Indians, generally urbanized or westernized (there need have been no visit to the UK).

English manufacture/manufacture *n.* [late 17C–early 19C] ale, beer or cider (cf. ENGLISH BURGUNDY). [SE; all these are native drinks, as opposed to wine or brandy]

English martini *n.* [19050s+] (US gay) tea; especially when spiked with gin.

English method *n.* [1960s+] (US gay) intercrural homosexual intercourse, i.e. non-penetrative rubbing between closed thighs (cf. PRINCETON RUB).

English muffins *n.* [1960s+] (US gay) a boy's buttocks. [the sexual image of the *English* + MUFFINS]

English pluck *n.* [late 19C] money, esp. as used for gambling. [fig. use; *pluck* = courage, thus phr. *have you any English pluck?*, have you the courage to gamble with me?]

English sentry *n.* [1960s+] (US gay) the erect penis. [it 'stands to attention' ? + reputation of Guardsmen for gay prostitution]

English winter *see* ENGLISH COLD.

English sunbathing *n.* [1970s+] (N.Z.) sitting fully-clothed in the sun. [the foolishness of recent immigrants from the UK]

enif *n.* [mid-19C] fine. [backsl.]

enin gens *n.* [mid-19C] 9 shillings (45p). [backsl.]

enin yeneps/yenneps *n.* [mid-19C] 9 pence. [backsl.]

enisel *n.* (drugs) morphine. [ety. unknown]

eno *n.* [mid-19C+] one. [backsl.]

enob *n.* [late 19C+] **1** a bone. **2** the penis. [backsl.]

enoch *n.*[1] [1970s] (juv.) a derog. term for a Black or coloured person. [*Enoch* Powell (1912–98), a UK politician notorious for his neg. attitude to racial integration]

enoch *n.*[2] [1990s] a towel. [rhy. sl. *Enoch Powell*; *see* ENOCH *n.*[1]]

enormous *adj.* [late 19C] (US) splendid.

enough to float a battleship *phr.* [mid-19C+] (US) a very large amount of alcohol.

enough to gag a maggot *phr.* [1940s+] (US) **1** something utterly repulsive. **2** something in great or overwhelming quantity.

enough to give you a fit on the mat *phr.* [1900s–10s] extremely funny indeed.

enough to make a Black man choke *phr.* [20C] a phr. indicating that something (usu. food and medicines but also of abstract objects, emotions etc) is unpalatable. [neg. stereotyping, on the basis that Blacks have a less refined palate]

enough to make/it would make a cat laugh *phr.* [mid-19C+] utterly hilarious, devastatingly funny.

enough to make a dog laugh *phr.* [17C–early 19C] extremely amusing.

enough to split the grain *phr.* [late 19C] enough to render one very drunk.

enough to swear by *phr.* [mid-18C–late 19C] a very small, but still perceptible amount.

ensign-bearer *n.* [mid-17C–early 19C] a red-faced drunkard. [the colours of the face resemble those of the Union Jack]

entered *adj.* [early 18C] (US) intoxicated.

enter for the gelding stakes, to *phr.* [late 19C] **1** to castrate someone. **2** to be a eunuch. [joc. use of racing imagery]

entertain the general, to *phr.* [20C] (US) to menstruate.

enthroned *adj.* [1950s–60s] (gay) searching for sex in public lavatories (cf. ABDICATED). [THRONE *n.* + a pun on QUEEN *n.*[1]]

enthusiastic amateur *see* AMATEUR.

enthuzimuzzy *n.* [late 19C] enthusiasm.

entire *adj.* [late 19C+] (Ulster) financially independent. [also in Lincolnshire dial.]

entire/extreme animal *n.* [mid-19C] absolutely everything, 'the lot'. [semi-euph. for WHOLE HOG]

entjie/endjie *n.* [1980s+] (S. Afr.) a cigarette end. [Afk. *end*, end + dim. sfx. *-ie*]

entrance *n.* [19C] the vagina (cf. BELLY DALE).

enzed *n.* [1910s+] (Aus./ N.Z.) New Zealand; thus *enzedder*, a New Zealander. [pron. of initial letters]

epar! *excl.* [1950s–70s] (US campus) a cry of distress used ironically. [reverse of SE *rape!* used fig.]

ephedrone *n.* [1980s+] (drugs) methicathinone.

ephus *n.* [1930s–50s] (US) the truth or a gimmick. [ety. unknown]

eppes/eppis/eppus *n.* [20C] **1** something, a little. **2** a somebody. **3** nothing. [Ger. *etwas*, something, thence Yid. *eppes*; like many Yid. terms *eppes* is capable of many uses, often ironic, and all dependent on context. It entered the sl. vocabulary via the underworld, which used it to mean low-class or worthless. Subseq. meanings have developed since]

eppes/eppis/eppus *adj.* [20C] debatable, worthless, unsatisfactory.

eppes/eppis/eppus *adv.* [20C] quite, perhaps, maybe, for some inexplicable reason.

Epsom races *n.* [mid-19C] a pair of braces. [rhy. sl.]

equalizer *n.* [1930s+] (US) a gun (cf. CONVINCER). [it reduces all before it to the same abject level]

equipment *n.* **1** [1940s+] the female breasts. **2** [1960s+] the male genitals (cf. ACCOUTREMENTS). [euph.]

equipped *adj.* [late 17C–18C; 1960s] **1** well-turned out, well-dressed. **2** (US Black) emotionally and socially poised. [20C use of (1) also mainly US Black]

-er *sfx.* [mid-19C+] used to create slangy formations of nouns by shortening the original noun and replacing the missing letters with *-er*. When the word is a monosyllable, this can be extended by the sfx. *-agger* or *-ugger*. [the 'Oxford *-er*' sfx. appeared 'early in the Queen's [Victoria] reign' (Ware) or was 'introduced from Rugby School into Oxford University slang, orig. at University College, in Michaelmas Term, 1875' (*OED*). The absence of any such terms from the seminal (and slang-laden) Oxford novel *The Adventures of Mr Verdant Green* (1853, by 'Cuthbert Bede') makes the later date far more likely. Strictly jargon, given its use at Oxford, it has moved into wider areas, typically *fresher*, a university freshman, *footer*, football, *soccer*, football and *rugger*, rugby. The extreme uses, e.g. *pragger-wagger*, the Prince of Wales and *wagger-pagger-bagger*, a waste-paper basket remain strictly Oxford and 1900s–20s Oxford at that. For a fuller discussion *see* M. Marples, *University Slang* (1950); *inter alia* he suggests the importation came not from Rugby but from Harrow]

erase *v.* [1950s+] to murder, to kill (cf. RUB OUT).

erb *n.* [1930s+] a wag, a humourist. [abbr. proper name H*erb*ert, which is seen to be 'funny']

erie *v.* [1940s] (US Und.) to overhear. [ON THE ERIE!]

erif *n.* [mid-19C) fire. [backsl.]

eriff *n.* [late 18C–19C] a young or novice criminal. [SE *eriff*, a two-year-old canary; the term migrated to US during the 19C]

-erine/-erino/-erina *sfx.* [late 19C+] (US) an intensifier applicable to various words, generally implying further excellence, appeal etc., e.g. PEACHERINO, very wonderful indeed.

erk *n.* [1940s+] a general term of contempt, an insignificant person. [orig. WW2 milit. use, either RN *erk*, a lower deck rating, or RAF *erk*, aircraftsman, second class]

erky *adj.* [1950s–60s] (Aus.) unpleasant, distasteful. [ERK + sfx. -*y*, but note *yuck*, a grunt of distaste]

ernie marsh *n.* [20C] the grass. [rhy. sl.]

-eroo *sfx.* [1940s+] (orig. US) a general intensifier, implying a greater flamboyance or exaggeration; allied to a variety of terms, e.g. BOOZEROO; FLOPEROO; SMACKEROOS; STINKEROO.

-eroonie/-aroonie/-oroonie *sfx.* [1960s+] (US) an intensifier, usu. pos. and added to various words, e.g. smackeroonie. [var. on -ERINE]

Errol Flynn *n.* [1940s+] a chin. [rhy. sl.; ult. Hollywood star *Errol Flynn* (1909–59)]

erth *n.*[1] *see* EARTH *n.*[1].

erth *n.*[2] [1980s+] (drugs) phencyclidine (cf. ACE *n.*[3]). [ety. unknown; ? SE *earth* but why?]

erth gens *see* EARTH GENS.

erth-pu *see* EARTH-PU.

erth sith-noms *see* EARTH SITH-NOMS.

erth yannops/yenneps *see* EARTH YANNOPS.

erupt Vesuvius *v.* [1990s] to masturbate.

ervine *n.* [1960s] (US Black) a policeman. [Los Angeles use; the *E* on number-plates that in L.A. signifies a police vehicle]

esaff *n.* [late 19C] the face. [backsl.]

escamao *adj.* [1960s+] (US) nervous, shaken up. [Sp. sl. *escamao*, 'losing it']

escargot *n.* [1980s] (US campus) a male walking arm in arm with his date. [Fr. *escargot*, a snail; the couple appear curled up as tightly as a snail in its shell]

esclop *n.* [mid-19C] the police (cf. SLOP *n.*[2]). [backsl., neither the *e* nor the *c* are pron.]

ese/essay *n.* [1990s] (US Black/Hispanic) a fellow Hispanic, esp. in the context of a street gang (cf. HOMEBOY). [Sp.]

esel/ezel *n.* [1910s] (S. Afr.) a fool, a simpleton (cf. ARSE *n.*[1]). [Afk. *ezel*, a donkey, an ass]

eskimo *n.* (US) a derog. term for a Jew. [rhy. sl. *eskimo* = IKEY-MO *n.*]

esky *n.*[1] [1910s+] (US) a derog. term for an Inuit, an Eskimo person or an Eskimo dog. [abbr. SE *Eskimo*]

esky *n.*[2] [1950s+] (Aus.) a portable drinks cooler, popularly filled with beer for cricket watching etc. [SE *eskimo* and thus chilliness]

esprit chick *n.* [1990s] (US teen) a girl who wears only designer clothing and looks down on others who dress differently. [the fashionable dress shop chain *Esprit* + CHICK *n.*[3] (1)]

espysay *n.* [late 19C] the Society for the Prevention of Cruelty to Animals. [initials SPCA, 'secretive in its nature, being created by people about horses and cattle, many of whom go about in savage fear of this valuable society' (Ware)]

esqueeze me *phr.* [1990s] (US campus) excuse me.

esqüintar *v.* [1960s+] (US) to leave. [Sp. lit. 'make one's squints']

esra *n.* [1980s+] (drugs) marijuana. [Turkish *esrar*, cannabis]

es-roph/es-roch *n.* [mid-19C] a horse. [backsl.]

essay *see* ESE.

essedartus *n.* [early 18C] a coachman. [Lat. *essedarius*, a fighter in a Gaulish war-chariot]

essence *n.*[1] [mid-19C] whisky. [SE *essence*, an extract obtained by distillation or otherwise from a plant]

essence *n.*[2] [1980s+] (drugs) MDMA. [ECSTASY]

essence of hickory *n.* [mid-19C] (US) a whipping with a hickory switch.

essence-peddler *n.* [mid-19C–1970s] (US) a skunk. [the skunk's notoriety as a smelly animal]

Essex calf *n.* [late 19C] a native of Essex, as used by those of Suffolk, who look down on their southern neighbours (cf. CALF *n.*[2]; ESSEX LION).

Essex lion *n.* [17C–mid-19C] **1** a calf. **2** pej. for a native of Essex, as used by those of Kent (cf. ESSEX CALF; ROMFORD LION; VALIANT AS AN ESSEX LION). [Essex was a popular source of cattle for the London meat markets]

Essex stile *n.* [late 18C–mid-19C] a ditch. [Essex being a low, marshy county, there are more ditches than stiles]

Establishment, the *n.* [mid–late 19C] (Aus.) the Fremantle Gaol. [SE *establishment*, an institution]

esther *n.* [1950s–60s] (camp gay) a Jewish homosexual male. [joc. ref. to the biblical *Esther*, who was a SE *queen*, thus pun on QUEEN *n.*[1]]

estuffa *n.* [1980s+] (drugs) heroin. [Sp.]

ET *n.* [1990s] (drugs) alpha-ethyltyptimine. [abbr.]

et-caetera/etcetera *n.* [late 16C–early 17C] the vagina (cf. POPERIN PEAR). [euph.]

eternity box *n.* [late 18C–20C] a coffin (cf. BOX *n.*[2]).

ethel *n.* [1920s+] a male homosexual (cf. AGNES). [the female name]

ether *n.* [1930s+] fig. use for communication through the radio or the wireless.

Ethiopian in the fuel supply *phr.* [20C] a self-consciously contrived euph. for NIGGER IN THE WOODPILE. [18C SE *Ethiopian*, a Black person]

Ethiopian paradise *n.* [20C] (US) the top gallery in a theatre (cf. BUZZARD ROOST *n.*[2]). [poor Black theatre-goers could usu. afford only the cheapest seats]

ethno *n.* [1970s+] (Aus.) immigrants to Australia, of various ethnic persuasions. [SE *ethnic* + sfx. -O]

ethy meat *n.* [20C] a Black woman. [SE *Ethiopian* + (DARK) MEAT]

-ette *sfx.* [late 19C+] an all-purpose dimin., used by the middle-classes in a generally twee manner, e.g. *smidgeonette*, a very, very small portion, *drinkette*, a very small measure of alcohol.

euchre *v.* **1** [mid-19C+] (US) to swindle, to trick, to cheat. **2** [1970s+] to destroy. [for ety. *see* EUCHRED]

euchred *adj.* [1930s+] (Aus.) exhausted, destitute. [the card-game *euchre* (orig. US) in which, if a player chooses to play a round and fails to take three tricks, they are 'euchred' (*OED*)]

European accentuation *n.* [1950s+] (gay) a tapered body with jutting buttocks. [? body-building use]

evaporate v. [early–mid-19C] to leave, to vanish, to escape.

evatch v. [mid-19C] to have. [backsl.]

eve n.[1] [18C–19C] a hen-roost. ['Som.(erset) slang' (*EDD*)]

eve n.[2] [1980s+] (drugs) MDEA, a synthetic hallucinogen similar to MDMA (cf. ECSTASY). [play on ADAM n.[4]]

even adv. [1980s+] (US) at all, used as a neg. emphasis.

even break n. [1910s+] (orig. US) a fair chance. [SE *even* + BREAK n.[2] (1)]

even-even adj. [20C] (US) equal (cf. EVEN STEPHEN).

evening n. [1960s] an *evening* paper. [abbr.]

evening! excl. [1910s+] good *evening*. [abbr.]

evening sneak n. [late 18C–early 19C] (Und.) a thief who works after dark (cf. MORNING SNEAK; UPRIGHT SNEAK). [SE *evening* + SNEAK n.[1]]

evening socket n. [1990s] the female genitalia. [the male 'plugs in' at night]

evening star n. [mid–late 19C] a prostitute (cf. FLASHTAIL; MOONLIGHTER; NIGHTBIRD; NIGHTCAP n.[1]; NIGHTHAWK n.; NIGHTIN-GALE n.; NIGHT POACHER; NIGHT SHADE; NIGHT TRADER; NIGHT WALKER; NOCTRESS; NOCTURNE; NYMPH OF DARKNESS; OWL n.).

evening wheeze n. [late 19C] false news, rumours. [SE *evening* + WHEEZE n.; the exciting but implausible stories used to sell evening papers]

even/good shake n. [1960s+] an equal chance (cf. FAIR SHAKE). [the shaking of dice]

even stephen/steven adj. [19C+] having fair shares (cf. EVEN-EVEN). [note Jonathan Swift, *Journal to Stella*, 20 January 1748: 'Now we are even, quoth Stephen, when he gave his wife six blows for one']

even terms phr. [1940s+] (Aus.) working for one's food.

ever been to flight school, boy? phr. [1990s] (US Black teen) a threat, a challenge to start fighting (cf. DO YOU LIKE HOSPITAL FOOD?). [the aggressor is about to make the opponent 'see stars' or 'fly through the air']

evergreen n. [1900s] (US) money (cf. FOLDING GREEN; GREEN BOYS; GREENIES n.[2]; GREENS n.[3]; GREEN SHIT; GREEN STAMP; GREEN THUMB; LEAN GREEN; LONG GREEN). [its colour]

evergreens n. [19C] the vagina (cf. BEAUTY SPOT n.[1]). [SE *ever* + GREENS n.[2]]

everlasting adj. [late 17C–1900s] (US) general intensifier, very, exceeding, excessive.

everlastingly adv. [late 17C–1900s] (US) beyond measure; immeasurably, excessively.

everlasting shoes n. [mid-19C] the feet.

everlasting staircase n. [mid-19C] the prison treadmill (cf. CUBIT; PERPETUAL STAIRCASE; STAIRS WITHOUT A LANDING; UNIVERSAL STAIRCASE; VERTICAL CARE-GRINDER; WHEEL OF LIFE). [invented by the builder William Cubitt (1785–1861) for use in prisons; it was improved by Colonel Chesterton, thus its expanded name *Colonel Chesterton's everlasting staircase*]

everlasting wound n. [mid-19C] the vagina (cf. AXE WOUND).

ever-loving n. **1** [1930s+] one's wife. **2** [1960s–70s] one's mind. [apparently coined and primarily used by Damon Runyon (1884–1946)]

ever so phr. [late 19C+] much, e.g. *thanks ever so*.

ever so very phr. [late 19C+] much. [ext. of EVER SO]

everton toffee n. [mid-19C] coffee. [rhy. sl.; like white coffee, this toffee is also made with cream or (later) evaporated milk. Note nickname for the British football club Everton, 'the Toffees']

everybody and his cousin phr. [mid-19C+] (US) absolutely everybody (cf. EVERYONE AND HIS BROTHER).

everyday chill n. [1990s] (US Black teen) the things one does every day to relax. [SE *everyday* + CHILL v.[3] (3)]

every dog and devil phr. [20C] (Irish) everyone.

every jack man see EVERY MAN JACK.

every last one phr. [late 19C+] (orig. US) every one without exception.

every living ass phr. [1940s+] (US) every single person. [play on SE + ARSE n.[1]]

every man jack/every jack man n. [early 19C+] every single one. [JACK n.[5] as generic for a man]

every man jag n. [19C] every single one (cf. EVERY MAN JACK).

every mother's son n. [late 16C+] each and every one.

everyone and his brother phr. [20C] a large number of people. [the implication is that the numbers are more than the speaker desires]

every postman on his beat phr. [1930s–40s] (US Black) kinky hair that stands up in odd strands or areas of the head.

every so often phr. [late 19C+] occasionally.

everything but the kitchen sink phr. [1940s+] used of an undertaking that requires whatever is available, no matter what it is, relevant or not.

everything cook and curry phr. [1950s+] (W.I. Rasta) all is well, all is taken care of. [culinary imagery]

everything in the book n. [1950s] (US) whatever is available, whatever is known.

everything in the garden is lovely phr. [1910s+] everything is perfectly satisfactory, all is well (cf. EVERYTHING'S NICE IN YOUR GARDEN).

everything is everything phr. [1990s] (US teen gang) everything is fine.

everything's nice in your garden phr. [late 19C] a phr. used to tease someone who seems overly pleased with their own situation (cf. ALL RIGHT FOR SOME; EVERYTHING IN THE GARDEN IS LOVELY). ['This is said to be derived from one of the young princesses (probably a daughter of the Princess Beatrice) who made this reply when something in her garden at Osborne was praised by Her Majesty' (Ware)]

every time! excl. [1920s+] (US) a general affirmative excl. (cf. RIGHT ON!; WAY TO GO!).

everywheres n. [mid-19C+] (US) everywhere.

Eve's custom house n. [late 18C] the vagina. [ext. of CUSTOM HOUSE]

evesdropper n. **1** [18C] a burglar who lurks outside a house waiting for the chance to break in while the owners are absent. **2** [mid-18C–early 19C] a robber of hen-houses. [pun on SE *eaves* + eavesdropper]

eve with the lid on phr. [1920s–30s] (US) apple pie. [the Garden of Eden story]

evif/ewif n. [mid-19C] the number five. [backsl.]

evil n.[1] [late 18C] a halter. [dial. *evil*, a swelling on the neck]

evil n.[2] [early 19C] one's wife (cf. ANCHOR n.[2]). [slang's usu. neg. image of marriage]

evil adj. [1980s+] excellent, wonderful, the best (cf. AWFUL adj.). [on bad = good pattern]

evilling n. [1930s+] (US Black) acting in a deliberately neg. manner, e.g. riotously, argumentatively, criminally. [SE *evil* + sfx. -*ing*]

evlenet gens n. [mid-19C] 12 shillings. [backsl.]

evlenet sith-noms n. [mid-19C] 12 months, usu. as a prison sentence. [backsl.]

evo n. [1990s] (Aus.) evening (cf. ARVO). [SE *ev(ening)* + sfx. -*o*]

ewe n. [late 18C] (Und.) a young and beautiful female member of a criminal gang.

ewe-mutton n. [18C] **1** an ageing prostitute. **2** an amateur prostitute. [SE *ewe* + BIT OF MUTTON n. (1)]

ewif see EVIF.

ewif gens n. [mid-19C] 5 shillings, a crown (25p). [backsl.]

ewif yeneps/yenneps n. [mid-19C] 5 pence. [backsl.]

ewscray v. [1930s–40s] (US) to go away, used as a command. [SCREW v.]

ex n. **1** [early 19C+] an ex-husband, ex-wife, ex-lover, the other half of a lapsed relationship. **2** [1900s–30s] (US prison) an ex-convict. [SE pfx. -ex, former, previous]

ex adj.[1] [20C] superlative, first-rate (cf. DEF; RAD adj.). [abbr. SE excellent]

ex adj.[2] [1950s+] angry, irritated. [x adj.]

ex! excl. [1980s+] (juv.) excellent! (cf. BRILL!). [abbr.; used in preparatory schools]

exactly adv. [mid-19C+] a term of agreement used in response to a previous statement, absolutely, completely; thus not exactly, not really, not at all, absolutely not.

exalted adj. [mid-17C–mid-18C] slightly drunk (cf. ELEVATED).

examine/inspect the equipment, to phr. [1990s] to masturbate. [euph.]

excellent adj. [1980s+] (US campus) extremely good or exciting. [popularized by the film Bill and Ted's Excellent Adventure (1988)]

exchange spit v. [1970s] **1** to kiss. **2** to have sexual intercourse.

exchequer n. [early–mid-16C] the vagina (cf. BANK n.[1]).

ex-con n. [20C] (orig. US) a former convict. [EX n. + CON n.[1] (6)]

excremental adj. [1960s+] euph. for SHITTY.

excused, to be v. [1950s+] (mainly school) euph. for to be allowed to go to the lavatory, usu. in interrog. phr. may I be excused?

excuse-me n. [1960s+] (S. Afr.) a member of the educated middle class. [their good manners]

excuse me while I whip this out phr. [1990s] (US Black teen) one's last words before commencing a fight. [this is one's fist or poss. a weapon]

excuse my French phr. [late 19C+] a genteel euph. automatically offered after the speaker has sworn in public (cf. PARDON MY FRENCH). [racial stereotyping; Anglo-Saxons blame the French for anything remotely 'dirty']

execs n. [late 19C+] the executives (of a firm or business). [abbr.]

execution day n. **1** [late 18C] washing day. **2** [20C] (US) Monday. [the washing is 'hanged' out to dry]

exercise the ferret, to phr. [1960s+] to copulate. [SE exercise + CHUTNEY FERRET]

exes n.[1] [mid-19C+] expenses. [abbr.]

exes/exis n.[2] [mid-19C+] the number six. [backsl.]

Exeter hall n. [19C] the vagina (cf. FUMBLER'S HALL). [a teasing allusion to Exeter Hall, best known for its temperance sermons and, later, as the first London site of a YMCA]

exflunct v. [mid-19C–1970s] (US) to destroy or overwhelm. [? SE fling]

exis see EXES n.[2].

exis-evif yeneps n. [mid-19C] 11 pence. [backsl.; lit. 'six plus five pence']

exis-ewif gens n. [mid-19C] 30 shillings, £1 10s (£1.50). [backsl.; lit. '6 times 5 shillings']

exis gens n. [mid-19C] 6 shillings (30p). [backsl.]

exis sith-noms n. [mid-19C] 6 months, usu. as a prison sentence. [backsl.]

exis yeneps/yenneps n. [mid-19C] sixpence (2½p). [backsl.]

expat n. [1960s+] **1** an expatriate, a UK citizen living abroad. **2** (W.I.) an immigrant, esp. a White foreigner, working in a local job. [abbr.]

expecting adj. [early 19C+] pregnant. [abbr. SE expecting a baby]

expect me when you see me phr. [1920s+] a phr. used to imply that the speaker is not certain of the time they will return.

expense n. [1940s] (US Black) a baby. [the cost of bringing up a child]

explore me! excl. [1910s] (US) used to express lack of knowledge (cf. SEARCH ME!).

explorers club n. [1970s+] (drugs) group of LSD users. [they go on a TRIP n.[3]]

express oneself v. [1980s+] to masturbate. [pun on SE express, make one's feeling felt/to press, squeeze or wring out]

exsie adj. [1990s] (Aus.) expensive.

extensive adj. [mid-19C] showy, vulgar. [euph.]

extinguish v. [late 19C+] to crush verbally, to reduce to silence.

extortion n. [late 19C] (US) the cost.

extra adj. [1940s–50s] (Aus.) extraordinarily good.

extract/take the Michael, to phr. [1950s+] a consciously 'genteel' version of TAKE THE MICKEY.

extract the urine, to phr. [1930s+] (orig. milit.) euph. for TAKE THE PISS.

extreme animal see ENTIRE ANIMAL.

e ya later phr. [1990s] (US teen) goodbye. [var. on see you later + joc. ref. to the drug ECSTASY or E]

eye n.[1] [1930s+] (US Und.) **1** a detective, a private eye. **2** a warder. **3** a look-out. [the logo of Pinkerton's detective agency]

eye n.[2] [1950s–70s] (US campus) a television set. [its monocular screen]

eyeball n.[1] [20C] (W.I.) the most beloved child in a family. [play on SE the apple of one's eye]

eyeball n.[2] [1950s+] a look or glance.

eyeball adj. [1950s+] (US) used of a personal inspection or eyewitness account.

eyeball v. **1** [mid-19C+] (orig. Aus.) to stare at, to ogle (cf. ORB; RECKLESS EYEBALLING). **2** (orig. US) [1940s+] to inspect, to examine. **3** [1970s] (US) to meet in person.

eyeballer n. [1950s+] (US) a know-it-all, esp. one who takes it upon themself to tell others what to do. [EYEBALL adj.]

eye booger n. [1980s+] (US campus) the small pieces of 'sleep' or mucus that collect in the corners of the eyes. [SE eye + BOOGER n.[1]]

eye candy n. [1980s+] (US) a piece of printed or televisual matter, esp. an advertisement, that pleases the eye (esp. in a sexual manner) but has no intrinsic worth (cf. ARM CANDY). [SE eye + candy]

eye doctor n. [1950s+] (gay) a male homosexual, i.e. one who practises anal intercourse. [BROWN EYE n.[2]/ROUNDEYE + SE doctor + pun on SE]

eye-eye! excl. [1940s+] look at that! what's all this! take a look around etc.

eyefuck v. [1910s+] (US) **1** to stare pointedly and lustfully at a sexually desirable person (cf. RECKLESS EYEBALLING). **2** to stare, without sexual overtones. [SE eye + FUCK v.[1]]

eyeful n. [1930s+] an attractive woman.

eyeglass weather n. [late 19C] foggy weather, in which one cannot see clearly. [one requires an eyeglass]

eye in the sky n. (orig. US) **1** [1960s+] a two-way mirror used for security in a casino. **2** [1970s+] a police or traffic helicopter.

eyelid movies n. [1970s+] (US) daydreams, fantasies enjoyed with the eyes closed, esp. as masturbation fantasies.

eye-limpet n. [late 19C] an artificial eye. [its sticks to one's eye socket]

eye-lotion n. [1940s] a very small amount of wine, enough to fill an eye-bath.

eye of one's arse n. [20C] (Irish) the anus. [ARSE n.[1]]

eye-opener n.[1] [19C] the penis (cf. COCK-OPENER).

eye-opener n.[2] **1** [early 19C+] (orig. US) the first drink of the day (cf. ALLEVIATOR). **2** [late 19C+] a surprise, a shock, not necessarily unpleasant. **3** [1910s] an attractive woman. **4** [1930s–70s] (drugs) the day's first dose of a drug. **5** [1980s+]

(drugs) crack cocaine. **6** [1980s+] (drugs) amphetamine (cf. A n.²). [all 'wake you up']

eye-popper *n.* [1940s+] (US) something sensational. [one's eyes *pop out of one's head*]

eyes *n.*¹ [20C] (US Und.) mirrors held through the bars of one's cell and used to survey the outer world. [the mirror extends the range of one's eyesight]

eyes *n.*² [1950s+] the nipples or female breasts (cf. HANDS n.²). [resemblance]

eyes catch fire/burn you/get red/red for *phr.* (W.I.) to become obsessed with at first sight and thus to desire to possess immediately (cf. SKIN CATCH FIRE). [? African langs., e.g. Yoruba *oju gba ina je*, lit. 'eye take eat fire', thus to crave something seen for the first time; Shona *kutsu ukisa ma ziso*, lit. 'make red both eye', thus one's eyes redden to get something]

eyes like pissholes in the snow *phr.* [20C] (orig. milit.) deeply sunken eyes, often bloodshot. [poss. the result of an excess of alcohol]

eyes make fire/make fire for *phr.* [20C] (W.I/Gren.) to be awaiting someone's arrival anxiously.

eyes set at eight in the morning *phr.* [early 17C] drunk (cf. EYES SET IN ONE'S HEAD). [one's eyes are staring in different directions]

eyes set in one's head *phr.* [early 17C] drunk (cf. EYES SET AT EIGHT IN THE MORNING).

eye that weeps most when best pleased *phr.* [19C] the vagina. [the secretions that indicate excitement]

eyetie *n.* [1920s+] a derog. term for an Italian (cf. ITIE). [exaggerated 'Italian' pron.]

eyeto *n.* [1940s+] (Aus.) an Italian. [EYETIE + sfx. -O]

eye-trouble *n.* [1980s+] (N.Z. prison) a propensity (real or imagined) for staring at other prisoners or at warders, usu. in challenging *phr. have you got eye-trouble?*, often the start of a fight.

eyewash *n.* **1** [late 19C+] (orig. milit.) rubbish, nonsense, humbug, anything done for appearance rather than effect (cf. BULL n.¹²). **2** [1920s–70s] cheap liquor. [the army use meant anything, e.g. washing the eyes, that is done for effect rather than for any practical purpose]

eyewater/devil's eyewater *n.* [early–mid-19C] **1** gin. **2** (US) illicitly distilled whisky (cf. PADDY'S EYEWATER).

ezel *see* ESEL.

F

F! *excl.* [1930s+] euph. for FUCK!; thus *f-ing*, FUCKING.

f.a. *see* FANNY ADAMS n.[2].

faastie *adj.* [1950s+] (W.I./Jam.) rude, impertinent, impudent (cf. FACETY). [? Surinam Creole *fiesti*, nasty, or FEISTY]

fab *adj.* [1960s+] a general term of approbation, first popularized by the Beatles *c.*1963 but still used, often with an ironic intonation. [abbr. SE *fabulous*, but Hancock suggests Sp. *fabulosa*, and sees it as orig. Polari]

fab! *excl.* [1960s+] a general excl. of approbation. [FAB adj.]

fabulous drop *n.* [1940s+] (Aus.) an attractive young woman. [the comparison is with a good drink, 'a good drop' (of liquor)]

face *n.*[1] **1** [16C–18C] a coin. **2** [mid-18C–mid-19C] credit at a public house (cf. RUN ONE'S FACE). [the face, usually royal, engraved on one of a coin's sides]

face *n.*[2] **1** [late 16C–early 17C] a grimace. **2** [mid-19C–1920s] (US) audacity, impudence. **3** [mid-19C+] (US) the mouth, as source of speech; thus *shut your face*. **4** [late 19C–1910s] (US) the mouth, as used for eating and drinking (cf. FEED ONE'S FACE). **5** [late 19C–1950s] (US) interference, nosiness; thus *stick one's face in*. **6** [late 19C+] a general term of greeting, e.g. *Hello, face*. **7** [1920s+] (Aus.) one's personal appearance. **8** [1930s–40s] (US Black) a stranger, esp. a White stranger. **9** [1940s+] (US) a cosmetic kit. **10** [1940s+] a person; esp. in police use, a known criminal. **11** [1960s+] a fellow member of a mod gang, esp. one who is considered particularly fashionable (cf. MOD n.[2]). **12** [1960s+] (US) fellatio or cunnilingus (cf. FACE ARTIST; GIVE FACE).

face *v.* **1** [1920s+] (Irish) of a man, to pay court to a woman. **2** [1980s+] (US campus) to outperform, to correct, to show up, to humiliate, to insult (cf. IN SOMEONE'S FACE). [15C SE *face*, 'to show a bold face, look big; to brag, boast, swagger' (OED)]

face! *excl.* [1980s+] (US campus) an excl. delivered to a person whom one has just insulted or humiliated. [FACE v.]

face-ache *n.* [1930s+] joc. form of address. [despite the apparent rudeness of the phr., the *ache* presumably comes f. laughter]

face and brace, to *phr.* [16C] to bluster, to defy, to bully verbally. [SE *face*]

face artist *n.* [1970s+] (US Und.) a fellator or fellatrix. [FACE n.[2] (12) + ARTIST n.[2]]

face bowl *n.* [1900s–50s] (US Black) a bathroom sink.

face cream *n.* [1980s+] (US gay) semen, esp. as when ejaculated onto a fellator's face. [note FACE n.[2] (12) + CREAM n.[1] (1)]

faced *adj.*[1] [1980s+] (US campus) humiliated, embarrassed. [FACE v.]

faced *adj.*[2] [1980s+] **1** (US teen) extremely drunk. **2** (drugs) stunned by the potency of a drug, usu. cannabis. [abbr. SHIT-FACED]

face fins *n.* [20C] a moustache, presumably a large one that protrudes on either side of the cheeks.

face fittings *n.* [20C] (Aus.) a beard and/or moustache (cf. FACE FUNGUS).

face-fucking *n.* [1970s+] fellatio in which one partner lies on their back with an opened mouth. [SE *face* + FUCKING n.]

face fungus *n.* [20C] male facial hair, i.e. a beard and/or moustache (cf. FACE FITTINGS).

face it out with a card of ten *see* BRAG IT OUT WITH A CARD OF TEN.

face like a bagful of spanners *phr.* [1970s+] used of someone who has a craggy, rough-looking face.

face like a stripper's clit *phr.* [1990s] a derog. description of the face of an unattractive woman.

face like the back of a bus/that would stop a bus *phr.* [1940s+] a very unattractive (usu. female) face.

face like the back of a tram *phr.* [1930s–40s] a very unattractive (usu. female) face.

face like the side of a house/rear end of a cow *phr.* [1940s+] a very unattractive (usu. female) face.

face like yesterday *n.* [1900s–10s] a very miserable-looking face.

face-plaster *n.* [1940s+] (Aus.) an alcoholic drink. [it 'bandages up' a miserable face]

face pussy *n.* [1980s+] (US gay) fellatio. [SE *face* + PUSSY n.[1]]

facer *n.*[1] **1** [late 17C–early 19C] a brimming glass. **2** [19C] a glass that holds a single dram of spirits. **3** [mid-19C] a glass of whisky punch. [all are poured into the face]

facer *n.*[2] **1** [early–mid-19C] a blow in the face. **2** [mid-19C+] an unexpected problem or obstacle, anything to which one must face up.

facer *n.*[3] [mid-19C] (US Und.) a criminal who stalls those in pursuit of their accomplices. [SE *face off*]

face rape *v.* [1980s+] (US campus) to kiss passionately. [on model of SE *date rape*]

face that would stop a bus *see* FACE LIKE THE BACK OF A BUS.

face the music, to *phr.* [mid-19C–1920s] **1** to deal stoically with a problem or difficult situation. **2** to take one's punishment. [SE post-1920s]

face the nation, to *phr.* [1970s+] (US Black) to perform cunnilingus (cf. FACE n.[2]).

facety *adj.* [1940s+] (W.I.) cheeky, impudent (cf. FAASTIE; FACEY). [SE *feisty* but ? note Surinam Creole *fiesti*, dirty, nasty, SE *fist*, a fart]

facey/facy *adj.* [early 17C+] cheeky, rude, impudent (cf. FACETY). [SE *face*, effrontery; 20C use is W.I. only]

facial *n.*[1] [1970s+] **1** a prostitute's client who likes the woman to sit on his face, sometimes after she has inserted a suppository or even when she is having intercourse with another man. **2** ejaculation in one's partner's face (cf. FACE CREAM). [SE *facial*, cosmetic treatment for the face]

facial *n.*[2] [1970s] (US campus) an insult, a rebuff. [? IN SOMEONE'S FACE]

facial v. [1970s+] **1** (US gay) to perform fellatio. **2** to ejaculate in one's partner's face. [FACIAL n.[1]]

factor see FATER.

-factor sfx. [1970s+] (US campus) in combination with a relevant noun, a quantity of, a degree of, e.g. dork-factor, the number of fools, dog-factor, the number of ugly women.

factory n.[1] [mid-19C+] (Und.) a large, forbidding Victorian police station in the London Metropolitan area. [resemblance to the architecture of 19C factories, ? + allusion to the 'manufacturing' of evidence]

factory n.[2] [1970s+] (drugs) a place where drugs are packaged, diluted or manufactured.

factotum n. [late 19C] the vagina. [SE factotum, a man of all work; a servant who has the entire management of his master's affairs]

facy see FACEY.

fad-cattle n. [19C] generic term for sexually available women. [dial. faddle, to make much of (a child) + SE cattle]

faddle n. [late 19C] **1** a trifling person. **2** a homosexual man. [Midlands dial. faddle, an over-particular, fussy person]

fade n.[1] [late 19C] (US) a former dandy, now fallen on hard times and thus less resplendent. [SE fade, faded glory]

fade n.[2] **1** [20C] (US Black) a derog. term for a White person. **2** [1970s+] (US Black) a Black person who becomes immersed in the White world and thus 'fades away' (cf. FADED BOOGIE). [SE faded, pale, wan]

fade/fade away n.[3] [1900s–60s] (US) a departure, an escape. [FADE v.[2] (1)]

fade n.[4] [1980s+] (US Black) short-cropped Black hair, pioneered by the hip-hop culture. [? it fades into the skull]

fade v.[1] **1** [late 19C+] (US) to put at a disadvantage. **2** [1920s] (US Und.) to hold up with a gun. **3** [1950s+] (US Black) to cause problems for someone, esp. in phr. don't fade me; thus have someone faded, to have someone at a disadvantage. **4** [1960s–70s] (US) to put up with, to manage something. **5** [1970s+] to surpass, to dismiss. **6** [1990s] (US Black/teen) to fool around or tinker with something or someone. [gambling use, either dice, to bet against the player holding the dice, or poker, to match the previous bet]

fade/fade away v.[2] **1** [20C] to leave, to vanish (cf. DO A GHOST). **2** [20C] (US) to die. **3** [1960s+] (US Black) to drop a topic of conversation, to change an unpalatable subject. **4** [1960s+] (US Black) to remain sufficiently silent not to be noticed. **5** [1980s+] (US campus) to become tired, to feel increasingly exhausted. [SE fade, to grow dim, faint or pale]

fade v.[3] [1990s] (US Black, rap music) to ignore, to erase, or get rid of. [SE fader, a slider on the mixing board; if one pulls the fader down it gradually reduces the volume; note also FADE v.[1]]

fade away n. see FADE n.[3].

fade away v. see FADE v.[2].

faded adj. [1980s+] (US Black) **1** drunk, under the influence of drugs. **2** unfashionable. **3** used to excess. [SE fade, to grow pale]

faded boogie n. [1950s] (US Black) **1** a Black informer. **2** a Black who apes Whites and loses his own ethnicity. [SE faded + BOOGIE n.[2]]

fade out n. **1** [1910s–60s] (US) a disappearance, a departure, an escape. **2** [1920s–50s] death. [film imagery + FADE v.[2]]

fade out v. [1920s–50s] (US) to die. [film imagery]

fadge n.[1] [late 18C–late 19C] a farthing. [pron.]

fadge n.[2] [1990s] the female genitalia. [there are various dial. uses that could fit, a small cake, an unkempt woman etc, but there is no positive link to any one]

fadger n. [late 19C–1910s] a farthing. [FADGE n.[1]]

fading game n. [1930s+] (US gambling) a dice game in which

players bet against each other rather than against the bank or house as in a casino (cf. HEAD AND HEAD GAME).

fadoodle n. [1910s–20s] a nothing, a trifle. [cited in Manchon; OED has one SE citation for 1670]

fadoodling n. [17C] euph. for sexual intercourse. [SE fadoodle, nothing, nonsense, a foolish trifle; the OED first and only use is 1670, but the term is used in Thomas Middleton's The Roaring Girl (1611) V.i when, midway through a scene in which the whole canting vocabulary is paraded and properly translated, the authors back away from explaining wapping (see WAP) and NIGGLING n., dismissing them as 'fadoodling, if it please you']

faff/faff about/around v. [late 19C+] to play around, to mess about, euph. for FUCK v.[2]. [echoic dial. faffle, to stutter or stammer, to utter incoherent sounds]

fag n.[1] [late 18C+] a bore, a chore, an unpleasant, tedious task (cf. FAGGED). [SE fag, to tire, to perform a wearisome task, ? ult. flag v., to droop, to tire; usu. considered UK, Thompson (1942) has it in US 1920s setting]

fag n.[2] **1** [early–mid-19C] (US) an errand boy or clerk. **2** [20C] (Aus.) a lawyer's clerk. [school use fag, a junior boy who performs (menial) tasks for his elders; ult. SE fag]

fag n.[3] [late 19C] a pickpocket. [? SE fag-end, the way a pickpocket tugs at handkerchiefs, watch-chains etc, or dial. fag, to cut corn with a sickle]

fag n.[4] [late 19C+] **1** a cigarette end. **2** a cheap cigarette. **3** any cigarette; thus fag-ash, cigarette ash, Fag-Ash Lil, a nickname for a woman who smokes heavily. [abbr. FAG END n. (2)]

fag n.[5] **1** [1920s+] (orig. US) a male homosexual (cf. AFGAY). **2** [1960s+] (US campus/teen) an offensive person. [abbr. FAGGOT n.[3]]

fag v.[1] [late 17C–19C] (Und.) to beat; thus fagging, a beating; fag the bloss, hit the wench, fag the fen, drub the prostitute. [FEAGUE]

fag v.[2] [late 18C–mid-19C] (US campus) to work hard academically. [FAG n.[1]]

fag/fag along v.[3] [20C] (US) to move quickly, to leave in a hurry. [? SE fag, to tire (of a situation)]

fag v.[4] [1920s–50s] to supply with a cigarette, to smoke a cigarette. [FAG n.[4]]

fag v.[5] [1960s] (US) a derog. term, meaning to engage in or subject another to homosexual practices. [FAG n.[5]]

fagan/fagin n. [1950s] the penis. [the character Fagin from Charles Dickens's Oliver Twist (1837–9); despite Fagin's poss. paedophilia and the use of 'fag', no specific gay context is implied]

fag-basher n. [1980s+] (US gay) an ostensibly heterosexual man who specializes in beating and terrorizing gay men (cf. GAY-BASHER; PAKI-BASHER; QUEER-BASHER). [FAG n.[5] + SE basher]

fag end n. **1** [early 18C+] orig. used of ropes, the end of, a part near the end of. **2** [mid-19C+] the butt of a cigarette. **3** [mid-19C+] a fragmentary part of a speech or conversation that one might overhear, just as it tails off (cf. PICK UP FAG ENDS).

fag-end man n. [1910s–20s] a man who collects cigarette ends from the pavement.

faggamuffin n. [1980s+] (Black) a homosexual Black person, usu. male (cf. AFGAY). [FAG n.[5] + RAGAMUFFIN]

fagged/fagged out adj. [late 18C+] exhausted. [FAG v.[2] + ? corruption of SE fatigued]

fagger/figger/figure n. [late 18C] a small boy used by robbers to enter a house through a window that would be too small to allow a man to climb through it (cf. DARKMANS BUDGE; TOOL n.).

fagging n. [18C] a thrashing, a beating. [FAG v.[1]]

fagging law see FIGGING LAW.

faggot n.[1] [late 17C–early 19C] a man mustered for duty in the army (and thus 'bound' to service) but not yet formally enlisted. [SE faggot, a bundle (usu. of sticks) bound together]

faggot *n.*[2] **1** [mid-19C–1930s] a general term of abuse, usu. of women or children. **2** [1960s+] (US teen/campus) an unattractive young woman. [for ety. *see* FAGGOT *n.*[3]]

faggot *n.*[3] [1910s+] (orig. US) **1** a homosexual man (cf. AFGAY). **2** [1950s] (US) a lesbian. [usu. seen as a US coinage, but *faggot* has an older, if debatable, UK etymology. One, somewhat fanciful, version suggests that a *faggot* was used in the burning of heretics, and thus became transferred to the name of an embroidered patch (like the pink triangles of the Nazi concentration camps) worn by unburned heretics; homosexuals are certainly considered as fig. heretics, therefore *faggot* means homosexual. More feasible is the descent from the 18C use of *faggot* as a woman (thus playing on homosexual effeminacy), especially in the derog. form of a 'baggage', which stems from the faggots that one had to haul to the fire. The abbr. *fag* may be linked independently to the British public school *fag*, a junior boy performing menial tasks and poss. conducting homosexual affairs with the seniors. Finally, there is the Yid. FAYGELE, meaning little bird (thus the synon. *birdie*), and thence homosexual]

faggot-lover *n.* [1960s+] (Aus./US) one who has no feelings of homophobia. [FAGGOT *n.*[3] + sfx. *-lover*]

faggot-master/faggoteer *n.* [19C] a pimp, a lecher. [FAGGOT *n.*[2] + sfx. *-master*]

faggoter *n.* [1960s+] (US Black) a pimp who specializes in selling the services of male homosexual prostitutes. [FAGGOT *n.*[3]]

faggy/faggoty *adj.* [20C] (orig. US) effeminate, homosexual. [FAGGOT *n.*[3] + sfx. *-y*]

fag-hag *n.*[1] [1940s+] (orig. US) **1** a woman, prob. heterosexual, poss. ageing, who courts and indulges the company of male homosexuals. **2** a heterosexual man, irrespective of age, who prefers the company of homosexuals to that of his peers. [FAG *n.*[5] + SE *hag*]

fag-hag *n.*[2] [1950s] (Can.) a woman who smokes excessively. [FAG *n.*[4] + SE *hag*]

fag-hag *v.* [1940s+] of a woman, to associate with and choose one's close friends from homosexual men. [FAG-HAG *n.*[1]]

fag-hole *n.* [1940s+] the mouth (cf. BACON HOLE). [FAG *n.*[4] + SE *hole*]

fag hots *n.* [1960s+] (gay) cheap pornography aimed at the male homosexual readership. [FAG *n.*[5] ? + HOT STUFF]

fagin *see* FAGAN.

fagingy-fagade *n.* [1920s] (US Black) a White person. [pig Latin version of FADE *n.*[2] (1)]

faglish *n.* [1980s+] (US gay) gay slang. [FAG *n.*[5] + SE *English*]

fagola *n.* [1960s] (US) a male homosexual (cf. AFGAY). [FAG *n.*[5] + sfx. *-OLA*; note FAYGELE]

fags! *excl.* [1920s] (Irish) a mild excl. [? SE *faith!*]

fag squeeze *n.* [1950s+] extortion based on the threat to reveal the victim's homosexuality. [FAG *n.*[5] + SQUEEZE *n.*[1]]

fag stag *n.* [1990s] (US) a heterosexual male who enjoys the company of homosexual men (cf. FAG-HAG *n.*[1]). [FAG *n.*[5] + STAG *n.*[5]]

fag tag *n.* [1950s+] (US campus) the small loop (ostensibly for hanging the shirt when no hanger is available) on the upper back of many shirts; such a loop, supposedly, can be used to hold a victim ready for buggery (cf. BUGGER'S GRIPS). [FAG *n.*[5] + SE *tag*]

fag your face! *excl.* [1980s] (US teen) a general term of dislike, a euph. for go fuck yourself! (cf. BAG YOUR FACE; FUG *n.*[2]).

fail *v.* [1980s+] (US campus) to fail to understand, to be unable to understand.

fail in the furrow *see* DIE IN THE FURROW.

fains!/fains I!/fain I!/fainits! *excl.* [mid-19C+] (juv.) a call for a truce during a game, or a statement that one is ineligible

for a given duty or command. [SE *fen*, to forbid, ult. ? f. *fend*, forbid]

fainting fits *n.* [1940s+] the female breasts (cf. THREEPENNY BITS). [rhy. sl. *fainting fit* = TIT *n.*[1]]

fainits! *see* FAINS!

faints, the *n.* [late 19C] a proclivity for fainting.

fair/fair-skin *n.* [20C] (US Black) a light-complexioned individual.

fair *adj.* [19C+] (Aus.) absolute, complete, usu. in combs, e.g. FAIR DINKUM!; FAIR DO'S!; FAIR SHAKES!

fair *adv.* [17C+] very, absolutely, e.g. *fair tasty*, *fair gorgeous*.

fair buck *n.* [1940s+] (N.Z.) a fair chance, usu. as excl. *fair buck!* be fair, give me a chance. [BUCK *n.*[5]]

fair cop *n.* [late 19C+] (orig. Und.) **1** a justifiable arrest; usu. in the tongue-in-cheek phr. *it's a fair cop guvnor, put the bracelets on …* (cf. BANG TO RIGHTS). **2** any situation seen as fair and about which there is no complaint. [SE *fair* + COP *v.*[1] (1)]

fair cow *adj.* [20C] (Aus./N.Z.) a general negative, applied to persons or things to which the speaker takes great exception, e.g. *fair cow of a day*, *he's a fair cow*.

fair crack of the whip *n.* [1920s+] (Aus.) an equitable opportunity, a reasonable chance.

fair crack of the whip! *excl.* [1960s+] (Aus.) be fair! give someone a chance!

fair crow *n.* [20C] (Aus./N.Z.) something inexpressibly tedious or baffling. [Aus. phr. *draw the crow*, to get the worst share or the worst job in any situation; the crow is a bird of traditionally bad omen]

fair deal *n.* [1920s+] (orig. US) an honest transaction, a fair bargain. [SE *fair* + DEAL *n.*[2]]

fair/square dinkum! *excl.* [late 19C+] (Aus.) honest! really! [SE *fair* + DINKUM *adj.*]

fair dos!/dues! *excl.* [mid-19C+] (Aus./N.Z.) a general statement of agreement, acceptance (cf. FAIR SHAKE OF THE DICE!). [SE *fair* + DO *v.*[3]]

fair enough! *excl.* [1920s+] a statement of acceptance, agreement.

fair few *n.* [late 19C+] (orig. Aus.) a good many (cf. FAIRISH). [understatement]

fair gang *n.* [19C] the gypsies. [? their regular appearances at fairs, but ? f. Faa, the Scot. gypsy equivalent of Smith]

fair/open go *n.* [20C] (Aus.) **1** any situation that meets a basic requirement of impartiality to all without fear of favour or prejudice. **2** a fair fight. [a call in a game of 'two-up' that indicates all relevant rules were satisfied and that the coins could be spun]

fair go! *excl.* [late 19C+] (Aus.) be reasonable! be fair!

fair-haired boy *n.* [20C] (US) an especial favourite, one who can, in supportive eyes, do no wrong (cf. WHITE-HEADED BOY).

fairish *adj.* **1** [mid–late 19C] in a fair manner. **2** [late 19C+] considerable in amount (cf. FAIR FEW).

fairish *adv.* **1** [mid–late 19C] to a fair degree. **2** [late 19C+] fairly large.

fair itch *n.* [late 19C–1930s] an absolute imitation.

fair nark *n.* [20C] (Aus.) something inexpressibly tedious or baffling (cf. FAIR CROW). [FAIR *adj.* + NARK *v.*]

fair one *n.* [1950s+] a (street gang) fight conducted under some sort of mutually recognized rules and poss. preceded by a verbal argument.

fair pop *n.* [late 19C+] a good opportunity, a fair chance. [SE *fair* + POP *n.*[5], *n.*[6]]

fair roebuck *n.* [early 18C] a woman at the peak of her beauty. [SE *fair roebuck*, a roebuck in its 5th year]

fair's fair *phr.* [late 19C+] a phr. used to state that each side must be fair to the other.

fair shake *n.* [early 19C+] a fair or acceptable situation. [abbr. FAIR SHAKE OF THE DICE!]

fair shake of the dice! *excl.* [early 19C+] (Aus.) be fair! (cf. FAIR DO'S!).

fair shakes! *excl.* [mid-19C+] (Aus.) a general statement of agreement, acceptance (cf. FAIR DINKUM!; FAIR DO'S!).

fair-skin *see* FAIR n.

fair suck/suck of the sauce bottle *n.* [1970s+] (Aus.) an equal opportunity, a fair chance.

fair suck of the sav *n.* [1980s+] (Aus./N.Z.) a fair or equal chance. [SE *sav*, a saveloy]

fair thing *n.* [1910s+] (Aus.) a sensible, judicious action or decision.

fair to middling *phr.* [mid-19C+] slightly better than average, usu. as an equivocal response to the question, 'How are you?'

fair treat *n.* [late 19C+] something or someone highly enjoyable or satisfactory, also used ironically to describe something or someone quite the opposite.

fair trod on *adj.* [late 19C] abused, treated very badly.

fair-weather drink *n.* [1970s] a small celebration before initiating some project or journey. [one toasts actual and fig. *fair weather*]

fairy *n.*[1] **1** [19C] a drunken old hag. **2** [mid-19C–1930s] (US) a young woman. **3** [20C] (N.Z.) a blonde-haired woman.

fairy *n.*[2] [late 19C+] (orig. US) a homosexual man (cf. PIXIE n.[1]). [a note in vol. VII of the *American Journal of Psychology* (1895) cites: 'the peculiar societies of inverts. Coffee-clatches, where the members dress themselves with aprons etc, and knit, gossip and crotchet; balls, where men adopt the ladies' evening dress, are well known in Europe. "The Fairies" of New York are said to be a similar secret organization']

fairy/fairy-twister *n.*[3] [late 19C] (Aus.) a fanciful tale, a 'tall story'. [SE *fairy-tale*]

fairy bower *n.* [20C] (Aus.) a shower of rain. [rhy. sl.]

fairydiddle *n.* [20C] (US) nonsense, rubbish. [SE *fadoodle*, nonsense]

fairy dust *n.* [1970s+] (drugs) phencyclidine (cf. ACE n.[3]; FERRY DUST). [play on ANGEL DUST]

fairy hammock *n.* [1990s] women's underwear, panties.

fairy hawk *n.* [1960s+] (US gay) one who attacks (and robs) homosexuals (cf. QUEER-BASHER). [FAIRY n.[2] + SE *hawk*, an aggressive person]

fairy lady *n.* [1940s–50s] (US) a lesbian. [FAIRY n.[2] + SE *lady*]

fairy loop *n.* [20C] (US) the small loop on the upper back of many shirts; such a loop, supposedly, can be used to hold a victim ready for buggery (cf. BUGGER'S GRIPS). [FAIRY n.[2] + SE *loop*; despite the link to homosexuality implicit in *fairy*, the term is sometimes capable of more fanciful interpretation, i.e. the practice cited in *DARE* as regards a Utah high school where 'a group of girls ... will run a contest. They were to pick a boy, usually in their class. The girl who gets the most of his "fairy loops" ... would be the one to marry him']

fairy powder *n.* [1930s–50s] (drugs) any form of powdered narcotic.

fairy-shaking *n.* [1990s] (US) blackmailing married men who frequent gay bars and similar centres. [FAIRY n.[2] + SHAKE DOWN v.[1]]

fairy snuff! *excl.* [20C] corruption of FAIR ENOUGH!

fairy's phonebooth *n.* [1960s+] (US gay) a public lavatory cubicle. [FAIRY n.[2] + SE *phonebooth*, but note BONE PHONE]

fairy-story/-tale *n.* [late 19C+] (orig. US) a fanciful, mendacious tale, often in aid of obtaining money or favours.

fairy's wand *n.* [1960s+] (US gay) any phallic object carried by a cruising gay man, e.g. a cigarette holder, a rolled umbrella (on a dry day), a long-stemmed rose (cf. PIXIE STICK). [FAIRY n.[2] + SE *wand*]

fairy-tale *see* FAIRY-STORY.

fairy-twister *see* FAIRY n.[3].

fake *n.*[1] **1** [19C] a dodge, a swindle, some form of fraudulent

money-making scheme. **2** [mid–late 19C] (US) an invented newspaper story or false rumour. **3** [late 19C–1930s] (US) an impostor or insincere person. **4** [late 19C–1940s] (US) cheap, esp. worthless, merchandise sold by street vendors. **5** [late 19C–1960s] (US) a confidence trickster. **6** [1920s] (US) a patent medicine. [FAKE v.[1]]

fake *n.*[2] [20C] (Ulster) cancer. [dial. *fake*, to hurt, *fakement*, pain]

fake *v.*[1] **1** [early 19C+] to steal, to rob. **2** [early 19C+] to shoot, to wound, to hit or cut. **3** [early 19C+] to cheat, to deceive, to swindle, to counterfeit; thus *faked/faked up*, counterfeit, spurious. **4** [late 19C+] (US) to malinger by feigning illness. [prob. fig. uses of FEAK; FEAGUE + Ger. *fegen*, to furbish up, clean, sweep]

fake *v.*[2] [early 19C] to hurt, e.g. *this shoe fakes my foot*, this shoe pinches my foot. [for ety. see FAKE n.[2]]

fake *v.*[3] **1** [early 19C] (Ling. Fr./Polari) to make, to do. **2** [late 19C–1900s] to dress the hair, to make up the face. [Ital. *faccio*, I make]

fake! *excl.* [1980s+] (US campus) an expression used by the twister that someone has been tricked or duped.

fake a cly, to *phr.* [19C] to pick a pocket. [FAKE v.[1] (3) + CLY]

fake and bake/fake bake, to *phr.* [1980s+] (US campus) to get a tan in a tanning booth (cf. FAKE-BAKE). [FAKE v.[1] (3) + SE *bake*]

fake a pin, to *phr.* [early 19C] (prison) to create a sore leg or to cut it, as if accidentally, in the hope of getting onto the doctor's list. [FAKE v.[1] (3) + PINS]

fake a poke, to *phr.* [late 19C] (Und.) to pick a pocket. [FAKE v.[1] (3) + POKE n.[2]]

fake a screeve, to *phr.* [19C] to write a begging letter. [FAKE v.[1] (3) + SCREEVE n.]

fake a screw, to *phr.* [19C] to make a skeleton key. [FAKE v.[1] (3) + SCREW n.[2]]

fake-ass *adj.* [20C] (US) fraudulent. [SE *fake* + sfx. -ASS]

fake away! *excl.* [early 19C] carry on! don't stop! [FAKE v.[3] + SE *away*]

fake-bake *n.* [1980s+] (US campus) **1** a tanning salon. **2** a fake tan. [FAKE AND BAKE]

fake bake *v.* *see* FAKE AND BAKE.

fake boodle *n.* [late 19C] (US) a roll of money in which small bills (or even paper cut to the right size) are surrounded, for ostentation's sake, by one large one. [SE *fake* adj. + BOODLE n.[1]]

fake down *v.* [mid-19C] (N.Z.) to carry out a crime. [FAKE v.[1] (1)]

fake it *v.* [1960s+] to pretend. [FAKE v.[3]]

fakeman-charley *see* FAKEMENT CHARLEY.

fakement *n.* [19C] **1** a false begging petition. **2** any act of robbery or swindling. **3** a forged signature. **4** a letter, a note. [FAKE v.[1] + sfx. -*ment*]

fakement charley/fakement chorley/fakeman charley *n.* [early–mid-19C] a private sign or mark. [FAKEMENT + CHARLIE n.[6]]

fakement dodge *n.* [mid-19C–1900s] the writing of spurious begging letters; thus *fakement dodger*, the individual who does so. [FAKEMENT + DODGE n.]

fake oneself *v.* [19C] to inflict wounds upon or otherwise disfigure oneself for a criminal purpose. [FAKE v.[1]]

fake one's slangs, to *phr.* [19C] to cut off one's chains or irons to make an escape from prison. [FAKE v.[1] + SLANG n.[2]]

fake on someone *v.* [1970s+] **1** (US Black/west coast) to ignore. **2** (US Black/east coast) to humiliate, to deceive. [FAKE v.[1] (3)]

fake out *n.* [1950s+] (US) a bluff, a deception, an unpleasant surprise. [FAKE OUT v.[1]]

fake out *v.*[1] [1940s+] (US) **1** to fool, to get the better of. **2** to sneak away.

fake out v.[2] [1990s] (US Black) **1** to ignore. **2** to humiliate, to deceive. [var. on FAKE ON SOMEONE]

fake out and out, to phr. [19C] to kill, to murder. [FAKE v.[1] (2) + SE out and out, complete, extreme]

fake pie n. [late 19C] (society) a pie made up of left-overs. [users are usu. somewhat impoverished and no longer very smart]

faker n.[1] **1** [17C–early 19C] a forger. **2** [late 17C–late 19C] a maker. **3** [mid-19C; 1900s] a thief. [Fr. faire, to make, ult. Lat. faceo; 20C use is US]

faker n.[2] **1** [mid-19C–1920s] a confidence trickster, a fraudster. **2** [mid-19C] a street salesman of cheap goods (cf. FAKIR). **3** [mid-19C] a pimp. **4** [mid-19C–1910s] (US) a thief. **5** [1910s–50s] (US) a person feigning illness or injury. [FAKE v.[1]]

faker/feager of loges n. [17C] a beggar, esp. one who backs up his fraudulent tales with especially created fake documents. [FAKER n.[2] + LOGES]

fake/work the broads, to phr. [mid-19C+] to cheat at cards, to perform the three-card trick. [FAKE v.[1] (3) + BROADS]

fake the duck, to phr. [mid-late 19C] to adulterate drink, to cheat, to swindle. [FAKE v.[1] (3) + SE (decoy) duck]

fake the funk, to phr. [1970s+] (US Black) to pose as more sophisticated than one actually is. [FAKE v.[1] (3) + FUNK n.[3]]

fake the rubber, to phr. [mid-19C] to stand treat. [FAKE v.[1] (3) + RUBBER n.[1] (2)]

fake the sweeteners, to phr. [mid-late 19C] to kiss. [FAKE v.[1] (3) + SWEETENERS]

fakir n. [mid-19C] a street salesman of cheap goods. [FAKER n.[2] (2); note the additional exotic tinge of SE fakir, a Muslim or Hindu holy mendicant (cf. ARAB n.[1])]

fal n. [late 19C] a young woman. [rhy. sl. fal = gal]

falairy adj. [20C] (Ulster) unpleasant. [SE floury]

falconer n. [16C] (Und.) a confidence trickster, spec. one who poses as a poor scholar and thus persuades his victims to put up money in order to back the printing of some spurious learned pamphlet.

fall n. (Und.) **1** [late 19C+] an arrest. **2** [late 19C+] a spell of imprisonment. **3** [1920s+] (US) the consequences, esp. blame taken on behalf of another (cf. FALL GUY; TAKE THE FALL).

fall v.[1] **1** [late 19C+] to be caught in illegal activities and subsequently arrested, tried and convicted. **2** [20C] (Aus.) to arrive suddenly, usu. of the police. [orig. UK but mainly US since the 1930s]

fall v.[2] [late 19C+] to become pregnant. [abbr. SE fall pregnant]

fall about v. [1960s+] (orig. US) to collapse in laughter.

fall all over oneself v. [late 19C+] to make extreme, if chaotic, efforts to achieve what one or another wants.

fall apart v. [late 19C+] to collapse emotionally, to lose control of one's feelings.

fall apart at the seams see COME APART AT THE SEAMS.

fall by v. [late 19C+] (orig. US Black) to visit without prior warning, to drop in (cf. FALL IN ; FALL UP).

fall down/fall down on v. [mid-19C+] (US) to fail, to blunder, to 'come to grief'.

fall-downs n. [late 19C] fragments of a pie that fall from the larger piece or slice when it is being cut up; plates of such fragments were sold at a halfpenny a plate in cookshops.

fall downstairs v. [20C] (US) to get a haircut. [Ger. die Treppe herunterfallen, to fall downstairs; the sl. is found in Ger. areas of the US]

fallen away from a horse-load to a cart-load, to have phr. [late 18C–mid-19C] to have put on weight.

fallen down and trod/trodden upon one's eye, to have phr. [late 18C–early 19C] to have a black eye.

fallen off the wagon phr. [20C] drunk (cf. ON THE WAGON).

fallen on adj. [1930s+] pregnant. [FALL v.[2]]

fall for v. [20C] **1** to fall in love with. **2** to be fooled by (a plan, a trick). **3** to become pregnant.

fall guy n. [20C] **1** (orig. US) a victim who is chosen or forced to suffer punishments or difficulties that are, in fact, due to another person (cf. PATSY n.). **2** (US) a person who is easily duped, a victim. [according to Bentley & Corbett there was a real-life fall guy, Albert Bacon Fall (1861–1944), who in 1922 took upon himself the entire blame for the Teapot Dome Scandal; despite the involvement of many top government officials, Fall was the only one to serve time, a sentence of one year and one day; this, however, does not match the OED first citation, 1906]

fall in v. **1** [late 19C+] (US Black) to arrive (cf. FALL BY; FALL UP). **2** [20C] (US) to go to bed.

fall in the furrow, to phr. [20C] to ejaculate. [SE fall in + FURROW]

fall in the shit, to phr. [mid-19C+] to find oneself in difficulties. [SE fall in + SHIT n.[1] (1)]

fall in the thick, to phr. [late 19C] to become very drunk.

fall money n. [late 19C+] (US prison) bail and legal fees, just in case one is arrested. [FALL n. (1) + SE money]

fall off the back of a lorry, to phr. [1950s+] an ironic reference to goods that are obviously stolen. [they didn't fall, 'they were pushed']

fall off the perch, to phr. [late 18C+] to die (cf. DROP OFF THE PERCH).

fall off the roof, to phr. [1960s+] **1** to be sexually incapacitated. **2** to be menstruating. **3** (US gay) to be in a nervous, irritable state.

fall off the wagon, to phr. [20C] to resume drinking after a period of abstinence. [play on ON THE WAGON]

fall on the wrong side of the hedge see BE ON THE WRONG SIDE OF THE HEDGE.

fall-out n. **1** [1950s+] (Aus.) the threat of pieces falling from an old, unsafe automobile. **2** [1960s+] (orig. Aus.) of a woman's breasts, their falling out of a badly secured or overly low-cut bikini or swimsuit. **3** [1970s] (US Black) a fainting fit.

fall out v. **1** [late 19C+] (US Black) to faint. **2** [1940s+] to be overcome with laughter (cf. FALL ABOUT). **3** [1940s+] to lose control of a situation. **4** [1940s+] to fall asleep. **5** [1970s] (US Black) to be surprised.

fall out of one's cradle/crib/high chair/off one's dinosaur, to phr. [20C] (US) a phr. used to imply that a joke is very old, usu. as the first time I heard that I fell ... .

fall/lean over backwards v. [1940s+] to go out of one's way to do something, usu. altruistically (cf. BEND OVER BACKWARDS).

fall over oneself v. [1920s+] to go out of one's way to do something (usu. altruistic) (cf. FALL OVER BACKWARDS).

fall through v. [1900s–30s] to miss or cancel an appointment.

fall to pieces, to phr. [20C] to go into labour, to give birth. [19C Leicester dial.; 1940s+ use is Aus.]

fall up v. [late 19C+] (US Black) to arrive, to turn up (cf. FALL BY; FALL IN).

false n. [1920s–30s] (US Black) a lie. [SE falsehood; note 16C–18C SE false, a lie, a deception]

false v. [1930s+] (Aus.) to lie, to deceive. [obs. SE false, to cheat, to betray, to defraud, to break one's word]

false! excl. [1980s+] (US campus) no! impossible! that's not true! [SE but note true/false answers required in various forms of examination]

false alarm n. [20C] (orig. milit.) the arm. [rhy. sl.]

false as a bulletin phr. [late 18C–early 19C] utterly unreliable, totally untrue. [joc. ref. to one's innate disbelief in any official announcements]

false face n. [1970s+] (US campus) a hypocrite, an insincere person.

false gig v. [1950s+] (Aus.) to pretend to be what one is not, to act under false pretences; thus *falsing*, shamming, malingering. [SE *false* + GIG v.[2]]

false hereafter n. [late 19C] (society) a bustle. [pun]

falsies n. [1940s+] pads placed in a brassiere that accentuate the shape and dimensions of otherwise diminutive female breasts.

fam/famm/fem n.[1] [late 17C–mid-19C] a hand. [abbr. FAMBLE]

fam n.[2] [1990s] (US Black/teen) the *family*. [abbr.]

fam v. [early 19C] to feel, to handle. [abbr. SE *famble*]

fam a dona/donna, to phr. [19C] to take liberties with a woman. [FAM v. + DONAH]

famble n. 1 [16C+] a hand (cf. FAM n.[1]). 2 [17C–19C] a ring. [? supposed 14C SE *famble*, to grope, to fumble, although *OED* first use is in the sense of verbal gropings, i.e. stuttering, rather than physical ones; none the less the roots (Du. *famle*, to grope, OE *folm*, a hand) indicate the manual clumsiness]

fambler n. [late 16C–early 17C] a dealer in fake 'gold' rings. [FAMBLE n. (2)]

famblers n. [17C] a pair of gloves. [FAMBLES]

fambling-cheat n. [16C] (Und.) a ring. [FAMBLE n. (2) + CHEAT, lit. 'hand thing']

fam-cloth n. [late 17C–18C] a handkerchief. [FAM n.[1] + SE *cloth*]

fam-grasp v. [late 17C–18C] to shake hands (and make up one's differences). [FAM n.[1] + SE *grasp*]

familiars n. [19C] lice (cf. BOSOM FRIEND).

family n.[1] 1 [18C+] the criminal fraternity; thus *family man*, *family woman*, a criminal (cf. JOHNSONS). 2 [20C] the American Mafia. 3 [1950s–60s] (US Black) a pimp and the women who work for him.

family n.[2] [1940s+] (US) crab lice. [note the prostitute's phr.: 'Sleep with that pig and you'll end up with a family to feed']

family n.[3] [1960s+] an intimate, whether related by blood or ties of friendship, usu. in phr. *he/she's family* etc.

family disturbance n. [19C] whisky. [the supposedly deleterious effects of alcohol on family life]

family hotel n. [mid–late 19C] a prison (cf. AKERMAN'S HOTEL). [FAMILY n.[1] + SE *hotel*]

family jewels n. [1960s+] the male genitalia (cf. BAUBLES).

family man/woman n. [late 18C–mid-19C] 1 a member of the criminal fraternity. 2 a receiver of stolen goods. 3 a thief. [ext. of FAMILY n.[1]]

family of love n. [late 17C–early 19C] prostitutes, considered as a group or occupation. [SE *family of love*, a 16C–17C religious sect, based in Holland, and very popular in England; its main tenets were that religion could best be realized through sex and that all governments, however tyrannical, must be obeyed]

family organ n. [1920s–50s] (US) the penis. [pun]

family people n. [late 18C–early 19C] thieves, robbers (cf. FAMILY MAN). [FAMILY n.[1] (1) + SE *people*]

family plate n. [19C] silver coins. [SE *family* + (*silver*) *plate*, silver coins]

family pound n. [late 19C] a family grave. [SE *family* + *pound*, an enclosure]

fam-lay n. [mid-18C–early 19C] shoplifting. [FAM n.[1] + LAY n.[4]]

famm see FAM n.[1].

famous adj. [early 18C+] excellent, grand, magnificent, splendid, 'capital'; thus *famously*, excellently etc.

famous dimes n. [1980s+] (drugs) crack cocaine. [ety. unknown]

famous last words! excl. [1940s+] don't you be so sure!; offered to a speaker who has just made an absolute promise as to some future event.

fam-snatcher n. [early 19C] a glove. [FAM n.[1] + SE *snatcher*]

fam-squeeze n. [early 19C] throttling. [FAM n.[1] + SE *squeeze*]

fan n.[1] [19C] the vagina. [FANNY]

fan n.[2] [19C] a waistcoat. [? the FANCY n.[1], who sported such garments, or its fan-like expanse across the frame]

fan v.[1] 1 [18C; 1920s] (US) to beat. 2 [mid-19C+] to conduct a search of a suspect's clothes or premises. 3 [mid-19C+] to pick pockets. 4 [mid-19C] to run one's hands over a potential victim's clothes to see if they have anything in their pockets that can be stolen. [all SE *fan*, to wave a fan; but note (1) underpinned by *fan*, to winnow or thresh corn; its 20C uses are US; (2) (3) (4) poss. link to FAM v.]

fan v.[2] 1 [mid-19C+] (US) to move around quickly, to run (cf. TURN ON THE FAN). 2 [mid-19C+] (US campus) to play truant, to miss a class. 3 [late 19C+] (US Black) to flaunt oneself deliberately to gain sexual interest (cf. FANFOOT).

fan v.[3] [1900s–50s] (US) to converse, to chat, usu. about sport. [SE *fan*, a supporter; ult. *fanatic*]

fan v.[4] [1970s+] (US) to calm someone down.

Fancy, the n.[1] [19C] 1 the sporting fraternity. 2 (Aus.) the underworld.

fancy n.[2] [early 19C+] a girlfriend (cf. FANCY PIECE; FANCY WOMAN).

fancy v. [late 19C+] to find attractive, esp. in phr. *I could fancy that*, used of a passing attractive member of the opposite sex. [SE *fancy*, to take a fancy to]

fancy! excl. [mid-19C+] an excl. of surprise. [abbr. of SE *fancy me! fancy that!*]

fancy bit n. [19C] the vagina (cf. FUNNY BIT). [euph.]

fancy bloke n. [early 19C+] a male lover, not always adulterous, but the relationship usu. refers to a married or older woman (cf. FANCY MAN n.[1]).

fancy cove n. [19C] a pimp, a procurer (cf. FANCY JOSEPH; FANCY MAN n.[1]). [FANCY n.[1] + COVE n. (1)]

fancy crib n. [20C] (US Black) a fashionable, chic, well-designed home. [SE *fancy* + CRIB n.[3] (4)]

fancy dan n. [1940s+] (orig. US) 1 a flashily dressed man, a dandy. 2 a ladies' man. 3 a showy but ineffective sportsman or worker. [SE *fancy* + *Dan* as generic for man]

fancy dude n. [20C] (US) anyone who acts in a superior or pretentious manner. [SE *fancy* + DUDE n.]

fancy-fagot n. [19C] a prostitute. [SE *fancy* + FAGGOT n.[2]]

fancy four n. [late 19C–1900s] a good quality of beer (cf. COLD FOUR). [SE *four-ale*, beer sold at 4 pence a quart]

fancy girl n. 1 [early 19C+] a man's girlfriend. 2 [early 19C+] the woman with whom a married man is having an affair (cf. FANCY MAN n.[1]). 3 [19C+] (US) a prostitute. [SE *fancy* + *girl*; note US use pre-Civil War *fancy girl*, a slave girl or woman used for the sexual enjoyment of her master]

fancy house n. [19C] a whore-house, a house of ill-repute, a brothel (cf. ACCOMMODATION HOUSE). [SE *fancy* + HOUSE n.[1]]

fancy joseph n. [19C] a pimp (cf. FANCY COVE). [SE *fancy* + generic use of Joseph or ? link to JOSEPH n. (1)]

fancy-lay n. [19C] the sport of boxing, prize-fighting. [FANCY n.[1] + LAY n.[4] (2)]

fancy man n.[1] [early 19C+] 1 a man who lives on the earnings of a prostitute (cf. FANCY COVE). 2 a male lover, not always adulterous, but the relationship usu. refers to a married or older woman (cf. FANCY BLOKE). [SE *fancy* + *man*, lit. one who is fancied]

fancy man n.[2] [early–mid-19C] a member of the fashionable sporting world. [FANCY n.[1] (1) + SE *man*]

fancy man n.[3] [1970s+] (US) a male homosexual or transvestite. [SE *fancy*, over-adorned, ornamental + *man*]

fancy one's chances, to phr. [20C] to feel confident of success.

fancy oneself v. [late 19C+] to have a (smugly) good opinion of oneself. [SE *fancy*, take a liking to]

fancy pants *n.* (orig. US) **1** [late 19C+] the social élite, the aristocracy (cf. HIGH HAT n.[2]; SILK STOCKINGS). **2** [1940s+] an overdressed man, erring towards the effeminate in this preoccupation. [SE *fancy* adj. + *pants*]

fancy pants *v.* [late 19C+] to act in an arrogant or supercilious manner. [FANCY PANTS n. (1)]

fancy piece *n.* **1** [early 19C] a prostitute, a mistress. **2** [1920s+] a girlfriend, a 'best girl'. [SE *fancy* adj. + PIECE n.[1]]

fancy sash *v.* [late 19C+] (Aus.) to hit. [rhy. sl. *fancy sash* = BASH v.[1]]

fancy smile *n.* [19C] a glass of whisky. [SE *fancy* + SMILE n.[1]]

fancy stroll *n.* [1980s+] (US Black) the main street on which the high life happens (cf. FUNKY BROADWAY). [SE *fancy* + STROLL]

fancy woman *n.* [early 19C+] **1** a mistress, a 'bit on the side'. **2** a man's favourite girl or woman (cf. FANCY n.[2]). **3** (US) a prostitute. [SE *fancy* v. + *girl*]

fancy work *n.*[1] [late 19C] prostitution; thus *take in fancy work*, to work secretly as a prostitute.

fancy work *n.*[2] [20C] the (usu. male) genitals and pubic hair.

fandangle *n.* [1940s+] (W.I.) **1** any form of fussy ornamentation, whether of clothes, buildings, automobiles etc. **2** stupidity, foolishness.

fandango girl *n.* [19C] (US) a prostitute. [SE *fandango*, a boisterous, energetic Spanish/Spanish-American dance, which was associated with dance-halls, which, in turn, were seen by their critics as quasi-brothels]

fanfoot *n.* [20C] (US Black) a promiscuous woman, one who openly seeks sex. [FAN v.[2] (3) + SE *foot*]

fanfuckingtastic *adj.* [1960s+] (orig. US) an intensified form of SE *fantastic* (cf. ABSOFUCKINGLUTELY; GUARANFUCKINGTEE).

fang *n.* **1** [mid-19C+] a tooth. **2** [1950s+] the penis; thus *bury the fang*, to have sexual intercourse. [SE *fang*, a tooth; the pointed tapering part of anything which is embedded in something else]

fang *v.*[1] [1960s] (Aus.) to drive fast. [abbr. of proper name of Spanish racing driver Juan *Fangio* (1911–95)]

fang *v.*[2] [1960s+] (Aus.) to demand money, to cadge, to beg for a loan; thus *put the fang on* (cf. PUT THE BITE ON). [FANG n. (1)]

fang artist *n.*[1] [1970s+] (Aus.) **1** one who is particularly adept at obtaining loans. **2** a glutton. **3** a lecher. [FANG v.[2] + ARTIST n.[2]]

fang artist *n.*[2] [1970s+] (Aus.) a lecher, a womanizer. [FANG n. (2) + ARTIST n.[2]]

fang-chovey *n.* [mid–late 19C] a dental surgery. [SE *fang* + CHOVEY]

fang-faker *n.* [late 19C] a dentist. [FANG n. (1) + FAKER n.[1] (2); cf. 20C milit. jargon *fang-farrier*, a dentist]

fangs *n.* [1950s–60s] (US jazz) the lips. [FANG n. (1)]

fanner *n.* [late 19C] (US) a brave, if ruthless, man. [FAN THE HAMMER]

fanning *n.* [mid-19C] a beating, a thrashing. [FAN v.[1] (1) + sfx. -ing]

fanny *n.*[1] **1** [mid-19C+] the vagina. **2** [20C] (US) one's self (cf. ARSE n.[1]). **3** [1920s+] (US) the buttocks. [ety. unknown. E.P. suggests link to *Fanny Hill*, the heroine of John Cleland's *Memoirs of a Woman of Pleasure* (1749)]

fanny *n.*[2] **1** [1910s+] verbal effusiveness, usu. nonsensical; thus *fanny merchant*, one who offers 'all talk and no action'. **2** [1920s+] lies, a cover story, esp. in phr. *a load of old fanny*.

fanny *n.*[3] [1950s+] (camp gay) a proper name, with its sl. allusions, used for a variety of camp nicknames, e.g. *Fanny Fed*, the FBI (cf. LILY n.[5]).

fanny *v.* [1930s+] to deceive or persuade by glib talk. [FANNY n.[2]]

fanny about *v.* [1970s+] to waste time, to act aimlessly. [FANNY v.]

fanny adams *n.*[1] [mid-19C] (orig. naval) tinned mutton (cf. HARRIET LANE). [the brutal murder and dismemberment of 8-year-old *Fanny Adams*, at Alton, Hampshire, on 24 August 1867; the murderer, one Frederick Baker, was hanged at Winchester on Christmas Eve; 5000 people watched the execution]

fanny adams/f.a. *n.*[2] [1910s+] euph. for FUCK-ALL, i.e. nonsense, rubbish (cf. SWEET FANNY ADAMS). [for ety. *see* FANNY ADAMS n.[1]]

fanny-artful/-fair *n.* [19C] the vagina. [ext. of FANNY n.[1] (1)]

fanny batter *n.* [1990s] vaginal secretions. [FANNY n.[1] (1) + SE *batter*]

fanny blair *n.* [mid-19C] the hair (cf. BARNET FAIR). [rhy. sl.]

fanny-fair *see* FANNY-ARTFUL.

fanny flange *n.* [1990s] the clitoris. [FANNY n.[1] (1) + SE *flange*]

fanny hat *n.* [1930s–60s] a trilby (cf. CUNT-HAT). [FANNY n.[1] (1) + SE *hat*; the dent in its crown]

fanny magnet *n.* [1980s+] anything that catches the female eye, e.g. a very attractive (young) man, an attractive motorcar. [FANNY n.[1] (1) + SE *magnet*]

fanny mound *n.* [1990s] the *mons veneris* or female pubic area. [FANNY n.[1] (1) + SE *mound*]

fanny pack *n.* [1990s] (US) a small pouch-like bag strapped around the wearer's waist (cf. ASS PACK). [FANNY n.[1] (1) + SE *pack*]

fanny rag *n.* [1940s+] (Aus.) a sanitary towel (cf. JAM RAG). [FANNY n.[1] (1) + SE *rag*]

fanny rat *n.* [1990s] the penis. [FANNY n.[1] (1) + SE *rat*]

fan one's ass, to *phr.* [1960s+] (US Black) to move one's buttocks in an exaggerated manner with the deliberate intention of attracting one's audience sexually; usu. of homosexuals (cf. FAN ONE'S PUSSY). [FAN v.[2] (3) + ARSE n.[1] (1)]

fan one's pussy, to *phr.* [1960s+] (US Black) of a woman, to flaunt oneself sexually (cf. FAN ONE'S ASS). [FAN v.[2] (3) + PUSSY n.[1]]

fanqui *n.* [mid-19C] (Anglo-Chinese) a European. [lit. 'foreign devil']

fantabulosa *adj.* [1950s+] excellent, perfect. [Polari; SE *fantastic* + *fabulous*]

fantabulous *adj.* [1950s+] incredibly wonderful. [SE *fantastic* + *fabulous*]

fantadlins *n.* [mid-19C] a pastry. [SE *tantoblin*, a sweet tart]

fantail *n.*[1] [mid-19C] a coal-heaver's hat, resembling a sou'wester; thus *fantail gentleman*, a coal-heaver. [naut. jargon *fantail*, 'the projecting part of the stern of a yacht or other small vessel when it extends unusually far over the water abaft the stern post' (*Century Dict.*, 1889)]

fantail *n.*[2] [1960s] (US prison) a highly promiscuous prison homosexual. [FAN (ONE'S ASS) + TAIL n.[1]]

fantail banger *n.* [late 19C] (Aus.) a morning coat. [FANTAIL n.[1] + BANGER n.[3]]

fantail-boy *n.* [early 19C] a dustman. [the sou'wester that was part of his 'uniform']

fantailer *n.* [early 19C] a person whose tail coat is excessively long. [SE *fantail*]

fantasia *n.* [1980s+] (drugs) **1** MDMA (cf. ECSTASY). **2** mescaline. **3** dimethyltryptamine. [the hallucinogenic effects]

fantastic *adj.* [1930s+] excellent, good beyond expectation. [loose use of the SE]

fan the air, to *phr.* [1920s] (US) to chatter, to gossip (cf. BACK THE BREEZE).

fan the breeze *phr.*[1] *see* BUST THE BREEZE.

fan the breeze, to *phr.*[2] [20C] to chatter, to gossip (cf. BACK THE BREEZE).

fan the fire, to *phr.* [1940s+] to chatter, to gossip (cf. BACK THE BREEZE).

fan the hammer, to *phr.* [late 19C] (US) to act in a brilliant but unscrupulous manner (cf. FANNER). [the action of fanning the hammer of a pistol or revolver in order to fire more speedily]

fantod/fantods *n.* [19C+] (US) **1** a feeling of uneasiness, a feeling of depression. **2** a feeling of excitement. **3** a minor or imaginary disease. **4** diarrhoea. [SE *fantod*, a crotchety way of acting; ult. ? f. *fantasy, fantastic*]

far and near *n.* [20C] beer. [rhy. sl.]

far away *adv.* [late 19C] in pawn; thus *far away*, to pawn. [the hymn 'There is a happy land,/Far, far away', which was often parodied in such lines as 'Where are my Sunday clothes?/far, far away']

far away! *see* FAR OUT!

farblondjet *adj.* [20C] (US) confused, lost, astray. [Yid. *farblondzhen*, to lose one's way, to go astray]

farchadet *adj.* [20C] confused, befuddled. [Yid. *fartschadat*, confused, ult. Slavic, *chad*, smoke, daze]

farcing *n.* [16C] (Und.) the picking of a lock. [SE *force*]

fardel *n.* [late 19C–1950s] (Irish) a farthing. [OE *féorða dæ'l*, fourth part]

farden *n.* [19C] a farthing. [pron.]

far-down *n.* [20C] (US) an Irish-American Catholic whose forebears come from Northern Ireland. [County *Down*, one of the 6 counties of Northern Ireland]

fare *n.* [1930s+] a male or female prostitute's client. [someone who 'pays for a ride']

far fucking out! *excl.* [1960s+] a general expression of pleasure, delight, appreciation etc (cf. FUCKING A!).

farger *n.* [late 16C–early 17C] (Und.) a false die. [play on SE *forger*]

far gone *adj.* [late 19C+] **1** exhausted, worn out. **2** mad, eccentric, insane. **3** drunk (cf. ADDLED).

farkakte *adj.* [1930s+] (US) unpleasant, disgusting. [synon. Yid.]

farm *n.[1]* [19C] a public house.

farm *n.[2]* [late 19C] a prison infirmary; thus *fetch the farm*, have oneself admitted to the infirmary. [SE *farm*, an institution for poor children]

farm *n.[3]* [1930s+] (US) a prison. [abbr. SE *work farm*]

farm *n.[4]* [1960s+] (US) a psychiatric institution. [abbr. FUNNY FARM]

Farm, the *n.[5]* [1960s+] (Aus.) Monash University, Melbourne (cf. SHOP n.[1]). [Monash, which opened in 1961 with 363 students, was originally set on a rural campus where cows still grazed and wildlife was a common sight]

farm *v.* [1970s+] (US campus) to drink alcohol. [one 'harvests' the CROP n.[3]]

farmer *n.[1]* [mid-19C] an alderman. [SE *farm*, to lease or let the proceeds or profits of customs, taxes etc for a fixed payment]

farmer *n.[2]* **1** [mid-19C+] (US) a derog. term for a peasant, an unsophisticated country person, whether an actual farmer or not. **2** [mid-19C+] a stupid or unsophisticated person. **3** [1940s+] (US Black) recently arrived southern farm workers who persist in their country ways despite the pressing sophistication of the northern cities.

farmer giles/farmers *n.* [1950s] (Aus.) haemorrhoids (cf. SEVEN DIALS). [rhy. sl. *Farmer Giles* = piles]

farmer's beef *n.* [20C] (US) illegally shot deer, butchered and eaten by its hunter (cf. CAMP MEAT).

farmer's haircut *n.* [20C] (US) a short haircut that leaves a white strip of skin showing between the bottom of the hair and the tanned portion of the neck. [the farmer's outdoor life gives the tan]

farmer's time *n.* [20C] (US) 30 minutes fast (cf. AFRICAN PEOPLE'S TIME).

farmer's wine/farm liquor *n.* [20C] (US) illicitly distilled whisky (cf. FIELD WHISKY). [joc. euph.]

Farmington *n.* [20C] (US campus/prep school) Miss Porter's School (for girls), Farmington, Connecticut.

farmisht *adj.* [20C] confused, mixed up. [Yid. *farmisht*, confused]

farm liquor *see* FARMER'S WINE.

farmyard confetti *n.* [1940s+] (Aus.) nonsense, rubbish (cf. COW CONFETTI). [euph. for BULLSHIT n.]

far out *adj.* [1950s+] (orig. US Black) excellent, wonderful, first-rate. [with its implication of 'other-worldliness' – and thus hallucinogenic drugs – the term became a staple of the White hippie vocabulary of the 1960s and faded, other than in ironic use, by the 1970s]

far out!/away! *excl.* [1960s+] amazing! remarkable! wonderful! [the mental 'space' entered under the influence of hallucinogens]

far out as Kit Logue *phr.* [20C] (Ulster) totally misdirected, absolutely wrong. [? anecdotal]

farputst *adj.* [20C] dressed up to excess. [Yid. *farpotshket*, sloppy, messy; ult. Ger. *Patsche*, a slap]

Farringdon hotel *n.* [mid-19C] the Fleet prison, in Farringdon Road, London EC4 (cf. AKERMAN'S HOTEL). [ironic euph.]

farshtinkener *adj.* [1940s+] (US) stinking. [Yid.; ult. Ger. *verstinken*, stink up]

fart *n.* **1** [late 14C+] an audible breaking of wind. **2** [mid-15C–late 17C] something worthless. **3** [1930s+] a fool, an unpleasant person, often older than the speaker; thus synon. *old fart* (cf. CUNT n.[2]; PRICK n.; SHIT n.[2]). [FART v.]

fart *v.* [14C+] to break wind. [cognate with various words in Teutonic and Indo-Germanic languages, e.g. Skrt. *pard*, MHG *verzen*, ON *freta*, Lith. *pérdzu*, Rus. *perdet*]

fart about/around *v.* [1930s+] to dawdle, to mess around (cf. BUGGER ABOUT; FUCK ABOUT). [fig. use of FART v.]

fart along *v.* [1990s] (US) to do something very slowly, without conviction. [fig. use of FART v.]

fart around *v.* *see* FART ABOUT.

fart-arse/-ass *n.* [1940s+] a general term of contempt, e.g. a fool, an incompetent. [fig. use of FART v. + ARSE n.[1]]

fart-arse/fart-arse about/around *v.* [1940s+] to dawdle, to mess around (cf. FART AROUND v.[2]).

fart-arsed/-assed *adj.* [1940s+] useless, incompetent, 'half-baked'. [FART-ARSE n.]

fart-arsed mechanic *n.* [1920s–30s] a clumsy incompetent. [FART-ARSED + SE *mechanic*]

fart box *n.* **1** [20C] the buttocks. **2** [1960s+] (US) the anus or rectum. [FART n. + SE *box*]

fart-catcher *n.* [late 18C] a footman. [FART n. + SE *catcher*; his being forced to walk closely behind his master or mistress]

fart-daniel *n.* [19C] the vagina. [? misprint for dial. *fare-daniel*, a sucking pig that is the youngest of a litter]

farteen *n.* [1960s] (Irish) anything totally insignificant (cf. NOT WORTH A ...). [NOT WORTH A FART IN A NOISEMAKER + Irish dimin. sfx. *-een*]

fart-head *n.* **1** [1960s+] (US) a contemptible person. **2** [1990s] a conservative, traditional old person. [FART n. + sfx. -HEAD (1) + play on FAT-HEAD]

farthing *n.* [mid–late 19C] worthlessness (cf. TOM-FARTHING). [SE *farthing*; thus the minimal value of the coin]

farthing dip *n.* [mid-19C] a piece of bread dipped in hot fat, sold by pork butchers for one farthing. [play on SE *farthing-dip*, a small candle]

farthing-faced *adj.* [late 19C+] mean-faced. ['as insignificant as a farthing' (Ware)]

farthing-faced chit *n.* [1900s] a small, pinch-faced, insignificant person. [FARTHING-FACED + SE *chit*, a brat]

farthing-taster n. [late 19C] the smallest available portion of ice-cream as sold by street vendors.

fartick/fartkin n. [19C] a small act of breaking wind.

farting adj. [1950s+] a general pej., piffling, trivial, irrelevant. [FART v. + sfx. -ing]

farting-crackers n. [late 17C–late 18C] (Und.) breeches, trousers. [FARTING + CRACKER n.²]

farting spell n. [19C+] a short space of time (cf. HAVE A FARTING SPELL). [FARTING + SE spell, a length of time; i.e. no more time than it takes to break wind]

farting strings n. [1980s+] a fig. part of the body, which can be damaged by some form of excess, usu. laughter, e.g. in phr. *If you don't stop that, I'll bust my farting strings!*

farting-trap n. [late 19C–1910s] (Anglo-Irish) a jaunting car, a light two-wheeled vehicle carrying 4 people, seated two on each side, back to back. [FARTING + SE trap]

fartkin see FARTICK.

fartknocker n. [20C] (US) **1** an obscure person. **2** a braggart. **3** one who does not know what they are talking about. [FART n. + SE knocker, i.e. one who knocks or makes farts]

fartleberries n. [late 18C+] pieces of excrement clinging to the anal hairs (cf. FART-O-BERRIES). [FART n. + joc. use of SE berries]

fart-o-berries n. [1990s] pieces of excrement clinging to the anal hairs (cf. FARTLEBERRIES).

fart-off n. [1940s+] (US) one who shirks responsibilities, a loafer (cf. FUCK-OFF n.). [fig. use of FART n.]

fart off v. [1940s+] (US) to idle, to avoid responsibilities (cf. FART ABOUT). [FART-OFF]

fart-sack n. [20C] a bed. [FART n. + SE sack]

fart-sucker n. [19C–1900s] a toady, a parasite. [fig. use of FART n. + SE sucker]

fart through silk, to phr. [1930s+] (US) to live prosperously, to feel happy, to be important (cf. SHIT IN HIGH COTTON).

fas' v. [1950s+] (W.I. Rasta) to be fast with, meaning to be rude, impertinent, to meddle with somebody's business, to be forward. [FAASTIE]

fashion arrest n. [1980s+] a fig. 'arrest' (most likely heavy verbal criticism) of one whose style is considered unacceptably unfashionable (cf. ARREST).

fashion criminal/mutant n. [1980s+] (US campus) one whose style is considered outside the bounds of acceptable fashion (cf. FASHION ARREST).

fashion police n. [1980s+] (US campus) a fantasy organization who are called upon, rhetorically, to deal with those who are judged to have offended against prevailing fashion codes.

fashion risk n. [1980s+] (US campus) an unattractive item of clothing.

fashion victim n. [1980s+] anyone seen as being overly obedient to the fast-changing fluctuations of fashion, esp. those who unquestioningly adopt its more ludicrous excesses.

fass adj. [20C] (US Black) promiscuous, amoral. [FAST adj.¹]

fast n. [1980s+] (drugs) amphetamine (cf. A n.²; SPEED n.²).

fast adj.¹ [early 19C+] **1** amoral, illegal, corrupt. **2** of a woman, promiscuous. ['A *fast* man – a person who, by late hours, gaiety and continual rounds of pleasure, lives too fast, and wears himself out ... a *fast* young lady is one who affects mannish habits, or makes herself conspicuous by some unfeminine accomplishment, – talks Slang, drives about in London, smokes cigarettes, is knowing in dogs, horses, &c.' (Hotten, 1867); the *Saturday Review* (28 July 1860) defines a *fast* woman as 'a woman who has lost her respect for men, and for whom men have lost their respect also']

fast adj.² [mid-19C] in financial difficulties.

fast adj.³ [late 19C+] (W.I.) **1** interfering, meddlesome (cf. GYPSY adj.). **2** cheeky, rude, impertinent. [FAASTIE]

fast adj.⁴ [20C] of dogs, copulating. [abbr. SE *stuck fast*, fastened together]

fast v.¹ [mid-19C] to be out of pocket. [FAST adj.²]

fast v.² [20C] (W.I.) to interfere, to meddle. [FAST adj.³]

fast alec/aleck n. [1930s] (US Black) anyone who moves fast. [var. on SMART ALEC]

fast and loose n. [late 16C] a gambling and cheating game, often practised by thimbleriggers, in which a garter is folded and held out to the punter who bets that by pricking with a pin they can hit the place where the material is folded. Almost inevitably they fail and lose their money (cf. FIND THE LADY; PRICK THE GARTER).

fast-ass adj. [1930s] (US) peremptory. [SE *fast* + sfx. -ASS]

fast black n. [1960s+] (society) a black London taxi.

fast buck n. [1940s+] (orig. US) money that is earned quickly, and poss. illicitly (cf. QUICK QUID). [SE *fast* + BUCK n.²]

fast-buck artist n. [1940s+] (US) anyone keen on (and successful in) making a great deal of money. [SE *fast* + BUCK n.² (1) + ARTIST n.²]

fastener n. [late 17C–early 19C] (Und.) an arrest warrant.

fast-fast adj. [20C] (W.I.) very fast. [redup.]

fast-fast mouth see FAST-MOUTH.

fast food sex n. [1980s+] (US gay) spontaneous, short-term sex, e.g. that enjoyed in lavatories, bath-houses and similar places of anonymous assignation.

fast fuck n. [20C] **1** sexual intercourse that, through various circumstances, has to be hurried and brief (cf. QUICKIE; WHAM-BAM-THANK-YOU-MA'AM). **2** of a man, one who is unable to delay his own orgasm until his partner is satisfied too; a premature ejaculator. [SE *fast* + FUCK n.¹]

fast house n. [mid-19C–1940s] (US) a brothel (cf. ACCOMMODATION HOUSE). [FAST adj.¹ + HOUSE n.¹]

fastidious cove n. [late 19C] a fashionable swindler, who poses as a member of the class he deceives. [ironic use of SE *fastidious* + COVE]

fast lane n. [1970s+] the active, competitive and ruthless world fought over by those of ambition and intent (cf. FAST TRACK).

fast-mouth/fast-fast mouth adj. [late 19C] (W.I.) cheeky, impertinent. [FAASTIE]

fast-sheet hotel n. [1940s+] (US) a cheap hotel that rents out its rooms by the hour to prostitutes and their clients or to illicit lovers (cf. HOT-PILLOW JOINT; HOT-SHEET HOTEL; NO-TELL HOTEL). [the pillows (and beds) are always in use]

fast-talker n. [1930s+] a confidence trickster (cf. FAST-TALKING CHARLIE).

fast-talking charlie n. [1950s+] (US Black) a Jew, esp. a Jewish storekeeper (cf. MR CHARLIE). [SE *fast-talking* + MR CHARLIE]

fast track n. [1960s+] **1** (US) those streets or blocks in a city where prostitutes work; esp. differentiating the East Coast cities from the slower world of the West, esp. California. **2** (orig. US) the lifestyle pursued by the ambitious and successful.

fast with someone phr. [20C] (W.I.) cheeky, impertinent. [FAASTIE]

fast/quick worker n. [1920s+] a successful womanizer, who achieves his seductions quickly. [modern use could extend to a sexually active woman, although the nature of male sexuality hardly calls for her to 'work' for sex]

fat/fatman/Harry Fat/Mr Fat n.¹ [late 19C–1950s] (Aus./N.Z.) a generic term for the business élite, the wealthiest members of the community.

fat n.² [1930s+] (Aus./N.Z.) an erection, esp. in phr. *crack a fat*.

fat adj.¹ [late 17C; mid-19C+] wealthy, rich; thus *fat cull*, a rich man. [the term faded in the UK by 1800 but reappeared in the US in the mid-19C and survives in US Black speech]

fat adj.[2] [1950s+] (US Black) pregnant.

fat adj.[3] [1990s] a general term of approval, first-rate, excellent (cf. PHAT adj.[2]).

fat ale n. [late 19C] strong beer (cf. THIN ALE).

fat and wide n. [20C] a bride. [rhy. sl.]

fat around the heart phr. [1930s] (US Black) cowardly. [fat around the heart clogs the arteries and makes one's blood, fig. courage, flow more slowly]

fat-arse/-ass n. [1930s+] a very fat person. [SE fat + ARSE n.[1]]

fat-arsed adj. [late 19C+] fat, large-buttocked. [for ety. see FAT-ARSE]

fat as a buggy-whip phr. [19C+] (US) very thin (cf. FAT AS A MATCH).

fat as a hen in the forehead/hen's forehead phr. [late 18C] thin (cf. FAT AS A MATCH).

fat as a match phr. [19C+] (US) very thin (cf. FAT AS A HEN IN THE FOREHEAD).

fat-ass adj. [1980s+] fat. [SE fat + ARSE n.[1]]

fat ass v. [1970s] (US) to loaf, to idle. [FAT-ARSE]

fat as Sir Roger phr. [late 19C] extremely fat. [the weighty Arthur Orton (1834–98), self-styled Sir Roger Tichborne, 'star' of the 1871 'Tichborne claimant' case]

fat bags n. [1980s+] (drugs) crack cocaine. [PHAT adj.[2] (2) + BAG n.[8]]

fat cat n. [1920s+] (orig. US) any successful, wealthy, influential person; recent UK use has tended to imply a degree of self-serving corruption to such individuals (cf. FAT n.[1]).

fatcha n. [20C] (Ling. Fr./Polari) the human face; thus fake the fatcha, to shave, to put on make-up. [Ital. faccia, face]

fat chance! excl. [mid-19C+] no chance at all (cf. FAT LOT; FAT SHOW!).

fat city n.[1] [1940s+] success, wealth, often from criminal activities. [SE fat, abundant, stimulating + sfx. -CITY]

fat city n.[2] [1970s+] (US campus) the process of gaining weight or the state of being fat. [SE fat, overweight + sfx. -CITY]

fat cock n.[1] [mid-19C] a fat old man. [SE fat + COCK n.[5]]

fat cock n.[2] [late 19C] the labia minora, esp. when prominent (cf. DOUBLE-SUCKER). [SE fat + COCK n.[2] (2)]

fater/fayter/factor n. (Und.) **1** [16C–early 17C] a cheat or impostor. **2** [18C–early 19C] a fortune-teller. [Fr. faiteur, maker; 'the Second (old) Rank of the Canting Crew' (B.E.)]

fat-face n. [mid-18C+] a general term of opprobrium.

fat-fancier/-monger n. [19C] a man who prefers plump women (cf. CHUBBY-CHASER).

fat-guts n. [late 16C–mid-19C] a term of abuse, used of one who has a fat stomach (cf. FULL-GUTS).

fat-head n. [mid-19C+] a fool, an idiot, often used affectionately as well as derog. [SE fat + sfx. -HEAD (1)]

father n. [mid-19C] **1** a receiver of stolen goods. **2** the owner of a common lodging house. [play on UNCLE n.[1] (3)]

father abraham n. [19C] the penis (cf. FATHER-OF-ALL).

father and mother of ... phr. [20C] a general intensifier, usu. ... of a thrashing, ... of a row.

father and mother stuff n. [1950s] (US teen) the attacking of 'civilians', i.e. non-gang members, women, children, the old.

Father Christmas n. [20C] a respected old man.

father confessor n. [19C] the penis (cf. CONFESSIONAL). [play on SE + ? ref. to popular image of the venal priest]

father-grabber see MOTHER-GRABBER.

father-grabbing see MOTHER-GRABBING.

father-of-all n. [19C] the penis (cf. FATHER ABRAHAM).

father something on someone v. [1910s+] to put the blame for something on someone else, to 'pass the buck'.

fat in the forehead phr. [20C] (Ulster) stupid.

fat in the head phr. [19C] stupid, foolish (cf. SOFT IN THE HEAD).

fat/all the fat is in the fire phr. [mid-16C–mid-19C] **1** used to indicate that a plan has failed. **2** used to indicate that the result of an action will be to provoke anger.

fat jack of the bone-house n. [mid-19C–1900s] a very fat man. [generic use of Jack + obs. SE bonehouse, the human body]

fat knot n. [1970s+] (US Black) a substantial roll of dollar bills (cf. KNOT n.[4]).

fat lip n. [1940s–60s] unpleasant talk (cf. FAT TALK).

fat lot n. [mid-19C+] not very much, if anything at all; often as phr. a fat lot of good/good that will do (cf. FAT CHANCE!). [an ironic reversal]

fatman see FAT n.[1].

fat meat n. [1940s–60s] (US Black) the truth. [phr. fat meat is greasy]

fat-monger see FAT-FANCIER.

fatmouth n. [20C] (US Black) a braggart, a boaster. [FATMOUTH v.]

fatmouth adj. [19C+] (orig. US Black) boastful, noisy, verbose. [FATMOUTH v.]

fatmouth v. [19C+] (orig. US Black) to argue, to answer back, to be cheeky, to talk excessively. [fig. use of SE or lit. trans. of Mandingo da-ba, big, fat mouth; thus fig. excessive talking]

fatness n. [19C] wealth.

fat one/fat 'un n.[1] [19C] an especially noisy breaking of wind.

fat one n.[2] [1950s–60s] (US) a $100 bill.

fats n. [1900s–30s] (US Black) generic term for jazz musicians.

fat's a-running phr. [late 19C] a phr. used to indicate that a loaded van is passing along the street and may be robbed, to the greatest possible extent, by opportunists.

fat scraps and glorious bits n. [17C] (Und.) a sound beating.

fat show! excl. [1930s+] (N.Z.) no chance at all (cf. FAT CHANCE!).

fatso n. [1940s+] (orig. US) a general derog. term addressed to a fat person.

fats or fems n. [1970s] (gay) fat or effeminate male homosexuals, as described in gay advertisements.

fat talk n. [1970s] (US Black) nonsense, rubbish (cf. FATMOUTH v.).

fat/phat tape n. [1990s] (US Black teen) an exceptionally good mix tape. [FAT adj.[3]/PHAT adj.[2] + SE tape]

fatter than a settled minister phr. [20C] (US) very fat. [derog. image]

fattoon n. [1950s] (W.I.) a very fat person. [SE fat + sfx. -oon; on model of octaron, quadroon etc]

fatty n.[1] [late 19C+] a fat person, esp. as a nickname.

fatty n.[2] [1980s+] (drugs) a particularly large marijuana cigarette (cf. BOMBER n.[1]).

fatty bum-bum n. [1950s+] (W.I./Gren., Trin.) a fat person, esp. a woman with large buttocks. [SE fatty adj. + BUM n.[2]]

fattymus/fattyma see FATYMUS.

fat 'un see FAT ONE.

fat will burn itself out of the fire phr. [late 19C] whatever the trouble is, it will pass (cf. FAT IS IN THE FIRE).

fatymus/fatyma/fattymus/fattyma n. [mid–late 19C] a fat man or woman. [cod-Latin]

faulkener/faulkner n. [late 17C–18C] **1** one who lures an innocent player into a crooked gambling game (cf. FALCONER). **2** a juggler, a tumbler. [? SE faulconer, who lures his hawks onto his hand or into a cage]

faulties n. [1990s] (US Black teen) a cellular telephone that is being used illegally. [SE faulty]

faust n. [1930s–40s] (US Black) **1** an ugly person of either sex. **2** a blind date. [? the fictional Dr Faustus]

faux n. [1980s+] (US campus) a mistake. [abbr. Fr. faux pas, a blunder]

faux v. [1980s+] (US campus) to make a mistake. [FAUX n.]

fave/fav *adj.* [1930s+] (orig. US) favourite.

fave rave *n.* [1960s+] (teen.) most favoured person, most enjoyable experience, preferred food etc.

favour *v.* [early 17C+] to look like, to resemble physically.

favourite vice *n.* [late 19C–1910s] one's preferred drink, usu. in phr. *what's your favourite vice?* what would you like to drink? (cf. POISON).

fawned-fam'd *see* FAWNIED.

fawney/fawny/forny/forney *n.* [late 18C–mid-19C] **1** a ring. **2** one who practises the fraud involving bogus jewellery; thus *fawney-man*, a seller of bogus jewellery (cf. FAWNEY-RIG; FAWNIED). [Irish *fáin(n)e*, a ring]

fawney-bouncing *n.* [late 18C–mid-19C] selling a ring to a victim; the justification for the sale is a supposed wager, which the seller can win only by selling the ring. [FAWNEY + SE *bounce*]

fawney-rig/-dropping *n.* [late 18C–mid-19C] 'A common fraud thus practised. A fellow drops a brass ring, double gilt, which he picks up before the party meant to be cheated, and to whom he disposes of it for less than its supposed, and ten times more than its real, value' (Grose, 1796). [FAWNEY + RIG *n.*[2] (2)]

fawney shop *n.* [mid–late 19C] (US) a shop selling fake or cheap jewellery. [FAWNEY + SE *shop*]

fawnied/fawned-fam'e *adj.* [late 18C–mid-19C] wearing more than one ring on a single finger. [FAWNEY]

fawny *see* FAWNEY.

fay/fey *n.* [1920s+] (US Black) a White person. [abbr. OFAY; given context, derog. or simply familiar]

fay broad *n.* [20C] (US Black) a light-skinned Black woman or a White woman. [FAY + BROAD *n.*[2] (2)]

faygele/feygele *n.* [20C] (US) a male homosexual (cf. AFGAY). [Yid. *feygele*, little bird + FAG *n.*[5]; Yid. *Feygel* is also a woman's proper name]

fayter *see* FATER.

f.b.i.! *excl.* [1990s] a general term of abuse, *fucking bloody idiot!* [abbr.]

f.d.r./roosevelt *n.* [20C] (US) an outdoor toilet (cf. FEDERAL BUILDING). [abbr. Franklin *D*elano *R*oosevelt (1882–1945); one of the projects of Roosevelt's New Deal WPA programme was the building in deprived rural areas of new outdoor toilets]

f.e. *n.* [1990s] (S.Afr.) a condom (cf. FRENCH LETTER). [abbr. *F*rench *e*nvelope]

feager of loges *see* FAKER OF LOGES.

feague *v.* [late 18C] to enliven, usu. of a horse (cf. FIG *v.*[3]). [SE *feague*, to beat, to whip, ult. Ger. *fegen*, to polish]

feak *n.* [early 19C] the posterior, the buttocks. [? link to FEAGUE]

fear! *excl.* [1980s+] (US campus) a negative response to anything the speaker finds distasteful, rather than actually frightening.

fearful *adj.* [late 19C–1920s] a general intensifier; thus *adv. fearfully*.

fearful frights *n.* [late 19C] a kick in the posterior.

fearnought *n.* [late 19C] a drink to boost one's morale (cf. DUTCH COURAGE).

feather *n.*[1] [18C] the pubic hair (cf. BADGER *n.*[7]).

feather *n.*[2] [20C] (tramp) a bed. [rhy. sl. *feather and flip* = KIP *n.*]

feather *v.* [20C] (US) to curry favour with, to toady to. [phr. *feather one's own nest*]

feather-bed *n.* [20C] (US) an extremely fat person. [resemblance]

feather bed *v.* [early 19C+] to make things (unfairly) easy for a friend, relation or confederate. [fig. use of the softness of the bed]

feather-bed and pillows *n.* [19C] a fat woman. [resemblance]

feather-bedding *n.* [early 19C+] the practice of making things easy for one's associates, handing out easy 'jobs for the boys'. [FEATHER BED]

feather-bed jig *n.* [late 18C–19C] sexual intercourse (cf. DANCE *v.*[1]).

feather-bed lane *n.* [late 17C–late 18C] a notably rough road or track. ['particularly that betwixt Dunchurch and daintrie' (B.E.)]

feather-bed soldier *n.* [19C] a womanizer, a lecher.

feather-driver *n.* [late 16C–early 17C] a clerk. [his quill pens]

feathered oof-bird *n.* [late 19C] a source or supplier of a large amount of money. [OOF]

featherhead *n.* (US) **1** [mid-19C+] a derog. term for a Native American. **2** [mid-19C+] a scatterbrain. **3** [20C] one who takes foolish chances. [SE *feather* + sfx. -HEAD (1)]

feather-legged *adj.* [20C] terrified, extremely frightened. [i.e. one's legs are shaking like feathers in the wind]

feather-merchant *n.* [1930s+] (orig. US milit.) **1** a physical weakling. **2** a foolish, silly person. **3** a shirker. [(1) his physical size; (2) and (3) he does not 'pull his weight']

feather-plucker *n.* [1940s+] a general term of abuse, usu. used to refer to someone unpleasant. [rhy. euph. for FUCKER]

feathers *n.*[1] **1** [mid-19C+] wealth, money. **2** [mid-19C+] (US) fancy clothes; thus *fine feathers*. [SE phr. *feather one's nest*]

feathers *n.*[2] [20C] (Aus.) facial hair.

feathers *n.*[3] [20C] (US) a bed; thus *a date with the feathers*, bedtime, *hit the feathers*, to go to bed.

feather up *v.* [20C] (US) to prepare to fight. [the action of birds]

feature *v.* [1930s+] (US) to note, to pay attention to, to understand; often as phr. *feature this*.

features *n.* [late 19C] a term of address, e.g. *Hello, features* (cf. FACE *n.*[2]).

feature with *v.* [1960s+] (orig. Aus.) to seduce a compliant woman. [coined by the Australian comedian and writer Barry Humphries (b.1934) for his strip character Barry Mackenzie]

feck *v.* (Irish/Scot) **1** [early 19C] to keep a look-out. **2** [late 19C+] to steal. [? OE *feccan*, to fetch; Ger. *fegen*, to plunder]

feck! *see* FUCK!

Fed/fed *n.* **1** [mid-19C] (US) a supporter of the Northern cause in the US Civil War, fighting for *fed*eral rather than states' rights. **2** [1920s+] (US) a member of the *Fed*eral Bureau of Investigation. **3** [1960s+] (Aus.) a *fed*eral police officer. **4** [1970s+] (Aus.) a member of the *Fed*eral government. [abbr.]

federal *adj.* [1990s] used of something of exceptional quality or of an extreme nature. [SE *federal*, pertaining to the federal, i.e. national rather than state (local) government]

federal building *n.* [20C] (US) an outdoor toilet (cf. F.D.R.).

federal joint *n.* [1950s+] (US Und.) a federal, rather than a state, prison. [SE *federal* + JOINT *n.*[3]]

federating *n.* [1900s–10s] (Aus.) having sexual intercourse. [SE *federate*, to join together]

fedex *n.* [1990s] (US Black teen) an individual who pays debts quickly. [popular abbr. for the *Fed*eral *Ex*press courier company]

fed up *adj.* [late 19C+] irritated, annoyed, bored; intensified as *fed up to the back teeth* and (orig. milit.) *fed up, fucked up and far from home* (cf. FULL UP *adj.*[1]).

fed with a fire-shovel *phr.* [late 18C] a phr. used of someone who has a notably wide mouth.

fedy *adj.* [1990s] (US Black) aggressive. [abbr. *Fed*eral (Bureau of Investigation)]

feeb *n.*[1] [mid-19C+] beef. [backsl.]

Feeb *n.*[2] [20C] (US) the FBI; thus [1940s+] *feebie*, an agent of the FBI.

feeb *n.*[3] [1910s+] a feeble, useless person. [FEEB *adj.*]

feeb *adj.* [1910s+] *feeble*. [abbr.]

fee-chaser n. [20C] (US derog.) a lawyer (cf. AMBULANCE-CHASER). [their supposed primary interest]

feed n. [early 19C+] food and drink, usu. as served in a meal, esp. a substantial one.

feed v. [1930s–40s] to bore. [FED UP]

feed a line, to phr. [1920s+] to deceive through a cunning story or excessive charm, to persuade, to talk smoothly. [SE feed + LINE n.¹]

feedback n. [1970s] (US) cheek, insolence.

feed bag n. [1960s+] (drugs) a container for marijuana.

feed box n. [20C] the mouth.

feeder n.¹ [late 18C–late 19C] (Und.) a silver spoon (cf. PAP FEEDER).

feeder n.² [1900s–20s] (US) the mouth or throat.

feeder-prigger n. [late 18C–late 19C] (Und.) a thief specializing in silver spoons. [FEEDER n.¹ + PRIG v.¹]

feed hot lead see FEED LEAD.

feeding n. [20C] (W.I.) 1 sexual intercourse. 2 a woman with whom a man wishes to have sex.

feeding adj. [1910s–30s] boring, disgusting. [FED UP]

feeding birk n. [late 19C] (Und.) a cookshop. [SE feeding + ? barrack]

feeding bottles n. [20C] the female breasts (cf. CREAM JUGS).

feed lead/hot lead v. [20C] (US) to shoot, usu. to shoot dead.

feed on v. [early 18C] to live off, to live at another's expense.

feed one's face, to phr. [20C] 1 to stuff oneself with food. 2 to indulge in oral intercourse.

feed one's pussy, to phr. [20C] of a woman, to have sexual intercourse. [SE feed + PUSSY n.¹; play on SE]

feed/give pap with a hatchet, to phr. [late 16C–early 18C] to perform a kind act in an unkind manner, to be 'cruel to be kind'. [SE pap, baby food; thus one feeds the baby (a kindness) with a hatchet (a cruelty)]

feed someone stuff, to phr. [1970s+] (US Black) to deceive, to pass on false (and self-serving) information.

feed the bears, to phr. [1970s+] (orig. used on Citizen's Band radio) to pay a parking fine, to get a parking ticket. [SE feed + BEAR n.⁸]

feed the ducks, to phr. [1990s] (US) to masturbate. [the similarity in hand motions]

feed the dumb glutton, to phr. [18C] to have sexual intercourse. [SE feed + DUMB GLUTTON]

feed the dummy, to phr. [19C] to have sexual intercourse. [for ety. see FEED THE DUMB GLUTTON]

feed the fishes, to phr. 1 [19C+] to die by drowning. 2 [20C] (US) to vomit, esp. over the side of a ship.

feed the goldfish/kippers, to phr. [20C] (US) to vomit, esp. over the side of a ship (cf. FEED THE FISHES).

feed the worms, to phr. [20C] to die. [although the image dates to the early 17C, the sl. use is modern]

feed with a spoon, to phr. [1910s–20s] to bribe.

feek n. [1990s] an extremely attractive woman. [? FUCK n.⁴]

feel n. [1930s+] an act of sexual groping (cf. COP A FEEL; FEEL UP). [FEEL v.]

feel v. [18C+] to caress sexually, whether or not the advance is desired.

feel a draught/draft, to phr. 1 [1920s+] to feel a general sense of hostility. 2 [1920s+] to feel insecure, esp. financially. 3 [1930s–40s] (US Black) to sense racial antagonism in one's conversation or dealings with Whites; thus drafty, unfriendly to Blacks. 4 [1930s–40s] (US Black) to warn one's friends that a White person has entered the room. [the phr. is generally credited to the jazz musician Lester Young (1909–59)]

feel all round/around my hat, to phr. [mid-19C–1910s] to feel unwell. [? ballad 'all round my hat I wears a green willow'; thus ? ref. to the green pallor of an ill complexion]

feel as if a cat had kittened in one's mouth, to phr. [16C+] to feel the nauseous after-effects of drinking on 'the morning after' (cf. MOUTH LIKE THE INSIDE OF …).

feel cheap v. [late 19C–1920s] to feel ill, esp. hungover; often as feel very cheap. [SE feel + CHEAP adj.]

feel day n. [1910s+] (Can.) heavy petting. [FEEL n. + SE day; a pun on SE field day]

feele/feelier/feelia n. [mid-19C] (Ling. Fr./Polari) a child; thus donah and feeles, a woman and (her) children, feele omi, a young (and poss. underage) man. [Ital. figlie, children]

feeler n.¹ [late 18C] (US) a knife or other pointed weapon. [the victim feels the point]

feeler n.² [late 19C] 1 a finger, usu. in pl. 2 a hand (cf. CLUTCH n.¹; GRAPPLER; GROPERS; PICKER; PICKERS AND STEALERS).

feel froggy/froggish v. [1970s+] (US Black) to feel like fighting; thus the challenge if you feel froggy/froggish, leap! [FROGGY adj.²]

feel funny v. 1 [early 19C+] to feel (unpleasantly) drunk. 2 [mid-19C+] to feel very emotional. 3 [late 19C+] to feel ill.

feel gay v. [19C–1910s] to feel amorous.

feel good v. [late 19C+] (orig. US) 1 to feel mildly drunk. 2 to feel in good spirits or health.

feelier/feelia see FEELE.

feelies, the n. [1940s+] (Aus.) petting in a darkened cinema. [FEEL n.]

feeling funny adj. [20C] drunk, out on a spree (cf. ABOUT RIGHT adj.¹; FEELING GOOD; FEELING NO PAIN; FEELING RIGHT ROYAL). [FEEL FUNNY]

feeling good adj. [1920s+] drunk, esp. in the earlier, more enjoyable stages (cf. ABOUT RIGHT adj.¹; FEELING FUNNY). [FEEL GOOD]

feeling no pain phr. [1940s+] drunk (cf. ABOUT RIGHT adj.¹; FEELING FUNNY). [i.e. anaesthetized by liquor]

feeling of oaks n. [late 17C–early 18C] sea-sickness. [the oak being the ship's timbers and deck]

feeling right royal phr. [late 19C+] drunk (cf. ABOUT RIGHT adj.¹; FEELING FUNNY).

feel in one's pocket for one's big hairy rocket, to phr. [20C] to masturbate.

feel like v. [late 19C+] (orig. US) to desire, to have an inclination for.

feel like a baby at a wedding, to phr. [1930s–40s] to feel superfluous (cf. FEEL LIKE A PORK CHOP AT A JEWISH WEDDING).

feel like a ball/bag of string, to phr. [1950s] (Aus.) to feel exhausted. [pun on Aus. phr. a ball of muscle, an energetic person, but note possible pun on phr. all wound up, emotional, tense]

feel like a boiled/fresh-boiled owl, to phr. [19C] (US) to be extremely hungover, to be very exhausted, run down.

feel like a boiled rag/piece of chewed rag/string, to phr. [20C] to feel ill.

feel like a fresh-boiled owl see FEEL LIKE A BOILED OWL.

feel like a million dollars, to phr. [1910s+] (orig. US) to feel excellent, very cheerful, extremely well, in the best of spirits.

feel like a piece of chewed rag/string see FEEL LIKE A BOILED RAG.

feel like a pork chop at a Jewish wedding, to phr. [1930s+] to feel superfluous (cf. FEEL LIKE A BABY AT A WEDDING).

feel like a stewed monkey, to phr. [19C] (US) to be extremely hungover, to be exhausted, to be run down.

feel like a warmed-up corpse, to phr. [1920s] to feel absolutely appalling, often used by those suffering from hangovers (cf. FEEL LIKE DEATH WARMED UP).

feel like death warmed up, to phr. [1930s+] to feel absolutely appalling, often used by those suffering from hangovers; thus look like death warmed up, to look terrible (cf. FEEL LIKE A WARMED-UP CORPSE).

feel like shit/shitty, to phr. [1940s+] to feel very bad, whether emotionally or physically. [SE *feel* + SHIT n.[1]]

feel like two dollars/two dollars worth of nothing, to phr. [1920s+] (US) to feel stupid, insignificant, depressed.

feel moldy v. [1980s+] (US campus) to feel humiliated, embarrassed. [SE *mouldy*]

feel much of an onion, to phr. [1910s–20s] to feel bored. [one is 'bored to tears']

feel no way, to phr. [1950s+] (W.I. Rasta) don't take offence, don't be sorry, don't worry.

feel one's keeping, to phr. [20C] (US) to be in good health. [SE *keeping*, taking care, maintaining in good condition]

feel one's oats, to phr. [mid-19C+] (orig. US) to feel aggressive, energetic, 'hot to trot'. [fig. use of SE *oats*, in their effect on a horse]

feel one's stuff, to phr. [1930s–40s] (US Black) to base one's actions or speech on one's most intense and sincere emotions.

feel one's way to heaven, to phr. [late 19C–1910s] to caress a woman, becoming increasingly intimate. [SE *feel one's way* + HEAVEN]

feel rough v. [1910s+] to feel very bad, whether emotionally or physically (cf. FEEL LIKE SHIT).

feel someone's collar, to phr. [1950s+] (Und.) to arrest, to place under suspicion (cf. PULL n.[2]; TUG n.[4]). [the physical act of grabbing a villain]

feel the draught, to phr. [1920s] **1** to be inconvenienced. **2** to have serious money problems.

feel the miss of, to phr. [late 19C] to long for something. [prior use was SE]

feel the thing, to phr. [20C] to feel 'just right'. [SE *feel* + REAL THING]

feel up v. [20C] to caress (usu. a woman) sexually (cf. FEEL v.).

feet-casements n. [mid-19C–1910s] boots, shoes (cf. TROTTER-BOXES). [SE *feet* + *casement*, a frame]

feet uppermost adj. [19C+] used to describe a woman lying supine, in the sexual 'missionary position'.

feeze/pheeze n.[1] [16C] sexual intercourse. [SE *feeze*, a sudden impact, a rub]

feeze/pheeze n.[2] [mid-19C] (US) a state of worry or alarm. [SE *feeze*, to frighten, to put into a state of alarm]

feeze/pheeze v. [16C] to have sexual intercourse. [SE *feeze*, to beat, to flog; ult. OE *fesian*, to drive]

fegary/figary/flagary n. **1** [17C] a prank, a freak, a whim, an eccentricity. **2** [early 18C–early 19C] as pl. trinkets, trifles, adornments of dress. [SE *vagary*]

fegary/flagary v. [early 19C] to concern oneself about trifles in dress. [FEGARY n. (2)]

feh/for true! excl. [20C] (W.I.) a general intensifier, in all honesty, without a doubt.

feist n. [20C] (US) a truculent, short-tempered person or animal. [FEISTY]

feisty adj. [late 19C+] (orig. US) **1** truculent, irascible, impertinent. **2** of young women, flirtatious (to a greater extent than the speaker sees as proper), showing off, putting on airs, of dubious morality. **3** (W.I. Rasta) impudent, rude, out of order, cheeky. [SE *fist*, a small dog; thus having the characteristics of such a yappy, snappy, energetic creature; the dog shares an ety. with 15C *fist*, a foul smell, the breaking of wind, but whether, as Wentworth & Flexner suggest, the dog was so named because one's own smells could be blamed upon it remains debatable. Equally feasible is the 19C suggestion that such dogs were not much bigger than a man's fist. Note dial. *feist*, to strut about, to flirt or show off]

feisty-breeches n. [19C+] (US) derog. epithet used between small boys. [SE *fist*, a stench, the breaking of wind + *breeches*]

feke n. [late 19C–1910s] methylated spirits; thus *feke-drinker*, a drinker of 'meths'. [*feke* = *fake*, i.e. fake alcohol]

felch v. [1960s+] (usu. gay) to lick out the semen from the anus of someone who has just enjoyed anal intercourse. [? echoic]

felcher n. [1990s] (gay) a man who ejaculates into another man's rectum and then eats all of what he has deposited there. [FELCH]

felch queen n. [1950s+] a male homosexual who is stimulated by faecal matter. [FELCH + QUEEN n.[1]]

felicia n. [1980s+] (US gay) a fellator. [SE *fellatio* ? + ref. to FELIX n.[2]]

felix n.[1] [1950s+] (W.I.) a very large, tough dumpling. [? the cartoon character *Felix* the Cat (1931), known for his toughness, or onomat., the dumpling makes a noise like 'flix' when one bites it]

felix n.[2] [1950s] the penis. [ety. unknown; ? a nonce-word coined by Colin MacInnes in his novel *Absolute Beginners* (1959)]

fellow, a n.[1] [mid-19C+] oneself, e.g. *a fellow ought to get drunk once in a while*.

fellow n.[2] [1930s–40s] (US Black) a White person. [deliberate reversal of dismissive White description of a 'Black fellow']

fellow n.[3] [1950s+] one's husband or regular male partner.

fellow commoner n. [late 18C] an empty bottle (cf. GENTLEMAN COMMONER). [orig. Cambridge Univ. use, as opposed to scholars, commoners were 'not in general considered as over-full of learning' (Grose, 1785)]

fellow-feeling n. [late 19C+] a ceiling. [rhy. sl.]

felon swell n. [early–mid-19C] (Aus.) a gentleman convict. [SE *felon* + SWELL]

felony shoes n. [1980s+] (US) any brand of the high-priced trainers (Nike, Adidas etc) worn by teenagers. [the term is implicitly racist, suggesting that the Black teenagers who particularly favour such footwear are automatically up to no good]

fem n.[1] *see* FAM n.[1].

fem n.[2] *see* FEMME.

fembo n. [1980s+] (US campus) a homosexual man. [SE *female* + BIMBO or ? proper name of the 1980s macho film hero *Rambo*]

feminine gender n. [late 19C] the vagina.

femme/fem n. (US) **1** [1920s+] a young woman. **2** [1960s+] an effeminate homosexual man. **3** [1960s+] a feminine lesbian. [Fr. *femme*, a woman; note West Point jargon *femme*, a young woman]

fen n. **1** [17C–late 18C] a prostitute; thus *fag the fen*, beat the prostitute. **2** [18C–early 19C] a madame, a procuress. **3** [late 18C] a receiver of stolen goods. [SE *fen*, a marshy bog; the image is of the 'dirtiness' of the prostitute or the receiver]

fen/fend v. [1920s–30s] (US Black) to de*fend*. [abbr.]

fen! excl. [early 19C] a call for a truce during a game, a statement that one is ineligible for a given duty or command (cf. FAINS!). [*fen*, to forbid, ult. ? f. *fend*, forbid]

fence n.[1] **1** [17C+] a receiver and seller of stolen property (cf. FENCE-SHOP). **2** [mid-19C] the place where stolen goods are kept (cf. FENCING CRIB; FENCING CULLY; FENCING KEN; FENCING MASTER). **3** [20C] (Aus.) a procurer of the sexually complaisant for customers who prefer something 'out of the ordinary'. [? as a middleman he provides a *fence* between the thief and the buyer of the goods]

fence n.[2] [1910s] (US) a man's detachable collar. [i.e. the collar provides a *fence* around the neck]

fence v. **1** [17C+] to buy and sell stolen property. **2** [late 17C] to spend money. [FENCE n.[1]]

fence con n. [20C] (US prison) an escapee, a prisoner who is planning an escape. [SE *fence* + CON n.[1] (6)]

fence-corner *adj.* [20C] (US) illegitimate; thus *fence-corner child*, an illegitimate child, *hatched on a fence post*, illegitimate.

fence-jumping *n.* [1990s] (N.Z.) race mixing. [farmyard imagery; i.e. a bull *jumping a fence* to reach the cows]

fence parole *n.* [20C] (US prison) the attempt to make an escape by climbing the prison fence or wall; such efforts, inevitably, lead to death.

fencer *n.* [mid-19C] a receiver and seller of stolen property. [FENCE n.¹ (1)]

fence rail *n.* [20C] (US) a very thin person. [dimensions of a fence rail]

fence-shop *n.* [late 18C] a shop where stolen property is on sale. [FENCE n.¹ (1)]

fencing *n.* [mid-19C+] receiving or dealing in stolen goods. [FENCE v. + sfx. *-ing*]

fencing crib *n.* [19C–1900s] the shop, house or room from which a receiver operates (cf. FENCE n.¹; DOLLYSHOP; LEAVING SHOP; SWAG-SHOP). [FENCING + CRIB n.³]

fencing cully *n.* [early 17C–18C] a receiver and seller of stolen goods. [FENCING + CULLY]

fencing ken *n.* [late 17C–19C] the shop, house or room from which a receiver operates (cf. FENCING CRIB). [FENCING + KEN n.¹]

fencing master *n.* [early 17C–late 18C] a receiver and seller of stolen goods. [FENCING + SE *master*]

fend *see* FEN v.

fender-bender *n.* **1** [1950s+] (drugs) a barbiturate capsule. **2** [1960s+] (US) a minor automobile accident. [SAmE *fender* (bumper) + *bender*; the effects of (1) are likely to cause (2)]

fend off *v.* [1930s] (N.Z.) to take, to steal. [one *fends off* the object from its owner so that one may keep it oneself]

Fenian/three cold Irish *n.¹* [late 19C] threepenny-worth of whisky and water (cf. HOME RULE). [a pun on 'three cold Irish', itself referring to the hanging of the Fenians Allen, Larkin and O'Brien for the 'Manchester Murder' of PC Brett in 1867 or for three men, also Fenians, hanged for the Phoenix Park murders of Lord Frederick Cavendish and Thomas Henry Burke, Under-Secretary for Ireland, on 6 May 1882]

Fenian *n.²* [1910s+] (Ulster) a Protestant term of abuse, used of Ulster Catholics/nationalists. [SE *Fenian*, a member of the mid–late 19C Fenian Brotherhood; ult. Irish *na Fianna*, the legendary warrior band led by Fionn Mac Cumhail]

fenky-fenky *adj.* [1940s+] (W.I.) **1** cowardly, effeminate, 'crybabyish'. **2** choosy, proud, snobbish. [? SE *finicky* + redup.]

fenneh *v.* [1950s+] (W.I. Rasta) to feel physical distress or pain. [Twi *fene*, to vomit; Fante *fena*, to be troubled; Lumba *feno*, to faint]

fen nightingale *n.* [late 18C–19C] a frog (cf. CAMBRIDGE NIGHTINGALE). [the large population of frogs in England's marshy fenlands]

ferchrissakes! *excl.* [20C] (orig. US) a mild oath, i.e. *for Christ's sake*.

feria *n.* [1960s+] (US) money. [SE *fare* + Hispanic sfx. *-ia*]

feringee *n.* [17C–19C] (Anglo-Ind.) a foreigner, a European. [Arabic *faranji*, a Frank, a European]

ferk *v.* [1920s+] euph. for FUCK (cf. FORK v.³).

ferme *n.* [early 17C–late 18C] (Und.) a hole; thus a prison, a cave. [Fr. *fermer*, to shut, to close]

fermedy/fermerly beggars *n.* [late 17C–early 18C] (Und.) beggars in general, other than those who parade their (faked) open sores. [? Fr. *fermer*, to close; i.e. their skin is 'closed' or 'shut']

fern *n.¹* [1950s+] **1** (US) the female genitals and pubic hair. **2** (US campus) the buttocks. [? ref. to SE *maidenhair fern*]

fern *n.²* [1980s+] (US campus) someone who clings to the styles of the 1960s. [image of flowers and 'love']

Fernandez talking *see* APPLETON TALKING.

ferninster *n.* [20C] (US) a devoted nay-sayer, one who consistently opposes. [dial. *fornenst*, opposite; ult. SE *foreign*]

ferret *n.¹* **1** [18C] a tradesman who entices the young and naïve to spend money on credit, then promptly duns them for his bill (cf. RABBIT SUCKER). **2** [early 18C–early 19C] a pawnbroker. **3** [late 19C] a young thief who gets into a coal barge and throws coal over the side to his confederates. [SE *ferret*, a thief, ult. Lat. *fur*, a thief + image of a SE *ferret*, a predator used in the hunting of rabbits (cf. CONY n.¹)]

ferret *n.²* [late 19C+] the penis. [SE *ferret*; like the animal, it burrows into holes]

ferret *n.³* [late 19C–1920s] (US) a detective. [SE *ferret* (out), to search]

ferret *v.* [late 17C–18C] to cheat, to defraud. [FERRET n.¹]

ferreting *n.¹* [16C] (Und.) a confidence trick that involves the offering of spurious credit and the subsequent profitable dunning of the victim who has taken it. [FERRET n.¹ (1) + sfx. *-ing*]

ferreting *n.²* [19C] sexual intercourse (cf. EXERCISE THE FERRET). [FERRET n.²]

ferricadouzer *n.* [19C+] a knock-out blow (cf. BANDOWZER). [Ital. *fare cadere*, to knock down + *dosso*, back, or Lat. *ferri*, iron + intensifier *ca* + *douse*, a heavy blow. Hancock suggests an origin in Polari]

ferry *n.* [20C] (Aus.) a prostitute (cf. BARRACK HACK). [many men get to 'ride on her']

ferryboat *n.* [20C] (US) a large, clumsy shoe (cf. CANAL BOAT n.²).

ferry dust *n.* [1980s+] (drugs) heroin. [? var. on FAIRY DUST]

ferschlugginer/furschlugginer *adj.* [1950s+] (US) confounded, darned, wretched. [Yid. *farshlogn*, worried, careworn]

fess *v.* **1** [19C+] to admit, to confess, esp. in phr. *fess up (to)*. **2** [19C+] (US campus) to fail in one's recitation, to admit that one has not prepared the lesson's work. **3** [1980s+] (US Black rap) to back down or decline. [abbr. SE *confess*]

fessor *n.* [1900s–30s] (US Black) **1** a pro*fessor*. **2** any intelligent man. [abbr.; (2) is fig. use of (1)]

-fest *sfx.* [1980s+] (orig. US) combined with a relevant noun, indicating a gathering or get-together (*see* synon. at BLABFEST). [abbr. SE *festival*]

festive *adj.* [late 19C] 'loud, fast, a kind of general utility word' (F&H).

fetch *n.¹* [19C] **1** a success. **2** a likeness; thus *the very fetch of*, the image of. [northern dial. *fetch*, an apparition, a double of a living person]

fetch *n.²* [19C] semen. [SE *fetch*, to draw forth]

fetch *n.³* [20C] (US Black) an illegitimate or abandoned child.

fetch *v.¹* [14C+] **1** to hit, esp. as *fetch someone one*. **2** [late 19C+] of a man, to ejaculate, to come to orgasm. [13C SE *fetch*, to give a blow]

fetch *v.²* **1** [mid-19C] to obtain a summons against someone (cf. FETCH LAW OF). **2** [late 19C+] to attract, to interest. **3** [late 19C+] to gain access to, to go to (esp. prison).

fetch a circumbendibus, to *phr.* [late 19C–1900s] to make a detour. [SE *fetch* + CIRCUMBENDIBUS]

fetch a howl, to *phr.* [late 19C] to cry out, to weep loudly.

fetch a Tyburn stretch, to *phr.* [16C] to be hanged (cf. MAKE A TYBURN SHOW; PREACH AT TYBURN CROSS). [TYBURN + SE *stretch*, the extension of the limbs]

fetch away *v.* [mid–late 19C] to divide, to separate, to take away (something) from.

fetch down *v.* **1** [18C] to bring down (with a gunshot etc). **2** [mid-19C] to force down prices.

fetched *adj.* [20C] (US) euph. for DAMNED.

fetch law of v. [early–mid-19C] to bring a court case or summons against.

fetch mettle v. [17C–early 19C] to masturbate. [SE *fetch*, to draw forth + METTLE]

fetch one's pennyworth out of, to phr. [late 17C–early 18C] to ensure that a person works hard for their wages, to get one's moneysworth out of.

fetch over the coals, to phr. [late 16C–early 18C] to reprimand (cf. HAUL OVER THE COALS). [the burning of heretics at the stake]

fetch someone a crack, to phr. [mid-19C] to hit someone.

fetch someone a lick, to phr. [19C+] (US) to attack, to hit, to beat up. [FETCH v.¹ + LICK n.²]

fetch someone a stinger, to phr. [late 19C] to hit someone a sharp blow. [FETCH v.¹ + STINGER n.¹]

fetch the brewer, to phr. [mid-19C] to become drunk. [SE *fetch*, impress, make interested]

fetch up v. **1** [mid–late 19C] to recuperate from an illness, to recover one's health. **2** [mid-19C+] (orig. US naut.) to arrive at a destination, intentionally or otherwise.

fete down v. [20C] (W.I.) to go on a (lengthy) spree. [SE *fête*, a party]

fete up v. [20C] (W.I.) to take out and entertain in the hope of persuading one's guest to agree with one's plans, esp. in a political or business context. [SE *fête*, a party]

fetti n. [1990s] (US Black teen) money. [abbr. SE *confetti*]

fettled adj. [19C] tipsy, drunk (cf. ABOUT RIGHT adj.¹). [SE phr. *in fine fettle* + note Cheshire dial. *fettled ale*, ale mulled with ginger and sugar]

few!, a excl. [late 18C–1950s] a deliberately down-played rejoinder to a suggestion that an event is worth noticing (cf. QUITE SOMETHING; RATHER!).

few bricks short/shy of a load, a phr. [1960s+] unintelligent, eccentric (cf. THREE BRICKS SHY OF A LOAD; TWO BRICKS SHORT OF THE LOAD). [for a full list of synon. phr. see NOT ALL THERE]

few pence short in the shilling, a phr. [1900s–60s] unintelligent, eccentric (cf. NOT ALL THERE).

fews and twos n. [1940s] (US Black) a very small amount of money.

few snags short of a barbie, a phr. [1980s+] (Aus.) eccentric, crazy (cf. NOT ALL THERE).

few tickers, a n. [1940s] (US Black) a few minutes. [SE *few* + TICK n.³]

fey see FAY.

fey cat n. [1940s–70s] (US Black) a White man. [FAY + CAT n.⁹]

feygele see FAYGELE.

f.f. see FIST-FUCKING.

F-40s n. [1980s+] (drugs) capsules of Seconal. [the pharmaceutical identification stamped on the capsule]

f.f.v. n. [20C] an important person or one who poses as such, often used teasingly or derisorily. [abbr. First Family of Virginia, a member of the founding families of Virginia; thus one of the élite. 'Used quite seriously in the South of the USA and satirically in the North' (Ware)]

f.h.b./f.h.o. phr. [1910s+] a phr. often used by a host/hostess when there is only enough food to feed the guests properly. [abbr. *family hold back/family hold off*]

fiasco n. [1920s+] a fiancé; occas. fiancée. [joc. mispron.]

fib n.¹ **1** [late 16C; mid-19C] a liar. **2** [early 17C+] a lie, usu. but not invariably, a trivial one. [? link to dial. *fible-fable*, a story, a fable]

fib n.² [early 19C] a blow, a punch. [FIB v.¹]

fib v.¹ [mid-17C–mid-19C] to beat, to thrash. [Lancs. dial.; thus boxing jargon *fibbing*, hitting with a succession of blows; *fibbing gloak*, a boxer, *fibbing-match*, a boxing-match]

fib v.² [late 17C+] (usu. juv.) to lie, usu. children's use. [FIB n.¹]

fibber n. [early 18C+] a liar; thus [mid-19C–1920s] *fibbery*, the telling of lies. [FIB n.¹ + sfx. *-er*]

Fibber McGee's closet n. [20C] (US) a very untidy room or cupboard. [*Fibber McGee*, a character in the radio show 'Fibber McGee & Molly' (1935–50); whenever he opened his closet door, the entire contents fell out]

fibbing n. [early 19C] prize-fighting, boxing; thus *fibbing gloak*, a boxer, *fibbing-match*, a prize-fight. [FIB v.¹]

fibre n. [1940s] (S.Afr.) a matchbox. [SE *wood fibre*]

fice/foyse n. [late 18C] a silent breaking of wind, 'more obvious to the nose than to the ears; frequently by old ladies charged on their lapdogs.' (Grose, 1796); thus the 19C US dial. *fice*, a small dog. [FOIST n.²]

ficky-fick/-ficky n. [20C] sexual intercourse. [pidgin var. of FUCK v.¹ + redup.]

fidas see FIETAS.

fiddle n.¹ [late 17C–early 19C] a writ of arrest. [the victim must 'face the music']

fiddle n.² **1** [late 18C] a swindler, a card-sharp. **2** [19C+] (orig. US) a swindle, a fraud. [SE *fiddle*, to swindle; the swindler can 'make people dance to his tune'. The term appears in 16C but is categorized as sl. only from mid-19C]

fiddle n.³ [19C] the vagina. [one 'plays on it']

fiddle n.⁴ [19C] a watchman's rattle (the precursor of the policeman's whistle). [? the noise, the watchman 'plays' his rattle]

fiddle n.⁵ [19C] a sixpence. [abbr. FIDDLER]

fiddle n.⁶ [mid-19C] a whip. [abbr. SE *fiddlestick*]

fiddle n.⁷ [20C] (Aus.) a maize grater. [resemblance/the movement of one's arm]

fiddle n.⁸ [1910s–20s] an unrewarding, annoying job of work. [FIDDLE v.² (2)]

fiddle n.⁹ [1930s] (N.Z.) a dressed hindquarter of mutton (cf. BANJO n.¹). [the shape]

fiddle v.¹ [early 17C] to take liberties with a woman.

fiddle v.² **1** [17C+] to cheat, to swindle. **2** [mid-19C+] to make one's living taking small jobs on the street, e.g. unloading a cart. **3** [late 19C] to drug liquor. **4** [late 19C+] to work as a petty thief. **5** [1940s+] to cheat on one's expenses. [FIDDLE n.²]

fiddle and flute n. [1930s+] (US) a suit (cf. WHISTLE AND FLUTE). [rhy. sl.]

fiddle-arse/-arse around v. [20C] (Aus.) to mess around, to waste time (cf. FIDDLE-FART; FIDDLE-FUCK). [SE *fiddle* + ARSE]

fiddle-bow n. [19C] the penis (cf. FIDDLESTICK). [it 'plays' the FIDDLE n.³]

fiddle-britches n. [20C] (US) anyone who is too clever for their own good.

fiddlecases n. [1940s] (US Black) shoes, esp. large ones. [resemblance]

fiddledeedee! excl. [late 17C+] a mild excl. denying the validity of the other speaker's remark (cf. FIDDLESTICKS!). [SE *fiddle* + a nonsense sfx.]

fiddle-diddle n. [19C] the penis. [FIDDLE n.³ + DIDDLE n.³]

fiddle-face n. [mid–late 19C] **1** one who has a wizened, drawn face. **2** one who has a miserable, 'long' face; thus *fiddle-faced*, wizened, miserable; foolish, empty-headed. [the long face resembles the shape of a violin]

fiddle-fart/fiddle-fart around v. [20C] to waste time, to shirk one's duties (cf. FIDDLE-ARSE). [? *fiddlefoot*, for a horse to make jumpy, skittish movements; thus *fiddlefoot*, to wander aimlessly]

fiddle-fuck/fiddle-fuck around v. [20C] to waste time, to shirk one's duties (cf. FIDDLE-ARSE). [SE *fiddle* + FUCK v.²]

fiddle-fucked adj. [1970s+] (US) damned, esp. in phr. *I'll be fiddle-fucked*. [SE *fiddle* + FUCK v.²]

fiddle-fucking adj. [1970s] elaboration of FUCKING adj.

fiddler n.¹ [mid-19C+] a cheat, a swindler. [FIDDLE v.² (1)]

fiddler *n.*[2] [mid-19C] **1** a farthing. **2** a sixpence. [FIDDLE n.[5]; ? the old custom of each couple at a dance paying the fiddler a farthing, and later sixpence]

fiddler's damn *see* TINKER'S CUSS.

fiddler's fare *n.* [early 17C] meat, drink and money (cf. FIDDLER'S MONEY; FIDDLER'S PAY; FIDDLER'S WAGES). [SE *fiddler* + *fare*, the wages paid to an itinerant fiddler]

fiddler's fuck *n.* [1950s+] (US) anything considered utterly insignificant, a 'damn', usu. in phr. *not make a fiddler's fuck*, to be worthless, pointless. [fig. use of sl.]

fiddler's green *n.* [19C] (orig. naut.) paradise, a place of unlimited rum, women and tobacco, i.e. 'nine miles this side (or the other side) of hell'.

fiddler's money *n.* [late 18C–19C] small change (cf. FIDDLER'S FARE). [fiddlers receive only very small wages]

fiddler's pay *n.* [late 17C] wine and thanks (cf. FIDDLER'S FARE). [i.e. no actual money]

fiddler's wages *n.* [16C] no wages at all, but simply a thank-you (cf. FIDDLER'S FARE). [ironic use of SE]

fiddles and flutes *n.* [20C] (Aus.) the boots. [rhy. sl.]

fiddlestick *n.* **1** [late 16C–early 17C] a sword. **2** [19C+] the penis (cf. FIDDLE-BOW). [resemblance]

fiddlesticks! *excl.* [17C+] nonsense! rubbish! [? FIDDLESTICK n. (2); thus cf. COCK n.[4] (2)]

fiddlestick's end *n.* [late 18C] nothing (cf. NOT CARE A FIDDLESTICK). [a SE *fiddlestick* ends in a point]

fiddley-did *n.* [1920s–70s] (Aus.) £1. [rhy. sl. *fiddley-did* = QUID]

fiddling *n.*[1] [mid-19C] **1** picking up a variety of odd jobs in the streets, holding horses, carrying parcels etc. **2** buying cheap and selling dear. [FIDDLE v.[2] (2)]

fiddling *n.*[2] [19C] gambling. [FIDDLE v.[2] (1)]

fiddling-stick *n.* [19C] the penis. [var. on FIDDLESTICK]

fiddly-fuck *n.* [1960s] (US) anything considered utterly insignificant. [var. on FIDDLER'S FUCK]

fidlam-ben/-cove *n.* [late 18C–mid-19C] (Und.) a petty thief, who will grab anything, irrespective of its value (cf. ST PETER'S SONS). [FIDDLE v.[2] + abbr. *'em* + BENE CULL]

fi-do-nie *n.* [1950s] (drugs) opium. [ety. unknown]

fie-fie *n.* [19C] a 'fallen' woman. [redup. excl. of *Fie!* on encountering such a person]

fie-fie *adj.* [19C] improper, of improper character. [FIE-FIE n.]

fie for shame *n.* [19C] the vagina. [the image of the vagina as something shameful; thus the common use, e.g. throughout E.P., of the euph. Lat. *pudendum* (lit. 'that of which one ought to be ashamed'), as the definition for the many sl. terms for the female genitals]

field artillery *see* ARTILLERY n.[3].

field colt/rabbit *n.* [20C] (US) an illegitimate child (cf. BRUSH COLT).

Field Lane duck *n.* [19C] a baked sheep's head (cf. CLARE MARKET DUCK; SNOB'S DUCK). [*Field Lane*, which once linked Holborn to Clerkenwell]

field nigger *n.*[1] [20C] (W.I.) a term of abuse for a deferential Black, who curries favour with Whites (cf. HOUSE NIGGER). [SAmE *field negro/nigger*, a Black slave who worked in the fields; this use is a paradox, or an erroneous def., since the usu. meaning is at next]

field nigger *n.*[2] [1960s] (US Black) working-class, street Blacks, as opposed to Black bourgeoisie. [the slavery era distinction between the rougher, less refined field workers and those who worked as 'house' servants]

field of wheat *n.* [20C] a street. [rhy. sl.]

field rabbit *see* FIELD COLT.

fields *n.* [1970s+] (drugs) LSD (cf. A n.[3]). [ety. unknown]

field whisky n. [20C] (US) illicitly distilled whisky (cf. FARMER'S WINE).

fiemies *n.* [20C] (S.Afr.) **1** whims, fads; thus *full of fiemies*, capricious, pernickety. [Afk. *fiemies*, whims]

fiend *n.*[1] **1** [late 19C–1910s] (US campus) a clever student. **2** [1960s] (US Black) a general term of praise for any person or thing. [on bad = good model]

fiend *n.*[2] **1** [late 19C+] (US drugs) an addict, esp. of opium. **2** [1960s+] someone who smokes marijuana alone (since smoking is usu. a communal experience). [contemporary use is always ironic]

fiender *n.* [1990s] (US) a drug addict. [ext. of FIEND n.[2]]

fiendish/fiendish-back *adj.* [1960s] (US Black) excellent, wonderful, admirable. [on bad = good model]

fiend on *v.* [1960s+] (US Black) to show off, to outdo a rival (cf. FONK v.; HIGH SIGN v.[2]; STYLE). [FIEND n.[1]]

fierce *adj.*[1] [20C] a general intensifier, whether positive or negative.

fierce *adj.*[2] **1** [1900s–50s] (US) very bad or unpleasant. **2** [1980s+] (US teen) a general adj. of approval: excellent, wonderful, first-rate. [(2) on bad = good model]

fiery lot *n.* [late 19C] a 'fast', 'sporting' man. [var. on HOT STUFF n.[2]]

fiery snorter *n.* [mid-19C] a drink-reddened nose.

fietas/fidas/vietas *n.* [1980s] (S.Afr.) Vredeorp/Pageview, i.e. Soweto District Six, an area from which the occupants were removed compulsorily under the Group Areas Act. [Afk. *fiela*, a backward, slovenly person + Du. *vielt*, a scoundrel ? and/or Zulu *i-vila*, a loafer]

fife and drum *n.* [1940s–50s] the buttocks, the posterior. [rhy. sl. *fife and drum* = BUM n.[2]]

fifi *n.* [1980s+] (US campus) an attractive, sexy young woman, who dresses to match but is, in the end, considered superficial. [? *Fifi*, the clichéd name of the typical sexy French maid of farce and fantasy]

fifi *adj.* [1960s+] (US prison) effeminate. [for ety. *see* FIFI n.]

fifi bag *n.* [1960s+] (US prison) a plastic sack that holds a towel soaked in warm water that is used as a substitute 'vagina' for masturbation. [FIFI adj. + SE *bag*]

fifi water *n.* [1970s+] (US prison) aftershave. [FIFI adj. + SE *water*; the presumed effeminacy of those who use it]

fifteen and two/fifteen-two *n.* [1940s+] (US) a Jew (cf. BOX OF GLUE). [rhy. sl.]

fifteen cents *n.* [1980s+] (US drugs) $15 worth of drugs.

fifteen puzzle *n.* [late 19C] absolute chaos, utter confusion. [SE *fifteen puzzle*, a popular puzzle, *c*.1879. Like a prototype Rubik's cube, it required players to arrange a set of numbered, moveable cubes in rows, each of which had to add up to 15]

fifteen-two *see* FIFTEEN AND TWO.

fifth *n.* [1930s+] (US) **1** a fifth part of a gallon of liquor. **2** a bottle containing such a part.

Fifth Avenoodles *see* AVENOODLES.

fifth calf *n.* [20C] (US) a superfluous person, one who does not fit in. [a cow's 4 udders; 4 calves can drink at a time, the fifth must wait its turn or force its way in]

fifth point of contact *n.* [1990s] (US) of a woman, the anus. [the other 4 points are mouth, nipples and vagina]

fifty *n.*[1] [1970s+] (Aus.) a pint of beer composed of 50% old beer and 50% new.

fifty *n.*[2] [1990s] (US Black) the police. [FIVE-OH]

fifty cent bag *n.* [1960s+] (US drugs) $50 worth of marijuana (cf. DIME BAG; NICKEL BAG).

fifty-eleven/-'leven *n.* [late 19C–1950s] (US Black) a large or infinite quantity (cf. ELEVENTY-ELEVEN; SEVENTY-'LEVEN).

fifty-fifty *n.* [1980s+] (gay) a sexual act in which the two partners alternately perform fellatio and sodomy on each other. [FIFTY-FIFTY adj.]

fifty-fifty *adj.* [1910s+] (orig. US) equal, of shares or of chances. [SE *fifty per cent*]

fifty-'leven see FIFTY-ELEVEN.

fifty-one n. [1990s] (drugs) **1** crack cocaine. **2** a cigarette made from a mix of marijuana and crack cocaine (cf. SLEEF). [ety. unknown]

fig/fig of Spain n.¹ [late 16C–19C] a coarse gesture of dismissal whereby one sticks one's thumb up between two forefingers (cf. GIVE THE FIG).

fig n.² [late 18C] a counterfeit coin. [phr. *not worth a fig*]

fig n.³ [mid-19C] the vagina (cf. APPLE n.¹⁰). [Ital. sl. *fica*, the vagina (lit. a fig)]

fig n.⁴ [1970s+] (N.Z. prison) a 1oz (28g) packet of prison-issue tobacco. [SNZE *fig*, tobacco, used as a unit of barter between settlers and Maoris in the mid-19C]

fig v.¹ [mid-16C–late 18C] to pick pockets. [SE *feague*, to overcome by trickery, to beat]

fig v.² [late 16C] 'to put something useless into a person's head. Low Cant' (Johnson, 1755). [? FIG. n.¹. The *OED* def. is Johnson's quote; the presumed implication is of fooling one's hearer with specious nonsense]

fig/fig a horse v.³ [mid-19C] 'to play improper tricks with [a horse] in order to make him lively' (Hotten, 1860). [FEAGUE]

figaries n. [late 19C] pranks, games, amusements. [FEGARY]

figaro n. [mid-19C–1920s] a barber. [Beaumarchais' comedy *Le Mariage de Figaro* (1784) and Mozart's opera *Le Nozze di Figaro* (1786)]

fig around v. [20C] (US) euph. for FRIG AROUND, itself a euph. for FUCK AROUND.

figary see FEGARY n.

fig-boy/figger n. [16C] (Und.) a pickpocket or cut-purse. [FIG v.¹ + SE *boy*]

figger see FAGGER.

figging/fagging law n. [16C–late 18C] (Und.) the art of picking pockets (cf. CHEATING LAW). [FIG v.¹]

figgins see FIGS.

fight n. [late 19C–1950s] (US) a party, a brawl. [abbr. BUN-FIGHT]

fight at the leg, to phr. [late 18C–19C] to take unfair advantage. [back-sword or single-stick rules, in which it is considered unfair to hold the opponent by the leg]

fight cunning v. [mid-18C–1900] to act smartly or astutely, to 'box clever'.

fight in armour v. [late 18C] to wear a condom (cf. IN ONE'S ARMOUR phr.¹).

fighting adj. [late 19C+] (orig. US) used of words or speeches to imply ferocity and aggression, e.g. *fighting talk*.

fighting drunk/tight adj. [20C] so drunk as to wish to fight, for no apparent reason, one's companions or some hapless stranger. [FIGHTING adj. + SE *drunk*/TIGHT adj.³]

fighting Irish n. [20C] (US) a boast. [racial stereotyping]

fighting mad adj. [late 19C+] (US) so angry as to wish to hit someone. [FIGHTING adj. + SAmE *mad*, angry]

fighting tight see FIGHTING DRUNK.

fightist n. [late 18C] a prize-fighter, a boxer. [SE *fight* + sfx. -*ist*]

fight like Kilkenny cats, to phr. [mid-19C+] to fight savagely and without restraint, to fight to the death. [one of a pair of cats fabled to have fought until only their tails remained. Brewer (1894) suggests that the first such fight came from Oliver Cromwell's troops in Ireland who, in the 1650s, would cruelly tie two cats together by their tails and hang them over a washing line; the maddened cats tore each other to pieces]

fight nob work, to phr. [early 19C] (Und.) to succeed without working in the respectable world (cf. NOB IT). [? to act like a NOB n.³]

fight off/up with v. [20C] (W.I.) to attack with unexpected aggression (cf. FIGHT UP ONESELF).

fight one's hat, to phr. [20C] (US) to struggle uselessly. [proverb, *if the hat fits, wear it*, the image is of struggling against a metaphorical 'hat that fits']

fight one's turkey, to phr. [20C] to masturbate (cf. ACCOST THE OSCAR MEYER).

fight the champ, to phr. [1980s+] to masturbate.

fight the old soldier, to phr. [late 17C] to malinger (cf. COME THE OLD SOLDIER).

fight the tiger, to phr. [mid-19C+] (US) to play the game of faro (cf. BUCK THE TIGER; TIGER DEN). [SE *fight* + TIGER n.³]

fight up oneself/with phr. [20C] (W.I.) to struggle for survival (cf. FIGHT OFF WITH; KILL OUT ONESELF).

fight up with see FIGHT OFF WITH.

fight-water n. [late 19C–1900s] (Can.) spirits. [their effect]

fight with the nails on your toes/with your own toenails, to phr. [1990s] (Irish) to be obsessively, continually aggressive.

fig-leaf n. [late 19C] an apron.

f.i.g.m.o. phr. [1960s+] *fuck it, got my orders* (cf. SNAFU phr.). [abbr.]

fig of Spain see FIG n.¹.

fig out v. [19C] to get dressed up in one's best clothes. [IN FULL FIG]

figs/figgins n. [late 19C] a grocer. [his stock]

figthing n. [late 18C] a counterfeit coin. [ext. of FIG n.²]

fig up v. [early 19C] to invigorate, to cheer up, to improve morale. [fig. use of FIG v.³]

figure n.¹ [late 18C] an untidy, unkempt person (cf. FIGURE OF FUN).

figure n.² see FAGGER.

figure n.³ [mid–late 19C] a sum of money, esp. a bill. [SE *figure*, a number]

figure/figure on v.¹ [late 18C] to total up (a bill or account) against.

figure v.² **1** [19C+] to consider, to feel, to estimate. **2** [20C] (orig. US) to work out as expected; esp. as *that figures*. **3** [20C] to think of a person or object in a given way; usu. *figure him/her for …* . [SE *figure*, to calculate, to ascertain, to understand]

figure-dancer n. [late 18C] a forger who specializes in altering the figures on banknotes, usu. adding a zero to make 10 into 100. [they make the 'figures dance' + pun on SE *figure-dancer*, one who performs in a figure-dance; i.e. a dance that offers representations of famous historical events]

figure-fancier n. [19C] a man who prefers plump women (cf. FAT-FANCIER).

figure-maker n. [late 19C] a womanizer. [SE *figure*, a woman's shape]

figure of fun n. [early 19C+] a ludicrous personage, an oddity.

figure on see FIGURE v.¹.

figure out v. [mid-19C+] (orig. US) to work out, to understand.

figure-six/figure-six curls n. [mid-19C] a hairstyle in which the hair is greased, twisted into spirals and then stuck to the face (cf. AGGERAWATOR).

fi-heath n. [mid-19C] a thief. [backsl.]

Fiji uncle n. [1900s–20s] (Aus.) a mythical figure, the human equivalent of Billy Bunter's never-materialized postal order, whose supposed wealth is ready and waiting to bail one out of any problems. [one's refs. to 'when my uncle in Fiji ...']

filbert n.¹ [late 19C–1930s] **1** the human head (cf. NUT n.³). [SE *filbert*, a hazelnut, which in France traditionally ripened on or near St Philibert's day, 22 August (Old Style)]

filbert n.² [1900s–10s] a fashionable dandy. [pun on KNUT; esp. in song 'Gilbert the Filbert/Colonel of the Knuts', featured in a 1914 version of *The Passing Show*]

filbert n.³ [1910s–50s] (US) a crazy person. [NUT n.²]

filch n. **1** [early 17C–late 18C] a short pole with a hook on one end, used to steal small, portable items from windows, stalls etc (cf. HOOKER n.[1]). **2** [17C] that which is stolen, the booty of a theft. [a cant word of no certain origin; despite a 40-year gap between printed first uses, it is poss. that *filch* n. (1) may have been the source of the v.]

filch v. [mid-16C+] **1** to steal. **2** to beat, to strike, to rob.

filcher n. [16C–late 18C] a thief. [FILCH v.]

filching-cove n. [17C–18C] a thief. [FILCH v. + COVE]

filching-mort n. [17C–18C] a female thief. [FILCH v. + MORT]

filchman n. [mid-16C–17C] a cudgel or staff. [FILCH n. (1)]

file n. **1** [mid-17C–19C] (Und.) a pickpocket. **2** [early 19C] an experienced fraudster or confidence trickster, also known as an *old file upon the town*. **3** [19C] an artful, cunning or shrewd person, a man, a 'fellow'; thus *old file*, an old and/or experienced person (cf. COVE). [ety. unknown; *OED* suggests abbr. 17C FOIL-CLOY, thence FILE-CLOY. Weekley offers link to Fr. *filou*, a pickpocket; E.P. suggests SE *file*, a metal tool used to cut through things, and *file*, a rascal; 18C Fr. argot also has *filer doux*, to flatter, wheedle, 'play the sleeping dog', i.e. lie in wait]

file v.[1] [late 17C–late-18C] to pick a pocket. [FILE n.]

file v.[2] [1930s+] (US campus) to throw away into a wastepaper bin (cf. CIRCULAR FILE)

file v.[3] [1960s] (US Black) to act in a brutal, cruel manner. [? 13C SE *file*, defile or f. SE *vile*]

file v.[4] [1970s] (US campus) to show off, dress up.

file a cly, to phr. [mid-18C–early 19C] to pick a pocket (cf. FILE-CLOY). [FILE v.[1] + CLY]

file-cloy n. [late 18C] a pickpocket. [FOIL-CLOY]

file lay n. [late 18C–early 19C] (Und.) pickpocketing. [FILE n. + LAY n.[4]]

file-lifter n. [late 17C–late 18C] a pickpocket. [FILE n. + SE *lifter*]

file one's fun-rod, to phr. [20C] to masturbate. [SE *file* + FUN-ROD]

file onto v. [1920s–30s] (Can.) to grab hold of, to seize.

filer n. [late 17C–early 18C] a pickpocket (cf. FILE-CLOY). [FILE v.[1]]

filet n. [1980s+] (US campus) a very attractive young woman (cf. BANANA n.[2]). [Fr. *filet de boeuf*, fillet steak ? + joc. ref. to LAY n.[2]]

filing-lay n. [18C] (Und.) pickpocketing. [FILE v.[1] + LAY n.[4]]

filiome adj. [mid-19C+] (Ling. Fr./Polari) of a child, under the age of consent. [FEELE + OMEE, lit. 'child-man']

filipinyock n. [20C] (US) a derog. term for a Filipino. [? *Filipino* + HUNYAK]

fillaloo n. [1910s–20s] a commotion, a row. [SE *hullaballo*]

fill a woman's pannier, to phr. [17C–18C] to impregnate a woman.

filled up adj. [20C] (Ulster) on the verge of tears. [one's eyes are filled with tears]

fillet of cod n. [1970s] a mild pej. [rhy. sl., *filet of cod* = SOD n.[1]]

fillet of veal n. [mid-19C] **1** the treadwheel. **2** a prison. [(1) rhy. sl.]

fillibrush v. [mid-19C] to flatter, to praise ironically. [? SE *filibuster*]

fill in v.[1] [1900s–40s] (US Und.) to join a criminal gang.

fill in v.[2] [1940s+] (orig. naut.) to beat up. [the image is of 'filling' one's victim's face with a fist]

fill in v.[3] [1950s+] (Aus.) to make pregnant; thus *filled in*, pregnant.

filling station n.[1] (US) **1** [20C] an urban description of a small town. **2** [1930s–40s] a place to eat or drink, esp. a nightclub. [SE *filling station*, a petrol or gas station. Apart from its filling station, such a town holds no use or appeal to a passing city-dweller]

filling station n.[2] [1970s+] (US Black) a liquor store. [pun]

fillmill n. [1940s] (US Black) a bar, a saloon. [SE *fill* + *mill*, a

building characterized by the task performed within it, in this case 'filling']

fill one's collar, to phr. [19C] (US) to perform adequately, to come up to expectations (cf. GET IN THE COLLAR; GO UP AGAINST THE COLLAR). [SE *fill* + *collar*, that part of a draft harness that fits the lower part of the neck. The image is of a draft horse pulling wagons as required]

fill one's pipe, to phr. [early 19C] to attain a comfortable life-style, to amass wealth. [one can lie back and smoke]

fill one's pipe and leave others to enjoy it, to phr. [early 19C] to amass a large fortune, then die, leaving it to be wasted by one's heirs. [FILL ONE'S PIPE]

fill one's shirt, to phr. [20C] (US) to eat heartily. [a full, bulging stomach fills one's shirt]

fill someone in on v. [1940s+] (orig. US) to inform, to explain. [i.e. to fill in blank spaces]

fill someone up v. [1970s+] (US Black) to gratify and satisfy completely; with obvious sexual overtones, although sex need not invariably be involved.

fill the bill, to phr. [late 19C+] (orig. US) **1** to suit ideally, to satisfy. **2** to work out, to be effective. [theatrical use, 'to excel in conspicuousness, as a star actor whose name is "billed" to the exclusion of the rest of the company' (F&H)]

fillupy/filluppey adj. [mid-19C] satisfying. [it 'fills you up']

filly n. **1** [17C+] a girl, a young woman (cf. FILLY-HUNTING). **2** [late 19C] (ballroom) a girl or woman who dances noticeably quickly. **3** [20C] (US) an illegitimate daughter (cf. COLT n.[4]). [SE *filly*, a young mare, a female foal]

filly and foal n. [late 19C] a couple who have left a larger group in search of privacy.

filly-hunting n. [19C] the pursuit of women. [FILLY + *hunting*]

film for your brownie n. [1990s] toilet paper. [pun on the Brownie (camera) + BROWNIE n.[5]]

filth n.[1] [late 16C] a prostitute (cf. FEN n.). [guilty equation of prostitution and dirt]

filth n.[2] [1960s+] (Und.) the police, esp. the CID (Criminal Investigation Department).

f.i.l.t.h. phr. [1980s+] used of one who is attempting to resuscitate their career, stalled in London, in the Far East. [abbr. *failed in London, try Hong Kong*]

filthily adv. [1920s–30s] very, extremely. [play on SE]

filthy, the n. [19C–20C] money. [phr. *filthy lucre*]

filthy adj. [20C] a general intensifier, e.g. *filthy rich*, *filthy temper* (cf. STINKING adj.[1]). [a quasi-adv. use, the equivalent of FILTHILY; the usage dates to mid-18C Oxon. dial. but became widespread only since 19C]

filthy fellow n. [19C] a term of mild affection.

filthy pillows n. [1990s] the female breasts.

filthy with adj. [20C] full with, over-loaded with, usu. money. [phr. *filthy rich*, but note FILTHY n.]

fimble-famble n. [mid-19C] a lame, prevaricating excuse. [the image is of fumbling weakly for the excuse]

fimpted adj. [20C] (US Black) very ugly. [ety. unknown]

fin n.[1] [late 18C+] the hand and sometimes the arm (cf. FLIPPER n.[1]; FOREFOOT; MITT n.; MITTEN n.; PAW n.). [SE refers only to fish]

fin n.[2] [mid-19C–1950s] £5, a £5 note. [abbr. FINNIP]

fin n.[3] [20C] (US Black) a female hip that resembles in its opulent curve the fins of a 1950s model automobile.

fin n.[4] **1** [1930s–40s] (US) a $5 bill (cf. FINNY). **2** [1930s+] (US Und.) a sentence of 5 years to life (cf. HANDFUL n.[2]; NICKEL n.[1]; POUND n.[2]). [abbr. FINNIF]

final n. [1930s] the fourth round of a pub drinking session (cf. A.B.F.; SWING OF THE DOOR).

final curtain n. [20C] death.

finale n. [1940s] (US Black) death.

final gallop n. [1990s] an orgasm. [horse-racing imagery]

final thrill n. [1940s] (US Black) death. [bravado]

finance n. [1900s–10s] a rich fiancé(e). [joc. mispron.]

financial adj. [1920s+] (Aus./N.Z.) in credit, solvent, 'in the black'.

find v. [mid-19C–1940s] to steal (cf. ACQUIRE).

find a clue, to phr. [1960s] (US Black) to become aware (cf. GET A CLUE).

find/have a miss/great miss/heavy miss of someone, to phr. [late 19C] to regret the absence loss disadvantage etc of someone; thus the neg. find no miss of … .

find an elephant in the moon, to phr. [late 17C–mid-19C] to delude oneself. [the astronomer Sir Paul Neal who believed, seeing a mouse in his telescope, that he could see an elephant in the moon]

find/grab a stump to fit/rest your rump phr. [1900s–60s] (US Black) an invitation to sit down.

find cold weather, to phr. [late 19C] to be thrown out of a public house.

finder n. **1** [mid-19C–1940s] a thief. **2** [mid-19C] one who gathers the scraps from the floors of a meat-market. [FIND]

finders keepers phr. [early 19C+] whoever finds something is entitled to keep it. [Scot. and northern dial. Proverbial phr. Losers seekers finders keepers or findee keepee, lossee seekee]

find fault with a fat goose, to phr. [late 17C–18C] to find fault for no apparent reason. [general opinion holds that the fatter the goose the better]

find fish on one's fingers, to phr. [late 16C–early 17C] to make up an excuse. ['something smells']

find no bones, to phr. [16C] to have or find no problems in a matter or situation (cf. MAKE NO BONES). [the bones that one finds in a cooked fish]

find one's sex and size, to phr. [20C] (W.I.) to mix with people of one's own age and class; thus not be sex and size with, not to fit in with on an age or social level. [shopping imagery]

find out/know where the barley grows, to phr. [20C] (W.I./Gren., Trin.) to be brought to one's senses, to realize what is really going on, usu. in a warning or threatening sense.

find the lady n. [mic-19C+] (criminal/gambling) the three-card trick, usu. played on the street, the 'lady' being a solitary queen alongside two nondescript cards (cf. FAST AND LOOSE; PEA AND THIMBLE; PRICK THE BELT; PRICK THE GARTER; THIMBLE-RIG; THREE-CARD MONTE).

find where you live!/your hole!/place!/yard! excl. [20C] (W.I.) an aggressive command, go home, go away (cf. ZANDOLI YOUR HOLE!).

find/go back to your bound-place! excl. [20C] (W.I.) go back to where you came from. [bound-place, that part of a sugar estate in which indentured labourers were confined on their arrival; thus the image is of poverty and lowly origins]

find your hole!/place!/yard! see FIND WHERE YOU LIVE!

fine adj. [1930s+] (orig. US Black) attractive, good-looking.

fine adv. [late 19C+] very well.

fine a fellow as ever crossed tit's back phr. [late 19C] an excellent person. [ety. unknown]

fine and dandy n. [20C] brandy. [rhy. sl.]

fine and dandy/all fine and dandy phr. [20C] excellent, perfect; often ironic. [SE all fine + DANDY adj.]

fine and mellow phr. [1930s–50s] (US Black) highly satisfying, very pleasant.

fine as a cow turd stuck with primroses phr. [late 18C] excellent, first-rate, very fine.

fine as a fiddle phr. [late 16C–late 18C] ideal, perfect, most opportune (cf. FIT AS A FIDDLE).

fine as a lord's/proud lord's bastard phr. [mid–late 17C] enjoying comfortable circumstances.

fine as fivepence/fippence phr. [late 18C] first-rate, excellent, very fine.

fine as frog hair phr. [20C] (US) feeling very well or very cheerful. [pun on SE fine, thin/fine, well]

fine as wine phr. (US Black) **1** [1930s+] satisfactory, pleasing. **2** [1970s+] referring to any particularly attractive man or woman.

fine banana n. [1930s–40s] (US Black) an attractive, light-skinned young woman. [FINE adj. + BANANA n.²]

fine brown frame n. [1930s–40s] (US Black) the figure of an attractive Black woman.

fine day/weather for ducks/the young ducks phr. [19C] used of a wet day.

fine dinner/fryer n. [1940s] (US Black) a good-looking Black woman. ['good enough to eat']

fine-fine adj. [20C] (W.I./Guyn.) in infinite and thus irritating detail. [redup.]

fine fryer see FINE DINNER.

fine-haired adj. [19C+] (US) **1** arrogant, conceited. **2** over-fastidious, pernickety.

fine madam n. [19C] a woman who considers herself 'above her station'.

fine morning to catch herrings on Newmarket Heath phr. [mid-17C–mid-18C] phr. used of a wet day (cf. FINE DAY FOR DUCKS).

fine Scot n. [early–mid-19C] a short-tempered person. [national stereotyping]

fine stuff n. [1980s+] (drugs) marijuana.

fine thing n. [1940s+] (Irish/US Black) an attractive woman (cf. FINE DINNER).

fine weather n. [1940s] (US Black/southern campus) an attractive woman (cf. FREEZING WEATHER).

fine weather for ducks/the young ducks see FINE DAY FOR DUCKS.

fine wirer n. [mid–late 19C] the most skilful grade of pickpocket, esp. one who steals from women. [? wire, a small implement, similar to a grappling hook, used to hook items from the victim's pocket]

finger n.¹ [mid-19C+] (orig. US) a measure of alcohol; thus three fingers of rye etc. [the width of a finger, measured against the side of the glass]

finger n.² **1** [late 19C] a policeman. **2** [late 19C] (Aus.) the manager or boss in a shearing shed. **3** [1910s+] an informer. **4** [1920s] (N.Z.) one's father, often ext. as old finger. **5** [1930s+] an unpopular person. **5** [1930s+] (US police) an identified suspect. [SE phr. point the finger at]

finger, the n.³ [late 19C+] (US) **1** an obscene gesture of contempt. **2** contemptuous or mocking treatment, esp. in phr. to give someone the finger.

finger n.⁴ [20C] (Aus.) an amusing person. [ety. unknown]

finger n.⁵ [1960s+] (US drugs) **1** a quantity of drugs smuggled into prison in a rubber finger. **2** a finger-shaped piece of hashish.

finger v.¹ [early 19C+] to indulge in sexual foreplay (cf. DIGITATE).

finger v.² **1** [late 19C+] (US Und.) to arrest. **2** [1930s+] (orig. US) to inform on, to point out, to tip off. [FINGER n.²]

finger and thumb n. [mid–late 19C] **1** rum. **2** a road. **3** a friend. [rhy. sl.; (2) Gypsy drum, a road; (3) CHUM n.¹]

finger artist n. [1940s–70s] (US Black) a lesbian. [FINGER v.¹ + ARTIST n.²; i.e. her manipulation of her partner's clitoris]

finger blasting n. [1990s] masturbation.

finger-bowl n. [1960s+] (Can.) an open-air cinema. [a pun on the various sporting 'bowls' + FINGER v.¹]

fingerer n. [16C] (Und.) **1** a pilferer, one who uses his fingers to remove small objects. **2** the accomplice of a team of cardsharps, the fingerer appears as an old, poor man and dresses accordingly; he then allows himself to be lured into some form of gaming by a group of young confederates, and, through his apparent inability to win, persuades their victim to bet and, inevitably, lose heavily.

finger fuck n. [1960s+] **1** the manual stimulation of the female genitals. **2** the manual stimulation of a man's anus. [FINGER FUCK v. (1)]

finger fuck v. **1** [late 18C+] to stimulate the vagina or anus. **2** [1960s+] of a woman, to masturbate (cf. DIGITATE). [SE finger + FUCK v.¹; an apparently unlikely early use is by Robert Burns in The Merry Muses of Caledonia (c.1793)]

finger fucking n. [mid-19C+] the use of one or more fingers to stimulate the clitoris or penetrate the vagina; popularly used in sexual foreplay (cf. FINGER PIE n.). [FINGER FUCK v.]

finger man n. [1910s+] (orig. US) a traitor, an informer. [FINGER n.² + SE man]

finger pie n. [1950s+] the manual stimulation of the female genitals (cf. CHERRY PIE; FUR PIE; HAIR PIE; HEARTHRUG PIE; MAGGIE'S PIE). [note FINGER v.¹]

finger pie v. [1950s+] of a woman, to masturbate. [FINGER PIE n.]

finger-pointing n. [mid-19C+] the making of (false) accusations.

finger-popping adj. [1950s–60s] (US) enjoying music intensely. [the 'popping' or snapping of one's fingers in time to the beat]

finger post n. [late 18C] a parson. [he points the way (that one should live one's life) but does not follow his own directions; 'like the finger post he points out a way he has never been, and probably will never go, i.e. the way to heaven' (Grose, 1785)]

fingers are made of lime-twigs phr. [late 16C–mid-18C] used of a thief. [lime-twigs are sticky]

finger-smith n. **1** [early 19C] a midwife. **2** [19C] a pickpocket (cf. FORK n.; FORKER). **3** [1950s] (W.I.) a thief. [SE finger + sfx. -smith, an adept, an expert]

finger the dog see FUCK THE DOG.

fingery-pokery n. [1990s] the act of masturbating a woman. [FINGER v.¹ + POKE v. + play on JIGGERY-POKERY]

finick n. [early 18C+] a faddy, 'picky' person. [Cheshire dial. finnick, a mincing, over-fastidious person]

finickerty adj. [1920s+] (orig. Aus.) picky. [FINICK n. + sfx. -erty]

finicky adj. [early 19C+] in the manner of an obsessive, petty person, concerned with minutiae and, as such, often irritating to others; thus ext. as finicky Dick. [FINICK n. + sfx. -y]

Finish, the n.¹ **1** [18C–19C] Carpenter's late-night coffeeshop, sited in Covent Garden opposite Russell Street, which closed only when the last customer had gone home into the dawn. **2** [19C] any late-night/early-morning café. [a place where one finishes one's night out]

finish n.² [early 19C] the end, the (disastrous) ultimate fate of a person, e.g. that affair will be the finish of her.

finish n.³ [1930s] (tramp) methylated spirits; thus finish-drinker. [? it finishes one off]

finish v. [19C+] to put an end to, to terminate, to destroy.

finisher n. [late 18C–late 19C] **1** something that puts an end to, discomfits or 'does for' someone. **2** something that settles a dispute.

finishing academy n. [18C] a brothel. [? pun on SE finish, to end a girl's education/to reach orgasm + ACADEMY]

finish one's circle, to phr. [20C] (US) to die. [Western jargon, orig. used of a dead cowman, whose jobs, when alive, included riding the boundaries of the ranch]

finish one's row, to phr. [20C] (US) to die. [the image is of a ploughman]

finito! excl. [1950s+] an excl. used to signify the end, a completion. [Ital. finito, finished]

fink n. **1** [late 19C+] a strike-breaker, a company policeman. **2** [20C] an unpleasant or contemptible person, one who cannot be trusted. **3** [1910s+] an informer, a detective. ['dating from the famous Homestead strike of 1892 is the odious fink. [It] according to one version was originally Pink, a contraction of Pinkerton, and referred to the army of strike-breakers recruited by the detective agency' (American Mercury, January 1926)]

fink/fink on v. [1920s+] to inform, to inform on. [FINK n.]

finkydiddle v. [late 19C–1940s] to indulge in foreplay (cf. FIRKYTOODLE). [ext. of DIDDLE v.²]

finnif/finuf n. [mid-19C+] (US) $5 (cf. FINNIP). [Yid. fünf, 5]

finnip/finnup/finn/finnio n. [mid-19C+] a £5 note; thus double finnip, long-tailed finnip, £10, half a finnip, £2 10s (cf. FIN n.²; FINNIF). [Yid. fünf, 5]

finny n. [mid–late 19C] a £5 note. [FIN n.²]

Finsbury bridge n. [1990s] the perineum in a man. [? anecdotal]

finuf see FINNIF.

fin up n. [1930s+] (US Und.) a sentence of 5 years to life (cf. HANDFUL n.²; NICKEL n.¹; POUND n.²). [FIN n.⁴ (2) + SE up (wards)]

fip n.¹ **1** [early 19C] (US) a 5-penny bit, the nickname for the Spanish half-real, worth about 4½ cents. **2** [19C] a threepenny bit. **3** [19C] any very small amount of money. [elision of SE fivepence]

fip n.² [19C] a drink of whisky. [its cost, 5 pence]

fipenny/fippenny n. [19C] a 5-penny coin.

fi'penny n. [early 19C–1910s] a clasp-knife. [use post-1860 is Aus.]

fippence n. [19C] a threepenny bit (cf. FIP n.¹).

fir n. [1980s+] (drugs) marijuana. [? resemblance to fir leaves]

fire n.¹ [19C] the vagina (cf. FIRELOCK).

fire n.² [19C] venereal disease. [the pain it causes]

fire n.³ **1** [mid-19C+] (US Und.) danger, esp. from the police; thus on fire, very dangerous. **2** [1940s] (US Black) a cigarette. **3** [1950s+] (US) matches or a cigarette lighter. **4** [1990s] (US Und.) a firearm.

fire n.⁴ [1980s+] **1** a mixture of crack cocaine and methamphetamine. **2** bad or weak crack cocaine. [? it burns the throat or play on BURN v.² (6)]

fire v.¹ **1** [late 19C+] (US) to ejaculate semen. **2** [20C] in sport, to play at maximum capacity. **3** [1950s+] (US Black) to strike a blow. [fig. uses of SE]

fire v.² [late 19C+] (orig. US) to dismiss from a job, throw out or expel. [pun on SE fire, discharge (a weapon)]

fire v.³ [20C] (W.I.) used in several phr. to denote aggressive or decisive action; thus fire a blow/box/chop/cuff/hand/kick/lash, to hit hard, fire yourself/your skin, hurry up. [SE fire, to stimulate, to inflame with passion]

fire v.⁴ [20C] (W.I.) **1** to obtain a drink, esp. of a barman, e.g. fire me a rum. **2** to drink strong liquor; thus fire a booze/a drink/a few/a rum/the grog, to take a drink.

fire v.⁵ [1940s+] (US) to light a cigarette.

fire v.⁶ [1980s+] (drugs) to inject a drug.

fire a blank/blanks, to phr. [1950s+] **1** of an impotent man or one who has had a vasectomy, to have intercourse despite one's inability to impregnate one's partner. **2** of a man, to have an orgasm without ejaculation (cf. FIRE A SHOT; SHOOT BLANKS v.²).

fire a good stick, to phr. [mid-19C] to shoot well.

fire a gun, to phr. [late 18C–mid-19C] **1** to lead up to a topic carefully. **2** to push a topic unsubtly into the conversation. [the firing of a warning gun + the suddenness of the explosion]

fi real *adv.* [1970s+] (W.I./UK Black teen) precisely or genuinely. [pron. of FOR REAL adv.]

fire-alarms *n.* [20C] the arms. [rhy. sl.]

fire a shot, to *phr.* [late 19C+] of a man, to reach orgasm (cf. FIRE A BLANK).

fire a slug, to *phr.* [late 18C] to drink a dram (cf. BALL OF FIRE n.[1]). [pun on *slug*, bullet/SLUG n.[1] (2) of liquor]

fire away! *excl.* [late 18C+] an instruction to start, usu. as 'start what you're doing', 'say your piece' etc (cf. AWAY adv.).

fire blanks *see* FIRE A BLANK.

firebox *n.* [late 19C] a constantly passionate man. [he is 'heated' with passion]

firebug *n.* [1960s+] (US) an arsonist. [SE *fire* + BUG n.[4]]

fire bur' me hand! *see* FIRE BURN ME HAND!

fire-burn *n.* [20C] (W.I.) a rowdy, riotous person. [such a person might, when enjoying himself, start a fire]

fire burn/bur' me hand! *exc..* [20C] (W.I.) an excl. indicating that a major fight is in the offing.

fire-catcher *n.* [1950s] (W.I.) old, ragged, workclothes. [such clothes are worth using only to light a fire]

fire down town! *excl.* [1950s] (W.I.) a call for speedy and generous service, esp. on arriving at a bar and calling for a quick round of drinks.

fired up *adj.* [19C] drunk (cf. ELEVATED).

fire-eater *n.*[1] **1** [mid-19C+] a braggart, an aggressive person always spoiling for a fight. **2** [mid-19C+] a noticeably courageous person, with the supposed daring of the performer. **3** [mid–late 19C] a quick worker.

fire-eater *n.*[2] [1920s+] (US) a firefighter.

fire-escape *n.* [mid-19C–1920s] a clergyman (cf. DEVIL-DODGER). [the *fire* is that of hell]

firefight *n.* [1980s+] (US Black) a street battle involving guns. [milit. jargon *firefight*, a battle between infantrymen on the ground]

fire in the air, to *phr.* **1** [19C] of a man, to have sexual intercourse. **2** [late 19C+] of a man, to ejaculate outside their partner's body.

fire into *v.* [20C] to approach sexually, to pick up, to seduce.

firelock/fireplace/firework *n.* [19C] the vagina, one of several terms that equate the vagina to a generator of venereal disease. [FIRE n.[1]]

fire on *v.* [1970s+] (US Black/campus) to disparage, to ridicule (cf. BLAZE ON). **2** to hit, to assault, usu. with a weapon.

fire on all cylinders, to *phr.* [20C] to work properly; thus *fire on one cylinder*, to work badly (cf. HIT ON ALL CYLINDERS). [automobile imagery]

fire one's peter, to *phr.* [20C] to masturbate. [SE *fire* + PETER n.[4]]

fireplace *see* FIRELOCK.

fireplug *n.* [19C] a man who is suffering from a venereal disease (cf. FIRESHIP). [FIRE n.[2] + pun]

fire power *n.* [20C] (US Black) physical strength and ability.

fire prigger *n.* [late 17C–18C] one who robs those who are otherwise preoccupied with watching their, or someone else's, home burn down. [SE *fire* + PRIG n.[1]]

fireproof *adj.* [late 19C+] (orig. US) invulnerable, guaranteed against failure.

fire queen *n.* [1980s+] (US gay) a militant gay activist. [SE *fire* + QUEEN n.[1]; they wish to 'set the world on fire']

fire-rage *n.* [20C] (W.I.) extreme anger, uncontrolled fury; thus *pick up someone's fire-rage*, to take someone's side in a quarrel as energetically as if it were one's own. **2** of a man, one who loses his temper easily, who 'flies off the handle'.

fireship *n.* [late 17C–late 18C] a diseased prostitute (cf. FIREPLUG). [FIRE n.[2] + pun]

fires of hell *n.* [19C] the vagina (cf. FIRE n.[1]; PUT THE DEVIL INTO HELL). [the image of the vagina as a threat and a source of evil]

fire-tail *n.* [20C] (W.I./Guyn.) of a woman, one who loses her temper easily (cf. FIRE-RAGE).

fire the flesh musket, to *phr.* [20C] to masturbate.

fire the hand cannon, to *phr.* [20C] to masturbate.

fire the question, to *phr.* [late 19C] (US) to make a proposal of marriage (cf. POP THE QUESTION).

fire the wobbly warhead, to *phr.* [1980s+] to masturbate.

fire up *v.*[1] (US) **1** [mid-19C–1900s] to begin, to get ready. **2** [1950s+] to start up a mechanical device, e.g. a car.

fire up *v.*[2] **1** [late 19C+] to light a pipe, cigarette or cigar. **2** [1960s+] to light a marijuana cigarette. [FIRE v.[5]]

fire up *v.*[3] [1940s+] (drugs) to pump the blood and heroin mixture out of the hypodermic into the vein or muscle.

fire up *v.*[4] [1970s+] (orig. US Black/campus) **1** to excite sexually. **2** to anger, to arouse emotionally. **3** to hit. **4** to have sexual intercourse.

firework *see* FIRELOCK.

fireworks *n.*[1] [mid-17C+] an emotional outburst, a state of intense excitement.

fireworks *n.*[2] (US) **1** [early–mid-19C] guns. **2** [mid-19C] (Und.) gunplay, shooting.

fire your tail! *excl.* [20C] (W.I.) get out! go away! [TAIL n.[1]]

firkin *adj.* [1970s+] euph. for FUCKING adj.

firkin of foul stuff *n.* [late 17C–18C] a very plain, fat, coarse woman.

firk the dude, to *phr.* [20C] to masturbate. [SE *firk*, to beat, to whip + DUDE n.[4]]

firkytoodle *v.* [17C] to indulge in foreplay. [FIRK + SE *toodle/tootle*, to play upon (cf. DIDDLE v.[2])]

firm *n.* [1960s+] a criminal gang, large or small.

firme *adj.* [1960s+] (US) a general term of high approval; also used as a magazine name in 1970s–80s. [Sp.]

firmota *n.* [1960s+] (US) a very attractive young woman. [FIRME]

firm up *v.* [1970s+] to consolidate one's position, to conclude an agreement or contract.

first base *n.* **1** [1920s+] (orig. US teen) a man's initial advances on a young woman, usu. implying the caressing of some part of the body or even the removal of some clothing; such a 'base' is always above the waist; thus *second base*, similar explorations of the breasts, *third base*, petting below the waist. **2** [1950s–60s] the start of something, usually applied in terms of failure when someone has failed to reach it, e.g. *he couldn't even get to first base*. [baseball jargon]

first base *v.* [1930s+] (US) to take one's first steps towards an objective. [FIRST BASE n.]

first belly pain *n.* [1950s] (W.I.) one's first-born child (cf. WASH-BELLY).

first bird *n.* [1920s+] (prison) one's first experience of a prison sentence. [SE *first* + BIRD n.[7]]

first/next cab off the rank *phr.* [1960s+] (Aus.) the speediest to react, the first one off the mark.

first cab on the rank *phr.* [1950s+] (Aus.) a prime suspect.

first chop *adj.* [19C] excellent, first-rate (cf. BRAHMA; CHEESE n.[1]; NO CHOP). [from Hind. *chhaap* meaning a print, and thus a seal, notably that which is placed on first-rate merchandise]

first-class *adj.* [mid-19C+] extremely good, 'first-rate'.

first-class *adv.* [mid-19C+] excellently, very well indeed.

first crack off the bat *phr.* [20C] at once, immediately, at the first attempt (cf. FIRST CRACK OUT OF THE BOX; FIRST DASH OUT OF THE BOX; FIRST SHOT OUT OF THE LOCKER).

first crack/cat out of the box *phr.* [20C] at once, immediately, at the first attempt (cf. FIRST CRACK OFF THE BAT).

first dash/pop/rattle out of the box *phr.* [20C] at once, immediately, at the first attempt (cf. FIRST CRACK OFF THE BAT).

first feel *n.* [1950s+] (W.I.) the first chance, the earliest opportunity.

first fleeter *n.* [mid-19C] (Aus.) one of the original emigrants from Britain to New South Wales. [SE *First Fleet*, the original fleet of ships, carrying mainly transported convicts, which arrived in New South Wales in 1788]

first floor *n.* [mid-19C+] the person who lives on the first floor, usu. in a lodging house or other rented accommodation.

first go-off, the *see* AT ONE GO-OFF.

first line *n.* [20C] (drugs) morphine. [SE *first*, best + *line* (of merchandise)]

first national bank *n.* [20C] (US) an outside lavatory (cf. F.D.R.; FEDERAL BUILDING). [the resentment of the farming community towards the banks, which regularly repossessed their land when times became hard]

first-nighter *n.* [1970s+] (US Black) a one-time sexual encounter, unlikely to be repeated.

first off *adv.* [late 19C+] (orig. US) at the outset, to start with.

first of May *n.* [mid–late 19C] the tongue. [rhy. sl. *first of May* = say]

first-rate *adv.* [mid-19C+] excellently, very well. [adj. use is SE]

firsts *n.* [1950s+] **1** the first chance, the first opportunity, often as excl. *firsts!* I want to do something first. **2** (US Black) any Blacks who are the first to take on a specific job in a formerly all-White world.

first shot out of the locker/box *phr.* [20C] at once, immediately, at the first attempt (cf. FIRST CRACK OFF THE BAT).

first thing *n.* [mid-19C+] the early morning.

first thing *adv.* [mid-19C+] in the early morning.

first thirty *n.* [1940s] (US Black) January. [although January has 31 days]

first-timer *n.* [late 19C+] (Aus. Und.) one who is serving their first sentence in prison.

first up *adv.* [20C] (Aus.) for the first time, at the first try.

fisgig/fizgig *n.* [early 19C] amusement gained at the expense of others. [SE *fizz*, animal spirits + *gig*, a frivolous person]

fish *n.*[1] [mid-18C+] a man, a person, esp. as qualified in various combs., e.g. [early–mid-19C] *loose fish*, [mid-19C] *cool fish*, [late 19C] *shy fish*, [20C] *poor fish* (cf. ODD FISH; QUEER FISH).

fish *n.*[2] [late 18C–early 19C] a sailor; thus *scaly fish*, a rough, blunt sailor.

fish *n.*[3] [mid–late 19C] (US) a gambling chip.

fish *n.*[4] **1** [mid-19C+] the vagina (cf. BEARDED CLAM). **2** [late 19C+] (US) a prostitute. **3** [late 19C+] (US) a derog. term for a woman. **4** [1940s+] (US gay) a heterosexual woman. **5** [1950s+] (US) a prison homosexual. **6** [1950s+] (W.I. Rasta) a gay person. **7** [1960s+] (US) a feminine lesbian (cf. FEMME). [(1) is derog. ref. to the supposed odour; (2)–(6) are ext. uses]

fish *n.*[5] **1** [mid-19C+] (Can./US prison) a new inmate; thus prison jargon *fish number*, the number issued to each prisoner by the US Department of Corrections. **2** [late 19C] (US campus) a newcomer. **3** [late 19C+] (US) any form of novice, esp. a gullible innocent. **4** [late 19C+] (US) a fool, a 'sucker'. [abbr. SE *fresh fish*]

fish *n.*[6] [1910s+] (US) a heavy drinker. [SE phr. *drink like a fish*]

fish *n.*[7] [1920s–40s] (US) a dollar.

fish *n.*[8] [1950s+] (W.I.) any form of sauce that accompanies the staple, some form of starch, which need not contain fish.

fish *n.*[9] [1950s+] (US) a Roman Catholic. [the Catholic tradition of abstaining from meat on Fridays]

fish *n.*[10] [1970s+] (US) a derog. term for a Newfoundlander (cf. FISH-EATER). [the staple industry]

fish *adj.* [mid-19C+] (US) fresh, uninitiated, new, esp. of a prisoner.

fish and find out! *excl.* [late 19C–1920s] a dismissive response given to a question that one does not wish to answer.

fish and shrimp *n.* [1940s–50s] a procurer, a pimp (cf. MCGIMP). [rhy. sl.]

fishbagger *n.* [late 19C] a suburbanite who works in the City. [they use their supposedly important briefcase to take home food, esp. cheap fish]

fish-broth *n.* [late 16C–early 17C] water, esp. when salted.

fish-eater *n.* [1950s+] **1** a Roman Catholic (cf. FISH *n.*[9]). **2** (Can.) an inhabitant of Nova Scotia (cf. FISH *n.*[10]).

fisher *n.*[1] [19C] a parasite, a toady. [they 'fish for compliments' or for favours]

fisher *n.*[2] [1910s–30s] a banknote (cf. ARCHER; FISHER'S FLIMSIES). [proper name of Sir Warren *Fisher*, secretary to the Treasury *c.*1919–33]

fisherman's daughter *n.* [late 19C] water (that which one drinks, rather than that making up lakes, rivers, seas etc). [rhy. sl.]

fisherman's luck *n.* [19C+] (US) no luck at all, bad luck. [popularly defined as 'a wet ass and a hungry gut']

fisher of fogles *n.* [early–mid-19C] a pickpocket, specializing in handkerchiefs. [SE *fisher* + FOGLE]

fisher's flimsies *n.* [1910s+] (Aus.) currency notes issued during the government of Prime Minister Andrew *Fisher* (1862–1928) (cf. ARCHER; FISHER *n.*[2]).

fish for food, to *phr.* [1940s–70s] (US Black) to gossip. [FOOD *n.*]

fish for zipper trout, to *phr.* [1990s] to masturbate.

fish-fosh *n.* [late 19C] kedgeree (cf. MEAT FOSH). [? redup.]

fish-head *n.*[1] **1** [20C] (US) a native of the west Florida coast. **2** [20C] anyone who lives alongside a river. **3** [20C] a West Indian. **4** [20C] a worker in a fish cannery. **5** [1970s+] an East Asian. [all uses are derog.; their consumption of and/or occupation with fish]

fish-head *n.*[2] [1950s] (W.I.) a bribe, a tip. [among the poor a fish-head was considered a treat or delicacy]

fish-hook *n.* [1920s+] a hand.

fish-hooks *n.* [late 18C+] the fingers. [the term, derived f. 19C naut. use, was UK and then moved to US Black use by 1930s]

fishing fleet *n.* [late 19C+] (society) those young women who visit Hong Kong, and once many more centres of the British Empire, esp. India, in the hope of catching a rich husband.

fish lips *n.* [1990s] the labia. [FISH *n.*[4] (1) + SE *lips*]

fish market *n.* [mid-19C–1900s] **1** the vagina (cf. BEARDED CLAM). **2** a brothel (cf. BUTTOCKING SHOP). [FISH *n.*[4] (1) + SE *market* + pun]

fish mitten *n.* [1990s] the vagina (cf. BEARDED CLAM). [FISH *n.*[4] (1) + SE *mitten*]

fishmonger *n.* [17C] a womanizer, a promiscuous man. [FISH *n.*[4] (1) + sfx. *-monger*]

fishmonger's daughter *n.* [late 16C–early 17C] a prostitute. [FISH *n.*[4] (1) + pun]

fish 'n' chip mob *n.* [1970s+] (society) anyone considered socially unacceptable. [Sandhurst jargon *fish 'n' chip mob*, unfashionable regiments]

fisho *n.* [1920s+] (Aus.) **1** a professional fisherman. **2** a fish-seller. [SE *fish* + sfx. *-O*]

fish or cut bait *phr.* [20C] either carry out what you're doing or let someone else more competent get on with it while you take a secondary role (cf. SHIT OR GET OFF THE POT!).

fish queen *n.* [1960s+] any man, homo- or heterosexual, who enjoys cunnilingus. [FISH *n.*[4] (1) + QUEEN *n.*[1]]

fish scales *n.* [1980s+] (drugs) crack cocaine. [? resemblance of the flakes of crack cocaine]

fish supper *n.* [1990s] sexual intercourse, esp. in the context of a conjugal right. [FISH *n.*[4] (1) + *supper* + pun on SE]

fishtail *v.* [1980s+] to suffer blackouts, seizures or convulsions following the inhalation of nitrous oxide (cf. DO THE FISH). [the image of a fish out of water, struggling for air]

fish-tank *n.* [1980s+] (US gay) the vagina of a heterosexual woman [cf. BEARDED CLAM]. [FISH *n.*[4] (1) + SE *tank* + pun]

fish wrapper *n.* [late 19C+] (orig. US) a newspaper. [the assumption that newspapers were good only for wrapping fish]

fishy *adj.*[1] [mid-19C+] suspect, dubious, unreliable, questionable. [the smell of rotting fish or the slipperiness of fresh fish]

fishy *adj.*[2] [mid-19C] looking ill, esp. around the eyes, after a drinking session. [one's eyes resemble those of a dead fish]

fishy *adj.*[3] [mid-19C+] (US) of whalers and professional fishermen, dedicated, steadfast (cf. SALTY). [the qualities of the work have transferred themselves to the man]

fishy about the gills *phr.* [late 19C] hungover (cf. GREEN ABOUT THE GILLS). [ext. of FISHY *adj.*[2]]

fist *n.* **1** [mid-15C; early 18C+] handwriting. **2** [early 19C+] an attempt, a try.

fist *see* FIST FUCK.

fist city/holler *n.* [20C] (US) a fist fight. [SE *fist* + sfx. -CITY/SE *hollow*; an imaginary place where quarrels are settled with the fists]

fist fuck/fist *v.* **1** [1960s] to masturbate. **2** [1970s+] (gay) to insert one's hand (and forearm) into someone's anus or vagina. [FIST-FUCKING *n.* (2)]

fist-fucker *n.* (US) **1** [1960s] an habitual masturbator. **2** [1970s+] (usu. gay) one who practises FIST-FUCKING. **3** [1970s] a generally unpleasant person.

fist-fucking/f.f. *n.* l. [1960s+] male masturbation. **2** [1970s+] (gay) the insertion of several or all the fingers and forearm into the anus of one's partner for purposes of sexual stimulation. [popular in the 1970s but latterly in decline through fears of injury and hence the possibility of spreading AIDS; also found in heterosexual sex, where the orifice is the vagina]

fist holler *see* FIST CITY.

fisting *n.* [1970s+] (usu. gay) the insertion of several or all the fingers and possibly the forearm into the anus or vagina of one's partner (cf. FIST-FUCKING).

fist it *v.* **1** [19C] for a woman, to caress a man's penis. **2** [mid-19C] (Aus./N.Z.) to eat with one's hands.

fist junction *n.* [1970s+] (US Black) that point of confrontation at which a physical fight takes over from mere words (cf. FIST CITY).

fist magnet *n.* [1990s] a punchable person (cf. BABE MAGNET).

fist one's mister, to *phr.* [20C] to masturbate.

fit *n.*[1] [1950s+] (drugs) the equipment (a needle, a spoon, a dropper) required for injecting narcotics (cf. BIZ *n.*[2]). [abbr. OUTFIT *n.*[2]]

fit *n.*[2] [1950s–60s] (US Black) a suit of clothes, esp. a well-cut garment. [abbr. SE *outfit*]

fit *adj.*[1] [late 19C] very well, healthy, usu. in response to the query 'How are you?'

fit *adj.*[2] [1980s+] (orig. Black) good-looking. [note agricultural use *fit*, of fruits and vegetables, ready to pick, full-grown, though not necessarily fully ripe]

fit *adv.* **1** [late 18C+] of things, likely. **2** [mid-19C+] of people, inclined, disposed.

fit! *excl.* [1950s+] (orig. W.I.) a general excl. of approval, excellent! first-rate! very good!

fit as a buck rat *phr.* [20C] (N.Z.) extremely healthy.

fit as a fiddle *phr.* **1** [late 16C–early 17C] ideal, perfect, most opportune. **2** [late 19C+] in peak condition, extremely healthy. [assonance]

fit as a fiddler *phr.* [20C] (Aus.) extremely healthy (cf. FIT AS A FIDDLE).

fit as a flea *phr.* [1960s+] (N.Z.) very healthy.

fit as a Mallee bull *phr.* [20C] (Aus.) extremely healthy, in perfect physical condition. [agricultural imagery]

fit as a pudding *phr.* [early 17C] very healthy.

fit as a trout *phr.* [1970s–80s] (N.Z.) very healthy.

fit end/ends to end, to *phr.* [late 19C–1900s] to have sexual intercourse.

fit in the arm *n.* [late 19C] a blow, a punch. ['In June 1897 one Tom Kelly was given into custody by a woman for striking her. His defence [was] that "a fit had seized him in the arm", and for months afterwards backstreet frequenters called a blow a fit' (Ware)]

fit like a ball of wax, to *phr.* [mid–late 19C] of clothes, to fit very tightly.

fit-me-tight *n.* [1960s] (Irish) a journeyman tailor.

fitness *n.* [1990s] (Black) an attractive (young) woman. [FIT *adj.*[2]]

fit the cap on, to *phr.* [mid-19C] to acknowledge that a given comment or allusion is applicable to oneself. [phr. 'when the cap fits, wear it']

fit the mitt, to *phr.* [1920s–40s] (US) to bribe; thus *fitted mitt*, an official who has been bribed. [fig. uses of MITT *n.*]

fit to ... *phr.* [early 18C+] **1** angry or troubled enough to (do something extreme). **2** exhausted enough to (collapse etc).

fit to a T, to *phr.* [late 18C+] to fit perfectly. [SE *fit* + the accuracy achieved by an architect's T-square]

fit to be tied *phr.* [mid-19C+] furious, enraged and in need, therefore, of restraint. [the image of one so hysterically furious that they need to be tied down]

fit to bust *phr.* [20C] emotionally moved, either to rage or ecstasy depending on context.

fit to kill *phr.* [early 19C+] (orig. US) a phr. used of something done to excess, esp. of one's dress.

fit-up *n.*[1] [mid-19C+] any temporary structure, esp. a stage, boxing-ring etc, which can be assembled, then knocked down for assembly at another venue. [orig. theatre use]

fit-up *n.*[2] [1930s+] (Und.) a false accusation or perjured evidence used to have an innocent suspect (albeit one who has a criminal record) arrested and found guilty. [FIT UP *v.*]

fit/fix up *v.* [1930s+] to incriminate by using false evidence, both physical and verbal (cf. FRAME *v.*[2]; STITCH UP).

fitz *n.*[1] [late 19C–1900s] the illegitimate child of a royal person. ['the Anglo-French word for "son"; chiefly Hist. in patronymic designations, in which it was followed by the name of a parent in the uninflected genitive. Some of these survive as surnames, e.g. Fitzherbert, Fitzwilliam etc; in later times new surnames of the kind have been given to the illegitimate children of royal princes.' (OED)]

fitz *n.*[2] [20C] (Aus./S.Afr.) a large sausage used for cutting into slices for sandwiches or to eat with salad. [? a brandname]

fitzroy cocktail *n.* [1920s+] (Aus./Melbourne) a drink based on methylated spirits with some form of mixer to mediate the taste. [*Fitzroy* is a suburb of Melbourne]

fitzroy Yank *n.* [1940s+] (Aus.) a relatively unsophisticated person who attempts to ape the supposedly smart style of an American (cf. WOOLLOOMOOLOO YANK). [for ety. *see* FITZROY COCKTAIL]

five *n.*[1] [late 19C+] **1** a 5-year prison sentence. **2** £5. [abbr.]

five *n.*[2] [1930s+] (US) a blow with the fist. [BUNCH OF FIVES]

five *n.*[3] *see* FIVE-OH.

five! *excl.* [1990s] (US teen) go away! leave me alone! [the 5 initial letters from *Get out of my face!*]

five-acre farm *n.* [mid-19C] an arm (cf. CHALK FARM). [rhy. sl.]

five-acre Tory *n.* [1980s+] (N.Z.) a very conservative small farmer.

five against one *n.* [20C] masturbation (cf. FIVE ON ONE). [five fingers v. one penis or vagina]

five and dime/ten *n.* [1900s–50s] (US) a small store where articles are all priced at 5 or 10 cents. [the original such store was that opened (1879) by F.W. Woolworth (1852–1919)]

five and dime *adj.* (US Black) **1** insignificant, paltry. **2** badly dressed, cheap, unattractive, sleazy. [FIVE AND DIME n.]

five and ten *n.*

five and ten *see* FIVE AND DIME n.

five annas/sixteen annas short of the rupee *phr.* [19C+] not very intelligent (cf. NOT ALL THERE).

five-barred gate *n.* [late 19C] a policeman. [the majority of policemen were recruited from the countryside, home of such gates]

five by five *n.* [1930s+] (Can./US Black) a short fat man (cf. MISTER FIVE BY FIVE). [his girth presumably equals his height]

five by two *n.* [1920s+] a Jew (cf. BOX OF GLUE). [rhy. sl.]

five-cent bag/paper *n.* [1960s] (US drugs) a small amount of heroin, less than 28g (1oz), sold for $5. [SE *five-cent* + BAG n.[8]/PAPER n.[2]]

five c note *n.* [1940s+] (US drugs) a $500 bill.

five-dollar bag *n.* [1960s] (US drugs) a bag of heroin costing $5 or $50. [SE *five-dollar* + BAG n.[8]]

five-finger discount *n.* [1960s+] (Aus./N.Z./US) the act and proceeds of shoplifting.

five-fingered exercise *n.* [1970s+] masturbation.

five-fingered widow *n.* [1970s+] masturbation (cf. DRY-MOUTHED WIDOW; MISS FIST).

five-finger mary *n.* [1970s+] the hand, as used for masturbation (cf. FIVE-FINGERED WIDOW; MISS FIST).

five fingers *n.* [mid-19C] in card-games, the 4 of trumps. [ety. unknown]

five fingers *adj.* [20C] (Irish) first-rate, excellent. [*five fingers* make a fig. whole hand]

five-finger/-knuckle shuffle *n.* [1990s] masturbation.

five-finger solo *n.* [1990s] masturbation.

five hundred *n.*[1] [20C] (US) the social élite, or those who think they are. [SE *the four hundred*, the members of New York's Social Register, as defined in 1892 by the social arbiter Ward McAllister (1827–95; sometimes known as *Mr Make-a-lister*) for Mrs Caroline Schermerhorn Astor (1792–1875). Mrs Astor had arranged a large ball, but found that her ballroom would hold a maximum of 400; McAllister thus cut the guest list to the supposed cream of New York society. A similar optimum guest list had already been seen in 1860 when McAllister's predecessor, Isaac Hull Brown, invited 400 top New Yorkers to meet the Prince of Wales at the Academy of Music on 14th Street, but it was the later party, and its exploitation in the media, that popularized the term]

five hundred *n.*[2] [1990s] (US Black) a BMW automobile. [a specific model number]

five in the south *n.* [20C] (US gambling) the point of 5 in craps dice.

five-knuckle shuffle *see* FIVE-FINGER SHUFFLE.

five-letter woman *n.* [1920s+] a prostitute, i.e. w-h-o-r-e or b-i-t-c-h (cf. FOUR-LETTER MAN).

five miles of bad road *see* TEN MILES OF BAD ROAD.

five o'clock *n.* [late 19C] afternoon tea. [obs. in English but perpetuated in synon. Fr. *le five o'clock* and in Romania, where the English term is used]

five-oh *n.* [1980s+] (US Black/teen) **1** the police. **2** a 5.0 litre Ford Mustang (used as a police vehicle in some areas). [1960s TV police show *Hawaii 5-0*]

502 *n.* [1990s] (US Black/teen) drunk driving. [California police code for the offence]

5150 *n.* [1990s] (rap music) an eccentric, a crazy person. [police code, an insane person is annoying the public]

five on one *n.* [20C] masturbation. [var. on FIVE AGAINST ONE]

five or seven *n.* [late 19C] a drunkard. [the popular sentence, a 5-shilling fine or 7 days in prison]

five over five *phr.* [late 18C] used of people who turn in their toes.

5% Nation *n.* [1990s] (US Black) a Black radical group, an offshoot of the Nation of Islam (cf. 85%). [it teaches that any large group of people, and more specifically, the African American nation, can be divided into three groups, the 85%, basically the ignorant masses that need to be led, the 5%, the people with true knowledge of self whose job it is to lead the masses and fight against the 10%, the people who have partial knowledge of self and use it to gain power and wealth by exploiting the 85%, also referred to as 'bloodsuckers of the poor'. The chosen percentages are those they feel are the percentages within the Black community. These numbers are neither universal (all though these groups do exist within any large group) nor unchangeable]

five pot piece *n.* [19C] two shillings and sixpence (2s 6d; 12½p). [orig. medical student use, f. the contemporary price of a quart or *pot* of mixed mild and bitter beer]

fiver *n.* **1** [mid-19C+] a £5 note, £5. **2** [late 19C+] (US) a $5 bill. **3** [late 19C] (US) a 5-year prison sentence. **4** [1930s+] £5000. **5** [1960s+] (US drugs) a quantity of heroin costing $5.

fives *n.*[1] **1** [17C] a foot. **2** [early 19C+] the hand, usu. when clenched in a fist (cf. BUNCH OF FIVES). **3** [late 19C] a street fight.

fives *n.*[2] [1960s] (drugs) 5mg Benzedrine or amphetamine tablets.

five-spot *n.* [20C] **1** a $5 or £5 note (cf. TEN-SPOT; TWENTY-SPOT). **2** a playing-card having 5 pips. **3** (US) a 5-year prison sentence. [SE *five* + SPOT n.[3]]

5000! *excl.* [1990s] (US Black/teen) goodbye, I'm off (cf. AUDI!). ['I'm outta here', which evolved to 'I'm Audi', and to *5000* after the Audi *5000* car]

five to six rush/swill *n.* [1950s–70s] (N.Z.) the nightly rush to the public house, caused by severely restricting licensing laws. [SE *five/six o'clock* + *rush/swill*]

five to two *n.* [20C] a Jew (cf. BOX OF GLUE). [rhy. sl.]

five to twos *n.* [1930s] shoes. [rhy. sl.]

fix *n.*[1] [19C] (orig. US) a dilemma, a problematic situation. [lit. the state in which one is 'fixed'; SE by 1900]

fix *n.*[2] [1920s+] (orig. US) any corrupt deal, a bribe, a favour; thus *put the fix in*, to ensure a plan or event favours whoever has paid the deal etc.

fix *n.*[3] **1** [1930s+] (drugs) an injection of narcotics (cf. FIX-UP). **2** [1960s+] (US) a compulsive desire or thrill. **3** [1990s] (drugs) heroin. [it 'fixes' one's emotional and/or physical state]

fix *v.*[1] (orig. US) **1** [early 18C+] to arrange, to prepare, to get ready. **2** [late 18C+] to bribe, to suborn. **3** [19C+] to take revenge upon, to get even with, to foil an antagonist's plans.

fix *v.*[2] [1930s+] (drugs) to inject oneself with narcotics.

fixed *adj.*[1] [late 19C+] (orig. US) **1** corrupted, bribed, 'squared', tampered with. **2** of a sporting contest, having had the result pre-arranged (to favour a group of gamblers). [FIX v.[1]]

fixed *adj.*[2] [1980s+] (drugs) using injectable narcotics. [FIX v.[2]]

fixed *adv.* [mid-19C] situated materially or financially, e.g. *how are you fixed?* how much money do you have?

fixed bayonet *n.* [19C] an erect penis (cf. BAYONET).

fixed up *adj.* [1990s] (S.Afr.) fine, good, worked out, happy, content (cf. SORTED).

fixer *n.*[1] [late 19C+] (orig. US) one who arranges or adjusts matters, a go-between, esp. in an illegal context. [SE *fix*/FIX v.[1]]

fixer *n.*[2] [1980s+] (US drugs) a drug dealer. [FIX v.[2]]

fixing *n.* [late 19C] (Aus.) strong drink. [it *fixes* one up]

fixings *n.*[1] [mid-19C+] (orig. US) food. [SE *fixing*, the garnishing of food]

fixings *n.*[2] [late 19C] furniture. [it is *fixed* in the house]

fixings *n.*[3] [1950s–60s] (US) sexual intercourse. [the couple are *fixed* together]

fix one's bones, to *phr.* [20C] (drugs) to take some heroin in order to ward off the pains of an unsatisfied heroin addiction. [the aching bones that are part of the symptoms of heroin withdrawal; note FIX v.²]

fix one's face, to *phr.* [1930s+] (orig. US) to apply one's make-up.

fix someone's clock, to *phr.* [19C+] (US) to thwart another's plans, to cause trouble for an enemy, to get even with (cf. FIX SOMEONE'S FLINT; FIX SOMEONE'S LITTLE RED FIRE ENGINE; FIX SOMEONE'S WAGON). [ironic use of SE *fix* + *clock*; the image is that the clock will indeed be 'fixed', but not in the way its owner desires]

fix someone's flint, to *phr.* [mid–late 19C] (US) to thwart another's plans, to cause trouble for an enemy, to get even with (cf. FIX SOMEONE'S CLOCK). [ironic use of SE *fix* + *flint*, the flint of a matchlock or musket]

fix someone's little red fire engine, to *phr.* [1960s+] (orig. US) to deal with, to take revenge on, to 'settle one's hash' (cf. FIX SOMEONE'S CLOCK).

fix someone's wagon, to *phr.* [1950s+] to thwart someone's plans (cf. FIX SOMEONE'S CLOCK). [ironic use of SE *fix* + *wagon*]

fix the old gum tree, to *phr.* [20C] (Aus.) of a former wanderer, to settle down at last.

fix-up *n.* **1** [mid–late 19C] (US) an alcoholic drink. **2** [1930s] (drugs) an injection of a narcotic drug. [FIX n.³ (1)]

fix up *v.*¹ **1** [mid-19C+] to set up a meeting (usu. for someone else); thus [20C] *fixed up*, having an appointment. **2** [late 19C+] to provide food, living quarters, accommodation etc for someone.

fix up *v.*² [1930s+] (US drugs) to inject heroin or morphine. [ext. of FIX v.²]

fix up *v.*³ *see* FIT UP.

fixy *adj.* [19C+] (US) fussy, esp. as regards one's clothes and appearance. [SE *fix oneself up*, to arrange one's clothes, to get ready]

fiz *n.*¹ [early 18C] the face. [SE *physiognomy*]

fiz *n.*² see FIZZ n.¹.

fizgig *n.*¹ *see* FISGIG.

fizgig/phizgig *n.*² [20C] (Aus.) a police informer. [? SE *fizgig*, a frivolous woman, one who 'gads about' and thus cannot be trusted]

fizz/fiz *n.*¹ **1** [mid-18C] a fuss, a commotion. **2** [mid-19C+] animal spirits, raw energy. **3** [mid-19C+] champagne, occas. lemonade and ginger beer mixed.

fizz *n.*² [1940s+] (Aus.) an informer. [abbr. FIZGIG n.²]

fizz around *v.* [1930s] to rush around energetically. [FIZZ n.¹ (2)]

fizzer *n.*¹ [mid–late 19C] anything excellent or first-rate. [FIZZ n.¹ (2)]

fizzer *n.*² [late 19C+] (Aus.) a wild scrub bull or bullock. [it *fizzes* with energy]

fizzer *n.*³ **1** [1910s+] (US) a firecracker that fails to go off. **2** [1950s+] (Aus.) a disappointing failure, a fiasco, a 'wash-out'. [FIZZLE v.]

fizzer/phizzer *n.*⁴ [1940s+] (Aus.) an informer. [FIZGIG n.²]

fizzical culturalist *n.* [1940s] (US Black) a bartender. [puns on SE *fizzy/physical*]

fizzies *n.* [1970s+] (drugs) methadone. [ety. unknown; play on SE *fizzy drink*; methadone is taken in liquid form]

fizzing *adj.* [mid-19C+] wonderful, excellent, first-rate. [? FIZZ n.¹; a euph. for FUCKING adj., but possibly an innocent ref. to the effervescence of champagne]

fizzing at the bung/bunghole/slit *phr.* [1990s] of a woman, sexually excited (cf. FOAMIN' AT THE GASH). [SE *fizzing*, effervescing + BUNG n.³/SLIT n.¹]

fizzle *n.*¹ [late 18C+] a breaking of wind. [16C SE *fizzle*, the

action of breaking wind silently. B.E. (?1690) defines '*fizzle*, a little, or low-sounding fart']

fizzle *n.*² [mid-19C] (US campus) a failure in recitation or examination. **2** [late 19C+] (orig. US) a failure.

fizzle/fizzle out *v.* [late 19C+] (orig. US) to peter out, to fail gradually but surely. [the sound of escaping air + FIZZLE n.²]

fizz out on *v.* [1940s+] (Aus.) to let down, to fail in a promise. [FIZZLE v.]

flaaitaal *see* FLY TAAL.

flab *n.* [1920s+] fat, fattiness. [onomat. for something hanging down; now nearly SE]

flaba-flaba *adj.* [1950s] (W.I.) **1** worthless, good-for-nothing. **2** stocky, short and thickset. [SE *flabby* + redup.]

flabagast *see* FLABBERGAST.

flabagasted *see* FLABBERGASTED.

flabbergast/flabagast *n.* **1** [20C] (US) an awkward, clumsy person. [FLABBERGAST v.]

flabbergast/flabagast *v.* [late 18C+] to astound, astonish, to confuse. [? SE *flabby* or *flap* + *aghast*; it was first mentioned in the *Annual Register* (1772) as a new piece of fashionable sl. It is possibly of dialectal origin; the *EDD* has it as a Suffolk word, while Scot. has *flabrigast*, to boast extravagantly and *flabrigastit*, worn out with exertion]

flabbergasted/flabagasted *adj.* [late 18C+] astonished, exhausted, annoyed or disgusted. **2** [20C] (US) euph. for *damned*. [FLABBERGAST v.]

flabby-knackers *n.* [1950s+] a term of affectionate ribaldry (cf. BUGGERLUGS). [SE *flabby* + KNACKERS]

flach *see* FLATCH.

flack *n.* see FLAK.

flack *v.* [1960s+] (US) to publicize. [FLAK]

fladge *n.* [1940s+] *flagellation*, only when used in a sexual context (cf. B & D). [abbr./pron.]

fladge queen *n.* [1940s+] (gay) a homosexual who enjoys flagellation, usu. as the 'victim'. [FLADGE + QUEEN n.¹]

flag *n.*¹ **1** [mid-16C–mid-19C] a groat, 4 pence. **2** [20C] (US) a $1 bill. **3** [1940s–60s] (Aus.) a £1 note. [(1) ? f. MLG *vleger*, 'a coin worth somewhat more than a Bremer groat'. (2) var. on (1) or abbr. JEWISH FLAG]

flag *n.*² [mid–late 19C] **1** an apron; thus *flag-flasher*, one who wears an apron when not actually working. **2** a sanitary towel.

flag *n.*³ [20C] (US Und.) the bottom row of cells in a prison block. [SE *flagstone*]

flag *n.*⁴ [1930s–50s] (US Und.) an assumed name, alias. [SE *flag of convenience*]

flag *n.*⁵ [1950s+] (drugs) the flow of blood from the vein into the syringe, where it blends with the narcotic/water mixture before being pumped back into the vein. [the blood 'waves' as it enters the syringe]

flag *n.*⁶ [1960s] (US) an erect penis; thus *grow a flag*, to have an erection.

flag *v.*¹ **1** [late 19C–1950s] (gay) to attract a stranger with the eyes or with a slight gesture of the head. **2** [late 19C+] (US) to signal an interest in someone in anticipation of romantic or sexual involvement or to accost. **3** [late 19C+] (US) to allow someone to pass by, esp. the intended victim of a pickpocket, to refuse service to in a bar, to avoid.

flag *v.*² **1** [1920s+] (US Und.) to be arrested. **2** [1970s+] (US campus) to fail a test or examination; thus to get a grade F in an examination. [? SE *wave the white flag*, to surrender + initial letters]

flag/flip/give/shoot a/the bone, to *phr.* [1960s+] (US) to make a gesture of contempt by raising the middle finger (cf. FLIP THE BIRD; GIVE SOMEONE THE FINGER). [the SE *bones* inside the finger]

flag-about *n.* [mid-19C] a street-walking prostitute. [? she waves her flag to attract customers or walks on *flag*stones]

flag a freight-train, to *phr.* [20C] (US) a phr. implying the subject's foolishness, usu. as *he/she hasn't enough sense to ...*.

flagary *see* FEGARY.

flag-flapper *n.* [1910s+] (Aus.) one whose noisy patriotism is surpassed only by the care with which they ensure their ineligibility for active service (cf. FLAG-WAGGER).

flag-flasher *n.* [mid-19C] any member of the services who wears their uniform despite being off duty and in civilian surroundings.

flagger *n.* [19C] a street prostitute (cf. FLAG-ABOUT). [SE *flag*, a paving stone, upon which she walks, ? + her *showing the flag*]

flagging *n.*[1] [late 19C+] (US) the refusing of service in a bar. [FLAG V.[1] (3)]

flagging *n.*[2] [1930s] (US) menstruation. [HAVE THE FLAG OUT]

flaggings *n.* [20C] (US) meat or any other foodstuff, usu. cold. [orig. tramp jargon; ? the *flagging down* by the tramp of a passing citizen, in the hope of getting a hand-out]

flaggin', saggin' and braggin' *phr.* [1990s] (US Black gang) a phr. describing means of identifying oneself as a member of a gang, esp. in prison. [spec. wearing the gang colours, wearing one's trousers low on the hips and boasting about one's exploits in the free world. Such activities are often specifically prohibited in prisons in the (vain) hope of minimizing inter-gang tensions]

flag/danger signal is up *phr.* [late 19C+] (US) used of a woman who is menstruating (cf. FLYING BAKER; FLY ONE'S FLAG; FLY THE RED FLAG).

flag of defiance is out *phr.* [late 17C–early 19C] used of someone who is drunk (cf. BLOODY FLAG IS OUT). [the aggressiveness that so often accompanies heavy drinking]

flag of distress *n.* [mid-19C] an advertisement or similar statement of charges for board and lodging. [those who have to pay suffer the distress]

flagon-wagon *n.* [1960s+] (N.Z.) a beer truck.

flags *n.* [mid–late 19C] clothes drying in the open air.

flag spot/stop *n.* [1930s–40s] (US Black) a bus stop. [SE *flag down*]

flag unfurled *n.* [mid–late 19C] a man of the world. [rhy. sl.]

flag-wagger/-waver *n.* **1** [late 19C+] overt and excessive imperialist patriotism, esp. as found during the Anglo-Boer Wars (cf. FLAG-FLAPPER). **2** [1920s+] (US) an enthusiastic patriot or a song, film or oration which arouses patriotic fervour.

flag-waver *n.* [20C] (US) an assistant to the boss. [such an assistant is given an order, he or she then communicates it to the rest of the workforce; the image is of semaphore flags]

flahoola *n.* [late 19C–1900s] (Irish) a fat, noisy, extremely vulgar woman. [Irish]

flail *n.* [1970s+] (US) a confused, anxiety-provoking activity. [SE *flail*, to act energetically but without direction]

flail *v.* [1980s+] (US campus) to fail a test through being flustered or over-pressured. [SE *fluster* + *fail*]

flak/flack *n.* **1** [1940s+] (orig. US) cheek, negative criticism, verbal attacks. **2** [1940s] interference, annoyance, problems. **3** [1940s+] (US show business) a publicity man/woman, a press agent. **4** [1970s+] a public relations man/woman, whose job is to catch adverse 'flak'. [SE *flak*, anti-aircraft fire, ult. the initials of the elements of Ger. f*liegerabwehrkanone* 'pilot-defence-gun']

flak catcher *n.* [1970s+] a civil servant or similar figure in private industry whose task is to intercept complaints, queries etc from the public, before such problems reach their superiors. [SE *flak*, anti-aircraft fire + *catcher*]

flake *n.*[1] [20C] (Aus.) shark meat, esp. as sold in fish 'n' chip shops. [SE *flake*, a thin broad piece peeled or split off from the surface of something]

flake *n.*[2] **1** [1950s+] (orig. US) a boring, unappealing, incompetent, undesirable person. **2** [1950s+] (US) an eccentric, crazy person. **3** [1960s] (US) a disappointment or failure. [FLAKY]

flake *n.*[3] [1980s+] (drugs) **1** cocaine, spec. pieces that are smaller than average (cf. ROCK n.[4]). **2** crack cocaine.

flake *v.*[1] [late 19C+] (Aus./Irish) to beat, to thrash.

flake/flake out *v.*[2] **1** [1930s+] to collapse, from exhaustion, or an excess of drink or drugs. **2** [1940s+] (US) to recline or lie down, to sleep. **3** [1960s] (US) to die. **4** [1960s+] to go crazy. **5** [1970s+] (US campus) to astound (cf. FREAK OUT). [for ety. see FLAKED OUT]

flake *v.*[3] [1970s] (US Und.) of police, to plant evidence. [FLAKE n.[2] (1), i.e. to act in that way]

flake/flake on *v.*[4] [1980s+] (US campus) to fail to keep an appointment or other commitment.

flaked *adj.* [1910s+] drunk (cf. FLAKO). [abbr. FLAKED OUT]

flaked out *adj.* [1940s+] **1** (orig. US) exhausted. **2** (US) unconscious, asleep, lying down, resting. [? SE *flag*, to grow weak, to become exhausted, or US commercial fishing jargon *on the flakes*, dead, laid out for burial; this refers to the laying out of split fish on wooden racks or *flakes*]

flake on *see* FLAKE v.[4].

flake off *v.* [1970s+] (US campus) **1** to depart, to go away. **2** to loaf, to idle.

flake out *see* FLAKE v.[2].

flakers *adj.* [1950s+] (orig. naut.) drunk. [FLAKE OUT + 'Oxford' sfx. *-ers*]

flakes *n.* [1970s+] (drugs) phencyclidine (cf. ACE n.[3]).

flakey *see* FLAKY.

flako *adj.* [1950s+] drunk. [FLAKED OUT]

flaky/flakey *adj.* [1960s+] (orig. US) **1** of a person, second-rate, unreliable, distasteful, possibly eccentric (cf. FLAKE n.[2]). **2** of an object, eccentric, crazy, outrageous, unusual, unreliable or erratic. [orig. baseball use. 'It's an insider's word ... It does not mean anything so crude as "crazy", but it's well beyond "screwball" and far off to the side of "eccentric"' *New York Times*, 26 April 1964; ? SE *fall/crumble into flakes*, i.e. to come apart]

flaky ho *n.* [1970s+] an unstable, unreliable prostitute, whose desire for clients and money is undermined by her inability to maintain a good front and economic and social discipline (cf. SLOUCH). [FLAKY + HO n.[1]]

flam *n.*[1] [mid-19C] a lie. [FLAM v.; but note FLIM-FLAM (although this is poss. a later coinage) + Scot. *flamfew*, a trifle, a trinket]

flam *n.*[2] [mid-19C] a ring. [? FAMBLE n.]

flam *v.* (US) **1** [17C–19C; 1980s+] to hoodwink, to deceive. **2** [mid-19C] (campus) to be attentive to a woman. **3** [1970s] to flirt with or be aggressively forceful towards someone. [SE *flam*, to deceive by a sham story or trick or by flattery]

flamboast *v.* [1990s] (US teen) to show off or flaunt material items. [FLAM v. (1) + SE *boast*]

flamdoodle *see* FLAPDOODLE n.[2].

flame *n.* [19C] venereal disease (cf. FIRE n.[2]). [the association of VD with heat]

flame *v.*[1] **1** [1950s+] to talk arrant and apparent nonsense about an otherwise interesting subject. **2** [1960s+] to exaggerate, to bore (cf. FLAM v.).

flame *v.*[2] [1960s+] to rant in an unacceptable manner, esp. to insult a specific individual, via a communications network, e.g. the Internet.

flame *v.*[3] [1960s+] **1** (US gay/campus) of a man (whether actually homosexual or not), to look exaggeratedly 'feminine' in dress and style; thus *flaming*, acting in an obviously homosexual manner. **2** (US gay) to wear make-up. [FLAMER n.¹ (2)]

flame v.⁴ [1980s+] to waste money, to spend to excess. [SE phr. 'burn money']

flame cooking n. [1980s+] (drugs) smoking freebase cocaine by placing the pipe over the gas burner of a domestic stove.

flame!/flaming hell! excl. [1920s+] a general excl.

flamer n.¹ **1** [19C+] an enthusiast. **2** [early–mid-19C] a conspicuous, ostentatious person who 'burns brightly'. **3** [1960+] (US campus) a blatantly unpleasant homosexual man (cf. FLAME v.³). [they all 'burn brightly', although (3) is underpinned by abbr. of *flaming faggot*]

flamer n.² [late 19C] a safety match burning with notably bright flame.

flamer n.³ (US campus) **1** [1930s+] a clumsy, embarrassing or highly unpleasant person. **2** [1970s+] anyone who commits a major social error; thus the error itself. [such blunders mean that one 'goes down in flames']

flames n. [19C+] a nickname for a redhead.

flamethrower n. [1980s+] (drugs) a cigarette laced with cocaine and heroin. [its fig. effect]

flaming n. **1** [1950s+] speaking incessantly and obsessively on a particular topic of little interest to anyone but oneself. **2** [1980s+] using computer 'bulletin boards' and other communications links to circulate obscene messages, pictures etc. [? gay use FLAME v.³, to act conspicuously]

flaming adj.¹ [late 18C–late 19C] excessively noticeable, flagrant, monstrous. [SE *flaming*, burning brightly]

flaming adj.² [1920s+] (orig. Aus.) a mild pej. [euph. FUCKING adj.]

flaming fury n. [1960s] (Aus.) an outside lavatory, the contents of which were periodically burned off.

flaming hell! see FLAME!

flammy adj. [1990s] (US Black teen) *flamb*oyant. [abbr.]

flanderkin n. [late 17C–early 19C] a notably fat man (cf. DUTCH BUILD). [proper name *Flanders* + sfx. *-kin*]

Flanders fortune n. [late 17C–18C] a relatively small fortune or inheritance. [stereotyping of the Dutch as mean, hypocritical or deceitful]

Flanders piece n. [late 17C–18C] a painting that looks good from a distance but not so good close to. [stereotyping of the Dutch as mean, hypocritical or deceitful]

Flanders reckoning n. [late 17C–18C] **1** a badly prepared account, or books that do not balance (cf. FLEMISH ACCOUNT). **2** spending money in a place that has no links to that where one received it. [stereotyping of the Dutch as mean, hypocritical or deceitful]

flange n. **1** [20C] the head of the penis. **2** [1990s] (orig. US) the vagina.

flanges n. [mid-19C] the fingers.

flank v. [mid-19C] (US) **1** to dodge, to evade. **2** to trick out of (cf. FLANKER). [SE *flank*, to go around the side]

flanker n. **1** [mid-19C–1900s] a blow or punch. **2** [mid-19C–1900s] a verbal response. **3** [1920s+] (orig. milit.) a trick, a swindle, a hoax; thus *do/pull/work a flanker*, to trick, to swindle. [SE *flank*, to go around the side]

flannel n.¹ **1** [18C–19C] heated gin and beer with nutmeg, sugar and spices (cf. HOT FLANNEL). **2** [early 19C] grog, punch or gin-twist, with a dash of beer. [SE *flannel*, a form of woollen cloth; the drinks 'keep one warm']

flannel n.² [1920s+] rubbish, nonsense, albeit plausible rubbish. [? 19C tradesmen's jargon *flannel*, the ornate, scroll-ridden letterheads with which tradesmen garlanded the invoices they sent to their aristocratic clients. There is no proof, however, that this is linked to the 20C use, albeit a similar one]

flannel v. [1940s+] to flatter, to curry favour, to talk nonsense in a soothing, plausible manner, esp. for the purposes of charming a woman one wishes to seduce. [FLANNEL n.²]

flannel face see FLANNEL MOUTH.

flannel feet n. [20C] (US) **1** large feet. **2** a clumsy person.

flannel-jacket n. [late 19C] a navvy, who wears such a garment.

flannel mouth/face n. **1** [19C+] (US) an Irishman. **2** [19C+] (US) a Pole. **3** [19C+] (US) a loudmouth, a braggart, one who talks too much and with too little sense. **4** [20C] (Can.) a well-spoken person. [FLANNEL n.² + SE *mouth/face*; (1) and (2) are considered derog.]

flannel-mouthed adj. [late 19C+] (orig. US) **1** having a large mouth. **2** talking thickly or with a brogue. **3** loud-mouthed. [FLANNEL MOUTH]

flap n.¹ **1** [17C] the vagina. **2** [17C] a prostitute. **3** [early–mid-17C] a promiscuous woman. **4** [1950s+] (US) the mouth. [(1) survived as Northumberland dial. until late 19C]

flap n.² **1** [early 17C] a cap. **2** [late 18C–1920s] any garment that has a pendant flap or flaps. **3** [1950s] an ear.

flap n.³ [late 19C] (Und.) strips of lead used on roofs. [? they *flap* about as one removes them]

flap n.⁴ [20C] excrement, esp. animal (cf. FLOP n.⁶). [? abbr. SE *flapjack*]

flap n.⁵ [1910s+] panic, excitement, commotion. [orig. WW1 milit. use]

flap n.⁶ [1950s–60s] (US) nonsense, rubbish. [abbr. FLAPDOODLE n.²]

flap v.¹ [mid-17C–mid-19C] to fall or throw oneself down suddenly. [? SE *flop*]

flap v.² [late 19C] to rob, to swindle; thus *flap the dimmock*, to pay (money) (cf. FLAP A JAY).

flap v.³ **1** [20C] to become over-excited, to lose control, esp. when faced with an unforeseen problem. **2** [1910s–40s] (US) to chatter (cf. FLAPJAW). [FLAP n.⁵]

flap a jay, to phr. [late 19C+] (Und.) to trick a simpleton, to swindle an innocent victim. [FLAP v.²]

flapdash adj. [1910s–20s] very clean, shiny. [? confusion of the two parts of *slapdash*, assuming the imagery to be of dusting]

flapdoodle n.¹ **1** [17C] the penis. **2** [19C] a sexually incompetent man, either one who is still too young to have had sex or one who is now too old to attempt it. [SE *flap*, something hanging down + DOODLE n.²]

flapdoodle/flamdoodle n.² [19C+] **1** (US) nonsense, rubbish; thus *flapdoodler*, a charlatan, a politician, a speaker of portentous but empty words. **2** (US Black) mischief, malicious behaviour. **3** a fuss, an uproar. [ety. unknown; the image is of flapping lips]

flapdragon n. **1** [17C] a derog. term for a German or Dutchman. **2** [late 17C–late 18C] venereal disease. [imagery drawn on SE *flapdragon/snapdragon*, a game 'in which they catch raisins out of burning brandy and, extinguishing them by closing the mouth, eat them' (Johnson, *Dictionary*, 1755). (1) supposes an image of the German or Dutchman as all display but no substance and races that for all their external show can be 'eaten up' by an Englishman; in (2) the 'heat' affects the penis]

flap/fling it in someone's face, to phr. [late 19C+] of a prostitute, to expose her genitals or breasts (cf. COCK IT UP AT).

flapjack invalid n. [late 19C] (US) one who is suffering from an excess of food and drink. [they are reduced to eating *flapjacks*]

flapjaw n. [20C] (US) a noisy talker, a braggart. [SE *flap* + *jaw*]

flap one's chops, to phr. [20C] to talk incessantly, to gossip (cf. FLAPPING AT THE JIBS). [SE *flap* + CHOPS]

flap one's jaw, to phr. [1930s+] (US) to talk idly, to gossip.

flap one's mouth, to *phr.* [1910s+] to chatter, to say more than is sensible or proper. [now mainly W.I. use]

flapper *n.*[1] **1** [17C] the penis. **2** [19C] an impotent old man. [FLAPDOODLE]

flapper *n.*[2] [19C] the hand (cf. FLAPPER-SHAKER).

flapper *n.*[3] (orig. US) **1** [late 19C–1910s] a very young prostitute (usu. in her early teens). **2** [late 19C–1930s] a flighty girl or young woman, usu. middle-class, in her late teens or very early 20s, who sported short, bobbed hair, lipstick and skimpy dresses and generally led a lifestyle as far as possible removed from that desired by her parents; thus combs. *flapper-seat*, a seat at the back of a bicycle to accommodate a young woman, *flapper vote*, a contemptuous expression for the parliamentary vote, which was granted to women aged 21 years in 1928 (the over-30s having been enfranchised in 1918) (cf. FLAPPER-BRACKET; JAZZ BABY). [various etys. have been offered, each of which may have some claim to accuracy: the Northumbrian dial. *flap*, an unsteady young woman; SE *flapper*, a young wild duck or partridge (which flaps its wings as it experiments with flying); SE *flap*, to act in an emotional manner, supposedly typical of such young women. Whatever the ety. the heyday of the *flapper* (2) was the 1920s, Scott Fitzgerald's 'Jazz Age', an era of which they were as emblematic as the 'swinging dolly-bird' of the 1960s]

flapper *n.*[4] [20C] (US) a large foot or the shoe that encases it.

flapper *n.*[5] [1930s+] (US Black) the mouth.

flapper-bracket *n.* [1930s] a motorcycle pillion (cf. PEACH-PERCH). [FLAPPER *n.*[3] / SE *bracket*]

flappers *n.* **1** [mid-19C; 1930s–40s] the arms. **2** [late 19C] exaggeratedly long, pointed shoes. **3** [1920s] (tramp) the boards carried by a 'sandwich-man'. **4** [1930s+] (US) the ears. [fig. uses of SE. (1) used in the UK 1830s–60s; then in US Black use]

flapper-shaker *n.* [19C] the hand; thus *flapper-shaking*, hand-shaking. [ext. of FLAPPER *n.*[2]]

flapper steaks *n.* [1940s] (US Black) pigs' ears (eaten as a 'soul food' dish). [FLAP *n.*[2]]

flapping *n.* [1910s+] any form of racing, e.g. horses or dogs, that is not subject to Jockey Club or National Hunt Committee regulations or, in greyhound racing, to those of the National Greyhound Racing Club.

flapping at the jaw *phr.* [1950s+] (US Black) talking wildly, out of control, in a panicky, unrestrained manner (cf. FLAPPING AT THE JIBS). [SE *flap* + *jaw*]

flapping at the jibs *phr.* [1950s+] (US Black) talking wildly, out of control, in a panicky, unrestrained manner (cf. FLAPPING AT THE JAW). [SE *flap* + JIB *n.*[1]]

flapping track *n.* [1910s+] a small, unlicensed racetrack for horses or dogs. [FLAPPING + SE *track*]

flaps *n.* [1960s+] **1** the ears, usu. large ones. **2** the labia (cf. PISS FLAPS). [note. juv. use *flap-ears*, nosy, inquisitive people]

flapsauce *n.* [20C] nonsense, rubbish (cf. FLAPDOODLE *n.*[2]).

flap shot *n.* [1970s+] in pornographic still or moving pictures, a close-up shot of the labia and open vagina. [FLAPS *n.* (2) + SE *shot*, a picture]

flap snot *n.* [1990s] vaginal secretions (cf. COCK SNOT). [FLAPS *n.* (2) + SNOT]

flaptabs *n.* [1950s+] the ears. [SE *flap* + TAB *n.*[1]]

flap takkie *v.* [1980s+] to masturbate. [SE *flap* + play on phr. *tread takkie*, to accelerate]

flap with a fox-tail, a *phr.* [mid-16C–early 18C] a contemptuous dismissal, a trivial rebuke. [the lightness of a SE *foxtail*]

flare *n.* [mid–late 19C] **1** a quarrel, an argument. **2** a spree, an outing. [FLARE-UP *n.*[1]]

flare *v.* [mid-19C] **1** to swagger. **2** to whisk out. **3** to steal by sleight of hand. [FLARE-UP *n.*[1]]

flare a handkerchief, to *phr.* [mid-19C] of a pickpocket, to remove a handkerchief from someone's pocket.

flared *adj.* [1960s+] (Can.) slightly drunk. [? abbr. FLARING (drunk)]

flare-up *n.*[1] **1** [mid-19C] an argument, a fight. **2** [mid-19C] a jovial social gathering.

flare-up *n.*[2] [1900s–20s] brandy. [its flammability]

flare up *v.* [mid-19C+] to lose one's temper (suddenly).

flare up! *excl.* [mid-19C] a cry of delight, triumph or defiance. [coined at the burnings that accompanied Reform Riots of 1832, esp. in Bristol]

flaring *adv.* [19C] very, extremely.

flash *n.*[1] **1** [early 17C–early 19C] a nouveau riche, an ostentatious swindler, a loud-mouthed bully. **2** [late 17C–19C] a generic term for the criminal underworld. **3** [late 17C–19C] cant or criminal slang; 'the classical language of the holy land; in other words, St Giles's Greek' (Moncrieff, *Tom & Jerry*).

flash *n.*[2] [late 17C–18C] a periwig; thus *rum flash*, a long, full, expensive wig, *queer flash*, an old, raggedy wig. [? its being worn by a FLASH *n.*[1], i.e. an ostentatious person]

flash *n.*[3] **1** [mid-19C+] (Und.) a large bundle of notes, esp. when used in a game of three-card monte to entice victims. **2** [late 19C] (Und.) imitation gold coins. **3** [1920s+] (US Und.) a piece of cheap but alluring jewellery that is used to lure a victim into some form of confidence trick. [abbr. FLASH ROLL]

flash *n.*[4] **1** [late 19C–1950s] (orig. US) a quick look around (cf. FLASH THE RANGE). **2** [1940s+] (orig. US) a brief glimpse, esp. when offered to a man by a woman inadvertently revealing her thighs, breasts or genitals. [(2) was initially a ref. to the conscious 'flashing' by stripteasers/burlesque artists]

flash *n.*[5] **1** [1920s+] (US) a burst of inspiration, a sudden idea. **2** [1930s–60s] (US) a surprising piece of news or a rumour.

flash *n.*[6] **1** [1920s+] (Aus.) one's personal appearance. **2** [1920s–50s] (US Und.) a suit of clothes. [SE *flash*, an ostentatious person]

flash *n.*[7] (drugs) **1** [1950s+] the instantaneous effect that follows the injection of a narcotic or other drug (e.g. Methedrine). **2** [1960s+] LSD (cf. A *n.*[3]).

flash *adj.*[1] **1** [18C–mid-19C] belonging to or connected with the underworld. **2** [early–mid-19C] amoral, promiscuous (cf. FAST *adj.*[1]). **3** [early–mid-19C] belonging to, connected with or resembling the world of 'sportsmen', esp. the patrons of the prize-fight 'ring'. [FLASH *n.*[1]]

flash *adj.*[2] **1** [late 18C+] ostentatious, showy. **2** [late 18C+] aping the manners of one's friends. **3** [late 19C+] (orig. Aus./N.Z.) fashionable, smart, chic. **4** [20C] cheeky. [FLASH *n.*[1]]

flash *adj.*[3] [19C] expert, understanding what someone else means, 'knowing the ropes', esp. of the underworld (cf. AWAKE; DOWN *adj.*[2]; FLY *adj.*[1]). [FLASH *n.*[1] (2)]

flash *adj.*[4] [19C–1900s] (Und.) counterfeit; thus *flash note*, a counterfeit banknote. [FLASH *n.*[3]]

flash *v.*[1] **1** [late 18C–late 19C] **1** to 'cut a figure', to show off, usu. one's material possessions and gross self-esteem. **2** (W.I.) to dress ostentatiously. [FLASH *n.*[1]]

flash *v.*[2] **1** [mid-19C+] to expose one's genitals, esp. in a public place. **2** [1960s+] (US) to expose a part of the body in a quick or provocative manner. [FLASH *n.*[4] (2)]

flash *v.*[3] [1960s+] (US) to experience the effects of taking a drug, esp. hallucinatory. [FLASH *n.*[7]]

flash *v.*[4] [1960s+] to realize, to think, usu. suddenly or spontaneously. [FLASH *n.*[5], compounded by drug imagery]

flash *v.*[5] [1970s+] (US campus) to vomit; also as *flash one's cookies* (cf. COOKIES *n.*[2]; FLIP ONE'S COOKIES).

flash *v.*[6] [1990s] (Black) to rush, to run away. [SE phr. *quick as a flash*]

flash a bit, to *phr.* [mid–late 19C] of a woman, to behave immodestly. [FLASH *v.*[2]]

flash a fawney, to phr. [19C] to wear a counterfeit ring. [FLASH v.¹ + FAWNEY n.]

flash alf n. [1900s–70s] a fashionable man (cf. FLASH HARRY). [FLASH adj.² + generic Alf]

flash as a rat with a gold tooth/Chinky's horse phr. [20C] (Aus.) extremely ostentatious.

flash a tattler, to phr. [late 18C–late 19C] to wear a watch. [FLASH v.¹ + TATTLER]

flashback n. [1960s+] (drugs) the repetition after the event of emotions and sensations, typically a recurrence without the presence of any drug of the hallucinations provoked by LSD, first experienced while using a drug.

flash case/crib n.¹ [early 19C] a public house frequented mainly by criminals (cf. FLASH-PANNY). [FLASH adj.¹ (1) + CASE n.²/CRIB n.³]

flash case n.² [1930s+] (US Black) a satchel or bag that contains illegal drugs or any other contraband. [FLASH adj.¹ (1) + SE case]

flash chant/chaunt n. [early 19C] a song filled with criminal slang (cf. FLASH SONG). [FLASH adj.¹ (1) + CHANT]

flash cove/covess n. [early 19C] 1 a thief (cf. FLASH GENTRY; FLASHMAN). 2 a landlord or landlady. [FLASH adj.¹ (1) + COVE/COVESS]

flash crib see FLASH CASE n.¹.

flash dona n. [late 19C] a showy, working-class woman. [FLASH adj.² (1) + DONAH]

flash drum n. [19C] 1 a criminal lodging house. 2 a brothel (cf. FLASH HOUSE; FLASH KEN). [FLASH adj.¹ (1) + DRUM n.²]

flashed-up adj. [20C] dressed up in one's best clothes. [FLASH adj.² (1)]

flasher n.¹ [late 19C+] an exhibitionist (cf. MEAT-FLASHER). [FLASH v.²]

flasher n.² [20C] (US) a spendthrift, one who shops ostentatiously. [FLASH v.¹ (1)]

flash gentry n. [18C] a thief (cf. FLASH COVE; FLASHMAN). [FLASH adj.¹ (1) + SE gentry]

flash girl n.¹ [19C] a showy dresser. [FLASH adj.² (1) + SE girl]
flash girl n.² [19C] a prostitute. [FLASH adj.¹ (2) + SE girl]

flash harry n. [1950s+] an ostentatious, loudly dressed and usually ill-mannered man. [FLASH adj.² + generic Harry; best known as the nickname of the conductor Sir Malcolm Sargent (1895–1967) and as the SPIV character played by George Cole (b.1925) in the 'St Trinian's' films in the 1950s]

flash house n. [mid–late 19C] 1 a public house frequented mainly by the underworld. 2 a brothel (cf. ACCOMMODATION HOUSE; FLASH DRUM). [FLASH adj.¹ (1) + HOUSE n.¹]

flashing n. [late 19C; 1960s+] indecent exposure. [FLASH v.²]

flashing adj. [1960s+] 1 intoxicated by a hallucinogenic drug, usu. LSD but also strong cannabis. 2 experiencing the recurrence of earlier hallucinations (cf. FLASHBACK). [FLASH v.³]

flash in the pan phr. 1 [early 19C+] an abortive effort or outburst. 2 [1980s+] sex without ejaculation. [SE phr. flash in the pan, an explosion of gunpowder without any communication beyond the touch-hole]

flash it v.¹ [late 18C–mid-19C] to show off. [FLASH v.¹]

flash it/one's meat v.² [mid-19C+] to reveal one's genitals. [FLASH v.² + MEAT n.]

flash it about/away v. 1 [mid-19C+] to act in a showy manner. 2 [1960s+] to show off one's money or wealth in an ostentatious manner. [FLASH v.¹]

flash jack n. [late 19C–1960s] (Aus.) a dandy, a swell, esp. in the context of a sheep station; thus flash jane, a showy woman. [FLASH adj.² + generic Jack]

flash ken n. 1 [late 17C–19C] a criminal lodging house. 2 [19C] a brothel (cf. FLASH DRUM). [FLASH adj.¹ (1) + KEN n.¹]

flash kiddy n. [early 19C] a dandified young thief (cf. ROLLING KIDDY). [FLASH adj.¹ (1) + KIDDY n.¹]

flash lingo n. [late 18C–19C] the jargon of the criminal underworld. [FLASH adj.¹ (1) + LINGO]

flashly adv. [early-mid-19C] 1 in an ostentatious, showy manner. 2 using the language of the criminal underworld (cf. CANT n.¹). [FLASH adj.¹]

flashman n. 1 [late 18C–late 19C] anyone conversant with the criminal world and thus its vocabulary. 2 [late 18C–late 19C] a thug employed by a brothel to deal with undesirables and drunks. 3 [late 18C–late 19C] a pimp. 4 [mid-19C] (US) a man-about-town, a loafer with no visible means of support but an endless appetite for good clothes, parties and places of entertainment; such a man lived by his wits and often off foolish women (cf. HOG IN TOGS). [FLASH adj.¹ (1) + SE man]

flash moll n. [19C] a prostitute (cf. FLASH GIRL n.²). [FLASH adj.¹ (2) + MOLL]

flash mollisher n. [early 19C] a female criminal or habitué of the underworld. [FLASH adj.¹ (1) + MOLLISHER]

flash notes n. [mid–late 19C] pieces of paper that at first glance look like banknotes. [FLASH adj.⁴ + SE notes]

flash of light n.¹ [late 19C+] a gaudily dressed woman. ['upon the model of a rainbow' (Ware)]

flash of light n.² [1970s+] a sight. [rhy. sl.]

flash of lightning n. [late 18C–mid-19C] a glass of gin. [SE flash + LIGHTNING n.¹ + play on SE]

flash on v. 1 [1920s+] (US) to catch sight of. 2 [1960s+] to have a sudden inspiration, memory, moment of absolute comprehension etc. [FLASH v.⁴]

flash one's gab, to phr. [early 19C] to talk, esp. to brag, to boast. [FLASH v.¹ + GAB n.]

flash one's gash, to phr. [1990s] (Aus.) of a woman, to expose her vagina as an incitement/invitation to intercourse (cf. AGILITY; FLASH THE UPRIGHT GRIN). [FLASH v.² + GASH n.¹]

flash one's meat see FLASH IT v.².

flash one's rags, to phr. [mid–late 19C] to show off one's bankroll. [FLASH v.¹ + RAGS n.¹]

flash one's sticks, to phr. [early-mid-19C] to draw but not to fire one's pistols. [FLASH v.¹ + STICK n.³]

flash one's ticker, to phr. [mid–late 19C] to take one's watch out frequently. [FLASH v.¹ + TICKER n.²]

flash-panny n. 1 [early 19C] a public house used primarily by criminals. 2 [mid-19C] a brothel. [FLASH adj.¹ (2) + PANNEY n.²]

flash piece n. [19C] a prostitute (cf. FLASH GIRL n.²). [FLASH adj.¹ (2) + PIECE n.¹]

flash roll n. [18C] a sum of money that is revealed as proof that a person, esp. a narcotics dealer or other criminal, is willing to do business; the money is 'flashed' before the client (cf. CALIFORNIA BANKROLL; FLASH CASE n.²). [FLASH adj.¹ (1) + SE bankroll]

flash song n. [early 19C] a song filled with criminal slang. [FLASH adj.¹ (1) + SE song]

flash-sport n. [1950s] (US Black) a notably stylish man. [FLASH adj.² + SPORT n.²]

flashtail n. 1 [18C] a prostitute (cf. BANG-TAIL n.¹). 2 [mid-19C–1920s] a prostitute who works at night (cf. EVENING STAR). 3 [1970s+] (US Black) any prostitute. [FLASH v.¹ + TAIL n.¹ (2)]

flash the ash, to phr. [20C] to hand around one's pack of cigarettes. [FLASH v.¹ + SE ash]

flash the dibs, to phr. [mid-19C–1920s] to spend one's money. [FLASH v.¹ + DIBBS]

flash the dicky, to phr. [mid-19C] to expose one's shirt-front. [FLASH v.¹ + DICKY n.¹]

flash the gab, to phr. [early 19C] to show off, to act ostentatiously. [FLASH v.¹ + GAB n.]

flash the gallery see FLASH THE RANGE.

flash the hash, to phr. [late 18C+] (Und.) to vomit. [FLASH v.¹ + SE hash, stew. 20C use is US]

flash the ivories, to *phr.* [early 19C+] to smile, to grin. [ext. of FLASH THE IVORY]

flash the ivory, to *phr.* [late 18C–late 19C] to smile, to grin. [FLASH v.[1] + IVORY n.[1]]

flash the meat, to *phr.* [16C] of a woman, to expose herself for sexual purposes. [FLASH v.[1] + MEAT n.]

flash the muzzle, to *phr.* [19C] to draw a pistol. [FLASH v.[1] + SE *muzzle*]

flash the patter, to *phr.* [19C] **1** to talk fast and meaninglessly. **2** to talk in cant (cf. PEDLAR'S FRENCH). [FLASH v.[1] + PATTER n.]

flash the range/gallery, to *phr.* [1950s+] (US prison) the scanning of the area outside one's cell by using a hand mirror to catch any reflections of approaching warders etc (cf. FLASH n.[4]). [SE *flash* + RANGE]

flash the red rag, to *phr.* [early 19C–1900s] to menstruate. [FLASH v.[1] + fig. use of RED RAG n.[2]]

flash the tongue, to *phr.* [19C] to talk fast and, usually, meaninglessly. [FLASH v.[1] + SE *tongue*]

flash the upright grin, to *phr.* [mid-19C–1920s] of a woman, to expose her vagina (cf. FLASH ONE'S GASH; VERTICAL SMILE). [FLASH v.[2] + UPRIGHT GRIN]

flash the wedge, to *phr.* [19C] (Und.) to dispose of one's 'swag' or booty. [FLASH v.[1] + WEDGE n.[1]]

flash toggery *n.* [early–mid-19C] smart clothes. [FLASH adj.[2] + TOGGERY]

flash up *v.* [20C] (US) of a woman, to dress showily, to use an excess of cosmetics. [FLASH v.[1]]

flashwoman *n.* [19C] a prostitute (cf. FLASHMAN). [FLASH adj.[1] (2) + SE *woman*]

flash yad *n.* [mid-19C–1900s] a pleasant day out. [FLASH adj.[2] + backsl. *yad* = day]

flashy blade/spark *n.* [early–mid-19C] a dandy. [FLASH adj.[2] + BLADE n.[1]/SE *spark*, a dandy]

flat *n.[1]* **1** [16C] (Und.) a type of false die, in which one side is fractionally shorter than the others (cf. BARRED). **2** [late 18C] a counterfeit coin.

flat/flatt *n.[2]* [mid-18C–late 19C] a peasant, a rustic and as such considered a fool or innocent; thus (Und.) *it's a good flat that's never down*, even the most naïve of dupes must realize what's happening eventually (cf. FLATTIE n.[1]). [antonym of SHARP n.[1]]

flat *n.[3]* [mid-19C] (US) a rejection. [SE *turn down flat*]

flat *n.[4]* [20C] (US) the truth. [abbr. *flat truth*]

flat *n.[5]* [1910s–30s] (US) a detective. [abbr. FLATFOOT n.[2] (5)]

flat *n.[6]* [1930s] (US Black) 5 cents, a nickel. [the thin, flat coin]

flat *n.[7]* [1950s] (US drugs) a thin packet of heroin. [its shape]

flat *n.[8]* [1960s+] a *flat* tyre. [abbr.]

flat *adj.[1]* **1** [early 19C+] without any money (cf. FLAT BROKE). **2** [19C+] total, complete.

flat *adj.[2]* [20C] (Aus.) exhausted, worn out. [abbr. FLAT OUT adj.[2]]

flat *v.* [19C] (US) to reject a suitor. [abbr. SE *turn down flat*]

flat arch *n.* [late 19C] a policeman (cf. FLATFOOT n.[2]; FLATHEAD n.[2]; FLATTER n.[1]; FLATTIE n.[3]). [the result of pounding the beat]

flat as a flounder *phr.* [17C–19C] very flat indeed. [the flat fish]

flat as a frying pan *phr.* [late 19C] very flat.

flat as a pancake *phr.* [17C+] very flat indeed.

flat as a tack *phr.[1]* [1950s+] (Aus.) at full speed. [SE *flat*, i.e. with the car's accelerator pressed to the floor]

flat as a tack *phr.[2]* [1960s+] (Aus.) very depressed. [FLAT adj.[2]]

flat-back *n.* [mid-19C] a bedbug (cf. B FLAT; MAHOGANY FLAT n.[1]). [ext. of FLATS n.[1]]

flatbacker *n.* [1940s+] (US Black pimp) a prostitute who specializes in quantity rather than quality in her clients. [she does no more than lie *flat on her back*]

flatbacking *n.* [1970s] (US Black) sexual intercourse. [the traditional 'missionary position']

flat bit *n.* [20C] (US Und.) a sentence served with no remission for good behaviour. [FLAT adj.[1] (2)]

flat blues *n.* [1970s+] (drugs) LSD (cf. A n.[3]). [packaging]

flatboat/flatboot *n.* [20C] (US) a large, clumsy shoe. [play on SE *flatboat*, a broad flat-bottomed boat, used for transport]

flat broke *adj.* [mid-19C] totally impoverished. [FLAT adj.[1] + BROKE]

flat-cap *n.* **1** [late 16C–early 18C] a citizen of London. **2** [late 17C–early 18C] a Billingsgate fishwife (cf. STRAW HAT). [the headgear]

flat-catcher *n.[1]* [early 19C+] **1** a confidence trickster, one who indulges in 'sharp practice'. **2** anything that will serve to dupe the public. [FLAT n.[2] + SE *catcher*]

flat-catcher *n.[2]* [mid-19C–1920s] a horse that looks good but fails to win races. [it is always caught and passed *in the flat*]

flatch/flach *n.* [mid-19C] **1** a half. **2** a halfpenny. [backsl.]

flat chicken *n.* [late 19C] stewed tripe. [? the taste, the consistency, the look]

flatch-kennurd *adj.* [mid-19C] tipsy, mildly drunk. [backsl.; lit. 'half-drunk']

flat chunks *n.* [1980s+] (drugs) crack cocaine mixed with Benzocaine.

flatch yenep/yennep/yennop *n.* [mid-19C] a halfpenny (cf. FLATCH). [backsl.]

flat-cock *n.* [late 18C–late 19C] a woman. [the anatomical difference]

flat fish/regular flat fish *n.* [early–mid-19C] a fool, a dullard. [SE *flat* + FISH n.[1] but ? a simple joc. use of SE]

flatfoot *n.[1]* [late 19C] (US) a man who stands firmly for one political party, come what may.

flatfoot *n.[2]* **1** [mid-19C] (US) a Black person. **2** [late 19C–1900s] a sailor. **3** [late 19C+] an infantryman. **4** [20C] (US) an Irish immigrant. **5** [1910s+] a policeman (cf. FLATTIE n.[3]). [all refer to marching or to walking in menial jobs]

flatfoot *n.[3]* [1910s–20s] a person who has flat feet.

flatfoot *v.* [1960s] (US) to down a glass of liquor in one gulp. [? after drinking one slaps the glass *flat* on the table or bar]

flat-footed *adj.[1]* [early 19C+] downright, positive, undeviating, straightforward. [FLATFOOT n.[1]]

flat-footed *adj.[2]* [mid-19C] (US) destitute, penniless. [FLAT adj.[1] + pun on SE]

flat-footed *adj.[3]* **1** [20C] (US) of food, plain, devoid of any further cooking or mixing. **2** [1950s–60s] insipid, maladroit.

flat-footed *adj.[4]* [20C] unprepared, caught unawares; thus *catch flat-footed*, to catch unawares.

flat-footed *adv.* [20C] (US) plainly, firmly, without adornment; thus *come out flat-footed*, to state an unequivocal opinion.

flat-footed Dutch *n.* [20C] (US) a German immigrant. [FLATFOOT n.[2] (4) + *Dutch*, i.e. *Deutsch*]

flat-footed in the corn-field *phr.* [20C] (US) utterly unsophisticated, completely ignorant.

flat-footer *n.* [late 19C–1900s] a pedestrian, a walker.

flat fuck *n.* [1960s+] (gay) sexual relations between two women, rubbing their bodies together (cf. DRY FUCK). [SE *flat* + FUCK n.[1]]

flat fuck *v.* [1960s+] of lesbians, to rub their bodies together for sexual stimulation. [FLAT FUCK n.]

flathead *n.[1]* [mid-19C+] (US) **1** a foolish, stupid person. **2** a Jew. **3** a Lithuanian. **4** an inhabitant of the Illinois-Ohio lowlands. **5** a German settler in Dakota or Wisconsin. [all uses are derog.]

flathead *n.[2]* [20C] a policeman. [var. on FLATFOOT n.[2]]

flat-iron n. [mid-19C] any wedge-shaped house, usu. at the diagonal confluence of two streets, esp. a public house sited on a corner. [note the *locus classicus* is New York's Flatiron Building, at the corner of Broadway and Fifth Avenue at 23rd Street]

flatite n. [1920s+] (Aus.) a flat-dweller. [SE *flat* + sfx. -*ite*, connected with or belonging to]

flat joint n. [late 19C+] a crooked gambling game or casino; orig. fair/carnival use, when a flat was a crooked or doctored 'wheel of fortune' (cf. SET JOINT). [SE *flat* + JOINT n.[3] (3); the flat surface that is vital to the playing of the sort of games, e.g. three-card monte, the shell game, featured at such places]

flatlander/flatter n. [20C] (US) an outsider, an incompetent person. [lit. one who comes from the flatlands, the plains and thus seen as inferior by those who live in the mountains]

flat-move n. [early 19C] (orig. Und.) any plan that fails. [SE *flat*, i.e. lifeless, disappointing + MOVE n. (1)]

flat out adj.[1] [late 19C+] straightforward, unadorned, blunt, esp. of speech (cf. FLAT-FOOTED adj.[3]).

flat out adj.[2] [20C] (orig. Aus.) exhausted.

flat out like a lizard drinking phr. [1940s+] (Aus.) moving or working at great speed.

flat out like a lizard on a log phr. [1940s+] (Aus.) lying flat out on one's face.

flats n.[1] [19C] bugs or lice (cf. CHITS).

flats n.[2] **1** [19C] playing cards. **2** [1960s+] plastic credit cards. [the shape; but note FLAT n.[1] for overtones of possible criminal use]

flats n.[3] **1** [late 19C] counterfeit money. [FLAT n.[1] (2)]

flats n.[4] [20C] (US Und.) the bottom row of cells in a prison block (cf. FLAG n.[3]). [19C SE *flat*, a floor or storey in a house]

flats and sharps n. [early 19C] edged weapons.

flat stick/tack/tap adv. [1970s+] (Aus./N.Z.) at top speed, at the limit of one's abilities or resources.

flatt see FLAT n.[2].

flatten v. **1** [late 19C] to get the better of. **2** [1960s+] to knock down (cf. IRON OUT v.).

flatter n.[1] [late 19C] a policeman (cf. FLATFOOT n.[2]).

flatter n.[2] see FLATLANDER.

flatters adj. [1950s+] absolutely penniless. [FLAT BROKE + 'Oxford' sfx. -*ers*]

flatter-trap n. [mid-19C] the mouth, esp. that of a sycophant or toady. [SE *flatter* + TRAP n.[3]]

flattie/flatty n.[1] [late 18C–19C] a dupe, a naïve countryman. [FLAT n.[2]]

flattie/flatty n.[2] [mid-19C+] a small, flat-bottomed sailing boat.

flattie/flatty n.[3] [1910s+] a police officer. [abbr. FLATFOOT n.[2] (5)]

flattie/flatty n.[4] [1980s+] (N.Z.) a *flat* tyre. [abbr.]

flatties n. [1940s+] low-heeled or flat shoes.

flat top n. [1950s+] a style of haircut.

flat to the boards phr. **1** [1920s+] at full speed. **2** [1960s+] (Aus./N.Z.) working to one's greatest extent, very busy. [SE *flat*, i.e. with the car's accelerator pressed to the floor]

flatty see FLATTIE.

flatty-gory n. [early 19C] a counterfeit coin. [FLAT n.[1] (2) + GOREE]

flatty-ken n. [mid-19C] a public house that is frequented by members of the underworld but of which the landlord remains oblivious of their activities. [FLATTIE n.[1] + KEN n.[1]]

flat-wheel n. [20C] (US) one who walks with a limp. [railroad jargon *flat wheel*, a car wheel that has worn flat spots on its tread and thus rolls slightly askew]

flava adj. [1990s] (US rap music) style (cf. FLAVOR n.[2]). [deliberate mis-sp.]

flavor n.[1] [1980s+] (US drugs) top quality cocaine. [abbr. SE *flavor of the month*]

flavor n.[2] [1990s] (US Black) **1** style. **2** attractiveness; thus an attractive young woman.

flavour of the month phr. [1970s+] a derisory reference to a contemporary and, it is presumed, short-lived fashion or fad. [orig. coined in 1946 as SE for varieties of ice-cream]

flaw v. [late 17C–early 18C] to make drunk.

flawed adj. **1** [late 17C–19C] drunk (cf. ADDLED). **2** [19C] of a woman, deflowered but still unmarried.

flaxation! excl. [late 19C] (US) euph. version of *damnation!* [ety. unknown]

flaxie n. [1910–20s] (N.Z.) a *flax*-cutter. [abbr.]

flay v. [late 19C] (US) to cheat someone of all their money by unfair means (cf. CLEAN OUT).

flay a flint, to phr. [mid–late 17C] to undertake the worst sort of meanness or excess to extract money from another person. [cf. SE *get blood from a stone*]

flaybottomist n. [late 18C] a schoolmaster (cf. BUM-BRUSHER).

flay the emperor, to phr. [1990s] to masturbate.

flay/flea the fox, to phr. [late 18C] to vomit (cf. WHIP THE CAT phr.[1]). [lit. trans. of Fr. sl. *écorcher le renard*]

flea and louse n. [mid-19C] a house, esp. a house with a bad reputation. [rhy. sl.]

fleabag 1 [mid-19C+] (orig. milit.) a sleeping bag or bed. **2** [late 19C+] a cheap hotel or lodging house (cf. BUGHOUSE). **3** [1930s+] (US) an ageing, ill dog. **4** [1960s+] (US) an old, worn-out prostitute who is forced to seek equally run-down clients, often on Skid Row, in cheap hotels etc. **5** [1960s+] (US Black) a troublesome, difficult person who tends, like fleas, to follow around and keep irritating the individual who has been made subject of their woes. [c.1910 there was an actual *Fleabag* in New York City, a cheap saloon at 241 Bowery]

flea box n. [late 19C+] a cheap hotel or lodging house (cf. BUGHOUSE).

flea circus n. [1920s+] (Aus.) a cheap, tawdry, run-down cinema (cf. FLEAPIT).

flea market n. [1920s+] a market specializing in junk, second-hand goods and similar bric-a-brac (but never food). [lit. trans. of Fr. *marché aux puces*]

fleapit n. **1** [1910s] a (run-down) flat. **2** [1930s+] a cheap, tawdry, run-down cinema.

flea powder n. [1980s+] (drugs) second-rate or poor quality drugs.

fleas and ants n. [20C] pants. [rhy. sl.]

fleas and itches/itchers n. [1960s] (Aus.) the cinema. [rhy. sl. *fleas and itches* = pictures]

fleas and scratches n. [20C] (Aus.) matches. [rhy. sl.]

flea the fox see FLAY THE FOX.

flea trap n. **1** [mid-19C] a cheap and dirty hotel (cf. BUGHOUSE). **2** [1930s+] (US) an ageing, ill dog (cf. FLEABAG).

fleece n. [19C] **1** the female pubic hair. **2** a generic term for women as sex objects, esp. in *fleece-hunter, fleece-monger*, a womanizer.

fleecer n. [20C] a confidence trickster. [SE *fleece*, to plunder, to rob heartlessly, to victimize]

fleecy-claimer n. [19C] a sheep-stealer.

Fleeter-Streeter n. [late 19C] 'a journalist of the baser sort, a spunging PROPHET; a sharking dramatic critic; a SPICY paragraphist; and so on' (F&H); thus *Fleet-Streetese*, 'the so-called English, written to sell by the Fleeter-Streeter, a mixture of sesquipedelians and slang, of phrases worn threadbare and phrases sprung from the kennel; of bad grammar and worse manners; the like of which is impossible outside Fleet Street, but which in Fleet Street commands a price, and enables not a few to live' (F&H). [*Fleet-Street* 'the estate of journalism, especially journalism of the baser sort' (F&H)]

fleet of blows/licks n. [20C] (W.I./Guyn., Trin.) a painful thrashing.

Fleet Street dove/houri n. [19C] a prostitute (cf. BANKSIDE LADY). [proper name *Fleet Street*, London EC4, the late 19C–1980s centre of London journalism, also celebrated for its population of prostitutes + SE *dove/houri*, a nymph of the Muslim paradise, thus a beautiful woman]

Flemington confetti n. [1920s+] (Aus.) rubbish, nonsense, 'tripe' (cf. COWYARD CONFETTI). [? *Flemington* racecourse, covered in torn-up betting slips etc at the end of a major meeting; or *Flemington* saleyards in Sydney and Melbourne]

Flemington races n. [1920s+] (Aus.) braces. [rhy. sl.]

Flemish account n. [late 17C–mid-19C] a badly prepared account or books that do not balance (cf. FLANDERS RECKON-ING). [the Flemish *livre* or pound was worth only 12 rather than 20 shillings; the main implication, however, is of the grasping stereotype attributed to any native of the Low Countries]

Flemo n. [20C] (Aus.) the suburb of *Flem*ington, northwest of Melbourne. [abbr. + sfx. -O]

flesh/flesh it v. [late 16C–late 19C] of a man, to have sexual intercourse. [SE *flesh*, to plunge one's weapon into flesh, to gratify one's lusts]

flesh!/flesh and fire! excl. [late 17C–early 18C] a blasphemous excl. [abbr. of SE *God's flesh!*]

flesh-and-blood n. [mid-19C] a drink composed of equal measures of port and brandy. [a loose approx. of the colours of the drinks]

flesh and fire! see FLESH!

fleshbag n. [early–mid-19C] a shirt.

flesh broker n. [late 17C–18C] **1** a match-maker. **2** a madame, a procuress (cf. FLESHMONGER; FLESH PEDDLER).

flesh-brokery n. [late 17C–18C] a brothel. [FLESH BROKER]

flesh hooks n. [17C] the hands (cf. BISCUIT HOOKS).

flesh it see FLESH.

fleshly part n. [19C] the vagina. [SE *fleshly*, sexual, carnal]

flesh market n. [mid-19C] a brothel (cf. BUTTOCKING SHOP).

fleshmonger n. [early–mid-17C] **1** a sexual athlete. **2** a pimp (cf. FLESH BROKER). [SE *flesh* + sfx. *-monger*]

flesh peddler n. **1** [late 17C–18C] a match-maker, a procuress (cf. FLESH BROKER). **2** [1930s+] (US) a film or theatrical agent.

flesh pencil n. [1990s] the penis.

fleshpot n. [1970s+] (US Black) a woman, viewed strictly (and thus offensively) as a sex object.

flesh-presser n. [1920s+] (orig. US) a politician who attempts to curry favour with the voters by shaking as many hands, kissing as many babies and patting as many backs as possible during a campaign (cf. GLAD HAND).

flesh-shambles n. [early 17C] a brothel (cf. FLESH-BROKERY; KILLING FLOOR). [SE *flesh* + *shambles*, a slaughterhouse]

flesh-tailor n. [17C] a surgeon.

fleshy bagpipes n. [1990s] the female breasts.

fleshy flugelhorn n. [1990s] the penis.

flex n. [1990s] **1** (US Black) guts, courage, integrity, energy. **2** (W.I./UK Black teen) a person's mannerism, idiosyncrasies etc.

flex v.[1] **1** [1960s+] (US prison) to get emotionally prepared for launching a gang fight (cf. PLEX). **2** [1990s] (US Black) to make others aware of one's potential for violence and willingness to use it; thus *on the flex*, acting in an excessively macho manner in the hope of impressing onlookers. **3** [1990s] to hit or to intimidate someone. [SE *flex one's muscles*]

flex v.[2] [1980s+] (US Black) to scratch records, i.e. to move the needle backwards and forwards across the record, thus repeating or distorting a chosen section. [the required flexing of the wrist]

flex/flex one's sex v.[3] [1990s] (US Black teen) to have an erection.

flex with v. [1990s] (Black) to associate with. [ext. of FLEX v.[1] (2)]

flick n.[1] [17C] a thief. [the word orig. appeared as *afflicke* (albeit at F in Rowlands' A–Z listing) and has always been assumed, by the *OED* and others, to have been a misprint of *a flick*. That said, it has no proven ety. and may indeed be one, equally incomprehensible word]

flick n.[2] [mid-19C–1930s] an amusing person, esp. as *old flick*.

flick n.[3] [1950s+] **1** a knife with a spring-loaded blade. **2** a razor blade with one side taped so that it can be held as a weapon. [abbr. SE *flick-knife*]

flick n.[4] [1960s+] (US Black) a photograph.

flick v.[1] [late 17C–early 19C] (Und.) to cut.

flick v.[2] [1970s+] (US Black) to fail deliberately to turn up for work or school.

flicker n. [late 17C–19C] (Und.) a glassful of alcohol; thus *rum flicker*, a large glass, *queer flicker*, an ordinary glass. [ety. unknown; ? one 'flicks' the contents down one's throat]

flicker v.[1] **1** [late 17C–early 19C] to grin, to laugh in someone's face. **2** [late 19C–1930s] (US Und.) to faint or pretend to faint, to die.

flicker v.[2] [19C] to kiss or caress a woman. [? the SE *flick* of the tongue or fingers]

flicker v.[3] [late 19C] to drink. [FLICKER]

flickers n. [1920s–30s] moving pictures, cinema films. [ext. of FLICKS]

flickertail n. [20C] (US) a native of North Dakota. [dial. *flickertail*, the ground squirrel, the state's best known native animal]

flick one's bic, to phr. [1970s] to stimulate the genitals with a hand (whether one's own or that of a partner). [SE *flick* + *bic*, a popular brand of pen]

flick one's wick, to phr. [1950s] (N.Z.) to hurry up. [the flicking of a cigarette lighter]

flicks n. [1920s+] a film or cinema (cf. FLICKERS). [early films jerked or 'flicked' slightly as they ran through the projector; mainly used historically/ironically post-1950s]

flick the bean, to phr. [1990s] of a woman, to masturbate. [SE *flick* + BEAN n.[3] (3)]

flick the dick, to phr. [1990s] of a man, to masturbate. [SE *flick* + DICK n.[5] (1)]

flier see FLYER.

flies' skating rink see SKATING RINK.

flif-floff adj. [1990s] (US teen) tousled or messy. [echoic]

flight deck n. [1980s] the female breasts. [? nonce-word created by Posy Simmonds for her raffish character Edmund Heap]

flight of steps see DOORSTEP.

flim n.[1] **1** [mid-19C+] a £5 note. **2** [1940s–50s] a 5-year prison sentence. [FLIMSY n.]

flim n.[2] [1910s–20s] a swindle, a fraud, a confidence trick. [abbr. FLIM-FLAM n.[1]]

flim v. [1910s–20s] to swindle, to defraud, to trick. [FLIM n.[2]]

flim-flam n.[1] **1** [mid-16C+] an idle tale, a piece of nonsense (cf. JIM-JAM; WHIM-WHAM). **2** [late 19C+] (orig. US) a confidence trick, a criminal hoax. [? ON *flim*, a lampoon, *flimska*, mockery]

flim-flam n.[2] [1970s] (US) the penis. [SE *flim-flam*, a trifle]

flim-flam v. [late 19C+] (US) to perpetrate a confidence trick or hoax. [FLIM-FLAM n.[1]]

flim-flammer n. [late 19C+] (US) a confidence trickster. [FLIM-FLAM v.]

flimp v. [mid–late 19C] **1** to steal, esp. watches, by snatching items from their owners (rather than carefully picking a pocket). **2** to have sexual intercourse (cf. BANG v.[1]). **3** to swindle, to cheat. [western Flemish *flimpe*, to hit in the face; *flimping* is equivalent to two-man mugging, one person pushes the victim from behind, the other robs him]

flimper *n.* [mid-19C] a mugger or thief, esp. of watches, working in a team, one man grabs the victim from behind, while the *flimper* steals his watch. [FLIMP v.[1]]

flimsy *n.* 1 [early 19C+] a banknote, esp. a £5 note. 2 [20C] (Aus.) a cheque. [the *flimsy* paper on which it is printed or written]

flimsy *v.* [late 19C] to copy out on tracing paper.

fling *v.* [mid-18C–mid-19C] to get the better of, to cheat, to deceive, esp. as *fling out of*. [SE *fling*, i.e. to fling money out of]

fling-dust/-stink *n.* [17C] a street-walking prostitute. [the dirt or dust that she stirs on her walk]

fling it in someone's face *see* FLAP IT IN SOMEONE'S FACE.

fling-stink *see* FLING-DUST.

fling the hatchet *see* THROW THE HATCHET.

fling the hoof *see* SLING THE HOOF.

fling the house out of the windows, to *phr.* [17C] to make a great deal of noise or disturbance in one's house.

flink *v.* (US) 1 [19C] to act like a coward, to shirk one's duties. 2 [20C] to play truant from school. [? SE *flinch*, to slink off, to sneak away]

flint *n.*[1] [late 18C–mid-19C] a worker who refuses to accept anything but full, union-negotiated wages (cf. DUNG). [the hardness of SE *flint*]

flint *n.*[2] [1970s] (US Black) a cigarette lighter. [the flint that it contains]

flip *n.*[1] [late 17C–late 19C] a mixture of beer and spirit sweetened with sugar and heated with a hot iron (cf. SIR CLOUDESLEY). [SE *flip*, to whip up]

flip *n.*[2] [late 19C+] a bribe or tip. [one 'flips' the recipient a coin]

flip *n.*[3] [1910s+] a short trip, orig. in an aeroplane, but also in other forms of conveyance. [SE *fillip*]

flip *n.*[4] 1 [20C] (Aus.) a person, a fellow. 2 [1910s] a triviality, an irrelevance. 3 [1940s–60s] an impudent, flippant, 'lightweight' person. 4 [1950s+] (US) an eccentric, a madman. 5 [1950s+] (US) a state of high excitement, delight or craziness.

Flip *n.*[5] [1920s+] (US) a derog. name for a *Filip*ino. [abbr.]

flip *n.*[6] [1940s+] (US prison) an informer (cf. FLIP v.[3]). [he 'flips over' on his fellow inmates]

flip *n.*[7] [1960s+] (US) a darn, a rap; thus *couldn't give a flip*. [euph. for FUCK n.[2]]

flip *n.*[8] [1980s+] (US Black) a passive male homosexual. [he 'flips over' for anal penetration]

flip *adj.* [1920s+] (orig. US) nonchalant, unconcerned, in control. [Devon dial. *flip*, glib, flippant]

flip *v.*[1] 1 [early–mid-19C] to shoot with a pistol or revolver. 2 [20C] (US) to steal a ride, esp. on a freight train. 3 [1930s] (US drugs) to make another addict unconscious in order to steal his drugs. 4 [1940s] (US Black) to reject someone. [SE *flip*, to strike at sharply]

flip *v.*[2] [late 19C+] (orig. Aus.) to masturbate. [SE *flip*, to give a flip with (the finger)]

flip *v.*[3] [1940s+] (US prison) to inform on a fellow inmate (cf. TURN OVER ON). [FLIP n.[6]]

flip *v.*[4] [1950s+] (orig. US) 1 to lose control, to get over-excited, often ext. in phr. *flip one's cork/frijoles/noodle/raspberry/stack* (cf. FLIP ONE'S TOP; FREAK). 2 to become drunk. [FLIP ONE'S WIG]

flip! *excl.* [20C] a euph. for FUCK!

flip a bitch, to *phr.* [1980s+] (US campus) to make an illegal U-turn. [BITCH n.[1] (1); the stereotype of the poor woman driver]

flip a bone *see* FLAG A BONE.

flip da/the scrip, to *phr.* [1990s] (US Black teen) to change completely, to take an utterly fresh direction. [SE *flip*, turn over + *script*]

flip-flap *n.*[1] 1 [mid-17C] the penis. 2 [late 19C] a broad fringe of hair falling across the forehead, esp. as used by street boys. [both 'flap' around]

flip-flap *n.*[2] [mid-19C] 'a kind of somersault in which the performer throws himself over on his hands and feet alternately'; also 'a peculiar rollicking dance indulged in by costers' (Hotten, 1864).

flip-flap *n.*[3] [late 19C] a type of firework. [echoic]

flip-flop *n.*[1] [20C] (US prison) 1 an individual who first gains parole and then returns to the same prison after breaking the terms of that parole or committing a new crime. 2 a bisexual.

flip-flop *n.*[2] [1960s–70s] mutual oral-genital stimulation (cf. SIXTY-NINE). [SE *flip-flop*, a somersault]

flip-flop *v.*[1] [1960s+] to indulge in gay sex. [SE *flip-flop*, to turn over, in this case for anal sex]

flip-flop *v.*[2] [1970s+] to change direction. [orig. computer use]

flip-flops *n.* [1920s+] (Aus.) bouncing breasts and the young women who have them. [the movement of the (unfettered) breast]

flip for *v.* [1950s+] (orig. US) to become fascinated, obsessed by. [FLIP v.[4]]

flip off *v.*[1] [1960s+] to masturbate (cf. BEAT OFF). [SE *flip*; note FLIP v.[2]]

flip off *v.*[2] [1960s+] to make an obscene, dismissive gesture by raising the middle finger from the otherwise clenched fist. [var. on FLIP THE BIRD]

flip one's bananas, to *phr.* [1970s] (US) to go suddenly insane. [SE *flip* + BANANAS adj.; note FLIP v.[4]]

flip one's bean/beanie, to *phr.* [1960s] (US) to go crazy, to lose emotional control. [SE *flip* + BEAN n.[4]]

flip one's cookies, to *phr.* [1950s+] to vomit (cf. TOSS ONE'S COOKIES). [SE *flip* + COOKIES n.[2]]

flip oneself off, to *phr.* [1930s+] (Aus.) to masturbate (cf. BEAT OFF).

flip one's gourd *see* BLOW ONE'S GOURD.

flip one's lid, to *phr.* [1940s+] (orig. US) to go crazy, to lose emotional control (cf. FLIP ONE'S TOP; FLIP ONE'S WIG). [SE *flip* + LID n.[1]]

flip one's top, to *phr.* [1940s–50s] (US Black) to go crazy, to lose one's temper (cf. BLOW ONE'S TOP; FLIP ONE'S LID). [SE *flip* + fig. use of *top*]

flip one's wig, to *phr.* [1930s+] (orig. US) to lose one's temper, to lose one's sanity (cf. FLIP ONE'S LID). [SE *flip* + WIG n.[1]]

flip-out *n.* [1960s+] (US) an eccentric, a madman. [FLIP OUT v.; one who has *flipped*]

flip out *v.* [1960s+] (US) to lose emotional control, to go mad (cf. FLIP ONE'S LID). [FLIP v.[4]]

flip over *v.* [1960s+] (gay) to make oneself available for anal intercourse (cf. FLIP-FLOP v.[1]). [SE *flip* + *over*]

flipper *n.*[1] [mid-19C+] the hand or arm (cf. FIN n.[1]). [reverse anthropomorphism]

flipper *n.*[2] [mid–late 19C+] (US) a pancake. [SE *flip*; one flips it over in the pan]

flipper *n.*[3] 1 [late 19C–1910s] (orig. US) a very young prostitute (cf. FLAPPER n.[3]). 2 [1960s] a friend.

flipper *n.*[4] [20C] (Irish) a messy, untidy man. [? he 'flips' things around]

flippers *n.* 1 [late 19C+] (US) the legs. 2 [1900s–40s] (US Black) the ears (cf. FLAPPERS).

flipping *adj.* 1 [1910s+] euph. for intensifier FUCKING; esp. in *flipping heck!* fucking hell! 2 [1960s+] (US campus) splendid.

flippy *adj.* [1950s–70s] crazy, eccentric. [FLIP n.[4] (4)]

flipside *n.* **1** [1950s+] the reverse. **2** [1980s+] (US gay) the anus. [rock music use, the 'other side' of a record, the B-side]

flip the bird, to *phr.* [1950s+] to make an obscene gesture (cf. FLAG A BONE; GIVE SOMEONE THE FINGER). [SE *flip* + BIRD n.[8] (2)]

flip the bishop, to *phr.* [late 19C+] to masturbate (cf. BANG THE BISHOP).

flip the bone *see* FLAG A BONE.

flip the scrip *see* FLIP DA SCRIP.

flipwreck *n.* [1940s+] (Aus.) **1** a person who has (supposedly) masturbated themselves into physical and mental decline. **2** a fool, an idiot. [FLIP v.[2]; pun on SE *shipwreck*]

flirt *n.[1]* [early 18C] a joke. [SE *flirt*, a smart tap or blow]

flirt *n.[2]* [early 19C] (US) a game of cards.

flirt-gill *n.* [late 16C–early 17C] a prostitute (cf. GILL-FLIRT). [SE *flirt* + *gill*, a lass, a wench]

flirtina cop-all *n.* [mid–late 19C] a prostitute. [play on SE *flirt* + fem. sfx. *-ina* + COP v.[1] + SE *all*]

flit *n.[1]* [1920s+] (US prison) prison-made coffee (cf. MOUTHWASH n.[2]; SPOW). [brandname *Flit*, an insect repellent spray]

flit *n.[2]* [1930s+] (US) **1** a male homosexual. **2** a silly person. [SE *flit*, a flutter, a light movement; the stereotypical effeminacy of male homosexuals]

flit *n.[3]* [1940s+] (US) drunkenness. [SE *flit*, a sudden movement]

flit *v.* [late 19C] (US) to run away, to escape.

flitter *n.* [19C] (US) the vagina (cf. APPLE n.[10]). [dial. *flitter*, a pancake]

flitter *v.* [1920s+] (Irish) to reduce to rags and tatters, both lit. and fig. [dial. *flitter*, to fluster]

flivver *n.* (US) **1** [1900s–60s] a failure, disappointment or something cheap and inferior. **2** [1910s] something or someone that has a negative influence on others. **3** [1910s+] a cheap automobile, spec. a Model T Ford. [ety. unknown; note US Navy 1920s use, 'a destroyer of 750 tons or less']

flo *see* AUNT FLO.

float *n.* [1960s] a small loan. [SE *float*, a sum of money in a shop used to provide change etc at the start of business]

float *v.[1]* **1** [late 19C] (US) to leave. **2** [late 19C+] (orig. US) to wander around. **3** [20C] (Aus.) to die. **4** [1910s+] to leave, to go.

float *v.[2]* [1950s+] (drugs) to experience the 'other-worldliness' that can accompany the use of certain drugs, typically cannabis and the hallucinogens (cf. FLY v.[3]). [play on SE *float*; one of a number of drug-related synon. that play on 'getting high']

float an air biscuit, to *phr.* [1990s] to break wind silently, but with a pervasive odour. [SE *float* + AIR BISCUIT]

float around *v.* [20C] to wander aimlessly. [ext. of FLOAT v.[1]]

floater *n.[1]* **1** [mid-19C+] (US) a migratory worker. **2** [1930s+] (prison) an old magazine, book or newspaper that is smuggled irregularly from cell to cell. **3** [1960s+] (gay) a gay prostitute who works only in towns where he is unknown and in which he does not live. [FLOAT v.[1]]

floater *n.[2]* **1** [mid-19C] a suet dumpling. **2** [late 19C+] (orig. US) a dead body found floating in water. **3** [20C] (Aus.) a meat pie floating in pea soup. **4** [20C] (N.Z.) a fried scone.

floater *n.[3]* [19C] the penis (cf. FLAPPER n.[1]).

floater *n.[4]* [1910s+] an error, a *faux pas*. [orig. Oxbridge use; ? corruption of *faux pas* as 'foper', thence 'floater'; SE *float*, to circulate a rumour]

floater *n.[5]* [1910s+] (US) **1** an official order to leave a town or district. **2** a sentence suspended on condition that the offender leaves the area.

floater *n.[6]* [1940s+] (Aus.) in two-up, a coin that fails to spin.

floater *n.[7]* [1970s] (US drugs) a Quaalude. [the sensations it creates in the user]

floaters/flying flies *n.* [1950s+] spots before one's eyes.

floating academy *n.* [19C] the prison hulks (cf. ADKINS'S ACADEMY). [SE *floating* + ACADEMY n. (4); run-down or part-derelict ships, no longer seaworthy, were recycled as prison ships, moored in the Thames estuary]

floating boat *n.* [1950s] (W.I.) cooked breadfruit. [? resemblance]

floating bullet *n.* [1940s+] (W.I.) a large, spherical cooked breadfruit. [? resemblance]

floating buoy *n.* [1950s] (W.I.) a dumpling made of flour and baking soda; it rises to the surface when cooking. [? resemblance]

float the note, to *phr.* [1990s] (US teen) to loan money to a friend to get them to participate in an activity. [SE *float*, to arrange a loan]

float-up *n.* [20C] (N.Z.) a casual approach to someone. [FLOAT UP]

float up *v.* [20C] (N.Z.) to approach casually, to stroll up. [FLOAT v.[1] (2)]

flob *v.* [1930s+] (mainly juv.) to spit. [echoic]

flock *n.* [1930s+] (US) those women currently working for a pimp (cf. STABLE).

flock/nest of sparrows flying out of one's backside *phr.* [1950s+] (Aus.) a phr. used to describe the sensation of the male orgasm, also as *geese/peacocks/swallows flying out* ... .

flock of starlings *n.* [1990s] small pieces of excrement.

flog *v.[1]* **1** [late 17C] (Und.) to whip. **2** [mid-19C] to beat, to surpass. **3** [20C] to masturbate. [(1) SE from 1800]

flog *v.[2]* **1** [late 18C+] to proceed by violent or painful effort, also as *flog on*. **2** [late 18C+] to obtain, usu. by violent effort. **3** [1970s+] (US) to hurry; thus *flog it*. [SE *flog*, to urge forward (a horse etc) by flogging]

flog *v.[3]* **1** [1910s+] to sell, currently non-specific, but orig. with criminal overtones (cf. KNOCK OUT). **2** [1980s+] (US) to advertise. [for ety. *see* FLOG v.[2]; here it is the merchandise that is being 'urged']

flogged at the tumbler *phr.* [late 17C–mid-18C] whipped at the cart's end, a judicial punishment (cf. SHOVE THE TUMBLER). [SE *flogged* + TUMBLER n.[2]]

flogger *n.[1]* [late 18C–early 19C] (Und.) a whip. [FLOG v.[1] (1)]

flogger *n.[2]* [20C] (Aus.) a morning coat. [pun on FLOGGER n.[1]: like a whip, esp. a cat-o-nine-tails, it has 'tails']

flogging *n.* [mid-19C+] saving up one's money carefully. [FLOG v.[2]]

flogging *adj.[1]* [late 19C] mean, grasping. [FLOGGING n.]

flogging *adj.[2]* [1920s+] (Aus.) euph. for FUCKING adj.

flogging-cove *n.* [16C–19C] **1** a beadle. **2** one who gives out corporal punishment as authorized by the courts. [FLOG v.[1] + COVE]

flogging cully *n.* [late 17C–late 18C] one who enjoys receiving a whipping as sexual stimulation. [FLOG v.[1] + CULLY]

flog my dolphin! *excl.* [1980s+] (US) a general excl. of surprise.

flog one's chops, to *phr.* [1940s+] (Aus.) to work very hard. [FLOG v.[1] + CHOPS n. (3)]

flog one's dong, to *phr.* [20C] to masturbate (cf. FLOG ONE'S DONKEY; FLOG ONE'S DUMBER BROTHER; FLOG ONE'S MUTTON; FLOG THE DOG; FLOG THE DOLPHIN; FLOG THE HOG; FLOG THE INFIDEL; FLOG THE LOG). [FLOG v.[1] + DONG n.[2]]

flog one's donkey, to *phr.* [late 19C+] to masturbate (cf. FLOG ONE'S DONG). [FLOG v.[1] + DONKEY n.[2]]

flog one's dumber brother, to *phr.* [20C] to masturbate (cf. FLOG ONE'S DONG). [FLOG v.[1] + joc. phr.]

flog one's dummy *see* BEAT ONE'S DUMMY.

flog one's mutton, to *phr.* [late 19C+] to masturbate (cf. ACCOST THE OSCAR MEYER; FLOG ONE'S DONG). [FLOG v.[1] + MUTTON n.[1] (2)]

flogster *n.* [late 19C+] one who enjoys flagellation for sexual purposes. [FLOG v.[1] + sfx. -STER]

flog the bishop *see* BANG THE BISHOP.

flog the clock, to *phr.* [late 19C] to move the clock's hands forward.

flog the daisy *see* BEAT THE DAISY.

flog the dog, to *phr.* [20C] to masturbate (cf. BEAT THE DOG; FLOG ONE'S DONG). [FLOG v.[1] + DOG n.[13]]

flog/stroke/swing the dolphin/finless dolphin, to *phr.* [1920s+] (orig. naut.) to masturbate (cf. FLOG ONE'S DONG).

flog the hog, to *phr.* [20C] to masturbate (cf. FLOG ONE'S DONG). [FLOG v.[1] + HOG n.[4]]

flog the infidel, to *phr.* [20C] to masturbate (cf. FLOG ONE'S DONG). [FLOG v.[1] + *infidel*, which is lit. 'unfaithful' to one's partner]

flog the log, to *phr.* [1950s+] to masturbate (cf. FLOG ONE'S DONG). [FLOG v.[1] + LOG n.[5]]

flood *v.* (US Black) **1** [1920s–30s] to have a menstrual period. **2** [1970s+] to have an erection, for the penis to 'flood' with blood.

flood-pants *n.* [20C] (W.I.) a (young) man's trousers that are too short and narrow (cf. BID-DIMS. [such trousers are ideal for walking through a flood – the legs are too short to get wet]

flooey! *excl.* [20C] (orig. US) an echoic excl. designed to resemble the sound of an explosion.

floor *n.* [mid-19C–1910s] **1** something that confounds or confuses. **2** a miscalculation, an error. [one is knocked to the SE *floor*]

floor *v.*[1] **1** [early–mid 19C+] to confuse, to confound, to puzzle, to defeat intellectually. **2** [early 19C+] to knock down, to defeat utterly. **3** [mid-19C] to drink alcohol. **4** [mid-19C] to finish properly, to do thoroughly. [boxing or wrestling imagery; SE *floor*, to knock to the ground]

floor *v.*[2] [1950s+] (orig. US) to make a car go faster by pressing the relevant pedal; thus *four on the floor*, a gearshift on the floor of the car, instead of on the steering wheel. [abbr. FLOOR-BOARD]

floorboard *v.* [1940s+] (US) to make a car go faster. [the pressing down on the accelerator pedal]

floorburners *n.* [1950s–70s] (US Black) shoes. [the idea of heat being generated by wildly dancing feet]

floored *adj.* **1** [early 19C] very drunk. **2** [early 19C+] astounded, amazed, confused. [FLOOR v.[1]]

floorer *n.* [mid-19C] a blow that will knock its recipient down; thus anything, e.g. a piece of bad news, that renders its recipient 'floored'. [FLOOR v.[1]]

floor fuck *n.* [1910s+] (orig. Aus.) sexual intercourse on the floor. [SE *floor* + FUCK n.[1]]

floor fuck *v.* [1910s+] (orig. Aus.) to have sexual intercourse on the floor. [FLOOR FUCK n.]

floor one's licks, to *phr.* [mid–late 19C] to surpass, to do very well. [FLOOR v.[1] + LICK n.[2]]

floor polish *v.* [1940s+] to defeat comprehensively (cf. MOP THE FLOOR WITH). [pun]

floozie/floosie *n.* [20C] (orig. US) a promiscuous young woman. [dial. *floosy*, flossy; thus soft. Note Irish *Floozie in the Jacuzzi*, the monument in O'Connell Street, Dublin, representing the spirit of the River Liffey]

floozie *adj.* [20C] (US) **1** showy, stylish. **2** over-dressed, over-made-up. **3** silly or light-headed. [FLOOZIE n.]

floozie up *v.* [20C] (US) to embellish, either of one's own appearance or by adding decoration to a garment (cf. TART UP). [FLOOZIE n.]

flop *n.*[1] [19C] (US campus) **1** any action by which someone else is deceived. **2** any form of cheating in an examination that leads to scoring high marks. [SE *flop*, i.e. one fig. lets something fall on the person one is cheating]

flop *n.*[2] [late 19C] a woman's hairstyle, in which the hair is worn low over the brow. [Ware notes the synon. *cretin* and *poodle* style]

flop *n.*[3] [late 19C–1910s] (US) a sudden political change of policy. [abbr. SE *flip-flop*]

flop *n.*[4] **1** [late 19C+] (orig. US) a failure, esp. of a film or stage play. **2** [1900s–30s] a weak, flabby person. **3** [1900s–30s] a fat, ungainly, slovenly person, esp. a woman (cf. FLOPPY n.[1]). **4** [1900s–30s] a dull, unpleasant person, a misfit, a failure. **5** [1900s–50s] (US Und.) an arrest. **6** [1950s+] (US prison) the rejection of one's application for parole (cf. KNOCKBACK n.[1]).

flop *n.*[5] **1** [1910s+] (US) a cheap room or bed (cf. FLOPHOUSE). **2** [1910s+] (US) a drunk who has passed out and as such a possible victim for a robber. **3** [1910s–50s] (US) a sleep, esp. a prisoner's last night in prison (cf. WAKE-UP n.[3]). **4** [1920s–50s] (US Und.) a helpless or sleeping beggar. **5** [1920s–60s] (US) an act of sexual intercourse (cf. FLOP A JUDY). **6** [1960s+] (Und.) anywhere a thief or gang can leave the loot so as to avoid detection during the immediate aftermath of a crime. [SE *flop*, to fall down in a heap]

flop *n.*[6] [1950s+] (US) excrement, esp. *cow-flop*. [Wilts. dial. *flop*, thick liquid]

flop *v.* **1** [mid-19C] (US campus) to cheat in an examination, esp. by faking sickness. **2** [mid-19C–1910s] (US) to knock down an opponent. **3** [late 19C–1960s] (US) to copulate (cf. FLOP A JUDY). **4** [20C] to fall asleep, to go to bed. **5** [1900s–70s] (US) to become enamoured of someone. **6** [1910s] (US Und.) to short-change. **7** [1910s–30s] (US) to fall to the ground for protection. **8** [1910s+] to collapse, to fail, esp. of a stage entertainment or similar undertaking.

flop about/round *v.* [late 19C+] to lie around.

flop a judy, to *phr.* [late 19C] to lay a woman down preparatory to intercourse. [FLOP v. (3) + JUDY n.[1]]

flop-ear *see* LOP-EAR.

floperoo *n.* [1950s+] (orig. US) an extreme failure, esp. a in show business context. [FLOP n.[4] (1) + sfx. -EROO]

flophouse *n.* [late 19C+] (US) **1** a lodging house or night shelter for tramps, down-and-outs, alcoholics etc. **2** a cheap restaurant or café. **3** a prison. [FLOP n.[5] (1) + SE *house*]

flop in *v.* [19C] of a man, to enter a woman before intercourse (cf. FLOP v.).

flop joint *n.* [late 19C+] (US) a tramp's lodging, a cheap hotel (cf. FLOPHOUSE). [FLOP n.[5] (1) + JOINT n.[3] (3)]

flop on the gills *n.* [mid–late 19C] a punch in the mouth. [Yorks. dial. *flop*, a blow, a slap]

flop out *v.* [1910s–20s] to knock down, to make someone fall into a heap. [Yorks. dial. *flop*, to strike with a sudden blow]

flopover *v.* [1960s+] to assume a position with the buttocks in the air or with the body bent at 45° and the hands thus supported by the knees, either of which will permit the easy introduction of the penis into the anus or vagina.

flopped out *adj.* [20C] (US) exhausted, tired out. [FLOP v. (4)]

flopper *n.* **1** [late 19C+] (US Und.) a criminal who pretends to have 'slipped' on a shop floor or 'been knocked down' by a slow-moving automobile; they then claim damages, usu. offering to take a quick cash payment rather than go to an insurance company. **2** [1910s+] (US Und.) a beggar who pretends to be crippled. **3** [1910s] (US Und.) a petty swindler. **4** [1910s–20s] a weakling, a spineless person. [FLOP v.]

flopper-stopper *n.* [1950s+] (Aus./US) a brassiere (cf. BOULDER-HOLDER).

floppy *n.*[1] [20C] (US) a fat, ungainly, slovenly person, esp. a woman. [FLOP n.[4] (3) + sfx. -y]

floppy *n.*[2] [1970s+] (S.Afr.) a derog. term for a Black person. [orig. Rhodesian milit. use, one who 'flops down dead' when hit by bullets; the targets of such bullets were invariably Black]

floptious *adj.* [20C] (Irish) generous. [? the gifts *flop* into the receiver's hand]

flop-whop *n.* [late 19C] a heavy fall. [echoic]

floral arrangement *n.* [1960s+] (US gay) a spintry, i.e. a circle of three or more people, hetero- or homosexual, all linked physically in mutual sex acts. [pun on DAISY CHAIN]

flor di cabbagio *n.* [late 19C+] a cheap cigar (cf. CABBAGE LEAF n.¹). [CABBAGIO PERFUMO]

florence *n.* [late 17C–18C] **1** a prostitute. **2** an untidily dressed young woman. [Northants. dial. *florence*, one who dresses untidily; whether this comes from the proper name and thus memorializes a long-forgotten woman is unknown]

florid *adj.* [late 18C–mid-19C] tipsy. [i.e. red-faced with the drink]

Florida *n.* [20C] (US prison) the solitary confinement/ punishment block. [the siting of such cells in the warmest areas of the prison, often underground]

Florida chicken *n.* [20C] (US) a turtle (cf. ADIRONDACK STEAK). [the abundance of the turtle, *Gopherus polyphemus*]

Florida snow *n.* [1980s+] (drugs) cocaine. [*Florida* + SNOW n.²; the centrality of Miami, Florida, to the cocaine trade]

florin *n.* [1990s] excrement (cf. BRAD; EARTHA; WILLIAM n.³). [rhy. sl. *florin* = 'two bob bit' = SHIT n.¹]

floss *n.* [1990s] (US) money. [ety. unknown]

flossed up *adj.* [1960s+] of a woman, made up, dressed up (cf. TARTED UP). [? FLOOZIE adj. or FLOSSY adj.]

flossie/flossy *n.* [late 19C+] (Aus./N.Z./S.Afr.) **1** a prostitute. **2** a girlfriend who is older than her partner. **3** an overdressed, over-affectionate woman. [FLOOZIE n.]

floss the cat, to *phr.* [1990s] of a woman, to masturbate. [SE *floss*, to clean the teeth with dental floss + CAT n.⁴]

flossy *n. see* FLOSSIE.

flossy *adj.* [late 19C+] (US) showy, slick, saucy, impertinent, ostentatious (cf. FLOOZIE adj.). [SE *floss*, silk used for embroidery]

flossy/flossy up *v.* [1950s+] (Aus.) to dress oneself up, esp. in a showy, excessive manner. [FLOOZIE v.]

floster *n.* [late 19C] a mixed drink consisting of sherry, soda-water, lemon, ice etc. [ety. unknown]

flounder *n.¹* [mid-19C+] a taxi-cab. [rhy. sl. *flounder and dab* = cab]

flounder *n.²* [mid-late 19C] a drowned man (cf. DAB n.³). [pun]

flounder *n.³* [1910s] (US) a Newfoundlander. [SE *flounder* n.; i.e. the fishing industry]

flounder mouth *n.* [20C] (US) a person with a notably large mouth. [SE *flounder*, a fish with a large mouth]

flour hungry *adj.* [1990s] used of a large woman. [phr. 'I had to roll her in flour and look for the wet patch']

flour mixer *n.¹* [20C] a non-Jewish woman. [rhy. sl. *flour-mixer* = Yid. *shikse*, a Gentile woman]

flour mixer *n.²* [1970s] an inoffensive man, a clerk. [? the presumed 'femininity' of the task, or the cartoon flour-mixer featured in a well-known advertisement]

flous *v.* [1900s–10s] (S.Afr.) to cheat, to trick, to put at a disadvantage. [Ger. *Flause*, deceit]

floush/go flouch *v.* [early 19C] to collapse. [echoic]

flow *v.* [1990s] (orig. US Black) to perform rap music, esp. in one's creation of lyrics, very well.

flower *n.¹* [20C] an effeminate male homosexual (cf. BUTTERCUP; LILY n.⁵; PANSY). [the 'feminine' image of flowers]

flower *n.²* [1960s] (drugs) marijuana.

flower-fancier *n.* [late 19C–1900s] a womanizer, a lecher, presumably specializing in 'flowers', i.e. virgins.

flower of chivalry *n.* [19C] the vagina (cf. BEAUTY SPOT n.¹). [pun on orig. use of SE *chivalry*, a body of men who ride; thus cf. RIDE v.¹]

flowerpot *n.* [19C] the vagina (cf. BEAUTY SPOT n.¹).

flowers *n.* **1** [mid–late 19C] euph. for menstruation. **2** [1970s+] (US) the vulva; thus *eat someone's flowers*, to perform cunnilingus. [prior use of (1) is SE since 15C]

flowers and frolics *see* FUN AND FROLICS.

flower tops *n.* [1960s+] (drugs) marijuana. [the most powerful part of the plant]

flowery dell *n.¹* [mid-19C] a room, especially a room in an inn. [pedlars' Ling. Fr.]

flowery dell *n.²* [1920s+] a cell. [rhy. sl.]

flowing hope *n.* [mid–late 19C] **1** the losers at a gaming table. **2** a gambler's last, despairing bet. [for ety. *see* FORLORN HOPE]

flub *v.* [1920s+] (US) **1** to botch, to bungle, to make a mess of. **2** to confuse. **3** to waste time, to fool around. [? link to FLUFF v.¹]

flubdub *v.* [20C] (US) to mess around, to waste time. [FLUB + redup. or ? DUB n.²]

flub the dub, to *phr.* [20C] (US) **1** (orig. milit.) to shirk, to evade one's duties. **2** to blunder, to fail in a task. **3** to masturbate. [FLUBDUB]

flue *n.¹* [1940s–50s] (prison) a warder. [rhy. sl. *flue* = SCREW n.²]

flue *n.²* **1** [early–mid-19C] a lift formerly in use in pawnbrokers' shops, up which the articles pawned were taken for storage (cf. SPOUT v.¹). **2** [late 19C+] (US) the vagina. **3** [20C] the anus. **4** [1970s+] (US Und.) the envelope supposedly containing money in a swindle. [SE *flue*, a chimney, thus any form of passage for conveying heat]

flue *v.* [late 19C] to put in pawn. [FLUE n.² (1)]

flue-faker *n.* [19C] **1** a chimney-sweep. **2** (racing) 'low sporting characters, who are so termed from their chiefly betting on the Great Sweeps' (sweepstakes) (Hotten, 1860). [SE *flue* + FAKER n.²]

fluence *n.* [1900s+] (Aus./N.Z.) **1** hypnotism (cf. PUT THE FLUENCE ON). **2** delicate, subtle influence, either in the context of business, politics etc or in actual physical acts, e.g. the spinning of a cricket ball.

fluff *n.¹* **1** [mid-19C] the female pubic hair (cf. BADGER n.⁷). **2** [1910s+] a young, attractive, but empty-headed woman, esp. in phr. *bit/piece of fluff*. **3** [1960s+] the passive partner in a lesbian couple (cf. FEMME). **4** [1970s+] (US Black) the vagina.

fluff *n.²* [1920s+] (Aus.) a railway ticket. [ety. unknown; ? link to FLUFF v.¹ (2)]

fluff *n.³* [1930s] (Aus.) rubbish, nonsense.

fluff *v.¹* **1** [mid–late 19C] of railway booking clerks, to give short change. **2** [mid-19C+] (orig. theatrical) to make a mistake. **3** [late 19C] to disconcert or put off a public speaker. **4** [1900s–50s] to bluff, to lie. **5** [1900s–50s] to falsify (accounts etc).

fluff *v.²* [1960s+] (N.Z. juv./US campus) to break wind. [echoic + SE *fluff*, a puff, an explosion]

fluffed *adj.* [mid-19C] drunk (cf. ADDLED). [FLUFF v.¹ (2)]

fluffer *n.¹* [late 19C] a drunkard. [FLUFFED]

fluffer *n.²* [1980s+] (US) a person employed on a film set to arouse an actor physically before filming a sexual episode. [SE *fluff*, a puff, a quick, short blast, a whiff, a slight explosion]

fluff in *v.* [late 19C] to deceive by smooth talk. [SE *fluff*, to puff]

fluffiness *n.* [late 19C] drunkenness. [FLUFFED]

fluff in the pan *n.* [mid–late 19C] a failure. [FLUFF v.¹ (2) + play on phr. FLASH IN THE PAN]

fluff it! *excl.* [mid-19C] take it away! I don't want it!

fluff off *v.¹* [1940s+] (US) to dismiss or reject. [SE *fluff*, to blow, to puff]

fluff off *v.²* [1950s+] to avoid work, to shirk. [? euph. for FUCK OFF v.]

fluffy adj. **1** [late 19C] drunk and incapable (cf. ADDLED). **2** [1990s] gentle, unaggressive, sympathetic (cf. SPIKY adj.). [SE *fluffy*, soft, covered in down]

flugens! excl. [19C+] a general, mild oath (cf. DICKENS; HELL!; TARNATION!). [ety. unknown; ? link to Ger.]

fluke n.[1] [early 19C] a gullible victim (cf. FLAT n.[2]). [SE *fluke*, a flat fish]

fluke n.[2] **1** [mid-19C+] an unforeseen success, a piece of unexpected good luck; thus *flukiness*, fortuitous good fortune. **2** [20C] (orig. US campus) a failure, a worthless person or thing. [? billiards jargon *fluke*, to succeed in a given shot more through luck than judgement; thus a player who wins through flukes cannot be judged as capable as one who wins through skill alone; ult. ety. unknown; ? link to dial. *fluke*, a guess]

fluke v.[1] [mid-19C+] to get a piece of good luck. [FLUKE n.[2]; the implication is always one of some degree of unfairness in such luck]

fluke v.[2] **1** [20C] to fail. **2** [20C] to steal. **3** [20C] to back out, to renege on a promise. **4** [1950s] (US) to die; thus *fluke out*.

fluky adj. **1** [mid-19C+] lucky. **2** [1910s+] (US) peculiar, bizarre. [FLUKE n.[2] + sfx. -y]

flumdiddle n. [1910s–20s] empty flattery, humbug. [FLUMMERY + DIDDLE n.[4]]

flumdoodle v. [1910s+] (Aus.) to cheat, to trick, to hoax (someone). [FLUMDIDDLE]

flummadiddle n. [19C+] (US) **1** nonsense, empty flattery, humbug. **2** something trivial or ridiculous. [? FLUMMERY + DIDDLE n.[4]. *Flummery* was also a variety of sweet dish; thus note *flummadiddle*, 'stale bread, pork-fat, molasses, cinnamon, allspice, [from which] a kind of mush is made, which is baked in the oven and brought to the table hot and brown' (Schele de Vere, *Americanisms*, 1872)]

flummergast v. [mid-19C] to astound, to astonish, to confuse. [FLUMMERY + FLABBERGAST]

flummery n. [mid-18C–early 19C] empty flattery, humbug (cf. FLUMDIDDLE; FLUMMADIDDLE). [later use is SE; for ety. see FLUMMADIDDLE]

flummocky adj. [late 19C] in poor taste. [FLUMMOX n.]

flummox n. [19C] (US) **1** a failure. **2** a stupid person. [FLUMMOX v.[1]]

flummox/flummux v.[1] [19C+] **1** to fool, to confuse, to overcome (by trickery). **2** to avoid. **3** to disappoint. **4** (US) to blunder, to fail. **5** to move in a clumsy manner. **6** to back down, to back out of a promise. [? dial. *flummocks*, to maul, to mangle; *flummock* n., a slovenly person or *flummock* v., to make untidy, to disorder, to confuse, to bewilder + onomat. element based on throwing down roughly and untidily. As such, the term is reminiscent of *flump*, a hummock, and *slommock*, a sloven]

flummox v.[2] [mid-late 19C] (US) to titivate one's hair. [fig. use of FLUMMOX v.[1]]

flummox by the lip, to phr. [19C] to talk down. [FLUMMOX v.[1]]

flummoxed adj.[1] [mid-19C+] **1** confused, let down, outwitted. **2** ruined. **3** drunk (cf. ADDLED). [FLUMMOX v.[1]]

flummoxed/flummuxed adj.[2] [mid-19C] (Und.) imprisoned for one month. [fig. use of FLUMMOX v.[1]; in tramp jargon *flummoxed* refers to a place that is unsafe to visit, the owners or guardians are likely to have one imprisoned]

flummut n. [mid-late 19C] a one-month prison sentence. [tramp/tinker use, *flummut*, a mark placed on a door to indicate a house that will be unfriendly; 'flummut, sure of a month in quod' (Mayhew)]

flummut adj. [mid-late 19C] dangerous. [FLUMMUT n.]

flummux see FLUMMOX v.[1].

flummuxed see FLUMMOXED adj.[2].

flump n. **1** [late 18C+] a sudden heavy fall. **2** [1990s] (US teen) the act of sitting down in a casual manner. [dial./echoic]

flump v. [late 18C+] to collapse or fall heavily. [FLUMP n.]

flunk n.[1] **1** [mid-19C–1960s] (US campus) a total failure in academic work, a grade F; thus a student who has failed. **2** [late 19C+] (US) a failure. **3** [late 19C+] (US) an idler, a loafer. [FLUNK v.]

flunk n.[2] [1920s–30s] (US Und.) the strongbox within a safe. [ety. unknown]

flunk/flunk out v. **1** [early 19C+] (US campus) to fail an examination. **2** [early 19C+] (US campus) to be dismissed or to dismiss on the grounds of academic failure. **3** [early 19C+] (US) to give in, back down or renege in a cowardly manner. **4** [late 19C+] (US) to blunder, to make a mistake. **5** [late 19C+] to embarrass someone (by an indiscreet remark). **6** [late 19C+] (orig. US) to do a skimpy, inadequate job. [? US dial. *flink*, ult. SE *flinch*, to act in a cowardly way, to shrink from one's duties; + 18C Oxford jargon (later sl.) *funk*, to exhibit a state of complete fear or panic]

flunky n.[1] **1** [19C+] (US campus) one who fails an examination (cf. FLUNK v.). **2** [20C] (US Black) a stooge. **3** [20C] (US) an assistant cook in a mining or lumber camp. [SE *flunkey*, servant]

flunky n.[2] [20C] a condom. [? joc. use of FLUNK n.[1]]

flurry one's milk, to phr. [early–mid-19C] to be worried, perturbed, annoyed. [SE *flurry*, to agitate]

flush n.[1] [1940s+] (W.I.) a 6-month prison sentence (cf. PINT; QUART n.[2]). [ety. unknown]

flush n.[2] [1960s+] (US) the lavatory.

flush/flush in the pocket adj.[1] [early 17C–late 18C] well-supplied with money. [SE *flush*, to burst with, usu. of a stream or river. The term remained sl. (the image being of a pocket running over with money) until 19C when it became SE]

flush adj.[2] [19C] drunk. [the level of the liquid that is *flush* with the rim of the glass]

flush v. [mid-19C] to whip; thus *flushed on the horse*, privately whipped in prison. [some punitive whipping was still carried out in public; the *horse* is a wooden frame to which the victim is secured]

flush a wild duck, to phr. [19C] to single out a woman in the hope of seducing her. [sporting imagery]

flustered adj. [late 17C–19C] drunk (cf. ADDLED). [17C SE *fluster*, to make half-tipsy]

flusticate v. [late 19C] to confuse. [SE *fluster*]

flustrate v. [early 18C] to confuse, to excite; thus *flustration*, excitement, confusion, bustle. [SE *fluster*]

flute n.[1] [early 18C] the Recorder of London. [pun on SE *recorder*, a flute-like instrument]

flute n.[2] **1** [19C+] the penis (cf. LIVING FLUTE; PINK OBOE; SILENT FLUTE; SKIN FLUTE). **2** [late 19C+] a policeman's whistle. **3** [late 19C] (US drugs) an opium pipe; thus *hit the flute*, to smoke opium.

flute n.[3] [mid-19C] a pistol. [resemblance]

flute v. [late 19C+] (Aus.) to talk incessantly; thus *pass the flute*, to let someone else speak, *hold the flute*, to monopolize the conversation, *on the flute*, talking continually. [SE *flute* v.]

flute! excl. [20C] (Irish) a general excl. of surprise, annoyance. [? euph. for FUCK!]

flute mute n. [1990s] a condom. [FLUTE n.[2] (1) + SE *mute*]

flute-player n. [1950s+] (US) a fellator or fellatrix (cf. CLARINET-PLAYER). [FLUTE n.[2] (1) + pun]

fluter n.[1] [late 19C+] (Aus.) an incessant talker. [FLUTE v.]

fluter n.[2] [1970s+] a fellator or fellatrix. [FLUTE n.[2] (1)]

flutter n.[1] [19C] any form of sexual experience; thus *be on the* *flutter*, to be a sexual sophisticate, *do/have a flutter*, to enjoy hedonistic rather than procreative intercourse, *have had a flutter*, to have lost one's virginity.

flutter *n.²* **1** [mid–late 19C] an attempt, a try. **2** [late 19C+] a bet, usu. presumed to be small, unless used ironically, usu. in phr. *have a flutter*. [the excitement that flutters one's heart or the punter fluttering their money at the bookmaker]

flutter *n.³* **1** [mid-19C] a spree, an adventure. **2** [mid–late 19C] a small, swift trip. **3** [mid–late 19C] a burst of speed.

flutter *v.¹* [mid–late 19C] to have sexual intercourse; thus *flutter a judy*, to pursue and/or seduce a woman (cf. JIGGLE).

flutter *v.²* [late 19C] **1** to enjoy oneself. **2** to gamble, to wager. [FLUTTER *n.²*]

flutter a skirt, to *phr.* [late 19C–1900s] to work as a prostitute.

flutterbudget *n.* [20C] (US) a particularly fussy person. [var. on FUSSBUDGET]

flutter someone's kidneys, to *phr.* [late 19C] to annoy, to disturb, to irritate.

flutter the ribands/ribbons, to *phr.* [mid-19C] to drive a coach.

flux *v.¹* [late 18C] to salivate. [SE *flux*, to make salivate, to purge]

flux *v.²* [late 18C] to cheat, to deceive. [SE *flux*, to confuse]

fly *n.¹* [late 18C] (Und.) a wagon. [SE *fly*, a fast carriage, a stage-coach]

fly *n.²* [mid-19C] a trick, a dodge. [SE *fly*; i.e. one is 'flying a kite']

fly *n.³* [mid-19C] a policeman. [pun on BLUEBOTTLE]

fly *n.⁴* [late 19C–1920s] (US) a plain-clothes policeman, a detective. [FLY adj. (3)]

fly *n.⁵* [late 19C] the act of tossing a coin. [SE *fly*, a throw, a toss]

fly *adj.* **1** [early–mid-19C] aware, knowledgeable; thus [mid-19C+] (orig. Aus.) *no flies on*, nothing slow or dull-witted, or nothing wrong with. **2** [mid-19C] dextrous, agile. **3** [mid-19C] smart, sharp, perspicacious. **4** [late 19C] of a woman, promiscuous, flirtatious. **5** [late 19C+] (US) insolent, brash. **6** [late 19C–1940s] (US) rebellious, uninhibited in behaviour. **7** [1970s+] (US campus) of a female, attractive, pretty, stylish. [Scots *flee*, aware; 20C US Black uses may be further influenced by Gullah *fly*, to be fast and ecstatic]

fly *v.¹* [mid-19C] to lift, to raise; thus *fly a window*, to open a (sash) window for the purpose of breaking into a house (cf. FLY THE MAGS). [note theatre jargon *fly*, to suspend scenery or lights from above the stage]

fly *v.²* **1** [mid-late 19C] to send quickly. **2** [mid-19C+] to go quickly, to rush, esp. in phr. *I must fly*, I must hurry away. [fig. uses of SE]

fly *v.³* [1950s+] (US drugs) to take or to be intoxicated by psychotropic drugs. [one gets 'high']

fly *v.⁴* [1980s+] to meet with approval. [the same metaphorical 'flag' as found in the SE phr. *run it up the flagpole and we'll see who salutes*]

fly a/the blue pigeon, to *phr.* [late 18C–mid-19C] to steal the lead from a church roof; thus *pigeon-flying*, conducting such thefts (cf. BLUE PIGEON). [FLY *v.²* + BLUE PIGEON]

fly a flag, to *phr.¹* **1** [20C] to betray one's personality, esp. in a situation, e.g. prison, where such honesty may be foolish. **2** [1990s] (US Black teen) to wear gang colours.

fly a flag, to *phr.²* [20C] (US) to be menstruating (cf. FLYING BAKER; HAVE THE FLAG OUT; PUT ONE'S FLAG OUT). [var. on FLY THE RED FLAG]

fly a kite, to *phr.¹* **1** [mid-19C] to obtain credit against bills, whether or not the 'paper' is valid or fraudulent (cf. RAISE THE WIND). **2** [late 19C] to raise money. **3** [1930s+] to pass a dud cheque, ext. as *fly a dodgy kite*. [SE *fly* + KITE *n.¹*]

fly a kite, to *phr.²* **1** [late 19C] to make public, to publicize. **2** [20C] (US) to show off, to make a big display. **3** [1920s+] to present a false front or a deceitful line of talk in order to persuade one's victim that one's intentions are other than they really are. **4** [1930s+] to sound out public opinion, by taking initial steps in a given project or idea.

fly a kite at, to *phr.* [mid-19C] to court, to pursue a woman.

fly a line, to *phr.* [mid-19C] to send a letter (cf. DROP A LINE). [FLY *v.²* + SE *line*, a short letter or note]

fly around *v.* [mid-19C] (US) to get busy, to rush about. [FLY *v.²* (2)]

fly around and tear one's shirt, to *phr.* [late 19C–1900s] to get on with things. [ext. of FLY AROUND]

fly a tile, to *phr.* [early 19C] to knock off a man's hat as a form of practical joke. [FLY *v.¹* + TILE]

fly-away *n.* **1** [late 19C] a tricycle. **2** [1910s–30s] (US) a deserter.

flyball *n.* [20C] (US) a male homosexual. [? pun on baseball jargon *flyball*, a ball that can be caught 'on the fly']

fly-blow *n.* [mid–late 19C] an illegitimate child. [BY-BLOW + ? SE *fly-blown*]

flyblow *v.* [20C] **1** (US) to gossip maliciously about an absent third party, to attack behind one's back. **2** (Aus.) to take money from someone, often by chicanery. [SE *flyblow*, the egg of a fly, which turns into a maggot that will, in this context, figuratively devour the victim's reputation or money]

fly-blown *adj.* **1** [19C] drunk. **2** [mid-19C–1920s] (Aus./N.Z.) ruined, penniless, without funds. **3** [late 19C] deflowered. **4** [late 19C] suspected of carrying venereal disease. **5** [late 19C] tired out, exhausted. [FLYBLOW *v.* (2) + fig. uses of SE]

flybog *n.* [1920s+] (Aus.) treacle, jam. [flies that land on jam tend to get stuck]

fly-boy *n.¹* **1** [late 19C+] (US Black) a shrewd, intelligent young man. **2** [late 19C+] (US Black) a sophisticated, stylish young man. **3** [1950s+] a 'wide boy', a SPIV. [FLY *adj.²*]

fly-boy *n.²* **1** [1910s] (Anglo-Irish) a British citizen who escaped to Ireland to avoid conscription in WW1. **2** [1940s+] (US) a pilot, civil or milit.; usu. with slight implication of disdain or dislike. [joc. uses of SE *fly* + *boy*]

fly-by-night *n.* **1** [late 18C+] one who defrauds the landlord by leaving his lodgings in the middle of the night, having failed to pay the rent. **2** [late 18C+] anyone dubious, crooked, criminal, esp. of a businessman who takes one's money but fails to provide any or at least adequate recompense. **3** [early–mid-19C] a sedan chair on wheels. [lit. one who 'flies by night'. Grose (1796) adds his punning joke: 'an ancient term of reproach to an old woman, signifying that she was a witch']

fly-by-night *adj.* [late 18C+] dubious, crooked, criminal. [FLY-BY-NIGHT *n.* (2)]

fly-by-night, pitch-by-day *phr.* [1950s] (W.I.) an idle, worthless person with no home.

fly-by-nights *n.* [1970s] tights. [rhy. sl.]

fly by the seat of one's pants, to *phr.* [1940s+] to fly an aircraft using natural ability and daring rather than instruments and technology; thus fig. to gamble with one's life, to take extravagant risks.

fly-cage/flycatcher/flytrap *n.* [19C] the vagina. [joc. use of SE ? + ref. to the FLY *adj.¹* young gentleman it ensnares]

flycar *n.* [1980s+] (US Black) a desirable automobile. [FLY *adj.²* + SE *car*]

flycatcher *n.¹* see FLY-CAGE.

flycatcher *n.²* [19C] a gawping fool. [his open mouth]

fly cemetery *n.* **1** [1930s+] (N.Z.) a pastry square filled with mincemeat. **2** [1930s+] (N.Z.) a raisin biscuit. **3** [1950s–60s] a steamed pudding with currants. [resemblance]

flychick *n.* [1930s–40s] (US Black) a young woman who enjoys parties and her social life (cf. FLY-GIRL *n.*[2]). [FLY *adj.*[2] + CHICK *n.*[3]]

fly cop *n.* (US) **1** [19C+] a plain-clothes policeman. **2** [mid–late 19C] an alert or experienced police officer. [FLY *adj.*[1] + COP *n.*[1]]

fly coy *v.* [1960s–70s] (US Black) suddenly to become reticent and coy (cf. FLY HOT). [SE *fly*, to become + *coy*]

fly crutch *n.* [1970s+] (US) any fashionable automobile (cf. AFROMOBILE). [FLY *adj.*[2] + CRUTCH *n.*[4]]

fly-disperser soup *n.* [mid-19C–1900s] oxtail soup (cf. FLY-SWISHER STEW). [the ox swishes its tail to get rid of clustering flies]

fly donah *n.* [late 19C] a cunning woman. [FLY *adj.*[1] + DONAH]

fly-dusters *n.* [late 19C–1900s] the fists.

flyer/flier *n.*[1] **1** [late 17C– late 18C] a shoe. **2** [mid-19C] a shoe that has been soled without having been welted. [? play on 'flying away' in one's footwear]

flyer/flier *n.*[2] (US) **1** [early 19C+] a wager or investment; thus *take a flyer*, to take a gamble, a risk. **2** [mid-19C+] a lark, a gambit.

flyer/flier *n.*[3] [mid-19C+] (Aus.) a fast-running kangaroo. [SE *fly*, to go fast]

flyer *n.*[4] [late 19C+] (US) **1** a small handbill or fly-sheet, esp. a 'wanted' poster issued by the police. **2** an arrest warrant.

flyer/flier *n.*[5] [1940s] (US Black) a hat. [? play on SKIMMER *n.*[1]]

flyer/flier *n.*[6] [1940s+] (US prison) suicide by throwing oneself from an upper gallery.

flyer/flier *n.*[7] [1960s+] (US campus) an idiotic or obnoxious person. [FLY A KITE *phr.*[2] (2), (3)]

flyer with the roof slightly higher *phr.* [1940s] (US Black/Harlem) a modified version of the traditional Stetson '10-gallon hat' and worn by fashionable Harlemites of the period. [FLYER *n.*[5]]

fly fishing *n.* [1990s] masturbation. [pun on SE *fly*, trouser buttons or zip]

fly-flapped *adj.* [late 18C] whipped at the cart's tail or in the stocks. [SE *fly-flap*, to beat, to whip, orig. to hit flies with a swatter]

fly-flapper *n.* [mid-19C–1920s] a heavy club.

fly-flat *n.* [mid-19C–1930s] a con-man's victim who believes himself to be cleverer than he actually proves. [FLY *adj.*[1] + FLAT *n.*[2]]

fly-girl *n.*[1] [19C] a prostitute. [FLY *adj.*[1] (4) + SE *girl*]

fly-girl *n.*[2] [1980s+] (US/UK Black) a smart, attractive woman. (cf. FLYCHICK). [FLY *adj.*[2] + SE *girl*]

fly high/fly rather high *v.* [mid–late 19C] to be (slightly) drunk. [note HIGH *adj.*[1]]

fly hot *v.* [1900s–30s] (US Black) suddenly to lose one's temper (cf. FLY COY; FLY OFF THE HANDLE). [SE *fly*, to become + HOT *adj.*[1] (2)]

flying *adj.* [1950s+] (drugs) under the influence of drugs (cf. FLOAT *v.*[2]). [one is 'high']

flying baker *adj.* [20C] (US) menstruating (cf. FLY A FLAG; FLY THE RED FLAG). [naut. jargon *baker*, B; the flag signifying the second letter of the alphabet is red]

flying bedstead *n.* [late 19C] a stall used by a bric-a-brac dealer.

flying blind *adj.* [20C] drunk (cf. FLYING HIGH). [pun on SE, but cf. BLIND *adj.*[1]]

flying camps *n.* [late 17C–18C] a group of beggars who work as a team at funerals. [SE *flying camp*, 'a little army of horse and foot, that keeps the field, and is continually in motion' (Phillips, *The New World of Words*, 1671)]

flying cat *n.* [late 17C–early 18C] (Und.) an owl. [its predilection for mice and other small rodents]

flying dustman *n.* [early 19C] a 'pirate' dustman, who collects garbage before the contracted dustman can arrive. [pun on the *Flying Dutchman*]

flying flies *see* FLOATERS.

flying fornicator *n.* **1** [1900s–30s] the last express train from London to a provincial town. **2** [1970s] (Aus.) the last train from Sydney to Wollongong on Saturday night, primarily patronized by young people. [the image of drunken couples necking on their way home]

flying fuck/shit *n.* [20C] an all-purpose negative epithet; usu. in comb., e.g. (*not*) *give a flying fuck*, (*go*) *take a flying fuck.*

flying giggers *n.* [late 18C] turnpike gates. [GIGGER *n.*[1]]

flying high *adj.* [20C] drunk (cf. FLYING BLIND). [fig. use of SE, but cf. HIGH *adj.*[1]]

flying horse *n.* [1950s] (W.I.) a bent pin or similar sharp object placed on a chair. [the person who sits on it 'flies']

flying knacker *n.* [mid–late 19C] a small-scale, travelling horseflesh butcher. [SE *flying*, moving fast + *knacker*]

flying lessons *n.* [20C] (US prison) the throwing of a guard or fellow inmate off the balcony of a cell tier.

flying pasty *n.* **1** [late 18C] a packet of excrement wrapped in paper and flung over a neighbour's wall. **2** [19C] (US prison) a similar package wrapped in newspaper and tossed out of one's cell window (cf. BROWN TROUT).

flying pasty shits *n.* [1980s+] (US campus) diarrhoea. [SE *flying* + *pasty*, a small pie + SHIT *n.*[1] (1)]

flying porter *n.* [late 18C] a cheat who approaches the victim of robbery, tells him that he can regain the stolen goods for him and demands a payment for fetching them. [SE *fly*, to run off]

flying saucer *n.*[1] **1** [1950s+] (orig. US) a diaphragm. **2** [1950s] (W.I.) a motorcycle policeman.

flying saucer *n.*[2] [1980s+] (drugs) the seeds of the plant *Ipomoea*, popularly known as morning glory. [their shape and their effect on the user]

flying shit *see* FLYING FUCK.

flying sixty-nine *n.* [20C] mutual oral-genital stimulation. [SE *flying* + SIXTY-NINE]

flying sixty-six *n.* [20C] oral sex. [rhy. sl. *flying sixty-six* = FRENCH TRICKS]

flying stationer *n.* [late 18C–late 19C] a street seller of cheap ballads, criminal 'confessions' and similar popular material (cf. RUNNING PATTERER; WALKING STATIONER). [SE *flying*, moving + *stationer*, a bookseller]

flying trapeze *n.* [late 19C+] cheese. [rhy. sl.]

fly in/up in one's head *v.* [20C] (W.I.) of alcohol, to go to one's head, to make one extremely and thus dangerously drunk.

fly-in-the-milk *n.* [20C] (US) a mulatto, a child of mixed Black and White parentage. [the black fly in the white milk]

fly jay *n.* [1970s+] (US Black) an attractive woman. [FLY *adj.*[2] + JAY *n.*[2]]

fly jerks *n.* [late 19C+] (Aus.) the small pieces of cork suspended from a hat to ward off flies (cf. JERKS *n.*[2]).

fly/Kentucky loo *n.* [late 19C] a form of betting, on the actions of flies, indulged in by students. [SE *fly/Kentucky* + *loo*, a card-game similar to whist. The participants stand around a table and each has a sugar lump daubed with a little honey in front of them; they then bet on which lump attracts a fly first]

fly low *v.* [20C] (US) to have one's trouser fly open. [pun]

fly machine *n.* [1980s] (S.Afr. Black) methylated spirits. [? the effect of the drink makes one 'fly']

fly-man *n.* **1** [19C] a shrewd, cunning, usu. criminal man. **2** [1920s] an expert thief. [FLY *adj.*[1] + SE *man*]

fly me! *excl.* [late 19C] a mild excl. [older *flay me!*]

fly member *n.* [late 19C] a smart, even cunning man, good at picking up on and exploiting the current fashions. [FLY adj.[1] + SE *member*]

fly Mexican airlines, to *phr.* [1960s+] (drugs) to smoke marijuana. [the easy access to marijuana in Mexico + flying 'high']

flymy *adj.* [mid-19C] sly, roguish, cunning. [FLY adj.[1] + SE *slimy*]

fly my kite *n.* [mid-19C] a light. [rhy. sl.]

fly off *v.* [20C] (US) to suffer from diarrhoea.

fly/go off at the deep end, to *phr.* [1910s+] **1** to lose control, to become extremely angry or depressed, to show any extreme of emotion. **2** to become emotionally involved with or obsessed by.

fly off/up in one's face, to *phr.* [20C] (W.I.) to lose control, to become extremely angry. [var. on FLY OFF THE HANDLE]

fly off the handle, to *phr.* [19C+] (orig. US) to lose control, to become extremely angry (cf. FLY HOT; FLY UP *v.*[1]; GO OFF THE HANDLE). [the image of an axe-head 'flying' from its handle]

fly one's mouth *see* RUN ONE'S MOUTH.

fly out of one's skin, to *phr.* [20C] (W.I.) to become violently excited.

fly-over people *n.* [20C] (US) inhabitants of those states of the US over which one passes in an aeroplane flying from coast to coast; formerly 'middle America'.

flypaper act *n.* [1900s–10s] the Prevention of Crimes Act, 1909; thus *on the flypaper*, subject to this Act, to be a criminal known to the police.

fly-pitch *n.* [1930s+] any form of street stall or other place where goods are sold in the open air; thus *fly-pitcher*, a street-seller. [FLY *v.*]

fly rather high *see* FLY HIGH.

fly rink *n.* [late 19C] a bald head. [the image of ice-skating flies]

fly slicer *n.* **1** [late 18C] a member of the Life Guards. **2** [19C] a cavalryman. ['from their sitting on horse-back, under an arch, where they are frequently observed to drive away flies with their swords' (Grose, 1785)]

fly speck/fly speck isle *n.* [20C] (Aus.) Tasmania; thus *fly-specker*, an inhabitant of Tasmania. [its relative size compared to Australia]

fly-swisher stew *n.* [1910s+] (Aus.) oxtail stew (cf. FLY-DISPERSER SOUP). [the function of the ox's tail]

fly taal/flaaitaal *n.* [1950s+] (S.Afr. Black) a form of urban slang used by street-wise young people (cf. TSOTSI). [FLY adj.[2] + Afk. *taal*, language]

fly the blue pigeon *see* FLY A BLUE PIGEON.

fly the coop, to *phr.* [mid-19C+] (US) **1** to leave, poss. suddenly. **2** to die. **3** to stop working. **4** to lose control, to lose one's temper. **5** to go wrong, to blunder.

fly the flag, to *phr.* [mid-19C] **1** of a prostitute, to walk the streets looking for trade. **2** to be menstruating (cf. FLY A FLAG).

fly the kite, to *phr.*[1] [mid-19C] to obtain credit against bills, whether or not the 'paper' is valid or fraudulent. [FLY A KITE phr.[1]]

fly the kite, to *phr.*[2] [mid-19C] to toss excrement from a window.

fly the mags, to *phr.* [early–mid-19C] (orig. Und.) to gamble by tossing halfpence, to play pitch and toss. [FLY *v.*[2] + MAG *n.*[1]]

fly the red flag, to *phr.* [20C] (Aus./US) to be menstruating (cf. FLY A FLAG).

fly the track, to *phr.* [19C+] (US) to abandon one's duties, to depart from an expected course of action (cf. GO OFF THE RAILS).

fly to flinders, to *phr.* [20C] (US) to lose one's temper (cf. GO TO PIECES). [SE *flinders*, fragments, splinters]

fly to the time of day, to *phr.* [early 19C] to be well aware of what is going on.

flytrap *n.*[1] **1** [18C+] the mouth. **2** [19C] a run-down hotel or similar establishment.

flytrap *n.*[2] *see* FLY-CAGE.

fly up/fly up in the air *v.*[1] [19C+] (US) to lose one's temper, to lose control (cf. FLY OFF THE HANDLE).

fly up *v.*[2] [20C] (US) to go to bed. [the action of chickens in 'flying up to the roost']

fly up in one's face *see* FLY OFF IN ONE'S FACE.

fly up in one's head *see* FLY IN ONE'S HEAD.

fly-up-the-creek *n.* [late 19C+] (US) **1** an inhabitant of Florida (cf. ALLIGATOR *n.*[3]). **2** a capricious person. **3** an immoral woman. [regional use *fly-up-the-creek*, a popular name of the small green heron (*Butorides virescens*), a native of Florida]

fly up with Jackson's hens, to *phr.* [late 16C–late 18C] to become bankrupt; thus *make one fly up with Jackson's hens*, to ruin someone financially. [? a long-lost anecdote]

f.o.! *excl.* [1940s+] (US) go away! leave me alone! [abbr. FUCK OFF!]

f.o.a.d *phr.* [1990s] *fuck off and die!* [abbr.]

foal *n.* [1990s] £10. [a play on a small PONY *n.*[2]]

foal and filly dance *n.* [late 19C] (society) a dance for young people only. [equine imagery]

foamin' at the gash *phr.* [1990s] of a woman, becoming damp with sexual arousal (cf. FIZZING AT THE BUNG). [SE *foam* + GASH *n.*]

foaming at the mouth *phr.* [1910s+] absolutely furious.

f.o.b. *n.* [1970s] **1** (N.Z.) a newly arrived coloured immigrant. **2** (US campus) an Asian not used to American ways. [abbr. *fresh off the boat*]

fob *n.* [late 17C–mid-19C] a trick, a deceit (cf. COME THE FOB ON). [the term was SE in 1622 (*OED* first citation) but sl. by late 17C; thus SE use *fob off*, to sidetrack, to put off with a lie or deceit]

fob *v.* **1** [late 17C–mid-19C] to trick, to deceive, to steal from. **2** [1900s–30s] (US Und.) to steal from a fob pocket.

f.o.b.b. *n.* [1970s] (US) a derog. acronym for a drunken, sluttish woman. [abbr. *fucked out boozy bitch*]

fobber *n.* [19C] a pickpocket who specializes in removing small change from the victim's fob pocket. [SE *fob*]

fob one off/out of *phr.* [mid-19C] to trick someone out of something. [FOB *v.*]

fobus *n.*[1] [17C] a general term of dislike. [ety. unknown; ? link to dial. *fobey*, an eccentric]

fobus *n.*[2] [late 19C] the vagina. [ety. unknown; ? link to SE *fob*, a small pocket]

fodder *n.*[1] [late 19C+] lavatory paper. [abbr. BUMFODDER]

fodder *n.*[2] [1940s+] food. [although it covered all forms of food in 11C–14C the SE is now only used for animal food]

fodder forker *n.* [20C] (US) a derog. term for a farmer, as seen by cowboys. [his usual task]

fofarrow *adj.* [19C] (US) arrogant, conceited, precious. [US pron. of Fr. *fanfaron*, a boaster, a braggart]

fofi-eye *n.* [20C] (W.I./Bdos., Guyn.) an eye with a discoloured, whitish eyeball. [ety. unknown; ? link to *fufu*, a plantain dough, which is white]

fog *n.* [late 18C] (Und.) smoke.

fog *v.* **1** [18C] to smoke a pipe. **2** [19C] to perplex, to confuse, to mystify. **3** [19C+] (US) to scold, to complain. **4** [19C+] (US) to go fast, to rush around, to chase. **5** [19C+] (US) to fire a gun rapidly. **6** [19C+] (US) to attack.

fog-bound *adj.* **1** [1920s–30s] slightly drunk (cf. ADDLED). **2** [1920s–40s] (US) confused, dazed.

fogey *n.* **1** [late 18C] an invalid soldier; thence the SE use, usu. with pfx. *old*, although from early 20C also *young*. **2** [late 19C] an old maid. [Fr. *fougeaux*, fierce, fiery or Scot. dial. *foggy*, fat, bloated. Note SE *fogram/fogrum*, an old-fashioned, out-of-date person]

fogey adj. see FOGY.

fogged adj. [mid-19C+] **1** drunk, tipsy (cf. ADDLED). **2** confused, bewildered. [FOG v. (2)]

foggy adj. **1** [early–mid-19C] drunk, tipsy (cf. ADDLED). **2** [20C] (US) confused, not very intelligent. [FOG v. (2)]

foggy bottom n. [1940s+] the US State Department. [derived both f. the name of an area of Washington, D.C., and from the 'foggy' obfuscations produced by its bureaucrats]

foghorn n. (US) **1** [20C] the nose (cf. BUGLE n.[1]). **2** [20C] one who talks too loudly. **3** [1910s–30s] a tuba or saxophone. [the noise it makes]

fog in v. [late 19C] (society) **1** to see a place by accident. **2** to achieve one's object by accident.

fogland n. [1910s] (Aus.) Britain; thus *fogtown*, London. [the weather and the contemporary smogs in London]

fogle n. [early–mid-19C] (orig. Ling. Fr./Polari) a silk handkerchief; thus *fogle-hunter*, a thief specializing in silk handkerchiefs. [? Ital. *foglia*, leaf; thus handkerchief or Fr. sl. *fouille*, a pocket; less likely is Ger. *vogel*, bird, and thus the 'bird's eye' pattern of some handkerchiefs]

fogle-hunting/-drawing n. [early–mid-19C] (orig. Ling. Fr./Polari) the stealing of silk handkerchiefs. [FOGLE]

fogmatic n. [mid-19C] (US campus) a bracing drink of alcohol (cf. ANTIFOGMATIC).

fogmatic adj. [mid-19C] (US campus) drunk. [FOGMATIC n.]

fogo n. [19C] a stench, esp. of breaking wind. [? SE *fog* + *hogo*, f. Fr. *haut gout*, high taste, i.e. a high or putrescent flavour, an offensive taste or smell, or *foh!*, an excl. of disgust]

fog out v. [1980s+] (US drugs) to fill a room or car with smoke.

fogram/fogrum n. [late 18C–late 19C] an antiquated or old-fashioned person, a fogy. [SE *fogram*, antiquated, out-of-date]

fogramite n. [late 18C–early 19C] a fogey. [FOGRAM + sfx. -ite]

fogrum see FOGRAM.

fogue v. [1920s–30s] (N.Z.) to stink. [FOGO]

fogus n. [late 17C–mid-18C] tobacco. [? SE *fog*, in this case that produced by a pipe]

fogy/fogey adj. [early 18C+] (orig. Scot.) old-fashioned, 'stuck-in-the-mud'. [FOGEY]

foil n. [1980s+] (Aus. drugs) a cannabis purchase wrapped in foil (cf. FOLD n.).

foil-/foyl-cloy n. [late 17C–early 18C] (Und.) a pickpocket. [? FILE n. (1) + CLOY]

foin n. [16C] (Und.) a cut-purse or pickpocket. [SE *foin*, a thrust with a pointed weapon]

foin v. [14C] of a man, to have sexual intercourse (cf. BANG v.[1]). [SE *foin*, to make a thrust with pointed weapon]

fois adj. [1980s+] (US campus) reminiscent of European style. [? Fr. *fois*, time, i.e. the perceived antiquity of such styles]

foist/foyst/fyst n.[1] (Und.) **1** [late 16C–late 17C] a pickpocket or cut-purse (cf. NIP n.[1]; STALL n.[1]). **2** [late 16C–late 17C] a card-sharp, a cheat. **3** [17C] a trick, a hoax. [FOIST v.[1]]

foist/foyst/fyst n.[2] [late 16C] a silent breaking of wind. [FOIST v.[2]]

foist/foyst/fyst v.[1] **1** [16C] to palm a false die so as to be able to introduce it into the game when required (cf. FLAT n.[1]). **2** [16C] to cheat by this means; thus *foist in*, to introduce a false die surreptitiously when palmed (cf. COG v.[1]). **3** [16C–19C] to pick a pocket. [prob. Du. dial. *vuisten*, to take in the hand, f. *vuist*, fist; the Du. means to play at a game in which one player holds some coins in his hand, and the others guess their number]

foist v.[2] [16C] to break wind silently (cf. FICE). [15C SE *fist*, to break wind; 16C SE *foist*, to smell or grow musty]

fold n. [20C] (US drugs) $25 worth of a given drug (cf. FOIL). [powdered narcotic drugs are sold in folds of paper]

fold v. [1980s+] (US campus) to become exhausted, to tire (cf. FOLDER). [poker imagery]

folder n. [1980s+] (US campus) one who tires easily; thus a poor companion for partying. [FOLD v.[2]]

fol-de-riddle-ido n. [late 19C–1920s] a trilby hat. [? SE *fol-de-rol*, a trifle]

fol-de-rol n. [late 19C] (US) a temporary, probably self-induced depression, pique. [SE *fol-de-rol*, a trifle]

folding/folding stuff n. [1920s+] (orig. US) paper money.

folding green n. [1970s+] (US Black) paper money, dollar bills.

folding stuff see FOLDING.

fold out v. [20C] (US) to go to bed. [the unfolding of one's bed-roll]

fold someone's ears, to phr. [1960s–70s] (US Black) to lecture or advise someone at great and serious length.

fold up v. **1** [1940s+] to collapse or to surrender, both under unbearable pressure (cf. FOLD v.). **2** [1980s+] (drugs) to withdraw from drug use. [poker use, *fold (up)*, to withdraw from a round of betting]

folks n. **1** [late 19C] (US Und.) fellow criminals (cf. FAMILY n.[1]). **2** [1990s] (US Black teen) fellow gang members, esp. used in prison where gang membership is, where possible, hidden from the authorities. [SAmE *folks*, one's family]

follies n. [1940s–50s] (prison) the Quarter Sessions. [ironic use]

follow a/march in the rear of a whereas, to phr. [late 18C–mid-19C] to become bankrupt. [notices of bankruptcy in the *London Gazette* invariably began with the word *Whereas*...]

follow-cat/-pot/-pup n. [20C] (US) one who tags along, whether so invited or not.

follower n. [mid-19C+] a man who courts a maidservant; thus the common admonition on hiring a cook or maid, *No followers*.

follower-upper/follyer-upper/follyinupper/folly-up n. (Irish) **1** [1940s–50s] a weekly cinema serial, usu. screened on Saturday mornings. **2** [1950s+] any form of sequel. [SE *follow-up*]

follow-foot monkey n. [20C] (W.I.) someone, often a young person, who 'apes' (as far as they can) the famous.

follow-foot monkey, to phr. [20C] (W.I.) to 'ape' the famous. [FOLLOW-FOOT MONKEY n.]

following that cloud phr. [1980s+] (drugs) searching for drugs. [the *cloud* of smoke, whether from marijuana or crack cocaine]

follow like a tantony pig, to phr. [late 18C] to follow closely. [ANTHONY]

follow-me-lads n. [mid-19C–1900s] curls that hang over a woman's shoulder (cf. FUCK-ME SHOES). [the apparent sexual invitation implicit in the hairstyle]

follow one's nose, to phr. [late 18C+] (US Black) to lead a law-abiding life, whatever temptations may exist to the contrary.

follow-pot/-pup see FOLLOW-CAT.

follow through v. **1** [20C] to ejaculate twice without withdrawal. **2** [1990s] to soil one's underwear by mistake.

follyer-upper/follyinupper/folly-up see FOLLOWER-UPPER.

fondle v. [19C] to have sexual intercourse.

fondle the fig, to phr. [1990s] of a woman, to masturbate. [FIG n.[2]]

fond of her mother phr. [1980s+] (gay) homosexual (cf. DOROTHY'S FRIEND). [a 'nudging' euph. emphasizing the supposed 'creation' of gay men by their suffocating mothers]

fond of meat phr. [19C+] used to describe a man who is fond of sex, esp. with prostitutes. [euph.; SE *fond* + MEAT n.]

fond of one's drops phr. [late 19C] used of a heavy drinker. [euph.]

fonfen n. [1960s–70s] the verbal trickery created by con-men to further a given fraud or trick. [Yid. *fonfer*, a cheat, one who deceives, fails to deliver on their promises?

fong/fong-eye *n.*[1] [1940s+] (N.Z.) **1** strong liquor. **2** methylated spirits as drunk by alcoholics. **3** a very heavy drinker.

fong *n.*[2] [1960s] (Irish) a kick. [? echoic]

fonged/fonged up/half-fonged *adj.* [1940s+] (N.Z.) drunk, tipsy. [FONG n.[1]]

fonk *n.* *see* FUNK n.[3].

fonk *v.* [1960s+] (US Black) to show off, to upstage others (cf. FIEND ON). [FONKY]

fonked out heavy *phr.* [1960s+] (US Black) very well dressed. [FUNK n.[3]]

fonk out *v.* [1960s+] (US Black) **1** to insult, to upstage, to humiliate, to attack verbally. **2** to praise. [FONK v.]

fonky *adj.* [1960s+] (US Black) positive or negative intensifier depending on context; thus exceptionally good or bad, smelling sweet or vile etc.

fonky-fresh *adj.* [1990s] (US Black) a general adj. of high praise, the most sophisticated, the smartest, the most attractive. [FONKY + FRESH adj.[3]]

fonky to the bone *phr.* [1940s+] (US Black) **1** exceptionally well dressed. **2** handsome. [FONKY + TO THE BONE]

food *n.* [1940s] (US Black) gossip (cf. FISH FOR FOOD). [something one 'chews' over]

foodie *n.* [1980s+] a gourmet, a food obsessive; one of a self-elected circle of London eaters, devoted to the best and newest in eating and drinking. [coined by food writer Paul Levy, 1981]

food inspector *n.* [1900s–50s] (Aus.) a tramp. [his 'inspection' of whatever food he can obtain]

fooey *see* PHOOEY.

foof *n.* [1980s+] (US campus) a superficial person. [? echoic of an insubstantial puff of wind]

foo-foo *n.*[1] [mid-19C+] **1** (orig. US) an effeminate or weak man. **2** (W.I.) a naïve, gullible, foolish person. [SE *fool* + redup.]

foo-foo *n.*[2] [1990s] the vagina. [ety. unknown; ? fig. use of FOO-FOO n.[1]]

foo-foo/fool-fool *adj.* [mid-19C+] (W.I.) **1** credulous, gullible. **2** oafish. 3 simple-minded, stupid. [FOO-FOO n.[1] (2)]

foo-foo dust/stuff *n.* **1** [1960s+] any form of talcum powder, baby powder etc (cf. FOO-FOO POWDER). **2** [1980s+] (drugs) heroin. **3** [1980s+] (drugs) cocaine. [var. on FOO-FOO POWDER]

foo-foo powder *n.* [1910s+] (US) talcum powder, baby powder, anti-louse powder etc. [orig. naut. jargon *foo-foo*, cologne; ult. FOO-FOO n.[1] (1)]

foo-foo stuff *see* FOO-FOO DUST.

fool *n.* [20C] anyone excessively enthusiastic about a given activity or topic; thus *dancing fool, singing fool*; often found as *a fool for ...* (cf. WRITING FOOL).

fool *adj.* [mid-19C+] (US) stupid, ludicrous, absurd. [prior SE use in UK]

fool *v.* [20C] (US) to curry favour with.

fool around *v.* **1** [1950s] (US Black) to tease. **2** [1970s+] to conduct a promiscuous sex life; thus the invitation *let's fool around*, a suggestion by one of a couple that they should abandon speech for (sexual) action.

fool away *v.* [20C] (US) to waste time or resources, to fritter away.

fooleries, the *n.* [late 19C–1920s] the amusements of April Fool's Day (1 April).

fool-finder *n.* [late 18C] a bailiff. [? because only fools are available when he comes to call]

fool-fool *see* FOO-FOO adj.

foolhead *n.* [19C+] a fool; thus *foolheaded*, stupid, foolish. [SE *fool* + sfx. -HEAD (1)]

foolish *adj.* [late 18C] used by prostitutes to distinguish a

casual customer from a more sophisticated client; thus the query, *Is he foolish or* FLASH?

foolish powder *n.* [1980s+] (drugs) **1** heroin. **2** cocaine. [their effects]

fool-maker/-sticker *n.* [19C] the penis. [the *fool* in this case is presumably a cuckolded husband]

fool-monger *n.* [late 16C–early 18C] **1** one who 'trades on' the credulity of fools, a swindler. **2** a gambler. [SE *fool* + sfx. -*monger*]

fool's gold *n.* [20C] (US Und.) fake jewellery. [SE *fool's gold*, iron pyrites, which fools novice miners into believing they have struck the real thing]

fool-sticker *see* FOOL-MAKER.

fool's wedding *n.* [19C] a party of women. [? proverbial]

fool-taker *n.* [late 16C] a dice- or card-sharp; thus *fool-taking*, the swindling of gamblers.

fool trap *n.* **1** [late 16C–early 18C] one who 'trades on' the credulity of fools, a swindler (cf. FOOL-MONGER). **2** [19C] the vagina. **3** [19C] a prostitute.

fool up *v.* [1950s] (W.I.) to deceive, to trick.

foont *see* FUNT.

foop *n.* [20C] a homosexual man (cf. FOOPER). [backsl. POOF]

foop *v.* **1** [1920s] (US Black) to dance uninhibitedly. **2** [1970s] (US campus) to engage in homosexual acts. [FOOP n.]

fooper *n.* [1970s] (US campus) a homosexual. [FOOP n.]

foot, the *n.* [1900s–50s] rejection, dismissal. [var. on BOOT n.[1]]

foot/footer/footy *v.* [17C] euph. for FUCK (cf. 'SFOOT!). [Fr. *foutre*, to fuck]

foot!/foot, foot! *excl.* [late 19C–1900s] go away! [usu. addressed to 'the respectably dressed person who wanders into strange and doubtful bye-ways' (Ware)]

foot ain't/don't deceive you *phr.* [20C] (W.I.) escaping, running as fast as possible.

footback *adv.* [19C+] travelling on foot (cf. ANKLE EXPRESS). [pun on SE *horseback*]

foot-back it *v.* [1930s] (Aus.) to travel by foot, with a pack on one's back (cf. FOOT-WALK IT).

football *n.* (drugs) **1** [1940s] a measure of one half grain of a narcotic. **2** [1940s–70s] (US) a capsule of a psychotropic drug.

footballer *n.* [1910s] (Aus.) **1** (Und.) a prison warder. **2** anyone who fights with their feet. [the use of the feet as an agent of violence]

footballs *n.* [1960s+] (drugs) amphetamine (cf. A n.[2]). [packaging]

football team *n.* [1940s–50s] a small, sparse moustache (cf. CRICKET TEAM). [it only has 11 (hairs) each side]

foot-bath *n.* [late 19C–1900s] an overfilled glass.

foot don't deceive you *see* FOOT AIN'T DECEIVE YOU.

footer *n.*[1] [mid-18C–mid-19C] a general term of contempt, a 'scurvy fellow', a 'low fellow'. [Fr. *foutre*, to fuck, thus cf. FUCKER]

footer *n.*[2] [late 18C–1940s] football. [SE *football* + 'Oxford' sfx. -*er*]

footer *v.*[1] *see* FOOT.

footer *v.*[2] [mid-19C] to idle around. [FOOTER n.[1]; thus cf. FUCK ABOUT v.[1]; FUCK OFF v.]

footermans *adj.* [1960s] (US West.) on foot. [20C and thus very late example of the 16C–17C -MANS sfx, e.g. CRACKMANS; DARKMANS]

foot, foot! *see* FOOT!

footie/footy *n.* [20C] **1** football (soccer). **2** (Aus./N.Z.) Australian Rules football.

foot-in-mouth disease *n.* [1960s+] the continual problem of making grossly tactless or embarrassing statements (cf. HOOF-AND-MOUTH DISEASE). [note the cod-academic synon. *dontopedology*]

foot is hot *phr.* [20C] (W.I./Trin.) used of one who is restless, esp. a woman.

foot is long *phr.* [20C] (W.I./Guyn.) said of one who has or can walk a long way in a relatively short time.

foot is too short *phr.* [20C] (W.I.) said of one who has missed their chance or has arrived too late, esp. for a meal.

foot it *v.* [1950s–60s] (US Black) to walk, esp. to walk a long way.

foot-kisser *n.* [20C] (US) a sycophant, a toady (cf. ARSE-LICKER).

foot land-raker *n.* [late 16C–early 17C] a highway robber (cf. FOOTPAD). [SE *foot* + LAND-RAKER]

footle *n.* [late 19C] nonsense, rubbish. [FOOTLE v.]

footle *adj.* [late 19C] paltry, trifling, insignificant. [FOOTLE v.]

footle *v.* [late 19C+] **1** to act or talk foolishly. **2** to potter around. [*OED* has 'of obscure origin' and suggests link to FOOTER v.², but *EDD* offers Nottingham dial. *footle*, to do anything in a feeble, ineffectual manner]

footless stocking without a leg, a *phr.* [late 19C] (Irish) nothing (cf. WHAT THE CONNAUGHT MAN SHOT AT).

footling *adj.* [late 19C+] incompetent, inadequate, mediocre. [FOOTLE v.]

footman's inn *n.* [early–mid-17C] **1** very poor lodgings. **2** a prison. [the poor status and negative image of the SE *footman*]

footman's maund *n.* [18C] a sore that counterfeits a kick or bite from a horse (cf. MASON'S MAUND). [SE *footman* + MAUND n.]

footmobile *n.* [1910s+] (US) transportation by foot (cf. ANKLE EXPRESS).

footpad *n.* [16C–19C] a highway robber, although not a highwayman, the former operated on foot, the latter from a horse. [SE *foot* + PAD n.¹]

foot-rot *n.* [late 19C] cheap (4 penny) ale. [? link to dial. *foot-ale*, in mining communities a miner uses his first day's pay to 'stand his foot-ale', i.e. buy drinks for his fellows]

foot-rotting *n.* [1930s+] (Aus.) idling away one's time in boredom.

footsack! *excl.* [mid-19C+] (S.Afr.) a general excl. of dismissal, go away! be off! get out! [anglicized version of VOET-SAK!]

foot-scamp *n.* [18C] a highway robber; thus *foot-scamping*, highway robbery. [FOOTPAD + SCAMP n.]

footsie *v.* [1950s+] (US) **1** to waste time. **2** to curry favour. [fig. uses of PLAY FOOTSIE]

footsie-footsie/footy-footy *n.* **1** [1930s+] the surreptitious nudging of someone's foot out of sight of anyone else, typically beneath a table; the contact is usu. a prelude to greater intimacy (cf. PLAY FOOTSIE). **2** [1950s+] (US) currying favour in an underhand way or to waste time by behaving coyly. [S.Afr. *voetsjie-voetsjie*]

footslogger *n.* **1** [20C] a pedestrian. **2** [1920s+] (Aus.) a policeman who walks his beat. [milit. use, an infantryman]

footslogging *n.* [1910s+] hard, exhausting and protracted walking. [orig. WW1 milit. sl.]

foot soldier *n.* [1980s+] (US gay) a male street prostitute.

footstool *n.* [early 19C–1900s] (US) the earth. [Isa. 66:1, 'Thus saith the Lord, The heaven is my throne, and the earth is my footstool']

foot the bill, to *phr.* [mid-19C+] (orig. US) to pay a bill. [SE *foot the bill*, to add up and set the sum at the foot of an account or bill]

foot up *v.* [late 19C] (US) to work out, to sum up a person. [the placing of the final result at the foot of a column of figures]

foot-walk it *v.* [1930s] (Aus.) to travel by foot (cf. FOOT-BACK IT).

foot-warbler/-wobbler *n.* [late 18C–early 19C] an infantryman, esp. as described by a cavalryman. [SE *foot* + *wobbler*]

footwasher *n.* [19C+] (US) a traditional, fundamentalist Baptist. [the religious rite whereby Primitive Baptists wash each other's feet, as commanded in John 13:14, 'If I then, your Lord and Master, have washed your feet, ye also ought to wash one another's feet']

foot, what you made for?/where you deh? *phr.* [20C] (W.I./Belz., Guyn.) an imaginary question asked by someone who is at the point of running away (in fright), i.e. foot, do your job!

foot-wobbler *see* FOOT-WARBLER.

footy *n. see* FOOTIE.

footy *adj.* **1** [18C–19C, UK; 19C+, US] insignificant, worthless, despicable, futile. **2** [19C+] (US) foolish, simple. [Fr. *foutu*, fucked]

footy *v. see* FOOT.

footy-footy *see* FOOTSIE-FOOTSIE.

fooy! *see* PHOOEY!

foozilow *v.* [late 19C] (Anglo-Ind.) to flatter. [Hind. *p'huslana*, to flatter or cajole]

foozle *n.¹* [mid–late 19C] (orig. sporting) a miss, a blunder. [FOOZLE v.]

foozle/fuzzle *n.²* [20C] (US) **1** a conservative, one who is behind the times (cf. FOGEY). **2** one who is easily tricked. [for ety. see FOOZLE v.; but note SE *fossil*]

foozle *v.* [19C+] **1** to perform clumsily, to bungle, to make a mess of. **2** (sporting) to miss a shot. [Ger. *fuseln*, to work too fast and thus badly]

foozle about/about with *v.* [1930s+] to fool around (with). [ext. of FOOZLE v.]

foozled/foozly *adj.* [late 19C+] blurred, spoilt. [FOOZLE v.]

foozler *n.* [late 19C] a bungler, one who does things clumsily. [FOOZLE v.]

foozly *see* FOOZLED.

fopdoodle *n.* [17C] a fool, a simpleton. [15C SE *fop*, a fool + DOODLE n.¹]

fopper *n.* [late 19C] a blunder, a mistake. [mispron. Fr. *faux pas*]

for Africa *phr.* [1970s+] (S.Afr.) a lot, a great many, a great deal.

forakers *n.* [mid-19C] the lavatory. [orig. Winchester School jargon ? synon. Lat. *forica* or SE *four acres*, i.e. a field (cf. BOG)]

for a kickers *see* FOR KICKERS.

for all one's natural *phr.* [20C] for ever. [abbr. *natural life*]

for a motherfucker! *excl.* [1960s+] (orig. US Black) an intensifying expletive; thus *he has guns for a motherfucker*, he has a great many guns, *I'm throwing bricks for a motherfucker*, I'm throwing bricks continually and passionately etc.

for beans *phr.* [1950s+] (orig. US) in no way whatsoever. [BEAN n.¹]

forbidden fruit *n.¹* [1930s–40s] (Irish) the 'Adam's apple' in the throat. [the biblical myth]

forbidden fruit *n.²* [1950s–60s] an underage sexual partner of either sex (cf. JAILBAIT).

force-meat ball *n.* [early 19C] anything essentially unpleasant, endured whether one likes it or not.

for Christ's sake! *excl.* [late 19C+] a now mildly blasphemous excl. of rage, annoyance, surprise, amazement.

for crap's sake! *excl.* [1930s+] (orig. US) a general excl. of annoyance, surprise etc. [euph. for FOR CHRIST'S SAKE!]

for cripes' sake! *excl.* [1960s+] a general excl. of annoyance, surprise etc. [euph. for FOR CHRIST'S SAKE]

for crying in a cemetery!/in the beer! *excl.* [20C] (US) euph. for FOR CHRIST'S SAKE (cf. FOR CRYING OUT LOUD!).

for crying out loud! *excl.* [1920s+] euph. for FOR CHRIST'S SAKE!

for days! *excl.* **1** [1950s+] (gay) an excl. implying shock or amazement. **2** [1950s–70s] (orig. US Black) a general intensifier implying an extreme, for a very long time, absolutely truthfully. [the orig. implication was of having sex continually, for day after day]

for ducks *phr.* [1900s–60s] (US) for no special reason. [ety. unknown]

fore and after *n.* [19C] a woman, usu. a prostitute, who is agreeable to group sex, involving vaginal (*fore*) and anal (*aft*) intercourse.

forebuttocks *n.* [early 18C] the female breasts (cf. TOP BALLOCKS).

forecaster *n.* [19C] the vagina (cf. FORECASTLE; FORE-COURT; FORE-HATCH; FORE-ROOM).

forecastle *n.* [19C] the vagina (cf. FORECASTER). [SE *forecastle*, the forward area of a ship]

fore coach-wheel *n.* [late 18C–19C] half-a-crown (12½p) (cf. COACH-WHEEL; HIND COACH-WHEEL). [the fore or front coach-wheels were smaller than those at the rear]

fore-court *n.* [19C] the vagina (cf. FORECASTER).

forefoot *n.* [16C] the human hand (cf. FIN n.¹).

foregather *v.* [18C] to have sexual intercourse. [SE *foregather*, to meet together, to associate with]

foregut *n.* [19C] the vagina (cf. FRONT GUT; GUT ENTRANCE). [SE *fore*, front + *gut*]

fore-hatch *n.* [19C] the vagina (cf. FORECASTER).

foreign *adj.* [1900s–40s] (US Black) referring to any form of sexual activity considered 'unnatural' (cf. ENGLISH; FRENCH; GREEK adj.²; SWEDISH). [the automatic xenophobia that attaches itself to fantasies about 'foreign' sexual practices]

foreigneering cove *n.* [late 19C] a foreigner. [SE *foreign* + COVE]

foreman *n.*¹ [early 17C] a goose. [the definition is assumed f. one use in Beaumont & Fletcher's *Philaster* (1622)]

foreman *n.*² [19C] the penis (cf. FOREWOMAN).

foreman of the jury *n.* [late 17C–early 19C] one who takes over the conversation. [a specific 'tavern term' drawn from the anonymous *The English Liberal Science, or a new-found Art and Order of Drinking* (1650)]

forenoon *n.* [19C] an alcoholic drink taken before breakfast.

fore-room *n.* [19C] the vagina (cf. FORECASTER).

foreskin hunter *n.* [19C] a prostitute.

forest *n.* [mid-19C+] the female pubic hair (cf. BUSH n.⁴).

forever gentleman *n.* [late 19C] (society) one in whom good breeding is ingrained, rather than the parvenu, in whom it is affected (cf. HALF-HOUR GENTLEMAN).

forewoman *n.* [mid-19C] the vagina (cf. FOREMAN).

for fair *adv.* [19C+] (US) completely, absolutely, altogether.

for-free *n.* [1940s] (orig. US) a prostitute who undercuts the going price, an amateur. [she effectively 'gives it away for free']

for fuck's sake! *excl.* [1960s+] a general excl. of exasperation (cf. FOR CHRIST'S SAKE!; FOR CRYING OUT LOUD!).

forge *n.* [19C] the vagina. [where the male 'rod' is softened]

forgers *n.* [late 16C] crooked dice.

forget it! *excl.* [1960s+] **1** an excl. implying absolute dismissal of a suggestion or concept. **2** (US Black) a euph. for *fuck it!* **3** an excl. implying that the previous speaker doesn't understand the gist of the conversation.

forget oneself *v.* [late 19C] of a child, to soil one's underwear, 'have an accident'.

forget you! *excl.* [1970s+] (US teen) impossible, out of the question. [euph. for FUCK YOU!]

forgive and forget *n.* [20C] (Aus.) a cigarette. [rhy. sl.]

for God's sake! *excl.* [mid-19C+] a once-blasphemous oath of irritation. [orig. 14C SE and used as an earnest appeal or exhortation]

for gosh sake! *excl.* [20C] (US) a euph. version of FOR GOD'S SAKE!

for greens *phr.* [mid-19C] (US) for fun, for no special reason.

for heaven's sake! *excl.* [20C] a euph. version of FOR GOD'S SAKE!

for it *phr.* [20C] (orig. milit.) in trouble, often as *in for it*.

fork *n.* **1** [late 17C–19C; 20C US] a pickpocket (cf. FINGERSMITH). **2** [18C] a spendthrift, a wastrel. [20C US also as *forks*]

fork *v.*¹ [late 17C–early 19C] to pick pockets, using the fore and middle fingers, extended like the tines of a fork, which are thrust into the pocket, then closed tight on any object within; this is then withdrawn between the 'fork'.

fork *v.*² **1** [mid–late 19C] to lay a woman down with spread legs preparatory to intercourse, also as *fork out*. **2** [late 19C+] (US) to mount a horse. **3** [20C] (Aus.) to ride a horse. [SE *fork*, the division of the legs where they join the torso]

fork *v.*³ [1950s] euph. for FUCK v.¹ (cf. FERK).

fork! *excl.* [early 19C+] give! (cf. FORK OVER). [abbr. FORK OUT; ult. FORKS]

fork and knife *n.* [late 19C+] **1** life. **2** a wife. [rhy. sl.]

for keeps *phr.* [mid-19C+] **1** for the duration, for a long time, for ever. **2** in absolute earnest.

forker *n.* [mid-19C] one of those 'who reside in seaports for the sake of stealing dockyard stores, or buying them, knowing them to be stolen' (Smyth, *Sailor's Word-book*, 1867).

fork-hooks *n.* [20C] (US) the fingers (cf. CUNT-HOOKS).

for kickers/a/the kickers *phr.* [1960s+] (US) for good measure. [KICKER n.⁴]

forklifts *n.* [1960s] (Aus.) a pair of cushions placed on the rear window of a car to be used for in-car sex (cf. HAWK ONE'S FORK). [SE *fork* n. + pun]

fork out/up *v.* [early 19C+] to pay, to donate. [FORKS]

fork over *v.* [early 19C+] to hand over, to give out. [FORKS]

forks *n.* **1** [18C–early 19C; 1940s] (orig. UK; US Black) the fingers, esp. the middle and forefingers (cf. FORK-HOOKS; MUCK-FORKS). **2** [early 19C] the hands.

fork up see FORK OUT.

for landsakes! *excl.* [mid-19C+] (US) a mild oath, euph. for *Lord's sake*.

for laughs *phr.* [1950s+] for fun, not to be taken seriously, often as *just for laughs*, *only for laughs* (cf. KICKS n.³).

forlorn hope *n.* [early 17C–late 18C] **1** the losers at a gaming table; thus **2** a gambler's last, despairing bet (cf. FLOWING HOPE). [Du. *verloren hoop*, a lost troop (of soldiers); the orig. 16C use described a band of skirmishers or assault troops who were sent ahead of the main force; this mutates into a desperate band of men and thence a desperate enterprise]

form *n.*¹ [late 19C] **1** liveliness, high spirits, conversational articulacy, esp. in phr. *in great form*. **2** habit, occupation, personality.

form *n.*² [late 19C+] (S.Afr.) a prison. [abbr. SE *reformatory*]

form, the *n.*³ [1930s+] the situation, the status quo, what is happening, how things are usually done; often in query, *what's the form?* [SE *form*, the proper way of doing things]

form *n.*⁴ [1950s+] (US) one's person as an object of sexual interest; thus *warm for someone's form*, sexually attracted to someone. [SE *form*, shape]

form *n.*⁵ [1950s+] **1** (Und.) previous convictions (cf. JACKET n.²; PEDIGREE; PREVIOUS; RAP SHEET). **2** character, style. [horse-racing use]

formula *n.* [1980s] (drugs) fake cannabis. [? SAmE *formula*, baby food, pap]

for my money see FOR ONE'S MONEY.

forney see FAWNEY.

fornicate the poodle, to *phr.* [1910s+] (US) to waste time (and loaf on the job) (cf. SCREW THE DOG). [euph. for FUCK THE DOG]

fornicating *adj.* [20C] euph. for FUCKING.

fornicating engine/member/tool *n.* [19C] the penis (cf. DEAREST MEMBER; FORNICATOR; GARDEN ENGINE; GARDENER n.²; GAYING INSTRUMENT; GENERATING PLACE, GENERATING TOOL; LOVE MACHINE; MACHINE n.¹; TOOL n.). [FORNICATING + ENGINE/MEMBER n.¹/TOOL n. (4)]

fornicator *n.* [19C] the penis; thus *fornicator's hall*, the vagina (cf. FORNICATING ENGINE).

fornicators *n.* [late 19C] trousers with a flap front rather than the modern fly. [their ease of exposure]

for nuts *phr.* [late 19C+] at all, in no way, e.g. *she can't cook for nuts*.

forny *see* FAWNEY.

for one's/my money *phr.* [mid-16C+] **1** what one would like, what one would choose. **2** in one's opinion, as far as one is concerned. [i.e. if one were having to pay or to wager]

for openers *phr.* [1960s+] to begin with.

for Pete's sake! *excl.* [1920s+] (orig. US) a euph. excl. used to indicate one's mild annoyance (cf. FOR THE LOVE OF MIKE!).

for real *adv.* [1950s+] (orig. US Black) honestly, sincerely, to be taken at face value.

for real? *phr.* [1990s] (US teen) used as a question to ask whether someone is teasing or telling the truth.

for skins *phr.* [20C] (Irish) at all, in any way. [SKIN n.²]

for starters *phr.* [1960s+] to begin with (cf. AS A STARTER).

for sure! *excl.* [late 19C+] certainly, definitely, absolutely. [the phr. gained a new lease of life as part of the Valley Girl vocab. of the early 1980s+]

Forsyte Saga *n.* [1970s] lager. [rhy. sl. John Galsworthy's early 20C literary saga of British business/social life]

fort/fortress *n.* [19C] the vagina.

fort bushy *n.* [20C] **1** the vagina. **2** (gay) the pubic hair. [FORT + BUSH n.⁴]

forteyed *adj.* [1990s] (US Black) drunk or intoxicated by a drug. [FORTY n.²]

Forth Bridge job *n.* [1970s+] anything that requires constant redoing, updating, amending. [the erroneous but trad. belief that the painting of Scotland's Forth Bridge is never finished – as soon as one end has been completed it is time to return to the other]

for the birds/strictly for the birds *phr.* [1950s+] (orig. US) trivial, worthless, appealing only to gullible people; coarsely ext. as *shit for the birds*.

for the fuck of it *phr.* [20C] for the fun of it. [fig. use of FUCK n.²]

for the good of the loo *phr.* [late 18C] for the good of all, for the benefit of the community. [SE *loo*, a card-game resembling whist; the game extends to its players and the plays, figuratively to the whole community]

for the hell/sheer hell of it *phr.* [1940s+] (orig. US) with no other justification than a (momentary) whim or self-indulgence.

for the jumps *see* IN FOR THE HIGH JUMP.

for the kickers *see* FOR KICKERS.

for the look of the thing *phr.* [late 19C+] for appearance's or form's sake.

for the love of Mike!/Pete! *excl.* [late 19C+] (orig. US) a euph. excl. of exasperation or surprise, for goodness' sake! (cf. FOR PETE'S SAKE!). [*Mike*, like *Pete*, is irrelevant, other perhaps than as a euph. for *Moses*]

for the ride *phr.* [1950s+] (orig. US) as a non-participant, as an observer only, esp. in phr. *be/come/go along for the ride*.

for the sheer hell of it *see* FOR THE HELL OF IT.

Forties *see* ROARING FORTIES.

Fortnum and Mason *n.* [late 19C] a large and sumptuous hamper, as provided by the famous London provisioners.

fortress *see* FORT.

for true *see* FEH TRUE.

fortune-biter *n.* [18C] a swindler, a confidence trickster. [SE *fortune* + BITE v.¹ (2)]

fortune cookie *n.* [1960s+] (Can.) a young woman, orig. typically from the chorus line, who swaps sexual favours for the monetary and material gifts of a (usually) older lover (cf. GOLD-DIGGER). [SE *fortune* + COOKIE n.²; pun]

fortune-teller *n.* [late 17C–18C] a trial judge (cf. CONJURER). [he tells you your *fortune*, i.e. your sentence]

forty *n.¹* [19C] (Aus.) a crook, a confidence trickster. [a Sydney gang of the mid-19C; poss. called the *Forty Thieves*, although that name may have been a subsequent journalistic invention]

forty/forty ounce *n.²* [1980s+] (US Black) a large bottle of beer. [its contents, *40 ounces* (1.1 litres) of beer]

forty *adj.* [mid-19C+] many. [thus orig. *OED* citation: 'I could beat forty of them' (Shakespeare, *Coriolanus*, 1607)]

forty acres *n.* [20C] (US) extremely large feet. [their supposed dimensions]

forty-ax *n.* [20C] (US) very strong coffee. [phr. *strong as 40 axes*, ult. ? AGGIE FORTIS, *aqua fortis*]

Forty-Deuce *n.* [20C] (US) 42nd Street from 8th Avenue to Times Square; the centre of New York's tourism, nightlife and underworld before its destruction by Disney's 'family' banalities (cf. DEUCE n.⁴). [SE *forty* + DEUCE n.² (2)]

forty-dog *n.* [1990s] (US Black) a 40-ounce (1.2-litre) bottle of beer (cf. SIXTY-FOUR). [FORTY n.² + SHORT DOG]

forty-eleven *n.* [20C] (US Black/W.I.) too many, an infinite number (cf. FIFTY-ELEVEN).

forty-faced *adj.* [late 19C] shameless; thus combs. *forty-faced liar, forty-faced flirt.* [? one has 'forty faces', none of them trustworthy, but note FORTY adj. + dial. *forty-legs*, a millipede, where *forty* is generic for 'many']

forty fits *n.* [late 19C+] an extreme loss of emotional control; thus *have forty fits*, to lose all control. [FORTY adj. + SE *fits*]

forty-five minute psychosis *n.* [1960s+] (drugs) dimethyltryptarine (DMT) (cf. BUSINESSMAN'S TRIP). [the short duration and intensity of the drug experience]

forty-foot *n.* [mid-19C] a short person.

forty-four *adv.* [20C] door-to-door. [rhy. sl.]

forty-guts *n.* [mid-19C] a fat man. [FORTY adj. + SE *guts*]

forty-jawed/-lunged *adj.* [19C] loquacious, talkative. [TALK FORTY TO THE DOZEN]

forty miles from nowhere *phr.* [20C] (US) far from what the speaker considers 'civilization', deep in the countryside.

forty miles of bad road *phr.* [1960s+] (US) a very unattractive person, sight or situation.

forty-niner *n.* [late 19C] (US) an early immigrant to California, drawn there because of the gold rush of 1849.

forty-pounder *n.* [19C] a policeman (cf. WEIGH FORTY). [the £40 cash bonus awarded to any policeman who secured a 'Tyburn ticket', i.e. captured a murderer]

forty-rod/forty-rod lightning *n.* [19C] cheap, strong whisky. [its strength; such whisky was jokingly said to be powerful enough to kill at a distance of 40 rods (about 17.7km/11 miles). Alternatively, its strength empowered the drinker to run at top speed for a similar distance, or the drinker is guaranteed to collapse if he attempts to walk much further than this]

forty-shilling word *n.* [1960s] (W.I.) an obscene word, for the use of which one can be fined 40 shillings or £2.

forty to the dozen *phr.* [mid-19C+] extremely fast (cf. TALK FORTY TO THE DOZEN). [SE phr. *nineteen to the dozen*]

forty ways from the jack *phr.* [20C] (US) (orig. gambling) in every way possible.

forty winks *n.* [early 19C+] a brief nap, often after a meal.

forwards *n.* [1970s+] (drugs) amphetamine (cf. A *n.*²). [it impels its users to action]

for yonks *adv.* [1980s+] for ages, for a very long time. [? SE *eons*]

foss *see* PHOS.

fossick/fossicker/night-fossick/night-fossicker *n.* [mid–late 19C] (Aus.) a thief who specializes in taking gold-dust or gold quartz. [SE *night* + SAusE *fossick*, to search for/pick up gold on the surface; ult. Warwicks dial. *fossick*, a troublesome person]

fossy jaw *see* PHOSSY JAW.

fotog *see* PHOTOG.

fou *adj.*¹ [late 17C+] drunk (cf. BITCH-FOU; GREETIN' FOU; PIPER FOU; PISSING FOU; ROARING FOU). [Scot. pron. of FULL *adj.*¹; note also FOUR *adj.*²]

fou *adj.*² [20C] (W.I.) crazy, mad. [Fr. *fou*, mad]

foul *adj.* [1910s–60s] a general negative, revolting, disgusting.

foul a plate with, to *phr.* [late 18C–early 19C] to share a meal with. [SE *foul*, to dirty]

foul ball *n.* [1990s] (US) an unpleasant, poss. criminal character. [baseball jargon *foul ball*, a ball struck so that it falls outside the lines drawn from the home base through the first and third bases]

fouled up *adj.* [1940s+] (US) **1** in a mess, in chaos, disorganized. **2** mistaken. **3** useless, worthless. [euph. for FUCKED UP]

foul-up *n.* [1940s+] (US, orig. milit.) **1** a state of confusion or chaos occasioned by bungling and/or ineptitude (cf. FUCK-UP *n.*). **2** the individual who causes or is capable of causing such chaos. [FOUL UP]

foul up *v.* [1940s+] (US, orig. milit.) **1** to ruin, to destroy, to blunder. **2** to fall into confusion, to fail through personal inadequacy, to get into trouble. [euphs. for FUCK UP]

foundling temper *n.* [late 19C] an extremely bad temper. ['proverbially said of the domestic servants poured upon London by the Metropolitan Foundling Hospital' (Ware)]

found on *adj.* [20C] (Irish) arrested for drinking in a public house after licensing hours. [police charge sheet, *found on licensed premises ...*]

foundry *n.* [late 19C] a shop, esp. a pork butcher's shop because of the noise of the sausage machine.

fountain of love *n.* [19C] the vagina (cf. DAMP *n.*).

fountain palaces/temples *n.* [late 19C] public conveniences.

four and nine/four and nine penny *n.* [mid-19C] a cheap hat (cf. GOSS). [the 1844 advertisement, which declared 'Whene'er to slumber you incline/Take a *short nap* at 4 and 9.']

four and one *n.* [1940s–50s] (US Black) the fifth day, i.e. payday, which is Friday.

four-and-twenty/four-and-twenty steps *n.* [1950s] (W.I.) an arrest, a trial (cf. ELEVEN STEPS). [ety. unknown; ? lit. the number of steps from a particular courtroom to the cells]

four-and-two *n.* [1930s] a sandwich. [? of the four sides of bread, only two are buttered]

four annas in the rupee *n.* [late 19C–1900s] a Eurasian quadroon. [16 annas = 1 rupee; thus 4 annas = one quarter]

four-bit *n.* [mid-19C+] (W.I.) one shilling and sixpence, post-1969 value 15 cents.

four bones *n.* [1920s] (Irish) the human body.

four-by *n.* [1990s] a 4-wheel-drive vehicle, usu. a form of Jeep, popular among drug dealers, rappers and their fans.

four-by-three *adj.* [1920s–30s] small, unimportant. [? the relatively small dimensions]

four by two *n.* **1** [1930s+] a Jew (cf. BOX OF GLUE). **2** (N.Z.) a prison warder. [rhy. sl.; (2) = SCREW *n.*² (2)]

four cautions, the *n.* [late 18C] 'I. Beware of a woman before. – II. Beware of a horse behind. – III. Beware of a cart sideways. – IV. Beware of a priest every way' (Grose, 1785).

four-cornered *adj.* [20C] (US prison) caught in the act (cf. DEADWOOD *adj.*²). [elaboration of SE *cornered*]

four corners *n.* [19C+] (US) a small, out-of-the-way place. [*four-corners*, a crossroads and thus a small settlement that might grow up around it]

four-eleven/411 *n.* [1990s] (US Black/campus) information; thus as an excl. give me the facts, give me some details. [the US phone number for information]

four-eleven-forty-four/4-11-44 *n.* [1960s] (Black) the penis (cf. NINE-INCH KNOCKER). [the 'lucky number' popularized by NUMBERS or POLICY bettors from late 19C+]

four-eyed *adj.* [mid-19C+] an insult aimed at those who wear spectacles.

four-eye puss *n.* [1940s] (W.I.) one who wears glasses. [FOUR-EYES + PUSS *n.*³]

four-eyes *n.* [mid-19C+] one who wears glasses; overtones also of distrust of anyone 'intellectual'.

4-F *adj.* [1940s+] (US) useless, inferior, weak. [milit. specification for anyone unfit to serve]

4-F club *n.* [1950s+] (US) a metaphorical 'club' based on the slogan 'find 'em, feel 'em, fuck 'em and forget 'em', the axiom for macho US youth in its dealings with women (cf. HUMP 'EM AND DUMP 'EM). [note Mae West in *I'm No Angel* (1933) tells her maid to 'find 'em, fool 'em and forget 'em' when it comes to men; the rap group NWA used 'find 'em, fuck 'em and flee' in 1991]

four-fingered shuffle *n.* [1980s+] masturbation (cf. KNUCKLE SHUFFLE).

four-flush *adj.* [late 19C] (US) cheating, crooked, untrustworthy. [FOUR-FLUSHER]

four-flush *v.* [late 19C+] (US) to cheat or bluff. [FOUR-FLUSHER]

four-flusher *n.* [late 19C+] (US) **1** a cheat, a bluffer. **2** a scrounger, one who fails to pay due debts. **3** a braggart, a boaster. [poker jargon; a real flush requires 5 cards of the same suit, 4 is merely a bluff]

four-foot amelia *n.* [1930s] (W.I.) a flimsy or roughly constructed bed.

four-Fs *n.* [1940s+] (US) a young man's guide to sexual ethics, 'find 'em, feel 'em, fuck 'em and forget 'em', sometimes amplified to *five Fs* by adding 'feed 'em' after 'find 'em' (cf. 4-F CLUB).

four-half *n.* [late 19C] a mix of ale and porter, sold at 4 pence a quart.

four-headed *adj.* [20C] (US Black) very clever, exceptionally intelligent (cf. TWO-HEADED). [for ety. *see* DOUBLE-HEADED]

four-legged fortune *n.* [late 19C–1910s] (society) a winning racehorse.

four-legged frolic *n.* [mid-19C] sexual intercourse. [note popular euph. for *the beast of two backs*]

four-letter man *n.* [1920s+] **1** (society) an unpleasant person; the 4 letters are perhaps *s-h-i-t* (as suggested by Manchon) or *c-u-n-t*. **2** (US) both as (1) and as *h-o-m-o* (cf. THREE-LETTER MAN).

four-letter word *n.* [20C] an obscenity, notably CUNT, FUCK, SHIT etc; thus six-letter word, BUGGER; and 10-letter word, COCKSUCKER etc. [euph.]

four-liner *n.* [late 19C] (society) something considered very important. [the '4-line whips' issued in Parliament]

four-oh-four/404 *n.* [1990s] (US teen) a fool. [computer use *404*, 'File Not Found' message on the Web]

four-one-one/411 *see* FOUR-ELEVEN.

fourpenny *n.* [late 19C–1900s] an ugly, worn-out old prostitute. [her price]

fourpenny cannon *n.* late 19C) a steak and kidney pie. [its shape or its consistency – a cannon ball]

fourpenny dark *n.* [1950s+] (Aus.) cheap red wine.

fourpenny one *n.* [20C] 'a clip round the ear-hole' (cf. GET A FOURPENNY ONE; GIVE A FOURPENNY ONE). [rhy. sl. *fourpenny bit* = hit]

fourpenny pit *n.* [late 19C] a fourpenny bit or groat, the predecessor of the threepenny bit.

four prices *adj.* [20C] (Ulster) very expensive. [? it costs fig. 'four times as much' as a normal item]

fourses *n.* [19C] a snack taken during the afternoon (cf. DEW-BIT; ELEVENSES). [SE *four o'clock*]

four sisters on thumb street *n.* [1970s+] (US Black) masturbation (cf. MISS FIST).

foursome *n.* [1990s] (US) 4 people involved in sex together; it can involve any combination of genders.

fourteen penn'orth *n.* [early 19C] a sentence of 14 years' transportation.

fourth *n.* [mid-19C] a lavatory. [? orig. used at Trinity, Cambridge, at that time the college privies were sited in the fourth court and thus an undergraduate who had temporarily gone there would write upon his door 'Gone 4'; alt. ety. suggests that one's morning went through 4 stages, chapel, breakfast, pipe, visit to the lavatory]

four thick *n.* [late 19C] beer sold at 4 pence a quart.

fourth of July *n.* [20C] a tie (cf. PECKHAM RYE). [rhy. sl.]

four-twenty/4:20 *n.* [1980s+] (US) marijuana. [police code or civil statute code for the smoking of marijuana]

four-wheeler *n.*[1] [19C] a beefsteak.

four-wheeler/four-wheel Christian *n.*[2] [1960s+] anyone (orig. Roman Catholic only) who only visits a church for weddings, christenings, funerals and other 'social' rather than purely religious events. [they drive to church]

four-/three-wheel skid *n.* [1930s+] a Jew. [rhy. sl. *four-/three-wheel skid* = YID]

foutra/foutre *v.* (16C) to have sexual intercourse (cf. FUCK v.[1]). [Fr. *foutre*]

fox *n.*[1] **1** [late 17C–18C] a cunning, duplicitous person. **2** [1970s+] (orig. US) a drinker who slips out of the bar when it is his turn to pay for a round. [stereotypical negative characteristics of the animal]

fox *n.*[2] [mid-19C] an artificial sore. [? SE *fox*, to fool]

fox *n.*[3] [late 19C+] (US) an inhabitant of Maine.

fox *n.*[4] **1** [1940s+] (orig. US Black) a girl, a woman, esp. an attractive one. **2** [1940s+] a womanizer (cf. WOLF n.[1]). **3** [1960s] (US prison) the passive partner in a lesbian relationship. **4** [1970s+] (US campus) a sexually attractive person of the opposite sex. [stereotypical positive characteristics of the animal + FOXY adj.[2]]

fox *v.*[1] **1** [early 17C+] to fool, to trick, to dissemble. **2** [late 17C–late 18C] to make drunk (cf. FOXED). [SE *fox*, to confuse]

fox *v.*[2] **1** [mid-19C] to observe surreptitiously. **2** [20C] (N.Z.) to be a voyeur, esp. when spying on couples in the open air.

fox *v.*[3] [mid-19C] to feign sleep (cf. FOX'S SLEEP).

fox and badger *n.* [1990s] the penis. [rhy. sl. *fox and badger* = TADGER]

fox bait *n.* [20C] (US) an old horse, ready for the knacker.

fox-drunk *adj.* [early 17C] drunk but still cunning. [SE *fox* as a symbol of cunning + *drunk*]

foxed *adj.* [early 17C–late 18C] drunk (cf. ADDLED). [FOX v.[1] (1)]

foxer *n.* [20C] (N.Z.) a voyeur, esp. one who spies on couples in the open air. [FOX v.[2] (2)]

foxhead *n.* [20C] (US) illicitly distilled whisky (cf. MOONSHINE; POPSKULL). [SE *fox*, to confuse + *head*]

foxing *see* FOX'S SLEEP.

fox's paw *n.* [late 18C] a mistake, a blunder. [Fr. *faux pas*]

fox's sleep/foxing *n.* [mid-19C] an air of indifference to what

is going on (cf. FOX n.[1]). [the belief that a fox sleeps with one eye open]

foxy *adj.*[1] [mid-19C] having red hair. [the fox's colouring]

foxy *adj.*[2] [1910s+] **1** (orig. US) attractive, sexy. **2** (US Black) splendid, good. [FOX n.[4] + sfx. -*y*]

foxy grandpa *n.* [20C] (US) a sly person, neither necessarily old or a grandfather. [the cartoon character *Foxy Granpa*, by C.E. Schultze (1866–1939), which appeared *c.*1900 and featured an adult who, in a reverse of the usual cartoon situation, played tricks on children]

foxy lady *n.* [20C] a male homosexual. [FOXY adj.[2] + SE *lady*]

foy *n.* [late 16C–early 17C] a swindler.

foy! *excl.* [late 17C] a general excl. [SE *fay*, faith]

foyl-cloy *see* FOIL-CLOY.

foyse *see* FICE.

foyst *see* FOIST.

f.p. *n.* [20C] (Und.) *false pretences,* thus fraud. [abbr.]

fraai *see* VRY.

fracture *v.* **1** [1940s+] to make one laugh, to amuse greatly, e.g. *that fractures me,* that's an amusing joke (cf. BREAK UP v.). **2** [1940s–70s] (US) to beat up, to trounce. **3** [1970s+] (US) to astonish, to disconcert.

fractured *adj.* [20C] very drunk (cf. BASTED).

fraho/frajo *n.* [1960s+] (US) **1** a cigarette. **2** (drugs) marijuana. [Sp.]

fraidy/fraidy-fraidy *adj.* [1950s] (W.I.) timid, fearful. [SE *afraid*]

fraidy-cat/-pants *n.* [19C] (juv.) a coward, a timorous person (cf. PAPBROEK; SCAREDY-CAT). [SE *afraid*]

fraidy-fraidy *see* FRAIDY.

frail *n.* **1** [mid-19C] a prostitute. **2** [20C] (orig. US) a girl, a woman. **3** [1950s] (US prison) a passive partner in a lesbian relationship. [the image of women as weaklings; thus Victorian euph. *the frail sisterhood,* prostitutes as a class]

frail eel *n.* [1940s–70s] (US Black) an attractive woman. [FRAIL + SE *eel,* an elusive creature which is hard to hold on to]

frajo *see* FRAHO.

fram *v.* [20C] (US) to beat, to strike, to attack. [? Midlands dial. *fram,* to be in a temper or passion]

frame *n.*[1] [20C] (Und.) the general situation, esp. that surrounding the suspects in a given crime (cf. IN THE FRAME).

frame *n.*[2] [1940s–50s] **1** (orig. US Black) the body. **2** (US Black) a suit of clothes.

frame *v.*[1] [1900s] (US) to dress. [SE *frame* (a picture)]

frame *v.*[2] **1** [1910s+] (orig. US) to trap a suspect (poss. innocent) by creating false evidence, witnesses etc. **2** [1920s–50s] (US) to trick or hoodwink. [FRAME-UP]

frames *n.* [1950s] (US Black) spectacles, glasses.

frame-up *n.* [1920s+] (orig. US) the concoction of criminal guilt or charges. [FRAME UP v.]

frame up *v.* (orig. US) **1** [1900s–20s] to form a plan of action, esp. in secret. **2** [1920s+] to concoct a false charge or accusation against, to devise a scheme or plot with regard to.

frammis *n.* [1950s+] (US) **1** any form of confidence trick. **2** a thingumibob. [? FRAME v.?]

France *n.* [1920s+] (W.I.) euph. for FUCK or *hell* (cf. GIVE FRANCE). [the basic use, *France!,* is as an oath, and refers to the horrors of WW1, when many West Indians fought and died in the trenches of Flanders. Other uses, all of which can be paralleled by a use of fuck and/or hell, include such phrases as *to France with that*; *get to France out of here*; *how/what/ when/who/why/where the France ...* and *give someone France.* The phrases may also have some background in the Du. *Loop naar de Franschen,* run to the French, i.e. go to the devil]

France and Spain *n.* [late 19C+] rain (cf. ALACOMPAIN). [rhy. sl.]

frances *n.* [20C] (US) the buttocks. [FANNY n.[1], of which it is the proper name]

franc-fileur *n.* [late 19C–1900s] (society) at a ball, a man who will not dance and refuses to talk to any woman for more than a moment. [Fr. *franc-fileur*, free runner]

franger *n.* [1970s+] (Aus.) a condom. [? FRENCH LETTER]

frangerlips *n.* [1990s] a general insult aimed at those with thick, puffy lips. [FRANGER + SE *lips*]

franklin teeth *n.* [1920s–30s] (Can.) projecting or 'buck' teeth. [the protruding grille of the Franklin automobile]

frank thring *n.* [1970s] (Aus.) a (wedding) ring. [rhy. sl.]

fransman/Frenchman/franse *n.* [1970s+] (S.Afr. Und.) an outsider, a convict who is not affiliated to a prison gang. [Afk. *fransman*, Frenchman, thus fig. a foreigner]

frantic *adj.* **1** [1900s] a general intensifier, terrific, awful. **2** [1950s] of a party, lively, frenetic. **3** [1950s–60s] exciting, amusing, enjoyable.

frantically *adv.* **1** [1900s] a general intensifier, terrifically, awfully. **2** [1950s] of a party, lively, frenetically. **3** [1950s–60s] excitingly, amusingly, enjoyably.

franzy house *n.* [20C] (US) **1** a brothel (cf. ACCOMMODATION HOUSE). **2** a psychiatric institution. [dial. *franzy*, SE *frenzy*, craziness, madness + HOUSE n.[1] used as sl. in **1** and as SE (*mad*) *house* in 2.]

frap *n.* [1990s] euph. for FUCK (all senses). [note dial *frap*, to strike to beat]

frapping *adj.* [1990s] euph. for FUCKING adj.

frapple *n.* [1990s] quick masturbation. [FRAP n. + dimin. sfx. -*ple*]

frat *n.* [late 19C+] (US) **1** a college *frat*ernity. **2** a member of a *frat*ernity. [abbr.]

fratdom *n.* [1980s+] (US campus) the world of fraternities. [FRAT + sfx. -*dom*]

frater *n.* [16C–early 18C] (Und.) a mendicant villain who poses as a friar and claims, as such, to beg alms for a hospital or charitable institution, specializing in poor, gullible women (cf. CANTING CREW). [Lat. *frater*, brother]

fratosoralingoid/fratosororalingoid *n.* [1990s] (US campus) an obnoxious fraternity or sorority member. [SE *fraternity* + *sorority* = SF sfx. -*lingoid*]

frat out *v.* [1970s] (US campus) to dress and act like a fraternity member. [FRAT]

frat rat *n.* [1970s] (US campus) a member of a fraternity. [FRAT + RAT n.[3]]

fratting *n.* [1940s+] essentially abbr. of SE *fraternizing*, but used as euph. for FUCKING n.[1], n.[2].

fratty *adj.* [1970s] (US campus) pertaining to fraternity life. [FRAT + sfx. -*y*]

fratty-bagger *n.* [1970s] (US campus) a stereotypical fraternity member. [FRATTY + fig. use of BAGGER n.[2]]

fray *see* VRY.

Fray Bentos *n.* [1960s] a typhoid victim. [brandname of a variety of corned beef imported from Uruguay; a bad consignment of corned beef led to a typhoid epidemic in Aberdeen in 1964]

frazer nash *n.* [1970s] an act of urination. [rhy. sl. *Frazer-Nash* = SLASH n.+; the Frazer-Nash was a sports car manufactured before 1940]

frazzle *n.* [mid-19C+] (orig. US) a state of emotional and/or physical exhaustion, esp. in phr. *worn to a frazzle*. [SE *frazzle*, a frayed end, a fragment, a shred]

frazzle *v.* [19C+] **1** to fray, to become unravelled, often used of a whip's end. **2** (US) to whip. **3** [20C] (Aus.) to rob. [East Anglia dial. *frazzle*, to wear away, to unravel, ult. SE *fray*]

frazzled/frazzled out *adj.* **1** [19C+] (orig. US) emotionally drained, physically exhausted. **2** [19C+] (orig. US) drunk.

3 [1980s+] (US drugs) under the influence of marijuana. [fig. use of FRAZZLE v. (1)]

frazzling *adj.* [20C] (US) a general intensifier, euph. for FUCKING.

freak *n.* **1** [late 19C] (US campus) a student who is exceptionally proficient in a subject. **2** [late 19C+] (US) an offensively eccentric or crazy person. **3** [20C] (orig. US Black) an effeminate man, a male homosexual. **4** [1960s+] one who enjoys non-standard sexual practices. **5** [1960s+] (US Black) a woman, usu. sexually aggressive and adventurous. **6** [1960s+] (orig. US) a young person devoted to the 'counter-culture' or 'alternative society'. **7** [1980s+] (US campus) an extremely beautiful, good-looking woman, usu. but not always a member of one's own peer group. [SE *freak*, a monstrosity (of nature), often as exhibited in a show. Note (6), like many parallel 'bad = good' usages, the young people in question adopted the name, synon. with 'extreme hippie', after they had been branded as 'freaks' by their critics]

freak *v.* [1960s+] (orig. drug/hippie) to worry, to disturb, to cause severe anxiety (the extent of the disturbance varies totally as to context). [abbr. FREAK OUT]

-freak *sfx.* [1970s] (orig. US campus) combining form that indicates an obsessive, one who is extremely interested in or overly fond of something, e.g. *health-freak*, *dope-freak* etc.

freak attack *n.* [1990s] (US teen) a state of extreme tension. [FREAK v. + SE *attack*]

freak-a-zoid *n.* [1990s] (US Black teen) an eccentric, an obsessive, a freak. [FREAK n. + SF sfx. -*azoid*]

freak daddy *n.* [1980s+] (US campus) an attractive man (cf. FREAK MAMA). [FREAK n. (7) + DADDY]

Freakeries, the *n.* [late 19C] Barnum's freak and acrobat shows, put on at Olympia (cf. COLINDERIES). [SE *freak*, a monstrosity + sfx. -*eries*]

freak fuck *n.* [1960s+] **1** any variation on 'straight' heterosexual intercourse, esp. anal intercourse. **2** (orig. US Black) a client who demands unusual or possibly physically dangerous services from a prostitute, often abbr. *freak*. [FREAK FUCK v.]

freak fuck *v.* [1960s+] (orig. US Black) **1** to engage in anal intercourse with a woman. **2** to engage in cunnilingus. [FREAK n. (4) + FUCK v.[1]]

freaking *n.* [1960s+] losing psychological control, whether enjoyably or otherwise, as the result of drugs, usu. hallucinogens (cf. FREAK OUT).

freaking *adj.* [1920s+] (US) euph. for FUCKING (cf. FRIGGING).

freakish *adj.* [1940s–50s] (US Black) homosexual, sexually deviant or lustful. [FREAK n. (3), (4)]

freak mama *n.* [1980s+] (US campus) an attractive woman, with overtones of sluttishness. [FREAK n. (4) + MAMA]

freak off *v.* **1** [1950s+] (US Black) to masturbate (cf. BEAT OFF). **2** [1960s–70s] (US Black) to express one's enjoyment. **3** [1960s–70s] to create something beautiful. **4** [1960s+] (US Black) to engage in unrestrained or unorthodox sexual activity. [FREAK v.]

freak-out *n.* [1960s+] **1** (orig. US drugs) any unpleasant experience caused by drug use, esp. with LSD. **2** anxiety, ranging from twinges of fear to a full nervous breakdown, varying as to context. **3** (US) a gathering of young people, esp. hippies, to enjoy music and take drugs together.

freak out *v.* [1960s+] **1** to worry, to disturb, to horrify – the level of trauma depends on context. **2** (US) to engage in unorthodox or unrestrained sexual activity (cf. FREAK OFF). **3** (US) to go crazy, wild or out of control with enthusiasm, or from fear or instability. **4** (US drugs) to experience an altered state of consciousness from the effects of a hallucinogenic drug, esp. an unpleasant effect.

freak trick *n.* [1960s+] (US prostitute) any customer who requires out-of-the-way sex or who attacks the woman physically. [FREAK n. (4) + TRICK n.[4] (2)]

freaky *adj.* [1960s+] odd, bizarre, unnerving. [FREAK n. + sfx. -*y*]

freckle *n.* [1960s+] (Aus.) the anus.

freckle-nature *n.* [1950s] (W.I.) an albino (cf. GLIMPSE; GREY NAYGA; GREY PUSS; NORWEGIAN; PATU-EYE; PUSS n.[5]; PUSS-EYE; QUAW; RIPE BANANA; SIDE-PORK; SPECKLE; WHITE KAFFIR; WHITE MAN n.[2]; WHITE-NAYGA; WHITEY-WHITEY).

freckle-puncher *n.* [1960s+] a male homosexual (cf. DUNG-PUNCHER). [FRECKLE + SE *puncher*]

fred *n.*[1] [1970s+] (Aus.) the average Australian (cf. ALF; OCKER). [the commonness of the name]

fred *n.*[2] [1980s+] (US campus) *n.* **1** a socially unacceptable person, a freeloader. **2** a fool (cf. BARNEY n.[5]). [the character *Fred Flintstone* in *The Flintstones* cartoon and film (1994)]

fred *v.* [1980s+] (US campus) to vomit. [echoic]

Fred Astaire *n.* [1940s+] (Aus.) **1** a chair. **2** the hair. **3** a dandy. [rhy. sl. (3) *Fred Astaire* = LAIR n.; ult. film star and dancer *Fred Astaire* (1899–1987)]

Fred Astaire *adj.* [1940s] (US campus) stylish. [rhy. sl.; for ety. see FRED ASTAIRE n.]

fred astaires *n.* [1940s] stairs (cf. DANCE v.[3]). [rhy. sl.; ult. Fred Astaire (1899–1987)]

Fred Karno's army *n.* [1910s–70s] a group of people considered incompetent. [the popular comedian *Fred Karno* (1866–1941), who fronted a series of slapstick mini-shows, often burlesquing music-hall. Orig. milit. use in WW1 for the 'New', i.e. conscripted, army and in WW2 for any platoon or section seen as inept]

fred nerk *n.* [1990s] (Aus.) an imaginary person, esp. one on whom the blame can be placed, e.g. in phr. *I suppose it was Fred Nerk* (who did it).

fred's *n.* [1970s+] (society) nickname for Fortnum and Mason, Piccadilly, London.

free *n.* [1960s+] (US prison) the free world, i.e. the world outside prison.

free *v.* [mid-19C] to steal, usu. a horse; thus *free a cat*, to steal a muff (cf. ACQUIRE). [ironic use of SE]

free-and-easy *n.* [mid–late 19C] **1** (US) a cheap brothel. **2** a convivial gathering for singing, at which one may drink, smoke etc.

freebase *n.* (drugs) **1** [1970s+] cocaine base, purified by ether and smoked rather than sniffed or injected. **2** [1980s+] crack cocaine.

freebase *v.* [1980s+] (drugs) to intensify the effect of cocaine by heating it in combination with ether or other chemicals before inhaling it (cf. BASE v.[2]; FREEBASING). [FREEBASE n.]

freebasing *n.* [1970s+] (drugs) intensifying the effect of cocaine by heating it in combination with ether or other chemicals before inhaling it. [SE *free*, to set free, to separate from + BASE v.[2]]

freebie *n.* [1940s+] (orig. US) any free sample, free trip, esp. press tours, promotions etc.

freebie *v.* [1940s+] (orig. US) of a prostitute, to provide sexual services without making a charge. [FREEBIE n.]

freedom cut *n.* [1960s+] (US Black/campus) a hairstyle for which normally short, curly Black hair is allowed to grow out in a bush around the head (cf. AFRO n.[2]). [the Afro cut was equated with a statement of Black freedom]

free-fishery *n.* [late 19C–1900s] the vagina (cf. BEARDED CLAM). [FISH n.[4] (1); but note SE *free fish*, a soft-bodied fish (as opposed to a crustacean)]

free-for-all *n.* [20C] (US) a sexually available woman.

free, gratis and for nothing *phr.* [late 18C+] absolutely free.

freeholder *n.* **1** [late 17C–18C] a man whose wife accompanies him to the tavern. **2** [late 19C–1900s] a prostitute's companion. [a specific 'tavern term' drawn f. *The English Liberal Science, or a new-found Art and Order of Drinking*; ? pun on SE *freeholder*, one who has land worth 40s (£2) a year; presumably one needed such income to buy a wife a drink]

free hotel/motel *n.* [20C] (US) a prison (cf. AKERMAN'S HOTEL). [i.e. one pays nothing for one's accommodation]

freelance *n.* [19C] an habitual adulteress, though not a professional prostitute.

freelance *v.* [1960s+] for a woman to work as a prostitute without being committed to a pimp.

freeload *v.* [1940s+] **1** to enjoy for free the pleasures that are primarily made available to a celebrity or laid on at an important event but become equally available to anyone who cares to struggle hard enough to grab them. **2** in general use, to define the taking of any benefits that one has not made due efforts to deserve. [backform. from FREELOAD n.]

freeloader *n.* [1930s+] (orig. US) a parasite, one who eats and drinks without spending any money; more recently those who form a celebrity's entourage and enjoy the crumbs from their various tables. [SE *free* + *load up*, to fill (oneself) up]

free lunch *n.* [1940s+] (US) something for nothing.

freeman *n.* [18C] an adulterer (cf. FREELANCE n.)

freeman of a corporation's work *n.* [late 18C] an unattractive, weak man. [SE *corporation*, the magistrates of a provincial town]

freeman of bucks *n.* [18C] an adulterer. [FREEMAN + pun on BUCK n.[1]]

freeman's/harry freeman's *n.* [1930s+] anything obtained for free, esp. as a bribe given to a corrupt policeman. [for ety. see DRINK AT FREEMAN'S QUAY]

freeman's key *n.* [late 19C–1910s] (Aus.) any situation in which payment, esp. for alcohol, can be put off. [corruption of/var. on. DRINK AT FREEMAN'S QUAY]

free motel see FREE HOTEL.

free object *n.* [19C] (Aus.) a 'civilian' settler who has not been transported. [pun on *free subject* (of His/Her Majesty)]

free of fumbler's hall *phr.* [late 17C–18C] referring to an impotent husband (cf. FUMBLER). [SE *free of* + FUMBLER'S HALL]

free of his/her patter *phr.* [late 19C] very talkative. [SE *free of* + PATTER n.]

free of sense as a frog of feathers *phr.* [20C] (Aus.) utterly stupid.

free of the bush *phr.* [late 19C] sexually intimate with a woman. [SE *free of* + BUSH n.[4]]

free-paper burn *phr.* [late 19C+] (W.I.) a phr. meaning that the holidays are over and one must return to work or school. [slavery days when a slave might get a 'free-paper' or pass to take temporary leave from the plantation; this was destroyed on their return]

free ride *n.* [20C] an easy time.

free school *n.* [1900s–40s] (US Black) a public school. [derog. phr. 'free schools, pretty yellow teachers and dumb Negroes' (Zora Neale Hurston, *American Mercury*, 1942)]

free shot *n.* [1970s+] the unpaid-for services of a prostitute.

free show *n.* [20C] the inadvertent revelation by a woman of her body, in all or part,– glimpsed by a passing man (cf. FLASH n.[4]).

Free State coal *n.* [late 19C] (S.Afr.) dried cow-dung, used as fuel.

freestyle *n.* [1990s] (US Black/teen) unwritten rap lyrics, using whatever comes to mind at the spur of the moment.

freestyle *v.* [1990s] (US Black/teen) **1** to create spontaneous rap rhymes, without prior preparation. **2** to act in a spontaneous manner, to live by one's own rules, wear one's own styles of clothes etc (cf. DO ONE'S THING).

free the slaves, to phr. [1990s] to masturbate.

free-traders n. [late 19C–1930s] women's knickers, open at the crotch. [the freedom of access to the vagina]

freeway freddie n. [1970s+] (US Black) a highway patrolman. [California use]

free, white and twenty-one/over twenty-one phr. [1920s+] (orig. US) phr. describing a free agent, one who is free to make their own decisions. [21 is the age of consent in many countries and US states]

free willy v. [1990s] to masturbate. [SE free + WILLIE n.[1] + pun on title of film (1993)]

freeze n.[1] [mid-17C–early 19C] a thin, hard cider, used by vintners; thus freezing vintner, a vinter who dilutes their wine.

freeze n.[2] **1** [1940s+] (orig. US) a snub, a rejection (cf. CHILL n.[1]; COLD SHOULDER). **2** [1930s+] (Aus.) a wife's deliberate withholding of sexual favours.

freeze n.[3] [1970s+] cocaine. [from the effects of the drug when inhaled or rubbed on the gums]

freeze v.[1] **1** [19C] to steal **2** [mid–late 19C] (US) to yearn for; thus froze for, desirous of. [FREEZE ON]

freeze v.[2] **1** [mid–late 19C] to exclude from society, business etc by intimidating, snubbing behaviour. **2** [20C] (US) to intimidate. **3** [1910s–60s] (US) to snub, to ignore. **4** [1930s+] (Aus.) of a woman, to refuse sexual favours. **5** [1970s+] (drugs) to renege on a drug deal

freeze v.[3] [1910s+] **1** to become silent, to quieten down, to refuse to answer questions or make conversation. **2** to stand absolutely still.

freeze! excl. [1910s+] don't move! stay where you are! [FREEZE v.[3] (2)]

freeze-/freezy-cat n. [20C] (US) one who has a low tolerance for cold weather. [on pattern of FRAIDY-CAT; SCAREDY-CAT]

freeze on v. [19C+] **1** to ignore, to snub, to reject. **2** (orig. US/Aus.) to take a tight grip of, to grasp.

freeze out v. [mid-19C+] (orig. US) to snub, to render socially unacceptable, to exclude from a (business) deal; thus freeze-out game, a deliberate exclusion.

freezer n.[1] **1** [late 18C+] a rebuff, a snub. **2** [mid–late 19C] a chilly look, a dismissive remark. [FREEZE v.[1]]

freezer n.[2] [20C] (Aus.) a prison (cf. COOLER n.[1]).

freeze to v. [late 19C] to be very keen on, to fancy greatly.

freezing weather n. [1930s–40s] (US Black) an unattractive woman (cf. FINE WEATHER).

freezy-cat see FREEZE-CAT.

French n.[1] [late 19C+] bad language; usu. in phr. excuse/pardon my French. [stereotyping]

French/French art n.[2] [late 19C+] fellatio. [FRENCH v.[1]]

French adj. **1** [mid-19C+] a racial stereotype used in various contexts, the English (and thus US) belief in 'gay Paree' and its supposedly sex-obsessed denizens has long equated 'French' with sexy or, pej., pornographic and 'dirty'. **2** [late 19C] (US) unfashionable, vulgar, distasteful.

French v.[1] [late 19C+] to fellate. [oral sex was generally seen as French 'perversion']

French v.[2] [20C] (US) to rearrange the bedclothes for a practical joke. [for ety. see APPLE-PIE ORDER]

French active n. [1950s+] (gay) the passive (sucked) partner in fellatio.

French art see FRENCH n.[2].

French article n.[1] [18C] brandy (cf. FRENCH CREAM; FRENCH ELIXIR; FRENCH LACE). [SE French + article]

French article n.[2] [mid-19C+] a French prostitute. [FRENCH adj. + ARTICLE]

French aunt n. [20C] (US) a flighty woman (cf. GERMAN AUNT). [FRENCH adj. + SE aunt]

French bath n. [1950s+] (gay) the use of perfumes as a deodorant in lieu of bathing. [stereotyping of the French as physically as well as morally dirty]

French bathe v. [1950s+] (gay) to use perfumes as a deodorant in lieu of bathing. [FRENCH BATH]

French blues n. [1960s] (drugs) a mix of methaqualone and amphetamine. [manufacturers Smith, Kline and French + BLUES n.[2] (2)]

French by injection phr. [1950s–60s] (gay) said of anyone considered particularly well-versed in fellatio (cf. DUTCH BY INJECTION). [FRENCH n.[2] + SE injection, i.e. by the penis]

French cannibal see FRENCH MEASLES.

French cap n. [1920s] (US) a condom.

French cream n. [18C] brandy (cf. FRENCH ARTICLE n.[1]). [France as the home of brandy; 'so called by the old tabbies and dowagers when they drink their tea' (Grose, 1796)]

French crown/goods/gout n. [late 17C–18C] venereal disease (cf. BARNWELL AGUE; BLOW WITH A FRENCH FAGGOT-STICK; FRENCH DISEASE; FRENCHIFIED; FRENCHMAN n.[1]; FRENCH MARBLES; FRENCH MEASLES; FRENCH PIG; FRENCH POX; KNOCKED WITH A FRENCH FAGGOT; NAPLES CANKER; NEAPOLITAN FAVOUR; SPANISH GOUT; SPANISH POX). [stereotyping of FRENCH adj. + joc. uses of SE crown, the ring of spots around the penis/goods/gout]

French culture n. [1960s+] fellatio, obs. except in homosexual contact advertisements (cf. AMERICAN CULTURE).

French deck n. [1960s+] (US) a pack of playing cards decorated with erotic pictures. [FRENCH adj. + SE deck]

French dip n. [1950s+] (gay) vaginal precoital fluid.

French disease n. [late 16C–late 18C] venereal disease, esp. syphilis (cf. FRENCH CROWN). [stereotyping]

French dressing n. [1950s+] (US gay) semen (cf. BABY GRAVY).

French elixir n. [19C] brandy (cf. FRENCH ARTICLE n.[1]). [France as the home of brandy]

French embassy n. [1960s] (US gay) any location, esp. a gym or YMCA, where homosexual activity is extensive and unchecked. [FRENCH v.[1] + pun on SE]

Frencher n.[1] [mid–late 19C] a Frenchman. [SE French]

Frencher n.[2] [20C] one who enjoys oral sex, usu. a man. [FRENCH v.]

Frenchery n. [mid-19C+] a brothel. [FRENCH adj. + sfx. -ery]

French-fried ice-cream n. [1950s+] (gay) semen (cf. BABY GRAVY). [FRENCH v.[1] + ICE-CREAM n.[2] + pun]

French fries/fries n. [1980s+] (drugs) crack cocaine.

French fuck n. [1930s+] (US) the rubbing of a man's penis between a woman's breasts. [FRENCH adj. + FUCK n.[1]]

French goods/gout see FRENCH CROWN.

French handshake n. [1970s] (US teen) a form of handshake signifying sexual interest or invitation. [FRENCH adj. + SE handshake]

French harp n. [late 19C–1940s] (US) a harmonica. [SE French + HARP n.[2]]

French head job n. [1940s+] fellatio. [FRENCH adj. + HEAD JOB]

frenchie/frenchy n.[1] [mid-19C+] a contraceptive sheath. [FRENCH LETTER + sfx. -ie]

frenchie n.[2] **1** [mid-19C+] (US) a Frenchman, a person of French descent, a French-Canadian. **2** [late 19C] anyone seen in the street and classified has foreign. **3** [late 19C+] a French person. **4** [20C] (W.I./St Kitts) a poor White, a descendant of the original French settlers on St Kitts who, as Roman Catholics, lost their status when the island was taken over by the Protestant British in 1690. [SE French + sfx. -ie]

frenchie/frenchy n.[3] [20C] (US) **1** a foolish man. **2** a flighty woman (cf. FRENCH AUNT).

frenchie/frenchy n.[4] [1990s] (N.Z.) a potato chip. [SE French fry]

frenchified adj. [late 17C–19C] **1** having venereal disease (cf. FRENCH CROWN). **2** usu. of a woman, sexually talented. [FRENCH adj. + sfx. -ified]

French inhale v. [1950s–60s] (US) to blow out cigarette smoke through the nose. [the supposed sophistication of the French]

French kiss n. [1920s+] a deep kiss, using the tongue as well as the lips (cf. SOUL KISS). [FRENCH adj. + SE kiss]

French kiss filter n. [1950s+] (gay) any filter-tipped cigarette.

French lace n. [19C] brandy (cf. FRENCH ARTICLE n.¹). [France as the home of brandy]

French language expert n. [1950s+] (gay) a fellator. [FRENCH adj.]

French language training n. [1950s+] (gay) teaching another person fellatio. [FRENCH adj.]

French leave n. [late 18C+] absenting oneself from a job or duty without prior permission. [negative national stereotyping]

French letter n. [mid-19C+] a contraceptive sheath; rare alts. are American/Italian/Spanish letter. [FRENCH adj. + SE letter; accepted as SE since 1950s]

French loaf n. [20C] £4. [rhy. sl. French loaf = backsl. rouf/roaf = 4]

French love n. [20C] fellatio. [FRENCH adj. + SE love]

Frenchman n.¹ **1** [17C] any foreigner. [generic use of the French foreign-ness]

Frenchman n.² [mid-17C–early 19C] a scholar of French.

Frenchman, the n.³ **1** [19C] syphilis. **2** [late 19C–1900s] a bottle of brandy. [the association of the disease and the drink with France]

Frenchman n.⁴ [20C] one who offers fellatio to others for cash. [FRENCH adj. + SE man]

Frenchman n.⁵ see FRANSMAN.

Frenchman, the n.⁶ [1990s] (US campus) heroin or any other form of illegal narcotic. [? film French Connection (1971)]

French marbles n. [late 16C] venereal disease, esp. syphilis (cf. FRENCH CROWN). [stereotyping]

French measles/cannibal n. [early 17C] venereal disease, esp. syphilis (cf. FRENCH CROWN). [stereotyping]

French passive n. [1950s+] (gay) the fellator (cf. FRENCH ACTIVE). [FRENCH adj. + SE passive]

French peasoup n. [19C+] (US/Can.) a French immigrant (cf. PEASOUPER n.²).

French photographer n. [1950s+] (gay) a homosexual photographer. [FRENCH adj. + SE photographer]

French pig n. [late 17C–18C] syphilis, esp. the syphilitic pustule or bubo (cf. FRENCH CROWN). [FRENCH adj. + PIG n.]

French postcard n. **1** [1910s+] (US) an erotic picture postcard. **2** [1950s+] (gay) an exciting prospective sexual partner. [FRENCH adj. + SE postcard]

French pox n. [early 16C–late 18C] venereal disease, esp. syphilis (cf. FRENCH CROWN). [stereotyping]

French prints n. [1950s+] (gay) unusual heterosexual pornography. [FRENCH adj. + SE prints]

French revolution n. [1950s–60s] (gay) the movement for homosexual rights. [FRENCH adj. + SE revolution; pun on SE]

French safe n. [1910s+] (Can./US) a condom (cf. FRENCH LETTER). [FRENCH adj. + SAFE n.]

French screwdriver n. [20C] a hammer (cf. BIRMINGHAM SCREWDRIVER). [supposed French inability to perform simple manual tasks]

French 75 n. [1930s–70s] (US) a cocktail of champagne, cognac, lemon juice and sugar. [a tribute to the large French gun, used in WW1]

French stuff n. [1950s+] (gay) **1** pornography. **2** any unusual sexual activity. [FRENCH adj. + SE stuff]

French tickler/tickler n. [1910s+] a contraceptive sheath with extra protrusions for added stimulation. [FRENCH adj. + SE tickler]

French tricks n. [mid-19C–20C] oral sex, of a man or a woman. [FRENCH adj. + SE tricks]

French vanilla n. [1990s] (US Black teen) a sexy White woman. [play on popular variety of ice-cream]

French walk n. [late 19C] (US) the posture assumed by those being thrown bodily out of a saloon (cf. SPANISH WALK). [a pun on FROG n.¹ + SE walk; unwelcome or obstreperous drinkers would be grasped by a couple of bouncers, held up with all 4 limbs spread out (like a frog) and tossed into the street]

French wank n. [1990s] the action of being masturbated between a woman's breasts (cf. FRENCH FUCK). [FRENCH adj. + WANK n.]

French way n. [20C] fellatio (cf. GO GREEK v.²; GREEK WAY; IRISH WAY). [FRENCH adj. + SE way]

Frenchwoman n. [1920s+] (W.I.) a fortune-teller. [fig. use of French to mean strange, mysterious]

Frenchy see FRENCHIE.

freney n. [late 18C–early 19C] (Irish) a one-eyed person. [the 18C highwayman James Freney, who had one eye]

fresh n. [1970s+] (drugs) phencyclidine (cf. ACE n.³).

fresh adj.¹ [mid-19C] tipsy, slightly drunk. [SE fresh wind, a light wind that is noticeable but that wouldn't blow one over]

fresh adj.² [mid-19C+] familiar, cheeky, over-intimate. [earlier meaning of naïve, 'green'; the implication is that such a person would innocently presume a greater intimacy than is acceptable]

fresh adj.³ **1** [20C] (W.I.) sexually aggressive, making open advances to the opposite sex. **2** [1980s+] (US Black/campus) smart, on the ball, aware, attractive; a general term of approval, varying as to context and applying to objects and events as well as people (cf. DEF).

fresh and fast/forward adj. [20C] (W.I.) **1** cheeky and impertinent. **2** sexually promiscuous. **3** of meat, smelling raw (although not stale). **4** of fish, smelling 'off'. **5** of popular music, in the latest style.

fresh bit n. [mid–late 19C] a sexually inexperienced woman. [SE fresh + BIT n.⁵]

fresh-cool adj. [1990s] (US Black) used to describe any superlative example, according to context. [FRESH adj.³ + COOL adj.³]

fresh cut n. [1980s+] (US Black) a short, neat haircut. [FRESH adj.³ + SE haircut]

fresher n. [late 19C+] (student) a student in their first term at a university. [one of the last survivors of the Oxford -er sfx., which once offered 'Pragger Wagger', the Prince of Wales, 'wagger pagger bagger', waste paper basket etc]

fresh fish n.¹ [mid-19C+] a new young prostitute. [SE fresh + FISH n.⁴]

fresh fish n.² [mid-19C+] a new recruit. [SE fresh + FISH n.⁵]

fresh greens n. [mid–late 19C] a new, young prostitute. [SE fresh + GREENS n.²]

fresh hide n. [1980s+] (US Black) a new lover or sexual partner. [SE fresh + HIDE n.²]

freshie n. [1990s] (Aus.) a freshwater crocodile. [SE fresh + sfx. -ie]

fresh lodger n. [20C] (Ulster) a loaf of bread.

fresh meat n. **1** [19C+] a newly fledged prostitute. **2** [mid-19C+] (US Und.) a new, young inmate, a potential victim of predatory prison homosexuals. **3** [late 19C+] a new sexual partner. [SE fresh + MEAT n; pun]

fresh of the irons phr. [late 17C–late 19C] newly graduated from university, just left school; thus inexperienced, brand-new. [SE leg-irons]

fresh on the graft phr. [late 19C] new to a job. [SE fresh + GRAFT n.²]

fresh out of phr. [20C] (US/Can.) absolutely bereft of; usu. used of some form of commodity.

fresh union adj. [1980s+] (US) clean, healthy. [? SAmE *union suit*, a suit of one-piece underwear]

fresh-up adj. [20C] (W.I.) **1** precocious. **2** sexually cheeky, suggestive. [FRESH adj.[3]]

freshwater n. **1** [mid–late 19C] an emigrant who works their passage rather than pay a fare. **2** [20C] (W.I./Trin.) a West Indian who visits America and comes back with a US accent.

freshwater mariner/seaman n. [late 17C–mid-19C] (Und.) 'their shippes were drowned in the playne of Salisbury' (Harman), such criminal beggars claimed to have suffered shipwreck or piracy and requested alms to return home (cf. FRESHWATER SOLDIER; WHIP-JACK).

freshwater soldier n. [16C] a professional beggar who trades on his spurious reminiscences of battles and campaigns of which, in fact, he has no personal experience (cf. FRESHWATER MARINER).

freshwater trout n. [1940s] (US Black) an attractive woman, usu. in a group. [play on FISH n.[4]]

fresh-whites n. [late 19C] a pallid complexion.

fress v. [20C] (orig. US) v. **1** to eat greedily, to snack. **2** to perform either form of oral intercourse, usu. cunnilingus. [Yid. *fress*, to eat]

fresser n. [20C] (US) **1** a glutton. **2** one who performs cunnilingus. [FRESS]

fret-kidney n. [mid–late 19C] a worrier (over trifles).

fret one's cream, to phr. [mid-19C] to worry.

fret oneself to fiddlestrings, to phr. [1910s–20s] to worry to excess.

fret one's fat, to phr. [late 19C] to worry.

fret one's giblets, to phr. [early–mid-18C] to worry.

fret one's gizzard/guts/kidneys, to phr. [mid-19C] to worry.

frey see VRY.

friar's balls n. [1930s+] (Aus.) the patent embrocation Friar's Balsam.

friar tuck n. [1940s+] sexual intercourse. [rhy. sl. *Friar Tuck* = FUCK n.[1]]

friar tuck v. [late 19C+] to have sexual intercourse. [FRIAR TUCK n.]

frick and frack n. [1980s+] (US Black) the testicles. [echoic of the sound of their knocking together; ult. *Frick and Frack*, the 1920s–30s Swiss comedy skating team, who performed in the US and Europe. They were famous for a routine where they would put the heels of their skates together, bend their knees and skate in large circles with their bodies leaning outwards]

fricking adj. [1930s+] euph. for FUCKING adj.

Friday face n. [late 16C–19C] a miserable or dour face; thus *Friday-faced*, miserable, gloomy. [Friday's traditional status as a day of abstinence either from all food or from meat]

fridge n. **1** [1910s+] (Aus.) a prison (cf. COOLER n.[1]; FREEZER n.[2]). **2** [1990s] a person, usually a woman who is frigid (cf. FREEZE n.[2]).

fried adj. **1** [1920s+] very drunk; thus *fried to the gills*, extremely drunk (cf. BOILED; STEWED adj.[1]). **2** [1960s+] (drugs) extremely intoxicated by a drug, usu. cannabis. **3** [1960s+] (US campus) angry. **4** [1980s+] (US) very tired, worn out. [fig. uses of SE]

fried carpet n. [late 19C] fish and chips. [? resemblance of the fried fish]

fried, dyed, laid/swooped to the side phr. [1970s+] (US Black) straightened Black hair that is attempting to emulate the texture and even colour of a White person's hair. [the three processes that are undertaken to straighten and arrange Black hair]

fried eggs n.[1] [20C] (Aus.) legs. [rhy. sl.]

fried eggs n.[2] [1930s+] small or undeveloped female breasts. [supposed resemblance]

fried rice n. [20C] (Aus.) the price. [rhy. sl.]

fried shirt n. [19C+] (US) a heavily starched shirt, a dress shirt (cf. BALDFACED SHIRT). [var. on BOILED SHIRT]

friend n.[1] [20C] (US Black) menstruation; thus euph. phr. *I have friends to stay*, I am menstruating.

friend n.[2] [1950s–60s] a prostitute's boyfriend or lover, but not necessarily her pimp.

friend n.[3] [1980s+] (drugs) fentanyl (cf. APACHE n.[2]).

friend-boy/-girl n. [1900s–40s] (US Black/southern) a boyfriend/girlfriend.

friend form n. [1950s+] (US prison) official papers that must be completed to facilitate outside visits to the inmates.

friend in need n. **1** [19C] a louse, usu. in pl. **2** [1970s+] (US Black) a sarcastic reference to anyone who is continually looking for loans, free hand-outs etc.

friendly fire v. [1980s+] to masturbate. [orig. milit. *friendly fire*, shots that are fired by one's own side]

friendly lead n. [late 19C] a subscription to help a unfortunate friend, usu. held by a 'whip-round' in a public house.

friendly pannikin n. [late 19C] (Aus.) a shared drink. [the *pannikin* or small tin container from which many Aus. 'diggers' ate and drank]

friendly road, the n. [1930s] (N.Z.) of workers, the decision to side with one's employer during an industrial dispute.

friend of Dorothy/Dorothy's see DOROTHY'S FRIEND.

fries see FRENCH FRIES.

frig n. **1** [late 18C–late 19C] an act of masturbation. **2** [late 19C–1920s] sexual intercourse. **3** [1940s–60s] a curse, as in phr. *not give a frig*. **4** [1940s+] euph. for FUCK. [FRIG v.]

frig v. **1** [late 16C+] to masturbate. **2** [early 17C+] to have sexual intercourse. **3** [late 17C–1950s] to cheat. **4** [late 18C+] to trifle or fool around (cf. DIDDLE v.[1]; FUTZ). **5** [1950s+] to perform lesbian sex, where the genitals are rubbed together. [Lat. *fricare*, to rub]

frig about/around v. [late 18C+] to trifle or fool around (cf. FRIG v.).

frigate n. [late 17C–18C] a woman (cf. FRIGATE ON FIRE; FRIGATE WELL RIGGED; LAND CARRACK; LIGHT FRIGATE; PINNACE). [SE *frigate*, a light, swift vessel; there may also be some punning connection to FRIG]

frigate on fire n. [early–mid-19C] a prostitute who has venereal disease. [FRIGATE + FIRE n.[2]]

frigate well rigged n. [late 17C–18C] an attractive, well-dressed woman. [FRIGATE + SE *well-rigged*]

frig-beard n. [16C] a degenerate, a seducer. [FRIG v. + SE *beard*; the image is of the adult, bearded male]

frigger n. [1950s] a general derog. term. [FRIG v.; semi-euph. for FUCKER]

frigging n. **1** [late 16C+] masturbation. **2** [late 19C+] the act of copulation (cf. FUCKING n.). [FRIG v.; first use in Florio (1598): '*Fricciare*, to frig, to wriggle, to tickle']

frigging adj. [20C] (orig. US) **1** euph. for FUCKING adj. **2** insignificant, petty, worthless. [FRIG v.]

frigging-A! see FUCKING-A!

friggle v. [19C] to masturbate. [FRIG v. + SE *wriggle*]

frig-/frigg-up n. [1940s+] (orig. Aus.) a disaster, a blunder, a mess (cf. BALLS-UP; COCK-UP; SCREW-UP). [FRIG v.; semi-euph. for FUCK-UP n.]

frig/frigg up v. [1930s+] (orig. Aus.) to make a blunder, to make a mess of. [semi-euph. for FUCK UP]

fright n. [mid-18C+] a person or thing of a shocking, grotesque, unkempt or ridiculous appearance.

frightener n. [1930s+] a scare.

frighteners n. [1930s+] threats, violence, anything that will terrify a given person into doing what is required (cf. PUT THE FRIGHTENERS ON).

frighten Friday n. [20C] (W.I.) a timid person. [SE *frighten*, frightened + FRAIDY, or *Man Friday*, the Black character in Daniel Defoe's *Robinson Crusoe* (1719)]

frighten into forty fits, to phr. [late 19C+] to terrify someone.

frighten the daylights/living daylights out of, to phr. [late 19C+] to terrify. [SE *frighten* + DAYLIGHTS n. (3)]

frighten the pants off see SCARE THE PANTS OFF.

frightful adj. [mid-18C+] a general intensifier, awful, terrible, annoying, shocking. ['A cant word among women for anything unpleasing' (Johnson)]

frightfully adv. [early 19C+] extremely, very much. [now only used ironically or in mockery of 'upper-class' usage]

frig off v. [20C] to masturbate, oneself or another (cf. BEAT OFF).

frig off! see FUCK OFF!

frig pig n. [late 18C–19C] a fussy, trifling person. [FRIG v. (4) + SE *pig*]

frigster/frigstress n. [late 16C–17C] a masturbator. [FRIG v. (1) + sfx. -STER/-*stress*]

frig/screw your buddy week n. [1960s] (orig. US milit. use) a response to any moment or act of betrayal, i.e. *I see, it's frig your buddy week* (cf. FUCK YOUR BUDDY WEEK).

fri-high-day n. [1990s] (US Black teen) a day devoted to drinking. [? play on FLY HIGH/FRY ONE'S BRAINS]

frijole-eater n. [20C] (US) a derog. term for a Mexican (cf. BEAN-EATER). [Mex. Sp. *frijol*, a bean + SE *eater*]

frikkie/frikky n. [1970s+] (S.Afr.) a condom. [? FRIG v.]

frildo adv. [1990s] (US Black teen) for real, though. [elided pron.]

frill n. [1930s–40s] a woman (cf. FRILLERY). [her clothing]

frilled lizard n. [20C] (Aus.) a bearded man.

frillery n. [19C] women's underwear; thus phr. *explore someone's frillery*, to caress a woman intimately (cf. FRILLIES).

frillies n. [20C] frilled feminine undergarments (cf. FRILLERY).

frills n. [mid-19C+] affectations of dress, speech, writing, painting or manner; ornamentation for its own sake.

frilly adj. [20C] (US) of a woman, arrogant, pretentious, snobbish.

frimped adj. [1940s] (US Black) ugly, unattractive. [? SE *frump*]

frios n. [1970s+] (drugs) marijuana laced with phencyclidine. [Sp.]

frip n. [1970s+] (US campus) a weak, ineffectual person. [? SE *frippery* or FRIPPING]

frippet n. [20C] a frivolous or showy young woman. [? *flibbertigibbet*]

fripping n. [1910s–20s] domestic bickering between husband and wife. [? SE *fripperies* or Lancs. dial. *frip*, something worthless]

frisco/frisko n.[1] [mid-17C] a term of endearment. [a 'frisky' person]

'Frisco n.[2] [19C+] (US) San *Francisco*. [abbr.]

'Frisco speedball/special n. [1960s–70s] (drugs) a drug cocktail containing LSD, cocaine and heroin.

frisk n. [early 19C+] sexual intercourse.

frisk/frisk in a hempen cravat v.[1] [18C] to be hanged. [SE *frisk* + HEMPEN CRAVAT]

frisk v.[2] **1** [late 18C+] (orig. Und.) to search, for weapons, illicit drugs, stolen goods etc. **2** [early 19C] to trick, to hoax. **3** [mid-19C–1930s] (US) to rob or steal, esp. from a sleeping or helpless person. [one's hands or schemes 'frisk' over the victim]

frisk v.[3] [19C] of a man, to have sexual intercourse; thus *frisking*, foreplay.

frisk and frolic n. [late 19C–1910s] carbolic (soap). [rhy. sl.]

frisk at the tables n. [late 19C] an evening's moderate gambling.

frisker n. [late 19C] a pilferer, a petty thief. [FRISK v.]

frisko see FRISCO n.[1].

frisky n. [late 19C+] whisky. [rhy. sl. + its effects on the drinker]

frisky adj. [late 19C] ill-tempered.

frisky powder n. [20C] (drugs) cocaine. [its effects]

frit n. [1940s–60s] (US) an effeminate male homosexual. [FRIT adj.; his supposed cowardice]

frit adj. [20C] frightened. [SE *fright*, to scare, to terrify]

frito n. [1950s–60s] (US) a derog. term for a Mexican or Spanish-American. [advertisements for *Frito Bandito* cornchips, which feature a stereotypical 'Mexican bandit']

frito toes n. [1980s+] (US campus) very smelly feet. [brandname *Fritos*, a US snack food]

fritz n.[1] [19C+] a German, esp. a German soldier. [Ger. dimin. of proper name *Friedrich*; the usage emerged c.1880 but came into widespread use during WW1, although it fell from favour afterwards]

fritz/pork fritz n.[2] [1910s] (Aus.) a large, but not especially spicy sausage. [Ger. name *Fritz*, linked to a German sausage]

frizzle n.[1] [18C] the vagina (cf. ACE OF SPADES). [abbr. OLD FRIZZLE]

frizzle n.[2] [mid-19C] champagne. [FIZZ n.[1] (3)]

fro n.[1] see FROE.

fro n.[2] [late 19C–1930s] (US Black) a damaged knife. [ety. unknown]

'fro see AFRO n.[2].

frock n.[1] [1900s–10s] a man wearing a frock-coat.

frock n.[2] [1980s+] the man who poses as a lesbian's 'husband' for the sake of 'passing' in an intolerant society (cf. BEARD n.[2]). [the image of the lesbian as a trouser-wearing woman for whom a frock is automatically unnatural]

frock and frill n. [late 19C–1900s] a chill. [rhy. sl.]

frock-hitcher n. [late 19C–1900s] a milliner.

froe/fro/vroe/vrow n. [early 17C–19C] a woman, esp. a prostitute (cf. VROW-CASE). [Du. *vrouw*, a woman]

frog n.[1] **1** [17C] a Dutch person. **2** [late 18C+] a French person. **3** [mid-19C+] (US) a contemptible person. **4** [1940s+] the French language. [orig. 14C SE *frog*, a contemptible or offensive person; used in early 17C to refer to Jesuits, then in 1650 to the Dutch, England's national enemy; when they were replaced by the French in the 18C, the definition changed accordingly]

frog n.[2] [mid-19C] (US) a policeman (cf. BEAR n.[8]; BULL n.[10]). [his sudden 'leaping' onto criminals]

frog n.[3] see FROG AND TOAD.

frog n.[4] [late 19C–1900s] a foot. [SE *frog*, an elastic, horny substance growing in the middle of the sole of a horse's hoof]

frog/frogskin n.[5] **1** [late 19C–1960s] (Aus.) a £1 note. **2** [20C] (US Black) a banknote, $1 bill (cf. SKIN n.[7]). [such notes were green; Franklyn (1961) suggests rhy. sl. *frogskin* = SE *sovereign*]

frog n.[6] **1** [1940s–70s] (US campus) a freshman. **2** [1960s+] (US campus) a grade of F. [initial letters]

frog n.[7] [1950s+] (Aus.) a condom (cf. FRENCH LETTER; FRENCH TICKLER; FROGSKIN n.[2]). [pun on FROG n.[1] (2)]

frog n.[8] [1990s] (US Black) a promiscuous person. [they 'hop' into bed with anyone]

frog and toad/frog n. [mid-19C+] the road. [rhy. sl.]

frog and toe n. [mid-19C] (US Und.) New York City. [ety. unknown]

frogeater n. [late 18C+] a French person (cf. FROG n.[1]).

froggee see FROGGIE.

frog eggs n. [1920s] (US) tapioca pudding (cf. FROG'S EYES; FROGSPAWN). [resemblance]

frog-/flat-footed adj. [late 19C–1900s] used of one who travels on foot.

froggie/froggy/froggee n. **1** [mid-19C+] (orig. US) a French person. **2** [1930s+] the French language. [FROG n.]

froggish *see* FROGGY adj.[2].

froggy *n. see* FROGGIE.

froggy *adj.*[1] [mid-19C+] French. [FROGGIE n.]

froggy/froggish *adj.*[2] [1970s+] (US Black) aggressive, belligerent, keen to fight, keen to start 'jumping'; thus *if you feel froggy, then leap*, if you want a fight, then let's get on with it.

frog in the throat *n.*[1] [20C] a boat. [rhy. sl.]

frog in the throat *n.*[2] [20C] (orig. US) (temporary) hoarseness, an irritation in the throat (cf. HAVE A DONKEY IN ONE'S THROAT). [SE *frog*, used of various afflictions, usu. swellings, of the throat]

froglanders *n.* [late 17C–early 19C] the Dutch. [SE *frogland*, marshy land that is full of frogs, orig. used of the Fens and of Holland]

frogmarch *v.* [mid-19C+] to carry someone face-down, one person holding onto each limb; used on drunks or recalcitrant prisoners.

frog's eggs/eyes *n.* [1910s+] (Aus./N.Z.) boiled sago (cf. FROG EGGS; FROGSPAWN).

Frogolia *n.* [1970s+] (N.Z.) a derog. term for France; thus *Frogolian*, a French person. [FROG n.[1] (3)]

frogskin *n.*[1] *see* FROG n.[5].

frogskin *n.*[2] [1920s+] (orig. Aus./N.Z.) a condom (cf. FROG n.[7]).

frogspawn *n.* [1950s–60s] (mainly school) sago or tapioca (cf. FROG EGGS).

frogsticker *n.* [19C+] (US) a long-bladed pocket-knife (cf. TOAD-STABBER).

frog's wine *n.* [mid-19C] **1** brandy. **2** gin. [FROG n.[1] + SE *wine*; brandy is always linked to France]

frogtown *n.* [19C+] (US) a small or out-of-the-way place. [the swampy, frog-ridden pond that is traditionally associated with such rural settlements]

frog up *v.* **1** [1920s–60s] (US Black) to cheat, to confuse, to trick. **2** [1950s–70s] (US) to waste time, to idle on the job. [stereotype of the French as cunning, deceitful and idle]

frolic pad *n.* [1940s] (US Black) a nightclub. [SE *frolic* + PAD n.[2]]

from *prep..* [20C] because of, as a result of; used in a variety of combs., e.g. *from hunger, from grief.*

fromage *adj.* [1990s] (US campus) objectionable (cf. CHEESE-BALL; CHEESEMAN). [Fr. *fromage*, cheese]

from a height/great height *phr.* [1970s+] intensely.

from Alice Springs to breakfast time *phr.* [1930s+] (Aus.) everywhere.

from arsehole to breakfast table *phr.* [1940s+] (N.Z.) completely, entirely. [ARSEHOLE]

from arsehole to breakfast time *phr.* [late 19C+] all the way, all the time.

from asshole to appetite *phr.* [late 19C+] (orig. Aus.) thoroughly, absolutely, totally.

from bitter creek *phr.* [late 19C] (US west) very tough. [the image of Bitter Creek, Wyoming, as an outlaw town]

from can to can't *phr.* [1960s–70s] (US) all day long. [the image of one's waning strength as the day continues]

from Chicago *adj.* [1980s+] (US campus) unaware of what's going on, behaving like an 'air-head'. [Chicagoans are seen as essentially provincial and unsophisticated]

from go to whoa *phr.* [1970s+] (Aus.) from start to finish.

from hell *adj.* [1980s+] (orig. US) appalling, very unpleasant, usu. with a noun, e.g. *the professor from hell, a game from hell.*

from hell to breakfast *phr.* [20C] (US) **1** in all directions, everywhere. **2** decisively, violently. **3** for a long time, for a long distance.

from here on out *phr.* [1940s+] henceforth, in the future.

from Mars *adj.* [1980s+] (US) weird, bizarre, eccentric. [the image of 'little green men']

from now on *n.* [20C] (US Und.) a life sentence (cf. ALL DAY).

from/in outer space *phr.* [1950s+] (US) crazy, insane, eccentric.

from soup to nuts *phr.* [20C] (US) from first to last, completely, comprehensively. [the image is of a meal]

from the bell *phr.* [1970s] (orig. US) from the beginning. [boxing imagery, a bell sounds the beginning of a new round]

from the drop *adv.* [20C] from the outset. [the drop of a flag that signals the start of a race]

from the gate *phr.* [1950s+] from the outset, from the beginning. [racecourse jargon]

from the get *phr.* [1970s] (US Black) from the very start. [abbr. FROM THE GIT-GO]

from the git-go *phr.* [1960s+] (orig. US Black) from the very start. [SE *get ready, get set, go!*]

from the ground up *phr.* [late 19C+] (orig. US) from the very beginning, from first principles, in essence.

from the rip *phr.* [1990s] (US Black) from the start (cf. JUMP STREET). [? RIP AND RUN]

from the same stable *phr.* [1950s+] (orig. US) from the same source.

from the sublime to the gorblimey/ridiculous *phr.* [20C] to the absolute extreme. [SE + GORBLIMEY!]

from the word go *phr.* [late 19C+] from the very beginning.

from this out *phr.* [mid-19C–1920s] henceforth, in the future.

from who laid the chunk *phr.* [20C] (US west) from time immemorial, for ever.

froncey *n.* [late 19C] a Frenchman. [mispron. of Fr. *Français*, Frenchman]

frone *n.* [1940s] (US Black) an unattractive woman. [? Ger. *Frau*, woman or SE *frown* + *crone*]

front *n.*[1] **1** [late 19C] (society) cheek, audacity. **2** [20C] a respectable appearance, a mask for illegal activities (cf. FRONT MAN). **3** [20C] (Und.) anything one needs, fancy clothes, a clever line of patter, a personal style, a mental attitude, for the successful promotion of one's schemes (cf. HAVE MORE FRONT THAN BRIGHTON BEACH).

front *n.*[2] **1** [late 19C–1920s] (US Und.) a watch and chain. **2** [1930s–60s] (US Black) a suit of clothes.

Front, the *n.*[3] **1** [1940s+] (gay) Piccadilly, Oxford Street. **2** [1950s] (teen) the main street of a gang's territory (cf. FRONT LINE).

front *v.*[1] **1** [late 19C–1910s] (US Und.) to aid a pickpocket by distracting the victim's attention. **2** [1930s+] (orig. US) to serve as a 'front (man)' in a variety of criminal contexts. [FRONT n.[1]]

front/front up *v.*[2] [1940s+] (Aus.) to appear in front of.

front *v.*[3] [1960s+] to advance either money or any other commodity (esp. drugs) as a loan or a sample of goods on offer; when buying drugs the seller may ask for the money to be 'fronted' so he in turn, can make a bulk purchase from his superior in the sales chain.

front *v.*[4] [1980s+] (orig. US Black) **1** to trick or deceive with glib verbosity for some gain, usu. monetary or sexual. **2** to pose as something one is not. **3** to show off. **4** (US Black/campus) to talk nonsense, to be 'all talk, no action'. [FRONT n.[1]]

fronta *n.* [20C] (W.I. Rasta) tobacco leaf used to roll a marijuana cigarette. [it provides a *front* to the marijuana within]

frontage *n.* [mid-19C+] the face (cf. FRONTISPIECE).

front attic *n.* [19C] the vagina (cf. FRONT BOTTOM; FRONT BUM; FRONT DOOR; FRONT ENTRANCE; FRONT GARDEN; FRONT GUT; FRONT PARLOUR; FRONT ROOM; FRONT WINDOW; PARLOUR).

front bottom *n.* [1990s] the vagina (cf. FRONT ATTIC).

front bum *n.* [1990s] the vagina (cf. FRONT ATTIC). [SE *front* + BUM n.[2]]

front door n. 1 [19C] the vagina (cf. DO A BIT OF FRONT-DOOR WORK; FRONT ATTIC). 2 [1900s–40s] (US Black) the female genitals (cf. BACK DOOR).

front-door mat n. [1940s] the female pubic hair. [FRONT DOOR + SE mat; pun]

front-door work n. [19C] sexual intercourse; thus do a bit of..., to have sexual intercourse. [FRONT DOOR + SE work]

front entrance n. [19C] the vagina (cf. FRONT ATTIC).

fronter n. [1970s+] (US Black) a show-off. [FRONT v.[4]]

front for v. [20C] to work as a decoy or a falsely respectable con-man (cf. FRONT-MAN). [FRONT v.[1]]

front garden/gate n. [19C] the vagina (cf. FRONT ATTIC).

front gut n. [19C] the vagina (cf. FOREGUT; FRONT ATTIC).

frontispiece n. [mid-19C] the face (cf. FRONTAGE).

front line n. [1970s+] 1 (W.I./UK Black teen) the main street or area, the main area of attraction or focus of activities. 2 (Black) that area of a city where the Black community is most likely to clash with the forces of White law and order, e.g. All Saints Road, Notting Hill, Railton Road, Brixton etc (cf. COMBAT ZONE).

front-man n. [1930s+] (orig. US) anyone who covers for illegal activities, posing as a 'legitimate' citizen. [FRONT v.[1] + SE man]

front money n. 1 [1940s–50s] (US) money to show and impress others. 2 [1960s+] (drugs) money advanced to a dealer for the purchase of drugs (cf. FRONT v.[3]).

front name n. [late 19C] a given or Christian name.

front on v. [1980s+] (US Black) to pretend, to deceive; the image of putting up a front. [FRONT v.[4]]

front parlour n. [19C] the vagina (cf. FRONT ATTIC; PARLOUR).

front room n. [early 19C] the vagina (cf. FRONT ATTIC).

fronts n. [20C] (US Black) clothes. [? show business jargon front, a large diamond tie pin or ring worn by vaudevillians to indicate prosperity]

front someone off v.[1] [1980s+] (US Black) 1 to reveal information about another person that puts that person in an embarrassing or otherwise difficult position. 2 to confront (someone) with talk about something they either should or should not have done. [SE confront]

front someone off v.[2] [1980s+] (US Black) to be attracted to the company of another person not so much for their personality as for the outward show and physical beauty in their reflected glory of which one can bask. [FRONT v.[4]]

front street n. [1960s+] (US Black) 1 the main street of a town, the street on which most of the (illegal) action takes place (cf. FAST TRACK). 2 the state of being on public display and thus open to attack, whether verbal or physical; a situation in which one must be responsible for one's words and deeds. [FRONT n.[1]]

front stuff n. [1930s+] a deceptive appearance, for the purpose of crime. [FRONT n.[1] + SE stuff]

front up v.[1] see FRONT v.[2].

front up v.[2] [1980s+] (N.Z. Und.) to appear in court. [i.e. in front of the judge]

front-wheel skid n. [1960s+] (derog.) a Jew (cf. FOUR-WHEEL SKID). [rhy. sl. front-wheel skid = YID]

front window n. [19C] the vagina (cf. FRONT ATTIC).

front windows n. 1 [mid-19C] the eyes (cf. WINDOWS). 2 [1900s–10s] spectacles.

front yard n. [20C] (US) the area of a town where the well-off citizens live (cf. BACK YARD).

frosh n. [1910s+] (US) 1 a college freshman. 2 a member of a freshman sports team. 3 (collective) freshmen. [freshman ? + Ger. dial. Frosch, frog, a grammar-school pupil]

frost n. 1 [late 19C] (orig. theatre) a failure. 2 [late 19C+] coolness (between two people).

frost bite me! excl. [1910s–20s] a general excl.

frost/cut a cake, to phr. [1900s; 1960s+] (US) to make a difference.

frost the pastries, to phr. [1990s] to masturbate.

frosty n. [1950s+] (US) a chilled glass or can of beer.

frosty adj. (US) 1 [late 19C] (US) very unfriendly. 2 [1970s+] cool, unemotional. 3 [1980s+] stylish, fashionable.

frosty face n. 1 [late 18C–19C] one whose face is pitted with smallpox scars. 2 [20C] (Ulster) the joker in a pack of cards.

frot n. [1970s+] the act of rubbing against a person for sexual pleasure. [for ety. see FROT v.]

frot v. [1970s+] to rub up against (for sexual pleasure and usu. in a clandestine manner). [Fr. frottage, rubbing (in a sexual context)]

froth n. [early 17C] beer.

froth and bubble n. [1960s+] (Aus.) 1 a racing double, the daily double. 2 trouble. [rhy. sl.]

frotting n. [1990s] the rubbing of bodies together for sexual pleasure. [FROT + sfx. -ing]

froudacious adj. [late 19C] (Aus.) absurd, ludicrous. [the erroneous comments made on Aus. (and N.Z.) by the historian J.A. Froude (1818–94)]

froust see FROWST.

frow n. [early 18C–mid-19C] 1 a woman. 2 a prostitute. [Du. vrouw or Ger. Frau, a woman]

frowst/froust n. [1900s–40s] the stuffy, close air of a room without adequate ventilation and that is used by too many people. [FROWST v.]

frowst/froust v. [late 19C] to lie around in a stuffy room. [dial. frowsty, fusty; having an unpleasant smell]

froyo n. [1990s] (US teen) frozen yoghurt. [abbr.]

frozen fruit n. [1960s+] (US gay) a sexually frigid gay man. [pun on SE frozen + FRUIT n.[2]]

frozen limit, the n. [1910s–20s] the absolute limit.

frozen/icy mitt n. [20C] (US) a rejection, an unfriendly reception (cf. COLD SHOULDER). [SE frozen/ICY + MITT n.]

fruit n.[1] 1 [late 19C–1920s] something or someone delightful or pleasant; thus old fruit, a good fellow. 2 [late 19C–1930s] (US) a dupe, an easy victim, one who is easily influenced. 3 [1990s] (US teen) an unintelligent, dull person. [? such a person is considered 'easy picking']

fruit n.[2] 1 [1910s–30s] a promiscuous woman. 2 [1930s+] a derog. term for a male homosexual (cf. FRUITCAKE n.[1]; FRUITER; FRUIT-FLY; FRUIT FOR MONKEYS; FRUIT-PLATE; TOOTI-FROOTI; VEGETABLE). [the 'softness']

fruit boots n. (US gay) 1 [1950s] white tennis shoes, white suede shoes. 2 [1960s+] 'Beatle boots' or any Italian-style shoes with pointed toes. [FRUIT n.[2] + SE boots; in more restrained eras, such shoes were seen as badges of effeminacy]

fruitcake n.[1] [1930s+] a male homosexual (cf. FRUIT n.[2]).

fruitcake n.[2] [1950s+] an eccentric, a peculiar person, esp. in phr. nutty as a fruitcake (cf. DATE n.[1]). [they are 'nuts']

fruiter n. [1910s+] (US) a male homosexual. [FRUIT n.[2] (2)]

fruit-fly n. [1950s+] 1 a homosexual man (cf. FRUIT n.[2]). 2 a woman who enjoys the company of homosexual rather than heterosexual men (cf. FAG-HAG n.[2]). [ext. of FRUIT n.[2]]

fruit for monkeys n. [1930s+] (US) (derog.) a homosexual man. [FRUIT n.[2] + SE monkey]

fruit for the monkeys n. [1950s+] (gay) the penis. [pun on BANANA n.[2] + FRUIT n.[2]]

fruit for the sideboard n. [1950s+] (Aus.) 1 'easy money', esp. as won while gambling. 2 a person who is seen as a source of 'easy money' (cf. FRUIT n.[1]). [the implication is of 'extras' or luxuries; fruit would normally be placed on the table and soon eaten]

fruitful vine n. [19C] the vagina (cf. BEAUTY SPOT n.[1]). [it 'bears flowers' (menstruation) every month]

fruit jar *n.* [20C] (US) illicitly distilled whisky; thus *fruit-jar nose*, a sore across the top of the nose, which has been irritated by the rubbing of the fruit jars from which the whisky is drunk. [SE *fruit jar*, in which the whisky is stored and from which it can be drunk]

fruit loop *n.*[1] [1980s+] **1** (US campus) the small loop (ostensibly for hanging the shirt when no hanger is available) on the upper back of many shirts; such a loop, supposedly, can be used to hold a victim ready for buggery (cf. BUGGER'S GRIPS). **2** (US) a homosexual man. [pun on the US breakfast cereal *Fruit Loops*/FRUIT n.[2]]

fruit loop *n.*[2] [1980s+] (US) a crazy or stupid person. [pun on the US breakfast cereal *Fruit Loops*/LOOPY]

fruit of the gibbet *n.* [late 19C] a hanged man (cf. TREE THAT BEARS FRUIT ALL YEAR ROUND).

fruit-plate *n.* [1930s+] (US) a male homosexual. [FRUIT n.[2] (2)]

fruit roller *n.* [1940s+] (US) a thug who specializes in mugging or beating up homosexuals. [FRUIT n.[2] + ROLL v.[1]]

fruit salad *n.*[1] [1960s+] (US drugs/teen) a random combination of any pills or capsules of drugs available, including psychotropic and medicinal, on which to get intoxicated. [pun on SE, suggested by the assorted colours]

fruit salad *n.*[2] [1980s+] (US gay) a group of gay men. [pun on FRUIT n.[2]]

fruit salad bowl *n.* [1980s+] (US drugs) a pipe or bowl filled with a mix of marijuana and hashish. [pun]

fruit that made man wise *phr.* [17C] sexual intercourse (cf. ADAM AND EVE phr.). [the eating of the apple in the Garden of Eden]

fruit tramp *n.* [20C] (US) a migratory worker who follows the fruit harvest; such people are not tramps as such, but simply move as the job demands.

fruity *adj.*[1] [20C] **1** sexually aroused. **2** full of a rich or strong quality, highly interesting, attractive or suggestive. [the fig. *fruit* is 'ripe' for enjoyment]

fruity *adj.*[2] [1920s+] (US) crazy. [FRUITCAKE n.[2]]

fruity *adj.*[3] [1940s+] (US) homosexual. [FRUIT n.[2]]

frum *adj.* [late 19C+] religious, orthodox (cf. LINK adj.). [Ger. *fromm*, pious, thence Yid. *frum*]

frummagemed *adj.* [late 17C–early 19C] choked, strangled, spoilt.

fruppencies *n.* [1970s] the female breasts (cf. THRUPS n.[2]). [Cockney pron. of SE *three-pences*]

frustrated *adj.* [20C] drunk. [? SE ADDLED].

fry *n.*[1] [late 19C] a policeman. [? SE *pry*]

fry *n.*[2] (drugs) **1** [1970s] LSD (cf. A n.[3]). **2** [1990s] (US) crack cocaine (cf. FRY ONE'S BRAINS). [they fig. *fry the brain*]

fry *v.*[1] (US) **1** [1910s+] to punish or be punished. **2** [1960s+] to ruin someone or to impair the mind. **3** [1960s+] to infuriate. [fig. uses of SE]

fry *v.*[2] [1920s+] (US Und.) to be electrocuted in the electric chair (cf. BAKE v.[1]).

fry *v.*[3] [1960s+] (US Black) to straighten the hair. [abbr. FRY ONE'S HAIR]

fry *v.*[4] [1980s+] (US drugs) to experience the effects of taking LSD. [FRY n.[2]]

fry daddy *n.* [1980s+] (drugs) **1** crack cocaine and marijuana. **2** a cigarette laced with crack cocaine. [FRY n.[2] (2) + DADDY n. (4)]

frying pan *n.*[1] [late 17C–19C] a large, silver pocket watch (cf. WARMING PAN n.[2]). [resemblance]

frying pan *n.*[2] [20C] an old man. [rhy. sl.]

frying-pan *adj.* [mid-19C] (Aus. Und.) small-time, petty. [shearer jargon *frying-pan brand*, a crude brand laid over the legitimate one by a cattle-thief; some rustlers literally used a red-hot frying pan]

frying size *n.* [19C+] (US) a young person, esp. a young woman (cf. CHICKEN n.[3]). [SE *frying size*, a young chicken which has reached the proper size for killing and then frying]

fry in one's own grease, to *phr.* [14C+] to suffer the consequences of one's own (foolish) actions.

fry-meat preacher *n.* [20C] (US) an unprofessional, part-time lay preacher (cf. CHICKEN-EATER). [dial. *fried meat*, bacon, served to the preacher in return for his sermon]

fry one's brains, to *phr.* [1960s+] to indulge in an excess of drugs.

fry one's hair, to *phr.* [1940s+] (US Black) to straighten one's hair (cf. CONK n.[3]).

fry/cook someone's bacon, to *phr.* [late 19C+] to cause difficulties or unhappiness for someone else.

f.s. *n.* [1960s+] a woman who offers oral sex. [abbr. *face sitter*]

f sharp *n.* [mid-19C] a flea. [play on B FLAT]

F-60s *n.* [1980s+] (drugs) Histadyl. [the pharmaceutical identification stamped on the capsule]

F-66s *n.* [1980s+] (drugs) Tuinal. [the pharmaceutical identification stamped on the capsule]

f.t.b. *phr.* [20C] a phr. used to denote that one has had more than enough to eat. [abbr. *full to bursting*]

f.t.d. *phr.* [1910s+] to waste time and loaf on the job (cf. FORNICATE THE POODLE). [abbr. FUCK THE DOG]

F-10 *n.* [1980s+] (drugs) a barbiturate. [the pharmaceutical identification stamped on the capsule]

f.t.w.! *excl.* [1970s+] (US, mainly bikers/campus) fuck the world! [abbr.]

fu *n.* [1960s+] (drugs) marijuana. [? Sp. *fumar*, to smoke]

fub *v.* [late 16C–mid-17C] to cheat, to impose upon. [FOB v.]

f.u.b.a.r. *phr.* (US) [1940s+] **1** (orig. milit.) extremely unhappy. **2** [1940s+] totally beyond repair and/or control (cf. SNAFU phr.). **3** [1940s+] (campus) very drunk. **4** [1970s+] (campus) very unattractive. **5** [1980s+] (drugs) completely intoxicated by a given drug. [abbr. *fucked up beyond all recognition*]

f.u.b.b. *phr.* [1950s+] (US, orig. milit.) in a very parlous state, whether from physical injury, emotional instability, the effects of drink and/or drugs (cf. SNAFU phr.). [abbr. *fucked up beyond belief*]

fubbery *n.* [early 17C] cheating, deception. [FOB v.]

fubbs *n.* [early 17C–18C] an affectionate term, applied to small children and women with whom one is in love. [thus later SE *fubsy*, plump, dumpy; allegedly coined by Charles II (r.1660–85) to describe the Duchess of Portsmouth; Grose (1785) cites this as sl.]

fubby/fubsy/fubsey *adj.* [late 17C–late 19C] pleasantly plump; thus *fubsiness*, fatness, plumpness.

f.u.b.i.s. *phr.* [1940s+] fuck you buddy, I'm shipping out (cf. FUCK YOU CHARLEY!; SNAFU phr.). [abbr.]

fubsy/fubsey see FUBBY.

fuck *n.*[1] **1** [late 17C+] an act of copulation. **2** [late 17C–1930s] copulation. [FUCK v.[1]]

fuck *n.*[2] [late 18C+] anything at all, usu. in neg. (i.e. nothing), e.g. *don't give a fuck, not matter a fuck*.

fuck, the *n.*[3] [mid-19C+] euph. for HELL, e.g. *why the fuck did your that? who the fuck wants to know? the fuck I care*.

fuck *n.*[4] [20C] a person (usu. a woman but covering both sexes since the 1970s) considered purely as a sex object; thus a *good/bad fuck*, someone who is seen as a sexual adept or incompetent (cf. BELT n.[1]).

fuck *n.*[5] [1920s+] a despicable person, usu. with qualifying adj., e.g. *dumb fuck, useless fuck*.

fuck *n.*[6] [1930s+] used as, like or than in comparisons, e.g. *as big as fuck, hurts like fuck, bigger than fuck*.

fuck *n.*[7] [1970s+] nothing, e.g. *I don't do fuck*.

fuck *n.*[8] [1970s+] a turn of ill-fortune, a piece of bad luck, e.g. *I lost the gig, ain't that a fuck*.

fuck *n.*[9] [1970s+] the essence, the spirit, e.g. *kick the fuck out of* (cf. DAYLIGHTS n.[3]; SHIT n.[1]).

fuck *n.*[10] [1980s+] indicating difference or importance, usu. in neg., e.g. *that don't make a fuck.*

fuck *adj.* [1940s+] (orig. US) as a description of something obscene or pornographic, e.g. *fuck movie* (cf. FUCK BOOK).

fuck *v.*[1] [late 17C+] to have sexual intercourse. [strictly, the ety. of *fuck* remains unknown, although the word has been linked to a supposed, if unsubstantiated, ME v. *fuken.* Neither Ger. *ficken*, nor the Fr. *foutre* (f. Lat. *fotuere*), both of which mean the same, can be linked semantically. Lighter notes MDu. *fokken*, to thrust, to copulate with; Nor. dial. *fukka*, to copulate, Swed. dial. *focka*, to strike, to push, to copulate + *fock*, the penis. Given the plethora of euphemisms equating intercourse or penetration with striking or hitting (BANG v.[1], SCREW v.[1], POKE v. etc), there may be some substance in E.P.'s suggestion of a root in the Lat. *pugnare*, to fight or strike. Considered (with CUNT n.[1] and the compound MOTHERFUCKER) as the ultimate in taboo terms, fuck is in fact SE, but has been listed as taboo, and thus as slang, since *c.*1690. The first print citation is dated 1503, in a line from the poetry of William Dunbar (?1456–?1513); the first dictionary listing is in Florio's *Worlde of Wordes* (1598): 'Fottere, to iape, to sard, to fucke, to swive, to occupy.' By the 18C, if printed at all, the form was usually *f—k*. The term returned to literary use with James Joyce's much-banned *Ulysses* (1922) but remained taboo in the popular media and in 'polite' speech. This position has been eroded ever since, with the term and its compounds appearing today in films, books and on television, although the press, especially the tabloids, pretend to a continuing squeamishness. 'Officially,' for all that the realities of everyday speech (irrespective of class) disprove the theory, *fuck* remains an outlaw in conversation]

fuck *v.*[2] **1** [mid-19C+] to harm irreparably, to cheat, to victimize, to betray, to deceive (cf. FRIG; FUCK OVER; SCREW v.[1]). **2** [1940s+] to trifle with, to 'mess around', to interfere (cf. FUCK AROUND). **3** [1980s] to use or exploit for one's benefit. [fig. use of FUCK v.[1]]

fuck *v.*[3] [1920s+] to stop, abandon or give up (on) (cf. CHUCK IT).

fuck *v.*[4] [1960s+] to blunder, to make a mess (of) (cf. FUCK UP).

fuck!/feck! *excl.* [1920s+] an excl. of anger, surprise, dismay, disbelief, resignation, esp. in combs. (cf. FUCK IT!; FUCK MY LUCK!; FUCK MY OLD BOOTS!; FUCK THAT!).

fuckability *n.* [1960s+] sex appeal. [FUCK v.[1] + sfx. *-ability*]

fuckable *adj.* **1** [late 19C+] sexually desirable (cf. FUCKY). **2** [1970s+] (US campus) sexually available. [FUCK v.[1] + sfx. *-able*]

fuck-about/-around *n.* [20C] a time-waster. [FUCK ABOUT v.]

fuck about/around *v.* **1** [20C] to mess about, to waste time, to fool around. **2** [20C] to annoy, to inconvenience, to waste someone's time (cf. ARSE ABOUT; DICK SOMEONE AROUND). **3** [1970s+] to astonish. [fig. use of FUCK v.[1] + SE *about/around*]

fuck a duck, to *phr.* [1930s+] to live a sexually promiscuous life.

fuck a duck! *excl.* [1940s+] an excl. of surprise, disbelief, dismissal or rejection. [cited occasionally as rhy. sl., but only by reduplication, and not a genuine version]

fuckaholic *n.* [1980s+] one who is obsessed with having sexual relations. [FUCK n.[1] + sfx. -OHOLIC]

fuck-all/shit-all *n.* **1** [late 19C+] none, nothing, often extended to *sweet fuck-all* (cf. DAMN-ALL). **2** [1920s+] a synon. for DAMN, e.g. *I don't give fuck-all.* **3** [1930s+] synon. for HELL, e.g. *who the fuck-all does he think he is?*.

fuck-all! *excl.* [1910s+] an ext. version of FUCK!

fuck else/-all else *n.* [1970s+] absolutely nothing, e.g. *there's fuck else to do around here.*

fuck/shag/screw anything on/with two legs/with a hole *phr.* [late 19C+] a phr. indicating male sexual omnivorousness and lack of discrimination. [the male equivalent of ANYTHING IN TROUSERS]

fuck-a-rama *n.*[1] [1960s+] (orig. US) a long sexual orgy (cf. FUCKATHON). [FUCK n.[1] + sfx. *-arama*]

fuck-a-rama *n.*[2] [1990s] an absolute disaster, utter chaos. [FUCK-UP + sfx. *-arama*]

fuck-a-rama! *excl.* [1990s] ext. of excl. FUCK!

fuck around *v.*[1] *see* FUCK ABOUT.

fuck around *v.*[2] [1930s+] to have a promiscuous sex life. [FUCK v.[1] + SE *around*]

fuck-around *see* FUCK-ABOUT.

fuckaround *n.* [1970s+] (US) bad treatment, 'messing about'; thus *play fuckaround*, to treat someone badly or contemptuously.

fuckarse/fuckass *n.* [1960s+] a general term of contempt (cf. FUCKHEAD; FUCKWIT). [FUCK v.[1] + ARSE n.[1]]

fuckathon *n.* [1960s+] (orig. US) a long sexual orgy (cf. FUCK-A-RAMA n.[1]). [FUCK n.[1] + sfx. *-athon*]

fuckation *n.* [mid–late 17C] sexual intercourse. [FUCK n.[1] + sfx. *-ation*]

fuck away *v.* [1970s+] to waste, to squander (cf. PISS AWAY). [fig. use of FUCK v.[1] + SE *away*]

fuckbag *n.* [1970s+] a general term of contempt for an unpleasant, disgusting person (cf. DIRTBAG). [FUCK n.[5] + BAG n.[7]]

fuck-beggar *n.* [18C] 'An impotent or almost impotent man whom none but a beggar-woman will allow to "kiss" her' (Grose, 1785) (cf. BUSS BEGGAR).

fuck book *n.* [1940s+] pornography (cf. STROKE BOOK). [FUCK adj. + SE *book*]

fuckboy *n.* **1** [1950s] one who is victimized by their superiors or associates. **2** [1970s+] a passive male homosexual, a catamite. [FUCK n.[1] + SE *boy*]

fuckbrain *n.* [1970s+] a fool, a simpleton; thus *fuckbrained*, stupid (cf. BAKEBRAIN). [FUCK n.[1] + sfx. *-brain*]

fuckchop *n.* [1990s] an imbecile, a stupid person. [FUCK n.[1] + CHOPS n. (3)]

fuckdust *n.* [20C] a general term of abuse. [FUCK n.[1] + SE *dust*]

fucked *adj.* **1** [1940s+] of things, broken, out of order, ruined, spoilt. **2** [1940s+] of people, exhausted, unhappy, wretched. **3** [1940s+] cheated, tricked, defeated, deceived. **4** [1960s+] intoxicated by a drug or drink (cf. FUCKED UP). **5** [1960s+] lacking in good sense, crazy. **6** [1960s+] very bad, offensive, rotten, unfair. **7** [1990s] psychologically maladjusted (cf. FUCKED UP). [fig. uses of FUCK v.[1]]

fucked by the fickle finger of fate *phr.* [1940s+] (orig. US) a victim of adverse circumstances, bad luck.

fucked duck *n.* [1930s–60s] (US) one who is about to die or doomed to die.

fucked off *adj.* [1940s+] annoyed, furious (cf. HACKED; PISSED OFF; TICKED OFF). [fig use of FUCK v.[1] + SE *off*]

fucked out *adj.* **1** [mid-19C+] exhausted by an excess of sex. **2** [1940s+] (orig. US) exhausted.

fucked over *adj.* **1** [1970s+] suffering (not always painfully) from the use of drugs or alcohol to excess (cf. FUCKED UP). **2** [1970s+] unpleasant, rotten. [fig use of FUCK v.[1] + SE *out*]

fucked up *adj.* **1.** [1930s+] of objects, intentions or plans, broken, wrecked, ruined. **2** [1940s+] of people, distressed, unhappy, mentally unstable. **3** [1940s+] suffering (not always painfully) from the use of drugs or alcohol to excess (cf. FUCKED). **4** [1940s+] (orig. US milit.) of people, badly hurt, wounded or killed. **5** [1940s+] worthless, contemptible, miserable. **6** [1940s+] an intensified var. of DAMNED. **7** [1980s+] exhausted, worn out. [fig use of FUCK v.[1] + SE *up*]

fucked up and far from home *phr.* [1930s+] in an utterly awful situation, miserable and lonely. [ext. of FUCKED UP; orig. milit. in the depths of misery, both physical and mental; f. the image of a seduced and abandoned woman]

fucked with no Vaseline *phr.* [1990s] suffering extreme physical or emotional pain. [the use of Vaseline to facilitate sexual (usu. anal) intercourse]

fuckee *n.* **1** the 'passive' or recipient person during copulation. **2** one who is treated badly (cf. FUCKED OVER). [the opposite of FUCKER; lit. 'one who is fucked']

fuck 'em all! *excl.* [1920s+] a general excl. of dismissal, bravado, 'to hell with them'. [the orig. words for the bowdlerized soldiers' song 'Bless 'Em All']

fucker *n.* **1** [16C+] one who has sexual intercourse. **2** [mid-19C–1900s] a lover. **3** [mid-19C–1900s] a pimp. **4** [late 19C+] a general term of abuse, e.g. *You stupid fucker!* **5** [late 19C+] a man, a fellow, with no particular abuse intended and even some degree of affection (cf. BUGGER n.[1]). **6** [1940s+] a difficult or irritating thing or task. **7** [1980s+] an extreme example, whether positive or negative. [FUCK v.[1]]

fuckery *n.* [19C] a brothel. [FUCK n.[1] + sfx. *-ery*; 'a place where an indicated article or service may be purchased or procured' (*OED*)]

fuckery *adj.* [20C] (W.I. Rasta) wrong, unfair.

fuck eye, the *n.* [1980s+] (US campus) a flirtatious, sexually encouraging glance (cf. FUCK-ME EYES). [FUCK n.[1] + SE *eye*]

fuckface *n.* [1960s+] (orig. US) a fool, an idiot, a generally contemptible person.

fuckfaced *adj.* [1940s+] **1** drunk. **2** bleary-eyed, half-awake. **3** having an ugly, miserable face.

fuckfest *n.* [1970s] (US) an orgy. [FUCK n.[1] + sfx. *-FEST*]

fuck-film *n.* [20C] a pornographic film (cf. SKIN FLICK). [FUCK adj. + SE *film*]

fuck/finger the dog, to *phr.* [1910s+] (US) **1** to idle, to waste time. **2** to blunder, to err (cf. SCREW THE DOG).

fuck-fist/-finger *n.* [late 19C–1900s] a male or female masturbator. [FUCK v.[1] + SE *fist*]

fuck flaps *n.* [1990s] the labia (cf. PISS FLAPS). [FUCK v.[1] + SE *flaps*]

fuckhead *n.* [1960s+] a fool, a complete idiot; the use of fuck merely intensifies the disdain by its own taboo status (cf. BOOFHEAD, DICKHEAD; FUCKWIT). [FUCK n.[1] + sfx. *-HEAD* (1)]

fuckheaded *n.* [1960s+] stupid, moronic, incompetent, contemptible (cf. FUCKFACED). [FUCKHEAD]

fuckhole *n.* **1** [late 19C+] the vagina. **2** [1950s+] an unpleasant, disgusting place (cf. ARSEHOLE OF THE UNIVERSE). **3** [1980s+] a contemptible, unpleasant person (cf. CUNT). [lit. + fig. uses of FUCK v.[1] + HOLE n.[1]]

fuck/fucked if *phr.* [1960s+] intensive form of *damned if*, e.g. *fuck if I'm going, fuck if I care.*

fuck-in *n.* [1960s–70s] (orig. US, mainly hippie) an orgy. [FUCK v.[1]; on the pattern of *love-in*]

fucking *n.*[1] [late 17C+] the act of copulation. [FUCK v.[1] + sfx. *-ing*]

fucking *n.*[2] [mid-19C+] harsh and/or unfair treatment. [FUCK v.[2] + sfx. *-ing*]

fucking *adj.* **1** [mid-19C+] a general intensifier, e.g. *fucking horrible, fucking stupid.* **2** [mid-19C+] implying a variety of negatives, e.g. vile, despicable, unpleasant, corrupt, dirty. **3** [1920s+] as infix. *-fucking-* (cf. ABSOFUCKINGLUTELY; FAN-FUCKINGTASTIC; GUARANFUCKINGTEE).

fucking-A *adj.* [1940s+] **1** excellent, superb, the best. **2** [1950s+] goddamned, damned (cf. FUCKING adj.).

fucking-A *adv.* **1** [1940s+] (orig. US) very little, as good as nothing, e.g. *I don't know fucking-A about it.* **2** [1960s+] generally used for emphasis; absolutely, very, utterly, completely e.g. *You're fucking-A right* (cf. FUCKING WELL).

fucking A! *excl.* [1970s+] an excl. used to denote astonishment, dismay, acceptance, praise, recognition.

fucking Ada! *excl.* [20C] a general excl. (cf. FUCKING A!). [the *Ada* is either a nonsense word or a euph. for the stronger alternative *fucking arseholes! fucking hell!* is a softer version; in all these cases the *fu* may be deliberately abandoned; thus *'kin' 'ell!* etc]

fucking-A well *adv.* [1970s] absolutely, very well, very much, extremely (cf. FUCKING WELL).

fucking hell! *excl.* [20C] an excl. of surprise, annoyance, wonder etc.

fuckingly *adv.* [1920s] extremely, very much, damned.

fucking Nora! *excl.* [1980s+] an excl. used to denote astonishment, dismay, acceptance, praise, recognition. [var. of FUCKING ADA!]

fucking off *n.* [1940s+] wasting time, idling, lazing about. [FUCK OFF v.]

fucking well *adv.* [1920s+] generally used for emphasis, absolutely, very well, very much, extremely. [FUCKING adj. + SE *well*]

fuckish *adj.* [late 19C+] keen to have sex (cf. FUCKY).

fuck it! *excl.* [19C] a general dismissive excl. (cf. TO HELL WITH IT!).

fuck job *n.* [1970s+] victimization, an act of victimization. [FUCK v.[2] + JOB]

fuck-knuckle *n.* [20C] (Aus.) a fool, an incompetent (cf. BUGGERLUGS). [a mix of FUCKWIT and KNUCKLEHEAD, the first of which implies plain stupidity, the second adds physical inadequacy]

fuck like a bunny, to *phr.* [20C] of a woman, to copulate enthusiastically.

fuck like a mink, to *phr.* [1910s+] (Aus.) of a woman, to copulate enthusiastically.

fuck like a rattlesnake, to *phr.* [20C] of a man, to copulate enthusiastically.

fuck like a stoat, to *phr.* [late 19C+] to copulate enthusiastically.

fuckload *n.* [1960s+] a great many, a large amount (cf. SHIT-LOAD).

fuck me! *excl.* **1** [1910s+] an excl. of surprise, astonishment; often as comb., e.g. *fuck me rigid! fuck me insensible!* (cf. FUCK MY OLD BOOTS!). **2** [1980s+] (US campus) an excl. of annoyance, of contempt, shut up! go away! you make me sick!

fuck-me *adj.* [1980s+] outrageous, esp. when extremely sexy (cf. FUCK-ME SHOES; GO-TO-HELL adj.).

fuck-me boots *n.* [1980s+] (US campus) high-heeled boots, esp. when worn with a mini-skirt (cf. FUCK-ME SHOES).

fuck-me eyes *n.* [1980s+] (US) flirtatious, sexually encouraging stares or glances (cf. FUCK EYE).

fuck me gently!/pink!/rigid! *excl.* [1910s+] a general excl. of surprise, alarm etc.

fuck me gently with a chainsaw *phr.* [1990s] a general expression of surprise or annoyance.

fuck me hard!/harder! *excl.* [1990s] (US) an expression used in response to an unwanted and undesirable action done to the speaker.

fuck me pink!/rigid! *see* FUCK ME GENTLY!

fuck-me shoes *n.* [1980s+] ankle-strapped, wedge-heeled shoes; also known as *follow me and fuck-me shoes* (cf. FOLLOW-ME-LADS; FUCK-ME BOOTS). [first worn, at least for mass delectation, by film star Joan Crawford (1906–77)]

fuck me with a limber prick! *excl.* [1990s] an excl. of discomfort, used after something unfortunate has occurred.

fuck Mrs Palmer, to *phr.* [1990s] to masturbate (cf. CONVERSE WITH HARRY PALM).

fuck muscle *n.* [1980s+] (US gay) the penis.

fuck my luck! *excl.* [1990s] I don't believe it!

fuck my old boots! *excl.* [1940s+] an excl. denoting one's astonishment; orig. milit. use, sometimes euph. as *seduce my ancient footwear* (cf. FUCK ME!).

fucknob *n.* [1990s] a fool, an unpleasant person (cf. FUCK-BRAIN; FUCKHEAD). [FUCK n.[1] + KNOB n.[1] (3)]

fuck-nutty *adj.* [1940s] obsessed with thoughts of sex. [FUCK n.[1] + NUTTY adj.[2]]

fucko *n.* [1970s+] a general term of address, with no specific overtones whether positive or negative (cf. BUCKO n.[1]; FUCKER). [FUCK n.[1] + sfx. -O]

fuck of a … *phr.* [1920s+] (orig. US) a large or notable amount of (cf. HELL OF A … ; STINK OF A …).

fuck-off *n.* [1940s+] a lazy or inefficient person, who prefers to *fuck off* rather than work. [FUCK OFF v.]

fuck off *v.* **1** [1920s+] to leave, to go away. **2** [1930s+] to annoy. **3** [1940s+] (orig. US) to waste time, to idle, to avoid one's duties; thus *fucking off*, wasting time, acting lazily. **4** [1960s+] to disregard, to brush aside, to put off. **5** [1970s+] to miss out on something through one's own or another's ineptitude.

fuck off! *excl.* [1920s+] either aggressive, 'go away!', or joc., 'don't be silly!', according to context; often compounded to *fuck off out of it!*

fuck one's fist, to *phr.* [20C] to masturbate.

fuck out *v.[1]* [1970s] to break down; thus *fucked out*, usu. of a man, exhausted by an excess of intercourse. [on pattern of SE *wear out*]

fuck out *v.[2]* [1980s+] to be sexually unfaithful. [to have sex 'out' of the house, 'out' of one's relationship]

fuck over *v.* [1960s+] **1** of people, to harm, to beat up, to hurt emotionally, to act cruelly, to interfere, to mess around with. **2** of ideas or objects, to adulterate.

fuck pad *n.* [1960s+] (orig. US) a room or apartment that a man keeps for seductions and sex (cf. BABE LAIR). [FUCK n.[1] + PAD n.[2]]

fuck palmela *v.* [1990s] to masturbate (cf. CONVERSE WITH HARRY PALM).

fuckpig *n.* [1960s+] a general term of derision; the implication is of grubbiness, slovenliness.

fuck-plug *n.* [1980s+] a contraceptive diaphragm. [FUCK n.[1] + SE *plug*]

fuckpole *n.* [1990s] **1** the penis. **2** a general term of dislike (cf. FUCKSTICK).

fuckpump *n.* [20C] a married man. [the monotonous regularity of his sex life]

fuck rubber *n.* [1980s] a contraceptive sheath. [FUCK n.[1] + RUBBER n.[5]]

fucksock *n.* [1990s] a sock used as a repository for the ejaculation that climaxes masturbation. [FUCK n.[1] + SE *sock*]

fucksome *adj.* [late 19C+] of a woman, sexually desirable (cf. FUCKABLE; FUCKY). [FUCK v.[1] + sfx. -*some*]

fuck someone's arse/ass off/brains out, to *phr.* [1950s+] **1** to copulate enthusiastically, from the male point of view; often in wishful phr. voiced by a young man watching a passing woman, *I could/I'd like to fuck the arse off that*. **2** to make one's partner the object of such enthusiastic or aggressive love-making. [despite the presence of ARSE n.[1], and the usu. male subjects of the phr., there is no implication of anal intercourse/homosexuality]

fuck someone's mind, to *phr.* [1960s+] to intimidate, astonish or confuse another or oneself. [FUCK v.[2] + SE *mind*]

fuckster *n.* [late 17C+] a promiscuous man. [FUCK v.[1] + sfx. -STER, implying agency or 'doing']

fuckstick *n.* **1** [1950s+] a worthless, contemptible or despicable person (cf. DICKHEAD; DORK n.[2]; PRICK n.). **2** [1960s+] the penis. [fig. + lit. uses of FUCK n.[1] + SE *stick*; cits. give this order, but presumably (2) actually predates (1)]

fuckstrated *adj.* [1980s+] (US campus) sexually frustrated. [FUCK n.[1] + SE *frustrated*]

fuckstress *n.* [19C] **1** a prostitute. **2** a female sexual sophisticate. **3** a nymphomaniac. [FUCK v.[1] + sfx. -*stress*, a female agent or 'doer']

fuck-struck *adj.* [1960s+] obsessed with sex (cf. FUCK-NUTTY). [FUCK n.[1] + SE *struck*]

fuck that! *excl.* [20C] a dismissive excl., often as a comb. e.g., *fuck that for a bowl of cherries, fuck that for a comic song, fuck that for a top hat* (cf. TO HELL WITH …). [fig. use of FUCK v.[1]]

fuck that/this for a game of soldiers! *excl.* [20C] an excl. of derision, indicating something is not working; often modified as 'blow this …', 'sod this …' etc.

fuck that/this for a lark! *excl.* [20C] **1** an excl. of derision, indicating something is not working. **2** don't expect me to get mixed up! that's a stupid idea! . [fig. use of FUCK v.[1]]

fuck that noise! *excl.* [1980s+] (US) forget it! rubbish! what a bore! [fig. use of FUCK v.[1]]

fuck the arse/ass off, to *phr.* [1960s+] of a man, to have sexual intercourse, usu. in an enthusiastic, animated manner; often in phr. *I could fuck the arse/ass off that*, aimed at a passing woman. [FUCK v. + ARSE n.[1] (1)]

fuck the begrudgers! *excl.* [1980s+] (Irish) a general excl. of defiance or scorn.

fuck/finger the dog/fuck the dog and sell the pups, to *phr.* (US) **1** [1910s+] to waste time and loaf on the job. **2** [1910s+] to bungle, to blunder. [var. on SCREW THE DOG]

fuck the duck, to *phr.* [1960s+] **1** to waste time. **2** to make a mistake (cf. FUCK THE DOG).

fuck them all but six/eight *phr.* [1910s+] (US, orig. milit.) a general oath of annoyance and hostility, often ext. with …*and save them for pallbearers*.

fuck this for a game of soldiers see FUCK THAT FOR A GAME OF SOLDIERS.

fuck this for a lark see FUCK THAT FOR A LARK.

fuck truck *n.* [1970s+] (Aus.) any vehicle, usu. a small van (possibly with a mattress in the back), in which a young man hopes to seduce women (cf. PASSION WAGON; SHAG-WAGON).

fuck udders *n.* [1990s] the female breasts.

fuck-up *n.* [1940s+] (orig. US) **1** an error, a mistake, bungling, incompetence. **2** a bungler, an incompetent, a hopeless failure. [FUCK UP]

fuck up *v.* **1** [late 19C+] to ruin, to destroy. **2** [1940s+] to confuse, to confound. **3** [1940s+] to blunder, to make a mistake (cf. ARSE UP). **4** [1960s+] (US Black) to fool around. **5** [1960s+] (orig. US Black) to hurt, to injure. **6** [1960s+] (orig. milit.) to kill, to thwart. **7** [1970s+] to make drunk or drugged. **8** [1980s+] to go wrong, to malfunction, to break down. [fig. use of FUCK v.[1]]

fuck up someone's pussy, to *phr.* [20C] (US Black) to interfere with a rival, a companion's efforts at seducing a woman. [FUCK UP + PUSSY n.]

fuckwad *n.* [1970s+] (US) a fool, a stupid or contemptible person. [FUCK v.[1] + WAD n.[5]]

fuckwank *n.* [1990s] a general term of derision, abuse. [FUCKER + WANKER]

fuck wise *v.* [1970s] (orig. US Black) to make a 'clever' comment that impresses no one, to pose as more sophisticated than one actually is (cf. CRACK WISE). [fig. use of FUCK v.[1] + WISE]

fuckwit *n.* [1960s+] **1** a fool; thus *fuckwitted* stupid (cf. FUCKHEAD). **2** a general term of derision, the implication is of stupidity. [FUCK v.[2] + SE *wit*]

fuck with *v.[1]* [1950s+] **1** to mess about with, to become involved with. **2** to interfere, often by physical or mental intimidation. **3** (US Black) to impress, to overwhelm, to manipulate (cf. FUCK ABOUT). [ext. of FUCK v.[2]]

fuck with v.[2] [1960s+] to copulate with (a partner is usu. cited). [FUCK v.[1]]

fuck without complications, to phr. [1990s] to masturbate.

fucky adj. [20C] nubile, ostensibly sexually enthusiastic; usu. of a woman. [FUCK v.[1] + sfx. -y]

fucky-fucky n. [19C] sexual intercourse; especially as used in Asia, often by prostitutes. [FUCK v.[1] + redup.]

fuck you! excl. [20C] a general excl. of dismissal, contempt, I don't believe you! go to hell! nonsense! don't make me laugh!

fuck you, Charley! excl. [19C] a general term of dismissal; often reversed as Chuck you, Farley!, but fooling no-one (cf. F.U.B.I.S.; FUCK YOU JACK, I'M ALL RIGHT!).

fuck you Jack, I'm all right! excl. [late 19C+] a general dismissive phr., don't bother me! I don't care! (cf. F.U.B.I.S.; F.U.J.I.A.M.A.). [orig. naut. catchphrase, denoting utter selfishness and disinterest in the plight of anyone else; general milit. use by WW1 and thence to civilians; the best known use is bowdlerized in the film title I'm Alright, Jack (1959), which burlesqued bloody-minded industrial relations]

fuck-you money n. [1980s+] a store of money that gives one the power of freedom from everyday constraints; i.e. one can tell one's employer, fuck you!

fuck your buddy week phr. [1950s+] (orig. US milit.) a response to any moment or act of betrayal; usu. as So it's fuck your buddy week then ... (cf. BUDDY-FUCK; FRIG YOUR BUDDY WEEK). [FUCK v.[2] + BUDDY n.]

fud n. [19C] the pubic hair. [dial. fud, a rabbit's tail]

fuddle n. **1** [late 17C–18C] drink, alcohol; thus on the fuddle, on a drunken spree (cf. FUDDLED). **2** [mid-18C–late 19C] intoxication, an intoxicated or generally muddled state.

fuddlecap n. [late 17C–18C] a drunkard. [FUDDLE]

fuddled adj. [late 17C+] drunk (cf. ADDLED).

fuddle-duddle n. [1950s] (Can.) euph. for FUCK n.[1].

fuddy-duddy/fud/fuddy-dud n. [20C] a fussy, pernickety, narrow-minded person, often with the assumption of their being old. [? Cumberland dial. duddy fuddiel, a ragged fellow]

fudge n.[1] [late 18C–mid-19C] nonsense, stupidity. [SE fudge! rubbish! bosh!]

fudge n.[2] [1970s+] (US) excrement, in association with homosexual practices; thus pack fudge, to perform anal intercourse. [SE fudge, a sweetmeat]

fudge v.[1] **1** [18C] to blunder, to err. **2** [mid-19C+] to lie, to 'tell stories'. [FUDGE n.[1]]

fudge v.[2] [1980s+] (US) to foul with excrement. [FUDGE n.[2]]

fudge! excl. [20C] euph for FUCK! (cf. SUGAR!).

fudge baby n. [1990s] a piece of excrement. [FUDGE n.[2] + SE baby]

fudge-nudger n. [1990s] a derog. term for a male homosexual, a sodomite. [FUDGE n.[2] + SE nudger]

fudge-packer n. [20C] (US) a derog. term for a homosexual man (cf. MUD-PACKER). [FUDGE n.[2] + SE packer]

fudge tunnel n. [1990s] the anus. [FUDGE n.[2] + SE tunnel]

fudgsicle n. [1960s+] (US) a Black person who is criticized by other Blacks as behaving in a 'White' manner (cf. OREO). [proprietary name of the Fudgsicle ice-cream-bar, although the bar is, in fact, all-chocolate; the usual image in such terms, e.g. APPLE n.[11], OREO, BANANA n.[2] (3), is of something that, while coloured outside, is White within]

fudwhumper n. [1990s] one who has sexual intercourse. [FUD + WHOMP n.]

fuel n.[1] [20C] food.

fuel n.[2] [1980s+] (drugs) **1** marijuana mixed with insecticides. **2** phencyclidine (cf. ACE n.[3]).

fuete n. [1980s+] (drugs) a hypodermic needle. [Cuban Sp. fuete, a whip]

fug n.[1] [late 19C+] (orig. public school) a thick, close, stuffy atmosphere, esp. as experienced in a smoky, unventilated

room; thus fugged, stuffy (cf. FUGGY). [? SE fog; note Lancashire dial. fug, stinking sweat, esp. accruing to the feet + Nor. dial. fugga, to spend one's time indoors]

fug n.[2] [1940s+] euph. for FUCK in all parts of speech and pron. as such (cf. FUGH). [FUG v.[2]]

fug v.[1] [late 19C+] to stay in a stuffy atmosphere. [FUG n.[1]]

fug v.[2] [1940s+] euph. for FUCK v. (all uses). [coined by Norman Mailer (b. 1923) as an all-purpose replacement for the taboo word in his book The Naked and The Dead (1948)]

fugazi adj. (US) **1** [1980s+] euph. for FUCKED UP. **2** [1990s] fake, artificial, false. [? Ital.]

fugel/fugle v. [early 18C–late 19C] to cheat, to deceive, to trick. [? Yorks. dial.]

fuggy adj. [late 19C–1920s] **1** of a place or room, close, stuffy, lacking in ventilation. **2** of people, preferring such an atmosphere. [FUG n.[1] + sfx. -y]

fugh n. [20C] euph. for FUCK and like it, used in a variety of meanings (cf. FUG v.[2]). [used mainly by its coiner Brendan Behan (1923–64) in his autobiography Borstal Boy (1958)]

fugitive from the chain gang n. [1960s+] (US gay) a man who has been one of a spintry. [play on DAISY CHAIN]

fugle see FUGEL.

fugly adj. [1970s+] (orig. US Black) very unattractive. [elision of fucking ugly]

fugo n. [17C–18C] the rectum (cf. FUG n.[1]). [FOGO; i.e. the smell of excrement]

f.u.j.i.a.m.a. phr. [1930s] written across an envelope back, fuck you Jack, I am all right. [abbr.; note US milit. f.u.j.i.g.m.o. fuck you Jack, I got my orders]

fulhams/fullams n. [16C–late 18C] (Und.) crooked dice that appear to be perfectly honest but have in fact been weighted with lead to ensure that they roll as the user wishes. [Fulham, southwest London, presumably a centre of their manufacture, although Walker recommends the King's Bench, the Marshalsea and, above all, 'Bird, in Holborn, is the finest workman.']

Fulham virgin n. [19C] a prostitute (cf. BANKSIDE LADY). [? the louche reputation of the nearby Cremorne Gardens]

fulke v. [early 19C] to have sexual intercourse (cf. FUCK v.[1]). [coined by Lord Byron in Don Juan (1819–24)]

fulker n. [mid–late 16C] a pawnbroker or moneylender. [Ger. fucker, fugger, a usurer, a great merchant]

full adj.[1] [1920s+] (orig. Aus./N.Z.) drunk (cf. FULL AS ...).

full adj.[2] [1960s+] absolute, complete, total (cf. FULL-ON).

fullams see FULHAMS.

full as ... phr. (Aus.) various phr. meaning very drunk, all starting with full as ... [early 16C–mid-17C] a tun, [18C] a goat, [late 19C+] a tick (cf. DRUNK AS A TICK), [1920s+] a goog/googy egg, a goose, a lord, [1940s+] a boot, [1950s] a bull, a fiddler, a fiddler's fart, an egg, [1960s] a bull's bum, [1960s+] a fairy's phone book, a seaside shithouse on Boxing Day, the family po, a state school/state school hat rack, two race trains, [1980s] the Bourke Street tram.

full as a boiled owl see DRUNK AS A BOILED OWL.

full-blown stallone n. [1990s] an erection. [rhy. sl. = BONE n.[6] (1); US film star Sylvester Stallone (b.1946), known for his macho 'hard' roles]

full bob adv. [17C–18C] suddenly, esp. in an unexpected collision. [SE full + bob, a blow (with the fist)]

full bottle, the n. [1960s+] (Aus.) an expert.

full-bottomed/-breeched/-pooped adj. [late 19C–1970s] having large buttocks.

full buf adj. [1980s] (US teen) dressed up in one's finery, 'dressed to kill'. [SE full + BUF]

full butt adv. [19C+] (US) **1** at full speed (cf. FULL SPLIT). **2** (W.I.) rushing forward without hesitation or thought. [the image of a charging bull, which 'butts' those in its way]

fuller's n. [1910s–20s] (N.Z.) a vaudeville, 'variety' show. [the *Fuller Bros.*, contemporary impressarios and owners of many theatres and cinemas]

fuller's earth n. [early 19C] gin. [SE *Fuller's earth*, 'a hydrous silicate of alumina, used in cleansing cloth' (*OED*); thus gin is a scourer and 'cleaner out']

full feather n. [early 19C+] (US) one's best clothes (cf. IN FULL FEATHER; IN FULL FIG).

full-fledged adj. [19C] of a virgin, ripe for defloration. [SE *full-fledged*, of a bird, fully feathered, grown to maturity]

full-growner n. [mid-19C] an adult.

full-guts n. [19C] a fat-stomached person; thus *full-gutted*, fat (cf. FAT-GUTS). [SE *full* + *guts*]

full hand n. [1940s+] **1** (Aus.) the equivalent of the US/UK 'full house' (one pair plus three of a kind) in poker. **2** a life sentence. **3** a simultaneous dose of both syphilis and gonorrhoea. **4** an infestation of both head and body lice.

full house n. [1920s+] a very busy time. [theatrical use]

fullie/fully n. [1980s+] (US gang) an automatic weapon, e.g. an Uzi, Glock or Tech Nine, as used in gang wars. [SE *fully automatic*]

full in the belly phr. [late 19C] pregnant (cf. FULL OF IT).

full in the hocks/pasterns phr. [late 19C] thick-ankled. [stable usage]

full in the waistcoat phr. [late 19C] fat.

full jerry n. [20C] (Aus./N.Z.) the whole truth, all the information, 'the facts'. [SE *full* + JERRY adj.]

full moon n. [1970s+] the bared buttocks, deliberately exhibited in public. [MOON v.² (2)]

full mouth n. [late 16C–early 17C] a talkative person.

fullmouth adj. [20C] (W.I.) bad-mannered, unrestrained. [image of 'talking with one's mouth full']

fullness/to the fullness adv. [1950s+] (W.I. Rasta) completely, absolutely, totally.

full of adj. [late 19C–1910s] (Aus.) thoroughly displeased by, 'fed up with'.

full of beans phr. **1** [mid-19C+] arrogant, esp. through the sudden or recent acquiring of wealth. **2** [mid-19C+] enthusiastic, excited, cheerful. **3** [1930s+] (US) nonsensical, rubbishy. [horse-racing jargon, referring to a sprightly horse]

full of bush fire phr. [20C] (Aus.) very energetic, active.

full of crap phr. [1930s+] (orig. US) contemptible, stupid, nonsensical. [CRAP n.³ (1)]

full of 'em phr. [late 19C–1900s] infested with fleas.

full of gifts as a brazen horse of farts phr. [late 18C] a phr. used of a notably mean person. [SE *gift*, a white spot beneath the fingernail, supposedly a sign of gifts or presents; the stingy man hoards such items for himself; a *brazen horse* is a bronze horse and as such does not fart]

full of glue phr. [1920s] (US) worthless, contemptible. [ety. unknown]

full of hop/hops phr. [1900s–20s] (US) behaving as if one were drugged, acting without sense. [HOP n.²]

full of it phr. **1** [late 19C] pregnant (cf. FULL IN THE BELLY). **2** [1940s+] of a person, lying, spinning a line, telling tales. [(2) euph. for FULL OF SHIT]

full of money as a toad is of feathers phr. [late 18C–19C] penniless, impoverished.

full of mouth/talk/tongue phr. [20C] (W.I.) **1** emptily boastful. **2** saucy, cheeky.

full of oneself phr. [late 19C+] self-obsessed, arrogant.

full of piss and vinegar phr. [20C] (orig. US) healthy in mind and body, full of energy and élan.

full of shit phr. [1950s+] **1** of a person, lying, spinning a line, telling tales of an experience. **2** unpleasant, distasteful. [SE *full* + SHIT n.¹]

full of talk/tongue see FULL OF MOUTH.

full on/on for it adj.¹ [mid-19C+] eager, enthusiastic, 'up for'.

full on adj.² [20C] (Aus.) having sex (cf. ON WITH).

full on adj.³ [1980s+] (US) complete, total, absolute (cf. FULL adj.²).

full on for it see FULL ON adj.¹.

full-pooped see FULL-BOTTOMED.

full quid/shilling/pound adj. [1920s+] (Aus./N.Z.) sensible, intelligent, aware, trustworthy, 'all there' (cf. NOT THE FULL QUID). [QUID/SE *shilling/pound*; lit. the 'whole pound']

full scream n. [20C] (US Black) total commitment, no holds barred.

full sheet n. [1950s+] (prison) a report against an officer for a serious offence against a prisoner. [the sheet of paper on which the complaint is written]

full shilling see FULL QUID.

full split adv. [19C] (US) at full speed (cf. FULL BUTT; LICKETY-SPLIT). [the person fig. 'splits' away from the place they have left]

full suit/suit of mourning phr. [mid-19C] having a pair of black eyes (cf. HALF-MOURNING). [the wearing of black as a sign of *mourning*]

full to the bung phr. [mid–late 19C] very drunk. [note FULL adj.¹]

full to the gills phr. [1910s+] (US) very drunk (cf. LIT TO THE GILLS).

full tour n. [1970s+] (US teen) a tedious experience (cf. THREE-HOUR TOUR). [the image of a bored group of students/tourists making their way round some less than thrilling 'attraction']

full treatment n. [1940s+] (orig. US) 'the works', the most complete way of dealing with something.

full two bob phr. [1960s+] (Aus.) worthwhile, as good as advertised. [lit. worth the two shillings that is charged]

full up adj.¹ [late 19C+] (Aus.) disgusted with, surfeited with. [var. on FED UP]

full up adj.² [20C] (W.I.) of an unmarried woman, pregnant.

fully n. see FULLIE.

fully v. [mid-19C–1930s] to commit for trial. [phr. *the prisoner was fully committed for trial*, commonly found in penny-a-line journalism]

fumbio adj. [1990s] (US teen) utterly disgusting, esp. with a disgustingly bad taste.

fumble v. [16C+] **1** to indulge in sexual foreplay. **2** to be impotent. [joc. uses of SE]

fumbler n. **1** [late 17C–18C] an impotent husband (cf. FREE OF FUMBLER'S HALL). **2** [early 18C] a young lecher. [FUMBLE v.]

fumbler's hall n. [late 17C–early 18C] **1** the vagina (cf. FREE OF FUMBLER'S HALL). **2** a metaphorical place where impotent men might be confined as punishment for their failings. [FUMBLER + SE *hall*]

fumo d'Angola n. [1960s+] (drugs) marijuana. [Port. the smoke of Angola]

f.u.m.t.u. phr. [20C] fucked up more than usual (cf. SNAFU phr.). [abbr.]

fumunda cheese n. [1980s+] (US campus) smegma (cf. COCK CHEESE). [SE *from under* (the foreskin)]

fun n.¹ [late 17C–18C] a cheat, a trick.

fun n.² [late 17C–18C] the buttocks, the backside. [SE *fundament*]

fun v. **1** [late 17C–18C] to cheat, to deceive; thus phr. *put the fun upon* to trick, to cheat. **2** [1970s+] to joke with, to tease. [FUN n.¹]

fun/flowers and frolics n. [20C] the testicles. [rhy. sl. *fun/flowers and frolics* = BALLOCKS n.]

fun and games n. [1950s] sexual play.

funbag n. [20C] a woman, with an assumption of sexual availability. [SE *fun* + BAG n.³]

funbags/funsacks *n.* [1960s+] the female breasts, esp. when large.

funch *n.* [20C] sexual liaisons at lunchtime (cf. NOONER). [FUCK *v.*[1] + SE *lunch*; the trad. genteel term is euph. SE *matinée*]

fungoo! *see* BAH-FUNGOO!

fungus *n.*[1] **1** [mid–late 19C] an old man. **2** [late 19C+] an unpleasant person.

fungus/fungus-features *n.*[2] [1920s+] a man with a heavy beard (cf. FACE-FUNGUS.

fun hatch *n.* [1990s] the vagina.

funk *n.*[1] [late 17C–18C] tobacco smoke. [the smell it gives off]

funk *n.*[2] [mid-18C+] **1** cowardice, terror; thus *funk it*, to avoid an issue or an act through fear. **2** [mid–late 19C] a coward. **3** [19C+] a black mood. [orig. Oxford Univ. use; ult. Flemish *fonck*, fear]

funk/fonk *n.*[3] [1950s+] (US Black) **1** the essence of being. **2** anything attractive or beautiful. **3** anything basic, elemental, earthy (cf. FONKY). **4** sweat generated during sex. **5** the odour of the male or female genitals.

fonk *v.*[1] [17C–19C] **1** to annoy someone by smoking or blowing smoke at them. **2** to smoke a pipe. **3** of a fire or stove, to smoke. **4** to cause an offensive smell (cf. FUNKY *adj.*[2]). **5** to stink through fear. [FUNK *n.*[1]]

funk *v.*[2] [early 18C+] **1** to act in a cowardly manner, to flinch or shrink through fear. **2** to try to back out of anything, to fight shy of, to wish or try to shirk or evade (an undertaking, duty etc). **3** to fear, to be afraid of someone. **4** to frighten or scare someone.

funked-up *adj.* [1990s] (US Black) excellent, splendid, first-rate. [FUNK *n.*[3]]

funker *n.*[1] **1** [18C] a petty criminal, rated as the lowest order of thieves. **2** [mid-18C+] one who is a coward, a weakling or a shirker. **3** [late 19C] a prostitute who quits the streets when the weather is bad. [FUNK *v.*[2]]

funker *n.*[2] [early–mid-19C] **1** a pipe, a cigar. **2** a fire. [FUNK *v.*[1]]

funkhole *n.* [1910s+] (orig. milit.) anywhere one can hide. [FUNK *v.*[2] + SE *hole*]

funk in the trunk *phr.* [1990s] (US Black teen) music issuing from one's car trunk or boot. [SE *funk music*, used as a generic; one's speakers are usually sited there]

funk on a dunk, to *phr.* [1990s] (US Black) to joke, to act insincerely. [FUNK *n.*[4] (3) + basketball jargon *dunk*; basketball star Shaquille O'Neal's dictum, *Don't fake the funk on a nasty dunk*]

funk the cobbler, to *phr.* [late 17C–early 19C] (juv.) to 'smoke out' a schoolmate, usu. with asafoetida. [FUNK *v.*[1]]

funky *adj.*[1] **1** [mid-19C] fearful, timid, nervous. [FUNK *n.*[2] + sfx. -*y*]

funky *adj.*[2] [20C] smelling very unpleasant. [FUNK *n.*[1] + sfx. -*y*]

funky *adj.*[3] [1950s+] fashionable, 'with it'. [FUNK *n.*[3] + sfx. -*y*]

funky *adj.*[4] **1** [1950s+] (orig. US Black) soulful, elemental. **2** [1970s+] pertaining to funk music. [FUNK *n.*[4] (3) + sfx. -*y*]

funky *adj.*[5] [1990s] (US teen) wrong, unsatisfactory. [FUNK *v.*[2] (3) + sfx. -*y*]

funky Broadway *n.* [1950s] (US Black) the main street of any town, where the high life is to be found (cf. FANCY STROLL). [FUNKY *adj.*[3] + *Broadway* as a generic]

funky dude *n.* [1950s] (US Black) a confidence trickster's victim, a dupe. [a reversal of the lit. meaning, i.e. a smart, fashionable city slicker]

funky fresh *adj.* [1980s+] (US Black) extremely smart, 'on the ball', aware, attractive. [ext. of FRESH *adj.*[3] (2)]

funnel *n.* [18C] the throat.

funnies *n.*[1] *see* FUNNY BUSINESS.

funnies *n.*[2] [20C] (US) comic strips in daily/weekly newspapers. [abbr. SE *funny papers*]

funniment *n.* [19C] the vagina. [FUNNY BIT + play on SE *fundament*]

funny *n.* [1950s+] a joke. [abbr. SE *funny story*]

funny *adj.*[1] [mid-18C] tipsy, slightly drunk. [SE *feeling funny*]

funny *adj.*[2] [20C] corrupt, fraudulent.

funny *adj.*[3] [1950s+] of a man, homosexual, effeminate. [abbr. fig. use of SE *funny one*, *funny fellow*]

funny as a bit of string *see* FUNNY AS A PIECE OF STRING.

funny as a box of worms *phr.* [20C] (N.Z.) very funny; often used ironically.

funny as a crutch *phr.* [1910s–60s] (US) **1** very funny. **2** not funny at all.

funny as a bit/piece of string *phr.* [1930s+] (N.Z.) highly amusing.

funny bird *n.* [late 19C] an odd, eccentric person (cf. QUEER BIRD). [SE *funny* + BIRD *n.*[3]]

funny bit *n.* [19C] the vagina (cf. FUNNIMENT).

funny-bunny *adj.* [1990s] (US) weird, odd, eccentric.

funny business/funnies *n.* [late 19C+] deceitful or underhand practices.

funny-face *n.* [1920s+] a term of affectionate address.

funny farm *n.* [1960s+] a psychiatric institution (cf. HAPPY HOUSE; LAUGHING ACADEMY].

funny-looking article *n.* [20C] an odd or eccentric-looking person.

funny man *n.*[1] [mid-19C+] a joker. [later 20C use often sarcastic and derog.]

funny man *n.*[2] [1970s+] (US Black) a homosexual man. [FUNNY *adj.*[3] + SE *man*]

funny money *n.* [1960s+] **1** (Und.) counterfeit money. **2** any money that has been gained illegally, usu. through some form of fraud. **3** tricks, deceits. [FUNNY *adj.*[2] + SE *money*]

funny pages *n.* [20C] those pages which newspapers reserve for comic strips.

funny peculiar or funny ha-ha? *phr.* [1930s+] asking the speaker whether 'funny' means odd or amusing.

fun of Cork, the *n.* [20C] (Aus.) a very jolly time. [imported by Irish immigrants]

fun of the fair *phr.* [mid-19C+] anything entertaining, enjoyable, emotionally stimulating, also used ironically. [fairground cry, 'roll up, roll up, all the fun of the fair!']

funsacks *see* FUNBAGS.

funt/foont *n.* [mid-19C+] £1. [Ger. *pfund*, thence Yid.]

fur *n.* **1** [18C+] the female pubic hair. **2** [18C+] the vagina (cf. BADGER *n.*[7]). **3** [1950s–60s] (US Black) a woman's wig. **4** [1960s] (US Black) a woman (cf. FURBURGER).

furbelow *n.* [18C–mid-19C] the female pubic hair. [SE *furbelow*, an adornment to a dress or other garment, ult. f. *falbala*, trimming for women's petticoats, scarves etc + pun on FUR + SE *below*]

furburger *n.* [1960s+] the vagina, esp. during the act of cunnilingus since then it is 'eaten' (cf. FINGER PIE; FUR PIE; HAIR *n.*[3]; HAIRBURGER; HAIR PIE). [play on SE *hamburger*]

furch *n.* [1920s] euph. spelling of FUCK (cf. FUG *n.*[2]; FUGH).

furioso *n.* [17C] a boaster, a braggart.

furk *n.* [1920s+] euph. spelling of FUCK *n.* (all senses)

furking *n.*, *adj.* [1920s+] euph. spelling of FUCKING (all senses).

furman *n.* [late 17C–18C] an alderman (cf. LAMBSKIN MAN). [SE *fur* + *man*; the fur trimmings that adorn his officials robes]

furmity-faced *adj.* [16C–17C] light-complexioned. [SE *frumenty*, hulled wheat (Lat. *frumentum*) boiled in milk and sweetened]

furnish *n.* [late 19C] an embellishment (to furnishing, clothing etc). [16C–17C SE]

furniture pictures *n.* [late 19C] mass-produced paintings of nondescript subjects, used purely as furniture and not as pictures in their own right.

furphy *n.* [1910s+] (Aus.) a groundless rumour. [proper name John *Furphy*, the proprietor of sanitary carts used by the Australian forces in WW1. The gossip and chat around these carts developed into the general word (cf. SCUTTLEBUTT). Furphy, a former ironfounder, made his carts of iron, and on them was inscribed 'Good, better, best,/never let it rest,/till your good is better/and your better best.' The same slogan was also inscribed in Pitman's shorthand. Note UK services, *Elsan gen*, a rumour, lit. news from the chemical toilet]

fur pie *n.* [20C] the female pubic hair and genitals (cf. FINGER PIE; FURBURGER). [FUR n. (1) + SE *pie*]

furrow *n.* [19C] the vagina (cf. AGREEABLE RUTS OF LIFE).

furry bicycle stand *n.* [1990s] the vagina. [FUR n. (1)]

furry front bottom *n.* [1990s] the female genitals. [FUR n. (1)]

furry hoop *n.* [20C] the vagina (cf. BLACK HOLE n.[1]; HOOP n.[3]). [FUR n. (1)]

furschlugginer *see* FERSCHLUGGINER.

further behind than Walla Walla *phr.* [1950s+] (Aus.) delayed, at a disadvantage. [proper name of the racehorse *Walla Walla*, celebrated for his ability to come from far behind and still win]

fur will fly *phr.* [19C+] noisy or argumentative conflict will occur. [animal imagery]

fury *n.* [19C+] euph. for HELL.

furze-bush *n.* [mid-19C] the female pubic hair. [SE *furze*, a spiny evergreen shrub with yellow flowers]

fusby *n.* [early 18C–mid-19C] a woman (in any negative context). [? FUBBY + FUSSOCK n.]

fuse *n.* [1970s] (S.Afr.) a cigarette. [the image of the cigarette as a lit. fuse attached to the 'bomb', i.e. the head]

fushme *n.* [mid–late 19C] 5 shillings (25p). [ety. unknown]

fuss *n.*[1] [mid-17C–early 18C] a lazy, fat woman. [abbr. FUSSOCK n.]

fuss *n.*[2] [late 18C] a social event that is crammed with people.

fuss *v.* (US) **1** [19C] to court, to date. **2** [20C] to quarrel, to pick a fight. [SE *make a fuss (of)*]

fuss-box *n.* [1910s–30s] a notably fussy person (cf. FUSSPOT).

fussbudget *n.* [20C] (US) **1** a particularly fussy person (cf. FLUTTERBUDGET; FUSS-BOX; FUSSPOT). **2** a bad-tempered person; also as *fuss-bug, fuss-butt, fuss-button, fuzz-button, fuzzy-dud*. [SE *fuss* + *budget*, one who embodies certain characteristics]

fussock/fuzzock/fussocks *n.* [late 17C–late 19C] a lazy, fat woman; thus *fat fussock*, a fat, strapping woman, *old fussock*, an ill-kempt old woman. [Yorks. dial. *fussock*, a stupid person, a coarse, fat woman; 'a lazy, fat-arsed bitch' (B.E.)]

fussock *v.* [1910s–20s] to make a fuss, to cause a commotion, to be noisy. [FUSSOCK n.]

fusspot *n.* [20C] a notably fussy person (cf. FUSS BOX; FUSS-BUDGET). [SE *fuss* + *pot*; one who has certain characteristics (cf. BARMPOT)]

fuss-up *n.* [1920s+] (Aus.) a fuss. [FUSS UP v.]

fuss up *v.* [20C] (US) to agitate, to annoy, to irritate, to disturb. [ext. of SE *fuss*]

fussy *adj.* [1920s+] of clothes, over-ornamented.

fustian *n.* [late 17C–early 19C] alcohol (cf. RED FUSTIAN; WHITE FUSTIAN).

fustilarian *n.* [late 16C–early 17C] 'a person, esp. a woman, of gross or corpulent habit; a fat, frowzy woman' (*OED*) (cf. FUSTILUGS).

fustilugs/fusty luggs *n.* [early 17C–mid-19C] 'a Fulsom, Beastly, Nasty Woman' (B.E.) [lit. 'dirty ears']

futhermucker *n.* [1960s–70s] (US) joc. reverse of MOTHERFUCKER.

futter *v.* [late 19C+] to have sex with. [Fr. *foutre*, to fuck; coined by Sir Richard Burton (1821–90) translator, *inter alia*, of the *Kama Sutra*]

future *n.* [1970s] (US campus) an unattractive man. [ety. unknown]

futy *n.* [20C] the vagina. [FUTZ n. (3)]

futz *n.* (US) **1** [1930s–50s] a fool, an unpleasant person. **2** [1940s+] euph. for FUCK. **3** [1940s+] the vagina (cf. FUTY; PFOTZ). [FUTZ v.]

futz/futz around *v.* [1920s+] (US) **1** to waste time, to mess around, to trifle with. **2** to treat with contempt. [Ger. *furzen*, to fart or Yid. *arumfartzen zikh*, to fart around; the term is also a euph. for FUCK AROUND]

futzer *n.* [1930s] a foolish or unpleasant person. [FUTZ n.]

futz off *v.* [1920s+] to leave, to go away. [var. on/euph. for FUCK OFF]

futz out *v.* [1960s] (US) to spoil, to confound. [var. on FUTZ UP]

futz up *v.* [1940s–60s] (US) to spoil, to confound. [FUTZ v. (2)]

fuz-chats *n.* [late 19C] (tramp) those who sleep in the open air. [SE *furze* + CHEAT]

fuzz *n.*[1] [1920s+] (orig. US) a policeman (cf. BUSY n.). [? SE *fuss*, which a policeman makes]

fuzz *n.*[2] [1980s+] the (female) pubic hair.

fuzz *v.*[1] [late 17C–early 18C] to make drunk, esp. as *fuzzed*, tipsy, drunk. [? SE *fuzz*, light, insubstantial particles; the obvious link, FUZZY, drunk, is a later coinage]

fuzz *v.*[2] **1** [mid–late 18C] to deal twice together with the same pack of cards, for luck's sake, at whist. **2** [late 18C–19C] to shuffle cards very carefully. [? onomat. sound of riffling cards, or SE *fuss*]

fuzz-brained *adj.* [20C] (US) stupid (cf. AMOEBA-BRAINED). [SE *fuzz(y)*, blurred + sfx. *-brained*]

fuzz bumper *n.* [1980s+] (US campus) a lesbian (cf. BUMPER n.[6]). [FUZZ n.[2] + SE *bumper*]

fuzzburger *n.* [1960s+] the vagina, esp. during the act of cunnilingus (cf. FURBURGER). [FUZZ n.[2] + play on SE *hamburger*]

fuzzies *n.* [1960s] (US) pubic hair. [FUZZ n.[2]]

fuzzle *see* FOOZLE n.[2].

fuzzock *see* FUSSOCK n.

fuzz tail *see* FUZZY TAIL.

fuzzy *n.*[1] *see* FUZZY-WUZZY.

fuzzy *n.*[2] [1940s+] a policeman. [FUZZ n.[1] + sfx. *-y*]

fuzzy *adj.* [late 18C+] drunk; thus *fuzziness*, drunkenness (cf. ADDLED).

fuzzy cup *n.* [1970s+] (US Black) the vagina (cf. SPLIT THE CUP). [FUZZ n.[2]]

fuzzy end of the lollipop *phr.* [1950s] (US) hostile or unfair treatment (cf. ROUGH END OF THE PINEAPPLE).

fuzzy lap flounder *n.* [1990s] (orig. US) the vagina (cf. BEARDED CLAM). [FUZZ n.[2]]

fuzzy/fuzz tail *n.* [1900s–10s] (US) the lowest category of vagrant or tramp. [? the way the fur of an angry or frightened animal bristles]

fuzzy-wuzzy/fuzzy *n.* [late 19C+] **1** a soldier's derog. nickname for a Sudanese warrior. **2** 'a coloured native of other countries, such as Fiji and New Guinea' (*OED*). [the Sudanese method of dressing the hair. After the late 19C, use is mainly historical]

f.y.f.i. *phr.* [1990s] for your fucking information, acronym often appended to memos in business. [abbr.]

f.y.o. *n.* [1980s+] (N.Z.) an invitation to a party at which the guests are asked to supply the drink. [abbr. fill your own; i.e. a beer flagon]

fy out *v.* [late 19C] to spy, to survey. [? SE *spy*]

fyst *see* FOIST.

G

G *n.*[1] [1920s+] (US) 1000 (usu. dollars or pounds) (cf. GEE n.[5]; K n.[3]; C n.[1]). [abbr. GRAND n.]

G, the *n.*[2] [1930s+] (US Und.) the US government. [abbr.]

g *n.*[3] [1940s–60s] (US) a cheating device. [abbr. GAFF n.[3]]

g *n.*[4] [1950s+] (drugs) **1** one grain, usu. of morphine. **2** one gram, orig. of heroin or cocaine, and latterly also of cannabis. [abbr.]

g *n.*[5] [1950s+] (US prison) prison-made cigarettes (cf. GIS n.[2]; PREMIUMS). [abbr. SE *generic*, no-brand]

g *n.*[6] [1950s+] (US Black) the female genitals, the vagina. [abbr. GOODIES n.[2]]

G *n.*[7] **1** [1980s+] (US Black) gangster (cf. GANGSTA n.). **2** [1980s+] (US Black) a friend, a partner. **3** [1990s] (US Black) a girlfriend. [abbr.; (2) is affectionate use of (1)]

g *adj.* [1980s+] (US teen) repellent, disgusting. [abbr. GROSS]

g *v.* [1990s] (US Black) to have sexual intercourse. [abbr. GET SOME]

gaan kak! *excl.* [1970s+] (S.Afr.) go to hell! [KAK n.; lit. 'go shit!']

gaan to bed *phr.* [1950s+] (W.I. Rasta) following a verb of liking or loving, it has a superlative meaning; can be used in any context, such as *I love hafu yam gaan to bed!*

gaats *see* GATS.

gab *n.* **1** [18C+] the mouth. **2** [late 19C+] idle chatter. [Scot. *gab*, the mouth]

gab *v.* [late 18C+] to talk. [GAB n.]

g.a.b.a. *n.* [1970s+] (Aus.) the outback. [abbr. the great *Australian bugger all*]

gaba *n.* [1950s+] (US teen gang) a White person. [abbr. Sp. *gabacho*, a White person]

gabba *n.* [1960s+] (S.Afr.) a friend. [Heb. *chaver*/Yid. *khaver*, a comrade]

gabber *n.* [late 18C–mid-19C] **1** talk, loquacity. **2** a chatterer. [GAB v.]

gabberlooney/gobberloony *n.* [20C] (Ulster) one who talks too much. [GAB n. ? + LOONY n.]

gabble *n.* [19C] a chatterer, a gossip. [GAB v. + sfx. -*ble*]

gabble *v.* [early 19C+] to chatter, to talk meaninglessly. [16C–18C SE; GABBLE n.]

gabble-grinder *n.* [19C] a chatterer (cf. GABBLE n.). [intensified by the 'grinding' of one's teeth]

gabbleblooter *n.* [20C] (Ulster) a loudmouth, a prattler. [SE *gabble* + BLOOTER]

gabbo *n.* [1930s–40s] (US) a chatterer. [GAB v. + sfx. -O]

gab-box *n.* [20C] (US) the mouth. [GAB n. + SE *box*]

gabby *n.*[1] *see* GABY.

gabby *n.*[2] [mid-19C+] (Aus.) water. [? Abor.]

gabby *adj.* [early 18C+] talkative. [GAB v. + sfx. -*y*]

gabby-guts *n.* [1940s] (Irish) an excessive talker. [GABBY adj. + sfx. -GUTS]

gabby row *n.* [20C] (US) the area of town where the poor live.

[GAB v. + SE *row*; the closeness of the houses leads to much neighbourly conversation]

gaberdine! *excl.* [1910s–30s] excellent! wonderful! [? Fr. *tres bien!* very good, presumably imported during WW1]

gabes *n.* [18C] a fool (cf. GABY). [East Suffolk dial. *gabes*, a fool, one who gapes or stares vacantly]

gabe's off-ox *n.* [late 19C+] a headstrong person (cf. ADAM'S OFF-OX). [lit. 'Gabriel's off-ox'; the offside ox of a pair is presumed to be the less tractable]

gabey *see* GABY.

gabfest/jabfest *n.* [late 19C+] (US) a gathering for talk; a spell of talking; a prolonged conference or conversation. [GAB v. + sfx. -FEST; *jab* is mis-sp. of *gab*]

gable/gable-end *n.* [late 19C] the head (cf. ATTIC).

gabriel *n.* **1** [1930s–40s] (US Black) a trumpet player. **2** [1930s–40s] (US Black) a puritan, a 'kill-joy', a 'bible-thumper'. **3** [1930s–50s] (prison) the chapel organist. [the archangel *Gabriel* who announces the 'last trump']

gabslick *n.* [20C] (Ulster) a talkative person. [GAB v. + SLICK]

gabster *n.* [19C] a chatterer, an idle talker. [GAB v. + sfx. -STER]

gab/gob string *n.* [late 18C] a bridle. [GAB n./GOB n.[1] + SE *string*]

gaby/gabey/gabby *n.* [18C] a fool (cf. GABES). [Yorks. dial. *gabes*, a fool, one who gapes or stares vacantly]

gack *see* GECK.

gad *n.*[1] [17C+] a euph. for God, used in a variety of oaths, which have become gradually milder as the decline of religiosity has robbed them of their import (cf. COCK n.[1]; GADSBOBS!; GADSBODIKINS!; GADSLID!; GADSNIGGERS!; GADSNOUNS!; GADSOKERS!; GADSPRECIOUS!; GADSWOONS!; GADZOOKERS!; GADZOOKS! GODSOOKERS!).

gad *n.*[2] [mid-19C] a loose woman, a slattern. [SE *gad*, to rush from place to place]

gadaha *n.* [20C] (W.I.) a fool, an idiot. [Hind. *gadha*, a donkey; used as a general derog. term by East Indians; the female version *gadahee* is more offensive]

gadderman *n.* [20C] (Ulster) a rogue. [Irish *cadramán*, a boor]

gadget/gidget *n.* [1940s+] (US) **1** the penis. **2** in pl. the male genitals (cf. ACCOUTREMENTS).

gadgy *n.* **1** [1910s+] any male. **2** [1960s+] (gay) a male prostitute's client (cf. JOHN n.[6]; TRICK n.[4]). [Rom. *gorgio*, a non-Gypsy male, and thus fig. in a sexual context a *straight*]

gadsbobs!/gadsbud! *excl.* [late 17C] a mild excl., lit. 'God's body!' (cf. GAD n.[1]).

gadsbodikins!/gadsbudlikins! *excl.* [early 17C] a mild excl., lit. 'God's little body!' (cf. GAD n.[1]).

gadsbud! *see* GADSBOBS!

gadsbudlikins! *see* GADSBODIKINS!

gadslid! *excl.* [late 16C–early 17C] a mild excl., lit. 'God's eyelid!' [GAD n.[1]]

gadsniggers!/gadsnigs! *excl.* [early–mid-17C] a mild excl.

(cf. GAD n.¹). [GAD n.¹ + *nigs/niggers*, 'not found in other contexts, and probably ... corrupt or fabricated' (*OED*)]

gadsnouns! *excl.* [mid–late 17C] a euph. for God and used as a mild excl., lit 'God's wounds' (cf. GAD n.¹).

gad's O! *n.* [late 19C] a mild oath, God's oath. [GAD n.¹]

gadso *n.* [17C–early 19C] **1** the penis (cf. CATSO). **2** a fool (cf. DICKHEAD). [Ital. *cazzo*, the penis]

gadso!/gad-so! *excl.* [late 17C–mid-19C] a general excl. [GAD n.¹, although there may be a link to GADSO!]

gadsokers!/gadsookers!/gadswookers! *excl.* [late 17C–early 18C] a euph. for God and used as a mild excl., lit. 'God's hooks' (cf. GAD n.¹).

gadsprecious! *excl.* [late 14C] a mild excl., lit 'God's precious (heart)!' (cf. GAD n.¹).

gadswoons! *excl.* [late 16C–mid-17C] a mild excl., lit 'God's wounds!' (cf. GAD n.¹).

gad the hoof, to *phr.* [mid-19C] to walk without shoes. [SE *gad*, to go from one place to another, to wander + HOOF]

gad up and down, to *phr.* [late 17C–early 18C] to go out gossiping. [SE *gad*, to move around]

gadzooks! *excl.* [17C+] a mild excl. or oath (cf. ADSZOOKS; GAD n.¹; GADZOOKS!). [lit. *God's hooks*; the relevance of hook is debatable, E.P. suggests *hocks* or *houghs*, bones; *hook* or *huck*, meaning hip-bones is also a candidate; in either case it must thus mean simply God's bones]

gadzooks! *excl.* [17C] lit. 'God's hooks'; a general oath, one of many ways of euphemizing God (cf. ADZOOKS!; GAD n.¹). [in this context *hooks* either means the nails used in the crucifixion or as HOOKS, hands]

Gaelically utter *n.* [late 19C] (society) a Scottish accent, esp. when modified to move in snobbish English circles.

Gaelick *n.* [1980s+] (US gay) a gay Irishman. [puns on SE *Gaelic* + *gay lick*]

gaff *n.*¹ **1** [mid-18C–early 19C] a fair. **2** [19C] a cheap music-hall or theatre. **3** [mid-19C] a show, an exhibition. **4** [1930s+] a house or shop, a home. **5** [1940s–50s] a prostitute's room, where she works, but usu. does not live. [Rom. *gav*, a town, esp. a market town]

gaff *n.*² **1** [early 19C] an outcry. **2** [mid-19C] humbug, nonsense (cf. GUFF). **3** [late 19C–1910s] (US) as *the gaff*, a dismissal. **4** [late 19C–1950s] (US) severe treatment, criticism, punishment or hardship; thus *get/give the gaff*, to suffer such treatment/criticism. **5** [20C] (Ulster) news, gossip. **6** [1910s–20s] talk (cf. GUFF v.¹). [? Fr. *gaffe*, a verbal blunder or Scot. *gaff*, to talk loudly and merrily or dial. *gaff*, loud, coarse talk. (1) ? also link to GAFF n.¹ (1), a fair, where 'outcry' would naturally be the order of any day]

gaff *n.*³ **1** [mid-19C+] a gimmick, a hidden trick. **2** [mid-19C+] a cheating device in gambling, orig. a small hook set in a ring used by a card-sharp. **3** [1930s+] (US Und.) a fraud, a racket. **4** [1940s–50s] (US) in pl. crooked dice. [SE *gaff*, a spur for a fighting cock + GAFF n.¹, a fair where such gambling was most likely to be found; post 19C use of (1) is only Aus.]

gaff *n.*⁴ [1960s] (US) the penis. [SE *gaff*, a barbed fishing spear, thus ? pun on FISH n.⁴]

gaff *adj.*¹ [19C] excellent, simple. [ety. unknown; ? link to dial. *gaff*, to laugh loudly]

gaff *adj.*² [1930s+] (US gambling) rigged. [GAFF n.³]

gaff *v.*¹ **1** [19C+] to talk loudly. **2** [1980s+] (US campus) to insult, to ignore. [GAFF n.²]

gaff *v.*² (gambling) **1** [19C+] to gamble, esp. to toss coins. **2** [19C+] (US) to cheat, to rig, to fix. **3** [1930s+] (US) to make a game crooked or dishonest, typically to tamper with a fruit machine or roulette wheel. [dial. + GAFF n.³]

gaff *v.*³ [mid–late 19C] to play or perform in a music-hall. [GAFF n.¹]

gaff *v.*⁴ [1970+] (US campus) to endure. [STAND THE GAFF]

gaffel *n.* [1980s+] (drugs) fake cocaine. [? GAFF adj.²]

gaffer *n.*¹ **1** [late 16C+] an old man. **2** [18C] a husband. **3** [mid-19C–1910s] (Anglo-Irish) a boy, a young fellow. [abbr. of *granfer*]

gaffer *n.*² **1** [19C] a boss or master, esp. of a show or circus. **2** [19C+] the 'straight' front man for any form of fraud or marginal business. **3** [1930s+] (US) a foreman, esp. an electrician. [GAFF n.¹; note Lincolnshire dial. *gaffman*, the bailiff or superintendent of a farm]

gaffer *n.*³ [early 19C] one who tosses up coins in a gambling game based on guessing heads or tails. [GAFF v.² (1) + sfx. *-er*]

gaffing *n.* [mid-19C] **1** tossing three coins in a hat in order to determine who pays for drinks; he who guesses right is exempt from payment. **2** coin-tossing, pitch-and-toss. [GAFF v.² + sfx. *-ing*]

gaffle *n.* [1990s] (US Black) defeat, failure, betrayal. [GAFFLE v.]

gaffle *v.* **1** [1950s+] (US Und.) to arrest. **2** [1970s+] (US) to snatch, to steal, to round up. **3** [1970s+] (US) to hoax, to deceive. **4** [1990s] (US teen) to ruin someone's plans. [GAFF v.²]

gaffled *adj.* [1990s] in an unfortunate condition. [GAFFLE v.]

gaffler *n.* [1990s] (US Black) a businessman, a thief. [GAFFLE v.]

gaffus *n.* [1960s+] (drugs) a hypodermic needle. [? SE *gaff*, a hook]

gaflooey *see* KERFLOOEY.

gag *n.* **1** [early 19C+] a joke, a deception, a tease. **2** [mid-19C] (US) a fool, a laughing stock. **3** [mid–late 19C] an ad-lib remark. **4** [mid-19C–1920s] (Und.) a lie, a deception. **5** [late 19C–1930s] (US) any form of behaviour or practice. **6** [1900s–10s] (US) a thing or aspect. **7** [1900s–20s] a plan, a scheme. [fig. uses of SE *gag*, something thrust into the mouth to procure the victim's silence. Note that Share suggests ON *gaghals*, with one's neck thrown back]

gag *v.* **1** [late 18C–1900s] to deceive, take in or impose upon (a person). **2** [mid-19C] to scold, to nag. **3** [mid-19C] to amuse. **4** [mid-19C–1910s] to ad lib. **5** [mid-19C+] to make a joke. **6** [late 19C] to inform against, to betray. **7** [1920s–30s] (tramp) to beg. [SE *gag*, to choke, to mute; the image is of making someone 'swallow' a lie or imposture]

gaga *n.*¹ [1930s+] an eccentric or senile person. [Fr. *gaga*, a senile person]

gaga *n.*² [1950s+] **1** an inexperienced, immature homosexual. **2** homosexual foreplay. [? play on the *ga-ga* noises of babytalk or GAGA adj. (3)]

gaga *adj.* **1** [late 19C+] drunk. **2** [1920s+] eccentric, senile. **3** [1920s+] ext. as *gaga over*, sentimental (about), infatuated (with). [GAGA n.¹]

gaga *v.* [1930s] (US) to act sentimentally. [GAGA n.¹ ? + the *ga-ga* noises of babytalk]

gage *n.*¹ **1** [mid-15C–late 18C] (Und.) a mug holding a quart (2pt/1.1l) of beer. **2** [17C–18C] any mug or container (cf. JOCKUM GAGE). **3** [late 17C–18C] a pipe, a pipeful of tobacco. **4** [late 17C–mid-19C] a small quantity; thus a *gage of tobacco*, a *gage of gin*. **5** [1930s–40s] (US) cheap whisky. [SE *gage*, a measure or, alternatively, a pledge, and thus, in the drinking context, a toast]

gage/gauge *n.*² [1930s+] (US drugs) marijuana. [modern ext. of GAGE n.¹ (3)]

gage/gauge butt *n.* [1950s+] (drugs) a marijuana cigarette. [GAGE n.² + BUTT n.²]

gaged/gauged *adj.* [1930s+] (US drugs) intoxicated by marijuana. [GAGE n.²]

gage of focus *n.* [late 17C–18C] a pipe, a pipeful of tobacco. [GAGE n.¹ (3); ? mis-sp. of FOGUS]

gagers/gaggers *n.*¹ [19C] (US) the eyes. [? they gauge the situation]

gagers *n.²* [1980s+] (drugs) methcathinone (cf. BATHTUB SPEED). [? it makes one SE *gag* or choke]

gage up *v.* [1930s+] (US Black) to smoke marijuana. [GAGE *n.²*]

gagger *n.¹* **1** [late 18C–mid-19C] a confidence trickster, a cheat, esp. when posing as a deaf-mute (cf. DUMMERER). **2** [mid-19C+] a tramp, a beggar. [GAG *v.*]

gagger *n.²* [1980s+] (US campus) a disgusting person or thing, lit. a 'sickener' [SE *gag*, to choke + sfx. *-er*]

gaggers *see* GAGERS *n.¹*.

gagging for it *phr.* [1980s+] usu. of a girl or woman, desperate for sex (cf. DRIPPING FOR IT). [SE *gag*, to choke]

gag me with a spoon! *excl.* [1980s+] (US teen) an expression of disgust.

gag on *v.* [late 19C] to inform against. [GAG *v.* (6)]

gah damn *see* GOR DAMN.

gaishen *see* GATION.

gait *n.* [mid-19C–1900s] (US) one's manner or way of being; thus *get a gait on*, to hurry. [SE *gait*, manner of walking or stepping, bearing or carriage while moving]

gak *see* GECK.

gal *n.* [late 18C+] a girl, a woman. [SE *girl*]

gal *v.* [1830s–1930s] (US) to court young women; thus *go a-gallin*, go courting. [GAL *n.*]

galé *n.* [20C] (W.I.) covered in scabs, itching, suffering from scabies, eczema or some other skin disease (cf. GALAY).

galah *n.* [1930s+] (Aus.) **1** a chap, a fellow. **2** a fool. [SE *galah*, the rose-breasted grey-backed Aus. cockatoo 'much given to chatter']

galah session *n.* [1950s+] (Aus.) an interval set aside regularly on the Flying Doctor radio network for anyone who wishes to exchange news and gossip rather than make emergency calls. [SAusE *galah*, the rose-breasted grey-backed Aus. cockatoo 'much given to chatter' + SE *session*]

galany/galaney *see* GALENY.

galay *v.* [20C] (W.I./Trin.) to hesitate, to speak or act indecisively (cf. GALÉ). [Fr. *galeux*, itching, suffering from scabies, thus the image is of one who is constantly scratching their head – in this context through perplexity. In 19C Fr. sl. the term, from the same basic meaning, also meant boss or master]

galbe *n.* [late 19C] (Und.) **1** an aggressive and frightening profile. **2** any physical deformity occurring above the knee. [Fr. *galbe*, 'in art, the general outline or form of any rounded object, as a head or vase; especially, in architecture, the curved form of a column, a Doric capital, or other similar feature' (*Cent. Dict.*, 1899)]

gal-boy *n.* **1** [19C+] (US) a tomboy (cf. HE-SHE). **2** [late 19C+] (US) a feminine young man, an effeminate homosexual boy (cf. GIRL-BOY). **3** [1950s] a passive male homosexual, a catamite (cf. FUCKBOY). [GAL *n.* + SE *boy*]

galee *n.* [late 19C] (Anglo-Ind.) bad language. [Hind. *gali*, abuse, bad language]

galeeny *see* GALENY.

galeery *adj.* [20C] (Ulster) foolish. [ety. unknown; ? link to ON *gola*, to howl or GALLEY *adj.*]

galen *n.* [late 19C] an apothecary. [*Galenus* (129–c.199 AD), the Greek physician, born at Pergamum in Asia Minor]

galena *n.* [19C] (US) salt pork. [*Galena*, Illinois, a centre of the pork rearing and packing industry]

galeny/galeeny/galany/galaney *n.* [late 18C–1900s] **1** a guinea-fowl. **2** any sort of fowl. [Sp. *gallina morisca*, a Moorish hen]

gal Friday *see* GIRL FRIDAY.

Galilee *n.* [1920s–50s] (US Black) the southern states. [? the image of '*Galilee* of the Gentiles' (Matt. 4:15), the 'gentiles' being White segregationists]

Galilee stompers *n.* [1950s+] (gay) sandals. [*Galilee* as metonymic for Jesus Christ, trad. pictured in sandals + SE *stompers*]

gall *n.* [late 19C+] (orig. US) impudence, arrogance, self-possession. [SE *gall*, bitterness of spirit, asperity, rancour]

galla *v.* [1960s+] (S.Afr.) to crave for, to desire very much, esp. of food. [Xhosa *ukurhala*, to be greedy for]

gallagher and sheehan *n.* [1910s] (US) a policeman. [pun on *Gallagher and Shean*, Irish/Jewish vaudeville stars, touring America from 1910–14. Gallagher was Ed Gallagher (*c.*1872–1929); Sheehan, spelled thus, was of course Irish – there weren't many Jews on the force – but the real Al Shean was the Marx Brothers' uncle, Al Schoenberg (1868–1949), and wrote their hit show *Home Again* in 1914]

gallersgood *n.* [late 19C] (Und.) anything considered so bad or useless that it is fit only for the gallows. [lit. SE *gallows good*]

gallery *see* SHOOTING GALLERY.

gallery 13 *n.* [20C] (US Und.) a prison cemetery (cf. MARBLE ORCHARD). [SE *gallery*, a floor of cells + the traditional bad luck associated with the number 13]

galley *n.* [20C] (Irish) fun, enjoyment. [Scot. *galliard*, cheerful, lively]

galley *adj.* [20C] (Irish) cheerful, lively. [GALLEY *n.*]

galley-packet *n.* [late 18C–late 19C] a false report, a rumour (cf. PACKET *n.¹*; SCUTTLEBUTT). [orig. naut. jargon *galley-packet*, rumours that emerge from talk in the ship's galley; ult. SE *packet*, a bundle of news]

galley-west *adv.* [19C+] (US) askew, crooked, scattered in all directions, usu. as *go galley-west*, *knock galley-west*. [Eng. dial. *colleywest(on)*, contrarily, askew; Collyweston is an actual village in Northamptonshire, although sources do not specify its particular skewedness; it is usu. found in relation to Collyweston roofing slates]

gallied *adj.* [early 19C–1940s] worried, hurried. [? dial. *gally*, to frighten, to alarm]

gallies *n.* [mid–late 19C] shoes. [? SE *galligaskins*, leggings or wide hose]

galligaskins *n.* [mid-18C–late 19C] a joc. term for any form of breeches. [SE *galligaskins*, a form of wide hose popular in the 16C–17C; later use is joc.]

gallihoot *see* GALLYHOOT.

gallimaufry *n.* **1** [late 16C–17C] a mistress. **2** [19C] the vagina. [SE *gallimaufry*, a mess or jumble (usu. of food)]

gallipot *n.* [late 18C–mid-19C] an apothecary. [SE *gallipot*, a small earthen glazed pot, esp. one used by apothecaries for ointments and medicines; *gallipot* itself means literally a pot that has been carried/imported in a galley]

gallivant *n.* [early–mid-19C] 'a nest of whores' (Jon Bee). [SE *gallivant*, to parade around in a showy fashion, esp. with persons of the other sex]

gallon distemper *n.* [early 19C–1900s] **1** a hangover. **2** delirium tremens. [SE *gallon*, joc. ref. to the amount one has drunk + *distemper*, mental or physical disease]

gallon head *n.* [20C] (US Black) **1** a person with a large head. **2** an intelligent person. [their skull could hold a gallon of liquid]

galloper *n.* [early–mid-19C] a blood horse, a hunter.

gallopers *n.* [1910s–30s] (US gambling) dice. [they tumble speedily over the table]

galloping *adj.* [late 18C+] (US) worsening or increasing.

galloping bones/cubes/horses/ivories *n.* [1920s+] (US gambling) dice. [SE *gallop* + BONE *n.¹*/SE *cube*/fig. use of SE *horse*/IVORY *n.¹* (2)]

galloping/crawling/mechanized/mobilized/travelling/walking dandruff *n.* [1920s–70s] (US) head lice.

galloping cubes *see* GALLOPING BONES.

galloping dominoes n. [1920s–70s] (US) dice. [SE gallop + DOMINO n. (2)]

galloping freckles n. [1920s] (US) head or body lice.

galloping goose n. [1920s–60s] (US) a train, car or plane that runs badly.

galloping horse n. [1980s+] (drugs) heroin. [ext. of HORSE n.[12]]

galloping horses see GALLOPING BONES.

galloping irons n. [1930s+] (Can.) spurs.

galloping ivories see GALLOPING BONES.

galloping snapshots n. [1920s–40s] (US) movie films.

gallop one's/the antelope/maggot, to phr. [mid-19C+] to masturbate (cf. TAKE ONE'S SNAKE FOR A GALLOP). [SE antelope/maggot n.]

gallop the old lizard, to phr. [20C] to masturbate. [SE gallop + LIZARD n.[3]]

gallous/gallus adj. [1910s] lively, spirited. [Scot. gallows, rascally, dissolute]

gallow-grass n. [late 16C–early 17C] hemp. [it is used for making hangman's ropes]

gallows n. see GALLOWS-BIRD.

gallows/gallus adj. [late 18C–1940s] a general intensive, very great, excellent, fine etc. [20C use is US; on pattern of BLOODY, i.e. fig. use of violence as synon. for extremism]

gallows/gallus adv. [late 18C–late 19C] extremely, very much, e.g. gallows poor, very poor. [GALLOWS adj.]

gallows apple n. [late 17C–early 19C] a candidate for the gallows (cf. JACK KETCH'S PIPPIN).

gallows-bird/gallows n. [late 18C–19C] **1** a thief or pick-pocket or one who associates with them (cf. SLIP-GIBBET). **2** the corpse of one who has been hanged. [the image is of one destined to 'fly' to the gallows]

gallows-looking adj. [early–mid-19C] fit for the gallows, having a hang-dog, run-down, shifty look.

gallowsness n. [mid-19C] mischief, perversity.

gallstone n. [1960s] (US) an irritating person.

galluptious adj. [mid-18C–1930s] (US) delightful, delicious. [var. on GOLOPSHUS + ? ref. to SE voluptuous]

gallus adj.[1] see GALLOWS adj.

gallus adj.[2] see GALLOUS.

gallus adv. see GALLOWS adv.

galluses n. [mid-19C+] (US) braces, suspenders. [play on SE gallows. Note US regional one-gallused, used of an impoverished rustic person]

gallyhoot/gallihoot v. [1940s–60s] (US) to go gallivanting. [SE gallivant + US regional scallyhoot, to be off, to 'skedaddle']

gallypot baronet n. [late 19C] an ennobled physician (cf. TWEEDLEDUM SIRS). [SE gallipot, a small earthen glazed pot, esp. one used by apothecaries for ointments and medicines + baronet]

gallyslopes n. [19C] leggings, gaiters. [SE galligaskins, wide breeches or hose]

gal officer n. [1940s–50s] (US Black) a lesbian. [GAL n. + SE officer]

galoot n. **1** [early–mid-19C] a soldier or a marine. **2** [19C+] (orig. US) an awkward or uncouth person, often used affectionately. [? pfx. ga- = KER- + Scot. loot, lout]

galoptious/galopshus see GOLOPSHUS.

gal's at the stockyards phr. [20C] (US) a woman is menstruating. [the blood flows at the SE stockyards]

gal-sneaker n. [late 19C] a seducer, esp. of other men's women. [GAL + SE sneaker]

galumptious see GOLOPSHUS.

galvanized adj. [late 19C–1930s] (US) in disguise. [joc. mispron.]

galvo n. [1970s] (Aus.) galvanized iron. [SE galv(anized) + sfx. -O]

Galway n. [late 19C–1920s] (US) a Catholic priest. [the birthplace of many such priests]

gam/gamb n.[1] **1** [late 18C+] a leg, esp. in 20C US a female leg; thus [late 18C] gam-case, a stocking (revived in 1940s among US Blacks), [early 19C] queer gams, bandy legs. **2** [1950s+] (Aus.) a tampon, a sanitary towel. [Fr. jambe, a leg or Ling. Fr. gamba, leg; (2) refers to the position of the vagina at the top of the legs]

gam n.[2] see GOM n.[2].

gam/gamb n.[3] [late 19C–1900s] (US) a gambler. [abbr.]

gam/gamb n.[4] [20C] an act of fellatio. [GAM v.[1]]

gam/gamb v.[1] [mid-19C+] to fellate. [abbr. GAMAHUCHE]

gam v.[2] **1** [mid–late 19C] (US) to chat, to pay a social call. **2** [1920s+] (US Black) to boast, to show off. [GAMMON v.]

gamahuche/gamaruche/gamaroosh/gamahoosh v. [mid-19C+] to perform oral sex, esp. fellatio. [? Gk. gamos, wedding or Northumbrian dial. rouched, wrinkled, puckered]

gamb see GAM.

gambetter v. [late 19C] to deceive, to hoax. [proper name (and negative reputation) of French politician Leon Gambetta (1838–82)]

gamble n. [early 19C+] a risk.

gambler n. **1** [17C] a confidence trickster who drops a supposedly valuable object, e.g. a ring, a wallet, and rather than claim it for himself, persuades a passer-by to buy it from him (cf. GOLD-DROPPER; SWEETENER n.[2]). **2** [mid-18C–19C] a cheating card- or dice-player. [Johnson (1755) cites it as 'a cant word, I suppose, for ... gamester' and defines it as 'a knave whose practice it is to invite the unwary to game and cheat them'. The cheating inference had worn off by early 19C; even so, the modern professional gambler is assumed to depend on skill, albeit honest, rather than on luck]

gamblous adv. [late 19C] (society) referring to gambling. [coined by Joseph Chamberlain (1836–1914) in a speech to the Eighty Club, 29 April 1885]

gambolier n. [mid-19C–1910] (US) a gambler. [joc. blend of SE gambol + gambler]

game n.[1] **1** [late 17C–early 19C] (Und.) a group of prostitutes, esp. in a brothel. **2** [mid-19C+] the world of prostitution, esp. in phr. on the game (cf. GAME PULLET).

game n.[2] [late 17C–early 19C] a fool, a simpleton, esp. a victim. [he provides a 'game' for his tormentors]

game, the n.[3] [late 17C+] an occupation, differing as to the group concerned; thus for lovers [17C+] sexual intercourse; for sportsmen [late 17C–early 18C] cock-fighting; for criminals [early 19C] robbery; for sailors [mid-19C] slave-trading; and for prostitutes [mid-19C+] commercial sex.

game n.[4] **1** [mid-19C] an amusing incident, a piece of fun, a 'lark'. **2** [mid-19C+] (US) a calling, business or interest, esp. in phr. what's your game? **3** [late 19C+] (US Und.) benefits or gains that, while illegally obtained, are seen as worth the poor reputation such actions might engender; thus have the game without the name. **4** [late 19C+] (US) a situation, a state of affairs. **5** [late 19C+] (US Black) any attempt to manipulate humanity for one's own ends, usually financial ones.

Game, the n.[5] [1930s+] (US Black) **1** the sophisticated, street-wise person's lifestyle. **2** prostitution and/or pimping. **3** deception, trickery (cf. GAME v.; RUN GAME ON). **4** courting the desired person with Black sl. talk. [(2) abbr. PUSSY GAME]

game adj. **1** [late 18C+] criminal or associated with the underworld; thus [late 18C–early 19C] game woman, a prostitute; [19C] game cove, an associate of thieves; [19C] game publican, a publican who affects not to notice the breaking of the law. **2** [late 18C+] of men, cunning, villainous. **3** [late 18C+] of women, promiscuous.

game v. **1** [late 17C+] to jeer, to mock, to delude (cf. GAME ON).

2 [late 19C+] (US Black) to manipulate humanity for one's own ends, usually financial ones; to trick, to deceive.

game as a meat ant *phr.* [1930s+] (Aus.) very brave. [SE *game*, enthusiastic, keen, 'up for' + *meat ant*, a large ant with a painful bite]

game as a pebble/piss ant *phr.* [late 19C+] (Aus.) brave, courageous. [SE *game* + *pebble/piss ant*, a large ant with a painful bite]

game as Ned Kelly *phr.* [1930s+] (Aus.) plucky, courageous, willing to go up against overwhelming odds. [SE *game* adj. + proper name *Ned Kelly* (1855–80), Australia's most celebrated bushranger, who ended his days on the gallows, remarking 'Such is life']

gameball *adj.* [1910s–20s; 1970s+] (Irish.) excellent, first-rate. [SE *gameball*, the final round in a game of handball]

gamecock *n.* [19C] a womanizer, a philanderer. [SE *gamecock*, a fighting cock]

game face *n.* [1980s+] (US Black) one's public face. [GAME n.⁴ + SE *face*]

game farming *n.* [1990s] (US teen) software pirating. [joc. use of *computer game* + *farming*]

game of nap *n.* [20C] **1** a cap. **2** excrement. [rhy. sl.; (2) *game of nap* = CRAP n.³ (1)]

game on *v.* [19C+] (US Black) to act deceitfully, to manipulate, to get an advantage over someone by underhand means. [GAME v. (2)]

game on! *excl.* [1980s+] **1** an excl. of excitement or anticipation, usu. about a possible sexual conquest or when a night out or drinking session is arranged. **2** an excl. of triumph at having sorted out initial arrangements. [darts jargon *game on!* the game is about to start]

game pullet *n.* [18C] a young prostitute (cf. CANARY n.²). [GAME adj. + *pullet*, a young chicken; the 'Game Chicken', however, was the nickname for the early 19C prize-fighter Henry 'Hen' Pearce]

game room *n.* [1960s+] in sado-masochistic sex, a torture chamber (cf. TOYS n.¹).

gamester *n.* [17C] a prostitute. [GAME n.¹ + sfx. -STER]

game-stock *n.* [1940s+] (W.I.) a risible figure, a laughing-stock. [SE *game*, an object of ridicule, laughing-stock]

gamfral/gamfril/gamful *see* GAMPH.

gaming *n.* [late 19C+] (US Black) playing a confidence trick on an innocent victim. [GAME v. (2)]

gam it *v.* [19C] to walk, to run (away). [GAM n.¹]

gammat *n.* [1950s+] (S.Afr.) **1** a Cape Malay, a 'coloured' person. **2** the stereotypical Cape Malay, esp. as the subject of jokes; thus *gamtaal*, *gammat-taal*, a street-gang argot, a mix of English, Afrikaans and Xhosa (cf. VAN DER MERWE). [proper name *Muhammad*]

gammon *n.¹* **1** [18C] the language or jargon of thieves, i.e. cant. **2** [18C] chatter. **3** [19C] nonsense, humbug; thus *gammoner*, *gammoning* (cf. APPLE SAUCE n.²). [GAMMON v.]

gammon *n.²* [1990s] the vagina (cf. BACON n.¹; BACON SANDWICH). [SE *gammon*, ham]

gammon *v.* **1** [late 17C–early 18C] to cheat (at a game). **2** [late 18C–19C] to deceive, to fool, to talk humbug, to pretend (cf. GIVE GAMMON; KEEP IN GAMMON). [? GAME v. or SE (*back*)*gammon* or fig. tying up of a *gammon* or ham]

gammon! *excl.* [19C] nonsense! humbug! rubbish! [GAMMON v. (2)]

gammon and patter *n.* [late 18C–19C] **1** criminal cant. **2** any form of jargon or 'professional slang'. [GAMMON n.¹ (1) + PATTER n.]

gammon and pickles/spinach *n.* [early 19C+] nonsense, rubbish, humbug (cf. ALFALFA n.). [pun on SE *gammon/* GAMMON n.¹ (3) + *pickles/spinach*]

gammoner *n.* [late 18C–19C] **1** one who covers for an

accomplice. **2** one who 'spins a yarn' or tells deceitful tales; thus a *prime gammoner*, an expert at such tale-spinning. [GAMMON v. (2)]

gammon lushy/queer *v.* [19C] to pretend to be drunk. [GAMMON v. (2) + LUSHY/QUEER]

gammon rasher *n.* [1970s] anything excellent, first-rate. [rhy. sl. *gammon rasher* = SMASHER n.² (1)]

gammon the draper, to *phr.* [early 19C] 'when a man is without a shirt, and is buttoned up close to his neck, to make an appearance of cleanliness' (Egan 1823). [GAMMON v. + SE *draper*]

gammon the twelve/twelve in prime twig, to *phr.* [early 19C] (Und.) to gain an acquittal in court; the implication is that the defendant has managed to fool the jurymen. [GAMMON v. (2) + SE *twelve*, generic for the jury]

gammy *n.¹* [mid-19C] a lame person. [GAMMY adj.²]

gammy *n.²* [late 19C] the cant or criminal language; thus *stoll the gammy*, to understand thieves' jargon. [? GAMMON AND PATTER]

gammy *n.³* [late 19C–1900s] (Aus.) a fool (cf. LAME n.). [GAMMY adj.²; he is mentally 'lame']

gammy *n.⁴* [20C] (US) grandmother. [SE *gammer*]

gammy *adj.¹* [mid-19C] (Und.) bad, usu. in combs. e.g. *gammy lour*, counterfeit coins; *gammy monicker*, a forged signature; *gammy stuff*, spurious soap or medicine; *gammy vial* (*ville*), a place where begging or hawking is prohibited. [? GAMMON v.]

gammy *adj.²* [late 19C+] lame, crippled, usu. as a *gammy leg*, a lame leg. [GAM n.¹ + sfx. -*y* but ? ext. of GAMMY adj.¹; note Share suggests Shelta *geamhchaoch*, bad]

gamocks *n.* [early 19C] pranks, wild games. [? SE *games*]

gamo/gammo *v.* [1910s+] to perform oral sex. [abbr. GAMAHUCHE]

gam on *v.* [1950s+] (Irish) to pretend. [GAMMON v.]

gamot *n.* [1980s+] (drugs) **1** morphine. **2** heroin. [ety. unknown]

gamp *n.* **1** [mid-19C–1920s] a monthly nurse, a midwife. **2** [mid–late 19C] an interfering busybody. [the fictional Sarah *Gamp*, created by Charles Dickens in *Martin Chuzzlewit* (1843–4)]

gamph/gamfral/gamfril/gamful *n.* [20C] a fool, a buffoon. [Scot. *gamf*, a fool, an idiot]

gan *n.* [16C–19C] the mouth, occas. the throat. [? Welsh *geneu*, Cornish *ganau*, mouth, Scot. *gane* or *ganne*, mouth, orig. of a fish; itself linked to Norw. *gan*, a fish-gill]

ganaglii *n.* [1940s+] (W.I.) a bully. [SE *gang*]

ganch/gaunch *n.* [20C] (Ulster) a fool, a boor. [Irish *gaimse*, a fool]

gander *n.¹* **1** [late 18C–19C] a husband (cf. GANDER MONTH). **2** [mid–late 19C] (US) a man or husband who is away from home, a 'grass-widower'. [reverse anthropomorphism]

gander *n.²* [early–mid-19C] a dandy, a fop. [Fr. *gandin*, a fop]

gander *n.³* [1910s+] a look, a survey; thus *cop a gander*, to take a look. [the bird's long neck]

gander *n.⁴* [1990s] juice. [play on pron. of nursery-rhyme 'goosey-goosey gander', i.e. 'juicy ...']

gander *v.* [1940s] (US Black) to walk. [early 19C SE *gander*, to wander aimlessly]

gander-faced *adj.* [late 19C] foolish-looking. [SE *gander*, the male goose]

gander-gut *n.* [mid-19C+] (US) one who is thin and awkward; thus *gander-gutted*, scrawny (cf. GANDER-LEGGED; GANDER-SHANKED). [SE *gander* + *gut*]

gander-legged *adj.* [19C] (US) thin-legged (cf. GANDER-GUT). [resembling the bird]

gander month/moon *n.* [late 18C–19C] the period immediately following childbirth; during this time it was considered acceptable for a man temporarily to abandon his domestic fidelity; thus *gander-moooner*, a man enjoying this privilege; *gander-party*, the male equivalent of a HEN-PARTY (cf. STAG-MONTH). [GANDER n.¹ + SE *month*]

ganderneck v. [1970s+] (US) to look at. [ext. of GANDER v.]

gander-shanked adj. [19C+] (US) referring to a thin, awkward person (cf. GANDER-GUT). [SE *gander* + SHANKS]

g and t n. [20C] *gin* and *t*onic (cf. B AND S; V.A.T.). [abbr.]

gandy dancer n. (US) **1** [20C] a petty crook, a tramp. **2** [20C] an Italian. **3** [1940s] a jitterbug. **4** [1990s] a womanizer, an active socialite. [railroad jargon *gandy dancer*, one who works in a railroad maintenance crew ult. the Gandy Mfg. Co., maker of railroad repair equipment. Such workers might spend their unemployed time tramping the country]

gang n. **1** [19C+] (US) a large amount of anything. **2** [1940s+] (orig. US) any social group (with no criminal overtones).

gang v. **1** [1900s–20s] (US) to attack or kill as part of a gang, to gang up on. **2** [1950s] to engage in multiple, non-consensual sexual intercourse with one woman as part of a gang (cf. GANGBANG v.).

ganga see GANJA.

gangbang/gang-screw n. **1** [1950s] (US drugs) a number of individuals taking drugs together. **2** [1950s+] the multiple rape of (usu.) a woman (cf. BANG n.²; GANGFUCK n.). **3** [1950s+] (US Black) a fight. **4** [1960s+] (US) a confusing or chaotic situation. **5** [1960s+] an orgy, in which there is no compulsion. [GANGBANG v.]

gangbang/gang screw v. **1** [1950s+] to engage in (usu. coerced) multiple sexual intercourse with one woman as part of a gang (cf. GANG v.). **2** [1960s+] (US) to belong to a gang or to engage in a gang fight. **3** [1970s+] (US) to victimize or destroy. [SE *gang* + BANG v.¹ (2)/SCREW v.¹]

gangbanger n. [1980s+] (US Black) a member of a teenage gang. [GANGBANG v. (2)]

gangbuster n. [1940s+] (US) an exciting and successful person, thing or event; thus *do/go gangbusters*, to be very successful. [COME ON LIKE GANGBUSTERS; i.e. someone or something that does so]

gangbusters adj. [1980s+] (US) rousing, inspiring. [GANGBUSTER n.]

gange see GANJA.

gangfuck n. [1940s+] the multiple rape of (usu.) a woman (cf. GANGBANG n.). [GANGFUCK v.]

gangfuck v. [1910s+] to engage in the multiple rape of (usu.) a woman (cf. GANGBANG v.). [SE *gang* + FUCK v.¹]

gang of adj. [1930s] (US Black) excellent.

gang roll n. [late 19C] (US) a sexual orgy or gang rape (cf. GANGBANG n. 1). [SE *gang* + ROLL v.]

gang-splash n. [1960s+] **1** (Aus.) a heterosexual orgy. **2** (US prison) a homosexual rape or orgy (see GANGBANG n.). [SE *gang* + SPLASH n.⁵]

gang screw see GANGBANG v.

gang-screw see GANGBANG n.

gang-shag n. [1920s+] **1** (orig. US) the mass rape of a single woman by a gang (cf. GANGBANG n.). **2** (US Black) a riotous, noisy party. [GANG SHAG v.]

gang shag v. [1920s+] (orig. US) of a gang, to engage in the mass rape of a single woman. [SE *gang* + SHAG v.¹]

gangsta/g-ster n. [1980s+] (US Black) a rebellious, nonconformist individual, who refuses to accept establishment (White) authority (cf. G n.⁷; HATA; O.G. n.²; PLAYA). [SE *gang ster*; the spelling is deliberately geared to emphasize the anti-establishment pose. The gangsta image, as propounded through rap music, offers an alluring mix of sex (often coerced), violence, drugs and illicitly gained money, but those same characteristics have made it a threatening force for conformists, whether Black or White]

gangsta adj. [1980s+] (US Black) used to describe the hedonist, violent lifestyle as epitomized in lyrics of 'gangsta' rappers. [GANGSTA n.]

gangsta bitch n. [1990s] (US) a woman who associates with a male gang and may participate in its activities. [GANGSTA n. + BITCH n.¹]

gangsta class n. [1980s+] (US Black) the style affected by a young street thug and/or drug dealer. [GANGSTA n. + SE *class*]

gangsta limp n. [1980s+] (US Black) a style of walking, characterized by a slight dip in the stride, adopted by young urban Black men (cf. AKIMBO v.). [GANGSTA n. + SE *limp*]

gangsta/gansta rap n. [1990s] (orig. US Black) a style of music that evolved in South Central Los Angeles. [GANGSTA n. + RAP n.⁵]

gangsta roll n. [1980s+] (US Black) a large wad of paper money (cf. CALIFORNIA BANKROLL). [GANGSTA n. + ROLL n.¹]

gangster n.¹ [1950s–60s] (US Black) marijuana. [? its rebel image, but note GANJA]

gangster n.² (US Black) **1** [1950s+] a troublemaker; an aggressive, abusive person. **2** [1980s+] (US Black) a rebellious, non-conformist individual (cf. GANGSTA n.).

gangster v. [20C] (US Und.) to take by force. [GANGSTER n.² (1)]

gangster doors n. [1970s+] (US Black) a 4-door saloon (cf. GANGSTER FRONT). [the car preferred by prominent ghetto criminals]

gangster front n. [1980s+] (US Black) a double-breasted suit (cf. DILLINGER FRONT). [GANGSTER n.² (2) + FRONTS; the style of suit worn by the (movie) gangsters of the 1920s–30s and adopted by latter-day ghetto criminals]

gangster lean n. [1970s+] (US Black) the supposedly sophisticated style of driving a car, with one's elbow out of the window and the body leaning in the same direction; thus fig., an attitude to life and a lifestyle (cf. GANGSTER RIDE).

gangster pills n. [1960s] (US Black) barbiturates. [? they slow down the gangster's natural energy]

gangster ride n. [1970s+] (US Black) an old-fashioned, large, poss. black car (cf. GANGSTER LEAN). [SE *gangster* + RIDE n.²]

gangsters n. [1990s] (orig. US) the female breasts. [? link to GANGSTER FRONT, which, with its wide lapels, emphasized the chest area]

gangster stick n. [1950s+] (US Black) a marijuana cigarette (cf. GANGSTER n.¹). [SE *gangster* + STICK n.¹¹; but note GANGSTER n.¹]

gangster walls n. [1970s+] (US Black) white-walled tyres. [SE *gangster* + (*white*)-*walls*; i.e. the style of wheel preferred by successful ghetto villains]

gang up/gang up on v. [1920s+] (US) to combine in a group, usu. against someone.

ganja/ganga/gange/ghanja/gunja n. [1950s+] marijuana, spec. that grown in Jamaica (cf. BLACK GANJA). [Hind. *ganja*, the hemp plant]

ganja stick n. [1950s] (W.I.) a device for smoking marijuana. [GANJA + SE *stick*]

gank/ganker n. [1980s+] (drugs) fake crack cocaine. [GANK v. (1)]

gank v. **1** [1980s+] to rob, to steal (cf. GAFFLE v.). **2** [1990s] (US Black teen) to shoot someone. [? SKANK]

ganker see GANK n.

gannet n. [1920s+] (orig. naut.) a glutton, a heavy eater. [SE *gannet*]

ganns n. [late 17C–18C] the lips. [GAN]

ganting n. [20C] (Scot.) begging (for). [SE *gant*, yawn or gape, thus a mouth hanging open]

ganymede n. **1** [16C] a young male homosexual, a catamite. **2** [17C–late 19C] a potboy. [*Ganymede*, in Greek mythology, the cup-bearer to Zeus]

gaolbait see JAILBAIT.

gaolbird/jailbird *n.* [17C–18C] a prisoner, a former prison inmate. [SE f. 1800; SE *gaol/jail* + BIRD n.[1] (2)]

gaoler's coach *n.* [late 17C–late 19C] a hurdle. [SE *hurdle* was a kind of frame or sledge on which traitors used to be drawn through the streets to execution; this remained part of the legal punishment for high treason till 1870]

gaolhouse lawyer *n.* [20C] (UK/US prison) any inmate who uses his incarceration to study law, both for his own use and to advise other prisoners; also in derog. sense to imply amateurishness and interference (cf. BARRACK-ROOM LAWYER; JAILHOUSE LAWYER).

g.a.p. *n.* [1960s+] (US) the *G*reat *A*merican *P*ublic. [abbr.]

gap *n.*[1] **1** [18C+] the vagina (cf. ARBOUR). **2** [late 19C+] the mouth.

gap *n.*[2] [1910s–40s] (US) a look, a glance. [GAP v.]

gap *v.* [1910s–40s] (US Und.) to stand and stare, esp. at a crime and not take part. [SE *gape*]

gape/gape over the garter *n.*[1] [mid-19C] the vagina (cf. ARBOUR). [SE *gape*, an opening]

gape *n.*[2] [1970s+] (US Black) anyone who is not part of the hip subculture and who thus 'gapes' in wonder or horror at its antics (cf. GAPESEED). [SE *gape*]

gape for gudgeons/give a gudgeon, to *phr.* [late 16C–late 19C] to be duped, fooled (cf. SWALLOW A GUDGEON). [GUDGEON]

gape over the garter *see* GAPE n.[1].

gaper *n.* **1** [1930s+] (US gamb.) a small mirror or similar used for cheating in card games. **2** [1940s] (US Black) a mirror, a looking-glass. [SE *gaper*, one that gapes; one that stares or gazes in wonder or curiosity]

Gaperies, the *n.* [1900s] Paris. [elision of the cliché *gay Paris* + sfx. *-eries*; plus an image of the gaping British visitor]

gapeseed *n.* [late 16C–mid-19C] **1** anything considered worthy of pause, an exciting event. **2** one who stares (with open mouth) (cf. GAPE n.[2]). [SE *gape* + *seed*. The term is usually derog.; such 'excitements' are presumed to appeal to the gullible or unsophisticated]

gapes, the *n.* [early–mid-19C] boredom, a fit of yawning.

gapia-mouth *n.* [20C] (W.I./US V.I.) one whose mouth hangs open or gapes. [SE *gape* + *mouth*, but note Du. *gapen*, one who yawns from hunger]

gap mouth *n.*[1] [1990s] (US Black) a person who likes to tell others how to conduct their lives. [SE *gap* + *mouth*]

gap mouth *n.*[2] [1990s] (US Black) a supposed expert in oral sex. [GAP n.[1] (2) + SE *mouth*]

gaposis *n.* [1940s+] (US) a lack of something, a gap. [SE *gap* + sfx. *-osis*]

gapped *adj.* [mid-18C–early 19C] defeated, vanquished. [SE *gapped*, broken through at intervals; full of holes or breaches]

gapper *n.*[1] **1** [1900s–50s] (US Und.) a foolish bystander. **2** [1930s+] (US prison) a mirror used as a periscope to watch a prison guard. [SE *gape*]

gapper *n.*[2] [1950s–60s] (US Black) a narcotic drug, usu. heroin. [the immediate effect of such a drug is to make one sleepy, thus one's mouth 'gapes' open]

gapper *n.*[3] **1** [1970s+] (US) a view of a fully exposed vulva. **2** [1980s+] the mouth. [GAPE n.[1]]

gappings *n.* [1930s–40s] (US Black) pay, wages, salary. [? phr. 'fill the gap']

gap-stopper *n.* **1** [18C] a pimp or whoremaster. **2** [19C] the penis (cf. CHINK-STOPPER). [GAP n.[1]]

gar *n.*[1] [16C] a euph. for God (cf. COCK n.[1]).

gar *n.*[2] [1960s+] (US) a derog. term for a Black person. [abbr. 'neegar', i.e. NIGGER n.]

garage door is open *phr.* [1960s–70s] (US) phr. used to warn a man that his fly is open (cf. BARN DOOR IS OPEN).

garb/garby *n.* [1910s–20s] (US) a sailor. [GOB n.[4]]

garbage *n.* **1** [16C] (Und.) stolen goods, esp. parcels or packages. **2** [20C] bad food. **3** [1950s+] (drugs) poor-quality or heavily adulterated drugs; orig. heroin, but since expanded to cover all drugs. **4** [1970s+] nonsense. **5** [1970s+] trivia, anything unimportant. [fig. uses of SE; note orig. 15C–19C SE *garbage*, 'the offal of an animal used for food; esp. the entrails. Rarely, the entrails of a man' (*OED*)]

garbage can *n.* [1920s–60s] (US) a disgusting person, esp. an old prostitute.

garbage heads *n.* [1980s+] (drugs) users who buy crack cocaine from street dealers instead of cooking it themselves. [GARBAGE n. (3) + sfx. -HEAD (2)]

garbage mouth *n.* [1970s] a regular, even obsessive user of obscenity or profanity.

garbage people *n.* [1990s] (US teen) unpleasant, incompetent, distasteful individuals.

garbage rock *n.* [1980s+] (drugs) second-rate or fake crack cocaine. [GARBAGE n. (3) + CRACK n.[17]]

garbage wagon *n.* [1950s+] a motorcycle that still retains its basic style and specifications, before being adapted for use by an outlaw motorcycle gang (cf. CHOPPER n.[6]).

garbar *n.* [20C] (W.I./Guyn. Trin.) nonsense, confusion; thus *make garbar*, to make trouble; *play garbar*, to play the fool. [Hind. *garbar*, disorder, chaos]

garbo *n.* [1950s+] (Aus.) a garbage man, dustbin man. [SE *garbage* + sfx. -O]

garbonzas *n.* [1980s+] (US) the breasts. [var. on GAZONGAS]

garbonzo *n.* [1980s+] (US) a crazy idiot (cf. TIT). [? GONZO]

garbroth *n.* [20C] (US) any poor or worthless person; often in phr. *mean as garbroth*, *poor as garbroth*. [lit. broth made from the *garfish*, generally seen as the food of the very poorest and as such not properly fit for human consumption]

garby *see* GARB.

garden *n.*[1] **1** [19C] the vagina (cf. BEAUTY SPOT n.[1]). **2** [19C+] pubic hair (cf. BUSH n.[4]).

Garden, the *n.*[2] [mid-19C] **1** Covent *Garden* market, London. **2** Covent *Garden* Theatre, London. [abbr.]

garden engine *n.* [19C] the penis (cf. FORNICATING ENGINE). [GARDEN n.[1] (1) + ENGINE]

gardener *n.*[1] [mid-19C] an insult hurled at a second-rate, incompetent coachman (cf. FARMER). [the relative status of their employment]

gardener *n.*[2] [mid-19C] the penis (cf. FORNICATING ENGINE). [which 'works' in the GARDEN n.[1]]

garden gate *n.*[1] [mid-19C] the *labia minora* (cf. GATE IN THE ORCHARD). [GARDEN n.[1]]

garden gate *n.*[2] [mid-19C+] a magistrate. **2** [1940s+] (bingo) the number 8 (cf. HARRY TATE). [rhy. sl.]

garden gates *n.* [20C] rates, taxes. [rhy. sl.]

garden gnome *n.* [1980s+] a comb. [rhy. sl.]

garden goddess/whore *n.* [early 19C] a Covent Garden prostitute.

garden gout *n.* [early 19C] venereal disease, whether syphilis or gonorrhoea. [abbr. *Covent Garden*, London, a centre for prostitution + SE *gout*]

garden house *n.*[1] [19C] **1** a brothel (cf. ACCOMMODATION HOUSE). **2** the house where one's mistress was kept. [? GARDEN n.[1] (1) or abbr. SE *Covent Garden* + HOUSE n.[1] (1)]

garden house *n.*[2] [20C] (US) an outside lavatory, a privy.

garden Latin *n.* [19C] very badly learned or written Latin. [SE *common-or-garden*, or that fig. learned by a gardener]

garden of Eden *n.* [16C–17C; 20C] the vagina (cf. BEAUTY SPOT n.[1]). [20C use is US Black]

garden of pleasure *n.* [19C] the vagina (cf. BEAUTY SPOT n.[1]).

garden padlock *n.* [17C–early 19C] a menstrual towel or napkin. [GARDEN n.[1]]

garden plant *n.* [20C] an aunt. [rhy. sl.]

garden rake *n.* [late 19C] a comb.

garden tool *n.* [1990s] (US campus) a sexually promiscuous woman, a 'whore'. [pun on HO n.¹/SE *hoe*]

garden violet *see* VIOLET.

garden whore *see* GARDEN GODDESS.

gargle *n.* [mid-19C+] **1** a drink. **2** strong drink in general; thus *gargle-house*, a public house. [orig. medical student use]

gargle *v.* [late 19C+] to have a drink. [GARGLE n.]

gargled *adj.* [mid-19C+] drunk. [GARGLE v.]

gargler *n.* [late 19C] the throat. [SE *gargle*]

Garibaldi biscuit *v.* [20C] to risk it. [rhy. sl.]

garlic-eater *n.* [mid-19C–1940s] (US) a derog. term for a Spanish, Portuguese or Italian person; thus *garlic-eating*, foreign (in a derog. context).

garlic-snapper *n.* [1940s] (US) an Italian.

garm *n.* [1990s] (Black) clothes, clothing. [abbr. SE *garment*]

garmouth *v.* [20C] (US) to boast, to brag, to make empty threats. [SE *gar*, a fish that is generally considered not worth eating other than in the direst extremity]

garn! *excl.* [late 19C+] a dismissive excl., used to indicate one's scepticism of the last statement. [Cockney pron. of *go on!*]

garnish *n.* [late 16C–early 19C] **1** money extorted from a new prisoner, either as a gaoler's fee or as drink-money for the other prisoners. **2** fetters. [SE *garnish*, to embellish, to add on. (1) the practice was abolished in 1824, after which time the term was restricted to SE. (2) although both Johnson (1755) and F&H both cite this meaning, it may have stemmed from a mis-reading of (1)]

garnish *v.* [mid-18C–19C] to fit a prisoner with fetters. [GARNISH n. (2)]

garret *n.* **1** [mid-19C+] the head (cf. ATTIC; QUEER IN THE GARRET). **2** [mid-19C+] (Und.) the fob pocket. **3** [mid-19C+] a woman's handbag. **4** [late 19C] the mouth.

garreteer/garreter *n.* [19C] a thief who specializes in entering houses via attics and skylights (cf. DANCER). [SE *garret* + sfx. *-eer/-er*, doer, agent]

garrison hack *n.* [19C] a prostitute (cf. BARRACK HACK). [ironic use of SE *garrison hack*, a regular attender at military balls. Such a woman, like the horse, can be 'ridden' by anyone]

garrot *n.* [1960s+] (W.I./UKVI) one who is not a native of the Virgin Islands, an outsider. [ety. unknown]

garrotting *n.* [mid-19C] among card-sharps, a method of cheating that involves hiding certain cards behind the neck, presumably slipped between the neck and the shirt collar.

garsoon/garsun/gorsoon *n.* [20C] (Irish) a boy, esp. in derog. contexts. [synon. Irish *garsún*, but note Fr. *garçon*, boy]

Gary Glitter *n.* **1** [1980s] (a pint of) bitter. **2** [1990s] the anus. [rhy. sl.; (2) *Gary Glitter* = SHITTER n.¹; ult. pop singer Gary Glitter, real name Paul Gadd (b.1940)]

gas *n.¹* **1** [late 18C+] idle or boastful talk, bombast, humbug. **2** [1910s+] energy; thus *out of gas*, tired out.

gas *n.²* [1930s+] (orig. Irish) **1** a very enjoyable, pleasant situation or experience. **2** someone who is very pleasing, exciting, impressive (cf. GREAT GAS).

gas *n.³* [1940s+] (US Black) hair that has been artificially straightened or 'processed' (cf. GAS-HEAD). [one's hair has been 'cooked']

gas *adj.* [1930s+] of objects or people, enjoyable, exciting, very pleasant. [GAS n.²]

gas *v.¹* [mid-19C+] to chatter, to talk inconsequentially and continually, to offer only 'hot air'. [SE *gas* n.]

gas *v.²* [1940s+] **1** to enjoy, to have a good time. **2** to impress or please enormously. **3** to excite or thrill. [GAS n.²]

gas *v.³* [1970s+] (US drugs) to sniff gasoline fumes.

gas and run, to *phr.* [1960s+] (US) to fill up or have one's car filled up by a garage attendant, then drive off before paying.

gasbag/gasman *n.* [late 19C+] a talkative person (cf. BAG OF WIND).

gaseous *adj.* (US) [1960s–70s] superlative, fantastic (cf. GASSY adj.²).

gasface *v.* [1990s] (US teen) to make faces at another. [? the image is of a user of laughing gas]

gas-guzzler *n.* [1970s+] the traditionally enormous US automobile, profligate of petrol and dwarfing its European rivals; symbolic of the 1950s, out of favour in the energy-conscious 1970s, it staged a brief renaissance in the early 1990s (cf. BOAT n.¹). [SAmE *gas*, gasoline, i.e. petrol + GUZZLE]

gash *n.¹* **1** [18C+] the vagina (cf. ARBOUR). **2** [18C+] any girl or woman. [as simple anatomy in the 18C, but 20C use is derog.; ? GASH adj.]

gash *n.²* [mid-19C] (US) the mouth.

gash *n.³* [1980s+] (drugs) marijuana.

gash *adj.* [1920s+] **1** extra, superfluous, spare. **2** (Aus.) a second helping. [? dial. *gaishen*, a skeleton, something or someone ridiculous, an obstacle]

gash *v.* **1** [1980s+] (US campus) to have sexual intercourse. **2** [1990s] to suffer from any form of sexually transmitted disease.

gas-head *n.* [20C] (US Black) one who has had their hair straightened with a 'process' haircut. [GAS n.² + SE *head*]

gash-eater *n.* [1970s+] one who performs cunnilingus. [GASH n.¹ + SE *eater*; note EAT v.³]

gash-hound *n.* [1970s+] a womanizer. [GASH n.¹ + sfx. -HOUND]

gashle *adv.* [late 19C+] (S.Afr.) gently, carefully. [Zulu/Xhosa *kahle*, sweetly, peacefully]

gas-house district *n.* [late 19C+] (US) a slum. [the original gas-houses that lined New York's East River between 14th Street and 22nd Street. The first gas-house appeared in 1842 and its peers followed over the next 50 years; the orig. Gas-house district covered 3rd Avenue to the river and 14th Street to 27th Street. The smell of leaking gas and the poor neighbourhood housing meant that few lived there by choice, but among those who did were the feared thugs of the Gas-house gangs]

gas jockey *n.* [1950s+] (US) a gas/petrol station attendant. [SE *gas* + JOCKEY n.² (2)]

gasket *n.¹* [1940s] (US) a doughnut or flapjack. [resemblance]

gasket *n.²* [1970s] (US drugs) anything used to seal a hypodermic needle to a syringe (cf. GEE n.⁷).

gaskins *n.* [late 17C–early 19C] breeches. [SE *galligaskins*, a form of wide hose popular in the 16C–17C]

gaslight *v.* [1950s+] (US) to confuse someone, causing them to feel insane. [the 1944 film of Patrick Hamilton's book *Gaslight* (1939), in which such deliberate cruelty forms the basis of the plot]

gasman *see* GASBAG.

gas-meter bandit *n.* [1960s+] a petty thief (cf. BALD-TYRE BANDIT). [the biggest 'job' he attempts is robbing the gas-meter]

gas monkey *n.* [1930s] (US) a gas/petrol station attendant (cf. GAS JOCKEY; GREASE MONKEY). [SE *gas* + MONKEY n.¹¹]

gasoline *n.* [1950s–60s] alcohol, esp. Jack Daniel whisky.

gasp *n.* [late 19C] a drink, a shot of liquor. [? the effect on one's throat]

gasp *v.* [late 19C] to drink a dram of spirits. [GASP n.]

gasp and grunt *n.* [1950s+] the vagina (cf. BERKELEY HUNT; GRUMBLE AND GRUNT). [rhy. sl. *gasp and grunt* = CUNT + ref. to the sounds of intercourse]

gasper *n.* **1** [1910s+] a cigarette, esp. a cheap brand (orig. Virginia rather than the more exotic Turkish tobacco). **2** [1970s+] (drugs) marijuana cigarette.

gasper stick *n.* [1970s+] (drugs) a marijuana cigarette. [GASPER n. (2) + STICK n.¹¹]

gas pipe n.[1] [mid-19C–1910s] (US) a talkative person (cf. GAS-BAG). [GAS v.[1] + SE *pipe*]

gas pipe n.[2] [1930s] (US) a slide-trombone.

gas pipes n. [late 19C] tight trousers (cf. DRAINPIPES).

gas round v. [late 19C–1910s] to ferret out information in a clandestine manner.

gassed adj.[1] [1910s+] drunk.

gassed adj.[2] [1950s] (US) delighted. [GAS v.[2]]

gassed-out adj. [1960s] (US) worn out. [? GAS v.[1], i.e. exhausted f. 'gassing']

gasser n.[1] **1** [19C] a loudmouth, a chatterer (cf. BAG OF WIND). **2** [1940s+] (Aus.) a cigarette (cf. GASPER). [GAS v.[1]]

gasser n.[2] **1** [1940s+] anything considered very enjoyable, superlative, first-rate. **2** [1950s–60s] a man or woman highly admired, considered to be the best. [GAS n.[2]]

gassy adj.[1] [mid–late 19C] **1** talkative, verbose, boastful. **2** irascible, likely to 'flare up' without warning (cf. GASEOUS). [fig. uses of SE + GAS v.[1]]

gassy adj.[2] (US) [1960s–70s] superlative, fantastic. [GAS n.[2] + sfx. -y]

gasumph *see* GAZUMP.

gas up one's head, to phr. [1980s+] (US drugs) to smoke crack cocaine. [SAmE *gas up*, to fill up with petrol]

gas wagon n. [1910s–20s] (US) a car. [SAmE *gas* + *wagon*]

gasworks n. [1990s] (Irish) an asthma inhaler.

gat n.[1] **1** [20C] (orig. US) a pistol or revolver. **2** [1920s] (US) a gunman. [*Gatling* gun]

gat n.[2] [1960s+] (S.Afr.) the anus, esp. as excl. (cf. ARSEHOLE n.). [Afk. *gat*, hole, vent]

gata n. [1970s+] (S.Afr.) **1** the police. **2** a prison warder. [Sotho sl. *legata*, a member of the police force, lit. 'catch a thief' or GAT n.[1] (1), from their guns]

gat-creeper n. [1980s+] (S.Afr.) a sycophant, a toady. [GAT n.[2] + SE *creeper*]

Gate, the n.[1] **1** [mid-19C] Billings*gate*. **2** [mid–late 19C] New*gate* prison. **3** [1950s+] Notting Hill *Gate*, London W11 (cf. GROVE n.). [abbr.]

gate n.[2] [1930s+] (US Black) a person, a man (cf. GATEMOUTH). [jazz jargon *gate*, a swing musician, ult. the 'swinging' of a gate + abbr. ALLIGATOR n.[4]; the term, at its peak 1935–43, was popularized by the comedian Jerry Colonna, who used it widely on Bob Hope's radio show]

gate n.[3] [1930s+] the mouth.

gate-crasher n. [1920s+] (orig. US) a person who gets into a social or public event without an invitation or admission ticket.

gatecrash v. [1920s+] (orig. US) to gain admission to a social or public event without an invitation or admission ticket. [GATE-CRASHER]

gate fever n. [1930s+] (prison) the nervous feeling that overtakes many prisoners as their sentence draws to its close; thus *gatey*, suffering from this 'disease'.

gate in the orchard n. [19C] the *labia minora* (cf. GARDEN GATE n.[1]).

gate is open *see* BARN DOOR IS OPEN.

gate money n. [1930s–60s] (US prison) money given to a prisoner on release.

gatemouth n. [1920s–40s] (US Black) **1** a person, a man (cf. GATE n.[2]). **2** a gossip, a loudmouth. [allegedly coined by jazz maestro Louis Armstrong (1901–71)]

gate of horn n. [19C] the vagina. [pun on SE *gate* + HORN n.[2]]

gate of life n. [late 18C] the vagina.

gates n. [1950s+] (W.I. Rasta) one's home (cf. YARD n.[4]). [i.e. one's front *gate*]

gates! excl. [1940s–50s] (US Black) an address between two males (cf. GATOR n.[3]). [GATE n.[2]]

gates of Rome n. [20C] home. [rhy. sl.]

gather-em-up/gather-up n. [1970s+] (Irish) a useless person. [Irish/Ulster *gather-up*, a rag-and-bone man]

gather straws *see* DRAW STRAWS.

gation/gaishen/gashun n. [20C] (Ulster) a very thin person. [Scot. Gael. *gaisean*, a stalk; thus a young boy]

gatkas n. [20C] trousers. [synon. Yid.]

gatling n. [late 19C–1960s] (US) a gun (cf. GAT n.[1]). [abbr. *Gatling gun*, a form of machine gun, invented by Dr R.J. *Gatling* (1818–1903), and first used in the American Civil War (1861–5)]

gato n. [1980s+] (drugs) heroin. [Sp.]

gator n.[1] [mid-19C+] (orig. US) an alli*gator*. [abbr.]

gator n.[2] [20C] (US) an inhabitant of Florida. [abbr. ALLIGATOR n.[3]]

gator n.[3] [1920s–40s] (orig. US Black) **1** a jazz fan (cf. CAT n.[9]; GATE n.). **2** any person considered to be in the swing of things. **3** a term of address used between two men (cf. GATES!). [abbr. ALLIGATOR n.[4]]

gator bait n. [1970s+] (US) a Black person. [abbr. ALLIGATOR BAIT n.[1]]

gator bit, the phr. [20C] (US) used of a menstruating woman. [GATOR n.[1] and the resulting blood]

gators n. [1950s+] (US Black) shoes made from alligator skin. [GATOR n.[1]]

gats!/gaats! excl. [1910s+] (S.Afr.) a general excl. of dismay, annoyance, surprise etc.; synon. with *God!* [euph. for Afk. *Gots*, God]

gatter n. [early–mid-19C] beer; esp. in phr. *shant of gatter*, a pot of beer. [ety. unknown; E.P. suggests poss. Ling. Fr. or mix of *agua* + *water*]

gattering n. [mid–late 19C] a public house. [GATTER]

gattes n. [1960s+] **1** (S.Afr. Black) the police. **2** (S.Afr. Jewish) an Afrikaaner. [? Sotho *gata*, to trample or Yid. *khates*, a bad person]

gat up v. [1920s–30s] (US Und.) to hold someone up with a gun. [GAT n.[1]]

gatvol adj. [1980s+] (S.Afr.) bored of, disgusted by, 'having a bellyful' of. [GAT n.[2] + Afk. *vol*, full]

gaubey n. [20C] (Irish) a gawper, one who looks on while others are doing something (cf. GABY). [Irish *gabhgaire*, an onlooker (at a card-game)]

gaudeamus n. [19C] **1** a student feast. **2** any form of party, merry-making. [Lat. *gaudeamus*, let us rejoice]

gaudy adj./adv. [late 19C–1920s] a general intensifier, very, extremely, but used only in negative sense, e.g. *not a gaudy lot*. [? euph. for BLOODY]

gauge n.[1] **1** [late 19C] extent; thus *get the gauge of*, to ascertain the extent; *that's about the gauge of it*, that seems a fair enough description. **2** [1970s] (US Black) the extent to which one is currently drunk.

gauge n.[2] *see* GAGE n.[2]

gauge n.[3] [1970s] (US Black) a shotgun. [abbr. *12-gauge*, a 12 bore]

gauge butt *see* GAGE BUTT.

gauged *see* GAGED.

gaul darned/gauldarned adj. [late 19C] (US) damned, cussed. [GOLDARNED]

gaulder/gulder n. [20C] (Ulster) a shout. [Scot. *gulder*, a noisy, energetic shout]

gaum n.[1] [18C+] intelligence. [dial. *gaum*, notice, heed, attention]

gaum/gaumhead n.[2] [20C] (US) a fool, a clumsy oaf. [dial. *gaumless*, stupid + sfx. -HEAD (1); note synon. dial. *gaumless-head*]

gaumy adj. [20C] (US) stupid, clumsy. [dial. *gaumless*, stupid + sfx. -y]

gaunch n.[1] *see* GANCH.

gaunch *n.*[2] [1950s] (US teen) an unpopular girl. [? GAUMY + GINCH]

gauzer/gawzer *n.* [20C] (Irish) a very pretty girl. [? SE *gorgeous* or *gaze*, to stare at]

gavacho *n.* [20C] (Hisp.Am.) a White person.

gavel and wig, to *phr.* [20C] to scratch (an itchy anus). [rhy. sl. *gavel and wig* = SE *twig*, i.e. the image of using a twig to do the scratching]

gavone *n.* [1920s+] an important man. [? JIBONE]

gaw/gawd/gor *n.* [late 19C+] mispron. of, or euph. for, God.

gawd aggie! *excl.* [20C] (Aus.) a general expletive of surprise, annoyance etc. [SE *God!* + proper name *Aggie*, i.e. Agatha]

gawdelpus/gordelpus/God-help-us *n.*[1] [late 19C+] **1** an irritating or helpless person; often used of a child, e.g. *You 'orrible little gawdelpus!* **2** a generally miserable looking person. [SE *God help us*; unstated is 'what shall we do about you?']

gawdelpus/gordelpus/God-help-us *n.*[2] [late 19C–1900s] an impoverished labourer. ['from his ordinary excl. "Gordelpus – what's a cove to do?"' (Ware)]

gawd forbid *n.* [late 19C+] a child (cf. GOD-FORBIDS *n.*[1]).

gawd/cor love-a-duck! *excl.* [20C] general expletives (cf. LORD LOVE-A-DUCK). [*gawd* is Aus. use, *cor* is general]

gawdsaker *n.* [1910s–50s] one who, in a state of panic, exclaims *For Gawd's sake, let's do something now.*

gawf *n.* [mid-19C] a red-skinned apple, considered inferior produce but capable, with judicious polishing, to be sold as something better. [? 'go for more' 'Gawfs are sweet and sour at once ... and fit only for mixing' (Mayhew)]

gawie *n.* [1960s+] (S.Afr.) a country bumpkin, an unsophisticated peasant. [Afk. *gawie*, lout]

gawk/gawkhead *n.* [17C–early 19C] **1** a peasant, a rustic. **2** a simpleton, a fool (cf. COUNTRY CRACKER). [Scot. *gowk*, cuckoo and thus fool or *gawk*, to stare at]

gawm *see* GOM *n.*[2].

gawney *n.* [18C] a fool. [Midl. dial. *gawney*, to stare vacantly]

Gawney Mac!/Jack! *excl.* [1980s+] (Irish) euph. for *Jesus!* (pron. 'Jaysus!').

gawp *n.* [early 19C+] a fool, a simpleton. [GAWP *v.*]

gawp *v.* [early 19C+] to stare. [obs. SE *galp*, to gape, yawn, orig. of animals]

gawsave *n.* [20C] the British national anthem. [the first line, '*God save* our gracious king/queen']

gawzer *see* GAUZER.

gay *n.*[1] [1940s+] a male homosexual. [GAY *adj.*[1] (3)]

gay *n.*[2] [1940s+] (Aus.) a dupe, a sucker, a gullible person. [GALAH *n.*[2]]

gay *n.*[3] [1960s] (Aus.) a party (cf. HALE AND HEARTY). [rhy. sl. *gay and hearty* = party]

gay *adj.*[1] **1** [18C–19C] promiscuous, dissipated. **2** [late 18C–late 19C] of a woman, leading an immoral life, working as a prostitute. **3** [1930s+] (orig. US) homosexual. [the use of *gay* as a self-description by homosexuals originated during WW2, probably an abbr. of US tramps' sl. GEYCAT, the young homosexual companion of an older tramp; the wider use in the heterosexual world did not begin until *c.*1970, with the emergence of the Gay Liberation Front, first in the US and subseq. in the UK. With the decline of derog. terms, such as QUEER, *gay* is now effectively SE]

gay *adj.*[2] **1** [19C–1900s] slightly drunk, tipsy (cf. ABOUT RIGHT *adj.*[1]). **2** [late 19C–1910s] (US) forward, impertinent, overfamiliar, esp. in phr. *get gay/gay with*, to be cheeky, impertinent (towards). [SE *gay*, cheerful]

gay *adj.*[3] [mid-19C–1910s] (orig. US) fine, first-rate.

gay *adj.*[4] [1970s+] (orig. US campus) a general pej.; stupid, ugly, eccentric. [a paradoxical use of the otherwise politically correct term *gay* as a derog., reminiscent of the trad. use of QUEER]

gay and frisky *n.* [20C] whisky. [rhy. sl.]

gay and hearty *n.* [20C] (Aus.) a party (cf. HALE AND HEARTY). [rhy. sl.]

gay-basher *n.* [1980s+] an ostensibly 'real man' who specializes in beating and terrorizing homosexual men (cf. FAG-BASHER). [GAY *n.*[1] + BASH *v.*[1]]

gay-bashing *n.* [1980s+] (orig. US) the homophobic beating up of homosexual men; thus *gay-bash*, to beat up homosexuals (cf. QUEER-BASHING). [GAY *n.*[1] + BASH *v.*[1]]

gay bit *n.* [mid–late 19C] a prostitute. [GAY *adj.*[1] (2) + BIT *n.*[3]]

gay boy *n.* [1950s+] (US) a male homosexual. [GAY *adj.*[1] (3) + SE *boy*]

gaycat *n.* (US) **1** [late 19C–1950s] a young or inexperienced tramp. **2** [late 19C–1950s] a hobo who accepts occasional work. **3** [1930s] a tramp's younger, homosexual companion. [var. on GEYCAT *n.*]

gaycat *v.*[1] [late 19C–1950s] (US) to act as a tramp's (homosexual) companion. [GEYCAT]

gaycat *v.*[2] [1920s–40s] (US Black) to have a good time. [SE *gay* adj. + CAT *n.*[5]]

gaychick *n.* [1980s+] (US gay) a lesbian. [GAY *adj.*[1] (3) + CHICK *n.*[3]]

gaydar *n.* [1980s+] (gay) the sensory perception that lesbians and gays have of detecting other gay people in their midst. [pun on GAY *adj.*[1] (3) + SE *radar*]

gay deceivers *n.* [1940s–50s] a padded brassiere that accentuates the shape and dimensions of otherwise diminutive female breasts (cf. FALSIES). [pun on original use, a deceitful rake]

gay girl/woman *n.* [mid-19C] a promiscuous girl or woman. [GAY *adj.*[1] (1) + SE *girl*]

gay gordon *n.* [20C] (US) a traffic warden. [rhy. sl.]

gay house *n.* [18C–1900s] a brothel (cf. ACCOMMODATION HOUSE). [GAY *adj.*[1] (2) + HOUSE *n.*[1] (1); later use is Aus. only]

gaying instrument *n.* [18C] the penis (cf. FORNICATING ENGINE). [GAY *adj.*[1] (1), (2) + SE *instrument*]

gaying it *n.* [18C] having sexual intercourse. [GAY *adj.*[1] (1), (2)]

gay in the arse/groin *phr.* [18C] promiscuous. [GAY *adj.*[1] (1), (2) + ARSE *n.*]

gay lady *n.* [mid-19C] a prostitute (cf. GAY GIRL). [GAY *adj.*[1] (2) + SE *lady*]

gayola *n.* **1** [1960s+] (US Und.) pay-offs and bribes made to police to permit running of gay clubs. **2** [1980s+] (US) a homosexual man. [sfx. -OLA; on pattern of SE *payola*]

gay tyke boy *n.* [mid-19C] a dog-fancier. [SE *gay* + TYKE *n.*[1]]

Gay White Way *n.* [1910s–20s] Broadway, New York City. [the term, in which *gay* is used in the conventional SE manner, i.e. cheerful, jolly, was a short-lived alternative to the longer-lasting GREAT WHITE WAY]

gay woman *see* GAY GIRL.

gazabo/gazabe/gazaybe/gazebo/gazee/gazooney *n.* [19C+] (Irish/US) an awkward, strange or stupid person (cf. GAZOB). [? Sp. *gazapo*, a sly fellow + SE *gaze*, i.e. their vacant stares]

gaze at the melody, to *phr.* [late 19C] **1** to deal stoically with a problem or difficult situation. **2** to take one's punishment. [play on FACE THE MUSIC]

gazebo *n.*[1] *see* GAZABO.

gazebo *n.*[2] [1900s] (US) the mouth. [SE *gazebo*, a form of garden hut, or a turret on the roof of a house]

gazee *see* GAZABO.

gazelle *n.* [late 19C–1940s] (US) a young woman.

gazer *n.* **1** [1930s–40s] (US Black) a flirtatious woman looking for a new partner. **2** [1930s–50s] (US Und.) a federal narcotics agent. [SE *gaze*, to stare at; in (1) the assumption being that she is *gazing* at other men in the hope of finding a new husband]

gazillion *n.* [1990s] (US teen) a very great number; too many to count (cf. SQULLION). [pfx. *ga-* (cf. KER-) + *zillion*]

gazing *n.* [1990s] (drugs) sitting around smoking cannabis, whether alone or with friends. [one gazes into the middle distance, lost in thought]

gazlon *n.* [20C] (Und.) a small-time, poss. timid thief. [Yid. *gozlin*, a swindler, an unethical person]

gazob *n.* [20C] (Aus.) a fool, simpleton. [? Sp. *gazapo*, a sly fellow, via GAZABO]

gazongas *n.* [20C] the female breasts, usu. large (cf. BAZONGAS; GAZONKAS; GAZUNGAS).

gazonkas *n.* [1990s] large female breasts. [ext. of GAZONGAS]

gazoo *n.* [20C] the anus. [var. on KAZOO n.]

gazook/gazoo/gazoop/gazoopus *n.* [1900s–40s] (US) a lout, a boor, a fool. [GAZABO]

gazookus *n.* (US) **1** [1920s] a thing; thus *the real gazookus*, the genuine article. **2** [1900s–40s] a lout, a boor, a fool (cf. GAZOOK). [ety. unknown]

gazookus *n.*[2] [1970s] (US) the vagina. [ext. of GAZOO]

gazoomph *see* GAZUMP.

gazooney *n.*[1] *see* GAZABO.

gazooney *n.*[2] (US) [1910s+] (tramp) a young, homosexual sidekick who accompanies a tramp (cf. GONSEL). [Anglo-Irish *gossoon*, ult. Irish *garsuin*, a boy, a lad]

gazoopie/gazupie *n.* [1970s] (US) a sex show. [GAZOOKUS n.[2]]

gazoopus *see* GAZOOK.

gazump / gasumph / gazoomph / gazumph / gezump / gezumph / guzzump *v.* [1920s+] **1** to swindle. **2** (orig. estate agent) to accept a stated price for one's property and then to raise that price, using as a threat a supposed, but usu. non-existent, 'offer' from elsewhere; alternatively, the seller accepts one price and then, tempted by a genuinely greater offer, dumps the first buyer without sorrow or ceremony (cf. GESSUMP); thus *gazumper*, a swindler. [? Yid. *gezumph*, to cheat or to overcharge]

gazungas *n.* [20C] the female breasts, esp. when large (cf. GAZONGAS). [BAZONGAS]

g.b. *n.*[1] [1930s+] (drugs) a barbiturate, a depressant. [GOOFBALL n.[1] (2)]

g.b. *n.*[2] [1950s] (W.I.) gym shoes or boots that lace at the front with buckles at the side. [GORBLIMEY]

g.b. *phr.*[1] [late 19C–1920s] (US) grand *bounce*, a forceful ejection or dismissal. [abbr.]

g.b. *phr.*[2] [1970s] (US campus) *good*bye. [abbr.]

g.b.! *excl.* [1950s] (W.I.) a mild euph. oath. [abbr. GORBLIMEY!]

g.b.h. *n.*[1] [1950s+] (orig. Und.) grievous *bodily harm*; thus fig. use, e.g. *g.b.h. of the brain*, pressure or strain; *g.b.h. of the ear*, excessive noise. [abbr.]

g.b.h. *n.*[2] [1980s+] (drugs) *gamma hydroxy butyrate*. [abbr., reversed for pun on G.B.H. n.[1]; developed in the US as an anaesthetic, it was picked up by body-builders as a growth-hormone stimulant. Its pleasurable side-effects brought it into recreational drug use, but these too led to its being banned]

G.D./G.d./g.d. *adj./adv.* [mid-19C+] (US) *God-d*amned; thus *g.d.f.*, *God-d*amned fool. [abbr.]

g.d.i. *n.* [1960s+] (US campus) a student who is not a fraternity or sorority member. [abbr. *God-d*amned *i*ndependent]

g'd up *adj.* [1990s] (US Black gang) dressed GANGSTA-style. [G n.[7]]

gé *n.* [1980s+] (S.Afr.) **1** a friend, a pal. **2** a tough, a thug. [Afk. *gê*, trash, rubbish]

geach *n.* [early 19C] a thief. [? Scot. *geck*, an act of deception; ult. Ger. *Gecken*, tricks]

geach *v.* [early 19C] to steal. [GEACH n.]

gear *n.*[1] **1** [late 17C–early 18C] trash, rubbish. **2** [late 19C+] dress, equipment. **3** [1930s+] stolen property. **4** [1930s+] an object or objects; things. **5** [1960s+] clothes, esp. fashionable clothes. **6** [1960s+] (drugs) drugs, esp. cannabis, heroin. [14C SE]

gear *n.*[2] [late 19C+] **1** the male genitals; thus [17C] *gear-itch*, lecherousness (cf. ACCOUTREMENTS). **2** the female genitals. [SE *gear*, accoutrements]

gear *n.*[3] [1930s+] (US prison) a homosexual (cf. GEARED). [fig. use of GEAR n.[1] (3), the gay man is 'stolen away' to become an object of gratification for others]

gear *n.*[4] [1950s+] (US) an important or influential person. [SE 16C–18C]

gear *adj.*[1] [1930s+] homosexual. [GEAR n.[3] + rhy. sl. *gear* = QUEER adj.[1] (2)]

gear *adj.*[2] [1950s+] excellent, wonderful, just right. [abbr. [1920s+] *that's the gear*, that's the stuff, and at peak popularity one of the Beatles' supposed favourite words; post-1960s use is ironic (cf. FAB)]

gearbox *n.* [1940s+] the female genitals. [GEAR n.[2] + BOX n.[6] (2); pun]

geared *adj.* [1930s+] (US Und.) sexually aberrant. [GEAR n.[3]]

geared up *adj.* **1** [1930s+] (US) intoxicated. **2** [1990s] (US Black) dressed up (cf. G'D UP). **3** [1990s] (US) very excited.

gearhead *n.* [1970s+] (US campus) an engineering student, someone mechanically minded. [mechanical sense of SE *gear* + sfx. -HEAD (1)]

gear job *n.* [1970s] (US prison) a homosexual. [GEAR n.[3] + JOB n.[6] (1)]

gears *n.* [1960s+] (W.I.) one's best clothing. [SE *gear*, apparel, attire + 1960s use of GEAR n.[1] (5)]

gear up *v.* [20C] to prepare oneself mentally and physically for dealing with the day.

geck/gack/gak/geek *n.* [20C] (Ulster) **1** a person who tells tales behind another's back, a gossip. **2** an odd, eccentric-looking person. [Scot. *geck*, to mock, to tease]

ged! *excl.* [late 17C–mid-18C] a euph. for God in a variety of oaths/excls., e.g. *ged's curse it!* *'fore ged!* (cf. ADAD!).

gedoente *n.* [1970s+] (S.Afr.) a fuss, a carry-on, a to-do. [Afk. *gedoente*, bustle]

gee *n.*[1] [19C] a horse. [abbr. GEE-GEE]

gee *n.*[2] *see* GUEE.

gee *n.*[3] **1** [late 19C+] (Aus.) one who 'gees up' the potential customers into a sideshow, strip-club etc (cf. AMSTER). **2** [1920s+] idle chatter, empty talk, 'blarney'. [GEE UP v.[1]]

gee *n.*[4] [1920s+] (US) a male, esp. a male friend. [GUY n.[2]]

gee *n.*[5] [1920s+] (US) 1000 (usu. dollars). [G n.[1]]

gee *n.*[6] [1930s–60s] (US drugs) opium. [initial letter of various opium-related words, e.g. GONG n.[2]; GOW n.[2]; GUM n.[3] or of SE *guy*, which is synon. with BOY n.[5], i.e. heroin; farther-fetched is poss. pun on SE *gee-up!*, used of horses, thus linked to HORSE n.[12], heroin]

gee *n.*[7] [1930s+] a paper 'collar' used by a drug user to secure the needle to eye-dropper prior to injecting the heroin/water solution (cf. BIZ n.[2]; GEEZE v.; JEEP n.[3]). [? ext. of GEE n.[6] but, despite dates, poss. abbr. GASKET n.[2]. Note unlike in the UK, where registered addicts (and via them other users) were allowed to use proper medical syringes, US users were forced to make their own WORKS n.[3], a do-it-yourself assemblage of a hollow needle and an eye-dropper]

gee *n.*[8] [1990s] (US Black) a girlfriend. [pron. of initial letter]

gee *n.*[9] [1990s] the vagina. [? Irish sl. *gowl*, the vagina, ult. Irish *gabhal*, the fork (of the body)]

gee *v.*[1] [late 17C–1910s] to fit, to suit, to behave as required or expected, usu. in phr. *it won't gee*, it doesn't suit, it doesn't work. [? pron. of initial letter of SE *go*]

gee *v.*[2] **1** [1930s+] to encourage, to persuade, to incite, esp.

when working as a showman's or market-trader's assistant. **2** [1930s+] to act as an *agent provocateur*, esp. when using entrapment for sexual crimes. **3** [1940s+] (prison) to inform against a fellow prisoner; thus *gee-er*, an informer. [GEE UP v.]

gee *v.*[3] [1970s+] (US Black) to have sexual intercourse. [? fig. use of GEE UP v., thus RIDE v.[1]]

gee!/jee! *excl.* [late 19C+] (US) a mild oath, euph. for *Jesus!* (cf. BEJABERS!).

geeba *n.* [1980s+] (US campus) marijuana (cf. CHEEBA).

geebung *n.* [mid-19C+] **1** (Aus.) an unsophisticated, uncultured, philistine native-born Australian, who values material gain above everything else. **2** a place-name for any out-of-the-way place. [SE *geebung*, a shrub or tree of the genus *Persoonia*; coined by D.H. Deniehy (1828–65) in 1859]

geech *n.* [1960s] (US) money. [? GEETUS]

geechee *n.* [20C] (US Black) a derog. term for anyone (typically a rural southerner, newly migrated to the urban north) whose speech is made incomprehensible by a heavy accent. [proper name *Geechee*, an inhabitant (usu. Black) of the coastal areas of Georgia, North Carolina or north Florida; the language such people speak is itself *Geechee*]

geechie *adj.* [20C] (US Black) unintelligible. [GEECHEE]

geed-up *adj.*[1] (US) [1900s–60s] crippled, in disrepair. [ety. unknown]

geed-up *adj.*[2] (US) [1920s–70s] **1** drunk (cf. ABOUT RIGHT adj.[1]). **2** excited or intoxicated by drugs. [? GEE-UP n. or (2) GEE n.[7]]

geedus *see* GEETUS.

gee for *v.* [1900s] (N.Z.) to support enthusiastically. [GEE UP v.]

gee-gee *n.*[1] [mid-19C+] a horse; often as *gee-gees*, horses, esp. those on racecourses; thus *play the gee-gees*, to gamble on horseraces. [SE *gee up!*]

gee-gee *n.*[2] [1920s] a man, a fellow. [GEEZER n.[1] (1)]

gee-gee *n.*[3] [1950s+] (US) the rectum or vagina. [? play on GEE-GEE n.[1]; i.e. it is 'ridden' during intercourse + note GEE n.[9]]

geek *n.*[1] **1** [late 19C+] (US) a clumsy, eccentric or offensive person. **2** [20C] a carnival freak who specialized in biting the heads off live chickens. **3** [1970s+] (US Black/teen) an eccentric, an intellectual. **4** [1980s+] (US teen) a vulgar, lower-class youth. **5** [1980s] a generally unpleasant person, irrelevant of class. **6** [1980s+] (US campus) one who is considered to devote too much time to their books; thus *geek out*, to work (too) hard. [dial. *geck*, a fool; 20C uses allegedly invented by one Wagner, of Charleston, West Virginia, who had a celebrated touring snake-eating act; his ballyhoo ran in part, 'Come and see Esau/Sitting on a see-saw/Eatin' 'em raw!']

geek *n.*[2] *see* GECK.

geek *n.*[3] [1910s+] (Aus.) a glance, a look. [Cornish dial. *geek*, to peer, to look intently]

geek *n.*[4] [1980s+] (drugs) a mix of crack cocaine and marijuana. [its effects are to render one a GEEK n.[1] (1)]

geek *v.* [20C] (Aus.) to stare at, to look at (cf. GIG v.[6]). [GEEK n.[3]]

geeked/geeked up *adj.* [20C] (US) naively excited or thrilled by something. [GEEK n.[1] (1)]

geekers *n.* [1980s+] (US drugs) a user of crack cocaine. [GEEK n.[4]]

geek it/out *v.* [1930s–50s] (US) to quit or back down. [GEEK n.[1]]

geek up *v.* [1980s+] (US) to frighten, to make nervous. [i.e. to render one a GEEK n.[1] (1)]

geeky *adj.* [1990s] (US campus) socially inept, overly studious. [GEEK n.[1] (6) + sfx. -*y*]

geeload *n.* [1990s] a large amount of anything. [? GEE! + SE *load*]

gee man *n.* [late 19C+] (Aus.) one who 'gees up' the potential customers into a sideshow etc (cf. GEE n.[3]).

gee mo nitty! *excl.* [1990s] (US Black) a general excl. of annoyance or bewilderment. [ety. unknown; ? ext. of GEE!]

gee one up *v.* [1990s] to inform against, to betray. [GEE v.[2] (3)]

geep/geepo *n.* [1940s+] (US) an obnoxious, inept or suspicious looking person. [? GEEK n.[1]]

geepie *n.* [1950s–60s] a youthful hipster (cf. TEENYBOPPER). [? ext. of GEEP; pron. with hard 'g' or echoic, i.e. the squeaky tones of the youthful enthusiast]

geepo *see* GEEP.

geese *n.* [20C] Jews. [deliberate mispron.]

geesefeathers *n.* [1910s–20s] (US) snow. [resemblance]

geetas/geetis *see* GEETUS.

geetoh *n.* [1960s–70s] GTO, a popular make of motorcar.

geetus/geedus/geetas/geetis/geets/gietus *n.* [1940s–60s] (US) **1** money. **2** power. [ety. unknown; ? SE *get us*]

gee-up *n.* [1920s+] (Aus.) a spree, any form of merry-making. [GEE UP v.]

gee up *v.* [late 19C+] **1** to encourage. **2** to provoke trouble deliberately, to tease maliciously; thus *geed up*, furious, very angry. [SE *gee up*, to urge a horse forward]

gee vet! *excl.* [20C] (S.Afr.) hurry up, get a move on, 'step on it!' [Afk. *gee vet*, to give grease]

gee whillikins!/gee whillikers!/gee whizzikers! *excl.* [mid-19C+] (mainly US juv.) a mild, euph. excl. (cf. BEJABERS!).

gee whiz! *excl.* [19C+] a euph. for *Jesus!* or *Jesus Christ!* and as such a mild excl. (cf. GEE WILLIKINS!).

gee whizzikers! *see* GEE WILLIKINS!

geewillies *n.* [20C] nerves, tension. [GEE! + WILLIES; ? underpinned by GEE WHILLIKINS!]

gee yen *n.* [late 19C–1930s] (US drugs) the residue that collects inside the stem of an opium pipe.

geez *n.* [1970s] a man, a fellow, a 'bloke'. [abbr. GEEZER n.[1] (1)]

geeze/geez *v.* [1960s+] (drugs) **1** to inject narcotics. **2** to inhale cocaine. [GEEZER n.[3]]

geezed *adj.* (US) **1** [1920s–50s] drunk. **2** [1930s–70s] intoxicated by a drug. [GEEZE v.]

geezer *n.*[1] [late 19C+] **1** a man, a 'bloke' (cf. JEEZER n.[1]). **2** [1940s+] a confidence trickster's victim. [dial. pron. of 15C *guiser*, a mummer (*OED*); E.P. wonders if Wellington's troops might not have picked it up from the Basque *giza*, a man, during the Peninsular War (1808–14)]

geezer *n.*[2] [1910s–40s] (US) a drink of whisky or strong alcohol. [Lincolnshire dial. *geezer*, a state of drunkenness]

geezer *n.*[3] (drugs) **1** [1920s+] an injection of a narcotic drug (cf. FIX n.[3]). **2** [1920s+] the equipment with which one injects. **3** [1960s+] (US) a heroin addict. [? GEE n.[6]]

geezer *n.*[4] [1980s+] (Irish) a cat. [ety. unknown; ? joc. use of GEEZER n.[1] (1)]

gefuffle *see* KERFUFFLE.

gegor *n.* [mid–late 19C] a beggar (cf. GAGGER n.[1]). [? GAGGER n.[1] (2)]

gehuncled *adj.* [1920s–60s] (US) crippled. [Ger. *gehunkelt*, hobbled]

geize *v.* [1980s+] (US campus) to drive or run extremely fast. [ety. unknown; ? link to GEEZE v.]

gek *adj.* [mid-19C+] (S.Afr.) foolish, obsessed, insane. [Du. *gek*, mad]

gel *v.* [1980s+] (US campus) **1** to relax. **2** to waste time, to loaf around (cf. JELL v.[1]). [SE *gel*, to solidify into a jelly-like substance; the image is of a jelly slowly melting]

geld *n.* [late 19C+] money (cf. DELOG). [Ger. *gelt*, gold; Yid. *gelt*, money]

gelly *see* JELLY n.[4].

gellyhead/jellyhead *n.* [1990s] (N.Z.) a fool. [SE *jelly*/(*jello*) + sfx. -HEAD (1)]

gel on *v.* [1980s+] (US campus) to break an appointment. [ext. of GEL v.]

gelt/gelter *n.* [late 17C+] money (cf. DELOG). [Yid. *gelt* money or Ger. *gelt*, gold; note S.Afr. colloq. *geld*, money f. Du.]

gem n. **1** [late 17C–early 18C] a (golden) ring; thus *rom-gem*, a diamond ring. **2** [19C] something greatly prized, a 'jewel', a 'treasure'.

gemini!/geminy!/jiminy! *excl.* [17C] a euph. for *Jesus!* and used as such in oaths (cf. BEJABERS!).

gemors n. [1970s+] (S.Afr.) **1** a mess, a confusion. **2** an insulting form of address. [synon. Afk.]

gen n.[1] [mid-19C] a shilling (5p) (cf. GENERALIZE n.; GEN-NET). [? abbr. *argent*, silver, or abbr. GENERALIZE, a supposed backsl. formation of *shilling*]

gen n.[2] [1940s+] information, facts; thus *gen up*, to inform; *genned up*, well informed. [? RAF *gen(eral information)* for all ranks]

gendarme n. [20C] a policeman. [Fr. *gendarme*, policeman]

gender-bender n. [1980s+] a synon. for a transvestite or a transsexual, bending or eroding the line between the two sexes. [SE ? + a pun on FENDER-BENDER; the term was popularized during the rise to fame of the pop star Boy George, whose outrageous clothes and ostentatious make-up managed to disturb many observers]

gender fuck v. [1960s+] (gay) of a man, to shock the heterosexual world by openly adopting women's clothes, blurring the assumptions about male/female separatism. [SE *gender* + FUCK v.[2]]

general n.[1] [late 19C–1900s] **1** a *general* servant, a maid-of-all-work. **2** a *general* stores. [abbr.]

general n.[2] [1960s] (US) the penis.

general n.[3] **1** [1950s+] (W.I. Rasta) a smart man, a 'cool operator'. **2** [1970s+] (S.Afr. Und.) a high rank in a prison gang (cf. CAPTAIN n.[3]). [SE]

General Booth n. [20C] a tooth. [rhy. sl.]

general election n. [20C] an erection. [rhy. sl.]

generalize n. [late 19C] a shilling (cf. GEN n.[1]). [? backsl.]

generalize v. [late 19C] (middle-class) to give or lend a shilling, usu. in phr. *can you generalize?* [GENERALIZE n.]

General Smuts n. [20C] the testicles. [rhy. sl. *General Smuts* = NUTS n.[2] (1); ult. S.Afr. *General* Jan Christian *Smuts* (1870–1950)]

generation tool *see* GENERATING TOOL.

generating place n. [19C] the vagina (cf. BABY CHUTE; FORNICATING ENGINE; GENERATING TOOL). [SE *generate*, to procreate]

generating/generation tool n. [19C] the penis (cf. FORNICATING ENGINE; GENERATING PLACE). [SE *generate*, to procreate]

generic n. [20C] (US) a Black person (cf. OFF-BRAND n.). [SE *generic*, not marked with the producer's brandname, and available at a lower price because of plain, cheap packaging]

Gene Tunney n. [1960s] (N.Z.) money. [rhy. sl.; ult. US boxer *Gene Tunney* (1898–1978)]

Geneva print n. [17C] gin; thus *read Geneva print*, to drink gin. [pun on *Geneva*, the kind of type used in a Geneva bible, the English translation of the Bible first printed at Geneva in 1560 + *Genever*, Dutch gin]

genga n. [1990s] an extremely unattractive woman. [? feminized version of *Genghis* Khan (c.1162–1227)]

genial adj. [1990s] excellent, first-rate, the best.

genials n. [1960s+] the genitals. [mispron.]

genitrave *see* GENNITRAF.

gen net/net gen n. [mid-19C] 10 shillings (50p) (cf. GEN n.[1]). [backsl.]

gennitraf/genitrave n. [late 19C] a farthing. [backsl.]

genol adj. [mid–late 19C] long. [backsl.]

gen out v. [1940s] (US) to figure out. [GEN n.[2]]

gent n.[1] **1** [late 18C+] (orig. US) a *gent*leman, a man, a fellow. **2** [mid-19C+] a *gent*leman, but only when 'applied derisively to men of the vulgar and pretentious class who are supposed to use the word, and as used in tradesmen's notices' (*OED*). [abbr.]

gent n.[2] [mid-19C] a mistress, usu. as *my gent*. [abbr. Fr. (*une femme) gentille*, a gentlewoman]

gent n.[3] [mid-19C+] (Ling. Fr./Polari) money, usu. silver. [Ital. *argento*, silver]

gentle annie n. [mid-19C+] an incline or small hill found on a small road or track. [? from lyrics to a contemporary popular song]

gentleman n. [19C] (US Und.) a crowbar (cf. ALDERMAN n.[2]).

gentleman commoner n. [late 18C] (orig. Oxon. jargon) an empty bottle. [the Oxford version of Cambridge's FELLOW COMMONER; commoners, as opposed to scholars, were seen as empty-headed]

gentleman in black/black pantaloons, the n. [mid–late 17C] the devil (cf. OLD GENTLEMAN IN BLACK).

gentleman in blue n. [late 19C] a policeman (cf. BLUE n.[3]). [the uniform]

gentleman in brown n. [late 19C] a bedbug (cf. BOSOM FRIEND).

gentleman in red n. [late 18C] a soldier.

gentleman of fortune n. [late 19C] a pirate. [pun on SE]

gentleman of the back door n. [late 18C–early 19C] a sodomite (cf. BACK-DOOR MAN n.[2]). [SE *gentleman* + BACK DOOR n.[1]]

gentleman of the first head/house n. [early–mid-17C] an upstart. [ety. unknown]

gentleman of the green-baize road n. [19C] a card-sharp. [the baize that covers card-tables]

gentleman of the nig n. [early 18C] a cutpurse. [SE *gentleman* + NIG n.[1] or NICK v.[1] (4)]

gentleman of the pad n. **1** [18C] a highwayman. **2** [early–mid-19C] a street-robber. [SE *gentleman* + PAD n.[1]]

gentleman of the road n. **1** [late 18C–early 19C] a highwayman. **2** [1940s–50s] (N.Z.) a tramp.

gentleman of the round n. [late 16C–early 17C] a discharged or invalided soldier who makes his living by begging. [? he 'does the rounds']

gentleman of the short staff n. [mid-19C] a constable. [his truncheon]

gentleman of the swag n. [1940s–50s] (N.Z.) a tramp (cf. SWAGMAN n.[2]). [SWAG n.[1] (7)]

gentleman of three ins n. [late 18C] 'In debt, in gaol, and in danger of remaining there for life; or, in gaol, indicted and in danger of being hanged in chains' (Grose 1796) (cf. GENTLEMAN OF THREE OUTS).

gentleman of three outs n. [late 18C] 'Without money, without wit, and without manners; some add another out, i.e. without credit' (Grose 1785) (cf. GENTLEMAN OF THREE INS). [variations include 'out of pocket, out of elbows, and out of credit' (Bulwer-Lytton, *Paul Clifford*, 1830); ... *of the four outs*, 'without wit, without money, without credit and without manners' (Hotten, 1864)]

gentleman outer n. [early 18C] a highwayman.

gentleman's n. [20C] (W.I.) a euph. for any form of venereal disease. [abbr. GENTLEMAN'S COMPLAINT]

gentleman's companion n. [late 18C–19C] a louse (cf. BOSOM FRIEND).

gentleman's complaint n. [1920s+] (W.I.) a euph. for gonorrhoea.

gentleman's/gent's gent n. [1920s–30s] a valet.

gentleman's master n. [18C] a highwayman. [his temporary ascendancy over his social betters]

gentleman's pleasure-garden n. [late 19C–1900s] the vagina (cf. BEAUTY SPOT n.[1]; PALACE OF PLEASURE; PLEASURE BOAT; PRIVY PARADISE).

gentleman usher n. [late 16C– early 17C] the penis.

gentleman who pays the rent n. [late 19C] (Irish) a pig (cf. MINT HOG).

gently Bentley! *excl.* [1940s–60s] a general excl. of restraint, 'hang on', 'take it easy', 'not too fast' etc. [BBC radio's weekly comedy *Take It From Here* (1940–60), used as catchphrase by Jimmy Edwards (1920–88), addressed to Dick *Bentley*]

gentoo/jentoe *n.* [late 19C+] (S.Afr.) a prostitute; thus *gentoo house*, a brothel, usu. entertained by a Malay band (cf. JINTOE). ['named for the *Gentoo*, a ship which arrived at Cape Town in the mid-19th century with a group of women passengers who became prostitutes; the countries of origin of the women and the ship, and the circumstances of their arrival at the Cape are obscure and in dispute' (*DSAE*). The main theories point to the UK, whose authorities sent out 46 women specifically recruited for the task, or the French]

gentry cove/cofe *n.* [mid-16C–mid-19C] (Und.) a nobleman, a gentleman. [SE *gentry* + COVE]

gentry cove's ken/gentry ken *n.* [mid-16C] (Und.) a nobleman's or gentleman's house. [GENTRY COVE + KEN]

gentry mort *n.* [mid-16C–mid-19C] (Und.) a noblewoman, a gentlewoman. [SE *gentry* + MORT]

gents *n.* [1930s+] the *gentleman's* lavatory (cf. LADIES n.¹). [abbr.]

gent's gent *see* GENTLEMAN'S GENT.

genuffel *v.* [1930s+] (S.Afr.) to flirt. [? backsl. 'loving']

Geoffrey Chaucer *n.* [20C] a saucer. [rhy. sl.; ult. *Geoffrey Chaucer* (*c.*1343–1400) author of *The Canterbury Tales*]

geography *n.*¹ [1920s–30s] the vagina (cf. ANTIPODES). [one 'explores' it; but note poss. link to GEOGRAPHY n.²]

geography *n.*² [1920s+] the lavatory. [euph.]

geometer *n.* [mid-17C–early 18C] a Jesuit. [SE *geometer*, one who studies, or is skilled in, geometry; the ref. is to Jesuitical skills]

Geordie *n.* **1** [mid-19C+] a Tynesider. **2** [1940s+] (Aus./N.Z.) a Scot. [proper name]

george *n.*¹ **1** [16C–17C] a noble (worth 6s 8d or one-third of a pound). **2** [mid-17C–early 19C] a half crown, 2s 6d (12½p). **3** a guinea (cf. YELLOW GEORGE). **4** [mid-19C] one (old) penny. [the image of St *George* engraved on the coin]

george *n.*² **1** [early-mid-19C] (N.Z.) a generic term for a Maori. **2** [1920s–50s] (Can.) a generic name for a nameless Black Pullman porter. [note RAF jargon *George*, a familiar form of address to any stranger; [1920s+] air crew jargon *George*, the automatic pilot in milit. and civil aircraft; N.Z. WW2 milit. *George*, an Egyptian]

george *n.*³ [1940s+] (US) a $1 bill (cf. ABRAHAM LINCOLN). [the portrait of *George* Washington on the note]

george *n.*⁴ [1940s+] (W.I.) a sore or swollen leg or foot; elephantiasis. [ety. unknown; but note the habit of giving pet names to parts of one's body, usu. the genitals]

george *n.*⁵ [1970s] (US prison) **1** a one-year prison sentence. **2** one of anything. [ety. unknown]

george *adj.* **1** [1900s–10s] (US Und.) wise, in the know; thus *be george*, to understand. **2** [1960s] (US) acceptable, satisfactory. [? var. on JERRY adj.]

George and Ringo *n.* [1960s] bingo. [rhy. sl.; the Beatles members *George* Harrison (b.1943) and *Ringo* Starr (b.1940)]

george and zippy *n.* [1980s] very cold. [rhy. sl. *George and Zippy* = NIPPY adj.²; puppets on the children's TV show *Rainbow*]

George Bernard Shaw *n.* [1940s–50s] a door. [rhy. sl.; the Irish-born playwright *George Bernard Shaw* (1856–1950)]

George Blake *n.* [1960s] a snake. [rhy. sl.; Soviet spy *George Blake* (b.1922)]

George Bohee *n.* [1900s–50s] tea. [rhy. sl.; the name of a once well-known banjo player, but note *bohea*, the best variety of black tea, from the Wu-i hills in north Fukien]

george called *phr.* [20C] (Aus./US) phr. indicating that a woman is menstruating (cf. AUNT MINNIE IS VISITING).

georged *adj.* [1960s] (US Black) seduced by a woman. [GEORGY]

George Gerrard *n.* [20C] (Aus.) a gross exaggeration. [the proper name of *George Gerrard*, a well-known (and presumably big-talking) character]

George Moore *n.* [1970s+] (Aus. sporting) a 4 in cricket (cf. DOROTHY DIX). [rhy. sl.; ? the Aus. jockey *George Moore* (b.1923)]

George Raft *n.* [1950s–60s] **1** a draught. **2** a banker's draft. **3** hard work, i.e. GRAFT n.¹. [rhy. sl.; ult. film star *George Raft* (1895–1980)]

George Robey *n.* [1910s–30s] (tramp) the road. [rhy. sl. *George Robey* = TOBY n.²; ult. comedian Sir *George Robey* (1869–1954)]

George the Third *n.* [1980s+] a third class degree (cf. RICHARD n.²). [rhy. sl.]

George Spelvin *n.* [20C] (US) an actor's pseudonym when playing a minor role. [created by the actor Edward Ables in 1906, when playing in *Brewster's Millions* on Broadway; also found as *Georgina Spelvin*, as used by the star of the 'art porn' film *The Devil in Miss Jones* (1972)]

George Washington *n.* [20C] (US) a $1 bill (cf. ABRAHAM LINCOLN).

georgia *n.* [1930s–60s] (US Black) a swindle, esp. that worked by a prostitute on a customer. [abbr. carnival use *Georgia scuffle*, a form of confidence trick]

Georgia *adj.* [20C] (US) a general derog. term, usu. found in a variety of combinations (cf. ALABAMA; ARIZONA; ARKANSAS). [the stereotyping of the state and its natives as poor and backward]

georgia *v.* [1930s–60s] (US Black) **1** to play a confidence trick on a person who has newly arrived from the south and is thus naïve as regards the northern, urban world. **2** to be seduced into a sexual liaison by a woman. [GEORGIA n.]

Georgia bacon *n.* [1950s] a turtle (cf. ADIRONDACK STEAK). [the availability of turtles in the state]

Georgia buggy *n.* [1910s+] (orig. US Black) a wheelbarrow (cf. IRISH BUGGY).

Georgia chicken *n.* [1970s] (US) salt pork (cf. ADIRONDACK STEAK).

Georgia ham *n.* [1940s–70s] (US) watermelon (cf. AUGUST HAM). [its popularity in Georgia + the pinkness of both foodstuffs]

Georgia ice-cream *n.* [1970s+] (US) grits.

Georgia major *n.* [20C] (US) a poser, a pretentious person, one who puts on airs. [GEORGIA adj. + SE *major*; a play on SAmE *Kentucky colonel*]

Georgia skin *n.* [1930s+] (US Black) a kind of card-game. [abbr. *Georgia skin game*, a card-game]

georgie/georgy *n.* [19C] (orig. Und.) a quartern loaf. [BROWN GEORGE n. (1)]

Georgie Best *n.* [1960s+] **1** a guest. **2** a (drunken) pest. [rhy. sl.; soccer star and fabled drinker George Best (b.1946)]

georgie bundle *n.* [20C] (W.I.) **1** a small bundle that nonetheless can hold one's few possessions. **2** a collection of odds and ends. [ety. unknown; ? anecdotal]

georgium sidus *n.* [late 19C] London south of the Thames, traditionally less fashionable than the north. [pun on Lat. *georgium sidus*, the planet Uranus, so named by its discoverer Sir William Herschel (1738–1822) in honour of George III; Uranus was then the furthest planet from the Earth and thus from 'civilization']

georgy *n. see* GEORGIE.

georgy *v.* [1950s] (US Black) **1** to trick or take advantage of a victim by using a variety of sexual lures. **2** to hire a prostitute and then leave without paying. [GEORGIA v.]

geranium *n.* [late 19C] a red nose.

gerbil *n.* [1980s+] (US) a stupid, insignificant or unpleasant person.

gerdoing!/gerdoying! *see* KERDOING!

geriatric *adj.* [1960s+] old, senile.

geriatricks *n.* [1950s+] (gay) ageing or old homosexuals. [pun on SE *geriatric* + TRICK n.⁴]

geri/gerri/gerry *n.* [1970s+] a term for the old (and middle-aged). [abbr. SE *geriatric*]

germ *n.* [1940s–70s] (US) a contemptible person.

Germaine Greer *n.* [1980s+] (Aus.) a beer. [rhy. sl.; the Australian writer *Germaine Greer* (b.1939)]

German *n.*¹ [late 19C] a German sausage, a wurst.

German *n.*² [1940s+] (W.I.) a poor White. [the early 19C settlement of German immigrants near Seaford Town, Westmoreland; their descendants still live there]

German aunt *n.* [20C] (US) a fat, frumpish woman (cf. FRENCH AUNT). [racial stereotyping]

German bands *n.* [20C] the hands. [rhy. sl.]

German comb *n.* [late 19C+] (US) the hand (cf. WELSH COMB). [the supposed lack of sophistication in German immigrants, who prefer their fingers to a comb]

German doggies *n.* [late 19C+] (N.Z.) the rolling of stones down a hill so as to persuade sheep to move down the hill. [? derog. ref. to German shepherding methods]

German duck *n.*¹ [18C–19C] half a sheep's head boiled with onions. [the popularity of the dish among the German sugar-bakers of London's East End]

German duck *n.*² [mid-19C] a bedbug. [orig. Yorks. dial.; ? racial stereotyping]

German flutes *n.* [mid-19C] a pair of boots. [rhy. sl.]

German goitre *n.* [20C] (US) a beer belly, a noticeable paunch (cf. MILWAUKEE GOITRE). [the stereotyped German capacity for beer]

German gospel *n.* [late 19C] vain boasting, megalomania, self-aggrandizement. [a speech delivered in November 1897 by Prince Henry of Prussia to his brother Kaiser Wilhelm II (1859–1941), which was full of such fulsome phrases as: 'The gospel that emanates from your Majesty's sacred person ...']

German helmet *n.* [1950s+] (orig. gay) the glans penis.

German marching pills *n.* [1950s+] (gay) amphetamines, esp. Methedrine, a German invention (cf. BOLIVIAN MARCHING POWDER). [used by Ger. soldiers, among others, in WWII and later conflicts]

German silver *n.* [late 19C+] anything that is sham, fake (cf. NICKEL-PLATE). [SE *German silver*, a white alloy consisting of nickel, zinc and copper]

gern *v.* [1990s] (US teen) to make fun of someone, to give someone a hard time about something. [? SE *gurn*, to make bizarre faces, ult. dial. *girn*, to grimace, to gnash the teeth]

Geronimo *n.* [1980s+] (drugs) a mixture of alcohol and barbiturates. [it leads one to excesses, supposedly similar to those of an Apache warrior]

Geronimo! *excl.* [1940s+] (US) (orig. Army) a cry made when leaping or about to start a fight. [proper name *Geronimo*, nickname of Apache leader, Goyathlay ('One Who Yawns') (1829–1909)]

gerook *n.* [1960s+] (S.Afr.) intoxicated by drink or a drug, usu. cannabis. [Afk. *gerook*, smoked]

gerri *see* GERI.

gerry *n.*¹ [16C] excrement. [ety. unknown; E.P. suggests Lat. *gero*, I carry. Note Devon dial. *gerred*, bedaubed, filthy]

gerry *n.*² *see* GERI.

gerry gan! *excl.* [16C] lit. 'shit in your mouth', thus shut up! be quiet! [GERRY n.¹]

gerry riddle *n.* [1930s+] (Aus.) a piddle, urination (cf. JERRY RIDDLE; JIMMY RIDDLE). [rhy. sl.]

gert and daisy *adj.* [20C] lazy. [rhy. sl.; ult. characters created on BBC radio in the 1930s by comediennes Elsie (d.1990) and Doris Waters (d.1978)]

gertcha!/gertcher! *excl.* [1920s+] a general excl. of dismissal, go away! be off! [*get away/along with you*]

gertie *n.* [1940s] a woman van-driver. [generic use of a 'typical' female name]

Gertie Gitana *n.* [20C] (Aus.) banana. [rhy. sl.; ult. music-hall star *Gertie Gitana* (1888–1957)]

gerund-grinder *n.* [early 18C–late 19C] a schoolteacher, esp. a pedant; thus *gerund-grinding*, instruction in Latin grammar, pedantic instruction generally; *gerund-grindery*, a classical school; *gerund-stone*, the imaginary grindstone of a *gerund-grinder*.

gerve *n.* [late 19C] (US) the breast-pocket in a jacket. [ety. unknown]

geseech *n.* [late 19C–1900s] the face. [? Yid. *gesicht*, face]

gessein *v.* [1940s–50s] (prison) to trick, to hoax, to dupe; thus *gesseiner*, valuables, belongings. [? Yid., but not Scot. *gess*, to leave clandestinely]

gessump *v.* [1940s–50s] (prison) to acquire anything by fraud or a confidence trick. [GAZUMP]

gestapo *n.* [1950s+] (US Black) the police. [fig. use of Ger. *Geheime Staatspolizei*, the *Gestapo*, the internal police force used by the German Nazi regime 1933–45]

gesuip *adj.* [1980s] (S.Afr.) drunk. [Afk. *suip*, to drink, used of an animal]

get *n.*¹ **1** [18C–19C] an idiot, a fool (cf. GIT). **2** [mid-18C–mid-19C] (US) a bastard child. [orig. 16C SE *get*, bastard, brat; the term lapsed into sl. by 18C]

get *n.*² [late 19C] a swindle, a trick, a means of defrauding a victim. [GET v.² (2)]

get *n.*³ [late 19C–1950s] (Und.) an escape. [abbr. SE *get away*]

get *n.*⁴ [20C] (US) the profit, the take, the booty of a robbery. [i.e. what the robbers ; 14C–17C SE]

get *v.*¹ **1** [mid-18C+] to start, to commence, with an implication of urgency, e.g. 'get moving', 'get walking' etc, esp. in excl. *get!* [20C] go away! be off! **2** [mid-19C+] (US) to go away.

get *v.*² **1** [mid-19C–1950s] (US) to succeed in killing for retribution, to 'do for'. **2** [mid-19C+] to trick, to cheat, to victimize. **3** [mid-19C+] to annoy, to irritate, esp. in phr. *that's what gets me.* **4** [late 19C] to corner someone, to get hold of, to track down. **5** [1910s+] (US) to get even with, to take vengeance on, e.g. *I'll get you, just wait and see.* **6** [1910s+] to attract, to enthral, to excite.

get *v.*³ [mid-19C–1900s; 1960s+] (orig. US) to be puzzled, to lack understanding.

get *v.*⁴ [late 19C] to eat a meal.

get *v.*⁵ **1** [20C] to understand, e.g. *I don't get it,* I don't understand; *now you get it,* now you understand. **2** (US) to reach the point or stage where, e.g. *I get where I see it all.* [abbr. *get the point of*]

get *v.*⁶ [1950s+] to notice, to look at, usu. as derog. imper. e.g. *get him!* look at him (isn't he stupid).

get a bang out of, to *phr.* [1920s+] to enjoy, to derive pleasure from, to get a thrill. [BANG n.⁵]

get a beat on, to *phr.* [mid-19C+] (US) to have at a disadvantage. [BEAT v.¹]

get/have a bee in one's bonnet, to *phr.* [mid-19C+] to become obsessed by a particular topic.

get a belly, to *phr.* [20C] (W.I.) to become noticeably pregnant.

get a bit, to *phr.*¹ [late 19C+] to obtain money. [SE *bit* (of money)]

get a bit, to *phr.*² [20C] to seduce. [BIT n.³]

get a bit of a pot *see* GET A POT.

get a bit on *see* GET ON v.¹.

get about *v.* [late 19C] of a man, to enter a woman.

get above oneself, to *phr.* [1920s+] to act in an arrogant manner, to be self-satisfied (cf. ABOVE ONESELF).

get a bug up one's ass *see* GET A HAIR UP ONE'S ASS.

get/pin/tie a can on, to *phr.* [1920s–50s] (US) to go on a drinking spree (cf. TIE ONE ON). [? SE *can*, a container for beer when taken home from a bar or public house]

get a capture, to *phr.* [1960s+] (Und.) to be arrested.

get a clue, to *phr.* **1** [1960s] (US Black) to become aware. **2** [1980s+] (US campus) to think sensibly or logically, not to be stupid or naïve.

get a crack at, to *phr.* [late 19C+] (US) to have a try at, to get a chance to do something.

get across *v.* [1920s–60s] **1** to irritate, to annoy. **2** (US Black) to succeed. **3** to seduce. **4** to acquire status.

get a cut, to *phr.* [20C] (Aus.) to obtain a job as a sheep-shearer.

get a dusty answer, to *phr.* [20C] to get a an unpleasant, intolerant response (cf. GIVE A DUSTY ANSWER). [DUSTY adj.[1]]

get a fair spin, to *phr.* [mid-19C+] to be treated fairly, to get a reasonable chance (cf. GIVE A FAIR SPIN). [the spin of a coin]

get a fall out of *see* TAKE A FALL OUT OF.

get a fifty, to *phr.* [20C] (Irish) to be rebuffed, rejected or 'stood up' by a woman. [Gaelic football, a form of penalty]

get a fourpenny one, to *phr.* [1930s+] to suffer physical harm, to be beaten up, spec. to be hit in the face (cf. GIVE A FOURPENNY ONE). [FOURPENNY ONE]

get a gage up, to *phr.* [1950s+] (drugs) to smoke marijuana. [GAGE n.[2]]

get a gift, to *phr.* [1950s] (drugs) to obtain drugs.

get/have a glow on, to *phr.* [1940s+] (orig. US) to get drunk. [the reddening of some drinkers' faces]

get a good ready, to *phr.* [mid–late 19C] (US) to be ready to start something.

get a green gown, to *phr.* [16C–19C] to lose one's virginity, usu. out of doors (cf. GREENS n.[2]). [the grass stains that come from lying on the ground; the dial. *get on the green gown*, however, means to be buried]

get a grip, to *phr.* [1970s+] (US campus) admonition to act in a responsible way, to get control.

get a grip on things, to *phr.* [1990s] to masturbate. [pun]

get a guernsey, to *phr.* (Aus.) to gain approval, to do well. [SAusE *guernsey*, a coloured shirt worn by Aus. Rules players; the award of one's team *guernsey* (like the UK 'get one's colours', 'get one's cap') that marks selection to a particular team]

get a gut *see* PUT ON A GUT.

get a haircut, to *phr.* [1900s–40s] (US Black) **1** to be cheated, robbed or in some way made to suffer by a woman. **2** to feel a soreness (or suffer an actual cut) in the penis on withdrawal after intercourse.

get a hair/bug up one's ass, to *phr.* [1940s+] **1** to be in a bad temper (cf. ALL HAIR BY THE NOSE). **2** to have an obsession.

get a handful of sprats/have a handful, to *phr.* [late 19C+] to grope a woman's genital area. [FISH n.[4] and similar terms meaning the vagina]

get a handle *phr.* [1960s+] (US) calm down, control yourself. [? abbr. *get a handle and turn yourself off*]

get a handle on, to *phr.* [1970s+] (orig. US) to understand, to work out, to gain control of a situation.

get a hand on it, to *phr.* [mid-19C+] to fondle a woman's genitals.

get a hard-on, to *phr.* [late 19C+] to have an erection (cf. GET A STAND; GET IT UP). [HARD-ON n.]

get/grab a hat, to *phr.* [1960s+] (US Black) to leave.

get a hump on, to *phr.* [late 19C+] (US) to hurry, to exert oneself (cf. BUST ONE'S HUMP).

get a hustle on, to *phr.* [1900s–30s] (US) to get moving, to get going, to get on with the job etc.

get a jag on, to *phr.* [late 17C+] to get drunk. [JAG n.[1] (1)]

get a job! *phr.* [1950s+] (US campus) find something constructive to do with yourself (cf. GET A LIFE!).

get a kick out of, to *phr.* to enjoy, to appreciate (cf. KICK n.[5]).

get a knob, to *phr.* [1950s–60s] (orig. milit.) to catch a venereal disease. [KNOB n.[1] (1)]

get a leg in, to *phr.* [late 19C+] to gain someone's confidence, to win over.

get a life! *excl.* [1980s+] a dismissive excl. used in any context where the speaker wishes to show disdain for the previous speaker and their ideas, suggestion or opinion.

get a line on, to *phr.* [20C] (orig. US) to understand, to acquire information about; thus *give a line on*, to impart information or knowledge. [LINE n.[1] (2)]

get all over *v.* [late 19C] to examine physically, to manhandle.

get a load of, to *phr.* [1920s+] (orig. US) to notice, to look at deliberately.

get a load of ...! *excl.* [1940s+] (orig. US) a demand that one's audience listen to something or notice an event; usu. in a sexual context, e.g. *get a load of that!* and usu. between males.

get a load on, to *phr.* [late 19C+] **1** to drink heavily; thus *have a load on*, to be very drunk. **2** to take a large amount of drugs. [SE *load*; earlier versions include [16C] *take a load* and [17C] *get a load*]

get along! *excl.* [late 19C+] **1** lit. go away! **2** fig. don't be silly, don't try to fool me.

get-along *n.* [20C] (US) a leg, esp. in phr. a *hitch in one's get-along*, a limp.

get/go along with you! *excl.* [mid-19C+] a general excl. of dismissal and ridicule, esp. as a response to what is seen as excessive or insincere flattery, don't be so silly! you can't fool me!

get a look at the elephant *see* SEE THE ELEPHANT.

get a manual! *excl.* [1980s+] (US campus) an admonition to find out what is going on.

get among frills/a woman's frills, to *phr.* [late 19C–1910s] to seduce a woman.

get among it *v.* [1910s+] (Aus.) **1** to make a large amount of money. **2** to seduce a woman.

get a move on, to *phr.* [late 19C+] (orig. US) to start moving, to hurry up, usu. as imper. *get a move on!*

get a name/name for, to *phr.* [20C] to get a reputation (usu. bad) for.

get an earful, to *phr.* [1910s+] to listen to, usu. in the context of a scolding or criticism.

get an edge on, to *phr.* [1920s+] to drink steadily, not to outright drunkenness but to preserve a feeling of general inebriation. [one is at the *edge* of inebriation]

get/have an encore, to *phr.* [20C] to have sexual intercourse very soon after one has concluded the initial bout.

get an eyeful, to *phr.* [1910s+] to have a good look at, to stare; often in the challenging phr. *got your eyeful?* aimed at one who is seen to be gazing over-intently at oneself or a (female) companion; a follow-up is 'Want a picture?'

get a nitch on *see* GET A SNITCH ON.

get a nut, to *phr.* [1990s] to have an orgasm. [NUT n.[11]]

get anything *v.* [late 17C+] to catch a venereal disease.

get a packet *see* COP A PACKET.

get/have a penn'orth of paradise, to *phr.* [mid-19C–1910s] to have a drink, usu. of gin. [the contemporary cost of a shot of gin, and its anaesthetic effects]

get a pick on, to *phr.* [20C] (Can.) to pick on, to quarrel with.

get a piece *phr.[1] see* BEG FOR A PIECE.

get a piece, to *phr.*[2] [1980s+] to seduce a girl or woman, to have sexual intercourse (cf. KNOCK OFF A PIECE; TEAR OFF A PIECE). [PIECE n.[1]]

get a pot/bit of a pot, to *phr.* [1920s+] to become obese. [POT n.[7]]

get/have a rat, to *phr.* [1900s–20s] (Aus./N.Z.) to act crazily in an eccentric manner; thus *give a rat*, to drive someone crazy.

get a scatter on, to *phr.* [1940s+] (Aus.) to lose touch with someone. [SE *scatter*, to become dispersed]

get a set on, to *phr.* [late 19C–1910s] (Aus.) to take against someone, to attack someone.

get a shift on, to *phr.* [1970s+] to hurry up.

get a shot of crack, to *phr.* [20C] (US) to have sexual intercourse. [CRACK n.[1]]

get a shot of leg, to *phr.* [1970s+] (US Black) to have sexual intercourse.

get/have a skinful, to *phr.* [late 18C+] to get drunk. [SE *skinful*, as much as one can drink]

get a smell of, to *phr.* [late 19C] to get a chance, to approach. [hunting imagery]

get/have a snitch/nitch on, to *phr.* [1930s–50s] to bear a grudge against, to take a dislike to. [SNITCH]

get a snootful, to *phr.* [1910s+] to get drunk. [SNOOT n. (1)]

get a spark up, to *phr.* [1930s+] (N.Z.) to strengthen one's spirits by taking a drink.

get a stand, to *phr.* [19C] to get an erection (cf. GET A HARD-ON). [(COCK)STAND]

get at *v.* **1** [early 19C+] to attack. **2** [early 19C+] to tease, to banter. **3** [mid-19C+] to corrupt, to bribe, to tamper with; thus *got at*, bribed, corrupted, subverted. **4** [late 19C–1920s] (US) to begin; to start work on, to turn one's attention to. **4** [late 19C+] to hint, to imply, usu. in phr. *what are you getting at?*

get a tickle, to *phr.* [1930s+] (Und.) to carry a successful crime or deal (cf. HAVE A NIBBLE). [SE *tickle*, i.e. the image of coaxing a result from ones' efforts]

get a time with, to *phr.* [20C] (W.I.) to seduce a woman.

get at the gee, to *phr.* [1920s–30s] to fool, to hoax. [GEE v.[2] (1)]

get away/away with *v.* [late 19C+] **1** to get the better of, to beat. **2** to carry off successfully, to attain one's goal (with the implication of slight underhandedness).

get away/away with you! *excl.* [1960s+] don't try to fool me; don't tell lies, don't make me laugh (cf. GET ALONG!).

getaway *n.* **1** [mid-19C–1920s] a sudden dash, esp. from the starting point in a game or sport. **2** [mid-19C+] (US Und.) a train or vehicle used for escape (cf. GETAWAY CAR). **3** [late 19C–1900s] (US) the very start. **4** [late 19C–1930s] (US) an escape. **5** [1920s+] an excuse.

getaway car *n.* [1930s+] (US) a car used by criminals escaping from a crime (cf. GETAWAY).

get away closer! *phr.* [late 19C] a paradoxical phr. requesting its object to 'keep on with what you're doing'.

get away with murder, to *phr.* [1910s+] to flout all proprieties with absolute success, to achieve the otherwise unacceptable.

get away with the baggage, to *phr.* [late 19C] (US) to commit a crime or some form of wrong-doing and escape undetected.

get a wet bottom *see* DO A WET BOTTOM.

get a wiggle on, to *phr.* [20C] (orig. milit.) to bustle, to hurry, to 'look lively'.

get a wriggle on, to *phr.* [1910s–60s] (Aus.) to move fast, to 'get a move on'.

get back *phr.* [1980s+] (US campus) alternative way of saying 'I'll see you later.'

get back! *excl.* [1980s+] (US campus) an expression of admiration. [the image of holding back people crowding to view something special]

get back at *v.* [late 19C+] (orig. US) to retaliate.

get back into your box! *excl.* [late 19C+] (orig. US) a general excl. of rebuke, be quiet! I don't want to know! that's quite enough of that!

get beans *v.* [late 19C–1910s] (orig. US) to be punished, to suffer. [? SE *bangs*, hits]

get beautiful *v.* [1980s+] (drugs) to use narcotics and enjoy the effects. [the illusory but alluring euphoria of drugs]

get before oneself *v.* [late 19C+] to boast, to threaten, to act angrily.

get behind *v.*[1] [late 19C] (US) to start smoking or drinking.

get behind *v.*[2] [1960s+] **1** to make a commitment to an idea, a job, a person etc. **2** to understand, to enjoy, to appreciate. [the image of putting one's weight behind; orig. hippie/drug use]

get behind oneself *v.* [late 19C+] to become forgetful.

get bent! *excl.* [1960s+] (US campus) a general excl. of dismissal or contempt (cf. GET FUCKED!; GO TO HELL!).

get brusher *v.* [1900s–30s] (Aus.) to be rejected to be snubbed. [BRUSH-OFF]

get busy *v.* **1** [20C] (orig. US) to become active. **2** [1990s] (US Black/teen) to have sexual intercourse. **3** [1990s] (US Black/teen) to eat.

get by *v.* [20C] **1** to avoid, to evade. **2** to survive without working. **3** to manage, to be acceptable to, to get away with.

get catch/ketch *v.* (W.I.) of an unmarried girl or woman, to become pregnant. [CATCH v.[3]]

get Chinese *v.* [1980s+] (US campus) to succumb heavily to a drug, usu. marijuana. [CHINESE adj.; the implication is of the 'skewed' aspect of the Chinese stereotype, rather than the effects of a drug]

get clear *v.* [1960s+] to work out a situation to its logical conclusion. [scientology jargon *clear*, the ultimate state of those who subject themselves to a scientology course]

get/have cold feet, to *v.* [late 19C+] to become scared, to back down on a previous promise or statement; the cold comes when one 'tests the water' of a situation and finds it chilly.

get comfortable *v.* [1990s] to masturbate.

get cracking *v.* [1930s+] to start work, to get on with anything speedily and efficiently. [cracking a whip over one's team of horses]

get down *v.*[1] [20C] (US) to place a bet. [the 'putting down' of one's wager]

get down *v.*[2] [1930s] (US) to perform fellatio or cunnilingus (cf. GO DOWN v.[6]).

get down *v.*[3] **1** [1960s+] (orig. US) to concentrate. **2** [1960s+] (orig. US) to commit oneself. **3** (orig. US) [1960s+] to do something especially well. **4** [1960s+] (orig. US) to have sexual intercourse. **5** [1970s+] (US Black) to fight. **6** [1970s+] (orig. US) to dance, to have a good time. [abbr. SE phr. *get down to business*]

get down *v.*[4] [1960s+] (US) to take a narcotic or other recreational drug, usu. heroin.

get down! *excl.* [1960s+] an excl. of encouragement, usu. in the context of a musical performance, whether live or created by a DJ playing records/tapes.

get down dirty/fonky/shitty *v.* [1970s+] (US Black) to become abusive, to cause trouble. [GET DOWN v.[3] (2) + SE *dirty/fonky/shitty*]

get down fine/get it down fine, to *phr.* [late 19C+] (US) to become skilful or knowledgeable.

get down fonky *see* GET DOWN DIRTY.

get down from the Y, to *phr.* [1970s+] (US Black) to fight. [ety. unknown]

get down heavy v. [1930s–70s] (US Black) to enjoy oneself, to enter wholeheartedly into the spirit of an occasion. [GET DOWN v.³ (2) + HEAVY adj.¹ (7)]

get down on v.¹ [late 19C] (US) to develop a dislike for or grudge against, to be hostile or oppressive to. [SE get + DOWN n.¹ (2)]

get down on v.² [20C] (Aus./N.Z.) to steal. [SE get down; i.e. bending down to pick something up]

get down shitty see GET DOWN DIRTY.

get down to/to it v. [20C] **1** to start committing oneself seriously, usu. to one's work. **2** to start talking about the crux of a topic. [GET DOWN v.³ (2)]

get down to brass tacks see COME DOWN TO BRASS TACKS.

get down to the nitty-gritty, to phr. [1960s+] (orig. US Black) to get down to essentials, to basics. [SE get down to + NITTY-GRITTY]

get down to tin tacks, to phr. [1920s–40s] to approach and deal with the central issues of a situation (cf. BRASS TACKS; COME DOWN TO BRASS TACKS). [coined and used only by the critic and playwright George Bernard Shaw (1856–1950)]

get 'em/them v. **1** [20C] to suffer delirium tremens. **2** [1910s+] to be mad. [them are the SHAKES]

get 'em off see GET IT OFF.

get even with v. [late 19C] to get revenge, to get one's own back. [SE in 20C]

get face v. [1960s+] (orig. US) to receive oral sex, usu. fellatio (cf. GIVE FACE). [FACE n.² (12)]

get fits v. [late 19C] to become angered by defeat. [SE fit, a seizure]

get fixed v. [1940s–50s] (US) to have sexual intercourse. [the image of 'fixing' or curing one's sexual frustration]

get fucked! excl. [mid-19C+] a general excl. of dismissal or contempt (cf. GET STUFFED!; GO AND FUCK YOURSELF).

get/turn funny v. [20C] **1** to reveal that one has been offended. **2** to act in an offensive manner; thus the threat don't get funny with me!

get gay/gay with v. [late 19C–1910s] (US) to tease, to provoke, to be flippant. [GAY adj.² (2)]

get ghost v. [1990s] (US Black) to act quietly, to 'keep a low profile'.

get-go see GIT-GO.

get going v. **1** [late 19C+] to drive someone into a temper, to make one lose control through teasing (cf. GET ONE AT IT). **2** to excite someone sexually.

get good to someone, to phr. [1990s] (US Black) to be carried away by one's enthusiasms while performing a task.

get gravel for one's goose, to phr. [1930s+] (US) to have sexual intercourse.

get head/skull v. [1990s] to receive oral sex, thus to be fellated. [HEAD n.⁸/SKULL n.⁵]

get hell v. [1930s+] to be severely told off or scolded.

get hep v. [1940s+] (orig. US) to see one's own interest, to learn what is going on, to become aware. [HEP adj.]

get her! excl. [1950s+] an excl. of derision, mockery (both affectionate and otherwise). [orig. camp gay, 'her' being someone acting exceptionally affectedly, but now general use]

get high v. [1930s+] (drugs) to experience a drug. [HIGH adj.¹ (2)]

get high behind v.¹ [20C] (US) **1** to hurry up, to get off to work. **2** to become impatient, to get angry.

get high behind v.² [1930s+] (drugs) to experience a drug. [HIGH adj.¹ (2)]

get hold of/have the wrong end of the stick, to phr. [mid-19C+] to have the facts wrong, to interpret a situation incorrectly; thus the reverse, get the right end of the stick, to get things right, to grasp the essence of the situation.

get home v.¹ [19C] **1** to bring a woman to orgasm. **2** to impregnate.

get home/get home to v.² [early 19C+] to make an impression on. [orig. boxing use, but latterly an emotional impression too]

get home with the milk, to phr. [late 19C+] to stay out all night and return only at dawn.

get horizontal v. [1970s+] (orig. US) **1** to lie down, to go to sleep. **2** to have sexual intercourse. **3** to drink or drug oneself into a stupor.

get horrors see DIG HORRORS.

get hot on v. [1920s] (US) to get busy, to put in an extra effort. [HOT adj. (3)]

get hot under the collar, to phr. [late 19C+] to become increasingly ill-tempered. [SE hot, angry passionate]

get hunk with v. [mid-19C–1940s] (US) to get even with. [SAmE hunk, in a safe or good position or condition, all right; ult. E.Fris. hunk, corner, nook, retreat, home in a game; thus SE adv. hunk, in a safe position all right]

get ideas in/into/have ideas in one's head, to phr. [mid-19C+] to fantasize, esp. about matters that are 'above one's station' or beyond one's abilities (often sexual).

get ignorant v. [20C] (W.I.) to lose one's temper, to be rude; thus get someone ignorant, to enrage, to infuriate.

get in v. [late 19C+] to hit, usu. as get in a couple of right-handers etc. [SE get a blow in]

get in/into a dog corn-piece, to phr. [1910s+] (W.I.) to get into difficulties. [dog is synon. with a guard or watchman, and if he catches you in his corn-piece or corn-field you are in trouble]

get in a gar hole, to phr. [20C] (US) to have bad luck (cf. GAR-BROTH). [angling jargon; a gar swims above the holes in which other, larger fish live; thus an angler who gets in a gar hole is fishing for a better fish but is having his bait intercepted by a gar]

get in bad/bad with v. [1910s+] to earn disfavour, to get into trouble (cf. GET IN GOOD).

get in deep v. [mid-19C+] to become heavily involved, usu. in either crime or love.

get in for it v. [1920s–30s] to establish oneself in a situation.

get in good/good with v. [1930s+] (US) to find favour with (cf. GET IN BAD).

get in line, to phr. [mid-19C+] to conform.

get in one's ass, to phr. [1960s] (US) to annoy, to irritate. [ARSE n.¹ (1)]

get in one's eye, to phr. [1970s+] (US Black) **1** to beat up. **2** to crowd, to encroach on someone's personal space. **3** to shout at someone from close quarters (cf. IN SOMEONE'S FACE). **4** to hit one in the face or eye.

get in one's hair, to phr. [mid-19C+] to annoy, to irritate. [the image is of lice]

get in on the ground floor, to phr. [late 19C+] to start at the beginning, to be present when a new project is in its infancy. [the emergent lift/elevator culture of the period]

get inside and pull the blinds down! excl. [late 19C] a mocking shout aimed at a poor horseman or woman.

get in the buggy/car, to phr. [20C] (US) to comply with requirements, to act as ordered (cf. STAY ON THE WAGON). [SE buggy, a coach or carriage/car]

get in the collar, to phr. [20C] (US) to start working, to work hard (cf. FILL ONE'S COLLAR; GO UP AGAINST THE COLLAR). [SE collar, the neckpiece of a draft harness; the comparison is to a hard-working draft horse]

get in there! excl. [1980s+] a general exhortation, typically of a man's friends who are watching his approaches to an unknown woman.

get in the ropes with, to phr. [20C] (W.I.) to start a quarrel, an argument. [boxing imagery]

get in the shit, to phr. [1940s+] to become involved in a situation; spec. US milit. use, to join a firefight or arrive on the front-line. [SHIT n.³]

get in the wind, to phr. [1950s–60s] (US Black) to leave, to depart quickly.

get into v.¹ [late 17C–early 19C] to put on one's clothes.

get into/in v.² [early 19C+] to penetrate either the vagina or anus (cf. GET IT IN; GET UP v.¹).

get into v.³ [1910s+] (orig. N.Z.) to attack, whether in a fight, or fig. food, a task etc.

get into v.⁴ [1960s+] to become aware of, to understand, to grow close to, to become involved in, to enjoy.

get into gear, to phr. [20C] (US) to get going, to get busy.

get into one's pants, to phr. [1960s+] to seduce.

get into one's ribs, to phr. [1930s+] to borrow money. [one's wallet is carried in a pocket near the ribs; coined by P.G. Wodehouse in *Uncle Fred in Springtime* (1939) and used exclusively by him thereafter]

get into trouble, to phr. [early 19C+] euph. phr. for suffering a variety of legal penalties, arrested, imprisoned, fined etc.

get in touch with one's inner-self, to phr. [1990s] to masturbate. [play on New Age vocab.]

get in wrong v. [1930s] to irritate, to annoy.

get it v. **1** [mid-19C+] (US) to be shot, wounded or killed. **2** [late 19C+] to be punished (cf. CATCH IT; GET IT HOT; GET IT IN THE NECK). **3** [late 19C+] to catch a venereal disease. **4** [1940s+] (US) to go at great speed. **5** [1960s+] (US) to be pleasing, attractive, used in negative contexts, e.g. *Sorry, but he just doesn't get it.*

get it? excl.¹ [20C] do you understand? esp. referring to the point of a joke. [GET v.⁵]

get it! excl.² [1980s+] (US campus) an excl. of encouragement.

get it down fine see GET DOWN FINE.

get it down one's neck, to phr. **1** [late 19C–1900s] to swallow. **2** [late 19C+] to take a drink.

get it every way, to phr. [20C] (orig. US) to do well, irrespective of circumstances.

get it hot v. [late 19C+] **1** to be punished severely. **2** to be scolded with great venom (cf. CATCH IT). [HOT adj.¹ (2)]

get it in v. [1920s+] **1** of a man, to enter a woman before sexual intercourse (cf. GET INTO v.²). **2** to seduce. ['it' being the penis; (2) is fig. use of (1)]

get it in for v. [late 19C+] to bear a grudge, to feel hostile towards (cf. HAVE IT IN FOR).

get it/there in one, to phr. [1930s+] to succeed in doing, in understanding etc at the first try, esp. in a sexual context.

get it in/up the ass/arse, to phr. [1940s+] (orig. US) to be attacked, victimized, killed (cf. GET SHAFTED).

get it in the neck, to phr. [late 19C+] (orig. US) **1** to be killed. **2** to be punished severely, to suffer badly (cf. CATCH IT; GET IT WHERE MAGGIE WORE THE BEADS; GET IT WHERE THE CHICKEN GOT THE AXE).

get it/'em/one off v. [1930s+] (US) to reach orgasm, to copulate, to derive pleasure.

get it off one's chest, to phr. [20C] to confess, to unburden oneself.

get it off with v. [1970s+] of a man, to have sexual intercourse (cf. GET OFF WITH).

get it on v.¹ [1950s+] (orig. US Black) **1** to start, to take positive action. **2** to seduce, to have sexual intercourse. **3** to start a fight (cf. GET DOWN v.³).

get it on/on with v.² [1960s+] to have sexual intercourse.

get it on someone cold, to phr. [1900s] (orig. US) to have at one's mercy, to have at a disadvantage (cf. HAVE SOMEONE COLD).

get it on the whisper, to phr. [1920s–50s] to buy on hire purchase. [the shame such purchases induced among those who were yet to succumb to life 'on the never-never']

get it together v. [1960s+] (orig. US Black) **1** to start a sexual relationship. **2** to make a decision, to take action. **3** to pull oneself together, to stop vacillating etc.

get it/one up v. [1940s+] (orig. US) **1** to achieve erection. **2** to maintain enthusiasm for an idea, situation etc (cf. HAVE A HARD-ON FOR).

get it up the ass see GET IT IN THE ASS.

get it wet v. [20C] of a man, to have sexual intercourse.

get it where Maggie wore the beads, to phr. [1900s–20s] to be hit or hurt, to suffer in the worst place, or fig. in the worst poss. way given the context (cf. GET IT IN THE NECK).

get it where the chicken got the axe, to phr. [1910s+] to suffer in the worst possible way, according to context (cf. GET IT IN THE NECK).

get Jack in the orchard, to phr. [19C] to penetrate a woman. [JACK n.⁸ + ORCHARD]

get jack of v. [late 19C+] (Aus.) to resent, to be bored with, to be fed up with. [JACK OF]

get jerry on/to, to phr. [1900s–40s] (US) to be aware of, to understand. [JERRY v.²]

get joined! excl. [1930s–70s] a dismissive, derisive excl. (cf. GET KNOTTED!; GET STUFFED!). [euph. for GET FUCKED!]

get juice out of a brickbat, to phr. [late 19C] (US Black) to perform the impossible.

get kailed up v. [1920s–30s] to get drunk. [KALIED]

get ketch see GET CATCH.

get kittens see HAVE KITTENS.

get knicked! see GET KNOTTED!.

get knocked v. [1930s+] (Aus.) to suffer a setback, a disappointment or defeat. [KNOCK v.² (1)]

get knotted!/knicked!/nicked! excl. [1930s+; 1970s+] go away! stop bothering me! [euph. for GET FUCKED!]

get/be left v. [late 19C+] (US) to be abandoned, esp. in a difficult situation.

get loose v. [1980s+] **1** to relax (cf. HANG LOOSE). **2** to throw some punches; also *get loose on*. **3** to dance, to have fun.

get lost! excl. [1940s+] a general excl. of dismissal, go away! be off! [Yid. *ver farvalgert*, disappear, move on, go away]

get low v. [1980s+] (US campus) to smoke marijuana. [a reverse pun on the usu. GET HIGH with other drugs, due to the relaxing effects of marijuana]

get meat for one's cat, to phr. [19C] to solicit. [MEAT n. (1) + CAT n.¹⁰]

get medieval on someone's ass, to phr. [1990s] (US Black/teen) to attack with extreme violence. [coined in Quentin Tarantino's film *Pulp Fiction* (1994)]

get me Steve? see GOT ME STEVE?

get misty v. [1996s+] to become sentimental. [abbr. *get misty-eyed*]

get money at the best, to phr. [19C] to live as a professional criminal.

get more butt than ashtrays, to phr. [1990s] of a man, to lead an active sexual life. [pun on BUTT n.¹/BUTT n.²]

get naked v. [1960s+] (US) **1** to get busy. **2** to enjoy oneself uninhibitedly.

get next to v. **1** [late 19C–1900s] (US) to get for oneself. **2** [1930s–70s] (US Black) to make a good impression, to curry favour with, to win over. **3** [1940s+] (US Black) to become lovers, to seduce. **4** [1950s–70s] (US Black) to feel friendly towards, to tolerate. **5** [1970s+] (US Black) to embarrass, to annoy, to anger. [all have image of drawing (too) close]

get nicked! see GET KNOTTED!

get no change out of, to phr. [mid-19C+] to receive no satisfaction from.

get no/not get any forrarder, to *phr.* [late 19C+] to make no progress. [SE *forward*]

get nowhere/not get anywhere *v.* [1920s+] (orig. US) to fail, despite one's best efforts.

get nowhere with/nowhere fast *v.* [1950s+] to get no satisfaction from, to make no headway with, esp. when one has made a special effort.

get off *v.*[1] [early 19C] to succeed in marrying off one's daughter(s).

get off *v.*[2] **1** [mid-19C+] to let off, to excuse. **2** [20C] to desist from harassing, to stop annoying (cf. GET OFF ONE'S BACK; GET OFF ONE'S CASE).

get off *v.*[3] [late 19C] (US) to steal.

get off *v.*[4] [late 19C+] (Aus.) (US) to make a joke, a witticism, e.g. *get off a good one.*

get off *v.*[5] **1** [1910s+] to strike up a relationship with a potential sexual partner (cf. GET OFF WITH). **2** [1990s] (Irish teen) to indulge in a formalized session of French kissing as a statement that the couple are interested in each other.

get off *v.*[6] **1** [1920s] (US Black) to achieve one's object. **2** [1930s+] (US) to improvise or play music skilfully. **3** [1970s+] (orig. US Black) to enjoy, to be stimulated by (cf. GET OFF ON *v.*[2]). **4** [1970s+] (orig. US) to achieve orgasm (cf. GET ONE'S ROCKS OFF). **5** [1970s+] to masturbate (cf. BEAT OFF).

get off *v.*[7] [1950s+] to succeed in getting a child to go off to sleep.

get off *v.*[8] [1960s+] (drugs) **1** to experience the effects of a drug (cf. TAKE OFF *v.*[4]). **2** to quit a drug addiction.

get off! *excl.* **1** [1950s+] a general excl. of disbelief. **2** [1950s+] stop it! **3** [1970s] (US campus) an expression of admiration.

get off/out at Broadgreen, to *phr.* [20C] to perform coitus interruptus, i.e. withdrawal well before ejaculation (cf. GET OFF AT EDGE HILL; GET OFF AT GATESHEAD; GET OFF AT HAYMARKET; GET OFF AT HILLGATE; GET OFF AT PAISLEY; GET OFF AT REDFERN; LEAVE BEFORE THE GOSPEL). [*Broadgreen* is the station before Edge Hill which is the station before Liverpool Lime Street]

get off/out at Edge Hill, to *phr.* [20C] to perform coitus interruptus (cf. GET OFF AT BROADGREEN). [*Edge Hill* is the station before Liverpool Lime Street]

get off/out at Gateshead, to *phr.* [20C] to perform coitus interruptus; spec. used by natives of Newcastle-upon-Tyne (cf. GET OFF AT BROADGREEN). [*Gateshead* is the railway station before Newcastle-upon-Tyne; note RN use *get off at Fratton* in which Fratton is the stop immediately before Bristol dockyard]

get off/out at Haymarket, to *phr.* [20C] to perform coitus interruptus (cf. GET OFF AT BROADGREEN). [used by the natives of Edinburgh, where *Haymarket* is the railway station immediately preceding their own]

get off/out at Hillgate, to *phr.* [1970s+] to perform coitus interruptus (cf. GET OFF AT BROADGREEN). [a real or notional bus-stop, immediately before one's actual destination]

get off/out at Paisley, to *phr.* [20C] to perform coitus interruptus (cf. GET OFF AT BROADGREEN). [used by Glaswegians, where *Paisley* is the railway station immediately preceding their own]

get off/out at Redfern, to *phr.* [1970s+] (Aus.) to perform coitus interruptus (cf. GET OFF AT BROADGREEN). [*Redfern* is the railway station immediately before Sydney Central]

get off it! *phr.* [1910s–20s] stop teasing! stop exaggerating! (cf. COME OFF IT!).

get off on *v.*[1] [1910s+] to insult, to get angry with (cf. SOUND OFF *v.*[2]).

get off on *v.*[2] [1960s+] (drugs) to experience the effects of a drug. **2** [1970s+] to enjoy, to be stimulated by, esp. sexually. [the image is of 'rising above' normal life (cf. HIGH n.[1])]

get off one's back, to *phr.* [late 19C+] to stop annoying someone, to stop nagging at or otherwise irritating someone.

get off one's bike, to *phr.* [1930s+] (Aus./N.Z.) to lose one's temper.

get off one's case, to *phr.* [1950s+] (orig. US Black) to stop harassing, to stop annoying.

get off the button, to *phr.* [1930s] (US) to experience orgasm, to relieve sexual tension. [the pressing of a button to trigger some kind of activity]

get off the dime/nickel, to *phr.* [1920s–30s] (US) **1** to leave to run off. **2** to move from a stationary position, esp. of a dancer. [the image of a person being stuck on a small spot, i.e. one the size of a *dime* or *nickel* coin]

get off the natural, to *phr.* [1960s] (US drugs) to become intoxicated.

get off the nickel *see* GET OFF THE DIME.

get off with *v.* **1** [1910s+] to seduce, to pick up and poss. go to bed with. **2** [1990s] to indulge in a petting session, but not in intercourse.

get on/get a bit on *v.*[1] [19C] to place a bet on a horse or dog. [a 'bit' of cash]

get on *v.*[2] [early 19C+] to relate to a person either positively or negatively, e.g. *get on well, get on badly.*

get on *v.*[3] [late 19C] of a man, to have sexual intercourse. [his 'mounting' of his partner]

get on *v.*[4] [late 19C+] to grow older. [abbr. SE *get on in years*]

get on *v.*[5] [20C] to leave, to depart. [abbr. SE *get on one's way*]

get on *v.*[6] [1960s+] (US Black) to get drunk, to take drugs.

get on *v.*[7] [1970s+] (US Black) to pursue a goal or aim.

get on at *v.* [late 19C+] to abuse, to scold, to nag (cf. GO ON AT).

get on dixie, to *phr.* [20C] (W.I.) to quarrel noisily, to become very angry (cf. DO DIXIE). [the energy and noise associated with *Dixieland* jazz]

get one at it *v.* [1940s+] to tease, to drive into a fury (cf. GET GOING).

get one down *v.* [late 19C] to make someone depressed. [DOWN adj.[1]]

get one going *v.* [late 19C+] to drink heavily. ['one' being a drinking session]

get one/them in *v.*[1] [20C] to order and pay for a round of drinks, esp. as excl. *get them in!*

get one in *v.*[2] [1920s+] (Aus.) to fool, to trick.

get one in a line, to *phr.* [early 19C] (Und.) to engage a victim in conversation while an accomplice is robbing them. [LINE n.[1] (1)]

get one in a string, to *phr.* [late 19C] (orig. US) to deceive someone over a period of time (cf. GET ONE IN A LINE; STRING ALONG).

get one in the gun, to *phr.* [20C] to get someone into trouble.

get one off *see* GET IT OFF.

get one off one's hands, to *phr.* [early 19C+] to get rid of a person who is a responsibility, esp. an unmarried daughter (cf. GET OFF *v.*[2]).

get one on *v.* [1970s] (US) of a man, to have an erection.

get one round the corner, to *phr.* [early–mid-19C] to infuriate on purpose.

get one's *v.* **1** [1910s+] (orig. US) to be killed, to die, usu. by accident or through violence. **2** [1960s+] (orig. US Black) to get one's share, usu. of material pleasures, to get what one deserves, usu. as *get mine.*

get one's act together, to *phr.* [1960s+] (orig. US Black) to calm down, to plan sensibly, to state a goal and aim for it (cf. GET ONE'S ARSE IN GEAR).

get one's African up, to *phr.* [20C] (US) to lose control, to lose one's temper (cf. GET ONE'S NIGGER UP). [racial stereotyping]

get one's angora, to phr. [1920s–40s] (US) to annoy, to irritate. [a pun on GET ONE'S GOAT]

get one's animal, to phr. [1920s] to annoy, to irritate. [play on GET ONE'S GOAT]

get one's arse/ass in an uproar, to phr. [1950s+] to get excited, to become emotionally overwrought.

get one's arse/ass on one's shoulders, to phr. [1930s+] (US) to become haughty, angry or excited but with no proper cause. [the shrugging gesture, which raises one's shoulders and thus, fig. one's posterior]

get one's arse/ass up, to phr. [late 19C+] (US) to annoy, to irritate, to infuriate (cf. GET ONE'S BACK UP).

get one's arse/ass in gear, to phr. to stop wasting time, to put some effort and commitment into one's activities, to start doing something useful and positive (cf. GET ONE'S ACT TOGETHER). [ARSE n.¹]

get one's ashes hauled, to phr. [20C] to have sexual intercourse. [? mispron. of ARSE/ASS]

get one's ass/tail in a crack, to phr. [1920s+] (US) to get into difficulties. [ARSE n.¹]

get one's ass in a sling, to phr. [1960s+] (US) to get into bad trouble, physical or otherwise. [ARSE n.¹]

get one's ass on one's shoulder, to phr. [1930s–50s] (US Black) to put on airs, to act in an arrogant manner. [ARSE n.¹ (5)]

get one's axle greased, to phr. [1960s] of a man, to have sexual intercourse.

get one's back up, to phr. [late 18C+] to annoy, to irritate, to infuriate (cf. GET ONE'S ARSE UP). [the feline habit of bristling the fur when annoyed or frightened]

get one's bait back, to phr. [1920s–50s] (US) to succeed in fathering a son. [fishing imagery]

get one's balls in an uproar, to phr. [1910s+] to become excited or agitated (cf. GET ONE'S BOWELS IN AN UPROAR; GET ONE'S KNICKERS IN A TWIST). [BALLS n.¹]

get one's balls off, to phr. [1960s+] (orig. US) of a man, to achieve orgasm (cf. GET ONE'S ROCKS OFF). [BALLS n.¹]

get one's banana peeled, to phr. [late 19C+] (orig. US) of a man, to have sexual intercourse. [BANANA n.²]

get one's batteries charged, to phr. [1930s+] (US) of a man, to have sexual intercourse.

get one's bitters, to phr. [early–mid-19C] (US) to get one's deserts. [SE bitter end]

get one's bowels in an uproar, to phr. [20C] to become excited or agitated (cf. GET ONE'S BALLS IN AN UPROAR).

get one's cards, to phr. [1920s+] to be dismissed from work; thus to give one one's cards, to dismiss. [the cards in question are insurance cards, P45 forms etc]

get one's checks, to phr. [late 19C] (US) to die (cf. CASH IN ONE'S CHECKS). [gambling imagery]

get/provide one's chump, to phr. [mid-19C–1910s] (Und.) to earn one's living. [? CHUMP n.² (2)]

get one's collar felt, to phr. [1950s+] (Und.) to be arrested.

get one's cookies, to phr. [1950s+] to have sexual intercourse; thus get one's cookies off, to come to orgasm. [COOKIES n.¹]

get/have one's corn ground, to phr. [early 19C] (US) to have sexual intercourse.

get one's dander up, to phr. [19C+] (orig. US) to lose one's temper. [? Rom. dander, to bite or ? f. fig. use of W.I. dander, the ferment created when working molasses]

get one's dandruff up, to phr. [20C] (US) to lose one's temper (cf. GET ONE'S DANDER UP). [joc. corruption of the common phr. + image of flecks of dandruff rising as one gesticulates with rage]

get one's dipper wet, to phr. [1980s+] (US) of a man, to have sexual intercourse (cf. DO A WET BOTTOM).

get one's ears chewed down/knocked down, to phr. [20C] (US) to be scolded severely (cf. FOLD SOMEONE'S EARS).

get one's ears lowered, to phr. [20C] (US) to get a haircut.

get oneself a banner, to phr. [20C] (US Und.) to move from the general prison population into protective solitary confinement (cf. CHECK IN v.; GET SLOUGHED UP; RULE 43). [SE banner = flag, a notation on one's prison file]

get oneself a cook, to phr. [20C] (US) of a man, to get married.

get oneself harnessed, to phr. [20C] to get married (cf. DOUBLE HARNESS; DOUBLETREE UP WITH).

get one's end away, to phr. [1970s+] to have sexual intercourse. [END n.³ (1); note milit. use ends away, having intercourse]

get one's end in, to phr. [1930s+] to have sexual intercourse (cf. GET ONE'S END AWAY). [END n.³ (1)]

get one set v. [late 19C+] (Aus.) to bear a grudge against someone, to have a score to settle with someone (cf. HAVE A SET ON).

get one's eyes together, to phr. [20C] (Ulster) to have a nap.

get one's face in a knot, to phr. [20C] (Aus.) to get angry, excited or over-emotional.

get one's feet muddy, to phr. [1960s+ to be in criminal trouble.

get one's feet under the old mahog, to phr. [late 19C+] to be living off another's bounty, to be living at another's expense. [HAVE ONE'S FEET BELOW THE MAHOGANY]

get one's feet under the table, to phr. [1920s+] **1** to establish friendly relations with someone. **2** of a man, to start living with a woman.

get one's finger out, to phr. [1940s+] to stop dawdling and lazing about and begin some constructive activity.

get one's fingers nipped, to phr. [late 19C+] to get into trouble.

get one's gallon, to phr. [1960s+] (Irish) to be dismissed from a job. [SE gallon, a container used by manual labourers for holding drinks]

get one's game together, to phr. [1960s+] (orig. US Black) to be in full control of a situation (cf. HAVE ONE'S ACT TOGETHER).

get one's gauge up, to phr. [1930s+] (US) **1** to excite or stimulate oneself, esp. from smoking marijuana or drinking alcohol. **2** to become angry. [GAGE n.²]

get one's goat, to phr. [20C] to annoy someone (cf. BURN SOMEONE'S GOAT; GET ONE'S ANGORA; GET ONE'S ANIMAL; GET ONE'S NANNY). [GET v.² (3) + SE goat; ? the goat's propensity to butt when in a bad temper]

get one's greens, to phr. [late 19C+] to have sexual intercourse; thus give one's greens, to consent to sexual intercourse. [GREENS n.²]

get one's gun/gun off, to phr. [1960s+] of a man, to ejaculate, to reach orgasm (cf. FIRE A SHOT; SHOOT). [GUN n.²]

get one's hackles up, to phr. [19C+] to become furious, to lose one's temper. [SE hackles, the long, prominent feathers on the tail of a fighting cock]

get one's hair cut, to phr. [20C] of a man, to visit a woman for the purpose of sexual intercourse. [HAIR n.³ (2), euph. with overtones of an adulterer's excuse]

get one's hat, to phr. [1940s–60s] (US Black) to leave, esp. to leave quickly.

get one's head bad/right, to phr. [1960s–70s] (US Black) to get drunk, to become intoxicated by drugs.

get one's head down, to phr. [1940s+] **1** to have some sleep. **2** (Aus.) to plead guilty in court.

get one's head straight, to phr. [1970s+] (US) to think clearly.

get one's head together, to phr. [1960s+] to sort oneself out, to calm down. [TOGETHER] get one's hips up/hips up on one's shoulders, to *phr.* [20C] (US Black) to get upset, annoyed, hurt (cf. GET ONE'S ASS ON ONE'S SHOULDERS).

get one's hole, to *phr.* [1960s+] of a man, to have sexual intercourse. [HOLE n.¹ (4)]

get one's hooks on/into, to *phr.* [1920s+] to grasp, to grab, to obtain, esp. when the object is most desired or currently held by a rival. [HOOKS]

get one's hump up, to *phr.* [mid-19C] to get in a temper, to become irritated (cf. GET THE HUMP). [the way a cat arches its back when angry or threatened]

get one's Irish up, to *phr.* [19C+] to lose one's temper (cf. AFRICAN; DUTCH; INDIAN; PADDY).

get one's jollies, to *phr.* [1950s+] 1 to enjoy oneself. 2 to have sex.

get one's jones off, to *phr.* [1960s+] (orig. US Black) to reach orgasm. [JONES n.²]

get one's kicks, to *phr.* [1950s+] (orig. US Black) to enjoy oneself (cf. GET ONE'S JOLLIES).

get one's kicks off, to *phr.* [1920s+] (US) to enjoy oneself. [KICK n.⁵]

get one's kit off, to *phr.* [1970s+] to take off one's clothes, to strip (cf. DROP ONE'S GEAR). [widely popularized by the spread of 1990s 'lad culture' and the magazines that pander to it]

get one's knickers in a twist, to *phr.* [1960s+] 1 to become excessively agitated over a problem or situation, to worry to extremes; thus *don't get your knickers in a twist*, stop getting so worried; *knicker-twisting*, agonizingly worrying (cf. GET ONE'S BALLS IN AN UPROAR). 2 to make a mistake, to be under a misapprehension, to 'get the wrong end of the stick'.

get one's knitting twisted, to *phr.* [1950s+] to become over-worried (cf. GET ONE'S KNICKERS IN A TWIST).

get one's lance waxed, to *phr.* [1980s] to have sexual intercourse (cf. LANCE n.]

get one's laundry in a bundle, to *phr.* [1960s+] (US campus) to get into an emotional state, to get upset (cf. GET ONE'S KNICKERS IN A TWIST).

get one's leg across/over, to *phr.* [early 18C+] 1 to seduce. 2 to have sexual intercourse.

get one's leg dressed, to *phr.* [18C] to have sexual intercourse (cf. GET ONE'S LEG ACROSS).

get one's leg over *see* GET ONE'S LEG ACROSS.

get one's licks, to *phr.* [mid-19C+] (US) to get one's chance, to get one's way. [LICKS n.² (1)]

get one's lines/wires crossed, to *phr.* [1930s+] to make a mistake in communication, to misunderstand. [telephonic imagery]

get one's mad up, to *phr.* [late 19C+] (US) to get very angry.

get/receive one's marching orders, to *phr.* [mid-19C+] (orig. US) to be dismissed, to be sent away.

get one's mind right, to *phr.* [1950s–60s] to think clearly, to agree with.

get one's monkey up, to *phr.* [early–mid-19C+] 1 to annoy someone, to infuriate someone. 2 to lose one's temper, to get into a bad temper; thus *my monkey's up*, I am very annoyed (cf. HAVE ONE'S MONKEY UP). [MONKEY n.⁶]

get one's nanny/nanny-goat, to *phr.* [1910s+] to annoy someone, to infuriate someone. [var. on GET ONE'S GOAT]

get one's nigger up, to *phr.* [20C] (US) to lose control, to lose one's temper (cf. GET ONE'S AFRICAN UP). [fig. use of NIGGER n.; racist stereotyping]

get one's nose, to *phr.* [1990s] (US Black) to have another person utterly dependent on oneself, typically in a one-sided love relationship (cf. HAVE ONE'S NOSE OPEN).

get one's nose cold, to *phr.* [1970s+] (drugs) to sniff cocaine. [the drug has a numbing quality, esp. if, as more than likely, it has been adulterated with procaine or Novocaine]

get one's nose painted, to *phr.* [20C] to get very drunk. [the colour is presumably red]

get/have one's nuff, to *phr.* [late 19C–1910s] (orig. milit.) to be drunk. [SE *enough*, i.e. too much]

get one's nuts off, to *phr.* [1930s+] (orig. US Black) to achieve orgasm, poss. through masturbation (cf. BEAT OFF). [NUTS n.² (1)]

get one's oats, to *phr.* [1920s+] to gain sexual release. [OATS n.¹]

get one's picture, to *phr.* [1920s] to be dismissed from a job. [? a picture on an identity card]

get one's pole varnished, to *phr.* [1980s+] to masturbate.

get/let one's rag out, to *phr.* [late 19C–1960s] 1 to lose one's temper (cf. LOSE ONE'S RAG). 2 to make someone else angry. [RAG n.⁴ (2)/RAG v.¹ (2)]

get one's respect, to *phr.* [1970s+] (US Black) to make sure that one is treated in the manner to which one feels one should be accustomed, esp. in prison.

get one's rocks off, to *phr.* 1 [1940s+] to have sexual intercourse, to experience orgasm (cf. GET ONE'S BALLS OFF). 2 [1940s+] to enjoy oneself. 3 [1940s+] to obtain any form of satisfaction. 4 [1960s+] to masturbate. [ROCKS n.³]

get one's rug beat, to *phr.* [1940s] (US Black) to have a haircut. [RUG n.³]

get one's shirt out, to *phr.*¹ [mid-19C] to become angry or to make another angry (cf. SHIRTY). [the disarrangement of one's clothes that may follow a fit of arm-brandishing fury]

get one's shirt out, to *phr.*² [mid-19C–1930s] to cause someone to lose all their money (through gambling) (cf. LOSE ONE'S SHIRT).

get one's shit together, to *phr.* [1960s+] (orig. US Black) to calm down, to plan sensibly (cf. GET ONE'S ACT TOGETHER). [SHIT n.⁶]

get one's shoes full, to *phr.* [20C] to become drunk. [the drink 'overflows']

get/put one's skates on, to *phr.* [late 19C+] (orig. milit.) to hurry up, to stop wasting time; often as imper.

get/put one's snout in the trough, to *phr.* [1940s+] 1 to act greedily and selfishly. 2 to drink beer or ale rather than spirits.

get one's soul in soak, to *phr.* [19C] to become very drunk (cf. LUBRICATED).

get one's swerve on, to *phr.* [1970s] (US Black) to have sexual intercourse.

get one's tail down, to *phr.* [mid-19C+] to act in a dejected manner, to lose heart. [reverse anthropomorphism]

get one's tail-feathers up, to *phr.* [20C] (US) to get annoyed, to lose one's temper (cf. LOWER ONE'S FEATHERS). [reverse anthropomorphism]

get one's thing off, to *phr.* [1970s+] (US Black) to gain pleasure from any act.

get one's tits in a knot, to *phr.* [1990s] (US) to be upset.

get one's wings, to *phr.* [1960s+] 1 (drugs) to start using heroin. 2 (Hell's Angels) to be initiated into an outlaw motorcycle club (cf. RED WINGS; BROWN WINGS). [play on USAF/RAF jargon *get one's wings*, to be commissioned as a pilot]

get one's wires crossed *see* GET ONE'S LINES CROSSED.

get one told, to *phr.* [1930s–50s] (US Black) to reprimand someone, to upbraid someone, to someone tell off.

get one up *see* GET IT UP.

get one wet *v.* [20C] (NZ) to gain an advantage over someone. [the image of dunking them in water]

get one wrong *v.* [1920s+] (orig. US) to misunderstand a person's meaning or intentions, to misinterpret someone.

get on it *v.* [20C] (orig. N.Z.) to go out on a drinking spree.

get on like a bushfire, to *phr.* [1940s] (Aus.) to get on well with someone, to make friends fast. [the speed with which a bushfire spreads]

get on one's arse/ass, to *phr.* [1950s+] to annoy.

get on one's back, to *phr.* [1920s+] (orig. Aus.) **1** to annoy, to harass (cf. GET OFF ONE'S BACK). **2** to tell off, to scold.

get on one's bike, to *phr.* [1980s+] to busy oneself, to get down to work. [popularized by a speech given by right-wing Employment Secretary Norman Tebbit (b.1931) at the Conservative Party Conference on 15 October 1981, in which he pointed out that his unemployed father – unlike that year's inner-city rioters – had not rioted in the 1930s but had 'got on his bike and looked for work']

get on one's brain *see* GET ON ONE'S NERVES.

get on one's case, to *phr.* [1950s+] (orig. US Black) to pester, to harass. [SE *case*, state of affairs, circumstance]

get on one's daily, to *phr.* [1930s+] to follow. [DAILY MAIL]

get on/stand on one's hind legs, to *phr.*[1] [late 19C+] to rise to speak usu. in a formal context. [a dog 'walking' on its back legs]

get on/stand on one's hind legs, to *phr.*[2] [late 19C+] to lose one's temper. [a rearing horse]

get on one's horse, to *phr.* [1940s+] (US) to get moving.

get on one's nerves/brain, to *phr.* [1950s+] to annoy, to irritate (cf. GET ON ONE'S PRICK; GET ON ONE'S QUINCE; GET ON ONE'S TIT; GET ON ONE'S TRIPE; GET ON ONE'S WICK; GET ON ONE'S WORKS).

get on one's own tail, to *phr.* [1910s+] (Aus.) **1** to become angry. **2** to become scared. [TAIL]

get on one's prick, to *phr.* [1940s+] to annoy, to irritate (cf. GET ON ONE'S NERVES). [PRICK n.]

get on one's quince, to *phr.* [1920s+] (Aus.) to annoy (cf. GET ON ONE'S NERVES).

get on one's tit/tits, to *phr.* [1940s+] **1** to infuriate, to annoy (cf. GET ON ONE'S NERVES). **2** (US) to pursue sexually (used by a woman of a pursuing man). [TIT n.[1] (1)]

get on one's tripe, to *phr.* [1930s+] (Aus.) to annoy or irritate someone (cf. GET ON ONE'S NERVES).

get on one's wick, to *phr.* [1940s+] to irritate, to annoy (cf. GET ON ONE'S NERVES). [rhy. sl. *Hampton Wick* = PRICK]

get on one's works, to *phr.* [1920s+] (Aus.) to annoy (cf. GET ON ONE'S NERVES).

get on some stiff time, to *phr.* [1930s–70s] (US Black) to succeed, esp. in an illicit, but profitable occupation. [ety. unknown]

get on stink, to *phr.* [20C] (W.I.) to behave badly, to start a noisy argument (cf. GIVE ONE STINK).

get on that *v.* [1940s] (Aus.) to understand, to look at.

get on the good foot, to *phr.* [1970s+] (US Black) **1** to correct what needs improving. **2** to do one's best, to 'put one's best foot forward'.

get on the home stretch, to *phr.* [late 19C] to be near achieving one's aim, the end of a piece of work, a journey etc. [horse-racing imagery]

get on the old fork, to *phr.* [late 19C–1900s] to have sexual intercourse. [SE *fork*, the fork of the body, where the legs divide from the torso]

get on the pole, to *phr.* [late 19C–1900s] to be approaching drunkenness. [UP THE POLE phr.[1]]

get onto *v.*[1] [late 19C+] **1** to suspect. **2** to interrogate, to pressurize. **3** to look, to observe.

get onto *v.*[2] **1** [late 19C+] (US) to understand. **2** [1910s+] (Aus.) to join in, to participate.

get-out *n.* [1940s–50s] (US Black) an outfit, a suit of clothes. [worn when one 'gets out' of the house]

get out *v.*[1] [early 18C+] to leave, usu. in imper. *get out!*

get out *v.*[2] [late 19C–1910s] to lengthen, e.g. *nights are getting out*. [note the synon. 'nights are drawing in']

get out *v.*[3] [1920s+] of a puzzle or game, to solve, to bring to an end. [? orig. patience, where one 'gets out' the last card]

get out *adv.* [mid-19C+] (US) to the utmost degree, esp. in phr. *all get out.*

get out! *excl.* [early 18C+] an excl. of dismissal, expressing one's disbelief or scepticism (cf. GET OUT OF HERE!).

get out at Broadgreen *see* GET OFF AT BROADGREEN.

get out at Edge Hill *see* GET OFF AT EDGE HILL.

get out at Gateshead *see* GET OFF AT GATESHEAD.

get out at Haymarket *see* GET OFF AT HAYMARKET.

get out at Hillgate *see* GET OFF AT HILLGATE.

get out at Paisley *see* GET OFF AT PAISLEY.

get out at Redfern *see* GET OFF AT REDFERN.

get out from under, to *phr.* [mid-19C+] (orig. US) to get away from a dangerous or awkward situation.

get out of bed on the wrong side/of the wrong side of the bed, to *phr.* [early 19C+] to be in a peevish, irritated mood. [what the *wrong side* of a bed is is hard to determine, but getting out that way supposedly causes ill-temper]

get out of here! *excl.* [1960s+] (orig. US Black) a general excl. of disbelief, dismissal, I don't believe you! you must be joking! don't be silly! who do you think you're fooling?

get out of it! *excl.* [20C] an excl. of dismissal or disdain, go away! don't be silly! don't make me laugh!

get out of one's face, to *phr.*[1] [1920s+] (orig. US Black) to stop pestering, esp. as imper. (cf. IN SOMEONE'S FACE).

get out of one's face, to *phr.*[2] [1960s+] to become intoxicated by drink or drugs. [OFF ONE'S FACE]

get out of one's pram, to *phr.* [1950s+] to lose one's temper.

get out of the rain, to *phr.* [20C] to leave at any sign of trouble.

get out of the shine! *excl.* [1920s–30s] get out of the light!

get out of town! *phr.* [1980s+] (orig. US Black/campus) a general excl. of disbelief, dismissal (cf. GET OUT OF HERE!).

get out one's mad, to *phr.* [1920s+] (Aus.) to lose one's temper.

get outside/outside of *v.* **1** [mid-19C+] (orig. US) to consume, to swallow, esp. a drink, e.g. *get outside a pint* (cf. PUT OUT OF SIGHT). **2** [late 19C+] (US) to understand, to learn, to master. **3** [late 19C+] of a woman, to have sexual intercourse.

get over *v.*[1] **1** [19C+] to take advantage of, to get around. **2** [late 19C–1910s] to astonish, to impress. **3** [late 19C–1910s] to seduce. **4** [1940s+] (US Black) to achieve a goal, to do well. **5** [1940s+] (Aus.) to intimidate. **6** [1980s+] (US prison) to improve one's own image/reputation by putting someone else at a disadvantage.

get over *v.*[2] [1970s+] (US Black) to have sexual intercourse. [the physical act of 'mounting' a woman]

get over her/the garter, to *phr.* [early 19C–1900s] to caress a woman sexually.

get over on *v.* [late 19C+] (US Black) to fool, to hoax.

get over the hump, to *phr.* [1950s–60s] (US Black) to overcome a difficulty, to move through a bad period in one's life.

get ox-tail soup, to *phr.* [mid–late 19C] (Irish) to maim cattle by cutting off their tails. [one of the ways in which Irish Fenians attacked English landowners]

get paddywhack the drumstick, to *phr.* [late 19C+] (Aus.) to get a spanking. [ext. PADDYWHACK v.]

get paid *v.* **1** [1980s+] (US campus) to engage in sex. **2** [1990s] (US Black) to obtain money, not necessarily by working for it.

get past/past with *v.* [1910s+] to get away with, to escape (moral) censure.

get past oneself *v.* [1910s+] **1** to get into a peevish, fractious mood. **2** to get over-excited (cf. ABOVE ONESELF; GET ABOVE ONESELF).

get plunked *see* PLUNK A BABY.

get points *v.* [late 19C] to have an advantage (cf. GIVE POINTS).

get previous *v.* [late 19C+] (orig. US) to act in a forward manner (cf. BIT PREVIOUS). [PREVIOUS adj. (3)]

get props v. [1990s] (US Black) to gain respect, admiration (cf. GIVE PROPS). [abbr. SE *proper respect*]

get/have/see rats v. **1** [mid–late 19C] (Aus./N.Z.) to feel unwell, 'out of sorts'. **2** [mid-19C+] to be very drunk.

get real v. [1980s+] (orig. US) to face facts, to abandon one's unreal fantasies (cf. GET A LIFE!; GET REAL!).

get real! *excl.* [1970s+] (US campus) an admonition to be serious, act maturely (cf. GET A LIFE!).

get religion v. [late 19C] (orig. US) to succumb to religious belief.

get right v. [1950s+] (US Black) to become drunk or intoxicated by drugs (cf. ABOUT RIGHT adj.[1]).

get ripped! *excl.* [1940s+] (Aus.) a general excl. of dismissal, be quiet! go to hell!

get rooted! *excl.* [1950s+] (Aus.) a strongly dismissive excl., euph. *fuck off! get fucked!* [ROOT v.[3] (1)]

get round v. **1** [mid-19C+] (orig. US) to trick, to fool. **2** [mid-19C+] to persuade, to 'con'. **3** to escape from an obligation or activity. **4** [late 19C+] to arrange events as one prefers them.

get set v. [late 19C+] to buckle down to one's work.

get shafted v. [1950s+] (orig. US) to be treated harshly or unfairly. [SHAFT v. (2)]

get shet of v. [mid-19C+] (US) to get rid of. [pron. of SE *shut*; thus synon. for GET SHUT OF]

get shit of v. [20C] to get rid of something or someone (cf. GET SHUT OF). [var. on GET SHOT OF]

get shot in the tail, to phr. [late 17C–early 18C] of a woman, to have sexual intercourse. [SE *shot* + TAIL n.[1]]

get shot of v. [mid-19C+] to get rid of something or someone (cf. GET SHUT OF).

get shut of v. [mid-18C+] to get rid of something or someone (cf. GET SHOT OF).

get skins/some skins v. [1990s] (US Black) to have sexual intercourse (cf. HIT SKINS).

get skull *see* GET HEAD.

get sloppy v. [1980s+] (US Black/campus) **1** to get drunk. **2** to have sexual intercourse.

get sloughed up v. [20C] (US Und.) to move from the general prison population into protective solitary confinement (cf. GET ONESELF A BANNER). [SLOUGHED]

get smart v. [20C] to act in an arrogant manner, usu. in phr. *don't get smart with me*.

get some v. [late 19C+] (orig. US) to have sexual intercourse (cf. GETTING ANY).

get some! *excl.* [1960s+] (US) a cry of encouragement, esp. to one participant in a fight or firefight. [as used in by US troops in the Vietnam War (1964–75)]

get some air, to phr. [1990s] (US Black) to leave.

get some boody/booty, to phr. (US Black) of a male, to have sexual intercourse. [BOODY n.]

get some brown/brown sugar, to phr. [1970s+] of a male homosexual, to have anal intercourse. [BROWN n.[3]]

get some cock, to phr. [1970s+] (US Black/South) of a male, to have sexual intercourse. [COCK n.[2] (2)]

get some cold comfort, to phr. [1980s+] to have sexual relations with a corpse.

get some dog *see* GO DOG-HUNTING.

get some duke, to phr. [1970s+] of a male homosexual, to have someone's fingers or fist pushed into one's anus. [DUKE n.[3] (1)]

get some ink, to phr. [1910s+] to receive coverage in the printed media for one's actions, speech etc.

get some kick, to phr. [1940s] (US Black) to obtain some money. [KICK n.[2]]

get some leg/big leg/soft leg, to phr. [1970s+] (US Black) of a male, to have sexual intercourse.

get some of this, to phr. [1990s] (US Black) to participate, to take a share of, usu. as imper. *get some of this!*

get someone's back, to phr. [1950s+] to look after someone, lit. to see that nobody is attacking from behind (cf. COVER SOMEONE'S ASS; WATCH SOMEONE'S BACK).

get someone's gun/gun off, to phr. [1940s+] to delight someone. [GUN n.[2]]

get someone's measure, to phr. [late 18C–mid-19C] to assess someone's character.

get someone's prat, to phr. [20C] (US) to irritate someone, to tease someone (cf. GET ON ONE'S ARSE). [PRAT n. (1)]

get someone's rattlie up, to phr. [20C] (Ulster) to infuriate, [dial. *rattlie*, a child's rattle]

get some pink, to phr. [1990s] (US) to have sexual intercourse (cf. PINK-EYE n.[2]). [note pornography trade jargon *pink*, the open vagina]

get some pussy, to phr. [1970s+] (US) of a male, to have sexual intercourse. [PUSSY n.[1] (1)]

get some rod, to phr. [1990s] (US campus) of a woman, to have sexual intercourse. [ROD n.[1]]

get some scrumptious, to phr. [1980s+] (US campus) usu. of a woman, to enjoy sexual relations with someone.

get some tail, to phr. [1970s+] (US) of a male, to have sexual intercourse. [TAIL n.[2]]

get/have something on one's brain/mind, to phr. [late 19C+] to be obsessed with.

get something on someone, to phr. [1920s+] (orig. US) to find out incriminating or otherwise negative information about someone, to gain an advantage over someone.

get someone/something straight, to phr. [1920s+] to explain to someone, to make things clear.

get somewhere v. [1930s+] to succeed, to gain one's desires.

get stoned v. [1950s+] **1** to become drunk. **2** to become intoxicated by a drug, usu. cannabis. [STONED]

get straight v.[1] [late 19C+] to overcome a temporary problem, usu. financial. [STRAIGHT adj.[1] (1)]

get straight v.[2] [1960s+] (US campus) to sober up, from either drink or drugs, esp. when overcoming an addiction. [STRAIGHT adj.[2]]

get stuck in v. [1940s+] **1** to begin, esp. of a meal or a job. **2** to fight.

get stuck into v. [1930s+] (orig. Aus./N.Z.) **1** to start a fight. **2** to start any form of activity; the implication is one of enthusiasm and activity. **3** to abuse verbally.

get stuffed! *excl.* [1940s+] a general excl. of dismissal (cf. GET FUCKED!).

get stupid v. [1990s] (US Black/teen) **1** to attend a party. **2** to become drunk or intoxicated by drugs.

getter n. [late 19C–1920s] (US Und.) a thief; thus *stone-getter*, a diamond thief.

get that across your chest! *excl.* [20C] an exhortation to start eating a dish.

get the air, to phr. [late 19C+] (US) to be dismissed or rejected, esp. in the context of a love affair (cf. GIVE THE AIR).

get the ambulance! *see* GET THE STRETCHER!

get the ass, to phr. [1970s+] (US Black/campus) to lose one's temper, to become annoyed. [abbr. GET THE RED ASS]

get the bass out of one's voice, to phr. [20C] (US prison) to stop acting aggressively. [one traditionally lowers one's voice when one is being verbally threatening]

get the belt, to phr. [1920s+] to be rejected, to be jilted. [BELT n.[1] (1)]

get the big one, to phr. [1920s] (US) to die.

get the bird/big bird, to phr. [early 19C+] **1** esp. theatrical use, to be jeered, mocked etc. **2** [late 19C+] to be dismissed, usu. from a job. [BIRD n.[8]; orig. 16C.; the hissing noise that geese, and an unappreciative audience, can make]

get the blue envelope, to *phr.* [1900s] (US) to be dismissed from one's job. [the packaging of a note of dismissal + BLUE *adj.*[1]]

get the boat, to *phr.* [mid-19C] to be sentenced to transportation overseas or a severe form of penal servitude.

get the bolt, to *phr.* [mid-late 19C] to be sentenced to penal servitude. [the *bolt* on one's cell door]

get the book, to *phr.* [1940s–50s] (prison) to become religious (cf. GET THE GLORY). [SE *book*, i.e. the Bible]

get the boot, to *phr.* [late 19C+] to be thrown out, both of a place or one's employment (cf. GET THE BOUNCE; GET THE BULLET; GET THE CANVAS; GET THE CHOP; GET THE EMPTY; GET THE FLICK; GET THE HOOF; GET THE KICK; GET THE ORDER OF THE BOOT; GET THE POKE; GET THE RUN; GET THE SACK; GET THE SHOOT; GET THE SLINGERS; GET THE SPEAR; GIVE THE BOOT). [one is 'kicked out']

get the bounce, to *phr.* [late 19C+] to be thrown out, both of a place or one's employment. [BOUNCE *n.*[4]]

get/put the breeze up, to *phr.* [1920s+] to worry, to disturb (cf. GET THE WIND UP).

get the bullet, to *phr.* [mid-19C+] to be thrown out, both of a place or of one's employment (cf. GET THE BOOT; SHAKE THE BULLET). [one is fig. 'shot']

get the bull's feather, to *phr.* [17C–early 19C] to be cuckolded, to be betrayed by one's lover or spouse (cf. HORN *n.*[4]). [phr. *a new feather made of an old horn*]

get the bum's rush, to *phr.* [late-19C+] (orig. US) to be thrown out, esp. of a saloon or place of entertainment. [BUM *n.*[3] + SE *rush*, a sudden onslaught; the origin of the phr. came in the saloons of late 19C New York where vagrants and other hungry people attempted to take advantage of the sometimes sumptuous free lunch counters, which were meant for drinkers only]

get/receive the canvas, to *phr.* [17C] to be dismissed from a job (cf. GET THE BOOT). [play on GET THE SACK, which was often made of canvas]

get the chop/chopper, to *phr.* [1940s+] **1** to be killed. **2** to be dismissed from one's job (cf. GIVE THE CHOP).

get the chuck, to *phr.* [late 19C+] to be dismissed, to be rejected (cf. GIVE THE CHUCK). [CHUCK *n.*]

get the chutes, to *phr.* [late 19C–1910s] (US) to be dropped, to be dismissed. [play on SE *parachute*]

get the cottonwood over, to *phr.* [19C] (US) to have an advantage over. [? the use of the cottonwood tree as an impromptu gallows]

get the dead wood/dead wood on, to *phr.* [mid-19C+] (US) to get the advantage of. [logging use, where a skilled axeman would cut a tree in such a way that he spared himself work by ensuring that any dead wood broke off by itself when the tree fell]

get/be handed the dirty end, to *phr.* [1920s+] to come off worst, to be treated unfairly.

get the dirty water off one's chest, to *phr.* [20C] to masturbate.

get the done, to *phr.* [20C] (W.I. teen) to be 'dropped' by a boy- or girlfriend; thus *give the done*, to end a relationship, to drop one's partner.

get the dope on, to *phr.* [20C] to find out about someone or something. [DOPE *n.*[3] (2)]

get the drawers, to *phr.* [20C] (US Black) to have sexual intercourse. [abbr. *get the drawers off*]

get the drop on, to *phr.* [mid-19C+] (orig. US) to obtain an (unfair) advantage over someone (cf. HAVE THE DROP ON). [DROP *n.*[2]]

get the elbow, to *phr.* [1970s+] to be rejected, to be dismissed. [ELBOW *n.*[3]]

get the empty, to *phr.* [late 19C] to be dismissed from one's job (cf. GET THE BOOT). [play on GET THE SACK, which is seen as empty of contents]

get the fat off, to *phr.* [20C] (Aus.) to relieve someone of their money, usu. by some form of trick or con-game. [the implication is that the victim can afford to lose, i.e. the excessiveness of SE *fat*]

get the flick, to *phr.* [1980s] (Aus.) to be dismissed from one's job (cf. GET THE BOOT). [a dismissive flick of the fingers]

get the fuck out!/get to fuck out! *excl.* [1950s+] **1** intensifier of 'go away!' (cf. FUCK OFF!). **2** intensifier of GET OUT OF HERE! and similar phr. of (joc.) disbelief.

get the fuck out my face! *excl.* [1990s] (US Black teen) go away!

get the g, to *phr.* [20C] (W.I.) to understand, to 'get the hang of'. [ety. unknown; ? the initial 'g' of *get*]

get the gate, to *phr.* [1910s+] (US) to be ejected, to be dismissed (cf. GIVE THE GATE).

get the g.b., to *phr.* [late 19C–1910s] (US) to be snubbed, to be ignored. [*get the* go *by* or grand *bounce*]

get the German soldier marching, to *phr.* [1980s+] to masturbate. [GERMAN HELMET]

get/have the gimmes, to *phr.* [1920s+] to be greedy, to be covetous. [SE *give me*]

get the glory, to *phr.* [1940s–50s] (prison) to become suddenly and fervently religious while serving a prison sentence (cf. GET THE BOOK).

get the glow, to *phr.* [late 19C–1900s] to blush.

get the goods on, to *phr.* [1940s+] (orig. US) to find out about, esp. to the subject's disadvantage (cf. HAVE THE GOODS ON). [GOODS *n.*[1]]

get the gooner, to *phr.* [1920s–30s] to be dismissed from a job (cf. GIVE THE GOONER). [SE *gone* or GONER]

get the gravel rash, to *phr.* [mid-19C] to be very drunk; thus *gravelled*, very drunk (cf. GRAVEL-GRINDER). [GRAVEL RASH]

get the gun, to *phr.* [1900s] (US) to die.

get the hang of, to *phr.* [mid-19C+] to work out, to learn the use of, to become familiar with. [orig. spec. to the use of tools]

get the hare's foot to lick, to *phr.* [19C] to get very little or nothing whatsoever. [the lack of meat on the hare's foot]

get the heck out of Dodge *see* GET THE HELL OUT OF DODGE.

get the heels on, to *phr.* [late 19C] (US) to succeed, to conquer. [the habit of sitting with one's feet proprietorially on a desk or table]

get the hell out of, to *phr.* [1910s+] (US campus) to leave, to depart, e.g. *if you don't want to stay here, then get the hell* ..., usu. with a place-name.

get the hell/heck out of Dodge, to *phr.* [1960s+] go away now! [the clichéd dialogue of a variety of Western films/TV series in which the 'baddie' is ordered, *Get the hell* ...]

get the hoof, to *phr.* [late 19C+] to be thrown out, both of a place or one's employment (cf. GET THE BOOT).

get the hook, to *phr.* [20C] (US) to be ejected. [the long pole or *hook* used to drag unpopular performers off stage; introduced in 1903 at Harry Minor's Bowery Theatre, New York City]

get the hot end of, to *phr.* [1900s] (US) to be victimized, to be given a hard time.

get the hump, to *phr.* [mid-19C+] **1** to be depressed, miserable. **2** to be over-sensitive or 'touchy' (cf. GET ONE'S HUMP UP). [HUMP *n.*[1]]

get the kick, to *phr.* [late 19C–1910s] to be dismissed from a job (cf. GET THE BOOT; GET THE KICK-OUT; GIVE THE KICK). [KICK *v.*[4] (2)]

get the knickers, to *phr.* [1930s+] (US prison) to get a life sentence (cf. KNICKERS AND STOCKINGS). [? play on NICK *n.*[7]/*n.*[8]]

get/take the knock, to *phr.* [late 19C–1910s] **1** to drink to excess. **2** to be dismissed from one's job.

get the lead, to *phr.* [19C] to be shot. [LEAD]

get the lead out/out of one's pants! *excl.* [1910s+] hurry up! stop dawdling! get on with it! [SE *lead* weighs one down]

get/know/have the length of one's foot, to *phr.* [late 16C–early 18C] to understand, to have worked out, to 'get the measure of'.

get/have the loan of, to *phr.* [20C] (Aus.) **1** to play a trick on. **2** to treat like a fool. [dial. *take the lend of*, to take advantage of, to cajole]

get the master over, to *phr.* [late 19C] to become superior, to act in a way superior to others.

get the message, to *phr.* [1950s+] to appreciate, to understand. [orig. jazz use, but now general]

get them *see* GET 'EM.

get them in *see* GET ONE IN v.[1].

get the miseries, to *phr.* [20C] **1** to be tetchy, to be irritated. **2** (US Black) to be in pain, to be ill.

get the mitten, to *phr.* [mid–late 19C] (US) to be turned down as a suitor (cf. GIVE THE MITTEN). [SE *mitten*, a glove; in this case the handshake is of farewell]

get the narkies on, to *phr.* [20C] to become domineering, to 'get on one's high horse'. [NARK n. (4)]

get the needle, to *phr.*[1] [mid-19C+] to be extremely annoyed. [NEEDLE n.[3]]

get the needle, to *phr.*[2] [mid-19C+] (gambling) to lose heavily. [SE *needle*, i.e. one is 'pricked']

get the net! *excl.* [1980s+] a joc., teasing comment aimed at someone whose behaviour is seen as strange or eccentric. [the image of the 'men in white coats' brandishing a net with which they capture the 'mad' person]

get the nips into, to *phr.* [1950s] (Aus.) to attempt to gain an advantage over someone. [SE *nip*, a pinch, a sharp bite]

get the order of the boot, to *phr.* [late 19C+] to be sacked from work (cf. GET THE BOOT). [a play on SE *Order of the Bath*]

get the picture, to *phr.* [1950s+] to understand, to appreciate.

get the pinchers into, to *phr.* [1920s] (N.Z.) to pressurize. [SE *pinch*]

get the pip, to *phr.* [late 19C+] to feel depressed, out of sorts, ill (cf. GIVE THE PIP). [PIP n.]

get the poke, to *phr.* [late 19C+] (Scot.) to be dismissed from one's job (cf. GET THE BOOT). [SE *poke*, a small bag or sack]

get the pricker, to *phr.* [1940s–60s] (Aus./ N.Z.) to get angry, to lose one's temper. [SE *pricker*, that which pricks or pierces]

get the rap, to *phr.* [1970s+] to be scolded, to be told off, to be blamed. [RAP n.[3] (1)]

get-there *n.* [19C+] (US) ambition, energy.

get there *v.* **1** [mid-19C+] of a man, to have sexual intercourse, esp. to deflower. **2** [late 19C+] (US) to attain a desired object, to be successful. **3** [late 19C+] to become intoxicated by drink or drugs. [fig. uses of SE]

get the red ass, to *phr.* [1960s+] (orig. US) to bear a grievance. [RED ARSE]

get there Eli/Ely, to *phr.* [19C] to do something well, to succeed in a notable manner (cf. GET THERE WITH BOTH FEET). [a racehorse named *Eli* or *Ely*]

get there in one *see* GET IT IN ONE.

get there with both feet, to *phr.* [19C+] (US) to do something well, to succeed in a notable manner.

get the run, to *phr.* [late 19C–1950s] to be dismissed from a job (cf. GET THE BOOT).

get the runaround, to *phr.* [1910s+] to be deceived, to be delayed, to be put off.

get the run on, to *phr.* [mid-19C] (US) to have at a disadvantage, to be in a position to laugh at.

get the sack, to *phr.* [mid-19C] **1** to be dismissed from a job

(cf. GET THE BOOT). **2** to be rejected by one's lover or sweetheart.

get the sads, to *phr.* [late 19C] to have 'a fit of the vapours', to become depressed. [SE *sad*]

get the shaft, to *phr.* [1950s+] (orig. US) **1** to treat unfairly or harshly. **2** to cheat, to deceive. **3** to take advantage of. **4** to slight or reject (cf. FUCK v.[2]; SHAFT v.). [SE *shaft*, a spear, a lance]

get the shillings ready, to *phr.* [late 19C] to get ready to hand out some money. [the mass of charities that took advantage of Queen Victoria's Diamond Jubilee in 1897, esp. the *Daily Telegraph*'s shilling lists, designed to help the London Hospital meet its debts]

get the shoot, to *phr.* [mid-19C–1900s] to be dismissed from a job (cf. GIVE THE SHOOT). [SE *shoot*]

get the shove, to *phr.* [late 19C+] to be dismissed from a job (cf. GIVE THE SHOVE). [SHOVE n.[2]]

get the show on the road, to *phr.* [1950s+] to start, to begin.

get the slingers, to *phr.* [1950s–60s] to be thrown out, to be dismissed from a job (cf. GET THE BOOT). [SE *sling*, to throw]

get the spear, to *phr.* [late 19C–1960s] (Aus.) to dismissed from a job (cf. GET THE BOOT).

get the spike, to *phr.* [late 19C] to be extremely annoyed (cf. GET THE NEEDLE).

get the spirit, to *phr.* [early 19C+] (US Black) **1** to become extremely religious. **2** to have an intense emotional experience.

get the stretcher!/ambulance! *excl.* [late 19C] an excl. used when seeing someone who is falling down drunk.

get/have the swap, to *phr.* [late 19C–1900s] to be dismissed from one's employment.

get the tom-tits, to *phr.* [1960s+] to become frightened. [rhy. sl. *tom-tits* = SHITS]

get the wind, to *phr.* [1970s+] (drugs) to smoke marijuana.

get the wind up, to *phr.* [1920s+] to become nervous. [abbr. *get the wind up one's trousers*]

get the works, to *phr.* [1920s+] (US prison) to receive a death sentence, to receive a very long sentence. [WORKS n.[2]]

get the wrong bull by the horns/tail, to *phr.* [late 18C+] to make a serious mistake (cf. GET THE WRONG PIG BY THE EAR; GET THE WRONG SOW BY THE EAR).

get/pull the wrong pig by the ear, to *phr.* [mid-16C–mid-17C] to make a mistake.

get the wrong sow by the ear, to *phr.* [late 18C+] to make a serious mistake, to get hold of the wrong person, to arrive at the wrong conclusion (cf. GET THE WRONG BULL BY THE HORNS).

get this! *excl.* [20C] now listen! this is amazing!

get through *v.* [1980s+] (drugs) to obtain drugs.

get through to *v.* [1930s+] to make oneself understood, esp. by someone who is 'slow on the uptake'.

getting any?/getting any lately? *phr.* [1940s+] (orig. Aus.) a popular greeting between men (cf. ANY). [the 'any' in question is, of course, sex]

getting much? *phr.* [1920s+] (US) a male-to-male greeting (cf. GETTING ANY?). [the 'much' is sex]

getting place, the *n.* [late 19C–1930s] (US Black) an abstract 'place' used in answer to a child's question, 'where did you get such-and-such?'

getting the mohawk *phr.* [1950s+] (US teen) building up one's irritation into a genuine bad temper (cf. INDIAN). [the stereotyping of Native Americans as unpredictably violent]

getting the job done *phr.* [1990s] masturbating.

get to *v.*[1] [late 19C] to start doing something. **2** [1910s+] (N.Z.) to attack physically. **3** [1920s+] to corrupt, to bribe, to influence (cf. REACH). **4** [1960s+] to effect, to influence emotionally, to worry. **5** [1960s+] to listen; thus *get to this*, listen to this. **6** [1960s+] to watch.

get to battle stations, to *phr.* [20C] to get ready, to prepare oneself.

get toco for yam, to *phr.* [20C] to be punished (cf. GIVE COCO FOR YAM). [TOCO; *for* in this context equals 'instead of']

get to first base, to *phr.* [1930s+] (orig. US) to make some preliminary headway, esp. in seduction. [FIRST BASE n.]

get to fuck!/get to fuck out of here!/it! *excl.* [1970s+] a harsh demand that one go away. [note synon. Scot. *awa' tae fuck!*]

get together *v.* **1** [1920s+] to act in concert, to help one another. **2** [1980s+] (US campus) to have sexual relations, with or without intercourse.

get to know yourself, to *phr.* [1990s] to masturbate.

get tongue-pie *v.* [1910s–20s] to receive a scolding. [TONGUE-PIE]

get tonked *v.* [1910s+] **1** to get punched. **2** to be completely defeated. [TONK v. (3)]

get to onest, to *phr.* [late 19C] (US) to run off, to escape. [SE *honest*; i.e. once one has escaped one is 'honest']

get tore in *v.* [1940s+] (Scot.) to fight vigorously. [TEAR INTO v. (2)]

get/go to the joint, to *phr.* [late 19C–1930s] (US) to come to the point, to achieve one's aim, esp. in a criminal context.

get tough/get tough with *v.* [1930s+] (orig. US) esp. of the criminals or the police, to act in an aggressive, harsh manner towards someone or something.

get under one's neck, to *phr.* [1930s+] (Aus.) to defeat or outwit someone. [horse-racing]

get under one's skin, to *phr.* (orig. US) **1** [20C] to annoy, to irritate. **2** [1920s+] to fascinate, esp. sexually. [insect infestation]

get-up *n.*[1] [mid-19C+] one's dress, esp. when special or 'best'.

get-up *n.*[2] [mid-19C+] (US) energy, spirit (cf. GET UP AND GO).

get-up *n.*[3] [1950s+] (US prison) the date of one's release as given by a parole board (cf. WAKE-UP). [the day on which one 'gets up' in prison but goes to bed free]

get-up *n.*[4] [1950s+] lies, a ruse, a subterfuge. [something 'got up' to allay suspicions or enquiries]

get up *v.*[1] [early 19C+] to penetrate sexually (whether by the vagina or anus) (cf. GET INTO v.[2]).

get up/up off *v.*[2] [1930s–50s] (US Black) **1** to experience the effects of a drug (cf. GET HIGH; GET OFF v.[8]). **2** to resist a way of doing things. **3** to give up something important or valuable.

get up! *excl.* [1980s+] (US campus) an expression of admiration.

get up and dust, to *phr.* [late 19C] (US) to run off quickly (cf. GET UP AND GO phr.). [DUST v.[3]]

get up and get/git, to *phr.* [19C+] (US) **1** to leave in a hurry, to move rapidly. **2** to act energetically.

get up and go *n.* [20C] (orig. US) energy, ambition, drive.

get up and go, to *phr.* [20C] (orig. US) to move fast, to get moving.

get up early/early in the morning, to *phr.* [18C+] to be clever, to be aware.

get up in a bunch, to *phr.* [1980s] (US) to get over-excited about something.

get up in someone's face, to *phr.* (orig. US Black) to argue, to confront face-to-face.

get up off the shoulder, to *phr.* [1990s] (US Black gang) to fight with one's fists (cf. GET ONE'S ASS ON ONE'S SHOULDERS; GET ONE'S HIPS UP ON ONE'S SHOULDERS).

get up on *v.* [1980s+] (US Black) to get excited by, to become interested in.

get up one's back, to *phr.* [1970s+] to annoy. [feline imagery]

get up someone's nose, to *phr.* [1930s+] (orig. US) to annoy, to irritate.

get up/go off/spin round on one's ear, to *phr.* [19C+] (US) to lose one's temper, to become violently angry, to get embarrassed.

get up steam, to *phr.* [late 19C+] to act energetically, to become interested in.

get up there *v.* [20C] (US) to grow old.

get up the yard! *excl.* [20C] (Irish) **1** an invitation to have sexual intercourse. **2** a general dismissive excl.

get up to *v.* [late 19C+] to perform an action, usu. mischievous, of dubious legality or in a sexual context.

get up to tricks, to *phr.* [19C] to work as a prostitute. [TRICK n.[4] (1) + play on SE]

get up with *v.* [1980s+] (US campus) **1** to have a romantic encounter. **2** to meet someone.

get weaving *v.* [1940s+] (orig. RAF) to stop wasting time, to hurry up.

get wet *v.*[1] **1** [late 19C–1940s] (Aus.) to lose one's temper, to become angry (cf. HAVE A WETTY). **2** [1920s–40s] (N.Z.) to get someone wet, to gain the upper hand over, to have at one's mercy. [? one gets wet with sweat]

get wet *v.*[2] [20C] **1** to murder, to kill. **2** to be wounded, to be stabbed. [KGB, CIA, MI6 jargon *get wet*, to kill; the blood that, figuratively at least, gets on one's hands]

get wise/wise to *v.* [late 19C+] (US) to become aware, to learn about. [WISE]

get with *v.* [1970s+] (orig. US Black) **1** to understand, to join in, to accept the party line, esp. as imper. *get with it!* join in, stop standing aside (cf. GET BEHIND v.[2]). **2** to have sexual intercourse. **3** to want sex with someone.

get with it! *excl.* [1990s] (US teen/campus) stop acting stupidly!

get with the program *phr.* [1980s+] (US campus) an admonition to act in a mature or responsible way. [the various '12-Step Programs', e.g. that promoted by Alcoholics Anonymous]

get wood *v.* [1990s] to achieve an erection. [WOOD n.[1] (2)]

get worked! *excl.* [20C] (Aus.) a general excl. of dismissal or contempt (cf. GET FUCKED!).

get you! *excl.* [1950s+] a teasing, mocking phr., used to deflate someone who is seen as showing off, overdressing etc.

get your brains/head examined, to *phr.* [1920s+] a general derisive phr. (cf. GO AND GET YOUR BRAINS EXAMINED).

gevalt *n.* [1930s+] (S.Afr.) a noisy argument, a row. [Yid. excl. *oi gevalt!*, ult. f. Ger. *Gewalt*, powers, force]

geycat *n.* [1930s] (US) a tramp's younger, homosexual companion. [ety. unknown; as the root of the homosexual use of GAY adj.[1] it is prob. a transitional development of SE *gay*, cheerful, happy + CAT n.[1] (5)]

geycat *v.* [1930s] (US) to loiter and chat in the street. [GEYCAT n.]

geyser *n.* [late 19C] a man. [var. on GEEZER n.[1]]

gezumph *see* GAZUMP.

gezunter *n.* [20C] a bettor. [rhy. sl. *gezunter* = PUNTER n.[1]]

g.f. *n.* [1920s–30s] (US) girl*f*riend. [abbr.]

g.f.o./g.f.u. *n.* [1940s+] (orig. milit.) a lazy, incompetent individual (cf. SNAFU phr.). [abbr. general *f*uck-*o*ff, general *f*uck-*u*p]

G-girl *n.* [1930s] (US) a female Government employee. [G-MAN]

G-guy *n.* [1930s] (US) an agent of the FBI. [Government employee = GUY n.[2] (1); var. on G-MAN]

g'hal *n.* [mid-19C+] (orig. US) a 'lad', a young rowdy. ['Irish' pron. of GAL n.; for background *see* B'HOY]

'Ghan *n.* [20C] (Aus.) an Af*ghan*. A term that is extended to cover Turks and Arabs; thus the *Ghan*, a train running between Port Augusta and Oodnadatta on the Central Australian Railway, its main passengers being Afghan camel teamsters, heading for their jobs. [abbr.]

ghanja *see* GANJA.

ghastly *adj.* [mid-19C+] of people, objects and circumstances, horrible, shocking, unpleasant, distasteful. [weak ext. of SE use]

G-heat *n.* [1930s–60s] (US) trouble from, or agents of, federal law enforcement agencies. [G-MAN + HEAT n.⁴]

ghee *n.*¹ *see* GUEE.

ghee *n.*² **1** [20C] (US) a man, a fellow (cf. GEE n.⁴). [SE *guy*]

ghee *n.*³ [1930s–60s] (US drugs) opium. [var. on GEE n.⁶; Spears (1986) suggests link to Hind. *ghee*, clarified butter, 'via China']

ghetto bird *n.* [1990s] (US Black) a helicopter. [the use of police surveillance helicopters above ghetto areas]

ghettoblaster/box/guitar *n.* [1980s+] a large stereo tape recorder-cum-radio carried by youths (cf. BEATBOX; BLASTER n.²; BOOFERBOX; BOOGIE BOX; BOOMBOX; BOX n.⁴; JAMBOX; JUNGLE BLASTER; SAN QUENTIN BRIEFCASE; THIRD-WORLD BRIEFCASE; THUNDERBOX; WOG BOX). [its orig. link to Black ghetto youths; thus derog. stereotyping]

ghetto star *n.* [1990s] (US gang) a leading gangster (cf. O.G.). [note STAR n.¹]

ghetto thing *n.* [1990s] (US Black) anything pertaining to Black cultural identity.

ghinny *n.* [late 19C+] (US) Italian (cf. GUINEA n.¹; GUINEA RED; GUINEA STINKER). [GINNY n.²]

ghinzo *see* GINZO.

ghoef *see* GOEF.

ghost *n.*¹ **1** [mid-19C] (US) a photograph. **2** [late 19C+] an individual who does the work on behalf of the person who is publicly credited (cf. GHOST JOB). **3** [1900s–20s] (US) a paymaster or cashier (cf. GHOST WALKS). **4** [1950s+] (US) a fictitious name created for fraudulent purposes. **5** [1960s+] (drugs) LSD (cf. A n.³). **6** [1970s+] (US Black) a White person.

ghost *n.*² [1960s] (Aus.) a creditor. [they give bad debtors an unpleasant fright when they appear]

ghost *n.*³ [1980s+] (US campus) an absentee, someone who has opted out of normal social life.

ghost *v.*¹ [late 19C+] (orig. US) to shadow, to follow surreptitiously.

ghost *v.*² [1970s+] (US/UK prison) to move a prisoner from one prison to another during the night, both departure and arrival taking place when the other prisoners are locked in their cells; thus *ghosting*, the late-night/early-hours transfer of prisoners from one prison to another with the intention of avoiding riots, frustrating external investigations etc. [such prisoners are 'spirited away']

ghost *v.*³ (US) **1** [1920s+] to write a book or article for someone else who takes the credit (cf. GHOST JOB). **2** [1980s+] to share lodgings or a hotel room with someone unbeknown to the proprietor.

ghostbusting *n.* [1980s+] (drugs) when taking a drug, usually heroin, cocaine or crack cocaine, searching for every particle of it. [play on 1984 film title *Ghostbusters*]

ghostface *n.* [1990s] (US/UK Black) a senior, experienced street hoodlum. [? the rap artist *Ghostface* Killa (Dennis Coles) of the Wu Tang Clan]

ghost job *n.* [1950s+] (US) material written by a ghost writer.

ghost move *v.* [1990s] (US Black) to move quickly.

ghosts *n.* [1990s] (drugs) white particles that resemble, but are not, crack cocaine (cf. GHOSTBUSTING).

ghost train *n.* [20C] (US Und.) the transfer of prisoners, under cover of night, from one gaol to another. [GHOST v.² + SE *train*]

ghost turds *n.* [1960s+] (US) fluff that collects under beds and furniture.

ghost walks, the *phr.* [early 19C+] (orig. theatre) a phr. indicating that weekly salaries are about to be given out. [the *ghost* is a joc. ref. to that of Hamlet's father]

ghoul *n.* (US) **1** [mid-19C–1920s] (police) a man who attempts

to blackmail a woman who is deceiving her husband. **2** [1930s+] a morgue attendant. **3** [1940s–70s] an unattractive looking woman.

ghoul *v. see* GOAL.

ghoulie *n.* [1960s+] (US) a low-budget horror film depicting excessive violence. [SE *ghoul*]

ghow *see* GOW n.².

g.i. *v.* [1940s+] to extinguish a cigarette before it is fully smoked, so that it can be re-lit later. [the practice of US soldiers or GIs]

gianluca *n.* [1990s] cocaine. [rhy. sl.; Italian footballer *Gianluca* Vialli (b.1965) = CHARLIE n.⁷ (1)]

giant-killer *n.* [1930s–40s] (US) whisky. [its illusory effects]

giant powder *n.* [late 19C–1940s] (US) a brand of dynamite. [the original tradename]

giare *see* MANGIARE.

g.i.b. *adj.* [1940s+] (orig. Aus./US) of a woman, *good in bed*. [abbr.]

gib *n.* [late 19C] a prison. [abbr. *Gibraltar*, orig. a convict settlement]

gibble-gabble *n.* [late 16C–mid-17C] nonsense. [GABBLE + redup.]

gibby *n.* [1960s+] (US Black) a reckless, foolhardy person. [Los Angeles use; ? dial. *gib*, a tom-cat]

gibface *n.* [mid–late 19C] an ugly person, esp. one with a heavy lower jaw. [dial. *gib*, a tom-cat]

giblets *n.* [mid-19C] **1** the intestines; thus an obese man.

gibroney *n.* [1960s] (US) an Italian. [? JIBONE]

gib teenuck *n.* [mid-19C+] a large vagina, lit. 'big cunt'. [backsl.]

gib teesurbs *n.* [mid-19C+] of a passing woman, big breasts. [backsl.]

gick *n.* **1** [1950s] (US) viscous matter (cf. GUCK). **2** [1990s] (Irish) anything disgusting, esp. excrement; thus *give one the gick*, to disgust. [var. on GUCK]

gick monster *n.* [1980s+] (drugs) a smoker of crack cocaine. [ety. unknown]

gicky *adj.* [1990s] (Irish) disgusting. [GICK n. (2)]

giddyap/giddyup *n.* [1920s–30s] (US) a racehorse. [SE *giddy-ap!* a sound made to urge a horse forward]

giddy goat *n.*¹ [20C] a fool. [abbr. PLAY THE GIDDY GOAT]

giddy goat *n.*² [1920s+] (Aus.) the tote, the totalizator. [rhy. sl.]

giddy gout *n.* [20C] (Aus.) a boy scout. [rhy. sl.; note popular juv. rhyme 'Giddy, giddy gout, your shirt is hanging out!']

giddy kipper *n.* [late 19C–1910s] a young man about town. [SE *giddy*, frivolous, excitable; thus essentially ludicrous persona]

giddy limit *n.* [late 19C+] the absolute extreme. [SE *giddy*, insane]

giddy whilk *see* WHILK.

giddyup *see* GIDDYAP.

giddy young whelk *n.* [late 19C–1910s] a young man about town (cf. GIDDY KIPPER). [SE *giddy*, frivolous, excitable + *whelp*, a child; *whilk* is a play on *whelp*]

gidget *see* GADGET.

gidgy *n.* [1950s–60s] (US) **1** an affectionate tickling under the chin or caressing, usu. directed at an infant. **2** any form of caressing. ['baby talk' *gidgy, gidgy, gidgy*]

gietus *see* GEETUS.

giffed *adj.* [1970s+] tipsy, drunk (cf. ABOUT RIGHT adj.¹). [abbr. *t.g.i.f.*, thank God it's Friday, i.e. time to stop work and go out for pleasure]

gift *n.* [early 19C+] anything seen as especially easy, requiring no effort to perform or obtain.

gifted *adj.* [1920s+] (Can.) homosexual (cf. SO). [an ironic use of the common suggestion that 'despite' being gay, so-and-so is 'very gifted']

gift of the gab

gift of the gab *n.* [late 18C+] articulacy, charm, persuasiveness. [orig. late 17C *gift of the gob*]

gift-of-the-sun *n.* [1980s+] (drugs) cocaine. [its origins in South America]

gift that keeps on giving, the *phr.* [1980s+] (US campus) venereal disease. [joc. use of an advertising slogan]

gig/gigg *n.*[1] **1** [late 17C–early 19C] the nose. **2** [mid–late 19C] the mouth. [? GIB-FACE]

gig *n.*[2] **1** [late 17C–18C] the female genitals. **2** [1920s+] (Aus.) a young woman. [? SE *gig*, a light carriage; thus something one 'rides']

gig *n.*[3] [late 17C–early 19C] a door. [GIGGER *n.*[1]]

gig *n.*[4] [mid–late 19C] a farthing. [? GRIG]

gig *n.*[5] [mid-19C–1910s] (US) a set of three numbers forming a bet in policy gambling.

gig *n.*[6] **1** [late 19C] one who wears spectacles. **2** [1920s+] (US) an eye (cf. GIG-LAMPS). **3** [1920s+] (Aus.) a look, a glance. [abbr. GIG-LAMPS]

gig/giggy *n.*[7] [20C] (Can.) the anus. [ety. unknown; ? link to GIG *n.*[2] + note late 17C *gig*, a hole in the ground for drying flax or gig]

gig *n.*[8] **1** [20C] (orig. US) business, state of affairs, occupation. **2** [1920s+] (orig. US) a musical performance at a particular venue. **3** [1950s+] (US teen) an event, a party. **4** [1950s+] (US Black) a jazz party or jam session. **5** [1950s+] (US Und.) a criminal job. **6** [1960s+] (US) one's special interest, practice or plan. **7** [1970s+] (US) a trick or swindle. **8** [1980s+] (US campus) a brief sexual entanglement (cf. ONE NIGHT STAND). [Lighter sees (1), and thus subseq. uses, as devel. of gambling use at GIG *n.*[5]]

gig *n.*[9] [1900s–40s] (US) a goading or gibing.

gig *n.*[10] **1** [1920s–30s] (US) a gigolo. **2** (Aus.) one who watches others working. **3** [1980s+] (US campus) a dedicated womanizer. [abbr. SE *gigolo*]

gig *n.*[11] **1** [1930s+] (Aus.) an informer. **2** [1930s+] (Aus.) a detective, an intrusive person. **3** [1950s+] (Aus. prison) a visitor, esp. a busybody. [abbr. FIZGIG *n.*[2]]

gig *n.*[12] [1940s+] (Aus.) a fool, an idiot. [UK dial. *gig*, a flighty fellow, a trifler]

gig *n.*[13] [1950s] (W.I.) a dumpling that resembles a top. [SE *gig*, a whipping top]

gig *v.*[1] [late 18C–early 19C] to hamstring (an animal). [ety. unknown]

gig *v.*[2] [late 19C+] (Aus.) to mock, to tease. **2** to irritate, to annoy. [? SE *gig*, to fool, to hoax]

gig *v.*[3] [1910s–60s] (US) to cheat or swindle. [? SE *gig*, to spear with a *gig*, a form of fish-spear]

gig/gig about *v.*[4] [1920s+] (Aus.) to look on when one ought to be working. [GIG *n.*[11]]

gig/gig around *v.*[5] [1930s+] **1** orig. music business, to play at a particular venue, to perform. **2** (US) to work, esp. at a number of short-lived jobs. [GIG *n.*[8] (2)]

gig *v.*[6] [1950s+] (Aus.) to look at, to stare. [GIG *n.*[10] (2)]

gig *v.*[7] [1980s+] (US campus) to have a single night's sex with someone. [GIG *n.*[8] (8)]

gigg *see* GIG *n.*[1].

gigger *n.*[1] [late 17C–18C] a door. [JIGGER *n.*[1]]

gigger *n.*[2] [late 19C] one who wears spectacles (cf. GIG-LAMPS). [the *locus classicus* was its use as the bespectacled Rudyard Kipling's schoolboy nickname and used as such for his fictional alter ego, 'Beetle', in *Stalky & Co.* (1899)]

giggle *n.* **1** [1940s–60s] a group of children or girls. **2** [1950s–60s] anything amusing, enjoyable, esp. if frowned upon.

giggle and titter *n.* [20C] bitter beer. [rhy. sl.]

gigglebox *n.* [1960s] (US) a girl or child who is prone to giggle (cf. GIGGLY-GUTS).

giggle dust *n.* [1990s] (US) (drugs) cocaine.

giggle/giggling academy *n.* [1940s+] (US) a psychiatric institution (cf. LAUGHING ACADEMY).

giggle-factory *n.* [1910s+] (Aus./N.Z.) a psychiatric institution.

giggle-grass *see* GIGGLEWEED.

giggle-house *n.* [20C] (Aus./ N.Z.) a psychiatric institution.

giggle-juice *n.* [1940s] (Aus.) alcohol (cf. GIGGLE-SOUP; GIGGLE-WATER).

gigglemug *n.* [late 19C] a face that is always smiling.

giggler/giglet/goglet *n.* [early 18C–19C] a young woman, esp. a prostitute (cf. GIGLOT). [SE *giggle* or ? GIG *n.*[2] (1)]

giggle-smoke *see* GIGGLEWEED.

giggle-soup *n.* [1930s–40s] (US) strong alcohol (cf. GIGGLE-JUICE).

gigglestick *n.*[1] **1** [20C] (US) the penis. [rhy. sl. (although not the rhy. sl. format of full phr.) = PRICK; the word may be equally placed among the various terms that equate penis with 'weapon']

gigglestick *n.*[2] **1** [1920s+] (Aus.) a swizzlestick, used for stirring cocktails. **2** [1930s+] cannabis (cf. GIGGLEWEED). [one of the drug's effects is to improve (or so it appears) one's sense of humour]

giggle-water *n.* [1920s+] (orig. US) **1** alcohol, esp. whisky or gin. **2** champagne (cf. BUBBLY WATER; GIGGLE-JUICE).

giggleweed/giggle-grass/giggle-smoke *n.* [1930s+] (drugs) cannabis (cf. GIGGLESTICK). [one of the drug's effects is to improve (or so it appears) one's sense of humour]

giggling academy *see* GIGGLE ACADEMY.

giggling-pin *n.* [20C] (US) the penis (cf. GIGGLESTICK *n.*[1]). [SE *pin* + the ability of the penis to make both partners 'giggle' during sex]

giggly-guts *n.* [1970s+] (US) a giggly person (cf. GIGGLEBOX). [SE *giggle* + -GUTS sfx.]

giggy *see* GIG *n.*[7].

gighead *n.* [1940s+] (Aus.) a fool, a simpleton. [GIG *n.*[12] + sfx. -HEAD (1)]

GI gin *n.* [1960s+] (orig. US milit.) cough syrup with a high alcohol content popular with addicts when heroin supplies are short.

gig-lamps *n.* [mid-19C+] spectacles; thus *gig-lamps*, the nickname of one who wears them (cf. GIGGER *n.*[2]). [SE *gig-lamps*, the two lights placed to either side of a gig or light carriage]

giglet *see* GIGGLER.

giglot *n.* [18C] a prostitute (cf. GIGGLER). [? GIG *n.*[2] (1)]

gigo *phr.* [1980s+] a phr. implying that one cannot expect poor input to produce, by some magic, excellent output. [computer jargon; abbr. *garbage in, garbage out*; pron. 'gyego']

gigolo *v.* [20C] (US Black) to steal a friend's lover, to cheat on one's lover or partner. [SE *gigolo*, a professional male dancing-partner or escort; a 'kept' man. Formed *c.*1920 as a masculine version of the French *gigole*, a tall, thin woman and hence a woman of the streets or public dance-halls. One 'who lives off women's money ... one of those incredible and pathetic male creatures, who, for ten francs would dance with any woman wishing to dance in the cafés, hotels, and restaurants of France' (*Woman's Home Companion*, 1922)]

gig on *v.* [20C] (US Black) to make a fool of, to deceive. [GIG *v.*[3]]

gigunda/gigundo/gigundus *adj.* [1970s] (US Campus) gigantic. [cod Latin]

GI haircut *n.* [20C] (US) a very short hair cut, imported into civilian life by former soldiers.

GI Jane *n.* [1940s+] (US) a female member of the armed forces (cf. GI JOE). [SAmE *GI* + generic use of *Jane*]

GI Joe *n.* [1930s+] (US) an American soldier (cf. GI JANE). [SAmE *GI* + generic use of *Joe*]

gilded moonshine *n.* [early 19C] sham IOUs or other bills of credit that have no actual financial backing.

gilhickie *n.* [1930s+] anything for which one has forgotten the name. [naut. use *gilguy*, a gadget + DOHICKEY]

gilks/gilkes/gilgks/gilkes for the jigger *n.* [17C] skeleton keys or picklock tools. [? GILT]

gill *n.*¹ [late 18C–1930s] **1** a fellow, a chap, esp. if gullible. **2** a general term for a man (cf. COVE n.¹; GLOAK).

gill *n.*² [late 18C+] (W.I.) one penny; then three-farthings (post-1969 value 2 cents).

gill-ale *n.* [late 17C–early 18C] ale used for medicinal purposes. [SE *gill*, a quarter of a pint, would be a suitably small measure]

gill-flirt *n.* [17C–19C] **1** a flirt, a tease. **2** a proud, vain woman (cf. FLIRT-GILL). [SE *gill*, a lass, a wench + *flirt*]

gillgadget *n.* [1930s+] (US) anything for which one has forgotten the name. [? naut. jargon *gilguy*, a gadget]

gillie potters *n.* [1950s+] **1** pig's trotters. **2** the human feet. [rhy. sl.; ult. proper name of comedian *Gillie Potter* (1887–1975)]

gilligan hitch *n.* [1930s–50s] (US Und.) a stranglehold. [US naut. jargon *gilligan hitch*, an out-of-the-ordinary or speedily tied knot]

gills *n.* **1** [late 18C+] the cheeks. **2** [19C] the corners of a stand-up shirt-collar (cf. STICK-UPS). [SE *gill*, a fish's breathing apparatus, situated on each side of the neck]

gilly *n.* [late 19C–1930s] (US) a yokel or simpleton (cf. GILL n.¹).

gillyflower *n.* [early 19C] a man who wore a yellow handkerchief round his neck. [SE *gillyflower*, the clove-pink (*Dianthus caryophyllus*)]

gilpin *n.*¹ [1930s] (US) a stupid or gullible person. [GILLY]

gilpin *n.*² *see* JOHN GILPIN.

gilt *n.*¹ (Und.) **1** [early 17C–late 18C] a burglar. **2** [late 17C–mid-19C] a skeleton key (cf. GILKS). [ety. unknown]

gilt *n.*² [late 17C–early 18C] 'a slut or light housewife' (B.E.). [? SE *gilt*, a young sow or female pig]

gilt *n.*³ [late 17C–19C] gold, money (cf. DELOG). [SE *gilt*, silver plate, ult. Ger. *gelt*, although this means gold]

gilt dubber *n.* [late 17C–18C] (Und.) an expert pick-lock (cf. RUM DUBBER). [GILT n.¹ (2) + DUBBER n.¹]

gilt-edged *adj.* [late 19C] first-rate, absolutely dependable. [lit. 'with gilded edges']

gilter *n.* [late 17C–mid-19C] a skeleton key. [GILT n.¹ (2)]

gilt-horn *n.* [18C] a complacent cuckold. [GILT n.² + HORN n.⁴; presumably he is paid for the 'use' of his wife]

gimbal-/gimber-jawed *adj.* [19C] very talkative. [SE *gimbal*, 'a contrivance by means of which articles for use at sea (esp. the compass and the chronometer) are suspended so as to keep a horizontal position. It usually consists of a pair of rings moving on pivots in such a way as to have a free motion in two directions at right angles, so as to counteract the motion of the vessel' (*OED*)]

gimcrack *n.* **1** [early 17C–late 18C] a fop, an affectedly showy person (cf. CRACK n.³; JEMMY; JIMCRACK; JIMCRACKER; JIM-DANDY). **2** [late 17C–18C] a pert young woman (cf. CRACK n.¹). **3** the female genitals. [SE *gimcrack*, a showy, but insubstantial trifle]

gi' me breeze *n.* [1950s+] (W.I.) ragged, torn, old work clothes (through which the wind blows).

gimix *n.* [1920s–40s] (US) a gadget. [SE *gimmicks*]

gimlet *n.* [1900s–30s] (Anglo-Irish.) a half-glass of whisky. [the *gimlet* cocktail, a mix of gin and lime juice, is SE]

gimme *n.* [1930s–60s] (Aus.) an acquisitive, greedy woman. [SE *give me*]

gimme *v.* [late 19C+] (orig. US) give me (cf. LEMME). [mispron. /sp. of SE *give me*]

gimme cap *n.* [20C] (US) a baseball cap carrying the logo of a sports team, manufacturer or other commercial institution. [SE *give me*; the practice of emblazoning objects with a logo

and offering them free in order to spread the brandname began with cigarette papers, which were given away free with the purchase of loose tobacco. Buyers would demand *Give me ... a pack of papers*, a cap or whatever is on offer]

gimme girl *n.* [1920s] (US) a greedy, materialistic young woman (cf. GIMME n.). [SE *give me* + *girl*]

gimmer *n.* [late 18C–late 19C] an old woman. [Scot. *gimmer*, a derog. term for a woman; ult. a young female sheep]

gimmick *n.* [1920s+] (orig. US) **1** a gadget; spec. a contrivance for dishonestly regulating a gambling game or an article used in a conjuring trick. **2** a tricky or ingenious device, gadget, idea, esp. one adopted for the purpose of attracting attention or publicity. **3** (US) a foolish person. **4** [1960s] (US) the penis. **5** [1960s+] (US drugs) a hypodermic needle or syringe. [ety. unknown, but note US journal *Words* (November 1936): 'The word gimac means "a gadget". It is an anagram of the word magic, and is used by magicians the same way as others use the word "thing-a-ma-bob".']

gimmick *v.* [1960s] (US) to adapt, to alter the function, typically of an electronic component. [GIMMICK n.]

gimmicks *n.* [1960s+] (drugs) the equipment used for injecting a narcotic drug (cf. BIZ n.²).

gimmie *n.* [1980s+] (drugs) a mixture of crack cocaine and marijuana. [? SE *give me*]

gimming *n.* [1940s] (US Black) staring at, gazing at. [GIMS]

gimp *n.*¹ [mid-19C+] **1** (US) courage, bravery, spirit (cf. GIMPY adj.¹). **2** (Irish) swagger, elegance. [Scot. *gimp*, slender, neat]

gimp *n.*² (US) **1** [1920s+] a crippled beggar or a limp (cf. GROPER n.¹; STUMPY n.²). **2** [1920s+] a fool. **3** [1980s+] (campus) a weakling, an inadequate. [? GAMMY n.]

gimp *v.* (US) **1** [1920s+] to limp. **2** [1960s] to cripple. **3** [1970s+] (campus) to ruin, to spoil. [GIMP n.²]

gimped in *adj.* [1970s+] (US campus) irregularly shaped, dented. [GIMP v. (3)]

gimped up *adj.* **1** [1940s+] (US) crippled, disabled. **2** [1970s+] (US campus) confused, at a loss, mixed up. [GIMP v.]

gimper *n.* **1** [1970s+] (US) a handicapped person. **2** [1980s+] (US) a news article of 'human interest' about death, injury or illness. [GIMP n.²]

gimp pram *n.* [1990s] a wheelchair. [GIMP n.² + SE *pram*]

gimp stick *n.* [1930s] (US) a crutch or walking-stick. [GIMP n.² + SE *stick*]

gimpy *n.*¹ [1920s+] a cripple. [GIMP n.²]

gimpy *n.*² [1970s] **1** a hippie, a 'longhair'. **2** (Aus.) a girlfriend. [ext. of GIMPY n.¹]

gimpy/gimpty *adj.*¹ [mid-19C] (US) spritely, brave, energetic. [GIMP n.¹]

gimpy *adj.*² **1** [1920s+] crippled. **2** [1970s] botched, second-rate. [GIMP n.²]

gims *n.* [1940s] (US Black) the eyes. [? misprint GLIM]

gin *n.*¹ **1** [19C+] a Black woman (cf. GIN-BANGER; GIN-BURGLAR; GIN-CUDDLER; GIN-JOCKEY; GIN-MASHER; GIN-SHEPHERD; GIN-STEALER). **2** [1960s+] (Aus.) any woman. [Dharuk *diyin*, woman; also (quite coincidentally) the abbr. for *Aborigine*]

gin *n.*² [1960s+] (US Black) a street fight; thus *gin time*, time to fight. [GIN v.]

gin *n.*³ [1980s+] (drugs) cocaine. [? play on SE *gin*, an engine; cocaine makes one 'work' faster]

gin *v.* [1930s–60s] (US Black) **1** to thrash, to beat. **2** to fight, to scuffle. **3** [1940s+] (US Black) to engage in sexual intercourse. [the threshing action of a cotton *gin*]

ginal/ginnal/jinal/jinnal *n.* [1920s+] (W.I./Jam.) a trickster, a confidence man. [an ironic play on SE *general*]

ginal/ginnal/jinal/jinnal *adj.* [1920s+] (W.I./Jam.) sharp, able to find a quick efficient solution to a problem; thus *ginal-ism* a philosophy that basically says that the end justifies any means, fair or foul. [? GINNAL n.]

gina la salsa n. [1950s+] (camp gay) an Italian male effeminate homosexual. [ext. of camp gay nickname *gina* + Sp. *salsa*, sauce]

gin and fog n. [1900s–40s] a hoarse or broken-down voice.

gin and French/It n. [20C] *gin and French* or *It*alian vermouth (cf. JINNIT n.[1]). [abbr.]

gin and fuck-it n. [1960s] a woman, usu. a foreign au pair or tourist, who can allegedly be seduced for the price of a drink in pubs where such young women congregate.

Gin and Gospel Gazette n. [mid-19C] the *Morning Advertiser* newspaper (cf. TAP-TUB). [its preoccupations]

gin and It *see* GIN AND FRENCH.

gin and Jag/Jaguar belt n. [1960s–70s] (Und.) **1** the wealthy Home Counties areas around London, esp. ripe for robbery; thus *gin and Jaguar bird*, a louche, raffish woman of this background, presumed, while probably married, not to be averse to something 'on the side'.

gin-and-tatters n. [late 19C] a heavy drinker whose clothes have been reduced to rags.

gin and tidy phr. [late 19C] neat. [JIM + SE *tidy*]

gin-banger n. [1910s] (Aus.) a man who sexually exploits Aborigine women (cf. GIN n.[1]). [GIN n.[1] + BANG v.[1] (2)]

gin barrel n. [mid-19C] (US) a drunk.

gin blossom n. [1930s] (US) a red nose or blotches resulting from drinking alcohol (cf. BRANDY BLOSSOM).

gin-bottle n. [late 19C] a 'dirty, abandoned, flabby, debased woman, generally over thirty; the victim of alcoholic abuse, within an ace of inevitable death' (Ware).

gin-bud n. [19C] a facial spot or ulcer resulting from excessive gin-drinking (cf. BRANDY BLOSSOM).

gin-burglar n. [1930s] (Aus.) a man who sexually exploits Aborigine women (cf. GIN n.[1]). [GIN n.[1] + *burglar*]

ginch n. [1950s+] **1** the vagina. **2** an attractive woman. **3** (gay) an attractive young man. [ety. unknown, but note dial. *ginch*, a small piece]

ginchy adj. [1950s+] attractive, sexy. [GINCH + sfx. -*y*]

gin-crawl n. [late 19C] a tour of public houses for the purpose of drinking a series of gins (cf. PUB-CRAWL).

gin-cuddler/-dozzler n. [1900s–10s] (Aus.) a man who sexually exploits Aborigine women (cf. GIN n.[1]). [GIN n.[1] + SE *cuddler/dozzler*, ety. unknown; ? SE *dazzle* or DO v.[2] (4)]

ging n. [20C] (Aus.) a catapult. [it 'gingers up' its targets]

gingambobs n. [late 18C–19C] **1** toys, baubles. **2** the testicles (cf. THINGUMBOBS). [SE *jiggumbob*]

ginge minge n. [1990s] ginger female pubic hair. [abbr. SE *ginger* + MINGE]

ginger n.[1] **1** [late 18C–mid-19C] a cock with reddish plumage. **2** [late 19C+] a red-haired or sandy-haired person.

ginger n.[2] [mid–late 19C] **1** high spirits, verve, vigour. **2** a showy, fast horse.

ginger/ginger beer n.[3] [1920s+] a male homosexual. [rhy. sl. *ginger beer* = QUEER n.[1]]

ginger n.[4] [1940s+] (Aus. juv.) a catapult. [for ety. *see* GING]

ginger/ginger girl/gingerer n.[5] [1940s+] (Aus.) **1** a prostitute who robs her customer of his wallet (cf. MURPHY GAME). **2** the act of robbing a prostitute's client; thus *gingering joint*, a brothel where such practices are common. [? back-form. of SE *gingerly*, with extreme caution, i.e. the caution necessary to effect the theft]

ginger v. [1930s+] (Aus.) of a prostitute, to rob a client. [GINGER n.[5]]

ginger ale n. [20C] **1** a gaol. **2** (N.Z.) bail. [rhy. sl.]

ginger beer n.[1] [late 19C] (Aus.) euph. for an alcoholic drink.

ginger beer n.[2] *see* GINGER n.[3].

ginger blue! excl. [late 19C] (US) an excl. used to mock one who is seen as behaving in a socially unacceptable way.

gingerbread n.[1] *see* GINGER-CAKE.

gingerbread n.[2] [late 17C–mid-19C] money; thus *have the gingerbread*, to be rich (cf. DELOG). [the gold colour]

gingerbread-office n. [17C] a privy. [the colour of excrement/urine]

gingerbread-trap n. [mid-19C] the mouth.

ginger-cake/gingerbread n. [19C+] (US) a mulatto. [the ginger-toned shade of the person's skin]

gingerer/ginger girl *see* GINGER n.[5].

ginger-hackled adj. [late 18C] red-haired. [cock-fighting jargon, *ginger*, a red cock]

ginger-nob n. [20C] a red-headed person.

ginger-peachy adj. [1950s–70s] (US) usu. ironic use, splendid.

ginger-pop n. [late 19C] a policeman. [rhy. sl. *ginger pop* = COP n.[1] (1)]

gingertown n. [19C–1930s] (US Black) the Black section of a town or city. [GINGER-CAKE]

ginger up v. [mid–late 19C] to enliven, to put spirit into. [SE f. 1890; f. the 18C technique of placing ginger in a horse's anus to make it more lively]

gingham n. [mid–late 19C] an umbrella, esp. one that is covered in gingham cloth.

gingleboy n. [19C] **1** a sovereign (£1 sterling). **2** any gold coin. [the noise it makes in one's pocket]

ginhead n. [1920s+] (US) a gin drinker. [SE *gin* + sfx. -HEAD (2)]

gin her up v. [late 19C] (US) to work hard, to infuse with energy. [SE *gin*, engine or abbr. GINGER UP]

gin-hunter *see* GIN-MASHER.

ginicomtwig v. [late 16C–early 17C] to have sexual intercourse (cf. THINGUMIBOB). [like THINGUMIBOB it could also mean a 'nameless item' and is thus also a euph.]

ginj v. [1940s] (W.I.) to fill with lies. [dial. *ginj*, to strangle, using a piece of wire; ult. fishing use *ginj*, to protect the line near the hook by twisting a piece of wire around it; thus, in turn, SE synon. *gange*]

gin-jockey n. [1950s+] (Aus.) a White man who enjoys sexual relations with Aborigine women (cf. GIN n.[1]). [GIN n.[1] + SE *jockey*]

gink n.[1] **1** [1910s+] (orig. US) a useless, stupid person. **2** [1910s+] (orig. US) a peasant. **3** [1940s+] (US) an East Asian (cf. CHING n.[1]). [? link to Scot. *gink*, trick]

gink n.[2] [1950s+] (Aus.) a look, a glance. [? GIG n.[10]]

gin ken n. [late 18C–mid-19C] a gin shop. [SE *gin* + KEN n.[1]]

ginky adj. [1960s–70s] (US) unfashionable or stupid looking. [GINK n.[1] (1)]

gin lane n. [mid-19C] **1** the mouth. **2** the throat (cf. BEER STREET). [presumably acknowledging William Hogarth's celebrated engraving of 1751]

gin-masher/-hunter n. [1900s–10s] (Aus.) a man who sexually exploits Aborigine women (cf. GIN n.[1]). [GIN n.[1] + MASHER]

gin-mill n. [mid-19C+] (US) a bar or night-club, orig. a speakeasy specializing in cheap, and probably adulterated, liquor (cf. BEER MILL; DRUNKERY). [SE *gin* + *mill* + pun on *gin*, a type of mill]

ginnal *see* GINAL.

ginned up adj.[1] [early 19C; 20C] drunk, tipsy (cf. ALED UP). [SE *gin*]

ginned up adj.[2] [1920s] (US) dressed up. [ety. unknown; ? GINGER UP or the image of one who frequents 'gin palaces']

ginney *see* GINNY n.[2].

ginnified adj. [late 19C] intoxicated by gin, or any other liquor.

ginning-up n. [1960s+] (Can.) a scolding, a telling-off. [fig. use of GIN v.]

ginny n.[1] [late 17C–18C] 'an instrument to lift up a Grate, the better to Steal what is in the window' (B.E.). [JEMMY, but note SE gin, engine, machine + dial. ginny, a simple form of crane]

ginny/ginney n.² [1900s–30s] (US Black) anyone with dark skin (cf. GHINNY). [? GUINEA n.¹]

ginny n.³ [1980s] (US Black) the vagina. [abbr.]

ginny adj. **1** [late 19C] of the liver or kidneys, adversely affected by excessive gin drinking. **2** [20C] very keen on gin. **3** [1920s] (US) tipsy. [SE gin]

ginny/guinea/jimmy gall n. [1900s–50s] (US Black) anywhere considered as far away, unpleasant and culturally alien (cf. BEE-LUTHER-HATCHEE). [proper name Guinea, a region in West Africa]

ginormous adj. [1940s+] incomparably huge. [orig. RAF sl. great + immense or giant + enormous]

gin-palace see GIN-TRAP.

gin-shepherd n. [20C] (Aus.) a White man who attempts to prevent miscegenation between his peers and Aborigine women. [GIN n.¹ + SE shepherd]

gin-shop/-sling see GIN-TRAP.

gin-slinger n. [late 19C] (US) a bartender.

gin-soak n. [1930s+] (US) an alcoholic, a gin-drinker. [SE gin + SOAK n.]

gin-spinner n. [late 18C–late 19C] **1** a distiller. **2** a dealer in spirits (cf. ALE-SPINNER). **3** a wine-vault.

gin-stealer n. [1920s] (Aus.) a man who sexually exploits Aborigine women. [GIN n.¹ + SE stealer]

gin-trap/-palace/-shop/-sling n. [early 19C] the mouth.

gin up v.¹ (US) [late 19C] to drink alcohol.

gin up v.² [1970s+] (US) to stir up, to enliven, to make ready. [GIN v.]

ginzo/ghinzo n. [1930s+] (US) **1** a derog. term for an Italian person or their language (cf. GHINNY). **2** any worthless person. [GUINEA n.¹]

gip see GYP.

gipe/gype n. [20C] (Ulster) **1** a fool. **2** a clumsy, awkward person. **3** a person with long legs. **4** a foolish young woman. [Scot. gipe, an awkward person, a fool]

gippo see GYPO.

gippy n. **1** [late 19C+] an Egyptian, esp. an Egyptian soldier. **2** [1910s] a gypsy. **3** [1920s] an Egyptian cigarette.

gippy tummy see GYPPY TUMMY.

gipsy and all combs. see GYPSY.

gipsy n. **1** [18C] a hussy. **2** [19C] a term of address to a woman, esp. one with a dark, i.e. 'gypsy', complexion.

giraffe v. [mid-19C] (US) to hoodwink; thus come/play the giraffe over, to fool someone. [US milit. giraffe, a form of game]

girl n.¹ **1** [late 18C+] one's sweetheart or girlfriend, esp. as best girl. **2** [late 18C–late 19C] a street-walking prostitute (cf. GIRL ABOUT TOWN). **3** [early 19C+] a mistress. **4** [19C+] (US) any Black woman, irrespective of age. **5** [1930s+] a male homosexual prostitute (cf. BOY n.⁶). **6** [1950s–60s] a queen of any suit in cards.

girl n.² [20C] (US Black) a general form of address between two women, neither of whom need, chronologically, be a girl (cf. MAN). **2** [1900s–20s] (US) used in direct address to a man, without homosexual implication.

girl n.³ (drugs) **1** [1940s+] cocaine (cf. BOY n.⁵). **2** [1970s+] heroin (cf. RED CHICKEN).

girl abductor n. [late 19C–1910s] (Aus.) a tram conductor. [rhy. sl.]

girl about town n. [19C] a streetwalking prostitute.

girl and boy n. **1** [mid-19C] a saveloy. **2** [20C] a toy. [rhy. sl.]

girl-boy n. (US) **1** [late 19C+] a feminine young man, an effeminate homosexual boy (cf. GAL-BOY). **2** [1960s+] (prison) a heterosexual prisoner engaging in homosexual acts.

girl-catcher n. [19C] the penis (cf. GIRLOMETER).

girlery n. [19C] a brothel (cf. BANGING-SHOP). [SE girl + sfx. -ery, the place where an occupation is carried on]

girlesk n. [1940s] (US) a show featuring striptease women. [SE girl + burlesque]

girl/gal Friday n. [1930s+] (orig. US) a female secretary or personal assistant. [Man Friday, Crusoe's servant in Daniel Defoe's Robinson Crusoe (1719) and thus fig. a male assistant]

girlfriend n.¹ **1** [1950s+] (S.Afr. Und.) the male lover of another prisoner. **2** [1980s+] a form of address between lesbians, not necessarily in a relationship. **3** [1980s+] a form of address between gay men.

girlfriend n.² [1980s] (US Black) cocaine. [GIRL n.³]

girl-getter n. [late 19C–1900s] an effeminate male. [? girl-begetter, an effeminate man would be unable to produce 'macho' boys]

girlie adj. **1** [late 19C+] a little girl, usu. as term of endearment. **2** [1920s+] (orig. US) use of a young woman employed in some form of the sex industry; thus girlie-magazine, a pin-up magazine; girlie-show, a strip show; girlie bar, a bar or 'nightclub' at which the hostesses may double as prostitutes.

girlometer n. [mid–late 19C] the penis (cf. GIRL-CATCHER).

girls, the n. [early 19C+] a generic term for prostitutes considered as a group.

girls and boys n. [20C] noise. [rhy. sl.]

girls are bandy at Urandangie, the phr. [1960s+] (Aus.) a phr. used to denote an unsatisfactory situation (cf. GOT THE ARSE AT BULLI PASS; IN JAIL AT INNISFAIL; THERE'S NO WORK IN BOURKE). [assonance]

girl's blouse see BIG GIRL'S BLOUSE.

girl-shop n. [late 19C] a brothel (cf. BANGING-SHOP).

girl show n. [late 19C] a ballet or review, usu. featuring chorus girls in revealing costumes (cf. LEG SHOW).

girls together/all girls together n. [1930s+] of a woman, on terms of close friendship with another woman or women.

girl-trap n. [late 19C] a dedicated womanizer.

GIs/GI trots n.¹ [20C] (US) diarrhoea; thus the GI pill, a pill designed to combat the malady (cf. APPLE-BLOSSOM TWO-STEP). [i.e. the food poisoning to which soldiers posted abroad might be susceptible]

GIs n.² [20C] (US prison) prison-made cigarettes, in a plain box with no brandname (cf. G n.⁵; PREMIUMS). [G.I., Government Issue]

gism see JISM.

gismo see GIZMO.

gissum see JISM.

git n. [1940s+] a fool, a worthless person. [GET n.¹]

git! excl. [mid-19C+] (US) go away! (cf. GET v.¹). [SE get away]

gitbox n. [1930s+] (US) a guitar (cf. GITFIDDLE). [orig. jazz jargon]

gitch n. [1990s] (Can.) male underpants. [ety. unknown; ? link to SE breech(es)]

git-down time n. [1950s+] (US) the start of a prostitute's working 'day', when she gets down to business.

git-'em-up guy n. [1920s–30s] a hold-up man, a robber. [his demand get your hands up!]

gitfiddle n. [1930s+] (US) a guitar (cf. GITBOX). [git (get) your fiddle and play]

git-/get-go n. [1960s+] (orig. US Black) the beginning, esp. in phr. from the git-go, from the beginning. [SE get going]

gitlet n. [20C] (US Black) an illegitimate child. [SE get + dimin. sfx. -let]

GI trots see GIS.

gitty-gap n. [1970s+] (US campus) a thing. [ety. unknown; ? nonsense word, like the synon. THINGUMIBOB]

give v.¹ [mid-19C+] to allow someone a specified, limited period of time, e.g. I'll give you 10 minutes.

give *v.*[2] **1** [late 19C+] to impart information, esp. in dismissive, sceptical phr. *what are you giving me?* or *don't give me that.* **2** [1930s+] (US) of a young woman, to be willing to engage in sexual intercourse; thus *to give out.* **3** [1950s+] (US) to give up, to surrender.

give *v.*[3] [20C] used as a reprimand in angry retorts, to indicate one's displeasure at the previous statement e.g. *I'll give you 'forgot'.*

give! *excl.* [late 19C+] (orig. US) explain! confess!

give a belly, to *phr.* [20C] (W.I.) to make a woman pregnant.

give a bit of hard for a bit of soft *see* GIVE HARD FOR SOFT.

give a bit/a piece of one's mind, to *phr.* [mid-19C+] to scold, to reprimand, to tell off.

give a black eye, to *phr.* [19C] to make inroads into, to finish, usu. of food or drink; thus *give the jelly and jam a black eye* (cf. GIVE A BOTTLE A BLACK EYE; GIVE SOMEONE A BLACK EYE). [fig. 'hurting' of the food or drink]

give a blow, to *phr.* [1960s+] (drugs) to blow marijuana smoke directly from the cigarette into someone else's mouth, achieved by reversing the joint in one's own mouth and blowing (cf. SHOTGUN v.). [abbr. BLOWBACK n.]

give a body, to *phr.* [1960s+] (Und.) to inform, to betray the names of one's criminal associates, usu. as exhortation, *Go on, John, give us a body (and we'll be kinder to you).*

give a bone *see* FLAG A BONE.

give a bottle a black eye, to *phr.* [late 18C] to drink a bottle almost to the bottom (cf. CRACK A BOTTLE; CRACK A TUBE; CRUSH A BOTTLE; GIVE A BLACK EYE; HIT THE BOOZE; HIT THE BOTTLE; HIT THE JUG; HIT THE SAUCE).

give absence without leave, to *phr.* [early 19C] to dismiss from employment. [play on milit. use]

give a cat's ass, to *phr.* [1990s] (US) to care about someone or something, usu. in neg. (cf. GIVE A DAMN; GIVE A FUCK; GIVE A SHIT).

give a curtain lecture/sermon, to *phr.* [late 17C–18C] for a wife to reprimand her husband after they have gone to bed (cf. CURTAIN LECTURE; GIVE A JUNIPER LECTURE). [the curtains in question are those of the four-poster bed]

give a damn, to *phr.* [mid-18C+] to care, usu. in neg. (cf. GIVE A CAT'S ASS).

give a dig about, to *phr.* [1910s–20s] to mock, to tease. [SE *dig*, a poke, a jab]

give a dusty answer, to *phr.* [20C] to give an unpleasant, intolerant response (cf. GET A DUSTY ANSWER). [DUSTY adj.[1]]

give a fair spin, to *phr.* [mid-19C+] to treat fairly, to give a reasonable chance (cf. GET A FAIR SPIN). [the spin of a coin]

give a flying fuck *see* GIVE A FUCK.

give a for instance, to *phr.* [1950s+] (orig. US) to give an example.

give a fourpenny one, to *phr.* [1930s+] to dole out physical harm, to beat someone up, spec. to hit them in the face (cf. GET A FOURPENNY ONE). [FOURPENNY ONE]

give a fuck/flying fuck/rusty fuck/two fucks, to *phr.* [1950s+] (orig. US) to care about, to be concerned, usu. in neg. use (cf. GIVE A CAT'S ASS).

give-a-fuck/-shit *n.* [1970s+] (US) the desire to do something, the state of being motivated towards, enthusiastic for.

give a green gown, to *phr.* [late 16C–early 19C] to have sex outdoors, possibly involving the loss of the woman's virginity (cf. GREENS n.[2]). [pun on SE *green*, with its general meanings of both countryside and innocence + the green stains that come from rolling on the grass]

give a gudgeon *see* GAPE FOR GUDGEONS.

give/lend a hole to hide it in, to *phr.* [late 19C+] of a woman, to permit sexual intercourse.

give a hot poultice for the Irish toothache, to *phr.* [19C] from a woman's point of view, to have sexual intercourse (cf.

GIVE JUICE FOR JELLY; GIVE MUTTON FOR BEEF; GIVE SOFT FOR HARD). [SE *hot poultice* + IRISH TOOTACHE]

give a jacket, to *phr.* [20C] (W.I./Jam.) for a married woman to conceive and bear a child by her lover and pass it off to her husband as his. [JACKET n.[1]]

give a juniper-/jiniper-lecture, to *phr.* [late 17C–18C] to tell off, to scold (cf. GIVE A CURTAIN-LECTURE). [the sharpness of the juniper-berry]

give aleck *v.* [mid-19C] (US) to thrash, to beat. [? pun on GIVE A LICK WITH THE ROUGH SIDE …]

give a leg-up, to *phr.* [late 19C+] to help someone over an obstacle, wall etc, both physical and fig.

give a lick with the rough side of one's tongue, to *phr.* [19C] to attack verbally. [pun on SE *lick*, a blow/*lick*, an act of licking]

give a little leg, to *phr.* [1960s–70s] to confuse, to tell tales. [var. on PULL SOMEONE'S LEG]

give and take *n.* [mid-19C+] **1** a cake. **2** a bundle of notes. [rhy. sl.; (2) is fig. use of (1), i.e. a 'cake' of notes]

give a packing-penny, to *phr.* [late 16C–late 18C] to dismiss, to 'send packing'.

give a pair of gloves, to *phr.* [late 18C] to give someone a bribe.

give a perm, to *phr.* [1980s+] (US campus) to perform oral sex. [SE *permanent wave*, a hairstyle + pun on BLOW JOB]

give a permanent wave, to *phr.* [20C] (US prison) to execute in the electric chair. [the effects of the electricity on the hair]

give a rusty fuck *see* GIVE A FUCK.

give a seeing-to, to *phr.* [20C] **1** to have sexual intercourse. **2** to beat up.

give a shit, to *phr.* [1970s+] **1** to care, usu. in neg. e.g. *I couldn't give a shit.* **2** (US) to not care, i.e. *I could give a shit* (cf. GIVE A CAT'S ASS). [(2) US use is usu. in the pos., with the neg. meaning]

give-a-shit *see* GIVE-A-FUCK.

give a shout, to *phr.* [20C] **1** to get in touch with. **2** (W.I./US) to pay a casual visit.

give a/sing a kyrie eleison to, to *phr.* [late 16C–early 17C] to scold, to 'tell off'. [Gk. *kyrie eleison*, Lord, have mercy]

give a squeeze, to *phr.* [1970s+] (Und.) to give a chance to. [? SE *squeeze*, i.e. the image of giving the other person an encouraging hug]

give a stuff, to *phr.* [1970s+] (Aus./N.Z.) to care, usu. in neg. (cf. GIVE A SHIT). [STUFF v.[3]; i.e. euph. for GIVE A FUCK]

give attitude/'tude *see* THROW ATTITUDE.

give a tumble, to *phr.* **1** [20C] to have sexual intercourse. **2** [1920s+] (US) to recognize, to acknowledge. **3** [1970s+] to try out, to experiment.

give away *v.* **1** [late 19C+] to betray. **2** [1940s+] (Aus.) to give up, to abandon, to forsake.

give-away *n.*[1] [late 19C+] a betrayal of a secret. [GIVE AWAY v. (1)]

give-away *n.*[2] [1930s+] (US) free samples and prizes.

give-away *adj.* [late 19C+] obvious, mistakable. [GIVE-AWAY n.[1]]

give-away cue *n.* [late 19C] a clandestine betrayal of a secret. [GIVE-AWAY n.[1]]

give a wigging, to *phr.* [early 19C] to reprimand, to scold. [WIG v.[1]]

give beans *v.* [late 19C+] (orig. US) to scold, to tell off (cf. BEANER n.[1]).

give beard/head for the washing, to *phr.* [17C] to give up without a struggle, to acquiesce tamely.

give bed-service, to *phr.* [20C] (W.I./Bdos.) for a woman to take part in a sexual relationship in return for material support.

give beef *see* CRY BEEF.

give bellows v. [20C] to get rid of, to send away (cf. BELLOWSED). [BELLOWS; the image is of blowing the unwanted person away]

give bondi/boondie/bundi/bundy v. [late 19C–1910s] (Aus.) to attack savagely. [SE *bondi*, a heavy Aboriginal club]

give bossooks v. [late 19C–1920s] to take revenge, usu. in threatening phr., e.g. *I'll give them*) *bossooks*. [? dial. *bossock*, to toss, to tumble]

give both barrels, to phr. [1950s] (US) to act or deal with in a very positive, uncompromising manner.

give brusher v. [late 19C+] (Aus.) **1** to obtain or borrow something (esp. money) and fail to return it. **2** to abandon a task. [BRUSH-OFF n.]

give bundi/bundy see GIVE BONDI.

give chi-ike with the chill off, to phr. [mid–late 19C] to scold, to reprimand. [CHI-IKE v. + *with the chill off*, i.e. HOT adj.[1]]

give coco for yam, to phr. [mid-19C] (W.I.) to give as good as one gets (cf. GET TOCO FOR YAM). [SE *coco(nut)* + *yam*]

give cold pig, to phr. [mid-19C] a 'joke' played on a late riser, the bedclothes are pulled back and water is poured on the sleeper (cf. CHOKING PIE). [cf. naut. jargon *cold norwester*, a bucket of seawater poured over a new recruit as an initiation ceremony]

give cone v. [1980s] (US teen) to fellate. [the image of licking an ice-cream cone]

give cuts v. [1980s+] (US campus) to let someone into a queue or line; thus *have cuts*, to get into the queue in a favourable position. [CUT IN]

give face v. [1960s+] (US) of either sex, to perform oral intercourse (cf. GIVE HEAD). [SE *give* + FACE n.[2] (12)]

give five/give someone five v. [1950s+] (orig. US) to slap hands in order to seal a bargain or to greet a friend; occas. ext. as *give ten*, to slap both hands (cf. SLAP FIVE). [the *five* fingers]

give France v. [20C] (W.I.) **1** to quarrel very bitterly. **2** to cause a good deal of trouble for someone. [FRANCE]

give gammon, to phr. [early 18C] (Und.) to stand next to a person while an accomplice picks their pocket (cf. KEEP IN GAMMON). [GAMMON v.]

give gas v. [mid-19C] (US) to scold, verbally abuse or ridicule (cf. TAKE GAS). [GAS n.[1] (1)]

give gip see GIVE GYP.

give good v.[1] [20C] (W.I.) to berate, to scold severely, to tell off.

give good v.[2] [1970s+] (US) used in phr. where a singular n. is used as a generic, e.g. *give good/great spiel*, to be notable for talking. [on model of orig. comb. GIVE HEAD]

give green rats, to phr. [19C] to slander someone in their absence, to backbite. [the link of *green* to envy/jealousy]

give gyp/gip, to v. [20C] to cause pain or trouble for someone. [GYP v.]

give haemorrhoids v. [1980s+] (US campus) to bother, to pester, to irritate. [a pun on PAIN IN THE ASS]

give hard for soft/a bit of hard for a bit of soft, to phr. [late 19C] from a man's point of view, to have sexual intercourse (cf. GIVE SOFT FOR HARD). [SE *bit* + HARD n.[3]/SE *hard* + SE *soft*]

give head v. [1940s+] (orig. US) to perform oral intercourse, usu. to fellate. [HEAD n.[8]]

give head for the washing see GIVE BEARD FOR THE WASHING.

give hell v. **1** [mid-19C+] to give someone a 'hard time', to scold severely. **2** [mid-19C+] (US) to hurt, to inflict punishment on.

give her a length, to phr. [1940s+] of a man, to have sexual intercourse (cf. SLIP HER A LENGTH).

give her a tail, to phr. [1960s+] of a man, to have sexual intercourse. [TAIL n.[1] (1)]

give her one v. [late 19C+] **1** to have sexual intercourse. **2** to kiss.

give horns v. [19C+] to cuckold (cf. HORNIFY). [HORNS]

give horrors v. [20C] (W.I.) to annoy, to infuriate, to disgust.

give hot beef see CRY BEEF.

give it a bone! excl. [late 19C+] shut up! stop talking! (cf. GIVE IT A REST!) [the silencing of a dog by giving it a bone; 20C use mainly N.Z.]

give it a burl, to phr. [1910s+] (Aus.) to give something a try (cf. BIRL). [Scot. *birl*, to spin, to twist]

give it a fly, to phr. [1910s+] (Aus.) to give something a try (cf. FLY A KITE phr.[2]; GIVE IT A BURL).

give it a go, to phr. [1910s+] (orig. Aus./N.Z.) to make an attempt, to give it a try.

give it all that, to phr. [1990s] to boast, to show off. [ALL THAT n.[2]]

give it an airing, to phr. [late 19C+] **1** take it away! **2** be quiet!

give it a name! phr. [1930s–50s] phr. used when one stands a round of drinks and asks the company what they would like (cf. NAME YOUR POISON!; NAME YOURS!).

give it a nudge/bit of a nudge, to phr. [1950s+] (Aus.) to drink to excess; thus *nudge*, to drink heavily, often with a specified drink, i.e. *nudge the nelly*, to drink too much cheap wine.

give it a pull, to phr. [20C] (Aus.) to stop, to desist. [? the pull on the reins that halts a horse]

give it a rest! excl. [20C] shut up! stop talking! (cf. GIVE US A REST!).

give it a tug, to phr. [1950s+] to masturbate.

give it away, to phr. [1940s+] (Aus.) to stop, to give up, to abandon.

give it a whirl, to phr. [late 19C+] (orig. US) try something out.

give it back to the Indians phr. [20C] (US) phr. used when anything fails or breaks. [negative racial stereotyping; Native Americans will accept any old rubbish]

give it hot/hot and strong, to phr. [late 17C+] to castigate severely.

give it one upon the rush, to phr. [early–mid-19C] to make an intense effort to leave or escape a place.

give it on the humble suit, to phr. [early 19C] to importune with great respect and self-abasement.

give it some wellie, to phr. [1970s+] to apply some force. [SE *wellington boot*; an extra image is from the 'wellie-chucking' contests that have become popular]

give it the big one, to phr. [1990s] to act in a verbally aggressive manner.

give it the boot, to phr. [1990s] to accelerate. [one pushes down on the accelerator with a boot or shoe]

give it the flick, to phr. [20C] (Aus.) to throw something away. [SE *flick*]

give it the gun, to phr. [1910s+] (orig. US) to accelerate, to drive a car or other vehicle fast. [GUN v.]

give it the herbs, to phr. [1930s+] (Aus.) to accelerate a car. [HERBS n.[2]]

give it to v. **1** [early 19C] (Und.) to rob. **2** [20C] of a man, to have sexual intercourse. **3** [1950s+] (US Und.) to murder, to execute.

give it up v. [1970s+] (US) **1** to accede to seduction. **2** to applaud, usu. in phr. *let's give it up for…* .

give it up! excl. [1970s+] **1** an aggressive demand from one male that another accept his advances, esp. in prison. **2** the same demand for sex, made from a man to a woman.

give jaro v. [20C] (N.Z.) to scold. [? Maori]

give jesse see GIVE ONE JESSE.

give jiggs v. [1910s–30s] (US) to keep a look-out; thus excl. *jiggers!* look out! run for it! [JIGGER n.[1] (4)]

give juice for jelly, to phr. [19C] from a woman's point of view, to have sexual intercourse (cf. GIVE A HOT POULTICE FOR THE IRISH TOOTHACHE; JELLY n.[1]).

give laldie/laldy *v.* [late 19C+] (Scot.) to be punished, to be beaten. [Scot. *laldy*, to punish]

give lamb and salad, to *phr.* [mid-19C–1900s] to beat, to thrash. [pun on LAM *v.*[1]]

give laugh for peas-soup, to *phr.* [20C] (W.I.) **1** for a visitor to act in a sufficiently entertaining manner to win an invitation to a meal. **2** to chat or gossip instead of getting on with one's work, thus using one's wit and charm to hide one's actual laziness.

give law *v.* [mid-19C] to give a chance. [sporting jargon *give law*, to give a hunted animal a chance of escape]

give leg bail, to *phr.* [mid-19C] to escape, to run away. [SE *leg* + *bail*, security given against the release of a prisoner pending their trial]

give leg bail and land security, to *phr.* [late 18C–mid-19C] to run away.

give/make/yield the crow a pudding, to *phr.* [late 16C–early 19C] **1** to hang on a gibbet. **2** to die. [SE *crow* + SE *pudding*, entrails, i.e. the crow will eat the entrails of the corpse]

give me fin on the soul side *phr.* [1940s–70s] (US Black) let's slap hands to seal the deal or bargain. [GIVE ME FIVE; FIN *n.*[1]]

give/slip me five! *excl.* [1910s+] (orig. US Black) let's slap hands to seal the deal or bargain; also as *give me five on the sly*, to slap hands behind one's back so as not to alert onlookers; *give me five on the black-hand side/the soul side*, to slap hands on the back (darker) side or the palm side of the hand (cf. GIVE SOME SKIN; SHAKE FIVE!; SLAP FIVE). [GIVE FIVE]

give me strength! *excl.* [1920s+] a 'prayer' uttered on hearing or encountering an especially stupid statement or action.

give mutton for beef, to *phr.* [19C] from a woman's point of view, to have sexual intercourse (cf. ACHING FOR A SIDE OF BEEF; GIVE A HOT POULTICE FOR THE IRISH TOOTHACHE). [MUTTON *n.*[1] (2) + BEEF *n.*[1] (3)]

given! *excl.* [1990s] (US campus) an expression of agreement. [SE *given*, something that is automatically accepted, 'taken as read']

give nature a fillip, to *phr.* [late 17C–18C] to indulge in hedonistic pleasures, notably women and wine.

give no change, to *phr.* [late 19C+] to reveal nothing, to give no satisfaction.

give off *v.* [20C] (Irish) to make a fuss (cf. GIVE OUT *v.*[1]). [fig. use of phr. *give out the hour*]

give one's best shot, to *phr.* [20C] to make one's best efforts. [SHOT *n.*[2]]

give one's bum an airing, to *phr.* [1940s–50s] to visit the lavatory. [BUM *n.*[2]]

give one's dog a swim, to *phr.* [20C] (Aus./S.Afr.) to have an excuse for doing something, to use an action as an excuse, *I'm just off to give the dog ...* .

give oneself a rope necklace, to *phr.* [1970s] (US Black) to commit suicide by hanging.

give one's gravy, to *phr.* [19C] **1** of a man, to reach orgasm. **2** of a man, to bring a partner to orgasm (presumably simultaneous with his own ejaculation). [GRAVY *n.*[1]]

give one's guts *see* COME ONE'S GUTS.

give one's left nut, to *phr.* [1950s+] (US) to yearn for, to desire. [fig. use of NUTS *n.*[2]]

give one's solemn, to *phr.* [late 19C–1910s] to swear upon one's 'solemn oath'.

give on/upon a man, to *phr.* [20C] (W.I.) for a woman to surrender herself to male advances.

give or take *phr.* [1950s+] phr. implying an estimation usu. of time number or weight, e.g. *give or take half an hour*, *give or take a couple of kilos*.

give out *v.*[1] [1960s+] (Irish) to make a fuss (cf. GIVE OUT THE PAY).

give out *v.*[2] **1** [1930s–40s] (US Black) to talk emotionally, to talk with great feeling. **2** [1930s+] of a young woman, to make herself available for sexual intercourse (cf. GIVE *v.*[2]). [fig. uses of SE]

give out the pay/yards, to *phr.* [1960s+] (Irish) to make a fuss (cf. GIVE OUT *v.*[1]).

give over! *excl.* [20C] (usu. northern) stop it!

give pap with a hatchet *see* FEED PAP WITH A HATCHET.

give points *v.* [late 19C] to permit an advantage to (cf. GET POINTS).

give props *v.* [1990s] (US Black) to applaud, to praise, to acknowledge as good (cf. GET PROPS; PROPS *n.*[2]). [abbr. SE *proper respect*]

give roast meat and beat with the spit, to *phr.* [late 17C–18C] to offer an apparent compliment and then to abuse its recipient.

give rounders *v.* [20C] (W.I./Trin.) to be evasive, to deceive, to deal with in an annoying manner. [SE *go round in circles*]

give skin-teeth *v.* [20C] (W.I.) **1** to smile falsely when one actually feels furious or embittered. **2** to laugh cynically. [fig. use of 'the skin of one's teeth' to mean superficiality]

give sky-high *v.* [late 19C] to reprimand severely. [var. on BLOW SKY-HIGH]

give soft for hard, to *phr.* [19C] from a woman's point of view, to have sexual intercourse (cf. GIVE A HOT POULTICE FOR THE IRISH TOOTHACHE; GIVE HARD FOR SOFT).

give some body, to *phr.* [1960s+] to accede to sexual advances. [BODY *n.* (2)]

give some flesh, to *phr.* [20C] (W.I.) ritual palm slapping that forms greeting between Blacks or Black and knowledgeable White (cf. GIVE SOME SKIN).

give some lip, to *phr.* [early 19C+] to be cheeky. [LIP *n.*[1] (1)]

give someone a bell, to *phr.* [1960s+] to call on the telephone (cf. BELL *v.*, GIVE ONE A BUZZ).

give someone a bit of hurry-up, to *phr.* [20C] (Aus.) to stimulate, to encourage to act more energetically.

give someone a black eye, to *phr.* [late 19C–1940s] to injure someone's reputation (cf. GIVE A BLACK EYE). [fig. 'hurting' of the reputation]

give someone a break, to *phr.* [1920s+] (orig. US) to give someone a chance, to let off, to excuse, to give an opportunity, esp. in excl. *give me a break!* [BREAK *n.*[2] (1)]

give someone a burst, to *phr.* [1940s+] to complain, to criticize, to remind strongly. [SE *burst of fire*]

give someone a buzz, to *phr.*[1] [1950s+] **1.** to call someone on the telephone (cf. GIVE A BELL). **2** to look up, to call at one's house. [BUZZ *n.*[2] (3)]

give someone a buzz, to *phr.*[2] [1950s+] to excite, to thrill (usu. sexually). [BUZZ *n.*[3] (2)]

give someone a chalk, to *phr.* [1910s–20s] to cheat, to swindle, to get the better of (cf. GIVE ONE CHALKS ON). [? SE *chalk up*]

give someone a coating, to *phr.* **1** [1930s+] to beat up, to thrash. **2** (Und.) to give someone a reprimand. [COAT *v.*]

give someone a cock's egg, to *phr.* [19C] to send on a fool's errand, esp. on April Fools' Day. [cocks do not lay; note East Anglian/Salop. dial. *cocks' eggs*, the small, yolkless eggs that hens sometimes lay. They are supposedly very unlucky and must never be brought into a house]

give someone a go *phr.*[1] *see* GIVE SOMETHING A GO.

give someone a go, to *phr.*[2] [1910s+] (Aus.) to give someone something to think about, to give 'a run for one's money'. [SE *go*, i.e. to get someone going]

give someone a hot time/hot time of it, to *phr.* [late 19C+] to make someone unhappy, to punish, to reprimand.

give someone a jolly, to *phr.* [late 19C] to applaud, to give someone a cheer.

give someone a jump, to *phr.* [20C] of a man, to have sexual intercourse. [JUMP n.[2] (1)]

give someone a leg/clean leg up, to *phr.* [late 19C+] to help someone, esp. to advance themselves professionally.

give someone a lift, to *phr.* [late 19C] to give someone a short, swift kick (cf. GIVE ONE A RISE IN THE WORLD). [the victim's body is 'lifted' through the air]

give someone/something a miss, to *phr.* [1910s+] to avoid seeing someone or doing something.

give someone a mouthful of moonshine, to *phr.* [late 18C–early 189C] to flatter. [MOONSHINE n. (1)]

give someone a piece, to *phr.* (W.I.) of a woman, to permit casual sexual intercourse. [PIECE n.]

give someone a pull, to *phr.* [1950s+] **1** to tell off, to reprimand. **2** to arrest. [PULL v.[1] (2)]

give someone a rise in the world, to *phr.* [1920s+] (Aus.) to kick someone's buttocks (cf. GIVE ONE A LIFT). [pun]

give someone a roasting, to *phr.* [late 19C+] to give someone a severe scolding. [ROAST v. (2)]

give someone a rolling, to *phr.* [1970s+] to attack, beat up and rob a gay man, to 'queer-bash'. [ROLL v.]

give someone a run for one's money, to *phr.* [late 19C+] to provide satisfaction, to give someone their 'money's worth', usu. fig. [note earlier racing sl. *have a run for one's money*, to have some kind of return or satisfaction for one's expenditure or exertions]

give someone a serve, to *phr.* [1960s+] (Aus.) to deal roughly with, to criticize or reprimand sharply. [SERVE OUT]

give someone a shirt full of sore bones, to *phr.* [18C] to beat, to thrash.

give someone a shot, to *phr.* [19C+] of a man, to have sexual intercourse. [SHOOT v.[3]]

give someone a snake, to *phr.* [late 19C–1920s] to annoy, to irritate.

give someone a song and dance, to *phr.* [late 19C+] (orig. US) to tell fanciful tales for the purpose of confusing or tricking the listener.

give someone a thrill, to *phr.* **1** [1910s+] to bring one's partner to orgasm. **2** [1920s+] of a man, to have sexual intercourse.

give someone a touch of them, to *phr.* [1920s+] (Aus.) to infuriate. ['them' = the SHITS]

give someone a tumble, to *phr.* [20C] to have sexual intercourse. [TUMBLE v.[1] (1)]

give someone beans, to *phr.* [mid-19C–1940s] (orig. US) to deal severely with, to punish heavily. [? SE *bangs*, hits]

give someone big rocks to hold, to *phr.* [20C] (W.I./Bdos.) for a woman to make a date with a man when she has no intention of keeping it, thus to trick a suitor in any way.

give someone cards and spades, to *phr.* [late 19C–1930s] to allow someone else an advantage. [card-playing imagery]

give someone chalks on, to *phr.* [late 19C+] to acknowledge someone else's superiority (cf. GIVE ONE A CHALK).

give someone change *v.* **1** [mid-19C] to do someone a service, often ironically, thus to pay one back [mid–late 19C] **2** to punish someone.

give someone curry/some curry/curried hell, to *phr.* [1930s+] (Aus.) to attack (verbally or physically), 'to make things hot' for someone (cf. MAKE IT HOT FOR). [SE *curry* is seen as 'hot', but note mid-19C Aus. pidgin *give one kurrajong*, to hang with a rope made from kurrajong fibre]

give someone diabetes/cavities, to *phr.* [1980s+] (US campus) to be excessively sweet. [SE *diabetes* results from an excess of sugar in the blood; tooth *cavities* from eating too many sweet things]

give someone down the banks, to *phr.* [1960s+] (Irish) to scold, to reprimand. [ety. unknown]

give someone down the country/river, to *phr.* [19C+] (US) to scold, to tell off, to reprimand. [ety. unknown]

give someone fits, to *phr.* [late 19C+] (orig. US) **1** to inflict a humiliating defeat on, to crush. **2** to scold vigorously, to reprimand. **3** to frighten.

give someone five *see* GIVE FIVE.

give someone grief *v.* [late 19C+] to make miserable, to harm in any way. [GRIEF n.[1]]

give someone jesse/jessie *v.* [mid-19C–1900s] to punish, to beat, to scold soundly. [play on Isa. 11:1 'There shall come forth a rod out of the stem of Jesse']

give someone kennedy, to *phr.* [mid-19C] to strike someone with a poker. [KENNEDY n. (2)]

give someone larry dooley, to *phr.* [1940s+] (Aus.) to beat someone, to punish. [Larry Foley, late 19C Aus. boxer; the phr. began by using the proper name, but soon replaced *Foley* by *dooley*]

give someone Moll Doyle, to *phr.* [mid-19C+] (Irish) to scold, to reprimand, usu. of a wife to a husband (cf. BY THE POWERS OF MOLL DOYLE). [*Moll Doyle's daughters*, a clandestine agrarian society, pitted against rapacious landlords and similar figures]

give someone oatmeal, to *phr.* [mid-18C–early 19C] to punish, to reprimand. [? OATMEAL]

give someone one *v.* [late 19C+] to hit, to have sexual intercourse, to kiss etc.

give someone one in the eye, to *phr.* [late 19C+] to hit, to reprimand, also in fig. use (cf. GIVE SOMEONE A BLACK EYE).

give someone one's fist, to *phr.* [early 19C–1900s] to shake hands, esp. as imper. *give me your fist!*

give someone onions *v.* [late 19C–1900s to attack physically. [one's watering eyes]

give someone rats *v.* [mid-19C+] (US) to give someone a hard time, to berate, to rebuke. [the neg. image of the rodent]

give someone rocks *v.* [1950s+] (US) to excite sexually, spec. to make a man have an erection (cf. GET ONE'S ROCKS OFF). [fig. use of ROCKS n.[3] (1)]

give someone's arse/ears a chance, to *phr.* [20C] a comment aimed at a talkative person, usu. prefaced by *Why don't you shut up and … .*

give someone scissors, to *phr.* [mid-19C–1900s] to treat someone badly, to pay someone back (for a slight or injury). [one fig. 'cuts them up']

give someone's ears a chance *see* GIVE SOMEONE'S ARSE A CHANCE.

give someone snuff, to *phr.* [late 19C] to punish, to reprimand. [SE *snuff*; the image is of beating someone to powder]

give someone some play, to *phr.* [1970s+] (US Black) to express sexual interest in, to flirt with.

give someone some stick, to *phr.* [1960s+] to threaten, to criticize roughly, to beat up; thus *get some stick*, to be on the receiving end of these attacks.

give someone something for themself, to *phr.* [late 19C] to thrash, to beat. [ironic]

give someone stink, to *phr.* [1940s] to give someone a 'hard time', to scold severely.

give someone that *v.* [1910s+] to acknowledge the other person's point, e.g. *I'll give you that.*

give someone the atmosphere, to *phr.* [1930s] (US) to turn down, to reject. [var. on GIVE THE AIR]

give someone the bag/belt/kickout/pike/road, to *phr.* [late 16C–early 19C] to dismiss, to discharge (cf. GIVE ONE THE BULLET; GIVE THE SACK). [SE *give* + SE *bag*, i.e. of possessions/BELT n.[1] (1)/SE *kick out/pike/road*]

give someone the belt/Lonsdale belt, to *phr.* [1930s+] (orig. Aus.) to get rid of, to throw out, to dismiss, to reject. [the *Lonsdale belt*; thus a pun on BELT v.; the belt itself, given to a boxing champion, is named for Hugh Cecil Lowther (1857–1944), 5th earl of Lonsdale]

give someone the blacks, to *phr.* [20C] (US) to ignore, to cut, esp. when snubbing a former friend. [SE *black look*]

give someone the brush/brush-off, to *phr.* [1920s+] (orig. US) to ignore, to snub. [BRUSH n.[1]; BRUSH OFF v.]

give someone the bullet, to *phr.* [mid-19C+] to dismiss from employment, to throw out (cf. GIVE ONE THE BAG). [BULLET n.[2] (1)]

give someone the business, to *phr.* [1940s+] (orig. US) **1** to kill. **2** to beat up, to assault. **3** to have sexual intercourse. **4** to tease, to taunt, to put at a disadvantage by one's own actions. **5** to deceive, to bamboozle. [BUSINESS]

give someone the buzz, to *phr.* [1930s–40s] to appraise, to look over, e.g. of a policeman looking at a person he sees as suspicious. [BUZZ v.[4]]

give someone the chop, to *phr.* [1940s+] **1** to kill or otherwise dispose of a person. **2** to fire from a job. [SE *chop*, to remove (one's head)]

give someone the cock, to *phr.* [20C] (W.I.) **1** to outsmart, to outwit by trickery or other unfair means. **2** to cause someone unexpected trouble (cf. FUCK AROUND; FUCK OVER). [COCK n.[2] (1)]

give someone the deep six, to *phr.* [1920s+] (US) to kill, to murder. [DEEP SIX]

give someone the dingbats, to *phr.* [1930s+] to make someone feel nervous. [DINGBATS]

give someone the dog to hold, to *phr.* [mid-17C–late 18C] to play a mean trick on someone (cf. HOLD THE BABY).

give someone the dust off, to *phr.* [20C] (US) to ignore, to snub (cf. GIVE ONE THE BRUSH). [DUST n.[3]]

give someone the finger, to *phr.* [1960s+] to make a manual gesture (the raised middle finger in the US, the V-sign in the UK) to imply derision and disdain (cf. FLAG A BONE). [FINGER n.[3]]

give someone the foot, to *phr.* [20C] (US) to throw out, to oust, to reject (cf. GIVE THE BOOT).

give someone the freedom of the world, to *phr.* [20C] to dismiss from a job. [irony]

give someone the glad eye, to *phr.* [1910s+] to give someone of the opposite sex a glance that implies sexual attraction. [GLAD EYE]

give someone the go-around, to *phr.* [20C] (orig. US) to reject, to avoid, to jilt.

give someone the go-by, to *phr.* [mid-17C+] **1** to avoid, to disregard deliberately. **2** to allow, to turn a blind eye. **3** to dismiss, to get rid of. [SE *go-by*, the action of going]

give someone the guy, to *phr.* [late 19C] to run away from. to 'give the slip'. [GUY n.]

give someone the highball, to *phr.* [20C] (US) to reject, to brush off, esp. to end a relationship or love affair. [? railroad jargon *highball*, a fast train; thus the individual who ends the affair is fig. 'taking a fast train' out]

give someone/put on the high hat, to *phr.* [1920s+] (orig. US) to act in a superior manner towards others (cf. HIGH HAT v.).

give someone the horse laugh, to *phr.* [late 19C–1920s] (US) to mock, to tease. [SE *horse laugh*, a loud coarse laugh]

give someone their gruel, to *phr.* [mid-19C] to kill (cf. SETTLE ONE'S HASH; TAKE GRUEL). [the thin SE *gruel* served to invalids]

give someone their running shoes, to *phr.* [1940s+] (orig. Aus./N.Z.) to dismiss from a job, as a lover etc. [US use added post 1960s]

give someone the kickout *see* GIVE SOMEONE THE BAG.

give someone the leather, to *phr.* [1930s] **1** to kick a person. **2** to beat with the fist, to punch. [the leather of (1) shoes, (2) boxing gloves]

give someone the leg *see* PULL SOMEONE'S LEG.

give someone the length of one's tongue, to *phr.* [19C+] to attack verbally.

give someone the loaf of bread, to *phr.* [1940s+] to hit with one's head (cf. GIVE ONE THE NUT). [rhy. sl. *loaf of bread* = head]

give someone the Lonsdale belt *see* GIVE SOMEONE THE BELT.

give someone the nut/put the nut on, to *phr.* [mid-19C+] to hit with one's head. [NUT n.[3] (1)]

give someone the office, to *phr.* [19C+] **1** to tip off, to give a warning. **2** (prison) to initiate a new prisoner into the rules and regulations, official and unofficial, of prison life. [OFFICE n.[3]]

give someone the old boracic, to *phr.* [20C] to deceive, to tell tales. [? Aus. POKE BORAK, ult. SE *barrack*, to jeer]

give someone the pike *see* GIVE SOMEONE THE BAG.

give someone the pink slip, to *phr.* [1950s+] (US) to hand over, to cede ownership of something to another person. [the pink slip that, in the US, proves ownership of a car]

give someone the pip, to *phr.* [late 19C+] to annoy or to infurate someone, or to be so annoyed oneself. [SE *pip*, a poultry disease, sometimes used of certain human diseases]

give someone the rinky-dink, to *phr.* [1920s–40s] (US) to cheat, to swindle. [RINKY-DINK adj.[2]]

give someone the road *phr.*[1] *see* GIVE SOMEONE THE BAG.

give someone the road, to *phr.*[2] [1910s+] (Can.) to ignore.

give someone the rub of the thumb, to *phr.* [mid–late 19C] to impart information to someone. [the gesture of rubbing one's thumb against the fore-finger]

give someone the runaround, to *phr.* [1910s+] (orig. US) to deceive, to delay, to put off, to avoid – all such efforts usu. in order to give oneself some form of advantage, breathing space etc (cf. GET THE RUNAROUND).

give someone the rush, to *phr.* [mid–late 19C] to sponge off someone for a lengthy period and top it off by successfully requesting a loan. [RUSH n.[1] (2)]

give someone the shits, to *phr.* [20C] to annoy, to infuriate someone. [fig. use of SHITS n.]

give someone the sick/sicks, to *phr.* [mid-19C–1920s] to disgust.

give someone the stiff, to *phr.* [early–mid-19C] to hand over any form of document – a summons, a bill etc. [STIFF n.]

give someone the threepennies, to *phr.* [late 19C+] to annoy, to irritate someone (cf. GET ON ONE'S TITS). [THREEPENNY BITS]

give someone the tom-tits, to *phr.* [1960s+] to annoy someone. [TOM-TITS]

give someone the works, to *phr.* **1** [1930s+] to put all one's efforts into communicating something, typically a sermon or political oration. **2** [1920s+] to harm, ranging from actual murder to beating up (cf. GIVE THE WORKS TO).

give someone what for/what's what v. [late 19C+] to reprimand severely, to inflict severe pain or chastisement, esp. of an errant child. [a response to presumed SE *query* 'what is that for?']

give some skin/plank/splib *phr.* [1950s+] (US Black) the ritual palm slapping that forms a greeting between Blacks or a Black and knowledgeable White; thus the greeting *give me some skin* (cf. GIVE FIVE; SLAP FIVE). [SE *skin*/SE *plank*/SPLIB n.[1]. The practice is of African origin; thus Temme *botme-der*, put skin and/or Mandingo *i golo don m bolo*, place your hand in my hand]

give some sugar, to *phr.* [1930s–50s] (US Black) to kiss, esp. as imper. *give me some sugar*, give me a kiss. [the 'sweetness' of the embrace]

give something/someone a go, to *phr.* [20C] (orig. Aus.) to try out, to take a chance on. [GO n.[3] (1)]

give something a miss *see* GIVE SOMEONE A MISS.

give the abdabs see COME THE ABDABS.

give the air, to *phr.* [late 19C+] (orig. US) to dismiss, to reject, esp. when ending a love affair (cf. AIR v.; GET THE AIR).

give the arse to, to *phr.* [1950s+] (Aus.) to treat with contempt. [ARSEN.[1] ? turning one's back, and thus one's buttocks, to someone]

give the avaunt, to *phr.* [late 16C–early 17C] to end someone away. [SE excl. *avaunt*, be off!]

give the bag to, to *phr.* **1** [late 16C+] to depart suddenly. **2** [late 18C+] to jilt or reject a suitor. [the handing over of a fig. bag of problems, responsibilities etc]

give/slip the berries to, to *phr.* [1920s–30s] (US) to deride, to insult. [RASPBERRY n.[1]]

give the bird, to *phr.* [mid-19C+] to express one's disapproval vocally, esp. by hissing (cf. GET THE BIRD). [the hissing is supposed to resemble that of a goose; orig./usu. theatrical, when the phr. began as GET THE BIRD/BIG BIRD, but also in general use]

give the boak, to *phr.* [1980s+] to make one sick. [SE *bolk*, to belch]

give the bone see FLAG A BONE.

give the boot, to *phr.* [late 19C+] to dismiss from a job, to throw out (cf. GET THE BOOT).

give/put/throw the boots to, to *phr.*[1] (US) **1** [late 19C+] to give a kicking to (cf. PUT THE BOOT IN). **2** [late 19C+] to victimize, to treat harshly.

give/put/throw the boots to, to *phr.*[2] [1930s+] of a man, to have sexual intercourse (cf. RIDE v.[1]). [horse-riding imagery]

give the bounce, to *phr.* [19C] (US) **1** to jilt. **2** to send away, dismiss from a job; thus *get the bounce*, to be dismissed. [BOUNCE n.[4]]

give the boys a treat, to *phr.* [late 19C+] for a girl or woman inadvertently to reveal her upper thighs or underwear, e.g. when getting out of a vehicle.

give the breeze, to *phr.* [1930s] (US) (orig. US) to dismiss, to reject, esp. when ending a love affair. [var. on GET THE AIR]

give the bucket, to *phr.* [mid-19C] to dismiss from a job. [var. on GIVE THE SACK]

give the business/business to, to *phr.* **1** [1920s+] (orig. US) to beat up, to kill. **2** [1940s+] (orig. US) to interrogate. **3** [1940s+] (orig. US) to tease, to humiliate, to scold. **4** [1940s+] (orig. US) to cheat, to hoax. **5** [1940s+] (orig. US) to cast flirtatious glances (at). [BUSINESS]

give the cheer, to *phr.* [late 19C] to greet, to welcome.

give the Chinaman a music lesson, to *phr.* [20C] a euph. for urinate. [the phr. reflects the *China* toilet bowl, and the *music* that is the 'tinkle' of the urine hitting it]

give the chop, to *phr.* [1940s+] to destroy, to abandon, to stop, to cut off (cf. GET THE CHOP). [SE *chop*, to remove (one's head)]

give the chuck, to *phr.* [late 19C+] to dismiss, to get rid of, to end a relationship (cf. GET THE CHUCK). [CHUCK n.]

give the chuck-up, to *phr.* [1910s–20s] of objects, to abandon, to give up on, to get rid of. [CHUCK UP v.[2]]

give the come-in, to *phr.* [1940s+] to stare amorously at (cf. GIVE THE COME-ON; GLAD EYE).

give the come-on, to *phr.* [20C] to entice, to lure, to stare amorously at (cf. COME-ON n.; GIVE THE COME-IN).

give the crock, to *phr.* [late 19C] to admit to defeat, to award a victory. [SE *crock*, a jug, i.e. to award a fig. cup as in a sporting victory]

give the dog a bone, to *phr.* [1980s+] to have sexual intercourse. [note DOG n.[12] + BONE n.[6] (1)]

give the done, to *phr.* [20C] (W.I./UKVI) to end a relationship. [SE *done*, over, finished]

give the double, to *phr.* [19C] to give the slip, to evade by stratagem. [SE *double*, to trace a winding, tortuous path; to evade]

give the drummer some *phr.* [1950s+] (US Black) ritual palm slapping that forms greeting between Blacks or Black and knowledgeable White (cf. GIVE SOME SKIN). [the drumming of one hand upon another]

give the duke, to *phr.* [1960s+] to slow hand-clap as a sign of disapproval of a sporting event. [DUKE]

give the elbow, to *phr.* [1970s+] to get rid of, to dismiss (cf. BIG E). [the image of jabbing someone in the ribs with one's elbow]

give the eye, to *phr.* [late 19C+] **1** to stare at. **2** to appraise sexually.

give the fence a run, to *phr.* [1970s+] (N.Z.) to fulfil one's sexual urges. [the image of a bull smashing through or jumping over a fence on the way to a cow]

give the fig, to *phr.* [late 16C–early 19C] to stick one's thumb up between two forefingers as a gesture of derision (cf. GIVE ONE THE FINGER). [FIG n.[1]]

give the fisheye, to *phr.* [1950s+] (US) to stare at in a hostile or threatening manner.

give the flat, to *phr.* [mid-19C] (US) to turn down a suitor. [SE *flat refusal*]

give the four-eleven/411, to *phr.* [1990s] (US Black) to give out information, to instruct. [? telephone code for directory enquiries]

give the gate, to *phr.* [1910s+] (US) to throw out, to reject, to dismiss (cf. GET THE GATE).

give the glad hand see GLAD HAND v.

give the glove, to *phr.* [20C] (US) to reject, to turn down, to dismiss (cf. HAND ONE THE MITT).

give the go, to *phr.* [late 19C+] (Aus./N.Z.) **1** to reject a suitor. **2** to give up a job, leave a country etc.

give the gooner, to *phr.* [1920s–30s] to dismiss someone from a job (cf. GET THE GOONER). [SE *gone* or GONER]

give the go-sign, to *phr.* [20C] (US) to dismiss, to reject, to brush off. [SE *go away*]

give the green light see GREEN LIGHT.

give the hand see GIVE THE MITT.

give the hard ass, to *phr.* [1970s+] (US) to give a hard time. [SE *hard* + ARSE n.[1]]

give the heat, to *phr.*[1] [1930s+] to murder, to kill. [HEAT n.[3]]

give the heat, to *phr.*[2] [1930s+] to make sexual advances. [HEAT n.[5] (1)]

give the hump, to *phr.* [mid-19C+] to annoy, to irritate. [HUMP n.[1]]

give the irrits, to *phr.* [20C] (Aus.) to annoy, to irritate. [abbr. SE *irritate*]

give the kick, to *phr.* [late 19C–1910s] to dismiss from a job (cf. GET THE KICK). [KICK v.[4] (2)]

give the laugh, to *phr.* [late 19C–1930s] (US) to jeer, to pour scorn.

give the licks of Lisbon, to *phr.* [20C] (W.I./Gun.) to berate, to scold severely, to tell off (cf. GIVE GOOD v.[2]). [SE *lick*, a blow; ? + ref. to Portuguese colonialism]

give the man the play, to *phr.* [1970s+] (US Black) to inform. [MAN n. + PLAY n.]

give them away with a pound of tea, to *phr.* [late 19C+] **1** a phr. used to deride something considered of little or no value; e.g. 'Expensive? He gives them away ... .' **2** an ironic reply by criminal to questions referring to the origins of obviously stolen goods in his possession. 'Stolen goods, officer? No. Give them away ... .'

give the miller, to *phr.* [mid-19C] to pelt someone with flour, grease or other rubbish.

give the mitt/hand, to *phr.* [1920s–40s] (US) to reject, esp. in the context of a proposal of marriage. [MITT n./SE *hand*; var. on GIVE THE MITTEN]

give the mitten, to phr. [mid–late 19C] (US) to reject a proposal of marriage (cf. GET THE MITTEN).

give old abdabs see COME THE ABDABS.

give the old man his supper, to phr. [19C] of a woman, to make herself available for sex. [OLD MAN n.[1]]

give/confer the order of the sack, to phr. [mid-19C+] to dismiss, to relieve of one's job (cf. BESTOW THE ORDER OF THE SACK; GET THE BOOT). [joc. amplification of SACK v.[2]]

give the pip, to phr. [late 19C] to irritate intensely (cf. GET THE PIP). [PIP n.]

give the rap, to phr. [1930s+] (US) to murder, to kill. [SE rap, a blow]

give the rounds of the kitchen, to phr. [late 19C+] (Aus.) to tell off, to scold..

give the run, to phr. [late 19C] to dismiss from a job.

give the sack, to phr. **1** [early 19C+] to dismiss from a job. **2** [late 19C–1920s] to reject (as a former lover or sweetheart). [current in Fr. f. 17C: 'On luy a donné son sac, hee hath his passport giuen him (said of a seruant whom his master hath put away)' (Cotgrave 1611). Note Du. iemand den zak geven, to give one the sack (already in MDu.), den zak krijgen, to get the sack.]

give the shoot, to phr. [mid-19C–1900s] to dismiss from a job (cf. GET THE SHOOT).

give the shove, to phr. [late 19C+] to dismiss from a job (cf. GET THE SHOVE). [SHOVE n.[2]]

give the show away, to phr. [mid-19C+] to betray a secret, to reveal one's or another's plans.

give the slip, to phr. [19C] to die. [SE give the slip, to elude, to run off]

give the snap away, to phr. [late 19C] to betray plans, to 'give the game away'. [? the snap of a finger that launches an action]

give the thumbs up, to phr. [1950s+] to approve, to answer positively, to encourage.

give the works to, to phr. [1920s+] (orig. US) **1** to harm, from actual murder to mere beating up. **2** to make an effort in a context, whether selling an item, shooting a line, criticizing etc. [WORKS n.[2]]

give/tell the works, to phr. [1920s–30s] to reveal everything. [WORKS n.[2]]

give three slips for a tester, to phr. [16C–mid-19C] to 'give the slip' (lit. to pass off three counterfeit twopenny pieces for a sixpence). [SLIP n.[1] + TESTER n. (1)]

give tongue-pie v. [1910s–20s] to give a scolding, to harangue. [TONGUE-PIE]

give turnips v. [early 19C] to abandon or jilt, esp. heartlessly, ruthlessly. [pun on TURN UP/SE turnip; note Suffolk dial. give cold turnips, to turn down a proposal of marriage/love]

give two fucks see GIVE A FUCK.

give-up n. **1** [1930s+] (US Und.) a payment made under duress. **2** [1940s] (US) submission, surrender.

give up v. [1930s+] **1** (Aus./US Und.) to betray, to inform against. **2** (US Und.) to pay money, esp. under duress.

give up on v. [1970s+] to lose one's faith, trust or belief in.

give up one's face, to phr. [1960s+] to permit oneself to indulge in oral intercourse at the insistence of a partner (cf. FACE ARTIST; FACE PUSSY; FACE THE NATION). [FACE n.[2] (12)]

give up one's halfpenny, to phr. [late 17C–late 18C] to vomit, after drinking to excess. [? the price one has paid for the drink]

give up rhythm, to phr. [1960s+] (US Black) for a woman, using body language, to indicate her sexual availability to a man with whom she is walking or dancing.

give up the ass, to phr. [1970s+] (US) to accede to seduction (cf. GIVE IT UP v.). [ARSE n.[1]]

give up the ship, to phr. to die (cf. COIL ONE'S ROPES).

give up the store, to phr. [20C] to surrender, to give in.

give us a rest! phr. [late 19C+] (US) stop talking, be quiet! (cf. GIVE IT A REST!).

give wings v. [1960s+] (drugs) to inject someone or teach someone to inject heroin. [one becomes HIGH]

give yourself a low five, to phr. [1980s+] to masturbate. [play on the raised-arm, palm-slapping rituals of the HIGH FIVE]

give Yul Brynner a high five, to phr. [1990s] to masturbate (cf. CHOKE KOJAK). [the film star Brynner (1915–85) was famously bald, thus cf. BALD-HEADED HERMIT]

givum's dead and lendum's very bad phr. [mid-19C] phr. used to turn down a request for loan. [play on SE give them + lend them]

gixie n. [16C] **1** a prostitute. **2** an affected, posing woman. [SE gixie, a woman]

giz n. **1** [1940s] (US) any small thing for which one has temporarily forgotten the correct name (cf. GIZMO). **2** [1970s+] (US) the vagina. **3** [1990s] an annoying thing, which is impossible to get rid of.

gizm see JISM.

gizmo/gismo n. [1940s+] (orig. US) **1** (drugs) the paraphernalia used for injecting narcotics. **2** any (small) thing for which one has temporarily forgotten the correct name, a gadget, a thingumajig. **3** [1940s] (US) the vulva or vagina. **4** [1940s] (US) the penis (cf. THINGUMMY). [ety. unknown]

gizzard n. **1** [mid-19C–1930s] (US) courage, guts. **2** [20C] the stomach, the solar plexus. **3** [1970s+] the throat. [10C SE gizzard, animal or insect stomachs, ult. Latin gicerium, the cooked entrails of a fowl]

gizzum see JISM.

gizzy n. [1980s] (US drugs) marijuana. [? GIZMO]

glab n. [19C+] (US) chatter, nonsense, gossip. [Scot. glabber, foolish, idle talk]

glabber v. [19C+] (US) to chatter, to jabber, to talk nonsense (cf. GLAB). [Scot. glabber, to chatter]

glacines n. [1970s+] (drugs) heroin. [Sp. ? glassine bags in which the drug is distributed]

glad n. [1920s+] a gladiolus (cf. CARNIE n.[1]). [abbr.]

glad adj. [19C+] tipsy, drunk (cf. ABOUT RIGHT adj.[1]).

glad-and-sorry system n. [1910s–40s] hire purchase. [the emotions it sequentially creates]

glad bag n. [1980s+] (US) a body bag. [play on tradename Glad Bags]

glad clothes see GLAD RAGS.

gladdie/gladi n. [1960s+] (orig. Aus.) a gladiolus (cf. CARNIE n.[1]). [abbr.]

glad eye n. [1910s+] a glance of sexual interest (cf. GIVE SOMEONE THE GLAD EYE; HARD EYES).

glad hand/mitt n. [late 19C+] an expression of effusive if insincere greeting, welcome. [SE glad + hand/MITT n.]

glad hand/give the glad hand v. [late 19C+] to welcome enthusiastically, even excessively and very likely insincerely; often used of politicians and similar professional charmers (cf. PRESS THE FLESH). [GLAD HAND n.]

glad-hander n. [20C] an enthusiastic, friendly but totally insincere person. [GLAD HAND v.]

gladiator school/kindergarten n. [1960s+] (US prison) a maximum-security prison.

glading n. [1960s+] (drugs) using inhalant. [GLAD RAG]

glad mitt see GLAD HAND n.

glad pad n. [1920s–40s] (US Black) a night-club, a dance-hall or similar establishment. [SE glad + PAD n.[2]]

glad rag n. [1960s+] (US drugs) **1** a rag soaked with an intoxicating chemical, the fumes of which one inhales. **2** one who sniffs such inhalants.

glad rags/clothes n. [20C] (orig. US) one's best and prob. gaudiest clothes.

glads *n.* [1950s+] (Aus.) *glad*ioli (cf. CARNIE n.¹). [abbr.]

Gladstone *n.* [late 19C] cheap claret. [Prime Minister William *Gladstone*'s reduction, in 1860, of the duty on French wine]

gladstonize *v.* [late 19C] to evade and prevaricate. [the alleged characteristics of Prime Minister William *Gladstone* (1809–98)]

glad stuff *n.* [1950s+] (drugs) any form of hard or narcotic drug. [the effects]

glad weeds *n.* [1970s] (US) formal dress wear (cf. GLAD RAGS). [SE *glad* + WEEDS]

gladys *n.* [1950s–60s] (camp gay) a fat, aggressive, ostentatious male homosexual. [the proper name, stereotypically associated with such a person]

glaik *see* GLEEK.

glam *adj.* [1930s+] (orig. US) glamorous; thus *glammy*, glamorous. [coined by US film magazines]

glamity *n.* [1980s+] (W.I./UK Black teen) **1** the vagina. **2** sexual intercourse (cf. PUNANY). [W.I. dial. *glami*, sticky and elastic; ult. SE *clammy*, wet, moist, sticky]

glamour boy/girl *n.* [1930s+] a glamorous young man or woman. [orig. used of RAF, esp. flying crews]

glamour pants *n.* [1930s–50s] an attractive young woman.

glamour puss *n.* [1950s+] an ostentatiously well-dressed, lavishly made-up etc (young) woman.

glamour up *v.* [1950s+] (US) to glamorize.

glam rock *n.* [1970s+] a form of rock music, esp. popular in the early–mid-1970s, featuring ostentatious clothes, make-up for both sexes and general air of androgyny; typified in the persona of David Bowie (b.1947), in his contemporary incarnation.

glam up *v.* [1950s+] to titivate oneself before a party, interview etc; thus *glammed up*, titivated (cf. TART UP).

glands *n.* (US) **1** [1910s–20s] the testicles. **2** [1970s+] breasts.

Glasgow baillie *see* GLASGOW MAGISTRATE.

Glasgow boat *n.* [late 19C+] (Anglo-Irish.) a coat. [rhy. sl.]

Glasgow kiss *n.* [20C] a head butt (cf. CHELSEA SMILE).

Glasgow magistrate/baillie *n.* [mid-19C] a salt herring (cf. ABERDEEN CUTLET). ['When George IV visited Scotland, a wag placed some salt herrings on the iron guard of the carriage belonging to a well-known Glasgow magistrate, who made one of a deputation to receive his Majesty' (Hotten, 1867). The *Scots Magazine* (December 1950) attributes the term to Walter Gibson, 'a merchant of Glasgow and Provost of that city in 1688']

Glasgows/Glasgow Rangers *n.* [1920s+] strangers, esp. as used by look-out men working with unlicensed street pitchmen. [rhy. sl.]

glasheen/glawsheen *n.* [20C] (Irish) a small glass of strong drink. [SE *glass* + dimin. sfx. *-een*]

glasier/glazier/glasyer *n.* [mid-17C–late 19C] (Und.) a thief who breaks into houses after removing an accessible window, or into shops by smashing the shop window. [SE *glasier*]

glasiers/glaziers/glasyers *n.* [mid-16C–late 18C] the eyes. [SE *glass*]

glass *n.*¹ [20C] (US Und.) a diamond; thus *genuine glass*, a very high quality diamond; *fake glass*, a worthless diamond.

glass *n.*² [1940s+] (drugs) a hypodermic needle. [early syringes were made of *glass*]

glass *n.*³ (drugs) **1** [1960s+] amphetamine (cf. A n.².). **2** [1980s+] methylamphetamine (cf. BOMBITA). [the shininess of the powder]

glass *n.*⁴ **1** [1940s+] (US) a glass of alcohol. **2** [1980s+] (Irish) a half-pint of stout or beer.

glass *adj.* [20C] (US, orig. boxing) used of any weak or vulnerable part of the body e.g. *a glass chin* (cf. GLASS JAW).

glass *v.* [1910s+] to hit in the face with a (broken) glass (cf. BOTTLE v.⁴).

glass brownies *n.* [1980s+] (drugs) cannabis.

glass case *n.* [mid-19C] a face. [rhy. sl.]

glass dick *n.* [1990s] (drugs) a pipe for smoking crack cocaine. [SE *glass* + fig. use of DICK n.² (1)]

glassed *adj.* [1910s+] (Und.) cut in the face or body by a jab or slash from a broken bottle. [GLASS v.]

glass eyes *n.*¹ [late 18C–19C] one who wears spectacles.

glass eyes *n.*² [1940s–50s] (drugs) a drug user. [the effect on one's eyes]

glass gun *n.* [1940s+] (drugs) a hypodermic needle (cf. GLASS n.²). [early syringes were made of *glass*; they gave one a SHOT n.⁵ (2)]

glasshouse *n.*¹ [1920s+] a military prison or guardroom. [the glass-roofed North Camp military prison at Aldershot]

Glass House, the *n.*² (US) **1** [1960s+] the Los Angeles County Jail. **2** [1980s+] the Ford Motor Co. Head Office, Michigan. [the design]

glasshouse *n.*³ [1990s] (drugs) a place where crack cocaine can be sold and/or smoked. [GLASS DICK + SE *house*]

glass jaw *n.* [20C] (orig. boxing) a conspicuously weak jaw, which breaks or fractures when hit and loses its possessor his fights.

glass of beer *n.* [late 19C+] an ear. [rhy. sl.]

glass of lunch/steak *n.* [1960s] (Aus.) a drink, a 'liquid lunch'.

glass of plonk *n.* [20C] the nose. [rhy. sl. *glass of plonk* = CONK n.² (1)]

glass of steak *see* GLASS OF LUNCH.

glass-work *n.* [late 19C] a method of cheating at cards in which the cheat uses a small convex mirror, concealed in the hand.

glassy alley, the *n.*¹ [1910s+] (Aus.) the best, the favourite, the most admired. [marbles use *glass alley*, a specially prized type of marble]

glassy/glassy eye *n.*² [1910s+] (Aus.) a cold, disdainful stare. [dead fish lying on the slab have 'glassy' eyes]

glayser *see* GLASIER.

glasyers *see* GLASIERS.

glaum *see* GLOM.

glawsheen *see* GLASHEEN.

Glaxo baby *n.* [1930s] (N.Z.) a young member of the special police used against strikers in Auckland. [brandname of *Glaxo*, a proprietary babyfood popular among the parents of these mainly middle-class young men]

glaze *n.* [late 17C–early 19C] a window; thus *on the glaze*, robbing jewellers' shops after smashing the windows (cf. GLASIER). [SE *glaze*, a vitreous composition used for glazing pottery etc]

glaze-ons *n.* [1960s] a spectacle-wearer.

glaze the donut, to *phr.* [1990s] of a woman, to masturbate.

glazier *see* GLASIER.

glaziers *see* GLASIERS.

glean *v.* [late 19C] euph. for steal. [SE *glean*, to gather, to harvest]

gleaner *n.* [19C] a thief. [GLEAN]

gleat/gleet *n.* **1** [early 18C+] urethritis. **2** [1940s+] (Aus.) venereal infection in the rectum. [OF *glette*, slime, filth, purulent matter]

gleef *n.* [1960s] (US) an idiot. [GLEEP]

gleek/glaik *n.* [1930s+] a glance, a quick look. [Scot. *glee*, a squint, a look behind]

gleek/glaik *v.* [1930s+] to glance quickly. [GLEEK n.]

gleep *n.* [1940s+] (US campus) an odd or stupid person. [ety. unknown; Lighter suggests 'perhaps intended to represent a Chinese person's' pron. of CREEP n. (1)]

gleep a cage, to *phr.* [1960s+] (US Und., motorcycle gang) to steal a car. [ety. unknown; ? link to CLIP v.[2] (3)]

gleet *see* GLEAT.

glengorm *n.* [20C] (Ulster) dirt, filth. [ety. unknown]

Glenn Hoddle *n.* [1970s+] something very easy. [rhy. sl. *Glenn Hoddle* = DODDLE n.; soccer star and latterly England team manager]

glib/glibb *n.* **1** [mid-18C] a ribbon. **2** [19C] the tongue; thus *slacken your glib*, loosen your tongue. [resemblance of (2) to (1); but note SE *glib*, voluble but essentially trivial]

glick/glic *adj.* [1980s+] (Irish) cunning, clever. [Irish *glic*, cunning, crafty]

glide *v.* [1990s] (US Black) to walk, to move, to arrive.

glim/glym *n.*[1] **1** [17C; late 19C–1960s] (US) a look, glimpse. **2** [late 17C–late 19C] a lantern, esp. a dark lantern used by thieves; thus *douse the glim*, turn out the light. **3** [late 18C+] the eye. **4** [mid-19C] a fake account of a dramatic fire, as sold in the streets. **5** [1910s–20s] a match. [SE *gleam*]

glim *n.*[2] [mid-18C] a fiery drink (cf. GUNPOWDER n.[2]; KNOCK-DOWN n.[1]; KNOCK-ME-DOWN n.[1]; RASHER OF BACON; RUSHLIGHT n.[1]; SLUG n.[1]; STRIP-ME NAKED n.[1]; TAPE; WILDFIRE). [fig. use of GLIM n.[1] (4)]

glim *n.*[3] [mid–late 19C] a venereal disease. [GLIM n.[1] (2), on pattern of FIRE n.[2], i.e. it 'burns']

glim *v.* **1** [late 17C–late 18C] (Und.) to burn on the hand, to brand. **2** [late 19C+] to see, to catch sight of. **3** [1910s–20s] (US Und.) to illuminate, to light. **4** [1950s] (US) to know (cf. GLOM). [GLIM n.[1]]

glim-fenders *n.* [late 17C–early 19C] **1** andirons. **2** (Und.) handcuffs. [(2) puns on (1) as 'hand irons']

glimflashy/glimflashly *adj.* [late 17C–early 19C] angry, impassioned. [one fig. *flashes* a GLIM n.[1]]

glim-gibber/-glibber *n.* [mid-19C] a jargon or professional slang. [? fig use of GLIM n.[1] (2) as generic for underworld + SE *gibber*, to mutter, to talk incomprehensibly]

glim-jack *n.* [late 17C–18C] **1** a link boy. **2** (Und.) a thief who works only at night. [GLIM n.[1] + generic proper name *Jack*]

glim-lurk *n.* [19C] (Und.) the pleading for alms after suffering a supposed fire. [GLIM n.[1] + LURK n.]

glimmer/glymmer *n.* **1** [16C+] (Und.) fire (cf. DEMANDER FOR GLIMMER; GLIM n.[1]). **2** [early 17C–mid-19C] a beggar, esp. one claims to have lost all his possessions in a fire (cf. GLIM-LURK; GLIMMERER). **3** [late 19C+] (US) a match, a locomotive headlight, a kerosene lamp, an electric light. **4** [1910s] (US) a cut gem. [SE *glimmer*, to shine, ult. Du./Ger. *glimmer*, to shine]

glimmerer/glimmering mort *n.* **1** [mid-16C–17C] a person, usu. a woman who gains entry to a house on the pretext of getting a light for the fire and, while inside, steals whatever she can. **2** [late 17C] one who deliberately sets fire to a house, hoping to take advantage of the confusion to steal. **3** [late 18C] a beggar who claims to have lost all their possessions as the result of a fire. [GLIMMER n. (1), (2) + MORT]

glimmers *n.* [late 18C+] the eyes. [ext. of GLIM. n.[1] (3)]

glimmie glide *n.* [20C] (Anglo-Irish.) the other side of a road, a field etc. [rhy. sl.]

glimming *n.* [late 19C–1940s] (US Black) watching, observing. [GLIM v. (2); note London cab-driver jargon, *glim*, to look for a cab]

glimpse *n.* [1950s+] (W.I.) an albino (cf. FRECKLE-NATURE). [albinos tend to have poor eyesight]

glims *n.* [mid-19C] (mainly US) spectacles, eye-glasses; thus *glim-faking* (Aus.), selling spectacles at inflated prices. [GLIM n.[1] (3)]

glim-stick *n.* [late 17C–early 19C] (Und.) a candlestick; thus *rum glimstick*, a silver candlestick, *queer glimstick*, a brass or pewter candlestick. [GLIM n.[1] + SE *stick*]

glint *n.* [20C] a look, a glimpse; thus *have/take a glint at* to observe, to glance at.

glisten *n.* [mid-19C] (US) a collective term for diamonds.

glistener *n.* [early 17C] a gold coin (cf. SHINERS).

glister *n.* [late 19C] a glass, a tumbler; thus a *glister of fish-hooks*, a glass of Irish whisky. [SE *glister*, a bright light, brilliance, lustre]

glitch *n.* [1970s+] a hitch, a snag, a malfunction. [Ger. *glitschen*, to slip, via Yid. *glitshen*, to slide or skid; orig. mainframe computer jargon *glitch*, 'a sudden interruption in electric service, sanity, continuity, or program function' *New Hacker's Dictionary* (1992). This was adopted *c.*1960 by astronauts, who gave it the more general def., and it moved into mainstream sl. with the spread of the personal computer culture]

glitter *n.* **1** [1950s+] (US prison) salt (cf. SNEEZE n.). **2** [1970s] (US) a collective term for diamonds. [both sparkle]

glitterati *n.* [1950s+] (orig. US) those fashionable writers, academics and sundry critics etc, who have transcended their usual obscurity into the dubious limelight of the New York and London gossip columns. [SE *glitter* + *literati*]

glitter gulch *n.* [1950s+] (US) the Las Vegas downtown casino area. [the lurid neon signs, hotel architecture etc]

glitz *n.* [1950s+] (orig. US) an extravagant but superficial display; thus *glitz up*, to make glitzy. [backform. f. GLITZY]

glitzy *adj.* [1950s+] fashionable, sophisticated, glamorous (cf. RITZY). [Ger. *glitzern*, glittering; or comb. of SE *glitter* + RITZY]

g.l.o. *phr.* [1990s] guest *list* only, used to describe an event so unappealing that one would only go if on the guest list, as it would not be worth paying for admission. [abbr.]

glo *n.* [1980s+] (drugs) crack cocaine. [ety. unknown; ? SE *glow*, the ROCKS n.[4] (3) are shiny]

gloak/gloach/gloque *n.* [18C–19C] a man, a fellow. [for ety. *see* BLOKE]

glob *n.* [20C] a mass or lump of some liquid or semi-liquid substance. [? *blob* + GOB]

globe *n.* [late 18C] a round, pewter pot.

globes *n.* [19C+] the female breasts.

globes of joy *n.* [1990s] the female breasts.

globetrotter *n.* [1960s] (drugs) a narcotics addict who is continually on the move, usu. in search of supplies.

globular *adj.* [20C] drunk. [? the sufferer is 'going round in circles']

glock *n.* [mid–late 19C] a fool. [Irish *gloichd*, a fool]

gloik *n.* [1910s+] (Aus.) a fool, a simpleton. [GLOCK]

glom/glaum *n.*[1] **1** [1930s+] (US) a hand (cf. HOOKS; MAULERS). **2** [1940s] (US) a look. [GLOM v.]

glom *n.*[2] [1930s+] (US) a fool. [? echoic of the solidity/dullness of the individual]

glom/glom onto/up *v.* **1** [late 19C+] (US) to grab, to steal. **2** [1910s+] (US) to arrest. **3** [1910s+] (US) to get, to obtain, to seize upon. **4** [1910s+] (US) to look, to see, to realize. **5** [1920s+] (US Und.) to pick fruit, crops. **6** [1930s+] (US) to eat greedily. **7** [1980s+] (US) to stick, to entangle. [Scot. *glaum*, to snatch, to grab, to seize with the jaws, to eat greedily]

glooms *n.* [1910s–70s] a bad mood, depression; thus a *gloom bug*, a depressed individual.

gloomy gus *n.* [20C] (US) a very unhappy, pessimistic person. [created *c.*1904 as a comic-strip character in *Happy Hooligan* by Frederick Burr Opper (1857–1937)]

gloop *see* GOOP n.[2].

gloopy *n.* [1990s] (US teen) something stupid. [fig. use of GLOP n. (3)]

glop *n.* **1** [1940s+] a liquid or viscous substance or mixture. **2** [1940s+] unappetizing food. **3** [1950s+] (US) silly nonsense. [onomat. of such a substance falling onto a hard surface;

coined by cartoonist Elzie Segar (1894–1938) as a sound made by the baby Swee'pea in the cartoon 'Popeye the Sailor']

glop v. [1990s] to masturbate. [GLOP n. (1)]

gloque see GLOAK.

glorified adj. [early 19C+] elevated above its usual station.

glorioski! excl. [1970s+] (US) an excl. used to express surprise. [ext. of GLORY!]

glorious adj. [late 18C–mid-19C] very drunk (cf. ABOUT RIGHT adj.¹).

gloriously adv. [late 18C+] extremely, usu. in phr. *gloriously drunk.*

glorious sinner n. [mid-19C] dinner. [rhy. sl.]

glory!/glory!/glory be! excl. [17C+] a euph. for *God* and used as such in a variety of mild oaths and exclamations.

glory be to Pete! excl. [1920s+] (Can.) a euph. for *God* and used as such in a variety of mild oaths and exclamations. [ext. of GLORY!]

glory hole n.¹ **1** [mid-19C] a small, holding cell in the court buildings, in which prisoners are kept during their trial. **2** [late 19C] a meeting place used by the Salvation Army. **3** [20C] (Irish) the space under the stairs (a place of punishment for badly behaved children). **4** [1960s+] (US) a bar frequented by homosexuals. [SE *glory hole*, anywhere in which things are heaped together without any attempt at order, ult. *glaur*, to make muddy]

glory hole n.² **1** [1920s+] (orig. US) the vagina (cf. BLACK HOLE n.¹). **2** [1940s+] (gay) a hole cut in the side of a public toilet cubicle; one man pushes his penis through while another, anonymous, man fellates him. [SE *glory*, splendour, magnificence, esp. as pun on *go to glory*, to ascend to heavenly bliss + *hole*]

glory pole n. [1950s] (US) the penis. [SE *glory* + POLE n.]

glory roll n. [1930s–40s] (US Black) a large bankroll, produced as often as possible in order to impress one's acquaintances (cf. CALIFORNIA BANKROLL). [SE *glory* + ROLL n.¹]

glossy n. [1960s+] a glossy magazine, usu. expensive women's fashion magazines, such as *Vogue* and *Harpers & Queen* (which has called itself 'the non-drip glossy', punning both on DRIP n.¹ = weakling, dullard and on gloss paint) (cf. SLICKS).

glouter n. [20C] **1** a sticky mess. **2** tapioca pudding. [? Scot. *cloiter*, a vile wet mess]

glove n.¹ [17C] some form of unspecified drinking-vessel. [the term is used in Thomas Dekker's book of 'manners', *The Guls Hornebooke* (1609), in a list of similar containers: 'hoopes, cans, half-canes, Gloues, Frolicks, and flap-dragons']

glove n.² [1950s+] (US) a condom.

glowing adj. [19C] drunk (cf. ABOUT RIGHT adj.¹).

glue n.¹ **1** [late 19C] gonorrhoea. **2** [late 19C] semen. **3** [late 19C+] thick soup. **4** [1940s–60s] (US) beer (cf. GLUED adv.¹). [(1) sticks to the ribs; (2) the thick yellow/white discharge]

glue n.² [late 19C–1940s] (US) money. [? one wishes to 'stick onto it']

glue v. [1920s–70s] (orig. US) **1** to steal. **2** to arrest.

glued adv.¹ [1940s–60s] (US) drunk. [GLUE n.¹ (3); i.e. the lassitude of a drunkard's speech and movements]

glued adv.² [1980s+] (US campus) stable, sane (cf. UNGLUED). [HAVE ONE'S HEAD GLUED ON]

gluehead see GLUEY.

glueneck n. [1920s–70s] (US) a prostitute (cf. GLUEPOT n.³). [GLUE n.¹ (2)]

gluepot n.¹ **1** [late 18C–19C] a parson. **2** [late 19C] a part of the road so muddy that vehicles stick in it. **3** [late 19C–1930s] (S.Afr.) a particularly pleasant public house. **4** [1920s] (US Und.) a post office. **5** [1920s–60s] (US) an old horse, suggested by use of horse carcasses in glue manufacture. [(1) he

'joins together' married couples, (3) one wishes to 'be stuck' there]

gluepot n.² [20C] the vagina. [rhy. sl. *gluepot* = TWAT]

gluepot n.³ [1920s] (US Und.) a prostitute (cf. GLUENECK).

gluepot has come unstuck phr. [late 19C] used of someone who smells of semen or recent intercourse. [GLUE n.¹ (2)]

glue the lady's eyes shut, to phr. [1990s] to masturbate.

gluey/gluehead n. [1960s+] (drugs) a person who sniffs glue. [SE *glue* + sfx. -HEAD (2)]

glug n. [1970s+] (US) a swig, a swallow. [echoic]

gluggar n. [20C] (Irish) a general term of abuse. [Irish *ubh ghlugair*, a rotten egg]

glum-pot n. [mid-19C] a miserable, sulky person (cf. BARM-POT). [SE *glum*]

glunch v. [1910s+] (Ulster) to grumble, to complain. [Scot. *glunch*, to grumble, to frown]

glut see GLUTTON.

glutes n. [1980s+] (US) the buttocks. [medical lat. *gluteus maximus*, one of the large muscles that form the buttock; ult. Gk. *glutos*, the rump]

glutton/glut n. [1970s+] (gay) a man obsessed with sex to the exclusion of other considerations.

glutton for punishment n. [1970s+] (gay) a fellator who continues sucking the penis even when orgasm has been reached.

glybe see GYBE n.

glym see GLIM n.¹.

glymmer see GLIMMER.

glype n. [20C] (Irish) a fool. [synon Scot. *glype*]

g.m. n. [1900s–50s] (US) a.m., the morning. [abbr. good morning]

G-man n. (US) **1** [1930s+] an FBI agent, lit. 'Government-man'. **2** [1940s+] a garbage man.

g.m.b.u./g.m.f.u. phr. [1940s+] a disaster, utter chaos. [abbr. grand military balls-up/grand military fuck-up]

gnarl/gnarl upon v. [early 19C] (Und.) to spy on, to inform against; thus *gnarling*, likely to act as an informer. [SE *gnar*; *gnarl*, to snarl]

gnarler/gnawler n. [early 19C; late 19C–1920s] **1** a small watchdog. **2** an informer. [GNARL]

gnarl upon see GNARL.

gnarly adj. (US) **1** [1980s+] a general term of disapproval, disappointment, annoyance. **2** [1990s] wonderful, first-rate, on 'bad = good' pattern. [SE *gnarly*]

gnasp v. [early–mid-18C] to annoy. [16C SE *gnasp*, to snap at]

gnat butter n. [1900s–40s] (US) **1** semen. **2** smegma (cf. DUCK BUTTER).

gnat's eyebrow/balls/bristle/eye/hair/heel/prick n. [20C] (US) something very small, esp. in phr. e.g. *down to a gnat's eyebrow*, to the finest detail, *sharp enough to split the hair on a gnat's ass*, extremely fine (cf. COCK'S HAIR).

gnat's piss n. [1950s+] a derog. description of any liquid, but esp. alcohol, that is weak, thin, tasteless etc.

gnat's prick see GNAT'S EYEBROW.

gnatter v. [19C] **1** to grumble, to complain, to be peevish or querulous. **2** to talk or gossip in an unfriendly manner.

gnawler see GNARLER.

gnaw the bone, to phr. [1990s] to perform fellatio (cf. GNAW THE 'NANA). [SE *gnaw* + BONE n.⁶]

gnaw the 'nana, to phr. [1960s+] to perform fellatio (cf. GNAW THE BONE). [SE *gnaw* + BANANA n.²]

gnome n.¹ [1950s+] (US) an insignificant person, esp. a low-level employee.

gnome n.² [1950s–60s] an international (esp. Swiss) banker. [coined on 12 November 1956 by Labour politician Harold Wilson (1916–95), referring to the economic problems that had plagued Britain in the wake of the Suez Crisis of earlier that year; he blamed them on the machinations of Swiss bankers and financiers, whose could manipulate the economies of nations, seemingly at will]

gnomon *n.* [late 16C–early 19C] the nose. [SE *gnomon*, 'a[n] ... object which serves to indicate the time of day by casting its shadow upon a marked surface; esp. the pin or triangular plate used ... in an ordinary sun-dial' (*OED*)]

gnostic *n.* [late 18C–early 19C] a 'knowing one', thus a cheat or sharper; thus *gnostically*, knowingly, artfully. [SE *gnostic*, an intellectual, one who possesses esoteric spiritual knowledge]

G-note *n.* [1930s+] (US) $1000 note. [G *n.*[1] + SE *note*]

go *n.*[1] **1** [late 18C+] the height of fashion. **2** [early 19C] a dandy, a fashionable man. [SE *go*, spirit, energy, dash]

go *n.*[2] [late 18C–1950s] **1** a measure (of alcohol), e.g. a *go of gin*; esp. a three-halfpenny bowl of gin and water, available at a *go shop*. **2** the vessel that contains such a measure. **3** a portion or measure of food.

go *n.*[3] **1** [late 18C+] an event, circumstances, a state of affairs, esp. as *rum go*, an odd situation; thus *what goes?* what's happening? **2** [late 18C+] an attempt, a try, e.g. *make a go of*. **3** [late 18C+] a success. **4** [early 19C+] a turn in a game, an opportunity to do something; thus *at/in one go*, at/in one attempt; *have a go*, take a turn; *have a go at*, make an attempt. **5** [late 19C+] a contest, a fight, esp. a boxing-match or a street fight. **6** [20C] an argument. **7** [1970s+] (Aus.) news, information.

go *n.*[4] [early 19C+] energy, spirit; thus *it's all go*, everything is very energetic, active.

go *n.*[5] [late 19C–1930s] a bargain, an agreement, a 'deal', usu. in phr. *it's a go.*

go *n.*[6] **1** [1930s] (US drugs) a very small quantity of drugs wrapped in paper. **2** [1980s+] (drugs) cocaine.

go *v.*[1] [17C+] to bet, to wager.

go *v.*[2] **1** [late 17C+] to succeed, to win approval or applause. **2** [mid-19C+] to be acceptable, to be permitted. **3** [late 19C+] (orig. US) to be accepted or carried into effect, to have authority or effectiveness, to be obeyed without question, esp. in phr. *what I say goes.* **4** [1910s+] to deal with, to find appealing or acceptable. **5** [1920s+] (US) to choose, esp. to become a member of; thus *go something.*

go *v.*[3] [18C] to have an orgasm (cf. COME *v.*[1]).

go *v.*[4] **1** [19C+] to tolerate, to bear, to put up with. **2** [late 19C+] to eat or drink, e.g. *I could go a couple of beers.*

go *v.*[5] [late 19C+] to match, to get along. [a pair of matched horses]

go *v.*[6] [late 19C+] for something to work out in a specific way, esp. of a political contest, e.g. *go Labour, go Republican.*

go *v.*[7] [20C] to *go* to the lavatory, used euph, esp. by children e.g. *Miss, I've got to go!* [abbr.]

go *v.*[8] [20C] usu. of a woman, to perform sexual intercourse, usu. in interrog. phr. used between two men, *Does she go?*

go *v.*[9] [1930s+] (Aus.) to attack, verbally or physically.

go *v.*[10] [1940s+] to say, to talk, e.g. *I go 'How are you', and he goes 'Lousy'... .*

go abroad *v.* [19C] to be transported. [ironic euph.]

go a bundle on, to *phr.* [1930s+] to support whole-heartedly, to be very fond. [fig. uses of GO *v.*[1] + BUNDLE *n.*[2]]

go a couple rounds with the ol' josh/champ, to *phr.* [20C] to masturbate.

go a-crash of, to *phr.* [20C] to assault. [SE *go* + pfx. *a-* (implying motion) + *crash* (into)]

go a cropper *see* COME A CROPPER.

go across the river, to *phr.* [19C] to die. [the mythological River Styx across which dead Greeks were supposedly ferried by Charon on their way to Hades]

goad *n.* [16C–early 18C] (Und.) a decoy at a horse-fair, 'they that stand by and cony-catch the chapman [merchant, trader], whether with out bidding, false praises etc.' Dekker *Lanthorn and Candlelight* (1608) [SE *goad*, a spur]

goadie *see* GODY.

go a fairy, to *phr.* [late 19C] to toss coins to see who buys a round of halfpennyworths of gin. [GO *v.*[1] + SE *fairy*, very small]

go aggro *v.* [1980s+] (US campus) to become aggressive. [AGGRO]

go-ahead *n.* **1** [mid-19C+] (US) progress, ambition, energy. **2** [1940s+] a command or permission to do something, esp. in phr. *give it/one the go-ahead.* [GO-AHEAD adj.]

go-ahead *adj.* [mid-19C+] (orig. US) progressive, enthusiastic to do well.

go ahead *v.* [1960s+] to authorize an action or a person to perform an action. [GO-AHEAD adj.]

go ahead like a whale, to *phr.* [late 19C] to throw oneself into something wholeheartedly (cf. WHALES ON). [the size of a whale]

go ahead up *v.* [1970s+] (US Black) to take part in some form of activity with another person.

goak *n.* [mid-19C–1930s] (Aus.) a prank, a practical joke. [SE *joke* + dial. *gowk*, a fool]

goal/ghoul/gool *v.* [1910s–70s] (US) to knock down, to stun, to defeat; thus *knock one for a goal*, to astonish. [SE *goal*; *ghoul/gool* are dial. prons.]

go all out *v.* [1930s+] to make one's best effort. [SE *go* + *all out*, completely]

go all out on *v.* [1930s] to trust completely. [betting imagery]

go all over town with, to *phr.* [1960s+] to lick and suck the partner's body, incl. the genitals and sometimes the anus (cf. AROUND THE WORLD). [the tongue 'travels' around the body. Usu. used by a prostitute as part of the 'menu' of paid services she can offer]

go all round the houses *see* GO ROUND THE HOUSES.

go all the way/the whole way, to *phr.* [1920s+] of a man, to achieve satisfactory seduction; of a woman, to be willing to permit this.

go all unnecessary *see* COME OVER UNNECESSARY.

go aloft *v.* [late 18C+] to die. [i.e. to heaven]

go alone *v.* [early 19C] to be wary or cautious, to be experienced.

go-along/-alonger *n.*[1] [mid-19C] (Und.) a fool. [he 'goes along' when someone orders him]

go-along *n.*[2] [mid-19C] a thief.

go along like sixty, to *phr.* [mid-19C+] to go at a good pace to move briskly (cf. SWING LIKE SIXTY). [? *60* miles an hour]

go along with you! *see* GET ALONG WITH YOU.

go a lower peg, to *phr.* [19C] to drink heavily. [the pegs that were once driven into a public house tankard to mark the amount drunk]

goamey *see* GOM *n.*[2].

go a million, to *phr.* [1910s+] (Aus./N.Z.) to be utterly lost, in a totally hopeless position, at a total disadvantage. [one has wagered and presumably lost 'a million']

go and boil your head *see* GO BOIL YOUR HEAD.

go and bust yourself! *excl.* [mid-19C+] a general excl. of dismissal or contempt.

go and eat coke! *excl.* [late 19C+] a general excl. of contempt or dismissal. [? punning on Marie Antoinette's supposed (but fictional) dismissal of the starving Paris mob, *Let them eat cake*]

go and fry your face! *excl.* [late 19C–1900s] a general excl. of dismissal or contempt.

go and fuck yourself! *excl.* [mid-19C+] a general excl. of dismissal or contempt (cf. GET FUCKED!). [FUCK *v.*[1]]

go and get cut! *excl.* [20C] (Aus.) a general excl. of dismissal or disdain.

go and get your brains examined! *excl.* [1920s+] an excl. used to someone who is seen as speaking or behaving foolishly (cf. GET YOUR BRAINS EXAMINED).

go and have a roll! *excl.* [early 19C+] go away! get lost!

go and jump in a lake! *see* GO JUMP IN A LAKE!

go and look at the crops, to *phr.* [mid-19C–1910s] to urinate, usu. as an excuse e.g. *I've just got to go and ... .*

go and piss up a shutter! *excl.* [1910s+] a general excl. of dismissal or contempt.

go and play trains with yourself! *excl.* [20C] a general excl. of dismissal or contempt.

go and scrape yourself! *excl.* [late 19C] a general excl. of dismissal or contempt (cf. GO SCRAPE!).

go and see uncle, to *phr.* [1900s–10s] to visit the lavatory (cf. AUNT n.^{2}).

go and sing 'sweet violets', to *phr.* [20C] to defecate. [euph.]

go and take a run against the wind! *excl.* [20C] (Anglo-Irish.) a general excl. of dismissal or contempt.

go and take a running/crawling/creeping jump/jump at yourself! *excl.* [1910s+] a general excl. of dismissal and distaste.

go animal *v.* [1960s] (US) to lose one's emotional control.

goanna *n.* [1910s+] (Aus.) a piano (cf. JOANNA). [rhy. sl.]

go a-padding *v.* [late 18C–early 19C] to rob on the highway. [PAD n.^{1}]

go ape/apeshit *v.* **1** [1950s+] (orig. US) to lose control, esp. of one's temper. **2** [1960s+] (orig. US) to malfunction. [APE adj./ APE-SHIT; the alleged 'craziness' of the animal. The specific ref. is prob. to the fictitious *King Kong*, created for the film in 1933]

go ape for/over *v.* [1960s+] to be obsessed with. [GO APE]

go a raker, to *phr.* [20C] (Aus.) to fall heavily. [RAKER]

go/run/rush around in circles, to *phr.* [1930s+] (orig. US) to move or act aimlessly or inconclusively.

go around the block, to *phr.* [1970s+] (US) to gain experience, esp. in phr. *X has been around the block* (*a few times*), X is experienced, esp. sexually.

go around the tower, to *phr.* [late 17C–18C] (Und.) to clip money. [proper name *Tower of London*, one of London's criminal centres]

go as if she cracked nuts with her tail, to *phr.* [late 17C–early 18C] of a woman, to be sexually enthusiastic. [SE *go* + TAIL n.^{1} (2); note GO v.^{8}]

go a snail's gallop, to *phr.* [mid-19C] to proceed very slowly. [orig. mid-16C dial]

goat *n.*^{1} **1** [late 17C+] a womanizer, a lecher. **2** [mid-19C] the buttocks. **3** [late 19C] (US Und.) a Catholic priest. **4** [late 19C–1950s] (US) a slow or worthless horse. **5** [1910s+] a dupe, a fool. **6** [1940s+] (US) an offensive old man. **7** [1960s+] (US campus) a student being initiated into a fraternity, a fraternity pledge; thus *goat room*, the room used for initiation. [the trad. characteristics of the animal, i.e. lechery, stubbornness etc]

goat *n.*^{2} **1** [late 19C+] (US) a *goatee* beard. **2** [late 19C+] (US) a *scapegoat*. [abbr.]

goat *n.*^{3} [1960s+] (US) a Pontiac GTO automobile. [pron./ reversal of GTO]

goat *v.* [mid-19C–1900s] to beat, to thrash. [COAT v.]

goat-and-galah *adj.* [1920s–50s] (Aus.) used of a small hotel, town or other place to indicate the lack of amenities. [the main inhabitants are *goats* and *galahs*]

goatees *n.* [1960s] (US gay) the testicles. [? GONADS + ref. to goatish lechery]

goat-fuck/-rope/-screw *n.* [1970s+] (orig. US milit.) a fiasco, a mess, chaos, confusion (cf. BEEN TO THREE COUNTY FAIRS AND A GOAT-FUCKING). [such a coupling is seen as an epitome of chaos]

go at full bang, to *phr.* [1910s–20s] to go at full speed.

goat-hair *n.* [1900s–50s] (US Black) homemade or bootleg liquor.

goat hill/town/woods/goat's gulch *n.* [20C] (US) an area of town where a certain class of people live, usu. the poor, but sometimes the better-off (cf. BILLY-GOAT ALLEY). [note. one such *goat's gulch* in Kansas was gentrified and re-nicknamed *Angora Heights*]

goat house *n.* [mid-19C] a brothel (cf. ACCOMMODATION HOUSE; GOATMILKER). [GOAT n.^{1} + HOUSE n.^{1}]

go at it hammer and tongs, to *phr.* [early 18C+] to approach an activity with maximum effort and energy; modern use esp. refers to sexual intercourse. [imagery of a blacksmith using a hammer to beat a piece of metal extracted with tongs from a furnace]

goatmilker *n.* [mid-19C] **1** the vagina. **2** a prostitute (cf. GOAT HOUSE). [GOAT n.^{1} + SE *milker*]

goat-mouth *n.* [20C] (W.I.) the ability that certain individuals supposedly posses to cause problems or frustrate the efforts of others; thus *put goat-mouth on*, to cause such problems, *goat-mouth bite you?* a question asked of one who seems unhappy or worried.

goat-rope *see* GOAT-FUCK.

goat roper *n.* [20C] (US) a peasant, a rural person, an unsophisticated person. [their stereotypical occupation]

goat-screw *see* GOAT-FUCK.

goat's gulch *see* GOAT HILL.

goat's jig *n.* [late 17C–18C] sexual intercourse (cf. DANCE v.^{1}). [the perceived sexuality of the goat]

goat skin *n.* [1960s+] (US gay) a long foreskin.

goat's nest *n.* [1950s] (US) a dirty, untidy place.

go at something baldheaded/go it baldheaded, to *phr.* [mid-19C+] (US) to put all one's efforts into, to commit oneself wholly – and totally disregard the possible consequences.

goat's toe *n.* [1920s+] (Ulster) an excellent, admirable outstanding person or object; thus *he's no goat's toe*, he's no fool (cf. CAT'S WHISKERS).

goat town *see* GOAT HILL.

go at two-forty/two-forty pace, to *phr.* [late 19C] (US) to move fast. [? milit. marching paces]

goat woods *see* GOAT HILL.

goaty *adj.* (US) **1** [1910s–50s] sexually frustrated. **2** [1910s–70s] irritated. [characteristics of the SE *goat*]

go-away *n.* **1** [mid-19C] (US Und.) a railroad train. **2** [late 19C] (society) the dress in which a bride departs from her reception to begin her honeymoon. **3** [1920s+] (Aus.) a train, a tram, a bus.

gob *n.*^{1} [mid-16C+] the mouth. [orig. northern dial.]

gob *n.*^{2} [19C+] a large amount, esp. as *gobs* (*of*). [16C SE *gob*, large amount of money]

gob *n.*^{3} **1** [early 19C+] a lump, a mouthful. **2** [mid-19C+] a lump or clot of some slimy substance. [the term appears mid-16C as SE; it gradually declined in status over the next 300 years]

gob *n.*^{4} [late 19C+] **1** a coastguard or a quarterdeck man. **2** (US) any sailor. [GOB n.^{1}. 'When a meeting takes place the men indulge in a protracted yarn and a draw of the pipe. The session involves a considerable amount of expectoration all round, whereby our friends come to be known as gobbies' (F&H)]

gob *n.*^{5} [late 19C+] (Und.) a theft carried out by a thief who spits on a man's coat, alerts him to the problem then robs him while pretending to 'help' him clean up. [GOB v. (2)]

gob *v.* **1** [18C–late 19C] to swallow in large mouthfuls, to 'choke down'. **2** [late 19C+] to spit. [GOB n.^{4}]

go-back *n.* [1920s+] (Aus.) a reply, a retort (cf. COME-BACK n.¹).

go back *v.* [1900s–50s] (US Black) for processed hair to return to its normal state.

go back from *v.* [mid-19C+] to retreat, to withdraw, to 'back down'.

go back on *v.* [mid-19C+] (orig. US) to reverse one's position, to break a promise.

go back to Africa, to *phr.* [20C] (W.I./Guyn.) for a light-skinned man to marry a woman whose complexion is much darker than his own.

go back to square one, to *phr.* [1930s+] to start again at the beginning. [? such board games as ludo or snakes and ladders where an unlucky throw of the dice can send one 'back to square one'; an alternative suggestion refers to the game of hopscotch, also based on squares]

go back to your bound-place! *see* FIND YOUR BOUND-PLACE!

go backwards *v.* [1900s] to visit an outdoor privy. [the position of the anus + the usu. siting of the privy at the back of the house]

go bag your head! *excl.* [mid–late 19C+] (US/Aus.) give in! back off! admit defeat! (cf. BAG YOUR FACE!). [BAG ONE'S HEAD]

go bail *v.* [late 19C] to be absolutely certain, to 'put one's money where one's mouth is'. [the presumption that one will only go bail for a person in whom one has faith]

go bald-headed at/for/into, to *phr.* [mid-19C+] to stake everything, to disregard consequences, to attack without care or thought.

go ballarat *v.* [late 19C–1920s] (Aus.) to drink alone (cf. BALLARAT). [? the minimal population of the town]

go ballistic *v.* [1980s+] (orig. US) to lose one's temper.

go ballocking *v.* [19C+] to have sexual intercourse. [BALLOCKS n.² (1)]

go bananas *v.* [1960s+] (orig. US) **1** to lose emotional control, to become obsessed by (cf. DRIVE BANANAS). **2** to delight in something absolutely, usu. as *go bananas over*. [image of an over-ripe banana that 'goes soft']

gob and rub, to *phr.* [1960s] to masturbate. [? GOB v. (2) + SE *rub*; spitting on the penis before masturbation]

go bang *v.* [1920s+] (Aus.) of a man, to have sexual intercourse. [BANG n.² + the 'explosion' of ejaculation]

go bark at the moon! *excl.* [1960s] go away! get lost! [note 16C *bark at the moon*, to complain uselessly, to make a pointless fuss]

gobber *n.* [1920s–30s] the mouth. [GOB n.¹]

gobberloony *see* GABBERLOONEY.

gobble *n.* [late 19C+] an act of fellatio. [GOBBLE v.]

gobble *v.¹* **1** [mid-19C–1900s] (US) to grab, to steal, to apprehend. **2** [1970s+] to fellate. [SE *gobble*, to eat food greedily]

gobble *v.²* [1920s–40s] (US Black) to chatter. [SE *gabble* ? + the turkey's *gobbling*]

gobble *v.³* [1970s] (US) to fail in the entertainment business. [i.e. to act like a TURKEY n.³ (1)]

gobble box *n.* [1970s] (US campus) television set. [var. on GOGGLE BOX]

gobbledygoo/gobbledgoo *n.¹* [1930s–40s] (US) a prostitute who performs fellatio. [SE *gobble* + GOO; note also GOBBLE v.¹ (2)]

gobbledygoo/gobbledgoo *n.²* [1940s+] (US) pretentious or nonsensical speech. [*gobbledegook*, coined in 1944 by Maury Maverick, chairman of US Smaller War Plants Committee in Congress, who suggested a link to the *gobbling* noises of a turkey; the term began as sl. but very quickly mutated into SE]

gobble-gobble *n.* [1920s–40s] (US Black) talk, chatter. [GOBBLE v.² + redup.]

gobblegoo *see* GOBBLEDYGOO.

gobble-gut *n.* [early–mid-17C] a glutton. [SE *gobble* + *gut*]

gobble hose *v.* [1980s+] to fellate. [SE *gobble*/GOBBLE v.¹ + HOSE n.¹ (1)]

gobble pipe *n.* [1930s] (US) a saxophone (cf. GOB-STICK).

gobbleprick *n.* [late 17C–18C] a sexually active woman. [SE *gobble*/GOBBLE v.¹ (2) + PRICK n. (2)]

gobbler *n.¹* [mid-16C–early 17C] a duck.

gobbler *n.²* **1** [19C] the mouth. **2** [mid-19C+] a voracious eater. **3** [1920s+] (US) an individual who performs oral sex (cf. BONE GOBBLER). [GOBBLE v.¹ (2)]

gobbler's knob/gobbler hill *n.* [1930s–70s] (US) generic nickname for anywhere considered far-away.

gobble the goo/gook/goop/goose, to *phr.* [1910s+] (orig. US) to fellate. [GOBBLE v.¹ (2) + GOO n./GOOK n.⁴/GOOP n.²/SE *goose*]

gobble up *v.* [mid-19C+] (US) to seize upon to snatch up, to lay hold of. [GOBBLE v.¹ (1)]

gob-box *n.* [18C] the mouth. [GOB n.¹ + SE *box*]

gobby *n.* [late 19C–1920s] a sailor. [GOB n.⁴ (2)]

gobby *adj.* **1** [early 18C+] talkative. **2** stupid. [GAB v. + sfx. -*y*]

go beard-splitting *v.* [18C] to have sexual intercourse. [BEARD-SPLITTER]

gobdaw *n.* [1960s+] (Irish) a gullible simpleton. [Irish *gabh-dán*, a gullible person]

go beat your meat! *excl.* [1930s+] (US) a general excl. of dismissal. [BEAT ONE'S MEAT]

go Bedford *n.* [mid-19C] a rich, throaty chuckle (cf. O. SMITH). [the contemporary actor Paul *Bedford* who issued such a trademark chuckle accompanied by the words 'I believe you my boy', a phrase he used in the hit melodrama *The Green Bushes*]

go bed-pressing *v.* [19C] to have sexual intercourse.

gobeen *n.* [1930s+] (Irish) a general term of abuse. [Irish *gob*, a beak + dimin. sfx. -*een*]

go before one's mare to market, to *phr.* [late 17C–mid-19C] to do absurd things.

go belly-bumping *v.* [19C] to have sexual intercourse; thus *get a belly-bumper/belly-buster*, to become pregnant.

go belly-up/belly-side-up *v.* [1920s+] **1** to go bankrupt. **2** to die. [the image of a dead fish, floating belly-up]

go below 14th street, to *phr.* [1960s] to engage in oral sex (cf. DOWNTOWN). [the ref. is to 14th Street, New York City, which divides downtown from midtown]

go bent *v.* [20C] **1** (Und.) for a witness to retract a previous statement (which would have helped the prosecution). **2** to turn to criminality. **3** (prison) for one's girlfriend to take up with someone else. [BENT adj. (3)]

go bent on *v.* [1950s+] (Und.) to let down, to desert. [BENT adj. (3)]

go/be off the handle, to *phr.* [mid-19C+] **1** to lose one's temper, one's emotional control (cf. FLY OFF THE HANDLE). **2** to die.

Go-between, The *n.* [late 19C] St Alban's Church, Holborn, London. [a court case of 1897 when a witness, asked what denomination this church was, replied 'It ain't Roman Catholic, and yet it's very High. It's a go-between' (Ware)]

go between the moon and the milkman, to *phr.* [late 19C] to abscond from a house or flat, taking one's furniture and possessions, but avoiding payment of any outstanding rent, utility bills etc (cf. SHOOT THE MOON). [i.e. to leave the house at or just prior to dawn]

go beyond *v.* [mid-19C] (Anglo-Irish.) to suffer judicial transportation. ['beyond' the world one knows]

gob-gobbler *n.* [1980s+] (US gay) a gay man who specializes in sailors as partners. [GOB n.² + GOBBLER n.² (3)]

go big licks, to *phr.* [1950s+] (Aus.) to enthuse over, to like very much. [SE *lick*, a hit]

go birds-nesting *v.* [20C] to have sexual intercourse. [euph.; BIRD n.⁵ + NEST n.¹]

gob-iron n. [1950s+] a mouth organ. [GOB n.[1] + SE *iron*]

go bitching v. [late 17C–mid-19C] to have sexual intercourse, esp. with a prostitute. [BITCH n.[1]]

gob job n. [1980s+] **1** fellatio (cf. BLOW JOB). **2** (US gay) fellatio performed on a sailor (cf. GOB-GOBBLER). [GOB n.[1] + JOB n.[5]; (2) adds pun on GOB n.[4] (2)]

go blah v. [20C] to have one's mind go momentarily blank. [SE *blah*, echoic of a nonsensical noise]

goblin n. [late 19C–1920s] a sovereign. [abbr. JEMMY O'GOBLIN]

go blind v. [20C] to masturbate. [mockery of the Puritan warning that those who masturbate will go blind]

goblin juice n. [1960s–70s] (US) whisky. [SE *gobble* + *juice*]

gob-lock n. [1990s] a fool. [GOB n.[1] + SE *lock*; their inarticulacy]

gob off! excl. [1990s] go away! (cf. BUGGER OFF!; FUCK OFF!; SOD OFF). [euph.]

go boil/go and boil your head! excl. [1930s] a generally dismissive excl., euph. for GO TO HELL!

goboon n. [1930s–40s] (US) a spittoon. [GOB v. (2) + sfx. *-oon*]

go Borneo v. [1970s+] (US campus) to get crazily drunk. [the presumed antics of the 'Wild Man of Borneo']

go-boy n. [1960s+] (Can./Irish) a young hoodlum, a juvenile delinquent.

gobshite n. **1** [late 19C–1910s] (US) an expectorated wad of tobacco. **2** [20C] a fool, a dupe. [lit. and fig. uses of GOB n.[1] + SHITE]

gobsmacked adj. [1980s+] flabbergasted, amazed, speechless. [orig. northern dial.; lit. SE *smacked* in the GOB n.[1]]

gob-stick n. (US) **1** [late 18C–19C] usu. pl., forks or spoons. **2** [1920s–50s] (orig. US) a clarinet or fife (cf. GOBBLEPIPE; LIQUORICE STICK). [GOB n.[1] + fig. use of SE *stick*]

gobstopper n.[1] [20C] the penis. [rhy. sl. *gobstopper* = CHOPPER n.[1] (3)]

gobstopper n.[2] [1920s+] a large, spherical sweet that one sucks, gradually reducing the size. [GOB n.[1] + SE *stopper*]

gob-string n. [late 18C] a bridle. [GOB n.[1]]

gob the knob, to phr. [1990s] (US) to perform fellatio. [GOB v.[1] + KNOB n.[1] (1)]

go bum-faking/-fighting/-tickling/-working v. [early–mid-18C] to have sexual intercourse. [BUM n.[2] + FAKE/SE *fight*/SE *tickle*/SE *work*]

go bung v. (Aus./ N.Z.) **1** [mid–late 19C] to die. **2** [late 19C+] to become bankrupt. **3** [late 19C+] to collapse, to break down, to fail. [Abor. *bong*, dead]

go bung into v. [late 19C] to smash into, to hit hard. [SE *bung*, into the very heart of things]

go bush v. (Aus.) **1** [20C] to go wild. **2** [20C] to seek the solitude and privacy of the bush. **3** [1910s+] to escape from prison and vanish. [SE *bush*, uncleared or untilled areas that are still in a state of nature]

go bushranging, to phr. to have sexual intercourse. [pun on SE + BUSH n.[4]]

go bust v. [late 19C+] of an individual firm or company, to lose one's money to become bankrupt. [BUST n.[1]]

go buttocking v. [18C] to have sexual intercourse (cf. BUTTOCK-BALL).

go buttock-stirring v. [late 18C–early 19C] to have sexual intercourse.

goby n. [1940s+] a middleman in criminal dealings, an underworld fixer (cf. GOFER). [SE *go-between*]

go-by-the-ground n. [late 17C–18C] a short person.

go by the number eleven bus, to phr. [late 19C] to walk (cf. GO BY WALKER'S BUS). [the two legs resemble the figure 11]

go by walker's bus, to phr. [late 19C] to go on foot (cf. GO BY THE NUMBER ELEVEN BUS). [pun on SE *walk*]

go by way of lothbury, to phr. [mid-16C–mid-17C] to hate, to dislike. [pun on *Lothbury* in the City of London/SE *lo(a)the*]

go callyhooting, to phr. [19C] (US) to be moving fast and noisily. [? SE *gallivanting* + a link to the *calliope* or street organ]

go-cart n. [1910s–70s] (US) a car.

go case/have a case on v. [mid-19C+] **1** to sleep with. **2** to have a semi-permanent relationship with. [CASE n.[2] or CASE n.[5]]

go caso v. [1900s–30s] to work as a genteel prostitute, from a flat rather than walking the streets. [CASE n.[2]]

go catch a horse, to phr. [20C] to urinate. [euph.]

go chase yourself! excl. [late 19C+] (US/Aus.) go away!

gock n. [1970s] (US) any form of sticky substance, ointment, cream (cf. GUCK). [onomat.]

go cockfighting v. [19C] to have sexual intercourse.

go cold at v. [1920s+] (Aus.) to scold, to blame, to reprimand.

go cold on v. [1920s+] to lose one's initial enthusiasm for a proposition, activity etc.

go commando v. [1970s+] (US campus) to go without underwear. [? tough commandos need no such 'soft' apparel]

go conk v. [1920s+] (Aus.) **1** usu. of machinery, to collapse, to break down, to malfunction (cf. CRUMP v.). **2** to die; thus *conked*, dead. **3** to fall asleep. [CONK OUT]

go cony-catching with a dead ferret see GO RABBIT-HUNTING WITH A DEAD FERRET.

go cook your own bush phr. [1970s] (W.I.) used to a sponger, go and eat in your own house.

go coolie-ing v. [late 19C–1900s] (S.Afr.) to hawk fruit and vegetables from a handcart. [SE *coolie*]

go crackers v. [1920s+] to go mad, become insane, eccentric. [CRACKERS adj.]

go crawl back in your hole! excl. [20C] a hostile excl. used when requesting someone to be quiet and go away.

go crawl up a hole! excl. [1940s+] (Aus.) a general excl. of dismissal or contempt.

go critical v. [1990s] to explode with emotion or rage. [nuclear physics; *go critical*, for the fissile material placed in a reactor or bomb to reach the minimum mass or size required to produce a chain reaction]

go crook on v. (Aus.) **1** [1900s] to act dishonestly. **2** [1910s+] to lose one's temper (with). **3** [1910s+] to break down, to stop working, to deteriorate. **4** [1910s+] to become ill. [CROOK adj. (3)]

go cunny-catching v. [18C] to have sexual intercourse (cf. CATCHING THE BIRD). [CUNNY + SE *catching*; pun on 16C Und. CONY-CATCHING]

God/God's used in a number of oaths that, when coined, had a good deal more resonance, given their blasphemous context, e.g. GODSOOKERS, GADZOOKS (cf. ADAD).

god n. [1980s+] (US campus) an exceptionally attractive male (cf. GODDESS).

go dance the kipples, to phr. [19C] to have sexual intercourse. [Scot. *kipple*, couple]

God-awful adj. [late 19C+] (orig. US) especially appalling.

god-bird n. [1950s] (W.I.) the much-loved and petted 'baby' of the family. [dial. *god-bird*, the youngest bird in a nestful]

God-blasted adj. [20C] a general oath (cf. DAD-BLASTED; DAD-GASTED).

God-blessed adj. [1980s+] (US) euph. for God-damned (cf. GOD-DAMN adj.).

God bless the duke of Argyle phr. [19C] a remark made on observing one's companion shrug their shoulders; the insinuation is that they have lice. [a row of iron posts erected in Glasgow by the contemporary duke. Grateful lice-ridden citizens were able to use them as scratching-posts. Another version suggests that the posts were erected around the duke's various estates; primarily for the benefit of sheep, they were adopted by verminous shepherds]

God-blind-me n. [1950s] (W.I.) flashy footwear (cf. G.B.!). [the ironic excl. by one who sees them]

God-botherer n. [1970s+] (Aus.) an evangelist (cf. GOD-HOPPER).

God-box n. **1** [1910s+] a church. **2** [1930s+] an organ.

go cony-catching with a dead ferret see GO RABBIT-HUNTING WITH A DEAD FERRET.

God-dam/-damn n. [early 19C+] a damn, usu. in phr. *I don't give a God-dam/good God-dam.*

God-damn/-damned adj. **1** [17C+] most damnable. **2** (US) [mid-19C+] exasperating, most strange.

God-dam!/-damn! excl. [early 19C+] a generally pej. excl. expressing anger, astonishment etc.

goddess n. [1980s+] (US campus) an ambitious, successful woman (cf. GOD).

goddess Diana n. [mid-19C] 6 pence (2.5p). [rhy. sl. *goddess Diana* = TANNER]

goddie n. [mid-19C+] a dog. [backsl.]

godfather/godfather-in-law n.[1] [late 16C–early 19C] a member of the jury.

godfather n.[2] [late 17C–18C] one who pays the bill after a meal or a session of drinking; thus *will you stand godfather and we will take care of the brat*, you pay now and we will repay you later.

godfer n. [late 19C] a badly behaved child. [SE *godforsaken*]

God-forbids n. [late 19C+] **1** children. **2** Jews. **3** a hat. [rhy. sl. *God forbids* = (1) kids; (2) YIDS; (3) LID n.[1] (1)]

God forgive him the prayers he said phr. [late 19C] phr. used when someone has been swearing long and loud.

Godfrey n. [20C] (orig. US) euph for *God* and used as such in various mild oaths, e.g. *by Godfrey! Godfrey mighty!*

God has gone to Jersey City phr. [1930s–40s] a mild oath, usu. in phr. *if I'm lying, then God has gone ... .*

God-help-us see GAWDELPUS.

God-hopper n. [1940s–50s] (US) an evangelist or very religious person (cf. GOD-BOTHERER).

God in heaven n. [20C] the number seven. [rhy. sl.]

God love her n. [1970s] one's mother. [rhy. sl.]

go doddling v. [19C] to have sexual intercourse. [SE *doddle*, to totter, to dawdle or ? DIDDLE n.[3] (2)]

go dog-hunting/get some dog, to phr. [1920s–30s] (US) of a man, to look for and successfully seduce a woman. [DOG n.[5] (6)]

go dog on v. [late 19C–1950s] (Aus.) **1** to let down. **2** to betray, to inform against (cf. DINGO). [DOG n.[8]]

go-down n. **1** [mid-17C–early 18C] a drink. **2** [1940s] (US Black) a basement flat or apartment (cf. GO-UP). [in (1) the liquor 'goes down', in (2) the human dweller or visitor]

go down v.[1] [early 17C+] to be accepted by, to be approved, to be allowed, usu. in phr. *go down well/badly with.*

go down v.[2] [late 19C] to rob, to steal from. [*go down* into the pockets]

go down v.[3] [late 19C–1930s] to become bankrupt.

go down v.[4] [20C] to be sent to prison. [*see* UP THE STAIRS]

go down v.[5] [20C] (W.I.) to be admitted to a mental hospital.

go down v.[6] [1900s–20s] to give birth. [? the child *goes down* from the womb; the mother *goes down* to the hospital]

go down/down on/down south v.[7] **1** [1910s+] (US) to perform fellatio or cunnilingus (cf. GET DOWN v.[2]). **2** [1960s+] (US) to copulate readily.

go down v.[8] **1** [1930s+] (orig. US Black) to happen, to take place, often of a fight or other dramatic encounter. **2** [1950s] (US street gang) to attack a rival gang.

go down for the gravy, to phr. [1950s+] to perform oral sex. [GO DOWN v.[6] + GRAVY n.[1]]

go down in flames, to phr. [1910s+] to fail to complete a task, despite one's best efforts. [the image of a downed aircraft]

go down in/in food v. [20C] (W.I./Bdos.) to eat ravenously.

go down/over like a lead balloon, to phr. [1950s+] (orig. US) usu. of an idea or suggestion, to find no favour or support whatsoever.

go down like flies, to phr. [20C] to collapse in the face of weapons, disease or adversity.

go down on v.[1] *see* GO DOWN v.[7].

go down on v.[2] **1** [1960s+] to cause someone trouble, to harm someone. **3** [1960s+] to fight with.

go down one v. [late 19C] to fail, to be conquered, to be beaten. [school use, where one *goes down* a place or class]

go down on one's bended, to phr. [1920s+] **1** to pray. **2** to beg (for forgiveness, etc, rather than money). [the missing word is 'knees']

go down south see GO DOWN v.[7].

go downstairs for breakfast, to phr. [1970s] (Aus.) to perform cunnilingus. [ext. of GO DOWN v.[7]]

go down the chute/chutes, to phr. [late 19C–1940s] (US) to be ruined, to meet with disaster (cf. GO DOWN THE TUBES).

go down the plughole/drain, to phr. [1930s+] to be wasted, to be lost for ever (cf. DOWN THE DRAIN). [the image of an emptying bath]

go down the river, to phr. [1900s–40s] (US, South) to go to the state prison in Mississippi (cf. SELL DOWN THE RIVER; UP THE RIVER).

go down the road, to phr. [1960s+] to pursue a policy or course of action, even if it proves unpleasant.

go down the Swanee, to phr. [1970s+] to be ruined to become bankrupt.

go down the tubes, to phr. [1960s+] (orig. US) to fail badly, to collapse completely (cf. GO DOWN THE CHUTE).

go down the weather, to phr. [late 17C–early 19C] to become bankrupt. [one suffers an 'ill wind']

go down the wind, to phr. [late 17C–early 19C] to be unfortunate (cf. GO UP THE WEATHER). [one suffers an 'ill wind']

go down to the ground, to phr. [17C] to defecate.

go down with a smacker, to phr. [late 19C] to fall flat on one's face or posterior. [one 'smacks' into the ground]

go down with barrel fever, to phr. **1** [18C+] to be drunk. **2** [20C] (Aus.) to suffer from delirium tremens. [BARREL FEVER]

God permit n. [late 17C–18C] a stage-coach. [such coaches were advertised as starting 'if God permit']

go drabbing v. [early 16C–19C] to have sexual intercourse. [DRAB n.[1] + sfx. *-ing*]

God save/God saves n. [1910s–30s] the British national anthem (cf. GAWSAVE). [it starts 'God save our gracious king/queen']

God save the queens n. [20C] vegetables. [rhy. sl. *God save the Queens* = SE *greens*]

God's bodikins!/bodykins! excl. [18C] a (blasphemous) oath, lit. 'God's little body'.

God's dines! excl. [late 16C–early 17C] a mild oath, usu. *by God's dines!* [? obs. SE *dignesse*, dignity]

God's drug n. [1940s+] (drugs) opium, morphine (cf. GOD'S OWN MEDICINE).

God's flesh n. [1950s+] (drugs) psilocybin/psilocin. [popular translation of Nahuatl *teonanacatl*, lit. *teotl*, God + *nancatl*, mushroom]

gods for clods n. [1970s+] (US campus) course in basic comparative religion (cf. AIDS FOR GRADES).

God's guts! see GOD'S TEETH!

God's in heaven n. [1940s+] (bingo) the number seven. [rhy. sl.]

God slot n. [1960s+] (orig. TV) that period of early Sunday evening TV viewing set aside by law for mandatory, if marginal, religious broadcasting.

God's medicine see GOD'S OWN MEDICINE.

God's mercy *n.* [19C] a dish of bacon and eggs served in a country inn. [the grace that preceded eating it]

God's off-ox *n.* [19C+] (US) a headstrong person; thus in phr. *as odd as God's off-ox*, extremely eccentric; *poor as God's off-ox*, very poor (cf. ADAM'S OFF-OX). [SE *off-ox*, the ox harnessed to the *offside* of the team]

godsookers *n.* [17C] a (blasphemous) oath, lit. God's wounds (cf. GAD n.¹; ZOUNDS).

Godsown/Godzone/Gordzone *n.* [1910s+] (N.Z.) New Zealand. [abbr. SE *God's own country*]

God's own ... *adj.* [1920s+] a general intensifier, e.g. *God's own row*.

God's own medicine/God's medicine *n.* [1940s+] (drugs) opium, morphine (cf. MOTHER NATURE'S OWN TOBACCO).

God squad *n.*¹ [1960s+] any form of proselytizing religious group (often evangelical), esp. as found within a university or similar institution.

God squad *n.*² [1990s] (US) the Endangered Species Committee. [they are accused of 'playing God' with nature]

God's quantity *n.* [1910s–20s] a large amount, an abundance.

God's teeth!/guts! *excl.* [1920s–50s] (US) an excl. used to express astonishment.

God's time *n.* [20C] (US) time as measured before the introduction during WW1 of Daylight Saving Time. [DST was ordained by the government; *God's time* by the passage of the sun]

God's trousers! *excl.* [1900s–50s] (Aus.) a mild oath.

go due north, to *phr.* [mid-19C] to become bankrupt. [the purpose-built debtor's prison, Whitecross Street Prison, is sited in what was then north London; its site is now covered by the Barbican development]

go Dutch *v.* **1** [1910s+] (orig. US) to share expenses, esp. of a meal (cf. ARKANSAW v.; DUTCH TREAT). **2** to commit suicide (cf. DO THE DUTCH ACT). [racial stereotyping of the Dutch]

gody/goadie *n.* [20C] (W.I.) a hugely swollen testicle, due to a rupture; known in med. jargon as *hydrocele*, a water tumour. [? SE *gourd*, a water carrier]

godzillion *n.* [1980s+] (US) an indescribably large number. [SE *God*/GOD'S (QUANTITY) + ZILLION]

go easy *v.*¹ [late 19C+] to act cautiously, to proceed with caution.

go easy/easy on/with *v.*² [late 19C+] to deal with someone kindly, to resist acting cruelly.

go easy *phr.* [1990s] (US teen) a phr. of farewell, take care, see you later.

go eat pussy! *excl.* [1950s+] (US Black) go away! leave me alone! (cf. EAT PUSSY). [SE *eat*/EAT v.³ + PUSSY n.¹ (1)]

goef/ghoef/goof *n.* [1960s+] (S.Afr.) a swim. [synon. Afk.]

goef/ghoef/goof *v.* [1960s+] (S.Afr.) to swim. [GOEF n.]

goer *n.* **1** [mid-19C+] an expert. **2** [late 19C–1950s] (Aus.) anything dependable, which can be counted on to work or succeed. **3** [1950s+] a promiscuous, sexually available woman. **4** [20C] an enthusiastic if not always competent amateur. [SE *go*; (3) GO v.⁸]

goers *n.* [19C] the feet. [they make one *go*]

goey *adj.* [1900s] enthusiastic, keen (cf. GOER). [SE *go* + sfx. -*y*]

go eyeball-to-eyeball, to *phr.* [1950s+] (US) to confront implacably and at close quarters. [the *locus criticus* was the remark made by US Secretary of State John Foster Dulles that after the US and USSR had 'gone eyeball-to-eyeball' during the Cuban missile crisis of 1962 'the other fellow just blinked']

go eyes out *v.* [late 19C+] (Aus./N.Z.) to weep excessively.

go facemaking *v.* [17C–18C] to have sexual intercourse. [the *face* is that of a newly conceived child]

go fanti *v.* [late 19C–1930s] to go crazy, to lose control, to go

on the rampage. [SE *go fantee*, for a White man to 'go native'; ult. *Fante*, the inhabitants of Ghana]

go-fast *n.* [1980s+] (drugs) methcathinone (cf. BATHTUB SPEED). [its effects]

go Federal *v.* [1990s] (US Black teen) to do well, to succeed. [the image of the Federal government and esp. Federal prisons as the most powerful institution in US]

gofer/gopher *n.* [1940s+] (orig. US) an assistant, errand boy or girl, anyone who is told to *go fer ...* some requirement (cf. GOBY).

goffel *n.* [1970s] (S.Afr. Coloured) an ageing prostitute.

goffer *n.* [late 19C–1900s] a blow, a punch. [? fig. use of RN *goffer*, mineral water or lemonade orig. that manufactured by *Goffe* & Sons Ltd. The image is of an angry person who is excited in the way that the bubbles in aerated water are. The mineral water use is extant in Aus.]

goffer *v.* [late 19C–1900s] to pull or crush a person's hat over their eyes, thus temporarily blinding them (cf. BONNET n.¹). [GOFFER n.]

goffo *n.* [1950s+] (Irish) a free ride on the back bumper of a car, unknown to the driver. [ety. unknown; ? SE *go for* (a *ride*)]

go fish *v.* [1960s+] (gay) **1** for an effeminate gay man to take the 'feminine', passive role during sex. **2** of a lesbian, to give cunnilingus. [FISH n.⁴]

go fishing *v.* [mid-19C+] to go out looking for a sexually obliging woman. [FISH n.⁴]

go flashing/fleshing it *v.* [mid–late 19C] to have sexual intercourse.

go fleshmongering *v.* [17C] to have sexual intercourse. [FLESHMONGER + sfx. -*ing*]

go flouch *see* FLOUSH.

go fly a kite *phr.* [1940s+] a suggestion that an unwanted person should go away (cf. FLY A KITE phr.²).

go for *v.*¹ **1** [late 19C+] to attack. **2** [late 19C+] (orig. US) to make an attempt.

go for *v.*² [late 19C+] (orig. US) **1** to enthuse over, to be keen on, to find sexually or otherwise attractive or appealing. **2** to accept, to believe, to be deceived.

go for *v.*³ [1920s+] to resemble, to 'pass' as.

go for *v.*⁴ [1960s+] to be in one's favour, to be favourable or advantageous to, esp. in phr. *have something going for one*.

go for a bo-peep, to *phr.* [1990s] (Aus.) to take a surreptitious look at.

go for a Burton, to *phr.* [1940s+] (orig. milit.) to die. [the precise ety. remains unknown but there are a number of suggestions. First is the elision of SE *burnt 'un*, i.e. a burning aircraft (and its pilot). E.P. (*DSUE* 1970), and Paul Beale (*DSUE* 1984) suggest: (1) a euph., going for a glass of Burton ale; (2) *Burton-on-Trent* as rhy. sl. for 'went', as in 'went west' (cf. GO WEST); (3) Burton ale is heavy, as is a burning aircraft as it crashes to the ground; (4) the tailors Montague Burton (cf. WOODEN OVERCOAT; WOODEN KIMONO); (5) during WW2 the RAF used a number of billiard halls, invariably sited above Burton shops, as medical centres, and those who attended such centres had 'gone for a Burton'. Other suggestions include the inter-war advertising campaign for Burton ales, bearing the copy line: 'He's gone for a Burton.' Another claim states that Burton's halls were used for morse aptitude tests, not medical checkups, thus the phr. meant failing such a test. Finally seafarers' jargon *burton*, the notoriously unsafe stowing of a barrel athwart rather than fore-and-aft; thus *going for a Burton* meant risking death]

go for a leslie, to *phr.* [1990s] of a woman, to urinate. [rhy. sl. *Leslie Ash* = SLASH n.⁴]

go for a skate, to *phr.* [1950s+] (N.Z.) **1** to fail. **2** to be brought up in court. [ext. of SKATE v. (1)]

go for a spin, to *phr.* [1900s–50s] to go out for a drive in a motor vehicle. [the spinning wheels]

go for a trip up the line *see* GO UP THE LINE.

go for a walk with a spade, to *phr.* [20C] to defecate in the open air.

go for bad, to *phr.* (US Black) to project a macho, tough image, whether of physical or emotional toughness. [BAD adj.]

go for broke, to *phr.* [1950s+] (orig. US) to commit oneself unreservedly, esp. in a gambling or betting context. [GO v.[1] + BROKE adj.]

go for channa, to *phr.* [20C] (W.I./Guyn.) to be absolutely wasted, esp. of money. [Hind. *chanaa*, chick-pea; thus the invested money has fig. turned into chick-peas]

go for it *v.* [1920s+] of a woman, to be sexually enthusiastic. [joc. use of SE but note GO v.[8] + IT n.]

go for it! *excl.* [1980s+] **1** an exhortation to make an effort, to overcome one's fears, to get on energetically. **2** (US campus) a general exhortation to those present, urging them to act crazily, the intention being thus to have fun.

go for/got to get mines, to *phr.* [1990s] (US Black teen) to look after oneself, to indulge one's own interests. [Black var. on SE *mine*]

go for one's life, to *phr.* [1920s+] (Aus.) to engage in an activity with vigour and enthusiasm.

go for one's quoits/the lick of one's coit, to *phr.* [1920s+] (Aus.) to run fast, to work hard, to make one's best effort. [? fig. use of QUOIT n.]

go for one's tea, to *phr.* [20C] to die (cf. HAND IN ONE'S DINNER PAIL; LAY DOWN ONE'S KNIFE AND FORK).

go for pink slips, to *phr.* [1950s+] (US) to race cars with the winner gaining the loser's vehicle. [the *pink* insurance *slip* that is proof of ownership]

go for six, to *phr.* [1940s] **1** to die, usu. as *gone for six*. **2** to be knocked down or knocked across a room. [cricketing imagery]

go for soul, to *phr.* [1930s–40s] (US Black) to be deeply moved.

go for sushi, to *phr.* [1980s+] (US campus) to kiss passionately. [TONGUE SUSHI]

go for the big spit *see* GO THE BIG SPIT.

go for/through for the doctor, to *phr.* **1** [1940s+] (Aus. orig. racing) for one rider and his mount to move significantly ahead of the field. **2** (Aus. gambling) to bet all one's money. [the image of rushing for (and paying a large fee to) a doctor]

go for the grouse, to *phr.* [1970s+] (Aus.) to look for whatever is seen as worthwhile. [GROUSE n.[3]]

go for the lick of one's coit *see* GO FOR ONE'S QUOITS.

go for the whole shot, to *phr.* [20C] to make an absolute commitment, to indulge oneself completely.

go for veg, to *phr.* [1970s] (US campus) to become drunk. [one becomes a fig. *vegetable*]

go-forwards *n.* [20C] (W.I.) a thong sandal that, if one does not keep walking forwards, is liable to fall off the foot.

go frig youself! *excl.* [1930s–50s] a general excl. of dismissal (cf. GO FUCK YOURSELF!). [FRIG v.]

go from the fists/shoulders/Y, to *phr.* [1970s+] (US Black) to fight. [Y, i.e. the shape of the two arms and the trunk]

go fry an egg! *excl.* [late 19C+] (US) mind your own business!

go fuck a duck! *excl.* [20C] an excl. of dismissal (cf. GO MILK A DUCK!)

go fuck your mother! *excl.* [1930s+] an all-purpose dismissive excl., generally seen as a supremely offensive remark (cf. MOTHERFUCKER).

go fuck yourself! *excl.* [late 19C+] a general excl. of dismissal (cf. GET FUCKED!; GO FRIG YOURSELF!).

gog *n.* [15C–16C] a euph. form of *God*, and used as such as in oaths (cf. COCK n.[1]).

go-getter *n.* [1920s+] (orig. US) an active, enterprising person.

gog-eye *n.* [20C] (Aus. juv.) a catapult.

gogga *n.* (S.Afr.) **1** [20C] an insect, a 'creepy-crawly'. **2** [20C] a term of affection aimed at a child or a small adult. **3** [1930s+] something menacing or frightening, a dangerous person or thing. [Nama *xo xo*, an insect]

goggle/goggle at *v.* [late 18C+] to stare at. [earlier use SE]

goggle box *n.* [1950s+] the television (cf. BOX n.[4]). [GOGGLE v. + SE *box*]

goggle-eyed *adj.* [late 19C–1910s] (US) wearing spectacles (cf. GOOGLE EYES).

goggler *n.* [early–mid-19C] **1** an eye. **2** a person with bulging 'goggle' eyes. [GOGGLE v.]

goggles *n.*[1] [early 18C–early 19C] **1** the eyes. **2** one who stares. **3** round spectacles. **4** in sing., the white of the eye.

goggles *n.*[2] [20C] the nickname of someone who wears spectacles.

goggy *n.* [1980s+] a school child who has been rejected by its fellows (cf. GUNK n.[1]; SPOD n.; WENDY; ZOID n.). [? GOGGLES]

go girl! *see* GO ON, GIRL!

go girling *v.* [mid-19C–1910s] to go out looking for female companionship and possible seduction. [SE *girl*]

goglet *see* GIGGLER.

go glimmering *v.* [late 19C–1940s] (US) to die away, to die out, to vanish. [SE *glimmer*, to give a weak, intermittent light]

gogo *n.* [20C] (US) the buttocks. [Louisiana-French]

go goosing *v.* [mid-19C+] to have sexual intercourse. [GOOSE v.[2]]

go great guns, to *phr.* [1910s+] to have a run of success, to advance rapidly towards success.

go Greek *v.*[1] [1970s+] (US campus) to join a college fraternity or sorority. [such institutions have Greek letters as their names]

go Greek *v.*[2] (US) [1980s] to engage in anal intercourse (cf. GREEK n.[5]; GREEK CULTURE; GREEK LOVE; GREEK SIDE; GREEK WAY). [GREEK adj.[2]; the identification of Greeks with sodomy]

go grunts *v.* [1960s] to defecate.

go/cry halves *v.* [late 18C+] to share, to divide equally; thus [1920s+] (Aus.) *on the halves*, sharing equally.

go hang *v.* [early 17C+] **1** of a plan, to collapse, to go wrong, to fail. **2** a dismissive phr. euph. for GO TO HELL!, GO TO THE DEVIL; thus *tell someone to go hang!*

go haywire *v.* [1920s+] (orig. US) to lose control, to go mad. [the baling wire used by US farmers to mend malfunctioning implements]

go Hollywood *v.*[1] [1970s+] to sodomize. [the presumption that such 'excesses' are quotidian pleasures in the movie capital]

go Hollywood *v.*[2] [1990s] (US campus) to lose emotional control, to act hysterically (cf. ACT UP). [the image of Hollywood as a centre of excessive (if faked) emotion]

go home *v.*[1] [late 19C] to die. **2** [1920s+] of an article of clothing, to wear out. [note SE phr. *go to one's last home*, to die]

go home *v.*[2] [20C] (W.I./Gren.) to defame a member of one's own or someone else's family.

go home by beggar's bush, to *phr.* [late 16C–19C] to be ruined. [to be reduced, like a beggar, to sleeping under a bush]

go home by Woodcock's cross, to *phr.* [17C] to regret one's actions, to fail badly; thus *go crossless home by Woodcock's cross*, to repent and then to be hanged (cf. COME HOME BY WEEPING CROSS). [ety. unknown; ? anecdotal]

go hostile at/on *v.* [1930s+] (Aus.) to become angry with. [orig. Aus./N.Z. milit. use]

go hunting *v.* [20C] to have sexual intercourse.

go in *v.* [mid–late 19C] to attempt, usu. as *go in and win*. [SE post-1890s]

go in a buster, to *phr.* [mid-19C–1920s] to spend regardless of the expense. [BUSTER n.³]

go in and out like a fiddler's elbow, to *phr.* [20C] to copulate enthusiastically and energetically.

go in a perisher, to *phr.* [mid–late 19C] (Aus.) to pursue one's course of action with maximum enthusiasm.

go in at *v.* [19C] to attack.

go in for *v.* (orig. US) **1** [mid–late 19C] of a man, to court a woman. **2** [mid-19C+] to approve of, to favour. **3** [mid-19C+] to specialize in. **4** [late 19C+] to announce one's candidature for. **5** [late 19C+] to attempt to obtain, to choose to wear.

going on have it *phr.* [1990s] (US Black) living in the swing of things, being chic or fashionable.

going-over *n.* (orig. US) **1** [late 19C+] a scolding, a telling-off. **2** [1910s+] (orig. US) an inspection. **3** [1940s+] a thrashing, a beating. [SE *go over*, to inspect, in lit. or fig. uses]

going to keep a piano shop? *phr.* [late 19C] a mocking phr. directed at anyone the speaker feels is over-well-dressed, even flashy. [the devotion to 'fashion' of piano salesmen]

go in lemons, to *phr.* [mid-19C+] (Aus.) to act enthusiastically (cf. PITCH IN LEMONS!). [LEMONS adv.]

go in stag, to *phr.* [early 17C] to go naked. [SE *stag*, of furs, raw, unseasoned]

go in the Marylebone/marrowbone stage *see* RIDE BY THE MARROWBONE STAGE.

go in the moon *see* GO TO THE MOON.

go in the tank/water, to *phr.* [20C] to surrender, to give up, esp. when such a surrender is by no means necessary. [fig use of boxing jargon *go in the tank*, to lose a fight deliberately; ult. SE *tank*, a swimming pool, thus synon. with TAKE A DIVE]

go into a flat spin, to *phr.* [1910s+] to lose perspective and orientation, to become very confused. [flying use]

go into a huddle, to *phr.* [1920s+] to hold a secret conference to consult specially about something. [US football use]

go into a sewer, to *phr.* [1980s+] (drugs) to inject a drug. [the less than 'clean' state of one's veins]

go into one, to *phr.* [1990s] (Black) to lose one's temper, to lose emotional control. [? 'one' being a rage, a tantrum]

go into orbit, to *phr.* [1960s+] to lose one's temper (cf. GO BALLISTIC).

go into the kitchen, to *phr.* [late 19C] to drink one's tea out of the saucer. [the vulgarity of such a way of drinking tea – seen as a servants' habit]

go into the pease-field, to *phr.* [late 17C–late 18C] to fall asleep. [pun on SE *pease/peace*]

go it *v.* [early 19C+] **1** to indulge to a reckless extent. **2** to commit oneself fully, usu. to a course of self-indulgent pleasure or as in a fight. **3** to move at great speed.

go it! *excl.* [mid-19C+] a general excl. of encouragement; in full *go it you cripples, crutches are cheap.*

go it alone, to *phr.* [mid-19C+] to act by oneself, without support or assistance.

go-it-alone *adj.* [mid-19C+] characterized by independent action.

go it baldheaded *see* GO AT SOMETHING BALDHEADED.

go it blind *v.*¹ [mid–late 19C] (US) to enter on an undertaking without proper preparation or planning.

go it blind *v.*² [late 19C+] to drink heavily. [BLIND adj.¹]

go it, boots! *excl.* [mid-19C–1910s] (US) a general cry of encouragement.

goiter *n.* [1980s+] (drugs) small 'sticks' of tobacco, which interfere with the quality of one's smoke when rolled together with cannabis. [SE *goiter/goitre*; they make a bulge in the cigarette]

goitre *n.* [1960s+] (Und.) a bulging wallet full of notes. [SE *goitre*, a swelling, sometimes very pronounced, of the thyroid gland]

go it strong/thick, to *phr.* [19C] to speak frankly, forcefully (cf. GO IT v.).

go jagging *v.* [20C] (Aus./N.Z.) to go visiting for the purpose of exchanging gossip. [? JAG v. or dial. *jag*, a journey; but note dial. *jag*, to tear roughly; i.e. the gossips 'tear someone to pieces']

go jesse *v.* [1950s+] (US) to act energetically, to be skilful to 'go great guns'. [adoption of *jesse*, as in GIVE ONE JESSE, to mean vigour, strength]

go jottling, to *see* DO A JOTTLE.

go jumming *v.* [17C] to have sexual intercourse. [JUMM v.]

go jump/go and jump in a lake! *excl.* [1910s+] a general excl. of dismissal or disdain.

go jump yourself! *excl.* [20C] (orig. US) a coarse dismissive excl; euph. for GO FUCK YOURSELF!

golblast! *excl.* [late 19C+] (US) a mild oath. [SE *God blast!*]

gold *n.*¹ [1940s+] (US Black) money (cf. DELOG).

gold *n.*² (drugs) **1** [1960s+] marijuana. **2** [1980s+] crack cocaine. [? its value]

goldarn/goldang/goldurn *adj.* [early 19C+] (US) euph. version of GOD-DAMN adj.; also as euph. for GOD-DAMN!

goldarned *adj.* [early 19C+] damned, cussed (cf. GAUL DARNED). [GOLDARN]

gold-backed ones/'uns *n.* [mid-19C] body lice (cf. BLACK CATTLE).

gold-badge man *n.* [20C] (US) a city detective.

Goldberg *n.* [1930s+] (US Black) any Jew, esp. the shop-owners of Harlem and other ghettos. [the stereotyped 'Jewish' surname and as such usu. derog.]

Goldberg's Green *n.* [1950s+] the London suburb of Golder's Green (cf. ABRAHAMSTEAD). [the large Jewish population in the district]

gold braid *n.* [1930s+] a collective noun for a number of senior military or prison officers. [the gold braid that adorns their caps]

goldbrick *n.* [mid-19C+] (US) **1** a shirker, a loafer, a lazy person. **2** a swindler. **3** one who obtains money without working for it; thus *goldbricking*, swindling, cheating. [the trick of selling a supposed 'gold' (in fact, painted lead) brick to the gullible. The scheme was originated by one Reed Waddell who sold his first brick for $4000 and thereafter never dropped his price below $3,500 – making an alleged $250,000 in 5 years]

goldbrick *v.* [mid-19C+] (US) **1** to shirk, to loaf, to act lazily. **2** to swindle. [GOLDBRICK n.]

goldbug *n.* [late 19C+] (US) a gold speculator. [SE *gold* + BUG n.⁴]

gold dig *v.* [1920s+] usu. of a woman, to obtain money and other gifts in exchange for sexual favours. [backform. GOLD-DIGGER]

gold-digger *n.* **1** [1910s–20s] (US) a prostitute. **2** [1910s+] (orig. US) a young woman, orig. typically from the chorus line, who swaps sexual favours for the monetary and material gifts of a (usually) older lover (cf. BIMBO n.; DIGGER n.⁵; SACK CHASER). [(2) faltered after WW2 but has been revived in US Black use]

gold-drop *n.* [late 18C] a gold coin.

gold-dropper/dropper *n.* [late 17C–early 19C] (Und.) a rogue who specializes in dropping something supposedly valuable where it will be found by a potential victim, who is either lured into a game or persuaded to buy the 'valuable', while the conman claims that although they should, by rights, share the profits, he will sell his share and let the victim have the whole benefit (cf. DROP-COVE; GAMBLER; GOLD-FINDER; MONEY-DROPPER; SWEETENER n.).

gold dust *n.* [1970s+] (drugs) **1** heroin. **2** cocaine (cf. GOLD SEAL; GOLD STAR n.²). [the high price of narcotics + ref. in (1) to the colour of, presumably, the Chinese (brown) variety]

gold dust twins *n.* [20C] (US) close friends. [the twin Black boys who featured in ads. for Gold Dust washing powder, *c.*1900; the slogan declared: 'Let the Gold Dust twins do your work']

golded *adj.* [1970s+] drunk (cf. ABOUT RIGHT adj.[1]). [? the golden colour of certain spirits/wines/beer]

golden *adj.* (US) **1** [1950s+] (US campus) fine, successful, secure. **2** [1980s+] lucrative.

golden, be *v.* [1980s+] (US campus) to be at one's peak, intellectually, emotionally, physically.

golden boy *n.* [1970s] (US) a gold-shield police detective (cf. GOLD STAR n.[1]).

golden chub *n.* [early 18C] a dupe, a fool. [a pun on the fish name; SE *golden* + CHUB n.[1]]

gold-end man *n.* [17C] an itinerant jeweller, a buyer of gold and silver.

golden doughnut *n.* [20C] the vagina (cf. APPLE n.[10]; BLACK HOLE n.[1]).

golden dragon *n.* [1980s+] (drugs) LSD (cf. A n.[3]). [? packaging]

golden girl *n.* [1970s+] (drugs) **1** heroin. **2** particularly high grade cocaine (cf. GOLDEN LEAF). [GIRL n.[3]; note heroin is otherwise BOY n.[5] (2), presumably the golden, i.e. brown, colour is more pertinent here]

golden googie *n.* [1900s–10s] (Aus./N.Z.) a golden coin, a sovereign. [SE *golden* + GOOG; ? ref. to 'the goose that laid the golden eggs']

golden grease *n.* [late 18C–mid-19C] a bribe (cf. PALM OIL). [SE *golden*, resembling gold in value + GREASE n.]

golden handcuffs *n.* [1970s+] (orig. US) financial perks, which keep employees attached to a firm.

golden handshake *n.* [1960s+] a bonus given as compensation for dismissal or compulsory retirement.

golden hello *n.* [1980s+] a signing-on bonus, given when starting a new job.

golden hind *adj.* [20C] blind. [rhy. sl. the name of the ship in which Francis Drake circumnavigated the globe in 1577–80)]

golden leaf *n.* [1920s–40s] (drugs) top-quality marijuana. [SE *golden*, resembling gold in value + LEAF n.[2]]

golden oldie *n.* [1960s+] anything vintage but still valued. [orig. used of rock 'n' roll records of 1950s–early 1960s, latterly in wider use, incl. refs. to people]

golden screw *n.* [1960s+] (US gay) anal intercourse culminating in urination rather than ejaculation (cf. GOLDEN SHOWER). [SE *golden*, yellow-coloured + SCREW n.[1] (2)]

golden shower *n.* [1960s+] **1** urolagnia. **2** (US gay) one who displays contempt for other people, i.e. he 'pisses on' them. [SE *golden*, yellow-coloured + *shower* n.]

golden shower queen *n.* [1960s+] a homosexual who enjoys being urinated on. [GOLDEN SHOWER + QUEEN n.[1]]

goldfinch *n.* [late 17C–early 19C] **1** a golden guinea or sovereign (cf. CANARY n.[4]). **2** one who always has money in his pocket or purse, thus a target of thieves. [play on the bird species]

goldfinch's nest *n.* [19C] the vagina (cf. BIRD'S NEST).

gold-finder *n.* **1** [early 17C–19C] a latrine cleaner (cf. GONG-FARMER; HONEY-DIPPER; JAKES-FARMER; NIGHTMAN; TOM TURDMAN). **2** [early 19C] a confidence trickster (cf. GOLD-DROPPER). [the colour of faeces; (cf. HONEY n.[5])]

goldfish *n.*[1] **1** [1920s–40s] (US) a beating of a prisoner to extract a confession, also the rubber hose used in such beatings. **2** [1950s–60s] (Black) a married woman, esp. one who is ripe for seduction; thus *fish for goldfish*, to seduce married women. [fig. uses of SE; (1) the prisoner is the isolated goldfish, the interrogators gather round; (2) the goldfish is trapped in its bowl, but apparently yearning for the world beyond]

goldfish *n.*[2] [1940s] **1** (US Black) sliced, canned peaches. **2** (Aus.) any form of canned fish. [orig. milit. use *goldfish*, herrings]

goldfish bowl *n.* [1930s+] (US) an interrogation room in a police station. [the isolation of the prisoner among their interrogators]

gold-hunters *n.* [mid–late 19C] (US) Californians. [the Gold Rush of 1849]

goldie locks *n.* [20C] (US) a uniformed police woman (cf. GOLD-BADGE MAN; MAMA BEAR). [play on the nursery rhyme *Goldilocks and the Three Bears* (thus cf. BEAR n.[8]) + play on SE *locks*, hair/*locks*, i.e. those of handcuffs/cell doors etc]

gold ring *n.* [20C] a king. [rhy. sl.]

gold seal *n.* [1970s+] (drugs) top quality hashish. [the block is stamped with a *gold seal*]

gold star/shield/tin *n.*[1] [1960s+] (US) a gold-shield police detective.

gold star *n.*[2] [1980s+] (drugs) **1** cocaine. **2** (drugs) marijuana (cf. GOLD DUST). [its price and colour]

gold tin see GOLD STAR n.[1].

goldurn *see* GOLDARN.

gold watch *n.* [19C+] Scotch whisky. [rhy. sl.; the orig. ref. was to the Waterbury watch]

go leather-stretching *v.* [late 16C–18C] to have sexual intercourse. [LEATHER n.[2] (1) + SE *stretch*]

go lemony at/with *v.* [1940s–50s] (Aus./ N.Z.) to lose one's temper with. [? the sourness of the fruit]

goles! *excl.* [early 18C–early 19C] a euph. for God and only found in phr. *by goles*, by God (cf. ADAD!).

golf ball *n.* [1980s+] (drugs) **1** a depressant. **2** a piece of crack cocaine. [joc. resemblance]

golfed *adj.* [1990s] (US campus) drunk. [? GOOF n.[2] (2)]

golgotha *n.* [mid-19C] a hat. [a pun on Gk. *golgotha*, the place of skulls]

go/come lickety-split, to *phr.* [1970s+] to give oral sex to a woman. [SE *lick* + SPLIT n.[7]]

go like a bat out of hell, to *phr.* [20C] (orig. US) to move exceptionally fast (cf. GO LIKE THE HAMMERS OF HELL).

go like a bird, to *phr.* [1940s+] of an automobile, to go fast and smoothly with no mechanical problems.

go like a bomb, to *phr.*[1] [1950s+] to go very fast.

go like a bomb, to *phr.*[2] [1950s+] to work out very successfully. [BOMB n.[1] (4)]

go like a cut cat, to *phr.* [1960s+] (N.Z.) to leave or run off at speed. [SE *cut*, castrated]

go like a dingbat, to *phr.* [1950s+] to go very fast. [DINGBAT n.[8] (2)]

go like a rabbit, to *phr.* [1950s+] of a woman, to copulate enthusiastically (cf. FUCK LIKE A BUNNY).

go like a train, to *phr.* [20C] **1** to go very fast. **2** of a woman, to be a very enthusiastic sexual partner (cf. GO LIKE A BAT OUT OF HELL; GO LIKE THE CLAPPERS; LIKE A BOMB).

go like a wanker's elbow, to *phr.* [1990s] to be extremely busy.

go like hell, to *phr.* [18C+] to go very fast.

go like hot cakes, to *phr.* [late 19C+] (orig. US) of a product or commodity, to sell out quickly.

go like the clappers, to *phr.* [1940s+] to run very fast; a euph. for GO LIKE HELL. [rhy. sl. *clappers* = bell = HELL; note RAF jargon *like the clappers of hell*, very fast]

go like the hammers of hell, to *phr.* [1950s+] to go very fast cf. GO LIKE A BAT OUT HELL; GO LIKE HELL).

goll *n.* [late 16C–early 17C] the hand. [ety. unknown; ? link to Irish *gabhlach*, a forked instrument used in fishing, used in modern Irish sl. as *golly-fishing*]

goll bing me! *excl.* [late 19C] (US) a euph. for *God damn me!*

gollier/gollywer *n.* [20C] (Irish) a lump of phlegm. [GOLLY v.]

gollion *n.* [20C] (Aus.) a lump of phlegm. [GOLLY v.]

golliwog n.[1] [1910s] a dog; thus *golliwogs*, greyhound racing. [rhy. sl. *golliwog(s)* = a *dog*; DOGS n.[2]]

golliwog n.[2] [1920s+] (Aus.) a large, hairy caterpillar. [it supposedly resembles the child's toy]

golliwog n.[3] [1930s+] a receiver of stolen property.

gollop n. **1** [19C+] (US) an amount, a portion. **2** [20C] a gulp. [SE *gulp* + *gobble*]

gollop v. [19C+] to swallow down greedily or hastily. [GOLLOP n.]

gollsocker see GOLLYWHOPPER.

gollumpus n. [late 18C–19C] a large, loutish, uncoordinated person. [? Scot. *golamus*, ungaily, large, unshapely]

golly n. [1960s+] a derog. term for a Black person. [SE *golliwog*; for the problems of the Robinson's jam/marmalade *golly* see my *Words Apart* (1996)]

golly v. [1930s+] (Aus.) to spit; thus *golly-gum*, chewing gum; *golly-pot*, a spittoon (cf. GOLLION). [? Scot. *golly*, to shout hoarsely; ult. Scot. *gollar*, to utter loud but thick and scarcely articulate sounds, to shout]

golly! excl. [mid-18C+] an extra-mild euph. for God, usu. child use only (cf. ADAD!). [E.P. suggests a Black origin, but the *OED* citation talks (G. White, *Journals*, 1775) of: 'Golly, a sort of jolly kind of oath, or asseveration much in use among our carters, & lowest people']

gollybuster see GOLLYWHOPPER.

gollywer see GOLLIER.

gollywhopper/gollsocker/gollybuster n. [20C] (US) an outstanding example of its kind. [GOLLY! + WHOPPER/SOCK v.[1]/BUSTER n.[2]]

gollywobbles n. [1940s+] (US) feelings of tension, fear or sickness, usu. seen as stemming from the stomach. [var. on COLLYWOBBLES]

gol-mol n. [mid-19C] (Anglo-Ind.) a disturbance, a commotion. [Hind. *golmaul*, confusion, disorder]

go loco v. (drugs) to smoke marijuana. [LOCO n. (3); LOCOWEED]

go-'long n. **1** [20C] (US Black) consequences, inevitable developments, circumstances; thus *caught in the go-'long*, to be a victim of circumstances. **2** [1920s–40s] (US Black) the police truck in which arrested people are taken to the local cells (cf. HURRY-UP). [one has no choice but to fig. or lit. *go along*]

go look at the crops, to phr. [20C] euph. excuse when one wishes to leave the room and urinate.

golopshus/goluptious/galoptious/galopshus/galumptious/goloptious adj. [mid-19C–1930s] delicious, flavoursome, luscious.

golpe n. [1970s+] (drugs) heroin. [Sp. *golpe*, a jolt, a blow]

goluptious see GOLOPSHUS.

g.o.m. n.[1] [late 19C+] grand old man. [coined for Prime Minister William Ewart Gladstone, (1809–98) but used more generally]

g.o.m. n.[2] [1940s+] (drugs) opium, morphine. [abbr. GOD'S OWN MEDICINE]

gom n.[1] [early–mid-19C] a euph. synon for God, and as such used in mild oaths (cf. COCK n.[1]). [Lancashire dial.]

gom/gawm/goamey/gam/gorm n.[2] [mid-19C+] (Irish) a painfully stupid or gullible person. [Irish *gamal*, a simpleton]

gom/gommie n.[3] [1960s+] (S.Afr.) a fool, an idiot; thus *gommy*, stupid, vulgar. [GOMTOR]

goma n. [1960s] (drugs) opium; black tar heroin. [Sp. *goma*, gum]

goma de moto n. [1980s+] (drugs) hashish. [Sp. *goma de moto*, gum of dust]

gombay n. [1940s+] (W.I.) a very dark-complexioned Black person. [dial. *gombay*, drum or drummer; ult. Kongo *nboma*, a goatskin drum]

gome n. [1980s+] (US campus) a devotedly hard worker. [GOMER]

gomer n.[1] [1960s+] (US) a fool, a rustic simpleton. [the proper name *Gomer Pyle*, a fictional T.V. comic yokel character; but cf. dial. *gaum*]

gomer n.[2] [1960s+] an old, dirty, difficult or chronically ill hospital patient. [abbr. *get out of my emergency room*]

gomeral/gomeril n. [20C] (Irish) a lout. [Irish *gomaral*, *gamal*, a lout, a boor; *gomeril* is also found throughout dial.]

gomer pyle n. [1980s] (US) a fool, a yokel (cf. GOMER n.[1]).

go milk a duck! excl. [20C] (US) an excl. of dismissal, euph. for GO FUCK A DUCK!

go mingo v. [mid-19C] to masturbate. [SE *go* + MINGO v.]

gommie see GOM n.[1].

gommy n. [19C] a dandy. [Fr. argot *gommeux*, pretty, fashionable]

go molrowing v. [mid–late 19C] to have sexual intercourse. [MOLROWER]

go motting v. [19C] to have sexual intercourse. [MOT n.]

gomtor n. [1960s+] (S.Afr.) an uncouth or common loutish person (cf. GOM n.[3]; GOPS). [synon. Afk.]

go much on v. [late 19C+] (orig. US) to like to enjoy; often in neg. form e.g. *I don't go much on that*.

go mulga v. [1950s+] (Aus.) to take to the bush, thus to go off by oneself. [MULGA]

gomus n. [mid-19C–1910s] (Anglo-Irish.) a fool. [GOM n.[2]]

gon n. (US) **1** [1910s–30s] a gun. **2** [1930s–60s] gonorrhoea. [pron./abbr.]

gonads n. (US) **1** [1910s+] the testicles; thus *have someone by the gonads*, to be in a controlling position (cf. GONIES). **2** [1970s] courage (cf. BALLS n.[1]). [SE *gonads*, any organ in an animal (as a testis or an ovary) that produces gametes]

go nap/nap on v. **1** [late 19C+] to commit oneself fully. **2** [1930s+] (Aus.) to not like. [racing use]

go native v. [late 19C+] to adopt the habits, dress etc. of local people when in a foreign country.

go naughty see DO THE NAUGHTY.

gonce/gons n. [late 19C–1930s] (Aus.) money. [? Yid. *gunz*, the lot]

gondolas n. [1920s–70s] (US) large clumsy shoes. [resemblance]

gone adj.[1] [19C+] (US) **1** used of one who is considered to be a lost cause, a hopeless case. **2** of a person or animal, dead or doomed. Both usu. in combs., e.g. GONE BEAVER; GONE CHICKEN; GONE COON; GONE GOOSE; GONE GOSLING; GONER. [fig. uses of *gone*, lost]

gone adj.[2] [mid-19C+] pregnant.

gone adj.[3] **1** [1920s+] drunk, intoxicated by a drug (cf. OUT OF IT phr.[2]). **2** [1930s+] insane, crazy, bizarre. **3** [1940s+] (orig. US Black) weird and wonderful, lost in music, drugs etc, esp. *gone cat*, *gone chick*. **4** [1950s+] a general intensifier, both positive and negative, extraordinary or thoroughly (cf. GONEST). [abbr. *gone out of this world*]

gone across/up adj. [20C] dead (cf. GONE OVERBOARD). [religious imagery, i.e. one has *gone across* the river Jordan or *gone up* to heaven]

gone a million phr. [20C] (Aus.) in a hopeless state. [? coined by the profligate John Scadden, Prime Minister of Western Australia, 1911–16]

gone and forgotten n. [20C] (Aus.) rotten. [rhy. sl.]

gone beaver n. [mid-19C+] (orig. US) one who is utterly doomed, without hope of escape. [GONE adj.[1] + SE *beaver*]

gone chicken n. [early 19C+] (US) (US) a doomed person, a 'lost soul' (cf. DEAD CHICKEN). [GONE adj.[1] (2) + CHICKEN n.[2]]

gone coon n. [mid-19C+] (orig. US) one who is utterly doomed, without hope of escape (cf. GONE GOOSE; GONE GOSLING). [GONE adj.[1] (2) + COON n. (1)]

gonef see GONNOF.

gone for a ride on padre's bike phr. [1950s+] (Aus.) a general answer to the question, 'Where is X?' (cf. HE WENT MAD AND THEY SHOT HIM).

gone for its tea phr. [1970s+] (Irish) **1** worn out, exhausted, of no further use. **2** vanished.

gone for the milk phr. [20C] (Irish) dead.

gone goose n. [early 19C+] (orig. US) a person or thing that is beyond all hope (cf. GONE COON). [note 19C naut. jargon gone-goose, a ship deserted or given up in despair]

gone gosling n. [mid-19C+] (orig. US) one who is utterly doomed, without hope of escape (cf. GONE COON). [GONE adj. [1] (2) + SE gosling]

gone in adj. [mid–late 19C] (US) exhausted (cf. ALL IN).

gone off one's dip phr. [late 19C–1910s] insane, eccentric. [? DIPPY]

gone on adj. [late 19C+] obsessed by, esp. when in love.

gone out adj. [1970s+] vacant, gormless (cf. LIGHTS ON AND NOBODY HOME).

gone over a goodish piece of grass phr. [late 19C] used of meat, esp. mutton, tough. [unlike a tender lamb, which is killed when young, mutton comes from a much older animal, which has spent much longer in the fields]

gone overboard adj. [20C] **1** dead. **2** (W.I./St Kitts) pregnant, the implication is unintentionally.

goner/gonner n. [mid-19C+] **1** one who is dead. **2** a doomed person, anyone who cannot avoid an unpleasant fate, one on the verge of death. [GONE adj.[1]]

gonest n. [1940s–50s] (US Black/beatnik) the most extraordinary, the most bizarre. [GONE adj.[3] (4)]

gonesville adj. [1950s+] **1** knocked out. **2** vanished, escaped, gone. [SE gone + sfx. -VILLE]

gone through the eddoes phr. (W.I./Bdos.) in a hopeless situation, in irretrievable difficulties (cf. CRAPAUD SMOKE YOUR PIPE). [SE eddoe, a root vegetable, smaller than a dasheen, and commonly used in making soup; phr. implies that one does not even have eddoes left for cooking]

gone to bed phr. [20C] dead. [rhy. sl.]

gone to Haslar phr. [1990s] insane (cf. CALLAN PARK; HASLAR NURSE). [RN psychiatric institution at Haslar, Gosport, Hampshire]

gone to hell see ALL TO HELL.

gone to Moscow phr. [1910s+] (Aus.) in pawn. [pun on mosk, to pawn]

gone to pot adj. [mid-19C+] **1** of a person, fallen in status, leading a degenerate life, dead. **2** of a thing, broken down, ceased from functioning properly or well. [GO TO POT]

gone to Rotisbone/Rot-His-Bone phr. [late 18C–early 19C] dead (cf. GO TO THE DIET OF WORMS). [pun on the religious colloquy or Diet of Ratisbon + lit. rot his bone]

gone to the dogs phr. [mid-19C+] in social decline, rundown, dirty, poss. living as a tramp. [GO TO THE DOGS]

gone to the pack phr. [mid-19C+] (Aus./N.Z.) in social decline, rundown, dirty and turned into a tramp. [var. on GONE TO THE DOGS]

gone to visit his uncle phr. [late 18C–19C] of a man who has deserted his wife soon after the marriage. [ironic euph.]

gone up see GONE ACROSS.

gone with the wind phr. [1930s+] vanished, esp. of money. [pun on the film title (1939)]

goney see GOONEY.

gong n.[1] [early 11C–late 16C] the privy. [OE gang, the act of walking or going; thus it is, however remotely, an ancestor of the child's plaint, 'I've got to go']

gong n.[2] [late 19C–1930s] (US drugs) **1** an opium pipe. **2** opium. **3** marijuana. [? transliteration of a Chinese word]

gong n.[3] [1910s+] (milit.) a medal. [Anglo-Ind. gong, a metal disc, not musical, used for striking the hour, thus imported by Indian Army veterans]

gong n.[4] [1930s] the bell (later replaced by a siren) on a police car.

gonga see GUNGA.

gonger n. [1910s+] (US drugs) an opium pipe; thus the dimin. gongerine, a small pipe. [GONG n.[2]]

gongers n. [1930s–40s] police patrolling in cars. [GONG n.[4]]

gong-farmer n. [mid-15C–late 16C] a cleaner-out of privies, a nightsoil man (cf. GOLD-FINDER). [GONG n.[1] + SE farmer]

gong girl n. [1930s] a woman who is picked up by a motorist, presumably for sex. [? gonged, of a motorist, pulled up by the police on some matter of road safety]

gong house n. [early 13C–late 16C] a privy (cf. GONG n.[1]).

gong-kicker/-beater n. [1930s–70s] (US) an opium smoker (cf. BEAT THE GONG; KICK THE GONG AROUND). [GONG n.[2]]

gongola n. [20C] (drugs) an opium pipe. [GONG n.[2]]

gongs n. [1950s] (US gay) the testicles. [they 'clang' together ? + GONADS]

gonicles n. [1950s] (US) testicles (cf. GONIES). [GONADS]

gonie n. [1960s+] (S.Afr.) a knife. [Angoni (Nyasaland) goni, to stab]

gonies n. [1990s] the male genitals. [GONADS]

gonif v. [mid–late 19C] (US) to steal. [GONNOF]

goniff see GONNOF.

go ninety v. [1990s] (US campus) to kiss passionately.

gonk n. [1960s] a contemptuous description of a prostitute's client. [the large cuddly homunculoid dolls briefly popular in 1960s]

gonkulator n. [1990s] a word used in place of the actual technical term for a mechanical device. [onomat. noise gonk + calculator]

gonna!/gonnas! excl. [1970s+] (S.Afr.) an general excl; euph for God!

gonner see GONER.

gonnof/gonef/gonnoph/gonoph/gonnif/gonov n. **1** [mid-19C+] a thief. **2** [late 19C–1930s] a scoundrel, fool. [Heb. gannabh, thief; Hotten (1860) suggests that the word is 'as old as Chaucer's time', but his ref. is to gnoff, a peasant, a lout, which comes from East Frisian knufe, lump and gnuffig, thick, rough, coarse, ill-mannered; note S.Afr. goniva, a stolen diamond]

go nowhere v. [1920s+] to be worthless, to be grossly inadequate.

gonov see GONNOF.

gons see GONCE.

gonsel/gonsil/gunsel/gonzel n. (US) **1** [1910s–40s] (tramp) a youth, a naïve boy. **2** [1910s–40s] (tramp) a young, homosexual sidekick who accompanies a tramp. **3** [1930s–70s] (US) a stupid or contemptible man. **4** [1950s+] an informer, a criminal, a gunman. [1. f. Ger. gänslein, a little goose, thence Yid. genzel, a man's young male lover, a catamite; the locus classicus is as the description of Elmer, the young, inadequate hoodlum of Dashiell Hammett's The Maltese Falcon (1930, film 1941); given that he is also a criminal's sidekick, the term is often mistranslated as 'gunman'. However, while Raymond Chandler is convinced of this, Lighter still quotes The Maltese Falcon as a source for gunsel, 'a gunman; thug', suggesting a root in GUN n.[8], gunman or GUN-SLINGER n. (1)]

gonus n. [mid-19C; 1980s+] (US campus) a fool, a stupid person. [GOONEY]

gonzel see GONSEL.

gonzo n. [1970s+] (orig. US) an anarchic eccentric. [GONZO adj.[1]]

gonzo adj.[1] [1970s+] eccentric, bizarre, extraordinary, boundsbreaking; esp. in comb. gonzo journalism, a form of extreme

'New Journalism', in which reporters, rather than taking the typical distanced, neutral position, interpolate their thoughts, emotions, and actions into the story. [GONE adj.³ (2) + CRAZO or cod Ital. sfx. -*zo* + pun on GUNG-HO; coined and pioneered as a journalistic form by US writer Hunter S. Thompson (b.1939) in *Rolling Stone* magazine 1970]

gonzo adj.² **1** [1970s+] finished, defeated, useless. **2** [1970s+] (US) drunk. [GONE adj.¹ (1)/GONE adj.³ (1)]

gonzoed adj. [1970s+] (US) very drunk or intoxicated. [GONZO adj.²]

goo n. [20C] (orig. US) **1** anything sticky or viscid, e.g. blood, semen, glue (cf. MAGOOZLUM). **2** sickly sentimentality, esp. in speech or writing. [? abbr. BURGOO]

goo/goob v. [20C] (Aus.) to spit out a lump of phlegm. [GOB v. (2)]

goob n.¹ *see* GOOBER n.¹.

goob n.² [1980s+] (drugs) methcathinone (cf. BATHTUB SPEED). [ety. unknown]

goober/goob n.¹ **1** [mid-19C+] an idiot, a fool, an incompetent (cf. DICKHEAD). **2** [1920s+] (US) the penis. **3** [1960s+] (US) a gob of phlegm. **4** [1970s+] (US campus) a small child. **5** [1970s+] (US campus) a small mole, spot or similar skin blemish. **6** [1980s+] (US campus) someone not attuned to the peer group norms. [fig. uses of *goober*, a peanut, thus an insignificant object; ult. f. African langs.]

goober n.² [mid-19C+] (US) an inhabitant of North Carolina, Arkansas or Georgia. [SAmE *goober*, a peanut, the state's main crop]

gooberbrain n. [1960s+] (US) a silly person (cf. BAKEBRAIN). [SAmE *goober*, a peanut + sfx. -BRAIN]

goober-grabber/-grubber n. [19C+] (US) an inhabitant of North Carolina, Arkansas or Georgia. [SAmE *goober*, the peanut, grown widely in all three states; the term means lit. 'one who grabs or digs peanuts']

gooberhead n. [20C] (US) a general derog. term, typically describing an eccentric, a fussy person, one who drives badly (cf. DICKHEAD). [SAmE *goober* + sfx. -HEAD (1)]

goob out v. [1980s] (US campus) to disgust, to repel. [GOOBER n.¹]

gooby n. [19C] a fool, a dullard. [GABY]

good n. **1** [mid-19C+] (orig. US) alcohol. **2** [1970s+] (drugs) phencyclidine (cf. ACE n.³)

good adj.¹ [early 19C] (Und.) a place or person that can be robbed easily; thus *good upon the crack*, easily broken into (cf. GOOD UPON THE STAR).

good adj.² [late 19C+] solvent, able to pay for or lend, usu. as *good for*.

good adj.³ [late 19C+] as *any/some/no good*, to some or no degree good.

good adj.⁴ [late 19C+] worthless or dead, esp. of an enemy or a criminal. [orig. used on frontier as *good Indian*, a dead Indian]

good a maid as her mother phr. [17C] a recently deflowered young woman.

good and phr. [late 19C+] (orig. US) a general intensifier, e.g. *good and ready, good and crazy*.

good and plenty n. [1980s+] (drugs) heroin.

good a piece as ever strode a pot n. [19C] an admirable woman, as good as one might find. [a woman 'bestrides' a chamberpot to urinate]

good as all get-out phr. [mid-19C+] (orig. US) excellent, wonderful, first-rate.

good as a shoulder of mutton for/to a sick horse phr. [mid-16C–mid-18C] absolutely useless.

good as caz phr. [early 19C] (Und.) easy, simple, referring to any projected fraud or robbery, or a person who is to be made a victim of either (cf. EASY AS PIE). [CAZ; *see* CASSAN]

good as ever pissed phr. [18C] of a person, as good as there has ever been. [PISS v.]

good as ever twanged phr. [late 16C–late 17C] of women, as good as one might wish, esp. in the sexual context. [TWANG]

good as wheat phr. [19C] excellent, wonderful, first-rate. [the positive image of wheat]

good at the game n. [19C] an enthusiastic, skilful lover. [GAME n.³]

good biz! excl. [late 19C–1910s] wonderful! excellent! [abbr. SE *good business!*]

good buddy n. **1** [1950s+] the popular form of address among users of Citizen's Band radios. **2** [1950s+] a CB radio user. **3** [1980s+] (US) a homosexual. [SE *good* + BUDDY n.]

good butt n. [1960s+] (drugs) marijuana cigarette. [SE *good* + BUTT n.²]

goodbye, Charlie phr. [1960s–70s] (US) the end, the finish, usu. in phr. *and it's goodbye. Charlie* (cf. GOODBYE, JOHN).

goodbye, John n. [late 19C–1900s] (US) the end (cf. GOODBYE, CHARLIE).

good cess to you! *see* BAD CESS TO YOU!

good Christmas! excl. [1920s+] a euph. var. of *good Christ!*

good deal! excl. [1940s+] (US) an expression of approval or congratulation, well done! that's wonderful!

good doer n. [1910s+] a smart person, who 'knows a thing or to'. [a play on *do-gooder*]

good dud n. [1980s+] (US campus) an unamusing joke. [SE *dud*, a failure, a 'flop']

good eating n. [1920s+] (Aus.) an attractive young woman. [the image is of food (cf. BANANA n.²); the sexual use of EAT is coincidental]

good egg n. [1900s+] **1** an admirable person. **2** as excl., that's good, that's lucky.

good evening, vicar phr. [20C] joking phr. used to acknowledge an audible breaking of wind.

goodfellas n. [1980s+] (drugs) fentanyl (cf. APACHE n.²). [ety. unknown; link to the film *Goodfellas* (1990)]

good few n. [early 19C+] a fair number, an unspecified but reasonably large quantity.

good-for n. [late 19C] (S.Afr.) an IOU. [it is GOOD adj.² for the debt]

good form n. [late 19C+] (society) anything that is seen as 'proper' or socially acceptable (cf. BAD FORM). [horse-racing use *form*, the state of a horse's health etc]

good for one! excl. [1910s+] well done!

good future! excl. [1980s+] (US campus) sarcastic response to the speaker's announcement of some form of menial employment, i.e. what a good job! aren't you lucky!

good Germans n. [1950s] (US) law-abiding, respectable, unquestioning people, irrespective of actual racial origins. [stereotype of Germans as law-abiding people who do not question authority]

good giggles n. [1970s] (drugs) marijuana. [its effect]

good girl/one n. [18C–late 19C; 17C–18C] a prostitute, a wanton. [ironic + she is *good for* sex]

good go n. [20C] (drugs) the proper amount of drugs for the money paid. [SE *good* + GO n.²]

good/great grief! excl. [1930s+] a general excl. of surprise and/or dismay. [dial.]

good gracious me! excl. [18C+] a mild oath (cf. GRACIOUS).

good guts n. [1930s+] (Aus.) the facts, the essential information. [SE *good* + GUTS n.³ (2)]

good guys n. [1960s+] friendly individuals, esp. those on one's side.

good hair n. [1900s–50s] (US Black) straight, soft hair (cf. BAD HAIR). [*good* as in superior, more acceptable, i.e. 'White']

good head n. **1** [19C+] an expert. **2** [1920s–60s] (US Und.) a trustworthy, admirable fellow.

goodie/goody n.[1] **1** [19C] a religious hypocrite. **2** [late 19C+] (orig. US) a good person, esp. in a film or story (cf. BADDIE).

goodie n.[2] [1970s+] a good thing, esp. in phr. *an oldie but a goodie*.

goodie and baddie n. [20C] an Irish person. [rhy. sl. *goodie and baddie* = PADDY n.[1] (1)]

goodies n. **1** [mid-19C+] sweetmeats, latterly any form of tasty food. **2** [1950s+] (US) the genitals of either sex. **3** [1950s+] (US) the female breasts (cf. APPLES n.[1]). **4** [1950s+] (US) sexual intercourse.

good ink n. [1910s+] (Aus./N.Z.) something agreeable, pleasant, usu. in phr. *that's good ink*. [? journalistic imagery]

good iron phr. [late 19C+] (Aus.) a general phr. of approval, congratulations. [quoits jargon *good iron*, a good throw]

good jump phr. [17C+] usu. of a woman, a sexually satisfying partner. [JUMP n.[2]]

goodle n. [1950s+] (Ulster) a lot. [SE *good deal*]

good lick n. [1960s+] (drugs) good drugs. [play on SE *lick*, a hit/HIT n.[4]/n.[5]]

good-looker n. [late 19C+] (orig. US) an attractive person, usu. a woman.

good luck see LUCK n.

good man, the n.[1] [18C+] the devil.

good man/goodman n.[2] **1** [late 18C] a boon companion, a rositerer. **2** [late 18C–early 19C] a gaoler.

goodman turd n. [17C] a derog. description of another person (cf. SHIT n.[2]). [GOODMAN + TURD]

goodness Agnes!/Agnes Brown!/Mable Agnes! excl. [20C] (US) a general excl. of surprise and/or pleasure (cf. GRACIOUS MISS AGNES!). [? *agnus dei*, the lamb of God and thus a euph. for God or Christ]

goodness gracious! excl. [19C+] a mild oath (cf. GRACIOUS).

good news n. [1970s+] a general term of approval, whether of people, things or events.

good night phr. [late 17C+] used to indicate incipient trouble or one's resignation in the face of a problem or disaster; thus [late 17C] *Pray my Lord let's have justice, or good night Nicholas*, elaborated in phr. [1910s+] *good night nurse*, [1910s+] *goodnight, Irene*, [1910s–30s] (N.Z.) *good night McGuinness*, [1930s+] *good night Vienna*. [fig. uses of SE, though Vienna *Goodnight, Vienna*, a romantic operetta by Eric Maschwitz and George Posford (1929)]

good night all phr. [1950s–60s] phr. used as an abrupt punctuation in order to change the subject of conversation (cf. THAT'S ALL SHE WROTE).

goodnight kiss n. [20C] urination. [rhy. sl. *goodnight kiss* = PISS n.]

good nose n. [late 17C–early 18C] something that smells very good.

good-o/good-oh adj. [20C] (orig. Aus./N.Z.) excellent, wonderful, as it should be.

good-o!/good-oh! excl. [20C] (orig. Aus./N.Z.) an excl. of approbation or assent. [usu. associated with somewhat dated schoolboy use]

good oil n. [1910s+] (Aus.) the honest truth, true facts (cf. DINKUM OIL).

good old adj. [mid-18C+] a general pfx. of approval and affection.

good old/ole boy n. **1** [19C+] (US) a man who embodies the traditional values of the southern White male country-dweller; used neutrally by those so defined (although there may be a slight implication of tolerable rascality), but usu. derog. or *good ole boy* at least ironic by outsiders for whom it is often a synon. for bigot/racist (cf. REDNECK). **2** [1980s] (US preppie) a student who is considered of the 'right type' by his peers. [SE *old boy*, a genial person, not unacquainted with the pleasures of the flesh]

good old brown n. [20C] (Can.) sodomy. [BROWN n.[3]]

good sort/old sort n. **1** [late 19C+] a generally admirable person. **2** [1920s+] a very pretty woman. **3** [1940s+] (Aus.) one who is attractive to the opposite sex; thus *drack sort*, one who is unattractive, *extra sort*, one who is extremely attractive. [SORT n.]

good ole boy see GOOD OLD BOY.

good one n.[1] see GOOD GIRL.

good one/'un n.[2] [19C+] **1** a joke. **2** an implausible statement, thus a lie.

good on the fang/tooth phr. [1940s+] (Aus.) used of one known as an enthusiastic eater.

good on the star adj. [early–mid-19C] (Und.) easy to open, usu. of a window. [the 'starring' of the window when one breaks the glass]

good on the tooth see GOOD ON THE FANG.

good on you! excl. [20C] (Aus./Irish) a general expression of approbation, thanks etc; also abbr. to *good*. [invariably linked to Aus., the term is equally common in Ireland. Share suggests that the origin lies in Irish *rinne sé mhaith orm*, lit. 'he made/did his good on me']

good pay, be v. [early 18C–1920s] to be trustworthy, esp. as regards paying one's debts.

good people n. [1950s+] **1** (US Und.) former criminals who have retired from their various specialities. **2** (US) one's peers.

good pup phr. [20C] (N.Z.) a general phr. of commendation, and approval, thus anything/anyone good, commendable.

goods, the n.[1] **1** [late 19C+] (orig. US) the real thing, the ideal thing or person; thus *deliver the goods*, to come up to expectations. **2** [late 19C+] information, usu. to be used in an unfriendly manner towards its subject; thus *get the goods on*, to find out (negative facts) about. **3** [late 19C–1930s] things or people, orig. used for racehorses and athletes.

goods n.[2] [20C] (US Und.) stolen goods, contraband; thus *catch with the goods*, to catch in the act.

good shake see EVEN SHAKE.

good ship Venus n. [20C] the penis. [rhy. sl.; ref. to the 'rugby song']

good shit n. [1960s+] (orig. US) anything of high quality, esp. drugs. [SHIT n.[5]]

good shot n. [mid-18C+] a good try, even though one may have failed.

good show! excl. [1940s+] a general excl. of approval or pleasure.

good stick n. [1950s+] (drugs) the short-lived bout of vomiting that can follow an injection of heroin.

good strange! excl. [early 18C] a mild oath., lit. 'God's strings'.

good stuff n. [1970s+] (US Black) **1** sexual sophistication. **2** effective, pleasant drugs. **3** success in a confidence trick, in deception.

good thing n. **1** [1910s+] (Aus./US) one who can easily be duped, a 'sucker'. **2** [1970s+] an advantageous opportunity, usu. in business.

good time n.[1] [1960s+] (US Und.) time off for good behaviour (cf. COPPER TIME). [SE *good* + TIME n.[1]]

good time n.[2] [1960s+] (US Black) an especially acceptable, likeable person (cf. GOOD NEWS).

good time n.[3] [1960s+] the penis. [its role in sex]

good-time Charlie n. [1920s+] a playboy, a dissolute man (cf. CHAMPAGNE CHARLIE). [SE *good time* + CHARLIE n.[6]]

good-time Jane n. [1940s–60s] (US) a sexually promiscuous woman. [SE *good time* + JANE n.[2]]

good 'un see GOOD ONE n.[2].

good value adj [1930s+] amusing, entertaining, worthwhile.

good voice to beg bacon phr. [late 17C–early 19C] a very unmelodious singing voice and therefore good only for begging.

good/great warrant n. [20C] (Irish) a good bet, a certainty. [SE *warrant*, a surety]

good woman n. [late 18C–19C] a common public house sign representing a woman without a head. [the implication is that her 'goodness' stems from the fact that bereft of a head she cannot scold. A similar sign depicts an *honest lawyer*, the absence of his head deprives him of the ability to lie]

good-woolled adj. [mid-19C] used of a plucky, spirited person. [Lincolnshire dial. *good-wooled*, said of a sheep that has a good fleece]

goody n. see GOODIE n.[1].

goody!/goody-goody! excl. [1920s+] (orig. Aus.) a general excl. of pleasure, satisfaction.

goodyear n.[1] [17C] venereal disease, esp. gonorrhoea. [? *gouge*, a slattern, a soldier's companion; ult. Fr. argot *gouge*, a slut]

goodyear n.[2] [1960s+] the ring of excess flesh around a portly stomach that may be seen in a kinder light by those who appreciate the Rubenesque figure (cf. BAGELS; LOVE HANDLES). [the *Goodyear* Rubber Company; a pun on SPARE TYRE]

good young man n. [late 19C] a hypocrite (cf. GOODIE n.[1]). [a lyric by music-hall star Arthur Roberts (1852–1933)]

goody two-shoes n. [1930s+] (US) a self-righteous person. [fairy-tale character]

gooey n. 1 [20C] (Aus.) a lump of phlegm (cf. GOLLION). 2 [20C] a man of weak character. 3 [1980s+] a pretty girlfriend. [GOOEY adj.]

gooey adj. 1 [20C] sticky, viscid. 2 [1940s+] sentimental, mawkish. [fig. uses of GOO + sfx. -y]

goof n.[1] 1 [1910s+] an eccentric, crazy person, a fool, a blunderer. 2 [1950s+] (US) a mistake. 3 [1950s+] (US) a joke, surprise; thus *goofs*, fun. 4 [1960s+] (US) something very unpleasant. [dial. *goof*, a fool, a clown, an oaf]

goof n.[2] [1930s–60s] (US) 1 (drugs) psychotropic drugs, esp. marijuana or barbiturates; thus *on the goof*, drowsy from the effects of a drug (cf. GOOFBALL). 2 alcohol. 3 a marijuana smoker. [GOOF v.[2]]

goof n.[3] see GOEF n.

goof v.[1] (US) 1 [1910s+] (US) to fool around, tease or taunt. 2 [1930s+] to dawdle, to waste time, to avoid work. 3 [1940s+] (Aus./US) to gawk, to stare mindlessly, esp. at the television; thus *goofbox*, a TV set. 4 [1940s+] to blunder, to make a mistake; thus *goof oneself*, to get into trouble. 5 [1950s+] (US) to mistreat, to victimize. 6 [1960s+] to make a mess of. [GOOF n.[1]]

goof v.[2] (US) [1930s+] to take drugs; thus *goofed up, on the goof*, under the influence of drugs. [GOOF n.[2]]

goof v.[3] see GOEF v.

goofball n.[1] 1 [1930s+] (drugs) cocaine and heroin. 2 [1950s+] a barbiturate, a tranquillizer. 3 [1950s+] (Aus.) a knock-out drop. [GOOF n.[2]; *OED*, citing *Am. Sp.* XIII (1938), claims 'marijuana' as a second def., but this may be an error, caused by the contemporary ignorance of drug terminology (the orig. source seems to be a *New Yorker* piece, published that year). The fact that the *OED* talks of a 'tablet' of marijuana only underlines the blunder]

goofball n.[2] [1940s+] (US) a silly, amusing, eccentric or insane person. [GOOF n.[1]]

goofball adj. [1940s+] crazy, eccentric. [GOOFBALL n.[2]]

goof bender n. [1940s+] (US) a period of letting one's hair down or acting absurdly just for fun. [GOOF n.[1] + BENDER n.[1]]

goof butt n. [20C] (drugs) a marijuana cigarette (cf. GOOFBALL n.[1]). [GOOF n.[2] + BUTT n.[2]]

goofed up adj. 1 [1940s+] (US) 1 inebriated with a drug, esp. barbiturates (cf. GOOFBALL n.[1]). 2 [1940s+] (US) drunk. 3 [1950s+] crazy, infatuated or bewildered. [GOOF v.[1]]

goofer/goopher n.[1] [1910s+] (US) a lout, an oaf, a clumsy fool. [GOOF n.[1]]

goofer n.[2] [1960s–70s] one who 'plays around' with drugs, esp. amphetamines or barbiturates. [GOOF v.[2] + GOOFBALL n.[1]]

goofer n.[3] [1960s+] a homosexual prostitute who will take active roles in fellatio or anal intercourse. [fig. use of GOOF n.[1] (1)]

goofers n. [1960s–70s] barbiturates (cf. GOOFBALL n.[1]).

go-off n. [mid-19C+] the starting time.

go off v.[1] 1 [mid–late 17C] to be disposed of at a sale. 2 [late 17C–19C] to die (cf. GO OFF WITH THE FALL OF A LEAF). 3 [mid-18C–late 19C] for a woman, to be married. 4 [early 19C+] to happen, to take place. 5 [mid-19C] to be disposed of, whether of persons or objects. 6 [late 19C–1910s] (society) to not take place, to fail to happen.

go off v.[2] [late 19C+] to lose freshness, to become increasingly rotten, usu. of fruit, meat or milk.

go off v.[3] (Aus.) 1 [1910s+] to be sent to prison. 2 [1920s+] to suffer a police raid, usu. because a hotel or public house is breaking local drinking laws. 3 [1940s+] to be fined.

go off v.[4] 1 [20C] (orig. Aus./N.Z.) to lose emotional control. 2 [1920s+] to have an orgasm (cf. COME OFF v.[1]). 3 [1970s+] (US Black) to do something exceptionally well. 4 [1980s+] (US campus) to become foolish or silly. 5 [1980s+] (US campus) to act intensely. 6 [1980s+] (US campus) to move from topic to topic while talking.

go off v.[5] [1930s+] to find a person or object unappealing, distasteful or tedious. usu. when one's feelings have been more positive before.

go off at v. [1940s+] (orig. Aus./N.Z.) to lose one's temper, to attack verbally, usu. at length.

go off at the deep end see FLY OFF AT THE DEEP END.

go off at half-cock/half-cocked, to phr. [mid-19C+] 1 to speak or act prematurely. 2 to talk foolishly, esp. when under the influence of one's emotions or of drink or drugs. 3 to work badly or inadequately. 4 to ejaculate prematurely. [SE *half-cock*, to put (a gun) at half-cock; (4) adds pun on COCK n.[2]]

go/run off at the lip/mouth, to phr. [20C] (US) to lose one's temper, to launch into a diatribe.

go off at the nail, to phr. [early 18C+] (Ulster) to become confused or flustered. [the image of two parts of a pair of scissors flying apart when the nail that links them snaps or falls out]

go off half-cocked see GO OFF AT HALF-COCK.

go off like a two-bob watch, to phr. [1970s] (Aus.) of a woman, to be highly sexed. [pun on SE *go off*/GO OFF v.[4] (2)]

go off on v. [1960s+] (US Black) to lose one's temper, to attack verbally, usu. at length (cf. GO OFF AT).

go off one's brain, to phr. [1940s+] (Aus.) to be extremely enthusiastic about something or someone.

go off one's burner, to phr. [late 19C–1910s] to go mad.

go off one's dot, to phr. [late 19C–1920s] to go mad. [DOTTY]

go off on one's ear see GET UP ON ONE'S EAR.

go off one's face, to phr. [1940s+] (Aus.) to burst into laughter.

go off one's napper, to phr. [late 19C] to go mad. [NAPPER n.[2] (2)]

go off pop/off pop at, to phr. [20C] (orig. Aus./N.Z.) to lose one's temper with. [SE excl. *pop!*]

go off song, to phr. [late 19C–1900s] of a usually pleasant or friendly person, to become surprisingly hostile. [the image of a cage-bird]

go off the boil, to phr. [20C] 1 to lose impetus, to lose enthusiasm. 2 to calm down. 3 of a woman, to lose her enthusiasm for sex.

go off the dome, to phr. [1980s+] (US Black) to create spontaneously, to compose lyrics out of one's head. [DOME n.[1]]

go off the hooks, to phr. [mid-19C+] to die.

go off the rails, to phr. [late 19C+] to err, to make a mistake (cf. FLY THE TRACK). [railway imagery]

go off the stocks, to phr. [mid-19C+] to die. [orig. naut. use stocks, the framework on which a ship or boat is supported while in process of construction]

go off twanging, to phr. [early 17C] to turn out very well. [TWANGING]

go off with the fall of the leaf, to phr. [late 18C–19C] to be hanged (cf. AUTUMN; DROP ONE'S LEAF; LEAFLESS TREE). [a pun on the leaves or hinged panels of the drop and the dead leaves that fall from a natural, rather than judicial 'tree'. Grose (1796) notes that 'criminals in Dublin being turned off from the outside of the prison by the falling of a board, propped up, and moving on a hinge, like the leaf of a table']

goofiness n. [1920s+] stupidity, foolishness. [GOOF n.[1]]

goof-off n. (US) **1** [1940s+] a loafer, idler. **2** [1960s+] an error or blunder. [GOOF OFF v.]

goof off v. [1940s+] **1** (orig. milit.) to act lazily, to mess around instead of working. **2** to blunder. **3** (US drugs) to go to sleep, esp. under the influence of drugs. [GOOF v.[1]]

goof on v. [1940s+] (US) **1** to laugh at, to find amusing. **2** [1950s] to get excited by. [GOOF v.[1]]

goo food n. [1980s] (US campus) Oriental food. [GOOK n.[3]]

goof out v. [1980s+] (US) to trick or fool. [GOOF v.[1]]

goof pill n. [1950s–70s] (drugs) a barbiturate (cf. GOOFBALL n.[1]).

goof-proof adj. [1970s+] (US) foolproof. [GOOF n.[1] + SE proof]

goof up n. [1930s+] (US) **1** a blunder. **2** a person who causes trouble for themselves. [GOOF UP v.]

goof up v. [1930s+] (US) to blunder, to spoil, to injure. [GOOF v.[1]]

goofus n. [1910s+] (US) an idiot. [GOOF n.[1]]

goofy adj. [1920s+] **1** stupid, uncoordinated, inept. **2** drunk (cf. ADDLED). [GOOF n.[1] + sfx. -y; the personification of the term (albeit anthropomorphic) is the eponymous Disney character]

goofy's goon n. [1980s+] (drugs) phencyclidine (cf. ACE n.[3]).

goog n.[1] [1920s–30s] (US) a black eye. [GOOGS]

goog/googie/googy n.[2] [1940s+] (Aus.) an egg. [Scot. goggie/ Irish gogaí, nursery term for an egg]

googeen adj. [20C] (Irish) usu. of a woman, fidgety. [synon. Irish guaigin]

googie/googy n.[1] [1930s] a fool. [GOO-GOO]

googie n.[2] see GOOG n.[2].

google-eyed adj. [1900s–70s] (US) wearing spectacles (cf. GOGGLE-EYED).

googly n. [20C] anything that poses a tough problem, esp. an awkward question that a person would rather not answer. [cricket jargon googly, an off-break that is delivered with what appears to the batsman as a leg-break action. Invented by the English bowler B.J.T. Bosanquet (1877–1936), it is also known as a bosie in Aus.]

goo-gobs n. [1930s–50s] (US Black) a very large or infinite amount. [ety. unknown; note SE googol, 10 to the 100th power]

goo-goo n.[1] [20C] (orig. US) anything sticky or viscid, e.g. blood, semen, glue (cf. MAGOOZLUM). [redup. of GOO n. (1)]

goo-goo n.[2] see GOO-GOO EYES.

goo-goo n.[3] (US) **1** [1900s–50s] a derog. term for an Asian or dark-skinned foreigner. **2** [1970s] an unintelligible foreign language. [GOOK n.[3]]

goo-goo n.[4] (US) [late 19C+] a supporter of political reform. [SE good government + GOODIE]

goo-goo n.[5] (US) [1930s] a silly fool. [? goo-goo noises of stupidity]

goo-goo v. [1900s–50s] (US) to make eyes at someone. [GOO-GOO EYES]

goo-goo eyes/goo-goo n. [20C] an amorous glance directed at a loved, or hopefully soon to be loved, one. [? GOGGLE, + the double 'o' is reminiscent of two rounded eyes; goo-goo is also

a classic piece of 'baby-talk' and as such reflects the infantility of such glances]

goo-goo watch n. [1930s–40s] (US Black) dawn and the period just preceding it. [ety. unknown]

googs n. [1920s–50s] (US) spectacles. [? play on GOO-GOO EYES]

googy n.[1] see GOOGIE n.[1].

googy n.[2] see GOOG n.[2].

googy eyes n. [1910s–20s] (US) amorous glances. [GOO-GOO EYES]

gooi n. [1940s+] (S.Afr.) a fling, a spree, a party. [GOOI v.]

gooi v. [1940s+] (S.Afr.) to throw, to fling, to give someone something. [Afk. gooi, to throw, fling]

gooi a canary, to phr. [1940s+] (S.Afr.) to whistle a warning. [GOOI v.]

gooi ankers v. [1980s+] (S.Afr.) to brake suddenly. [GOOI v. + Afk. sl. ankers, the brakes]

gooi a spasm, to phr. [1980s+] (S.Afr.) to react with joy or enthusiasm. [GOOI v. + SE spasm]

gooi a U-ie, to phr. [1980s+] (S.Afr.) to make a U-turn (cf. THROW A U-IE). [GOOI v. + SE U]

gooi grief v. [1940s+] (S.Afr.) to annoy someone (cf. GIVE SOMEONE GRIEF). [GOOI v. + SE grief]

gooi pomp v. [1980s+] (S.Afr.) to have sexual intercourse. [GOOI v. + POMP n.[1]]

gooi tackie v. [1980s+] (S.Afr.) to accelerate (cf. BURN RUBBER). [GOOI v. + SAfrE tackie, a tyre]

gook n.[1] [19C] a street-walker. [? GOWK]

gook n.[2] [1910s+] (US) a dull, stupid, foolish person. [? GINK n.[1] (1)]

gook n.[3] **1** [1920s+] (orig. US milit.) a derog. term for any foreigner esp. Oriental, e.g. (in order of use) Filipino, Japanese, Korean, Vietnamese (cf. CHING n.[1]). **2** [1940s+] any foreign language. [ety. unknown; ? GOO-GOO n.[3] + goo-goo, baby-talk, a ref. to the incomprehensibility of Oriental languages in Western ears; or nursery excl. of disgust, gucchh! denoting Western distaste for the omnivorousness of some Oriental cuisines; neither seems very likely]

gook n.[4] **1** [1940s+] (US) slimy, sticky, dirty viscid matter, also distasteful food. **2** [1980s+] (US) anything unpleasant. [ext. of GOO n. (1)]

gook wagon/car n. [1950s–60s] (US) an inferior car over-decorated with chrome and accessories. [GOOK n.[3], as synon. for a taste for gaudiness and excess]

gooky adj. [1960s+] (US) unpleasantly sticky or awkward. [GOOK n.[4] + sfx. -y]

gool see GOAL.

goola n.[1] [1900s–40s] (US Black) a piano. [ety. unknown]

goola n.[2] [1940s] (US) the anus. [Ital. culo, the anus]

goola box n. [1940s–50s] (US Black) a jukebox or 'nickarola'. [GOOLA n.[1] + SE box]

goolies n. [1930s+] **1** testicles **2** (Aus.) a stone or pebble. [? Hind. golí, a bullet, ball or pill or dial. gullies; given the common equation of the male genitals with weaponry, one might also note dial. gully, a large knife, although that would more properly represent the penis; also note New South Wales Aborigine goolie, a stone]

gooly v. [1990s] (US teen) to walk and dance at the same time. [? GOOLA n.[1] or 1960s dance step, the wully-gully]

goom n. [1960s+] (Aus.) **1** methylated spirits, as an alcoholic's drink. **2** a drinker of methylated spirits. [? Jagara goom, water]

goombah/gumbah n. **1** [1950s+] (US, orig. Ital. Am.) a close male friend. **2** [1950s+] (US) a stupid person. **3** [1960s+] (US) a thug, a gangster. **4** [1990s] (US campus) an outsider, social outcast. [Italian compare, godfather, one of the names (see Mario Puzo, The Godfather, 1969) used for a leader of the Italian-American Mafia]

goom-/goon-bye! excl. [1900s–60s] (US) good-bye.

goomer *n.* [1960s+] (US) a fool, a failure (cf. GOOF n.[1]). [GOMER]

goomy *n.* [1960s+] (Aus.) a drinker of methylated spirits. [GOOM]

go on *v.*[1] [early 19C+] (orig. US) to like, to approve; thus neg. phr. *not go much on*, to disapprove.

go on/go on about *v.*[2] [late 19C+] to talk continuously, repetitively and often tediously; thus *going on* (*about*), talking in this manner.

go on *v.*[3] [1940s+] to use as a basis for one's opinions, calculations, usu. in phr. *something/nothing to go on*.

go on! *excl.* [late 19C+] an excl. used to imply incredulity.

goon *n.*[1] (US) **1** [1920s+] a stolid, stupid person. **2** [1930s+] a thug (cf. HEAVY n.[2]). **3** [1930s+] non-union labour used for strike breaking, intimidation etc. **4** [1940s] (US) a derog. term for a Black person. [? cartoon character, Alice the *Goon* from the comic *Thimble Theatre* (1919) by E.C. Segar (1894–1938). Given the implication of stupidity, note gooney, a fool, ult. OE *ganian*, to gape]

goon/goon crystal/goon dust *n.*[2] [1970s+] (drugs) phencyclidine (cf. ACE n.[3]). [its effects may turn the user into a GOON n.[1] (1)]

goon *n.*[3] [1980s] (Aus.) a flagon of cheap wine. [? mispron./abbr. SE *flagon* or GOOM]

go on a boonie, to *phr.* [1980s+] (US campus use) to go on a picnic in which sex is likely to be involved. [BOONDOCKER]

go on about *see* GO ON v.[2].

go on a date with handrea and palmela, to *phr.* [1990s] to masturbate (cf. CONVERSE WITH HARRY PALM). [puns of female names *Andrea/Pamela* and *hand/palm*]

go on a date with rosy palm and her five daughters, to *phr.* [20C] to masturbate (cf. CONVERSE WITH HARRY PALM). [ROSY PALM AND HER FIVE LITTLE SISTERS]

go on a fishing expedition, to *phr.* [1930s+] to interrogate others for information, 'tips' etc. [pun on SE *fishing*, angling/ *fishing*, looking for information]

go on/have/take a lark, to *phr.* [19C] to have fun esp. at the expense of others. [LARK n.[1]]

go on and on *v.* [late 19C+] to nag. [GO ON v.[2]]

go on a sleigh ride, to *phr.* [1920s+] (drugs) to inhale cocaine. [pun on SE *snow*/SNOW n.[2]]

go on at *v.* [late 19C+] to scold, to abuse, to nag; thus *going on at*, nagging, telling off (cf. GET ON AT). [note W.I. use *go on* to argue fiercely]

go on/out on a tear, to *phr.* [mid-19C+] (orig. US) to go out on a spree. [TEAR n.]

goon-bye *see* GOOM-BYE.

goon-child *n.* [1940s–70s] (US) a stupid or silly person. [GOON n.[1] + SE *child*]

goon crystal/dust *see* GOON n.[2].

gooned/gooned out *adj.* [1960s+] (US) intoxicated on drugs or by alcohol. [GOON n.(1)]

go one-on-one *v.* [1960s+] (orig. US) to have a direct confrontation with another person. [ONE-ON-ONE]

go one scone-hot, to *phr.* [1930s+] (Aus.) **1** to lose one's temper with. **2** to tell off severely. [SCONE]

go one's death, to *phr.* [mid-19C] (US) to do one's utmost for, to risk one's all on, to bet to the limit.

gooney/goonie/goney *n.* **1** [19C+] (US) a fool, an idiot. **2** [1920s+] (US) a foreigner, an enemy, esp. a Chinese communist soldier. [GOON n.[1]]

go on, girl!/go girl! *excl.* [1990s] (orig. US Black campus) an excl. of encouragement among young women.

goonhead *n.* [1980s+] (US) a fool. [GOON + sfx. -HEAD (1)]

go on Hobbes's voyage, to *phr.* [18C] to have sexual intercourse. [pun on the last words of the political philosopher Thomas Hobbes (1588–1679): 'I am about to take my last voyage, a great leap in the dark']

goonie *see* GOONEY.

go on one's face *see* RUN ONE'S FACE FOR.

go on peewee's little adventure, to *phr.* [1980s] (US) to masturbate. [the comedian *Pee-Wee* Herman (b.1952), whose career was truncated when he was caught in a pornographic film theatre]

goon squad *n.* [20C] **1** a group of thugs, usu. organized for a specific purpose – strike-breaking, extortion etc. **2** (US prison) a team of inmates recruited to help the authorities discipline their fellow prisoners. [GOON n.[1] + SE *squad*]

go on the account, to *phr.* [early 19C] to become a pirate. [SE phr. *on one's own account*, in one's own interest]

go on the bum, to *phr.* [20C] (orig. US) to go begging, living as a tramp. [BUM n.[3]]

go on the burst, to *phr.* [19C] to go out on a binge of food and drink. [BURST n. (2)]

go on the cousin sis, to *phr.* [1920s+] to get drunk. [rhy. sl. *Cousin Sis* = PISS n.]

go on the drag, to *phr.* [late 18C] to follow a cart or wagon in order to rob it (cf. VAN DRAGGER). [SE *drag*, a wheeled vehicle]

go on the dub, to *phr.* [late 17C–18C] (Und.) to break into a house using a picklock or skeleton key. [DUB n.[1]]

go on the dummy, to *phr.* [1930s–70s] (US) to stop talking, to be quiet. [DUMMY n.[1]]

go on the hop *see* PLAY THE HOP.

go on the lap, to *phr.* [late 19C–1900s] to drink a good deal of strong liquor. [LAP n.]

go on the letter Q, to *phr.* [early 19C] (Und.) to hoax, to defraud (cf. ON THE BILLIARD SLUM). [a pun on *Q*/(billiard) cue]

go on the lob, to *phr.* [late 18C–early 19C] to play a confidence trick on shopkeepers by asking for change for a high-value coin but then switching coins to make a profit. [LOB n.[1]]

go on the loose, to *phr.* [19C] to have sexual intercourse. [ON THE LOOSE]

go on the piss, to *phr.* [20C] to go out drinking (cf. ON THE PISS). [PISS n.]

go on the/stand a shout, to *phr.* [late 19C+] to go out drinking, to buy a round of drinks. [SHOUT n.[1]]

go on the sneak, to *phr.* [late 17C–late 19C] (Und.) to go out working as a sneak-thief or petty pilferer. [SNEAK n.[1]]

go on the stitch *see* STITCH v.

go on the town, to *phr.* [19C+] to go out on a spree, to enjoy a good time. [18C SE *on the town*, in the swing of fashionable life; the 19C use implies that those so occupied are not fashionable, although they are aiming to get their share of urban pleasures, smart or not]

go on the track, to *phr.* [late 19C+] (Aus.) to travel as a tramp through the outback. [TRACK n.[2]]

go on tick, to *phr.* [late 17C] to run up debts. [TICK n.[2]]

go on, twist my arm *phr.* [1950s+] a joking pretence that the speaker has to be persuaded into doing something (esp. taking a drink) that is, in fact, very appealing and will require no second thoughts on doing it.

goonus *n.* [19C] (usu. US campus) a fool, a simpleton. [cod Latin for GOONEY n. (1)]

go on with the funeral, to *phr.* [late 19C] (US) to carry on with what one is doing.

goony *adj.* [1930s+] (US) silly. [GOON n.[1] + sfx. -y]

goop/goopy *n.*[1] [20C] (orig. US) a fool, an idiot, a boor. [? var. on GOOF n.[1]; coined by Gelett Burgess (1866–1951) in 1900 for a 'race' of fantasy childlike creatures]

goop/gloop *n.*[2] **1** [1910s+] (US) any slimy, sticky viscous matter, esp. hair oil, sticky sweets, cosmetics. **2** [1940s+] (US) (orig. milit.) napalm. [GOO n.]

goop *v.* [1960s+] (US) to perform fellatio or cunnilingus; thus *gobble the goop*. [ext. of GOO n.]

goopheads *n.* [1940s+] (US) acne, pimples. [GOOP n.[2]]

goopher *see* GOOFER n.[2].

goopy *adj.* (US) **1** [20C] sticky. **2** [20C] lacking in energy, exhausted. **3** [1950s+] silly. [GOOP n.[1] + sfx. -*y*]

goorie/goory *n.* [1930s+] (N.Z.) a general term of abuse. [Maori *goorie*, a mongrel dog]

goose *n.*[1] [late 16C–mid-19C] a tailor's iron. [the shape of its neck]

goose *n.*[2] **1** [17C+] a fool. **2** [late 19C] a woman. **3** [late 19C] sexual intercourse. **4** [20C] (US campus) a socially unacceptable person.

goose *n.*[3] [mid-19C–1920s] a scolding, a reprimand (cf. BIRD n.[8]). [theatrical use, *get the goose*, to be hissed]

goose *n.*[4] [late 19C+] a Jew. [? pron. of *goose* as *joose*, i.e. Jews]

goose *v.*[1] **1** [mid-19C] to ruin, to spoil. **2** [late 19C] to make a fool of. [GOOSE n.[3]]

goose *v.*[2] **1** [late 19C+] to pursue women, to womanize. **2** [late 19C+] to poke or tickle a person in the genital or anal area, usu. by a man to a woman. **3** [late 19C+] to have sexual intercourse. **4** [late 19C+] to perform anal intercourse. **5** [1930s+] (US) to press, to push, to provoke, to enliven. **6** [1940s+] (US) to accelerate a car; thus *goose up*, to move forward a short distance. **7** [1960s+] (US campus) to grasp someone's testicles from behind, as a prank. [GOOSE n.[2]]

goose *v.*[3] [late 19C] (US) to repair or enlarge boots by putting in or adding pieces of leather (a process known as 'footing'). [ety. unknown]

goose and duck *n.* **1** [late 19C+] sexual intercourse. **2** [20C] a truck. [rhy. sl.; (1) *goose and duck* = FUCK n.[1]]

gooseberries *n.* [20C] a small boy's testicles (cf. APRICOTS). [supposed resemblance]

gooseberry *n.*[1] [18C] a fool. [punning on the popular dessert, a *gooseberry fool*, which is also SOFT]

gooseberry/gooseberry-picker *n.*[2] [mid-19C+] an unwanted chaperon, esp. a third party who is not wanted by or feels uncomfortable being with the couple. [? *gooseberry-fool* or their excuse for following the couple round a garden: 'I'm just picking gooseberries']

gooseberry *n.*[3] [1940s] (US) a small piece of excrement around the anus. [var. on DINGLEBERRY n. (2)]

gooseberry *v.* [1920s–40s] (US Und.) to steal clothes from a clothes-line (cf. GOOSEBERRY LAY). [GOOSEBERRY BUSH n.[2]]

gooseberry bush *n.*[1] [19C] the pubic hair (cf. BEAUTY SPOT n.[1]). [ext. of BUSH n.[4]; it is this bush, of course, rather than the fruiting variety, beneath which a child is allegedly born]

gooseberry bush *n.*[2] [mid-19C–1940s] (Und.) a clothes-line from which clothes may be stolen. [GOOSEBERRY LAY]

gooseberry-eyed *adj.* [late 18C–late 19C] having eyes that look like boiled gooseberries, grey and lifeless.

gooseberry grinder *n.* [late 18C–19C] the buttocks, esp. in phr. *ask Bogey the gooseberry grinder*, euph. for 'ask my arse' (cf. ASK BOGY!). [ety. unknown' ? ref. to the effect on the digestion and thus defecation of unripe gooseberries]

gooseberry lay *n.* [mid-19C–1940s] (Und.) the stealing of linen drying in the open air by tramps and thieves (cf. GOOSEBERRY BUSH n.[2]). [? as easy as picking gooseberries]

gooseberry-picker *see* GOOSEBERRY n.[2].

gooseberry pudding/pudden *n.* [mid-19C] a woman, esp. as the *old gooseberry*, one's wife. [rhy. sl. *pudding* pron. 'pudden']

gooseberry ranch *n.* [1930s–70s] (US) a brothel. [GOOSING RANCH]

gooseberry tart *n.* [mid-19C–1930s] the heart (cf. RASPBERRY TART n.[1]). [rhy. sl.]

gooseberry wig *n.* [late 18C] a large, frizzled wig. [? its resemblance to a gooseberry bush]

goose-bumper *n.* [1980s+] (US) a horror film. [the tension gives watchers GOOSE BUMPS]

goose bumps *n.* [20C] gooseflesh, the rough pimply condition that can be produced by cold or a sudden attack of nerves. [skin in such a condition supposedly resembles the flesh of a plucked goose]

goose-cap *n.* [16C–mid-18C; 19C] a fool, an idiot, a numbskull. [GOOSE n.[2] (1) + SE *cap*, head. Coined in the UK, it had lapsed by the 18C but was picked up in the US during the 19C]

goosed *adj.* [1920s+] ruined, finished. [GOOSE v.[1]]

goose-drownder/drowner *n.* [1920s+] (US) very heavy rain.

goose egg *n.*[1] [late 19C+] zero, nothing. [the shape of the egg resembles a zero; note cricket jargon a *duck('s egg)*, a score of nothing]

goose egg/gooser *n.*[2] [20C] (US) an illegitimate child. [a euph.]

goose egg *n.*[3] [20C] (US) a large bruise that comes up on the head after striking it or being struck a blow. [joking resemblance]

goose flat *see* GOOSE TOWN.

goosefoot *n.* [late 19C] (US) a man who stands firmly for one political party, come what may (cf. FLATFOOT n.[1]).

goose girl *n.* [1910s] a lesbian. [synon. Fr. argot *gousse*; ? ult. Fr. argot *gousser*, to eat; but note GOOSE n.[2](2)]

goosegog/goosegob *n.* [late 19C+] a gooseberry (cf. STRAWBUG). [abbr.]

goose-grease *n.* [late 19C] vaginal secretions.

goose hangs/honks high *phr.* [19C+] (US) all is well, everything is prosperous. [the image of a goose hanging in the larder, a token of rural prosperity]

goosehead *n.* [late 19C–1910s] (US) an idiot. [GOOSE n.[2] + sfx. -HEAD (1)]

goose hollow *see* GOOSE TOWN.

goose honks high *see* GOOSE HANGS HIGH.

goose nibble *see* GOOSE TOWN.

gooser *n.*[1] [mid-19C] a knock-out blow. [? such a blow COOKS ONE'S GOOSE]

gooser *n.*[2] **1** [late 19C] the penis (cf. BACON n.[1]). **2** [20C] (Can.) a pederast. [GOOSE v.[2]]

gooser *see* GOOSE EGG. n.[2].

goose's gazette *n.* [early–mid-19C] a foolish story. [GOOSE n.[2] + SE *gazette*]

goose shearer *n.* [18C–19C] (Und.) a confidence trickster. [such a villain 'shears' a gullible GOOSE n.[2]]

goose's neck *n.*[1] [late 19C] the penis; thus *have a bit of goose's neck*, to have sexual intercourse (cf. BACON n.[1]). [supposed resemblance]

goose's neck *n.*[2] [20C] a cheque. [rhy. sl.]

goose town/flat/hollow/nibble *n.* [20C] (US) the poor part of town. [geese might be running free in such an area]

goose tracks *n.* [late 19C] (US) illegible handwriting.

goosey/goosy *adj.* [mid-19C+] nervous, jittery, on edge.

goosie *n.* **1** [1960s+] (S.Afr. prison) the passive, 'female' partner of a homosexual couple. **2** a girl, a girlfriend. [GOOSE n.[2]]

goosing ranch *n.* [1920s–30s] (US) a brothel. [GOOSE v.[2]]

goosing slum *n.* [mid–late 19C; 1950s] (US) a brothel. [GOOSE v.[2] + SLUM n.[2] (1)]

goosy *see* GOOSEY.

gooter *n.* [1980s+] (Irish) the penis. [ety. unknown]

go out *v.*[1] **1** [19C] (Und.) to work as a thief. **2** [20C] (Aus./US Black) to die. **3** [1980s+] (US Black) to act, to behave. [fig. uses of SE; post-1940s use of (2) is mainly US Black]

go out *v.*[2] [1930s+] (orig. US) to faint, to lose consciousness, esp. phr. *go out like a light*.

go out foreign, to *phr.* [late 19C] (Und.) to emigrate under suspicious circumstances.

go out for one's tea, to *phr.* [1970s] (Ulster) **1** to go on a paramilitary operation that might lead to one's death. **2** to be subjected to a beating or some other form of punishment by a paramilitary group.

go out like a sucker, to *phr.* [1980s+] (US Black) to die as a result of one's involvement in gangs, drug use and similar activities. [SUCKER; the implication, little heeded, is that involvement in such activities is pointless]

go out the back door, to *phr.* [1960s+] (US prison) to back down under pressure.

go out with the blades, to *phr.* [late 19C–1900s] (Aus.) to become obsolete. [shearing jargon *blades*, hand-held shears, discarded by most shearers in the early 20C]

go over *v.*[1] **1** [late 19C] to rob, after running one's hands over and through the victims' clothes. **2** [1910s+] to inspect.

go over *v.*[2] [late 19C–1920s] (US Und.) to be sent to prison.

go over *v.*[3] [1910s+] (Aus.) of a man, to become a homosexual. [fig. in *go over to the other side* in one's sexuality]

go over big, to *phr.* [1910s+] (orig. US) to be notably successful.

go overboard *v.* [1930s+] **1** to commit oneself completely, often as *go overboard for …* . **2** to behave immoderately, to display excessive enthusiasm.

go over like a lead balloon *see* GO DOWN LIKE A LEAD BALLOON.

go over like a million bucks, to *phr.* [20C] to succeed absolutely, to do very well.

go over the highside, to *phr.* [1990s] (US) **1** to lose control, to lose one's composure. **2** to show off. [HIGHSIDE v.]

go over the hill, to *phr.*[1] [1950s+] (US) to get married. [image of couple vanishing from everyday 'single' life into the world of matrimony]

go over the hill, to *phr.*[2] [1960s] (US) to go mad.

go over the hill, to *phr.*[3] [1960s+] (US prison) to escape. [orig. escaping outdoors work gangs, using hills as cover from one's pursuers]

go over the hump, to *phr.* [1930s] (US tramp) to cross the Rockies on one's trek from east coast to west.

go over the range, to *phr.* [1930s–40s] (Aus.) to die.

go over the score/have a few over the score, to *phr.* [mid-18C+] to drink too much.

go over the top, to *phr.* [1910s–20s] to do something dangerous or remarkable. [WW1 imagery; the 'top' was that of a trench]

go over the wall, to *phr.* **1** [1910s+] to go to prison. **2** [1930s+] (orig. US) to escape from prison. **3** [1940s+] to leave a religious order also as *jump over the wall, leap over the wall.* **4** [1970s] to defect to another country. **5** [1960s+] to go mad. [lit. and fig. uses of SE]

goozer *n.* [1980s+] (Irish) a kiss. [? GUZZLE v. (4)]

goozie/gozzie *n.* [late 19C+] (Aus.) a gooseberry.

goozle/goozlem/goozle pipe/goozler *n.* [19C+] (US) **1** usu. of an animal, the windpipe. **2** of a human, the throat, the Adam's apple. [GUZZLE n.]

goozlum *n.* [20C] (US) any viscous, treacly substance, often describing a food. [GOO n.]

go pear-shaped *v.* [1980s+] of plans or schemes, to fail or collapse. [the image of a solid rectangle 'slipping down' into a pear shape, thus 'the bottom drops out']

go pfft/phffft/phut *v.* [1930s–50s] to come to an abrupt end; esp. of a couple, to divorce. [echoic of the noise of air escaping from a deflated, popped balloon; coined by columnist Walter Winchell (1897–1972)]

gopher *n.*[1] [mid-19C] (US) **1** an Arkansan. **2** a Floridian. **3** a Minnesotan. [SE *gopher*, a burrowing rodent of the genera *Geomys* and *Thomomys*, native to these states]

gopher *n.*[2] **1** [mid-19C] (US) a louse. **2** [mid–late 19C] (US) a primitive form of plough. **3** [mid-19C+] (US) an offensive or

stupid person. [the image is of the animal's burrowing or its role as vermin]

gopher *n.*[3] [late 19C–1930s] (US Und.) a member of a notorious New York City street gang. **2** a thug, a gangster. [the Gophers, whose 'turf' encompassed New York's 'Hell's Kitchen' (the West side between 42nd Street and 14th Street), used the area's cellars and basements as their preferred hideouts]

gopher/gopher-man *n.*[4] [late 19C–1930s] (US Und.) **1** a robber who specializes in safes, strongboxes or bank vaults. **2** a safe-cracker. [like the animal, he 'burrows']

gopher *n.*[5] *see* GOFER.

go phut *see* GO PFFT.

go pile driving, to *phr.* [20C] to have sexual intercourse.

go pill *n.* [1950s–60s] (US) a pill or capsule of amphetamine (cf. A n.[2]). [amphetamines give one energy and 'go']

go piss up a rope! *excl.* [20C] (orig. US) a general excl. of dismissal. [PISS v. + SE *rope*]

go places *v.* [1920s+] (orig. US) **1** to succeed, to do well. **2** to wander about, to travel; thus *go places and see things.*

go pop like a paper bag, to *phr.* [1950s+] to copulate with great enthusiasm (cf. POP ONE'S CORK).

go postal *v.* [1990s] (US teen) to lose one's temper, to lose control of one's emotions. [coined to reflect a spate of mass killings (of fellow workers) by disgruntled postal employees]

go prick scouring, to *phr.* [17C–19C] of a man, to have sexual intercourse. [PRICK n. + SCOUR v.[2](5)]

gops/gopse *n.* [1960s+] (S.Afr.) **1** the backwoods, a backward, rural area. **2** [1960s+] (S.Afr.) an uncouth or common loutish person (cf. GOMTOR). [ety. unknown]

go quim-sticking/wedging *v.* [19C] of a man, to have sexual intercourse. [QUIM n. + SE *stick* v.]

gor *see* GAW.

gor! *see* COR!

go rabbit-hunting/cony-catching with a dead ferret, to *phr.* [late 17C–early 19C] to set out on a task with the wrong or inadequate tools.

gorb/gorby-guts *n.* [late 19C+] (Irish) a glutton. [dial. *gorb*, a gluttonous person or animal; ? ult. Scot. *gorb*, an unfledged bird]

Gorbachev! *excl.* [1990s] (US campus) a response to a sneeze. [a play on the trad. *Gesundheit* + a ref. to the former USSR leader *Mikhail Gorbachev* (b.1931)]

Gorbals kiss *n.* [1930s+] a head butt (cf. CHELSEA SMILE). [ironic use of SE]

gorblimeries *n.* [late 19C] Seven Dials, London. [its Cockney/villainous population, for whom GORBLIMEY! is a regular excl. Note a parallel use as an adj.: 'the Gorblimey aspect of history, the feelings of the ordinary man on the spot at the time' (*Oxford Magazine*, 27 February 1958)]

gorblimey *n.* [1910s+] a rakish cap. [orig. milit. use. 'A "Gorblimey" was the common colloquial term for an unwired, floppy, field-service cap worn by a certain type of subaltern in defiance of the Dress Regulations. Lines from a song, popular before the War, ran: "He wears Gorblimey trousers/ An a little Gorblimey 'at".' (Fraser & Gibbons); ult. f. GORBLIMEY!]

gorblimey!/gor blimey! *excl.* [late 19C+] a mild, euphemistic oath, lit. 'God blind me!' (cf. COR BLIMEY!; COR LUMME!).

gorby drops *n.* [1980s+] a form of BLOTTER n.[2] ACID n.[3] imprinted with a portrait of Mikhail Gorbachev (b.1931), last president of the Soviet Union. [devotees were especially keen on that portion of the picture bearing Gorbachev's birthmark, which stands out on his balding forehead]

gorby-guts *see* GORB.

gor/gah damn *n.* [late 19C–1910s] jam. [rhy. sl.]

gordelpus *see* GAWDELPUS.

Gordon & Gotch *n.* [20C] a watch. [rhy. sl.; the firm of book and periodical importers]

Gordon Bennett! *excl.* [late 19C+] a euph. for GORBLIMEY! [either f. James *Gordon Bennett* (1795–1872), the founding editor of the New York *Herald*, or his similarly named son (1841–1918)]

Gordon Hutter *n.* [1930s–40s] (N.Z.) butter. [rhy. sl.; ult. the contemporary racing and wrestling commentator *Gordon Hutter*]

gore *n.* [1920s–30s] (US) juicy gossip, scandal. [SE *gore*, blood]

goree/gory *n.* [late 17C–18C] money (cf. DELOG). [proper name of *Fort Goree*, on the Gold Coast, a centre for slave trading and gold]

gorge *n.* [19C] **1** a heavy meal. **2** a glutton. [SE *gorge*, to eat to excess]

gorge out *v.* [20C] (US campus) to commit suicide by jumping from a high cliff. [SE *gorge*, a ravine with rocky walls]

gorger *n.*[1] [mid-19C] an employer. [? SE *gouge*, to cheat, to impose upon]

gorger *n.*[2] [mid-19C] **1** a dandy, an exceptionally well-dressed man. **2** any man, irrespective of appearance. [? SE *gorgeous* or Rom. *gorgio*, a non-Romany]

gorgon *n.* [1950s+] (W.I. Rasta) outstanding dreadlocks. [the mythical Gorgon, whose hair was made of writhing snakes]

gorgonzola *adj.* [1920s+] (Aus.) very good. [play on CHEESE *n.*[1]]

goric *n.* [late 19C–1950s] (drugs) opium. [SE *paregoric elixir*, a camphorated tincture of opium flavoured with aniseed and benzoic acid; opium and heroin addicts use paregoric when stronger drugs are unavailable]

gorill *n.* [mid-19C–1940s] (US) **1** a guerilla. **2** a thug. [abbr.]

gorilla *n.*[1] **1** [mid-19C+] (US) a thug, a ruffian, a violent person. **2** [1960s+] (US) a prostitute's customer who likes to beat up the woman. **3** [1970s] (US campus) an unattractive, often overweight young woman. **4** [1970s+] (US) something or someone irresistible or posing difficulty, often modified as *600-pound gorilla, 800-pound gorilla* etc. **5** [1980s+] a monster success, a smash hit. [the image of the animal as a brutal monster; note the conundrum: Where does a 500-pound gorilla sleep? Anywhere it wants to]

gorilla *n.*[2] [1950s+] (US drugs) a severe heroin addiction. [SE *gorilla*, i.e. the size of the primate]

gorilla *n.*[3] [1970s] £1000. [twice the size of a MONKEY *n.*[4]]

gorilla *v.* [1960s+] (US Black) to use violence, to rape. [GORILLA *n.*[1] (1)]

gorilla biscuits/tabs *n.* [1970s+] (drugs) phencyclidine (cf. ACE *n.*[3]). [? the drug turns a user into a GORILLA *n.*[1] (1)]

gorilla burger *n.* [1990s] the vagina.

gorilla in the washing machine, to *phr.* [1970s] (US Black) to perform cunnilingus.

gorilla pills *n.* [1980s+] (drugs) barbiturates (cf. IDIOT PILLS; KING KONG PILLS). [? the drug turns a user into a GORILLA *n.*[1] (1)]

gorilla pimp *n.* [1960s+] (US Black) a pimp who controls his prostitutes by threats and actual violence (cf. SUGAR PIMP). [GORILLA *n.*[1] (1) + SE *pimp*]

gorilla salad *n.* [1960s+] (US gay) the pubic hair, esp. if luxuriant.

gorilla tabs *see* GORILLA BISCUITS.

gork *n.* [1980s+] (US campus) an inadequate, an incompetent. [GEEK *n.*[1] + DORK *n.*[2]; note hospital jargon *gork*, an imbecile or comatose patient, f. acro. *God only really knows*]

gorked *adj.* [1970s+] (US) mindless, dumb. [GORK]

gorm *see* GOM *n.*[2].

gorm *v.*[1] [late 19C–1920s] (orig. US) to eat heartily. [SE *gormandize*]

gorm *v.*[2] [1910s+] to stare at. [dial. *gaum*, to stare vacantly]

gorm/gawm *adj.* [mid-19C+] God-damn. [euph.]

gormagon *n.* [18C] a man on horseback with a woman riding side-saddle behind him. [? SE *gorgon* + *dragon*, the nonsense word was supposedly 'Chinese'. 'A monster with six eyes, three mouths, four arms, eight legs, five on one side and three on the other, three arses, two tarses, and a **** [cunt] upon its back' (Grose, 1785). Note mid-18C secret society, the Gormogons, a short-lived imitation of the Freemasons]

gormed *adj.* [mid-19C] euph. for GOD-DAMNED *adj.* [coined by Charles Dickens for Mr Peggotty in *David Copperfield* (1850)]

gormy-ruddles *n.* [19C] the stomach, the intestines. [SE *gormy ruttles*, 'the strangles', i.e. horses' quinsies or tonsillitis]

gornet *n.* [20C] (Ulster) a fool. [fig. use of SE *gurnard*]

go rocky *v.* [late 19C+] to go wrong. [ROCKY *adj.*]

go round *v.* [late 19C+] to make an informal or spontaneous visit. [note theatrical jargon *go round*, to visit a performer in their dressing-room, usu. after the show]

go round the corner, to *phr.* [late 19C+] to visit the lavatory. [euph.]

go round/all round the houses, to *phr.* [1960s+] to take a circuitous route; also in fig. use.

go round the traps, to *phr.* [1930s–60s] (Aus.) to make a tour of inspection. [the image is of a farmer, gamekeeper or poacher touring the traps set to catch game]

go round with, to *phr.* [20C] to fight with.

gorp *v.* [20C] (US) to eat nosily, greedily. [? onomat.]

gorrel *n.* [1980s+] (S.Afr.) the throat. [Afk. *gorrel-(pyp)*, the throat]

gorry! *excl.* [19C+] (orig. US) a euph. for God and used as such in various mild excls., e.g. *gorry mighty!* (cf. ADAD!; BEDAD!; BY GORRY!).

gorsoon *see* GARSOON.

go rubber walls, to *phr.* [1960s–70s] (gay) to go mad. [the *rubber walls* used in padded cells]

go rude at, to *phr.* [1970s+] (N.Z.) to insult, to attack verbally.

go rumping *v.* [19C+] of a man, to have sexual intercourse.

go rump splitting, to *phr.* [19C] of a man, to have sexual intercourse.

gory *n.*[1] *see* GOREE.

gory *n.*[2] [early 19C] a person, a fellow (cf. COVE; GILL *n.*[1]; GLOAK). [ety. unknown]

go scrape! *excl.* [17C] go away! (cf. GO AND SCRAPE YOURSELF!). [? trans. of Fr. *envoyer au grat*, to dismiss from employment, lit. 'to send grazing']

go see a man, to *phr.* [19C] to take a drink. [euph.]

gos/gosse *n.* [mid-16C–mid-17C] a term of address. [SE *gossip*, a friend, a chum]

gosh *n.* [mid-18C+] euph. for God., usu. in combs. e.g. *gosh-awful*, *gosh-darned* or excl. *by gosh!*, *my gosh!* (cf. COCK *n.*[1]).

gosh! *excl.* [mid-18C+] an extra-mild euph. for God!; by 20C usu. in juv. use (cf. ADAD!).

gosh all! *excl.* [19C+] (US) an euph. for *God almighty!* usu. in combs, e.g. *gosh all fish-hooks! gosh all hemlock/s! gosh all Potomac! gosh all Tarnation!*

gosh-almighty *adj., excl.* [19C+] a euph. used in excl. and mild oaths, lit. *God almighty*.

gosh-damned!/-danged! *excl.* [19C+] (US) a euph. used in excl. and mild oaths, lit. GOD-DAMNED!

gosh-darn!/-dern! *excl.* [19C+] (US) a euph. used in excl. and mild oaths, lit. GOD-DAMN!

gosh-darned/-derned *adj.* [19C+] (US) a euph. for GOD-DAMNED (cf. DOSH-BURNED).

gosh-ding! *excl.* [mid-19C+] (US) a mild oath, euph. for GOD-DAMN!

gosher *n.* [late 19C–1910s] a heavy punch. [? it makes the recipient say GOSH!]

go shit in your hat! *excl.* [1920s+] (US) a general term of abuse; an extended version is *go shit in your hat, pull it over your head and call it flowers* (cf. SHIT IN YOUR HAT!).

go shoe the goose! *excl.* [late 16C–18C] go away! be off!

Go-Shop, the *n.* [late 18C–early 19C] the Queen's Head tavern, Duke's Court, Bow Street, London WC2. [GO n.²]

go sixteen annas, to *phr.* [1900s–30s] (Anglo-Ind.) to go very fast, at full speed. [*16 annas* make a full rupee]

go snacks *v.* [mid-17C–mid-19C] to divide up, to hand over a share of the loot (cf. SNACK v.¹).

go snip *v.* [mid-17C–mid-18C] to share, to divide up. [SE *snip*, to cut]

go soak your head *phr.* [late 19C+] (US) an abusive, dismissive remark.

go solid *v.* [late 19C] (US) to unite, to act together.

go some *v.* [1910s+] (orig. US) to go fast, to work hard, to do well.

go somewhere *v.* [1920s+] to go to the lavatory. [euph.]

go south *v.*¹ [19C+] (US) **1** to be defeated, to lose. **2** to abscond with, to run off.

go south/go way down south in Dixie *v.*² [1950s] (US) to perform cunnilingus or anilingus. [*south* being 'down' the body]

go spare *v.* **1** [1940s] to be unemployed. **2** [1950s+] to lose one's temper, to act crazily. [SPARE adj.]

go sparrow-catching, to *phr.* [19C] to work as a prostitute. [? the Cockney *sparrow*]

gospel according to St Jeames *n.* [late 19C] (society) snobbery. [William Thackeray's character Jeames Yellowplush, a servant noted for his crawling to his social superiors and the narrator of *The Yellowplush Papers* (1837–8)]

gospel bird *n.* [20C] (US Black) a chicken (cf. CHAIRBACKER). [the practice of rewarding itinerant preachers with a chicken dinner]

gospel-cove *n.* [1900s–10s] (Aus.) a clergyman. [SE *gospel* + COVE]

gospel gab *n.* [late 19C] supposedly pious, but actually empty, hypocritical talk about religion. [SE *gospel* + GAB n.]

gospel-grinder/-peddler/-postillion/-shark/-slinger *n.* [mid-19C–1940s] **1** (US) a preacher (cf. GOSPEL-SHARP). **2** an evangelistic missionary or tract-distributor, a Sunday School teacher.

gospel mill/shop *n.* [19C] (US) a chapel, a church (cf. GIN-MILL). [SE *gospel* + *mill*, a place where a given industry is performed/*shop*]

gospel of gloom *n.* [late 19C] (society) the Aesthetic Movement, whose advocacy of drab interior decoration was regarded by its critics as distinctly gloomy.

gospel of the tub *n.* [mid-19C–1910s] (society) the mania for cold baths that afflicted Britain in the 19C and has not yet, in certain quarters, been properly abandoned.

gospel-peddler *see* GOSPEL-GRINDER.

gospel-pipe *n.* [1910s–20s] (US) the penis. [it 'preaches' to the vagina]

gospel-postillion/-shark *see* GOSPEL-GRINDER.

gospel-sharp/-shooter/-slinger/-whanger *n.* [19C+] (US) **1** a preacher. **2** an unctuous, self-satisfied, smug person.

gospel shop *see* GOSPEL MILL.

gospel-slinger *see* GOSPEL-SHARP.

gospel-whanger *see* GOSPEL-SHARP.

goss/gossamer *n.*¹ [mid-19C] a hat (cf. FOUR AND NINE). [SE *gossamer hat*, fashionable *c.*1830 and costing 4s 9p (23½p)]

goss *n.*² [1980s+] news, information, *gossip*. [abbr.]

goss *v.* [mid-19C–1900s] (orig. US) to beat, to dole out punishment; thus *give goss*, to beat, to dole out punishment; *get goss*, to receive a beating. [? Virginia dial. *give gorse*, to thrash]

gossamer *see* GOSS n.¹.

gosse *n. see* GOS.

gosse! *excl.* [18C] a euph. used in mild oaths, lit. God! (cf. ADAD!).

gossip pint-pot *n.* [late 16C] a hard drinker. [SE *gossip*, a friend, a companion + *pint-pot*]

go star-gazing/star-gazing on one's back, to *phr.* **1** [late 18C–mid-19C] for a woman, to have sex in the open air. **2** [1990s] of a woman, to have sexual intercourse. [the earlier use, which had languished, has recently reappeared, although without any 'open air' implication]

go steady *v.* [late 19C+] (orig. US) to maintain a regular relationship.

go steady with one's right hand, to *phr.* [1970s+] (US) to masturbate. [ironic use of GO STEADY]

goster *n.* [20C] (Irish) chat, conversation. [Irish *gastaire*, a chatterer; note UK-wide dial. *gauster, goster*, to gossip, to talk, to waste time chatting]

go straight *v.* **1** [mid-19C] to behave honourably. **2** [1940s+] to give up crime. **3** [1960s+] to give up drugs. **4** [1960s+] (gay) to abandon homosexuality. [STRAIGHT adj.¹]

go strumming *v.* [19C] to have sexual intercourse. [STRUM v.]

go tail-tickling/twitching *v.* [late 17C–early 18C] of a man, to have sexual intercourse. [TAIL n.¹ (2) + SE *tickle/twitch*]

gotcha *n.* [1960s+] (US) a sudden humiliation, esp. the inadvertent exposure of the buttocks or genitals. [SE *got you!*]

gotcha!/gotcher! *excl.* [1930s+] I have got you! [SE *got you!*; the *locus classicus* was the 1982 *Sun* newspaper headline *Gotcha!* on the drowning of the crew of the Argentine warship *General Belgrano*]

gotcha back *phr.* [1990s] (US campus) an expression of support. [lit. 'I've got your back']

gotcha covered *phr.* [1990s] (US campus) an expression of support. [lit. 'I've got you covered']

gotcher! *excl.*¹ *see* GOTCHA!

gotcher! *excl.*² *see* GOT YOU!

gotch-gutted *adj.* [late 18C–19C] pot-bellied. [dial. *gotch*, a pot-bellied jug]

got 'em bad *phr.* [late 19C+] used of one who is suffering from bad nerves, intense (if irrational) terror or delirium tremens.

goth *n.* **1** [mid-19C] a fool. **2** [1980s+] (teen/campus) a subgroup of PUNK rock fans who dress in austere black and enjoy correspondingly austere music. [SE *Goth*, one who behaves like a barbarian; a rude, uncivilized or ignorant person]

go the big figure *see* COME THE BIG FIGURE.

go the/go for the big spit, to *phr.* [1950s+] (Aus.) to vomit.

go the bundle, to *phr.* [1930s+] **1** (orig. US) to bet heavily, to bet one's entire funds. **2** to be very fond of. [BUNDLE n.²]

go the complete/entire swine, to *phr.* [late 19C–1920s] to do thoroughly, to go all the way, to commit oneself unreservedly. [var. on GO THE WHOLE HOG]

go the entire/extreme animal *see* GO THE WHOLE ANIMAL.

go the gamble, to *phr.* [late 19C] to make a bet.

go the grope *see* COME THE GROPE.

go the hang-out road, to *phr.* [1960s+] to tell the complete truth. [LET IT ALL HANG OUT]

go the hops, to *phr.* [1940s–50s] (Aus.) to enjoy drinking beer. [metonymy of SE *hops*, the basic constituent of beer]

go the knock on, to *phr.* [1910s+] (Aus.) to steal. [KNOCK v.¹ (2)]

go the knuckle, to *phr.* [1940s+] (Aus.) to have a fist-fight. [KNUCKLE n.¹ (2)]

go the length of a ... , to *phr.* [late 19C] to lend, the amount being specified at the end, e.g. *go the length of a quid*.

go the limit, to *phr.* **1** [20C] to commit oneself unreservedly (cf. GO FOR BROKE). **2** [1920s+] to have or permit sexual intercourse.

go the nigger route, to *phr.* [1990s] (US Black) to act in a manner that underpins the negative White stereotypes of the Black man. [NIGGER]

go the pace, to *phr.* [19C] to proceed with reckless vigour of action, to indulge in dissipation, to 'go it'.

go the whole/entire/extreme animal, to *phr.* [mid–late 19C] (US) to go on to the end, to do completely and exhaustively. [var. on GO THE WHOLE HOG]

go the whole coon, to *phr.* [late 19C] (US) to go on to the end, to do completely and exhaustively (cf. GO THE WHOLE HOG). [SE *racoon*]

go the whole critter, to *phr.* [mid-19C] (US) to do thoroughly, to go all the way, to commit oneself unreservedly. [var. on GO THE WHOLE HOG]

go the whole figure, to *phr.* [mid-19C–1900s] (US) to risk or do everything possible (cf. BIG FIGURE).

go the whole hog, to *phr.* [mid-19C+] (orig. US) to do thoroughly, to go all the way; thus various derivs., *whole-hogger, -hoggery, -hoggism, -hoggite, whole-hogging* (cf. GO THE WHOLE SHOOT). [? to eat a complete pig]

go the whole shoot, to *phr.* [late 19C+] to commit oneself wholeheartedly (cf. GO THE WHOLE HOG). [var. on WHOLE BANG SHOOT]

go the whole shot, to *phr.* [1950s+] (orig. US) to commit oneself unreservedly (cf. GO FOR BROKE). [SHOT n.² (2)]

go the whole way see GO ALL THE WAY.

gothic *adj.* [early 18C–early 19C] ill-behaved, uncouth. [SE *Goth*, a barbarian]

go thorough-stitch/thorough-stitch with, to *phr.* [early 19C–1900s] to perform something thoroughly, to carry it out completely. [tailors' jargon *go thorough-stitch*, to finish a job that has been begun]

go through *v.*¹ **1** [mid-19C–1910s] (US) to thrash, to suffer, to be defeated. **2** [late 19C] (US/Aus.) to rob, after searching the victim's clothes (cf. GO OVER). **3** [20C] (orig. US) to search. **4** [1920s+] (Aus.) to give up, to desist. **5** [1940s+] (orig. milit.) to desert one's responsibilities, to shirk one's work.

go through *v.*² [late 19C+] to have sexual intercourse, sometimes extended to *go through like a dose/packet of salts* (cf. BANG v.¹).

go through/through on *v.*³ [1930s+] (Aus.) **1** to leave, esp. without giving prior warning. **2** to go absent without leave. **3** to escape from prison or abscond while on bail (cf. SHOOT THROUGH).

go through changes, to *phr.* [1950s+] (orig. US Black) to undergo alterations in one's emotional or mental state or attitudes (cf. CHANGES; PUT THROUGH CHANGES). [jazz use *changes*, a chord sequence, thence adopted by hippies/drug users/New Agers in the late 1960s+]

go through for *v.* [1930s+] (US) to study a course at college or university.

go through for the doctor see GO FOR THE DOCTOR.

go through Hades with one's hat off, to *phr.* [late 19C] (US) to act courageously, to show no fear. [SE *Hades*, hell]

go through like a Bondi tram see SHOOT THROUGH LIKE A BONDI TRAM.

go through on see GO THROUGH v.³.

go through one for a short cut, to *phr.* [1980s+] (Irish) to criticize severely.

go through the card, to *phr.* [1960s+] to cover comprehensively and completely. [betting use, to bet on every horse in a race]

go through the flint mill, to *phr.* [20C] (US) to endure a series of problems, to suffer badly (cf. GO THROUGH THE HACKLES). [SE *flint mill*, a crushing machine used in making Portland cement]

go through the hackles, to *phr.* [20C] (US) to suffer, to

endure an excess of bad luck (cf. GO THROUGH THE FLINT MILL). [SE *hackle*, a flax-comb an instrument set with parallel steel pins for splitting and combing out the fibres of flax or hemp]

go through the hoop, to *phr.* [20C] (orig. milit.) to have a difficult time (cf. HOOP IT). [circus imagery]

go through the motions, to *phr.* [1920s+] to make a pretence of enthusiasm, effort, commitment etc when performing a tedious or unappealing task. [orig. milit. when men being trained without proper equipment, e.g. a rifle, were told to 'go through the motions']

go through the ox house to bed, to *phr.* [late 17C–early 19C] to be cuckolded. [phr. used of an old man with a young wife, *ox* refers to the cuckold's HORNS]

go through the ring, to *phr.* [mid-19C] to become bankrupt. [one fig. jumps through a *ring* or hoop]

go through the roof, to *phr.* [1950s+] to lose one's temper.

go through without a water-bag, to *phr.* [1940s–50s] (Aus.) to rush, to be in a very great hurry.

got it bad *phr.* [1910s+] used of one who is sexually infatuated.

got/get me Steve? *phr.* [1910s] (Aus.) are you with me?, do you understand?

go to Abney Park, to *phr.* [late 19C–1920s] to die. [*Abney Park* cemetery in Stoke Newington, north London. Founded in 1840, it succeeded Bunhill Fields as the centre of non-conformist burials. Among those buried there is General William Booth (1829–1912), founder of the Salvation Army]

go to/come from Bangkok, to *phr.* [1990s] to masturbate. [pun on placename and *bang one's cock*]

go to bat, to *phr.*¹ [late 19C+] to take action, to involve oneself with a specific task or job, to take a stance. [baseball (or cricket in UK) imagery]

go to bat *phr.*² see COME TO BAT.

go to Bath, to *phr.* [mid-17C–19C] to take up life as a beggar; thus excl. *go to Bath (and get your head shaved)*, go away, you're insane. [the rich pickings that were supposedly to be obtained from Bath's fashionable wealthy population. Bath, with its spas, attracted the mad as well as the rich and their parasites]

go to bed in one's boots, to *phr.* [late 19C–1900s] to be very drunk.

go to Bible class, to *phr.* [late 19C] (orig. printing) to get a pair of black eyes. [the rowdiness and horseplay of a printer's *chapel* or workshop]

go to blazes! *excl.* [mid-19C+] an excl. of dismissal, both of the person and their opinion or statement (cf. GO TO HELL!; GO TO HELL AND HELP YOUR MOTHER MAKE BITCH-PIE!; GO TO HELL, HULL AND HALIFAX!; GO TO HONG KONG; GO TO JERUSALEM!). [BLAZES, euph. for hell, where the fires of perdition burn]

go to blows, to *phr.* [1970s+] (US Black) to fight.

go to buck, to *phr.* [early 18C] of a woman, to have sexual intercourse. [BUCK v.¹]

go to Buenos Aires, to *phr.* [1900s–30s] to become a prostitute. [the association of 'White slavery' with South America]

go to buggery! *excl.* [1920s+] a general excl. of dismissal (cf. BUGGER OFF!).

go to Chicago, to *phr.* [late 19C] (US) to run away, esp. to avoid one's debts. [New York businessmen who found themselves in trouble tended to run to Chicago or at least announce it as their destination]

go to church, to *phr.* [late 16C–early 17C] to get married.

go to Copenhagen/Denmark, to *phr.* [1950s+] (gay) to have a sex change operation (cf. COPENHAGEN CAPON; DANISH PASTRY). [the ref. is to the pioneering operation undergone in Denmark in 1952 by Christine (formerly George) Jorgensen]

go to father! *excl.* [late 19C–1900s] a general excl. of dismissal; euph. for GO TO HELL!

go to foreign parts, to *phr.* [mid-19C] to be transported as a convict. [euph.]

go to France, to *phr.* [20C] (W.I.) a general phr. of dismissal; euph. for GO TO HELL! [FRANCE]

go to glory, to *phr.* [early 19C+] to die.

go to grass, to *phr.* **1** [19C+] (US) to die, to be ruined. **2** [19C+] (US) to be knocked down. **3** [mid-19C–1900s] of a limb, to waste away. [fig. uses of SE *go to grass*, of an animal, to be put to pasture]

go to grass! *excl.* [19C+] (US) a dismissive excl. either demanding that the subject leaves or suggesting that their statement is nonsense; also as *go to grass and eat hay!*. [? a comparison of the subject with a farm animal or with King Nebuchadnezzar, whose madness was denoted by his appetite for grass]

go to grass with one's teeth upward, to *phr.* [19C] **1** to be buried. **2** to die.

go to Hairyfordshire, to *phr.* [mid-19C] to have sexual intercourse. [HAIRYFORDSHIRE]

go to Hanover! *excl.* [18C] a general dismissive excl., go to hell! [the 18C dislike of its Hanoverian monarchs]

go to heaven in a string, to *phr.* [late 16C–early 18C] to be hanged; thus *feel like going to heaven in a string*, to be so deliriously happy as not to mind even the possibility of imminent death. [orig. applied in 16C to the Jesuits whose faith could bring them judicial death]

go to heaven in a wheelbarrow, to *phr.* [17C] to go to hell. [the popular image of the devil taking away a scolding wife in a wheelbarrow]

go-to-hell *adj.* [early 19C+] outrageous, extreme.

go to hell! *excl.* [mid-18C+] a general excl. of dismissal (cf. GO TO BLAZES!).

go to hell and help your mother make bitch-pie! *excl.* [mid-18C–late 19C] intensified version of GO TO HELL!

go to hell and pump thunder! *excl.* [late 19C] an excl. of derision and dismissal.

go to hell, Hull and Halifax! *excl.* [16C+] a general excl. of dismissal (cf. HALIFAX). [the 16C prayer 'from hell, Hull and Halifax Good Lord deliver us', which refers to the Halifax Gibbet Law under which a prisoner was executed first and his guilt or innocence ascertained afterwards]

go to hell in a hand-basket, to *phr.* [1990s] (US) to come to a bad end.

go to hell or Connaught! *excl.* [mid-17C–late 19C] an excl. of aggressive dismissal, go where you want but don't expect me to be bothered. [a law, passed in 1654, forcing Irish land-owners out of Ulster, Munster and Leinster]

go to Hong Kong, to *phr.* [late 19C–1910s] to go away, to 'go to hell'.

go to it *v.* [mid-18C+] to get on with things, to get to work.

go to Jericho, to *phr.* [late 18C–early 19C] to become drunk. [fig. use of *Jericho* as a place of exile]

go to Jerusalem, to *phr.* [mid-18C–early 19C] to get drunk (cf. GO TO JERICHO; GO TO PUTNEY). [? drunkenness being 'the promised land']

go to Jerusalem! *excl.* [19C] a mild oath, wishing that someone would go away, whether actually or figuratively (cf. GO TO BLAZES!).

go to market, to *phr.*[1] [late 19C] to make an attempt, to try. [used mainly of horses until early 20C]

go to market, to *phr.*[2] [late 19C+] (Aus.) **1** to lose one's temper, to behave irritably. **2** to make a fuss, to let off steam (cf. GO TO TOWN).

go-to-meeting bags *n.* [mid-19C] one's best trousers. [GO-TO-MEETING-CLOTHES]

go-to-meeting-clothes *n.* [18C+] (US) one's best clothes. [those garments one wore to go to a church meeting or similar formal occasion]

go to Mexico, to *phr.* [1950s+] (US) to become drunk. [for US teenagers brief trips across the border usu. implied non-stop excess]

go to noggin-staves, to *phr.* [mid–late 19C] to be ruined financially (cf. GO TO STICKS). [SE *noggin*, a vessel made of wood (holding nearly a quart/1.14 litres; ult. synon. Irish *noigin*) + *stave*, a piece of wood used in the making of a barrel]

go to one's chest, to *phr.* [1910s+] of objects or events, to irritate, to annoy.

go to one's dig, to *phr.* [late 19C+] (Aus.) to go home. [DIGS *n.*[1]]

go to Peckham, to *phr.* [early–mid-19C] to sit down to eat. [pun on *Peckham*, a district in south London/PECK *v.*[1] + SE *ham*]

go to peg trantum's, to *phr.* [late 17C–early 19C] to die. [note East Anglian dial. *peg trantum*, a tomboy]

go to picket-hatch grange *see* GO TO THE MANOR OF PICKED HATCH.

go to pieces, to *phr.* **1** [mid-19C–1900s] to give birth. **2** [mid-19C+] to collapse emotionally (cf. ALL TO PIECES).

go to pigs and whistles, to *phr.* [late 18C–mid-19C] (Scot.) to be ruined financially. [Scot. 'pigs and whistles, a mass of foolish, inconvenient furniture or nick-nacks' (*EDD*)]

go to pot, to *phr.* [mid-19C+] **1** to fall on hard times, to be ruined economically or morally, voluntarily or otherwise. **2** to die. [fig. uses of SE *pot*; (1) the cutting up of whole pieces of meat for the stewing pot; (2) 'the classic custom of putting the ashes of the dead in an urn' (Hotten, 1867)]

go to pot! *excl.* [mid-19C+] a general excl. of dismissal. [GO TO POT *phr.* (1)]

go to Putney/to Putney on a pig, to *phr.* [mid-19C] to get drunk (cf. GO TO JERUSALEM).

go to quat, to *phr.* [19C] to defecate. [? SE *squat*]

go to rest in a horse's nightcap *see* DIE IN A HORSE'S NIGHTCAP.

go to ruggins', to *phr.* [early 19C] to go to bed. [? the rug that served as a blanket]

go to school at Bromley, to *phr.* [1920s] (W.I.) not to go to school at all and thus become a rough, ignorant person. [the celebrated Bridgetown dance band, named for its leader, and its association with hedonistic fun]

go to school in August, to *phr.* [20C] (W.I.) to be uneducated, to display one's ignorance. [*August* is a school holiday]

go to see the doctor *see* GO TO THE DOCTOR.

go to shut-eye land, to *phr.* [1940s] (W.I.) to die.

go to sleep, to *phr.* [20C] to die. [perhaps the ultimate of such euphemisms and equally popular when *putting an animal to sleep*]

go to sticks/sticks and staves, to *phr.* [mid-19C] to be ruined financially (cf. GO TO NOGGIN-STAVES).

go to the bad, to *phr.* [mid-19C+] to adopt a life of crime or at least one that is seen as outside society's acceptable norms.

go to the Bahamas, to *phr.* [20C] (US Und.) to be sent to solitary confinement (cf. BERMUDAS). [the distance of the Bahamas from the mainland]

go to the basket *see* BROUGHT TO THE BASKET.

go to the baths, to *phr.* [1980s+] (US) to lose badly, esp. in business, sport, gambling. [var. on TAKE A BATH *phr.*[1]]

go to the bow-wows/bugs *see* GO TO THE DOGS.

go to the cleaners, to *phr.* [1930s+] (orig. US) to lose badly, esp. in sport, gambling or business (cf. TAKE A BATH). [antonym of TAKE SOMEONE TO THE CLEANERS]

go to the devil, to *phr.* late 18C+] to fall into disreputable habits, often as [orig. 14C+] imper. excl. *go to the devil!*

go to/go to see the doctor, to *phr.* [1980s+] (US campus) to drink alcohol. [the supposedly restorative effects of alcohol]

go to the diet of worms, to *phr.* [late 18C–early 19C] to die (cf. GONE TO ROTISBONE). [pun on the proper name *Diet of Worms*, the meeting (1521) between Emperor Charles V and Martin Luther that effectively launched the Protestant Reformation + the action of worms on the dead body]

go to the dogs/bow-wows/bugs, to *phr.* [mid-19C+] to decline socially, to become rundown, dirty and turn into a tramp. [the sending of run-down horses to the knackers, thence to become dogs' meat]

go to the grass, to *phr.* [1900s] (N.Z.) to run off, to abscond.

go to the joint *see* GET TO THE JOINT.

go to the kaffirs, to *phr.* [1980s+] (S.Afr.) to deteriorate, to GO TO THE DOGS. [KAFFIR]

go to the manor of picked hatch/picket-hatch grange, to *phr.* [late 18C–early 19C] to visit a brothel (cf. GO TO WESTMINSTER FOR A WIFE). [SE *pickt hatch*, a hatch with pikes, commonly used as a brothel-sign. The original such address was a tavern-cum-brothel in Turnmill Street, Clerkenwell, London]

go to the mat, to *phr.* [20C] (US) to commit oneself wholeheartedly, to go all out. [wrestling imagery]

go to/hit the mattress/mattresses, to *phr.* [1970s+] (orig. US Und.) to hide, to take refuge, esp. when under siege from another gang. [the practice of sleeping on mattresses in one's hide-out, rather than in one's bed at home. Orig. a US Mafia usage, the phr. was widely popularized by the success of Mario Puzo's book *The Godfather* (1969) and the films that followed]

go to/in the moon, to *phr.* [1930s] (Ulster) to lose one's temper.

go to the pack, to *phr.* [1910s+] (Aus.) to decline, socially, economically etc (cf. GO TO THE DOGS).

go to the pot, to *phr.* [mid-19C] to die (cf. GO TO POT phr.).

go to the races, to *phr.* [20C] to die (cf. HANG UP ONE'S HARNESS; JUMP THE LAST HURDLE). [euph.]

go to the ranch, to *phr.* [1990s] (US gay) to go crazy. [the ranch-style 'homosexual healing centres' advocated by anti-gay campaigner Anita Bryant]

go to the school of placebo, to *phr.* [mid-14C–late 16C] to be a toady or sycophant (cf. AT THE SCHOOL OF PLACEBO). [PLACEBO/Lat. *placebo*, I shall please]

go to the spot, to *phr.* [mid-19C–1920s] to suit the circumstances, to be absolutely satisfactory in the context (cf. HIT THE SPOT).

go to the wrong shop *see* COME TO THE WRONG SHOP.

go to town/to town on, to *phr.* [1930s+] (orig. US) **1** to make a great fuss about, to concentrate on. **2** to enjoy greatly. [a rural sensibility that equates such activities with urban life]

got out of pawn *phr.* [20C] born. [rhy. sl.]

go to visit one's uncle, to *phr.* [late 18C] to abandon one's wife shortly after the marriage ceremony. [euph; but note RAF jargon *go uncling*, to pursue a married woman; her children call the suitor 'uncle']

go to Westminster/Paul's/Saint Paul's for a wife, to *phr.* [late 17C–early 19C] to visit a brothel. [16C proverb: 'Who goes to Westminster for a wife, to St Paul's for a man or to Smithfield for a horse, may meet with a horse, a knave and a jade.' Despite the supposed difference indicated in the proverb, Old St Paul's Cathedral was also well-known for the raffish individuals who frequented its purlieus]

gotrocks *n.* [20C] (US) a rich person. [SE *got* + ROCKS n.[1] + link to the millionaire Rockefeller family]

go tromboning *v.* [20C] to have sexual intercourse (cf. BAGPIPING). [the physical action]

go trumpet-cleaning *v.* [late 19C] to die. [the trumpeter in question being the angel Gabriel]

gotta love that *phr.* [1990s] (US campus) an expression of approval of another's good fortune.

gotter-dam-merung *n.* [mid-late 19C] (society) coarse swearing. [a pun on Richard Wagner's *Ring* cycle of operas, first performed in London in 1862]

got the arse at Bulli Pass *phr.* [1960s+] (Aus.) phr. used to denote an unsatisfactory situation (cf. GIRLS ARE BANDY AT URANDANGIE). [ARSE n.]

gotto *n.* [1940s] (W.I.) a rope-soled shoe. [? SE *got to*, i.e. poverty dictates that one has no choice but to buy such cheap footwear]

got to get mines *see* GO FOR MINES.

go tummy tickling, to *phr.* [mid-late 19C] to have sexual intercourse.

got up *adj.* dressed up particularly smartly for some occasion; thus ext. in phr. *got up regardless, got up to kill, got up to the knocker, got up to the nines.*

got-up *n.* [late 19C–1910s] an upstart.

got up like a pox-doctor's clerk *phr.* [1930s+] describing someone who is very smartly (too smartly?) dressed.

go/turn red as a turkey-cock, to *phr.* [mid-19C+] (mainly Aus./N.Z.) to blush.

go twat faking/raking, to *phr.* [1900s–20] of a man, to have sexual intercourse. [TWAT + FACE v./RAKE v.]

go twatting *v.* [1900s–20] of a man, to have sexual intercourse. [TWAT]

got you!/gotcher! *excl.* [1940s+] I understand, I'm 'with you'. [SE *got you!*]

got your eye full? *phr.* [1950s+] addressed to someone who is staring, with the undoubted suggestion that they should stop at once; it can be followed with 'Want a picture?'

gouch/gouch out *v.* [1980s] to fall asleep or collapse, whether through exhaustion or an excess of drink or drugs. [ety. unknown; ? link to GOW n.[2] (1) or joc. ref. to the clichéd image of a sleeping *gaucho*]

gouchy *adj.* [20C] (Scot.) depressed. [? Scot. *gowk*, to stare vacantly]

gouda, gouda, gouda *n.* [1990s] (US campus) an unappealing, unpopular person (cf. CHEDDAR). [SE *gouda*, a popular Dutch cheese; thus one who is CHEESY]

gouge *n.* [mid-late 19C] (US) a swindle, a cheat. [SE *gouge*, to cheat]

gouge *v.* [1980s+] (US campus) to take something from another person, to cheat out of, to insult; thus excl. *gouge!* uttered after a successful insult or theft.

gouger *n.* [1960s+] (Irish) a thug, a lout. [SE *gouger*, one who gouges out another's eye in a fight]

goul *n.* [1960s–70s] (US) the anus (cf. GOOLA n.[2]). [Ital. *culo*, the anus]

goulash *n.* [1920s–50s] (US) nonsense. [? bridge use *goulash*, a re-deal of unshuffled cards after the hands have been thrown in without bidding, thus fig. a mess]

go under *v.* [late 19C] **1** (US) to die. **2** to go bankrupt.

go under one's neck, to *phr.* [1950s+] (Aus.) to take someone else's prerogative, to steal someone's idea, to stop someone else's intended actions. [horse-racing imagery]

go under petticoating, to *phr.* [19C] to have sexual intercourse.

go under the house, to *phr.* [1970s] (Black) to perform cunnilingus (cf. GO UP HER PETTICOATS).

go-up *n.* [1920s–50s] (US Black) an upstairs flat or apartment (cf. GO-DOWN n.).

go up *v.*[1] [early 19C] to be killed or hanged, to die, to be done for; esp. phr. *to be gone up.*

go up *v.*[2] [mid-19C] (US) to be ruined, to be destroyed, to become bankrupt.

go up *v.*[3] [late 19C+] (orig. US) to be sent to prison. [abbr. GO UP THE RIVER]

go up *v.*[4] [1960s+] (US drugs) to become intoxicated by psychotropic drugs. [one gets HIGH adj.[1]]

go against the collar, to *phr.* [19C+] (US) to work hard, esp. in a difficult or inconvenient situation (cf. FILL ONE'S COLLAR; GET IN THE COLLAR). [SE *collar*, the neckpiece of a draft harness; the comparison is to a hard-working draft horse]

go up a log, to *phr.* [1910s+] (Aus.) to hide. [the activity of a snake or lizard]

go up a tree, to *phr.* [1910s+] (Aus.) to fall off one's horse (cf. RIDE UP A GUMTREE).

go up Green River, to *phr.* [mid–late 19C] (US) to die; thus *send up Green River*, to kill. [the *Green River* brand of knife, made in Texas]

go up her petticoats, to *phr.* [19C] to have sexual intercourse (cf. GO UNDER PETTICOATING).

go up in a balloon, to *phr.* [mid–late 19C] (US) to be ruined, to come to nothing.

go up in the air, to *phr.* [19C+] to lose one's temper.

go up one! *excl.* [late 19C] a general compliment. [school use, whereby the successful pupil goes up a place or class]

go up Salt River, to *phr.* [1940s] (US Black) to die. [? the salty tears of the mourners and/or the bitterness of death]

go upside one's head, to *phr.* [1950s+] (US Black) to hit in the face, to beat up (cf. RUN UP SIDE O' ONE'S HEAD).

go upstairs out of the world, to *phr.* [late 17C–early 18C] to be hanged. [? the steps to mount the gallows]

go up the bad-eye, to *phr.* [1990s] to have anal intercourse.

go up the chute, to *phr.* [1950s+] to have anal intercourse. [POOPCHUTE]

go up the council, to *phr.* [1990s] to have anal intercourse. [rhy. sl. COUNCIL GRITTER = SHITTER n.[1]]

go up the flume, to *phr.* [mid–late 19C] (US) **1** to suffer a disaster. **2** to be exhausted, to be worn out, to be dead (cf. UP THE FLUE). [mining jargon *flume*, an artificial stream that brings water to a mine]

go up the ladder to bed/rest, to *phr.* [late 16C–19C] to be hanged (cf. CLIMB THREE TREES WITH A LADDER; MOUNT THE LADDER; WALK UP LADDER LANE AND UP HEMP STREET).

go up/for a trip up the line, to *phr.* [1920s–30s] to go to prison (cf. GO UP THE RIVER).

go up the old dirt road, to *phr.* [1910s+] to perform anal intercourse. [DIRT ROAD n.[2]]

go up the rainbow, to *phr.* [1970s] to reach orgasm. [the end of the *rainbow* as being supposedly heaven]

go up the river, to *phr.* [late 19C+] to go to prison; thus phr. to get oneself into trouble (cf. GO DOWN THE RIVER). [the Hudson River, which leads to Sing-Sing, New York State's main prison]

go up the wall, to *phr.* [1950s+] to lose one's temper (cf. CLIMB THE WALLS).

go up the weather, to *phr.* [late 17C–early 19C] to do well (cf. GO DOWN THE WIND).

gourd *n.*[1] [16C] (Und.) crooked dice, which have been hollowed out to affect the throw. [the hollow centre of the plant or OF *gourd*, a swindle]

gourd *n.*[2] [1970s+] **1** (esp. drugs) the head (cf. OUT OF ONE'S GOURD). **2** (US campus) a stupid, empty-headed person.

gourd-head *n.* [mid-19C–1970s] (US) a blockhead, a fool. [GOURD n.[2] + -HEAD (1)]

Gourock ham *n.* [mid-19C] a salt herring (cf. ABERDEEN CUTLET). [*Gourock*, on the Clyde 40km (25 miles) from Glasgow, was once a fishing port]

gov *n.* [mid-19C+] (US) a state *governor*. [abbr.]

go vaulting *v.* [late 16C–late 17C] to have sexual intercourse.

govern *v.* [1960s+] **1** to take the active role in sexual intercourse (cf. CATCH v.[6]). **2** to engage in sado-masochism.

government bad bargain *n.* [20C] a long-lived pensioner who draws a pension for a very long time.

government/governor's beef/cow/yearling *n.* [20C] (US) a deer that has been illegally shot by poachers (cf. CAMP MEAT).

government grapes *n.* [1990s] temazepam (cf. JELLIES). [their being issued on a National Health Service prescription and the similarity of the pills to grapes]

government house *n.* [late 19C–1950s] (Aus./N.Z.) the house of a plantation or estate owner or manager.

government-inspected meat *n.* [1990s] (US gay) a gay man serving in the US armed forces.

government man *n.* [19C] a prisoner.

government rag *n.* [mid-19C] (N.Z.) a paper currency worth 5/-, issued in 1844 by Governor Fitzroy. [SE *government* + RAG n.[1] (2)]

government securities *n.* [mid–late 19C] handcuffs or fetters. [pun]

government signpost *n.* [mid-19C] the gallows. [its points the way to the next world]

government stroke *n.* [mid-19C] (Aus.) **1** lazy working. **2** relief work, subsidized by the state. [the deliberately minimal rate of work put out by convict labourers]

government yearling *see* GOVERNMENT BEEF.

governor *n.* **1** [early 19C+] a father. **2** [early 19C+] an employer, a superior. **3** [mid-19C+] a general term of address to any strange man. **4** [mid-19C+] an acknowledged expert.

governor's beef *see* GOVERNMENT BEEF.

govy/govey *n.* [1900s] a *governess*. [abbr.]

gow *n.*[1] (US) [1900s–50s] a prison. [abbr. HOOSEGOW]

gow/ghow *n.*[2] (US drugs) **1** [1920s+] opium, heroin or morphine. **2** [1940s] a pleasurable drug experience. [Chinese *yao-kao*, opium; ult. *yao*, drug + *kao*, an oily, fatty substance, esp. an unguent]

gow *n.*[3] [1960s] (US prison) sauce. [? GOO n. (1)]

go walking *v.* [20C] to go rotten. [the foodstuff is not walking, but the maggots are]

go wax a gaza *phr.* [20C] (Irish) a dismissive phr. [lit. 'go climb a gas lamp']

go way down south in Dixie *see* GO SOUTH v.[2]

gowed/gowed up *adj.* [1910s–60s] (US) very intoxicated by alcohol or drugs. [GOW n.[2]]

go wenching *v.* [early 17C–early 18C] to have sexual intercourse. [ext. of SE *wenching*, associating with common women]

Gower Street dialect *n.* [mid-19C] a form of sl. whereby the user transposes the initial letters of adjacent words. [for ety. *see* MARROWSKYING]

go west *v.* [late 16C+] to die, to end, to collapse; thus *gone west*, dead. [the image of the setting sun, going down in the west + the drive west that took a condemned criminal along Holborn from Newgate prison to the 'triple tree' at Tyburn (today's Marble Arch)]

go whack *v.* [mid-19C] to take one's share. [WHACK n.[2]]

gowhead *n.* [1930s] (US) a drug addict. [GOW n.[2] + sfx. -HEAD (2)]

go when the wagon comes, to *phr.* [1940s] (US Black) of a situation, to be out of control. [the only solution will be when the metaphorical police wagon arrives and arrests all concerned]

go with *v.* **1** [late 19C+] to have an affair or relationship with someone, to have sexual intercourse with. **2** [1960s+] to accept and act upon a plan or suggestion.

go with a roar, to *phr.* [mid-19C–1900s] to be conspicuously successful.

go with a swing, to phr. [1970s+] of a party, show or entertainment, to pass off highly successfully and enjoyably.

go without a passport, to phr. [mid-19C] (US) to commit suicide. [the 'passport' is presumably the funeral ritual]

go with the flow, to phr. [1960s+] to accept a situation and make no attempt to alter it, to act passively. [a mass popularization of the more complex dictum of US psychologist Carl Rogers (1902–87), who saw life as 'floating with a complex streaming of experience']

gow job n. (US) **1** [1940s] a 'hot rod' car modified for high performance. **2** (campus) a flashily dressed girl. [? SE go or fig. use of GOW n.²]

gowk n.¹ [19C] a tramp. [GOOK n.¹]

gowk n.² [19C] (prison) one who is ignorant of the tricks and stratagems of prison life. [Scot. gowk, a fool]

gowl n. [late 19C+] (Irish) **1** the vagina (cf. FORK n.). **2** a fool. [Irish gabhal, a fork, a junction]

gowl v. [late 19C+] (Irish) to shout, to howl. [ON gaula, bark, roar, or SE yowl]

go working the double oracle/the hairy oracle, to phr. [late 18C–mid-19C] to have sexual intercourse. [SE work + DUMB/HAIRY ORACLE]

gowster n. [1930s–60s] (US drugs) an opium addict or habitual user of marijuana, heroin etc. [GOW n.² + sfx. -STER]

goy n. [late 19C+] a gentile, a non-Jew. [Heb. goy, a nation, thence Yid.; pl. goyim]

go Yarmouth v. [20C] to go mad (cf. CALLAN PARK). [orig. naval jargon f. the RN Hospital at Great Yarmouth]

goyno see GUINO.

gozz n. [1980s] a long gossip on the telephone. [SE gossip]

gozzie see GOOZIE.

gozzle n. [1900s–70s] (US) the throat. [GOOZLE; GUZZLE n. (1)]

gozzle v. [1940s–50s] (US) to throttle. [GUZZLE v. (2)]

g.p. n. [1940s+] (US) general principles. [abbr.]

g.p.o. n. [1990s] (Aus.) a flaccid penis (cf. BACCHUS MARSH). [abbr. the General Post Office in Melbourne, Australia. The ref. is to the fact that when one has a BALLARAT, one's penis is fully erect thus the Melbourne GPO, many miles from Ballarat, is logically its opposite]

g.q. adj. [1980s+] (US campus) fashionably dressed. [ref. to GQ or Gentleman's Quarterly magazine]

graal/grawl n. [20C] (Ulster) a growing boy, a young lad. [fig. use of Scot. grawl, a young salmon]

grab n. **1** [mid-18C+] an arrest, a theft; thus put the grab on, to steal or kidnap (cf. PULL; TUG n.⁴). **2** [mid-late 19C; 1950s] a policeman. **3** [1900s–30s] (US) a hand. **4** [1940s–50s] (prison) one's pay. [fig. uses of SE]

grab v.¹ **1** [18C+] to steal, to take or obtain for oneself. **2** [mid-18C+] to arrest. **3** [1910s+] (US) to capture, to kidnap, to abduct. **4** [1910s+] to appeal to, esp. as how does that grab you? how do you like that? **5** [1920s+] (US) to catch a train or taxi. **6** [1940s+] (US) to grasp, to comprehend. **7** [1960s+] (US) to irritate. **8** [1970s+] (US) to make a turn in a vehicle. [fig. uses of SE]

grab/grab on v.² [1980s+] (US campus) to make sexual advances towards, to neck. [ext. of GRAB v.¹]

grab a handful of, to phr. [1910s+] (US) **1** (hobo) to steal a ride. **2** to take, to steal, to secure for oneself.

grab a hat see GET A HAT.

grab-all n. **1** [late 19C] a bag to carry odds and ends. **2** [20C] (US) a greedy person.

grab a root, to phr. [mid-19C+] (US) to hold tight, to get busy, to go ahead.

grab a sit-down, to phr. [1970s–80s] (US Black) to take a seat, often as an invitation to a guest or visitor.

grab-ass v. [1920s+] to play around, to mess about; thus grab-assing, fooling around. [SE grab + ARSE/ASS]

grab a stump to rest your rump see FIND A STUMP TO FIT YOUR RUMP.

grab-bag n. [mid-19C+] a random collection of items, ideas, people etc. [orig. US carnival grab-bag, the equivalent of 'lucky dip', a bag containing various articles, into which one may dip on payment of a small sum]

grabber n. **1** [mid-late 19C] (Und.) a garrotter. **2** [mid-19C] (US Und.) a thief. **3** [mid-19C+] a hand. **4** [1910s–20s] a pickpocket. **5** [20C] (US) a selfish or greedy person. **6** [1960s+] (US) something that seizes the attention.

grabbers n. [early 19C+] the fingers, the hands. [GRABBER n. (3)]

grabble v. [late 18C–19C] to snatch, to grab, to seize; thus grabble the bit, to snatch someone's money. [OED lists it as SE (ult. synon. Du. grabbelen), although it cites Grose (1796)]

grabbling irons see GRAPPLING IRONS n.².

grabby adj. [1910s+] greedy, avaricious. [SE grab + sfx. -y]

grabhooks n. [1910s–40s] (US) the hands or fingers. [GRAB v.¹ + HOOKS]

grabilicious adj. [1950s+] (W.I. Rasta) covetous (cf. GRAVALICIOUS). [SE grab + delicious]

grab-it-and-growl/-gallop n. [20C] (US) a diner, a lunch counter. [the speed of one's eating]

grab joint n. [1900s+] (US) a snack bar, cafeteria. [GRAB v.¹ + JOINT n.³]

grab on v.¹ [mid-19C] to survive, to get along.

grab on v.² see GRAB v.².

grab one's dick, to phr. [1980s+] (US Black) to boast, to brag. [fig. use of GRAB v.¹ + DICK n.⁵ (1)]

grab sky v. [1990s] (US) to put one's hands in the air.

grab the flab/slab, to phr. [1990s] to masturbate.

grace before meat n. [late 19C] a kiss (presumably as a preliminary to intercourse). [SE grace + MEAT n.]

grace-card n. [mid-19C] (Irish) in cards, the six of hearts. [ety. unknown]

Gracemans n. [17C] (Und.) 'Gracious' (Gracechurch) Street market, the corn and hay market of medieval London. [abbr. Gracechurch + sfx. –MANS]

gracing/greycing n. [1920s–30s] greyhound racing. [contraction of SE]

gracious! excl. [18C+] a mild oath (cf. GRACIOUS ME!; GOODNESS GRACIOUS!; GRACIOUS ALIVE!; GOOD GRACIOUS ME!).

gracious alive! excl. [19C+] a mild oath (cf. GRACIOUS).

gracious me! excl. [19C+] a mild oath (cf. GRACIOUS).

gracious Miss Agnes! excl. [20C] (US) a general excl. of surprise and/or pleasure (cf. GOODNESS AGNES!). [? agnus dei, the lamb of God and thus a euph. for God or Christ]

gracious to goodness adj. [1900s–40s] (US Black) excessive, far too much.

grad n. [late 19C+] a graduate. [abbr.]

grade v. [1920s–30s] (US) to succeed in seducing someone. [the seducer 'makes the grade']

grade A n. **1** [1920s+] (orig. US) the very best. **2** [1940s–50s] (US) an order of milk in a snack bar. [the US division of milk into three classes: Grade A for infants and children; Grade B for adults only; Grade C for cooking purposes only]

graduate n. [late 19C] **1** an up-market prostitute. **2** a clever, cunning man.

graduate v. **1** [late 19C+] to increase, through knowledge and sophistication, one's status within the ranks of one's peers in the streets and the criminal milieu. **2** [1960s+] (drugs) to stop using drugs altogether or to progress to stronger drugs. [modern use of (1) mainly US Black]

graf-head n. [1980s+] (orig. US Black) a graffiti-artist. [SE graffiti + sfx. -HEAD (2)]

graft n.¹ **1** [mid-19C–1920s] corruption. **2** [late 19C–1940s] (US) an easy job or sinecure. **3** [1900s–50s] the proceeds of corruption, political bribery etc. **4** [1920s+] (Und.) one's criminal speciality. [? link to GRAFT n.¹ or fig. use of SE *graft*, to insert or fix in or upon something]

graft n.² [mid-19C+] efforts, hard work, usu. physical, labouring work. [fig. ? SE *graft*, the depth of earth that may be thrown up at once with a spade]

graft v.¹ [late 17C–18C] to cuckold. [SE *graft*, to fix onto, in this case the cuckold's HORNS]

graft v.² **1** [mid-19C–1910s] to live as a professional criminal (cf. GRAFTER n.²). **2** [1900s–10s] to acquire political gain though bribery or extortion. [GRAFT n.²]

graft v.³ [mid-19C+] to work hard, to make an effort, to struggle. [GRAFT n.¹]

grafted adj. [late 17C–18C] cuckolded. [GRAFT v.¹ + sfx. -ed]

grafter n.¹ [mid-19C+] a hard worker, one who perseveres. [GRAFT v.³]

grafter n.² [mid-19C+] (orig. US) **1** a pickpocket, a thief. **2** a swindler, esp. one who works at a fair, carnival, mock-auction etc. [GRAFT v.²]

grafty adj. [20C] (US Black) mean, stingy, miserly. [? GRAFT n.¹ (1) + sfx. -y]

g-rag n. [1960s] (drugs) a cloth wrapped round an opium pipe. [? GUM n.³ or GOW n.² + SE *rag*]

gram n. **1** [late 19C–1960s] a tele*gram*. **2** [1950s–70s] a gramophone. [abbr.]

gram-fed adj. [late 19C] (Anglo-Ind.) getting the best of everything, living 'in the lap of luxury'. [SE *gram*, chick-pea, usu. as *gram-flour*, an ingredient of Indian cooking]

grammel v. [20C] (Irish) to grope for, to fumble at. [? SE *grope* + *fumble*]

gramp/gramps n. [1910s+] a grandfather (cf. BUMPS n.¹). [dial.]

grand n. [1920s+] (orig. US) 1000, usu. dollars or pounds (cf. G; K).

grand adj.¹ [early 19C+] a general term of approval, magnificent, splendid.

grand adj.² [20C] (W.I.) proud but impoverished, unwilling to take charity no matter how much it might be needed (cf. POOR-GREAT).

grand adv. [late 18C] in an excellent, well-funded manner (cf. LARGE adj.).

grand as ninepence phr. [mid-19C] first-rate, excellent.

grand bag n. [1970s] (gay) a large scrotum. [SE *grand* + BAG n.¹ (2)]

Grand Canyon/Lincoln Tunnel n. [1960s+] (US gay) a loose anus; thus *Grand Canyon Suite*, noisy, sloppy-sounding anal intercourse.

Grand Central Station n. [1960s+] (US gay) the scarred arm of a long-term heroin user. [pun on the numerous SE *tracks*/TRACKS]

grand charge n. [20C] (W.I.) an empty bluff, loud but hollow boasting. [Fr. *grand*, great, big + *charge*, exaggeration]

grand charge v. [20C] (W.I.) to present a false but self-aggrandizing image. [GRAND CHARGE n.]

granddad/grandpa n. [20C] any old man, there is no need for a blood relationship.

grand-daddy n. [1950s+] the extreme example, the most outstanding (of a kind) (cf. MOTHER n.⁶).

grand duchess n. [1950s+] (gay) **1** a heterosexual woman who occupies pride of place in a homosexual male coterie. **2** an experienced, older, sophisticated homosexual man. [on the model of QUEEN n.¹]

grandfather/grandmother n.¹ [20C] (W.I.) a general intensifier, used respectively in Guyn. and Bdos, added to a noun; thus *a grandmother of a ...* .

grandfather n.² [20C] the penis. [rhy. sl. *grandfather clock* = COCK n.² (1)]

grandies n. [1990s] (N.Z.) *grand*parents. [abbr.]

grandma/grandmama/grandpa/grandpapa n.¹ [mid-18C+] affectionate substitutes for SE *grandmother*, *grandfather*.

grandma/grandma George n.² [late 19C+] (US) menstruation; thus *grandma's coming*. [euph.]

grandma n.³ [1940s+] (US) the lowest gear of a vehicle. [the image of a slow-driving grandmother]

grandma change n. [1930s–40s] (US Black) a very rich person (cf. MONEY'S MAMMY).

grandma George see GRANDMA n.².

grandmama see GRANDMA n.¹.

grandmother see GRANDFATHER n.¹.

grandpa n.¹ see GRANDMA n.¹.

grandpa n.² see GRANDDAD.

grandpapa n.¹ see GRANDMA n.¹.

grand quay n. [mid-19C–1910s] (US Und.) a state prison. [? SE *dock*]

grand slam n. [1910s+] an absolute and overwhelming success. [bridge use *grand slam*, taking all 13 tricks]

grandstand v. [late 19C+] to make oneself conspicuous, to show off. [sporting imagery, the performance is in front of the grandstand]

grandstand-artist/-jockey/-player n. [late 19C+] an exhibitionist, a show-off. [GRANDSTAND v. + ARTIST n.¹ + JOCKEY n.² (2)/ SE *player*]

grand strut n. [mid-19C] used of various fashionable promenading areas of London, i.e. Rotten Row or the Broad Walk in Hyde Park, Bond Street, W1. [SE *grand* + *strut*]

grand theft n. [1960s] (US Black) a large amount of stolen money. [US legal jargon *grand theft* synon. for *grand larceny*, the theft of sums exceeding a figure established by local penal codes]

grand tour n. [1980s+] (US campus) the traditional tour undertaken by recently graduated US college students in Europe. [SE *grand tour*, a similar tour undertaken esp. during 18C–19C by England's young aristocrats]

grand Turk n. [mid-19C] a boastful, arrogant person. [SE *Grand Turk*, the Sultan of Turkey]

granger n. [late 19C–1910s] (US) a farmer or countryman. [SAmE *Granger*, a member of the Patrons of Husbandry (a farmers' organization]

granite boulder n. [late 19C+] a shoulder. [rhy. sl.]

granite-boy n. [mid-19C+] a native of New Hampshire, known for its granite quarries.

granite jug n. [1930s–50s] Dartmoor Prison, west Devon. [SE *granite* + JUG n.¹ (1)]

grannam n.¹ [mid-16C–18C] corn (cf. BITE ONE'S GRANNAM). [SE *grain/grannary*]

grannam n.² [late 16C–early 19C] grandmother. [SE *granddam*]

grannam-gold/grannam's gold n. [late 17C–18C] old, hoarded coin. [SE *grandam*, grandmother + SE *gold*; lit. 'grandmother gold']

grannie see GRANNY n.³.

granny n.¹ **1** [late 18C; 1970s+] an old woman. **2** [mid-19C–1910s] (Aus.) nonsense, rubbish, 'old wives' tales'. **3** [mid-19C+] (orig. naut. jargon) a badly tied knot which will not hold. **4** [20C] a fussy person, not necessarily old or female. **5** [1920s–60s] (US) menstruation (cf. GRANDMA n.²). **6** [1940s–50s] (UK Und.) a legitimate business that serves only as a front for criminal activities. **7** [1970s+] (US) the lowest (thus slowest) gear of a vehicle (cf. GRANDMA n.³). [all based on the stereotyped characteristics of a SE *granny/grandmother*]

granny n.² [mid-19C] knowledge, importance, pride; thus *take the granny off*, to humiliate, to 'bring down a peg'. [? the supposed experience of a grandmother, or phr. *teach your grandmother to suck eggs*]

granny/grannie *n.*[3] [mid-19C] (US) a dollar. [ety. unknown]

Granny *n.*[4] [20C] (Aus.) the *Sydney Morning Herald*. [? its style and attitudes]

granny *v.*[1] **1** [mid-19C] to swindle, to cheat. **2** [20C] to defeat comprehensively, to allow one's opponent no score at all. **3** [1910s–20s] to disguise oneself. [the wolf's disguise in the story of 'Little Red Riding Hood']

granny *v.*[2] [mid-19C] to recognize, to understand.

granny-bashing/-battering *n.* [1970s+] violence towards an elderly member of one's family, esp. one's grandmother.

granny chills *see* GRANNY GRUNT n.[1].

granny-dodger *n.* [1960s+] **1** (US Black) a contemptible person. **2** (US prison) a rapist of elderly women; thus *granny-dodging*.

granny-dumping *n.* [1990s+] (US) the abandonment of an elderly relative in a hospital or nursing home by younger family members (cf. LEGION OF THE LOST).

granny grunt/chills *n.*[1] [20C] (US) a stomach ache, menstruation (cf. GRANNY RAG).

granny grunt *n.*[2] **1** [20C] a fussy, irritating person, although not necessarily female or old (cf. GRUNT). [rhy. sl. *granny grunt* = CUNT n.[2]]

granny grunt *n.*[3] [1930s–40s] (US Black) a mythical figure to whom otherwise unanswerable questions are referred.

granny lane *n.* [1970s+] (US) the right or slow lane of a high-way (cf. HAMMER LANE; SANDWICH LANE). [the stereotyped cautious driving of old women]

granny rag *n.* [20C] (US) homemade tampons, made of pieces of cloth (cf. GRANNY GRUNT n.[1]).

granny's coming *phr.* [20C] (Aus./US) phr. indicating that a woman is menstruating (cf. GEORGE CALLED). [GRANNY n.[1] (5)]

granny's wrinkle *n.* [20C] a winkle (a form of crustacea). [rhy. sl.]

granola/granola-groid *n.* [1980s+] (US campus) a natural-looking person who pursues a healthy lifestyle (cf. CRUNCHY). [the supposedly healthy US cereal CRUNCHY GRANOLA]

granty *n.* [mid-19C+] (Aus./N.Z.) a grandmother.

grape, the *n.* [late 19C+] any form of liquor, wine and spirits. [this metonymy has been recorded in SE since 1636]

grape-cat *n.* [1940s] (US Black) an alcoholic who prefers wine to other drinks; thus the female version, *grape-chick*. [SE *grape* + CAT n.[9]/CHICK n.[4]]

grapefruit *n.* [20C] the female breasts (cf. APPLES n.[1]). [resemblance]

grape juice *n.* [late 19C+] (US) wine.

grape-monger *n.* [early 17C] a wine-drinker.

grape-nut *n.* [1980s+] (US campus) one who identifies with the styles and concerns of the 1960s. [the healthiness of the breakfast cereal, *Grape-Nuts*]

grape on the business *n.* [1940s+] (Aus.) **1** a puritan (cf. BLUE STOCKING). **2** a bore, one who depresses or irritates the company by their presence (cf. GOOSEBERRY n.[2]). [? SE phr. *sour grapes*]

grape parfait *n.* [1960s+] (drugs) LSD (cf. A n.[3]). [when packaged in purple pills]

grapes *n.*[1] **1** [20C] the female breasts (cf. APPLES n.[1]). **2** [1930s–60s] (Aus./US Black) haemorrhoids. [resemblance]

grapes *n.*[2] [1960s–70s] (US Black) money. [the 'richness' of wine]

grapeshot *adj.* [19C] drunk (cf. CUPSHOT). [SE *grape*, the main constituent of wine]

grape society *n.* [1930s–50s] (US Black) an ironic dignification of a group of wine-drinkers standing around on a street-corner. [GRAPE + play on SE 'great society']

grapes of wrath *n.* [1940s] (US Black) wine. [the biblical use + the then-recent publication of John Steinbeck's novel *The Grapes of Wrath* (1939)]

grape-stomper *n.* [1950s+] any person of Mediterranean origin, e.g. Italian, French, Spanish, Portuguese, Greek. [the viticulture practised in these countries]

grape up *v.* [20C] (US) to toady, to curry favour (cf. APPLE UP).

grapevine *n.*[1] [mid-19C+] a network of unofficial sources, rumours, half-truths etc, which seems to spread the news around a circle or group faster than any sanctioned announcement (cf. BUSH TELEGRAPH).

grapevine *n.*[2] [20C] a washing-line. [rhy. sl.]

grapevine cinch *n.* [late 19C] (US) a certainty. [GRAPEVINE n.[1] + CINCH n.[1]]

grapevine telegraph *n.* [mid-19C–1970s] (US) a network of unofficial but often highly efficient communications. [GRAPEVINE n.[1] + BUSH TELEGRAPH]

grapevine wireless *n.* [1930s] (US) a network of unofficial but often highly efficient communications. [GRAPEVINE n.[1] + SE *wireless*]

grapey *adj.* [mid-19C] (US) grumpy. [? through an excess of the GRAPE n.]

graph *n.* [1970s+] (US) a para*graph*. [abbr.]

grappler *n.* [mid-19C] a hand (cf. FEELER n.[2]). [SE *grapple*]

grapplers *n.* [mid-19C] the fingers (cf. CUNT-HOOKS).

grapples *n.* [mid-late 19C] the hands. [SE *grapple*]

grapple the gorilla, to *phr.* [1980s+] to masturbate.

grapple the rails *n.* [18C] a glass of rough whisky. [its effects; one hangs on to keep upright]

grappling hooks *n.* [late 19C–1910s] (US) fingers or hands (cf. CUNT-HOOKS).

grappling irons *n.* [early–mid-19C] handcuffs.

grappling/grabbling irons *n.*[2] [mid-19C] the fingers (cf. CUNT-HOOKS). **2** [late 19C] (US) spurs.

grass *n.*[1] [mid-19C+] green vegetables, esp. asparagus. [asparagus use SE in 18C]

grass *n.*[2] [late 19C–1900s] sexual intercourse. [var. on GREENS n.[2]]

grass *n.*[3] [1910s] **1** hair; thus *cut the grass*, to cut the hair. **2** pubic hair (cf. BUSH n.[4]).

grass *n.*[4] [1930s+] marijuana (cf. BUSH n.[6]; WEED n.[1]).

grass *n.*[5] [1930s+] an informer. [rhy. sl. *grasshopper* = SHOPPER]

grass *v.*[1] **1** [late 19C–1900s] to kill, to defeat. **2** [late 19C+] to knock down. [abbr. SEND TO GRASS]

grass *v.*[2] [1930s+] to inform, to tell tales, to betray. [GRASS n.[5]]

grass *v.*[3] [1930s–40s] (US Black) to have sexual intercourse outdoors, esp. lit. on the grass.

grass before breakfast *n.* [mid-18C–mid-19C] (Irish) a duel. [? *grace before breakfast*]

grass-eater *n.* [1970s+] (US) a policeman who accepts small bribes; thus *grass-eating* (cf. MEAT-EATER).

grasser *n.* [1940s+] an informer. [GRASS n.[5]]

grass-fighter *n.* [1950s+] (Aus.) **1** a bare-knuckle boxer. **2** one who fights in public rather than in the prize-ring. **3** anyone known for losing their temper and brawling in public. [fighting on the grass rather than on canvas]

grasshead *n.* [1960s] (drugs) a heavy smoker of marijuana. [GRASS n.[4] + sfx. –HEAD (2)]

grasshopper *n.*[1] **1** [mid-19C–1910s] a waiter at a tea-garden. **2** [20C] (Aus.) a waiter at a picnic. [he 'hops across the grass']

grasshopper *n.*[2] [late 19C] a thief. [? he 'hops' from theft to theft]

grasshopper *n.*[3] **1** [late 19C–1950s] a policeman. **2** [1940s+] an informer. [GRASS n.[5]]

grasshopper *n.*[4] [1930s+] a marijuana user (cf. GRASSHEAD). [GRASS n.[4] + pun]

grasshopper n.[5] [1950s+] (Aus.) a tourist, esp. one who is visiting Canberra (cf. LOCUST n.[2]). [from their descending on a town or tourist site like a plague of hungry insects]

grass in the park n. [20C] an informer. [rhy. sl. *grass in the park* = NARK n.[1]]

grass sandwich n. [1910s–50s] (US) an alfresco act of sexual intercourse.

grassville n. [early 19C] the countryside (cf. DEUSEAVILLE).

grass widow n. **1** [16C–19C] a discarded mistress. **2** [19C+] (orig. Anglo-Ind.) a woman whose husband is temporarily absent (cf. SOD WIDOW; WIDOW BEWITCHED). [(1) A mistress is one who is enjoyed on a temporary straw-mattress or actually in/on the grass, rather than in the feather-filled matrimonial bed; *widow* is ironic, although it denotes that her 'husband' has gone; (2) phr. *out to grass*]

grass widower n. [20C] a man whose wife is temporarily absent. [GRASS WIDOW n. (2)]

grata n. [1970s+] (drugs) marijuana. [Sp.]

gratters n. [1900s–10s] (school/university) congratulations. [abbr. SE + 'Oxford' sfx. *-er*]

graum v. [1950s] (US) to worry; thus *the graums*, worries, depression, 'the blues'. [ety. unknown]

gravalicious adj. [1950s+] (W.I. Rasta) covetous (cf. GRABILICIOUS). [SE *greedy* + *avaricious*]

grave-digger n.[1] [late 19C] (Anglo-Ind.) strong drink. [alcohol often proved fatal to White men in India]

grave digger n.[2] [20C] the spade suit in cards. [resemblance]

grave digger n.[3] [20C] a Black person. [rhy. sl. *grave digger* = NIGGER + ref. to SPADE]

gravel n. **1** [1900s–30s] (US) granulated sugar. **2** [1980s+] (drugs) crack cocaine. [consistency]

gravel v. [19C] **1** to confound, to confuse. **2** (US) to annoy, to irritate. [the rubbing action of *gravel* e.g. on the bottom of a boat]

gravel-agitator n. [late 19C+] (US) an infantryman (cf. GRAVEL CRUSHER; GRAVEL-GRINDER n.[2]). [his marching and drilling]

gravel-crusher n. (Anglo-Irish.) **1** [late 19C+] a tramp. **2** [late 19C+] (US) an infantryman (cf. GRAVEL-AGITATOR). **3** [20C] a heavy boot, typically worn by a farmer or agricultural worker.

gravel-digger n. [mid-19C] an agile dancer.

gravel-grinder n.[1] [mid-19C] a drunkard (cf. GET THE GRAVEL RASH). [their drunken falling to the ground]

gravel-grinder n.[2] [late 19C+] (US) an infantryman (cf. GRAVEL-AGITATOR).

gravel rash n. [mid-late 19C] abrasions caused by a fall on a gravely or uneven surface, esp. in the context of drunkenness (cf. GET THE GRAVEL RASH).

gravel-train/-wagon n. (US) **1** [1910s] (Und.) a go-between of lobbyists who buy up legislators. **2** [1910s–30s] a sugar bowl (cf. GRAVEL n.).

grave noddy n. [early 18C] an unpleasant person. [SE *grave*, serious + NODDY n.[1]]

grave rat n. [mid-19C] (US) a medical student. [his stealing of corpses for dissection]

graves n. [1910s–20s] long, dirty finger-nails. [they are filled with dirt]

Gravesend bus n. [late 19C–1910s] a hearse. [pun on the town of *Gravesend*/the gravel is at 'the end of the line']

Gravesend sweetmeats n. [mid-19C] shrimps. [*Gravesend*, a town on the Thames estuary]

Gravesend twins n. [mid-19C] solid pieces of excrement. [the sewerage outfall at *Gravesend*]

gravestones n. [20C] (US) **1** prominent front teeth. **2** false teeth. [resemblance]

graveyard n.[1] **1** [19C] the mouth. **2** [20C] (US) prominent front teeth. **3** [20C] (US) false teeth. [the supposed resemblance of the teeth to tombstones]

graveyard n.[2] see GRAVEYARD SHIFT.

graveyard n.[3] [1980s+] (US) the least desirable seats in a restaurant. [they represent social 'death']

graveyard juice n. [1940s–50s] (US) whisky. [the fatal effects of excessive drinking]

graveyard shift/graveyard n. [20C] the overnight shift, the late shift. [usu. in the context of paid employment, but also used of gamblers, prostitutes and any other late-night 'workers']

graveyard stew n. [20C] (US) milk toast. [such toast is generally given to the ill; thus the idea that once his or her appetite has been reduced to such a meal the sufferer has nowhere to go but the graveyard]

graveyard widow n. [20C] (US) an actual widow, whose husband is dead (cf. GRASS WIDOW; SOD WIDOW).

graviers n. [16C] (Und.) crooked dice. [perhaps f. Fr. *grave*, heavy, given that the weight of crooked dice was generally affected in one way or another; however the *OED* suggests poss. alternative sp., notably *graniers* (cited in Thomas Dekker, *The Bellman of London*, 1608), which offers no obvious origin]

gravney n. [mid-late 19C] a ring. [ety. unknown]

gravy n.[1] [mid-18C+] **1** semen; thus [19C] *gravy-giver*, the penis (cf. BABY GRAVY; BULL FUCK; FUCK). **2** vaginal secretions.

gravy n.[2] **1** [1910s+] (orig. US) money, esp. profit when easily acquired, a tip or bonus, some that comes 'on top of' something that is already very good (cf. GRAVY TRAIN). **2** [1910s+] (orig. US) extras, perquisites. **3** [1940s+] (Aus.) any form of tinned food.

gravy n.[3] **1** [1960s+] (drugs) the mix of blood and heroin solution that is created in a hypodermic syringe before it is reinjected into the vein; it can coagulate while in the syringe and, when this happens, must be heated before the injection. **2** [1980s+] heroin.

gravy adj. [1970s+] a general term of approbation, easy, privileged, wonderful, perfect.

gravy boat n. [1940s+] (US) a sinecure, a simple, substantially profitable situation from which one can benefit easily. [var. on GRAVY TRAIN]

gravy-eyed adj. [late 18C–19C] bleary-eyed, having mucus-filled eyes.

gravy-giver n. [19C] **1** the vagina (cf. GRAVY-MAKER). **2** the penis. [GRAVY n.[1] + SE *giver*]

gravy-maker n. [19C] the vagina (cf. GRAVY-GIVER). [GRAVY n.[1] + SE *maker*]

gravy-rider n. [1920s–50s] (US) a person with an easy job. [GRAVY n.[2]]

gravy ring n. [20C] (Ulster) a doughnut. [resemblance to a ring of gravy staining a cloth]

gravy street n. [1970s] (US) an easy, profitable or successful situation (cf. EASY STREET). [GRAVY n.[2] + SE *street*]

gravy train n. [1920s+] (orig. US) a sinecure, a simple, substantially profitable situation from which one can benefit easily; thus *ride the gravy train*, to obtain easy financial success. [GRAVY n.[2] + SE *train*]

grawl see GRAAL.

gray/grey adj.[1] the spelling of gray/grey remains debatable; according to the *OED* there have been various choices over the years, but there seems to have been little real consistency. For the purposes of this dictionary, and based as far as possible on the pre-eminent style of the respective countries, **gray** will be used for US terms and **grey** for UK/Aus. and other 'Commonwealth' uses.

gray/grey adj.[2] [1950s+] (orig. US Black) used of a White person, esp. when racist, usu. in combs. e.g. *gray cat*, a White man, *gray broad*, a White woman (cf. BLANCO). [by 1980s also used for light-skinned Latinos; colour, but also f. what Blacks perceive as the 'colourless' behaviour and character of Whites, esp. the middle-classes]

gray as a badger/grannam's cat see GREY AS A BADGER.

grayback n. (US) **1** [early 19C] a professed Christian. **2** [mid-19C+] a head or body louse. **3** [mid–late 19C] a Confederate soldier in the US Civil War. [colour of the uniform or, for lice, the body]

graybar hotel n. [1970s+] (US) prison (cf. AKERMAN'S HOTEL; GRAYSTONE COLLEGE). [its *grey* walls and steel *bars*]

grayboy n. [1950s+] (US Black) a White man. [GRAY adj.^{2} + SE *boy* + conscious counter to the racists' 'black boy']

gray dog n. [1970s+] (US Black) the police. [GRAY adj.^{2} + DOG n.^{8}]

grayhair n. [1980s+] (US campus) an old person (cf. BLUE-HAIR).

graymail n. [1960s+] (US) a threat to reveal classified information in court as a form of legal blackmail. [on pattern of *gray imports*, imports that are not illegal as such but that sidestep a country's customs duties]

gray matter n. [late 19C–1910s] (US) intelligence (cf. GREY MATTER).

graymite n. [late 19C] (US) a vegetarian. [abbr. of *Graham-ite*, from Sylvester Graham (1794–1851), an advocate of vegetarianism]

gray mule n. [1900s–10s] (US) corn whisky or gin (cf. WHITE MULE). [MULE n.^{2}]

gray-rock hotel see GRAYSTONE HOTEL.

grays see SCOTCH GREYS.

graystone college/hotel/gray-rock hotel n. [1930s–60s] (US Und.) prison (cf. GRAYBAR HOTEL).

graze n. [1960s+] (S.Afr.) food.

graze v. [20C] (US prison) to eat prison food (cf. CHUCK; JUG UP; SCORF). **2** [1960s+] (S.Afr) to eat.

graze on the plain, to phr. [mid-19C–1900s] to be dismissed.

grazie! excl. [1980s+] (US campus) thanks. [synon. Ital.]

greapha see GREEFO.

grease n.^{1} **1** [late 18C+] money, esp. when given as a bribe or paid as protection money. **2** [mid-19C+] flattery. **3** [1940s+] (US) political influence.

grease n.^{2} **1** [late 18C–1960s] rancid butter, butter, margarine. **2** [1950s–60s] (Aus.) butter or margarine. **3** [1960s+] (gay) any form of lubricant – KY Jelly etc – that facilitates anal intercourse. [dial, referring to rancid or second-rate butter; there is no pej. in Aus. use]

grease n.^{3} [1920s+] (US Und.) nitroglycerine.

grease n.^{4} [1920s–30s] (US) opium. [the viscosity of the drug; note ety. of GUM n.^{1}]

grease n.^{5} [1920s–70s] (US Black) a Black man.

grease n.^{6} [1950s+] (US Black/campus) a meal, food.

grease n.^{7} [1960s+] **1** motorcycle riders (Rockers, as opposed to Mods), also collectively as *the grease*. **2** (US) working-class White youth, member of a hot-rod, motorcycle or juvenile gang. [abbr. GREASER n.^{4} (2)]

grease v.^{1} **1** [16C+] to corrupt, to bribe, to smoothe over problems, esp. f. authorities (cf. GREASY CHIN). **2** [17C] to cheat, to deceive. **3** [18C+] to curry favour with, to toady to.

grease/grease down v.^{2} [1920s+] (orig. US Black) to eat, esp. to eat voraciously or to eat highly greasy food. [GREASE n.^{6}]

grease v.^{3} [1960s+] (orig. milit.) to kill (cf. GREASE-GUN).

grease/grease down v.^{4} [1980s+] (US campus) to have sexual intercourse. [vaginal secretions and/or semen]

grease/stuff a fat pig/sow in the arse/tail, to phr. [late 17C–early 19C] to give money to a rich man or woman. [ext. of GREASE v.^{1} (1)]

grease a man in the fist, to phr. [18C] to bribe someone. [GREASE v.^{1}]

grease and lease, to phr. [1960s+] (gay) to have anal intercourse.

greaseball n. [1920s+] (orig. US) **1** a derog. description of any Latin race, Greeks, Puerto Ricans, various South Americans etc (cf. GREASER; SPIC). **2** (US) a short-order cook. **3** (US) any filthy or offensive person.

greaseburger n. [1960s+] (US) a very greasy or unappetising hamburger.

grease-burner n. [1920s–60s] (US) a cook (cf. GREASE POT).

greased adj. [1920s–50s] (US) drunk.

greased lightning n. [mid-19C+] very high speed, usu. in phr. *like greased lightning*.

greased mitt n. [1920s–40s] (US) anyone who has been bribed. [SE *greased* + MITT n.]

grease-gun n. [1960s+] an automatic weapon (cf. GREASE v.^{3}). [it goes as fast as 'greased lightning']

grease-hand/-palm n. [1970s] (W.I.) a bribe. [GREASE n.^{1} + SE *hand/palm*]

greasehound n. [1920s–40s] (US) a mechanic (cf. GREASE MONKEY; GREASE PUSHER).

greasies n. [1980s] (N.Z.) fish and chips or some form of takeaway food.

grease job n.^{1} [1940s+] (US) insincere flattery. [GREASE v.^{1} + JOB n.]

grease job n.^{2} [1950s+] anal intercourse using Vaseline, KY Jelly or a similar lubricant. [GREASE n.^{2} + JOB n.]

grease joint n. [1910s+] (US) **1** a hamburger or hot dog stand. **2** a cheap or inferior restaurant (cf. GREASY SPOON). [SE *grease* + JOINT n.^{3}]

grease monkey n. [1940s+] a mechanic (cf. GREASEHOUND). [SE *grease* + MONKEY n.^{11}]

grease off v. [late 19C+] to slip away.

grease one's chops, to phr. [1920s–70s] (US Black) to eat, esp. to eat highly greasy food. [ext. of GREASE v.^{2} + CHOPS]

grease one's/the gills, to phr. [late 17C–1900s] to eat heartily and substantially. [GREASE v.^{2} + SE *gills*]

grease one's pipe, to phr. [20C] to masturbate (cf. CLEAN ONE'S RIFLE). [SE *grease* + PIPE n.^{8}]

grease one's pole, to phr. [1990s] to masturbate. [SE *grease* + POLE n.]

grease one's skates, to phr. [1920s+] (Aus.) to get ready, to make a quick getaway.

grease one's throat/tonsils, to phr. [late 19C+] (US) to drink alcohol.

grease patty n. [20C] (US prison) prison-cooked, chicken-fried steak (cf. GREASEBURGER).

grease pit n. [1950s–70s] (US drugs) anywhere a drug seller sets up their business. [GREASE n.^{4}]

grease pot n. [1910s–60s] (US) a prison or camp cook (cf. GREASE-BURNER).

grease-pusher n. [1950s] (US) a mechanic (cf. GREASEHOUND).

greaser n.^{1} [mid-19C+] (orig. US) a derog. term for a Mexican and thus a member of another Latin race (cf. GREASEBALL).

greaser n.^{2} [20C] (US) **1** an objectionable person. **2** a sycophant. [GREASE v.^{1} + sfx. *-er*]

greaser n.^{3} [1920s–70s] (US Black) an enthusiastic eater, esp. of soul food. [GREASE v.^{2}]

greaser n.^{4} [1950s+] **1** a 1950s Teddy Boy, his hair larded with Brylcreem or a similar unguent. **2** [1960s+] (US) a member of a motorcycle gang (cf. ROCKER) or (Calif.) a hotrodder. **3** (US campus) an old-fashioned person, whose style harks back to 1950s youth cults. [the greasiness of the youths' hair (and the motors with which they tinker)]

greaser n.^{5} [1950s+] (N.Z.) a fall, a setback, esp. in phr. *come a greaser*, to fall (lit. or fig.).

greaserita n. [mid-19C] (US) a Mexican woman. [GREASER n.^{1} + Sp. fem. sfx. *-ita*]

grease someone's boots v. [late 16C–mid-19C] to toady to, to flatter. [GREASE v.[1] (3)]

grease someone's hide, to phr. [late 19C] (US) to whip someone.

grease someone's palm, to phr. [early 19C+] to bribe (cf. ANOINT A PALM). [GREASE v.[1]; devel. of early 16C+ *grease one's hand*]

greasespot n. (US) **1** [mid-19C+] an infinitesimally tiny quantity. **2** [late 19C+] the fig. state to which one is reduced either after losing a violent fight or suffering extremely hot weather.

grease stop n. [1980s+] (US) a stop for refreshment during a bus or car journey. [GREASE n.[6] ? + GREASE JOINT]

grease the dukes/dukes of, to phr. [mid–late 19C] to bribe someone. [SE *grease*/GREASE v.[1] + DUKES]

grease the gash, to phr. [20C] of a woman, to masturbate. [SE *grease* v. + GASH n.[1]]

grease the gills see GREASE ONE'S GILLS.

grease the rails/track, to phr. [1910s–50s] (US) to be run over by a train. [ironic use of SE]

grease the weasel, to phr. [1990s] (US teen) to have sexual intercourse. [SE *grease* + WEASEL n.[4]]

grease the wheel, to phr. [mid-19C–1900s] to have sexual intercourse.

grease-trap n. [1980s] (US) a lunch counter.

grease-trough n. [1940s] (US) a lunch counter.

grease-wagon n. [1980+] (US) a cheap restaurant or mess-hall.

greasy n.[1] (Aus./N.Z.) **1** [mid-19C+] a cook (cf. SLUSHY). **2** [1920s–30s] a butcher. **3** [1960s+] a seller of fast or take-away food.

greasy n.[2] see GREASY MOP.

greasy n.[3] [1950s+] a shearer. [SE *greasy*, wool that has not yet been cleaned]

greasy adj.[1] [1970s] (US Black) anything that is simultaneously appalling and appealing. [fatty food is both tasty and bad for one's health]

greasy adj.[2] [1970s] (US drugs) anything concerning drugs and their sale. [GREASE n.[4]]

greasy aces n. [1930s] (US gambling) specially doctored aces, which are thus made easier to recognize.

greasy as a butcher's apron, as phr. [1940s–60s] (N.Z.) very greasy or slippery.

greasy bag n. [1970s] (US drugs) a bag in which heroin is transported and/or sold (cf. SKID BAG). [GREASE n.[4] + BAG n.[8]]

greasy chin n. **1** [mid-18C–early 19C] a treat given to parish officers in recompense for registering the birth of a bastard (cf. EAT A CHILD). **2** [mid-19C] a dinner. [the effects of the treat or dinner]

greasy corner n. [20C] (US) any poor area or settlement, esp. that occupied by Blacks and poor Whites. [SE *greasy*, i.e. the stereotypically pork-based diet of such poor groups]

greasy fingers n. [1930s–40s] (US Black) a pickpocket. [objects 'stick' to such fingers]

greasy grind n. [mid-19C+] hard, continuous, wearing work, esp. academic work (cf. GRIND n.[1]).

greasy guts n. [1940s] (US) a fat person. [SE *greasy* + -GUTS sfx.]

greasy junkie n. [1960s] (US drugs) a heroin addict who maintains their own supplies by running errands for dealers or by prostitution. [SE *greasy*, i.e. they 'slither around' + JUNKIE]

greasy Mac n. [1980s] (US) any fast-food restaurant. [proper name *McDonalds*, purveyors of fast-food; devel. of GREASY SPOON]

greasy mop/greasy n. [20C] (Aus.) a policeman. [rhy. sl. *greasy mop* = COP n.[1]]

greasy/dirty spoon n. [1920s+] a cheap café or restaurant (cf. GREASY MAC; SLOPPY JOE'S). [the state of its cutlery and the texture of its product]

greasy spot on the road n. [20C] (US) a small town or hamlet (cf. WIDE PLACE IN THE ROAD). [the oily patches outside the gas stations where cars would stop + the implied insignificance of a habitation that represents no more than a dirty mark]

great adj.[1] [early 19C+] wonderful, excellent.

great adj.[2] [20C] (Irish) close, very friendly; thus *great with*, close to, esp. of lovers.

great adj.[3] [20C] (W.I.) proud but impoverished, unwilling to take charity no matter how much it might be needed. [abbr. POOR-GREAT]

great! excl. [1960s+] an excl. of approval (cf. GREAT adj.[1]).

great as shirt and shitten arse phr. [late 18C] very intimate, as close as possible.

great balls of fire! excl. [20C] (orig. US) an excl. of surprise, amazement.

great bear n. [1980s+] (drugs) fentanyl (cf. APACHE n.[2]). [ety. unknown; ? its strength]

great bounce n. [late 19C] (US) death. [SE *great* + BOUNCE n.[4]]

great Caesar!/Jehosaphat!/sun! excl. [late 19C+] mild oaths, all euphs. for *great God!*

great Caesar's ghost! excl. [19C+] a mild oath.

great divide, the n. **1** [mid-19C] the vagina (cf. ANTIPODES). **2** [1930s+] (Aus.) the cleavage between a woman's breasts. [pun on the *Great Divide*, in the Blue Mountains, or the US equivalent in the Rocky Mountains, cited in the celebrated poem 'Eskimo Nell']

greatest, the phr. [1940s+] (US) excellent.

greatest thing since sliced bread see BEST THING SINCE SLICED BREAD.

great gas! excl. [1910s+] (Irish) an excl. used of something extremely enjoyable. [SE *great* + GAS n.[2]]

great grief! see GOOD GRIEF!

great gun n. **1** [19C+] an important, powerful, influential person, usu. a man (cf. BIG GUN). **2** [1910s–20s] a cheerful rogue.

great guns adv. [late 18C+] energetically, successfully, violently, loudly, esp. in phr. *go great guns* and, in ref. to gale-force winds, to *blow great guns*.

great guns! excl. [19C+] (US) a general excl. of surprise or annoyance; also as *great guns and little fishes! great guns and little pistols!* (cf. YE GODS AND LITTLE FISHES!).

great horn spoon n. [mid-19C+] God, usu. in the oath *By the great horn spoon!* [ety. unknown; ? the use of spoons made of buffalo horn]

great house n. [mid-19C] the workhouse. [its size in comparison with the homes its inmates might have had]

great I am, the n. [20C] used of a self-important person. [the *locus classicus* is in the career of the US confidence trickster Guy Ballard, who set up a whole cult under the title 'The Great I Am', which mulcted the deserving gullible of hundreds of thousands of dollars of 'love gifts' in 1934–9]

great Jehosaphat! see GREAT CAESAR!

great joseph n. [late 18C] an overcoat. [the biblical *Joseph*'s 'coat of many colours']

great jumping Judas! see BY THE JUMPING JUDAS!

great Kiwi clobbering machine see CLOBBERING MACHINE.

great national indoor game see NATIONAL INDOOR GAME.

great on phr. [late 19C+] expert in, knowing a great deal about. [var. on SE *great at/*IN]

great priest n. [18C–19C] (Scot.) constipation. [Scot. *priest*, a strong but ineffectual desire to defecate; ? SE *pressed* or link to QUAKER]

great scott! excl. [19C+] a mild oath. [? euph. for *great satan* or *good God!*]

great seizer *n.* [late 19C] (US) a sheriff. [a pun on *great Caesar*, the sheriff 'seizes' wrongdoers]

great shakes *adj.* [early 19C+] very good, admirable, usu. in neg. *no great shakes*.

great shot *n.* [1920s+] (orig. US) a superior person or one who claims to be (cf. BIG SHOT).

great snakes! *excl.* [19C+] (orig. US) a mild oath.

great sun! *see* GREAT CAESAR!

great tobacco *n.* [20C] (drugs) opium.

great warrant *see* GOOD WARRANT.

great whipper-in *n.* [mid-19C–1920s] a personification of death. [hunting jargon *whipper-in*, a huntsman's assistant who keeps the hounds from straying by whipping them back into the pack]

great white chief *n.* [1910s+] the senior figure in any business, institution or organization. [a play on the 19C Native American name for the US president; orig. applied to a Civil Service head of department]

great white father *n.* [1930s–40s] (US Black) ironic description of any White authority-figure, esp. the US president. [19C SE *white father*, a White man, esp. in Africa, who controls and/or protects members of a Black race]

Great White Way *n.* [20C] (US) Broadway, New York City, esp. its theatrical district around Times Square (cf. GAY WHITE WAY). [SE *great* + *white way*, a street lit with electric lights. The first *white way* was a stretch of Broadway between 14th Street and 23rd Street, on which electric lights were introduced on 20 December 1880. As used with its qualifying adj., the term was coined by Oscar Gude, a New York advertising man who pioneered the use of electrical advertising, starting with a sign erected over Madison Square in 1892 and began erecting signs in Times Square (then Longacre Square) in 1900. His first use of the term came in 1901. Alternatively, it derives f. the title of Albert Bigelow Paine's novel, *The Great White Way* (1901), although this story, set in the Antarctic, referred not to light but to snow. The link, supposedly, came when a reporter viewed mid-town Broadway under a blanket of snow]

grebo *n.* [1980s] a British youth cult featuring a cultivatedly sordid appearance, a boorish manner and devotion to heavy metal music. [? *greb*, a general term of abuse used in north of England schools since 1930s]

Grecian *n.* [mid-19C] an Irish immigrant; thus *Grecian accent*, the brogue. [? the use of GREEK n.² as a generic for 'foreign']

Grecian *v.* [1940s] (W.I.) for a woman to walk in a self-consciously 'stylish' manner, either arrogantly or proudly (cf. CUT GRECIAN).

Grecian bend *n.* **1** [late 19C] a particular, stooping style of walking adopted by fashionable women (*c.*1872–80), in which the body bends forward from the hips (cf. ALEXANDRA LIMP). **2** [late 19C] (US) a bustle; thus *Grecian bender*, one who wears a bustle. [orig. Eton College sl., referring to a typically scholarly stoop]

Grecian bender *n.*¹ [late 19C] a revolver. [ety. unknown]

Grecian bender *n.*² [late 19C] 'the bends' or caisson disease. [play on GRECIAN BEND]

greeby *adj.* [1940s–60s] (US teen) ugly, unattractive. [? var. on SE *grubby*; note GREBO]

greedhead *n.* [1970s+] (US) an avaricious person. [SE *greed* + sfx. -HEAD (2)]

greedy *adj.* [1990s] bisexual. [i.e. one who is 'not satisfied' with attraction to one sex]

greedy-gut/-guts *n.* [16C+] a glutton, a selfish person. [SE; *greedy-gut* is 16C–18C UK, US subseq.; *greedy-guts* is 18C+ UK, 19C+ US]

greefo/greefa/grifo/griefo/greapha *n.* [1930s+] marijuana.

[Mex. Sp. cab (sl.) *grifo*, under the influence of marijuana; the original use of *grifo* is tangled or frizzy hair; thus the image of mental fuzziness/frizziness]

Greek *n.*¹ **1** [16C+] a cunning, sly individual, esp. a gambler or swindler. **2** [early 19C+] a derog term for an Irish immigrant to the US or UK. [the use of Greek as generic for a 'foreigner'; in the UK an automatically suspect figure; 20C use of (1) is derog.]

Greek *n.*² [early 17C+] unintelligible language, esp. cant or sl., esp. in phr. *it's all Greek to me* (cf. CHOCTAW).

Greek *n.*³ [1930s+] (US campus) a member of a college fraternity or sorority (cf. GO GREEK v.¹). [the use of *Greek* letters as the names of such societies]

Greek *n.*⁴ [1930s+] **1** a person who engages in anal intercourse, not necessarily but usu. a homosexual. **2** anal intercourse; often used on a prostitute's 'bill of sale'. [the identification of Greeks with homosexuality]

Greek *adj.*¹ [mid-19C] Irish. [GRECIAN]

Greek *adj.*² [1930s+] a generic term for homosexual (cf. GO GREEK v.²; GREEK n.⁵). [GREEK n.⁴]

Greek *v.* [1930s+] (gay) to engage in pederasty. [GREEK n.⁵]

Greek back *see* MEDITERRANEAN BACK.

Greek culture *n.* [1930s+] anal intercourse, usu. in homosexual advertisement use (cf. AMERICAN CULTURE; ATHENIAN; GREEK LOVE). [the ethnic cliché that categorizes all (ancient) Greeks as sodomites]

Greek fashion *see* GREEK WAY.

greeking *n.* [early 19C] cheating at cards. [? racial stereotyping]

Greek lightning *see* JEWISH LIGHTNING.

Greek love *n.* [1930s+] (gay) pederasty (cf. GREEK CULTURE; GO GREEK v.²). [euph.]

Greek's, the *n.* [1940s+] (Aus.) generic term for any small café (cf. GREEK SHOP). [Greek immigrants, who specialize in such establishments]

Greek sauna *n.* [1990s] placing one's partner's head under the duvet after breaking wind.

Greek shop *n.* [1920s+] (S.Afr.) a local corner store, often owned by an immigrant Greek family (cf. GREEK'S). [the equivalent of the stores owned by Koreans in the US and by exiled Ugandan Asians in the UK]

Greek side *n.* [1930s+] (gay) the buttocks (cf. GO GREEK v.²). [GREEK adj.² + SE *side*]

Greek trust *n.* [20C] (US) an absolute lack of trust. [Virgil's maxim *Timeo Danaos et dona ferentis* ('I fear the Greeks bearing gifts')]

Greek way/fashion *n.* [20C] **1** (gay) pederasty. **2** anal intercourse (cf. FRENCH WAY). [GREEK adj.²]

green *n.*¹ [mid–late 19C] an unsophisticated, naïve person. [SE *green*, naïve]

green *n.*² [late 19C+] (US) money, dollar bills (cf. ALFALFA n.; GREENBACK n.²; LEAN GREEN).

green *n.*³ (US drugs) **1** [1950s+] marijuana, esp. of inferior quality. **2** [1970s+] phencyclidine (cf. ACE n.³). **3** [1980s+] ketamine (cf. K n.⁴).

green *n.*⁴ [1990s] (US Black) a bottle of beer. [the colour of the glass]

green *v.* [late 19C] to deceive, to hoax, to swindle, to render gullible. [SE *green*, naïve]

green *adv.* [1910s+] (US) utterly.

green about the gills *phr.* [late 19C+] ill (cf. BLUE ABOUT THE GILLS; FISHY ABOUT THE GILLS). [one's complexion, lit. or fig.]

green and yellow fellow *n.* [late 19C] a male homosexual (cf. GREENERY-YALLERY). [SE *greenery-yallery*, of, pertaining to, or affecting the colours green and yellow, in accordance with the style or fashion of the Aesthetic Movement and thus, in short, affected]

green apple n. [1960s–70s] (US) a naïve person (cf. GREENBEAN n.[1]; GREENHORN; GREEN PEA). [ext. of GREEN n.[1]]

green-apple quickstep/-trots/-two-step n. [1950s+] (US) diarrhoea (cf. APPLE-BLOSSOM TWO-STEP).

green apron n. [mid-17C–early 18C] a lay preacher. [female Quaker preachers wore a *green apron*]

green as duckweed phr. [late 19C] very naïve, innocent, foolish.

green-ass adj. [1940s+] (US) naïve, inexperienced. [SE *green* + sfx. -ASS]

greenback n.[1] [late 18C–late 19C] a frog.

greenback n.[2] **1** [mid-19C+] (US) $1 bill, usu. in pl. (cf. GREEN n.[2]). **2** [20C] (Aus.) £1 note. [colour]

greenback v. [1970s] (US) to pay, esp. a bribe. [GREENBACK n.[2]]

green-bag n. [late 17C–late 19C] **1** a lawyer. **2** in phr. *what's in the green bag?* 'what is the charge to be preferred against me? [the green cloth that was traditionally used to make lawyers' bags, used to carry briefs and other documents. 'These gentlemen carry their clients' deeds in a green bag; and, it is said, when they have no deeds to carry, frequently fill them with an old pair of breeches ... to give themselves the appearance of business' (Grose). *Green bags* were replaced by *blue bags* (barristers) and *red bags* (King's or Queen's Counsel)]

green banana n. [1930s–40s] (US Black) a young, light-skinned woman. [SE *green*, naïve + BANANA [2] (2)]

greenbean n.[1] [1950s+] (US) a naïve person (cf. GREEN APPLE). [SE *green*, naïve]

greenbean/greenfly n.[2] [1980s+] (S.Afr.) a township municipal policeman. [colour of the uniform]

green belly n. [1950s] (US) a novice, an unsophisticated person, esp. a new arrival in the city from the country (cf. GREENHORN). [SE *green*, naïve]

green boys n. [mid-19C] paper money, notes (cf. GREEN n.[2]; GREENBACK n.[2]). [the colour of dollar bills]

greenbud n. [1980s+] (US drugs) marijuana that is green, usually of a superior quality. [SE *green* + BUD n.[3]]

green cart n. [1930s+] (Aus.) a vehicle, actual or metaphorical, in which people are taken to a mental hospital (cf. BLACK MARIA).

green cloth n. [late 19C] a billiards/snooker table. [abbr. *board of green cloth*, the green baize with which it is covered]

green death n. [1960s–70s] (US campus) sickness and diarrhoea, supposedly caused by student canteen food. [play on SE *Black Death*]

green door n. [1960s–70s] (US Und.) the door of the execution chamber in New York state prisons.

green dragons n. [1970s+] (drugs) **1** barbiturates. **2** amphetamines. **3** LSD. [(1), (2), the colour of the pills; (3) a type of LSD distributed on squares of blotter stamped with a *green dragon*]

greener n.[1] **1** [late 19C+] (US) a novice, an innocent, one who has newly arrived (cf. GREENHORN). **2** [late 19C] an inexperienced workman used as a strike-breaker. [SE *green*, naïve]

greener n.[2] [1940s+] (US) $1 bill (cf. GREEN n.[2], GREENBACK n.[2]). [the colour of dollar bills]

greener n.[3] see GREENIE n.[2].

greenery n. [1990s] (Black) marijuana.

greenery-yallery adj. [late 19C] (society) pertaining to the Aesthetic Movement whose preferred colours were green and yellow (cf. GREEN AND YELLOW FELLOW). [thus W.S. Gilbert, *Patience* (1880) 'A greenery-yallery, Grosvenor Gallery, Foot-in-the-grave young man!']

greenfinch n. [mid-19C] a member of the Pope's Irish guard. [*green* being the national colour of Ireland]

greenfly see GREENBEAN n.[2].

green frog n. [1980s] (drugs) depressant.

greengages n. [late 19C+] wages. [rhy. sl.]

green goddess n. [1930s–50s] (drugs) marijuana. [the colour of the marijuana leaves and the pleasure of the drug]

green gold n. [1980s+] (drugs) cocaine. [? SE *green gold*, an alloy of gold and silver; high quality cocaine sparkles]

green goods n. **1** [late 19C–1930s] (US Und.) counterfeit banknotes. **2** [1980s+] (drugs) paper currency. [the colour of the bills]

green goose n. [16C] a young, innocent girl, soon to be made into a prostitute. [SE *green goose*, a gosling, a young goose; a simpleton or SE *green* + GOOSE n.[2]]

greengrocery n.[1] [mid-19C] **1** the vagina (cf. CABBAGE n.[7]). **2** a brothel (cf. BANGING-SHOP; BUTTOCKING SHOP). [GREENS n.[2] + a ref. to the essentially commercial element of the place]

greengrocery n.[2] [1920s–30s] an illicit bar or 'speakeasy' (cf. GROCERY n.[3]). [euph.]

green grove n. [19C] the pubic hair (cf. BUSH n.[4]). [GREENS n.[2]]

green handshake n. [1970s] (US) a bribe, a tip, a bonus (cf. GOLDEN HANDSHAKE). [? it makes others 'green with envy']

greenhorn n. [late 17C+] a novice, an unsophisticated person, esp. a new immigrant or a new arrival in the city from the country (cf. GREEN APPLE; GREEN BELLY; GREENER n.[1]; GREENIE n.[1]; GREENLAND n.[2]). [15C SE *greenhorn*, a young animal, spec. an ox with 'green' or young horns. The term is first used in a military sense, describing a new recruit. Grose (1785) defines it as 'an undebauched young fellow, just initiated into the society of bucks and bloods'. Its post-19C use has been mainly US]

green hornet n. **1** [1940s–70s] (US drugs) amphetamine (cf. A n.[2]). **2** [1960s] (US) a New York City police patrol car, sugg. by colour scheme of the time. **3** [1960s] (Can. Und.) a Toronto motorcycle policeman. [the colour of the pill or uniform + ref. to the NBC radio series *The Green Hornet*]

greenhouse n.[1] [1900s–20s] (Irish) a public lavatory.

greenhouse n.[2] [1980s+] (drugs) a place known for selling drugs, esp. marijuana. [GREEN n.[3] + pun on SE]

greenhouse special n. [1990s] (drugs) marijuana, cultivated in one's own greenhouse.

greenie n.[1] [late 17C+] a novice, an unsophisticated person, esp. a new arrival from the country. [abbr. GREENHORN]

greenie/greener/green tiger n.[2] [1970s+] (S.Afr.) a 10-rand note. [the colour]

greenie n.[3] [1970s+] (Aus./N.Z.) an environmentalist, a conservationist. [the *Green* party]

greenie n.[4] [1980s+] **1** (US campus) beer, spec. Heineken lager, which comes in predominantly green-labelled bottles or cans. **2** (US teen) a lump of phlegm.

greenies n.[1] [1960s] (US) envy. [one is 'green with envy']

greenies n.[2] **1** [1940s+] (US) dollar bills (cf. GREENBACK n.[2]). **2** [1970s+] (society) money. [the colour. Like so many similar class usages, the -*ie* sfx. in the UK usage underlines the lifelong addiction to nursery language]

greenies n.[3] [1970s] (US) green vegetables. [SE *greens*]

greenies n.[4] [1980s+] (drugs) amphetamines (cf. A n.[2]; GREEN DRAGONS; GREEN HORNET).

greening n. [1910s–20s] an obsession; thus *have a greening for*, to be obsessed by someone.

Greenland n.[1] [mid–late 19C] (US) Ireland; thus *Greenlander*, an Irish person; *from Greenland*, used of an unsophisticated, ignorant person.

Greenland n.[2] [mid-19C] the fig. world of innocence; thus *greenlander*, a gullible, innocent person (cf. GREENHORN). [GREEN adj. + SE *land*]

green leaves n. [1980s+] (drugs) phencyclidine (cf. ACE n.[3]).

green light/give the green light v. [1970s+] to give permission, to allow. [traffic lights/railway signals imagery]

green-light hotel *n.* [1950s] (US) a prison or police station (cf. AKERMAN'S HOTEL). [the green light that marks its address]

green man *n.* [20C] a public house urinal. [the common pub name + the common painting of such urinals green]

greenmans *n.* [17C] fields, countryside. [SE *green* + sfx. -MAN]

green meadow *n.* [mid-19C] the vagina (cf. CABBAGE n.⁷).

Green Mountain boys *n.* [late 19C] (US) natives of Vermont. [lit. meaning of Vermont, France *verts monts*, green mountains]

green niggers *n.* [20C] (US) Irishmen. [similar inferior status to a Black NIGGER but *green*, i.e. Irish from the national colours]

green one *n.* [1910s] (US) $1 bill (cf. GREEN n.²; GREENIES n.²; LONG GREEN). [the colour]

green pea *n.* [1910s–70s] (US) a naïve person (cf. GREEN APPLE). [SE *green*, naïve]

greens *n.*¹ [early 18C] chlorosis. [abbr. of the synon. nickname *green sickness*]

greens *n.*² [mid-19C+] sexual intercourse. [GET A GREEN GOWN; GIVE A GREEN GOWN]

greens/green stuff *n.*³ [late 19C+] paper currency, notes (cf. GREEN n.²). [the colour]

greens *n.*⁴ [1930s+] wages. [rhy. sl. *greengages* = wages]

greens *n.*⁵ [1990s] (drugs) marijuana (cf. GREEN n.³).

greens and brussels *n.* [20C] muscles. [rhy. sl.]

green shit *n.* [1950s–70s] (US Black) money. [SE *green* + SHIT n.³; although in this context *shit* = stuff; cf. CRAP n.¹; DUST n.¹]

green stamp *n.* (US) **1** [1950s+] $1 bill; thus *green stamps*, money. **2** [1970s+] a traffic offence summons. [play on *Green Shield* trading stamps, issued in 1960s]

green stuff *n.*¹ see GREENS n.³.

green stuff *n.*² [1940s+] (US Black) marijuana (cf. BROWN STUFF; GREEN n.³; GREENS n.⁵).

green tea *n.* [1980s+] (drugs) phencyclidine (cf. ACE n.³). [? rhy. sl. or the common mixing of the drug with parsley, which may resemble marijuana, i.e. TEA n.²]

green thumb *n.* [1970s+] (US Black) one who has the knack of making money. [GREEN n.² + SE *thumb*; play on the more usual gardeners' 'green fingers']

green tiger see GREENIE n.².

green verbs *n.* [20C] (W.I.) poorly spoken, ungrammatical English, esp. when used by one who would be expected to speak correctly. [SE *green*, unripe, immature, thus unsophisticated]

green wedge *n.* [1970s+] (drugs) LSD (cf. A n.³). [? packaging]

green weenie *n.* [1940s+] (US orig. milit.) anything bad; thus *eat/get/have had the green weenie*, to be killed. [SE *green*, of food, decaying, 'off' + WEENIE n.¹]

green welly brigade *n.* [1970s+] the rural upperclasses. [the green wellingtons (rather than the more common black variety) that such people tend to wear]

Greenwich barber *n.* [late 18C–19C] a seller of sand from the Greenwich sandpits. [such retailers 'shaved' the sand for their product]

Greenwich goose *n.* [late 18C–19C] a pensioner of Greenwich Royal Naval Hospital, founded in 1692 by Queen Mary. [proper name *Greenwich* + SE *goose*]

greeny *n.*¹ [late 17C+] a novice, an unsophisticated person (cf. GREENHORN). [SE *green*, naïve]

greeny *n.*² [1990s] (US drugs) the best grade of marijuana. [GREEN n.³]

greet *n.* [20C] (US) a *greet*ing; thus *greets*, greetings. [abbr.]

greeter/greta *n.* [1950s–60s] (drugs) marijuana. [? GREEFO]

greetin' fou *adj.* [17C+] very drunk, lit. crying drunk (cf. BITCH-FOU). [Scot. *greet*, to cry + FOU]

greg/grig *v.* [1950s+] (Irish) to tease. [Irish *griog*, to tease]

grego *n.* [19C] a rough greatcoat, with a hood. [SE *grego*, a coarse jacket with a hood, worn in the Levant, ult. Lat. *Graecus*, Greek]

gregorian tree *n.* [late 18C–19C] the gallows (cf. DEADLY NEVERGREEN). [pun on proper name *Gregory* Brandon; for details *see* GREGORY]

gregory *n.* [early 17C] a hangman (cf. DERRICK n.). [*Gregory* Brandon, who worked as executioner under James I, to be succeeded by his son Richard, better known as 'Young Gregory']

Gregory Peck *n.* [1950s+] the neck. [rhy. sl.; proper name of US actor *Gregory Peck* (b.1916)]

gregory pecks *n.* [1950s+] (Aus.) spectacles, glasses. [rhy. sl. *gregory pecks* = SPECS; for details *see* GREGORY PECK]

gregory peg *n.* [20C] (Aus.) the leg. [rhy. sl.; pun on GREGORY PECK + SE *peg-leg*]

gremlin *n.* [1920s+] an unidentified source of trouble or malfunctioning. [? SE *goblin*; orig. use in 1929 refers to troublesome or unimportant officers. Popularized through WW2 RAF use, where the meaning was as above, although one citation claims the term was invented in WW1 by the Royal Flying Corps]

greng-greng *n.* [20C] (W.I./Trin.) coarse, short hair. [Twi *greng*, rough, rugged, coarse]

greta see GREETER.

grette *n.* [1960s] (US campus) a ci*garette* (cf. CIG; CIGGIE). [abbr.]

grey *n.* **1** [early 19C–1940s] a halfpenny or other coin, having two heads or two tails, esp. as used in cheating games. **2** [mid-19C] money in general. [(1) Rom. *gry*, a horse, thus linked to PONY n.², 20C use mainly Aus.; (2) the colour of 'silver' coins once they have been some time in circulation]

grey *adj.* [1960s+] dull, boring, earnest, hard-working, esp. university use.

grey/gray as a badger/grannam's cat *phr.* [early 18C–late 19C] having the white or grey hairs of advancing age.

greybacks/grey-backed 'uns *n.* [19C] lice (cf. BLACK CATTLE).

greybeard *n.* [late 18C–19C] an earthenware jug used in public houses. [such jugs had the figure of a man with a large beard stamped on them. The name was also used for Dutch earthenware jugs, used for smuggling gin along the east coast]

grey biscuit *n.* [1980s+] (drugs) MDMA (cf. BISCUIT n.⁷; DISCO BISCUIT; ECSTASY). [the colour of the tablet]

grey bomber see GREY GHOST.

greycing see GRACING.

greycoat *n.* [1900s] (Aus. Und.) a prisoner. [the prison uniform]

grey-coat/grey-coated parson see GREY PARSON.

grey death *n.* [1960s+] (Aus. Und.) weak prison stew.

greyers see GREYS n.³.

grey gal *n.* [1950s+] (Black) a White woman (cf. BROWN GAL). [GRAY adj.²]

grey ghost/meanie/bomber *n.* [1960s+] (Aus.) a parking policeman (cf. BLUE MEANIE). [the colour of the uniform]

greyhound *n.* [1970s+] (N.Z.) a very thin hand-rolled cigarette. [SE *greyhounds* are very thin dogs]

greyhound *v.*¹ [1940s–50s] (US Black) to run fast.

greyhound *v.*² [1960s] (US Black) to pursue White sexual partners (cf. COCK HOUND; PUSSY HOUND). [GRAY adj.² + SE *hound* v.]

grey mare *n.*¹ [late 18C–19C] a wife, esp. if she is the dominant partner in the marriage. [16C proverb *the grey mare is the better horse*]

grey mare *n.*² [20C] the fare. [rhy. sl.]

grey matter *n.* [19C] the human brain (cf. GRAY MATTER). [its colour]

grey meanie see GREY GHOST.

grey nayga/owl *n.* [1960s] (W.I.) an albino (cf. FRECKLE-NATURE). [GRAY adj.² + NAYGA/SE *owl*]

grey nurse *n.* [20C] (Aus.) a purse. [rhy. sl.]

grey/grey-coat/grey-coated parson *n.* [late 18C–19C] a farmer who rents out the tithes normally due to a vicar or rector. [*grey* as 'light' black' in an adj. use of 'black', referring to matters clerical. The use of *grey* to mean amateur or partial is similar to 20C *grey import*, an unofficial, but not actually illegal import, typically of computer hardware manufactured elsewhere that has yet to become available in the country in which it is sold]

grey puss *n.* [1950s+] (W.I.) an albino (cf. GREY NAYGA). [GRAY adj.² + PUSS n.]

greys *n.¹* see SCOTCH GREYS.

greys, the *n.²* [mid-19C–1920s] a fit of yawning, a feeling of laziness, lassitude.

greys/greyers *n.³* [1900s–40s] grey flannel trousers, once a staple of the 'off-duty' uniform of the British middle-class male. [SE *grey* + 'Oxford' sfx. *-er*]

grey shields *n.* [1970s+] (drugs) LSD (cf. A n.³). [packaging]

grey-white nigger *n.* [1950s] (W.I.) a mulatto. [GRAY adj.² + NIGGER]

grick *n.* [early 19C] a farthing. [var. on GRIG n.]

grid *n.* [1920s+] a bicycle. [abbr. GRIDIRON; post-1940s use mainly Aus.]

griddle *n.* [late 19C–1900s] a violin. [? rhy. sl. *griddle = fiddle*]

griddle *v.* [mid-late 19C] to beg, to peddle, to scrounge, esp. as a street-singer.

griddler *n.* [mid-late 19C] **1** a street singer who performs without benefit of a lyric sheet. **2** a wandering tinker. [GRIDDLE v.]

griddling homey/polone *n.* [late 19C+] a male or female violinist. [Polari; GRIDDLE n. + OMEE/PALONE]

g-ride *n.* [1990s] (US Black) any type of automobile favoured by teen gangs, usu. stolen. [G n.² + RIDE n.²]

gridiron *n.¹* [early 19C] (Anglo-Irish) a public house sweetheart. [? she is 'hot stuff']

gridiron *n.²* [mid-19C] a county court summons. [the arms of the City of Westminster, which resemble a *gridiron*]

gridiron *n.³* **1** [late 19C] the bars on a prison-cell window. **2** [20C] a bicycle. **3** [late 19C–1930s] (US) a football field. [resemblance to SE *gridiron*; subseq. use of (3) is SE]

grief *n.¹* [late 19C+] misery, problems, troubles; thus *bring/come to grief*, to cause or to experience unhappiness, troubles.

grief *n.²* [1980s+] (Aus. drugs) marijuana. [abbr. GREEFO]

grief *v.* [1970s+] (US campus) to trouble, to bother, to annoy.

griefer *n.* [1910s+] (US drug) a habitual marijuana user. [GRIEF n.]

griefo see GREEFO.

grievous *n.* [1940s–50s] (Aus.) *grievous* bodily harm. [abbr.]

griff *n.¹* see GRIFFIN n.³.

griff *n.²* [1980s+] (drugs) marijuana (cf. GREEFO).

griff *n.³* [late 19C+] information, news. [abbr. GRIFFIN n.⁴]

griff *v.* [mid-19C–1920s] (Anglo-Ind.) to cheat, to fool. [GRIFFIN n.³; i.e. his innocence]

griffin *n.¹* **1** [18C–19C] a fool. **2** [early 19C–1920s] a menacing woman, a 'gorgon'. [SE *griffin*, a mythical animal usually represented as having the head and wings of an eagle and the body and hind-quarters of a lion]

griffin *n.²* [mid-19C] an umbrella. [ety. unknown; as used by 'fast' young men in London]

griffin/griff *n.³* [mid-late 19C] (Anglo-Ind.) **1** a cadet newly arrived from the UK. **2** any novice or newcomer. [orig. denoting a newcomer to the Indian Army or Civil Service; thus a general term for a novice, a newcomer, a naïve. Y&B note an actual Admiral *Griffin* 'who commanded in the Indian seas

from November 1746 to June 1748, and was not very fortunate' but accept earlier uses]

griffin *n.⁴* [late 19C+] news, reliable information, a tip (in betting), a hint (cf. GRIFF n.³). [? pun on GRIFFIN n.³ (2); in modern use mainly as Liverpool dial.]

griffmetoll *n.* [mid-late 18C] (Und.) a sixpence. [ety. unknown]

griff sense *n.* [1940s+] a pickpocket's ability in assessing a potential victim's personality. [GRIFF n.³ + SE *sense*]

grifo see GREEFO.

grift *n.* [1910s+] **1** corruption. **2** the proceeds of corruption, political bribery etc. [GRAFT n.²]

grift *v.* [1910s+] to work as a confidence trickster or petty thief. [GRIFT n.]

grifter *n.* [1910s+] (US) a small-change swindler, confidence man, any form of non-violent criminal or thus any small-time gambler, living primarily on his wits. [GRIFT v.]

grig *n.* [mid-17C–mid-19C] a farthing (cf. GIG; JIGG); in pl. money, cash. [ety. unknown, but all meanings of SE *grig* (a dwarf, a short-legged hen etc) imply diminutive size. Johnson suggests that its original meaning was 'anything below the natural size']

grig *v.* see GREG.

grik *n.* [1970s+] (US) a Greek. ['foreign' pronunciation]

gril *n.¹* [1970s+] (S.Afr.) a shiver, a shudder, 'the creeps'. [Afk. *gril*, shudder]

gril *n.²* [1990s] (US campus) an affectionate term of address between women.

grill *n.¹* **1** [1940s] (US Black) the stomach. **2** [1980s+] (US Black/teen) the face or mouth.

grill *n.²* [1950s+] (Aus.) a southern European immigrant, esp. a Greek. [the near-monopoly of Greeks on the running of small cafés]

grill *v.* [late 19C+] to interrogate; thus *on the grill*, under close interrogation.

grilled cheese *n.* [1980s+] (US drugs) cannabis. [? a supposed similarity in smell]

grimacious *adj.* [1980s+] (Irish) unpleasant, terrible. [on pattern of BODACIOUS]

grim and gory *n.* [20C] (Aus.) a story. [rhy. sl.]

grimbo *n.* [1980s+] (US campus) a contemptible person. [SE *grim* + BIMBO/DUMBO]

grimmy *n.* [1960s–70s] a middle-aged woman. [? SE *grim-faced*]

grin, the *n.¹* [early 19C] an interrogation. [SE *grin*, a snare]

grin *n.²* [1960s+] (US) amusement; thus *for grins*, for fun.

grinagog/grinagog, the cat's uncle *n.* [mid-16C–late 18C] a simpleton who has a fixed grin on his face. [SE *grin* + *agog*]

grin at the daisy roots, to *phr.* [late 19C] (Anglo-Ind.) to be dead. [one is 'looking upwards' at the soil that covers one's coffin]

grincome / grincombe / grincam / grincom / grincum / grinkcome / grinkum. *n.* [17C] syphilis. [var. on CRINKUM]

grind *n.¹* **1** [mid-19C–1920s] (US) a swindle. **2** [late 19C] (US campus) a satirist. **3** [late 19C–1930s] (US campus) a joke, usually personal.

grind *n.²* **1** [mid-19C+] hard, continuous, wearing work, esp. academic work. **2** [late 19C+] (US campus) a student who studies constantly. **3** [late 19C+] (US campus) a demanding instructor. **4** [late 19C+] (US campus) a demanding course.

grind *n.³* **1** [late 19C+] an act of sexual intercourse; thus *on the grind*, having sexual intercourse (cf. BASH n.²; HONE n.). **2** [late 19C+] a girl or woman regarded as a sex object, further qualified as a *good grind, bad grind*. **3** [1970s] masturbation.

grind *v.¹* **1** [mid-17C+] to have sexual intercourse, also *do/have a grind*; of a man, *grind one's tool* (cf. BANG v.¹). **2** [1920s+] (US) to rotate the hips in a sensuous manner while dancing.

3 [1950s+] to rub one's body, especially the genital area, against one's partner while dancing. **4** [1970s+] to masturbate. [note Florio, *Worlde of Wordes*, 1598: 'Macinio, the grinding or greest. Also taken for carnall copulation']

grind v.[2] **1** [mid-19C+] to work hard, esp. at an unrewarding but necessary task. **2** [late 19C] to tire, to exhaust. **3** [late 19C] to cause someone to work hard. **4** [late 19C+] to devote an unreasonable amount of time and effort to one's studies.

grind v.[3] [late 19C] to ridicule, to satirize. [GRIND n.[2]]

grind v.[4] [1980s+] (US campus) to eat, to have some food. [SE *grind one's teeth*]

grind coffee v. [1930s–60s] (US) **1** to rotate one's hips in a manner suggestive of copulation. **2** to rotate one's hips during intercourse. [ext. of GRIND v.[1] (2), (3)]

grinder n.[1] [mid-19C] a coarse gesture, which involves placing the tip of one's thumb on one's nose and using the other hand to work an imaginary coffee-grinder; the gesture is used to refute what the subject feels is an unjustified attack on their credulity.

grinder n.[2] [mid-19C+] a highly diligent student. [GRIND n.[1] (2); their 'nose is to the grindstone']

grinder n.[3] [19C] a private tutor. [GRIND n.[1] (3)]

grinder n.[4] [20C] (Aus.) a small coin. [ety. unknown; ? link to SE *grin*, to work someone hard for very little pay]

grinder n.[5] [1950s+] (US) a striptease artist. [GRIND v.[1] (2)]

grinder n.[6] [1950s+] (US) a large sandwich made of two slabs of bread cut lengthwise from the loaf and containing a variety of ingredients (cf. HERO n.[1]; HOAGIE; SUBMARINE n.[2]). [? the need to grind one's teeth as one chews into the over-sized sandwich]

grinder n.[7] [1960s+] (US Midwest) a Slovenian. [dial. *griner*, *greiner*, ult. Ger. *Krainer*, a Slovenian inhabitant of Carniola in the former Austro-Hungary]

grinders n. [late 17C+] the teeth. [their function and f. 14C SE *grinder*, a molar; the term moved into sl., always as a plural, during 17C]

grind house n.[1] [20C] **1** a cinema. **2** a second-rate cinema, rarely showing any first-run feature films. [SE *grind*; (1) the physical turning of the early projectors, similar to the rotation of the arm of a coffee grinder; (2) the second-rate films, which a studio simply 'grinds out']

grind house n.[2] see GRIND JOINT.

grinding n. [1990s] (US Black teen) selling drugs of any kind on the street. [SE *grind (it) out*]

grinding-house n.[1] **1** [17C–18C] a house of correction. [SE *grind*; a ref. to the work one does as part of one's punishment]

grinding-house/-shop n.[2] [19C] a brothel (cf. ACCOMMODATION HOUSE; BANGING-SHOP; BUTTOCKING SHOP). [GRIND v.[1] + HOUSE n.[1]/SE *shop*, a place of business or work]

grinding tool n. [19C] the penis; thus *grind one's tool*, to copulate. [GRIND v.[1] + TOOL n.[4]]

grind joint/house n.[1] (US) [1920s+] an entertainment establishment that uses a front-man to solicit customers and runs continuous performances. [SE phr. *grind it out*]

grind joint/house n.[2] (US) [1960s+] a brothel (cf. ACCOMMODATION HOUSE; BANGING-SHOP). [GRIND v.[1] + HOUSE n.[1]]

grindo/grindoff n. [late 19C] a miller. [name of a character in Pocock's play *The Miller and His Men* (1813); ult. SE *grind*]

grind one's coffee, to phr. [1920s] (US) to have sexual intercourse. [GRIND v.[1]; pun]

grinds n. [1980s+] (US campus) food. [GRIND v.[4]]

grind show n. [1920s–50s] (US) an entertainment show that runs continuously (cf. GRIND JOINT n.[1]). [SE *grind* + *show*]

grindsman n. [20C] (W.I. Rasta) one who displays great prowess in bed. [GRIND v.[1]]

grind someone's jaw see TIGHTEN SOMEONE'S JAW.

grindstone n. [mid-19C+] the vagina. [GRIND v.[1]; pun]

gringa n. [20C] (US Hispanic) a White woman. [synon. Sp.]

grin in a glass case, to phr. [late 18C–19C] to be anatomized. [many criminals were dissected after their execution and their skeletal remains preserved under glass in hospitals]

grin in the canyon see YODEL IN THE CANYON.

grinkcome/grinkum see GRINCOME.

grin like a basket of chips phr. [late 18C–early 19C] to grin broadly (cf. HOMELY AS A BASKET OF CHIPS; POLITE AS A BASKET OF CHIPS). [SE *basket* + *chips*, small pieces of wood sawn or chiselled off by a carpenter; f. an older Salop. saying, *smile like a basket of chips*]

grin like a street-knocker, to phr. [mid-19C+] to grin broadly. [? one's teeth shine like a well-polished knocker]

grinning bear n. [1950s] (US) the vulva.

grinny bin n. [1970s] (US) a psychiatric institution. [the inmates whose fixed smiles fail to reflect their inner turmoil]

grin up the valley, to phr. [1960s+] to perform cunnilingus (cf. YODEL IN THE CANYON).

grip n.[1] [late 19C–1900s] a place, a town or city. [ety. unknown]

grip n.[2] [late 19C+] (orig. US) a small, hand-held bag or case. [abbr. SE *gripsack*]

grip n.[3] **1** [1900s–50s] (Aus.) a steady job, regular employment. **2** [1970s+] (US Black) an expense, a problem. **3** [1990s] (US Black) money. [one either grips onto it, or it has one in its grip]

grip n.[4] [1990s] (US Black) the male genitals.

grip v.[1] [1960s] (US Black) to boast and then to retreat from one's claims. [? GRIPE v.[2]]

grip v.[2] [1960s+] (US prison) to curry favour with a more powerful inmate or with the authorities (cf. STROKE v.[3]).

gripe n.[1] [mid-16C–early 17C] (Und.) any cheating gamester, spec. the member of a team who makes bets with the victim (cf. VINCENT'S LAW). [SE *gripe*, the act of grasping]

gripe n.[2] [1920s+] (US) a complaint or tedious person or thing; thus *gripe session*, an airing of complaints. [SE *gripe*, to grip, to grasp]

gripe v.[1] [1900s–20s] (US) to disgust. [SE *gripes*, the pains of colic, of which one complains]

gripe v.[2] **1** [1920s+] (orig. US) to complain, to make a fuss. **2** (US) to anger, annoy. [SE *gripe*, to distress]

griped adj. [1920s–60s] (US) angry. [GRIPE v.[2]]

gripe-fist/-money/-penny n. [19C, 17C, 19C] a moneylender, a miser. [GRIPE n.[1] (3)]

gripe one's soul/cookies, to phr. [1930s+] (US campus) to anger or disgust greatly. [GRIPE v.[2] (2) + SE *soul*/joc. use of SE *cookies*, i.e. one's being oneself]

gripe-penny see GRIPE-FIST.

griper n.[1] **1** [late 18C] (US) an annoying thing. **2** [1930s] (US) a moaner, a complainer. [GRIPE v.[2]]

griper/gripper n.[2] [early 19C+] (Irish) a bailiff. [SE *griper*, one who grasps]

gripes n.[1] [late 17C–18C] a miser, a banker, a usurer. [SE *gripe*, to grasp; ? underpinned by SE *gripe*, a vulture]

gripes n.[2] [mid-19C] of humans, stomach-ache. [SE *gripe*, a spasm of pain]

gripper n.[1] see GRIPER n.[2].

gripper n.[2] [late 19C] a miser (cf. GRIPES n.[1]; GRIPE-FIST).

grippers n. [1940s] (US Black) shoes, esp. new ones (cf. GROUND GRABBERS).

gripples n. [20C] (US Black) the anus. [SE *gripple*, a small ditch or trench, ult. synon. 11C *grip*]

gripsack n. [late 19C–1940s] (US) a holdall, a traveller's handbag.

grip the gold, to phr. [1990s] to masturbate.

grip the pencil, to phr. [1990s] to masturbate.

grip the tip, to phr. [1990s] to masturbate.

grisly *adj.* [1980s+] (US teen) awful, disgusting, generally distasteful.

gristle *n.* [19C] the penis. [SE *gristle-bone*, any part of the body consisting of gristle]

gristle-gripper *n.* [1990s] the vagina. [GRISTLE + SE *gripper*]

grit *n.*[1] [19C] (US) solidity or strength of character, spirit, pluck, stamina; thus *be the grit*, to be the 'right sort', the 'genuine article'.

grit *n.*[2] [mid-19C] (US) land or property. [SE *grit*, the ground; SE in 20C]

grit *n.*[3] [1940s–60s] (US Black) food. [SE *hominy grits*, a staple of Black and White food in the US South]

grit *n.*[4] 1 [1960s+] (US orig. Black) a White person, esp. a southerner or redneck. 2 [1980s] (US campus) a working-class White student. [for ety. *see* GRIT n.[3]]

grit *n.*[5] [1980s+] (drugs) crack cocaine.

grit *v.* (US Black) [1960s–70s] to eat. [GRIT n.[3]]

gritch *v.* [1970s+] (US campus) to nag, to complain. [GRIPE v.[2] (1) + BITCH v.[2] (2)]

gritchy *adj.* [1970s+] (US campus) irritable, grouchy. [GRITCH v. + sfx. -y]

grit on *v.* [1970s] (US Black) to stare in a rude manner. [SE *grit*, coarse, tiny particles of stone or sand; one's stare grates on its target]

grit out *v.* [1980s+] (US) to endure hardship. [GRIT n.[1]]

grits *n.* [1990s] (US Black) 1 any form of food (cf. GRIT n.[3]). 2 money. 3 one's business. [lit. + fig. uses of SE *grits*, coarse oatmeal, a traditional African-American food]

grit-sucker *n.* [19C+] 1 a poor White (cf. CLAY-EATER; CLOVER-EATER). 2 a general derog. term. [the impoverished diet, extending as far as the literal 'eating dirt' by such individuals]

gritty *adj.*[1] [mid-19C–1950s] (US) determined, firm, plucky. [subseq. use is SE; GRIT n.[1] + sfx. -y]

gritty *adj.*[2] 1 [late 19C] impoverished, penniless. 2 [1950s+] in 'straitened circumstances'.

gritty whiskers *n.* [20C] the stubble on an unshaven male face.

grizzle *n.* [early 18C] 1 a grumbler, a whinger. 2 a fit of whinging, grumbling or sulking, a peevish mood. [GRIZZLE v.]

grizzle/grizzle one's guts *v.* [mid-19C+] to whine, to cry slightly but continually, usu. of a child. [despite the lack of citations (the first is in a ballad recorded in 1842), the v. is prob. contemporary with GRIZZLE n.]

grizzly *n.* [mid–late 19C] (US) a brute. [SE *grizzly bear*]

groak/growk *n.* [20C] (Ulster) a child who sits watching others eating, in the hope of being asked to join them. [synon. Scot. *groak*]

groan and grunt *see* GRUMBLE AND GRUNT.

groan-box *n.* [1900s–50s] (orig. US Black) a musical instrument, esp. an accordion, radio or juke box.

groaner *n.* [late 18C–19C] (Und.) a pickpocket who specializes in robbing members of a church congregation. [his exaggeratedly enthusiastic, albeit completely spurious devotions, which draw the congregants' attention away from his actual purpose]

groaner *n.* 1980s+] (US) a bad pun or joke. [the groan from the person told the joke]

groatable *adj.* [early 18C] (US) drunk. [? SE *groats*, hulled and/or crushed grain of various kinds; poss. used in brewing; or SE *groat*, fourpence, the price of a drink]

groaty *adj.* (US teen/campus) disgusting, unpleasant (cf. GRODY; GROTTY). [SE *grotesque*]

grob *adj.* [1940s+] (S.Afr.) unpleasant, coarse. [Ger./Yid. *grob*, loutish, vulgar, coarse]

groceries *n.*[1] 1 [19C] the vagina (cf. APPLE n.[10]; CABBAGE n.[7]). 2 [1980s+] (US gay) the male genitals. [GREENS n.[2]]

groceries/grocery *n.*[2] [mid-19C–1910s] sugar, esp. when added to a hot alcoholic drink.

groceries *n.*[3] [1980s+] (drugs) 1 a cache of marijuana. 2 crack cocaine. [euph.]

grocer's cart *n.* [20C] (Aus.) the heart. [rhy. sl.]

grocer's shop *n.* [1970s] an Italian. [rhy. sl. *grocer's shop* = WOP n.]

grocery *n.*[1] [mid-18C–early 19C] small change. [? its suitability for buying groceries]

grocery *n.*[2] *see* GROCERIES n.[2].

grocery *n.*[3] [1920s–30s] a speakeasy (cf. CONFECTIONARY; DELICATESSEN; GREENGROCERY n.[2]). [the term had been used as euph. for a legal liquor store or small bar in 19C]

G-rock *n.* [1980s+] (drugs) one gram of crack cocaine. [G. n.[2] (2) + ROCK n.[4]]

grockle *n.* [1960s+] 1 a tourist. 2 (society) an outsider, with overtones of unpleasantness and boorishness. [the term originated in the West Country, specifically in Torbay, where a local remarked that the stream of visitors to the town resembled little Grocks (the celebrated clown *Grock*, real name Charles Adrien Wettach, 1880–1959), but spread throughout Britain's holiday resorts where the local people thus derided the flocks of annual visitors to their area]

grody *adj.* [1980s+] (US teen) disgusting, unpleasant. [GROTTY, ult. SE *grotesque*]

grody to the max *adj.* [1980s] (US teen) extremely or even more, disgusting. [GRODY + TO THE MAX]

groe *n.* [1990s] (US) a derog. term for a Black person. [abbr. SE *Negro*; esp. New England use]

grog *n.* 1 [mid-18C+] alcohol, orig. rum but soon generic for any intoxicating liquor, whether beer or spirits. 2 [late 19C] a party at which grog is drunk. [abbr. SE *grogram*, a coarse fabric of silk, of mohair and wool, or of these mixed with silk. Orig. applied as a nickname to Admiral Vernon, known as 'Old Grog', from the fact of his wearing a grogram cloak. The name was transferred to the mixture of rum and water, which in August 1740 he ordered to be served out instead of the RN's usual issue of neat spirit]

grog *v.* [1950s+] (Aus.) to drink; thus *grog on*, to drink for a lengthy period, *grog up*, to drink excessively, *grogging*, drinking. [GROG n.]

grogan *n.* [1990s] a large piece of excrement. [ety. unknown]

grogans *n.* [1910s–20s] (US) muttonchop sidewhiskers. [generic Irish family name *Grogan*. Such whiskers were popular among Irish-Americans]

grog artist *n.* [1990s] (N.Z.) a heavy drinker, a drunkard (cf. BOOZE ARTIST). [GROG n. + sfx. -ARTIST]

grog blossom *n.* [18C+] a red face caused by the bursting of blood-vessels through excessive, long-term drinking (cf. BRANDY BLOSSOM). [GROG + SE *blossom-faced*, having a red, bloated face]

grog-den *see* GROG-SHOP.

grog-fight *n.* [mid–late 19C] (orig. milit.) a drinking party (cf. BUNFIGHT). [GROG + SE *fight*]

grogged *adj.* [mid–late 19C] tipsy. [GROG + sfx. -y]

groggery *n.* [early 19C+] (US/N.Z.) a saloon, a public house (cf. GROG-SHANTY; GROG-SHOP). [GROG]

grogging *n.* [late 19C] adulteration. [SE *grogging*, extracting spirits from an empty cask by soaking the interior with hot water; ult. GROG, i.e. watered-down rum]

groggy *n.* [late 19C] (US) 1 a grog seller. 2 an opponent of prohibition. [GROG + sfx. -y]

groggy *adj.* [mid-19C+] 1 drunken, tipsy (cf. ALED UP). 2 weak, unsteady, semi-conscious. [GROG + sfx. -y; f. orig. meaning of drunken]

grogham *n.* [late 18C–19C] (Und.) an old horse. [ety. unknown]

grog-hole *n.* [mid-19C] (US) a public house (cf. GROG-SHOP). [GROG + SE *hole*]

grog-mill *n.* [1940s] (US) a rough or illicit drinking place. [GROG n. + pattern of GIN-MILL]

grog-on/-up *n.* [1950s+] (Aus./N.Z.) a drinking session, a party. [GROG n.]

grog-shanty *n.* [mid-19C+] (US/Aus./NZ) a public house (cf. GROG-HOLE; GROG-SHOP. [GROG + SE *shanty*]

grog-shop/-den *n.* [mid–late 19C] a public house (cf. GROG-GERY; GROG HOLE; GROG-SHANTY). [GROG n. + SE *shop*]

grog-up *see* GROG-ON.

grog watch *n.* [late 19C] (US) a watch set forward in time, thus closer to the next drinking hour. [GROG n.]

groid *n.* [1970s+] (US South, campus) a Black student. [abbr. *Negroid*]

groin/growne/groyne *n.* [1930s+] (Und.) any ring containing a gemstone, esp. a diamond. [ety. unknown; *OED* links it to the body's physical *groin*, but the link seems unlikely]

grok *v.* [1960s+] in popular hippie and mystic use, to appreciate, to understand and experience completely, usu. in phr. *grok the fullness.* [coined by SF author Robert Heinlein (1907–88) in *Strangers in a Strange Land* (1961)]

grommet *n.* [late 19C–1940s] (US) **1** the vagina. **2** the anus. [SE *grommet*, a ring of rope, a washer]

gronked *adj.* [1960s+] (US) drunk, passed out, tired out, fast asleep. [? echoic of snoring]

grooby *adj.* [1940s–60s] (US) wonderful, excellent, first-rate. [GROOVY adj.² (1)]

groody *n.* [1990s] (US teen) one's breast.

grooly *adj.* [1920s–70s] sinister; thus *grool*, a sinister person. [SE *gru(esome)* + *(gris)ly*]

groomed to zoom *phr.* [1970s] (US campus) well dressed.

grootbek *n.* [1940s+] (S.Afr.) a braggart, a boaster (cf. BIG-MOUTH). [Afk. *groot*, big + *bek*, mouth]

groot krokodil *n.* [1980s+] (S.Afr.) **1** anyone considered to be acting in a ferocious or relentless manner. **2** the nickname of Prime Minister P.W. Botha (b.1916). [Afk. *groot krokodil*, great crocodile, and as such parodying the reverse anthropomorphic titles given to African chiefs]

grootpraat *n.* [1940s+] (S.Afr.) boasting, bragging. [Afk. *groot*, big + *praat*, talk]

groove *n.¹* [1920s–60s] (US Black) the vagina (cf. AGREEABLE RUTS OF LIFE). [physiognomy]

groove *n.²* [1930s+] (orig. US jazz) **1** a way of life, of thinking and dealing with people, events etc. **2** a delight, a pleasure, anything enjoyable; thus *in the groove*, happy, in control, fashionable, chic.

groove *n.³* [1960s+] (US) a record or cassette recording.

groove *v.* [1930s+] **1** to enjoy, to give pleasure; thus *grooviness*, pleasure, enjoyment. **2** (US) to play jazz or (latterly) rock music. [GROOVE n.²]

groove behind/on *v.* [1950s+] to enjoy or appreciate a situation or other stimulus. [ext. of GROOVE v.]

grooved *adj.* [1960s+] very pleased, very happy. [GROOVE v.]

groove on *see* GROOVE BEHIND.

groover *n.* [1960s+] a person, neutral when coined in the 1960s but by 1980s+ slightly derisory, since the term, and by extension the person described, is *de facto* old-fashioned. [GROOVE v.]

grooving *n.* [1980s+] (drugs) having an enjoyable time while using a drug. [GROOVE v.]

groovy *adj.¹* [late 19C] staid, conservative. [SE *groove*, a routine life]

groovy *adj.²* **1** [1930s–60s] **1** delightful, wonderful, pleasant, enjoyable etc. **2** [1980s+] (US teen) passé, out-of-date, esp. when referring to the tastes and styles of the 1960s, during which time (1) was the only accepted meaning.

groovy chick *n.* [1960s+] an attractive girl. [GROOVY adj.² + CHICK n.³]

grope *n.* [1940s+] (US) a welcome or unwelcome fondling or handling of the breasts, buttocks or genitals. [GROPE v.]

grope *v.* [14C–18C; 1920s+] **1** to fondle or touch the breasts, buttocks or genitals of someone, esp. a potential partner in order to assess response to one's advances. **2** to kiss passionately.

grope for Jesus, to *phr.* [late 19C] to pray in public. [the Salvation Army's early prayer meetings, when congregants were urged to 'grope for Jesus!']

grope for trout in a peculiar river, to *phr.* [early 17C] to have sexual intercourse. [coined by Shakespeare in *Measure for Measure* (1604)]

groper *n.¹* **1** [late 17C–mid-19C] a blind man, both actually and in the game of Blind Man's Buff. **2** [18C–19C] a midwife. **3** [late 19C] (US) a blind beggar (cf. GIMP n.²; STUMPY). [SE *grope*]

groper *n.²* [late 18C] a pocket (cf. GROPUS). [one gropes in it for money]

groper *n.³* [1920s+] (Aus.) a Western Australian; thus *Groperland*, Western Australia, *Groperlander*, an inhabitant of West Australia. [abbr. SAND-GROPER]

groper *n.⁴* [1980s+] (US drugs) a deep inhalation of cannabis from a pipe. [it tends to be followed by a coughing fit as one's lungs grope for air]

groperess *n.* [mid-19C] a blind woman. [GROPER n.¹ + fem. sfx. -*ess*]

gropers *n.* [19C] the hands (cf. FEELER n.²).

groping *n.* [1940s+] sexual stimulation, often unwanted. [GROPE v. (1)]

gropus *n.* [mid-19C] a coat pocket (cf. GROPER n.²). [one has to grope into its depths to find small items]

gross *adj.* [1970s+] (orig. US teen and campus) disgusting.

grossed *adj.* [1960s] (US campus) disgusted. [GROSS OUT]

grossed-out *adj.* [1970s+] (US campus) repelled, appalled. [GROSS OUT]

grosser *n.* [1970s+] (US) a disgusting or ugly person. [GROSS]

gross out *v.* [1980s+] (orig. US campus) to disgust, to shock; thus excl. *gross me out!* that really disgusts me! [GROSS adj.]

grostulation *n.* [1990s] (US) the contractions of the rectum during anal sex. [GROSS adj.]

grosvenor squares *n.* [1970s] flares (flared trousers). [rhy. sl.]

grot *n.* **1** [1940s+] (N.Z.) a lavatory; thus an act of defecation or a piece of excrement. **2** [1960s+] (Aus.) a dirty, untidy person. [abbr. GROTTY]

grot *adj. see* GROTTY.

grote *n.* [late 19C–1910s] an informer.

Grotsend-on-Sea *n.* [1970s+] a generic name for an unappealing, small town. [GROTTY + play on Southend-on-Sea, Essex, and similar towns]

grotto *n.* [19C] the vagina (cf. ARBOUR).

grotty/grot *adj.* [1960s+] disgusting, unattractive (cf. GROATY; GRODY; SCROTTY). [SE *grotesque*; especially popular during the Beatlemania era of the early 1960s]

grouce *see* GROUSE adj.

grouch *n.* [late 19C+] (US) **1** a bad temper. **2** a grumpy, complaining person. [? backform. f. GROUCHY]

grouch *v.* [1910s+] (US) to mope, to grumble, to complain. [GROUCH n.]

grouch-bag *n.* [20C] **1** a hidden pocket or purse, in which money can be secured. **2** the money hidden in it; thus *grouch money*, savings. [the image, among the actors who coined the term, of one who saved as a GROUCH n.]

grouch-box/-pot *n.* [late 19C+] (US) a grumpy, irritable person (cf. FUSS-POT). [GROUCH n. + SE *box/pot*]

groucho n. [20C] an electrician. [rhy. sl. *Groucho Marx* = SPARKS n.[2]; ult. US comedian Groucho Marx (1890–1977)]

grouch-pot see GROUCH-BOX.

grouchy adj. [late 19C+] ill-tempered, sour. [? *OED* suggests a root in GROUCH n., but Lighter prefers the reverse and roots *grouchy* in SE *grudge*, synon. dial. *grutch* or Yorks./US dial. *grouty*, grumpy]

grounation n. [1950s+] (W.I. Rasta) a large, island-wide meeting-cum-celebration for Rastas. [? ety. unknown; ? Fr. *grosnation*, a great nation or fig. use of SE *groan*, i.e. shout out + sfx. *-ation*]

ground n. [1950s+] (W.I. Rasta) one's home.

ground apple n. [1940s] (US Black) a rock, a stone (cf. ALLEY-APPLE n.[1]).

groundbags see GROUNDPADS.

ground ball n. [1990s] (US) anything easy or simple. [baseball jargon *ground ball*, a ball the rolls along the ground and is thus easy to gather]

ground biscuit n. [1920s+] (US) a brick or stone when used as a missile (cf. ALLEY-APPLE n.[1]).

ground control n. [1960s+] (drugs) a guide or caretaker during a hallucinogenic experience. Such a person is either not taking the drug or a veteran user. [SE *ground control*, a ground-based individual who communicates with an astronaut]

grounded, be v. 1 [1930s+] (US) to be suspended from work. 2 [1950s+] (orig. US teen) to be stopped from enjoying some normal right or pleasure; the sufferer is usu. confined to their home. [SE *grounded*, used of an aircraft that cannot fly]

grounder n.[1] 1 [late 19C] a knock-down blow. 2 [1970s+] (US drugs) a barbiturate. [they lit. and fig. *knock one to the ground*]

grounder n.[2] [1930s] (US) a cigarette that is picked up from the ground to be smoked.

ground grabbers n. [1930s–40s] (US Black) shoes, esp. new ones (cf. GRIPPERS).

ground-hog n.[1] [1910s–50s] (US) a sausage, a frankfurter, a hot dog.

ground-hog n.[2] [1920s+] (US) 1 any worker whose occupation keeps them on the ground. 2 a caisson worker, working under compressed air, digging and laying the foundations of bridges etc (cf. SAND-HOG). 3 [1960s+] (Can.) a meteorologist.

groundhog case n. [late 19C–1950s] (US, West) a tight corner, an inescapable situation. [imagery of the trapped animal]

groundnut/ground-seed n. [mid-19C] (US) a rock or stone (cf. GROUND APPLE).

groundpads/groundbags n. [1930s–40s] (US Black) 1 feet. 2 shoes (cf. GROUND GRABBERS). 3 socks.

groundpad spade n. [1940s] (US Black) a shoehorn. [GROUNDPADS + SE *spade*]

ground-parrot n. [late 19C] (Aus.) a small farmer (cf. COCKATOO n.[2]; COCKY n.[2]).

ground-pounder n. [1940s+] (US) an infantry soldier (cf. GRAVEL-AGITATOR).

ground rations n. [1930s–40s] (US Black) sexual intercourse. [pun]

grounds n. [1960s] (drugs) the residue left after an injection of heroin.

ground-seed see GROUNDNUT.

ground-sweat n. [late 16C–mid-19C] a grave; thus *take a ground-sweat*, to be buried.

ground zero n. [1950s+] the basic position, the start, the essentials. [milit. use.]

grouper see GROUPIE n.[1].

group grope n. [1960s+] an orgy. [SE *group* + GROPE n.]

group gropes n. [1970s] (US campus) encounter groups.

groupie/groupy/grouper n.[1] [1960s+] 1 a young girl who associates herself with rock bands, offering her body in return for a share of their celebrity (cf. BAND MOLL). 2 anyone, male or female, who is an obsessive fan; the adoration need not run to sex, nor are the subjects necessarily rock stars. [SE *group*, a pop/rock band]

groupie n.[2] [1960s+] a devotee of group sex. [SE *group*, a collection of people]

grouse n.[1] [mid-19C+] a young woman (cf. BIRD n.[4]). [SE *grouse*, the small game bird]

grouse n.[2] [1910s–20s] a complaint; thus *grouser*, a complainer. [GROUSE v.]

grouse, the n.[3] [1920s+] (Aus./N.Z.) the best, the ultimate, the ideal. [GROUSE adj.]

grouse n.[4] [1960s+] (Aus. Und.) a tailormade, rather than a prison-issue cigarette. [GROUSE adj.]

grouse/grouce adj. [1930s+] (Aus./N.Z.) wonderful, attractive, excellent, an all-purpose term of approval. [ety. unknown; ? UK dial. *crouse*, happy, lively, pleased]

grouse v. 1 [late 19C] (orig. milit.) to grumble, to complain. 2 [1950s+] (US) to engage in sexual activity. [? OF. *groucier*; *groucher*, to murmur, grumble]

grouse gear n. [1950s+] (Aus.) teen expression for a particularly attractive woman. [GROUSE adj. + GEAR n.[1] (4) but note GEAR n.[2] (2)]

grout-bag n. [late 19C–1910s] (teen) a very hard worker (cf. GRIND n.). [SAmE *grout*, to grumble, to sulk]

grouter n. [20C] (Aus.) a piece of good luck, an unfair advantage; esp. in phr. *come in on the grouter, run the grouter*. [ety. unknown; ? Yorks. dial. *grout*, to rummage or root about]

grouter v. [20C] (Aus.) to get hold of something through luck rather than judgement, to take advantage of a situation. [GROUTER n.]

grouthead n. [late 19C–1900s] (US) a fool, a simpleton. [SAmE *grout*, grumble + sfx. -HEAD (1)]

grouty adj. [19C+] (US) grumpy, irritable; thus *the grouties*, ill temper. [? GROUCHY]

Grove, the n. [1950s+] (orig. Black) Ladbroke *Grove*, London W11/W10 (cf. GATE n.[1]). [abbr.]

grove v. [1960s+] to have taken great pleasure in something. [GROOVE v.]

grovel v. [1980s+] (US campus) to neck, to enjoy sexual relations, esp. with someone who is not one's regular partner.

grovel, grovel phr. [1960s+] used when one wants to make an apology but hopes good humour can still prevail.

grove of eglantine n. [19C] the pubic hair (cf. BUSH n.[4]). [SE *elegantine*, the sweetbriar]

grove/shady grove of the evangelist n. [mid-19C–1910s] St John's Wood, London NW8 (cf. APOSTLE'S GROVE). [pun; the area was well-known for its up-market courtesans and 'kept women']

grover n. [1980s] (US) $1000 bill (cf. ABRAHAM LINCOLN). [the head of US President *Grover* Cleveland (1837–1908), which is printed on the bill]

grow horns v. [1970s+] (US campus) to become angry. [the horns are those of a bull rather than of a cuckold]

growk see GROAK.

growl n. [1940s+] (Aus.) 1 the vagina. 2 women, viewed as sex-objects. 3 sexual intercourse. [abbr. *growl and grunt* (see GRUMBLE AND GRUNT)]

growl and grunt see GRUMBLE AND GRUNT.

growl at the badger, to phr. [1990s] to perform cunnilingus (cf. GROWL IN HER BUSBY). [SE *growl* + BADGER n.[7] (2)]

growl-biter n. [late 19C+] one who performs cunnilingus. [GROWL n. (1) + SE *bite*]

growl-biting n. [late 19C+] cunnilingus. [for ety. see GROWL-BITER]

growler *n.*[1] **1** [early 19C+] a dog. **2** [early 19C+] a cannon. **3** [1960s] (US) a police car siren. [they all 'growl']

growler *n.*[2] **1** [mid–late 19C] a 4-wheeled cab; thus *work the growler*. **2** [late 19C–1910s] hiring a cab to accompany one on a 'pub-crawl'. [either a pun on SE *sulky* (although this was a one-horse, two-wheeled vehicle) or the creaks and rattles of the cab or the stereotypically poor temper of the driver]

growler *n.*[3] [late 19C+] (US) a container, usu. a covered pail with a carrying handle, in which beer is purchased at a tavern, then brought home for consumption (cf. RUSH THE GROWLER). [ety. unknown; ? the growling, grating noise of the can as it slid, full of beer, across the bar, or the 'growling' or grumbling of the children who were sent on the errand or the drunken arguing that ensued among recipients of the liquor]

growler *n.*[4] **1** [1970s+] (US campus) a lavatory. **2** [1980s] (US) a prison. [the noise, either of someone straining to defecate or of incarcerated prisoners]

growler *n.*[5] [1990s] the vagina. [GROWL AND GRUNT]

growler-shover *n.* [late 19C–1910s] a cab driver. [GROWLER *n.*[2] + SE *shove*]

growlery *n.* [mid-19C] a private sitting-room, a 'den'. [coined by Charles Dickens in *Bleak House* (1852–3)]

growlies *n.* [1980s+] (US drugs) the craving for food while smoking marijuana (cf. MUNCHIES). [one's stomach rumbles or 'growls']

growl in her busby, to *phr.* [1930s] to perform cunnilingus (cf. GROWL AT THE BADGER). [SE *growl* + BUSBY]

grown-ass *adj.* [1930s] (US Black) adult, mature, grown-up. [SE *grown* + sfx. -ASS]

growne *see* GROIN.

grownies *n.* [1970s+] adults. [SE *grown-ups* + *groan*]

grown man's dose *n.* [mid-19C+] a large measure of alcohol.

grow up! *excl.* [1930s+] used contemptuously to anyone, adult or child, who is behaving immaturely.

groyne *see* GROIN.

grualt *n.* [1990s] (US teen) a mixture of GRUNGE and alternative music. [pron. 'grult']

grub *n.*[1] [mid-17C+] **1** food. **2** a meal. [one has 'grubbed it up']

grub *n.*[2] [mid-19C+] (US campus) a hard worker, one who works to the exclusion of other interests. [he 'grubs up' facts]

grub *n.*[3] [mid-19C+] a dirty, unkempt person, esp. a child. [20C use is Aus.; SE *grub*, the larva of an insect]

grub *n.*[4] [1940s–50s] (Aus.) tuberculosis. [SE *grub*, the larva of an insect]

grub *v.*[1] **1** [18C–19C] to eat. **2** [19C] to provide with food. [GRUB *n.*[1]]

grub *v.*[2] **1** [mid-19C+] (US campus) to study hard. **2** [1960s+] to kiss passionately. **3** [1970s] to eat heartily. **4** [1980s+] to engage in sex.

grub *v.*[3] [late 19C+] to beg, to scrounge.

grub along *v.* [late 19C+] to subsist, to struggle along. [GRUB *v.*[3]]

grub and bub *n.* [19C] food and drink (cf. GRUBBERY). [GRUB *n.*[1] + BUB *n.*[2]]

grubbed up *adj.* [1960s] (US) unkempt, dirty. [GRUB *n.*[3]]

grubber *n.*[1] **1** [19C] a promiscuous woman (cf. DIRTY LEG). **2** [1900s] (US) a beggar. **3** [1940s+] (US) a disgusting person (cf. HOG-GRUBBER). [GRUB *n.*[3]]

grubber *n.*[2] [late 19C] (US campus) a diligent student. [GRUB *v.*[2]]

grubber *n.*[3] [19C] an eater, esp. as *heavy grubber*, a glutton. [GRUB *v.*[1]]

grubber *n.*[4] [20C] (Aus.) a hospital, spec. a vagrants' casual night shelter or workhouse. [GRUB ALONG + SE *grub*, an insect larva, thus a disease]

grubbery *n.* [19C] **1** food. **2** a public meal. **3** a cookshop. **4** a dining room. [GRUB *n.*[1]]

grubbies *see* GRUBS.

grubbing *n.* [19C] eating. [GRUB *v.*[1]]

grubbing-crib/-ken *n.* [mid-19C] **1** a cookshop; **2** a workhouse; thus *grubbing-crib fencer*, the proprietor of an eating house. [GRUBBING + CRIB *n.*[3]/KEN]

grubbins *n.*(US) **1** [mid-19C] food. **2** [1910s] (Und.) money. [GRUB *n.*[1]]

grubble *v.* [1960s] (orig. US) to rummage around, to search at random. [GRUB *v.*[3] + SE *scrabble*]

grub-box *n.* [mid-19C] the mouth (cf. GRUB-MILL; GRUB-SHOP; GRUB-TRAP). [GRUB *n.*[1]]

grubby *n.* [1940s] (US campus) an ostracized student. [GRUB *n.*[2]]

grub-crib *n.* [mid-19C] an eating house (cf. GRUB-SHOP). [GRUB *n.*[1] + CRIB *n.*[3]]

grub hooks *n.* [1920s+] (US) fingers or hands. [GRUB *n.*[1] + HOOKS]

grub-liner/-rider *n.* [1900s–60s] (US) an itinerant, out-of-work cowboy who subsists on hand-outs; thus *ride the grub line*, to travel around seeking work (cf. GRUB-RIDER). [GRUB *n.*[1] + fig. use of cowboy jargon *line*, the boundary of a ranch]

grub-mill *n.* [late 19C+] (US) the mouth (cf. GRUB-BOX). [GRUB *n.*[1] + SE *mill*]

grub on *v.* [1980s+] (US campus) to eat. [GRUB *v.*[1]]

grub-pile *n.* [late 19C–1930s] (US West.) a meal. [GRUB *n.*[1] + SE *pile*]

grub-rider *see* GRUB-LINER.

grubs/grubbies *n.* [1960s+] (US campus) old or comfortable, informal clothes. [SE *grubby*]

grubshite *v.* [late 18C–19C] to foul, to make dirty. [SE *grubby* + SHIT *v.*[1]]

grub-shop *n.* [mid-19C] **1** an eating house. **2** the mouth (cf. GRUB-BOX). [GRUB *n.*[1] + SE *shop*]

grub-slinger *n.* [1910s] (US) a cook (cf. GRUB-SPOILER). [GRUB *n.*[1] + SE *slinger*]

grub-spoiler *n.* [late 19C–1930s] (US) a cook. [GRUB *n.*[1] + SE *spoiler*]

grubstake *n.* **1** [late 19C+] (orig. US) enough money to buy one a meal. **2** [1930s+] an advance or loan to provide an author funds with which to work. [GRUB *n.*[1] + SE *stake*, the sum of money one places on a bet; immediate root is US mining jargon *grub stake*, 'the outfit, provisions etc furnished to a prospector on condition of participating in the profits of any find he may make; a lay-out' (Century Dictionary)]

grubstake *v.* [late 19C+] (orig. US) to provide one with sufficient money with which to eat, live etc. [GRUBSTAKE *n.*]

grub-stakes *n.* [late 19C+] (orig. US) food. [GRUBSTAKE *n.*]

Grub Street news *n.* [late 17C–18C] rumours, lies. [proper name *Grub Street*, the notional home of hack journalism. There actually was a Grub Street, possibly named for a Mr Grubbe, near Moorfields in the City of London; it was renamed Milton Street in 1830. Andrew Marvell coined the phr. to epitomize the world of hackery. Grub Street, according to Johnson (1755), was 'much inhabited by writers of small histories, dictionaries, and temporary poems']

grub-trap *n.* [mid-19C] the mouth (cf. GRUB-BOX). [GRUB *n.*[1] + TRAP *n.*[3]]

grub up! *excl.* [1950s+] an excl. denoting that it is time to eat, the food is ready. [GRUB *n.*[1]]

grue *adj.* [1920s+] nervous, afraid. [SE *gruesome*]

gruel *n.*[1] [late 18C–late 19C] punishment; thus *have/get one's gruel*, to receive one's punishment, to get killed, *take one's gruel*, to receive and accept punishment, to *give someone his gruel*, to punish. [the thin gruel one receives in prison]

gruel *n.*[2] [late 19C] (US) sentimental, 'thin' poetry.

grueller *n.* [mid-19C] a problem, a 'poser'. [SE *gruel*, to punish, to exhaust]

gruesome *adj.* [1930s+] (US) awful, unattractive.

gruesome and gory *n.* [20C] the penis. [rhy. sl. *gruesome and gory* = CORIE]

gruesome twosome *n.* [1940s+] **1** (US Black) a couple in a steady relationship. **2** two teenage girls sharing a very close friendship.

grulch *n.* [20C] (Irish) a small stocky person, usu. somewhat uncouth and less than amicable. [synon. Scot. *grulsh*]

grumble/groan/growl and grunt *n.* [1930s+] **1** the vagina (cf. BERKELEY HUNT). **2** sexual intercourse (cf. MAKE HER GRUNT). [rhy. sl. *grumble and grunt* = CUNT]

grumble and mutter *n.* [20C] a bet. [rhy. sl. *grumble and mutter* = FLUTTER n.[2]]

grumble-guts *n.* [late 19C+] an habitual complainer. [Yorks. dial.; note synon. Lancashire dial. *grumble-belly*]

grumble in the gizzard, to *phr.* [late 18C–1900s] to be annoyed, but to keep one's feelings to oneself.

grumbler *n.* [early 19C] fourpennyworth of grog. [? some *grumbles* at the price; the drink makes one's stomach *grumble*]

grumbles, the *n.* [mid-19C] bad temper, sulkiness; thus *be all on the grumbles*, to be in a bad mood.

grumbletonian *n.* [late 17C–mid-19C] a constant grumbler, esp. as regards the 'state of the country'. [a pun on two late 17C religious sects, the Muggletonians (founded 1651 by Lodowicke Muggleton) and Grindletonians (? the Yorks. village of Grindleton); the term was used first as specific political jargon *c.*1690 when the 'Court Party' apostrophized as *grumbletonians* their 'Country Party' rivals, whom, they claimed, resented their personal ambitions being thwarted]

grummet *n.* **1** [19C] the vagina (cf. BLACK HOLE n.[1]). **2** [19C] sexual intercourse. **3** [1960s+] (orig. N.Z. surfers) a woman, esp. as a sex object. **4** [1980s+] (N.Z. juv.) someone or something disliked. [SE *grummet*, a ring of rope, a washer]

grump *n.* [20C] a bad-tempered, surly person. [dial.]

grumper *n.* [1970s] (US) the buttocks. [? SE *rump*]

grumpus *n.* [1980s+] (US) a bad-tempered person. [SE *grumpy*]

grunch *n.* [1960s+] sticky, dirty, unpleasant substances. [GRUNGE n.]

grunch! *excl.* (US campus) a general excl. of annoyance or disgust. [GRUNCH n.]

grundle *v.* [1990s] (US) the perineum. [ety. unknown]

grundy *n.* [16C] usu. of men, a short, fat person. [? Du. *grundje*, *grontje*, groundling]

grunge *n.* (orig. US) **1** [1960s+] sticky, dirty, unpleasant substances (cf. GRUNCH n.). **2** [1960s+] a general term of abuse, a repugnant, odious, dirty or boring person. **3** [1970s+] a form of rock music, epitomized by the work of the Seattle band Nirvana, but first used in relation to the New York Dolls, *c.*1973 (also known, among many rivals, as the 'godfathers of PUNK'). **4** [1980s+] the fashion style that developed out of the rock music.

grunge *v.* [1960s+] **1** to whine, to complain. **2** to assault, to attack, to terrify. [? GRIPE v.[2] (1) + WHINGE]

grunged-out *adj.* [1980s+] (US) dirty, messy, unappetizing, unappealing. [GRUNGY]

grungehole *n.* [1980s] (US) a dirty room or place. [GRUNGE n. + HOLE]

grungey *see* GRUNGY.

grungies *n.* [1980s+] (US campus) dirty laundry. [GRUNGE n.]

grungy/grungey *adj.* **1** [1960s+] dirty, messy, unappetizing, unappealing. **2** [1980s+] dressed in the style of GRUNGE n. (4). [SE *grubby* + SE *dingy*]

grunt *n.*[1] [20C] (US) an ill-tempered, constantly complaining person (cf. GRANNY GRUNT n.[2]).

grunt *n.*[2] [1920s+] (US) a slice of ham or pork (cf. GRUNTER n.[1]).

grunt *n.*[3] **1** [1940s+] (US) excrement. **2** [1960s] (US Black) a bowel movement. [the sounds of defecation]

grunt *n.*[4] **1** [1950s+] (US) the bill, for food, drink. **2** [1960s+] (US campus) food, esp. snack food.

grunt *n.*[5] **1** [1960s+] (US) a combat soldier, a Marine soldier or a non-flying Airforce officer. **2** [1970s+] (US) any person doing menial work (cf. GRUNT WORK). **3** [1970s+] (US) a stupid or unpleasant person. [? the soldier's endless complaining; the Vietnam era successor to the DOUGHBOY n.[1], thus used in civilian senses]

grunt *n.*[6] [1990s] an extremely unattractive woman. [play on PIG n.[1]]

grunt *v.* (US) **1** [1930s–40s] to do menial work. **2** [1960s] to defecate. [the sound of a person straining]

grunter *n.*[1] **1** [mid-16C–18C] a pig (cf. GRUNTING-CHEAT). **2** [mid-16C–18C] pork (cf. GRUNTING PECK). **3** [late 17C–18C] a sucking pig.

grunter *n.*[2] **1** [late 18C–early 19C] a shilling (5p). **2** [mid-19C] sixpence (2.5p) (cf. HALF A HOG; PIG n.[2]; SOW'S BABY). [play on HOG n.[1] (1)]

grunter *n.*[3] [early 19C] a policeman. [pun on PIG n.[3]]

grunter *n.*[4] **1** [1910s–20s] an automobile. **2** [1930s] (US) a professional wrestler.

grunter *n.*[5] [1940s+] (Aus.) prostitute. [? the (simulated) grunts of passion with which she embellishes her services]

grunter *n.*[6] [1980s+] an old person out of sympathy with current youth enthusiasms (cf. CRUMBLY). [their grunts of complaint]

grunter's gig *n.* [late 18C–19C] the flesh of a smoked pig's face. [GRUNTER n.[1] + GIG n.[1]]

grunter's muns *n.* [early 18C] the flesh of a smoked pig's face (cf. GRUNTER'S GIG). [GRUNTER n.[1] + MUNS]

grunt horn/iron *n.* [1920s–30s] (US) a tuba.

grunting-cheat/-chete *n.* [mid-16C–early 18C] (Und.) a pig (cf. GRUNTER n.[1]; GRUNTING PECK). [SE *grunt* + CHEAT]

grunting peck *n.* [mid-17C–mid-19C] pork, bacon or any pig-meat (cf. GRUNTING CHEAT). [GRUNTER n.[1] + PECK n. (1)]

grunt iron *see* GRUNT HORN.

gruntling *n.* [late 17C–early 18C] (US) a pig (cf. GRUNTER; GRUNTING-CHEAT).

grunt work *n.* [1970s+] (US) menial work, drudgery. [GRUNT v. + SE *work*]

grush/grushie *v.* [1970s+] for children to scramble for a handful of small change tossed to them, typically after a wedding. [synon. Scot. *grush*]

G-shot *n.* [1950s+] (drugs) small dose of drugs used to hold off withdrawal symptoms until a full dose can be taken. [it SE *gees* one up]

g.s.p. *n.* [1990s] (US Black) anyone who treats one badly or contemptuously, people who act against your interests. [abbr. golden shower *people*, i.e. those who, in sl. 'piss on you' (cf. GOLDEN SHOWER)]

g-ster *n. see* GANGSTA n.

G-string *n.* [1970s+] (US Black) any device – a tampon, towel etc – used to staunch the flow of menstrual blood. [SE *G-string*, the minimal 'loin-cloth' worn by striptease artists etc]

g.t.f.o.o.m.w. *phr.* [1990s] get *the fuck out of my way.* [abbr.]

g.t.h.! *excl.* [1910s] (US) go *to hell!* [abbr.]

g-thang/g-thing *n.* [1990s] (US Black) **1** anything that is seen as a male preserve. **2** anything that concerns a street thug. **3** a 'girl-thing'. [note (1) anglicized as 'it's a guy thing', as used in *FHM* magazine advertisements in 1996]

g.t.t. *phr.* [late 19C] (US) gone *to Texas*; the sign affixed to the door of an absconding businessman. [abbr.]

güantes *n.* [1960s+] (US) hitting someone. [Sp. *güantes*, gloves]

guaranfuckingtee/guarandamntee v. [1940s+] an intensified form of SE *guarantee*, with the infix of FUCKING/DAMN (cf. ABSOFUCKINGLUTELY; FANFUCKINGTASTIC).

Guat n. [20C] (W.I.) a *Guate*malan. [abbr.]

guava n.[1] [1970s+] (S.Afr.) the buttocks, the posterior (cf. SLIP ON ONE'S GUAVA). [resemblance]

guava n.[2] [1980s] (S.Afr.) South African version of the YUPPIE. [abbr. grown/growing *up and very ambitious*]

gub n. [1970s+] (Aus. Aborigine) a White man (cf. MR GUB). [? SE *garbage* or SE *government*]

guban n. [20C] (Irish) a general term of abuse, esp. an unpleasantly negative critic whose attacks are not based in actual expertise or knowledge. [Irish *gobán*, an old-fashioned incompetent tradesman]

gubbins n. [1910s+] **1** an indefinite noun for any nameless object. **2** a fool, a simpleton. [SE *gubbins*, fragments, esp. of fish; fish-parings]

gubbrow v. [late 19C] (Anglo-Ind.) to bully, to confuse, to worry. [Hind. *gabrao*, to dumbfound]

Gucci n. [20C] (US Black) a poser. [brandname *Gucci*, much beloved by those who rate their own value in terms of the designer labels they can flaunt]

guck n. [1940s+] (orig. US) any form of sticky substance, ointment, cream (cf. GOCK). [echoic]

gucky n. [1970s+] (society) deliberate mispronunciation of Gucci, a favourite designer label for such speakers.

gucky adj. [1960s+] (society) of an event or person as much as of food or drink, sickening, likely to make one vomit. [GUCK + sfx. *-y*]

gud n. [late 17C–mid-18C] God, as used in oaths (cf. COCK n.[1]).

guddha n. [mid-19C–1900s] (Anglo-Ind.) a fool. [synon. Hind. *gadha*]

gudgeon n. [late 16C–mid-19C] a gullible person, one who will 'swallow' anything (cf. GAPE FOR GUDGEONS; SWALLOW A GUDGEON). [SE *gudgeon*, a small freshwater fish, often used as bait]

guee/gee/ghee n. [mid-19C–1900s] (US) a derog. term for a Portuguese person. [abbr.]

guerrilla n. [mid–late 19C] (US) a swindler, a crooked gambler.

guesser n. [[1900s] (N.Z.) a dishonest racing tipster, hired by bookmakers to persuade punters to bet on useless horses.

guessing-stick n. [1950s–70s] a slide-rule; thus [1980s+] *guessing box*, a handheld electronic calculator.

guest of the cross-legged knights, to be phr. [18C–early 19C] to go without one's dinner (cf. DINE WITH DUKE HUMPHREY). [the effigies in the Round Church in the Temple, London]

guff n.[1] [late 19C+] insolence, lies, nonsense, twaddle. [SE *guff*, a puff, a whiff]

guff n.[2] [20C] a fart. [dial. *guff*, an offensive smell]

guff v.[1] [late 19C] (US) to chat. [GUFF n.[1]]

guff/guff off v.[2] [20C] (Aus.) to shirk, to act lazily. [? dial. *guff*, to talk nonsense, to babble]

guffin n. [mid–late 19C] a clumsy fool (cf. GUFFOON). [northern dial.]

guff off see GUFF v.[2].

guffoon n. [late 19C] (Irish) a clumsy fool (cf. GUFFIN).

guggle n. [17C–19C] the windpipe, the throat. [SE *guggle*, to make a gurgling sound, like that of water pouring from a narrow-necked bottle]

guggy n. [20C] (Irish) an egg (cf. GOOG n.[2]). [Irish *gogaí*, nursery term for an egg]

guided missile n. [1970s+] (US Black) the erect penis.

guide-post n. [late 18C–1900s] a clergyman. [he is supposed to guide the congregation to heaven]

guido/guidette n. [1980s+] (US campus) someone acting in an ostentatiously masculine (or feminine) manner. [Ital.

proper name *Guido*; the initial ref. was to the young working-class Italians who live outside Manhattan and come into the city for their entertainment]

guilderhead n. [1970s+] (Ulster) a stupid, clumsy person. [Scot. *guildie*, 'a tall, black-faced, gloomy-looking man' (*EDD*)]

guilt trip n. [1970s+] (US) imposed guilt, esp. on another. [SE *guilt* + TRIP n.[3]]

guilt trip v. [1970s+] (US) **1** to feel guilty. **2** to impose feelings of guilt on someone else. [GUILT TRIP n.]

guinea n.[1] (US) **1** an Italian person, usu. an immigrant to the US (cf. GHINNY). **2** [20C] various other non-Anglo nationalities, usu. Mediterranean, e.g. a Greek, a Portuguese, a Jew. **3** [20C] a foolish man. [18C *guinea*, a Black. The original guineas were Black slaves from the Guinea Coast of Africa, and the term gradually evolved to mean anyone with a notably dark complexion, although it is rarely if ever used to mean a Black in 20C other than in the SE *Guinea Negro*, a mixed-race group native to Maryland, Virginia and West Virginia, who call themselves *Our People* or *Melungeons*]

Guinea n.[2] [20C] (US) euph. for hell, e.g. *phr. go to Guinea* (cf. GINNY GALL). [the far distance of African Guinea]

Guinea n.[3] [20C] (US) a euph. for God, e.g. *swear to Guinea!* [the common use of words with the initial G in this way, e.g. GOSH, GORRY]

guinea bird n. [early 19C] (W.I.) an African-born Black person; so called by the Creoles, who were born in the West Indies. [the state of Guinea]

guinea cadillac n. [1970s] (US) a powered tricycle used in the construction industry to convey concrete on a building site. [GUINEA n.[1] + ironic use of SE *Cadillac*; many big city construction workers are Italians]

guinea-dropper n. [late 17C–early 18C] a confidence trickster who drops counterfeit guineas to ensnare the gullible (cf. GOLD-FINDER n.[2]; RING-DROPPER]

guinea football n. [20C] (US) a large firecracker (cf. DAGO BOMB). [GUINEA n.[1] + SE *football*; i.e. the popularity of fireworks in the Italian community]

guinea gall see GINNY GALL.

guinea gold adj. [18C] sincere, perfect (cf. GOREE). [the golden guineas of the 18C, which were made from Guinea gold]

guinea hen n. [late 16C–early 18C] a courtesan, a prostitute. [pun on SE *guinea hen*/SE *guinea* + HEN n., i.e. a girl who costs a guinea]

guinea pig n. **1** [mid-18C–mid-19C] a general term of opprobrium. **2** [mid-19C] anyone whose fee comes to one guinea (£1.05), e.g. a doctor. **3** [late 19C–1910s] anyone working only part-time, e.g. a company director who only attends board-meetings, a clergyman serving as a deputy. **4** [1970s] (US Und.) an informer, a stool pigeon. [all puns on SE with ref. to their availability for money]

guinea red n. [20C] (US) cheap red wine, possibly homemade (cf. DAGO RED; GHINNY). [GUINEA n.[1] + SE *red* (*wine*); the making of wine by Italian immigrants (and their descendants)]

guineas n. **1** [19C] money of any denomination. **2** [1970s] (US campus) money. [SE *guinea*, a pre-decimal coinage sum worth £1 1s (1.05p)]

guinea ship n. [1920s+] (W.I.) a crowd, a large number of people. [SE *Guinea ship*, a ship bringing slaves – in terribly crowded conditions – from West Africa]

guinea stinker n. [late 19C+] a cheap, malodorous cigar supposedly preferred by Italian-Americans (cf. GHINNY). [GUINEA n.[1] + STINKER n.[1] (3)]

guinea to a gooseberry phr. [late 19C–1900s] the longest possible odds, thus an absolute certainty. [var. on LOMBARD STREET TO A CHINA ORANGE]

guinea trade n. [early 19C] the work of anyone acting as a deputy or locum. [pun on SE *Guinea trade*]

guino/goyno n. [1980s+] (Irish) money. [? SE *guinea*]

guintzer n. [20C] (Aus.) a person, a 'chap'. [GEEZER n.¹ (1) or Yid.]

guinzo n. [19C+] (US) Italian. [GUINEA n.¹]

Guitar Town n. [1970s] (US) Nashville, Tennessee. [the 'home of country music']

guiver/guyver/gyver n.¹ [mid-19C+] (Aus./N.Z.) flattery, insincerity, pretension. [Heb. pride]

guiver n.² [late 19C] a hairstyle, in which the hair is brushed forward over the forehead, affected by Cockney dandies; thus *guiver-lad*, a working-class dandy.

guiver adj. [late 19C] fashionable, smart. [GUIVER n.²]

guiver v. **1** [late 19C] to cheat, to trick. **2** [20C] (Aus./N.Z.) to pretend, to put on airs. [GUIVER n.¹]

gulder see GAULDER.

gulf n. [19C] the vagina (cf. ARBOUR).

gull n. [late 16C–late 19C] a trickster, a cheat. [GULL v.; note *gull*, simpleton, dupe is SE]

gull v. [late 16C–late 19C] to deceive, to fool. [? SE *gull*, a fledgling; thus an innocent. The image is compounded by that of the feeding of the open-mouthed young bird, voraciously swallowing whatever is offered, which in turn echoes SE *gull*, to swallow hungrily]

gulley-/gully-raker n. [19C] **1** the penis. **2** a man having sexual intercourse. **3** a womanizer (cf. KENNEL-RAKER). [? GULLY n.²+ SE *raker* or SAusE *gully-raker*, a cattle whip, a cattle thief]

gull-finch n. [17C] a simpleton, a fool. [SE *gull*, a simpleton, a dupe + *finch*]

gull-groper n. [16C–mid-19C] (Und.) a money-lender who specializes in loaning money – often to gamblers – and then defrauding them by avoiding repayment when due, but rather entrapping them in a legal suit, the only resolution of which is the handing over not of the original loan, but of land or valuables that are worth much more. [GULL + SE *grope*; 19C nautical jargon has *gull-sharper*]

gull-groping n. [16C–18C] the swindling of a fool or innocent. [GULL-GROPER]

gullion n. [20C] (Ulster) a muddy hole, an open sewer. [Irish *góilín*, a creek]

gulliver n. [1990s] (US teen) one who travels a lot. [the book *Gulliver's Travels* (1727) by Jonathan Swift]

gully/gully hole n.¹ [19C] **1** the throat. **2** the vagina (cf. BLACK HOLE n.¹). [(1) food and drink pour down the throat, as they might down a gully; (2) one of many terms equating the vagina with a hole]

gully n.² [1990s] (Black) a woman. [pron. of *girlie* but note GULLY n.¹(2)]

gully v. [mid-19C–1900s] to trick, to fool. [GULL v.]

gully dirt n. [20C] (US) a worthless, contemptible person, one who fails to fit the local norms; esp. in phr. *sorry as gully dirt*.

gully-groper n. [late 19C] (Aus.) a long cattle-whip.

gully-gut n. [mid-16C–19C; 1930s+] a glutton. [20C use is US Black; one can pour food and drink down someone]

gully-jumper n. [20C] (US) a farmer, a peasant (cf. APPLE-KNOCKER n.²).

gully-raker n.¹ see GULLEY-RAKER.

gully-raker n.² [mid-19C] (Aus.) **1** a long whip used to drive cattle. **2** a cattle thief; thus *gully-raking*. [the *gullies* or narrow valleys where the cattle he steals collect]

gully-washer n. [20C] (US) a heavy downpour of rain.

gully-whumper n. [1950s] (US) a surprising example. [SE *gull* + WHOMP v.; i.e. something that will shock a fool]

gulpin n. [mid-19C] a fool. [he will 'gulp down' anything; orig. naut. jargon for a Royal Marine; note Irish *guilpin*, a lout, Scot. *gulpin*, a simpleton, a gullible fool]

gulpy adj. [late 19C–1900s] gullible. [SE *gull* + *gulp*]

gum n.¹ **1** [mid-18C–early 19C] impertinent, abusive talk, chatter. **2** [mid-19C] (US) a trick or deception; thus *come the gum over*, to hoodwink. **3** [1920s–30s] (US) a sneak thief (cf. GUMSHOE). [SE *gum*]

gum n.² [19C+] euph. for God (almighty) and used in various phr., esp. by *gum!* (cf. COCK n.¹). [*God*, or abbr. *God almighty*]

gum/guma n.³ [1930s+] (drugs) opium. [its stickiness]

gum n.⁴ [1980s+] (Irish) taste for, desire. [Scot. *gum*, the palate]

gum v.¹ [mid-19C] (US) to cheat, to delude, to humbug. [GUM n.¹ (2)]

gum v.² (US) **1** [20C] to mess up, spoil; thus *gum the game*, *gum up the works*. **2** [1930s+] to talk nonsense.

gum v.³ [1980s+] (US gay) for a person using dentures to remove them before performing fellatio.

guma see GUM n.³.

gumbah see GOOMBAH.

gumball/gumball light/machine n. [1970s+] **1** (US) the flashing light on a police car. **2** a police car (cf. BUBBLE-GUM MACHINE). [joc. equation of the shape]

gum-beat n. [1940s–50s] (US) frivolous, tedious chatter, complaining. [BEAT ONE'S CHOPS]

gum-beating n. [1930s+] (orig. US) incessant, frivolous, tedious chatter (cf. BEAT ONE'S CHOPS).

gum-beater n. [1940s–70s] (US) a chatterer or complainer (cf. GUM-BEAT). [BEAT ONE'S CHOPS]

gumbler see KNULLER.

gumboot n.¹ see GUMSHOE n.

gumboot n.² [1990s] (N.Z.) rough, forthright, mainly rural language, i.e. that of fishermen, roustabouts etc. [the SE *gum-boots* they are seen as wearing]

gumbrain/gumhead n. [1950s+] (US) an idiot (cf. BAKE-BRAIN). [GUM v.² + sfx. -BRAIN]

gum-bumping n. [20C] (US) arguing. [BEAT ONE'S GUMS]

gumby n.¹ [1960s+] a fool, an idiot. [the character in BBC TV's *Monty Python's Flying Circus* (1969–74); echoic of his monosyllabic incoherence]

gumby n.² [1980s] (US campus) a large quantity.

gumbyhead n. [1980s+] (US campus) someone who does something stupid. [GUMBY n.¹ + sfx. -HEAD (1)]

gum-chum n. [1940s] an American soldier stationed in the UK. [his plentiful supplies of chewing-gum]

gum-digger n. [1930s+] (Aus./N.Z.) a dentist; thus *gum-digging*, dentistry.

gumdrop n. [1970s+] (drugs) **1** barbiturate, esp. seconal. **2** any kind of drug available in pill or capsule form.

gumdrop adj. [late 19C] (US) sweet and silly. [play on SE]

gum-flapping n. [1990s] empty, boastful chatter. [BEAT ONE'S GUMS]

gumfoot see GUMSHOE n.

gumfudgeon n. [mid-19C] (US) nonsense. [ety. unknown]

gum game n. [mid–late 19C] (US) a trick or dodge; thus *come the gum-game*, to deceive, to subject to trickery. [the activity of the opossum, which, in its efforts to elude the hunter, climbs to the very top of a gum tree, thus taking itself beyond the hunter's reach and, since it was hunted at night, beyond his eyesight]

gum-gardening n. [1990s] working as a dental hygienist (cf. GUM-DIGGER).

gumhead see GUMBRAIN.

gum heel n. [1960s+] (US prison) a policeman (cf. GUMSHOE; RUBBER HEEL).

gumjob n. [1980s+] (US) fellatio (cf. GUM v.³). [var. on BLOW JOB]

gummagy/gummidgy adj. [mid-19C] used of peevish, self-pitying, and pessimistic people. [*Mrs Gummidge*, a character in Dickens' *David Copperfield* (1850)]

gummed adj. [late 19C] (US) old, geriatric. [old people tend to lose their teeth]

gummer n.[1] [mid–late 19C] an old, toothless pit-bull or other fighting dog.

gummer n.[2] [1990s] (US) an act of fellatio from an old, toothless person (cf. HUMMER n.[6]).

gummidgy see GUMMAGY.

gummy n.[1] **1** [19C] a fool, a tedious person. **2** [mid-19C+] a toothless person.

gummy n.[2] [late 19C] a dandy, a swell. [Fr. *gommeux*, dandy]

gummy n.[3] [1950s+] (N.Z.) a *gumboot*. [abbr.]

gummy adj.[1] [mid-18C–mid-19C] puffy, swollen, esp. of the ankles of a horse or human, also of a clumsy drunkard. [orig. dial.; ult. ety. unknown]

gummy adj.[2] [1980s+] (US drugs) used of one who has become lethargic after smoking cannabis. [the rubberiness of their movements]

gummy! excl. [late 19C+] a mild oath. [var. of BY GUM!]

gump n.[1] **1** [18C+] a fool; thus *gump-headed*, foolish. **2** (US prison) a passive homosexual, the target of predatory prison homosexuals. [Yorks. dial. *gump*, homely, parochial, awkward, well-meaning; the role of a pathetic *gump* was adopted as a trademark by the 20C UK comedian Norman Wisdom (b.1915)]

gump n.[2] [1910s+] (US) a chicken, a fowl; esp. a sick or dying chicken given by a dealer to a begging tramp. [? its innate stupidity; ? link to Scots *gump*, an over-grown child]

gump n.[3] [1940s–60s] intelligence, native wit. [abbr. GUMPTION]

gumption n. [early 18C+] intelligence, natural wit, shrewdness. [18C dial. *gawm*, understanding, thus ? *gawmtion* (*gawm* also gives *gormless*, stupid, doltish) or Scot. *rumgumption*/*rumblegumption*, common sense]

gumptious adj. [19C+] **1** ambitious, aggressive. **2** proud, conceited. **3** excellent, first-rate. [GUMPTION]

gum-puncher n. [20C] a dentist (cf. GUM-SMASHER; GUMTICKLER n.[1]).

gums n. [mid–late 19C] (US) rubber-soled shoes. [*elastic gum*, India rubber]

gumshoe/gumboot/gumfoot/gumshoer n. [20C] **1** a private detective or police officer. **2** (US) a sneak thief or prowler. [lit. or fig. rubber-soled shoes used for creeping around, whether as investigator or thief]

gumshoe v. [1950s+] to creep around, esp. used of policemen or private detectives. [GUMSHOE n.]

gumshoe artist n. [1930s+] (US) a plain-clothes detective. [GUMSHOE n. + ARTIST n.[2]]

gumshoer see GUMSHOE n.

gum-smasher n. [mid-19C–1920s] a dentist (cf. GUM-PUNCHER).

gumshoe worker n. [1900s] (US) a private detective, a policeman. [GUMSHOE n. + SE *worker*]

gumsuck v. [19C+] (orig. US campus) to kiss (cf. SUCK FACE). [SE *gum* + *suck*]

gum-sucker n. [mid–late 19C+] (Aus.) **1** a European native Australian (esp. a Victorian) or a Tasmanian. **2** a fool or simpleton. [the proliferation of gum trees]

gum-sucking see JOWL-SUCKING.

gum-tickler n.[1] [early 19C] (orig. US) a dentist (cf. GUM-PUNCHER).

gum-tickler n.[2] [early–mid-19C] (US) an alcoholic drink.

gum up the works, to phr. [1910s+] to make a mess, to cause an obstruction. [GUM v.[2]]

gun n.[1] [mid-17C–late 18C] a flagon of ale; thus *in the gun*, drunk. ['perhaps from an allusion to a vessel called a *gun*, used for ale in the universities' (Grose, 1785)]

gun n.[2] **1** [late 17C; 19C+] the penis (cf. ARSE-OPENER; BAZOOKA;

HOGLEG; PEACEMAKER n.[1]; PIECE n.[4]; PISTOL; ROD n.[1]; SHOOTING IRON; SHOOTING STICK). **2** [late 19C] a general pej. term, e.g. a 'rascal', a 'terror'; thus [1920s] *great gun*, a cheery scamp. **3** [late 19C+] (US drugs) a hypodermic syringe; thus *gun-toter*, one who uses such a syringe (cf. ARTILLERY n.[1].). **4** [20C] an important person (cf. BIG GUN). **5** [1910s+] (US) throttle power; thus *give her the (full) gun*, to accelerate; *cut the gun*, turn off the motor. **6** [1920s+] (US) a camera, esp. a film camera.

gun n.[3] **1** [late 17C–late 18C] a lie. **2** [early 18C] a strange and unaccountable story.

gun n.[4] [18C–early 19C] a tobacco pipe.

gun n.[5] [mid-19C–1930s] a thief. [abbr. GONNOF]

gun n.[6] [late 19C+] gonorrhoea. [abbr./pron.]

gun n.[7] [late 19C+] (Aus./N.Z.) the fastest shearer in a shed (cf. DRUMMER n.[4]). [he SE *shoots down* the sheep]

gun n.[8] [1930s+] (US) a gunman, a gangster, esp. in phr. *hired gun*, a professional gunman who kills, wounds or merely intimidates as required by his employer. [metonymy]

gun v.[1] **1** [19C] to stare at, to look over, to examine. **2** [early 19C+] (Und.) to watch, to look out for; thus *on the gun*, on the look-out. **3** [1930s–40s] (US Black) to stare aggressively or pointedly (cf. GUN FOR). [the aggression of the stare equates with a pointed gun]

gun v.[2] **1** [mid-19C–1930s] (Und.) to steal; thus *on the gun*, to be engaged in theft. **2** [late 19C+] (US) to shoot someone. [lit. or fig. use of a weapon]

gun v.[3] [1910s+] to rev an engine hard. [GUN n.[2] (5)]

gun artist n. [1920s] (US) a Western gun-fighter (cf. GUN DOG). [SE *gun* + ARTIST n.[2]]

gunboat n.[1] [late 19C] (US) an armed stage-coach.

gunboat n.[2] [1920s–70s] (US tramp) a water bucket made from a gallon can. [its unwieldiness]

gunboat n.[3] (US) [1940s] a river-boat being used as a brothel. [GUN n.[1] (1) + SE *boat* + pun]

gunboats n. [mid-19C+] (US) big shoes. [SE *gunboat*, considered oversized and awkward by sailors, as are the shoes]

gun boss n. [1940s] (US) the leader of a gang of Western gunmen.

gun-bull n. [1920s–60s] (US) an armed prison guard. [SE *gun* + BULL n.[10]]

gun-case n. [mid–late 19C] a judge's tippet, a scarlet cloth from the right shoulder to the left side, held in by the sash or girdle. [resemblance to the way in which one wears a SE *guncase*]

Gundaroo bullock n. [20C] (Aus.) cooked koala meat. [*Gundaroo*, a town in southeast New South Wales]

gundiguts n. [late 17C–early 19C] a fat person. [Scot. *gundie*, greedy + -GUTS sfx.]

gun dog n. [1940s–50s] (US) a Western gun-fighter (cf. GUN ARTIST). [SE *gun* + DOG n.[4]]

gun down v. [1960s+] (US) to reject a suitor or to refute facts.

gun-fanner n. [1900s] (US) a Western gun-fighter. [gunfighters supposedly 'fanned' the hammer of their pistol to increase the speed of shooting]

gun-fighter n. (US) **1** [1950s+] a wild, undisciplined fighter. **2** [1960s+] an aggressively forceful political candidate or campaigner.

gun-flint n. [late 19C] (US) a native of Rhode Island. [trad. nickname]

gun-foot n. [1940s] (W.I.) long trousers, esp. narrow ones (cf. BID-DIMS). [the narrow, tubular trousers, reminiscent of a shotgun barrel]

gun for v. [20C] (orig. US) **1** to look for someone with the intent of creating some form (violent or otherwise) of confrontation. **2** to be sexually interested in a person. [the image of a Western gun-fighter pursuing a victim or rival]

gunga/gonga/gunger *n.* [1940s+] (N.Z.) the anus. [? GONG n.[1], but note Kipling poem 'Gunga Din' (1892): 'though I've belted you and flayed you...', i.e. on the backside]

Gunga Din *n.* **1** [20C] the chin (cf. ERROL FLYNN). **2** (Aus.) gin. [rhy. sl.]

gun gang *n.* [20C] (US Und.) the chain gang. [they work 'under the gun']

gunge *n.*[1] **1** [1960s+] a sticky mess, poss. when in the form of gravy or sauce, but equally often merely resembling such foods (cf. GRUNGE n.). **2** [1960s+] (US) a skin irritation of the male genitals, a mythical disease believed to make a man rot from his genitals outwards, prevalent among soldiers in Vietnam.

gunge *n.*[2] [1970s+] (US drugs) potent marijuana or heroin (cf. GANJA; GUNJEH). [abbr. GUNGEON]

gunge *v.* [1960s+] to clog up with a sticky or messy substance, to become clogged up. [GUNGE n.[2]]

gunjeh *n.* [late 19C] (US drugs) potent marijuana or heroin (cf. GUNGE n.[1]). [var. on GANJA]

gungeon/gungion/gungun *n.* [1940s+] potent marijuana, usu. from Mexico or Africa (cf. BLACK GUNGEON). [? GANJA]

gunger *see* GUNGA.

gung-ho *adj.* [1940s+] (orig. US) often of soldiers or sportsmen, enthusiastic, usu. aggressively so. [Chinese *keng ho*, awe-inspiring (lit. 'more fiery'). The term was initially popularized as the motto of the US Marine Corps Second Raider Battalion, introduced there in 1942 by Lieut. Col. Evans F. Carlson]

gung-ho *adv.* [1940s+] enthusiastically, vigorously. [GUNG-HO adj.]

gungion/gungun *see* GUNGEON.

gungy *adj.* [1960s+] **1** sticky, messy, slimy. **2** second-rate, inferior; of food, spoilt. [GUNGE n.[2] (1)]

gun hand *n.* [1950s+] (US) a gun-fighter. [on model of SE *farm hand*]

gun happy *adj.* [1950s+] (US) prone to frequent shooting of guns (cf. TRIGGER HAPPY).

gunhawk *n.* [1940s+] (US) an expert gun-fighter (cf. GUN-SHARP).

gunja *see* GANJA.

gunjie *n.* [1990s] (Native Aus.) a White person. [ety. unknown]

gunk *n.*[1] **1** [20C] (Ulster) an unpleasant shock, a major disappointment. **2** [1940s+] (US) nonsense. **3** [1960s+] (US) a fool, a dullard (cf. GONK). **4** a school child who has been rejected by its fellows (cf. GOGGY). [? Irish *gonc*, to snub, to rebuff]

gunk *n.*[2] [1930s+] (orig. US) a viscous or liquid substance (cf. GOO; GUNGE). [orig. a proprietary name patented in 1932 by A.F. Curran Co. for 'liquid soaps and liquid cleaners for hard surfaced materials or articles']

gunk up *v.* [1960s+] (US) to mess up with viscous or liquid substances. [GUNK n.[2]]

gunky *adj.* [1970s+] (US) messed up with or looking like gunk. [GUNK n.[2] + sfx. -y]

gun-maker *n.* [1900s–30s] (US) (Und.) an older thief who instructs young criminals, esp. pickpockets. [GUN n.[5] + pun]

gun moll *n.* [1900s–40s] a female, gun-carrying gangster or female accomplice of a gun man. [SE *gun* + MOLL]

gun-mouth/gun-mouth pants *n.* [20C] (W.I.) a (young) man's trousers that are too short and narrow (cf. BID-DIMS).

gunner *n.*[1] [early 18C] 'Those who recount strange Accidents and Circumstances which have no Manner of Foundation in Truth, when they design to do Mischief are comprehended under the Appellation of Gunners ... The Gunner is destructive, and hated' (*The Tatler* no. 88, 1709) (cf. GUNSTER).

gunner *n.*[2] (US campus) **1** [1920s–60s] a zealous woman-chaser. **2** [1970s+] a very competitive student. [SE *gun for*]

gunner *n.*[3] [1930s] the person who is throwing the dice in a game of dice craps (cf. SHOOTER).

gunny *n.*[1] [1930s] (US) a gunman, a gangster. [SE *gun*]

gunny *n.*[2] [1960s] (drugs) marijuana. [GUNGEON]

gunpoke/gunpoker *n.* [1900s–30s] (US) a gun-fighter. [on model of *cowpoke*]

gunpowder *n.*[1] [late 17C–early 19C] an old woman. [presumably a cantankerous one who 'goes off with a bang'. In *Henry IV Pt 1* Shakespeare uses the term in such a manner to describe the irascible 'gunpowder Percy']

gunpowder *n.*[2] **1** [mid-18C] a fiery drink (cf. GLIM n.[2]). **2** [1900s–30s] (US Black) gin. [the short-lived 18C UK use was revived in US Black use in 20C]

gunpowder tea *n.* [mid-19C] (US) gunfire. [note British Army sl. *gunfire*, an early morning cup of tea served out to troops before going on first parade]

guns *n.* [1950s+] **1** (US prison) fists. **2** (US campus) biceps. **3** (US Black) the female breasts (cf. ARTILLERY n.[3]).

gunsel *see* GONSEL.

gun-sharp/shark *n.* [20C] (US) an expert gun-fighter. [on model of SE *cardsharp/shark*]

gunshot *n.* [1980s+] reversing a cannabis cigarette, placing the lit end between one's lips, then exhaling the smoke into another person's mouth (cf. BLOWBACK n.; SHOTGUN).

gunslick *n.* [1930s–50s] (US) an expert gun-fighter (cf. GUN-SHARP; GUNSLINGER). [SE *gun* + SLICK adj.]

gun-slinger *n.* **1** [1930s+] (US) a gunman, esp. in the (fictional) 'Wild West'. **2** [1990s] (US campus) a woman who rejects a man's attention rudely. [both 'shoot down' their target]

gunsmith *n.* **1** [mid-19C] a thief. **2** [1930s] (US) an older thief who trains young criminals (cf. GUN-MAKER). [GUN n.[5]]

gunster *n.* [early 18C] 'Those who recount strange Accidents and Circumstances which have no Manner of Foundation in Truth, ... when they endeavour only to surprise and entertain, they are distinguished by the Name of Gunsters ... the Gunster [is] innocent, and laughed at.' (*The Tatler* no. 88 1709) (cf. GUNNER n.[1]).

gun talk *n.* [1920s] (US) thieves' cant. [the language of those who carry guns]

gunterpake *n.* [20C] (Ulster) a fool. [ety. unknown; ? link to Scot. *gant*, to gape]

gun-thrower *n.* [1910s–50s] (US) a gun-fighter as found in the real/fictional 'Wild West'.

gun-tosser *n.* [1950s] (US) a gun-fighter as found in the real/fictional 'Wild West'.

gun-toter *n.* [1920s–30s] (US) a gun-fighter as found in the real/fictional 'Wild West'.

guntz *n.*[1] [1950s+] the whole lot. [synon. Ger. *ganz*]

guntz *n.*[2] [1980s] (US) a worthless person. [abbr. GONSEL]

gun up *v.* [1960s+] (US prison) to get oneself ready for a fight. [GUNS n. (1), although many fights employ some form of knife]

gun-wadding *n.* [1910s–50s] (US) soft white bread.

gunyah *n.* [late 19C] (Aus.) a White person's hut or house. [SA *gunyah*, an aboriginal hut or other dwelling; as sl. the term is thus derisively racist]

gunzel *v.* (US Black) to fight. [? misreading of GONSEL]

gup/gup-gup *n.*[1] [mid-19C] gossip. [Hind. *gap*, prattle, which borrowed in turn from the Turkish *gep* or *geb*, word, saying or talk and the Persian *guftan* or *guptan*, to say. The word made its way to the UK *c.*1868, the year in which a highly critical account of South Indian society was published, under the pseudonym of 'Gup']

gup *n.*[2] [1930s–40s] (Aus.) a fool, a simpleton. [? GUP n.[1] or SE *gulp*]

guppie *n.* [1980s+] (US gay) gay urban professionals, or gay YUPPIES. [abbr.]

gup-gup see GUP n.[1].

guppy adj. [1930s+] (Aus.) silly, foolish. [GUP n.[2]]

guppy-gobbler n. [1960s] (US) a catholic (cf. MACKEREL-SNAPPER). [the Catholic 'fish-day' of Friday]

gurgle n. [20C] (Aus./US) liquor, a drink. [SE gurgle, to swallow]

gurk v. [1920s+] **1** to belch. **2** (Aus.) to break wind. [echoic]

gurly adj. [20C] boisterous, ill-tempered. [synon. Scot.]

gurrawaun n. [mid-19C] (Anglo-Ind.) a coachman. [Hind. gari, a cart or carriage]

gurrell n. [mid-19C] a fob, a small pocket either in the waistband of the breeches or, latterly, in the waistcoat. [? link to dial. gorrell; gurrel, a glutton, a fat-stomached person]

gurrier n. [1950s+] (Irish) a street urchin. [? Fr. guerrier, a fighter; ? link to Fr. argot guéri, free]

gurry n. [16C] diarrhoea. [JERE]

gush n.[1] **1** [mid-19C] a whiff, a smell. **2** [mid-19C] (US) a good deal of a commodity. [both 'gush out']

gush n.[2] [mid-19C] an objectionably effusive or sentimental display of feeling, esp. as spoken. [GUSH v.]

gush v. [mid-19C+] to speak in a cloying sentimental manner; thus gushing, an extravagant display of feeling or sentiment.

gusher n. [mid-late 19C] one who talks to excess, uttering usu. insincere and sentimental remarks. [GUSH v.]

gusset n. [17C] **1** a woman. **2** the vagina. [SE gusset, a triangular piece of material sewn into garments to make it easier to move, typically at the armpit or the crotch]

gusseteer n. [19C] a womanizer. [GUSSET]

gusset-nuzzler n. [1990s] a lesbian.

gusset of the arse n. [late 18C–early 19C] the cleft of the buttocks.

gusset typing n. [1990s] female masturbation; thus [1990s] gusset typist, a woman who masturbates.

gussie n. **1** [late 19C+] (Aus.) a male homosexual. **2** [1900s–40s] (US) a weak, effeminate man. [proper name Augustus, seen as stereotypically effeminate]

gussied up adj. [1940s+] dressed up, esp. for a night out (cf. DOLLED OUT). [? GUSSIE]

gussies n. [1950s] women's lace underwear. [the tennis player 'Gorgeous Gussie' Moran, who favoured such knickers]

gussy up v. [1940s+] to smarten up, to dress up. [GUSSIE; the implication is usu. of excessive smartness and, in a man, effeminacy]

gusto n.[1] [1960s+] (US Black) beer. [SE gusto as used in the 1966 advertising slogan for Schlitz beer, 'Schlitz. Grab for the gusto!' an abbr. of the orig. line 'You only go around once in life, so grab for all the gusto you can']

gusto n.[2] [1980s+] (US Black) money.

gut n.[1] **1** [19C] gluttony. **2** [19C] a glutton. **3** [1910s–20s] (US Und.) a sausage.

gut n.[2] **1** [1910s+] (orig. US campus) an easy task. **2** [1910s+] (US campus) an easy course. **3** [1920s+] (US) a certainty. [SE gut; i.e. the use of the instincts rather than that of the brain in performing the task (1) or course (2), or in making the assessment (3)]

Gut, the n.[3] [1940s+] Strait Street, Valetta, the centre of Malta's red-light district.

gut n.[4] [1960s+] (US) the main street; thus shoot/drag the gut, to drive along or cruise the main street. [SE gut, a narrow passage or lane]

gut adj. **1** [1910s+] (US campus) easy. **2** [1950s+] (orig. US) based on instinct, feeling. **3** [1960s+] of fundamental importance. [one knows 'in one's guts']

gut v. [17C–1900s] **1** to eat like a glutton. **2** to empty, esp. in phr. [18C–20C] gut a quart pot, to drink the pot to the dregs; [late 17C–19C] gut a house, to empty a house of its furnishings.

gutache/guts-ache n. [early 19C+] a stomach-ache.

gut bomb n. [1960s+] (US) a very greasy hamburger or similar food. [its deleterious effects]

gutbucket n.[1] **1** [late 19C–1960s] (orig. US Black) a very basic, raw, unsophisticated style of jazz (cf. BARRELHOUSE adj.). **2** [1930s–60s] (US Black) a bucket used to carry food or drink, thus inferior liquor. **3** [1940s–50s] (US Black) a low place or dive. **4** [1960s+] (US) a washtub bass. **5** [1970s] a jazz musician. [lit. + fig. derivations of saloon use gutbucket, the small bucket to catch drippings or 'gutterings' from the barrels that is found in cheap bars and saloons. Such jazz was played in these 'low' saloons]

gutbucket n.[2] **1** [1930s+] (US) a pompous fat person. **2** [1940s] (US) a toilet. **3** [1950s+] (US) the belly.

gut-burner see GUT-WARMER.

gut-buster n. **1** [1950s+] (N.Z.) a very steep hill. **2** [1980s+] (US) a very funny joke eliciting hysterical laughter. [it 'busts one's guts']

gut-butcher see GUT-REAMER.

gut check n. [1970s+] (US) a quick reassessment of strategy and stiffening of morale. [orig. sporting use]

gut-eater n. [1920s–60s] (US West) a Native American. [their taste for offal, despised by Whites]

gut entrance n. [19C] the vagina (cf. BELLY DALE).

gut food n. [1930s–40s] (US Black) fallen arches, i.e. flat feet. [ety. unknown]

gutfoundered adj. [mid-17C–late 18C] extremely hungry. [SE gut + founder]

gut-fucker/-monger/-sticker n. [late 19C–1900s] a sodomite (cf. GUT-REAMER). [SE gut + FUCKER/sfx. -monger/SE sticker]

gut-head n. [early 17C] one who is stupefied by an excess of food. [GUT n.[1] + sfx. -HEAD (2)]

gut-heater see GUT-WARMER.

gut-hooks n. [1930s+] (US) spurs.

gut it v. [1910s+] (US campus) to stay up all night working without any amphetamines for stimulation but purely through strength of will and character. [GUTS]

gutless adj. [20C] cowardly; thus gutless wonder, a total coward.

gut-monger see GUT-FUCKER.

gut/guts out v. [1960s+] (US) to endure courageously. [GUTS]

gut-piece n. [1960s] (US) the abdomen.

gut plunge on butch n. [1920s–40s] (US) scrounging for meat from a butcher's shop by a tramp.

gut pudding n. [19C] a sausage. [sausages were orig. encased in animal gut]

gut-puller n. [mid-late 19C] a poulterer.

gut-reamer/-butcher/-stretcher/-stuffer n. [1920s–30s] (US) a pederast (cf. GUT-FUCKER).

gut-ripper n. [1930s–40s] (US) any kind of knife used as a weapon.

gut-robber n. [20C] (US) a cook, esp. a bad one. [orig. logging jargon]

gutrot n. [20C] **1** cheap wine or spirits. **2** unpalatable food. [its presumed effect on one's innards]

guts n.[1] **1** [late 14C+] the stomach. **2** [late 17C+] a notably fat person; thus tub of guts, a grossly obese person. **3** [late 17C+] a glutton. **4** [mid-18C+] insides, contents.

guts n.[2] **1** [early 19C+] energy, vigour, power in performance. **2** [19C+] courage, bravery, staying power (cf. BELLY).

guts n.[3] **1** [late 19C; 1960s+] the source of true feelings; thus at gut level, instinctively. **2** [20C] (orig. Aus.) the facts, the information, esp. good guts, reliable information. **3** [20C] the essence of a matter, the underlying meaning.

guts n.[4] [1910s–30s] (US Und.) the undercarriage of railroad trains on which tramps hitched a ride.

guts v. [late 19C+] (Aus.) to overeat. [GUTS n.[1]]

-guts *sfx.* [late 16C+] a person (cf. BLABBERGUTS; CLEVERGUTS; DOUBLE GUTS; DOUGHGUTS; FAT-GUTS; FULL-GUTS; FORTY-GUTS; GABBY-GUTS; GIGGLY-GUTS; GREASY GUTS; GREEDY-GUT; GRUMBLE-GUTS; GUNDIGUTS; GUZZLE GUTS; LUSTY-GUTS; POSSUM-GUTS; POT-GUTS; PUFF GUTS; ROTTEN-GUTS; RUSTY-GUTS; SHEEP-GUTS; SKIN-A-GUTS; WIMP-GUTS; WORRYGUTS). [metonymy]

gutsache see GUTACHE.

guts and garbage *n.* [late 18C–mid-19C] a very fat man or woman.

guts ball *n.* [1960s+] (US) **1** any kind of fiercely aggressive and competitive ball game. **2** any action requiring aggression, courage and determination. [GUTS n.⁴]

gutsball *adj.* [1960s+] (US) plucky, courageous. [GUTS BALL n.]

gut-scraper *n.* [late 18C–19C] a fiddle player, a violinist (cf. TORMENTOR OF CATGUT). [the violin's catgut strings]

gutser/gutzer *n.*[1] [20C] (Aus.) **1** a heavy fall, a collision; thus *come a gutser*, to trip over and fall; *bring one a gutser*, to engineer someone's downfall. **2** a disappointment, a let-down.

gutser/gutzer *n.*[2] [1910s+] a greedy person. [GUTS n.¹]

gutsful *n.* [1920s+] (orig. Aus./N.Z.) a sufficiency, quite as much of anything as one wants or cares to take (cf. BELLYFUL). [GUTS n.¹ + SE *full*]

gutsful of grunts *phr.* [1910s+] (Aus.) an unpleasant person.

guts high see GUTS UP.

gut-shoot *v.* [mid-19C+] (US) to shoot in the stomach; thus *gut-shot*, wounded in the stomach.

gutso *n.* [1950s+] a fat person. [GUTS n.¹ (2) + sfx. -O]

guts out see GUT OUT.

gutstick *n.* [1970s] (US Black) the penis (cf. GUT WRENCH).

gut-sticker see GUT-FUCKER.

gut-stretcher see GUT-REAMER.

gut-struggle *n.* [1920s] (US) a dance that involves the partners being physically very close.

gut-stuffer see GUT-REAMER.

guts up *v.* [mid-19C+] (Aus.) to eat. [GUTS v.]

guts up/high *adj.* [1950s+] (US) fearless. [GUTS n.²]

gutsy *n.* [late 19C+] a fat man. [GUTS n.¹ (2)+ sfx. -y]

gutsy *adj.* [late 19C+] **1** tough, spirited, brave; thus *gutsiness*, courage, spirit. **2** greedy, very hungry. [GUTS n.² + sfx. -y]

gutta-percha *n.* [late 19C–1910s] (Aus.) an inhabitant of the state of Victoria. [? the prevalence of the gutta-percha tree (*Isonaudra Gutta*) in the state]

gutted *adj.*[1] [early 19C–1900s] impoverished, without money.

gutted *adj.*[2] [1960s+] deeply disappointed, sick and tired, fed up, utterly depressed. [abbr. of phr. *sick to one's guts*, the term originated in prison use, but has become widespread since mid-1970s]

gutter *n.*[1] [19C] the vagina (cf. ARBOUR).

gutter *n.*[2] [1960s+] (drugs) a vein into which a drug is injected.

gutter alley *n.* [17C–19C] the throat (cf. GUTTER LANE).

gutter-blood *n.* [mid-19C] **1** a lout, a hoodlum. **2** a parvenu, a vulgar man who puts on airs. [SE *gutter*, low class + BLOOD n.¹]

gutter-chaunter *n.* [mid–late 19C] a street-singer. [SE *gutter* + CHANTER n.²]

gutter-gripper *n.* [1950s+] (Aus.) a motorist who drives with one hand stuck through the open window, gripping the gutter that runs around the car's roof.

gutter hotel *n.* [late 19C] (tramp) the open air.

gutter hype/junkie *n.* [1930s–40s] (drugs) an addict who relies on others to obtain drugs. [SE *gutter*, low class + HYPE n.² (2)/JUNKIE]

gutter-kid *n.* [late 19C] a street urchin.

gutter lane *n.* [late 17C–18C] the throat. [? proper name

Gutter Lane, a small street in 17C London and the source of phr. *go down Gutter Lane*, to be a drunkard or glutton. E.P., however, suggests links to Lat. *guttur*, the throat and to Devon dial. *gutter*, to eat greedily, as well as to GUTTLE and GUZZLE]

gutter-merchant *n.* [1910s–20s] an itinerant street salesman.

gutter-prowler *n.* [19C] a small-time thief.

gut through *v.* [1970s+] (US) to endure courageously (cf. GUT OUT). [GUTS n.²]

guttie/gutty *n.* [19C] **1** a glutton. **2** a very fat person. **3** (Irish) one who has no redeeming features, a street urchin. [GUTS n.¹]

gutties *n.* [20C] (Ulster) plimsolls, trainers. [SE *gutta-percha*, a tree (*Isonaudra Gutta*) the juice of which is used in the manufacture]

guttle *v.* [early 18C] to drink alcohol. [synon. dial.]

gutty *n.* see GUTTIE.

gutty *adj.*[1] (US Black) [1930s–40s] raw, unsophisticated (cf. STREET n.³). [SE *gutter*, thus the lifestyle of those who lived 'in the gutter']

gutty *adj.*[2] [1940s+] tough, spirited, brave. [GUTSY adj.]

gut-wagon *n.* [1920s+] (US) a truck that carries cattle carcasses.

gut-warmer/-burner/-heater *n.* [1940s+] (US) a strong alcoholic drink.

gut-winder *n.* [mid-19C] (US) a bullet wound in the abdomen.

gut-wrench *n.* [1940s+] (US) the penis (cf. GUTSTICK).

gutzer see GUTSER.

Guv *n.* [mid-19C+] a general term of address, usu. to someone seen as or actually higher in the social order (cf. GOVERNOR; GUVNOR).

guvnor/guvner *n.* [mid-19C+] **1** a boss, an important, influential person. **2** a general term of address (cf. GUV).

guy *n.*[1] **1** [19C] a fool. **2** [early 19C] a dark lantern; thus *stow the guy*, cover or douse the lantern. **3** [mid-19C] a crimp, one who tricks men into joining the navy. **4** [mid-19C–1910s] (US) a comical fellow, a smart aleck. **5** [mid-19C–1910s] (US) a trick or hoax. **6** [late 19C–1930s] an act of running off, of leaving surreptitiously, usu. in phr. *do a guy, give the guy to*, to slip away (cf. GUY-A-WHACK adj.). [fig. uses of the neg. image of *Guy* Fawkes (1570–1606), leader of the Gunpowder Plot of 1605]

guy *n.*[2] **1** [late 19C+] (US) a man or boy; thus *the main guy*, the man in authority. **2** [1920s+] (US) a woman. **3** [1970s+] (US) an object, thing or an animal. **4** [1980s+] a general term of address, orig. among young UK Blacks, and now in general teen use (cf. MAN).

guy *n.*[3] [late 19C+] a walk, thus an expedition or journey. [rhy. sl. *Guy Fawkes* = walk]

guy *n.*[4] [20C] (US) euph. for God (cf. GORRY; GOSH).

guy *n.*[5] **1** [1910s+] (Aus.) a fool. **2** [1980s+] (US campus) an incompetent, an inadequate (cf. NERD). [parody of the usual male characteristics]

guy *adj.* [1990s] (US) particularly or only of interest to men; thus *it's a guy thing*.

guy/guy off *v.* [late 19C] to run off, to go away. [GUY n.¹ (6)]

guy-a-whack *n.* [1910s+] (Aus.) a defaulting bookmaker. [GUY n.¹ (6)]

guy-a-whack *adj.* [20C] (Aus.) useless, incompetent. [ety. unknown; *AND* suggests ext. of GUY n.¹ (6) + *a-whack* as var. on SE *away*]

guy-a-whack *v.* [late 19C–1910s] (Aus.) to run off, to leave quickly. [GUY n.¹ (6)]

guyver see GUIVER.

guzinters *n.* [1910s+] (Aus.) an animal's innards. [SE *goes into* the animal]

guzunder *n.* [20C] a chamberpot. [it *goes under* the bed]

guzzery *n.* [late 19C+] (US) a cheap saloon (cf. GROGGERY; GUZZLE SHOP).

guzzle *n.* [late 17C+] **1** the throat (cf. GOOZLE). **2** a swig, a gulp. **3** liquor; thus *guzzling*, drinking heavily. **4** beer. [? OF *gosiller*, to vomit or to chatter + OF *gosier*, throat]

guzzle *v.* **1** [mid–late 19C] to swindle. **2** [1900s–60s] to strangle, to throttle, to murder. **3** [1930s] (Und.) to arrest. **4** [1930s] to indulge in sexual foreplay, to 'neck'. [lit. + fig. uses of GUZZLE *n.*]

guzzled *adj.* [1930s] (US) drunk. [GUZZLE *n.*]

guzzle guts *n.* [late 18C–early 19C] a drunkard. [GUZZLE *v.* (1) + sfx. -GUTS]

guzzler *n.* [1920s] (US) a hopeless case.

guzzle shop/guzzlery *n.* [late 19C+] (US) a cheap saloon or bar. [GUZZLE *v.* (1) + SE *shop*]

guzzump *see* GAZUMP.

g.v. *n.* [1900s–10s] a governor. [abbr.]

gwaai *n.* [1980s+] (S.Afr.) **1** tobacco. **2** a cigarette, a 'smoke'. [Zulu *ugwayi*, tobacco, snuff]

gwaan! *excl.* (W.I./UK Black teen) a term of encouragement and appreciation, i.e. go ahead! get going! [lit. *go on!*]

gwat *n.* [1990s] term used to describe a woman's genitalia. [? link to TWAT]

gweeb/gweep/gweebo *n.* [1970s+] (US campus) a person entirely lacking in social skills and style. [var. of DWEEB]

gweva *n.* [1960s+] (S.Afr. township) a bootlegger (cf. MAILER). [Xhosa *igweva*, an illicit diamond buyer]

gwimp *n.* [1970s] (US campus) a socially inept person. [GWEEB + WIMP *n*]

G-woman *n.* [1980s+] (US) a female F.B.I. agent (cf. G-MAN).

gybe/glybe *n.* [mid-16C–18C] a written paper, esp. a counterfeit pass or license, carried by many of the mendicant villains (cf. BENE-GYBE; JARKMAN). [ety. unknown; E.P. suggests Ger. *schreiben*, a writing; if so then also ? SE *scribe*]

gybe *v.* [late 17C–18C] to whip, to beat; thus *gybed*, whipped. [SE *gybe*, for a sail to swing from one side to the other]

Gyle *n.* [late 19C] the Ar*gyle* Rooms, Windmill Street, London. [abbr.]

gymnasium *n.* [17C] the vagina (cf. APHRODISIACAL TENNIS COURT).

gym rat *n.* [1970s+] (US) a gym and basketball enthusiast. [SE *gym* + RAT *n.*[3] (5)]

gynae *n.* [1940s+] **1** *gynae*cology. **2** a *gynae*cologist. [abbr.]

gyp/gip *n.* (orig. US) **1** [late 19C+] a thief. **2** [1910s+] an act of deception, a fraud or hoax. **3** [1910s+] a cheat, one who fails to pay his due debts. [abbr. SE *gypsy* and as such an ethnic slur]

gyp/gip *v.* (orig. US) **1** [late 19C+] to cheat, to deceive, to renege on one's debts. **2** [1910s] to steal. **3** [1920s] to disappoint. **4** [1970s] to play truant from school. [GYP *n.*]

gyp artist *n.* [20C] a swindler. [GYP *n.* + ARTIST *n.*[1]]

gype *see* GIPE.

gyp joint/flap *n.* [1930s+] (US) anywhere, esp. a club, bar

etc, where the unwary will be swindled (cf. CLIP-JOINT). [GYP *v.* + JOINT *n.*[3]]

gyp moll *n.* [20C] (US) a female swindler. [GYP *v.* + MOLL]

gypo/gyppo/gyppy/gippo/jippo *n.* **1** [20C] gypsy, usu. derog. **2** [1920s–60s] (US) contract work. [abbr. The implication of (2) is that like a gypsy the worker fulfils the contract then moves on. Note UK services sl. *gyppo*, gravy, grease, stew; S.Afr. milit. *gyppo*, to shirk duty]

gypper *n.* [late 19C+] a gypsy.

gyppery *n.* [20C] (US) dishonest activity, swindling (cf. GYP RACKET). [GYP *v.* + sfx. -*ery*]

gyppo/gyppy *see* GYPO.

gyppy/gippy tummy *n.* [1940s+] stomach troubles, diarrhoea; orig. that contracted in Egypt, but now extended to any such problems that UK tourists experience abroad or in ethnic restaurants at home (cf. APPLE-BLOSSOM TWO-STEP; DRIPPY TUMMY).

gyp racket *n.* [20C] (US) swindling, fraud. [GYP *v.* + RACKET]

gyp sheet *n.* [1970s] (US) a crib sheet. [GYP *v.* + SE *sheet*]

gypsie lee *n.* [1930s+] (Aus.) tea (cf. ROSIE LEA). [rhy. sl.]

gypsies *n.* [1970s+] (US sex industry) prostitutes who travel around for trade or who live in trailer parks.

gypsy/gipsy *n.* [1940s+] (US) **1** an independent trucker or the truck he owns. **2** an independent cab-driver or taxicab. **3** a prostitute who travels around for trade or lives in a trailer park.

gypsy/gipsy *adj.* [20C] (W.I.) interfering, irritatingly inquisitive. [the neg. image of the Romanies]

gypsy/gipsy in the parlour *phr.* [20C] (US) something suspicious, something not as it should be, someone attempting to deceive the speaker (cf. NIGGER IN THE WOODPILE). [negative racial stereotyping]

gypsy's/gipsy's *n.* [20C] urination. [rhy. sl. *gypsy's kiss* = PISS]

gypsy's/gipsy's deal *n.* [20C] (US) a business deal that never actually materializes. [neg. stereotype of a gypsy]

gypsy's/gipsy's ginger *n.* [20C] a pile of human excrement found out of doors. [neg. stereotyping]

gypsy's/gipsy's leave *n.* [20C] departure without warning and without settling one's debts (cf. FRENCH LEAVE). [neg. stereotype of gypsy habits]

gypsy's/gipsy's warning *n.*[1] [mid-19C+] no warning at all. [neg. stereotyping]

gypsy's/gipsy's warning *n.*[2] [mid-19C+] morning. [rhy. sl.]

gysm *see* JIZZUM.

gytch *v.* [1950s] (US) to steal. [ety. unknown]

gyte *n.* [19C] (Scot.) a child. [pron. of SE *goat*]

gyve *n.*[1] [late 18C] the vagina. [? dimin. of SE *gyve*, a shackle, a fetter]

gyve *n.*[2] [1960s+] (drugs) a marijuana cigarette. [JIVE *n.*[2]]

gyvel *n.* [18C–19C] (Scot.) the vagina. [? GYVE *n.*[1]]

gyver *see* GUIVER *n.*[1].

gyvo *n.* [1930s+] (Aus.) flattery, insincerity, pretence (cf. GUIVER *n.*[1]).

gyzm *see* JISM.

H

H *n.*[1] [mid-19C+] (US) hell. [abbr.]
H *n.*[2] [1930s+] (drugs) *heroin* (cf. c n.[2]; E; M n.[2]). [abbr.]
H *n.*[3] [1980s+] (US drugs) hashish. [abbr.]
ha/haha *n.* [1980s+] (US campus) a can of beer. [abbr. BREWHA]
hab *n.* [20C] (Can.) a derog. term for a share-cropper, a tenant farmer. [Fr. *habitant*, an inhabitant. The name was adopted deliberately by the Montréal Canadiens, to display their pride as French, rather than British, Canadians]
habdabs *see* ABDABS.
habe *n.* [1960s+] habeas corpus, an order compelling its subject to attend court (cf. HAPUS CAPUS). [abbr. legal jargon]
haberdasher of pronouns/nouns and pronouns *n.* [late 17C–19C] a schoolmaster. [the expanded version is 17C–18C only]
habit *n.* [late 19C+] (drugs) drug addiction. [note that earliest citations are more SE than sl., e.g. in 1887, 'May he continue to wage war against [Chinese opium dens] until the habit has been swept entirely out of existence', a phr. adopted by drug users since the 1910s]
habitual *n.* [late 19C] an *habitual* criminal, drunkard etc. [abbr.]
ha-bloody-ha!/ha-fucking-ha! *excl.* [1950s+] a sarcastic 'fake' laugh, underlining how very unfunny one finds a situation or statement.
hab-nab/hab-nabs/hab or nab *adv.* [mid-16C–mid-19C] at random, hit or miss. [ME *habbe*, have and *nhabbe*, have not. The *OED* offers this ety, but notes that while the phonology seems correct 'there is a long gap in the history, between the general disappearance of the *habbe* forms of the verb in ME and the first examples of *hab-nab*']
habra, dabra and the crew *phr.* [20C] (W.I./Bdos) everybody one can think of, a large, undifferentiated crowd (cf. HAIAH AND KAIAH AND BUDDY-BORN-DRUNK; HE, SHE AND THINGAMERRY; NEPSHA AND KAIAH; PHILIP AND CHEYNEY; TOM, DICK AND HARRY). [? SE *abracadabra*]
hache *n.* [1980s+] (drugs) heroin. [Sp. *hache*, the letter H]
hachi *n.* [1950s+] (orig. US milit.) the penis; thus *eat/suck a hachi!* go to hell! [Jap. *shakuhachi*, 50cm (20in); imported by US veterans of the Korean War (1950–53)]
hack *n.*[1] **1** [late 17C–19C] the driver of a hackney carriage. **2** [early 18C+] a reporter, a journalist, formerly derog. but recently popular, if tongue-in-cheek. **3** [mid-18C–mid-19C] a prostitute. **4** [1920s+] (US) a taxicab. [abbr. SE *hackney* carriage/cab-driver. (2) and (3) are fig. use: both are 'for hire']
hack *n.*[2] **1** [19C+] an embarrassment, an embarrassing situation. **2** [19C+] an annoying characteristic. [SE *hackneyed*, banal, lacking novelty]
hack *n.*[3] [mid-19C+] (US) an attempt, a try. [SE *hack*, to chop (at)]
hack *n.*[4] **1** [1910s–60s] (US) an ambulance. **2** [1910s–60s] (US) a hearse. **3** [1910s–60s] (US) an old, dilapidated boat. **4** [1960s+] (US) a motorcycle sidecar. [SE *hackney carriage*]

hack *n.*[5] [1910s+] **1** (US/Can.) a night watchman, a prison guard. **2** (US Black) a generic term for any White person. [SE *hack*, a night watchman; or HAWK n.[2]]
hack *v.*[1] **1** [late 19C+] (US campus) to socialize, to waste time, to idle. **2** [1940s–60s] (US) to neck, to kiss, to engage in sexual activity.
hack *v.*[2] [late 19C+] to irritate, to annoy, esp. in phr. *hack off*, to annoy (cf. HAWK v.[3]). [SE *hack*, to chop]
hack *v.*[3] [late 19C+] (US) to ride in or drive a hackney coach or taxicab. [HACK n.[1] (4)]
hack *v.*[4] [1910s+] (US) to accomplish; thus *hack it*, to cope, endure, manage. [SE *hack*, to cut through]
hack *v.*[5] [1970s] (US Black) to watch closely. [? HAWK v.[2] (1)]
hack *v.*[6] [1970s] (US campus) to vomit. [SE *hack*, to cough]
hack *v.*[7] (orig. computing jargon) **1** [1970s+] to tinker with a computer system for pleasure and as a proof of one's expertise. **2** [1980s+] to gain unauthorized access to a computer system (and possibly use that access for illegal activities). [HACK n.[3] + SE *hack*]
hack around/about/off *v.* [late 19C+] **1** (US campus) to socialize, fool about. **2** (US) to joke, to tease. **3** (US) to waste time. [HACK v.[1]]
hacked/hacked off *adj.* (US) **1** [late 19C–1910s] exhausted. **2** [1930s+] very angry. [HACK v.[2]]
hackems *n.* [1960s+] (Aus.) hostilities, conflicts. [SE *hack*, to chop (at)]
hacker *n.*[1] [1910s+] (US prison) a prison guard. [HACK n.[5]]
hacker *n.*[2] [1930s+] (US) a taxi-driver (cf. HACKIE). [HACK n.[1] (4)]
hacker *n.*[3] [1960s+] a run of the mill, average person. [HACK n.[1]; the implication is of a 'jack-of-all-trades']
hacker *n.*[4] (orig. computer jargon) **1** [1970s+] an enthusiast for programming or using computers as an end in itself. **2** [1980s+] one who uses their skill with computers to try to gain unauthorized access to computer systems. [HACK v.[7]]
hackette *n.* [1970s+] a female journalist. [HACK n.[1] (2) + dimin. female sfx. *-ette*]
hack hand *n.* [1940s] (US) a commercial truck-driver. [HACK n.[1] (4) + SE *hand*, a worker]
hackie *n.* [late 19C+] (US) taxi-driver. [HACK n.[1] (4)]
hacking *n.* (orig. computing jargon) **1** [1970s+] the use of a computer for the sheer pleasure in computing. **2** [1980s+] the unauthorized accessing of computer systems. [HACK v.[7]]
hack it *v.* [20C] to manage, to tolerate, to bear a difficulty, to solve a problem, to succeed; thus *hack it out*, *hack it over*, to work out, to make a plan. [HACK v.[4]]
hackle *n.* [mid-19C] courage, pluck; thus *show hackle*, to be willing to fight (cf. COCK OF A DIFFERENT HACKLE). [SE *hackles*, the long, shining feathers on the necks of certain birds, typically the domestic cockerel]
hackle *v.* [1950s+] (W.I. Rasta) to bother, worry, trouble. [? HASSLE ? + SE *get one's hackles up*]

hackles *n.* [late 19C–1920s] whiskers. [SE *hackles*]

hackle up *adj.* [20C] (W.I.) **1** of people, physically deformed. **2** of things, torn, damaged, untidy. [? SE *hacked*, chopped up]

hackle up *v.* [20C] (W.I./Baha.) to beat up. [? SE *hack*, to chop up]

hackling *n.* [1950s+] (W.I. Rasta) bothering, worrying, troubling. [HACKLE V.]

hackney/hackster *n.* [late 16C–late 17C] a prostitute (cf. BARRACK HACK; GARRISON HACK; HACK n.¹). [14C SE *hackney horse*, a run-of-the-mill horse, i.e. not a warhorse or hunter, which was used for everyday riding and subsequently typified as the sort of horse available for hire]

Hackney marsh *n.* **1** [late 19C–1950s] a glass (of alcohol). **2** [20C] spectacles, glasses. [rhy. sl.; *Hackney marsh* = glass; *Hackney marshes* = glasses]

hack off *v.*¹ *see* HACK AROUND.

hack off *v.*² [20C] **1** to annoy, to irritate. **2** to confuse, to embarrass. [HACK V.², but note dial. *hake*, to tease, to worry + *hock*, to jeer]

hack one's mack, to *phr.* [20C] to masturbate. [SE *hack*; assonance, but note MACK]

hack pilot/pusher *n.* [1930s+] (Aus./US) a taxi-driver (cf. HACKIE). [HACK n.¹ (4) + SE *pilot/pusher*]

hack rack *n.* [1970s] (US) a taxicab stand. [HACK n.¹ (4) + SE *rack*]

hackslaver *v.* [19C] to stutter. [SE *hack*, to stammer + *slaver*, to salivate]

hackster *see* HACKNEY.

hack the hog, to *phr.* [20C] to masturbate. [SE *hack* + HOG n.⁴]

hackum *n.* [18C] a braggart (cf. CAPTAIN HACKUM). [SE *hack*, i.e. he fig. *hacks about* him]

had *adj.* **1** [early 19C+] seduced. **2** [mid-19C+] tricked, hoaxed, deceived. [HAVE V.]

haddit *see* HAD IT.

haddock *n.* [early–mid-19C] **1** a purse; thus *haddock stuff'd with beans*, a purse full of guineas. **2** (US) money. [the once popular belief that assigned the dark marks on the shoulders of a haddock to the impression left by St Peter's finger and thumb, when he took the tribute-money out of the fish's mouth at Capernaum. Thus 16C proverbial phrase, to *bring haddock to paddock*, to spend or lose everything]

haddock and cod *n.* [20C] an irritating person, also as an affectionate name for a child. [rhy. sl. *haddock and cod* = SOD n.]

haddock pastie *n.* [1990s] the female genitals and pubic hair (cf. BEARDED CLAM). [one of several terms that link the female genitals to fish (cf. FISH n.⁴)]

haddums/had 'em *n.* [late 17C–late 18C] venereal disease. [the punning phr. 'been at had 'em and come home by Clapham' (cf. CLAP n.)]

ha'd/ha-d/ha-dee *n.* [mid-19C–1960s] one halfpenny (pron. 'hay-dee'). [SE *half a d.* (a penny)]

had it/haddit *adj.* [1970s+] (N.Z.) useless, second-rate. [HAVE HAD IT V.]

hadland *n.* [late 16C–mid-17C] one who has lost land that they once possessed.

had your pennorth or do you want a ha'penny change? *phr.* [1920s+] a phr. addressed to a person one feels is staring rudely (cf. GOT YOUR EYE FULL?).

haematoid *adj.* [1920s] a consciously 'clever' euph. for BLOODY. [SE *haematoid*, resembling blood, characterized by the presence of blood]

haemorrhage *n.* [1900s–30s] (US) tomato ketchup. [SE *haemorrhage*, a flow of blood]

haemorrhage *v.* [1920s+] (US) to get exceedingly angry or excited; thus *have a haemorrhage*, to be furious.

haemorrhoid/hemo *n.* [1960s+] (US campus) an annoying person. [pun on a PAIN IN THE ASS]

haemorrhoid hitman *n.* [1990s] a homosexual man. [SE *haemorrhoid* + HITMAN]

haffie *n.* **1** [1920s+] (US) a half-share (cf. HALVERS). **2** [1970s] (S.Afr.) a 375ml half-bottle of spirits or wine (cf. HALF-JACK n.³).

ha-fucking-ha! *see* HA-BLOODY-HA!

hag *n.* [1920s–50s] (US campus) an unattractive or sexually promiscuous young woman; thus derog. *hag party*, a party for women.

hag *v.* [19C] (US) **1** to provoke, to annoy. **2** to complain. **3** to bring bad luck upon. [SE *hag*, to torment or terrify as a hag]

hagarian *adj.* [1940s+] (W.I.) oafish, uncouth, rough. [SE *hog*]

haggard *n.* [late 16C] (Und.) a potential dupe who refuses to fall into the trap that has been prepared. [SE *haggard*, an intractable person (esp. a woman) who refuses to abandon their own desires. Orig. applied to a wild falcon that would not be tamed]

haggerawator *see* AGGERAWATOR.

Haggisland *n.* [late 19C+] Scotland. [SE *haggis*, the 'national' dish, which was once equally popular in England]

hagride *v.* [1900s–40s] (US Black) to harass verbally, esp. when the target is asleep, to nag, to criticize. [SE *hag*, to torment or terrify as a hag + RIDE V.⁴]

hagsmash *n.* [20C] (Ulster) a botched, inadequate piece of work. [SE *hog* + *smash*]

ha-ha *n.*¹ [late 19C–50s] (US) a laugh of ridicule or derision.

ha-ha *n.*² [1970s] (US campus) beer. [abbr. BREWHA]

ha-ha *n.*³ [1970s+] (drugs) marijuana. [abbr. marijuan*a*]

haha *see* HA.

ha-ha pigeon *n.* [1930s+] (Aus.) a kookaburra or laughing jackass.

haiah and kaiah and buddy-born-drunk *phr.* [20C] (W.I./Bdos) everybody one can think of, a large, undifferentiated crowd (cf. HABRA, DABRA AND THE CREW).

hail *n.* **1** [1930s–50s] (US) ice cubes, as in a drink. **2** [1980s+] (drugs) crack cocaine.

hail *excl.* [1950s+] (W.I. Rasta) a general excl. of greeting.

hail and rain *n.* [1920s–70s] a train. [rhy. sl.]

hail Columbia/Columbus *n.* [19C+] (US) **1** a punishment, a telling-off, a scolding. **2** euph. for *hell*. [*Hail Columbia*, a patriotic song publ. in 1798 by Joseph Hopkinson (1770–1842)]

hailer *n.* [1950s+] (Irish) the prayer 'Hail Mary'.

hail Mary *adj.* [1980s+] (US) desperate, last resort. [a Catholic prayer for spiritual help. Note football/basketball jargon *hail Mary*, a very long throw, often the last of the game, which is most likely to succeed through divine intervention]

hail smiling morn *n.* [1970s+] an erection (cf. COLLEEN BAWN). [rhy. sl. *hail smiling morn* = HORN n.² (2)]

hailstorm *n.* [mid-19C] (US) a cocktail made with crushed ice.

hail up *v.* [late 19C–1900s] (Aus.) to stay at an inn or similar lodging.

haim/hame *n.* [1940s+] (US Black) a job, usu. tedious or unpleasant. [ety. unknown]

haincty *see* HINCTY.

Haines!/Hanes! *excl.* [mid–late 19C] (orig. US) a warning shout. [MY NAME IS HAINES]

haint'ing/ain'ting *n.* [20C] (US) a rustic, a peasant. [rustic pron. of SE *hasn't* as *hain't* and *isn't* as *ain't*]

hair *n.*¹ [mid-19C+] (US) a curative drink for a hangover. [abbr. HAIR OF THE DOG]

hair *n.*² [mid-19C+] (US) the scalp, as a trophy in phr. *lift or raise hair*.

hair *n.*³ [late 19C+] **1** pubic hair. **2** a generic for the female sex; thus *after hair*, in search of sex, *bit of hair*, sexual intercourse, *hair-monger*, a womanizer, *plenty of hair*, large numbers of women, *put down some hair*, of a man, to have sexual intercourse.

hair *n.*[4] [20C] (Ulster) a hair-pulling fight between women.

hair *n.*[5] [1950s+] (US campus) courage, masculine prowess. [the image of the hairy-chested macho man. Note US sports use [1960s] *show hair*, for a sportsman to play aggressively and well]

hair/hairy about the heels/fetlocks *phr.* [late 19C+] of poor breeding, socially inferior (cf. HAIRY-HEELED). [bloodstock use]

hair and hide/hide and hair/hide and tallow *phr.* [20C] everything, entirely, completely. [butcher/slaughterhouse jargon, the whole animal]

hairbag *n.* (US) 1 [1950s+] a veteran police officer. 2 [1970s+] an unpleasant, disgusting person (cf. HAIRBALL).

hairball *n.* [1980s+] a general term of derision for a situation or person (cf. HAIRBAG). [SE *hairball*, a mass of hair found in the stomachs of various animals, e.g. a cat]

hairburger *n.* [1980s+] (US) the female genitals (cf. FUR-BURGER; HAIR *n.*[3]; HAIR PIE). [HAIR *n.*[3] (1) + sfx. *-burger*]

hairburner *n.* [1980s+] (US gay) a gay male hairdresser.

hair court *n.* [19C] the female pubic hair (cf. HAIRYFORDSHIRE; HAIRY ORACLE; HAIRY RING). [SE *hairy* + *court*]

hair-curler *n.* [19C] (US) alcohol. [its effects]

haircut *n.*[1] [late 19C] (US) a blow over the head.

haircut *n.*[2] [1940s–50s] (prison) a short term of imprisonment, in a local prison from a few weeks up to 2–3 months or in a convict prison for 3–5 years. [the relatively short period and the cutting of one's hair on arrival in prison]

haircut *n.*[3] [1960s] (US Und.) a verbal telling off. [euph.]

hair-divider/-splitter *n.* [20C] the penis (cf. ARSE-OPENER; BEARD-SPLITTER). [HAIR *n.*[3] (1) + SE *divider*]

haired up *adj.* [20C] (US) annoyed, furious, upset. [GET A HAIR UP ONE'S ASS]

hair fairy *n.* [1960s+] (US) an effeminate male homosexual, with long or styled hair. [SE *hair* + FAIRY *n.*[2]]

hairhead *n.* [1970s+] (US) a long-haired man, a hippie. [SE *hair* + sfx. -HEAD (2)]

hair-hopper *n.* [1980s] (US) a woman who frequently changes her hairstyle. [she *hops* from style to style]

hair in the butter *n.* [20C] (US) a delicate situation. [var. on SE *fly in the ointment*]

hair-monger *n.* [late 19C] a womanizer. [HAIR *n.*[3]]

hair of the dog *n.* [mid-19C+] a hangover cure that consists of drinking more of the alcohol that created the hangover (cf. HAIR *n.*[1]). [var. on HAIR OF THE SAME WOLF; abbr. phr. *the hair of the dog that bit you*]

hair of the same wolf *n.* [17C] a hangover cure that consists of drinking more of the alcohol that created the hangover (cf. HAIR OF THE DOG). [the alcoholic 'wolf' that has 'bitten' the sufferer]

hair pie *n.* [1930s+] (orig. US) 1 the vagina (cf. HAIRBURGER). 2 cunnilingus (cf. FINGER PIE *n.*). [HAIR *n.*[3] (1) + SE *pie* (which one can EAT *v.*[3]), plus pun on SE *hare pie*; one of many slang examples of equating sex with food]

hairpin *n.* (US) 1 [late 19C] a fool, a simpleton. 2 [1910s] a thin person. 3 [1920s–50s] (US) a woman. 4 [1950s–70s] (US gay) a homosexual; thus *drop hairpins*, to hint that one is homosexual.

hair-raiser *n.* [late 19C+] an exciting or terrifying adventure story or film.

hair-splitter *see* HAIR-DIVIDER.

hair to sell *phr.* [late 19C] used of a woman who is willing to prostitute herself. [HAIR *n.*[3] (1)]

hairy *n.*[1] [20C] (Glasgow) a poor woman. [the premise is that a better off woman would wear a hat and hide her hair]

hairy/hairyback *n.*[2] [1960s+] (S.Afr.) an Afrikaner. [a hairy back is seen as an image of animality]

hairy *n.*[3] [1980s+] (drugs) heroin. [pron. 'hair-o-in']

hairy *adj.*[1] 1 [mid-19C+] difficult. 2 [late 19C] excellent, first-rate. 3 [1920s+] (orig. Irish) impressive, sometimes used as an intensive. 4 [1940s+] (US) bad or unsatisfactory. 5 [1960s+] weird, complicated. 6 [1960s+] dangerous, exciting. 7 [1960s+] (US) stylish, excellent. [abbr. HAIRY-ARSED, use both pos. and neg.]

hairy *adj.*[2] [mid-19C+] of a woman, desirable, sexy; thus *feel hairy*, to feel sexually inclined.

hairy *adj.*[3] [20C] annoyed, furious, upset. [GET A HAIR UP ONE'S ASS]

hairy *adj.*[4] [1900s] ill-bred, bad-mannered. [HAIR ABOUT THE HEELS]

hairy *adj.*[5] [1940s–50s] old-fashioned, out-of-date (cf. HAVE HAIR ON IT).

hairy about the heels/fetlocks *see* HAIR ABOUT THE HEELS.

hairy-arsed/-assed *adj.* [1960s+] 1 veteran, mature. 2 overtly, aggressively masculine. [SE *hairy* + ARSE *n.*[1]]

hairy-arsed/-assed *adv.* [1960s+] madly, wildly, extremely. [for ety. *see* HAIRY-ARSED *adj.*]

hairy axe wound/cheque book *n.* [1990s] the female genitals.

hairyback *see* HAIRY *n.*[2].

hairy bit *n.* [mid-19C+] a sexually attractive woman. [HAIR *n.*[3]]

hairybottom *n.* [1990s] a general term of derision or dislike.

hairy buffalo *n.* [1960s+] (US) a strong mixed alcoholic drink, esp. when used to uninhibit women at parties.

hairy cheque book *see* HAIRY AXE WOUND.

hairy cup/goblet *n.* [1990s] the vagina.

hairy doughnut *n.* [1990s] the vagina (cf. DOUGHNUT *n.*[3]).

hairy eyeball, the *n.* [1960s+] (US) a hostile look.

hairyfordshire *n.* [mid-19C+] the vagina (cf. HAIR COURT). [pun on SE *Herefordshire* and the pubic HAIR *n.*[3]; *ford* also points to those words that equate the vagina with a stream or river (cf. DAMP *n.*)]

hairy goat *n.* [1940s] (Aus./N.Z.) a horse that runs badly in a race; thus *run like a hairy goat*.

hairy goblet *see* HAIRY CUP.

hairy-heeled *adj.* [late 19C+] of poor breeding, socially inferior (cf. HAIR ABOUT THE HEELS). [bloodstock use]

hairy lasoo *n.* [1990s] the vagina.

hairy Mary *n.*[1] [1960s+] (US gay) a masculine homosexual. [SE *hairy* + MARY *n.*[3]]

hairy Mary/Molly *n.*[2] [1960s+] (Irish) the female genitals.

hairy oracle *n.* [late 18C–mid-19C] the female pubic hair (cf. HAIR COURT; ORACLE *n.*[2]).

hairy ring *n.* [19C] the female pubic hair (cf. HAIR COURT). [SE *hairy* + RING *n.*[1] (1)]

hairy sausage *n.* [1990s] the penis (cf. BACON *n.*[1]).

hairy toffee *n.* [1990s] anal hairs coated in faeces.

hairy wheel *n.* [mid-19C+] 1 (Aus.) the pudendum (cf. HAIRY RING). 2 the male genitals.

Haiti *n.* [19C+] (US) that area of a town where the Black population lives. [proper name]

ha-ja *see* HALF-JACK *n.*[3].

hakim *n.* [mid-19C] (Anglo-Ind.) a doctor. [Arabic *hakim*, wise, learned, a philosopher, a physician; ult. f. *hakama*, to exercise authority; thus to know, be wise or learned]

halal *n.* [1990s] a derog. term for a Muslim, esp. a Pakistani immigrant. [Arabic *halal*, lawful; in this context ritually slaughtered meat, eaten by Muslims]

halari *n.* [20C] (W.I.) a low-class woman given to fighting. [*halari*, a nosiy brown bird]

hale and hearty *n.* [1970s+] a party (cf. GAY AND HEARTY). [rhy. sl.]

half n.[1] **1** [late 19C+] ½ pint (280ml) of beer, ½ gill (70ml) of spirits; esp. in phr. *a swift half* (of beer). **2** [1940s–70s] 10 shillings (50p) (cf. HALF-A-BAR). **3** [1950s+] (drugs) ½ ounce, 0.5 gram. [abbr.]

half n.[2] [20C] in telling the time, an elision of *half-past* ..., e.g. *half-ten*, *half-four*.

half-a-bar/-sheet n. [20C] formerly 10 shillings, currently 50p. [SE *half* + BAR n.[2] (1)/SHEET n. (2)]

half-a-bean/-quid n. [late 18C–1900s] a half-sovereign, a half-dollar (cf. HALF-BEAN). SE *half* + BEAN n.[1]]

half-a-borde see HALF-BORDE.

half-a-brewer adj. [late 19C] drunk.

half-a-bull/half-bull/half-bull white n. [mid-19C] half-a-crown, 2s 6d (12½p). [SE *half* + BULL n.[3] (1)]

half-a-c n. [1950s+] (US drugs) $50 bill. [C n.[1] (2)]

half-a-caser n. [late 19C–1910s] (Aus.) half-a-crown, 2s 6d (12½p). [SE *half* + CASER n.[1]]

half-a-cock n. [mid-19C+] £5. [rhy. sl.; SE *half* + COCK AND HEN n. (1)]

half-a-couter see HALF-COUTER.

half-a-crack n.[1] [19C] a very short time. [CRACK n.[6]]

half-a-crack n.[2] [1930s–50s] half-a-crown, 2s 6d (12½p). [SE *half* + corruption of SE *crown*]

half-a-crown n. [1940s+] (bingo) the number 26. [SE *half-a-crown*, in pre-decimal coinage 2s 6d (12½p)]

half-a-crowner/half-crowner n. [late 19C] any publication costing 2s 6d. [SE *half-a-crown*, in pre-decimal coinage 2s 6d (12½p)]

half-a-dollar n.[1] see HALF-DOLLAR.

half-a-dollar n.[2] [20C] a collar. [rhy. sl.]

half-a-foot n. [1920s+] (W.I.) a person with a wooden leg.

half-a-football field n. [1980s+] (drugs) 50 rocks of crack cocaine. [a football field is 100 yards (91m) long]

half-a-grunter see HALF-GRUNTER.

half-a-hog/half-hog n. [late 17C–mid-19C] sixpence (cf. GRUNTER n.[2]).

half-a-idiot see HALF-IDIOT.

half-a-job n. [late 17C–18C] half a guinea. [JOB n.[2]]

half a man n. [1970s+] (US Black) a passive homosexual (cf. FLIP n.[8]).

half a mo n. [1910s–30s] a cigarette. [? the delaying excuse, 'Half a mo, I'm just having a fag']

half a mo phr. [late 19C+] wait a moment, hang on. [abbr. SE *half a moment*]

half and between adj. [20C] (Ulster) **1** of a person, slightly mad, eccentric. **2** neither one thing nor another.

half-and-half n.[1] [18C+] a mixture of ale and porter.

half-and-half n.[2] **1** [19C+] (US) a half-breed, a person of mixed race. **2** [1930s–60s] (US Black) a hermaphrodite. [half-Black/half-White; half-man/half-woman]

half-and-half n.[3] [1930s+] as offered by a prostitute, fellatio plus full intercourse.

half-and-half adj. [1930s+] (US campus) bisexual.

half-and-half coves/boys/men n. [mid-19C] would-be dandies who fail to make the grade. [SE *half-and-half* + COVE/ SE *boys/men*]

half-and-halfer n. [late 19C+] a person or object that cannot easily be categorized, 'neither one thing nor the other'.

half-and-half men see HALF-AND-HALF COVES.

half-an-hour n. [late 19C–1930s] (Aus.) flour. [rhy. sl.]

half-a-nicker see HALF-NICKER.

half-a-note n. [20C] 10 shillings (50p) (cf. HALF-NOTE). [abbr. *half a pound-note*; the 10s itself was also a note]

half-an-ounce n. [late 18C–19C] half-a-crown, 2s 6d (12½p). [the contemporary measurement of silver at 5s an ounce]

half-a-quid see HALF-A-BEAN.

half-arsed see HALF-ASSED.

half-a-sheet see HALF-A-BAR.

half-ass n. [1920s+] (US) a stupid, incompetent person. [SE *half* + ARSE n.[1]]

half-assed/-arsed adj. [mid-19C+] (orig. US) careless, inadequate, incompetent, second-rate. [SE *half* + ARSE n.[1]]

half-assed/-arsed adv. [mid-19C+] (orig. US) carelessly, incompetently. [HALF-ASSED adj.]

half-assed-backwards adj. [1920s+] (US) back-to-front (cf. ARSE ABOUT FACE).

half-a-stretch n. [mid-19C+] (Und.) 6 months' imprisonment. [SE *half* + STRETCH n.[2]]

half a stretch away n. [1930s–40s] (US Black) the distance of half a city block. [SE *stretch*, a distance]

half-a-surprise n. [late 19C–1900s] a single black eye. [Charles Coborn's song lyric (c.1886), 'Two lovely black eyes/ Oh what a surprise']

half-a-thick see HALF-THICK.

half a tick n. [late 19C+] a very short time (cf. TICK n.[3]).

half-a-tosheroon/-tusheroon n. [mid-19C] half-a-crown, 2s 6d (12½p). [SE *half* + TOSHEROON]

half-away adj. [20C] (Ulster) insane. [on the NOT ALL THERE model]

half-a-yard n. [1920s+] (US) $50. [SE *half* + YARD n.[2] (1)]

half-baked n. [late 19C–1930s] (Aus.) an immature person. [HALF-BAKED adj.]

half-baked adj. [mid-19C+] **1** silly, foolish. **2** incompetent, inadequate, below standard.

half-bean n. [early–mid-19C] half a sovereign, 10 shillings. [var. on HALF-A-BEAN]

half-borde/half-a-borde n. [late 16C–late 18C] a sixpence (2.5p). [SE *half* + BORD]

half-brass n. [1940s+] a woman who associates with the prostitute milieu but is not a 'working girl' herself (cf. HALF-SQUARE). [SE *half* + BRASS n.[4]]

half-bull/half-bull white see HALF-A-BULL.

half-canned adj. [1920s+] tipsy rather than wholly drunk. [SE *half* + CANNED adj.[1]]

half-case/caser n. [19C] **1** half-a-crown, 2s 6d (12.5p) (cf. HALF-OXFORD). **2** (US) half a dollar (cf. HALF-DOLLAR). [SE *half* + CASER n.[1]]

half-century n. [late 19C–1930s] (US) a $50 note. [SE *half* + CENTURY]

half-cocked adj.[1] [early 19C+] (orig. US) second-rate, not fully capable, unfinished; thus *go off half-cocked*, to start without proper planning, to fail to turn out properly. [SE *cock*, to pull back the hammer on a gun]

half-cocked adj.[2] [20C] mildly drunk (cf. COCKED; HALF-CUT adj.[2]; HALF-GONE; HALF-SHOT adj.[2]; HALF-SLEWED).

half-copper n. [19C] (N.Z.) a halfpenny. [SE *half* + COPPER n.[2]]

half-couter/half-a-couter n. [mid-19C] half a sovereign, 10 shillings (cf. HALF-BEAN). [SE *half* + COUTER]

half-cracked adj. [19C] slightly insane, not wholly balanced (cf. HALF-GONE; HALF-THERE). [SE *half* + CRACKED adj.[1] (1)]

half-crowner see HALF-A-CROWNER.

half-crown word n. [late 19C–1960s] a long and supposedly 'difficult' word (cf. FORTY-SHILLING WORD; SEVENTY-FIVE CENT WORD). [the image of a *half-crown* (2s 6d/12½p) as a large sum of money]

half-cut adj.[1] [19C] (US) crude, uncultivated. [SE *half-cut quality*, those who look down on everyone, other than those who look down on them]

half-cut adj.[2] **1** [late 19C+] (Aus.) foolish, silly. **2** [20C] more than mildly drunk but not yet incapable (cf. HALF-COCKED adj.[2]; HALF-HIGH). [SE *half* + CUT adj.[1]]

half-dollar/half-a-dollar n. [late 19C+] half-a-crown, 2s 6d (12½p) (cf. HALF-CASE). [a period when £1 sterling was worth around $4, i.e. 5 shillings (25p) to a dollar]

halfer *n.* [1930s–40s] (US) a half-dollar coin.

half-flash and half-foolish *phr.* [early 19C] (Und.) one who exists on the fringes of the underworld and pretends to a far greater involvement than they actually have. [FLASH adj.[3]]

half-fonged *see* FONGED.

half-foolish *adj.* [mid-19C] ridiculous.

half-G (drugs) (US) $500. [SE *half* + G n.[1]]

half-go *n.* [late 19C–1900s] three pennyworth of spirits, usu. mixed with water. [SE *half* + GO n.[2]]

half-gone *adj.* [19C] **1** simple, stupid (cf. HALF-CRACKED). **2** drunk (cf. HALF-COCKED adj.[2]).

half-grunter/half-a-grunter *n.* [mid-19C] sixpence (cf. HALF-A-HOG). [SE *half* + GRUNTER n.[2] (1)]

half-half-and-half *adj.* [late 19C] drunk.

half-hard *adj.* [20C] **1** of the penis, semi-erect. **2** not very intelligent.

half-high *adj.* [20C] (US) tipsy, mildly drunk (cf. HALF-CUT adj.[2]). [SE *half* + HIGH]

half-hitch *v.* [1970s+] (N.Z.) to steal. [rhy. sl. *half-hitch* = SNITCH v. (3)]

half-hog *see* HALF-A-HOG.

half-horse, half-alligator *n.* [19C] (US) a notably tough man, esp. a river-boatman (cf. ALLIGATOR n.[1]). [characteristics of the animals]

half-hour gentleman *n.* [late 19C] (society) a parvenu, one in whom breeding is at best an affectation (cf. FOREVER GENTLE-MAN).

half-hundred *n.* [1970s+] (N.Z.) a £50 note.

half-idiot/half-a-idiot *n.* [20C] (W.I./Bdos.) a complete fool.

halfie *n.* [1940s–60s] (Aus.) a half-caste.

half-inch *n.* [1950s+] (W.I.) an inferior workman. [HALF-INCH adj.]

half-inch *adj.* [1950s+] (W.I.) inadequately equipped for a job. [? ref. to the size of one's penis]

half-inch *v.*[1] [1910s+] (N.Z.) to approach slowly. [ext. of SE *inch forward*, to move very slowly]

half-inch *v.*[2] [1920s+] to steal. [rhy. sl. *half-inch* = PINCH]

half in two, to *phr.* [late 19C–1930s] (US Black) to break in two.

half-iron *n.* [1940s+] a man who enjoys the company but not the specific predilections of homosexuals. [SE *half* + IRON HOOF]

half-jack *n.*[1] *see* JACK n.[11].

half-jack *n.*[2] [mid–late 19C] 10 shillings (50p), half a sovereign. [SE *half* + JACK n.[11]]

half-jack/ha-ja *n.*[3] [1960s+] (S.Afr.) **1** a 375ml half-bottle of spirits or wine. **2** brandy (cf. MAHOG n.[2]).

half-James/Jane/Ned *n.* [mid–late 19C] 10 shillings (50p) (cf. HALF-A-BAR; HALF-JACK n.[2]). [SE *half* + JAMES n.[3]/JANE n.[1]/NED n.[1] (1)]

half-lo *n.* [1970s+] (US drugs) 15 packs of heroin, each weighing about 1g and thus equivalent to ½ ounce, a typical purchase made by a small pusher. [SE *half-load*]

half-man *n.* [20C] (US Black) a half-bottle of spirits, esp. whisky. [Scot. *halfman*, half a bottle of spirits]

half-moon *n.*[1] **1** [17C] the female genital area. **2** [18C–19C] a wig. [resemblance]

half-moon *n.*[2] [1960s+] (drugs) **1** a piece of hashish moulded in a half-moon shape. **2** a piece of peyote cactus. [resemblance]

half-mourning *n.* [mid-19C] a single black eye (cf. IN MOURN-ING). [play on FULL SUIT OF MOURNING]

half-nab/-nap *n.* [18C–early 19C] 'hit or miss', haphazard. [HAB-NAB]

half-Ned *see* HALF-JAMES.

half-nelson *adj.* [1920s] half-drunk. [? pun on BLIND DRUNK and the blind eye of Lord Nelson (1758–1805)]

half-nicker/half-a-nicker *n.*[1] [20C] a vicar. [rhy. sl.]

half-nicker/half-a-nicker *n.*[2] [1930s+] a 10-shilling note (50p). [SE *half* + NICKER]

half-note *n.* [20C] (Aus.) a 10-shilling note. [abbr. HALF-A-NOTE]

half-off, half-on *adj.* [late 19C] tipsy, semi-drunk (cf. HALF-HALF-AND-HALF).

half-one *n.* [1930s] (Irish) a small glass of whisky.

half-ounce *v.* [20C] **1** to beat up. **2** to cheat, to short change. [rhy. sl. *half-ounce* = BOUNCE v.[1], v.[2]]

half-ounce of baccy *phr.* [1970s+] a derog. term for a person of Indian, Pakistani, Bangladeshi or Ugandan Asian blood. [rhy. sl. *half-ounce of baccy* = PAKI]

half-ouncer *n.* [20C] a security man at a nightclub, dance-hall or similar place. [rhy. sl. *half-ouncer* = BOUNCER n.[1] (7)]

half-Oxford *n.* [late 19C] half-a-crown, 2s 6d (12½p). [SE *half* + OXFORD SCHOLAR n. (1)]

half past *adj.* [mid-19C] of age, and a half; thus *half past seven*, seven and a half.

half past a colored man *phr.* [1940s] 12:30am; usu. in answer to one who asks what time it is.

half past a monkey's ass *phr.* [1970s] (US Black) half past 12. [a coarse rejoinder to a question (as to time) that one cannot be bothered to answer]

half past eight *phr.* [1980s] (US) sneaky, shady. [ety. un-known]

half past kissing time/kissing time and time to kiss again *phr.* [18C–19C] catchphrase used in answer to the query, 'What time is it?'

half past nines *n.* [late 19C] women's outsize footwear. [a size that was then considered large, even for a man's foot]

half past two *n.* [20C] a Jew (cf. BOX OF GLUE). [rhy. sl.]

halfpenny dip *n.* [mid-19C+] a ship. [rhy. sl.]

halfpenny howling swell *n.* [late 19C] an imitation dandy, a pretentious man. [HOWLER n.[2]]

halfpenny stamp *n.* [20C] a tramp. [rhy. sl.]

half-pie *adj.* [1920s–50s] (Aus./N.Z.) imperfect, mediocre (cf. HALF-BAKED).

half-piece *n.* [1950s+] (drugs) ½ ounce (14g) of heroin or cocaine. [SE *half* + PIECE n.[1] (5)]

half-pint *n.* [late 19C+] (US) a short person or child (cf. HALF-PORTION).

half-portion *n.* [1910s–40s] a diminutive person (cf. HALF-PINT).

half-quarter *n.* [1980s+] (US drugs) one-eighth of an ounce (3.5g) of cannabis.

half-quid *n.* [20C] 10 shillings (50p). [SE *half* + QUID]

half-rats *adj.* [late 19C] tipsy, mildly drunk (cf. RAT-ARSED; RATTED).

half-rinsed *adj.* [1910s+] (Aus./N.Z.) tipsy, semi-drunk. [RINSE v.]

half-rocked *adj.* [mid-19C] incompetent, inadequate, foolish (cf. HALF-BAKED). [? one who has not been fully rocked in the cradle and is thus still infantile]

half seas over *phr.* [late 17C+] drunk (cf. AFLOAT). [either naval imagery, an unstable boat is more likely to ship water, or Du *op-zee zober*, overseas strong beer (cf. UPSEE)]

half-section *n.* [1950s+] (S.Afr.) a friend. [orig. UK Services]

half set *n.* [1950s–60s] (mainly drugs) an unacceptable offer, usu. in the context of a drug deal.

half-shake *n.* [20C] (N.Z.) a moment, a very short time.

half-shaved *adj.* [early–mid-19C] (US) drunk. [SE *half* + SHAVED]

half-shot *adj.*[1] [early 19C+] (orig. US) second-rate, not fully capable, unfinished (cf. HALF-COCKED adj.[1]).

half-shot *adj.*[2] [mid-19C+] (orig. US) tipsy, mildly drunk (cf. HALF-COCKED adj.[2]). [SE *half* + CUPSHOT]

half-slewed adj. [early 19C+] tipsy, half-drunk (cf. HALF-COCKED adj.[2]). [SE half + SLEWED]

half-slick/-smart adj. [1920s–60s] (US) stupid or reckless.

half-snags n. [late 19C] half-shares in something. [SE snag, to catch onto or SNAG v. (1)]

half-square n. [1910s] (Aus.) a sexually experienced woman, positioned in the contemporary moral spectrum between an all-out prostitute and a respectable woman (cf. HALF-BRASS). [SE half + SQUARE n.[5] (1)]

half-squarie n. [1910s–50s] (Aus.) a demi-mondaine, an 'amateur' prostitute. [HALF-SQUARE]

half-stamp n. [20C] a tramp. [rhy. sl.]

half step, to phr. [1940s+] **1** (US Black/Und.) to make a feeble effort. **2** (US Black) to act in an inappropriate or ineffectual manner. **3** to loaf, to idle. [milit. half-step, a form of slow marching]

half-stepper n. [1950s+] (US prison) one who promises things, but never properly achieves them, thus one who cannot be depended upon. [HALF STEP]

half-/half-way strainer n. [late 19C–1920s] (US) a social climber. [dial. half-strain, a mongrel, half-strained gentry, shabby-genteel individuals]

half the bay over phr. [late 19C] drunk (cf. AFLOAT).

half-there adj. [19C] simple, stupid (cf. HALF-CRACKED). [i.e. 'not all there']

half-thick/half-a-thick/half-thick 'un n. [late 19C–1900s] (N.Z.) a half-sovereign, 10 shillings. [SE half + THICK 'UN]

half-tiz n. [late 19C–1900s] (N.Z.) threepence. [SE half + TIZZY n.[1]]

half-tore adj. [20C] (Ulster) tipsy, half-drunk. [SE half + TORE UP]

half-track n. [1980s+] (drugs) $125 worth of crack cocaine. [rhy. sl.]

half-way house n. [1940s+] (bingo) the number 50. [there are 100 numbers available to the caller]

half-way strainer see HALF-STRAINER.

half-wheel n. [1960s] (N.Z.) half-a-crown, 2s 6d (12½p). [SE half + WHEEL n.[1] (1)]

half-wide adj. **1** [16C] immoral. **2** [19C+] reasonably intelligent, aware of what goes on and thus, in certain contexts, corruptible (cf. WIDE BOY). [SE half + WIDE]

halfy n. [1910s–50s] (US) a legless beggar. [he has only 'half' his body]

half-yenork n. [mid-19C] half-a-crown, 2s 6d (12½p). [SE half + YENORK]

half your luck! excl. [1930s+] (Aus.) signifying envy, jealousy of the person addressed, i.e. I wish I had ... .

Halifax n. [17C+] euph. for SE hell, often in phr. go to Halifax (cf. GO TO HELL, HULL AND HALIFAX).

Halifax mutton n. [late 19C+] (W.I.) salt codfish (cf. ABERDEEN CUTLET). [its being imported from Halifax, Nova Scotia]

Hall, the n.[1] [mid-19C] Leadenhall Market. [orig. used as the market for 'foreigners', i.e. out-of-Londoners, the Hall burnt down in 1666 and was rebuilt as a meat, poultry, fish and vegetable market. The current buildings date f. 1881]

hall n.[2] [1920s–30s] (US Und.) alcohol. [abbr. DR HALL]

hallan/halland shaker n. [16C+] a 'sturdy' or able-bodied and possibly violent beggar. [Scot. hallan, the partition of a cottage wall, especially when it cut off the front door from the fire + SE shaker]

hallelujah n. [20C] (US) a partial euph. for SE hell.

hallelujah-hawking n. [1910s+] (Aus.) working as a door-to-door evangelist. [SE hallelujah + hawk, to peddle]

hallelujah-lass n. [late 19C+] a young woman Salvationist.

hallelujah stew n. [20C] the stew served out at Salvation Army hostels.

halligator n. [late 19C] a herring. [pun on SE alligator]

hall of fame n. [late 19C–1910s] (US Und.) a rogues' gallery.

halloo-wach n. [1980s+] (drugs) amphetamine (cf. A n.[2]). [ety. unknown]

halter n. [mid-16C–mid-19C; 20C] the noose used in a judicial hanging (cf. HALTER-SACK). [20C use is US]

halter-broke adj. [20C] (US) timid, submissive, unadventurous. [SE halter broken, of a horse, accustomed to the halter]

halter-sack n. [early 17C] a villain whose destination will be the gallows. [the noose is the halter, their body the sack]

halvers n. [19C+] equal shares; thus go halvers, to divide equally, halvers! I demand half shares.

halvies/halvsies n. [19C+] equal shares (cf. HALVERS).

halvsies n. [1980s] the sexual act of SIXTY-NINE.

ham n.[1] **1** [mid-19C+] an incompetent, esp. one who poses as more expert than his performance – often in sport – shows him to be (cf. HAMFATTER). **2** [1940s–50s] (US) an inexpert or over-theatrical performance. [theatrical use ham, a melodramatic, ranting, over-acting actor; ult. abbr. hamfatter, a second-rate and thus impoverished actor who was forced to rub hamfat over their face, as a base for the powder that was then applied, rather than being able to afford sweeter smelling oils]

ham n.[2] [late 19C–1920s] (US) an incompetent boxer, a poor fighter. [HAM + SE ham-fisted]

ham n.[3] [1910s+] an amateur telegraphist, subseq. an amateur radio operator (cf. RADIO HAM). [? SE amateur + ham-fisted]

ham adj. [1940s–60s] clumsy, ineffective, incompetent. [HAM n.[1]]

ham v. [1910s–60s] (US Und.) to walk. [the trad. HAM actor whose company gets stranded on the road, forcing him to walk to the city]

ham and n. [late 19C–1950s] (US) an order of ham and eggs.

ham and beef n. [mid-19C] (prison) the chief officer. [rhy. sl.]

ham and egg phr. [20C] (US) unskilled. [HAM AND EGGER]

ham and egger n. [20C] (US orig. boxing) an ordinary, run-of-the-mill person or an incompetent individual. [SE ham and eggs, the image is of its commonness]

ham and eggs n. [1950s+] (orig. Aus.) legs (cf. BACON AND EGGS). [rhy. sl.]

ham-bags n. [late 19C–1910s] women's knickers. [SE ham, the thigh and buttock + bags]

hambo n. [1920s–40s] (US) a posing incompetent, esp. on stage. [HAM n.[1] (1) + HAMBONE n.[1] (1)]

hambone n.[1] **1** [late 19C–1910s] a second-rate actor. **2** [late 19C–1910s] (US) a bad 'nigger minstrel'. **3** [1950s+] (US) a show-off. [HAM n.[1]]

hambone n.[2] [late 19C+] (US Black) shorthand for the Black cultural experience. [the stereotyped Black diet is pig-based]

hambone n.[3] [20C] the penis (cf. BACON n.[1]).

hambone n.[4] **1** [20C] a telephone. **2** [1930s] (US) a trombone. [rhy. sl.]

hambone adj. [late 19C+] referring to Blacks. [HAMBONE n.[2]]

hambone v.[1] [20C] (US) to live frugally. [? a bone from which nearly all of the meat has been chewed]

hambone v.[2] [20C] (Aus.) of a man, to strip off his clothes in public, usu. at a drunken party.

hambone v.[3] [1960s+] (US) **1** to trick, to cheat. **2** to show off. [HAMBONE n.[1]]

hambones n. [1900s] (US) the knees. [SE hams, the buttocks, the thighs]

ham buggy n. [1970s] (US Black) a hamburger. [pron.]

Hamburg n. [late 19C] (Anglo-Ind.) a bazaar rumour. [the role of Hamburg as a trading entrepôt and thus centre of gossip]

hamburger n.[1] [1940s+] (US) a stupid or worthless individual, e.g. he has no more brains than a ... .

hamburger *n.*[2] [1940s+] (US) mangled flesh, remains. [note Hamburger Hill, the Vietnam War battle of Ap Bia (1969), thus nicknamed because large numbers of US troops were killed and wounded]

hamburger *n.*[3] [1980s+] (drugs) MDMA (cf. ECSTASY). [? the round shape of the tablet]

hamburgerhead *see* HAMHEAD.

hamburger heaven *n.* [1940s–50s] (US) any small diner serving hamburgers. [the name of a chain of New York City restaurants]

hamburger helper *n.* [1980s+] (drugs) crack cocaine. [the resemblance to SE *hamburger helper*, i.e. MSG (monosodium glutamate), which looks like white crystals]

hamburger shot *n.* [1990s] close-up photographs of the vagina, as displayed in 'men's magazines' (cf. PINK *n.*[5]). [the supposed resemblance of the vagina to raw meat]

ham-cases *n.* [late 18C–19C] breeches, trousers (cf. HAM-BAGS). [? Rom. *hamyas*, knee breeches or SE *ham*, the thigh and buttock + *cases*]

hame *see* HAIM.

hamfat *n.*[1] [1900s] (US) a derog. term for a Black person. [the stereotypical pig-based Black diet]

hamfat *n.*[2] [1900s–30s] (US Black) a mediocrity, whether a person or thing (cf. HAMFATTER). [ext. of HAM *n.*[1]]

hamfat *n.*[3] [1950s] (US Black) euph. for SE *hell*.

hamfatter *n.* **1** [late 19C–1950s] (US) an ineffective actor or performer, a mediocre jazz musician (cf. HAMFAT *n.*[1]). **2** [1930s] (US) a loudly dressed and loudly decorated dandy. [HAM *n.*[1]]

ham-frills *n.* [1900s–20s] women's running shorts (cf. HAM-BAGS; HAM-CASES).

hamhead/hamburgerhead *n.* [1910s–50s] (US) a fool (cf. MEATHEAD). [SE *ham/hamburger* + sfx. -HEAD (1)]

ham-hock *n.* [1980s+] (US) a Black person. [stereotypical Black food]

ham-hocks *n.* **1** [20C] the legs (cf. HAMS). **2** [1930s–40s] (US Black) the female legs or ankles (cf. HOCKS).

ham howitzer *n.* [1990s] the penis (cf. BACON BAZOOKA).

hamilton *n.* [1940s+] (US) $10 note (cf. ABRAHAM LINCOLN). [the portrait of US politician Alexander Hamilton (1755–1804) on the note]

ham it up *see* HAM UP.

hamlet *n.* [late 17C–late 19C] (Und.) a high constable. [note Yorks. dial. *play Hamlet with*, to 'play the devil' with]

hamma/hammer *n.* [1950s–60s] (US Black) a very attractive Black woman, occas. extended to men. [? they 'knock one on the head'; but note HAMMERS]

ham-match *n.* [late 19C–1900s] a stand-up luncheon. [SE *ham* + fig. use of *match*, a contest]

hammer *n.*[1] **1** [late 17C–19C; 1930s+] the penis; thus *how's your hammer hanging?* a joc. greeting between men. **2** [1930s+] a thug. **3** [1970s+] (US) the accelerator; thus *put the hammer down*, to accelerate. [later use of (1) is US Black]

hammer *n.*[2] [19C] **1** a strong puncher. **2** a bodyguard.

hammer *n.*[3] **1** [mid–late 19C] an unashamed lie. **2** [late 19C+] an unjust or carping criticism.

hammer *n.*[4] *see* HAMMER AND TACK.

hammer *n.*[5] *see* HAMMA.

hammer/hammer and nail *v.*[1] [20C] to follow. [rhy. sl. *hammer and nail* = TAIL]

hammer *v.*[2] [1940s+] to beat up, to hurt physically, to defeat comprehensively; thus *hammering*, a comprehensive beating. **2** [1970s+] to copulate vigorously with.

hammer *v.*[3] [1960s–70s] (US Und.) to solicit money for drinking. [SE *hammer (away)*, to persist]

hammer *v.*[4] **1** [1970s+] (US) to drive at maximum speed.

2 [1980s+] (US campus) to drink fast, usu. beer (cf. HAMMERED). [HAMMER *n.*[1] (3)]

hammer a job, to *phr.* [1940s+] (Irish) to have sexual intercourse (cf. HAMMER *v.*[2]).

hammer and nail *see* HAMMER *v.*[1].

hammer and saw *n.* [1920s] (US) a policeman. [rhy. sl. *hammer and saw* = officer of the law]

hammer and sickles *n.* [1990s] (drugs) MDMA (cf. ECSTASY). [packaging]

hammer and tack/hammer *n.* **1** [late 19C+] (Aus./N.Z.) a sixpence. **2** [1920s+] the road. **3** [1950s+] the human back. **4** [1980s+] (Aus./N.Z. drugs) heroin. [rhy. sl. *hammer and tack* = (1) ZAC; (2) the *track*; (4) SMACK *n.*[5] (1)]

hammer ass *v.* [1950s+] (US) to work very hard. [SE *hammer* + ASS]

hammered *adj.* **1** [1950s+] very drunk (cf. BASTED). **2** [1980s+] (US drugs) extremely intoxicated by a drug. [fig. uses of SE *hammer*]

hammered down *adj.* [20C] (US) stunted, short and squat, insignificant. [the image is of one who has been pounded down]

hammer-/hoe-handle *n.* [1920s–50s] (US) the penis. [supposed resemblance]

hammerhead *n.*[1] [1970s+] (US campus) anyone stupid and obstinate; thus *hammerheaded*, stupid, stubborn (cf. BEETLE-HEAD). [SE *hammer* + sfx. -HEAD (1); but note HAMMER *n.*[1] (1) thus cf. DICKHEAD]

hammerhead *n.*[2] [1990s] the penis. [joc. use of SE or HAMMER *n.*[1] (1) + SE *head*]

hammer into *v.*[1] [mid-19C+] to succeed, after much effort, in imparting some information or knowledge.

hammer into *v.*[2] [1940s+] to attack, to beat up. [HAMMER *v.*[2] (1)]

hammerish *adj.* [late 18C–early 19C] very well aware (cf. DOWN AS A HAMMER).

hammer lane *n.* [1970s+] (US) the left, or overtaking, traffic lane (cf. GRANNY LANE). [HAMMER *n.*[1] (3) + SE *lane*]

hammer man *n.* [1920s–70s] (US Black) **1** an authoritarian figure. **2** the penis (cf. HAMMER *n.*[1]).

hammer on *v.* [late 19C–1920s] to reiterate, to nag.

hammers *n.* [1960s+] (US Black) women's thighs (cf. HAMMA).

hammy *adj.* [late 19C+] **1** typical of bad acting. **2** sentimental, false, bogus. [HAM *n.*[1]]

h.a.m.n.i.f. *phr.* [1990s] (US Black teen) a threat of violence, *how about my nine in your face?* (cf. NINE). [abbr.]

hamps *n.*[1] *see* HAMPSTEADS.

hamps *n.*[2] [1990s] (US Black/drugs) a Hav-a-Tampa cigar (cf. BLUNT *n.*[2]). [as used for rolling marijuana cigarettes]

Hampshire hog *n.* [early 18C+] **1** a nickname for an inhabitant of Hampshire. **2** a dish of boiled bacon and vegetables. [the popularity of hogs in the county, which was thus also known as *Hoglandiad*.]

Hampstead donkeys *n.* [mid–late 19C] lice.

Hampstead Heath sailor *n.* [late 19C] a very poor sailor, no sailor at all (cf. DRY-LAND SAILOR). [apart from the Round Pond and a number of bathing pools, the Heath is dry land]

hampsteads/hamps *n.* [mid-19C+] the teeth. [rhy. sl. *Hampstead Heath* = teeth]

Hampton/Hampton Wick *n.* [late 19C+] **1** the penis (cf. HAMPTON ROCK). **2** a fool. [rhy. sl. *Hampton Wick* = PRICK *n.*]

Hampton Court *n.* [20C] salt. [rhy. sl.; Cockney pron.]

Hampton rock *n.* [late 19C+] the penis. [rhy. sl. *Hampton rock* = COCK *n.*[2]]

Hampton Wick *see* HAMPTON.

hams *n.* **1** [early 18C–early 19C; 1930s–40s] the legs. **2** [late 18C–19C] breeches, trousers (cf. HAM-CASES). [(1) obs. UK use revived by US Black]

ham scam *n.* [1920s–30s] (US Black) a tough time, a difficult period in one's life. [HAM adj. + SCAM n.]

ham-scram *n.* [1940s] (US Black) a tough time, a difficult period in one's life (cf. HAM SCAM). [note dial. *hamstram*, a difficulty]

ham shank *n.* [1990s] masturbation (cf. BARCLAY'S). [rhy. sl. *ham shank* = WANK n.]

hamshank *n.* [1940s–60s] an American. [rhy. sl. *hamshank* = YANK n.]

ham shanker *n.* [1990s] **1** a masturbator. **2** an unpleasant, stupid, despised person. [rhy. sl. *ham shanker* = WANKER]

ham-snatcher *n.* [1960s+] (US Black) a looter, breaking into stores during urban riots.

hamster *n.* [1990s] (US) a Black person (cf. HAMBONE n.[2]). [SE *ham* + sfx. -STER]

ham up/ham it up *v.* [1930s+] (orig. US) to act in an exaggerated manner, to ruin a situation by foolishly excessive behaviour. [HAM n.[1]]

hanced *adj.* [17C] tipsy (cf. ELEVATED). [SE *enhanced*]

hancock *n.* [1920s] (US) one's signature. [abbr. JOHN HANCOCK n.]

hancock *v.* [1920s] (US) to sign, to affix one's signature. [HANCOCK n.]

hand *n.*[1] [late 18C+] **1** a person, often as *cool hand*, *loose hand* (cf. CUSTOMER). **2** an expert, usu. combined with defining adj., i.e. *old Africa hand*, *poor hand at computing*. [metonymy]

hand *n.*[2] [20C] (Irish) a butt, a victim. [dial.]

hand *n.*[3] [1960s+] (S.Afr. drugs) a small measure of marijuana (cf. ARM n.[3]). [SE *handful*]

hand *v.*[1] [late 19C–1940s] (US) to inflict a blow, to impress upon, to conquer. [one hits with the hand]

hand *v.*[2] [late 19C+] (US) to tell with intent to deceive, e.g. *hand one a line of nonsense/of bull*.

hand! *excl.* [1990s] (US campus) used to wish that someone will *have a nice day*. [abbr.]

hand and pocket shop *n.* [late 18C–19C] an eating house where one must pay cash and credit is not available. [one must put one's *hand in one's pocket*]

hand and fist *phr.* [20C] drunk. [rhy. sl. *hand and fist* = PISSED adj.[1]; never truncated]

hand artillery/cannon *n.* [1920s–30s] (US) a pistol.

handbag *v.* [1980s+] to attack, esp. of a woman. [the ideologically inspired aggressiveness of the former British Prime Minister Margaret Thatcher (b.1925), who was seen, cartoonishly, as hitting opponents with her omnipresent handbag]

handball *n.*[1] [1980s+] (US gay) the insertion of one's hand and forearm into the partner's anus or vagina (cf. FIST-FUCK). [SE *hand* + BALL v.[4] + pun]

handball *n.*[2] [1980s+] (drugs) crack cocaine. [ety. unknown]

hand-basket portion *n.* [late 18C–19C] a woman whose family continually give money to her husband. [note 16C SE *handbasket sloy*, a unpleasant epithet for a woman]

handbook *n.* [late 19C–1970s] (US) a small bookmaker or illegal betting establishment. [SE *hand* + BOOK n.[2]]

H & C *n.* [1960s+] (drugs) heroin and cocaine. [H n.[2] + C n.[2]]

hand cannon *see* HAND ARTILLERY.

handcuff *n.* [1920s–40s] (US Black) an engagement ring, a wedding ring. [a negative view of marriage]

-handed *sfx.* [20C] (Und.) the size of a gang of criminals can be two-, three-, four-, team- or mob-handed.

handed the dirty end *see* GET THE DIRTY END.

hand fucking *n.* [1960s+] (US Black) male masturbation (cf. FIST-FUCKING; HAND SHANDY).

handful *n.*[1] [late 19C+] a difficult person, usu. a child.

handful *n.*[2] [1930s+] (Und.) a 5-year prison sentence. [the hand's 5 fingers]

handful of gimme and a mouthful of much obliged *phr.* [1920s+] (US) one who expects generosity but offers little or insincere thanks in return.

hand gallop *v.* [1970s] to masturbate.

hand gig *n.* [1960s+] (gay) a homosexual prostitute who specializes in masturbating his clients or joining in mutual masturbation with them.

H & H *phr.* [1980s] (US preppie/campus) of sexual or romantic partnerships, *hot and heavy*. [abbr.]

handicap *n.* [20C] venereal disease. [rhy. sl. *handicap* = CLAP n.]

hand in one's checks, to *phr.* [mid-19C+] (US) to die (cf. CASH IN ONE'S CHECKS). [gambling imagery]

hand in one's chips, to *phr.* [late 19C+] to die (cf. CASH IN ONE'S CHECKS). [var. on CASH IN ONE'S CHIPS]

hand/pass/turn in one's dinner pail, to *phr.* [1920s+] **1** to die. **2** to resign from one's job.

hand is long/hand is longer than one's foot *phr.* (W.I.) a phr. used to reprimand someone who has a reputation for petty thieving.

hand it to *v.* [20C] (orig. US) to accept someone else's achievements (esp. when one has no real respect for the individual concerned and the acceptance is reluctant), usu. in phr. *I've got to hand it to …* .

hand jig *n.* [1930s–60s] (US prison) masturbation, usu. of one prisoner by another (cf. HAND JOB). [SE *hand* + *jig*, a fidgety movement]

hand jive, to *phr.* **1** [1950s+] (US) to slap the hands in time to the rhythm of music. **2** [1970s+] (US) to masturbate, usu. someone else (cf. HAND JOB v.).

hand job *n.* **1** [1930s+] masturbation, often offered in a prostitute's price list. **2** [1970s+] (US) an act of insincere flattery. **3** [1980s+] (US) an obnoxious person (cf. WANKER).

hand job *v.* [1960s+] (US) to masturbate. [HAND JOB n. (1)]

handkerchief-head *n.*[1] [20C] (US Black) a subservient, role-playing, White-stereotyped Black woman, the female version of an UNCLE TOM n. (cf. AUNT JANE n.[2]). [the covering of one's expensively straightened hair with a handkerchief. Black militants of the 1960s, who advocated the AFRO n.[2] as a symbol of emancipation, saw such hairstyles as selling out to White standards]

handkerchief-head *n.*[2] [1990s] (US) a derog. term for an Arab (cf. TOWELHEAD). [SE *handkerchief* + sfx. -HEAD (3); the *keffiyeh* head-dress worn by Arabs]

handle *n.*[1] **1** [18C–mid-19C] the nose. **2** [1960s+] (US) the penis.

handle *n.*[2] [mid-19C+] a name, a nickname, a title (esp. as spoken rather than written); thus *a handle to one's name*, a title, an honorific.

handle *n.*[3] [20C] (Aus./N.Z.) a glass of beer. [? the handle that draws the beer or that of the glass]

handle *v.* **1** [19C] to have sexual intercourse (cf. FONDLE). **2** [19C] to masturbate. **3** [1910s] (US) to manhandle. [euph.]

handlebars/long handlebars *n.* [20C] (US) long underwear.

handle of one's face *n.* [early 18C] the nose. [HANDLE n.[1] (1)]

handles *n.* **1** [1980s+] (US campus) a ring of excess fat around one's stomach, a 'spare tyre' (cf. LOVE HANDLES). **2** [1980s+] (US) the female breasts.

handle the ribbons, to *phr.* [19C] to drive a coach and horses (cf. FLUTTER THE RIBANDS).

handle with kid gloves, to *phr.* [20C] to treat carefully, gently.

handle like a foot *n.* [early 18C] clumsy, badly shaped handwriting. [SE *hand*, a style of writing]

hand-me-downs *n.* [mid-19C+] second-hand clothes, either given free or bought at a second-hand shop (cf. REACH-ME-DOWN). [such clothing is 'handed down' from one owner to the next]

hand-me-down shop *n.* [late 19C] an illicit pawnbrokers.

hand-mucker *n.* [1930s+] a card cheat who specializes in palming cards, then holding them out of the game until they become useful to him (cf. HOLD-OUT ARTIST).

hand-out *n.* [late 19C+] (US) food or money given to a beggar.

hand out *v.* [late 19C–1930s] (US) to impart information that is insincere or aiming to impress.

hand out a line, to *phr.* [1920s+] to deceive through a cunning story or excessive charm (cf. FEED A LINE). [SE *hand out* + LINE n.¹ (3)]

hand over fist *phr.* [early 19C+] **1** in large quantities, usu. of the making of money. **2** very quickly. [naut. jargon, referring to the pulling on, or climbing of, ropes]

hand over the baby, to *phr.* [1930s+] to pass on an unpleasant or wearisome responsibility.

hand queen *n.* [1960s+] (US gay) one who prefers being masturbated to other forms of sex. [SE *hand* + QUEEN n.¹]

hand-reared *adj.* [20C] possessed of a large penis (cf. BRING UP BY HAND; TAKE ONESELF IN HAND).

hands *n.*¹ [20C] (a piece of) meat. [rhy. sl. *hands and feet* = meat]

hands *n.*² [1980s+] (US campus) the female breasts (cf. EYES n.²).

hand-saw *n.* [mid-19C] a street seller of cutlery, razors and knives (cf. CHIVE-FENCER).

handshake *n.* [1930s+] a tip or bribe, given surreptitiously (cf. GOLDEN HANDSHAKE; GREEN HANDSHAKE).

handshake *v.* [1910s–60s] (US) to curry favour.

handshaker *n.* **1** [late 19C–1920s] (US) an insincere person (cf. HANDSHAKE v.). **2** [late 19C] (US) a swindler.

hand shandy *n.* [20C] the act of masturbation. [SE *shandy*, a fizzy drink combining beer and lemonade]

hand shandy *v.* [20C] to masturbate. [HAND SHANDY n.]

hand shoe *n.* [late 19C–1960s] (US) a glove.

hands-off *adj.* [20C] a way of doing things that distances the performer from the subject of the action.

hands off! *excl.* [mid-16C+] leave it alone! do not touch!

hands off cocks/your cocks, feet in socks/your socks! *phr.* a joc. wake-up cry, orig. RAF, but general in the services, institutions and similar sites of dormitory accommodation.

hand/han solo *n.* [1990s] masturbation (cf. DO THE HAN SOLO). [pun on the character Han Solo in the *Star Wars* films of the 1970s–80s]

handsome *n.* [1940s+] (orig. US) a general term of address, the subject may or may not actually be attractive.

handsome! *excl.* [20C] a general term of approval, excellent, wonderful (cf. SWEET adj.³). [16C SE *handsome*, becoming, courteous, gracious]

handsome harry *n.* [1930s+] a womanizer, esp. one whose seductive 'line' cannot be trusted.

hand someone something on a platter/silver platter, to *phr.* [1910s+] to give someone something (concrete or fig.) without calling for any effort on the receiver's part (cf. HAND SOMETHING TO SOMEONE ON A PLATE).

hand someone the cold and frosty, to *phr.* [1920s+] to treat disdainfully and coldly (cf. COLD SHOULDER).

hand someone the mitt, to *phr.* [20C] (US) to reject, to turn down, to dismiss (cf. GIVE THE GLOVE). [SE *hand* + MITT n.]

handsome ransome *n.* [1930s] (US Black) a large sum of money.

hand something to someone on a plate, to *phr.* [1930s+] to give someone something (concrete or fig.) without calling for any effort on the receiver's part.

handstaff *n.* [mid-19C+] the penis (cf. HANDLE n.¹). [SE *handstaff*, the handle of a flail]

hand's turn *n.* [19C+] a stroke of work; thus *at every hand's turn* (US), often, frequently, continually.

handsupper *n.* [1940s+] (S.Afr.) a traitor. [those Boers who surrendered, i.e. *put their hands up*, at the end of the Anglo-Boer Wars (1880–1, 1899–1902)]

hand to fist *phr.* [mid-17C–early 19C] one after another.

hand-to-gland combat *n.* [20C] masturbation. [pun on SE *hand-to-hand combat*]

hand-to-hand man *n.* [1980s+] (drugs) transient dealers who carry small amounts of crack cocaine.

hand-warmers *n.* [1920s+] (Aus.) the female breasts.

hand/handy work *n.* [20C] masturbation.

handy *adj.* [late 19C+] useful, admirable. [var. on SE]

handy for *phr.* [1960s+] convenient for, near to. [synon. 19C SE *handy by*, *handy to*]

handyman *n.* [1950s+] a man who, unable to bring his partner to orgasm through intercourse, uses his fingers to bring her to the desired climax.

handy wagon *n.* [1920s–30s] (US) a police patrol car. [its SE *handiness* for making arrests]

handy work *see* HAND WORK.

Hanes! *see* HAINES!

hang *n.*¹ [mid-19C+] euph. for DAMN!; thus *not give a hang*, not to care at all.

hang *n.*² [1950s+] (US Black) a job, esp. one that may not be ideal but supports one's living. [SE *hang*, to hold on to]

hang *n.*³ (US campus) **1** [1980s+] a loiterer, someone who spends a lot of time at a place. **2** [1980s+] a place suitable for loiterers to gather. **3** [1990s] (US) a social occasion, a rock or other concert, a party. **4** [1990s] time spent hanging around. [HANG AROUND; HANG OUT v.¹ (5)]

hang *v.*¹ [mid–late 19C] to be in difficulties; thus *hanging*, in great difficulties. [sporting jargon a *hanging man* is one who is facing great problems, usually in the form of debts]

hang *v.*² [20C] (US) to impose upon, to blame, to make a criminal charge against.

hang *v.*³ [20C] (US) to behave, usu. in combs., e.g. HANG LOOSE; HANG TOUGH v.

hang *v.*⁴ [1950s] (US) to murder.

hang *v.*⁵ [1950s–60s] (US drugs) **1** to be under the influence of drugs. **2** to be in need of some drugs.

hang *v.*⁶ [1960s+] to endure, to suffer, to handle pressure. [abbr. HANG IN v.; HANG TIGHT]

hang *v.*⁷ [1960s+] (orig. US) to turn a corner in a motorcar, as in *hang a left*, *hang a right*.

hang *v.*⁸ [1970s+] (US) to pass forged or worthless cheques, usu. in phr. *hang paper*.

hang *v.*⁹ [1980s+] to loiter, to stand around aimlessly (cf. HANG OUT v.¹).

hang *v.*¹⁰ [1980s+] (US teen) to play basketball. [the apparent hanging in the air that accompanies a jump for the hoop]

hang! *excl.* [1960s+] (S.Afr.) a general excl. (cf. HELL!). [HANG n.¹]

hang a bootie! *excl.* [1980s+] (US campus) **1** good luck! **2** wait! [(2) joc. pron. of HANG ABOUT!]

hang about! *excl.* [1960s+] wait a minute! don't go!

hang about *see* HANG AROUND.

hang a hat on *see* PUT A HAT ON.

hang a jacket on, to *phr.* [1950s+] (US prison) for one inmate to accuse another of informing. [SE *hang* + JACKET n.²]

hang a lilly, to *phr.* [1960s+] to turn left (cf. HANG A LOUIE; HANG A RALPH). [HANG v.⁷ + the initial letter of *lilly*]

hang a louie, to *phr.* [1960s+] to turn left. [HANG v.⁷ + the initial letter of *louie*]

hang an arse, to *phr.* [late 18C] to hang back, to be afraid to go forwards.

hang a pin, to *phr.* [1930s+] (US) to give one's girlfriend one's fraternity pin to wear as a sign of engagement or exclusive dating relationship.

hangar n. [1970s] (US) the fly of the trousers. [the image of the penis as a 'flying machine']

hangara see HANG OF A.

Hangar Lane n. [20C] pain. [rhy. sl.]

hang a ralph/ralphie, to phr. [1960s+] to turn right (cf. HANG A LOUIE). [HANG v.[7] + the initial letter of *ralph*]

hang around/about v. [late 19C+] (orig. US) to wait about, to linger in one place.

hang a shanty on, to phr. [1940s] (Aus.) to give someone a black eye. [SE *shanty*, a bruised eye]

hangashun adj. [20C] (Aus./N.Z.) a general intensive, meaning something extreme or large (cf. HANGAVA). [phonetic sp. of nonce-form *hangation*]

hang a U-ie/U-ey/yewie/youee phr. [1960s+] (orig. Aus.) to make a U-turn. [U-IE]

hangava adj. [20C] (Aus./N.Z.) a general intensive, meaning something extreme or large of its kind (cf. HANGASHUN; LIKE HANG). [SE *hang of a*, thus euph. for HELL OF A]

hang a yewie/youee see HANG A U-IE.

hang black, to phr. [20C] (US Black) to associate primarily, if not wholly, with one's Black peers. [HANG OUT v.[1] (5) + SE *Black*]

hang bluff n. [mid-19C] snuff. [rhy. sl.]

hang by one's eyebrows/eyelashes, to phr. [19C] to maintain a position with the greatest difficulty.

hang dog adj. [1940s+] (W.I.) plentiful. [? US phr. *till the last dog is hung*, till everything is used up]

hang-down n. [20C] the penis (cf. HANG-OUT n.[2]). [its flaccid posture]

hanger n. [1980s+] (US Und.) a wallet protruding from a pocket or purse, thus ripe for pickpocketing. [SE *hang*, to dangle]

hangers n. 1 [late 19C–1910s] gloves, esp. when held in the hand for ornamental purposes. 2 [1930s+] (Aus./US) the female breasts.

hang in n. [1930s+] (US) influence.

hang in/in there v. [1930s+] 1 to maintain a position, usu. with implication of pressures to surrender. 2 used as a farewell (cf. STICK WITH IT).

hangin', bangin' and slangin' phr. [1990s] (US Black gang) a phr. used to describe the GANGSTA lifestyle, associating with one's friends and fellow gangsters, fighting with other gangs and selling drugs. [HANG OUT v.[1] (5) + BANG v.[6] + SLANG v.[3]]

hang-in-chains n. [late 18C–19C] a villain, a desperate looking person. [the corpses of villains were traditionally hanged in chains as an 'awful warning' to passers-by]

hanging n. [late 19C] (Aus.) a perquisite, a bonus, an 'extra'.

hanging adj. [20C] (Irish) drunk.

hanging bee n. [mid-19C–1910s] (US) a public hanging.

hanging cheat n. [16C–19C] the gallows. [SE *hanging* + CHEAT n.; lit. 'hanging thing']

hanging johnny n. [19C] the flaccid penis.

hanging out n. [1980s+] (N.Z. drugs) suffering from withdrawal symptoms. [HANG OUT v.[2]]

hanging salad n. [1990s] the male genitals.

hang in the bellropes phr. [mid-18C–late 19C] to postpone marriage even after the banns have been read in church.

hang in the hedge phr. [late 17C–early 18C] to be undecided, usu. of a lawsuit.

hang it all on one's back, to phr. [20C] of a woman, to display wealth through extravagant dress and jewellery.

hang it easy! phr. [1950s–60s] (US) take it easy!

hang it in your ass! excl. [1950s+] (US) an excl. of contempt, often accompanied by a gesture, the right forefinger is hooked over the left thumb, which in turn makes a circle with the left forefinger.

hang it on v. [early 19C] 1 to protract, to put into abeyance. 2 to cohabit with a woman, to form a temporary sexual relationship. [the image is of hanging something on a peg and forgetting it]

hang it on the limb/a bush phr. [1930s–50s] (US prison) to escape from prison. [ety. unknown; ? image of a member of a work gang removing his prison uniform and hanging it from a tree or bush before running]

hang it out phr. 1 [late 19C–1940s] (Aus.) to endure. 2 [1960s+] (US) to run a risk, risk one's life. [euph. for HANG ONE'S ASS OUT]

hang it up v.[1] see HANG UP v.[2].

hang it up v.[2] [20C] to give up trying, to accept defeat, to acknowledge that a target will never be achieved (cf. HANG UP ONE'S HAT). [the image of hanging up something that is no longer in use]

hang-loose adj. [1950s+] (orig. US) very informal. [HANG LOOSE]

hang loose v. [1950s+] (orig. US) to relax, to take things as they come (cf. HANG TOUGH v.).

hang loose! excl. [1950s+] (orig. US) an imper. excl. relax! enjoy yourself! don't worry! [HANG LOOSE]

hangman n. [late 19C] (N.Z./W.I.) a reprobate, a ruffian. [i.e. one who ought to be hanged]

hangman's wages n. [late 18C–19C] 13½ pence, 1s 1½d (cf. LOONSLATE). [the equivalent of a Scot. mark, the sum instituted as the executioner's fee by James VI of Scotland (1566–1625; also James I of England). It was divided into one shilling for the execution and three halfpence for the rope]

hang of a/hangara/hangura phr. [1940s+] (orig. N.Z.) a general intensifier, e.g. *a hang of a headache* (cf. HELL OF A).

hang on! excl. [1930s+] a general excl. requesting a pause in either activity or speech.

hang on by the/one's eyebrows phr. [20C] 1 to persevere despite every difficulty, to be extremely tenacious. 2 to be very near death, ruin or defeat.

hang on by the/one's eyelashes phr. 1 [mid-19C+] 1 to persevere despite every difficulty, to be extremely tenacious. 2 [20C] to be very near death, ruin or defeat.

hang on by the/one's eyelids phr. 1 [late 18C–mid-19C] to persevere despite every difficulty, to be extremely tenacious. 2 [20C] to be very near death, ruin or defeat.

hang on by the splashboard, to phr. [late 19C–1900s] to jump on a bus or tram as it is moving off. [SE *splashboard*, a board fixed over or beside a wheel to intercept splashings]

hang one on v.[1] [1900s–50s] to hit someone, to have a fight. [a punch, a blow]

hang one on v.[2] [1940s+] to be drunk. [a drunken spree]

hang one's ass out, to phr. [1960s+] (US) to run a risk, to risk one's life. [SE *hang* + ARSE n.[1]]

hang oneself out v. [1990s] (US Black) to take a risk. [the image of hanging out over a long drop]

hang one's hat, to phr. [1940s+] to live, to stay.

hang one's hat up, to phr. [mid-19C–1900s] to become engaged; thus *hang one's hat up to*, to make advances towards, in the hope of eventual marriage; *hanging one's hat up*, engaged.

hang one's jib, to phr. [late 18C–19C] to look miserable, lit. to 'hang one's underlip'.

hang one's latchpan, to phr. [late 19C–1900s] to look miserable. [SE *latchpan*, a pan to catch the drippings from roasting meat. In this context the 'drippings' are presumably tears]

hang one's lip, to phr. [20C] (US) to be in a bad temper, to sulk. [the position of the pouting lower lip]

hang one's meat, to phr. [1900s–10s] (US) of a man, to urinate.

hang one's mouth where the soup drips, to *phr.* [20C] (W.I.) to curry favour with whichever political party is currently in power, irrespective of one's own political beliefs (if any). [the image of collecting whatever hand-outs are on offer]

hang on Sloopy, Sloopy hang on *phr.* [1990s] (US Black teen) don't give up, help is on the way. [the chorus of the pop song 'Hang on Sloopy' (1965) by the McCoys]

hang on someone's bra strap, to *phr.* [1990s] (US Black) of a woman, to impose upon or bother another woman.

hang/hold onto your hat! *phr.* [1910s+] (orig. US) be prepared for a shock.

hangout/hang-out *n.¹* **1** [mid-19C+] a lodging, a place of residence. **2** [late 19C+] a place where a group tends to meet (cf. HANG n.³). [HANG OUT v.¹]

hang-out *n.²* **1** [1980s+] the penis (cf. HANG DOWN). **2** [1980s+] a general term of abuse, applied equally to either sex.

hang out *v.¹* **1** [early 19C+] to live. **2** [mid-19C+] to meet, to collect together at a regular venue (cf. HANG AROUND; KICK BACK v.²). **3** [1910s+] to exist, to be situated, to be available. **4** [1910s+] (Aus.) to endure (cf. HANG IN). **5** [1950s+] to idle away time with friends.

hang out *v.²* [1980s+] (N.Z. drugs) of an addict, to be desperate for drugs. [i.e. have one's tongue hanging out for]

hang out a flag of distress see SHOW A FLAG OF DISTRESS.

hang out big bootie, to *phr.* [1980s+] (US campus) to be in the way, esp. to park one's car in such a way that it causes an obstruction. [pun on the car *boot*/BOOTIE]

hang out cool, to *phr.* [1970s+] (US) to take it easy. [HANG OUT v.¹ + COOL adj.³]

hang out one's shingle, to *phr.* [mid-19C+] (US) to establish oneself in business by hanging up or otherwise affixing a nameplate or signboard. [SAmE *shingle*, a small signboard]

hang out the bloody flag see BLOODY FLAG IS OUT.

hang over the stretcher, to *phr.* [1910s–20s] to overeat. [SE *hang over* + STRETCHERS]

hang slack, to *phr.* [1990s] to relax, to take things as they come (cf. HANG LOOSE).

hang-slang about *v.¹* [mid-19C–1900s] to attack verbally. [SLANG v.¹ (3)]

hang-slang about *v.²* [1920s] to loiter with illicit intent. [HANG AROUND + assonance; note SE *sling*, to throw, in this case to throw oneself around]

hang/leave someone out/up to dry, to *phr.* [1970s+] (orig. US) to treat particularly harshly; to make an example of someone.

hang someone's ass, to *phr.* [1960s] (US) to defeat thoroughly, to trounce. [SE *hang* + ARSE n.¹]

hang someone to the wall, to *phr.* [20C] to punish severely. [the victim is tied against a wall for a beating]

hang the moon, to *phr.* [20C] (US) to be very important; thus *think one hung the moon*, to think very highly of oneself. [only someone very important, e.g. God, could have *hung the moon* in the sky]

hang the old man, to *phr.* [20C] to masturbate. [SE *hang* + OLD MAN n.¹ (3)]

hang/tie the rap on, to *phr.* [1930s+] to impute a crime to a criminal (whether or not they are actually implicated). [SE *hang/tie* + RAP n.³]

hang tight *v.* [1940s+] (US) to sit, to wait, esp. under pressure. [HANG v.³ + TIGHT adj.⁴]

hang tough *n.* [1930s+] a tough character. [HANG TOUGH v.]

hang tough *adj.* [1930s+] stubborn. [HANG TOUGH v.]

hang tough *v.* [1930s+] to behave in an aggressive, tough manner, to persist in a course of action whatever the problems; thus *hang tough tit*, to stick to a decision (cf. HANG LOOSE). [HANG v.³ + TOUGH adj. (1)]

hang-up *n.¹* **1** [mid-16C–mid-17C] one who is to be hanged. **2** [late 19C] one who is in serious trouble, whether criminal or financial. **3** [1970s] (US prison) a suicide.

hang-up/hangup *n.²* **1** [1940s+] (orig. US) a problem, a delay, **2** [1950s+] neurosis, obsession. [one's mind gets fig. 'hung up' on the problem or emotion]

hang up/it up *v.¹* [early 18C–late 19C] to offer credit, to defer payment, to record as a debt (cf. ON THE SLATE). [the placing of records of debt on a piece of paper nailed to a tavern or shop wall]

hang up *v.²* **1** [19C] to buy on credit. **2** [late 19C–1950s] to charge exorbitantly. **3** [late 19C–1940s] (US) to pawn. [HANG UP v.¹]

hang up *v.³* **1** [mid-19C–1910s] to rob in the street, to garrotte, to 'mug'. **2** [1940s–50s] (US) to place under arrest. **3** [1950s+] to distress, to annoy.

hang up *v.⁴* [mid-19C+] (Aus.) to tether one's horse. [one hangs the reins on a hitching post. Note UK taxi jargon *hanging it up*, loitering around a theatre or similarly lucrative place waiting for a fare]

hang up *v.⁵* **1** [mid-19C+] (US) to stop work, to retire, to quit. **2** [late 19C] (US) to be quiet, to stop talking. [HANG UP ONE'S HAT]

hang up *v.⁶* [1910s+] to end a telephone call. [one *hangs up* the receiver]

hang up one's boots, to *phr.* [mid-19C+] **1** to die (cf. JUMP THE LAST HURDLE; TAKE THE LONG COUNT). **2** to retire. [var. on. HANG UP ONE'S HAT]

hang up one's fiddle, to *phr.* [mid-19C] (US) **1** to stop what one is doing. **2** to retire. **3** to die (cf. HANG UP ONE'S HAT).

hang up one's harness/tackle, to *phr.* [19C] **1** to retire. **2** to die.

hang up one's hat, to *phr.* [mid-19C+] **1** to live. **2** to die. **3** to retire.

hang up one's jock, to *phr.* [1950s+] (US) **1** to retire. **2** to be killed. [SE *hang up* + JOCK n.² (2)]

hang up one's tackle see HANG UP ONE'S HARNESS.

hang up the gloves, to *phr.* [1940s+] (US) to retire from one's profession. [orig. prize-fighting jargon]

hang up the ladle, to *phr.* [18C] to get married. [the bride brings kitchen implements to hang in her new home]

hang up the spikes, to *phr.* [1940s+] (US) to retire from baseball, football etc. [the spiked shoes worn by such athletes]

hangura see HANG OF A.

hang with *v.* [1970s+] (US) **1** to associate with, to spend time with (cf. HANG AROUND). **2** to handle a situation (cf. HANG IN v.; HANG TIGHT).

hank *n.¹* [late 18C–early 19C] the baiting of an animal; thus *Smithfield hank*, an ox rendered furious by over-driving and barbarous treatment, *hank*, to bait, *hanker*, one who takes part in a baiting. [? SE *hank*, a restraint, a power of check or dial. *hank*, a cluster, a gang]

hank *n.²* [early 19C] a break from work, gained by pretending to be feeling unwell or some other small lie. [dial. *hank*, a hook, a loop; i.e. one is fig. 'hung on a hook', rather than moving back to work]

hank *n.³* [1930s] nonsense. [ety. unknown; ? dial. *be in a hank*, to be confused, mixed up]

hank *n.⁴* [1980s+] (US campus) a slut, a promiscuous woman (cf. SKANK n.¹).

hank *v.¹* [early 19C–1910s] to tease, to bait, to persecute. [HANK n.¹]

hank *v.²* [late 19C] to hesitate, to draw back. [SE *hank*, a restraining or curbing hold]

hankie-head *n.* [1970s+] a derog. term for an Arab (cf. RAGHEAD n.¹ (2); TOWELHEAD). [SE *hankie* + sfx. -HEAD (3); the *keffiyeh* head-dress]

hanktelo *n.* [late 17C–early 19C] a fool, a simpleton. [ety. unknown]

hankypanky/hanky panky/hanky pank *n.* **1** [mid-19C+] trickery, deceit, esp. of a sexual nature (cf. HOCUS-POCUS n.¹; HOOTCHY-KOOTCHY n.). **2** [20C] (US) silly talk. **3** [20C] (US) a carnival game. [? Rom. *hakk'ni panki*, or redup. of the *hanky* (handkerchief) used by a conjuror in some tricks. Thus note theatrical jargon *hank-panky bloke*, a conjuror]

hankypanky *adj.* [20C] (Aus.) cranky, silly. [HANKYPANKY n.]

hanky-spanky *adj.* [late 19C] stylish, fashionable, well cut. [HANKYPANKY n. + SPANKING adj.]

Hannah *n.* [19C+] (US) **1** proper name that is the subject of various phr., e.g. *that's what's the matter with Hannah*, a general phr. of agreement or certainty, *since Hannah died, since Hannah was a rag doll*, for a very long time, *dead as Hannah Emerson*, totally dead, *he/she doesn't amount to Hannah*, referring to a worthless individual. **2** as euph. for *God* and used in various mild oaths, such as *so help me Hannah!*

hannah cook *phr.* [19C+] (US) a general phr. implying unimportance or insignificance, e.g. *not give a hannah cook, not worth a hannah cook*. [naut. jargon *hand or cook*, a lowly ranked seaman who had no specific job or qualification and could thus be used either as a crewman or a cook, according to the captain's wishes]

Hanover jack *n.* [late 19C] an imitation sovereign. [? counterfeit sovereigns produced in Germany and bearing the head of James II or *Jac(obus)*; they were infiltrated into England and circulated during the reign of William III (r.1689–1702)]

Hans *n.* [late 16C–19C] **1** a Dutchman. **2** a German. [the common name; 20C use is (2) only]

Hans Carvel's ring *n.* [late 18C] the vagina. ['Hans Carvel, a jealous old doctor, being in bed with his wife, dreamed that the Devil gave him a ring, which, so long as he had it on his finger, would prevent his being made a cuckold, waking, he found he had got his finger the Lord knows where' (Grose)]

hansel and gretel *n.* [20C] a kettle. [rhy. sl.; the fairy-tale characters]

hanseller *n.* [mid-19C] a street salesman, a 'cheap jack'. [SE *handseller*, which Hotten cites as sl.]

Hans-en-Kelder *n.* [mid-17C–18C] an unborn child, often used as a toast (cf. JACK IN THE LOW CELLAR). [joc. use of Du. *Hans-en-Kelder*, Jack in the cellar]

han solo *see* HAND SOLO.

hansom cab *n.* [20C] (Aus.) a scab, a non-unionist. [rhy. sl.]

hansom cabs *n.* [20C] body lice (cf. BEATTIE AND BABS). [rhy. sl. *hansom cab* = CRAB n.²]

hans wurst *n.* [20C] (US) a fool, an idiot. [Ger. proper name *Hans* + *Wurst*, a sausage or salami]

hanyak *n.* [1980s+] (drugs) smokeable methamphetamine. [ety. unknown]

hap/haps *n.* **1** [1950s+] (US Black) abbr. of happening; thus *what's the haps?* used as a greeting; *no haps*, no indeed. **2** [1970s+] (S.Afr.) a bite, a mouthful, a morsel. [synon. Afk.]

ha'penny *n.* [20C] the pudendum (cf. NINEPENCE). [usu. middle-class euph.]

ha'penny boy *n.* [1960s+] (Irish) a worthless, unimportant person.

ha'penny place *n.* [1960s+] (Irish) a worthless, unimportant place, position or status.

hap-harlot *n.* **1** [mid-16C–mid-18C] a rug. **2** [19C] women's undergarments. [SE *hap*, to cover + *harlot*, a knave, a rascal]

ha'porth *n.* [20C] a very small, negligible amount. [lit. 'halfpenny-worth']

ha'porth of liveliness *n.* **1** [mid-19C] any musical entertainment. **2** [late 19C] an idler, a dawdler.

happa *n.* [1980s+] (US campus) a person who is half-Asian. [Jap. *hampa*, half]

happen *v.* **1** [1940s+] (orig. US music industry) to attract publicity and be successful. **2** [1980s+] (US) to appear, function or work.

happen for someone with something, to *phr.* [1960s+] to turn out successfully or happily.

happen-in *n.* [1940s] (US) a casual, spontaneous visit (cf. DROP-IN n.¹).

happening *adj.* [1970s+] fashionable, chic, up-to-the-minute. [rarely used 1980s + other than ironically/historically]

happenings *n.* [1950s+] **1** (US) goings-on, esp. those of an intimate nature. **2** (US drugs) any illicit narcotics.

happy *adj.* [18C+] drunk (cf. ABOUT RIGHT adj.¹). [euph.]

-happy *sfx.* [1940s+] (orig. milit.) slightly insane as a result of a circumstance, e.g. *demob-happy, bomb-happy*.

happy as a boxing kangaroo in fog time *phr.* [20C] (Aus.) very discontented, very unhappy.

happy as a box of birds *phr.* [20C] (Aus.) in very high spirits. [the chirping of birds]

happy as a clam *phr.* [mid-19C+] (US) very happy, totally satisfied.

happy as a flea at a dog show *phr.* [1990s] (N.Z.) very happy.

happy as a nun weeding the asparagus *phr.* [1910s+] (Can.) very cheerful (with obvious sexual overtones given the 'phallic' asparagus).

happy/comfortable as a pig/pigs in shit *phr.* [late 19C+] very happy, utterly contented.

happy as a sick eel on a sandspit *phr.* [1940s+] (N.Z.) very unhappy.

happy as Larry *phr.* [20C] (Aus.) perfectly happy, quite content. [ety. unknown; 'possibly but not certainly commemorating the noted Australian pugilist Larry Foley (1847–1917)' (Baker, 1966)]

happy as pigs in shit *see* HAPPY AS A PIG IN SHIT.

happy bag *n.* [1970s+] (Und.) the bag in which a shotgun is carried on an armed robbery; the gun makes the victim 'happy' to pass over his money.

happy box *n.* [1980s+] (S.Afr.) wine sold in 2.5- or 5-litre (4½–8¾ pint) containers, placed in a cardboard box (cf. CHATEAU CARDBOARD).

happy camper *n.* [1980s+] (US campus) one who is perfectly satisfied with their life and the circumstances in which they find themselves; also as neg., *not a happy camper*, a dissatisfied, unhappy person; the deliberate levity of the phrase may hide a genuinely deep unhappiness/dissatisfaction.

happy cigarette *n.* [1960s+] (drugs) a marijuana cigarette.

happy-clappies *n.* [1980s+] (orig. S.Afr.) members of an evangelical church, whose services involve a good deal of 'audience participation', e.g. singing, responding, clapping the hands. [a derog. term that emphasizes the differences between the lower- and lower-middle-class evangelicals and the middle- and upper-class Church of England]

happy days *n.* [1920s–30s] a mixture of strong ale and beer. [? its effect]

happy days! *excl.* [1910s+] a common toast.

happy dosser *n.* [late 19C–1900s] a homeless person. [ironic; such a down-and-out was, unless fuelled by a good deal of alcohol, far from 'happy']

happy dust *n.* [1910s+] (orig. US drugs) cocaine; thus *happy dusters*, cocaine users.

happy Eliza *n.* [late 19C–1900s] a female Salvationist. [the relentless good humour of such individuals; *Eliza* is generic for a Salvation Army girl]

happy farm *n.* [1970s+] (US) a psychiatric institution. [var. on FUNNY FARM]

happy-gas *n.* [1930s–40s] (US) laughing gas or nitrous oxide.

happy grass *n.* [1960s+] (US drugs) marijuana. [among its effects is the promotion of laughter]

happyhands n. [1950s] (US campus) a young man who is rebuffed for making unwanted physical advances to a woman.

happy herb n. [1980s+] (Aus. drugs) cannabis. [var. on HAPPY GRASS]

happy home see HAPPY HOUSE.

happy hour n.[1] [1950s+] (orig. US) a period, 1 or poss. 2 hours, when a pub or bar offers drinks at half price, usu. about 6pm; the assumption is that those customers who arrive for the cheap drinks will become sufficiently tipsy to stay on for the more expensive ones. [orig. US Navy term for a scheduled period of time for entertainment and refreshment]

happy hour n.[2] [1950s+] (Aus.) a shower. [rhy. sl.]

happy hours n. [1950s+] flowers. [rhy. sl.]

happy house/home n. [1960s+] a psychiatric institution (cf. FUNNY FARM).

happy hunting grounds n. [19C] (orig. US) **1** death. **2** the vagina. [Native American imagery]

happy juice n. [1920s–50s] (US) good humour resulting from alcohol or drug intoxication.

happy lamp n. [1990s] the penis. [the image of Aladdin rubbing the magic lamp]

happy pill n. [1950s+] a tranquillizer or stimulant.

happy powder n. [1970s+] (drugs) cocaine (cf. HAPPY DUST).

happy returns n. [late 19C–1920s] (Aus.) the act of vomiting. [pun]

happy sack n. [1990s] the testicles.

happy shack n. [1970s] (US Black) a liquor store. [HAPPY adj.]

happy shop n. [1960s–70s] (US Black) a liquor store. [HAPPY adj.]

happy stuff n. [1920s+] (US) cocaine (cf. HAPPY DUST).

happy trail n. [1990s] (US) line of chest hair down the middle of a man's torso leading to the penis.

happy trails n. [1970s+] (drugs) cocaine. [the 'lines' of cocaine set out on a mirror]

happy valley n. [20C] the female genitals. [note milit. use *happy valley*, first an area of the Somme battlefield and, later, anywhere that is suffering heavy bombing]

happy wagon n. [20C] (US) a prison or police van. [ironic]

happy water n. [20C] (US) alcohol, liquor. [HAPPY adj.]

haps see HAP.

hapus capus n. [19C] a prison inmate who has made himself into a self-taught lawyer, to pursue his own case, combat prison corruption or help his fellow inmates (cf. JAILHOUSE LAWYER). [Lat. *habeas corpus*, thou (shalt) have the body (in court). The prerogative writ *habeas corpus ad subjiciendum*, requiring the body of a person restrained of liberty to be brought before the judge or into court so that the lawfulness of the restraint may be investigated and determined. This writ is seen as the basis of all open, honest and democratic legal systems]

haramzada/haramzadeh n. [mid-19C] (Anglo-Ind.) a scoundrel. [Pers. *haramzada*, misbegotten, 'son of the unlawful']

harbour/harbour of hope n. [19C] the vagina (cf. ARBOUR).

harbour light phr. [late 19C+] all right, usu. as phr. *all harbour*. [rhy. sl.]

harbour of hope see HARBOUR.

harch off v. [1940s+] (Aus.) to abandon, to leave. [orig. milit. use; ? parade-ground pron. of 'march' as 'harch']

hard n.[1] **1** [late 17C–19C] sour or stale beer. **2** [mid-19C+] cash, money (cf. SOFT MONEY). **3** [late 19C+] hard labour in prison. **4** [late 19C–1910s] on the railways, third class. **5** [late 19C–1930s] plug tobacco. **6** [1950s+] (US) cider or whisky. **7** [1960s+] (US/N.Z. drugs) hard drugs.

hard, the n.[2] [mid-19C+] whisky. [HARD STUFF]

hard n.[3] [late 19C+] an erection. [abbr. HARD-ON]

hard n.[4] [late 19C+] a thug, a hoodlum. [abbr. HARD MAN]

hard adj. [1930s+] **1** tough, aggressive, violent. **2** (orig. US Black/teen) on bad = good model, excellent, fashionable, admirable.

hard adv. [mid-19C–1910s] very, extremely.

hard/tough act to follow phr. [1960s+] (orig. US) anything or anyone seen as difficult to emulate or rival.

hard-arse see HARD-ASS.

hard-arsed adj. [mid-19C+] **1** tough, uncompromising, cruel. **2** mean, miserly (cf. TIGHT-ARSED).

hard as a goat's knees phr. [1940s+] (Aus.) extremely hard.

hard as Brazil phr. [mid–late 17C] extremely hard. [SE *Brazil*, a hard, red wood]

hard as lard phr. [1940s–60s] (US Black) excellent, wonderful, as good as one could desire (cf. HEAVY LARD). [assonance]

hard ass, to phr. **1** [1940s+] (US) to bully, to treat severely. **2** [1950s+] (US) to endure. [one has, fig. a *hard* ARSE n.[1]]

hard-ass/-arse adj. [late 19C; 1950s+] tough, no-nonsense, uncompromising. [SE *hard* + sfx. -ASS]

hard as the hobs of hell phr. [19C] (US) very hard (cf. HINGES OF HELL). [orig. in a song detailing the miserable life endured by Irish immigrant quarrymen in the US; the *hobs of hell* refers to the bread baked by the boss's wife]

hard-back adj. [20C] (W.I.) **1** approaching middle-age or older. **2** used of one who ought to know better. [the onset of back problems with advancing age]

hard-baked adj. **1** [mid–late 19C] constipated. **2** [mid-19C] (orig. US) stern, unrelenting.

hardball n. [1980s+] (US drugs) a mixture of heroin and cocaine. [SE *hard drugs* + SPEEDBALL n.[1] (3)]

hardball v. [1970s+] (orig. US) to act aggressively towards, to coerce or intimidate (cf. PLAY HARDBALL). [the hard balls used in professional baseball, as opposed to softball]

hardball it see PLAY HARDBALL.

hard bargain n. [mid-19C+] a lazy person, one who cannot be disciplined.

hard bit n.[1] [1950s+] (US prison) an unpleasant time in prison because of one's personality, one's crime (which may alienate other prisoners), inability to adapt etc. [SE *hard* + BIT n.[7]]

hard bit n.[2] [20C] an erect penis.

hard body n. [1980s+] (US) a physically trim, sexually attractive person.

hard-boiled adj. [1910s+] tough, mean, unpleasant.

hard-boiled hat n. [late 19C+] (US) a stiff hat.

hard-boiled shirt n. [1900s–10s] (US) a stiff, starched detachable shirt front. [ext. of BOILED SHIRT]

hard bop n. [1950s–60s] (orig. US) a variety of jazz that links blues to bop and resembles the earlier form, hot jazz; thus *hard bopper*, a fan of the form.

hard candy n. [1960s+] (drugs) heroin. [SE *hard* (*drugs*) + (NOSE) CANDY]

hard case n. **1** [mid-19C+] (orig. US) a tough, ruthless person. **2** [late 19C+] (Aus./N.Z.) someone with a closed mind (no matter how tolerant they might believe themselves to be). **3** [late 19C+] (Aus./N.Z.) a witty and amusing daredevil. **4** [late 19C+] (Aus./N.Z.) a sexually available woman. [SE *hard* + CASE n.[4]]

hard chaw n. [20C] (Irish) a tough person, an irrepressible joker (cf. HARD CASE). [SE *hard* + *chaw*, chew]

hard cheese/Cheddar phr. [mid-19C+] bad luck, usu. as *hard cheese on ... , hard cheese for ... .*

hardcore n.[1] [1960s+] the strongest varieties of pornography, usually featuring uncensored still or moving pictures of intercourse, plus such personal choices as paedophile shots, bestiality, extreme sado-masochism etc.

hardcore n.² [1970s+] the US branch of PUNK rock; *-core* is an all-purpose rock music suffix, it includes *thrashcore*, *grindcore, dancecore*. [HARDCORE n.¹. 'If you worship non-sense Heavy Metal bands, like whacking out 30-minute long songs with wind down riffs and useless guitar wanking, plus crave to be "hip" and have journos licking your scrotum, call yourself grindcore; … grungecore … much the same as [grindcore] with absolutely zero musical skill and unwashed underwear' (*Britcore, The Street Suss Encyclopedia*, 1990)]

hardcore adj.¹ [1960s+] (orig. US) a general term of approval, serious, experienced, committed, full-time; the implication is that the word, act or person thus qualified is the ultimate of the type. [HARDCORE n.¹]

hardcore adj.² [1990s] (US teen) true to what you believe. [HARDCORE adj.¹]

hard-cutting adj. [1940s] (US Black) extremely good, fashionable. [var. on HARD-HITTING]

hard daddy n. [1960s+] (US prison) a butch lesbian. [SE *hard* + DADDY n. (9)]

hard dick n. [1970s+] (US) a tough guy. [SE *hard* + DICK n.¹]

hard doer n. [20C] (Aus.) **1** a character, an eccentric, one who never gives up despite any circumstances. **2** an amusing fellow, a 'good sport'. [ext. of DOER n. (2)]

hard down adj. [1930s] (US Black) truthful, genuine, dependable.

hard-down adv. [1930s] (US Black) really, truly, genuinely.

hard drink n. [late 16C–early 18C] stale, sour drink. [HARD n.¹ (1)]

hard-ears n. [late 19C+] (W.I.) disobedience. [HARD-EARS adj.]

hard-ears adj. [late 19C+] (W.I.) obstinate, stubborn (cf. HARD-ASS; HARD-NOSE n.).

hardegat n. [1950s+] (S.Afr.) an obstinate person. [HARDEGAT adj.]

hardegat adj. [1950s+] (S.Afr.) stubborn. [Afk. *harde*, hard + GAT n.²]

harder than pulling a soldier off your sister phr. [20C] very difficult indeed.

hard eyes n. [1960s+] (US) unpleasant look, disapproving stare (cf. GLAD EYE).

hard guy n. [1910s+] (US) a criminal character, a 'tough guy'.

hard hair n. [1950s+] (US Black/W.I.) a Black person's naturally kinky hair (cf. BAD HAIR).

hard hat n. [1950s+] (US) a construction worker. [the essential part of his 'uniform']

hardhead n.¹ (US) **1** [mid-19C–1950s] a White native of rural Tennessee or Kentucky. **2** [20C] a Dutchman. **3** [20C] a German. **4** [20C] an Englishman. **5** [20C] a primitive Baptist. [the stereotyped hard-headedness, whether emotional or physical, of all these groups]

hardhead n.² **1** [1930s+] (Aus.) a villain, a criminal (cf. HARD CASE). **2** [1940s+] (US) a rebellious, non-conformist Black person (cf. BAD-ASS NIGGER). [such a name does reinforce the White cliché that one can never knock out or hurt a Black man by hitting him on his head because it is too solid to damage]

hard head makes a soft behind, a phr. [late 19C–1940s] (US Black) stubbornness can lead to unpleasant consequences.

hard hit n. [1970s] an act of defecation. [rhy. sl. *hard hit* = SHIT n.¹]

hard-hitter n. [late 19C–1910s] (Aus./N.Z.) a bowler hat (cf. BENDIGO; BOXER n.¹; HARD-KNOCKER; HARD-PUNCHER).

hard-hitting adj. [1940s] (US Black) smart, fashionable (cf. HARD-CUTTING).

hard horse n. [19C] (US) a brutal, tyrannical person.

hard hustle n. [1950s+] (US) any form of complex and thus potentially highly lucrative confidence trick. [SE *hard* + HUSTLE n.]

hard John n. [1930s–40s] (US Black) an FBI agent. [SE *hard* + JOHN n.³]

hard-knocker n. [late 19C–1940s] (N.Z.) a bowler hat. [var. on HARD-HITTER]

hard labour n.¹ [20C] a neighbour. [rhy. sl.]

hard labour n.² [1990s] masturbation.

hard leg n. [1940s+] (US Black) **1** a tough man or boy. **2** a man who devotes all his time and energies to pursuing the street life and the world of strictly male endeavour – pimping, HUSTLING etc. **3** an ugly woman, esp. an old, worn-out prostitute.

hardlegs n. [1960s] (US Black) a boy. [HARD LEG]

hard line n. [1980s+] (drugs) crack cocaine. [SE *hard drugs* + LINE n.⁴]

hard lines n. [early 19C+] bad luck, misfortune. [? biblical use of *lines* as one's 'lot in life', i.e. Ps. 16:6: 'The lines are fallen unto me in pleasant places; yea, I have a goodly heritage']

hard lot n. [mid–late 19C] (US) a rough, aggressive individual. [SE *hard* + *lot*, a person]

hard man n. [1950s+] **1** a thug, a professionally violent person. **2** one who has a high opinion of his own powers, usu. physical.

hard money n. [1970s+] cash, coins, change (cf. SOFT MONEY).

hard morris n. [1940s+] (W.I.) a tough fighter. [? anecdotal; i.e. proper name *Morris* or SE *morris* (dancing), i.e. the 'dancing' around of a fighter]

hardmouth n. [20C] (W.I.) one who argues and resists when it is time to repay a loan or to pay a bill.

hardmouth v. [1940s+] to attack verbally, to slander (cf. BADMOUTH v.)

hard mouthful n. [20C] the erect penis, presumably in the context of fellatio.

hard neck n. [late 19C+] cheek, impudence, thus a person who displays such characteristics (cf. BRASS NECK).

hard-nose n. [20C] (orig. US) **1** a mean, unpleasant person; thus *get the hard-nose*, to become angry or irritated (cf. HARD-ASS). **2** (gambling) a bettor who will never let himself become excessively in debt to his bookmaker

hard-nose adj. [20C] tough, uncompromising. [HARD-NOSE n.]

hard-nosed adj. [1920s+] (orig. US) **1** stubborn, unyielding, extreme. **2** common-sense, sensible, e.g. *hard-nosed practicalities*.

hard nut n. [late 19C+] a tough person, a dangerous enemy, anything difficult to achieve. [abbr. phr. *hard nut to crack*]

hard oil n. [1910s–40s] (US) butter, margarine, lard. [*hard oil*, any form of grease, used for lubrication, that will not flow; orig. used in WW1 for butter]

hard-on n. **1** [late 19C+] an erection; thus *have a hard-on for*, to want something very much, to like or dislike a person particularly. **2** [1930s+] used as term of address, usu. sarcastic and referring to someone's high self-esteem. **3** [1960s+] (US) a despicable individual or difficult task.

hard-pan adj. [19C] (US) fundamental, conservative; thus *get down to hard-pan*, to get down to basics, to come down to fundamentals. [SE *hardpan*, hard compacted soil or subsoil]

hard-pay man n. [1950s] (W.I.) a bad debtor, either through his inability or unwillingness to pay.

hard-puncher n. [mid–late 19C] a fur cap typically worn by a London tough (cf. BENDIGO; HARD-HITTER). [his wearing it identifies him as a thug]

hard-pushed adj. [mid-19C] in poor economic circumstances, in difficulties.

hard put to it phr. [late 17C+] in financial difficulties.

hard rock n.¹ [1940s+] (US Black) a tough person, both emotionally and physically.

hard rock n.² [1980s+] (drugs) crack cocaine.

hardrock adj. (US) **1** [1920s+] craggy, physically tough. **2** [1960s+] a general term of approval (cf. HARDCORE adj.[1]).

hard-rock hotel n. [1940s–70s] (US) a prison (cf. AKERMAN'S HOTEL). [the stones from which it is built ? + the rocks that prisoners are made to break]

hard root n. [19450s+] (Irish) a tough, devil-may-care individual.

hard row to hoe, a phr. [mid-19C+] (orig. US) a difficult situation to pursue.

hard-run adj. [late 19C] in poor financial circumstances. [one is exhausted by a fig. SE *hard run*]

hards n. [early 19C] *hard* times. [abbr.]

hardscrabble adj. [19C] (US) tough, challenging. [SE *hard* + *scrabble*, a difficult struggle for survival; *hardscrabble* is often used as the fig. name for any barren location, where survival is achieved only through the greatest efforts]

hard scran! excl. [mid-19C+] (Aus.) bad luck (to you)! (cf. BAD SCRAN). [fig. use of SCRAN n.]

hard-shell n. **1** [mid-19C–1910s] (US) a member of the primitive Baptist Church (cf. HARDHEAD n.[1]). **2** [mid-19C–1970s] (US) an uncompromising conservative person.

hardshell adj. [19C+] (US) uncompromising, fundamentalist, unswervingly conservative (cf. HARDCORE adj.[1]). [SE *hard* + *shell*, having a hard shell, e.g. a clam, a crab]

hard shot/thing n. **1** [late 19C+] (Aus./N.Z.) someone with a closed mind (no matter tolerant they might believe themselves to be). **2** [late 19C+] (Aus./N.Z.) a witty and amusing daredevil. **3** [late 19C+] (Aus./N.Z.) a sexually available woman. [HARD CASE]

hard skull-fry n. [1940s–50s] (US Black) a straightened or 'processed' hairdo that is covered in hair-oil or cream. [the hot lye that is placed on the head to straighten one's hair]

hard spiel n. [1930s–40s] (US Black) Black slang, jive talk. [SE *hard* + SPIEL n.]

hardstep n. [1990s] a kind of music originating out of London and combining rave and ragga (cf. JUNGLE n.[3]).

hard stuff n. **1** [late 18C–1940s] money in the form of coins, as opposed to notes. **2** [early 19C+] spirits, as opposed to beer. **2** [1950s+] (drugs) hard drugs, i.e. narcotics, as opposed to soft, i.e. tranquillizers, cannabis etc.

hard tack n. [early 19C–1900s] inadequate rations. [naval use *hard tack*, ship's biscuits, coarse food]

hardtail n. **1** [1910s–30s] (US) a mule. **2** [1930s–70s] (US) an experienced man. [SE *hard* + TAIL n.[1] (1)]

hard talk v. [20C] to employ pressure tactics in a sales pitch.

hard thing see HARD SHOT.

hard thomas n. [1950s] (W.I.) a stubborn man. [? biblical doubting *Thomas*]

hard ticket n. (US) **1** [late 19C+] a thug, a hoodlum. **2** [20C] a difficult situation. **3** [1960s+] (Irish) a humorist, an eccentric.

hard time n. [20C] (Und.) a long or severe prison sentence; thus *hard-timer*, a prisoner. [SE *hard* + TIME n.[1]]

hard time, to phr. [1960s+] (US) to harass.

hard times n. [19C] (US) a cheap, poor quality fabric, which resembles heavy wool but is not much better than cotton shoddy and used for the cheapest of clothes; thus *hard times party*, someone who wears worn-out or seedy clothes. [SE *hard times*, a period of poverty]

hard titty see TOUGH TITTY.

hard-up n.[1] [mid-19C+] **1** a smoker of cigar or cigarette ends. **2** a cigarette or cigar end. **3** a collector of cigar or cigarette ends. **4** a cigarette made of discarded ends. [those who smoke them are HARD-UP adj.[1]]

hard up n.[2] [1930s] the erect penis. [var. of HARD-ON n. (1)]

hard up/hard-up adj.[1] [early 19C+] impoverished; thus [mid-19C+] *hardupness, hardup(p)ishness*, poverty.

hard-up adj.[2] **1** [late 19C] drunk. **2** [1930s+] (US) in need of sexual gratification. **3** [1950s+] (W.I.) unable to attract a steady partner. [ext. of HARD UP adj.[1], but in (2) note HARD n.[3]]

hard up for phr. [mid-19C] badly at a loss for.

hard walk n. [late 19C] a swaggering walk affected by New York's 'Bowery Boys' (and girls). [HARD adj. + SE *walk*]

hardware n. **1** [early 19C–1960s] strong liquor, whisky. **2** [mid-19C–1960s] (US) coins, cash. **3** [mid-19C+] (Und.) guns, ammunition, safe-cracking equipment and other 'tools of the trade'. **4** [1940s–50s] jewellery. **5** [1990s] (drugs) isobutyl nitrite.

hardware bloke n. [late 19C–1910s] a native of Birmingham, known for its manufacture of pots, pans and other hardware; thus *Hardware Village*, Birmingham. [SE *hardware* + BLOKE n. (1)]

hard way n. [20C] (gambling) the making of an even point in a dice game by throwing a pair rather than two separate numbers.

hard word n. [late 19C–1910s] (Anglo-Irish) a tip-off, a warning; thus *give one the hard word*, to warn.

hare and hound adj. [20C] round. [rhy. sl.]

hare it v.[1] [late 19C] to retrace one's steps. [the zigzag, backwards-and-forwards course of a hare when attempting to elude a pursuer]

hare it v.[2] [20C] to run or move very fast. [the animal's speed]

harelip v. [20C] (US) to destroy, to disfigure, to discomfit, esp. in phr. *harelip the government, harelip the governor*. [SE *harelip* in the general sense of disfigurement]

haricot n.[1] [late 19C–1900s] the penis. [rhy. sl. *haricot bean* = BEAN n.[3] (1)]

haricot n.[2] [1960s+] (Aus.) a male homosexual. [rhy. sl. *haricot bean* = QUEEN n.[1]]

harker n. [mid-19C] (US) an ear. [SE *hark*, to listen]

hark-from-the-tomb n. [19C+] (US) a severe scolding, a telling off, a reprimand. [such an admonition fig. comes from grim spirits of the afterlife]

hark-ye v. [late 18C–19C] to borrow money. [the image is of drawing one's target to one side and whispering a request for a loan]

Harlem adj. [late 19C+] (US) used in derog. senses to emphasize the neg. stereotypes of Afro-Americans as lazy, larcenous, stupid, vulgar etc. [proper name *Harlem*, the centre of New York City's Black community]

Harlem/Mexican credit card n. [1950s+] (US) a piece of hose used to siphon petrol from another car into the tank of one's own (cf. ARKANSAS CREDIT CARD). [negative racial stereotyping]

Harlem oil n. [late 19C–1940s] (US) a medicine based on a mixture of kerosene or petroleum and sugar and used for children.

Harlem sunset n. [1940s] (US) blood pouring from razor slashes (cf. JIG CUT). [the stereotyped use of razors in Black-on-Black fights]

Harlem taxi n. [1960s] (US police) a large, fin-tailed, brightly coloured car.

Harlem toothpick n. [1930s–40s] (US Black) a knife (cf. ARKANSAS TOOTHPICK).

harlequin n. [19C] a sovereign (cf. RAINBOW n.[1]). [SE *Harlequin*, a character in English pantomime who wears particoloured, bespangled tights; the shininess, and thus the colours reflected in it]

harlequin Jack n. [late 19C] a show-off, both in manner and in dress. [SE *Harlequin* + JACK n.[5]]

harman/harman-beck n. [mid-16C–early 19C] a constable. [ety. unknown; ? *OED* suggests elision of SE *hard-man*; E.P. prefers *ha-man*, i.e. one who shouts *ha!*, stop; ult. dial. *har*, stop! + SE *beck*, beak]

harmans/hartmans *n.* [16C–late 17C] the stocks. [fig. use of HARMAN or ? SE *hard* + sfx. -MANS, thus lit. a 'hard state of being']

harmola *n.* [1940s–50s] a second-rate boxer. [SE *harm* + sfx. -OLA, which tends to imply some jocularity, in this case as regards the fighter's potential for causing harm]

harmony hair spray *n.* [1970s+] the act of ejaculating into a woman's hair. [the brandname of the popular hair spray]

harmufrodite/harumphrodite *n.* [late 19C+] an hermaphrodite. [mispron. of SE]

harness *n.* [late 19C+] (US) clothes, esp. a uniform; thus *Sunday harness*, one's best clothes (cf. HARNESS BULL).

harness bull/cop *n.* [20C] (US Und.) a uniformed police officer. [SE *harness*, i.e. the Sam Browne belt some forces in the US favour]

Harold Holt *n.* [1970s+] (Aus.) **1** salt. **2** a bolt, an act of absconding; thus *do a Harold Holt*, to abscond. [rhy. sl.; ult. Aus. Prime Minister *Harold Holt* (1908–67), who died in mysterious circumstances, apparently drowned in the Bass Strait]

Harold Lloyd *see* LLOYD.

Harold Macmillan *n.* [1950s–60s] a villain. [rhy. sl.; ult. Prime Minister *Harold Macmillan* (1894–1986)]

Harold Pinter *n.* [1960s+] a splinter. [rhy. sl.; ult. dramatist *Harold Pinter* (b.1930)]

harolds *n.* [20C] **1** trousers. **2** (Aus.) knickers. [rhy. sl. *Harry Taggs* = BAGS n.[1]]

harp *n.*[1] **1** [late 18C–mid-19C] the 'tail' (reverse side) of coin. **2** [late 19C+] (US) an Irish person. [the 'national instrument'; the reverse of a coin once pictured Hibernia and her harp]

harp *n.*[2] [late 19C+] (orig. US) a harmonica, mouth organ. [abbr. MOUTH HARP]

harp *v.* [1960s] (US Black) to recite one of a variety of purpose-written 'tales', usu. recounting the exploits of some mythical gangster-cum-sexual athlete (cf. SIGNIFY v.). [the image of the harpist playing and singing folk-tales]

harper *n.* [late 19C+] a penny. [the Irish coin has a harp on it]

harpic *adj.* [1930s+] crazy, insane. [the eponymous lavatory cleanser, which uses the advertising slogan 'clean AROUND THE BEND']

harpoon *n.* **1** [late 19C–1950s] (US) ridicule or victimization. **2** [20C] the penis (cf. BAYONET) **3** [20C] a hypodermic syringe, as used by drug addicts (cf. WORKS n.[3]).

harpoon *v.* **1** [mid-19C+] (US) to ridicule, to victimize. **2** [1960s] (US) to copulate with a woman; thus *throw the harpoon in/into.* [HARPOON n. (1), (2)]

harp six *adv.* [20C] (Ulster) head-over-heels, esp. to *go down harp six*, to fall head-over-heels. [the *harp* engraved on the reverse of Irish coins]

harpy *n.* [1970s] (US Black) a lesbian. [SE *harpy.* 'A fabulous monster, rapacious and filthy, having a woman's face and body and a bird's wings and claws, and supposed to act as a minister of divine vengeance' (*OED*); in Homer the Harpies personified hurricanes and whirlwinds]

harriet lane *n.* [late 19C–1930s] Australian chopped meat (cf. FANNY ADAMS n.[1]). [proper name *Harriet Lane*, the victim of the murderer Wainwright]

Harrington *n.* [early–mid-17C] a farthing. [Sir John *Harrington* (1561–1612) obtained a patent from James I to mint farthings]

harry *n.*[1] [late 18C–19C] a countryman, a peasant (cf. COUNTRY HARRY). [proper name, used as a generic; thus *Tom, Dick and Harry*.]

harry *n.*[2] [1960s+] (drugs) heroin (cf. CHARLIE n.[2]). [initial letters]

harry *adj.* [1990s] foolish. [rhy. sl. *harry and billy* = silly]

harry bluff *n.* [late 19C–1920s] snuff. [rhy. sl.]

harry casual *n.* (S.Afr.) a laid-back, easy-going, unambitious person. [a joke proper name]

harry common *n.* [late 17C–18C] a womanizer. [generic use of proper name *Harry* + SE *common*]

Harry —ers *phr.* [1940s+] a verbal style, orig. in services, affected in 1950s by society and now widespread if obs., in which various words are prefixed by *Harry* and suffixed by *-ers*, e.g. *Harry flakers*, tired out (cf. FLAKED OUT), *Harry crashers*, asleep (cf. CRASH v.[4]) etc.

Harry Fat *see* FAT n.[1].

harry freeman's *see* FREEMAN'S.

harry-harry *n.* [1940s+] (W.I.) rum. [ety. unknown]

harry huggins *n.* [20C] a fool, an idiot. [rhy. sl. *Harry Huggins* = MUGGINS]

Harry James *n.* [1950s] the nose. [the trumpet played by US bandleader *Harry James* (1916–83)]

harry johnson *n.* [1990s] masturbation by one's partner. [the initials *h.* and *j.*, also those of HAND JOB]

Harry Lauder *n.* [20C] a prison warder. [rhy. sl.; ult. the Scot. music-hall star *Harry Lauder* (1870–1950)]

Harry Lime *n.* [1950s–70s] time. [rhy. sl.; ult. *Harry Lime*, the anti-hero of the film *The Third Man* (1949)]

harry monk *n.* [20C] semen. [rhy. sl. *Harry Monk* = SPUNK n.]

Harry Randall *n.* [20C] **1** handle. **2** candle (cf. JACK RANDALL). [rhy. sl.; ult. the music-hall comedian *Harry Randall* (1860–1932)]

Harry Tate *n.* [20C] **1** (bingo) the number 8. **2** a state of nerves. **3** a plate. **4** in pl. Weights, i.e. *Player's Weights* cigarettes. [rhy sl.; ult. *Harry Tate* (1872–1940); note also WW1 milit. use *Harry Tate's Cavalry*, the Yeomanry (cf. FRED KARNO'S ARMY), *Harry Tate's Navy*, the Royal Naval Volunteer Reserve, the Fleet Auxiliary and the Motor Boat Reserve]

Harry Tate *adj.* [20C] **1** late. thus **2** incompetent, disorderly, amateur. [HARRY TATE n.]

harry, tom and dick *adj.* [20C] sick. [rhy. sl.]

Harry Wragg *n.* [20C] a cigarette. [rhy. sl. *Harry Wragg* = FAG n.[4]; ult. *Harry Wragg*, the jockey and trainer whose career peaked in the 1930s]

harsh *adj.*[1] [1980s+] (US campus/teen) very unpleasant, exceptionally rude, ill-mannered, extremely bad; thus *harsh on*, to treat unfairly, to give a hard time to.

harsh *adj.*[2] [1980s+] (US drugs) used of marijuana that, whether through strength or dryness, makes one cough.

harsh *v.* **1** [1980s+] (US campus) to mistreat, to be very unfair towards; thus *harsh me out!* that's very unfair! **2** [1990s] (US) to ruin, damage.

harsh on *v.* [1980s+] (US campus) to criticize, to belittle. [ext. HARSH v.]

hartmans *see* HARMANS.

harumphrodite *see* HARMUFRODITE.

harum-scarum *adj.* [late 17C+] wild, reckless, careless. [SE *hare*, to run wildly + *scare*]

harum-scarum *adv.* [late 17C+] wildly, giddily, uncontrollably. [HARUM-SCARUM adj.]

harvest *v.* [late 19C] (US) to guard, to watch over.

harvest moon *n.* [20C] a derog. term for a Black person. [rhy. sl. *harvest moon* = COON]

harvey *n.* [1950s–60s] a man or woman who acts in a stupid or naïve fashion; sometimes abbr. as *Harve*. [? the film *Harvey* (1950) starring James Stewart as a drunk]

harvey nichol *n.* [1920s+] a problem, a difficult situation. [rhy. sl. *harvey nichol* = PICKLE n.[1] (4)]

Harvey Nichols *n.* [20C] pickles. [rhy. sl.; the store in Knightsbridge, London SW3]

harvy *n.* [mid-19C] (US campus) a *Harv*ard student. [abbr.]

has *n.* [1990s] (drugs) *has*hish. [abbr.]

has-beens n. [20C] (usually prison) greens, vegetables. [rhy. sl.]

hash n.[1] **1** [19C+] food or a meal, often of reheated left-overs. **2** [mid-19C+] a mess, esp. in *make a hash of*, make a mess, often of one's speech. [SE *hash*, a mess or jumble]

hash n.[2] [1940s+] (drugs) hashish. [abbr.]

hash v. [late 19C+] (US campus) to wait on tables in a college or local cafeteria/bar, usu. as a part-time job to help pay for fees; abbr. *sling hash*, to work as a waiter/waitress in a café (cf. HASHER). [HASH n.[1] (1)]

Hashbury n. [1960s] (US) the Haight-Ashbury area of San Francisco. [HASH n.[2] + *Haight-Ashbury*]

hash-cake n. [20C] a cake of any sort into the ingredients of which hashish has been mixed; such cakes, thanks to the cooking process, render the hashish a good deal more potent than simply smoking it (cf. SPACE-CAKE). [HASH n.[2] + SE *cake*]

hash dispensary n. [late 19C] (US) a boarding house (cf. HASH-HOUSE). [HASH n.[1] (1) + SE *dispensary*]

hasher n. [20C] (US) a waiter or waitress. [HASH n.[1] (1)]

hashery see HASH-HOUSE.

hash factory/foundry n. [mid-19C–1930s] (Aus./N.Z./US) a cheap café or restaurant, a 'greasy spoon' (cf. HASH DISPENSARY; HASH-HOUSE). [HASH n.[1] (1) + SE *factory/foundry*]

hash/hesh girl n. [1970s+] (S.Afr.) a woman who frequents shebeens (drinking clubs) to rob the male patrons. [? Zulu *héshe*, swooping onto, or *heshe*, a hawk]

hash-head n. [1950s+] (US) a habitual user of hashish. [HASH n.[2] + sfx. -HEAD (2)]

hash hook n. [1910s–20s] (US) a fork (cf. GRUB HOOKS). [HASH n.[1] (1) + SE *hook*]

hash hound n. [1910s–40s] (US) anyone notably keen on their food, a glutton. [HASH n.[1] (1) + sfx. -HOUND]

hash-house/hashery/hash-joint n. [mid-19C+] (US/Aus.) **1** a cheap café or restaurant (cf. HASHER). **2** a boarding house, a cheap hotel. [HASH n.[1] (1) + SE *house*]

hash-house Greek n. [20C] the jargon of US fast-food restaurants and cafés. [HASH-HOUSE + GREEK; such jargon included *slaughter in the pan*, beefsteak, *red mike with a bunch o' violets*, corned beef and cabbage, *two of a kind*, fishballs and a *sheeny funeral with two on horseback*, roast pork and boiled potatoes]

hash-joint see HASH-HOUSE.

hashmagandy n. [1910s+] (Aus./N.Z.) a basic stew, served on sheep stations and in the army. [? SE *salmagundi*, a dish composed of chopped meat, anchovies, eggs, onions with oil and condiments]

hash-monster n. [1980s+] (US drugs) a crumb of hashish burned on the point of a pin; the smoke is trapped in a container and then inhaled through a straw. [HASH n.[2] + SE *monster*]

hashover n. [1960s+] the after-effects of an evening's heavy indulgence in smoking hashish. [play on the drinkers' *hangover*]

hash-slinger n. [mid-19C+] (US) **1** a short-order cook. **2** a college student waiter in a mountain resort hotel. [HASH n.[1] (1) + SE *slinger*]

hash-up n. [late 19C+] (orig. US) a meal, usu. of whatever ingredients are available, or of reheated, recooked left-overs. **2** fig. any thing that has been speedily thrown together or reworked. [HASH n.[1] (1)]

hash up v. [20C] **1** (US) to plan (cf. COOK UP v.[1]). **2** to spoil, to ruin, to make a mess of. [HASH n.[1] (1)]

hasie n. [1960s+] (S.Afr.) a male homosexual. [Afk. *haas*, hare]

hasikara n. [20C] (W.I.) a noise, a commotion; thus *make hasikara*, to cause an argument, to make trouble, to make a noise. [? Hind. *hasiikara*, ludicrous, ridiculous]

Haslar nurse n. [1990s] a nightstick (cf. GONE TO HASLAR). [RN psychiatric institution at Haslar, Gosport, Hampshire]

hassle n. [1940s+] (orig. US) a dispute, a quarrel, a problem, a nuisance, anything requiring irritating effort.

hassle v. [1940s+] **1** (orig. US) to annoy, to nag, to pressurize. **2** (US) to quarrel. [Cumbrian dial. *hassle*, to hack or cut at with a blunt edge, using a sawing motion]

hassle out/with v. [1960s+] (US) **1** to sort something out through discussion. **2** to struggle with something. [HASSLE v.]

hasta! excl. [1990s] (US campus) goodbye, see you later (cf. HASTA LA BYE-BYE!; HASTA LA PASTA!). [Sp. *hasta la vista*, see you later; ? popularized by the use of 'Hasta la vista' (usu. after an act of extreme violence) by film star Arnold Schwarzenegger in *Terminator 2* (1991)]

hasta la bye-bye! excl. [1990s] (US teen) see you later (cf. HASTA!). [Sp. *hasta la vista* + SE *bye-bye*]

hasta la pasta! excl. [1990s] (US campus) see you later, goodbye (cf. HASTA!). [play on Sp. *hasta la vista*]

haste! excl. [1950s+] (Aus.) stop it! look out! (cf. CAVE!).

haste it up! excl. [1940s] (Aus.) shut up! hurry up and finish – what you're saying is boring!

hasty banana! excl. [1940s+] (US) goodbye (cf. BANANAS!). [a play on Sp. *hasta la vista*]

hasty pudding n.[1] [late 18C–late 19C] a muddy road. [SE *hasty pudding*, a pudding made of flour stirred into boiling milk or water to the consistency of a thick batter]

hasty pudding n.[2] [mid–late 19C] a bastard, an illegitimate child. [pun; the couple have been 'hasty', the child is the 'pudding']

has your bottle fallen out? phr. [1940s+] are you afraid? [BOTTLE n.[3]]

hat n.[1] **1** [mid-18C–mid-19C] the vagina. **2** [early 19C–1900s] a prostitute. **3** [20C] (US) a general term for sexual intercourse. **4** [1940s–50s] (US Black) a woman, esp. a wife or sweetheart; thus *wear a hat*, to be married or have a girlfriend. [abbr. OLD HAT n.; it too is 'frequently felt' (Grose, 1796)]

hat n.[2] [late 19C–1910s] a condition, a 'state'; thus *get into a hat*, to get into difficulties, *deuce of a hat*, a bad situation.

hat n.[3] [20C] (US) a contraceptive. [note Yid. *Schmeckeldecke*, a condom, lit. 'cock ceiling']

hat n.[4] [1990s] (US campus) a fraternity member. [? some form of headgear relating to their status]

hata n. [1990s] (orig. US Black) a hater, usu. in phr. *playa hata*. [deliberate mis-sp. of SE]

hat and coat n. [20C] a boat, esp. a refrigerated cargo ship. [rhy. sl.]

hat and feather n. [20C] weather. [rhy. sl.]

hat and scarf n. [20C] a bath. [rhy. sl.]

hatch n.[1] **1** [1900s–10s] (US) a prison. **2** [1910s+] (US) a psychiatric institution; thus *hatch up*, to commit to a psychiatric institution (cf. BOOBY-HATCH).

hatch n.[2] [1920s+] (US, orig. naut.) the throat or mouth; thus *down the hatch*, a drinking toast.

hatched-faced adj. [late 17C+] usu. of a woman, ugly (cf. HATCHET-FACE). [SE *hatchet-faced*, having a long, thin face]

hatched, matched and dispatched phr. [20C] the births, marriages and deaths announcements in *The* (London) *Times*; listings under adoptions were proposed as 'attached'.

hatchet n. **1** [mid-19C+] (US) the female genitals. **2** [late 19C–1950s] an ugly or debauched woman.

hatchet-face n. [late 17C–mid-18C] an ugly person, usu. used of a woman.

hatchet job n. [1940s+] **1** (orig. US) a particularly vicious piece of criticism, slanderous gossip etc. **2** (US campus) a broken date.

hatchet man n. **1** [late 19C+] (US Und.) a man who is used to punish, or even murder, selected victims on the orders of his boss. **2** [late 19C+] anyone who takes on, or is told to take on, unpleasant tasks, such as, in a company, firing members of staff, broaching distasteful but necessary topics etc. **3** [1940s+] a person who is willing to perform a hatchet job in support of a cause or political party. [SE *hatchet man*, a Chinese assassin, who uses a hatchet]

hatchet-thrower *n.* [1930s–40s] (US Black) a derog. term for a Spanish-speaking man living in Harlem. [Hispanic 'Indians' were equated with Native Americans]

hatchi *n.* [1960s+] (lesbian) the vagina. [? SE *hatch*]

hatching jacket *n.* [1940s–70s] (US) a maternity garment.

hatchway *n.* (orig. naut.) **1** [early–mid-19C] the mouth. **2** [mid–late 19C] the vagina.

hate someone's guts, to *phr.* [20C] to loathe, to detest.

hat holder *see* HAT PEG.

hat job *see* HEAD JOB.

hat peg/holder *n.* [18C; 1930s–60s] the head (cf. HAT RACK). [upon which one 'hangs one's hat'; the obs. UK use was revived by US Black use]

hat rack *n.* **1** [18C; 1930s–60s] the head (cf. HAT PEG). **2** [18C] a thin, scrawny person. **3** [20C] (Aus./US) a scraggy animal, usu. a horse.

hats *n.* [1960s] (drugs) LSD (cf. A n.³). [ety. unknown]

hat size *n.* [1990s] (US Black) one's self-image, usu. the implication is of an exaggerated one.

hatter *n.* [mid-19C+] (Aus.) an eccentric. [? mining jargon *hatter*, a miner who works independently rather than in a partnership, but note MAD AS A HATTER]

hat time *n.* [20C] (US Black) the end of a day's work, thus used as synon. for *goodbye*. [note prison farm jargon *hat time*, the moment when the captain takes off his hat and waves it to signal the end of the chain gang's working day]

hat trick *n.* [1950s+] a remarkable achievement, usually involving three consecutive successes. [orig. a 19C cricket term, adopted by other sports]

hatty/hutty *n.* [19C] (Anglo-Ind.) an elephant. [Hind. *hathi*, an elephant]

hat up *v.* [1960s] (US Black) to leave, to exit. [one puts on one's hat]

haugh *see* HOUGH.

haul *n.* **1** [late 18C+] (orig. US) a large amount of loot or profit. **2** [mid-19C–1920s] (US) a robbery. **3** [late 19C+] a round-up of suspects, criminals, also as *haul in*.

haul *v.* **1** [late 17C–mid-18C] to pester, to irritate. **2** [late 18C–late 19C] to call to account, to bring up for a reprimand (cf. HAUL OVER THE COALS).

haul!/haul it! *excl.* [20C] (US/W.I.; orig. naut.) go away!, get out! (cf. HAUL ASS; HAUL ONESELF).

haul and pull *adj.* [20C] (W.I.) messy, confused, upset. [HAUL AND PULL phr.]

haul and pull, to *phr.* [20C] (W.I.) to upset, to make a mess of, to confuse.

haul ass/arse/tail, to *phr.* **1** [1910s+] (orig. US) to leave, to escape, to run off, as excl. *haul ass!* let's go, hurry up! get out of here! the phr. has created several euphs., e.g. *haul bottom*, *haul it*, *haul pork* (cf. HAUL BUGGY; HAUL FREIGHT). **2** [1910s+] to increase one's efforts, to work harder. **3** [1990s] (US) to be extremely successful. [SE *haul* + ARSE n.¹/TAIL n.¹ (3)]

haul buggy, to *phr.* [20C] **1** to leave, to escape, to run off. **2** to increase one's efforts, to work harder. [euph. for HAUL ASS]

haul buns/butt, to *phr.* [1960s+] (US) **1** to leave, to escape, to run off. **2** to increase one's efforts, to work harder. [SE *haul* + BUNS n.²/BUTT n.¹; euph. for HAUL ASS]

haul-cly *n.* [18C] a pickpocket; thus *haul a cly*, to pick a pocket. [SE *haul* + CLY]

haul-devil *n.* [mid-19C–1900s] a clergyman.

haul freight, to *phr.* [20C] euph. for HAUL ASS.

haul it! *see* HAUL!

haul off *v.* **1** [mid-19C+] to get ready, to leave, often as *haul off and … .* **2** [mid-19C+] (US) to prepare to strike a blow. [the image is of drawing back slightly before acting]

haul one's ashes, to *phr.* [20C] to have sexual intercourse. [GET ONE'S ASHES HAULED]

haul oneself/one's tail/skin, to *phr.* [20C] (W.I.) to leave, esp. as imperative, *haul yourself!* get the hell out! (cf. HAUL ASS). [SE *haul* + TAIL n.¹ (3)/SE *skin*]

haul one's own ashes, to *phr.* [20C] (US) to masturbate. [GET ONE'S ASHES HAULED]

haul one's skin/tail *see* HAUL ONESELF.

haul/pull over the coals, to *phr.* [mid-18C+] to reprimand. [the punishment meted out to heretics; the coals would have been burning]

haul someone off *v.* [1960s+] to hit someone with a fist.

haul tail *see* HAUL ASS.

haul/tote the mail, to *phr.* [20C] (US) to go or run fast. [the image of the indomitable US mailman]

haul-up *adj.* [20C] (W.I.) unhealthy-looking, sick-looking. [the position of one's arms and shoulders, huddled against the pain or cold]

haul up *v.* [late 19C+] to round-up suspects or criminals.

havage *n.* [early–mid-19C] a family or group of criminals. [southwest dial. *havage*, a lineage, a family tree]

have *n.¹* [mid-19C+] one who 'has', usu. money (cf. HAVE-NOT).

have *n.²* **1** [late 19C+] a swindle, a hoax. **2** [20C] a disappointment. [HAVE v.]

have *v.¹* [late 16C+] to seduce, usu. a woman.

have *v.²* [late 16C+] to receive punishment, whether verbal or physical.

have *v.³* [early 19C+] to make an incontrovertible point in an argument or dispute, to place in a situation from which there is no escape.

have *v.⁴* [late 19C+] to deceive, to trick, to cheat (cf. HAD).

have *v.⁵* [1920s+] to represent as doing something.

have *v.⁶* [1970s+] (orig. US) to kill, to injure, used in pass. only.

have a baby, to *phr.* [1950s+] to experience fright, shock or fury (cf. HAVE KITTENS).

have a bad cold, to *phr.* **1** [mid-19C–1910s] to be in debt; thus *have a very bad cold*, to leave one's lodgings without paying the rent (cf. CATCH A COLD; COLD IN HAND). **2** [19C+] a euph. synon. for having venereal disease.

have a bad marble, to *phr.* [1920s–50s] (Aus.) to be in a disadvantageous position (cf. HAVE A GOOD MARBLE). [horse-racing use, to be in a bad position at the starting gate; ult. MAKE ONE'S MARBLE GOOD]

have a bag, to *phr.* [1970s] (US Black) to have a problem; thus *have a bag and a half*, to have a very great problem. [fig. use of BAG n.⁷]

have a bag on, to *phr.* [1940s+] (US) to be drunk (cf. IN THE BAG phr.³). [BAG n.⁶]

have a ball, to *phr.* [1940s+] **1** (orig. US) to enjoy oneself. **2** to masturbate.

have a banana, to *phr.* [1910s+] to have sexual intercourse. [lines from the song *Berlington Bertie*, 'When they ask me to dine I say "No./I've just had a banana with Lady Diana."/I'm Berlington Bertie from Bow.' Whether the *double entendre*, with its ref. to socialite goddess Lady Diana Cooper, was deliberate is unknown]

have a bar on, to *phr.* [20C] to have an erection. [BAR n.⁵]

have a bash, to *phr.* [1950s+] to make an attempt. [BASH n.² (3)]

have a bee in one's bonnet *see* GET A BEE IN ONE'S BONNET.

have a beer in, to *phr.* [1900s] (N.Z.) to be very drunk.

have a bellyfull/bellyful of, to *phr.* [mid-19C+] to lose patience, to become infuriated by irritating repetition, f. mental, rather than physical satiety.

have a belly like a poisoned pup's, to *phr.* [1920s–30s] to be pot-bellied. [the dead animal swells up]

have a berry, to *phr.* [1990s] to have homosexual anal intercourse. [BERRY n.²]

have a Bex, to *phr.* [1990s] (Aus.) to relax. [*Bex*, a tranquilizing drug]

have a big date with rosy palm, to *phr.* [20C] to masturbate (cf. CONVERSE WITH HARRY PALMER).

have a bird, to *phr.* [1980s] (US) to become very angry. [BIRD n.⁸]

have a bit of beef, to *phr.* [late 19C] to have sexual intercourse (cf. ACHING FOR A SIDE OF BEEF; DO A BIT OF BEEF). [BEEF n.¹ (2), (3)]

have a bit of bum, to *phr.* [late 19C+] to have sexual intercourse. [BIT OF BUM]

have a bit of cauliflower, to *phr.* [18C] to have sexual intercourse (cf. CAULIFLOWER n.²; DO A BIT OF CAULIFLOWER). [*cauliflower*, a large white wig 'such as is worn by the dignified clergy'; it came to mean vagina, according to Grose, after a woman used the term in court and was duly reproved by a the Judge 'saying she might as well call it artichoke. Not so my lord replied she; for an artichoke has a bottom but a **** and a cauliflower have none']

have a bit of cock, to *phr.* [20C] to have sexual intercourse. [COCK n.²]

have a bit of creamstick, to *phr.* [19C] to have sexual intercourse. [CREAMSTICK]

have a bit of cunt, to *phr.* [late 17C+] to have sexual intercourse. [CUNT n.¹ (3)]

have a bit of curly greens, to *phr.* [late 19C+] to have sexual intercourse. [GREENS n.²]

have a bit of fish/fish on a fork, to *phr.* [mid-19C+] to have sexual intercourse. [FISH n.⁴ (1)]

have a bit off the chump end, to *phr.* [20C] to have sexual intercourse. [SE *chump-end*, the thick end of a loin of mutton]

have a bit of fun/fun with, to *phr.* [late 19C+] to have sexual intercourse. [euph.]

have a bit off *see* HAVE IT OFF v.².

have a bit of giblet pie *see* DO A BIT OF GIBLET PIE.

have a bit of gut stick, to *phr.* [1970s] of a woman, to have sexual intercourse. [GUT-STICK]

have a bit of jam, to *phr.* [1960s+] to have sexual intercourse. [JAM n.³]

have a bit of keifer, to *phr.* [late 19C+] to have sexual intercourse. [*khyfe*, a woman as sex object; poss. from the Arabic *keyif*, 'the amiable beauty of a fair woman']

have a bit of meat, to *phr.* [late 19C+] to have sexual intercourse (cf. BIT OF MEAT). [MEAT n. (1)]

have a bit of mutton, to *phr.* [mid-16C+] to have sexual intercourse (cf. BIT OF MUTTON). [MUTTON n.¹]

have a bit of pork, to *phr.* [18C+] to have sexual intercourse (cf. BIT OF PORK; PORK v.). [PORK n.¹]

have a bit of quimsy, to *phr.* [19C] to have sexual intercourse. [QUIM n.]

have a bit of rattle, to *phr.* [late 19C–1920s] to have some money. [RATTLE n. (3)]

have a bit of rough, to *phr.* [mid-19C+] to have sexual intercourse. [BIT OF ROUGH n.¹]

have a bit of skirt, to *phr.* [20C] to have sexual intercourse. [BIT OF SKIRT]

have a bit of split mutton, to *phr.* [18C–1900s] to have sexual intercourse. [SPLIT MUTTON]

have a bit of sugar stick, to *phr.* [19C] to have sexual intercourse.

have a bit of summer cabbage, to *phr.* [19C] to have sexual intercourse. [CABBAGE n.⁷ + play on GREENS n.²]

have a bit on, to *phr.* [late 19C+] to make a bet to wager money on. **2** [mid-19C] to be drunk.

have a blow-through, to *phr.* [late 19C+] to have sexual intercourse.

have a blue fit, to *phr.* [1940s+] (N.Z.) to lose emotional control. [SE *blue fit*, an apoplectic fit]

have a bottom-wetter *see* DO A BOTTOM-WETTER.

have a brass neck, to *phr.* [20C] to be impudent, rude (cf. BRASS-NECK).

have a brick in one's hat, to *phr.* [mid–late 19C] (orig. US) to be extremely drunk (cf. TOP-HEAVY).

have a broadway *see* HAVE A MAIN STREET.

have a bug on, to *phr.* [1930s] (US) to be in a bad temper. [BUG n.⁵ (4)]

have a bug up one's ass, to *phr.*¹ [1940s+] (US) **1** to be acting nervously, to fidget. **2** to be in a bad mood. [SE *bug*, an insect]

have a bug up one's ass, to *phr.*² [1940s+] (US) to be obsessed by something. [SE *bug*/BUG n.⁵ (4)]

have a bun/one in the oven, to *phr.* [1940s+] to be pregnant (cf. HAVE A COOKIE IN THE OVEN; HAVE A DUMPLING ON).

have a burr up one's ass, to *phr.* [1960s+] (US) to be very short-tempered.

have a busy foot, to *phr.* [1920s+] (Aus.) of a horse, to be a fast mover.

have a buzz on, to *phr.* [mid-19C+] (orig. US) to be drinking and mildly intoxicated but not drunk. [BUZZ n.⁵ (1)]

have a cab, to *phr.* [late 19C] to be drunk. [the phr. is used to the drunkard, advising him not to try walking home]

have a calf, to *phr.* [1970s] (US) to lose control, to have an emotional fit (cf. HAVE KITTENS). [CALF n.¹ (2)]

have a canary, to *phr.* [1960s+] (Irish) to have an emotional outburst (cf. HAVE A HAIRY CANARY).

have a case on *see* GO CASE.

have a catfish death, to *phr.* [20C] to drown oneself.

have a c.b., to *phr.* [1980s+] (US campus) of a woman, to get extremely excited sexually or otherwise. [abbr. *clitoris* BONER n.³]

have a cherry, to *phr.* [1920s+] (US) **1** of a woman, to maintain one's virginity. **2** usu. of men, to deflower. [CHERRY n.¹ (1)]

have a chicken dinner, to *phr.* [1980s+] (US gay) to fellate an underage boy. [CHICKEN n.⁵ + pun]

have a Chinaman on one's back, to *phr.* [1930s–40s] to be addicted to narcotics, esp. heroin (cf. HAVE A MONKEY ON ONE'S BACK phr.²). [the Chinese origin of opium, the base of heroin]

have a chip at, to *phr.* [1910s–20s] to tease, to make fun of. [CHIP v.¹]

have a chip on one's shoulder *see* CARRY A CHIP ON ONE'S SHOULDER.

have a clear-out, to *phr.* [1920s+] to defecate. [the implication is subseq. to a bout of constipation]

have a cob on, to *phr.* [1930s+] to be in a bad temper, to be annoyed. [? dial. *cob*, to strike or *cob* a lump, a large piece, thus cf. CARRY A CHIP ON ONE'S SHOULDER]

have a collar on, to *phr.* [late 19C] to put on airs. [working-people rarely wore collars on an everyday basis]

have a colt's tooth, to *phr.* [late 14C–19C] esp. of an old man, to have youthful desires that belie one's real age. [SE *colt's tooth*, the first set of a horse's teeth]

have a conversation with the one-eyed trouser snake, to *phr.* [1960s+] to masturbate. [ONE-EYED TROUSER SNAKE]

have a cook, to *phr.* [20C] to have a look. [rhy. sl.]

have a cookie in the oven, to *phr.* [1960s] (US) to be pregnant. [US var. of HAVE A BUN IN THE OVEN]

have a cow, to phr. [1960s+] (US) to lose emotional control, to have a fit (cf. HAVE A CALF; HAVE KITTENS).

have a crack, to phr. [mid-19C+] (orig. US) to attempt, to have a try, 'have a shot'. [CRACK n.[14]]

have a crow to pick/pluck/pull, to phr. [16C–18C] to have an embarrassing or contentious subject to discuss (cf. PICK A BONE WITH).

have a cub, to phr. [1930s–40s] (US gambling) to stack a deck of cards (cf. CUB n.[1]).

have a cup of tea, to phr. [1960s+] (US gay) to have sex in a public lavatory.

have/have had/have got a cup too much, to phr. [mid-17C–19C] to be drunk.

have a cut, to phr. [late 19C+] (Aus.) to try, to make an attempt. [SE cut, a blow]

have a cut off the joint, to phr. [20C] of a man, to have sexual intercourse. [CUT OFF THE JOINT]

have a dab, to phr. [late 19C–1900s] to try, to make an attempt. [SE dab, a light blow]

have a dash, to phr.[1] [1920s+] to try, to make an attempt (cf. HAVE A LASH; HAVE A PELT AT). [DASH n.]

have a dash/dash of lavender, to phr.[2] [1950s+] to be marginally homosexual. [LAVENDER]

have a date with fisty palmer, to phr. [1990s] to masturbate (cf. CONVERSE WITH HARRY PALM). [play on SE fist + palm]

have a derry on, to phr. [late 19C+] (Aus.) to be prejudiced against (cf. DERRY n.[1]). [abbr. derry down = DOWN ON]

have a dirty nose, to phr. [late 16C] to be a good drinker.

have a doctor's appointment, to phr. [1980s+] (US campus) to drink alcohol (cf. GO TO THE DOCTOR).

have a dog tied up, to phr. [20C] (Aus./N.Z.) to be indebted, esp. at a hotel. [the image of having left one's dog while moving on elsewhere]

have a dose of the balmy, to phr. [late 19C] to sleep. [BALMY n.]

have a double shot, to phr. [20C] of a man, to ejaculate twice during the same session of love-making.

have a downer on, to phr. [1910s–30s] to bear a grudge towards. [DOWNER n.[2]]

have a down on, to phr. [mid-19C+] (orig. Aus.) to feel hostile towards, to be prejudiced against. [DOWN n.[1] (2)]

have a drop in one's eye, to phr. [late 17C–early 18C] to be tipsy.

have a dumpling on, to phr. [late 19C] to be pregnant (cf. HAVE A BUN IN THE OVEN).

have a dust, to phr. [1970s+] (drugs) to sniff cocaine. [DUST n.[6] (2)]

have a face as long as a fiddle, to phr. [early 19C] to look dismal (cf. FIDDLE-FACE).

have a face as long as a Lurgan spade, to phr. [late 19C+] (Irish) to look miserable. [Irish lorgán spáid, a spade handle]

have a face like a coastguard station, to phr. [1940s+] to have a chilly, 'stony' face. [pun on STONY]

have a face like a milkman's round, to phr. [1950s+] to look miserable. [play on SE long, i.e. distance/long face]

have a face like a yard of pump-water, to phr. [20C] to look miserable. [for ety. see HAVE A FACE LIKE A MILKMAN'S ROUND]

have a face on, to phr. [late 19C+] 1 to be ugly, e.g. she's got a face on her … . 2 to be in a troubled, nervous mood.

have a face-ticket, to phr. [1920s] to hold a season-ticket usu. for the London Underground or local commuter lines. [note late 19C use, to be sufficiently well known to the janitors of the British Museum Reading Room that one does not need to show one's pass]

have a farting spell, to phr. [20C] to lose one's temper, to lose control.

have a feel till Friday, to phr. [1960s] to enjoy what's on offer for the time being. [the available 'feel' is better than a merely promised 'fuck']

have a few, to phr. [20C] (orig. Aus.) to have a few drinks; thus have a few too many, to be drunk.

have a few in, to phr. [1940s+] to have a drink.

have a few of one's pages stuck together, to phr. [20C] to be stupid, to be foolish (cf. NOT ALL THERE).

have a few over the score see GO OVER THE SCORE.

have a field day, to phr. [early 19C+] 1 to have a task or problem turn out to be infinitely simple. 2 to have great and unopposed success. [milit. field day, a military review, military exercises]

have a fishy eye, to phr. [mid-19C+] 1 to have a glazed eye, 2 to look suspiciously at. [the image of a dead fish on a slab]

have a fit/fit in the arm, to phr. [late 19C] to aim a punch a blow. ['one Tom Kelly' who was tried for striking a woman; 'his defence before the magistrate took the shape of a declaration that "a fit had seized him in the arm"' (Ware)]

have a flea in one's ear, to phr. [mid-15C+] 1 to be reprimanded. 2 to be angry. 3 to fail in one's intentions.

have a flutter see DO A FLUTTER.

have a flutter for, to phr. [late 19C] to attempt, to try to obtain. [FLUTTER n.[2]]

have a fly at, to phr. [1910s+] (Aus.) to have a try, to make an attempt (cf. GIVE IT A FLY).

have a foot in the dish, to phr. [mid-17C–late 18C] to get a share of, to become involved in.

have a full bag on, to phr. [1990s] to have gone without ejaculation for a long period. [SE full + BAG n.[1] (2)]

have again v. [20C] (W.I./Gren.) to have as much as one desires.

have a game at/play at pully-hawly, to phr. [late 18C–20C] to have sexual intercourse. [colloq. pully-hawly, a rough and tumble]

have a gecko at, to phr. [1970s+] (US) to take a look at, to glance at. [play on DEKKO + ? TAKE A GANDER]

have a glow on see GET A GLOW ON.

have a good/long innings, to phr. [mid-19C+] 1 to be lucky, to make plenty of money. 2 to live a long time. [cricketing imagery]

have a good marble, to phr. [1920s–50s] (Aus.) to be in an advantageous position (cf. HAVE A BAD MARBLE). [horse-racing, to be in a good position at the starting gate; ult. MAKE ONE'S MARBLE GOOD]

have a g.p. on, to phr. [1900s–30s] to be sexually obsessed with. [abbr. grande passion]

have a grand finale, to phr. [1990s] to ejaculate on one's partner's face.

have a grape on, to phr. [1920s+] (Aus.) to feel hostile towards someone (cf. HAVE A TOBY ON). [? SE sour grapes]

have a guest in the attic, to phr. [20C] to be eccentric, to be insane (cf. QUEER IN THE ATTIC). [ATTIC]

have a gut like a crane, to phr. [1920s+] (Aus.) to be very thirsty. [the bird's habits]

have a haemorrhage, to phr. [1920s+] (US) to become furious (cf. BURST A BLOOD-VESSEL).

have a hair across one's ass, to phr. [1910s+] (US) to be manly, courageous. [fig. use of ARSE n.[1]]

have a hair crossed, to phr. [20C] (US) to be over-sensitive, to be touchy (cf. ALL HAIR BY THE NOSE).

have a hairy canary, to phr. [1960s+] (US) to have a temper tantrum, an emotional outburst (cf. HAVE A CANARY). [euph. var. of GET A HAIR UP ONE'S ASS]

have a half-nelson on, to phr. [late 19C–1950s] (US) to be in firm control of. [wrestling jargon half-nelson, a hold in which one arm is thrust under the corresponding arm of the opponent and the hand placed on the back of his neck]

have a ham shank, to *phr.* [20C] to masturbate (cf. ACCOST THE OSCAR MEYER). [rhy. sl. *ham shank* = WANK v.]

have a handful *see* GET A HANDFUL OF SPRATS.

have a hank on, to *phr.* [late 17C–19C] to have the advantage over, the implication is of potential blackmail. [SE *hank*, a restraining or curbing hold]

have a hard-on for, to *phr.* [20C] **1** to care deeply about, to be extremely concerned about (cf. GET IT UP). **2** to dislike intensely, of both persons and objects. [fig. use of HARD-ON]

have a hate on, to *phr.* [1930s+] (Aus./US) to dislike intensely.

have a head full of proclamations, to *phr.* [late 17C–18C] to have one's head full of nonsense.

have a head like a beaten favourite/robber's dog/twisted sandshoe, to *phr.* [1960s+] (Aus.) to be ugly or unattractive.

have a head like a drover's dog, to *phr.* [1940s+] (Aus.) to be suffering a very bad hangover.

have a head like a robber's dog/twisted sandshoe *see* HAVE A HEAD LIKE A BEATEN FAVOURITE.

have a head on, to *phr.* **1** [mid-19C+] to have a hangover. **2** [late 19C–1900s] to be aware, to be alert. [SE *have a head/ smart head on one's shoulders*]

have a heart! *excl.* [1910s+] have pity, don't be cruel, be reasonable.

have a hearty-choke for breakfast, to *phr.* [late 18C–late 19C] to be hanged, also extended as *have a hearty-choke for breakfast and/with caper sauce*; thus *artichoke and an oyster*, a pre-hanging breakfast (cf. TAKE A VEGETABLE BREAKFAST). [pun on SE *artichoke* + *caper*; pun on *hoist*]

have a heat on, to *phr.* [1910s–30s] to be drunk or intoxicated by drugs. [HEAT n.[1] (1)]

have a hit on, to *phr.* [1970s+] of a project or person, to make an impact, to come into conflict with.

have a hot-mouth, to *phr.* [20C] (W.I./Guyn.) to answer cheekily, to talk back.

have a hot pie, to *phr.* [1990s] to be defecated upon by one's partner, as a sexual stimulus.

have a hot stomach, to *phr.* [late 18C–19C] to pawn one's clothes to get money for buying liquor; also extended as *have so hot a stomach as to burn the clothes off his back*. [one is warm enough without the pawned garments and one's stomach is HOT adj.[1] for drink]

have a hummer going, to *phr.* [1960s+] (US) to be drunk. [HUMMER n.[7]]

have a hump in one's back, to *phr.* [1990s] (US Black) of a man, to be in the middle of sexual intercourse. [the physical movement of 'missionary position' intercourse]

have air and exercise, to *phr.* [late 18C–early 19C] to be whipped at the cart's tail as a judicial punishment (cf. SHOVE THE TUMBLER).

have a jack, to *phr.* [1970s+] (N.Z.) to take a look.

have a jag on, to *phr.* [late 17C+] to be in a state of drunkenness. [JAG n.[1]]

have a J. Arthur, to *phr.* [1950s+] to masturbate. [J. ARTHUR]

have a jaw like a sheep's head, to *phr.* [late 19C] to be all talk and no action.

have a joey in the pouch, to *phr.* [1950s–60s] (Aus.) to be pregnant. [SE *joey*, a baby kangaroo]

have a knocker on the front door, to *phr.* [late 19C] to achieve respectability.

have a lam on, to *phr.* [20C] to be in a bad temper. [LAM n.[2]]

have a lark *see* GO ON A LARK.

have a lash, to *phr.* [1940s+] (Aus./N.Z.) to take part in, to make a try at (cf. HAVE A DASH phr.[1]). [SE *lash*, a whip-crack]

have a lash at, to *phr.* [late 19C+] (Aus.) to attack, to fight. [*lash*, a whip-crack]

have/take a lend/loan of, to *phr.* [1910s+] to treat someone like a fool.

have a line on, to *phr.* [20C] to understand, to know what is happening. [racing jargon *the line*, the daily details of the horses running and the odds on them]

have a little visitor, to *phr.* [1920s+] of a woman, to be menstruating. [a genteel euph.]

have a live sausage for supper, to *phr.* [19C] of a woman, to have sexual intercourse. [LIVE SAUSAGE]

have all one's buttons on, to *phr.* [late 19C–1900s] to be 'sharp', to know what is going on, to be impervious to hoaxers.

have all one's chairs, to *phr.* [1960s] to be sane, to be rational, to be 'all there'.

have all one's change about one, to *phr.* [late 19C+] to be aware, to know what is going on.

have all one's work cut out *see* HAVE ONE'S WORK CUT OUT.

have all that/more than one can carry, to *phr.* [20C] to be very drunk.

have a long innings *see* HAVE A GOOD INNINGS.

have a loose connection, to *phr.* [1970s] (US) to be eccentric, to be mad (cf. HAVE A SCREW LOOSE).

have a loose leg, to *phr.* [20C] (Irish) to be free to live one's life without restraint.

have a lot on one's plate, to *phr.* [1920s+] to be overburdened with duties, worries, responsibilities etc.

have a lump of jaw on, to *phr.* [late 19C] to be talkative.

have a mad on/mad on with, to *phr.* [mid-19C+] (orig. US) to be annoyed with. [MAD n.]

have a main street/broadway, to *phr.* [20C] (US) to have a large vagina (cf. MUCH-TRAVELLED HIGHWAY).

have a miss/great miss/heavy miss of someone *see* FIND A MISS OF SOMEONE.

have a monkey on one's back, to *phr.*[1] [mid-19C] to be angry.

have a monkey on one's back, to *phr.*[2] [1940s+] to be addicted to narcotics, esp. heroin. [ety. unknown; the image is of a monkey, clawing at the sufferer]

have a moustache, to *phr.* [20C] to perform cunnilingus. [joc. use of SE *moustache* as the female pubic hair]

have a mouth like a cow's cunt, to *phr.* [late 19C] to be very talkative.

have a mouth like the bottom of a bird-cage/parrot-cage, to *phr.* [1920s+] to be suffering the physical results of a night's drinking; also as *one's mouth feels like … .* [the filthiness of the cage]

have a mouth like the inside of an Arab's armpit/ underpants, to *phr.* [1940s+] to be suffering ghastly physical feelings as are concomitant with a hangover. [stereotyping of Arabs as dirty]

have an aching tooth, to *phr.* [16C] to desire, usu. sexually (cf. IRISH TOOTHACHE). [pun]

have an Anglo-Indian back, to *phr.* [20C] (Can.) of a young woman, to have leaves adhering to her back after a stroll in the woods with her boyfriend. [the idea of 'Red Indians' having sex in the open-air]

have an appointment, to *phr.* [20C] (US campus) to go out drinking (cf. GO TO THE DOCTOR). [the euph. excuse offered, usu. to one's female partner, traditionally cast as the inhibitor of such excursions]

have an arm-wrestle with your one-eyed vessel, to *phr.* [1990s] to masturbate (cf. ONE-EYED TROUSER-SNAKE). [assonance]

have an axe/axes to grind, to *phr.* [early–mid-19C] (orig. US) to have one's own interests at heart, to desire revenge; thus *axe-grinders*, ideologically motivated or self-interested grumblers. [coined as US pol. jargon and SE by 1850s]

have an egg in the nest, to *phr.* [20C] (US Black) to be pregnant (cf. HAVE A BUN IN THE OVEN).

have an encore *see* GET AN ENCORE.

have a nibble, to *phr.* [late 19C] **1** to have the best of a bargain. **2** to have a good job. **3** (Und.) to score a success, whether with a bet or a crime (cf. GET A TICKLE).

have a nickel in that dime, to *phr.* [1970s+] (US Black) to have an interest in a state of affairs. [i.e. to invest 5 cents (a *nickel*) in a larger investment of 10 cents (a *dime*)]

have an in *v.* [1960s+] **1** to have special contacts. **2** (Und.) to have contacts in a place – e.g. a bank – that is to be robbed.

have an itch in the belly, to *phr.* [mid-17C–late 19C] of a woman, to feel amorous (cf. ITCH; ITCHER; ITCHING JENNY; PLAY ITCH-BUTTOCKS).

have an itchy back, to *phr.* [1920s+] (Aus.) of a woman, to desire sexual intercourse (presumably in the 'missionary' position). [the idea that women often initiate sex with the request 'scratch my back']

have an M under the girdle *see* CARRY AN M UNDER THE GIRDLE.

have an oar in every man's boat, to *phr.* [mid-16C] to interfere in other people's business (cf. PUT IN ONE'S OAR; SHOVE ONE'S OAR IN).

have a nose of wax, to *phr.* [early 19C] to be gullible, to be impressionable. [SE *nose of wax*, an impressionable person]

have a nose on, to *phr.* [1940s–70s] (Aus./N.Z.) to bear a grudge against someone, to take offence (cf. HAVE A SNOUT ON SOMEONE).

have another guess coming, to *phr.* [20C] (US) to be wrong, to be mistaken.

have a notice to quit, to *phr.* [early–mid-19C] to have a terminal illness.

have ants in one's pants, to *phr.* [1930s+] (orig. US) to be restless, nervous, twitchy, (sexually) excited (cf. ANTS).

have a one night stand with yourself, to *phr.* [1990s] to masturbate. [ONE NIGHT STAND]

have a packet *see* COP A PACKET.

have a paper asshole, to *phr.* [1940s–50s] (US) to be a weakling, to be a coward (cf. KEEP A TIGHT ASSHOLE). [ARSEHOLE n.]

have a pelt at, to *phr.* [1920s] have a try at, to make an attempt (cf. HAVE A DASH phr.[1]). [SE *pelt*, an act of throwing]

have a penn'orth of paradise *see* GET A PENN'ORTH OF PARADISE.

have a peppermint in one's speech, to *phr.* [late 19C] to stammer, to stutter.

have a piece/piece of, to *phr.* [early 19C+] of a man, to seduce a woman, to have sexual intercourse (cf. GET A PIECE phr.[2]).

have a pile, to *phr.* [late 19C+] (Can.) to be in serious trouble. [? a pile of SHIT n.[4]]

have a pink fit, to *phr.* [1930s+] to lose control of one's emotions (cf. HAVE A HAEMORRHAGE).

have a plaster for every sore, to *phr.* [20C] (W.I.) to have an excuse ready for any situation.

have a plum in the mouth, to *phr.* [1920s+] to speak in what is considered an affected, upper-class British accent; thus *plum-in-the-mouth*, affectedly upper-class in speech (cf. PLUMMY adj.).

have a poor way on one, to *phr.* [20C] (Ulster) to be impoverished.

have a pop/pop at, to *phr.* [late 19C+] to try, to make an attempt. [POP n.[6]]

have a pot in the pate, to *phr.* [mid-17C–mid-18C] to be drunk. [lit. a 'tankard in the head']

have a put-in, to *phr.* [19C] to have sexual intercourse. [the insertion of the penis]

have a rag on every bush, to *phr.* [mid-19C–1920s] of a man, to pursue a number of women at the same time.

have a rat *see* GET A RAT.

have a rattle, to *phr.* [20C] of a man, to have sexual intercourse. [RATTLE v.[2] (2)]

have a ring through one's nose, to *phr.* [1970s+] (US Black) to be obsessed, to the point of foolishness, with one other person, usu. a lover, by whom one can be led.

have a roll/roll in the hay, to *phr.* [1920s+] to have sexual intercourse. [ROLL IN THE HAY]

have a roll on, to *phr.* [late 19C–1910s] (teen) to swagger, to put on airs.

have/take a run, to *phr.* [late 19C] to go for a 'constitutional', i.e. a walk for one's health.

have a run for it, to *phr.* [late 19C–1910s] to make a fight.

have/take a screw at, to *phr.* [1910s+] (orig. Aus.) to stare at in aggressive manner; thus *who you screwin'?* as a ritual challenge to a fight. [SCREW v.[3]]

have a screw loose, to *phr.* [early 19C+] to be eccentric, insane or retarded.

have a see, to *phr.* [mid-19C–1930s] to take a look at, to glance at.

have/take a set on, to *phr.* [mid-19C+] (Aus./N.Z.) to bear a grudge against, to have a score to settle with. [SE *set against*]

have a sheet short, to *phr.* [1910s+] (Aus.) to be mentally deficient; also as *short of a sheet of bark.*

have a sherman, to *phr.* [1980s+] to masturbate. [rhy. sl. *sherman tank* = WANK v.]

have a shit haemorrhage, to *phr.* [1950s] to be absolutely terrified (cf. SHIT A BRICK). [the loss of sphincter control that can accompany great fear]

have a shot at, to *phr.*[1] [early 19C+] to make an attempt, to have a try. [SHOT n.[2]]

have a shot at, to *phr.*[2] [mid-19C+] (Aus.) to make a sneering remark in someone's direction, to try to provoke. [SHOT n.[4]]

have a shot in the locker, to *phr.* [mid-19C+] to maintain one's potency or ability, sexual and otherwise. [fig. use of naut. jargon *shot in the locker*, something kept in reserve]

have a shy for, to *phr.* [1920s+] (Aus.) to search for. [SE *shy*, as throw, thus an attempt to hit]

have a sight at, to *phr.* [mid-19C] to make a rude gesture, i.e. 'to place the thumb against the nose ... closing all the fingers except the little one, which is agitated in token of derision' (Hotten, 1860) (cf. HOOKEY WALKER!).

have a skinful *see* GET A SKINFUL.

have a slap at, to *phr.* [late 19C+] to make an attempt, to have a try (cf. HAVE A CRACK; HAVE A DASH phr.[1]). [SE *slap*, a light blow]

have a slash, to *phr.* [20C] to urinate (cf. HAVE A SPLASH; SPLASH ONE'S BOOTS). [SLASH n.[4]]

have a smell of oneself, to *phr.* [20C] (Irish) to have a high opinion of oneself.

have a smell/sniff of the barman's/barmaid's apron, to *phr.* [1920s+] to be drunk.

have as much idea/idea of it as a donkey has of Sunday, to *phr.* [late 19C] to have no idea at all.

have as much wit as three folks/two fools and a madman, to *phr.* [late 17C–early 19C] **1** to be a fool. **2** to be clever.

have a sniff of the barman's apron *see* HAVE A SMELL OF THE BARMAN'S APRON.

have a snitch on *see* GET A SNITCH ON.

have/take a snout on someone, to *phr.* [1940s–70s] (Aus./N.Z.) to bear a grudge against someone, to take offence (cf. HAVE A NOSE ON). [SE *snout*, nose; they get 'up one's nose']

have a soft spot for, to *phr.* [late 19C+] to favour someone, even if such favouritism is neither sensible nor approved.

have a soul above buttons, to *phr.* [late 18C–mid-19C] to see oneself realistically or otherwise as superior to the situation in which one currently exists. [orig. use by George Colman in *New Hay at Old Market* (1795): 'My father was an eminent

Button-maker ... but I had a soul above buttons ... I panted for a liberal profession']

have a spark in one's throat, to *phr.* [early 18C–early 19C] **1** to be continually thirsty. **2** to be keen on, to be enthusiastic.

have a spiral swallow, to *phr.* [1920s] to have a large capacity for alcohol. [water runs down a plughole in a spiral]

have a splash, to *phr.* [20C] of a man, to urinate (cf. HAVE A SLASH; SPLASH ONE'S BOOTS).

have a spring at one's elbow, to *phr.* [mid-17C–mid-18C] to be a dice gambler (cf. ELBOW SHAKER n.[1]). [the movement of one's elbow in shaking the dice cup]

have a spur in one's head, to *phr.* [late 18C] 'To express the Condition of an Honest Fellow and no Flincher under the Effects of good Fellowship he is said to [have] ... Got a spur in his head' (*Gentleman's Magazine* XL, 1770).

have a stick up one's ass, to *phr.* [1960s+] to be totally and irredeemably boring; such a stick would render one physically, and thus mentally, rigid. [SE *stick* + ASS]

have a sticky palm, to *phr.* [mid-19C+] **1** to be a habitual thief. **2** to be susceptible to bribes.

have a stomach on one's chest, to *phr.* [late 19C] to have something, presumably food, lying heavily on one's stomach.

have a swelled/swollen head, to *phr.* **1** [late 19C+] to feel tipsy, drunk. **2** [20C] to be arrogant, conceited.

have a taffy pulling contest, to *phr.* [20C] (US) to masturbate. [SAmE *taffy* = UK *toffee*]

have a thing about, to *phr.* [1930s+] (orig. US) to be obsessed with, esp. to be sexually obsessed.

have a thing with, to *phr.* [1960s+] to have a love affair with.

have a tile loose, to *phr.* [mid-19C] to be eccentric or foolish (cf. NOT ALL THERE; SHINGLE SHORT).

have a tin ear, to *phr.* [1920s+] to have no ear for music, to be tone deaf.

have a tip on, to *phr.* [1900s–20s] to be drunk. [TIP n.[1]]

have a toby on, to *phr.* [1920s+] (Aus.) to feel kindly or friendly towards (cf. HAVE A GRAPE ON). [TOBY n.[5]]

have a tongue/tongue in one's head, to *phr.* [late 19C+] to be sarcastic. [SE *have a sharp tongue*]

have a tongue too long for one's teeth/mouth, to *phr.* [mid–late 19C] to be indiscreet.

have a toot, to *phr.* [1930s–40s] to take a drink. [TOOT n.[1] (2)]

have a trial at Stafford Court, to *phr.* [early 17C] to be beaten, to be thrashed (cf. STAFFORD LAW). [pun on SE *staff*]

have a trout in the well, to *phr.* [1940s] (Irish) to be pregnant.

have a tug, to *phr.* [1950s+] (Aus.) to masturbate (cf. TUG ONE'S SLUG). [TUG n.[3]]

have a tug o' war with ol' cyclops, to *phr.* [1990s] to masturbate.

have a turn, to *phr.* [late 19C] to fight.

have a vacant spot, to *phr.* [late 19C–1900s] to be stupid, i.e. 'not all there'.

have a wet arse and no fish, to *phr.* [late 19C+] to have been out on a fruitless errand. [the image of fishing; successful or not, one is still likely to get wet]

have a wetty, to *phr.* [1940s+] (Aus.) to work oneself up into a rage. [GET WET v.[1]]

have/take a whack at, to *phr.* [late 19C+] (orig. US) to make an attempt or attack upon. [WHACK v.[1]]

have a whack attack, to *phr.* [1970s+] to masturbate. [WHACK (OFF) + play on McDonalds' hamburger's coinage, *Mac attack*, a sudden craving for a hamburger]

have a white coat, to *phr.* [late 19C] to be drunk. [ety. unknown; ? joc. ref. to the white coats of those who 'take away' sufferers from delirium tremens]

have a white feather, to *phr.* [late 18C–late 19C] to be a coward. [cock-fighting jargon; a white feather denoted that a cock was not of the true gaming breed; the term had become

SE by WW1 when it 'enjoyed' wide use; the better known *show the white feather* had become SE by late 19C]

have a white swelling, to *phr.* [late 18C–early 19C] to be pregnant. [18C medical jargon *white swelling*, a watery tumour found on a joint]

have a wink in one's eye, to *phr.* [mid-19C–1900s] (Aus.) to feel sleepy.

have a wolf in the stomach, to *phr.* [late 18C–20C] to suffer the pangs of intense hunger.

have a woman round the corner, to *phr.* [1970s+] to maintain a mistress.

have axes to grind *see* HAVE AN AXE TO GRIND.

have bad typee for, to *phr.* [20C] (W.I./Guyn.) to be sexually obsessed with. [Carib.E. *typee*, an infatuation, an obsession]

have ballast on board, to *phr.* [late 19C+] to be drunk (cf. CARRY BALLAST).

have balls on one like a scoutmaster, to *phr.* [1930s+] (Can./N.Z.) to have large testicles. [BALLS n.[1] (1); the popular image of the infinitely rampant paedophile scoutmaster]

have bats in the belfry, to *phr.* [late 19C+] to be eccentric, to act crazily (cf. ATTIC; BAT-HOUSE). [the image is of infestation of the brain]

have beans up one's nose, to *phr.* [20C] (US) to have ulterior motives, to act in a deceptive or dishonest manner (cf. PUT BEANS UP ONE'S NOSE).

have beat on *v.* [20C] to have an erection.

have been after the girls, to *phr.* [mid–late 19C] to have contracted a venereal disease. [euph.]

have been around *v.* [1920s+] **1** to be experienced in life. **2** to be experienced sexually; if used of a woman, usu. derog.

have been around the block, to *phr.* [1940s+] to be sexually experienced.

have been around the track, to *phr.* [20C] to be sexually experienced; if used of a woman (the usu. form) derog.

have been in the sun, to *phr.* [mid-18C] to be drunk (cf. HAVE THE SUN IN ONE'S EYES). [euph.]

have been served with a writ of fieri facias, to *phr.* [late 16C–18C] to have a red face. [legal jargon *fieri facias*, 'a writ wherein the sheriff is commanded that he cause to be made out of the goods and chattels of the defendant the sum for which judgement was given' (Blackstone); for sl. use this is punningly mispronounced as 'fiery face']

have been to barking creek, to *phr.* [early–mid-19C] to have a very bad cough (cf. MEMBER FOR BARKSHIRE). [pun]

have been to Blackwall, to *phr.* [mid–late 19C] to have suffered a black eye. [pun]

have been standing too long in the sun *see* HAVE THE SUN IN ONE'S EYES.

have big eyes, to *phr.* [1940s+] (US) to be particularly interested (cf. HAVE EYES FOR).

have blood like gnat's piss, to *phr.* [1900s–10s] to be extremely frightened. [the insect's blood is seen as weak]

have boiled pig at home, to *phr.* [late 18C–early 19C] to be the master in one's own home. [according to Grose (1785), an allusion to a 'well-known' (but unspecified) poem and story]

have brass in one's face, to *phr.* [20C] to be impudent, forward, shameless. [BRASS NECK + SE *bold as brass*, shameless]

have bread and cheese in one's head, to *phr.* [mid-17C–mid-18C] to be drunk.

have breath strong enough to carry coal, to *phr.* [late 19C] (orig. US) to be very drunk.

have broken knees, to *phr.* [late 19C] of a girl or woman, to have been deflowered or seduced (cf. BROKEN-LEGGED). [euph]

have bugs in the/one's head, to *phr.* [20C] (orig. US) to be mentally unstable (cf. BUGGED adj.[2]; BUGS). [BUG n.[5] (4)]

have but a mile to midsummer, to phr. [mid–late 15C] to be eccentric, to be verging on insane. [the popular image of 'midsummer madness']

have buttered eggs in one's breeches, to phr. [mid-17C–18C] to soil one's trousers through a sudden attack of terror.

have by the nuts, to phr. [1940s+] (orig. US) to have at one's mercy. [NUTS n.²]

have by the short and curlies, to phr. [1940s+] to have someone at an extreme disadvantage, to control completely (cf. HAVE BY THE SHORT HAIRS; HAVE BY THE WOOL). [the image of grasping the victim's pubic hair]

have by the short hairs, to phr. [late 19C+] **1** to have someone at an extreme disadvantage, to control completely (cf. HAVE BY THE SHORT AND CURLIES). **2** [1920s+] (Aus.) to know a subject extremely well.

have by the toe, to phr. [mid-16C–mid-17C] to hold securely (cf. HOLD BY THE TOE).

have by the wool, to phr. [20C] to have someone sexually enslaved (cf. HAVE BY THE SHORT AND CURLIES). [WOOL n.²]

have calluses on one's feet, to phr. [20C] (US) to be illegitimate (cf. BORN WITH BURNED FEET). [the phr. describes a child that is born less than 9 months after its parents were married; such a child has calluses from making the usual 9-month 'journey' in a somewhat shorter time]

have caught a fox, to phr. [17C–19C] to be drunk (cf. HUNT A TAVERN FOX; HUNT THE FOX). [CATCH A FOX]

have cavities, to phr. [1980s+] (US campus) to consider something or someone extremely sweet.

have champagne taste/tastes and mauby pocket/pockets, to phr. [20C] (W.I.) to attempt to live beyond one's means. [SE + *mauby*, a bitter-sweet non-alcoholic drink made from the fermented bark of the mauby tree, *Colubrina arborescens* (Rhamnaceae). Sweetened it makes a refreshing drink; unsweetened it can be used medicinally. The phr. points up the difference between the sophisticated (and costly) wine and the simple (and free) folk remedy]

have claws for breakfast, to phr. [mid-19C] to be whipped with the cat-o'-nine-tails. [CLAW OFF]

have cobwebs, to phr. [1980s+] (US campus) to have lived a celibate life for a long time.

have cobwebs in one's throat, to phr. [19C] to feel thirsty (for alcohol); thus *cobweb throat*, the dry throat that accompanies a hangover.

have cold feet see GET COLD FEET.

have cork eye, to phr. [1930s+] (Aus.) to stare aggressively at someone. [ety. unknown; ? link to CORKED]

have corns in the head, to phr. [mid-18C–mid-19C] to be drunk. [play on SE *corns/corn* as used in brewing]

have cramp in one's kick, to phr. [late 19C] to be mean. [SE *cramp* + KICK n.⁴]

have crap in one's blood, to phr. [1950s] (US) to be a coward. [CRAP n.³ (1)]

have death adders in one's pocket, to phr. [1920s+] (Aus.) to be a miser, to spend only reluctantly (cf. DEATH ADDER).

have donkey in one's throat, to phr. [late 19C] to have phlegm caught in one's throat (cf. FROG IN THE THROAT n.²).

have dook on it, to phr. [20C] (Aus.) to shake hands in order to seal a bargain. [DUKE v.]

have down chill, to phr. [20C] (US) to know something thoroughly (cf. HAVE DOWN COLD). [CHILL adv.]

have down cold, to phr. [20C] (US) to know something thoroughly (cf. HAVE DOWN CHILL). [COLD adj.¹ (1)]

have drink taken, to phr. [1920s+] to have consumed alcohol and in consequence to be drunk. [the somewhat portentous phr. underpins the likely inability of the drunken speaker to pronounce it properly]

have drunk of sauce's cup/eaten sauce, to phr. [early 16C] to be abusive. [SE *saucy*, insolent]

have ears, to phr. [1940s–50s] (US Black) to listen.

have eaten sauce see HAVE DRUNK OF SAUCE'S CUP.

have egg on one's face, to phr. [1950s+] (US) to be embarrassed, to look foolish.

have everything v. [1920s+] to possess every kind of attraction, advantage, requirement etc.

have eyes for, to phr. [1930s+] (US) to desire, wish for, usu. sexually.

have eyes for fluff, to phr. [1960s] (gay) for a 'masculine' lesbian to be looking for a 'feminine' partner. [HAVE EYES FOR + FLUFF n.¹ (4)]

have eyes like a shithouse rat, to phr. [1910s+] to have shifty, but acute eyes.

have eyes like cod's ballocks, to phr. [20C] to have popping eyes.

have fat nuts, to phr. [1980s+] (US Black) to use violence, to be a violent person. [NUTS n.²]

have feathers in one's hair, to phr. [20C] (US) to be sleepy. [FEATHER]

have fireworks on the brain, to phr. [late 19C–1900s] to be emotionally disturbed.

have fish-hooks in one's pockets, to phr. [1910s+] (US) to be particularly mean and miserly. [one's pockets are lined with fish-hooks but note FISH-HOOKS, fingers]

have five minds to, to phr. [20C] (W.I.) to be strongly inclined to do something (usu. rash). [var. on SE *be in two minds*]

have got a cup too much see HAVE A CUP TOO MUCH.

have got it by the throat see HAVE THE GAME BY THE THROAT.

have got knock in the cradle, to phr. [late 17C–18C] to be stupid; thus occas. *knock in the cradle*, a fool.

have got something on someone, to phr. [late 19C+] to have someone at a disadvantage, to know something about someone.

have got something on the winkle, to phr. [1920s+] to be obsessed by something (cf. GET ON ONE'S WICK). [fig. use of WINKLE]

have got the game by the throat see HAVE THE GAME BY THE THROAT.

have got them/them all on, to phr. [late 19C] to be very well dressed, often to excess.

have gravy on one's grits, to phr. [1930s+] (US Black) to be enjoying a materially successful life. [the image of a brimming plate]

have gum-leaves growing out of one's ears, to phr. [1920s+] (Aus.) to be a countryman, thus to be naïve, foolish, gullible. [the plentiful gum-trees found in the outback]

have guts in one's brains, to phr. [mid-17C–early 18C] to be sensible, to show some intelligence. [SE *guts*, courage, spirit]

have had a cup too much see HAVE A CUP TOO MUCH.

have had a flutter, to phr. [mid–late 19C] to have lost one's virginity, to be sexually experienced (cf. DO A FLUTTER phr.¹). [FLUTTER n.¹]

have had enough phr. [late 19C+] drunk, e.g. *you've had enough.*

have had it v.¹ **1** [19C+] to have been seduced. **2** [1930s+] to have failed, to have broken down, collapsed, died. **3** [1930s+] to be in trouble, esp. in the minatory phr. *you've had it*, you're in serious trouble.

have had it v.² [1940s+] (orig. N.Z.) to have finished with, to have had a surfeit of, to be tired or bored of, often ext. as *have had it up to here.*

have had it/had it in a big way v.³ [1940s+] 'to have no chance whatever of having or doing something; to have had one's (adverse) fate finally decided, to be defeated; to be dead, to have been killed; to be ruined, broken down, useless; to have had enough' (*OED*)

have had it up to here v. [1940s+] to be exasperated, to have lost all one's patience.

have had it with v. [1940s+] to be annoyed with, to have lost patience with, e.g. *I've had it with you.*

have had more — than someone has had hot dinners, to *phr.* [1960s+] a general phr. used to imply the expertise of the named person in a certain area of life, esp. of sexual experience.

have had one or two, to *phr.* [late 19C+] to be drunk. [euph. understatement]

have had one's chips *see* HAVE ONE'S CHIPS.

have had the cotton, to *phr.* [1970s] (US) to be doomed. [ety. unknown]

have hair on it, to *phr.* [20C] of a joke, to be old, to be out of date, no longer to be funny. [the way mould appears on ancient, rotting fruit or vegetables, but note SE *hoary*, white with age, musty and mouldy]

have hair on one's chest, to *phr.* [1950s+] to be brave, to be plucky.

have heads on them like boils/mice *phr.* [1940s+] (Aus.) of a hand at cards, a succession of good throws of the dice or a group of important and powerful people, to be strong.

have her country cousins *see* COME HER COUNTRY COUSINS.

have hollow legs, to *phr.* [late 19C+] to be able to consume large amounts of food without apparently putting on any weight.

have hot balls, to *phr.* [1980s+] (US campus) to be drunk, usu. as *—'s balls are hot*. [SE *eyeballs*]

have hot pants, to *phr.* [1920s+] (orig. US) 1 to be worried, anxious, 2 to be sexually eager. [SE *hot*/HOT adj.[1] (1)]

have hot pudding for supper, to *phr.* [19C+] of women, to have sexual intercourse. [PUDDING n.]

have ideas in one's head *see* GET IDEAS IN ONE'S HEAD.

have in one's eye, to *phr.* [late 18C–mid-19C] to be considering, to have in mind.

have in/in some liquor/rum v. [20C] (W.I.) to be drunk.

have it v. [20C] to have sexual intercourse. [note music-hall song 'A Little of What You Fancy ...': 'I always hold with having it if you fancy it,/If you fancy it, that's understood .../'Coz a little of what you fancy does you good']

have it away v. [1960s+] to have sexual intercourse, sometimes extended as *have it away together* (cf. HAVE IT IN; HAVE IT OFF v.[2]).

have it away/take it on one's toes, to *phr.* [1950s+] to escape from prison or impending arrest (cf. TOES LIVELY).

have it away with *phr.*[1] [1920s+] to steal an object.

have it away with *phr.*[2] [1950s+] to copulate with someone.

have it/them bad v. [late 19C+] to be experiencing something. e.g. illness, sexual obsession, love, delirium tremens, intensely.

have it coming, to *phr.* [late 19C+] to deserve, to merit; usu. 'it' is unpleasant.

have it/someone covered, to *phr.* [1950s+] (orig. US Black) 1 to have a situation well under control. 2 to understand a person and accept their position.

have it in v. [late 19C+] to have sexual intercourse (cf. HAVE IT AWAY; HAVE IT OFF v.[2]).

have it in for v. [early 19C+] to bear a grudge, to feel hostile towards.

have it knocked, to *phr.* [late 19C+] to have a problem, and esp. life in general, absolutely under control. [KNOCK v.[2] (2)]

have it made/made in the shade, to *phr.* [1940s+] (orig. US) to be in an excellent situation, to have no problems. [? tramp use *made*, lucky]

have it off v.[1] [1920s+] 1 (Und.) to carry out a successful crime. 2 (Und.) of police, to make a successful raid and arrest.

have it off/a bit off v.[2] [1940s+] 1 to copulate (cf. COME OFF v.[1]). 2 to masturbate (cf. BEAT OFF).

have it on one's dancers, to *phr.* [1950s+] (Und.) to run away, to escape (cf. HAVE IT AWAY). [DANCERS n. (2)]

have it out *see* HAVE OUT.

have it out of someone, to *phr.* [late 19C+] to punish, to exact compensation from.

have it so good, to *phr.* [1940s+] (orig. US) to have a variety of advantages; usu. in neg. use. [the *locus classicus* is British Prime Minister Harold Macmillan's speech on 20 July 1957: 'Let's be frank about it. Most of our people have never had it so good. Go around the country, go to the industrial towns, go to the farms, and you'll see a state of prosperity such as we have never had in my lifetime – nor indeed ever in the history of this country. What is beginning to worry some of us is "Is it too good to be true?" or perhaps I should say "Is it too good to last?"']

have it taped, to *phr.* [1910s+] (orig. milit.) to have something worked out, assessed fully etc. [SE *tape*, to measure with a tape]

have it till hell wouldn't, to *phr.* [20C] (US) plentiful, abundant, also as *till hell wouldn't sneeze at it*

have it up her, to *phr.* [late 19C+] to have sexual intercourse (cf. HAVE IT IN).

have jam on it, to *phr.* [1910s+] to have things very easy. [JAM n.[2]]

have kangaroos in one's top paddock, to *phr.* [20C] (Aus.) to be eccentric, to be mentally unstable.

have kidney trouble, to *phr.* [1960s+] (gay) to frequent public lavatories for sex. [one's excuse for making so many visits to the lavatory]

have/get kittens, to *phr.* [20C] to worry to excess, to throw a fit, to succumb to one's emotions, to lose one's temper, often through worry or fear (cf. HAVE A BABY; HAVE A COW; LAY AN EGG). [the nervousness of a pregnant cat]

have larks for breakfast/supper, to *phr.* [1910s] (Ulster) to be especially eloquent. [larks are trad. good singers]

have lead in one's pencil, to *phr.* [1920s+] (orig. US) 1 to be potent (cf. HAVE NO LEAD IN ONE'S PENCIL). 2 to have an erection.

have legs v. [late 19C+] to be considered fast. [note media jargon *have legs*, of a TV programme, book etc, to be a potential success]

have legs on one's belly, to *phr.* [1940s+] (N.Z.) to be a sycophant, a toady. [they facilitate one's 'crawling']

have long eyes/raw eyes, to *phr.* [20C] (W.I.) to be covetous for (cf. LONG OUT ONE'S EYE ON).

have lunch downtown, to *phr.* [1920s+] to engage in oral sex. [LUNCH n.[2] (2) + DOWNTOWN]

have maggots in one's head, to *phr.* [late 19C–1900s] to be eccentric, to be irritable (cf. MAD AS A MAGGOT).

have malt above the water, to *phr.* [19C] to be drunk. [proverbial phr.]

have malt above the wheat, to *phr.* [mid-16C] to be drunk (cf. HAVE MALT ABOVE THE WATER). [proverbial phr.]

have mind, to *phr.* [20C] (W.I.) to possess courage, to be brave.

have missile lock, to *phr.* [1980s+] (US campus) to target another person, either though love or hate. [milit. jargon *missile lock*, to aim a missile electronically so that it follows a specific target until its destruction; popularized through the film *Top Gun* (1986)]

have more arse than a toilet seat, to *phr.* [1960s+] of a man, to have an active, even excessive, sex life (cf. MORE PRICKS THAN A SECONDHAND DART BOARD). [ARSE n.[1]]

have more arse than Jessie *see* HAVE MORE HIDE THAN JESSIE.

have more front than Brighton beach, to *phr.* [1930s+] to be exceptionally cheeky, daring. [pun on SE (*sea-*) *front*/FRONT n.[1]]

have more front than Foy and Gibson's *see* HAVE MORE FRONT THAN MYERS.

have more front than Harrods, to *phr.* [1970s] to be audacious, outspoken, extremely cheeky. [pun on SE *front* (of Harrods, a very large London department store)/FRONT n.[1]]

have more front than Myers/Foy and Gibson's, to *phr.* [1950s+] (Aus.) to be audacious, outspoken, extremely cheeky. [pun on SE *front* (of the large department stores in Melbourne and Adelaide)/FRONT n.[1]]

have more guts than brains, to *phr.* [17C] to be foolish but determined in one's stupidity.

have more hide/arse than Jessie, to *phr.* [1950s+] (Aus.) to be immensely cheeky. [a favourite elephant *Jessie* (1872–1939), which could be visited at the Taronga Park Zoo]

have more kid in him than a goat in the family way, to *phr.* [1930s+] (Aus.) to be an incurable joker or 'kidder'. [pun on KID v./SE *kid*]

have more points/points to one than a porcupine, to *phr.* [20C] (Aus.) to have a number of good points to one's character.

have more than one can carry *see* HAVE ALL THAT ONE CAN CARRY.

have mousetraps/scorpions/snakes in one's pocket, to *phr.* [1920s+] (Aus.) to be extremely mean (cf. DEATH ADDER). [one dare not, therefore, put one's hand in one's pocket to extract money]

have ne'er/never a face but one's own, to *phr.* [late 17C–early 18C] to be penniless. [the 'faces' are those on coins]

have negative clues, to *phr.* [1980s+] (US campus) to have no idea of what is going on, to be totally devoid of common sense. [var. on NOT HAVE A CLUE]

have never a face but one's own *see* HAVE NE'ER A FACE BUT ONE'S OWN.

have no butter in one's eyes, to *phr.* [early–mid-19C] to be well aware, to have no illusions.

have no head, to *phr.* [late 19C] to be hare-brained, to be irresponsible.

have no lead in one's pencil/ink in one's pen, to *phr.* [1920s+] to be impotent. [HAVE LEAD IN ONE'S PENCIL]

have no life, to *phr.* [1980s+] (US campus) to exist in an aimless manner, to have no purpose in life (cf. GET A LIFE!).

have no more wit than a coot, to *phr.* [16C] to be foolish, stupid (cf. COOT n.[1]). [the coot, synon. with the *Foolish Guillemot*, is seen in pvbs. as a foolish bird]

have no skin on one's face, to *phr.* [20C] (Irish) to have no shame. [? without skin one cannot blush]

have-not *n.* [mid-19C+] one who is materially unsuccessful (cf. HAVE n.[1]).

have no time for, to *phr.* [1910s+] to be intolerant of, to be uninterested in.

have no virtues, to *phr.* [late 19C] to have abstained from all life's hedonistic pleasures.

have off *v.* [1930s–40s] (US Black) to berate, to attack verbally. [HAVE v.[2]]

have-on *n.* [late 19C] a swindle, a hoax. [HAVE v.[4]]

have one beat, to *phr.* [20C] (US) to defeat, to get the better of, to baffle, to confuse, often in phr. of resignation, *beats me*.

have one foot in the grave, to *phr.* [17C+] to be dying (cf. ON ONE'S LAST LEGS).

have one for the worms, to *phr.* [late 19C–1930s] to have a drink of alcohol. [the assumption that drinking will, eventually, prove fatal]

have one in the box, to *phr.* [late 19C+] to be pregnant (cf. HAVE A BUN IN THE OVEN).

have one in the oven *see* HAVE A BUN IN THE OVEN.

have one more time, to *phr.* [1910s] (US) to have a very good time.

have one more wrinkle in one's arse, to *phr.* [late 18C–mid-19C] to have gained a fresh piece of knowledge. ['Every fresh piece of knowledge being supposed by the vulgar naturalists to add a wrinkle to that part' (Grose, 1796); note *wrinkle*, a tip, a clever trick, a short-cut]

have one mother too many, to *phr.* [20C] to be illegitimate. [a bastard should not have any mother at all, i.e. should have been left unconceived]

have one on the city, to *phr.* [19C] (US) to have a drink of water. [the city-run water supply]

have one over *v.* [1970s+] **1** to seduce. **2** to deceive, to defraud, to trick.

have one's act together/down, to *phr.* [1960s+] (orig. US Black) to be in full control of a situation, whether emotional, social, sexual, financial etc (cf. HAVE ONE'S GAME UPTIGHT; HAVE ONE'S SHIT TOGETHER).

have one's arse/ass, to *phr.* [1950s+] to reprimand severely, to punish. [ARSE n.[1] (1)]

have one's ass in the wind, to *phr.* [1960s+] (US) to be exposed to trouble or danger.

have one's back, to *phr.* [1980s+] to take care of, to look after. [the image of guarding one's back from attack]

have one's back scratched, to *phr.* [mid–late 19C] to suffer a judicial flogging (cf. HAVE CLAWS FOR BREAKFAST). [one is *scratched* by the cat-o'-nine-tails]

have one's back teeth afloat, to *phr.* (orig. US) **1** [late 19C+] to be very drunk (cf. AFLOAT). **2** [1960s+] to be desperate to urinate.

have one's back teeth awash/under water, to *phr.* [1900s–10s] to be drunk (cf. AFLOAT).

have one's back teeth underground, to *phr.* [1900s–10s] to have eaten to satiation or excess.

have one's back teeth under water *see* HAVE ONE'S BACK TEETH AWASH.

have one's ballocks in the right place, to *phr.* [20C] to be deserving of praise, commendation, approval by one's fellows. [BALLS n.[1]]

have one's balls under one's chin, to *phr.* [1930s–60s] (US) to be terrified. [a coarser version of SE *have one's heart in one's mouth*]

have one's barrel full, to *phr.* [late 19C] (US) to be drunk.

have one's beer goggles on, to *phr.* [1980s] (US campus) to find someone attractive because of the influence of alcohol. [BEER GOGGLES]

have one's belly boil, to *phr.* [20C] (W.I./Gren.) to be very frightened.

have one's belly full, to *phr.* [late 18C] to be pregnant.

have one's belly touching one's back, to *phr.* [20C] (W.I.) to be absolutely starving.

have one's boots on/laced, to *phr.*[1] [1940s–60s] (US Black) to be wise, sophisticated, intelligent. [one is thus ready to confront the world]

have one's boots on, to *phr.*[2] [1980s+] (US Black) to use a condom. [BOOT n.[3] (5)]

have one's brains on ice, to *phr.* [1930s] to be very calm.

have one's bread buttered on both sides, to *phr.* [mid-17C+] to enjoy great (and unexpected) good fortune.

have/have had one's chips, to *phr.* [1930s+] to have died (cf. CASH IN ONE'S CHECKS). [gambling use]

have one's clock stopped, to *phr.* [late 19C] to have been denied credit. [pun on no more TICK n.[2]]

have one's cock caught in a zipper, to *phr.* [1970s+] to be in very bad trouble. [COCK n.[2]]

have one's cock on the block, to *phr.* [1970s+] (orig. US) to be facing serious problems. [COCK n.²]

have one's comb cut, to *phr.* [mid-19C] to be disgraced. [cock-fighting jargon]

have one's corn ground *see* GET ONE'S CORN GROUND.

have one's cut, to *phr.* [late 19C+] of a man, to have sexual intercourse. [CENTRAL CUT]

have one's ducks in a row, to *phr.* [1970s+] (US) to have one's affairs in order (cf. LINE UP ONE'S DUCKS). [? image of the mother duck and her attendant ducklings]

have one's ears flapping, to *phr.* [1920s+] to be listening attentively.

have oneself *v.* 1 [1920s+] to indulge oneself, to provide for oneself, usu. in phr., e.g. *have oneself a good time*, *have oneself some fun*. 2 [1980s+] (US Black) to masturbate.

have one's eye in a sling, to *phr.* [late 19C] to be depressed, crushed, defeated (cf. GET ONE'S ASS IN A SLING).

have one's eye on the ball, to *phr.* [20C] to be alert and aware (cf. KEEP ONE'S EYE ON THE BALL). [sporting imagery]

have one's eyes opened, to *phr.* [20C] to be drunk. [one's wild, unfocused stare]

have one's face at half-past eight, to *phr.* [20C] to look miserable. [the corners of the mouth point down, as would the hands of the clock]

have one's face made of a fiddle, to *phr.* [early 19C] to be irresistibly charming.

have one's feet below the mahogany, to *phr.* [mid-19C] to be living off another's bounty, to be living at another's expense. [SE *mahogany*, a dining table]

have one's fighting clothes on, to *phr.* [20C] (US) to be ready to quarrel, to be spoiling for a fight.

have one's finger in the mortar, to *phr.* [mid-17C–mid-18C] to dabble in the building trade.

have one's finger on the trigger, to *phr.* [1990s] a threat, i.e. one is prepared to shoot if necessary.

have one's finger up one's arse/ass, to *phr.* [1940s+] to idle, to loiter, to stand around doing nothing (cf. PULL ONE'S FINGER OUT). [ARSE n.¹]

have one's foot in the road, to *phr.* [20C] (US) to spend a good deal of time away from home, to travel frequently.

have one's foot on the rail, to *phr.* [20C] (US) to drink heavily. [the 'rail' is that of a bar]

have one's game uptight, to *phr.* [1960s+] (orig. US Black) to be in full control of a situation (cf. HAVE ONE'S ACT TOGETHER).

have one's garret unfurnished/empty, to *phr.* [late 18C] to be a fool.

have one's glasses on, to *phr.* [1930s–40s] (US Black) to pose as an intellectual, to lay down the law. [stereotyped association of spectacles with intelligence]

have one's greens, to *phr.* [late 19C+] to have sexual intercourse (cf. GREENS n.²).

have one's hair raised, to *phr.* [late 19C] (US) of two women, to fight. [women stereotypically pull hair during a brawl]

have one's hand out, to *phr.* [late 19C+] to beg, to scrounge.

have one's hat nailed to the ceiling, to *phr.* [1910s–30s] (US) to be fellated. [the excitement so produced]

have one's head glued on, to *phr.* [20C] to be mentally balanced, emotionally controlled.

have one's head screwed on/screwed on right/the right way, to *phr.* [early 19C+] to be aware, to understand, to know what's what (cf. HAVE A SCREW LOOSE).

have one's head up one's arse/ass, to *phr.* [1940s+] (orig. US) to be completely and deliberately stupid.

have one's head wedged, to *phr.* [1960s+] (US) to be very stupid. [it is wedged 'up one's ass']

have one's heart/hand on one's halfpenny, to *phr.* [16C+] to be dead-set on, to want something obsessively, to have one's 'eye on the main chance'. [image of a child clutching its money, ready to be spent on a promised pleasure]

have one's heart in one's boots, to *phr.* [mid-17C+] to be depressed, frightened.

have one's heart in one's mouth, to *phr.* [mid-16C+] to be terrified, to be very apprehensive.

have one's heart up *see* BRING ONE'S HEART UP.

have one's hip boots on, to *phr.* [1930s–50s] to be sophisticated, aware. [pun on SE *hip*/HIP adj.]

have one's jawing-tackle on board, to *phr.* [early 19C–1910s] to be impudent, to be cheeky. [JAW v.¹]

have one's jaws tight, to *phr.* [1990s] (US Black) to be angry. [the facial expression; cf. SE *tight-lipped*]

have one's legs open, to *phr.* [1930s–50s] (US Black) of a woman, to behave in a promiscuous manner.

have one's mind in the mud, to *phr.* [1900s–40s] (US Black) to be thinking vulgar or lustful thoughts.

have one's monkey up, to *phr.* [mid-19C] to be angry (cf. GET ONE'S DANDER UP; GET ONE'S MONKEY UP; PUT SOMEONE'S MONKEY UP). [MONKEY n.⁶]

have one's mouth full of pap, to *phr.* [late 18C–early 19C] to act in a childish manner. [SE *pap*, baby food]

have one's mouth on, to *phr.* [1930s–40s] (US Black) to gossip, to criticize someone in their absence (cf. BADMOUTH).

have one's mouth paved, to *phr.* [early 18C] to have a mouth inured to hot food or drink.

have one's nose in parenthesis, to *phr.* [late 18C–early 19C] to have one's nose pulled. [SE *parenthesis*, an interlude, a hiatus]

have one's nose in the air, to *phr.* [20C] to act in a snobbish, superior manner (cf. HIGH HAT n.²). [the tilted nose intends to avoid noxious smells]

have/put one's nose in the manger, to *phr.* [mid-19C–1920s] to eat heartily.

have one's nose open, to *phr.* [1950s+] (US Black) 1 to produce sexual excitement in another person (cf. GET ONE'S NOSE). 2 to be infatuated with another person. [both uses imply heavy breathing]

have one's nose up someone's arse/ass, to *phr.* [1970s+] to act sycophantically, to toady (cf. BROWN NOSE v.).

have one's nuff *see* GET ONE'S NUFF.

have one's number come up, to *phr.* [20C] to die (cf. CASH IN ONE'S CHECKS).

have one's porch light out, to *phr.* [20C] to be stupid, to be mentally deficient; thus the reverse, *put on one's porch light*, to sit up and take notice (cf. LIGHTS ON BUT THERE'S NOBODY HOME).

have one's pots on, to *phr.* [19C] to be drunk (cf. POTTED adj.²).

have one's sails high, to *phr.* [1940s–50s] (US Black) to be drunk (cf. THREE SHEETS IN THE WIND).

have one's shirt in the wind, to *phr.* [late 19C] to have one's shirt visible through a hole in the seat or sticking out through one's fly.

have one's shite *phr.* [late 19C+] (Irish) an indication of rejection, i.e. one is due to suffer. [fig. use of SHITE n.]

have one's shit together/down, to *phr.* [1960s+] (orig. US Black) to be in full control of a situation (cf. HAVE ONE'S ACT TOGETHER). [SHIT n.³]

have one's shutters up, to *phr.* [late 19C] to act in a surly manner.

have one's sitting breeches on, to *phr.* [late 18C–1900s] to outstay one's welcome.

have one's stuff out the window, to *phr.* [1900s–30s] (US Black) to be cautious, to be prepared for trouble.

have one's tail in the water, to phr. [mid-19C–1900s] to be well off, to be thriving. [ety. unknown]

have one's tail out, to phr. [late 19C–1910s] to be angry. [the waving of a cat's tail, which supposedly denotes aggression]

have one's tit in a tight crack, to phr. [1920s+] (Can.) to find oneself in trouble, in an unpleasant situation (cf. HAVE ONE'S TIT IN A WRINGER). [TIT n.[1] (1)]

have one's tit in a wringer, to phr. [1960s+] (US) to be in difficulties, to be foolish. [TIT n.[1] (1)]

have one's tits on, to phr. [1990s] (US) to be patient. [TIT n.[1] (1); var. on KEEP ONE'S HAIR ON]

have one's tongue hanging out, to phr. [late 19C+] to be eagerly expectant.

have/take one's whack, to phr. [mid-19C+] to take one's share. [WHACK n.[2] (1)]

have one's wires crossed, to phr. [20C] to act in an eccentric or unstable manner. [electrical imagery]

have one's wool shorn, to phr. [1920s+] (Aus.) to have a haircut.

have one's/all one's work cut out, to phr. [mid-19C+] to be forced to make a great effort to be occupied with as much as one can handle.

have one too many, to phr. [20C] to be drunk. [euph.]

have only fifty cards in one's deck, to phr. [1920s–40s] (US) to be stupid, unintelligent (cf. NOT ALL THERE).

have on one's high-heeled shoes, to phr. [19C+] (US) to be arrogant, self-important, snobbish (cf. HIGH-HEELED).

have on the raws, to phr. [late 19C] to tease, to touch an emotionally sensitive spot. [SE raw]

have on the stick, to phr. [late 19C–1910s] to make fun of. [? the image of a toy 'monkey on a stick']

have on toast, to phr. [late 19C+] to have at a complete disadvantage. [the victim becomes no more than a figurative 'mouthful' to be chewed up at the aggressor's leisure, like a mouthful of toast]

have out/have it out v. [early 19C+] to have a frank, argumentative discussion, to air an otherwise 'difficult' topic. [imagery of exposing the problem to fig. 'open air']

have papers/paper on, to phr. [1940s+] (US Black) to be legally married. [one's marriage certificate]

have pepper in the nose, to phr. [late 14C] to act in a supercilious arrogant and rough manner.

have plenty of stir on, to phr. [late 19C–1900s] to be very well off. [? dial. stir/stirabout, a stew, i.e. one is well fed; or SE stir, a commotion, i.e. one is busy with making money]

have rats see GET RATS.

have raw eyes see HAVE LONG EYES.

have red-eye for/red one's eye/red-eye after, to phr. [20C] (W.I.) to become obsessed with at first sight and thus to desire to possess immediately (cf. EYES CATCH FIRE; LOOK WITH RED-EYE). [the red eyes that are trad. associated with madness]

have red sails in the sunset, to phr. [20C] of a woman, to be menstruating.

have rheumatism in the shoulder, to phr. [late 18C] to be arrested. [the pain engendered by the hand that grasps one's shoulder]

haverel/haveril n. [20C] (Irish) an ignorant man, a slatternly woman. [synon. dial. haverel; ult. SE haver]

have scorpions in one's pocket see HAVE MOUSETRAPS IN ONE'S POCKET.

have seen the cheque, to phr. [late 19C] to have exact knowledge, to have proof.

have seen the French king, to phr. [17C] to be drunk.

have shit on one's liver, to phr. [1930s+] (Aus.) to be in a bad temper. [SE liverish, testy]

have shut up shop-windows, to phr. [late 17C–mid-19C] to declare oneself bankrupt.

have smallpox, to phr. [20C] (US Und.) to be wanted on an arrest warrant.

have snakes in one's boots, to phr. [late 19C] (US) to be suffering delirium tremens. [SNAKES]

have snakes in one's pocket see HAVE MOUSETRAPS IN ONE'S POCKET.

have some v. [1980s+] (US campus) combined with a relevant noun to mean to notice the large amount of, e.g. have some babes, look at all the pretty young women. [the implication being that there are so many/there is so much that anyone can take a share]

have someone cold, to phr. [1920s+] (orig. US) to have at one's mercy, to have at a disadvantage (cf. GET IT ON SOMEONE COLD). [COLD adv.]

have someone covered see HAVE IT COVERED.

have someone for breakfast, to phr.[1] [mid–late 19C] (US, West.) to discover a murdered body when one wakes in the morning. [ironic]

have someone for breakfast, to phr.[2] [20C] to be able to achieve a task, defeat a rival etc.

have someone in v. [1940s+] (orig. US) to swindle, to cheat, to deceive (cf. HAVE-ON).

have someone in your craw, to phr. [20C] (W.I.) to harbour ill-feeling towards someone. [SE craw, the throat]

have someone mapped, to phr. [20C] to have someone completely and accurately assessed, to work out another's movements and attitudes.

have someone on v.[1] [mid-19C+] to tease, to hoax, to engage someone's attention with the longer term intention of deceiving them; thus have someone on, to swindle, to cheat.

have someone on v.[2] (Aus./N.Z.) **1** [1940s–60s] to accept sexually. **2** [1940s+] to prepare oneself to fight, to accept a challenge. **3** [1950s+] to attack physically. [dial.]

have someone on a string, to phr. [early 19C+] **1** to hoax, to trick, to fool. **2** to keep in suspense.

have someone set, to phr. [1910s+] (Aus.) to have someone marked down for punishment or revenge. [abbr. SE set down]

have someone over a barrel, to phr. [1930s+] to put at a great disadvantage, to inconvenience deliberately. [? 19C barrel punishment, lashing someone across a barrel and whipping them]

have someone pegged, to phr. [1920s+] (US) to categorize, to form an opinion of. [PEG v.[6]]

have someone's guts for garters, to phr. [1930s+] to punish comprehensively, to hurt.

have someone's number, to phr. [mid-19C+] (orig. US) **1** to understand another person absolutely, for all their possible evasions and excuses (cf. PEEP SOMEONE'S HOLE-CARD). **2** to be aware, to be alert, to see through someone's pretences.

have someone sussed, to phr. [1970s+] to see through someone's duplicity, to know what someone is up to. [SUSS OUT]

have someone's weights up, to phr. [1970s+] (N.Z.) to have the measure of a person. [horse-racing imagery]

have someone thick, to phr. [late 19C–1900s] to make someone drunk. [THICK HEAD n.[1]]

have someone waxed, to phr. [1900s] to have someone at a disadvantage (cf. HAVE A NOSE OF WAX).

have some rabbit in one, to phr. (US Black/Und.) **1** to be an habitual absconder from institutions or situations. **2** to be sexually active. [both meanings derive f. the alleged habits of rabbits]

have something v. [1910s+] to have a valid point or opinion; thus one has something there, one may well be right.

have something above the ears, to phr. [1920s–60s] to be intelligent. [i.e. one's brain]

have something down v. [1940s+] (orig. US Black) to be aware of the situation, to know what is going on. [DOWN adj.[2]]

have something going, to *phr.* [1960s+] to be involved in a close relationship, usu. sexual.

have something going for oneself, to *phr.* [1960s+] to be in a good situation, to have circumstances working in one's favour.

have something on someone, to *phr.* [20C] (orig. US Und.) to have someone at a disadvantage, usu. through incriminating or negative information.

have something on one's brain *see* GET SOMETHING ON ONE'S BRAIN.

have taken ugly pills, to *phr.* [1950s+] (Can.) to be unpleasant, aggressive, unattractive etc.

have the bags/bags off, to *phr.* [mid-19C] to be well-off, to be rich (cf. BREECHED).

have the ball at one's feet, to *phr.* [mid-19C+] to have a thing or situation in one's power. [soccer imagery]

have the big one, to *phr.* [1970s] (US) to die of a heart attack. [euph.]

have the bot, to *phr.* [1940s+] (Aus./N.Z.) to be sick, to be out of sorts, moody or disagreeable. [N.Z. medical jargon *bot*, a germ, a sufferer from tuberculosis ult. *bot(t)*, 'a parasitical worm or maggot'; now restricted to the larvae of flies of the genus *Oestrus*' (*OED*)]

have the Britts/Britts up, to *phr.* [1940s] (Aus.) to be in a nervous state. [abbr. JIMMY BRITTS]

have the bulge on, to *phr.* [mid-19C+] (US) to have an advantage over, to be in a superior position.

have the cheek-ache, to *phr.* [late 19C] to blush.

have the darling pea, to *phr.* [mid-19C+] (Aus.) to act eccentrically. [SAusE *Darling pea*, a variety of *Swainsona*, a herb that can cause cattle to suffer from stiffness of limbs, muscle tremor and uncoordination]

have the dead needle *see* HAVE THE NEEDLE.

have the deadwood on, to *phr.* [19C+] (US) to have at a disadvantage, to control, esp. through the possession of incriminating information (cf. HAVE THE WOOD ON). [? the shooting in the back of Marshall James Butler by 'Wild Bill' Hickok in the town of Deadwood, South Dakota on 2 August 1876 (whether this really was his hand remains in dispute); or 10-pin bowling, if after one pitch a single pin is left lying in front of those that have not been knocked down, hitting that 'dead wood' will knock it into the others, successfully knocking them all down]

have the decorators in, to *phr.* [mid-19C+] of a woman, to be menstruating (cf. HAVE THE PAINTERS IN). [euph.; the colour they 'paint' is of course blood-red]

have the dick, to *phr.* [1970s] (Aus.) to be finished, to be permanently damaged. [DICKED]

have the dingbats, to *phr.* [1910s+] (Aus.) **1** to be mad, stupid, eccentric. **2** to be a victim of delirium tremens. [DINGBATS]

have the drop on, to *phr.* [mid-19C] to place someone else at a disadvantage, in any confrontation, physical, mental, financial etc (cf. GET THE DROP ON). [DROP n.²]

have the fiddle but not the stick, to *phr.* [19C] to have the ability to do something, but still lack the intelligence to do it properly.

have the flag out, to *phr.* [20C] of a woman, to be menstruating (cf. FLYING BAKER; FLY THE RED FLAG). [the flag in question is, presumably, that indicating quarantine]

have the frost, to *phr.* [late 19C–1910s] to be unemployed. [FROST n. (1)]

have/have got the game/it by the throat, to *phr.* [1940s+] (Aus.) to have the situation under control.

have the game sewn up, to *phr.* [1920s] (Aus.) to be in a position where one can only win, to be 'on a sure thing'.

have the gimmes *see* GET THE GIMMES.

have the goods on, to *phr.* [late 19C+] **1** to place someone else at a disadvantage, in any confrontation, physical, mental, financial etc. **2** to have information, whether or not actually injurious, about someone (cf. GET THE GOODS ON). [GOODS n.¹ (2)]

have the grindstone on one's back, to *phr.* [18C–19C] of a man, to fetch the nurse for one's wife's confinement.

have the horn, to *phr.* [late 19C+] to be in a state of sexual arousal (cf. HORNY adj.). [HORN n.² (2)]

have the hots for, to *phr.* [1940s+] (orig. US) **1** to desire sexually. **2** to become enthusiastic, excited. [HOTS n.¹]

have the inside track, to *phr.* [late 19C–1950s] to be privy to exclusive information. [late 20C use is SE; note racing jargon *inside track*, the truth]

have the kick, to *phr.* [late 19C–1910s] to be lucky. [football imagery]

have the laugh of, to *phr.* [20C] to outwit, to get the better of.

have the length of one's foot *see* GET THE LENGTH OF ONE'S FOOT.

have the loan of *see* GET THE LOAN OF.

have the map of Ireland written all over one's face, to *phr.* [1960s+] to be unmistakably Irish.

have them bad *see* HAVE IT BAD.

have the monkies, to *phr.* [1950s–60s] (US) of a woman, to be menstruating; also as *her monkey's sick*; *her monkey's got a haemorrhage*. [mispron. of *monthlies* but note MONKEY n.¹⁰]

have the morbs, to *phr.* [late 19C] to feel depressed. [SE *morbid*]

have the needle/dead needle, to *phr.* [mid-19C+] to be very angry (cf. GET THE NEEDLE phr.¹).

have the painters in, to *phr.* [mid-19C+] of a woman, to be menstruating (cf. HAVE THE DECORATORS IN). [euph.]

have the pants, to *phr.* [late 19C] to be exhausted. [one *pants* when out of breath through exertion]

have the pasties, to *phr.* [1980s+] (US campus) to have diarrhoea. [FLYING PASTY SHITS]

have the pencil put on one, to *phr.* [1920s–30s] (US prison) to be reported to the prison authorities. [one's name is written down]

have the perpetual, to *phr.* [late 19C] to be vigorous, go-getting. [SE *perpetual motion*]

have the quandongs, to *phr.* [late 19C+] (Aus.) to behave stupidly, to be stupid. [QUANDONG]

have the rabbits, to *phr.* [late 19C+] (Aus.) to be exceptionally stupid. [the assumed stupidity of rabbits]

have the rag on, to *phr.* [1950s+] **1** of a woman, to be menstruating. **2** to act foolishly or eccentrically, to be annoyed. [JAM RAG]

have the Richard, to *phr.* [1960s+] (Aus.) to be finished or exhausted, to be irreparably damaged (cf. HAVE THE DICK). [theatrical rhy. sl. *Richard III* = BIRD n.⁸]

have the slows, to *phr.* **1** [mid-19C+] to suffer some form of imaginary disease to which one attributes lassitude, inactivity etc. **2** [1970s+] (drugs) to be very intoxicated, at which point life outside one's head seems to crawl by.

have the stick, to *phr.* [1950s+] (Aus.) to be finished, to be permanently damaged. [rhy. sl. *have the stick* = HAVE THE DICK]

have the stroke, to *phr.* [1920s] (US) to be in charge. [? rowing use]

have the sun in one's eyes/have been standing too long in the sun, to *phr.* [mid-19C] to be drunk. [euph. play on BLIND DRUNK]

have the swap *see* GET THE SWAP.

have the tiger by the tail, to *phr.* [1900s–40s] to endure, to survive.

have the urge for a surge, to *phr.* [1990s] to masturbate. [assonance]

have the woefuls, to *phr.* [late 19C] to feel miserable or depressed.

have the wood on, to *phr.* [1920s+] (Aus./N.Z.) to have the upper hand over, to hold at a disadvantage. [abbr. HAVE THE DEADWOOD ON]

have the worse end of the staff, to *phr.* [mid-16C–late 19C] to be treated unfairly (cf. GET HOLD OF THE WRONG END OF THE STICK).

have the wrong end of the stick *see* GET HOLD OF THE WRONG END OF THE STICK.

have tickets on, to *phr.* [20C] (Aus.) to be very fond of someone; thus *have tickets on oneself*, to be vain, to be conceited. [i.e. one would pay to see them/oneself]

have tight cheeks, to *phr.* [1950s+] (US Black) to be angry. [the taut cheeks that indicate tension]

have-to *n.* [20C] (US) anything inescapable, esp. something that is forced upon one by social convention; thus *have-to wedding*, a wedding that is arranged after the putative bride is found to be pregnant.

have to be *v.* [1960s+] must be.

have tongue enough for two sets of teeth, to *phr.* [late 18C–mid-19C] to be overly talkative.

have too much on one's plate, to *phr.* [20C] to be overburdened, esp. with work or commitments.

have to rights, to *phr.* [mid-19C+] to settle with, to get even with, to conquer.

have to see a man about a dog *see* SEE A MAN ABOUT A DOG.

have two hands alike, to *phr.* [20C] (Irish) to fail to pay one's way. [? neither is in one's pocket]

have two left shoes, to *phr.* (US Black) to be absolutely wrong.

have two penn'orth of rope, to *phr.* [1920s–30s] to have this bare minimum of sleeping accommodation. [TWOPENNY ROPE]

have two shirts and a rag, to *phr.* [late 17C–late 18C] to be reasonably well-off, to be comfortable.

have under one's belt, to *phr.* **1** [early 19C] to have in one's stomach. **2** [1930s+] (orig. Aus.) to have to one's credit, to have stored away. [the image is of eating a good meal and storing energy]

have what it takes, to *phr.* [1930s+] to possess the requisite characteristics, commodities, money etc.

have whiskers/whiskers on it, to *phr.* [1920s+] to be old, to be out of date. [the bacteria that develop on old food, or an old, whiskery man]

have wind in one's jaws, to *phr.* [1950s–60s] (US Black) to be extremely annoyed.

have windmills in the head, to *phr.* [late 18C–early 19C] to entertain crazy notions to fantasize. [Don Quixote's 'tilting at windmills']

havey cavey/havy cavy *adj.* [late 18C–19C] **1** higgledy-piggledy, confused, doubtful; thus *on the havey-cavey*, questioning, doubting. **2** drunken. [dial.]

havil *n.* [late 18C–mid-19C] (Und.) a sheep. [ety. unknown; dial. *havil*, a small crab]

Hawaiian disease *n.* [20C] (gay) the absence of women, or *lakanuki*.

Hawaiian eye *n.* [1970s+] (gay) the anus. [play on the eponymous 1960s television programme]

Hawaiian sunshine *n.* [1960s+] (drugs) LSD (cf. A n.³).

Hawaiian time *n.* [20C] (US) flexible time, a general disregard for punctuality (cf. AFRICAN PEOPLE'S TIME). [racial stereotyping]

hawbuck *n.* [early 19C] a country bumpkin, a lout (cf. HICK n.; HOB; HODGE). [? SE *haw*, hedge + *buck*, a man]

Hawcubite/Hawkubite *n.* [early 18C] one of a band of dissolute young men infesting the streets of London in the early 18C; a street-bully, a ruffian (cf. SCOURER; TITTERY-TU). [? SE *hack about*; but note *Brewer* (1894): 'The succession of these London pests after the Restoration was … The Muns, the Tityre-Tus, the Hectors, the Scourers, the Nickers, then the Hawkubites (1711–14), and then the Mohocks – most dreaded of all. (Hawkubite is the name of an Indian tribe of savages)']

haw-haw toff *n.* [late 19C] a dandy, an aristocrat. [his 'haw-haw' laugh + TOFF]

hawk *n.*¹ **1** [mid-17C–early 19C] a cardsharp, a confidence trickster (cf. PIGEON n.²; ROOK n.¹; WARE THE HAWK!). **2** [1970s+] (US) a robber or mugger. [HAWK v.]

hawk *n.*² **1** [18C+] a bailiff, a constable, a police officer; thus excl. *ware hawk*, a cry of warning. **2** [20C] (US Black) a prison officer (cf. HACK n.⁵).

hawk *n.*³ [1930s+] (US Black) chilly winter winds, esp. as experienced in northern cities, esp. as *the hawk* (cf. MR WIND).

hawk *n.*⁴ [1960s–70s] (drugs) **1** LSD. **2** an LSD user. **3** an LSD seller.

hawk *n.*⁵ [1960s+] **1** (S.Afr.) a 'masculine' male homosexual (cf. HASIE; RABBIT n.⁵). **2** (US) a person, esp. in public office, government or business, who advocates an aggressive policy. **3** (US) an older male homosexual with a preference for young boys (cf. CHICKEN-HAWK).

hawk *v.*¹ [mid-19C] **1** to act as a decoy, esp. for a card-sharper or a cheapjack. **2** (US) to pounce upon, to capture, esp. of a criminal seizing upon a victim (cf. WARE THE HAWK!).

hawk *v.*² **1** [19C+] (US Black) to keep a suspicious and close watch on. **2** [1960s–70s] to walk quickly. **3** [1980s+] (US) to pilfer, steal. **4** [1990s] to stare down someone.

hawk *v.*³ [20C] to irritate, to annoy. [var. on HACK v.²]

hawk *v.*⁴ [1980s+] (US campus) to participate in an athletic activity for fun.

hawk and pigeon *n.* [late 19C] a sharper and his victim. [HAWK n.¹ + PIGEON n.²]

hawker *n.* [1970s+] (US) a gob of expectorated phlegm. [SE *hawk*, to spit, to cough up]

hawker *v.* [1970s+] (US) to cough up phlegm. [HAWKER n.]

hawkesbury rivers *n.* [20C] (Aus.) the cold shivers. [rhy. sl.]

hawk-eye *n.* [mid-19C+] a native or inhabitant of Iowa, popularly called the Hawk-eye State.

Hawkins/'awkins *n.*¹ [late 19C–1900s] a superior costermonger. [the line by music-hall star Albert Chevalier (1862–1923): 'And 'Enery 'Awkins is a first-class name']

Hawkins *n.*² [late 19C–1900s] a severe disciplinarian. [the 'hanging judge' Sir Frederic *Hawkins*]

Hawkins/Mister Hawkins *n.*³ [1930s+] (US Black) very cold weather. [HAWK n.³]

hawk it *v.* [late 19C+] to work as street prostitute. [abbr. HAWK ONE'S FORK]

hawk one's brawn, to *phr.* [1970s+] (Aus.) to work as a prostitute (cf. HAWK ONE'S BROWN; HAWK ONE'S FORK). [SE *hawk*, to seel + *brawn*, a form of potted pork]

hawk one's brown, to *phr.* [20C] to work as a male prostitute (cf. HAWK ONE'S BRAWN; HAWK ONE'S FORK). [SE *hawk*, to sell + BROWN n.³]

hawk one's fork, to *phr.* [20C] (Aus.) to work as a prostitute; the 'fork' is the juncture of the legs and thus the vagina. [SE *hawk* + *fork*, the crutch]

hawk one's meat, to *phr.* [19C] to display one's body (cf. AIR THE DAIRY). [SE *hawk* + MEAT n. (1)]

hawk one's mutton, to *phr.* [19C+] of either sex, to work as a prostitute. [SE *hawk* + MUTTON n.¹]

hawk one's pearly, to *phr.* [1970s+] to act in a promiscuous manner, to offer one's body for sexual enjoyment. [SE *hawk* + rhy. sl. *pearly king* = RING n.¹]

hawks *n.* [mid-19C] an advantage.

hawkshaw *n.* [1950s+] (esp. W.I.) a detective. [*Hawkshaw the Detective* created by Henry Cecil Bullivant in such books as *The Ticket-of-Leave Man* (1935), itself taken f. *The Ticket-of-Leave Man* (1863), a play by the English dramatist Tom Taylor (1817–1880); also in the comic strip *Hawkshaw the Detective* by the American cartoonist Gus Mager (d.1956)]

hay *n.*[1] [20C] a bed, in the context of a place for sexual intercourse; thus *great in the hay*, an above-average sexual performer. [the use of hay for stuffing mattresses]

hay *n.*[2] [1930s+] a small sum of money; usu. in phr. *that ain't hay*, remarking on a substantial sum.

hay *n.*[3] [1930s+] (drugs) marijuana.

Hay and Hell and Booligal *see* HAY, HELL AND BOOLIGAL.

haybag *n.* [19C+] (US) a fat old woman, often a slovenly drunkard; thus ext. as *old haybag*. [US milit. jargon *haybag*, a camp-follower]

hay-band *n.* [mid-19C] a second-rate cigar. [SE *hay*, the supposed content + the cigar-band]

hay burner *n.*[1] [20C] (US) a tobacco pipe.

hay burner/motor *n.*[2] **1** [20C] (Aus./US) a horse. **2** [1940s] (US) a Western film. [the animal's food]

hay burner *n.*[3] [1930s+] (US) a smoker of marijuana. [HAY *n.*[3]]

hay butt *n.* [1950s+] (drugs) marijuana cigarette. [HAY *n.*[3] + BUTT *n.*[2]]

hay eater *n.* [late 19C–1930s] (US Black) a White person. [? derog. ref. to White farmers]

hayfoot *n.* [1900s–50s] (US) a farmer (cf. APPLE-KNOCKER *n.*[2]).

hay-footed *adj.* [1900s–50s] (US) rustic, unsophisticated. [HAYFOOT]

hayhead *n.* [1940s–50s] (US) a smoker of marijuana. [HAY *n.*[3] + sfx. -HEAD (2)]

Hay, Hell/Hay and Hell and Booligal *phr.* [late 19C+] (Aus.) a mythical place that is beyond all the bounds of civilization and devoid of any proper comforts. [*Booligal*, a town in western New South Wales]

haylee *n.* [1940s–50s] tea (cf. ROSIE LEA). [rhy. sl.]

haymaker/old haymaker *n.*[1] [mid-19C–1920s] (US) the sun. [its beneficial effect on crops]

haymaker *n.*[2] [mid-19C–1950s] a farmer (cf. APPLE-KNOCKER *n.*[2]). [his job]

haymaker *n.*[3] [20C] a swinging, roundhouse punch, which counts more on energy and ire than on skill and direction (cf. HAYPITCHER). [the image of a man swinging a scythe to cut hay]

Haymarket hector *n.* [19C] a pimp. [proper name *Haymarket*, the centre of 19C London prostitution + HECTOR]

Haymarket ware *n.* [19C] prostitutes in general (cf. BANKSIDE LADY). [London's Haymarket, a centre of 19C prostitution]

hay motor *see* HAY BURNER *n.*[2].

haypile *n.* [1900s–30s] (US) a bed or mattress.

hay-pitcher *n.* [19C] a farmer, a peasant (cf. APPLE-KNOCKER *n.*[2]).

hay-pounder/hay-shagger/hay-shaker *n.* [20C] (Aus./N.Z./US) a farmer, a simple peasant (cf. APPLE-KNOCKER *n.*[2]).

hayseed *n.* [19C+] (Aus./N.Z./US) a farmer, a simple peasant (cf. APPLE-KNOCKER *n.*[2]). [naut. phr. *he hasn't got the hayseed out of his hair*]

hay-shagger/hay-shaker *see* HAY-POUNDER.

haystack *n.* [20C] the back of a building etc. [rhy. sl.]

haystack agreement *n.* [20C] (US) a secret agreement or understanding. [the participants fig. retiring behind a haystack to converse in secret]

haystack kid *n.* [20C] (US) an illegitimate child. [such a child is conceived in a haystack]

hay-tosser *n.* [1900s–20s] (US) a farmer (cf. APPLE-KNOCKER *n.*[2]).

haywire *adv.* **1** [1920s+] (orig. US) obsessed, crazy, out of control. **2** [1920s+] (US) out of order, impaired, ruined. [SE *hay wire*, which flails around when cut]

hazard-drum *n.* [mid-19C] a casino, a gambling house. [SE *hazard*, a gambling game + DRUM *n.*[2]]

haze *n.* [1960s+] (drugs) LSD (cf. A *n.*[3]). [abbr. PURPLE HAZE + its effect]

hazel *n.* [1970s+] (drugs) heroin. [its colour]

hazeler *n.* [20C] (Irish) a countryman. [the *hazel* rods used to drive cattle]

hazel-gild *v.* [late 17C–early 19C] to beat with a hazel rod (cf. HAZEL OIL). [B.E. has sp. *hazel-geld*, but this may be a printer's error]

hazel oil/oil of hazel *n.* [late 18C–19C] a beating, often as phr. *anoint with oil of hazel*, to beat. [a variety of sap supposedly contained in a green hazel rod, which adds vigour to a beating]

hazy *adj.* [mid-19C] tipsy, drunk (cf. WOOZY).

h.b.i. *n.* [1940s–50s] (Und.) *house breaking implements*. [abbr.]

H caps *n.* [1960s–70s] (drugs) heroin. [H *n.*[2] + CAP *n.*[4]]

h.c.l. *phr.* [1910s+] (US) *high cost of living*. [abbr.]

h.d. *phr.* [1980s+] (US campus) a man who lives off a woman. [abbr. *husband dependent*]

he/him *n.* [19C+] the penis. [the dating is almost random, as E.P. says, this personification is 'prob. almost immemorial']

head *n.*[1] [19C] a lavatory, a privy. [naut. jargon *head* or *heads*, the ship's lavatory, which was originally sited at the 'head' of a ship, near the bowsprit]

head *n.*[2] [mid-19C] a postage stamp. [the monarch's head appears on all UK stamps]

head *n.*[3] [mid-19C] (US) the mouth, as source of offensive language; thus *shut your head*, shut up.

head *n.*[4] [late 19C+] a hangover, e.g. *I've got an awful head this morning* (cf. BACK *n.*[2]; BIG HEAD *n.*[2]). [abbr. SE *headache*]

head *n.*[5] [late 19C+] (Aus.) **1** a professional gambler. **2** a long-term prisoner. [? HARDHEAD *n.*[2] (1)]

head *n.*[6] [1920s–30s] (US Und.) an illegal immigrant. [? such immigrants were counted as 'heads']

head *n.*[7] [1930s+] (US) a sexually appealing young woman.

head *n.*[8] [1940s+] oral intercourse, usu. fellatio, but also cunnilingus, esp. in phr. *give head*, to perform oral sex.

head *n.*[9] [1950s+] (US) the erect penis.

head *n.*[10] [1950s+] (orig. US drugs) **1** the regular user of any kind of drug; thus ACID-HEAD etc. **2** a drug-induced state (cf. HIGH).

head *n.*[11] [1960s+] (US campus) a person. [ext. of HEAD *n.*[10]]

head *n.*[12] [1960s+] (US) facial appearance, usually constructed with 'bad', e.g. *she's got great tits, but that's a bad head*.

head *n.*[13] [1970s] (US) beer.

-head *sfx.* **1** [17C+] in a variety of combs. in which *-head* is linked to a noun to create a term meaning fool or idiot; the implication is that the head is shaped like or otherwise resembles the noun (cf. AIRHEAD; APEHEAD; APPLEHEAD; ASSHEAD; BALLOON-HEAD; BANANAHEAD; BEAN-HEAD; BEEF-HEAD; BEETLE-HEAD; BLOCKHEAD *n.*[1]; BLUBBER-HEAD; BOMBHEAD *n.*[1]; BONEHEAD *n.*[1]; BOOFHEAD; BOTTLEHEAD; BOWHEAD; BOXHEAD; BRASS-HEAD; BUBBLEHEAD; BUCKETHEAD; BUFFLEHEAD; BUGHEAD; BULLET-HEAD; BULL-HEAD *n.*[1]; BURRHEAD *n.*[2]; BUSH-HEAD *n.*[1]; BUTTERHEAD; BUTT-HEAD; CABBAGE-HEAD; CEMENT-HEAD; CHOWDER-HEAD; CHUCKLE-HEAD; CLOTH-HEAD; CLUCKHEAD *n.*[1]; CLUNKHEAD; COCKHEAD; COCONUT HEAD *n.*[1]; CORKHEAD; COTTONHEAD; CRAPHEAD; CRAZY-HEAD; CRUDHEAD; CUNTHEAD; DEADHEAD *n.*[2]; DICKHEAD; DIP-HEAD; DOPEHEAD *n.*[2]; DOSSHEAD; DOUGH-HEAD; DOUGHNUT-HEAD;

DUDHEAD; DULLHEAD; DUNCEHEAD; DUNDERHEAD; FART-HEAD; FAT-HEAD; FEATHERHEAD; FOOLHEAD; FUCKHEAD; GEARHEAD; GELLYHEAD; GIGHEAD; GOOBERHEAD; GOONHEAD; GOOSEHEAD; GOURD-HEAD; GROUTHEAD; GUMBYHEAD; HAMHEAD; HAMMERHEAD n.[1]; HOLLOW-HEAD; HONCH-HEAD; HOSEHEAD; JERKHEAD; LARDHEAD; LEADHEAD; LEATHERHEAD n.[1]; LOGGERHEAD; LUGHEAD; LUMPHEAD; LUNKHEAD; MALLETHEAD; MARBLEHEAD n.[2]; MEATHEAD; MELONHEAD; MOLLY-HEAD; MUDDLE-HEAD; MUD-HEAD; MUFFIN-HEAD; MUMMYHEAD; MUSCLEHEAD; MUSH-HEAD; MUTTHEAD; MUTTON-HEAD; NIBHEAD; NOODLEHEAD; NUMBHEAD; NYAAMS HEAD; ONIONHEAD n.[1]; PECKERHEAD; PESTLEHEAD; PIGHEAD; PINHEAD n.[2]; PISS-HEAD n.[1]; POO-HEAD; POOPHEAD; POTATO-HEAD; POTHEAD n.[1]; PRAWNHEAD; PUDDING-HEAD; PUMPKIN HEAD; PUPPET-HEAD; PUTTY-HEAD; RAT'S HEAD; ROCKHEAD; RUBBLEHEAD; SAP-HEAD; SCAMHEAD; SCUMHEAD; SHITHEAD; SHOVELHEAD; SHREWD-HEAD; SMEGHEAD; SOCKHEAD; SPACKAHEAD; SPUNK-HEAD; SQUAREHEAD n.[1]; STUPE-HEAD; TACK-HEAD; TIMBER-HEAD; TOOLHEAD; WETHEAD; WOODHEAD). **2** [20C] an habitual user, a devotee, usu. of a drug or of drink or a particular music or performer (cf. ACID-HEAD; A-HEAD; BASE-HEAD; BEERHEAD; BLOCKHEAD n.[2]; BOOZE-HEAD; BOTTLEHEAD; BREADHEAD; BUDHEAD; C-HEAD; CHIPHEAD; CLUCKHEAD n.[2]; COKE-HEAD; CRACKHEAD; CUBEHEAD; DOPEHEAD n.[1]; DOWN-HEAD; DREDGE-HEAD; DRUGHEAD; GARBAGE HEADS; GINHEAD; GOWHEAD; GRAF-HEAD; GREEDHEAD; GUT-HEAD; HAIRHEAD; HASH-HEAD; HAYHEAD; HEAT-HEAD; HIT-HEAD; HOP-HEAD n.[1]; HOP-HEAD n.[2]; HORSE-HEAD; JAKEHEAD; JARHEAD n.[2]; JICK HEAD; JUGHEAD n.[2]; JUICE-HEAD; JUNKHEAD; LIQUORHEAD; LUSH-HEAD; METALHEAD; METH-HEAD; MUGGLEHEAD; PETROL-HEAD; PILL-HEAD; PIPE-HEAD; PISS-HEAD n.[2]; POTHEAD n.[2]; SMACK-HEAD; TEA-HEAD; WEEDHEAD; WHISKY-HEAD; WINEHEAD (cf. ARTIST n.[2])). **3** [20C] (US derog.) a person of a specific (and alien) ethnic origin (cf. BUDDHAHEAD; CHILE-HEAD; HANDKERCHIEF-HEAD n.[2]; HANKIE-HEAD; NAPPY HEAD; POPEHEAD; RAG-HEAD n.[1]; TACO-HEAD; TOWEL-HEAD).

headache n. **1** [1930s] (US) one's wife or girlfriend. **2** [1930s+] (orig. US) a problem, a cause of anxiety, a worry.

headache stick n. [1910s–70s] (US) a stick used as a club.

head and head game n. [20C] (gambling) a dice game in which players bet against each other rather than against a bank (as in a casino game).

head and heels n. [1960s–70s] (US gay) a young, inexperienced homosexual. [one has to lift the boy by his *head and heels* to position him for sex]

head-banger n. **1** [1970s+] in the music business, a fan of loud, monotonous, 'heavy metal music', usu. a youth who plays a make-believe (or even cardboard) guitar and shakes his head violently as he watches or listens to his heroes; thus *headbanging music*. **2** [1980s+] a psychotic, a randomly, obsessively violent person, someone who cannot control his temper.

headbeater/headbuster n. [1950s+] (US Black) a brutal police officer (cf. HEADWHIPPER).

head-beetler n. [mid-19C+] **1** a foreman. **2** 'the bully of the workshop, who lords it over his fellow-workmen by reason of superior strength, skill in fighting &c' (Hotten, 1864). [SE *beetle*, any implement used in a variety of industrial processes for crushing, bruising, beating, flattening, or smoothing]

headbin n. [20C] (Ulster) a unstable person, an eccentric. [var. on HEADCASE]

headbone n. [20C] (US Black) the skull.

head bully/cully of the pass/passage bank n. [late 17C–early 19C] a gang boss or top criminal who levies a tax on all games of chance in the area of which he is in control. [BULLY n.[1] + PASS-BANK]

head bummaroo, the n. [mid-19C–1940s] the chief, the person in charge. [? BUMPER n.[1] (2)]

headbuster see HEADBEATER.

head-candler n. [1950s–60s] (US) a psychotherapist; thus *head-candling*, psychotherapy (cf. HEAD DOCTOR; HEAD-FEELER; HEAD-PEEPER; HEAD-SHRINKER; HEAD-TRIPPER; SHRINK n.[1]). [SE *head + candle*, to test an egg for freshness]

headcase n. [1960s+] **1** an eccentric, bizarre person. **2** someone undergoing, or in need of, psychiatric treatment. [SE *head* + CASE n.[6]]

headcheese n.[1] [20C] smegma (cf. CHEESE n.[2]). [its odour and its appearance near the head of the penis]

headcheese n.[2] [20C] an important, powerful influential person. [SE *head* + (BIG) CHEESE]

headcheese n.[3] [1950s+] (US Black) pork luncheon meat. [SE *headcheese*, brawn]

head-chick n.[1] [1930s–40s] (US Black) a female lover, a favourite girlfriend. [SE *head* adj. + CHICK n.[4]]

head-chick n.[2] [1930s–40s] (US Black) an expert fellatrix. [HEAD n.[8] + CHICK n.[4]]

head cook and bottle-washer see CHIEF COOK AND BOTTLE-WASHER.

head cully of the pass see HEAD BULLY OF THE PASS.

head devil n. [mid-19C–1910s] (US) the boss.

head doctor n. [1950s+] (US) a psychiatrist, a psychotherapist (cf. HEAD-CANDLER).

head drugs n. [1960s+] (drugs) amphetamines (cf. A n.[2]). [they affect the head (though so do all drugs)]

header n.[1] **1** [early 19C] a blow to the head. **2** [mid-19C+] a head-first dive into water.

header n.[2] [1960s+] (Irish) a psychotic, unstable person (cf. HEADBIN; HEADCASE).

header n.[3] [1970s+] (US) an act of oral copulation. [HEAD n.[8]]

head-feeler n. [1940s] (US) a psychotherapist (cf. HEAD-CANDLER).

headfuck v. [1970s+] (orig. US) to confuse, to mislead, to disorientate (cf. MINDFUCK v.). [SE *head* + FUCK v.[2]]

headfucker n. [1970s+] (drugs) an especially powerful drug, esp. an hallucinogen.

head game n. [1970s+] (orig. US) psychological trickery and manipulation, usu. hostile or negative in intent (cf. MIND GAME).

head gasket n. [1960s+] (US) a condom. [HEAD n.[9] + SE *gasket*]

head hen n. [1930s–40s] (US Black) a landlady.

head hunt v. [1940s+] (US Black) to look for trouble, to start a fight.

head hunter n.[1] [1980s+] (US) an aggressively selfish and single-minded individual.

head hunter n.[2] [1980s+] (US) one who performs oral sex, esp. in exchange for drugs. [HEAD n.[8] + SE *hunter*]

heading n. [1940s–50s] using the top of the head to butt someone in a fight (cf. NUTTING).

head is not sweet phr. [20C] (W.I.) **1** of old people, suffering dizzy spells. **2** of young people, mentally unstable.

head/hat job n. [1950s+] (orig. US) fellatio (cf. FRENCH HEAD JOB). [HEAD n.[8] + SE *job*]

head jockey n. [1950s+] a man who performs cunnilingus. [HEAD n.[8] + SE *jockey*]

head knock n. [1930s–40s] (US Black) God, Jesus. [the image of the deity 'knocking' and summoning one to heaven/hell]

headknocker n. (US) **1** [late 19C+] a boss. **2** [1960s+] a brutal policeman (cf. HEADBEATER).

headlamps n.[1] [1970s+] (US) the eyes (cf. HEADLIGHTS n.[1]).

headlamps n.[2] [1990s] the female breasts (cf. HEADLIGHTS n.[1]).

head lar n. [20C] (Irish) the man in charge. [SE *head* + LAIR n.]

headlight n. [1930s–40s] (US) a light-skinned Black person (cf. HIGH YELLOW). [the golden colour]

headlights n.[1] (US) **1** [late 19C+] the eyes (cf. HEADLAMPS n.[1]). **2** [20C] spectacles, glasses, esp. tinted or dark glasses. **3** [20C]

(US) diamonds. **4** [20C] the female breasts, esp. when prominent and well shaped (cf. HEADLAMPS n.²). **5** [1920s] (US) eggs. [supposed resemblance]

headlights n.² [1960s+] (drugs) LSD (cf. A n.³). [it *lights up* one's head]

headliner n. [20C] (orig. US show business) an important, powerful, influential person.

head/big nigger in charge n. [1930s+] (US Black) a sarcastic ref. to any Black authority-figure (cf. BLACK NIGGER IN CHARGE; H.N.I.C.). [the implication being that, given institutional racism, the authority lies in the title not in the actual job. According to Darryl Pinckney (*NYRB*, December 1995) the phr. was coined for the authoritarian Black rights campaigner Booker T. Washington (1856–1915)]

head over teakettle phr. [20C] head-over-heels (cf. ARSE OVER KETTLE).

head over turkey phr. [20C] (Aus./N.Z.) head-over-heels. [SE *head* + TURKEY n.³]

head-peeper n. [1980s] (US) a psychotherapist (cf. HEAD-CANDLER).

head-piece n. **1** [late 16C+] the head, the mind. **2** [20C] (Irish) an intelligent person; thus *have the head-piece on one*, to be intelligent.

headquarters n. [1920s–50s] (US Black) a person with a particularly prominent skull. [pun]

head queen n. [1940s–70s] (US gay) a male homosexual who frequents public toilets in search of sex. [HEAD n.⁸ + QUEEN n.¹]

head rails n. [mid-18C–mid-19C] the teeth.

head robber n.¹ [late 19C] a boxer, a prize-fighter. [he 'takes your head off']

head robber n.² [late 19C] a butler. [SE *head*, chief + *robber*; used by those with a low opinion of servants]

heads n.¹ [19C] (orig. naut.) a latrine. [HEAD n.¹]

heads n.² [1950s+] (US) *head*lights. [abbr.]

heads n.³ [1990s] (US Black) one's children.

heads and tails n. [late 19C–1950s] (Aus.) the act of SIXTY-NINE.

head-serag/-serang n. [mid-19C–1900s] (Anglo-Ind.–Bengali) an overseer, a foreman. [Pers. *sarhang*, a commander, an overseer]

head-set n. [1970s+] (US) a state of mind, a mood. [var. on SE *mind-set*]

head shop n. [1960s] (orig. US) a shop specializing in drug paraphernalia. [HEAD n.¹⁰ + SE *shop*. The first such emporium was San Francisco's Psychedelic Shop, which flourished in the mid-1960s]

headshot n. [1990s] (US Black teen) **1** a shot to the head from any firearm. **2** in rap music, freestyle rapping.

head-shrinker/headshrink n. [1950s+] (orig. US) a psychoanalyst, a psychotherapist; thus *headshrinking*, psychoanalysis, psychotherapy (cf. HEAD-CANDLER).

heads I win, tails you lose/and tails you lose phr. [mid-19C+] come what may, I shall win.

head smack n. [1960s+] (US) a dose of heroin inhaled through the nose. [SE *head* + SMACK n. + play on SE]

head smack v. [1960s+] (US) to inhale heroin through the nose. [HEAD SMACK n.]

head space n. [1990s] (US) a state of mind, a mood (cf. HEAD-SET).

headsplitter n. [mid-19C+] (US) strong whisky, esp. when illegally distilled (cf. BUSTHEAD).

headstaggers n. [20C] (Irish) mental illness or instability. [SE *head* + *staggers*, a disease of horses]

head stick n. [1920s–30s] (US Black) a wooden grave marker.

heads-up adj. [1930s+] (US) alert and skilful, esp. in sport.

heads up! excl. [1910s+] shout by look-outs for illegal street

traders or street gamblers to warn of an approaching policeman.

head-the-ball n. [1990s] (Irish) a fool. [the image of one who has headed the ball so often that their brains are scrambled]

head-to-head adj. [1970s+] at close-quarters.

head-topper n. [mid-19C] a wig.

head trip/h.t. n. **1** [1960s+] (US) (orig. drugs) a drug-induced fantasy, reverie. **2** [1970s+] (US) something requiring challenging thought. **3** [1980s+] (US) deception or flattery. [SE *head* + TRIP n.]

head trip v. [1960s+] (orig. US) to daydream, usu. under the influence of drugs. [HEAD TRIP n. (1)]

head-tripper n. [1970s+] (US) a psychotherapist (cf. HEAD-CANDLER).

head up v. [1990s] (US Black gang) to start a fight. [HEAD UP adv.]

head up adv. [20C] in direct confrontation.

head up and tail up phr. [19C+] (US) cocky, brash, lively, also as *head up and tail over the dashboard*, *head up and tail a-rising*.

headwhipper n. [1950s+] (US Black) a police officer (cf. HEADBEATER).

heady adj.¹ [late 17C–early 18C] drunk (cf. ABOUT RIGHT adj.¹). [SE *heady*, intoxicating, stupefying]

heady adj.² [20C] (mainly Aus./N.Z.) ingenious, shrewd. [the contents of one's head]

Healtheries, the n. [late 19C] the Health Exhibition, held in London in 1884 (cf. COLINDERIES).

heap n.¹ **1** [mid-17C–18C;19C+] a large amount, often of money. **2** [early 19C+] a woman, usu. with some derog. adj., e.g. *lazy heap*, *fat heap*. [SE *heap*, a pile, a mass]

heap n.² **1** [1920s+] (orig. US) an old or unreliable car. **2** [1940s+] (US) an old aeroplane. [abbr. *heap of scrap*, *heap of junk*]

heap adv. [early 19C+] (orig. US) very, much. [supposedly a representation of the speech of Native Americans]

heaped adj. [17C] involved in sexual intercourse. [SE *heap*, to pile on top]

heap o'coke/heapy n. [20C] a man, a person. [rhy. sl. *heap o'coke* = BLOKE]

heaps n. [mid-17C+] a large quantity, many, an abundance.

heap sight n. [late 19C–1910s] (US) a great deal.

heapy see HEAP O'COKE.

hear v. [1960s+] (US) to understand, to agree with someone completely. [SE *hear*, with an implication, the product of drugs/New Age philosophizing, of a deeper understanding than the pure SE implies]

hear a bird sing, to phr. [late 16C–early 17C] to discover a secret.

hearing n. [early 19C] a scolding, telling-off. [HEAR OF IT]

hearing cheats n. [mid-16C–19C] (Und.) the ears. [SE *hearing* + CHEAT]

hear it on the street phr. [20C] to pick up a rumour, to hear the latest gossip.

hear of it v. [late 16C–mid-17C] to be called to account, to be summoned to explain oneself.

hear one's belly knocking against one's backbone, to phr. [20C] to be extremely hungry, to be on the verge of starvation (cf. MY BELLY THINKS MY THROAT'S BEEN CUT).

hearse n.¹ (US) **1** [late 19C] a police patrol wagon. **2** [20C] an ambulance. **3** [20C] a large automobile.

hearse/hearse-driver n.² [late 19C] (US) a pessimistic person. [the popular image of undertakers]

hear someone's horn, to phr. [1940s–60s] (US) to hear and acknowledge the importance of what someone is saying.

heart n. [1930s+] (orig. US Und.) courage, bravery, spirit (cf. BALLS n.¹; BELLY; GUTS n.²; PLUCK n.¹). [metonymy]

heart *adv.* [1900s] (Ulster) very, extremely.

heart and dart *n.* [mid-19C–1920s] a fart. [rhy. sl.]

heart and lung *n.* [1920s] (US) the tongue. [rhy. sl.]

heartbalm *n.* [1920s–30s] alimony (cf. HEARTSEASE). [cynical use of SE]

heartbeat *n.*[1] [1930s] (US campus) a love- or sex-object (cf. HEART-THROB).

heartbeat *n.*[2] [1980s+] (US) a split second; thus *in a heartbeat*, without hesitation.

heartbreaker *n.* [16C] a curled love-lock (cf. AGGERAWATOR). [its supposed effect on the opposite sex]

heartbreak hotel *n.* [1980s+] (US) a prison. [sugg. by 1956 song 'Heartbreak Hotel' by Elvis Presley]

heartburn *n.* [late 19C–1920s] a bad cigar. [its effects]

hear the bear growl, to *phr.* [mid-19C] (US) to expose oneself to danger, to go into battle.

hearth rug *n.* [1910s–50s] **1** a fool, a simpleton (cf. STEAMER n.[2]). **2** a bedbug. [rhy. sl.; (1) *hearth rug* = MUG n.[5]]

hearthrug pie *n.* [1950s–60s] sexual intercourse on the sitting-room floor (cf. FINGER PIE). [SE *hearthrug* + PIE]

hearthstone *n.* [late 19C] butter, which is spread on a thick slice of bread (cf. DOORSTEP).

heart/hearts of oak *adj.* [20C] out of funds, impoverished. [rhy. sl. *heart/s of oak* = BROKE]

heart of the roul/rowl *n.* [1960s+] the best person. [? Scot. *rail, raul*, a line; corruption of SE *royal*]

heart-on *n.* [1980s+] (drugs) an inhalant. [play on HARD-ON + the stimulating effect on the heart]

hearts *n.* [1960s–70s] (drugs) amphetamine (cf. A n.[2]). [abbr. PURPLE HEARTS]

hearts-and-flowers *n.* [1930s+] (orig. US) mawkish sentimentality.

heartsease *n.* [late 17C–early 19C] **1** a 20-shilling piece (cf. HEARTBALM). **2** a measure of gin. [both 'ease the heart' in their separate ways]

hearts of oak *see* HEART OF OAK.

heart-starter *n.* [1990s] (Aus.) the first alcoholic drink of the day (cf. ALLEVIATOR).

heart-throb *n.* [1920s+] someone (or either sex) who thrills the heart, a lover, esp. used of film stars and other entertainers (cf. HEARTBEAT n.[1]).

heart-to-heart *n.* [1910s+] (US) an intimate talk.

hearty *n.* [mid-19C–1910s] strong drink (cf. ABOUT RIGHT adj.[1]).

hearty *adj.* [mid-19C–1910s] drunk. [HEARTY n.]

heat *n.*[1] **1** [1900s–60s] (US) drunkenness. **2** [1930s–70s] (US tramp) the crude alcohol that is drunk in solution as a substitute for alcohol (cf. CANNED HEAT). **3** [1970s+] (drugs) the heating of powdered heroin before smoking it (cf. CHASE THE DRAGON).

heat *n.*[2] [1920s+] (orig. Und.) intensive police activity of any kind, pressure, esp. on criminals from the police. **2** [1930s+] the police. [? they 'cast light' on things or 'warm things up']

heat *n.*[3] [1920s+] (US) weapons, arms (cf. HEATER).

heat *n.*[4] [1930s+] (US) **1** problems, difficulties, trouble. **2** blame, sarcasm, intense criticism (cf. STEAM n.[2]).

heat *n.*[5] (US) **1** [1940s–60s] sex appeal, pornography; thus *give the heat*, to make sexual advances. **2** [1980s+] popularity. **3** [1980s+] anger, excitement. [HOT adj.[1]]

heated *adj.* [1980s+] (US campus) drunk. [HEAT n.[1]]

heater *n.* **1** [1900s–30s] (US) an overcoat. **2** [1910s+] (US) a cigar. **3** [1920s+] a pistol, revolver (cf. HEAT n.[3]). **4** [1930s–60s] (US) the female genitals.

heat-head *n.* [1920s+] (US) a consumer of crude alcohol (cf. CANNED HEAT). [HEAT n.[1] (2) + sfx. -HEAD (2)]

heathen chinee *n.* [19C] (US) a Chinese person. [coined 1870 by US writer Bret Harte [1836–1902] in his poem 'Plain Language from Truthful James', better known, from this coinage, as 'The Heathen Chinee': 'For ways that are dark/ And for tricks that are vain,/The heathen Chinee is peculiar']

heathenish *adj.* [late 16C–late 19C] abominable, disgusting, offensive. [the antonym of SE *Christian*]

heathen philosopher *n.* [late 17C–early 19C] a ragged vagrant, whose flesh can be seen through his garments. [image of Greek philosophers who traditionally scorned the niceties of dress]

heather *n.* [1980s+] (US campus) a superficial young woman, pretty but lacking in intelligence. [film *Heathers* (1988)]

heat-seeking missile/moisture missile *n.* [1990s] (US campus) the penis (cf. PORTABLE POCKET ROCKET).

heat's on *phr.* [1920s+] the police are exerting exceptional pressure on the community. [HEAT n.[2]]

heave *n.*[1] [19C] a flagrant attempt to deceive, to swindle, to persuade.

heave *n.*[2] [1990s] (US) **1** a hide-out. **2** a place where one sleeps.

heave *v.*[1] [mid-16C–early 19C] to rob (cf. HEAVE A BOUGH; HEAVE A CASE). [SE *heave*, lift and carry away]

heave *v.*[2] [20C] to vomit. [the sensation in one's stomach]

heave a Havana *phr.* [1990s] to defecate. [the similarity of a piece of excrement to a cigar]

heave a bough *phr.* [mid-16C–18C] (Und.) to rob or rifle a booth. [HEAVE v.[1] + SE *bough*, booth]

heave a case *phr.* [18C–late 19C] to rob a house. [HEAVE v.[1] + CASE n.[2]]

heave-ho *n.* **1** [late 19C+] rejection, ejection, often as *the old heave-ho*. **2** [1940s+] (US) an act of vomiting. [naut. jargon *heave-ho!*, a sailor's cry when hauling on the anchor cable, pulling in sails and performing similar strenuous tasks. In this case the task was that of the BOUNCER n.[1], who grasped his victim by the scruff of the neck and the seat of the trousers and tossed him through the saloon door]

heave in/into sight, to *phr.* [early 19C+] (orig. naut. jargon) to appear.

heaven *n.* [18C] the vagina (cf. HELL n.[1]).

heaven and hell *n.*[1] **1** [20C] a smell. **2** [1940s] a projectile shell. [rhy. sl.]

heaven and hell *n.*[2] [1970s+] (drugs) phencyclidine (cf. ACE n.[3]). [the unpredictability of its effects]

heaven-born, the *n.* [19C] (Anglo-Ind.) senior members of the Indian Civil Service (cf. MANDARIN). [? Chinese honorific]

heaven dust *n.* [1970s+] (drugs) **1** heroin. **2** cocaine. [SE *heaven*, i.e. the effects + DUST n.[6]]

heaven-eleven *n.* [20C] (US gambling) the point of 11 in craps dice. [*heaven*, since if the shooter throws 11 on the first throw the bet is won]

heavenly *adj.* [late 19C+] wonderful, splendid.

heavenly plan *n.* [late 19C–1900s] (Aus.) a man. [rhy. sl.]

heavens! *excl.* [late 19C+] a mild oath.

heavens above *n.* [20C] love. [rhy. sl.]

heavens to Betsy!/Murgatroyd! *excl.* [20C] (US) a general excl. of shock, horror, surprise.

heaver *n.*[1] **1** [late 17C–19C] (Und.) the female breast. **2** [18C–19C] a person in love. **3** [20C] (US Black) a self-styled great lover, esp. of the more earthy, animalistic type. [the cliché, the breast *heaves* with emotion]

heaver *n.*[2] [1910s–20s] a coin of small value, usu. a penny. [rhy. sl. *coal-heaver* = STIVER]

heaves *n.* [late 19C+] stomach cramps.

heave up/throw up Jonah, to *phr.* [mid-19C–1910a] (US) to be violently sick. [the biblical story of Jonah and the whale]

heavies *n.*[1] [1970s+] (Und.) the Special Branch. [abbr. HEAVY MOB]

heavies *n.*[2] [1980s+] (N.Z.) threats. [HEAVY v.]

heavy/heavy cheer n.[1] [early–mid-19C] a mixture of porter and beer (cf. HEAVY WET n.[1]). [SE *heavy* + cheer, happiness, contentment, esp. as a result of drinking alcohol]

heavy n.[2] **1** [late 19C–1920s] (US) an actor playing a serious or tragic part in a melodrama. **2** [1910s–20s] (US campus) a girlfriend, an important date. **3** [1920s+] a thug, a villain, esp. a violent criminal (also as portrayed in cinema and theatre). **4** [1920s+] violent crime, armed robbery. **5** [1920s–40s] (US) a large, fat man. **6** [1920s+] (US) an important or powerful person (cf. BIG SHOT). **7** [1950s+] (drugs) a hard drug (heroin, cocaine) rather than a soft one (cannabis etc).

heavy adj.[1] **1** [mid–late 19C] (US) of an object or idea, remarkable in a positive or negative way. **2** [mid-19C+] (US) of a person, powerful, wealthy, influential, popular. **3** [mid-19C+] ponderously dignified; stern, repressive, unbending, esp. as *heavy father, heavy uncle*. **4** [20C] thuggish, violent. **5** [1930s+] intense, urgent. **6** [1930s+] shocking, frightening, threatening. **7** [1930s+] meaningful, important, emotionally strong; a general intensifier, esp. loved by late 1960s hippies and radicals, varying as to context.

heavy adj.[2] **1** [20C] (W.I.) physically attractive. **2** [20C] (W.I.) enthusiastic. **3** [1940s+] (US Black) wonderful, amazing, admirable. **4** [1960s+] (US Black) highly intelligent. **5** [1940s+] very passionate.

heavy adj.[3] [mid-19C+] (US) in possession of a great deal of money, flush. [the weight of one's purse or wallet]

heavy adj.[4] [1950s] (US drugs) in possession of drugs. [the fig. 'weight' of the drugs]

heavy v. [1950s+] to threaten, to menace. [HEAVY n.[2] (3)]

heavy-arse n. [late 19C+] a lazy person. [HEAVY-ARSED]

heavy-arsed adj. [17C–18C] apathetic, lazy. [SE *heavy* + arse; thus pamphlet, *Shove to Heavy-Arsed Christians* by Richard Baxter (1615–91)]

heavy baggage n. [late 18C–19C] women and children. [they weigh down the man who is in pursuit of pleasure or focused on work]

heavy cavalry/dragoons/horsemen n. [mid-19C–1900s] bedbugs (cf. LIGHT INFANTRY; LIGHT TROOPS; SCOTCH GREYS).

heavy cheer see HEAVY n.[1].

heavy date n. [20C] a more than usually important meeting with one's boy- or girlfriend.

heavy dragoons see HEAVY CAVALRY.

heavy-duty adj. **1** [1930s+] (orig. US) intense, serious, committed (cf. HEAVY adj.[2]). **2** [1970s+] (US) tough, unpleasant (cf. HEAVY adj.[1]). **3** [1970s+] (US) terrific, first-rate (cf. HEAVY adj.[2]). **4** [1980s+] (US drugs) strongly addictive (cf. HEAVY adj.[4]). [SE *heavy-duty*, hard-wearing]

heavy-foot n. [1930s] (US Und.) a plain-clothes detective. [identified as such by his shoes]

Heavy Gang, the n. [1980s+] (Irish) a special, extra-tough, section of the Garda Síochána.

heavy grubber n. [mid-19C] an enthusiastic eater. [SE *heavy* + GRUBBER n.[3]]

heavy heat stretch n. [1940s] (US Black) summer.

heavy hitter n. **1** [1970s+] an important, influential person, esp. in the worlds of business or politics (cf. BALL-PARK FIGURE). **2** [1970s+] (US) a violent criminal, a hired thug. **3** [1980s] (US) an alcoholic. [baseball imagery + (3) HIT THE BOOZE]

heavy horsemen n.[1] [mid-19C] Thames thieves who pose as dock-hands to enter ships and steal the cargoes (cf. LIGHT HORSEMEN).

heavy horsemen n.[2] see HEAVY CAVALRY.

heavy lard n. [1940s] (US Black) **1** any impressively, convincingly told story (cf. HARD AS LARD). **2** a 'tall story', a dramatic but unfeasible story.

heavy lump n. [1940s] the fashionable area of contemporary

Harlem, New York City, otherwise known as Coogan's Bluff, between Amsterdam and Edgecombe Avenues, between 138th and 155th Streets. [pun on SUGAR HILL]

heavy man n. [1920s+] a thug, a criminal who is prone to use violence. [HEAVY n.[2] (3)]

heavy manners n. [1970s+] (orig. W.I. then UK Black) any form of oppression or repression experienced by Blacks (esp. at the hands of the police; thus *under heavy manners*, under strict discipline. [HEAVY adj.[1] + SE *manners*; also used by the authorities to denote their own firm measures in the fight against crime]

heavy metal! excl. [1970s+] (Ulster) an excl. of surprise or amazement. [? SE *heavy metal* music or euph. for Holy Mother!]

heavy mob n. [1950s+] (Und.) **1** a gang of thugs. **2** physically tough police officers used in violent situations. **3** officers from the Flying Squad and, formerly, the Special Patrol Group.

heavy number n. [1970s+] anything or anyone seen as serious, important etc. [HEAVY adj.[1] + NUMBER n.[3]]

heavy/hot on hand phr. [mid-19C–1900s] hard to control. [horse-riding imagery]

heavy soul n. [1950s] (drugs) heroin. [its long-term effects]

heavy stuff n. [mid-19C] portentous moralizing, esp. by a father (cf. COME THE HEAVY FATHER).

heavy sugar n. [1920s] (US) a large amount of money; thus *heavy sugar papa*, a sweet old man with a fat purse. [HEAVY adj.[1] (2) + SUGAR n.[1]]

heavy/howling swell n. [mid–late 19C] a dandy, an aristocrat or one who tries to pose as one. [HEAVY adj.[1]/HOWLING + SWELL n.]

heavyweight n. **1** [late 19C+] an important person with power and influence. **2** [1910s+] (US Und.) a violent criminal. **3** [1970s] (US) a fat person, esp. a fat woman.

heavy wet n.[1] **1** [early–mid-19C] a mixture of porter and beer. **2** [early–mid-19C] malt liquor. **3** [mid-19C–1900s] a heavy drinking bout. ['the more a man drinks of it, the heavier and more stupid he becomes' (Hotten, 1867)]

heavy wet n.[2] [1930s–40s] (US Black) a downpour, a rainstorm.

Hebe/Hebie/Heeb n. [1920s+] (orig. US) a derog. term for a Jew. [abbr. *Hebrew*, a Jew]

hebe n. [early–mid-18C] the pubic hair. [*Hebe*, the mythological goddess of youth and spring and cup-bearer of Olympus; note SE *Hebe*, a barmaid]

Hebie see HEBE.

he-blow n. [1980s+] (US gay) a gay Jewish man. [a pun on SE *Hebrew* + BLOW v.[6]]

Hebrew n. [17C–early 19C] unintelligible language (cf. CHOCTAW; GREEK n.[2]).

he can put his shoes under my bed any time phr. [20C] a complimentary ref. by a woman about an attractive man.

heck! excl. [18C+] euph. for HELL!

hecka adv. [1980s+] (US campus) very (cf. HELLA). [HECK!]

heck-of-a-no! excl. [1990s] (US teen) a statement of absolute rejection, an emphatic negative, esp. when one is being pressurized to do something against one's will. [HECK!]

he-coon n. [1910s–50s] (US) an important, powerful man. [SE *he* + COON n. (2)]

he could make me write bad checks phr. [1980s+] (US campus) a comment made by a woman about on an especially attractive man.

he could sleep on a clothes-line phr. [mid-19C+] a phr. used to describe someone who is capable of dealing with difficult or challenging circumstances. [note George Orwell's refs. to the ropes slung across rooms in the cheapest tramps' lodgings, on which impoverished men could lean and thus, if fortunate, sleep]

hectic *adj.* [20C] exciting, disturbing, in a state of feverish excitement or activity.

hector *n.*[1] [mid-17C–mid-19C] a blustering, swaggering bully, a thug (cf. HAYMARKET HECTOR). [an ironic use of the Trojan hero *Hector*, son of Priam and Hecuba, husband of Andromache, 'the prop or stay of Troy']

hector *n.*[2] [19C+] (US) used in a variety of phr., e.g. *dead as Hector, mad as Hector, meaner than Hector.* [? euph. for HELL]

he'd drink the stuff if he had to drain it through a shitty cloth *phr.* [1920s+] (Can. use) used of an unregenerate drunkard.

he'd fuck anything with a hole in it *phr.* [20C] said of an indiscriminately promiscuous man.

hedge *n.* [20C] (Und.) the crowd that gathers round illicit street traders or gamblers.

hedge *adj.* [16C] a general pej., used in a number of compounds (cf. HEDGE-BIRD; HEDGE-CREEPER; HEDGE-PRIEST; HEDGE-WHORE). [SE *hedge*, implying dirty, inferior, lit. plying one's trade beneath a hedge]

hedge and ditch *n.* [late 19C+] **1** a market pitch. **2** a cricket or football pitch. [rhy. sl.]

hedge-bird *n.* [16C–17C] a general derog. term esp. for a tramp or vagrant, i.e. one who lives or might as well live in a hedge (cf. HEDGE-CREEPER; HEDGE-PRIEST; HEDGE-WHORE). [HEDGE adj. + SE bird/BIRD n.[2]]

hedge-bit *n.* [19C] a low-grade prostitute who carries on operations in the open air. [HEDGE adj. + BIT n.[3]]

hedge-creeper *n.* [16C–early 18C] **1** a petty thief who steals laundry from the hedges on which it is laid to dry. **2** a prostitute, presumably working in the countryside (cf. HEDGE-WHORE). [obs. SE *hedge-creeper*, a sneak thief, a creeping rogue]

hedge-docked *adj.* [19C] seduced, esp. deflowered, in the open air. [SE *hedge* + DOCK v.[1]]

hedgehog *n.*[1] [19C] an unattractive woman (cf. BAT n.[3]).

hedgehog *n.*[2] [mid-19C] veal. [the two meats are supposedly not dissimilar when cooked]

hedgehog *n.*[3] [20C] a derog. term for a foreigner, esp. a Black or Asian person. [rhy. sl. *hedgehog* = WOG n.[1]]

hedge-hopping *n.* [1910s+] flying an aeroplane as close as possible to ground and 'hopping' over the trees.

hedge on the dyke *n.* [19C] the female pubic hair. [*dyke* is SE; there is no ref. to lesbianism]

hedge-popping *n.* [mid-late19C] shooting small birds perched on hedges, in adults considered unsportsmanlike and the pursuit of boys only; thus *hedge-popper*, one who shoots in this manner. [SE *hedge* + POP v.[1] (1)]

hedge-priest *n.* [16C–early 18C] (Und.) a priest, or a beggar who poses as such, who works in rural areas, ministering to other beggars and the local peasantry; the implication is that such clergy were not true priests (cf. BARNYARD PREACHER). [HEDGE adj. + SE *priest*]

hedger *n.* [late 19C] one who 'hedges' or secures their bets.

hedge-tavern *n.* [late 17C–18C] a low tavern, often the home of criminals, card-sharps and similar underworld figures. [HEDGE adj. + SE *tavern*]

hedge-whore *n.* a prostitute who plies her trade in the open air (cf. STAR-GAZER). [HEDGE adj. + SE *whore*]

he'd worry the dog *phr.* [late 19C] said of a person whose appearance or behaviour would terrify even a dedicated guard-dog.

heeb see HEBE.

heebie-jeebies/heebs/heebies, the *n.* [1920s+] (orig. US) **1** unpleasant fantasies, nameless terrors, anything the mind can conjure up to produce nerves and fear (cf. JEEBIES). **2** the

physical and mental symptoms that accompany heroin withdrawal. **3** a hangover. [? ety. unknown, although the *heebie-jeebie*, a dance popular *c*.1926, was alleged to have taken its name f. the incantations of an Indian witch-doctor before making a human sacrifice. More likely it is a nonce coinage by the US cartoonist Billy Derbeck and first noted in his strip *Barney Google* in the *New York American* on 26 October 1923]

heefus *n.* [1950s–60s] (US) sexual intercourse. [ety. unknown; ? SE *heave*]

hee-haw *n.* [20C] (US) **1** a donkey. **2** loud, offensive laughter esp. if scornful. [the traditional transliteration of the donkey's bray]

hee-haw shoes *n.* [1960s] large, clod-hopping shoes, the sort a donkey-minding rustic would choose.

heel *n.* [1910s+] (orig. US) **1** a petty criminal (cf. HEEL-THIEF). **2** a dishonest, untrustworthy person, esp. one who treats women badly. [? *down-at-heel* or the image on an unwanted person, continually at one's heels]

heel *v.*[1] **1** [mid-18C+] to arm oneself with a firearm. **2** [1900s–40s] (US) to lend money. [cock-fighting jargon *heel*, to arm a game-cock with a gaff or spur]

heel *v.*[2] **1** [mid-19C+] (US) to run away, to escape, to walk quickly; thus *heel it*. **2** [1910s–30s] (US Und.) to walk stealthily, to stalk, to steal sneakily. [SE *heel*]

heel *v.*[3] **1** [late 19C+] (US) to court, to flatter for personal advantage. **2** [1930s+] (US) to cheat a hotel or similar establishment by sneaking in another person without registering. [HEEL n.]

heel-and-toe *v.* [late 19C+] (US) to run or walk quickly; thus *take it on the heel-and-toe*, to escape.

heel-ball *n.* [1990s] (Irish) busy, energetic. [SE *heel-ball*, a shoemaker's tool]

heel-beater *n.* [1920s] (US) a dancer (cf. HOOFER).

heeled *adj.*[1] [mid-19C+] (orig. US) armed. [SE *heeled*, used of a fighting cock, which had sharpened spurs tied to its heels]

heeled *adj.*[2] (orig. US) **1** [late 19C+] prepared, well provided for, wealthy, rich. **2** [1960s+] in possession of drugs. [abbr. SE *well-heeled*]

heeler *n.* **1** [mid-19C–1910s] (US Und.) a criminal's unskilled accomplice, a hired thug. **2** [late 19C–1950s] (US) a hanger-on who performs tasks for a politician or political party in the hope of personal aggrandizement. **3** [1930s+] (US Und.) a sneak thief (cf. HEEL n.). **4** [late 19C–1920s] a lurch to one side. [SE *heel*, of a dog, to follow at the heels]

heel-licker *n.* [20C] (US) a toady, a sycophant (cf. ARSE-LICKER).

heel on *v.* [1910s+] (US Black) to leave, to depart.

heeltap *n.* [late 18C–mid 20C] the liquor left at the bottom of a glass; thus [19C+] *no heeltaps!*, [mid-18C–mid-19C] *take off your heeltap!* drain your glasses. [SE *heel-tap*, a layer of leather used in making a shoe heel]

heel-thief *n.* [1930s–40s] (US) a petty criminal (cf. HEEL n.).

heft *n.* [19C] the bulk, the mass, the main part. [SE *heft*, weight, heaviness, ponderousness]

he goes for my money *phr.* [mid-16C–mid-17C] he is the ideal person, he is the one for me.

heifer *n.* **1** [early 19C+] a woman, a girl. **2** [late 19C+] (US Black) an unattractive, obese woman (cf. COW n.[1]; MULLINGAR HEIFER). **3** (US Black) an immoral woman, esp. one who chooses to defy the current moral codes. **4** [1970s+] (US campus) any woman, but esp. a fat one.

heifer-dust *n.* **1** [1920s–30s] (US) Bull Durham brand tobacco. **2** [1920s+] (US) nonsense, rubbish (cf. BULLSHIT n.; HEIFER DUST ACT). **3** [1920s+] (Aus.) a girl or woman (cf. HEIFER). [SE *heifer* + *dust*, rubbish, garbage]

heifer-dust act n. [20C] (US) an arrest and interrogation by the police. [HEIFER DUST n. (2) + SE *act*]

heifer-paddock n. [late 19C] (Aus.) a girls' school. [HEIFER + SE *paddock*]

heigh-ho n. [mid-19C] (Und.) stolen yarn. [the SE excl. *heigh-ho* was used to indicate to a potential buyer that such yarn was on offer]

heighty-toity see HIGHTY-TIGHTY.

Heinie n.[1] [20C] a derog. term for a German. [Ger. proper name, *Heinz*, but note HEINIE n.[3]]

heinie n.[2] [20C] (US) a very short haircut. [? the popularity of crewcut hair among Germans]

heinie n.[3] [1910s+] (US) the buttocks. [euph. dimin. of SE *hind end* or *hinder parts*]

Heinie n.[4] [1970s+] (US) a bottle or can of *Heine*ken lager beer. [abbr.]

heinie highway n. [20C] (US) the anus (cf. HERSHEY HIGHWAY). [HEINIE n.[3]]

heinous adj. [1970s+] (US campus) terrible. [intensified use of SE]

Heinz n. 1 [1920s+] (orig. US) a mongrel. 2 [1940s+] (bingo) the number 57. 3 (gambling) any combination bet. [the *57 varieties* offered by H.J. Heinz]

heist n. [1920s+] (US Und.) a robbery. [HEIST v.]

heist/hist v. [1920s+] (US Und.) to steal, to hold up; thus *heist artist/guy/man*, a thief or armed robber. [var. on HOIST v.[1]]

heister n. [1920s+] a robber, a hold-up man. [HEIST v.]

hel-bat n. [mid-19C] a table. [backsl.]

held at the long saw phr. [mid–late 18C] kept in suspense.

helen n. [1970s+] (drugs) heroin. [the initial letter]

Helen!/Helena!/Helen Blazes!/Helen Maria!/Helena Montana! excl. [20C] (US) euph. for HELL! and used in various mild oaths.

helium-brain/-head n. [1930s+] (US campus) a silly person (cf. AIRHEAD; BAKEBRAIN). [SE *helium* + sfx. *-brain/-HEAD* (1)]

hell n.[1] [18C] the vagina (cf. HEAVEN). [misogyny + phr. PUT THE DEVIL INTO HELL]

hell n.[2] [mid-19C+] a casino, a gambling house. [the puritan terror of such places]

hell n.[3] [1920s+] (US Black) an expert, an admirable or impressive person; thus (on *bad* = *good* model) a general term of approval.

hell v. 1 [mid-17C] to place in hell or in a situation similar to hell, to cause one to have their hell. 2 [mid-17C] to make into a hell. 3 [mid-17C] to scold, to reprimand, to 'give one hell'. 4 [late 19C+] to hurry, to go 'hell for leather', to 'fly' around (esp. in some activity disapproved of by the speaker).

hell, the phr. [19C+] a general intensifier to express anger, annoyance, impatience, also (ironically) disbelief or contempt.

hell! excl. [mid-19C+] a general expletive.

hella adv. [1980s+] (US campus) very, extremely, really (cf. HECKA). [HELL n.[3]]

hellacious adj. [1920s+] (US) wonderful, amazing, extraordinary. [HELL n.[3] + BODACIOUS]

hell-all/hell-in-all n. [1960s+] (US) absolutely none, nothing whatsoever. [var. on DAMN ALL]

hella mile phr. [late 19C–1920s] (US) terrible, hellish (cf. HELL ON WHEELS).

hell and gone phr. [1910s+] (US) far away, godforsaken.

hell and half Georgia n. [20C] (US) an extremely large area; the second half of the phr. varies according to the speaker's locality, e.g. *hell and part of Groton*, *hell and half of New York state*.

hell and scissors n. [20C] (W.I./Guyn.) any form of dramatic, exciting, threatening or frightening situation, typically an argument.

hell and spots n. [20C] utter destruction. [var. on HELL AND TOMMY]

hell/devil and tommy n. [mid-19C+] utter destruction, esp. as *play hell and tommy*, to cause absolute chaos; also used as an oath *hell and tommy!* [? proper names Henry VIII ('Hal') (r.1509–47) and Thomas Cromwell ('Tommy') (*c*.1485–1540), the chief engineers of the English Reformation, or SE *hell and torment*]

hell and tommy! excl. [mid-19C+] a general excl. [ext. of HELL!]

hell around v. [late 19C+] (US) to cause trouble or a disturbance. [PLAY HELL]

hell beating tanbark phr. [19C+] (US) very fast, usu. as *quicker than hell beating tanbark*.

hell-bender n. [19C+] (US) a formidable, outrageous thing or individual. [fig. use of US dial. *hellbender*, the American salamander or alligator]

hell-bending adj. 1 [late 19C+] (US) hellish, arduous. 2 [1910s+] (Can.) hellfire evangelistic preaching.

hellbent adj. [mid-19C+] (orig. US) determined, stubbornly. [lit. 'determined on hell']

hellbent for breakfast see HELL FOR BREAKFAST.

hellbent for election/Sunday phr. [20C] (US) hurriedly, recklessly (cf. HELL FOR BREAKFAST; HELL FOR LEATHER). [HELLBENT + fig. uses of *election/Sunday*; the enthusiasm of politicians for the fruits of power/workers for their day of rest]

hell-broth n. [mid–late 19C] bad liquor. [SE *hell-broth*, 'a decoction of infernal character or prepared for an infernal purpose' (*OED*)]

hell buster n. [1910s–30s] (orig. US) an amazing, riotous or violent thing or person.

hell-cart n. [mid–late 17C] a hackney carriage. [? its lack of comfort]

hell-cat n. [late 17C–18C] used of a man, 'a very Lewd Rake-helly Fellow' (B.E.). [used of a woman, and dating to early 17C, is SE]

hell-dodger n. [20C] (US) a sanctimonious Christian.

hell-driver n. 1 [late 17C+] a coachman who drives recklessly. 2 [20C] a similarly inclined car-driver.

hell dust n. [1960s+] (drugs) heroin. [SE *hell* + DUST n.[6]]

heller n. 1 [late 19C+] one who lives an unfettered, undisciplined and adventuresome life. 2 [late 19C+] (US) a very difficult, formidable or exciting thing or person. 3 [1970s+] (US campus) an exciting, dramatic party. [HELL OF A person, HELL OF A good time]

hell-fire adv. [mid–late 18C] a general intensifier, extremely, very much.

hell-fired adj. [19C+] (orig. US) a general intensifier (cf. ALL-FIRE).

hell for adv. (US) 1 [mid-19C+] intent on, insistent upon. 2 [1950s+] as a general intensifier.

hell/hellbent for breakfast phr. [20C] rushed, hurriedly, at top speed. [var. on HELLBENT FOR ELECTION]

hell for leather phr. [19C+] very fast, at top speed, rip-roaring (cf. HELL FOR BREAKFAST). [the leather refers to the phrase's origin in riding and refers to the harness]

he'll fuck/shag/screw anything on two legs phr. [late 19C+] a phr. indicating male sexual omnivorous and lack of discrimination; the male equivalent of ANYTHING IN TROUSERS. [FUCK v.[1]; SHAG v.[1]; SCREW v.[1]]

hellified adj. [1980s+] (US Black) extreme, excessive.

hellifying adj. [1970s] (US) wonderful or very bad (cf. HELLACIOUS).

hell-in n. [1960s+] (S.Afr.) a fury, a temper.

hell-in adj. [1960s+] (S.Afr.) furious, angry.

hell in, the adv. [1960s+] (S.Afr.) furiously, angrily, e.g. *he's going the hell in on everyone today*.

hell-in-all *see* HELL-ALL.

hellish *adj.* [mid-18C+] a general intensifier, e.g. *hellish bad*, *hellish cold*.

hellishing/hellishun *adj.* [1930s+] (usu. Aus./N.Z.) a general intensifier.

hell is popping *phr.* [late 19C+] (US) all hell is breaking out.

hellite *n.* [mid-19C] a professional gambler. [HELL n.²]

hellity-split *see* LICKETY-SPLIT.

hell-master *n.* [1980s+] (US campus) an over-bearing, bullying person. [i.e. a fig. 'devil']

hell mend him! *excl.* [late 19C+] (Can.) a mild, if heart-felt curse.

hell night *n.* [1940s+] (US campus) the night of initiation into a fraternity or sorority (cf. HELL WEEK). [the initiatory rituals, known as hazing, that accompany such an event]

hello! *excl.¹* [20C] (US) euph. for HELL!

hello!/hello Mary! *excl.²* [1950s–60s] a cry of surprise to no one in particular when a beautiful woman is seen.

hello! *excl.³* **1** [1980s+] (US campus) a general excl. of surprise and disbelief, I don't believe this! what's happening? this is bizarre! **2** [1990s] (US teen) dismissive excl., implying that the individual at whom it is aimed should stop talking foolishly, obscurely or saying things in which they patently do not believe.

hello beautiful/handsome *phr.* [1930s+] (orig. US) greetings exchanged between boys and girls.

hell of a ... *phr.* **1** [late 17C+] hellish, awful; also as *one hell of a ...* . **2** [mid-19C+] (orig. US) extraordinary, surprising (as often pos. as neg.) (cf. HELLUVA; STINK OF A ...).

hell of a note *n.* [late 19C+] (US) very bad news.

hello-girl *n.* [late 19C+] (US) a female telephone operator. [she answers all calls with *Hello*]

hello Mary! *see* HELLO! excl.².

hell on *adj.* **1** [mid-19C–1960s] (US) very fond of. **2** [1940s+] (US) very hard on, opposed to.

hell on stilts *phr.* [19C+] (US) very fast (cf. HELL BEATING TANBARK).

hello, nurse! *excl.* [1990s] (US teen) a comment made on seeing an attractive member of the opposite sex.

hell on wheels *phr.* [mid-19C+] (orig. US) anyone or anything regarded as the equivalent of hell, usu. referring to character, speed or enthusiasm.

hellpig *n.* [1980s+] (US campus) an unattractive, fat woman. [SE *hell* + PIG n.¹]

hell-raking *adj.* [17C+] dramatically violent, chaotic; thus *hell-raker*, a violent, forceful or exuberant person or thing. [backform. of SE *rakehell*]

hell-roaring *adj.* [late 19C+] (US) wild, out of control.

hell-robber *n.* [1930s+] (US) a Christian evangelist.

hell's a-popping/hellzapoppin' *phr.* [late 19C+] (orig. US) a general phr. of intensification, implying aggression, chaos, forcefulness.

hell's bells *n.¹* [mid–late 19C] (US) 'the daylights', 'the stuffing', as in *I'll knock hell's bells out of you!*

hell's bells *n.²* [1980s] (US campus) somewhere considered very far away (cf. BEHIND GOD'S BACK).

hell's bells *adv.* [1930s+] (US) headlong, at great speed.

hell's bells!/fire!/teeth! *excl.* [1920s+] a general mild. excl., usu. implying irritation or disappointment.

hell's bottom/hollow/point *n.* [20C] (US) any disreputable or out-of-the-way area (cf. HELL'S HALF ACRE).

he'll screw anything on two legs *see* HE'LL FUCK ANYTHING ON TWO LEGS.

hell's delight *phr.* [early 19C+] pandemonium, chaos.

hell's fire! *see* HELL'S BELLS!

he'll shag anything on two legs *see* HE'LL FUCK ANYTHING ON TWO LEGS.

hell's half acre *n.* [19C+] (orig. US) *n.* any disreputable area or place, esp. the slum area of a town or a low-class dance-hall or bar; thus *all around/over hell's half-acre*, all over the place, everywhere (cf. HELL'S BOTTOM).

hell's hollow *see* HELL'S BOTTOM.

hell's kitchen *n.* [mid-19C+] (US) a generic term for any urban slum area, esp. one that serves also as a lower class entertainment centre, or any dangerous or seedy place. [proper name *Hell's Kitchen*, the Irish-Black slum area that covered part of the West Side of New York City from *c.*1850 to 1910, bounded by the Hudson River and 8th Avenue, it ran from 39th Street to 59th Street. The name may have applied initially only to a single tenement or it may have been picked up from the name of a saloon in the red-light area of Corlear's Hook (cf. HOOKER n.²). The toughest part of Hell's Kitchen was known, at least to the writer O. Henry, as the *stovepipe*, a narrow enclave running along 11th and 12th Avenues]

hell's mint of *phr.* [late 19C–1910s] (US) a large quantity.

hell's own *adj.* [late 19C+] (orig. US) used as a general intensifier.

hell's point *see* HELL'S BOTTOM.

hell's teeth! *see* HELL'S BELLS!

hell-stick *n.* [20C] (US) a sulphur match.

hell to pay *phr.* [19C+] serious consequences will follow.

hell to pay and no pitch hot *phr.* [18C+] a situation in which one faces unspecified but substantial problems in the future, caused by an action in the present (cf. DEVIL TO PAY AND NO PITCH HOT). [the myth of the 'Faustian bargain']

hell to pay *see* THERE'LL BE HELL TO PAY.

hell-to-split/-toot *adv.* [19C+] (US) at breakneck speed.

helluva *adj.* [1950s+] (orig. S.Afr.) a general intensifier. [mispron. of HELL OF A]

hell week *n.* [1930s+] (US campus) the period of initiation for pledges to a college fraternity (cf. HELL NIGHT).

hell west and crooked/winding *phr.* [19C+] (orig. US) in all directions, disarray, confusion (cf. HIGH, WEST AND CROOKED).

hell with, the *phr.* [1930s+] (orig. US) a dismissive phr. used of people, events, objects.

hell with it!, the *excl.* [20C] a mild oath of annoyance or dismissal.

hell with the lid off *phr.* [late 19C+] (US) something extremely difficult or hard to bear.

hellzapoppin' *see* HELL'S A-POPPIN'.

helmet *n.* **1** [1950s+] the glans penis (cf. GERMAN HELMET). **2** [1990s] (US Black teen) a condom.

helo *n.* [1960s+] a *heli*copter. [abbr.]

helpa *n.* [mid-19C] an apple. [backsl.]

helpers *n.* [1960s] (US drugs) amphetamine pills (cf. A n.²). [? the Rolling Stones' song 'Mother's Little Helper' (1966)]

helpless *adj.* [mid-19C+] very drunk.

helter-skelter *n.* **1** [1940s] an air-raid shelter. **2** [1950s+] a bus shelter. [rhy. sl.]

he-male *n.* [late 19C] a manly man.

he-man *n.* (drugs) fentanyl (cf. APACHE n.²). [its confidence-boosting effects]

hem-haw *v.* [1930s+] (US) to mutter, to mumble, to be indecisive. [SE *hem* + *haw*, representations of a speaker's clearing his throat]

hemlock steak *n.* [20C] (US) deer that has been illegally shot by poachers (cf. CAMP MEAT). [SAmE *hemlock*, the North American tree (*Abies canadensis*), which is seen as resembling the common hemlock plant]

hemo *see* HAEMORRHOID.

hemp *n.* [late 19C+] (drugs) marijuana.

hemp *v.* [mid-19C] (US) to hang, to choke to death.

hemp cravat *n.* [late 18C–mid-19C] a hangman's noose (cf. HEMPEN COLLAR; HEMPEN CRAVAT; HEMPEN HABEAS; HEMPEN QUINSY;

HEMPEN TIPPET; HEMPEN WIDOW; HEMP FEVER; HEMP PARTY; WEAR A HEMPEN NECKTIE).

hempen collar *n.* [18C] a hangman's noose (cf. HEMP CRAVAT).

hempen cravat/garter/necktie *n.* [late 17C–18C] the hangman's noose (cf. DANCE ON NOTHING phr.[2]; HEMP COLLAR).

hempen habeas *n.* [late 17C–18C] a hangman's noose (cf. HEMP CRAVAT; WOODEN HABEAS). [SE *hempen* + pun on *habeas corpus*, lit. 'thou shalt have the body'; a writ whereby an accused and imprisoned person must be brought before the court and the reason for his imprisonment justified]

hempen necktie *see* HEMPEN CRAVAT.

hempen quinsy *n.* [late 17C–18C] death by hanging (cf. HEMP CRAVAT). [SE *hempen* + *quinsy*, a form of tonsillitis]

hempen tippet *n.* [late 16C–early 17C] a hangman's noose (cf. HEMP CRAVAT; TYBURN TIPPET).

hempen widow *n.* [late 17C–18C] a woman whose husband is hanged (cf. HEMP CRAVAT).

hemp fever *n.* [late 18C–1930s] execution by hanging (cf. HEMP v.; HEMP CRAVAT).

hemp party/stretching *n.* [19C+] (US) a hanging, esp. a lynching (cf. HEMP CRAVAT; HEMP FEVER; WAG HEMP IN THE WIND). [the hempen rope]

hemp's grown for you, the *phr.* [17C] a warning phr. implying that the person in question is bound to end on the gallows if they pursue their current lifestyle.

hemp stretching *see* HEMP PARTY.

hems *n.* [20C] *haemorrhoids*. [abbr.]

hen *n.* **1** [17C] a prostitute. **2** [17C] a mistress. **3** [early 17C+] a woman, usu. over 30. **4** [20C] (Scot.) a term of address to a woman. **5** [20C] (W.I./Tbgo.) a male homosexual.

hen *v.* [19C] to act cautiously. [the timidity of the fowl]

hen/hens and chickens *n.* [mid-19C] large and small pewter pots.

hen apple/berry *n.* [1930s–60s] (US) an egg (cf. HEN FRUIT).

hencackle *n.* [1930s+] (N.Z.) a trifle, anything unimportant. [mountaineering jargon *hencackle*, an easy climb]

henchman *n.* [1950s–60s] (US) a friend.

hen college *n.* [1920s–40s] (US) a women's college.

hen-fest *n.* [20C] (US) a women-only party or gathering (cf. HEN PARTY). [HEN n. (3) + SE *fest*]

hen frigate *see* HEN HOUSE.

hen/hen's fruit *n.* [mid-19C+] (US) chicken's eggs (cf. BUM-DROPS; HEN APPLE).

heng-pan-nail *n.* [20C] (W.I.) **1** unpressed clothes. **2** ready-made clothes, rather than individually tailored garments. [W.I. pron. of SE *hang upon a nail*, whether in one's house or in the shop]

hen-headed *adj.* [20C] (US) stupid, foolish, scatter-brained. [characteristics of the barnyard fowl]

hen house/frigate *n.*[1] [late 18C–19C] any house where the wife rather than the husband rules (cf. SHE HOUSE). [note naut. jargon *hen frigate*, a ship where the captain's wife travelled with her husband]

hen house *n.*[2] **1** [late 19C] a woman's hostel or lodging house. **2** [1900s–40s] (US prison) a women's prison.

hen-hussy *n.* [20C] **1** (US) a man who is seen to be over-involved in household affairs and similar 'women's concerns'. **2** (US Black) an effeminate man. [dial. *hen hussy*, a woman who looks after the poultry]

hen is on, a *phr.* [late 19C–1940s] (US) something important is to happen.

hen of the game *n.* [19C] a prostitute. [HEN n. (1) + GAME n.[1]]

hen party *n.* [late 19C+] a women-only get-together (cf. BITCH PARTY; HEN FEST). [HEN n. (3) + SE *party*]

henpeck *n.* [late 18C; 1920s+] a nagged husband. [backform. of HEN-PECKED]

henpeck *v.* [late 17C–mid-19C] of a woman or wife, to dominate her partner. [backform. of HEN-PECKED]

hen-pecked *adj.* [late 17C+] used of a man, usu. married, who is persecuted by the woman with whom he lives (cf. PUSSY-WHIPPED).

hen pen *n.* [20C] (US Und.) a woman's prison. [HEN n. (3) + PEN n.[3]]

henpicking *n.* [1980s+] (drugs) searching on hands and knees for crack cocaine. [the image of a hen pecking for food]

henry *n.*[1] [20C] (US) a Ford automobile. [Henry Ford I (1863–1947), the patriarch of the automobile assembly line]

henry *n.*[2] [1960s+] (drugs) heroin (cf. BIG HARRY; HELEN). [initial letter]

henry/Henry VIII *n.*[3] [1980s+] (drugs) an eighth of an ounce of a drug, e.g. cannabis or cocaine. [abbr. *Henry VIII*]

Henry! *excl.* [20C] (US) a mild oath, euph. for HELL!

henry halls *n.* [1950s+] the testicles. [rhy. sl. *Henry Halls* = BALLS n.[1] (1); ult. popular UK bandleader Henry Hall (1898–1989)]

henry hase *n.* [early 19C] a banknote, usu. defined as to its amount, e.g. a *£10 Henry Hase*. [the signature of the banking official]

henry melville *n.* [late 19C] the devil. [rhy. sl.; ult. the G.R. Sims ballad 'Tottie' (1887): 'What the Henry Melville/Do you think you're doing there?'; ? elision of *henry melville* = *hell*]

henry nash *n.* [20C] cash (cf. OSCAR NASH; SAUSAGE AND MASH; SMASH n.[3]). [rhy. sl.]

Henry III/the Third *n.* [1950s+] a piece of human excrement (cf. RICHARD n.[2]). [rhy. sl. *Henry the Third* = TURD]

Henry VIII *see* HENRY n.[3].

hens and chickens *see* HEN AND CHICKENS.

hen's fruit *see* HEN FRUIT.

hen-skin *n.* [late 19C–1950s] (US) a cowboy's blanket or underwear.

hen's race *n.* [20C] (Ulster) a very short distance.

hen tracks *n.* [19C] (US) illegible handwriting (cf. CHICKEN SCRATCH n.[1]).

hep *n.* [1960s+] *hepatitis*. [abbr.]

hep *adj.* [20C] aware, sophisticated, in the know; thus *hepped on*, enthusiastic about (cf. HIP adj.). [first used among jazz fans of the 1940s, but rooted in the 19C SE *hep*, shrewd, which comes in turn from *Hep!*, the exhortation of the ploughman or driver urging his horses to 'Get up!' and get lively]

hep-/hip-cat *n.* [1930s+] (US Black) **1** a jazz or swing fan. **2** an aware, sophisticated person. [HEP adj. + CAT n.[9]]

hepkitten *n.* [1970s] (US) a young woman who is a fan of swing music. [joc. dimin. of HEP-CAT]

hepped up *adj.* [1930s+] (US) excited or intoxicated by drugs or alcohol. [HEP adj.]

hepster *n.* [1930s–50s] a jazz or swing fan. [HEP-CAT n. (1)]

hep to the jive *phr.* [20C] aware, informed, sophisticated, in the know. [HEP adj. + JIVE n.[1]]

her *n.*[1] [1970s+] (drugs) cocaine (cf. HIM n.[2]). [GIRL n.[3]]

her *n.*[2] [1990s] (US) the wife (cf. HER INDOORS).

herb/herbs/herba *n.*[1] [1950s+] (US Black/W.I. Rasta/drugs) marijuana. [orig. used in Jamaica, the religious role of marijuana for Rastafarians is emphasized in the 'natural' image of *herb*, also known as the 'herb of meditation' + a poss. ref. to Ps. 104:14, 'He causeth the grass to grow for the cattle, and herb for the service of man']

herb *n.*[2] [1990s] (US Black) an unsophisticated person, one who has no knowledge of street life. [? abbr. HERBERT or he is SE *green*]

herb *v.* [1990s] (US Black) to rob. [? the victim is a HERB n.[2]]

herba *see* HERB n.[1].

herbalz *n.* [1990s] (US Black) semen. [ety. unknown]

herb and a' *phr.* [1980s+] (drugs) marijuana and alcohol.

Herbert/'erbert n. [20C] a simple person; thus *Herbert music*, music-hall jokes mixed with rock music.

herbie's bonnet/herbie's beetle's bonnet n. [1990s] the female genital area, esp. when shaved. [*Herbie*, the star of the eponymous films (1968–80) was a Volkswagen, 'Beetle'; the similarity of the car's curving bonnet]

herbs n.[1] see HERB n.[1].

herbs n.[2] [1950s+] (Aus.) **1** a car's speed, power, responsive to the accelerator. **2** enthusiasm, praise, 'wind-up'. [ety. unknown; ? fig. use SE *herbs*, which 'spice up' a dish]

herd/herd of camels n. [1930s–40s] (US Black) a pack of Camels cigarettes. [pun]

herd v. [1920s+] (US) to drive a car or other vehicle.

herder n. [20C] (US prison) a prison guard who works in the prison yard, controlling the prisoners. [SE *herd*, to drive and control animals]

herd of camels see HERD n.

here and there n. **1** [20C] a chair. **2** [1930s] (Aus.) hair. [rhy. sl.; never truncated]

here-and-thereian n. [late 18C–19C] a wanderer, a nomad. [he wanders *here and there*]

Herefordshire weed n. [mid-19C] an oak tree. [the commonness of the tree in that county]

here goes! excl. **1** [early 19C+] an excl. voiced on starting to do something, esp. if the action is potentially dangerous or risky. **2** [early 19C+] a popular toast (cf. HERE'S HOW!).

here's how! excl. [20C] popular toast when drinking (cf. HERE GOES!).

here's looking at you! excl. [20C] a toast before drinking. [immortalized (and clichéd) after Humphrey Bogart's rendition in the film *Casablanca* (1941)]

here's mud in your eye! excl. [1910s+] a toast when drinking. [orig. milit. use; thus ref. ? to the muddy trenches of WW1]

here's your hat and what's your hurry phr. [20C] (Irish) a phr. used to encourage a guest to leave.

here to stay phr. [1930s+] permanent, established.

here we go/here we go again phr. [1950s+] often stated with some resignation and implying distaste for some form of repetitious activity, speechifying etc.

here we/you are phr. [mid-19C+] this is what you want.

her highness/royal highness n. [late 19C+] used by a man as a sarcastically 'respectful' description of his wife; the implication is of laziness (cf. HIS HIGHNESS).

her indoors n. [1970s+] one's wife (cf. HER n.[2]). [coined by Leon Griffiths in the *Minder* series on Thames TV, 1979; note Jap. *uichinomono*, wife, lit. 'the one inside']

herkin the gherkin n. [20C] masturbation. [var. on JERK ONE'S GHERKIN]

herky-jerky adj. [1940s+] (US) awkward, uneven, foolish.

her ladyship/his lordship n. [late 19C+] ironic ref. to any individual; the social status is irrelevant.

Her/His Majesty's/king's/queen's bad/hard bargain phr. [late 18C+] a worthless soldier (cf. HARD BARGAIN). [his service does not justify his pay]

Her/His Majesty's carriage n. [late 19C] a prison van.

Her/His Majesty's naval police n. [late 19C] sharks. [by swimming near warm-water ports they prevent sailors from attempting to desert ship by swimming ashore]

Her/His Majesty's School for Heavy Needlework n. [1940s+] prison (cf. IRONMONGERY DEPARTMENT).

herman the one-eyed German n. [1990s] (US campus) the penis (cf. ONE-EYED TROUSER SNAKE).

hermit n. [mid-16C] (gypsy) a highwayman.

Her Mope-Eyed Ladyship n. [late 17C–early 18C] fortune, chance, 'Lady Luck'. [SE *mope-eyed*, shortsighted or blind in one eye]

herms n. [1980s] (drugs) phencyclidine (cf. ACE n.[3]). [ety. unknown]

hero/hero sandwich n.[1] [1950s+] (US) a large sandwich made of two slabs of bread cut lengthwise from the loaf and containing a variety of ingredients (cf. GRINDER n.[6]). [? the idea that one needs be a hero to eat one, or an ironic comment on the qualities (eating rather than fighting) of an 'Italian hero']

hero/heroina n.[2] [1980s+] (drugs) heroin. [conscious or unconscious ref. to Gk. *heros*, a hero, the root of the SE term]

herone n. [1980s+] (drugs) heroin. [? Sp.]

hero of the underworld n. [1980s+] (drugs) heroin (cf. HERO n.[2]).

her royal highness see HER HIGHNESS.

herp n. [1970s+] (US) genital herpes.

herped adj. [1970s+] (US) carrying the virus for herpes.

herring n.[1] [19C+] (US) a foolish, offensive or inconsequential person. [? backform. of HERRING-GUTTED adj. (2) or the commonness of the fish]

herring n.[2] [1930s] (US) $1. [FISH n.[6]]

herring and kipper n. [20C] a striptease artiste, i.e. a stripper. [rhy. sl.]

herring choker n. [late 19C+] **1** (US) a Scandinavian-born immigrant (cf. HERRING DESTROYER; HERRING SNAPPER). **2** (Can) nickname for a native or inhabitant of the Maritime Provinces. [their consumption of herrings]

herring destroyer n. [late 19C+] (US) a Scandinavian-born immigrant (cf. HERRING CHOKER).

herring-gutted adj. **1** [18C–early 19C] used of a thin person (cf. SHOTTEN HERRING). **2** [mid-19C–1940s] cowardly, 'gutless'.

herring-Jew n. [1960s] (W.I.) a derog term for a Jewish or Syrian immigrant, who founded their fortunes on peddling salt-fish.

herring pond n. [late 17C+] n. the sea. esp. the Atlantic; thus *be sent across the herring pond* or *cross the herring pond at the King's expense*, to be transported (albeit to Botany Bay, Australia, rather than America).

herring snapper n. [late 19C+] (US) a Scandinavian-born immigrant (cf. HERRING CHOKER).

hers and hims n. [Aus.) hymns. [rhy. sl.]

Hershey adj. [1970s+] (US) used in ref. to the anus and thus male homosexuality. [brand name of *Hershey Bars*, a popular US chocolate bar]

Hershey/Hershey bar highway/road n. [1970s+] (US) the anus. [HERSHEY]

Hershey in a straw n. [1990s] a self-administered suction enema. [HERSHEY]

Hershey road see HERSHEY HIGHWAY.

Hershey squirt/squirts n. **1** [1970s+] (US) diarrhoea. **2** [1980s+] (US campus) faecal stains on one's underwear due to liquid emitted when breaking wind or through a badly cleaned anus. [HERSHEY]

Hertfordshire kindness n. [late 17C–early 19C] a favour that is granted in return for one favour received, repaying one positive gesture with another; the phr. particularly refers to an exchange of congratulatory toasts. [apparently a custom among Hertfordshire people]

he-say-she-say/he-said-she-said n. [1960s–70s] (US Black) gossip, chatter, loose talk.

hesh n. [20C] a male homosexual (cf. HE-SHE; HIMMER; OMEE-POLONE; SHE-HE; SHE-MALE; SHE-MAN). [SE *he* + *she*]

he-she n. [late 19C; 1960s+] a transvestite, transsexual or homosexual person (cf. HESH).

he, she and thingamerry phr. [20C] (W.I./Bdos) everybody one can think of, a large, undifferentiated crowd (cf. HABRA, DABRA AND THE CREW).

hesher n. [1980s+] (US campus) a fan of heavy metal music. [? *heavy metal* + *thrash*]

hesh girl see HASH GIRL.

hesitation marks n. [1960s+] **1** scars on one's wrist denoting a failed or insufficiently committed suicide attempt. **2** (US gay) excessive weight, since such a weight gain can supposedly turn body-conscious gay men to thoughts of suicide.

hessian n. [20C] (US) **1** a troublesome, mischievous person, esp. a fussy woman. **2** a mischievous, ill-behaved child. [SE *Hessian*, a Hessian mercenary employed by the British during the American War of Independence (1775–83); thus a general term of derision. Note also the *hessian fly*, supposedly imported by the Hessian troops, the larvae of which devastate wheat crops]

hessle n. [20C] (drugs) heroin. [? HASSLE n.; i.e. the problems involved in buying it, the addiction etc]

het n. [1970s+] (orig. gay) a *hetero*sexual. [abbr.]

hetero n. [1930s+] (orig. gay) *hetero*sexual. [abbr.]

het up adj. [19C+] (orig. US) tense, nervous, angry. [SE *heat*, thus lit. 'heated up'; in general use 14C–16C but subseq. in dial. or sl. only]

hevethee n. [late 19C–1920s] a thief. [centre slang; created by rearranging the syllables or constituent parts of a word]

he went mad and they shot him phr. [1950s+] (Aus.) a general answer to the question, 'Where is X?' (cf. GONE FOR A RIDE ON THE PADRE'S BIKE).

hewgag n. [mid-19C+] (US) **1** a bugle or trumpet. **2** a battle cry. [SE *hewgag*, a toy musical instrument; ult. orig. unknown; ? *gewgaw*, a jew's harp']

he-whore n. [20C] a male homosexual prostitute.

he who smelt it, dealt it phr. [1960s+] a phr. used to disclaim all responsibility for having farted; often used as a rejoinder to the query WHO CUT THE CHEESE?

he wouldn't go out to a dog-tucker's picnic phr. [1980s+] (N.Z.) a phr. used to describe a dedicated recluse. [DOG-TUCKER]

he wouldn't say 'shit' even if his mouth were full of it phr. [20C] (Can.) a phr. used of an especially mealy-mouthed, hypocritical person.

he wouldn't work in an iron lung phr. [1940s+] (Aus.) said of someone who is totally lazy. [the purpose of an iron lung is to perform the patient's breathing for them]

he would skin a turd phr. [late 19C+] (Can.) said of particularly mean person (cf. SKIN A LOUSE).

hex n. [late 19C+] a curse, a spell. [HEX v.]

hex v. [mid-19C+] (orig. US) to curse, to cast a spell against. [Pennsylvania Ger./Yid. *hexe*, a witch]

hey n. [1960s+] (US) euph. for SE *hell*; thus *what the hey*, what the hell.

hey-diddle-diddle n. [1950s] **1** urination. **2** middle. **3** fiddle. [rhy. sl.; (1) *hey-diddle-diddle* = PIDDLE]

hey-nonny-no n. [late 16C–mid-18C] the vagina. [used in SE as a chorus in various songs/ballads + SE *nonny-no*, a trifle, a 'nothing']

hey Rube! excl. [late 19C+] **1** a call for help. **2** a fight, orig. between circus or carnival people and local townspeople. [SE *hey!* excl. + RUBE n.[1]. *Hey Rube!* was the traditional rallying cry of circus or carnival employees when faced with any trouble from locals]

hey-wow n. [1980s+] (US campus) someone who clings to the styles of the 1960s. [mockery of the hippie's cries of 'Hey, wow, man, can you dig that ...' etc]

H/H abbr. [1960s+] used in sex contact advertisements, *high heels*.

hi! excl. [mid-19C+] (orig. US) hello!

hiccius doccius adj. [18C] drunk. [SE *hiccius doccius*, a juggler, ult. ? real Lat. *hicce est doctus*, this or here is the learned man, or cod Lat. formula used, like the conjuror's *abracadabra* to accompany a juggling trick. Note SE *hiccup*]

hice yourself! excl. [20C] (W.I.) get up and get out! (cf. PICK UP YOURSELF!). [Scot. *hoise*, to lift up, to raise (cf. HEIST)]

hick n. **1** [late 17C+] any inhabitant of the countryside, a peasant, a farmer (cf. HAWBUCK). **2** [late 17–mid-18C] a potential victim, a gullible simpleton. **3** [1960s+] (US) a Puerto Rican. [popular corruption of the personal name *Dick*, seen as generic (cf. HARRY n.[1]; TOM n.[1])]

hick adj. [20C] (US) unsophisticated, naïve. [HICK n. (1)]

hickery-pickery n. [19C] a nickname for the plant *Hiera picra*, 'a purgative drug composed of aloes and canella bark, sometimes mixed with honey and other ingredients' (*OED*) (cf. HICRA-PICRA; HIGRY-PIGRY).

hickey n.[1] [late 19C+] (N.Z./US) any small, otherwise nameless object. [abbr. DOHICKEY]

hickey n.[2] **1** [1910s+] (US) a pimple, a boil. **2** [1940s+] (US campus) a love bite, usu. on the neck. **3** [1940s+] (US) the penis. **4** [1960s+] (US) a bruise, a bump. [ety. unknown]

hickey n.[3] [1940s+] (Aus.) any inhabitant of the countryside, a peasant, a farmer. [HICK n. (1)]

hickey adj. [late 18C+] drunk, tipsy. [SE *hiccup*]

hickey hockey n. [20C] (Aus.) a jockey. [rhy. sl.]

hickory v. [20C] (US) to whip, to thrash. [SE *hickory*, a walking-stick of hickory wood]

hickory-dock n. [20C] clock. [rhy. sl.]

hickory oil/tea n. [1900s–40s] (US) a whipping. [SE *hickory* (*stick*) + joc. use of *oil/tea*]

hickory towel n. [mid-19C+] (US) a hickory switch (cf. OAKEN TOWEL).

hicra-picra n. [mid-19C] a nickname for the *Hiera picra*, 'a purgative drug composed of aloes and canella bark, sometimes mixed with honey and other ingredients' (*OED*) (cf. HICKERY-PICKERY).

hicksam n. [late 17C+] any inhabitant of the countryside, a farmer. [ext. of HICK n. (1)]

hicksius doxius/hictius-doctius adj. [18C] drunk. [var. on HICCIUS DOCCIUS]

hickster n. [1990s] a gullible, unsophisticated person. [HICK n. (1) + sfx. -STER]

hicktown/hicksville n. [20C] (US) a small town (cf. JAY-TOWN). [HICK n. (1) + SE *town*/*ville*]

hicky adj. [mid-19C+] (US) countrified, rural, unsophisticated. [HICK n. (1)]

hid adj. [1980s+] (US campus) very ugly. [abbr. SE *hideous*]

hidden treasure n. [20C] the landlady's husband, who never appears.

hiddy adj. [1980s+] (US campus) drunk. [SE *hideously*]

hide n.[1] **1** [17C+] the human skin, thus one's life, esp. in phr. *save one's hide* etc. **2** [1930s+] (US derog.) a horse. **3** [1930s–50s] (music) drums. **4** [1950s–60s] (US) a wallet. [SE 11C–late 16C]

hide n.[2] **1** [18C] the female genitals. **2** [20C] (US) a woman, usu. considered as a sex object. **3** [20C] (US) an old crone, a hag, an ugly old woman. [SE *hide*, to secrete]

hide n.[3] [1910s+] (usu. Aus./N.Z.) impudence, effrontery, cheek (cf. HAVE MORE HIDE THAN JESSIE). [fig. use of HIDE n.[1]]

hide v.[1] [late 18C] (W.I.) to murder, dismember and bury secretly. [a practice carried out on 18C plantations to discipline rebellious slaves]

hide v.[2] [mid-19C+] to thrash, to flog. [SE *hide*/HIDE n.[1] (1), the human skin]

hide and hair see HAIR AND HIDE.

hide and seek n. [20C] cheek. [rhy. sl.; never truncated]

hide and tallow see HAIR AND HIDE.

hideaways n. [1930s–40s] (US Black) pockets. [one *hides* one's money etc]

hide-beater n. [1930s–40s] (US) a drummer. [HIDE n.[1] (3) + SE *beater*]

hi-de-hi … ho-de-ho *phr.* [1940s+] popular style of greeting and the requisite response. [orig. used by US bandleader Cab Calloway in 'The Hi-De-Ho Man' but popularized in the BBC-TV's situation comedy, *Hi De Hi!* (1970s–80s), which was set in a 1950s holiday camp]

hide one's/the baloney, to *phr.* [1920s+] (US) to have sexual intercourse (cf. HIDE THE SALAMI). [BALONEY n.²]

hides *n.* [1930s–50s] (US Black) drums. [HIDE n.¹ (3)]

hide the baloney *see* HIDE ONE'S BALONEY.

hide the salami/hot dog, to *phr.* [1980s+] (US) to have sexual intercourse; usu. phr. *play hide the salami* (cf. BURY THE BRISKET; HOT DOG n.¹).

hide the sausage, to *phr.* [1940s+] (Aus.) to have sexual intercourse (cf. BURY THE BRISKET; HIDE THE SALAMI; SINK THE SAUSAGE).

hide the weenie/wienie, to *phr.* [1910s+] (US) to have sexual intercourse (cf. BURY THE BRISKET; HIDE THE SALAMI).

hide-up *n.* [1920s+] (Aus.) a hide-out.

hide won't hold hay/shavings/shucks *phr.* [20C] (US) a phr. used as a threat, usu. as *beat him so his hide … .*

hidey!/hidey herb!/i.d. herb! *excl.* [1920s+] (Aus.) a general greeting, how are you? how do you do? [HI! + HOWDY]

hidey-hole *n.* [19C+] (US) a retreat or refuge, a small hiding place.

hi-diddle-diddle *n.* [1950s] **1** the middle. **2** urination. **3** a fiddle. [rhy. sl.; (2) *hi-diddle-diddle* = PIDDLE]

hi-diddle-diddle *v.* [20C] (Aus.) to piddle, to urinate. [rhy. sl.]

hiding *n.* [early 19C+] a thrashing; thus fig. a severe sporting defeat. [HIDE v.²]

hiez-haad *adj.* [20C] (W.I. Rasta) thick-skulled, stubborn, unwilling or unable to hear. [pron. of *ears-hard*]

higgledy-piggledy *adv.* [late 17C–late 19C] thrown together, out of order, jumbled up. [the way in which pigs huddle together in the stye. Johnson saw *higgledy* as based in *higgle*, a confused mass, but *OED* prefers the development via *pig*: *pigly*, *higly-pigly*]

high *n.* **1** [1940s+] (drugs) the euphoric, pleasurable state induced by taking drugs. **2** [1960s+] (US) something that induces an intoxicated state. **3** [1970s+] a general feeling of well-being, esp. in phr. *on a high*, feeling very happy and positive.

high *adj.*¹ **1** [17C+] intoxicated with drink or poss. religious/spiritual enthusiasm. **2** [1930s+] intoxicated with drugs. **3** [1970s+] very enthusiastic about or taken with something.

high *adj.*² [mid-19C–1940s] (US) impressive, attractive, splendid; thus *how's that for a high?* what do you think of that?

high *adj.*³ [late 19C] often of a prostitute, suffering from venereal disease. [SE *high*, of meat, slightly tainted but still desirable]

high *adj.*⁴ [1950s] (drugs) pure. [such a drug has a *high percentage* of the stated drug, rather than the cut]

high *adj.*⁵ [1950s] (W.I.) fashionable, stylish.

high and dry *phr.* [mid-19C] belonging to the Church of England, Anglican (cf. BROAD AND SHALLOW; LOW AND SLOW). [abbr. *High Church*]

high and goodbye *n.* [1950s] (US Black) an unreliable person. [? HI + SE *goodbye*]

high as a cat's back *phr.* [mid-19C+] (US) drunk (cf. HIGH adj.¹). [pun on SE *high*/HIGH adj.¹]

high as a fiddler's fist *phr.* [1950s–60s] (US) drunk. [HIGH adj.¹]

high as/higher than a Georgia pine *phr.* [1930s–40s] (US Black) very drunk. [pun on SE *high*/HIGH adj.¹]

high as a kite *phr.* [1930s+] **1** very drunk. **2** intoxicated by a drug. [play on SE + rhy. sl. *high as a kite* = TIGHT]

high as Lindbergh *phr.* [1930s–40s] (US) drunk. [pun on SE *high*/HIGH adj.¹; Charles *Lindbergh* (1902–74), the first person to fly the Atlantic solo]

high as nine *phr.* [mid-19C–1940s] (US) absolutely splendid. [ety. unknown; trad. image of *nine* as a lucky number]

high as ninety *phr.* [mid-19C] (US) drunk. [HIGH adj.¹; the use of *ninety* may be ext. of trad. image of *nine* as a lucky number]

high ass *adj.* [1930s+] (US) haughty. [SE *high* + ASS]

high as the hair on a cat's back *phr.* [20C] (US) very expensive.

highball/highboy *n.* [late 19C–1940s] (US) whisky and soda. [? the tall or *high* glass in which it is served]

highball *v.*¹ [1910s+] (US) **1** to leave at high speed. **2** to speed things up (cf. BALL THE JACK).

highball *v.*² [1920s–30s] (US Black) to make a gesture with one's hand. [railway use *highball*, to give a signal to proceed]

highballer *n.* [1910s+] (US) one who moves fast, works hard. [HIGHBALL v.¹]

highbeams *n.* [1980s+] (drugs) the wide eyes of a person on crack cocaine. [SE *highbeams*, automobile headlights when they are not dipped]

high-bellied/high in the belly *adj.* [mid–late 19C] in the last stages of pregnancy.

high bicycle *n.* [1930s] (US) a famous or self-important person.

highbinder *n.* (US) **1** [early 19C+] (Und.) a prison inmate. **2** [early/mid-19C] a rowdy person, a vandal. **3** [19C] a gangster, a thug. **4** [late 19C] a member of a secret society supposedly existing among the Chinese in the US for the purpose of blackmailing, extortion and murder. **5** [late 19C–1950s] a criminal, a swindler, a fraudulent politician. [SE *high*, haughty, pretentious, arrogant + BENDER n.¹ (1), a hard drinker or drinking spree. Note, however, *high-binder*, an early 19C New York City gang, composed originally of butchers' boys and simultaneously known as the *Hide-binders*; ult. f. the similarly named mid-19C Chinese secret society, supposedly terrorizing fellow-Chinese throughout the US]

high blood *n.* [20C] (US Black) *high blood* pressure. [abbr.]

high blower *n.* [late 18C–early 19C] a broken-down horse (cf. PIPER n.¹; ROARER n.²). [its heavy breathing]

high boy *n.* [18C] a High Churchman, and thus usu. a supporter of Jacobitism (cf. HIGH AND DRY).

highboy *see* HIGHBALL n.

highbrow *n.* [late 19C+] (orig. US) a clever person, an intellectual, depending on context there is often a nuance of jealous attack. [a large forehead supposedly indicates great intelligence]

high brown *n.* [1900s–60s] (US) a mulatto woman or girl (cf. HIGH YELLOW).

high collar and short shirt *n.* [late 19C] an imitation dandy.

high/tall cotton *n.* [1930s+] (orig. US Black) the good life, the materially successful life (cf. LOW COTTON; SHIT IN HIGH COTTON).

high-daddy *adj.* [19C+] (US) slick, deceptive, excellent, pleasing. [SE *high* + DADDY n. (4)]

high dive *v.* [1930s+] (US) to pickpocket. [SE *high* + DIVE v.¹]

high diver *n.*¹ [1930s+] one who performs cunnilingus. [DIVE v.²]

high diver *n.*² [1930s+] (US) a pickpocket. [HIGH DIVE v.]

high eating *n.* [late 18C–19C] 'eating skylarks in a garret' (Grose, 1796). [? no more than Grose's punning joke]

high-end *adj.* [1970s+] (US) expensive or first-class.

higher than a cat's back *phr.* [mid-19C–1940s] (US) very tall, very high.

higher than a Georgia pine *see* HIGH AS A GEORGIA PINE.

higher than Gilderoy's kite *phr.* [19C+] (US) extremely high. [*phr. to be hung higher than Gilderoy's kite*, to be punished more savagely than one's fellow-criminals. The 17C Scot. robber *Gilderoy* of whom a ballad notes: 'Of Gilderoy sae fraid they ware/They bound him mickle strong,/Tull Edenburrow they led him thair,/And on a gallows hong;/They hong him high abone the rest, ...' so high that he resembled 'a kite in the air']

highfalutin *adj.* [mid-19C+] (orig. US) snobbish, pompous. [SE *high* + unknown *falutin*; ? f. *floating, flighting* or *flown*; Hotten suggests Du. *verlooten*, to go and cast lots; other poss. etys. include Yid. *hifelufelem*, extravagant, boastful talk; Cohen (1989) suggests US milit. jargon *high saluting*, saluting in accordance with military training (crisply, with a sharp snap of the wrist) rather than the somewhat lackadaisical salute of everyday milit. practice]

high five *v.* **1** [1970s+] to greet someone by raising the arm and ritualistically slapping each other's palm (cf. SLAP FIVE). **2** [1990s] to slap hands at waist height (cf. LOW FIVE). [orig. used in sports as a greeting or sign of congratulations]

high-flier *see* HIGH-FLYER.

high fly *n.* [19C] showing off, acting in a superior, arrogant manner.

high-flyer/-flier *n.*[1] **1** [late 17C] a daring adventurer. **2** [late 17C–19C; US 20C] a pretentious or fashionable strumpet, a promiscuous woman. **3** [late 17C–19C] a 'swell' beggar, who poses as a fashionable gentleman. **4** [late 17C–19C] a begging-letter writer. **5** [18C] a patron of the gallery at a theatre. **6** [18C] a pretentious or exaggerated statement. **7** [18C–19C] a piece of hurried revision. **8** [mid-19C] a genteel beggar or swindler (cf. ON THE HIGH FLY). **9** [late 19C–1900s] a gentleman who has fallen on hard times. **10** [20C] (US) an important person or one who poses as such. **11** [1970s+] (orig. US Black) one who lives well, one who enjoys material or professional success.

high-flyer/-flier *n.*[2] [late 17C–early 18C] a High Churchman, a Tory.

high flying *n.* [20C] (US) immorality, hedonism, extravagance.

high-go *n.* [mid-19C] a frolic, a spree. [SE *high* + GO n.[3]]

high-grade *adj.* [late 19C+] (US) first-rate, excellent, superior.

high guy *n.* [late 19C+] (US) an important person. [SE *high* + GUY n.[2]]

high hat *n.*[1] [late 19C–1930s] **1** (US drugs) a large opium pill, costing $1 (cf. PIN-HEAD n.[1]). **2** a glass of whisky and soda (cf. HIGHBALL n.). [? its supposed resemblance]

high hat/hatter *n.*[2] [1920s+] (orig. US) **1** a member of the social élite (cf. FANCY PANTS). **2** an arrogant, superior person, a snob. [the *high hat* or top hat they were presumed to wear]

high hat *v.* [1920s+] (orig. US) to act in a superior manner towards others, to snub; thus *give/put on the high hat*, to put on airs. [HIGH HAT n.[2]]

high-hatted *see* HIGH-HATTY.

high hatter *see* HIGH HAT n.[2].

high-hatty/-hatted *adj.* [1920s+] (orig. US) snobbish, stuck up. [HIGH HAT n.[2]]

high-headed/-heeled *adj.* [19C+] (US) arrogant, haughty, self-important. [orig. used of horses, referring to the way a horse carries its head high]

high-heeled time *n.* [19C+] (US) an exciting or enjoyable time.

high-heeler *n.* [1920s] (US Und.) a female beggar. [? SE *high* + HEELER n.]

high in the belly *see* HIGH-BELLIED.

high in the instep *phr.* [mid-16C–late 18C] over-proud, arrogant.

high in tooth *phr.* [late 19C] arrogant, boastful. [? the 'long

teeth' of the old, whose gums have shrunken and whose tones may tend to the superior]

high jinks *n.* [late 18C–19C] a gambler who drinks with his victim in order to render the latter more malleable. [SE *high jinks*, any form of game, usually involving some form of forfeit, that is played by drinkers]

high jive *v.* [1930s+] (US) to tease. [ext. of JIVE v.[1]]

high jump *n.* [1920s+] serious problems (cf. IN FOR THE HIGH JUMPS). [horse-racing imagery]

high-kicker *n.* [19C+] (US) a dissolute person. [image of a troublesome horse that kicks out]

high-kilted *adj.* [19C] (Scot.) indecorous. [wearing the kilt or petticoat high or tucked up]

highland fling *n.* **1** [20C] (Aus.) string. **2** [1960s+] in cards, the king. [rhy. sl.]

highland fling *v.* [1950s] to sing; thus *highland flinger*, a singer. [rhy. sl.]

highlands *n.* [20C] (US) the prosperous parts of a town, where the wealthy élite live. [the way in which the wealthy gravitated to the high ground in an era when the lowlands, usu. near the river, had a higher incidence of disease]

high law *n.* [16C] (Und.) highway robbery (cf. CHEATING LAW). [SE *highway*]

high lawyer *n.* [16C] a highwayman (cf. MARTIN; OAK n.[1]; SCRIPPER). [HIGH LAW]

high living *n.* [late 18C–19C] esp. of a thief, living in a garret or cockloft, i.e. a very small room immediately above the garret. [pun]

high lonesome *n.* [19C+] (US) a solo drinking spree (cf. HIT THE HIGH LONESOME).

high-lows *n.* [mid-19C] laced boots that reach the ankles. [such footwear stands between low shoes and high boots]

highmadandy *n.* [20C] (Ulster) someone who has more money than brains. [SE *high* + *dandy*]

high maggie *see* HIGH NELLIE.

high maintenance *adj.* [1990s] (US) emotionally demanding. [pop. by the film *When Harry Met Sally* (1989)]

high men *n.* [late 16C–late 18C] crooked dice that will always produce a high number.

high mucky-muck / -muckety-muck / -muckty-muck / -micky-doodle / -monkey-monk *n.* [19C+] (US) a superior or important person, whether in fact or through pretension (cf. CHIEF MUCK OF THE CRIB). [Chinook jargon *hiu*, plenty + *muckamuck*, food]

high nellie/maggie *n.* [20C] (Irish) an old-fashioned ladies' bicycle.

high noon *n.* [1950s] a spoon. [rhy. sl.; ult. the film *High Noon* (1952)]

high nose *n.* [20C] (US) arrogance, snobbery. [the subject's sticking their nose in the air]

high-nosed *adj.* [mid-19C–1920s] arrogant, supercilious. [HIGH NOSE]

high octane *n.* [1990s] (US) very strong alcohol or caffeinated coffee, as opposed to de-caffeinated coffee, *low octane*.

high old time *see* HIGH TIME.

high on *adj.* [1930s+] (orig. US) enthusiastic about.

high on oneself *phr.* [1930s+] (US) conceited, arrogant, snobbish.

high on the hog *phr.* [20C] (orig. US) living a comfortable, secure and well-off life (cf. CHOPPING HIGH; LIFE OF RILEY). [that area of the animal from which come the choicest cuts of pork and its by-products]

high pad *n.* **1** [mid-16C–17C] the highway (cf. HIGH-TOBY; MAIN TOBY). **2** [late 17C–19C] a highwayman (cf. PADDER). [SE *high* + PAD n.[1]]

high pike *n.* [mid-19C] an exorbitantly high price. [SE *pike*, the toll paid at a turnpike]

highpockets *n.* [1910s+] (orig. US) a tall man.
high-powered *adj.* [1940s–50s] (US Black) stylish.
high pressure *n.* [1920s] (US) a boss, a powerful man.
high priest of Paphos *n.* [19C] a womanizer, a promiscuous man. [*Paphos*, the city in southwestern Cyprus, where it is claimed that Aphrodite, the Greek goddess of love, was born]
high prime *v.* [19C–1920s] (US Black) to show off (cf. HIGH SIGN v.).
high-rented *adj.*[1] [mid-19C] hot.
high-rented *adj.*[2] [mid-19C] of a villain, extremely well known to the police. [pun on SE *hot*/HOT adj.[2] (2)]
high-rider *n.* [1980s+] (US) a young, esp. working-class, man whose car is modified so that its rear is higher than the front (cf. LOWRIDER n.[2]).
high roll *v.* [1980s+] (US) to act boldly or aggressively. [HIGH ROLLER]
high roller *n.* **1** [late 19C+] one who spends extravagantly, one who gambles for high stakes. **2** [1930s] (US Black) a type of hat worn by gamblers. **3** [1970s] (US) an expensive prostitute. **4** [1980s+] (W.I./UK/US Black teen) a materially successful person, usu. a rich ghetto drug dealer, as used by the Los Angeles gang, the Crips (cf. BALLER). [SE *high* + *roller*, a dice-player.]
high Russian *n.* [1960s+] (gay) simultaneous anal and oral sex (cf. LOW GREEK).
high school harry *n.* [1950s+] (US campus) an immature male student.
high-season brown *n.* [1900s–30s] (US Black) a beautiful, brown-skinned woman.
high-shoe *n.* [late 17C–19C] a rustic, a peasant; thus *high shoon*, countrified, gullible. [? the heavy footwear favoured by country-dwellers]
high shot *n.* [1920s+] (orig. US) a superior person or one who claims to be superior. [var. on BIG SHOT n.]
highside *v.* [1960s] (US Black) to behave in an arrogant, boastful manner, to show off.
high-siding/-steppin' *adv.* [1960s+] (US Black) showing off, bragging, often in the ostentatious display of jewellery, expensive clothes, cars etc. [HIGHSIDE]
high sign *n.* [late 19C+] (orig. US) a warning, a recognition signal, a secret sign, esp. when denoting one's membership of a group; a signal that the 'coast is clear'.
high sign *v.* **1** [late 19C+] (US) to warn, to give a sign of recognition, to signal that there is no danger. **2** [1970s+] (US Black) to show off, to upstage (cf. HIGHSIDE). [HIGH SIGN n.]
high-sniffing *adj.* [1900s] arrogant. [the sniffing nose is also 'in the air']
high steam *adj.* [1940s] (W.I.) very good, superior. [? SE *high esteem*]
high-stepper *n.*[1] [mid–late 19C] a fashionably dressed or smoothly mannered person. [20C use is SE; orig. of a horse that lifts its feet high when walking or trotting]
high-stepper *n.*[2] [20C] pepper. [rhy. sl.]
high-steppin' *see* HIGH-SIDING.
high-stomached *adj.* [mid-16C–late 18C] haughty, arrogant.
High Street, China *phr.* [20C] a far-away, fantasy place.
highstrikes *n.* [mid-19C–1910s] hysterics. [mispron.]
hightail/hightail it *v.* [1910s+] (orig. US) to leave quickly, to run off, to escape. [reverse anthropomorphism]
high tec *n.* [1980s+] (drugs) alkyl nitrites. [play on SE *high tec(hnology)*]
high tide *see* HIGH WATER n.
high time/high old time *n.* [late 19C+] (US) an uproarious time, a spree.
high-/main-toby/high-toby-splicer *n.* [early–mid-19C] **1** highway robbery. **2** the highway, the main road (cf. HIGH PAD; LOW-TOBY).

high-toby-gloak/-tober-gloak *n.* [late 18C–mid-19C] a mounted highwayman (cf. TOBY-GILL). [HIGH-TOBY + GLOAK]
high-toby-man *n.* [late 18C] a highwayman (cf. PLY THE TOBY; RIDE THE TOBY). [HIGH-TOBY + SE *man*]
high-toby spice *n.* [early–mid-19C] the highway. [HIGH-TOBY + SPICE n.]
high-toby-splicer *see* HIGH-TOBY.
high tone *v.* [19C+] (US) to snub, to ignore. [HIGH-TONED]
high-tone *n.* [19C+] (US) an important person, a pretentious person. [HIGH-TONED]
high-toned *adj.* [19C+] (US) **1** superior, high quality. **2** standoffish, snobbish.
high-top fade *n.* [1990s] a style of haircut favoured by young Blacks. [SE *high* + *top* + FADE n.[3]]
high-topper *n.* [mid–late 19C] a dandified thief. [fig. use SE]
highty-tighty/heighty-toity *n.* [late 17C–late 18C] a promiscuous girl. [first cited in *B.E.* (1699) – who spells it 'hightetity' – it seems to predate synon. HOITY-TOITY n., but *OED* notes the contemporary pron of 'oi' as 'igh', as in oil = ile, boil = bile, and thus sees it as no more than 'a variant']
highty-tighty *adj.* [late 17C–19C] aloof, snobbish, supercilious (cf. HOITY-TOITY adj.).
highty-tighty! *excl.* [mid-18C–mid-19C] an excl. of disdain, annoyed surprise, infuriation.
high-up *n.* [1920s+] (orig. US) the boss, the leader, anyone senior to or more powerful than the speaker.
high up on the stick, to be *phr.* [early 19C] to have reached the top of one's profession.
high-wall job *n.* [20C] (Und.) breaking and entering a factory or any similar building surrounded by a high wall (cf. SECOND-STOREY MAN).
high water/tide *n.* [late 18C–19C] financial security. [the image is, however, of impermanence: like the real high water, such an economic 'tide' will ebb in time]
highwater *adj.* [20C] (US) used to describe trousers that are too short.
highwaters *n.* [20C] (US) trousers that are too short. [HIGHWATER]
high-water mark/tidemark *n.* [late 19C+] a dirty mark showing the limit to which a person has washed.
highway *n.* [20C] the vagina (cf. ALLEY n.[1]).
high, west and crooked *phr.* [19C+] (orig. US) in all directions, disarray, confusion (cf. HELL WEST AND CROOKED).
high, wide and handsome *phr.* [20C] (orig. US) happy, pleasant, carefree, performing well and easily.
high yellow/yaller/yalla/deep yellow *n.* [1920s+] a mulatto woman or girl. [her complexion]
higry-pigry *n.* [late 18C] a nickname for the *Hiera picra*, 'a purgative drug composed of aloes and canella bark, sometimes mixed with honey and other ingredients' (*OED*) (cf. HICKERY-PICKERY).
hijack/hi-jack *n.* **1** [late 19C] (US) the robbery of tramps as they sleep in the 'hobo jungles'. **2** [late 19C] (orig. US) a hold-up followed by the theft of goods (often exercised by one criminal upon another). [according to Cohen (1989) based on *high jack*, zinc ore, a term used *c.*1899 in the mines of Webb City, Missouri, then the world's greatest lead/zinc mine. This zinc ore was more valuable than the basic lead among which it was found, and miners would steal it to further enrich themselves. The term was virtually SE by 1900, as are the later meanings referring to the holding up of vehicles, including aircraft, and the killing or ransoming of their occupants]
hijack/hi-jack *v.* **1** [1900s] (US) to subject to extortion. **2** [1920s+] (US) to remove or move a person against their will. [HIJACK n.]

hi jimmy knacker n. [20C] tobacco. [rhy. sl.; ult. the name of an old street game]

hijo! excl. [1950s+] (US) a general excl. [Sp. hijo, son (of a …)]

hike n. [late 19C] (US) a derog. term for an Italian immigrant. [? comb. of KIKE n. + HUNKY n.[1] (1)]

hike v. [mid-19C+] **1** to raise. **2** to drag. **3** to store up, to put away, esp. a valuable object. [dial.]

hike off v. **1** [late 18C–mid-19C] (Und.) to leave (cf. HIT THE ROAD; TAKE A HIKE). **2** [late 18C–mid-19C] (Und.) to arrest. **3** [1950s] (US) to trick or cheat. [dial. hike, to run off with, to snatch]

hiker n. [1900s–30s] (US) a small-town marshal.

hikori n. [20C] (drugs) peyote. [? Amerindian]

hikuli n. [20C] (drugs) peyote. [? Amerindian]

hilda handcuffs n. [1980s+] (camp gay) a policeman (cf. BRENDA n.[2]; LILLY LAW).

hilding n. [16C] a prostitute. [SE hilding, a contemptible, worthless person of either sex; a good-for-nothing]

hill n. [20C] (US) a cemetery (cf. MARBLE HILL; STILL HILL).

hill and dale n. [1940s+] confidence trickery. [rhy. sl. hill and dale = TALE n.]

hilljack n. [20C] (US) a hillbilly, a country yokel. [SE hill + JACK n.[4]]

hillman hunter n. [20C] a customer. [rhy. sl. the motorcar Hillman Hunter = PUNTER n.[1]]

hill-top literature n. [late 19C] good advice. [the warnings that, in the early days of cycling, were posted at the top of hills, warning cyclists of the incline and/or dangerous curves ahead]

him n.[1] see HE.

him n.[2] [1960s–70s] (drugs) heroin (cf. HER n.[1]; HOMBRE n.[2]). [BOY n.[5]]

himbo n. [1980s+] a gigolo (cf. TOYBOY). [him + BIMBO; allegedly coined in Tatler magazine]

himmer n. [1950s] a male homosexual (cf. HESH). [SE him; Rodgers suggests an old joke, the punchline of which puns on SE hymn/him]

hinchinarfer n. [late 19C] a grumpy, gruff-voiced woman. [SE inch and a half, the supposed length of her husband's penis – her grumpiness is due to sexual frustration]

hincty/hinckty/haincty n. [1920s+] (US Black) **1** a snob, an arrogant, self-opinionated person. **2** a White person (cf. HONKIE). [HINCTY adj.]

hincty/hinckty/haincty adj.[1] [1920s+] (US Black) **1** snobbish. **2** derog. ref. to any Black abandoning racial pride for attempts to ape White manners or styles (cf. DICTY; SEDDITY; UPPITY). [ety. unknown; a suggestion that the word is an elision of HANDKERCHIEF-HEAD n.[2] has no linguistic backing; ? note Lincolnshire dial. hinch, meanness, miserliness]

hincty adj.[2] see HINKY.

hind n. [1930s–40s] (US Black) the buttocks, the posterior. [abbr. behind]

hind coach-wheel n. [late 18C–19C] a 5-shilling piece (25p), a crown (cf. COACH-WHEEL; FORE COACH-WHEEL). [the 'hind' or rear coach-wheels are larger than the front ones]

hinder end/parts/world n. [19C+] the buttocks, the posterior (cf. HINDER ENTRANCE; HINDERS). [SE hind end + dial. hinder]

hinder entrance n. [19C] the buttocks (cf. HINDER END).

hinder parts see HINDER END.

hinders n. [late 19C–1930s] the buttocks (cf. HINDER END).

hinder world see HINDER END.

Hindoo/Hindu n. **1** [19C] (S.Afr.) Europeans who came from India to recuperate their health. **2** [1900s–10s] (US) a person with special ability, a wizard. [facet. uses of SE Hindoo/Hindu, a follower of Hinduism and thus, broadly, an Indian]

hind paw n. [1920s] a foot, a leg.

hind-shifters n. [mid-19C] the feet or heels, esp. as a pair of … .

hindside n. [20C] the buttocks, the posterior (cf. BACKSIDE; HINDER END).

hindside-backaways/backwards adv. [20C] (US) back to front.

hindside-before adv. [20C] (US) back to front.

hindside of nowhere n. [20C] (US) a particularly out of the way place (cf. ARSE-END OF THE UNIVERSE).

Hindu see HINDOO.

Hindustani jig n. [1960s+] (gay) anal intercourse. [? a supposed predilection of Hindus for sodomy]

hinge n. [1930s+] (US) a look.

hinge-jaw n. [20C] (US) one who talks too much (cf. RATCHET JAW).

hinges n. [20C] (US) the joints of the human body; thus one's hinges are creaking, one is getting old.

hinges/hobs/hugs of hell phr. [20C] (US) a general phr. of intensification, esp. as black as the hinges of hell, hot as the hinges of hell (cf. HARD AS THE HOBS OF HELL). [SE hinge/hob, a griddle (but note play hob, play the devil)/hug]

hinky adj. **1** [1950s+] (US) scared, jumpy, nervous. **2** [1960s] (US) very cheap, petty. **3** [1970s+] (US police) suspicious. [Scot. hink, a hesitation, a misgiving]

hinky-dinky adj. **1** [1900s–40s] (US) little, short in stature. **2** [1910s–30s] (US) excellent. [the nickname of Michael 'Hinky Dink' Kenna (1858–1946), alderman and politician of Chicago]

hinterland n. [late 19C] the buttocks, the posterior.

hip/hips/hipp/hipps/hyps, the n. [18C–19C] neuroses, misery, esp. when brought on by excessive drinking; thus [early 18C] hippish, [late 19C] hippy, miserable, low-spirited. [SE hypochondria]

hip adj. **1** [20C] sophisticated, aware, in tune with events, ideas and situations. **2** [1940s+] (US Black) splendid, enjoyable. **3** [1940s–50s] (US) insolent, cheeky. **4** [1940s+] (US) infatuated, excited. [HEP or Wolof hepi, to see or hipi, to open one's eyes. As abbr. for HIPSTER the word had a more specific meaning to jazz buffs/beatniks of 1950s, but now the general use is predominant]

hip v.[1] [mid–late 19C] to depress. [HIP n.]

hip v.[2] [1920s+] to initiate, to explain, to tell. [HIP adj. (1)]

hip-/hop-and-drop, to phr. [20C] (W.I.) to limp, either because of a temporary injury or a permanent deformity.

hip at the clinch n. [20C] (Ulster) one who has a limp.

hip-cat see HEP-CAT.

Hip City n. [20C] (US Black) Cleveland, Ohio.

hip deep to a tall Indian phr. [20C] (US) very deep, often used of water, snow (cf. ASS-HIGH TO A TALL INDIAN).

hip-disease n. [1920s+] (Aus.) the habit of carrying a hipflask.

hip-flipper n. [1920s–30s] (US) an oriental dancer. [coined by columnist Walter Winchell (1897–1972)]

hip-hitter n. [1960s] (gay) a male homosexual. [the physical movements of anal intercourse]

hip-hop n. [1970s+] (orig. US Black) the singing or chanting of the lyrics of a RAP song against a heavy bass line, usually produced by a drum machine or synthesizer. [coined either by D.J. Hollywood, who pioneered the hip-hop style of singing at Club 371 in Harlem, New York, spec. in the scat-rap 'Hip hop de hippy hop the body rock' or by DJ Kool Herc in 1968 (Alex Pate USA Weekend magazine 1993) or 1975 (George). While the terms hip-hop and rap are used interchangeably, the former gives more emphasis to the words, while the latter will often feature a more elaborate, even dominant backing track]

hip-hop *adj.* [1970s+] (orig. US Black) pertaining to the hip-hop/rap lifestyle and attitudes.

hip/hyp Michael, your head's on fire! *excl.* [mid-18C–19C] an excl. aimed at any passing red-headed man.

hipidity *n.* [1970s] (US campus) a usu. young person, preaching a philosophy of 'love and peace', backed by wide spectrum drug use, esp. cannabis and hallucinogens. [HIPPIE n.² (3)]

hip inside/outside *n.* [mid-19C] (Und.) inside and outside coat pockets.

hipped *adj.*¹ **1** [early 18C+] miserable, unhappy, in low spirits (cf. HIP n.). **2** [early 18C+] angry, irritated. **3** [1900s–30s] (US) defeated, done for. [*hip* or *hyp*, abbr. SE *hypochondria*]

hipped *adj.*² [1920s–40s] (US Und.) carrying a gun or hip-flask. [SE *hip*]

hip-peddler *n.* [1900s–40s] (US) a prostitute.

hipped on *adj.* **1** [late 19C+] interested in, obsessed by, aware of. **2** [1920s+] (US) aware and informed; thus *hipped to the jive/tip*, well informed. [HIP adj. (1)]

hippie *n.*¹ [20C] (W.I./Guyn.) a half-bottle. [a bottle small enough to be kept in one's hip pocket]

hippie/hippy *n.*² **1** [1940s–60s] (US Black) one who poses (without little or no success) as a HIPSTER. **2** [1950s+] (orig. US) a sophisticated, cool, 'hip' person. **3** [1960s+] (orig. US) a (usu.) young person, preaching a philosophy of 'love and peace', backed by a wide spectrum of drug usage, esp. of cannabis and hallucinogens. [like many terms, *hippie* crossed from the Black to White worlds; unlike most, however, it altered its meaning, in this case from negative to, in peer-group eyes at least, positive. Since the 1960s/early 1970s the negative image has returned, although not as a failed *hipster* but as a 1960s throwback]

hippie crack *n.* [1980s+] nitrous oxide (cf. LIQUID CRACK). [HIPPIE n.² (3) + CRACK n.¹⁷]

hippies *n.* [1940s–50s] (N.Z.) a man's brief swimming trunks. [SE *hip*]

hippo *n.*¹ [19C+] (US) a mild depression. [SE *hyp*, abbr. *hypochondriac*]

hippo *n.*² [1970s+] (S.Afr.) an armoured police vehicle. [abbr. SE *hippopotamus*]

hippodrome *n.* [late 19C] (US sporting) any race or sporting contest in which the result has been fixed in advance. [SE *hippodrome*, a course or circus for horse-races and chariot-races]

hippodrome *v.* [late 19C] (US sporting) to fix a sporting competition. [HIPPODROME n.]

hipp/hipps *see* HIP n.

hippy-dippy *adj.* [1960s+] eccentric with added overtones of hippiedom. [HIPPIE n.² (3) + DIPPY]

hips *see* HIP n.

hipster *n.* [1930s+] (orig. US Black) one who espouses the fashionable Bohemian stance of the period; the essence was a conscious downplaying of emotional display, a stance possibly facilitated by heroin addiction. [HIP adj. (1) + sfx. -STER; Black use dropped by 1940s]

hipsters *n.* [1960s+] the accumulations of fat around the thighs and stomachs of the overweight. [SE *hip*]

hipsy hoy *n.* [20C] a boy. [rhy. sl.]

hiram *n.* [20C] (US) a rustic, a peasant. [proper name, used in the Old Testament and thus popular among Puritan immigrants]

hiray/hirey *n.* [20C] money. [? SE *hire*]

hired gun *n.* [1950s+] (orig. US) in business, an executive who is hired for the performance of a particularly tough task. [the imagery of cinema Westerns; the task performed, he may well 'ride off into the sunset']

hi-res *adj.* [1930s+] (US) fine, satisfactory, admirable. [abbr.

SE *high resolution*, used to define image quality on a video monitor]

hirey *see* HIRAY.

hironpon *n.* [1980s+] (drugs) smokeable methamphetamine. [? brandname]

hirsute oyster *n.* [1990s] the vagina. [play on BEARDED CLAM]

his balls are bigger than his brains *phr.* [1940s+] said of a man who rushes into situations without thinking. [BALLS n.¹ (1)]

his dibs *n.* [1920s–30s] a wealthy person. [a pun on HIS NIBS + DIBS]

his hair grows through his hood *phr.* [mid-15C–early 18C] used of someone considered to be 'on the road to ruin'. [the significance of so unkempt an appearance]

his gills *n.* [late 19C–1910s] (Aus.) a self-important person, an authority, 'his nibs'.

his highness/royal highness *n.* [late 19C+] used by a woman as a sarcastically 'respectful' description of her husband; the implication is of laziness (cf. HER HIGHNESS).

his knabs *see* HIS NABS.

hi si *n.* [1950s] (US) high society. [phonetic abbr.]

his lordship *see* HER LADYSHIP.

His Majesty's bad bargain *see* HER MAJESTY'S BAD BARGAIN.

His Majesty's carriage *see* HER MAJESTY'S CARRIAGE.

His Majesty's naval police *see* HER MAJESTY'S NAVAL POLICE.

His Majesty's School for Heavy Needlework *see* HER MAJESTY'S SCHOOL FOR HEAVY NEEDLEWORK.

his morning and evening song do not agree *phr.* [late 18C–mid-19C] his statements are inconsistent.

his nabs/knabs *n.* [late 18C–19C] himself. [? NEB]

his name is Dennis *phr.* [19C+] (US) a phr. indicating failure, also abbr. as *Dennis* (cf. HIS NAME IS MUD). [whaling jargon *dennis*, a whale that has been harpooned and is on the verge of death]

his name is mud *phr.* [19C+] a phr. implying failure or disgrace following some objectionable or foolish act (cf. HIS NAME IS DENNIS; MUD n.¹).

his nibs *n.* [early 19C+] **1** himself. **2** an employer, a superior. **3** a self-important person (cf. HIS DIBS). [NIBS n.²]

his royal highness *see* HIS HIGHNESS.

his shoe pinches him *phr.* **1** [18C] he is drunk. **2** [20C] he (probably) has a large penis. [euphs.; (2) the premise that large feet or a large nose equate with a large penis]

his stockings belong to two parishes *phr.* [late 18C–mid-19C] said of one who is wearing odd stockings.

hissy *n.* [20C] (US) a tantrum, an outburst of bad temper; thus ext. as *hissy fit.* [? SE *hysterical* or *hiss*]

hist *adj.* [1980s+] (US campus) finished, over, completed. [SE *history*]

hist *v. see* HEIST v.

hist! *excl.* [1980s+] (US campus) goodbye! [SE *history*]

historical *adj.* [late 19C] (society) old-fashioned.

history *adj.* **1** [1970s+] (orig. US) out-of-date, no longer relevant, dead. **2** [1980s+] (US) leaving, used as a term of farewell, i.e. *I'm history.*

history of the four kings *see* BOOK OF THE FOUR KINGS.

his wife keeps the key *phr.* [late 19C] a phr. used of one who has to sneak out to the pub surreptitiously.

hit *n.*¹ [19C–1950s] (US gambling) a winning series of numbers in gambling.

hit *n.*² **1** [1940s–60s] (US Und.) a prison sentence or denial of parole. **2** [1960s+] (US Und.) an arrest. [HIT v.¹]

hit *n.*³ **1** [20C] an attempted crime, esp. a robbery. **2** [1950s+] (Und.) a murder, esp. a gangster killing. **3** [1960s+] (US Und.) an attack against a rival gang.

hit *n.*⁴ **1** [20C] a single drink of alcohol. **2** [20C] a swig. **3** [1930s+] (drugs) a purchase of a drug. **4** [1950s+] (drugs) a puff on a marijuana cigarette. **5** [1950s+] (drugs) a portion of any drug, a tablet of amphetamine or barbiturate; an injection or a line of heroin or cocaine etc. **6** [1960s+] (drugs) the act of injecting a narcotic drug (cf. RUSH n.²). **7** [1980s+] (drugs) a puff on a crack cocaine pipe. [HIT v.²]

hit n.⁵ [1960s+] a kiss. [rhy. sl. *hit and miss* = *kiss*]

hit n.⁶ [1970s+] (US) an instance, an attempt or time (cf. POP n.⁶).

hit v.¹ **1** [19C] (US) to send to prison. **2** [1950s+] (US Und.) to raid an establishment.

hit v.² **1** [mid-19C+] to use or consume drugs or alcohol. **2** [1940s+] (drugs) to inject narcotics, esp. for the drug to register its immediate effect on the user. **3** [1960s+] (drugs) to adulterate drugs before selling them (cf. CUT v.¹²).

hit v.³ [late 19C+] to arrive at, to use.

hit v.⁴ **1** [late 19C+] (US) to beg, to ask, to accost. **2** [1990s+] (US Black/drugs) to call someone on a pager.

hit v.⁵ [late 19C+] (US campus) to pass an exam with a high grade.

hit v.⁶ [1930s+] (orig. US) **1** to pay, to hand over money. **2** to give someone a drink. **3** to deal out a card, esp. in imper. *hit me!* give me another card.

hit v.⁷ (US) **1** [1940s+] to have sexual intercourse with a woman (cf. HIT IT; HIT SKINS). **2** [1940s+] to kill, to assassinate. **3** [1950s+] to rob, to hold up.

hit v.⁸ [1940s+] to switch on or off, to apply the brakes of a vehicle.

hit a big one, to phr. [1940s+] (US) to wander unintentionally into trouble.

hit a home run, to phr. [1980s+] (US campus) to engage in sex (cf. SCORE v.¹). [baseball imagery]

hit a house, to phr. [20C] (US prison) to search a cell. [HIT v.¹ (2) + HOUSE n.¹ (5)]

hit a knot, to phr. [20C] (US) to snore. [the sound made when a saw hits a knot while cutting timber]

hit a lick/hit a lick at a snake, to phr. [1920s+] (US) to make an effort; usu. in negative combs. implying laziness on behalf of the subject of the phr. e.g. *He hasn't hit a lick all week.* [SE *hit* + LICK n.]

hit-and-get n. [1920s+] (US Und.) the passing off of a confidence trick in a town and then immediately leaving that town. [HIT n.³ + GET v.¹]

hit and miss n. [1960s+] **1** a kiss. **2** urination. [rhy. sl.; (2) *hit and miss* = PISS n.]

hit and missed adj. [1960s+] drunk. [rhy. sl. *hit and missed* = PISSED; unlike most rhy. sl. this phr. is always used in full]

hit and run adj. [20C] cheated, deceived. [rhy. sl. *hit and run* = DONE adj.¹ (1)]

hitch n.¹ [19C+] (US milit.) **1** a term of enlistment in one of the US armed forces. **2** a period of employment of any sort. [SE *hitch*, a temporary fastening, as with a loop or knot]

hitch n.² [late 19C+] **1** (US) an effort, an attempt. **2** help through a difficulty, temporary assistance. [SE *hitch*, a short abrupt movement, pull or push]

hitch n.³ [1930s+] an act of hitchhiking, e.g. *I got a hitch up to London.* [HITCH v.²]

hitch v.¹ [19C+] (US Black) to start fighting. [? abbr. *hitch up one's sleeves*]

hitch v.² [1930s+] to *hitch*hike. [abbr.]

hitched adj. [mid-19C+] (US) married. [SE *hitch*, to fasten, esp. in a temporary way]

hitchhiker on the Hershey highway phr. [20C] (US) a homosexual man. [SE *hitchhiker* + HERSHEY HIGHWAY]

hitchhike to heaven, to phr. [1990s] to masturbate.

hitchhike under the big top, to phr. [1990s] to masturbate.

hitch horses/horses together v. [19C+] (US) **1** to agree

upon. **2** to marry (cf. HITCH-UP). [hitching two horses to the same post]

hitchpussy n. [1980s+] (US gay) a gay hitchhiker. [HITCH v.² + PUSSY n.¹]

hitch teams v. [19C+] to get married (cf. HITCH HORSES). [rural imagery]

hitch-up n. [19C] (US) a marriage (cf. HITCH HORSES; HITCH TEAMS).

hitch up v. [late 19C] (US) to start, to set off. [the *hitching up* of one's team to a wagon or coach before setting off on a journey]

hitch up the reindeers, to phr. [1980s+] (drugs) to inhale cocaine. [play on the relationship of reindeer to SNOW n.³ (1)]

hitey-titey adj. [1950s+] (W.I. Rasta) aloof, snobbish, super-cilious (cf. HOITY-TOITY adj.). [HIGHTY-TIGHTY adj.]

hit for v. [20C] **1** to purchase, esp. drugs. **2** to borrow money; thus *hit for a loan* (cf. HIT ON). [HIT v.⁴]

hit for six, to phr. [20C] to assert oneself decisively in an argu-ment, to destroy any form of opposition. [cricket imagery, a hit for 6 is the highest scoring single shot that can be played]

hit gut v. [1990s] (US campus) to engage in sex (cf. HIT SKINS).

hit-head n. [1980s+] a user of crack cocaine (cf. ACID-HEAD; HITTER n.²). [HIT n.⁴ + sfx. -HEAD (2)]

hit her up v. [20C] (US) to accelerate, to go fast.

hit house n. **1** [1930s] (US Black) an illegal bar that sells contraband liquor (cf. NIP JOINT). **2** [1950s+] (drugs) a house where users go to inject narcotics and leave the owner drugs as payment. [HIT n.⁴ + SE *house*]

hit it v. [1990s] (US Black) **1** to have sexual intercourse (cf. HIT SKINS). **2** to smoke crack cocaine. [HIT v.², v.⁷]

hit it off v. [late 18C–late 19C] to establish a relationship, to become friendly, to get on well. [20C use is SE]

hit it/things up v.¹ [20C] to behave in an aggressive, noisy manner.

hit it/hit it up v.² [20C] (US) to get on with, to establish good relations (cf. HIT IT OFF). [dial. *hit it*, to agree]

hit it with v. [20C] (Aus.) to get on with, to establish good relations (cf. HIT IT OFF).

hit lady see HIT WOMAN.

Hitler boot n. [1940s] (W.I.) a shoe made from old automobile tyres and very common during WW2 (cf. JUMP-AND-JIVE). [Adolf *Hitler* (1889–1945), dictator of Nazi Germany]

hit list n. [1970s+] **1** a list of those scheduled for assassination. **2** any list that details tasks that are to be carried out. [HIT v.⁷ (1) + SE *list*]

hit man n. [1960s+] (orig. US) a hired or 'contract' killer. [HIT v.⁷ (1) + SE *man*]

hit-mark n. [1960s+] (drugs) a scar from injecting a narcotic drug (cf. TRACKS). [HIT n.⁴ (6) + SE *mark*]

hit me! excl. [1930s+] (orig. US gambling) an invitation to the dealer to give one another card. [HIT v.⁶]

hit me and cut the rap! excl. [1960s+] (US teen) stop talking and just do what you came to do, give me what I want etc. [HIT v.⁶ + CUT v.⁵ + RAP n.⁴]

hitmeister n. [1980s+] (US drugs) a small pipe made from 3mm (1/8in) brass fittings used for burning roaches and small chunks of marijuana. [HIT n.⁴ (7) + sfx. -*meister*, an expert, the supreme example]

hit on v. **1** [1940s+] (orig. US Black) to make advances to, to seduce. **2** [1940s+] in pimp use, to attract a woman to one's team of prostitutes. **3** [1950s+] (US Black) to ask, to approach, usu. against the subject's wishes. **4** [1960s+] (US) to attempt to swindle or victimize. [HIT v.⁴]

hit on all cylinders, to phr. [20C] to work properly (cf. FIRE ON ALL CYLINDERS). [SE *hit* + automobile imagery]

hit one's head on the ceiling, to phr. [1970s] (US campus) to make a mistake.

hit one's hobbles, to *phr.* [1950s+] (Aus.) to make a comeback. [racing use *hit the hobbles*, for a horse to keep galloping despite a hobble chain]

hit one's kick, to *phr.* (Aus.) to open one's wallet, e.g. to pay for a round drinks. [SE *hit* + KICK n.⁴]

hit on rosy palm, to *phr.* [20C] to masturbate (cf. CONVERSE WITH HARRY PALM). [VISIT ROSY PALM AND HER FIVE DAUGHTERS]

hit on the head by the tavern bitch *phr.* [17C–18C] drunk (cf. BITTEN BY THE TAVERN BITCH).

hit on the master vein, to be *phr.* [16C] to become pregnant (cf. MASTERPIECE). [SE *master-vein*, a major vein, usu. the carotid artery or jugular vein]

hit or miss *n.* [late 19C+] an act of urination (cf. HIT AND MISS). [rhy. sl. *hit or miss* = PISS n.]

hit paydirt *v.* [1950s+] (US) to be successful (cf. PAYDIRT). [gold-mining imagery]

hits *n.* [1960s+] LSD (cf. A n.³). [HIT n.⁴]

hit skins *v.* [20C] to have sexual intercourse (cf. BUMP BELLIES). [note PNG Tok Pisin *paitim bun*, to have sex, lit. 'hit bones']

hit someone up *v.* [1980s+] (US Black) to approach, to speak to, to question.

hit someone with the book, to *phr.* [1960s+] (Aus.) to discipline heavily, to reprimand severely. [var. on THROW THE BOOK AT; the 'book' is the 'book of rules' that one has contravened]

hit some shit, to *phr.* (US Black) to encounter problems. [SE *hit*, encounter + SHIT n.³]

hitsville *n.* [1960s] the fig. world of success. [SE *hit*, a successful record + sfx. -VILLE]

hitter *n.¹* [1960s+] a success, a star, usu. with overtones of violence or criminality. [SE *hit*, a success + HIT v.⁷]

hitter *n.²* [1980s+] (drugs) 1 a user of crack cocaine (cf. HIT-HEAD). 2 a small crack pipe, designed for only one puff. [HIT v.²]

hit the air, to *phr.* [1920s–50s] (US) to leave, to depart (cf. HIT THE BREEZE).

hit the ball, to *phr.¹* [20C] (US) to leave quickly (cf. BALL THE JACK). [railway jargon *highball*, a signal directing the train to go at full speed; thus *highball*, to go fast]

hit the ball, to *phr.²* [1910s+] (US) to work hard, to be diligent at a job. [sporting imagery]

hit the books, to *phr.* [1960s+] (US campus) to study hard (cf. BEAT THE BOOKS).

hit the booze/bottle/jug, to *phr.* [late 19C+] (orig. US) to drink heavily (cf. HIT THE POT; HIT THE SAUCE). [BOOZE n./SE *bottle/jug*]

hit the breeze, to *phr.* [20C] (N.Z./US) to depart, to travel, to run fast (cf. PUNCH THE BREEZE).

hit/pad/pound the bricks, to *phr.* [1930s+] (orig. US) 1 to exit, to leave for the street, to start walking. 2 to be discharged from a prison sentence. 3 to go on strike. 4 to walk the streets all night, through homelessness (cf. BEAT THE BRICKS).

hit the bung, to *phr.* [1930s] (US) to get drunk. [HIT v.² (1) + SE *bung*]

hit the button, to *phr.* [20C] to talk aptly, to speak pertinently.

hit the can, to *phr.* [1950s+] (Aus.) to pay for a round of drinks (cf. HIT THE DECK phr.²; KICK THE TIN; TOUCH ONE'S SKY. [SE *hit* + *can*, a beer container]

hit the ceiling, to *phr.* [1910s+] (orig. US) 1 to lose one's temper (cf. HIT THE ROOF). 2 to increase to a new level. 3 to become shocked.

hit the deck, to *phr.¹* [1910s+] 1 to fall down. 2 to throw oneself deliberately to the ground. 3 to go to bed. 4 to get up from one's bed. [SE *hit* + DECK n.¹]

hit the deck, to *phr.²* [1950s+] (Aus.) to pay for a round of drinks (cf. HIT THE CAN; KICK THE TIN; TOUCH ONE'S SKY).

hit/take the deep six, to *phr.* [1960s+] (US) to die. [DEEP SIX]

hit the dirt, to *phr.* [20C] (US) to throw oneself to the ground.

hit the dust, to *phr.* [1910s] (US) to set off, to get going (cf. HIT THE GRIT; HIT THE PIKE; HIT THE ROAD; HIT THE STREET; HIT THE TRAIL).

hit the fan, to *phr.* [1940s+] (US) of trouble or scandal, to erupt, to become public; thus *the egg has hit the fan*, the trouble has started. [WHEN THE SHIT HITS THE FAN]

hit the gas, to *phr.* [1920s+] (US) to accelerate in a motorcar. [HIT v.⁸ + SAmE *gas(olene)*]

hit the gong, to *phr.* [1930s+] (drugs) to smoke opium (cf. HIT THE PIPE). [HIT v.² + GONG n.²]

hit the gow, to *phr.* [1930s+] (drugs) to smoke opium (cf. HIT THE PIPE). [HIT v.² + GOW n.²]

hit the grit/turf, to *phr.* [19C+] (US) 1 to leave, to get moving, to travel fast (cf. HIT THE DUST). 2 to die.

hit the ground, to *phr.¹* [late 19C+] (US) to leap or jump, esp. from a moving train.

hit the ground, to *phr.²* [1960s] (US) to be released from prison.

hit the ground running, to *phr.* [1960s+] to start a task with maximum energy and commitment.

hit the hay/haystack, to *phr.¹* [1910s+] to go to sleep (cf. HIT THE SACK).

hit the hay, to *phr.²* [1950s+] (drugs) to smoke marijuana. [HAY n.³]

hit the headlines, to *phr.* [1930s+] (US) to become famous.

hit the high lonesome, to *phr.* [19C+] (US) to set off on a solo trip (cf. HIGH LONESOME).

hit the high spots, to *phr.* [1910s+] 1 to go to excess or extremes, to rise to a very high level. 2 to go out for an evening's dining and dancing. 3 (Can.) to tackle only superficial issues.

hit the hike *see* HIT THE ROAD.

hit/strike the jackpot, to *phr.* [1930s+] (orig. Aus./N.Z.) to have very good luck, esp. when unexpected (cf. CRACK THE JACKPOT).

hit the jug *see* HIT THE BOOZE.

hit the kellicks, to *phr.* [1940s+] (Aus.) to put the brakes on (cf. ANCHORS). [SE *killick*, an anchor; orig. a stone on a rope used to anchor a boat in place]

hit the lolly *see* DO THE LOLLY.

hit the mainline, to *phr.* [1950s+] (drugs) to inject a drug (cf. MAINLINE v.).

hit the mattress *see* GO TO THE MATTRESS.

hit the needle, to *phr.* [1950s+] (drugs) to inject a drug. [the hypodermic needle]

hit the pavement, to *phr.* [1930s+] 1 to be ejected, esp. from a nightclub or other place of entertainment. 2 to be dismissed from one's job.

hit the pike, to *phr.* [1900s] (US) 1 to leave (cf. HIT THE DUST). 2 to leave one's job. [PIKE n.¹ (3)]

hit the pipe, to *phr.* (US drugs) 1 [late 19C+] to smoke opium. 2 [1980s+] to smoke crack cocaine.

hit the pit, to *phr.¹* [20C] (US Und.) to be imprisoned.

hit the pit, to *phr.²* [1950s+] (drugs) to inject a drug. [abbr. SE *armpit*, where the veins are easily accessed]

hit the pot, to *phr.* [1900s–30s] (US) to drink excessively (cf. HIT THE BOOZE). [SE *pot*, a tankard]

hit the road/hike, to *phr.* [late 19C+] (orig. US) to leave, to set out on a journey; thus imper. *hit the road/hit the road, Jack*, get out, go away (cf. HIT THE DUST).

hit the rods, to *phr.* [1920s–50s] (US) to ride freight trains as an itinerant worker or tramp. [ROD]

hit the roof, to *phr.* [1920s+] to explode with temper, to become extremely annoyed. [var. on HIT THE CEILING]

hit the sack, to *phr.* [late 19C+] to go to sleep (cf. HIT THE HAY; HIT THE TICK; SACK OUT). [SACK n.²]

hit the sauce, to *phr.* [1940s+] (orig. US) to drink to excess (cf. HIT THE BOOZE). [SAUCE n.[1] (3)]

hit the sheets, to *phr.* [1970s+] **1** (US) to go to bed. **2** (US) to have sexual intercourse. **3** (US gay/lesbian) to be passive to the overtures of another woman.

hit the shucks, to *phr.* [20C] (US) to go to bed, to go to sleep (cf. HIT THE HAY; HIT THE SACK; HIT THE TICK). [dial. *shuck*, a corn husk, with which old mattresses were sometimes filled]

hit the sidewalks, to *phr.* [20C] (US) to walk the streets searching for a job (cf. HIT THE BRICKS).

hit the silk, to *phr.* [1940s–50s] (US) to bail out of an aeroplane using a parachute. [the silk that makes the parachute canopy]

hit the skids, to *phr.* [1920s+] (orig. US) to enter into a period of economic decline. [ON THE SKIDS]

hit the slit, to *phr.* [20C] of a woman, to masturbate. [SLIT n.[1] (1)]

hit the spot, to *phr.* [20C] to suit the circumstances, to be absolutely satisfactory in the context.

hit the steel *see* HIT THE TIES.

hit the street, to *phr.* [1960s] (orig. US) to leave, to go out for the night (cf. HIT THE BRICKS; HIT THE ROAD).

hit the stuff, to *phr.* [1930s] (drugs) to smoke opium (cf. HIT THE PIPE). [STUFF n.[5]]

hit the tarpot, to *phr.* [1940s+] (N.Z.) to pursue a Maori woman. [TARPOT]

hit the tick, to *phr.* [20C] (US) to go to bed, to go to sleep. [SE *tick*, a mattress cover]

hit the ties/steel, to *phr.* [20C] (US) to walk along railway tracks, esp. after quitting one's job in a work camp and following the spur back into town. [SE *tie*, a railway sleeper]

hit the toe *see* TAKE TO THE TOE.

hit the trail, to *phr.* [19C+] (orig. US) to leave (cf. HIT THE DUST).

hit the turf *see* HIT THE GRIT.

hit the wind, to *phr.* [20C] (US Black) to leave quickly, to run away.

hit things up *see* HIT IT UP v.[1].

hitting it up *phr.* [late 19C+] (US) drinking heavily. [HIT v.[2] (1)]

hitting up n. [1940s+] (drugs) injecting drugs. [HIT v.[2] (2)]

hit under the wing *phr.* [mid-19C] drunk (cf. WINGED adj.[1]).

hit up v.[1] [late 19C–1920s] (US) to drink (cf. HIT THE BOOZE). [HIT v.[2] (1)]

hit up/hit up the hypo v.[2] [late 19C] (US drugs) to inject cocaine. [HIT v.[2] (2) + HYPO]

hit up v.[3] [20C] (US) to visit.

hit up v.[4] [1950s+] (US) to inject a drug. [HIT v.[2] (3)]

hit up for v. [1910s+] (Aus./N.Z.) to ask someone for something, usu. money. [HIT v.[6]]

hit with the stupid stick, to be *phr.* [1970s] (US Black) to be stupid (cf. BEAT WITH THE UGLY STICK).

hit woman/lady n. [1970s+] (US) a female hired killer. [fem. version of HIT MAN]

hit-your-back n. [20C] (US) a native of Virginia (cf. SOREBACK). [the supposed hospitality of Virginians, an attitude that is underlined by their constantly slapping one another's backs in camaraderie]

hive n. [mid–late 19C] the vagina (cf. BEEHIVE n.[1]; HONEYPOT). [as a receptacle for HONEY n.[2]]

hive off v. [20C] (Aus.) to leave. [SE *hive off*, to break away from a group]

hiver n.[1] [19C] (US) a prostitute. [SE *hive* (*off*) of bees, to swarm; the image is of whores 'swarming like bees' to the newly settled Western towns]

hiver n.[2] [1980s+] a derog. term for a person with AIDS. [SE *HIV* (human immuno-deficiency virus)]

h.n. *see* HOUSE NIGGER.

h.n.i.c. *abbr.* [1930s+] (US Black) a sarcastic ref. to any Black authority-figure (cf. BLACK NIGGER IN CHARGE). [abbr. HEAD NIGGER IN CHARGE]

ho/hoe n.[1] **1** [1950s+] (orig. US Black) a prostitute. **2** [1950s+] (US Black/campus) a promiscuous or seductively dressed young woman. **3** [1950s+] a generic term describing any woman. **4** [1950s+] a person indiscreet in sexual matters. **5** [1990s] (US Black) a sexually promiscuous man. [Black pron. of SE *whore*. (3) is ostensibly neutral, but the undertones of its ety. still make it controversial]

ho n.[2] [1980s+] (drugs) cannabis. [? it is available to anyone with the money; it is a soft, thus 'feminine' drug compared to harder, 'male' narcotics]

ho v. [1990s] (US Black teen) to sell out, to prostitute oneself. [HO n.[1]]

hoag *see* HOGO.

hoagie n. [20C] (US) a large sandwich consisting of a sliced French loaf filled with a variety of fillings (cf. GRINDER n.[6]). [as named in Pennsylvania and New Jersey]

hoax n. [late 18C–early 19C] a deception, a fraud, a 'tease'. [? SE *hocus*, to trick. Although this ety. seems highly likely, there are no 18C citations and thus 'no direct evidence of connection' (*OED*). Subseq. use is SE]

hoax v. [late 18C–early 19C] to deceive, to ridicule; thus *hoax a quiz*, to tease an eccentric person. [HOAX n.]

hob n. [late 17C–19C] a rustic, a simpleton (cf. HAWBUCK). [early use is SE. Corruption of proper name *Robin* or *Robert*]

hob and nob, to *phr.* **1** [mid-18C–mid-19C] to invite to drink, and then to clink glasses (cf. HOB NOB). **2** [mid–late 19C] to fraternize, to be on intimate terms. [lit. 'to lay heads together']

hobbes! *excl.* [1980s+] (US campus) a general excl., really! honest! on my honour! [? joc. ref. to the US comic strip *Calvin and Hobbes* (1980s)]

hobbinol n. [late 17C–19C] a rustic, a simpleton. [HOB + NOLL]

hobble n. [late 18C–mid-19C] a difficult situation, from which it is hard to extricate oneself (cf. HOBBLED; IN A HOBBLE). [Scot. *habble*, a difficulty, a perplexity]

hobble v. **1** [18C] (Und.) to steal, to arrest (cf. HOBBLED). **2** [late 19C–1910s] (US) to restrain. [SE *hobble*, orig. of an animal, to restrain]

hobbled *adj.* [early 19C] arrested, committed to trial; thus *hobbled upon the legs*, transported, sent to the hulks. [SE *hobble*, to tie up an animal]

hobbledegee/hobbledejee n. [late 18C–19C] a jog trot, a pace between a walk and a run. [SE *hobble*, to limp, to walk unsteadily]

hobbledehoy n. [mid-17C–late 19C] an awkward, clumsy youth, between boyhood and manhood. [? SE *hobble*, to move clumsily + excl. *hoy*! (Skeat); or HOB (E.P.)]

hobbledejee *see* HOBBLEDEGEE.

hobby n. [mid-19C] (US) an English translation of a text in a foreign language. [play on PONY n.[3]]

hobby bobby n. [1980s] a special constable. [SE *hobby* + BOBBY n.[1] (1)]

hobby horse n.[1] [late 16C–early 17C] a prostitute, a promiscuous woman. [she can be 'ridden' by all and sundry]

hobby horse n.[2] [late 16C–early 17C] a fool, a jester. [SE *hobby horse*, the performer, in a morris dance, who manipulates, with much capering, the wicker horse that is part of the trad. 'cast']

ho-bitch n. [1990s] (US campus) a general negative when applied to any woman. [HO n.[1] + BITCH n.[1]]

hob-job n. [late 19C] an unskilled job, an odd job, e.g. holding horses, carrying parcels. [HOB + SE *job*]

hob-jobber n. [mid–late 19C] a man or boy walking the streets on the look out for small jobs. [HOB-JOB]

hobnail *n.* [late 17C–19C] a rustic, a simpleton (cf. HIGH-SHOE; HOB). [the heavy footwear, studded with hobnails, used by country-dwellers]

hobnailed *adj.* [18C] rustic, boorish. [HOBNAIL]

hobnail express *v.* [1950s+] (N.Z.) to walk, to travel by foot.

hob nob *v.* [late 18C–19C] to invite to drink and then to clink glasses; thus as *hob nob/hob a nob*, a toast (cf. HOB AND NOB). [according to Grose (1785), the custom dates to the late 16C: 'When great chimnies were in fashion, there was at each corner of the hearth ... a small elevated projection, called the *hob*, and behind it a seat. In winter time the beer was placed on the hob to warm; and cold beer was set on a small table, said to have been called the *nob*, so that the question, Will you have hob or nob, seems only to have meant Will you have warm or cold beer?' Skeat opts for AS *hab*, have and *nabban*, not have, thus 'take it or leave it', i.e. the choice is yours]

hobnobs *n.* [1990s] (Irish) members of the upper classes. [NOB n.³]

hobo *n.*¹ [late 19C+] (US) a tramp, a vagrant, an itinerant worker, often using the US rail system as a means of free transport. [ety. unknown; claims have been made for *hoe-boy*, a migrant farm-worker and the cry *Ho, boy!* used regularly by northwestern railway mail handlers *c.*1880–90]

hobo *n.*² [1910s] (US) the penis. [fig. use of HOBO n.¹; i.e. it 'wanders around']

hobo *v.* [late 19C+] (US) to live or travel as a tramp (cf. HOBO n.¹).

hobo cell *n.* [1900s] (US) the iron cage in a prison for locking up minor offenders. [HOBO n.¹]

hobo cocktail *n.* [1940s] (US) a glass of water, esp. when requested (rather than alcohol) in a restaurant. [HOBO n.¹ + SE *cocktail*]

Hoboken *n.* [20C] (US) **1** an insignificant, out-of-the-way place. **2** hell. [proper name of *Hoboken*, New Jersey; poss. f. an imagined identification with HOBO although the name is, in fact, Indian]

ho boots *n.* [1970s+] (US Black) ostentatiously sexy, high, tight, high-heeled woman's boots (cf. FUCK-ME SHOES). [HO n.¹ + SE *boots*]

hobosex *n.* [1990s] sex with a number of strangers in a short period of time; thus *hobosexual*, one who enjoys such random adventuring. [HOBO n.² + SE (*hetero*)*sexual*]

hob's knob *n.* [20C] (US) the smart, rich area of a town (cf. NOB HILL).

hobs of hell *see* HINGES OF HELL.

hobson-jobson *n.* [mid-17C–1920s] (Anglo-Ind.) an Indian festival, esp. that of the Muharram procession celebrating the first month of the Muslim year, and the martyrdom of Hasan and Husain, grandsons of Muhammad. [the corruption by British soldiers of the cries of *Ya Hasan! Ya Husayn!* ('O Hasan! O Husain!'). The phr. is best known as the title of *Hobson-Jobson*,'a glossary of colloquial Anglo-Indian words and phrases, and of kindred terms', by Yule & Burnell (1886), and the phr. 'the law of Hobson-Jobson ... used of the process of adapting a foreign word to the sound-system of the adopting language' (*OED*)]

hobson's choice *n.* [20C] the human voice. [rhy. sl. f. SE *Hobson's choice*, no choice at all. Named for Tobias Hobson or Jobson (d.*c.*1630), the Cambridge carrier (commemorated by John Milton (1608–74) in two epitaphs), who let out horses and is said to have compelled customers to take the horse that happened to be next to the stable-door or to go without; orig. *Hodgson's choice* and cited as such by Ernest Weekley as occurring in 1617, 13 years before Hobson's death]

hocake *n.* [1990s] (US Black) the vagina (cf. APPLE n.¹⁰). [HO n.¹ + SE *cake*; it is something to EAT v.³]

hoch *see* HOUGH.

hock *n.*¹ [18C–20C] the foot, the foot and ankle. [SE *hock*, the joint in the back leg of a quadruped]

hock *n.*² [20C] a male homosexual. [rhy. sl. *hock* = COCK n.² (1)]

hock *v.*¹ **1** [late 19C+] (orig. US) to pawn (cf. PUT AWAY v.²). **2** [1930s–70s] (US) to steal (cf. IN HOCK). **3** [1960s] (N.Z.) to get hold of, to obtain. [Du. *hok*, hutch, hovel, prison; sl. credit, debt]

hock *v.*² [1970s] (US) to kick (cf. HOCK n.¹).

hock-dockies *n.* [mid-19C] shoes (cf. HOPPER-DOCKERS). [HOCK n.¹ + redup.]

hockelty *n.* [mid–late 19C] (US) in faro, the last card remaining in the box after the deal has been made. [ety. unknown]

hocker *n.* [1960s] (US teen) a gob of phlegm or spit. [SE *hawk*, to clear one's throat of phlegm]

hocker *v.* [1990s] to hock, to hawk up. [HOCKER n.]

hockey *n. see* HOCKIE n.

hockey *adj.* [late 18C–19C] drunk, spec. with strong, stale beer known as *old hock*. [such beer was traditionally served at harvest-homes or harvest-suppers, celebrating the successful completion of the annual harvest. The beer was sold cheap to the farmer]

hockey *v. see* HOCKIE v.

hockey box *n.* [1970s–80s] (US) the buttocks. [HOCKIE n. (1) + SE *box*]

hockey puck *n.* [1960s+] (US) a stupid person. [coined in 1963 by US comedian Don Rickles]

hockey stick *n.* [1940s+] (N.Z.) a mutton chop.

hockie/hockey/hocky *n.* **1** [19C+] excrement, both human and animal. **2** [1930s–60s] (US) nonsense, lies (cf. BULLSHIT n., CRAP n.³; SHIT n.¹). [? CACKY]

hockie/hockey/hocky *v.* [19C+] to excrete. [HOCKIE n.]

hock-pintled/-pointed *adj.* [18C–19C] suffering from penile strabismus, lit. 'a squint of the penis', i.e. a painful condition in which the penis is painfully bent out of shape (cf. HOOK-POINTED). [SE *hock* + PINTLE]

hocks *n.* [mid-19C] the feet; thus *curby hocks*, round or clumsy feet. [SE *hock*, a joint in the back leg of a quadruped, between the knee and the fetlock, which points backwards; *curby* f. curb, a disease of horses manifested in a swelling on the hock]

hockshop *n.* [mid-19C+] the pawnbroker's shop. [HOCK v.¹ (1) + SE *shop*]

hocky *n. see* HOCKIE n.

hocky *adj.* [1970s] (US campus) unpleasant, nasty. [HOCKIE n.]

hocky *v. see* HOCKIE v.

hocus *n.*¹ **1** [mid-17C–early 18C] a juggler, a magician, a charlatan. **2** [mid-17C–late 18C] juggling, imposture. [abbr. HOCUS-POCUS n.¹]

hocus *n.*² **1** [19C] drugged liquor. **2** [20C] (drugs) opium, morphine, heroin or cocaine. **3** [1980s+] (drugs) marijuana. [fig. use of HOCUS n.¹]

hocus *adj.* [early 18C–early 19C] drunk. [abbr. HOCUS-POCUS n.¹]

hocus *v.* **1** [mid-19C] to drug a person with a mixture of snuff and beer before robbing them. **2** [1940s–50s] (US gambling) to make dice crooked. [SE *hocus*, to confuse]

hocus-pocus *n.*¹ **1** [late 17C–18C] a juggler. **2** [early 18C+] a juggler's trick; thus any form of imposture, trickery. **3** [early 18C] an astrologer. [SE *hocus-pocus*, nonsense incantation used by jugglers to accompany a trick or piece of sleight of hand; itself, according to Archbishop Tillotson (1630–94), Lat. *hoc est corpus*, this is the body: 'In all probability those common juggling words of hocus pocus are nothing else but a corruption of hoc est corpus, by way of ridiculous imitation of the priests of the Church of Rome in their trick of Transubstantiation' (Serm. xxvi., 1742). About 1620 a popular juggler worked under the name of Hocus Pocus, accompanying his tricks with the line 'Hocus pocus, tontus talontus, vade celeriter jubeo']

hocus-pocus n.² **1** [19C] drugged alcohol. **2** [1980s+] marijuana. [fig uses of HOCUS-POCUS n.¹; they all 'confuse' the mind]

hocus-pocus n.³ [1930s–50s] (US Und.) a purse or wallet. [joc. play on POKE n.² (1)]

hocus-pocus adj. [18C] drunk. [HOCUS-POCUS n.¹]

hod/brother hod n. [late 18C] a bricklayer's mate or labourer. [the hod they carry]

hodad/ho-daddy/hodag n. [1980s+] (US) a stupid, obnoxious person. [surfing jargon hodad, a non-surfer, thus a fool; ult. ety. unknown; poss. greeting Ho! Dad]

hoddie n. [1920s+] (Aus.) a bricklayer's mate, a hod-carrier. [the hod he carries]

hoddy-doddy n. [16C–18C, US 19C–20C] **1** a fool, a simpleton. **2** a short, squat person; thus rhy. phr. hoddy doddy/all arse and no body. [dial. hoddy-doddy, a snail]

hoddy peak n. [16C] **1** a fool, a simpleton (cf. HODDY-DODDY). **2** a cuckold. [dial. hoddy-doddy, a snail; in (2) the snail's horns become those of the cuckold + SE peak, head]

hodge n. [late 17C–19C] a rustic, a simpleton (cf. HAWBUCK). [corruption of proper name ROGER]

hodmandod n. [late 17C–19C] **1** a snail. **2** a crippled or deformed person; thus hodmandod, short and clumsy. [SE hodmandod, any form of shelled snail]

hod of mortar n. [mid-19C] a pot of porter. [rhy. sl.]

hoe see HO n.¹.

hoe-handle see HAMMER-HANDLE.

hoe into v. [1930s+] (Aus.) to begin a task with energy and enthusiasm.

h.o.g. n. [late 19C] (US) high old genius. [abbr.; a satire on such honorifics as G.O.M., grand old man, coined for Prime Minister W.E. Gladstone (1809–98) but also a nudge towards SE hog]

hog n.¹ **1** [17C–19C] 1 shilling (5p). **2** [18C–19C] sixpence (2½p). **3** [19C–20C] half-a-crown, 2s 6d (12½p). **4** [mid-19C] (US) a 10-cent piece. **5** [20C] (US) $1. [picture of a pig engraved on the coins]

hog n.² **1** [late 19C+] (US) an engine used for hauling freight cars (cf. PIG). **2** [1950s+] (orig. Hell's Angels) a motorcycle (usu. a Harley-Davidson) modified and cut down for outlaw gang use (cf. GARBAGE WAGON). **3** [1950s–60s] (US Black) any large automobile, esp. a Cadillac Milner. **4** [1970s+] (US) any large vehicle or aircraft that uses quantities of fuel (cf. GAS-GUZZLER). [fig. ref. to the size and power of a hog]

hog n.³ **1** [20C] (US) a miser, a mean person. **2** [1950s+] (drugs) anyone who uses more narcotics than the speaker does. [HOG v.²]

hog n.⁴ [1960s+] (US) the penis. [HOG v.¹]

hog n.⁵ [1960s+] (US) a derog. term for a policeman. [devel. of PIG n.³ (1)]

hog n.⁶ [1960s–70s] (US prison) a tough prisoner who survives hardship stoically. [the toughness of the animal]

hog n.⁷ [1970s+] (US campus) a male term for an unattractive woman (cf. DOG n.⁵).

hog n.⁸ [1970s+] (drugs) phencyclidine (cf. ACE n.³). [the original use of phencyclidine (PCP) as an animal tranquilizer, often of pigs]

hog v.¹ **1** [19C] to have sexual intercourse. **2** [1960s] (US prison) to subject to assault, esp. homosexual rape. [the puritan image of 'swinishness' allied to sex]

hog v.² **1** [late 19C+] (orig. US) to grab for oneself, to act greedily or selfishly. **2** [mid–late 19C] (US) to defraud, to cheat. **3** [mid-19C+] (US) to steal. [the neg. image of the animal]

hog-age n. [20C] (US) male adolescence. [the behaviour of the young men concerned]

hog and a kye n. [mid-19C] one shilling and sixpence (1s 6d/7½p). [HOG n.¹ (1) + KYE]

hog and hominy n. [late 18C+] (US) pork with hominy grits or cornbread.

hogan-magan/hogen-mogen n. **1** [late 17C–early 18C] a Dutchman. **2** [mid-17C–mid-18C] an important person or one who presumes himself to be one. **3** [mid-17C–mid-18C] strong, intoxicating drink. [Du. Hoogmogendheiden, lit. 'High Mightinesses', the title of the States-General]

hogan-magan/hogen-mogen adj. [mid-17C–early 18C] pretentious, high and mighty. [HOGAN-MAGAN n.]

hogan-mogan rug n. [mid-17C] a strong drink. [HOGAN-MOGAN adj. + 17C SE rug, a strong drink]

hogans n. [1960s+] (US) **1** female breasts. **2** (campus) a mouthful, used as a unit of measurement when describing the size of a woman's breasts. **3** a young woman. [? fig. use of SE hog, to eat greedily]

hogan's alley n. [20C] (US) a mess. [? the cartoon series Hogan's Alley (generally known as The Yellow Kid) created by R.F. Outcault (1863–1928); the storyline is set in the Manhattan slums]

hogan's ghost! excl. [20C] (Aus.) a general expression of amazement. [? an unknown anecdote]

hogan's goat phr. [20C] (US) smelly, malodorous, usu. as stinks like hogan's goat. [a fanciful animal owned by a fictitious Irishman]

hog at/up v. [20C] (W.I.) **1** to speak roughly to, to humiliate verbally. **2** to eat ravenously.

hog-caller n. (US) **1** [20C] a loud and piercing scream, akin to those used by farmers calling their pigs. **2** [1940s–60s] (US) a loudspeaker.

hog dollar n. [20C] (US) $1 (cf. HOG n.¹). [the picture of a pig engraved on the coin]

hog down v. [1960s+] (US) to eat or drink greedily. [the neg. image of the animal]

hog-drunk adj. [1950s–60s] (US) very drunk. [the neg. image of the animal]

hogen-mogen see HOGAN-MAGAN.

hoger see HOGO.

hog-eye/hog's eye n. **1** [1910s–60s] (US) the female genitals. **2** [1990s] the anus. **3** [1990s] the urethral hole in the head of the penis (cf. JAP'S EYE). [supposed resemblance]

hog-fat n. [1920s+] (Aus.) a useless person, a parasite, a 'good-for-nothing'.

hog feed n. [19C+] (US) food considered unfit for human consumption, whether on grounds of taste or actual rottenness (cf. RABBIT FOOD).

hogged up adj. [1990s] of a man, sexually frustrated. [HOG v.¹]

hoggenheimer n. [1910s] (S.Afr.) generic name for the stereotypical Jewish capitalist (esp. as based on Johannesburg); thus Hoggie. [a 1902 stage character, amplified into a cartoon character created c.1913 by D.C. Boonzaaier of Die Burger]

hogger n.¹ [late 19C+] (Irish) a street-corner idler. [the image of the lazy hog]

hogger n.² [1960s+] (US campus) a fat, homely young woman. [HOG n.⁷]

hogger n.³ [1980s+] (US) the penis. [HOG n.⁴]

hoggins/'oggins n. [20C] a due share in pleasure, usu. sexual pleasure. [SE hoggings, i.e. a pig's portion]

hoggish/hoggy adj. [20C] (US) **1** greedy, avaricious. **2** stupid. [the neg. image of the animal]

hog-grubber n. **1** [late 17C–18C] a mean, miserly, sneaking person. **2** [late 17C–19C] a disgusting, filthy person. [HOG n.³/fig use of SE hog, a disgusting person + GRUBBER n.¹, n.²]

hoggy *see* HOGGISH.

hog heaven *n.* [late 19C+] (US) a state of bliss or blissful ignorance (cf. IN HOG HEAVEN AND JOHN CROW PARADISE).

hog in armour *n.* [mid-17C–late 19C] a well-dressed lout, of either sex. [SE *hog*]

hog in togs *n.* [mid-19C] (US) a man-about-town, a loafer with no visible means of support but an endless appetite for good clothes, parties and places of entertainment (cf. BROADWAY JOE; FLASHMAN). [SE *hog* + TOGS. Such a man lived by his wits, often off foolish women, and worked, if at all, as a ROPER n.² or SHILL n.² for a gambling house or similar establishment]

hog island/town/waller *n.* [20C] (US) generic term for any small, impoverished, out-of-the-way settlement (cf. HOBOKEN; PODUNK). [i.e. a 'pigstye']

hog it *v.* [1910s–20s] to sleep deeply, esp. when accompanied by snores. [the snores resemble a hog grunting]

hog-killing *n.* [late 19C–1910s] (US) an unexpected or large financial profit. [the hog, born on the farm, costs nothing; killing it provides food etc]

hog-killing *adj.* [mid-19C–1930s] (US) wild, rowdy, violent or enjoyable. [for ety. *see* HOG-KILLING TIME]

hog-killing time *n.* [20C] (US) a boisterous party, a celebration. [trad. throwing of a party to coincide with the annual killing of a farm's hogs]

hogleg *n.* (US) **1** [19C+] a large handgun. **2** [1940s] the penis (cf. GUN n.²; PEACEMAKER n.¹). [resemblance; the nickname of the Colt Single-Action Army, also known as the *Peacemaker* and launched in 1870]

hogmagundy *n.* [19C] (Scot.) sexual intercourse. [? HOG v.¹ + SE *salmagundi*]

hogmanay *n.* [19C] (Scot.) a promiscuous woman. [? the New Year's celebrations on Hogmanay or the *Hogmanay cake*, trad. given away at Scot. New Year]

hogmarket somebody *n.* [late 19C] (W.I.) an ill-mannered person (cf. HAGARIAN). [they have porcine manners]

hogo/hoag/hoger *adj.* [late 18C+] stinking, esp. of rotting meat. [20C use Ulster only; Fr. *haut goût*, a 'high' flavour, thus also SE *high*]

hog out *v.* [1980s+] (US) to overeat massively. [var. on PIG OUT]

hog pen *n.* [1920s–40s] (US Black) a disgusting or filthy place.

hog ranch *n.* [late 19C+] (US) a brothel (cf. CHICKEN RANCH). [derog. use of SE; ? an actual brothel thus named]

hog-rich *adj.* [1980s] (US) very wealthy. [one has had one's 'snout in the trough']

hog-rubber *n.* [early 17C] a rustic, an ignorant peasant. [lit. 'one who rubs hogs']

hogs *n.* [1970s+] (US Black) the police. [var. on PIG]

hog's eye *see* HOG-EYE.

hog-shearing *n.* [late 17C–18C] futile labour, much effort and little reward. [pvb.: 'Great cry and little wool, as the man said when he sheared his hogs']

hog-stomp *see* HOG-WRESTLE.

hogstye of Venus *n.* [19C] the vagina. [the 'hoggishness' of sexual intercourse]

hog-thomas *n.* [20C] (W.I.) a crude, loud person. [SE *hog* + THOMAS n.²]

hog town *see* HOG ISLAND.

hog up *see* HOG AT.

hog waller *see* HOG ISLAND.

hogwash *n.* **1** [late 18C–early 19C] thick and bad beer. **2** [19C+] nonsense, rubbish (cf. BELLY WASH n.²; PIGSWILL). [fig. uses of 15C *hogwash*, the swill of a brewery, which was given to the pigs]

hogwash! *excl.* [19C] rubbish! [HOGWASH]

hog-whimpering *adj.* [20C] (US) extremely drunk.

hog-wild *adj.* [20C] (US) out of control.

hog-wrestle/-stomp *n.* [20C] (US) a noisy, inelegant, low-class dance.

ho gya/ho-gya/hogya *adj.* [mid–late 19C] (Anglo-Ind.) in trouble, confused, lost for words, esp. in anglicized phr. *that won't hogya*, that won't do. [ety. unknown; ? Hind.]

h.o.h.a. *phr.* [20C] (Irish) a street challenge, esp. from a weaker to a stronger person or group. [abbr. *hit one, hit all*; pron. 'haitch-oh-haitch-ay']

hoha *n.* [1970s] (N.Z.) an annoying person. [HOHA adj.]

hoha *adj.* [mid-19C+] (N.Z.) irritated, tetchy, 'fed up'. [synon. Maori]

ho-hum *adj.* [1920s+] non-committal, inconclusive. [SE *ho-hum*, tedious, quotidian]

hoick *n.* [late 19C+] a sudden jerk, a wrench. [HOICK v.¹]

hoick *v.*¹ [late 19C+] **1** to lift or hoist, with a jerk or snatch. **2** to drag out of. [? SE *hike*, drag]

hoick *v.*² [20C] (Aus.) to spit. [SE *hawk*]

hoist *n.*¹ **1** [early 18C+] (Und.) the act of shoplifting or breaking into houses. **2** [late 18C+] a pickpocket. **3** [1930s+] (US) a hold-up or hijacking. **4** [1960s+] (US) the proceeds of a theft. [HOIST v.¹]

hoist *n.*² (US) **1** [mid-19C–1960s] a kick, a prod, a fall. **2** [1940s] a raise, an increase.

hoist *v.*¹ **1** [18C+] to break into, to rob. **2** [late 18C–early 19C] (Und.) to turn a man upside down and shake him until the money falls out of his pockets (cf. REVERSE). **3** [mid-19C+] (UK/US Und.) to shoplift. **4** [1920s+] (US Und.) to commit an armed robbery or a hold-up. **5** [1970s] (US gambling) to defeat soundly. **6** [late 19C–1910s] (US) to kick or thrash someone. **7** [late 19C–1910s] (US gambling) to raise one's opponent's bet in poker. [SE *hoist*, to raise]

hoist *v.*² [mid-19C+] to drink; thus *hoist/hoist a few*, to have a drink/drinks, *on the hoist*, out drinking. [one *hoists* one's elbow]

hoister *n.*¹ [early 18C+] **1** (orig. Und.) a pickpocket. **2** (Und.) a shoplifter. [HOIST v.¹]

hoister *n.*² [late 19C–1900s] a drunkard. [HOIST v.²]

hoist-in *n.* [mid-19C–1910s] a drink. [HOIST v.²]

hoisting *n.* [mid-19C] shoplifting (cf. HOOK v.¹). [HOIST v.¹]

hoisting engineer *n.* [1920s–30s] (US) a drunkard. [HOIST v.² + pun]

hoist-lay *n.* [mid–late 19C] **1** shoplifting. **2** robbing a man by holding him upside down and shaking the money out of his pockets. [HOIST n.¹ + LAY n.⁴]

hoist-merchant *n.* [19C] a shoplifter. [HOIST n.¹ + MERCHANT]

hoist one *v.* [mid-19C+] to have a drink. [HOIST v.²]

hoist tail *v.* [1940s] (US) to get going, to set off. [reverse anthropomorphism]

hoist the blue flag, to *phr.* [late 18C] to take on the running of a public house (cf. ADMIRAL OF THE BLUE). [the blue apron traditionally worn by the publican]

hoitch *n.* [1980s+] (US campus) an unpopular, unpleasant woman. [HO n.¹ + BITCH n.¹]

hoity-toity *n.* [early 18C–early 19C] a promiscuous woman (cf. HIGHTY-TIGHTY n.). [SE *hoity-toity*, giddy behaviour, flightiness; *see also* ety. of HIGHTY-TIGHTY n.]

hoity-toity *adj.* [early 18C+] aloof, snobbish; also used as excl. to express surprise or disdain. [SE *haughty* + redup, though Weekley notes that the synon. mid-17C phr. *upon the hoyty-toyty* has poss. link to walking on a high wire]

ho-jo *n.* [1960s+] (US) a *Howard Johnson's* motel or a take-away meal from a Howard Johnson's restaurant. [abbr.]

hoke *v.* [1920s+] (US) to flatter, to string along, to hoax. [abbr. HOKUM]

hokey *n.* [late 19C–1910s] a prison. [? rhy. on CHOKY/POKEY]

hokey *adj.* [1920s+] (US) fake, false. [HOKUM]

hokey-pokey *n.*[1] **1** [mid–late 19C+] swindling and other illicit activities. **2** [late 19C+] nonsense. [for ety. *see* HOCUS-POCUS]

hokey-pokey *n.*[2] **1** [late 19C+] a cheap kind of ice-cream, sold by street vendors. **2** (N.Z.) a toffee-like sweet. [street cry 'hokey-poky, a penny a lump!' The ices were sold by Italian organ-grinders at one penny or a halfpenny each, but despite the popular ety., it does not come f. Ital. *o che poco!* 'o how little!']

hokey-pokey *n.*[3] [20C] (US) a local or county prison. [HOKEY n. + POKEY n.]

hokey-pokey *adj.* [late 19C] duplicitous, untrustworthy, swindling. [HOKEY-POKEY n.[1]]

Hokitika swindle *n.* [1930s+] (N.Z.) a bar game, based on betting on a sequence of numbers, e.g. on a £1 note, to determine who will buy the round of drinks. [proper name *Hokitika*, a town on the west coast of New Zealand + SE *swindle*]

hokum *n.* [20C] (orig. theatrical) sentimental or melodramatic speechifying or 'business'; thus used generally. [? HOCUS-POCUS + BUNKUM. Orig. theatrical jargon *hokum*, to use comedy or sentimentality to appeal to an unsophisticated audience]

hokum-snivvy *n.* [20C] (US) a stew or boiled dinner made of unspecified ingredients. [fig. use of HOOKEM-SNIVEY n.]

ho layer *n.* [1980s+] (US Black) **1** one who conducts most of (or all) his sex-life with prostitutes. **2** a womanizer, a ladies' man. [HO n.[1] + LAY v.]

hold *v.*[1] [18C+] to conceive a child. [the embryo is 'held' in the womb]

hold *v.*[2] [20C] (US) to restrain someone, esp. from speech, e.g. 'that'll hold you', that will keep you quiet.

hold *v.*[3] **1** [1930s+] to be in possession of drugs, esp. for selling. **2** [1970s+] (US Und.) to be armed.

hold a candle, to *phr.* [late 19C] to act humbly. [abbr. HOLD A CANDLE TO THE DEVIL phr.[1]]

hold a candle to the devil, to *phr.*[1] [late 18C–early 19C] to be civil to someone out of fear. [the tale of the old woman, who, not knowing whether she was destined for heaven or hell, lit tapers to both St Michael and to the devil in the hope of making friends in both places]

hold a candle to the devil, to *phr.*[2] [19C] to be actively wicked. [lighting a candle as a gesture of worship]

hold aces/every ace/an ace full, to *phr.* [late 19C+] (US) to be in total control. [poker use]

hold a tangi, to *phr.* [20C] (N.Z.) to feel bad about. [Maori *tangi*, a formal lamentation, a dirge]

hold big rocks, to *phr.* [20C] (W.I.) to be left waiting for someone who does not turn up.

hold by the toe, to *phr.* [mid-16C–mid-17C] to hang on to securely (cf. HAVE BY THE TOE).

hold court in the street, to *phr.* [1960s+] (US) to engage in a gun battle on the street (with the implication that one would rather die than face prison).

hold down *v.*[1] **1** [late 19C–1910s] (US) (tramp) to ride atop a freight car. **2** [late 19C+] to keep a job for some time. **3** [1980s+] (US campus) to wait, esp. as imp. *hold down!* (cf. HOLD HARD!).

hold down *v.*[2] [20C] (W.I.) **1** of a woman, to control one's partner, esp. to stop him from having other sexual relationships. **2** of a man, to assault a woman sexually.

hold everything! *see* HOLD IT!

hold foot *v.* [20C] (Ulster) to sustain, fig. to keep up with.

hold hard/on *v.* [mid-18C+] to stop, usu. in imper. *hold hard!* (cf. HOLD DOWN v.[1]). [orig. referring to holding a horse's reins]

holding *adj.* **1** [late 19C+] well-off financially. **2** [1930s+] (drugs) in possession of drugs, esp. for dealing, selling (cf. ANYWHERE). [fig use of SE *hold*/HOLD v.[3]]

hold it!/everything! *excl.* [late 19C+] stop what you're doing, be quiet etc. [the subject is supposed to freeze in position. E.P. suggests orig. painters' jargon]

hold it down! *excl.* [20C] be quiet!

hold light *v.* [20C] to have only a little money, to be out of pocket. [HOLD v.[3] + SE *light*]

hold on *see* HOLD HARD.

hold one's ass, to *phr.* [1960s+] (US) to be patient. [fig. use of ARSE n.[1]]

hold/keep one's guts, to *phr.* [late 19C+] to remain silent under questioning.

hold one's hair on *see* KEEP ONE'S HAIR ON.

hold one's head, to *phr.* [20C] (US Black) to be patient, to restrain oneself. [? the holding of a horse's head]

hold one's horses, to *phr.* [mid-19C+] (orig. US) to slow down, to show restraint, often as excl. (cf. HOLD YOUR POTATO).

hold one's mud, to *phr.* [1960s+] (US Black) to keep one's own counsel, to keep quiet.

hold one's noise, to *phr.* [mid-19C] to stop talking, esp. as imper. *hold your noise!* shut up!

hold one's own *v.* [20C] to masturbate. [pun]

hold one's water, to *phr.* [20C] to be patient, to remain calm, esp. in imper. *hold your water!* calm down! (cf. HOLD ONE'S HORSES; HOLD THAT MULE; HOLD YOUR GALLUSES; HOLD YOUR KITTIES; HOLD YOUR PANTS ON; LOOK TO ONE'S WATER). [fig. ref. to restraining oneself from urinating]

hold one's whid, to *phr.* [mid-19C] to be quiet. [WHID]

hold onto the slack, to *phr.* [mid-19C] to be lazy, to skulk around. [naut. imagery, holding the slack of a sail requires no real effort]

hold onto your hat! *see* HANG ONTO YOUR HAT!

hold out *v.* [mid-19C] (US) to live, to reside.

hold-out artist *n.* [1950s+] a gambler or cheat who will never admit how much money they have made out of a game. [SE *hold out* + ARTIST n.[2]]

hold out on *v.* [20C] (orig. US) to withhold something from someone.

hold over someone *v.* [mid–late 19C] (US) to have an advantage over someone.

hold paper on, to *phr.* [1960s+] to stand as a creditor to someone. [PAPER n.[1]]

hold someone's hand, to *phr.* [1930s+] to give comfort or moral support to someone, to back someone up.

hold someone's hind leg, to *phr.* [19C] (US) to act as best man at a wedding. [? the holding of a horse's hind leg to restrain or steady it during mating]

hold someone with their bill in the water, to *phr.* [late 16C–late 17C] to keep someone in suspense.

hold sticks to/with *v.* [19C] to compete on equal terms.

hold that mule! *excl.* [20C] be patient, remain calm (cf. HOLD ONE'S WATER).

hold the baby, to *phr.* [late 19C+] to be left to clear up a problem, to take an unpleasant responsibility (cf. GIVE SOMEONE THE DOG TO HOLD).

hold the bag, to *phr.* **1** [mid-18C+] to take responsibility; esp. (Und.) for a villain to be left with full responsibility for a crime in which his associates have not been legally involved. **2** [1950s] (drugs) to be in possession of a quantity of drugs, to deal drugs. [SE *bag*, but note BAG n.[8]; the 18C–mid-19C use is properly 'give one the bag to hold' but the meaning is identical]

hold the blow! *excl.* [18C+] be quiet! (cf. HOLD YOUR JAW!). [BLOW v.[1] n.[1]]

hold the bold, to *phr.* [1990s] to masturbate.

hold the can, to *phr.* [1920s+] to take responsibility, usu. unwanted (cf. HOLD THE BABY). [var. on CARRY THE CAN FOR]

hold/mind the fort, to *phr.* [1930s+] to look after, to take care of, esp. in another person's absence.

hold the lantern, to *phr.* [20C] (Aus.) to stand by relaxing while another person actually works. [song lyric 'I hold the lantern while mother chops the wood']

hold the mayo, to *phr.* [1990s] to masturbate. [the resemblance of semen to *mayo(nnaise)* + pun on short-order cooking phr. *hold the mayo*, don't add mayonnaise]

hold them in the road *phr.* [20C] (US) goodbye, safe journey. [orig. use as directed to the driver of a team of animals]

hold the phone, to *phr.* [20C] to wait, to delay, to 'hang on', esp. as imper. *hold the phone!* [telephone imagery]

hold the sausage hostage, to *phr.* [1990s] to masturbate (cf. ACCOST THE OSCAR MEYER).

hold tight! *excl.* [1910s+] stop! don't move! [orig. a bus- or tram-driver's shout]

hold-up *n.* **1** [late 19C–1950s] (US) an instance of extortion. **2** [late 19C+] (orig. US) an armed robbery or robber. [HOLD UP v.[1]]

hold up *v.*[1] **1** [mid-19C+] to commit an armed robbery. **2** [late 19C] to cheat. **3** [late 19C–1950s] (US) to demand, esp. to charge an exorbitant price. [the demand that victims should hold up their hands]

hold up *v.*[2] [mid–late 19C] (US) to give in, submit, surrender. [16C Scot. use]

hold up *v.*[3] [mid-19C+] (joc.) to lean against, to support. [the pretence of 'holding up' the structure against which one leans]

hold up one's clothes/dress at, to *phr.* [20C] (W.I.) of a woman, to raise her skirts and expose her buttocks as a gesture of derision.

hold with *v.* [late 19C+] to agree with.

hold your ... for combs. with *hold your ... see also* combs. with HOLD'S ONES ... .

hold your galluses, to *phr.* [20C] to be patient, to remain calm (cf. HOLD ONE'S WATER). [SAmE *galluses*, suspenders (UK braces)]

hold/stop your jaw! *excl.* [18C+] be quiet! (cf. HOLD THE BLOW; HOLD YOUR MOUTH!).

hold your kitties, to *phr.* [20C] to be patient, to remain calm (cf. HOLD ONE'S WATER).

hold your mouth! *excl.* [18C+] be quiet! (cf. HOLD YOUR JAW!).

hold your pants on, to *phr.* [20C] to be patient, to remain calm (cf. GET ONE'S KNICKERS IN A TWIST).

hold your potato, to *phr.* [mid-19C+] (orig. US) to slow down, to show restraint (cf. HOLD ONE'S HORSES). [ety. unknown]

hold your shirt! *excl.* [20C] calm down! (cf. KEEP ONE'S SHIRT ON).

hold your whiz! *excl.* [late 19C–1920s] be quiet! shut up! [WHIZ n.[1]]

hole *n.*[1] **1** [late 14C+] the anus. **2** [late 16C+] the vagina (cf. BLACK HOLE n.[1]). **3** [mid-19C+] the mouth, esp. in imper. *shut your hole!* (cf. BACON HOLE). **4** [20C] sexual intercourse; thus *get one's hole*, to have sex. **5** [1940s+] (US) a woman or a prostitute. **6** [1960s+] (US) a passive homosexual man (cf. HOLER).

hole *n.*[2] **1** [mid-16C+] (prison) the punishment cells. **2** [early 17C+] derog. description of any small, dirty, clandestine place, presumably one where illegal occupations were planned or carried out (cf. DIVE). **3** [1920s+] (US campus) a student's room. **4** [1930s+] (US) a subway station. **5** [1940s+] (US) a space or slot. [the orig. Hole was found in the Counter or Compter debtors' prison in Wood Street, London, where it was the nickname for that cell, a notably squalid one, in which the poorest prisoners were confined. The rich enjoyed the 'masters' side', while the middle classes went to the

'knights' side'; all were entered in the prison's Black Book. William Fennor's *Counter's Commonwealth* (1617) gives an extensive survey of life within the prison]

hole, the *n.*[3] [20C] (US) euph. for hell.

hole *n.*[4] [1930s] (tramp) a shilling (5p).

hole *n.*[5] [1930s+] a difficult situation, a fix, a scrape, a mess.

hole and corner work *n.* [mid–late 19C] sexual intercourse. [HOLE n.[1] + pun]

hole card *n.* [1920s+] (orig. US) a secret, which can be either a weakness that, once discovered, can be exploited, or a hidden strength; thus *peep one's hold car*, to elicit a person's secrets. [poker jargon *hole card*; the card that, in 5-card stud, is dealt face down]

holed *adj.* [late 19C+] of a man, enjoying sexual intercourse. [HOLE n.[1] (2)]

hole-filler *n.* [1990s] a male homosexual. [HOLE n.[1] (1) + SE *filler*]

hole/hole out in one *v.* [1910s+] (Aus.) to become pregnant after one's first sexual intercourse, esp. one's marriage night. [golfing imagery]

hole in one! *excl.* [1970s+] absolutely correct! [golf imagery]

hole in one's head *phr.* [1920s–50s] (US) a lack of common sense, usu. in phr. *need something/someone like a hole in the head*, used of something of no use whatsoever. [joc. use of SE. but note Yid. *ich darf es vi a loch in kop*, 'I need that like a hole in the head']

hole in the ground *n.* [20C] £1 sterling. [rhy. sl.]

hole in the wall *n.* **1** [19C] (US) an illicit liquor store or bar (cf. BLIND PIG). **2** [mid-19C+] a small, insignificant, remote place. **3** [1930s+] a tiny, cramped apartment. **4** [1980s+] an automatic teller machine (ATM), installed in the external wall of a bank or building society branch. [either f. the holes in the walls of English debtor's prisons, through which the inmates could obtain supplies and money to alleviate their situation, or f. the small shops and similar establishments found in the broad stone walls of fortified medieval cities. *Hole in the wall* became a generic term, although the US West had its *Hole in the Wall*, an outlaw hideaway in the gorges and cliffs that straddle the Wyoming, Colorado and Utah state lines (a sometime refuge for Butch Cassidy and Sundance Kid and the real-life Wild Bunch), while 1860s New York City boasted the *Hole in the Wall* on Water Street, where its proprietor, Gallus Meg (a monstrous Englishwoman), bit the ears off ill-behaved customers and preserved her trophies in a pickle jar displayed behind the bar]

hole in the wall *adj.* [19C+] (orig. US) second-class, inferior. [HOLE IN THE WALL n.]

holemonger *see* HOLER.

hole of content *n.* [19C] the vagina (cf. BLACK HOLE n.[1]). [pun on SE *whole of content*]

hole of holes *n.* 19C] the vagina (cf. BLACK HOLE n.[1]).

hole out in one *see* HOLE IN ONE.

holer/holemonger *n.* **1** [16C+] a womanizer, a successful seducer. **2** [19C] a male prostitute. **3** [19C] a pimp (cf. MEAT-MERCHANT). **4** [late 19C] a prostitute. [13C–15C SE *holour*, a fornicator or whoremonger and, as such, applied to men only. HOLE n.[1] + SE sfx. *-monger*]

-holer *sfx.* [20C] (US) applied to an outside lavatory or privy and denoting the number of seats available, e.g. *one-holer, two-holer* etc.

holes and poles *n.* [1960s+] (US campus) sex education classes. [HOLE n.[1] + POLE n.]

hole time *n.* [20C] (US prison) time spent in the punishment cells. [HOLE n.[2] (1) + TIME n.[1]]

hole up *n.* [late 19C+] a hide-out. [HOLE UP v.]

hole up *v.* [late 19C+] **1** to settle. **2** to take up residence, with a poss. but not invariable implication of hiding away or taking refuge. [SE *hole up*, (of an animal) to retire to a hole for hibernation or security]

holey dollar *see* HOLY DOLLAR.

holier-than-thou *adj.* [1910s+] sanctimonious.

holing *n.* [19C] womanizing. [HOLE n.¹ (4)]

hol' it dung! *excl.* [1980s+] (W.I./UK Black teen) keep it a secret, keep it quiet, take care. [Black pron. of HOLD IT DOWN!]

holla/holler boys, holla/holler *n.* [late 19C+] a collar. [rhy. sl.]

holland *phr.* [1940s+] an affectionate message, written on envelopes of love letters (cf. SWALK). [abbr. *here our love lies and never dies*]

hollanders *n.* [late 19C] (south London) a pointed waxed moustache. [Mr W. Holland, lessee of Covent Garden, who had 'the finest pair of black-waxed sheeny moustaches ever beheld' (Ware)]

Holland tape *n.* [mid-18C] gin (cf. BIT OF TAPE).

Hollard Street *n.* [1940s–70s] (S.Afr.) the Johannesburg Stock Exchange (cf. DIAGONAL STREET). [its address]

holler *n.* [late 19C+] (US) **1** a complaint, a fuss. **2** (Und.) information given to the police. [HOLLER v.]

holler *v.* **1** [mid-19C–1920s] to surrender, to admit defeat (cf. HOLLER CALF-ROPE). **2** [late 19C+] to shout, to scream, to complain. **3** [1980s+] (US Black) to ridicule, to abuse. [SE *holler*, to scream, shout or complain]

holler bloody murder *see* HOLLER MURDER.

holler boys, holler *see* HOLLA BOYS, HOLLA.

holler/say calf-rope, to *phr.* [19C] (US; orig. West, South) to give in, to surrender, to admit defeat, esp. in children's games.

holler copper *v.* [1930s+] to inform (cf. CRY COPPER). [SE *holler* + COPPER n.³]

holler/shout for murder, to *phr.* [20C] (W.I.) to make a loud noise, to shout in order to attract attention.

holler murder/bloody murder *v.* [mid-19C+] (US) to raise an outcry.

holler New York, to *phr.* [1960s+] (US) to vomit. [echoic]

holler uncle *see* CRY UNCLE.

hollow *n.* [20C] (US) in a variety of combs, describing an area of a town; usu. combined with a ref. to poor or foreign groups, e.g. *dead man's hollow, frog hollow, Irish hollow, piggy hollow, punkin hollow, skunk hollow, sleepy hollow, smoky hollow, snuff hollow*.

hollow *adv.* [mid-17C+] completely, utterly, esp. in phr. *beat hollow*, to trounce completely.

Holloway *n.* [mid-19C–1920s] the vagina (cf. BLACK HOLE n.¹). [pun on 'hollow way']

Holloway castle *n.* [late 19C] Holloway prison (cf. NORTH CASTLE). [before its mid-20C remodelling the gateway of the original Holloway prison (now England's main women's prison) had 'castellated' architecture, copied in part from Caesar's Tower, Warwick Castle. The pub across the road is still called the Holloway Castle]

Holloway, Middlesex *n.* [mid-19C–1900s] the stomach. [Holloway, London N7/N19; puns on both words]

hollowhead *n.* [mid-19C+] (US) an idiot. [SE *hollow* + sfx. -HEAD (1)]

hollow leg *n.* [1920s+] (US) a capacity for heavy drinking, a heavy drinker; thus *hollow-legged*, used of a serious drinker.

hollow log *n.* [1970s] (Aus.) a racing dog. [rhy. sl.]

Hollyweird *n.* [1970s+] (US) Hollywood, California. [the neg. image of the film capital]

Hollywood hustler *n.* [1950s+] (US) a male homosexual. [SE *Hollywood*, seen as a 20C 'Sodom' + HUSTLER]

Hollywood stew *n.* [20C] (US prison) creamed cod fish.

Hollywood stop *see* CALIFORNIA STOP.

Hollywood swoop *n.* [1970s+] (US Black) an automobile manoeuvre whereby one cuts in front of another vehicle,

stopping one's own car and thus forcing the other vehicle to halt. [such manoeuvres are reminiscent of, or learned from, film or TV police chase sequences]

holmes! *excl.* [1980s+] (US campus) affectionate diminutive of HOMEBOY (cf. HOMES). [note also note NO SHIT, SHERLOCK!]

hols *n.* [20C] holidays. [abbr.]

holstein *n.* [1950s+] (Can.) a black and white police car. [the colours of *Holstein* cattle]

holus-bolus *adv.* [mid–late 19C] in a mess, jumbled up. [mock Latin or a ponderous pun on Gk. *holos bolos*, the whole lump]

holy alls *phr.* [20C] (Irish) the end result.

holy balls! *excl.* [1940s+] (orig. US) an excl. of shock, surprise, annoyance etc. [SE *holy* + BALLS n.¹]

holy bilge water!/cats!/Egypt!/gee!/gosh!/heck!/hoptoads!/snakes! *excl.* [20C] a mild excl. of surprise, dismay, alarm. [despite the use of *holy*, none is blasphemous]

Holy City *n.* [1900s] (Aus.) Adelaide, South Australia. [the city's many churches; thus the alternative nickname the *city of churches*]

Holy Cod *n.* [late 19C–1920s] Good Friday. [a mockery of religious fish-eating]

holy cow! *excl.* [1920s+] (orig. US) an excl. of surprise (cf. HOLY CROW!).

holy crap! *excl.* [1960s+] (US) a general excl. of amazement, surprise, annoyance etc. [SE *holy* + CRAP n.³]

holy cripes! *excl.* [20C] a general excl. of surprise, alarm etc. [SE *holy* + CRIPES!]

holy crow! *excl.* [1960s+] (US) a phr. of amazement, surprise (cf. HOLY COW!).

holy/holey dollar *n.* [mid-19C] (Aus.) a silver dollar out of which a circle has been punched (cf. DUMP n.¹).

holy dooley! *excl.* [20C] (Aus.) a general expression of surprise. [? link to GIVE SOMEONE LARRY DOOLEY]

holy dorito *n.* [1990s] the vagina (cf. APPLE n.¹⁰). [brandname of the US snack food]

holy Egypt! *see* HOLY BILGE WATER!

holy father *n.* [late 18C–19C] 'A butcher's boy of St Patrick's Market, Dublin or any other Irish blackguard' (Grose, 1785). [SE *holy father*, the Pope]

holy fly! *excl.* [20C] (Irish) a mild oath.

holy friar *n.* [20C] a liar. [rhy. sl.; never truncated]

holy fuck! *excl.* [1940s+] (orig. US) a general excl. used to express surprise, astonishment. [SE *holy* + FUCK!]

holy gee! *see* HOLY BILGE WATER!

holy ghost *n.* **1** [20C] (Aus.) the post, the mail. **2** [20C] the post, i.e. the start-line for a horserace. **3** [1950s+] toast. [rhy. sl.]

holy ghosts *n.* [20C] (Aus.) fence posts. [rhy. sl.]

holy ghost shop *n.* [late 19C] a church.

holy gosh! *see* HOLY BILGE WATER!

holy ground, the *n.* [late 18C+] (orig. US) a red-light district or slum (cf. HOLY LAND). [SE *holy ground*, an area within church jurisdiction in which villains or persecuted people could gain sanctuary. The slums and criminal ghettos were often impervious to the law]

holy heck! *see* HOLY BILGE WATER!

holy herb/weed *n.* [1950s+] marijuana (cf. HERB n.¹). [the use of marijuana as sacramental by Rastafarians]

holy hoptoads! *see* HOLY BILGE WATER!

Holy James Street! *see* JAMES STREET!

holy joe *n.* [mid-19C+] **1** anyone of a religious bent. **2** a clergyman, esp. in the services or in a prison. **3** a prudish, sanctimonious, narrow-minded puritan (cf. JOEY n.²). [orig. naut. jargon]

holy kicker! *excl.* [late 19C+] an excl. of surprise, shock or wonder (cf. HOLY SMOKE!).

holy lamb *n.* [late 18C–19C] a complete and utter villain. [a pun on Lat. *agnus dei*, the lamb of God, used as the first words of the Catholic mass. The term lamb was given to the particularly violent troops led by the soldier of fortune Colonel Percy Kirke in 1684–6. Their flag carried an image of the paschal lamb, known in heraldry as the *holy lamb*, and the troops were known as 'Kirke's lambs'. Lambs also referred to gangs of thugs used to intimidate voters at 19C elections, e.g. the 'Nottingham lambs', which flourished 1860–70]

holy land *n.* **1** [mid-19C] the area around St Giles, London, including Seven Dials (cf. HOLY GROUND; PALESTINE IN LONDON; ROOKERY). **2** [late 19C] any area of a city populated by or frequented by Jews. **3** [late 19C] (Aus.) Tasmania.

holy mackerel! *see* HOLY SMOKE!

holy/old mackinaw! *excl.* [1900s–70s] (US) a mild excl.

holy Mary *n.* [1950s+] (Irish) of men or women, a religious hypocrite, one who pretends to great and showy religiosity.

holy moly! *excl.* [1940s+] (US juv.) a general excl. of amazement or shock. [var. on HOLY MOSES! The catchphrase favoured by the comic-book character Captain Marvel]

holy Moses *n.* [early 17C] a cuckold. [paintings of Moses displaying him with a part-halo, the curves of which resemble horns protruding from his head]

holy Moses! *excl.* [early 17C+] a general excl. of amazement or shock (cf. HOLY MOLY!).

holy nail *n.* [late 19C+] legal bail. [rhy. sl.]

holy poker *n.* [mid-19C+] the penis.

holy poker! *excl.* [20C] (Irish) a mild oath. [the instrument of punishment used in Purgatory]

holy roller *n.* (US) **1** [mid-19C+] a member of a Pentecostal church. **2** [1970s+] a sanctimonious person or a religious fundamentalist. [their physical twitchings and 'rollings' at the height of their apparent religious ecstasy]

holy shit! *excl.* [1950s+] a general excl. of surprise or astonishment. [SHIT n.[1]]

holy show *n.* [20C] (Irish) the cause of a scandal or embarrassment, esp. in phr. *make a holy show of oneself*, to behave in such a manner.

holy show! *excl.* [mid-19C–1900s] a mild oath. [? the resurrection of Christ]

holy smoke *n.* [20C] **1** coke, the fuel. **2** Coke, the drink Coca-Cola. [rhy. sl.]

holy smoke!/mackerel! *excl.* [late 19C+] an excl. of surprise, shock, wonder or amazement.

holy snakes! *see* HOLY BILGE WATER!

holy terror *n.* [late 19C+] a person of exasperating habits or manners.

holy water *n.*[1] [20C] water that has been laced with whisky.

holy water *n.*[2] [20C] a daughter. [rhy. sl.]

holy-water sprinkler/stick *n.* [19C] a spiked club. [it sprinkled not water but blood]

holy weed *see* HOLY HERB.

holy Willie *n.* [20C] a sanctimonious, hypocritically pious person. [the subject of Robert Burns's poem 'Holy Willie's Prayer' (1785)]

hombre *n.*[1] **1** [mid-19C+] a man. **2** [1990s] (US campus) a male friend. [Sp. *hombre*, man, but widely popularized through 20C spread of the Hollywood Western film]

hombre *n.*[2] [1980s+] (drugs) heroin (cf. BOY n.[5]; HIM n.[2]). [Sp. *hombre*, a man]

hombrecitos *n.* [1960s+] (drugs) psilocybin. [Sp. *hombrecitos*, little men; ? those that one sees after taking the hallucinogen]

home *n.* **1** [1940s+] (US Black) a friend, often used in direct address. **2** [1980s+] (US campus) person from the same home town, friend (cf. HOMES; HOMEY n.[3]). [abbr. HOMEBOY]

home and dried/dry *phr.* [late 19C+] **1** safe and sound. **2** accomplished without having to have made any real effort. [image of a car driven home and washed/covered up]

home and hosed/home with a rug on *phr.* [1940s+] (Aus./N.Z.) **1** safe and sound. **2** accomplished without having to have made any real effort.

homebake *n.*[1] [1980s+] (drugs) phencyclidine (cf. ACE n.[3]).

homebake/bake *n.*[2] [1980s+] (Aus./N.Z. drugs) the manufacture of homemade heroin or morphine from codeine phosphate. [HOMEBAKE v.]

homebake/bake *v.* [1980s+] (Aus./N.Z. drugs) to manufacture homemade heroin or morphine from codeine phosphate; thus *homebaker*, one who does this; *homebaking*, the process. [the use of heat in the manufacturing process]

homebird *n.* **1** [mid–late 19C] a hen-pecked husband. **2** [1950s+] (orig. US) one who prefers their home to venturing anywhere more exciting or challenging.

home biscuit *n.* [1980s+] (US campus) a friend.

homeboy *n.* **1** [late 19C+] someone who stays mainly at home. **2** [late 19C+] a neighbourhood person (cf. HOMEGIRL). **3** [late 19C+] a good friend (compare Yid. *landsman*). **4** [late 19C+] a naïve person, newly arrived in the city from the countryside (cf. DOWN-HOMER; HOME FOLKS). **5** [1950s+] (S.Afr.) someone who came to the city from the same rural or provincial area as oneself. **6** [1950s–60s] (Irish) an ex-inmate of a religious institution. **7** [1970s+] (US Black) a young Black or Hispanic member of a street gang (cf. BOY n.[7]). **8** [1980s+] (US Black) a fellow Black person. [now almost exclusively a Black term, *homeboy* orig. in the South *c.*1930 and was used by all races before it migrated, with the Black population, to the urban ghettos]

homechop *n.* [1980s+] (US campus) a friend, usu. of opposite sex. [? SE *home* + *lambchop*]

home cooking *n.* [1930s–40s] (US Black) anything outstanding, wonderful or first-rate. [the presumed excellence of home cookery]

homee *see* OMEE.

home folks *n.* [19C+] (US) **1** one's immediate or extended family. **2** people from the area in which one grew up, from one's home community (cf. DOWN-HOMER; HOMEBOY).

home for lost frogs/fogs *n.* [1930s+] England. [its damp and misty climate, although ? ref. to FROGS, e.g. the French who are just across the Channel]

homegirl *n.* [1930s+] (orig. US Black) **1** a woman from one's home town or neighbourhood (cf. HOMEBOY). **2** a close female friend.

homegrown *n.* [1960s+] (drugs) marijuana that has been grown at home (cf. HOMESTONE). [such marijuana was usu. seen as inferior before the introduction of new techniques, e.g. hydroponics, that have revolutionized the former cottage industry over the last 20 years]

home guard *n.* [20C] (US) **1** a regular worker, one who stays on one job in one locality rather than a transient (cf. BOOMER n.[2]). **2** a beggar or tramp who stays in one place.

homeland *n.* [1960s+] (US Black) the Black area of a city (cf. HOMEBOY).

homely as a basket of chips *phr.* [early 19C] (US) plain (cf. GRIN LIKE A BASKET OF CHIPS).

home on the pig's back *phr.* [1910s+] (Aus./N.Z.) very contented, happily or successfully placed, having arrived at a successful conclusion.

home on the range *n.* [20C] (Aus.) small change. [rhy. sl.]

home piece *n.* [1970s+] (US) **1** (prison) a fellow inmate who was already a friend before imprisonment. **2** a friend (cf. HOMEBOY).

homer *n.* (US) **1** [late 19C+] in sports, a referee who favours the home team. **2** [1980s+] a friend (cf. HOMEBOY).

home rule n. [late 19C–1900s] whisky. [play on FENIAN n.[1]]

home rulers n. [late 19C] baked potatoes, cooked and sold in the street. [? the stereotypical Irish diet of potatoes. The period saw a major agitation by nationalists in favour of Irish Home Rule]

home run n. [1960s+] (US) sexual intercourse. [baseball imagery]

homes n. [1930s+] (US) affectionate diminutive of HOMEBOY, usually as a term of address, e.g. *Hey, homes ... .*

home skillet n. [1980s+] (orig. US Black) a fellow Black person. [var. on HOMEBOY]

home slice n. [1990s] (US Black teen) a fellow Black person. [var. on HOMEBOY]

home squeeze n. **1** [1920s+] (orig. US) one's most favourite person, usu. a lover (cf. MAIN SQUEEZE). **2** [1980s+] (orig. US Black) one's wife or regular partner. [SE *home* + SQUEEZE n.[6]]

homestone n. [1980s+] (US drugs) marijuana grown on private premises (cf. HOMEGROWN). [SE *home* + STONED]

home sweet home n. [late 19C–1920s] the vagina.

home with a rug on see HOME AND HOSED.

homework n. [1930s+] (orig. US) **1** petting, necking. **2** a girl-friend.

homey/homie n.[1] [mid-19C–1910s] (N.Z.) a native-born Briton who emigrates to New Zealand (cf. HOMIE n.[2]). [SE *home country*]

homey n.[2] see OMEE.

homey n.[3] see HOMIE n.[3].

homey n.[4] [1980s+] (orig. US Black) an affectionate dimin. of HOMEBOY (cf. HOMIE n.[2]).

homey adj. see HOMY.

homey don't play dat phr. [1990s] (US campus) a phr. indicating one's refusal to cooperate with, consent to or accept something. [the catchphrase of the character Homey the Clown in the TV show *In Living Color*]

homicide n. **1** [1950s] (US) someone or something formidable. **2** [1990s] (US drugs) a cocktail of heroin and/or cocaine plus various prescription drugs, incl. scopolamine, used to increase the heart-rate, a sea-sickness remedy and dextromethorphan, usually used as a cough medicine. The effects are generally negative, including paranoia, hallucinations and memory loss, and can lead to death, usu. by heart attack.

homie n.[1] see HOMEY n.[1].

homie n.[2] [20C] (US) **1** a *homosexual*. **2** an affectionate dimin. of HOMEBOY (cf. HOMEY n.[4]). [abbr.]

homie/homey n.[3] [1920s+] (Aus./N.Z.) an Englishman; a British immigrant, esp. one newly arrived (cf. HOMEY n.[1]).

hominy gazette n. [1950s+] (Aus. prison) internal prison rumours (cf. BUSH TELEGRAPH). [the main constituent of prison meals. Note Aus. prison sl. *hominy bus*, the bus that runs between Darlinghurst Prison and Long Bay Prison, *hominy pimples*, an itchy rash, prevalent in summer, which prisoners ascribe to the monotonous diet, *hominy cock/prick*, poss. real, poss. fantasy 'penis' made by stuffing a sock with hominy and used by women prisoners for masturbation]

homo n.[1] [mid-19C] a man (cf. OMEE). [Ling. Fr.]

homo n.[2] **1** [1920s+] a male homosexual. **2** [1980s+] (US campus) a weakling, an inadequate (cf. GAY n.[2]). [abbr. of SE; in (2) no specific sexuality is implied]

homo adj. [1920s+] homosexual. [HOMO n.[2] (2)]

homoney n. [18C] **1** a woman. **2** a wife. [Lat. *homo*, a man]

homosexual adj. [1980s+] (US campus) eccentric, odd, strange (cf. GAY adj.[4]; HOMO n.[2]). [no specific sexuality is implied]

homy/homey adj. [mid-19C] feeling like home, thus comfortable, secure.

hon n. [20C] (US) a general term of endearment, affection. [abbr. HONEY n.[4]]

honch n.[1] [1970s] (US drugs) heroin.

honch n.[2] [1990s] **1** an eccentric. **2** a cripple. [SE *hunch*]

honched adj. [1990s] unwell, unhappy. [HONCH n.[2]]

honch-head n. [1990s] a fool, an eccentric. [HONCH + sfx. -HEAD (1)]

honcho n. **1** [1940s+] (orig. US) a leader, employer, boss, the head person of any job or other situation. **2** [1960s+] (US) a fellow man. [Jap. *han'cho*, group leader; imported to West by US forces in Korea]

honcho v. [1940s+] (orig. US) to lead, to direct others in a task or plan. [HONCHO n.]

hondoo n. [1910s] (US) the vagina. [ety. unknown]

hone n. [17C] the vagina (cf. GRIND n.[3]; WHETTING STONE). [SE *hone*, a whetstone used to grind knives]

hone v. [20C] (US) **1** to pine for, to yearn after. **2** to look for, to search out. [OF *hogner*, *hoigner*, to grumble, mutter or murmur, to whine like a child, or dog]

hone out v. [1980s+] (US campus) to eat voraciously. [? one has *honed* the edge of one's appetite]

honest? excl. [mid-19C+] do you really mean it? are you joking? etc.

honest Injun/Indian excl. [mid-19C+] (orig. US) on my honour. [the term was orig. sarcastic (Indians being seen as essentially dishonest) but became used at face value, esp. by children]

honest john n. [late 19C+] (US) an honest citizen, a hard-working person. [SE *honest* + JOHN n.[1]]

honestly! excl. [20C+] an excl. of annoyance, exasperation.

honest-to-God/-goodness adj. [1910s+] genuine, sincere.

honest to John phr. [1950s+] (US) honestly, sincerely. [euph. var. on HONEST-TO-GOD]

honest trout n. [early 18C] an honest, respectable woman (cf. TRUSTY TROUT). [SE *honest* + TROUT n.[2]]

hone the cone, to phr. [1990s] to masturbate.

honey n.[1] [19C+] (US) one whose personality makes them hard to associate with but who has no appreciation of the fact. [abbr. *she's a honey but the bees don't know it*]

honey n.[2] [19C+] semen (cf. BABY GRAVY).

honey n.[3] [mid-19C–1910s] (US) **1** money. **2** (drugs) currency.

honey n.[4] **1** [late 19C+] (orig. US) anyone or anything good of its kind. **2** [20C] an attractive young woman (cf. BANANA n.[2]). **3** [20C] a mistress. **4** [1970s+] (US campus) a female term for an endearing, attractive man.

honey/honeydew n.[5] [1920s+] (US) human excrement (cf. HONEY-BUCKET; HONEY-CART; HONEY-DIPPER; HONEY HOUSE; HONEY-WAGON).

honey n.[6] [1920s] money. [rhy. sl. *pot o' honey*]

honey/honey up v. [19C+] to cajole, to flatter, to sweet talk. [abbr. HONEYFUGGLE v. (4)]

honey altar n. [1990s] the vagina, esp. in context of cunnilingus (cf. APPLE n.[10]).

honey around see HONEY UP v.[2].

honey-baby n. [1940s–50s] a general term of affection, usu. for a girl or woman.

honey blunts n. [1990s] (drugs) marijuana cigars sealed with honey. [SE *honey* + BLUNT n.[2]]

honey-bucket/honeypot n. [1930s+] a bucket used for night-soil. [HONEY n.[5]]

honey-bum n. [1940s–50s] (Aus.) a passive homosexual. [SE *honey* + BUM n.[2]]

honey-bun/-bunch n. [20C] a general term of affection.

honey-cart n. [1920s+] (US) a vehicle for collecting human excrement. [HONEY n.[5]; the term has been adopted by airlines, railway companies and other owners of public transport that provide mobile lavatory facilities]

honey-chile n. [1920s+] (US) a general term of affection, usu. in Southern and/or Black use. [SE *honey-child*]

honey-cooler *n.* [mid-19C–1900s] (US) an extraordinary person or thing. [ety. unknown]

honeydew/honey dip *n.*[1] [20C] (US) whisky.

honeydew *n.*[2] *see* HONEY n.[5].

honeydew *n.*[3] *see* HONEY-DO.

honey-digger *see* HONEY-DIPPER.

honey dip *n.*[1] *see* HONEYDEW n.[1].

honey dip *n.*[2] [1990s] (US Black) a pretty young woman with a golden-brown complexion.

honey-dipper/-digger *n.* [1920s+] a latrine cleaner; thus *honey-dipping*, the removal of excrement or sewage (cf. GOLD-FINDER). [HONEY n.[5]]

honey-do/honeydew *n.* [1990s] (US) a household chore. [domestic imperatives, starting with *Honey, do ...*]

honey-fall *n.* [mid-19C] a piece of good luck.

honeyfoogler *n.* [19C+] (US) a flatterer. [HONEYFUGGLE v. (4)]

honeyfuck *n.* [1950s+] **1** a very sexy woman. **2** a prepubescent girl, viewed as a sex object. [HONEYFUCK v.]

honeyfuck *v.* [1950s+] (US) **1** to have sexual intercourse in innocent or idyllic circumstances. **2** to have sex with a pre-pubescent girl. [HONEY n.[4] + FUCK v.[1]]

honeyfuggle *v.* (US) **1** [early 19C+] to swindle, to trick, to fool. **2** [19C] to cuddle up to, whether physically or figuratively; vars. include *honeyfackle, honeyfugle, honeyfogle*. **3** [19C] to lure, to entice. **4** [19C–1940s] to sweet talk, to flatter. **5** [1950s+] to have sex with a pre-pubescent girl (cf. HONEYFUCK v.). [dial. *connyfogle*, to entice by flattery, to hood-wink or dial. *gallyfuggle* to deceive or trick]

honey hill *n.* [20C] (US) the poor area of a town. [? HONEY n.[5]]

honey house *n.* [20C] (US) a privy or outside lavatory. [HONEY n.[5] + SE *house*]

honey it up *see* HONEY UP v.[2].

honeymoon *n.* [1950s+] (drugs) the early use of heroin, before actual addiction, during which period the user can stop without any real physical or mental pain.

honeymoon cystitis *n.* [1960s+] a vaginal infection that supposedly stems from intensive intercourse, which, in turn, is supposedly the staple of honeymooning couples.

honey oil *n.* [1990s] (drugs) ketamine, an inhalant (cf. K n.[4]).

honeypot *n.*[1] [early 18C+] the vagina (cf. APPLE n.[10]; BEEHIVE; HIVE). [Puxley (1992) suggests rhy. sl. *honey pot* = TWAT, but the chronology militates against this]

honeypot *n.*[2] *see* HONEY-BUCKET.

honeypot *n.*[3] [1930s+] (Aus.) jumping into a swimming pool with one's knees drawn up and one's hands clasped around them.

honey-thighs *n.* [1920s+] (orig. US) a general term of affection from a man to a woman.

honey up *v.*[1] *see* HONEY V.

honey up/around/it up *v.*[2] [20C] (US) to toady to, to act the sycophant, to flatter (cf. HONEY V.; HONEYFUGGLE).

honey-wagon *n.* [20C] (US) **1** a manure cart used for cleaning out barns. **2** a garbage wagon. **3** (US) a vehicle used to spread manure on a field. **4** (US) a vehicle for collecting human excrement. [HONEY n.[5] + SE *wagon*]

Hong Kong *n.* [20C] a smell. [rhy. sl. *Hong Kong* = PONG n.[3]]

Hong Kong dog *n.* [20C] a form of stomach problem picked up by visitors to Hong Kong (cf. APPLE-BLOSSOM TWO-STEP).

hong-yen *n.* [1900s–30s] (drugs) heroin in pill form. [? *hong* + YEN n.]

honk *n.*[1] *see* HONKIE.

honk *n.*[2] [1920s+] (orig. Aus.) an unpleasant smell. [? Maori *haunga*, ill-smelling]

honk *n.*[3] **1** [1940s–60s] a wild, uproarious party. **2** [1970s+] (US) country and western or honky-tonk music. [abbr. HONKY-TONK]

honk *n.*[4] [1960s–70s] (US) the penis. [its ? similarity to a HONKER n.[1] (2), nose]

honk *n.*[5] [1980s+] (US drugs) an inhalation of cocaine, heroin. [HONK v.[4]]

honk *v.*[1] **1** [1920s+] (orig. Aus.) to smell unpleasant, to stink, intensified as *honk like a gaggle of geese*. **2** [1970s+] (US campus) to be very offensive or unattractive.

honk *v.*[2] **1** [1940s+] (US) to talk loudly in a boastful manner. **2** [1960s+] to vomit. [SE *honk*, to make a honking noise]

honk *v.*[3] [1960s+] (US) to squeeze the penis or breast (cf. HONKER n.[3]; HONK JOB; HOOTER n.[3]). [the image of squeezing or 'honking' an old-fashioned horn or hooter]

honk *v.*[4] [1960s–70s] to inhale or snort a narcotic. [HONKER n.[1] (2)]

honk *v.*[5] [1970s+] **1** to have sexual intercourse, to seduce. **2** (US campus) to be sexually aroused. **3** (US Und.) to kill someone.

honked off *adj.* [1950s+] (US campus) angry. [HONK v.[2]]

honked up *adj.* [1960s+] (US campus) excited. [HONK v.[2]]

honker *n.*[1] **1** [mid-19C+] (US) a goose. **2** [1940s+] the nose (cf. BUGLE n.[1]). **3** [1960s+] (US) a player of a brass instrument. [SE *honk*]

honker *n.*[2] [1970s+] (US) a very fast vehicle (cf. HONK IT ON).

honker *n.*[3] **1** [1970s+] a large penis. **2** [1970s+] (US) the female breasts, esp. if large. [HONK v.[3]]

honker *n.*[4] **1** [1970s+] (US campus) an offensive or unattractive person. **2** [1980s+] (US teen) anyone considered odd or eccentric. [HONK v.[1]]

honker *n.*[5] [1980s+] (US) a gob of phlegm. [HONK v.[2] (2)]

Honkers *n.* [1920s+] Hong Kong, usu. among UK ex-patriates stationed or working in the Far East. [*Hong Kong* + 'Oxford' sfx. *-ers*]

honkers *adj.* [1950s+] drunk (cf. HONKING adj.[1]). [HONK v.[2] (2)]

honkie/honk/honkey/honky *n.* [1940s+] (US Black) **1** a White person, occas. a light-skinned Latino; thus *Honkie Town*, the predominantly White area of a town (cf. SUPER-HONKIE). **2** an ice-cream bar. [abbr. BOHUNK; the Black use is a devel. of the White HUNKY, the orig. name for Poles who worked in Chicago stockyards. The change of the White 'u' to the Black 'o' supposedly accentuates the Black desire, embodied in the Black militants of the 1960s, to distance themselves as far as possible from the object of their hate]

honking *adj.*[1] [1940s+] very drunk (cf. HONKERS adj.). [HONK v.[2] (2)]

honking *adj.*[2] [1990s] (US campus) enormous, huge. [? var. on HULKING]

honking brown *n.* [1940s] (US Black) an ostentatious tan-coloured suit of clothes. [HONK v.[2]]

honk it on *phr.* [1960s+] (US) to drive or go at top speed. [? the *honking* of the horn that accompanies such a progress]

honk job *n.* [1970s] (US) the act of squeezing someone's penis or breast. [HONK v.[3]]

honkoe *n.* [1950s–60s] (Aus.) a general term of abuse. [? HONKIE, but with no racial overtones or HONK v.[1]]

honk off *v.*[1] [1950s+] (US campus) to anger, to annoy. [HONK v.[1]]

honk off *v.*[2] [1960s+] (US) to leave, to get out.

honk on *v.* [1970s] (US campus) to go away, to leave one alone (cf. HONK OFF v.[2]). [? HONK IT ON]

honky *see* HONKIE.

honky-tonk *n.*[1] [late 19C+] **1** a seedy bar which may also offer music, gambling, prostitutes. **2** a small town. [the *honky-tonk* piano that was often a feature of such establishments. The UK comedian Dick Emery (1918–83) used 'hello honky-tonk/tonks' as a catchphrase, but it has not survived his death, other than in the context of his career]

honky-tonk *n.*[2] [20C] (Aus.) cheap wine. [rhy. sl. *honky-tonk* = plonk]

honky-tonk *v.* [late 19C+] (US) to go out on the town. [HONKY-TONK *n.*[1]]

honour bright/honour *phr.* [early 19C+] a phr. used to confirm the honesty or sincerity of one's statement.

honyock/honyocker *n.* [20C] (US) **1** rustic, peasant. **2** an ignorant, inexperienced or unsophisticated person, a low-class person. [var. on HUNYAK]

hoo *see* HOOHA.

hooa *see* HOOER.

hooch *n.*[1] [19C+] (orig. US) **1** alcohol, liquor. **2** any inferior alcoholic drink (esp. whisky) in Alaska and the Can. northwest. **3** (US prison) illicitly distilled liquor, often made from surprisingly unorthodox ingredients; thus [1920s+] (US) and [1930s+] (S.Afr.) *hooched*, tipsy. [*hoochinoo*, an alcoholic liquor made by Alaskan Indians, esp. the Hoochinoo people]

hooch *n.*[2] *see* HOOTCHY-KOOTCHY n.

hooch/hoochie *n.*[3] [1970s+] (US drugs) cannabis. [adoption of HOOCH n.[1]]

hooch dog *n.* [1980s+] (US campus) marijuana cigarette. [HOOCH n.[3]]

hoochie *see* HOOCH n.[3].

hoochie-coochie / hootchie-cootchie / hootchy-cootchy man / woman *n.* [late 19C+] (US Black) a practitioner of voodoo. [HOOTCHY-KOOTCHY + SE *man/woman*]

hoochie/hootchie/hootchy mama *n.* [1980s+] (US Black) a promiscuous girl or woman. [HOOTCHY-KOOTCHY n. (2)]

hoochie-pap *n.* [1920s] (US Black) **1** the buttocks, the posterior. **2** copulation. [? the exaggerated movement of the buttocks when dancing the *hoochie-coochie*]

hood *n.*[1] **1** [late 19C+] (US) a gangster, a thug. **2** [1960s+] (Aus.) the police. [abbr. HOODLUM]

hood *n.*[2] [1950s+] (W.I. Rasta) the penis. [? its foreskin]

hood *n.*[3] [1960s+] **1** (US Black) the area in which one lives, one's home ground. **2** (US prison) a friend who has come from one's own neighbourhood (cf. HOMEY n.[4]). [abbr. SE *neighbourhood*]

hoodickie/hoodackie *n.* [1940s+] (N.Z.) an otherwise nameless object, often a gadget. [DOHICKEY]

hoodie/hoody *n.* [1980s+] (orig. US) a *hood*ed sweatshirt, as worn by many young people, esp. those involved in rap music, as a semi-uniform (cf. CAGGIE). [abbr.]

hoodle *v.* [20C] (US) to cobble together, to botch up, to perform a bad job. [Ger. *hudeln*, to do something incompetently]

hoodlelacky *n.* [1940s–50s] (N.Z.) an otherwise nameless object, often a gadget.

hoodlum *n.* [late 19C+] (orig. US) **1** an unpleasant person or a street ruffian. **2** a thug or gangster. [ety unknown. The term was coined in San Francisco *c.*1870–2 and spread across the US by the end of the decade, generating a number of popular etymologies. Among them, according to H.L. Mencken (1880–1956), is the idea of a local newspaperman who, keen to coin a term to describe the street gangs that were plaguing the city's streets, decided simply to reverse the name of a leading gangster, one Muldoon. This created *noodlum*, and a printer's error, substituting 'h' for 'n', did the rest. Other theories include a reference to a gang rallying-cry, 'Huddle 'em!', and to roots in the Bavarian dialect term *Hodalump*, which carries exactly the same meaning, in various terms in Spanish and among US Indian languages. There is also the wonderfully unlikely linkage put forward by B&L that the term is based on the pidgin English *hood lahnt*, lazy. It is tempting to bring in the near-synon. SE *hooligan*, but that word was British and was noted only when it began appearing in London police reports *c.*1898]

hoodlum wagon *n.* [late 19C–1960s] (US) a police patrol wagon.

hoodman *n.* **1** [18C–early 19C] blind. **2** [19C] drunk; thus *hoodman blind*, very drunk. [*hoodman*, the blinded player in a game of *hoodman-blind*, the older name of *blind man's buff*]

hoodoo *n.* **1** [late 19C] (US) a party or celebration. **2** [late 19C+] (US) a curse, jinx, run of bad luck. [SE *hoodoo*, the practice of witchcraft]

hoodoo *v.* [20C] (US) to cheat, to deceive, to take advantage of. [HOODOO n. (2)]

hood rat *n.* [1990s] (US Black teen) an unattractive woman. [HOOD n.[3] + SE *rat*]

hoody *n. see* HOODIE.

hoody *adj.* [1960s+] (US) acting in a thuggish manner. [HOODLUM]

hooer/hoor/hooa/hua *n.* [1930s+] (Aus.) a term of general disapproval, applied to either sex (cf. BASTARD). [lit. *whore*]

hooey *n.* **1** [1910s+] rubbish, nonsense (cf. HOOHA). **2** [1980s+] (US) excrement (cf. HOOHAH). [? Rus. (translit.) *hooey*, sl. for penis, i.e. cock, thus load of old cock]

hoof *n.* [late 16C+] the human foot.

hoof/hoof it *v.*[1] **1** [late 17C+] to walk, to go on foot. **2** [mid-19C+] to kick. **3** [20C] to run. **4** [1920s+] to dance. [HOOF n.]

hoof/hoof out *v.*[2] [late 19C+] to throw out, to expel (cf. GET THE HOOF). [one is kicked with the HOOF n.]

hoof-and-mouth-disease *n.* [1940s–60s] (US) the act of talking too much. [var. on FOOT-IN-MOUTH DISEASE]

hoof-covers *n.* [late 19C] (US) a boot or shoe.

hoofer *n.* [1910s+] (US) a dancer, a chorus–girl. [HOOF n.]

hoofing *n.* **1** [late 17C+] travelling on foot. **2** [20C] (orig. US) dancing. [HOOF n.]

hoof it *see* HOOF v.[1].

hoofler *n.* [20C] (Irish) a general term of abuse. [HUFFLE]

hoof out *see* HOOF v.[2].

hoof the pad, to *phr.* [mid-19C–1920s] (Aus.) to live as a tramp, to go on the tramp (cf. PAD THE HOOF). [HOOF v.[1] (1) + PAD]

hoogie/hoogy *n.* [1940s+] (US Black) a derog. term for a White person, a racist (cf. HONKIE; HOOSIER).

hooha/hoohah/hoo *n.* **1** [1910s+] an uproar, commotion. **2** [1940s+] (orig. milit.) nonsense, rubbish, twaddle. **3** [1980s+] (US) an important or self-important person. [Yid. *hu-ha*, a hullabaloo]

hoohah *n.* [1920s+] a lavatory. [? fig. use of HOOHA, although E.P. notes a suggestion that brackets the *hoo* of effort and the *ha* of relief that accompany defecation]

hoojacky/hoojay/hoojit *n.* [1940s+] (N.Z.) an otherwise nameless object, often some form of gadget.

hoo-jahs, the *n.* [1930s+] (Aus./US) delirium tremens (cf. HEEBIE-JEEBIES).

hoojay/hoojit *see* HOOJACKY.

hook *n.*[1] *see* HOOKER n.[1].

hook *n.*[2] **1** [early 19C+] a finger, usu. pl., thus a hand. **2** [mid-19C+] the pickpocket who actually steals the wallet, money etc rather than his various accomplices (cf. WIRE n.[2]). **3** [late 19C+] (Aus.) any expert thief, esp. a pickpocket. **4** [1940s+] (Irish) a confidence trickster, a cheat. **5** [1990s] (US Black/Und.) the police.

hook *n.*[3] [late 19C+] **1** a catch, a drawback. **2** a gimmick or angle. **3** an imposture. [late 20C use is US Black]

hook *n.*[4] **1** [20C] (orig. Aus.) a spur, usu. in pl. **2** [1910s–60s] (US prison) a straight razor used as a weapon.

hook *n.*[5] [1930s+] (US) an influential patron, political influence.

hook *n.*[6] [1950s+] (drugs) an addiction. [HOOK v.[5] (1)]

hook *n.*[7] **1** [1940s+] (US) a jack or 7 in poker. **2** [1960s+] (US campus) the grade C; thus *hook and a half*, the grade B+ (cf. CAT n.[12]; HOOK v.[10]). [the shape of the letter or number]

hook n.[8] [1960s+] (US Black) a derog. term for a Jew (cf. HOOK-NOSE). [the popular stereotype of hook-nosed Semites]

hook n.[9] [1970s+] (US gang) a weakling, a conformist, esp. a non-gang member. [? HOOK n.[8], the stereotypically studious Jew is seen as unlikely to join a gang]

hook n.[10] [1970s+] (US campus) the telephone. [one 'hangs it up'; early models had a hook on which the receiver was hung]

hook adj. [1980s+] (US Black) physically attractive (cf. HOOKED adj.[1]).

hook v.[1] [early 17C–late 19C] to steal, to pilfer, esp. by cutting a hole in a shop window and 'fishing' for its contents with a hook on a string (cf. HOOKER n.[1]). [SE *hook*]

hook/hook it v.[2] 1 [mid-18C] to run off, to escape, to go about one's own business (cf. HOOK OFF). 2 [late 19C+] (US) to play truant (cf. PLAY HOOKEY). [SE *hook*, move with a sudden twist or turn]

hook v.[3] [18C+] to fool, to practise a confidence trick upon. [SE *hook*, ensnare]

hook v.[4] 1 [early 19C+] to attract, esp. into marriage. 2 [1980s+] to attract, to catch the eye of. 3 [1980s+] (US Black) to search for.

hook v.[5] 1 [20C] (drugs) to addict someone to drugs. 2 [1920s+] (US) to arrest, to catch in a crime.

hook/hook up/up with v.[6] 1 [20C] to marry. 2 [20C] to meet, join, to ally oneself to. 3 [1980s+] (US campus) to find a partner for romance or sex. 4 [1980s+] to kiss passionately. 5 [1980s+] (US) to provide or give something to someone.

hook v.[7] [1920s+] (Aus.) to punch.

hook v.[8] 1 [1930s+] (US) (orig. tramp) to steal a ride on a train, to hitchhike. 2 [1980s+] (US campus) to engage in love making. [HOOK ONTO]

hook v.[9] [1940s+] to engage in prostitution. [HOOKER n.[2]. While there appears to be no evidence of this use before 1940s, it seems unlikely that the word was not in unrecorded use as much as a century earlier]

hook v.[10] [1970s+] (US campus) to get a grade C. [HOOK n.[7] (2)]

hook-and-eyes/-eyers/hooker n. [20C] (US) nickname for the Amish, whose beliefs forbid them the use of buttons.

hook and snivey/snivvy see HOOKEM-SNIVEY.

hook down v. [20C] to swallow.

hooked adj.[1] 1 [mid-late 19C] tricked, fooled, deceived. 2 [1990s] (US Black/campus) physically attractive.

hooked/hooked on adj.[2] [1920s+] addicted to, usu. of narcotic drugs but fig. uses also, e.g. *hooked on someone*, obsessed with someone

hooked on adv [20C] (Aus.) of a woman, 'picked up' in the street or in some other informal situation.

hooked up adj.[1] [1920s] dead. [one has been *hooked up* to heaven]

hooked up adj.[2] [1930s+] (US) well-dressed or intelligent. [*hooked up* with what is fashionable, interesting]

hooked up adj.[3] [1980s+] (US Black) dating, 'going steady'. [SE *hook up*, to join with]

hookem-snivey / hookum-snivey / hook and snivey / snivvy / hook 'em snivey / hookem-snivvy / hook um snivey n. 1 [late 18C–19C] a trick or deceit, spec. a contrivance for undoing the bolt of a door from the outside (cf. HOKUM-SNIVVY; HOOK n.[3]). 2 [late 19C] nobody. [abbr. of Und. phr. *hook and snivey, with nix the buffer*, a criminal trick designed to feed a dog (cf. BUFE) and an additional man for nothing (cf. NIX n.)]

hookem-snivey / hookum-snivey / hook and snivey / snivvy / hook 'em snivey / hookem-snivvy / hook um snivey adj. [mid–late 19C] deceitful, tricky.

hookem-snivey / hookum-snivey / hook and snivey / snivvy / hook 'em snivey / hookem-snivvy / hook um snivey v. [mid–late 19C] to deceive, esp. by faking an illness.

hooker/hook n.[1] 1 [mid-16C–19C] a thief who uses a pole with a hook at one end to 'fish' items from open windows, unguarded market stalls, passing carts etc (cf. ANGLER; CANTING CREW). 2 [late 17C–early 18C] a confidence trickster. 3 [late 19C] a pickpocket, esp. of watches. [HOOK v.[1]]

hooker n.[2] [mid-19C+] (orig. US) a prostitute. [SE *hook*, to catch, to lure, to entice. Popular ety. suggests the denizens of *Corlear's Hook*, known as *The Hook*, a red-light area on the New York City waterfront. The view is sanctified by Bartlett's *Dictionary of Americanisms* (1859), which defines *hooker* as 'a resident of The Hook, i.e. a strumpet, a sailor's trull'. However, the term appears at least 10 years earlier, not only in the US, where it has always been more popular, but in the UK, as noted by Mayhew (1849). Thus the ety. is probably the SE, but with strong reinforcement f. the geographical ref.]

hooker n.[3] [19C+] (US) a drink, a measure of liquor (cf. HOOTER n.[2]). [HOOK DOWN]

hooker n.[4] see HOOK-AND-EYES.

hooker n.[5] [1930s–40s] (US Und.) a warrant for an arrest.

hooker n.[6] [1960s+] (US) a trick or concealed drawback. [HOOK n.[3]]

hookey/hooky walker! excl. [19C] 1 an expression of incredulity, nonsense! rubbish! (cf. WALKER!). 2 go away! be off! [? according to J.B. the proper name of *John Walker*, 'an outdoor clerk' at Longman, Clementi and Co.'s in Cheapside; Walker had a hooked or crooked nose and was used by the 'nobs of the firm' to spy on his fellow employees. Those upon whom he spied naturally declared that his reports were nonsense and since there were more of him than them, they tended to prevail. Hotten (1867) offers an alternative view, and a third can be found in *Notes & Queries* iv. 425]

hookface see HOOKNOSE.

hook house n. [late 19C+] (US) a brothel (cf. ACCOMMODATION HOUSE). [HOOKER n.[2] + HOUSE n.[1]]

hook in v. [1910s+] (US) to get introduced to or put in touch with, involved in.

hook it see HOOK v.[2].

hook jack v. [mid-19C–1900s] (US) to play truant (cf. PLAY HOOKEY). [for ety. see HOOK v.[2]]

hook, line and sinker phr. [mid-19C+] absolutely, completely. [fishing imagery]

hooknose/hookface n. [mid-19C] a derog. term for a Jew (cf. HOOK n.[8]). [physiological stereotyping]

hook off v. 1 [late 19C] to steal. 2 [1940s+] (N.Z.) to escape, to run off (cf. HOOK v.[2]).

hook one's bait/mutton, to phr. (Aus. N.Z.) to escape, to run off (cf. HOOK v.[2]).

hook onto v. [late 19C+] to attach oneself to someone, to follow about.

hook-pointed adj. [19C] of the penis, semi-erect (cf. HOCK-PINTLED). [the curved shape; *pintled* is Scot. use]

hooks n. [early 19C+] the fingers, the hands (cf. FORK-HOOKS; LUNCH HOOKS; THIEVING HOOKS). [HOOK n.[2] (1)]

hooks and crooks n. [19C] (US) letters, writing (cf. POTHOOKS AND HANGERS). [the shapes of the letters + pun on SE phr. *by hook or by crook*]

hook shop n. [mid-19C+] a brothel (cf. BUTTOCKING SHOP). [HOOKER n.[2] + SE *shop*]

hookum-/hook um snivey see HOOKEM-SNIVEY.

hook-up n. 1 [1980s+] (US campus) an ability to get proper connections with certain people or things. 2 [1900s–50s] (US) a connection, esp. political. 3 [1980s+] (US) a sexual or romantic relationship or the person with whom one has a relationship.

hook up/up with v.[1] see HOOK v.[6].

hook up v.[2] [1990s] (US teen) to get more than one is entitled to, to get something for free (cf. HOOKED UP adj.[2]). [one is 'hooking up to' fashionable people, occupations etc]

hook up v.[3] [1990s] (US Black) to create something according to one's own taste, e.g. clothing, house decoration, holiday plans.

hooky n.[1] [mid-19C+] (US) truanting. [abbr. PLAY HOOKEY]

hooky n.[2] [1930s] (US Und.) a thief. [HOOK n.[2]]

hooky adj. [1970s+] illegal. [HOOK v.[1] + pun on BENT]

hooky v. [mid-19C+] to play truant. [HOOKY n.[1]]

hooky party n. [1990s] (US Black) a group of teenagers who skip school to drink malt liquor or liquid crack cocaine. [PLAY HOOKEY]

hooky walker! see HOOKEY WALKER!

hooley n.[1] **1** [late 19C] a fur-lined and fur-collared overcoat. **2** [1960s] (US) a worthless person. [Mr *Hooley*, a noted millionaire; his luck ran out in 1898 when he was declared bankrupt and the term, initially admiring, became more ironic]

hooley n.[2] [20C] a rip-roaring party. [? Irish *ceilidh*, a gathering for the playing of music, telling of tales and general conversation (pron. 'kayley'). Share, however, opts for Anglo-Ind *hooly*, ult. Hind. *holi*, the Hindu spring festival in honour of Krishna]

hooley v. [late 19C] to prosper, to follow success with success. [HOOLEY n.[1]]

hoolihan n. [20C] (US) a riotous event, a boisterous party. [HOOLIHAN v.]

hoolihan v. [20C] (US) to have a very good time, esp. of a cowboy 'painting the town red'. [*Hoolihan*, an Irish surname, thus the stereotyped image of the riotous Irish ? + SE *hooligan*]

hoon n. **1** [1930s+] (Aus./N.Z.) a procurer of prostitutes, but not a pimp to a specific woman or women. **2** [1930s+] (Aus./N.Z.) a show-off with limited intelligence. **3** [1930s+] (Aus./N.Z.) a flashy lout or hooligan. **4** [1930s+] (Aus./N.Z.) one who drives in a dangerous, showing-off manner. **5** [1980s+] (N.Z.) an exploit that involves 'hoonish', i.e. exhibitionist, loutish behaviour. [ety. unknown. Baker suggests, esp. for (2), a contraction of Jonathan Swift's *houyhnhnm* (the anthropomorphic horses of *Gulliver's Travels*, 1726), but they are seen as intelligent beings. It is their human slaves, the *yahoos*, who are the fools – and noted as such in dictionaries. Note also N.Z. WW2 use by religiously motivated conscientious objectors to describe those with political or humanitarian agendas]

hoon bin n. [1980s+] (N.Z.) an enclosure where drunken sports supporters are detained during a match. [HOON + SIN BIN n.[1]]

hoonchaser n. [1980s+] (N.Z.) a policeman. [HOON + SE *chaser*]

hoondom n. [1980s+] (N.Z.) the world of loutish exhibitionists. [HOON + sfx. -*dom*]

hoonery n. [1980s+] (N.Z.) loutish behaviour. [HOON + sfx. -*ery*]

hoonish adj. [1980s+] (N.Z.) of a person or their behaviour, exhibitionist, loutish. [HOON]

hoon it up v. [1980s] (N.Z.) to have a noisy, boisterous party. [HOON]

hoop n.[1] [1900s–40s] (US Black) a ring, e.g. a wedding ring. [SE 16C–19C]

hoop n.[2] [1930s+] (Aus.) a jockey. [the hooped 'colours' worn by some jockeys]

hoop n.[3] [1930s+] **1** the vagina (cf. BLACK HOLE n.[1]; FURRY HOOP). **2** the anus. **3** (US prison) sodomy (cf. RING n.[1]).

hoop/hoops n.[4] [1970s+] (US teen) the game of basketball.

[the basketball *hoop*, thus the basketball film *Hoop Dreams* (1994)]

hoop v.[1] [late 18C–19C] to beat. [fig. SE *put through the hoop*]

hoop v.[2] [1970s+] (US) to play basketball. [HOOP n.[4]]

hoop v.[3] [1980s] (US) to vomit. [echoic]

hoopdee see HOOPTIE.

hoopdie swoop v. [1970s+] (US Black) to move in on and pick up a man or woman with great speed and efficiency. [? SE *hoopla!* + *swoop*]

hoop down/out v. [1980s] (US) to play top-class basketball. [HOOP n.[4]]

hooped/hoopsy coopsy adj. [1940s+] (N.Z.) drunk. [? ref. to a barrel *hoop*]

hoop it v. [20C] (orig. milit.) to have a difficult time (cf. GO THROUGH THE HOOP).

hoopla n. [20C] fuss, commotion. [SE *hoop-la!* an expression accompanying a sudden movement, esp. of some trick on stage or in a circus ring; ult. Fr. *houp-là!*]

hoople n.[1] [1920s–30s] (US Und.) a ring. [Du. *hoepel*, a hoop, orig. used in New York City]

hoople n.[2] [1920s+] (US) a fool, an idiot. [? *Major Hoople*, a US cartoon strip character]

hoop one's barrel, to phr. [late 18C–19C] to beat. [HOOP v.[1]]

hoop out see HOOP DOWN.

hoops see HOOP n.[4].

hoop-stick n. [late 19C] the arm.

hoop stretcher n. [1990s] a male homosexual (cf. KID STRETCHER). [HOOP n.[3] (2) + SE *stretcher*]

hoopsy coopsy see HOOPED.

hooptie/hoopty/hoopdee n. **1** [1960s–80s] (US orig. Calif.) a car, esp. the latest model. **2** [1990s] (US Black) a worn-out, falling-to-pieces automobile (cf. BUCKET n.[2]; RAGGEDY-ASS RIDE).

hoopty-mack n. [1990s] (US Black) a woman who has been singled out for potential seduction. [HOOPDIE SWOOP + MACK n.]

hoor see HOOER.

hoorah n.[1] see HURRAH n.

hoorah n.[2] **1** [1980s] (US) a damn. **2** [1990s] (US Black) loud talking, noise. [SE excl. *hoorah!*]

hoorah adj. see HURRAH adj.

hoorah/hooraw v. see HURRAH v.

hooray fuck! excl. [1950s+] (N.Z.) used as a farewell to someone one dislikes or has just been insulting. [SE *hooray* + FUCK!]

hooray/hoorah henry n. [1930s+] a rich young man given to much public exhibitionism, drunkenness and similar antisocial activities, all based on an excess of snobbish self-esteem (cf. MAYFAIR MERCENARY; PREPPIE; SLOANE RANGER). [despite the term's virtually invariable appearance in a UK context, it was coined in the US. Damon Runyon, 'Tight Shoes' in *Colliers*, 18 April 1936: '[Calvin Colby] is without doubt strictly a Hoorah Henry, and he is generally figured as nothing but a lob as far as ever doing anything useful in this world is concerned']

hooride v. [1990s] (US Black) **1** to act in a rowdy manner. **2** to shoot, to assassinate. [SE excl. *hoorah!*]

hooroo! excl. [1910s+] (Aus.) **1** goodbye. **2** hoorah! hooray! [SE excl. *hoorah!*]

hooroosh/hurroosh n. [mid-19C+] (orig. US) an uproar, a great fuss. [SE *hurrish*, *hurroosh*. 'To drive with the cry "hurrish!" or "hurroosh!"' (OED). ? ult. *hooray!*]

hoosegow n. [20C] (US) **1** a prison. **2** an outhouse, a privy. [Sp. *juzgado*, a tribunal or court of justice]

hoosh n. [1900s–20s] **1** a form of thick soup, as eaten by arctic explorers. **2** (Can.) corned beef hash and potatoes. [? Inuit term]

hoosh v. **1** [1900s–40s] of animals and people, to herd, to drive. **2** [1950s] to rush around. [*hoosh!*, excl. used when driving animals]

hooshgod *n.* [20C] (Can.) a cook. [HOOSH n. + SE *God*]

hoosheroon *see* HOOSIEROON.

hoosier *n.* [19C+] **1** (US) a peasant, a rustic simpleton. **2** a native of Indiana. **3** an amateur or novice. **4** (US Und.) a gullible person. **5** (US Black) a White person, esp. a racist (cf. CRACKER n.[4]; HONKIE; PECKERWOOD; WHITE TRASH). [Cumbrian dial. *hoozer*, something large of its kind; ? a ref. to the size of the corn-fed country farm-boys]

hoosieroon/hoosheroon *n.* [mid–late 19C] (US) a native of Indiana. [HOOSIER]

hoot/hootoo/hout/hutu *n.*[1] [late 19C+] money. [Maori *utu*, money paid as recompense]

hoot *n.*[2] **1** [late 19C+] (orig. US) a very small amount. **2** [19C+] (orig. US) anything or anyone considered unimportant, insignificant, esp. in phr. *not give a hoot*, not care at all. **3** [19C+] (US) a tot of liquor, a drink. [? fig. use of SE *hoot*, an abrupt, sharp cry]

hoot *n.*[3] [1920s+] (orig. US) a most amusing experience (cf. HOWL n.). [HOOT v.[1] or ? SE *hoot*, a sharp cry or excl.]

hoot *n.*[4] [1940s+] (US) a party. [abbr. HOOTENANNY]

hoot *v.*[1] [1920s+] **1** to laugh loudly. **2** (US) to talk loudly and to excess. **3** (US) to cough. **4** (orig. Aus.) to smell badly, to stink. [SE *hoot*, to shout, to call out]

hoot *v.*[2] [1960s+] to have a good time, to carouse. [HOOT n.[3]]

hoot-and-holler *n.*[1] [20C] (US) an out-of-the way place. [pun on *holler/hollow* as a name + the need to *hoot and holler* to make oneself heard from an out-of-the-way place]

hoot-and-holler *n.*[2] [20C] (US) a nickname for the religious Holy Rollers. [their noisiness]

hootch *n.* [1960s+] (orig. US milit. in Vietnam) any form of shelter from a peasant hut, to a bunker, to an office building.

hootchie-cootchie man/woman *see* HOOCHIE-COOCHIE MAN.

hootchie mama *see* HOOCHIE MAMA.

hootchy-cootchy man/woman *see* HOOCHIE-COOCHIE MAN.

hootchy-kootchy/hooch *n.* **1** [late 19C+] (orig. US) a form of highly suggestive belly-dance, usu. performed at carnivals. **2** [1980s+] (US) sexual activity (cf. HANKYPANKY; OOTCHIMA-GOOTCHI). [ety. unknown; perhaps no more than a showman's idea of an 'exotic' or 'Oriental' name, the vowels of which suggest the sinuous gyrations of the dancer]

hootchy-kootchy *adj.* [late 19C+] (orig. US) erotic, suggestive, sexy. [HOOTCHY-KOOTCHY n.]

hootchy mama *see* HOOCHIE MAMA.

hooted *adj.* [late 19C–1930s] (US) drunk. [HOOT n.[2] (3)]

hootenanny *n.* **1** [1920s+] (US) an imaginary object (cf. DINGUS; THINGUMMABOB; THINGUMMAJIG). **2** [1920s+] a general term of abuse. **3** [1920s+] nonsense, rubbish, anything insignificant, euph. for *a damn* and used similarly, e.g. *I don't give a hootenanny* (cf. HOOT n.[2]). **4** [1940s+] (US) a party. **5** [1960s+] (US) a performance of folk music. **6** [1980s+] (US) a commotion. [ety. unknown]

hooter *n.*[1] [19C] (US) an insignificant amount. [HOOT n.[2]]

hooter *n.*[2] [late 19C] (US) a drink (cf. HOOKER n.[3]).

hooter *n.*[3] **1** [1950s+] the nose (cf. BUGLE n.[1]). **2** [1970s+] the female breast (cf. HONKER n.[3]). **3** [1980s+] (US) a woman with large breasts. [the supposed resemblance to an old-fashioned automobile *hooter*]

hooter *n.*[4] [1970s–80s] (US) a telephone.

hooter *n.*[5] [1980s+] (US) a breaking of wind. [HOOT v.[1]]

hooter *n.*[6] **1** [1980s+] (drugs) a marijuana cigarette. **2** [1980s+] (N.Z. drugs) a tube (generally of rolled cardboard) used to inhale smoke from heated drops of cannabis oil.

hoot him! *excl.* [1920s–30s] (Aus.) a derisory cry at a passer-by deemed worthy of verbal attack.

hoot in hell *phr.* [19C+] (US) the least bit. [ext. of HOOT n.[2] (2)]

hootoo *see* HOOT n.[1].

hooty *adj.* [1920s] (US) angry. [HOOT v.[1]]

hoove *n.* [1990s] (US Black) a casual, 'amateur' prostitute. [? HO n.[1] + SE *half*]

hoover *n.* [1930s] (US) an outside lavatory, a privy (cf. F.D.R.). [US President Herbert Hoover (1874–1964), during whose administration (1929–33) the US suffered the worst privations of the Depression]

hoover *adj.* [1930s] a generic adj. used in a variety of combs., all referring to events or objects engendered by the poverty that accompanied the Great Depression, e.g. *Hooverville*, a shanty town, *Hoover blankets*, newspapers used to wrap up in for warmth (cf. HOOVER HOG). [for ety. *see* HOOVER n.]

hoover/hoover up *v.* [1970s+] (orig. US) to inhale drugs, to eat or drink, to snatch, to fellate, all in a greedy or vigorous manner. [sugg. by the brandname of *Hoover* vacuum cleaners, used generically as meaning to vacuum, thus to 'suck up']

hoover buggy/cart/wagon *n.* [20C] (US) any makeshift vehicle horsedrawn and dedicated to hauling hay. [HOOVER adj. + SE *buggy, cart, wagon*]

hoover dust *n.* [20C] (US) cheap tobacco. [HOOVER adj. + SE *dust*]

hoover gravy *n.* [20C] (US) particularly thick gravy, often virtually all a family had to eat. [HOOVER adj. + SE *gravy*]

hoover flag *n.* [1930s] (US) empty pockets turned inside out. [HOOVER adj. + SE *flag*]

hoover hog *n.* [1940s+] (US) **1** a wild rabbit. **2** (Texas) an armadillo, a cheap form of meat for poor farmers during the Depression. [HOOVER adj. + SE *hog*]

hoover pork *n.* [20C] (US) sow belly. [HOOVER adj. + SE *pork*]

hoover's ham *n.* [20C] (US) salt pork. [HOOVER adj. + SE *ham*]

hoover wagon *see* HOOVER BUGGY.

hoowah *n.* [1950s+] a prostitute. [the New York City pron. of SE *whore*]

hoozie/hosie *n.* [1970s] (US) a sexually promiscuous woman or prostitute. [SE *whore*/HO n.[1] + FLOOZIE]

hop *n.*[1] **1** [mid-18C+] a dance; thus *hop-merchant*, a dancing master. **2** [late 19C–1950s] (US) an organized dance, held in a dance-hall and frequented by lower-class young people (cf. RACKET n.[2]).

hop/hops *n.*[2] [late 19C+] **1** opium. **2** heroin. **3** any type of illicit drugs. **4** a regular drug user (cf. HOP FIEND; HOP-HEAD). [ety. unknown; ? Chinese term]

hop *n.*[3] [1910s+] a policeman. [abbr. JOHN HOP]

hop *n.*[4] [1920s+] (US/Aus./N.Z.) beer. [SE *hops*, the main constituent of beer]

hop *n.*[5] [1930s+] (US) a bellhop. [abbr.]

hop *v.* **1** [20C] (US) to jump onto a moving vehicle, esp. a train, to get a lift or ride, to catch a train or aeroplane. **2** [1920s+] (US) to engage in sexual intercourse (cf. HOP ON).

hop-and-drop *see* HIP-AND-DROP.

hop a/the twig, to *phr.* **1** [late 18C–early 19C] (Und.) to run away. **2** [late 18C+] to die (cf. DROP OFF THE TWIG).

hop bail *v.* [1900s–50s] (US) to forfeit one's bail by fleeing.

hopeful *n.* [early 18C+] an optimist; thus *young hopeful*, a neophyte, a beginner, often used ironically.

hope-to-die *adj.* (US Black) closest, most trusted, best. [abbr. *hope to die if ...*]

hope to hell *see* WISH TO HELL.

hope to my die! *excl.* [20C] (US) a strong excl. used to underline the veracity or sincerity of the speaker's statement. [*hope to die + I hope I may die*]

hope to tell you! *excl.* [20C] (US) a strong excl. used to underline the speaker's statement.

hop fiend *n.* [late 19C–1920s] a drug user (cf. HOP-HEAD n.[1]). [HOP n.[2] + SE *fiend*]

hop-fighter *n.* [1910s] (US drugs) an opium smoker (cf. BOOZE-FIGHTER). [HOP n.^{2} + SE *fighter*]

hop harry *n.* [1920s–40s] (Aus.) a bowler hat. [play on SE *hop*, to move/*bowl*, to move]

hop-head *n.*^{1} [20C] (drugs) **1** a heroin addict. **2** the user of any drug (cf. ACID-HEAD). [HOP n.^{2} + sfx. -HEAD (2)]

hop-head *n.*^{2} **1** [20C] (US/N.Z.) a drunk or a beer-drinker. **2** [1940s–50s] (N.Z.) an alcoholic. **3** [1940s+] (N.Z.) a wild, eccentric person (US) a German-American. [HOP n.^{4}/SE *hops* + sfx. -HEAD (2)]

hop-head *n.*^{3} [20C] delirium tremens (cf. WHISKY-HEAD). [SE *hops*/HOP n.^{4} + HEAD n.^{4}]

hop in *v.*^{1} [19C] to arrive, to turn up. [var. on SE *pop in*]

hop in/into *v.*^{2} [1940s–50s] (Aus.) to fight, to attack.

hop in for one's chop, to *phr.* [1960s+] (Aus.) to seize one's opportunity. [HOP IN v.^{1} + CHOP n.^{5}]

hop into *v.*^{1} *see* HOP IN v.^{2}.

hop into *v.*^{2} [1960s+] (Aus.) to start, to begin, e.g. *hop into the grub*, to start eating, often used as an invitation or imper.

hop into bed with, to *phr.* [1950s+] to have casual or spontaneous sexual intercourse with.

hop it! *excl.* [20C] go away! run along! etc.

hop joint *n.*^{1} [late 19C+] a room or apartment where patrons gather to smoke opium or, more recently, to take heroin (cf. SHOOTING GALLERY). [HOP n.^{2} + JOINT n.^{3} (3)]

hop joint *n.*^{2} [1910s+] (US) a saloon bar. [HOP n.^{4} + JOINT n.^{3} (3)]

hop juice *n.* [late 19C] (US) beer. [HOP n.^{4} + JUICE n.^{3}]

Hopkins *see* MR HOPKINS.

hop-merchant *n.* **1** [late 17C–late 18C] a dancing master (cf. CAPER MERCHANT). **2** [19C] a fiddler. [HOP n.^{1} (1) + MERCHANT]

hop off *v.*^{1} **1** [late 18C] to die. **2** [20C] to leave.

hop off *v.*^{2} [20C] **1** (Ulster) to attack violently, using the fists. **2** (Irish) to tease; thus *have a hop of*, to make fun of.

hopola *n.* [1990s] (US Black) a woman (cf. HOP ON A BABE). [HOP ON + sfx. -OLA]

hop on *v.* [20C] to have sexual intercourse.

hop on a babe, to *phr.* [1990s] (US campus) to have sexual intercourse; the implication is that the man, lacking greater finesse, has made a pounce (prob. when drunk) to initiate the activity. [HOP ON]

hop one's frame, to *phr.* [1910s–40s] (N.Z.) to move, to make a sudden journey.

hop out *v.* [20C] (Aus.) to challenge someone to fight.

hop out! *excl.* [20C] (Aus.) are you ready to fight? (cf. FEEL FROGGY).

hop pad *n.* [1920s–40s] (drugs) a room or apartment where patrons gather to smoke opium or to take heroin (cf. SHOOTING GALLERY). [HOP n.^{2} + PAD n.^{2}]

hopped/hopped up *adj.* (US) **1** [20C] (drugs) under the influence of drugs. **2** [1920s+] excited, impatient. **3** [1940s+] of a car, improved beyond its basic specifications. **4** [1940s–50s] embellished, jazzed up. [lit. + fig. uses of HOP n.^{2}]

hopper *n.* **1** [mid-19C–1910s] the mouth. **2** [1970s+] (US) a toilet.

hopper-arsed *adj.* [late 17C–18C] large-buttocked. [SE *hopper* + ARSE]

hopper-dockers *n.* [early 19C] shoes. [ety. unknown; ? var. on HOCK-DOCKIES]

hop-picker *n.* [late 19C] a prostitute (cf. HOPPING WIFE). [? euph.]

hopping *adj.* [late 19C–1920s] (US) furious. [abbr. SE *hopping mad*]

hopping around like a gin at a christening *phr.* [1960s+] (Aus.) on one's best behaviour, esp. when slightly nervous, socially uncomfortable (cf. DEMURE AS A WHORE AT A CHRISTENING). [GIN n.^{1}]

hopping giles *n.* [late 18C–19C] a lame, limping person (cf. MR HOPKINS). [proper name *St Giles*, the patron saint of cripples]

hopping Jesus *n.* [mid-19C–1920s] a limping person (cf. CREEPING JESUS).

hopping pot *n.* [late 19C+] the lot. [rhy. sl.]

hopping wife *n.* [late 19C] a prostitute (cf. HOP-PICKER).

hoppin' john *n.* [mid-19C+] (US) a dish of pork, rice and peas seasoned with chilli.

hop it and scram *n.* [20C] ham. [rhy. sl.]

hoppo *n.* [early 18C–19C] (Anglo-Chinese) **1** a customs man. **2** a customs house and the business transacted within it. [Chinese *hoo-poo*, the Board of Revenue; thus *hoopoo-man*, revenue official]

hop-pole *n.* [mid-19C] a tall, thin person.

hoppy *n.*^{1} **1** [mid–late 19C] a dancing master. **2** [late 19C] a fiddler. [HOP n.^{1}]

hoppy *n.*^{2} [late 19C–1900s] (US) a lame person. [they *hop* along]

hoppy *n.*^{3} [20C] (drugs) orig. an opium addict, a drug addict (cf. ACID-HEAD; HOP-HEAD n.^{1}). [HOP n.^{2}]

hoppy *n.*^{4} [1960s] a flea.

hoppy *adj.*^{1} **1** [mid-19C+] lame, limping. **2** [1930s+] lively, full of movement.

hoppy *adj.*^{2} [1940s] (US drugs) characteristic of, or relevant to, drugs or drug-taking. [HOP n.^{2}]

hops *n.*^{1} *see* HOP n.^{2}.

hops *n.*^{2} **1** [late 19C–1900s; 1960s+] beer. **2** [1900s] (US prison) tea. [SE *hops*; later use of (1) is Aus/N.Z./US Black]

hops *n.*^{3} [1990s] (US Black) the ability to jump high during a game of basketball.

hop stick *n.* [1930s] (US drugs) **1** orig. an opium pipe. **2** a cannabis cigarette. [HOP n.^{2} + SE *stick*/STICK n.^{14}]

hop talk *n.* [late 19C+] (US) foolish or exaggerated talk. [HOP n.^{2} + SE *talk*; the implication is that such talk is promoted by opium smoking]

hop the ball, to *phr.* [20C] (Irish) to make a provocative remark. [Gaelic football *hop the ball*, to set the game in motion]

hop the charley, to *phr.* [late 19C] to play truant (cf. HOP THE WAG). [var. on PLAY THE CHARLEY WAG]

hop the coop, to *phr.* [mid-19C+] to escape, from any form of confinement, not necessarily prison. [SE *hop* + COOP n.^{1}]

hop the perch, to *phr.* [late 19C+] to die (cf. DROP OFF ONE'S PERCH; HOP A TWIG).

hop the twig *see* HOP A TWIG.

hop the wag, to *phr.* [mid-19C+] to play truant from school (cf. PLAY THE HOP). [PLAY THE WAG]

hop toy *n.* [late 19C–1950s] (drugs) a container used for smoking opium. [HOP n.^{2} + SE *toy*]

horace *n.* [1900s–30s] a joc. form of address to an office-boy. [generic use of proper name]

horchin *n.* [20C] (Ulster) an unpleasant person. [SE *urchin*]

horizontal *n.* **1** [late 19C–1910s] an up-market prostitute, a kept woman. **2** [1920s+] (US) sexual intercourse (cf. HORIZONTAL BOP). [Fr. *grande horizontale*; she is, of course, 'horizontal' on a bed or *chaise longue*]

horizontal barn-dancing *see* HORIZONTAL DANCING.

horizontal bop *n.* [1980s+] (US) sexual intercourse (cf. HORIZONTAL DANCING; HORIZONTAL REFRESHMENT; HORIZONTAL RELAXATION; HORIZONTALS). [SE *horizontal* + BOP n.^{1}]

horizontal dancing / barn-dancing / mambo / polka / polo / rhumba / rumble / twist and shout *phr.* [1950s+] sexual intercourse (cf. HORIZONTAL BOP). [all modern vars. on HORIZONTAL REFRESHMENT]

horizontalize *v.* [1980s+] (US) to have sexual intercourse. [HORIZONTAL n. (2)]

horizontal mambo/polka/polo *see* HORIZONTAL DANCING.

horizontal refreshment *n.* [late 19C+] sexual intercourse (cf. HORIZONTAL BOP).

horizontal relaxation *n.* [1940s+] (Aus./N.Z.) sexual intercourse (cf. HORIZONTAL BOP; HORRY).

horizontal rhumba/rumble *see* HORIZONTAL DANCING.

horizontals *n.* [1920s–30s] (US) sexual intercourse (cf. HORIZONTAL BOP). [HORIZONTAL n. (2)]

horizontal twist and shout *see* HORIZONTAL DANCING.

horizontal worker *n.* [20C] (US) a prostitute. [HORIZONTAL n. (1)]

hork *v.*¹ [1980s+] (US campus) to steal, to take without permission, to borrow without asking. [? HOICK v.¹]

hork *v.*² [1990s] (US) to spit. [SE *hawk*, to clear the throat of phlegm, to spit]

Horlicks *n.* [1980s] (society) a mess. [brandname of a late-night drink]

hormone *n.* [1980s+] (US campus) a sexually aggressive person, whether verbally or physically.

hormone fix *n.* [1980s+] (US campus) any form of sexual encounter, from the most marginal to full intercourse. [SE *hormone* + FIX n.³]

hormone queen *n.* [1960s–70s] (US) a male transvestite who takes oestrogen. [SE *hormone* + QUEEN n.¹]

hormones *n.* [1980s] (US) courage, guts.

horn *n.*¹ [18C+] (US) a drink. [SE *horn*, a drinking vessel made from a horn]

horn *n.*² [late 18C+] **1** the penis. **2** an erection (cf. BUGLE n.²). **3** sexual excitement or lust. [resemblance to an SE *horn*]

horn *n.*³ **1** [mid-19C+] the nose (cf. BUGLE n.¹). **2** [1940s+] (US) a telephone.

horn *n.*⁴ [20C] (W.I.) adultery; thus *take a horn*, to accept that one's partner is having/has had an affair without making an issue out of it. [HORNS]

horn *n.*⁵ [1930s+] (orig. jazz) **1** a trumpet. **2** any kind of wind instrument.

horn *n.*⁶ [1980s+] (drugs) a pipe for smoking crack cocaine.

horn/horn with *v.*¹ [20C] (W.I.) to be unfaithful to one's husband, wife or lover by having sex with or dating another person. [the cuckold's HORNS]

horn *v.*² [1950s+] (US drugs) to inhale a narcotic.

hornbug *n.* [1950s] (US) a sex maniac. [HORN n.² + BUG n.⁴]

horn-child *n.* [20C] (W.I.) the offspring of an adulterous relationship. [HORN n.⁴ + SE *child*]

horn colic *n.* [late 18C–1950s] an involuntary erection (cf. IRISH TOOTHACHE). [HORN n.² + SE *colic*]

horndog *n.* [1980s+] (US campus) a sexually aggressive person. [HORN n.² + DOG n.⁵ (7)]

horndog *v.* [1980s+] (US campus) to pursue sexually. [HORNDOG n.]

horned-up *adj.* [1960s+] (US) sexually excited. [HORN n.²]

horner-man *n.* [20C] (W.I.) a man who has a reputation for cuckolding others. [HORN n.²]

hornet *n.* [mid-19C] an unpleasant, ill-tempered person. [note ironic Gloucestershire dial. phr. 'mild as a hornet']

hornets *n.* [mid-19C] (US) bullets. [their sound]

hornety *adj.* [mid-19C] angry. [HORNET]

horney *n.* [mid-19C+] (Und.) a policeman. [dial. *horney*, the Devil + constable]

horn-grower/-merchant *n.* [18C] a married man. [HORNS; he is likely to 'wear the horns' of cuckoldry]

hornies, the *n.* [1970s+] (US) sexual desire. [HORNY adj.]

hornification *n.* [late 18C+] an erection; thus *hornify*, to become erect. [HORN n.²]

hornified *adj.* [late 18C–19C] cuckolded. [HORNS]

hornify *v.* [19C] to cuckold (cf. GIVE HORNS). [HORNS]

horn in/in on *v.* [1910s+] (US) to intrude, interfere. [SE *horn*]

horning *n.*¹ [late 19C] boasting, showing off. [SE *horn*, as blown by a huntsman]

horning *n.*² [1950s+] (drugs) **1** heroin. **2** inhaling a narcotic. [HORN v.²]

horn in on *see* HORN IN.

horn-mad *adj.* **1** [late 18C–19C] extremely jealous, esp. as a victim of cuckoldry. **2** [18C–1950s] lecherous, maddened by lust; thus *horn-madness*, the condition of lustfulness, *horn-madded*, lustful. [SE *horn-mad*, enraged, the image is a horned beast that is ready to gore anyone in its way, but note HORNS, HORN n.²]

horn-merchant *see* HORN-GROWER.

horn movie *n.* [1950s+] a pornographic film. [HORN n.²]

horn off/out *v.* [late 19C–1910s] (US) to impose upon, to force someone. [fig. to use one's horns]

horn-pills *n.* [20C] aphrodisiacs or supposed ones (cf. BACK-UP PILLS). [HORN n.² + SE *pills*]

horns *n.* [mid-15C+] a generic term for cuckoldry (cf. GIVE HORNS; HORNIFY). [the obvious link is to HORN n.², the penis, but the term apparently comes from an old German farming practice of grafting the spurs of a castrated cock on the root of the severed comb. These transplants would grow into horns, sometimes several inches long. The German word *hahnreh* or *hahnrei*, meaning cuckold, originally meant capon, a castrated cock]

horn-sticks *n.* [1960s+] celery. [the theory that celery is aphrodisiac]

horns-to-sell *n.* [18C–mid-19C] a promiscuous wife. [HORNS]

hornswoggle *n.* [19C+] (US) nonsense, humbug; thus *hornswoggler*, a fraud, a cheat.

hornswoggle *v.* [19C+] (US) **1** to embarrass, to confuse, to disconcert. **2** to cheat, to swindle (cf. BUMSWIGGLE; HONEYFUGGLE).

hornswoggled/cornswoggled *adj.* [19C+] (US) euph. for DAMNED (cf. BUMSWIGGLED; BUMSWIZZLED).

horn-thumb *n.* [16C] a cutpurse. [the sheath of horn worn by a cutpurse to protect his thumb from the knife-blade]

horn with *see* HORN v.¹.

horn work *n.* [late 18C–19C] cuckoldry. [HORNS]

horny *n.* [early 19C+] (Aus.) a cow, a bullock; thus *horney-steerer*, a bullock-driver. [orig. Scot.]

horny *adj.* **1** [late 19C+] sexually eager, aroused. **2** [1930s+] sexually arousing, erotic, pornographic, e.g. a *horny picture*. [HORN n.²]

horrible *n.* [1920s–50s] (Aus.) a rascal, a villain; a Bohemian, one who acts without regard for social convention (cf. LARRIKIN).

horrible *adj.* [early 17C+] a general intensifier, e.g. *horrible bad* (cf. AWFUL adv.; GHASTLY; TERRIBLE).

horrid *adj.* **1** [mid-17C+] offensive, detested, objectionable; thus *horridly*, offensively. **2** [late 18C] semi-drunk, tipsy.

horrid horn *n.* [mid–late 19C] (Anglo-Irish) a fool. [Erse *omadhun*, a fool]

horries *n.* (S.Afr.) **1** [1950s+] delirium tremens. **2** [1970s+] a phobia, a visceral fear. [Afk. *horries*, DTs, but note HORRORS]

horror-bollocks *n.* [1940s+] (orig. services) a term of affectionate address, usu. used among men (cf. BUGGERLUGS). [SE *horror* + BALLOCKS n.²]

horrors, the *n.* **1** [mid-18C+] a fit of depression (cf. BLUES). **2** [19C] a hangover. **3** [mid-19C+] delirium tremens, ext. as [late 19C–1900s] *blue horrors*; [1900s–20s] (Anglo-Irish) *cast-iron/stonewall horrors*. **4** [1960s+] hence unpleasant experiences (usu. paranoid fantasies) brought about occas. by the effects of smoking cannabis or from taking a hallucinogen.

horrorshow *adj.*¹ [1950s+] (US) unpleasant, disgusting or embarrassing.

horrorshow *adj.*[2] [1990s] (US teen) extremely good. [on *bad* = *good* model, HORRORSHOW adj.[1] , but note use in Anthony Burgess, *A Clockwork Orange* (1961), where it means excellent and is based on Rus. *horosho*]

horry *n.* [1940s+] (Aus./N.Z) sexual intercourse (cf. HORIZONTAL RELAXATION). [abbr. HORIZONTAL]

hors d'oeuvres *n.* [1970s+] (drugs) barbiturates or amphetamines (cf. A n.[2]). [SE *hors d'oeuvres*, the first dish of a meal, usu. of mixed items and intended to whet the appetite; a prelude to stronger, more exotic pleasures]

horse *n.*[1] 1 [mid-late 18C] a lottery ticket that is hired out by the day. 2 [late 19C+] (US gambling) a selection of 4 numbers to be played simultaneously. 3 [late 19C] (US) a queen in cards.

horse *n.*[2] [late 18C-mid-19C] work charged for before it is executed. [abbr. HORSEFLESH]

horse *n.*[3] [19C] £5 sterling. [? play on PONY n.[2]]

horse/hoss *n.*[4] 1 [19C+] (US) a strong, athletic man or an admirable, good fellow. 2 [mid-19C+] (US) a form of address by one man to another (cf. OLD HORSE). 3 [mid-19C] (US) one's husband. 4 [mid-19C+] a fine specimen, usu. constructed with of. 5 [late 19C-1910s] a student of remarkable ability.

horse *n.*[5] 1 [19C+] (US) a joke, esp. a joke at someone else's expense. 2 [late 19C-1910s] (US campus) horseplay, fun. 3 [1900s-40s] (US) nonsense, rubbish (cf. HORSESHIT). [? SE *horse laugh*]

Horse, the/Old Horse, the *n.*[6] [mid-19C] Horsemonger Lane prison, Southwark, London. [erected 1799 as a model prison, it lasted until 1880s. It was outside this prison on 13 November 1847 that Charles Dickens witnessed the public hanging of the murderers Frederick and Maria Manning]

horse *n.*[7] [late 19C-1910s] (US campus) a literal translation used in preparing a lesson (cf. ANIMAL n.[3]). [play on PONY n.[3]]

horse *n.*[8] [1920s+] (US) a prostitute, one of a group of women working for a pimp. [she is part of his STABLE]

horse *n.*[9] [1940s-60s] (US) a motorcycle.

horse *n.*[10] [1950s-60s] (US Black) a knife. [ety. unknown]

horse *n.*[11] [1950s+] (US prison) a visitor or prison warder who is willing to smuggle contraband in and out of prison (cf. MULE n.[3]).

horse/hoss *n.*[12] [1950s+] (drugs) heroin. [the initial letters]

horse *n.*[13] [1960s+] (Can. prison) a smooth piece of wood with a string attached. [ety. unknown]

horse *n.*[14] [1960s+] venereal disease, spec. gonorrhoea. [rhy. sl. *horse and trap* = CLAP n.]

horse *v.*[1] [17C; 1950s+] to have sexual intercourse (cf. RIDE v.[1]).

horse *v.*[2] [late 18C-19C] to flog, to whip. [the victim is placed across a wooden frame or 'horse']

horse *v.*[3] [19C+] (US) to yearn for, to want eagerly, to lust after. [? a horse straining at the bit or dial. *horse*, for a mare to be in heat]

horse *v.*[4] 1 [mid-19C] to work very hard, to work harder than a fellow. 2 [20C] (US) to haul or drag with great effort. [the animal's strength]

horse *v.*[5] 1 [mid-late 19C] to swindle, to cheat. 2 [late 19C-1960s] (US) to trick, to deceive, to tease.

horse *v.*[6] [late 19C-1910s] (US campus) to study with the help of a translation. [HORSE n.[7]]

horse *v.*[7] 1 [20C] to joke, to mess about. 2 [1930s+] (US) in a vehicle or plane, to change direction abruptly. [HORSE AROUND]

horse and cart *n.* 1 [late 19C] the heart. 2 [20C] (Aus.) the start. 3 [1970s+] a fart. [rhy. sl.]

horse and cart, to *phr.* [1970s] to fart. [rhy. sl.]

horse and carriage *n.* [20C] a garage. [rhy. sl.]

horse and foal *n.* [20C] (Aus.) the dole. [rhy. sl.]

horse and horse *phr.* [mid-19C-1950s] (US) dead even, esp. in gambling. [horse-racing imagery]

horse and trap *n.* 1 [20C] excrement (cf. PONY n.[3]). 2 [1960s+] venereal disease, spec. gonorrhoea (cf. HORSE n.[14]). [rhy. sl. *horse and trap* = (1) CRAP n.[3] (1); (2) = CLAP n.]

horse and trough *n.* [20C] a cough. [rhy. sl.]

horse apple/biscuit/doughnut/dumpling *n.* [20C] (US) a piece of horse excrement found lying in the road (cf. ALLEY-APPLE).

horse apples *n.* [1920s+] (US) nonsense (cf. HORSESHIT).

horse around *v.* 1 [20C] to joke, to mess about. 2 [1950s+] (US) to make sexual advances to, to indulge in sexual horseplay (cf. STUD v.). 3 [1950s+] (US) to be keen on becoming married. 4 [1950s+] (US) to sleep around, to philander.

horseback opinion *n.* [19C+] (US) a casual judgement, an off-hand opinion (cf. BALL-PARK FIGURE). [a man estimating the extent of his land by riding round it on horseback but making no accurate measurements]

horse biscuit *see* HORSE APPLE.

horse-bite *n.* [1940s+] a rough pinch on the thigh.

horse/monkey blanket *n.*[1] [late 19C+] (US Black) (orig. milit.) an overcoat.

horse/money/saddle blanket *n.*[2] [20C] (US) a griddle cake (cf. BLANKET ON THE COALS).

horse buss *n.* [late 18C-19C] 1 a loud smacking kiss. 2 a bite (cf. HORSE KISS). [SE *horse* + *buss*, a kiss, ult. earlier *bass*]

horse chaunter *n.* [mid-19C] a crooked horse dealer (cf. CHANTER).

horsechips *n.* [1960s] (US) nonsense (cf. HORSESHIT). [SE *horse chips*, horse droppings]

horsecock *n.*[1] [1920s-50s] (US) nonsense (cf. HORSESHIT). [SE *horse* + COCK n.[4] (2)]

horsecock *n.*[2] 1 [1940s+] (US) a sausage, salami. 2 [1940s+] (US) a large penis. [SE *horse* + COCK n.[2] (1)]

horse-collar *n.* 1 [19C] the vagina, esp. when considered larger than average (cf. DONKEY'S YAWN). 2 [1900s-10s] (US) a zero, esp. in sport. 3 [1940s-50s] (Can./US) a clerical or man's high collar. [supposed resemblances]

horse cop *n.* [1940s-70s] (US) a mounted police officer. [SE *horse* + COP n.[1]]

horsecrap *n.* [1930s-70s] (US) nonsense (cf. HORSESHIT). [SE *horse* + CRAP n.[3] (2)]

horsed *adj.* [late 17C-late 19C] 1 flogged. 2 held on another person's back before receiving a flogging. [HORSE v.[2]]

horse dookie *n.* [1970s] (US) nonsense (cf. HORSESHIT). [SE *horse* + DUKIE n.[2]]

horse doughnut/dumpling *see* HORSE APPLE.

horsed up *adj.* [20C] (US) of a woman, showy, overdressed, over made-up. [ASTOR'S PET HORSE]

horse-faker *n.* [late 19C] a horse dealer. [SE *horse* + FAKER n.[2]]

horsefeathers *n.* [1920s+] (orig. US) nonsense, rubbish (cf. BULLFEATHERS; HOTSY-TOTSY). [euph. for HORSESHIT; supposedly coined by the comic strip artist William de Beck]

horseflesh *n.* [late 17C] work that is charged for before it is actually done. [ult. SE phr. *dead horse*, anything that is beyond saving or use and cannot be revived. The work, which will bring in no further money, is no more use than a 'dead horse']

horse-/hoss-fly *n.* [mid-19C-1930s] (US) a fellow.

horse foaled by an acorn *phr.* [mid-17C-mid-19C] the gallows. [which are made of wood]

horse fuck *n.* [1970s] sexual intercourse with the man using rear entry (cf. DOGFUCK n.[1]). [SE *horse* + FUCK v.[1]]

horse-fucking *adj.* [1960s] (US) very large.

horse godmother *n.* [late 18C-19C] a large masculine woman, 'a gentlemanlike kind of lady' (Grose, 1785).

horse-head *n.* [1950s] (US) a heroin addict (cf. ACID-HEAD). [HORSE n.[12] + sfx. -HEAD (2)]

horse heads *n.* [1970s+] (drugs) amphetamines (cf. A n.²). [? packaging or like the celebrated severed horse's head in a film-maker's bed in the book/film *The Godfather* (1969/1972), the drug makes one 'jump out of bed']

horse heavy *n.* [1940s] (US Black) a fat person.

horse-high, bull-strong, pig-tight *phr.* [20C] (US) totally secure, esp. used of financial dealings. [19C agricultural jargon referring to the qualities required of a 'lawful fence'; it required 5 strands of wire, must be too high to be jumped by a horse, too strong to be butted down by a bull and too tight to be wormed through by a pig. Some versions added *goose-proof*, many substitute *hog* for *pig*]

horse hockey *n.* [1960s+] (US) nonsense (cf. HORSESHIT). [SE *horse* + HOCKIE n. (2)]

horse hooey *n.* [1980s+] (US) nonsense (cf. HORSESHIT). [SE *horse* + HOOEY n.]

horse it *phr.* **1** [late 19C] (US) to walk fast. **2** [20C] to work hard. [the strength and stamina of the animal]

horse kiss *n.* [late 17C–late 18C] a rough, heavy kiss (cf. HORSE BUSS). [the image is of a horse's mouth, with large teeth and lips]

horse-leech *n.¹* [late 16C–mid-17C] a quack doctor. [SE *horse-leech*, a veterinary surgeon]

horse-leech *n.²* [mid-17C] a prostitute. [SE *horse-leech*, a sucking worm]

horseman *n.¹* [18C+] a promiscuous man, a philanderer. [HORSE v.¹; his 'riding' of women]

horseman *n.²* [20C] (Can. Und.) a Mountie, a member of the Royal Canadian Mounted Police (RCMP).

horse manure *n.* [1920s+] (US) nonsense, rubbish; also as excl. (cf. HORSESHIT). [euph.]

horse-marine *n.* [mid-19C] an awkward person. [traditional sailors' disdain for the poor seamanship of the Royal Marines]

horsemeat *n.* **1** [1920s] (US) corned beef. **2** [1980s+] (US gay) a large penis (cf. BACON n.¹; DINK n.³; HORSECOCK n.²). [the low opinion in which the meat is held]

horse-milliner *n.* [19C] a saddle and harness maker.

horse-nails *n.* [mid-19C] money (cf. BRADS; RIVETS). [SE *horse-nail*, a nail used to secure a horseshoe]

horse of another colour *phr.* [19C] a very different topic. [SE by 20C]

horse opera *n.* **1** [mid-19C–1940s] (US) a show featuring trained horses. **2** [1920s+] (orig. US) a Western, whether on film or television (cf. SAGEBRUSHER). [on model of SOAP OPERA]

horse piss/pee *n.* [20C] (US) weak coffee or weak beer (cf. GNAT'S PISS; SHEEP-WASH).

horse-protestant *n.* [20C] (Irish) **1** the country gentry. **2** in pl. Protestants in general. [as opposed to the Catholic peasantry]

horseplayer *n.* [1930s+] a gambler on horse-races.

horse-pox *n.* [mid-17C–18C] an especially severe strain of venereal disease, esp. as used in excl.

horse pucky *n.* [1970s+] (US) nonsense; also as excl. (cf. HORSESHIT, HORSE HOCKEY). [SE *horse* + PUCKY]

horseradish *n.* [1920s–60s] (US) nonsense; also as excl. (cf. HORSESHIT). [euph.]

horses *n.¹* [late 19C+] (US gambling) mis-spotted dice in craps. [abbr. *horse dice*]

horses *n.²* [20C] horsepower. [abbr.]

horses! *excl.* [1920s] (US) an excl. used to express anger or disappointment. [abbr. HORSESHIT]

horses and carts *n.* [20C] darts. [rhy. sl.]

horse's arse/ass *n.* [mid-19C+] **1** a fool, an idiot (cf. DICKHEAD; HORSE'S HANGDOWN). **2** a general term of abuse.

horse's hangdown *n.* [20C] a fool, an idiot (cf. DICKHEAD;

HORSE'S ARSE). [SE *hangdown*, i.e. the animal's penis, thus cf. DORK n.²; PRICK]

horse-shed *v.* [19C+] (US) to attempt to influence another person's opinion, esp. in political matters; thus *horseshedder*, one who tried to influence opinions. [SE *horse-shed*, into which a political campaigner might take a potential supporter for a chat and possibly a quiet drink or even the passing of a small bribe]

horseshit *n.* **1** [1920s+] horse dung. **2** [1920s+] rubbish, nonsense (cf. BULLSHIT n.; HORSEFEATHERS). **3** [1940s] (US) a damn, e.g. *that isn't worth horsehit.* [SE *horse* + SHIT n.]

horseshit *adj.* [1930s+] (US) contemptible, offensive, worthless. [HORSESHIT n.]

horseshit *v.* [1950s+] (US) to lie, to flatter. [var. on BULLSHIT v.]

horseshit! *excl.* [1960s+] (US) an excl. of disgust, disappointment. [HORSESHIT n.]

horseshit luck *n.* [1970s] (US) surprising and exceptional good luck. [the superstition that stepping in horse droppings betokens good luck]

horseshoe *n.¹* [18C–1900s] the female genitals. [resemblance]

horseshoe *n.²* [1910s–20s] (US) a propensity for good luck. [the trad. association of horseshoes and luck]

horse's hoof *n.* [1950s+] a male homosexual (cf. IRON HOOF). [rhy. sl. *horse's hoof* = POOF n.]

horse-skinner *n.* [1920s–50s] (Can.) one who drives horse teams.

horse's meal *n.* [late 18C–late 19C] a meal that has no accompanying drink, alcoholic or otherwise. [cf. synon. Scot. and Yorks. dial. *horse-feast*]

horse's neck *n.¹* [20C] (orig. US) ginger ale flavoured with lemon peel, with or without whisky, brandy or gin. [ety. unknown; Lighter (1997) suggests a link to HORSE'S NECK n.² or to HORSE'S ASS, but gives no reason]

horse's neck *n.²* [1920s–70s] (US) a fool, an idiot, a general term of abuse. [partial euph. for HORSE'S ASS]

horse's nightcap *n.* [late 18C–early 19C] the cap pulled over the condemned man's head before his death (cf. DIE IN A HORSE'S NIGHTCAP).

horse's ovaries *n.* [1930s–70s] (US) hors d'oeuvres. [intentional malapropism]

horse sovereign *n.* [late 19C] a sovereign coin decorated by Benedetto Pistrucci (1784–1855) with effigies of St George and the Dragon (cf. DRAGON n.²).

horse's patoot/patootie *n.* [1980s+] (US) a fool, an idiot, a general term of abuse. [partial euph. for HORSE'S ASS]

horse thief *n.* [1920s+] (US) a dishonest person.

horse tracks *n.* [1970s+] (drugs) phencyclidine (cf. ACE n.³).

horse tranquillizer *n.* [1970s+] (drugs) phencyclidine (cf. ACE n.³). [the legitimate use of the drug as an animal tranquillizer]

horsewomen *n.* [20C] masculine lesbians. [they 'ride' their partner]

horsey *adj.* [20C] (US) **1** amorous, lustful, frolicsome. **2** impatient, rude, peremptory. [HORSE v.³]

hortical *adj.* [1950s+] (W.I./UK Black teen) genuine, sincere, respected (cf. ARTICAL). [? SE *exhort*]

hortical don *n.* [1950s+] (W.I. Rasta) respected, acclaimed person. [HORTICAL + DON n.¹]

hortus *n.* [18C] the vagina. [Lat. *hortus*, a garden]

hose *n.¹* **1** [1920s+] (US) the penis. **2** [1960s] (US) a prostitute's pimp. **3** [1980s] (US campus) a boyfriend. [joc. uses of SE; but (2) ? HO n.¹]

hose *n.²* [1980s+] (US campus) a promiscuous woman. [? HO n.¹ or HOSE v.¹ (2)]

hose *v.¹* **1** [1920s] (US campus) to curry favour with. **2** [1930s+] to copulate with (always from a man's point of view). **3** [1960s+] (gay) to sodomize. [HOSE n.¹]

hose *v.*² **1** [1910s+] to fire at with a machine gun. **2** [1920s+] (US orig. police/Und.) to beat with a rubber hose, to punish. **3** [1940s+] (US) to cheat, to victimize. [SE *hose* (*down*)]

hosebag *n.* [1970s] (orig. US campus) a promiscuous woman. [ext. HOSE n.²; ? + pun, she is a 'bag' for the male HOSE n.¹]

hosebeast *n.* [1990s] (US) a sexually promiscuous person. [HOSE n.² + BEAST n.²]

hosed *adj.* [1990s] (US Black) in trouble, in difficulties. [HOSE v.² (3)]

hosed and shod *phr.* [late 17C–mid-18C] born to wealth and power, usu. in phr. *come in hosed …* .

hosed out *adj.* [1960s] (US) exhausted. [SE *hose*]

hose down *v.* [1910s+] (orig. milit.) to fire at, usu. with automatic weapons or aircraft weapons. [HOSE v.² (1)]

hosehead *n.* [1980s+] (US campus) a stupid person. [SE *hose* + sfx. -HEAD (1)]

hose in *v.* [1980s+] (N.Z.) to win easily (cf. HOSE OUT).

hose job *n.* [1970s+] (US) fellatio. [HOSE n.¹ (1) + JOB n.⁵]

hoseman *n.* [1970s] (US) an exceptionally virile man (cf. COCKSMAN). [HOSE n.¹ (1) + sfx. -*man*]

hose monster *n.* [1980s+] (US) a sexually promiscuous person. [HOSE n.² + SE *monster*]

hose off *v.*¹ [1950s+] (N.Z.) to annoy, to infuriate.

hose off *v.*² [1980s] (US) to get out, to send off. [? play on PISS OFF]

hose off! *excl.* [1980s] (US) go away! be off! [HOSE OFF v.²]

hose one's hole, to *phr.* [20C] of a woman, to masturbate. [? by using the stimulating qualities of a shower head]

hose-out *n.* [1930s] (US campus) a useless person. [HOSE n.¹; thus cf. DORK n.²; DICKHEAD; PRICK or the image of a hose that is out of water]

hose out *v.* [1970s+] (N.Z.) to beat comprehensively (cf. HOSE IN).

hose queen *n.* [1980s+] (US campus) a sexually promiscuous woman. [HOSE n.² + QUEEN n.²]

hoser *n.* [1980s+] (Can./US campus) **1** a womanizer. **2** a fool, an idiot, an uncultured, boorish person (cf. DORK n.²; DICKHEAD; PRICK). [HOSE n.¹]

ho shit *n.* [1990s] (US Black teen) women's clothing that is seen as overtly sexy. [HO n.¹ + SHIT n.⁶; not necessarily pej.]

hosie *see* HOOZIE.

hospitable roofer *see* ROOFER n.².

hospital game *n.* [late 19C] soccer or football. [the broken limbs that accompany it]

hospital heroin *n.* [1950s+] (drugs) Dilaudid. [a synthetic opiate used in hospitals as a substitute for heroin]

hoss *n.*¹ *see* HORSE n.⁴.

hoss *n.*² *see* HORSE n.¹².

hoss-fly *see* HORSE-FLY.

hoss it *v.* [1960s–70s] (US campus) to walk hurriedly. [the animal's speed]

hostie *n.* [1960s+] (Aus.) air *hostess* (cf. STEW n.⁴). [abbr.]

ho stroll *n.* [1960s+] (US Black pimp) the street or streets in a town or city where prostitutes work regularly (cf. BRICKS; STROLL; TRACK n.²). [HO n.¹ (1) + STROLL n.]

hot *n.*¹ [mid–late 19C] beer mixed with gin.

hot *n.*² **1** [20C] (US) a hot meal; thus *hot up*, to heat up (usu. leftovers) (cf. THREE HOTS AND A COT). **2** [1910s–20s] (US) sexual intercourse.

hot *adj.*¹ **1** [14C+] sexually aroused, sexually available. **2** [late 16C+] furious, extremely angry. **3** [late 16C+] zealous, eager, enthusiastic. **4** [17C+] reckless, boisterous. **5** [mid–late 19C] lively, energetic. **6** [mid-19C–1950s] (US) highly amusing, esp. if ironic, ludicrous; thus a *hot one*. **7** [late 19C+] attractive, pleasurable, a general term of approval. **8** [late 19C+] urgent, pressing, poss. dangerous. **9** [late 19C+] of books, films etc, erotic, sexually stimulating, pornographic. **10** [1920s+]

orig. applied by men to women, sexy, sexually attractive. **11** [1930s+] (US) fast or powerful. **12** [20C] very popular or promising, thus commercially successful.

hot *adj.*² (Und.) **1** [17C+; mid-19C+] dangerous, thus unsafe for criminal activity. **2** [early/mid-19C+] known to or wanted by the police, suspect. **3** [early–mid-19C+] of goods, stolen. **4** [1920s+] of money or documents, forged or counterfeit. **5** [1920s–60s] (US Und.) of a house or place, occupied while being robbed. [(1) orig. SE]

hot *adj.*³ **1** [18C+] (US) drunk, usu. in combs. e.g. *hot as a red wagon*, *hotter than love in haying-time*, *hotter than a skunk*. **2** [19C] suffering from venereal disease or pubic lice. **3** [1930s+] (US drugs) of an injection or drug, likely to cause death (cf. HOT-SHOT n.³). **4** [1940s+] (US) radioactive. **5** [1950s+] (US) of a part of body, an organ, seriously physically infected.

hot *adj.*⁴ [mid-19C+] **1** of a sportsman, playing well, on top form, also used fig. of any contestant, in business etc. **2** of a gambler enjoying a run of luck; thus *hot favourite*, the person or animal most likely to win a race or other sporting contest. **3** (US) first-rate, later used ironically, not so good. **4** very adept, skilful (cf. HOT ON; HOT STUFF).

hot/hot up *v.*¹ [late 19C+] **1** to heat, to warm up. **2** of events, to become more exciting, more dramatic.

hot *v.*² [1920s] to tell off, to reprimand.

hot *v.*³ [1990s] to indulge in joy-riding of stolen cars. [HOTTING]

hot *adv.* [late 19C+] ardently, eagerly, violently, severely, angrily. [HOT adj.¹]

hot air *n.* [late 19C+] (orig. US) nonsense, rubbish, empty chatter; thus *hot-air artist*, *hot-air merchant*, one who indulges in talk of this kind.

hot and cold *n.*¹ [20C] gold. [rhy sl.]

hot and cold *n.*² [1970s–80s] (US drugs) a combination of heroin and cocaine. [initial letters, pus fig. ref. to the effects of the drugs]

hot and heavy, like a tailor's goose *phr.* [late 17C–18C] a phr. applied to a passionate lover. [SE *goose*, a tailor's iron, the neck of which supposedly resembles that of the bird; ? + the hissing noise it makes when the heated iron meets the dampened cloth]

hot-and-nice *n.* [1940s] (W.I.) a meat patty.

hot and strong *phr.* [late 19C+] severe, intense, usu. in phr. *give/get it hot and strong*, to deliver or receive a severe punishment.

hot-arsed/-assed *adj.* [17C+] of a woman, lecherous, lascivious. [HOT adj.¹ + ARSE n.¹]

hot as a fire-cracker *phr.* [1910s+] (Can.) sexually promiscuous. [HOT adj.¹]

hot as floogies *phr.* [20C] (US) extremely hot (cf. FLUGENS!). [*floogy* = *floozy*, a 'hot', i.e. a sexually active woman]

hot as/hotter than a fresh-fucked fox in a forest fire *phr.* [1950s+] (US) extremely hot, whether as to temperature or sexuality.

hot as a three-dollar pistol *phr.* [20C] (US) very hot. [play on SE *hot*/HOT adj.² (3)]

hot-ass *adj.* [late-20C] superlative. [SE *hot* + ARSE n.¹]

hot-assed *see* HOT-ARSED.

hot baby *n.* [1900s] (US campus) a student who excels in a certain subject. [HOT adj.¹ + BABY n.²]

hot-backed *adj.* [17C] of a woman, promiscuous, sexually voracious (cf. HOT-ARSED).

hotbed *n.* [1920s+] (US) **1** a bed in a cheap rooming-house that could be hired for 25 cents for 8 hours (cf. HOT-SHEET HOTEL). **2** a cheap rooming-house. [the beds are continually occupied]

hot beef/meat/mutton *n.* [19C] a promiscuous woman (cf. ACHING FOR A SIDE OF BEEF). [HOT adj.¹ + BEEF n.¹/ MEAT/ MUTTON n.²]

hot beef! *excl.* [mid–late 19C] a cry of alarm, synon. with and rhyming on SE 'stop thief!' (cf. CRY BEEF).

hot beef injection *see* BEEF INJECTION.

hot/pepper belly *n.* [20C] (US) a Mexican. [racial stereotyping, Mexicans like hot, peppery food]

hot biscuit *n.* [1980s+] (US) something exciting.

hot blanketer/blanketeer *n.* [late 19C] one who pawns their blankets on a daily basis to provide money for food. [the blankets are still *hot* from being slept in]

hot book *n.* [1940s+] (US) a pornographic magazine, book. [HOT adj.^{1} + SE *book*]

hot-bot/lady hot-bot *n.* [20C] a promiscuous, sexually voracious woman (cf. HOT-ARSED; HOT-BACKED). [HOT adj.^{1} + SE *bottom*]

hot box *n.* **1** [20C] (US) the female genitals. **2** [1930s–60s] (US) a sexually promiscuous woman. [HOT adj.^{1} (1) + BOX n.^{6}]

hot box *v.* **1** [1940s] (drugs) to hold onto a marijuana cigarette for too long before passing it. **2** [1980s+] (US drugs) to fill a small sealed room with the smoke of cannabis or crack cocaine.

hot boy *n.* [1960s] (W.I.) a fashionable young man, a 'young blood'. [HOT adj.^{1} + SE *boy*]

hot buns *n.* [1980s+] (US gay) the buttocks, esp. when attractive. [HOT adj.^{1} + BUNS n.^{2}]

hot button *n.* [1970s+] (US) something that affects someone, provoking a response.

hot cack *adj.* [20C] (Aus.) very good. [SE *hot* + CACK n.^{1}; ? euph. of SHIT-HOT]

hotcakes *n.* [1980s+] (drugs) crack cocaine.

hot card *n.* [late 19C–1920s] (US) a provocative, lively person. [HOT adj.^{1} + CARD n.^{3}]

hotch *v.* [20C] to swarm with, to burst with. [Scot. *hotch*]

hotcha *n.* **1** [1930s+] (orig. US) hot jazz music, any flashy, exciting entertainment. **2** [1990s] (US) an exciting, attractive young woman. [HOTCHA!]

hotcha! *excl.* [1930s+] (orig. US) an excl. of enthusiasm and approval, esp. in phr. *with a hey nonny-nonny and a hotcha-cha.* [onomat.]

hot chair *n.* [1920s+] (US) the electric chair (cf. HOT SEAT; SIZZLE SEAT).

hot cock *n.* [1940s+] (Aus./US) nonsense, rubbish. [SE *hot* + COCK n.^{4} (2)]

hot coppers *n.* [19C] **1** a mouth and throat parched through excessive drinking. **2** a hangover (of which a dry throat is a primary symptom). [SE *hot* + *copper*, a large saucepan used for boiling either food or laundry]

hot corner *n.* [mid–late 19C] a difficult situation in which one finds oneself threatened, bullied or otherwise under attack. [HOT adj.^{2} + SE *corner*]

hot crate *n.* [1930s+] (Aus./US) a stolen car. [HOT adj.^{2} + CRATE n.^{1}]

hot cross bun *n.* [20C] **1** a gun. **2** (Aus.) the sun. **3** a son. [rhy. sl.]

hot cross bun *phr.* [20C] on the run. [rhy. sl.]

hot cup of tea *phr.* [late 19C–1910s] a sexually attractive woman (cf. CUP OF TEA n.^{2}; HOT STUFF).

hot damn!/dang! *excl.* [1930s+] (US) a general excl., usu. implying pleasure rather than fury.

hot diggety!/diggety dog! *excl.* [1920s+] (US) a general excl. of pleasure or surprise (cf. HOT ZIGGETY!).

hot dinner *n.* [20C] a winner. [rhy. sl.]

hot dog *n.*^{1} **1** [late 19C+] (orig. US) a spiced, heated sausage or frankfurter, served on a split roll and garnished, traditionally, with sauerkraut and mustard (cf. NEW YORK TUBE STEAK). **2** [1920s+] the penis (cf. BACON n.^{1}). [SE since *c.*1939, when it was served under that name by the Coney Island Chamber of Commerce to President Franklin D. Roosevelt and his guests,

King George VI and Queen Elizabeth of England, the hot dog started life as slang. It probably comes from heavy-handed mid-19C humour focusing on the supposed use of horse- and dog-meat as sausage filling, a concept that was accentuated by the 1843 scandal concerning the use of dog-meat for human consumption. The image was intensified by the use (*c.*1860) by German immigrants of *Hundewurst*, dog sausage, to mean smoked frankfurter sausages (larger sausages were *Pferdwurst*, horse baloney). The dachshund, of course, is a 'sausage dog']

hot dog *n.*^{2} [late 19C+] (orig. US campus) one who is particularly proficient at an occupation or activity, esp. a successful gambler. [HOT adj.^{1} + DOG n.^{9}]

hot dog *adj.*^{1} **1** [late 19C–1920s] (orig. US campus) good, excellent. **2** [1920s+] (US) showy, flamboyant. [HOT DOG n.^{2}]

hot dog *adj.*^{2} [1960s–70s] (US prison) pornographic. [HOT adj.^{1} (9)]

hot dog *v.* [1960s+] to chase, to harass. [HOT DOG n.^{2}]

hot dog!/hot doggies! *excl.* [20C] (orig. US campus) an expression of delight or strong approval (cf. HOT DIGGETY!).

hot-dogger *n.* [20C] (US teen/campus) **1** a show-off, a braggart. **2** a successful, talented individual. [HOT DOG n.^{2}]

hot dog stand is open *phr.* [20C] (US) a warning to a man that his trouser-fly is open. [HOT DOG n.^{1} (2)]

hot dope *n.* [1950s+] (drugs) heroin. [HOT adj.^{2} + DOPE n.^{1} (8)]

hot duke *v.* [1970s+] (Aus.) to fool, to take advantage by trickery (cf. HOTPOINT). [HOT adj.^{1} + DUKE n.^{3}]

hotel *n.* **1** [19C] the vagina (cf. COCK INN). **2** [mid-19C+] (US) a prison (cf. AKERMAN'S HOTEL).

hotel beat *n.* [late 19C] one who stays in hotels and then leaves without paying the bill. [SE *hotel* + BEAT v.]

hotel crowbar *n.* [1920s+] (Can.) a local prison (cf. AKERMAN'S HOTEL). [you need a *crowbar* to leave]

hot de garvie/garvey *n.* [1900s] (N.Z.) the Wellington prison. [its governor, one *Garvey*]

hotel de gink *n.* [1930s+] (US) (orig. among tramps) a lodging house. [SE *hotel* + GINK n.^{1}]

hotel-de-loose *n.* [late 19C] (US) a brothel. [pun on *hotel de luxe*/the *loose* women]

hotel warming-pan *n.* [19C] a hotel chambermaid (cf. SCOTCH WARMING-PAN). [her supposed sexual availability]

hot enchilada *see* HOT TACO.

hot enough to fuck *phr.* [1960s+] (US) very angry, furious. [FUCK v.^{1}]

hot fat *n.* [1990s] semen (cf. HOT MILK).

hot fat injection *n.* [1950s] (Aus.) sexual intercourse (cf. HOT MEAT INJECTION). [FAT n.^{2}]

hot flannel *n.* [18C–19C] heated gin and beer with nutmeg, sugar and spices.

hot-fling *n.*^{1} [20C] a particularly active bout of sex. [HOT adj.^{1} + SE *fling*, a fit of self-indulgence. Note 16C *fling*, to wriggle the buttocks during sex]

hot-fling *n.*^{2} [1990s] (US Black) an exciting sexual encounter with a new partner. [HOT FLING n.^{1}]

hot foot *n.* [late 19C+] (US) a malicious trick played on an unsuspecting sleeper. Matches are thrust end-first into the gap between the upper and sole of the shoe (or between naked toes if vulnerable); the matches are lit, and the shoe 'catches fire' or the flesh is painfully singed]

hot foot/hot foot it *v.* [late 19C+] (orig. US) **1** to rush around, to hurry, to run. **2** to chase away.

hot for/on *adv.* [1940s+] (orig. US) enthusiastic, keen on, esp. sexually. [HOT adj.^{1}]

hot ice *n.* [1990s] (drugs) smokeable methamphetamine. [SE *hot* + ICE n.]

hot in the biscuit *adj.* [1960s–70s] (US) very angry, furious (cf. DROVE; GEED-UP adj.^{2}). [HOT adj.^{1} + BISCUIT n.^{1}]

hot/light/warm in the tail *phr.* [late 17C–early 18C] wanton, promiscuous. [HOT adj.[1]/LIGHT adj./WARM adj. + TAIL n.[1]]

hot item *n.* [1980s+] (US) a couple having a romantic relationship. [SE *hot* + ITEM n. (3)]

hot-knife *v.* [1980s+] (drugs) to smoke cannabis from a heated knife; the fumes are sucked up through a broken-off milk-bottle neck.

Hotlanta/Hot Town *n.* [1970s+] (US) Atlanta, Georgia. [the city's actual and fig. temperature]

hot-lips *n.* [1920s+] (US) a nickname applied to someone with a reputation for passionate kissing.

hotload *n.*[1] [1970s+] (US) a powerful firearm cartridge.

hotload *n.*[2] [1980s+] (drugs) an overdose. [HOT adj.[2] + LOAD n.[7]]

hot lot *see* HOT MEMBER.

hot lot it *v.* [1970s] (US) to go at great speed.

hot-making *adj.* [1930s] embarrassing. [one's cheeks 'burn']

hot/red hot mama/mamma *n.* **1** [late 19C–1930s] a flighty young woman (cf. FLAPPER n.[3]). **2** [1920s–40s] (orig. US Black) a large, hedonistic woman, often an habitué of saloons, bars and nightclubs. [HOT adj.[1] + MAMA; note the entertainer Sophie Tucker (1884–1966), who billed herself as 'the last of the red hot mamas']

hot meat injection *n.* [1930s+] sexual intercourse (cf. BAY-ONET; BEEF INJECTION; HOT FAT INJECTION). [MEAT n.]

hot member/lot *n.* **1** [19C] a debauchee, a degenerate (cf. HOT 'UN). **2** [19C] one who flaunts convention. **3** [late 19C] a troublesome, quarrelsome person. **4** [late 19C–1910s] (US) a sexually attractive woman, also a prostitute. **5** [late 19C–1910s] (US) the penis (cf. DEAREST MEMBER). [HOT adj.[1] + SE *lot*]

hot milk *n.* [19C] semen (cf. HOT FAT).

hot minute *n.* [1930s+] (US) a moment.

hot needle burning thread *phr.* [20C] (W.I.) a phr. used to describe anything done in a hurry.

hotnot *n.* [1940s+] (S.Afr.) a derog. term for a Black person. [SE *Hottentot*]

hot number *n.* [late 19C+] a sexually attractive woman, also her telephone number, esp. if written on the wall of a phone booth. [HOT adj.[1] + NUMBER n.[1] + pun]

hot nuts *n.* [1930s+] (US) usu. of a man, strong sexual desire. [HOT adj.[1] + NUTS n.[2]]

hot off the bat *see* RIGHT OFF THE BAT.

hot oil *n.*[1] [1960s] (US) a predicament. [var. on HOT WATER]

hot oil *n.*[2] [1980s] (US Black) a self-opinionated person, an important person (cf. BIG SHOT n.; HOT-SHIT n.; HOT-SHOT n.[2]; HOT STUFF n.[1]).

hot on *adv.*[1] [late 19C+] **1** very severe towards. **2** very skilful at. [HOT adj.[1]]

hot on *adv.*[2] *see* HOT FOR.

hot on hand *see* HEAVY ON HAND.

hot on someone's tail *see* ON SOMEONE'S TAIL.

hot pants *n.* **1** [1920s+] (US) strong sexual desire, also a sexually eager woman. **2** [1960s–70s] (US) extreme keenness.

hot patootie *n.* [1910s–70s] (US) an attractive young woman. [var. on HOT POTATO n.[2]]

hot-pillow joint *n.* [1940s+] (US) a cheap hotel that rents out its rooms by the hour to prostitutes and their clients or to (illicit) lovers (cf. FAST-SHEET HOTEL). [the pillows (and beds) are always in use]

hot place *n.* [19C+] (US) euph. for HELL.

hotpoint *v.* [1970s+] (Aus.) to fool, to take advantage by trick-ery; thus *hotpointer*, one who does this. [the trickster *points out* something that is supposedly HOT adj.[1]]

hot poop *n.* [1960s+] the latest news or gossip. [HOT adj.[1] + POOP n.[4]]

hot pot *n.*[1] [late 17C–18C] a hot drink made of ale and brandy (cf. HUCKLE-MY-BUFF; HUGGLE-MY-BUFF).

hot pot *n.*[2] [1920s–30s] (US Black) a sexually promiscuous woman. [she is always 'on the boil']

hot potato *n.*[1] [late 19C] a waiter. [rhy. sl.; Cockney pron. 'pertater']

hot potato *n.*[2] [late 19C+] (US) a admirable, clever or ener-getic person. [HOT adj.[1] + POTATO n.[2]]

hot potato *n.*[3] [1950s+] (orig. US) a problem, a difficult per-son, a trying situation, anything those concerned would pre-fer not to handle.

hot potato *adv.* (Aus.) later. [rhy. sl.; Aus. pron. 'pertater']

hot property *n.* [1950s+] a success, a sensation.

hot prowl *n.* [1930s+] (US police/Und.) a burglary while the occupants of the building are present. [HOT adj.[2] + SE *prowl*]

hot puppy!/puppies! *excl.* [1920s+] (US) an excl. of pleasure. [var. on HOT DOG!]

hot rock *v.* [1980s+] (drugs) to drop burning lumps of can-nabis from a cigarette onto one's clothes. [HOT ROCKS n.[2]]

hot rocks *n.*[1] **1** [1920s] (US campus) someone or something splendid. **2** [1940s+] (US) esp. of a man, strong sexual desire. **3** [1950s] (US) as a form of address. [HOT adj.[1] + ROCKS]

hot rocks *n.*[2] [1980s+] (Aus. drugs) hot ash, sucked through a pipe, which burns one's throat.

hot-rod *n.* **1** [1940s–50s] a car modified for speed and flashi-ness (cf. SPEED SHOP). **2** [1950s+] (US) an aggressive, unruly young man. [HOT adj.[1] + ROD n.[4]/n.[1]. Subseq. use of (1) is SE]

hot-rod *adj.* [1950s+] (US) energetic, aggressive. [HOT-ROD n.]

hot roller *n.* [1970s+] (US police) a stolen car, esp. while being driven. [HOT adj.[2] + ROLLER n.[2]]

hot roll with cream *phr.* [late 19C+] sexual intercourse. [HOT adj.[1] + ROLL n.[2] + CREAM n.[1]; pun on SE]

hots, the *n.*[1] [1940s+] sexual desire. [HOT adj.[1]]

hots *n.*[2] [1980s+] (US campus) electric hair rollers. [abbr. SE *hot rollers*]

hot scone *n.* [1920s+] (Aus.) a policeman, a detective. [rhy. sl. *hot scone* = JOHN n.[3]]

hot seat/squat *n.* [1920s+] (US) **1** the electric chair (cf. BAR-BECUE n.[3]; HOT CHAIR; SIT IN THE HOT SEAT). **2** an unpleasant situ-ation, esp. in a courtroom or public enquiry.

hot session *n.* [1920s–60s] (US) orig. sexual intercourse, a good time. [HOT adj.[1] (1) + SE *session*]

hot sex on a platter *phr.* [1990s] **1** (US Black teen) a very sexy woman. **2** overtly or excessively sexy clothes (cf. HO SHIT).

hot sheet *n.* [1920s+] (US police) a list of stolen property and of crimes under investigation. [the items that are HOT adj.[2]]

hot-sheet hotel/motel *n.* [1940s+] (US) a hotel that rents out some or all of its rooms to prostitutes, adulterous couples and others who wish to use the beds for short periods rather than for overnight accommodation (cf. FAST-SHEET HOTEL). [such beds are in near-continuous occupation and thus stay warm]

hot-shit *n.* [1950s+] (orig. US) an important person or some-one who thinks they are (cf. HOT OIL n.[2]). [HOT adj.[1] + SHIT n.[9]]

hot-shit *adj.* **1** [1960s+] (US) splendid. **2** [1970s+] (US) offensively self-conceited. [HOT-SHIT n.]

hot-shit! *excl.* [1940s+] (US) an expression of excitement, enthusiasm.

hot-shit for *phr.* [1970s+] (US) keen or enthusiastic. [HOT-SHIT!]

hot-shot *n.*[1] [late 19C–1920s] (US) a cutting or sarcastic remark. [HOT adj.[1] + SHOT n.[4]]

hot-shot *n.*[2] [1920s+] (orig. US) an important, influential per-son or one who believes that they are (cf. HOT OIL n.[2]). [note 17C *hot-shot*, one who discharged his firearm too enthusi-astically]

hot-shot *n.*[3] [1930s+] (drugs) the substitution of cyanide or battery acid for white powdered heroin; when injected by the addict, it causes instant death and leaves no trace. [HOT adj.[2] + SHOT n.[5]]

hot-shot n.[4] [1960s] (US) bad homemade liquor, bootleg whisky. [whisky distilling jargon *hot shot*, the first drops of distilled liquor in a batch to be produced]

hot-shot adj. [1920s] (orig. US) conceited, self-opinionated, ostentatious. [HOT-SHOT n.[2]]

hotshot charlie n. [1940s–70s] (US) a nickname for a brash, egotistical young man. [HOT-SHOT adj. + CHARLIE n.[6]; coined in Milton Caniff's comic strip 'Terry and the Pirates' (1940s+)]

hot-shot in a mustard-pot, to be a phr. [17C] to be or to esteem oneself an important man (cf. HOT-SHOT n.[2]).

hot-shot indeed, to be a phr. [17C] to be an important man (cf. MUSTARD POT).

hot sketch n. [1910s–30s] (US) **1** an attractive young woman. **2** an amusing thing. [HOT adj.[1] + SE *sketch*, a drawing]

hotsmoke n. [1980s+] (drugs) the smoking of crack cocaine.

hot spit n. [1930s+] (US) anything good, exciting, sexually attractive (cf. HOT-SHIT; HOT STUFF n.[2]).

hot spot n. [1930s+] (US) a popular, fashionable nightclub, bar. [HOT adj.[1] + SPOT n.[6]]

hot squat see HOT SEAT.

hot stepper n. [20C] (W.I./UK Black teen) a prison-breaker, a fugitive from prison or a penal institution. [he runs off 'as if his feet were on fire']

hot stick n. [1950s+] (drugs) a marijuana cigarette. [HOT adj.[2] + STICK n.[14]]

hot-stopping n. [mid-19C] hot spirits and water.

hot stuff n.[1] [mid-19C–1920s] (US) spiced rum, strong alcohol.

hot stuff n.[2] [late 19C+] (orig. US) **1** something or someone considered first-rate, excellent (cf. HOT OIL n.[2]). **2** an attractive woman. **3** a clever, intelligent person (cf. FIERY LOT). [HOT adj.[1] + SE *stuff*]

hot stuff n.[3] [1920s+] (US) stolen goods. [HOT adj.[2] (3) + SE *stuff*]

hot stuff! excl. [late 19C+] form of address, often implying that the person in question has a higher opinion of themself than does the audience. [HOT STUFF n.[2]]

hot supper n. [1930s–60s] (US Black) a switch-blade knife or flick-knife. [? used for robberies it will obtain one the money for food]

hotsy-totsy adj. [1920s+] (orig. US) excellent, satisfactory, just right. [ext. of HOT adj.[1]; coined by cartoonist William 'Billie' de Beck, *c*.1926]

hot taco/enchilada n. [1970s] (US) a passionate young woman, esp. Hispanic (cf. HOT TAMALE). [one of several terms that equate women with food (cf. BANANA n.[2])]

hot-tailed adj.[1] [late 17C–early 18C] infected with venereal disease. [HOT adj.[3] (2) + TAIL n.[1]]

hot-tailed adj.[2] [1960s+] of a woman, lecherous, lascivious (cf. HOT-ARSED). [HOT adj.[1] + TAIL n.[1]]

hot tamale n. **1** [late 19C–1930s] (US) a clever person, often used ironically. **2** [late 19C+] (US) an attractive, sexy, young woman (cf. HOT TACO).

hot tamale! excl. [1940s+] (US) an excl. of excitement, pleasure.

Hottentot n. **1** [late 17C+] (S.Afr.) a derog. term for a Black person. **2** [late 19C–1910s] used in the East End of London to denote a stranger; thus cry *Hottentots!* strangers coming! **3** [late 19C–1910s] a fool, a simpleton. [proper name Hottentot, possibly meaning 'stutterer' or 'stammerer'. 'One of the two sub-races of the Khoisanid race (the other being the Sanids or Bushmen), characterized by short stature, yellow-brown skin colour, and tightly curled hair. They are of mixed Bushman-Hamite descent with some Bantu admixture, and are now found principally in South-West Africa' (*OED*). Since 18C the term has been used abusively, to describe someone 'uncivilized' and of inferior intelligence and culture]

Hottentot apron n. [20C] elongated labia (cf. BOON LIP). [the physical characteristics of 'Hottentot' women]

Hottentots n. [20C] the buttocks. [the nakedness of African tribespeople]

hotten up one's copper, to phr. [20C] (N.Z.) to have something warm to eat and drink (cf. HOT COPPERS).

hotter n. [1990s] one who indulges in the taking and driving away (and often destruction) of cars. [HOTTING]

hotter than a fresh-fucked fox in a forest fire see HOT AS A FRESH-FUCKED FOX IN A FOREST FIRE.

hotter than French love phr. [20C] (US) of weather, extremely hot. [racial stereotyping]

hot ticket n. [1960s+] (US campus) a person, event or object that is currently fashionable or stylish. [orig. theatre use, a successful show or performer]

hottie n.[1] [20C] (orig. Aus.) a *hot*-water bottle. [abbr.]

hottie n.[2] [20C] (Aus.) a very unlikely story. [HOT adj.[1] (6)]

hottie n.[3] [1990s] (US Black) a good-looking or promiscuous member of the opposite sex. [HOT STUFF n.[2] (2)]

hot tiger n. [mid-19C] a mixture of hot-spiced ale and sherry, originated at Oxford University.

hotting n. [1990s] the vogue term for what used, prosaically, to be known as *joy-riding*, or, in legal parlance, *taking and driving away*. [HOT adj.[1] + adj.[2]; the 'hotter' steals a high performance car, drives it off and, often to the cheers of an appreciative crowd, puts it, and his own driving skills through their paces, emphasizing skids, spins and hand-brake turns – the stuff of film car chases]

hot toddy n. [20C] a body. [rhy. sl.]

hot tomato n. [1920s–30s] (US) a smart fellow.

hot to trot phr. [1950s+] **1** enthusiastic for sex. **2** eager to leave, to be moving.

Hot Town see HOTLANTA.

hot 'un n. [19C] a debauchee, a degenerate (cf. HOT MEMBER). [HOT adj.[1] + SE *one*]

hot up see HOT v.[1]

hot water n. [16C+] difficulties, problems (cf. BOIL).

hot wheels n. [1960s+] a stolen car or cars. [HOT adj.[2] + WHEELS n.[1]]

hot-wire v. [1950s+] (orig. US) to start a car without an ignition key by making the required connection between two wires. [the electric spark thus produced is 'hot']

hot with n. [mid-19C] hot spirits and water with sugar (cf. COLD WITHOUT).

hot ziggety! excl. [1900s–50s] (US) used to express excitement, enjoyment. [var. on HOT DIGGETY!]

houdini n.[1] [20C] (US campus) someone who avoids work. [joc. ref. to Harry *Houdini* (1874–1926), US conjuror and escape artist]

houdini/houbini n.[2] [1980s+] (US drugs) marijuana. [escapologist Harry *Houdini* (1874–1926); the smoker 'escapes' reality]

hough/haugh/hoch/huff n. [20C] **1** a thigh. **2** a mess. [SE *hough*, the hollow part of the human knee joint; the adjacent section of the thigh]

houghmagandy n. [20C] (Ulster/Scot.) adulterous sexual intercourse. [? *hough*, the hollow part of the human knee joint; the adjacent section of the thigh + *canty*, cheerful, lively, brisk; but note ? fig. use of HASHMAGANDY]

hou jou bek! excl. [1910s+] (S.Afr.) shut your trap! [Afk. *bek*, a animal's mouth, when used of human it is sl.; note Fr. *ferme ta gueule*, shut your gob, in which *gueule*, usu. of an animal is sl. when used of human]

hoult n. [20C] (Irish) **1** a sexually attractive woman, often qualified as a *fine/great/good hoult*. **2** sexual intercourse. [pron. of SE *hold* n.]

hound n.[1] [1950s+] (US Black) a Grey*hound* Corporation bus. [abbr.]

hound n.[2] [1960s] (US) 'the daylights', 'the stuffing'; thus *kick/knock the hound out of.*

hound n.[3] [1980s+] (US Black) an indiscriminatingly promiscuous man. [abbr. PUSSY-HOUND]

hound adj. [1950s–60s] (US prison) cowardly (cf. DOG n.[5]). [the neg. characteristics of a dog]

hound v. [1980s+] (US campus) to have sex with (cf. DOG OUT).

-hound sfx. [1910s+] an enthusiast, usu. for 'pleasures of the flesh' (cf. ASS-HOUND; BOOZE HOUND; COCK-HOUND; COKEHOUND; CUNT-HOUND; DICKHOUND; GASH-HOUND; HASH HOUND; LUSH HOUND; PLEASURE HOUND; PUSSY-HOUND; SAUCE-HOUND; SMOKE-HOUND; SMUT-HOUND).

hound dog n.[1] [20C] (US) a person of mixed race. [dial. *hound dog*, a mongrel]

hound dog n.[2] [20C] (US) one who hangs around when he or she is not wanted.

houndish adj. [20C] (W.I./Guyn.) shamelessly gluttonous. [SE *hound*, a glutton, but the noun form is rarely found]

Hounslow Heath n. [mid-19C] the teeth. [rhy. sl.]

hour-grunter n. [early 18C] a watchman. [watchmen patrolled the streets, calling out the time]

house n.[1] **1** [19C+] a whore-house, a house of ill-repute, a brothel (cf. ACCOMMODATION HOUSE) **2** [late 19C] a poor-house, a workhouse. **3** [late 19C–1930s] (society) a group of guests at a ball or dance who sit, eat and dance within their own circle only. **4** [20C] (US Und.) a police station. **5** [1970s+] (US Und.) a single prison cell (cf. DEN n.[2]; PAD n.[2]).

House, the n.[2] [late 19C] the London Stock Exchange.

house n.[3] [1990s] the most popular form of contemporary dance music, originated at Chicago's Warehouse Club and spread across the Western world; a direct descendant of disco, it features what critics dismiss as similarly mindless rhythms and banal lyrics, with the sole difference that electronic special effects (synthesizers, sampling, drum machines) have replaced the original instrumental playing (cf. ACID HOUSE PARTY).

house v.[1] [1980s+] **1** (US Black/rap music) to take for oneself, to steal. **2** [1990s] (US teen) to give, to take, to bring. [SE *house*, to take into a house]

house v.[2] [1980s+] (US Black/rap music) to excite and impress an audience. [? SE *bring down the house*]

house v.[3] **1** [1980s+] (US) to outdo, to defeat. **2** [1990s] (US) to attack someone violently. **3** [1990s] (US Black) to take over, to exert one's authority. [? fig. to send someone back to their house, and exclude them from street life]

house v.[4] [1990s] (US Black) to go, to come or move towards.

house-a-blazes adv. [1940s] (W.I.) utterly, completely.

house ape n. [1960s+] (US) a small child.

house-bit/-piece n. [mid-19C–1910s] a servant who doubles as a lover. [SE *house(maid)* + BIT n.[3]/PIECE n.[1]]

house-farmer see HOUSE-KNACKER.

house fee n. [1980s+] (drugs) a fee charged for entry into a room or apartment where one can smoke crack cocaine. [CRACK HOUSE + SE *fee*]

house for rent n. [18C–19C] **1** a widow's weeds (cf. APARTMENT TO LET; SIGN OF A HOUSE TO LET). **2** the widow herself. [a widow becomes 'vacant' for a new (male) 'tenant']

house hop n. [1930s+] (orig. US Black) a party at which the guests buy their refreshments to help pay the rent (cf. RENT PARTY). [SE *house* + HOP n.[1]]

house-keeper n. [1930s–40s] **1** a servant who doubles as a lover (cf. HOUSE-BIT). **2** a kept mistress.

house-knacker/-farmer n. [late 19C] a landlord. [SE *house-knacker*, one who buys old houses to strip out their materials or to convert them for profitable use]

housemaid's knee n. [1970s] the sea. [rhy. sl.]

houseman/house-man n. [1900s–20s] (US) a burglar. [his specializing in house-breaking rather than safe-cracking etc]

house mother n. [1960s+] in the sex industry, a madame. [HOUSE n.[1] (1) + SE *mother*]

house nigger/h.n. n. [1970s+] (US Black) **1** a Black person employed, often as the 'token nigger', i.e. token Black worker, in a mainly White organization. **2** a Black person who is seen as preferring White friends and opinions to those of their own community (cf. FIELD NIGGER n.[1]). [the slavery-era division between 'house' and 'field niggers', i.e. those who worked as indoor servants and those who worked in the fields; the former were seen as 'softer' than the latter]

house of civil reception n. [late 18C] a brothel (cf. ACCOMMODATION HOUSE).

House of Commons n. [late 18C–mid-19C] a privy, a lavatory (cf. HOUSE OF LORDS). [HOUSE (OF EASEMENT) + COMMONS; pun]

house of countless drops n. [1930s–40s] (US Black) a bar that sells grilled food as well as the usual liquor.

house of D n. [1960s+] (US prison) a *house of d*etention. [abbr.]

house of easement n. [17C] a privy (cf. CHAPEL OF EASE).

house of fraser n. [20C] a razor, either as a weapon or for shaving. [rhy. sl.; usu. as 'howser']

House of Lords n.[1] [early 19C+] the lavatory (cf. HOUSE OF COMMONS).

House of Lords n.[2] [20C] cords, i.e. corduroy trousers. [rhy. sl.]

house of noodles n. [mid-19C] the House of Lords. [NOODLE n.[1]]

house of office n. [17C] a privy (cf. LITTLE OFFICE).

house of pain n. [1940s] (US Black) the dentist's.

house of sale n. [late 16C–early 17C] a brothel (cf. ACCOMMODATION HOUSE). [HOUSE n.[1] (1)]

house of waste n. [late 18C–early 19C] a tavern. [the moral standpoint]

house party n. [20C] (US Black) a party held in a private house, for which an admission fee (to cover food and drink) is paid (cf. HOUSE-RENT PARTY; RENT PARTY).

house piece n. (drugs) a gift of crack cocaine, esp. when brought to the host of a party. [SE *house* + PIECE n.[5]]

house-plant n. [1910s+] (US) an indolent person who does nothing but sit around.

house-rent party/shake/stomp/strut n. [20C] (US Black) a party held in a private house, for which an admission fee is paid (cf. HOUSE PARTY).

house that Jack built n.[1] [mid–late 19C] a prison. [the generic hangman *Jack Ketch*]

house that Jack built n.[2] [1920s+] (Aus.) the Government Savings Bank in Sydney.

house-trashing n. [1980s+] (N.Z.) a party held by tenants who are leaving a house or flat, in which the fixtures and fittings are deliberately destroyed (cf. DEMOLITION PARTY).

house to let see APARTMENT TO LET.

house under the hill n. [19C] the vagina (cf. DOWN BELOW; SHOOTER'S HILL). [the image of the vagina as being 'down there' and beneath the fig. *hill*, or pubic mound; note Aubrey Beardsley's title for his sole and unfinished erotic novel *Under the Hill* (1898)]

housewife n. [19C] the female genitals. [metonymy]

housewife's hour n. [1960s+] (US gay) the afternoon, esp. as used for masturbation since nothing else is happening.

house without chairs n. [1920s–40s] (US Black) a temporarily unfurnished apartment or house.

housewives' choice n. [1950s+] a voice. [rhy. sl.; ult. the BBC radio programme]

housey-housey adj. [20C] lousy, i.e. unwell. [rhy. sl.]

hout see HOOT n.[1].

houthern n. [20C] (Ulster) a slovenly, untidy woman.

houtkop n. [1950s+] (S.Afr.) a blockhead, a fool, thus a general term of abuse for a Black person; often abbr. to *hout*, *houtie*. [Afk. *hout*, wood + *kop*, head]

how? prep. [mid-19C] (US) used as a synon. for 'what?' when one fails to hear a statement properly.

how about my forty-five up your ass? phr. [1990s] (US Black teen) a rejoinder to the threat HOW ABOUT MY NINE IN YOUR FACE?

how about my nine in your face? phr. [1990s] (US Black teen) a threat, demanding either obedience or silence. [NINER]

how about that?/that then? phr. [1930s+] an interrog. phr. calling for agreement that something is worthy of praise or approval.

howard's way adj. [1990s] homosexual. [rhy. sl. *Howard's Way* = gay; ult. the British 1980s TV series, *Howard's Way*]

how are they hanging? phr. [1970s+] jocular man-to-man greeting (cf. GETTING ANY?). ['they' are testicles]

how are we? phr. [20C] joc. form of greeting. [? echoing the cheery 'bedside manner' used by doctors]

how are you blowing? phr. [1920s] (Irish) a general term of informal greeting.

how are you diddling? phr. [1970s] a general term of informal greeting. [? DIDDLE v.¹]

how are you going? phr. [1930s+] (orig./mainly Aus.) a general phr. of greeting.

how are you hitting them? phr. [late 19C+] (US) a phr. of greeting, how are you? [sporting imagery]

how are you off for soap? phr. [mid–late 19C] a general phr. of greeting, i.e. *how are things? how are you doing?*

how are you popping?/popping up? phr. [late 19C–1940s] (Aus.) a general phr. of greeting, how are you doing? how are you feeling?

how came you so?/Lord, how came you so? phr. [19C] drunk (cf. HOW-COME-YE- SO). [? a blasphemous ref. to a biblical quotation]

how—can you get? phr. [1950s+] (orig. US) how far will you go? what is your limit? [defined by the specific adj.]

how come? phr. [mid-19C+] (US) why?

how-come-ye-so phr. [19C–1910s] (US) **1** slightly tipsy, mildly drunk (cf. HOW CAME YOU SO?). **2** pregnant.

how does that grab you? phr. what do you think of that? [a slightly aggressive implication, a challenge is assumed]

how does that hang? phr. [1980s+] (US Black) what do you think?

how do/how-do phr. [late 19C+] a general term of greeting. [SE *how do you do?*]

how-do-you do n. [mid-19C+] **1** a shoe. **2** a problem, a difficulty, a fuss; usu. as *a fine how-do-you do*. [rhy. sl.; (2) *how-do-you do* = STEW n.]

how do you like me now? phr. [1990s] (drugs) crack cocaine. [? the allegedly instant addictiveness of the drug. Despite its justifiably bad reputation, consumption transcends warnings]

how do you like them apples? phr. [1920s+] (US) an ironic, rhetorical demand, 'What do you think of that then and what are you going to do about it?' The implication is that whatever one thinks, one can do nothing.

how do you sell your string? phr. [mid-19C] a phr. used to disabuse someone who appears to be taking the speaker for a fool.

howdy doody! excl. [1950s+] (US) a general greeting. [SE *how do you do?* + the NBC-TV puppet Howdy-Doody, launched 27 December 1947]

howd'ye do/dos n. [19C] a shoe, shoes. [rhy. sl.]

howdzacky n. [1940s+] (N.Z.) an otherwise unnamed object, esp. a gadget.

however adv. [mid-19C+] how, in any circumstances or way whatsoever?

how goes? phr. [1930s] a general phr. of greeting.

how goes the enemy? phr. [mid-19C] what time is it? [the image of passing time as the enemy of life]

how high is a Chinaman? phr. [20C] the answer to a statement or question which the speaker considers to be absurd or unanswerable. [pun on the supposed Chinese name *How Hi*]

howish adj. [mid-18C–early 19C] vaguely out of sorts, not wholly well.

how is that for high? phr. [late 19C–1920s] (orig. US) an excl. used to invite admiration. ['a low game known as Old Sledge, where the high depends, not on the card itself but on the adversary's hand. Hence the phrase means, What kind of an attempt is that at a great achievement?' (Schele de Vere, *Americanisms*, 1872)]

howitzer n. [late 19C–1960s] (US) a large pistol or revolver (cf. CANNON n.¹). [SE *howitzer*, a light cannon]

howl n. **1** [late 19C+] (US) a noisy objection, a complaint. **2** [1920s+] a highly amusing story, situation or experience (cf. HOOT n.³).

howl v. **1** [20C] (US) to celebrate wildly. **2** [1980s] (US 'preppie') to mock, to tease. [fig use of SE; (2) the 'howls of derision' that accompany such teasing]

howler n.¹ [mid-19C+] a notable blunder (esp. in an examination), a gross error, a social solecism. [such errors 'howl out' for notice]

howler n.² [late 19C] a dandy, a fop, a fashionable dresser (cf. HALFPENNY HOWLING SWELL). [his clothes and personality 'howl' for attention]

howler n.³ [late 19C] a heavy fall, a bad accident; thus *come/go a howler*. [one 'howls' with pain]

howler n.⁴ [1950s+] (US) a siren.

howling adv. **1** [mid-19C+] extremely, obviously (cf. HOWLER n.¹). **2** [late 19C+] to the highest degree. [the subject 'howls' its badness]

howling bags n. [mid-19C] 'trousers of an extensive pattern, or exaggerated fashionable cut ... when the style has been very "loud"' (Hotten, 1860). [SE *howl* + BAGS n.¹]

howling-stick n. [mid–late 19C] a flute.

howling swell see HEAVY SWELL.

how low can you go? phr. [1990s] (US Black) a general teasing taunt, i.e. how good a lover are you? how long can you last?

how many f's are there in 'go away' phr. [1990s] (US teen) remark indicating that someone should leave. [euph. for FUCK OFF!]

how much? excl. [mid-19C+] an excl. of incredulity, a demand for further detail or information, esp. when what has been offered seems unbelievable; it need have no ref. to price, but is delivered in response to what the listener considers to be a far-fetched statement.

how rudeness! excl. [1980s+] (US campus) how rude!

hows n. [20C] (drugs) morphine. [? coded enquiry: 'How's you going to act? do you have any drugs?']

how's about/how's about that phr.¹ [1930s+] a general phr. implying that something is good, pleasing or surprising.

how's about phr.² [1950s+] a general interrog., e.g. *how's about a drink? how's about a bit of supper?* [in 1970s–80s the phr. was adopted almost as his own property by UK disc jockey Jimmy Savile (b.1926), who also talks not of boys and girls but of 'guys and gals']

how's high? phr. [late 19C] (US) how are you?

how's it going? phr. [20C] a general phr. of greeting.

how's it hanging? phr. [20C] a man-to-man greeting, what are you up to? how are you? (cf. HOW ARE THEY HANGING; HOW'S YOUR HAMMER HANGIN'?). ['it' being the penis]

how's she cutting? *phr.* [1980s+] (Irish) a general phr. of greeting. ['she' being some form of agricultural implement]

how's that for high? *phr.* [19C+] (US) a phr. synon. with *what do you think of that?*

how's the body? *phr.* [1940s–50s] (Anglo-Irish) how are you?

how's things? *phr.* [20C] how are you?

how's tricks? *phr.* [1910s+] a phr. of greeting (cf. WHAT'S HAPPENING?).

how's-yer-father *n.* [20C] **1** sexual intercourse. **2** nonsense, rubbish. **3** occas. use as a general euph., *swear like how's yer father*, i.e. swear 'like fuck'. [coined in a music-hall sketch performed by the comedian Harry Lauder (1870–1950) and popularized by services during WW1]

how's your ass? *phr.* [1960s+] (US) a general excl. of greeting. [ARSE n.¹]

how's your bod? *phr.* [1970s+] (orig. US) how are you (feeling)? [BOD n.]

how's your hammer hangin'? *phr.* [1990s] (US) a phr. used to inquire about someone's state of well being; the typically facetious answer being: 'A little to the left and in the dirt.' (cf. HOW ARE THEY HANGING, HOW'S IT HANGING?). [HAMMER n.¹]

how's your rotten/dirty rotten form? *phr.* [1940s+] (Aus.) a phr. used to someone who has just proved themselves successful, had a piece of luck etc.

how/what/who/why the blazes *phr.* [mid-19C+] a general excl. [ref. is to the flames of hell]

how to go! *see* WAY TO GO!

how will you have it? *phr.* [late 19C+] a general invitation to take a drink.

howzit? *excl.* [1970s+] (S.Afr.) hello, how are you?; thus *howzit for/with something?* how about something? i.e. may I have something? shall we do something?

hoxter *n.* [early–mid-19C] an inside pocket. [SE *oxter*, the armpit]

hoy *n.* [early 19C] (US) lit. and fig. uses, rubbish, nonsense (cf. HOOEY).

hoy *v.*¹ (Aus.) **1** [1920s+] to drag. **2** [1930s+] to get rid of, to discard. [dial. *hoy*, to throw, to heave/SE *haul*]

hoy *v.*² [1950s+] (Aus.) to call. [excl. *hoy!*]

h.p. *n.* [1990s] (US Black teen) the *H*unter's *P*oint area of San Francisco. [abbr.]

h.q. *n.* [1980s+] (US drugs) an eighth of an ounce (3.5g) of cannabis. [abbr. *half-q*uarter]

h.r.n. *n.* [1980s+] (drugs) *h*e*r*oi*n*. [abbr.]

h.t. *see* HEAD TRIP n.

h town *n.* [1970s+] (US) any town whose name begins with H.

hua *see* HOOER.

hub *see* HUBBY.

hubba *n.*¹ [1940s+] a lively, energetic spirit. [HUBBA! HUBBA!]

hubba *n.*² [1980s+] (drugs) crack cocaine (cf. ROCK n.⁴). [fig. use of HUBBA! HUBBA! to denote its energizing effect]

hubba! hubba!/hubba-hubba!/hava-hava! *excl.* [1940s+] (US teen) term of approval, esp. when directed at a passing girl. [SE *hubba! hubba!*, a college cheer]

hubba, I am back *n.* [1980s+] (US drugs) crack cocaine. [rhy. sl.; HUBBA! HUBBA! + joc. ref. to clichéd line 'Honey, I'm home']

hubba pigeon *n.* [1980s+] (US drugs) a user of crack cocaine reduced to searching for small pieces of the drug, left lying on the floor after a police raid. [HUBBA, I AM BACK + SE *pigeon*, pecking for food in the street]

hubbie *see* HUBBY.

hubble *n.* [20C] (Ulster) fuss and bother. [? abbr. HUBBLE-BUBBLE]

hubble-bubble *n.* [late 18C–19C] confusion, chaos; thus *hubble-bubble fellow*, a fool. [SE *hubble-bubble*, the confused noise emanating from a person talking so fast as to be incomprehensible]

hubble de shuff *adv.* [late 18C–19C] confusedly, chaotically. [milit. jargon *fire hubble de shuff*, fire quickly and irregularly. ? the orig. root of both in 16C northern dial. *hubbleshow*, a hubbub, a disturbance]

hubbly-bubbly *n.* [1980s+] (S.Afr. drugs) a water pipe, used for smoking cannabis. [the noise of the bubbling liquid]

hubby/hub/hubbie *n.* **1** [late 17C+] a husband. **2** [1980s+] (US campus) a steady boyfriend. [abbr./corruption of SE]

hubshi *n.* [mid-19C+] (Anglo-Ind.) anyone or anything with tight kinky hair, esp. a Black person but also used of animals. [Arab. *habashi*, an Abyssinian, an Ethiopian, a Black person in general]

hubs of Hades *phr.* [20C] (US) a general phr. of intensification (cf. HINGES OF HELL).

huck *n.* (US) **1** [late 19C–1910s] a fellow. **2** [1920s+] a Black person (cf. HUCKLEBERRY n.²). [? proper name *Huckleberry Finn*, hero of Mark Twain's novel *The Adventures of Huckleberry Finn* (1884)]

huckle *n.* [1900s] (US) an effeminate male homosexual. [? dial. *huckle*, to bend the body; he 'bends over' for penetration]

huckle *v.*¹ [early 18C] to chatter, to gossip. [? dial. *huckle*, to bend the body, as one might during intimate conversation]

huckle *v.*² [1950s+] **1** to be seized. **2** to be arrested. [? dial. *huckle*, to stoop, to bend the body]

huckleberry *n.*¹ [19C+] (US) a small amount, degree, or extent.

huckleberry *n.*² **1** [mid-19C+] (US) a fellow, boy. **2** [late 19C+] (US) a person of little importance. **2** [1920s+] nickname for a Black person (cf. HUCK). [SE *huckleberry*, a sweetheart. (2) and (3) influenced by proper name *Huckleberry Finn*, hero of Mark Twain's novel of 1884]

huckleberry, the *n.*³ [late 19C+] (US) bad treatment (cf. RASPBERRY n.¹).

huckleberry *n.*⁴ [1980s+] (US drugs) a very compact marijuana bud 5cm (2in) or less in length. [resemblance to the fruit]

huckleberry above/over one's persimmon *phr.* [early 19C+] (US) **1** beyond one's capabilities, esp. when the task cited is, in fact, simple (cf. ABOVE ONE'S BEND; PASS ONE'S PERSIMMON). **2** superior, to a single degree, to what it is compared with. [proverbial phr.; the disparate 'status' of the fruits]

huckleberry finn *n.* [20C] (Aus.) gin. [rhy. sl. ult. the novel *The Adventures of Huckleberry Finn* (1884) by Mark Twain]

huckle-my-buff/-butt *n.* **1** [18C–19C] a drink made by heating beer, eggs and brandy together (cf. HOT POT n.¹). **2** [20C] (US) bourbon and milk poured over crushed ice, recommended as a hangover cure. [dial. *huckle*, to jog along, thus lit. 'jog my skin/my buttocks']

huddle *v.* [18C] to have sexual intercourse. [dial. *huddle*, to hug]

hue *v.* (Und.) **1** [late 17C–18C] to beat, to whip. **2** [19C] to hit with a cudgel. [SE *hue*, colour (of the flesh after a beating), or SE *hue*, to assail, to drive, or *hew*, to cut with blows]

huey/hughey *n.*¹ [mid-19C] (tramp) a town or village. [? SE *hue*, to chase with shouts, or *hue and cry*; such fates might befall a hapless tramp]

huey *n.*² *see* HUGHIE.

huff *n.*¹ [mid-19C] **1** a dodge or trick. **2** a bad temper. [SE *huff*, to puff, to blow up]

huff *n.*² [late 19C] **1** the buttocks (cf. DUFF n.²). **2** the vagina. [play on SE *huff*, the buttocks are 'blown up' flesh]

huff *n.*³ *see* HOUGH.

huff *n.*⁴ [1960s+] (drugs) a solvent, an inhalant.

huff *v.*¹ [late 17C–19C] **1** to scold, to reprove, to bully (cf. BULLY HUFF; CAPTAIN HUFF; HUFF AND DING). **2** to annoy, to offend. [SE *huff*, to blow]

huff v.[2] [early 19C] to throw one's arms over a victim's shoulders and then take the money from his pockets; the assault requires two partners, one to grab and one to rifle the clothes. [SE *huff*, to bully, to hector; note 1910s–20s milit. sl. *huff*, to kill]

huff v.[3] [1960s+] (drugs) to sniff solvents or similar volatile substances; thus *huffing*, inhaling. [HUFF n.[4]]

huff! excl. [late 15C–late 16C] 'an exclamation attributed to a swaggerer or bully, esp. when introduced on the stage' (*OED*). [imitative of a blast of air through some form of orifice]

huffa! excl. [early 16C–early 17C] a general excl.

huff and ding, to phr. [late 17C–early 18C] to swagger and boast (cf. BULLY HUFF; CAPTAIN HUFF; HUFF AND DING; HUFFCAP; HUFFER n.[1]; HUFF-SNUFF). [HUFF v.[1] + DING v.[1]]

huffcap n. 1 [late 16C–late 19C] a form of strong ale. 2 [early 17C–early 18C] a swaggerer, a blusterer. [HUFF v.[1] + SE *cap*, i.e. that which raises the cap. The bully set his cap at a swaggering angle]

huffer n.[1] [17C] a bully, a braggart, a boaster (cf. HUFF AND DING). [HUFF v.[1]]

huffer n.[2] [1960s+] (drugs) an inhalant abuser. [HUFF v.[3]]

huffle v. [18C] to perform *coitus in axilla*, i.e. intercourse in which the penis is placed within the clenched armpit (cf. BAGPIPING; HOOFLER). ['a piece of bestiality too filthy for explanation' (Grose)]

huff-snuff n. [16C] a bully, a braggart (cf. HUFF AND DING). [his swaggering, threatening presence]

hufty-tufty/huftie-tuftie n. [late 16C–early 17C] a swaggering, boastful individual. [HUFF v.[1] + redup.]

hug, the n. [mid-19C] (Und.) the act of garrotting; thus *hugging*, garrotting, *put on the hug*, to garrotte. [SE *hug*, to grasp tightly]

hug-booby n. [early 18C] (pej.) a married man. [punning on BOOBY n.[1] (a fool) and BOOBY n.[3] (the breast)]

hug centre n. [late 19C–1900s] (orig. US) anywhere popular for public love-making, e.g. Hyde Park. [love-making in the 19C rather than 20C sense]

hug drug n. [1980s+] (drugs) MDMA (cf. ECSTASY). [its effects; the drug makes users want to touch everyone around them]

huge adj. [mid-19C; 1990s] (US) wonderful, great, impressive.

huggle-my-buff n. [mid-18C] a form of mixed, hot drink (cf. HOT POT n.[1]).

huggy-bear n. [1960s+] (US) a cuddly person.

hughey see HUEY n.[1].

hughie/huey n. [1950s+] (Aus.) the act of vomiting (cf. BUICK; CRY HUGHIE). [echoic]

hugh prowler n. [16C] a generic nickname for a small-time thief. [generic use of proper name *Hugh* + SE *prowler*]

hugmatee n. [late 17C–early 18C] a type of ale. [? SE *hug me t'ye*, hug me to you]

hugmetight n. [20C] (Ulster) 1 a woollen vest. 2 a shawl that can be fastened across the body.

hugs and kisses n. [20C] one's wife. [rhy. sl. *hugs and kisses* = MISSUS]

hugs of hell see HINGES OF HELL.

hugsome adj. [late 19C+] sexually attractive. [SE *hug* + sfx. -*some*]

hug the hog, to phr. [1990s] to masturbate. [SE *hug* + HOG n.[4]]

hug the porcelain god/goddess see KISS THE PORCELAIN GOD.

hula-hoop v. [1990s] of a woman, to masturbate.

hula raider n. [1990s] a male homosexual. [abbr. SE *hula-hoop* + *raider*; thus cf. HOOP STRETCHER]

hulk n. [1980s+] (US) a large, muscular man. [SE *hulk*, a big, unwieldy person; popularized by the 1962 comic-book character, the *Incredible Hulk*, created by Stan Lee and Jack Kirby]

hulked adj. [1980s+] (US campus) angry. [HULK n.; the *Incredible Hulk* would turn into his superhero form only when emotionally aroused]

hulking adj. [late 17C+] unwieldy, heavy, lumpish (cf. HULKY). [HULK n.]

hulky adj. [late-18C–late 19C] bulky, lumpish, outsized (cf. HULKING). [HULK n.]

hull n. [1910s–30s] (US) a saddle. [SE *hull*, that which encases, e.g. a peapod]

hullaballoo n. [mid-18C–late 19C] uproar, confusion, noisy chaos. [SE in 20C; redup. *halloo-baloo*. Ware suggests an origin in Fr. *hurluberlu* and *OED* notes, but rejects, another Fr. use, the hunting cry *bas le loup!* bring down the wolf!]

hull-cheese n. [17C] malt liquor and water; thus *eat hull-cheese*, to become drunk. [orig. Yorks. dial. *hull-cheese*, 'the strong ale of Hull' (*EDD*)]

hull down adv. [19C+] (US) completely, utterly. [naut. jargon *hull down*, of a ship that is so far away that its hull has disappeared beneath the horizon]

hulling n. [1980s+] (drugs) using others to get drugs. [SE *hull*, a covering, an outer case]

hullo my buck! excl. [late 19C] a general term of address between men. [SE *hello* + BUCK n.[1]]

hully n. [1970s+] (US Black) an especially fat person.

hully-gully n. [1960s+] (W.I.) 1 a young ruffian. 2 a playboy. [SE *hully-gully*, a form of dance, based on the *frug*; thus a fan of the dance]

hulverhead n. [17C–19C] a fool. [Norfolk dial. *hulver*, holly; the wood of a holly bush is notably hard]

hum n.[1] [late 17C–18C] strong beer. [abbr. HUMMING ALE]

hum n.[2] [early 18C+] speed, energy, enthusiasm. [HUM v.[1]]

hum n.[3] 1 [mid-18C–late 19C] nonsense, a trick, a hoax; a whispered lie. 2 [1910s–30s] (Aus.) a cadger, a scrounger; thus *on the hum*, begging, cadging. [abbr. SE *humbug*]

hum n.[4] [late 19C+] an unpleasant smell. [HUM v.[3]]

hum n.[5] [1940s+] (US) euph. for HELL.

hum n.[6] [1960s+] (US) fellatio. [abbr. HUMMER n.[6]]

hum n.[7] [1970s+] (US drugs) a mild intoxication from drug use (cf. BUZZ n.[5]).

hum v.[1] [mid-18C+] to be active, to be getting about one's business energetically, to go fast.

hum v.[2] 1 [mid-18C–mid-19C] to trick, to hoax, to humbug. 2 [1910s–30s] (Aus.) to scrounge, to borrow with no intention of giving back. 3 [1960s+] (US Und.) to arrest on false charges (cf. HUMBLE). [HUM n.[3]]

hum v.[3] [late 19C+] to smell disgusting. ['the humming of fermentation in an active manure heap' (Ware)]

humble n. 1 [1940s+] (US Und.) a false charge. 2 [1950s+] (US Black) a self-defeating act.

humble as a dead nigger phr. [mid-19C] (US) totally subservient, utterly cowed.

hum-box n. [late 18C–mid-19C] a pulpit. [the preacher's droning tones]

humbug n.[1] [mid-18C+] 1 a trick, a hoax, an imposture. 2 the person who employs such ploys. [ety. unknown. 'The facts as to its origin appear to have been lost, even before the word became common enough to excite attention' (*OED*). Hotten (1859) traces the first use back to *c*.1735, finding it in Ferdinando Killigrew's *The Universal Jester* (the *OED* dates this edn. to 1754), where it is cited in list of 'merry conceits, facetious drolleries, &c., clenchers, closers, closures, bon-mots and humbugs'. He also notes that the mid-18C radical Orator Henley was sometimes nicknamed 'Orator Humbug'. As to ety., he suggests either *hum* or the German town of Hamburg 'from which town so many false bulletins and reports came during the war in the last century'. After 1800 its use spread 'in periodical literature, and in novels not written by squeamish or over-precise authors']

humbug n.[2] **1** [mid-19C+] (US; later use US Black) anything worrying, complicated, unpleasant, offensive, troublesome or a misunderstanding. **2** [1960s+] (US Black) a fight. **3** [1970s] (US Und.) a false arrest on trumped-up charges (cf. HUM v.[2]; HUMBLE). [fig. uses of HUMBUG n.[1]]

humbug v.[1] [mid-18C+] to cheat, to delude, to deceive (cf. HUMBUG ABOUT; HUMBUG INTO; HUMBUG OF). [HUMBUG n.[1]]

humbug v.[2] [1960s+] (US Black) to fight, to act tough; thus *humbugger*, a thug, a fighter; *humbugging*, fighting, brawling. [HUMBUG n.[2]]

humbug! excl. [early 19C+] nonsense! rubbish! [HUMBUG n.[1]]

humbug about v. [19C] to play the fool. [HUMBUG v.[1]]

humbugger n. [mid-18C–late 19C] **1** a cheat. **2** a hoaxer. **3** one who 'plays about' all the time. [HUMBUG v.[1]]

humbugging n. [mid-18C+] hoaxing, swindling, deceiving. [HUMBUG v.[1] + sfx. -*ing*]

humbug into v. [19C+] to persuade into doing something. [HUMBUG v.[1]]

humbug of v. [mid-18C–mid-19C] to cheat out of. [HUMBUG v.[1]]

hum cap n. [late 18C–19C] very old, very strong beer (cf. HUMMING ALE; PHARAOH n.[1]).

humdinger n. [20C] (orig. US) a remarkable and excellent event or person (cf. WHOPCACKER). [? HUMMER n.[3] + DINGER n.[3]. Note. the earliest (print) use includes a hyphen, i.e. *hum-dinger*]

humdinging adj. [20C] extraordinary. [HUMDINGER]

humdrum n. **1** [17C–early 19C] a wife, a husband. **2** [early 18C–19C] a parson (cf. HUM-BOX). [SE *humdrum*, a dull, monotonous person; ult. SE *hum*, to murmur on]

humdudgeon/humdurgeon n. [late 18C] an imaginary illness; thus *humdurgeoned*, annoyed. [? HUMBUG n.[2] + SE *dudgeon*, ill humour]

humgumptious adj. [mid-19C] artful, cunning, knowing. [fanciful formation]

hum-job n. [1960s+] (US) fellatio. [HUMMER n.[6] + JOB n.[5]]

hummer n.[1] **1** [late 17C–early 19C] an obvious lie. **2** [1930s+] (US police/Und.) an arrest on false or petty charges. **3** [1950s–70s] (US Black) something deceptive, a minor or insignificant mistake.

hummer n.[2] [mid-18C–early 19C] a cheat, an imposter. [HUMBUG n.[1]]

hummer n.[3] [20C] **1** [late 17C] a very energetic, active person. **2** [late 17C+] something or someone exceptional of its type (cf. HUMDINGER). **3** [1980s+] (US) a thing, device (cf. GIZMO). [HUM v.[1]]

hummer n.[4] **1** [1910s–40s] (Aus.) a scrounger. **2** [1960s–70s] (US campus) a stupid or inconsequential person. [HUM n.[4]]

hummer n.[5] **1** [1930s–60s] (Und.) an arrest on trumped up charges. **2** [1940s–50s] (US Black) a minor error. [HUMBUG n.[2] (3)]

hummer n.[6] [1960s+] (US) fellatio, esp. when the testicles are held in the mouth and the woman hums (cf. HUM n.[6]).

hummer n.[7] [1960s+] a heavy drinking session. [? link to HUM n.[1]]

humming n. [early 19C] teasing, hoaxing, fooling. [HUM v.[2]]

humming adj. **1** [late 17C–early 18C] of liquor, strong, frothing; thus *humming punch*, *humming stuff* (cf. HUMMING ALE). **2** [mid-17C–late 19C] notably large or active, energetic, intense.

humming adv. [18C] exceedingly, very much so.

humming ale/tipple n. [late 17C–18C] strong beer (cf. HUM CAP). [HUMMING adj. + SE *ale*]

humming bird n. [late 19C–1930s] (US prison) **1** a type of torture using electricity. **2** the electric chair.

humming October n. [early 18C–late 19C] very strong ale, made from the new season's hops (cf. OLD OCTOBER). [HUMMING (ALE) + SE *October*]

humming tipple see HUMMING ALE.

hummum n. [late 17C–19C] a brothel. [Arabic *hammamm*, a hot or Turkish bath. The original *Hummum* was set up in Covent Garden in 1631; it later became a hotel]

humongous / hunungous / humongoid / humungo adj. [1960s+] (orig. US) enormous, outsized, huge. [sugg. by SE *huge/monstrous/tremendous*]

hump n.[1] [late 19C+] a fit of bad-humour, a sulk. [abbr. SE phr. *hump the back*, to sulk]

hump n.[2] [20C] (US) euph. for DAMN, e.g. *I don't give a hump*.

hump n.[3] [1910s+] (US Und.) the midpoint of one's prison sentence.

hump n.[4] [1910s+] (orig. US) **1** sexual intercourse (cf. BLOW ONE'S HUMP). **2** a woman, considered purely as a sexual object (cf. FUCK v.[1]; SHAG n.[1]). [HUMP v.[1]]

hump n.[5] **1** [1920s+] (US) a Camel (brandname) cigarette. **2** [1930s+] (Aus.) a camel. [the animal's defining aspect]

hump n.[6] [1930s+] **1** a contemptible person, esp. a man. **2** a general term for a person, basically a peasant or manual worker (cf. HUMPER). [? HUMP v.[2]]

hump v.[1] [late 18C+] to have sexual intercourse. [the *hump* in the man's back, when in the 'missionary position' (cf. BANG v.[1]). The term starts in the UK, dies out by the early 19C, then to the US, and back to the UK in the mid-20C]

hump v.[2] **1** [19C+] (US) to exert oneself, to work hard, to hurry (cf. GET A HUMP ON). **2** [early 19C+] to take pride in oneself, to fancy oneself. **3** [mid-19C+] to carry heavy objects; esp. in milit. use, patrolling with a heavy pack, weapon, supplies etc; esp. popular in Aus. **4** [mid-late 19C] to botch, to spoil. **5** [late 19C–1920s] (orig. Aus.) to tramp, to trudge, to go on foot. **6** [20C] (US) to act lazily, to loaf around, to be idle. **7** [1960s+] (US) to victimize. [lit + fig. uses of SE *hump*, to make a hump in one's back, f. effort, ill-temper etc]

hump day/night n. [1950s+] (US) Wednesday, the middle of the week. [SE *hump*, the critical point of an undertaking. Once Wednesday has passed one is coasting 'downhill' towards the weekend]

hump 'em and dump 'em phr. [1980s+] a popular male catchphrase suggesting that seduction and then abandonment are the best ways of relating to women (cf. 4-F CLUB). [HUMP v.[1] + DUMP v.[1] (2)]

humper n. [1960s+] **1** a carrier of heavy objects, esp. in rock music use for those who lift a band's equipment. **2** (US) an irritating thing. **3** (US) a hard-working person. [HUMP v.[2] (3), (4) and (6)]

hump house n. [1920s] (US) a brothel (cf. ACCOMMODATION HOUSE). [HUMP v.[1] + HOUSE n.[1]]

humping adj. **1** [1940s+] (US) a general intensifier, pos. or neg. according to context. **2** [1980s+] (US Black) very attractive. [HUMP v.[1]; thus a partial euph. for FUCKING adj.]

hump it v. [late 19C–1920s] **1** to die. **2** to leave. [HUMP v.[2]]

hump night see HUMP DAY.

hump-nutty adj. [1920s] (US) obsessed with sex. [HUMP v.[1] + NUTTY]

hump one's drum/bluey/swag, to phr. [mid-19C+] (Aus./N.Z.) to walk from place to place carrying a pack on one's back. [HUMP v.[2] + DRUM n.[3]/BLUEY n.[2] (1)/SWAG n.[1] (7)]

hump one's hose, to phr. [20C] to masturbate. [HUMP v.[1] + HOSE n.[1]]

hump one's swag see HUMP ONE'S DRUM.

hump the horn, to phr. [20C] to masturbate. [HUMP v.[1] + HORN n.[2]]

humpty n. [1970s+] sexual intercourse (cf. RUMPY-PUMPY). [HUMP v.[1]]

humpty adj.[1] [20C] sexually excited. [HUMP v.[1]]

humpty adj.[2] [20C] irritated, tetchy. [HUMP n.[1]]

humpty/humpty-dumpty *adj.*[3] [1920s+] (US) incompetent, foolish, ridiculous. [abbr. the nursery-rhyme character Humpty-Dumpty, who despite his posturing 'fell off a wall']

humpty-doo *n.* [1930s+] (Aus.) drunk (cf. UMPTY-DOO). [HUMPTY adj.[3]]

humpty-dumpty *n.*[1] [late 17C–19C] a hot drink made of ale and brandy boiled together. [redup.; the two liquors are 'humped together']

humpty-dumpty *n.*[2] **1** [late 18C–late 19C] a short, squat person. **2** [1920s–30s] an outright failure. **3** [1950s+] (US) an incompetent person, esp. in sport. [the nursery-rhyme character]

humpty-dumpty *adj. see* HUMPTY adj.[3].

humpy *n.*[1] **1** [mid–late 19C+] a hunchback. **2** [1930s–40s] (Aus.) a camel (cf. HUMP n.[5]). [their defining physical characteristic]

humpy *n.*[2] [1960s+] (Aus. surfing) an ideal surfing wave. [its back is suitably 'humped']

humpy *adj.*[1] [1900s] depressed, miserable. [HUMP n.[1]]

humpy *adj.*[2] **1** [1960s+] sexually attractive (cf. FUCKY). **2** [1970s+] (US gay) good looking. [HUMP v.[1]]

humpy-pumpy *see* RUMPY-PUMPY.

hums *n.* [late 18C] a parson (cf. HUMDRUM). [his droning sermons]

humungo *see* HUMONGOUS.

hun *n.*[1] [late 19C] an attractive, wonderful thing or person. [abbr. HONEY n.[4]]

Hun *n.*[2] [late 19C+] a derog. term for a German, the German army. [Ger *Hunnen*, one of an Asiatic race of warlike nomads, who invaded Europe *c.*375, and under their leader Attila (*c.*406–453), overran much of Europe *c.*450. The original Huns were the Chinese *Hiong-nu* or *Han*. The modern use originated during WW1 and stemmed directly from the speech made by Kaiser Wilhelm II to German troops setting sail for China on 27 July 1900: 'No quarter will be given, no prisoners will be taken. Let all who fall into your hands be at your mercy. Just as the Huns a thousand years ago ... gained a reputation in virtue of which they still live in historical tradition, so may the name of Germany become known in ... China that no Chinaman will ever again even dare to look askance at a German']

hun *n.*[3] [late 19C+] *hundred*, $100. [abbr.]

hunch *n.* [mid-19C+] (US) a hint, a suggestion, a premonition. [20C use effectively SE]

hunchy *n.* [1910s–30s] (Aus.) a camel. [its hump]

hundred-and-seventy-fiver *n.* [1990s] (gay) a homosexual. [paragraph 175 of the German Penal Code of 1871 outlawed homosexual practices; thus a *175er* in late 19C Germany was someone violating this paragraph]

hundred-pounder *n.* [1980s] (US drugs) a 100mg tablet of Demerol.

hundred to thirty *phr.* [1970s] dirty. [rhy. sl.]

hung *adj.*[1] [17C+] **1** having a large penis. **2** having large breasts.

hung *adj.*[2] [1940s+] (US) suffering from a hangover. [SE *hung over*]

hung *adj.*[3] [1950s+] (orig. US) **1** desperate, needy; **2** depressed or upset. **3** obsessed or infatuated. [HUNG UP]

hungarian *n.* [early 17C] a hungry person, a glutton. [pun on SE *hungry* + racial slur]

hungarian *adj.* [late 17C–early 17C] thievish, marauding, needy, beggarly. [for ety. *see* HUNGARIAN n.]

hung beef *n.* [early 19C] a dried bull's penis, esp. when used as a whip.

hunger street *n.* [20C] (US) the poor area of a town (cf. HUNGRY-GO-NAKED PLACE; HUNGRY HILL).

hung for *adj.* [1950s+ (US teen) in need of, lacking. [HUNG UP adj. (5)]

hung for bread *adj.* impoverished, out of money. [HUNG FOR + BREAD n.[1]]

hung like a bull/mule/show dog/stallion/stud *phr.* [1960s+] a man with a large penis (cf. HUNG LIKE A HORSE).

hung like a doughnut *n.* [1960s+] (US gay) a woman, i.e. one who has a vagina (a hole). [play on HUNG LIKE A HORSE]

hung like a field mouse *see* HUNG LIKE A MOUSE.

hung like a horse *phr.* [1960s+] possessing a large penis (cf. HUNG LIKE A BULL; HUNG LIKE A JACK DONKEY). [HUNG adj.[1] (1)]

hung like a mouse/field mouse *phr.* [1960s+] possessing an extremely small penis. [play on HUNG LIKE A HORSE]

hung like a jack donkey *phr.* [1960s+] possessing a large penis (cf. DONKEY-DICKED; DONKEY-RIGGED; HUNG LIKE A HORSE). [HUNG adj.[1] (1)]

hung like a mule/show dog/stallion/stud *see* HUNG LIKE A BULL.

hung like a stud mosquito *phr.* [1960s+] (US) possessing a very small penis.

hung low *adj.* [1990s] (US Black) equipped with a notably large penis. [HUNG adj.[1] (1)]

hung out *adj.* [1980s+] **1** (drugs) addicted. **2** obsessed with, fascinated by.

hungries *n.* [1960s+] an appetite (cf. MUNCHIE). [SE *hungry*]

hungry *adj.* **1** [late 16C+] ambitious, enthusiastic, driven. **2** [mid-19C+] (Aus.) mean, grasping, stingy; often used as a nickname, e.g. Hungry Scott. **3** [1970s+] (US campus) sexually excited.

hungry-belly *adj.* [20C] (W.I.) esp. of children, starving, malnourished.

hungry croaker *n.* [1950s+] (drugs) a doctor who, for one reason or another, is willing to prescribe drugs for any user who asks for them (cf. WRITING DOCTOR). [HUNGRY adj. + CROAKER n.[3]]

hungry enough to eat the arse out of a dead skunk *phr.* [20C] (Can.) very hungry.

hungry-go-naked place *n.* [20C] (US) the poor area of a town (cf. HUNGER STREET; HUNGRY HILL).

hungry hill/gulch/hollow/ridge/street *n.* [20C] (US) the poor area of a town (cf. HUNGER STREET; HUNGRY-GO-NAKED PLACE).

hungry mile *n.* [1930s–60s] (Aus.) a stretch of Sussex Street, Sydney, frequented by dockers in search of work.

hungry ridge/street *see* HUNGRY HILL.

hungry track *n.* [late 19C+] (Aus.) a section of the road on which a vagrant finds it hard to find either food or work.

hung to *adj.* [1950s–60s] (US Black) obsessed with.

hung up *adj.* **1** [late 19C] (society) self-obsessed, snobbish. **2** [late 19C+] delayed or hindered. **3** [20C] desperate, poor, in trouble. **4** [1940s+] (orig. US) unhappy, depressed, neurotic, anxious. **5** [1950s+] (orig. US) obsessed or infatuated.

hung up on *adj.* [1950s+] obsessed with, esp. in love with someone. [ext. of HUNG UP (5)]

hunk *n.*[1] **1** [19C+] (US) a country bumpkin, a peasant, a farmer. **2** [late 19C+] a dull, slow, stupid person (cf. LUMMOCKS). **3** [1920s+] (US) sexual intercourse, thus a sexual partner, usu. a woman. **4** [1940s+] a large man or woman. **5** [1940s+] (US) a sexually attractive woman. **6** [1940s+] (US) an attractive, rugged, well-built man, possibly somewhat unintelligent (cf. BEEFCAKE). [19C US dial. *hunk*, bulk; a large body]

hunk *n.*[2] [late 19C+] (US) an immigrant from Central Europe, i.e. a Hungarian, Lithuanian, Slav, Pole; thus *hunky town*, the area of a town in which such immigrants congregate (cf. BOHUNK). [HUNKY n.]

hunk *adj.* [mid-19C–1900s] (US) satisfactory, fine (cf. ALL HUNK). [fig. use of Du. *hunk*, home, e.g. a place of safety or security, as used in juv. games]

hunkamo *n.* [1990s] (US Black) a White person. [HUNKY n.]

hunker *n.* [1950s–60s] a jack-of-all-trades, one who runs errands (cf. GOFER). [? HUNKY adj.]

hunker *v.* [20C] (Ulster) to act as a parasite, to curry favour with. [one fig. *hunkers* down awaiting orders]

hunkersliding *n.* [19C] (US) acting unfairly, deceitfully. [Scot. *hunkersliding*, dishonourable or shifty conduct]

hunkie *see* HUNKY.

hunko *adj.* [1950s+] (US) of someone's physique, short, stocky. [HUNKY adj.]

hunk of ass/arse/butt/skirt/tail *see* PIECE OF ASS.

hunks *n.* **1** [early 18C–late 19C] a miser, also a surly person. **2** [19C+] (US) a worthless, good-for-nothing person. [ety. unknown; ? anecdotal from a *Mr Hunks*]

hunks *adj.* [1930s+] (orig. US) wonderful, fine, perfect (cf. HUNK adj.). [fig. use of Du. *hunk*, home, e.g. a place of safety or security, as used in juv. games]

hunkum-bunkum *adj.* [mid-19C–1910s] (US) excellent (cf. HUNKY-DORY). [? HUNKY adj.]

hunky/hunkie *n.* **1** [late 19C+] (US) an immigrant from Central Europe, i.e. a Hungarian, Lithuanian, Slav, Pole; thus *Hunky Town*, the area of a town in which such immigrants congregate (cf. HUNK n.[2]). **2** [1920s+] (US) a derog. term for a Black person. **3** [1950s+] (US Black) a derog. term for a White person (cf. HONKIE). [abbr. BOHUNK]

hunky *adj.*[1] **1** [mid-19C+] (US) excellent, satisfactory, lucky, pleasurable, in good condition, 'safe and sound'. **2** [late 19C–1910s] (US) friendly, ingratiating. [abbr. HUNKY-DORY]

hunky *adj.*[2] [1970s+] of a man, good-looking, well-built. [HUNK n.[1] (6)]

hunky-doodle *adj.* [1900s] (US) fine, satisfactory. [var. on HUNKY-DORY]

hunky-dory *adj.* [mid-19C+] (orig. US) wonderful, excellent, first-rate. [Du. *hunk*, home (in a game; the word was first used by youngsters in New Amsterdam and thence New York); thus giving the adv. *hunk*, in a safe position, all right; *dory*, ety. unknown; ? redup.]

hunky-dunky *adj.* [1950s+] (US) fine, excellent. [var. on HUNKY-DORY]

hunky-fucking-dory *phr.* [1970s+] (US Black) wonderful, excellent, first-rate. [for ety. *see* HUNKY-DORY. According to Major (1994), Black users prefer this augmented version of the basic (and White) term]

hunt *v.* **1** [20C] (Aus.) to drive away, to chase off. **2** [1990s] (US campus) to search for a partner for romance or sex.

hunt-about *n.* [mid-19C–1920s] **1** a prostitute. **2** an interfering, meddlesome gossip.

hunt a gowk *n.* [20C] (Ulster) one who can be sent on a fool's errand. [SE *hunt* + SE *gowk*, a cuckoo, a fool]

hunt a placebo, to *phr.* [late 15C–late 16C] to be a toady or sycophant (cf. AT THE SCHOOL OF PLACEBO). [PLACEBO]

hunt a tavern fox, to *phr.* [mid–late 17C] to get drunk. [pun on SE *fox*/FOXED]

hunter *n.*[1] [19C] the penis (cf. CRACK-HUNTER; CRANNY-HUNTER; CUNNY-CATCHER; NIMROD n.[1]).

hunter *n.*[2] [1980s+] (drugs) cocaine. [ety. unknown]

hunter-pitching *n.* [mid–late 19C] the game of cock-shy, a fairground game, which involved throwing broomsticks at a cock; if the thrower could knock the cock over and then grab it before it regained its feet he would win the bird.

hunt grass *v.* **1** [mid–late 19C] (US) to be knocked down (cf. GO TO GRASS). **2** [mid–late 19C] (US) to be extremely confused.

hunting *n.* [late 18C–19C] (Und.) searching for a victim whether for a theft, a confidence trick etc.

hunting licence *n.* [20C] (US prison) a commitment to kill an inmate, often ordered by a gang leader (cf. CONTRACT).

hunt one's hole, to *phr.* [mid-19C–1910s] (US) to run away, to seek refuge.

hunt's breakfast powder *n.* [mid-19C] roasted corn. [so called from its being the favourite breakfast of the radical 'Orator' Henry Hunt (1773–1835)]

hunt the anchovy, to *phr.* [1960s+] to perform cunnilingus (cf. BEARDED CLAM).

hunt the dummy, to *phr.* [19C] to steal pocket-books. [SE *hunt* + DUMMY n.[2]]

hunt the elephant *see* SEE THE ELEPHANT.

hunt the fox, to *phr.* [late 16C–17C] to be drunk (cf. HUNT A TAVERN FOX). [pun on SE *fox*/FOXED]

hunt the same old coon, to *phr.* [late 19C] (US) to persist in doing the same thing.

hunt the squirrel, to *v.* [18C–mid-19C] for two coachmen to attempt to upset each other's vehicles as they race along a public road. [the coaches veer from side to side a does a frightened squirrel]

hunt up a cow *see* CHASE UP A COW.

hunungous *see* HUMONGOUS.

hunyak *n.* **1** [20C] (US) an immigrant from central or eastern Europe, e.g. a Hungarian or Pole (cf. BOHUNK; HUNK n.[2]; HUNKY n.). **2** [20C] (US) an ignorant, inexperienced or unsophisticated person, a low-class person (cf. HONYOCK). **3** [1920s+] (US) a yokel, country man or a lout. [? *Hun*(*garian*) + (Pol)*ack*]

hura *n.* [1960s+] (US) the police. [Sp.]

hurdy-gurdy *n.* [mid-19C+] (US) a dance-hall, a dancer in a dance-hall; thus *hurdy-gurdy house*, *hurdy-gurdy girl*. [SE *hurdy-gurdy*; onomat. f. the sound of the instrument]

hurkaru *n.* [mid-19C] (Anglo-Ind.) a messenger. [Hind. *harkara*, messenger, emissary, spy]

hurkle *v.* [20C] (Ulster) to look on rather than offer help when others are working. [dial. *hurkle*, to crouch, to squat, to shrink from the cold]

hurl *v.* [1960s+] (Aus./S.Afr.) to vomit (cf. CHUCK v.[2]).

hurl a monkey wrench into the machinery *see* THROW A MONKEY WRENCH INTO THE MACHINERY.

hurler *n.* [20C] (Irish) a measure of whisky. [? SE *hurl*, to toss, i.e. what is tossed into the glass]

hurley foot *n.* [20C] (Irish) a club-foot. [? Irish game of *hurley*/*hurling*, in which the ball is hit with a stick or club]

hurrah/hoorah *n.* [mid-19C+] (US) a boisterous party, a ruckus. [SE *hurrah!*]

hurrah/hoorah/hooraw *v.* [20C] (US) **1** to tease, to harass. **2** to cause a commotion, to raise a ruckus. [HURRAH n.]

hurrah/hoorah *adj.* [mid-19C+] (US) wild and disorderly. [HURRAH n.]

hurrah boys *n.* [19C–1920s] (US) college students. [the ritualized college cheers popular among students]

hurrah clothes *n.* [20C] (US) one's best clothes, one's 'Sunday suit'. [SE *hurrah!*; i.e. the wearing of such clothes to events at which one may applaud]

hurrah's nest *n.* [19C] (US) a confused, tangled or disorderly mess, a state of confusion or disorder. [*hurrah*, an imaginary bird]

hurricane *n.* [mid-18C–early 19C] a crowded, fashionable assembly held in a private house.

hurricane deck *n.* [mid-19C–1910s] (US) the back of a horse or mule. [SE *hurricane-deck*, a light upper deck on a steamer]

hurricane lamp *n.* [20C] tramp. [rhy. sl.]

hurroosh *see* HOOROOSH.

hurry-buggy *n.* [1920s–30s] a police van (cf. HURRY-UP; HURRY-UP VAN; HURRY-UP WAGON). [it 'hurries' one to prison]

hurry-come up *n.* [1930s–40s] (W.I.) a parvenu, esp. with overtones of a bad reputation.

hurry-scurry/-skurry *n.* [mid-18C–late 19C] hurry, confusion, the hurrying and disorderly rushing of a number of people. [SE *hurry* + *scurry*]

hurry-scurry/-skurry *adj.* [mid-18C–late 19C] hurried, disorderly. [HURRY-SCURRY *n.*]

hurry-scurry/-skurry *adv.* [mid-18C–late 19C] in a confused, hurried manner, of people running pell-mell in a variety of directions. [HURRY-SCURRY *n.*]

hurry-up *n.* [1940s+] a police car (cf. HURRY-BUGGY).

hurry up the cakes, to *phr.* [mid–late 19C] (US) to go quickly.

hurry-up van *n.* [1950s] a police van (cf. HURRY-BUGGY). [the speed with which it is driven]

hurry-up wagon *n.* [19C+] a police van (cf. HURRY-BUGGY). [the speed with which it is driven]

hurry-whore *n.* [early–mid-17C] a street-walker (cf. SHORT TIME). [the speed with which she deals with a customer]

hurt *v.*[1] (US) **1** [1930s+] of an inanimate object, to cause problems for, to injure. **2** [1940s] (US) to complain. **3** [1950s] (Und.) to wound severely, to kill (cf. PUT A HURTING ON).

hurt *v.*[2] [1950s+] (drugs) of a drug addict, to suffer the lack of their drug of choice.

hurt for *v.* [20C] to want something desperately, usu. to alleviate current unhappiness.

hurtin' for certain *phr.* [1950s+] (US Black) **1** distressed, in trouble. **2** ugly, very unattractive. [HURTING]

hurting/hurting for *adj.* (US) **1** [1940s+] short of money. **2** [1950s+] generally miserable or in trouble. **3** [1950s+] (drugs) urgently needing narcotics to sustain one's regular dosage. **4** [1950s+] in financial difficulties.

hurting dance *n.* [1950s+] (orig. US) sadness, frustration, jealousy, usu. in a relationship in which one person has another *doing a hurting dance.*

hurting for *see* HURTING.

hurt in the head, to *phr.* [18C] to cuckold. [i.e. to 'put HORNS on']

hus *see* HUSS.

husband *n.* [1960s+] the supposedly 'aggressive' partner of a homosexual couple.

husband and wife *n.* [20C] a knife. [rhy. sl.]

husband's tea *n.* [mid-19C] very weak tea. [? a husband's inadequacy as opposed to that of a lover]

hush *n.* **1** [18C+] a bribe (cf. HUSH MONEY). **2** [1940s+] silence, quietness, calm, esp. in phr. *let's have a bit of hush*, used to quieten a crowd or audience.

hush *v.* [late 18C–19C] (Und.) to murder.

hush-crib *see* HUSH-SHOP.

hush-house *n.* [1920s] (US) a speakeasy. [coined by columnist Walter Winchell (1897–1972) but note HUSH-SHOP]

hush-hush *n.* [1930s–40s] (US Und.) a pistol with a silencer. [SE *hush-hush*, most secret, undercover + ref. to HUSH *v.*]

hush money *n.* [early 18C+] a bribe paid to ensure that embarrassing facts are suppressed.

hush mouth *n.* [1940s] (US Black) a sip of whisky.

hush puppy *n.* [1980s+] a YUPPIE. [rhy. sl.]

hush-shop/-crib *n.* [mid-19C] an unlicensed beer or liquor shop (cf. HUSH-HOUSE). [the sales are made 'on the hush']

husk *v.* [1940s] (US Black) to undress, to strip (cf. HUSKINGS). [SE *husk*, to remove a shell]

huskings *n.* [1940s] (US Black) a pile of clothes, esp. those discarded immediately after undressing. [HUSK]

Husky/husky *n.* [late 19C] (US) a derog. term for an Inuit. [SE *husky*, an Eskimo/Inuit dog]

huskylour *n.* [late 18C–19C] (Und.) a guinea. [SE *husky*, dry (as a corn husk) + LOUR; thus lit. 'dry money', i.e. hard cash]

huss/hus *n.* **1** [1950s] (US Black) a fellow, a man, used in direct address. **2** [1960s] (US Black) a smart, stylish man's suit. [abbr. HUSTLER]

huss/hus *adj.* [1950s] (US Black) smart, fashionable stylish. [HUSS *n.* (2)]

hussy *see* HUZZY.

hustle *n.* **1** [1940s+] (US Und.) a swindle, a hoax, a get-rich-quick scheme. **2** [1940s+] (US) flattery, deception. **3** [1940s+] (US Black) a job, a means of earning a living. **4** [1970s+] (US) a means of seduction, a pass. [HUSTLE *v.*]

hustle *v.* **1** [19C] to have sexual intercourse (cf. BANG *v.*[1]). **2** [19C+] to practise swindling or petty theft. **3** [mid-19C+] (US) to use initiative to obtain or secure. **4** [late 19C+] (US) to work hard, to make an effort (cf. HUSTLER). **5** [late 19C+] (US) to sell goods, esp. in an aggressive manner; thus combs. *hustle hash*, to work as a waiter or waitress, *hustle shoes*, to work as a shoe-shine, *hustle sheets*, to sell newspapers. **6** [late 19C+] (US) to work as a prostitute (cf. HUSTLER). **7** [20C] (US) to cadge, to beg. **8** [1930s+] (US) to deceive or to con (cf. HUSTLER). **9** [1940s+] (US) to make sexual advances. **10** [1950s+] (US drug) to attempt to obtain drug customers. **11** [1960s+] (drugs) to offer a sale of drugs to someone. [SE *hustle*, to push around or against, to jostle; ult. Du. *husselen, hutselen*, to shake, to toss]

hustle-buggy *n.* [1920s–30s] (US) a police car. [HUSTLE *v.* + SE *buggy*]

hustle one's bustle, to *phr.* **1** [1930s–40s] to work as a prostitute. **2** [1970s] to hurry.

hustler *n.* **1** [early 19C] (Und.) one of a pickpocket gang. **2** [late 19C–1910s] (US) a hard-working, ambitious person, also an energizer, one who exhorts his fellows to harder work, greater commitment. **3** [late 19C–1930s] (US) a racetrack tout. **4** [late 19C+] a gambler or player of pool, bowling etc, who uses skill and possibly cheating to make a living against lesser opponents. **5** [20C] (W.I.) a confidence man, a well-dressed beggar. **6** [1910s+] (Und.) a pimp. **7** [1920s+] (US) a prostitute of either sex. **8** [1930s+] (US gay) a male prostitute with homosexual clients. **9** [1970s+] (US campus) a man who succeeds in seducing women, a womanizer. [HUSTLE *v.*]

hustlers don't call showdowns *phr.* [1960s+] (US Black) one who is on the receiving end of a hand-out does not cause trouble because that might terminate the flow of free gifts. [HUSTLER]

hustling *n.* **1** [early 19C+] bag-snatching (cf. MUGGING). **2** [1920s+] working as a prostitute. **3** [1960s+] cadging, begging. **4** [late 19C+] selling objects, ideas, one's services etc in an aggressive manner. [HUSTLE *v.*]

hustling-ass *adj.* [1980s+] (US Black) aggressively self-aggrandizing, hard-working, self-promoting etc. [HUSTLE *v.* + ARSE *n.*[1]]

hustling broad/woman *n.* [1930s+] (US Und.) a female prostitute (cf. HUSTLER). [HUSTLE *v.* + BROAD *n.*[2]/SE *woman*]

hutch *n.* [1940s] (US) a police station.

hutch up *v.* [1930s+] to move up, along, esp. in a confined space (cf. OOCH). [synon. Yorks. dial.]

hutchy *adj.* [20C] of atmosphere, stale, frowzy. [as in the inside of a *hutch*]

hutty *see* HATTY.

hutu *see* HOOT *n.*[1].

huxter *n.* [20C] (Ulster) a decaying, dilapidated house or property. [SE *huckster*, a middleman, a small businessman, one who will cheat to make money]

huzzy/hussy *n.* [18C–early 19C] a small container of needles, thread and similar useful items. [SE *housewife*; note synon. naval jargon *huzzif*]

hyatari *n.* [1950s+] (drugs) peyote. [ety. unknown; ? a Mexican Indian lang.]

Hyde Park *n.* [20C] an informer. [rhy. sl. *Hyde Park* = NARK n.[1] (1)]

Hyde Park railings *n.* [late 19C] a breast of mutton. [the row of bones that make up such a breast resemble the fencing of the London park]

hydrant *n.* [1900s–40s] (US) tears, weeping.

hydraulic *n.* [1970s+] (Aus.) a light-fingered person, who'll 'lift anything that isn't nailed down'. [pun on SE *hydraulic jack*]

hydraulic *adj.* [1970s+] (Aus.) used of a petty thief or shoplifter. [HYDRAULIC n.]

hydro *n.* [1980s+] (US drugs) **1** hydroponically grown marijuana. **2** crack cocaine. [(1) abbr.; (2) ? the chemical process used in manufacturing crack]

hydroplug *n.* [1980s+] (US drugs) a pipe for smoking marijuana.

hyena *n.* [mid-19C–1950s] (US) a lazy or stupid person.

hyke *v.* [late 19C] to attract someone's attention, to shout after someone. [CHI-IKE]

hykey *n.* [mid–late 19C] pride. [? fig. use of HIKE v. (1)]

Hymie *n.* [20C] **1** (orig. US) a derog. term for a Jew. **2** a derog. nickname for a German. [the stereotypical Jewish name *Hyman*/Ger. name *Herman*]

Hymietown *n.* [1980s+] (US) a derog. nickname for a New York City. [HYMIE n. (1) + SE *town*]

hymns and prayers *n.* [late 19C+] usu. unmarried men and women. [SE *his* and *hers* but note pun on the woman who is 'praying' for a husband]

hype *n.*[1] (US Und.) **1** [1910s+] a short-change swindle in which the criminal persuades a shopkeeper that he has paid with a larger denomination note than he actually has, thus gaining extra change (cf. BILL n.[4]). **2** [1920s+] (US) a swindle, a confidence trick, fraud, lies or exaggeration. **3** [1920s+] (US) an exorbitant increase in prices. **4** [1950s+] publicity, promotion, especially wild statements guessing about something's nature (whether positive or negative). **5** [1960s+] any contrived situation or scheme designed to fleece a victim. [SE *hyperbole*]

hype *n.*[2] **1** [1910s+] (US drugs) a hypodermic syringe or injection. **2** [1920s+] (US drugs/Und.) a heroin or morphine addict. **3** [1970s] (pimp) a prostitute who works simply to support her narcotic addiction. [abbr. SE *hypodermic* (syringe)]

hype *adj.* **1** [1970s] (US) fraudulent. **2** [1980s+] (US campus) uptight, upset, jittery, nervous, worried. **3** [1980s+] (US Black/Rap) splendid, exciting, cool or attractive. [HYPE n.[1]]

hype *v.*[1] **1** [1910s+] (US Und.) to operate a short-change racket, to swindle, to cheat. **2** [1930s+] (US Black) to fool or cajole, to outsmart. **3** [1940s+] (orig. US) to promote a person or commodity through an excess of overzealous, grandiose publicity, esp. in rock or show business use. [HYPE n.[1]]

hype/hype up *v.*[2] **1** [1930s+] (drugs) to inject a drug. **2** [1940s+] to work up one's emotions, to become stimulated, to make more exciting. [HYPE n.[2]]

hyped *adj.* [1920s+] intoxicated by narcotic drugs. [HYPE v.[2]]

hyper *n.* [1910s–30s] (US Und.) one who works the short-change racket. [HYPE n.[1]]

hyper *adj.* [1940s+] **1** tense, over-emotional. **2** betraying one's feelings, esp. towards an attractive person. [abbr. SE *hyperactive*]

hyper *v.* [late 19C–1950s] (US) to hurry, to run. [abbr. SE *hyperactive*]

hyper down *v.* [1980s] (US) to calm down. [abbr. SE *hyperactive*]

hyperdrive whore *n.* [1980s+] (US campus) a highly promiscuous woman (cf. TURBOBITCH; TURBOSLUT). [SE *hyperdrive*, an SF coinage to indicate ultra-fast speeds + *whore*]

hyperjacks *n.* [1980s+] (drugs) ampoules of heroin. [HYPE v.[2] + JACK n.[28]]

hype stick *n.* [1910s] (US drugs) a hypodermic needle. [HYPE n.[2] (2) + STICK v.[6]]

hype up *see* HYPE v.[2].

hyp Michael, your head's on fire! *see* HIP MICHAEL, YOUR HEAD'S ON FIRE!

hypnotist *n.* [1980s+] (US campus) crazy person. [HYPE v.[2] (2) + pun]

hypo *n.*[1] **1** [18C–19C] a feeling of mild depression, of being out of sorts (cf. HIPPO n.[1]). **2** [late 19C+] (orig. US) a hypochondriac. [abbr. SE *hypochondriac*]

hypo *n.*[2] [20C] (drugs) **1** a drug addict. **2** a hypodermic syringe. [HYPE n.[2]]

hypo *v.* **1** [1920s+] to administer a hypodermic injection. **2** [1930s+] (US) to promote or enhance, to stimulate enthusiasm. [HYPE v.[2]]

hypocon/hyppocon *n.* [early 18C] *hypochon*dria. [abbr.]

hypogastrian cranny *n.* [mid-17C] the vagina. [the Greek *hypogastrium*, that section of the body below the belly and above the privates]

hyppocon *see* HYPOCON.

hyps *see* HIP n.

hy-yaw! *excl..* [mid-19C] (Anglo-Chinese) a common excl., equivalent to UK *oo-er!* [Chinese *ai-yah!*]

I

I *n.*[1] [mid-19C+] (US, mainly South/Midwest) used in a variety of combs. to express *God* or *Jesus*, e.g. *I golly! I Godfrey!* (cf. ADAD!).

i *n.*[2] [1910s] (US) an *i*dea. [abbr.]

I ain't no joke *phr.* [1990s] (US Black teen) a minatory phr. designed to warn any possible attacker of one's own powers.

I am back *n.* [1980s] (drugs) crack cocaine. [rhy. sl. = CRACK *n.*[17]]

I am sure/I'm sure *phr.*[1] [mid-19C+] a phr. used at the end of a sentence to imply **1** I don't know. **2** I am sure of that.

I am sure *phr.*[2] [1980s] (US teen) 'I am sure that you are wrong ... that I don't want to do what you suggest' etc; intensified as *I am so sure.*

I and I *phr.* [1960s+] (W.I. Rasta/UK Black teen) **1** us, we, you and I. **2** a Rastafarian.

Ian Rush *n.* [1980s] a brush. [rhy. sl.; footballer *Ian Rush* (b.1961)]

I ask you *phr.* [mid-19C+] a phr. implying one's distaste for what has just been stated; often prefixed by *well ... .*

I beg your parsnips *phr.* [late 19C–1920s] joc. mispron. of SE *I beg your pardon.*

I believe you, thousands wouldn't *phr.* [1920s+] a teasing response to what is seen as an unlikely statement.

I bet you say that to all the girls/boys *phr.* [1930s+] a teasing phr. orig. used by women to men but latterly by either sex; it follows a compliment or 'line'.

i.b.m. *n.* [1960s+] (US) a small penis. [abbr. *i*tty *b*itty *m*eat]

I can hardly wait *see* I CAN'T HARDLY WAIT.

I can't handle this *phr.* [1960s+] (orig. US teen) a general phr. indicating apprehension, disentanglement from a difficult situation, popular among drug users who are finding an experience too intense.

I can't/can hardly wait *phr.* [1930s+] an ironic phr. used to imply one's distaste for a promised future occurrence.

I caught that ill vibe *phr.* [1990s] (US Black teen) I was tricked. [CATCH *v.*[1] (4) + ILL *adj.* + VIBE *n.*]

ice *n.*[1] (US) **1** [late 19C+] profit from the illegal sale of tickets for the theatre, cinema etc. **2** [1940s–50s] protection money (cf. JUICE *n.*[1]).

ice *n.*[2] [20C] (orig. US) jewellery, esp. diamonds.

ice *n.*[3] **1** [20C] (US) a cool reception, a brush-off (cf. COLD SHOULDER). **2** [1990s] (US Black) an emotionless person, one who has no qualms about saying and doing what they feel.

ice *n.*[4] (US Black) **1** [1960s+] something or someone excellent. **2** [1990s] courage. [fig. uses of COOL *adj.*[3]]

ice *n.*[5] (US drugs) **1** [1970s+] amphetamines (cf. A *n.*[2]). **2** [1970s+] cocaine. **3** [1980s+] methylamphetamine (cf. BOMBITA).

ice *v.*[1] (US) **1** [20C] to ensure victory, orig. in a sporting contest. **2** [1930s] to pay bribes or protection money. [ICE *n.*[1] (2)]

ice *v.*[2] **1** [1930s+] to snub, to treat coldly. **2** [1930s+] (prison) to place in solitary confinement. **3** [1940s+] to murder, to kill

(cf. CHILL *v.*[2]). **4** [1960s+] (US Black) to reject, to turn down. **5** [1970s+] to break an appointment with, to abandon or cancel a plan or scheme. **6** [1990s] to hide. [fig. uses of PUT ON ICE]

ice *v.*[3] [1980s+] to complete, to round off. [SE *to put the icing on the cake*]

iceberg *n.* **1** [mid-19C+] an unemotional person. **2** [1930s+] (Aus.) anyone who enjoys an early morning swim in the icy ocean waters.

iceberg slim *n.* [1960s] (US Black) a pimp. [ICEBERG; more immediately the street name of Robert *Iceberg Slim* Beck, one-time pimp and author of a series of autobiographical books; such GANGSTA RAPPERS as Ice T (real name Tracy Marrow) took their names from his]

icebox *n.* (US) **1** [late 19C+] an unemotional person, esp. a sexually unresponsive woman. **2** [1920s+] a prison. **3** [1920s+] a solitary confinement cell.

ice-cream *n.*[1] [1920s+] (US drugs) cocaine, morphine, heroin, crack cocaine. [the whiteness of the drugs and the pleasure they give]

ice-cream *n.*[2] [1960s+] semen (cf. BABY GRAVY).

ice-cream *n.*[3] [1970s] (Black teen) a White person.

ice-cream eater *n.* [late 19C–1930s] (US drugs) a person who uses opium occasionally rather than being addicted to it (cf. CHIPPY HABIT; ICE-CREAM HABIT). [on the premise that one likes ice-cream but doesn't want it all the time]

ice-creamer *n.* [1950s+] (Aus.) an Italian. [the stereotyped occupation of Italian immigrants]

ice-cream freezer *n.* [20C] a male person. [rhy. sl. *ice-cream freezer* = GEEZER *n.*[1]]

ice-cream habit *n.* [1980s+] (drugs) the irregular use of an otherwise addictive drug (cf. ICE-CREAM EATER). [SE *ice-cream* + HABIT; on the premise that one likes ice-cream but doesn't want it all the time]

ice-cream machine *n.* [20C] the penis (cf. CREAMSTICK).

ice-cream man *n.* [1990s] (US Black/drugs) a seller of crack cocaine. [ICE-CREAM *n.*[1] + pun]

ice-cream pants *n.* [1900s–50s] (US) lightweight, light-coloured summer trousers. [the colour]

ice-cream suit *n.* [late 19C+] (orig. Aus./US) a white linen suit. [the colour]

ice cube *n.* [1980s+] (drugs) crack cocaine (cf. ICE *n.*[5]; ICE-CREAM *n.*[1]).

iced *adj.*[1] [20C] (US prison) placed in the punishment block, in solitary confinement. [ICE *v.*[2] (2) + chilly conditions in the cells]

iced *adj.*[2] [1950s+] (drugs) intoxicated by cocaine. [ICE *n.*[5]]

iced *adj.*[3] [1980s+] (US campus) abandoned, let down. [PUT ON ICE]

iced to the eyebrows *phr.* [20C] extremely drunk.

ice jack *n.* [1910s–20s] an ice-cream salesman. [SE *ice* + generic use of proper name]

ice maiden *n.* [1950s+] a 'cold' or unresponsive woman.

iceman *n.*[1] (US) [1920s–50s] a diamond thief. [ICE *n.*[2] + sfx. *-man*]

iceman *n.*[2] [1940s+] an emotionless man. [ICE *n.*[3] (2) + sfx. *-man*]

iceman *n.*[3] [1970s+] a paid killer, a 'hit man'. [ICE *v.*[2] (3) + sfx. *-man*]

ice-o *n.* [1920s+] (Aus.) an iceman. [SE *ice* + sfx. -O]

ice palace *n.* [1940s+] (US Black) a jewellery store. [ICE *n.*[2] + SE *palace*]

ice queen *n.* [1980s+] a cool, apparently emotionless woman.

ice wagon *n.* [late 19C–1920s] (US) a slow-moving person or vehicle.

ichiban *adj.* [1950s+] (US) the best (cf. NUMBER ONE *n.*[2]). [Jap. *ichiban*, number one, orig. picked up by US troops serving in the Korean War (1951–3)]

icing *n.* [1980s+] methylamphetamine (cf. BOMBITA). [ext. of ICE *n.*[5] (3)]

icing expert *n.* [1960s+] (gay) a fellator. [ICE-CREAM *n.*[2] + SE *expert*]

ick *adj.* [1960s+] (US) sickly, over-sentimental, distasteful. [abbr. ICKY *adj.*]

icky *n.* [1930s–40s] (US Black) a stupid person, one who is conventional. [ICKY *adj.*; thus lit. one who likes only bad, 'sweet' jazz]

icky/icky-boo/icky-poo *adj.* [1930s+] (orig. US) **1** of a person or an object (typically a film or play), sickly, over-sentimental. **2** (mainly teen) distasteful, nauseating, unpleasant. **3** (mainly teen) of food, sticky, sweet. [abbr. SE *stick*/echoic + 'baby-talk' sfx. *-boo/poo*]

icky-poo *adj.* [1920s+] (children's) disgusting, nasty, unpleasant, usu. with overtones of stickiness.

I could care less *see* I COULDN'T CARE LESS.

I could do that/her a favour *phr.* [1940s+] remark made by a man of a passing female. [the *favour* would, of course, be sexual]

I could do that before breakfast *phr.* [20C] (Aus.) a phr. implying that a task requires no real effort.

I could do that with my prick out *phr.* [1930s+] a phr. used to emphasize the ease of a task (cf. DO IT ON ONE'S DICK). [PRICK]

I could do with *phr.* [late 18C+] a phr. implying that one could make use of, or profit from something; 'I would be glad to have', 'I need'.

I could eat a horse and chase the jockey *phr.* [1990s] (Aus.) I am ravenously hungry.

I could eat the hind leg off a donkey *phr.* [20C] I am extremely hungry.

I couldn't care less/I could care less *phr.* [1940s+; 1960s+] (UK/US) a statement of absolute indifference, although the opposite sentiment, albeit hidden, may be the true one; sometimes extended (in N.Z.) as *I couldn't care less if the cow calves or breaks a leg.*

I could shit through the eye of a needle *phr.* [late 19C+] used by a sufferer from diarrhoea.

I could struggle *phr.* [late 19C] a phr. indicating that one would like a drink. [joc. understatement of one's enthusiasm]

I could use/I'd crawl three miles over broken glass to use her shit for toothpaste *phr.* [1950s+] a hugely exaggerated phr. implying the extent of one's infatuation.

icy *adj.* [1940s] (US) emotionless (cf. COOL *adj.*[3]).

icy mitt *see* FROZEN MITT.

icy pole *n.* [1980s+] (Aus.) an ice-cream. [the temperature and shape]

icy pop *n.* [1990s] (US campus) beer. [SE *icy* + POP *n.*[2] (2)]

i.d. *n.* [1920s+] (US) the penis. [abbr. SE *identification*; a pun on the phr. *Let's see your I.D.*]

i.d. *v.* [1940s+] (orig. US) to *id*entify. [abbr.]

Idaho rainstorm *n.* [1910s+] (US) a dust storm (cf. ARIZONA CLOUDBURST).

i.d.b. *phr.*[1] [1920s] a general insult. [abbr. *ignorant Dutch bastard*]

i.d.b. *phr.*[2] [1980s] used by privileged young men to describe their occupation. [abbr. *in daddy's business*]

I'd crawl three miles over broken glass to use her shit for toothpaste *see* I COULD USE HER SHIT FOR TOOTHPASTE.

iddy/iddy boy *n.* [20C] a derog. name for a Jew. [abbr. YID]

idea!/very idea, the! *phr.* [1910s+] a phr. implying one's (supposed) shock or disgust on hearing a proposition (usu. accredited to women, esp. working-class or lower middle-class women).

idea box/pot *n.* [late 18C–19C; 1930s+] (UK/US) the brain, the head, knowledge (cf. KNOWLEDGE BOX). [defunct UK use revived by US Black use]

ideal home *n.* [1950s+] a comb. [rhy. sl.]

idea pot *see* IDEA BOX.

I desire *n.* [mid-19C] a fire. [rhy. sl.]

I'd have done it for half a farthing *phr.* [late 19C–1920s] it would have taken very little persuasion to make me do it.

i.d. herb! *see* HIDEY!

I didn't come down in the last rain/shower/shower of rain *phr.* [20C] (Aus.) a phr. used when claiming a greater degree of experience or knowledge than that with which one is being credited.

I didn't fall off a Christmas tree *phr.* [20C] I'm not stupid, don't take me for a fool.

I didn't know you cared *phr.* [1940s+] an ironic phr. that implies one's acknowledgement that the last speaker was being insulting.

idiot box/idiot *n.* [1950s+] (orig. US) the television, implying that TV watchers are less than normally intelligent. [note TV jargon *idiot girl*, the girl who holds up cue cards for an announcer or other performer]

idiot fringe *n.* [late 19C] a popular hairstyle for girls and young women.

idiot juice *n.* [1970s] (US drugs) a mixture of nutmeg and water, used mainly in prisons. [its effects]

idiot light *n.* [1960s+] a warning light, usu. red, that goes on when a fault occurs in a mechanical or electrical device.

idiot oil *n.* [1980s+] alcohol (cf. IGNORANT OIL). [its effects]

idiot pills *n.* [1980s+] (drugs) barbiturates, any strong sedatives (cf. GORILLA PILLS). [their effects]

idiot-proof *adj.* [1980s+] of a machine or a mechanical process, supposedly calculated to be comprehensible to even the least technologically minded person.

idiot spoon *n.* [1940s–60s+] (US) a shovel (cf. IDIOT STICK; IDIOT TOOL). [the supposed intelligence of those that wield them]

idiot stick *n.* [1930s+] (US) a shovel (cf. IDIOT SPOON). [the supposed intelligence of those who wield them]

idiot tool *n.* [1980s+] (US) a shovel (cf. IDIOT SPOON). [for ety. *see* IDIOT STICK]

idiot tube *n.* [1960s–70s] (US) a television. [IDIOT (BOX) + TUBE *n.*[3]]

Idle Hall *n.* [20C] (W.I.) a notional place used fig. to mean a state of unemployment; thus *work at Idle Hall*, to be unemployed (cf. KICKSTONE & CO.; WALKER & CO.).

idles, the *n.* [17C] laziness, esp. in the guise of an illness; often as *sick of the idles.*

idleset *n.* [20C] (Ulster) a fat stomach. [it is evidence of one's idleness]

I don't believe this! *excl.* [20C] an excl. of disbelief that extends beyond mere lack of simple credence into a denial that one could ever have landed in such a mess, that others could have created such horrors, that such stupidity could exist etc.

I don't care if I do *see* I DON'T MIND IF I DO.

I don't give a fuck phr. [20C] an intense version of I COULDN'T CARE LESS. [note, however, one-time late 18C use in a poem 'The Discontented Student'; the word is not spelt out, but the rhyme and the context ensure that the absentee can only be 'fuck']

I don't know phr. [1980s+] (orig. US teen) an all-purpose phr. that is used less as a definite statement than as an alternative to 'er' or 'Y'know' as a sentence-breaker; usu. pron. *dunno*.

I don't make the fries phr. [1990s] (US teen) a phr. used to express the fact that one does not have any influence on the outcome of life. [the image of a worker in a junk-food restaurant]

I don't mind/care if I do phr. [mid-19C] a phr. offering the speaker's thanks in response to an offer of food or drink or some similar invitation.

I don't rightly know phr. [mid-19C+] I am not fully sure.

I don't think phr. [mid-19C+] an ironic phr. used at the end of a declaratory statement as a means of negating whatever has just been said, e.g. *She's a real sweetie. I don't think* (cf. NOT!).

I don't want to know phr. [1940s+] a phr. implying the speaker's refusal to acknowledge some unpalatable fact or piece of information.

idrin n. [1950s+] (orig. W.I. Rasta) one's fig. 'brothers'. [W.I. pron. of SE *brethren*]

iez-haad adj. [1950s+] (W.I. Rasta) thick-skulled, stubborn, unwilling or unable to hear. [W.I. pron. 'ears-hard']

i'facins!/i'facks! see I'FECKS!

i'fecks!/i'fackins!/i'facks! excl. [early 18C] a mild excl., lit. 'in faith'.

if ever! excl. [early 19C+] would you believe it? is it possible?

if ever there was phr. [early 19C+] an assertion that the person or thing referred to is a perfect or undoubted example of its kind.

iffy adj. [1930s+] (orig. US) marginal, not wholly acceptable, unpalatable. [SE *if*]

if his cap be made of wool phr. [17C–18C] certainly, without any doubt.

if I'm lying I'm dying/flying phr. [1930s+] (US Black) a phr. implying the speaker's attestation of absolute honesty and good faith.

if it ain't you, it's somebody/someone else phr. [1930s+] (US Black) a phr. in which the speaker indicates a belief that trouble is imminent.

if it had been a bear it would have bit you phr. [17C+] a phr. used to ridicule someone who can't see something that is right in front of them.

if it moves, salute it; if it don't, paint it phr. [1940s+] (orig. milit.) supposedly the advice for a successful (services) career. [carried into civilian life by WW2 veterans]

if it were raining pea soup I'd get hit on the head by a fork phr. [1940s+] (Aus.) a general expression of continual bad luck.

if my aunt had been a man, she'd have been my uncle phr. [mid-17C+] a phr. used as a rejoinder to a speaker who has just finished a long and laborious explanation of the obvious.

if poss phr. [late 19C+] *if possible*. [abbr.]

if their brains were gas, they couldn't power a flea's motorcycle around the inside of a Cheerio phr. [1970s] (US Black) statement underlining the absolute stupidity or inadequacy of the person so assailed.

...if they're/it's a day phr. [mid-19C+] a phr. indicating that a person's or object's age is at least the number stated, e.g. *He's fifty if he's a day*.

if they're big enough, they're old enough phr. [1960s+] a phr. used among men to suggest that, whatever actual age a

girl is, if she has reached puberty biologically (menstruation, body shape etc), she is old enough for intercourse.

if they're big/old enough to bleed, they're big/old enough to butcher/fuck phr. [1960s+] a phr. used among men to suggest that if a girl is old enough to menstruate she is old enough for intercourse.

if they had the flu they wouldn't give you a sneeze phr. [1930s+] a phr. used to describe someone's extreme meanness.

if you ask me phr. [20C] in my opinion. [abbr. SE *if you ask me my opinion*]

if you can't beat 'em, join 'em phr. [20C] a statement of cynical resignation, not to mention the justification for a number of otherwise self-abasing acts.

if you can't be good, be careful! see BE GOOD!

if you can't do the time, don't do the crime phr. [20C] (orig. Und.) don't take an action if you cannot deal with the concomitant responsibilities. [TIME n.[1]; orig. Und. but used fig. in the wider world]

if you don't mind phr. [late 17C+] a phr. used as a form of reproof, esp. to someone who barges in, pushes one aside etc.

if you go says Bob Munro phr. [1950s+] (N.Z.) a general phr. of encouragement at the outset of a project, competition etc. [ety. unknown; ? anecdotal or simply assonant]

if you like phr. [20C] a phr. implying one's reluctant agreement.

if your aunt had balls, she'd be your uncle phr. [20C] a phr. used as a rejoinder to a speaker who has just finished a long and laborious explanation of the obvious (cf. IF MY AUNT HAD BEEN A MAN, SHE'D HAVE BEEN MY UNCLE).

ig/igg n. [1960s–70s] (US Black) a snub, a rejection. [IG v.]

ig/igg v. [1940s+] (orig. US Black) to *ig*nore deliberately, to snub (cf. DIS). [abbr.]

igaretsay n. [1940s+] (orig. US) a cigarette. [pig Latin]

iggy adj. [1910s] (US) *ig*norant. [abbr.]

ightna n. [late 19C] night. [backsl.]

ig man n. [20C] (US Black) an *ig*norant *man*, a fool. [abbr.]

ignant adj. [1940s+] (US Black) an *ig*norant, stupid person. [abbr./pron. of SE *ignorant*]

ig'nant oil see IGNORANT OIL.

ignite n. [1980s+] (US Black) whisky (cf. BALL OF FIRE n.[1]). [it sets the drinker 'on fire']

ignite the lightsaber, to phr. [1980s+] to masturbate (cf. DO THE HAN SOLO). [a ref. to the swordlike weapons in the *Star Wars* films of the 1970s–80s]

igno n. [1970s+] (US) a fool. [abbr. SE *ignoramus*]

ignorance n. [1940s+] (W.I.) extreme anger that threatens the other person.

ignorant adj. [1940s+] **1** angry, irascible, short-tempered. **2** arrogant, ill-natured, bullying. [dial. *ignorant*, uncouth, ill-mannered]

ignorant as Paddy's pig n. [1970s+] (N.Z.) very stupid. [PADDY n.[1] (1); thus neg. racial stereotyping]

ignorant/ig'nant oil n. [1960s+] (US Black) alcohol (cf. IDIOT OIL). [its effects]

ignorant stick n. [1950s+] (US) a shovel. [var. on IDIOT STICK]

I got it like that phr. [1990s] (US Black teen) a phr. indicating that one is doing well.

I guess phr. [early 19C+] (orig. US) I imagine, I assume, I am fairly certain; often in reply to a question as 'I suppose you are right'.

I guess yes! excl. [late 19C] (US) yes indeed! absolutely!

igxagxa n. [1950s+] (S.Afr. Black) **1** a poor White. **2** one who falls between two ethnic cultures. [Xhosa *ukugxagxa*, one who has become poor and squalid]

I hate it/that phr. [1980s+] (US campus) a sarcastic expression of pleasure.

I hear better cock crow *phr.* [20C] (W.I.) a phr. used to dismiss someone, esp. in authority, whose word has proved hollow or who has gone back on a supposedly firm promise or agreement.

I hear you *phr.* [1960s+] an emphatic way of saying 'I understand', 'yes'. [note jazz use of *hear*, to become emotionally involved with the music, to concentrate absolutely on what one is hearing]

i jacks! *see* BY JACKS!

ijuwishi *n.* [1960s+] (S.Afr. Black) expensive clothing. [JEWISH n.]

Ike *n.* [late 19C+] (US) **1** an ignorant rustic male (cf. JAKEK n.¹; RUBE n.¹). **2** a self-important, pretentious person (cf. BIG IKE). [abbr. the 'rural' name *Isaac*]

ikey *n.*¹ **1** [mid-19C] a derog. term for a Jew. **2** [late 19C–1910s] the 'inevitable' nickname for a Jew or one who has 'Jewish' features. **3** [late 19C–1910s] one who plays a duplicitous 'sharp' trick. **4** [20C] a pawnbroker (irrespective of racial origin). [abbr. IKEY-MO n.; lit. or fig. refs. to stereotyped Jewish characteristics]

ikey *n.*² [1910s+] (S.Afr.) a student of the University of Cape Town; thus *Ikeys*, the university itself (cf. MATIE). [proper name *Isaac*, thus ? f. IKEY-MO n.; despite the obvious racial implication, the term is regularly used in sports reports without further comment]

ikey *v.* [1950s–60s] (US) to cheat financially (cf. JEW). [IKEY-MO n.]

ikey-mo *n.* **1** [early 19C] a derog. term for a Jew; thus the various stereotypes. **2** [mid-19C+] a Jewish receiver, moneylender, pawnbroker. **3** [mid-19C+] a loafer, a layabout. **4** [mid-19C+] a tip, information. **5** [mid-19C+] (Aus.) a bookmaker. [SE *Isaac* + *Moses*, two typical Jewish given names; note Kentish dial. *ikey*, proud]

ikey-mo *adj.* **1** [late 19C+] artful, crafty, knowing. **2** [late 19C+] having a good opinion of oneself, stuck-up. **3** [1960s] dandified (cf. JEWISH adj.²). [IKEY-MO n.]

ikeyness *n.* [late 19C+] Jewishness, i.e. the derog. stereotypes: artfulness, craftiness, greed, financial chicanery etc. [IKEY-MO n. + sfx. *-ness*]

I kid you not *phr.* [1950s+] (orig. US) a phr. implying that the speaker is being absolutely serious.

ilie *adj.* [1950s] (W.I. Rasta) describes something valuable, exalted, sacred. [lit. use of SE *highly*]

I like it, but it doesn't like me *phr.* [late 19C+] a phr. that refers to food and/or drink that, while delicious, has a deleterious effect on the consumer.

I like that! *excl.* [20C] an ironical expression of surprise or disgust at someone's impudence, conceit, untruthfulness etc.

ill *adj.* (US Black teen) **1** [1970s+] aggressive, offensive, bad. **2** [1990s] bizarre, surprising. **3** [1990s] on the bad = good paradigm, wonderful, first-rate (cf. AWFUL adj.). **4** [1990s] angry, frustrated. [fig. uses of SE *ill*, unwell]

ill *v.* (orig. US Black teen) **1** [1980s+] to act crazily, aggressively, wildly. **2** [1990s] to do something very well. [ILL adj.]

I'll be a Chinaman! *excl.* [20C] a mild oath (cf. I'M A DUTCHMAN!).

I'll be a dirty word! *excl.* [20C] a mild oath. [lit. + fig. use of SE *dirty word*]

I'll be a Dutchman! *see* I'M A DUTCHMAN!

I'll be a lowdown son of a bitch! *see* I'LL BE A SON OF A BITCH!

I'll be a marble/marble up on another's taw *see* I'LL BE ONE MARBLE ON ANOTHER'S TAW.

I'll be a monkey's uncle! *phr.* [1920s+] a general expression of surprise.

I'll be a son/lowdown son of a bitch! *excl.* [20C] a general excl. of surprise or annoyance.

I'll be blowed! *excl.* [late 19C+] a general excl. of surprise, shock etc. [euph.]

I'll be consarned! *excl.* [19C+] a mild oath.

I'll be cow-kicked! *excl.* [20C] (US) a euph. for *I'll be damned!* Often as comb. *cow-kicked by a jackass* or *cow-kicked by a mule*.

I'll be darned! *excl.* [late 18C+] a mild oath, euph. for *I'll be damned!*

I'll be dicked! *excl.* [1960s] (US) a general excl. of surprise, amazement. [fig. use of DICK v.²]

I'll be go-to-hell! *excl.* [1930s+] (US) an excl. of astonishment. [GO-TO-HELL adj.]

I'll be hanged! *excl.* [early 18C+] a general excl. of surprise, annoyance or impatience.

I'll be jiggered! *excl.* [mid-19C+] a general excl. of surprise. [JIGGER v.¹]

I'll be John Browned! *excl.* [1900–30s] (US) a joc. euph. for I'LL BE HANGED. [the abolitionist *John Brown* (1800–59), who was hanged for his part in the attack on Harper's Ferry, Virginia]

I'll be one/a marble/marble up on another's taw *phr.* [early 19C] a phr. meaning 'I'll get even'. [for ety. *see* I'LL BE ONE UP ON YOUR TAW PRESENTLY]

I'll be one up on your taw presently *phr.* [late 18C–19C] a threatening phr. meaning 'I'll deal with you in due course'. [marbles imagery; SE *taw*, the large marble with which a player shoots]

I'll be shot if ...! *excl.* [mid-18C–mid-19C] a strong expression of denial or refusal; thus synon. *I'll see you shot first!*

I'll be/I'm sniggered! *excl.* [mid-19C] a general oath; basically a euph. for *I'll be damned* (cf. JIGGERED adj.²).

I'll be switched! *excl.* [mid-19C–1940s] an excl. of irritation, surprise, denial. [SE *switch*, to thrash]

I'll bet *phr.* [late 19C+] a phr. used to imply (depending on context) the speaker's enthusiastic or sceptical response to what they have just heard.

I'll be there *n.* [20C] a chair. [rhy. sl.]

I'll buy that *phr.* [20C] (Aus./Can.) a phr. indicating agreement, 'I'll go along with that.'

I'll eat my hat *phr.* [19C+] a statement of utter disbelief. *If such and such is true/happens, I'll ...*.

illegit *adj.* [1910s+] *illegit*imate. [abbr.]

illegitimate *n.*¹ [19C] (Aus.) a free, i.e. non-convict, Australian settler. [paradoxically, a *legitimate* settler was a criminal who had been sentenced to transportation]

illegitimate *n.*² [mid-19C] a poor class of costermonger looked down on by the mainstream costers, selling pea soup, sweetmeats, spice-cakes etc.

illegitimis non carborundum/nil carborundum illegitimi *phr.* [1940s+] (orig. milit.) don't be overcome by the pressures created by one's superiors. [i.e. 'don't let the bastards grind you down'; the 'Latin' translation is hardly accurate]

ill fortune *n.* [late 17C–early 19C] ninepence (a coin). [unfortunate in that it is not a whole shilling]

I'll freeze, Bill *phr.* [20C] (US teen) a polite rejection of an offer or suggestion, 'thank you, but no'.

I'll give you Jim Smith! *excl.* [late 19C] a threat to give someone else a beating. [*Jim Smith* was a contemporary pugilist]

I'll go hopping to hell *phr.* [20C] a phr. implying the speaker's amazement, approval or admiration, often with pfx. *well ...*.

illing/illin' *adj.* [1980s+] (orig. US Black/teen) **1** acting or thinking wildly, aggressively, crazily. **2** annoyed, unhappy. **3** in a difficult or unpleasant situation, under severe stress. [ILL v. (1)]

I'll knock out your eight eyes *phr.* [late 18C] a threat, commonly used by Billingsgate fishwives. ['a common Billingsgate threat from one fish nymph to another: every woman, according to the naturalists of that society, having eight eyes, viz. two seeing eyes, two bub-eyes (cf. BUBBIES), a bell-eye (SE *belly*), two popes-eyes (f. SE *pope's eye*: the lymphatic gland in a leg of mutton, regarded as a delicacy; here presumably the urinal and anal orifices), and a ***-eye' (Grose 1796) (the censored term remains mysterious, it is, presumably, a ref. to the vagina)]

I'll make you sing/sing o-be-joyful on the other side of your mouth *phr.* [late 18C–early 19C] a general threat of violence (cf. SING O-BE-JOYFUL). ['o-be-joyful' implies hymn-singing]

I'll murder you *phr.* [1930s+] a usu. joking threat, e.g. *If you tell anyone, I'll murder you.*

I'll pay that *phr.* [1930s+] (Aus.) **1** a phr. used to acknowledge that the speaker has been tricked or 'had'. **2** a phr. used to acknowledge the telling of a good joke or funny story.

ill piece *n.* [1950s+] (gay) an unattractive and therefore unpopular homosexual. [SE *ill* + PIECE n.¹]

I'll put the smack down on yo azz beeyach! *phr.* [1990s] (US Black teen) a general statement of aggression, lit. 'I shall hit you'. [pron. of SE *your* + ASS (*see* ARSE n.¹) + BITCH n.¹]

I'll say *phr.* [1920s+] (orig. US) absolutely, definitely, I couldn't agree more.

I'll see about it *phr.* [mid-19C+] a deliberately vague promise in order to avoid answering a specific request straightaway.

I'll see you further/further first *phr.* [mid-19C+] a phr. implying one's total disagreement, 'I absolutely will not'.

I'll tell you what *phr.* [late 16C+] 'I'll tell you what it is' or 'I'll tell you something'.

I'll tickle your tail *phr.* [late 19C+] a threat of violence, though often teasing or joc.

illuminated *adj.* [1920s+] drunk. [play on LIT UP]

illustrated shirt *n.* [mid-19C] a coloured shirt, as favoured by costermongers.

I'll warrant/warrant you *phr.* [late 18C+] 'I assure you', 'I'll be bound'.

illywhacker *n.* [1940s+] (Aus.) a professional confidence man, esp. an itinerant following fairs and country shows. [SPIELER]

ill-willie *adj.* [20C] (Ulster) uncooperative. [SE *ill will*]

i.l.u.v.m. *phr.* [20C] *I love you very much*; written on the envelopes of love letters (cf. BOLTOP). [abbr.]

I'm a coon *phr.* [1930s] a phr. used to refute a suggestion or hypothesis (cf. I'M A DUTCHMAN). [COON n.]

I'm/I'll be a Dutchman *phr.* [early 19C+] a phr. used to refute a suggestion or hypothesis, usu. preceded by *If that's ... then I'll be ...*.

I'm afloat *n.* [20C] **1** a boat. **2** a coat. [rhy. sl]

image *n.* [mid-19C+] a person attracting amused, affectionate or contemptuous glances, a 'sight', esp. qualified as *old image*, *little image* etc.

imaginitis *n.* [1940s+] a tendency to fantasize, to imagine things. [SE *imagine* + sfx. -ITIS, implying an illness or medical condition]

i-man *pron.* [1950s+] (W.I. Rasta) I, me, mine (cf. I AND I).

imbo *n.* [1930s–50s] (Aus.) a fool, a simpleton (cf. IMBY). [SE *imbecile* + sfx. -O]

imbuggerance *n.* [1960s+] (Aus.) irrelevance. [phr. *I don't give a bugger*]

imby *n.* [1980s] (US) a fool (cf. IMBO). [SE *imbecile*]

I'm easy *phr.* [1940s+] (orig. Aus.) I don't mind, I'm satisfied whatever the outcome.

imey-wimey *n.* [1920–30s] (US Black) a meek-sounding, whining voice. [? SE *whine* or elision of *I ... me ... why me?* + onomat.]

I'm from Missouri *phr.* [20C] (US) a phr. used to denote one's scepticism and suspicions. [orig. *I come from Missouri. You have got to show me*; the image is of the cautious countryman refusing to fall for the wiles of the city slicker. The phr. was popularized, though not actually coined, by Missouri Congressman Willard D. Vandiver (1854–1932)]

I'm history *phr.* [1990s] (US teen/campus) I'm leaving, goodbye.

imma/immy *n.* [1920s+] a marble. [SE *immy*, a choice marble made in imitation, as of a cornelian or an agate; ult. SE *imitation*]

immense *adj.* [mid-18C–1900s] extremely good, first-rate, splendid.

immense *adv.* [mid-18C] splendidly, well.

immensikoff *n.* [late 19C–1910s] a bulky, fur-lined overcoat. [coined by the music-hall star Arthur Lloyd (1840–1904), who called himself *Immensikoff* and appeared on stage in such a coat to sing, *c.*1868, his hit 'The Shoreditch Toff']

immies *n.* [1940s+] (US) **1** the game of marbles. **2** the eyes. [SE *immy*, a highly rated marble, made to resemble a semi-precious stone, e.g. cornelian, agate]

immigrant chic *see* PORTAGEE COLONIAL.

immo *adj.* [1940s–60s] (US Black) *im*itation, counterfeit. [abbr.]

immortal *adj.* **1** [mid-16C–early 17C] superhuman, inhuman, excessive. **2** [mid-19C] (US) wonderful, excellent.

immortally *adv.* [late 19C] infinitely, superlatively. [IMMORTAL adj.]

immy *see* IMMA.

I'm not made of money! *see* DO YOU THINK I'M MADE OF MONEY?

I'm not out for chocolates, just for grapes *phr.* [1900s–10s] no thanks.

I'm not so green as I'm cabbage-looking *phr.* [late 19C] don't take me for a fool, I may look stupid, but I'm not. [SE *green*, naïve]

imoogie *see* MOEGIE.

I'm outtie *phr.* [1990s] (US teen) I'm leaving (cf. AUDI). [lit. *I'm out of here*]

impale *v.* [19C] to have sexual intercourse (cf. BANG v.¹).

imperence *n.* [mid-18C–mid-19C] impudence, impertinence; thus *imperent*, impudent. [SE *impudence*]

imperial pop *n.* [late 19C] ginger beer. [POP n.² + the fact that the Emperor Napoleon III (r.1852–70) declared it to be his favourite drink]

impimpi *n.* [1960s+] (S.Afr.) a police informer (cf. PIMP n.²). [SE *pimp* or Zulu *umbimbi*, a conspiracy or *iphimpi*, a species of cobra]

impixlocated *adj.* [1930s] tipsy. [SE *intoxicated* + PIXILLATED]

implement *n.* [late 17C–18C] a fool who is persuaded to take part in a dangerous or foolhardy enterprise (cf. TOOL n.).

import *n.* [1920s+] (US campus) a date or partner brought from elsewhere (outside the college town itself) to attend a party or dance.

importance *n.* [late 17C–1910s] one's wife. [abbr. COMFORTABLE IMPORTANCE]

impos *adj.* [1920s] *impos*sible. [abbr.]

impost-taker *n.* [late 17C–early 19C] one who lends money to losing gamblers, taking advantage of their desperate need for new funds to extort the highest possible interest. [SE *impost*, a tax or customs levy + *taker*]

impudence *n.* [mid-18C–late 19C] the penis.

impudent stealing *n.* [late 18C–19C] 'Cutting out the backs of coaches and robbing the seats' (Grose 1796).

impure *n.* [18C] a prostitute.

imshee!/imshi!/imshy! *excl.* [1910s+] (orig. milit.) be off! go away! [Arab. *imshi*, go away, adopted by WWI troops serving in the Middle East]

I'm sniggered *see* I'LL BE SNIGGERED.

I'm so *n.* [1930s] whisky. [rhy. sl.; *I'm so frisky* = SE *whisky*]

I'm so hungry I could eat a shit sandwich – only I don't like bread *phr.* [1950s+] (Aus.) a phr. implying the intensity of one's starvation.

I'm sure *see* I AM SURE phr.[1].

I'm sure I don't know *phr.* [mid-19C+] a phr. used assertively, i.e. to add emphasis to one's earlier statement.

I'm talking to the butcher, not the block *phr.* [20C] a dismissive phr. used to silence an interruption by someone the speaker does not consider worthy of an audience.

I'm telling you *phr.* [1930s+] an emphatic statement that there is no need for discussion or argument.

I'm there *phr.* [1990s] (US campus) an expression of support.

I must break you *phr.* [1990s] (US Black teen) a general phr. used to threaten an opponent or rival.

I must have killed a Chinaman *phr.* [late 19C+] (Aus.) a phr. used on experiencing any form of bad luck. [the stereotyping of the Chinese as capable of bringing on ill luck]

I'm willing *n.* [20C] a shilling (5p) (cf. ABRAHAM'S WILLING). [rhy. sl.]

in *n.* [1920s+] (orig. US) a means of infiltrating otherwise closed groups, usu. those holding power and influence (cf. ON THE IN).

in *adj.* **1** [mid-19C+] fashionable. **2** [20C] guaranteed of success in a given project (cf. IN LIKE FLYNN). **3** [20C] (US) being part of a closed or influential group, often through the payment of bribes, wielding of influence etc. **4** [1920s+] socially acceptable. **5** [1960s+] (drugs) connected with drug suppliers.

in a bad skin *phr.* [late 18C–19C] bad-tempered, 'out of sorts' (cf. IN A GOOD SKIN).

in a bad way *phr.* [20C] suffering problems, difficulties.

in a big way *phr.* [late 19C+] (orig. US) very much, extremely, intensely.

in a box *phr.* [mid-19C+] in difficulties, in a confused state of mind, in a quandary; thus *in the same box*, sharing the same problems.

in a brace/couple of shakes *phr.* [early 19C+] immediately. [SE *brace*, a pair]

in a cat's ass *phr.* [1950s] (orig. US) completely impossible, absolutely not! I don't believe you! go away! (cf. IN A PIG'S ASS).

in a coon's age *phr.* [mid-19C+] (US) over a very long period (cf. COON'S AGE). [the lifespan of a raccoon]

in a couple of shakes *see* IN A BRACE OF SHAKES.

in a crack *phr.* [late 18C–late 19C] very soon, in a moment. [CRACK n.[6]]

in a cross *phr.* [1950s–60s] (US Black) in trouble, at a disadvantage, usu. in the phr. *put in a cross*, to put into a difficult situation.

in a delicate condition/state of health *phr.* [mid-19C; 20C] euph. for pregnant.

in a fix *phr.* [20C] (US) pregnant. [FIX n.[1]]

in a flea's leap *phr.* [mid-19C] immediately.

in a fling *phr.* [mid-19C–1900s] in a fit of temper. [SE *fling*, a spree]

in a good skin *phr.* [late 18C–19C] good-humoured, cheerful (cf. IN A BAD SKIN).

in a hobble *phr.* [18C–19C] in trouble, perplexed, committed for trial (cf. HOBBLE n.). [Scot. dial. *habble*, a difficulty, a perplexity]

in a hog's horn *phr.* [mid–late 19C] (US) never, not at all (cf. IN A PIG'S ASS).

in a horn *phr.* [19C+] (US) a general phr. of dismissal (cf. IN A PIG'S ASS). [? dial. *in a horn*, expression of incredulity]

in a jam *phr.* [1910s+] (orig. US) facing a problem, in difficulties. [SE *jam*, the position of being jammed or stuck]

in a jerk *phr.* [mid-18C–early 19C] very quickly.

in a jiffy *phr.* [late 18C+] very quickly, in a moment. [JIFFY]

in a kick *phr.* [mid-19C] in a moment, very soon (cf. IN A JIFFY).

in alt *adj.* [mid-18C–early 19C] haughty, arrogant. [musical jargon *in alt*, in the octave above the treble stave beginning with G, i.e. a high tone]

in a man's beef, to be *phr.* [late 18C–early 19C] to wound a man with a sword (cf. IN A WOMAN'S BEEF). [BEEF n.[1] (1)]

in a merry pin *phr.* [late 18C–early 19C] almost drunk, tipsy (cf. ABOUT RIGHT adj.[1]). [a variety of tankard, used in the north, which was divided by silver pins set at equal distances from top to bottom. The custom was for a drinker to drink down to the next pin, then pass it on. If he drank too far, he had to go on to the next pin, and if he missed this one, to continue until the next. The drunker one became, the less capable one was of assessing the proper measure to drink and so the process continued]

in a minute *phr.* [1980s+] (US Black) a phr. of farewell, goodbye (cf. LATER!).

in a muck *see* ALL OF A MUCK.

in-and-in *n.* [1930s] (Und.) that moment in a swindle when the swindler seems to risk their money along with that of the dupe. [both have put their money *in* the swindle]

in-and-out *n.[1]* [late 19C] a pauper who alternates between living in a workhouse and street begging. [*in* and *out* of the workhouse]

in-and-out *n.[2]* [20C] **1** the nose. **2** a cigarette. **3** a bottle of stout. **4** a tout, a racecourse tipster. [rhy. sl.; (1) SE *snout*; (2) SNOUT n.[2]]

in and out like a fiddler's elbow *phr.* [20C] rapid and enthusiastic copulation.

in-and-out man *n.* [1950s+] (Und.) an opportunist thief, who goes quickly *in and out* of the house he is robbing.

in-and-out-of *n.* [1940s] (US Black) a door.

in-and-out shop *n.* [20C] a shop in a corridor along which are displayed the items for sale.

in anger *adv.* [1970s+] seriously, properly, earnestly (rather than casually or as a practice).

in a pickle *phr.* [mid-19C+] in a mess, in difficulties. [PICKLE n.[1]]

in a pig's ass!/ear!/eye!/neck!/poke!/tonsil!/wig! *excl.* [20C] (orig. US) completely impossible, absolutely not! I don't believe you! go away! [US rural catchphrase *in the pig's ass*, referring to bestiality and, as such, the subject of a variety of coarse jokes, which depend on the mistaken orifice (the anus rather than the vagina) and the mistaken object of affection (the pig rather than the woman)]

in a Portuguese pignot *phr.* [1940s] confused, esp. of one who is telling a story but constantly loses their thread.

in a pucker *phr.* [mid-18C–late 19C] in a state of excitement. [one's face puckers up when expressing excitement]

in a shake/shake of a hand *phr.* [early 19C] at once, immediately, very quickly (cf. IN HALF A SHAKE; IN A BRACE OF SHAKES).

in a sling *phr.* [1960s] (US) in difficulties (cf. PUT SOMEONE IN A SLING).

in/up arsehole street *phr.* [1950s+] in difficulties, facing problems (cf. IN SHIT STREET). [ARSEHOLE n.]

in a spot *phr.* [1920s+] in trouble, in difficulties. [abbr. SE *in a spot of bother*]

in a stew *phr.* [late 19C–1910s] sweating heavily, bathed in perspiration.

in a stink *adj.* **1** [late 17C+] awful, terrible. **2** [mid-19C+] (orig. US) extraordinary, surprising (as often pos. as neg.).

in a sweat *phr.* [1920s+] anxious, worried.

in a twink *phr.* [1930s+] in a very short time (cf. IN A JIFFY). [TWINK n.[1]]

in a way *phr.* [mid-19C+] in an emotional 'state'.

in a woman's beef, to be *phr.* [late 18C–mid-19C] to have sexual intercourse with a woman (cf. ACHING FOR A SIDE OF BEEF; IN A MAN'S BEEF). [BEEF n.[1] (2)]

in bad bread *phr.* [late 18C] in trouble, in a difficult situation.

in bad loaf *phr.* [late 18C–mid-19C] in trouble, in a difficult situation. [var. on IN BAD BREAD]

in bad shape *phr.* [mid-19C+] in a troubled or depressed state.

in bed with *phr.* [1970s+] (orig. US) allied or associated with, usu. implying nefarious activities.

in-between *n.* [20C] (Aus.) a male homosexual. [rhy. sl. *in between* = QUEEN n.[1]]

in-betweens *n.* [1960s+] (drugs) depressants, amphetamines (cf. A n.[2]).

in bondage *phr.* [20C] (US Black) indebted to, or under the control of, with a biblical implication.

in Bushey Park *see* AT BUSHEY PARK.

in cack street *see* IN SHIT STREET.

in cahoots with *phr.* [19C] (orig. US) in partnership with, usu. implying a slightly disreputable or surreptitious alliance. [? Fr. *cahute*, cabin, or *cohorte*, company; other suggestions include US *cahot*, a pothole, or the *pfx.* KER– + *hoot*, albeit the latter remains inexplicable]

Inca message *n.* [1970s+] (drugs) cocaine. [the relation of cocaine to South America]

incandescent belt, the *n.* [1920s–50s] (US) Broadway, NYC. [coined by columnist Walter Winchell (1897–1972)]

inch *n.* [19C] the penis. [it *inch*es in]

inch *v.* [1990s] (US campus) to steal. [abbr. HALF-INCH v.[2]]

in chancery *adv.* [late 19C] in an awkward situation (cf. PUT IN CHANCERY).

inch and pinch, to *phr.* [20C] (Ulster) to live frugally.

in check *adj.* [1990s] (US teen) under control. [SE *check*, to restrain]

incident *n.* [late 19C] (orig. US) an illegitimate child. [euph.]

in clover *adj.* [late 18C+] in comfort (cf. ON CLOVER).

in co *phr.* [early–mid-19C] (US) along with, *in co*mpany with. [abbr.]

incog *adj.*[1] [late 17C–early 18C] *incog*nito. [abbr. SE *incognito*, disguised]

incog *adj.*[2] [19C] drunk (cf. COGE IT, COGUEY). [Scot. dial. *cogue*, a drinking vessel or dram]

incognita *n.* [mid–late 19C] a courtesan, a high-class prostitute (cf. ANONYMA). [Lat. *incognito*, unknown]

in collar *adj.* [late 19C] employed (cf. IN HARNESS). [the image is of a horse in its working harness]

in Crab Street *phr.* [early 19C] annoyed, irritated (cf. CRABBED). [CRAB v.[1]]

increase *n.* [20C] a new baby.

in cuerpo *adj.* [mid-18C] naked. [a borrowing of the Sp. phr. *in cuerpo*, in the body, to mean without the cloak or upper garment, in order to show the shape of the body; used as such by contemporary men-about-town]

in deadly suspense *phr.* [late 18C–early 19C] hanged. [pun]

in dead trouble *phr.* [1930s+] (orig. milit.) in severe trouble. [DEAD adv. + SE *trouble*]

indeed and indeed *phr.* [late 17C–mid-19C] really and truly, absolutely.

indescribables *n.* [late 18C–19C] trousers (cf. DON'T-SPEAK-OF-'EMS).

index *n.* **1** [early 19C] the nose. **2** [1930s–40s] (US Black) the face.

india *n.* [1950s–60s] (camp gay) a plain man, with homely, peasant features. [Sp. *india*, a peasant woman]

Indian *n.*[1] (US) **1** [mid-19C–1960s] an uncouth, rowdy person, irrespective of actual race. **2** [mid-19C+] a person; esp. as *big Indian*, an influential, important person. **3** [late 19C+] a quick temper, esp. in the phr. *get one's Indian up*, to lose one's temper (cf. AFRICA). [note B&L differentiate: 'to say that one has his "*Indian*" up,' implies a great degree of vindictiveness, while *Dutch* wrath is stubborn but yielding to reason']

Indian *n.*[2] [late 19C] (US) whisky. [since 1920s it is illegal in Can. to sell liquor to Native Americans living on reserves or settlements]

Indian *n.*[3] [late 19C] a cent. [a picture of a Native American was engraved on the reverse]

Indian *n.*[4] [1950s+] (gay) a man who uses make-up (cf. WAR-PAINT).

Indian *n.*[5] [1960s+] an Indian meal (cf. CHINESE n.).

Indian burn *see* CHINESE BURN.

Indian coffee *n.* [mid-19C+] (US) coffee made from reheated grounds. [the assumption being that 'Red Indians' deserved nothing better]

Indian dick *n.* [1980s] (Aus.) a thin sausage. [SE (Asian) *Indian* + DICK n.[5] (1)]

Indian giver *n.* [mid-18C+] (US) **1** one who when giving, expects a gift in return. **2** one who first gives, then takes back a gift. [the racist stereotype of the untrustworthy 'Red Indian']

Indian haircut *n.* [20C] (US) scalping. [the stereotype of the warlike 'Red Indian', tomahawk in hand]

Indian hay *n.* [1930s+] marijuana. [SE *Indian hemp* + HAY n.[3]]

Indian hunting *n.* [early 19C] (US) a fight between two men. [ety. unknown]

Indian liquor/rum/whisky *n.* [19C] (US) the lowest quality spirits (cf. INDIAN COFFEE). [the assumption that anything could be palmed off on 'Red Indians']

Indian pow-wow *n.* (US) [20C] a noisy discussion or gathering. [racist stereotyping]

Indian rub *n.* [1980s+] (US) a means of causing pain by rubbing the knuckles hard across someone's skull (cf. DRY SHAVE v.[2]; DUTCH RUB). [a supposed Native American punishment]

Indian rug *n.* [1960s+] (gay) a cheap wig done in braids. [SE *Indian* + RUG n.[3]]

Indian rum *see* INDIAN LIQUOR.

Indian side *n.* [1920s+] (US, mainly West.) **1** the right-hand side, esp. of a horse. **2** the wrong way of going about things (cf. SIWASH SIDE). [the Indian practice of mounting a horse from the right, as opposed to Whites who mounted from the left]

Indian time *n.* [1960s+] (US, mainly West.) unpunctuality, a relaxed attitude to time-keeping (cf. AFRICAN PEOPLE'S TIME). [racial stereotyping]

Indian up *v.* [19C+] (US) to sneak up without alerting one's targets. [racial stereotyping]

Indian whisky *see* INDIAN LIQUOR.

India rubber *see* RUBBER n.[2].

India wipe *n.* [late 18C] a handkerchief made of Indian (Asian) cotton.

indicated *adj.* [1910s+] seeming like a good idea, judged necessary, e.g. *a large meal was indicated*.

indie *n.*[1] [1920s+] (orig. US) abbr. for *indie*pendent, used initially of cinemas and production companies and, latterly, of small record companies. [abbr.]

Indie, the *n.*[2] [1980s+] abbr. for the *Independent* newspaper, thus the *Sindie* for the *Independent on Sunday.*

in difficulty *adj.* [19C] drunk. [euph.]

indispensables *n.* [mid-19C] trousers (cf. DON'T-SPEAK-OF-'EMS).

Indo *n.* **1** [1960s–70s] (orig. Aus.) Indonesia. **2** [1980s+] (drugs) marijuana. [abbr. *Indonesia*]

in dock *adj.* [late 18C+] **1** out of work, out of circulation. **2** of an object, undergoing repair. **3** of a person, in hospital. [fig use of SE *dry dock* where ships are laid up for repairs]

Indonesia/Indonesian bud *n.* [1980s+] (US drugs) **1** marijuana (cf. INDO n.). **2** the state of intoxication caused by marijuana, irrespective of origin.

indoor aviator *n.* [1930s–40s] (US) an elevator operator.

indoor golf *n.* [1920s–50s] (US) craps dice (cf. ABYSSINIAN POLO).

indoor money *n.* [1960s+] (Und.) a reserve of cash for use in day-to-day life rather than the proceeds of a robbery.

indoor sledging *n.* [20C] sexual intercourse (cf. INTERIOR DECORATING).

indorse *v.* [18C] to sodomize. [SE *in* + *dorse*, the back]

indorser *n.* [late 18C–19C] a male homosexual. [INDORSE v.]

indorse with a cudgel, to *phr.* [late 18C–19C] to thrash, to beat with a stick. [SE *indorse*, stamping the flesh of one's victim]

in dry dock *phr.* [1920s–30s] **1** of a person, out of work, out of circulation. **2** of an object, undergoing repair. [ext. of IN DOCK]

in duck's guts, to be *phr.* [20C] (W.I.) to be in a hopeless situation, to be in irretrievable difficulties (cf. CRAPAUD SMOKE YOUR PIPE).

indulge *v.* [early 18C+] to eat or drink to excess.

industrial *adj.* [1980s+] (US campus) extremely masculine. [the image of an industrial worker as a 'real man']

industrial debutante *n.* [1980s+] (US) a prostitute who specializes in attending US business conventions.

in dutch *adj.* [early 19C+] (US) in trouble, out of favour. [one who has fig. succumbed to the DUTCH ACT]

ineffable, the *n.*[1] [19C] the vagina (cf. DOWN BELOW). [lit. the 'unspeakable']

ineffable *n.*[2] [mid-19C] **1** anyone who cannot be named or mentioned. **2** a supreme dandy.

ineffables *n.* [mid-19C] trousers (cf. DON'T-SPEAK-OF-'EMS).

in effect mode *phr.* [1990s] (US Black teen) to be in a relaxed, stress-free state of mind.

inexplicables *n.* [mid-19C] trousers (cf. DON'T-SPEAK-OF-'EMS).

inexpressibles/innominables *n.* [late 18C–19C] trousers (cf. DON'T-SPEAK-OF-'EMS; UNMENTIONABLES). [euph.; note 20C Romanian *indispensabili*, underpants]

i-ney! *excl.* [1950s+] (W.I. Rasta) a greeting. [ety. unknown]

infanteer *n.* [1910s+] an infantryman.

infantry *n.* [mid-19C] children. [pun on SE *infant*]

infernal *adj.* [mid-18C?–late 19C] a general term of abuse or condemnation; thus *infernally*, detestably, confoundedly.

in fine fettle *phr.* [19C+] in good spirits, in good physical condition. [Lancashire dial. *fettle*, dress, case, condition]

in fine twig *phr.* [early 19C] splendidly, admirably. [SE *fine* + TWIG n.[1]]

in flagrante *phr.* [early 17C+] caught in the act, in the throes of, usually sexual intercourse. [Lat. *in flagrante delicto*, lit. in flagrant lust]

inflash *v.* [1990s] (US) to inform, to explain. [FLASH v.[4]]

info *n.* [1910s+] *information* (cf. INS). [abbr.]

in for/in for it *adj.* **1** [17C–18C] in trouble, facing punishment (cf. FOR IT). **2** [19C] drunk. **3** [mid-19C+] willing, committed to, eager. **4** [1910s–20s] of a woman, pregnant. [(1) SE post 1800]

in for one's chop *phr.* [1920s+] (Aus./N.Z.) out for oneself, for one's own profit or advantage. [CHOP n.[3]]

in for patter *phr.* [mid-19C] facing trial. [the *patter* is that of the judge, counsel, witnesses etc, dismissed as such by the prisoner]

in for the high jump/for the jumps *phr.* [1920s+] in serious trouble. [? steeplechasing; or of trouble so bad that one will

metaphorically have to 'jump very high' to get over it; but ? image of death by judicial hanging]

in for the plate *phr.* [late 18C–early 19C] suffering from venereal disease. [a rather laboured derivation f. horse-racing jargon. Horses that qualify for the *plate* (the main race) have first won the *heat*; symptoms of VD include inflammation, i.e. *heat*]

in for the rope *phr.* [late 19C–1910s] due to be hanged.

in front *see* UP FRONT adj.

in front *see* UP FRONT adv.

in front *adv.* [1960s+] in advance, beforehand (cf. FRONT v.[3]; UP FRONT adv.).

in full blast *see* AT FULL BLAST.

in full dig *phr.* [mid-19C–1900s] earning one's full pay. [one 'digs' out one's pay]

in full effect *phr.* [1990s] (orig. US Black) present, going on, happening.

in full feather *phr.* [mid-19C+] in top condition, very cheerful, rich. [FULL FEATHER]

in full fig *phr.* [19C+] dressed up. [SE *fig out*, to dress up, but note FEAGUE; FIG v.[4]]

in full jerry *phr.* [late 19C+] knowledgeable, informed. [JERRY adj.]

in full swing *phr.* [mid-19C] totally committed, very successful.

ing-bing *n.* [1920s–40s] (US) a fit, an emotional outburst. [? var. on WING-DING]

ingler *n.* [17C] a horse thief who toured country fairs looking for victims. [? dial. *ingle*, to fondle; thus he 'fondles' the horse to persuade it to go with him. Note SE *ingle*, a catamite]

in goat heaven and kiddie kingdom, to be *phr.* [20C] (W.I./ Bdos.) to be in a state of absolute bliss (cf. IN HOG HEAVEN AND JOHN CROW PARADISE).

ingogo *n.* [1970s+] (S.Afr.) a cheap prostitute. [Zulu *ingogo*, a half-crown or 25 cents]

in good arrow *phr.* [late 19C+] throwing well, fig. feeling well. [ARROW]

in good nick *phr.* [20C] of a person or thing, in good condition. [NICK n.[2]]

in good/proper fettle *phr.* [late 19C–1910s] drunk (cf. IN FINE FETTLE). [Lancashire dial. *fettle*, dress, case, condition]

ingoted/ingotted *adj.* [mid–late 19C] very rich. [SE *ingot*, a brick of gold or silver]

in great/high force *phr.* [mid-19C] displaying oneself as an articulate and entertaining conversationalist or orator.

in great snuff *see* IN HIGH SNUFF.

in great spout *phr.* [late 18C] in high spirits.

in guts gully *phr.* [20C] (W.I.) in serious difficulties (cf. GUTTED adj.[1]).

inhale *v.* **1** [1950s+] to drink. **2** [1980s+] (US campus) to eat very fast.

in half a shake *phr.* [1930s+] immediately.

in harness *adj.* [20C] employed, in work (cf. IN COLLAR). [working horse imagery]

in heat *adj.* [1910s+] (US gambling) on a winning streak. [one is HOT adj.[4]]

in high feather *phr.* [early–mid-19C] rich (cf. IN FULL FEATHER).

in high force *see* IN GREAT FORCE.

in high/great snuff *phr.* [mid-19C–1930s] **1** elated, very happy. **2** healthy, in good shape. [SE *snuff*, a fit of temper, emotion]

in hock *adj.* **1** [mid-19C+] indebted to, owing both money and metaphorical debts. **2** [mid-19C–1910s] in prison. **3** [late 19C+] in pawn. [Du. *hok*, hutch, hovel, prison; but note gambling jargon *in hockelty*, the last card in the box is the *hockelty card*, which is described as *in hock*, and a player who bets on it is at a disadvantage and thus *in hock*, at risk of losing their bets]

in hog heaven and john crow paradise, to be *phr.* [20C] (W.I./Bdos.) to be in a state of absolute bliss (cf. IN GOAT HEAVEN AND KIDDIE KINGDOM).

in hot ashes *phr.* [20C] **1** nervous, excited, apprehensive. **2** in trouble.

in huckster's hands *phr.* [late 18C–19C] in a bad way, in difficulties. [SE *huckster*, a small trader; the sufferer presumably owes money to such a trader]

in hugger-mugger *adv.* [mid-19C] secretly, clandestinely. [SE *hugger-mugger*, concealment, secrecy]

Iniskillen men *n.* [late 17C–18C] a derog. term for the militia. [the original *Iniskillen* regiment distinguished itself in Ireland; the militia was less impressive, 'soon raised, as soon set down' (B.E.)]

in it *adj.* **1** [mid-19C+] conforming to one's ideas and attitudes, worthy of notice, often as *not in it*. **2** [late 19C+] in trouble. **3** [1920s+] (Aus.) agreeing to participate, taking a share.

in it for one's health *phr.* [20C] (orig. US) something that is done for self-gratification only; usu. in neg. sense, as in *I'm not in it …* .

iniversal *adj.* [1960s+] (W.I./UK Black teen) universal. [the substitution by Rastafarians of 'i' for 'you' or the sound 'u']

in jail at Innisfail *phr.* [1960s+] (Aus.) a phr. used to denote an unsatisfactory situation (cf. GIRLS ARE BANDY AT URANDANGIE).

Injun *n.* [early 19C+] (US) a Native American.

ink *n.*[1] **1** [1910s–70s] (Aus./N.Z./US) a cheap red wine. **2** [1920s–40s] strong, bitter coffee. **3** [1950s+] a mention in the newspapers. **4** [1980s+] a tattoo. [colour, although *DNZE* suggests rhy. sl. for (1)]

ink *n.*[2] [1910s–30s] (US) a derog. term for a Black person, esp. with a very dark complexion (cf. INKY-DINKY). [the blackness of SE *ink*]

ink *v.* **1** [1940s+] (orig. US) to sign a contract. **2** [1980s+] (US) to get a tattoo. [INK *n.*[1]]

ink-bottle *n.* [late 19C] a clerk. [note Royal Navy jargon *ink-slinger*, the purser's clerk]

inkbug *n.* [mid-19C] (US) a derog. term for a Black person.

inked *adj.* [late 19C+] (Aus./N.Z.) drunk; thus *inky*, in a state of drunkenness. [SE *ink*, i.e. the dark colour of wine or whisky]

in kinks *adj.* [20C] (Irish) doubled up with hysterical laughter.

ink-jerker *n.* [mid-19C–1910s] (US) a writer, esp. a journalist (cf. INK-SLINGER).

ink-slinger *n.* [mid-19C+] (orig. US) a writer, esp. a journalist; thus *ink-slinging*, the profession of writing or journalism (cf. INK-SPLASHER).

ink-spiller *n.* [late 19C] a clerk.

ink-splasher *n.* [1900s–20s] (US) a writer, esp. a journalist (cf. INK-SLINGER).

inkspot *n.* [1910s–60s] (US) a Black person, usu. derog.

inkwell *n.* [1970s] (US) the vagina (cf. BLACK HOLE *n.*[1]).

inky/inky-poo *adj.* [1900s–60s] (Aus.) drunk. [INKED]

inky blue *n.* [1970s+] influenza. [rhy. sl. *inky blue* = flu]

inky-dinky *n.* [1900s–40s] (US Black) a particularly dark-skinned person. [note the popular fictional schoolboy Billy Bunter's Indian rajah friend, nicknamed *Inky*]

inky-poo *see* INKY.

inky smudge *n.* [late 19C–1930s] a judge. [rhy. sl.]

inlaid/well-inlaid/inlayed/well-inlayed *adj.* [late 17C–early 19C] rich, well-off. [SE *inlaid*, ornamented, usu. with precious metals]

in lavender *adj.* [mid-19C] hidden from the police. [LAY UP IN LAVENDER]

in like Flynn *phr.* [1950s+] (orig. US) a dead certainty, esp. in

areas of sexual conquest. [the alleged sexual prowess of the actor Errol *Flynn* (1909–59)]

in low tide, to be *phr.* [late 17C–19C] to be in financial difficulties. [the image of one's vessel being stranded by low tide]

in lug *adj.* [mid-19C] in pawn. [LUG CHOVEY]

in lumber *adj.* **1** [early 19C+] (mainly Aus.) jailed, in prison. **2** [1930s–60s] in trouble, often extended to *in dead lumber*. [fig. uses of LUMBER *n.*[1]]

in lust *adj.* [1960s+] (US) sexually attracted to another's body, rather than in love.

in more strife than a pork chop at a synagogue/than a pregnant nun *phr.* [1950s+] (Aus.) in very great difficulties, in a most embarrassing situation.

in more trouble than Brown *phr.* [20C] (W.I.) in a good deal of trouble or embarrassment, to be seriously embarrassed. [? a lost anecdote]

in Morocco *adj.* [mid-19C] stripped, naked. [coined as supposed 'gypsy slang' by H.W. Longfellow (1807–82); ? a pun on *buff*, which can refer, like *morocco*, to leather and can also mean naked in the phr. *in the buff*]

in mothballs *phr.* [1940s+] (orig. US milit.) laid up, put out of use or action for a long time (cf. OUT OF MOTHBALLS).

in mourning *adj.* **1** [late 19C+] (society) having dirty fingernails, edging the hands like the black border of mourning paper; thus [20C] *you're in mourning for the cat*, you have dirty fingernails. **2** [mid-19C+] having a black eye; thus *have one's eyes in mourning*, to have a pair of black eyes (cf. FULL SUIT OF MOURNING; HALF-MOURNING). [the wearing of black as a sign of *mourning*]

in my other hose *phr.* [late 16C–early 17C] a phr. used to express one's disbelief or refusal (cf. NOT IN THESE TROUSERS).

in my stars! *excl.* [17C] a mild oath (cf. MY STARS!).

inna *adj.* [20C] (W.I./UK Black teen) inside, in the, in.

innards *n.* [1930s+] the innermost workings, the essence, the mechanism of an engine or other mechanical device. [SE *inwards*]

inner man *n.* [mid-19C] the stomach, one's appetite (for food).

innie *n.* [1970s+] (US) an indented navel (cf. OUTIE *n.*[2]).

in nigger heaven *phr.* [1900s] (US) enjoying oneself. [stereotyping of 'happy darkies']

innocent *n.*[1] [20C] a prisoner. [since the prisoner is locked up they cannot be accused of any subsequent crimes until release]

innocent *n.*[2] [1960s] (US Black) ironic ref. to White liberals wishing to become involved in the Black struggle. [the usual liberal disavowals of racism, prejudice, the responsibility for slavery etc]

innocent of *adv.* [early 18C+] devoid of, completely without.

in no hurry, to be *phr.* [mid-19C+] to take one's time, esp. in ironic use, e.g. *well, she was in a real hurry to help out, wasn't she*.

innominables *see* INEXPRESSIBLES.

in on *adj.* [1910s+] involved with, esp. a plan or scheme, legal or otherwise.

in on a good thing, to be *phr.* [1970s+] to be placed advantageously as regards a plan or business deal. [GOOD THING *n.* (2)]

in once *phr.* [late 19C–1900s] at the first attempt.

in one's *phr.* [mid-19C–1940s] (US) part of one's circumstances, e.g. *none of that in mine*, no thank you. [phr. *in one's life*]

in one's ackee/salt *phr.* [1940s+] (W.I.) energetic, cheerful (cf. FULL OF BEANS). [these positive emotions arise from being well-fed on *ackee*, a popular W.I. fruit of the *Blighia sapida* tree, usu. accompanied by saltfish]

in one's ale/ales *phr.* [late 16C–early 17C] drunk (cf. IN ONE'S CUPS).

in one's altitudes *phr.* [17C–late 18C] drunk (cf. ELEVATED).

in one's armour *phr.*[1] [17C–early 19C] drunk, 'pot-valiant' (cf. DUTCH COURAGE).

in one's armour *phr.*[2] [late 18C] using a condom; thus phr. to *fight in armour*, to have intercourse using a condom.

in one's beer *phr.* [late 17C–18C] drunk.

in one's birthday suit *phr.* [late 18C+] euph. for naked. [one is born naked]

in one's book *phr.* [1950s+] in one's opinion, to one's way of thinking.

in one's brown *phr.* [1980s+] (Irish) a phr. of dismissal, contempt, general negation, e.g. *'I mean it, I really do', 'Bollocks!, you do in your brown!'* (cf. UP ONE'S ARSE). [BROWN n.[3] (2)]

in one's corner *phr.* [1940s+] (orig. US) on one's side. [boxing imagery]

in one's cups *phr.* [early 18C+] drunk.

in one's gears *phr.* [late 17C–early 18C] 1 dressed, ready. 2 ready to get to work. [SE *gear*, apparel or dress]

in one's glory *phr.* [late 19C] extremely happy and satisfied.

in one's/the nip *phr.* [20C] (Irish) stark naked. [? NIPPY adj.; i.e. one suffers from the cold]

in one's pots *phr.* [early 17C] drunk. [SE *pot*, a tankard]

in one's royal *phr.* [20C] (W.I.) very drunk. [? Carib.E *royal/rial*, arrogant, high and mighty]

in one's salt *see* IN ONE'S ACKEE.

in one's skin *phr.* [early 18C] a non-committal answer when asked where someone is.

in one's socks *phr.* [early 19C+] a phr. used to refer to one's height, e.g. *six foot two in his socks*.

in one's Sunday best, to be *phr.* [late 19C] to have an erection. [pun on the SE *starched*, i.e. stiffened clothing/penis]

in on one's fourth, to be *phr.* [late 19C–1900s] to be very drunk. [? one's fourth glass]

in on the act, to be *phr.* [1940s+] to be involved, often used in the phr. *get in on the act*, to become involved, to interfere.

in/into orbit *phr.* (orig. US) 1 [1960s+] in a state of high excitement, whether of delight or of anger. 2 [1960s+] doing very well. 3 [1970s+] a state of intoxication from drugs or alcohol. [one is extremely HIGH adj.[1] + ref. to the Sputnik of 1957 and subseq. circumnavigations of the earth]

in outer space *see* FROM OUTER SPACE.

in over one's head *phr.* [1940s+] over involved.

in Paris *adj.* [late 19C] (society) eloped. [Paris was a popular destination for such romantic flights]

in pickle *adj.* [late 17C–18C] venereally diseased (cf. MOTHER CORNELIUS' TUB; POWDERING TUB). [the contemporary cure for VD, which involved sitting in a 'sweating tub']

in pig *adj.* [1940s+] pregnant. [joc. use of SE, which refers only to swine]

in plant *adj.* [mid-19C] (Aus.) hidden away. [PLANT v.[1]]

in proper fettle *see* IN GOOD FETTLE.

in pull *adj.* [early–mid-19C] under arrest. [PULL v.[1] (2)]

in queer *adj.* [late 19C+] in trouble with the authorities. [abbr. IN QUEER STREET]

in Queer Street *phr.* [early 19C+] in trouble, esp. financial (cf. IN SHIT STREET). [*Queer Street* begins as a fig. 'place' where the only 'dwellers' are problems and difficulties; the financial aspect, now dominant, was added in mid-19C]

in quick sticks *phr.* [mid-19C+] hurriedly, quickly; thus imper. [20C] (Aus.) *quick sticks!*, hurry up!

in rag order *phr.* [1980s+] (Irish) in dire straits, in a mess. [SE *ragged*]

ins *n.* [1960s] (US) *informations* (cf. INFO). [abbr.]

insane *adj.*[1] [mid-19C+] idiotic, utterly senseless, irrational, obsessive, e.g. *insane lust for ...* .

insane *adj.*[2] [1940s+] (orig. US Black) wonderful, admirable, excellent (cf. MENTAL adj.). [on bad = good model]

in schtook *see* IN SHTUCK.

insects/insects and ants *n.* [20C] 1 trousers. 2 knickers, i.e. underwear. [rhy. sl. *insects and ants* = pants]

in shit/cack street *phr.* [1920s+] (orig. US) in difficulties, facing problems (cf. IN ARSEHOLE STREET; IN QUEER STREET; UP SHIT CREEK WITHOUT A PADDLE). [SHIT n.[4] (2)/fig. use of CACK n.[1] (1)]

in shtuck/shtook/stook/schtook *adj.* [20C] in trouble. [Yid. *shtook*, difficulties]

inside/insides *n.*[1] [mid-18C+] the stomach, the intestines.

inside *n.*[2] [late 18C–late 19C] one who rides inside a passenger coach or similar vehicle.

Inside, the *n.*[3] [late 19C+] (Aus.) central Australia; thus *insider*, one who lives there.

inside *n.*[4] [1920s+] (US) information, esp. when privileged.

inside *adj.* [late 19C+] in prison.

inside and outside! *excl.* [early–mid-19C] a popular toast (cf. TIGHT CUNTS AND EASY BOOTS!). [abbr. *inside of a cunt and outside of a jail!*]

inside job *n.* [20C] a crime that has been committed with the aid or cognizance of an employee of the company or servant of the house in question.

inside lining *n.* [mid-19C–1930s] a meal or the eating of any foodstuff.

inside man *n.* [1930s+] (Und.) 1 a tipster who locates prospects for robbers or safe-blowers. 2 anyone involved in a crime, usu. a large-scale robbery of a firm or private house, who is employed on site and helps the robbers with information etc. 3 in a three-card monte team, an accomplice who poses as a normal bettor but acts only to encourage the real victims of the game.

inside of *phr.* [mid-19C+] within a period of time, during, e.g. *inside of a week*, before a week has passed (cf. IN THE INSIDE OF).

insider *n.* [mid-19C+] a pocket or wallet. [it is *inside* one's pocket]

insiders *n.* [1940s–40s] (US Black) pockets.

insides *see* INSIDE n.[1].

inside stand *n.* [1930s+] (Und.) anyone involved in a crime (cf. INSIDE MAN).

in smoke *phr.* [1920s+] (Aus.) in hiding. [the obscurity cast by a pall of smoke]

in someone's ass *phr.* [1960s] (US) nagging (cf. IN SOMEONE'S SKIN phr.; ON SOMEONE'S DICK). [ARSE n.[1]]

in someone's blood *phr.* [20C] (W.I.) in hot pursuit.

in someone's crack *phr.* [1980s+] (US campus) inquisitive, over involved. [CRACK n.[1] (5)]

in someone's face *phr.* [1950s+] (orig. US Black) aggressive, confrontational, e.g. *in your face music, in your face fashion*; thus *get in one's face*, to confront, to provoke (cf. ATTITUDE; FACE v.). [basketball use, when a defensive player crowds his opposite number. The term, while ostensibly unappealing, is considered positive by its primary users, the young]

in someone's skin *phr.* [20C] (W.I.) harassing, nagging (cf. IN SOMEONE'S ASS).

in spades *adj.* [1920s+] (orig. US) to the greatest extent, very much, extremely, any form of intensifier; thus *you can say that in spades*, you couldn't be more right. [in cards *spades* are the highest suit]

inspector *n.* [1930s–40s] (US) an itinerant worker. [he moves from job to job, 'to see what they are like']

inspector of city buildings *n.* [1920s+] (Aus.) one who is unemployed and not especially keen on finding work (cf. INSPECTOR OF PUBLIC BUILDINGS). [for ety. *see* INSPECTOR]

inspector of manholes *n.* [1930s+] a male homosexual. [pun on SE *manhole/man hole*, i.e. the male anus]

inspector of pavements/the pavement *n.* [late 18C–mid-19C] one who stands in the pillory (cf. SUPERINTENDENT OF THE

PAVEMENT; SURVEYOR OF THE HIGHWAYS). [the posture one has to adopt]

inspector of public buildings n. [late 19C–1910s] an unemployed person (cf. INSPECTOR OF CITY BUILDINGS). [for ety. see INSPECTOR]

inspector of the pavement see INSPECTOR OF PAVEMENTS.

inspect the equipment see EXAMINE THE EQUIPMENT.

inspired adj. [late 19C+] drunk (cf. ABOUT RIGHT adj.[1]). [euph.]

instant boot camp n. [20C] (US campus) the act of vomiting. [BOOT v.[7] + pun on milit. boot camp, a notably vile environment]

instant zen n. [1960s+] (drugs) LSD (cf. A n.[3]). [the contemplative world of Zen Buddhism]

in stook see IN SHTUCK.

instrument n. [late 16C–17C] the penis (cf. ARSE-OPENER; GAYING INSTRUMENT).

in Swell Street see LIVE IN SWELL STREET.

in synch adj. [1970s+] fig. in tune with (cf. OUT OF SYNCH). [SE phr. in synchronization, of sound, usu. in films]

intelligence department n. [1910s–20s] the head.

intended n. [mid-18C+] one's future husband or wife.

intense adj. [1980s+] (US campus) **1** very good, excellent. **2** very difficult.

intense! excl. [1980s+] (US campus) a general excl. of approval. [INTENSE adj.]

intentions n. [late 18C–late 19C] one's purposes in respect of a proposal of marriage.

intercoursed adj. [1970s] exhausted, utterly tired. [euph. for FUCKED adj. (2)]

interesting condition/situation n. [early 19C+] euph. for pregnancy, usu. in the phr. she is in an … .

interior/interiors n. [mid-19C+] the internal parts of the body, esp. the digestive system.

interior decorating n. [1980s+] (society) sexual intercourse during the day.

interiors see INTERIOR.

international milk thief n. [1970s+] (police) ironic term for any petty villain.

international nigger n. [1950s–60s] (US Black) a person who dresses in expensive, imported clothes. [NIGGER n.]

interplanetary mission n. [1990s] (drugs) of a user, making the rounds of CRACK HOUSES in the hope of getting some drugs. [the 'mission' is to get HIGH adj.[1]]

in the altogether phr. [late 19C+] naked. [abbr. SE altogether naked/nude]

in the arms of Morpheus phr. [19C+] asleep (cf. IN THE ARMS OF MURPHY). [Morpheus, the Roman god of dreams]

in the arms of murphy phr. [mid-19C] asleep (cf. IN THE ARMS OF MORPHEUS). [a pun on the classically based arms of Morpheus, the Greek god of sleep or dreams]

in the bag phr.[1] [1920s+] (orig. US) **1** secured, made certain. **2** of a sporting contest, the outcome has been made certain by the giving of bribes, doping of one or more contestants, horses etc.

in the bag phr.[2] (orig. US) **1** [1920s+] in debt. **2** [1960s] in trouble, facing difficulties. [? BAG v.[7]]

in the bag/wrapper phr.[3] [1940s] (orig. US) drunk; thus half in the bag, beginning to become drunk (cf. HAVE A BAG ON). [BAG n.[8]/SE wrapper]

in the barrel phr. [1930s–40s] (US) **1** in debt, bankrupt. **2** dismissed or likely to be dismissed from one's job (cf. OUT IN THE WATER).

in the black phr. [20C] in credit, financially secure (cf. IN THE RED). [the pre-computer-era practice of writing up credit accounts in black ink and debits in red ink]

in the blowing of a match phr. [late 19C] immediately.

in the blue phr.[1] [1920s–30s] far away, off in the distance. [SE the wild blue yonder]

in the blue phr.[2] [1920s+] (Aus.) **1** in debt, in difficulties. **2** out of control. [BLUES n.[1]]

in the blue phr.[3] [1940s] working as a policeman. [the uniform]

in the blues phr. [19C] suffering from delirium tremens (cf. IN THE HORRORS). [BLUE DEVILS n.[1] (2)]

in the bol phr. [1980s] naked. [abbr. BOLLOCKY NAKED]

in the book phr. [1950s+] recorded, in existence. [the Book of Life]

in the box seat phr. (Aus.) [20C] in full control, in a position of dominance, power (cf. IN THE DRIVING SEAT). [SE box seat, the driving seat in a horse-pulled coach]

in the breeze see ON THE BREEZE.

in the briers phr. [16C–18C] in trouble, in difficulties (cf. IN THE CACTUS). [SE brier, a thorny, prickly bush, thus implying difficulty]

in the buff phr. [mid-17C+] naked. [the colour of 'white' flesh]

in the cactus phr. [1920s+] (Aus./N.Z.) in difficulty (cf. IN THE BRIERS).

in the can phr. [1920s+] (US) finished, successfully completed. [a completed film is placed in film cans ready for distribution to the cinemas]

in the car phr. [20C] (US Und.) on good terms (cf. OUT OF THE CAR). [CAR]

in the cart phr. [late 19C+] **1** in trouble, in difficulties; thus put in the cart, to trick, to deceive. **2** aware, in the know.

in the catching up of a garter phr. [late 17C] very quickly, in an instant.

in the cellar phr. [20C] **1** in sports, at the bottom of a league or similar points table. **2** miserable, feeling low, 'down in the dumps' [note P.G. Wodehouse (1881–1975) coinage 'down among the wines and spirits']

in the chair phr. [1960s+] buying a round of drinks. [SE in the chair, acting as chairperson of a meeting]

in the chips phr. [1930s+] (orig. US) financially secure, well-off. [CHIPS n.[2]]

in the clart phr. [1970s] in trouble, lit. 'in the shit'. [dial. clart, viscous sticky mud or filth]

in the clear phr. (orig. US) **1** [20C] free from suspicion, out of reach of punishment or prosecution. **2** [1920s+] in profit.

in the closet phr. [1950s+] (orig. US) **1** used of a gay man/woman who has yet to reveal their sexuality in public. **2** hidden away.

in the clouds phr. [mid-17C–mid-19C] obscure, mystical, fanciful, unreal.

in the club phr. [20C] pregnant. [the club in question is the PUDDING CLUB]

in the cold phr. [1910s+] (Aus.) in prison (cf. ICEBOX).

in the cooler phr. [late 19C–1900s] (US) in reserve (cf. ON ICE phr.[1]).

in the crapper phr. [1940s] (US) finished, failed, rejected, abandoned, rendered useless (cf. IN THE DUMPER). [fig. use of CRAPPER n.[3]]

in the crown office phr. [late 17C–early 18C] tipsy. [play on SE crown (of the head), which suffers]

in the dark phr. [late 19C] (US) black coffee. [the colour of the coffee]

in the days of Queen Dick/reign of Queen Dick phr. [late 18C+] never (cf. QUEER AS DICK'S HATBAND). [Dick, i.e. Richard, being a man there could not be a Queen Dick]

in the death phr. [1950s–60s] in the end.

in the ditch phr. [1980s+] (US) extremely drunk. [the image of a drunk driver steering off the road and into a ditch]

in the dogbox phr. [1950s+] (N.Z.) out of favour, in disgrace. [for ety. see IN THE DOGHOUSE]

in the doghouse *phr.* [1930s+] (orig. US) in trouble, out of favour. [SAmE *doghouse*, a dog kennel; i.e. in disgrace and so consigned to the dog's kennel rather than one's own home]

in the driving seat *phr.* [20C] in control, running things, on top of a situation (cf. IN THE BOX SEAT). [the controlling position in a vehicle]

in the dumper *phr.* [1980s+] **1** out of favour, rejected, thrown away. **2** lost, ruined, good for nothing (cf. IN THE CRAPPER). [fig. use of DUMPER *n.*[1]]

in the dwang *phr.* [1990s] (S.Afr.) in trouble, in difficulties, constrained. [Afk. *dwing*, to force; but note dial. Scot. *dwang*, to struggle, to oppress]

in the familiar way *phr.* [late 19C] pregnant. [play on IN THE FAMILY WAY]

in the family way *phr.* [18C+] pregnant.

in the firing line *phr.* [1910s+] open to problems, likely to face difficulties (cf. IN THE GUN *phr.*[2]).

in the first flight *phr.* [mid–late 19C] at the front, in the lead.

in/up the flue *phr.* **1** [mid-19C–1900s] in pawn. **2** [mid-19C–1900s] physically or mentally run down. **3** [mid-19C–1900s] dead. **4** [1930s] pregnant. [the FLUE *n.*[2] or SE *spout* (cf. UP THE SPOUT), a lift used in pawnbrokers' shops, up which the articles pawned were taken for storage; (2), (3) and (4) are fig. use of (1)]

in the frame *phr.* (Und./police) under suspicion, usu. with some grounds, of having committed a crime. [racetrack use, the *frame* holds the numbers of the winning horses in a race + FRAME-UP]

in the full of one's shirt *phr.* [20C] (Irish) in good form.

in the glue *phr.* [1960s+] (US) in trouble, in difficulties.

in the grand secret *phr.* [18C–19C] dead.

in the grease *phr.* [1920s–60s] (US) in serious trouble.

in the gun *phr.*[1] [late 17C–early 19C] drunk, tipsy. [GUN *n.*[1]]

in the gun *phr.*[2] **1** [1910s–20s] (Aus.) facing dismissal from one's job. **2** [1920s+] (Aus.) unpopular, of ill repute, in trouble, likely to attract criticism or punishment (cf. IN THE FIRING LINE). [one is 'under fire']

in the hard/hard card *phr.* [early 19C–1920s] cash down, no credit.

in the hell *phr.* [mid-19C+] (orig. US) used to intensify a variety of prepositions, such as what, why, where, how, who, when; e.g. *what the hell?*

in the hole *phr.* [20C] in debt, owing, usu. connected with gambling.

in the horn *phr.* [late 19C] a general term, implying disbelief (cf. IN A PIG'S ASS; LIKE HELL). [ety. unknown]

in the horrors *phr.* [19C] suffering from delirium tremens. [HORRORS *n.* (3)]

in the hospital *phr.* [1900s–20s] (US) in prison. [euph.]

in the hot seat *phr.* [1930s+] to be in a difficult, poss. embarrassing, certainly demanding position. [HOT *adj.*[2] + ref. to HOT SEAT *n.* (2)]

in the house *phr.*[1] [1980s+] lit., present and fig., aware, 'on the ball' etc.

in the house *phr.*[2] [1980s+] (orig. US Black/teen) excellent. [ext. of IN THE HOUSE *phr.*[1]]

in the house-roof *see* AT THE HOUSE-ROOF.

in the housetop *see* AT THE HOUSETOP.

in the inside of *phr.* [late 19C+] within or before time (cf. INSIDE OF).

in the jigs *phr.* [1970s+] very drunk. [JIGGERED *adj.*[2] (3)]

in the know *phr.* [late 19C+] privy to secret, privileged information.

in the lime *phr.* [1940s] (Aus.) conspicuous, popular, heavily advertised. [SE *limelight*]

in the long grass *phr.* [20C] lying low, esp. of someone one hasn't seen for some time; thus *wait for someone in the long grass*, to lie low, to maintain a 'low profile'.

in the lurch *n.* [20C] (Aus.) a church (cf. LEAN AND LURCH; LEFT IN THE LURCH; ROCK AND LURCH). [rhy. sl.]

in the middle *phr.* [1930s+] (orig. US) in trouble, in a dangerous or difficult situation.

in the middle of nowhere *phr.* [1950s+] in a remote or inaccessible place.

in the mix *phr.* [1990s] (US Black) involved, esp. in gang activities. [record industry jargon]

in the money *phr.* [20C] rich, successful in a wager. [*run in the money*, a racing term for those horses that finish 1–2–3, thus paying out to those who bet on them]

in the mood *n.* [20C] food. [rhy. sl.]

in the nick *phr.*[1] [late 17C–18C] fashionable, in the height of fashion. [SE *nick*, the mark, the exact point aimed at]

in the nick *phr.*[2] [1940s+] (N.Z.) naked, esp. in the context of swimming. [? SE *naked*]

in the nip *see* IN ONE'S NIP.

in the nooer *phr.* [1970s] (Aus.) in difficulties (cf. UP SHIT CREEK WITHOUT A PADDLE). [SE *manure*]

in the nuddy *phr.* [1950s+] (orig. Aus.) naked, in the nude.

in the nude *n.* [1970s] food. [rhy. sl.]

in the ozone *phr.* [1970s+] (US) dazed or intoxicated by drugs or drink.

in the park *see* AT BUSHEY PARK.

in the peek *phr.* [1940s–50s] (prison) in an observation cell, into which prisoners are placed if, for instance, they have smashed up their cells or shown other signs of instability.

in the picture *phr.* [1940s+] aware of what is happening; often as *put in the picture*, to inform.

in the pink *phr.* [mid-18C+] extremely fit, well and cheerful. [abbr. *in the pink of condition*; ult. SE *pink*, the finest example of excellence, extending the colloq. 'flower of excellence/perfection', itself based on SE *pink*, the *Dianthus plumarius*, a popular garden flower]

in the pipeline *phr.* [1960s+] about to happen, in process (cf. IN THE WORKS).

in the pits *phr.* [20C] depressed, miserable (cf. DOWN IN THE DUMPS).

in the poo/pooh *phr.* [1960s+] (Aus.) in difficulties (cf. UP SHIT CREEK WITHOUT A PADDLE). [POO *n.*[1]]

in the pudding club *phr.* [1930s+] pregnant; thus *put in the pudding club*, to make pregnant; *join the pudding club*, to become pregnant. [PUDDING CLUB]

in the race *phr.* [1940s–50s] (Aus.) having an opportunity of doing well; thus *not in the race*, hopeless, without a chance.

in the rats *phr.* [19C+] insane, mad, esp. when suffering delirium tremens from an excess of alcohol (cf. RATHOUSE; RATS IN THE ATTIC). [RATS]

in the raw *phr.* [1930s+] (orig. US) naked.

in the raz *phr.* [1940s+] (Aus.) naked. [var. on IN THE RAW]

in there *adj.* **1** [1930s–60s] (orig. US Black) involved, aware, informed; doing well prospering. **2** [1950s+] sexually successful, thus *phr. you're in there*, you'll find no problems with seduction (cf. IN THERE!). **3** [1950s+] (US campus) pleased and excited. **4** [1950s+] (US Black) looking attractive.

in there! *excl.* [1950s+] a cry of encouragement from one male to another, when he sees the latter making advances to a woman or girl, esp. as *get in there!* [IN THERE *adj.* (2)]

in the red *phr.* [1920s+] **1** in debt. **2** 'in the money' (cf. IN THE BLACK). [the inking of old accounts, *red* for profit, *black* for loss]

in the reign of Queen Dick *see* IN THE DAYS OF QUEEN DICK.

in the right ball-park *phr.* [1950s+] (orig. US) approximately accurate (cf. BALL-PARK FIGURE). [SE *ball-park*, a baseball stadium]

in the rude *phr.* [1950s+] naked. [a genteel euph.]

in the saddle *phr.* **1** [20C] having sexual intercourse. **2** [1990s] in charge, in control.

in the shit *phr.* [mid-19C+] in serious trouble, extended as *in deep shit*. [SHIT n.⁴ (2)]

in the skins *phr.* [1990s] (US Black) having sexual intercourse. [HIT SKINS]

in the soup *phr.* [late 19C+] (orig. US) in trouble, in difficulties.

in the spoon *phr.* [20C] (drugs) using drugs (cf. OUT OF THE SPOON). [SPOON n.²]

in the spud line *phr.* [1930s+] pregnant.

in the straight *phr.* [20C] out of one's difficulties, e.g. after financial struggles. [*straight and narrow* rather than *the straight* in horse-racing]

in the straw *phr.* [mid-19C+] in labour, giving birth. [18C SE *straw* as the stuffing of a bed, but note the defunct practice of laying straw in the street outside the house of a woman in labour in order to quieten the passing traffic; 20C use mainly Aus.]

in the street *phr.* [1960s–70s] (US Black) openly, publicly.

in the stretch *phr.* [20C] almost complete. [horse-racing term *the stretch*, the last part of the course]

in the suds *phr.* [late 18C–late 19C] in trouble, in a disagreeable situation. [SE *suds*, filth, muck]

in the swim *phr.* **1** [mid-19C] keeping out of the hands of the police. **2** [mid–late 19C] moving in smart, fashionable circles. [(2) SE f. 1900]

in the tank *phr.* [20C] drunk. [SE *tank*, a swimming pool; one is 'sodden' with liquor]

in the tin *phr.* [1940s+] (Aus.) in trouble, in a tight spot. [fig. use of SE *tin can*]

in the toot *phr.* [1960s+] in trouble, facing problems. [fig. use of TOOT n.² (1)]

in the true Mesopotamia ring *phr.* [late 19C–1900s] a phr. indicating that something is 'pleasing, high-sounding and incomprehensible' (E.P.). ['The allusion is to the story of an old woman who told her pastor that she "found great support in that comfortable word "Mesopotamia"' (Brewer 1894)]

in the twinkling of a bedpost/a bed-staff *phr.* [mid-19C] very quickly, in a moment (cf. IN A TWINK).

in the wars *phr.* [mid-19C+] in trouble, having problems, suffering physical attacks; thus *have been in the wars*, to have suffered an accident or been physically assaulted.

in the wind *phr.* [20C] (US prison) free.

in the works *phr.* [1940s+] about to happen, in process (cf. IN THE PIPELINE).

in the worst way *phr.* [1910s+] (US) very much indeed.

in the wrapper *see* IN THE BAG *phr.*³.

in the wrong box *phr.* [mid-16C+] out of one's element, incorrect. [? a mix-up among apothecary's boxes]

intimate *n.* [19C] a shirt. [the shirt's proximity to one's body]

in Tip Street *phr.* [late 19C] well-off, generous. [SE *tip*, a gratuity]

into *adj.*¹ [mid-19C+] fighting (cf. GET INTO v.³; GET STUCK INTO).

into *adj.*² [late 19C+] owing money to.

into *adj.*³ [1960s+] aware of, interested in, involved with, attracted to; thus *be into*. [abbr. *deeply into* or similar; a hippie phrase that emerged during the late 1960s and thence proceeded to general speech as well as use in a variety of New Age therapies]

into/right up one's barrow *phr.* [20C] (Aus.) absolutely one's business, very much one's concern.

into orbit *see* IN ORBIT.

in town *adj.* [early 19C] well-off, having plenty of money.

intro *n.* [1920s+] an *intro*duction, whether to a person or to a piece of writing, music etc. [abbr.]

introduce Charley/Charlie, to *phr.* [20C] of a man, to have sexual intercourse. [CHARLEY n.³]

introduce her to Fagan/Fagin, to *phr.* [1950s] of a man, to have sexual intercourse (cf. BURY OLD FAGIN). [FAGAN]

introduce the shoemaker to the tailor, to *phr.* [late 19C] to kick someone on the seat of their trousers.

in trouble *adj.*¹ [late 19C+] of a woman, pregnant and unmarried. [euph.]

in trouble *adj.*² [late 19C] serving a sentence in prison. [euph.]

in tucks *adj.* [20C] reduced to helpless laughter (cf. CREASED).

in two ticks *phr.* [20C] very quickly, virtually immediately (cf. TICK n.³). [SE *tick*, the movement of a clock, i.e. seconds]

in two twos *phr.* [mid-19C+] at once, very quickly. [20C use Aus.]

in two-ups *adv.* [1930s+] (Aus.) very quickly. [the game of *two-up*, based on tossing coins]

invasion *n.* [1980s+] (US campus) in comb. with a relevant noun, denoting a quantity, a large number, e.g. *hunk invasion*, a lot of handsome boys.

invertebrated *adj.* [1980s+] (US campus) drunk (cf. LEGLESS). [SE *invertebrate*, without a backbone, i.e. one has collapsed]

invigorator *n.* [mid-19C+] a drink (cf. ALLEVIATOR).

invite *n.* [early 19C+] an *invit*ation. [abbr.]

in with *adj.* **1** [late 17C–19C] intimate with. **2** [mid-19C–1900s] suspicious of a person, getting even with. **3** [mid-19C+] fashionable, socially aware. **4** [late 19C] in comparison with, compared with. [(1) SE post-1800]

in wrong *adj.* (US) **1** [1900s–50s] in trouble, unpopular. **2** [1910s–20s] wrong, erroneous.

in your arse! *excl.* [20C] (W.I.) a phr. used to add emphasis to what has been said, synon. with 'by God', 'for God's sake'. [ARSE n.¹]

in your dipper! *excl.* [1920s–30s] (N.Z.) a general excl. of rejection, dismissal (cf. UP YOURS!).

in your dreams! *excl.* [1980s+] (orig. US) a dismissive excl. (cf. DREAM ON!)

in your eye! *excl.* [late 19C+] (US) an excl. of general derision, dismissal, contempt. [sl. *in a pig's eye!* (*see* IN A PIG'S ASS)]

in your grannie's/granny's *phr.* [20C] (Irish) a state of absolute comfort, both physical and psychological.

I promise you *phr.* [late 15C+] I am confident, I am sure, believe me.

ipsal dixal *n.* [mid-19C–1900s] an unsupported statement. [Lat. *ipse dixit*, an unproved statement, a dictum, lit. 'he himself said it']

ipse *n.* [early 18C] a variety of ale. [Lat. *ipse*, itself; thus 'the very thing'. Note the Umbrian wine *Est! Est! Est!*, lit. 'It is, it is, it is!', i.e. it is the best/the thing]

ipsydinxy *n.* [mid-19C] (US) whisky. [? echoic of the slurred tones of a drinker]

I.Q. *n.* [1960s] (US) a signature. [play on I.D. v.]

ira *n.* [1970s] (gay) hair. [EP suggests 'centre slang', but ? missp. of RIAH]

I refer you to Smith *phr.* [late 19C] a phr. that implies the other speaker is lying or at least exaggerating. [a character named Smith, a congenital liar, in the play *The Prodigal Father* (1897)]

irey/irie *adj.* [1950s+] (W.I. Rasta) pleasing, powerful, euphoric; orig. in the context of the sensations that followed smoking cannabis. [HIGH adj.¹]

Irish *n.* [mid-19C+] (orig. US) temper (cf. AFRICA).

Irish *adj.* [18C+] a general negative racial epithet (cf. CHINESE adj.; FRENCH adj.; JEW adj.; MEXICAN adj.). [the stereotypical Irishman or woman is stupid, short-tempered, violent (whether on the street or in the home), addicted to potatoes, keen on brawling and usually employed in a menial, labouring task, often rural; all these traits are reflected in the combs.

that follow, and all combs. with *Irish* should be assumed to be derog. (if seen as joc. by the coiner/speaker) unless otherwise stated]

Irish ambulance *n.* [1910s–30s] (US) a wheelbarrow (cf. IRISH BABY BUGGY; IRISH BUGGY; IRISH CHARIOT; IRISH LOCAL).

Irish apple *n.* [late 18C+] a potato (cf. IRISH APRICOT; IRISH FOOTBALL; IRISH GRAPE; IRISH LEMON; IRISH ROOT; MUNSTER PLUMS). [stereotype of the potato as an Irish staple]

Irish applesauce *n.* [1960s] (US) mashed potatoes.

Irish apricot *n.* [late 18C–19C] a potato (cf. IRISH APPLE).

Irish arms *n.* [20C] thick legs. [racial stereotyping]

Irish assurance *n.* [late 18C–19C] boldness, shamelessness. [like the Greek myth, which proclaims that being dipped in the River Styx gives a child invulnerability, 'so it is said, that a dipping in the River Shannon totally annihilates bashfulness' (Grose 1785)]

Irish baby buggy *n.* [1910s+] (US) a wheelbarrow (cf. IRISH AMBULANCE).

Irish banjo/spoon *n.* [20C] a spade, a shovel.

Irish beauty *n.* [20C] a woman with a pair of black eyes.

Irish bouquet *n.* [1960s–70s] (US) any form of projectile, usu. a stone or brick (cf. IRISH ROSE n.²).

Irish buggy/pluggy *n.* [20C] (US) a wheelbarrow (cf. IRISH AMBULANCE).

Irish by birth but Greek by injection *n.* [1960s+] a male homosexual (cf. GREEK adj.²).

Irish cabbage *n.* [1960s] (US) the traditional St Patrick's Day meal of corned (salt) beef, cabbage and Irish potatoes (cf. IRISH TURKEY).

Irish caviar *n.* [1930s] (US) Irish stew.

Irish channel *n.* [1900s] the throat. [down which alcohol flows]

Irish chariot *n.* [1900s–40s] (US) a wheelbarrow (cf. IRISH AMBULANCE).

Irish cherry *n.* [1930s] (US) a carrot.

Irish chicken *n.* [1920s–30s] (US) pork (cf. ADIRONDACK STEAK).

Irish clubhouse *n.* (US) **1** [1900s] a police station. **2** [1960s] (gay) a refined house of prostitution.

Irish cocktail *n.* [1980s] (US) a drink containing a substance that causes unconsciousness. [play on MICKEY FINN]

Irish comics/funnies *n.* [20C] the obituary columns in a newspaper. [supposed Irish illiteracy]

Irish compliment *n.* [mid-19C+] a back-handed compliment (cf. JEW'S COMPLIMENT).

Irish confetti *n.* **1** [mid-19C+] bricks, esp. as thrown during riots (cf. ALLEY-APPLE n.¹). **2** [20C] (gay) semen spilled extravagantly. [IRISH adj. + pun on SE *confetti*. From *c.*1832, in the era before asphalt, New York streets were paved with bricks]

Irish dip *n.* [1960s+] (gay) sexual intercourse.

Irish dividend *n.* (US) **1** [mid-19C+] a non-existent or fictitious profit, a deficit, a stock assessment. **2** [1920s] (US Und.) a shake-down by the police.

Irish draperies *n.* [late 19C] cobwebs.

Irish evidence *n.* **1** [late 18C–19C] a perjuring witness. **2** [1960s] (gay) pendulous breasts.

Irish fan *n.* [1920s–60s] (US) a spade, a shovel.

Irish favourite *n.* [1920s] (US) an emerald.

Irish flag *n.* [20C] (US) a diaper, a nappy.

Irish football *n.* [1970s] (US) a potato (cf. IRISH APPLE).

Irish fortune *n.* [19C] the vagina (cf. ROCHESTER PORTION; TETBURY PORTION; TIPPERARY FORTUNE; WHITECHAPEL PORTION).

Irish funnies *see* IRISH COMICS.

Irish goose *n.* [mid-19C] (US) cooked codfish (cf. ABERDEEN CUTLET).

Irish grape *n.* [1940s–70s] (US) a potato (cf. IRISH APPLE).

Irish hint *n.* [mid-18C+] (US) a very broad hint. [the supposed stupidity of the Irish]

Irish hoist *n.* [20C] a kick in the behind. [the stereotypically boorish, brawling Irishman]

Irish horse *n.* **1** [mid-18C–late 19C] tough, undercooked salt beef (cf. ADIRONDACK STEAK). **2** [1950s+] (gay) an impotent penis.

Irish hurricane *n.* [early 19C+] a flat calm.

Irish inch *n.* [1970s–80s] (US) the erect penis. [a slur on Irish penis size]

Irish jig *n.* [20C] **1** wig. **2** a cigarette. [rhy. sl.; (2) CIG]

Irish King *n.* [1960s] (N.Z.) something one needs; usu. in phr. *buggered for the want of an Irish King.*

Irish lace *n.* [19C] a spider's web.

Irish lasses *n.* [20C] glasses. [rhy. sl.]

Irish legs *n.* [late 18C–19C] heavy female legs.

Irish lemon *n.* [late 19C] (US) a potato (cf. IRISH APPLE).

Irish local *n.* [20C] (US) **1** a wheelbarrow (cf. IRISH AMBULANCE). **2** a hand-car, propelled by pushing a handle backwards and forwards. [SAmE *local*, a local train line]

Irishman's coat of arms *phr.* **1** [mid-18C–mid-19C] a black eye. **2** [early 19C] (US) two black eyes and a bleeding nose.

Irishman's dinner *n.* [19C] a fast. [stereotype of the stupid Irishman, but note Irish Famine 1845–51]

Irishman's harvest *n.* [19C] the orange season. [used by London costermongers; indigent Irishmen presumably picked up rotten oranges]

Irishman's necktie *n.* [late 19C] (US) a rope.

Irishman's nightingale *n.* [1900s] (US) a bullfrog (cf. CAMBRIDGE NIGHTINGALE).

Irishman's pocket *n.* [20C] (US) a pocket that is both large and empty.

Irishman's rest *n.* [late 19C] mounting a ladder carrying a hod of bricks.

Irishman's/Irish sidewalk *n.* [mid-19C] (US) the street. [racial stereotyping; either the loathed Irish ought to walk in the street, rather than on the pavement where more civilized people walked, or they were too stupid to know the difference]

Irish marathon *n.* [20C] an extended session of lovemaking.

Irish mile *n.* [late 19C+] a 'country mile', i.e. a mile that twists and turns and thus seems much further.

Irish pasture *n.* [20C] (US) a fainting fit, esp. a pretended one. [? SE *posture*]

Irish pennants *n.* [late 19C+] untidy ropes on board a ship (cf. DUTCH PENNANTS).

Irish pluggy *see* IRISH BUGGY.

Irish promotion *n.* **1** [late 19C+] a cut in one's pay (cf. IRISH RISE). **2** [20C] (gay) masturbation.

Irish rifle *n.* [19C] a small toothcomb.

Irish rise *n.* **1** [late 19C+] sexual detumescence (cf. IRISH TOOTHACHE). **2** [late 19C+] a cut in one's pay; in US as *Irish raise* (cf. IRISH PROMOTION).

Irish root *n.* [19C] **1** the penis. **2** a potato (cf. IRISH APPLE).

Irish rose *n.*¹ [20C] the nose. [rhy. sl.]

Irish rose *n.*² [1930s] (US) a stone, for throwing (cf. IRISH BOUQUET).

Irish screwdriver *n.* [20C] a hammer (cf. BIRMINGHAM SCREWDRIVER).

Irish shave *n.* [20C] the act of defecation.

Irish shift/switch *n.* [1930s–60s] (US) political hypocrisy. [the supposed propensity of Irish politicians to blow with the prevailing wind. Given the year of first use – 1960 – the Irish in question may have been the Kennedys, whose scion John was elected president that year]

Irish sidewalk *see* IRISHMAN'S SIDEWALK.

Irish spoon *see* IRISH BANJO.

Irish stew *adj.* [20C] **1** true, esp. in the phr. *too Irish stew.* **2** blue. [rhy. sl.]

Irish switch *see* IRISH SHIFT.

Irish toothache/i.t.a./paddy's toothache *n.* [19C] **1** an erection (cf. HORN COLIC; IRISH RISE n.[1]; TOOTHACHE). **2** pregnancy.

Irish toothpick *n.* [1920s] (US) **1** a pickaxe. **2** (gay) the erect penis (cf. IRISH TOOTHACHE).

Irish toyle *n.* [16C–18C] (Und.) a mendicant villain who posed as a tinker or pedlar to fool their victims. [IRISH + SE *toil*, a net or trap]

Irish turkey *n.* [1910s+] (US) corned (salt) beef and cabbage (cf. ADIRONDACK STEAK). [popularized by its use in the *Jiggs and Maggie* comic strip]

Irish twins *n.* [20C] two siblings born within a 12-month period. [the stereotypical fecundity – and lack of contraceptive practice – of Irish families]

Irish virgin *n.* [20C] (US) one who is a virgin and is likely to remain one. [? pious Irish virgins who become nuns]

Irish wager *n.* [late 18C–early 19C] a rump of beef and a dozen bottles of claret, a then popular bet in Ireland (cf. RUMP AND A DOZEN).

Irish wake *n.* [20C] any boisterous occasion and not necessarily a wake (cf. PADDY FUNERAL).

Irish wash *n.* [20C] the turning or reversing of a garment or other object to hide rather than actually remove the dirt.

Irish way *n.* [20C] heterosexual anal intercourse (cf. FRENCH WAY). [the belief that pious Catholics used anal intercourse as their sole means of contraception]

Irish wedding/wedding *n.* **1** [late 18C–19C] a brawl, 'where black eyes are given instead of favours' (Grose 1796). **2** the emptying of a cesspool. **3** [20C] (gay) masturbation (cf. IRISH PROMOTION; IRISH RISE).

Irish whist *n.* [19C] sexual intercourse; thus *play Irish whist*, to have sexual intercourse (cf. IRISH TOOTHACHE).

iris out *v.* [1920s+] to leave unobtrusively. [film jargon *iris out*, to contract the picture to the dimensions of a small dot and thence a blank screen]

iron *n.*[1] [late 17C–early 18C; 1930s+] the penis (cf. BETHLEHEM STEEL; PINK STEEL). [later use is US]

iron *n.*[2] **1** [late 18C–mid-19C] money. **2** [1900s–10s] (US) $1 in cash (cf. IRON BOY; IRON MAN). [the metal coins]

iron *n.*[3] **1** [mid-19C+] (US) a gun. **2** [1930s+] (US) a discontinued model of motor car, a rundown, dilapidated car. **3** [1940s+] a housebreaker's implement, a crowbar. **4** [1960s–70s] (US) a motorcycle. **5** [1960s+] (US) weights, as used in body-building exercises, esp. in the phr. *pump iron*, to exercise with weights; thus *iron freak*, a weight-lifting enthusiast.

iron *n.*[4] [1930s+] a male homosexual. [rhy. sl. *iron hoof* = POOF n.]

iron *v.* **1** [late 19C+] to kill. **2** [1950s] (Aus.) to defeat in a fight.

iron-bound *n.* [late-19C–1910s] a hard-baked pie.

iron-bound hat *n.* [late 18C–19C] a silver-laced hat.

iron boy *n.* [1910s–20s] (US) $1 (cf. IRON n.[2]).

iron butterfly *n.* [1950s+] an old-fashioned hypodermic syringe made of metal and glass. [shape; the curved finger-holes are the 'wings' of the butterfly]

iron cow *n.* [19C] a village pump.

iron cross *n.* [1960s+] (US Black) extremely unfavourable circumstances from which it is hard to extract oneself. [SE *cross*, a burden]

iron cunny *n.* [1950s] (W.I.) a tough sugar candy, extremely hard to chew (cf. BUSTA BACKBONE). [SE *iron* + *candy*]

iron dollar *n.* [1900s–20s] (US) $1 in cash (cf. IRON n.[2]).

iron doublet *n.* [17C–18C] a prison.

iron duke *n.* [late 19C+] a lucky chance. [rhy. sl. *iron duke* =

FLUKE n.[2]; the orig. *Iron Duke* was the Duke of Wellington (1769–1852)]

iron eye, the *n.* [1940s] (US) a hard and hostile stare.

iron feed *n.* [1940s] (W.I.) corn meal cooked with rice. [such a starchy dish is very 'hard']

iron gaiters/garters *n.* [early-mid-19C] leg-irons.

iron hat *n.* [1910s–30s] (US) a derby hat. [note WW1 US milit. *iron derby*, a steel helmet]

ironhead *n.* [1910s+] (US) a fool; thus *iron-headed*, stupid. [the hardness of iron]

iron hoof *n.* [1930s+] (US) a male homosexual (cf. IRON n.[4]). [rhy. sl. *iron hoof* = POOF n.]

iron hoop *n.* [late 19C–1910s] soup (cf. LOOP-THE-LOOP n.[1]). [rhy. sl.]

iron horse *n.* [20C] **1** a racecourse. **2** a toss (note Cockney pron. *torss*), also as *the iron*, *the ironing*. [rhy. sl.]

iron horse *v.* [20C] to toss. [IRON HORSE n. (2)]

iron house *n.* [1920s+] (US Und.) **1** a punishment cell. **2** a prison.

iron jaws *n.* [1980s+] (US gay) an exceptionally competent fellator (cf. RAW JAWS).

iron louie *n.* [late 19C] (US) $1 (cf. IRON n.[2]).

iron lung *n.* **1** [1940s] a deep shelter in the London underground. **2** [1950s] the Central Line, in its extension from Shoreditch to Essex. **3** [1960s+] (Irish) an aluminium keg of beer, usu. Guinness.

iron man *n.* **1** [20C] (US) $1 (cf. IRON n.[2]). **2** [1950s–70s] (orig. Aus.) £1 note. **3** [1960s] (US) $1000. [the metal coins]

ironmongery *n.* [late 19C+] firearms, weapons (cf. IRON n.[3]).

ironmongery department, the *n.* [1940s+] prison (cf. HER MAJESTY'S SCHOOL FOR HEAVY NEEDLEWORK). [the iron bars; pun]

iron out *v.* [20C] **1** to correct a situation, to put things right. **2** to overwhelm in a fight (cf. FLATTEN v.). [fig. uses of SE]

iron parenthesis *n.* [early 19C] a prison (cf. WOODEN PARENTHESIS). [it provides a *parenthesis* in one's on-going life]

iron pile *n.* [20C] (US Und.) **1** a prison. **2** the weight-lifting and body-building facilities in a prison. [IRON n.[3] (5) + SE *pile*]

irons *n.* [1920s+] utensils, knife and fork. [abbr. EATING IRONS]

iron some wrinkles, to *phr.* [1990s] to masturbate.

iron tank *n.* [20C] a bank. [rhy. sl.]

iron the yard, to *phr.* [1920s–40s] (US Black) to sweep the yard.

irrigate one's canal, to *phr.* [late 18C+] to drink.

irrigate one's tonsils, to *phr.* [mid-19C–1910s] (orig. US) to drink, usu. alcohol.

irvine *n.* [20C] (US Black) the police. [? joc. use of proper name]

irving *n.* [20C] (US) a dull, uninformed, obnoxious person (cf. MELVIN n.). [? *Irving* seen as a quintessential 'nerd' name]

isabella/isabeller *n.* [mid-19C] an umbrella. [rhy. sl.]

isadora *n.* [1960s–70s] (camp gay) a long scarf. [the demise of dancer *Isadora* Duncan (1878–1927), who was throttled to death when her long scarf was caught in a car's rear wheel]

is all *phr.* [1950s+] abbr. of *that is all.*

I say! *excl.* [late 19C–1930s] a general excl. of surprise, disagreement or to attract attention.

isda *n.* [1980s+] (drugs) heroin. [? Sp.]

I see *phr.* [early 19C+] I agree.

i-shence *n.* [1950s+] (W.I. Rasta) marijuana. [SE *essence*]

ish kabibble *phr.* [1910s+] (US) it is of no importance to me, 'I should worry'. [for etym. *see* ABIE KABIBBLE]

ishkimkisk *adj.* [18C–late 19C] drunk. [Shelta]

I shot one lightly and one died politely *phr.* [1930s–40s] (US Black) a phr. implying that the speaker has had the better of an opponent, verbally or physically.

I should be so lucky! *excl.* [20C] intimating envy on behalf of a speaker who has just been informed of another's luck, also used ironically (cf. HALF YOUR LUCK!). [the word-pattern implies a Yid. origin]

I should cocoa! *excl.* [1930s+] you must be joking! don't make me laugh! [rhy. sl. *cocoa* = SE *say so*; esp. popular in BBC Radio's *Billy Cotton Bandshow* in the 1950s]

I should imagine *see* I SHOULD THINK.

I shouldn't wonder if *phr.* [mid-19C+] I should not be surprised if; often abbr. *shouldn't wonder*.

I should smile *phr.* [late 19C] (US) an ironic response to an implausible suggestion.

I should suppose *see* I SHOULD THINK.

I should talk! *excl.* [1970s+] an excl. used to stress that one speaker is in no position to criticize another.

I should think/imagine/suppose *phr.* [mid-19C+] a phr. used to imply one's strong affirmation of what has just been said; thus abbr. of *I should think I did do ...* .

I should worry *phr.* [20C] I don't care (cf. ISH KABIBBLE). [Yid.]

is it? *phr.* [1960s+] (S.Afr.) a non-committal colloq. expression used to convey polite disbelief, astonishment, 'Really?' 'You don't mean to say?'.

is it buggery!/fuck!/hell!/shit! *excl.* [20C] an excl. used to stress one's disbelief, derision and general negative attitude.

Island, the *n.* [20C] the Isle of Wight and, thus the prisons of Parkhurst or Camp Hill, both of which are situated on the island.

island nigger *n.* [1980s+] (US) a derog. term for a Puerto Rican. [SE *island* + NIGGER n.; the premise being that, as foreigners and non-Whites, Puerto Ricans are *de facto* NIGGERS]

isle of fling *n.* [late 19C–1900s] a coat. [ety. unknown; ? one 'flings' it over one's shoulders]

isle of France *n.* [mid–late 19C] a dance. [rhy. sl.]

Isle of Man *n.* [20C] a pan. [rhy. sl.; never shortened]

Isle of Wight *phr.* [20C] **1** light. **2** all right. [rhy. sl.]

ism and skism/isms and skisms *n.* [1990s] (W.I./UK Black teen) a phr. that denotes society's ways, class consciousness, sub-systems and/or classifications.

isn't that special *phr.* [1980s+] (US campus) a dismissive phr. implying that *that* is not special at all (cf. BIG DEAL!).

Israelite *n.* [1940s] (US Black) a Jew.

isro *n.* [1970s] (US) a bushy hairstyle worn by White people, often curly-headed Jews. [SE *Israel* + AFRO n.[2]]

Issachar *n.* [18C] a donkey, an ass (cf. BALDWIN). [use of proper name for animal]

issue *n.* [1910s+] (Aus.) everything, the lot, all there is, often as *the whole issue*.

issues *n.* [1980s+] (drugs) crack cocaine. [ety. unknown]

I suppose *n.* [mid-19C+] a nose. [rhy. sl.]

is your father a glazier? *phr.* [mid-18C–1910s] a rude phr. used to embarrass one who is obstructing one's view.

it *n.*[1] **1** [late 16C+] sexual intercourse. **2** [mid-19C+] the male or female genitals. **3** [late 19C] a chamberpot. **4** [late 19C–1920s] (US) a fool or an unpleasant person. **5** [late 19C+] (US) money. **6** [20C] a ref. to a casual, picked-up partner as opposed to a lover. **7** [20C] a cover-all for such special qualities that are required for social or professional success. **8** [1920s] sex appeal. **9** [1960s+] (US Black) the quintessence of Black spirit, sensitivity etc. [(1) first (non-sl.) use cited 1611 in Cotgrave]

it *n.*[2] **1** [late 19C+] as an indefinite object, used with a v., e.g. *walk it, cab it*. **2** [late 19C+] (orig. US) the ultimate, usu. when applied to a person, e.g. *he really thinks he's it*.

i.t.a. *see* IRISH TOOTHACHE.

ital/i-tal *adj.* **1** [1950s+] (orig. W.I. Rasta) essential, basic, *echt* Rastafarian. **2** [1950s+] (W.I. Rasta) vital, organic, natural, wholesome, referring both to a way of cooking and of life. **3** [1960s+] (W.I./UK Black teen) of food, natural, unprocessed (fresh vegetables, fruits etc) or prepared without salt. [SE *vital* + Rastafarian use of pfx. *i-*]

Italian *n.* [1990s] (US) anger, bad temper (cf. AFRICA). [stereotyping]

Italian airlines *n.* [1950s+] (gay) walking (cf. JEWISH AIRLINES; POLISH AIRLINES). [the stereotyped inefficiency of Italian air companies]

Italian hero *n.* [20C] (US) a large sandwich made of two slabs of bread cut lengthwise from the loaf and containing a variety of ingredients (cf. GRINDER n.[6]). [its 'heroic' size, or ? f. stereotype of Italians as placing sexual – the phallic sandwich – above martial prowess]

Italian quarrel *n.* [late 19C] death, murder, poisoning, treachery. [stereotyping; the image is of the corrupt Borgia family]

Italian salute *n.* [1940s+] (US) an obscene gesture of contempt or derision; one arm is bent and the fist and forearm thrust upwards while the other hand grasps the forearm or bicep. [the gesture originated in Italy and was imported by immigrants]

Italian special/straws *n.* [20C] (US) pasta, spaghetti.

it/that all depends *phr.* [late 19C+] a temporizing phr. for perhaps, possibly, probably; thus *it all depends what school you went to*, used by those who are unsure as to the proper pronunciation of a (foreign) word and thus offer both variations.

italy *phr.* [1940s] *I trust and love you*, written on envelopes of love letters (cf. BOLTOP). [abbr.]

itch *n.* [17C+] sexual excitement (cf. HAVE AN ITCH IN THE BELLY; ITCHER; ITCHING JENNY; PLAY ITCH-BUTTOCKS).

itch and scratch *n.* [20C] a match. [rhy. sl.]

itcher *n.* [late 17C–early 18C] the vagina (cf. ITCH). [the vagina is supposedly a sexually voracious organ always in need of being touched]

itching jenny *n.* [19C] the vagina (cf. ITCH). [the vagina is supposedly a sexually voracious organ always in need of being touched; note JENNY n.[5] despite dates]

itchland *n.* **1** [late 17C–early 19C] Wales. **2** [early 18C–early 19C] Scotland (cf. ITCH; SCRATCHLAND). [derog. stereotyping of Wales and Scotland as a land of overt sexuality or of infestations of body-lice]

itch the ditch, to *phr.* [1990s] of a woman, to masturbate. [SE *itch* + DITCH n.[1]]

itchy eye *n.* [1990s] (US) haemorrhoids. [SE *itchy* + ROUNDEYE; a typical symptom is an itching sensation of the sphincter]

item *n.* **1** [19C] (US) a hint, an inkling, a piece of information. **2** [1930s+] (US) a person. **3** [1980s+] (orig. US) a couple. [the exploits of such fashionable individuals provide items for newspaper gossip columnists]

I thought you thought *phr.* [1990s] (US teen) a phr. used to state the obvious.

itie *n.* [1920s+] (orig. US) Italian (cf. EYETIE). [exaggerated 'Italian' pronunciation]

-itis *sfx.* [20C] used humorously to create imagined 'diseases', e.g. *Zeppelinitis*, a fear of aerial bombardment during WW1; *danceitis*, an obsession with dancing; *workitis*, a pathological dislike of work. [SE *-itis*, used with the proper noun to create the name of a disease, often an inflammation of the part in question, e.g. arthritis, nephritis]

it isn't done *see* IT'S NOT DONE.

it isn't true *phr.* [1960s+] a phr. used to intensify the extent of the original statement; thus to an unbelievable extent, e.g. *he's so fat, it isn't true*.

it is to laugh *phr.* [late 19C–1960s] (US) it is very ironic.

it just/only goes to show *phr.* [1920s+] 'that proves ...'.

it/that licks me *phr.* [late 19C] that defeats me, I cannot explain it. [LICK v.]

it'll all come out in the wash *phr.* [20C] problems etc will all be made clear in due course, no matter how daunting at present. [sometimes prefaced by 'never mind' or 'don't worry']

it'll be all right on the night *phr.* [late 19C+] don't worry, all will be well. [orig. theatre use, the *night* is the first night of a performance – the traditional belief is that a bad dress rehearsal ensures a great first night]

it'll cost ya! *see* COST YA!

it looks like rain *phr.* [20C] (Und.) an arrest, poss. of the speaker, seems likely.

it must be jelly, 'cos jam don't shake like that *phr.* [1920s–40s] (US Black) a phr. used between males to express their appreciation of an especially attractive female.

it only goes to show *see* IT JUST GOES TO SHOW.

it's a bastard/proper bastard *phr.* [late 19C+] (orig. Aus.) a phr. for anything considered unpleasant, excessively challenging etc.

it's a breeze *phr.* [20C] a phr. indicating that something is easy. [BREEZE n.[4]]

it's a case of spoons with them *phr.* [mid-19C–1920s] a phr. used of a couple who are obviously in love. [SPOON n.[1] + a pun on the *case of spoons* one might receive as a wedding gift]

it's a deal *phr.* [late 19C+] a phr. indicating agreement, 'that's agreed', 'that's settled'.

it's a dog's life *phr.* [20C] said of an unpleasant situation or of one's whole wretched existence.

it's a fair cow *phr.* [late 19C+] (orig. Aus.) a phr. for anything considered unpleasant, excessively challenging etc (cf. IT'S A BASTARD). [COW n.[2]]

it's a fair old/proper/right bugger *phr.* [mid-19C+] said of anything considered unpleasant, excessively challenging etc.

it's a fine day for travelling *phr.* [20C] (Aus.) a phr. used in the Outback to signify that one has received notice to quit. [ironic use of SE]

it's a free country *phr.* [mid-19C+] a catchphrase asserting a person's rights as an individual, implying that the action proposed is not illegal.

it's a gas *phr.* [1960s+] (teen) a phr. indicating that everything is fine, 'it's all wonderful'. [GAS n.[2]]

it's a gig *phr.* [1920s+] (Aus.) a general term of satisfaction, congratulation or praise. [GIG n.[8] (1)]

it's a go *phr.* [20C] (Aus./N.Z.) a phr. used to indicate agreement, 'that's settled' (cf. IT'S A DEAL). [GO n.[5]]

it's a licker to me *see* LICKS ME.

it's all betty *phr.* [mid-19C–1920s] a general phr. of distress, it's a disaster, we've failed etc. [ALL MY EYE AND BETTY MARTIN]

it's all bob *phr.* [16C+] (Und.) everything is safe, the bet is secured (cf. BOB'S YOUR UNCLE). [BOB adj.]

it's all happening! *excl.* [1960s] there is much activity or success, everything is working out as desired.

it's all right for you/for you to laugh *phr.* [1940s+] a phr. of jealousy or envy, directed at another whose fortune seems better than one's own (cf. ALL RIGHT FOR SOME).

it's a new one on me *phr.* [20C] that's the first I have heard of it, I've never seen, heard or experienced that before.

it's/that's an idea *phr.* [1910s+] an idea worth considering.

it's an old ... custom *phr.* [1930s+] a phr. used to justify a practice, usu. in the workplace, that would otherwise be condemned, abandoned etc had it not been established over a long period; usu. *an old Spanish custom.*

it's a peg *phr.* [1930s+] (Aus.) a phr. used to indicate pleasure, that's wonderful, excellent etc. [ety. unknown]

it's a proper bastard *see* IT'S A BASTARD.

it's a proper/right bugger *see* IT'S A FAIR OLD BUGGER.

it's a term of endearment among sailors *phr.* [20C] euph. for BUGGER n.[1].

it's a thought *phr.* [1960s+] a phr. used to indicate that the speaker will think about or consider something further.

it says *phr.* [late 19C+] used of a book, newspaper or some other form of supposedly authoritative print, to mean *the book/magazine/journal says.*

it's been real *phr.* [1970s+] (US campus) a farewell, an acknowledgement of what has just been experienced, e.g. a meeting; also used ironically.

it's dogged as does it *phr.* [late 19C–1940s] a phr. stating that persistence always wins through in a given endeavour. [SE *dogged*, persistent, obstinate, stubborn]

it's going to rain *phr.* [1950s–60s] a phr. used to indicate boredom, e.g. *I think it's going to rain*, indicating that it is time to leave a dull gathering or party. [euph.]

it shouldn't happen to a dog *phr.* [1940s+] a general comment of commiseration or complaint.

it's my way or the highway *phr.* [1980s+] (US) do as I say or you will suffer. [the image of a boy tossing a girl out of his car, some way from home, after she has refused to have sex]

it's/that's news to me *phr.* [late 19C+] that is the first knowledge I have of it, I did not know that.

it's no hanging matter *phr.* [late 19C+] an assurance that something is unimportant.

it's not/it isn't done *phr.* [late 19C+] a general phr. implying that an action is quite unacceptable, or is beyond the bounds of 'civilized' behaviour.

it's not the bull they're afraid of, it's the calf *phr.* [20C] (Aus.) of women, it's not intercourse they dislike, it's the thought of possible pregnancy.

it snowed *phr.* [late 19C] (orig. US) a phr. denoting the occurrence of problems, disasters.

it's one/two/three o'clock at the button factory *phr.* [20C] advice to a man that his fly is open.

it's one/two/three o'clock/o'clock at the water-works *phr.* [1910s+] advice to a man that his fly is open.

it's snowing down south *phr.* [1940s+] (Aus.) a phr. used to tell a woman that her slip is showing. [the ship is seen as generically white]

it stands to sense *phr.* [mid-19C] it seems sensible, it stands to reason.

it's/it was the beer talking *phr.* [1920s+] **1** the excuse, usu. in a public house, for breaking wind. **2** an excuse for any excessive talk or actions when drunk, either at the time or when sober on reflection (cf. APPLETON TALKING).

it's this way *phr.* [20C] (orig. US) a phr. used to introduce an explanatory sentence.

it's two/three o'clock at the button factory *see* IT'S ONE O'CLOCK AT THE BUTTON FACTORY.

it's two/three o'clock/o'clock at the water-works *see* IT'S ONE O'CLOCK AT THE WATER-WORKS.

it's your baby *phr.* [1920s+] a phr. used to disclaim responsibility for a problem, 'that's your problem'. [BABY n.[2] (5)]

it's your corner *phr.* [20C] a phr. indicating it's your turn to pay, usu. in a pub. [? CORNER n. or a play on SE *round*]

it's your little hip pocket *phr.* [1950s+] (US Black) you're in great trouble. [? the keeping of one's wallet in the hip pocket]

it takes all sorts *phr.* [late 19C] an abbr. of the pvb. *it takes all sorts to make a world.*

it takes one to know one *phr.* [late 19C+] a phr. upbraiding someone for possessing the exact characteristics they are criticizing in another.

it takes two to tango *phr.* [20C] **1** sexual intercourse, esp. adulterous, requires two people; not just a lustful male is implied. **2** applied to a situation where one party is getting the blame but both are equally responsible.

itty *v.* [1990s] (US teen) to leave. [? SE (get) *out of* (here)/SPLIT v.[1] (2)]

it was the beer talking *see* IT'S THE BEER TALKING.

it won't wash *phr.* [mid-19C+] that won't work, that won't stand proper investigation. [dying, when a poor or badly applied dye will vanish in the wash]

it would make a cat laugh *see* ENOUGH TO MAKE A CAT LAUGH.

it would make a stuffed bird laugh *phr.* [late 19C] (US) said of anything considered totally absurd.

itzy house *n.* [1930s] (US) a psychiatric institution. [? DITZY adj.[1]]

Ivan *n.* [1970s] a generally stupid east European person. [*Ivan*, a stereotypical Slavic/Russian name]

I've got a feeling in my water *phr.* [late 19C+] I sense something instinctually. [ref. to an era when the state of one's urine was seen as a guide to one's overall health]

I've got him! *excl.* [late 19C] now I understand!

I've got the time if you've got the money *phr.* [1910s+] a joc. phr. delivered to one who asks 'Have you got the time?'. [the supposed conversation between a streetwalker and her client who has asked, as a way of initiating their relationship, 'Do you have the time?']

ivory/ivories *n.*[1] **1** [late 18C+] the teeth. **2** [mid-19C+] dice; thus *rattle the ivories*, throw dice. **3** [late 19C+] (US) poker chips. **4** [late 19C–1950s] billiard balls. **5** [1940s+] (US Black) piano keys. [lit. or fig. uses of SE *ivory* used in manufacturing all these items]

ivory *n.*[2] [mid-19C] a season ticket for the railways, places of entertainment etc. [such 'tickets' were made from a small slab of ivory]

ivory *adj.* [1990s] (US) White, Caucasian. [the whiteness]

ivory-bender *n.* [1920s] (US) a piano-player. [the ivory keys of a piano]

ivory box *n.* [late 18C+] the mouth. [IVORY n.[1] (1) + SE *box*]

ivory-carpenter/-picker/-puller/-snatcher *n.* [1940s–50s] (US) a dentist. [IVORY n.[1] (1)]

ivory dome *n.* **1** [20C] a bald-headed person (cf. CHROME DOME). **2** [1910s–20s] (US) a fool; thus *ivory-domed*, stupid.

ivory float *n.* [1920s] (US) a coat. [rhy. sl.]

ivory gate *n.* [19C] the vagina (cf. BELLY DALE).

ivory-hammerer/-spanker *n.* [late 19C+] a pianist (cf. IVORY HOUND; IVORY-POUNDER; IVORY-THUMPER; IVORY-TICKLER). [the *ivory* keys of a piano]

ivory hound *n.* [1930s] (US) a piano player (cf. IVORY-HAMMERER). [the *ivory* keys]

ivory pearl *n.* [1930s–60s] a girl. [rhy. sl.]

ivory-picker *see* IVORY-CARPENTER.

ivory-pounder *n.* [20C] (US) a piano player (cf. IVORY-HAMMERER). [the *ivory* keys]

ivory-puller/-snatcher *see* IVORY-CARPENTER.

ivory-spanker *see* IVORY-HAMMERER.

ivory-thumper *n.* [1910s+] (US) a piano player (cf. IVORY-HAMMERER). [the *ivory* keys]

ivory-tickler *n.* [1920s–40s] (US) a piano player (cf. IVORY-HAMMERER). [the *ivory* keys]

ivory-turner *n.* [early–mid-19C] a skilful dice-player. [IVORY n.[1] (2) + pun]

ivy cottage *n.* [late 19C+] an outside lavatory.

I want to know! *excl.* [mid-19C–1920s] an excl. of interest, amazement, i.e. 'well, well!'

I wish you may/don't you wish you may get it? *phr.* [mid-19C] an ironic phr. implying the speaker's lack of interest in, or backing for, another's success.

I wonder *phr.* [mid-19C+] a phr. used to imply incredulity, second thoughts, reserved judgement.

I wouldn't be in it *phr.* [1940s+] (Aus.) I wouldn't join in, take part.

I wouldn't fuck her with a borrowed prick/your prick *phr.* [20C] a general term of masculine distaste, spoken on seeing what is considered an unattractive or unpleasant woman (cf. I WOULDN'T TOUCH IT WITH A TEN-FOOT BARGEPOLE).

I wouldn't have/take it as a gift *phr.* [mid-19C+] a phr. implying one's absolute rejection of whatever is offered, irrespective of the terms proposed.

I wouldn't kick her out of bed *phr.* [20C] referring to an attractive woman; a comment usually made by one of a group of young men observing a passing woman.

I wouldn't know *phr.* [20C] a statement of dismissal, disinterest (cf. DON'T ASK ME).

I wouldn't piss on them if they were on fire *phr.* [1960s+] a phr. implying the speaker's absolute contempt or loathing for the person thus decried.

I wouldn't take it as a gift *see* I WOULDN'T HAVE IT AS A GIFT.

I wouldn't touch it with a ten-foot/the end of a barge-pole *phr.* [late 19C+] I refuse to have the least thing to do with it.

I wouldn't trust ... *phr.* used in a variety of contexts to imply one's absolute lack of faith in the person who is its object; e.g. [early 19C] *he may be trusted alone*, the implication being '...but not if allowed in company'; [mid-19C] *I wouldn't trust them as far as I could fling a bull by the tail*; [late 19C+] *I wouldn't trust them as far as I could throw them*; [20C] *I wouldn't trust them as far as I could throw an anvil in a swamp*; [20C] *I wouldn't trust them with a kid's money-box* (with a an added ref. to financial improbity); [20C] *I wouldn't trust them with our cat* (the distrust is compounded by an implication of sexual perversion).

ixnay *prep.* [1920s+] (US) no. [dog Latin, the reverse of *nix*]

izm *n.* [1980s+] (US drugs) cannabis. [ety. unknown]

J

j *n.*[1] [late 19C] a gullible fool, a sucker. [abbr. JUGGINS]

j *n.*[2] [1970s+] (drugs) a cannabis cigarette. [abbr. JOINT *n.*[4] (2)]

j.a. *n.* [1990s] (US) a Japanese-American. [abbr.]

Ja/Jam-down *n.* [20C] (W.I. Rasta) Jamaica (cf. JAMDUNG). [abbr.]

jaap/japie *n.* **1** [1940s+] an Afrikaner. **2** [1960s+] (S.Afr.) a peasant, a rustic, an unsophisticated person. [Afk. *jaap*, f. proper name *Jacob*, a typical 'country' name. *DSAE* claims that 'no examples of the word in use by non-South Africans have been found', but cf. YARPIE, common in Aus., albeit transliterated]

jab *n.*[1] **1** [20C] (US) an attempt, a try (cf. STAB *n.*[1]). **2** [1980s+] (US) an act of copulation.

jab *n.*[2] **1** [1910s+] (orig. milit.) an inoculation, any form of injection, esp. against diseases such as TB and polio. **2** [1920s+] (drugs) an injection of a narcotic drug.

jab *v.* **1** [1920s+] (drugs) to inject drugs. **2** [1980s+] (US campus) of a man, to have sexual intercourse.

ja-baas *n.* [1960s+] (S.Afr.) a servile, subservient Black. [Afk. *ja baas*, yes, master]

jabber *n.*[1] [early 18C+] **1** gossip. **2** unrestrained, even unintelligible talk.

jabber *n.*[2] [1900s] (US prison) a prize-fighter. [one who SE *jabs*]

jabber *v.* **1** [late 15C+] to gossip. **2** [late 15C+] to talk in an incomprehensible manner. **3** [early 16C–mid-19C] to talk a foreign language. [JIBB *v.*]

jabberknowl/jabbernowl *see* JOBBERKNOWL.

jabez *v.* [1910s–20s] to play an underhand trick. [*jabez*, a typical rural name; thus peasant cunning]

jabfest *see* GABFEST.

jab job *v.* [1950s+] (drugs) to inject a drug. [SE *jab* + JOB *n.*[5]]

jabone *see* JIBONE.

jaboney *see* JABRONIE.

jabongoes *n.* [1960s] (US) the female breasts. [nonce-word, var. on BAZONGAS]

jabonie *see* JABRONIE.

jabooby *n.* [1950s+] (drugs) marijuana. [? play on JOINT *n.*[4] (2)]

jabronie / jaboney / jabonie / jarboni / jumbloney *n.* [1930s+] (US) **1** a newly arrived foreign immigrant, a 'greenhorn' (cf. JIBONE). **2** an inexperienced, inept, unsophisticated person (cf. JADROOL).

jack *n.*[1] [mid-16C] a very small amount, the least bit. [ety. unknown]

jack *n.*[2] **1** [late 17C–18C] a farthing. **2** [19C+] £1. **3** [late 19C+] (US) money. [ety. unknown]

Jack *n.*[3] **1** [late 17C–mid-18C] a Jacobite, i.e. an adherent of James II of England after his abdication (1688), or of his son, the Old Pretender (James Stuart), and grandson, the Young Pretender (Charles Edward Stuart). **2** [mid-19C] (US) a *Jack*sonian Democrat, i.e. a supporter of Andrew Jackson, 7th President (1767–1845). [abbr.]

jack *n.*[4] [18C–19C] a sailor. [abbr. JACK TAR *n.* (1)]

jack *n.*[5] [mid-18C; 1940s+] a man or boy. [20C usage is US Black]

jack *n.*[6] [late 18C–early 19C] a lavatory (cf. AJAX). [JAKES]

jack/jack lantern/jacklight *n.*[7] [late 18C+] (US) a light used for hunting by night (cf. JACK DEER; JACK-HUNTER). [the light momentarily stuns the prey, giving the hunter time to shoot; also used in fishing, when the powerful light shines through the water to the fish below]

jack *n.*[8] **1** [19C] an erection (cf. WHEN THE JACK TAKES THE ACE). **2** [19C+] the penis (cf. ABRAHAM). **3** [1950s+] copulation. [SE *jack*, a device for lifting things]

jack *n.*[9] **1** [19C+] (US) a flap*jack*. **2** [early–mid-19C] a *jack*-boot. **3** [late 19C] a *jack*al. **4** [20C] (US/Can.) a lumber*jack*. [abbr.]

jack *n.*[10] [early 19C] a post-chaise, a travelling carriage seating two or four, with the coachman or postilion riding one of the horses (cf. JACK BOY *n.*[1]). [ety. unknown, but note SE *jack*, used for a variety of machines]

jack/half-jack *n.*[11] [mid-19C] a counter, similar in size and shape to a sovereign or half-sovereign, used in gambling houses and casinos.

jack *n.*[12] [mid–late 19C] (Anglo-Ind.) a native soldier. [*Jack-Sepoy*, 'kindly, rather than otherwise' (Y&B)]

jack *n.*[13] [mid-19C+] a detective (cf. JOHN *n.*[3]). [orig. northern dial., now general]

jack *n.*[14] [mid-19C+] (US) a fool. [abbr. SE *jackass*]

jack/jacky *n.*[15] [late 19C–1950s] (Aus.) a kookaburra. [SE *laughing jackass*]

jack *n.*[16] [late 19C+] (US) a general term of address to a man (cf. JOHN *n.*[1]).

jack *n.*[17] [late 19C+] the anus. [abbr. JACKSIE]

jack *n.*[18] [20C] nothing. [abbr. JACKSHIT *n.*]

jack *n.*[19] [20C] syphilis. [abbr. JACK IN THE BOX *n.*[3]]

jack/country jack *n.*[20] [20C] (US) a rustic, a peasant. [JAKE *n.*[1]]

jack *n.*[21] **1** [20C] (US) illegally distilled liquor, based on various fruits and vegetables and usu. specified as such, e.g. *tater jack* (potatoes), *prune jack*, *raisin jack*. **2** [20C] (W.I.) illegally distilled rum. **3** [1930s+] methylated spirits, used as a drink.

jack *n.*[22] [20C] (US) a mugger, a thief (cf. JACK BOY *n.*[2]). [abbr. JACK ROLLER *n.*[1]]

jack *n.*[23] **1** [20C] (Aus.) a black*jack* or cosh. **2** [1930s] (US) the card-game black*jack*. [abbr.]

jack *n.*[24] [20C] (Aus.) a double-headed penny. [? JACK *n.*[2]]

jack *n.*[25] [1900s] horseflesh that has been washed to remove its salty flavour. [ety. unknown; ? joc. ref. to a JACK *n.*[4] who will be eating it]

jack *n.*[26] [1900s] (US campus) a translation or hidden notes. [? play on SE *jackass*, i.e. the sort of student who requires a crib]

jack n.[27] [1940s+] (Aus.) a non-union labourer, a strikebreaker, spec. a member of the Permanent and Casual Waterside Workers' Union. [rhy. sl. *Jack McNab* = SCAB n. (4); ? anecdotal]

jack n.[28] [1950s+] a pill of heroin in which the drug is issued to registered addicts. [rhy. sl. *jack and jill* (usu. pl.) = pill(s)]

jack, the n.[29] [1950s+] (Aus.) venereal disease. [rhy. sl. *jack in the box* = POX n.[1]; but note JACK IN THE BOX n.[3]]

jack n.[30] [1970s] a bar. [rhy. sl. *jack tar* = bar]

Jack/Jack D/Jack's n.[31] [1970s+] (US) Jack Daniel's brand of whisky.

jack adj. [1980s+] flashy, ostentatious. [abbr. NEW JACK]

jack v.[1] [mid-19C+] (US) to hunt deer at night, illegally, with the aid of a light; thus *jacker*, one who hunts in this way (cf. JACK n.[7]).

jack v.[2] **1** [1930s+] (US Und.) to beat with a blackjack. **2** [1960s] (US prison) to serve a prison sentence.

jack v.[3] [1970s+] (US drugs) to inject a drug, esp. to draw a portion of blood, which mixes with the drug and then to reinject the mixture, repeating the process several times. [JACK UP v.[8]]

jack v.[4] [1980s+] **1** (orig. US) to steal, to hijack, to take forcibly. **2** (drugs) to steal someone else's drugs.

jack act v. [1960s+] (Irish) to play the fool. [SE *jackass*]

jack adams n. [late 17C–19C] a fool; thus *jack adams' parish*, Clerkenwell. [? anecdotal]

jack-a-dandy n.[1] [late 17C–18C] an insignificant person (cf. JACK OF DANDY). [SE pfx. *jack*, a person, esp. in derog. or contemptuous contexts + *dandy*]

jack-a-dandy n.[2] [late 19C+] brandy. [rhy. sl.]

jackal v. [1990s] (US) to masturbate. [var. on JACK OFF v.[1]]

jackanape n. [1960s] (US Black radical) an undisciplined, albeit enthusiastic member of a radical movement, one who finds it hard to put the general good before their own pleasures. [SE *jackanapes*, a tame ape or monkey, and thus someone who acts like one. The orig. use (in a poem of 1449) was as a nickname of William de la Pole, Duke of Suffolk (murdered 1450), whose badge was a clog and chain, such as was attached to a tame ape]

jack an' danny n. [1990s] the vagina. [rhy. sl. *jack and danny* = FANNY n.[1] (1)]

jack and jill n. [20C] **1** a hill. **2** a bill. **3** a till. **4** a pill, esp. of heroin (cf. JACK n.[28]). **5** (Aus.) a fool. [rhy. sl.; (5) *jack and jill* = DILL]

jack and shit see JACKSHIT n.

jackanory n. [20C] **1** a children's story. **2** a lie, i.e. a 'tall story'. [rhy. sl.]

jackaroo/jackeroo n. [mid-19C+] (Aus.) **1** a White man living beyond the bounds of 'civilization'. **2** a man newly arrived from Britain to gain experience in the bush. [Jagara *dhugai-tu*, a wandering White man]

jack around v. [1960s+] **1** to mess about, usu. with sexual, adulterous overtones. **2** (US campus) to tease. **3** (US) to treat badly, with deceit or contempt (cf. JERK AROUND).

jack ashore adj. [late 19C] larky, excited, tipsy. [JACK TAR and his habits when in port]

jackass brandy n. [1920s] (US) home-distilled brandy. [US West *jackass*, second-rate, irregular]

jackass rope n. [1950s+] (W.I. Rasta) home-grown tobacco, twisted into a rope (cf. JACKASS BRANDY).

jack-at-a-pinch n. **1** [late 17C–early 19C] a temporary clergyman, hired when the regular incumbent is absent. **2** [mid-19C] one whose assistance is required only in an emergency. [generic use of SE *jack*, a man, usu. derog. + phr. *at a pinch*]

Jack Benny n. [20C] a penny. [rhy. sl.; ult. US comedian *Jack Benny* (1894–1974)]

jack blunt n. [late 19C–1910s] a blunt person. [generic use of SE *jack*, a man + *blunt*]

jack boots n. [early–mid-19C] the 'boots' or bootboy at an inn. [generic use of SE *jack*, a man + *boots*]

jack boy n.[1] [early 19C] a postilion, one who rides one of a carriage's leading horses rather than riding on the box. [JACK n.[10] + SE *boy*]

jack boy n.[2] [1980s+] (US police) a hold-up man. [JACK n.[32] + SE *boy*]

jack bragger n. [late 16C] a boaster, a braggart. [generic use of SE *jack*, a man + *bragger*]

jack bumps n. [1960s+] (US) acne, allegedly caused by masturbation. [JACK OFF v.[1]]

Jack D see JACK n.[31].

jack dandy n. [mid-19C] brandy (cf. FINE AND DANDY n.; JACK-A-DANDY n.[2]). [rhy. sl.]

jackdaw n. [mid-19C+] a jaw. [rhy. sl.]

jack deer n. [late 18C+] (US) deer shot, illegally, by one who hunts at night, using a light to stun the prey. [JACK n.[7]]

jack-deuce adj. [1930s] (US) at an angle or slanted.

jack/john/tom drum's entertainment phr. [late 16C–mid-17C] a rough reception, esp. the throwing out of an unwelcome guest. [they are 'drummed out' of the house]

jacked adj.[1] **1** [late 18C–19C] of a horse, spavined. **2** [late 19C+] (Aus.) angry, annoyed, tired of.

jacked/jacked up adj.[2] [1930s+] (US drugs) **1** under the influence of a drug, either narcotic or pharmaceutical, or of alcohol. **2** excited, exhilarated (cf. HYPED; WIRED adj.[1]). [JACK UP v.[8]]

jacked adj.[3] [1980s+] (US campus) happy, satisfied, excited (cf. JAKED adj.[2]). [SE *jacked up*]

jacked in adj. [1940s+] given up, abandoned. [JACK IN]

jacked it adj. [late 19C] died. [fig. use of JACK IN]

jacked off adj. [1980s+] (US) enthusiastic, very keen.

jacked out adj. [1970s+] (US campus) annoyed, irritated, angry. [JACKED adj.[1]]

jacked up adj.[1] **1** [mid–late 19C] ruined, given up, abandoned. **2** [1900s–10s] (US) pregnant.

jacked up adj.[2] [20C] (US Und.) charged with an offence. [? JACK n.[18]]

jacked up adj.[3] [20C] (Aus.) infected (usu. with venereal disease). [JACK n.[19]]

jacked up adj.[4] see JACKED adj.[2].

jacked up adj.[5] [1960s+] (N.Z.) arranged, sorted out, 'fixed'. [JACK ONESELF UP]

jacked up adj.[6] [1970s+] (US teen) upset, anxious, waiting anxiously for time to pass. [JACKED adj.[1]]

jackeen/Dublin jackeen n. [mid–late 19C] (Anglo-Irish) **1** a Dubliner. **2** a self-assertive but worthless person. [generic use of SE *jack*, a man + dimin. sfx. *-een*]

jacker n. [1980s+] (US) a hijacker. [JACK v.[4] (1)]

jackeroo n. see JACKAROO.

jackeroo v. [mid-19C+] (Aus.) to pick up experience (cf. JACKAROO).

jackery n. [late 19C–1900s] (Aus.) a popular station-hand; usu. in pl. [JACKAROO]

jackery-pokery see JIGGERY-POKERY.

jacket n.[1] [20C] (W.I.) **1** a child fathered by a woman's lover rather than by her husband. **2** any child who has no 'official' father; thus *wear a jacket for*, for a husband to accept the child as his own. [the image is a jacket 'dressing up' a man and thus conferring respectability on the child]

jacket n.[2] (US Und.) **1** [1930s+] a bad reputation. **2** [1950s+] the police/prison file on a criminal, recording previous convictions etc, one's criminal record (cf. FORM n.[1]; PEDIGREE; PREVIOUS n.; RAP SHEET).

jacket *n.*³ [1950s+] (drugs) Nembutal, a tranquillizer. [abbr. YELLOW JACKETS]

jacket *n.*⁴ [1960s+] (US) a condom.

jacket *v.*¹ [early 19C] to 'remov[e] a man by underhand and vile means from any birth or situation he enjoys, commonly with a view to supplant him' (Vaux).

jacket *v.*² [mid-19C] to beat, to thrash (cf. TRIM SOMEONE'S JACKET). [Lincolnshire/Sussex dial.]

jacket *v.*³ **1** [mid-19C] (US Und.) to identify a suspect. **2** [1970s+] (US prison) to be labelled untrustworthy by fellow prisoners.

jacket *v.*⁴ [late 19C] to threaten someone with confinement in a lunatic asylum. [the threat is of the *strait-jacket*]

jacket and vest *n.* [1910s–30s] the West End of London. [rhy. sl.]

jacketing *n.* [mid–late 19C] a thrashing, a beating. [JACKET *v.*²]

jackey *n.* [late 18C–mid-19C] gin (cf. CAT'S WATER). [? name of a gin distiller]

jack flash *n.* [1960s+] (Aus.) hashish. [rhy. sl.? + ref. to Rolling Stones' song 'Jumping *Jack Flash*' (1968)]

jack fool *n.* [17C] a foolish person (cf. JACK-PUDDING). [SE *jack*, generic for a man + *fool*; the term survived in 1940s Kansas dial.]

jack-gagger *n.* [19C] (US) a pimp who is also married to the prostitute he exploits. [? JACK *n.*¹⁶ + GAGGER *n.*¹]

jack gentleman *n.* [late 17C–18C] a man of low birth or manners who has pretensions to be a gentleman, an insolent fellow, an upstart. [SE *jack*, generic for a man, esp. derog. + *gentleman*. *Jack-gentlewoman* exists, but rarely]

jackhammer *n.* [1980s+] (US gay) the erect penis. [play on SE; note HAMMER *n.*¹ (1)]

jackhammer *v.* [1990s] to masturbate. [JACKHAMMER *n.*/JACK (OFF) *v.*¹ (1)+ HAMMER *n.*¹ (1)]

jackhandle *n.* [1960s] (US) an erect penis.

jack-hold-my-staff *n.* [17C] a servile attendant (cf. JOHN-HOLD-MY-STAFF). [SE *jack*, generic for a man, esp. derog. + phr. *hold my staff*]

jackhouse see JAKEHOUSE.

jack-hunter *n.* [late 18C+] (US) someone who hunts by night, using a light to stun the prey. [JACK *n.*⁷]

Jackie/Jacky Howe *n.* [1930s+] (Aus./N.Z.) a navy blue or black woollen singlet worn by Aus. and N.Z. shearers and bushmen. [proper name of *Jackie Howe* (1855–1922), an Australian shearer who in 1892 established a world shearing record by shearing 321 merino sheep with hand shears in 8 hours 40 minutes]

Jackie Robinson *n.* (US Black) **1** [1940s+] any Black person who is the first to gain entry to a profession. **2** [1960s] the penis (cf. ABRAHAM). [proper name of *Jackie Robinson* (1919–72), who in 1947 became the first Black man to play in major league baseball (for the Brooklyn Dodgers)]

jackies *n.*¹ [1930s+] (Aus.) Native Australians, Aborigines. [abbr. JACKY JACKY *n.* (1)]

jackies *n.*² [1940s] American sailors. [JACK TAR *n.* (1)]

Jackie Trent *adj.* [1990s] corrupt, untrustworthy. [rhy. sl. *Jackie Trent* = BENT *adj.*]

jack in/it in *v.* [1940s+] to stop doing something, to give in. [? *jack*, to give up suddenly, to relinquish, to abandon or CHUCK *v.*²]

jack in a box *n.* [late 16C–mid-19C] a cheat, spec. a thief who deceives tradesmen by the substitution of identical boxes, his own filled with gold pounds, that with which the tradesman finds himself left filled with silver shillings.

jacking off *n.* [20C] (gambling) **1** racking up the pool balls. **2** shaking dice with a movement that might be seen as resembling masturbation. [JACK OFF *v.*¹ (1)]

jack-in-office *n.* [late 17C+] an officious petty official, their assumed power of inverse proportion to the actual importance of their job (cf. JACK-OUT-OF-OFFICE). [SE *jack*, generic for a man, usu. derog. + *office*]

jack in the bean stack *phr.* [1950s–60s] (US Black) an adventurous, daredevil person. [assonance/play on the fairytale character *Jack in the Beanstalk*]

jack in the box *n.*¹ [mid-16C–late 17C] the consecrated host. [a blasphemous joke]

jack in the box *n.*² [late 17C–early 18C] a street pedlar. [the box of goods that is carried]

jack in the box *n.*³ [late 19C+] venereal disease (cf. BAND IN THE BOX). [rhy. sl. *jack in the box* = POX *n.*¹]

jack in the box *n.*⁴ [late 19C+] the penis. [it 'pops up']

jack in the box *n.*⁵ [1970s+] (US Black) the state of having one's penis inside one's partner's vagina. [JACK *n.*⁸ + BOX *n.*⁶ (2)]

jack in the box, to *phr.* [20C] (US Und.) to break and enter a house or apartment.

jack in the low cellar *n.* [mid-18C] an unborn child. [trans. of Du. HANS-EN-KELDER]

jack in the pulpit *n.* [19C] a pretender, an upstart. [SE *jack*, generic for a man, usu. derog. + *pulpit*, i.e. one who sets themselves up as a preacher, lit. or fig.]

jack in the water *n.* [mid–late 19C] a waterman's attendant, who helps passengers on and off boats. [SE *jack*, generic for a man, usu. derog. + *water*]

jack iron *n.* [20C] (W.I.) a form of unlicensed and very potent rum, distilled secretly in the countryside (cf. BUSHIE; JACK *n.*²¹).

jack it *v.* [late 19C–1900s] to die. [abbr. JACK IN]

jack it in see JACK IN.

jack it up someone's ass, to *phr.* [1960s+] (US) to punish or victimize someone. [SE *jack*, to force up + ARSE *n.*¹]

jack job *n.* [1970s+] (US campus) unfair treatment. [JACKSHIT]

jack jones *n.* [20C] alone, usu. in phr. *on your jack*. [rhy. sl.]

Jack Ketch *n.* [mid-18C+] the hangman (cf. DERRICK *n.*; JACK KETCH'S KITCHEN; JACK KETCH'S PIPPIN). [proper name of the common executioner *Jack Ketch* (c.1663–86). Partly on account of his barbarity at the executions of Lord Russell, the Duke of Monmouth and other political offenders, and partly perhaps from the obvious links with the SE *catch*, his name became widely known. When it was given to the hangman in the puppet-play of *Punchinello*, which arrived from Italy shortly after his death, his immortality was assured]

Jack Ketch's kitchen *n.* [18C] that room in Newgate prison where the hangman boiled the quarters of those dismembered for high treason. [JACK KETCH + SE *kitchen*]

Jack Ketch's pippin *n.* [late 17C–early 19C] a candidate for the gallows (cf. GALLOWS APPLE; JACK KETCH). [JACK KETCH + PIPPIN]

jack-knife face *n.* [mid-19C+] (US) a thin, pointed face.

jack lantern see JACK *n.*⁷.

jack lattin/latten *n.* [20C] (Irish) a threat of punishment, esp. in phr. *I'll make you dance jack lattin/latten for that.* [*John Lattin* of Morristown House, Co. Kildare, won a bet after dancing, as wagered, a distance of over 32km (20 miles), changing his dance-step every furlong]

jackleg *n.* [mid-19C+] (US) an incompetent, unskilled or unprincipled worker or professional person, esp. a quack doctor, a crooked lawyer, a hypocritical preacher. [the generic male name *jack* + sfx. *-leg*; on model of *blackleg*]

jackleg/jakeleg/jack-legged *adj.* [mid-19C+] (US) **1** untrained, unprofessional, dishonest. **2** thrown-together, makeshift. [US dial. *jackleg*, unskilled, ult. UK dial. *jack-a-legs*, a large clasp knife, as used by a second-rate carpenter]

jackleg *v.* [mid-19C+] (US) to act in an incompetent, unskilled or unprincipled way. [JACKLEG *n.*]

jacklight see JACK n.[7].

jackman n. [mid-16C–mid-19C] (Und.) a mendicant villain who used his abilities of reading and writing to forge counterfeit begging licences (cf. JARKMAN). [apparently derived f. a misspelling of JARKMAN as printed in the 1575 edn. of Awdelay (1561)]

jack Mormon n. **1** [mid–late 19C] a non-Mormon who sympathizes with the Mormons. **2** [20C] an apostate Mormon. [? JACK(LEG) n. + *Mormon*]

jack move n. [1980s+] (US Black) a wild, foolish, eccentric move or type of behaviour. [JACK n.[18] + MOVE n. (2)]

jack mum n. [20C] (Irish) a discreet person, esp. in the phr. *between you and me and jack mum*. [SE *jack*, generic for a man, esp. derog. + MUM adj.]

jack nasty n. [mid-19C] a sneaking, slovenly person. [SE *jack*, generic for a man, usu. derog. + *nasty*]

jack nasty face n. [mid-19C] the vagina (cf. JACK NASTY). [punning on the general use, 'a dirty fellow, seldom seen' (J.B.). Note merchant navy jargon *jack nasty face*, a cook's assistant, or anyone considered ugly]

jack nohi n. [1940s+] (N.Z.) an inquisitive person, a 'nosey parker'. [HAVE A JACK + Maori pron. of NOSEY]

jack 'n' the beanstalk, to phr. [1990s] to masturbate. [pun on JACK (OFF) v.[1] (1) + fairy-tale *Jack and the Beanstalk*]

jacko n. [1940s] (Aus.) a kookaburra (cf. JACK n.[15]). [SE *jack*, a laughing jackass or kookaburra]

jack of adj. [late 19C+] (Aus.) bored with, tired of (cf. JACKED adj.[1]). [JACK UP v.[1]]

jack of/on both sides n. [mid-16C–late 19C] a neutral, one who sides first with one party and then with the other. [SE *jack*, generic for a man, usu. derog.]

jack-of-clubs n. [19C] a good fellow, man. [generic use of proper name + SE *club*, a social centre; also play on SE]

jack of dandy n. [early 18C] a fop, a dandy. [var. on JACK-A-DANDY n.[1]]

jack of dover n. [late 14C–17C] a sole. [play on SE *jack*, generic for a man + *Dover sole*]

jack-off n. **1** [1930s+] a pej. form of address, lit. a masturbator. **2** [1950s+] (US) an act of masturbation. [JACK OFF v.[1] (1)]

jack off v.[1] **1** [1930s+] to masturbate (cf. BEAT OFF). **2** [1940s+] (US) to fool around (cf. GOOF OFF). **3** [1960s+] (US) to take advantage of, to deceive or tease someone. [JACK n.[8] + JERK OFF v.[1]/v.[2]]

jack off v.[2] [1950s+] (drugs) to pump backwards and forwards with the plunger of the hypodermic without finally injecting the blood and heroin mix into the arm. [the up-and-down gesture of masturbation and the figurative 'jacking off' instead of reaching a climax]

jack of legs n. [late 18C–19C] **1** a tall, long-legged man. **2** an outsize clasp-knife. [folk legend of *Jack of Legs*, a supposed giant, some 4.3m (14ft) tall, who is allegedly buried in the churchyard at Weston, Hertfordshire. A large thigh bone, excavated in the graveyard, was given to the naturalist Sir John Tradescant (1608–62)]

jack of spades n. [20C] dark glasses. [rhy. sl. *jack of spades* = SHADES n.]

jack of the clockhouse n. [16C] (Und.) a confidence trickster, specializing in selling supposedly purpose-written pamphlets, poems etc, which flatter the vanity of the purchaser but which are, in fact, mass-produced with a personalized dedication tacked on. [SE *jack of the clockhouse*, which 'goes upon screws, and his office is to do nothing but strike'; the actual *jack* was a figure of a man which strikes the bell on the outside of a clock]

jack on both sides see JACK OF BOTH SIDES.

jack/jerk one's jaw/jaws, to phr. [1960s+] (US) to chatter at length.

jack oneself v. [1930s+] to masturbate. [JACK (OFF) v.[1] (1)]

jack oneself up, to phr. [1940s+] (N.Z.) to settle in; thus to make oneself or someone else at home.

jack out v. [mid-19C] (US) to knock unconscious.

jack out of doors n. [late 16C] a vagrant, one who has been thrown out of his house. [SE *jack*, generic for a man, usu. derog.]

jack-out-of-office/-service n. [mid-16C–late 18C] one who has been dismissed from his job (cf. JACK-IN-OFFICE; JOHN-OUT-OF-OFFICE). [SE *jack*, generic for a man, usu. derog.]

jack poke n. [1930s–40s] (US) a slow, listless person. [SE *jack*, generic for a man, usu. derog. + POKE (ALONG)]

jack policy/system n. [1940s+] (Aus.) absolute selfishness. [FUCK YOU JACK, I'M ALL RIGHT!; despite the fact that here 'jack' is not the speaker]

jackpot n.[1] [late 19C+] (US) **1** a dilemma, a difficult situation, trouble. **2** an arrest. [sources claim a link to poker's *jackpot*, a large 'pot' of money, but there seems no real proof]

jackpot n.[2] [1980s+] (drugs) fentanyl (cf. APACHE n.[2]). [its effects]

jackpot v.[1] [20C] (US prison) to fight (cf. SCUFF UP). [JACKPOT n.[1]]

jackpot v.[2] [1970s+] (US Und.) to chat, to gossip, to reminisce. [abbr. of gambling *cut up jackpots*, to reminisce over card-games]

jack pudding n. [late 17C–19C] a jester or clown, travelling with a mountebank or itinerant quack (cf. JACK ADAMS; JACK FOOL). [SE *jack*, generic for a man, usu. derog. + innate humour of a *pudding*]

jackrabbit n. **1** [late 19C–1960s] (US) a mule. **2** [1970s+] (US prison) an escaped convict.

jackrabbit v. [1970s+] (US) to run, escape. [JACKRABBIT n. (2)]

jackrabbit parole n. [1970s+] (US prison) an escape from prison (cf. BUSH PAROLE). [JACKRABBIT n. (2)]

jack randall/randle n. [mid-19C] a candle (cf. HARRY RANDALL). [rhy. sl.]

jack rees n. [20C] (Aus.) fleas. [rhy. sl.]

jack robinson n. [19C] the penis (cf. ABRAHAM). [Grose (1785) suggests a real 'Jack Robinson ... a very volatile gentleman of that appellation, who would call on his neighbours, and be gone before his name could be announced']

jackroll v.[1] [1910s+] to rob one's companions while they are drunk or sleeping. [SE *jack*, generic for a man + ROLL v.[1]]

jackroll v.[2] [1990s] (S.Afr.) to abduct, then rape a woman, usu. a schoolgirl, to gang-rape; thus *jack-rolling*, abducting and raping. [despite logical link to JACK-ROLL v.[1], *DSAE* suggests a song by Womack & Womack, with lyrics 'Love is just a ballgame, sometimes you lose – jackroll']

jack roller n.[1] [20C] (US) a robber who specializes in stealing from drunk, drugged or otherwise incapacitated victims. [JACKROLL v.[1]]

jack roller n.[2] [1990s] (S.Afr.) an individual, usu. one of gang, who abducts and rapes women. [JACK-ROLL v.[2]]

Jack's see JACK n.[31].

jacks n. [20C] a detective. [JACK n.[13]]

jack's alive/jacks/jax n. [1920s+] 5, esp. as £5 note. [rhy. sl.]

jack sauce n. [late 16C–early 18C] a saucy or impudent fellow. [SE *jack*, generic for a man + *sauce*]

jack scratches n. [20C] (Aus.) matches. [rhy. sl.]

jack's delight n. [19C] a prostitute. [JACK TAR + SE *delight*]

jack shay v. [20C] (Aus.) to stay. [rhy. sl.; ? anecdotal]

jack shea n. [late 19C] (Aus.) a tin container, holding a quart (1.2 litre) of liquid, used for brewing tea and, when empty, containing a smaller vessel for drinking the tea. [? rhy. sl. *jack shea* = tea (in Irish pron. 'tay')]

jackshit/jack shit/jack and shit n. **1** [1960s+] (orig. US) absolutely nothing, always used with a qualifying neg. v., e.g.

you don't know jack shit about ... (cf. DICK SHIT). **2** [1970s+] (US) nonsense (cf. BULLSHIT n.). **3** [1970s+] (US) a stupid, contemptible person (cf. JACK n.¹⁴). [JACK n.¹ + SHIT n.⁴]

jackshit *adj.* [1990s] (US) worthless, useless, negligible. [JACK-SHIT n.]

jacksie *n.* **1** [late 19C+] the anus; thus *up your jacksie*, a derog. response to an unpalatable idea or opinion. **2** [20C] (Aus.) a brothel. [ety. unknown; ? link to JACK n.⁸]

jack smithers *n.* **1** [1900s–30s] (Aus.) a drink taken by one who is drinking alone. **2** [1930s+] a solitary drinker. [? anecdotal]

jack snip *n.* [late 19C–1900s] a second-rate tailor. [SE *jack*, generic for a man, usu. derog. + *snip*]

jackson *n.* [1930s–40s] (US) a form of address between men. [ext. of JACK n.¹⁶]

jack sprat *n.*¹ [late 16C–19C] a small person, a dwarf. [the name survives mainly in the nursery rhyme, which itself post-dated it. Its first appearance in print was *c.*1570, while the nursery rhyme was first published in 1639]

jack sprat *n.*² [20C] **1** fat (on meat). **2** a brat, an irritating small child. [rhy. sl.]

jack squat *n.* [1980s+] (US) a partial euph. for JACKSHIT n.

jack stickler *n.* [mid-16C–mid-17C] a meddlesome or interfering person, a busybody. [SE *jack*, generic for a man, usu. derog. + *stickler*]

jack straw/jackstraw *n.* [late 16C–late 17C] a nonentity, lit. a 'man of straw'. [SE *jack*, generic for a man, usu. derog. + *straw*, and ref. to *Jack Straw*, leader of the failed Peasants' Revolt, 1381]

jack straw's castle *n.* [19C] the vagina. [JACK STRAW; the image of the vagina as a trifle, a nothing, is common in slang]

jacksy jockey *n.* [1990s] an aficionado of anal sex (whether hetero- or homosexual). [JACKSIE n. (1) + JOCKEY n.² (2)]

jacksy-pardo/jacksy-pardy/jaxey/jaxie *n.* [mid-19C+] the anus. [vars. on JACKSIE n. (1)]

jack system *see* JACK POLICY.

jack tar *n.* **1** [late 18C+] a sailor. **2** [19C] a hornpipe. [SE *jack*, generic for a man + *tar*, i.e. the 17C naut. practice of smearing canvas breeches with tar to provide a primitive form of waterproofing. The term gradually evolved into SE during the 19C]

jack the contract, to *phr.* [1910s+] (Aus.) to give up or leave a job when it proves too difficult (cf. JACK IN). [JACK UP v.¹+ SE *contract*]

jack the corn, to *phr.* [1990s] to masturbate.

jack the dancer *n.* [20C] (Aus.) cancer. [rhy. sl.]

jack the dog, to *phr.* [1940s] (US) **1** to waste time, to loaf on the job. **2** to bungle, to blunder (cf. FUCK THE DOG; SCREW THE DOG). [JACK (OFF) v.¹ (2) + SE *dog*]

jack the Jew *n.* [19C] a receiver of stolen goods, usu. of the least valuable type. [racial stereotyping]

jack/jam the joystick, to *phr.* [1990s] to masturbate. [JACK (OFF) v.¹ (1) + JOYSTICK n.¹ (2)]

jack the lad *n.* [1950s+] **1** a show-off, anyone particularly pleased with themself and keen to ensure that everyone knows it. **2** a priapic 'robot' made from a cigarette packet. [SE *jack*, generic for a man + SE *lad*]

jack the lad *phr.* [20C] bad. [rhy. sl.]

jack the painter *n.* [mid–late 19C] (Aus.) a strong, coarse green tea, which stained the drinker's lips. [the stain it leaves on the cup or teapot or its smell, supposedly similar to paint]

Jack the Ripper *n.* [20C] **1** a kipper. **2** a slipper. [rhy. sl.; ult. *Jack the Ripper*, the late 19C mass-killer. (1) like his victims, kippers are slit open]

jack the sack, to *phr.* [1990s] to masturbate. [JACK (OFF) v.¹ (1) + (NUT)SACK]

jack the slipper *n.* [late 19C] a prison treadmill.

jack up *n.* [1940s+] (Aus.) an argument, a dispute, a refusal to cooperate, esp. at work or in the office. [JACK UP v.² (4)]

jack up *v.*¹ [late 19C] to give up, esp. a love affair (cf. JACK IN). [note dial. uses; to give up anything in a bad temper (Sussex); to become bankrupt or insolvent (Leicester)]

jack up *v.*² [late 19C+] to collapse, to become bankrupt, to be completely exhausted.

jack up *v.*³ **1** [late 19C+] to ruin, to exhaust completely. **2** [20C] (Und.) to plead 'not guilty'. **3** [20C] (US/W.I./Trin./Tob.) to scold, to tell off severely, to annoy. **4** [1940s+] (Aus.) to refuse to carry out an instruction, to refuse to work, to offer resistance.

jack up/up on *v.*⁴ [late 19C+] to show disapproval, to withdraw one's cooperation; thus *jacked up/up on*, annoyed with, disenchanted.

jack up *v.*⁵ [late 19C+] (US) to criticize, to rebuke, to discipline or call to account.

jack up *v.*⁶ **1** [20C] (orig. US) to raise, to increase, e.g. to raise rents. **2** [1940s+] (N.Z.) to arrange, to organize, to put right, to spruce up.

jack up *v.*⁷ [1910s–60s] (US) to urge, incite.

jack up *v.*⁸ [1950s+] (US drugs) to inject narcotics (cf. JACK OFF v.²).

jack up *v.*⁹ [1960s+] (US Black) **1** to assault, to attack, to beat up, to hold up, to mug (cf. JACK v.²). **2** [1960s+] to have sexual intercourse. **3** [1960s+] of the police, to interrogate; to stop and search.

jack up *v.*¹⁰ [1990s] (US) to vomit.

jack up on *see* JACK UP v.⁴.

jack weight *n.* [late 18C–19C] a fat man. [SE *jack*, generic for a man, usu. derog. + SE *weight*]

jack white is out of jail *phr.* [20C] (US) used to worn a man that his shirt-tail is untucked.

jack-whore *n.* **1** [late 18C–mid-19C] a large, tough prostitute. **2** [mid-19C–1920s] a womanizer. [SE *jack*, generic for a man, usu. derog. + *whore*]

jack with the feather/a plume of feathers *n.* [late 16C–early 17C] an insignificant, unimportant person (cf. PLUME OF FEATHERS). [generic use of proper name *Jack* + image of the pointless embellishment of the feathers]

jacky *n.*¹ [late 18C–early 19C] (Aus.) gin (cf. JACK n.²¹). [? a gin distiller]

jacky *n.*² *see* JACKY JACKY.

jacky *n.*³ *see* JACK n.¹⁵.

jacky howe *see* JACKIE HOWE.

jacky jacky/jacky *n.* [mid-19C+] **1** (Aus.) a White man's derog. name for an Aborigine, the 'typical' Aborigine (cf. JACKIES n.¹). **2** a coconut. [generic use of SE *jack* + redup.]

jack your jizz, to *phr.* [1930s+] to masturbate. [JACK (OFF) v.¹ (1) + JIZZ n.]

jacky raw *n.* [20C] (Aus.) a new immigrant (cf. JOHNNY RAW). [JACKAROO? + generic use of SE *jack* + *raw*]

jacky rue *n.* [20C] (Aus.) a squatter. [? JACKY RAW + JACKAROO]

jacob *n.*¹ **1** [late 18C–early 19C] a ladder. **2** [late 18C–early 19C] (Und.) a thief who uses a ladder. **3** [19C] the penis (cf. ABRAHAM). [the biblical story of *Jacob*'s ladder. In (3) the penis 'climbs up' the vagina]

jacob *n.*² [late 18C–19C] a fool (cf. DICKHEAD). [pun on JAY n.3 (1) or J n.¹]

jacob *n.*³ [late 18C–19C] a jay (the bird).

jacobite *n.* [late 17C–19C] a shirt collar, a fake shirt. [? the 'false' claims of the *Jacobites* to the British throne]

jacob's ladder *n.* [19C] **1** (orig. theatre) a 'ladder' in a pair of tights or stockings. **2** the vagina (cf. JACOB n.¹). [one 'climbs' up it]

jacobus *n.* [early 18C] a guinea. [the Lat. name *Jacobus*, (King) James I (r.1603–25) inscribed on it]

jacque's n. [16C] a privy, a lavatory (cf. AJAX).

Jacques Cousteau job n. [1980s+] a dive, in football. [*Jacques Cousteau* (1910–97) the aquanaut + JOB n.[5]]

jade n. [19C] (Aus.) a prison sentence of between 4 and 12 months. [? one becomes SE *jaded*]

jadrool n. [1960s+] (US, esp. Ital. Amer.) a stupid or unpleasant person (cf. JABRONIE). [ety. unknown]

jaffle n. [1960s+] (Aus.) a toasted sandwich. [brandname of a sandwich toaster, reg. in 1965 by Hi-Craft Manufacturing Co. Pty. Ltd]

jag n.[1] **1** [late 17C+] a drunken spree. **2** [18C+] a drink. **3** [1950s+] the taking of a drug, usu. narcotic, but also cannabis or LSD.

jag n.[2] **1** [late 19C+] (US) a period of indulgence, a fit, a spree of any kind. **2** [1910s+] (orig. US) a breakdown, an emotional collapse, often as a *crying jag*, lengthy and profound sobbing. [dial. *jag*, as much liquor as one can hold, a 'load']

jag n.[3] [20C] (US) a strange or stupid fellow (cf. JAG-OFF). [JACK n.[14]]

Jag n.[4] [1950s+] a *Jaguar* motorcar. [abbr.]

jag v.[1] [mid-19C+] (S.Afr.) to hunt, to chase. [Du. *jagen*, to hunt]

jag v.[2] **1** [late 19C] to assault with a knife. **2** [1960s] (US) to copulate with a woman. [dial. *jag*, to cut roughly]

jag v.[3] [late 19C+] (N.Z.) to depress, to irritate. [JAG n.[2] (2)]

jag v.[4] [1980s+] (drugs) to maintain one's drugged or drunken state. [JAG n.[1]]

jagabat n. [20C] (W.I.) a prostitute or notably promiscuous woman. [? Hind. ? *jaggery*, sugar, sweet + *bat*, language]

jagged adj. **1** [mid-18C+] drunk. **2** [1930s+] intoxicated by drugs. [JAG n.[1]]

jagger n. [mid-19C] a gentleman. [Ger. *Jäger*, a sportsman]

jaggers n. [late 19C–1900s] a messenger boy. [one *Jaggers* who made a celebrated, spur-of-the-moment journey from London to Chicago]

jag-off n. **1** [1930s+] (US) a masturbator. **2** [1930s+] (US) an idiot, dolt. [JACK-OFF n.]

jag off v. **1** [1950s–60s] (US drugs) to inject a narcotic, esp. slowly. **2** [1960s+] (US) to masturbate (cf. BEAT OFF). **3** [1970s+] (US) to fool around or to tease someone. [JACK OFF v.[2]/v.[2]]

jags adj. [20C] (S.Afr.) randy, lecherous. [Afk. *jags*, of an animal, in season, on heat]

jag snakes n. [late 19C] (US) hallucinations from delirium tremens. [JAG n.[1] + SE *snakes*]

jague n. [mid-17C–mid-19C] a ditch. [? JAKES, since both are seen as repositories of filth]

Jah n. [1960s+] (W.I./UK Black teen) God, as used by Rastafarians. [contraction of SE *Jehovah*]

jail v. [1960s+] (US) to spend time in prison, spec. to create the best possible situation for oneself given the overriding circumstances (cf. JAILING).

jailbait n. **1** [1930s+] (US) a young person who is a troublemaker and thus likely to be sent to prison. **2** [1930s+] (orig. US) an under-age, and thus illegal, sexual partner of either sex, although usu. teenage girls. **3** [1960s–70s] (US) a charge of statutory rape (cf. GAOLBAIT).

jailbird see GAOLBIRD.

jailhouse daddy n. [1950s–60s] (US prison) a dominating male homosexual prisoner who exploits or protects his partner. [SE *jailhouse* + DADDY n. (8)]

jailhouse lawyer n. [19C+] (US Und.) a prison inmate who has made themself into a self-taught lawyer, either to pursue their own case, combat prison corruption or help fellow inmates (cf. BARRACK-ROOM LAWYER; GAOLHOUSE LAWYER).

jailhouse salute n. [1970s] (US) an obscene gesture (cf. ITALIAN SALUTE).

jailhouse turnout/j.t.o. n. [1960s] (US) a prisoner who is

forced to engage in homosexual practices or who becomes a homosexual while in prison. [TURN OUT v.[4]]

jailic n. [1970s+] (Irish) Irish as learned while imprisoned in the prison at Long Kesh, Belfast. [SE *jail* + *Gaelic*]

jailing adj. (US prison) accustoming oneself to life in jail and adapting one's lifestyle to make one's time there as tolerable as possible.

jaina n. [1960s+] (US) a girlfriend. [Sp.]

jake/country jake n.[1] [mid-19C+] (US) a farmer, a rustic (cf. ALVIN). [the 'rural' proper name *Jacob*]

jake/jakers/jakey n.[2] [1920s–30s] (US) **1** Jamaica ginger, a drink with intoxicating properties. **2** methylated spirits used as an alcoholic drink; thus *jake-drinker*, a meths drinker, *jakeleg*, paralysis of the leg or legs caused by an excess of jake, *jakeleg liquor/whisky*, 'bad' liquor or whisky (which may well cause paralysis). [abbr. The drink was esp. popular during Prohibition (1919–33)]

jake n.[3] [1970s] (US) coffee. **2** [1980s] (US) a New York City police patrolman. [? (2) drinks so much of (1)]

jake adj. [1910s+] **1** (Aus./N.Z./US) satisfactory, as required, esp. in phr. *she's/she'll be/we're jake*, it's fine, it/things will be fine, we are fine. **2** (US Und.) aware, in the know. [? SE *chic*]

jake v. [1990s] (US campus) to cancel an appointment without prior notice, to drop out of an arrangement. [? SE *jerk* oneself out of]

jakealoo see JAKELOO.

jaked adj.[1] [late 19C+] (Aus.) broken. [JACKED adj.[1]]

jaked adj.[2] [1980s+] (US campus) excited, happy, thrilled (cf. JACKED adj.[3]). [JAKE adj.]

jake flake n. [1950s+] (US Black) anyone interested in themselves above anything or anyone else. [JAKE n.[1] + FLAKE n.[2]]

jakehead/jakehound n. [1920s–30s] (US) an addict of Jamaica ginger. [JAKE n.[2] + sfx. -HEAD (2)/-HOUND]

jakehouse/jackhouse n. [16C] a privy, a lavatory (cf. AJAX). [JAKES + SE *house*]

jake leg v. [1990s] (US) to tease, playfully deceive. [Tennessee dial. *jack leg*, the loss of motor control of the limbs caused by drinking poisonous bootleg liquor]

jakeleg see JACKLEG adj.

jakeloo/jakealoo/jakerloo adj. [1910s+] (Aus./N.Z.) excellent, wonderful, very good. [JAKE adj.]

jakers see JAKE n.[2].

jakes n. [early 16C–1900s] a lavatory (cf. AJAX). [? *jack's* or *jack's place*; using SE *jack* as generic for a man. Note synon. 1930s + Virginia dial. *jack-house*]

jakes-farmer n. [late 16C–mid-17C] a man employed to clean out privies (cf. GOLD-FINDER). [JAKES + SE *farmer*, one who cleanses]

jakey n. see JAKE n.[2].

jakey adj. [late 19C+] (US) unsophisticated, gauche, rustic, characteristic of a country person. [JAKE n.[1]]

jakkitch n. [late 19C] (provincial) a general pej. [? proper name of the hangman JACK KETCH]

jalobies n. [1960s+] nipples (cf. JABONGOES). [ety. unknown]

jalopy n. [1920s+] (orig. US) **1** a decrepit car. **2** a worthless or unattractive person or object. [ety. unknown; ? Sp.; echoic of the car's unsteady progress]

jam n.[1] **1** [19C] (US) a social gathering or party. **2** [1930s+] (US Black) a party with music. [SE *jam*, a crush. Note 19C SE *crush*, a party]

jam n.[2] **1** [mid-19C] anything easy. **2** [late 19C+] profit, an advantage, anything seen as easy (cf. BLUE PIGEON). [orig. sporting jargon *real jam*, anything exceptionally good]

jam n.[3] **1** [mid–late 19C] an attractive woman (cf. BANANA n.[2]). **2** [late 19C] sexual intercourse with a woman. **3** [1980s+] (US Black) the vagina (cf. APPLE n.[10]). [JAM TART]

jam *n.*[4] [late 19C+] (Aus.) affectation, pretentiousness; thus *put on the jam*, to act in an affected manner, *jammy*, affected. [the image of spreading jam on bread]

jam *n.*[5] **1** [late 19C+] a problem, a difficult situation, usu. *in a jam*. **2** [1920s–30s] (US) a disagreement or a fight. [SE *jam*, a crush]

jam *n.*[6] **1** [1920s+] (US Black) swing or other popular music, recording or song. **2** [1990s] (US Black/campus) music, a tune, a song, a performance of jazz, rock or rap music with a dance routine. [ety. unknown; ? link to JAM *n.*[1]]

jam *n.*[7] (drugs) **1** [1960s–70s] (US Black) cocaine. **2** [1970s+] amphetamine (cf. A *n.*[2]). ['it gets you in a jam' (Spears, 1986)]

jam *n.*[8] **1** [1960s+] menstrual blood. **2** [1960s+] (US Black) semen (cf. BABY GRAVY). **3** [1970s] (US gay) faeces (cf. EAT JAM).

jam *n.*[9] [1960s+] (gay) **1** a heterosexual man. **2** foreplay between two homosexual men. [abbr. for *just a man*, but this may be a camp joke and the real ety. is unknown]

jam *n.*[10] [1980s+] (Ulster) a second-rate teacher. [abbr. *junior assistant mistress*]

jam/jam-up *adj.*[1] **1** [19C+] (orig. US) splendid, fine, excellent, first-rate. **2** [early 19C–1940s] thorough. [SE *jam*, as in phr. 'put jam on it']

jam *adj.*[2] [1930s+] (US gay) heterosexual. [JAM *n.*[9]]

jam *v.*[1] [mid-18C–early 19C] to hang. [one's head is 'jammed' into the noose; ? ref. to the original method of hanging, jamming the neck into a forked piece of wood]

jam *v.*[2] **1** [mid-19C+] to injure, to damage by striking or crushing. **2** [20C] (W.I.) to strike hard and suddenly. **3** [1960s+] (US Black) to confront, to fight, to overcome or defeat, to arrest. **4** [1960s+] to put in an unfavourable position.

jam *v.*[3] **1** [1930s+] (W.I./US Black) to play or, of an instrument or of music in general, to be played so as to encourage vigorous dancing; thus *jamming*, dancing in an abandoned manner. **2** [1930s+] (orig. US) of musicians, to play together without set scores or arrangement for the pleasure and the spontaneous music thus created **3** [1970s+] (US campus) to dance, to have a good time, to perform well. **4** [1970s+] (US Black) to talk forcefully, esp. in a group. [? Wolof *jama*, a crowd, a gathering; by 1860s a gathering of slaves getting together for pleasure and dancing]

jam *v.*[4] [1960s+] (US teen) to leave, to exit fast. [? SE *jam* one's foot on the accelerator]

jam *v.*[5] [1960s+] (US Black) to have sexual intercourse. [JAM *n.*[3]]

jam *v.*[6] [1960s–70s] (US Black) to sniff cocaine. [JAM *n.*[7] (1)]

jam *v.*[7] **1** [1970s+] (US Black/campus/drugs) to have fun, a good time, also by taking drugs. **2** [1980s+] (US campus) to do very well. [ext. of JAM *v.*[3] (3)]

Jamaica discipline *n.* [1960s+] (gay) a wife's denial of sexual favours to her husband. [? pun on *do you make her*]

Jamaican coat-of-arms *n.* [1940s+] (W.I.) a dish of rice-and-peas. [rice-and-peas is the Jamaican national dish]

Jamaica rum *n.* [20C] a thumb. [rhy. sl.]

jam and fritters *phr.* [late 19C] a real treat (cf. REAL JAM).

jamas *n.* [1960s] pyjamas (cf. JAMS *n.*[3]).

jam back *v.* [1930s–70s] (US Black) to dance.

jambas *n.* [1960s+] theft, robbery. [Sp.]

jamberoo *n.* [late 19C–1900s] (Aus.) a drunken spree. [SE *jamboree*]

jambone *adj.* [1980s+] (US) worthless, contemptible. [? var. on JIBONE]

jamboree *n.* **1** [mid-19C+] (orig. US) a spree, a noisy revel. **2** [late 19C–1920s] (US) a disturbance or fight. [best known in 20C as a SE description of any large Boy Scout rally, the first of which, the International Rally of Boy Scouts, was held in 1920]

jambox *n.* [1980s+] (US campus) a portable stereo tape deck (cf. GHETTOBLASTER). [JAM *v.*[3] (3) + BOX *n.*[4] (5)/SE *box*]

jam cecil *n.* [1960s+] (drugs) amphetamine (cf. A *n.*[2]). [? JAM *n.*[7] (2) + CECIL]

Jam-down *see* JA.

jam duff *n.* [20C] a male homosexual. [rhy. sl. *jam duff* = PUFF *n.*[3]]

Jamdung *n.* [1950s+] (W.I./Jam.) Jamaica (cf. JA). [SE *jam*, press + *dung* (W.I. pron.), down; refers to oppression of the Jamaican proletariat]

james *n.*[1] [19C] a housebreaker's implement. [play on the nickname *Jemmy*/JEMMY *n.*[4]]

james *n.*[2] [early 19C–1910s] a cooked sheep's head (cf. BLOODY JEMMY). [JEMMY *n.*[2] (1)]

james *n.*[3] [mid-late 19C] a sovereign (cf. JACK *n.*[11]; JANE *n.*[1]). [orig. use as 16C *James Royal*, a Scot. silver coin of James VI of Scotland (r.1567–1603), the sword dollar]

james bong *n.* [1980s+] (US drugs) that person in a group who is the most intoxicated or most visibly intoxicated by a drug, usu. cannabis. [pun on BONG *n.* and the fictional spy *James Bond*]

james earl dog *n.* [1980s+] (US campus) a marijuana cigarette. [? ref. to *James Earl Ray* (1928–98), the alleged killer of Martin Luther King in 1968]

James Hunt *n.* [20C] audacity, cheek, 'front'. [rhy. sl.; ult. UK motor racing champion *James Hunt* (1947–93)]

James Street!/Holy James Street! *excl.* [20C] (Irish) a general excl. [*James Street*, Dublin, site of the Guinness brewery]

jamette *n.* [20C] (W.I.) **1** a prostitute. **2** a woman widely recognized to be promiscuous. [? Fr. sl. *jeanette*, a prostitute, or Fr. *diamètre*, diameter, i.e. the line between two halves of the social world]

jam fag *n.* [1950s] a homosexual with no other sexual interests. [JAM *n.*[8] (2) + FAG *n.*[5]]

jam house *n.* [1960s–70s] (US Black) a place where cocaine can be both purchased and then snorted in convivial surroundings (cf. CRACK HOUSE). [JAM *n.*[7] (1) + SE *house*]

jamie duff *n.* [mid-late 19C] a professional mourner. [? an undertaker's name]

jam it *v.*[1] [1930s+] to listen to music. [JAM *v.*[3]]

jam it *v.*[2] [1960s+] to drive a car or bike fast. [JAM *v.*[4]]

jam it! *excl.* [1950s+] (Aus./US) a threatening excl. [abbr. *jam it up your ass!*]

jam jar *n.* [1930s+] a motorcar. [rhy. sl.]

jammed *adj.* **1** [mid-18C–19C] (Und.) hanged, murdered, killed. **2** [late 19C+] (US Und.) in trouble with the law, arrested. **3** [1920s] (US) drunk or intoxicated. **4** [1970s+] (US) troubled, upset. [JAM *n.*[5]]

jammed out *adj.* [early 19C–1940s] (US) dressed up. [JAM *adj.*[1]]

jammer *n.* [1980s+] (US) a player of music. [JAM *v.*[3]]

jammie *see* JAMMY *n.*[1].

jammies *n.* [1950s+] pyjamas. [abbr.]

jammiest bits of jam *n.* [late 19C] extremely attractive young women. [JAM *n.*[3]]

jammin' *adj.* [20C] (W.I. Rasta) having a good time, dancing calypso/soca. [JAM *v.*[3]]

jamming *n.* [20C] (W.I.) severe criticism, physical assault. [JAM *v.*[2] (2)]

jamming *adj.* [1980s+] (orig. US Black) exciting, pleasing, excellent, the best. [JAM *v.*[7]]

jammiwam *v.* [1990s] (US teen) to play music together, to have a good time. [JAM *v.*[3] + redup.]

jammy/jammie *n.*[1] [1960s+] (S.Afr.) a motorcar. [abbr. JAM JAR + dimin. sfx. *-ie*]

jammy *n.*[2] [1980s+] a tampon. [JAM RAG]

jammy *n.*[3] [1980s+] (US Black) **1** the penis. **2** a handgun, a pistol. [? JIMMY *n.*[6]]

jammy *adj.*[1] [mid-19C+] easy, simple, lucky, profitable. [JAM *n.*[2]]

jammy *adj.*[2] [1960s+] (Aus.) unwashed. [lit. covered in jam]

jamoke/jamocha/jomoke *n.*[1] [late 19C+] (US) coffee. [*Java* + *Mocha* coffee beans]

jamoke *n.*[2] [1940s+] (US) a stupid or objectionable fellow. [a WW1 soldier's nickname; on the basis of the first citation (it is spelled *jamocha*) there is an apparent link to JAMOKE *n.*[1] but no obvious reason]

jamoke *n.*[3] [1960s] (US) the penis. [ety. unknown; ? ext. of JAMOKE *n.*[2] on pattern of DORK *n.*[2] etc, where the term means both a fool and a penis]

jam out *v.* [1980s+] (US campus) to listen to music. [JAM *v.*[3]]

jam pies *n.* [1990s] the eyes. [rhy. sl.]

jampot *n.*[1] [late 19C] (Aus.) a high collar. [resemblance]

jampot *n.*[2] [late 19C+] the vagina (cf. APPLE *n.*[10]). [JAM *n.*[8] (1)]

jampot *n.*[3] [1970s+] (US Black) the anus. [JAM *n.*[8] (3)]

jam rag *n.* [1960s+] a tampon, a sanitary towel. [JAM *n.*[8] (1) + RAG *n.*[9]]

jam roll *n.* [1970s+] **1** (prison) parole. **2** the dole. [rhy. sl.]

jams *n.*[1] [late 19C–1910s] **1** delirium tremens. **2** a hangover. [abbr. JIM-JAMS *n.*[1] (1)]

jams *n.*[2] [1950s] (US Black) long-playing records. [JAM *v.*[3]]

jams *n.*[3] **1** [1960s+] long and baggy shorts or swimming trunks. **2** [1960s+] pyjamas. [abbr.; (1) are seen as pyjama-like]

jam session *n.* [1920s+] (orig. US) an informal gathering, a get-together, esp. of musicians, a group discussion. [jazz use *jam session*, an impromptu concert. The first session, according to Mezz Mezzrow (*Really the Blues*, 1946), took place in late 1927 at 22 North State Street, Chicago, in the cellar of the Three Deuces speak-easy. Among those playing were Bix Beiderbecke, Bing Crosby and Mezzrow himself]

jam someone up *v.* (US Black) **1** [1960s+] to rape. **2** [1960s+] to beat, to overpower. **3** [1970s+] to talk forcefully, to challenge, to confront. [SE *jam*, to press, to squeeze, to push]

jam supper *n.* [1990s] performing cunnilingus on a menstruating woman. [JAM *n.*[8] (1) + SE *supper*]

jam tart *n.* **1** [mid–late 19C] a mart. **2** [19C+] a sweetheart, a girlfriend. **3** [20C] the heart, whether anatomically or as a card suit. [rhy. sl.]

jam the joystick see JACK THE JOYSTICK.

jam-up *adj. see* JAM *adj.*[1].

jam up *v.* [1980s+] (US campus) to give someone a hard time, to put on the spot.

jam-up and jelly-tight/jelly-tight *phr.* [1960s+] (US Black) splendid, first-rate. [JAM *adj.*[1] + JELLY *n.*[1] (2); the overall implication is sexual]

jan *n.* [17C] (Und.) a purse. [ety. unknown; ? Rom.]

jane *n.*[1] [19C] a sovereign (cf. JACK *n.*[11]; JAMES *n.*[3]; JIMMY *n.*[1]). [SE *jane*, a small silver coin from Genoa, introduced into England towards the end of the 14C]

jane *n.*[2] **1** [mid-19C+] a woman, a sweetheart, a girlfriend (cf. JILL; JILLAROO). **2** [1950s+] (US) a women's lavatory (cf. JOHN *n.*[10]). **3** [1950s–60s] (camp gay) the embodiment of one's feminine side (cf. SAM *n.*[4]). [generic use of the proper name]

jane *n.*[3] [1960s+] (drugs) marijuana. [abbr. MARY JANE *n.*[2]]

ja-nee! *excl.* (S.Afr.) **1** [1940s+] a non-committal excl. used when one wishes to avoid controversy. **2** [1970s+] an excl. used to express resignation, reluctant acquiescence. **3** [1970s+] an excl. used to express emphatic approval, 'that's a fact', 'I'll say that is', 'that's right'. **4** [1970s+] an excl. used to indicate the contradictory, paradoxical nature of a situation. **5** [1980s] an excl. used to indicate that one understands but disagrees with the previous speaker. [Afk. *ja*, yes + *nee*, no]

Jane Q Public/Citizen *n.* [1970s+] (US) the average, typical woman (cf. JOHN Q PUBLIC).

Jane Russell *n.* [20C] a mussel. [rhy. sl.; ult. film star *Jane Russell* (b.1921)]

Jane Shore *n.* [mid–late 19C] **1** the floor (cf. RORY O'MORE). **2** a prostitute. [rhy. sl.; ult. *Jane Shore* (d.1527), mistress of Edward IV]

janet *n.* [1980s+] (drugs) a quarter ounce of cannabis. [rhy. sl.; *Janet* Street-Porter (b.1944), a UK TV personality]

janey mack! *excl.* [1970s+] (Irish) a general excl., euph. for *Jesus Christ!* (cf. BEJABERS!).

janga-manga *n.* [1940s] (W.I.) a person of the lowest class. [? *jangga*, a river prawn, eaten by poor peasants + *manga* = Fr. *manger*, to eat]

jangle *n.* [mid-19C+] (US) a quarrel, an argument. [JANGLE *v.*]

jangle *v.* [mid-19C+] (US) to quarrel, to argue.

jankie/janky *n.* [1990s] (US Black) bad luck. [? SE *Yankee*, i.e. a neg. comment on White people]

janky *adj.* [1990s] (US Black teen) second-rate, inferior, unpleasant. [JANKIE *n.*]

jannie *n.* [1980s+] (US drugs) a meticulously rolled, large cannabis cigarette that burns smoothly. [? abbr. MARY-JANE *n.*[2]]

jannock *adj.* [19C] sociable, fair-dealing, honest; thus *die jannock*, to die bravely. [dial.]

janusmug *n.* [19C] a receiver of stolen goods. [*Janus*, the Roman god with two faces or MUGS *n.*[1] (1)]

j.a.p. *n.* [1970s+] (US) a rich, spoiled Jewish girl (cf. B.A.P.; JEWISH PRINCESS). [abbr. *J*ewish-*A*merican *p*rincess]

jap *n.*[1] **1** [late 19C–1940s] (US) a derog. term for a Black person. **2** [1950s–70s] (US street gang) a surprise attack by a teenage gang. **3** [1960s+] (US campus) an unexpected test, a bad surprise. [? lingering dislike of the Japanese as America's 'traditional enemy', esp. in the context of the surprise attack on Pearl Harbor in WW2]

Jap *n.*[2] [late 19C+] a derog. term for a *Jap*anese person. [abbr.]

jap *v.* [1940s+] **1** (US) to attack, esp. of street gangs, to ambush one's rivals. **2** to undermine someone's plans or efforts, to queer someone's pitch. [JAP *n.*[1]]

japan *v.* [late 18C–19C] to ordain a priest. [SE *japan*, to make black and glossy. The ref. is to the black clerical garb. Note Aus./US prison use *japanned*, said of a convict who has been converted by the chaplain]

Japanee *n.* [mid-19C+] (US) a derog. term for a *Jap*anese person (cf. CHINEE *n.*[1]). [abbr.]

Japanese knife-trick *n.* [late 19C–1900s] eating from one's knife. [the image is of chopsticks]

Japanese roller skate *n.* [1970s+] (US) a small car of Japanese manufacture.

Japanese triad *n.* [1960s+] sexual relations between one woman and two men. [stereotyping of Japanese sexual tastes]

japanning *n.* [1900s] (Aus.) stealing cash-boxes. [the *japanned* surface of such a box]

Jap crock *n.* [late 19C] (society) Japanese porcelain. [abbr. SE *Japanese* + *crockery*]

jape *v.* **1** [late 14C–late 16C] to seduce a woman. **2** [mid-15C–late 16C] to have sexual intercourse. [in 1599 *jape* appears in Florio alongside the first ever listing of *fuck*. Note its survival in 20C in certain US states, esp. North Carolina, Virginia and in the Appalachians]

japers! *excl.* [20C] (Irish) a general excl., euph. for JESUS! (cf. BEJABERS!).

Jap hash *n.* [20C] (US) chow mein. [*chow mein*, itself an ersatz form of Chinese food, invented for Western consumers, has nothing to do with Japanese cuisine]

japie *n.*[1] *see* JAAP.

japie *n.*[2] [1950s+] (Aus.) a South African. [JAAP]

Jap/Asian moll *n.* [1970s+] (N.Z.) a prostitute who specializes in Asian or Japanese customers. [JAP n./SE *Asian* + MOLL n. (1)]

jap out *v.* [1960s+] (US campus) to fail to keep an appointment, to renege. [JAP n. (2)]

jappa-jappa *adj.* [20C] (W.I.) rough, indifferent, esp. of work or personal appearance. [? Yoruba *jaba-jaba*, higgledy-piggledy, Krio *jagbajagba*, worthless stuff]

Jappo/Jappy *n.* [1940s–50s] (US) a derog. term for a *Jap*anese person. [abbr.]

Jap scrap *n.* [1980s+] (US campus) a motorcycle or appliance made in Japan.

Jap's eye *n.* [1990s] the male urethral opening at the end of the penis (cf. HOG-EYE). [its resemblance to a 'slit eye' and thus racial stereotyping]

Jap-slap *v.* [1980s+] (US) to slap someone suddenly, also used fig. [racist stereotyping of the Japanese as specialists in surprise attacks, e.g. Pearl Harbour]

Japstick *n.* [1950s–60s] (gay) the penis of an Asian man. [JAP n.[2] + STICK n.[1] + pun on the brandname *Chapstick*]

Jap wise *adj.* [20C] (US) partially, insufficiently informed. [? stereotype of Japanese stealing Western skills and reproducing the form but still lacking the innate knowledge that helped create them]

jar *n.*[1] **1** [20C] (Anglo-Irish) a stone hot-water bottle. **2** [1920s+] a glass of beer.

jar *n.*[2] [1940s–50s] fake jewellery, usu. so well made that it can pass for real; thus *do a jar up*, to trick a sucker into buying it. [? SE *jargoon*, a zircon or fake diamond]

jar *n.*[3] [1960s+] (drugs) a quantity of pills, usu. 500 or 1000 (cf. LID n.[4]). [the amount in the jars supplied to pharmacists]

jarboni *see* JABRONIE.

jarbox/jawbox *n.* [20C] (Ulster) the kitchen sink. [Scot.]

jargonelle *n.* [18C] the penis (cf. POPERINE PEAR). [SE *jargonelle*, an early-ripening brand of pear, originally limited to what gardeners condemned as a second-rate variety. It may be pure coincidence that in Fr. the fruit is known as *Cuisse Madame*, lady's thigh]

jargoozle *v.* [late 19C–1900s] to confuse, to trick. [SE *jargogle*, to confuse + BAMBOOZLE]

jarhead *n.*[1] (US Black) **1** [1930s–40s] a Black man. **2** [1940s+] a fool, a slow, stupid person. [US dial. *jarhead*, a mule (despite the obvious link to a *jar* of liquor); ult. f. pron. of *jawhead*]

jarhead *n.*[2] [1980s] an alcoholic, a heavy drinker. [SE *jar* (of liquor) + sfx. -HEAD (2)]

jark *n.* **1** [mid-16C–mid-19C] (Und.) a seal. **2** [19C] any trinket worn on a watch-chain. **3** [19C] a safe-conduct pass. **4** [19C] a watch (cf. YACK). [ety. unknown]

jark it *v.* [mid-19C] to run away. [? fig. use of SE *jerk*]

jarkman *n.* [mid-16C–mid-19C] (Und.) a mendicant villain who used his abilities of reading and writing (Latin) to forge counterfeit begging licences (cf. CANTING CREW; GYBE n.; PATRICO). [JARK N. (1) + sfx. -MAN]

jar loose *v.* [late 19C–1940s] (US) to let go, to leave.

jaro/jyro *n.* [20C] a telling off, a scolding. [Maori *whauran*, to scold]

jar of jam *n.* **1** [20C] a pram. **2** [1930s] a tram. [rhy. sl.]

jarpot *n.* [1990s] (US campus) particularly strong marijuana. [? it *jars* one's brain]

Jarrahland *n.* [20C] (Aus.) the state of Western Australia; thus *jarrah-jerker*, anyone who works in the bush. [SAusE *jarrah*, a type of eucalyptus found in Western Aus.]

jarred *adj.*[1] [1980s+] drunk. [JARHEAD n.[2]]

jarred *adj.*[2] [1990s] (US teen) emotionally disturbed, upset. [SE *jar*]

j. arthur *n.* [1940s+] **1** a bank (cf. ARTHUR). **2** masturbation (cf.

BARCLAY'S). **3** a fool. [rhy. sl. *j. arthur rank* = WANK n.; ult. the cinema magnate *J. Arthur* Rank (1888–1972)]

jarvey/jarvis/jervis *n.* [late 18C–19C] **1** a hackney coachman; thus *jervis' upper benjamin*, a coachman's greatcoat. **2** [late 18C–19C] the coach itself. **3** [19C] (US) a waistcoat. [proper name *Jarvis*]

jarvey *v.* [late 18C–19C] to drive a hackney coach. [JARVEY n.]

jarvis *see* JARVEY n.

jasbo *see* JAZZBO.

jasey/jazey *n.* [late 18C–19C] a wig, esp. one made of worsted; thus *bloke with the jasey*, a judge. [? proper name *Jersey*, a type of flax used in the making of a certain type of wig]

jasm *n.* [mid–late 19C] (US) spirit, energy (cf. JISM).

jason's fleece *n.* **1** [16C] (Und.) the gold pieces that are used to trap the victim in a money-switching fraud (cf. JACK IN A BOX n.[2]). **2** [late 17C–18C] a citizen who has been swindled of their money. [the Greek myth, where *Jason* stole the Golden Fleece + a pun on SE *fleece*, to strip someone of their money or possessions]

jasper *n.* (US) **1** [mid-19C+] a man, esp. a rustic, a peasant. **2** [1920s–30s] a Black person (cf. JAZZBO). **3** [1950s+] (US prison/Black) a lesbian. [the proper name]

jass *see* JAZZ v.[1]

jassack/jass-onkey *n.* [mid-19C+] (US) a mule. [SE *jackass* + *donkey*]

jaul *see* JOL.

java *n.* [mid-19C+] (US/Can.) coffee (cf. JAMOKE n.[1]). [Java coffee beans]

jaw *n.* **1** [mid-18C+] talk, conversation, a speech; thus *hold/stop your jaw*, stop talking. **2** [1970s] (US) sexual intercourse. [JAW v.[1]]

jaw *v.*[1] **1** [mid-18C+] to talk, to argue. **2** [19C+] to address censoriously or abusively, to scold or lecture. [SE *jaw*]

jaw *v.*[2] [mid–late 19C] to go. [? Rom. *java*, I go or Hind. *jao*, go]

jaw-ass *v.* [1960s+] (US) to talk at length. [JAW v.[1] + ARSE v.]

jawaub/juwaub *n.* [mid-19C] (Anglo-Ind.) a dismissal, a rejection. [Hind. *jawaub*, an answer]

jawbation *n.* [17C] a tedious scolding; thus *jawbatious*, tedious, argumentative, ill-humoured (cf. JAW n.; JOB n.[1]; JOBATION).

jawblock *v.* [1940s] (US Black) to talk. [one 'blocks one's jaw' with words]

jawbone *n.*[1] **1** [mid-19C–1970s] (orig. Can./US) credit. **2** [late 19C+] (US) empty talk, exaggerated promises that are not kept. **3** [1960s+] (US) political persuasion. [the verbal persuasiveness required to get goods on credit, to make political speeches etc]

jawbone *n.*[2] [mid-19C] (US) **1** a castanet. **2** a Jew's harp.

jawbone *adj.* [mid-19C–1970s] (orig. Can./US) on credit. [JAWBONE n.[1]]

jawbone *v.* **1** [late 19C–1970s] to persuade someone into extending credit, to sell or buy on credit. **2** [1940s+] to talk, to chatter. **3** [1960s+] (US) to persuade, esp. in politics.

jawbone breaker/doctor *see* JAWBREAKER n.[2]

jawbone time *n.* [1950s+] (US Und.) time spent in jail awaiting sentencing (cf. BACK TIME). [JAWBONE n.[1] (2); the judge is still talking about how many years to give the guilty person]

jawboning *n.* [1960s+] (US) a political or industrial tactic whereby a negotiator or leader attempts to talk two warring sides out of making unreasonable demands. [JAWBONE v. (3)]

jawbox *see* JARBOX.

jawbreaker *n.*[1] [mid-19C+] a word that the speaker considers so long or complex that its pronunciation threatens to be harmful (cf. JAW-TWISTER).

jawbreaker / jawbone breaker / jawbone doctor *n.*[2] [1930s+] (US) a dentist (cf. JAW CRACKER; JAWSMITH).

jaw-breaking *adj.* [19C] of words and speech, hard to pronounce. [JAWBREAKER n.¹]

jaw cove *n.* [mid-19C] (US Und.) **1** a lawyer. **2** an auctioneer. [JAW v.¹ + COVE]

jaw cracker/puller *n.* [1930s+] (US) a dentist (cf. JAWBREAKER n.²).

jawelnofine *phr.* [1980s+] (S.Afr.) a general response (usu. ironical and resigned) to any form of information, 'fair enough', 'what can I say? that's life.' [Afk. *ja*, yes + SE *well* + *no* + *fine*; coined by R.J.B. Wilson, broadcaster with South African Broadcasting Association]

jawfest *n.* [1900s–30s] (US) a long chat or talking session. [JAW n. (1) + sfx. -FEST]

jaw-flapping *n.* [1950s+] (US) empty chatter.

jawing *n.* **1** [late 18C–late 19C] talk, a conversation. **2** [19C–1920s] a telling-off, a scolding. [JAW v.¹]

jawing-tackle *n.* [early–mid-19C] (US) the mouth, the tongue, as used in talking (cf. JAW-TACKLE). [JAW v.¹ (1)]

jaw-jacking *n.* [1960s+] (US Black) voluble or excessive talking (cf. RUN OFF AT THE MOUTH). [US Black pron. of *jaw-jerking/-jerking off*, i.e. 'verbal masturbation']

jaw-jaw *v.* [1950s+] to talk, to converse, to discuss. [JAW v.¹ (1) + redup. Note Prime Minister Harold Macmillan's dictum delivered at Canberra, 30 January 1958: 'Jaw-jaw is better than war-war']

jawkins *n.* [mid-19C] a club bore. [used in clubs and taken f. William Thackeray's *Book of Snobs* (1848), where it is the name of one such character]

jawl *see* JOL.

jaw-mag *n.* [late 19C] talk, conversation, a speech. [JAW n. (1) + MAG n.²]

jaw-me-dead/-dad *n.* [late 18C–1900s] a chatterer. [JAW n. (1); lit. someone who will talk one to death]

jawn *n.* [1980s+] (US campus) something that causes happiness, joy or excitement (cf. CHUMPIE). [ety. unknown]

jawn *adj.* [1990s] (US teen) used of someone or something considered to be the absolute best, the ultimate, the finest.

jawp *v.* [19C] **1** to talk. **2** to inform. **3** to confess. [Scot. *jawp*, to make a light splashing sound]

jaw puller *see* JAW CRACKER.

jaws *n.*¹ [1940s+] (US) the vaginal labia. [the myth of the *vagina dentata*]

jaws, the *n.*² [1960s+] (US) anger. [? the grinding of one's teeth]

jawsmith/jaw-smith *n.* **1** [late 19C–1940s] (US) a talkative person, a demagogue. **2** [1930s–40s] (US) a dentist.

jaw-tackle/jaw-tackle fall *n.* [mid-19C–1910s] (US) the mouth, the tongue, as used in talking (cf. JAWING TACKLE). [JAW v.¹ (1) + SE *tackle*]

jaw-twister *n.* [mid-19C+] a word that the speaker considers so long or complex that its pronunciation threatens to be harmful (cf. JAWBREAKER n.¹).

jax *see* JACK'S ALIVE.

jaxey/jaxie *see* JACKSY-PARDO.

jaxy/joxy *n.* [20C] the female genitals. [? JACKSIE]

jay *n.*¹ [early 16C–early 17C] a cheeky chatterer. [SE *jay* (*Garrulus glandarius*), a bird noted for its noisiness]

jay *n.*² [16C–1970s+] a showy or flashy woman, a prostitute. [SE *jay* (*Garrulus glandarius*), a bird noted, *inter alia*, for its noisiness and bright colouring. 20C use is US Black]

jay *n.*³ (US) **1** [late 19C–1940s] a rustic, a simpleton, a novice, a newcomer. **2** [late 19C] (college) a person who does something disagreeable or foolish. [16C SE *jay*, a simpleton; ult. SE *jay* (*Garrulus glandarius*) a bird that is typified as noisy and boorish towards other birds]

jay/jaybird *n.*⁴ [1960s+] (drugs) a marijuana cigarette. [play on J n.²]

jay *adj.* [late 19C–1950s] (US) worthless, unsophisticated; thus *jay town*, a backward, provincial township. [JAY n.³ (1)]

jay *v.* [1990s] (US) to steal. [JAYHAWK v.]

jaybird *n.*¹ [late 19C+] (US) a rustic, a simpleton, a novice, a newcomer. [JAY n.³ (1)]

jaybird *n.*² *see* JAY n.⁴.

jaybird *adj.*¹ [late 19C+] (US) inferior, contemptible. [JAY n.³]

jaybird *adj.*² [1960s+] (US) stark naked (cf. JAYBIRD-NAKED). [abbr. NAKED AS A JAYBIRD]

jaybird-naked *adj.* [1940s+] (US) stark naked. [NAKED AS A JAYBIRD]

jayhawk *n.* **1** [late 19C+] (US) a rustic, a simpleton, a novice, a newcomer (cf. JAY n.³). **2** [20C] (US) a mythical bird used as an emblem of Kansas (cf. JAYHAWKER). **3** [1950s] (US) a Kansan (cf. JAYHAWKER). [(3) combines (1) + (2)]

jayhawk *v.* [mid-19C+] (US esp. army, orig. Civil War) to raid, to plunder, to steal, to operate as a guerrilla soldier. [neg. image of the SE *jay*, the bird]

jayhawker *n.* **1** [mid-19C+] (US) a native of Kansas. **2** [late 19C–1950s] (US) a rustic, a simpleton. [the alleged similarity of Kansans – raping and pillaging during the US Civil War (1861–5) – to the SE *jay*, noted for its aggressive, bullying relations with other birds]

jayhoo *see* JEHU.

jay house *n.* [late 19C–1900s] (US) a brothel, esp. one that specializes in exploiting out-of-town innocents and tourists to the big city (cf. ACCOMMODATION HOUSE). [JAY n.³ + HOUSE n.¹]

Jays *n.* [20C] (Irish) members of the Society of Jesus, the Jesuits.

jay smoke *n.* [1960s+] (drugs) marijuana. [JAY n.⁴]

jaytown *n.* [20C] (US) a small town (cf. HICKTOWN). [JAY n.³ (1) + SE *town*]

jazey *see* JASEY.

jazz *n.*¹ **1** [late-19C–1930s] (orig. US Black) sexual intercourse. **2** [1910s+] (US) spirit, energy, excitement. **3** [1930s] (US) semen (cf. JISM). **4** [1950s+] (US) thing, stuff. [ety. unknown; ? Mandingo *jasi*, to act in an out-of-the-ordinary manner or late 19C Fr. *jaser/jazer*, to copulate. The best suggestions link the term to the African West Coast, whence many slaves were imported. There, it meant 'hurry up' and was used as such in Creole dial. to name the fast, syncopated music that emerged in New Orleans in the late 19C. Today *jazz* is generally associated with a musical style, which remains its SE def. It had first appeared in New York in 1915, pioneered by the Original Creole Band of Freddie Keppard (1890–1933). Few registered that show, but far more acknowledged a second arrival, in 1917, played by Nick LaRocca's Original Dixieland Jazz Band at the smart Reisenweber's restaurant. None the less there were those, both Black and White, who acknowledged the background. As *Étude* magazine put it in 1924: 'If the truth were known about the origin of the word "Jazz" it would never be mentioned in polite society.' In 1927 America's *Journal of Abnormal & Social Psychology* declared that 'the word jazz ... used both as a verb and as a noun to denote the sex act ... has long been common vulgarity among Negroes in the South']

jazz *n.*² [1910s+] (US) misleading, untrue, empty or pretentious talk, nonsense. [fig. use of JAZZ n.¹]

jazz/jass *v.*¹ **1** [late 19C+] (orig. US Black) to have sexual intercourse. **2** [1910s+] (US) to enliven, to inspire, to excite (cf. JAZZ UP). [JAZZ n.¹]

jazz *v.*² [1910s+] (US) **1** to mess up, to confuse, to tease. **2** to lie, to deceive. [JAZZ n.²]

jazz around *v.* [1910s–60s] to fool about, to idle, to lead a fast life, mainly in pursuit of sex. [JAZZ v.¹ + SE *around*]

jazz baby n. [late 19C–1930s] a flighty young girl, usu. middle-class, in her late teens or very early 20s, who sported short, bobbed hair, lipstick, skimpy dresses and generally led a lifestyle as far as possible removed from that of her parents (cf. FLAPPER n.³). [SE *jazz*/JAZZ n.¹ + BABY n.² (1); whether the jazz refers to sex or music, or to something of both, remains debatable. Note Merrill and Jerome's popular US song, 'Jazz Baby' (1919)]

jazzbo/jazz-bo/jasbo n. [1910s+] (US) **1** a fellow, a man, esp. a fashionable young man (cf. JELLY BEAN n.¹). **2** slapstick comedy. **3** a dissolute person. **4** a Black vaudeville performer, esp. in a 'black and white minstrel' show. **5** the finale of a vaudeville bill, when all the acts joined together on stage (according to the composer John Philip Sousa (1854–1932), this is the original source for *jazz*). **6** a Black person, esp. a man or soldier (cf. JIGABOO n.¹). [? proper name *Jasper* or SE *jazz*/JAZZ n.¹ + SE *boy*]

jazzed adj. [1910s+] (US campus) excited, thrilled, pleased; thus *unjazzed*, depressed. [JAZZ v.¹ (2)]

jazzed up adj. [1910s–60s] (US) intoxicated by drugs or alcohol. [JAZZ v.¹ (2)]

jazzer n. [1910s+] (orig. US) **1** a jazz musician. **2** a jazz fan. [SE *jazz*]

jazzhound n.¹ [1920s] (US) a jazz enthusiast. [SE *jazz* + sfx. -HOUND]

jazzhound n.² [1920s] (US) a sexually promiscuous man. [JAZZ n.¹ (1) + sfx. -HOUND]

jazz house n. [1920s] (US) a brothel (cf. ACCOMMODATION HOUSE). [JAZZ n.¹ (1) + HOUSE n.¹]

jazzing n.¹ [1910s+] (US) playing jazz music. [SE *jazz*]

jazzing n.² [1950s] (US) having sexual intercourse. [JAZZ n.¹ (1)]

jazz mag n. [1990s] an 'adult' pornographic magazine. [JAZZ n.¹ (1) + MAG n.³ (1)]

jazz one's joy stick, to phr. [1990s] to masturbate. [JAZZ v.¹ (1) + JOYSTICK n.¹ (2)]

jazz up v. [1910s+] to brighten up, to improve, to make more gaudy. [JAZZ v.¹ (2)]

jazzy adj. (US) **1** [1910s+] bright, lively, exciting. **2** [1920s+] ostentatious, brash. [SE *jazz*. Both defs. refer to the music and its image rather than to the sl. use]

j.b. n.¹ [1930s] a hat made by the *John B.* Stetson Company. [abbr.]

j.b. n.² [1940s+] (US) a Black person. [abbr. *jet black*; also a pun on *j.c.* or *jaycee*, a respectable, middle-class White person]

J. Carroll Naish n. [1970s] urination. [rhy. sl. *J. Carroll Naish* = SLASH n.⁴; ult. US actor *J. Carroll Naish* (1900–73)]

j.c.l. n. [1940s+] (US) a novice. [abbr. JOHNNY-COME-LATELY]

j.d. n. **1** [1950s+] *juvenile delinquent*. **2** [1970s] (US Und.) *John Doe*. **3** [1970s+] *Jack Daniels* whisky (cf. JACK n.³¹). [abbr.]

jeames n. [mid-19C] the *Morning Post* newspaper. [deliberately tortured pron. of proper name *James* and thus a generic term for a footman or a pej. for a flunkey. This in turn based on Thackeray's servant *Jeames* in the *Diary of C. Jeames de la Pluche, Esq.* (1846). Until it was swallowed up by the *Daily Telegraph* (in 1937), the ultra-conservative *Morning Post* was the paper of choice for the British upper classes]

jean-baptiste n. [late 19C+] a French Canadian. [the 'typical' name]

jean potage n. [19C] (US) a French-born immigrant (cf. PEA-SOUP). [Fr. *Jean potage*, John(ny) soup]

jeasley/jeasly see JEEZLY.

Jebby n. [1940s+] (US) a Jesuit. [abbr.]

'jects n. [1990s] (US Black teen) something that is cheap. [abbr. of housing *projects*, considered to be the lowest form of housing]

Jedburgh/Jedwood/Jeddart justice n. [18C–early 19C] **1** execution before a trial (cf. CUPAR JUSTICE). **2** severe and often arbitrary justice as administered by petty local magistrates. [the level of *justice* meted out in the courts of *Jedburgh*]

jee! see GEE.

jeebies/jeeby n. [1930s+] (US) unpleasant fantasies, nameless terrors, anything the mind can conjure up to produce nerves and fear. [abbr. HEEBIE-JEEBIES]

jee gee n. [1960s+] (drugs) heroin. [? DUJI]

jeek adj. [1980s+] (US campus) smartly dressed, stylish, fashionable (cf. G.Q.). [pron. of *GQ* or *Gentleman's Quarterly* magazine]

jeems! excl. [mid-19C+] (US) used in mild oaths as euph. for JESUS! (cf. BEJABERS!).

jeep n.¹ **1** [1930s–50s] (US) a cartoon character, a small animal. **2** [1930s+] (US) a stupid, inept or inexperienced person. **3** [1940s] (US Black) a drunkard. [Eugene the *Jeep*, an animal with amazing powers, created in 1936 by E.C. Segar (1894–1938) and incorporated in his cartoon *Popeye*]

jeep n.² [1930s+] any form of vehicle. [general *purpose* vehicle; but supposedly influenced by E.C. Segar's cartoon character, Eugene the *Jeep* (cf. JEEP n.¹)]

jeep n.³ [1960s] (drugs) a paper 'collar' used by a drug user to secure the needle in an eye-dropper before injecting the heroin/water solution (cf. GEEZE). [var. on GEE n.⁶]

jeepers! excl. [1920s+] (orig. US) a mild oath, euph. for JESUS! (cf. BEJABERS!).

jeepers creepers! excl. [20C] euph. for *Jesus Christ!*; usu. as a mild oath (cf. BEJABERS!).

jeer see JERE.

Jeese! see JEEZ!

jeeter n. [1930s–60s] (US) a rustic, a peasant. [*Jeeter* Lester, the poor White peasant protagonist of Erskine Caldwell's novel *Tobacco Road* (1932)]

jeetled adj. [20C] (Ulster) exhausted. [Scot. *jeetle*, to delay, to idle]

jeez!/jeeze!/jeese! excl. [1920s+] (orig. US) a mild excl., euph. for JESUS! (cf. BEJABERS!).

jeezer n.¹ [1970s] (US) a man, fellow. [GEEZER n.¹ (1)]

jeezer n.² [1980s] (US) something remarkable. [it makes one exclaim JESUS!]

jeezle!/jeezle-peezle! excl. [1970s+] a mild oath, euph. for JESUS! (cf. BEJABERS!).

jeezly/jeasley/jeasly adj. **1** [1920s+] (US) darned, DAMNED. **2** [1990s] (US) inferior. [var. on JESUSLY!]

jeezy-peezy adj. [1960s] (US teen) very easy (cf. EASY-PEASY).

jeff n. [1930s+] (US Black) **1** a derog. term for a White rustic, a peasant, esp. a Southerner. **2** a White person, esp. if a racist. **3** a dull, stupid person, a pest. [abbr. proper name *Jefferson Davis* (1808–89), president of the Confederate States 1861–5. Note mid-19C circus jargon *tight-jeff*, a tight-rope, *slack-jeff*, a slack rope]

jeff v. **1** [20C] (US Und.) to lie. **2** [20C] (US prison) to tease, to joke with. **3** [1960s] (US Black) to talk, to chatter, esp. to seduce, to fool or deceive with a 'line'; thus *tight jeff*, well-rehearsed patter, *slack jeff*, spontaneous ad-libbed chatter. **4** [1960s+] (US Black) to behave obsequiously towards Whites, to humiliate oneself (cf. TOM v.). [abbr. proper name *Jefferson Davis* (1808–89), president of the Confederate States during the US Civil War 1861–5]

jeff artist/hat n. [1930s+] **1** (US) a liar, a confidence trickster. **2** (US Black) a Black person who behaves subserviently towards Whites. [JEFF n. + ARTIST n.¹/SE *hat*]

jeff davis v. [1960s] (US Black) **1** to talk, to chatter, esp. to seduce, to fool. **2** [1960s+] (US Black) to behave obsequiously towards Whites, to humiliate oneself (cf. JEFF v.). [abbr. proper name *Jefferson Davis* (1808–89), president of the Confederate States during the US Civil War 1861–5]

jeffer *n.* [1960s+] a rustic, a peasant. [JEFF n.]

jefferson airplane *n.* [1980s+] (US drugs) a split match that is used as an improvised holder for the last fraction of a marijuana cigarette. [*Jefferson Airplane*, one of the most successful 'psychedelic bands' of the 1960s]

jeffey *see* JIFFY.

jeff hat *see* JEFF ARTIST.

jeffing *n.* (US Black) **1** [1950s] working a confidence trick, fooling a victim. **2** [1970s] acting subserviently towards Whites (cf. TOMMING n.²). [JEFF v.]

jeffy *see* JIFFY.

jeflon *n.* [1980s+] (US campus) someone who is unaware of what is going on. [JEFF n. (3) + brandname *Teflon*, a nonstick coating for cookware]

jehoshaphat! *excl.* [mid-19C+] used in a variety of mild oaths; euph. for JESUS! (cf. BEJABERS!; JERUSALEM!).

jehu/jayhoo *n.* [1900s–40s] (US) a rustic, simpleton. [the 'rustic' name *Jehu*? + JAY n.³ (1)]

jekyll *n.* [1930s–40s] (S.Afr.) a brandy and Coca-Cola. [*Dr Jekyll and Mr Hyde* (1866), the story by R.L. Stevenson; the phr. reverses the actual tale, where Dr *Jekyll* is the good figure, i.e. the soft drink, and Mr *Hyde* is the villain, i.e. the alcohol]

jekyll and hyde *adj.* [1920s+] crooked, fake, spurious, counterfeit. [rhy. sl. *jekyll and hyde* = SNIDE adj.]

jekyll and hydes *n.* [20C] (Aus.) trousers. [rhy. sl. *jekyll and hydes* = STRIDES]

jel/jell *n.* [1980s] (US teen) an appalling, unacceptable person. [abbr. JELLO BRAIN]

jeldi *see* JILDI n.

jell *n.¹* [1950s+] (Aus.) a coward (cf. JELLY BELLY).

jell *n.² see* JEL.

jell *v.¹* [1930s+] (US campus) to idle, to loaf around, to relax (cf. GEL v.; JELLY v.²). [SE *gel*, to set solid]

jell *v.² see* JELLY v.².

jell/jell out *v.³* [1980s+] (US campus) to relax by doing nothing, to calm down (cf. JELL v.¹). [to turn into *Jell-O/jelly*]

jell around *see* JELLY v.².

jellied *adj.* [20C] under the influence of tranquillizers. [JELLIES]

jellied eels *n.* [20C] wheels, i.e. transport. [rhy. sl.]

jellied out *adj.* [1930s] (US campus) dressed up. [JELLY BEAN n.¹ (5)]

jellies *n.* [1980s+] (drugs) temazepam (cf. JELLY n.⁶).

jello/jello-brain *n.* [1980s+] (US campus) **1** a foolish, scatter-brained person whose brain is like jelly. **2** an older person. [*Jell-O* the brandname of a gelatine dessert/+ sfx. *-brain*]

jello squad *n.* [1980s+] (US campus) an imaginary gathering or club of all those students considered beyond the social pale of their peers on campus. [JELLO + SE *squad*]

jell out *see* JELL v.³.

jelly *n.¹* **1** [17C–19C] semen (cf. BABY GRAVY). **2** [1920s+] (US Black) the penis or the vagina (cf. APPLE n.¹⁰; JELLY BABY n.¹; JELLY BAG; JELLY BOX; JELLY ROLL n.). **3** [1920s+] (US Black) sexual intercourse (cf. GIVE JUICE FOR JELLY).

jelly *n.²* [19C–1940s] (US Black) a tough, virile man. [? 17C–18C SE *jelly*, seminal fluid or dial. *jelly*, upright, worthy]

jelly *n.³* [late 19C–1930s] a buxom, pretty young woman. [she 'wobbles']

jelly/gelly *n.⁴* [1930s+] (US) a close friend, esp. a girlfriend or boyfriend. [abbr. JELLY ROLL n.]

jelly *n.⁵* [1940s+] (orig. Aus.) *geli*gnite. [abbr./pron.]

jelly *n.⁶* [1970s+] (drugs) cocaine (cf. JELLIES).

jelly *v.¹* **1** [1930s–50s] (US) to dance (cf. JELLY ASS; JITTERBUG v.). **2** [1950s] (US Black) to have sexual intercourse (cf. JELLY ROLL v.). **3** [1970s–80s] (US street gang) to beat someone up.

jelly/jell/jell around *v.²* [1930s+] (US campus) to idle, to relax, esp. at a soda fountain or caf□ (cf. GEL v.; JELL v.¹; JELLY-DATE).

jelly ass *v.* [1930s–50s] (US) to dance (cf. JELLY v.¹). [? the shaking of one's ARSE n.¹]

jelly baby *n.¹* [1920s+] secretions from the anus or vagina during or after intercourse. [JELLY n.¹]

jelly baby *n.²* [1960s+] (drugs) amphetamine (cf. A n.²). [var. on JELLY BEAN n.² (1)]

jelly bag *n.* [17C] **1** the testicles. **2** the vagina (cf. APPLE n.¹⁰). [JELLY n.¹]

jelly ball *n.* [1970s] (US) a weak-willed person.

jelly bean *n.¹* **1** [1910s–50s] (US) a sweetheart. **2** [1910s+] (US) a foolish, inept or effeminate person. **3** [1910s+] an unpleasant, weak or dishonest person, esp. a pimp. **4** [1920s–30s] a highschool student, esp. one devoted to pleasure rather than work. **5** [1920s–50s] a fashionably dressed young man, a womanizer (cf. JAZZBO; SHEIK). **6** [1930s–50s] (US Black) a term of address.

jelly bean *n.²* **1** [1900s] (US campus) a painkiller. **2** [1960s+] (drugs) any form of pill, e.g. a barbiturate, an amphetamine. [the drugs resemble sweets]

jelly beans *n.* [1990s] (drugs) crack cocaine. [JELLY BEAN n.² (1); although there is no actual similarity of crack cocaine to sweets]

jelly belly *n.* **1** [late 19C+] a fat person. **2** [1930s+] (Aus.) a coward.

jelly box *n.* [1920s+] (orig. US) the vagina (cf. APPLE n.¹⁰). [JELLY n.¹ + SE *box*/BOX n.⁶ (2)]

jelly-/bean-/cake-/coke-date *n.* [1920s–40s] (US campus) a date to take a girlfriend to the soda fountain or similar, where one sits and chats. [the relevant SE *food* + DATE n.³]

jelly-dog *n.* [late 19C] a harrier; thus *jelly-dogging*, hunting with a harrier. [the dog's use in hunting hares, which, when caught, killed and cooked, are served with redcurrant jelly]

jellyfish *n.* [1930s] a weak, ineffectual, cowardly person.

jellyhead *see* GELLYHEAD.

jelly roll *n.* (US Black) **1** [late 19C+] a lover, a spouse. **2** [1920s–40s] the female genitals (cf. APPLE n.¹⁰). **3** [1920s+] sexual intercourse. [SAmE *jelly roll*, a doughnut, which has a hole at its centre]

jelly roll *v.* [1920s+] (US Black) to have sexual intercourse. [JELLY ROLL n.]

jelly roller *n.* [1960s] (US Black) a womanizer, a seducer. [JELLY ROLL v.]

jelly sandwich *n.* [1970s] (US Black) a sanitary towel. [JELLY n.¹ (2) + SE *sandwich*]

jelly snatchers *n.* [1970s] (US Black) the hands. [JELLY n.¹ + SE *snatchers*]

jelly-tight *see* JAM-UP AND JELLY-TIGHT.

jem *n.¹* [late 18C–19C] (Und.) a jewel, a gold ring. [SE *gem*]

jem/jembo *n.²* [1940s+] (Irish) a generic name for a Dubliner. [abbr. JEMMY n.¹]

jemima *n.¹* **1** [late 19C] a servant girl. **2** [late 19C–1900s] a chamberpot. **3** [late 19C–1920s] a dressmaker's dummy. [generic use of proper name; the removal of (2) is one of the servant's (1) tasks]

jemima *n.²* [1950s+] (gay) the Black female genitals. [AUNT JEMIMA, the stereotypical Black 'mammy']

jemima! *excl.* [mid-19C+] (US) euph. for JESUS!; used in a variety of mild oaths.

jemimas *n.* [1900s+] elastic-sided boots. [ety. unknown; ? a brandname or link to JEMMY adj.¹ (3)]

jemima suit *n.* [1990s] a leather or rubber item of clothing with strategically placed holes over the erogenous zones. [ety. unknown]

jeminy-o! *excl.* [mid-19C] a general excl., euph. for JESUS! (cf. BEJABERS!).

jem mace *n.* [20C] face (cf. CHEVY CHASE). [rhy. sl.; ult. the prize-fighter *Jem Mace* (1831–1910)]

jemmy *n.*[1] 1 [mid-18C–early 19C] a dandy. 2 [mid-late 18C] a light cane, as carried by a dandy. 3 [mid-19C–1910s] a shooting coat, a great coat. [16C SE *gim*, smart, spruce and thus ? linked to Scot. *jimp*, slender]

jemmy *n.*[2] [mid-19C] 1 a sheep's head (cf. BLOODY JEMMY). 2 a large human head. [ety. unknown]

jemmy *n.*[3] [mid-late 19C] (Aus.) an immigrant. [? abbr. JIMMY GRANT]

jemmy/jenny *n.*[4] [mid-19C+] (Und.) a house-breaker's short crowbar (cf. BESS *n.*[1]; JAMES *n.*[1]).

jemmy *adj.*[1] 1 [mid-late 18C] clever, 'sharp'. 2 [mid-18C–mid-19C] dandified, e.g. a *jemmy fellow*, a smart, well-turned out, dandified man, *jemminess*, neatness, smartness, *jemmily*, smartly. 3 [mid-19C] smart, of superior class. [JEMMY *n.*[1]]

jemmy *adj.*[2] [mid-19C–1900s] rubbishy, nonsensical (cf. ALL JEMMY!).

jemmy jessamy *n.* [mid-18C–mid-19C] a smart, well-turned-out fellow. [JEMMY *n.*[1] + JESSAMY]

jemmy jessamy *adj.* [mid-18C–mid-19C] smart, well-turned-out.

Jemmy/Jimmy O'Goblin *n.* [mid-19C+] (orig. theatre) a sovereign. [rhy. sl.]

Jemmy/Jimmy O'Goblins *n.* [mid-19C+] money (cf. JEMMY O'GOBLIN). [rhy. sl. *Jemmy O'Goblins* = sovereigns]

jemson/jimmison *n.* [1920s–50s] (US) the penis. [? SE *jimsonweed*, i.e. the penis also grows]

jeng-jeng *n.* [20C] (W.I./Jam., Bel.) 1 anything considered worthless, a useless collection of bits and bobs. 2 of things or of personal appearance, a general state of confusion. [Carib.E. *jege*, rags, tatters ? + Ngombe *jengé*, disorder]

jeng-jeng *adj.* [20C] (W.I./Jam., Bel.) disreputable, unpleasant. [JENG-JENG *n.*]

jennie lee/jenny lea *n.* [20C] 1 a flea. 2 a key. 3 tea (cf. ROSIE LEA). [rhy. sl.]

jenny *n.*[1] [18C+] a donkey (cf. BALDWIN). [post-18C uses are US]

jenny *n.*[2] *see* JEMMY *n.*[4].

jenny *n.*[3] [late 19C] (US) a young woman. [dial. *jenny*, a country girl]

jenny *n.*[4] [late 19C–1920s] a hot-water bottle. [? abbr. SE, it *generates* warmth; note TV/film jargon *jenny*, an operator]

jenny *n.*[5] [1990s] (US) the vagina. [abbr.]

jenny/jenny-ass/jinny-wing *adj.* [20C] (Irish) of a man, effeminate.

jenny *v.*[1] [late 19C] (Und.) to understand. [ety. unknown; ? link to JERRY *adj.*]

jenny/jinny *v.*[2] [20C] of a woman, to nag, to henpeck. [SE *jenny*, used as a pfx. denoting the female sex]

jenny-ass *see* JENNY *adj.*

jenny darby *n.* [mid-19C] a policeman (cf. JOHNNY DARBY). [*gendarmes* + ref. to DARBIES]

jenny hills *n.* [late 19C] pills. [rhy. sl.; ult. UK music-hall star *Jenny Hill* (1851–96)]

jenny lea *see* JENNIE LEE.

Jenny Lind *n.*[1] [mid-19C] a 'wide-awake' hat. [for ety. *see* JENNY LIND *n.*[2] and note Yorks. dial. *Jenny Lind pie*, a bone pie]

Jenny Lind *n.*[2] [20C] wind, either in the context of weather or the human stomach; thus *Jenny Lindy*, windy. [rhy. sl.; ult. the Swedish soprano *Jenny Lind* (1820–87)]

jenny linda/linder *n.* [mid-19C] a window. [rhy. sl.; *see* JENNY LIND *n.*[2]]

jenny wine *n.* [20C] (Irish) one who abstains from alcohol, a teetotaller. [? JENNY *adj.*]

jenny wren *n.* [20C] Ben Truman beer. [rhy. sl.]

jentoe *see* GENTOO.

jere/jeer *n.*[1] [16C] (Und.) a piece of human excrement (cf. JEREPECK). [Rom. *jeer*, excrement]

jere/jeer *n.*[2] [20C] a homosexual. [? rhy. sl. *jere* = QUEER *n.*[1]]

jereboam *n.* [mid-19C] a chamberpot (cf. JERRY *n.*[3]).

jeremiah *n.* [1930s] a fire (cf. ANNA MARIA). [rhy. sl.]

jeremiah *v.* [late 19C–1930s] to complain. [proper name *Jeremiah*, the biblical prophet]

jeremiah-mongering *n.* [late 19C] (society) needless pessimism. [JEREMIAH *n.* + sfx. *-monger*; coined to describe those who proclaimed that after the fall of Khartoum in 1885 all was over for the Empire and thus Britain]

Jeremy Beadle *n.* [20C] irritation, annoyance. [rhy. sl. *Jeremy Beadle* = the NEEDLE *n.*[3]; ult. the UK TV entertainer]

jeremy diddler *see* DIDDLER *n.*[1].

jere-peck *n.* [17C] a sewer. [JERE *n.*[1] + *peck*, a vessel or container]

jericho *n.* 1 [mid-17C–late 19C] a place of retirement, banishment or concealment, a far-distant place, esp. in phr. *let someone go to jericho*. 2 [mid-18C–late 19C] a privy, an outside lavatory. [anecdote in 2 Sam. x.5 when David ordered his servants to stay in that city until their beards were grown]

jerk *n.*[1] 1 [1930s+] (US) a male masturbator. 2 [1930s+] (orig. US) a fool, an idiot, a failure. [JERK OFF *v.*[1]; (1) may be earlier]

jerk *n.*[2] [1940s+] (US) an ice-cream soda or soda-fountain clerk. [abbr. SAmE *soda jerk*]

jerk *v.*[1] 1 [mid-18C–early 19C] to accost. 2 [late 18C–19C] to write or utter. 3 [1910s+] (US) to dismiss, to disqualify, to withdraw. 4 [1980s+] (US) to cheat, to mistreat. 5 [1980s+] (US campus) to mess around, to annoy deliberately, to harass (cf. JERK AROUND).

jerk *v.*[2] [mid-19C+] (US) to draw a gun or weapon.

jerk *v.*[3] 1 [mid-19C+] (US) to take, to snatch. 2 [late 19C+] (US) to draw beer, soda etc from a tap.

jerk *v.*[4] [late 19C+] to masturbate. [abbr. JERK OFF *v.*[1]]

jerk *v.*[5] [1910s–20s] (US drugs) to inject a drug (cf. JACK OFF *v.*[2]).

jerk a gybe, to *phr.* [mid-17C–early 18C] (Und.) to forge a licence. [JERK *v.*[1] (2) + GYBE *n.*]

jerk a knot, to *phr.* [1940s+] (US) to hit or punch someone. [SE *knot*, a lump or bruise]

jerk around *v.* 1 [1930s+] (US) to treat badly. 2 [1960s+] (US) to tease someone, to fool around, to mess about.

jerk-ass *n.* [1960s+] (US) a contemptible idiot. [JERK *n.*[1] (2) + ARSE *n.*[1]]

jerk/snatch bald-headed *v.* [mid-19C–1930s] (US) to treat roughly, to manhandle.

jerk chin music, to *phr.* [19C] (US) to chatter, to gossip. [JERK *v.*[1] (2) + CHIN MUSIC]

jerked/jerked up/off *adj.* [1950s+] (US) exceedingly stupid. [JERK-OFF *n.*[2] (1)]

jerker *n.*[1] 1 [mid-late 19C] a drinker. 2 [1920s] (US) a soda-fountain clerk. [JERK *v.*[3] (2)]

jerker *n.*[2] [late 19C] a chamberpot. [? JERE *n.*[1]]

jerker *n.*[3] [1940s+] a masturbator, esp. one who frequents striptease shows or similar. [JERK OFF *v.*[1]]

jerkface *n.* [1970s] (US campus) a foolish, dull person (cf. JERKHEAD). [JERK *n.*[1] + sfx. *-face*]

jerkhead *n.* [1980s+] (US) a stupid, contemptible person (cf. JERKFACE). [JERK *n.*[1] + sfx. *-HEAD* (1)]

jerking *n.* [late 19C+] masturbation. [JERK OFF *v.*[1]]

jerking each other off *phr.* [20C] (Aus.) indulging in mutual flattery (cf. UP EACH OTHER). [fig. use of JERK OFF *v.*[1]; the image is of mutual masturbation]

jerking off the jelly juice *phr.* [1990s] masturbation. [JERK OFF *v.*[1] + JELLY *n.*[1] (1)]

jerk-nod *n.* [mid-19C] a donkey (cf. YEKNOD). [backsl.]

jerko *n.* [1940s+] (US) a stupid, contemptible person. [JERK n.¹ + sfx. -o]

jerk-off *n.*¹ [1920s+] (US) an act of masturbation. [JERK OFF v.¹]

jerk-off *n.*² **1** [1930s+] (US) a useless, despised person, a lazy incompetent (cf. JACK OFF v.¹). **2** [1970s+] (US) a fraud, a pretence. [fig. uses of JERK-OFF n.¹]

jerk-off *adj.* [1930s+] (US) stupid, worthless, despicable. [JERK OFF v.²]

jerk off *v.*¹ [late 19C+] to masturbate (cf. BEAT OFF).

jerk off *v.*² **1** [1940s+] (US) to mess around, to waste time or energy. **2** [1960s+] (US) to get away. **3** [1960s+] (US) to tease, to cheat, to treat badly, to infuriate someone. **4** [1960s+] (US) to fiddle with an object, to interfere maliciously. [fig. uses of JERK OFF v.¹]

jerk one's gherkin, to *phr.* [20C] to masturbate (cf. PUMP ONE'S PICKLE).

jerk one's jaw *see* JACK ONE'S JAW.

jerk one's jelly / joystick / juice / mutton / rod / rope / turk / turkey, to *phr.* [late 19C+] to masturbate (cf. ACCOST THE OSCAR MEYER; JERK OFF v.¹). [SE *jerk* + JELLY n.¹ (2)/JOYSTICK n.¹ (2)/JUICE n.² (2)/MUTTON n.² (2)/ROD n.¹ (1)/SE *rope*/TURKEY (NECK)]

jerk over *v.* [1980s+] (US) to spoil, to upset, to botch up. [var. on JERK OFF v.²]

jerks *n.*¹ **1** [19C] a hangover. **2** [late 19C] (US) delirium tremens, acute anxiety or religious fervour (cf. JUMPS).

jerks *n.*² [20C] (Aus.) the pieces of cork that are suspended from a hatbrim to distract flies. [abbr. FLY JERKS]

jerk-silly/-simple *adj.* [1930s+] (US) mentally unbalanced, supposedly from chronic masturbation. [JERK OFF v.¹]

jerk someone around, to *phr.* [1960s+] (orig. US) to waste someone's time, to irritate. [fig. use of JERK OFF v.¹]

jerk someone's chain, to *phr.* [1960s+] to annoy, to distract forcefully, to taunt (cf. JERK SOMEONE'S DICK). [as an owner drags on a dog's lead to control it]

jerk someone's dick, to *phr.* [1980s+] to annoy, to distract forcefully, to taunt (cf. JERK SOMEONE'S CHAIN). [SE *jerk* + DICK n.²]

jerk the cat, to *phr.* [early 17C] to vomit (cf. SHOOT THE CAT). [var. on WHIP THE CAT phr.¹ (2)]

jerk the cly, to *phr.* [17C–18C] (Und.) to be whipped at the post. [SE *jerk* + CLY n.]

jerk the tinkler, to *phr.* [mid-19C] to ring a bell. [SE *jerk* + TINKLER n.²]

jerk to Jesus, to *phr.* [late 19C] (US) to execute by hanging.

jerk town *n.* [1900s–50s] (US) a small provincial or rural town. [abbr. JERKWATER TOWN]

jerk up *v.* **1** [mid-19C] (US) to arrest. **2** [1900s–10s] (US) to reprimand. **3** [1990s] (US) to impose upon (cf. JERK AROUND). [fig. uses of SE; but note JERK OFF v.²]

jerkwad *n.* [1990s] (US) a masturbator. [JERK (OFF) v.¹ + WAD n.⁵]

jerkwater *adj.* **1** [late 19C+] (US) small-time, second-rate, mediocre. **2** [1980s+] (US) slow-witted, foolish. [backform. JERKWATER TOWN]

jerkwater town *n.* [20C] (US) a small, insignificant town (cf. TANK TOWN; WHISTLE STOP). [such towns were known only for the trackside water tower and a trough from which a train could scoop or *jerk water* from between the tracks without actually stopping. An alternative ety., based on earlier railroad practice, suggests that the crew had actually to leave the train and *jerk* the *water* in buckets from local wells, then run with it to the waiting locomotive. A further suggestion cites buckets that were attached to the locomotive by a leather strap and that were used to *jerk* the *water* from streams running alongside the track]

jerkweed *n.* [1990s] (US) a stupid, contemptible person. [JERK(-OFF) n.² + (DICK)WEED]

jerky *adj.* [1930s+] (US) silly, idiotic. [JERK n.¹ (2)]

jerrawicke *n.* [mid-19C] (Aus.) Australian-brewed beer. [? dial. *jerry beer*, second-rate beer]

jerry *n.*¹ [19C] (Und.) a fog, a mist. [ety. unknown]

jerry *n.*² [19C] (Und.) a watch; thus *jerry-getting*, *jerry-nicking*, *jerry-stealing*, watch stealing. [? link to JERRY n.⁴, they are both round]

jerry *n.*³ [mid–late 19C] a cheap tavern (cf. JERRY SHOP). [abbr. TOM AND JERRY SHOP]

jerry *n.*⁴ [mid–late 19C] a round felt hat. [abbr. SE *jerry hat*]

jerry *n.*⁵ [mid-19C+] **1** a chamberpot. **2** a lavatory. [abbr. SE *jereboam*, a double magnum of wine]

jerry *n.*⁶ [late 19C] a moment of recognition or discovery. [JERRY v. (2)]

jerry *n.*⁷ [late 19C–1910s] a second-rate builder who erects badly built houses with inferior materials. [abbr. SE *jerry builder*, itself ? a Merseyside building firm]

Jerry *n.*⁸ [1910s+] a derog. name for a German. [abbr.]

jerry *adj.* **1** [late 19C+] aware, knowledgeable, informed (cf. IN FULL JERRY). **2** [1900s–30s] (US) good, fine. [JERRY v. (2)]

jerry *v.* **1** [mid–late 19C] to tease, to chaff, to sneer at. **2** [late 19C+] to understand, to work out, to recognize, to discern. [? abbr. JERRYCUMBLE, as rhy. sl. for TUMBLE v.² (1)/RUMBLE v.²]

jerry-come-tumble *n.* [mid–late 19C] a lavatory. [JERRY n.⁵ + JERRY-GO-NIMBLE]

jerrycumumble/jerrymumble *v.* [late 18C–19C] **1** to shake about, to tumble. **2** to 'tumble' to, i.e. to understand, to work out. [? rhy. sl. (1) SE *tumble*, (2) TUMBLE v.²]

jerry-diddle *n.*¹ [late 19C+] a violin. [rhy. sl. *jerry-diddle* = fiddle]

jerry-diddle *n.*² [20C] (Aus.) a drink 'on the house'. [? the implication that the publican is 'fiddling' himself out of a profit]

jerry-go-nimble *n.* [mid-19C] diarrhoea. [JERE n.¹ + SE *go nimble*]

jerry lynch *n.* [mid-19C–1900s] a pickled pig's head. [? anecdotal]

jerrymumble *see* JERRYCUMUMBLE.

Jerry O'Gorman *n.* [20C] a Mormon. [rhy. sl.]

jerry riddle *n.* [mid-19C] urination (cf. GERRY RIDDLE). [rhy. sl. *jerry riddle* = piddle]

jerry rumble *v.* [1900s] (N.Z.) to discover, to understand. [JERRY adj. + RUMBLE v.²; ? rhy. sl. *jerryrumble* = TUMBLE v.²]

jerry shop *n.* [mid-19C] **1** a cheap tavern (cf. JERRY n.³). **2** a pawnbroker. [TOM AND JERRY SHOP]

jerry sneak *n.*¹ [late 18C–mid-19C] a hen-pecked husband. [*Jerry Sneak*, a character in *The Mayor of Garratt* (1764) by Samuel Foote, who is dominated by his wife]

jerry sneak *n.*² [19C] a thief who specializes in stealing watches. [JERRY n.² + SE *sneak*]

jerry to *adj.* [20C] (orig. US) alert to or aware of, seeing one's own interest. [? JERRYCUMUMBLE v. (2)]

jerry wag *n.* [mid-19C] a tipsy individual, out on a spree; thus a *jerry-wag shop*, a coffee stall, much frequented by such people. [JERRY n.³ + SE *wag*]

jersey *n.* [late 19C–1910s] (Aus.) a red-head. [Cheshire dial. *jersey*, 'a contemptuous term for a head of hair' (*EDD*)]

Jersey city *n.* [1950s–60s] (US) a female breast (cf. BRADFORD CITIES). [rhy. sl. *Jersey City* = TITTY n.²]

Jersey highball *n.* [1940s] (US Black) cow's milk. [SE *jersey* (cow) + HIGHBALL n.]

Jersey lightning *n.* [mid-19C–1960s] (US) a strong kind of apple-jack, peach brandy or illicitly distilled whisky. [made in New Jersey]

jerseys *n.* [1960s+] the female breasts (cf. BRADFORD CITIES). [rhy. sl. *Jersey Cities* = *titties* (*see* TITTY n.²)]

Jersey side *n.* [1940s] (US Black) the wrong side, the inferior type etc. [the position of New *Jersey*, the 'wrong' side of the Hudson River from Manhattan]

Jersey side of the snatch play *phr.* [1940s] (US Black) over 38 years old. [JERSEY SIDE + SNATCH PLAY; lit. on the wrong side of one's sexual peak]

Jerusalem! *excl.* [mid-19C+] used in a variety of mild oaths; euph. for JESUS! (cf. BEJABERS!; JEHOSHAPHAT!).

Jerusalem artichoke *n.* [20C] a donkey (cf. JERUSALEM CUCKOO). [rhy. sl. *Jerusalem artichoke* = MOKE n.² (1)]

Jerusalem-by-the-sea *see* JERUSALEM THE GOLDEN.

Jerusalem cricket! *excl.* [mid-19C–1900s] (US) a mild oath, i.e. *Jesus Christ!* (cf. BEJABERS!).

Jerusalem cuckoo *n.* [20C] a mule (cf. JERUSALEM ARTICHOKE). [its 'hee-haw' bray is presumably reminiscent of the cuckoo's 'cuc-oo']

Jerusalem-on-sea *see* JERUSALEM THE GOLDEN.

Jerusalem parrot *n.* [20C] a flea.

Jerusalem pony *n.* [19C+] a donkey (cf. BALDWIN; KINGSWOOD LION; ROMFORD LION). [according to the Bible, Christ rode into Jerusalem on a donkey]

Jerusalem screw *n.* [1920s+] (Aus.) an extremely harsh prison warder. [WW1, when the Australian military police based in Jerusalem were taught by the British Army the best methods of breaking even the most recalcitrant prisoners]

Jerusalem slim *n.* [1920s–70s] (US tramps) Jesus Christ. [proper name *Jerusalem* + nickname *slim*]

Jerusalem the golden/-by-the-sea/-on-sea *n.* [1950s+] Brighton. [the large number of Jews who retire to Brighton and other towns along Britain's south coast]

jerve *n.* [mid-19C–1950s] (US Und.) a waistcoat or waistcoat watch pocket; thus *jerver*, a pickpocket. [abbr. *jervis* (*see* JARVEY n.)]

jervis *see* JARVEY n.

jessamy *n.* [mid-18C–mid-19C] a fop or dandy (cf. JEMMY n.¹). [SE *jessamine*, jasmine. Lit. a man who scents himself with perfume or who wears a sprig of jessamine in his buttonhole; the implication is of effeminacy as well as dandyism. The term forms part of an ascending scale of fashionableness, notably the 'Greenhorn, Jemmy, Jessamy, Smart, Honest Fellow, Joyous Spirit, Buck, and Blood', cited as such by the editor and essayist John Hawkesworth (1715–73) in his journal *The Adventurer* (1753)]

jesse *n.* [1910s–30s] (US Und.) a bluff or threat. [? US outlaw *Jesse James* (1847–82)]

Jesse James killer *n.* [1940s] (US Black) any heavy, sticky hair pomade, usu. with a distinctive smell. [? Robert Ford, killer of the outlaw *Jesse James*, was a former member of his gang; thus a traitor and a 'slimy' figure]

jessie *n.*¹ [1920s+] **1** a male homosexual (cf. AGNES). **2** a weakling, an ineffectual person (cf. BIG GIRL'S BLOUSE; NELLIE n.¹). [use of generic female name]

jessie *n.*² [1940s] (US Black) a red-haired girl or woman. [JERSEY]

jesta *see* DIGESTER.

jester *v.* [1970s] (W.I.) to play the fool.

Jesuit *n.* [mid-16C] a male homosexual. [the contemporary suspicion of Jesuits, who were thus branded with a suitably repellent image]

Jesus *adj.* **1** [1920s+] (US) a derog. term for ardently Christian (cf. JESUS STIFF). **2** [1960s] (W.I.) a general intensifier, e.g. *not one Jesus shilling*, not one DAMNED/cursed shilling.

Jesus! *excl.* [late 14C+] a general and blasphemous oath (cf. BEJABERS!).

Jesus boots/shoes/slippers *n.* [1940s+] (orig. US) footwear, usu. sandals. [Christ is traditionally portrayed as wearing sandals]

Jesus Christ on a raft! *excl.* [20C] a mild excl. (cf. CHRIST ON A BIKE!).

Jesus freak *n.* [1960s+] (orig. US) a fervent or evangelical Christian; usu. used contemptuously. [JESUS adj. + sfx. -FREAK]

Jesus H Christ! *excl.* [late 19C+] a mild oath (cf. BEJABERS!). [the H is redundant other than for rhythm, although *DARE* suggests a link to *IHS*, the monogram for Jesus]

Jesus kate! *excl.* [20C] (Irish) a general excl.; euph. for JESUS CHRIST! (cf. BEJABERS!).

jesusly! *excl.* [19C] (US) darned, DAMNED (cf. JEEZLY). [SE *Jesus*]

Jesus shoes/slippers *see* JESUS BOOTS.

Jesus stiff *n.* [20C] (US Und.) a religious person (cf. PSALM-SINGING MUZZLER). [JESUS adj. + STIFF n.⁴]

Jesus tonight! *excl.* [20C] (Irish) a general excl., euph. for *Jesus Christ!* (cf. BEJABERS!).

Jesus wept! *excl.* [1920s+] a general and blasphemous oath (cf. BEJABERS!).

jet *n.*¹ [18C] **1** a parson (cf. AUTEM JET). **2** a lawyer. [the *jet* black gown]

jet *n.*² [1980s+] (drugs) ketamine (cf. K n.⁴). [its effect on the mental process]

jet *v.* [1960s+] (US Black/campus/teen) to leave in a hurry, to move very fast (cf. FLY v.²; MOTOR v.).

jet fuel *n.* **1** [1970s+] (US) a very strong alcoholic drink made from mixing spirits etc. **2** [1970s–80s] (drugs) phencyclidine (cf. ACE n.³).

jet one's juice, to *phr.* [late 19C–1900s] of a man, to achieve orgasm (cf. JIT ONE'S MUCK). [SE *jet* + JUICE n.² (2)]

jeune siècle *n.* [late 19C–1900s] (society) those who are considered *fin de siècle*, i.e. advanced, modern or decadent in their behaviour. [Fr. *jeune siècle*, 'young century']

Jew/Jewish *adj.* [16C+] in slang, reflecting centuries of Christian teaching, the Jew is grasping, avaricious, wealthy, untrustworthy, deceitful and mean (as well as circumcised and abstaining from pork). Thus virtually all combs. with *Jew/Jewish* are derog. and play on these stereotypes (cf. IRISH adj.).

Jew *n.* **1** [17C+] a mean person, a skinflint. **2** [1940s–50s] (US Black) the boss, irrespective of their actual religion. **3** [1950s+] (W.I.) any rich person, presumably White but with no religious overtones, other than the worldwide derog. stereotype.

jew/jew down/up *v.* [early 19C+] to cheat financially. [racial stereotyping; the cheater need in no way be Jewish]

Jew/Jew's bail *n.* [late 18C–19C] insufficient bail (cf. QUEER BAIL). [the belief that while Jews will offer bail in any situation, they will not be there to pay it if the criminal absconds]

Jew-boy *n.* [late 18C+] a young Jewish man. [SE by late 19C, and then usu. derog; not initially derog., although note the US use of *boy* to address Blacks]

Jew buggy *see* JEW CANOE n.¹.

Jewburg *n.* [1900s–50s] (S.Afr.) Johannesburg; thus *Jewburger/Jewburgher*, a rich Johannesburg merchant (cf. JEW YORK; YIDNEY). [the city's large Jewish population + a pun on the usual nickname, *Jo'burg*]

Jew butter *n.* [20C] (US) goose or chicken dripping. [the popularity among Jews of *schmaltz*, fat as a spread]

Jew canoe/Jew buggy/Jewish submarine *n.*¹ [1930s+] (US) a Cadillac.

Jew canoe *n.*² [1980s] (society) a Jaguar (cf. JEW'S BENTLEY). [SE *Jew* + CANOE n.]

Jew cheque *n.* [1980s+] (US) any form of cheque that is obtained through fraud, e.g. on Social Security. [the stereotyping of Jews as devious money-makers]

Jew chum n. [1930s–50s] (Aus.) a Jewish refugee from Germany or central Europe (cf. REFUJEW).

jew down see JEW v.

jewel/jewels n. **1** [late 18C+] the male genitals (cf. FAMILY JEWELS). **2** [19C–1920s] (US/Irish-Amer.) a fellow, a man.

jewellery n. [mid-19C–1920s] (US prison) handcuffs, shackles, chains.

jewels see JEWEL.

Jewey see JEWY.

Jew-fencer n. [mid-19C] a Jewish street-seller.

Jew flag see JEWISH FLAG.

Jew food n. [20C] ham. [in mockery of the Jewish dietary prohibition on all pork products]

Jewie n. [late 19C+] (Anglo-Irish) a Jew.

jewish n. [1960s+] (S.Afr. Black) smart, expensive clothing. [racial stereotyping, the invariably rich Jew]

Jewish adj.¹ see JEW adj.

jewish adj.² [1960s+] (S.Afr. Black) of clothes or other material objects, smart, expensive, chic. [JEWISH n.]

jewish v. [1960s+] (S.Afr. Black) to dress someone up in smart clothes. [JEWISH n.]

Jewish airlines n. [1960s+] (gay) walking (cf. ITALIAN AIRLINES). [Jews are too mean to pay airfares]

Jewish Alps n. **1** [20C] (US) Washington Heights, New York City, home of many successful Jews (cf. SWISH ALPS). **2** [1960s+] (US) the Catskill Mountain resort area, patronized by Jewish New Yorkers (cf. BORSCHT BELT).

Jewish-American princess see JEWISH PRINCESS.

Jewish by hospitalization phr. [1950s+] (gay) circumcised but not Jewish.

Jewish compliment see JEW'S COMPLIMENT.

Jewish corned beef n. [1960s] a circumcised penis (cf. JEWISH NATIONAL; JEW'S LANCE).

Jewish/Jew flag n. [1910s–50s] (US) a currency note. [the avaricious Jew has no nation, only money; the same image as of the Communist derog. phr. 'rootless cosmopolitans']

Jewish foreplay n. [1950s+] (US) the man pleads for sex, his partner refuses all physical contact. [the supposed frigidity of the JEWISH PRINCESS]

Jewish forest n. [20C] in poker, three threes. ['mittel-European' pron. 't'ee t'rees']

Jewish joanna see JEW JOANNA.

Jewish/Greek lightning n. [20C] deliberate arson in order to gain the insurance on an otherwise unprofitable business.

Jewish national n. [1950s+] (US gay) a circumcised penis (cf. JEWISH CORNED BEEF). [the ref. is to the *Hebrew National* brand of kosher salami]

Jewish nightcap n. [1950s] a foreskin.

Jewish overdrive n. [20C] (US) freewheeling down hills to save petrol (cf. MAORI OVERDRIVE; MEXICAN OVERDRIVE; PORTAGEE OVERDRIVE). [the stereotyped meanness of Jews]

Jewish Oxo n. [20C] money. [*Oxo*, the brandname of a beef extract. Like the kitchen stand-by, money makes 'gravy']

Jewish penicillin n. [1960s+] (US) chicken soup. [despite its essentially humorous content, the term has some medical reality. The effect of hot soup on the mucous membranes is to make them work harder and thus help clear the nose of the blocking that comes with a cold]

Jewish piano/pianola n. **1** [20C] a taximeter. **2** [1930s+] a cash register (cf. JEWISH TYPEWRITER; JEW JOANNA; YIDDISHER PIANO). [racial stereotyping]

Jewish prince n. [1980s+] (US) a (middle-class) a Jewish man who is spoiled or dominated by his mother (cf. JEWISH PRINCESS).

Jewish/Jewish-American princess n. [1970s+] (US) a young, conceited, (middle-class) Jewish woman (cf. J.A.P; JEWISH PRINCE).

Jewish renaissance n. [1950s+] (gay) over-elaborate furniture in doubtful taste (cf. JEWY LOUIS).

Jewish/Yiddish screwdriver n. [20C] a hammer (cf. BIRMINGHAM SCREWDRIVER). [the supposed inability of stereotypically cerebral/entrepreneurial Jews to perform manual tasks]

Jewish sidewalls n. [1950s–60s] (US) white rubber sidewalls, glued onto otherwise black tyres in an attempt to make them look more fashionable. [stereotyped Jewish meanness]

Jewish standard time see JEWISH TIME.

Jewish submarine see JEW CANOE n.¹.

Jewish time/standard time n. [1950s+] (US) unpunctuality time (cf. AFRICAN PEOPLE'S TIME). [the supposed propensity of Jews to arrive late for any meeting or appointment]

Jewish typewriter n. [20C] a cash register (cf. JEWISH PIANO). [racial stereotyping, the Jew as moneygrabber]

Jewish waltz n. [1980s+] (US) deal-making, haggling. [racial stereotype]

Jew/Jewish joanna n. [1900s] **1** a cash register (cf. JEWISH PIANO). **2** a taximeter. [SE *Jewish* + JOANNA]

Jew joint n. [20C] (US) a second-hand clothes store. [SE *Jew* + JOINT n.³ (3)]

jewlark v. [mid-19C+] (US) to flirt, to court. [SE *gill/jill*, a girl or woman + LARK v.]

jewlarker n. (US) **1** [mid-19C+] a sweetheart, a beau. **2** [late 19C–1900s] a dandy. [JEWLARK]

Jewman n. [20C] (Irish) a moneylender.

Jew's bail see JEW BAIL.

Jew's balls n. [1970s] (US Black) a pawnbroker. [the three balls that signify a pawnbroker and the fact that most Harlem pawnbrokers were Jews]

Jew's Bentley/Rolls Royce n. [1930s+] a Jaguar motorcar (cf. JEW CANOE n.²). [the stereotyped association of Jaguars and *nouveaux riches* Jews]

Jew's/Jewish/Judische compliment n. **1** [mid-19C+] a large penis but no money or presents. **2** [1950s–70s] (gay) a circumcised penis. [the premise of (1) is that the penis is free, but to the stereotypically mean Jew, presents involve losing money]

Jew's eye n. [late 18C–19C] something valuable or desirable, usu. as *worth a Jew's eye*. [? Ital. *gioie* or Fr. *joaille*, a jewel or, given the prevailing stereotype, the medieval practice of extorting money from the Jewish community on pain of threatened torture, which may or may not have involved blinding]

Jew shave n. [20C] (US) covering one's face with talcum powder instead of shaving. [traces of a beard that still remain on some swarthy Jewish men's faces despite their shaving]

Jew sheet n. [1950s+] (gay) an account, often imaginary, of money lent to friends.

Jew's lance n. [1950s+] (gay) a Jewish circumcised penis (cf. JEWISH CORNED BEEF).

Jew's poker n. [20C] the gentile who, in religious households, is brought in to light the fires on the Sabbath. [the lighting of fires (and in more recent years, the turning on of electric lights), is among many prohibitions against 'work' on the Sabbath. The Yid. term for the same individual is *shabbas goy*, Sabbath gentile]

Jew's Rolls Royce see JEW'S BENTLEY.

Jew town n. [20C] (US) a Jewish community within an urban area (cf. BEAN TOWN n.²).

jew up see JEW v.

Jewy/Jewey adj. [late 19C–1930s] an 'inevitable' nickname for a Jew, esp. when surnamed Moss.

Jewy Louis n. [1970s+] (society) a flashy, vulgar style of interior decoration, poss. featuring (fake) Louis XV or Louis XVI furniture.

Jew York n. [20C] (society) New York (cf. JEWBURG). [the large Jewish population in that city]

jezabel n. [19C] the penis. [proper name *Jezabel*, wife of Ahab king of Israel, in SE a wicked, impudent, or abandoned woman]

jib/jibb n.¹ **1** [mid-19C] (tramp) the tongue. **2** [20C] (US Black) the mouth. **3** [20C] (orig. US Und.) speech, impudent talk. [Rom. *chib*, *jib*, the tongue; Hind. *tschib*, language; dial. *jib*, the underlip; thus the mouth]

jib/jibber n.² [mid-19C] a worn-out horse, an uncooperative horse. [SE *jib*, of a horse, to back away, to refuse to go forward]

jib n.³ [late 19C] (society) an opera hat, i.e. 'flat-folding "chimney-pot" hat, closed by springs set in centre of vertical ribs' (Ware). [proper name *Gibus*, the Fr. inventor]

jib v.¹ [mid-19C+] to depart quietly, to slip away. [? JIB n.²]

jib v.² [1960s+] (US Black) to talk at length or nonsensically. [JIB n.¹]

jiba/jibba/juba n. [19C+] (US Black) leftovers. [SE *giblets*; the slave term for left-overs from the White masters' table]

jibb n.¹ see JIB n.¹.

jibb n.² [1980s+] (US drugs) a gram of hashish. [ety. unknown; ? SE *jib*, the 'arm' of a crane; thus pun on getting one HIGH adj.¹]

jibb v. [19C+] to talk, to chatter. [JIB n.¹]

jibba see JIBA.

jibber n.¹ see JIB n.².

jibber n.² [20C] (Irish) a coward. [fig. use of JIB n.²]

jibbernoll n. [early 18C] a fool, a simpleton. [var. on JOBBERKNOWL n.]

jibber the kibber n. [late 18C–19C] a device used deliberately to wreck ships for the potential plunder. [a lantern is tied to a horse's neck and the horse itself has one foot tied. The movement this produces appears, from out on a dark sea, to resemble a moving ship's light. Ety. unknown; E.P. suggests *jibber*, to confuse, but it does not appear until 1824; *jib*, for a horse to move in fits and starts, is also 19C; ?17C dial. *jibby-horse*, a flashy, showy woman is East Anglian, but Grose (1785) links such wrecking to 'our western coasts'; *kibber* may be reduplication, it may relate to Cornish dial. *kib*, to steal]

jibb in v. [1960s+] to talk one's way in, esp. into an otherwise paying venue, to GATECRASH. [JIBB v.]

jib-jibe n. [1960s+] (US Black) talk that goes in one ear and out the other (cf. JI-JIBE). [JIB v.²]

jib jobs n. [1990s] excrement. [? var. on BIG JOBS]

jiblet n. [1960s+] (drugs) barbiturate. [ety. unknown]

jibone/jabone/jiboney n. [1920s+] (US) **1** a novice, an innocent, a newly arrived immigrant. **2** a heavy, a thug, a muscleman, as which (1) was often used (cf. JABRONIE). [? Milanese *giambone*, ham, cf. JAMBONE]

jibs n.¹ [20C] (US Black) the lips, the mouth or the teeth. [JIB n.¹]

jibs n.² **1** [1950s+] (US Black) the buttocks. **2** [1980s+] (US) a woman's breasts. [SE *jib*, a protruding sail at the bow of the ship]

jick n. [1920s–40s] (US Black) alcohol, esp. bootleg alcohol. [JIGGER n.³]

jickajog n. [late 17C–mid-19C] a shoving, a commotion (cf. JIG-A-JIG). [echoic of the action]

jick head n. [1940s] (US Black) a drunkard. [JICK + sfx. -HEAD (2)]

jif adj. [1990s] (US teen) smart, first-rate, excellent. [SE *jiffy*, a brief space of time; the image is of 'sharpness']

jiffy/jiff/jeffey/jeffy n. [late 18C+] a moment, a very short time, almost invariably in phr. *in a jiffy*, occasionally *in a jiff*,

also intensified as *half a jiffy*. [the variations *jeffey*, *jeffy* are 19C only]

jig n.¹ [late 16C–mid-19C] a trick, a swindle; thus [late 18C+] *the jig is up*, the game is up. [late 16C SE *jig*, a comical performance, usu. given in the interval or at the conclusion of a play]

jig n.² [18C] a joking, mocking nickname for a person. [SE *jig*, a lively dance; a general name for a mechanical device]

jig n.³ [1920s+] (orig. US) a derog. term for a Black person. [abbr. JIGABOO n.¹]

jig v. [1960s+] (US) to bother, to irritate. [SE, *jig* someone around]

jigaboo n.¹ [1920s+] (orig. US) a derog. term for a Black person (cf. JIGGER n.⁹). [either SE *jig*, a dance, ult. Fr. *giguer*, to leap, to gambol, to frolic (the classic 19C Black stereotypes); or modelled on SE *bugaboo*, which, in the 13C, was the name of a demon, and since the 18C, the fear of demons in general; or Bantu *tshikabo*, a meek and servile person, used as derog. by slaves. Paradoxically, the first use of *jigaboo* – in the song 'I've got rings on my fingers' in the show *The Midnight Sons* (1909; music Raymond Hubbell) – appears to have referred to Asians. Certainly the show was set in India, although the line 'Mistress Mumbo Jumbo Ji-ji-boo J O'Shea' would imply that the writer was of the 'they all look alike to me' persuasion]

jigaboo n.² [1980s+] (US drugs) a cannabis cigarette. [JIGABOO n.¹ + CIG]

jigaboo joy shop n. [1920s–50s] (US) an automobile supply store specializing in cheap but ostentatious chrome accessories (cf. NIGGER BAIT). [JIGABOO n.¹; stereotyping of the tastes of Black car buyers]

jig-a-jig/jig-jig/jig-a-jog n. [mid-19C+] sexual intercourse, often found in pidgin slangs (cf. JIGGY-JIG). [redup. indicative of the movements of copulation]

jigamaree/jiggamaree n. **1** [early 19C–1900s] (US) a thing, a gadget, a fanciful contrivance. **2** [mid-19C] a cunning trick. **3** [mid-19C] anything the speaker considers ridiculous or worthless. [var. on JIGUMMIBOB]

jig around v. **1** [20C] to wander around, to loiter. **2** [1960s] to prance, to strut, to swagger.

jig-chaser n. [20C] (US) a White person who pursues the company of Blacks. [JIG n.³ + SE *chaser*]

jig cut n. [1940s–50s] (US) a razor or knife slash (cf. HARLEM SUNSET). [JIG n.³ + SE *cut*; the stereotype of the knife-wielding Black]

jigg n. [19C] a farthing. [ety. unknown; ? link to GRIG n.]

jig gallery n. [1960s–70s] (US) the 'gods', the uppermost balcony in a theatre or cinema (cf. BUZZARD ROOST n.²). [JIG n.³ + SE *gallery*]

jiggalorum n. [early 17C] a trifle, a fanciful thing. [on pattern of JIGGUMBOB]

jiggamaree see JIGAMAREE.

jigged adj. **1** [20C] (Aus.) broken, useless. **2** [1900s] (US) darned, DAMNED. [JIG v.]

jigger n.¹ **1** [mid-16C–mid-19C] (Und.) a door. **2** [mid-16C+] (Und.) a key. **3** [18C–1920s] a doorkeeper. **4** [1920s–70s] (US prison/Und.) a look-out man (cf. JIGGER! excl.²; JIGGER MAN). [? link to Lancashire dial. *jigger*, a narrow entry between houses, although the cant very likely preceded it]

jigger n.² [19C+] a man. [euph. for BUGGER]

jigger n.³ (US) **1** [early–mid-19C] a clandestine, illicit still. **2** [early–mid-19C] bootleg liquor (cf. JIGGER STUFF). **3** [mid-19C+] a drink of spirits, a dram. **4** [mid-19C+] a small glass or metal cup, a measure used in mixing cocktails (now SE). **5** [mid-19C+] a whisky cocktail. [SE *jig*, to shake]

jigger n.⁴ [mid-19C] **1** the penis (cf. DOJIGGER). **2** [mid-19C–1930s] the vagina. [? JIGGER n.¹ (2) or SE *jig*, to move up and down]

jigger/jiggie/jiggus *n.*⁵ **1** [mid-19C–1900s] (US) a thing, a gadget, any small, mechanical contrivance (cf. DOHICKEY; DO-JIGGER). **2** [1950s+] (Aus. Und.) an improvised radio receiver, used in prison. [ety., unknown; ? fig. uses of SE *jig*, to dance]

jigger/jiggers *n.*⁶ [late 19C] (US) a policeman. [JIGGER! excl.]

jigger *n.*⁷ **1** [late 19C–1900s] (US hobo) a fake sore, wound or bandage to elicit sympathy. **2** [late 19C–1910s] (US) a scoop of ice-cream. **3** [1900s] (US) a tattoo. [ext. of JIGGER *n.*⁵ (1)]

jigger *n.*⁸ [late 19C+] a prison or cell. [GIGGER *n.*¹; 20C uses are US]

jigger *n.*⁹ [1920s+] (orig. US) a derog. term for a Black person (cf. JIGABOO *n.*¹).

jigger *v.*¹ **1** [mid-19C] to shake or jerk rapidly. **2** [mid-19C+] to break, to destroy, to ruin (cf. JIGGERED *adj.*²). **3** [late 19C–1930s] (US) to fool, to cheat, esp. in passive. [SE *jig*, to move around]

jigger *v.*² [late 19C] to lock up, to imprison. [GIGGER *n.*¹]

jigger *v.*³ [1910s] (US) to tattoo. [JIGGER *n.*⁷ (3)]

jigger *v.*⁴ [1960s] (US prison/Und.) to act as a look-out. [JIGGER *n.*¹ (4)]

jigger!/jiggers! *excl.*¹ [early 19C+] used as a vaguely indecent oath, e.g. as *by jiggers! jigger it! I'll be jiggered! be jiggering well careful* etc (cf. BEJABERS!). [? a euph. for JESUS!, although usu. used in v. forms]

jigger!/jiggeroo!/jiggers! *excl.*² [1910s–30s] (US) a warning that someone hostile, e.g. the police, a teacher, one's parents, is coming (cf. GIVE JIGGS; JIGS!). [? euph. of JESUS!]

jigger-dubber *n.* [late 18C] a turnkey. [JIGGER *n.*¹ (3) + DUB *n.*¹]

jiggered *adj.*¹ [early 19C] **1** contraband, smuggled. **2** secret. [JIGGER *n.*³]

jiggered *adj.*² [mid-19C+] **1** euph. for DAMNED, with some feeling of confusion; thus *I'll be jiggered.* **2** exhausted, worn out, often as *jiggered up.* **3** drunk. [JIGGER *v.*¹ (2)]

jigger-foot market *n.* [1940s+] (W.I.) a market popular among the very poorest people. [Carib.E *jigger-foot*, a foot infested with *jiggers* or larval mites, which lay their eggs beneath the skin. The poor are often prone to such infestation]

jigger man *n.* [1920s–70s] (US prison/Und.) a look-out man (cf. JIGGER *n.*¹).

jiggeroo *see* JIGGER! *excl.*².

jiggers *see* JIGGER *n.*⁶.

jiggers! *see* JIGGER!

jigger stuff *n.* [early 19C] a secret still (cf. JIGGER *n.*³). [the JIGGER *n.*¹ (2) that unlocks the place where the still is kept]

jigger-worker *n.* **1** [mid-19C–1900s] a seller of illicitly distilled spirits. **2** [late 19C] a drinker of such illegal spirits, esp. whisky. [JIGGER *n.*³ + SE *worker*]

jiggery-/jackery-pokery *n.* [late 19C+] tricks, lies, underhand activities in general. [synon. dial. *jiggery-pokery*, ? ult. Scot. *joukery-pawkery*, a trick]

jigget *v.* [late 17C–late 19C] to move about with a jerky or shaky motion, to hop or skip about, to shake up and down, to fidget. [dimin. of SE *jig* v.]

jiggie *see* JIGGER *n.*⁵.

jiggle *v.* [19C] to have sexual intercourse; thus *jiggly*, of a woman, amorously inclined (cf. JIG-A-JIG; JIGGLING BONE).

jiggle and jog *n.* [1970s] a Frenchman. [rhy. sl. *jiggle and jog* = FROG *n.*¹ (2)]

jigglers *n.* [1970s] (Und.) skeleton keys for use on pin tumbler locks. [SE *jiggle*, i.e. using the sleight of hand required to turn the lock, but note JIGGER *n.*¹]

jiggle show *n.* [1970s+] (US) a television show featuring actresses in sexually titillating clothing.

jiggling bone *n.* [19C] the penis (cf. BONE *n.*⁶; DOJIGGER). [JIGGLE + SE *bone*]

jiggumbob *n.* [mid-19C–1940s] (US) something strange, peculiar, unknown. [var. on THINGUMABOB]

jiggus *see* JIGGER *n.*⁵.

jiggy *n.* [1990s] (US Black) the police (cf. JIGGER! excl.²). [JIGGER *n.*⁶]

jiggy *adj.* [1930s+] (US) crazy, nervous, fidgety. [SE *jig*, to move around]

jiggy-jig *n.* [19C] (Anglo-Ind.) sexual intercourse (cf. JIG-A-JIG). [E.P. quotes 'a Hindi-English dictionary', which defines it as an 'exclamation of delight used by Indian women during sexual intercourse']

jig-jagging *n.* [1900s–20s] (US Black) dancing with absolute abandonment. [SE *jig* v.]

jig-jig *see* JIG-A-JIG.

jig juice *see* JIG WATER.

jiglets *n.* [late 19C–1910s] (US) oneself, as in *his jiglets* (cf. NIBS). [ety. unknown; ? fig. use of SE, *giblets*, i.e. generic use of one's innards as one's whole being]

jigs! *excl.* [1920s–40s] (US) a cry of warning. [abbr. *jiggers!* (*see* JIGGER! excl.²)]

jig town *n.* [1920s+] (US) a Black community within an urban area (cf. BEAN TOWN *n.*²). [JIG *n.*³ + SE *town*]

jigwalker/jigwawk *n.* [late 19C–1930s] (US) a derog. term for a Black person (cf. JIGABOO *n.*¹). [JIG *n.*³ + play on SE *jaywalker*]

jig water/jig juice *n.* [late 19C+] (US) alcohol, spirits. [JIG *n.*³ + SE *water/juice*; stereotyped fondness of Blacks for alcohol]

jigwawk *see* JIGWALKER.

ji-jibe *n.* [20C] (US Black) talk, unimportant chatter (cf. JIB-JIBE). [JIB *v.*²]

jildi/jeldi/jildy/juldie *n.* [late 19C+] haste, speed, esp. in the phr. *on the jildi*, in a hurry, quickly, *move a jildi*, hurry up, *jildi!* hurry up! get on with it! [Hind. *jaldi*, quickness]

jildi/jildy *adv.* [late 19C+] quickly. [JILDI n.]

jill *n.* [1930s+] (US) a young woman (cf. JANE *n.*²).

jillaroo *n.* [1940s+] (Aus.) **1** a White woman newly arrived in Australia, a White woman living in the bush (cf. JANE *n.*²). **2** a land girl. [play on JACKAROO]

jillion *n.* [1930s+] (orig. US) an indefinite, extremely large number; thus *jillionaire*, an extremely wealthy person. [on model of SE *million, trillion*]

jill off *v.* [1980s+] (orig. US gay) of a woman, to masturbate. ['feminized' version of JACK OFF *v.*¹ (1)]

jills *n.* [1900s–40s] the self, used with possessive pron., e.g. *my jills*, I, *his jills*, he. [Shelta; used mainly in show business]

jilt *n.*¹ **1** [late 17C–19C] a prostitute. **2** [late 17C–mid-19C] a tease, a flirt. [SE *jilt*, 'a woman who gives her lover hopes, and deceives him' (Johnson); ult. *gillet/jillet*, a loose or wanton woman]

jilt *n.*² [mid-19C–1900s] a crowbar, housebreaking tools in general. [GILT *n.*¹ (2)]

jilt *v.* [mid-19C–1900s] (orig. US) to break into a house or to enter a building under false pretences – both for the purpose of theft. [JILT *n.*²]

jilter *n.* [mid-19C] (orig. US) a sneak thief. [JILT *v.*]

jim *n.*¹ [19C+] jewellery, diamonds. [SE *gem* or a play on TOM *n.*¹²]

Jim *n.*² [late 19C+] **1** (US Black) a title for a fellow Black man, usu. used as shorthand for making a gesture of friendship. **2** (S.Afr.) a derog. all-purpose generic name for Black men (cf. JACK *n.*⁵; JACK *n.*¹⁶).

jim *n.*³ [1900s–20s] (Aus.) £1. [? abbr. *jimmy o'goblin* (*see* JEMMY O'GOBLIN)]

jim *n.*⁴ [1970s] a man who likes to watch prostitutes at work (or just a 'dirty old man' who frequents 'adult' bookshops, stripshows etc) but offers no actual sexual threat. [generic use of proper name]

jim *n.*⁵ [1980s+] (US Black) a condom (cf. JIMMY CAP).

jim/jim up *v.* [20C] (US) **1** to spoil, ruin or botch. **2** to fool around. [? JIM *n.*², if so, a racist slur; cf. AFRICAN ENGINEEER-ING]

jimber-jawed *adj.* (US) **1** [mid-19C+] having a projecting lower jaw. **2** [20C] lopsided, askew. [SAmE *gimbal-jawed*]

jim britts *see* JIMMY BRITTS.

jim brown *n.* [late 19C+] town, i.e. the West End of London. [rhy. sl.]

jimbrowsky/jim browski *n.* [1980s+] (US Black) the penis. [? JIMMY *n.*⁶ (1)]

jimbugg *n.* [mid-19C] (Aus./N.Z.) a sheep. [Abor. *jombok*, a sheep]

jimcrack *n.* [1900s–50s] (US) a fop, an affectedly showy person. [GIMCRACK *n.* (1)]

jimcracker *n.* [mid-19C–1960s] (US) a remarkable person or thing. [GIMCRACK *n.* (1)]

Jim Crow *n.*¹ **1** [early 19C+] a complaisant, subservient Black person (cf. UNCLE TOM). **2** [mid–late 19C] a type of comb with long teeth. **3** [1910s+] White racist discrimination against Blacks and the *Jim Crow* laws that embody it. [early 19C Kentucky plantation song with the chorus 'Jump *Jim Crow*' and the 'black face' entertainer Thomas Dartmouth Rice (1808–60), who first performed it in Louisville in 1828]

jim crow *n.*² [mid-19C] a street clown (cf. BILLY BARLOW *n.*¹). [rhy. sl. *jim crow* = *saltimbanco*, a street clown]

jim crow *adj.* [mid-19C+] (US) **1** for or of use by Blacks only. **2** racially prejudiced against Blacks. **3** small-time, incompetent, fraudulent. [JIM CROW *n.*¹ (3)]

jim-dandy *n.* [late 19C+] (US) an excellent person or thing. [? 1844 song 'Dandy Jim ob Caroline'. The song, apparently written by a Black rather than White author, trumpets the admirable qualities of this especially 'dandy nigger'. Alternatively, dial. *gim/jim*, neat, spruce + DANDY *adj.*; *gim* ult. ? Scot. *jimp*, slender, delicate, graceful. Cohen (1989) suggests that the popularization of the term may have come through its use in baseball *c.*1890s]

jim-dandy *adj.* [late 19C+] (US) excellent, satisfactory (cf. DANDY *adj.*; JEMMY *adj.*¹). [JIM-DANDY *n.*]

jim fish *n.* [1930s+] (S.Afr.) a derog. term of address to a Black man (cf. JIM CROW *n.*¹). [? the character *Jim Fish*, who was used in miners' training films in the 1940s as an example of what not to do]

Jim Gerald *n.* [20C] (Aus.) *The Herald* newspaper. [rhy. sl.]

jim-hickey *n.* [late 19C–1900s] an excellent or admirable person. [? JIM-DANDY *n.*+ DOHICKEY]

jiminetty! *excl.* [20C] (US) used in mild oaths as euph. for JESUS! (cf. BEJABERS!). [var. on JIMINY]

jiminy! *see* GEMINI!

jiminy cricket!/crickets!/Christmas!/criminy! *excl.* [mid-19C+] (orig. US) euph. for *Jesus Christ!* (cf. BEJABERS!).

jim-jam *n.* **1** [mid-16C–late 19C] a fanciful or trivial article, a knick-knack. **2** [1990s] (Aus.) nonsense, rubbish. [ety. unknown, but of similar pattern to FLIM-FLAM *n.*¹; WHIM-WHAM]

jim-jam *v.* [1940s–50s] (US Black) to sing, dance and play music, to have a lively party. [? JIM CROW *n.*² + JAM *v.*³]

jim-jams *n.*¹ **1** [mid-19C–1950s] (orig. US) delirium tremens, a hangover (cf. JAMS *n.*¹). **2** [late 19C+] 'nerves', apprehension, a fit of depression. **3** [late 19C] odd manners, personal peculiarities. [ety. unknown]

jim-jams *n.*² [20C] pyjamas, usu. children's use. [abbr.]

jim johnson *n.* [1970s] (US) the penis (cf. ABRAHAM). [ext. of JOHNSON *n.*¹ (1)]

Jim Jones *n.* [1990s] (drugs) marijuana laced with cocaine and phencyclidine. [the cult leader Rev. *Jim Jones* (1933–78), whose 'act of revolutionary suicide' in November 1978 led to the mass-poisoning of some 913 of his followers with Kool-Aid spiked with cyanide at their home in Jonestown, Guyana]

Jim Jones *v.* [1990s] (US Black) to poison. [for ety. *see* JIM JONES *n.*]

jimkwim *see* DR JIM.

jimmie/jimmy howe *n.* [1930s+] (Aus./N.Z.) a navy or black woollen singlet worn by Aus. and N.Z. shearers and bushmen. [var. on JACKIE HOWE]

jimmies *n.*¹ **1** [20C] (US) pyjamas (cf. JIM-JAMS *n.*²). **2** [1920s–70s] (US) candy that is sprinkled on ice-cream.

jimmies *n.*² *see* JIMMY BRITTS.

jimmison *see* JEMSON.

jimmunt *see* DR JIM.

jimmy *n.*¹ [late 17C–late 19C] a guinea. [abbr. JEMMY O'GOBLIN; note ety. at JACOBUS]

jimmy *n.*² [early 19C+] (mainly US) a short house-breaker's crowbar (cf. JEMMY *n.*⁴).

jimmy *n.*³ *see* JIMMY GRANT.

jimmy *n.*⁴ [1930s+] an act of urination. [abbr. JIMMY RIDDLE]

jimmy *n.*⁵ [1950s+] (US) a car manufactured by the *General Motors Corporation*.

jimmy *n.*⁶ **1** [1980s+] the penis (cf. JAMMY *n.*³). **2** [1990s] (US Black/campus) a condom (cf. JIMMY CAP). [? JIMMY *v.*¹ (2); note that (2) is not considered authentic by rap aficionados since it appeared to have been coined by a White and thus 'fake' rapper]

Jimmy *n.*⁷ [1980s+] (mainly Scot.) used as a term of address to a person whose actual name one does not know. [generic use of the name]

jimmy *adj.* [19C–1900s] (US) exact, fit, stylish, fashionable. [? JEMMY *adj.*¹; 16C SE *jump*, exact, precise, coinciding; 1750 *OED* 'a jemmy fellow']

jimmy *v.*¹ **1** [mid-19C+] (US Und.) to break into. **2** [1910s] (US) to copulate. **3** [1910s–40s] (US Und.) to injure, wound or spoil. **4** [1920s] (US) to cheat. [JIMMY *n.*²]

jimmy *v.*² [1930s+] to urinate. [JIMMY RIDDLE]

jimmy/jim britts/jimmies *n.* [1940s+] (Aus.) diarrhoea. [rhy. sl. *jimmy britts* = SHITS; ult. proper name of *Jimmy Britt* (1879–1940), a US-born boxer who toured Australia during WW1]

jimmy cap/hat *n.* [1980s+] (US Black) a condom (cf. JIM *n.*⁵). [JIMMY *n.*⁶ (1) + SE *cap*]

jimmy dancer *n.* [20C] (Aus.) cancer. [rhy. sl.]

jimmy dog *n.* **1** [20C] (Irish juv.) the penis. **2** [1980s+] (US campus) a marijuana cigarette. [ety. unknown]

jimmy gall *see* GINNY GALL.

jimmy grant/jimmy *n.* [mid-19C–1940s] (Aus./N.Z./S.Afr.) an immigrant. [rhy. sl.]

jimmy green *adj.* [20C] naïve, gullible. [SE *green*, naïve; note *Jimmy*, the 'inevitable' nickname for men surnamed *Green* in the British Army/Royal Navy]

jimmy green on *phr.* [20C] susceptible, gullible. [SE *green*, naïve]

jimmy hat *see* JIMMY CAP.

jimmy hills *n.* [20C] pills. [rhy. sl.; ult. UK TV soccer pundit *Jimmy Hill*]

jimmy hix *n.* **1** [1910s+] (US gambling) the point of 6 in craps dice. **2** [1940s–50s] (Und.) an injection of narcotics. [rhy. sl.; (2) *jimmy hix* = FIX *n.*³]

jimmy hope *n.* [1910s+] (US prison) soap. [rhy. sl.]

jimmy howe *see* JIMMIE HOWE.

jimmy joint *n.* [1980s+] (US Black) the penis (cf. JIMMY CAP). [JIMMY *n.*⁶ (1) + JOINT *n.*⁵ (1)]

jimmy lee *n.* [20C] (Aus.) tea (cf. ROSIE LEA). [rhy. sl.]

Jimmy Logie *n.* [1950s] a piece of nasal mucus. [rhy. sl. *Jimmy Logie* = BOGEY *n.*⁵; ult. soccer star *Jimmy Logie*]

jimmy low *n.* [late 19C] (Aus.) a eucalyptus tree. [? a local New South Wales 'character']

jimmy mason *n.* [20C] a basin. [rhy. sl.]

Jimmy Nail *n.* [1990s] **1** mail. **2** a sale. [rhy. sl.; ult. UK actor and singer *Jimmy Nail* (b.1954)]

Jimmy O'Goblin *see* JEMMY O'GOBLIN.

Jimmy O'Goblins *see* JEMMY O'GOBLINS.

jimmy prescott *n.* [mid–late 19C] a waistcoat (cf. CHARLIE PRESCOTT). [rhy. sl.]

jimmy protector *n.* [1980s+] (US Black) a condom. [JIMMY n.⁶ (1) + SE *protector*]

jimmy riddle *n.* [1930s+] an act of urination (cf. GERRY RIDDLE). [rhy. sl. *Jimmy Riddle* = PIDDLE]

jimmy rollocks *n.* [20C] the testicles (cf. TOMMY ROLLOCKS). [rhy. sl. *jimmy rollocks* = *bollocks* (see BALLOCKS n.)]

jimmy rounds *n.* [early 19C] Frenchmen. [Fr. *je me rends*, the cry supposedly offered by hapless French sailors when faced with the might of the RN]

jimmy/jim/joe/johnny skinner *n.* [20C] dinner. [rhy. sl.]

jimmy's lightning *n.* [1990s] deliberate arson of one's own home or place of business in order to secure a fraudulent insurance claim (cf. JEWISH LIGHTNING). [the traditional Glaswegian term of address JIMMY n.⁷]

jimmy-swing *n.* [1940s+] (W.I.) a poor, common young man. [note *Captain Swing* 'the Kent rick-burner' who terrorized farmers *c.*1830 in an attempt to put off the spread of farm machinery that was seen as a threat to farm-workers' livelihoods]

jimmy/johnny woodser/woods *n.* (Aus./N.Z.) **1** [late 19C+] anyone who drinks alone, a drink that is taken by oneself; thus *jimmy woodsing*, drinking by oneself (cf. DICK SMITH). **2** [1930s+] a solitary person, an orphan. [a character in a poem by B.H.T. Boake, pub. in *The Bulletin* (7 May 1892): 'At the thought the hearts beats quicker/Than an old Bohemian's should ... /I'll go and have a liquor/With the genial "Jimmy Wood".' Poss. a genuine person, a loner named Jim Woods]

Jimmy Young *n.* [20C] **1** a bribe. **2** the tongue. [rhy. sl.; (1) *Jimmy Young* = BUNG n.¹ (4); ult. the singer turned radio personality *Jimmy Young* (b.1923)]

jimped-up *adj.* [1900s] (US) affected in dress or manners. [Scot. *jimp*, slender, neat, elegant]

jimplecute/jimpricute *adj.* [1900s] elegant, handsome, neat (cf. GIMCRACK; JEMMY adj.¹; JIM-DANDY adj.). [? dial. *jimpsey*, neat, smart, pretty]

jim-rags *n.* [late 19C] (Aus.) tiny pieces, shreds, esp. in the phr. *kick someone to jim-rags*. [dial. *jamrags*, tatters, rags]

jims *n.* [late 19C–1920s] (Aus.) **1** a fit of 'nerves' or depression. **2** delirium tremens. [abbr. JIM-JAMS n.¹]

jimsecute *n.* [mid–late 19C] (US South) a sweetheart. [? dial. *jimpsey*, neat, smart, pretty + SE *cute*]

jim skinner *see* JIMMY SKINNER.

jimswinger *n.* [late 19C–1940s] (US, mainly southern Black) a tailcoat. [? JIM n.² (1), a generic Black name + the swinging of the coat's tails]

jim town *n.* [1940s–60s] (US) **1** a shanty town. **2** the poor (thus often Black or Hispanic) part of a town (cf. BEAN TOWN n.²). [? *gimcrack* or JIM n.² (1)]

jim up *see* JIM v.

jim-whizzed *adj.* [late 19C] (US) euph. for DAMNED, usu. in the phr. *I'll be jim-whizzed!* [fanciful; ? link to JESUS!]

jinal *see* GINAL.

jing *n.* [1970s+] (US campus) money (cf. CHINK n.¹). [it 'jingles' in one's pocket]

jing-bang *n.¹* [mid–late 19C] the whole lot, as in phr. *the whole jing-bang* (cf. WHOLE BANG SHOOT).

jing-bang *n.²* [1940s+] (W.I.) **1** a noisy, dirty crowd. **2** a low-class, rough, noisy person. **3** a promiscuous woman. [JING-BANG n.¹ + echoic of the noise and crush of the crowd/the careless lifestyle of the individuals]

jing-jang *n.* [1950s+] (US gay) **1** the penis. **2** the vagina. **3** sexual intercourse. [echoic of the movements of sex]

jingle *n.¹* [mid-19C] (US) spirit, energy.

jingle *n.²* [late 19C–1920s] (US) an alcoholic drink. [? the rattle of ice-cubes in one's glass]

jingle *n.³* [20C] (orig. Aus.) money (cf. JING; JINGLE-BOY). [its noise in one's pocket]

jingle *n.⁴* [1940s+] (US) a telephone call.

jingleberry *n.* [1930s–50s] (US) a testicle (cf. APRICOTS). [var. on DINGLEBERRY n. (1)]

jingle-box *n.* [late 17C–early 19C] a leather drinking vessel, decorated with silver bells, popular among heavy drinkers.

jingleboy *n.* [early 17C–late 19C] a golden sovereign (cf. BOY n.¹; JINGLE n.³). [the noise a number of them makes in a purse or pocket]

jingle-brained *adj.* [1920s] (US) foolish (cf. AMOEBA-BRAINED). [JINGLE-BRAINS]

jingle-brains *n.* [late 17C–early 19C] a fool, a dunce (cf. BAKE-BRAIN).

jingled *adj.* [late 19C–1930s] (US) drunk. [JINGLE n.²]

jingler *n.¹* [16C–19C] a crooked horse-dealer. [SE *jingle*; thus the noise of the harness, but perhaps more f. a further SE meaning, to play with words, verbal facility being the stock-in-trade of the horse-trader]

jingler *n.²* [late 19C–1920s] (US) usu. pl., money, coins (cf. JINGLE n.³). [abbr. JINGLE-BOY]

jingling *adj.* [1990s] (US Black) sexy, attractive, usu. of a woman.

jingling johnny *n.¹* [20C] the musical instrument known as a Chinese pavilion or Chinese crescent. [it 'consists of a pole, with several transverse brass plates of some crescent or fantastic form, and generally terminating at top with a conical pavilion or hat. On all these parts a number of very small bells are hung which the performer causes to jingle' (*Grove's Dictionary of Music*). A later Aus. version, which uses bottle tops tacked loosely onto an old broomstick, is the *lagerphone*]

jingling johnny *n.²* [1900s–30s] (Aus.) **1** hand shears. **2** a hand-shearer. [the clicking noise of the shears]

jingo *n.* [1980s+] (drugs) a cannabis cigarette. [play on JOINT n.⁴ (2)]

jings!/by jings! *excl.* [late 18C+] (orig. and usu. Scot.) used as a mild oath (cf. BEJABERS!). [euph. for JESUS!]

jink *n.* [late 19C] money (cf. CHINK n.¹; CHING n.²; CHINKERS; CLINK n.²; JINGLE-BOY). [the noise of one coin hitting another]

jink *v.* [1920s+] (Aus.) to swindle. [Scot. *jink*, to dodge]

jink one's tin, to *phr.* [mid-19C–1930s] **1** to pay out money. **2** to rattle one's change. [SE *jink*, to rattle with a metallic sound + TIN n.¹]

jinks the barber *n.* [mid-19C] (middle-class) a secret informant, a gossip (cf. POSTMAN'S SISTER). [the stereotype of the chatty barber]

jinky *adj.* [1950s–60s] (US Black) difficult, problematical, unpleasant. [SE *jinx*]

jinnal *see* GINAL.

jinna rumble *n.* [1940s] (W.I.) makeshift crutches, made of sticks and used to help walking. [ety. unknown]

jinnit *n.¹* [20C] a cocktail of gin and Italian vermouth. [abbr./pron. of *gin and it* (see GIN AND FRENCH).

jinnit *n.²* [20C] (Irish) a mule. [Sp. *jinete*, a light horseman]

jinny *n.* [1920s–40s] (US) a speakeasy or unlicensed drinking place. [the *gin* available there]

jinny *v. see* JENNY v.².

jinny-wing *see* JENNY adj.

jintoe n. [late 19C+] (S.Afr.) a prostitute. [for ety. *see* GENTOO]

jip n.[1] [mid-19C] (US) a derog. term for a woman, esp. a Black woman. [? US sporting jargon *gyp*, a bitch (dog); ult. abbr. *gypsy*, used as a popular dog's name]

jip n.[2] [1940s+] (Aus.) energy, 'pep'. [? GIVE GYP]

jip/jip-job adj. [20C] (Ulster) badly done, poorly produced, botched. [dial. *jip*, to trick, to cheat]

jippo see GYPO.

jirk-nod see YERKNOD.

Jis n. [16C] Jesus, esp. in mild oaths, e.g. *by Jis!* (cf. BEJABERS!).

jis v. [1980s+] (US campus) to ejaculate. [JISM n. (2)]

jislaaik! excl. [1950s+] (S.Afr.) a general excl., the meaning of which varies as to context and the speaker's mood, usu. surprise, but also annoyance, grievance, dismay. [? *Jesus*; pron. 'yis-like']

jism / jizzum / jiz / jizz / gism / gissum / gizm / gizzum / gyzm / chism n. (orig. US) 1 [mid-19C+] energy, spirit. 2 [late 19C+] semen. 3 [1930s+] (mainly south) gravy (cf. BULL FUCK). [ety. unknown; Ki-Kongo *dinza*, the life force; note northeast US dial. *jasm*, energy]

jit n.[1] [1900s–40s] (US) a nickel, a 5-cent coin. [thus colloq./SE *jitney*, an omnibus, which orig. carried passengers for 5 cents a trip]

jit n.[2] [1930s–40s] (US) a Black person. [? fig. use of JIT n.[1], i.e. a virtually worthless person]

jit n.[3] [1970s] (US campus) semen (cf. JITBAG). [var. on JISM n. (2) ? + the SE *jet* of ejaculated semen]

jitbag n. [1990s] a condom. [JIT n.[3] + SE *bag*]

jitney n. 1 [1900s–70s] (US) a 5-cent piece, a nickel (cf. JIT n.[1]). 2 [1910s–60s] (US) a small, cheap car or vehicle. 3 [1910s+] (US) a bus charging a fixed fare. [the 5-cent fare charges on the original *jitney* omnibuses. *DARE* quotes a source claiming *jitney* to be 'Jewish slang', but there is no evidence]

jitney adj. [1910s–40s] anything cheap, improvised or ramshackle; thus *jitney bus*, any form of cheap, ramshackle transport, often a private car; [1910s–30s] *jitney dance*, a pay-per-dance or 'taxi-dance' dance-hall. [JITNEY n.]

jitney v. [1910s+] (US) to travel by bus or small vehicle. [JITNEY n.]

jitney girl n. [1950s] (US) a prostitute who drives around in her own car soliciting customers. [JITNEY n. (2) + SE *girl*]

jit one's muck, to phr. [late 19C–1900s] of a man, to achieve orgasm (cf. JET ONE'S JUICE; MUCK n.[6]). [SE *jet* + SE *muck*]

jits n. [1930s+] (US) *jit*ters, i.e. anxiety, nervousness. [abbr.]

jitterbug n. 1 [1930s–40s] (orig. US) a nervous person. 2 [1940s+] (US) an adolescent who is naïve or foolish. 3 [1960s+] (US Black) a voluble, indiscreet person, a chatterer. 4 [1960s+] (US Black) a youth who lives a street life but is not invariably a criminal. [JITTER(S) + BUG n.[5] (2); app. coined 1934 by US band leader Cab Calloway (1907–94); *jitterbug*, the dance and a dancer is SE]

jitterbug v. 1 [1940s–70s] (US) to fool around. 2 [1950s–60s] (US) to participate in gang fighting. 3 [1950s–70s] (US Black) to saunter, to swagger. [JITTERBUG n.]

jitterdoll/jitterjane n. [1940s] (US Black) a woman who loves to dance. [for ety. *see* JITTERBUG n.]

jitter joint n. [1940s] (US) a cheap dance-hall. [JITTER(BUG) + JOINT n.[3]]

jitters, the n. 1 [1920s+] extreme nervousness, a state of emotional and often physical tension, agitation. 2 [1930s–40s] (US) a hangover, delirium tremens. [supposedly f. the Spoonerism 'bin and *jitters*' for 'gin and bitters' and orig. used of one who has drunk too much of that mixture]

jittery adj. [1930s+] nervous, tense, 'on edge'. [JITTERS]

jive n.[1] 1 [1920s+] (orig. US Black) nonsense, rubbish, insincere or pretentious talk (cf. ALL THAT JAZZ). 2 [1920s+] (US) as *jive* (*talk*), Afro-American slang, esp. as coined in Harlem

and thence used by jazz musicians. 3 [1920s–60s] (US Black) sexual intercourse, also a sex partner. 4 [1930s+] (US) anything, stuff, goings-on, situation. [? Wolof *jev*, gossip, false talk, trickery or SE *jibe*, to scoff, to sneer]

jive n.[2] [1930s+] (drugs) 1 heroin. 2 cannabis. 3 recreational drugs in general. [fig. uses of JIVE n.[1] (4)]

jive n.[3] [1960s+] (US Black) a deceitful, arrogant or pretentious person. [abbr. JIVE-ASS n.[1]]

jive adj. [1920s+] (orig. US Black) a generally neg. term, applicable to a range of dubious actions, fake, phoney, deceitful, unappealing, hypocritical, insincere etc (cf. JIVE-ASS adj.). [JIVE n.[3]]

jive v.[1] (orig. US Black) 1 [1920s–60s] to engage in sexual intercourse (cf. JAZZ). 2 [1920s+] to talk nonsense, to deceive, trick or flatter by apparently empty chatter; thus *jive about with*, *give some jive*, to play with, to mess around. 3 [1920s+] to idle, to loaf about. 4 [1930s+] (US) to tease, to make fun of (cf. JIVE AROUND). 5 [1930s+] to play or dance to jive music, to have a good time. 6 [1960s+] to saunter, to swagger, to dodge (cf. JITTERBUG v.). [JIVE n.[1]]

jive v.[2] [1940s+] to fit in, to make sense, to agree, esp. in neg. uses, e.g. *that don't jive*, that doesn't make sense. [SE *jibe*]

jive and juke, to phr. [1970s+] (US campus) to have a very good time. [JIVE v.[1] (5) + JUKE v.[3]]

jive around v. [1930s+] (US) to tease, to make fun of. [JIVE v.[1] (4)]

jive-ass n.[1] [1960s+] (orig. US Black) a deceitful, arrogant or pretentious person (cf. JIVE TURKEY). [JIVE n.[3] + sfx. -ASS]

jive-ass n.[2] [1960s+] (US) one who loves fun or excitement. [JIVE v.[1] (5) + sfx. -ASS]

jive-ass adj. [1960s+] (orig. US Black) deceitful, pretentious, arrogant, insincere. [JIVE-ASS v.[1]]

jive-ass v.[1] [1960s+] (orig. US Black) 1 to talk nonsense. 2 to swagger, to boast. [JIVE n.[3] + sfx. -ASS]

jive-ass v.[2] [1960s+] (orig. US Black) to dance. [JIVE v.[1] (5) + sfx. -ASS]

jive doojee n. [1950s+] (drugs) heroin. [JIVE adj. + DUJI]

jive hand n. [1970s+] (US Black) an undesirable situation that puts one person at an unfair disadvantage, one is dealt 'a bad hand'. [JIVE adj. + SE *hand*, the cards that one has been dealt]

jiver n. [1920s–50s] (US Black) a trickster, a deceiver, a flatterer, an insincere person. [JIVE v.[1] (1)]

jive stick n. [1950s+] (drugs) a marijuana cigarette. [JIVE n.[2] (2) + STICK n.[4] (2)]

jivetime adj. [1960s+] (US Black) insincere, dishonest, stupid. [JIVE n.[3] + ? pun on the radio daypart *drivetime*]

jive turkey n. [1970s+] (US Black) an insincere, deceitful, dishonest person (cf. JIVE-ASS n.[1]).

jive up v. [1940s+] (US) to falsify, to fabricate. [JIVE v.[1]]

jivey adj.[1] [1940s+] (US) redolent of jive music, lively, aware. [JIVE v.[1] (5)]

jivey adj.[2] [1960s+] (US) pretentious, insincere, phoney, hypocritical etc. [JIVE n.[3]]

jiz n. see JISM.

jiz/jizz v. [late 19C+] (orig. US) to ejaculate. [JISM n.]

jizrag n. [1990s] a handkerchief or similar piece of material into which one masturbates. [JISM + SE *rag*]

jizz n. see JISM.

jizz v. see JIZ v.

jizzbag/jizzbucket n. [1980s+] a contraceptive sheath (cf. SCUMBAG). [JISM n. + SE *bag/bucket*; note BAG n.[5]]

jizzbags n. [1990s] the testicles. [JISM n. + SE *bag/*BAG n.[1] (2)]

jizzbucket see JIZZBAG.

jizzlob v. [1990s] to masturbate. [JISM n. + SE *lob*, to throw]

jizzum see JISM.

j.o. *n.* [1990s] (US Black) a job. [abbr.]

j.o. *v.* [1950s+] in sex industry, to masturbate. [abbr. JERK OFF]

jo *n.* [20C] (Can.) a ban*jo*. [abbr.]

jo *v.* [early 19C; 1950s+] (US) **1** to spoil, exhaust. **2** (gambling) to rig a game. [? abbr. SE *joke*]

joan *n.* **1** [late 17C–18C] a homely woman. **2** [18C–19C] a fetter, also ext. as *Darby and Joan*. [the commonness of the proper name]

joanie *adj.* [1980s] (US teen) out-of-date, unfashionable. [? the character *Joanie* in the sitcom *Happy Days*, set in late 1950s and early 1960s]

joaning/joining *n.* [1930s+] (US south, Black) indulging in a ritualized exchange of insults (cf. DOZENS). [ety. unknown, but note dial. *Joan Blunt*, an outspoken woman]

joan on *v.* [1930s+] (US Black) to indulge in a ritualized exchange of insults. [JOANING]

joanna *n.* [mid-19C+] a piano. [rhy. sl.; the single 19C citation is for *joano*; *joanna* appears *c.*1910]

Joan of Arc *n.*[1] **1** [20C] a park. **2** [20C] a lark, a situation; thus *sod this for a Joan of Arc*. **3** [1940s–50s] (Aus.) a shark. [rhy. sl.; ult. *Joan of Arc* (*c.*1412–31)]

Joan of Arc *n.*[2] [1950s–60s] (camp gay) an ostentatious, camping homosexual. [pun on the *faggots*/FAGGOTS *n.*[3] (1) with which St Joan (*c.*1412–31) was burned]

job/jobe *n.*[1] **1** [17C] a tedious scolding. **2** [late 19C] a henpecked husband (cf. JAW *n.*; JAWBATION; JOBATION). [the biblical proper name *Job*, who received a lengthy telling-off from his supposed 'comforters']

job *n.*[2] [late 17C–early 19C] a guinea (cf. HALF-A-JOB). [? 15C SE *job*, a small compact portion of some substance; a piece, lump (cf. THICK 'UN)]

job *n.*[3] [18C+] (Und.) any form of criminal activity, esp. a robbery, often with a qualifying name, e.g. *the Barclays Bank job*.

job *n.*[4] [late 19C+] a bowel movement; thus *do a job*, to defecate (cf. BIG JOBS; JOBBIE *n.*[2]). [euph.]

job *n.*[5] [late 19C+] a type, a variety or a procedure, e.g. *the desk was a teak-oiled job*, *his moustache was a bushy brown job*, *a boob job*, *a nose job* (cf. BLOW JOB; BOOB JOB; GOB JOB; HAND JOB).

job *n.*[6] **1** [1920s+] (orig. US) a person of either sex, e.g. a *cute little job*, a *first-class job*. **2** [1930s+] (Aus.) a drunkard. **3** [1930s+] (Aus.) a fool, a poor worker.

job *n.*[7] [1920s+] (orig. US) an aircraft, a motorcar or any other vehicle.

job *adj.* [1970s+] (UK/US police) anything involved in police work, i.e. *a job dog*, *a job car* etc. [all police work is known as the *job* and the magazine of the Metropolitan Police is *The Job*]

job *v.*[1] **1** [mid-16C+] to have sexual intercourse; thus *jobbing*, sexual intercourse. **2** [late 18C+] (US) to poke, to thrust sharply. **3** [1940s+] (Aus.) to hit, to beat up. [SE *job*, to pierce, to thrust something into]

job/jobe *v.*[2] [late 17C–mid-19C] to scold, to tell off. [JOB *n.*[1] (1)]

job *v.*[3] [mid-19C+] to finish. [SE *job*, to do a piece of work]

job *v.*[4] **1** [late 19C+] to cheat, to betray, to 'frame up'. **2** [1960s] (US) to steal.

jo-bag *n.* [1960s+] a condom. [JOHNNIE *n.*[11] + SE *bag*/BAG *n.*[5]]

jobanjeremiah *n.* [late 19C] an especially depressed, and depressing, person. [biblical figures *Job* and *Jeremiah*, both synonymous with misery and complaint]

jobation *n.* [late 18C–19C] a tedious scolding. [JOB *n.*[3]; the lengthy scolding given to *Job* by his supposed 'comforters'; ? + link to JAW *n.*]

jobbard *n.* [16C] a fool, a simpleton (cf. JOBBERKNOWL *n.*). [Fr. *jobe*, silly + synon. *jobard*]

jobbed *adj.* [mid-19C+] **1** concluded, finished (cf. JOB'S JOBBED). **2** (Und.) accused or 'framed' on false evidence. [JOB *v.*[3]]

jobber *n.* [1920s–70s] (US) a job, employment, a difficult chore.

jobberknowl/jobbernowl/jabberknowl/jabbernowl *n.* [late 16C–late 19C] a fool, a blockhead. [? JOBBARD + NOLL; mid-19C+ uses are US]

jobberknowl/jobbernowl/jabberknowl/jabbernowl *adj.* [late 16C–late 19C] stupid, blockheaded. [JOBBERKNOWL *n.*]

jobbie/jobby *n.*[1] [mid-19C+] (orig. Scot.) **1** a piece of excrement, a turd. **2** a general term of abuse. [note W.I. use, for children only]

jobbie *n.*[2] **1** [1900s–40s] (US) a man or woman (cf. JOB *n.*[6]). **2** [1960s+] (US) a thing (cf. JOB *n.*[5]).

jobby *see* JOBBIE *n.*[1].

jobby jouster *n.* [1990s] a male homosexual. [JOBBIE *n.*[1] (1) + joc. use of SE *jouster*]

job description *n.* [1990s] (US) personal responsibility, usu. in neg. contexts, *that's not my job description*.

jobe *n. see* JOB *n.*[1].

jobe *v. see* JOB *v.*[2].

job's jobbed *phr.* [mid-19C+] that piece of work is finished (cf. JOBBED). [JOB *v.*[3]]

Job's ward *n.* [late 18C–early 19C] the venereal disease ward at St Bartholomew's Hospital in London. [the suffering therein]

Job's wife *n.* [19C] a scolding, promiscuous woman. [the biblical story of *Job*]

jobsworth *n.* [1970s+] a minor factotum whose only status comes from enforcing otherwise petty regulations. [the inevitable rejoinder, *It's more than my job's worth to …*]

Joburg/Jo'burg *n.* [late 19C+] (orig. milit.) Johannesburg, South Africa (cf. JOEYS).

Jock *n.*[1] **1** [18C–19C] a Northcountry seaman, esp. a collier. **2** [20C] a Scot. [the stereotypical Scot. given name *Jock*, f. *John*]

jock *n.*[2] **1** [late 18C+] the genitals, both male and female (cf. JAXY; JOCK-PIECE; JOCKUM; JOCKY). **2** [1920s+] an athletic supporter or 'jock strap'. **3** [1950s+] (US campus and sports) a sportsman (cf. ROCKS FOR JOCKS). **4** [1960s+] (US campus) a politically conservative, White, middle-class young man. **5** [1960s+] (US campus) a devoted and diligent student, e.g. *math jock*, *computer jock*. **6** [1980s+] (US) a stupid, unimaginative person, a nerd. [(1) the word vanished from the mainstream but remains in US Black in the late 20C]

jock *n.*[3] **1** [early 19C+] a *jockey*. **2** [1940s+] (orig. US) a disc *jockey*. [abbr.]

jock *n.*[4] [late 19C] food. [use extended into various industrial jargons in the mid-20C]

jock *n.*[5] [1970s+] (US) a worker, an operator, e.g. *construction jock, elevator jock*. [abbr. JOCKEY *n.*[2] (2)]

jock *adj.* [1970s+] (US) athletic, sporty. [JOCK *n.*[2] (2), (3)]

jock *v.*[1] [late 17C–19C; 1960s+] to have sexual intercourse. [JOCK *n.*[2] (1)]

jock *v.*[2] [1960s+] (US) to engage in athletics. [JOCK *n.*[2] (2), (3)]

jock *v.*[3] [1980s+] (US Black) to steal. [? JACK *v.*[4]]

jock *v.*[4] **1** [1980s+] (US Black) to imitate, to irritate, as in the phr. *on one's jock*, being pursued, harassed. **2** [1980s+] (US Black teen) to idolize, to put on a pedestal, to try constantly to impress or emulate. **3** [1990s] to toady to, to act sycophantically. [fig. use of JOCK *n.*[2] as an object of desire]

jockam *see* JOCKUM.

jock and boxer *n.* [20C] (gay) a young man and his older friend. [the names of two varieties of underwear]

jock and doris *n.* [20C] a drink, usu. of whisky. [Scot. *deoch-an-doris*, a parting drink or stirrup cup, which, by ancient custom, must be taken standing and need not be paid for]

jocker *n.* **1** [late 19C+] (US) a tramp who travels with a younger partner, working for him and possibly acting as his catamite (cf. GONSEL). **2** [late 19C+] (US) a male homosexual, the 'husband' of the couple. **3** [20C] one who performs anal intercourse. **4** [1910s+] (US prison) a predatory homosexual, who forces his attentions on younger/weaker prisoners. **5** [1960s–70s] (US) a lecher. [JOCK v.¹]

jockey *n.*¹ [17C] the penis. [JOCKUM]

jockey *n.*² **1** [mid-19C–1940s] an accomplice or assistant, usu. of a driver of a cab or utility vehicle. **2** [20C] a worker in a particular job, e.g. *swab jockey*, washer-up, *pump jockey*, petrol pump attendant, *grunt-and-squeal jockey*, a stock hauler, *juice jockey*, a gasoline-truck driver, *suicide jockey*, a nitro-glycerine hauler, *disc jockey*. **3** [20C] a user of drugs or one who is habituated, e.g. *hop-jockey*, drug addict, *horse-jockey*, heroin user. **4** [1910s+] any form of driver, esp. of cabs, buses.

jockey *n.*³ [1950s] (gypsy) a general term of address, e.g. *Hello jockey…*.

jockey *n.*⁴ [1960s+] (US) a masculine lesbian.

jockey *v.*¹ [early 18C+] to struggle for a place, esp. the lead in a race. [racecourse use]

jockey *v.*² [1940s+] (US) to drive a vehicle, to pilot a plane.

jockeying *n.* [late 19C] racing carriages along the streets of London.

jockey's whip *n.* [1940s–60s] a bed, a sleep. [rhy. sl. *jockey's whip* = KIP n.¹ (4)]

jock-gagger *n.* [early 19C] a pimp, one who lives off a prostitute. [JOCK n.² (1) + GAGGER n.¹ (1)]

jock major *n.* [1960s+] (US campus) a student who majors in physical education. [JOCK n.² (2), (3)]

jocko *n.* [1910s+] (US) a stupid or contemptible man or boy. [generic use of name *Jock* but ? dial. *jockey*, a peasant, a countryman]

jock-piece *n.* [1920s] (US) the penis. [JOCK n.² (1) + SE *piece*]

jock rot *n.* [1980s+] (US) a skin infection of the genital area. [JOCK n.² (1) + SE *rot*]

jocks *n.*¹ [late 19C–1920s] (US) used in mild oaths, typically *by jocks, i jock* (cf. BEJABERS!). [euph. for JESUS!]

jocks *n.*² [1950s+] (Aus.) men's underwear. [abbr. SE *jockey shorts*]

jocksniffer *n.* [1960s+] (US) a (presumably male) sports groupie who likes to hang around sports stars. [joc. use of JOCK n.² (2) + SE *sniffer*]

jockstrap *n.* [1960s+] (US) a stupid, insignificant fellow.

jockum/jockam *n.* [16C] the penis (cf. JOCK n.²). [ety. unknown]

jockum cloy *v.* [late 17C–early 19C] of a man, to have sexual intercourse (cf. JOCK n.²). [JOCKUM + fig. use of CLOY v.]

jockum gage *n.* [17C–18C] a chamberpot; thus *rum jockum gage*, a silver chamberpot. [JOCKUM + GAGE n.¹ (2)]

jockum-gagger *n.* [late 18C–early 19C] a man who lives on his wife's prostitution. [JOCKUM + GAGGER n.¹ (1), lit. 'penis-beggar']

jocky *n.* [late 17C+] the penis (cf. JOCK n.²). [JOCKUM]

jodie/jody/joe the/de grinder *n.* [1930s+] **1** (US Black) the mythical seducer, *Joe del/the grinder*, who specializes in married women or those with boyfriends. **2** derided by US troops, prisoners and other isolated men, the lover who takes the 'girl you've left behind'. **3** (US) (used derog. by soldiers) a male civilian; thus *jody clothes*, men's civilian clothes. [generic use of proper name *Joe* + GRIND v.¹ (1)]

jodrell *n.* [1950s+] **1** masturbation (cf. BARCLAY'S). **2** a tired-out old prostitute. [rhy. sl. *Jodrell Bank* = WANK n.]

jods *n.* [1950s+] *jod*hpurs. [abbr.]

jody the grinder *see* JODIE THE GRINDER.

joe *n.*¹ *see* JOE MILLER.

joe *n.*² [mid-19C] (Aus.) a policeman (cf. JOE GOSS; JOEY n.³). [JOE n.⁵]

joe/joe house *n.*³ [mid-19C–1930s] (US campus) a privy, an outside lavatory (cf. JOHN n.¹).

joe *n.*⁴ **1** [mid-19C+] (W.I.) sixpence (post-1969 value 5 cents). **2** [1930s] (N.Z.) one penny.

joe *n.*⁵ [mid–late 19C] (Aus.) a term of abuse hurled at anyone who was not a miner (cf. JOE v.). [Victorian goldfield jargon *joe*, a trooper enforcing the regulations laid down by Gov. Charles *Joseph* LaTrobe (1801–75); *AND* adds cit., noting that LaTrobe himself was not actually unpopular]

joe *n.*⁶ [20C] (gambling) the point of 4 in craps dice. [JOEY n.¹ (1)]

joe *n.*⁷ [20C] **1** a generic name for a person, e.g. *joe average*, *joe citizen*, the average man in the street; also one who has a job or position, e.g. *joe plainclothes*, a plain-clothes policeman, *working joe* one who is employed etc (cf. JOE BLOW; JOE COLLEGE; JOE PUBLIC). **2** a stupid or offensive person. **3** (US) a likeable person, often used in direct address. [*The Swell's Night Guide* (1846) defines *joe* as 'an imaginary person, nobody']

joe *n.*⁸ *see* JOE GURR.

joe *n.*⁹ *see* JOE BLAKE.

joe *n.*¹⁰ [1930s+] (US) coffee. [Java]

joe *n.*¹¹ [1960s] (US) a Navajo Indian. [abbr. of proper name]

joe *n.*¹² [1960s+] (N.Z.) a general term of abuse. [rhy. sl. *Joe Hunt* = CUNT n.²]

joe *n.*¹³ [1960s+] (Can.) a French Canadian. [generic use of proper name]

joe *n.*¹⁴ [1970s] (US campus) beer. [ext. of incorrect understanding of JOE n.¹⁰]

joe *adj.*¹ **1** [1900s–20s] (US) aware, in the know (cf. JERRY adj.; JOE HEPadj.; JOSEPH adj.). **2** [1950s–60s] (US) used for anything exceptionally strong, large or extraordinary. [ety. unknown, but note northern dial. *to be joe*, to the master, presumably a generic use of the name]

joe *adj.*² [1990s] (US) tedious or inconsequential. [? JOE n.⁷ (2)]

joe/joey *v.* [mid–late 19C] (Aus./N.Z.) **1** to abuse. **2** to warn. [JOE n.⁵; goldfields jargon, thus a cry of *joe!/joey!* warned that a trooper was approaching]

joe baxi *n.* [20C] a taxi. [rhy. sl.]

joe blake/joe *n.* **1** [late 19C+] cake. **2** [20C] a stake, a bet. **3** [1940s+] (Aus.) a snake. **4** [1940s+] (Aus.) steak. [rhy. sl.]

joe blakes *n.* (Aus./N.Z.) **1** [late 19C+] the shakes. **2** [1940s+] snakes (which one sees), delirium tremens. **3** [1960s+] in phr. *out the joe*, passed out drunk. [rhy. sl.]

joe blake the Bartlemy, to *phr.* [mid-19C] to visit a prostitute. [? rhy. sl. *joe* blake = FAKE v.¹ (3) + Bartlemy = Bartholomew Fair]

joe bloe *see* JOE BLOW.

joe bloggs *n.* [1940s+] a generic name used for any otherwise unnamed man (cf. JOE BLOW; JOE DOAKES).

joe blow/bloe *n.* [1940s+] (Aus./US) any man (cf. JOE BLOGGS; JOE DOAKES). [orig. the horn player in a band, who 'blows']

joe bonce *n.* [1930s+] a ponce, a procurer of prostitutes (cf. ALPHONSE n.²). [rhy. sl.]

joe brown *n.* [1960s+] town. [rhy. sl.]

joe buck *n.* [1930s+] (Aus.) an act of copulation. [rhy. sl. *joe buck* = FUCK n.¹]

joe chilly *n.* [1990s] (US Black) icy winter winds, esp. as experienced in northern cities (cf. HAWK n.³). [JOE n.⁷ + SE *chilly*]

joe chink *n.* [1970s] (US drugs) a heroin addiction. [JOE n.⁷ + CHINK n.³; the link of heroin (or properly opium) to the Orient]

joe college *n.* [1930s+] (US) a college boy, esp. one who is self-satisfied and self-indulgent. [JOE n.⁷ + SE *college*]

joe/johnny/Mr cool *n.* [1970s+] (US) a mythical character who embodies whatever qualities are currently seen as 'cool'. [JOE n.[7] + COOL adj.[3]]

joe crap *see* JOE SHIT.

joe-dandy *adj.* [late 19C–1940s] wonderful, excellent, superlative. [var. on JIM-DANDY adj.]

joe de grinder *see* JODIE THE GRINDER.

joe doakes *n.* [1920s+] (US) any anonymous man (cf. JOE BLOW).

joe gardiners *n.* [1950s] (Aus.) boots. [proper name of *Joe Gardiner Ltd*, a boot- and shoe-maker of Sydney]

joe goss *n.* [20C] (Aus./US) **1** the boss. **2** a policeman (cf. JOE n.[2]). [rhy. sl., ? *Joe Goss*, a late-19C US prize-fighter]

joe gurr/joe *n.* [20C] prison. [rhy. sl. *Joe Gurr* = STIR n.[1]]

joe heath's mare *n.* [20C] (W.I.) a workhorse; thus *like joe heath's mare*, exerting oneself, behaving in an excited manner. [ety. unknown; presumably anecdotal]

joe hep/hip/hept *n.* [20C] (US) an aware, wise person. [JOE n.[7] + HEP adj./HIP adj./HIPPED ON]

joe hep/hip/hept *adj.* [20C] (US) aware, wise. [JOE HEP n.]

joe hoke *see* JOE ROKE.

joe hook *n.* **1** [1930s] a villain, a crook. **2** [1930s+] a book (cf. JOE ROOK). [rhy. sl.]

joe hope *n.* [20C] (Aus.) soap. [rhy. sl.]

joe house *see* JOE n.[3].

joe hunt *n.* [20C] **1** a fool. **2** a general derog. term. [rhy. sl. *joe hunt* = CUNT n.[2]; (1) abbr. to *joey*; (2) never truncated]

joe job *n.* [1980s] (US campus/teen) a menial, low-paid task. [JOE n.[7] (1) + SE *job*]

joe jorgensen *n.* [1950s] (Aus.) one who kicks while fighting. [proper name *Joe Jorgensen*, a well-known goal kicker for Balmain Aus. Rules Football team]

Joe Loss *n.* [20C] a toss, as in a *damn*. [rhy. sl.; ult. UK bandleader *Joe Loss* (1909–90)]

Joe Louis *n.* [1940s] **1** (W.I.) a large, solid cake (cf. CREPE SOLE). **2** (US) 'bad' or homemade liquor. [proper name of US heavyweight champion *Joe Louis* (1914–81); the size of (1); the strength of (2)]

joe lunchpail/lunchbox/lunchbucket *n.* [1960s+] (US) an ordinary working man. [JOE n.[7] + SE *lunchpail/lunchbox/lunchbucket*]

Joe MacBride *n.* [20C] sexual intercourse. [rhy. sl. *Joe MacBride* = RIDE n.[3] (1)]

Joe McGee *n.* [1920s–70s] (US) a stupid, unreliable person. [? anecdotal]

Joe Manton/manton *n.* [19C] a fowling-piece. [proper name *Joe Manton*, a celebrated London gunsmith]

joe marks *n.* [1930s–40s] (Aus.) sharks (cf. JOAN OF ARC n.[1]). [rhy. sl.]

joe maxi *n.* [1990s] (Irish) a taxi (cf. JOE BAXI). [rhy. sl.]

Joe Miller/joe *n.* [early 19C–1920s] **1** a joke, esp. an old 'chestnut'. **2** a joke-book; thus *I don't see the Joe Miller of it*, I don't see what's funny about it. [proper name of *Joe Miller* (1684–1738), a comedian whose name was attached to the bestselling *Joe Miller's jests, or the Wit's Vade-mecum*, written by John Mottley and published in 1739, after Miller's death]

joe morgan *n.* [1940s] (Aus.) an organ (cf. MOLLY O'MORGAN). [rhy. sl.]

joe morgans *n.* [1920s] (N.Z.) delirium tremens. [? anecdotal]

Joe O'Gorman *n.* [late 19C+] a foreman. [rhy. sl.]

joe poke *n.* [late 19C] a *J*ustice of the *P*eace. [abbr.]

joe public *n.* [1940s+] (orig. US) the general public (cf. MR AVERAGE). [JOE n.[7] + SE *public*]

joe rocks *n.* [20C] (Aus.) socks. [rhy. sl.]

joe roke/hoke *n.* [late 19C+] (US) smoke. [rhy. sl.]

joe/johnny ronce *n.* [1930s+] a ponce, procurer (cf. ALPHONSE n.[2]). [rhy. sl.]

joe rook *n.* [1930s+] a book (cf. JOE HOOK). [rhy. sl.]

joe rourke *n.* [20C] a fork. [rhy. sl.]

joes *n.* [1910s+] (Aus.) **1** a fit of depression. **2** an attack of nerves. [abbr. rhy. sl. *joe blakes* = SHAKES]

joe sad *n.* [1920s+] (US Black) a miserable or unpopular person. [JOE n.[7] + SE *sad*/SAD adj.]

joe savage *n.* [mid-19C] a cabbage. [rhy. sl.]

Joe Schmo/Schmoe/Shmo/Shmoe *n.* [1950s+] (orig. US) anyone, 'Mr. Average'. [JOE n.[7] + SCHMO]

joe shit/joe shit the rag man/joe crap *n.* [1940s+] (US) an extremely contemptible person, a nobody. [JOE n.[7] + SHIT n.[1]/CRAP n.[3]]

Joe Shmo/Shmoe *see* JOE SCHMO.

joe six-pack *n.* [1970s+] (US) an ordinary, beer-drinking man. [JOE n.[7] + SE *six-pack*]

joe skinner *see* JIMMY SKINNER.

joe soap *n.* [1930s+] **1** a self-description, e.g. *joe soap here* ... . **2** any man. **3** a fool, a gullible individual. [rhy sl. *joe soap* = DOPE n.[2]]

joe strummer *adj.* [20C] unpleasant, disappointing. [rhy. sl. *Joe Strummer* = BUMMER n.[3]; *Joe Strummer* (b.1952) was a member of the early punk band, *The Clash* (1977–86)]

joe the grinder *see* JODIE THE GRINDER.

joey *n.*[1] **1** [mid-19C] a fourpenny piece, a groat. **2** [1930s–40s] a threepenny bit. [radical politician *Joseph Hume* MP (1777–1855), who encouraged the introduction of the coin. The term was coined by the London cabbies, who lost money by the coin's invention, when the *joey* replaced the sixpence as the usual payment for shorter journeys]

joey *n.*[2] **1** [mid-19C] a hypocrite, a humbug. **2** [20C] an excuse, a small 'white' lie. [? HOLY JOE]

joey *n.*[3] [mid–late 19C+] (Aus.) **1** a policeman (cf. JOE n.[2]). **2** in the goldfields, an outsider. [JOE n.[5]]

joey *n.*[4] **1** [late 19C–1930s] a circus clown. **2** [1990s] (US) a stupid person. [abbr. proper name Joseph Grimaldi, the British clown (1779–1837)]

joey *n.*[5] (Aus.) **1** [20C] a sodomite, an active male homosexual. **2** [1970s] (gay) a young male prostitute. [SAusE *joey*, a young kangaroo]

joey *n.*[6] [20C] the menstrual period. [euph.]

joey *n.*[7] [20C] a weakling, a foolish, inadequate person. [rhy. sl. *joey hunt* = CUNT n.[2]]

joey *n.*[8] [1910s+] (Aus.) a worthless cheque. [like SAusE *joey*, a young kangaroo, it 'bounces']

joey *n.*[9] [1940s–50s] (US Black) a White person. [ety. unknown; ? generic use of proper name]

joey *n.*[10] [1940s–50s] (prison) any form of contraband, letters, parcels etc, smuggled into a prison. [ety. unknown; ? link to JOEY n.[3] (1)]

joey *n.*[11] [1980s] (Aus.) a White child (cf. KANGA n.[3]; SKIPPY n.[3]). [SAusE *joey*, a young kangaroo]

joey *v. see* JOE v.

Joeys/Johies/Jozi *n.* [1970s+] (S.Afr.) Johannesburg. [abbr.]

joe zilch/zilsch *n.* [1920s] (US) the average, otherwise unnamed man. [JOE n.[7] + ZILCH n.[1] (2)]

jo-fired *adj.* [early–mid 19C; 1980s+] (US) a general intensifier, complete, absolute, very much. [var. on ALL-FIRE]

jogar/jogah *n.* [1920s+] a busker. [JOGAR v.]

jogar/jogger *v.* [mid-19C+] (Ling. Fr./Polari) to sing, to play, to entertain; thus *jogari/joggering omee/polone*, an entertainer. [Ital. *giocare*, to play]

jogue *n.* [early 19C] (Und.) one shilling; thus *five jogue*, 5 shillings etc. [the term survives in 20C market traders' jargon *joag*]

jogul *v.* [mid-19C] to play a game, esp. a card-game. [Sp. *jugar*, to play]

Johies *see* JOEYS.

john n.[1] **1** [late 18C] generic term for a man (cf. JOHNNIE n.[2]). **2** [19C–1900s] a male servant. **3** [early 19C+] a general term of address, orig. of White men by immigrants etc, irrespective of actual name, e.g. *Hello, John, got a new motor* etc (cf. JACK n.[16]). **4** [late 19C+] (S.Afr.) generic term for any male Black servant. [commonness of the name; note police/legal jargon *John Doe*, any anonymous male suspect, victim etc]

John n.[2] [19C] (US) an Englishman. [abbr. JOHN BULL]

john n.[3] [early 19C+] a policeman (cf. JOHN BLUEBOTTLE; JOHNDARM; JOHN DUNN n.[2]; JOHN ELBOW; JOHN HOP; JOHN LAW; JOHN NABS; JOHNNY n.[2]; JOHNNY-BE-GOOD; JOHNNY DARBY; JOHNNY GALLAGHER; JOHNNY HAM; JOHNNY LAW; JOHNNY TIN PLATE; JONNOP). [abbr./mispron. of Fr. *gendarme*]

john n.[4] [mid-19C–1930s] a derog. term for a Chinese man. [abbr. JOHN CHINAMAN]

john n.[5] [late 19C] (US) money. [abbr. JOHN DAVIES]

john n.[6] **1** [late 19C+] (US Und.) an easy victim, a sucker. **2** [late 19C+] (US Und.) any law-abiding man. **3** [20C] (orig. US) a prostitute's client. **4** [1940s–60s] (US Black) a gullible White man. [ext. of JOHN n.[1]]

john n.[7] [20C] a skilled, professional tramp. [ext. of JOHN n.[1] (1); such a top-class tramp is well dressed and thus resembles a 'normal' citizen]

john n.[8] [1900s–50s] (US) a jack in poker. [punning on the name *Jack*]

john n.[9] [1910s+] the penis (cf. ABRAHAM). [abbr. JOHN THOMAS n. (2)]

john/john-house n.[10] [1930s+] (orig. US college) the lavatory (cf. AJAX; JOE n.[3]). [? abbr. CUZ JOHN]

john n.[11] [1950s] (US) the menstrual period. [JOEY n.[6]]

john n.[12] **1** [1950s+] (gay) an older man who supports a younger one without actually sharing a long-term relationship with him. **2** [1960s+] (US gay) among lesbians, a man who associates with female homosexuals. [ext. use of JOHN n.[1] (1)]

john n.[13] [1960s+] a condom. [JOHNNIE n.[11]]

john n.[14] [1980s] (US) one's signature. [abbr. JOHN HANCOCK n.]

john n.[15] [1980s] an arrest. [rhy. sl. *John Bull* = PULL n.[2] (1)]

john among the maids n. [19C] a whoremonger, a promiscuous man. [JOHN n.[1] (1)]

john-and-john n. [late 18C–mid-19C] a male homosexual. [i.e. twice JOHN n.[1] (1)]

john b n. [1930s] (US) a hat made by the *John B.* Stetson Company (cf. J.B. n.[1]). [abbr.]

john bluebottle n. [20C] a policeman. [JOHN n.[3] + BLUEBOTTLE]

john brown/D/esquire/handle/Q/rogers/smith/willy n. [1960s] (US) one's signature. [all vars. on JOHN HANCOCK n.]

john-brown/-browned adj. [1950s+] (US) damned. [JOHN BROWN v.]

john brown v. [mid–late 19C] (US) to execute by hanging; thus *be john-browned*, to be 'hanged' or damned. [the hanging of the US abolitionist *John Brown* (1800–59)]

john-browned see JOHN-BROWN adj.

john/johnny bull n.[1] [late 18C+] an Englishman, the British, Great Britain. [first used to name a character in John Arbuthnot's *The History of John Bull* (1712), in which he also coined *Nic Frog* + *Louis Baboon*, for the Dutch- and Frenchman respectively]

john bull n.[2] [20C] **1** an arrest. **2** a seduction, or the hope of it; thus *go out on the John Bull*, to go out looking for sex. [rhy. sl. *john bull* = PULL n.[2]]

john bull adj. [1960s+] (Aus.) drunk. [rhy. sl. *john bull* = FULL adj.[1]]

john/johnnie/johnny Chinaman/Chinee n. [19C] a derog. term for a Chinese man. [assonance]

john crow n. (W.I.) a general derog. description of a person. [*john crow*, the carrion crow]

john D see JOHN BROWN.

johndarm n. [mid-19C] a policeman (cf. JOHN n.[3]). [pron. Fr. *gendarme*]

john davies, the n. [late 19C] (US) money (cf. READY JOHN). [ety. unknown; ? anecdotal]

john dillon n. [1930s+] (N.Z.) one shilling (5p) (cf. ABRAHAM'S WILLING). [rhy. sl.]

john drum's entertainment see JACK DRUM'S ENTERTAINMENT.

john dunn n.[1] [late 19C] (Aus.) £1. [rhy. sl. *john dunn* = one]

john dunn n.[2] [1930s+] (Aus.) a policeman (cf. JOHN n.[3]). [mispron. of Fr. *gendarme*]

john elbow n. [20C] a policeman (cf. JOHN n.[3]). [he grabs one by it]

john esquire see JOHN BROWN.

john farmer n. [1900s–70s] (US) an ordinary farmer. [JOHN n.[1] + SE *farmer*]

john fortnight n. [late 19C] the tallyman, who visits debtors every fortnight to pick up their regular down-payment on goods purchased on credit.

john gilpin/gilpin n. [1950s] (W.I.) a large cutlass with a curved back and flared blade. [? tradename, but note the 'trusty sword' carried by the eponymous hero of William Cowper's poem 'John Gilpin' (1783)]

john hall n. [1920s] (US) alcohol. [var. on HALL n.[2]]

John Hancock n. [late 19C+] (US) one's signature, esp. on some form of legal or otherwise official document (cf. ALEXANDER HAMILTON n.[2]; JOHN n.[14]; JOHN BROWN n.; JOHN HENRY n.[3]). [the particularly large signature of *John Hancock* (1737–93) on the US Declaration of Independence, 1776]

John Hancock v. [late 19C+] (US) to sign one's name. [JOHN HANCOCK n.]

john handle see JOHN BROWN.

john henry n.[1] [late 19C–1940s] (US Black) a hard-working Black man, tough and indomitable in the face of appalling challenges. [the mythical hero of a popular 19C work song]

john henry n.[2] [late 19C+] the penis (cf. ABRAHAM). [var. on JOHN THOMAS n. (2)]

john henry n.[3] [20C] (US) one's signature, esp. on some form of legal or otherwise official document. [var. on JOHN HANCOCK n.]

john-hold-my-staff n. [late 17C] a servile attendant (cf. JACK-HOLD-MY-STAFF).

john/johnny hop/hopper n. [1910s+] a policeman (cf. JOHN n.[3]). [rhy. sl. *john hop* = COP n.[1]]

john-house see JOHN n.[10].

john is/johnny's dead/out of jail! excl. [1950s+] (teen) your slip is showing. [var. on CHARLIE'S DEAD]

john-john n. [1980s+] (Black) a motorcar. [? echoic of a running car]

john law n. [late 19C+] (US orig. Und.) a policeman, esp. a senior one (cf. JOHN n.[3]).

john nabs n. [20C] a policeman. [JOHN n.[3] + NAB v.[1]]

johnnie/johnny note that wherever I have source material, I have given alternative spellings; in those cases where there is a single spelling, I have given only the one I found. The alternative may, none the less, exist.

johnnie/johnny n.[1] [mid-17C] a sweetheart, a lover.

johnnie/johnny n.[2] **1** [late-17C+] a generic term for a man (cf. JOHN n.[1]). **2** [mid-19C+] used in direct address to any man, name unknown. **3** [late 19C] an idle, vacuous young aristocrat, a smart young man about town.

johnnie/johnny n.[3] [19C] **1** an inexperienced youngster, a raw recruit, a new hand. **2** (esp. Aus.) a new immigrant. [abbr. JOHNNY RAW]

johnnie/johnny n.[4] [early 19C+] (Anglo-Irish.) a half-glass of whisky. [synon. Scot. use]

johnnie/johnny *n.*[5] **1** [mid-19C] a Confederate soldier (cf. JOHNNY REB). **2** [mid-19C–1940s] a soldier in the Indian Army. **3** [late 19C–1910s] a Gurkha. **4** [1910s] a Turk. **5** [1910s–40s] an Arab. **6** [1950s+] an onion-seller from Brittany. **7** [1980s] (S.Afr. Black) a soldier. [generic (and slightly contemptuous) use of proper name]

johnnie/johnny *n.*[6] [late 19C+] (Aus.) a kookaburra (cf. JACK n.[15]).

johnnie/johnny *n.*[7] [late 19C+] the corner, esp. a public house on a corner. [abbr. JOHNNY HORNER]

johnnie/johnny *n.*[8] [1930s] a sanitary towel (cf. JOHN n.[11]).

johnnie/johnny *n.*[9] [1930s] (US) a jack in poker. [JOHN n.[8]]

johnnie/johnny *n.*[10] [1930s+] the penis (cf. ABRAHAM). [JOHN n.[9]]

johnnie/johnny/johnny bag *n.*[11] [1960s+] a condom (cf. RUBBER JOHNNY). [JOHN n.[13]]

johnnie Chinaman/Chinee *see* JOHN CHINAMAN.

johnny *see also* JOHNNIE.

johnny *n.*[1] [mid-19C] a rustic simpleton (cf. JOHNNY CAKE; JOHNNY RAW).

johnny *n.*[2] [mid-19C–1930s] a policeman (cf. JOHN n.[3]).

johnny *n.*[3] [mid-19C; 1930s+] (US) a lavatory (cf. JOHN n.[10]).

johnny *n.*[4] [1900s] (Aus.) the government (cf. JOHNNY GOVERNMENT).

johnny- *pfx.* [19C+] used as a pfx., as in *johnny-darkie*, *johnny-gyppo* etc. [modern use tends to be facetious/ironic]

johnny all sorts *n.* [late 19C] (Aus.) a general dealer, usu. in second-hand goods. [JOHNNIE n.[2] + SE *all sorts*]

johnny-at-the-rat-hole *n.* [1900s–30s] (US) an exceptionally enthusiastic, greedy person; thus *play johnny-at-the-rat-hole*, to eavesdrop, to interfere in other people's affairs (cf. JOHNNY-ON-THE-SPOT).

johnny bag *see* JOHNNIE n.[11].

johnny-bait *n.* [1960s] (US) an under-age, and thus illegal, sexual partner; used of either sex, although more often of teenage girls (cf. JAILBAIT). [? JOHNNIE n.[10] + SE *bait*]

johnny-be-good *n.* [1970s–80s] (US Black) the police (cf. JOHN n.[3]). [JOHNNY n.[2] + play on rock song 'Johnny B. Goode' (1958)]

johnny bliss *n.* [20C] (Aus.) an act of urination. [rhy. sl. *johnny bliss* = PISS n.]

johnny bull *see* JOHN BULL n.[1].

johnny bum *n.* [late 18C–19C] a donkey. [a euph. for *Jack-ass*]

johnny cake *n.* **1** [mid-19C] (US) a countryman, esp. a New Englander. **2** [19C+] (US/Can.) a French-born immigrant.

Johnny Cash *n.* [1960s+] **1** urination. **2** (Aus.) hashish. [rhy. sl.; (1) = a SLASH n.[4]; ult. US country singer *Johnny Cash* (b.1932)]

johnny Chinaman/Chinee *see* JOHN CHINAMAN.

johnny-come-lately *n.* [mid-19C+] a novice, an unsophisticated person, a recent arrival or recruit. [JOHNNIE n.[1] + SE *come lately*]

johnny congress *n.* [early 19C] (US) the US Congress. [JOHNNY- pfx. + SE *Congress*]

Johnny Cool *see* JOE COOL.

Johnny Cotton *adj.* [20C] rotten (cf. DR COTTON). [rhy. sl.]

Johnny Crapose/Crapo/Crappo/Crapeau *n.* [late 19C] a Frenchman. [JOHNNY- pfx. + Fr. *crapaud*, a toad]

johnny darbies *n.* [mid-19C+] handcuffs (cf. DARBIES).

johnny darby *n.* [mid-19C+] a policeman (cf. JENNY DARBY; JOHN n.[3]). [added pun on Fr. *gendarme*, a policeman]

johnny gallagher *n.* [20C] (US) a policeman (cf. JOHN n.[3]). [the traditional association of the police with the Irish]

johnny gee *n.* [1930s] (N.Z.) methylated spirits, as drunk by alcoholics. [? GEE UP]

johnny government *n.* [1900s] (Aus.) the government, esp. as a tax-gatherer. [JOHNNY- pfx. + SE *government*]

johnny ham *n.* [1930s] (US) a detective (cf. JOHN n.[3]). [? JOHNNY LAW + PIG n.[3]]

johnny hop/hopper *see* JOHN HOP.

johnny horner *n.* [late 19C+] the corner, esp. a public house on a corner (cf. JOHNNIE n.[7]; ROUND THE JOHNNY). [rhy. sl.]

johnny house *n.* [1930s+] (US) a privy, an outside lavatory (cf. JOHN n.[10]).

johnny-jump-up *n.* [20C] (Irish) a bottle of cider. [joc. ref. to its effects]

johnny-just-come/just-come *n.* [20C] (W.I.) a newcomer (cf. JOHNNY NEWCOME; JOHNNY RAW). [JOHNNIE n.[3] + SE *just come*]

johnny law *n.* [1920s+] (US) a policeman (cf. JOHN n.[3]).

johnny newcome *n.* **1** [early 19C–1940s] a newcomer or novice (cf. JOHNNY-JUST-COME). **2** [mid–late 19C] a newborn child. [JOHNNIE n.[3] + SE *new come*]

johnny on the coals *n.* [mid-19C] (US) a countryman, esp. a New Englander (cf. JOHNNY CAKE). [the role of *johnny cakes* (small flat cakes of cornbread) in the local diet]

johnny-on-the-spot/-on-the-job *n.* [late 19C+] (US) a reliable, punctual or decisive person (cf. CHARLIE-ON-THE-SPOT; JOHNNY-AT-THE-RAT-HOLE).

johnny-popper *n.* [1990s] a form of high-powered, if rudimentary catapult, based on a rubber condom taped to a plastic bottle, which, with its bottom cut out, forms a basic barrel; a small stone or slug is placed in the condom, which is pulled back and fired, at high speed, through the plastic 'barrel'. [JOHNNIE n.[11] + POP v.[1]]

johnny rann *n.* [20C] food (cf. TOMMY O'RANN). [rhy. sl. *Johnny Rann* = SCRAN]

johnny raper *n.* [20] (Aus.) newspaper. [rhy. sl.]

johnny raw *n.* [19C] **1** an inexperienced youngster, a raw recruit, a new hand, a novice. **2** (esp. Aus.) a new immigrant (cf. JACKY RAW; JOHNNY-JUST-COME). [JOHNNIE n.[3] + SE *raw*]

johnny reb *n.* [late 19C+] (US) a Southerner, esp. a fighter for the Confederacy. [JOHNNY n.[1] + SE *rebel*]

johnny ronce *see* JOE RONCE.

Johnny Russell *n.* [late 19C] (Aus.) bustle, hustle, esp. in the phr. *on the Johnny Russell*, bustling about. [rhy. sl.; ult. ? politician Lord *John Russell* (1792–1878)]

johnny rutter *n.* [late 19C–1930s] butter. [rhy. sl.]

johnny's dead *see* JOHN IS DEAD.

johnny's out of jail *see* JOHN IS DEAD.

johnny skinner *see* JIMMY SKINNER.

johnny tin plate *n.* [20C] (US) a rural sheriff (cf. JOHN n.[3]). [a mocking allusion to his badge]

johnny walker *n.* [20C] **1** a talker, a garrulous person. **2** an informer. [rhy. sl.]

johnny warder *n.* (Aus.) **1** [late 19C] a drunken layabout. **2** [1910s–30s] anyone who drinks alone, a drink that is taken by oneself (cf. JIMMY WOODSER). [proper name of *John Ward* who kept a public house in Sussex Street, Sydney, in which he allowed such people to drink]

johnny wet-bread *n.* [20C] (Irish) a teasing rather than aggressive term of mockery. [anecdote of a Dublin beggar who moistened his bread in the city's fountains]

johnny whop-straw *see* WHOP-STRAW.

johnny woods/woodser *see* JIMMY WOODSER.

John O'Brien *n.* [1900s–20s] (US) **1** a freight train. **2** an empty safe. [ety. unknown; ? anecdotal]

John O'Groat *n.* [20C] a coat. [rhy. sl.]

John O'Groats *n.* [20C] sexual satisfaction. [rhy. sl. *john o'groats* = OATS n.[1]]

john-out-of-office *n.* [mid-16C] one who has been dismissed from his job (cf. JACK-OUT-OF-OFFICE).

john plush *n.* [mid-19C–1920s] a footman. [his *plush* uniform]

john Q *see* JOHN BROWN.

John Q Public/Citizen n. [1930s+] the average, law-abiding citizen (cf. JANE Q PUBLIC). [JOHN n.¹ ? + ref. to US President *John Q(uincy) Adams* (1767–1848)]

John Roberts n. [late 19C] enough alcohol to last a drinker from Saturday night to Sunday night. [*John Roberts*, MP, the author of the Sunday Closing Act, which was applied to Wales]

john rogers n. see JOHN BROWN.

John Rogers phr. [20C] used in mild oaths as euph. for HELL! [proper name of Protestant martyr *John Rogers* (d.1555)]

john roper's window phr. [mid-16C–mid-19C] the hangman's rope. [pun]

john roscoe see ROSCOE.

john selwyn n. [1980s] **1** an unpleasant reaction to drugs. **2** any unpleasant experience or person. [rhy. sl. *John Selwyn Gummer* = BUMMER n.³; *John Selwyn* Gummer (b.1939), UK Conservative politician]

john smith see JOHN BROWN.

johnson n.¹ **1** [mid–late 19C; 1960s+] the penis (late usage esp. US Black). **2** [1970s] (US) a dildo. [analogous with JOCK n.² or JACK n.⁸; later use ? link to boxing champion Jack *Johnson* (1878–1946)]

johnson n.² [1960s] a pimp; a man living off a prostitute's earnings. [JOHNSONS n.¹ ? + ref. to JOHN n.⁶]

johnson n.³ **1** [1970s+] (US) a thing. **2** [1980s] the buttocks. [generic use of the common surname]

johnson n.⁴ (US drugs) **1** [1970s+] marijuana. **2** [1980s+] crack cocaine. [ext. of JOHNSON n.³ (1)]

johnson bar n. **1** [1900s–10s] (US) a penis (cf. JOHNSON n.¹). **2** [1960s–70s] (US) a dildo (cf. JOHNSON n.¹). [? railroad jargon *johnson bar*, the reverse bar of an early 20C locomotive]

johnson-boys/-brothers see JOHNSONS n.¹.

johnson family n. [late 19C+] (US) a generic term for the world of professional criminals. [var. on JOHNSONS n.¹]

johnson-man see JOHNSONS n.¹.

johnson rod n. [1940s+] (US) an imaginary part of an engine, as in a car, blamed for a malfunction. [? railroad jargon *johnson bar*, the reverse bar of an early 20C locomotive]

johnsons/johnson-boys/-brothers/-man n.¹ [late 19C+] (US) a generic term for the world of professional criminals (cf. JOHNSON FAMILY). [? the commonness and thus potential anonymity of the name; or railroad jargon *johnson bar*, the reverse bar of an early 20C locomotive, used as a weapon or cosh]

johnsons n.² [1970s] (US) a woman's breasts. [ety. unknown; ext./misreading of JOHNSON n.¹]

john stagger-back n. [20C] (W.I.) a variety of codfish fritter, so tough and chewy that one 'staggers back' when one bites it.

John T./Paul/Sam/O. Henry n. [1910s+] one's signature. [on pattern of JOHN HANCOCK.; despite *O. Henry* (the writer) these are generic uses of fictional names]

john thomas n. **1** [mid-19C] a liveried servant. **2** [mid-19C+] the penis (cf. ABRAHAM; MAN THOMAS; THOMAS n.¹). [? like the former, the latter 'stands' in the presence of a lady]

John Wayne n. [1960s+] (US) anything seen as heroic, macho, manly. [suggestive of heroic film characters played by the Hollywood actor *John Wayne* (1907–79)]

John Wayne adj. [1960s+] (US) heroic, macho, manly. [JOHN WAYNE n.]

John Wayne v. [1970s+] (US) to act decisively, daringly, in an attacking manner. [JOHN WAYNE n.]

john willie n. [19C] the penis (cf. ABRAHAM; JOHN THOMAS; WILLIE).

john willy see JOHN BROWN.

join-boy n. [1940s+] (S.Afr.) a newly recruited miner. [? Fanakalo *joyin*, a contract + SE *boy*]

joined adj. [late 19C] married. [note JOIN GIBLETS]

joiner n. [late 19C+] (orig. US) one who delights in joining a number of societies, groups and other organizations.

join/mix giblets v. [18C] **1** to have sexual intercourse (cf. DO A BIT OF GIBLET PIE; JOIN PAUNCHES; JUMBLE-GIBLETS; JUMBLER; NAIL TWO WAMES TOGETHER; RUB OFFAL; TROUBLE GIBLETS). **2** to cohabit without being married. [the *OED* offers SE *join giblets*, to marry, but the citation implies that this might possibly have been a mistakenly delicate translation of a piece of 18C coarseness]

join in n. [20C] (Ulster) a pool or 'kitty' of money to provide a round of drinks.

join out the odds, to phr. [1950s] (US Und.) to become a pimp. [circus jargon *join out*, to work as an employee or associate; thus he is working 'on the side of' the odds or fig. betting against the customer]

join paunches v. [18C] to have sexual intercourse (cf. JOIN GIBLETS).

joint n.¹ [late 19C–1900s] a wife. [JOINED]

joint n.² [late 19C–1920s] (Aus.) a person, a fellow, a 'chap'. [briefly Cockney in the late 19C; ? the 'other half' of JOINT n.¹]

joint n.³ **1** [late 19C–1950s] (US) an opium den. **2** [late 19C+] (orig. Und.) a swindling set-up or a place to be robbed. **3** [20C] (US) any place, esp. a bar or club, a brothel, a gambling establishment. **4** [1930s+] (US) as *the joint*, prison. **5** [1980s] (US) a detoxification facility. [according to the *OED* the orig. use applied spec. to Chinese-run opium dens and thence to illicit saloons; in both cases the *joint* was seen as a gathering place for criminals, a low-life nuance that remains with the word, even in its more general sl. use]

joint n.⁴ (drugs) **1** [1920s+] (US) an opium pipe or hypodermic syringe and other drug paraphernalia. **2** [1930s+] a marijuana or hashish cigarette. [(1) the 'joining' of the opium and its pipe; (2) the 'joining' of the drug with tobacco to make the cigarette; by the 1990s the drug reference had become sufficiently common for the word to be used almost without comment or identifying quotation marks]

joint n.⁵ **1** [1930s+] (US) the penis. **2** [1970s] (US) the vagina. [? the physical connection or joining that is basic to sexual intercourse]

joint n.⁶ [1950s+] (US) a gun. [? fig. use of JOINT n.⁵]

joint n.⁷ **1** [1970s+] (US Black) something excellent, as in the phr. *the serious joint*, the real thing. **2** [1980s+] (US Black) an artistic creation, typically a record or film. [? fig use of JOINT n.³; popularized by film-maker Spike Lee (b.1956) who credits his films 'Another Spike Lee Joint'; now used by many HIP-HOP n./RAP n.⁵ artists to describe their records and tapes]

join the angels, to phr. [19C+] to die.

join the club! excl. [1960s+] an excl. of sympathy offered to a speaker who has just recounted an unfortunate or unpleasant experience (cf. JOIN THE CROWD!).

join the crowd! excl. [1970s+] an excl. used to make it clear to one who is complaining that their problems are by no means theirs alone (cf. JOIN THE CLUB!).

join the gang, to phr. [late 19C] to become a professional thief.

join the great majority, to phr. [20C] to die, thereby joining all the dead of thousands of years of humanity (cf. LEAVE THE MINORITY).

join the household brigade, to phr. [late 19C] of a man, to get married. [pun]

jointman n. [20C] (Can./US prison) any prisoner who flatters or toadies to the authorities (cf. CENTERMAN; STATE CON). [JOINT n.³ (4) + SE *man*]

joint of beef n. [20C] the chief, i.e. the boss. [rhy. sl.]

jointwise adj. [20C] (US prison) well-adjusted to prison life, capable of sustaining one's existence in prison (cf. CONWISE). [JOINT n.³ (4) + sfx. -WISE]

jojee n. [1950s+] (drugs) heroin. [var. on DUJI]

jo-jo n. **1** [late 19C–1900s] (Aus.) a man with a very heavy beard and side-whiskers. **2** [1900s–60s] (US) a funny character. [*Jo-Jo*; (1) a Russian 'dog-man' who was exhibited as a sideshow freak in Melbourne, c.1880; (2) a dog-faced boy exhibited by P.T. Barnum (1810–91)]

jojo n. [1960s+] (US Black) the penis. [? JOHN n.⁹; JOHNSON n.¹]

jo-jos n. [1960s+] (Can. prison) a bulky coat without pockets. [ety. unknown]

joke over phr. [1960s+] a phr. used by the victim of a practical joke who wishes to indicate that they are not amused.

joker n. **1** [early 19C+] (orig. Aus.) a man, a person, usu. with implications of incompetence. **2** [mid-19C+] (US) any thing or situation that poses a problem, a hidden catch. **3** [20C] (W.I.) anyone who is given authority but performs their work with irritating incompetence, thus 'a disgrace to one's profession'. [they make a joke of the situation]

jol/jaul/jawl n. (S.Afr.) **1** [1950s+] a good time, merry-making, enjoyment, entertainment. **2** [1970s+] a party, a festival or other social occasion. **3** [1980s+] a joke, a stunt, a game. **4** [1980s+] a holiday, a trip taken for pure enjoyment. [Afk. *jol*, a dance, a party]

jol/jaul/jawl v. (S.Afr.) **1** [1940s+] to go out. **2** [1940s+] to stroll, to run, to depart, to look for some fun or entertainment. **3** [1960s+] to have an affair with, to flirt, to 'carry on'. **4** [1970s+] to tease, to joke. **5** [1970s+] to play, to frolic, to have fun, to 'party'. [JOL n.]

jola n. [1950s+] (W.I.) an over-sized handbag. [Carib.E *jola*, a large jute sack]

joller n. (S.Afr.) **1** [1960s+] a hedonist. **2** [1960s+] one who frequents 'unsavoury' bars, dance-halls and similar places of low-life entertainment. **3** [1980s+] one who attends a party, concert or social gathering. **4** [1980s+] a player of a game. [JOL v. + sfx. -er]

jolling n. (S.Afr.) **1** [1960s+] flirting. **2** [1980s+] merry-making, 'partying'. [JOL v. + sfx. -ing]

jollo n. [20C] (Aus.) a party, a celebration, usu. involving drinking. [SE *jollification*]

jollocks/jollux n. [mid-18C–early 19C] **1** a parson. **2** a fat person. [SE *jolly*, but note dial. *jollus*, fat, fleshy, *jollock*, jolly, hearty]

jollop n.¹ **1** [1920s+] a purgative, a medicine. **2** [1920s+] strong liquor or a measure of liquor. [SE *jalap*, a purgative drug obtained from the tuberous roots of *Exogonium* (*Ipomoea*) *purga*]

jollop n.² [1990s] ejaculate, semen. [dial. *jollop*, a wet mess (of food)]

jollop v. [1990s] to ejaculate. [JOLLOP n.²]

jollux see JOLLOCKS.

jolly n.¹ [late 18C–19C] the head. [abbr. JOLLY-NOB]

jolly n.² [19C] a marine; thus *tame jolly*, a militiaman, *royal jolly*, a royal marine. [*OED* suggests n. use of SE *jolly*, cheerful, gallant, brave etc, but Bowen (*Sea Slang*, 1929) says it was adapted from the nickname of the City Trained Bands (which may also have come from SE]

jolly n.³ **1** [mid-19C] praise, esp. when spoken for an ulterior and/or criminal purpose. **2** [mid-late 19C] a cheer. **3** [late 19C] a sham purchaser, who praises up inferior goods in order to facilitate their sale to an innocent buyer (cf. CHUCK A JOLLY). [SE *jolly*]

jolly n.⁴ [mid-19C] an accomplice. [? they 'jolly one along']

jolly n.⁵ **1** [mid-late 19C] a ruckus, a fracas. **2** [mid-late 19C] the person who encourages or initiates a ruckus. **3** [late 19C–1900s] (US) a deception or hoax. **4** [late 19C+] (US) light-hearted teasing, bantering, often as *the jolly*.

jolly n.⁶ [late 19C] **1** a cheer. **2** a party, a merry-making. [(2) SE *jollification*]

jolly n.⁷ **1** [late 19C+] a thrill of pleasure or excitement. **2** [1960s+] (US) an orgasm (cf. GET ONE'S JOLLIES).

jolly adj.¹ [19C] tipsy, drunk (cf. ABOUT RIGHT adj.¹).

jolly adj.² [mid-19C+] big, great, plump.

jolly v. **1** [mid-19C–1900s] (orig. US?) to tease roughly, to chaff, to abuse, to trick. **2** [mid-19C] to make a sham bid at an auction. **3** [mid-19C+] to treat someone in an agreeable manner, with the intention of keeping them happy and/or obtaining a favour from them; esp. in the phr. *jolly up*, *jolly along*. **4** [late 19C] to cheer. **5** [late 19C] (US campus) to have a good time.

jolly adv. [mid-19C+] **1** extremely, very, esp. when used ironically. **2** [late 19C+] exceedingly pleasant, agreeable, delightful. [SE 14C–19C]

jolly bag n. [1980s+] (US) a condom.

jolly beans/pills n. [1960s+] (drugs) amphetamine (cf. A n.²).

jolly boys n. [late 19C] 'a group of small drinking vessels connected by a tube, or by openings one from another' (F&H). [the effect of using such a vessel]

jolly d! excl. [20C] (juv.) wonderful, excellent, fantastic. [? abbr. SE *jolly delightful*]

jolly dog n. [late 18C–mid-19C] a boon companion. [SE *jolly* + DOG n.⁹; later use is SE]

jolly for v. [mid-19C–1920s] to support one's friend with teasing and banter. [JOLLY v.]

jolly for polly phr. [20C] sexually available. [SE *jolly* + rhy. sl. *polly* = LOLLY n.²]

jolly green n. [1960s+] (drugs) marijuana. [GREEN n.³ (1) + ref. to *Jolly Green Giant* brand of packaged vegetables]

jolly joker n. [20C] a poker. [rhy. sl.]

jolly member n. [19C] the penis (cf. DEAREST MEMBER).

jolly nob n. [late 18C–19C] the head (cf. JOLLY n.¹). [SE *jolly* + NOB n.¹ (1)]

jollyo n. [1970s] a celebration. [SE *jolly*/JOLLY n.⁶ + sfx. -O]

jolly pills see JOLLY BEANS.

jolly pop/popper n. [1950s+] (drugs) a casual user of heroin. [SE *jolly* + POP v.⁶ (1)]

jolly roger n. [20C] a lodger. [rhy. sl.]

jolly tit n. [early 18C] a pleasant companion. [SE *jolly* + TIT n.³ (3)]

jolly-up n. **1** [1900s–20s] a drinking bout, a spree. **2** [1920s+] an informal dance, a party. **3** [1920s–50s] a good time. [JOLLY n.⁶]

jolly utter adj. [late 19C] appalling, unspeakable. [JOLLY adv. + SE *utter*; coined by W.S. Gilbert in *Patience* (1881), his satire on the Aesthetic Movement]

Jolson story n. [1970s] the penis. [rhy. sl. *Jolson story* = CORIE. *The Jolson Story*, a biopic of the singer Al *Jolson* (1886–1950), was released in 1946]

jolt n.¹ **1** [20C] (US drugs) a measure of a drug as taken by a user, esp. an injection of a narcotic (cf. BANG n.⁶; SHOT n.⁵). **2** [20C] a stiff drink of spirits, esp. brandy, whisky or bourbon. **3** [1920s+] the effects of a drug or alcohol, a kick.

jolt n.² [1910s+] (US Und.) a prison sentence, usu. with the number of years specified, e.g. a *seven-year jolt*.

jolt v. **1** [19C] to have sexual intercourse. **2** [1920s+] (Aus.) to hit someone. **3** [1950s+] (US drugs) to inject a drug.

jolterhead/jolthead n. [late 18C–19C] a fool, a stupid person. [dial; ult. ? SE *jowl*, a bump on the head]

jomer n. [mid-19C] a girlfriend (cf. BLOWER n.¹). [? Rom./Polari]

jomoke see JAMOKE n.¹.

jonah n. [mid-19C+] one who brings bad luck or one who suffers severe misfortune. [the biblical story of *Jonah and the Whale*]

jonah v. **1** [late 19C+] to bring bad luck. **2** [1960s] (US Black) to trick, to swindle. [JONAH n.]

jonah's whale n. [late 19C–1910s] a tail. [rhy. sl.]

jonathan n. [late 18C–mid-19C] (US) a New Englander. [the popularity of the name]

jonathan ross n. [20C] a drink, spec. beer. [rhy. sl. ? Ross = SE *toss* (*it back*) or play on TOSSER n.¹; ult. Jonathan Ross, UK TV personality]

jones n.¹ **1** [1950s+] (US drugs) drug addiction, esp. to heroin. **2** [1960s+] (US drugs) heroin addict, the symptoms of heroin withdrawal (cf. JONESING). **3** [1970s+] pleasurable drug-induced feelings. **4** [1970s+] (US) a strong craving or habit, whether for cigarettes, food, a person or anything, e.g. a *love jones*, a *chocolate jones*. [the common family name; its link to craving remains unexplained]

jones n.² [1960s+] **1** (US Black) the penis (cf. GET ONE'S JONES OFF). **2** sexual intercourse.

jones n.³ [1970s+] (US Black) a Black person. [generic use of surname]

jones-boy see JONES-MAN.

joneser n. [1980s+] (US) an addict, esp. of cocaine. [JONES n.¹]

jonesing/jonesing out n. [1970s+] (US drugs) experiencing withdrawal symptoms. [JONES n.¹]

jones-man/-boy n. [1970s+] (US Black/drugs) a heroin dealer. [JONES n.¹ + SE *man/boy*]

jonestown n. [1980s+] drug addiction (cf. JIM JONES n.). [JONES n.¹ + ref. to the 'revolutionary suicide' of 913 cultists, followers of the Rev. Jim Jones, at his settlement of *Jonestown*, Guyana, in 1978]

jong n. (S.Afr.) **1** [early 17C–late 19C] a Black servant (cf. SE *boy*). **2** [early 19C] an informal mode of address, irrespective of sex. **3** [20C] a derog. term for a Black man. [Cape Du. *jongen*, a young lad]

jong! excl. [1950s+] (S.Afr.) an excl. of surprise, delight, exasperation, approval etc.

joning see JOANING.

jonna see JONNOP.

jonnick adj. [late 19C+] (Aus.) fair, genuine, honest, truthful. [dial. *jannock*, fair, straightforward]

jonnop/jonna n. [early 19C+] a policeman (cf. JOHN n.³). [elision of JOHN HOP]

jonto n. [1940s] a person, a fellow.

joog see JUKE v.

joogie n. [1970s] (US Black) a Black person, occas. derog. use. [? JUKE n. + BOOGIE n.²]

jook n.¹ [late 19C+] (W.I.) **1** a stab or poke. **2** an injection. [JOOK v.²]

jook n.² *see* JUKE n.

jook v.¹ *see* JUKE v.

jook v.² [late 19C+] (W.I. Rasta) to pierce or stick, as with a needle, thorn or a long pointed stick (cf. JUKE v.). [var. on JUKE v.² (1); note South Carolina dial. *joog/jook*, to prick, to poke, to stab]

jook v.³ [20C] (W.I./UK Black teen) to have quick, casual sexual intercourse, esp. when the man is keen but the woman is reluctant (cf. JUKE v.). [fig. use of JOOK v.²]

jookass n. [19C+] (US Black) a jackass.

jook joint see JUKE JOINT.

jook-halter n. [19C] (Ulster) one who has only just escaped hanging. [Scot. *jouk*, to trick + SE *halter*]

jook house see JUKE JOINT.

jooking n. [20C] sexual intercourse. [JOOK v.³]

jook it v. [late 19C–1940s] (US Black) to play piano in a cheap bar or brothel (cf. JUKE v.³).

jook out someone's eye, to phr. [1950s+] (W.I.) to cheat in a business deal (cf. DIG OUT SOMEONE'S EYE). [fig. use of JOOK v.²]

jooks n. [1990s] (Black) a fool (cf. PRICK). [JUKE v.¹ (2)]

jook-the-beetle n. [20C] (Ulster) **1** a bad cook. **2** a lump in mashed potatoes. [fig. use of Scot. *jouk*, to trick + *beetle*, a hammer, in this case a masher for the vegetables]

jook-the-bottle n. [20C] (Ulster) a teetotaller. [fig. use of Scot. *jouk*, to trick + SE *bottle*]

joombye n. [1990s] (Scot.) semen. [ety. unknown; ? Scot. word; or link to JAM n.⁸]

joram/jorum n. [mid-18C–mid-19C] a drink. [*joram*, a drinking bowl, ? ult. the biblical name *Joram* who 'brought with him vessels of silver, and vessels of gold, and vessels of brass' (2 Sam. 8:10)]

jordan/jordain/jurden n.¹ [early 15C–mid-18C] a chamber-pot. [origin unknown, one theory suggested that the term abbr. *Jordan-bottle* – a bottle of water brought from the River Jordan by crusaders or pilgrims – but this ignores the orig. form of the word, as found in *Prompt. Parv.* (1440) *inter alia*, *jurdanus*, which has no links to *Jordanes*, the contemporary Lat. for the Jordan. An earlier SE use was a kind of pot or vessel formerly used by physicians and alchemists; such pots might often have held urine for analysis; thus leading to the sl. term]

jordan/jordain n.² [late 17C–mid-19C] a blow with a staff. [ety. unknown; ? f. use of 'go over the Jordan' as euph. for die; such a blow might kill the recipient]

jorum see JORAM.

j.o. scene n. [1960s+] **1** masturbation. **2** mutual masturbation. [JERK-OFF n.¹ + SCENE n. (4)]

Jose n. [1970s+] (US) a term for a Puerto Rican, usu. derog. [a common given name among Hispanics]

Joseph n. [late 17C–19C] **1** a woman's overcoat; thus *rum Joseph*, a first-rate overcoat (cf. BEN n.²). **2** a bashful young man. [both are biblical: (1) Joseph's 'coat of many colours'; (2) Joseph who fled from Potiphar's wife]

joseph adj. [1900s–20s] (US) aware, in the know (cf. JERRY adj.; JOE HEP adj.). [ext. of JOE adj.¹]

josh n.¹ **1** [mid-late 19C] a fool, a dullard. **2** [late 19C+] (US) a good-natured joke or piece of banter. [JOSKIN; (2) JOSH v.]

Josh n.² [mid-19C–1900s] (US) a rustic, simpleton (cf. ALVIN).

josh v. [mid-19C+] (US) **1** to ridicule or tease. **2** to indulge in teasing or banter. [proper name *Josh* Billings (Henry Wheeler Shaw, 1818–85), an American humorist]

josh! excl. [mid-19C] (US) a cry of encouragement. [JOSH n.¹]

josher n. [late 19C–1900s] (Aus.) an immoral old woman. [? JOSH v. or play on Suffolk dial. *josh*, an old cow]

joskin n. [early 19C–1960s] **1** an old man, old gaffer. **2** a country bumpkin (cf. ALVIN). [dial. *joss*, bump + SE *bumpkin*; 20C use is US]

joss n. [1910s+] luck; thus *good joss, bad joss*. [pidgin *joss*, a Chinese god; ult. Port. *deos* and Javanese *dejos*]

josser n.¹ [early 19C–1960s] an old man (cf. JOSKIN).

josser n.² **1** [late 19C] a swell, a grandee. **2** [late 19C] an ageing roué. **3** [late 19C+] (Aus.) a clergyman, a minister (cf. JOSSMAN). [pidgin *joss*, a Chinese god or idol; ult. Port. *deos* and Javanese *dejos*]

josser n.³ [late 19C] an outsider. [Polari]

josser n.⁴ [late 19C–1910s] one who begs for loans, a 'sponge'. [var. on PROSSER]

josser n.⁵ [late 19C–1940s] **1** a simpleton, a fool. **2** a chap, a fellow. [note circus/Rom. *josher, josser*, an outsider, an amateur]

joss-house n. [late 19C+] (Aus.) a church. [JOSSER n.² (2)]

jossman n. [late 19C–1960s] a clergyman, esp. a missionary (cf. JOSSER n.²). [SE *joss-man*, a priest of a Chinese religion, ult. *joss*, a Chinese idol or image; thus luck (f. Pidgin version of Port. *deos*, god). Note RN use *jossman*, Plymouth gin, which carried a picture of a monk on the bottle]

jossop *n.* [1930s+] gravy. [ety. unknown; ? link to JOLLOP n.[1]; ? ult. ME *jussell*, a broth]

jostle *v.* **1** [late 18C–1960s] (Und.) to cheat. **2** [1960s+] (US Und./police) to pickpocket. **3** [1990s] to masturbate.

jostler *n.* [1920s–60s] (US Und./police) a pickpocket or petty thief. [JOSTLE v. (2)]

jots *n.* [1930s–60s] (US) bread. [ety. unknown]

jouk *see* JUKE n.

joukoutoo *pron.* [20C] (W.I.) a derog. pron., even you, unimportant you; thus, as adj., insignificant, unimportant. [Fr. *jusqu'à vous*, as far down (socially) as you]

jounce *v.* [19C] of a man, to have sexual intercourse (cf. BANG v.[1]). [SE *jounce*, to shake]

jour *n.* [19C] a *jour*neyman worker, e.g. a printer, a cabinet-maker. [abbr.]

journey *n.* [late 19C] a spell of work, a time or occasion.

journeyman soul-saver *n.* [mid–late 19C] a scripture-reader.

journey's end *n.* [1930s] prison. [a play on *Journey's End* (1929), a play by R.C. Sherriff]

journo *n.* [1960s+] (orig. Aus.) a journalist. [abbr. SE + sfx. -O]

Jove *n.* [late 16C+] used in mild oaths and excls. as euph. for the otherwise blasphemous *God*. [the Latinized version of the Greek Zeus, 'king of the gods']

jow *v.* [mid-19C] to go away, to leave; usu. as imper. *jow!* go away! be off! [Hind.]

jowl-/gum-sucking *n.* [mid–late 19C] kissing.

joxy *see* JAXY.

Joy, the *n.*[1] [late 19C+] (Anglo-Irish) Mount*joy* Prison, Dublin. [abbr.]

joy *n.*[2] [1950s+] (drugs) **1** marijuana. **2** heroin. [the effects]

joy bang *n.* [1950s+] (drugs) an occasional injection of a narcotic by anyone who is not addicted (cf. JOY POP). [SE *joy* + BANG n.[6]; such an injection would usually be subcutaneous rather than intravenous]

joy bone *n.* [1980s] (US) the penis (cf. JOY BOX).

joy box *n.* **1** [1930s–40s] (US Black) a radio or a piano. **2** [1970s] (US) the vagina (cf. JOY BONE).

joy boy *n.* [20C] **1** a male homosexual (cf. TOY BOY). **2** (US) a foolish joker, or (ironically) a bad-tempered person. [note Mr *Joyboy*, the US mortician, in Evelyn Waugh *The Loved One* (1948)]

joy button/buzzer *n.* [1970s+] (US) the clitoris. [note BUTTON n.[3] (2)]

joy dust *n.* [1930s+] (US drugs) heroin, morphine or cocaine (cf. JOY FLAKES; JOY POWDER). [SE *joy* + DUST n.[6]]

joy flakes *n.* [1950s+] (US drugs) heroin, morphine or cocaine (cf. JOY DUST). [note FLAKE n.[3]]

joy girl *n.* [1910s–60s] (US) a prostitute.

joy hemp/roots *n.* [1940s] (US Black) marijuana (cf. JOY SMOKE; JOY WEED).

joy hole *n.* [1930s+] (US) the vagina (cf. BLACK HOLE n.[1]). [note HOLE n.[1] (2)]

joy house *n.* [1910s–70s] (US) a brothel (cf. ACCOMMODATION HOUSE). [note HOUSE n.[1]]

joy jelly *n.* [1970s+] (US) fruit-flavoured vaginal lubricant jelly.

joy joint *n.* [late 19C–1920s] (US) a saloon bar. [SE *joy* + JOINT n.[3] (3)]

joy juice *n.* (US) **1** [1910s+] liquor, alcohol (cf. JOY WATER). **2** [1950s+] (Black/campus) beer. **3** [1950s+] (drugs) liquid amyl nitrite (cf. AIMIES n.[2]). **4** [1960s+] a depressant. **5** [1980s+] semen. [note JUICE n.[1]; JUICE n.[3]]

joy knob *n.* [1950s+] (US) the penis. [note KNOB n.[1] (1)]

joy plant *n.* [20C] (drugs) opium.

joy pop/shot *n.* [1920s–70s] (drugs) an occasional injection of a narcotic by anyone who is not addicted (cf. JOY BANG). [SE *joy* + POP n.[8]/SHOT n.[5] (2)]

joy pop *v.* [1920s–70s] (drugs) to inject narcotic drugs irregularly. [JOY POP n.]

joy-popper *n.* [1930s+] (drugs) an occasional taker of illegal drugs, esp. injectable narcotics (cf. JOY-RIDER n.[2]). [JOY POP n.]

joy popping *n.* [1920s–70s] (drugs) the occasional use of drugs. [JOY POP n.]

joy powder *n.* [1920s+] (US drugs) heroin, morphine or cocaine (cf. JOY DUST).

joy prong *n.* [1910s–70s] the penis (cf. JOYSTICK n.[1]). [SE *joy* + PRONG n.]

joy-rider *n.*[1] [1920s–30s] (US) a legless beggar who transports themself on a skateboard.

joy-rider *n.*[2] [1930s–60s] (US drugs) an occasional narcotic drug user (cf. JOY-POPPER).

joy roots *see* JOY HEMP.

joy shot *see* JOY POP.

joy smoke *n.* [1930s–60s] (drugs) marijuana (cf. JOY HEMP). [note SMOKE n.[2] (2)]

joystick *n.*[1] **1** [1910s–20s] the control lever of an aeroplane or other vehicle. **2** [1910s+] (orig. US) the penis. [play on *joystick*, the control lever of an aeroplane and on SE *joy* + *stick*. (1) SE by 1950s, since when it has been extended to cover an external control device used in playing computer games; Puxley suggests rhy. sl. *joystick* = PRICK n., but this is unlikely]

joystick *n.*[2] **1** [1930s] (drugs) an opium pipe. **2** [1960s+] a marijuana cigarette. [note STICK n.[11]]

joy trail *n.* [1970s+] the vagina (cf. ALLEY n.[1]).

joy water *n.* [1900s–20s] (US) alcohol (cf. JOY JUICE).

joy weed *n.* [1930s–40s] (US drugs) marijuana (cf. JOY HEMP). [note WEED n.[1] (4)]

joxer *n.* [20C] (Irish) **1** an idler. **2** one who is out of work. [? northern dial. *jock*, a seaman]

Jozi *see* JOEYS.

J school *n.* [1950s+] (US campus) a *school* of journalism. [abbr.]

j.s.t. *phr.* [1960s+] (US) *Jewish Standard Time*, derog. only if used by a non-Jew (cf. AFRICAN PEOPLE'S TIME). [abbr.]

j.t. *n.* [mid-19C+] the penis. [abbr. JOHN THOMAS]

j.t.o. *see* JAILHOUSE TURNOUT.

juanita *n.* [1950s+] (drugs) marijuana. [play on the Sp. name *marijuana*, lit. 'Mary Jane']

Juan Valdez *n.* [1950s+] (drugs) marijuana (cf. JUANITA). [play on the *juana* part of the Sp. word]

juba *see* JIBA.

jubbies *n.* [20C] breasts. [? SE *chubby*]

jube *n.* [1930s+] a ju*jube*. [abbr.]

jubilee *n.* [late 19C] the buttocks, the posterior. [coined by the *Sporting Times* at the time of Queen Victoria's Golden Jubilee (1887) + a play on the 'arse-end' of the century]

jubilee mutton *n.* [late 19C–1920s] (Irish) very little, a very small portion. [the meagre portions of *mutton* that were distributed in 1897 as part of Queen Victoria's Diamond *Jubilee* celebrations]

Judaic superbacy *n.* [late 19C] a Jew dressed in 'all the glory of his best clothes' (Ware). [the implication is of flashiness and vulgarity]

judas *n.* [20C] (US Und.) the spyhole set into a solid cell door. [SE *judas-hole*; *judas-slit*, a peep-hole; ult. the biblical *Judas*, the betrayer of Christ]

judas-haired *adj.* [mid-19C] **1** red-haired. **2** deceitful. [the biblical *Judas* was supposedly red-haired]

judas priest! *excl.* [1910s+] (orig. US) euph. for *Jesus Christ!* (cf. BEJABERS!; BUDDHIST PRIEST!).

jude *n.* [late 19C] a prostitute. [JUDY n.[1]]

judge *n.*[1] (Und.) **1** [19C] an experienced criminal. **2** [1950s+] (S.Afr.) a senior figure in a prison gang, among whose tasks is to authorize the assassination of a fellow prisoner.

judge *n.*² [mid–late 19C] (US) used in direct address to a man whose real name is unknown.

judge *n.*³ [1960s+] (Aus.) a manual labourer who shirks on the job (cf. LONDON FOG *n.*²). [such a person is 'always sitting on a case']

judge *v.* [1950s+] (W.I. Rasta) to wear one's everyday or ordinary clothes or shoes in the yard or in the bush. [ety. unknown; ? the idea of a judge refusing to relinquish their robes]

Judge Dredd *n.* [1990s] the head. [rhy. sl.]

Judge Lynch *n.* [mid-19C–1940s] (US) lynch law. [SE *lynch law*, ult. the court held by *Captain William Lynch* (1742–1820) of Pittsylvania in Virginia *c.*1776–80]

judgin' *adj.* [20C] (W.I. Rasta) ref. to everyday or ordinary clothes or shoes worn in the yard or in the bush, as in *judgin' boot.* [JUDGE *v.*]

Judi Dench *n.* [1990s] a stench, a stink. [rhy. sl.; the UK actor Dame *Judi Dench* (b.1934)]

Judische compliment *see* JEW'S COMPLIMENT.

judy *n.*¹ [19C+] (orig. Und.) **1** a ludicrous-looking woman. **2** a woman, irrespective of looks. **3** a promiscuous woman (cf. JUDE). [*Punch*'s wife *Judy* in the puppet-show 'Punch and Judy'; 20C use mainly in Liverpool dial. + Aus.]

judy *n.*² [mid-19C] (orig. US) a fool. [? Punch and *Judy*]

judy/jupe balls *n.*³ [20C] (US Und.) a particularly unappealing item of food served to prisoners in solitary confinement; the meal consists of a ground patty, approx. 10 × 10 × 8cm (4 × 4 × 3in), which is composed of the entire meal's ingredients put together through a blender; it is traditionally burned on the outside and raw within. [ety. unknown]

judy *n.*⁴ [1930s+] a duodenal ulcer. [abbr. *duode*nal]

judy and punch *n.* [20C] lunch. [rhy. sl.]

judy-slayer *n.* [late 19C] a successful ladies' man. [JUDY *n.*¹ + SE *slayer*; play on SE *lady-killer*]

judy with the big booty *phr.* [1970s+] (US Black) a fat woman. [JUDY *n.*¹ + BOOTY *n.* (3)]

juff *n.* [late 19C+] the buttocks, the posterior (cf. CHUFF *n.*²). [? Fr. *joues*, cheeks]

jug *n.*¹ **1** [early 19C+] prison; thus as *the jug*, solitary confinement, *jugged*, in prison (cf. STONE JUG *n.*¹). **2** [mid-19C] the mouth, esp. as a receptacle for alcoholic drink (cf. GROG-SHOP; SLUICE-HOUSE; SLUICERY). **3** [mid-19C+] (US) a bank. **4** [1900s–60s] (US) a safe. **5** [1920s+] (US) a bottle of whisky or wine. **6** [1930s+] a female baby (cf. TEAPOT *n.*³). **7** [1950s+] a drink, esp. a pint of beer. **8** [1940s+] (US campus) a detention. **9** [1970s] (US drugs) a bottle of a drug in liquid form.

jug *n.*² [late 19C–1950s] a fool, a gullible person. [abbr. JUGGINS]

jug *n.*³ [1900s] (Und.) one shilling (5p). [JOGUE]

jug *n.*⁴ [1930s+] (US) a carburettor. [resemblance]

jug *v.*¹ *see* JUKE v.

jug *v.*² **1** [mid-19C+] to imprison, to incarcerate. **2** [late 19C] to deceive, either jokingly or through some form of illegality. **3** [late 19C+] (US campus) to be put on detention.

jug *v.*³ [1970s+] (N.Z.) to hit or slash with a beer bottle. [SNZE *jug*, a litre bottle of beer]

jug and pail *n.* [20C] jail. [rhy. sl.]

jug-bitten *adj.* [early 17C] drunk (cf. JUG-BROKE; POT-SHOT).

jug-broke *adj.* [mid-17C] drunk (cf. JUG-BITTEN).

jugelow *n.* [early 19C] (Und.) a dog. [Rom. *guggal*, a dog; note market traders' jargon *juck, juckle*, a dog]

jug-fuck *n.* [1980s+] (US) an awful mess or terrible situation. [such an image, copulation with a jug, is seen as absurd]

jugg *see* JUKE v.

jugged *adj.* **1** [early 19C+] imprisoned. **2** [1920s–70s] (US) drunk. [JUG *n.*¹ (1), (5)]

jugger *n.* **1** [1920s–60s] (US Und.) a bank robber. **2** [1930s]

(US Und.) a banker. **3** [1960s–70s] (US) a drunk (cf. JUGGED). [JUG *n.*¹ (1), (5)]

juggins *n.* [late 19C] a fool, a dupe, esp. someone who is so foolish that they can be prevailed upon to buy every round of drinks (cf. BILLY MUGGINS). [var. on MUGGINS *n.*¹. Note Henry Ernest Schlesinger Benzon, better known to London's sporting fraternity as the *Jubilee Juggins*. Benzon, the son of a Birmingham umbrella frame-maker, went through an inheritance of £250,000 (a massive sum at the time) in less than two years. His last pennies went in 1887, the year of Queen Victoria's Golden Jubilee, thus earning him his nickname. Only the kindness of his fellow patrons of the raffish Romano's Restaurant in the Strand, who established a fund that sustained him on £7 a week for life, saved him from absolute penury]

juggins' boy *n.* [late 19C] 'the sharp and impudent son of a stupid and easily ridiculed father' (Ware). [JUGGINS + SE *boy*]

juggins-hunting *n.* [late 19C] looking for someone who will pick up one's bar bill. [JUGGINS + SE *hunting*]

juggle/juggler *n.* [1960s+] (drugs) **1** an addict who sells drugs to help finance their own addiction. **2** a teenaged street dealer, now usu. of crack cocaine. [they juggle the packets or vials of drugs from hand to hand as they await a customer]

juggle *v.* **1** [late 19C–1930s] (US) to manhandle, esp. large things. **2** [1960s+] (US drugs) to sell drugs, esp. to support one's own habit. **3** [1990s] (Black) to do any form of illicit business.

juggler *see* JUGGLE n.

juggler's box *n.* [late 18C–early 19C] (Und.) a machine used to brand criminals on the hand.

juggling law *n.* [late 16C] (Und.) criminality as it pertains to the corrupt practice of certain games, e.g. dicing or skittles. [SE *juggling* + LAW *n.*¹]

jug-handles/-lugs *n.* [20C] sticking out ears. [joc. use of SE/ LUG *n.*¹]

jughead *n.*¹ (US) **1** [late 19C+] a fool. **2** [1910s+] a mule. **3** [1910s+] a general term of abuse. [? JUGGINS; orig. use denoted a horse or mule with a large chunky head; such a head supposedly denoted stubbornness and stupidity]

jughead *n.*² [1960s–70s] a drunkard (cf. JUGGER). [JUG *n.*¹ + sfx. -HEAD (2)]

jugheaded *adj.* [1930s–40s] (US) stupid. [JUGHEAD *n.*¹ (1)]

jughouse *n.* [1930s–60s] (US) a prison. [JUG *n.*¹ (1) + SE *house*]

jug-loops *n.* [mid–late 19C] loops of hair brought forward over the temples and curled. [such loops resemble the handle of a jug]

jug-lugs *see* JUG-HANDLES.

jugs/milk jugs *n.*¹ [1950s+] (orig. US) the female breasts, esp. when large (cf. CREAM JUGS). [abbr. SE *milk jugs*]

jugs *n.*² [1960s+] (drugs) vials of amphetamine and later of crack cocaine (cf. A *n.*²; JUGGLE n.).

jug-up *n.* [1960s+] (Can. prison) mealtime. [JUG UP v.]

jug up *v.* [20C] (US prison) to eat prison food (cf. CHUCK *v.*⁴; GRAZE v.; SCORF *v.*¹). [JUG *n.*¹ (1)]

juice *n.*¹ **1** [early 16C–early 17C] the profits of a profession or office. **2** [late 17C; 1930s+] (later use US) money, esp. from bribery, corruption, loan-sharking. **3** [1930s+] (US) interest on a debt or loan (cf. VIGORISH). **4** [1930s+] (US) political or criminal influence; anything involving corruption, pay-offs, favours. **5** [1940s–50s] protection money. **6** [1950s+] (US gambling) a bookmaker's percentage. **7** [1980s+] recognition, publicity, respect. [its 'lubricant' properties]

juice *n.*² **1** [late 17C+] spirit, vitality, energy, usu. sexual. **2** [early 18C+] semen or vaginal fluid. **3** [1930s+] (US) blood. **4** [1970s+] (US) 'the daylights', or a fig. use of urine, i.e. PISS *n.* as in such phr. as *knock/scare the juice out of* (cf. DAY-LIGHTS). **5** [1980s+] (US Black) sexual intercourse.

juice *n.*[3] **1** [late 17C+] alcohol, wine. **2** [early 19C+] (orig. Aus., then US) alcohol. **3** [20C] petrol. **4** [20C] (US Und.) any form of alcohol illicitly made inside a prison. **5** [1930s+] (US) whisky or any other strong liquor. **6** [1950s+] any form of drugs, esp. heroin or methadone in liquid, phencyclidine, crack cocaine. **7** [1970s+] (S.Afr.) methylated spirits, as drunk by alcoholics (cf. VLAM). **8** [1970s+] steroids.

juice *n.*[4] **1** [late 19C+] electricity. **2** [1920s–50s] (US Und.) nitroglycerine. [fig. use of JUICE n.[2] (1)]

juice *n.*[5] [1920s–60s] (Irish) twopence. [pron. of DEUCE n.[2] (1)]

juice *n.*[6] **1** [1930s–60s] (US) flattering talk. **2** [1980s+] (US) gossip. [both 'lubricate' communication]

juice *n.*[7] [1930s+] a gun. [fig. use of JUICE n.[1] (4)]

juice *n.*[8] [1960s+] enjoyment, satisfaction, stimulation.

juice *v.*[1] **1** [late 19C+] (US) to drink alcohol, to get drunk. **2** [1910s–70s] (US) to milk a cow, also used facetiously. **3** [1920s–30s] to rain. [JUICE n.[3]]

juice *v.*[2] **1** [1920s+] (US) to electrocute, to kill or torture with electricity. **2** [1960s+] (US Black) to intensify, to augment, to liven up, to excite. [JUICE n.[4]]

juice *v.*[3] **1** [1950s] to bribe, esp. in context of organized crime paying off the authorities. **2** [1950s+] to add interest to a loan, debt. [JUICE n.[1]]

juice *v.*[4] [1970s+] (US Black/campus) to have sexual intercourse. [JUICE n.[2]]

juice *v.*[5] [1980s+] (drugs) to take methadone. [JUICE n.[3] (6)]

juice a woody, to *phr.* [1990s] to masturbate. [SE *juice* (*up*) + WOODIE n.[3]]

juice box/can *n.* [1940s–60s] (US) a battery. [JUICE n.[4] + SE *box/can*]

juiced/juiced up *adj.*[1] [1940s+] (orig. US) drunk or intoxicated by drugs. ext. as *juiced to the skin*. [JUICE n.[3]]

juiced/juiced up *adj.*[2] [1970s+] (US) **1** excited, nervous. **2** of a woman, sexually aroused. [JUICE n.[2]]

juice-freak *n.* [1970s] (US campus) a person who drinks, as opposed to taking drugs (cf. JUICE-HEAD). [JUICE n.[3] + sfx. -FREAK]

juice harp *n.* [1920s] a harmonica, a Jew's harp. [pron.]

juice-head/-hound *n.* [1920s+] (US) a heavy drinker, an alcoholic. [JUICE n.[3] + sfx. -HEAD (2)]

juice house *n.* [1920s+] (US Black) a liquor store. [JUICE n.[3] + SE *house*]

juice joint *n.*[1] [late 19C+] (US) a tavern, a bar, any establishment selling liquor (cf. ALKY JOINT). [JUICE n.[3] + JOINT n.[3] (3)]

juice joint *n.*[2] [1940s+] (US gambling) a crooked gambling establishment operating electronically controlled games. [JUICE n.[1] + JOINT n.[3] (3)]

juice joint *n.*[3] [1980s+] (drugs) a marijuana cigarette sprinkled with crack cocaine. [fig. use of JUICE n.[3] (6) + JOINT n.[4] (2)]

juice man *n.*[1] [1920s–50s] (US) an electrician. [JUICE n.[4] + SE *man*]

juice man *n.*[2] [1950s+] (US Und.) the collector of loans for an illegal money-lender. [JUICE n.[1] + SE *man*]

juiceoline *n.* [1970s] (US) gasoline. [JUICE n.[3] (3) + SE (*gas*)*oline*]

juice one's fruit, to *phr.* [1980s+] to masturbate (cf. ADJUST THE BOWL OF FRUIT). [brandname *Juicy Fruit*, a popular variety of chewing gum]

juice one's joystick, to *phr.* [1910s+] to masturbate. [JUICE (UP) + JOYSTICK n.[1] (4)]

juice pot *see* JUICER n.[2].

juicer *n.*[1] [1920s+] (US) an electrician (cf. JUICE MAN). [JUICE n.[4]]

juicer/juice pot *n.*[2] [1930s+] (US) a carburettor (cf. JUG n.[4]). [JUICE n.[3] (3) + SE *pot*]

juicer *n.*[3] [1960s+] (US) a heavy drinker, an alcoholic. [JUICE n.[3]]

juicer *n.*[4] [1980s+] (drugs) a woman who barters sex for drugs,

esp. crack cocaine (cf. DOGGING n.[1]; DUFFER n.[6]; STRAWBERRY n.[2]). [JUICE n.[3] (6)]

juice the plum, to *phr.* [1990s] to masturbate (cf. ADJUST THE BOWL OF FRUIT).

juice up *v.* [1990s] **1** to become damp with sexual arousal. **2** to stimulate one's female partner to sexual arousal. [JUICE n.[2] (2)]

juicily *adv.*[1] [1910s+] vigorously, excellently. [JUICY adj.[1] (3)]

juicily *adv.*[2] [1960s+] suggestively. [JUICY adj.[3]]

juicy *adj.*[1] **1** [early 17C–late 19C] wealthy. **2** [early 17C–late 19C] intellectually stimulating. **3** [1910s] excellent, first-rate. [in all cases the implication is one of 'suitable for sucking dry']

juicy *adj.*[2] [mid–late 19C] of weather, raining, very wet.

juicy *adj.*[3] [late 19C+] suggestive, racy, sexy. [JUICE n.[2] (2)]

juicy about *phr.* [1920s+] (Aus.) aware of. [fig. use of JUICY adj.[3]]

juicy fruit *n.*[1] [1930s] (US Black) a male homosexual. [JUICY adj.[3] + FRUIT n.[2] (2); also a pun on the epon. chewing gum brandname]

juicy fruit *n.*[2] [1950s+] (Aus.) sexual intercourse. [rhy. sl. *juicy fruit* = ROOT n.[1] (4)]

juicy-spicy *n.* [mid-19C] (US, Texas) a boyfriend, the object of a young woman's affections. [JUICY adj.[3] + SPICY (3)]

ju-ju *n.* (drugs) [20C] **1** any drugs in capsule form. **2** [1940s–60s] a marijuana cigarette. [SE *ju-ju*, a charm, an amulet, a fetish; the image is of the exoticism of drugs + (2) abbr. SE *marijuana*]

jujubes *n.* [1970s+] the female breasts (cf. APPLES n.[1]; CREAM JUGS). [SE *jujube*, a suckable lozenge, flavoured so as to represent the jujube fruit (*Zizyphus vulgaris*). Jujube is a very much altered form of the orig. Gk. *zizuphon*]

juk *n.* [1940s+] (W.I.) **1** a stab. **2** a hypodermic injection. [var. on JOOK n.[1]]

juk *v.* [1940s+] (W.I.) **1** to pierce, to prick, to stab. **2** to have sexual intercourse. **3** to increase power, to boost. [Fulani *jukka*, to poke, to knock down, to spur]

juke/jook/jouk *n.* **1** [1930s+] (orig. US Black) any establishment offering drink, food, music or dancing. **2** [1930s+] (orig. US Black) cheap, raucous music played at similarly inclined roadhouses, cafés and brothels. **3** [1940s+] (US) a jukebox. [? Gullah *jook/joog house*, a disorderly house, a house of ill-repute; ? ult. Bambara (dial. of Mandingo) *jugu*, wicked, violent]

juke/jook/joog/jug/jugg *v.*[1] **1** [16C; mid-19C+] to evade, to dodge, to avoid. **2** [mid-19C; 1960s+] (US) to trick, to cheat, to victimize (cf. FUCK ABOUT). **3** [20C] (Ulster) to play truant. **4** [20C] (Ulster) to swindle. [? Scot. *jouk*, to trick, esp. for (3), (4)]

juke/jook/joog/jug/jugg *v.*[2] **1** [late 19C+] (orig. W.I./US Black) to stab, poke or punch. **2** [1940s+] (orig. W.I./US Black) to have sexual intercourse. [? Bantu *juka*, Wolof *dzug*, thence to Gullah *juke*, *joog*, disorderly, wicked]

juke/jook/joog/jug/jugg *v.*[3] [1930s+] (orig. US Black/campus) **1** to dance, to party, to play music, to frequent dance-halls etc. **2** to have a good time (cf. JIVE AND JUKE).

juke/jook joint/house *n.* [1930s+] (US) a cheap roadhouse or brothel, esp. an establishment providing food, drink and music for dancing (cf. ACCOMMODATION HOUSE; JUMP JOINT). [JUKE n. + JOINT n.[3] (3)]

juke up *v.* [late 19C+] to improve, to boost. [JUKE v.[2]]

juk-maka *n.* [1940s] (W.I.) a cunning person. [JUKE v.[2] (1) + *maker*. He is 'sharp enough to prick a thorn' (Cassidy & LePage)]

jukrum *n.* [late 17C–early 19C] **1** a seal. **2** a licence. [JARK]

juldie *see* JILDI n.

Julius Caesar *n.*[1] [19C] the penis (cf. ABRAHAM).

Julius Caesar *n.*² [20C] **1** a cheeser, i.e. 'cheesecutter' cap. **2** a freezer. [rhy. sl.]

julk *v.* [mid-19C] of a caged songbird, to sing. [? link to East Anglian dial. *julk*, to make a sound like liquor shaken in a cask that is not quite full]

jum *n.* [1980s+] (drugs) **1** a sealed plastic bag containing crack cocaine. **2** an outsize vial of crack cocaine (cf. JUMBO n.³). [JUMBO adj.]

jumbie *n.* [20C] (W.I.) a ghost or spirit, a duppy. [? one of several Bantu languages incorporating *nsmabi*, God or devil]

jumble *n.*¹ [early–mid-19C] a bumpy ride in a coach or carriage.

jumble *n.*² [1950s–60s] a White person. [pron. of *John Bull*; used by West African immigrants/students in UK and popularized in the books of Colin MacInnes (1914–76)]

jumble *v.* **1** [16C] to have sexual intercourse (cf. JUMBLE-GIBLETS). **2** [late 18C–early 19C] to go for a bumpy drive.

jumblefuck *v.* [1930s] (US) to participate in an orgy or group sex. [var. on CLUSTERFUCK n.]

jumble-giblets *n.* [17C] the penis; thus *do/perform a jumble-giblets*, to have sexual intercourse (cf. JOIN GIBLETS; JUMBLE v.).

jumble-gut lane *n.* [late 17C–early 19C] a rough, badly-maintained road (cf. JUMBLE n.¹).

jumbler *n.* [17C–18C] a womanizer, a promiscuous man (cf. BEARD-JAMMER). [JUMBLE v. (1)]

jumbloney *see* JABRONIE.

jumbo *n.*¹ **1** [19C+] a large and clumsy person. **2** [1940s+] (N.Z.) the buttocks, the posterior. **3** [1940s+] a fool, simpleton. [? *Mumbo-Jumbo*, a West African (Mandingo) deity. Popular ety. links the term to *Jumbo*, the celebrated elephant of the Regent's Park Zoo, sold to Barnum and Bailey's Circus in 1882. However, the Zoo opened in 1828 and Jumbo and a female, Alice, did not arrive until 1863. *OED*'s first citation, from *Badcock*, is 1823 and thus the term was initially applied to the elephant rather than, as is assumed, vice versa]

jumbo *n.*² [late 19C] the Elephant and Castle public house in south London (cf. ANIMAL n.²).

jumbo *n.*³ [1980s+] (drugs) an outsize vial of crack cocaine. [JUMBO adj.]

jumbo *adj.* [20C] very large. [JUMBO n.¹ (1)]

jumbo's trunk *adj.* [late 19C] drunk (cf. ELEPHANT'S TRUNK). [rhy. sl.]

jumbuck *n.* [mid-19C+] (Aus./N.Z.) **1** a sheep (cf. JIMBUGG). **2** a fool, a simpleton. [Native Australian *jombok*, a sheep; *DNZE* prefers mispron. of SE *jumpup*]

jumm *adj.* [20C] (Ulster) used of something that is large but unwieldy and as such virtually worthless. [Scot. *jumm*, a clumsily built, awkward-looking house]

jumm *v.* [17C] to have sexual intercourse. [abbr. JUMBLE v. (1), but note dial. *jum*, a sudden jolt]

jump, the *n.*¹ **1** [late 16C–early 17C] (Und.) a robbery carried out around dusk by a number of rogues, who mill about, walking slowly along a street and opening every accessible window they can, grabbing whatever they can reach and moving on. **2** [late 18C] a robbery that uses a man posing as a lamp-lighter, who can lean his ladder against a house without suspicion, climb it and enter through any window he can open. **3** [19C] a ground-floor back window. **4** [19C] (Und.) a robbery that involves breaking in through a ground-floor back window (cf. BACK-JUMP n.¹).

jump *n.*² **1** [17C+] an act of sexual intercourse. **2** [1930s–40s] (US) a sexually promiscuous woman. **3** [1950s+] (US) a gang fight.

jump, the *n.*³ [mid-19C+] (US) the beginning, the outset; thus *at/from/on jump/the jump*, from the start (cf. JUMP STREET).

jump *n.*⁴ **1** [late 19C–1900s] (US) liveliness, energy. **2** [1920s+] (orig. US) a journey, esp. from coast to coast or city to city; thus (tramp) a free trip on a train. **3** [1930s+] (orig. US Black) a party where the guests buy their refreshments to help pay the rent (cf. JUMP JOINT; RENT PARTY). **4** [1950s–80s] (US Black) a dance party (cf. HOP n.¹).

jump *n.*⁵ [1970s+] (W Aus.) a public house bar. [one 'jumps up' to get a drink there]

jump *v.*¹ **1** [17C+] to have sexual intercourse (cf. GIVE SOMEONE A JUMP; JUMP UP AND DOWN). **2** [mid-19C+] to ambush, to make a surprise attack. **3** [mid-19C] (US, orig. west) to rob, unlawfully to take possession of another's property etc. **4** [mid-19C+] to beat up. **5** [late 19C+] (US) to rebuke, to criticize. **6** [late 19C] (Aus.) to arrest. **7** [late 19C] (S.Afr.) to seize goods wrongfully. **8** [1980s+] (US campus) to seduce.

jump/jump someone's/on someone's bones *v.*² **1** [mid-19C+] of a man, to have sexual intercourse. **2** [1980s] to attack.

jump *v.*³ **1** [mid-19C+] (US) to leave, to abscond, to quit, from duty or to avoid payment. **2** [1920s+] (US) to leave a job. [SE *jump ship*]

jump *v.*⁴ [20C] (W.I.) to startle, to surprise. [SE *make* (one) *jump*]

jump *v.*⁵ [1910s+] (Aus.) to understand, to work out. [? play on SE *jump to a conclusion*]

jump *v.*⁶ [1930s+] to fail to stop at a red traffic light or stop signal, usu. in phr. *jump the lights*.

jump *v.*⁷ *see* JUMP THE GUN.

jump *v.*⁸ [1930s+] (orig. US) **1** of a place of entertainment, e.g. a nightclub, to pulsate with energy, to be full of excitement. **2** to dance, to have fun.

jump/jump off *v.*⁹ [1940s+] (US Black) **1** to occur, to happen. **2** to act, to behave.

jump *v.*¹⁰ [1950s+] (Ulster) to convert from Catholicism to Protestantism for the material advantages such a change would confer.

jump all over *v.* [1930s+] (orig. US) to attack verbally, to berate (cf. JUMP DOWN SOMEONE'S THROAT; JUMP UP). [note synon. US dial. uses *jump out, jump up*]

jump-and-jive *n.* [1940s] (W.I.) a shoe made from old automobile tyres and very common during WW2 (cf. HITLER BOOT). [SE *jump* + JIVE n.¹ (5)]

jump at *v.* **1** [mid-19C+] to grab an opportunity enthusiastically and speedily. **2** [late 19C] to guess.

jump back! *excl.* [1960s+] (US Black/campus) an expression of astonishment.

jump bad *v.* [1940s–70s] (orig. US Black) to misbehave. [JUMP v.⁹ (2) + BAD adj.]

jump bail *v.* [mid-19C+] (orig. US) to leave the country and thus avoid a possible prison sentence while remanded on bail before trial. [JUMP v.³ + SE *bail*]

jump city *n.* [1980s+] (US) the start, esp. in phr. *from jump city*, from the very beginning (cf. JUMP STREET). [JUMP n.³ + sfx. -CITY]

jump-down *n.* [late 19C–1900s] (Can.) somewhere at the very extreme of 'civilization'. [? where one *jumps down* from the wagon at the end of one's journey]

jump down someone's throat, to *phr.* [early 19C+] to become furious with someone, often for no apparent reason (cf. JUMP ALL OVER).

jumped in port *phr.* [1930s–40s] (US Black) newly arrived.

jumper *n.*¹ [early–mid-19C] a Scot. coin, worth 10 pence. [the image of a man on horseback carried on one face of the coin]

jumper *n.*² **1** [early–mid-19C] a flea. **2** [20C] a travelling bus or rail inspector. **3** [1960s+] (US) one who makes a suicide jump from a height.

jumper *n.*³ [mid-19C] (Can.) a light buggy, a basic form of sledge. [it *jumps over* the bumps]

jumper *n.*[4] [mid–late 19C] (Aus.) one who jumps a mining claim. [JUMP v.[1] (3)]

jumpers *n.* [1960s+] (US Black) gym shoes. [their use in basketball]

jump in *v.* [1980s+] (US Und.) **1** to initiate into a street gang. **2** to be initiated into a street gang (cf. COURT IN). [JUMP v.[1] (4). The initiation involves the new member being beaten up by one or more of their putative peers]

jumping *adj.*[1] [early 19C+] (orig. US) used as the first half of a number of combs. that make up mild, euph. oaths, e.g. *jumping beans, catfish, fire, gee whillikers, grasshoppers, hyenas, jacks, jeepers, Jehovah, Jehu, jemima jane, jenny, Jerusalem, jews, jews harps, Joseph, Judas.*

jumping *adj.*[2] [1930s+] (orig. US) lively, energetic, exciting (cf. BUMPING n.[2]). [JUMP v.[8]]

jumping cat *n.* [1950s+] (US Black) **1** a sophisticated, poised older person. **2** anyone successful in their occupation, legitimate or criminal. [JUMPING adj.[2] + CAT n.[9]]

jumping jack *n.* [20C] the black ball in snooker. [rhy. sl.]

jumping Jehoshaphat!/Jupiter! *excl.* [20C] one of a variety of phr. that euphemize the once blasphemous JESUS! (cf. BEJABERS!).

jumping Moses! *excl.* [late 19C+] (US) a mild oath, great heavens! (cf. BEJABERS! JUMPING JEHOSAPHAT!).

jumping powder *n.* [early–mid-19C] a stimulant, esp. that taken (usu. in liquid form) by huntsmen or steeplechasers.

jump in the box, to *phr.* [1960s+] (Aus.) to give Queen's evidence. [one 'jumps' into the witness box]

jump joint *n.* **1** [1930s+] (orig. US Black) a party where the guests buy their refreshments to help pay the rent (cf. JUMP n.[4]). **2** [1930s+] (US) a cheap roadhouse or brothel, esp. an establishment providing food, drink and music for dancing (cf. JUKE JOINT). [JUKE n. + JOINT n.[3] (3)]

jump-off *n.* [1910s+] (orig. US/Can. milit.) the outset, the beginning (cf. JUMP-OUT).

jump off *v. see* JUMP v.[9].

jump on/upon *v.* [1910s+] to attack, verbally or physically, someone who is seen to have exposed themselves to such an assault by their behaviour or their weakness.

jump one's bill, to *phr.* [late 19C] (US) to abscond, esp. from a hotel or lodging, without paying one's bill. [JUMP v.[3] (1) + SE *bill*]

jump one's horse over the bar, to *phr.* [late 19C–1930s] (Aus.) to barter one's horse for liquor.

jump on someone's bones *see* JUMP v.[2].

jump-out *n.* [20C] (Aus.) the beginning. [var. on JUMP-OFF]

jump out *v.*[1] [1980s+] (US Black) to be unfaithful.

jump out *v.*[2] [1990s+] (US Und.) to expel from a street gang, a ritual that involves beating up the departing member. [the opposite of JUMP IN]

jump over the doorstep/hoop/traces *see* JUMP THE BROOMSTICK.

jumps, the *n.* **1** [late 19C–1940s] (orig. US) delirium tremens. **2** [late 19C] excitement, 'the fidgets'. **3** [1950s+] (US) nervousness (cf. JITTERS). [fig. uses of SE]

jump salty *v.* [1930s+] (orig. US Black) to be annoyed or irritated, to take offence. [JUMP v.[9] (2) + SALTY]

jump ship *v.* [1930s+] (US) to quit, to renege. [SE *jump ship,* for a sailor to leave the ship (at a port) before the voyage has finished]

jump someone's bones *see* JUMP v.[2].

jump someone's hand, to *phr.* [1980s+] (US Black) to threaten or victimize someone. [JUMP v.[1] + fig. use of SE *hand* (*of cards*)]

jump steady *n.* [1930s+] (US Black) alcohol, which ensures that one keeps 'jumping'.

jump steady *v.* [1900s–50s] (US Black) to act properly, to be

honest, usu. in context of a sexual relationship. [JUMP v.[9] (2) + SE *steady*]

jump street *n.* [1970s+] (US) the start, esp. in phr. *from jump street,* from the very beginning (cf. JUMP CITY). [JUMP n.[3]]

jump the broomstick / broom / besom / bucket / ditch / fence / puddle / over the doorstep / hoop / traces, to *phr.* [17C+] to enter into a common-law marriage; no civil or religious ceremony is undertaken, but the couple 'make their vows' by jumping over a broomstick or any of the other obstacles/implements. [the uses are all fig. in 20C although they were once actual actions]

jump the gun/jump, to *phr.* **1** [1930s+] to act prematurely. **2** [1940s+] to have extramarital sex or to have become pregnant before one's marriage. [fig. use of sporting jargon; in a false start a competitor will set off before the starting pistol has been fired]

jump the joint, to *phr.* [1910s] (Aus.) to take command. [ext. use of SAusE *jump,* to take possession of a parcel of land, esp. in a deceitful or illegal manner + JOINT n.[3] (3)]

jump the last hurdle, to *phr.* to die (cf. HANG UP ONE'S BOOTS). [sporting imagery]

jump the rails, to *phr.* [20C] to lose control, to disappear. [horse-racing imagery]

jump the rattler, to *phr.* [late 19C] (Aus.) to travel on the railway without paying (cf. BATTLE THE RATTLER).

jump through one's ass, to *phr.* [1960s+] (US) to panic, to lose control, to be terrified. [SE *jump* + ARSE n.[1]]

jump through one's asshole, to *phr.* [1970s+] (US) to throw a tantrum. [SE *jump* + ARSEHOLE]

jump to/to it *v.* [1910s+] to obey at once, to act smartly. [milit. use]

jump up/up on *v.* [mid–late 19C] to criticize harshly (cf. JUMP ALL OVER). [ext. JUMP v.[1] (5)]

jump-up *n.*[1] [1910s+] (Aus.) a paste made of flour, water and sugar. [? it jumps in the pan]

jump-up *n.*[2] [1950s+] (W.I.) a wild dancing party. [orig. held as a funeral wake, but now in general use; note US *jump-up/jump-up song,* a lively song with ad hoc lyrics, often extemporized from various proverbial sayings]

jump up and down *v.* [1970s+] (US Black) to have sexual intercourse.

jump-up merchant/man *n.* [1940s+] one who steals from lorries, trucks etc. [SE *jump up* + MERCHANT; he 'jumps up' on the back]

jump up my ass! *excl.* [1970s] (US) a coarse, derisive retort.

jump up on *see* JUMP UP.

jump upon *see* JUMP ON.

jump up someone's ass, to *phr.* [1970s+] (US) to attack, verbally or physically. [SE *jump* + ARSE n.[1]]

Junction, the *n.* [20C] the area of south London near Clapham Junction railway station.

junebug *n.* [mid-19C–1950s] (US Black) a boy who is named after his father. [SE *junior boy*]

june too-too *n.* [late 19C] Queen Victoria's Diamond Jubilee, 22 June 1897. [apart from the spelling out of *22,* there is a dig at the contemporary Aesthetic Movement, which was *too-too* sensitive]

jungle *n.*[1] **1** [late 19C–1920s] (US) the backwoods, the suburbs. **2** [20C] (W.I.) an area in West Kingston, Jamaica. **3** [20C] (US) a prison. **4** [1910s+] (US) that area of a town or city where criminals, tramps and vagrants congregate; also as *hobo jungle*; thus *jungle buzzard, jungle hound, jungle stiff,* one who frequents such centres, *jungled up,* living together in such an area.

jungle *n.*[2] [20C] (US) a derog. term for a Black person. [racist stereotyping]

jungle n.[3] [1990s] (W.I./UK Black teen) a kind of music originating in London and combining *rave* and *ragga*, with emphasis on a very fast drum beat.

junglebird n. [1920s–30s] (US) a tramp. [JUNGLE N.[1] + BIRD n.[2]]

jungle blaster n. [1990s] (US) a large, portable stereo. [JUNGLE n.[1] + (GHETTO) BLASTER]

jungle bunny n. [1950s+] a derog. term for a Black person. [their alleged origins in the *jungle*]

jungle fever n. [1950s+] **1** (US) the desire of Whites (usu. men) to have sex with Black partners. **2** (US Black) the desire of Blacks to have White partners. [the term, generally outlawed as racist in White use, changed its emphasis with the release of Spike Lee's film *Jungle Fever* in 1991]

jungle juice n. **1** [1940s+] (orig. Aus.) any form of strong, home-distilled liquor, often made of jungle-grown fruits and plants, herbs etc by soldiers with no 'regular' drinks. **2** [1970s] (US) men's aftershave that supposedly enhances virility and sexual appeal. [SE *jungle* + JUICE n.[3]]

jungle meat n. [1960s+] (gay) a Black man's penis. [JUNGLE n.[2] + MEAT n. (2); alleged origins in the *jungle*]

jungle mouth n. [1970s+] (US campus) bad breath. [on pattern of SE *jungle rot*, US milit. *jungle mouth*, very bad halitosis suffered by soldiers patrolling in the jungle]

jungle sex n. [1990s] an intense, rough and speedy bout of sexual intercourse. [the image of 'Black natives' and their lusts; thus racial stereotyping]

jungle telegraph n. [1940s+] a network of gossip and rumour that brings news (often inaccurate) before the official sources (cf. BUSH TELEGRAPH).

jungli adj. [1900s–20s] (Anglo-Ind.) uncouth, unsophisticated. [Urdu *jungli*, of the jungle]

junglist n.[1] [20C] (W.I./Jam.) someone who comes from the JUNGLE area in West Kingston, Jamaica. [JUNGLE n.[1] (2)]

junglist n.[2] [1990s] (W.I./UK Black teen) a lover of JUNGLE music. [JUNGLE n.[3]]

jungly adj. [1980s+] (society) disorganized, chaotic, less than smart. [racist stereotyping]

junior jumper n. [1990s] (US Black) a juvenile (under 16) who commits rape and robbery (cf. R AND R). [SE *junior* + JUMP v.[1]]

juniper/juniper juice n.[1] [19C+] gin. [SE *juniper*, its primary constituent]

juniper n.[2] [late 19C–1940s] (US) a rustic (cf. HAYSEED).

juniper juice see JUNIPER n.[1].

junk n.[1] **1** [mid-18C–mid-19C] salt beef (cf. OLD HORSE n.[2]). **2** [mid–late 19C] poor or indigestible food (cf. JUNK FOOD). [naut. jargon *junk*, old or second-rate cable or rope; ? + overtones of SE *junk*, a lump, a chunk]

junk n.[2] **1** [late 19C+] (orig. US) possessions, stuff or any unspecified objects that may be recyclable but equally possibly worthless, used dismissively of objects that are in fact sound but that the speaker no longer likes. **2** [20C] (Aus.) the dregs of a bottle or glass of alcohol. **3** [1900s–20s] (US Und.) jewellery. **4** [1910s+] (US) rubbish, nonsense. **5** [1930s] (US) cheap or inferior liquor.

junk n.[3] [1910s+] (drugs) opiates esp. heroin. [SE *junk*, rubbish (cf. SHIT n.[5]) + ref. to SE *junk*, a form of Chinese sailing boat]

junk n.[4] [1950s+] (Aus.) a heroin addict. [abbr. JUNKIE]

junk, the n.[5] [1990s] (US campus) the very best. [on bad = good pattern or on image of JUNK n.[3] as being the ultimate in drugs]

junk v. [late 19C+] to reject, to throw away, to abandon. [JUNK n.[2] (1)]

junk box see JUNKER n.[2].

junk buzzard n. [1970s] (US) an extremely contemptible person, usu. a drug addict. [JUNK n.[3] + SE *buzzard*]

junked/junked up adj. [1930s+] (US drugs) intoxicated by drugs. [JUNK n.[3]]

junker n.[1] [1920s–40s] (US) a drug addict. [var. on JUNKIE]

junker/junk box n.[2] [1940s+] (US) a near-derelict but just drivable second-hand car, one step from the junkyard. [JUNK n.[2] (1)]

junket around, to phr. [20C] (Aus.) to play the fool. [SE *junket*, to go on an excursion, a spree]

junkette n. [1960s+] (drugs) a young female heroin addict. [JUNK(IE) + fem. sfx. -*ette*]

junk food n. [1970s+] **1** the products of the burgeoning world of 'fast-food' restaurants such as McDonalds, Burger King, Spudulike etc. **2** anything considered as lacking in 'nutrition', usu. cultural. [JUNK n.[2] + SE *food*; the implication, and to many palates, the actuality, is that such food is indeed *junk*, i.e. rubbish]

junk hawk n. [1970s+] (US drugs) a heroin user whose entire existence centres on the drug. [JUNK n.[3] + SE *hawk*]

junkhead n. [1960s–70s] (US drugs) a drug addict or drug dealer. [JUNK n.[3] + sfx. -HEAD (2)]

junkie n. [1920s+] (drugs) **1** a heroin addict. **2** (rare) a heroin seller. **3** an addict of any sort, e.g. *vinyl junkie*, a collector of vinyl (rather than cassette or CD) recordings. [JUNK n.[3]]

junk in one's/the trunk phr. [1990s] (US) large buttocks. [JUNK n.[2] (1) + SAmE *trunk*, the 'boot' of a car]

junkman n. [1950s+] (US drugs) a heroin dealer (cf. DOPEMAN). [JUNK n.[3] + SE *man*]

junko n.[1] [1970s+] (US) a person who deals in second-hand goods. [SE *junk*]

junko n.[2] [1970s+] (US) a drug addict (cf. JUNKIE). [JUNK n.[3]]

junk tank n. [1960s+] (US police) a cell reserved for drug abusers and alcoholics. [JUNK n.[3] + TANK n.[2], with pun on DRUNK TANK]

junkyard dog n. [1980s+] (US) a politician who is adept at investigating corruption. [SE phr. *meaner than a junkyard dog*]

jupe balls see JUDY n.[3].

jurden see JORDAN n.[1].

jurk n. [19C] a seal, a licence. [var. on JARK]

jury leg n. [late 18C–early 19C] a wooden leg. [ety unknown; ? on pattern of naut. jargon *jury-rigged* or *jury-mast*, temporary rigging or a temporary mast, a short-term arrangement that replaces equipment swept away in a gale or after a battle]

just adv. [20C] absolutely, definitely, very.

just as cheap phr. [1950s+] (W.I. Rasta) just as well.

just as I feared n. [20C] a beard. [rhy. sl. f. Lewis Carroll limerick: 'There was an old man with a beard/Who said "It is just as I feared"']

just a tick phr. [late 19C+] wait a moment. [TICK n.[3] (2)]

just-come see JOHNNY-JUST-COME.

just come up phr. [20C] naïve, gauche, inexperienced, stupid (cf. SE *green*). [the image is of a young plant's first shoots]

just escaped phr. [20C] used of someone who is seen as acting eccentrically. [the 'escape' is from a fig. lunatic asylum]

just fallen off the cabbage truck phr. [1980s] (US) very naïve, unsophisticated. [play on SE *green*, naïve]

just fancy that! excl. [20C] an excl. of reluctant belief or incredulity, 'can you imagine?', 'would you believe?'

just for the hell of phr. [1930s+] for fun, for devilry, for no rational reason, for 'kicks'.

justice-clerk n. [early 18C] the 9 of diamonds (cf. CURSE OF SCOTLAND). [*the curse of Scotland*, the nickname of Lord *Justice-Clerk* Ormistone, who was instrumental in the vicious suppression of the 1715 Jacobite rebellion]

just like a bear/bear's daughter – ain't got a quarter phr. [1920s–40s] (US Black) miserable, out of sorts, dejected (cf. CAN'T GO NO FURTHER JUST LIKE A BEAR'S BROTHER).

just like downtown *phr.* [1990s] (US teen) a phr. of satisfaction when a plan works out as required. [SAmE *downtown*, the business and administrative centre of a US city]

just like mother makes it *phr.* [1910s+] perfect, ideal, often, but not necessarily, referring to food or drink.

just my handwriting *phr.* [1930s+] I can do that, that's exactly what I like.

just nicely *adj.* [1930s+] tipsy (cf. ABOUT RIGHT adj.¹). [abbr. SE *just nicely drunk*]

just quietly *phr.* [1910s+] (Aus./N.Z.) just between you and me, confidentially.

just-raped look *n.* [1980s+] of a woman, a sluttish, provocative style of dressing (cf. WANNABE RAPED LOOK).

just seven *n.* [1970s+] (gambling) the point of 7 in craps dice.

just the glassy *phr.* [1900s–50s] (Aus.) wholly satisfactory, just as required (cf. JUST THE SHINER). [SE *glassy*, of a surface, smooth, unruffled, absolutely flat]

just the hammer *phr.* [mid-19C+] ideal, perfect, exactly what is wanted. [Stock Exchange/auction-house imagery]

just the job *see* JUST THE TICKET.

just the shiner/shining *phr.* [1920s+] (Aus.) exactly what one requires. [var. on JUST THE GLASSY]

just the shiny/shiny shilling/shiny bob *phr.* [1970s+] (Aus.) a general term of approval.

just the shot *phr.* [1910s+] (Aus.) exactly what one requires (cf. JUST THE GLASSY; JUST THE SHINER). [SHOT n.² (3)]

just the ticket/job *phr.* [mid-19C+] perfect, ideal, exactly as desired and required. [? a winning lottery ticket, or SE *ticket*, the list of candidates put forward by a political party/SE *job*]

justum *n.* [16C] the vagina. [? Lat.]

just what the doctor ordered *phr.* [1910s+] anything perfect, ideal, excellent; with extra implication of acting as a cure for previous problems.

jutland *n.* [19C] the buttocks. [their 'jutting out' from the body]

juve/juvie/juvey *n.* **1** [1930s+] (US) a *juve*nile delinquent. **2** [1960s+] (US) a *juve*nile court or detention establishment. **3** [1960s+] (US) *Juve*nile Hall, reform school. [abbr.]

juwaub *see* JAWAUB.

jyro *see* JARO.

K

K *n*.[1] [20C] a *k*nighthood. [abbr.]

K *n*.[2] [1960s+] a homosexual. [abbr.; deliberately illiterate 'kweer', i.e. QUEER n.[1]]

K *n*.[3] [1960s+] 1000, esp. as $1000 or £1000. [abbr. SE *kilo*, 1000 grams; since 1980s *K* has replaced the former equivalent G n.[1]]

K *n*.[4] (drugs) **1** [1970s+] a *k*ilogram of any illicit drug. **2** [1980s+] *k*etamine hydrochloride, a mildly hallucinogenic drug, developed as a battlefield anaesthetic, associated chemically with phencyclidine (PCP) and often used as a legal substitute for MDMA (cf. BUMP n.[4]; CAT VALIUM; GREEN n.[3]; HONEY OIL; JET n.[2]; PURPLE n.; SPECIAL K; SPECIAL LA COKE; SUPER ACID; SUPER C). **3** [1980s+] phencyclidine (cf. ACE n.[3]).

K! *see* KAY!

k.a. *n*. [1950s+] (Aus.) a know-*a*ll. [abbr.]

kaalgat *adj*. [1960s+] (S.Afr.) naked. [Afk. *kaal*, bare + GAT n.[2]]

kaalvoet *adj*. [late 19C+] (S.Afr.) barefoot. [synon. Afk.]

KaaPee *n*. [1980s+] (S.Afr.) the Conservative Party. [Afk. Konserwaitiewe *P*arty]

kaartjie *n*. [1950s+] (S.Afr. drugs) a very small measure of cannabis. [Afk. *kaartjie*, a ticket, a card, in turn f. UK *card*, a small measure of opium or Mex. Sp. *cachuca*, a capsule of drugs, which is f. Chilean sl. *cachuca*, a small comet]

kaaskop *n*. [1970s+] (S.Afr.) a Dutchman. [Afk. *kaas*, cheese + *kop*, head]

kabac genals *n*. [late 19C–1900s] backslang (cf. KABGNALS).

kaba-kaba *n*. [20C] (W.I.) a low-class, worthless, rough person. [KABA-KABA adj.]

kaba-kaba *adj*. [20C] (W.I.) **1** of people, slovenly, ill-kempt, boorish-looking. **2** of animals and things, cheap, worthless. [Yoruba *kaba-kaba*, orig. used of speech to mean haltingly, then second-rate, of inferior quality]

kabayo *see* CABALLO.

kabeezer *n*. [1960s] (US) **1** the head. **2** the face (cf. BEEZER n.[1]). [CABEZA]

kabgnals *phr*. [late 19C] backslang (cf. KABAC GENALS). [the word itself is *backslang* spelt backwards and its use – spoken very quickly – is a coded way of asking, 'Do you understand backslang, and shall we use it for this conversation?']

kabillion/kajillion/kazillion *n*. [1980s+] (US) an uncountable large number. [pfx. KER- + play on SE (*m*)*illion*]

kabitz *see* KIBITZ n.

kabitzer *see* KIBITZER.

kablooey!/kaflooey! *excl*. [20C] an onomat. term indicating an explosion (cf. KERFLOOEY!; KERPLOOEY!). [pfx. KER- + BLOOIE!]

kabloom! *excl*. [1970s] an onomat. term indicating a large explosion (cf. KABOOM!). [pfx. KER- + SE *boom*/*bloom*]

kaboodle *see* CABOODLE.

kaboom! *excl*. [1940s+] an onomat. term indicating a loud noise or explosion (cf. KABLOOM!). [pfx. KER- + SE *boom*]

kabosh *see* KIBOSH n.

kabuki *n*. [1980s+] (drugs) a crack cocaine pipe made from a plastic rum bottle and a rubber sparkplug cover. [ety. unknown]

kabump! *excl*. [1970s+] an onomat. term indicating the noisy landing of one object or person on another. [pfx. KER- + SE *bump*; note *belly-cabump*, (US) to throw oneself face-down onto a sled preparatory to sliding down a hill]

kachew!/kerchew! *excl*. [20C] an onomat. term indicating the sound of a sneeze. [pfx. KER- + SE (*ti*)*shoo*]

kaching! *excl*. [1980s+] an onomat. term indicating the noise of a metal object striking another and giving a sharp, bell-like note. [pfx. KER- + SE *ching*]

kack *n*. (US Black) **1** [1900s–50s] an important person. **2** [1920s–30s] a snobbish person. [CACK n.[3]]

kadi/kady/katy *n*. [19C+] a hat (cf. CADY). [? Rom. *stadi*, a hat]

kadoodle *v*. [late 19C] (US) to hang around, to frequent, to wander about. [pfx. KER- + TODDLE]

kadooment *n*. [20C] (W.I.) **1** noise, confusion. **2** usu. as *Kadooment*, open-air fun and excitement. [dial. '*k*, look + *do*(*o*)*ment*, 'doings', disturbance, entertainment; thus lit. 'look, excitement!']

kady *see* KADI.

kafferboetie *see* KAFFIRBOETIE.

kaffer-op-sy-plek *phr*. [1980s+] (S.Afr.) a phr. used to state the philosophies of apartheid and of the belief in Black inferiority/White superiority. [Afk. *kaffer-op-sy-plek*, the Black man in his place]

kafferpak *n*. [1930s+] (S.Afr.) a thorough beating, a thrashing, a comprehensive defeat. [Afk. *kaffer*, KAFFIR n. + *pak*, a hiding]

kaffir *n*. **1** [early 17C+] (S.Afr.) a derog. term for a Black person. Like *nigger*, *Jewish*, *Chinese*, *Mexican* etc, the term is used in a wide variety of combs., all of which are *de facto* insulting, including [late 18C+] *kaffir corn*, a form of sorghum; [early 19C+] *kaffir bread*, the Encephalartos (a form of mollusc); [mid-19C+] *kaffir dog*, a species of long-tailed, sharp-muzzled, lean dog, popular among indigenous Africans; [mid-19C+] *kaffir sheeting*, a coarsely woven, thick cotton fabric used for clothes or cheap curtains; [late 19C] *kaffir beer*, a drink made from fermented prickly pears and honey; [late 19C+] *kaffir piano*, any of a number of multistringed wooden percussion instruments. **2** [mid-19C–1900s] a pimp, an unpleasant person (cf. AF n.[2]). [Arab *kefir*, an infidel; orig. a Xhosa-speaking African and by extension, any African; orig. (early 17C+) seen as a simple description of a given ethnic group, the term became insulting and abusive and its use is now actionable]

kaffir *adj*. (S.Afr.) **1** [early 17C+] in combs. meaning of or pertaining to Black people. **2** [1930s–60s] bad, unreliable. [KAFFIR n. (1)]

kaffir appointment *n*. [1950s+] (S.Afr.) an appointment for which one fails to arrive on time (cf. AFRICAN PEOPLE'S TIME). [KAFFIR n. (1) + SE *appointment*]

kaffirboetie/kafferboetie *n.* [1930s+] (S.Afr.) a White sympathizer with Black causes (cf. NIGGERLOVER). [KAFFIR n. (1) + BOET]

kaffir's tightener *n.* [mid-19C] (S.Afr.) a large, heavy meal. [KAFFIR n. (1) + TIGHTENER; such a meal supposedly satisfies even an African]

kaffir taxi *n.* [1980s+] (S.Afr.) brandy plus Coca-Cola or some other sweet fizzy drink. [? it 'gets you going']

kaffir tobacco *n.* [1960s+] (S.Afr. drugs) marijuana.

kaflooey! *see* KABLOOEY!

kaflunk!/kerflunk! *excl.* [1980s+] an onomat. term indicating something solid falling to the ground. [pfx. KER- + SE *flunk*]

kafoom! *excl.* [1960s] an onomat. term indicating the sound of an explosion (cf. KABLOOM!; KABOOM!). [pfx. KER- + *foom*, echoic of an explosion]

kafooster *n.* [1970s] (US) useless talk, idle chatter. [? pfx. KER- + PHOOEY!]

kagg *see* CAG n.

kagou *adj.* [20C] (W.I./Trin.) looking miserable, unenthusiastic, 'sorry for oneself'. [Fr. *cagot*, sanctimonious]

kahoonas *n.* [1990s] large female breasts (cf. BAZONGAS). [joc. use of KAHUNA]

kahuna *n.* [1980s+] (US) an important person or thing, an expert, often in the phr. *the big kahuna*. [Hawaiian *kahuna*, priest or wise man, orig. used for an expert surfer]

kaifa *see* KYFER.

Kaintuck *see* KENTUCK.

kaiser baby *n.* [1920s–30s] (US Black) a woman who leaves home and returns married to a successful, wealthy (and usu. White) husband. [SE *kaiser*, a metaphor for power]

kajees *n.* [1980s+] (drugs) cannabis. [ety. unknown]

kajillion *see* KABILLION.

kak *n.* **1** [18C+] excrement (cf. CA-CA; YACKUM). **2** [1970s+] (S.Afr.) rubbish, nonsense (cf. BULLSHIT n.; CACK n.¹; CRAP n.²). [SE *cack*, to excrete; for S.Afr. Du. *kak*, excrement; both ult. Lat. *cacare*, to defecate]

kak *adj.* [1970s+] (S.Afr.) unpleasant, nasty (cf. CRAPPY). [KAK n.]

kak *v.* **1** [1960s+] (US) to vomit. **2** [1980s+] (S.Afr.) to defecate. [KAK n.]

ka-ka/kaka *see* CA-CA.

kaka *n.²* [1970s] (US drugs) **1** heroin. **2** fake heroin. [play on SHIT n.⁵]

kaka queen *n.* [1950s–60s] (gay) one whose sexual preferences involve excrement, a coprophage (cf. FELCH). [CA-CA + QUEEN n.¹]

kaker *n.* [1960s+] **1** anything unpleasant or distasteful. **2** cannabis (cf. SHIT n.⁵). [Yid. *kaker*, excrement]

kakker-boosah *n.* [19C] prematurely voided excrement. [CA-CA; KAK n. + *boosah*, ety. unknown]

kakpot *n.* [1970s+] (S.Afr. Und.) a latrine. [KAK n. + SE *pot*]

kaks *n.* [20C] (Irish) the testicles. [ety. unknown; ? link to KAK n. or KECKS]

kaksonjae *n.* [1980s+] (drugs) smokeable methamphetamine. [ety. unknown; pig Latin]

Kalahari oysters *n.* [1920s+] (S.Afr.) a hangover cure consisting of two raw eggs with a layer of (hot) sauce between them (cf. PRAIRIE OYSTER). [the *Kalahari* desert]

Kalahari wishing well *n.* [1970s+] (S.Afr.) an outdoor privy (cf. LONG DROP).

kale/kale seed *n.* [20C] (US) money (cf. ALFALFA n.). [its greenness connotes the vegetable, but ? note COLE]

kali/cooly *n.* [1950s+] (W.I. Rasta) marijuana. [ety. unknown; ? link to COOL adj.⁴ or Carib.E *coolie weed*, a variety of fern and thus a play on WEED n.¹]

kalied/kaylied *adj.* [1930s+] drunk (cf. GET KAILED UP). [? SE *alcohol* + *alkali*]

kali mist *n.* [1990s] (drugs) marijuana. [KALI]

kali-water *n.* [1970s+] champagne (cf. BUBBLY WATER). [KALIED]

kalumpus! *excl.* [mid-19C] an onomat. term indicating the noise made when an object falls onto a hard surface. [pfx. KER- + SE *lump*]

kamma *adj.* [20C] (S.Afr.) esp. of emotions or illness, fake, trumped up, spurious. [Nama *khamo*, like, similar]

Kanaka *n.* [mid-19C+] **1** (Aus.) a Pacific Islander, esp. one brought to Australia as an indentured labourer on the Queensland cotton or sugar plantations. **2** a Hawaiian. [Hawaiian *kanaka*, man]

Kanakaland *n.* [late 19C–1940s] (Aus.) Queensland. [KANAKA]

Kanakalander *n.* [late 19C–1940s] (Aus.) a Queenslander. [KANAKALAND]

kanakas *n.* [20C] (Aus.) the testicles. [a play on KANAKA + KNACKERS]

kanga *n.¹* [1950s+] (Aus.) **1** money. **2** a prison warder. [rhy. sl. *kangaroo* = SCREW n.⁵/SCREW n.² (2)]

kanga *n.²* [1970s] (orig. Aus.) a pneumatic drill. [abbr. SE *kangaroo*, which also 'jumps up and down']

kanga *n.³* [1980s] (Aus.) a White child (cf. JOEY n.¹¹). [the TV series *Skippy, the Bush Kangaroo*]

kangaroo *n.¹* [mid-19C+] (US) an Australian.

kangaroo *n.²* [late 19C] a thin, slope-shouldered person. [the supposed resemblance to the animal]

kangaroo *n.³* [20C] a Jew (cf. BOX OF GLUE). [rhy. sl. *kangaroo* = JEW]

kangaroo *n.⁴* [1900s–30s] (US) a 'kangaroo court', an irregular court, esp. one set up by prisoners or strikers.

kangaroo *n.⁵* [1920s+] a prison warder (cf. KANGA n.¹). [rhy. sl. *kangaroo* = SCREW n.² (2)]

kangaroo *n.⁶* [1980s+] (drugs) crack cocaine (cf. KANGAROO v.). [it makes you 'jump up and down']

kangaroo *v.* **1** [20C] (US) to convict unjustly, orig. as in a 'kangaroo court' (cf. KANGAROO n.⁴). **2** [1950s–60s] (US Black) to make one hyperactive, often used of a drug. **3** [1970s+] of a car, to jerk along rather than run smoothly, thus *kangaroo start*, a jerky, shuddering start, typically that of a learner driver. [the bounding motion of the animal]

kangaroo droop *n.* [late 19C] (Aus.) a short-lived feminine affectation in which the hands were held palm-down at the breast, a pose reminiscent of the kangaroo (cf. ALEXANDRA LIMP).

kangaroo it *v.* [1920s+] (Aus.) to defecate in a squatting position. [KANGAROO SHIT]

kangaroo shit *n.* [1920s+] (Aus.) defecation in a squatting position.

kangarooster *n.* [1920s+] (Aus.) an amusing or eccentric person. [SE *kangaroo* + sfx. -*ster*]

kangaroo straight *n.* [1950s+] (US) a poker hand which resembles a straight but has a card or cards missing, thus a worthless hand. [suggested by the gaps or 'jumps']

Kangaroo Valley *n.* [1960s+] Earls Court, London, base for many expatriate Australians. [KANGAROO n.¹]

kango *n.* [1940s+] an Australian (cf. KANGAROO n.¹). [SE *kangaroo*]

kangol *n.* [1990s] (US Black/teen) a beret. [the brandname of a popular make]

kangse/koks/konks *n.* [20C] (W.I.) a light blow, usu. given to a child and usu. on the head. [? dial. *conk*, a blow on the nose]

kangse *v.* [20C] (W.I.) to hit lightly. [KANGSE n.]

kani *n.* [1940s+] (W.I.) **1** a bad cough, usu. with a temperature.

2 a person who is suffering this (cf. CON n.³). [SE *consumption*, 19C name for tuberculosis]

kanits n. [mid-19C] a stink. [backsl.]

kanitseno n. [mid-19C] a stinker, lit. 'stinking one'. [backsl.]

kanker/canker n. [1930s+] a Jew. [abbr. KANGAROO n.³]

Kansas City roll see CALIFORNIA BANKROLL.

Kansas neck-blister n. [late 19C] (US) a Bowie knife (cf. ARKANSAS TOOTHPICK).

Kansas yummy n. [1960s+] (US) a young woman who proves hard to seduce; she need not necessarily come from Kansas, but the implication is of small-town/rural innocence and morality. [*Kansas* + YUMMY n.¹]

kanurd/kennurd adj. [mid-19C] drunk. [backsl.]

kapella n. [mid-19C+] (Ling. Fr./Polari) a hat, a cap. [Ital. *capella*, a hat, a cap]

kapello n. [mid-19C+] (Ling. Fr./Polari) a coat. [Ital. *capello*, a coat]

kaplooey! see KERPLOOEY!

kaplunk!/kerplunk! excl. [late 19C+] an onomat. term indicating one object hitting another with a dull thump, or a solid object falling into liquid. [pfx. KER- + SE *plunk*]

kapow!/kapowie!/kerpow! excl. [1930s+] an onomat. term indicating a sudden noise or shock, typically an imitation of a handgun firing. [pfx. KER- + SE *pow!*, echoic of a blow or sudden noise]

kappie n. [1980s+] (S.Afr.) a member of the *Kappie Kommando*, an ultra-conservative Afrikaner women's organization. [Afk. *kappie*, a large cloth sunbonnet, part of the traditional wear of Afk. women]

kaps n. [1970s+] (drugs) phencyclidine (cf. ACE n.³). [? SE *capsules*]

kapswalla v. [late 19C] (US Und.) to steal. [Native American use]

kaput adj. [late 19C+] out of order, utterly ruined or exhausted. [Ger. *kaputt* and Fr. (*être*) *capot*, (to be) without tricks in the card-game of piquet]

karachi n. [1980s+] (drugs) heroin. [proper name *Karachi*, Pakistan, a major source of heroin]

karibat n. [mid-19C] (Anglo-Ind.) food. [Hind. *karibat*, curry and rice, thus generic term for food]

kark see CARK v.

karma n. [1960s+] (US) an emotional or spiritual state of being, either good or bad, orig. used by hippies, from Hindu and Buddhist beliefs. [Skrt. *karma*, fate, action]

karsy/karsey/karzey/kazi n. [1960s+] **1** a lavatory. **2** any messy or otherwise unappealing place that resembles a lavatory (cf. CARSEY). [CASE n.² (4)/Ital. *casa*, house]

kaschnickered adj. [1970s] (US Black) drunk. [pfx. KER- + ? SHICKERED]

kashoom! excl. [1970s+] an onomat. term indicating speedy movement. [pfx. KER- + SE *shoot/zoom*]

kasj see CAS.

kasouse! see KERSOUSE!

kasplat! see KERSPLAT!

kass kass n. [1950s+] (W.I. Rasta) a quarrel or contention. [SE *curse/cuss* + redup. or Twi *kasa kasa*, to dispute verbally]

kat n. [16C] a prostitute (cf. KATE n.¹). [abbr.; generic use of proper name *Katherine*]

kate n.¹ [16C] (Scot.) a prostitute. [generic use of proper name]

kate n.² [late 17C–early 19C] **1** a skeleton key. **2** a pick-lock. [the dimin. of the SE name *Katherine*, and on the model of other burglars' tools, e.g. BETTY n.¹; JEMMY n.⁴]

Kate, the n.³ [1940s] the British army. [abbr. KATE CARNEY]

kate and sidney/sydney n. [20C] steak and kidney. [rhy. sl.]

Kate Carney/Karney n. [late 19C+] the British army. [rhy. sl.; ult. music-hall singing star *Kate Carney* (1869–1950)]

kath see KATHLEEN MAVOURNEEN n.¹.

kathleen maroon n. [1910s+] (Aus.) a three-year prison sentence. [KATHLEEN MAVOURNEEN n.¹]

kathleen mavourneen/kath n.¹ (Aus.) **1** [20C] an indeterminate period of time. **2** [1910s+] a prison sentence of indeterminate time. **3** [1910s+] an habitual criminal. **4** [1920s] a pack. [the song 'Kathleen Mavourneen', the chorus of which runs 'It may be for years, it may be forever'; (4) presumably refers to the way a vagrant carries his pack]

kathleen mavourneen n.² [20C] (Aus.) the morning. [rhy. sl.]

kathleen mavourneen system n. [1920s–30s] (Aus.) hire purchase. [business jargon *Kathleen Mavourneen*, a defaulting debtor; ult. KATHLEEN MAVOURNEEN n.¹]

katonk n. [1940s+] (US, Hawaiian) a Japanese-American from the US rather than from Hawaii (cf. BUDDHAHEAD). [the theory, propounded by Hawaii-born Japanese, that tapping their heads would give the sound *katonk* like that of a coconut]

katootin'! excl. [1920s+] (US) intensifier, as in *durn katootin' right*. [pfx. KER- + TOOTING adj.]

katowse n. [mid-19C] (US) a row, a rumpus. [Ger. *getöse*, a rumpus]

katterzem n. [late 19C] (Scot.) a parasite, a hanger-on. [Fr. *quatorzième*, fourteenth (the 14th at table is there purely to stop there being unlucky 13 and is thus socially dispensable)]

katy n.¹ see KADI.

Katy n.² [late 19C–1960s] (US) the Missouri, Kansas and Texas Railroad. [initial letters]

Katy bar the door/gate phr. [20C] (US) used as a warning, to indicate impending danger. [adoption of a popular US fiddle tune, thus entitled]

katzenjammer n. [mid-19C+] (US) **1** a hangover or its symptoms. **2** anxiety or jitters. [Ger. *katzen*, cats + *jammer*, distress, wailing]

kawhallop see KERWHALLOP.

kay n. [1980s+] (S.Afr.) one kilometre. [K n.³]

kay!/K! excl. [1950s+] (US) all right, in order. [abbr. OK!]

kaya n. [1980s+] (drugs) marijuana. [orig. Jam. use; ety. unknown; ? link to Carib.E. *kayakiit*, a form of medicinal herb, thus note HERB n.¹]

kaycuff foe! excl. [20C] go away! [backsl. FUCK OFF!]

kayf see CAFE.

kaylack v. [mid-19C+] to talk. [backsl.]

kaylied see KALIED.

kayo/k.o. adj. [1910s+] (US) all right, in order. [joc. reversal of OK adj.]

kayo v. see K.O. v.¹.

kaze see CASE n.¹.

kazi see KARSY.

kazillion see KABILLION.

kazoo n. [1960s+] the anus, the buttocks, the vagina or penis; thus *up the kazoo* (cf. GAZOO). [? KEISTER n.]

k.b.¹ n. [20C] (prison) a rejection, esp. of parole. [abbr. *knockback*]

k.b.² n. [1960s+] (S.Afr.) *kaffir beer* (a form of beer brewed with malted sorghum millet). [abbr.; the initials are preferred to the offensive term KAFFIR n. (1)]

k.b. v. [20C] to reject. [abbr. *knock back*]

K-blast n. [1970s+] (drugs) phencyclidine (cf. ACE n.³). [K n.⁴ (3) + SE *blast*]

k.b.o. phr. [1940s] keep buggering on, i.e. persevere, stick to the job. [abbr.]

K-boy n. [1940s+] (US) a king in cards. [SE *k(ing)* + *boy*]

K.C. n. [late 19C+] (US) *Kansas City*, Missouri. [abbr.]

k.c. brown see CASEY BROWN.

kcirp see CURP.

k-chung! excl. [1940s+] an onomat. term indicating the

sound of an object colliding with another, probably metal, one. [pfx. KER- + SE *chung*]

k'daar *see* KY'DAAR.

keaster *see* KEISTER n.

kebab one's fist, to *phr.* [1990s] to masturbate.

keck *n.* [late 19C–1910s] (US) a pocket. [KICK n.[4]]

keck-handed *adj.* [late 19C+] left-handed. [dial.; note SE *cack-handed*, maladroit]

kecks/keks *n.* [19C+] **1** knickers. **2** trousers (cf. KICKS n.[1]; KICKSIES). [orig. Liverpool use]

kedger *n.* [19C] a beggar who gains money for performing small jobs; thus *kedger's coffee-house/hotel*, a centre for beggars. [Cockney pron. of SE *cadger*]

kee *see* KEY n.[4].

keeber *n.* [1980s] (US Black) a White person. [ety. unknown]

keech/keegh/keek *n.* [1970s+] **1** excrement. **2** something distasteful, disgusting. [Scot. *keech*, excrement]

keechters *n.* [1990s] the posterior, the backside. [KEECH]

keed *n.* [1920s+] (US) a child. [SE *kid*]

keegh/keek *see* KEECH.

keel *n.* [late 19C+] the buttocks (cf. POOP n.[1]; STERN). [naut. imagery; *keel*, the bottom of a boat]

keel-haul *v.* [mid-19C+] to treat badly, to punish, to beat. [naut. jargon *keel-haul*, 'To haul (a person) under the keel of a ship, either by lowering him on one side and hauling him across to the other side, or, in the case of smaller vessels, lowering him at the bows and drawing him along under the keel to the stern' (*OED*)]

keel-hauling *n.* [1940s+] (W.I.) a flogging. [KEEL-HAUL + JOC. use of KEEL]

keelie *n.* [mid-19C+] (Scot.) a street thug. [Scot. *keelie*, a kestrel]

keel off/out *v.* [20C] (W.I.) **1** to collapse. **2** to die (cf. KEEL OVER).

keel over/up *v.* **1** [mid-19C–1900s] (US) to knock down or to kill. **2** [mid-19C+] (orig. US) to collapse, to fall over (cf. COIL ONE'S ROPES). [naut. jargon *keel over*, for a boat to capsize and thus reveal her keel]

keen *adj.* [late 19C+] (US) splendid, competent, sharply dressed etc; thus *keen society*, high society.

keen as mustard *phr.* [late 19C+] very enthusiastic. [pun on *keen*, sharp/*keen*, enthusiastic]

keener/keenie *n.* [mid-19C+] (US) a hard bargainer, a cheat, a card-sharp. [SE *keen* + sfx. *-er*]

keen gear *n.* [1990s] (US teen) something good or fabulous. [KEEN + GEAR n.[1] (4), (5)]

keenie *see* KEENER.

keeno *adj.* [1910s+] excellent, wonderful, first-rate etc. [ext. of KEEN]

keen on *adj.* [early 18C+] interested in, esp. in pursuit of love or sex.

keep *v.* [early 18C–late 19C] to live at, to dwell. [14C–late 17C SE *keep*, to stay or remain in a place]

keep a cart on the wheel, to *phr.* [late 19C–1920s] to sustain a situation.

keep a fuss, to *phr.* [20C] (W.I.) **1** to make a noise or a disturbance. **2** to quarrel loudly.

keep ahead of the game, to *phr.* [1970s+] to have a situation under control. [GAME n.[4]]

keep a lamp lit, to *phr.* [20C] (US) to keep a look-out.

keep a nestling, to *phr.* [late 17C–early 18C] to be restless, uneasy. [imagery of a worried mother bird]

keep an ironmonger's shop by the side of a common/a common where the sheriff sets one up, to *phr.* [late 18C–early 19C] to be hanged in chains.

keep a rut, to *phr.* [late 17C–early 19C] to cause trouble. [SE *rut*, noise, disturbance]

keep a stiff lip, to *phr.* [1970s+] (US Black) to keep quiet, to maintain a secret. [SE *keep a stiff upper lip*]

keep a straight face, to *phr.* [late 19C] to restrain oneself from laughing.

keep a swannery, to *phr.* [late 18C–early 19C] to boast, to boost one's own achievements. [the mocking phr. 'all his geese are swans']

keep a tight asshole, to *phr.* [1940s+] (orig. US milit.) to maintain emotional control. [ARSEHOLE; the propensity of intense fear to loosen one's bowels]

keep at the stick's end, to *phr.* [late 19C–1920s] to snub, to keep 'at arm's length'.

keep bachelor's hall, to *phr.* [mid-18C–late 19C] (orig. US) to set up home as a bachelor (cf. BACH v.).

keep banker's hours, to *phr.* [20C] to act lazily. [the relatively brief periods (although expanded recently) during which a bank remains open for public business]

keep cases on *v.* [late 19C–1930s] (US) to watch closely. [CASE v.[1]]

keep cave *v.* [mid-19C+] (school) to keep a look-out. [Lat. *cave*, beware; but Ware suggests *K.V.* as in *on the qui vive*, on the look-out]

keep/lay chick/chickie *v.* [1940s+] (US) to maintain a look-out (during a crime). [SE *keep* + CHICK n.[3]]

keep company/company with *v.* [early 18C–mid-19C] to associate with, esp. as a lover.

keep cool *v.* [1940s+] (orig. US Black) to keep calm, to restrain one's emotions. [SE *keep* + COOL adj.[3]]

keep dark/it dark *v.* [mid-19C+] to keep secret, to hide away (esp. of information).

keep dead *v.* [1960s+] (US) to stay silent.

keep dick *v.* [20C] (Ulster) to keep a look-out. [DICK v.[1]]

keep down *v.* [20C] (Aus.) to maintain one's job despite the problems entailed. [SE *hold down*]

keep down the census, to *phr.* [19C] **1** to masturbate (cf. BEQUEATH ONE'S GENES). **2** to procure an abortion.

keeper *n.* [20C] any form of weapon (cf. CONVINCER). [SE; it keeps one safe]

keep in a tow-line *see* KEEP IN TOW.

keep in gammon, to *phr.* [early 19C] (Und.) to engage a person's attention while a confederate is robbing them (cf. GIVE GAMMON). [GAMMON v.]

keeping cully *n.* [late 17C–early 19C] **1** 'One that maintains a Mistress and parts with his money very generously to her' (B.E.). **2** 'One who keeps a mistress, as he supposes, for his own use, but really for that of the public' (Grose 1785). [SE *keep* + CULLY]

keeping the passover *phr.* [late 19C] (W.I.) spreading out one's clothes for an airing. [orig. known as *hold a Rag Fair* or *hold a Monmouth Street*. The association of Jewish old-clothes sellers with Monmouth Street led to the introduction of *Passover*, the Jewish spring festival commemorating the Exodus from Egypt; presumably + added ref. to the 'passing over' of the fresh air]

keep in the pin, to *phr.* [mid-19C] to abstain from drinking. [SE *keep* + *pin*, one of a set of pegs fixed on the inside of a large drinking vessel, possibly used to indicate the amount each drinker is allowed as the vessel is handed from person to person]

keep in tow/on a string/in a tow-line, to *phr.* [early 19C] (Und.) to keep someone in suspense.

keep in with *v.* [late 16C+] to remain on good terms with.

keep it clean, to *phr.* [1920s+] to avoid obscenity or 'dirty' stories, esp. as imper. *keep it clean!* (cf. KEEP THE PARTY CLEAN).

keep it out! *excl.* [1970s+] mind your own business! ['it' is one's nose]

keep it/things under one's hat, to *phr.* [late 19C+] to act discreetly, to keep a secret, esp. in imper. *keep it under your hat!*

keep it up *v.* [late 18C–mid-19C] to prolong a debauch. [pun on SE *keep it up*, to maintain an erection]

keep-miss/-woman *n.* [20C] (W.I.) a kept woman. [SE *keep* + *miss/woman*]

keep mum *v.* [late 18C+] to keep quiet; thus 1940s exhortation to secrecy, *be like Dad, keep Mum.* [SE *keep* + MUM adj.]

keep nikko *v.* [1980s+] (Irish) to keep a look-out. [? link to NICK n.³; i.e. prepared to run off]

keep nit *v.* [1930s+] (Aus.) to act as look-out; thus *nitkeeper*, a look-out. [var. on KEEP NIX]

keep nix *v.* [mid-19C+] to keep a look-out (cf. KEEP NIT). [SE *keep* + NIX!; 20C use is mainly juv.]

keep off the grass, to *phr.* [late 19C] to act cautiously.

keep on and on, to *phr.* [1970s+] to nag (cf. GO ON AND ON).

keep on a string *see* KEEP IN TOW.

keep one's best eye peeled *see* KEEP ONE'S EYE PEELED.

keep one's cock up, to *phr.* [1970s] (US) to stay cheerful, despite possible adversity; 'never say die!' (cf. KEEP ONE'S PECKER UP). [COCK n.² (1)]

keep one's cool, to *phr.* [1950s+] (orig. US) to remain calm, despite circumstances to the contrary. [COOL n.²]

keep one's corners up, to *phr.* [19C+] (US) to work carefully and meticulously, to take special trouble. [the image of ploughing or sowing right up to the corners of a field]

keep one's dick in one's pants, to *phr.* [20C] to act calmly, often as imper. *keep your dick in your pants!* calm down! [DICK n.⁵ (1)]

keep one's ear to the ground, to *phr.* [1940s+] (orig. US) to be on the look-out, to take note of developments.

keep oneself to oneself *v.* [mid-18C+] **1** to lead a solitary life. **2** to resist interfering in the business of others.

keep one's end up, to *phr.* [mid-19C+] to do one's duty, to carry out one's share. [cricket imagery, or f. helping lift a heavy weight]

keep one's eye on the ball, to *phr.* [20C] to stay alert and aware (cf. HAVE ONE'S EYE ON THE BALL). [sporting imagery]

keep one's eye/best eye/eyes peeled, to *phr.* [mid-19C+] (orig. US) to be on one's guard, to act cautiously.

keep one's eye skinned, to *phr.* [mid–late 19C] (orig. US) to pay the closest attention to what is happening. [var. on KEEP ONE'S EYE PEELED]

keep one's feet in one's pants, to *phr.* [1960s] (US Black) to keep calm, to restrain one's emotions.

keep one's fingers crossed, to *phr.* [1920s+] (Aus.) to hope for success or good luck.

keep one's guts *see* HOLD ONE'S GUTS.

keep/hold one's hair on, to *phr.* [19C+] to keep calm, to keep one's temper (cf. KEEP YOUR HAIR ON!). [? the image of tearing out one's hair when in a rage, or (though probably a folk ety. at best) the need of members of US pioneering wagon trains to keep calm in the face of an Indian attack. (Were they to panic, they might well be scalped, thus losing their hair)]

keep one's hand in, to *phr.* [mid-18C–late 19C] to maintain one's skills (in a job). [20C use is SE]

keep one's nose clean, to *phr.* [mid-19C+] (orig. milit.) **1** to avoid alcohol. **2** to lead a law-abiding, upright life. **3** to resist interfering in things that are not one's business.

keep one's nose down, to *see* KEEP ONE'S NOSE TO THE GROUND.

keep one's nose to the ground/nose down, to *phr.* [20C] to search keenly. [canine imagery]

keep one's pants on, to *phr.* [1930s+] (orig. US) to act in a sensible, calm manner, to keep one's temper.

keep one's pecker up, to *phr.* [mid-19C+] to stay cheerful, despite possible adversity; 'never say die!' (cf. KEEP ONE'S COCK

UP). [PECKER n.² (1); despite chronological impossibility, popular ety. usu. links phr. to PECKER n.² (2)]

keep one's shirt on, to *phr.* [mid-19C+] to keep one's temper.

keep one's tache on, to *phr.* [late 19C–1910s] (Anglo-Ind.) to keep calm, to keep one's temper (cf. KEEP ONE'S HAIR ON). [EP ingeniously suggests roots in Hind., in Welsh gypsy jargon and a reference to a hair-restorer ('Tatcho'); the prosaic reality is more likely an abbr. of *moustache*]

keep one's tail quiet, to *phr.* [20C] (W.I.) to stay where one is, to keep quiet, to stay out of trouble. [TAIL n.¹]

keep one's trap shut, to *phr.* [late 18C+] to be quiet. [TRAP n.³]

keep one's wig cool, to *phr.* [1910s+] to remain calm.

keep on keeping on, to *phr.* [1960s+] (orig. US Black) to persist in one's efforts (cf. TRUCKING n.¹).

keep on taking the tablets *see* KEEP TAKING THE TABLETS.

keep out of the rain, to *phr.* [late 19C+] (orig. Aus.) to avoid trouble.

keep sheep by moonlight, to *phr.* [late 18C–early 19C] to hang in chains. [the gibbet was often on a heath or moorland where sheep might be wandering; the corpse provided a fig. 'shepherd']

keep shoatie *v.* [20C] (Scot.) to keep a look-out. [presumably SHUTEYE, but rather than closing the eyes, one is keeping them wide open; also Scot. *shut-eye*, a trick or swindle]

keepsies! *excl.* [1950s+] (US, usu. juv.) an excl. staking a claim, esp. a claim of first rights to something (cf. BEANS!).

keep someone back and belly, to *phr.* [late 18C–late 19C] to look after, to clothe and feed.

keep someone guessing, to *phr.* [late 19C+] (orig. US) to keep someone in a state of uncertainty.

keep someone on the jump, to *phr.* [20C] to keep someone in a state of uncertainty, esp. as regards their employment. [SE *keep* + ON THE JUMP]

keep someone's nose to the grindstone, to *phr.* **1** [19C+] to make someone work hard, to treat someone harshly. **2** [late 19C+] to work long and hard.

keep someone straight, to *phr.* [mid-19C] to keep a person informed. [STRAIGHT adj.¹]

keep stum/stumm *v.* [20C] to keep quiet, to say nothing. [STUMM AND CRUM]

keep tabs on, to *phr.* [late 19C+] (orig. US) to keep under surveillance, to take note of. [TAB n.²]

keep/keep on taking the tablets *phr.* [1960s+] carry on with one's prescribed medicine; a phr. used in response to a statement that implies madness or eccentricity on behalf of the speaker.

keep the anchors on *see* PUT THE ANCHORS ON.

keep the ball rolling, to *phr.* [mid-19C+] to maintain the progress of a situation.

keep the bone green, to *phr.* [20C] (Ulster) **1** to postpone settling an argument. **2** to confront someone.

keep the cap on the bottle, to *phr.* [20C] to suppress the publication of facts or information deleterious to oneself.

keep the cork on, to *phr.* [20C] to maintain control of one's emotions.

keep the devil out of one's clothes, to *phr.* [19C] (US) to fight against poverty. [? trans. of a synon. Du. phr., imported by settlers]

keep the doctor, to *phr.* [late 19C] to sell adulterated alcohol. [SE *doctor*, to adulterate + ? implication that one's customers will require a *doctor*]

keep the door, to *phr.* [late 18C–mid-19C] to run a brothel. [euph.]

keep the faith, to *phr.* [1960s] (US Black) to stay loyal, to keep struggling with.

keep the faith! *excl.* [1960s] (US Black) stay loyal, don't desert us. [best known in the slogan *keep the faith, baby*, popularized by the controversial US Congressman Adam Clayton Powell Jr (1908–72)]

keep the line, to *phr.* [early 19C] to behave properly. [hunting jargon *keep one's own line*, to ride straight]

keep the lines open, to *phr.* [20C] to maintain communication. [telephone imagery]

keep the party clean, to *phr.* [1930s+] to avoid obscenity or 'dirty' stories (cf. KEEP IT CLEAN).

keep the tambourine a-rolling, to *phr.* [mid-19C] to keep things cheerful, lively. [the use of the instrument to provide merry music]

keep things under one's hat *see* KEEP IT UNDER ONE'S HAT.

keep tout *v.* [early–mid-19C] to spy on, to keep a look-out. [TOUT]

keep-up *n.* [1970s+] (US Black) anyone who looks after the home, spec. a maid. [SE *keep up appearances*]

keep up to the collar, to *phr.* **1** [mid–late 19C] to stay hard at work, or to make someone else stay hard at work. **2** [1910s–20s] to be overwhelmed by one's work. [the *collar* is that of a horse, linked to a cart]

keep up with the Joneses, to *phr.* [1910s+] to maintain one's social position, to ensure that one does not let one's neighbours or peers 'get ahead'. [generic use of *Jones* as anyone else]

keep-woman *see* KEEP-MISS.

keep your hair/wool on! *excl.* [mid-19C+] calm down, don't lose (emotional) control (cf. KEEP ONE'S HAIR ON).

keep your hand on your ha'penny till the right man turns up *phr.* [1900s–20s] advice to young women to retain their virginity until the advent of 'Mr Right'. [HA'PENNY]

keep your wool on! *see* KEEP YOUR HAIR ON!

keep yow *v.* [1940s+] (Aus.) to keep a look-out, esp. in a criminal context. [*yow*, onomat. for a cry of alarm]

keeshkas *see* KISHKES.

keester *n. see* KEISTER *n.*

keester *v. see* KEISTER *v.*

keet *n.* [mid-19C+] (Aus.) a para*keet*. [abbr.]

keeva *adj.* [1990s] (US campus) excellent, worthy of admiration. [ety. unknown]

keffal/keffel *n.* [late 17C–late 19C] (Und.) a horse. [Welsh *ceffyl*, a horse; its use often implied that the horse was second-rate]

keg/beer keg *n.*[1] [late 19C+] (US) the stomach.

keg *n.*[2] [1940s+] (Aus./N.Z.) beer, a barrel of beer. [abbr. SE *beer keg*]

keg *v.*[1] [late 18C–mid-19C] (US) to abstain from drinking alcohol. [KEG *n.*[2]; the image is of leaving the beer in the keg]

keg *v.*[2] *see* CAG *v.*

keg! *excl.* [1990s] (US campus) an excl. of approval. [the identification of beer-drinking with happiness, excellence]

keg fly *n.* [1980s+] (US campus) someone who hovers around the beer keg at parties. [on pattern of BARFLY]

kegger *n.* [1960s+] (US campus) a party featuring a large supply of beer. [SE *keg*/KEG *n.*[2]]

kegging *n.* (N.Z.) **1** [1910s+] buying alcohol legally, and then taking it to a teetotal or 'dry' area of the country for consumption. **2** [1970s+] indulging in a keg-party, i.e. a party where kegs of beer are consumed. [KEG *n.*[2]]

kegging *adj.* [1990s] (US campus) excellent, worthy of admiration. [KEG!]

keg it up *v.* [1990s] (N.Z.) to drink, usu. in a party or public house. [KEG *n.*[2]]

kegmeg *n.* **1** [mid-19C] tripe (cf. CAGMAG); thus *kegmeg shop*, a tripe shop. **2** [late 19C] an intimate conversation. [SE *kegmeg*, rotten meat or a tough old goose; (2) ? pun on TRIPE *n.*[2] or a moral disapproval of the 'rotten-ness' of gossip]

keifer *see* KYFER.

keister/keaster/keester/keyster/kiester *n.* (US) **1** [late 19C+] a suitcase, a satchel, a handbag, a salesman's sample case. **2** [late 19C+] a burglar's bag of safe- or house-breaking tools. **3** [1910s–50s] (Und.) a safe, a strongbox. **4** [1930s+] the anus, the buttocks. **5** [1930s–60s] sexual intercourse with a woman. **6** [1930s–60s] (esp. prison) anal copulation; thus *keister bandit*, a homosexual. **7** [1940s–60s] a prison. **8** [1960s+] one's self (cf. ARSE *n.*[1]). [Ger. *kiste*, a box, a case + Ger. sl. the rump]

keister/keester *v.* [20C] (US, esp. prison) **1** to hide something in the rectum; thus *keister plant*, drugs hidden in the rectum. **2** to sodomize. **3** to betray, to harm. [KEISTER *n.* (4); (3) is fig. use of (2)]

Keith Moon *n.* [20C] an eccentric, a loon. [rhy. sl.; ult. rock drummer *Keith Moon* (1947–78)]

keks *see* KECKS.

kelch *see* KELT.

kelder *n.* [mid-17C–mid-19C] the stomach, the womb (cf. HANS-EN-KELDER). [Du. *kelder*, a cellar]

kell *n.* [20C] (Ulster) a ring of dirt that reveals an unwashed neck. [northern dial. *kell*, the equivalent of SE *caul*]

kelly *n.*[1] [20C] (Aus.) an axe; thus *swing kelly*, to swing an axe (cf. DOUGLAS). [brandname of *Kelly* Axe Manufacturing Co., Charleston, West Virginia]

kelly *n.*[2] [20C] a crow. [Cumbrian dial. *kelp*, a young crow]

kelly *n.*[3] [1900s–70s] (US) a man's hat. [pun on a *Derby hat*; ? rhy. sl. DERBY KELLY]

kelly *n.*[4] [1940s–50s] (Aus.) a bus or tram inspector. [the bushranger Ned *Kelly* (1855–80); like him the inspectors pounce suddenly on their victims]

kelly ned *n.* [20C] (Aus.) the head. [rhy. sl.; ult. the bushranger *Ned Kelly* (1855–80)]

kelly's eye *n.* [1920s+] (bingo) the number one (cf. BUTTERED SCONE *n.*[2]). [? a lost anecdote]

kelp/calp *n.*[1] [mid-18C–mid-19C] a hat. [Turkish *calpac*, a Turkish and Tartar felt cap]

kelp *n.*[2] [20C] a self-conscious, awkward teenager, usu. a girl. [? Scot. *gilpp*, a growing girl]

kelp *v.* [early–mid-19C] to raise one's hat to an acquaintance. [KELP *n.*[1]]

kelper *n.* [1960s+] a Falkland Islander. [the *kelp* (large seaweeds) found on the islands + sfx. *-er*]

kelsey *n.* [1950s–70s] (US Black) **1** a prostitute. **2** a popular hairstyle, favoured by many prostitutes. [(2) orig. carnival use; presumably a punning ref. to (TIGHT AS) KELSEY'S NUTS]

kelt/kelch/kelsey/keltch/keltz *n.* [1900s–60s] (US Black) **1** a White person. **2** a Black person 'passing' as White. [? Scot. *kelt*, a homespun cloth, usu. of black and white wool mixed, once used for outer garments by country people]

kelter *n.* [late 18C–early 19C] money, cash. [northern dial.]

keltz *see* KELT.

kembla grange/kembla *n.* [1950s+] (Aus.) small change. [rhy. sl.]

kemels *n.* [1940s] (US Black) shoes. [? brandname]

kemesa *see* CAMESA.

kemo sabe *n.* [1930s+] (US) a friend, used in direct address. [the 'Native American' term for the loyal Indian companion, Tonto, in the *Lone Ranger* radio and television series created by George Trendle in 1933]

kemp/kimp *n.* [1950s–70s] (US) a car. [ety. unknown]

ken *n.*[1] [16C–late 19C] (Und.) a house (cf. BOUSING-KEN; SMUGGLING-KEN; STALLING-KEN; TOOTING-KEN). [poss. abbr. SE *kennel* (in a non-canine mode) or f. Hind. *khan(n)a*, a house or room, which is also found in combs., e.g. *buggy-khanna* (coach house) or *bottle-khanna* (drinking house); Hotten (1867) attributes it to 'Gypsy and Oriental' and notes that 'all slang and cant words which end in -*ken* are partly of Gypsy origin' on which basis E.P. opts for a root in Rom. *tan*, a place; the term vanished from sl. *c*.1860, but has survived in market-traders' jargon]

Ken *n.*[2] [1980s+] (US campus) a painstakingly fashionably dressed and groomed man (cf. BARBIE n.[3]). [the popular toy]

ken-burster *n.* [late 17C–18C] a house-breaker (cf. KEN-MILLER). [KEN n.[1] + SE *burster*]

ken-cracker *n.* [late 18C–mid-19C] a house-breaker (cf. KEN-MILLER). [KEN n.[1] + SE *cracker*]

Ken Dodd *n.* [20C] a large roll of banknotes. [rhy. sl. *Ken Dodd* = WAD n.[1]; ult. comedian *Ken Dodd* (b.1931)]

ken dodds *n.* [20C] the testicles (cf. KEN DODD). [rhy. sl. *ken dodds* = CODS n.[1]]

kenird *adj.* [late 19C] drunk (cf. KANURD). [backsl.]

ken-miller *n.* [late 17C–early 19C] a house-breaker (cf. KEN-CRACKER). [KEN n.[1] + MILL v.[1]]

kennedy *n.* [mid-19C] **1** a poker (cf. NEDDY n.[3]). **2** a blow inflicted with a poker. **3** (fig.) the penis. [proper name *Kennedy*, a man who allegedly suffered thus in London's St Giles slums]

kennedy *v.* [mid-19C] to strike or beat to death with a poker (cf. GIVE SOMEONE KENNEDY). [KENNEDY n.]

kennedy rot *n.* [20C] (Aus.) a sot. [rhy. sl.]

kennedy swoop *n.* [1970s+] (US Black) a hairstyle in which Black hair is straightened, then brushed to one side in a manner loosely resembling the hairstyles of John *Kennedy* (1917–63) and Robert *Kennedy* (1925–68).

kennel *n.* [late 17C–19C] the vagina (cf. BEST IN CHRISTENDOM).

kennel raker *n.* [19C] the penis. [KENNEL + SE *raker*]

kennetseeno *adj.* [mid-19C] putrid, stinking, 'off'. [backsl.]

kennick *n.* [mid-19C] a mixture of criminal cant and the slang talked in a lodging house. [KEN n.[1] ? + model of *Celtic*]

Kennington Lane *n.* [20C] pain. [rhy. sl.]

kennuck *n.* [mid–late 19C] a penny. [? KILKENNY n.[2]]

kennurd *see* KANURD.

keno! *excl.* [mid-19C–1920s] (US) used to express excitement or success (cf. BINGO!). [used in game of *keno* to describe a winning set of numbers]

Kenso *n.* [1940s+] (Aus.) **1** Kensington, a suburb of Sydney. **2** the University of New South Wales at Kensington. [*Kens*(*ington*) + sfx. -O]

kent *n.* [19C] any variety of coloured handkerchief; thus also *kent clout, kent rag*. [ety. unknown; ? as favoured in *Kent*, the UK county]

Kentish Town *n.* [20C] a penny (cf. CAMDEN TOWN). [rhy. sl. *Kentish Town* = BROWN n.[2]]

Kent-Street ejectment/distress *n.* [late 18C–early 19C] the removal of the front door when tenants are more than two weeks in rent arrears. [Kent Street, Southwark, where the landlords originated the practice]

Kentuck/Kaintuck *n.* [19C+] (US) a Kentuckian. [abbr.]

Kentucky bite *n.* [mid-19C] (US) a cutting bite to the ear or nose during a fight. [regional stereotyping]

Kentucky blue *n.* [1960s+] (drugs) a variety of marijuana grown in Kentucky. [joc. ref. to *Kentucky blue grass*]

Kentucky breakfast *n.* [late 19C+] (US) **1** popularly defined as 'three cocktails and a chew of terbacker'. **2** a bottle of bourbon, a three-pound steak and a setter dog; the dog is there to eat the steak. [the supposed favourite breakfast of the classic 'Southern gentleman']

Kentucky loo *see* FLY LOO.

Kentucky oysters *n.* [late 19C+] (US, mainly Black) chitterlings, pig intestines. [regional stereotyping]

Kentucky treat *n.* [1910s+] (US) a supposed 'treat' for which everyone present has to contribute (cf. DUTCH TREAT). [regional stereotyping]

kenz *adj.* [20C] (W.I./USVI) gullible, simple-minded, easily fooled. [Scot. *kensy*, a general term of abuse for a rough, rude person]

keo/keo-boy *n.* [20C] (Ulster) **1** an entertaining, if less than respectable, individual. **2** a term of abuse, a contemptible person. **3** a womanizer. **4** a trickster. [Scot. *kiow-ow*, a trifle in speech or conduct]

keptie *n.* [1930s–60s] (US) a mistress, a kept woman. [SE *kept* + fem. sfx. -*ie*]

ker- *pfx.* [mid-19C+] (orig. US) a pfx. used in a wide variety of combinations to indicate the sound of falling, of collision or of movement; other synon. pfxs. include *ca-, che-, co-, com-, con- cor-, cul-, cur-, ga-, k'-, ka-, ke-, ki-, ko-*. [most dictionaries (*OED*, Webster, F&H, *DAE*) link the pfx. to onomatopoeia, but beyond that the precise meaning of *ker-* becomes more problematical. A range of possibilities is listed by George Cohen, whose detailed analysis is recommended for further study (Cohen 1985, pp.1–28): (1) f. simple onomatopoeia. (2) f. Ger. past participle pfx. *ge-*. (3) f. dial. *cur-/car-* and Gaelic *car-*, wrongly, confusedly; ult. f. Gaelic *car*, a twist, a turn. (4) the initial *crrr-* pron. of words such as *crash* and *crunch* (Cohen's own belief)]

kerb *see* CURB.

kerbam! *excl.* [20C] an onomat. term indicating a sudden noise or sharp shock. [pfx. KER- + SE *bam*]

kerb and gutter *n.* [20C] (Aus.) butter. [rhy. sl.]

kerbang! *excl.* [20C] an onomat. term indicating a sudden sharp noise or explosion. [pfx. KER- + SE *bang*]

kerb boy *n.* [20C] a street-seller of trifles, e.g. combs, thread etc.

kerb-crawling *n.* [1970s+] driving a car slowly along the edge of the pavement in areas where prostitutes are known to operate, to make a pick-up; this practice often leads to men approaching women who are not prostitutes.

kerbiff! *excl.* [20C] an onomat. term indicating a sudden blow. [pfx. KER- + BIFF n.[1]]

kerbim! *excl.* [mid-19C+] an onomat. term indicating a sudden blow (cf. CO-BIM!). [pfx. KER- + SE *bim*]

kerblam! *excl.* [late 19C+] an onomat. term indicating a sudden shock or explosion. [pfx. KER- + SE *blam*]

kerblinketyblank! / kerblinketyblink! / kerblinketyblunk! *excl.* [late 19C] an onomat. term indicating annoyance, irritation. [pfx. KER- + BLANKETY-BLANK]

kerblip! *excl.* [20C] an onomat. term indicating the noise of something hitting the (soft) ground. [pfx. KER- + SE *blip*]

kerblump! *excl.* [1940s+] an onomat. term indicating the noise of a solid object hitting the (soft) ground (cf. KERPLUMP!). [pfx. KER- + SE *bump/blump*]

kerbolluxed *adj.* [20C] messed up, confused, with overtones of attendant noise. [pfx. KER- + BOLLOXED]

kerbonk! *excl.* [1980s+] an onomat. term indicating the noise of a solid object hitting (or being hit by) another one. [pfx. KER- + BONK n.]

kerboodle *see* CABOODLE.

kerbside virginia *n.* [20C] a cigarette rolled from discarded cigarette ends (cf. KERBSTONE MIXTURE).

kerbstone *see* CURBSTONE.

kerbstone broker *see* CURBSTONE BROKER.

kerbstone canary *see* CURBSTONE CANARY.

kerbstone justice *see* CURBSTONE JUSTICE.

kerbstone language *n.* [1900s] (N.Z.) coarse language; i.e. that 'of the gutter'.

kerbstone mixture *see* CURBSTONE MIXTURE.

kerbstone philosopher *see* CURBSTONE PHILOSOPHER.

kerbstone sailor *see* CURBSTONE SAILOR.

kerbstone setter *see* CURBSTONE SETTER.

kerchew! *see* KACHEW!

kerchug! *excl.* [1930s+] an onomat. term indicating the sound of an ailing motor engine turning over. [pfx. KER- + SE *chug*]

kerchunk!/cajunk!/cashunk! *excl.* [late 19C+] an onomat. term indicating the sound of a solid object hitting the ground or two solid objects colliding (cf. CACHUNK!). [pfx. KER- + SE *chunk*]

kerdash! *excl.* [mid-19C] (US) an onomat. term indicating the sound of an object hitting a liquid. [pfx. KER- + ? SE *splash*]

kerdiff! *excl.* [mid-19C] (US) an onomat. term indicating a sudden shock or noise. [pfx. KER- + *diff*, echoic of a sudden noise]

kerdoing!/gerdoing!/gerdoying!/kerdoink!/kerdoying! *excl.* [1950s+] an onomat. term indicating a sudden noise. [pfx. KER- + *doing*, echoic of a sudden noise]

kere gee *n.* [late 19C] vim, vigour, 'get-up-and-go'. [? Fr. *qui vive*]

kerel *n.* (S.Afr.) **1** [early 19C+] a chap, a fellow. **2** [early 19C+] a boyfriend. **3** [early 19C+] a tricky, cunning person. **4** [late 19C+] a term of address to a man. **5** [1970s+] the police. [OE *ceorl*, a countryman, a common man]

kerflap! *excl.* [1930s+] an onomat. term indicating a sudden shock or gesture. [pfx. KER- + SE *flap*]

kerflip! *excl.* [1930s+] an onomat. term indicating the sound of a solid body hitting a soft one or hitting liquid. [pfx. KER- + SE *flip*]

kerflooey/gaflooey *n.* [1910s+] nonsense, rubbish; thus *go kerflooey*, to go to pieces. [pfx. KER- + FLOOEY!]

kerflooey! *excl.* [1910s+] an onomat. term indicating a sudden explosion (cf. KABLOOEY!; KERPLOOEY!). [pfx. KER- + FLOOEY!]

kerflop! *excl.* [late 19C+] an onomat. term indicating the sound of a solid body hitting a soft one or hitting liquid. [pfx. KER- + SE *flop*]

kerflummox/curflummux/kerflumix *v.* [mid-19C–1900s] (US) to fall heavily, to confound, to flabbergast. [pfx. KER- + FLUMMOX]

kerflummox!/kerflumix! *excl.* [mid-19C–1900s] (US) an onomat. term indicating the sound of a heavy fall. [pfx. KER- + FLUMMOX]

kerflunk! *see* KAFLUNK!

kerfuffle/cufuffle/gefuffle *n.* [late 19C+] (orig. US) a fuss, a row, a confusion. [Scot. *curfuffle*, a fuss, a row]

kerfuffle valve *n.* [1970s+] (Aus.) a make-believe 'valve' within the human body, supposedly under stress when one lifts heavy objects. [joc. use of KERFUFFLE + SE *valve*]

kerlaraping *n.* [late 19C] cavorting, jumping around excitedly. [pfx. KER- + ? *larrup*, to thrash]

Kermit the Frog *n.* [1970s] a lavatory. [rhy. sl. *Kermit the Frog* = BOG *n.*; ult. *Kermit the Frog*, a character in *The Muppet Show* (1976–81)]

kero *n.* [1930s+] (Aus.) **1** kerosene. **2** beer. [abbr. SE *kerosene*; (2) implies a form of 'fuel']

kerplonk! *excl.* [1960s+] an onomat. term indicating the sound of a heavy object hitting a solid surface. [pfx. KER- + SE *plonk/plunk*]

kerplooey!/kaplooey! *excl.* [1930s+] an onomat. term indicating the noise made by the explosion of something soft and messy, e.g. a large fruit or a living body (cf. KERFLOOEY!). [pfx. KER- + SE *plooey*]

kerplop! *excl.* [late 19C+] an onomat. term indicating the sound of a solid body falling into liquid or of a bubble bursting in liquid. [pfx. KER- + SE *plop*]

kerplump! *excl.* [1950s+] an onomat. term indicating the sound of a solid body hitting a soft surface. [pfx. KER- + SE *plump*]

kerplumpus! *excl.* [mid-19C] an onomat. term indicating the sound of a solid body hitting a soft surface. [ext. of KERPLUMP!]

kerplunk! *see* KAPLUNK!

kerpow! *see* KAPOW!

kerried *adj.* [1970s+] exhausted, tired out. [rhy. sl. *Kerry Packered* = KNACKERED; ult. Aus. media magnate *Kerry Packer* (b.1937)]

Kerry security *n.* [late 18C] any form of bond or oath that has been sworn in return for money. [? stereotyping of Kerrymen as corrupt]

Kerry witness *n.* [late 18C] a witness who is happy to swear to anything (for a price) (cf. KERRY SECURITY). [? stereotyping of Kerrymen as corrupt]

kershewey! *excl.* [1940s+] (US) euph. interj., the equivalent of *by Christ* or *by Jesus*. [pfx. KER- + ? *Jesus*]

kershlunk! *excl.* [1940s+] an onomat. term indicating the clandestine, slinking movement of an animal or human, e.g. *The cat went kershlunk into the bushes.* [pfx. KER- + *slunk/slink*]

kerslam! *excl.* [late 19C] an onomat. term indicating a sudden noise or action. [pfx. KER- + SE *slam*]

kerslap! *excl.* [mid-19C+] an onomat. term indicating a sudden noise or, usu., action. [pfx. KER- + SE *slap*]

kerslash! *excl.* [mid-19C] (US) an onomat. term indicating a sudden crash, as caused by tripping over an object. [pfx. KER- + SE *slip/crash*]

kerslesh! *excl.* [mid-19C] (US) an onomat. term indicating movement at speed. [pfx. KER- + SE *slash*]

kersling! *see* KERSLUNG!

kerslosh! / coslush! / kerslush! / kersplosh! / kerswosh! / kerwash! / kerwosh! *excl.* [mid-19C+] an onomat. term indicating movement through a wet or soft substance, or the falling of a solid object into such a substance, e.g. viscous mud. [pfx. KER- + SE *slosh/splosh/slush/wash*]

kerslung!/kersling! *excl.* [mid-19C] an onomat. term indicating a sudden movement. [pfx. KER- + SE *slung/sling*]

kerslush! *see* KERSLOSH!

kersmack! *excl.* [1930s+] an onomat. term indicating a sudden movement or a sharp blow. [pfx. KER- + SE *smack*]

kersmash!/casmash! *excl.* [mid-19C+] an onomat. term indicating a sudden crash or collision. [pfx. KER- + SE *smash*]

kersouse!/kasouse!/kesouse! *excl.* [mid-19C] an onomat. term indicating a fall into liquid. [pfx. KER- + SE *souse*]

kersplash! *excl.* [late 19C+] an onomat. term indicating a fall into liquid. [pfx. KER- + SE *splash*]

kersplat!/kasplat! *excl.* [1980s+] an onomat. term indicating a fall onto a soft surface, esp. with concomitant mess, e.g. a stunt-man's dive into a stall of soft fruit and vegetables. [pfx. KER- + SPLAT!]

kersplosh! *see* KERSLOSH!

kerswallop!/kerswollop! *excl.* [mid-19C] (US) an onomat. term indicating a fall or flop. [pfx. KER- + SE *swallop*]

kerswish! *excl.* [1940s+] an onomat. term indicating a swishing noise. [pfx. KER- + SE *swish*]

kerswollop! *see* KERSWALLOP!

kerswop! *excl.* [mid-19C] an onomat. term indicating a fall into liquid. [pfx. KER- + SE *swop*]

kerswosh! *see* KERSLOSH!

kerterver *see* CATEVER.

kertever cartzo *n.* [mid-19C] venereal disease. [Ling. Fr. *cattivo cazzo*, lit. 'bad cock']

kerthud! *excl.* [1940s+] an onomat. term indicating the dull noise of a solid object landing on a solid surface. [pfx. KER- + SE *thud*]

kerthump! *excl.* [late 19C+] an onomat. term indicating a sudden dull noise. [pfx. KER- + SE *thump*]

kerumph!/kerump! *excl.* [20C] an onomat. term indicating an exclamation or sudden shock. [pfx. KER- + SE *crump*]

kerwash! *see* KERSLOSH!

kerwhackety! *excl.* [1940s+] an onomat. term indicating noisy, stumbling, erratic progress. [pfx. KER- + SE *whack/ racket*]

kerwhallop/kawhallop *v.* [mid-19C+] to hit hard and suddenly, to smack (cf. CHEWALLOP). [pfx. KER- + SE *wallop*]

kerwhallop/kawhallop *adv.* [20C] (US) precisely, exactly (cf. SLAM-BANG adj.). [pfx. KER- + SE *wallop*]

kerwhammy! *excl.* [1940s+] an onomat. term indicating the sound of a sudden collision. [pfx. KER- + WHAM!]

kerwhop!/cawhop! *excl.* [mid-19C+] an onomat. term indicating the noise of a solid body falling onto a solid surface. [pfx. KER- + SE *whop*]

kerwoosh! *excl.* [20C] an onomat. term indicating speedy movement. [pfx. KER- + SE *whoosh*]

kerwosh! *see* KERSLOSH!

keskydee *see* KISKEEDEE.

kesouse! *see* KERSOUSE!

ketchup *n.* **1** [20C] (Aus.) beer. **2** [1940s–70s] (US) blood. [(1) the colour of 'brown sauce'; (2) the colour of tomato ketchup]

kettle *n.*[1] [17C] the vagina. [the image of a vagina as a receptacle; note the repertoire of bawdy songs in which wandering tinkers 'mend' ladies' *kettles*]

kettle *n.*[2] **1** [early–late 19C] (US) a steam engine. **2** [mid-19C+] a pocket watch; thus *red kettle*, a gold watch, *white kettle*, a silver watch. **3** [1920s+] a wrist watch. [the original large circular pocket watches resembled kettles]

kettle/kettle on a hob *n.*[3] [late 19C+] one shilling (5p). [rhy. sl. *kettle on a hob* = BOB n.[3]]

kettle *n.*[4] [20C] a pet name for someone called Bob. [rhy. sl. *kettle on a hob* = *Bob*]

kettle *v.* [1920s–30s] (US) esp. of a horse, to frighten or become frightened. [? dial. *kittle*, to arouse, to stimulate, to prick]

kettlebelly *n.* [late 19C–1920s] (US) a fat person.

kettle brandy *n.* [late 19C–1900s] tea, esp. as drunk at tea parties (cf. PRATTLE BROTH; SCANDAL-WATER).

kettle-de-benders *see* KITTLY-BENDERS.

kettledrum *n.* [mid–late 19C] an afternoon tea party on a large scale. [a play on the omnipresent tea kettle + *drum*, 'an assembly of fashionable people at a private house, held in the evening, much in vogue during the latter half of the 18th and beginning of the 19th century … later, an afternoon tea party, formerly sometimes followed by the larger assembly' (*OED*)]

kettledrums *see* CUPID'S KETTLEDRUMS.

kettle on a hob *see* KETTLE n.[3].

Kevin *n.* [1980s+] (upper and middle classes) a derog. name for lower-middle- or working-class youths, whom they regard as overly flashy and socially unacceptable (cf. SHARON). [the commonness of the name]

kew *n.* [mid–late 19C] a week; thus *skew*, weeks. [backsl.]

kewl *adj.* [1990s] (US teen) a general term of approval. [COOL adj.[3]]

kewpie *n.* [1990s] (Aus.) a prostitute. [rhy. sl. *kewpie doll* = MOLL]

key *n.*[1] [18C] the penis (cf. PICKLOCK). [the complement to the KEYHOLE]

key, the *n.*[2] [20C] (Aus./N.Z.) a declaration that one is an habitual criminal, thus the indefinite detention that, following the Habitual Criminals Act (1905) was mandatory for such individuals, who would first serve a specified sentence, then, subject to behaviour etc. would begin the indefinite 'key'. [SE *throw away the key*]

key/keys *n.*[3] [20C] (US prison) a prison warder. [metonymy SE *key*, which they carry]

key/kee/ki *n.*[4] [1960s+] (drugs) one *ki*lo of marijuana, hashish or any other drug. [abbr.]

key *adj.* [1980s+] (US campus) excellent, admirable. [SE *key*, central, vital]

key *v.* [1980s+] (US campus) to scratch an automobile with a key or other pointed object.

keyhole *n.* [late 19C–1920s] the vagina. [KEY n.[1] + SE *hole/* HOLE n.[1] (2)]

keyhole a round-tripper, to *phr.* [1930s–40s] (US Black) to witness a remarkable event.

keyhole-whistler/-whisperer *n.* [mid-19C–1920s] one who sleeps in barns or outhouses, thus a tramp or vagrant (cf. SKIPPER-BIRD). [those inside the adjacent house hear whispering/whistling through the keyhole]

keyholing *n.* [1950s–60s] singing and playing at public house doors.

key in *v.* [1950s+] to focus on. [film jargon; the *key light* focuses directly on a single actor]

key of the door *n.* [1950s+] (bingo) the number 21. [the traditional year of 'coming of age' and getting one's own front-door key]

keynod *see* YERKNOD.

keys *see* KEY n.[3].

keyster *see* KEISTER n.

Keystone *n.* [1910s+] a policeman. [Hollywood's *Keystone Cops*, a group of comical, incompetent policemen created by director Mack Sennett (1884–1960) in 1912. They featured in a number of films made by his Keystone Studios]

key winder *n.* [1910s] (US) a girl; thus *stem winder*, a boy. [SE *key winder*, a watch that is wound up with a key (ref. to KEY n.[1]); *stem winder*, a watch that requires no key]

k-foot *n.* [1940s+] (W.I.) knock-knees (cf. CAPITAL K).

k.g. *n.* [1950s+] (US Und.) a *k*nown *g*ambler. [abbr.]

k.g.b. *n.* [1980s+] (US drugs) a variety of especially potent marijuana. [abbr. *k*iller *g*reen *b*ud]

khabbar *see* KUBBER.

khaki *n.*[1] [late 19C] pease pudding; thus *cannon and khaki*, a globular steak pudding and a lump of pease pudding on the side. [the colour of the food]

khaki *n.*[2] [1940s+] (S.Afr.) a non-Nationalist White South African, usu. of English background. [Boer War sl. *khaki*, an English soldier]

khaki buttonhole *n.* [1990s] the anus. [the colour and shape]

khakis *n.* [1990s] *khaki* shorts. [abbr.]

khaki-wacky *n.* [1940s] (US) a woman who is enamoured of men in military uniform. [SE *khaki* + WHACKY adj.]

K-hole *n.* [1980s+] (drugs) a period of confusion that follows the use of ketamine (cf. K n.[4]). [the 'hole' in one's life]

khubber *see* KUBBER.

Khyber/Khyber Pass *n.* **1** [late 19C] a glass. **2** [1940s+] the buttocks. [rhy. sl. (2) *Khyber Pass* = ARSE n.[1]]

khyfer *see* KYFER.

ki *n.*[1] [1940s–50s] (prison) cocoa. [orig. naut. use; supposedly dial. *kyish*, muddy-looking, brown, but *EDD* has no listing]

ki *n.*[2] *see* KEY n.[4].

ki *n.*[3] [1990s] (drugs) phencyclidine (cf. ACE n.[3]). [ety. unknown]

kibbitz *see* KIBITZ v.

kibbitzer *see* KIBITZER.

kibbles & bits *n.* [1980s+] (US Black) **1** cheap food. **2** (drugs) small crumbs of crack cocaine. **3** used of a man who has small genitals. [the brandname of a petfood]

kibitz/kabitz *n.* [1930s+] (US) tedious chatter, unwanted advice. [KIBITZ v.]

kibitz/kibbitz *v.* [1920s+] **1** to watch (a gambling game) and to comment/advise but not to participate. **2** to chat, to gossip, to pester, to cajole. [Ger. *Kiebitz*, a lapwing or pewit, a noisy and inquisitive bird; thus *kiebitzen*, to look over a cardplayer's shoulder; popularized by Yid. speakers]

kibitzer/kibbitzer/kabitzer *n.* [1920s+] **1** one who looks over a card-player's shoulder, advising and interfering with the game. **2** anyone who butts in or meddles, offering usu. unwanted advice (cf. BAGGAGE n.³; BACK-SEAT DRIVER). [KIBITZ v.]

kibo *see* KYBO.

kibosh/kabosh/kybosh *n.* **1** [late 19C+] rubbish, nonsense, humbug. **2** [late 19C] the height of fashion. **3** [1940s–50s] an 18-month prison sentence. [? Heb. or Yid. *kabas, kabasten,* to suppress (B&L, but rejected by Rosten 1968); but note intensifying pfx. KER- + BOSH n.¹; KYE + BOSH n.¹, i.e. 18 pence, and thus synon. with 'a fourpenny one' (*see* E.P. *DSUE* 8th edn. Appendix for further theories)]

kibosh/kybosh *v.* [late 19C+] to finish off, to destroy; thus *on the kibosh,* ruined (cf. PUT THE KIBOSH ON). [KIBOSH n.]

kick *n.*¹ **1** [late 17C–19C] the current fashion; thus *all the kick,* the present vogue; *high kick,* the height of fashion. **2** [1940s+] a fashion, a fad; thus *on a/the … kick,* e.g. *on a writing kick, on the religion kick* etc. [ety. unknown; ? fig. use of SE *kick,* with the image of the sharp impact thereof]

kick *n.*² [early 18C+] **1** sixpence; thus *two-and-a-kick,* half-a-crown (25p). **2** money in general. [rhy. *six = kick,* but not rhy. sl. as such]

kick, the *n.*³ [mid-19C–1900s] a dismissal, 'the sack'; thus *get/give the kick,* to be dismissed or to dismiss. [SE *kick*; one is lit./fig. 'kicked out']

kick *n.*⁴ [mid-19C+] a pocket, esp. in trousers. [Ware suggests Und. only]

kick *n.*⁵ **1** [mid-19C+] a stimulating or intoxicating effect, usu. from alcohol or drugs (cf. BUZZ n.⁵; HIGH n.; RUSH n.²). **2** [mid-19C+] the sensation any place or situation produces. **3** [1910s+] (orig. US) a thrill, amusement or excitement.

kick *n.*⁶ **1** [mid-19C+] a moment (cf. JIFFY; TICK n.³). **2** [1950s+] (US Black) generally any little thing or situation.

kick *n.*⁷ [mid-19C+] (orig. US) a complaint; thus *kicker,* a complainer, a whinger. [i.e. a 'kick against the pricks']

kick *n.*⁸ **1** [late 19C–1900s] a chance, a 'go'. **2** [1910s–60s] (US) something ironic, a twist. **3** [1940s+] a trick, a 'line'.

kick *n.*⁹ **1** [1950s] (W.I.) gin or whisky (cf. WHITE MULE). **2** [1950s+] (US drugs) any kind of psychotropic drug. [KICK n.⁵ (1)]

kick *n.*¹⁰ [1950s–60s] (US) a fit, as in *a laughing kick.* [one 'kicks up one's legs']

kick *n.*¹¹ [1990s] (US) the beat or rhythm in rock music.

kick *adj.* [1920s+] (US drugs) describing anything relating to coming off an addiction, e.g. *kick ward,* a hospital ward reserved for recovering addicts. [KICK v.⁷]

kick *v.*¹ [early 18C+] to die (cf. KICK OFF; KICK THE BUCKET). [? abbr. KICK THE CLOUDS]

kick *v.*² [18C+] to leave, to walk, to wander aimlessly (cf. KICK AROUND v.¹; KICK IT v.³). [the image is of kicking stones etc; the combs. are more usu. from the early 19C+]

kick *v.*³ [late 18C–mid-19C] **1** to demand money, work etc. **2** to appeal to, to dun a person for something, to obtain something by asking.

kick *v.*⁴ **1** [19C] to rid oneself of something, to reject a lover. **2** [late 19C] to dismiss from a job. [abbr. SE *kick out*]

kick *v.*⁵ **1** [mid-19C+] (US) to complain or protest. **2** [1980s+] (US campus) to be difficult, to prevail over something or someone. [KICK n.⁷]

kick *v.*⁶ [late 19C] (US) to amuse or entertain one's audience. [KICK n.⁵]

kick *v.*⁷ [1920s+] (orig. US drugs) to stop taking an addictive drug. [abbr. KICK THE HABIT]

kick *v.*⁸ [1950s] (US drugs) to inject a drug. [KICK n.⁹ (2)]

kick/kick to *v.*⁹ [1980s+] (US Black) **1** to inform, to explain the facts. **2** to do something in a committed manner.

kick *v.*¹⁰ [1980s+] (US Black/rap) to raise, increase or produce, as of a recording, sound or volume. [one fig. *kicks* the volume, price etc upwards]

kick *v.*¹¹ [1980s+] (US) to do something that causes excitement, to have fun. [KICK n.⁵ (3)]

kick *v.*¹² [1980s+] (US campus) to have a strong smell, usually a foul odour.

kick *v.*¹³ [1990s] (US Black/Und.) to kill, to murder.

kick *v.*¹⁴ [1990s] (US) to get along well with someone. [KICK ALONG]

kick about *v.* [mid-19C+] (orig. US) to make a fuss, to complain. [KICK v.⁵]

kick a brown dog *see* CHOCK A BROWN DOG.

kick along *v.* [1970s+] (Aus.) to survive reasonably easily, to get along well (cf. KICK v.¹⁵).

kick and buck *n.* [1920s] (W.I.) a water tank or cistern made of clay that has been *kicked* and *bucked* (pounded) until it is absolutely water-tight.

kickapoo/kickapoo juice *n.* [1950s+] (US) strong alcohol, esp. home brewed. [coined in 1941 by cartoonist Al Capp in his strip *L'il Abner,* in ref. to patent medicines of 1900s named after the *Kickapoo,* the Algonquian Indians]

kick around *v.*¹ [mid-19C+] **1** [mid-19C+] to hang about, to wander aimlessly (cf. KICK v.²). **2** [1930s+] to discuss a topic or idea.

kick/kick it around *v.*² [1930s–40s] (US) to carouse, to have a good time.

kick-ass/-butt *adj.* (US) **1** [1960s+] powerful, aggressive, thuggish or violent. **2** [1980s+] terrific, exciting. [KICK ASS v.]

kick ass/arse/butt *v.* **1** [1950s+] (orig. US) to beat someone up, to fight. **2** [1970s+] (US campus) to have a good, if boisterous, time. **3** [1980s+] (US campus) to do well, to make a successful effort. [lit. + fig. uses of SE *kick* + ARSE n.¹/BUTT n.¹]

kick away the prop, to *phr.* [18C] to suffer execution by hanging. [the removal of the ladder, cart, stool etc on which the victim stands]

kickback *n.* **1** [1910s+] (US) a repercussion, usu. neg. **2** [1930s+] a commission on a payment made by the payee to the customer, usu. a genteel euph. for a bribe (cf. DRAWBACK n.²). **3** [1930s+] (orig. US Und.) a payment (prob. illegal) made to a person who has facilitated a deal, a transaction, someone's appointment to a job etc.

kickback *adj.* [1980s+] (US) relaxing, calm, low-key. [KICK BACK v.²]

kick back *v.*¹ [1910s+] (US) **1** to return something, such as money or stolen goods, to the original owner. **2** to pay a bribe.

kick back *v.*² [1970s+] (orig. US Black) to laze around, to relax (cf. CHILL v.³). [KICK v.² + (LAID-)BACK]

kick back *v.*³ [1980s+] (US) to drink (cf. KNOCK BACK v.²).

kickback place *n.* [1990s] (US Black gang) anywhere one can relax, away from the stresses and threats of the streets. [KICK BACK v.² + SE *place*]

kick before the hotel door, to *phr.* [late 18C–mid-19C] to be hanged (cf. AKERMAN'S HOTEL). [HOTEL n.¹ (2); public hangings were performed outside the prison where the malefactor had been held]

kick brass/dust/hell/sands *v.* [20C] (W.I.) to make a fuss, to cause a commotion. [? var. on KICK ASS v.]

kick butt *see* KICK ASS v.

kick coming, a *phr.* [late 19C] **1** a problem in the offing. **2** an effort.

kick down/kick down to *v.* [20C] **1** (US) to give something to, to hand over. **2** (US Black) to set a person up in the drug business.

kick dust *see* KICK BRASS.

kicker *n.*¹ [mid-19C] a dancing-master.

kicker *n.*² [late 19C+] (US) in poker, a bluff hand, with one high card. [? KICK n.⁴; i.e. if the bluff works one will fill one's pockets]

kicker n.³ [late 19C–1930s] (US) one who complains or grumbles. [KICK v.⁵]

kicker n.⁴ [1940s+] (US) a thrill. [KICK n.⁵]

kicker n.⁵ [1940s+] (US) a consequence or hidden twist. [KICK n.⁸]

kicker n.⁶ [1980s+] (orig. US) the last, most problematical piece of information. [it *kicks* the rest along]

kicker n.⁷ [1980s+] (US) a cowboy or one who poses as such. [abbr. SHITKICKER]

kicker n.⁸ [1990s] (US) a chaser, as in drink or drugs.

kickeraboo v. [mid-19C] (W.I.) to die. [pron. of KICK THE BUCKET]

kickers n. **1** [mid-19C+] the feet. **2** [1940s+] shoes. **3** [1940s+] (US) boots with pointed toes, made from rare or exotic reptile skins (e.g. armadillo, alligator, snake); such boots are used specifically for dancing.

kick flavor v. [1990s] (orig. US) to perform rap music.

kick game v. [1980s+] (US Black) to use any means whereby one attempts to gain economic, psychological or other advantages over a rival or victim.

kick hell see KICK BRASS.

kick hell out of see BEAT HELL OUT OF.

kick in v.¹ **1** [late 19C+] (US Und.) to smash one's way through a door, to break in and burglarize. **2** [1990s] (US Black) to start a fight.

kick in v.² [20C] **1** to begin. **2** to take effect, to start to work. [? orig. used for drugs, thus KICK n.⁵]

kick in/kick in with v.³ [20C] **1** to contribute money. **2** to pay one's share.

kick in v.⁴ [20C] (US) to die. [ext. of KICK v.¹]

kick in v.⁵ [1930s+] (US) to speak up, to tell the truth.

kicking/kickin' adj. [1980s+] excellent, wonderful, first-rate. [KICK n.⁵]

kicking/kickin'/kickin' it/kicking it n. [1980s+] (orig. US Black/teen) lying around, wasting time, relaxing, socializing. [abbr. KICK AROUND v.¹; KICK BACK v.²]

kick in someone's gallop, a phr. [20C] (Ulster) a weakness of character; thus *put a kick in someone's gallop*, to ruin someone's plans, to 'put a spoke in their wheel'. [riding imagery]

kick in the arse/ass/balls see KICK IN THE PANTS.

kick in the guts, a phr. **1** [late 18C–early 19C] a dram of gin. **2** [1920s+] a setback or disappointment (cf. KICK IN THE PANTS).

kick in the pants/arse/ass/balls/head, a phr. [1920s+] **1** a setback, a grave disappointment. **2** anything that urges one on to greater effort, commitment etc. [note 19C citation of a 'kick ... in the breech']

kick into dry goods, to phr. [late 19C] (US) to get dressed.

kick in with see KICK IN v.³.

kick it v.¹ [mid-19C+] to die (cf. KICK v.¹; KICK OFF v.²). [abbr. KICK THE BUCKET]

kick it v.² **1** [1930s+] to play music. **2** [1980s+] (US Black) to chatter, to gossip, to relax (cf. KICK BACK v.²). [abbr. KICK (it) AROUND v.²]

kick it v.³ [1980s+] to have an affair over and above one's primary, monogamous relationship. [KICK v.¹¹]

kick it v.⁴ [1980s+] (US) to associate with, to get on well with someone (cf. KICK ALONG).

kick it! excl. [1930s+] a general exhortation, often in the context of playing music.

kick it around see KICK AROUND v.².

kick it live, to phr. [1980s+] (US Black) to talk, to chatter, to gossip. [KICK IT v.² (2)]

kick it to someone, to phr. [1990s] (US Black) to give something to someone or let someone have something (cf. SOCK IT TO).

kick loose v. [1940s+] to release, to make available, to let go.

kick mud v. [1950s–70s] (US Black) **1** to perform hard, dirty work. **2** to work as a street prostitute. [back form. of MUD-KICKER]

kick-off n. [20C] the beginning, the start. [KICK OFF v.¹]

kick off v.¹ [20C] (orig. US) to begin, to start, to set in motion. [soccer imagery]

kick off v.² **1** [20C] to die. **2** [1910s–20s] (US) to kill.

kick on v. [1940s+] (Aus.) to struggle on despite the neg. odds.

kick one's heels, to phr. [mid-18C+] to be kept waiting (cf. COOL ONE'S TOES).

kick out v.¹ **1** [late 19C+] to die (cf. KICK OFF v.²). **2** [1910s–20s] to run away. **3** [1910s+] to get out of bed. [(1) 20C use only W.I.]

kick out v.² [1970s+] (US) **1** to pay up or to produce (cf. KICK IN v.³). **2** to fail.

kick out a hind leg, to phr. [late 18C–early 19C] to bow in an unsophisticated 'rustic' manner.

kick over v. [1920s–30s] (US Und./police) to raid an establishment or place (cf. KICK IN v.¹).

kick pad n. [1950s–60s] (US drugs) a detoxification centre or hospital. [KICK v.⁷ + PAD n.²]

kicks n.¹ [late 17C–19C] breeches, thus trousers (cf. KECKS; KICKSIES). [ety. unknown; ? link to UK dial. *kecks*, the (dried) hollowed-out stem of an umbelliferous plant, e.g. a teazle; such stalks were used as candlesticks, water-pipes etc, and the link to trousers, themselves 'hollow stalks', seems feasible]

kicks n.² [late 19C–1930s; 1960s+] (US Black/campus) shoes; in later usage, athletic shoes.

kicks n.³ [1910s+] (orig. US) thrills, pleasure. [KICK n.⁵]

kick sands see KICK BRASS.

kicksees/kickseys see KICKSIES.

kick-shoe n. [19C] a dancer.

kicksies/kicksees/kickseys n. [early 18C–mid-19C] trousers (cf. KECKS); thus *kicksies-builder*, a tailor. [for ety. *see* KICKS n.¹]

kicksing n. [20C] (W.I.) making fun of, not taking seriously. [KICKS n.³]

kick someone for v. [late 18C–mid-19C] to ask someone for money, to borrow money.

kick someone into touch, to phr. [1980s+] to dismiss, to throw away. [soccer imagery (cf. PLAY AWAY)]

kick someone's ass/butt, to phr. [1950s+] (orig. US) to give someone a beating, to defeat someone.

kick someone's bum see TOE SOMEONE'S BUM.

kick someone's lung out, to phr. [late 19C–1900s] to criticize someone harshly, to attack someone verbally.

kick start v. [1950s+] to set going with an initial sudden impetus. [from the kick-starting of a motorcycle]

kickster n. [20C] (W.I.) a jester, a joker, an irresponsible person. [KICKS n.³]

kick stick n. [1950s–60s] (drugs) a marijuana cigarette. [KICK n.⁵ + STICK n.¹¹]

Kickstone & Co. n. [20C] (W.I.) a notional firm or business, used fig. to mean a state of unemployment (cf. IDLE HALL). [one is idly 'kicking stones' around]

kick stones v. [20C] (W.I.) to be unemployed (cf. IDLE HALL). [KICKSTONE & CO.]

kicksy adj. [mid-19C] troublesome, disagreeable. [Ger. *keck*, bold or SE *kick*]

kick the ballistics, to phr. [1990s] (US Black) to explain a situation, to inform. [KICK v.⁹ + BALLISTICS]

kick the bejazus out of, to phr. [mid-19C+] to beat up thoroughly. [BEJAZUS!; euph. of KICK THE SHIT OUT OF]

kick the bucket/can, to phr. [16C+] to die. [the contemporary method of slaughtering a pig, in which the animal is suspended from a beam by the insertion of a piece of bent wood (a 'bucket') behind the tendons of its hind legs; the dying animal naturally kicks out at the bucket. Alternatively, and rather less likely, the story of an ostler working at an inn on the Great North Road who killed himself by hanging; to gain the necessary drop he stood on a bucket, kicking it away as required]

kick the cat, to phr. [late 19C] to vent one's frustrations. [the cat being the 'lowest' member of the household and thus most likely to suffer such abuse]

kick the clouds/wind, to phr. [late 18C–early 19C] to be hanged.

kick the gong around, to phr.[1] [late 19C–1930s] (drugs) to use drugs, esp. opium, heroin or morphine (cf. BEAT THE GONG). [GONG n.[2]]

kick the gong around, to phr.[2] [20C] (US) to masturbate. [play on KICK THE GONG AROUND phr.[1]]

kick the habit, to phr. [1930s+] (drugs) to stop taking an addictive drug, usu. heroin. [KICK v.[7] + HABIT n.]

kick the hell out of see BEAT HELL OUT OF.

kick/knock the shit out of, to phr. [1950s+] to beat severely (cf. BEAT THE SHIT OUT OF). [SHIT n.]

kick the stuffing out of, to phr. [late 19C+] to maltreat, to beat up severely.

kick the tin, to phr. [1960s+] (Aus.) to make a financial contribution, esp. to buying a round of drinks. [fig. use of SE kick + tin]

kick the wind see KICK THE CLOUDS.

kick through/through with v. [1910s+] (US) to pay up, to come across with. [KICK IN v.[3]]

kick to see KICK v.[9].

kick to the curb, to phr. [1990s] (US Black) to reject someone, esp. to bring a relationship to an end.

kick-up n. **1** [late 18C–early 19C] (orig. US) a dance, a party. **2** [late 18C–1930s] an argument, a disturbance. **3** [20C] (US prison) a prison riot (cf. BINGO n.[2]; ROCKIN' n.).

kick up v. [mid-19C+] to cause trouble, to react unfavourably, usu. as kick up a fuss, kick up a row, kick up a shindy, kick up a stick.

kick up bobsy-die, to phr. [1930s+] (N.Z.) to make a fuss, a commotion. [dial. bobs-a-dying, a great fuss, pandemonium]

kick up a breeze, to phr. [late 18C+] to make a fuss, to cause trouble.

kick up a dido, to phr. [20C] to make a noisy fuss. [DIDO n.]

kick up a lark, to phr. [early–mid-19C] to cause a commotion. [LARK n.[1]]

kick up daisies see PUSH UP DAISIES.

kick up dust, to phr. **1** [19C] to die. **2** [mid–late 19C] (US) to cause a commotion.

kick up hell's delight, to phr. [20C] (Can.) to cause a great deal of trouble or disturbance.

kick up jack see CUT UP JACK.

kick/lay/topple/turn up one's heels, to phr.[1] [late 16C+] to die.

kick up one's heels, to phr.[2] [20C] to enjoy oneself, to have a good time. [the image of dancing, or of a horse freed from its harness]

kick up sand, to phr. [1950s–60s] (US Black) to make a fuss, to complain. [? the famous 'Charles Alas' advert, in which the bully kicks sand into the weakling's face]

kick upstairs v. [late 17C+] to promote an official or executive who cannot actually be dismissed but whose value in their current role is no longer useful to the organization.

kick with the left foot, to phr. [1930s+] (N.Z.) to be a Roman Catholic. [LEFT-FOOTER + rugby imagery]

kicky adj.[1] [mid-19C+] (orig. US) notable for complaints, filled with complaints. [KICK v.[5]]

kicky adj.[2] [1940s+] (US) exciting, lively. [lit. providing or creating a KICK n.[5] (3)]

kid n.[1] **1** [17C–late 18C] a child. **2** [early 19C] (Und.) a child of either sex, esp. a juvenile thief, known as 'the kid ...' (their surname). **3** [19C+] a friend or fellow, often used in direct address. **4** [late 19C–1970s] (US prison) a catamite. **5** [20C] (US) a young woman, used affectionately, esp. in direct address. **6** [1920s+] (orig. US) as one's kid, one's younger sibling. [SE kid, a young goat; (1) SE f. 19C]

kid n.[2] [late 19C+] **1** teasing, mockery, chaff. **2** nonsense, rubbish; usu. as no kid, I am not telling. [KID v.]

kid adj. (orig. US) **1** [late 19C+] younger, as in kid brother. **2** [1910s+] pertaining to, or fit for children, as in kid stuff. [KID n.[1]]

kid v. [early 19C+] to tease, to pretend, to fool; used in phr. [1920s+] I'm not kidding, no kidding, I kid you not, I'm telling (you) the truth; who are/do you think you're kidding, who do you think you're fooling (because it certainly isn't me)? [? to treat as a KID n.[1] or to COD v.]

kid along v. [1920s+] **1** to tease, esp. with a long and apparently feasible story. **2** to deceive, to hoax. [ext. of KID v.]

kid blister n. [20C] (Aus.) a sister. [rhy. sl.]

kid-catcher n. [late 19C] a truant officer, employed by the London School Board to track down those refusing to attend school. [KID n.[1]+ SE catcher]

kidded adj. [late 19C–1900s] pregnant. [KID n.[1]]

kidder n.[1] **1** [late 17C–mid-19C] a tradesman's tout (cf. BARKER n.[1]; CLICKER n.[1]). **2** [early 19C+] a teaser, a joker, a hoaxer; thus ext. as [20C] (Aus.) kidder from Kidderville. [KID v.]

kidder n.[2] **1** [mid-19C+] Kidderminster. **2** [late 19C] a carpet made in Kidderminster. [abbr.]

kidderbunk n. [1940s] a boy, a youth. [KID n.[1]]

kiddey see KIDDY n.[1].

kiddey-nipper see KIDDY-NIPPER.

kiddie dope n. [1960s+] (drugs) prescription drugs. [KID n.[1] + DOPE n.[1] (17); the implication that any drugs the doctor is willing to prescribe are probably only good for children]

kiddie/kiddy porn n. [1970s+] pornography that features the sexual exploitation of young (sometimes very young) children. The practice has been going on for very many years; the term emerged into wider use during the mid-1980s. [KID n.[1] + SE porn(ography)]

kiddier n. [mid-19C] a pork butcher. [? SE kidney]

kiddily adv. [mid-19C] fashionably or showily; thus kiddily togged, smartly dressed. [KIDDY n.[2]]

kidding on the square/level phr. [20C] (US) teasing with underlying serious intent. [KID v.]

kiddish adj. [late 19C] childish. [KID n.[1]]

kiddiwink n. [20C] a young child. [ext. of KID n.[1]]

kiddken see KIDKEN.

kiddleywink/kidleywink n. **1** [early 19C] a place. **2** [mid-19C] a village shop. **3** [mid-19C] a public house or tavern (cf. TIDDLEYWINK n.[1]). **4** [mid-19C–1900s] a prostitute, who is likely to be found in a public house. **5** [20C] a child (cf. KIDDIWINK). [dial. kidleywink, an unlicensed beer house]

kiddo n. [late 19C+] (orig. Aus./N.Z.) a child, esp. as a greeting, Hey, kiddo. [KID n.[1] + sfx. -o]

kiddy/kiddey n.[1] **1** [late 18C–mid-19C] a man. **2** [late 18C–mid-19C] a fashionable, flashy young man, a rake, a pimp or a thief; thus [early 19C] rolling kiddy, a dandy-cum-thief, or a dandy who dresses like a smart thief. **3** [early 19C+] (later usage US Black) a friend or fellow. **4** [mid-19C–1900s] a pimp. **5** [mid-19C] a stage-coach driver. **6** [mid-19C–1910s] a child. [fig./joc. uses of KID n.[1]]

kiddy n.[2] [mid-19C] a hat fashionable among small-time but dandified thieves. It featured a broad ribbon passing through a large buckle at its front. [KIDDY n.[1]]

kiddy *adj.* [late 18C–mid-19C] well-dressed, fashionable, flashy. [KIDDY n.[1]]

kiddy *v.* [mid-19C] to hoax, to humbug, to subject to confidence trickery. [KID v. or KIDDY n.[1]]

kiddyish *adj.* **1** [late 18C–mid-19C] stylish, showily dressed. **2** [mid-19C] frolicsome, jovial. [KIDDY n.[1]]

kiddy-/kiddey-nipper *n.* [late 18C–19C] a variety of pickpocket who cuts the pockets out of clothes to steal their contents. [KIDDY n.[1] + NIPPER n.[1]; note tailors' jargon *kiddey-nipper*, an out-of-work tailor who sneaks up on his working peers, and while they sit cross-legged and concentrating on their work, snips out their waistcoat pockets, stealing whatever is in them]

kiddy porn *see* KIDDIE PORN.

kideo *n.* [1980s+] (orig. US) a videotape recording aimed specifically at children. [KID n.[1] + SE *video*]

kidflick *n.* [1970s+] (orig. US) a film or video recording aimed at the child audience. [KID n.[1] + FLICK n.[4] + play on SKIN FLICK]

kidger *n.* [20C] (Irish) a term of endearment to a young boy. [KID n.[1]]

kidken/kiddken *n.* [mid-19C] a lodging house frequented by young criminals. [KID n.[1] + KEN n.[1]]

kid lay *n.* [late 17C–early 19C] (Und.) robbery that involves waylaying messenger boys and similar youngsters, and defrauding them of the goods they are carrying by offering them money to run a quick errand and promising, during their absence, to look after the goods. [KID n.[1] + LAY n.]

kid leather *n.* [mid-19C] a very young prostitute (cf. KID STRETCHER). [KID n.[1] + LEATHER n.[2]]

kidlet/kidlets *n.* [late 19C+] a small child or an affectionate term for a young woman. [KID n.[1] + dimin. sfx. *-let*]

kidling *n.* **1** [early 19C] a young thief, esp. if the father is already 'in the trade'. **2** [late 19C] a baby, an infant. [KID n.[1] + dimin. sfx. *-ling*]

kidlywink *see* KIDDLEYWINK.

kidman's blood mixture/joy *n.* [1930s] (Aus.) treacle (cf. BULLOCKY'S DELIGHT). [proper name of Sir Sidney *Kidman* (1857–1935) a large-scale grazier]

kidment *n.* [mid-19C] **1** a handkerchief which is attached to the pocket from which it is protruding, so that a pickpocket, however careful, alerts the handkerchief's owner when an attempt is made to remove it. **2** any inducement to dishonesty or crime. **3** a fictitious story or any form of statement written with the intent of deception. **4** a begging letter. [KID v. + sfx. *-ment*]

kidna?/kitna? *excl.* [mid-19C] (Anglo-Ind.) how much? [? Hind.]

kidnap *v.* [late 17C–early 19C] to steal children, esp. for use as servants or labourers on the plantations, thus *kidnapper*, one who kidnaps. [KID n.[1] + NAP v.; SE by mid-19C]

kidney-bruiser / -buster / -crusher / -rider / -rotter *n.* [1950s+] (Aus./N.Z.) a frameless pack that, without any support, bangs on one's back and kidneys.

kidney-buster *n.* (US) **1** [1930s] a large penis (cf. KIDNEY-PRODDER; KIDNEY-WIPER; LIVER-DISTURBER; LUNG-DISTURBER). **2** [1930s–40s] a vehicle that gives a bumpy ride.

kidney-crusher *see* KIDNEY-BRUISER.

kidney-foot *n.* [mid-19C–1930s] (US) a flat-footed person. [resemblance]

kidney-pie *n.* [1930s] (Aus./N.Z.) flattery, humbug, deceit. [pun on SE *kidney*/KID v.]

kidney-prodder *n.* [1960s] (US) a large penis (cf. KIDNEY-BUSTER).

kidney punch *n.* [20C] lunch, usu. as a *bit of kidney*. [rhy. sl.]

kidney-rider/-rotter *see* KIDNEY-BRUISER.

kidney scrape *v.* [1990s] to indulge in anal sex (cf. KIDNEY-BUSTER).

kidney-wiper *n.* [late 19C–1960s] (US) a large penis (cf. KIDNEY-BUSTER).

kidology *n.* [1970s+] the art of teasing or fooling a victim, esp. with the intent of obtaining something from them. [KID v. + sfx. *-ology*; thus note the nonce-word coined by Terry Pratchett (b.1948), *headology*, using one's head rather than force to get what one wants]

kid on *v.* [mid-19C+] **1** to encourage someone else to do something. **2** to tease, to deceive (cf. KID ALONG).

kid oneself/kid oneself up *v.* [mid-19C+] to delude oneself. [KID v.]

kid-rig *n.* [18C–early 19C] (Und.) the robbery of children sent out on errands (their parcel or the money with which they have been entrusted is taken either by guile or by force). [KID n.[1] + RIG n.[2]]

kids *n.* [late 19C] kid gloves. [abbr.]

kid's eye *n.* [early–mid-19C] fivepence. [orig. Scot.]

kid-simple *n.* [1960s+] (gay) an obsessive lover of young boys. [KID n.[1] + SE *simple*]

kidsman *n.* [mid-19C] one who trains boys to steal and pick pockets. [KID n.[1] + SE *man*]

kid someone up a quintree, to *phr.* [1930s–50s] (N.Z.) to fool someone completely.

kid's stuff *see* KID STUFF n.[1].

kidstakes! *excl.* [1910s+] (Aus./N.Z.) nonsense! rubbish! 'fiddlesticks!' [rhy. sl. *kidstake* = fake or KID n.[2] + SE *stake*, a wager]

kid stretcher *n.* [19C] a paedophile (cf. HOOP STRETCHER; KID LEATHER). [KID n.[1] (1) + SE *stretcher*]

kid/kid's stuff *n.[1]* [1920s+] (orig. US) anything considered childish and/or insignificant. [KID n.[1] + SE *stuff*]

kid stuff *n.[2]* [1980s+] **1** pornography that features the sexual exploitation of young children (cf. KIDDIE PORN). **2** the children who are exploited in such pornography. [euph. use of KID STUFF n.[1]]

kid the pants off, to *phr.* [1930s+] to tease mercilessly. [ext. of KID v.]

kidult *n.* [1980s+] (US) any form of entertainment, usu. film, videotape or television, geared to attract both child and adult audiences. [KID n.[1] + SE *adult*]

kid-walloper *n.* [late 19C–1940s] a schoolmaster. [KID n.[1] + SE *walloper*, Yorks. dial.; 20C use mainly Aus.]

kief *see* KIF.

kielbasa *n.* [1970s+] (US) a penis (cf. BACON n.[1]; CUDDLE THE KIELBASA). [Polish *kiełbasa*, a highly seasoned garlicky sausage, usu. poached before it is eaten]

kiester *see* KEISTER n.

kif/kief *n.* [1950s+] (drugs) a variety of hashish produced in Morocco. [Arabic *kaif*, the state of bliss reached after smoking hashish]

kif/kief/kiff *adj.* [1970s+] (S.Afr.) a general term of approval meaning wonderful, first-rate, excellent. [fig. use of KIF n.; note Afk. *gif*, poison; the similarity in pron. has led to POISON adj., and the nickname for marijuana, DURBAN POISON]

kife *n.[1]* [mid-19C+] a bed. [? var. on KIP n. (2)]

kife *n.[2] see* KYFER.

kife *v.* **1** [late 19C+] to have sexual intercourse. **2** [1930s+] (US) to cheat or to steal (cf. FUCK ABOUT; FUCK OVER). [KYFER]

kiff *see* KIF adj.

kiffle *v.* [20C] (Ulster) to procrastinate, to act hesitantly, to potter about. [? Scot. *kiffle*, a slight cough]

kike/kyke *n.* [late 19C+] (orig. US) **1** a derog. name for a Jew, esp. an East European late 19C immigrant to US rather than the older, German immigrants of earlier decades. **2** a grasping, dishonest if also shrewd person (irrespective of race). [poss. rhyming with the common Jewish name *Ike*, i.e. Isaac (cf. IKEY MO); or f. Yid. *kikel*, a circle, the mark used by some illiterate

Jewish immigrants rather than a cross when signing papers at Ellis Island, New York City, c.1900, or f. common sfx. -ki, -ski, which was found in many European Jewish names. P. Tamony (*Maledicta* I, 2, 269ff) rejects these, preferring Ger. *kieken*, to peep. In this case the ref. is to the (predominantly Jewish) US clothes manufacturers who 'peeped' at smarter European fashions and produced mass-market knock-offs for popular, poorer customers]

kike *adj.* [20C] (orig. US) Jewish. [KIKE n.]

kike it *v.* [20C] (US) to walk. [KIKE n.; the stereotypically mean Jew prefers not to pay fares]

kikey *adj.* [1930s+] (orig. US) Jewish. [KIKE n.]

ki-ki/kiki *n.* [1930s–60s] (US) **1** a bisexual. **2** a homosexual who is equally happy in active or passive sex roles. **3** a lesbian. **4** a male homosexual who engages in oral and genital sex simultaneously. [play on QUEEN n.¹ or CHICHI adj.]

kiko *v.* [1940s+] to say so, usu. as *I should/should bloody kiko.* [Cockney pron. 'sye so']

kileery *see* CALEERY.

kilkenny *n.*¹ [late 17C–early 19C] a frieze coat. [proper name *Kilkenny*, a county and city in Leinster in the Republic of Ireland; *frieze* is a variety of coarse woollen cloth usu. made in Ireland]

kilkenny *n.*² [late 19C+] a penny. [rhy. sl.]

kill *n.*¹ **1** [1930s–60s] (US) a murder. **2** [1940s–50s] (US Black) a killer.

kill *n.*² [1980s+] (drugs) high-grade, strong marijuana; thus *smoke some kill.* [abbr. KILLER WEED]

kill *adj.* [1980s+] (US) fashionable, smart, sophisticated. [abbr. KILLER adj.; on bad = good pattern]

kill *v.*¹ (orig. US) **1** [early 19C+] to consume, to eat or drink. **2** [late 19C+] to finish, esp. a drink.

kill *v.*² (orig. US) **1** [mid-19C+] to amaze or delight, esp. an audience. **2** [1930s+] to convulse with laughter, to delight, to bowl over; esp. as *that kills me* (cf. KILLING adj.²). [(1) note earlier SE use in 17–18C, usu. as *kill one with ...* or *kill at first sight*]

kill *v.*³ **1** [late 19C+] (orig. US) to suppress information. **2** [20C] (US campus) to pass an exam, to do well, esp. easily. **3** [1920s+] (orig. US) to cut the engine of a vehicle or machine. **4** [1920s+] to turn off lights, esp. in TV or film studios. **5** [1970s+] (US campus) to fail, to do badly. **6** [1990s] (US) to get rid of or remove an item, usu. of clothing or food.

kill-a-ho *adj.* [1990s] (US Black teen) used of the lyrical style of rap bands who specialize in extreme misogynism. [lit. *kill a whore*]

kill a snake/tree, to *phr.* [19C] to urinate (cf. SHOOT A LION).

kill-calf/-cow *adj.* [early 19C] murderous. [SE *kill-calf/-cow*, a butcher]

kill-cobbler *n.* [early–mid-18C] gin. [? the propensity of shoemakers for gin-drinking]

kill-cow *n.* [mid-19C–1900s] an unrestrained braggart. ['I could kill a cow with one blow']

kill-cow *adj. see* KILL-CALF.

kill-crazy/-simple *adj.* [1930s+] (orig. US) obsessed with murdering, desperate to kill.

kill-devil *n.*¹ **1** [mid-17C–19C] (US) rum, or newly made rum, also known as *rumbullion.* **2** [mid-19C–1960s] (US) strong alcohol, esp. whisky. **3** [1950s] (US, Ozarks) very strong tobacco.

kill-devil *n.*² [early 18C–19C] a gun. [late 19C use is US]

killed *adj.* [1980s+] (US) intoxicated by drugs or alcohol. [KILL v.² (2)]

killed off *adj.* [19C] **1** lying under the table after drinking too much. **2** dragged out from one's recumbent position.

killer *n.*¹ **1** [20C] (orig. US) an outstanding, if slightly menacing, person. **2** [1940s+] the 'clincher', the final word in an

argument. **3** [1940s+] (orig. US) something very difficult to manage.

killer *n.*² [1920s+] (Aus.) a womanizer. [abbr. LADY-KILLER]

killer *n.*³ [1940s–50s] (drugs) **1** marijuana. **2** phencyclidine (cf. ACE n.³).

killer *adj.* (orig. US) **1** [1970s+] terrific, amazing, effective (cf. KILL adj.; KILLER-DILLER adj.). **2** [1980s+] ghastly, terrible.

killer beans *adj.* [1990s] (US teen) a general expression of approval meaning really wonderful, absolutely excellent. [ext. of COOL BEANS!]

killer-diller *n.* [1930s+] (orig. US) a ladies' man. [KILLER n.² + redup.]

killer-diller/thriller-diller *adj.* [1930s+] (orig. US) excellent, wonderful. [redup. of KILLER adj.]

killer joint *n.* [1970s+] (drugs) phencyclidine (cf. ACE n.³). [the strength]

killers *n.* [late 18C] the human eyes.

killer weed *n.* [1960s+] (drugs) **1** marijuana. **2** phencyclidine (cf. ACE n.³). [SE *killer* + WEED n.¹ (4); orig. a non-sl. epithet applied to discourage use, now used ironically]

kill-grief *n.* [early–mid-18C] gin or rum. [its emotional anaesthesia]

killin' fields *n.* [1990s] (US Black teen) East Oakland. [the frequency of random killings, usu. gang or drug-related, in the area; ult. the title of the film *The Killing Fields* (1984)]

killing *n.* [late 19C+] (US) a great success, usu. financial. [now SE]

killing *adj.*¹ **1** [mid-18C–early 20C] fashionable, stylish. **2** [late 19C+] (orig. US) fascinating, very interesting, wonderful. [17C SE *killing*, captivating, bewitching]

killing *adj.*² [mid-19C+] extremely funny (cf. KILL v.²).

killing floor *n.* [1970s+] (US Black) anywhere used for the purpose of sexual intercourse (cf. SLAUGHTERHOUSE n.³).

kill it *v.*¹ [1910s+] (orig. US) to stop talking; usu. as imper. *kill it!*, shut up!

kill it *v.*² [1990s] to masturbate (cf. KILL OFF; KILL SOME BABIES). [the waste of procreative possibility]

killjoy *n.* [1940s] (US Black) a policeman or any authority figure.

kill-me-quick *n.* **1** [mid-19C–1910s] (US) whisky. **2** [late 19C–1900s] (Aus.) a form of fritter. **3** [1940s+] (S.Afr.) a form of strong liquor drunk in the townships, made of bread, syrup, brown sugar, yeast and bran. [the effect of such food or drink]

kill off *v.* [1990s] to masturbate (cf. KILL IT v.²).

kill one's dog, to *phr.* [mid-18C] to be drunk, to drink heavily.

killout *n.* [1930s–40s; 1980s+] (US Black) a fascinating person, an enthralling topic or thing. [var. of KILLER n.¹]

kill out oneself *v.* [20C] (W.I.) to exhaust oneself.

kill-priest/-preacher *n.* [late 18C–19C] port wine, also whisky (cf. KILL-THE-BEGGAR). [the clergy's supposed partiality to the drink]

kill-simple *see* KILL-CRAZY.

kill some babies, to *phr.* [20C] (US) to masturbate (cf. BEQUEATH ONE'S GENES; KILL IT v.²).

kill/stomp someone's buzz, to *phr.* [1980s+] (US campus) to depress someone, to destroy someone's enjoyment or pleasure, to disappoint someone (cf. BUZZKILL). [SE *kill* + BUZZ n.⁵]

kill-the-beggar *n.* [19C] rough whisky (cf. KILL-PRIEST).

kill who? *excl.* [late 19C] a defiant response to a threat (cf. YOU AND WHOSE ARMY?).

Kilmarnock whittle *n.* [late 19C+] (Scot.) a person of either sex who is engaged to be married. [dial. *whittle*, a blanket; thus the term may refer to the practice of *bundling*, unmarried couples sleeping together, albeit fully dressed]

kilt adj. [late 18C+] (Irish) suffering, whether mentally or physically. [hyperbolic use of SE killed]

kiltie/kilty n. [mid-19C–early 20C] a Scottish soldier. [his SE kilt]

k.i.m.b.a. phr. [1990s] (US Black teen) kiss my Black ass. [abbr. Note Joyce, Ulysses (1922) KMRIA, Kiss My Royal Irish Arse]

kimbaw v. [late 17C–early 19C] to cheat, to rob, to deceive (cf. CROSS v.²). [SE akimbo, crossed or crooked]

Kimberley adj. [20C] (Aus.) a general derog. name used in various combs., e.g. Kimberley mutton, roast goat, Kimberley oyster, a meat fritter. [Kimberley, an area of northwest Australia]

kimible n. [1960s+] (US Black) an exaggerated, identifiable pimp walk (cf. AKIMBO v.). [? SE (arms) akimbo]

kim-kam adj. [late 16C–early 19C] crooked, awry, out of order. [dial. cam, crooked, awry + redup.; ult. Welsh cam, crooked, awry, false]

kimp see KEMP.

kin n. [late 19C–1900s] (US) a miser. [SE skinflint]

kinat/canat/kinnat/kinnatt n. [20C] (Irish) an impertinent, conceited youngster. [Irish cnat, a gnat]

kinchin/kinchen n. [mid-16C–late 19C] (Und.) a (small) child. [Ger. Kindchen, MDu. kindeken, a little child]

kinchin/kitchin co n. [16C] (Und.) a child who has been brought up to thieving as a profession, 'an idle rungate boy' (Awdeley) (cf. CANTING CREW; KINCHIN COVE). [KINCHIN + co = COVE]

kinchin cove n. **1** [late 17C–18C] a little man. **2** [late 17C–18C] a child brought up as a thief. **3** [mid-19C] a man who robs children. [KINCHIN + COVE]

kinchin/kynchin lay n. [mid–late 19C] street stealing from children. [KINCHIN + LAY]

kinchin/kitchin mort n. [mid–late 16C] **1** a beggar's child. **2** (Und.) a young, virgin girl, destined to be a prostitute or beggar's companion: 'she is brought at her full age to the UPRIGHT MAN to be broken, and so she is called a DOXY, until she comes to the honour of an ALTHAM' (Awdeley) (cf. CANTING CREW). [KINCHIN + MORT]

kincob n. [mid-19C] (Anglo-Ind.) uniform, fine clothes, richly embroidered dresses. [Hind. or Gujerati kamkhâb, gold brocade; note 13C camocca, damasked silk, f. Pers. kamkha, ult. Chinese kin-kha, gold cloth]

kind, the n. (US) **1** [1960s+] anything good such as food, drugs or liquor. **2** [1980s+] (drugs) superior quality cannabis (cf. DA KINE). [Hawaiian surf sl. da kine, anything of which one forgets the precise name]

kinda/kinder n. [1950s+] (Aus.) the kindergarten class in a primary school (cf. KINDIE). [abbr.]

kinda phr. see KIND OF.

kinder see KINDA n.

Kinder Eggs n. [1990s] (drugs) MDMA (cf. ECSTASY). [brandname of a popular sweet]

kindergarten see GLADIATOR SCHOOL.

kindheart n. [17C] a dentist.

kindie/kindy n. [1960s+] (Aus./N.Z.) a kindergarten (cf. KINDA n.). [abbr.]

kindness n. [late 19C–1920s] (US Black) a sexual favour; thus to do a kindness, to indulge sexually.

kind of/kinda phr. [early 19C+] to some extent, in a way (cf. SORT OF).

kindy see KINDIE.

'kin'ell! excl. [20C] an excl. of surprise, annoyance, wonder etc. [abbr. FUCKING HELL!]

King n.¹ [late 19C+] (S.Afr.) King William's Town, Eastern Cape; once capital of the provinces of Queen Adelaide and British Kaffraria.

king n.² [1980s+] (US campus) used with a suitable noun or verb to denote the best of something, e.g. surfer king, toking king.

King n.³ [1990s] (US Black) Burger King (cf. B.K.).

king adj. [1960s+] (Aus.) excellent, wonderful, perfect.

king! excl. [1960s+] (Aus.) brilliant! wonderful! [KING adj.]

king bee n. [mid-19C+] (orig. US) the most important person of a group or organization.

King Billy n. [mid-19C+] (Aus.) **1** a generic term for any Aboriginal leader. **2** any Aboriginal singled out from the rest. [King William IV of England (r.1830–7)]

king canutes see DAISY ROOTS.

king daddy n. [1990s] (US teen) the very best of a person, place or thing; thus the female counterpart queen mama. [note DADDY n.]

king death n. [20C] bad breath. [rhy. sl.]

king dick n.¹ [late 19C+] a brick; thus king dickie, a brickie, a bricklayer. [rhy. sl.]

king dick n.² [20C] (Aus.) the leader, the boss, the 'guv'ner'. [generic use of proper name]

king dick adj. [20C] stupid, dull. [rhy. sl. king dick = THICK adj.¹]

kingdom come n.¹ **1** [late 18C+] the 'after-life'; thus send to kingdom come, to kill. **2** [20C] (US) an infinitely remote time or place. [the phr. 'thy kingdom come' in the Lord's Prayer]

kingdom come n.² **1** [20C] rum. **2** [1970s] the buttocks. [rhy. sl.; (2) kingdom come = BUM n.²]

kingfish n. [1930s+] (US) a political leader or 'boss'. [the original Kingfish was the populist Governor and Senator Huey P. Long (1893–1935) of Louisiana; Long, who declared that he 'looked around at the little fishes present and said "I'm the Kingfish"', fought his campaigns on the slogan 'Everyman a King but no man wears a crown'. The name was also given to a character in the hit US radio show Amos 'n' Andy]

king-hell adj. [1960s+] (orig. US) formidable, impressive.

king hit n. (Aus.) **1** [1910s+] a knock-out or knock-down blow. **2** [1910s+] a thug, a bully; thus king-hit artist, king-hit merchant, one who specializes in thuggery. **3** [1940s+] a surprise punch. [SE king, supreme, extreme + hit]

king hit v. [1910s+] (Aus.) to knock down. [KING HIT n.]

king ivory n. [1980s+] (drugs) fentanyl (cf. APACHE n.²). [? its colour]

King Kong n. **1** [1930s–60s] (US Black) cheap, potent, homemade whisky (cf. KONG). **2** [1970s] (US drugs) a strong addiction (cf. GORILLA n.²). [the name of the fictitious monster ape, who 'starred' in the film King Kong (1933)]

King Kong pills n. [1980s+] (drugs) barbiturates (cf. GORILLA PILLS). [the film King Kong (1933), in which the monster ape is knocked out, albeit by gas, not pills]

King Lear n. **1** [late 19C+] an ear. **2** [20C] a male homosexual. [rhy. sl. (2) King Lear = QUEER n.¹]

king of clubs n. [19C] a promiscuous man, a womanizer. [SE king + CLUB n. (2)]

king of Spain n. [20C] (Aus.) rain. [rhy. sl.]

king of Spain's trumpeter n. [late 18C] a donkey. [pun on SE Don Key/donkey]

kingpin n. [mid-19C+] (orig. US) the central figure, the most important figure in an organization or team. [US use is late 19C, then Aus. early 20C, UK 1950s+; SE kingpin, synon. with kingbolt, the most important or largest bolt in a mechanical structure, itself linked to kingpost, the central post that holds up a roof-truss]

king pippin n. [1910s+] an important, outstanding person. [SE king + PIPPIN]

kings!/kings on! excl. [1950s+] (US, usu. juv.) a claim, esp. a claim of first rights to something (cf. CHECKS!).

kings and queens *n.* [20C] baked beans; thus *kings on holy ghost*, baked beans on toast. [rhy. sl.]

king's bad bargain *see* HIS MAJESTY'S BAD BARGAIN.

king's books *n.* [mid-17C–early 19C] a pack of cards (cf. DEVIL'S BOOKS). [SE *king's books*, taxation lists; gamblers are 'taxed' when they lose]

King's College *n.* [late 18C] the King's Bench prison (cf. CITY COLLEGE).

king's cruse! *see* KING'S EX!

king's elevator, the *n.* [1950s+] (US) total victimization. [pun on ROYAL SHAFT]

King's English *n.* [1920s–60s] (US Black) standard American English.

king's ex!/sax!/cruse! *excl.* [mid-19C+] (juv.) a traditional cry requesting a pause in a combative game. [SE *excuse* or f. the 'X-ed' or crossed (thus *cruse*) fingers that allow players to stand (temporarily) outside the game]

king's habit *n.* [1980s+] (drugs) cocaine. [SE *king* + HABIT; i.e. the cost]

King's Head Inn/Chequer Inn in Newgate Street *n.* [late 18C–early 19C] Newgate prison.

king shit/spit *n.* [1940s+] (orig. US) an arrogant, self-opinionated person (cf. LADY MUCK; SHIT n.⁹). [SE *king* + SHIT n.²]

kingsman *n.* [mid–late 19C] **1** a silk handkerchief in a variety of colours, as worn by costermongers of both sexes (cf. BILLY n.⁴). **2** a silk handkerchief with a green base and a yellow pattern; thus *kingsman of the rortiest*, a very gaudy variety.

kings on! *see* KINGS.

king's peg *n.* [late 19C+] a champagne cocktail, champagne mixed with brandy (cf. BOY n.⁴). [SE *king* + PEG n.; the ref. is presumably to Edward VII's appetite for the wine]

king's pictures *n.* [late 17C–18C] money (cf. QUEEN'S PICTURES). [the royal features are engraved or printed on money]

king spit *see* KING SHIT.

king's plate *n.* [early 19C] chains, fetters. [the ult. royal control of the prisons and police]

king's proctor *n.* [20C] a doctor. [rhy. sl.]

king's sax! *see* KING'S EX!

Kingswood lion *n.* [early 19C] a donkey (cf. JERUSALEM PONY). [the village of Kingswood, known for the keeping of donkeys by the colliers who lived there]

King Tut's revenge *n.* [1970s+] (US) diarrhoea contracted in the Middle East (cf. APPLE-BLOSSOM TWO-STEP).

kinifee *n.* [1950s–60s] (Aus. teen) a knife. [exaggeratedly lit. pron. of SE *knife*]

kink *n.¹* **1** [early 19C–1920s] (US) a tricky or surprising aspect of something. **2** [19C–1920s] (US) a whimsical idea, a slight eccentricity. **3** [1930s+] (Aus.) a good idea. [SE *kink*, a sudden bend in an otherwise straight line]

kink/kinkhead *n.²* [mid-19C–1940s] (US) a derog. term for a Black person; thus *come the kink*, to steal a Black slave from the country, and dispose of them in town (cf. KINKYHEAD). [typically 'kinky' Black hair]

kink *n.³* [1910s–50s] (US Und.) **1** a criminal, later esp. a car thief. **2** a non-criminal tramp or a criminal who specializes in a style of theft different from that practised by the speaker.

kink *n.⁴* **1** [1950s+] a perversion, esp. in sexual activity. **2** [1960s+] a sexually abnormal person, an eccentric.

kinkhead *see* KINK n.².

kinko *n.* [1960s+] (US) an eccentric (cf. WEIRDO n.). [KINK n.¹ + sfx -O]

kinky *n.¹* [1920s–40s] (US) one who has kinky hair, thus usu. a Black person (cf. KINKYHEAD). [SE *kink*]

kinky *n.²* [1920s–40s] (US Und.) anything that has been obtained dishonestly, esp. a stolen car. [KINKY adj.²]

kinky *n.³* [1950s+] a sexual eccentric. [KINKY adj.³]

kinky *adj.¹* **1** [mid-19C+] (US) odd, bizarre, eccentric. **2** [late 19C–1910s] immoral or unladylike. **3** [1900s–40s] (US) of livestock, frisky. [SE *kink*, a bend]

kinky *adj.²* **1** [1900s–70s] (US Und.) dishonest or criminal. **2** [1920s–50s] (Und.) corrupt. [var. on BENT adj. (3)]

kinky *adj.³* [1950s+] sexually perverse, esp. sadomasochistic; thus *kinky boots*, thigh-high boots, worn by women and associated with the traditional 'dominatrix' figure. [KINK n.⁴]

kinkyhead *n.* [mid-19C–1950s] (US Black) one who has kinky hair (cf. KINKY n.¹).

kinnat/kinnatt *see* KINAT.

Kinsey 6 *n.* [1950s] (gay) a person who is completely homosexual, as opposed to one with some bisexual inclinations. [the categorization by sexologist Alfred Kinsey in his book *Sexual Behavior in the Human Male* (1947), popularly known as the 'Kinsey Report']

kin teet *adj.* [1950s] (W.I.) dead. [the skin (*kin*) has drawn back from the teeth through *rigor mortis*]

'kin teet' *v. see* SKIN TEETH v.

kioodle *see* KIYOODLE.

kip *n.* **1** [mid-18C+] a brothel; thus *kip-keeper*, a brothel-keeper, a madame; *kip-shop*, a brothel. **2** [mid-19C+] a bed. **3** [late 19C+] the place where one sleeps, one's home. **4** [late 19C+] sleep, a nap. **5** [late 19C] a lodging house, a hotel room. **6** [late 19C+] (Anglo-Irish) a job. **7** [1920s] (US Und.) a nightwatchman, thus *kipped*, guarded by a nightwatchman. [Danish *kippe*, hut, a low alehouse, *horekippe*, a brothel]

kip *v.* **1** [early–mid-19C] to play truant. **2** [late 19C+] to lodge, to sleep. **3** [1900s] (US teen/Und.) to sleep on the streets. [KIP n.]

kipe/kype *v.* [1930s+] (US) to steal. [? dial. *kip*, to take property through fraud or violence]

kiphouse *see* DOSSHOUSE.

kip-in *adj.* [20C] easy, undemanding. [KIP v.; lit. 'sleep-in']

kip in *v.* [late 19C+] to be quiet, to stop talking. [fig. use of KIP v.]

kipper *n.¹* [20C] anywhere one can sleep, a 'dosshouse'. [KIP v.]

kipper *n.²* [1900s–50s] a person, esp. a young or small person, a child. [an affectionate nickname]

kipper *n.³* [1940s+] (Aus.) an Englishman, an English immigrant. [SE *kipper*, a herring which, after processing, has become 'two-faced with no guts']

kipper *n.⁴* [1950s] the vagina (cf. BEARDED CLAM; KIPPER BOX). [the identification of the vagina with FISH n.⁴]

kipper *n.⁵* [1960s] a notably wide-ended tie. [the shape supposedly resembled that of the fish]

kipper *v.* [1920s+] to ruin someone else's chances. [? a herring is 'ruined' by kippering]

kipper and bloater *n.* [1970s] **1** a motor. **2** a photo. [rhy. sl.]

kipper and plaice *n.* [20C] the face. [rhy. sl.]

kipper box *n.* [1990s] an unwashed vagina (cf. BEARDED CLAM). [KIPPER n.⁴ + BOX n.⁶]

kipper feast *n.* [1990s] cunnilingus. [KIPPER n.⁴]

kippers *n.* [20C] (a pair of) slippers. [rhy. sl.]

kipping *n.* [1950s] (Aus.) masturbating. ['two-up' use *kip*, the piece of wood on which the pennies are placed before throwing them into the air; like other similarly shaped objects it can be synon. for the penis]

kipping-house/kippings *n.* [1920s–30s] a common lodging house. [KIP n.]

kippy *adj.* [1910s–80s] (US) attractive, striking, lively. [ety. unknown]

kipsie/kypsey *n.¹* [mid-19C] a wicker basket, usu. to hold cherries. [SE *keep*]

kipsie/kypsey *n.²* [1910s+] (Aus.) a cheap lodging house. [KIP n.]

kirb *n.* [mid-19C] a brick. [backsl.]

kirk-buzzer *n.* [19C] a pickpocket who specializes in the robbery of church congregations (cf. AUTEM-DIVER). [Scot. *kirk*, church + BUZZER n.[1]]

kirker *n.* [late 17C–late 19C] (Scot.) a member of a church or religious group; thus *Auld Kirker*, *Free Kirker*. [Scot. *kirk*, a church]

kirking/kirkling *n.* [mid-19C] the practice of breaking into churches (cf. CRACK A KIRK; DEAD LURK). [Scot. *kirk*, a church]

kishkes/keeshkas/kishka/kishkas *n.* [20C] (orig. US) **1** the guts, the stomach. **2** courage, pluck. [Yid. *kishkes*, intestines]

kiskeedee/keskydee *n.* [mid-19C] (US) a French-speaking person. [Fr. *qu'est-ce qu'il dit?*, what is he saying?]

kisky *adj.* [mid-19C] drunk, tipsy. [? rhy. sl. *kisky* = whisky or Rom. *kushto*, feeling good or happy (cf. CUSHTY)]

kiss *n.* **1** [1910s–20s] (US) a drink from a bottle (cf. KISS THE BABE). **2** [1920s+] (US teen) a blow or hit.

kiss *v.*[1] **1** [19C] to have sexual intercourse. **2** [19C] to fellate or perform cunnilingus. **3** [1910s+] (US) to hit or strike hard. [euph.; note Fr. *baiser*, lit. to kiss, in sl. to have sexual intercourse]

kiss *v.*[2] [1970s+] (US teen) to reject, to do without etc. [abbr. KISS OFF v./SE *kiss goodbye*]

k.i.s.s.! *excl.* [1960s+] (US) *k*eep *i*t *s*imple, *s*tupid. [abbr.; orig. milit. usage, later general, also popular in drug rehabilitation circles]

kiss and cuddle *n.* [20C] a muddle. [rhy. sl.]

kiss-arse/-ass *n.* [1910s+] (orig. US) a toady, a sycophant (cf. ASS-KISSER). [KISS ARSE v.]

kiss-arse/-ass *adj.* [1910s+] (orig. US) sycophantic. [KISS ARSE v.]

kiss/lick/suck arse/ass/butt *v.* [1910s+] (orig. US) to be subservient, to toady, to act as a sycophant. [SE *kiss* + ARSE n.[1]/BUTT n.[1]]

kisscurl *n.* [19C] a small twisted curl worn on the temple. [SE in 20C, when it has tended to refer to a single curl worn over the brow]

kisser *n.*[1] **1** [mid-19C+] (orig. boxing) the mouth. **2** [20C] the face. **3** [1920s–30s] (gypsy) a baby.

kisser *n.*[2] **1** [20C] a male homosexual. **2** [1950s+] a toady, a sycophant. [abbr. ASS-KISSER]

kiss goodbye *v.* [1900s–40s] to reject, to do without.

kissing-crust *n.* [late 19C] **1** the soft part of a loaf, where it has been touching another loaf while cooking and has not therefore become crisp. **2** the 'under-crust' in a pudding or pie. [SE *kiss*, to touch]

kissing-trap *n.* [19C] (orig. prize-ring) the mouth (cf. KISSER n.[1]). [SE *kiss* + TRAP n.[3]]

kiss it/me where the sun don't shine! *excl.* [1940s+] (orig. US) a general excl. of derision or dismissal. [semi-euph. for KISS MY ARSE!]

kiss kiss *phr.* [1990s] (US campus) goodbye. [the kisses offered on saying goodbye]

kiss mary *v.* [1960s] to smoke marijuana. [SE *kiss* + MARY (JANE) n.[2]]

kiss me hardy *n.* [20C] a measure of Bacardi rum. [rhy. sl.]

kiss me neck! *phr.* [1950s+] (W.I. Rasta) a common excl. of surprise. [euph. for KISS MY ARSE!]

kiss-me-quick *n.*[1] **1** [mid-19C] a small hat, worn by women and fixed to the back of the head. **2** [20C] a small hat sold at the seaside which may even bear the legend '*Kiss Me Quick!*' [its size and position presumably left more room for kissing than larger, veiled pieces of millinery]

kiss-me-quick *n.*[2] [20C] **1** the penis. **2** a fool. [rhy. sl. *kiss-me-quick* = PRICK n.]

kiss me where the sun don't shine! *see* KISS IT WHERE THE SUN DON'T SHINE!

kiss/suck my arse!/ass! *excl.* [mid-16C+] a general statement of contempt or dismissal; often ext. as *kiss my ass in Macey's window*. [note Chaucer, *Miller's Tale* (1386): 'But with his mouth he kiste hir naked ers']

kiss my arse fellow *n.* [late 18C–early 19C] a sycophant.

kiss my ass! *see* KISS MY ARSE!

kiss my foot! *excl.* [late 19C+] (Aus.) a general statement of contempt or dismissal. [euph. var. on KISS MY ARSE!]

kiss my parliament! *excl.* [late 17C] a general statement of contempt or dismissal. [euph. var. on KISS MY ARSE!]

kiss my tail! *excl.* [late 18C–late 19C] a general statement of contempt or dismissal. [var. on KISS MY ARSE!; TAIL n.[1]]

kiss my tuna! *excl.* [1980s] (US teen) an all-purpose excl. of rejection. [var. on KISS MY ARSE!; TUNA, thus the implication is that the oral sex that is invited is *de facto* distasteful]

kiss of death *n.* [1940s] a person or object, contact with whom or which invariably proves fatal – metaphorically if not practically. [the original *kiss of death* is presumed to be that given by Judas to Christ]

kiss of life *n.* [20C] one's wife. [rhy. sl.]

kiss off *n.* **1** [1920s+] (US) a dismissal, a rejection. **2** [1930s+] (US) a conclusion, a farewell, a termination (usu. with sense of one party compelling it on the other). **3** [1940s+] death.

kiss off *v.* **1** [1930s+] to reject, to ignore, to spurn, esp. a lover; thus excl. *kiss off!*, go away, don't talk rubbish! **2** [1940s] (US) to murder or to die.

kiss one's ass goodbye, to *phr.* [20C] to give up completely, to abandon all hope. [ARSE n.[1]]

kiss oneself goodbye, to *phr.* [20C] to commit suicide.

kiss someone's ring, to *phr.* [1930s+] to fawn, to act the sycophant, to toady. [SE *kiss the ring*, to pay homage, but note RING n.[1] (2)]

kiss teet/teeth *v.* [1950s+] (W.I. Rasta) to make a hissing noise of disapproval, dislike, vexation or disappointment.

kiss the babe/baby, to *phr.* [mid-19C–1910s] (orig. US) to take a drink.

kiss the baby, to *phr.*[1] [20C] (US Und.) to face a certain term of imprisonment. [such a prisoner would have to kiss their baby goodbye]

kiss the baby/baby in the boat, to *phr.*[2] [1930s] to perform cunnilingus (cf. BABY IN THE BOAT).

kiss the clink/counter, to *phr.* [mid–late 18C] to be confined in either of these prisons. [SE *kiss* + CLINK n.[1]/SE *counter*, a prison attached to a city court]

kiss the cross, to *phr.* [1920s+] (Aus.) to be knocked out. [SE *cross*, a blow in boxing + pun on religious use]

kiss the dog, to *phr.* [1930s] (US Und.) of a pickpocket, to steal from a person while face-to-face.

kiss the dust, to *phr.* [20C] (orig. US) to die.

kiss the hare's foot, to *phr.* [17C–18C] to be too late. [? the foot is the last part of a hare to be seen as it vanishes]

kiss the maid, to *phr.* [late 17C–18C] to be executed on a primitive form of the guillotine. [SE *maiden*, a form of early guillotine used at Edinburgh in late 16C; occas. applied to the Halifax gibbet]

kiss the parson's wife, to *phr.* [late 18C] to be lucky in the choosing of or betting on horses. [the belief that those who wish for such luck must 'kiss the parson's wife']

kiss the pope's toe, to *phr.* [late 18C] to show one's respect to the pope by kissing the golden cross of the sandal of his right foot. [only sovereigns were excluded from making this obeisance]

kiss/bow to/hug/pray to the porcelain god/goddess, to *phr.* [1960s+] (US campus) to vomit (cf. DRIVE THE PORCELAIN BUS). [the 'porcelain god' being the lavatory bowl]

kiss the worm, to *phr.* [1970s+] to fellate.

kiss-up *n.* [1950s+] a sycophant. [KISS UP TO]

kiss up to *v.* [1950s+] to toady to (cf. KISS ARSE v.).

kissyface n. [1950s+] (US teen/campus) the act of kissing.

kissy-kissy n. [1980s+] (US) sycophantic behaviour. [KISS ARSE v.]

kit n.[1] [early 18C–early 19C] a dancing-master. [SE *kit*, a small fiddle, esp. popular among dancing-masters; ult. ? Gk. *cithara*]

kit n.[2] [18C–mid-19C] a number of things or persons viewed as a whole, a set, a lot, a collection (cf. WHOLE KIT AND CABOODLE).

kit n.[3] [19C] the penis (cf. ACCOUTREMENTS).

kit n.[4] [1940s+] (N.Z.) a shopping basket.

kit n.[5] [1960s+] clothing; thus *get one's kit off*. [SE *kit*, the uniforms used for various sports]

kit n.[6] [1980s+] (drugs) the equipment, such as a syringe or a spoon, required for injection of a narcotic (cf. OUTFIT; WORKS).

kit and caboodle see WHOLE KIT AND CABOODLE.

kit and killybang/cargo/crew/parcel/posse/tolic/tuck phr. [mid-19C+] (orig. US) the lot, everything there is (cf. WHOLE KIT AND CABOODLE).

kitchen n. 1 [mid-19C] the vagina (cf. OVEN; ROASTING JACK). 2 [late 19C+] the stomach (cf. VICTUALLING DEPARTMENT).

kitchen-bitch/-crumb/-key n. [20C] (W.I.) a man who hangs around the kitchen instead of going out and doing 'man's things' (cf. AUNTIE-MAN).

kitchen Latin n. [mid-18C+] bad Latin, mangled Latin (cf. APOTHECARIES' LATIN). [the second-rate Latin spoken by monastery servants, poor priests etc.]

kitchen mechanic n. [late 19C–1960s] (US) a cook or washer-up (cf. K.M.).

kitchen range n. [20C] small change. [rhy. sl.]

kitchen sink n. 1 [20C] a stink. 2 [20C] (Aus.) a drink. 3 [20C] a derog. term for a Chinese person. [rhy. sl.; (3) = CHINK n.[3]]

kitchen stoves n. [20C] (Aus.) cloves. [rhy. sl.]

kitchin co see KINCHIN CO.

kitchin mort see KINCHIN MORT.

kite n.[1] 1 [mid-16C–early 17C] a despicable person, one who preys on others. 2 [mid-19C–1990s] the stomach. 3 [late 19C–1950s] (US) a prostitute or promiscuous woman. 4 [late 19C] (US) the human face. [SE *kite*, a bird of prey (*Milvus ictinus*); (2) the stomach as an 'eater'; (4) the position of the 'eating' mouth in the face]

kite n.[2] 1 [mid-19C+] (US/Can. prison) a contraband letter or note smuggled into or out of prison. 2 [mid-19C+] (US prison) any form of written document, memo etc used within a prison. 3 [19C+] a dud cheque (cf. KITE v.[2]). 4 [1910s+] (Aus. prison) a newspaper. 5 [1970s] (US Und.) a complaint to the police about some form of illegal operation, often from a gambler who has been fleeced. 6 [1970s+] (US campus) an inveterate drug user, who stays *high as a kite*. [SE *kite*, the toy; in (3) a 'bouncing' cheque 'flies away']

kite n.[3] [20C] (Irish) the anus. [? dial. *kite*, the stomach/KITE n.[1] (2)]

kite v.[1] [mid-19C] to wander around. [SE *kite*, i.e. one is 'gliding' like a kite]

kite v.[2] 1 [mid-19C+] to pass a dud cheque; thus *kite-dropper*, one who passes dud cheques (cf. KITE-FLYER). 2 [1920s+] to smuggle letters in and out of prison. [KITE n.[2] (3), (1)]

kite around v. [mid-19C+] to rush about. [ext. of KITE v.[1]]

kite-flyer n. [1920s+] a passer of dud cheques. [KITE n.[2] (3)]

kite-flying n. 1 [19C+] raising money by persons colluding in the exchange of accommodation bills or cheques on different banks, in none of which they possess sufficient funds. 2 [mid-19C] raising money by transferring accounts between banks and creating an illusory balance against which one cashes cheques. 3 [mid-19C+] passing forged, stolen or unbacked cheques. [KITE n.[2] (3)]

kite-man n. [1920s+] a criminal who specializes in cheque fraud. [KITE n.[2] (3) + sfx. -*man*]

kiter n. [1930s+] a criminal who specializes in cheque fraud. [KITE n.[2] (3) + sfx. -*er*]

kite-string n. [1970s+] (N.Z.) a close attachment, an 'apron-string'.

kite with no string, a phr. [1930s+] (US Black) 1 an airmail letter. 2 any form of communication, incl. e-mail. [SE *kite*; such a 'kite' flies off into the sky; note KITE n.[2]]

kit has come phr. [late 19C+] a menstrual period has begun (cf. GEORGE CALLED). [euph.]

kit-kat shuffle n. [1990s] female masturbation (cf. FIVE-FINGER SHUFFLE; KNUCKLE SHUFFLE). [KITTY n.[2]]

kitmegur/kitmutgar n. [mid-19C] (Anglo-Ind.) an under-butler, a footman. [Hind. *khidmatgar*, an under-butler; lit. 'one who renders service']

kitna? see KIDNA?

kitskonstabel n. [1980s+] (S.Afr.) a special constable, only partially trained, used to keep order in townships during a state of emergency. [Afk. *kits*, instant + *konstabel*, constable]

kitt n. [1980s+] (drugs) cannabis. [ety. unknown; ? misuse of KIT n.[6] or KIF n.]

kitted-up adj. [1960s+] dressed, clothed. [KIT n.[5]]

kitten n.[1] [early 19C] a pint or half-pint pot. [i.e. a small CAT n.[3]]

kitten n.[2] [1920s+] (US Black) a young, inexperienced girl (cf. KITTY n.[2]).

kitten v. [late 19C–1900s] of a woman, to go into labour.

kitten hammock n. [1990s] a bra. [CATS AND KITTIES + SE *hammock*]

kittens' noses n. [1990s] female nipples. [supposed resemblance]

kitteys see KITTIES.

kittie n. [19C] a prostitute (cf. JUDY n.[1]; MAGGIE n.[1]). [the popular name + ref. to CAT n.[10]; KITTY n.[2]; PUSSY n.[1] etc]

kitties/kitteys n. [late 18C] one's furniture or household effects. [? SE *kit*; note the first citation in Grose (1785) in which kit is defined as 'the whole of a soldier's necessaries, the contents of his knapsack']

kittle pitchering n. [late 18C–early 19C] a way of cutting off a boring talker by continually interrupting them with small queries. [Scot. *kittle*, to puzzle with a question, a riddle etc + *pitcher*, to throw in]

kittly-benders/kettle-de-benders n. [mid-19C] (US) 1 thin ice which bends under one's weight. 2 the sport of running over this. [SE *kittly*, requiring great caution or skill, unsafe to meddle with, risky]

kitty n.[1] 1 [19C–1940s] a prison, a lock-up. 2 [late 19C] the 'pool' in card-games. [Northumbrian dial.; ? f. *kidcote*, the name of the prison in various northern towns, incl. York and Lancaster. In (2), SE in 20C, the money is fig. 'imprisoned' while the hand is played]

kitty n.[2] 1 [20C] the vagina (cf. CAT n.[10]). 2 [1930s+] (US Black) a young, inexperienced girl. 3 [1970s+] a woman, esp. in a sexual context (cf. PUSSY n.[1]). [SE *Kitty*, the dimin. of the female name *Katherine*]

kitty/kitty-cat n.[3] [1930s–70s] (US Black) a Cadillac.

kitty n.[4] [1950s–60s] (US) a young man. [CAT n.[9]]

kitty-cat see KITTY n.[3].

kittywampus/kitty-ki-wampus adj. [1940s+] (US) aslant, skewed (cf. CATAWAMPUS adj.[3]). [SAmE *kitty-corner* + WAMPUS]

kivey n. [mid-19C–1920s] a man. [presumably a dimin. of COVE, though poss. linked to Lat. *civis*, a citizen]

Kiwi n. [1910s+] a New Zealander. [the national bird]

kiwi grace n. [1970s+] a name for the excl. '2, 4, 6, 8, bog in, don't wait!'; i.e. an allusion to the New Zealander's enthusiasm/greediness for food. [SE *kiwi*, generic for N.Z. + *grace* (before meals)]

kiwi green *n.* [1970s+] (N.Z. drugs) locally grown marijuana. [SE *kiwi*, generic for N.Z. + GREEN n.³ (1)]

kiwi haircut *n.* [1960s+] (N.Z.) a 'short-back-and-sides' haircut. [SE *kiwi*, generic for N.Z. + *haircut*]

ki-yi *n.* (US) **1** [late 19C–1910s] a noisy dog. **2** [late 19C–1940s] a contemptible fellow, a cur. [echoic]

kiyoodle/kioodle/kyoodle *n.* (US) **1** [late 19C+] a small noisy dog. **2** [late 19C–1960s] a worthless fellow. [? echoic or SE *cur*]

k.j. *n.* [1970s+] (drugs) phencyclidine (cf. ACE n.³). [abbr. KRYSTAL (JOINT)]

klaat! *excl.* [20C] (W.I.) a general excl. of anger. [BLOOD-CLAAT]

kleenex *n.*¹ [1980s+] (US) a juvenile word used for sex, because 'You pick it up, blow, and throw it away' (cf. DIXIE CUP n.²) . [*Kleenex*, a popular brand of paper handkerchief]

kleenex *n.*² [1990s] (drugs) MDMA (cf. ECSTASY). [*Kleenex*, a popular brand of paper handkerchief; i.e. it 'blows one's mind']

kleinhuisie *n.* [1960s+] (S.Afr.) an outdoor privy. [Afk. *klein*, small + *huis*, house, lit. 'little house']

klep/klepper *n.* [late 19C–1970s] a thief. [SE *kleptomaniac*]

klep/klepper *v.* [late 19C–1970s] to steal. [KLEP n.]

klepto *n.* [1920s+] a *klepto*maniac, an obsessive shoplifter. [abbr.]

klick *n.* [1960s+] (orig. US milit.) a kilometre. [abbr.]

klingon *n.* [1980s+] (drugs) a crack cocaine addict (cf. BEAM ME UP, SCOTTY!). [play on *cling on* (to every morsel of crack) and the 'spaced-out' state in which they live; the *Klingons* are the 'bad guys' in the TV series *Star Trek* (from 1966)]

klip *v.* [late 19C] (S.Afr.) to place a stone under a vehicle's wheel to stop it running away downhill. [Afk. *klip*, a small rock]

klobber *see* CLOBBER n.

klondike *n.* [20C] (US prison) the punishment cells (cf. HOLE n.²). [the *Klondike*, site of the Alaskan gold rush in the late 19C; miners worked alone and in darkness]

klondike *adj.* [late 19C] mad. [the 19C Alaskan gold rush on the *Klondike* river, which rendered diggers mad with greed]

klonkie *n.* [1950s+] (S.Afr.) a young Black boy. [Afk. *klein-jong*, servant-boy]

kloop *n.* [mid–late 19C] an onomat. term describing the sound of a cork being withdrawn from a bottle.

klootchman/klootch *n.* [mid-19C+] (US, mainly Pacific northwest) **1** a Native American woman. **2** any woman. [Chinook jargon *klootchman*, a woman]

klucker/kluxer *n.* [mid-19C+] (US Black) a member of the racist Ku Klux Klan.

kludge *n.* [1960s+] anything thrown together more by luck than judgement and with little style or sophistication. [computer jargon; note Ger. *kluge*, smart, witty. Coined by J.W. Granholm (*Datamation*, n.d.) and defined by him as 'an ill-assorted collection of poorly matching parts, forming a distressing whole']

klunk *n.* [1940s+] (US) a fool. [CLUNK n.²]

klunk out *v.* [1970s] (US) to break down (cf. CLUNKER n.¹). [var. on CONK OUT]

klutz *n.* [1950s+] (orig. US) a stupid, clumsy, socially inept person (cf. KLUTZY). [synon. Yid.; ult. Ger. *klotz*, a log, a lump of wood]

klutz *v.* [1950s+] (orig. US) to bungle or botch. [KLUTZ n.]

klutzy *adj.* [1950s+] (orig. US) clumsy, inept (cf. SCHLEPPY). [KLUTZ n.]

kluxer *see* KLUCKER.

k.m. *n.* [late 19C–1940s] (US) a chef or washer-up. [abbr. KITCHEN MECHANIC]

k.m.a.! *excl.* [late 19C–1920s] (US) a general statement of contempt or dismissal. [abbr. *kiss my ass!* (*see* KISS MY ARSE!)]

knabs *see* NABS.

knack *n.* [19C] the penis. [? KNACKERS]

knacked *adj.* [1980s+] exhausted, utterly tired-out. [abbr. KNACKERED]

knacker *n.* [mid-19C] a worn-out horse, fit only for slaughter (cf. ROARER n.²; SCRUB n.; WHISTLER n.²; WIND-SUCKER). [SE *knacker*, a horse-slaughterer]

knacker *v.* **1** [mid-19C+] (Aus.) to castrate. **2** [late 19C+] to kill, to ruin, to tire (cf. KNACKERED). [KNACKER n.]

knackered *adj.* [1950s+] **1** worn-out, exhausted. **2** of machinery, broken, irreparable. **3** stopped from doing what one wishes, thwarted. [KNACKER v.]

knackering *adj.* [1950s+] exhausting, debilitating. [KNACKER v.]

knackers/knacks/nackers *n.* [mid-19C+] the testicles. [dial.]

knackety/knacky *see* NAUKY.

knap *n.* [mid–late 19C] a mock blow; thus *give/take the knap*. [SE *knap*, to strike]

knap *v.* [19C] (Und.) to steal, to take, to receive; thus *knap a clout*, to steal a handkerchief, *knap seven penn'orth*, to receive a 7-year sentence, *knap the glim*, to catch venereal disease, *knap the swag*, to grab the plunder. [var. on NAP v.¹]

knap a jacob from a danna-drag, to *phr.* [early 19C] (Aus. Und.) 'This is a curious species of robbery ... ; it signifies taking away the short ladder from a nightman's cart, while the men are gone into a house, the privy of which they are employed emptying, in order to effect an ascent.' (Vaux). [KNAP v. + JACOB n.¹+ DUNNAKEN + DRAG n.¹]

knap of the case, the *phr.* [mid-16C] (Und.) the head of the house. [? SE *knap*, the crest or summit of a hill, but *OED*, which includes it as a derivative, notes 'doubtfully placed here']

knapped *adj.* [early–mid-19C] (Und.) pregnant. [fig. use of KNAP v.]

knapper *n.* [mid-18C–mid-19C] the knee. [dial.]

knapper's poll *n.* [late 18C–early 19C] (Und.) a sheep's head. [NAP n.⁴ + POLL n.¹]

knapping-jigger *n.* [mid-19C] (Und.) a turnpike gate; thus *dub at the knapping-jigger*, to pay at the turnpike gate. [KNAP v. + JIGGER n.¹]

knapsack descent *n.* [late 19C] a family in which one or both sides are, traditionally, professional soldiers.

knap the ding, to *phr.* [early–mid-19C] to take or steal what has already been stolen. [KNAP v.]

knap the rust, to *phr.* [19C] to lose one's temper. [KNAP v. + SE *rusty*, of horses, refractory]

knap/nab/nap the stoop, to *phr.* [mid-19C] to be placed in the pillory. [fig. use of KNAP v. + SE *stoop*, the position into which the prisoner is forced]

knark *n.* **1** [mid-19C] 'a hard-hearted or savage person' (Hotten 1859). **2** [mid-19C+] a police informer. [var. on NARK n.]

knave in grain *n.* [late 17C–early 19C] a miller. [the miller is traditionally dishonest]

knave's grease *n.* [late 16C–early 17C] a flogging.

knawky *see* NAUKY.

knead one's dough, to *phr.* [1990s] to masturbate.

knead one's knockwurst, to *phr.* [1990s] to masturbate (cf. ACCOST THE OSCAR MEYER).

knee *v.* [1930s+] to hit someone in the testicles with one's knee.

kneecap *v.* [1970s+] to exact an extra-legal 'punishment' esp. beloved of, and poss. introduced by, the IRA, whereby victims are shot through the kneecaps and, while painfully crippled, are not actually killed.

knee-drill *n.* [late 19C] insincere praying, presumably on one's knees. [esp. the prayers one needed to offer when claiming free food, drink and lodging from the Salvation Army]

knee-high to a grasshopper/duck/toad *phr.* [early 19C+] (orig. US) very short (cf. ASS-HIGH TO A TALL INDIAN).

knee-knockers *n.* [1960s+] (US) knickerbockers or men's knee-length shorts.

kneel at the altar, to *phr.* [1960s+] (US prison) to fellate.

kneesies *n.* [1950s+] (US) amorous knee contact, usu. covertly under a table (cf. PLAY FOOTSIE).

knee-slapper *n.* [1960s+] (US) an uproarious joke, often used ironically. [such a joke makes the listener slap their knee with delight]

knees up *n.* [1940s+] a party, a celebration. [the Cockney popular song 'Knees up Mother Brown!']

knee-trembler *n.* [late 19C+] sexual intercourse when both partners are standing up, popular with cheap prostitutes or with couples who have nowhere to lie down; thus *do a knee-trembler*, to have intercourse standing up (cf. PERPENDICULAR; STAND-UP n.¹).

knee-walking/knee-walking drunk *adj.* [1970s+] (US) very drunk.

knicker bacon *n.* [1990s] the labia (cf. BUM BACON).

knickers!/knickers to you! *excl.* [1970s+] a general excl. meaning rubbish!, you must be joking! etc; general negation of the preceding speaker's opinion, demand etc. [? euph. for KNACKERS! or use of *knickers* as a juv. 'obscenity']

knickers and stockings *n.* [1930s] a term of imprisonment (cf. GET THE KNICKERS). [ety. unknown]

knickers bandit *n.* [1960s+] **1** one who steals from washing lines (cf. HEDGE CREEPER; LULLY PRIGGER; SNOW DROPPING). **2** a general term for a small-time petty criminal (cf. BALD-TYRE BANDIT).

knick-knack *n.¹* [19C] the vagina (cf. DOWN BELOW; NICK-NACK n.¹). [SE *knick-knack*, a pleasing or curious trifle]

knick-knack *n.²* see NICK-NACK n.².

knick-knacked *adj.* [1970s] absolutely exhausted. [KNACKERED]

knick-knacker *n.* [1960s–70s] (US) a fussy, officious person. [SE *knick-knack*, one whose mind is limited by their obsession with trivia]

knicks *n.* [late 19C+] **1** *knick*ers. **2** *knick*erbockers. [abbr.]

knife *n.* [late 19C] a shrewish, nagging woman. [like a knife, she is 'into' her victim with 'sharp' remarks]

knife *v.* [late 19C+] (US) to attack, either verbally or in print, in an underhand manner.

knife and fork *n.* [20C] pork. [rhy. sl.]

knife it! *excl.* [mid-19C] stop!, don't go on! [i.e. cut it short]

knife-man *n.* [1960s+] a surgeon.

knifer *n.* [late 19C–1920s] a fraud and cadger.

knife-thrower *n.* [1900s] (US) a waiter or waitress. [the laying of tables]

kniff-knaff *n.* [late 17C] a joke, a jest. [? link to Scot. *kniff*, lively, alert]

knight *n.* [late 16C+] an all-purpose appellation, linked to a variety of occupations (cf. KNIGHT OF THE ...).

knight and barrow pig *n.* [late 18C–early 19C] someone with ideas above their station. [phr. *more hog than gentleman*]

knight of Hornsey *n.* [mid-17C–early 19C] one whose job involves digging with a fork (cf. KNIGHT OF THE FORKED ORDER). [the tines of the fork are its 'horns']

knight of industry/the industry *n.* [mid-17C–mid-18C] a cheating gambler. [he 'works' his victims]

knight of St Nicholas *n.* [late 17C–18C] a wandering criminal beggar (cf. KNIGHT OF THE BLADE n.¹).

knight of the ... *phr.* 'Various jocular (formerly often slang)

phrases denoting one who is a member of a certain trade or profession, has a certain occupation or character etc. In the majority of these the distinctive word is the name of some tool or article commonly used by or associated with the person designated, and the number of such phrases may be indefinitely increased.' (*OED*) While the earlier (16C–18C) terms definitely have this occupational basis, the later (19C) ones tend to use the occupation in more of an ironic or joking sense.

knight of the awl *n.* [mid-19C] a cobbler (cf. KNIGHT OF THE LAPSTONE).

knight of the blade *n.¹* [late 17C–18C] **1** a wandering villain, posing as a soldier and living on his wits. **2** a bully.

knight of the blade/blades/bright blade/shining sword/sword *n.²* [late 19C] (Aus.) a shearer.

knight of the brush *n.* [late 19C] an artist.

knight of the brush and moon *n.* [mid-19C] a drunkard. [? SE *brush* that was once used as the sign of a tavern; or a real or generic public house name]

knight of the cleaver *n.* [19C] a butcher.

knight of the cloth *n.* [late 18C–mid-19C] a tailor.

knight of the collar *n.* [mid-16C–mid-17C] one who has been hanged.

knight of the cue *n.* [late 19C] a billiard-player.

knight of the elbow *n.* [late 17C–mid-18C] a card-sharp, a cheating gambler (cf. ELBOW SHAKER n.¹).

knight of the field *n.* [16C–early 17C] a tramp, a vagrant.

knight of the forked order/order of the fork *n.* [mid-17C–mid-18C] one whose job involves digging with a fork.

knight of the golden grummet *n.* [1970s+] (US Und.) one who enjoys anal intercourse. [naut. jargon *grummet* = rope ring + *gold* = excrement]

knight of the grammar *n.* [late 17C–mid-18C] a teacher.

knight of the green cloth *n.* [late 19C–1920s] (orig. US) a gambler.

knight of the gusset *see* BROTHER OF THE GUSSET.

knight of the hod *n.* [mid-19C] a bricklayer.

knight of the industry *see* KNIGHT OF INDUSTRY.

knight of the jemmy *n.* [late 19C] (society) a burglar.

knight of the knife *n.* [17C] a cutpurse. [KNIGHT + SE *knife*]

knight of the lapstone *n.* [mid-19C] a cobbler (cf. KNIGHT OF THE AWL).

knight of the napkin *n.* [mid–late 19C] a waiter.

knight of the needle *n.* [late 18C–late 19C] a tailor (cf. KNIGHT OF THE SHEARS; KNIGHT OF THE THIMBLE).

knight of the order of the fork *see* KNIGHT OF THE FORKED ORDER.

knight of the pad *n.* [mid-17C–mid-19C] a highwayman (cf. SQUIRE OF THE PAD). [KNIGHT + PAD n.¹]

knight of the pen *n.* [mid–late 19C] a clerk.

knight of the pencil *n.* [late 19C–1920s] a bookmaker.

knight of the pestle *n.* [17C–19C] an apothecary.

knight of the petticoat *n.* [late 19C–1900s] a man employed as 'muscle' by a brothel.

knight of the pigskin *n.* [late 19C] a jockey.

knight of the pisspot *n.* [late 19C] a doctor, an apothecary.

knight of the pit *n.* [late 19C] a fan of cock-fighting.

knight of the post *n.* [16C] (Und.) a notorious perjurer, one who earns a living by giving false evidence. [prob. meaning a whipping-post or pillory]

knight of the quill *n.* [late 17C] an author.

knight of the rainbow *n.* [late 18C–early 19C] a footman. [the colours of the uniform, which would represent those of the person served]

knight of the road *n.* **1** [mid-17C–mid-19C] a highwayman. **2** [late 19C] (Aus.) a bushranger. **3** [late 19C+] a commercial traveller. **4** [1920s+] (mainly Aus.) a tramp. **5** [1970s] a truck-driver.

knight of the scran-bag *n.* [19C] a beggar, a cadger. [SCRAN-BAG]

knight of the shears/sheers *n.* [late 18C–late 19C] a tailor (cf. KNIGHT OF THE NEEDLE).

knight of the shining sword *see* KNIGHT OF THE BLADE n.².

knight of the spigot *n.* [early 19C] a publican, an inn-keeper.

knight/squire of the gusset *n.* [19C] a pimp, a procurer (cf. BROTHER OF THE GUSSET).

knight of the sword *see* KNIGHT OF THE BLADE n.².

knight of the thimble *n.* [late 18C–late 19C] a tailor (cf. KNIGHT OF THE NEEDLE).

knight of the trencher *n.* [late 18C–early 19C] a great eater.

knight of the triple tree *n.* [late 17C] a prisoner (presumably one who is due to be hanged). [TRIPLE TREE]

knight of the vapour *n.* [17C] a smoker; also known, by the coiner John Taylor the Water Poet (*c.*1578–1653), as *gentlemen of the whiffe, esquires of the pipe*.

knight of the wheel *n.* [late 19C] a cyclist.

knight of the whip *n.* [19C] a coachman.

knight of the whipping-post *n.* [19C] a sharper, a cheating gambler.

knits *n.* [1960s–70s] (US Black) knitwear, esp. garments expensively imported from Italy.

knitting *n.* [1940s] girls or women considered collectively. [the 'feminine' occupation]

knitty *see* NITTY adj.

knob *n.*¹ **1** [mid-17C; 1920s+] the penis. **2** [late 17C+] the head (cf. NOB n.¹). **3** [1990s] (US teen) a general term of abuse.

knob *n.*² **1** [mid-19C] a swindling fairground game, also called 'under and over'. **2** [1920s–40s] (Aus./N.Z.) a double-headed penny, esp. as used in the game of two-up, produced by filing down standard coins and welding them together (cf. GREY n.). [KNOB n.¹ (2)]

knob *n.*³ [1930s–40s] (US Black) a shoe. [? the shape of the toecap]

knob *v.* **1** [early 19C] to hit in the face or head. **2** [20C] usu. of a man, to have sexual intercourse (cf. BANG v.¹). [KNOB n.]

knobber *n.* **1** [1970s+] (US) a male homosexual transvestite prostitute. **2** [1980s+] (US campus) fellatio (cf. PUT SOME SLOBBER ON THE KNOBBER). **3** [1990s] (US) a stupid, obnoxious person. [KNOB n.¹ (1)]

knobbies *see* KNOBS.

knobbly-knee *n.* [20C] a key. [rhy. sl.]

knobby *see* NOBBY adj. (2), (4).

knob cheese *see* KNOB CHEESE.

knob-end *n.* [20C] a general derog. term (cf. KNOBHEAD). [KNOB n.¹ (1) and SE *end*; lit. the glans penis]

knob-gobbling *n.* [1960s+] fellatio; thus *knob-gobbler*, a fellatrix or fellator. [KNOB n.¹ (1) + GOBBLE v.¹ (2)]

knobhead/knobknot *n.* [1920s+] (orig. US) a stupid person (cf. KNOB-END). [KNOB n.¹ (1) + sfx. -HEAD (1)/SE *knot*]

knob-job *n.* [1960s+] (orig. US) fellatio (cf. BLOW JOB). [KNOB n.¹ (1) + JOB n.⁵]

knob jockey *n.* [1990s] a general insult, implying that the male subject is a masturbator or a homosexual. [KNOB n.¹ (1) + JOCKEY n.²]

knobknot *see* KNOBHEAD.

knob on to *v.* [late 19C–1920s] to pay court to, to conceive a passion for. [? SE *knob*, which is attached to a door or KNOB n.¹ (1)]

knob polisher *n.* [1960s+] a young male prostitute. [KNOB n.¹ (1) + pun]

knobs/knobbies *n.* **1** [1930s+] the female breasts. **2** [1940s+] (US Black) the knees. **3** [1960s] (US Black) stylish, up-to-date shoes with shined toecaps.

knob-shiner *n.* [1990s] **1** a masturbator. **2** a general term of abuse (cf. WANKER). [KNOB n.¹ (1) + SE *shiner*]

knob snot *n.* [1990s] ejaculate (cf. COCK SNOT). [KNOB n.¹ (1) + SNOT n.]

knobstick *n.* [mid-19C] a strike-breaker (cf. SNOBSTICK). [SE *knobstick*, a club with a rounded head, used by strike-breakers as a weapon]

knob-thatcher *n.* [early–mid-19C] a wigmaker. [KNOB n.¹ (2) + SE *thatcher*]

knob-twister *n.* [1980s] (Aus.) a bookmaker. [the knobs on the betting board]

knock *n.* **1** [16C; 20C] a promiscuous woman. **2** [18C+] the penis. **3** [1900s–10s] (US) a prison sentence. **4** [1950s+] sexual intercourse; thus (Aus.) *do a knock with*, to have sexual intercourse with; *on the knock*, working as a prostitute (cf. BASH n.²). [20C use of (1) is Aus.]

knock *v.*¹ **1** [late 16C+] to have sexual intercourse (cf. BANG v.¹). **2** [late 18C+] (Und.) to rob, to steal; thus [late 18C] *knock the lobb*, breaking and entering; [1920s+] *knock a peter*, break into a safe. **3** [19C+] (US/Aus.) to kill, to shoot dead, later usage in phr. *knock yourself*, to commit suicide. **4** [mid-19C+] (orig. US) to disparage, to criticize. **5** [late 19C–1940s] (US) to inform on. **6** [1920s+] (Aus.) to flirt with a woman. **7** [1940s+] to cheat, to defraud, esp. to obtain credit which one has no intention of honouring. **8** [1940s+] (US) to arrest. **9** [1940s–70s] (US) to earn.

knock *v.*² **1** [early 18C+] to strike with astonishment, alarm or confusion, to confound. **2** [mid–late 18C] to excel, to surpass. **3** [mid-19C+] to impress highly, to elicit great admiration, to make a big impression, esp. of new fashions, entertainments. [subseq. uses of (2) are SE]

knock *v.*³ [1940s+] (US) to give, as in *knock me a kiss*.

knocka *see* KNOCKER n.⁹.

knock-about/-around *n.* **1** [late 19C+] (Aus.) a tramp, a vagrant. **2** [20C] (W.I.) the lowest type of prostitute. [KNOCK ABOUT v.]

knockabout *adj.* [late 19C+] (orig. theatrical) noisy, violent, rambunctious.

knock about *v.* [mid-19C+] to travel around rather than settle down.

knockabout man/hand *n.* [1930s+] (Aus.) **1** a layabout, an idler. **2** a thief, esp. a pickpocket.

knock about the bub, to *phr.* [late 18C–mid-19C] to circulate the bottle, to pass the drink around. [SE *knock about* + BUB n.²]

knock acock *v.* [19C] to amaze, to shock, to 'knock sideways' (cf. KNOCK INTO A COCKED HAT). [abbr. COCK-EYED adj.¹; note SE *acock*, defiantly]

knock a joe, to *phr.* [1900s–40s] (US Black) to mutilate oneself in order to escape hard labour in prison or on the chain gang. [ety. unknown]

knock a line with *see* DO A LINE WITH.

knock all of a heap, to *phr.* [early 19C+] to overturn, to destroy.

knock all to rags, to *phr.* [late 19C] (US) to knock senseless.

knock all to sticks *see* BEAT ALL TO STICKS.

knock along *v.* **1** [late 19C+] (orig. Aus.) to idle, to wander. **2** [late 19C+] to travel around rather than settle down (cf. KNOCK ABOUT v.). **3** [1970s+] to manage, to subsist.

knock andrew *n.* [late 18C] the penis. [? a misprint for NOCKANDRO]

knock a nod, to *phr.* [1920s–40s] (US Black) to go to sleep. [NOD n.]

knock anthony *see* CUFF ANTHONY.

knock-around *n. see* KNOCK-ABOUT n.

knockaround *adj.* [1940s+] (US) having worldly or criminal experience. [KNOCK AROUND v.]

knock around v. [mid–late 19C] (orig. US) to wander, to travel aimlessly (cf. LICK ABOUT). [20C use is SE]

knock at the door see KNOCK ON THE DOOR.

knockback n.[1] [late 19C+] a rejection. [KNOCK BACK v.[3]]

knockback n.[2] [1940s+] (prison) the rejection of one's application for parole (cf. FLOP n.[4]).

knock back v.[1] **1** [20C] to cost, e.g. *that'll knock you back a bit.* **2** [1910s+] to fine someone.

knock back v.[2] [20C] to eat, to drink, esp. to finish off one's drink.

knock back v.[3] [1930s+] (orig. Aus./N.Z.) to reject.

knock-beetle n. [20C] (Ulster) one who allows themselves to be victimized. [Scot.]

knock boots/knock boots with v. [1980s+] (US Black/campus) to have sexual intercourse (with). [SE *knock* + BOOTY n.]

knock cold/dead v. [mid-19C+] **1** to knock unconscious. **2** to astound, to amaze.

knock commission out of, to phr. [1940s+] to damage a vehicle by excessive use. [ext. of SE *out of commission*, out of order]

knock cuckoo, to phr. [1920s–30s] (US) to knock out. [SE *knock* + CUCKOO adj.]

knock dead see KNOCK COLD v.

knock dog v. [20C] (W.I.) to idle, to do nothing. [the image of lying around like a dog]

knock-down n.[1] [late 17C–19C] strong ale or liquor. [its effects]

knock-down/knock-down and drag-out n.[2] [early 19C+] (orig. US) a vicious fight in which one participant is knocked unconscious; thus fig. an acrimonious but non-violent dispute (cf. DRAG-OUT).

knock-down n.[3] **1** [mid-19C+] (Aus./N.Z./US) an introduction, esp. a formal introduction of a man to a woman in whom he is interested; thus *give one a knock-down*, to give one an introduction. **2** [1930s–60s] (US) information (cf. LOWDOWN).

knock-down n.[4] [1950s] (Aus.) a loan. [? abbr. KNOCK-DOWN MONEY]

knock down v.[1] [mid-18C–mid-19C] to choose, to nominate someone. [the chairman at a dinner knocking with a hammer before announcing a speaker]

knock down v.[2] **1** [mid-19C+] to lower prices. **2** [mid-19C+] (US) to embezzle, to steal from a firm's takings. **3** [1920s+] (US) to earn or obtain money, usu. for work, or by requesting a loan or gift.

knock down v.[3] [mid-19C+] (orig. US) to sell by auction (cf. KNOCK OFF v.[2]). [the use of the auctioneer's hammer, now SE]

knock down v.[4] **1** [mid-19C+] (Aus./N.Z.) to spend all of one's money on a celebration; thus *knock down a cheque*, to spend an entire season's pay cheque on a single drinking bout (cf. KNOCK UP A CHEQUE). **2** [1950s+] (US) to drink (cf. KNOCK BACK v.[2]).

knock down v.[5] [20C] (Aus.) to make an introduction; thus *knock one down to*, to introduce, e.g. *knock me down to that daisy*, introduce me to that girl. [KNOCK-DOWN n.[3]]

knock down v.[6] [1950s+] (Can.) to act lazily, to shirk one's work.

knock down v.[7] [1990s] (US prison) to serve a sentence.

knock-down and drag out see KNOCK-DOWN n.[2].

knock-down money n. [mid-19C; 1980s+] (US) tips or gratuities. [? SE *knock-down*, a reserve price at an auction]

knocked adj. [19C+] under control, at one's mercy, e.g. *I've got it knocked.* [KNOCK v.[2] (2)]

knocked down for crop/the crop phr. [early–mid-19C] condemned to execution by hanging. [ironic use of KNOCK DOWN v.[2] + CRAP n.[2]]

knocked off one's pins phr. [late 19C+] utterly astounded. [PINS]

knocked out adj. **1** [late 19C] (US) bankrupt. **2** [late 19C+] exhausted. **3** [1940s+] (US) heavily intoxicated. **4** [1940s+] (US) stylish, excellent.

knocked over adj. [late 19C] dead, very ill.

knocked up adj. [mid-19C+] **1** tired, jaded, used up. **2** (orig. US) pregnant.

knocked with a French faggot phr. [late 17C–18C] referring to one whose nose has been eaten away by syphilis (cf. BLOW WITH A FRENCH FAGGOT-STICK; FRENCH CROWN). [stereotyping of FRENCH adj. + SE *faggot*, a stick]

knock 'em/knock 'em cold, to phr. [1910s] to make a success, to score a 'hit', to amaze. [thus music-hall song 'Wotcher!, or Knocked Them in the Old Kent Road']

knock-'em-down n. [early 16C] a fiery drink (cf. KNOCK-ME-DOWN). [its effects]

knock 'em down, to phr. [late 19C] to be given applause.

knock-'em-down business n. [late 19C] the profession of auctioneering. [KNOCK DOWN v.[3]]

knock-'em/-me-downs n. **1** [early 19C] a coconut shy. **2** [mid-19C] skittles, esp. as played in a public house.

knock-'em-stiff n. [19C] (US) strong whisky. [STIFF adj.[1]]

knock endways v. [mid–late 19C] to astound, to astonish, to shock profoundly (cf. KNOCK SIDEWAYS).

knocker n.[1] [17C] a promiscuous man, a whoremonger (cf. BEARD-JAMMER). [KNOCK v.[1] (1)]

knocker n.[2] **1** [early 17C–mid-19C] an outstandingly attractive person (cf. STUNNER). **2** [1940s+] (US) the top person, the person in authority, often in comb., e.g. *head knocker, top knocker.* [KNOCK v.[2]; their 'striking' appearance]

knocker n.[3] [18C+] the penis (cf. KNOCK n.). [KNOCK v.[1] (1)]

knocker n.[4] [early 19C] a form of pendant to a wig, similar to a pigtail. [its similarity to a door-*knocker*]

knocker n.[5] [late 19C] (Aus.) common sense. [ety. unknown; ? link to Yid. *naches*, pleasure]

knocker n.[6] [late 19C+] (orig. US) a critic, esp. one who relishes making neg. comments. [KNOCK v.[1] (4)]

knocker n.[7] [20C] (US Und.) an informer or complainant. [KNOCK v.[1] (5)]

knocker n.[8] [1940s+] a gambler who refuses to pay their debts (which cannot be enforced legally in the UK). [KNOCK v.[1] (7)]

knocker/knocka n.[9] [1990s] (US Black) a fool. [? KNUCKLE-HEAD]

knocker and knob n. [20C] a job. [rhy. sl.]

knocker-face/-head n. [late 19C–1920s] an ugly face, or the person who 'owns' it.

knocker-off n. [1920s+] a thief. [KNOCK OFF v.[5]]

knockers n.[1] [19C] small curls worn flat on the temples, a fashionable hairstyle at that time (cf. AGGERAWATOR). [abbr. NEWGATE KNOCKER]

knockers n.[2] **1** [late 19C+] the testicles. **2** [1930s+] (orig. US) the female breasts. [they knock against each other/the body]

knocker-worker n. [20C] a door-to-door pedlar.

knock fairly silly, to phr. [late 19C] to overcome almost to the point of annihilation. [joc. understatement]

knock for a/the loop, to phr. [1920s+] to astound, to astonish, to devastate (cf. KNOCK SOMEONE DOWN WITH A FEATHER). [one is fig. knocked 'head-over-heels']

knock for a row of ashcans, to phr. [1940s] (N.Z.) to impress greatly.

knock for a row of stumps/latrines, to phr. [1910s–30s] (US) to hit or knock someone senseless.

knock for six, to phr. [late 19C+] **1** to defeat heavily. **2** to astound, to astonish (cf. BOWL SOMEONE OVER). [cricketing imagery]

knock for the loop see KNOCK FOR A LOOP.

knock hell/the hell out of, to *phr.* [late 19C+] (orig. US) to beat severely (cf. BEAT HELL OUT OF).

knock her dead one on the nose each and every double trey, to *phr.* [1940s] (US Black) to get a pay cheque every sixth day (or the sixth day of every week?).

knock-in *n.* [mid-late 19C] **1** the game of loo. **2** a hand at cards. [ety. unknown; ? one 'knocks in' or plays one's cards]

knock in *v.* [mid-late 19C] (coster) to make money. [the money is 'knocked in' to the coster's pocket]

knocking *n.* [late 16C+] sexual intercourse. [KNOCK v.[1] (1)]

knocking company *n.* [1940s-60s] a hire-purchase company. [KNOCK v.[1] (8)]

knocking dog *adj.* [20C] (W.I.) plentiful, in abundance, usu. of cheap items on sale at a market. [ety. unknown]

knocking-house *see* KNOCKING-SHOP.

knocking it back with a stick *phr.* [1940s+] (Aus.) a phr. used by a man who wishes to boast of the success of his sex life; usu. in answer to a question, e.g. 'Getting any?'.

knocking-jacket *n.* [1900s] a nightdress. [KNOCK v.[1] (1)]

knocking-joint *see* KNOCKING-SHOP.

knocking on/knocking on a bit, to be *phr.* [1930s+] to be growing older, usu. of a middle-aged or old person.

knockings *n.* [1990s] information, facts. [? KNOCK-DOWN n.[3] (2)]

knocking-shop/-house/-joint *n.* [mid-late 19C; 1960s+] a brothel (cf. ACCOMMODATION HOUSE; BUTTOCKING SHOP). [KNOCK v.[1] (1) + SE shop/HOUSE n.[1]/JOINT n.[3]]

knock into *v.* **1** [late 19C+] to run into. **2** [1910s+] (Aus.) to fight with.

knock into a cocked hat/fits/the middle of next week, to *phr.* [early 19C+] (orig. US) to overturn, destroy or beat thoroughly or completely.

knock into a mish, to *phr.* [mid-19C] (N.Z.) to overcome, to surpass. [SE mishmash]

knock into horse-nails, to *phr.* [late 19C–1900s] to defeat heavily.

knock into the middle of next week *see* KNOCK INTO A COCKED HAT.

knock it down *v.* [late 19C–1900s] to signify one's approval by hammering on the table or stamping on the floor.

knock it off *v.* **1** [19C+] to complete or dispose of something easily or quickly. **2** [20C] to stop doing something.

knock it off! *excl.* [late 19C+] stop it! be quiet! shut up!

knock it on the head, to *phr.* [late 19C+] to stop doing something, to finish a task. [? the final blow of a hammer that drives in a nail]

knock it out *see* KNOCK OUT v.[3]

knock! knock! *phr.* [1930s+] a phr. used as an introduction to 'knock-knock jokes', a form of joke which goes 'Knock, knock.' 'Who's there?' followed by a punning riposte.

knockman *see* KNOCKO.

knock-me *see* KNOCK-ME-SILLY.

knock-me-down *n.* [mid-18C–early 19C] a fiery drink (cf. GLIM n.[2]). [var. on KNOCK-'EM-DOWN n.]

knock-me-down *adj.* [late 18C] violent, aggressive or overpowering.

knock-me-downs *see* KNOCK-'EM-DOWNS.

knock-me-silly/knock-me *n.* [20C] (Aus.) a billy (used to boil water). [rhy. sl.]

knocko/knockman *n.* [1980s+] (US Black) a police officer, esp. a member of the drugs squad. [the knocking at one's door or on one's skull]

knock-off *n.[1]* [late 19C+] (orig. US) time to leave work, the end of the day. [KNOCK OFF v.[1]]

knock-off *n.[2]* **1** [1920s+] (US Und.) an underworld killing. **2** [1930s+] a robbery; thus *on the knock-off*, working as a

thief. **3** [1950s+] something that has been stolen. **4** [1950s] (US Und.) a police raid. [KNOCK OFF v.[5]; (1) is v.[4]]

knock-off *n.[3]* [1960s+] a fake, a copy; used in the fashion trade to describe cheap copies of 'designer' garments, cheap reproductions of antiques etc. [KNOCK OFF v.[3]]

knock off *v.[1]* **1** [mid-17C+] to stop work. **2** [early 18C; 1930s–40s; 1980s+] to die. **3** [late 18C+] to bring to an end abruptly, to conclude speedily. **4** [late 18C–19C] to abandon, to cease from. **5** [early 19C; 1920s+] to consume, esp. a drink (cf. KNOCK BACK v.[2]). **6** [late 19C+] (US) to abstain or give up a habit.

knock off *v.[2]* **1** [mid-18C–late 19C] (orig. US) to assign to a bidder at auction (cf. KNOCK DOWN v.[3]). **2** [1950s+] (Aus./N.Z.) to sell, to dispose of. [20C use is SE]

knock off *v.[3]* **1** [early 19C+] to do quickly and perfunctorily. **2** [1920s–40s] (US) to acquire money, usu. easily.

knock off *v.[4]* **1** [late 19C] (N.Z.) to dismiss from a job. **2** [late 19C+] (orig. US) to kill, to murder (cf. BUMP OFF). **3** [1930s+] (orig. US) to seduce, to have sexual intercourse (often adulterous or purely hedonistic).

knock off *v.[5]* **1** [1910s+] (orig. Und.) to steal, to burglarize. **2** [1920s+] (orig. US police) to raid, to seize stolen goods or to arrest.

knock off a piece, to *phr.* [20C] to seduce a woman (cf. SAW A CHUNK). [KNOCK OFF v.[4] + PIECE n.[1]]

knock off hen tracks on a rolltop piano, to *phr.* [1940s] (US Black) to use a typewriter to compose a personal letter. [? typewriters were usually reserved for business use]

knock off one's perch, to *phr.* [1910s+] **1** to upset. **2** to conquer. **3** to kill (cf. TURN OVER THE PERCH).

knock off the hooks, to *phr.* [mid-19C–1920s] (US) to kill, to murder.

knock one out *v.* [1990s] to masturbate. ['one' is an orgasm]

knock oneself out *v.* [1940s+] (orig. US) to have a very enjoyable time, to 'let oneself go', to amaze oneself.

knock one's own thing, to *phr.* [20C] (W.I./Belz.) to masturbate (cf. DO ONE'S OWN THING).

knock one's wig, to *phr.* [1940s] (US Black) to comb one's hair.

knock on/at the door, a *phr.* [20C] (bingo) the number 4. [rhy. sl.]

knock on together *v.* [20C] to have an affair.

knock on wood, to *phr.* [20C] to masturbate. [WOOD n.[2]]

knockout *n.* **1** [late 19C+] a person or thing of outstanding quality, attractiveness or excellence. **2** [1930s+] a pleasant, gratifying surprise.

knockout *adj.* (orig. US) **1** [late 19C+] stupefying or liable to cause unconsciousness. **2** [1920s+] excellent, wonderful, the very best. [KNOCKOUT n.]

knock out *v.[1]* **1** [mid-19C+] to earn a sum of money; e.g. *knock out £200 per week*. **2** [mid-19C+] to do roughly or quickly, esp. of writing (cf. BASH OUT). **3** [late 19C+] to obtain for oneself, e.g. *knock out some sleep*. **4** [late 19C+] to sell.

knock out *v.[2]* **1** [late 19C] to kill someone. **2** [late 19C] to make someone bankrupt. **3** [late 19C–1950s] (US) to deprive someone, esp. of money. **4** [late 19C] to fail an examination candidate. **5** [late 19C+] (orig. US) to surprise, overcome or defeat. **6** [late 19C+] (esp. US Black) to impress, to overwhelm, to delight. **7** [1930s–40s] (US Und.) to arrest. **8** [1940s–70s] to steal, esp. to steal everything from the place one is robbing.

knock out/knock it out *v.[3]* [1960s+] **1** (US Black) to have sexual intercourse. **2** to do anything quickly, with neither style nor concentration.

knockout! *excl.* [late 19C+] wonderful! perfect! [KNOCKOUT adj.]

knock out an apple, to *phr.* [19C] to father a child. [KNOCK OUT v.[1]]

knock-out drops *n.* **1** [late 19C+] chloral hydrate mixed into a drink to render an innocent victim unconscious (cf. MICKEY FINN). **2** [late 19C–1900s] a soothing linctus, usu. based on laudanum or opium, used to soothe fractious young children. **3** [1910s+] (Aus.) drugged or adulterated liquor.

knock out of the box, to *phr.* [late 19C+] (US) to defeat, to overcome, to kill. [baseball jargon]

knock out one's link, to *phr.* [mid-18C] to be very drunk. [? SE *link*, 'a torch...formerly much in use for lighting people along the streets' (*OED*)]

knock-over *n.* **1** [1920s+] (US police) an armed robbery. **2** [1920s+] (Aus.) a substantial, if surprising, success. **3** [1970s] (US) an easy task.

knock over *v.*[1] **1** [19C+] (US) to murder, to kill. **2** [mid-19C; 1970s+] (US) to defeat or abuse through violence. **3** [1920s+] (orig. US) to rob or steal, usu. with violence. **4** [1920s+] (US Und./police) to raid, to arrest. **5** [1920s+] (US Und./police) to punish a prisoner. **6** [1940s–60s] (US) to seduce, to have sexual intercourse.

knock over *v.*[2] [mid-19C–1950s] (US) to drink (cf. KNOCK BACK v.[2]).

knock over *v.*[3] [late 19C–1900s] **1** to die. **2** to give way.

knock over a/the doll, to *phr.* [1950s] (Aus.) to take the consequences for an act.

knock rotten *v.* [1910s+] (Aus.) to kill, to stun.

knock saucepans/smoke out of, to *phr.* [late 19C–1900s] (Aus.) **1** to attack aggressively. **2** to overcome completely.

knock/scare seven bells out of, to *phr.* **1** [1920s+] to beat viciously. **2** [1940s+] to terrify. [orig. naut.]

knock shingles/the roof in, to *phr.* [1960s+] (US) to snore. [the similarity of the noise]

knock shop *n.* [1960s+] (Aus.) a brothel (cf. KNOCKING-SHOP). [KNOCK v.[1] (1) + SE *shop*]

knock sideways *v.* [1920s+] to astound, to astonish, to shock profoundly (cf. KNOCK ENDWAYS).

knock silly *v.* [mid-19C+] (orig. US) to daze or even knock unconscious in a fight.

knock smoke out of *see* KNOCK SAUCEPANS OUT OF.

knock someone down *v.* [late 19C+] (US) to introduce someone. [KNOCK DOWN n.[3]]

knock someone down with a feather, to *phr.* [1920s+] to surprise completely, to astound.

knock someone off the Christmas tree, to *phr.* [20C] (US) to amaze, to astonish. [ref. to the trad. fairy on the top]

knock someone's block off, to *phr.* [20C] to injure someone physically, usu. in the form of a threat, *I'll knock ... .* [SE *knock* + BLOCK n.[1] (2)]

knock/put someone's dick in the dirt, to *phr.* [1970s+] (US) **1** to knock down. **2** to defeat, to punish. [DICK n.[5]]

knock someone's eye out, to *phr.* [20C] (US) to be stunningly attractive.

knock someone's hat off, to *phr.* [1940s+] to astonish, to amaze.

knock someone sick, to *phr.* [1910s–20s] to amaze, to astonish.

knock/beat someone's jock off, to *phr.* [1950s+] (US) to overcome completely. [SE *knock* + JOCK n.[2] (2)]

knock spots off/out of, to *phr.* [mid-19C+] (orig. US) to beat thoroughly, to surpass, to excel.

knock stiff *v.* [mid-19C–1920s] (US) **1** to knock unconscious or to shoot. **2** to amaze or impress. [SE *knock* + STIFF adj.[1]]

knock the ass/arse off/out of, to *phr.* [20C] (orig. US) to thrash severely, to defeat comprehensively. [SE *knock* + ARSE n.[1]]

knock the back out of, to *phr.* [1990s] to express a desire to indulge in a sexual act with a member of the opposite sex, e.g.

I'd knock the back out of that! [KNOCK v.[1] (1) + SE *back*; ult. euph. for FUCK SOMEONE'S ARSE OFF]

knock the bejazus out of, to *phr.* [date] to beat severely (cf. KNOCK THE STUFFING OUT OF). [SE *knock* + BEJAZUS!]

knock the bottom out of, to *phr.*[1] [late 19C] to render invalid, to ruin, to undermine (cf. KNOCK THE END IN).

knock the bottom out of *phr.*[2] *see* KNOCK THE STUFFING OUT OF.

knock the corners off, to *phr.* [1900s] (N.Z.) to punish violently.

knock the dew off the lily *see* SHAKE THE DEW OFF THE LILY.

knock the drawing-room out of, to *phr.* [20C] (N.Z.) to harden, to toughen up.

knock the dust off the old sombrero, to *phr.* [20C] (US) to perform oral sex.

knock the end in/off, to *phr.* [late 19C–1920s] to ruin a situation (cf. KNOCK THE BOTTOM OUT OF phr.[1]).

knock the filling out of *see* KNOCK THE STUFFING OUT OF.

knock the hell out of *see* KNOCK HELL OUT OF.

knock the hindsight off, to *phr.* [mid-19C–1950s] (US) to dispose of, to demolish completely.

knock the hindsights out of, to *phr.* [19C] (US) to deal a heavy blow to, to beat up.

knock the inside out of *see* KNOCK THE STUFFING OUT OF.

knock the jive out, to *phr.* [1940s] (US Black) to play the piano. [JIVE v.[1] (5)]

knock the lining out of *see* KNOCK THE STUFFING OUT OF.

knock them cold/dead, to *phr.* [1920s+] of a performer or performance, to devastate an audience with excellence (cf. KNOCK 'EM COLD).

knock the roof in *see* KNOCK SHINGLES IN.

knock the shit out of *see* KICK THE SHIT OUT OF.

knock the socks off, to *phr.* [mid-19C+] (orig. US) to defeat comprehensively (cf. BEAT THE BAGS OFF).

knock the stuffing / bottom / filling / inside / lining / wadding out of, to *phr.* [late 19C+] to beat severely (cf. BEAT THE STUFFING OUT OF; KNOCK THE BEJAZUS OUT OF).

knock the tar out of *see* BEAT THE TAR OUT OF.

knock the wadding out of *see* KNOCK THE STUFFING OUT OF.

knock the wool out of one's head, to *phr.* [1900s] (N.Z.) to wake up; to think (or make someone else think) clearly.

knock up *v.*[1] [early 18C+] to waken. [knocking on the bedroom door]

knock up *v.*[2] **1** [mid-18C–19C] to injure, to impair, to wear out. **2** [early 19C+] (orig. US) to make pregnant.

knock up *v.*[3] **1** [early 19C+] to earn a living, usu. with a noun, e.g. *knock up a crust.* **2** [late 19C] to put together spontaneously, to arrange at short notice.

knock up a cheque, to *phr.* [late 19C–1940s] (Aus.) to earn money for one's labour (cf. KNOCK DOWN v.[4]). [KNOCK UP v.[3] + *cheque*]

knockwurst *n.* [1970s] (US) the penis (cf. BACON n.[1]). [Ger. *Knockwurst*, a sausage]

knock yourself out! *excl.* [1940s+] (US) have a good time!

knot *n.*[1] [mid–late 19C] the swelling at the base of the head of the penis.

knot *n.*[2] [1910s+] (Aus.) a pack; thus *carry/push the knot*, to travel with a pack. [the *knots* that secure the pack or SWAG n.[1] (7)]

knot *n.*[3] [1950s–70s] (US Black) the head, esp. one that appears impenetrable by sense. [SE *knot*, an especially hard mass of wood]

knot *n.*[4] [1970s+] (US Black) a substantial roll of dollar bills (cf. FAT KNOT).

knothead *n.* **1** [1910s+] (US) a mule or stubborn animal. **2** [1920s+] a fool. [SE *knot*, an imperfection in a piece of

wood + sfx. -HEAD (1). Such spots are harder than the surrounding wood]

knot-/knotty-headed *adj.* [1920s+] stupid. [KNOTHEAD]

knothole *n.* [1940s] (US Black) a doughnut.

knotty! *excl.* [1970s+] (W.I. Rasta) used as a greeting or
farewell. [the knotted DREADLOCKS that betoken a Rasta-
man]

knotty ash *n.* [1980s] cash. [rhy. sl.; ref. to the problems of
comedian Ken Dodd (cf. KEN DODD) and his taxes]

knotty-headed see KNOT-HEADED.

**know A/great A from a bull's foot/gable-end/windmill,
to** *phr.* [20C] (W.I.) to be aware, intelligent, 'on the ball'. [var.
on NOT KNOW B FROM A BULL'S FOOT]

know-all *n.* [late 19C+] an extremely clever person, esp. one
who likes to impress others with their knowledge (cf. KNOW-
IT-ALL; KNOW-IT OF KNOW-ALL PARK].

know all the answers, to *phr.* [1930s+] to be intelligent,
fully knowledgeable or expert but usu. used in a sarcastic
manner (cf. KNOW-ALL).

know a man by his headmark, to *phr.* [18C–19C] to
recognize that a man is being cuckolded. [SE phr. *know by
one's headmark*, to recognize by one's appearance; in this
case the 'headmark' is his HORNS]

know an ace more than the devil see KNOW ONE POINT MORE
THAN THE DEVIL.

know a thing or two, to *phr.* [mid-19C+] to be aware, to be
knowledgeable.

know a trick worth two of that, to *phr.* [late 16C+] to be
cleverer, better informed or more efficient.

know backwards *v.* [20C] to know perfectly.

know beans *v.* [mid-19C–1910s] (US) to be well aware, to be
knowledgeable (cf. NOT KNOW BEANS). [abbr. KNOW HOW MANY
BEANS MAKE FIVE]

know from nothing, to *phr.* [1930s+] (US) to be ignorant;
usu. as *not know from nothing.*

know great A from a bull's foot see KNOW A FROM A BULL'S
FOOT.

know how many beans make five, to *phr.* [19C+] to be alert,
to be aware of facts or information.

know how many go to a dozen, to *phr.* [late 19C] to be
aware, alert, 'on the ball' (cf. KNOW HOW MANY BEANS MAKE
FIVE).

knowing *adj.* [mid-19C] stylish, fashionable, i.e. knowing
what is in style.

knowing as Kate Mullet *phr.* [late 19C–1900s] stupid.
[*Mullet* was a murderess, supposedly 'hanged for a fool']

know-it-all *n.* [19C+] **1** a clever person, esp. one who is 'too
clever for their own good' (cf. KNOW-ALL). **2** a braggart, a show-
off.

know it all, to *phr.* [late 19C+] to assume one's own perfection
and to ignore one's own deficiencies; usu. in phr. *he/she
knows it all* or *they know it all.*

know-it of know-all park *n.* [1910s+] a show-off, a braggart
(cf. KNOW-ALL).

knowledge box *n.* **1** [late 18C+] the head or the mind (cf. IDEA
BOX). **2** [20C] (US) a school. [UK use of (1) faded by early 19C
but revived in US Black use by 20C]

know like the back of one's hand, to *phr.* [1940s+] to know
perfectly.

known *n.* [mid-19C] a well-known person. [on the pattern of
SE *unknown*]

**know no more about it than the moon knows about
Sunday, to** *phr.* [late 19C] to know nothing whatsoever.

know one point/trick/an ace more than the devil *phr.*
[late 17C–mid-18C] to be extremely cunning.

know one's apples see KNOW ONE'S ONIONS.

know one's book, to *phr.* [late 19C–1900s] **1** to have the

correct information. **2** to make a decision. **3** to see what one
can gain.

know one's goulash, to *phr.* [1920s] (US) to know one's own
business. [var. on KNOW ONE'S ONIONS]

know one's onions/apples/oats/oil, to *phr.* [1920s+]
(orig. US) to be well informed, to be aware (cf. KNOW ONE'S
STUFF).

know one's shit, to *phr.* [1990s] (US) to be very competent
(cf. HAVE ONE'S SHIT TOGETHER). [SE *know* + SHIT n.[3]]

know one's stuff, to *phr.* [1920s+] to be accomplished in
one's own particular pursuit (cf. KNOW ONE'S ONIONS).

know one thing and that ain't two, to *phr.* [late 19C] to be
absolutely sure about something.

know one trick more than the devil see KNOW ONE POINT
MORE THAN THE DEVIL.

know on which side one's bread is buttered, to *phr.*
[16C–19C] to look after oneself.

know someone's number, to *phr.* [1910s+] to understand
another person, to assess a situation (cf. PEEP SOMEONE'S HOLE-
CARD).

know someone when, to *phr.* [1960s+] (orig. US) a phr. used
to imply one's prior knowledge of a person, esp. when their
life was somewhat or even radically different, e.g. *Don't come
the virtuous husband with me, I knew you when ... .*

know the dish, to *phr.* [1980s+] (US Black) to be aware of the
embarrassing truth. [DISH n.[1] (2)]

know the ins and outs of a duck's bum/cat's arse, to *phr.*
[late 19C] to know all the details; thus *want to know the ins
and outs ... , to* be very inquisitive.

know the length of one's foot see GET THE LENGTH OF ONE'S
FOOT.

know the ropes, to *phr.* [mid-19C+] to understand how to do
a task. [sailing imagery]

know the score, to *phr.* [1930s+] to understand a situation,
to know what is going on. [sporting imagery]

know the time of day, to *phr.* [mid-19C+] to be well aware of
what is going on (cf. KNOW WHAT TIME IT IS).

know the words and music, to *phr.* [1950s+] (gay) to understand and partake in the gay sub-culture.

know two of that, to *phr.* [late 19C+] to know something
much better.

know what goes what's what see KNOW WHAT'S WHAT.

know what I mean *phr.*[1] see NUDGE, NUDGE, WINK, WINK.

know what I mean? *phr.*[2] [1960s+] an almost transparent
interj., used as much for punctuation as for explication (cf.
LIKE; YOU KNOW).

know what I mean, Vern? *phr.* [1980s+] (US campus)
Do you understand? [ref. to a nationwide advertising cam-
paign]

know what o'clock it is, to *phr.* [19C+] to be aware, to know
what is going on (cf. KNOW WHAT TIME IT IS).

know what's what/what goes, to *phr.* [mid-16C+] to be
aware of the facts, to be abreast of a situation. [SE *know* +
WHAT'S WHAT]

know what time it is, to *phr.* [mid-19C+] to be *au fait*, aware,
STREETWISE (cf. KNOW THE TIME OF DAY).

know where the barley grows see FIND OUT WHERE THE
BARLEY GROWS.

know where the bodies are buried, to *phr.* [20C] to have
special knowledge of a situation, esp. of its less appealing
side, giving one power over those who nominally control it.
[the threat, rather than the use, of blackmail]

knuck *n.* **1** [early 19C–1900s] a pickpocket or thief (cf.
KNUCKLER; KNUCKLING COVE). **2** [1960s] (US Black) a fist fight.
[SE *knuckle/knuckles*]

knuck *v.* [early 19C–1900s] to pick pockets. [abbr. KNUCKLE v.[1]]

knuckle *n.* **1** [late 18C–mid-19C] a pickpocket; thus [early–

mid-19C) *go on the knuckle*, to work as a pickpocket. **2** [1930+] a fight, violence; thus *go the knuckle/knuckles*, to fight. [SE *knuckle*]

knuckle *v.*[1] [late 18C–early 19C] to steal, to pick pockets 'after the approved method' (Hotten 1859); thus *knuckle a wipe*, steal a handkerchief (cf. KNUCKLER). [KNUCLE n.; 'the approved method,' according to Vaux, implies the robbery of notes and cash rather than less valuable items]

knuckle *v.*[2] [late 19C] to hit.

knuckle *v.*[3] [late 19C–1950s] (US) to give in, to confess. [abbr. SE *knuckle under*]

knuckleburger *n.* [1970s+] (US) a punch in the mouth (cf. KNUCKLE SOUP). [SE *knuckle* + (*ham)burger*; a play on KNUCKLE SANDWICH]

knuckle-buster *n.* [1930s–60s] (US) a crescent wrench (tool). [the hazard of its use]

knuckle-dabs/-confounders *n.* [late 18C–early 19C] hand-cuffs.

knuckleduster *n.* **1** [mid–late 19C] a metal instrument, traditionally brass, that covers the knuckles, thus strengthening them when delivering a blow. **2** [late 19C+] a large, gaudy, flashy ring. [(1) SE f. 1900]

knucklehead *n.* [1930s+] (orig. US) a term of abuse, a description for any foolish, stupid, slow person. [knuckles pressed to the forehead imply the intensity of thought for one who is not overly bright]

knuckleheaded *adj.* [1930s+] (orig. US) stupid. [KNUCKLE-HEAD]

knucklenob *n.* [1950s+] (US) a stupid person (cf. KNUCKLE-HEAD). [SE *knuckle* v. + NOB n.[1] (1)]

knuckler *n.* [mid-19C] a pickpocket (cf. KNUCKLE n.). [KNUCKLE *v.*[1]]

knuckles *n.*[1] [late 18C–early 19C] (Und.) the top rank of pick-pockets. [KNUCKLE n.]

knuckles *n.*[2] [1960s–80s] (US) a knuckleduster, 'brass knuckles' (cf. KNUCKS n.).

knuckle sandwich *n.* [1960s+] (orig. US) a blow from a fist (cf. KNUCKLEBURGER; SLICE OF KNUCKLE PIE).

knuckle shuffle *n.* [1990s] masturbation (cf. FIVE-FINGER SHUFFLE; KIT-KAT SHUFFLE).

knuckle soup *n.* [mid-19C] (US) a punch in the mouth (cf. KNUCKLEBURGER).

knuckle the bone, to *phr.* [1990s] to masturbate. [SE *knuckle* + BONE n.[6]]

knuckle to *v.* [mid-19C+] to surrender, to accept something one dislikes but is not strong enough to fight. [var. on SE *knuckle under*]

knuckle-up *n.* [1940s+] (N.Z.) a fist fight.

knuckle up *v.* [1990s] (US Black teen) to prepare to fight, by closing and raising one's fists.

knuckling cove *n.* [early 19C] a pickpocket (cf. KNUCKLE n.). [KNUCKLE *v.*[1] + COVE n.]

knucks *n.* **1** [mid-19C–1950s] (US) the knuckles. **2** [late 19C+] (orig. US) brass knuckles, worn over the fist to ensure victory in a fist fight (cf. KNUCKLEDUSTER).

knuller/gumbler *n.* **1** [mid-19C] a chimney sweep who goes from house to house offering his services. **2** [mid-19C–1900s] a clergyman. [OE *cynllan*, to knell; the old-fashioned sweep rang a bell to announce his progress along a street]

knut *n.* [1910s–20s] a dandy, a very well-dressed, fashionable (if not overly intelligent) young man (cf. FILBERT n.[2]).

k.o. *adj. see* KAYO adj.

k.o./kayo *v.*[1] **1** [20C] (orig. US) to knock out. **2** [1970s+] (US campus) to defeat. [abbr.]

k.o. *v.*[2] [1970s+] (US campus) to die. [KICK OFF v.[2]]

koala *n.* (Aus.) **1** [1940s+] a diplomat, who is immune from Aus. law. **2** [1970s+] an unappreciative man (cf. WOMBAT n.[2]).

[(1) the koala is an officially protected creature; (2) ? his immunity from criticism despite his rudeness]

koboko *see* BOKO.

kochonni *n.* [20C] (W.I./St Lu./Dmnca) a piece of junk, anything worthless or useless. [Fr. *cochon*, a pig; note synon. Yid. *chaserei*, lit. 'pig things']

kocks newnes! *excl.* [mid-19C] var. on the blasphemous oath, *God's wounds!* [euph.]

k.o.'ed *adj.* [1960s–70s] (US) very drunk or intoxicated (cf. KNOCKED OUT).

koelie *see* COOLIE n.[1].

koffie-moffie *n.* [1980s+] (S.Afr.) a male flight attendant. [Afk. *koffie*, coffee + MOFFIE]

Kofifi *n.* [1950s] (S.Afr. township) Sophiatown, a Black residential area of Johannesburg, razed during the 1950s after the forcible removal of its inhabitants. [? Sotho (*le)fifi*, darkness, (*se)fifi*, corpse or (*bo)fifi*, mourning]

kojak *v.* [1970s+] (US teen) to find a parking space in an area where such discoveries are at best rare. [US TV show *Kojak* (1973–7) whose epon. hero possessed this facility]

kojak's rollneck *n.* [1990s] the glans or bell-end of the penis. [the TV detective *Kojak*, played by bald actor Telly Savalas (1925–94), often sported such clothing (cf. KOJAK)]

kojak with a Kodak *n.* [1970s] (US) a policeman manning a radar speed trap. [the TV show *Kojak* + the make of camera]

kojo *n.* [20C] (W.I.) a tough and violent person, usu. from a rural area (cf. CUFFEE). [Fante *Kodwo*, a male born on a Monday]

koki/cokey *n.* [1990s] (S.Afr.) a fibre-tipped colouring pen. [proprietary name *Koki*]

koko *see* COCO n.[2].

kokomo *n.* [1980s+] (drugs) crack cocaine. [play on COKE n.[1] (1)]

koks *see* KANGSE n.

kombo *see* COMBO n.[1].

komra *see* CAMBRA.

kong *n.* [1930s+] (US Black) home-distilled whisky. [the film *King Kong* (1933); thus denoting great strength]

kongkongsa *adj.* [20C] (W.I.) deceitful, hypocritical, biased. [Twi *kongkongsa*, double-dealing, duplicity, betrayal]

kongo *see* CONGO n.[1].

koniacker/coniacker *n.* [mid–late 19C] (US) a counterfeiter. [? CONY n.[1]]

konk *n. see* CONK n.[2].

konk *v. see* CONK v.[2].

konk-buster *see* CONK-BUSTER.

konks *see* KANGSE n.

konky *see* CONKY.

kooch *see* KOOTCH.

kook/kuke *n.* **1** [1950s+] (US) a crazy person, an eccentric, albeit an acceptable one (cf. KOOKABOO). **2** [1960s+] (US campus) an annoying or mistaken person. **3** [1960s–70s] (US/S.Afr.) a novice. [? CUCKOO n.[1] but popularized following the late-1950s US TV show *77 Sunset Strip* in which the supposedly (by 1958 standards) 'eccentric' character Gerald Lloyd Kookson III ('Kookie'), played by actor Edd Byrnes, became a teenage idol]

kooka *n.* [1930s+] (Aus.) a *kooka*burra. [abbr.]

kookaboo/cuckaboo *n.* [1950s+] (US) a crazy person (cf. KOOK). [? SE *kookaburra*, the Australian 'laughing' bird/cuckoo]

kooked-up *adj.* [1950s+] (US) crazy, eccentric. [KOOK]

kookie house *see* KOOKY HOUSE.

kooky *adj.* [1950s+] (orig. US) odd, eccentric (with overtones of charm). [KOOK]

kooky/kookie house *n.* [1950s] (US) a psychiatric institution. [KOOKY + SE *house*]

kool see COOL adj.³.

kools n. [1970s+] (drugs) phencyclidine (cf. ACE n.³). [play on cigarette brandname *Kool*]

kool toul! excl. [mid-19C] look out! [backsl.]

koosh see CUSH n.².

koota/kooti/kuti n. [late 19C+] (N.Z.) a body louse. [for ety. see COOTIE n.²]

kootch/kooch n. [1940s–70s] (US) a form of highly suggestive belly-dance, usu. performed at carnivals; thus *kootcher*, a dancer. [HOOTCHY-KOOTCHY n.]

kootee n. [mid-19C] (Anglo-Ind.) a house. [Hind. *kot*, a fort, a citadel]

kooti see KOOTA.

kopat v. [1990s] (US teen) to understand. [? Fr. *comprendre*, to understand]

kopgee/kop-jee n. [late 19C] the head. [Du. *kopje*, a mound or low hill]

kopjie-walloper n. [late 19C] (S.Afr.) a diamond-buyer (often Jewish) who traded directly with miners on their claims; this practice was outlawed by the Diamond Trade Act (1882). [Du. *kopje*, a hill + SE *wallop*, to thrash]

kosh adj. [late 19C+] honest, legitimate, above-board. [abbr. KOSHER adj.¹]

koshe n. [1980s+] (US campus) acceptable, satisfactory, as required. [Yid. *kosher*, according to Jewish dietary laws; pron. rhymes with 'gauche']

kosher adj.¹ **1** [late 19C+] honest, legitimate, above-board. **2** [1970s] (US) Jewish. [fig. uses of Yid. *kosher*, acceptable according to the Jewish dietary laws; ult. Heb. *k(sh(r)*]

kosher/kosher style adj.² [1960s+] (gay) circumcised. [the role of ritual circumcision in Judaism]

kosher delicatessen n. [1960s+] (gay) Israel. [everyone one EATS v.³ will be KOSHER adj.², i.e. Jewish]

kosher dill n. [1960s+] (gay) a circumcised penis.

kosher nosher n. [1980s+] (US gay) a coterie of gay Jewish men. [pun on *Cosa Nostra* + Yid. *kosher*, religiously acceptable to Jews + Yid. *nosher*, an eater]

kosher style see KOSHER adj.².

kotch see COTCH v.³.

koté-si-koté-la see COTÉ-SI-COTÉ-LA.

kouchie see CUTCHIE.

kowtow chow n. [1980s+] (US gay) the act of performing fellatio while kneeling in front of one's partner. [SE *kowtow*, lit. 'knock the head', 'the Chinese custom of touching the ground with the forehead in the act of prostrating oneself, as an expression of extreme respect, submission, or worship' (*OED*) + CHOW n.¹]

k.p. n. [1940s+] (Aus.) a prostitute. [abbr. police jargon *known prostitute*]

kraak v. [1950s+] (S.Afr.) to speed, to go fast, esp. on a motorbike (cf. CRACK ALONG). [Afk. phr. *gaan dat dit so kraack*, 'go like the blazes']

krag n. [1950s+] (S.Afr.) energy, strength, 'oomph'. [Du. *kracht*, power, strength]

kratz v. [1960s] to make a mess, to blunder. [ety. unknown; ? Ger./Yid.]

kraut n. **1** [mid-19C+] orig. US a derog. name for a German. **2** [1940s+] the German language. [*Sauerkraut*, a form of pickled, shredded cabbage, supposedly loved by the nation]

kraut-eater n. [mid-19C–1930s] (US) a derog. term for a German. [KRAUT + sfx. -*eater*]

krauthead/kraut stomper n. [1910s+] (US) a derog. term for a German. [KRAUT + sfx. -HEAD (3); SE *stomper*]

krautland n. [1950s+] (orig. US) a derog. name for Germany. [KRAUT + SE *land*]

kraut stomper see KRAUTHEAD.

krazin n. [1960s+] (US campus) a load of utter rubbish, absolute nonsense. [ety. unknown; ? play on SE *crazy*]

kreskin v. [1970s] (US teen) to prophesy, to work out intuitively, to foresee. [US TV magician *Kreskin*]

krex v. [1930s+] (US) to grumble, to fret, to complain (cf. KVETCH v.). [ety. unknown]

krexy adj. [1930s+] (US) pettish, cranky. [KREX]

kris' see CRIS'.

krissy/kroes/kroesie n. [1940s+] (S.Afr.) frizzy hair. [Afk. *kroes*, frizzy]

kroeskop n. [1910s+] (S.Afr.) one who has frizzy or tightly curled hair, thus a derog. term for Africans in general. [Afk. *kroes*, frizzy + *kop*, head]

kron n. [1990s] (US) a handgun. [a brandname]

kronk see CRONK.

krop n. [mid-19C] pork. [backsl.]

krud see CRUD n.¹.

kruger-spoof n. [late 19C] lying. [the contemporary antipathy to the Boers and their leader Paul *Kruger* (1825–1904) + SPOOF n.¹]

krunk n. [1990s] (US) an all-purpose euph. used in place of an obscenity, usu. SHIT. [ety. unknown]

krunk v. [1990s] to have sexual intercourse. [joc. use of SE *crunch*]

kryptonite n. [1980s+] (drugs) crack cocaine. [SE *kryptonite*, the mineral that weakens even Superman's powers]

krystal/krystal joint n. [1970s] (drugs) phencyclidine (cf. ACE n.³; CRYSTAL T). [var. on CRYSTAL JOINT]

kubber/khabbar/khubber n. [mid-19C] (Anglo-Ind.) news. [Hind. *khabar*, news; esp. news of local game suitable for hunting]

ku bomvu!/kumbomvu! excl. [1970s+] (S.Afr.) a warning shout that indicates the presence or proximity of police; usu. used by illicit liquor makers. [Nguni *ku bomvu*, it is red, thus 'red alert']

kugel n. [1960s+] (S.Afr.) the daughter of wealthy parents, whose main interest is her wardrobe, appearance, boyfriend (as an acquisition not a person) and the expenditure of money (cf. BAGEL n.¹; J.A.P.). Such girls, as the etymology implies, are Jewish; Black and Boer versions are *ebony-kugel* and *boere-kugel* respectively; thus *kugelese*, the jargon spoken between such young women. [Yid. *kugel*, a sweet or savoury casserole or pudding]

kuka/kungse n. [20C] (W.I.) a piece of excrement, a TURD. [var. on CA-CA]

kuke see KOOK.

kumba n. [1980s+] (drugs) marijuana. [ety. unknown]

kumbomvu! see KU BOMVU!

kumquat n. [1980s+] (US) a young woman (cf. BANANA n.²). [equation of the fruit with femininity]

kungse see KUKA.

kunumunu n. [20C] (W.I.) a stupid man, esp. one who is controlled by a woman; an imbecile. [Yoruba *kunun*, bashful, lacking in self-confidence]

kuri n. [20C] (N.Z.) **1** a mongrel, a badly-behaved dog. **2** a second-rate racehorse. **3** a contemptible, unpopular person (cf. GOORIE). [Maori *kuri*, a dog]

kurl the mo see CURL THE MO.

kurl-the-mo see CURL-THE-MO. ok ld

kurve n. [late 19C+] a prostitute. [Yid. *kurveh*, a prostitute; ult. Heb. *kurve*, a strange woman who approaches too close]

kutcha see CUTCHA.

kuti see KOOTA.

kuzat n. [1960s–70s] (S.Afr. township) money. [ety. unknown]

kvell v. [1960s+] to boast, to feel proud or happy, to gloat. [Yid.; ult. Ger. *quellen*, to gush, to swell]

kvetch *n.* [1960s+] a nag, a whiner, a complainer. [KVETCH v.]

kvetch *v.* [1950s+] (orig. US) to complain, to delay, to nag. [Yid. *kvetsh*; ult. Ger. *quetschen*, to squeeze, to press]

kvetchy *adj.* [1950s+] irritable, whiny. [KVETCH v.]

kwaal *n.* [1960s+] (S.Afr.) an illness, a complaint. [Afk. *kwaal*, a complaint]

kway *n.* [1940s+] (Aus.) **1** a general thief, with no real speciality. **2** a man who lives on money taken from a procurer. [? SE *take away*]

kwela-kwela *n.* (S.Afr. Black) **1** [1950s+] a police or prison wagon. **2** [1980s+] a minibus taxi. [the shouts of Nguni *kwela! kwela!*, get on! get on!; ult. Nguni *kwela*, climb in/on]

kwy *n.* [late 19C] death. [pron. of Lat. *quietus*, death]

k.y. *n.* [1960s+] (US drugs) the Federal Narcotics Hospital, Lexington, Kentu*cky*. [abbr.]?

k.y. *adj.* [1970s] (US Black) **1** describing anything which provides assistance or facilitates an action or task. **2** slippery or smooth in the physical sense. **3** comfortable. [the proprietary name of *KY* Jelly]

ky'daar/k'daar *n.* [1980s+] (S.Afr.) a tourist. [Afk. *kyk daar*, look there]

kybo/kibo *n.* [1960s–70s] (US) a privy. [KHYBER]

kybosh *see* KIBOSH.

kye *n.* [19C] one shilling and sixpence. [ety. unknown; E.P. suggests the Yid. *kye*, 18; but this is not cited in Rosen]

kyfer/kaifa/keifer/khyfer/kife/kyfering *n.* [late 19C+] **1** the vagina. **2** women regarded as sex objects; thus *kyfermashing*, pursuing women; *bit of kyfer*, a woman, a 'bit of skirt'. **3** money. [Arabic *kaif*, absolute enjoyment, perfect contentment, thus 'that which pleases one', one's delight; the word is the root of KIF, a type of hashish, and also meant the pleasure engendered by cannabis]

kyke *see* KIKE n.

kylege *n.* [1980s] (Black) money. [ety. unknown; ? ext. of KYE]

kynchin lay *see* KINCHIN LAY.

kyoodle *see* KIYOODLE.

kype *see* KIPE.

kypher/khyfer *v.* [late 19C] to dress one's hair. [Fr. *coiffeur*]

kypsey *see* KIPSIE.

kyuter *see* CUTER.

L

L *n.*[1] [mid-19C] (US) a $50 banknote. [Roman numeral *L*, 50]

l *n.*[2] [1980s+] (drugs) **1** LSD (cf. A *n.*[3]). **2** marijuana. [abbr.; (2) LOC n. (1)]

L.A. *n.*[1] [1900s–30s] (US) *Los Angeles*. [abbr.; later use is SE]

l.a. *n.*[2] [1990s] (drugs) *long-a*cting amphetamine (cf. A *n.*[2]). [abbr.]

la/lah *n.* [1990s] (US Black) marijuana. [ety. unknown]

la! *see* LAWKS!

laad-mi-don *n.* [1940s+] (W.I.) **1** the poorhouse, the alms-house. **2** a tuberculosis sanatorium. [lit. 'Lord, me done (for)']

laaitie *see* LIGHTIE.

laama *n.* [1940s+] (W.I.) clothing worn for celebrations and other special occasions. [lit. *Lord! Ma'am*, the expression uttered on seeing such finery]

laanie/lahnee/lani/lanie/larney *n.* [1970s+] (S.Afr.) **1** a boss, an employer. **2** a White person, a rich person. [ety. unknown, but ? Fr. *l'orné*, the ornate one, or Malay/Hind. *rani*, a queen]

laanie/lahnee/lani/lanie/larney *adj.* [1970s+] (S.Afr.) **1** showy, arrogant. **2** moneyed. **3** intellectually sophisticated. [LAANIE n.]

lab *n.* [1950s+] (orig. Can./US) a *Lab*rador dog (cf. DACHS). [abbr.]

laba/laba-laba *n.* [1950s+] (W.I.) a chatterbox, a gossip, a talkative person. [BLAB v.; BLABBER n.]

laba-laba *v.* [1960s] (W.I.) to chatter, to gossip, to betray secrets. [LABA n.]

labber-mouth *n.* [20C] (W.I.) a chatterer, a talker. [BLABBER-MOUTH]

labdick *n.* [20C] a policeman. [abbr. *L*othian *a*nd *B*orders Constabulary, and presumably a link to DICK n.[6] (1)]

label *n.* [1920s–50s] (US) a person's name (cf. HANDLE n.[2]).

lab hound *n.* [1970s+] (US) a person who frequently volunteers to be used in psychology experiments. [SE *lab*(oratory) + sfx. -HOUND]

labonza *n.* [US] **1** [1930s+] the pit of the stomach. **2** [1950s+] the buttocks. [? Ital. *la pancia*, the paunch]

labour, the *n.* [1930s+] the labour exchange, the employment exchange, the job centre.

labour gone in Maxwell Pond *see* MONEY GONE IN MAXWELL POND.

labret *n.* [1990s] in body piercing, a stud through the bottom lip. [SE *labret*, an ornament inserted in the lip]

labrick/laverick *n.* [late 19C] (US) an idiot. [? dial. *laverick*, a lark or a hare]

labrish *n.* [1940s–50s] (W.I.) gossip, chatter. [BLAB v.]

labrish *adj.* [1940s–50s] (W.I.) talkative, gossipy. [LABRISH n.]

labrish *v.* [1940s–50s] (W.I.) to tell tales, to gossip (cf. LABA n.; LABBER-MOUTH)

labrisher *n.* [1940s] (W.I.) a chatterer, a telltale. [LABRISH v.]

lab wretch *n.* [1980s+] (US) a person who undertakes unpleasant laboratory tasks. [SE *lab*(oratory) + *wretch*]

lac/lack/lahk *n.*[1] [mid-19C] (Anglo-Ind.) very many, a great deal, often in pl. [Hind. *lakh*, 100,000 rupees]

lac *n.*[2] [1980s+] (US Black) a Cadil*lac*. [abbr.]

lacatan *n.* [1950s] (W.I.) a short, stoutish person (cf. LANGULALA). [SE *lacatan*, a type of small banana]

lace *n.*[1] [1960s+] (US gay) the foreskin; thus *lace queen*, one who prefers uncircumcised males. [abbr. LACE CURTAIN n.[2]]

lace *n.*[2] [1970s+] (drugs) a mixture of cocaine and marijuana. [ety. unknown]

lace *v.* **1** [1970s] (US) to swindle (cf. STITCH UP). **2** [1980s+] to shoot (cf. STITCH).

lace curtain *n.*[1] [20C] beer, orig. spec. Burton's beer. [rhy. sl.]

lace curtain/curtains *n.*[2] [1960s+] (gay) a long foreskin.

lace-curtain Irish *n.* [1920s+] (US) genteel, petit-bourgeois Irish-Americans (cf. SHANTY IRISH). [they adorn their windows with such items]

lace curtains *n.*[1] [1910s–30s] (US) a beard.

lace curtains *n.*[2] *see* LACE CURTAIN n.[2].

laced *adj.*[1] **1** [late 17C–early 18C] of coffee, sugared. **2** [late 17C+] of a drink, mixed or combined with something. **3** [1980s+] (US) drunk, intoxicated (cf. ALED UP). [SE *laced*, of a plant, entwined; (1) SE in 20C; (3) one's blood is *laced* with alcohol]

laced/laced by the neck *adj.*[2] [1970s+] (US Black) extremely sophisticated. [image of lace-ornamented garments]

laced mutton *n.* [17C–mid-19C] **1** a prostitute. **2** a woman dressed to appear younger than her years (cf. MUTTON DRESSED AS LAMB). [SE *lace* + MUTTON; the lacing is that of stays or corsets, embellishing a young, or disguising an ageing, figure. Poss. a pun on the culinary term 'lacing' (making incisions into) a duck or chicken's breast, but this meaning is slightly later]

lace into *v.* [early 19C+] to attack, to beat, to thrash. [ext. of SE *lace*, to thrash; note dial. phr. *lace one's jacket*, to beat]

lacing *n.* [late 17C–early 19C] a flogging. [LACE INTO; but ? SE *lash* or f. the whip's cord, which resembles a lace]

lack *see* LAC n.[1].

lackanooky/lakanuki *n.* [1940s+] (US) ill-health caused by lack of sexual activity. [the respelling of a Polynesian word + play on SE *lack of* + NOOKIE n.]

lackey-dog *n.* [1940s+] (W.I.) a skulking hanger-on. [ext. of SE *lackey*]

lackin *n.* [mid–late 19C] a wife. [ety. unknown]

la cosa *n.* [1970s+] (US drugs) heroin. [Sp. *la cosa*, the thing]

lacy-pants *n.* [20C] (US) a flashily dressed person (cf. FANCY PANTS n.).

Lad, the *n.*[1] [20C] (Irish) cancer. [euph.]

lad *n.*[2] [20C] (Irish) **1** an inanimate object. **2** a penis. **3** a fox.

ladder *n.* [16C] the gallows (cf. CLIMB THREE TREES WITH A LADDER; MOUNT THE LADDER; WALK UP LADDER LANE AND DOWN HEMP STREET). [metonymy]

la-di-da see LA-DI-DAH v.

la-di-dah n.[1] [mid-19C+] a snob. [LA-DI-DAH adj. (1)]

la-di-dah n.[2] [1970s] **1** a car. **2** a cigar. [rhy. sl.]

la-di-dah adj. [mid-19C+] **1** stuck up, arrogant, snobbish. **2** effeminate, affected. [the supposed excl. of La-di-dah! in the face of information, experience etc]

la-di-dah/la-di-da v. [1900s–30s] to use affected manners or speech. [LA-DI-DAH adj.]

ladies n.[1] [1930s+] a ladies' lavatory (cf. GENTS). [abbr.]

ladies n.[2] [1960s+] (US Black) a generic term for prostitutes. [euph.]

ladies' boarding house n. [mid-19C–1900s] a brothel (cf. ACCOMMODATION HOUSE). [euph.]

ladies' college n. [18C] a brothel (cf. ACADEMY). [euph.]

ladies' delight/plaything/treasure n. [19C] the penis. [note ety. of DILDO]

ladies' lollipop n. [19C] the penis (cf. LOLLIPOP n.[1]; SUGAR-STICK; SWEETMEAT n.[3]; TUMMY BANANA).

ladies' plaything see LADIES' DELIGHT.

ladies' tailor n. [19C] a womanizer, a promiscuous man. [the in-and-out 'sewing' motion of intercourse]

ladies' treasure see LADIES' DELIGHT.

ladle v. [19C] to talk slowly and solemnly. [the image of carefully doling out soup]

lad of wax n. [late 18C–1900s] **1** a cobbler (cf. COCK-A-WAX). **2** a boy, a weak or unimportant man.

lady n.[1] **1** [late 17C–19C] a crooked or hunchbacked woman (cf. LORD). **2** [late 19C; 1960s+] (US) one's girlfriend. **3** [1930s (US prison)] one's effeminate homosexual partner. **4** [1960s+] (US Black) an independent, high-class prostitute. **5** [1970s+] (US) a prostitute belonging to a pimp.

lady n.[2] [20C] a queen in a pack of playing cards.

lady n.[3] [1970s+] (drugs) **1** cocaine (cf. GIRL n.[3]). **2** the pipe used for smoking base or crack. [LADY SNOW n.[2]; WHITE LADY n.[2]]

Lady, the n.[4] [1980s] (US) the Statue of Liberty.

lady abbess see ABBESS.

Lady Berkeley n. [19C] the vagina (cf. BERKELEY HUNT; LADY JANE). [ult. rhy. sl. BERKELEY HUNT = CUNT n.[1]]

ladybird n. [16C+] a prostitute. [SE ladybird, a sweetheart]

Lady Blamey n. [1940s] (Aus.) a drinking vessel made of half a beer bottle with the cut edge rounded by sandpaper. [Lady Blamey, widow of Sir Henry Blamey (1884–1951), who taught soldiers how to cut a beer bottle in two by winding a kerosene-soaked string around it, setting the string alight and then plunging the bottle into cold water, where it broke cleanly]

lady caine n. [1980s+] (drugs) cocaine (cf. LADY SNOW n.[2]; WHITE LADY n.[2]).

lady-cracker/-fart/-finger n. [1940s+] (US) a small firecracker. [image of femininity as small]

Lady Dacre's wine n. [early 19C] gin. [ety. unknown; ? anecdotal]

lady-fart see LADY-CRACKER.

ladyfied adj. [early 17C–late 19C] affecting the airs of a fashionable lady.

lady-finger n.[1] [1940s–70s] (US) a cowardly man. [the softness of female hands]

lady-finger n.[2] see LADY-CRACKER.

lady/old lady five fingers n. [20C] masturbation (cf. MISS FIST; WIDOW FIVE-FINGERS).

lady flower n. [mid-19C] (US) the vagina. [euph. coined by Walt Whitman (1819–92)]

lady from Bristol n. [20C] (Aus.) a pistol. [rhy. sl.]

lady from the ground up n. [late 19C] (US) a woman who is drunk and disorderly (cf. PERFECT LADY).

Lady Godiva n. [20C] £5. [rhy. sl. FIVER n. (1)]

lady hot-bot see HOT-BOT.

Lady Jane n. [mid-19C+] the vagina (cf. LADY BERKELEY). [euph. use of proper name]

lady-killer n. [early 19C+] a man who considers himself to be irresistible to women.

lady love v. [1930s+] to engage in lesbian behaviour.

lady-lover n. [1930s+] a lesbian.

lady muck n. [1950s+] an arrogant, pretentious woman of any class (cf. KING SHIT; LORD MUCK).

lady of the lake n. [18C] a prostitute (cf. LAKER LADY). [SE lake, to play amorously, ? ult. LARK v.]

lady right n. [mid-19C+] the perfect girlfriend or lover (cf. MR RIGHT).

lady's low toupee n. [19C] the pubic hair.

lady snow n.[1] [1950s–70s] (US Black) a respected upper-class White woman. [SE lady + SNOW n.[4] (3)]

lady snow n.[2] cocaine (cf. LADY CAINE). [SE lady + SNOW n.[3] (1)]

lady's waist n. [1930s–40s] (Aus.) **1** a slender beer glass, with an hour-glass shape. **2** the drink served in such a glass.

lady ware n. [19C] the penis (cf. WARE). [SE lady + ware, goods]

lag n.[1] **1** [16C–18C] a bundle of clothes for washing (cf. LAG OF DUDS). **2** [mid-16C–late 19C] water. **3** [late 16C–19C] urine. **4** [17C] weak liquor. [? SE lage, to wash, OF l'aige/l'aigue, water]

lag n.[2] **1** [early 19C+] a convict who has been transported or sentenced to penal servitude (cf. OLD LAG). **2** [1910s–30s] (US Und.) a term of transportation or penal servitude (cf. LAGGING). [LAG v.[2]]

lag/lag-a-bag/lag-lost n.[3] [20C] (Ulster) a lazy person. [Scot. lag/lag-a-bag/lag-lost, a lazy person]

lag v.[1] [mid-16C–mid-19C] to urinate. [LAG n.[1] (3)]

lag v.[2] **1** [early–mid-19C] to sentence to transportation for over 7 years. **2** [mid–late 19C] to arrest, to apprehend. **3** [mid-19C+] to imprison. **4** [late 19C+] (Aus.) to inform on. [14C SE lag, to carry off, to steal]

lag-a-bag see LAG n.[3].

lage/lagge n. [16C] (Und.) water (cf. LAG n.[1]). [LAG n.[1] (2)]

lage of duds n. [16C–19C] a bundle of clothes for washing. [LAG n.[1] (1) + DUDS n. (2). Harman's orig. definition is 'a buck of clothes', f. SE buck, a washtub, and thus a 'washtub's measure of clothes', buck contemporaneously meant lye, which would be used in the washing process]

lag fever n. [early 19C] a spurious illness feigned in order to avoid transportation (cf. LAG SHIP). [LAG n.[2] + SE fever]

lagg v. [mid-19C] (US) to execute by hanging. [? misreading of LAG v.[2]]

lagge see LAGE.

lagged adj.[1] [mid-19C] (US) hanged. [LAGG]

lagged adj.[2] [mid-19C+] imprisoned, transported. [LAG v.[2]]

lagger n.[1] [early–mid-19C] a sailor. [? LAG n.[1] (2)]

lagger n.[2] **1** [early 19C] a convict. **2** [mid-19C+] a police informer. [LAG n.[2]; 20C use of (2) is Aus.]

lagger n.[3] [20C] (Ulster) anything sticky or greasy, e.g. porridge or mud. [Scot. lagger, a muddy place]

lagging n. [early 19C+] (Und.) **1** any prison sentence. **2** a sentence of more than three years' imprisonment; thus [early 19C] lagging matter, any crime punishable by transportation (cf. LAGGING DUES). [LAG v.[2]]

lagging dues n. [19C] transportation; e.g. lagging dues will be concerned, this person is liable to be transported. [LAG v.[2] (1)]

lagging gage n. [18C–19C] a chamberpot. [LAG v.[1] + GAGE n.[1] (2)]

lagging station n. [20C] (prison) a prison for long-term prisoners. [LAG v.[2]]

L.A. glass see L.A. ICE.

lag-lost see LAG n.[3].

lag ship n. [early 19C] a ship used for the transportation of convicts to Australia (cf. LAG FEVER). [LAG n.[2] (1) + SE ship]

Lah *n.*[1] [1970s+] (US) Los Angeles (cf. LA-LA LAND *n.*[1]).

lah *n.*[2] *see* LA n.

lahdee/lahdi *adj.* [1930s+] smart, fashionable. [abbr. LA-DI-DAH adj.]

lahk *see* LAC n.[1].

lahnee *see* LAANIE.

lahteeache! *excl.* [mid-19C+] all right. [backsl.]

L.A. ice/glass *n.* [1990s] smokeable methamphetamine. [L.A. n.[1]+ ICE n.[5]]

laid *adj.*[1] [1960s+] (US Black) intoxicated by alcohol or drugs (cf. LAID-BACK; LAID OUT adj.[1]).

laid *adj.*[2] [1970s+] (US Black) **1** fashionably dressed. **2** fashionably decorated (cf. LAID OUT adj.[2]).

laid-back *adj.* **1** [1960s+] soothing, peaceful, passive (cf. MELLOW adj.). **2** [1970s+] intoxicated by drugs or alcohol (cf. LAID adj.[1]).

laid crib *n.* [1960s] (US Black) an attractive, well-furnished home. [LAID adj.[2] + CRIB n.[3] (7)]

laid out *adj.*[1] [1920s+] (US) drunk (cf. BASTED). [i.e. one is 'dead' drunk]

laid out *adj.*[2] [1960s+] (US Black) well-dressed. [ext. of LAID adj.[2] (1)]

laid, relaid and parlayed *phr.* [1950s+] (US) **1** having had frequent sexual intercourse. **2** deceived, cheated. [LAY v.[1] + joc. uses of SE]

laid to the bone *phr.*[1] [1960s–70s] (US Black) drunk (cf. LAID OUT adj.[1]). [ext. of LAID adj.[2] (1)]

laid to the bone *phr.*[2] [1960s–70s] (US Black) **1** well-dressed. **2** of clothes, cut so well they seem a second skin (cf. LAID OUT adj.[2]).

laid to the natural bone *phr.* [1970s+] (US Black) naked. [LAID TO THE BONE phr.[2] + SE *natural*, unadorned]

laid up in Job's dock, to be *phr.* [late 19C–early 19C] to be treated in hospital for a venereal disease. [SE *laid up* + JOB'S WARD]

laigz *n.* [1940s+] (W.I.) **1** a trick. **2** influence. [? fig. use of SE *legs*; or *lag*, used in games as 'a chance, an opportunity']

laimeter/lamester/lameter/lamitor *n.* [20C] (Ulster) one who is feeling unwell. [Scot. *lamiter*, a lame person, a cripple]

lain *see* LANE n.[3].

lair/lare *n.* [1920s+] (Aus.) a show-off, one who dresses flashily (cf. LARRIKIN.). [backform. f. LAIRY]

lair *v.* [1920s+] (Aus.) **1** to dress flashily, to dress up. **2** to act in a showy manner. [LAIR n.]

lairize *v.* [1930s+] (Aus.) to brag, to boast, to show off (cf. LAIR UP). [ext. of LAIR v.]

lair/lare up *v.* [1920s+] (Aus.) to brag, to boast, to show off (cf. LAIRIZE). [ext. of LAIR v.]

lairy/lary *adj.* **1** [mid-19C+] knowing, conceited, cheeky. **2** [late 19C+] (Aus.) flashy, ostentatious, showy. [LEERY adj.]

lakanuki *see* LACKANOOKY.

lakbay diva *n.* [1990s] (drugs) marijuana. [ety. unknown; pig Latin for 'black weed']

laker lady *n.* [18C] a prostitute. [for ety. *see* LADY OF THE LAKE]

lakes/lakes of Killarney *adj.* [20C] **1** mad, eccentric. **2** two-faced, untrustworthy. [rhy. sl., *Lakes of Killarney* = (1) BARMY; (2) CARNEY adj.]

lakesy *adj.* [20C] insane, eccentric. [LAKES]

Lake Wendouree *v.* [1990s] (Aus.) to have just ejaculated (cf. BACCHUS MARSH). [*Lake Wendouree*, situated at the centre of Ballarat, Australia; the lake is wet, as is one's penis]

la-la *n.* [1960s+] (Aus.) a lavatory. [abbr./redup.]

lala/la-la *see* LOLLA.

La-La Land *n.*[1] [1970s+] (orig. US) Los Angeles. [L.A. n.[1] but note LA-LA LAND n.[2]]

la-la land *n.*[2] [1980s+] (US) a fantasy world; thus *in la-la land*, out of touch with reality, drugged or drunk.

lalapalooza *see* LALLAPALOOSA.

lal brough/lally *n.* [1900s] snuff. [rhy. sl.; *Lal* = dimin. of *Alice*, the image is of an old lady, 'Lal Brough', taking snuff]

lal-lah *see* LOLLA.

lallapaloosa/lalapalooza/lallapalooza/lollapaloosa/lollapalooza *n.* [late 19C+] (orig. US) something or someone outstandingly good, stylish or pleasing of its kind (cf. HUMDINGER; LOLLA; LULU).

lallie/lallette/lally/lyle *n.* [1950s+] (Ling. Fr./Polari) a leg, usu. in pl. [? shared initial letters]

lall-shraub *n.* [late 18C–1920s] (Anglo-Ind.) claret, red Bordeaux. [Hind. *lal-sharab*, red wine]

lally *n.*[1] *see* LULLY.

lally *n.*[2] *see* LAL BROUGH.

lally *n.*[3] *see* LALLIE.

lallycooler *see* LOLLYCOOLER.

lallygag/lollygag *v.* [mid-19C+] (US) **1** to fool around, to kiss and cuddle. **2** to dawdle, to dally. [ety. unknown, ? link to dial. *lolly*, the tongue]

lam *n.*[1] [late 19C+] (US) an escape from prison (cf. TAKE IT ON THE LAM). [LAM v.[2] (1)]

lam *n.*[2] [1910s–30s] (US) a punch or blow. [LAM v.[1] (1)]

lam/lamb *v.*[1] **1** [late 16C+] to beat or strike; thus *lamming*, a beating (cf. LAMBASTE; LAMB-PIE). **2** [mid–late 19C] (US) to defeat in a fight. [linked to ON *lemja*, to lame, as a result of a beating]

lam/lamb *v.*[2] **1** [late 19C+] (US Und.) to run away, to escape from prison. **2** [1930s] (US) to chase. [? early 19C Und. *lammas*, to depart, to leave, or as abbr. of *slam*; thus pun on BEAT IT. Major (1994) suggests link to Igbo *lam*, to leave, which would be interchangeable in the eyes of US Black slave owners]

lamb *n.* **1** [late 17C–late 19C] a simpleton, a fool, esp. one easily cheated of their money (cf. CALF n.[1]; CALF-LOLLY). **2** [1900s–50s] (mainly US prison) a young homosexual boy (cf. CHICKEN n.[5]). **3** [1950s+] (US Black) an innocent.

lamb *v. see* LAM v.

lambaste *v.* [mid-17C–mid-19C] to beat, to thrash. [LAM v.[1] (1) + SE *baste*, to thrash, to cudgel]

lamb cannon *n.* [1990s] the penis (cf. BACON BAZOOKA).

lamb down *v.* (Aus./N.Z.) **1** [mid-19C+] to persuade someone to spend all their money on alcohol. **2** [late 19C–1910s] to squander one's earnings on drink. [shearing jargon *lamb down*, to tend ewes at lambing time, usu. used by shearers and other rural workers]

lambe/lambiche *n.* [1960s+] (US) a toady. [Sp. *lambe*, licker]

Lambeth *v.* [late 19C] to wash. [the well-known public bath-house in Lambeth]

Lambeth Walk *n.* [20C] the chalk used in billiards. [rhy. sl.]

lambiche *see* LAMBE.

lambing-down shanty *n.* [20C] (Aus.) a rural tavern. [LAMB DOWN + SE *shanty*]

lambing-down shop *n.* [late 19C–1900s] (Aus.) a public house. [LAMB DOWN + SE *shop*]

lam black *n.* [1930s] (US Black) a very dark-skinned person (cf. LAMPBLACK). [? LAM v.[1]; thus the bruises make one's skin even darker, or SE *lampblack*, carbon residue, often used for blacking up]

lamborghini *n.* [1990s] (drugs) a crack pipe made from a plastic rum bottle and a rubber sparkplug cover. [a make of luxury sports car]

lamb-pie *n.* [late 17C–early 19C] a beating, a flogging. [a pun on the SE/LAM v.[1] (1)]

lambsbread *n.* [1950s+] (W.I./Rasta) a form of high-quality marijuana. [? a form of plant, cf. SE *lamb's lettuce*, corn salad]

lamb's fry *n.* [20C] (Aus.) **1** a necktie. **2** an eye, usu. used in the pl. [rhy. sl.]

lamb skin-it *n.* [mid-19C] the card game *lansquenet* (cf. SKIN-THE-LAMB n.¹).

lambskin man *n.* [late 17C–early 19C] a judge. [the ermine-bordered robes]

lamb's leg/tail *n.* [20C] (US) a piece of mucus running from one's nose. [resemblance]

lame *n.* **1** [1950s+] (orig. US Black) an unsophisticated person or a fool (cf. LAMEBRAIN). **2** [1950s+] (US prison) a weakling. **3** [1960s] (US drugs) a tobacco cigarette. **4** [1960s+] (US Und.) a non-criminal and so a possible victim. [LAME adj.]

lame *adj.* **1** [mid-19C+] (US) bankrupted by gambling (cf. LAME DUCK). **2** [20C] drunk. **3** [1930s+] (orig. US Black) naïve, clumsy, socially inept. **4** [1950s+] (US Black) contemptible.

lame as a tree *phr.* [late 19C] very lame. [the wooden crutch or even wooden leg such a lame person might require; note also 16C SE *tyre*, a leper]

lame as St Giles Cripplegate *phr.* [17C–19C] very lame indeed. [the patron saint of the disabled and so the popularity of his church (founded in 11C) among those afflicted]

lamebrain *n.* [1910s+] (orig. US) a fool, a simpleton; thus *lamebrained*, stupid, foolish (cf. BAKEBRAIN; LAMEHEAD; LAME-O). [SE *lame* + sfx. -*brain*]

lame duck *n.* **1** [mid-18C+] a defaulter on the Stock Exchange. **2** [19C+] any weak, handicapped or useless person, so falling behind their peers. **3** [mid-19C+] (US, orig. political) a defeated politician who is working out a period of office, esp. a president who has been defeated in the presidential election in November but does not leave office – in which all decisions are now *de facto* irrelevant – until January; this usage can extend to any similarly placed officials. **4** [late 19C–1900s] (Aus.) a rascal. **5** [late 19C–1920s] (US) a person who is unable to pay their debts.

lamehead *n.* [1970s] (US) a fool (cf. LAMEBRAIN). [SE *lame* + sfx. -HEAD (1)]

lame-o/lamo *n.* [1970s+] (US campus) a general term of contempt or disparagement, a weakling, an inadequate, one not attuned to the prevailing styles and priorities (cf. LAMEBRAIN; LAME n. (1) + sfx. -O)

lamer *n.* [1990s] (US teen) a general term of contempt, disparagement. [LAME n. (1)]

lames *n.* [1950s+] (US Black) a general term of contempt, disparagement. [LAME n.; on pattern of HOMES]

lame scene *n.* (US Black) a disappointing, boring event, typically a tedious party. [LAME adj. (3) + SCENE]

lamester/lameter *see* LAIMETER.

l.a.m.f. *phr.* [1960s] (US gang) *like a motherfucker*; when added to a gang name it implies the toughness and aggressiveness of the person so defined. [abbr.]

laminated *adj.* [1980s+] (US campus) phoney, false. [pun on PLASTIC adj.]

Lamington *n.* [late 19C–1940s] (Aus.) a Homburg hat. ['a soft felt hat with a curled brim and a dented crown, first worn at Homburg, once a fashionable health-resort' (*OED*). Aus. use plays on SAusE *lamington*, a square of sponge cake coated in chocolate icing and desiccated coconut, ult. Baron Lamington (1860–1940), governor of Queensland]

lam into *v.* [late 19C+] to beat up. [ext. of LAM v.¹; the term began life as UK sl. but crossed the Atlantic to reappear in criminal milieux]

lamitor *see* LAIMETER.

Lammermoor lion *n.* [18C–mid-19C] (Scots) a sheep (cf. COTSWOLD LION).

lammister *see* LAMSTER.

lammy *n.* [mid-19C] a blanket. [SE *lambskin*. Note naut. jargon *lammy*, a duffel coat]

lamo *see* LAME-O.

lamous *adj.* [1910s] (US tramp) cheap, inferior, esp. of jewellery. [? the name of a Chicago company that made fake jewellery]

lam out *v.* [late 19C] to strike out at, to hit (cf. LAM INTO). [LAM v.¹]

lamp *n.* **1** [19C+] an eye; thus *queer lamp*, a blind, sore or squinting eye. **2** [1920s–40s] (US) a look or glance. [(1) often in pl., note Shakespeare (*Comedy of Errors*, 1590): 'My wasting lampes some fading glimmer left']

lamp *v.*¹ **1** [early 19C+] to beat, to strike, to thrash. **2** [1950s] (W.I.) to trick, to deceive. [? LAM v.¹]

lamp *v.*² **1** [1910s+] (orig. US) to look at, to assess visually. **2** [1980s+] (US Black/campus) to loiter, to 'hang out', to relax while others panic. [LAMP n.; the image of (2) is watching while others do]

lamp along *v.* [mid-19C] (Irish) to go along at a great pace. [a *lamplighter* works quickly]

lampblack *n.* [1930s–40s] (US Black) a very dark-skinned Black person (cf. LAM BLACK).

lamper *n.*¹ [1920s–30s] a teasing name for a tall, thin person. [LAMP-POST]

lamper *n.*² [1950s] (W.I.) a confidence trickster. [LAMP v.¹ (2)]

lamp of light *n.* [19C] the penis (cf. LAMP OF LOVE; LIGHT THE LAMP).

lamp of love *n.* [19C] the vagina (cf. LAMP OF LIGHT).

lamp oil *n.* [1940s–50s] (US) whisky. [? it 'lights you up']

lamp-post *n.* [late 19C+] a teasing name for a tall, thin person (cf. LAMPER n.¹).

lamps *n.* [mid-19C] spectacles (cf. GIG-LAMPS).

lamster/lammister *n.* [20C] (US Und./prison) an escapee, a fugitive. [LAM v.² (1)]

Lancashire lass *n.* [late 19C+] a drinking glass. [rhy. sl.]

Lancashire lasses *n.* [20C] glasses (spectacles). [rhy. sl.]

lance *n.* **1** [late 16C–early 17C] the penis (cf. BAYONET; LANCE IN REST; LANCE OF LOVE). **2** [1950s] (US drugs) a hypodermic needle.

lance *v.* (US) **1** [1900s] to swindle. **2** [1960s] of a man, to have sexual intercourse.

lance in rest *n.* [late 16C–early 17C] the erect penis (cf. BAYONET; LANCE n.). [joc. use of SE *lance in rest*, a lance fixed to a pocket-like contrivance on the right side of the cuirass so it will not be driven back on impact]

lance-knight/lanceman/lance-prigger *n.* [late 16C–mid-17C] a highwayman. [? Ger. *Landsknechte*, a mercenary soldier who, when not actually fighting, terrorized civilians]

lance of love *n.* [19C] the penis (cf. BAYONET; LANCE n.).

lancepresado/lanspresado *n.* [late 17C–late 18C] one who comes into company, esp. in a tavern or public house, with only a few pence in their pocket. [Fr. *lancepessade*, 'the meanest officer in a foot-company' (Cotgrave 1611), used in English as a synon. for *lance-corporal*, the lowest rank of NCO]

lance-prigger *see* LANCE-KNIGHT.

land *n.* [20C] (Irish) a disappointment, a letdown. [SE *land(ed) a blow*]

land *v.*¹ [mid-19C] to help someone out, to 'set them on their feet']

land *v.*² [late 19C+] to hit, i.e. to land a blow on; thus *land one on*.

land carrack *n.* [19C] a prostitute (cf. FRIGATE). [SE *land* + *carrack*, a large ship; she 'sails' the streets]

landed estate *n.* [19C–1900s] **1** a cemetery; thus (WW1 milit.) *become a landowner*, to die. **2** dirt beneath the fingernails.

landlady *n.* [late 19C+] (US) a madam, a proprietress of a brothel. [euph.]

land-leaper/-loper *n.* [late 14C–early 17C] a criminal vagabond, subsisting on pilfering and often disguised with fake sores and similar blandishments (cf. LAND-LUBBER). [SE *land* + *leap*/Du. *loopen*, to run]

landlord halo *n.* [1980s+] (US) a notably dim light in the hallway of a slum apartment block.

land-lubber *n.* [late 17C–early 19C] a wandering tramp, a vagrant (cf. LAND-LEAPER. [SE *land* + LUBBER]

land navy *n.* [mid-19C+] beggars who pose as impoverished seamen (cf. DRY-LAND SAILOR; FRESHWATER MARINER; TURNPIKE SAILOR).

Land o' Cakes *n.* [18C–late 19C] Scotland (cf. MARMALADE COUNTRY).

land of darkness *n.* [1930s–40s] (US Black) the Black district of any city.

land of fruit and nuts *n.* [1940s–50s] (US) California. [the state's supposed over-representation of homosexuals (FRUIT n.²) and eccentrics (NUT n.⁶)]

land of hope *n.* [20C] soap (cf. CAPE OF GOOD HOPE n.²). [rhy. sl.]

land of the hard *n.* [1990s] (US Black teen) one's own neighbourhood. [HARD adj.; used in the hope of boosting one's own status by living there]

land on *v.* [1910s+] (US) to reprimand severely.

land on/sight a pebbly beach, to *phr.* [late 19C–1900s] to be short of money; thus *pebbly-beached*, out of pocket (cf. STONE-BROKE).

land on one's feet, to *phr.* [1950s+] to survive a difficult situation.

Land o' Scots *n.* [late 19C] heaven. [ety. unknown]

land pike *n.* [mid–late 19C] (US) a wild hog (cf. LAND-SHARK).

land-pirate *n.* [late 17C–19C] a highwayman, a wandering thief (cf. LAND-LEAPER).

land-raker *n.* [late 16C–mid-18C] a vagrant, a tramp (cf. LAND-LEAPER; LAND-LUBBER). [SE *land* + *rake*, to search]

landsakes! *excl.* [late 19C+] (mainly US) a mild oath. ['Lord's sake!']

land security *n.* [mid-18C–19C] unauthorized absence (cf. GIVE LEG BAIL AND LAND SECURITY).

land's end! *excl.* [1980s+] (US campus) an all-purpose excl. [var. on LANDSAKES!]

land-shark *n.* **1** [19C] a money-lender, a usurer (cf. SHARK). **2** [19C] a custom house officer. **3** [mid–late 19C] (US) a wild hog.

landsman *n.* [late 19C+] a fellow countryman, esp. a fellow Jew (cf. PAISAN). [Yid.]

land someone in the shit, to *phr.* [mid-19C+] to bring trouble to someone else. [SE *land* v. + SHIT n.¹]

land someone with *v.* [20C] to burden someone with, to pass on responsibility.

lane, the *n.*¹ [mid-16C+] the throat (cf. GUTTER LANE; NARROW LANE; RED LANE; RED LION LANE).

Lane, the *n.*² [mid-19C] **1** Drury Lane Theatre (cf. GARDEN n.²). **2** Petticoat Lane Market (Middlesex St, London E1).

lane/lain *n.*³ [1930s–60s] (US Black) **1** a peasant, a rustic. **2** an unsophisticated person. **3** a male. **4** a new inmate in a prison. [? one who lives in a country lane or var. pron. of LAME n.; the image of (4) is of their lack of knowledge of prison life]

Lane Cove *n.* [20C] (Aus.) a stove. [rhy. sl.]

langel *n.* [20C] (Ulster) a tall, thin person. [dial. *langel*, tether or rope for restraining an animal]

langer *n.* [1980s+] (Irish) the penis. [? joc. var. of SE *long one* or link to LANGOLEE]

langered/langers *adj.* [20C] (Irish) drunk. [Scot. *langer*, weariness]

langolee *n.* [mid–late 19C] the penis. [Welsh *trangluni*, tools]

langret *n.* [16C] a type of false die, in which one side is

fractionally longer than the rest (cf. BARRED). [15C Eng. and 15–19C Scot. variant sp. of *lang*, long]

langtries *n.* [late 19C] attractive eyes. [Lillie *Langtry* (1853–1929), a beauty and popular singer]

language *n.* [mid-19C+] bad language, obscenity.

language! *excl.* [mid-19C+] be quiet!, shut up! (cf. CONVERSATION). [abbr. *Mind your bad language!* or some similar restraint]

language of flowers *n.* [late 19C] a fine of 10 shillings or a sentence of 7 days in jail. [a contemporary Bow Street magistrate, Mr Flowers, 'a very popular and amiable magistrate at this court' (Ware), or a play on the SE *language of flowers*, a method of expressing sentiments by means of symbolic flowers]

langulala *n.* [1940s+] (W.I.) a very tall, thin person (cf. LACATAN). [Hausa *langalanga*, a tall, thin person]

lani/lanie *see* LAANIE.

lank *adj.*¹ [late 19C–1930s] (US) hungry. [SE *lanky*]

lank *adj.*² (S.Afr.) **1** [1970s+] a general term of approval, usu. from children or young people. **2** [1970s+] plenty, lots of. **3** [1980s+] very. [Afk. phr. *lank nie sleg nie*, not bad at all]

lanky *n.* [mid-19C+] a nickname for a tall, thin person.

Lanna Macree's/Lanty McHale's dog *n.* [20C] (Irish) a time-server, one who befriends whoever they happen to be with (cf. BILLY HARRAN'S DOG). [? anecdotal]

lanspresado *see* LANCEPRESADO.

lanter *v.* [early 19C] (US) to hang from a lamp-post. [Fr. revolutionary exhortation *à la lanterne!*, 'string 'em up!']

lanty *v.* [20C] (Ulster) to scold; thus *give someone lanty*, to tell off, to give someone a hard time. [Scot. *lant*, to jeer at, to make a fool of]

Lanty McHale's dog *see* LANNA MACREE'S DOG.

lanyard *n.* [1990s] the penis. [joc. use of SE + pun on YARD n.¹]

lap *n.*¹ **1** [mid-16C] buttermilk or whey or any thin, non-alcoholic drink. **2** [mid-16C–1950s] liquor in general (cf. GO ON THE LAP). **3** [late 16C–mid-19C] soup. **4** [late 19C] tea. [SE *lap*, to drink]

lap *n.*² [late 16C] the vagina. [euph.; but note SE *lap*, a fold of flesh]

lap *n.*³ [late 19C] a tail coat. [SE *laps*, the 'skirts' of a coat]

lap/lap up *v.*¹ **1** [late 19C+] to drink alcohol, esp. greedily. **2** [1920s+] to enjoy greatly. [fig. use of SE/LAP n.¹]

lap/lap up *v.*² [1920s+] to perform cunnilingus. [LAP n.²/CUNT-LAPPER]

lap-clap *n.* [17C–mid-18C] **1** sexual intercourse. **2** conception; thus *get a lap-clap*, to become pregnant. [SE *lap* + *clap*, a blow]

lap-ears *n.* [mid-19C] (US campus) a notably religious student (cf. DONKEY n.¹). [SE *lop-ears*, a donkey]

lap feeder *n.* [late 19C–1900s] a silver tablespoon. [LAP n.¹]

lapful *n.* [19C–1920s] **1** a husband. **2** a lover. **3** an unborn child. [LAP n.²]

lapland *n.* [mid–late 19C] **1** the vagina. **2** the world of women. [LAP n.²]

lap-lover *n.* [1990s] one who enjoys cunnilingus. [LAP n.² + SE *lover*]

lapper *n.*¹ [early 19C–1900s] **1** alcohol. **2** a hard drinker. [LAP n.¹ (2)]

lapper *n.*² [mid-19C] (US) the tongue.

lapper *n.*³ [1920s+] one who performs cunnilingus (cf. CUNT-LAPPER). [LAP v.²]

laprogh *n.* [late 19C] (tinker) **1** a goose or duck. **2** a bird of any type. [Shelta]

lap the gutter, to *phr.* [19C] to drink. [SE *lap* + either GUTTER ALLEY or GATTER]

lap up *see* LAP v.

larceny *n.*[1] [1920s+] (US Und.) an inclination towards theft, a liking for theft; thus *larceny in his heart*.

larceny *n.*[2] [1940s–60s] (US Black) unpleasant, antagonistic thoughts or feelings. [use of SE *larceny*, 'the ... taking and carrying away of the personal goods of another with intent to convert them to the taker's use' (*OED*), as a generic for evil]

larceny *v.* [1940s–60s] (US Black) to feel bad towards, to suspect. [LARCENY *n.*[2]]

larceny shoes *n.* [1980s+] (US) elaborate, high-priced trainers. [as a status symbol of (orig.) Black teens, such shoes are allegedly the badge of criminality; thus a racist slur]

lard *n.* (US) **1** [1920s+] human fat (cf. TUB OF LARD). **2** [1920s–50s] butter or margarine.

lard-ass *n.* [1930s+] (US) **1** a lazy, good-for-nothing person. **2** an overweight person; thus *lard-assed*, fat-buttocked. [SE *lard* + ARSE *n.*[1]; i.e. someone who sits on their posterior and does nothing but cultivate lard]

lard-belly *n.* [1930s–40s] (US) an obese person.

lard-bladder *n.* [late 19C–1920s] an obese person.

lard-bucket *n.* [20C] a fat person (cf. BUCKET OF LARD).

lard-butt *n.* [1960s+] (US) an obese person. [SE *lard* + BUTT *n.*[1] (1)]

lardhead *n.* **1** [1930s+] (US) a stupid person. **2** [1980s+] (Aus.) a fool, a simpleton. [SE *lard* + sfx. -HEAD (1)]

lard-king *n.* [late 19C] (US) one who has made their fortune through the processing and selling of pork products.

lardo *n.* [1980s+] (US) a fat person, usu. used in direct address. [SE *lard* + sfx. -O]

lardy-dardy *adj.* [late 19C] affected, supercilious, foppish. [LA-DI-DAH *adj.*]

lardy-dardy *v.* [late 19C] to act in a supercilious manner. [LARDY-DARDY *adj.*]

lare *see* LAIR *n.*

lareover/layer-over/layover *n.* [late 17C–18C] a word that is substituted for one that is considered indecent. [it is 'laid over' the taboo term]

lare up *see* LAIR UP.

large/large one *n.* [1970s+] (US) $1000, usu. as *15 large ones* etc.

large *adj.* **1** [1930s–40s] (US Black) successful, exciting (cf. LIVE LARGE). **2** [1950s+] (W.I./Rasta) respected. **3** [1990s] (US teen) impressive.

large *adv.* [mid-19C+] unrestrained, excessively enjoyable, in a self-indulgent manner (cf. LIVE LARGE); thus *dress large*, to dress in an ostentatious manner; *play large*, to gamble heavily; *talk large*, to boast.

large dooey *n.* [1920s–30s] a large cup of tea. [DOOE; the 'cuppa' cost 2d., but E.P. notes the typical café menu, 'tea 1d, large do. (i.e. ditto) 2d']

large for *adj.* [1960s+] (US) enthusiastic. [LARGE *adj.*]

large for *adv.* [1960s+] (US) enthusiastically. [LARGE *adv.*]

large-head *n.* [late 19C] (US) a drunkard. [SE *large* + sfx. -HEAD (1)]

large house *n.* [mid–late 19C] the workhouse (cf. BIG HOUSE *n.*[1]).

large one *see* LARGE *n.*

large order *n.* [1900s–50s] a serious amount, a major demand (cf. TALL ORDER).

largie *n.* [1970s+] (W.I./Bdos.) a 750ml (26fl oz) bottle of rum (cf. BIGGIE *n.*).

lark *n.*[1] **1** [early 19C+] any form of activity, occupation. **2** [early 19C+] a frolic, a game; thus *larkiness*, a propensity for such pleasures; *larkish*, *larksome*, *larky*, frolicking around or 'up for' such amusements. [? northern dial. *lake*, to play (although its Yorks. pron. might well have sounded more like 'lark') or SE *skylark*, to play tricks, to indulge in rough horse-play]

lark/larky *n.*[2] [mid–late 19C] (US) a fellow, a man. [play on BIRD *n.*[2] (1)]

lark *v.* **1** [19C] to play tricks, to play around. **2** [19C] to masturbate. **3** [mid-19C] to tease. [LARK *n.*[1] (2)]

larker *n.* [mid-19C] one who is given to enjoying themselves at others' expense. [LARK *v.* (1), (3)]

larkin *n.* [early–mid-17C] a very strong, spiced punch, created in the Raj. [Y&B 'are in the dark' as to the origin; they suggest (1) Robert *Larkin* (*fl.* early 17C) an employee of the East India Co.; (2) a ref. in Hakluyt to '*larnike* = drinke', which takes them to Javan *larih*, to pledge, to invite to drink at an entertainment + Malay *larih-larahan*, mutual pledging to drink]

larking *n.*[1] [late 18C–19C] fellatio, cunnilingus. [Grose included the term in his first edn. (1785) as 'a lascivious practice that will not bear explanation'; he omitted it from subsequent edns. It reappears in F&H, who label it 'venery' and define it as 'irrumation'. E.P., in his edition of Grose's 3rd edn. (1796), notes its absence and glosses it as 'irrumation, cunnilingism']

larking *n.*[2] [19C] **1** fun, enjoyment; thus *down to larking*, the excuse offered by one who claims that they were convicted unfairly. **2** masturbation. [LARK *v.*]

larky *see* LARK *n.*[2].

larky-boy *n.* [20C] (Irish) a mischief-maker. [LARK *n.*[1] (2)]

larney *see* LAANIE.

larrikin *n.* [mid-19C+] (orig. Aus.) a rascal, a villain, a Bohemian, one who acts without regard for conventions; thus *larrikin push*, a street gang; *larrikiness/larrikina*, a female larrikin; *larrikinism* (cf. CABBAGE-TREE MOB). [? Warwickshire/Worcestershire dial. *larrikin*, a mischievous or frolicsome youth. Other theories include elision of LEARY + KINCHIN or dial. *larack*, to lark/lark about]

larro *n.* [20C] fellatio, usu. between male homosexuals. [backsl. *larro* = *oral* (*sex*)]

larrup *v.* [early 19C+] to flog, to beat, to thrash; thus *larrupping*, a sound thrashing. [? orig. Suffolk dial., ult. ? *lee-rope* or a variation on SE *lather* or *leather*, to beat + *wallop*]

larruping/tad-larruping *adj.* [early 19C+] (US) very good, excellent, esp. of food. [fig. use of LARRUP *v.*; cf. LASHINGS]

larry *n.*[1] [mid-19C–1900s] (US) deception. [? LAIRY; LEERY]

larry *n.*[2] [20C] (Irish) a fool. [Irish *learaire*, a lounger, an idler]

larry-doo *n.* [late 19C] (Aus.) a thrashing. [GIVE SOMEONE LARRY DOOLEY]

Larry Dugan's eye water *n.* [late 18C–19C] blacking. [*Larry Dugan*, a well-known Dublin shoe-black]

larstins/larstings *n.* [1910s+] (Aus.) elastic-sided boots. [? abbr. SE *elastics*]

lary *see* LAIRY.

las *n.* [1970s+] (S.Afr.) money, esp. as a loan or a contribution. [colloq. Afk. *las*, to increase]

laser lips *n.* [1970s+] (US campus) a person with orthodontic braces (cf. METAL-MOUTH; TIN GRIN; TINSEL TEETH; TWINKLE TEETH).

lash *n.*[1] **1** [late 18C] (US) a sword. **2** [1910s+] (Aus.) violence. **3** [1920s+] (Aus.) a trick. **4** [1920s+] (Aus./Irish) a try, an attempt; thus *give it a lash*, to have a try. [SE *lash*, a whip]

lash *n.*[2] [1980s+] alcohol. [var. on LUSH *n.*[1]]

lash *v.*[1] [1950s] (W.I.) to have sexual intercourse, esp. in a vigorous manner (cf. LASHER *n.*[2]). [SE *lash*, to whip]

lash *v.*[2] [1980s+] (N.Z. Und) to fail to humour a debt. [SE *lashes*, neglect in the performance of a legal duty]

lash *v.*[3] [1990s] (US) to urinate. [? SLASH *v.*[4]]

lasher *n.*[1] [20C] (Irish) an attractive woman, a beauty. [? SE *luscious*]

lasher *n.*[2] [1950s] (W.I.) a womanizer, a sexual athlete (cf. COUNT LASHER; LASH LARUE). [LASH *v.*[1]]

lasher *n.*[3] [1980s+] (N.Z. Und) one who does not pay their debts. [LASH *v.*[2]]

lash in v. [20C] (Irish) to spend money without restraint. [SE *lash out*]

lashings n. [mid-19C+] (orig. US) lots, an abundance; thus [1930s+] (Irish) *lashings and leavings*, plenty and then some to spare. [16C SE *lashing out*, lavishing, squandering]

lash larue n. [1950s] (W.I.) a womanizer, a sexual athlete (cf. COUNT LASHER). [LASH v.[1], but also as pun on proper name of US entertainer *Lash LaRue* 'King of the Bullwhip']

lashool adj. [late 19C] (tinker) pleasant. [Shelta]

lash-up n. [late 19C+] an object, organization, idea etc that is essentially amateur and homemade, but adequate for the time being. [orig. naut.]

las mujercitas n. [1960s+] (drugs) psilocybin. [fig. use of Sp. 'little wives'; ? the shape of the mushrooms resembles small breasts]

lason sa daga n. [1980s+] (drugs) LSD (cf. A n.[3]). [parallel initials but ety. unknown]

lassitudinarian n. [late 19C] a constitutionally lazy person. [SE *lassitude*, laziness + pun on *valetudinarian*]

last n.[1] [early 19C+] the end of one's relationship with someone, or dealings with something; thus *you've not heard the last of this* ... .

last n.[2] [1900s] a person's most recent comment, joke or escapade (cf. LATEST).

last bit of the family plate n. [late 19C] the last silver coin in one's pocket.

last-call look n. [1980s+] (US campus) the desperate, searching look that comes over men who hear the call for 'last orders' and have still not found a woman to take home.

last card of the pack n. **1** [mid-19C–1910s] the human back. **2** [20C] dismissal from employment. [rhy. sl.; (2) *last card in the pack* = SACK n.[3]]

last debt n. [1940s] (US Black) death; thus *pay one's last debt*, to die.

last farewell/goodbye/muster/round-up n. [20C] death.

last heartbeat n. [1940s] (US Black) a lover, a sweetheart. [? an exaggerated phr. of love; 'I will love you until my last heartbeat']

last mile n. [1930s+] (US prison) the final walk of a condemned man from death row to the execution chamber (cf. LAST WALTZ).

last muster see LAST FAREWELL.

last out n. [1940s] (US Black) death.

last round-up see LAST FAREWELL.

last shake of the bag n. [19C+] one's youngest child. [BALL-BAG n. (1) + bingo imagery]

last waltz n. [20C] (US prison) a condemned man's final walk to the execution chamber (cf. LAST MILE).

lasty adj. [20C] (Irish) lasting, enduring.

lat see LATS.

latch n.[1] [late 18C–mid-19C] (US) a buckle or breast-pin. [i.e. it secures one's clothes]

latch n.[2] [1960s–70s] (US Black) a parasite, a beggar. [SE *latch on to* + *leech*]

latch v. **1** [early 18C–19C] (Und.) to let in. **2** [1950s] (US campus) to embrace.

latched adj. [1930s+] (US) married.

latch for the gate to your front yard n. [1930s–40s] (US Black) fly buttons or a collar pin (cf. LATCH n.[1]).

latch-key n. [late 19C] (Irish police) a crowbar. [its use when evicting defaulting tenants]

latch on v. [1910s+] to understand, to 'pick up on'.

latchpan n. [mid-19C] the lower lip; thus *hang one's latch-pan*, to sulk, to pout. [SE *latchpan*, a dripping pan, lit. a 'catching pan']

late adj.[1] [1960s+] of a woman, whose menstrual period has failed to occur at the expected time.

late adj.[2] [1980s+] (US campus) not catching the punch line of a joke until some time after the joke was told.

late! excl. [1990s] (US teen) see you later! (cf. LATER!).

late bird n. [late 19C] one who tends to get up late (cf. EARLY BIRD n.[1]). [SE *late* + BIRD n.[3]]

late black n. [1930s–40s] (US Black) a very dark night, with neither moon nor stars.

late-night n. [1980s+] (US campus) a party, usually at a fraternity house, that does not start until after the bars and clubs close.

later!/later on!/lates! excl. [1940s+] (orig. US Black) see you later! goodbye!

later for that phr. [1940s+] (orig. US Black) a phr. of dismissal, 'I can't be bothered (now)'.

later for you! excl. [1940s+] (orig. US Black) shut up! go away! to hell with it! (cf. LATER!).

later on! see LATER!

later, tater phr. [1970s] (US campus) a farewell (cf. LATE!; LATER!).

lates! see LATER!

latest n. [1900s] a person's most recent comment, joke, escapade etc (cf. LAST n.[2]).

latest hot drop n. [1950s+] (Aus.) the latest trend or fashion.

latest thing on the beach phr. [1950s] (Aus.) a general phr. of approval.

lath and plaster n. [mid-19C] a master, an employer. [rhy. sl.]

lather/lathering n.[1] [late 18C–late 19C] a scolding, a beating. [SE in 20C]

lather n.[2] [19C–1900s] semen.

lather v. [late 18C–late 19C] **1** to thrash. **2** to defeat. [SE in 20C]

lather a bar of soap, to phr. [1920s–50s] (US) to masturbate.

lathered adj. [1910s–40s] (Aus.) drunk. [SE *lather*, a state of agitation]

lathering see LATHER n.[1].

lather-maker n. [19C] the vagina. [LATHER n.[2]]

lat-house see LATS.

Latin n. [mid-17C] alicante wine (cf. ENGLISH n.[1]; SPANISH n.[2]). [SE *Latin*, one of the communities in Europe e.g. Spain, the manufacturer of *alicante*]

Latin mystery n. [20C] a doctor's prescription. [the medical Lat. in which it is written]

latitat n. [mid-16C–mid-19C] an attorney, a lawyer. [Lat. *latitare*, to lie concealed; thus legal jargon *latitat*, 'a writ which supposed the defendant to lie concealed and which summoned him to answer in the King's Bench' (*OED*)]

latro! excl. [1990s] (US campus) farewell. ['Italianized' version of LATER!]

lats/lat/lat-house n. [1920s+] (orig. milit.) a *lat*rine. [abbr.]

lattie/latty see LETTY.

laugh and joke n. [late 19C–1950s] a smoke. [rhy. sl.]

laugh and scratch, to phr. [1980s+] (drugs) to inject a drug, usu. heroin. [what one does when the injection takes effect]

laugh and titter n. [20C] a pint of beer. [rhy. sl. *laugh and titter* = bitter (beer)]

laughing adj. [1930s+] (orig. milit.) safe, secure; usu. in such phr. as *you're laughing* or *I'm laughing*.

laughing academy/farm/house/school n. [1940s+] (US) a psychiatric institution (cf. FUNNY FARM).

laughing boy n. [20C] an ironic nickname given to someone who seems consistently, or even temporarily, miserable and in low spirits. [? Gilbert & Sullivan song 'A Laughing Boy But Yesterday' in *The Yeoman of the Guard* (1888), about a miserable person]

laughing farm see LAUGHING ACADEMY.

laughing gear/tackle n. [1970s+] the mouth. [SE *laughing* + GEAR n.[1] (4)/SE *tackle*]

laughing grass n. [1950s+] (orig. US drugs) marijuana (cf. LAUGHING WEED). [SE *laughing* + GRASS n.⁴; i.e. its effects]

laughing house/school see LAUGHING ACADEMY.

laughing-sided boot n. [1930s+] (Aus.) an elastic-sided boot. [adopted from Aborigine mispron. of SE]

laughing soup/water n. [20C] (US) an alcoholic drink, esp. champagne (cf. BUBBLY WATER).

laughing tackle see LAUGHING GEAR.

laughing water see LAUGHING SOUP.

laughing weed n. [1920s+] (US drugs) marijuana (cf. LAUGHING GRASS). [SE *laughing* + WEED n.¹ (4); i.e. its effects]

laugh like a drain, to phr. [1940s+] to laugh uproariously. [the supposed equivalence of the laughter and gurgling of water down a drain]

laughs and smiles n. [20C] (Aus.) haemorrhoids. [rhy. sl. = piles]

laugh that off! phr. [1910s–60s] (US) a sarcastic retort meaning that the listener will have to take one seriously.

launch n. [late 18C–19C] childbirth, esp. the actual labour. [SE but with ? implication of dial. *launch*, to groan]

launching pad n. [1950s–60s] (US drugs) a room, flat or house where drug addicts can go to inject (cf. BASING GALLERY). [SE *launch* + PAD n.² (2); pun]

launch the tadpoles, to phr. [1990s] to masturbate. [under a microscope sperm resemble tadpoles]

launder v. [1970s+] to decriminalize money that has been gained through criminal activities by 'washing' it through a legitimate business, such as a casino or bank (cf. DIRTY MONEY). [the 'dirty' money is invested or deposited and is withdrawn 'clean' of any association with crime]

laundress n. [19C] a prostitute. [euph.]

laundromat n. [1980s+] a business, such as a casino, in which money that has been gained through criminal activities can be decriminalized or LAUNDERed. [SE *Laundromat*, a 'do-it-yourself' laundry shop]

laundry n. (US) **1** [1950s+] clothes that are being worn; thus *drop one's laundry*, to undress. **2** [1970s] a woman.

laundryman n. [late 19C+] (US) a Chinese man. [the stereotyping in the USA of Chinese immigrants as laundry workers]

lauras n. [1930s+] (Can.) chocolates. [a brand of chocolates made by the firm *Laura* Secord, named for a heroine of the war of 1812]

Laurel and Hardy n. [20C] a Bacardi (rum). [rhy. sl.; ult. comedians Stan *Laurel* (1890–1965) and Oliver *Hardy* (1892–1957)]

lav n. [1910s+] *lavatory*. [abbr.]

lavender adj. [1920s+] (orig. US) a euph. for homosexual and anything referring to homosexuals (cf. PINK adj.³).

lavender boy n. [1920s+] a male homosexual. [LAVENDER + SE *boy*]

lavender cove n. [19C] a pawnbroker. [LAY UP IN LAVENDER + COVE]

lavender cowboy n. [1990s] a male homosexual. [LAVENDER + SE *cowboy*]

lavender law n. [1920s+] legal issues, practice and study pertaining to the gay and lesbian community. [LAVENDER + SE *law*]

laverick see LABRICK.

la vida loca phr. [1960s+] (US gang) the gangster lifestyle of the Mexican barrios of the US, esp. Los Angeles. [Sp. *la vida loca*, the crazy life; coined by the Mexican immigrant gangs, starting with the *pachucos* of the 1930s–40s and the *cholos* of 1950s–60s, who initiated the gang style, subsequently picked up by Black teens and their elders]

lavo n. [1920s+] (Aus.) the *lavatory*. [abbr. + sfx. -O]

la vogue n. [1980s+] (US campus) a restroom or public lavatory for women. [? *Vogue* magazine; i.e. the use of the restroom for waking up, etc.]

lavvy n. [20C] (mainly Scot.) a *lavatory*. [abbr.]

law n.¹ [mid-late 16C] (Und.) a type of criminal activity (cf. FIGGING LAW; LAY n.⁴ (2); LIFTING LAW; VINCENT'S LAW). [OF *lei*; ult. Lat. *legem*, law]

law, the n.² [early 19C+] (orig. US) the police. [metonymy]

law n.³ [1940s+] a police officer, e.g. *Mark was busted by half a dozen law*. [the article is deliberately omitted]

law, the n.⁴ [1970s+] (US Black) the penis. [macho imagery]

law! excl. [late 16C+] a mild excl. of surprise or amazement (cf. LAWKS!). [euph. for SE *Lord!*]

law dog/hound n. [late 19C+] (US) a police officer. [note DOG n.⁷ (4)]

lawdy!/lordy! excl. [mid-19C+] a mild excl.

lawful blanket n. [19C] a wife. [SE *lawful* + fig. use of *blanket*]

lawful jam n. [late 19C–1900s] one's wife. [SE *lawful* + JAM n.³]

lawful lady n. [mid-19C–1920s] (US Black) one's legal wife.

lawful picture n. [17C–18C] a coin, usu. in pl., money. [the engraving on coins or picture on notes]

law hound see LAW DOG.

lawks!/lawk!/la! excl. [late 18C+] used as a euph. for SE *Lord* in a variety of mild oaths, esp. *lawks-a-mercy!*, Lord have mercy! [note synon. US South *lawsy*]

lawks-a-mussy! excl. [late 19C+] a mild oath, lit. 'Lord have mercy!'

lawless adj. [20C] (W.I.) **1** irresponsible, troublesome. **2** of a woman, promiscuous, unrestrainedly vulgar. **3** of speech, smutty, dirty. **4** sitting with the legs sprawled apart.

lawless as a town bull phr. [late 17C–early 19C] of a man, extremely promiscuous. [TOWN BULL]

lawman n. [1950s+] a law-enforcement officer.

lawn n.¹ [early 19C] (Und.) a white cambric handkerchief. [SE *lawn*, a form of fine linen, resembling cambric]

lawn n.² [1950s+] (gay) pubic hair, and if it is shaved it is a *mowed lawn* (cf. BUSH n.⁴).

lawn mower n. [1930s] (US Und.) a machine gun.

law sakes! excl. [mid-19C+] (US) a mild oath, lit. 'for the Lord's sake!'

law's-a-me! excl. [late 19C] (US) a mild oath, 'Lord save me!'

law sharp n. [late 19C–1930s] (US) a lawyer. [SE *law* + SHARP n.¹]

law station n. [1950s] a police station. [LAW n.² + SE *station*]

lawt adj. [mid-19C] tall. [backsl.]

law you there! excl. [17C] a general oath.

lay n.¹ [17C] (Und.) buttermilk. [Fr. *lait*, milk]

lay n.² **1** [mid-17C; 1920s+] (orig. US) sexual intercourse. **2** [1930s+] a person with whom one has sexual intercourse, or a promiscuous woman, usu. qualified as *a good lay*, *a bad lay*, *an easy lay* etc. [LAY v.¹]

lay n.³ [18C] a chance. [SE *lay*, to wager]

lay n.⁴ **1** [early 18C–1940s] any form of enterprise, business or occupation. **2** [early 18C+] (Und.) any kind of criminal activity, usually modified by a participle that denotes the speciality, e.g. CHIVING LAY; CLOUTING LAY; CRACK LAY; KID LAY (cf. LAW). **3** [late 18C–late 19C] the life and practice of crime as in *the lay* (cf. ON THE LAY). **4** [early 19C] stolen goods. **5** [late 19C–1940s] (US) one's hidden intention or aim. **6** [mid-19C–1950s] (Und.) a place considered for robbing. **7** [mid-19C–1950s] (US) a state of affairs. [OF *lei*, law, which itself is the root of the synon. LAW n.¹]

lay n.⁵ [mid-19C] **1** a piece, a portion, e.g. a *lay of pannum*, a piece of bread. **2** goods. [? SE *lay*, to place; i.e. that which is laid on the table, counter etc]

lay n.⁶ **1** [1910s–30s] (US) a place to sleep, a bed. **2** [1920s–30s] (US drugs) the act of lying down and smoking opium.

lay v.¹ **1** [? mid-17C–mid-18C; 19C+] to have sexual intercourse with. **2** [1960s+] to make oneself available for sexual relations.

lay v.² [late 17C+] to watch for, to survey (cf. ON THE LAY). [abbr. SE *lay in wait*]

lay v.³ **1** [mid-19C–1950s] (US) to knock someone unconscious (cf. LAY OUT v.¹). **2** [20C] (US Black) to over-indulge in drugs or drink to such an extent that one is laid on one's back. **3** [1970s] (US Black) to idle, to relax (cf. LAY BACK IN THE CUT).

lay/lay paper v.⁴ [late 19C–1900s] (US Und.) to pass counterfeit money or stolen cheques.

lay a batch/patch, to phr. [1960s+] (US) to make tyre marks by accelerating fast in a car (cf. LAY 'EM DOWN v.²).

layabout n. [1930s+] a voluntarily unemployed male, usu. involved in some minor criminality.

lay a/in water, to phr. [15C–early 17C] to put off judgement, esp. to put it off for too long. [SE *lay a/in water*, to render worthless]

lay a leg on/over see LIFT A LEG ON.

lay an egg, to phr. [1920s+] **1** to fail completely, esp. in show business. **2** (Aus.) to worry (cf. HAVE KITTENS). [RAF sl. *lay an egg*, drop a bomb. The link with US BOMB n.¹ (5) may be coincidental. Note *Variety* headline the morning after the 1929 Crash, 'Wall Street Lays an Egg']

lay a patch see LAY A BATCH.

lay a rap on, to phr. [20C] (orig. US) to persuade. [LAY ON + RAP n.⁴]

lay back n. [1980s+] (drugs) a depressant. [LAY BACK v.]

lay back/low/up v. [1960s+] (US Black) **1** to relax (cf. LAY BACK IN THE CUT). **2** to do nothing specific. **3** to have sexual intercourse (cf. LAY v.¹).

lay back and front shops into one, to phr. [late 18C–early 19C] to remove the physical division between the vagina and the anus (cf. LAY PIT AND BOXES INTO ONE). [thus described by Grose (1785); presumably, since he refers to 'an operation in midwifery' he means episiotomy, the widening of the vulval orifice to facilitate childbirth]

lay back in the cut, to phr. [1960s+] (US Black) **1** to lie in ambush, whether actually or fig. **2** to relax.

lay bones v. [20C] (US juv.) to act as a look-out, to warn of the approach of an adult. [i.e. one is standing still]

lay bread on v. [1930s+] to give some money to. [LAY ON + BREAD n.¹ (2)]

lay bricks v. [1930s] (US) to have sexual intercourse (cf. LAY SOME PIPE). [LAY v.¹]

lay-by n. [20C] (Aus.) a deposit on and the subsequent purchasing by instalments of an article in a shop. [the shop 'lays' the article 'by'; i.e. on one side]

lay by the heels, to phr. [18C–mid-19C] **1** to place in the stocks. **2** to imprison.

lay cane upon Abel, to phr. [late 18C] to beat, to thrash. [pun on the biblical brothers *Cain* and *Abel*]

lay chick/chickie see KEEP CHICK.

lay/sit chilly v. [1970s+] (US) to lie low. [SE *lay/sit* + CHILLY adj.]

lay dead v. [1960s+] (US Black) **1** to wait. **2** to do nothing, to stop everything.

lay-down n.¹ [mid-19C–1930s] a sleep, a place to sleep.

lay-down n.² [1930s+] (US) a certainty. [one can lay down money on it]

lay down v.¹ [20C] (US prison) to place in the punishment cells. [punishment cells were so cramped there was barely enough room to stand upright]

lay down v.² [20C] to outline, to present a theory (cf. LAY ON; LAY OUT v.¹).

lay down v.³ [1970s+] to accept, to acquiesce.

lay down! excl. [1920s–30s] (US) be quiet! shut up!

lay-down joint n. [1930s+] (US drugs) a place to smoke opium (cf. LAY n.⁶). [SE *lay down* + JOINT n.³ (3)]

lay-down merchant n. [1950s+] a criminal who specializes in the distribution (*laying-down*) of counterfeit banknotes. [LAY v.⁴ + MERCHANT]

lay down one's bone, to phr. [20C] (Ulster) to work very hard. [synon. SE *put one's back into*]

lay down one's knife and fork, to phr. [mid-19C+] to die (cf. HAND IN ONE'S DINNER-PAIL).

lay/lie down on the job, to phr. [1920s+] (orig. Aus.) **1** to act lazily. **2** to do a job badly.

lay down some cow, to phr. [1970s+] (US Black) to walk, esp. to walk so much that one's shoes are worn out. [the leather soles]

lay down the law, to phr. [mid-18C+] to make dogmatic statements, esp. during an argument.

lay 'em down v.¹ (US) [1930s–40s] to die. [one 'lays down' one's body]

lay 'em down v.² (US) [1940s+] to drive very fast. [the pressing down of the accelerator]

layer n. [1930s–50s] (US) a currency note.

layer-over see LAREOVER.

lay five see SLAP FIVE.

lay for v. [mid-19C+] (US) to wait for someone, invariably with the intention of harming them. [SE *lay in wait*]

lay in v.¹ [late 19C+] **1** to attack. **2** to eat voraciously (cf. LAY INTO).

lay in v.² [1950s+] (US prison) to stay in one's cell when one might usually be out of it.

layin' and playin' phr. [1970s+] (US Black) of a man, idling around the house, usu. with one's female partner.

laying hen n. [20C] a farmer's wife who has a job. [her contribution to the farm economy]

lay/cast in someone's dish, to phr. [mid-16C–mid-19C] to object to a characteristic in someone else. [var. on synon. SE phr. meaning to impute to, to charge upon]

lay into v. [mid-19C+] **1** to attack physically. **2** to start eating in a voracious manner (cf. LAY IN v.¹).

lay in water see LAY A WATER.

lay iron v. [1930s–50s] (US Black) to tap-dance, esp. as a professional. [the metal cleats on a tap-dancer's shoes]

lay it v. [1930s–50s] (US) to play jazz music well.

lay it on v. [1930s+] (US) to act or work efficiently or energetically.

lay it on someone v. [1930s+] (orig. US) **1** to criticize, to berate. **2** to inform, to pass on information.

lay it on the line, to phr.¹ [1940s] (US) to have sexual intercourse. [ext. of LAY v.¹ (1)]

lay/put it on the line, to phr.² [1940s+] to be absolutely honest, to declare one's feelings, one's attitude.

lay it on thick/with a trowel, to phr. [mid-19C+] to exaggerate, to make too much of a fuss. [painting or plastering imagery]

lay it out v. [1960s+] of a homosexual of either sex, to admit and poss. flaunt one's sexual preference (cf. LAY IT ON THE LINE phr.¹).

lay/lie low v.¹ [late 19C+] to hide oneself away, to keep a low profile.

lay low v.² see LAY BACK v.

lay me in the gutter n. [1910s–20s] butter. [rhy. sl.]

lay-off n. (US) **1** [late 19C+] a respite from work. **2** [1930s–40s] a stop-over during a long journey. [(1) is now SE]

lay off v. **1** [mid-19C–1920s] (orig. US) to take time off work. **2** [20C] (US) to stop being annoying or interfering. **3** [1920s+] (orig. US) to abstain from using or consuming something.

lay off! excl. [20C] a warning, an excl. telling someone to stop doing something. [LAY OFF v. (2)]

lay off to someone v. [1910s–20s] to make an attempt to impress someone.

lay off with v. [1940s–50s] (Aus.) to have sex with. [ext. LAY v.¹ (1)]

lay on v. [1930s+] (orig. US Black) **1** to give, esp. drugs. **2** to tell, to impose facts upon.

lay one on someone, to phr. [1960s+] (US) to hit or beat someone.

lay one's legs on one's neck/the ground, to phr. [17C–late 19C] to run off, to leave very quickly.

lay one's racket, to phr. [1930s–40s] (US Black) **1** to reveal one's real agenda, usu. a confidence trick or hoax. **2** to tease. [SE lay(out) + RACKET n.¹ (1)]

lay someone trigging, to phr. [late 18C–mid-19C] to knock someone down. [? SE trig, the starting line of a race or that from which bowlers deliver the bowl; or SE trig, in good physical condition, strong, sound]

lay/be on the jack, to phr. [19C] to beat or scold severely (cf. ON THE JACK).

lay on the shelf, to phr. [late 18C–19C] to pawn something (cf. LAY UP IN LAVENDER). [an ironic ref. to SE use, to put away for later]

lay on to be v. [1930s+] to pretend to be, to claim to be. [LAY ON v.]

layout n.¹ [mid-19C–1920s] (US) an association of persons, such as a gang or team.

layout n.² (US) [mid-19C–1950s] **1** a plan, a scheme. **2** [late 19C–1950s] an apartment, a house.

layout n.³ [late 19C–1980s] the various accoutrements – pipe, box, needle etc – required for smoking opium (cf. KIT n.⁶; LAY n.⁶; OUTFIT n.²; WORKS n.³). [the 'kit' is 'laid out' in front of the user before smoking]

layout n.⁴ [1990s] (US Black) an undemanding, easy job.

lay out v.¹ **1** [early 19C–1910s] (US) to defeat or overcome. **2** [mid-19C–1940s] (US) to kill. **3** [mid-19C+] (orig. US) to knock someone out in a fight. **4** [1900s–60s] (US) to scold or reprimand. **5** [1920s–30s] (US Black) to stop what one is doing, esp. suddenly. **6** [1920s–30s] (US Black) to avoid someone, to step aside. **7** [1960s–70s] (US) to amaze or astound.

lay out v.² [1970s] (US campus) to sunbathe.

layout across the drink n. [1940s] (US Black) Europe. [LAYOUT n.² (2) + DRINK n.¹]

lay out cold, to phr. [early 19C+] (orig. US) **1** to knock out. **2** to astound, to amaze (cf. KNOCK COLD v.).

lay out in lavender, to phr. [1940s+] (US) to scold severely, to indulge in a verbal battle.

lay out like a carpet, to phr. [1900s–50s] (US) to knock unconscious. [ext. of LAY OUT v.¹ (3)]

layover n. see LAREOVER.

lay over v.¹ [mid-19C–1920s] (US) to surpass, to excel.

lay over v.² [late 19C] (US) to miss, to allow to pass by, to postpone.

lay paper see LAY v.⁴.

lay pit and boxes into one, to phr. [late 18C–early 19C] to remove the physical division between the vagina and the anus (cf. LAY BACK AND FRONT SHOPS INTO ONE). [orig. theatrical jargon. 'A simile borrowed from the playhouse, when for the benefit of some favourite player, the pit and boxes are laid together' (Grose)]

lay rubber v. [1970s+] (US) to drive off at speed, spinning the wheels as one accelerates away. [the rubber leaves a mark on the road]

lay some on me! excl. [1950s+] (US Black) an invitation to swap ritual hand slaps as a form of greeting.

lay some pipe, to phr. [1930s+] (US) to have sexual intercourse, whether vaginal or anal (cf. LAY BRICKS).

lay the dust, to phr. [1910s+] to take a drink of alcohol. [the image of wetting one's dusty throat]

lay the hip, to phr. [1930s–70s] (US) to smoke opium. [the usu. posture for smoking opium is to lie on one's side]

lay the leg, to phr. [1910s+] **1** to have sexual intercourse. **2** (US prison) to sodomize. [ext. of LAY v.¹ (1)]

lay the lip, to phr. [1970s+] (US) to fellate.

lay them down v. [mid–late 19C] to play cards.

lay the make/make on, to phr. [1960s+] (US) to become sexually aggressive (cf. PUT THE MAKE ON). [SE lay + MAKE n.³ (2)]

lay/roll them in the aisles, to phr. [1940s+] (orig. theatre) to be a great success, to reduce people to uncontrollable laughter (cf. ROLLING IN THE AISLES).

lay the note, to phr. [1920s–70s] (US Und.) to swindle, to short-change (cf. LAY v.⁴).

lay the scene on, to phr. [1950s+] to explain, to outline a situation. [LAY ON v. + SCENE]

lay the stool's foot in water, to phr. [18C–mid-19C] to prepare for the arrival of guests. [ety. unknown]

lay tight v. [1940s+] (US Black) to stay calm, to retain one's grip of a situation.

lay two ways, to phr. [1960s–70s] (US Black) to short-change or otherwise rob someone in an ostensibly honest exchange of money.

lay-up n. **1** [late 19C] a drink of alcohol. **2** [1930s] a term in jail.

lay up v.¹ **1** [late 19C] (US) to die. **2** [1930s+] (US) to hide (cf. LAY DEAD). **3** [1930s+] to rest.

lay up v.² see LAY BACK v.

lay up in lavender, to phr. **1** [late 17C–18C] to pawn. **2** [early 19C–1910s] to put out of harm's way. [ironic use of SE lay up in lavender, to put aside carefully for future use. Lavender was then, as now, kept with stored linen and other fabrics]

lay up one's heels see KICK UP ONE'S HEELS phr.¹.

lay up with v. [1920s+] (US) to have sexual intercourse with. [LAY v.¹]

laziosis n. [20C] (W.I./Guyn./Belz.) laziness. [SE lazy + a play on sfx. -osis used in words that name illnesses, e.g. tuberculosis]

lazy as a Maori dog phr. [1950s] (N.Z.) very lazy (cf. CUNNING AS A MAORI DOG). [racially derog. comparison]

lazy as Joe the marine phr. [19C] a phr. used of a notably lazy person (cf. LAZY AS LUDLAM'S DOG). [pvb. as lazy as Joe the Marine who laid down his musket to sneeze]

lazy as Ludlam's dog phr. [mid-19C] a phr. used of a lazy person (cf. LAZY AS JOE THE MARINE). [pvb. as lazy as Ludlam's dog, which leaned its head against the wall to bark]

lazy body n. [1980s+] (W.I./UK Black teen) a slob, someone who is averse to physical exercise and exertion.

lazybones n. **1** [late 16C+] an idler, a loafer. **2** [late 18C–19C] an implement resembling a pair of tongs that old, ill or fat people use to pick things up.

lazyboots n. [19C] a lazy person. [on the pattern of SLYBOOTS]

lazy-dazy adj. [1940s+] (Aus.) lazy.

lazy Laurence/Lawrence/Larrence n. [mid-18C–1900s] the embodiment of laziness; thus [19C] get Laurence, Laurence has got me, I am feeling lazy; touch of Laurence, laziness; have Laurence on one's back, to be lazy. [the probably apocryphal tale of the martyred St Lawrence who refused to make a sound as he was roasted to death, causing his executioner to suggest that far from being stoic, he was too lazy]

lazy-legs n. [19C] an idler, a loafer (cf. LAZYBONES).

lazy lob n. [20C] a semi-erect penis. [SE lazy + LOB n.²]

lazy-man's load n. [late 18C–19C] an excessively heavy load carried to avoid a second trip.

l.b. *n.* [1960s+] (drugs) one pound weight (cf. OZ). [1*lb*; pron. 'el-bee']

l.b.j. *n.* [1960s+] (drugs) **1** LSD (cf. A n.³). **2** phencyclidine (cf. ACE n.³). **3** heroin. [? joc. ref. to US President *Lyndon Baines Johnson* (1908–73)]

l.b.w. *see* LEG BEFORE WICKET.

l.c. *adj.* [1990s] *lower class* (cf. L.M.C.; M.C.; U.C.; W.C.). [abbr.]

l.d. *n.* [1960s+] (US Black) a Cadillac *Eld*orado. [abbr.; pron. 'el-dee']

lead/lead plum/lead sandwich *n.* [mid-19C+] (US) **1** a bullet. **2** a gun (cf. LEAD-PUSHER; LEADEN PILL).

lead a cat and dog life, to *phr.* [mid-16C+] of a married couple, to quarrel incessantly (cf. AGREE LIKE CAT AND DOG).

lead a gay life, to *phr.* [mid–late 19C] to work as a prostitute, to lead an immoral life. [GAY *adj.*¹ (1)]

lead apes in hell, to *phr.* [late 16C–mid-19C] to become an old maid; thus *ape-leader*, an old maid. ['Rather thou shouldest leade a lyfe to thine owne lyking in earthe, than ... leade Apes in Hell' (John Lyly, *Euphues*, 1579); ult. pvb. *women dying maids lead apes in hell*]

lead balloon *n.* [1950s+] (US) a failure (cf. GO DOWN LIKE A LEAD BALLOON).

lead down *v.* [1960s+] (orig. milit.) to fire at. [one uses leaden bullets]

leaden favour *see* LEADEN PILL.

Leadenhall market sportsman *n.* [late 19C] a landowner who sells game to the poulterers of London's Leadenhall Market.

leaden pill/favour *n.* [late 19C] a bullet (cf. LEAD; LEAD-PUSHER).

leadfoot *n.* [1930s+] (US) a fast driver. [LEAD FOOT v. (1)]

lead foot *v.* (US) **1** [1930s+] to drive a vehicle very fast. **2** [1950s] to move slowly and clumsily. [SE *lead + foot*; (1) refers to the heaviness of a foot on the accelerator, (2) the heaviness that slows one down]

lead-footed *adj.* [1930s+] (US) **1** speeding. **2** slow, clumsy. [LEAD FOOT v.]

leadhead *n.* [1950s+] (US) an idiot. [SE *lead* + sfx. -HEAD (1)]

leading article *n.*¹ **1** [mid–late 19C] the nose. **2** [mid-19C–1900s] the vagina.

leading article *n.*² [late 19C] the best bargain in the shop, which should lead the buyer on to a more expensive purchase.

leading card *n.* [late 17C+] an example or precedent. [card-playing jargon; the card that is led sets the initial betting standard for a round of play]

lead me to it! *excl.* [20C] a phr. used of any situation that is considered easy or enjoyable.

lead off *v.* [1930s+] (orig. milit.) to lose one's temper.

lead on, Macduff *phr.* [late 19C+] a phr. exhorting someone else to take the initiative. [corruption of 'lay on, Macduff' in Shakespeare's *Macbeth*, V:iii (1605–6)]

lead pill *n.* [mid-19C–1950s] (US) a bullet (cf. LEAD; LEADEN PILL).

lead pipe *n.* [20C] (US prison) prison-cooked spaghetti (cf. SPA-GAG-ME).

lead-pipe cinch *n.* (US) **1** [late 19C] a firm grip. **2** [late 19C+] an absolute certainty, an easy task. [the solidity of a SE *lead pipe* + CINCH n.¹ (1)]

lead plum *see* LEAD.

lead poisoning *n.* [late 19C+] (US) shotgun shells, revolver bullets, esp. when lodged in a victim's body.

lead-pusher/-spitter/-squirt *n.* [mid-19C+] (US) a gun (cf. LEAD).

lead sandwich *see* LEAD.

lead sheet *n.* [1930s–40s] (US Black) an overcoat or other outer garment. [musical jargon *lead sheet*, a sheet of music containing the melodic line and lyric only]

lead sled *n.* [1950s+] (US) a slow vehicle.

lead someone by/on/with a string, to *phr.* [late 19C+] to have someone utterly under one's control.

lead-spitter/-squirt *see* LEAD-PUSHER.

lead the llama to the lift shaft, to *phr.* [1990s] to have sexual intercourse.

lead towel *n.* **1** [mid-18C–early 19C] a pistol. **2** [early 19C] a bullet (cf. OAKEN CUDGEL).

lead up the garden path, to *phr.* [1920s+] to trick, to deceive deliberately, to tease. [the image is of luring a woman up the garden path and so out of sight of the house in order to attempt seduction]

lead with one's chin, to *phr.* [1940s+] (orig. boxing) to act incautiously, to act without restraint. [in boxing such a technique would leave one dangerously vulnerable]

leaf *n.*¹ (US) **1** [1920s–30s] a $100 bill. **2** [1920s+] a $1 bill (cf. ALFALFA n.).

leaf *n.*² (US drugs) **1** [1940s+] cocaine. **2** [1960s+] marijuana. [the plants from which they are taken]

leaf freak/peeper *n.* [1960s+] (US) a tourist drawn to New England in order to enjoy its spectacular autumn leaves. [SE *leaf* + sfx. -FREAK/SE *pepper*]

leafless tree *n.* [early–mid-19C] the gallows (cf. DEADLY NEVERGREEN).

leaf of the old author *n.* [19C] a drink, esp. of brandy (cf. LINE OF THE OLD AUTHOR). [? the *old author* being God]

leaf peeper *see* LEAF FREAK.

leak *n.*¹ *see* LEEK.

leak *n.*² [late 18C–late 19C] the female genitals.

leak *n.*³ **1** [1910s+] (orig. US) the act of urination; thus *take/spring a leak*, to urinate. **2** [1920s+] (Aus.) an informer. **3** [1930s+] (Aus.) a trick, a dodge.

leak *n.*⁴ *see* LEAKY HOLLA.

leak *v.*¹ **1** [late 16C+] to urinate. **2** [late 19C+] (US) to weep.

leak *v.*² **1** [mid-19C+] to reveal a secret unintentionally. **2** [late 19C] (US) to lie. [(1) is now SE]

leakhouse/leakery *n.* [1940s+] (Aus.) a lavatory. [LEAK n.³ (1) + SE *house*]

leaky *adj.*¹ **1** [late 17C+] unable to keep a secret. **2** [late 19C] talkative when drunk. [LEAK v.²]

leaky *adj.*² [20C] (US) tearful, weepy. [LEAK v.¹]

leaky bladder *n.* [20C] a stepladder. [rhy. sl.]

leaky holla/leak *n.* [1980s+] (drugs) phencyclidine (cf. ACE n.³). [ety. unknown]

lean *adj.*¹ [late 19C] of employment, unremunerative. [SE *lean*, *thin*]

lean *adj.*² [1990s] (drugs) under the influence of cannabis. [? abbr. LEAN AND MEAN]

lean and fat *n.* [mid-19C] a hat. [rhy. sl.]

lean/long and linger *n.* [1920s] (US) a finger. [rhy. sl.]

lean and lurch *n.* [mid-19C] a church (cf. IN THE LURCH; LEFT IN THE LURCH; ROCK AND LURCH). [rhy. sl.]

lean and mean *phr.* [1970s+] (US) **1** used to describe something that is plain but efficient. **2** fit, ready for action. [SE *lean* + MEAN adj. (3)]

lean-away *n.* [late 19C–1900s] (Aus.) a drunkard.

lean green *n.* [1970s+] (US teen) money (cf. GREEN n.²; GREENBACK n.²).

leaning house *n.* [1970s+] (US Black) a brothel or a place where illicit meetings, drug sales etc take place (cf. ACCOMMODATION HOUSE).

lean into *phr.* [20C] (Irish) to pressurize, to threaten (cf. LEAN ON v.).

lean on *v.* **1** [1920s+] (orig. US) to pressurize, to persuade, poss. with violence or threats of violence (cf. LEAN INTO). **2** [1950s+] (orig. US) to beat up. **3** [1960s+] (US Black) to disparage or ridicule.

lean over backwards *see* FALL OVER BACKWARDS.

lean trot *n.* [1960s+] (Aus.) a spell of bad luck or unfortunate experiences. [SE *lean* + TROT n.² (5)]

leap *v.* [18C–19C] to have sexual intercourse (cf. JUMP v.¹). [SE *leap*, of an animal, to copulate]

leap and you will receive *phr.* [1970s+] (US Black) a ritual challenge to a fight.

leap at a crust, to *phr.* [mid-17C–mid-18C] to be starving.

leap at a daisy, to *phr.* [mid-16C–early 17C] to be hanged. [the grass surrounding the gallows]

leap at Tyburn, to *phr.* [late 17C–early 19C] to be hanged.

leaper *n.* [1960s+] **1** (drugs) any form of stimulant, amphetamine etc. **2** a dud cheque, drawn against inadequate funds (cf. BOUNCE v.²).

leapfrog *n.* [1970s] a client who hires a number of prostitutes to play leapfrog while he watches.

leapfrog milk *n.* [1970s+] (US) the wine Liebfraumilch.

leap from the leafless tree, to *phr.* [early–mid-19C] to be hanged. [SE *leap* + LEAFLESS TREE]

leaping *adj.* [1920s–50s] (US drugs) under the influence of drugs.

leaping dominoes *n.* [1920s] (US) dice or the game of craps.

leaping house *n.* [18C] a brothel (cf. ACCOMMODATION HOUSE). [LEAP v. + SE *house*]

leaping lena *n.* [1910s–50s] (US) a small car. [its bumpy motion]

leaping lizards! *excl.* [1920s–70s] (US) an excl. expressing surprise. [coined in comic strip *L'il Orphan Annie* by Harold Gray (1894–1968)]

leap in the dark/up a ladder *n.* [18C–late 19C] sexual intercourse.

leaps *n.* [1920s–70s] (US drugs) withdrawal symptoms. [the fits that may be part of withdrawal]

leap the besom/broom/broomstick/sword, to *phr.* [17C+] to enter into a common-law marriage; no civil or religious ceremony is undertaken, but the couple 'make their vows' by jumping over a broomstick or any of the other obstacles/implements (cf. JUMP THE BROOMSTICK). [the uses are all fig. in 20C although they were once actual actions]

leap up a ladder *n. see* LEAP IN THE DARK.

leap up a ladder, to *phr.* [17C–early 18C] to be hanged (cf. TAKE A LEAP IN THE DARK).

lea-rigs *n.* [late 18C] the vagina. [SE *lea-rig*, a ridge left in grass at the end of a ploughed field]

learn a new way, to *phr.* [1960s+] of a heterosexual man, to turn to homosexuality.

learning shover *n.* [late 19C] a teacher.

learn manners in Seville, to *phr.* [1910s–20s] to learn acceptable, if rather juvenile, manners. [pun on *Seville/civil*]

learn one's Ps and Qs, to *phr.* [early–mid-19C] **1** to learn one's letters. **2** to learn manners. [(1) lit. use of SE; (2) abbr. *pleases* and *thank-yous*]

leary *adj.* **1** [late 18C+] bright and alert, and so suspicious of someone (cf. LAIRY). **2** [1920s–30s] (US Und.) of goods, damaged. [LEERY]

leary bloke *n.* [mid-19C] a showy dresser. [LEARY + BLOKE n. (1)]

leary cove *n.* [early 19C] one who is well versed in the criminal world (cf. FLY adj.; WIDE-AWAKE adj.). [LEARY adj. + COVE]

least *n.* [1950s] (US Black) a mediocre or dull person or event. [the opposite of MOST]

leather *n.¹* **1** [14C] the skin; thus *lose leather*, to rub off skin while riding. **2** [1910s–30s] (US) meat.

leather *n.²* **1** [mid-16C+] the vagina (cf. SKIN n.⁴; SKINCOAT). **2** [mid-16C+] a promiscuous woman; thus *labour leather*, to have sexual intercourse; *nothing like leather*, there is

nothing as good as sex (cf. STRETCH LEATHER). **3** [1940s+] (US) the anus.

leather *n.³* **1** [mid-18C+] a wallet. **2** [1910s–30s] (US) a whip. **3** [1920s+] (US) a holster. **4** [1920s+] (US) a shoe. **5** [1920s+] (US) a boxing glove (cf. THROW LEATHER). **6** [1920s+] (US) a saddle; thus *fork leather*, to ride a horse; *hit leather*, to ride off; *pull/hunt leather*, to grasp the saddle while riding a bucking horse. **7** [1930s] (US Und.) a pickpocket. **8** [1930s–40s] (US) a brutal kicking with a boot or shoe.

leather *adj.* [1960s+] (orig. US gay) pertaining to leather fetishism in attire and behaviour (cf. LEATHER BAR; LEATHER BOY).

leather *v.¹* [late 18C+] to beat, to kick. [LEATHER n.³ (4)]

leather *v.²* [1930s+] (gay) to perform anal intercourse. [LEATHER n.² (3)]

leather and prunella *phr.* [late 19C] something to which one is utterly indifferent. [a corrupt use of Alexander Pope's lines 'Worth makes the man, and want of it, the fellow, The rest is all but leather or prunella' (*Essay on Man* (1734) iv. 204). The lines refer to the way in which clothes – leather for a cobbler, prunella for a parson's worsted gown – can define social standing. Ware defines it as 'flimsy' and suggests the ety. f. phr. all *lather and prunella*, whipped cream and damson purée, a very light dessert]

leather bar *n.* [1960s+] (US gay) a bar frequented by leather fetishists and sadomasochistic male homosexuals. [LEATHER adj.]

leather-bottom *n.* [20C] a civil servant who is totally dedicated to work and thus never leaves their desk.

leather boy *n.* [1960s+] (gay) a male leather fetishist homosexual. [LEATHER adj.]

leather-dresser *n.* [19C] the penis (cf. LEATHER-STRETCHER).

leathered *adj.* [1990s] having consumed a large volume of alcohol in a very short time. [fig. use of LEATHER v.¹]

leather-face *n.* [late 19C] (US) an emotionless individual.

leather freak *n.* [1960s+] (US) a leather fetishist. [SE *leather* + sfx. -FREAK]

leather glommer *n.* [1930s] (US) a pickpocket's assistant. [the pickpocket 'lifts' the LEATHER n.³ (1), while the assistant GLOMs or grabs it and takes it away]

leatherhead *n.¹* **1** [early 17C+] a fool, a stupid person. **2** [mid–late 19C] (US) an inhabitant of Pennsylvania. [SE *leather* + sfx. -HEAD (1)]

leatherhead/leatherneck *n.²* [mid-19C–1950s] (US) a policeman. [the protective leather helmets worn by the police, or the leather badges that New York's first policemen wore]

leatherhead *n.³* [1920s] (US) a louse. [their seeming indestructibility]

leather-headed *adj.* [late 18C–19C] foolish, stupid. [LEATHERHEAD n.¹ (1)]

leathering *n.* [late 18C+] a beating, a flogging. [LEATHER v.¹]

leather lane *n.* [19C] the vagina (cf. ALLEY n.¹). [LEATHER n.² (1) + pun on the *Leather Lane* market, off Holborn, London]

leather-lane *adj.* [early 19C] second-rate, poorly made. [the *Leather Lane* market, off Holborn, London]

leather medal *n.* [mid-19C–1940s] (US) a fig. medal for failure, laziness, the booby prize. [a 'real' medal is metal]

leather-merchant *n.* [19C] a pickpocket. [LEATHER n.³ (1), (7)]

leathern conveniency *n.* [late 18C–early 19C] a stage-coach. [orig. 17C Quaker jargon]

leatherneck *n.¹ see* LEATHERHEAD n.².

leatherneck *n.²* [late 19C–1960s] (orig. Aus.) a roustabout. [the effects of the sun on skin]

leatherneck *n.³* [20C] (UK/US) a marine. [early US marine uniforms had a leather neckband]

leather piece n. [1960s+] (US Black) any garment, esp. a coat, made of leather.

leather queen n. [1960s+] (orig. US gay) a male homosexual who likes dressing in leather and may also enjoy sadomasochism. [LEATHER adj. + QUEEN n.¹]

leathers n. **1** [mid–late 19C] anyone wearing leather leggings or breeches. **2** [1960s+] leather garments, esp. as worn by motorcyclists.

leatherskin n. [mid–late 19C] (US) a derog. name for a Native American.

leather-stretcher n. [19C] the penis (cf. LEATHER-DRESSER). [LEATHER n.² (1) + SE stretcher]

leave v. [mid-19C+] (mainly US) to allow, to permit.

leave be v. [early 19C+] to leave alone, to leave in peace.

leave before the gospel, to phr. [20C] to practise coitus interruptus (cf. GET OFF AT BROADGREEN). [i.e. before the church service is fully over]

leave for dead, to phr. [late 19C+] to defeat absolutely, to leave far behind in any form of competition.

leave go/hold/loose v. [mid-19C+] to let go of.

leave in the air, to phr. [1960s+] to leave unresolved.

leave it out! excl. [1970s+] stop doing that!

leave loose see LEAVE GO.

leave off! excl. [late 19C+] stop it! (esp. in sense of stop telling lies).

leave one's trademark on someone see DRAW ONE'S TRADEMARK ON SOMEONE.

leave one's visiting-card, to phr. [1940s+] (orig. milit.) to leave unpleasant evidence (orig. some form of milit. destruction) of one's having been in a place.

leave shaping v. [20C] (W.I.) to outsmart, to fool. [the image is of cricket: a batsman is still shaping up to play the ball when it passes the bat and bowls him]

leave someone cold, to phr. [mid-19C+] to fail to excite or interest one.

leave someone hanging, to phr. [1990s] (US Black) to reject or ignore a proffered handshake or to refuse to indulge in the ritualizing hand-slapping used as a greeting.

leave someone in their glory, to phr. [late 19C] to leave someone by themself.

leave someone out to dry see HANG SOMEONE OUT TO DRY.

leave someone the bucket, to phr. [20C] (US prison) to leave jail. [the bucket used a chamberpot that prisoners must empty each morning]

leave the dead at someone, to phr. [20C] (W.I.) to abandon when in difficulties, to 'leave holding the baby'. [image of abandoning a corpse]

leave the key under the door, to phr. [early 18C–mid-19C] to declare oneself bankrupt. [one leaves the key under the door of one's business and starts avoiding one's creditors]

leave the minority, to phr. [late 19C] to die (cf. JOIN THE GREAT MAJORITY).

leave the world with cotton in one's ears, to phr. [19C] to be hanged (cf. DIE WITH COTTON IN ONE'S EARS). [proper name Cotton, a 19C Newgate chaplain who would preach a last sermon to the condemned man]

leave town v. [1900s–50s] (US Black) to die.

leave yer 'omer n. [late 19C] a very attractive man. [one for whom one would 'leave your home']

leaving shop n. [mid–late 19C] **1** an unlicensed pawnshop. **2** the vagina. [both places where something is left, deposited]

leb/Lebanese n.¹ [1960s+] (drugs) Lebanese hashish, usu. qualified as Red Leb, Lebanese Gold.

Leb n.² [1980s+] (US) a Lebanese. [abbr.]

lech see LETCH.

lechery-layer n. [early 18C] a prostitute (cf. LETCH n.). [SE lechery + LAY v.¹]

lecky n. [1960s+] electricity, esp. as a utility; thus fiddle the lecky, to cheat on one's electricity bill. [abbr.]

lecky adj. [1960s+] electric; thus lecky blanket, lecky kettle. [abbr.]

led by the head of one's dick phr. [1990s] (US Black) of a man, blinded by sexual desire. [fig. use of DICK n.⁵ (1)]

led captain n. [17C–mid-19C] **1** a toady or sycophant, 'an humble dependent in a great family, who, for a precarious subsistence, and distant hopes of preferment, suffers every kind of indignity' (Grose 1785). **2** a pimp. [SE led horse, a riderless horse that is often seen in the retinues of the rich and powerful, underlining the extent of their possessions, and the fact that they have them, even if they are of no real use; Grose adds that 'the small provision made for officers of the army and navy, in time of peace, obliges many ... to occupy this wretched station]

leek/leak n. [early 18C] a Welsh person. [a national emblem]

Leekshire n. [18C–19C] Wales.

leeky store n. [1970s] (US Black) liquor store. [pron. of SE]

Lee Marvin n. [20C] starving. [rhy. sl.; US film star Lee Marvin (1924–87)]

leen n. [1990s] (US Black/drugs) mescaline. [abbr.]

leer n. [late 18C–late 19C] a newspaper. [? LURE or Sp. leer, to read]

leery adj. **1** [early 18C+] guarded, suspicious, alert. **2** [late 18C+] cunning, underhand (cf. LAIRY; LEARY). **3** [late 19C–1910s] (US) hungover, drunk. **4** [1960s+] bad-tempered, disagreeable, cheeky. [? SE leer, looking askance, sly]

left adv. [late 19C–1910s] (US) at a disadvantage, defeated; esp. in get left, to be placed at a disadvantage.

left and right n. [late 19C+] a fight. [rhy. sl.]

left-field adj. [1960s+] (US) unorthodox; thus out of left field, out/off in left field, eccentric, out of the ordinary, bizarre. [baseball imagery]

left-footer/-hander n. [1930s+] a Roman Catholic, but used in reverse by Catholics who define themselves as right-handers; thus dig with the left foot, to be a Catholic. [? turf-cutting spades, as used by Catholics, having the lugs – that piece upon which the foot presses down – on the left of the haft. Note Pennsylvania use left-winger, a Roman Catholic]

left-handed adj. **1** [late 19C–1940s] undesirable, illicit, evil. **2** [1920s–70s] (US) homosexual. [lit. trans. of Lat. sinister]

left-handed compliment n. [1910s+] an insincere or 'back-handed' compliment, a remark that 'damns with faint praise'. [LEFT-HANDED adj. (1) + SE compliment]

left-handed monkey wrench n. [1910s+] (US) an imaginary tool that an inexperienced worker is sent to find as a prank.

left-handed sugar bowl n. [1950s+] (US) a chamberpot.

left-handed wife n. [late 18C–1930s] a mistress. [anything left-handed is de facto suspect. Grose (1796) adds the German custom whereby 'when a man married his concubine, or a woman greatly his inferior, he gave her his left hand']

left-hander see LEFT-FOOTER.

left in the lurch n. [late 19C+] a church (cf. IN THE LURCH; LEAN AND LURCH). [rhy. sl.]

left-off n. [late 19C+] a cast-off.

left off! excl. [1960s–70s] (US campus) a joc. reversal of RIGHT ON!

left raise n. (US Black) **1** [1930s–40s] the left-hand side of one's body plus the relevant limbs. **2** [1930s–40s] the left. **3** [1940s–50s] a pocket, presumably on the left of one's jacket or trousers.

left, right and centre phr. [1940s+] (orig. milit.) of the way in which one will suffer, comprehensively, to a great extent. [the accuracy of a bombing raid, which hits left, right ...]

lefty n. (orig. US) **1** [late 19C+] a left-handed person. **2** [1930s+] a left-wing political radical.

leg *n.*[1] [19C–1930s] a cheating racehorse gambler; thus *leggism*, the characteristics of such a gambler. [abbr. BLACKLEG n.[1] (1)]

leg *n.*[2] [mid-19C] a round or rubber of a card-game; thus *leg-and-leg*, a situation in which each player in the game has won a leg. [orig. naut. use as 'a run made on a single track' (Webster 1897)]

leg *n.*[3] **1** [mid–late 19C] a footman. **2** [1970s] (US) an errand boy. [metonymy]

leg *n.*[4] [20C] (Irish) influence; thus *have a good/great leg of someone*, to have influence with, to be 'well in' with them.

leg *n.*[5] **1** [1940s+] a promiscuous woman (cf. DIRTY LEG). **2** [1960s+] (US Black/campus) a woman (cf. ANKLE n.). **3** [1960s+] female sexuality. **4** [1960s+] sexual intercourse (cf. LEG BUSINESS). [both metonymic + poss. euph.]

leg *v.*[1] **1** [17C+] to run (cf. LEG IT v.[1]). **2** [late 19C] to trip someone up by seizing their leg. **3** [1960s] (US Und.) to shoplift by hiding goods between the legs.

leg *v.*[2] [1920s+] (US) to make or distribute illicitly distilled whisky. [abbr. SE *bootleg*]

leg *v.*[3] [1970s] (US Black) to have sexual intercourse. [LEG n.[5]]

legal eagle *n.* [1930s+] (orig. US) a lawyer, with the implication of being an astute one (cf. LEGAL BEAGLE). [rhy. sl., albeit internal]

legal beagle *n.* [1940s+] (orig. US) a lawyer, esp. an assiduous one (cf. LEGAL EAGLE).

leg art *n.* [1940s–50s] pictures of women revealing their legs (cf. CHEESECAKE n.[1]; LEG DRAMA).

leg bags *n.* [late 18C–late 19C] stockings or trousers (cf. BAGS n.[1]; LEG SACKS).

leg bail *n.* [mid-18C–19C] unauthorized absence (cf. GIVE LEG BAIL).

leg before wicket/l.b.w. *n.* [20C] a ticket, both lit. and fig.; thus *not the l.b.w.*, 'not the ticket'. [rhy. sl., usu. abbr. as *l.b.w.*]

leg-breaker *n.* [1970s+] (US Und.) a hired thug.

leg business *n.* **1** [late 19C–1930s] sexual intercourse (cf. LEG v.[3]). **2** [mid–late 19C] (US) the ballet.

leg drama *n.* [late 19C] any form of show, whether a musical or full-scale striptease, in which the focus is on a woman's legs (cf. LEG ART; LEGGY; LEG PIECE; LEG SHOP; LEG SHOW).

leg em pone *n.* [16C–17C] the payment of money, cash down. [the first two words of the fifth division of Ps. 119, which begins the psalms at Matins on the 25th day of the month, associated with 25 March, the year's first quarter day and thus the first major payday of the calendar]

leger *n.* [late 16C] (Und.) **1** a coal merchant who gives short weight. **2** a London coal merchant who buys wholesale in the country and then retails the coal in London, pretending to be from the country himself. [Fr. *léger*, light; presumably country coal was considered better quality]

legering *n.* [late 16C] (Und.) the giving of short measure by colliers. [LEGER n. (1)]

legged *adj.* [mid-19C] chained.

legger *n.*[1] [late 18C–1900] one who pretends to be selling smuggled goods, but is in fact selling old or shop-worn stock, obtained cheaply. [? he produces such goods from his breeches' pockets or his boot-tops]

legger *n.*[2] [20C] (Irish) a departure on foot; usu. as *do a legger*.

leggings *n.* [20C] (W.I.) greens and root vegetables used in soup. [Fr. *legume*, a vegetable]

leggins *n.* [1930s+] (US gay/prison) copulation when the penis is rubbed between the legs of the sexual partner.

leggner *n.* [1940s–50s] (prison) a 12-month sentence. [pun on STRETCH n.[2]/SE *stretch a leg*]

leggo! *excl.* [late 19C+] (orig. US) **1** let go! **2** [late 19C+] a shout of warning, let's go! run for it! [mispron./mis-sp.]

leggo beas' *adv.* [1950s+] (W.I. Rasta) wild, disorderly. [LEGGO-BEAST n.]

leggo-beast *n.* [1940s+] (W.I.) **1** a tramp. **2** a person, usu. a woman, with loose morals. **3** a prostitute. [SE *let go*, uncontrolled, without an owner + *beast*]

leggy *adj.* (orig. US) **1** [mid–late 19C] of a stage show that features the display of female legs (cf. LEG DRAMA). **2** [1920s+] of a woman, having particularly attractive legs. The adj. is esp. loved by tabloid newspapers who offer *leggy lovely* as a noun. **3** [1940s+] sexually attractive.

legion of the lost *n.* [1950s–60s] those elderly or mentally unstable patients who have been abandoned by family and friends (cf. GRANNY-DUMPING).

legit *adj.* [late 19C+] (orig. US) *legit*imate, and as such the description of anything that, in context, might be considered as otherwise; thus *on the legit*, conducting an honest life/business etc. [abbr.]

legit! *excl.* [1990s] (US teen) an excl. of approval, acceptance, 'you're OK', 'that's acceptable'. [LEGIT adj.]

legit *v.*[1] [mid-19C+] to run away. [LEG v.[1] (1)]

legit *v.*[2] [1980s+] to have sexual intercourse (cf. GET ONE'S LEG OVER).

legitimacy *n.* [19C] (Aus.) the state of emigrating to Australia as a convict (cf. ILLEGITIMATE n.[1]; LEGITIMATE n.[2]). [one had 'legal reasons' for the trip]

legitimate *n.*[1] [early 19C] a sovereign (money). [? as opposed to a forgery]

legitimate *n.*[2] [19C] (Aus.) a settler who arrived in Australia as a transported convict (cf. ILLEGITIMATE n.[1]; LEGITIMACY). [such settlers had 'legal reasons' to make the trip]

legless *adj.* [1970s+] drunk to the extent of probably falling over (cf. BADERED).

leg-lifter *n.* [early 18C–late 19C] a promiscuous man, a womanizer; thus *leg-lifting*, casual sexual intercourse. [LIFT ONE'S LEG]

leg man *n.*[1] [1940s+] (US) an assistant. [they run errands]

leg man *n.*[2] **1** [1950s+] a man who prefers a woman's legs to any other part of her anatomy (cf. ARSE MAN). **2** [1970s] (US campus) a womanizer.

leg of beef *n.* [20C] a thief (cf. HOT BEEF!). [rhy. sl.]

leg of mutton *n.*[1] [mid-19C] a sheep's trotter.

leg of mutton *n.*[2] [20C] a button. [rhy. sl.]

leg of mutton in a silk stocking *n.* [late 17C–20C] a woman's leg (cf. MUTTON IN LONG COATS). [note MUTTON n.[2]]

leg of the law *n.* [19C] a lawyer. [var. on LIMB OF THE LAW]

leg-opener *n.* [1950s+] (orig. Aus.) a drink given to a woman in the hope of getting her drunk enough for seduction (cf. COCK-OPENER).

legover *n.*[1] [20C] (Irish) assistance, help. [image of giving someone a *leg over* a stile or gate]

legover *n.*[2] [1940s+] (orig. milit.) sexual intercourse; thus *give/have a bit of legover*, to have sexual intercourse. [back form. f. GET ONE'S LEG OVER]

leg piece *n.* **1** [late 19C] any form of stage performance featuring the female leg, e.g. a burlesque show (cf. GIRL-SHOW; LEG DRAMA). **2** [1910s–20s] the ballet (cf. LEG BUSINESS).

leg pull *n.* [late 19C+] a good-natured hoax or tease. [PULL SOMEONE'S LEG]

leg pull *v.* [1990s] (US teen) to make a joke. [LEG PULL n.]

legs *n.* [19C+] a tall, thin person. [i.e. all *legs*, no body]

leg sacks *n.* [1930s–40s] (US Black) socks (cf. LEG BAGS).

legs eleven *n.* [1940s+] (bingo) the number 11. [resemblance]

legshake artist *n.* [20C] (orig. Aus.) a pickpocket. [ARTIST n.[2]]

leg-shaker *n.* [late 19C–1900s] a dancer.

Legshire *n.* [19C] the Isle of Man. [the three linked legs that make up its armorial bearing]

leg shop n. [late 19C] (US) a theatre devoted to burlesque, i.e. the display of women's legs (cf. LEG DRAMA).

leg show n. [mid-19C+] (orig. US) any form of show, whether a musical or full-scale striptease, in which the focus is on a woman's legs (cf. GIRL-SHOW; LEG DRAMA).

legs right up to her ass/arse phr. [1930s+] (orig. US) a male description of a woman with exceptionally long and attractive legs. [SE legs + ARSE n.¹]

legume n.¹ [1980s+] (US drugs) a piece or 'button' of peyote cactus. [Fr. legume, a vegetable]

legume n.² [1980s+] (US campus) a lazy person, one who lies around doing nothing (cf. COUCH POTATO). [Fr. legume, a vegetable]

leg work n. [20C] **1** intercourse between the thighs or the buttocks (without penetration of the anus). **2** (US tramp) any job that requires a great deal of walking.

leg worker n. [1930s] (US) a street prostitute.

leisure hours n. [late 19C] flowers. [rhy. sl.]

lekker adj. [mid-19C+] (S.Afr.) **1** an all-embracing term of approval. **2** tipsy, slightly drunk. [Du. lekker, pleasant, tasty]

lel/lell v. [mid–late 19C] to arrest, to seize. [? Scots tell, to take aim; note market traders' use, to summons, to prosecute]

lem v. [1980s+] (US drugs) to smoke up and go directly to sleep. [? LEMON n.¹ (1), i.e. one who refuses to socialize]

lemme v. [late 19C+] (orig. US) let me (cf. GIMME v.). [mispron./mis-sp.]

lemon n.¹ **1** [mid-19C] a person of a sour disposition. **2** [20C] anything undesirable, esp. of a woman. **3** [1910s] a disappointment, anything worthless or fraudulent. **4** [1920s+] (US) a defective car; thus the lemon law, a law that provides redress for buyers of substandard or defective cars. **5** [1950s+] (US drugs) a diluted or poor-quality drug, esp. poor heroin. **6** [1980s+] (Aus.) a lesbian (cf. FRUIT n.²). [images of the lit. + fig. sourness of the fruit]

lemon n.² [20C] a victim, a fool. [? pun on SUCKER n.¹]

lemon n.³ [1930s+] (US Black) **1** the female pubic hair. **2** the vagina (cf. APPLE n.¹⁰). **3** the male genitals (cf. SQUEEZE ONE'S LEMON). [? all can be 'squeezed'; orig. use as euph. in blues lyrics]

lemon n.⁴ [1900s–50s] (US Black) a light-skinned Black person. [the colour]

lemon n.⁵ [1920s–50s] the head. [the shape]

lemon n.⁶ [1930s] (US) an informer. [such a person can be 'squeezed' by an interrogator]

lemon n.⁷ [1960s+] a piece of excrement. [rhy. sl. lemon curd = TURD n. (1)]

lemon 714 n. [1990s] (drugs) phencyclidine (cf. ACE n.³). [ety. unknown]

lemonade n.¹ [1970s] (US) urine (cf. SQUEEZE ONE'S LEMON). [the colour + LEMON n.³ (3)]

lemonade n.² [1980s+] (Aus.) a lesbian. [ext. of LEMON n.¹ (6)]

lemon and dash n. [1950s+] a public lavatory. [rhy. sl. lemon and dash = wash/SLASH n.⁴]

lemon and lime n. [20C] time. [rhy. sl.]

Lemon Avenue n. [1920s+] (Aus.) the fig. name for the 'spiritual home' of censorious or socially repressive people. [LEMON n.¹ (1); their lips are eternally pursed with disapproval, as if they had just sucked a lemon]

lemon curd n. [20C] **1** a piece of excrement. **2** a derog. term for a person. **3** a woman. [rhy. sl. lemon curd = (1) + (2)TURD n.; (3) BIRD n.⁵ (1)]

lemon-eater/-pelter/-sucker n. [1960s+] (US derog.) an English person (cf. LIMEY n.). [LEMON n.¹ (1) + SE eater/pelter, one who skins or peels/sucker, the English are seen as sour]

lemoner n. [1970s+] (Irish) a disappointment, something depressing. [LEMON n.¹ (3)]

lemon-game n. [20C] (US) a way of cheating at pool, whereby a victim is enticed into the game and allowed to win. Once they are sufficiently confident to bet heavily their opponent has a 'run of luck' and takes all their money.

lemon-pelter see LEMON-EATER.

lemons n. [1940s+] (US) the female breasts (cf. APPLES n.¹).

lemons adv. [mid-19C–1900s] (Aus.) energetically, enthusiastically. [the 'sharpness of the fruit]

lemon squash n. [20C] (Aus.) a wash. [rhy. sl.]

lemon-squash party n. [late 19C] (orig. Oxford University) a temperance meeting. [the rejection of any drink but this]

lemon-squeezer n.¹ [1940s+] (Aus./N.Z.) a hat with a peaked crown and broad, flat brim worn by Aus. and N.Z. soldiers (cf. CHEESE-CUTTER). [resemblance]

lemon-squeezer n.² [1970s+] a man. [rhy. sl. lemon squeezer = GEEZER n.¹ (1)]

lemon-sucker n.¹ [1920s–60s] (US) an effeminate man. [? LEMON n.³ (1) + SE sucker; or his stereotypically pursed lips]

lemon-sucker n.² see LEMON-EATER.

lemon tea n. [20C] urination. [rhy. sl. lemon tea = PEE n.¹]

lemony adj. [1940s–50s] (Aus./N.Z.) angry, irritated; thus go lemony at, to become annoyed with. [the 'sharpness' of the fruit]

lend n. [16C+] a loan, e.g. give us a lend of your barrow.

lend a hole to hide in see GIVE A HOLE TO HIDE IT IN.

lend his arse and shit through his ribs, to phr. [late 18C–mid-19C] used of anyone who lends money without worrying about a security, e.g. he would lend his arse and shit through his ribs.

lend us your breath to kill Jumbo phr. [late 19C] a teasing ref. to another person's bad breath (cf. JUMBO n.¹). [Jumbo, the London Zoo elephant who arrived in 1863 and proved one of the Zoo's main attractions until he was sold to P.T. Barnum's Circus in 1882]

length n. [mid-19C] 6 months' imprisonment. [horse racing imagery, a length is half a STRETCH n.²]

Len Hutton n. [20C] a button. [rhy. sl., ult. cricketer Len Hutton (1916–90)]

lenny the lion n. [20C] a homosexual. [rhy. sl. Lenny the Lion = IRON n.⁴]

leño n. [1950s+] (US drugs) marijuana, a marijuana cigarette (cf. STICK n.¹⁴). [Sp. leño, a stick of wood]

leños n. [1990s] (drugs) phencyclidine (cf. ACE n.³). [ety. unknown; presumably linked to LEÑO]

lens n. [1990s] (drugs) LSD (cf. A n.³). [SE lens, i.e. the visual distortions that can accompany the LSD experience]

lens v. [1980s+] (US) to film a movie.

lens lizard n. [1920s+] (US) a photographer, a film-maker.

Leo Sayer n. [1990s] an all-day drinking session. [rhy. sl. = all-dayer; ult. pop star Leo Sayer (b.1948)]

leo-time n. (US teen) August. [the astrological sign Leo]

Leperland n. [late 19C] (Aus.) a nickname for Queensland (cf. LEPER LINE). [its population of lepers]

leper line n. [1950s+] (West. Aus.) a line running across Western Australia at 20¡S. [the W.A. Native Australian Welfare Act (1955), which sought to prevent the spread of leprosy by forcing all sufferers to move to a place south of that parallel]

lepping adj. [20C] (Irish) **1** angry. **2** throbbing painfully. [fig. uses of SE leap]

leprosy n. [1930s–40s] (Aus.) cabbage. [ety. unknown]

leracam/lur-a-cham n. [mid-19C] a mackerel. [backsl.]

lerricompoop v. [17C] to have sexual intercourse. [? link to LERRICOMTWANG or dial. lerry, a whim, a caprice]

lerricomtwang n. [mid–late 17C] a fool, a simpleton. [the chorus of a contemporary popular song]

les/lesbo/lez/lezbo n. [1920s+] (orig. US) a lesbian (cf. LESB; LESBIE; LESLIE n.¹; LESO; LEZZER; LEZZIE). [abbr.]

lesb n. [1940s–50s] a *lesb*ian (cf. LES). [abbr.]

lesbie/lesby n. [1950s+] a *lesb*ian; thus the punning phr. *lesby friends* (cf. LES). [abbr.]

leslie n.[1] [1950s+] (Aus.) a lesbian (cf. LES). [abbr. + a name that serves for men and women]

leslie n.[2] [1990s] the vagina. [rhy. sl. *Leslie* Ash, a popular TV actress. = GASH n.[1] (1)]

leso/lezo/lezzo n. [1940s+] (Aus.) a *lesb*ian (cf. LES). [abbr. + sfx. -O]

'less/less conj. [late 19C+] (mainly US) un*less*. [abbr.]

less of your lip! see NOT SO MUCH OF YOUR LIP!

less than nothing n. **1** [20C] (US Black) a derog. term for a passive homosexual (cf. HALF A MAN). **2** [1980s+] (gay) a weak gay man, unable to look after himself.

less than no time phr. [mid-19C+] very quickly, almost immediately.

let a brewer's fart grains and all, to phr. [late 18C–19C] to foul one's trousers.

let alone phr. [early 19C+] not to mention.

letari see LETTARY.

letch/lech n. **1** [late 18C+] a strong sexual desire. **2** [1940s+] (orig. US) a *lech*er. [abbr.]

letch/lech v. [20C] to lust, crave. [LETCH n.]

letching-piece n. [20C] a promiscuous woman. [PIECE n.[1]]

letchwater n. [19C] semen. [LETCH n. + SE *water*]

let-down n. [mid-19C+] a disappointment.

let down for someone's chimer, to phr. [1940s] (US Black) to steal a watch.

let down someone's blind, to phr. [1910s–20s] to make clear that someone is dead.

let down the bars, to phr. [mid–late 19C] (US) to bring to a halt, to interfere. [the image is of a portcullis descending to block an entrance]

let 'em all come! excl. [late 19C+] a defiant excl. daring one's opponents, present or otherwise, to do their worst.

let 'em trundle! excl. [late 17C–mid-18C] go away! be off!

let 'er Gallagher!/go! see LET HER GO!

let George do it phr. [1910s+] (US) let someone else do the work or take the responsibility. [GEORGE n.[2] + WW2 phr. *let George do it, I can't be bothered*]

let go v. **1** [late 19C+] to reach orgasm. **2** [1990s] (US campus) to relax.

let go phr. [1910s–20s] not to mention, all the more reason, e.g. *let go you didn't even turn up*. [i.e. *let* that fact *go* without comment or action]

let go a razzo, to phr. [19C] to break wind. [RASPBERRY TART n.]

lethal weapon n. [1980s+] (drugs) phencyclidine (cf. ACE n.[3]).

let her flicker phr. [1940s–50s] (Aus.) a phr. used at the start of some operations, usu. as *OK, let her flicker ... .* [running a reel of movie film]

let her/'er go!/Gallagher! excl. [late 19C–1930s] (Aus./US) go ahead! [? assonance of proper name]

let her rip! excl.[1] [mid-19C+] (orig. US) to allow anything, real or fig., to go at full speed, to remove any impediment to progress. [? f. steamboat engines that exploded or *ripped* when under excessive pressure. The phr., according to Ware, was common among their captains when urging the crew to put on full steam when racing against a rival boat]

let her/him rip! excl.[2] [20C] the hell with her!/him! [let them rest *in* peace]

let her sling! see SLING YOURSELF!

let him rip! see LET HER RIP! excl.[2].

let-in n. [1910s–20s] **1** a robbery. **2** a hoax. **3** an illegal victimization. [LET IN v.]

let in v. [mid-19C] to cheat, to defraud, to victimize. [image of falling through ice]

let into v. [mid-19C] to attack physically.

let into the secret, to phr. [late 17C–early 18C] to draw a victim into betting on a crooked race or game and then to defraud them.

let it all hang out, to v. [1960s+] (orig. US Black) to cast aside any restraints, to do what one wants. [a musicians' term, this migrated to White hippie use and thence, like a number of similar terms, to the jargon of 'new therapies']

let it ride, to phr. [20C] to ignore, to forget. [dice or roulette gambling where a winning bet is not picked up from the table but left to be gambled again]

let it slide phr. [20C] don't bother, it doesn't matter (cf. SLIDE v.[4]).

let it soak see SOAK IT.

let it sweat phr. [1920s+] stop worrying or interfering, just let things turn out as they will.

let leap a whiting, to phr. [mid-16C–late 18C] to let an opportunity slip. [fishing imagery]

let loose the juice, to phr. [1990s] to masturbate. [SE *let loose* + JUICE n.[2] (2)]

let me alone for that! phr. [late 17C–late 19C] a general phr. of reassurance, 'you can trust me' or 'don't worry, everything will be fine'.

let me die!/be hanged!/perish! excl. **1** [late 17C–mid-19C] a general phr. of assurance, self-justification, *let me die if I lie!* **2** [mid-19C–910s] a phr. used when one is laughing without restraint, as in 'if you go on I'll die of laughter'.

let me hold some change phr. [1960s+] (US Black) please give me some money.

let me perish! see LET ME DIE!

let off a little nigger, to phr. [late 19C+] (US) a derog. phr. meaning to act in a crazy, uninhibited way, to let off steam (cf. ACT THE NIGGER). [racist stereotyping]

let off steam see BLOW OFF STEAM.

let on v. [mid-19C+] **1** to admit, to confess. **2** to pretend, to pose.

let one go/fly/off/rip, to phr. [1970s+] (US campus) to break wind (cf. LET GO A RAZZO).

let oneself loose, to phr. [late 19C+] to speak openly, candidly.

let one's game slip, to phr. [1960s+] (US Black) to lose control of a situation or plan. [GAME n.[5]]

let/take one's hair down, to phr. **1** [mid-19C+] (orig. US) to relax one's inhibitions. **2** [1930s+] to admit to being gay (cf. UNPIN ONE'S BACK HAIR).

let one's horse out of the stable, to phr. [1950s–60s] to urinate (cf. WATER THE HORSES).

let one's rag out see GET ONE'S RAG OUT.

let-out n. **1** [late 19C+] (Anglo-Irish) a spree, an entertainment. **2** [1920s+] an excuse, an alibi.

let out v. **1** [early 19C+] to reveal a secret. **2** [late 19C+] to ride a horse fast. **3** [late 19C+] (orig. US) to exonerate from blame or guilt. **4** [1920s] to sing enthusiastically. **5** [1930s+] accelerate or drive a car fast.

let out a reef or two, to phr. [late 19C+] (orig. naut.) to unbutton one's waistcoat or trousers after a heavy meal. [SE *reef*, one of the horizontal portions of a sail which can be rolled or folded in order to regulate the amount of canvas exposed to the wind]

let out at v. [20C] (Aus.) to aim a blow at.

let rip v. [late 19C+] to 'let fly', to let go, esp. with great energy and force.

let run a milestone, to phr. [late 17C] (gaming) to let a die roll some distance.

let's be having you! phr. [20C] time to start work, get out of bed etc.

let's boogie phr. [1980s+] (US teen) let's go, let's be off. [fig. use of BOOGIE v.]

let's face it *phr.* [20C] let us accept the facts.

let's go hangin' *phr.* [1990s] (US teen) let's go somewhere and do nothing in particular. [HANG OUT v.[1]]

let slide *v.* [1950s+] (orig. US) to overlook, to forgive (cf. SLIDE v.[4]).

let slip at *v.* [mid-19C] to attack physically.

let's lose Charley *phr.* [1950s–60s] a term used among intimates who want to get rid of a bore in their company.

let someone down easily, to *phr.* [mid-18C+] to treat someone kindly and considerately when one has to deliver bad or disappointing news.

let someone down gently/softly, to *phr.* [early 19C+] to treat someone kindly and considerately when one has to deliver bad or disappointing news.

let someone have it, to *phr.* [mid-19C+] (orig. US) to hit to kill, esp. with gunfire.

let someone in for *v.* [early–mid-19C+] to involve, usu. in unfortunate circumstances, such as financial ruin or a criminal prosecution.

let someone in on *v.* [1940s+] to impart otherwise secret or privileged information.

let someone off easy *v.* [early 19C+] to deal with someone kindly, to resist acting cruelly (cf. GO EASY v.[2]).

lets out her fore room and lies backwards/lies backwards and lets out her fore room, she *phr.* [late 18C–early 19C] of a woman, allegedly working as a prostitute.

let's rejoice *n.* [20C] (Aus.) the voice. [rhy. sl.]

let's vamos! *excl.* [1980s+] (US campus) let's go! [SE *let's* + Sp. *vamos*, let's go]

let's you and me *phr.* [1920s+] (US) why don't we ... ?

lettary/letari *n.* [late 19C–1930s] (tramp) a lodging (cf. LETTY). [Ital. *letto*, a bed]

letter *n.* [1910s+] (US) a letter worn on one's clothing that indicates success in college sports.

letterbox *n.* [1990s] a passive homosexual (cf. MANCUNT; POSTMAN).

lettered *adj.* [early 18C–early 19C] (Und.) branded on the hand (cf. CHARACTERED).

letter-fencer *n.* [late 19C] a postman. [SE *letter* + joc. use of FENCER]

letter from home *n.* **1** [1930s+] (US) anything that provokes nostalgia. **2** [1950s–60s] (US Black) a watermelon. [the stereotypical link of watermelons and life 'down home']

letter-racket *n.* [early 19C] (Und.) the sending of fake begging letters. [SE *letter* + RACKET n.[1] (1)]

letters *n.* [late 19C+] the abbr. following a person's name that signify qualifications, honours and institutions, often expanded as *letters after one's name.*

let the air out of, to *phr.* [1950s] (US) to let down, to deflate emotionally.

let the badger loose, to *phr.* [1970s] (US, West) to celebrate wildly, to 'let off steam'. [the 'sport' of badger-baiting]

let the best dog leap over the stile first, to *phr.* [18C–19C] to allow the best qualified or most suitable person take the lead. [pvb.]

let the daylight into/through, to *phr.* [early 18C–1920s] to shoot, to stab, often ext. as [mid-19C+] *let the daylight into the victualling department,* [mid-19C+] *let the daylight into the luncheon reservoir.*

let the deal go down, to *phr.* [1940s–60s] (US Black) to allow events to proceed without dishonesty or deceit. [card-playing imagery]

let the dog see the rabbit, to *phr.* [1930s+] to give someone a chance to get on with a task.

let the hide go with the tallow, to *phr.* [20C] (US) to ignore small details while concentrating on the overall picture. [for ety. *see* LET THE TAIL GO WITH THE HIDE]

let the milk down, to *phr.* [1970s+] (US) to reveal the facts.

let the priest say mass *phr.* [20C] (Irish) a phr. used to reprimand someone who keeps interrupting or offering unwanted suggestions.

let the tail go with the hide, to *phr.* [20C] (US) to ignore small details while concentrating on the overall picture (cf. LET THE HIDE GO WITH THE TALLOW). [butchers'/slaughterhouse jargon; it implies the throwing in of the relatively worthless tail with the valuable hide]

letting the finger ride the thumb *phr.* [18C] getting drunk. [? FINGER AND THUMB or SUPERNACULUM]

lettuce *n.*[1] [20C] money in notes, sometimes ext. as *lettuce leaves* (cf. ALFALFA n.). [the colour]

lettuce *n.*[2] [1990s] the female genitals; thus *shake the lettuce,* to urinate. [var. on CABBAGE n.[7]]

letty/lattie/latty *n.* [mid-19C–1950s] (Ling. Fr./Polari) a bed; thus *letties,* lodgings, accommodation. [Ital. *letto,* a bed]

let up on *v.* [mid-19C+] (orig. mainly US) to reject, to snub, to have nothing to do with.

leucoddy *n.* [mid-19C+] the human body. [Polari]

levanter *n.* [early 18C–late 19C] an absconder, esp. one who runs off after placing a losing bet. [*Levant,* the Middle East. The image is of running off to foreign parts; ? + f. stereotype of 'oily Levantine']

levanting/running a levant *n.* [early 19C] betting without sufficient funds to cover one's losses. [SE *levant,* to run off without paying one's debts, ult. Sp. *levantar,* to lift up, but note racial stereotyping, *Levantine* = Jew = crooked]

level *n. see* LEVEL BEST.

level *adj.* [late 19C+] (orig. US) honest, trustworthy, true.

level *v.* [1920s+] (orig. US) **1** to admit, to confess. **2** to be honest (cf. ON THE LEVEL).

level best/level/dead level best *n.* [19C+] (orig. US) one's very best efforts (cf. LEVEL WORST). [note that *level best* is SE in UK but sl. in US]

level vibes *phr.* [1980s+] (W.I./UK Black teen) a satisfactory situation, peace and quiet. [SE *level* + VIBE n.]

level worst *n.* [19C] (US) one's worst attempt or effort. [reverse of LEVEL BEST]

leven *n.* [mid-19C] the number 11. [Hotten (1859) credits this to backsl.]

leventy-leven *adj.* [1970s] (US Black) a large, unspecified number.

leven yenneps/nevele yeneps *n.* [mid-19C] 11 shillings (55p). [backsl.]

levite *n.* [mid-17C–mid-19C] a priest or parson. [SE *Levite,* a member of the ancient Hebrew tribe of Levi, one of the two tribes authorized to serve as priests in the Temple]

levy *n.* [19C] **1** (US) 12 cents. **2** one shilling (5p). [abbr. (e)*leven cents,* which was the value of the Spanish *real,* formerly accepted as currency in US]

levy *v.* [20C] to masturbate (cf. BARCLAY'S). [rhy. sl. *Levy and Frank* = WANK v., ult. the name of a London restaurateur]

lewdie *n.* [1970s] a married woman who frequents singles' bars looking for brief encounters. [SE *lewd*]

lewd infusion *n.* [1920s–30s] sexual intercourse. [the infusion of semen]

lewis and witties *n.* [1940s–50s] (Aus.) the female breasts. [rhy. sl. *Lewis and Witty,* a well-known Melbourne department store = TITTY n.[2]]

lewis cornaro *n.* [early 19C] a drinker of water. [the name of a man renowned for his consumption of water]

lex *n.*[1] [1980s+] (US Black) a *Lex*us motorcar, one of the high-status cars preferred by the rap/hip-hop community. [abbr.]

lex *n.*[2] [1990s] (Black) a Ro*lex* watch. [abbr.]

lex-luther *n.* [1990s] (US Black teen) a *Lex*us automobile, a coveted status symbol. [LEX n.[1] + pun on *Lex Luthor*, an enemy of the comic superhero Superman]

lez/lezbo *see* LES.

lezo *see* LESO.

lezzer *n.* [1950s+] (Aus./Irish/US) a *les*bian (cf. LES). [abbr.]

lezzie/lezzy *n.* [1930s+] a *les*bian (cf. LES). [abbr.]

lezzo *see* LESO.

lezzy *see* LEZZIE.

l.f. *see* LONG FIRM.

lib *n.* [1970s+] (orig. US) *lib*eration, usu. in gender political contexts and thus abbr. for 'liberation movement', e.g. *Women's Lib, Gay Lib.* [abbr.]

lib *v.* [16C–late 18C] **1** (Und.) to lie down (cf. LIBKEN). **2** to sleep together. [ety. unknown]

lib-beg / libbedge / libbege / libedge / lyb beg / lybbeg / lyb bege *n.* [16C–mid-19C] a bed (cf. LIG n.[1]). [LIB v. + sfx. *-age*]

libben *n.* [late 17C–mid-19C] a private house (cf. LIBKEN). [LIB v.]

libber *n.[1]* [20C] (Irish) an untidy, slovenly person. [Irish *leadhb*, a strip, a rag, a slovenly person]

libber *n.[2]* [1970s+] (orig. US) a feminist, a member of the Women's Liberation Movement. [usu. derog. when used by men]

libe *n.* [1910s+] (US campus) a *lib*rary. [abbr.]

libe *v.* [1910s+] (US campus) to study in a library. [LIBE n.]

libedge *see* LIB-BEG.

liberate *v.* [1940s+] to steal (cf. ACQUIRE). [esp. in 1960s radical use, on the Proudhon principle that 'property is theft' but likewise with a degree of irony/self-mockery given the 1960s obsession with 'freedom' and 'the revolution'. With further irony, the 'radical' use stems f. WW2 'liberating forces' who 'freed' commodities as well as people]

liberty *n.* [1910s–40s] **1** (US) money. **2** (US, esp. Black) a quarter, a 25-cent coin.

libken/libkin/lipken/lybkin *n.* [16C–early 19C] (Und.) a house, a lodging. [LIB v. + KEN n.[1]]

library *n.[1]* **1** [mid–late 17C] a drinking club, a friendly gathering. **2** [20C] a book borrowed from a lending library. **3** [1960s+] (US) an adult bookstore.

library *n.[2]* [1930s+] (US) an outdoor privy. [the old catalogues, newspapers etc that are often left there as lavatory paper]

libs *n.* [1990s] *lib*erties. [abbr.]

lick *n.[1]* **1** [mid-18C+] a slight and hasty wash (cf. LICK AND A PROMISE). **2** [mid-18C+] a quick tidy-up. **3** [mid-18C+] a casual amount of work. **4** [mid-19C+] a bit, a cursory amount. **5** [mid-19C+] (Aus./N.Z./US) a short sprint. [? East Anglian dial. *lick-up*, a miserably small pittance of any thing]

lick *n.[2]* **1** [late 18C+] an effort, an attempt. **2** [1930s–50s] (US Black) a plan, an idea. **3** [1930s+] (US Und.) a theft. **4** [1990s] (Black) an attempt, a 'go'; thus *one-lick*, once only. [SE *lick*, a blow]

lick/lick-arse/lick-me-lug *n.[3]* [20C] (Irish) a toady, a sycophant (cf. ARSE-LICKER). [SE *lick* + ARSE n.[1]LUG n.]

lick, the *n.[4]* [1940s+] (orig. W.I.) the very best, the supremely fashionable.

lick *n.[5]* [1950s+] a particular phrase of music, i.e. a *guitar lick*.

lick *v.* **1** [mid-16C+] to beat, to thrash; thus *lick out of*, to change someone's character/beliefs/actions by a threat of violence, to 'knock it out of' someone. **2** [19C+] to defeat, to overcome, to be victorious. **3** [mid-19C+] (US) to move fast, also as *lick it*. [SE *lick*, a blow; (2) generally restricted to W.I. use in 20C, esp. in combs. *lick up*, stir up; *lick down*, knock or fling to the ground; *lick 'way*, strike or cut off (as in a tree branch)]

lick about/around *v.* [20C] (W.I.) to live an unsettled life (cf. KNOCK ABOUT). [SE *lick*, a blow]

lick a box, to *phr.* [1990s] (orig. W.I./Trin.) to perform cunnilingus. [SE *lick* + BOX n.[6] (2)]

lick and a promise *n.* [late 19C+] a quick, if not well-performed, piece of work.

lick and a smell *n.* [mid-18C+] a very small portion. [the image is of a dog licking its empty bowl]

lick an' pran, to *phr.* [1950s+] (W.I.) to tidy up. [LICK AND A PROMISE]

lick around *see* LICK ABOUT.

lick-arse *n. see* LICK n.[3].

lick arse *v. see* KISS ARSE.

lick boots *v.* [late 19C+] to act in a servile manner. [note late-18C synon. *lick the shoe*]

licked *adj.* [mid-19C+] beaten, utterly defeated. [SE *lick*, to beat]

licker *n.[1]* [18C–19C] anything that is exceptional in size, power etc (cf. BUMPER n.[1]). [SE *lick*, to beat]

licker *n.[2]* [1970s+] (US Black) the tongue.

lickerish/likki-likki/likky-likky *adj.* [1950s+] (W.I./UK Black teen) never satisfied and wanting everything; gluttonous and aggressively greedy, esp. for food. [SE *lick*]

lickety-split/hellity-split *adv.* [mid-19C+] (orig. US) fast, with some onomat. overtones, also as *lickety-click, -cut, -liner, -smash, -switch, -wallop* (these forms faded by late 19C).

lick-finger *n.* [early 17C–early 18C] a cook. [note Ben Jonson's *Staple News* (1625): 'Lick-finger, a Master Cooke']

licking *n.* [mid-18C+] a beating, a defeat. [LICK v.]

licking *adj.* [late 19C] a general intensifier, e.g. huge, excellent etc (cf. STONKING; THUMPING; WHACKING adj.; WHOPPING).

licking-match *n.* [1910s] (W.I.) a brawl. [LICK v.]

licking-post *n.* [mid-19C+] (US) **1** a gathering place. **2** a point of argument or dispute. [regional AmE *licking-post*, a salt lick used by cattle]

lick into fits, to *phr.* [late 19C] to beat comprehensively. [LICK v. + SE *fits*]

lick into shape, to *phr.* [mid-19C+] (orig. US) to prepare, to get ready, esp. if the person or object is far from ready when one starts the 'licking'. [LICK v. + fig. use of SE *shape*]

lick log *v.* [1990s] (US) to perform fellatio. [SE *lick* + LOG n.[5]]

lick man *n.* [1990s] (Black) the main man, the most important person. [one who gives out LICKS n. (2)]

lick me! *excl.* [1970s+] (US campus) a dismissive, abusive excl., such as 'shut up, you make me sick!' (cf. EAT MY SHORTS!; LICK MY FROTH!; LICK MY LOVE PUMP!).

lick-me-lug *see* LICK n.[3].

lickmouth *n.* [20C] (W.I.) cheap, nasty gossip. [LICK ONE'S MOUTH]

lick my froth! *excl.* [1980s] (US teen) a general term of abuse or dismissal (cf. KISS MY TUNA!). [? inference of sexual secretion/fluids]

lick my love pump! *excl.* [1980s+] (US campus) a dismissive, abusive excl., such as 'shut up! you make me sick!' (cf. LICK ME!). [SE *lick* + LOVE PUMP]

lick of the tarbrush *see* TOUCH OF THE TARBRUSH.

lick one's/the eye, to *phr.* [1910s–20s] to be happy, to be joyful.

lick one's lips, to *phr.* [1990s] of a woman, to masturbate.

lick one's mouth, to *phr.* [20C] (W.I.) to carry around or to impart negative gossip. [the participants lick their lips in pleasure]

lick on the whip *see* DRINK ON THE WHIP.

lick-over *n.* [1960s+] (US) a quick, cursory clean (cf. LICK AND A PROMISE).

lick pap together, to *phr.* [20C] (W.I./UKVI) to come from the same impoverished background.

lickpot *n.* [20C] (W.I.) the first finger. [14C–15C SE. Other finger names are *longman* (middle finger), *ring-man* (third or ring-finger), *little man* (little finger) and *big tom* (the thumb)]

licks *n.* **1** [18C+] hits, blows. **2** [18C+] orders (cf. LICK MAN). **3** [1990s] (US Black) robbery. [(1) and (2) now mainly UK Black]

lick shot *v.* [1980s+] (W.I./UK Black teen) to fire a shot from a real or imaginary gun to signal appreciation of music or an event. [fig. use of LICK v. + SE *shot*]

lickskillet *n.* [late 19C–1950s] (US) a contemptible person. [SE *lick* + *skillet*; cf. SE *lickspittle*]

licks like fire *n.* [20C] (W.I.) **1** a savage beating. **2** an overwhelming victory. [LICK v.]

licks me *phr.* [late 19C+] it's too much for me; I can't work it out (cf. BEATS ME). [LICK v.]

lick-spigot *n.* [18C–19C] a fellatrix. [SE *lick* + SPIGOT]

lick the chops, to *phr.* [1930s–40s] (US Black) of musicians, to tune up before a performance. [pun on SE phr./LICK v. + CHOPS]

lick the dick, to *phr.* [1980s+] to masturbate. [LICK v. + DICK n.⁵ (1)]

lick the eye *see* LICK ONE'S EYE.

lick the holy ground, to *phr.* [1990s] to perform cunnilingus.

lick thumbs *v.* [20C] (Ulster) to seal a bargain. [the action thus involved; the equivalent of spitting one one's palm and similar gestures of commitment]

lick-twat *n.* [17C–19C] a person who performs cunnilingus. [SE *lick* + TWAT n. (1)]

licky-licky *adj.*¹ [1920s+] (W.I.) fawning, flattering, obsequious. [abbr. LICK ARSE v. (*see* KISS ARSE v.)]

licky-licky *adj.*² [1920s+] (W.I.) pernickety, choosy, esp. as to one's food. [taking tentative licks rather than bites]

licorice stick *see* LIQUORICE STICK.

lid *n.*¹ **1** [late 19C+] a hat (cf. SKIDLID). **2** [late 19C+] (orig. US) the head. **3** [1960s] (US) fellatio (cf. HEAD n.⁸).

lid, the *n.*² [20C] (orig. US) a restraint, protection or confidentiality, or the lack of it; usu. in the phr. *keep the lid on*, to keep it secret; *blow the lid off*, to reveal secrets.

lid *n.*³ [1920s–60s] (US Black) **1** the sky. **2** one's mind.

lid *n.*⁴ [1960s+] (drugs) a quantity of marijuana, about 22g (¾oz) or 40 cigarette's-worth, and often considered the equivalent of 1oz (28g). [the quantity of the drug that fills the *lid* of a tin of a popular brand of tobacco]

lido *n.* [1980s+] (US drugs) crack cocaine. [ety. unknown; ? Sp.]

lid-proppers *n.* [1960s+] (drugs) amphetamines (cf. A n.²). [they keep one awake, and 'prop up one's eyelids']

lie-and-story *n.* [1940s+] (W.I.) gossip, slander.

lie at rack and manger, to *phr.* [late 17C–18C] to live hard. [SE *rack and manger*, the frame that holds an animal's food and the stable in which it is kept; thus lit. to live like an animal]

lie by the wall, to *phr.* [15C–late 17C] to be dead.

lie doggo *v.* [late 19C+] to remain hidden and quiet, just like a stalking dog.

lie-down *n.* **1** [mid-19C+] a rest on a bed or similar object. **2** [1930s+] (orig. US) a protest that involves participants lying on the ground and refusing to move.

lie down on the job *see* LAY DOWN ON THE JOB.

lie-in *n.* **1** [mid-19C+] an extra portion of sleep, after one would normally have to get up. **2** [1960s–70s] (orig. US) a protest that involves participants lying on the ground and refusing to move (cf. LIE-DOWN).

lie in state, to *phr.* [early 18C–19C] of a man, to lie in bed with two or three women. [ironic use of SE; the man is 'dead' after his sexual exertions]

lie like a bastard, to *phr.* [1960s+] to tell bare-faced lies.

lie like a flatfish, to *phr.* [1960s] to lie skilfully and continually. [pun]

lie like a pig, to *phr.* [20C] (Aus.) to tell plausible lies.

lie like truth, to *phr.* [mid-19C] to lie in a plausible manner, often used of cheapjacks and other street salesmen.

lie low *see* LAY LOW v.¹.

lie made of whole cloth/out of the whole stuff *n.* [17C] an absolute and uncompromising lie, a bare-faced lie. [SE *whole cloth*, a bolt of cloth that has yet to be cut up]

lie on *v.* [late 16C] to have sexual intercourse (cf. LIE WITH).

lie on one's face, to *phr.* [late 19C] to drink very heavily until one collapses.

lie out *v.* [20C] (Ulster) to play truant.

lie rough *v.* [late 17C–18C] to go to sleep without first removing one's clothes.

lies backwards and lets out her fore room *see* LETS OUT HER FORE ROOM AND LIES BACKWARDS.

liesca *n.* [1980s+] (US drugs) marijuana. [Sp.]

lieutenant *n.* [1990s] (US drugs) a senior member of a gang of crack sellers who buys from the wholesaler and distributes to the lowest level of dealer.

lieuy *see* LOOEY n.².

lie with *v.* [late 16C] to have sexual intercourse with (cf. LIE ON).

lie with a latchet *n.* [early 17C–early 19C] an absolute and uncompromising lie. [SE *lie* + *latchet*, a binding, i.e. the lie is 'tied tight' and cannot be uncovered]

life, the *n.*¹ (orig. US) **1** [20C] the world of prostitution. **2** [1910s] (Und.) the criminal underworld. **3** [1940s+] (US Black) the subculture of crime, pimping, drug dealing etc that makes up the alternative world of the streets (cf. LA VIDA LOCA). **4** [1950s+] (gay) the world of homosexuality. **5** [1960s] (drugs) the world of drug addiction.

life *n.*² [20C] imprisonment for a life sentence. [abbr. SE *life sentence*]

life! *excl.* [early 17C] a euph. oath. [abbr. *God's life!*]

life and death *n.* [20C] breath. [rhy. sl.]

lifeboat/lifesaver *n.* [1900s–30s] (US prison) a pardon or the commutation of a sentence.

lifejacket *n.* [1980s+] (US campus) a condom.

life of Larry *phr.* [1960s+] (Irish) the good life, a comfortable existence. [? HAPPY AS LARRY]

life of Riley *n.* [1910s+] the good life, a comfortable existence. [? one of a number of late 19C songs. However, the first known use is in 'My Name is Kelly' (1919), written by H. Pease. The relevant line runs 'Faith and my name is Kelly Michael Kelly,/But I'm living the life of Reilly just the same']

life on the instalment plan *n.* [20C] (US Und.) a succession of sentences as served, with periods of freedom, by a recidivist.

life preserver *n.*¹ [mid-19C–1910s] the penis (cf. BAT n.⁷). [SE *life preserver*, a loaded bludgeon]

life preserver *n.*² [1940s] (US) a doughnut. [resemblance to SE *life preserver*, a life-buoy]

lifer *n.*¹ **1** [mid-19C] one who has been transported for life. **2** [mid-19C] a life sentence. **3** [mid-19C] a prisoner serving a life sentence. **4** [1980s+] (US campus) an ironic term for someone who has committed a trivial offence. [SE *life sentence*]

lifer *n.*² [1960s+] (US, orig. milit.) **1** a career soldier. **2** a pej. term for anyone who appears excessively keen on discipline and its administration on their peers. **3** a person unwilling to change their way of life, esp. a drug addict. **4** one who intends to stay in the same job or career until retirement. [SE *life sentence*]

lifer dog *n.* [1980s+] (US) a usu. pej. term for a person who is obsessively committed to their career. [LIFER n.² + DOG n.⁵]

lifesaver *see* LIFEBOAT.

life's dainty *n.* [19C] the vagina. [euph.]

Liffey water *n.* [late 19C+] porter. [rhy. sl.; the orig. ref. was to Guinness, brewed near the River Liffey in Dublin]

lift *n.*[1] **1** [late 16C–mid-19C] theft, burglary. **2** [late 16C–mid-17C] (Und.) a thief of parcels or packages; 'he that stealeth or prowleth any plate, jewels, bolts of satin, velvet or such parcels from any place ...' (Greene 1591b). **3** [1910s–20s] a punch. **4** [1940s+] (orig. US) the effects of intoxication from alcohol or drugs (cf. BUZZ n.[5]; HIGH n.; KICK n.[5]).

lift *n.*[2] [17C] a crutch (cf. LIFTER n.[1]).

lift *v.*[1] **1** [late 16C+] (Und.) to steal. **2** [1910s+] to pick pockets. **3** [1940s+] (esp. Ulster army and police) to arrest. [orig. SE, esp. for cattle thieving]

lift *v.*[2] **1** [late 19C] (US) to raise someone's bet in a poker game. **2** [1930s–50s] to have an erection. **3** [1950s+] (US) to drink (cf. LIFT ONE'S HAND TO ONE'S HEAD).

lift *v.*[3] [20C] (Ulster) to understand.

lift/lay a leg on/over, to *phr.* [18C] to have sexual intercourse (cf. GET ONE'S LEG OVER).

lift a rope, to *phr.* [1950s+] to be in a job. [orig. naut. use]

lift arse on *v.* [20C] to have sexual intercourse. [ARSE n.[1]]

lift doesn't reach the top floor *phr.* [1990s] a phr. describing a fool; one of several implying that something is lacking (cf. NOT ALL THERE).

lifted *adj.* [1940s+] (US) intoxicated by alcohol or drugs (cf. HIGH adj.[1]).

lifted and laid *phr.* [20C] (Ulster) favoured unfairly.

lifter *n.*[1] [late 17C–late 18C] (Und.) a crutch (cf. LIFT n.[2]).

lifter *n.*[2] [late 18C–1930s] (US Und.) a shoplifter. [LIFT v.[1]]

lifter *n.*[3] [late 19C] (US) a heavy blow. [lit. *lifting* the victim off their feet]

lifting *n.* [mid-16C+] shoplifting. [LIFT v.[1]]

lifting law *n.* [mid-16C] (Und.) the stealing of parcels or packages. [LIFT v.[1] + LAW n.[1]]

lift-leg *n.* [early 18C–mid-19C] strong ale. [? its amorous effects (cf. PLAY AT LIFT-LEG)]

lift one's game, to *phr.* [1960s+] (US Black) to improve one's situation financially, emotionally etc. [SE *lift* + GAME n.[4]]

lift one's hand to one's head, to *phr.* [late 18C–19C] to drink, esp. to excess (cf. BEND ONE'S ELBOW).

lift one's heels, to *phr.* [18C–19C] of a woman, to lie down preparatory to sexual intercourse (cf. LITTLE MISS ROUNDHEELS).

lift one's leg, to *phr.* [early 18C–late 19C] of either sex, to have sexual intercourse (cf. LIFT ONE'S HEELS).

lift pill *n.* [1960s–70s] (US drugs) an amphetamine pill (cf. A n.[2]). [lit. it gives one 'a lift']

lift skirts *n.* [mid-19C] a promiscuous woman, a prostitute (cf. LIGHT SKIRTS).

lift the little finger/elbow/hand, to *phr.* [18C] to drink.

lift the lizard, to *phr.* [1990s] to masturbate. [SE *lift* + LIZARD n.[3]]

lifty *n.* [1930s+] (Aus.) a lift attendant.

lig *n.*[1] [early 18C–mid-19C] a bed. [? dial. *lig*, to lie down or LIBBEG]

lig/liggety *n.*[2] [1940s+] (Ulster) a fool (*lig* is male, *liggety* female). [Scot. *lug*, a fool]

lig *n.*[3] [1960s+] anything easy or free (cf. DOSS n.[2]; LIGGER).

lig *v.* [1960s+] to sponge, to 'freeload', to GATECRASH functions or parties, esp. those connected with show business. [backform. of LIGGER]

ligby *n.* [17C] a mistress. [? LIG n.[1]]

liggen *v.* [17C] to sleep. [dial. *liggen*, to lie down]

ligger *n.* [1960s+] a hanger on, esp. in show business, a 'freeloader'. [ety. debatable: acro. of *least important guest* or SE *linger*, to hang around, or Banffshire dial. *lig*, to gossip, to talk too much. Most likely it is dial. *lig*, to lie around. The

term became widespread in the early 1970s, but dates at least to 1960 when Colin MacInnes (1914–76) used it in his essay 'The Other Man']

liggety *see* LIG n.[2].

light *n.*[1] [mid-19C] credit; thus *strike a light*, to open a line of credit; *get a light*, to obtain credit; *have one's light put out*, to have one's credit stopped. [orig. printers' use; ? to cast a *light* on one's financial 'darkness']

light *n.*[2] [20C] (W.I.) insanity, craziness; thus *have a light*, to be crazy. [? SE *light-headed*]

light *adj.* **1** [mid-18C; 1930s+] (US) intoxicated, esp. by drugs. **2** [1950s+] (orig. US Black) short of money. **3** [1960s+] (US Black) stupid. **4** [1960s+] weak. [fig. uses of SE *light*, as in 'light in the head', 'light in the pocket']

light *v.* [20C] (US Black) to enlighten someone with general or specific knowledge. [SE *enlighten*]

light and dark *n.* [late 19C+] a park. [rhy. sl.]

light blue *n.* [18C] gin (cf. BLUE RIBBON).

light bread *n.* [1940s–50s] (US Black) white bread.

light cavalry *n.* [19C] body lice (cf. LIGHT TROOPS).

light drip-drizzle *n.* [1940s] (US Black) a light spring shower.

lighten the load, to *phr.* [1980s+] to masturbate (cf. SHOOT ONE'S LOAD).

lighten up *v.* **1** [1940s+] to act more cheerfully, to cheer up. **2** [1940s+] to reduce verbal or psychological pressure. **3** [1960s+] (orig. US Black) to calm down, to cease from an action. [orig. SE 15C]

light feeder *n.* [mid-19C–1900s] a silver spoon. [ety. unknown; ? the light reflecting off the silver]

light finger *v.* [1950s+] (US) to steal, to pilfer. [backform. of SE *light-fingered*]

light-food *n.* [late 19C] chewing tobacco.

lightfoot *n.* **1** [20C] a male homosexual (cf. LIGHT IN THE LOAFERS). **2** [1970s–80s] (US Black) a neophyte to the raffish world of the streets, one who leads a sheltered life and does not properly participate in the tougher ghetto world. [i.e. one who does not 'tread heavily' in society + the presumed effeminacy of homosexual men]

light frigate *n.* [late 17C–19C] a prostitute (cf. FRIGATE; LAND CARRACK; LIGHT HEELS; LIGHT HORSE; LIGHT HOUSEWIFE; LIGHT O' LOVE; LIGHT SKIRTS). [pun on SE *light frigate*, a light, swift vessel + FRIG v. (2)]

lighthead *n.* [19C] a fool, a simpleton. [SE *light* + sfx. -HEAD (1)]

light heels *n.* [early 18C–19C] a promiscuous woman, a prostitute (cf. LIGHT FRIGATE).

light horse *n.* **1** [17C] a courtesan (cf. LIGHT FRIGATE; PRETTY HORSE BREAKER). **2** [early 18C] a highwayman.

light horsemen *n.* [mid-19C] '"Light Horsemen" would look out for a lighter having valuable goods on board, and at night, stealing up quietly, would cut her adrift, then following her, as she floated down with the tide, would by-and-by rescue her, and bring her back, claiming salvage' (*Daily News*, 9 January 1899) (cf. HEAVY HORSEMEN n.[1]).

lighthouse *n.* **1** [19C] an especially prominent nose, esp. when reddened by years of drinking. **2** [late 19C–1920s] (US Und.) a look-out man or a person who procures customers for a brothel. **3** [1900s–10s] (N.Z.) an illicit dealer in alcohol who carries supplies around and canvasses potential customers.

light housewife *n.* [late 17C–mid-19C] a prostitute (cf. LIGHT FRIGATE).

lightie/laaitie/lighty *n.* **1** [1940s+] (S.Afr.) a child. **2** [1970s+] (S.Afr. Und.) young men used for sexual purposes by older prisoners. [SE *light-weight*]

light infantry *n.* [mid-19C] fleas (cf. HEAVY CAVALRY).

light in the loafers/on her feet *phr.* [1950s+] (US) homosexual. [the image is of the stereotyped effeminate male, tripping along]

light in the tail *see* HOT IN THE TAIL.

light into *v.* [late 19C+] (Irish/US) **1** to attack verbally, to criticize. **2** to tackle, to attack, whether food or a task.

light lady *n.* [late 17C–19C] a prostitute (cf. LIGHT FRIGATE).

lightly, slightly and politely *phr.* [1930s–40s] (US Black) smoothly, effortlessly.

lightly sprung *adj.* [1980s+] mentally unstable.

lightmans *n.* [mid-16C–mid-19C] (Und.) the day (cf. DARK-MANS). [SE *light* + sfx. -MANS]

lightning/liquid lightning *n.* [1] **1** [late 18C–19C] gin (cf. FLASH OF LIGHTNING). **2** [mid-19C+] (US) whisky or any form of cheap spirits.

lightning *n.* [2] **1** [late 19C] (US) electricity. **2** [late 19C] (US) a telegraph (cf. LIGHTNING JERKER n.[1]). **3** [1970s+] (US drugs) amphetamine or crack cocaine.

lightning *adj.* [mid-19C+] (US) extraordinary, formidable.

lightning jerker *n.*[1] [late 19C–1910s] (US) a telegraph operator. [the use of electricity in the telegraph system]

lightning jerker/squirter *n.*[2] [1910s–40s] (Aus.) a telegraph operator. [for ety. *see* LIGHTNING JERKER n.[1]]

lightning water *n.* [mid-19C+] (US) strong whisky (cf. LIGHTNING n.[1]).

light of *adj.* [1920s+] lacking, usu. money, e.g. *I'm a bit light of a couple of quid* (cf. LIGHT ON).

light off *v.* [late 19C+] to have an orgasm. [SE *light off*, to ignite as an explosive]

light of love *n.* [1940s–50s] (prison) a prison governor. [rhy. sl. *light of love* = abbr. *gov*]

light o' love *n.* [late 17C–18C] a prostitute (cf. LIGHT FRIGATE). [euph.]

light on *adj.* [1940s] (Aus.) lacking, usu. money (cf. LIGHT OF).

light on her feet *see* LIGHT IN THE LOAFERS.

light out *v.* [mid-19C+] (US) to leave, to escape. [? naut. use *light out*, to move something along, e.g. a sail]

light piece *n.* [late 19C–1920s] (US tramp) a dime (10 cents) or quarter (25 cents). [the silver, i.e. light colour, of the coins]

light pockets *n.* [1940s+] (US) an impoverished person.

lights *n.*[1] [19C] a fool (cf. CRUISING WITH ONE'S LIGHTS ON; LIGHTS ON BUT THERE'S NOBODY HOME). [SE *lights*, offal, often considered an inedible piece of the animal]

lights *n.*[2] [early 19C+] the eyes. [20C usage is usu. US Black]

light skirts *n.* [19C] a prostitute (cf. LIFT SKIRTS; LIGHT FRIGATE).

light someone up *v.* [1920s] (drugs) to give someone a portion of cocaine.

lights on but there's nobody home *phr.* [1970s+] insane, mentally deficient, vacant (cf. NOBODY AT HOME).

lights out *n.* [20C] death. [a fig. evocation of the end of the day in a dormitory or barracks]

light stuff *n.* [1940s–50s] (drugs) any non-addictive drugs, e.g. cannabis.

light the candle, to *phr.* [1990s] of a woman, to masturbate. [the use of a candle as a substitute dildo]

light the lamp, to *phr.* [late 19C–1920s] of a woman, to have sexual intercourse (cf. LAMP OF LIGHT).

light-timbered *adj.* [late 17C–mid-19C] **1** of a person, slender, thin. **2** of a person, weak.

light time *n.* [20C] (US Und.) an uneventful time in prison (cf. EASY TIME).

light troops *n.* [19C] body lice (cf. LIGHT CAVALRY).

light up *v.*[1] **1** [mid-19C+] to light a pipe, cigar or cigarette. **2** [1920s+] (US drugs) to take cocaine. **3** [1930s+] (US drugs) to smoke marijuana. **4** [1980s+] to smoke a crack pipe.

light up *v.*[2] **1** [1930s+] (US Black) to hit or attack someone (cf. LIGHT INTO). **2** [1940s–50s] to reach orgasm (cf. LIGHT OFF). **3** [1950s+] (US) to shoot, to destroy with gunfire. **4** [1960s] (US) to arouse sexually. **5** [1980s+] (US Black) to dominate, esp. in sports.

light up and say 'tilt', to *phr.* [1950s+] to register by one's expression or reaction that something is wrong. [pinball imagery; when a player pushes the table too enthusiastically, lights flash, the table 'dies' and a sign declares 'Tilt']

lightweight *n.* **1** [late 19C+] (orig. US) an insignificant person, a weakling. **2** [1970s–80s] (US Black) one who leads a sheltered life and does not properly participate in the tougher ghetto world (cf. LIGHTFOOT). **3** [1990s] one who cannot equal their peers in the sphere of drinking or taking drugs.

lightweight *adj.* [19C+] (US) insignificant, unimpressive. [now SE]

light wet *n.* [19C] gin (cf. HEAVY WET n.[1]; WET n.[1]). [SE *light* + WET n.[1]]

light woman *n.* [late 17C–mid-19C] a prostitute (cf. LIGHT FRIGATE).

lighty *see* LIGHTIE.

like *adv.* **1** [late 18C+] used to express 'kind of', 'in a way' or 'so to speak' when used postpositively, as in *he ran down the road like, and* ... . **2** [1940s+] (orig. US Black/beatnik) to express 'approximately', 'just about' or poss. to draw attention to the subject matter when used prenominally, as in *it takes like ten minutes; I feel, like, sick* (cf. SORT OF THING). **3** [1950s+] (orig. US jazz/beatnik/hippie/teen) usu. used as an interjection or excl. to introduce or draw attention to what follows, or to indicate uncertainty, or simply as a meaningless filler as in *Like man, it's out of sight, Like he drove so fast* ... (cf. YOU KNOW).

like a ... *phr.* a variety of similes, all of which are fig./joc. uses of SE and of slang.

like a baby's arm with an apple/orange in it *phr.* [1930s+] a phr. used to describe an extra-large penis.

like a baby's arm holding an apple/orange *phr.* [1930s+] a phr. used to describe an extra-large penis.

like a baby's bottom *phr.* [1920s+] smooth, featureless.

like a bandit *phr.* [1970s+] (US) enthusiastically, very fast, very successfully.

like a bat out of hell *phr.* [1920s+] (orig. US) moving very quickly.

like a beer bottle on the Coliseum *phr.* [1940s+] (Aus.) conspicuous (cf. LIKE A LILY ON A DUSTBIN; LIKE A SHAG ON A ROCK).

like a big dog *phr.* [1980s+] (US campus) intensely.

like a blink *phr.* [1900s–30s] immediately, very quickly.

like a blue-arsed baboon/striped-assed ape *phr.* [1950s+] headlong, very fast.

like a bomb *phr.* [1950s+] (orig. US) very fast.

like a bump on a log *phr.* [mid-19C–1930s] (US) stupidly silent or inarticulate.

like a butterfly on heat *phr.* [1970s] (orig. gay) dithering frantically.

like a cat on a hot tin roof *phr.* [20C] nervous, agitated (cf. LIKE A HEN ON A HOT GRIDDLE).

like a cat on hot bricks *phr.* [mid-19C+] very nervous.

like a cock-maggot in a sink-hole *phr.* [late 19C–1920s] very angry, infuriated.

like a cow with a musket *phr.* [late 19C–1910s] very clumsy.

like a doctor *phr.* [1990s] (US teen) a phr. used of someone who pulls something off with ease or with a great deal of panache.

like a dog in shoes *phr.* [19C] (Anglo-Irish) a phr. used of someone who is making a pattering sound as they move.

like a dose of salts *phr.* [19C+] very quickly; usu. as *go through you like a dose of salts*.

like a dream *phr.* [1940s+] easily, effortlessly, without difficulty.

like a duck on a dough-pile *phr.* [late 19C] (US) heavily, solidly; thus *landed like a duck* ... .

like a Durham steer in a ploughed field *phr.* [late 19C] (US) very clumsily.

like a fart in a bottle/colander *phr.* [late 19C+] twitchy, nervous, agitated.

like a fart in a gale/wind-storm *phr.* [20C] (Can.) utterly useless, helpless.

like a fish on a hook *phr.* [20C] (Aus.) a phr. used to describe one who has been caught in an inescapable situation.

like a fly in a glue-pot *phr.* [mid-17C–late 19C] very nervous, twitchy excited.

like a fly in a tar-box *phr.* [mid-17C–late 18C] very nervous, twitchy excited.

like a good 'un *phr.* [mid-19C+] enthusiastically, keenly.

like a gravedigger *phr.* [late 18C] extremely busy. [phr. 'up to the a-se in business, and don't know which way to turn' (Grose)]

like a hen on a hot griddle *phr.* [20C] (US) in an agitated or nervous manner (cf. LIKE A CAT ON A HOT TIN ROOF).

like a hog on ice *phr.* [late 19C] (US) unsteadily, clumsily.

like a house on fire/afire *phr.* [early 19C+] very fast, very energetically.

like a lily on a dustbin/a dirt tin *phr.* [1930s+] (Aus.) utterly incongruous (cf. LIKE A BEER BOTTLE ON THE COLISEUM).

like all nature *phr.* [mid-19C] (US) with maximum energy, 'like blazes', 'like anything'.

like a midshipman with money in both pockets *phr.* [mid-19C] extremely unlikely, very odd.

like a miller's mare *phr.* [17C] clumsily. [the supposed inability of millers to judge horseflesh]

like a mojo *phr.* [1980s+] (US Black/campus) a great deal. [MOJO n.[1] (1)]

like a monkey on a stick *phr.* [late 19C+] behaving in an eccentric, bizarre manner.

like a monkey with a tin tool *phr.* [mid-19C] impudent, cheeky, self-satisfied.

like a nigger girl's left tit *phr.* [20C] (orig. US) used of something that, punningly, is 'neither right nor fair'. [alt. versions, varying as to chronology, substitute the name of a contemporaneously celebrated Black woman]

like an owl in an ivy-bush *phr.* [late 18C–19C] used of a narrow-faced man who has a large wig or very bushy hair, or of a woman with frizzy hair.

like a nun in a knocking shop *phr.* [late 19C+] utterly incongruous.

like anything *phr.* [mid-18C+] very much so (cf. AS ANYTHING).

like a pakapoo/pakapu ticket *phr.* [1950s+] (Aus.) said of anything untidy, complex, incomprehensible (cf. PACK OF POO TICKETS). [Chinese pidgin *pak-ah-pu ticket*, a form of betting slip used by Chinese gamblers; properly known as *pai-ke-p'iao*, lit. 'white pigeon ticket', it was a small square of paper marked with 80 Chinese characters; the gambler chose some of these, usu. 10, and, depending on how many matched that day's winning combination, would make a small profit for their sixpenny stake]

like a pearl in a half-storm *phr.* [late 19C] impossible to find.

like a pimple on a cow's/bull's arse/pig's bum *phr.* [20C] utterly insignificant.

like a possum up a gum-tree *phr.* [late 19C–1950s] (Aus.) absolutely content, perfectly happy.

like a rat up a drainpipe *phr.* [1960s+] (orig. Aus.) very quickly, usu. used in a sexual context.

like a rope-dancer's pole with lead at both ends *phr.* [late 18C–early 19C] a phr. used of a person considered very stupid and slow.

like a sailor on a water-cart *phr.* [20C] useless, inadequate, ineffective.

like as an apple to an oyster/lobster *phr.* [mid-16C–late 17C] utterly different.

like as fourpence to a groat *see* NEAR AS FOURPENCE TO A GROAT.

like a shag on a rock *phr.* [1930s+] (Aus.) conspicuous; also various phr. denoting solitariness, e.g. *lonely/miserable as a shag on a rock.* [SE *shag*, a cormorant]

like a shot *phr.* [early 19C+] immediately, as fast as possible.

like a snob's cat – all piss and tantrums *phr.* [early–mid-19C] a general phr. of derision or disdain. [SE *snob*, a bootmaker]

like as not *phr.* [late 19C+] very likely, almost certainly; often as *most like as noti; very like as not.*

like a spare prick at a wedding *phr.* [20C] absolutely useless, often preceded by *standing around* ... (cf. USELESS AS A SPARE PRICK AT A WEDDING). [PRICK n. (1); the assumption is that only the bridegroom is necessary]

like a striped-assed ape *see* LIKE A BLUE-ARSED BABOON.

like a stunned mullet *phr.* [1950s+] (Aus.) dull, stupefied.

like a tooth-drawer *phr.* [mid-17C–early 18C] very thin. [SE *tooth-drawer*, an instrument used by a dentist for extractions]

like a Trojan *phr.* [mid-19C+] in a staunch, determined manner (although moral excellence is not indispensable, as one can *lie like a Trojan*).

like a trooper *phr.* [early 18C+] vigorously, energetically; thus *swear like a trooper, eat like a trooper, lie like a trooper.*

like a two-year-old *phr.* [1910s+] in a sprightly, lively manner. [the ref. is to a two-year-old racehorse rather than a human baby]

like a Whitechapel needle *phr.* [mid–late 19C] very sharp, very fast. [the area's sweatshops]

like a winter's day – short and dirty *phr.* [late 18C+] a pej. description for an unpopular person.

like Barney's brig *phr.* [20C] (US) completely disorganized (cf. BARNEY'S BULL). [orig. naut. and ext. in full by 'both main tacks over the foreyard' – the original *Barney* was presumably an incompetent sailor]

like billy-o/billy-ho *adv.* [late 19C+] a general intensifier and expression of energy or effort, most enthusiastically, strenuously, speedily (cf. AS ANYTHING). [dial., euph. for 'bloody hell']

like bingo *adv.* [1930s] a general intensifier and expression of energy or effort, most enthusiastically, strenuously, speedily (cf. LIKE BILLY-O). [BINGO!]

like black ants on soursop *phr.* [20C] (W.I.) a phr. used of a person seen as walking in a proud, haughty manner. [black ants move with their hind parts cocked in the air]

like blazes *adv.* [early 19C] energetically, passionately. [euph. for 'like hell']

like blue murder *phr.* [mid-19C+] very quickly, at top speed. [BLUE MURDER]

like buggery *adv.* [1930s+] a general intensifier, usu. neg. (cf. LIKE HELL).

like cow buss rope *phr.* [20C] (W.I.) very angrily, highly enraged. [Carib.E.; *buss* = SE *burst/bust*]

like crap! *excl.* [1940s] (US) a general intensifier, usu. neg. (cf. LIKE HELL).

like crazy *adv.* [1920s–70s] intensely, excessively, obsessively, esp. as an answer to 'Do you like ... ?' '*Sure, like crazy.*'

like death to a dead cat/African/nigger *phr.* [early 19C–1920s] (US) a phr. used of someone who is holding on without the slightest weakening, e.g. *he's holding on like death ... .*

like Edgware Road *phr.* [20C] a phr. describing tight trousers. [because 'that's got no ballroom either'; pun on SE *ballroom* + BALLS n.[1] (1)]

like enough *adv.* [mid-16C–late 19C] very likely, almost certainly.

like five hundred *adv.* [19C] (US) to excess, very much so, intensely. [on model of LIKE SIXTY]

like forty *adv.* [mid-19C+] (US) with great force, with absolute commitment. [on model of LIKE SIXTY]

like fuck *adv.* [20C] intensely, very much.

like fuck! *excl.* [20C] an excl. of denial or negation, usu. as *like fuck I will!* (cf. DID I FUCK!; LIKE HELL!).

like fucking hell *phr.* [late 19C+] in no way whatsoever, absolutely not.

like fun *adv.* [early 19C+] vigorously, energetically, quickly.

like fury *adv.* [mid-19C] (US) furiously, 'like mad'.

like grim death *adv.* [early 19C+] (orig. US) with absolute tenacity; usu. in the phr. *hang on like grim death.*

like grub *phr.* [late 19C] keenly, enthusiastically. [SE *grub*, to dig, to root up]

like hang *phr.* [20C] (Aus./N.Z.) a general intensive phr. (cf. HANGASHUN; HANGAVA).

like heaven *adj.* [1990s] (US) bald. [like heaven, a bald head has 'no parting']

like hell *adv.* **1** [mid-19C+] recklessly, intensely, very much. **2** [late 19C+] an ironic excl. of negation and denial, usu. as *like hell I will* (cf. LIKE FUCK!).

like herrings in a barrel *phr.* [late 19C–1910s] very crowded.

like hi *phr.* [1990s] (US campus) hello.

like hog under saddle *phr.* [20C] (W.I.) ridiculous, absurd, ludicrous.

like Hunt's dog will neither go to church nor stay at home *phr.* [late 18C–19C] a description of 'discontented and whimsical persons' (Grose 1785). [a Shropshire labourer by the name of Hunt whose mastiff was neither happy at home where he howled whenever his master left for church or at the church where he refused to enter]

like it or lump it, to *phr.* [late 16C+] to accept a situation, willingly or not; usu. as *You'll have to like it or lump it*, or sometimes the euph. phr. *If you don't like it you'll have to do the other thing.*

like it's/something is going out of style *phr.* [1960s+] very enthusiastically.

like nobody's business *phr.* [1930s+] **1** in no ordinary way, exceptionally. **2** very well, excellently, very quickly.

like old boots *phr.* [mid–late 19C] a general intensifier, e.g. *fight like old boots*, to fight enthusiastically.

like old gooseberry *phr.* [late 18C–late 19C] very fast. [OLD GOOSEBERRY]

like one thing *phr.* [1940s+] (Aus.) very much so (cf. LIKE ANYTHING).

like peas *adj.* [20C] (W.I.) plentiful, abundant.

like peas *adv.* [20C] (W.I.) plentifully, abundantly.

like pie *adv.* [late 19C] energetically, vigorously. [? enthusiastic eating]

like poison *phr.* [mid-19C+] very much; usu. in phr. *to hate like poison*, to detest.

liker *n.* [1990s] one who has particular homosexual predilections. [abbr. for *a liker of boys and young men*]

like St Paul's *phr.* [20C] (Aus.) a phr. used to describe tight trousers. [? because 'there's no standing room inside']

like shit *adv.* [20C] very fast, enthusiastically.

like shit off a shovel *phr.* [1930s+] prompt, immediate, fast.

like shot off a shovel *phr.* [1920s+] (Irish) prompt, immediate, fast.

like sixty *adv.* [mid-19C+] (orig. US) with great force or vigour, at a great speed (cf. LIKE FORTY). [? SE *like sixty men*]

like snuff at a wake *phr.* [20C] (Irish) **1** very quickly. **2** in large amounts.

likes of, the *phr.* [mid-17C+] such (a person) as; often used in a pej. context, e.g. *you shouldn't mix with the likes of him.*

like something is going out of style *see* LIKE IT'S GOING OUT OF STYLE.

like steam *adv.* [1920s+] (Aus.) very quickly, very easily, energetically.

like stink *adv.* [1920s+] intensely, furiously. [? euph.]

like stink on shit *phr.* [1950s–60s] (US Black) very close, extremely intimate.

like taking candy from a baby *phr.* [20C] (US) extremely easy.

like that *phr.* [1970s+] (US, mainly South) a euph. for pregnant (cf. THAT WAY adj.[2]).

like the cocky on the biscuit tin *phr.* [1980s+] (Aus.) useless, impotent, a non-participant. [the old tins of Arnott's biscuits had a picture of a cockatoo, which was thus 'on' the tin but not 'in' it]

like the devil had an auction/a fit *phr.* [20C] (US) a remark offered when faced with a particularly untidy house.

like the hammers of hell *phr.* [20C] very quickly.

like thirty cents *phr.* [late 19C+] (US) cheap, worthless, esp. as *feel like thirty cents.*

like to *phr.* [early 19C+] on the verge of, almost ready to.

like to meet her in the dark *phr.* [late 19C] a phr. used of a plain woman who presumably has a good figure; usu. as *I'd like to … .*

like two apples in a bag *phr.* [1950s+] (orig. US) a ref. to well-formed buttocks, irrespective of sex.

like two cents *phr.* [1920s–50s] (US) worthless (cf. LIKE TWO PENNORTH OF TRIPE).

like two pennorth of tripe *phr.* [20C] useless, worthless, unpleasant (cf. LIKE TWO CENTS).

like whelks behind a window-pane *phr.* [1990s–10s] a phr. describing the eyes of a person who wears very thick glasses.

like white on rice *phr.* [1980s+] (US Black) very closely. [rice is white itself]

like winking *adv.* **1** [early 19C+] very quickly. **2** [mid-19C] vigorously, energetically.

like winky *adv.* [early 19C–1920s] very quickly. [abbr. LIKE WINKING]

liking white meat [1990s] preferring sexual encounters with young (underage) boys. [the tenderness of young SE *chicken*/CHICKEN n.[5] (2)]

likkered *adj.* [mid-19C+] (US) drunk. [SE *liquored*]

likki-likki/likky-likky *see* LICKERISH.

lil/lill *n.* **1** [early–mid-19C] a book; a pocket-book or wallet. **2** [mid-19C] a £5 note. **3** [1900s] any banknote. [Rom. *lil*, a book, a paper]

l'il abners *n.* [1940s+] (US) square-toed shoes. [those worn by the hero of the cartoon strip *L'il Abner* (1934–79), created by Al Capp]

lilac *adj.* [1960s+] effeminately homosexual (cf. LAVENDER). [SE *lilac*, a colour seen as stereotypically homosexual]

lilacs *n.* [late 19C–1910s] (US) sideburns or sideboards (cf. SIDELILACS). [the supposed similarity of a bushy sideburn to a lilac flower]

Lilian Baylis's leg *n.* [late 19C+] meat loaf, jam roly-poly (cf. BABY'S HEAD). [proper name *Lilian Baylis* (1874–1937), theatrical manager and founder of the Old Vic and Sadler's Wells theatres]

lilies-of-the-valley *n.* [1990s] (gay) haemorrhoids. [supposed resemblance]

lill *see* LIL.

lilley and skinner *n.* [20C] dinner. [rhy. sl.; ult. *Lilley and Skinner*, the London shoe shop]

lill for loll/law *phr.* [15C–17C] tit for tat.

lillian *n.* [1980s+] (gay) the police (cf. LILY LAW). [camp feminization]

Lillian Gish *n.* [1920s+] **1** (Aus.) a dish. **2** a fish. [rhy. sl. *Lillian Gish* (1899–1993), the film star]

lillies *n.* [1910s–30s] (US) a White person's hands; thus *lily-presser*, a handshaker (cf. LILYWHITES).

lilly *n.* [1970s+] (drugs) Seconal. [the manufacturer's name on the pill, branded as *Lilly F-40*]

lilly law *see* LILY LAW.

lilt *n.* [20C] (Ulster) one who acts foolishly or carelessly. [Scot. *lilt*, to dance]

lily *n.*[1] [late 19C–1950s] (US) anything remarkable or particularly outstanding (cf. LULU n.[1]).

lily *n.*[2] [1910s–20s] a livid bruise.

lily *n.*[3] **1** [1920s] (US Und.) a gullible person. **2** [1920s–30s] (US) a virgin. **3** [1920s+] a derog. term for an effeminate man or a homosexual, esp. one who fears to reveal his sex life. [the purity or innocence of the flower]

lily *n.*[4] [1940s+] (US) a penis, usu. with ref. to urination or masturbation (cf. SHAKE/KNOCK THE DEW OFF THE LILY).

lily *n.*[5] [1950s–60s] (camp gay) a proper name used for a variety of camp nicknames (cf. AGNES; BUTTERCUP; LILY LAW).

lily *n.*[6] [1960s+] (US Black) a White person (cf. BLANCO). [SE *lilywhite*. Note 14C SE *lily*, a person or thing of exceptional whiteness, fairness or purity]

lily-benjamin *n.* [mid-19C] a white greatcoat or overcoat. [SE *lily*, white + BENJAMIN]

lily/lilly law *n.* [1940s+] (US gay) the police (cf. BRENDA n.[2]; HILDA HANDCUFFS; TERESA TRUNCHEON). [female proper name *Lily* + LAW n.[2]]

lily of lagoona *n.* [20C] (Aus.) **1** a schooner, which in Aus. is a tall beer glass. **2** beer. [(1) rhy. sl.; (2) is from (1)]

lily-shallow *n.* [early–mid-19C] a low-crowned white hat, esp. as worn by a coachman. [SE *shallow*, low + *lily*(*white*)]

lilywhite *n.*[1] **1** [late 17C–early 19C] a chimney-sweep. **2** [late 17C–early 19C] a Black person (cf. CHIMNEY CHOPS; SNOWBALL n.[1]). **3** [20C] (US Black) a White person who claims superiority on the grounds of their colour. [(1) and (2) a heavy joke at the expense of the soot-blackened sweep or Black-skinned individual]

lilywhite *n.*[2] [late 19C–1900s] a young male homosexual (cf. LILY n.[3]; LILY n.[5]).

lilywhite *adj.*[1] [20C] (US) bigoted against or segregated from Black people. [LILYWHITE n.[1] (3)]

lilywhite *adj.*[2] [1960s+] (Aus./mainly surfing) cowardly. [? the lack of suntan, but note LILY n.[3] (3)]

lilywhite groat *n.* [mid-19C–1910s] a shilling (5p). [the coin was silver]

lilywhites *n.* **1** [1920s–70s] (US Black) bedsheets. **2** [1930s–70s] (orig. US) a White person's hands (cf. LILLIES).

lima *n.* [1980s+] (drugs) marijuana. [ety. unknown; ? imported from *Lima*, Peru]

limb *n.*[1] [early 11C–late 19C] the penis. [euph.]

limb *n.*[2] [early 17C–mid-19C] a mischievous boy, a 'young rascal'. [a *limb of Satan*]

limb *n.*[3] [1930s+] (Aus.) a policeman. [abbr. LIMB OF THE LAW n. (2)]

limber-jack/-jim *n.*[1] [mid-19C–1930s] (US) a small whip, usu. used to beat children. [SE *limber up*, to make pliant + generic use of proper names]

limber-jack/-jim *n.*[2] [1900s–20s] (US) a loose-jointed person, a contortionist. [SE *limber*, lithe, nimble + generic use of proper names]

limbie/limby *n.* [1910s+] (N.Z.) one who has lost a leg, usu. in battle. [SE *limb*]

limbo *n.* **1** [late 16C–1910s] prison. **2** [late 17C] pawn. [SE *limbo*, 'a region supposed to exist on the border of Hell as the abode of the just who died before Christ's coming, and of unbaptized infants' (*OED*)]

limb of the bar *n.* [early–mid-19C] a barrister. [LIMB OF THE LAW n. (1)]

limb of the law *n.* [mid-18C–mid-19C] **1** a second-rate attorney or any legal functionary, incl. the police (cf. LIMB OF THE BAR). **2** [1930s+] (Aus.) a policeman. [SE *limb*, an extension, a branch]

limbo *n.* [1970s+] (drugs) marijuana from Colombia.

limbo room *n.* [1960s+] (Can. prison) a place where corporal punishment is administered to prisoners. [SE *limbo*]

Limburger *n.* [late 19C–1950s] (US) a derog. name for a German. [however *Limburger* is a Dutch/Belgian cheese, not a German one]

limby *see* LIMBIE.

lime *n.* [1970s+] (orig. W.I.) a spontaneous, unorganized social gathering, usu. of young people. Often qualified by its focus, e.g. *beach lime*, a beach get-together; a *roti lime*, a gathering to eat roti; thus punning phr. *this lime has no juice*, this get-together is boring. [LIME v.]

lime *v.* [1970s+] (orig. W.I.) to sit around and relax with friends or family; thus *liming*, hanging around, chatting (cf. BASE OUT). [? LIMEY n. (2), i.e. the groups of US sailors who frequented the Trinidad red-light areas during WW2. Also US teen use in the 1990s]

lime acid *n.* [1960s+] (drugs) LSD (cf. A n.[3]).

limehouse *v.* [1930s] to use coarse, abusive language, esp. in a political speech. [the proper name *Limehouse*, then a rough area of East London and one in which the Liberal leader David Lloyd George made a notably acerbic speech on 30 July 1909, in which he attacked the aristocracy, financial magnates etc]

limehouse cut *n.* [20C] a paunch. [rhy. sl. *Limehouse cut* = SE *gut*]

lime juice *n.* **1** [mid–late 19C] (Aus.) an immigrant from England; thus *hasn't got the lime-juice off, smelling of lime-juice* etc used of newly arrived immigrants. **2** [1950s] (US) English, English idiom. [LIME-JUICER n.]

lime-juicer *n.* **1** [mid–late 19C] (Aus.) an immigrant from England. **2** [mid-19C–1950s] (US) an English or British person or sailing ship. [the former habit of serving sailors lime-juice as a preventative against scurvy on long voyages]

lime-juicer *adj.* [mid-19C–1950s] (US) English, British. [LIME-JUICER n.]

limer *n.* [1970s+] (W.I.) a layabout, an idler. [LIMEY n. (2)]

lime-twig *n.* [17C] a thief (cf. LIME-TWIGS). [SE *lime-twig*, a twig smeared with birdlime for catching birds; thus a snare]

lime-twigs *n.* [16C] (Und.) playing cards, as used by a confidence trickster or card-cheat. [SE *lime-twig*, a twig smeared with birdlime for catching birds; thus a snare]

limey *n.* **1** [late-19C+] (orig. Aus.) an English person or sailing ship. **2** [1940s+] (W.I.) a derog. term for a disreputable White person of lower class (cf. LIME-JUICER n.). [the former habit of serving sailors lime-juice as a preventative against scurvy on long voyages]

limey *adj.* [late-19C+] (orig. Aus.) English, British. [LIMEY n.]

limey land *n.* [1910s–70s] (US) England. [LIMEY n. + SE *land*]

limit, the *n.* [late 19C–1930s] (US) something splendid or fine.

limited, the *n.* [late 19C+] (US) a type of US mail train in which only a limited number of passengers is conveyed. [SAmE *limited mail*]

limo/limmo *n.* [1920s+] (orig. US) limousine. [abbr.]

limousine liberal *n.* [1970s+] a liberal, the intensity of whose pronouncements on social problems are in direction proportion to their own ability to escape such an existence (cf. BOLLINGER BOLSHEVIK).

limp-dick/-prick n. [20C] an inadequate person, a weakling. [SE *limp* + DICK n.⁵ (1)/PRICK n.]

limp-dick/-prick adj. [20C] inadequate, weak. [LIMP-DICK/-PRICK n.]

limping Jesus n. [19C] a lame person (cf. HOPPING JESUS).

limp-prick see LIMP-DICK.

limp wrist/wrister n. [1950s+] (orig. US) a male homosexual. [his extravagantly effeminate gestures]

limp-wristed adj. [1950s+] (orig. US) weak, effeminate, homosexual. [LIMP WRIST n.]

limp wrister see LIMP WRIST.

lina n. [1990s] (drugs) cocaine (cf. LINE n.⁴). [Sp. *lina*, a line]

lincoln n. [1960s–70s] (US) a $5 note. [ABRAHAM LINCOLN]

lincoln and bennett n. [late 19C] (society) a first-class hat. [the makers' name]

Lincoln's Inn n. **1** [mid-19C+] a hand (cf. BRASS BAND; MARY ANN; ST MARTIN'S LE GRAND). **2** [late 19C] a £5 note. **3** [late 19C+] gin (cf. BRIAN O'LINN; BUNG IT IN; GUNGA DIN; HUCKLEBERRY FINN; NEEDLE AND PIN; VERA LYNN). [rhy. sl.; (1) = FIN n.¹, (2) = FIN n.²]

Lincoln Tunnel see GRAND CANYON.

line n.¹ **1** [mid-19C–1910s] a hoax, a trick; thus *get someone in a line*, to mock, to tease. **2** [late 19C+] (orig. US) a useful tip, a piece of information, usu. acquired confidentially. **3** [1910s+] (orig. US) a smooth verbal style aimed at seduction or at persuading someone else to accept an idea or plan, esp. in sexual or business contexts; thus *feed one a line*, *do a line with* (cf. SHOOT A LINE). [fig. use of SE *line* + abbr. *a line of talk*]

line n.² [late 19C+] (US) a red-light district. [orig. police jargon; lit. a *line* of buildings]

line n.³ [1930s+] (US Black) **1** money. **2** the cost or price of an item. [? BOTTOM LINE]

line n.⁴ (drugs) **1** [1930s+] the main vein in the arm used to inject heroin (cf. MAINLINE n.). **2** [1950s] injected heroin. **3** [1950s+] a small marijuana cigarette. **4** [1960s+] a portion of heroin or cocaine scraped into a line across a mirror in order for it to be sniffed into the nostril.

line n.⁵ [1940s+] (Aus.) a woman, usu. with a defining adj., e.g. *good line*, *nice line*, *slashing line*.

line v. **1** [16C] to seduce. **2** [1940s] (US) to copulate, used of both men and animals. [14C SE *line*, to copulate]

lined adj. [late 19C] married. [the couple have signed on the dotted *line*]

line haul n. [1930s+] (US) a scheduled truck route.

linen/linen-draper n. [mid-19C+] a newspaper. [rhy. sl. *linen-draper* = newspaper]

linen-armourer n. [late 17C–18C] a tailor.

linen-draper see LINEN.

linen-lifter n. [1980s] (Aus.) a womanizer (cf. PANTS MAN).

Linenopolis n. [late 19C] Belfast (cf. COTTONOPOLIS). [its one-time manufacturing base]

line of the old author n. [late 17C–18C] a drink, esp. of brandy (cf. LEAF OF THE OLD AUTHOR).

line one's jacket, to phr. [late 17C–early 19C] to fill one's stomach.

line out v. [1920s+] (US) to scold, to discipline, to punish; thus *lining out*, a scolding.

liner n. [20C] (Irish) a substantial meal (cf. TIGHTENER). [it *lines* one's stomach]

lines n.¹ [19C] a marriage certificate. [abbr. SE *marriage lines*]

lines n.² [1970s+] (US Black) **1** words in general. **2** persuasive patter aimed at seduction. [LINE n.¹ (3)]

line-shooter n. [1940s+] one who talks pretentiously or boasts. [SHOOT A LINE]

line someone with licks, to phr. [20C] (W.I.) to administer corporal punishment. [SE *lick*, a blow]

line the flue, to phr. [1900s–40s] (orig. US West, mainly Black) to eat.

line-up n. **1** [1910s+] gang-rape. **2** [1950s+] a police identification parade.

line up v.¹ **1** [1900s–60s] (US) to associate, to join up with. **2** [1940s+] (Aus.) to accost, to approach.

line up v.² **1** [20C] (orig. US) to arrange, to organize, to plan in advance. **2** [1930s+] (US) to arrange an illicit and profitable deal.

line up v.³ **1** [1910s+] (US) to subject to or (rare) to be subjected to a gang rape. **2** [1920s] (US) to rob.

line up on v. [1910s+] **1** to gang rape. **2** (gay) to gang fellate or sodomize. [ext. of LINE UP v.³ (1)]

line up one's ducks, to phr. [1970s+] (US) to set one's affairs in order (cf. HAVE ONE'S DUCKS IN A ROW).

line up to v. [1920s+] (Aus.) to accost. [ext. of LINE UP v.¹ (2)]

ling n. **1** [19C] the vagina or the female sexual odour; thus *ling-grappling*, sexual intercourse (cf. BEARDED CLAM). **2** [1920s+] (Aus.) a stench. [20C use of (1) is also Aus. E.P. notes the old music-hall song, *c*.1835, which tells the tale of a woman attempting to buy a fish, the name of which she has forgotten and runs in part: 'Then the girl shoved her hand 'neath her clothes in a shot/And rubbed it about on a certain sweet spot;/Then, blushing so sweetly, as you may suppose, she put her hand up to the fishmonger's nose./The fishmonger smelt it, and cried with delight,/ ... /"I'll tell you directly, you wanted some *ling*"']

ling-grappler n. [19C] a womanizer. [LING n. (1) + SE *grappler*]

lingo n. **1** [mid-19C+] (orig. Ling. Fr./Polari) a language, esp. slang. **2** [1900s] (US) insincere talk, a yarn, an excuse. [Ital. *lingua*, language]

linguist n. [1950s+] (Aus.) a cunni*linguist*. [abbr.]

link n. [1990s] (drugs) the money handed over in a drug deal. [play on CONNECTION n.]

link adj. [late 19C] (Jewish/Cockney) unorthodox, irreligious (cf. FRUM). [Ger. *links*, left, in the sense of left-handed = unorthodox, unnatural]

linkman n. [late 19C] a general servant. [ext. of SE *linkman*, one who carries a *link* or torch]

linthead/lintbrain n. (US) **1** [1930s–60s] an insignificant or lower-class person. **2** [1960s+] a stupid person. [SE *linthead*, a worker in a cotton mill]

lint-scraper n. [mid–late 19C] a junior surgeon.

lion n.¹ **1** [18C] a spy employed by an influential and powerful man (cf. TIGER n.¹). **2** [late 18C] a prosperous citizen or merchant; thus its use in late 18C–early 19C in Oxon. sl. for a visitor to the university (his female companions were *lionesses*). **3** [early 19C] a fashionable person, a 'man-about-town' (cf. SEE THE LIONS).

lion n.² [1950s+] (W.I. Rasta) an outstanding Rastafarian, a great soul. [the *lion of Judah*, a central Rasta symbol]

lion v. [1920s+] (Aus.) to frighten, to intimidate. [reverse anthropomorphism]

Lionel Blair n. [1970s+] a chair. [rhy. sl., entertainer *Lionel Blair*]

lionel blairs n. [1970s+] flares, flared trousers. [rhy. sl., entertainer *Lionel Blair*]

lioness n. [19C] a prostitute (cf. POLECAT).

lion's lair n. [20C] a chair. [rhy. sl.]

lion's roar n. [20C] a snore. [rhy. sl.]

lip n.¹ **1** [early 19C+] cheek, impertinence. **2** [1920s+] (US) a lawyer, esp. in criminal practice (cf. MOUTHPIECE). [(2) the concept of 'talking back' (as in cheekiness) in defence of a client]

lip n.² [late 19C+] (US) musical ability, esp. as a player of brass instruments, thus its later usage as 'a brass player'.

lip v. **1** [late 18C–late 19C] to sing; thus *lip us a chant*, sing us a song. **2** [late 19C] to speak. **3** [late 19C+] to insult, to abuse, to be impudent. **4** [20C] (Ulster) to eat.

lip action *see* LIP DANCING.

lip and lagging/lippin-leggin *adj.* [20C] (Ulster) full to the brim. [Scot. *laggen*, the projecting part of the stave at the bottom of a barrel]

lip-burner *n.* [1950s] (US) a very short cigarette butt.

lip dancing/action/music *n.* [20C] (US) oral sex.

lip fart *n.* [1920s+] (US teen) a farting noise made with the lips (cf. RASPBERRY n.¹).

lip fart *v.* [1920s+] (US teen) to make a rude farting noise with the lips (cf. BLOW A RASPBERRY). [LIP FART n.]

lip in *v.* [late 19C–1940s] (US) to butt into a conversation impolitely. [LIP n.¹ (1)]

lipish/lippish *adj.* [mid-19C] impudent, cheeky (cf. LIPPY adj.).

lipken *see* LIBKEN.

lipkisser *n.* [1960s+] (US) a man who enjoys cunnilingus. [Lat. *labia*, lips]

lip-lock *n.* [1970s+] (US) **1** a fig. tight hold with the mouth. **2** fellatio. **3** a passionate kiss.

lip music *see* LIP DANCING.

lip off *v.* [1940s+] (US) to talk rudely, cheekily or provocatively. [LIP v. (3)]

lippin-leggin *see* LIP AND LAGGING.

lippish *see* LIPISH.

lippy *n.* [1950s+] *lip*stick. [abbr.]

lippy *adj.* [mid-19C+] cheeky, talkative, loudmouthed. [LIP n.¹ (1)]

lip read *v.* [1970s] to kiss.

lip rug *n.* [1970s] (US Black) a moustache. [SE *lip* + RUG n.³]

lips *n.* [1990s] (US Black) the vagina (cf. NETHER LIPS). [Lat. *labia*, lips]

lip service *n.* [1970s] fellatio (cf. LIP DANCING).

lipstick *adj.* [1980s+] (orig. US) of a lesbian, feminine and smart in appearance.

Lipton's orphan *n.* [late 19C–1900s] a pig. [the imagery employed in a celebrated billboard used by *Lipton's* grocers]

Lipton's/Lipton tea *n.* [1960s+] (US drugs) inferior quality cannabis. [pun on SE *tea*/TEA n.² (1)]

lip-wrestle *n.* [1990s] (US) passionate kissing.

liq *n.* [1970s+] (US Black) a *liq*uor store. [abbr.]

liquefied *adj.* [1930s+] drunk.

liqueur of four ale *n.* [late 19C] bitter beer.

liquid *n.* [1960s+] LSD dissolved into a liquid form (cf. A n.³).

liquidate *v.* **1** [mid-19C] (US) to pay one's debts. **2** [1930s+] (orig. US) to kill someone. [(1) is SE in UK. (2) euph. used during the Stalinist era in the former USSR]

liquid cosh *n.* [1970s+] (prison) major tranquillizers used to calm rebellious or 'difficult' prisoners.

liquid courage *n.* [1940s+] (US) courage due to the consumption of alcohol (cf. DUTCH COURAGE).

liquid crack *n.* [1990s] (US Black) malt liquor (cf. HIPPIE CRACK). [SE *liquid* + CRACK n.¹⁷; the ref. is to the strength of the drug and of the beer]

liquid crime/death/fire *n.* [19C] strong, potent alcohol, esp. whisky.

liquid gold *n.* [1980s+] (drugs) alkyl nitrites.

liquid laugh *n.* [1960s+] (orig. Aus.) vomit.

liquid lightning *see* LIGHTNING n.¹.

liquid lunch *n.* **1** [1960s+] (orig. Aus.) a meal that consists of alcohol. **2** [1990s] a self-administered suction enema (cf. HERSHEY IN A STRAW).

liquid X *n.* [1980s+] (drugs) gamma hydroxy butyrate. [joc. use of *X* to glamorize the drug as mysterious (cf. G.B.H.²)]

liquor *n.* **1** [mid–late 19C] (US) a drink; thus *what's your liquor?*, what will you have to drink? **2** [late 19C] the water used by unscrupulous publicans to adulterate beer.

liquored up *adj.* [1920s+] (US) drunk.

liquorhead *n.* [1920s+] (US) a drunkard. [SE *liquor* + sfx. -HEAD (2)]

liquorice/licorice stick *n.* **1** [1930s+] (US) a clarinet. **2** [1980s+] (US gay) a Black man's penis (cf. BLACK JACK n.⁷).

liquor one's boots, to *phr.* **1** [early 18C] to cuckold. **2** [late 18C–19C] to drink before leaving on a journey. [note synon. 19C Roman Catholic jargon 'to deliver extreme unction'; i.e. the anointing with holy oil of one who is at the point of death]

liquor someone's hide, to *phr.* [late 17C–early 18C] to thrash, to give a beating (cf. LIQUOR UP v.¹). [pun on LICK v. (1)]

liquor's/whisky's talking *phr.* [1920s+] a situation in which indiscretions and/or garrulous speech are put down to drunkenness (cf. APPLETON TALKING).

liquor-up *n.* [mid–late 19C] (US) a drink.

liquor up *v.*¹ [late 17C–late 18C] to beat, to thrash (cf. LIQUOR SOMEONE'S HIDE). [pun on LICK v. (1)]

liquor up *v.*² **1** [18C–19C] to ply with drink, to supply with alcohol. **2** [mid–late 19C] to drink alcohol; thus *liquorer*, a hard drinker; *liquoring*, drinking.

lisp and stutter *n.* [20C] (Aus.) butter. [rhy. sl.]

lispers *n.* [late 18C–mid-19C] the teeth.

listen *v.* [1900s–30s] (US) to sound; as in *that listens well*.

listener *n.* [early 19C] (orig. boxing) the ear.

listen good *v.* [1910s–30s] (US) to sound promising (cf. LOOK GOOD).

listen to oneself, to *phr.* [late 19C] (Irish) to think.

listing to starboard *adj.* [19C+] tipsy, drunk (cf. ROLLING adj.³; SLEWED). [naut. imagery]

listman *n.* [1920s–30s] a ready-money bookmaker. [the list of prices exhibited]

lit *n.*¹ **1** [mid-19C+] *lit*erature. **2** [late 19C+] *lit*erary, esp. in combs. *lit. crit.*, literary criticism; *lit. ed.*, literary editor; *lit. supp.*, literary supplement. [abbr.]

Lit/Lith *n.*² [1920s+] (US) a *Lith*uanian. [abbr.]

lit *adj.*¹ **1** [1910s+] drunk (cf. LIT UP). **2** [1980s+] (US drugs) extremely intoxicated by a drug.

lit *adj.*² [1960s+] (US Black) having been shot. [? the flash of the shot]

literature *n.* [late 19C+] any form of printed material.

lith *see* LIT n.².

little and large *n.* [20C] margarine. [rhy. sl. *little and large* = MARGE n.¹]

little audrey *n.* [1970s] in darts, the bull's-eye. [? + ref. to a vagina]

Little Barbary *n.* [late 17C–18C] Wapping, home of the Radcliffe Highway, once London's tough port area. [for ety. *see* BARBARY COAST]

little barn *n.* [20C] (US) an outside lavatory (cf. LITTLE HOUSE).

little bit off the top *phr.* [1910s+] (Aus.) slightly insane. [pun on hairdressing use]

little black book *n.* [20C] the volume in which every bachelor supposedly keeps lists of available and willing women.

little bomb *n.* [1980s+] (drugs) amphetamine, heroin or a depressant. [trans. of BOMBITA]

Little Bo-Peep *n.* [late 19C+] sleep (cf. BO-BEEP). [rhy. sl.; ult. the nursery rhyme]

little boy blue *n.*¹ [20C] a prison warder. [rhy. sl. *little boy blue* = SCREW n.² (2)]

little boy blue *n.*² [1960s+] (US Black) the police (cf. BLUE n.³). [the colour of their uniforms]

little boy in the boat *n.* [20C] the clitoris (cf. BABY IN THE BOAT).

little boy's room *n.* [1930s+] (orig. US) a coy euph. for a men's lavatory (cf. LITTLE GIRL'S ROOM).

little breeches/britches n. [late 18C+] an affectionate term of address to a small boy. [UK use ends/US commences in mid-19C]

little britches n. [1980s+] (US gambling) the point of three in craps dice (cf. LITTLE FOUR; LITTLE JOE n.[1]; LITTLE JOSIE; LITTLE PHOEBE). [ety. unknown]

little brother n. [mid-19C+] the penis.

little brown jug n. [20C] **1** an electric plug. **2** a bath plug. **3** a tampon. [rhy. sl.; (3) is fig. use of SE *plug*]

little casino n. **1** [1900s–50s] (US) an insignificant person. **2** [1960s+] (US) gonorrhoea. [SE *casino*, a card game in which the ten of diamonds, called *great casino* counts two points, and the two of spades, called *little casino*, counts one; (2) compares gonorrhoea with syphilis, which would be a 'greater' form of VD]

little charmer n. [late 19C+] an attractive young woman.

little clergyman n. [late 18C–19C] a young chimney-sweep. [blackened clothes]

little conversation n. [late 19C–1900s] violent swearing (cf. LANGUAGE!).

little dabbler n. [1970s–80s] the decimal halfpenny, an anomalous coin discarded in 1984. [DABBLER]

little davy n. [17C+] the penis.

little deers n. [late 19C] (US) young women who are involved in some way with the stage. [double pun on *little dear* and *deer* as a fem. version of STAG n.[5] (1), i.e. the single men who frequent the theatre]

little devil n. [17C+] a term of mildly reproving affection.

little end of nothing phr. [early 19C+] (US) anything very insignificant, utterly unimportant; also intensified as *little end of nothing sharpened/whittled down to a point*.

little end of the horn phr. [19C+] (US) failure; usu. in the phr. *come out of the little end of the horn*. [the *Horn of Plenty*, which in mythology was one of the horns of the goat Amalthea by which the infant Zeus was suckled, and hence a symbol of fruitfulness and plenty. Its large end is depicted as pouring forth its bounty]

little eva n. [1960s–70s] (US Black) a loud-mouthed White woman.

little fish n. [early 19C+] (US) an unimportant person. [reverse of BIG FISH n. (1)]

little four n. [20C] (US gambling) the point of 4 in craps dice (cf. LITTLE BRITCHES).

little friend n. [1920s+] (orig. Can./Aus.) menstruation; thus *my little friend has come*, I am menstruating. [the ref. is to the welcome appearance of a period as a sign that, had one been worried, one was not pregnant]

little gentleman in the black velvet coat n. [18C–19C] a mole. [the Jacobite phrase, often used as a toast, referring to the belief that the death in 1702 of William III (their conqueror) was caused by his horse's stumbling over a molehill]

little girl's room n. [1940s+] a coy euph. for the lavatory (cf. LITTLE BOY'S ROOM).

little go n. **1** [late 19C] (Und.) one's first experience of prison. **2** [1960s] (US) an unimportant, unexciting or incomplete attempt at a task or performance. [Oxford University jargon *little go*, the first public examination (usu. taken during or at the end of one's first year and now known as *prelims*) as opposed to finals or *great go*]

little green men n. [1950s+] a popular description of the putative inhabitants of outer space. [note the *OED*'s first citation for the phr. is not strictly SF, but certainly fantastical, Rudyard Kipling's *Puck of Pook's Hill* (1906)]

little grey cells n. [1920s+] the human brain. [coined by crime writer Agatha Christie in *The Mysterious Affair at Styles* (1920) and always associated with her fictional sleuth Hercule Poirot]

little grey home in the west n. [1910s–50s] a vest. [rhy. sl.]

little house n. [late 19C+] (Aus./N.Z./US) an outside lavatory (cf. LITTLE BARN).

littlie n. [1960s+] (Aus./N.Z.) a child. [SE *little* + N.Z. sfx. *-ie*, equivalent of Aus. sfx. *-o*]

little jobs n. [20C] (juv.) urination (cf. BIG JOBS). [euph.]

little Joe/little Joe from Kokomo n.[1] [late 19C+] (gambling) the point of 4 in craps dice (cf. LITTLE BRITCHES).

little joe/little joe in the snow n.[2] [1920s+] (drugs) cocaine (cf. SNOW n.[3]).

little john n. [1980s+] (N.Z. drugs) a cannabis cigarette made from two papers. [ety. unknown]

little josie n. [20C] (gambling) the point of 4 in craps dice (cf. LITTLE BRITCHES).

little lowie n. [1940s] an unprofessional prostitute, who fails to take her work seriously. [SE *little* + LOWIE]

little madam/proper little madam n. [mid-19C+] a very young girl who acts, and considers herself, both older than her years and superior to her peers.

little mama n. [19C+] (US Black) an attractive Black woman.

little man n. [20C] **1** the penis. **2** the clitoris (cf. BABY IN THE BOAT).

little mary n. [1900s–20s] the stomach. [coined by Sir James Barrie (1860–1937) in his play *Little Mary*, 'a nursery name that the child-doctor invents as a kind of polite equivalent to what children ordinarily allude to as their "tum-tum"' (*Punch*, 14 October 1903)]

Little Miss Muffet, to phr. [20C] to get rid of, to ignore. [rhy. sl. *Little Miss Muffet* = STUFF IT!]

Little Miss Roundheels n. [1950s+] a promiscuous woman (cf. LIGHT FRIGATE; SHORT-HEELED WENCH). [note Robert Greene in *The Blacke Bookes Messenger* (1592): 'the commonest harlot and hackster ... and with the lightnes of hir heeles bring me in the some crownes']

little more! excl. [1950s+] (W.I. Rasta) a general excl. of farewell, 'see you later!'.

little nell n. [20C] a bell, usu. a doorbell. [rhy. sl.]

little nigger n. [20C] (US) in poker, a game in which the low spade splits the pot (cf. BIG NIGGER).

little office n. [18C+] the lavatory (cf. LITTLE BARN; LITTLE HOUSE). [ext. of OFFICE n.[2]; 20C use is Aus./US]

little old adj. [late 19C+] (US, mainly South/Midwest) used variously to express contempt, familiarity or affection.

little old man in the boat n. **1** [late 19C–1900s] the navel. **2** [20C] the clitoris; thus *sink the little man in the boat*, to have sexual intercourse (cf. BABY IN THE BOAT).

little ones n. [1980s+] (drugs) phencyclidine (cf. ACE n.[3]). [ety. unknown]

little pal see LITTLE SISTER.

little peter n. [20C] a gas or electricity meter. [rhy. sl.; note PETER n.[3]]

little phoebe n. [20C] (US gambling) a throw of 5 in craps (cf. LITTLE BRITCHES).

little ploughman n. [19C] the clitoris (cf. BABY IN THE BOAT). [? pun on SE *plough*/PLOUGH v.[1]]

little pretty n. [1970s] (US Black) an attractive male.

little quid n. [18C] the Devil. [SE *little* + Lat. *quid*, what, which thing]

little rabbits have big ears phr. [20C] a phr. used when one is talking indiscreetly in front of children. [var. on pvb. 'little pitchers have big ears']

little red ridings n. [1950s–60s] stolen goods. [rhy. sl. *Little Red Riding Hood*s]

little red wagon n. [1930s–60s] (US Black) a problem, a difficulty; usu. in the phr. *that's your little red wagon*.

little Rome n. [1960s] Liverpool, UK. [the substantial Roman Catholic community]

little school n. [1920s] (US Und.) a juvenile reformatory. [in contrast to an adult prison, *big school*]

little season n. [late 19C] (society) the social events of the spring, which precede 'the Season', the events of which tend to take place in the summer.

little shame tongue n. [19C] the clitoris. [trans. of synon. Ger.]

little shot n. [1930s+] (US) an insignificant person. [reverse of BIG SHOT]

little sister/pal n. [19C] the vagina.

little smack n. [1900s–20s] a half-sovereign (50p). [? its relatively muted smack into the palm, compared with the full sovereign]

little smoke n. [1960s+] (drugs) **1** marijuana. **2** psilocybin/psilocin.

little snakesman n. [late 18C–19C] a small boy in a gang of burglars who is put through a narrow opening into a house, then lets the gang in (cf. DIVER; FAGGER; SNAKESMAN). [SE *little* + SNAKESMAN]

little stranger n. [20C] an unborn foetus, esp. one that is illegitimate or of unknown paternity.

little titch/titchy adj. [20C] itchy. [rhy. sl.; ult. music-hall comedian Harry Relph (*Little Titch*) (1868–1928)]

little wack/whack n. [late 19C] a small measure of spirits. [SE *little* + WHACK n.²]

little woman n. [mid-19C+] one's wife.

lit to the gills phr. [20C] drunk. [ext. of LIT UP adj. (1)]

lit up adj. **1** [late 19C+] (orig. US) drunk. **2** [1920s] (US) showily dressed up. **3** [1920s+] (orig. US) under the influence of a drug.

lit up like a Christmas tree phr. [20C] very drunk. [ext. of LIT UP adj. (1)]

lit up like Broadway/Main Street/Times Square phr. [20C] very drunk. [ext. of LIT UP (1)]

litvak n. [late 19C+] a Jew whose family come from Lithuania and are therefore considered lower-class by Jews from Poland (cf. POLACK).

live adj. **1** [mid-19C+] (orig. US) alert, energetic. **2** [1970s+] excellent, first-rate, thrilling; thus *a live one*, an admirable person or object. [the image of a live performance]

live at Easy Hall, to phr. [20C] (W.I.) to live comfortably (cf. EASY STREET).

live at the sign of the cat's foot, to phr. [late 18C] of a man, to be dominated by one's wife (cf. PUSSY-WHIPPED).

live at the sign of the Queen's Head/in Queen Street, to phr. [late 18C–mid-19C] of a man, to be dominated by one's wife.

live at your aunt/nennen, to phr. [20C] (W.I.) to find it hard to make enough money to live, to subsist, to suffer great hardship (cf. CATCH HELL v.). [W.I. *nennen*, a godmother]

live bache v. [late 19C] (society) of a man, to live alone, as a bachelor.

live blanket n. [1990s] (W.I./UK Black teen) a human body, particularly when covering another, as in sexual intercourse.

live eels n. [mid-19C] fields. [rhy. sl.]

live high on the hog, to phr. [1940s+] (orig. US) to live in general and to eat in particular with great self-indulgence.

live horse n. [mid-19C] work done and not charged for. [antonym of DEAD HORSE n.¹]

live in a good paddock, to phr. [1950s] (N.Z.) to live comfortably. [farming imagery]

live in high wood, to phr. [mid–late 19C] to hide out. [an actual *High Wood*, to which London villains would escape]

live in Queen Street *see* LIVE AT THE SIGN OF THE QUEEN'S HEAD.

live in Swell Street, to phr. [early 19C–1900s] to live a prosperous, respectable, secure life (cf. EASY STREET; FAT CITY; SWELL STREET). [SWELL adj. + SE *street*]

live in someone's ear, to phr. [20C] (Irish) to live on very intimate terms.

live it up v. [1950s+] (orig. US) to have a good time, to enjoy oneself.

live large v. [1970s+] (US Black) to live extravagantly and ostentatiously (cf. LIVE LOW). [SE *live* + LARGE adv., coined as the motto of 'The Executioner', hero of the action adventure series by Don Pendleton, first publ. 1969]

live low v. [1980s+] (US Black) **1** to have a poor standard of living (cf. LIVE LARGE). **2** to feel depressed.

live meat wagon n. [1920s+] (US) an ambulance (cf. COLD MEAT CART). [ext. of MEAT WAGON n. (1)]

livener n. [late 19C–1900s] the first drink of the day, used as a 'pick-me-up' (cf. ALLEVIATOR). [SE *enliven*]

live off the land, to phr. [late 19C+] (Aus.) to live as a tramp.

live off the smell of an oil/oily rag, to phr. [mid-19C] (Aus./N.Z.) to subsist on a bare minimum of material wants.

live-on n. [late 19C] an attractive young woman. [a husband could *live on her earnings*; the image is of her (unrealized) potential as a prostitute]

live one n. **1** [late 19C+] (US) a notable, popular or well-respected individual. **2** [late 19C+] (Und.) the ideal victim for a proposed hoax, fraud or other deceit. **3** [1960s+] (gay) a generous rich client for a prostitute. [LIVE adj.]

live ones n. [1980s+] (drugs) phencyclidine (cf. ACE n.³).

live on the skin of a rasher, to phr. [Irish] to live very frugally.

live out v. [late 19C] (US) to be in domestic service. [one *lives out of one's own home*]

live out of one's suitcase/trunks/boxes, to phr. [20C] to live a peripatetic life, with no opportunity to settle in one place.

liver n. [late 19C+] a bout of ill temper; thus *liverishness* (cf. BACK n.²).

live rabbit n. [19C] the penis; thus *have a bit of rabbit pie, skin the live rabbit*, to have sexual intercourse (cf. HAVE A BIT OF RABBIT PIE).

liver-chops n. [mid-19C] **1** large, dark lips. **2** a person with thick, dark lips, often used in direct address (cf. LIVER-LIPS). [SE *liver* + CHOPS n. (1)]

liver-disturber/-lifter n. [late 19C] (US) a very large penis (cf. KIDNEY-BUSTER).

liver-faced *see* WHITE-LIVERED.

liver-jerker n. [late 19C–1900s] a tricycle.

liver-lifter *see* LIVER-DISTURBER.

liver-lips n. [1910s+] (US Black) **1** large, dark lips. **2** a person with thick, dark lips, often used in direct address (cf. LIVER-CHOPS).

Liverpool kiss n. [1940s+] (US) a blow to the mouth or face (cf. GLASGOW KISS; GORBALS KISS). [orig. naut.]

liver-shaker n. [late 19C–1910s] a riding hack.

liver-spot n. [1940s+] (W.I.) a mulatto.

liver-string n. [20C] (W.I./Guyn.) a notional source of one's energy; thus *work out one's liver-string*, to exhaust oneself through hard labour.

livery adj. [1930s+] suffering problems with one's liver, so tetchy, irritable. [cf. SE *liverish*]

live sausage n. [19C] the penis (cf. BACON n.¹).

live shallow v. [late 19C] for a villain to live quietly, 'in retirement', when wanted by the police.

live square v. [1950s+] (Aus.) to lead a respectable life. [SE *live* + SQUARE adj. (1)]

livestock n. **1** [late 18C–1910s] lice, fleas, any bodily infestation (cf. BLACK CATTLE; GOLD-BACKED ONES; GREYBACKS; HAMPSTEAD DONKEYS; SADDLEBACK). **2** [mid-19C] (US) slaves. **3** [1920s–50s] (US) women as objects of sexual interest, or prostitutes.

live tally v. [mid-19C–1900s] (mainly north) to cohabit, to live as man and wife without an actual marriage; thus *tally-ho*, living in this manner (cf. TALLY-HUSBAND; TALLY-WIFE). [SE *tally*, one of two corresponding parts]

live till they sun you, to phr. [20C] (W.I.) to live to a great old age. [the image is of an old person being placed to sit quietly in the sun]

live under the cat's foot, to phr. [late 18C] of a man, to be dominated by one's wife (cf. LIVE AT THE SIGN OF THE QUEEN'S HEAD; PUSSY-WHIPPED). [CAT n.¹ (3)]

live up to one's blue china, to phr. [late 19C–1910s] to live up to or beyond one's means. [the gentility implied by a collection of blue china]

live up to the door/knocker, to phr. [mid-19C–1900s] to live up to one's means.

live wire n. [late 19C+] a lively, energetic person (cf. SPARK PLUG).

live with v. [1930s+] to tolerate, to put up with.

livid adj. [1910s+] (orig. US) furious, overcome with rage.

living end n. [1950s+] the extreme, the absolute limit.

living flute n. [19C+] the penis (cf. FLUTE n.²).

living fountain n. [mid-17C] the vagina (cf. DAMP n.).

living off the tit phr. [1960s+] living in luxury, overly protected. [TIT n.¹ (1); i.e. 'breast-fed']

living sauce n. [1990s] semen (cf. BABY GRAVY).

living with mother now phr. [late 19C] a phr. used by women to reject offers of marriage or of an affair. [the chorus of a 'doubtful' (Ware) music-hall song]

Liz see LIZZIE n.².

lizard n.¹ [mid-19C+] an inhabitant of Alabama. [lizards are common in the state]

lizard n.² **1** [late 19C] (Aus./N.Z.) a shepherd, a musterer, a mender of boundary fences (cf. SNAIL). **2** [1900s–60s] (US) an old or useless racehorse. **3** [1910s+] a smooth and highly plausible fortune-hunter or womanizer who works his charms in the lounges of hotels, an adventurer. **4** [1920s+] (US) a contemptible person. **5** [1980s+] (US Black) a young woman.

lizard n.³ [1960s+] (Aus./US) the penis; thus (Aus.) *give the lizard a run*, to have sexual intercourse; (US) *leak one's lizard*, to urinate; *stroke/whip one's lizard*, to masturbate (cf. BLEED THE LIZARD; DRAIN ONE'S LIZARD; GALLOP THE OLD LIZARD; MILK THE LIZARD; PET THE LIZARD).

-lizard sfx. [1920s+] (US) used in combs. to describe a person with a particular habit or type of behaviour; thus *chow-lizard*, a person who eats a lot; *couch-lizard*, a person who frequently lies necking with his girlfriends on a couch etc (cf. LOUNGE LIZARD).

lizarding n. [1970s] (Aus.) lazing. [the way a lizard basks in sun]

lizards n. [1950s–70s] (US Black) lizard-skin shoes.

lize n. [mid-19C] (US) a generic name for New York's 'Bowery g'hals', the female accomplice/equivalent of MOSE n.¹ (cf. 'ARRY). [for ety. see MOSE n.¹]

lizzie/Lizzie n.¹ **1** [late 19C] (orig. US) an effeminate youth (cf. MARY-ANN; NANCY; NELLIE) **2** [1900s–20s] (US campus) a young woman. **3** [1940s+] a lesbian.

lizzie/Lizzie/liz/Liz n.² **1** [1910s] (US) an aeroplane. **2** [1910s] (US) as *the Lizzie*, the Cunard liner Queen Elizabeth. **3** [1910s+] (orig. US) an early Model Ford car, spec. the Model T, known as the *tin Lizzie*. [affectionate use of the female name]

lizzie/Lizzie n.³ [1930s] cheap Portuguese wine. [abbr. *Lisbon*, the Portuguese capital]

lizzie v. [1910s+] (US) to drive an early Model Ford car, spec. the Model T. [LIZZIE n.² (3)]

lizzie up v. [1910s+] (US) to act as a homosexual. [LIZZIE n.¹ (1)]

l.l. n.¹ [late 19C] (Dublin) a superior brand of whisky. [abbr. *lord lieutenant*]

l.l. n.² [1990s] (drugs) marijuana. [play on the name of rap singer *L.L. Cool J*/COOL adj.⁴ + J. n.²]

llello n. [1990s] (US Black) hello. [mispron.]

lloyd/Harold Lloyd n. [1910s+] a piece of celluloid used for picking Yale locks (cf. LOID n.; SHIM n.³). [rhy. sl. *Harold Lloyd* = LOID n.; ult. silent film star *Harold Lloyd* (1893–1971)]

l.m.c. adj. [1990s] *lower middle class* (cf. L.C.). [abbr.]

Lo/Mr Lo/Mrs Lo n. [mid-19C+] (US) a Native American. [pun on the line 'Lo, the poor Indian' in Pope's *Essay on Man* (1733)]

'lo! excl. [1920s+] hel*lo*. [abbr.]

load n.¹ [early 18C+] a heavy responsibility. [abbr. colloq. phr. 'a load on one's mind']

load n.² **1** [mid-18C–mid-19C] (Und.) one's personal possessions or money, also the proceeds of a crime. **2** [1940s+] (US) a very fat person.

load n.³ [19C+] (orig. Aus.) a bout of venereal disease (cf. DOSE n.⁴); thus *loaded*, venereally diseased. [SE *loaded*, to be burdened with, to be weighed down. Note late 19C use of *load*, measles, smallpox]

load n.⁴ **1** [mid-19C+] (US) faeces, a bowel movement; thus *drop one's load*, to defecate. **2** [1920s+] (US) an ejaculation of semen or an orgasm (of either sex) (cf. SHOOT ONE'S LOAD). **3** [1970s+] (US Black) the intense urge to have sex. **4** [1970s+] (US Black) a large amount of semen in the testes.

load n.⁵ **1** [1930s+] (orig. US) utter nonsense. **2** [1940s+] (US) a stupid, ridiculous or contemptible person (cf. CROCK OF SHIT). [abbr. *load of garbage*, *load of shit* etc]

load n.⁶ **1** [1930s+] (US) an old, discontinued model or a run-down, dilapidated vehicle or a stolen car (cf. HEAP n.²). **2** [1990s] (US Black) an automobile.

load n.⁷ [1950s+] (drugs) 25 or 30 packs of heroin held together in a bundle, the equivalent of an ounce weight (cf. HALF-LO).

load v. [late 19C–1950s] (US) to lie, to deceive.

loaded adj.¹ **1** [late 19C+] (orig. US) drunk (cf. GET IN ONE'S LOAD; WELL-LOADED). **2** [1920s+] (orig. US) intoxicated with a drug. **3** [1920s+] (US) laced with alcohol, drugs or poison. **4** [1940s+] (orig. US) rich, either in actual cash or simply, esp. in prison use, in possessions such as tobacco.

loaded/loaded for bear adj.² **1** [late 19C+] (US) fully prepared for all problems, esp. the hardest ones, thus also fully armed and equipped for conflict. **2** [late 19C–mid-20C] (US) drunk. **3** [late 19C–mid-20C] (US) holding a good poker hand. [hunting use, bear-shooting requires heavy armament]

loaded gun n. [1980s+] (US gay) the penis before ejaculation of its 'load' of semen.

loaded to ... phr. [late 19C+] synonyms for drunk, incl. *loaded to the barrel*, *... the earlobes*, *... the gills*, *... the guards*, *... the gunnels*, *... the hat*, *... the muzzle*, *... the Plimsoll Mark*, *... the tailgate*.

loadie n. [1970s+] (US campus) a habitual drinker or drug user. [LOADED adj.¹]

load in v. [late 19C] to drink.

load of n. [20C] a great deal of, a lot of, usu. in combs. to form dismissive phr.; thus *load of crap*, *load of old cobblers*, *load of old cods*, *load of old wank* etc.

load off one's behind n. [1920s+] a defecation. [pun]

load off one's mind n. [1920s+] **1** a haircut. **2** a defecation. [puns]

load of hay n. [mid-19C] a day. [rhy. sl.]

load of mischief n. [late 18C–early 19C] one's wife, when carried upon one's back.

load of reg n. [20C] a load of rubbish, nonsense. [abbr. milit.

regimental, a stickler for discipline, esp. petty, nonsensical rules]

load on _n._ [mid-19C+] (US) a drunken state. [LOADED adj.[1]]

loads of _n._ [early 17C+] many, a great quantity, esp. of a desirable commodity (cf. DEAD LOADS).

load the cannon, to _phr._ [1980s+] to masturbate (cf. ARMING THE CANNON). [CANNON n.[1] (2)]

load up _v._[1] [20C] to get drunk, to use a drug; also as _load up on_ a drink or drug.

load up _v._[2] [1930s+] (Aus./N.Z.) to infect with venereal disease. [LOAD n.[3]]

loaf _n._[1] [mid-19C] (orig. US) **1** the act of loafing, idling; thus (US) _loaf-day_, a day when no regular work is done. **2** any occupation deemed to require minimal if any effort. [LOAF v.[1] (1), but note Sw. _lofdag_, Du. _verlofdag_, a leave-day, a holiday]

loaf _n._[2] [1910s+] a head, esp. brains, intelligence; thus _use one's loaf_, to act sensibly, often as imper. _use your loaf!_ [rhy. sl. _loaf of bread_]

loaf _n._[3] [1990s] (drugs) marijuana. [? resemblance of a block of marijuana to a loaf of bread]

loaf _v._[1] **1** [19C] (orig. US) to idle, to relax. **2** [mid–late 19C] (US campus) to steal. [ety. unknown; the posited link to Ger. dial. _lofen_, to run, cannot be sustained. (1) 20C SE]

loaf _v._[2] [20C] (Irish) to head-butt. [LOAF n.[2]]

loafer _n._ (orig. US) **1** [19C] an idler. **2** [early 19C+] a beggar, a cadger or a ruffian. [LOAF v.[1]]

Loaferies, the _n._ [late 19C] the Whitechapel Workhouse. [LOAF v.[1] (1) + sfx. _-eries_, the ref. is to the uncharacteristic kindness shown by its staff to those who were forced to live on its charity. A pauper could loaf around, rather than be forced to work, pray or otherwise justify their existence. This extended to their attempt, in 1898, to abandon the pej. name 'Workhouse']

loafing _n._ **1** [19C] lounging, relaxing. **2** [early 19C+] begging, cadging. [LOAF v.[1]]

loaf of bread _phr._ [1930s] dead. [rhy. sl.]

lo and behold _n._ [20C] a plunging neckline. [the neckline is _lo(w)_ and one _beholds_ the breasts]

loaner _n._ [1920s+] (US) a temporary replacement for an item being repaired. [SE _loan_]

loan shark _n._ [20C] a supplier of private loans at maximum interest; thus _loan sharking_, the practice of lending money at usurious rates, esp. by organized crime syndicates (cf. SHARK).

lob _n._[1] **1** [18C] a snuffbox, any box. **2** [early 18C–mid-19C] a till, a cash register; thus _dip/frisk/pinch/sneak a lob_, to rob a till; _make a good lob_, to take a large amount of money from the till. **3** [19C–1900s] a fortune, a large amount of money; thus (Und.) a haul. **4** [mid-19C–1900s] the head. **5** [1940s–50s] (prison) pay.

lob/lobb _n._[2] [18C+] the penis, esp. when half- or fully erect (cf. LOBCOCK). [SE _lob_, something pendulous]

lob/lobb _n._[3] [20C] a dull, stupid person (cf. LOBBY; LOOBY). [16C SE/dial. _lob_, a country bumpkin. Note Yid. _lobbes_, rascal + Du. _lobbes_, a clown]

lob, the _n._[4] [20C] the lavatory. [? ext. of LOB n.[1] (1)]

lob _v._[1] [early 19C] to droop, to allow to hang heavily. [16C–18C SE]

lob/lob in _v._[2] **1** [1910s+] (Aus.) to arrive, to turn up. **2** [20C] to commence having sexual intercourse. [SE _lob_, to move heavily or clumsily]

lobb _see_ LOB n.[2], n.[3].

lobby _n._ [19C] a fool (cf. LOB n.[3]; LOOBY). [SE _lob_, a country bumpkin]

lobby-gow _n._ **1** [late 19C–1970s] (US) a hanger-on, a messenger, an errand boy, esp. one who frequents or works in an opium den or brothel, or a tourist guide in Chinatown,

New York City. **2** a Chinese police informer. **3** an insignificant person. [SE _lobby_ + GOW n.[2] (1)]

lobby louse/lizard _n._ [1930s] (US) a person who loiters in hotel lobbies, usu. harassing guests (cf. LOUNGE LIZARD).

lobcock _n._ **1** [16C] a fool (cf. DICKHEAD). **2** [late 18C+] a large, flaccid penis (cf. LAZY LOB). **3** [18C–19C] a penis suffering from penile strabismus (cf. HOCK-PINTLED). [LOB n.[2] + COCK n.[2] (1)]

lob-crawler/-sneak _n._ [mid–late 19C] (US) a thief who specializes in robbing shop tills; thus _lob-crawling_, committing such robberies. [LOB n.[1] (2)]

lob in _see_ LOB v.[2].

lobkin _n._ [late 18C–early 19C] a lodging house. [LIBKEN]

loblolly _n._ **1** [late 16C–late 18C] a thick gruel, both a peasant and a naut. dish, and also used as a simple medicine (cf. LOBSCOUSE). **2** [early 17C–late 19C] a bumpkin, a peasant, a boor. **3** [early 19C] (W.I.) a weakling. **4** [mid-19C–1940s] (US) a mud hole. **5** [20C] (US) a fat person. [? echoic but note dial. _lob_, to bubble while boiling, esp. of a thick substance like porridge + Devon dial. _lolly_, broth, soup or other food boiled in a pot]

lobo _n._ [1940s] (US Black) an unattractive woman. [SE _lobo_, grey wolf, thus synon. DOG n.[5] (6)]

lob onto _v._ [1920s+] (Aus.) to get hold of or find out through a stroke of luck.

lobs _n._[1] [mid-19C] an under-gamekeeper. [? LOB n.[3]]

lobs _n._[2] [mid-19C] (tramp) talk, conversation. [Rom. _lavaw_, words]

lobs! _excl._ (juv.) **1** [mid-19C] a warning shout that heralds an approaching master (cf. CAVE!). **2** [1910s–20s] a call for truce during a game. [ety. unknown]

lobscouse _n._ [18C+] a sailor's dish consisting of meat stewed with vegetables and ship's biscuit, which is the totemic dish of Liverpool (cf. SCOUSE n.[1]; SCOUSER n.[2]).

lob-sneak _see_ LOB-CRAWLER.

lob's pound _n._ **1** [late 16C–early 19C] a prison. **2** [17C] the vagina. [LOB n.[1] (1) + SE _pound_, an enclosure, but note LOB n.[2]]

lobster _n._[1] **1** [mid-17C–late 19C] a soldier (cf. BOILED LOBSTER; BOIL ONE'S LOBSTER; LOBSTER-BACK; LOBSTER-BOX; RAW LOBSTER; UNBOILED LOBSTER). **2** [mid-19C+] (US) a slow-witted, awkward or gullible person; a fool, a dupe; a bore. [(1) orig. f. the full suits of armour worn by the Roundheads in Cromwell's New Model Army (spec. Hazelrigg's cuirassiers); then f. the red coats worn by British soldiers of the period; (2) the slow movements of the crustacean, but note LOB n.[3]]

lobster _n._[2] [1970s] (US Black) a rich person. [the role of lobsters as luxury food]

lobster _n._[3] [1990s] a general term of abuse. [one who has 'a tail full of meat and a head full of shit']

lobster-back _n._ [early–late 19C] a British soldier. [ext. of LOBSTER n.[1] (1)]

lobster-box _n._ [early 19C] **1** a transport ship. **2** a military barracks. [LOBSTER n.[1] (1) + SE _box_]

lobster-palace society _n._ [1890s] (US) the world of wealth if not of social position. [_lobster-palace_, one of the elegant, expensive new restaurants that emerged in New York City, which specialized in lobsters and attracted the rich and famous]

lobster-pot _n._ [19C] the vagina (cf. BEARDED CLAM).

lobster-shift/-trick _n._ [1940s+] (US) a late-night work shift. [the slow pace of the crustacean; i.e. such a shift, usu. between 2.00a.m. and 9.00a.m. is rarely busy]

lobstertails _n._ [1940s–60s] (US Black) **1** a case of venereal disease. **2** a case of body lice.

lobster-trick _see_ LOBSTER-SHIFT.

loc _n._ [1990s] (US Black) marijuana. [abbr. LOCOWEED]

loc/lok _adj._[1] [1990s] (US Black) **1** crazy, mad, whether because of taking drugs or one's emotional state; thus *loc-ed up*, emotional. **2** armed. [LOCO adj.; the image of (2) is of one who, once armed, will do something 'crazy']

loc *adj.*[2] [1990s] (US Black) *loc*al, from the neighbourhood. [abbr.]

loc *v.* [1990s] (US Black) to smoke marijuana. [LOC n. (1)]

local, the *n.*[1] [1930s+] the nearest public house, or that which the speaker uses regularly; thus *my local*.

local *n.*[2] [1970s] (US) an act of a prostitute masturbating a customer.

local *adj.* [1940s+] (S.Afr.) eccentric, crazy (cf. LOC adj.[1]). [LOCO adj.]

local talent *n.* [1970s+] the attractive women in a neighbourhood. [SE *local* + TALENT n. (2) + pun]

local yokel *n.* [1950s+] (US) a naïve and foolish small-town or country man.

location joke! *excl.* [1980s+] (US campus) you had to be there!

loced out *see* LOC'D OUT.

locie/loci/lokey/lokie *n.* [1930s+] (Can./N.Z./US) a *loco*motive. [abbr.]

lock *n.*[1] **1** [late 17C–early 19C] a place for storing stolen goods (cf. LOCKUP). **2** [late 17C–early 19C] a receiver of stolen goods. **3** [19C] the vagina. [SE *lock*, an enclosure; (2) from (1)]

lock *n.*[2] **1** [early 18C–early 19C] a chance; thus *stand a queer lock*, to have a poor chance. **2** [early 18C–early 19C] character, e.g. *stand a queer lock*, to bear an indifferent character. **3** [1930s+] (US) a certainty (cf. CINCH n.[1]). **4** [1960s+] (US) complete control over something. [SE *lock*, a grip or trick in wrestling]

lock *n.*[3] [20C] (Ulster) a small quantity, e.g. of food; thus *brave lock*, *quare lock*, a substantial amount. [orig. dial.]

lock *v.* **1** [1930s+] (US prison) to occupy a cell. **2** [1960s+] of a pimp, to ensure a whore's fidelity, emotional and economic (cf. BONDS). **3** [1970s+] (US Und.) to imprison.

lock-all-fast *n.* [late 17C–late 18C] a receiver of stolen goods (cf. LOCK n.[1]).

lock assholes/asses *v.* [1950s+] (US) to fight (cf. SNAP ASSHOLES). [ARSEHOLE n./ARSE n.[1]]

lockdown *n.* [20C] (US prison) an instance of the entire prison population being confined to the cells and deprived of exercise or association.

locked *adj.* [20C] (Irish) drunk. [SE *locked*, i.e. shut off from coherent thought or action]

locked-up *adj.* [1950s–60s] engaged, booked, spoken for.

locker *n.*[1] [early 18C] (Und.) one who leaves goods at a house in the country or a small town and borrows money on them, pretending that they have been made in London, i.e. that they are valuable.

locker *n.*[2] **1** [19C] the vagina (cf. KEYHOLE; LOCK n.[1]; LOCK OF LOCKS). **2** [mid-19C+] (US) the stomach.

locker room *n.* [1980s+] (drugs) isobutyl nitrite. [its association with all-male amusements]

locket *see* LUCY LOCKET.

lock into *v.* [20C] to become part of a plan, a group etc, to join.

lock it in cruise mode, to *phr.* [1980s+] (US campus) to focus attention on a stranger in a group for romantic or sexual reasons. [CRUISE v.[1] (1) + SF imagery]

lock off *v.* [20C] (W.I.) to put a choke-hold on someone's neck in order to immobilize and then rob them; also known as *choke-and-rob*.

lock of locks *n.* [18C] the vagina (cf. JIGGER n.[4]; KEYHOLE; LOCK n.[1]; LOCKER n.[2]; MACHINE n.[1]).

lock one's barn door, to *phr.* [1960s+] (US) to fasten one's trouser fly.

lock on with *v.* [20C] (Aus.) to fight.

locks *n.* [1950s+] (orig. W.I.) the long knotted hair that is the best-known and typical badge of Rastafarianism.

locksman *n.* [1950s+] (orig. W.I.) a Rastafarian. [LOCKS + SE *man*]

locksmith's daughter *n.* [late 18C–late 19C] a key.

lockup *n.* **1** [mid-19C] (US) a jail. **2** [20C] (US Und.) the punishment cell or cells (cf. HOLE n.[2]). [20C use of (1) is SE]

lock up *v.* **1** [1910s+] (US) to be in complete control and thus assured of victory. **2** [1940s] (US Black) to have under one's complete control, to possess absolutely.

lock-up chovey *n.* [early 19C] a covered cart in which travelling hawkers carry their goods around the country. It can be locked to secure the stock. [SE *lock up* + CHOVEY]

loco *n.* **1** [mid-19C+] (US) a lunatic. **2** [1960s+] (US teen gang) a Mexican-American gang member (cf. LA VIDA LOCA). **3** [1960s+] (US drugs) marijuana (cf. LOCOWEED). [Sp. *loco*, crazy]

loco *adj.* [late 19C+] (orig. US) insane, crazy. [abbr. *locoweed*, a narcotic weed that affects cattle in the Southwest US; ult. Sp. *loco*, insane, crazy]

locomo *v.* [1990s] (US teen) to leave the area. [LOCOMOTE]

locomote *v.* [early 19C] (US) to move around from place to place. [backform. f. SE *locomotion*]

locomotive *n.*[1] [18C] a drink made of Burgundy, curaçao, egg yolks, honey and cloves all heated together. [? play on SE, i.e. it 'gets one moving']

locomotive *n.*[2] [1900–50s] (orig. US campus) 'a cheer characterized by a slow beginning and a progressive increase in speed and used esp. at school and college sports events' (Webster 1966). [SE since the 1960s]

locomotives *n.* [mid-19C] the legs.

locomotive tailor *n.* [late 19C] a travelling workman.

loc out *v.* [1980s+] (US Black) to drive crazy, to make exciting. [LOC adj.[1]]

loc'd out/loced out/loqued out *adj.* [1980s+] (US Black) crazy, under stress. [LOC OUT]

locoweed *n.* [1930s+] (US drugs) marijuana. [Sp. *loco*, crazy, the erroneously presumed effects of cannabis + *locoweed*, milkvetch, or any other plant of the genus *Oxytropis*, which causes erratic behaviour, impaired coordination and poss. lethargy in livestock]

locs *n.*[1] [1990s] (US Black) locks, i.e. the softer, straighter curls known as Jheri curls (cf. CURL n.[2]; LOCKS). [pron. with a long 'o']

locs *n.*[2] [1990s] (US Black) sunglasses. [LOC adj.[1]; i.e. the image of the sunglass-wearer as tough, dangerous and ready for any action – no matter how 'crazy']

locura *n.* [1960s+] (US) the state of being a gang member (cf. LA VIDA LOCA). [Sp. *locura*, craziness]

locus *n.* [late 17C] anything stupefying; thus (W.I.) *locus-ale*, an intoxicating drink made of the scum of the sugar cane. [? Sp. *loco*, mad, i.e. the effects of the drink]

locus *v.* [mid–late 19C] **1** to stupefy with drink; thus *locus away*, to steal something when the victim is drunk. **2** to trick, to fool. **3** to render a victim unconscious with chloroform, usu. to rob them or carry them aboard a ship in need of crew. [? rhy. with *hocus*, though not proper rhy. sl. or LOCUS n.]

locust *n.*[1] **1** [mid-19C] (US) a policeman. **2** [mid-19C–1930s] (US police) a billy club or stick. [SE *locust wood*, from which the clubs were made]

locust *n.*[2] **1** [late 19C] (society) an extravagant person who throws away any left-overs, rather than saving them for possible reuse. **2** [1970s] (Aus.) a tourist (cf. GRASSHOPPER n.[5]).

loddy *n.* [early 19C] laudanum or tincture of opium.

lodger *n.* [mid–late 19C] an unimportant, insignificant person.

lodgers *n.* [late 19C–1910s] head lice, rats and mice, any kind of vermin.

lodgings *n.* [19C] the vagina.

lodging-slum *n.* [early 19C] (Und.) the hiring of expensive lodgings with the intention of stealing the furniture etc that one finds there. [SE *lodging* + SLUM n.¹ (4)]

lofty *n.* [20C] a nickname both for a very tall and a very short man.

log *n.*¹ [late 19C] (Aus.) a prison or lock-up. [the earliest such prisons in Aus. were built of logs]

log *n.*² **1** [1930s] (US drugs) an opium pipe. **2** [1970s+] a large marijuana cigarette (cf. STICK n.¹⁴). **3** [1970s+] (US drugs) phencyclidine (cf. ACE n.³).

log *n.*³ [1950s–60s] (US) a bar. [the wood from which it is constructed]

log *n.*⁴ [1970s+] a piece of excrement; thus *lay a log*, to defecate (cf. BUILD A LOG CABIN).

log *n.*⁵ [1970s+] (US) the penis (cf. FLOG THE LOG; SLOG THE LOG).

log-cabin raider *n.* [1990s] a male homosexual. [LOG n.⁵]

loge *n.* [late 17C–18C] (Und.) a watch. [Fr. *horloge*, watch]

loges *n.* [17C] (Und.) a faked pass or warrant (cf. FAKER OF LOGES). [Gk. (((o(, logos, a word]

logey *n.* [20C] (Irish) a heavy, fat person. [SE *log*]

loggerhead *n.* [late 17C+] a fool, a dullard; thus *logger-headed*, dull, stupid. [post-18C use is US, f. SE *logger*, something heavy or clumsy + sfx. -HEAD (1)]

loggo *n.* [mid-19C–1900s] logs, esp. as a street cry *Any loggo?*

logie *n.* [mid-19C] sham jewellery. [theatre jargon *logie*, prop jewels, made mainly of zinc, invented by one David *Logie*]

logi-logi/logo-logo *n.* [1950s] (W.I.) a stupid, oafish person. [? SE *log*]

log-juice *n.* [mid-19C] a cheap port wine. [the use of SE *logwood* (used in dyeing and in medicine as astringent) to adulterate port]

log of wood *n.* [1950s+] (Aus.) a dull, stupid person.

logo-logo *see* LOGI-LOGI.

logor *n.* [1980s+] (drugs) LSD (cf. A n.³). [ety. unknown; ? Sp.]

log-pusher *n.* [1990s] a male homosexual (cf. BEACHCOMBER n.²). [LOG n.⁵]

log-rolling *n.* [early 19C+] (orig. US) the corrupt giving of mutual aid, esp. in professional contexts (e.g. a critic consistently pushing a novelist friend). [the habit among early American settlers of communities or neighbours helping one another with the annual heavy tasks occasioned by logging]

logs *n.* [late 19C–1900s] (Aus.) a lock-up, a prison. [LOG n.¹]

log the dog/hog, to *phr.* [1990s] to masturbate. [DOG n.¹²/HOG n.⁴]

log-town *n.* [1950s+] (US) a small, insignificant town. [the orig. 19C *log-towns*, made up of buildings constructed of logs]

logy *adj.* [1980s+] (US drugs) lethargic after smoking cannabis. [LOG n.² (2), but note US regional *logy*, slow, lethargic, stupid, ult. synon. dial. *louggy, loogy*]

loho *n.* [1930s+] (drugs) marijuana. [Sp. *loco*, crazy]

loid *n.* [1950s+] cellu*loid* or a piece of plastic, such as a credit card, used to slip open Yale-style locks when housebreaking (cf. LLOYD; SHIM n.³). [abbr.]

loid *v.* [1950s+] to gain entry by means of a strip of celluloid (cf. SHIM v.). [LOID n.]

loincloth age *n.* [1990s] prehistory.

loiner *n.* [1940s+] an inhabitant of Leeds, West Yorkshire. [Marples, *University Slang* (1950), suggests a possible corruption of late 19C–1910s *oiner*, f. Gk. *oinidzein*, to smell of wine, and as such a term used to disparage 'town' people by students]

lok *see* LOC adj.¹.

lokey/lokie *see* LOCIE.

loksh *see* LUKSHEN.

Lola Montez *n.* [mid-19C] (Aus.) a drink made of Old Tom, ginger, lemon and hot water. [*Lola Montez* (1818–61), an Irish dancer and courtesan, who toured Australia in 1855]

lolla/lala/la-la/lal-lah *n.* [late 19C+] (US) something or someone outstandingly good, stylish or pleasing (cf. HUMDINGER; LULU). [ety. unknown; ? abbr. of LALLAPALOOSA]

lollapaloosa/lollapalooza *see* LALLAPALOOSA.

lollied *adv.* [1960s–70s] informed against, betrayed to the police. [? LOLLIPOP v.¹]

lollies *n.* **1** [mid-19C+] (Aus.) all sweets, except for ice lollies. **2** [20C] the female breasts, which can, like a sweet, be sucked (cf. APPLES n.¹; DOLLIES n.²). [abbr. SE *lollipop*]

lollion *n.* [20C] (Ulster) a fat, clumsy person. [? SE *loll*]

lollipop *n.*¹ **1** [19C] the penis (cf. LADIES' LOLLIPOP). **2** [1960s+] the penis or vagina in the context of oral sex (cf. APPLE n.¹⁰).

lollipop *n.*² **1** [mid-19C–1950s] a woman, esp. an attractive one. **2** [20C] (US) one's sweetheart, usu. used as a term of affection. **3** [1920s–60s] (US) an effeminate man or a homosexual. **4** [1960s+] one's special favourite, the prize article in a collection. [all are 'sweet']

lollipop *n.*³ [20C] a monetary tip. [rhy. sl. *lollipop* = DROP n.⁵]

lollipop/lolly *n.*⁴ [20C] a policeman. [rhy. sl. *lollipop* = COP n.¹]

lollipop *n.*⁵ **1** [1940s+] (US Black) a gullible person who has been 'sucked', i.e. taken advantage of (cf. SUCKER n.¹). **2** [1950s] an older man who is happy to indulge a younger woman, whether or not he receives any favours in return (cf. SUGAR DADDY).

lollipop *v.*¹ [20C] to inform, to betray. [rhy. sl. *lollipop* = SHOP v.¹ (2)]

lollipop *v.*² [1950s+] (US Black) to take advantage of someone. [LOLLIPOP n.⁵ (1)]

lollipop man/woman *n.* [1960s+] a man or woman who supervises children crossing the road near a school. [the sign on a pole that they carry, now SE]

lollipop stop *n.* [1980s+] (US gay) a lavatory, esp. one where one can get quick, anonymous sex. [LOLLIPOP n.¹]

lollipop woman *see* LOLLIPOP MAN.

lollop *n.* [late 19C] an insignificant, lazy person. [LOLLOP v.]

lollop *v.* [late 18C+] to lounge, to sprawl. [SE *loll*]

lolloper *n.* [1910s+] (US) anything or anyone exceptional in quality, size, character etc (cf. LALLAPALOOSA; WALLOPER n.³).

lolloping *n.* [mid-18C+] lazing, loafing, idling. [LOLLOP v.]

lollopy *adj.* [mid-19C+] lazy. [LOLLOP v.]

lollos *n.* [1950s] (Aus.) the female breasts, esp. when large. [the Ital. film star *Gina Lollobrigida* (b.1927), who was also known as 'La Lollo']

lolly *n.*¹ [mid-19C] the head. [SE *loll*; orig. boxing use]

lolly *n.*² [mid-19C] money. [? rhy. sl. *lollipop* = cop = copper]

lolly *n.*³ *see* LOLLIPOP n.⁴.

lolly *n.*⁴ [1960s] (US) the anus, esp. in derisive excl. *up your lolly!* [ety. unknown]

lolly *n.*⁵ [1990s] an annoying, depressing person. [? LOLLY n.¹, thus cf. DICKHEAD; DORK n.²; WEENIE n.¹ (4)]

lollycooler/lallycooler *n.* [late 19C+] (US) someone or something successful, admirable (cf. LALLAPALOOSA).

lollygag *n.* **1** [mid-19C+] foolishness, nonsense, empty chatter. **2** [20C] flirting, love-making. **3** [1940s] a wastrel, an irresponsible person. [LOLLYGAG v.²]

lollygag *v. see* LALLYGAG.

lolly scramble *n.* [1960s+] an undignified struggle, for money, power, influence, fame etc. [SNZE *lolly scramble*, the tossing of a handful of *lollies*, i.e. sweets, for children to grab]

lolly up *v.* [1950s+] to inform to the police. [rhy. sl. *lollipop* = SHOP v.¹ (2)]

lollywater *n.* [1950s+] (Aus./N.Z.) a soft, non-alcoholic drink. [SE *lollipop* + *water*]

lolpoop *n.* [late 17C–late 18C] a lazy, idle drone. [SE *loll*]

lombard *n.* [1980s] *loads of money but a right dickhead* (cf. BUPPIE). [an acronymic pun on the 17C Lombards, natives of Lombardy who provided Europe, including London, with its leading bankers. One of a rash of acronyms coined during the mid-1980s, *lombard* described many of the newly rich young men who populated the City of London]

Lombard fever *n.* [late 17C–early 19C] idleness, indolence, laziness, 'the idles' (Grose). [dial. *lomber*, to idle. The *OED* links the term to dial. *fever-lurden, fever-lurgan, fever-lurgy, fever-largie*, all meaning the same. Its first citation comes from the dialectologist John Ray (1627–1705)]

Lombard Street to a Brummagem sixpence *phr.* [19C] the longest possible odds, an absolute certainty (cf. ALL THE WORLD TO A CHINA ORANGE; LOMBARD STREET TO A CHINA ORANGE; LOMBARD STREET TO AN EGGSHELL; LOMBARD STREET TO NINEPENCE).

Lombard Street to a china orange *phr.* [mid-19C+] the longest possible odds, an absolute certainty (cf. ALL THE WORLD TO A CHINA ORANGE; LOMBARD STREET TO A BRUMMAGEM SIXPENCE). [Lombard Street, a centre of London banking since the 12C + SE *china orange*. The sweet orange (*Citrus aurantium*) was first sold in London in the mid-17C and by the 19C it was used figuratively to mean anything of minimal value. The bet wagers the wealth that is available in the street's banks against the almost valueless orange]

Lombard Street to an eggshell *phr.* [mid-18C] the longest possible odds, an absolute certainty (cf. ALL THE WORLD TO A CHINA ORANGE; LOMBARD STREET TO A BRUMMAGEM SIXPENCE).

Lombard Street to ninepence *phr.* [early 19C] the longest possible odds, an absolute certainty (cf. ALL THE WORLD TO A CHINA ORANGE; LOMBARD STREET TO A BRUMMAGEM SIXPENCE).

Londonderry *n.* [mid-19C+] sherry. [rhy. sl.]

London fog *n.*[1] [late 19C–1910s] a dog. [rhy. sl.]

London fog *n.*[2] [1960s+] (Aus.) any manual worker who does not perform their share of the work (cf. JUDGE *n.*[3]). [such a person 'will not lift']

London ivy *n.* [late 19C] **1** dust. **2** fog. [both tend to obscure what they 'grow on']

London ordinary *n.* [mid-19C] Brighton beach.

London particular *n.*[1] [19C] a type of Madeira wine, imported especially for London merchants.

London particular *n.*[2] [mid-19C+] a London fog or smog (cf. LONDON IVY). [? the pale yellow colour of LONDON PARTICULAR *n.*[1] or f. the image of such a fog appearing only in London]

London smoke *n.* [late 19C] (society) a yellowish colour, like the polluted London smogs.

London taxi *n.* [20C] the anus. [rhy. sl. *London taxi* = JACKSIE]

London to a brick *phr.* [1960s+] (Aus.) a certainty, the longest possible odds (cf. ALL THE WORLD TO A CHINA ORANGE; BET LONDON TO A BRICK). [BRICK *n.*[4]]

Londrix *n.* [mid-19C] London. [? Fr. *Londres*, London]

lone duck/dove *n.* [late 19C–1900s] **1** a former 'kept woman' who is now a common prostitute. **2** a prostitute working in a brothel (cf. QUIET MOUSE).

lone hand *n.* [1920s–30s] (US Und.) a thief who operates alone (cf. LONE WOLF).

lonely art *n.* [20C] masturbation. [apart from its obvious connotations, note the pun on 'lonely heart']

lonelyhearts *n.* [20C] (US Und.) prisoners who maintain a correspondence with people outside prison.

lonely in the weather *n.* [1950s] (W.I.) a tall, thin person. [their head is 'in the clouds']

lone man/woman *n.* [late 19C–1930s] (US) an unmarried man or woman.

lone ranger *n.* [20C] a chance, an opportunity. [rhy. sl. *lone ranger* = SE *danger*]

lone wolf *n.* [1900s–50s] (orig. US police/Und.) a criminal who works alone, not necessarily a recluse, but not permitting anyone to penetrate their façade. [thus SE use, a solitary person, usu. male]

lone wolf it *v.* [1900s–50s] (orig. US) to live or act alone. [LONE WOLF]

lone woman *see* LONE MAN.

long *n.*[1] [1930s–40s] (US) a long-barrelled revolver (cf. SHORT *n.*[3]).

long *n.*[2] [1990s] (US Black) money. [abbr. LONG GREEN *n.* (1)]

long *adj.*[1] **1** [mid-18C+] of numbers, large; thus *long odds*, high odds; *long price*, a high price; *long purse*, riches; *long shillings*, good wages. **2** [1940s+] (US Black) of money, large amounts (cf. LONG *n.*[2]; LONG GREEN).

long *adj.*[2] [mid-19C+] of banknotes, being in small denominations (cf. SHORT *adj.*[1]). [orig. cashiers' jargon, small denominations mean more notes, which take a *longer* time to count]

long *adj.*[3] [1910s–20s] of liquor, watered down. [LONG DRINK]

long *adj.*[4] **1** [1910s+] abundant. **2** [1910s+] (Und.) used to describe a prisoner who still has most of their sentence to serve (cf. SHORT *adj.*[3]). **3** [1950s+] (US drugs) of a drug addiction, severe; thus a *long jones*, a severe habit.

long acre *n.* [mid-19C] a baker. [rhy. sl.]

long and linger *see* LEAN AND LINGER.

long and narrow, like a Welsh mile *phr.* [late 18C–19C] said of anything that is thus shaped. [like a *country mile*, a *Welsh mile* is proverbially longer than its actual measure pronounces]

long and short *n.* [20C] port (wine). [rhy. sl.]

longas *n.* [1950s] (W.I.) a very tall man. [? SE *long* + ARSE *n.*[1]]

long bacon *n.* [20C] the gesture of 'thumbing one's nose'; thus *make/pull long bacon*. [BACON *n.*[1] (1)]

long beer *n.* [mid-19C+] a glass of beer or of a soft drink, as opposed to wine or spirits (cf. LONG DRINK).

long belly/gut *n.* [1950s] (W.I.) a greedy person.

long-belly/-guts *adj.* [1950s] (W.I.) gluttonous, greedy, usu. of a man or a child. [LONG BELLY *n.*]

long-bench *see* LONG-METER.

long bit *n.*[1] [1930s–50s] **1** (US Und.) a sentence of 10 years or more (cf. BIG BIT). **2** any term of imprisonment over 38 months that must be completed before becoming eligible for parole. [SE *long* + BIT *n.*[7]]

long bit *n.*[2] [mid-19C–1950s] (US) 12½ or 15 cents, in contrast to a dime or SHORT BIT. [BIT *n.*[1] (4)]

longbow man *n.* [late 17C–mid-19C] a liar. [DRAW A LONGBOW]

long boy *n.* [1960s+] (US) a large sandwich made of two slabs of bread cut lengthwise from the loaf and containing a variety of ingredients (cf. HERO *n.*[1]; SUBMARINE *n.*[2]).

long-bread/-cash/-dough *n.* [1940s+] (US Black) a large amount of money (cf. LONG GREEN).

long clay *n.* [mid-19C] a churchwarden pipe.

long con *n.* [1930s+] (orig. US Und.) any confidence trick or cheat that is carefully planned for perfect execution (cf. SHORT CON).

long-cork *n.* [early 19C] claret. [the length of cork used for such wine]

long crown *n.* [mid-19C] a clever person. [pvb. 'that caps long-crown, and he capp'd the devil'; i.e. one who has a SE *long crown*, a large skill – and supposedly a large brain]

long dedger *n.* [mid-19C+] (Ling. Fr./Polari) the number 11. [Ital. *undici*, 11]

long dong silver *n.* [1980s] (US) the penis. [DONG *n.*[2]+ pun on the fictional pirate Long John Silver, the anti-hero of R.L. Stevenson's *Treasure Island* (1883)]

long-dough *see* LONG-BREAD.

long drink *n.* [mid-19C+] a glass of beer or a soft drink, as opposed to wine or spirits (cf. LONG BEER; SHORT n.[1]) [note Trollope, *West Indies* (1859) 'A long drink is taken from a tumbler, a short one from a wine-glass']

long drink of water *n.* [late 19C–1900s; 1930s+] a very thin person (cf. LONG THIN STREAK OF PISS). [Scot. *drink*, a lanky overgrown person; ult. ON *drengr*, a young, unmarried man; 1930s+ use is US]

long drop *n.* [1970s+] (S.Afr.) an outdoor privy.

long ear *n.* **1** [mid-19C] a clever person (cf. LONG CROWN). **2** [mid–late 19C] (US campus) a sober, religious student. **3** [1930s–50s] (US) an eavesdropper.

longears *n.* [late 19C–1960s] (US) a mule, a donkey.

long-eye *n.*[1] **1** [mid–late 19C] the vagina. **2** [20C] (W.I.) a promiscuous woman.

long-eye *n.*[2] [20C] (W.I.) greed, covetousness; thus *put one's long eye on*, *throw long eye on*, to covet, to desire for oneself.

long face *n.* [late 18C+] a miserable or solemn appearance.

long-faced chum *n.* [late 19C] a horse (cf. LONG-HAIRED CHUM).

long fifteen *n.* [early 17C] 'some class of lawyers' (*OED*). [ety. unknown]

long firm/l.f. *n.* [mid-19C+] (Und.) a fraudulent scheme whereby a firm is set up, small orders placed and paid for to establish good credit, then a massive order is made, its contents quickly sold off, often below par, and the firm vanishes, the warehouse is shut down and the debt, this time huge, is never paid (cf. ORDER-RACKET).

long foot *adj.* [20C] (W.I.) long-legged.

long ghost *n.* [mid-19C–1900s] a tall, awkward person.

long goodbye *n.* [1950s+] death. [the title of a Raymond Chandler novel publ. in 1953]

long-grain rice *n.* [1940s+] (W.I.) a boiled green banana. [similar shape, if different size]

long gut *see* LONG BELLY.

long-guts *see* LONG-BELLY.

long green *n.* **1** [late 19C+] (US) money, paper money, esp. in large amounts (cf. ALFALFA n.). **2** [1960s] (US drugs) a kind of marijuana. [the colour of dollar bills/marijuana]

longhair *n.* **1** [1920s+] (orig. US) an intellectual or artist. **2** [1930s+] (US) a performer or *aficionado* of classical music. **3** [1950s+] (US) classical music. **4** [1960s+] (US) a hippie or a politically liberal person. [stereotyped image of an intellectual as bearded, sandalled and hirsute]

longhair *adj.* [1920s+] (US) intellectual, usu. pej. [LONGHAIR n.]

longhaired *adj.* **1** [1910s+] (orig. US) intellectual, aesthetic, always pej.; thus *longhaired music*, the classics etc. **2** [1910s] (esp. milit.) of a man, female-looking; as in *longhaired bunkie*, a longhaired buddy (cf. LONG-HAIRED CHUM n.). [LONGHAIR n.]

long-haired chum *n.* [late 19C] **1** a horse (cf. LONG-FACED CHUM). **2** a young woman, a girlfriend.

long handlebars *see* HANDLEBARS.

long-handled spoon *n.* [1920s] (US) a spade.

long-handles/long-handled underwear *n.* [1940s+] (Can./US) long woollen winter underwear, combinations (cf. LONG JOHNS). [late 19C *long-handled hose*]

long-head *n.* [late 18C–late 19C] (US) an astute, shrewd person. [SE *long* + *head*]

long-headed *adj.* **1** [early 19C+] discerning, shrewd. **2** [late 19C+] obstinate. [LONG-HEAD]

long-heel *n.* [1950s+] (US/mainly South) a Black person. [supposed physiological characteristic]

longhorn *n.* [late 19C–1940s] (US/mainly West) a tough, Texan old-timer or cowboy (cf. SHORTHORN). [the *longhorn cattle* that were found in Texas]

long house *n.* [1900s–40s] (US Black) a brothel (cf. ACCOMMODATION HOUSE). [a typical brothel of the period had a

long central corridor with a number of small bedrooms arranged along either side]

longies *n.* **1** [1910s–60s] long trousers. **2** [1940s+] (orig. US) long woollen winter underwear, combinations (cf. LONG JOHNS).

long in the arm *phr.* [late 19C–1910s] a phr. used to describe an habitual thief.

long in the hips *phr.* [19C] broad-buttocked.

long in the mouth *phr.* [mid-19C–1920s] tough.

long john *n.* [1960s+] (US) a sandwich consisting of a small sausage that is put into a much longer bun or roll.

long johns *n.* [1940s+] (orig. US) long woollen winter underwear, combinations (cf. LONGIES).

long jump *n.* [1920s–60s] a hanging; thus *take the long jump*, to be hanged.

long lady *n.* [late 19C] a farthing candle.

long legs *n.* [18C+] a tall person.

long-lick *n.* [late 19C] (US) molasses.

long meg *n.* [late 17C–early 19C] an exceptionally tall woman; thus *as long as Meg of Westminster* (cf. LONG SHANKS). [proper name of a celebrated late 17C woman, *Long Meg* of Westminster]

long-meter/-bench *n.* [20C] (W.I.) a boring, long-winded speaker. [? *long meet her*, i.e. one who won't go away/one who sits next to you on the *bench* and will not leave]

long-mouth *n.* [20C] (W.I.) a glutton, one who is constantly hungry.

longneck *n.*[1] [late 19C+] (Aus.) a camel.

longneck/longnecker *n.*[2] [20C] **1** (US, mainly Texas) a round bottle of whisky. **2** (Aus./US) a beer bottle. [the shape of the respective bottles]

long nine *n.* [mid–late 19C] (US) a cigar. [? nine inches long]

long on *adj.* [20C] well supplied with, expert in.

long out *v.* [20C] (W.I.) to purse one's lips or stick out one's tongue in a gesture of deliberate rudeness.

long out one's eye on, to be *phr.* [20C] (W.I.) to be covetous for (cf. HAVE LONG EYES).

long paddock *n.* [1920s+] (Aus./N.Z.) the road.

long-playing record *n.* [1960s+] a chatterer, a gossip.

long-pull *n.* [late 19C] an over-measure in a public house. [the *pull* is of the handle of the beer pump]

Long's *n.* [late 19C] Short's Winehouse, in the Strand opposite Somerset House, London.

longs *n.* [1920s+] long trousers. [the slightly joc. antonym of SE *shorts*]

longs-and-shorts *n.* [mid-19C] cards purpose-made for cheating.

long shanks *n.* [late 17C–20C] a notably tall man (cf. LONG MEG).

long-shoe/long-shoe game *n.* [1950s–80s] **1** (US Black) a sophisticated, urbane pimp or swindler. **2** the profession and lifestyle of pimping. [the style of footwear preferred by US Black pimps in the 1960s and 1970s]

long shoes *n.* [1950s–80s] (US Black) success; thus *wear long shoes*, to be successful.

longshore lawyer *n.* [early 19C] a corrupt, ruthless lawyer. [SE *longshore*, tough, villainous]

long shot *n.* [late 19C+] (gambling) a wild guess, an adventurous attempt, a slim chance. [SE *long* + SHOT n.[2] (2); the inaccuracy of shooting at a distant target, thus a bet laid at long odds on an unlikely contender]

long slab *n.* [20C] a very tall, thin woman.

long-sleeved top *n.* [late 19C–1910s] a silk hat.

long-sleever *n.* [late 19C+] (Aus.) a drinking glass of the largest size (cf. DEEP NOSER; DEEP SINKER). [SE *long* + SLEEVER]

long soup *see* SHORT SOUP.

long spit *see* BIG SPIT.

long stale drunk n. [late 19C] a hangover, the depression that follows a bout of heavy drinking.

long stomach n. [late 18C–early 19C] **1** a voracious appetite. **2** a greedy eater.

long streak of misery n. [late 19C+] a very tall person, esp. one with a mournful, depressed air (cf. LONG THIN STREAK OF PISS).

long strokes n. [20C] the initial stage of sexual intercourse (cf. SHORT STROKES).

long suit n. [late 19C+] anything in which one feels esp. secure or capable. [card-playing imagery, now SE]

long tail n. [20C] (Aus.) treacle. [ety. unknown; ? the slow progress of treacle off the spoon]

long-tailed bear n. [late 19C] a lie. [a bear has no tail]

long-tailed beggar n.[1] [mid-19C] a cat. [the supposed story of a sailor who came home after his first voyage unable to remember the name of cat and asked his mother 'What's she called, that 'ere long-tailed beggar?']

long-tailed beggar n.[2] [1900s] a large denomination sterling note (cf. LONG-TAILED 'UN).

long-tailed finnup n. [mid–late 19C] a large denomination sterling note. [LONG-TAILED 'UN + FINNIP]

long-tailed 'un n. [mid-19C+] a large denomination sterling note, £10, £20, £50; thus *long-tailed*, of more than £5 face value.

long tea n. [18C] urine (cf. TEA n.[1]).

long thin streak of piss n. **1** [1900s–10s] one who over-estimates their own importance or abilities. **2** [20C] an un-flattering description of a tall, thin person.

long tickey/tickey-wire n. [1970s] (S.Afr.) a coin on a thread that can be used to operate a telephone kiosk, then retrieved and used again. [SE *long* + TICKEY n. (1)]

long time no see phr. [20C] (orig. US) a general greeting meaning 'I haven't seen you for a long time'.

long tom n. **1** [late 19C] the penis. **2** [1900s] (N.Z.) a long-handled shovel.

long-tongue adj. [20C] (Irish/W.I.) talkative, indiscreet. [LONG-TONGUED]

long-tongued adj. [late 18C–early 19C] of a chatterer, a gossip, one who is unable to keep a secret; thus *as long-tongued as Granny*. ['Granny was an (actual) ideot (*sic*) who could lick her own eye' (Grose)]

long town n. [19C] (Anglo-Irish) London. [? its geographical dimension]

long 'un n.[1] [18C+] a tall person (cf. SHORT 'UN).

long 'un n.[2] [late 19C] a pheasant. [the length of its tail]

long underwear n. [1930s–60s] (US) jazz music popularized for 'easy listening', also classical music. [? play on LONGHAIR n.]

long-winded adj. **1** [late 19C+] used of one who takes a long time to do something. **2** [1950s+] used of a man who takes a long time to reach orgasm.

long-winded paymaster n. [late 17C–early 19C] (Und.) one who extends lengthy credit.

long word n. [mid-19C+] any statement that implies a long time, e.g. *never is a long word*.

loo n.[1] [late 19C+] the lavatory. [? Fr. *l'eau*, water. The *bordalou*, a portable commode, resembling a sauce boat and carried by 18C ladies in their muff. SE *leeward*, the side of a ship turned away from the wind and as such the side over which one would urinate/defecate. An abbr./pun on *Waterloo*, whether the station or the battle it commemorates]

Loo, the n.[2] [late 19C–1950s] (Aus.) Wooloomoo*loo*, a tough, working-class suburb of Sydney. [abbr.]

loo n.[3] [1960s+] (US) a police or fire lieutenant. [US pron. of *loo*-tenant]

looby n. [14C–late 19C] a fool, a dullard; thus *loobily* (cf. LOB n.[3]; LUBBER). [dial.]

loocha/loocher n. [19C] (Anglo-Ind.) 'a blackguard libertine, a lewd loafer' (Y&B). [synon. Hind. *luchcha*]

looder n. [late 19C+] (Irish) a blow. [Irish *licedar*/Scot. *lowder*, a blow]

looey n.[1] *see* LOOIE n.[1].

looey/lieuey/looie n.[2] [1970s+] (US) a lump of expectorated phlegm. [echoic]

loof-faker n. [mid-19C] a chimney-sweep. [backsl. *loof* = flue + FAKER n.[1] (2)]

loogan/loogin/lugan n. [1920s–30s] (US) a fool, a new-comer, a petty crook or ruffian. [? typical 'Irish' surname and thus based on neg. racial stereotyping]

loogie n. [1980s+] (US) a gob of phlegm (cf. LOOEY n.[2]; LOUIE n.[5]; LUNGER).

loogin n.[1] *see* LOOGAN.

Loogin n.[2] *see* LUGEN.

looie/looey/louie n.[1] [1910s+] (US milit.) lieutenant. [US pron.]

looie n.[2] *see* LOOEY n.[2].

look after number one, to phr. [early 18C+] to take care of oneself, irrespective of others. [NUMBER ONE n.[1]]

look-a-here! excl. [1930s+] (US) an imper. calling on one's attention, esp. before delivering some reprimand or lecture (cf. LOOK HERE!).

look alive/slimy v. [mid-19C+] to hurry up, esp. as imper.

look as if one hasn't got the right change, to phr. [late 19C] to be enraged, to look furious (cf. LOOK LIKE ONE LOST A POUND AND FOUND SIXPENCE).

look at every woman through the hole in one's prick, to phr. [late 19C+] of a man, to regard every woman as a sex object.

look at/read the maker's name, to phr. [19C] to drink heavily. [the name is found on the bottom of an upturned glass]

look at the ceiling, to phr. [20C] of a woman, to have sexual intercourse in the missionary position.

look back v. [late 19C] to indulge in nostalgia, regrets etc.; usu. in phr. *never looked back*, to progress from that time on.

look big v. [late 17C+] to act in what one hopes is an impressive manner.

look blue v. [17C+] **1** to be astonished or surprised. **2** to look miserable, to look nervous. [BLUE adj.[1] (1), (2)]

look bullets v. [mid-19C] (US) to stare at aggressively.

look dead and done-for, to phr. [late 19C+] to look utterly miserable.

look down one's nose at, to phr. **1** [early 19C+] to disdain, to despise, to snub. **2** [1910s–30s] (US) to look unhappy, embarrassed, to give in to someone else. [fig. uses of SE; 'at' is a mid-19C addition. (2) the lowering of one's eyes]

lookee here! *see* LOOK HERE!

looker n. (orig. US) **1** [late 19C+] an attractive woman. **2** [1970s] a client who wishes only to look at a prostitute, who is usu. naked, and occas. fondle her breasts. **3** [1970s] a voyeur.

lookers n. [20C] (US) the eyes.

look for a piece *see* BEG FOR A PIECE.

look for gapeseed, to phr. [late 16C–mid-19C] to be inattentive, to let one's mind wander. [GAPESEED]

look for maidenheads, to phr. [late 19C] to search for the unattainable or something very hard to find.

look for one's swag straps, to phr. [late 19C+] (Aus./N.Z.) to start thinking of leaving one job and going in search of another. [one is about to strap on one's SWAG and get moving]

look for what one ain't put down, to phr. [20C] (W.I.) to be a professional thief.

look goats and monkeys at, to *phr.* [mid-18C–late-19C] to gaze lecherously at, to leer. [the trad. propensities of these two animals]

look good *v.* [1910s+] (orig. US) to appear promising.

look/lookee here! *excl.* [mid-19C+] an imper. calling on one's attention, esp. before delivering some reprimand or lecture.

lookie-lou/looky-loo *n.* [1980s+] (US Black/campus) an inquisitive person, a peeping Tom.

look-in *n.* **1** [late 18C+] a brief visit. **2** [mid-19C+] a chance, an opportunity, usu. with the implication of ultimate success.

look in *v.* [1920s–50s] to watch television. [a descendent of the earlier SE *listen in*, to listen to the radio]

looking as if one couldn't help it *phr.* [late 18C–early 19C] looking like a fool or simpleton.

looking glass *n.*[1] [early 17C–mid-19C] a chamberpot. [one's reflection in the urine, as well, possibly, as the attention paid by contemporary physicians to the urine itself. Thus the 18C riddle: 'Q. Why is a Chamber-Pot call'd a Looking-Glass? A. Because many rarely see their Faces in any other']

looking glass *n.*[2] [1960s] (US) the buttocks, the posterior. [rhy. sl. *looking glass* = ARSE *n.*[1] (1)]

looking like death warmed over/up *phr.* [1930s+] looking extremely ill, usu. very pale.

looking lively *adj.* [mid-19C+] drunk (cf. ABOUT RIGHT *adj.*[1]).

look into the whites, to *phr.* [late 19C] to be on the verge of fighting. [the two adversaries are staring into each other's eyes]

lookism *n.* [1970s+] (orig. gay) evaluating a stranger purely on the basis of their physical appeal or lack of it. [generally seen as non-politically correct and thus pej.]

look like a kookaburra that has swallowed the kangaroo, to *phr.* [1930s+] (Aus.) to look elated, to look very happy.

look like a monkey fucking a football, to *phr.* [1960s+] (US) to look utterly absurd.

look like a tooth-drawer, to *phr.* [17C] to appear very thin and undernourished. [derog. image of dentists]

look like a wet week, to *phr.* [20C] to look utterly wretched.

look like bull-beef, to *phr.* [late 17C–early 19C] to look stern, grim and threatening.

look like death eating a sandwich, to *phr.* [1940s+] (US) to look very ill, very emotional or very tired.

look like God's revenge against murder, to *phr.* [late 18C–early 19C] to look furious; later as abbr. *look like murder*.

look like Jock Blunt, to *phr.* [early 18C–early 19C] for one's face to betray one's disappointment. [JACK BLUNT]

look like one lost a pound and found sixpence/a halfpenny, to *phr.* [19C+] to look notably downcast (cf. LOOK AS IF ONE HASN'T GOT THE RIGHT CHANGE).

look-look *v.* [20C] (W.I.) to gaze about in a furtive manner, to peep.

look marlin spikes/spikes at, to *phr.* [early–mid-19C] to glare at, to 'look daggers' at. [SE *marlin spike*, an iron tool tapering to a point, used to separate the strands of rope in splicing]

look nine ways for Sunday/nine ways at thrice, to *phr.* [16C+] to squint (cf. LOOK SEVEN WAYS FOR SUNDAY).

look old *v.* [late 19C] to act severely or cautiously.

look on with/over *v.* [late 19C] to read a book while someone else is reading it.

look-out *n.* [mid-18C+] (orig. US) a problem, a responsibility; usu. as *that's their look-out*.

look over the wood, to *phr.* [late 18C–early 19C] to mount the pulpit, to preach. [the wooden pulpit]

look parsnips *v.* [mid-19C] to look displeased, to look sour.

look round the clock, to *phr.* [late 19C] (US) to look old.

looksee *n.* **1** [late 19C+] a glimpse, a glance; thus [1920s] (US) *looksee man*, a tourist or sightseer. **2** [1920s–60s] (US) a doctor's licence to practise. [? Pidgin]

looksee *v.* [mid-19C+] (orig. US) to make an inspection, to have a look, to glance at.

look seven ways for Sunday, to *phr.* [late 19C+] to squint. [var. on LOOK NINE WAYS FOR SUNDAY]

look sharp *v.*[1] [early 19C+] to hurry up, to get on with, esp. as imper. (cf. LOOK ALIVE). [SE *sharp*, quick-witted]

look sharp *v.*[2] [1920s+] to dress smartly, fashionably. [SHARP *adj.*]

looks like a wet weekend, it *phr.* [20C] (orig. Aus.) used by a woman announcing, or registering, the onset of a menstrual period.

looks like he wouldn't piss if his pants were on fire, he *phr.* [20C] a phr. used of an especially dull, stupid-looking person.

looks like it *phr.* [mid-19C+] it would appear, it seems.

look slimy *see* LOOK ALIVE.

look slippery! *excl.* [late 19C–1920s] (orig. RN) hurry up!, get on with it! (cf. LOOK SLIPPY!).

look slippy! *excl.* [late 19C+] hurry up! get on with it! (cf. LOOK SLIPPERY!).

look spikes at! *see* LOOK MARLIN SPIKES AT.

look story! *excl.* [20C] (W.I.) a general excl. of dismissal or contempt, how absurd!

look through a glass, to *phr.* [19C] to be drunk (cf. LOOK AT THE MAKER'S NAME).

look through a hempen window, to *phr.* [17C] to be hanged.

look through one's fingers, to *phr.* [late 19C] (Irish) to pretend ignorance, to evade one's responsibilities.

look through the wood, to *phr.* [late 18C–mid-19C] to stand in the pillory.

look to one's water, to *phr.* [mid-16C–late 18C] to follow one's movements, to watch closely (cf. WATCH ONE'S WATERS).

look towards *v.* [mid-19C] to drink a health.

look-up *n.* [1910s–20s] a brief visit (cf. LOOK-IN). [backform. f. LOOK UP *v.*[1]]

look up *v.*[1] [late 18C+] to visit.

look up *v.*[2] [early 19C+] (orig. commercial) usu. of a situation, to improve, to be getting better.

look upon a hedge, to *phr.* [1930s] to urinate.

look/see what the cat's brought in *phr.* [1920s+] a dismissive, disdainful, teasing phr.; thus *looks like something the cat brought in*, phr. used to describe an unkempt or unappealing person.

look what the wind's blown in *phr.* [1920s+] a facetious greeting to a new arrival, or a remark to a companion concerning that arrival.

look who's talking! *phr.* [1940s+] a phr. used to stress that one speaker is in no position to criticize another.

look with red-eye/red-eye at, to *phr.* [20C] (W.I.) to become obsessed with at first sight and thus to desire to possess immediately (cf. EYES CATCH FIRE; HAVE RED-EYE FOR).

looky here! *excl.* [1920s+] (US) an imper. calling on one's attention, esp. before delivering some reprimand or lecture (cf. LOOK HERE!).

looky-loo *see* LOOKIE-LOU.

looloo *n.*[1] *see* LULU *n.*[2].

looloo *n.*[2] [late 19C+] (US gambling) a remarkable poker hand that beats a royal flush. [? LULU *n.*[1] (3)]

loon *n.* [early 19C+] a fool, an idiot. [Lat. *luna*, moon; such people are supposedly 'moonstruck'. Note mid-15C+ SE *loon*, a worthless person, a rogue, an idler]

loon/loon about *v.* [1960s+] to act crazily or irresponsibly. [LOON *n.*]

looney see LOONY.

looney/loony tune *n.* [1960s+] a crazy person, a lunatic. [*Looney Tunes*, the series of film cartoons created for Warner Bros. by the team of Hollywood animators Hanna-Barbera and released 1930–69, then shown on TV from 1950s; the term was popularized by another Hollywood star, Ronald Reagan, to describe such figures as Libyan leader Colonel Gaddaffi]

looney/loony tune *adj.* [1960s+] insane, irrational. [LOONEY TUNE n.]

loonie *n.* [1980s+] (Can.) the Can. $1 coin, introduced in 1987. [the representation of a *loon* or diver on its reverse]

loon pants/loons *n.* [1970s+] trousers with enormous flared bottoms, esp. beloved of early 1970s hippies. [LOON v. + PANTS n.¹ (2)]

loon pipe *n.* [1990s] the anus.

loons see LOON PANTS.

loonslate/loonslatt *n.* [late 17C–18C] one shilling and one penny-halfpenny, 1s 1½d (cf. HANGMAN'S WAGES; SLAT n.¹). [? LOON n. + SLAT n.¹ (1); lit. 'a fool's half-crown']

loony/looney/luny *n.* [mid-19C+] (orig. US) a fool, an eccentric. [SE *lunatic*]

loony/looney *adj.* [mid–late 19C+] (orig. US) eccentric, insane. [LOONY n.]

loony bin/farm *n.* [1910s+] a psychiatric institution (cf. LOONY HOUSE; LOONY PEN). [LOONY n.]

loony bird *n.* [1960s–70s] (US) a crazy person. [LOONY adj. + BIRD n.²]

loony doctor *n.* [1910s+] a psychoanalyst, a psychiatrist. [LOONY n. + SE *doctor*]

loony farm see LOONY BIN.

loony house *n.* [1950s+] (US) a psychiatric institution (cf. LOONY BIN). [LOONY n. + SE *house*]

loony pen *n.* [1980s+] (US) a psychiatric institution (cf. LOONY BIN). [LOONY n. + SE *pen*]

loony tune see LOONEY TUNE.

loop *v.* [1920s+] (US) to go on a drinking spree. [SE *loop*, i.e. one's drunken meandering]

looped *adj.* (US) **1** [1930s+] drunk (cf. LOOP-LEGGED). **2** [1970s+] infatuated with something or someone, or demented. [one is 'going round in circles']

loopie/loopy *n.* [1970s+] (N.Z.) a tourist. [the 'looping' movement used in swatting sand flies + LOOPY adj. (1); i.e. the quality of questions they ask local people]

loop-legged *adj.* [1940s+] (US) drunk.

loop off *v.* [early–mid-18C] to run away. [? SE *lope off*]

loop-the-loop/loopy the loop *n.¹* **1** [1910s+] soup (cf. IRON HOOP). soup. **2** [1920s] (US) a finger ring or hoop. [rhy. sl.; *loopy* is Aus. use]

loop-the-loop *n.²* [1970s+] mutual oral-genital stimulation (cf. SIXTY-NINE).

loopy *n.* see LOOPIE.

loopy *adj.* [1920s+] (orig. naut.) **1** eccentric, crazy. **2** drunk (cf. LOOPED). [? LOOBY or Scot. *loopy*, cunning]

loopy the loop see LOOP-THE-LOOP n.¹.

loor see LOUR.

loose *adj.¹* **1** [late 19C] of an appointed time, not punctual, round about, e.g. *a loose midday*. **2** [1950s+] (US) unperturbed, casual, relaxed (cf. HANG LOOSE).

loose *adj.²* **1** [1960s+] (US campus) drunk. **2** [1990s] (US Black) out of control.

loose a fiver, to *phr.* [late 19C] to have to pay heavily for one's pleasures.

loose as a goose *phr.* [1930s+] (US) very loose, in any sense (cf. LOOSEY-GOOSEY).

loose ball *n.* [1970s+] (Irish) an opportunity to pick up free drink. [soccer imagery]

loose bit of goods *n.* [late 19C] a flighty young woman who has 'abandoned the proprieties' (Ware) (cf. BIT OF GOODS). [SE *loose* + BIT OF GOODS]

loose-bodied gown *n.* [16C] a prostitute (cf. LOOSE-COAT GAME). [metonymy]

loose-box *n.* [mid-19C] a brougham or similar vehicle owned by a kept woman or well-off prostitute (cf. MOT-CART). [SE *loose box*, a stall in which a horse can move around freely + pun on euph. *loose woman*]

loose cannon on a rolling deck *n.* [1970s+] (orig. US) an unstable person, one who may well be dangerous to others.

loose-coat game *n.* [16C] prostitution (cf. LOOSE-BODIED GOWN).

loose end *n.* [late 19C–1910s] a dissolute person (cf. LOOSE FISH).

loose ends *n.* [1970s+] (US Black) spare money available for loans.

loose fish *n.* **1** [early 19C] a prostitute. **2** [early–mid-19C] one who has no settled way of life. [note whaling jargon *loose fish*, a whale that is fair game for anybody who can catch it]

loose French *v.* [late 19C] to swear (cf. EXCUSE MY FRENCH). [SE *loose off* + FRENCH n.¹]

loose goose *n.* [1950s+] (US) a person or thing that is loose, in any sense (cf. LOOSE AS A GOOSE).

loose-hung *adj.* [early 19C–1920s] used of an unstable character (cf. LOOSE IN THE BEAN).

loose in her rump see LOOSE IN THE RUMP.

loose in the bean *phr.* [1920s] (US) eccentric, crazy (cf. LOOSE-HUNG; OFF ONE'S BEAN). [SE *loose* + BEAN n.⁴]

loose in the hilt *phr.* **1** [mid-17C–early 18C] maritally unfaithful. **2** [19C] suffering from diarrhoea.

loose in the/her rump *phr.* [18C–mid-19C] of a woman, wanton, promiscuous. [SE *loose* + *rump*]

loose-legged *adj.* [19C] suffering from diarrhoea.

loose link *n.* [1980s+] (US Black) an informer.

looseners *n.* [1920s–30s] (US) prunes. [their trad. role in curing constipation]

loosen someone's hide, to *phr.* [1900s] to thrash, to flog.

loosen up *v.* [20C] (orig. US) **1** to relax, esp. as an imper. **2** to spend money. [(1) fig. use of SE; (2) to loosen one's purse-strings]

loose screw *n.* [early 19C+] an eccentric. [HAVE A SCREW LOOSE]

loose up top *phr.* [late 19C+] mad, eccentric. [HAVE A SCREW LOOSE]

loosey-goosey *adj.* [1960s+] (US) very loose, in any sense (cf. LOOSE AS A GOOSE).

loosies *n.* [1980s+] (US Black) cigarettes bought unpackaged.

loot *n.¹* **1** [late 18C–mid-19C] plunder, booty. **2** [1930s+] money. [(1) SE by late 19C, f. Hind. *lut*, plunder, ult. Skrt. *lotra*, plunder. Note also Anglo-Ind. *lootie-wallah*, a plunderer or bandit]

loot *n.²* [late 19C+] (US) a lieutenant. [abbr. pron.]

loothy *n.* [20C] (Irish) a large, ungainly man. [Irish *liœtar*, big, ungainly]

lop/lophead *n.¹* **1** [20C] (US Und.) a fool. **2** [1970s+] (US) a contemptible fellow. [LOB n.³]

lop *n.²* **1** [1920s–30s] (Anglo-Irish) a penny. [ety. unknown, ? link to dial. *lop*, a flea, i.e. the coin's innate worthlessness]

lop cock *n.* [1930s–40s] (US) a circumcised penis (cf. SNIP-COCK). [SE *lop*, to cut off + COCK n.² (1)]

lop down *v.* [mid–late 19C] (US) to sit down, to lie down. [East Anglian dial. *lop*, to droop]

lope *v.* [late 18C+] **1** to run, to run away. **2** to steal. [SE *loup*, to leap]

lop-ear/flop-ear *n.* [mid-19C+] (US) a nickname for an inhabitant of Oregon. [? the prevalence of rabbits in the state]

lop-eared *adj.* [mid-19C+] (US) exceptionally stupid or gullible. [the *lop-ears* of an animal, but ? LOB n.[3]]

lophead *see* LOP n.[1].

lope the mule/the pony, to *phr.* [1930s+] (US) to masturbate.

loppy *n.* [late 19C–1930s] (Aus./N.Z.) a handyman on a rural station, a roustabout. [? dial. *lop*, to idle, to hang about or f. SE *loppy*, infested with 'lops' or fleas]

loppy dust *n.* [1980s+] (drugs) cocaine. [LOP n.[1]]

loqued out *see* LOC'D OUT.

lor!/lors! *excl.* [mid-19C+] an abbr. version of LORD!, used in a variety of excl. and mild oaths (cf. LAWKS!).

lor-a-mussy! *excl.* [19C] a mild oath, 'Lord have mercy!'

lord *n.* [late 17C–20C] a hunch-backed or badly crippled man (cf. LADY n.[1]). [Gk. *lordos*, bent backwards; thus the medical term *lordosis*, anterior curvature of the spine]

Lord, how came you so? *see* HOW CAME YOU SO?

Lord John Russell *n.* [mid-19C] a bustle. [rhy. sl., ult. British politician *Lord John Russell* (1792–1878)]

lord knows how/what/where/why, the *phr.* [late 17C+] a phr. implying amazement, incredulity or plain ignorance.

Lord Lovat *v.* [20C] to get rid of, to throw away (cf. LITTLE MISS MUFFET). [rhy. sl. *Lord Lovat* = SHOVE IT!]

lord love-a-duck! *excl.* [1910s+] a mild excl. of surprise etc (cf. GAWD LOVE-A-DUCK!).

lord lovell *n.* [mid-19C+] a shovel. [rhy. sl.; 20C use is US]

lord love us!/you! *excl.* [late 19C+] a mild oath.

lord love your heart! *excl.* [mid–late 19C] a mild oath.

Lord Mansfield's teeth *n.* [late 18C–early 19C] the *chevaux de frize* or row of spikes embedded into the top of the wall of the King's Bench prison. [*Lord Mansfield* (1733–1821), Lord Chief Justice of the Court of Common Pleas]

lord mayor *n.* [late 19C] a large crowbar. [on pattern of ALDERMAN n.[2]]

lord mayor *v.* [20C] to swear. [rhy. sl.]

lord mayor's coal *n.* [mid-19C] a piece of slate.

lord mayor's fool *n.* [mid-19C] 'a personage who likes everything that is good, and plenty of it' (Hotten 1864). [pvb. 'like My Lord Mayor's fool, full of business and nothing to do']

lord muck *n.* [1930s+] a hypothetical aristocrat, snobbish and conspicuous in his contempt for lesser mortals, but since he is lord of 'muck' he is, in fact, no better than they are (cf. CHIEF MUCK OF THE CRIB; LADY MUCK).

Lord Northumberland's arms *see* NORTHUMBERLAND ARMS.

lord of the manor *n.* [mid–late 19C] a sixpence. [rhy. sl. *lord of the manor* = TANNER]

lord right *n.* [mid-19C+] the ideal lover, husband or boyfriend (cf. MR RIGHT).

Lord Sutch *n.* [20C] **1** the clutch. **2** the crotch. [rhy. sl.; ult. popstar/politician 'Screaming *Lord Sutch*' (b.1940)]

Lord Wigg *n.* [1960s] a pig. [rhy. sl.; ult. UK politician George Wigg (1900–83)]

lordy! *see* LAWDY.

lordy me! *excl.* [late 19C+] a euph. for *Lord help me!*

lorette *n.* [mid-19C] a euph. term for prostitute, borrowed from France. [the *lorettes*, a class of courtesan that was based near the Church of Notre Dame de Lorette ('the Paris Pimlico' *Barrère*) in Paris]

lorna doone *n.* [20C] a spoon. [rhy. sl., ult. the novel *Lorna Doone* (1869) by R.D. Blackmore]

lorry/lurry up *v.* [1940s+] (Irish) to beat, to thrash. [Irish *lïœradh*, a beating]

lors! *see* LOR!

Los *n.* [1910s–30s] (US) *Los* Angeles. [abbr.]

los *adj.* [1950s+] (S.Afr.) usu. of a woman, promiscuous. [Afk. *los*, loose]

los *v.* [1980s+] (S.Afr.) to let go, often as excl. [Afk.]

lose *v.* **1** [mid-19C+] (US) to vomit (cf. LOSE A DINNER; LOSE A MEAL; LOSE IT; LOSE ONE'S DOUGHNUTS; LOSE ONE'S LUNCH). **2** [mid-19C+] to suffer a miscarriage, to have a still-birth or have one's child die very early in life. **3** [late 19C+] (US) to kill. **4** [late 19C–1910s] (US) to evade. **5** [1930s+] [(orig. US) to get rid of, to dispose of.

lose a cartful and find a waggon-load, to *phr.* [late 19C] to become fat.

lose a dinner, to *phr.* [1950s+] (Aus.) to vomit (cf. LOSE).

lose a meal, to *phr.* [1940s+] (Aus.) to vomit (cf. LOSE).

lose it *v.* [1970s+] **1** to lose control temporarily; in an extreme case to have an actual mental breakdown, to go mad. **2** (US campus) to be surprised, to be shocked. **3** (US campus) to vomit (cf. LOSE).

lose leather *v.* [late 18C–19C] to become saddle-sore from excessive riding.

lose move *n.* [1980s+] (US campus) a stupid action. [SE *lose*, to fail, to be defeated + MOVE n.]

lose one's arse, to *phr.* [late 18C–mid-19C] to be careless; usu. in phr. *he/she'd lose their arse if it were loose*. [ARSE n.[1]]

lose one's ass, to *phr.* [1950s+] (US) to fight, to brawl, to argue vehemently. [ARSE n.[1]]

lose one's ballast, to *phr.* [late 19C–1950s] to lose control emotionally. [in a ship the ballast keeps the vessel 'on an even keel']

lose one's block *see* DO IN ONE'S BLOCK.

lose one's bottle, to *phr.* [20C] to back down, to turn cowardly. [SE *lose* + BOTTLE n.[3]]

lose one's britches, to *phr.* [20C] to lose a good deal of money, usu. through betting (cf. LOSE ONE'S SHIRT).

lose one's cool, to *phr.* [1960s+] (orig. US) to lose one's dignity or self-possession, to lose one's temper. [SE *lose* + COOL n.[2] (2)]

lose one's dip, to *phr.* [1900s] (US) to lose one's composure. [fig. use of DIP n.[7]]

lose one's doughnuts, to *phr.* [1940s+] (US campus) to vomit (cf. BLOW ONE'S DOUGHNUTS; LOSE).

lose one's gender, to *phr.* [1960s+] (gay) to abandon homosexuality to become a heterosexual.

lose one's gourd *see* BLOW ONE'S GOURD.

lose one's grip, to *phr.* [late 19C+] (orig. US) to lose one's composure, to lose one's sanity.

lose one's hair, to *phr.* [1930s] to lose one's temper.

lose one's jock, to *phr.* [1960s+] (US) to be fooled. [fig. use of SE *lose* + JOCK n.[2] (2)]

lose one's legs, to *phr.* [mid–late 18C] to be drunk.

lose one's lunch, to *phr.* [1940s+] (US campus) to vomit (cf. BLOW ONE'S LUNCH; LOSE).

lose one's marbles, to *phr.* [1920s+] to go mad, to lose control (cf. SHOOT OUT ONE'S MARBLES). [SE *lose* + MARBLES n.[5]]

lose one's mess, to *phr.* [1990s] to ejaculate.

lose one's rag, to *phr.* [1950s+] to lose one's temper (cf. GET ONE'S RAG OUT). [SE *lose* + RAG n.[4]]

lose one's ring, to *phr.* [late 19C–1900s] to lose one's virginity. [SE *lose* + RING n.[1]]

lose one's rudder, to *phr.* [20C] to be drunk and thus lose one's sense of direction.

lose one's shirt, to *phr.* [1930s+] to lose a good deal of money, usu. through gambling or other speculation (cf. LOSE ONE'S BRITCHES).

lose one's vest, to *phr.* [19C] to lose one's temper (cf. SHIRTY).

lose one's wool, to *phr.* [early 19C–1940s] to lose one's temper; thus [late 19C+] *keep one's wool on*, to keep one's temper (cf. KEEP ONE'S HAIR ON).

lose out on *v.* [late 19C+] **1** to fail. **2** to be fooled, to be swindled, to miss an opportunity.

loser *n.* **1** [1910s+] (US) a convicted prisoner, one who served a jail sentence (cf. THREE-TIME LOSER). **2** [1930s+] (orig. US) a disappointment, a problem, an obstacle. **3** [1950s+] (orig. US) a failure, esp. a socially inadequate person.

loser *adj.* [1970s+] (US) second-rate, useless. [LOSER n.]

lose the ball, to *phr.* [1970s+] to find oneself in an increasingly difficult situation, to lose control of one's life, work, relationships etc (cf. LOSE IT v.). [sporting imagery]

lose the combination, to *phr.* [late 19C–1910s] to miss the meaning or point (cf. LOSE THE PLOT).

lose the match and pocket the stakes, to *phr.* [19C] of a woman, to have sexual intercourse. [the male is seen as the 'winner'; the stakes are his ejaculated semen]

lose the number of one's mess, to *phr.* [mid-19C] to die (cf. COIL ONE'S ROPES). [naut. imagery]

lose the plot, to *phr.* [1980s+] to lose one's way in a situation, to miss the meaning or point.

lose the run of oneself, to *phr.* [1970s+] (Irish) to lose one's self-control. [Irish *ná bí ag rith leat féin mar sin*, lit. 'don't be running with yourself like that']

loskop *n.* [1950s+] (S.Afr.) a forgetful, scatty person. [Afk. *los*, loose + *kop*, head]

loskop *adj.* [1950s+] (S.Afr.) crazy, forgetful, eccentric. [LOSKOP n.]

lossie *n.* [1950s+] (S.Afr.) a promiscuous woman. [LOS adj.]

lost a button *phr.* [19C+] eccentric, crazy (cf. BUTTONS n.¹; BUTTON SHORT; NOT ALL THERE).

lost and found *n.* [20C] £1. [rhy. sl.]

Lost Wages *n.* [1960s+] (US) Las Vegas. [an intentional malapropism]

lot, the *n.*¹ [mid-19C+] all, the complete amount, everything that is/was available, e.g. *he's scoffed the lot.*

lot *n.*² [late 19C–1900s] the male genitals. [ext. of LOT n.¹]

lot *n.*³ [20C] an event, a circumstance, a happening; thus ironic *that was a nice lot, that was.*

loteby/ludby *n.* [14C] a mistress (cf. LIGBY). [SE *lote*, to skulk or hide]

lothario *n.* [late 17C+] a libertine, a rake. [in the cast list of Sir William D'Avenant's play *The Cruel Brother* (1627) is a 'Lothario, a frantic young gallant'. The name was used again by Nicholas Rowe in *The Fair Penitent* (1703), and the term's popularity stems from the latter, in which he is characterized as 'The Gay Lothario']

lotion *n.* [mid–late 19C] a drink.

lot lizard *n.* [1980s+] (US) a prostitute who works at truck stops. [SE (*parking*) *lot* + LIZARD n.² (5)]

lot of, a *phr.* [1940s–60s] (US Black) exceptionally good, skilful, esp. of musical ability. [abbr. SE *whole lot of*]

lot of nature *phr.* [1990s] (US Black) a high sex drive (cf. NO NATURE). [NATURE n. (2)]

lots *n.* [early 19C+] very many, a large number, usu. as *lots of.*

lotsa *n.* [1920s+] (orig. US) very many, a large number. [pron. of LOTS of]

lotta *n.* [1940s+] (orig. US) very many, a large number. [pron of LOTS of]

lotties *n.* [late 19C–1910s; 1990s] the female breasts. [? the music-hall singer *Lottie* Collins (1866–1910)]

lotties and totties *n.* [late 19C] prostitutes as a group. [theatrical jargon *lotties and totties*, out of work young actresses, in turn f. common names]

Lotusland *n.* [1980s+] (US) Los Angeles (cf. LA-LA LAND). [SE *lotus-eating*; i.e. the indolent lifestyle associated with California]

lou *see* LOUIS n.¹.

loud *adj.* **1** [mid-17C+] usu. of smell, strong or foul. **2** [mid–late 19C] vulgar, showy. [(1) orig. literary; (2) SE by 20C]

loudmouth *n.* [1930s+] (orig. US) **1** a braggart, a boaster. **2** a lawyer.

loudmouth *v.* [1930s+] (US Black) to speak abusively.

loud one *n.* [late 17C–mid-19C] a gross lie.

loud pedal *n.* [1940s+] (Aus.) the accelerator pedal in a car. [borrowed from the piano]

loudspeaker *n.* [1930s] (US) a loudmouth, boaster.

loudtalk *v.* [1930s+] (US Black) to talk in a way that confronts or embarrasses one's hearers. [LOUD-TALKING]

loud-talking *n.* [1930s+] (US Black) deliberately antagonistic, confrontational talk.

louie *n.*¹ *see* LOOIE n.¹.

louie *n.*² [1960s+] (Aus.) a fly. [the Mortein commercials of 1960s+ which featured *Louie the Fly*]

louie *n.*³ [1960s+] in driving, a left turn (cf. HANG A LOUIE). [the initial letter]

Louie/louie *n.*⁴ **1** [20C] (US) $1. [joc. use of proper name, although there appears to be no specific reason]

louie *n.*⁵ **1** [1970s] (US campus) a punch with the fist. **2** [1970s+] a gob of phlegm (cf. LOOGIE). [echoic]

louies/louis *n.* [1980s+] (US) the luxury luggage manufactured by *Louis* Vuitton. [abbr.]

louis/lou *n.*¹ **1** [1920s–30s] (US) a pimp (cf. ALPHONSE n.³). **2** [1990s] (US campus) an unattractive man. [stereotyping of the proper name]

louis *n.*² [1980s+] (drugs) sixteenth of an ounce (2g) of cannabis. [play on French king, Louis XVI (r.1774–93)]

louis *n.*³ *see* LOUIES.

lounce *n.* [19C] (mainly naut.) a ration of food. [SE *allowance*]

lounge-lice *n.* [1930s+] (Aus.) a womanizer, an adventurer. [var. on LOUNGE LIZARD n. (1)]

lounge lizard *n.* [1910s+] **1** a fortune-hunter or womanizer who works his charms in the lounges of hotels (cf. BOUDOIR BANDICOOT; PARLOR LIZARD; SALOON BAR COWBOY). **2** a poor or miserly man who would rather court a woman in her own house than take her out on the town.

lour/loor/loure/lower/lowre/lowrie *n.* [mid-16C–late 19C] money (cf. GAMMY adj.¹; LURRY). [Fr. *louier*, a reward, then 14C SE *lower*, a reward; cf. Rom. *loor*, to plunder, and *luripen*, booty]

Lou Reed *n.* [20C] amphetamine (cf. A n.²). [rhy. sl. *Lou Reed* = SPEED n.²; ult. rock star Lou Reed (b.1942)]

louse *n.* [mid-17C+] an extremely contemptible or untrustworthy individual.

louse *v.* [1940s–50s] (Aus.) to pilfer (cf. LOUSER). [LOUSE n.]

-louse *sfx.* [1920s+] (US) used in combs. to refer to a despicable person, a waster, a hanger-on (cf. LOBBY LOUSE). [used with qualifying n.]

louse around *v.* [1910s+] (US) to idle, to loiter, to waste time. [northern UK dial. *lowse*, stop working]

louse bag *n.* [late 18C–early 19C] a wig or a bag worn over the hair (cf. LOUSE LADDER; LOUSE TRAP n.¹; LOUSE WALK).

louse cage *n.* (US) **1** [late 19C–1920s] a cheap hotel or lodging house (cf. BUGHOUSE; LOUSE HOUSE; LOUSE TRAP n.²). **2** [1920s–60s] a bunkhouse.

loused *adj.* [1950s+] (drugs) covered by sores and abscesses from repeated use of unsterile needles.

louse house *n.* [late 18C–1930s] a prison or a seedy hotel or lodging house (cf. BUGHOUSE; LOUSE CAGE).

louse ladder *n.* **1** [late 18C–19C] a ladder, i.e. 'a stitch fallen in a stocking' (Grose 1785). **2** [1900s] bushy sidewhiskers (cf. LOUSE BAG).

louseland *n.* [late 17C–18C] Scotland; thus *Scotch louse-trap*, a comb (cf. ITCHLAND). [a derog. suggestion that Scotland is infested with vermin]

louser *n.* **1** [1930s+] (orig. US) a contemptible individual.

2 [1940s–50s] (Aus.) a petty thief. [LOUSE n.; also Irish use 1960s+]

louse someone around, to phr. [1910s+] (US) to mistreat someone. [i.e. to act like a LOUSE n.]

louse someone up v. [1930s+] (orig. US) to cause a person difficulties, to cause trouble.

louse trap n.[1] [late 18C–mid-19C] **1** a toothcomb (cf. LOUSE BAG). **2** a sideburn or sidewhisker.

louse trap n.[2] [1910s–40s] a cheap hotel or lodging house (cf. BUGHOUSE; LOUSE CAGE).

louse-up n. [1970s+] (US) a situation or thing that is a mess or that is troublesome. [LOUSE UP v.]

louse up v. [1930s+] (orig. US) **1** to make a mess of, to ruin, usu. deliberately. **2** to blunder, to fail.

louse walk n. [mid-19C] a back-hair parting (cf. LOUSE BAG).

lousing n. [1960s+] (Irish) hanging around on street corners. [LOUSER]

lousy adj.[1] [14C+] a general intensifier, usu. with derog. implications. [fig. use of SE louse]

lousy adj.[2] [1940s–50s] (Aus.) mean, tight-fisted (cf. LOUSY WITH). [fig. use of SE louse]

lousy adv. [14C+] a general intensifier, usu. with derog. implications. [fig. use of SE louse]

Lousy Anna n. [1940s+] (US) a derog. name for Louisiana.

lousy-looked adj. [early 18C] a general epithet of abuse. [lit. 'looking lice-ridden']

lousy lou n. [20C] the 'flu, influenza. [rhy. sl.]

lousy with adv. [mid-19C+] full of, abundant with (a commodity, type of person etc).

love n.[1] [early 19C+] anything pleasant, attractive, e.g. it's a real love.

love n.[2] see LOVE UP n.

love n.[3] [1980s+] (drugs) crack cocaine.

love v. see LOVE UP v.

love affair n. [1970s+] (drugs) a mixture of heroin and cocaine. [pun on BOY n.[5] + GIRL n.[3] (1)]

loveage n. [mid-19C] a drink consisting of the dregs collected from the overflow from the pouring taps, the ends of spirit bottles and similar leavings, which was sold cheaply in gin-shops, particularly to women (cf. ALL NATIONS). [SE lovage, a cordial based on the herb lovage (Ligusticum scoticum)]

love and hate n. [20C] weight. [rhy. sl.]

love and kisses n. [20C] one's wife. [rhy. sl. = missus]

love and marriage n. [20C] a carriage. [rhy. sl.]

love apples n. [19C; 1980s+] the testicles (cf. APRICOTS). [note Fr. pomme d'amour; Ger. liebesapful, the fruit of the tomato]

love arm n. [1990s] the penis (cf. LOVE BONE; LOVE MUSCLE).

love boat n. [1980s+] (US drugs) **1** marijuana dipped in formaldehyde. **2** phencyclidine (cf. ACE n.[3]).

love bone n. [1960s+] (US Black) the penis (cf. LOVE ARM).

love box n. [1980s+] (US) the female genitals. [SE love + BOX n.[6] (2)/SE box]

love button n. [1990s] (US) the clitoris.

love canal n. [1980s+] (US) the vagina. [+ pun on 1993 ecological abuse of the Love Canal, New York]

love chocolate n. [1980s+] a White person who specializes in Black partners (cf. LOVE VANILLA). [SE love + CHOCOLATE n.[1]]

love-curls n. [mid-19C] a hairstyle in which the hair is cut short and worn low over the forehead.

love custard n. [1990s] semen (cf. BABY GRAVY; CUSTARD).

love dart n. [19C] the penis (cf. BAYONET).

loved it! phr. [1980s+] (US campus) an expression of elation.

love dove n. [1990s] (drugs) MDMA (cf. DOVE; ECSTASY). [the tablets are branded with a small dove of peace]

love drug n. [1980s+] (drugs) MDMA (cf. ECSTASY). [among the drug's primary effects is a sense of world-embracing benevolence]

love 'em and leave 'em n. [late 19C+] a philanderer, a womanizer (cf. 4-F CLUB). [SE love them and leave them]

love 'em and leave 'em phr. [late 19C+] philandering, womanizing, e.g. he's the love 'em and leave 'em sort. [LOVE 'EM AND LEAVE 'EM n.]

love envelope n. [1980s+] (US gay) a condom (cf. LOVE GLOVE).

love flesh n. [19C] the vagina.

love gap see PASSION GAP.

love glove n. [1980s+] (US) **1** a condom (cf. LOVE ENVELOPE). **2** the vagina.

love gun n. [1970s+] (US) the penis. [ext. of GUN n.]

love handles n. [1960s+] the excess flesh around a portly stomach that may be seen in a kinder light by those who appreciate the Rubenesque figure (cf. BAGELS).

love hole n. [1980s+] (US) the vagina (cf. BLACK HOLE n.[1]).

love-in n. [1960s+] (US) **1** a group gathering to express mutually loving feelings. **2** an orgy. **3** positive, optimistic relations.

love it to death, to phr. [1960s+] **1** to enjoy or to love to extremes. **2** in ironic use, to deplore.

love juice n. [late 19C+] **1** semen. **2** vaginal secretions.

love lane/love-lane n. [mid-19C] the vagina (cf. ALLEY n.[1]).

love letter n. [1940s] (US Black) **1** a bullet. **2** a stone or rock thrown at someone (cf. IRISH CONFETTI).

lovelies/lovely/lovely high n. [1970s+] (US drugs) marijuana laced with phencyclidine (PCP).

lovely n.[1] [1930s+] a pretty young woman, a word esp. popular with tabloid press, seaside entertainers etc. [SE lovely adj.]

lovely n.[2] see LOVELIES.

lovely adj. [early 17C+] delightful, really excellent.

lovely dripping phr. [1930s+] a general phr. implying excellence, absolute approval.

lovely drop n. [1930s] a fine example of, a tasty bit of (cf. NICE DROP).

lovely grub! excl. [1950s+] implies approval of whatever is being considered, whether actual food or not.

lovely high see LOVELIES.

lovely jubbly! excl. [1980s+] a general excl. of approval. [the term originated in BBC TV's sitcom Only Fools and Horses c.1987, and like some other terms in that series, e.g. DIPSTICK, is synthetic rather than spontaneous. Its main role is to imply long-rooted sl., but it is in fact ult. euph.]

lovely money n. [1930s+] a good deal of money.

love machine n. **1** [1960s+] the penis (cf. FORNICATING ENGINE). **2** [1970s+] (US) a sexually virile man, a womanizer (cf. SEX MACHINE).

love muffin n. [1980s+] (US) a sexually attractive person (cf. STUD-MUFFIN).

love muscle n. [1950s+] (US) the penis (cf. LOVE ARM).

love nest n. (US) **1** [1950s+] an apartment used by lovers. **2** [1950s+] a drive-in film, known as a venue for teenage love-making. **3** [1990s] the vagina.

love off v. [20C] (W.I./Jam.) to make obvious sexual advances towards.

love pearls/pills n. [1980s+] (drugs) alphaethyltyptamine. [? the effects]

love-penny n. [early 18C] a miser.

love pills see LOVE PEARLS.

love-pot n. [19C] a drunkard (cf. TOSSPOT).

love pump n. [1980s+] (US) the penis. [popularized by the film This is Spinal Tap (1984)]

lover n.[1] [20C] (US) a pimp. [euph.]

lover n.[2] [1910s+] (orig. US) an affectionate general term of address, though no actual love affair need be implied.

lover-boy/-man n. [1950s+] a womanizer; the term is often used (esp. by women) ironically.

lover's nuts/balls/knots n. [1940s+] (US) aches in the

testicles caused by sexual stimulation without ejaculation. [SE *lover* + NUTS n.²/BALLS n.¹ (1)/*knots*]

lover's tiff *n.* [20C] venereal disease. [rhy. sl. *lover's tiff* = SYPH]

love shack *n.* [1960s+] (orig. US) **1** a room or apartment that a man keeps for seductions and sex (cf. FUCK PAD). **2** a lover, an object of sexual desire (and conquest). [(2) is fig. use of (1)]

love's harbour *n.* [19C] the vagina (cf. ARBOUR).

love's paradise *n.* [19C] the vagina.

love spuds *n.* [1990s] the testicles. [SE *love* + SPUD n.¹]

lovesteak *n.* [1980s+] (US campus) the penis (cf. BACON n.¹).

love stick *n.* [1920s+] (US) the penis (cf. LOVE TRUNCHEON).

love torpedo *n.* [1990s] the penis.

love trip *n.* [1980s+] (drugs) a mixed dose of MDMA and mescaline.

love truncheon *n.* [1990s] the penis (cf. LOVE STICK).

love up/love *n.* [late 19C+] (US) a caress, a hug. [LOVE UP v.]

love up/love *v.* [late 19C+] (US) to caress, to hug, to embrace.

love vanilla *n.* [1980s+] a Black person who specializes in White partners (cf. LOVE CHOCOLATE).

love weed *n.* [1930s+] (US drugs) marijuana. [SE *love* + WEED n.¹]

lovey-dovey *n.* **1** [late 19C+] a term of endearment. **2** [1940s+] (US) lovemaking. [SE *love* + redup. + image of billing and cooing turtle-doves]

lovey-dovey *adj.* [late 19C+] **1** affectionate. **2** maudlin and sentimental. [LOVEY-DOVEY n.]

loving *adj.* [1940s+] (US) used as a euph. for FUCKING adj. (cf. MOTHERLOVING).

loving it *phr.* [1980s+] in a positive or pleasing situation. ['it' is life]

low *n.* [1970s+] (US drugs) a bad reaction to a drug. [opposite of HIGH n. (1), and slightly contrived]

low *adj.* [mid-19C+] of religious beliefs, Low Church (Nonconformist) as opposed to High Church (Anglican).

low and slow *phr.* [mid–late 19C] a phr. used to describe the Low Church or Nonconformism (cf. HIGH AND DRY).

lowbrow *n.* [20C] (orig. US) an uncultured person who is considered to have mass-market, undemanding and non-intellectual tastes (cf. HIGHBROW; MIDDLEBROW).

lowbrow *adj.* [20C] (orig. US) pertaining to mass-market values. [LOWBROW n.]

low cotton *n.* [1940s+] (US) low spirits, depression; esp. in the phr. *feel in low cotton*, to feel dejected, miserable.

low countries *n.* [18C] the female genitals (cf. LOWLANDS; NETHERLANDS). [the 'geography' of the body + a pun on *country*/CUNT n.¹ (1)]

Low Country soldier *n.* [17C] a good drinking companion. [the characteristics of those who have soldiered in the Low Countries or of Dutch troops]

lowdown, the *n.* [20C] (orig. US) privileged information, intimate details, 'the inside story'.

lowdown *adj.* (US) **1** [mid-19C+] mean, contemptible, unpleasant. **2** [1960s+] depressed, impoverished, out of luck.

low-downer *n.* [mid–late 19C] (US Black) a poor White person. [LOWDOWN adj. (1)]

lower *see* LOUR.

lower a glass, to *phr.* [late 19C+] to take a drink, to empty a glass (or bottle) by drinking its contents.

lower mouth *n.* [mid-19C] the vagina (cf. BEST LEG OF THREE).

lower one's feathers, to *phr.* [19C] (US) to back down from a challenge (cf. GET ONE'S TAIL-FEATHERS UP). [bird imagery]

lower than a snake's belly *phr.* [1930s+] (Aus.) as low as one can go.

lower than the belly of a cockroach *phr.* [20C] used of a person categorised as the lowest of the low.

lower/drop the boom/boom on, to *phr.* [late 19C+] (US) **1** to hit hard. **2** to give up on. **3** to take decisive action against.

4 to reprimand severely, to put an end to someone's mis-behaviour. [naut. imagery]

lower wig *n.* [19C] the pubic hair (cf. NETHER BEARD).

lowey *n.* [1970s–80s] (Aus.) a young woman who is dedicated to hedonism, the equivalent and accomplice of a REV-HEAD. [? LOWHEEL]

low five *n.* [1980s+] (US Black) a palm-/hand-slapping ritual, with the hands held low rather than the usual HIGH FIVE.

low-flung *adj.* [mid-19C] (US) of low character or social position.

low Greek *n.* [1960s+] (gay) heterosexual intercourse (because the vagina is lower than the anus); thus homosexual intercourse is *high Greek* (cf. HIGH RUSSIAN).

lowheel *n.* [1930s–60s] **1** a prostitute or promiscuous woman (cf. LITTLE MISS ROUNDHEELS; LOWIE). **2** a down-and-out, a tramp. [the state of one's shoes after constantly walking the streets]

lowie *n.* [1930s–60s] a prostitute or promiscuous woman (cf. LOWHEEL).

lowing cheat/chete *n.* [16C] (Und.) a cow, a calf (cf. BLEATING CHEAT). [SE *lowing* + CHEAT, lit. 'lowing thing']

low in the lay *phr.* [mid-19C–1910s] extremely poor. [SE *lay low*, to knock down]

low in the saddle *phr.* [20C] (orig. US) drunk and thus slumped over. [cowboy imagery]

lowland *n.* [1930s–60s] (US Black) the area of a city, usu. the south, where the Black ghetto is generally sited.

lowlands *n.* [late 18C–mid-19C] the female genitals (cf. LOW COUNTRIES; NETHERLANDS).

lowlife *n.* [1910s+] (orig. US) a contemptible person, esp. a criminal.

lowlife *adj.* [1910s+] (orig. US Black) unpleasant, aggressive. [LOWLIFE n.]

low men *n.* [late 17C–18C] fixed dice that will always show low numbers (cf. UPHILLS).

low neck and short sleeves *n.* [1960s+] (gay) a circumcised penis. [the foreskin is the 'sleeves']

low on *adj.* [1960s+] deficient in, short of.

low on the totem pole *phr.* [1940s+] inferior, second-rate, a junior or uninfluential position at work; thus [1970s+] abbr. *low on the totem*. [an image of Native American hierarchy]

low pad *n.* [late 17C–18C] (Und.) a footpad. [SE *low* + PAD n.¹ (1)]

low pro *n.* [1990s] (US Black) a *low pro*file (cf. DOWN LOW). [abbr.]

low quarters *n.* [1930s–40s] (US Black) Oxford shoes, with laces over the instep.

low rate *v.* [20C] (US South/Black) to attack verbally, to criticize, to denigrate.

lowre *see* LOUR.

low rent *n.* [1960s+] (US campus) a worthless individual, or a promiscuous woman who sleeps around. [LOW RENT adj.]

low rent *adj.* [1950s+] (orig. US) cheap, distasteful, unfashionable.

lowride *v.* [1950s+] (US) to cruise the streets in a low-slung, customized car. [LOWRIDER n.²]

lowrider *n.¹* [1930s+] (US Black) a pimp. [his fig. 'lowriding' in the area of morals + ethics]

lowrider *n.²* [1950s+] (US) **1** a customized car that has been 'chopped and channelled' to lower the suspension and give it a generally sleeker look (cf. RANFLA). **2** the driver of such a car. [since the driving of such cars is illegal, they are fitted with hydraulic systems to adjust the height of the car while driving, making it appear to bounce]

lowriding *n.* [1970s+] (US) cruising the streets in a low-slung, customized car. [LOWRIDE v.]

lowrie *see* LOUR.

low-run *adj.* [1950s+] (W.I.) untrustworthy, hypocritical.

low tide/low water *n.* [late 17C–19C] financial difficulty.

low-toby *n.* [mid-19C] highway robbery by footpads (rather than mounted highwaymen) (cf. HIGH PAD; HIGH-TOBY).

low-toby-man *n.* [19C] a footpad (cf. HIGH-TOBY-MAN).

low water *see* LOW TIDE.

lox *n.* [1960s+] (US) a fool (cf. LUMMOX).

lox jock/lox jockey *n.* [20C] (US) a Jew (cf. CAMEL CHASER; COW JOCKEY; PLOW JOCKEY; SWAB JOCKEY). [Yid. *laks*, thence SE *lox*, smoked salmon, served with cream cheese and bagels, a favourite Jewish dish]

loz *n.* [1990s] (drugs) 1oz (28g) of cannabis. [? misreading of the numeral 1, pron. as the letter 'l' + *oz*, abbr. for one ounce]

L-7/l-seven *n.* [1950s+] (US Black/teen) a conventional, tedious person, unsympathetic to teen interests. [the L and the 7 when put together form a SQUARE n.⁵; the word can be accompanied by using thumb and forefinger extended at right angles, forming an L and a 7, and when the two are combined they form a square]

L-7/l-seven *adj.* [1950s+] (US Black/teen) unfashionable, unsophisticated (cf. SQUARE adj.). [L-7 n.]

l.t.r. *n.* [1970s+] a *l*iving *t*ogether *r*elationship, marriage in all but the legalities. [abbr.]

L train *n.* [1990s] (US Black) a late-night New York subway train.

lubage *n.* [1990s+] (US campus/drugs) marijuana. [SE *lub*(*ricate*) + sfx. -AGE]

lubber *n.* [14C–19C] a fool; thus [16C–19C] SE *lubberland*, an imaginary land of plenty without labour; a land of laziness (cf. ABBEY-LUBBER). [? OF. *lobeor*, a swindler or parasite, ult. *lober*, to deceive, to sponge upon or to mock; it is the basis of the 16C nautical *land-lubber*, a landsman or incompetent sailor. The clumsiness implicit in the nautical use implies a further link to LOB n.³; ult. from a variety of Teut. forms all meaning heavy or clumsy]

lube *n.* **1** [1940s+] (Aus.) a drink. **2** [1970s+] (US) a lubricated condom (cf. LUBIE). [SE *lubrication*]

lube *v.* [1930s+] **1** to keep happy, to entertain. **2** to bribe, to tip. [fig. uses of SE *lubricate*]

lube job *n.* [1940s+] (US) oral or sexual intercourse. [the fluids thus generated + pun]

lube the tube, to *phr.* [1990s] of a woman, to masturbate. [SE *lubricate* + SE *tube*]

lubie *n.* [1970s+] (US) a lubricated condom (cf. LUBE n.).

lubra *n.* [1960s+] (Aus.) a woman. [Abor. *lubra*, a woman]

lubricate *v.* **1** [mid-18C–early 19C] to have sexual intercourse (cf. LUBE JOB). **2** [late 19C+] to ply with drink. **3** [1920s] to bribe.

lubricated *adj.* [1920s+] (orig. US) drunk (cf. ALED UP; GET ONE'S NECK IN SOAK; MELTED; SATURATED; SAUCED; SOAKED; SODDEN; SOUSED).

lubricator *n.* [mid–late 19C] (US) a derog. name for a Mexican (cf. GREASER n.¹).

luck/good luck *n.* [late 18C–early 19C] stepping into a heap of excrement. [pvb. 'Shitten luck is good luck']

luck/luck it *v.* [1930s+] to take a chance or to succeed or manage something through luck, to come up with a stroke of luck.

luck boy *see* LUCKY BOY.

luck in/into *v.* [1920s+] (orig. US) **1** to experience good luck. **2** to succeed through good luck.

luck it *see* LUCK v.

luck of a fat priest/pox doctor, the *phr.* [mid-19C+] very good (and fortuitous) luck; a phr. used of anyone with such luck, e.g. *he has the luck of a . . .* .

luck of Eric Connolly *phr.* [1940s–60s] (Aus.) a description of any lucky person. [proper name of *Eric Connolly* (d.1944), known as an exceptionally lucky gambler]

luck out *n.* [1940s+] (orig. US) a piece of good luck. [LUCK OUT v.]

luck out *v.* [1940s+] (orig. US) to strike lucky (cf. LUCK OUT n.; LUCK UP ON).

luckpenny *n.* [20C] (Irish) a token sum of money handed back to the buyer/seller on the completion of a deal. [on the same principle as that of never giving an empty wallet as a present]

luck through *v.* [1930s+] (US) to succeed or manage by good luck.

luck up on *v.* [1930s+] (US Black) to become lucky (cf. LUCK OUT v.).

lucky bag *n.* [19C] the vagina. [fairground jargon *lucky bag*, a 'lucky dip']

lucky/luck boy *n.* [late 19C+] (US) a crooked professional gambler.

lucky dips *n.* [20C] chips, french fries. [rhy. sl.]

lucky for some *n.* [20C] (bingo) the number 13.

lucky piece *n.* [late 19C+] an illegitimate child (usu. a son) born to a poor mother and wealthy father who does not live with his 'family' but provides for them generously.

lucky pierre *n.* [1940s+] **1** the man in a sexual threesome of two women and one man. **2** (gay) the middle man in a 'sandwich' of three sexually entwined men. [? the punchline of a joke]

lucky shop *n.* [1970s+] (Aus.) a Totalizator Agency Board (TAB) betting shop in Victoria.

Lucozade *n.* [1950s+] a Black person. [rhy. sl.; the brandname of the tonic drink *Lucozade* = SPADE]

lucy *n.*¹ [1950s–60s] (US camp gay) one who has a 'loose asshole'.

lucy *n.*² **1** [1950s+] (US) sweet wine. **2** [1950s+] marijuana. **3** [1990s] (US Black) a cigarette. [they all help one become SE *loose*; i.e. less tense, less stressed]

lucy in the sky with diamonds *n.* [1960s] LSD (cf. A n.³). [the title of Beatles song (1967), the initial letters (and the psychedelic lyrics) of which left no one in doubt – for all the band's disclaimers – as to its subject]

lucy law *n.* [1960s+] (gay) the police (cf. LILY LAW).

lucy locket/locket *n.* [20C] a pocket (cf. PENNY LOCKET). [rhy. sl.]

lud! *excl.* [early 18C–late 19C] a form of *Lord!* and similarly used in mild oaths.

ludby *see* LOTEBY.

lude/ludes *n.* [1970s+] (US drugs) methaqualone, or other depressant drugs; thus *ludehead*, a habitual user of the drug. [brandname *Quaalude*, manufactured until 1983]

lude out *v.* [1980s+] (US campus) to become unable to function, usually because of drugs. [LUDE]

ludes *see* LUDE.

Ludgate bird *n.* [17C] a bankrupt, one who has been imprisoned for bankruptcy. [*Ludgate* Prison, which housed mainly debtors]

Lud's bulwark *n.* [late 17C–early 19C] Ludgate prison. [statues of the mythical King *Lud* and his sons used to stand on this old London gate, which the king had supposedly erected in 66BC, but it was more likely a Roman gate. Brewer suggests Ludgate comes from OE *ludgeat*, a postern, while E.P. opts for Norse *ludden*, thick, broad]

luego! *excl.* [1980s+] (US campus) goodbye. [Sp. *hasta luego*]

luff *n.* [mid-19C] speech, talk. [echoic of a puff of wind; i.e. that expelled while talking]

l.u.g. *n.* [1980s+] (orig. US campus) a female student who is not necessarily a lesbian, but who experiments with feminism and lesbian politics and culture. [abbr. *l*esbian *u*ntil *g*raduation]

lug *n.*¹ [late 16C+] an ear. [Scot./northern dial.]

lug *n.*² [1920s+] (orig. US) **1** a large, stupid man. **2** a lout, a sponger. [SE *lug* v., to drag, to haul. Such a heavyweight would need to be dragged along, mentally or physically. Note Scot. *luggie*, awkward, sluggish]

lug *n.*[3] **1** [late 19C–1920s] (US) an act of pride, a display of affectation. **2** [1960s+] (US Black) an act of disparagement, of severe criticism (cf. DROP A LUG ON; PUT THE LUG ON phr.[2]). [Scot./northern dial.]

lug *v.*[1] [late 19C+] to escort someone, to bring along a companion. [SE *lug*, to drag]

lug *v.*[2] **1** [1920s–40s] (orig. US) to beg. **2** [1960s+] (US Black) to berate, to criticize harshly (cf. DROP A LUG ON; PUT THE LUG ON phr.[1]). [LUG n.[1]]

lug *v.*[3] [1970s] (US Und.) to beat up (cf. PUT THE LUG ON phr.[2]). [? LUG n.[1], as in *OED*; however Lighter (1997) suggest that this *lug* could poss. be a separate word]

lug *v.*[4] [1970s+] (US prison) to make into a homosexual. [PUT THE LUG ON phr.[2]]

lugan *n.*[1] *see* LOOGAN.

Lugan *n.*[2] *see* LUGEN.

lug-bite *n.* [late 19C] (Aus.) to cadge, to ask for a loan; thus *lug-biter*, a cadger. [LUG n.[1]]

lug chovey *n.* [mid-19C] a pawnshop. [IN LUG + CHOVEY]

Lugen/Loogin/Lugan/Lugie/Lugun *n.* [1940s+] (US) a Lithuanian or person of Lithuanian background. [? LOOGAN or *Lithuanian*]

luggage *n.*[1] [20C] the male genitals. [pun on BAG n.[1] (2)]

luggage *n.*[2] [1970s] (US teen) bags under the eyes. [pun on SE *bags*]

lugger *n.*[1] **1** [1920s+] (US Und.) an accomplice who makes contact with an intended victim or punter, also in a shoplifting team (cf. BOOSTER n.[2]). **2** [1920s+] (US Und.) the accomplice (there are usually two) who helps the actual thief remove the stolen goods from the store. **3** [1960s+] (Can. prison) a smuggler of contraband in or out of the prison. [LUG v.[1] + sfx. -*er*]

lugger *n.*[2] [1940s–50s] (Aus.) **1** a shameless beggar. **2** a nag. [LUG v.[2]]

luggers *n.* [mid–late 19C] earrings. [LUG n.[1]]

lughead *n.* [1950s+] (US) a stupid person. [LUG n.[2] (1) + sfx. -HEAD (1)]

lughole *n.* [20C] an ear. [dial./LUG n.[1]]

Lugie *see* LUGEN.

lug out *v.* [late 17C] to draw a sword. [SE *lug*, to drag (out)]

lugow *v.* [19C–1930s] (Anglo-Ind.) to fasten, to place. [Hind. *lugana*, to attach, to join, to fix]

lugs *n.* [late 19C–1920s] (US) affected manners, posing; often with *put on* ... (cf. PILE ON LUGS).

lug someone's ear, to *phr.* [20C] (Aus.) to attempt to borrow money. [SE *lug*, to drag, to pull]

Lugun *see* LUGEN.

luke *n.*[1] [mid-19C] nothing. [? northern dial.]

luke *n.*[2] [1950s+] a Black person. [abbr. rhy. sl. *lucozade* = SPADE]

lukshen/loksh *n.* [20C] (US) an Italian, as used by Jews (cf. SPAGHETTI n.[1]). [Yid. *lokshen*, noodles]

lull *n.* [mid-17C] ale. [SE *lull*, a soothing drink]

lullaby *n.* [mid–late 19C] the penis. [it 'puts one to sleep']

lullaby-cheat *n.* [late 17C–early 19C] a child. [SE *lullaby* + CHEAT n., lit. 'lullaby-thing']

lully/lally *n.* [mid-16C–late 19C] **1** (Und.) wet or drying linen. **2** a shirt. [? SE *laundry* or *lilywhite*]

lully prigger *n.* [late 16C–late 19C] one who steals from washing lines or from wherever washing has been put out to dry (cf. HEDGE-CREEPER; KNICKERS BANDIT; SNOW-DROPPING). [LULLY + *prigger* (see PRIG n.[1])]

lulu *n.*[1] **1** [mid-19C+] (orig. US) anything remarkable, exceptional, wonderful (cf. LALLAPALOOSA; LOLLA). **2** [late

19C+] (orig. US) a disaster, an abject failure or a foolish person. **3** [late 19C+] (US gambling) a remarkable poker hand that beats a royal flush. [ety. unknown; (2) is ironic use of (1)]

lulu/looloo/luluh *n.*[2] **1** [mid-19C–1930s] (orig. US) a girlfriend, a gangster's girlfriend. **2** [1950s] a silly young woman. [the proper name, seen as somewhat exotic]

lulu *n.*[3] [late 19C+] the lavatory. [LOO n.[1]]

luluh *see* LULU n.[2].

lumb *n.* [18C] (Und.) too much. [? LUMBERED adj.[1]]

lumber *n.*[1] **1** [early 17C–mid-19C] a pawnshop (cf. IN LUMBER; LUMBERED adj.[2]). **2** [mid-18C+] a house or room, esp. one used for storing stolen goods. **3** [mid–late 19C] anywhere frequented by confidence tricksters and similar villains. **4** [1940s–50s] the flat from which a prostitute works, but does not occupy as a home. [17C SE *Lombard*, a bank, money-changer's or money-lender's office, a pawnshop. The Lombards, or natives of Lombardy, were celebrated bankers; thus the medieval *Lombard Room*, where pawnbrokers and bankers stored their pledges]

lumber/lumber sauce *n.*[2] [1930s–60s] (US) a toothpick. [SE *lumber*, wood]

lumber *n.*[3] [1960s+] **1** sexual play, petting. **2** (mainly Scot.) a prospective sexual partner, a casual pick-up. [? dial. *lumber*, mischief]

lumber *n.*[4] [1970s+] (US) the penis (cf. LOVE STICK). [pun on WOOD n.[2]]

lumber *n.*[5] [1970s+] (US drugs) unwanted twiggy stems in marijuana.

lumber *v.*[1] **1** [19C] to pawn. **2** [early 19C+] (Aus.) to arrest, to imprison. [LUMBER n.[1]]

lumber *v.*[2] **1** [1930s+] (mainly Scot./Ulster) to fondle sexually, to have intercourse. **2** [1930s+] to court, to 'chat up'. **3** [1950s] to persuade, to trick. [LUMBER n.[3]]

lumbered *adj.*[1] [mid-18C+] burdened with, trapped. [SE *lumber*, to weigh down, to fill up with; ult. *lumber*, useless, space-consuming objects]

lumbered *adj.*[2] **1** [early 19C+] pawned. **2** [mid-19C+] imprisoned. **3** [1950s+] short of money, indebted. [LUMBER v.[1]]

lumberer *n.*[1] **1** [mid-18C] a poor prostitute (cf. BULKER n.[1]). **2** [mid-18C–early 19C] a tramp, a vagrant. [SE *lumber*, i.e. they are forced to sleep on piles of timber]

lumberer *n.*[2] **1** [late 19C] a swindling tipster. **2** [late 19C] a pawnbroker. **3** [1900s–40s] a prostitute who specializes in robbing her clients. [LUMBER v.[1]]

lumber gaff *n.* [1930s–50s] the flat from which a prostitute works but which she does not occupy as a home. [LUMBER n.[1] (4) + GAFF n.[1] (5)]

lumber out *v.* [20C] (Aus.) to throw out, to eject. [LUMBER v.[1]]

lumber sauce *see* LUMBER n.[2].

lumber-shover *n.* [19C] a workman in a timber-yard.

lumme! *excl.* [late 19C+] an excl. of surprise, shock, disbelief. ['Lord love me!]

lummocks/lummox *n.* [early 19C+] a large, heavy or clumsy person, an ungainly or stupid lout (cf. HUNK n.[1]). [dial. *lummock*, to move heavily or clumsily]

lummy *adj.* [19C] excellent; thus *lummy lick*, a delicious mouthful. [Yorks. dial.]

lump *n.*[1] [mid-19C] (US) a gold coin.

lump *n.*[2] [mid–late 19C] a lot, a large quantity.

Lump, the *n.*[3] [mid-19C–1930s] the workhouse, the casual ward, esp. the Marylebone workhouse, ext. as *Lump Hotel* (cf. PAN n.[2]; SPINNIKEN). [? its occupants are 'lumped together']

lump *n.*[4] [late 19C–1920s] (US) semen; thus *blow one's lump*, to ejaculate.

lump *n.*[5] [20C] (US) a parcel of food given to a tramp or vagrant. [dial. *lump*, a luncheon]

lump *n.*[6] [1980s+] (US campus) a lazy idler.

lump *v.*[1] [late 18C+] (orig. US) to accept something, however grudgingly, that has to be endured; usu. as *lump it* (cf. LIKE IT OR LUMP IT). [SE *lump*, to look sulky or disagreeable]

lump *v.*[2] **1** [mid-19C+] (US) to beat. **2** [1950s+] to hit someone over the head with a lump of stone or a brick. [SE *lump*, to beat or thresh]

lump *v.*[3] [late 19C+] to haul about, to carry a heavy weight. [LUMPER *n.*[2]]

lump *v.*[4] [1970s+] (US) to defecate.

lump *v.*[5] [1980s+] (US campus) to act lazily, to do nothing. [LUMP *n.*[6]]

lump and bump *n.* [late 19C–1930s] a fool, a simpleton. [rhy. sl. *lump and bump* = CHUMP *n.*[2]]

lumper *n.*[1] **1** [late 18C] a riverside thief. **2** [late 18C–mid-19C] the lowest order and more contemptible species of thief who lurk and grab whatever they can, regardless of value. **3** [mid-19C] a seller of goods under false pretences, the old made to look new, the weak, strong etc (cf. DUFFER *n.*[1]).

lumper *n.*[2] **1** [late 18C+] a contractor or a worker who loads and unloads heavy cargo, orig. ship's cargo. **2** [mid-late 19C] a small contractor, a middleman, an exploitative factory owner. [LUMP *v.*[3]]

lumper *n.*[3] [mid-19C] a militiaman. [his stolidity and/or the weight of his equipment and pack; note dial. *lumper*, of a horse to walk heavily; of a man, to stumble]

lumper *n.*[4] [1970s+] (US) a piece of excrement. [SE *lump*]

lumpers *n.* [1950s–60s] a lump sum paid as unemployment compensation.

lumphead *n.* [1950s–60s] (orig. US) an absolute fool, an idiot, an incompetent (cf. LUNKHEAD). [SE *lump* + sfx.-HEAD (1)]

lumping *adj.* [early 18C+] large, heavy, unwieldy; often as *lumping great...* (cf. STUMPING).

lumping pennyworth *n.* [late 17C–mid-19C] a good bargain; thus [late 18C–early 19C] *get/have a lumping pennyworth*, to marry a fat woman.

lump into *v.* [late 19C+] to work with enthusiasm, energy; thus *lump into it!* [LUMP *v.*[2]]

lump of bread *n.* [1910s–20s] the head. [rhy. sl.]

lump of coke *n.* [mid-19C] a man, a person. [rhy. sl. *lump of coke* = BLOKE *n.* (1)]

lump of ice *n.* [late 19C] advice. [rhy. sl.]

lump of lead *n.*[1] [mid-19C] the head. [rhy. sl.]

lump of lead *n.*[2] [20C] (Aus.) bread. [rhy. sl.]

lump of school *n.* [late 19C] a fool. [rhy. sl.]

lump of soap *n.* [late 19C–1900s] a woman (cf. BIT OF SOAP). [SE *lump* + SOAP]

lump of stone *n.* [late 19C] (Und.) a local prison (i.e. one outside London).

lumps *n.*[1] [1930s+] (US) a beating, punishment, blame or criticism, usu. constructed with a prn. and *give/take/get*.

lumps *n.*[2] [1990s] (US) the female breasts.

lump the lighter, to *phr.* [late 18C–late 19C] to be transported. [fig use of SE *lump*, to load + *lighter*, a vessel used for loading/unloading ships]

lumpy *adj.* [early–mid-19C] tipsy, slightly drunk. [dial. *lumpy*, awkward, sluggish]

lumpy chicken *phr.* [1960s+] (orig. US milit.) loud and clear. [initial letters]

lumpy-roar *n.* [mid-late 19C] a grandee, an aristocrat, 'a swell of the first water' (Ware). [Fr. *l'empereur*, emperor, which gained popularity during the visit to the UK of Napoleon III in 1853]

lun *n.* [late 18C–early 19C] Harlequin, the *commedia del arte* stock character. [? LOON *n.*]

lunan *n.* [mid-19C] (tramp) a woman. [Rom. *loobni*, a prostitute]

lunar *n.* [1900s–50s] a look, a glance; thus *take a lunar*, to glance at. [abbr. SE *lunar observation*]

lunar *adj.* [19C] moonstruck (cf. LOONY adj.).

lunatic soup *n.* [1930s+] (Aus./Irish/N.Z.) **1** cheap alcohol. **2** methylated spirits as drunk by alcoholics (cf. MADMAN'S BROTH).

lunch *n.*[1] **1** [1900s–10s] (US) the stomach. **2** [1910s+] (US) the contents of the stomach (cf. LOSE ONE'S LUNCH). **3** [1960s+] something/someone who is destined to suffer or be physically hurt. [(3) is only good to serve as food for some large predator]

lunch *n.*[2] [1940s+] **1** the penis. **2** oral intercourse (cf. EAT *v.*[3]; FRESS).

lunch/lunchie *n.*[3] [1960s+] (US campus) a dull, stupid person (cf. LUNCHY). [OUT TO LUNCH]

lunch *v.*[1] [late 19C] to provide someone with lunch.

lunch *v.*[2] **1** [1950s] (US campus) to spoil, ruin or fail. **2** [1980s+] (US campus) to procrastinate. **3** [1990s] (US teen) to act in a silly manner. [OUT TO LUNCH]

lunch at the lazy Y, to *phr.* [1950s+] (US) to perform cunnilingus (cf. EAT AT THE Y). [the Y refers both to the spread legs and to the YMCA/YWCA]

lunchbag/lunchbox/lunchbucket/lunchsack *n.* [1960s+] (US campus) a dull, foolish person (cf. LUNCH *n.*[3]). [one who is OUT TO LUNCH]

lunch-basket/-wagon *n.* [1910s+] the stomach (cf. LUNCH *n.*[1]).

lunchbox *n.*[1] see LUNCHBAG.

lunchbox *n.*[2] [1970s] (US Black) the stomach.

lunchbox *n.*[3] [1980s+] the male genitals, esp. when large and prominent beneath tight shorts or trousers (cf. LUNCH *n.*[2]; SNACK *n.*[3]).

lunchbucket *n.* see LUNCHBAG.

lunchbucket *adj.*[1] [1950s+] (US) middle-class, blue-collar. [LUNCHPAIL *n.*[1]]

lunchbucket *adj.*[2] [1950s+] (US) stupid, dull, uninspiring (cf. LUNCHBAG). [ext. of LUNCH *n.*[3]]

lunchcounter/lunchpail *n.* [1960s] (US) the female breasts. [their provision of milk]

lunched-out *adj.* [1980s+] (US) dazed, unaware, stupid. [OUT TO LUNCH]

lunch gut *n.* [1950s+] (drugs) the vomiting that may follow an injection of heroin (cf. DUMP *n.*[4]).

lunch hooks *n.* [late 19C+] (orig. US) the hand or fingers (cf. BISCUIT HOOKS). [SE *lunch hook*, a hook used to remove meat from the pot]

lunchie see LUNCH *n.*[3]

lunchmeat *n.* **1** [1950s+] (US campus) a stupid, contemptible person (cf. LUNCH *n.*[3]). **2** [1980s] (US) nonsense. **3** [1990s] (US) stupidity. **4** [1990s] (US) a victim.

lunchpail/lunchpailer *n.*[1] [1950s+] (orig. US) a blue-collar worker (cf. LUNCHBUCKET adj.[1]). [metonymy]

lunchpail *n.*[2] see LUNCHCOUNTER.

lunchpail *n.*[3] [1960s+] (US campus) a stupid, contemptible person. [ext. of LUNCH *n.*[3]]

lunchpailer see LUNCHPAIL *n.*[1].

lunchsack see LUNCHBAG.

lunch-wagon see LUNCH-BASKET.

lunchy *adj.* [1960s+] (US campus) **1** dull, stupid, absent-minded. **2** carefree, light-hearted, jokey. **3** unfashionable, out of style. [OUT TO LUNCH]

lung *n.* [1980s+] (drugs) a form of pipe used for smoking cannabis. [a 2-litre plastic bottle with a polythene bag attached to the bottom, when the bag is pulled out of the bottle the smoke fills it up]

lung *v.* [1980s+] (drugs) to smoke cannabis using a purpose-built 'pipe' constructed from a bottle and a polythene bag. [LUNG *n.*]

lung-box *n.* [mid–late 19C] the mouth.

lungbuster *n.* [1980s] (Aus.) a cigarette.

lung-disturber *n.* [20C] the penis (cf. KIDNEY-BUSTER).

lung-duster *n.* [1920s–40s] (US Black) a cigarette.

lunger *n.* (US) **1** [late 19C+] one who is suffering from lung disease or has been wounded in the lungs. **2** [1930s+] a mouthful of spit, a gob of phlegm (cf. LOOGIE).

lung hammock *n.* [1980s+] (US) a brassiere (cf. LUNGS n.²).

lungie *n.* [early 17C] a lout. [? dial. *lungie*, a guillemot, which scavenges on the beach]

lungs *n.*¹ [late 17C–mid-18C] a powerfully-voiced person.

lungs *n.*² [1950s+] (orig. US) the female breasts (cf. LUNG HAMMOCK; LUNG SHOT; PANTERS).

lung shot *n.* [1950s+] a photograph of a woman's breasts, used for softcore pornography. [LUNGS n.² + SE *shot*]

lung warts *n.* [1940s+] (US) the female breasts (cf. LUNGS n.²).

lunk *n.* [mid-19C+] (US) **1** a fool. **2** an oaf, a curmudgeon. [abbr. LUNKHEAD]

lunk *adj.* [late 19C+] (Irish) **1** of weather, close, sultry. **2** of a person, feeling ill. [Scot. *lunkie*, close, ult. Norwegian *lunke*, a tepid degree of heat]

lunker *n.*¹ [mid-19C+] (US) an animal or fish considered more than usually large for its species. [ety. unknown]

lunker *n.*² [1970s+] (US) a dilapidated motor car. [? CLUNKER n.¹]

lunkhead *n.* [mid-19C+] (orig. US) an absolute fool, an idiot, an incompetent. [? SE *lump* + sfx. -HEAD (1)]

lunky *adj.* [1940s+] (US) stupid. [LUNKHEAD]

luny *see* LOONY n.

luokal-mediocal *n.* [1950s] (W.I.) an undependable, untrustworthy person. [W.I. pron. of SE *local mediocre*]

luppies *n.* [1980s+] (US gay) lesbian urban professionals, i.e. lesbian yuppies (cf. GUPPIES). [abbr.]

luptious *adj.* [late 19C–1900s] delicious, luscious, lovely. [SE *voluptuous + delicious*]

lur-a-cham *see* LERACAM.

lurch *n.* [16C+] a cheat or swindle, often ext. as *give the lurch*; thus *in one's lurch*, at a disadvantage; *have/take at/in lurch*, to have at a disadvantage. [LURCH v.]

lurch *v.* [16C+] to deceive, to get the better of. [MHGer. *lurz*, left, wrong, thence *lurzen*, to deceive. The Ger. appears to have been adopted into Fr. as *lourche*, the name of a game similar to backgammon, and in its heyday equally popular in Britain, in which a *lurch* meant a game in which one player defeats an opponent to a score of zero. Those who lose a game of whist without scoring five are *lurched*]

lurcher *n.* [20C] **1** (Aus.) a rascal, a villain. **2** (Aus.) a Bohemian, one who acts without regard for social convention. **3** (Ulster) one who lurks around waiting for an advantage to present itself. [LARRIKIN]

lurcher of the law *n.* [late 18C–early 19C] the lowest rank of bailiff, a 'bum bailiff' (cf. BANDOG). [dial. *lurch*, lurk or slink about]

lure *n.* [late 17C–18C] 'an idle pamphlet' (B.E.) (cf. LEER). [SE *lure*, anything that tempts or entices]

lured *adj.* [20C] (Ulster) happy, cheerful.

lurgi/lurgy *n.* [1950s+] any unspecified but deleterious disease or ailment; esp. as the minatory phr. *dreaded lurgi*. [apparently coined by the writers of *The Goon Show* (1953–60), but the *EDD* cites *lurgy*, idleness, loafing + *lurgy-fever*, the 'disease' of idleness. The *OED* adds the synon. *fever-lurden, fever-lurgan*, ult. SE *fever* + *lurdan*, 'a general term of opprobrium, reproach, or abuse, implying either dullness and incapacity, or idleness and rascality; a sluggard, vagabond, "loafer"']

lurk *n.* **1** [mid-19C] (Und.) a form of fraud in which one pretends some form of distress in order to raise money from the credulous; thus [mid-19C–1900s] *go on a lurk*, get money through false pretences. **2** [mid-19C+] a hideaway, a meeting place; thus *servant lurk*, a public house where duplicitous servants meet criminals to plan mutually beneficial robberies. **3** [late 19C+] (Aus./N.Z.) a dodge, racket or scheme; thus *up to all lurks*, wide-awake, cunning. **4** [late 19C+] (Aus./N.Z.) a job. **5** [20C] (Aus.) a hanger-on, an eavesdropper. [SE *lurk*, to hide oneself, to lie in ambush, to remain furtively or unobserved about one spot]

lurk *v.* [1960s] (US Black) to go riding in a stolen car. [SE *lurk*; i.e. one tends to adopt a 'low profile' while driving in this way]

lurker *n.* **1** [mid-19C] a criminal beggar who travels the country showing off various forged certificates referring to losses in fires, shipwrecks or similar disasters and hoping thereby to get financial aid (cf. COUNTERFEIT CRANK; DOMMERER; SILVER BEGGAR). **2** [20C] (Aus.) a petty criminal. [LURK n. (1)]

lurkie *n.* [1940s+] (Aus.) a cunning, knowing, 'wide-awake' person, up to any trick. [LURK n. (3)]

lurking *n.* [mid-19C] (Und.) **1** stealing. **2** fraudulent begging, following the occupation of a fraudulent beggar. [LURK n. (1)]

lurkman *n.* [1930s+] (Aus.) **1** a confidence trickster. **2** a petty criminal. [LURK n. (1) + sfx. -*man*]

lurkola *n.* [1950s+] (Aus.) the practice (ostensibly illegal and generally denied by its practitioners) of bribing (with cash or kind) those with access to the public to tout a product. [LURK n. (1) + sfx. -OLA]

lurky *adj.* [1970s+] (US campus) seedy, untrustworthy, weird. [SE *lurk*]

lurp *n.* [1990s] (US teen) an extremely clumsy or awkward person. [play on SE *lunch*]

lurries *n.* [mid–late 17C] a quantity of valuables, e.g. watches and rings. [LURRY]

lurry *n.* [mid–late 17C] money. [LOUR]

lurry up *see* LORRY UP.

lus *n.* [1970s+] (S.Afr.) a yearning, a longing; thus *be lus for*, to long for. [Afk. *lus vir*, desirous of]

lush *n.*¹ **1** [late 18C+] alcohol, esp. beer. **2** [mid-19C+] a drunkard (cf. ALDERMAN LUSHINGTON). **3** [mid-19C+] a drinking spree. [LUSHINGTON, but note Ger. *Loschen*, strong beer, Shelta *lush*, to eat and drink]

lush *n.*² [mid–late 19C] (US Und.) money. [? SE *luscious*]

lush *n.*³ **1** [1940s–50s] (US gay) an extremely attractive heterosexual. **2** [1980s+] (US campus) an attractive woman. [SE *luscious*]

lush *n.*⁴ [1940s–60s] (US) a victim or fool. [fig. use of LUSH n.¹]

lush *adj.*¹ [early 19C+] drunk. [LUSH v.¹]

lush *adj.*² [1910s+] of a woman, very sexually attractive, esp. if voluptuous. [SE *luscious*]

lush *adj.*³ [1930s–40s] (US) wealthy. [LUSH n.²]

lush *v.*¹ **1** [19C] to ply with drink, to make drunk. **2** [early 19C+] to drink. [LUSH n.¹]

lush *v.*² *see* LUSH ROLL.

lush at Freeman's Quay *see* DRINK AT FREEMAN'S QUAY.

lush betty *n.* [mid-19C] (US) a whisky bottle (cf. BLACK BETTY). [LUSH adj.¹ + proper name *Betty*; ? anecdotal ref. to a once well-known prostitute or drinker]

lush cove *n.* [mid-19C] a drunkard. [LUSH adj.¹ + COVE]

lush/lushing crib *n.* [19C, 1970s] a saloon or bar (cf. LUSHING KEN). [LUSH n.¹ + CRIB n.³ (2)]

lush dip *n.* *see* LUSH WORKER.

lush dip *v.* *see* LUSH ROLL.

lush dive *see* LUSH JOINT.

lush drum *n.* [mid-19C] (US) a saloon or bar (cf. LUSH JOINT). [LUSH n.¹ + DRUM n.²]

lushed up *adj.* [1920s+] **1** drunk (cf. LUSH n.¹; LUSH adj.¹) **2** intoxicated by drugs. [LUSH v.]

lusher *n.* (US) **1** [late 19C–1920s] a heavy drinker (cf. LUSH n.¹). **2** [1910s–30s] a prostitute who preys on drunken customers (cf. LUSH ROLL). [LUSH v.¹]

lushery *n.* [late 19C] (US) a saloon or bar (cf. LUSH CRIB).

lush-head *n.* [1930s–60s] (US) a drunkard (cf. WINEHEAD). [LUSH + sfx. -HEAD (2)]

lush hound *n.* [1930s–40s] a drunkard (cf. BOOZE HOUND). [LUSH n.¹ + sfx. -HOUND]

lush-house *n.* [late 19C–1920s] a bar or saloon (cf. LUSH CRIB).

lushie *n.*¹ *see* LUSHY COVE.

lushie *n.*² *see* LUSHY n.

lushing *adj.* [mid–late 19C] used of a person who enjoys drinking. [LUSH v.¹]

lushing crib *see* LUSH CRIB.

lushing/lush ken *n.* [late 18C–19C] an alehouse, saloon or bar (cf. LUSH CRIB). [LUSH n.¹ + KEN n.¹]

lushing-man *n.* [mid-19C–1900s] (mainly US) a drunkard. [LUSH v.¹ + SE *man*]

Lushington/lushington *n.* [19C] a drunkard; thus *dealing with Lushington, Alderman Lushington is concerned, voting for the Alderman, Lushington is his master*, to be drinking too much (cf. ALDERMAN LUSHINGTON). [either LUSH n.¹, the proper name *Lushington* (a brewer) or f. 'The "City of Lushington" which, according to the *OED*, 'was the name of a convivial society (consisting chiefly of actors) which met at the Harp Tavern, Russell Street, until about 1895. It had a "Lord Mayor" and four "aldermen", presiding over "wards" called Juniper, Poverty, Lunacy, and Suicide. On the admission of a new member, the "Lord Mayor" ... harangued him on the evils of excess in drink.' The society was founded *c.*1750]

lush it *v.* [early 19C+] to drink. [LUSH v.¹]

lush it around/up *v.* [1950s+] (US) to become drunk. [LUSH v.¹]

lush joint/dive *n.* [late 19C+] a saloon, a bar (cf. LUSH DRUM) [LUSH n.¹ + JOINT n.³ (3)]

lush ken *see* LUSHING KEN.

lush merchant *n.* [late 19C+] (Aus.) a drunkard. [LUSH n.¹ + MERCHANT]

lush-out *n.* [early 19C–1900s] a drinking bout. [LUSH n.¹]

lush panny *n.* [19C] a bar, a saloon, a tavern (cf. LUSH CRIB; LUSHING KEN). [LUSH n.¹ + PANNEY n.²]

lush roll/lush/lush dip *v.* [1910s–60s] (orig. US) to rob a drunk; thus *lush roller*, one who robs drunks (cf. LUSH WORKER). [LUSH n.¹ + ROLL v.¹]

lush stash *n.* [1900s–40s] (US Black) a bar, a tavern. [LUSH n.¹ + STASH n.²]

lush thrush *n.* [1940s–50s] a very attractive young woman. [LUSH adj.² + SE *thrush*]

lush-toucher *n.* [1900s–20s] (US) a person who robs a drunk (cf. LUSH ROLL; LUSH WORKER). [LUSH n.¹ + SE *toucher*]

lush trotter *n.* [19C] (US) a boy or girl who is sent to the saloon to bring back beer either for their parents or for working men who cannot leave their jobs (cf. RUSHER n.²). [LUSH n.¹ + SE *trotter*, a runner]

lush up *v.* **1** [late 19C+] to become drunk. **2** [1920s+] to ply with drink. **3** [1960s] to provide with a luxurious standard of living. [LUSH v.¹]

lushwell *n.* [1960s+] (US) a heavy drinker. [LUSH n.¹ + fig. use of SE *well*]

lush worker/dip *n.* [20C] (US) one who robs drunks, esp. in subways. [LUSH n.¹ + WORKER n.¹]

lushy/lushie *n.* [1940s] (US Black) a drunkard. [LUSH n.¹]

lushy *adj.* [early 19C–1940s] drunk, tipsy. [LUSH n.¹]

lushy cove/lushie *n.* [early–mid-19C] a drunkard. [LUSH n.¹ + COVE]

lust dog *n.* [1970s+] (US campus) a male term for an allegedly promiscuous woman.

lust with *v.* [1980s+] (US campus) to feel sexual attraction toward.

lusty cod *see* COD n.⁴.

lusty-guts *n.* [16C] a promiscuous man, a womanizer (cf. LUSTY LAWRENCE).

lusty lawrence *n.* [16C] a womanizer, a promiscuous man. [? pun on LAZY LAWRENCE]

lute *n.*¹ [19C] the penis; thus *play a lute solo*, to masturbate (cf. FLUTE n.²). [an 'instrument' upon which one 'plays']

lute *n.*² [20C] (US) a *Lut*heran. [abbr.]

luvvie/luvvy *n.* **1** [1960s+] a general term of affectionate greeting. **2** [1980s+] a slightly derog. synon. for an actor or actress, esp. of the more demonstrative and overtly emotional type. [their stereotyped effusive cries of 'Luvvy! Darling!' on meeting]

lux *v.* [1970s+] (N.Z.) to vacuum a carpet etc. [abbr. brandname *Electrolux*]

l.v. *n.* [1990s] (US Black teen) the *L*ake*v*iew area of San Francisco. [abbr.]

lyb beg/lybbeg/lyb bege *see* LIB-BEG.

lybkin *see* LIBKEN.

lyesken chirps *n.* [18C–late 19C] (tinker) fortune-telling. [Shelta]

l.y.k.a.h. *phr.* [20C] (Irish) *l*eave *y*our *k*nickers *a*t *h*ome, written by men on the back of letters to their loved one (cf. BOLTOP). [abbr.]

lyle *see* LALLIE.

Lymps, the *n.* [mid-19C] the O*lymp*ic Theatre, London (cf. GARDEN n.²; LANE n.²). [abbr.]

lyp *v.* [mid-16C–late 17C] to lie down (cf. LIB v.).

lyrebird *n.* [late 19C+] (Aus.) a liar, a mimic. [pun on SE *lyrebird*]

lyrics *n.* [1980s+] (Black) fantasies, wild talk.

lyricsing *n.* [1980s+] (UK Black) chatting up, sweet-talking (cf. BUMCHAT).

M

M *n.*[1] [mid-16C–early 19C] a master or mistress. [abbr.]

M *n.*[2] (drugs) **1** [1910s+] morphine. **2** [1960s–70s] marijuana. **3** [1980s+] MDMA (cf. ECSTASY). [abbr.]

ma *n.*[1] **1** [mid-19C+] one's wife. **2** [1940s+] one's mother. **3** [1940s+] a term of address to a middle-aged or older woman, or to any woman in authority.

ma/mother *n.*[2] [1950s+] a derog. title put before a man's name to imply his homosexuality.

ma. *adj.* [late 18C+] (esp. public school) major, i.e. elder, esp. used to differentiate brothers, e.g. *Grabber ma* (cf. MI.). [abbr.]

Maalox moment *n.* [1990s] (US campus) a time of stress. [the proprietary antacid *Maalox*; the phr. was coined for an advertising campaign]

ma and pa store *n.* [20C] (US) a small corner store selling necessities, traditionally owned and run by a family (cf. MOM AND POP STORE).

maat/maatie/maatjie *n.* [20C] (S.Afr.) a friend, a chum, a pal. [Du. *maat*, a friend]

mab *n.*[1] [late 18C–early 19C] a prostitute; thus *mab up*, to dress carelessly (cf. MOB *n.*[2]). [SE *mab*, a slattern]

mab *n.*[2] [mid-19C] a cab. [rhy. sl.]

Ma Bell *n.* [1940s+] (US) the American Telephone & Telegraph Inc. (orig. *Maw Bell*). [SE *ma*, i.e. mother + the earlier firm, the *Bell* Telephone Company]

Mac/mac *n.*[1] **1** [17C+] a Celtic Irishman. **2** [17C+] a Scottish man. **3** [20C] (Can.) McMaster University, Hamilton, Ontario. **4** [1910s+] (US) a general term of greeting with no specific ref. to Scottish men implied. [Irish/Gaelic *mac*, son]

mac *n.*[2] [late 19C+] (W.I.) one shilling (post-1969 value 10 cents). [abbr. MACARONI *n.*[3]]

Mc- *pfx.* [1980s+] (orig. US campus) used to emphasize the mediocre or mass-market quality of the added n. (cf. MCJOB; MCNEWS). [*McDonalds*, the chain of fast-food restaurants, notorious for the tedium and low wages of their jobs]

macadam *n.* [1950s] (W.I.) a codfish fritter. [SE *macadam*, a type of road made of compacted layers of stone, invented by *John Loudon McAdam* (1756–1836). The fritter is hard and flat like the road]

macadocious *see* MACKADOCIOUS.

McAlpine fusilier *n.* [1960s+] a building labourer, a navvy. [*McAlpine*, a leading UK construction company]

mac-and-fip *n.* [1940s+] (W.I.) one shilling and three pence (post-1969 value 12.5 cents). [MACARONI *n.*[3] + FIP *n.*[1]]

macaroni *n.*[1] **1** [18C] a jolly fool, esp. an Italian one. **2** [mid-19C+] an Italian. [note synon. US regional use *macaroni-smacker*, *macaroni-snapper*]

macaroni *n.*[2] [late 18C–early 19C] a fop, a dandy, thus *macaroni-stake*, a horse-race ridden by a 'gentleman jockey' (cf. MACAROON *n.*[1]). [the *Macaroni Club*, 'which is composed of all the travelled young men who wear long curls and spying-glasses' (Horace Walpole ed., *Letters of Earl Hertford*, 1764).

The travelling, suggests the *OED*, probably gave the members a taste for foreign foods, hence the name]

macaroni *n.*[3] [early 19C+] (W.I.) one shilling (post-1969 value 10 cents). [? the tip commonly proffered by a dandy or MACARONI *n.*[2]]

macaroni *n.*[4] [mid-19C+] £25. [rhy. sl. *macaroni* = PONY *n.*[2] (1)]

macaroni *n.*[5] [1920s+] (Aus.) nonsense, meaningless talk (cf. APPLE SAUCE *n.*[2]). [joc. use of SE but note rhy. sl. *macaroni* = PONY *n.*[5] = *pony and trap* = CRAP *n.*[3] (2)]

macaroni *n.*[6] [1960s+] (US) the middleman, usu. a pimp, who stands between the client and prostitute. [joc. ext. of MACK *n.*[1] (1)]

macaroni *n.*[7] [1970s] information. [ety. unknown]

macaroni *n.*[8] [1970s+] a piece of human excrement; thus the act of defecation. [supposed resemblance]

macaroni queen *n.* [1980s+] (US gay) a non-Italian gay man who prefers Italian partners. [MACARONI *n.*[1] (2) + QUEEN *n.*[1]]

macaroni with cheese *n.* [1970s+] (US Black) someone involved in a wide variety of activities such as pimping, drug-selling and gambling games. [play on MACARONI *n.*[6]]

macaroon *n.*[1] [early 17C–early 19C] **1** a buffoon, a blockhead, a dolt. **2** a fop, a dandy (cf. MACARONI *n.*[2]).

macaroon *n.*[2] [20C] a Black person. [rhy. sl. *macaroon* = COON *n.* (3)]

macca-man *n.* [1970s] (W.I.) a tough, strong, efficient man. [dial. *macca*, a prick, a thorn, but note MACK MAN]

McCoy *adj.* [1920s–40s] (US) genuine. [REAL MCCOY]

McDaddy *see* MACK DADDY.

mace *n.* **1** [mid-18C–1930s] a swindle, a fraud, confidence tricks. **2** [late 18C–19C] a confidence trickster, a swindler, 'a rogue assuming the character of a gentleman, or opulent tradesman, who under that appearance defrauds workmen, by borrowing a watch, or other piece of goods till one [that] he bespeaks is done [swindled]' (Grose, 1785) (cf. MACER). [ety. unknown; ? SE *mace*, a club, but con-men do not require violence]

mace *v.* **1** [late 18C+] to sponge, to swindle. **2** [late 18C+] to fail to pay one's debts; thus *give on the mace*, *strike the mace*, *work the mace*, to obtain goods by persuading the shopkeeper to extend credit that one has no intention of paying. **3** [1900s–50s] (US) to beg or demand money from. [MACE *n.*]

mace-cove *n.* [early 19C] a confidence trickster, a swindler. [MACE *n.* (2) + COVE]

mace-gloak *n.* [early 19C] a confidence trickster, a swindler. [MACE *n.* (2) + GLOAK]

maceman *n.* **1** [19C] a confidence trickster (cf. MACE *n.*). **2** [mid-19C] one who defaults on their debts. **3** [late 19C] an élite criminal (cf. SWELL-MOBSMAN). [MACE *n.* (2) + sfx. -*man*]

macer *n.* [early–mid-19C] **1** a swindler. **2** a thief, a villain. [MACE *n.* (2)]

mace the rattler, to phr. [late 19C] to travel by train without buying a ticket. [MACE v. + RATTLER n.[1]]

McFly n. [1980s+] (US campus) a fool, an empty-headed person; thus *McFly!* wake up! [the character George *McFly* in the *Back to the Future* films (1985, 1989)]

MacGimp/McGimp/MacGimper/magimp n. [1950s–60s] (US) a pimp (cf. FISH AND SHRIMP). [rhy. sl.]

McGoogle n. [1930s] (US Und.) the big boss. [joc. use of supposed proper name]

MacGorrey's Hotel n. [late 19C] Chelmsford prison, Essex (cf. AKERMAN'S HOTEL). [the name of a contemporary governor]

MacGuffin n. [1950s+] (US) a gimmick, key element or a device in a story or plot, from which the whole drama develops. [coined in 1939 by film-maker Alfred Hitchcock to describe an aspect of his technique in creating suspense films]

mach see MACON.

machine n.[1] **1** [mid-18C; 1950s+] the penis (cf. FORNICATING ENGINE). **2** [late 18C] a condom. **3** [late 19C] the vagina.

machine n.[2] **1** [late 19C–1940s] (N.Z.) a totalizator. **2** [20C] (US) an automobile. **3** [1970s+] (US campus) a motorcycle.

-machine sfx. [1930s+] (US) combining form that indicates an enthusiast, a devotee, e.g. *sex-machine, rap-machine*.

machinery n. **1** [1930s+] (US drugs) the equipment used for injecting a narcotic (cf. BIZ n.[2]). **2** [1980s+] (drugs) marijuana.

macho adj. [1970s+] (US campus) aggressively masculine; thus *macho man*, a self-consciously 'masculine' man, a pose adopted by both hetero- and homosexual men. [Sp. *macho*, masculine, vigorous]

macing n.[1] [19C] a severe thrashing. [the prize-fighter Jem *Mace* (1831–1910)]

macing n.[2] [19C+] cheating, esp. at three-card monte. [MACE v.]

McJob n. [1980s+] (orig. US) a pointless, menial job with no prospects or job satisfaction (cf. MCPAPER). [brandname *Mc*Donald's + SE *job*, coined by Douglas Coupland in his book *Generation X* (1991), 'low-pay, low-prestige, low-benefit, no-future jobs in the service industry'. The use of McDonald's refers both to the type of job, which epitomizes those available in the fast-food chain, and to what critics see as the disposable, tasteless, non-nutritional quality of the food the chain sells]

mack n.[1] **1** [late 19C+] (US Und.) a pimp. **2** [1960s+] (US Black) a person who deceives or tries to charm a member of the opposite sex with seductive words (cf. SHOOT ONE'S BEST MACK). **3** [1960s+] a clever, influential person, a smooth operator. [early 15C–mid-17C SE *mackerel*, a pimp, pander or procuress, ult. Fr. *maquereau*, a pimp + ? Du. *makelaar*, a broker]

mack, the n.[2] [1960s+] seductive, manipulating talk. [MACK n.[1] (2)]

mack n.[3] [1970s+] (US Black) a French kiss. [MACK n.[1] or abbr. SE *smack*]

mack adj. (US Black) **1** [1960s] masculine in appearance and behaviour. **2** [1960s+] anything pertaining to a pimp, such as attitude, philosophy, automobile or clothes. [MACK n.[1] (1)]

mack v.[1] **1** [late 19C+] to work as a pimp. **2** [1960s+] (US Black) to talk seductively, to flirt. **3** [1960s+] (US Black) to lie or exaggerate in order to deceive, exploit or influence someone. **4** [1960s+] (US Black) to swagger, to walk rhythmically. **5** [1960s+] (US gay) of lesbians, to act in a masculine manner. **6** [1990s] (US Black) to be successful. [MACK n.[1]]

mack v.[2] [1970s+] (US Black) to French kiss. [MACK n.[3]]

macka n. [1980s+] (drugs) amphetamine (cf. A n.[2]). [ety. unknown; ? var. on MACON]

mackadocious/macadocious adj. [1980s+] (US Black) excellent, the very best. [MACK adj. + sfx. -*ocious*]

mack daddy/McDaddy n. (US Black) **1** [1950s+] a successful

pimp or criminal. **2** [1950s+] an important, influential Black man, a power in the community (cf. BIG DADDY). **3** [1990s] a handsome, virile man. **4** [1990s] a very successful or skilful man. [MACK n.[1] + DADDY n. (7); thus 'The Great *MacDaddy*', protagonist of an African-American rhyme of 1950s]

mack down v. [1970s+] (US campus) to eat (cf. MAC ON; MAC OUT). [*Mc*Donald's hamburgers]

macked out adj. [1930s+] (US) stylishly or flashily dressed. [MACK v.[1]]

macker n.[1] [1930s–40s] (Aus.) a pony, a horse. [ety. unknown]

macker n.[2] [1930s+] (US Und.) a pimp. [MACK n.[1] (1)]

mackerel n. **1** [late 18C–early 19C] a prostitute. **2** [mid-19C–1920s] (US) a worthless or stupid man. **3** [1930s+] (US Und.) a pimp. [Fr. *maquereau*, a pimp + MACK n.[1]]

mackerel-backed adj. [late 17C–early 19C] long-backed, tall and thin.

mackerel-snapper/-eater/-gobbler/-smacker/-snatcher n. [mid-19C; 1920s+] (orig. US) a Roman Catholic. [the role of fish in the religion]

mackery n. [1930s+] (US) pimping. [MACK n.[1] (1)]

mackie n. [1940s+] a bottle of *Mackeson stout*. [abbr.]

macking n. [1930s+] (US Black) **1** working as a pimp. **2** making verbal advances to someone with a view to seduction. [MACK v.[1]]

mack man n. [1950s+] (US Black) a pimp; thus *hard-mack*, a pimp who rules through threatened or actual violence; *sweet mack*, a gentle pimp who prefers to use charm (cf. SUGAR PIMP). [MACK n.[1] + SE *man*]

mack on/to v. [1970s+] (US Black/teen) to make a verbally forceful attempt to seduce a person, to flirt heavily. [ext. of MACK v.[1] (2)]

McMuff n. [20C] (US) the vagina. [MUFF n.[1]+ pun on *Egg Mc-Muffin*, a McDonald's hamburger chain product]

McNews n. [1990s] (US campus) CNN headline news, seen as only superficial. [on the model of MCJOB]

maco/mako n.[1] [20C] (W.I.) a gossip, a busybody. [Fr. *macommère*, my child's godmother, thus my very good friend]

maco/mako n.[2] [20C] (W.I.) **1** an effeminate man. **2** a peeping Tom. **3** a fool, an idiot. [? Fr. *maquereau*, a pimp]

maco/mako adj. [20C] (W.I.) inquisitive, gossipy, meddlesome; thus *maco-man, maco-woman*. [MACO n.[1]]

maco/mako v. [20C] (W.I.) **1** to interfere in other people's affairs. **2** to act as a voyeur (cf. MAKU). **3** to gossip scandalously. [MACO n.[1]]

macon/maconha/mach n. [1960s+] (drugs) marijuana. [Brazilian Port. *maconha*, marijuana]

mac on v. [1980s+] (US campus) to eat (cf. MACK DOWN). [*Mc*Donald's hamburger chain, and its major seller, the *Big Mac*]

maconha see MACON.

mac out v. [1980s+] (US teen) to overeat, to gorge oneself, esp. on JUNK FOOD (cf. MACK DOWN). [the McDonald's hamburger chain]

McPaper n. [1990s] (US campus) **1** a sloppily written, poorly researched piece of work (cf. MCJOB). **2** the notoriously banal *USA Today*. [pfx. MC- + SE *paper*]

McQ n. [1980s] a brief but enjoyable act of sexual intercourse. [abbr. SE meaningful + QUICKIE]

macrophiliac n. [1990s] (US teen) a devotee of Apple's Macintosh computer (as opposed to the IBM clones that rival it). [play on Apple *Mac* + SE *necrophiliac*]

McTavish n. [1960s] (US) a nickname for anyone of Scot. background.

macumeh see MAKOMÉ.

mad n. [mid-19C+] (US) madness, insanity, temper.

mad adj.[1] [mid-19C+] (US/W.I.) sufficiently aroused to do something drastic. [obsolete SE usage]

mad *adj.*² [1930s+] generally intensifying adj. of approval, whether of objects, e.g. *a mad hat* or of persons, e.g. *you mad bastard* (cf. CRAZY adj.¹; MENTAL adj.). [the term received something of a revival in hip-hop/teen use in 1990s]

mad/madd *adj.*³ [1990s] (US Black) a lot of, very much, e.g. *mad piles of cash* (cf. CRAZY adj.²).

mad *v.* [mid-19C+] (US/W.I.) to exasperate, to drive mad with jealousy. [obs. SE usage]

madam *n.*¹ **1** [late 16C–early 19C] a courtesan, a kept woman, a prostitute. **2** [19C] a general term of contempt for a woman, esp. one whose lifestyle does not reflect her self-appraisal.

madam *n.*² [early 18C+] the proprietor of a male or female brothel. [? reflecting a prejudice against foreigners; i.e. the adoption of Fr. *madame*]

madam *n.*³ [mid–late 19C] a handkerchief. [? its ostensible respectability]

madam *n.*⁴ [1920s+] nonsense, rubbish, esp. in phr. *a load of old madam*. [? the fawning shopkeeper who calls every customer *madam*]

madam *v.* [1930s] to tell the tale, to 'pitch a line'. [MADAM n.⁴]

madame bishop *n.* [early 19C–1910s] (Aus.) a mixed drink consisting of port, sugar and nutmeg. [? SE *bishop*, mulled and spiced port. The popular ety. based on a link to the proper name of an Aus. hotel-keeper is prob. specious]

Madame de Luce *n.* [1930s+] deceptive talk. [rhy. sl. *Madame de Luce* = SPRUCE]

Madame Van *n.* [late 17C–early 18C] a prostitute. [? a real-life whore or madam or (given the contemporary role of the Dutch as 'national enemy') f. the common *van* pfx. used in Du. surnames]

mad as ... *phr.* [1910s+] (Aus.) completely deranged, utterly furious. Variations include *mad as a beetle, ... Chinaman, ... dingbat, ... goanna, ... gum-tree full of galahs, ... meat axe, ... snake.*

mad as a buck *phr.* [late 16C–early 17C] very angry.

mad as a cut snake *phr.* [1910s+] (Aus.) completely deranged, utterly furious (cf. SILLY AS A CUT SNAKE).

mad as a hare/March hare *phr.* [14C–15C] very crazy. [the hare's sexual excitement, which peaks in March]

mad as a hatter *phr.* [mid-19C] very mad, utterly insane (cf. HATTER). [the use in 18C of mercurous nitrate in the tanning of felt hats. This was absorbed by the hatters, in whom the effects could produce mental problems]

mad as a maggot *phr.* [20C] (N.Z.) very crazy (cf. HAVE MAGGOTS IN ONE'S HEAD; MAGGOTY).

mad as a March hare *see* MAD AS A HARE.

mad as a meat axe *phr.* [1920s+] (Aus./N.Z.) **1** very angry. **2** completely insane.

mad as a weaver *phr.* [17C] very crazy. [proverbial wisdom associates weavers and insanity]

mad as a wet hen *phr.* [early 19C+] extremely angry.

mad as hops *phr.* [mid-19C+] (US) extremely excited. [the fermenting process]

mad as May butter *phr.* [17C] very crazy. [the warmth of May makes the making of butter esp. difficult]

mad as mud *phr.* [1920s] absolutely furious. [assonance]

madball *adj.* [1960s+] (US) crazy (cf. ODDBALL adj.; SCREWBALL adj.).

Madchester *n.* [1980s+] Manchester. [the brief but well-publicized period (*c.*1989–92) when Manchester, rather than London, dominated teen fashion, music and choice of drug consumption. *Mad* refers to the use of MDMA (cf. ECSTASY), the drug of choice in the city's clubs]

madd *see* MAD adj.³.

madder than a cow's tit on a cold day *phr.* [1970s] (US) extremely angry.

maddie *n.* [1980s+] (S.Afr.) the White mistress of a house, the employer of domestic servants. [abbr. SE *madam*]

maddikin *n.* [late 18C–mid-19C] the vagina. [? MADGE-KEN]

mad dog *n.*¹ **1** [late 16C–early 17C] strong ale. **2** [1970s] (US campus) cheap wine, esp. the brand Mogen David 20/20. **3** [1970s] (drugs) phencyclidine (cf. ACE n.³). [the effects]

mad dog *n.*² [20C] (Aus.) an unsettled debt that the debtor refuses to pay, esp. at a public house.

mad dog *n.*³ [1970s+] (US Black) a rebel, a non-conformist, one who refuses to accept their role in society (cf. BAD NIGGER).

mad dog *v.* [1990s] (US Black/prison) to stare at intensely and threateningly (cf. BAD EYE). [SE *mad dog*, such animals fix their targets with an unwavering, aggressive stare]

maddy *adj.* [20C] (W.I.) crazy, insane, unstable. [SE *mad*]

made *adj.*¹ **1** [late 17C–19C] stolen (cf. MAKE v.¹). **2** [1950s+] (US) cheated, tricked. **3** [1950s+] (US) recognized, identified (cf. MAKE v.⁴).

made *adj.*² [1900s–50s] (US Black) usu. of girls or women, describing someone who has had their hair straightened (cf. MAKE v.⁷).

made in Germany *phr.* [late 19C] third-rate, valueless. [the UK was swamped with an influx of cheap German-produced goods at end of the 19C. This phr. was printed on any such goods by law]

made man *n.* [1950s+] (US Und.) a formally initiated member of the US Mafia.

made of money *phr.* [mid-19C+] very rich.

made up *adj.* [20C] (Irish) lucky, secure, well-off.

madge *n.*¹ *see* MADGE HOWLET.

Madge *n.*² [1950s–60s] (camp gay) a tasteless person. [joc. use of female proper name]

madge-cove *n.* [early 18C–mid-19C] a homosexual man (cf. MADGE-CULL). [? *Madge*, abbr. Margaret, thus cf. AGNES and similar uses of female names to denote male homosexuality + COVE]

madge-cull *n.* [late 18C–mid-19C] a homosexual man. [var. on MADGE(-COVE) + CULL n.¹ (4)]

Madge Howlet/Howlett/madge *n.* [late 18C–19C] the vagina (cf. MADGE-KEN). [dial. *madge howlet*, a barn owl]

madge-ken *n.* [late 18C–mid-19C] the vagina. [MADGE (HOWLET) + KEN n.¹]

mad haddock *n.* [20C] (Aus.) an exceptionally eccentric person. [? play on ODD FISH]

madhatter *n.*¹ [1920s+] (Aus.) a solo prospector, living out in the desert and characterized by surliness, taciturnity and general misanthropy (cf. DEATH ADDER). [SE *mad* + HATTER]

madhatter *n.*² [1990s] (US teen) someone who sells drugs. [MAD AS A HATTER]

madison *n.* [1990s] any form of neck piercing. [ety. unknown; ? anecdotal]

madly *adv.* **1** [mid-18C+] passionately, fervently. **2** [late 19C+] extremely, very.

madman *n.* [1970s] (drugs) phencyclidine (cf. ACE n.³). [melodramatic assessment of the effects]

madman's broth *n.* [1950s] (Aus.) brandy (cf. LUNATIC SOUP).

mad mick *n.* (Aus.) **1** [20C] the penis. **2** [1910s–30s] a pick. [rhy. sl.; (1) *mad mick* = PRICK n. 2)]

mad money *n.* **1** [1920s+] (orig. US) money carried by a woman for an emergency, such as being abandoned far from home by her boyfriend when she hasn't agreed to sex (cf. VEX-MONEY). **2** [1950s+] (US) savings set aside for some spontaneous, unscheduled expenditure, usu. on pleasure. [in (1) the 'madness' is in the anger of the boyfriend; in (2) it is in the spending]

mad nurse *n.* [mid-18C] a nurse who attends mental patients.

madonna *n.* [1990s] in body piercing, a beauty spot stud in the upper lip. [? the pop singer *Madonna* (b.1959)]

mad Tom *n.* [late 17C–early 19C] a beggar who counterfeits madness, the 18th rank of criminal beggars (cf. CANTING CREW; TOM OF BEDLAM). [? a real-life mad beggar or TOM n.[1]]

Mad Town *n.* [1980s+] (US) *Mad*ison, Wisconsin. [abbr.]

madza/medza/medzer/midzer *n.* [mid-19C+] (Ling. Fr./ Polari) a half; thus *madza beargured*, half-drunk, *madza round the bull*, half a pound of steak. [Ital. *mezzo*, a half]

madza caroon *n.* [mid-19C] half a crown, 2s 6d (12½p). [MADZA + CAROON]

madza poona *n.* [mid-19C] a half-sovereign. [MADZA + SE *pound*]

madza saltee *n.* [mid-19C] one halfpenny. [MADZA + SALTEE]

Mae West *n.* [1930s–40s] a female breast. [rhy. sl.; ult. Hollywood star *Mae West* (1892–1980)]

m.a.f. *adj.* [1990s] extremely annoyed. [abbr. *mad as fuck*]

mafeesh!/mafish! *excl.* [late 19C–1930s] (orig. milit.) used in a variety of negative senses to mean done with, nothing doing, go to hell! [colloq. eastern Arab. *mafis*, there is nothing]

mafficking *n.* [late 19C–1910s] celebrating in the streets in an uproarious manner, esp. during a national celebration, general street rowdyism. [the lifting of the siege of *Mafeking* on 17 May 1900, a major date in the Boer War]

mafia *n.* [1950s+] (W.I. Rasta) big-time criminals. [borrowing of US/Ital. use]

mafish! *see* MAFEESH!

mag/magg *n.*[1] [late 18C–mid-19C] **1** a halfpenny. **2** a penny. [MAKE n.[1]]

mag *n.*[2] [late 18C+] **1** talk, chatter. **2** a chatterer. [SE *magpie*, post-19C use mainly Aus.]

mag *n.*[3] **1** [19C+] a *mag*azine. **2** [1970s+] (US) a *mag*num pistol. [abbr.]

mag *n.*[4] [late 19C] the face. [? var. on MUG n.[1]]

mag *v.* **1** [early 19C] to scold. **2** [early 19C] (Scot.) to steal. **3** [early 19C–1900s] to chatter, to talk. **4** [mid–late 19C] (Und.) to cheat through insincere talk. **5** [20C] (Aus.) to talk at, to nag. [MAG n.[2]]

maga *adj.* [1950s+] (W.I. Rasta) thin. [SE *meagre* or Fr. *maigre*, thin]

maga dog *n.* [1950s+] (W.I. Rasta) a mongrel. [MAGA + SE *dog*]

magageba *n.* [1970s+] (S.Afr. Black) money. [? Zulu *amakhekheba*, flat, rigid objects]

magazine *n.* [1920s] (US Und.) a 6-month jail sentence. [? the time it takes to read one]

Magdalen marm *n.* [late 19C] a servant who was recruited from the Magdalen home for 'fallen women' in Blackfriars Road, Southwark. [many employers felt that such servants made only second-rate workers because they had been treated too kindly at the refuge]

mageegle *v.* [20C] (Ulster) to confuse, to bewilder. [Scot. *maggle*, mangle]

magflying *n.* [mid–late 19C] playing pitch and toss. [MAG n.[1] + FLY v.[2] (1)]

magg *see* MAG n.[1].

maggie *n.*[1] **1** [17C; 1930s] a prostitute (cf. JUDY n.[1]; KITTY n.[2]). **2** [19C] a generic term for a woman. [proper name *Maggie*, abbr. Margaret]

maggie *n.*[2] [19C] a former inmate of the *Mag*dalen Asylum, Leeson Street, Dublin. [abbr.]

maggie *n.*[3] [20C] (Ulster) in cards, the ace or queen of hearts. [proper name *Maggie*, abbr. Margaret]

maggie *n.*[4] [20C] (Aus.) a *mag*pie. [abbr.]

maggie/maggie ann/maggy/maggy anne *n.*[5] [1910s+] (orig. milit.) margarine. [pron.]

maggie *n.*[6] [1940s+] (W.I.) a handcuff, a manacle, usu. in pl.

maggie and jiggs *n.* [1950s–60s] (US) an outdoor privy. [the 'lead characters' in a long-running US strip cartoon]

maggie ann *see* MAGGIE n.[5].

maggieman *n.* [20C] (Irish) a fairground showman. [Irish *margadh*, a fair]

maggie rab/rob/robb *n.*[1] [19C] (Scot.) a bad halfpenny. [MAG n.[1] + SE *rob*; play on proper names]

maggie rab/rob/robb *n.*[2] [19C] (Scot.) a nagging, unpleasant wife. [MAG v. (1) + SE *rob*; ply on proper names]

maggies *n.* [20C] (Aus.) women's underpants. [rhy. sl. *maggie moores* = drawers]

maggie's pie *n.* [20C] (US Black) the female genitals. [var. on MAGPIE'S NEST]

magging *n.*[1] [early–mid-19C] chattering, talking. [MAG v. (3)]

magging *n.*[2] [mid–late 19C] confidence trickery, swindling. [MAGSMAN n.[1]]

maggot *n.*[1] **1** [late 17C+] a contemptible person. **2** [1980s+] (US Black) a White person. **3** [1980s+] (Aus.) a general term of abuse. **4** [1980s+] (US police) a criminal, esp. a drug dealer.

maggot *n.*[2] [20C] the penis. [a *maggot* burrows into flesh]

maggot *n.*[3] [1980s+] (US campus) a very lazy person, esp. one who stays in bed all day. [they 'burrow' beneath the sheets]

maggot boiler *n.* [late 18C–early 19C] a tallow chandler. [the maggots that were found in the tallow or animal fat that was used as the basis for candle-making]

maggot-brained *adj.* [early 18C] a general epithet of abuse.

maggoty/maggotty *adj.* **1** [late 17C–early 19C] eccentric, whimsical. **2** [20C] (Aus.) ill-tempered, irritable. **3** [20C] (Irish) dirty, disgusting. **4** [1920s+] (US/Irish) drunk. **5** [1990s] (US) crazy, insane. [the image of a rotting brain]

maggy/maggy anne *see* MAGGIE n.[5].

maggy ryan *n.* [1980s+] (Irish) margarine. [pron.]

magic/magic dust *n.* [1980s+] (drugs) phencyclidine (cf. ACE n.[3]; ANGEL DUST). [SE *magic* + DUST n.[6] (4)]

magic *adj.* [1950s+] excellent. [a term that has spread from London working-class use into far wider currency]

magic dust *see* MAGIC n.

magic mushroom *n.* [1960s+] a psilocybe mushroom, a hallucinogen somewhat milder than LSD.

magic smoke *n.* [1980s+] (drugs) marijuana.

magic wand *n.* [1960s] the penis. [either a tribute to masculine power or the myth that sexual intercourse somehow puts an end to quarrels]

magiffer *see* MAGOOFER.

magimp *see* MACGIMP.

magistrate *n.* [mid-19C] a herring. [abbr. GLASGOW MAGISTRATE]

magistrate's court *n.* [20C] a measure of spirits, as bought in a public house. [rhy. sl. *magistrate's court* = SHORT n.[1]]

magnet *n.* [18C] the vagina. [its allure]

magnificents *n.* [mid-19C] a mood of haughty indignation.

magnolia curtain *n.* [1940s] (US Black) the Mason-Dixon (40°N) line that divides the American north and south. [SE *magnolia*, generic synon. for the South + play on *Iron Curtain*]

magnolious *adj.* [mid-19C+] (US) magnificent, splendid, large; thus *magnoliousness*, the fact or quality of being *magnolious*. [elaboration of SE *magnificent*]

magnoon *adj.* [1910s+] (Aus./N.Z.) crazy, eccentric. [Arab. *magnoon*, eccentric]

magoo, the *n.*[1] [1930s+] (US) **1** sex appeal. **2** the thing, the situation. [usage infl. by 1932 Broadway comedy *The Great Magoo* by Hecht and Fowler and the character *Mr Magoo* in UPA Studios cartoon series shown on children's television in the 1970s]

magoo *n.*[2] **1** [1940s+] (US) an important person. **2** [1940s+] (US) a foolish person. **3** [1980s+] (US campus) a driver, usu. old and male, who drives very slowly and thus impedes the faster car behind. [MAGOO n.[1]]

magoofer/magiffer n. [1950s–60s] (US) a pimp. [var. on MACGIMP, but note MAGOO n. (2)]

magoozlum n. [1920s+] (US) rubbish, trash (cf. GOO-GOO n.¹). [? Hollywood jargon magoo, the gooey ingredient of 'custard pies']

magpie n.¹ [mid-19C] a halfpenny. [ext. of MAG n.¹]

magpie n.² (Aus.) **1** [early 17C–1920s] an Anglican bishop. **2** [mid-19C] convict clothing (coloured yellow and black). **3** [1910s+] a nickname for a South Australian. **4** [1980s] a half-caste. [(1) the black chimere and white rochet forming his ordinary ceremonial attire; (3) the black and white colouring of the bird; the ref. is to the convict clothes worn by early settlers]

magpie's nest n. [20C] (US Black) the female genitals (cf. MAGGIE'S PIE.)

magsman n.¹ [mid-late 19C] the king of the 19C swindlers, a fashionable swell who appeared as sophisticated a figure as those on whom he preyed (cf. MEGSMAN). [? Yid. machas, a great man]

magsman n.² [1930s+] (Aus.) a chatterbox, a talker. [MAG v. (3)]

mag-stake n. [mid-late 19C] money obtained by trickery or fraud. [MAGSMAN n.¹ + SE stake]

magtig!/magtie! excl. [mid-19C+] (S.Afr.) a general excl., the equivalent of Lawdy! or Lawks! [Afk. allemagtig, almighty]

maguffy n. [20C] (W.I.) **1** one who thinks that they are more important than they really are. **2** anything large and pretentious. [? a real name, but note the film jargon MACGUFFIN]

mahaha see MAHULA n.

maharishee n. [1960s+] (drugs) marijuana. [proper name Maharishi Mahesh Yogi (b.1911), a popular 1960s guru, espoused by the Beatles and others in search of raised consciousness]

Mahatma Gandhi n. [20C] **1** brandy. **2** shandy. [rhy. sl., ult. Ind. freedom fighter Mahatma Gandhi (1869–1948)]

mahcheen n. [mid-19C] (Anglo-Chinese) a merchant. [Chinese pron. of SE]

mahog n.¹ [late 19C+] (US) a bar counter. [abbr. MAHOGANY n.² (2)]

mahog/mahoga n.² [1960s+] (S.Afr. Black) brandy (cf. HALF-JACK n.³). [abbr. SE mahogany, thus the colour of the wood and the drink]

mahogany n.¹ [late 18C–mid-19C] **1** a Cornish drink made of gin and treacle. **2** a strong mixture of brandy and water. [the colour]

mahogany n.² **1** [mid-19C+] a table, esp. a dining table (cf. MAHOGANY TREE). **2** [late 19C+] (US) a bar counter.

mahogany flat n.¹ [mid-19C–1900s] a bedbug. [late 19C+ use is US; SE mahogany + FLAT-BACK]

mahogany flat n.² [1970s] (US Black) an expensive, well-furnished and situated apartment or home. [SE mahogany, as a symbol of luxury + flat]

mahogany gaspipe n. [20C] the intonations of the Irish language. [a joc. rendering of its sound]

mahogany slosh n. [late 19C–1910s] tea from a cook-shop or coffee-stall. [play on SE mahogany + SLOSH n.¹; its colour and taste]

mahogany top n. [mid-late 19C] a red-head. [the colour of the wood/hair]

mahogany tree n. [mid-19C] a dining table (cf. MAHOGANY n.²).

Mahometan gruel n. [late 18C–early 19C] coffee. [its origins and popularity in the Middle East]

mahoska, the n. [1930s+] (US Und.) anything illicit, esp. drugs, money, a weapon, stolen goods etc. [? Irish mo thosca, my business; thus cf. cosa nostra, 'these things of ours', a synon. for the Sicilian/US mafia]

mahula/mahaha n. [1920s–40s] (US) nonsense. [MAHULA adj.]

mahula adj. [1920s+] (US) bankrupt or ruined. [Yid. mekhule, Heb. mechula, spoiled, bankrupt]

maiden n. [late 19C–1910s] (Aus.) **1** cloves. **2** peppermint. [ety. unknown; ? a local plant name]

maiden's blush n. [1940s+] (Aus.) **1** ginger beer and raspberry cordial. **2** port and lemonade (cf. BARMAID'S BLUSH n.¹). [the colour]

maiden sessions n. [late 18C–early 19C] a legal sessions where no prisoners are sentenced to death. [SE maiden, a form of early guillotine]

maiden's water n. [late 19C] any weak drink, usu. beer (cf. MAID'S WATER).

Maiden Town n. [early 18C–late 19C] Edinburgh. [legend that the maiden daughter of a Pictish king fled there for protection during a civil war]

maiden-wife-widow n. [late 17C–late 18C] a bride, now a widow, whose husband died before consummating their marriage.

Maid Marian n. [16C] a prostitute. [the morris dancing tradition of having that character played by a local prostitute]

maids adorning n. [mid-19C] the morning. [rhy. sl.]

maid's meat see BOY'S MEAT.

maid's ring n. [late 19C] a hymen. [SE maid + RING n.¹ (1)]

Maidstone jailer n. [mid-19C] a tailor. [rhy. sl.]

maid's water n. [late 19C+] (Aus.) any weak drink, esp. tea (cf. MAIDEN'S WATER).

mail n.¹ [1940s+] (S.Afr.) a carrier for an illicit grog-shop.

mail n.² [1960s+] (Aus.) a rumour, a report, racing tip (cf. MULGA WIRE).

mail n.³ [1990s] (US Black teen) money. [? like the US mail it 'gets through anywhere']

mail v. [1970s+] (S.Afr.) **1** to send someone to buy liquor illicitly. **2** to act as a go-between in such a purchase (cf. MAILER). [MAIL n.¹]

mailer n. [1950s] (S.Afr. Und.) a middleman in the illicit liquor trade (cf. MAIL n.¹). [MAIL v.]

mail-order adj. [1920s–50s] (US) second-rate, inferior.

mail-order cowboy n. [1920s–40s] (US) a would-be cowboy who has the clothes but is otherwise spurious.

main n., v. see MAINLINE n., v.

main adj. [late 19C+] (US) used to describe a person or thing with power or importance, usu. in combs., as in the main cheese, the main cop etc (cf. MAIN DRAG; MAIN MAN; MAIN SQUEEZE etc).

main alley n. [20C] (orig. US tramp) the main street (cf. MAIN DRAG; MAIN STEM).

main avenue n. [19C] the vagina (cf. ALLEY n.¹).

main bitch/girl/ho/stuff/woman n. [1940s+] (US Black) **1** the favourite prostitute among those a pimp controls. **2** a man's favourite girlfriend (cf. MAIN QUEEN; MAIN SQUEEZE). [MAIN adj. + BITCH n.¹ (1)/SE girl/HO n.¹ (1)/STUFF n.⁴/SE woman]

main chance n. [late 17C] (orig. Und.) the principle opportunity one may have for making money, attaining a goal, taking advantage of one's rivals etc; thus one who has an eye for the main chance, a smart operator.

main drag n. **1** [mid-19C+] the main street (cf. MAIN ALLEY; MAIN STEM). **2** [1930s–40s] (US Black) 7th Avenue in Harlem, New York. [MAIN adj. + DRAG n.⁶ (1), a road or street, also note drag (oneself along), to make one's way wearily, tiredly. The term referred orig. to a town or city's centre of tramp or vagrant life but was extended and then transferred to the main street, whether or not frequented by vagrants. Despite its almost invariably US use today, the term started in the UK and is cited as such by Mayhew (1861–2)]

main drag of many tears *n.* [1940s] (US Black) 125th Street Harlem, New York. [MAIN DRAG + SE, the bars and theatres on 125th St (Harlem's main street) where otherwise depressed and frustrated people can attempt to drown their sorrows]

main finger *n.* [late 19C–1920s] (US) the boss.

main girl *see* MAIN BITCH.

main guy *n.* [late 19C+] (US) the boss. [MAIN adj. + GUY n.²]

main ho *see* MAIN BITCH.

Mainiac *n.* [mid-19C+] (US) a native of Maine. [pun on SE *maniac*]

main kazoo/kazaam *n.* [20C] (US) a person of importance. [MAIN adj. + play on the self-aggrandizing names of various US societies, esp. the *kleagles* etc of the Ku Klux Klan]

main kick *n.* [1930s–40s] (US Black) 1 one's favourite activity. 2 the stage or theatre. 3 an addiction to drugs. 4 alcohol. [MAIN adj. + KICK n.⁵ (3)]

mainland *n.* [1940s+] (N.Z.) the South Island.

mainlander *n.* [1940s+] (Aus.) one who lives on the mainland of Australia (rather than Tasmania).

ma-in-law *n.* [1950s+] mother-in-law.

mainline/main *n.* [1930s+] (orig. US drugs) the vein into which an addict injects narcotics.

mainline/main *v.* [1930s+] (orig. US drugs) to inject narcotics directly into a vein (cf. SKINPOP v.). [MAINLINE n.]

mainliner *n.* [1930s+] (orig. US drugs) a drug addict who injects narcotics into the vein. [MAINLINE v.]

main man *n.¹* [1950s+] (orig. US Black) 1 one's best friend. 2 a hero. 3 a lover, a sweetheart. 4 any important person, e.g. a chief prison warder or a managing director.

main man *n.²* [1960s+] (S.Afr.) a local hero, esp. in a school or college (cf. MAIN MAN n.¹).

main on the hitch *n.* [1940s] (US Black) a woman's favourite man, esp. her husband. [MAIN (MAN) n.¹ (3) + HITCHED]

main ou *n.* [1970s+] (S.Afr.) a local hero, esp. in a school or college. [MAIN (MAN) n.² + OU]

main queen *n.* [1940s+] (US Black) one's girlfriend or wife (cf. MAIN BITCH; MAIN SQUEEZE). [MAIN adj. + QUEEN n.² (1)]

mainsheet *n.* [late 19C] (W.I.) rum and water. [naut. imagery]

main squeeze *n.* 1 [late 19C+] (US) the boss, the foreman, any important person. 2 [1920s+] (orig. US) one's most favoured person, usu. a lover (cf. HOME SQUEEZE; MAIN BITCH; MAIN QUEEN). [SE *main* + SQUEEZE n.⁷]

mainstay *n.* [1980s] (US drugs) a dealer's most trustworthy friend or lover. [ext. of SE]

main stem *n.* 1 [late 19C–1930s] (US) a person of importance, the boss. 2 [20C] (US Black) the elite, the upper class. 3 [20C] the main street of a town (cf. MAIN DRAG). [SE *main stem*, the central trunk]

main stuff *see* MAIN BITCH.

main thrill *n.* [1930s–40s] (US Black) 1 the main street (cf. MAIN DRAG). 2 one's drug of choice (cf. MAIN KICK).

main-toby *see* HIGH-TOBY.

main vein *n.* [1950s+] the vagina.

main woman *see* MAIN BITCH.

maître d'/de *n.* [1950s+] (orig. US) the *maître d'*hôtel. [abbr.]

majat *n.* [1950s+] (S.Afr. drugs) the third and lowest grade of marijuana on sale in S.Afr. [? Malay *madat*, opium]

majita/majika, *n.* [1950s+] (S.Afr. Black) a streetwise young man (cf. WISE GUY), also as a term of address. [the film *The Magic Garden* (1951), which depicts, *inter alia*, the life of such a youth]

major *adj.* [1970s+] (US teen) 1 all-purpose term of great approval (cf. SERIOUS). 2 large, extreme.

major-league *adj.* [1940s+] (orig. US) very important, the most powerful, highly impressive (cf. MINOR-LEAGUE). [baseball imagery]

Major Loder *n.* [late 19C] (society) (whisky and) soda (cf. ROSIE LODER). [rhy. sl., use of proper name *Major Eustace Loder*, owner of the racehorse Pretty Polly]

majorly *adv.* [1980s+] (orig. US campus) extremely, very much, primarily. [MAJOR]

Major Mitchell *v.* [20C] (Aus.) to ride a zigzag course, to meander aimlessly, to get lost. [proper name *T.L. Mitchell* (1792–1855), Surveyor-General of New South Wales]

major nasty *adj.* [1970s+] (US Black/teen) very unpleasant, very difficult. [MAJOR adj. (2) + NASTY n.²]

major operation *n.* [1930s+] the act of 'cutting someone dead'.

Major Stevens *n.* [20C] (betting) evens. [rhy. sl.]

major-time *adj.* [1990s] (US Black) large, very important. [MAJOR + (BIG-)TIME]

make/mec *n.¹* [16C–early 19C] a halfpenny (cf. MAG n.¹; MAGPIE n.¹). [Midlands/northern dial.]

make *n.²* 1 [mid–late 19C] a successful robbery or swindle. 2 [1910s–60s] (US Und.) the proceeds of a theft. [MAKE v.¹]

make *n.³* 1 [1940s+] (orig. US) a promiscuous woman or girl, one who can be seduced easily (cf. EASY MAKE). 2 [1960s+] (US) kissing, necking, a seduction (cf. ON THE MAKE phr.²). [MAKE v.³ (3)]

make *n.⁴* [1950s+] (US) a description or an identification of a suspect, esp. through fingerprinting, photofit or other forms of police records. [MAKE v.⁴]

make *v.¹* [late 17C–19C] to steal (cf. MADE adj.¹).

make *v.²* [mid-19C+] (US) to consider, to regard, to estimate as.

make *v.³* 1 [mid-19C+] to attain a goal, to promote, to make successful, e.g. *make the team*, *make a club*. 2 [late 19C+] to catch, e.g. *make a plane*, *make a train*. 3 [1910s+] (US) to seduce, to have sexual intercourse with (cf. MAKE TIME WITH; PUT THE MAKE ON). 4 [1930s+] (US) to succeed in getting something, constructed with 'for', e.g. *to make a croaker for a reader*, to persuade a doctor to write a prescription for narcotics.

make *v.⁴* [20C] 1 (US police/Und.) to witness or observe, to recognize, to identify a suspect, also as *make one for*, to recognize someone as. 2 (US Und.) to prove someone guilty in court (cf. BANK v.³). [abbr. SE *make an identification*]

make *v.⁵* [1910s+] (US) to meet with, to attend, to go to.

make *v.⁶* [1910s–50s] (US) to understand or to empathize with (cf. DIG v.⁶).

make *v.⁷* [1940s+] (US Black) to straighten one's hair (cf. MADE adj.²).

make *v.⁸* [1940s+] (US, mainly south) to distil liquor illicitly.

make *v.⁹* [1950s+] to enlist someone as an official member of the US Mafia (cf. MADE MAN).

make *v.¹⁰* [1950s–70s] (US) to bear or endure.

make a bad fall *see* MAKE A GOOD FALL.

make a balls of, to *phr.* [late 19C+] to make a mistake, to get into trouble. [BALLS-UP n.]

make a balls-up, to *phr.* [1910s+] (orig. milit.) to blunder. [BALLS-UP n.]

make a barney balls of oneself, to *phr.* [1940s+] (Irish) to make a fool of oneself. [ext. of MAKE A BALLS OF]

make a big feller/fellow of oneself, to *phr.* [1940s+] (Aus.) to pose as a generous, magnanimous person.

make a bitch of, to *phr.* [early 19C+] to bungle, to blunder, to ruin. [BITCH n.¹ (5)]

make a blue fist of, to *phr.* [mid-19C] (US) to blunder, to make a mess of. [neg. and ext. var. on MAKE A GOOD FIST OF]

make a bolt of it, to *phr.* [mid–late 19C] to run off, to escape. [SE *bolt*]

make a bomb, to *phr.* [1950s+] to become very rich. [BOMB n. (2)]

make a box of, to *phr.* [1920s+] (Aus.) to make a mess of. [? BALLOCKS n.¹ (2)]

make a break, to *phr.* [mid-19C+] (orig. US) to escape or attempt to escape from prison. [BREAK n.[3]]

make a bridge of someone's nose, to *phr.* [late 18C] to miss out a person during the passing of a bottle around the table.

make a car, to *phr.* [1950s+] to break into a parked car in order to steal any valuables left inside it. [MAKE v.[3] (4) + SE *car*]

make a clean breast of, to *phr.* [mid–late 18C] to confess, to own up unreservedly (cf. COME CLEAN). [19C+ use is SE; synon. with phr. 'getting it off one's chest']

make a clean job of, to *phr.* [late 19C–1910s] (US) to do a thorough job of.

make a coffeehouse of a woman's cunt, to *phr.* [late 18C] to perform coitus interruptus, i.e. 'to go in and out and spend nothing' (Grose 1796). [pun; the popularity of SE *coffeehouses* as social centres, rather than places for eating and drinking]

make a cow's of, to *phr.* [1970s] to make a mess of. [abbr. *cow's arse*]

make a crush on, to *phr.* [1920s] (US) to make a good impression on.

make a day/day of it, to *phr.* [early 19C+] to devote a day to a single pursuit, usu. pleasurable and usu. other than one's regular employment; thus also *make a night*.

make a die of, to *phr.* [early 17C–late 19C] to die. [? pun on MAKE A DAY ('day' = 'die' in Cockney pron.)]

make a dog's dinner out of, to *phr.* [1930s+] to make an appalling mess of.

make a do of, to *phr.* [20C] (Aus/N.Z.) to succeed at, to 'make a go' of.

make a fashion arrest, to *phr.* [1980s+] (US campus) to denigrate someone's dress sense, esp. behind the subject's back.

make a Federal case of/out of, to *phr.* [1950s+] to take very seriously, esp. when the speaker feels that the problem is really minor, 'to make a mountain out of a molehill'. [in the US legal system the Federal, rather than state, legislature often implies greater severity]

make a foreskin cone, to *phr.* [1990s] to masturbate.

make a get, to *phr.* [20C] (Aus./N.Z.) to leave quickly, to run off. [abbr. SE *getaway*]

make a good/bad fall, to *phr.* [late 19C–1920s] to have a piece of good or bad luck.

make a good/poor fist of, to *phr.* [early 19C+] to make a good or bad attempt at. [FIST n. (2)]

make a go of, to *phr.* [1920s+] to succeed (despite odds). [GO n.[3] (2)]

make a hack of, to *phr.* [late 19C] to wear the same dress every day. [fig. use of SE *hack*, a horse for ordinary riding, as distinguished from cross-country, milit., or other special riding]

make a hames, to *phr.* [1930s+] (Irish) to bungle, to make a mess. [SE *hames*, the two pieces of metal placed on each side of a horse's collar; though why then a 'mess'?]

make/take a hand of, to *phr.* [20C] (Irish) to tease, to mock, to make fun of. [HAND n.[2]]

make a hare of, to *phr.* [mid-19C+] (Anglo-Irish) to make someone look foolish; to expose someone's ignorance. [the image of a *hare* as a foolish creature]

make a Hebrew congee/leg, to *phr.* [late 17C] to make a formally courteous farewell. [*Hebrew*, i.e. Jewish + SE *congee*, ceremonious dismissal and leave-taking/SE *leg*]

make a hit, to *phr.* [mid-19C+] (orig. US) to make a favourable impression. [SE *hit*]

make a hole in, to *phr.* [mid-17C–19C] to use up a great deal of, esp. money or a dish of food. [20C use is SE]

make a hole in one's manners, to *phr.* [mid–late 19C] to behave rudely.

make a hole in someone's reputation, to *phr.* [mid-19C+] to seduce a woman.

make a hole in the water, to *phr.* [late 19C] to commit suicide by diving or jumping into water and drowning.

make a job of, to *phr.* [20C] (Aus.) to beat up, to defeat severely. [var. on DO A JOB ON]

make a joe of oneself, to *phr.* [1960s+] (N.Z.) to make a fool of oneself. [JOE n.[12]]

make a judy/judy fitzsimmons of oneself, to *phr.* [mid-19C+] to play the fool. [ety. unknown; ? anecdotal]

make a kick, to *phr.* [mid-19C+] to raise an objection, to complain. [KICK n.[7]]

make a killing, to *phr.* [late 19C+] (orig. US) to make a profit by gambling, whether at the races, on the stock market, in a casino etc. [KILLING n.]

make a kirk and a mill of, to *phr.* [early 18C–late 19C] (Scot.) **1** to make one's best of. **2** to put to whatever use one pleases, to do with however one wishes. [Scots. *kirk*, a church]

make a leg, to *phr.* [1900s] of a woman, to show one's legs. [a pun on SE *make a leg*, to bow]

make all split, to *phr.* [late 16C–early 17C] to cause a disturbance, to make a commotion.

make all the right noises *see* MAKE THE RIGHT NOISES.

make a long arm, to *phr.* [late 19C+] to stretch out one's arm to grab something.

make a long nose, to *phr.* [mid-19C] to thumb one's nose (cf. SIGHT n.[1]).

make a loose, to *phr.* [early 18C] to make one's escape.

make a mash, to *phr.* [late 19C–1920s] (US) to seduce someone (cf. MASHER). [MASH v.[1]]

make a May-game of, to *phr.* [late 17C–18C] to play games with, to trick or deceive. [the traditional Mayday pastimes]

make a meal of, to *phr.* [1960s+] to make a great deal of fuss about, to go into over-elaborate descriptions, esp. of something distasteful; thus *don't make a meal of*, don't make a fuss about.

make a mess of, to *phr.* **1** [early 19C+] to bungle, to blunder. **2** [1910s+] to beat completely or easily.

make a milk run, to *phr.* [1990s] (US gay) to hang around a men's lavatory looking for sex. [MILK v.[3]]

make a monkey out of, to *phr.* [late 19C+] (orig. US) to make a fool of, to make someone look stupid.

make a muck of, to *phr.* [20C] to make a mess of, to perform a task badly.

make a napkin of one's dishclout, to *phr.* [mid-18C–early 19C] **1** to marry one's cook. **2** to make a foolish, unsuitable marriage. [the cook wields the *dishcloth*, the wife the *napkin*]

make an exhibition of oneself, to *phr.* [mid-19C+] to make oneself seem stupid by a piece of foolish, ostentatious behaviour.

make an eyeball *see* SHOOT AN EYEBALL.

make an honest woman of, to *phr.* [early 17C+] to marry. [the assumption is that there has already been some form of 'illicit' (in religious terms) pre-marital relationship]

make a noise, to *phr.* [late 19C+] to break wind. [euph.]

make a noise like a ... *phr.* [20C] pretend to be, a command that is rendered humorous through its impossibility, e.g. *go into the changing room and make a noise like a cricket bat*. [the original (perfectly serious) use apparently came in Baden-Powell's *Scouting for Boys* (1908), in which scouts in danger of detection are advised to take cover and 'make a noise like a (say) thrush']

make an omelette, to *phr.* [1920s+] to make a blunder, to commit a social solecism.

make an out, to *phr.* [mid-19C–1940s] to be successful (cf. MAKE OUT v.[1]).

make a pass, to _phr._ [1920s+] **1** (orig. US) to approach with amorous intentions (cf. MAKE A PLAY FOR). **2** to approach, usu. with some form of business proposition. **3** to attempt to harm or attack.

make a payday, to _phr._ [1940s] (US Black) to obtain money in any way other than working at a legitimate job.

make a pearl on the nail, to _phr._ [late 16C–18C] to upend one's emptied glass onto the left thumbnail, thus proving that one has drunk every drop (cf. SUPERNACULUM). [SE _pearl_, a drop of liquid]

make a pig of oneself, to _phr._ [1940s+] (orig. US) to act in a gluttonous manner, to be extremely greedy.

make a piss stop, to _phr._ [1980s+] to visit the lavatory, esp. to stop drinking in order to do so. [PISS n.]

make a pit stop, to _phr._ [1980s+] **1** to visit the lavatory, esp. to stop drinking in order to do so. **2** to stop what one is doing to take a drink. [joc. use of motor-racing jargon]

make a splash/shine _see_ CUT A SPLASH.

make a placebo _see_ MAKE PLACEBO.

make a plan, to _phr._ [20C] (S.Afr.) to think of, to arrange, to work out. [Afk. _'n plan maak_, to devise a scheme; the phr. is used in response to any situation, whether important or utterly trivial]

make a play for, to _phr._ [20C] to make sexual advances towards someone, to attempt seduction. [PLAY n.[1]]

make a poor fist of _see_ MAKE A GOOD FIST OF.

make a punch, to _phr._ [1900s–10s] (Aus.) to make a killing in the goldfields, stock market etc.

make a rendezvous with Mrs Hand, to _phr._ [1980s+] to masturbate (cf. CONVERSE WITH HARRY PALM).

make a rise, to _phr._ [mid-19C–1940s] (Aus.) to do moderately well, to make a small success.

make a run, to _phr._ [1960s+] to go out to buy a commodity, esp. drugs, but also groceries, liquor etc.

make a sale, to _phr._ [1930s+] (Aus.) to vomit.

make a sandwich, to _phr._ [1970s+] to make a sexual position in which two men are having simultaneous vaginal and anal intercourse with a woman.

make a settlement in tail _see_ MAKE SETTLEMENT IN TAIL.

make a six-fist, to _phr._ [1990s] to masturbate. [the enclosed penis being the sixth 'finger']

make a solo flight, to _phr._ [1990s] to masturbate (cf. PLAY A FLUTE SOLO; PLAY AN ORGAN SOLO; PLAY A SOLO ON ONE'S MEAT WHISTLE).

make a sow's ear of, to _phr._ [1940s+] to make a mess of. [a play on the pvb. 'make a silk purse out of a sow's ear' + PIG'S EAR n.[2]]

make a speak, to _phr._ [early 19C] (Und.) to commit a robbery. [SPEAK v.]

make ass _v._ [1980s+] (US Black) to get going (cf. MAKE IT v.[4]). [MAKE v.[3] + ARSE n.[1]]

make a stag/make to wear the stag's crest, to _phr._ [late 16C–mid-17C] of a woman, to cuckold one's husband. [punning use of the stag's horns/HORNS]

make a straight coat-tail, to _phr._ [mid-19C–1920s] (US) to run, to hurry. [one's tails are blown out by the wind of one's progress]

make a strike, to _phr._ [mid-19C+] to be lucky, to be successful. [skittles/bowling imagery]

make a ten-strike, to _phr._ [late 19C–1940s] (US) to do well, to succeed. [bowling use _ten-strike_, the knocking over of all 10 pins]

make a/the pot with two ears, to _phr._ [late 17C] to set one's arms akimbo. [resemblance]

make a time, to _phr._ [late 19C] (US) to make a fuss. [? SE _difficult/hard time_]

make a touch, to _phr._ [late 19C+] (orig. US) to borrow money, esp. when the donor is less than enthusiastic. [TOUCH n.[1] (2)]

make a trip, to _phr._ [late 18C–early 19C] to be mother to a bastard child. [play on BREAK AN ANKLE]

make a Tyburn show, to _phr._ [late 18C–early 19C] to be hanged. [TYBURN, 18C London's main site of public hangings]

make a welter, to _phr._ [1910s+] (Aus.) to make a fuss, to make an issue out of something. [dial. _welter_, something exceptionally big or heavy of its kind]

make a wry mouth, to _phr._ [17C] to be hanged. [the rictus of suffocation, ult. SE _make a wry mouth_, to grimace with disapproval]

make babies, to _phr._ [1960s+] (orig. US) to have sexual intercourse. [a coy euph.]

make bacon, to _phr._ [1970s+] (US) to have sexual intercourse. [the first recorded 'citation' (Lighter, 1994) is of a T-shirt picturing copulating pigs, captioned 'Making Bacon', but note PORK v.; PORK SWORD etc]

make bank, to _phr._ [1990s] (US Black) to make money.

make beef, to _phr._ [19C] to leave, to run off. [BEEF v.[1]]

make bloody carpet bags of, to _phr._ [late 19C] (orig. US then imported to Liverpool) to mutilate with a cut-throat razor, to beat severely, to thrash. [SE _carpet bags_ are often red]

make book/book on, to _phr._ [1940s+] **1** to run a bookmaking operation. **2** to wager (on), to gamble (on) (also fig.).

make brick walls, to _phr._ [late 19C+] to swallow one's food without chewing it.

make bush, to _phr._ [20C] (US prison) to escape (cf. BUSH PAROLE). [one escapes into the bushes]

make butter and cheese, to _phr._ [mid-17C] to confound, to bamboozle. [the churning action that turns the former into the latter]

make change, to _phr._ [1950s+] (US Black) to work or otherwise obtain money for staying alive.

make children's shoes, to _phr._ [17C–19C] to fool, to trifle with, to belittle. [Norfolk dial.]

make cold meat of _see_ MAKE MEAT OF.

make/spin crooked spindles, to _phr._ [late 16C–early 17C] of a woman, to commit adultery, to cuckold one's husband. [the abandonment of proper wifely tasks]

make down _v._ [late 19C–1900s] to alter a garment so that a smaller person can wear it.

make ducks and drakes of _see_ PLAY DUCKS AND DRAKES WITH.

make easy _v._ [late 18C] to kill. [ironic use of SE _easy_, free of care and discomfort]

make faces _v._ [late 18C–early 19C] to father children; thus _face-making_, sexual intercourse.

make feet for children's shoes/stockings, to _phr._ **1** [late 18C–mid-19C] to have sexual intercourse. **2** [1930s+] (US Black) to be pregnant.

make fist-kabobs _v._ [1990s] to masturbate.

make foot/pick up one's foot/put one's foot in one's hand/take foot/take up one's foot and run _v._ [20C] (W.I.) to flee in panic.

make for _v._ [20C] to identify. [ext. of MAKE v.[4]]

make for a stash, to _phr._ [1950s+] to steal the drugs another addict has hidden so as to use them oneself. [MAKE v.[3] (4) + STASH n.]

make four eyes, to _phr._ [1940s] (W.I.) of two people, to gaze at one another.

make free with both ends of the busk, to _phr._ [late 18C–late 19C] of a man, to caress a woman intimately. [SE _busk_, a corset, spec. its stiffening and supporting whalebone or other agent]

make friendly, to _phr._ [1990s] (US campus) to have passionate sexual intercourse.

make friends with Big Ed, to phr. [1990s] to masturbate. [pet name for the penis]

make fun v. [19C] to drink.

make gallows-apples of, to phr. [early–mid-19C] to hang. [the victim hangs from the TRIPLE TREE]

make her grunt, to phr. [20C] of a man, to have sexual intercourse (cf. GRUMBLE AND GRUNT).

make ignorant v. [1940s+] (Und.) to irritate, to annoy. [SE make + IGNORANT adj.]

make indentures with one's legs, to phr. [17C] to stumble drunkenly. [the custom of indenting the top edges of legal documents]

make instant pudding, to phr. [1990s] to masturbate.

make it v.[1] **1** [mid-19C+] to subsist, often as phr. just barely making it, also used in greeting, as in How you making it? **2** [late 19C+] to be successful; thus make it big, make it good.

make it v.[2] **1** [late 19C+] to have sexual intercourse. **2** [1950s+] (US) to have an orgasm.

make it v.[3] [1950s–70s] (US drugs) to take drugs, esp. opiates.

make it v.[4] [1950s+] to move, to get on, to run off (cf. MAKE ASS).

make it snappy! excl. [1920s+] get on with it! hurry up!

make it warm/warm for, to phr. [late 19C+] to punish, to make life difficult for someone.

make leg v. [late 19C] to become prosperous. [var. on MAKE UP ONE'S LEG]

make like a ... v. **1** [late 19C+] (orig. US) to imitate, to pretend to be, to behave like or as if; thus make like a chicken, ... duck. **2** [1950s+] (US) as part of a number of phrs. all of which mean 'go away', 'get lost', e.g. make like a fart and blow away, ... dragster and lay rubber, ... drum and beat it, ... banana and split, ... cow pat and hit the trail, ... paper doll and cut out, ... tree and leave, ... rubber and roll on. [an extensive selection can be found in MAL IV, 1, pp.40–42]

make like a baby and head out, to phr. [1980s+] (US campus) to leave.

make like an alligator and drag ass, to phr. [1950s+] (US) to leave. [joc. extension of DRAG-ASS]

make lip music, to phr. [20C] (US Black) to talk in Black slang.

make love to the porcelain goddess, to phr. [1960s+] (US campus) to vomit (cf. DRIVE THE PORCELAIN BUS).

make mac/mack with v. [1960s+] **1** (US Black) to flirt with a young woman using the style and language of a pimp (cf. MACKING). **2** (US campus) to flirt, to pick up a woman. [MACK n.[1]]

make meat/cold meat of v. [mid-19C+] (orig. US) to kill (cf. MAKE MINCEMEAT OF).

make mice-feet o' v. [18C–19C] (Scot.) to destroy completely.

make mincemeat of v. [18C+] to beat up, to destroy.

make mutton of v. [late 19C–1900s] to kill, to murder.

make nice v. (US) **1** [1950s+] often as admonition, to be friendly or considerate, to behave oneself. **2** [1990s] to curry favour, to act in a friendly manner (whether or not one means it). [trans. of Yid./Ger. usage]

make no bones, to phr. [mid-16C+] **1** to deal with something promptly, to make no excuses (cf. MAKE NO KNOBS). **2** to speak frankly and openly. [15C find no bones, find no problems, offer no difficulties. The original image was of finding bones in meat jelly or aspic]

make noises about v. [1970s+] to discuss, with the implication that one wishes to take some form of action.

make no knobs, to phr. [late 17C–late 18C] to act immediately, to resist one's scruples. [var. on MAKE NO BONES]

make no never mind, to phr. [late 19C+] (orig. US) to be utterly unimportant.

make on v. [20C] (juv.) to pretend.

make one v. [1950s+] **1** (prison) to plan and effect an escape, also as phrs. make one out, make one with, to commit a crime or to escape in partnership with one or more other people. **2** (Und.) to put together plans for a crime, esp. a robbery, and then carry out that crime. ['one' is either an escape or a plan]

make one's alley good, to phr. [1920s+] (Aus.) to exploit a situation, to improve one's position (cf. MAKE ONE'S MARBLE GOOD). [SE alley, a marble; thus orig. marbles jargon]

make one's bones, to phr. [1950s+] (US Und.) to arrange and carry out one's first contracted murder.

make oneself scarce, to phr. [late 18C+] to slip away, to hide.

make oneself right see MAKE SOMEONE RIGHT.

make/take one's eye/eyes pass somebody, to phr. [20C] (W.I./Guyn.) to speak disrespectfully to one who ought to be treated respectfully.

make one's head, to phr. [late 18C] (Irish) to acquire a tolerance or 'head' for drink.

make one's jack, to phr. [late 18C–late 19C] (US) to prosper, to make one's fortune. [JACK n.[2] (2)]

make one's love come down, to phr. [1950s–60s] (US Black) to stimulate one sexually, to come to orgasm.

make one's lucky see CUT ONE'S LUCKY.

make one's marble good, to phr. [1920s+] (Aus./N.Z./S.Afr.) to make a good impression on someone, to ingratiate oneself, to improve one's position (cf. MAKE ONE'S ALLEY GOOD).

make one's rep, to phr. [1950s] (US Und.) to establish oneself as a successful, respected criminal. [REP n.[2]]

make one's tucker see EARN ONE'S TUCKER.

make-out n. **1** [1950s+] (US campus) one who is good at seducing others (cf. MAKE-OUT ARTIST). **2** [1970s+] (US) romantic and sexual behaviour. [MAKE OUT v.[1]]

make out v.[1] **1** [mid-19C+] (orig. US) to get along, to make the grade, to succeed. **2** [1930s+] (US) to seduce a woman. **3** [1940s+] (US) to indulge in hetero- or homosexual foreplay or petting but not necessarily intercourse.

make out v.[2] [late 19C+] to arrive at a conclusion; thus how do you make that out? how do you reach that conclusion?

make-out artist n. [1930s+] (US) a ladies' man, a successful seducer. [MAKE OUT v.[1] (2) + ARTIST n.[2]]

make out with yourself v. [1950s+] (US) to masturbate. [MAKE OUT v.[1]]

make over v. [20C] (US Black) to flatter.

make pee-pee, to phr. [1920s+] (usu. juv.) to urinate. [PEE n. + redup.]

make placebo/a placebo v. [mid-14C–late 17C] to be a toady or sycophant (cf. AT THE SCHOOL OF PLACEBO). [PLACEBO]

make pots and pans, to phr. [19C] to spend heavily, to use up one's money and start begging. [? the selling of pots and pans by a tinker]

make prick juice, to phr. [1990s] to masturbate. [PRICK n. (2) + JUICE n.[2] (2)]

maker n. [19C+] a forger, a counterfeiter (cf. QUEER COLE).

make rat/rat in v. [20C] (W.I.) to sneak into without paying, to GATECRASH. [Fr. Creole faire (le) rat, to act like a rat; ult. the neg. stereotype of the rat]

make roast meat for worms, to phr. [late 16C–18C] to kill (cf. FEED THE WORMS).

make settlement/a settlement in tail, to phr. [late 17C–early 18C] of a man, to have sexual intercourse. [pun on legal jargon entail, 'to attach as an inseparable appendage to, upon, an estate or inheritance' (OED) + TAIL n.[1] (1)]

makes ill music phr. [early 18C] a phr. used of unwelcome news, e.g. that makes ill music here. [SE ill, bad + fig. use of music]

make someone creak in their shoes, to phr. [late 19C] to terrify, to frighten someone. [? here creak = quake]

make someone jump, to *phr.* [20C] (W.I.) to keep someone in a state of anxiety or fear.

make someone piss, to *phr.* [late 17C] to annoy, to infuriate, to disgust someone.

make someone/oneself right, to *phr.* [1950s+] (US Black) to feel good, esp. as a result of drug use.

make someone's bristles rise, to *phr.* [late 19C] to irritate, to infuriate someone (cf. PUT SOMEONE'S BACK UP). [animal imagery]

make someone scream, to *phr.* [1980s+] (US campus) to have sexual intercourse with someone (cf. MAKE HER GRUNT). [the screams are of orgasmic bliss]

make someone's day, to *phr.* [20C] to delight someone, to act in such a way as to make someone happy; thus *make one's evening, make one's night.*

make someone sit up, to *phr.* [late 19C+] to astound, to shock, to galvanize someone into action.

make someone's nose swell, to *phr.* [mid-18C] to make someone jealous. [SE *put someone's nose out of joint*]

make someone spin, to *phr.* [20C] (W.I.) to give someone a hard time, to 'lead someone a dance'.

make someone tick, to *phr.* [1930s+] to stimulate, to motivate someone.

make someone tired, to *phr.* [late 19C+] (orig. US) to irritate someone.

make something talk, to *phr.* [1920s+] to operate a piece of machinery with more than average skill.

make soup *v.* [1990s] to masturbate.

make standing room for, to *phr.* [late 19C] of a woman, to permit sexual intercourse. [COCKSTAND; STAND n.[2] (1)]

make strange, to *phr.* [20C] usu. of a child, to act in an awkward or embarrassing manner.

make style *v.* [20C] (W.I.) **1** to behave in an exhibitionist manner to attract attention (cf. CUT STYLE). **2** to be overly fussy, fastidious.

make/turn the air blue/turn blue, to *phr.* [late 19C+] to swear, to use obscenities (cf. BURN IT BLUE). [BLUE adj.[3]]

make the bald man puke/sick, to *phr.* [1990s] of a man, to masturbate.

make the beast with two backs/two-backed beast, to *phr.* [early 17C+] to have sexual intercourse. [the first cited use of the phr. is by Shakespeare, in *Othello* (1604); it also occurs in Fr., where Rabelais uses *faire la bête à deux dos*]

make the blind see, to *phr.* [1980s+] (US gay) to fellate an uncircumcised penis. [BLIND adj.[3]]

make the cheese more binding, to *phr.* [1920s+] (US) to make matters worse.

make the chimney smoke, to *phr.* [mid-19C+] of a man, to give one's partner an orgasm.

make the crow a pudding *see* GIVE THE CROW A PUDDING.

make the cut, to *phr.* [1990s] to succeed. [golf jargon *make the cut*, to score sufficiently well in a preliminary round to proceed to the later stages of a competition; those that fail to make a set figure (the *cut*) are eliminated]

make the feathers/fur fly, to *phr.* [19C+] (orig. US, fig.) 'to claw, to scratch, to wound severely' (Bartlett, 1848). [the image of birds or cats fighting]

make the fist, to *phr.* [1960s–70s] (US Black) to give a Black Power salute, with the arm raised at an angle and the fist clenched.

make the fur fly *see* MAKE THE FEATHERS FLY.

make the hooded cobra spit, to *phr.* [1990s] to masturbate.

make the legal move, to *phr.* [1950s+] (US teen) to get married.

make the nut, to *phr.* [1960s+] (US) to achieve a target, to have a sufficiency. [NUT n.[7] (2)]

make the pot with two ears *see* MAKE A POT WITH TWO EARS.

make the right/all the right noises, to *phr.* [1950s+] to talk in bland, unaggressive, ameliorative terms, sincerely or otherwise.

make the rooster crow, to *phr.* [1990s] to masturbate.

make the scene, to *phr.* **1** [1930s+] to understand, to appreciate a situation, to experience something. **2** [1950s+] to go somewhere. **3** [1950s+] to be involved in a particular situation, esp. one that features fashionable, smart people. [SCENE n.]

make the scene with the magazine, to *phr.* [1900s] to masturbate. [joc. use of MAKE THE SCENE + assonance, with ref. to the 'men's magazines' used for stimulation]

make the skies look blue, to *phr.* [mid-17C–mid-18C] to carouse, to enjoy oneself. [blue skies are equated with happiness]

make the turn, to *phr.* [1980s+] (drugs) to withdraw from drug use.

make the two-backed beast *see* MAKE THE BEAST WITH TWO BACKS.

make things hum, to *phr.* [late 19C+] to excite or stir things up. [the sound of an agitated wasps' nest]

make time with, to *phr.* [1930s+] (US) to make advances, to court, to flirt (cf. MAKE v.[3]; PUT THE MAKE ON).

make to wear the stag's crest *see* MAKE A STAG.

make tracks, to *phr.* [mid-19C+] to run away, to escape.

make-up *n.[1]* **1** [mid-19C–1920s] anything, esp. a meal, thrown together from odds and ends or left-overs. **2** [late 19C–1950s] one's appearance, looks and dress.

make-up *n.[2]* [1930s+] (US campus) a re-sit, a second examination for a student who has failed to pass it at the first attempt. [one *makes up* for the previous failure]

make-up *n.[3]* [1950s] (drugs) **1** an injection of heroin. **2** the need to find more drugs. [MAKE v.[3] (4)]

make up one's leg, to *phr.* [late 19C] (coster) to make money (cf. MAKE LEG). ['the time of smalls, stockings and buckled shoes, when making up the leg was a necessary prelude to going into society' (Ware)]

make up one's mouth, to *phr.* [late 19C] to earn one's living. [SE phr. *make up one's mouth*, to conclude a meal with something especially tasty]

make up to *v.* [early 19C+] to 'make love to', to 'chat up'.

make V *v.* [early 17C] to make a V-sign with the first and second fingers of the hand, which implies that the target of the gesture is a cuckold.

make wallpaper/be a wall-prop *v.* [1900s–20s] to be a 'wallflower' at a dance or other social occasion. [one merely provides background for the more enthusiastic participants]

make waves, to *phr.[1]* [1970s+] to cause trouble, esp. in an otherwise calm situation; thus *don't make waves*, don't make a fuss.

make waves/for the man in the boat, to *phr.[2]* [1990s] of a woman, to masturbate (cf. BABY IN THE BOAT; MAN IN THE BOAT).

makeweight *n.* [late 18C–early 19C] **1** a small candle. **2** a small person.

make whoopee, to *phr.* [1920s+] to go out on a spree, to enjoy oneself uproariously (cf. GO ON A TEAR; TAKE A FLIER). [SE *make* + WHOOPEE; the coinage seems to have been in G. Kahn's 1928 song 'Makin' Whoopee', 'Another bride, another June, Another sunny honeymoon, Another season, another reason for making whoopee!']

make with *v.* [1930s+] (orig. US) to use, to affect, to pose as. [Yid. *macht mit*, make with]

make yes of it, to *phr.* [1910s–20s] to agree.

-making *sfx.* [1920s+] used with a variety of nouns, e.g. *blush-making, shy-making, sick-making*, sometimes prefixed by 'too'. [mainly 1930s and general middle-/upper middle-class use, but disinterred regularly by readers of the novels of Evelyn Waugh, esp. *Vile Bodies* (1930)]

making a trundle for a goose's eye *phr.* [mid-19C] one of many responses used to defer a 'difficult' question as to 'what one has been doing?' (cf. MAKING A WHIM-WHAM FOR A GOOSE'S EYE; WEAVING DOLLS' EYES).

making a whim-wham for a goose's eye/to bridle a goose *phr.* [mid-19C] one of many responses used to defer a 'difficult' question as to 'what one has been doing?' (cf. MAKING A TRUNDLE FOR A GOOSE'S EYE; WEAVING DOLLS' EYES).

making Ms and Ts *phr.* [late 18C–mid-19C] becoming drunk (cf. MOLL THOMPSON'S MARK). [a pun on the letters *M* and *T*, i.e. 'empty']

makings *n.* **1** [mid-late 19C] wages, lit. 'what one makes'. **2** [20C] (orig. US) tobacco and cigarette papers. **3** [1960s+] (drugs) the tobacco, cannabis and cigarette papers required for the production of a cannabis cigarette.

mako *see* MACO.

makomé/macumeh/makoumé *n.* [20C] (W.I.) an effeminate man. [Carib.E *makomé*, one's child's godmother, usu. an elderly female friend; ult. Fr. *macommère*]

maku *n.* [20C] (W.I.) **1** an effeminate man. **2** a peeping tom. **3** a fool, an idiot (cf. MACO n.²). [? Fr. *maquereau*, a pimp]

Malabar Hilton *n.* [1980s+] (Aus. Und.) Long Bay prison, New South Wales (cf. AKERMAN'S HOTEL).

malaky *see* MALARKEY.

malalapipe *n.* [1970s+] (S.Afr.) a homeless child beggar (cf. STROLLER). [Zulu *umalalepayipini*, 'one who sleeps in a pipe']

malaria *n.* [1980s] (US Black) sweat. [SE *malaria*, a disease characterized by a high fever]

malarkey / malaky / malarky / mallarkey / mullarkey *n.* [1920s+] (orig. US) **1** nonsense, foolishness, 'messing about'. **2** a fool. [? Irish *mullachán*, a strongly built boy, thus a ruffian]

malavogue/malivogue *v.* [20C] (Irish) to beat, to manhandle. [ety. unknown; a nonce-word]

Malawi grass *n.* [1980s+] (drugs) marijuana from Malawi; thus *Malawi cob*, marijuana from Malawi bundled in a shape reminiscent of a cigar. [SE *Malawi* + GRASS n.⁴/COB n.³]

malazanas *n.* [1960s–70s] (S.Afr. township) money. [ety. unknown; ? an African language]

malco *n.* [1980s+] a general term of abuse (cf. MONG n.²; SPAS n.). [abbr. SE *malcoordinated*]

maleesh *phr.* [1910s+] (Aus./N.Z.) a phr. used to indicate one's lack of interest /dismissal of an idea or thing. [Egyptian Arabic *ma'lesh*, no matter, never mind]

male-mules *n.* [16C] the testicles. [play on SE; pos. used only in Urquhart's trans. of Rabelais]

malflor *n.* [1960s+] (US) a lesbian. [Sp. lit. 'an evil flower', but note Sp. *marimacho*, a tomboy]

malfunction junction *n.* [1940s] (US) a major congestion, usu. a traffic jam.

malhavelins *see* MANAVILINS.

malicious *adj.* [20C] (W.I.) **1** tiresomely inquisitive. **2** offensively meddlesome with the aim of causing harm.

malivogue *see* MALAVOGUE.

malkin *n.* [late 17C–18C] the vagina (cf. CAT n.¹⁰; ROUGH MALKIN). [Scot. *malkin*, a cat. *Grimalkin* is often the name of a witch's feline familiar, while *malkin* itself also means hare, suggesting a link to the rabbit, a traditionally 'sexy' animal, that may or may not be coincidental]

malkin-trash *n.* [late 17C–early 19C] an ill-dressed person. [SE *malkin*, an untidy woman, a slattern]

mallacky *n.* [20C] (Irish) cat excrement. [Irish *meallach*, lumpy, globular]

mallarkey *see* MALARKEY.

mallee root *n.* [1940s+] (Aus.) a prostitute. [rhy. sl., ult. Abor. *mallee*, eucalyptus]

mallet *n.* [1970s–80s] (US Black) the police. [their image as a repressive agency]

mallet *v.* [1970s+] to hit, to beat up.

mallethead *n.* [1950s+] (US) a stupid person. [SE *mallet* + sfx. -HEAD (1)]

malleting bout *n.* [early–mid-19C] a fist-fight. [var. on HAMMER n.²]

malley *n.* [mid-19C] (Anglo-Ind.) a gardener. [Hind. *mali*, a gardener]

Malley's cow *n.* [1950s] (Aus.) one who has left, gone away. [the story of one *Malley* who was supposed to look after a cow. When his boss returned to find Malley but no cow and asked what had happened, he received the reply 'she's a goner']

mall rat/mallie *n.* [1980s+] (US) a young person who spends the day hanging around shopping malls (cf. ALLEY RAT). [SE (*shopping*) *mall* + RAT n.³ (1)]

Malt *n.* [late 19C–1960s] a *Malt*ese. [abbr.]

malt *v.* [early 19C] to drink (cf. SHOVEL OF MALT). [SE *malt*, a component of beer]

malted *adj.* [19C] drunk, tipsy (cf. ALED UP). [MALT v.]

Malteser *n.* [1950s–60s] a Maltese. [the brandname of the popular sweet]

malthorse *n.* [early 17C–1900s] a native of Bedford. [the high quality malt produced by Bedfordshire barley]

maltooler *n.* [mid-late 19C] a pickpocket specializing in stealing from women travelling on buses. [MOLL n. (1) + TOOL v.³]

maltoot/maltout *n.* [late 18C–late 19C] a marine. [? Fr. *matelot*, a sailor]

maltpie *n.* [early 17C] alcohol.

maltworm *n.* [early 18C] a heavy drinker. [play on SE *maltworm*, a malt-infesting weevil]

malty *adj.* [early–mid-19C] drunk (cf. ALED UP). [MALT v. + sfx. -y]

malty-cove *n.* [19C] a beer-drinker. [MALTY + COVE]

mama *n.* **1** [1910s+] (orig. US Black) a woman. **2** [1910s+] (orig. US Black) esp. in direct address, a girlfriend or wife. **3** [1940s–70s] (US) an effeminate male homosexual. **4** [1950s+] (Hell's Angel) a woman who rides with the Hell's Angels and is available for communal sex and allied indignities but is distinguished from the *old ladies* (the actual girlfriends of the riders); the term is an abbr. of *Let's go make someone a mama*. **5** [1950s+] a feminine lesbian (cf. PAPA). **6** [1970s+] anything considered very powerful, large or admirable.

mama bear *n.* [1970s+] (US) a policewoman, esp. in the Highway Patrol. [SE *mama* + BEAR n.⁸]

mamacita *n.* [1970s+] (US) an attractive young woman. [Sp., lit. 'little mother']

mama coca *n.* [1970s+] (drugs) cocaine. [lit. 'mother coca']

mama-huncher *n.* [20C] euph. for MOTHERFUCKER.

mama-jabber *n.* [20C] euph. for MOTHERFUCKER.

mama-jabbing *adj.* [20C] euph. for MOTHERFUCKING adj.

mama-man *n.* [1940s+] (W.I.) **1** a man who does women's work. **2** an unmanly man (cf. AUNTIE-MAN).

mama's boss *n.* [1930s–40s] (US Black, usu. male usage) a husband.

mama smokey *n.* [1970s+] (US) a policewoman. [SE *mama* + SMOKY n.²]

mammaries *n.* [1970s+] the female breasts (cf. MAMS). [SE *mammary gland*]

mammock *v.* [mid-19C+] (US, mainly west and south) **1** to tear into pieces, to mangle. **2** to beat, to thrash; thus *mommicking*, a thrashing. **3** to mess up, to confuse (cf. BOLLIX v.). [dial. *mammock*, to pull about, to mess]

mammy *n.* [19C+] (US Black) the ideal Black woman as

stereotyped by Whites. Such women would typically be employed as nannies or cooks in White households.

mammy *adj.* [1930s+] (US Und.) abundant, esp. in phr. *money's mammy*, a great deal of money (cf. LONG *adj.*[4]). [the image of maternal, i.e. *mammy's* abundance, of love, food etc]

mammy-dodger *n.* [1920s–30s] (US Black) euph. for MOTHERFUCKER.

mammy-dodging *adj.* [20C] euph. for MOTHERFUCKING *adj.*

mammy-jammer *n.* [20C] euph. for MOTHERFUCKER.

mammy-jamming *adj.* [20C] euph. for MOTHERFUCKING *adj.*

mammy-rammer *n.* [20C] euph. for MOTHERFUCKER.

mammy-ramming *adj.* [20C] euph. for MOTHERFUCKING *adj.*

mammy-tapper *n.* [20C] euph. for MOTHERFUCKER.

mammy-tapping *adj.* [20C] euph. for MOTHERFUCKING *adj.*

mampala/-man/maparla/-man *n.* [20C] (W.I.) an effeminate man, a homosexual man who plays the 'female' role in sex. [Sp. *mampolón*, a cock, but not a fighting cock, thus a weakling]

mams *n.* [1970s+] the female breasts. [abbr. SE *mammaries*]

mamzer/momser/momza/momzer *n.* [1950s+] a catch-all term implying everything from great affection to deep dislike (cf. BASTARD; BUGGER *n.*[1]). [Heb. *mamzer*, a bastard, adapted in Lat. and thus used throughout the Middle Ages. The modern use, however, is related to Yid., and imported by Jewish immigrants to US and UK]

man *n.*[1] [late 14C+] **1** used emphatically in direct address. **2** used in direct address, without emphasis, to acknowledge a shared social or cultural identity (later usage sometimes includes women, children and animals). [Major (1994) suggests that the term was adopted by US Blacks to counter the common White use of 'boy' when addressing Blacks]

man *n.*[2] **1** [early 19C] the head of a coin (cf. WOMAN). **2** [1910s–60s] (US) $1 (cf. IRON MAN). [the picture, usu. of a male monarch, that was engraved on most coins]

man, the *n.*[3] **1** [20C] (US) any man or group in charge, a commanding officer, a prison warden, a policeman, one's boss etc. **2** [1920s+] (US) the penis. **3** [1940s+] (orig. US) a drug dealer. **4** [1950s+] (US Black) the White ruling class. **5** [1950s+] (US Black) the US Government. **6** [1970s+] (US) God.

man *n.*[4] [1930s–40s] (US Black) a pint bottle of liquor; thus *half-a-man*, a half-pint.

man *adj.* [20C] (W.I.) very expensive, usu. in phr. *something is a man*. [SE *man*, to mean something powerful, strong]

man *v.* [mid-19C] to have sexual intercourse.

man! *see* MAN ALIVE!

-man/-mans *sfx.* [16C] a state of being or a thing (cf. CRACKMANS; CRAGMANS; DARKMANS; HARMANS; LIGHTMANS; RUFFMANS; TOGEMANS). [the *OED* cites it as 'unexplained' but E.P. (*DSUE* 8th edn., 1984, *Origins*, 4th edn., 1966) suggests links with Lat. *mens*, mind, Fr. sfx. *-ment*, SE *man*, a human being or Skrt. *-moni*, mood or mind]

manablins *see* MANAVILINS.

man a-hanging *n.* [1970s] (US Black) a person in trouble (cf. MAN HANGING).

man alive *phr.* [20C] the number 5. [rhy. sl.]

man alive!/man! *excl.* [early 19C+] a mild oath of surprise, astonishment etc (cf. SNAKES ALIVE!).

man and wife *n.* [1900s–10s] a knife. [rhy. sl.]

manavilins / malhavelins / manablins / manarolins / manavalins/menavelings *n.* [mid-19C–late 19C] odds and ends, bits and pieces, typically of food or small change (cf. BLUE PIGEON). [ety. unknown, but note contemp. naut. jargon *manarvel*, to pilfer small stores]

man-better-man *phr.* [20C] (W.I.) a phr. used to issue a definite challenge to fight, with the implication of finding out who is the 'better man'.

man-box *n.* [mid-19C] a coffin.

man-catcher / -getter / -grabber / -hunter / -shark *n.* [1920s–50s] (US) a labour recruiter, an employment agency.

manchester *n.*[1] [early 19C] the tongue. [? Scot. *mang*, talk and/or f. Rom. *mag*, to beg]

Manchester *n.*[2] [20C] (Aus./N.Z.) household linen; thus *Manchester department* in shops. [the days when *Manchester* was 'Cottonopolis', the textile capital of the globe]

Manchester-bred *adj.* [mid-19C] physically strong, mentally weak. [the descriptive rhyme 'long in the arms and short in the head']

Manchester Cities/manchesters *n.* [20C] (Aus.) the female breasts (cf. BRADFORD CITIES). [rhy. sl. *Manchester City* = TITTY *n.*[2]]

Manchester sovereign *n.* [mid-19C–1930s] one shilling (5p) (cf. BRUMMAGEM BUTTON). [the implication is of cheapness, from Manchester's reputation for mass production]

mancunt *n.* [1990s] a passive homosexual. [SE *man* + CUNT *n.*[1] (1)]

mandarin *n.* [20C] **1** a senior civil servant. **2** a senior politician or commentator (cf. HEAVEN-BORN). [Port. *mandarim*, itself ult. Skrt. *mantrin*, counsellor. The term was adopted in China to describe the 9 grades of Chinese officials, each of which was distinguished by a particular kind of 'button']

mandingo *n.* [1960s+] (US Black) a tough, physically strong, virile African-American man. [proper name *Mandingo*, a member of the peoples of the upper Niger in West Africa, whose ranks supplied many slaves; more immediately a ref. to the book title *Mandingo*, concerning the stereotypical 'Black buck' slave and his effect on women, both Black and White]

M & Ms *n.* [1970s+] (drugs) barbiturates, amphetamines, drugs available as pills. [the US-originated sweet]

man-down! *excl.* [1990s] (US Black teen) the police are coming! [MAN *n.*[3] (1) + COME DOWN *v.*[2] (2)]

mandozy *n.* [mid-19C] **1** a powerful blow. **2** a term of endearment among London Jews. [the Jewish prize-fighter *Daniel Mendoza (1764–1836)*]

mandrake *n.* [early 17C+] a sodomite, a male homosexual. [SE *mandrake*, 'Any plant of the genus *Mandragora* ... characterized by very short stems, thick, fleshy, often forked, roots, and fetid lance-shaped leaves. The mandrake is poisonous, having emetic and narcotic properties, and was formerly used medicinally. The forked root is thought to resemble the human form, and was fabled to utter a deadly shriek when plucked up from the ground' (*OED*)]

M and S/Marks/Marks and Sparks *n.* [1950s+] nickname for Marks & Spencer group of department stores. [abbr.; note the firm's house magazine is called *Sparks*]

man dumpling *n.* [1950s] (W.I.) a very large dumpling. [the implication is either of being as big as a man, or a man-sized portion]

mandy/manny *n.* [1960s+] a Mandrax or methaqualone tablet. [the spelling 'manny' seems to appear only in Fabian & Byrne, *Groupie*, 1969, and was coined by them as a deliberate euph.]

man-eater *n.* **1** [mid-19C] (Anglo-Ind.) a horse that tends to bite people. **2** [20C] a sexually predatory woman. **3** [1940s+] a homosexual man. [orig. naut. use, a particularly disciplinarian officer, ult. SE, a man-eating tiger]

maneen *n.* [1910s+] (Irish) a little man. [SE *man* + dimin. sfx. *-een*]

manfat *n.* [1990s] semen.

man for my money *phr.* [mid-19C+] the one I prefer, my choice.

mang *v.* [early–mid-19C] to talk; thus *mangsman*, a lawyer. [Scot. or Rom. *mag*, to beg]

mangarly/manjarie n. [mid-19C+] (Ling. Fr./Polari) food. [Ital. *mangiare*, to eat]

mange n. [late 19C] food. [Ital. *mangiare*, to eat]

mange v. [1980s+] (US campus) to eat. [Ital. *mangiare*/Fr. *manger*, to eat]

man-getter see MAN-CATCHER.

mangiare/giare v. [mid-19C+] (Polari) to eat. [Ital. *mangiare*, to eat]

mangle n.[1] [19C] the vagina (cf. CATCH 'EM ALIVE-O).

mangle n.[2] [1940s+] (Aus.) a bicycle. [supposed resemblance]

mangle and wringer n. [20C] a singer. [rhy. sl.]

mangled adj. [1980s+] (US campus) dishevelled, unkempt.

mangle the midget, to phr. [1990s] to masturbate.

mangoes n. [1980s+] (US) the female breasts (cf. APPLES n.[1]).

man-grabber see MAN-CATCHER.

mangy adj. **1** [late 19C+] contemptible. **2** [20C] (Irish) mean, grasping, avaricious. [SE *mangy*, squalid, shabby, lit. 'scabby']

man hanging n. [mid-19C] a person in difficulties, esp. one who is prepared to go to any lengths to remedy their situation (cf. MAN A-HANGING). [when someone is hanging, any alternative must be an improvement]

Manhattan silver/white n. [1970s+] (drugs) an imaginary brand of marijuana, silver/white because its seeds have grown in darkness, after being flushed away into the sewer system (cf. NEW YORK CITY SILVER).

manhole n.[1] **1** [20C] the vagina (cf. CATCH 'EM ALIVE-O). **2** [1980s+] (US gay) a passive partner in anal intercourse.

manhole n.[2] [1970s] (US Black) a bar, a saloon, a club etc, esp. for men only.

manhole cover n.[1] [20C] a brother. [rhy. sl.]

manhole cover n.[2] [1940s+] (Aus./US) a sanitary towel. [MANHOLE n.[1] (1) + SE *cover*]

manhole covers with custard n. [1940s+] bread pudding. [supposed resemblance]

manhole inspector n. [1990s] a male homosexual. [heavy puns]

man-hunter n.[1] [late 19C] a woman, esp. a widow or spinster.

man-hunter n.[2] see MAN-CATCHER.

manicou-man n. [20C] (W.I.) an effeminate man. [? Carib.E. *manicou*, a 'nocturnal, foul-smelling marsupial rodent the size of a cat' (Allsopp); the young of this creature hang onto their mother for transportation]

manifest n. [1930s] (US) a fast freight train (cf. REDBALL). [the *manifest* of the goods it carries]

man in blue n. [late 19C] a policeman (cf. BLUE n.[3]).

man in the boat n. [late 19C+] the clitoris (cf. BABY IN THE BOAT).

man in the gap phr. [20C] (Irish) one who bravely and successfully defends a cause or position.

man in the moon n.[1] [mid-19C] the nickname for the person, necessarily anonymous and quick to disappear, who pays out bribes at elections.

man in the moon n.[2] [20C] a fool, an eccentric. [rhy. sl. *man in the moon* = LOON n.]

manipulate the mango, to phr. [1990s] to masturbate.

manjarie see MANGARLY.

mankie/manky adj. [1940s+] (orig. Ling. Fr./Polari) unpleasant, disgusting, poss. smelly. [? Ital. *mancare*, to lack, to want or ? Fr. *manqué*, lost]

man-killer n. [late 19C–1900s] porter, stout, any black beer. [the effect of such sweet, heavy beers on one's weight and thus health]

manky see MANKIE.

manmanpoul n. [20C] (W.I.) **1** a person who fusses excessively. **2** a gullible fool. [Fr. *maman poule*, mother hen]

man muscle n. [1970s+] (US Black) the penis.

manne, die n. [1960s+] (S.Afr.) a local hero, esp. in a school or college (cf. MAIN MAN n.[2]; MAN n.[3]). [Afk. *man(ne)*, man]

mannish adj. [mid-19C+] (US/W.I.) usu. of young people, forward, impertinent (cf. WOMLISH). [i.e. a child acting beyond its years]

mannish water n. [20C] (W.I./Jam.) goat-head soup, a highly seasoned, peppery soup made from the head and offal of a goat, eaten on festive occasions. The soup is linked to virility in and with placating the spirits of the dead in Tob. [the association of the soup with virility]

manny see MANDY.

mano n. [1960s+] (US Hispanic) used in direct address, man (cf. MAN n.[1]).

manoeuvre the apostles, to phr. [late 18C+] to manipulate one's accounts to pay off one debt while incurring another. [pun on popular phr. *to rob Peter to pay Paul*]

man of business n. [20C] (W.I.) a woman's lover on whom she relies for various favours. [Carib.E. *man of business*, a handyman]

man of many morns n. [18C–1900s] (Scot.) a procrastinator.

man of remnants n. [1910s–20s] a tailor.

man of the world n. [late 19C] a professional thief.

man of war n. [18C–19C] the Fleet prison, London (cf. NEVER WAG; NUMBER 9). [its site, on the east bank of the Fleet River; the image is of an anchored warship]

man on the moon n. [1960s+] a spoon. [rhy. sl.]

manor n. [1920s+] (usu. police) an area of operations, one's home base (cf. BEAT n.[1]).

man outside Hoyt's n. [1930s+] **1** (Aus.) the source of all rumours. **2** (Aus. Und.) the source of any stolen property that the police might find with a receiver. [the commissionaire *outside Hoyt's* Theatre, Melbourne, a gorgeously uniformed individual]

man o' war n. [20C] a bore. [rhy. sl.]

man pains n. [1990s] (US Black teen) injuries suffered while doing 'manly' things, i.e. lifting a trunk, playing football etc.

manpower v. [1940s+] (Aus./N.Z., mainly historical) to conscript for non-military work, e.g. fruit-picking, as part of the war effort.

man root n. [19C] the penis (cf. IRISH ROOT; OLD ROOT; ROOT n.[1]; STALK n.[1]; TAIL n.[1]).

-mans see -MAN.

man-shark see MAN-CATCHER.

man's milk n. [1990s] semen.

mantalini n. [mid-late 19C] a male milliner. [Mr *Mantalini*, the milliner in Charles Dickens's *Nicholas Nickleby* (1839)]

mantee n. [1930s–40s] a masculine lesbian; thus *mantee walk*, to swagger, *mantee voice*, a deep voice. [? Fr. *mintée*]

man the cannon, to phr. [1980s+] to masturbate. [CANNON n.[1] (3)]

man the cockpit, to phr. [1980s+] to masturbate.

man thomas n. [early 17C–early 19C] the penis (cf. JOHN THOMAS).

manto n. [20C] a woman, a girl. [? dial. *manto*, a lady's gown, ult. Fr. *manteau*, a gown; thus by metonymy, its wearer]

manton see JOE MANTON.

man-trap n.[1] **1** [late 18C] a widow. **2** [late 18C–early 19C] the vagina (cf. CATCH 'EM ALIVE-O). **3** [1910s+] an attractive and available woman.

man-trap n.[2] [late 19C–1900s] a piece of excrement. [rhy. sl. *man-trap* = CRAP n.[3] (1)]

manual compliment/subscription n. [19C] a blow. [pun on SE *sign-manual*]

manual labour n. [1990s] masturbation.

manual override n. [1990s] masturbation.

manual subscription see MANUAL COMPLIMENT.

manufacture see ENGLISH MANUFACTURE.

man upstairs, the *n.* [1960s+] God (cf. UPSTAIRS n.²).

manure *n.* [1920s–60s] (US) nonsense. [euph. for BULLSHIT n.]

man who rides the screaming gasser *phr.* [1930s–40s] (US Black) a policeman in a patrol car.

man with a headache stick *n.* [1950s–60s] (US Black) a policeman. [his nightstick/truncheon]

man with a paper ass/asshole *n.* [1950s+] (US Black) a talkative fool – all talk and little or no action. [ARSE n.¹/ ARSEHOLE]

man with fuzzy balls *n.* [1960s–80s] (US Black) a White man. [BALLS n.¹; note the theory that FUZZ n.¹ derives from this]

man with no hands *n.* [1940s+] (Aus.) a miser.

man with the book of many years *n.* [1940s] (US Black) a judge.

Maori *adj.* [20C] (N.Z.) not a sl. term as such, *Maori* (cf. CHINESE adj.; IRISH adj.) has been stereotyped as an all-purpose shorthand for stupid, lazy, or primitive. It is used as such in the combs. that follow.

Maori cannon *n.* [1930s–40s] (N.Z.) a badly played shot in billiards or snooker. [racist stereotyping]

Maori car *n.* [1980s] (N.Z.) an old or broken-down vehicle. [racist stereotyping]

Maori day off *n.* [1980s] (N.Z.) unauthorized absence from the workplace. [racist stereotyping]

Maori half-crown *n.* [1950s–70s] (N.Z.) a penny. [racist stereotyping; the half-crown (12.5p) was worth 30 pennies]

Maori holiday *n.* [1970s+] (N.Z.) the day after payday. [racist stereotyping]

Maori mustang *n.* [1970s+] (N.Z.) the Mark II Ford Zephyr. [the *Mustang* is a much sought-after sports car; the *Ford* is definitely not]

Maori overdrive *n.* [1970s+] (N.Z.) sliding one's car downhill with the engine off and the gears in neutral (cf. JEWISH OVER-DRIVE; MEXICAN OVERDRIVE). [racist stereotyping]

Maori P.T. *n.* [mid-19C+] (N.Z.) taking it easy and doing nothing. [racist stereotyping]

Maori roast *n.* [1970s+] (N.Z.) fish and chips or some form of fast food. [racist stereotyping]

Maori weed *n.* [20C] (N.Z.) a wild horse.

map *n.* **1** [late 19C+] the human face. **2** [1920s–60s] (US Und.) a bank cheque, usu. a fraudulent one.

map *v.* [1980s+] (US Black) to hit, esp. to hit in the face. [MAP n. (1)]

maparla/-man *see* MAMPALA.

maphepha/mephepha *n.* (S.Afr.) **1** [1970s+] a rand. **2** [1970s+] money in general. **3** [1980s+] an official document, 'papers'. [Xhosa *amaphepha*, papers]

map of ... *phr.* [1900s–40s] (US) a phr. used with the name of a country to refer to typical facial features, e.g. a Jew will have *a map of Jerusalem all over his face.*

map of England/Ireland *n.* [1960s+] a semen stain on a sheet. [note synon. Fr. *carte de France*]

map of tassie *n.* [1990s] (Aus.) the female genitals and pubic hair. [the supposed similarity of this shape to the outline of a map of Tasmania]

mapusa/mapuza *n.* [1970s+] (S.Afr. Und.) the police. [? Afr. pron. of SE *police*]

maracas *n.* [1940s+] (US) the female breasts. [? the musical instrument; i.e. one 'plays' on them]

marathons *n.* [1970s+] (drugs) amphetamines (cf. A n.²). [their effect on one's stamina]

marble *v.* [late 19C] (US) to leave, to go. [SE *marble*, that rolls along]

marble arch *n.* [mid-19C] the vagina (cf. ADAM'S OWN ALTAR; BELLY DALE). [lit. euph.]

marble city *n.* [1900s–40s] (US Black) a cemetery (cf. MARBLE HILL; MARBLE ORCHARD).

marble dome *see* MARBLEHEAD n.².

marble halls *n.* [20C] the testicles. [rhy. sl. *marble halls* = BALLS n.¹ (1)]

marblehead *n.¹* [19C] a Greek. [the many marble statues of Greece]

marblehead/marble dome *n.²* [1910s–50s] (US) an idiot. [SE *marble* + sfx. -HEAD (1)]

marble heart *n.* [late 19C–1930s] (US) a rejection. [play on COLD SHOULDER n.]

marble hill *n.* [20C] (US) a cemetery (cf. HILL; MARBLE CITY).

marble orchard/town *n.* [1920s+] (US) a cemetery (cf. MARBLE HILL). [note film title *Gardens of Stone* (1987), referring to the Arlington National Cemetery]

marbles *n.¹* [19C] venereal buboes or pocks. [? Fr. *morbilles*, small blisters]

marbles *n.²* [mid-19C–1930s] furniture. [Fr. *meubles*, furniture]

marbles *n.³* [mid-19C+] the testicles. [resemblance, but note MARBLE HALLS]

marbles *n.⁴* **1** [mid-19C+] personal possessions, esp. money used as gambling stakes. **2** [1950s+] money; thus *big marbles*, a large sum of money.

marbles *n.⁵* [20C] (orig. US) mental faculties, brains, common sense, usu. in phr. *lose one's marbles*, to go mad. [despite orig., ? link to MARBLES AND CONKERS]

marbles and conkers *adj.* [20C] eccentric, crazy. [rhy. sl. *marbles and conkers* = BONKERS]

marbles to manslaughter *phr.* [mid-19C] used of someone who is open to anything, *from marbles to manslaughter*. [the terms are used to symbolize opposite extremes]

marble town *see* MARBLE ORCHARD.

marble upon your taw *see* ONE UPON YOUR TAW.

marching dust *see* MARCHING POWDER.

marching money *n.* [20C] (Aus.) daily travel allowance. [19C milit. jargon *marching money*, money used to pay for a soldier's meals during a march]

marching powder/dust *n.* [1980s+] (US drugs) cocaine, as in *Bolivian/Peruvian marching powder.*

march in the rear of a whereas *see* FOLLOW A WHEREAS.

marchioness *n.* [mid-19C] a maid-of-all-work. [character in Charles Dickens's *Old Curiosity Shop* (1841)]

Marco Polo *n.* [1980s+] (US gay) an Italian gay man. [Ital. explorer *Marco Polo* (1254–1324)]

marcus clark *n.* [20C] (Aus.) a shark. [rhy. sl.]

mard-arse *n.* [20C] a sulky person (cf. CANDY-ASS n.¹). [dial. *mardy*, sulky, in turn f. dial. *mar*, to spoil or over-indulge a child + *arse*, used as general pej. rather than actual physical description]

mare *n.* [14C–18C; 1930s+] an ill-tempered, unpleasant woman (cf. BITCH n.¹; COW n.¹).

mare's nest *n.* [1950s–70s] (N.Z.) a bar set aside for women and their escorts (cf. CAT'S BAR).

mare with two/three legs *n.* [17C–mid-19C] a gallows (cf. HORSE FOALED BY AN ACORN; THREE-LEGGED MARE).

marg *see* MARGE n.¹.

margarine mess *n.* [late 19C–1900s] a yellow cab, running in London in the 1890s (cf. BUTTER BEAUTY).

Margate sands *n.* [20C] hands. [rhy. sl.]

marge/marg/marj *n.¹* [1920s+] margarine.

marge *n.²* [1950s+] (US gay) a feminine or passive lesbian (cf. NELLIE n.¹). [the proper name]

margery *n.* [mid-19C+] a homosexual man (cf. AGNES). [the proper name]

margery jane *n.* [1900s–10s] margarine.

margery-prater *n.* [16C–early 19C] a hen. ['Here's Grunter and Bleater,/with Tib of the Buttry,/And Margery Prater,/ all drest without sluttry' (Richard Brome, *The Joviall Crew,*

1641). *Prater* comes from her constant clucking or 'prating', while *margery* echoes dial. *margery daw*, jackdaw and *margery howlet*, an owl]

mari *n.* [1930s–50s] (drugs) *mari*juana, a *mari*juana cigarette. [abbr.]

maria monk *n.* [late 19C+] **1** courage. **2** semen. [rhy. sl. *maria monk* = SPUNK *n.*]

maricon *n.* [1960s+] (Mexican/US) a homosexual. [Sp.]

Marie Corelli *n.* [1970s] television. [rhy. sl. *Marie Corelli* = TELLY; ult. *Marie Corelli*, pseudonym of romantic novelist Marie Mackay (1855–1924)]

marigold/marygold *n.*[1] [mid-19C] **1** a gold coin (cf. CANARY *n.*[4]). **2** £1 million.

marigold *n.*[2] [1970s] (drugs) marijuana. [SE *marijuana* + ACAPULCO GOLD]

marihoochie/marihooch/marihootee/marihootie *n.* [1960s+] (drugs) marijuana. [joc. mispron.]

marinate *v.*[1] [late 17C] to transport overseas as a punishment; thus *marinated*, transported to a foreign penal colony. [pun on SE *marine*]

marinate *v.*[2] [1990s] (US teen) to idle, to loaf; thus *marinating*, idling, 'hanging out'. [pun on SE *marinate*, to pickle or tenderize in wine and vinegar, herbs and spices]

marine officer/recruit *n.* [late 18C–early 19C] an empty bottle (cf. DEAD MARINE). [orig. used by sailors who saw their officers as useless, amplified by William IV (r.1830–7), who used the term in a wardroom, explaining that, like officers, the empty bottles had done their duty and were ready to do it again]

marish and parish *phr.* [20C] (W.I./Bdos., Guyn., Trin.) everyone. [SE *marish*, a marsh + *parish*, a local governmental sub-division. Allsopp presumes some lost UK dial. phr. transported to W.I.]

mariweegee *n.* [1970s+] (drugs) marijuana. [joc. mispron.]

marj *see* MARGE *n.*[1].

marjie *n.* [1940s+] (Aus.) margarine (cf. MARGE *n.*[1]).

mark *n.*[1] [mid-18C–late 19C] one's preference, one's style. [SE *mark*, a distinctive characteristic]

mark *n.*[2] **1** [mid-18C+] (orig. Und.) the potential and actual victim of a con-man, a gullible person. **2** [mid-18C+] (Und.) an item to be stolen, a place to be robbed. **3** [mid-18C+] (tramp) a good place to beg. **4** [mid-19C+] (Aus.) a person, usu. in the context of their financial probity, specified as a *good mark* or *bad mark*. **5** [1920s] a newcomer to the world of prostitution. **6** [1920s–30s] (tramp) a generous giver. **7** [1960s+] (US) a prostitute's customer. [SE *mark*, to note down, i.e. one who is noted down as a possible victim]

mark *n.*[3] [mid-19C–1930s] a humorist. [? *Mark* Lemon (1809–70), the co-founder and first editor of *Punch* (1841)]

mark *v.* **1** [1940s+] (US Und.) to select a prospective victim (cf. PUT THE FINGER ON). **2** [1950s–60s] (US Black) to tease, to mock.

marked with a T *phr.* [late 19C] known as a thief. [the ancient habit of branding convicted thieves with a *T*]

marker *n.*[1] **1** [mid-late 16C] (Und.) that member of a pickpocketing team who takes the stolen item from the person who actually picks the pocket. **2** [1960s+] (US Black) the bait that lures a victim into some form of swindle or other fraud.

marker *n.*[2] [late 19C–1900s] (US) something worthy to be compared.

marker *n.*[3] [late 19C+] (orig. US) an IOU for a gambling debt. [it has been 'marked down']

market dame *n.* [early 18C] a prostitute. [euph., the market being that of Covent Garden]

mark foy *n.* [1940s+] (Aus.) a boy. [rhy. sl.; the name of late 19C London firm of carters or f. a well-known Sydney department store]

marking M *n.* [late 19C] (Irish) rapidity, speed of action. [the Virgin *M(ary)*]

mark it *v.* [late 19C+] to be careful, to watch out.

mark it up *see* MARK UP *v.*[1].

mark of the beast *n.* [18C] the vagina. [the popular (male) image of the satanic vagina]

mark on *n.* [late 19C] someone who has a pronounced taste in a commodity or is an expert in an occupation, e.g. *a mark on strawberries*, *a mark on swearing*. [they 'make their mark']

mark one *adj.* [1920s] first-rate, the best.

Marks *n.*[1] *see* M AND S.

marks *n.*[2] [1950s+] (drugs) the signs of narcotic injections (cf. TRACKS).

Marks and Sparks *see* M AND S.

marksman *n.* [20C] (Irish) one who cannot write and must therefore sign with a mark.

mark someone's card, to *phr.* **1** [mid-19C+] to watch someone, to place someone under surveillance, to pick someone out as a potential victim. **2** [1940s+] to explain, to point out, to warn. **3** [1960s+] to categorize. **4** [1960s+] to realize, to see and understand. [racecourse use, tipsters *mark race-cards with their selections*]

mark up/it up *v.*[1] [late 19C+] to put on one's credit, usu. in a public house (cf. WALL IT). [*mark up* on a slate]

mark up *v.*[2] [1970s+] to bruise, to leave scars after a fight.

Marlboro country *n.* [1960s+] (US) the remote countryside. [suggested by the landscapes featured in advertisements for *Marlboro* cigarettes]

marley *n.* [mid–late 19C] a *marble*. [abbr.]

marley stopper *n.* [mid–late 19C] one who is splayfooted. [MARLEY + SE *stopper*]

Marmalade Country *n.* [late 19C] (orig. music-hall) Scotland (cf. LAND O'CAKES). [the popularity of Scot. marmalades]

Marmite driller/miner *n.* [1990s] a male homosexual. [pun on BROWN *n.*[3] and SE *brown*, the colour of *Marmite*, a popular spread in the UK]

Marmite motorway *n.* [1990s] the anal passage (cf. BOURNEVILLE BOULEVARD; HERSHEY HIGHWAY). [for ety. *see* MARMITE DRILLER]

marm poosey/marm-puss *n.* [late 19C] a flashily dressed public house landlady. [SE *ma'am* + PUSSY *n.*[1], orig. tailors' use *marm-pussy*, one's wife]

maroon *n.* [1940s+] (US) a stupid person. [SE *maroon*, a former slave]

marquis *see* MARQUIS OF LORNE.

Marquis of Granby *n.* [mid-19C] a bald-headed man. [many public house signs show a bald *Marquis of Granby*]

Marquis of Lorne/marquis *n.* **1** [mid-19C] the penis. **2** [1960s+] an erection. [rhy. sl. *Marquis of Lorne* = HORN *n.*[2]]

marquis of marrowbones *n.* [late 16C–17C] a lackey, a servant. [SE *marquis* + MARROWBONES *n.* (1)]

marriage face *n.* [late 19C] (middle-class) a miserable face. [the bride's tearfulness through leaving her family or at the thought of the married life to come]

marriage gear *n.* [mid-19C] the penis and testes (cf. WEDDING KIT).

marriage music *n.* [late 18C–early 19C] the sound of wailing children.

married *adj.* **1** [late 18C–early 19C] used to describe convicts who have been chained together for the purposes of moving them from one place to another. **2** [1980s+] (US campus) in a long-term relationship.

marrowbone and cleaver *n.* [mid-19C] the penis (cf. ARSEOPENER).

marrowbones *n.* **1** [mid-16C–1900s] the knees; thus *bring someone down on their marrowbones*, make someone beg forgiveness (cf. MARQUIS OF MARROWBONES). **2** [early 17C–mid-19C] the fists when used as weapons.

marrow-pudding *n.*[1] [mid-19C] the penis (cf. MARROWBONE AND CLEAVER).

marrow-pudding *n.*[2] [mid-19C] a foetus, usu. in phr. *bellyful of marrow-pudding*, pregnant.

marrowskying/mowrowsky/medical Greek *n.* [mid-19C] a form of slang whereby the user transposes the initial letters of adjacent words (cf. GOWER STREET DIALECT). [? proper name of a Polish count, possibly Count Joseph Boruwlaski. Popularized by medical students at University College in Gower Street, London]

marry! *excl.* [mid-14C–mid-18C] **1** a mild oath. **2** in answering a question, implying surprise that it should be asked, 'why, to be sure' (cf. MARRY COME UP!). [SE *the Virgin Mary*]

marry brown bess, to *phr.* [late 19C] to serve as a soldier. [SE *marry* + BROWN BESS n.]

marry come up! *excl.* [late 16C–mid-18C] an excl. used to express indignant or amused surprise or contempt; ext. [late 17C–late 18C] as *marry come up, my dirty cousin!*, used to tease one who is putting on airs (cf. MARRY!). [synon. with HOITY-TOITY adj. or the modern GET YOU!]

marry Mistress Roper, to *phr.* [mid-19C] to enlist in the Royal Marines. [the flogging at the 'rope's end' that a recruit would have to endure and because such recruits handle the ships' ropes 'like girls']

marry the Devil's daughter/and live with the old folks, to *phr.* [late 18C–20C] to marry a termagant.

marry the widow, to *phr.* **1** [early 19C] to be hanged. **2** [late 19C–1900s] to make a mess of things. [trans. of Fr. sl. *épouser la veuve*, to be guillotined, lit. 'to marry the widow']

marry up *v.* [late 17C–late 19C] to tie up or preoccupy in matrimony.

Mars and Venus *n.* [20C] the penis. [rhy. sl.]

Mars bar *n.* [1970s+] a scar. [rhy. sl.]

marse *n.* [20C] (W.I.) anyone in authority. [ironic use of the old slave pron. of *master*]

marshall *n.* [mid-19C] a £5 note (cf. ABRAHAM LINCOLN). [proper name *Marshall*, chief cashier of the Bank of England, whose name appeared on the notes, *c*.1870]

marshmallow *n.*[1] [1960s+] (US) a soft, weak person.

marshmallow/marshmallow reds *n.*[2] [1970s+] (drugs) depressants, barbiturates. [they soften one's emotions]

marshmallow *adj.* [1960s+] (US) sentimental. [MARSHMALLOW n.[1]]

marshmallow reds *see* MARSHMALLOW n.[2].

marter *n.* [late 16C] **1** a bargainer. **2** a receiver of stolen goods. [SE *mart*, to bargain, to do business]

martian *n.* [1970s+] (US) an eccentric person. [SE *martian*, i.e. they come from/live in 'outer space']

martin *n.* [16C] the victim of a team of confidence tricksters (cf. HIGH LAWYER). [? SE *martin*, a species of bird. It is supposedly lucky for a martin to nest in the eaves of one's house; possibly in this case it is the sharpers who see the appearance of such a *martin* as lucky for themselves]

martin drunk *adj.* [19C] drunk. [SE *St Martin's evil*, drunkenness]

martingale *v.* [19C] (gambling) to double the stakes every time one loses, 'to double stakes constantly, until luck taking one turn only, repays the adventurer all' (Jon Bee). [SE *martingale*, a restraining strap that prevents the horse from rearing or throwing back its head; thus fig. to 'ride one's luck']

martinis *n.* [1980s+] (gay) the arms. [ety. unknown]

Martin-le-Grand *n.* [mid–late 19C] a hand. [rhy. sl.; ult. London street name]

Martin Place *n.* [1930s+] (Aus.) the face. [rhy. sl., ult. proper name *Martin Place*, Sydney]

Martin Place *adj.* [1930s+] (Aus.) in the context of the city, decadence or corruption, or what is seen as such by country people. [proper name *Martin Place*, Sydney; the image of the 'big city' as *de facto* wicked]

martin's *see* ST MARTIN'S.

martin's hammer knocking at the wicket *phr.* [18C–19C] pregnant with twins. [*Father Martin*, a man armed with a staff; link to twins is unknown]

martooni *n.* [1950s+] (US) a martini cocktail. [a 'drunken' pron. of SE]

martyr *n.* [1940s] (Irish) a tormentor. [OF *martire*, to torture]

Marty Wilde *n.* [20C] mild (beer). [rhy. sl.; ult. pop singer *Marty Wilde* (b.1936)]

marv *n.* [1930s+] (US campus/teen) a highly intelligent person, a scholar. [MARV adj.]

marv/marvy *adj.* [1930s+] (US) wonderful, the best, outstanding. [abbr. SE *marvellous*]

marvel *v.* [mid–late 19C] (US) to leave, esp. quickly. [ety. unknown]

marvelious *adj.* [1920s–50s] marvellous. [joc. mispron. of SE]

marvin *see* MELVIN n.

marvy *see* MARV adj.

marwooded *adj.* [late 19C] hanged. [the name of a contemporary hangman, *William Marwood* (1820–83). Marwood invented the drop, thus speeding up the execution process by snapping the neck, rather than choking the victim to death]

mary *n.*[1] **1** [early 19C+] (Aus./N.Z.) an Aboriginal native woman; thus pidgin *White mary*, a White woman. **2** [1920s–70s] (S.Afr.) an Indian woman, usu. a fruit or vegetable hawker (cf. SAMMY n.[2]). **3** [1940s+] (S.Afr.) any Black woman, esp. a domestic servant. [generic use of one of the most common of female proper names]

Mary *n.*[2] [1920s+] (US gay) the most popular camp proper name; typically in phr. *get you Mary!* (cf. AGNES; MARY ANN n.[1]). [the commonness of the name, but also offering a touch of Mariolatry]

mary *n.*[3] [1940s] (US drugs) **1** marijuana (cf. AUNT MARY n.[2]). **2** morphine. [(1) trans. of Sp.; (2) simply the initial letter *M*]

Mary! *excl.* **1** [mid-14C+] a general excl. **2** [20C] a clichéd, camp homosexual excl. (cf. MARY n.[2]).

mary and johnny *n.* [1940s+] (drugs) marijuana. [play on Sp. which translates as 'mary' and 'jane']

mary ann *n.*[1] **1** [late 19C+] an effeminate male homosexual (cf. AGNES). **2** [late 19C–1910s] a dressmaker's dummy. [joc. uses of proper name]

mary ann *n.*[2] [20C] **1** a fan. **2** a hand. [rhy. sl.]

mary ann/maryanne *n.*[3] [1920s–50s] (drugs) marijuana (cf. AUNT MARY n.[2]).

mary banger *n.* [20C] an extremely plain, dowdy woman (cf. MARY HICK).

mary blaine/blane *n.* **1** [mid–late 19C] a railway train. **2** [mid-19C–1900s] rain. [rhy. sl.]

mary blaine/blane *v.* [mid–late 19C] to travel by train. [rhy. sl.]

Mary Decker *n.* [1980s] (S.Afr. Black) **1** a black taxi. **2** a fast armoured police vehicle (cf. ZOLA BUDD). [proper name of US athlete *Mary Decker* Slaney (b.1958)]

mary ellen *see* MARY FIST.

mary ellens *n.* [20C] the female breasts. [rhy. sl. *mary ellens* = MELONS]

mary fist/ellen/five-fingers/palm *n.* [1940s+] (US) the hand, as used in male masturbation; thus *married to mary fist*, addicted to masturbation (cf. MISS FIST).

mary frances *n.* [20C] euph. for MOTHERFUCKER. [euph. using the initial letters]

marygold *see* MARIGOLD n.[1].

mary green *n.* [20C] in cards, the queen. [rhy. sl.]

mary hick *n.* [20C] a plain, dowdy woman (cf. MARY BANGER).

mary j. *see* MARY JANE n.²

mary jane *n.*¹ [mid-19C–1930s] the vagina.

mary jane/j./jonas *n.*² [1920s+] (orig. US) marijuana, cannabis (cf. AUNT MARY n.²). [lit. trans. of Sp.]

Maryland farmer *n.* [20C] euph. for MOTHERFUCKER.

Marylebone kick *n.* [mid-19C] a kick to the stomach. [? a speciality of the area's thugs]

marylou *n.* [20C] glue. [rhy. sl.]

mary palm *see* MARY FIST.

mary poppins *n.* [1960s] (US) the female breasts. [joc. use of film title *Mary Poppins* (1964)]

mary walkers *n.* [late 19C] (US) trousers. [Dr *Mary Walker* (1832–1919), US campaigner for rational dress for women who would lecture on her subject wearing men's evening dress]

mary warner *n.* [1930s–70s] (orig. US drugs) marijuana (cf. AUNT MARY n.²). [pron.]

mary weaver *n.* [1930s–70s] (drugs) marijuana (cf. AUNT MARY n.²). [pron.]

mary worthless *n.* [1940s+] (gay) an ageing, unattractive male homosexual. [pun on the camp term MARY n.² + popular US cartoon *Mary Worth*, launched 1938]

mascot *adj.* [1950s+] (W.I. Rasta) used of one who is of inferior status. [the diminutive size of a traditional mascot, e.g. the small boy who parades with a soccer team]

maserati *n.* [1980s+] (drugs) an improvised crack cocaine pipe, using a spark-plug cover and a plastic bottle (cf. LAMBORGHINI). [fig. use of the automobile name]

masers *n.* [1960s+] a *Mase*rati car. [abbr.]

mash *n.*¹ **1** [late 19C–1910s] a person with whom one is infatuated; thus *on the mash*, looking for an opportunity of seduction, *have a mash on*, to make advances towards. **2** [late 19C+] (US) an infatuation, a crush on someone. [MASH v.¹]

mash *n.*² [late 19C+] a dandy. [abbr. MASHER]

mash *n.*³ [1920s+] *mash*ed potatoes, esp. in phr. *sausage and mash*. [abbr.]

mash *n.*⁴ [1920s+] (Aus.) sentimental nonsense. [? MUSH n.¹ (2)]

mash *v.*¹ **1** [late 19C+] (orig. US theatrical) to make oneself attractive to a member of the opposite sex, to flirt with, to succeed in seduction; thus *mashing*, seducing, making advances (cf. MASHED adj.¹). **2** [1950s] (W.I.) to seduce, to rape (cf. MASH THE FAT). **3** [1980s+] (US campus) to kiss, to neck. [? SE *mash*, to crush, to pulp, thus to render 'soft', note Rom. *mash*, to allure, to entice]

mash *v.*² **1** [late 19C+] (US) to beat someone up. **2** [1930s+] to give one what is due; thus *mash it on me*, give it to me, *mash me a fin*, loan me $5. **3** [1930s+] (US Black) to pass over stolen or contraband goods.

mash dog! *excl.* [20C] (W.I.) a general phr. of irritation and dismissal, get out! get out of my way! [Carib.E. *mash*, a call to a dog, meaning go or walk]

mash down *v.* [20C] **1** to apply pressure, to press down on. **2** (W.I. Rasta) to destroy.

mashed/mashed on *adj.*¹ [late 19C–1950s] (US) infatuated, sexually or romantically obsessed (by). [MASH v.¹]

mashed *adj.*² **1** [1940s+] (US) drunk. **2** [1980s] (drugs) under the influence of cannabis. [SE *mashed*, crushed; but Spears (1986) suggests link of (1) to SE *mash*, the basis of whisky]

mashed on *see* MASHED adj.¹

masheen *n.* [18C] (tinker) a cat. [Shelta]

masher *n.* [late 19C+] (US) a man who forces his unwanted attentions on women, a 'lady-killer'; thus *masher blue*, a shade of blue favoured by such men for their waistcoats, *masherdom*, *mashery*, the world of mashers, *mashing*, elegant flirtation. [MASH v.¹]

masher *adj.* [late 19C–1910s] flashy, dandified, fashionable. [MASHER n.]

mashers *n.* [1930s+] (W.I.) cheap shoes, sold initially with rope soles, then with pieces of car tyre. [? they 'mash' the ground]

mashers corners *n.* [late 19C] (society) the opposite prompt (O.P.) and prompt side (P.S.) entrances to the stalls at the Gaiety Theatre, London. [the MASHERS and STAGE-DOOR JOHNNIES could best ogle the chorus-girls from the front stalls]

mash flat, to *phr.* [1940s] (W.I.) to accelerate a car. [*mashing* the accelerator pedal]

mash it up *v.* [1950s+] (W.I. Rasta) to achieve a huge success.

mash-mash *n.* [1940s] (W.I.) small change. [onomat. for the noise it makes in one's pocket]

mash note *n.* [late 19C+] (US) a love letter. [MASH n.¹ + SE *note*]

mash one's sore toe, to *phr.* [1950s] (W.I.) to embarrass.

mashonisa *n.* [1970s+] (S.Afr. township) a money-lender. [? Zulu *mashonisa*, a cause of one's losing heavily]

mash that! *excl.* [late 19C] be quiet! hold your tongue! [? Fr. *macher*, to chew (on)]

mash the fat, to *phr.* [1970s+] (US Black) to have sexual intercourse.

mash-tub *n.* [19C] a brewer. [note the defunct newspaper the *Morning Advertiser* was known as the 'Morning Mash-tub' because of its brewery interests]

mashugga *see* MESHUGA.

mash up *v.* **1** [late 19C+] (orig. US/W.I.) to destroy, to break, to beat up. **2** [1920s+] (W.I.) to get oneself into trouble. **3** [1920s+] (W.I.) to cause trouble.

mash-up *adj.* [late 19C+] (orig. US/W.I.) badly broken or bent, damaged beyond repair. [MASH UP v. (1)]

mash with *v.* [1980s+] (US campus) to kiss, to neck. [MASH v.¹ (3)]

mashy *adj.* [late 19C] affectionate towards, amorous towards (cf. MASHED adj.¹). [MASH v.¹]

Mas John/Messjohn *n.* [mid-17C–early 19C] a derog. term for a Scot. Presbyterian minister, as opposed to an Anglican or Roman Catholic. [*Mas*, master; the hostility is underlined by the abbr.]

masked man *n.* [1980s+] (US campus) a male homosexual. [? ref. to TV's famous masked lawman, The Lone Ranger]

maskee! *excl.* [mid-19C] (Anglo-Chinese) never mind, it's not important, no matter. [? Port. *mas que*]

mason *n.*¹ [mid-18C] one who acquires goods fraudulently by giving a bill that they do not intend to honour. [the stereotyping of Freemasons as dishonest]

mason/mason line *n.*² [19C+] (US Black) a town's main street, esp. when it delineates the line between the Black and White communities. [proper name *Mason-Dixon line*, dividing the US north and south along the 40th parallel]

masonics *n.* [late 19C] (society) secrets. [Freemasonry, 'not that there are either secrets or rites in Freemasonry – at all events in England – where combined secrets are neither wanted nor expected' (Ware)]

mason line *see* MASON n.²

masonry *n.* [late 19C] secret signs and passwords. [the traditional image of 'secretive' Freemasons]

mason's maund *n.* [late 17C–early 19C] a fake sore, placed above the elbow and counterfeiting a broken arm (cf. FOOTMAN'S MAUND). [SE *mason* + MAUND n. (2)]

ma's plaster *n.* [20C] (Irish) a whiner, a whinger. [one who needs a fig. *plaster* from their *ma*, i.e. mother]

mass *n.* [1990s] (W.I./UK Black teen) money, currency. [ety. unknown]

massacree/massacrate *adj.* [1910s] (Irish) a general term of abuse, e.g. *that massacree dog!* [SE *massacre*]

massacree v. [18C–1920s] (US) to massacre, murder, victimize or cruelly humiliate.

massa-day n. [1960s+] (W.I.) **1** the era of slavery. **2** the imperial era between slavery and W.I. independence. [coined by Guyn. P.M. Eric Williams (1911–81) in 1961: 'Massa is the symbol of a bygone age. Massa Day is a social phenomenon. Massa Day Done denotes a political awakening and a social revolution.' Note Papua/New Guinea Tok Pisin *taim bilong masta*, the era of imperialism]

massage v.[1] [1920s+] (orig. US) **1** to beat, to injure, to kill. **2** of the police, to beat up a suspect during an interrogation.

massage v.[2] **1** [1960s+] to manipulate initially unpalatable facts or figures to create a required positive impression, profit statement etc. **2** [1970s+] to flatter, to manipulate someone. [(2) SE phr. *massage someone's ego*]

massage the frankfurter, to phr. [1950s] (Aus.) to masturbate (cf. ACCOST THE OSCAR MEYER).

massage the one-eyed monk, to phr. [1990s] to masturbate (cf. BANG THE BISHOP).

massa planter n. [1960s–70s] (US Black) one's boss, esp. when White. [ironic use of 19C *massa*, master]

mass coolies adj. [1990s] (US teen) very cool. [MASS(IVE) adj. + COOL adj.[3]]

Massey-Harris n. [20C] (Aus./Can.) cheese. [pun on the *Massey-Harris* self-binder (an early combine harvester); the ref. is to the 'binding' effects of cheese on the digestion]

massive n. [1980s+] (W.I./UK Black teen) a group of people who stick together and have shared social interests, such as a dance-hall crowd; often specified by a geographical name, e.g. the *Peckham massive*, the *Tottenham massive* (cf. CREW).

massive adj. [1950s+] (orig. W.I. Rasta) **1** respected; ext. as *massive large* for emphasis. **2** a general term of great approval.

mass tom n. [1940s] (W.I.) a shark. [lit. 'master tom'; thus joc. use of proper name]

Ma State n. [1900s–50s] (Aus.) New South Wales; thus *ma stater*, a native of New South Wales. [*ma*, mother; thus the 'mother state'. New South Wales is the oldest Aus. state]

master adj. [20C] (US Black) the absolute best.

master bacon v. [1990s] to masturbate. [pron.]

master blaster n. [1980s+] (drugs) a large amount of freebase cocaine. [MASTER + BLAST v.[4] (3)]

mastercan n. [19C] a chamberpot. [SE *master* + CAN n.[1] (1)]

master-dog n. [20C] (US Black) the supreme authoritarian figure (usu. a White man) within an institutional hierarchy.

Master John Goodfellow/Thursday n. [19C] the penis. [generic use of *John* + SE *goodfellow*, a jovial companion; ety. of *Thursday* unknown]

master member n. [19C] the penis (cf. DEAREST MEMBER).

master of ceremonies n.[1] [mid-17C] as a tavern term, 'he that stands upon his strength, and begins new healths'; i.e. gets up and proposes a succession of toasts (*The English Liberal Science* ... , 1650).

master of ceremonies n.[2] [19C] the penis.

master of misrule n. [mid-17C] an uproarious drunkard, i.e. 'He that flings Cushions, Napkins, and Trenchers about the room' (*The English Liberal Science* ... , 1650).

master of the black art n. [16C] any beggar, irrespective of their 'speciality'.

master of the mint n. [late 18C–early 19C] a gardener. [a pun on the SE *herb*]

master of the novelties n. [mid-19C] a playful drunkard, i.e. 'he that is first to begin new frolicks' (*The English Liberal Science* ... , 1650).

master of the rolls n. [late 18C–early 19C] a baker. [pun]

master of the wardrobe n. [late 18C–early 19C] one who pawns their clothes to get money for drink. [pun]

masterpiece n. [18C] the vagina. [joc. use of SE + pun on SE *master* + *piece*/PIECE n.[1]]

masterpiece of night work n. [late 19C] a good-looking prostitute.

Master Reynard n. [19C] the penis. [SE *Reynard*, a nickname for a fox; like the animal the penis 'gets into' a NEST n.[1]]

mat n.[1] *see* MOT n.

mat n.[2] *see* DOORMAT.

mat n.[3] [1910s–30s] (US) a *matinée* performance. [abbr.]

mat n.[4] [1940s] **1** (US) a prostitute or sexually promiscuous woman. **2** (US Black) one's regular sweetheart, one's wife. [abbr. SE *mattress*]

match *see* MATCHBOX n.[2].

matchbox n.[1] **1** [1920s+] a very small house. **2** [1980s+] (Und.) an easily robbed target. [both are flimsy; (1) is also small]

matchbox/match n.[2] [1950s+] (US drugs) **1** $10 worth of marijuana, orig. an actual matchbox full, by 1990s more like a thimbleful. **2** approx. 10g (½oz) of marijuana (cf. LID n.[4]).

matchstick n. [1950s+] a nickname for a very thin person; thus *matchstick with the wood shaved off*, an exceptionally thin person.

mate n. **1** [mid-19C+] (orig. Aus.) a general term of address to a man, usu. by a man (cf. BUSTER n.[8]). **2** [late 19C+] a friend; thus (Aus.) *mate up*, to befriend. [orig. used as sailor's jargon]

mateloe *see* MATLOW.

matelot n. [20C] (orig. RN) a sailor (cf. MATLOW). [Fr. *matelot*, a sailor]

mater n. [mid–late 19C] (usu. juv.) one's mother, often as *the mater* (cf. PATER). [Lat. *mater*, mother]

materials n. [late 19C] (Irish) the ingredients of a whisky punch.

maternal n. [mid-19C] one's mother (cf. GOVERNOR). [? abbr. SE *maternal parent*]

matey/maty n.[1] [early 19C+] a pal, a chum, a companion, often as a term of address.

matey/maty n.[2] [mid-19C] a hospital or usu. workhouse matron. [abbr.]

matey/maty adj. [early 19C+] friendly. [MATEY n.[1]]

'matic n. [1990s] (W.I./UK Black teen) an auto*matic* weapon. [abbr.]

-matic sfx. [1980s+] (US campus) a sfx. indicating intensity or repetition, e.g. *cram-o-matic*.

matie n. [20C] (S.Afr.) a student at Stellenbosch University in the Western Cape (cf. IKEY n.[2]). [MAAT]

matilda n. [late 19C+] (Aus.) a tramp's pack; thus *matilda up*, carrying a pack, *matilda-bearer*, *matilda-carrier*, *matilda-hawker*, *matilda-lumper*, *matilda-man*, *matilda-waltzer*, a vagrant (cf. CARRY MATILDA; WALTZ MATILDA).

matineers n. [late 19C] frequenters of theatrical matinées.

matlow/mateloe n. [20C] a sailor (cf. MATELOT). [Fr. *matelot*, a sailor]

mat-man n. [1920s+] (orig. US) a wrestler. [the SE *mat* on which he fights]

matric n. [1950s+] (S.Afr.) the last year (class 10) of school, the *matric*ulation class. [abbr.]

matriculate v. [1970s] (US campus) to start on a trip.

matrimonial n. [19C] sexual intercourse in the 'missionary position'. [seen as the usual practice of married couples]

matrimonial peacemaker n. [late 18C–early 19C] the penis (cf. WIFE'S BEST FRIEND).

matrimony n. [19C] a mixture of two sorts of food or drink. [lit. a 'marriage']

matsakaw n. [1970s] (drugs) heroin. [ety. unknown]

matter of form phr. [early 19C] a merely formal affair, a point of ordinary routine, therefore of no particular importance. [SE *matter of form*, a formal, set procedure]

matter will keep cold, the *phr.* [late 17C–early 18C] said of something that can be left unresolved for a while (cf. PUT ON ICE).

mattress *n.*[1] (US) **1** [1920s] a beard. **2** [1930s] pubic hair.

mattress *n.*[2] [1960s+] (US) a woman as a sexual partner (cf. MAT n.[4]; MATTRESSBACK). [the man 'lies' on her]

mattressback *n.* [1960s+] (US) a sexually promiscuous woman (cf. MAT n.[4]; MATTRESS n.[2]).

mattress-muncher *n.* [1960s+] (orig. Aus.) a passive homosexual man (cf. PILLOW-BITER). [his response to anal intercourse]

mattress polo *n.* [1930s–60s] (US) sexual intercourse.

maty *see* MATEY.

maud/maude *n.* [1940s+] **1** a male prostitute. **2** a dowdy male homosexual (cf. AGNES). [play on the female proper name]

maud and ruth *n.* [1970s] the truth. [rhy. sl.]

mauger/mauga/maugre/mawgre *adj.* [20C] (W.I.) thin, scrawny. [Du. *mager*, lean or Fr. *maigre*, thin]

Maui wauie/wowie *n.* [1970s+] (US drugs) potent marijuana from Hawaii. [*Maui*, a Hawaiian island + SE *wow!*, an excl. of pleasure or astonishment]

maul *v.* [late 19C; 1940s+] (US campus) to have a very passionate petting session.

maul and wedges *n.* [mid-19C] (US) one's possessions, one's goods. [SE *maul*, a hammer]

mauldy *adj.* [1910s–20s] (Aus.) left-handed. [? MAULEY n. (1)]

mauled *adj.* [late 17C–mid-19C] very drunk (cf. BASTED).

mauler *n.* **1** [early 19C+] the hand, the fist. **2** [early 19C+] brass knuckles. **3** [1920s–30s] (US) a boxer. [SE *maul*, to handle roughly]

mauley/maulie/mawley/morley *n.* **1** [late 18C–1950s] the hand (cf. MAULER). **2** [mid-19C] a finger, usu. in pl. **3** [mid-19C+] a signature. **4** [mid-19C+] handwriting. [SE *maul*, to handle roughly or Shelta *malya*, ult. transposition of Gaelic *lamh*, hand]

mau-mau *v.* [1960s–70s] (US) of Black or minority activists, to harass the White establishment for their community's gain, esp. by taking advantage of liberal guilt. [proper name *Mau-Mau*, Kenyan guerrillas of 1950s who spearheaded the drive to free their nation from British rule. The term is best-known in the title of Tom Wolfe's essay *Mau-Mauing the Flak-Catchers* (1970)]

mauming and glauming *phr.* [mid-18C] pawing in an amorous or sexual manner. [? SE *maul* + Scot. *glaum*, to snatch at]

maund *n.* [16C] (Und.) **1** begging. **2** a specific begging ruse, e.g. a fake sore (cf. FOOTMAN'S MAUND; MASON'S MAUND). [MAUND v.]

maund/maund it/mawnd *v.* [16C–early 19C] (Und.) to ask or require. [? Fr. *mendier/quémendier*, to beg, ult. Lat. *mendicus*, a beggar, the root of the SE *mendicant*. Note Rom. *mang*, to beg]

maund abram *v.* [16C] to beg while posing as a madman. [MAUND v. + ABRAM adj.]

maunder *n.* [late 17C–mid-19C] a beggar. [MAUND v.]

maunder *v.* [early 17C–late 18C] to beg; thus *maunder on the fly*, to beg in the streets, *maundering*, begging, prone to begging. [MAUND v.]

maundering broth *n.* [late 18C–early 19C] a scolding (cf. IN THE SOUP). [dial. *maunder*, to grumble, to threaten]

maunding-cove *n.* [early 17C–late 18C] a beggar. [MAUND v. + COVE]

maund it *see* MAUND v.

maurice *n.* [1970s] (US Black) a policeman. [ety. unknown; ? anecdotal]

maux *see* MAWKES.

maven/mayvin *n.* [1950s+] (US) an expert, a connoisseur. [Heb. *mavin*, understanding]

maw *n.* [mid-19C+] **1** the mouth. **2** the vagina (cf. BLACK HOLE n.[1]). [SE *maw*, an animal's stomach, 20C use mainly US Black]

maw-dicker *n.* [1960s+] (US, mainly southwest) a general term of extreme dislike (cf. MOTHERFUCKER). [dial. *maw*, mother + DICK v.[2]]

mawgabraw! *excl.* [20C] (Irish) a general excl. of abuse, usu. delivered as a parting shot, i.e. go to hell! [Irish *magh go brách*, the field for ever]

mawgre *see* MAUGER.

mawkes/maux *n.* [late 16C–early 19C] **1** a prostitute. **2** a slatternly woman. [MALKIN]

mawkin *n.* [20C] (Ulster) a simpleton. [Scot. *mawkin*, a half-grown girl]

mawkish *adj.* [early 18C] slatternly. [MAWKES]

mawley *see* MAULEY.

mawnd *see* MAUND v.

maw-wallop *n.* [late 18C–early 19C] a disgusting dish of food, enough to make the eater vomit. [SE *maw*, stomach + *wallop*, a churning and bubbling, a blow]

maw-wormy *adj.* [mid–late 19C] **1** hypocritical. **2** pessimistic, fault-finding, nagging. [proper name *Mawworm*, a character who epitomized hypocrisy, in Bickerstaffe's play *The Hypocrite* (1769), ult. *maw-worm*, a stomach worm]

max *n.* **1** [early–mid-19C] gin, esp. high-quality gin. **2** [mid–late 19C; 1960s+] (US campus) the maximum score or achievement in an examination, the student who achieves this. **3** [1940s+] (US Und.) the maximum sentence for an offence. **4** [1960s+] (US) a maximum security jail. **5** [1970s] (US campus) the highest level of degree. **6** [1990s] (drugs) gamma hydroxy butyrate, GBH, dissolved in water and mixed with amphetamines. [all uses of SE *maximum*]

max/maximum *adj.* [1970s+] (US) superlative, outstanding.

max *v.* **1** [mid-19C–1930s] (US campus) to achieve a maximum score or grade in an examination. **2** [1970s+] to serve the full length of a jail sentence. **3** [1970s+] to give one's maximum effort. **4** [1970s+] (US) to exceed the limit (cf. MAXED). **5** [1970s+] (US Black/campus) to have a very good time (cf. MAX AND RELAX; MAX OUT v.[2]).

max/maximum *adv.* [1970s+] (US) extremely, at the maximum, at most.

max and relax, to *phr.* [1980s+] (US Black/campus) to take life easy, to enjoy oneself; esp. in phr. *maxin' and relaxin'*. [MAX v. (5) + SE *relax*]

maxed *adj.* **1** [19C+] drunk or highly intoxicated (cf. ABOUT RIGHT adj.[1]; MAXED OUT). **2** [1980s+] (US) utterly exhausted, drained of energy. **3** [1980s+] (US) full to maximum capacity.

maxed out *adj.* [1970s+] very drunk or highly intoxicated (cf. ABOUT RIGHT adj.[1]). [MAX OUT v.[2]]

Max Factor *n.* [20C] (esp. fig.) an actor, i.e. one who fakes illness or injury, a footballer who 'dives' etc. [rhy. sl.; brandname *Max Factor*, a leading producer of cosmetics and make-up]

max fuckter *n.* [1950s–60s] (gay) make-up. [brandname *Max Factor*, a leading producer of cosmetics]

maxi/maxy *n.* [1940s+] (W.I.) one shilling (5p). [abbr. SE *maximum*; ? an obsolete maximum fare on a form of public transport]

maxie *n.* [mid-19C] (Scot.) a major mistake, a serious blunder. [Lat. *maximus*, the greatest]

maximum *see* MAX adj., adv.

maxing *n.* [1970s+] relaxing. [MAX AND RELAX; MAX OUT v.[2] (3)]

Max Miller *n.* [20C] a pillow. [rhy. sl. Cockney pron. 'piller'; ult. comedian *Max Miller* (1895–1963)]

max out *v.*[1] [1960s+] (US prison) to complete one's sentence without gaining any remission for good behaviour. [MAX v. (2)]

max out v.² **1** [1970s+] to indulge to extremes. **2** [1980s+] (US) to succeed. **3** [1980s+] to relax. [MAX v. (5)]

max walls n. [20C] the testicles. [rhy. sl. *max walls* = BALLS n.¹ (1); ult. comedian *Max Wall* (1908–90)]

Maxwell House n. [1960s+] a mouse. [rhy. sl., the popular brand of instant coffee]

maxy *see* MAXI.

mayate n. [20C] (US) a Black person. [? Sp.]

May bees don't fly all the year long *phr.* [mid-18C+] a response to someone who continually uses the statement *it may be* ... to preface their statements.

Maybelline waste n. [1990s] (US campus) a disappointing social event. [*Maybelline*, a brandname of cosmetics; i.e. it was not worth getting made-up]

Mayfair mercenary n. [1980s] a young woman whose indeterminate class is transcended by her beauty and her ambition to climb in society, often the 'mistress', 'girlfriend' or 'companion' of a successful, wealthy man (cf. HOORAY HENRY). [*Mayfair*, an exclusive area of London + SE *mercenary*, coined in *Harpers & Queen* c.1980]

may I be shot!/shot if ...! *excl.* [mid-19C+] a general oath.

may I die! *excl.* [18C] a general oath.

may I gasp my last!/last if ...! *phr.* [late 19C–1930s] a general oath intended to emphasize the truth of one's statements.

may I never do an ill turn! *excl.* [18C] a general excl. of emphasis.

maymay-lippy *adj.* [20C] (W.I. Antg.) talkative, gossipy. [? SE *mama* + LIPPY *adj.*]

ma-yo n. [1970s] (drugs) cannabis. [? Chinese]

mayo n.¹ [1940s+] (drugs) cocaine, heroin. [? misreading of MA-YO]

mayo n.² [1950s+] (orig. US) mayonnaise. [abbr.]

maypop n. [1980s+] (US Black) a very worn tyre. [pun. on SE *may pop*/US dial. *maypop*, the passion flower]

Maytag n. [1970s+] (US prison) a weak male prisoner who is abused by other inmates, forced to do their menial chores and poss. raped. [the *Maytag* brand of home appliances]

mayvin *see* MAVEN.

may your chooks turn into emus and kick your shit-house down *phr.* [1980s+] (Aus.) used to convey one's extreme annoyance with another's actions or words.

may your prick and purse/your purse never fail you *phr.* [early 18C–mid-19C] a popular toast.

may your rabbits flourish *phr.* [1920s] (Aus.) a phr. of supposed goodwill, though rabbits are one of Australia's most loathed pests.

mazard/mazzard n. **1** [16C–19C] a drinking vessel. **2** [16C–19C] the head. **3** [16C–19C] the face. **4** [early 19C] (Anglo-Irish) the 'head' of a coin. [SE *mazer*, a hard wood (usu. but not invariably maple) used as a material for drinking cups]

mazard/mazzard v. [early 17C] to hit on the head. [MAZARD n. (2)]

mazarine n. [late 18C] a common councilman of London. [the *mazarine* (a deep rich blue) gown he wore]

mazawattee n. [20C] a potty. [rhy. sl.]

Mazda Lane n. [1920s–50s] (US) Broadway, New York. [*Mazda*, a major brand of lightbulb; coined by columnist Walter Winchell (1897–1972)]

mazeh/mazehette n. [1980s+] (US campus) a very attractive man or woman. [Heb. *mah ze?*, what is this?]

mazel/muzzle n. [20C] good luck. [synon. Yid.]

Mazola party n. [1960s+] (US) a party of two or more people who cover their bodies in vegetable oil to engage in sexual activity and intercourse. [*Mazola*, a brand of vegetable oil + SE *party*]

mazoo/mazoola n. [1940s–60s] (US) money. [abbr. MAZUMA]

mazoom n. [1900s–20s] (US) money. [abbr. MAZUMA]

mazuma n. [late 19C+] money (cf. MAZUZU). [Yid., ult. Heb. *mazuma*, prepared, ready]

mazuzu n. [1960s–70s] (S.Afr. township) money. [? an African word or var. on MAZUMA]

mazzard *see* MAZARD.

m.b. n. [1930s+] (Aus.) *M*elbourne *B*itter; thus *suffer from m.b.*, to be drunk. [abbr. brandname]

m.b. coat n. [mid-19C] a long coat worn by clergymen (cf. M.B. WAISTCOAT). [abbr. *m*ark of the *b*east; the 'beast' in this context was Popery]

mbongo n. [1910s+] (S.Afr.) a political stooge or apologist, a 'yes-man'. [Nguni *imbongi*, a praise-singer]

m.b. waistcoat n. [mid-19C] a kind of waistcoat with no opening in front, worn by Anglican clergymen (cf. M.B. COAT). [orig. worn by tractarians only, c.1840, but later adopted by other clergymen]

M.C./emcee n. [1980s+] (orig. US Black) **1** the lead singer of a RAP band; thus *M.C. Noise* (cf. RAP n.⁵). **2** one who is in charge, a leader, a boss. [lit. *m*aster of *c*eremonies, orig. 1930s]

m.c. *adj.* [1990s] middle class (cf. L.C.).

m.c.p. n. [1970s+] male chauvinist pig. [abbr.; much beloved by early 1960s–70s feminists but now obs. apart from among tabloid journalists and very late arrivals]

mc2 *adj.* [1980s+] (US campus) overly studious, over-devoted to books and uninterested in parties, drink, drugs and other forms of pleasure. [the shorthand for Einstein's theory of relativity + pun on SQUARE adj. (2)]

m.d./M.D. n. [1970s] (US campus) cheap liquor. [abbr. MAD DOG n.¹ (2)/*Mo*gen *D*avid, a cheap wine]

m.d.g. *phr.* [1980s+] (US campus) strong physical attraction. [abbr. *m*utual *d*esire to *g*rope]

m.d.l. n. [1990s] a person, usu. a woman, who dresses younger than her years. [abbr. MUTTON DRESSED AS LAMB]

me *prn.* [1990s] used at the end of a sentence to indicate preference, e.g. *I like lard, me.*

...me *phr.* [1950s+] (orig. US) used with a relevant n. to denote an imperative, e.g. *pen me*, hand me a pen. [the *locus classicus* comes in the film *The Sweet Smell of Success* (1957) where the venal columnist J.J. Hunsecker confirms his absolute power over the venal, scrabbling press agent Sidney Falco with the command, *Match me, Sidney*, i.e. Light my cigarette]

meadow mayonnaise n. [1930s+] (Aus.) nonsense, rubbish. [euph. pun on BULLSHIT n.]

meadow muffin n. [1970s+] (US) a lump of manure (cf. ALLEY APPLE n.²).

mealer n. [late 19C] **1** one who pledges to drink alcohol only with meals. **2** one who has meals at one place but lives elsewhere, a 'table-boarder'.

mealie/mealie-muncher n. [1970s] (S.Afr.) an Afrikaner. [S.Afr.E. *mealie*, maize + SE *muncher*]

meal-mouth n. [late 17C–18C] one who demands money, but in a sly, sheepish manner. [SE *mealy-mouth*, one who fears to speak their mind]

meals on wheels n. [1960s+] (US gay) teenagers cruising the streets in their cars.

meal ticket n. [late 19C+] (orig. US) **1** anyone good for the price of a meal. **2** anyone who provides money or a livelihood for someone else, who thus needs to make less effort (cf. MEAT TICKET).

mealy-mouth n. [1930s–40s] (US) a customer in a café or restaurant who continually makes complaints. [SE + pun on *meal*]

mealy-mouth v. [early 17C+] to speak in a duplicitous, deceptive, insincere manner. [SE *mealy*, soft-spoken, one who 'minces' matters, ult. SE *meal*, powder]

mean *adj.* **1** [early 19C+] (US) of people and things, poor in quality or condition, comparatively worthless (cf. MEAN WHITE). **2** [mid-19C–1910s] (US) unwell, in low spirits. **3** [late 19C+] (US) aggressive, unpleasant. **4** [late 19C+] (orig. US) pettily unpleasant or disobliging; thus *feel mean*, to feel ashamed of one's unpleasant conduct. **5** [1910s+] (orig. US) very good, very clever, adroit, with implications of 'so good it's unfair', on the 'outlaw' premise of bad = good (cf. AWFUL adj.). **6** [1930s+] (US Black) exceptionally attractive or stylish. **7** [1980s+] (drugs) either very high or very poor in quality.

mean as a louse *phr.* [late 19C] extremely mean. [SE *mean*]

mean as catshit and twice as nasty *see* MEAN AS PIGSHIT AND TWICE AS NASTY.

mean as/meaner than dirt *phr.* [19C] (US) very mean, very unpleasant to others. [MEAN adj. (4)]

mean as pigshit/catshit and twice as nasty *phr.* [1930s+] extremely ungenerous (cf. MEANER THAN CATSHIT). [SE *mean*]

mean as Pusley *phr.* [late 19C] (US) very cruel. [MEAN adj. (3) + ? anecdotal ref. to an unknown *Pusley*]

mean business, to *phr.* [mid-19C+] to be totally committed, to be utterly earnest.

me-and-you *n.[1]* [20C] **1** (bingo) the number two (cf. DIRTY OLD JEW). **2** sexual intercourse. [rhy. sl.; (2) *me and you* = SCREW n.[1] (2)]

me-and-you *n.[2]* [1930s–40s] a menu. [a play on words rather than rhy. sl.]

me and you *phr.* [1940s–50s] (US Black) an invitation to start fighting; esp. in phr. *it's gonna be me and you.*

mean enough to kill his grandmother *phr.* [20C] (US) a phr. describing a notably unpleasant person; variations include *push his grandmother downstairs, rob his grandmother's grave, steal the pennies off his grandmother's eyes, take the fillings out of his grandmother's teeth.* [MEAN adj. (3)]

mean enough to steal acorns from a blind hog *phr.* [late 19C] (US Black) possessing the characteristics of 'poor White trash', i.e. stupid, rustic, unsophisticated. [MEAN adj. (3)]

meaner than catshit/cat dirt/cat dung/cat manure/cat's tail *phr.* [20C] (US) description of an notably unpleasant person. [MEAN adj. (3)]

meaner than dirt *see* MEAN AS DIRT.

mean green *n.* [1980s] (drugs) phencyclidine (cf. ACE n.[3]). [SAmE *mean*/MEAN adj. (7) + *green*, the colour of the marijuana or parsley with which the drug is often mixed]

mean-hair *adj.* [1960s+] (gay) unpleasant, cruel. [SAmE *mean* + fig. use of *hair*]

meanie *n.* [1930s+] a spoilsport (cf. BLUE MEANIE). [MEAN adj. (3)]

mean machine *n.* [1980s+] (US) a fast or stylish car. [MEAN adj. (6) + MACHINE n.[2] (2)]

mean-mouth *v.* [1960s+] (US) to attack verbally, to slander (cf. BADMOUTH v.).

mean white *n.* [late 19C] (US Black) an extremely unpleasant White person (cf. MEAN ENOUGH TO STEAL ACORNS FROM A BLIND HOG).

meany *n.* [1920s+] (usu. juv.) a mean, tight-fisted person. [SE *mean*]

measle *v.* [20C] (Ulster) to cause red blotches on one's legs by sitting too close to the fire. [Du. *maschelen*, red blotches caused in this way]

measles *n.[1]* [mid-19C] a meat stew. [supposed resemblance of the meat to spotty flesh; note contemp. US Navy *measles*, salt pork]

measles *n.[2]* [mid-19C] venereal disease, esp. syphilis. [syphilis can also produce a rash]

measly *adj.* [mid-19C+] contemptible, petty, miserable-looking. [SE *measles*]

measure *v.* [1900s–40s] (US Und.) to strike hard (cf. MEASURE OUT). [? SE *measure* out blows]

measure a twig, to *phr.* [late 17C–mid-19C] to do something absurd. [the impossibility of measuring something so gnarled and irregular as a twig]

measured for a new overcoat, to be *phr.* [1930s–40s] (US) to be buried. [ref. is to a WOODEN OVERCOAT]

measured for a new umbrella, to be *phr.* [late 19C] (US) **1** to appear in new but ill-fitting clothes. **2** to pursue a policy of doubtful wisdom. [joc./fig. uses of SE]

measure out *v.* [late 19C] to knock down. [SE *measure one's length*, to fall prostrate]

measures *see* MEDZERS.

measure someone's dick, to *phr.* [1960s+] to put someone under suspicion, to check records on a suspect. [SE *measure* + DICK n.[5] (1)]

meat *n.* **1** [late 16C+] a body, usu. a woman's, as an object of sexual pleasure; thus *fond of meat*, amorously inclined. **2** [late 16C–18C; 20C] the penis (cf. BACON n.[1]). **3** [late 16C+] the vagina (cf. BACON SANDWICH). **4** [18C–1920s] a prostitute; thus *fresh meat*, a novice prostitute, *raw meat*, a woman *in flagrante delicto*, the *price of meat*, the cost of a prostitute. **5** [mid-19C+] (orig. US) one's body or flesh. **6** [mid-19C+] prey, as in *he's my meat* referring to a potential victim (cf. DEAD MEAT). **7** [late 19C+] (orig. US) a person of another race as an object of sexual gratification, constructed with a colour; thus *dark meat, White meat*. **8** [late 19C+] (orig. US) a person who fits the bill, meets one's needs. **9** [1900s–50s] (US) a corpse (cf. MEAT HOUSE). **10** [1950s+] (US) an inferior person, poss. physically robust but mindless or gullible, thus often used to describe sportsmen. **11** [1990s] (N.Z.) a sporty, macho man, who places physical development above intelligence.

meat and drink *n.* **1** [19C] drunken love-making. **2** [late 19C] (W.I.) strong drink in general, but spec. liquor thickened with egg yolks.

meat and two veg *n.* [1990s] the penis and testicles (cf. MEAT; OKRA AND PRUNES; THREE-PIECE SET; WATCH AND SEALS).

meat and two veg *phr.* [20C] plain, unadorned, 'no-frills'. [the stereotypically basic dish, roast meat, potatoes and cabbage]

meat axe *n.* (US) **1** [early–mid-19C] used in similes, e.g. *savage as a meat axe*. **2** [1970s] the penis (cf. ARSE-OPENER; BACON BAZOOKA).

meat axe *n.* [1940s+] (Aus./N.Z.) an eccentric, a mad person. [backform. f. MAD AS A MEAT-AXE]

meatbag *n.* [19C] the stomach (cf. BREAD-BAG).

meatball *n.[1]* **1** [1930s+] (US) an Italian. **2** [1930s+] (US) a stupid person. **3** [1950s+] (US) a prostitute's customer. [the stereotyped partiality of Italians for the dish; (2) and (3) are fig. ext. + ref. to MEATHEAD]

meatball *n.[2]* [1940s+] (US Und.) a minor or false criminal charge. [ety. unknown; ? the commonness, thus unimportance of the food]

meatball *adj.[1]* [1940s+] (US Und.) used of a criminal charge for a petty crime. [MEATBALL n.[2]]

meatball *adj.[2]* [1960s] (US) stupid. [MEATBALL n.[1] (2)]

meatbeater *n.* [1990s] one who masturbates excessively; thus a general term of abuse. [BEAT ONE'S MEAT]

meatbrain *n.* [1980s+] (orig. US) a fool (cf. BAKEBRAIN; BEEF-BRAIN).

meat cart/crate *n.* [1930s] (US) a hearse (cf. COLD MEAT CART).

meat-cleaver *n.* [20C] the penis (cf. ARSE-OPENER; BACON BAZOOKA; MARROWBONE AND CLEAVER).

meat crate *see* MEAT CART.

meat curtains *n.* [1990s] the female vaginal lips or *labia majora* (cf. BACON SANDWICH).

meat-drink-washing-and-lodging *n.* [early–mid-18C] gin. [its image as a universal panacea]

meat-eater *n.* [1970s+] (US Und.) a police officer who, not content with the payoffs, bribes and perks that are freely offered, actively compels people to offer him such monies (cf. GRASS-EATER).

meater *n.* [late 19C] a coward. ['said of a dog who only bites meat, that is to say, one who will not fight' (Ware)]

meat fancier's *n.* [19C] a brothel (cf. BUTTOCKING SHOP). [MEAT n. (1) + SE *fancier*]

meat-flasher *n.* [late 19C–1910s] an exhibitionist, one who exposes themself indecently; thus *meat-flashing*, exhibitionism. [MEAT n. (2) + SE *flasher*]

meat fosh *n.* [late 19C] hash, stew. [var. on FISH-FOSH]

meat grinder *n.* (US) **1** [1940s–50s] a car with a loud engine. **2** [1950s+] any tough situation or place in which an elimination process is being carried out, such as training.

meathead *n.* [1910s+] (US) **1** a stupid person. **2** a general term of abuse; thus *meat-headed*, foolish (cf. BEEF-BRAIN). [SE *meat* + sfx. -HEAD (1), implying that solid flesh, rather than brains, occupies one's skull]

meathook *n.* **1** [mid–late 19C] a curl on the temple, then fashionable among London cockneys; thus *meathooks*, curls in general (cf. AGGERAWATOR). **2** [1910s+] (Aus./US) the arm. **3** [1970s] (US) the penis.

meathooks *n.* [1910s+] (US/Aus.) the fingers, the hands.

meathound *n.* **1** [1930s–60s] (US) a lecher. **2** [1960s] (US Black) one who indulges in oral sex (cf. CANNIBAL n.²). [MEAT n. (1) + sfx. -HOUND; they EAT v.³ their partner]

meat house *n.* **1** [late 19C–1960s] a brothel (cf. ACCOMMODATION HOUSE; BUTTOCKING SHOP). **2** [1930s] (US police) a morgue. [MEAT n. (1), (9) + HOUSE n.¹]

meat injection *n.* [1980s+] (US) an act of intromission of the penis (cf. BEEF INJECTION). [MEAT n. (2) + SE *injection*]

meat-in-the-pot *n.* [mid-19C+] (US, mainly West.) a rifle, a shotgun, a revolver. [its use in obtaining food]

meat lance/spear/stick *n.* [1970s+] (US) the penis (cf. BACON BAZOOKA). [MEAT n. (2) + SE *lance/spear/stick*]

meat market *n.¹* **1** [late 19C+] a rendezvous for prostitutes of either sex. **2** [1950s+] anywhere that people gather for the primary purpose of finding sexual partners, often used in universities to describe first-year parties. **3** [1970s+] (US) any situation or place where people are regarded as commodities, such as a recruiting agency or a modelling agency. [MEAT n. (1); in (2) note synon. 1910s US *meet market*]

meat market *n.²* [late 19C+] the female breasts. [MEAT n. (1)]

meat-merchant *n.* [late 19C] a prostitute (cf. MEAT-MONGER). [MEAT n. (3)]

meat-monger *n.* [late 18C–19C] a womanizer, a philanderer (cf. MEAT-MERCHANT). [MEAT n. (2) + SE *monger*]

meat pie *n.* [20C] **1** a fly. **2** a trouser fly. [rhy. sl.]

meat pie bookie *n.* [1910s–20s] (Aus.) a small-time bookmaker. [the cheapness of *meat pies*]

meat puppet *n.* (US) **1** [1980s+] a gullible person. **2** [1990s] the penis. [MEAT n. (6), (2) + SE *puppet*, both 'jump up and down']

meat rack *n.* [1950s+] (orig. gay) a place, such as a bar or a particular street, where homosexuals display their charms to potential customers. After the 'singles bar' explosion of the 1970s, the term was extended to heterosexuality. [pun on SE/ MEAT n. (1), (2)]

meat/money shot *n.* [1960s+] in pornographic still or moving pictures, a close-up of the genitalia, male or female. [MEAT n. (2), (3)/SE *money* + SE *shot*; money refers to the commercial potential of such shots + phr. ON THE MONEY]

meat spear/stick *see* MEAT LANCE.

meat ticket *n.* [1930s] **1** anyone good for the price of a meal.

2 anyone who provides money or a livelihood for someone else, who thus needs to make less effort. [var. on MEAL TICKET]

meat tool *n.* [1960s+] (US) the penis. [MEAT n. (2) + TOOL n. (2)]

meat trap *n.* [mid–late 19C] (US) the mouth.

meat wagon *n.* **1** [1920s+] (US) an ambulance. **2** [1940s+] a vehicle used for conveying prisoners to and from court, police stations, prisons etc, a general police van. **3** [1940s+] (US) a hearse. [MEAT + SE *wagon*]

meat water *n.* [1940s+] (W.I.) stock, soup.

meat whistle *n.* [1940s+] (US) the penis, esp. as an object of fellatio.

meat-works *n.* [1940s] (Aus.) a brothel. [MEAT n. (3) + SE *works*]

meaty *adj.* [early 19C+] sexually attractive. [MEAT n. (1)]

mebbe *adv.* [mid-19C+] maybe. [mispron.]

mec *see* MAKE n.¹.

meccano set *n.* [1950s] (N.Z. prison) the portable, silver-painted, steel gallows, moved and erected as and when required. [*Meccano*, a popular construction kit used by children]

mech *n.* [1950s+] (orig. RAF) a mechanic. [abbr.]

mechanic *n.* **1** [20C] (orig. US) a professional cheat at cards or dice (cf. ARTIST n.¹). **2** [20C] any notably successful player. **3** [20C] (W.I.) a trick, a contrivance, usu. involving some form of physical activity. **4** [1940s–70s] (US Und.) a pickpocket or safe-breaker. **5** [1970s+] a hired killer.

mechanical digger *n.* [20C] a derog. term for a Black person. [rhy. sl. *mechanical digger* = NIGGER]

mechanics' avenue/alley/street *n.* [1920s–60s] (US) a poor or run-down part of a town or city. [SE *mechanic*, a manual labourer + SE *avenue/alley/street*]

mechanized dandruff *see* GALLOPING DANDRUFF.

meckem-peckam *adj.* [1940s+] (W.I.) fault-finding, very hard to satisfy. [? SE *make* + *pernickety*]

mecks *n.* [mid–late 19C] wines and spirits. [ety. unknown]

med *n.* **1** [mid-19C+] a medical student; thus [1940s+] *med college*, medical school, *med business*, medical business. **2** [1940s+] a doctor. **3** [1940s+] medicine. **4** [1940s+] medical school.

medal showing! *excl.* [mid-19C+] your fly is undone.

meddle/meddle with *v.* [1970s+] (US campus) **1** to have sexual intercourse. **2** to be intimate, but not spec. on a sexual level. [14C–17C SE *meddle*, to have sexual intercourse]

meddlesome mattie *n.* [1940s+] (US) an interfering, nosy person. [the poem 'Meddlesome Matty' (1804) by Ann Taylor]

meddle with *see* MEDDLE.

meddling duchess *n.* [late 19C] any interfering upper-class woman who interests herself, doubtless on self-proclaimedly philanthropic grounds, in lives that do not concern her.

medic *n.* **1** [17C; mid-19C+] (orig. US) a physician. **2** [early 19C+] (orig. US) a medical student. [mid-16C–late 17C SE]

medical *n.* [early 19C–1900s] a doctor or a student of medicine.

medical Greek *see* MARROWSKYING.

medicine *n.* **1** [mid–late 19C; 1980s+] (US) an intoxicating drink (cf. LOTION; POISON n.¹). **2** [mid-19C+] sexual intercourse. **3** [late 19C–1930s] (US) information, knowledge.

medicine *adj.* [late 19C–1930s] (US) persuasive. [the soothing effects of SE *medicine*]

medicine man *n.* [late 19C+] a doctor, with slight implications of possible quackery. [a joc. play on SE *medicine man*, a magician or shaman among Native Americans]

medicine sharp *n.* [late 19C–1910s] (US) a physician. [SE *medicine* + SHARP n.¹ (2)]

medico *n.* [mid-19C–1950s] **1** a doctor. **2** a medical student. [SE late 17C–mid-19C]

medieval *adj.* [late 19C+] barbaric, illiberal, cruel; thus *phr.* [1990s] *get medieval on one's ass*, to treat with extreme savagery. [the stereotype of the Middle Ages as symptomatic of such excesses; the phr. was coined in the Quentin Tarantino film *Pulp Fiction* (1994)]

medina *n.* [1990s] (US Black/rap music) a nickname for Brooklyn. [? as opposed to Mecca, presumably Manhattan, but note Arab. *medina*, the Arab section of a town]

Mediterranean/Greek back *n.* [1970s+] (Aus.) a supposedly fake illness or incapacity, used to justify malingering, apparently by Italians, Greeks, Yugoslavs and others seen as lazier than 'White' Australians (cf. M.G.A.).

medium *n.*[1] [20C] (Irish) the Irish language. [SE *medium of communication*]

medium *n.*[2] [1950s–70s] (Irish) an indeterminate measure, approx. 0.3l (a half-pint) of beer.

medlar *n.* [late 18C–early 19C] the vagina (cf. APPLE n.[10]).

med-man *n.* 1 [1930s–40s] (US) a quack or a patent *med*icine seller. 2 [1940s+] a doctor. [abbr.; (2) SE *medicine man*]

meds *n.* [1970s+] (US) *med*ication. [abbr.]

medusa *n.* [1990s] (US Black teen) a woman who is beautiful from the neck down. [the mythical Greek goddess *Medusa*, a beautiful woman whose hair was live snakes and whose face turned one to stone]

medza/medzer *see* MADZA.

medzers/measures *n.* (Ling. Fr./Polari) money. [abbr. MADZA CAROON; *measures* is mispron.]

meeja *n.* [1980s+] generic for the print and electronic media, seen as a social group. [joc. mispron. of SE *media*]

me elbow! *excl.* [1910s+] (Irish) a general excl. of incredulity, dismissal. [euph. of MY ARSE! excl.[1]]

meemies/mimis *n.* [1920s+] (orig. US) hysteria (cf. SCREAMING MEEMIES). [note WW2 US milit. sl. *screaming meemie*, the German *nebel-werfer*, a multi-barrelled mortar]

meep! *excl.* [1970s+] (US teen) an expression used on seeing anything overwhelmingly joyful that just makes one want to smile from ear to ear. [? coined by cartoonist Edward Barker in *The Boggies* series for the *Observer c.*1972]

meet *n.* 1 [mid-19C+] (orig. US) a meeting, appointment, esp. for illicit purposes such as drug selling. 2 [20C] (US) a gathering for the purpose of an activity, usu. sport, e.g. *a swim meet*, also a conference or convention. [(1) now SE]

meet hell *v.* [20C] (W.I.) to find it hard to make enough money to live, to subsist, to suffer great hardship (cf. CATCH FRANCE).

meet mary palm and her five sisters, to *phr.* [1950s+] to masturbate (cf. CONVERSE WITH HARRY PALM).

meet rosie hancock, to *phr.* [1950s+] to masturbate (cf. CONVERSE WITH HARRY PALM). [pun on name/SE *hand* + COCK n.[2] (1)]

meet with mother thumb and her four daughters, to *phr.* [20C] to masturbate (cf. CONVERSE WITH HARRY PALM).

meet your right-hand man, to *phr.* [1990s] to masturbate.

me for *phr.* [20C] (orig. US) I want.

meg *n.*[1] [late 17C–mid-18C] a guinea. [generic use of MAG n.[1] (1) as any coin]

meg *n.*[2] [late 18C–late 19C] a halfpenny, a cent or small coin. [MAG n.[1] (1) or MAKE n.[1]]

meg *n.*[3] [1930s–40s] a *meg*aphone. [abbr.; note film jargon *meg*, to direct a picture, *megger/megaphoner*, a film director]

meg/megg/meggie/meggs *n.*[4] [1940s–50s] (drugs) marijuana. [var. on MAGGIE n.[5]]

meg *v.* [late 19C] to swindle; thus *megging*, swindling.

mega *adj.* [1960s+] (orig. US teen) 1 of an object, superlative, excellent, extra-special. 2 of an object, huge, enormous, substantial. 3 of a person, very well known or very successful, also later used predicatively e.g. *the movie was mega*. [adopted Greek pfx. *mega-*, great]

megablast *n.* [1990s] 1 (drugs) a very deep inhalation of a cannabis cigarette. 2 an extremely exciting, satisfying experience. [MEGA + BLAST n.[2]]

megabuck/megabucks *n.* [1940s+] (US) an enormous sum of money, usu. in context of film or book deals. [MEGA + on model of nuclear *megadeath*, one million deaths, one *megabuck* = $1 million]

megg/meggie/meggs *see* MEG n.[3].

megilla/megillah *n.* [1950s+] 1 a long, tedious or complicated story, a complicated state of affairs, a long explanation. 2 the lot, everything; usu. as *the whole megillah*. [Yid. *gantse Megillah*, a whole (tedious) story, ult. Heb. *megillah*, roll, scroll. In standard use the term refers to 5 O.T. books – the *S. of S.*, *Ruth*, *Lam.*, *Eccles.* and *Esther* – that are traditionally associated with certain festivals, esp. the Book of Esther, read at Purim]

megsman *n.* 1 [mid–late 19C] the king of the 19C swindlers (cf. MAGSMAN n.[1]). 2 [mid-19C+] a petty criminal, a cheat. [MEG v.]

mehawn! *excl.* [1930s+] (Ulster) nonsense! rubbish! [Irish *mo thón*, my arse!]

meig *n.* [20C] (US) a nickel, a 5-cent coin. [var. on MEG n.[2] (2)]

meisensang *n.* [mid-19C] (Anglo-Chinese) a missionary. [Chinese pron. of SE *missionary*]

-meister *sfx.* 1 [1980s+] (orig. US) master, i.e. expert; used in comb. with a relevant n. to denote the leader of a profession, although the praise may often be tinged with irony. 2 [1990s] (US campus) used in comb. with a personal name or first syllable of a name. [Ger. *meister*, master, Yid. *meyster*, master]

mejoge/midjic *n.* [mid–late 18C] one shilling (5p). [Shelta]

mek-mek *n.* [1940s+] (W.I.) 1 a pernickety person, a fault-finder. 2 a quarrel, quarrelling. [SE *make* (*a fuss*) + redup.]

mek-mek *adj.* [1940s+] (W.I.) quarrelsome. [MEK-MEK n. (2)]

mek-mek *v.* [1940s+] (W.I.) to hesitate, to be indecisive, to make a half-hearted attempt. [MEK-MEK n. (1)]

melancholy hat *n.* [late 16C] 1 a mourning hat. 2 a smart, fashionable hat.

Melbourne/Port Melbourne Pier *n.* [1940s+] (Aus.) an ear. [rhy. sl.]

melia/millia murder! *excl.* [mid-19C+] (Irish) a general excl. of surprise, horror, regret. [Irish *míle murdar*, lit. 'a million murders', thus 'horror of horrors!']

melkpens *n.* [1970s] (S.Afr.) a young, naïve and inexperienced person. [Afk. *melk*, milk + *pens*, stomach]

mellish *n.* [early 19C] a sovereign. [? Lat. *mel*, honey, thus the image of money as a 'sweetener']

mellow *n.*[1] [late 17C] a smooth drink.

mellow *n.*[2] 1 [1950s+] (US Black) a favourite boy- or girl-friend, a good friend of either sex. 2 [1970s+] (US) a state of calm relaxation. [MELLOW adj. (5), (6)]

mellow *adj.* 1 [late 17C–18C] pleasantly drunk (cf. ABOUT RIGHT adj.[1]). 2 [1930s+] (US Black) relaxed and comfortable. 3 [1930s+] (orig. US Black) perfect, fine. 4 [1940s+] (US Black) attractive, stylish (cf. MELLOW-BACK). 5 [1940s+] (US Black) of a friend, close, intimate. 6 [1960s+] calm, peaceful, unconcerned with the material or painful, a state often induced by smoking cannabis (cf. LAID-BACK).

mellow-back *adj.* [1950s–60s] (US Black) fashionable, chic, well-dressed. [MELLOW adj. (4) + SE *back*]

mellow-Black *n.* [1930s–40s] (US Black) an attractive young Black woman. [MELLOW adj. (4) + SE *Black*]

mellow drag with the sag *n.* [1930s–40s] (US Black) a suit featuring an exaggeratedly long jacket. [MELLOW adj. (4) + DRAG n.[7] (1)]

mellow drug of America *n.* [1960s+] MDA (3,4-methylenedioxyamphetamine), an hallucinogenic that resembles LSD in its effects; it has the same chemical formula as MDMA, but is not identical (cf. ECSTASY). [MELLOW adj. (6)]

mellow out v. [1960s+] (orig. US) to calm oneself down, to calm someone down, to relax, esp. under the influence of drugs. [MELLOW adj. (6)]

mellow roof n. [1930s–40s] (US Black) the human head. [MELLOW adj. (2) + ROOF n. (2)]

mellows n. [1940s–50s] (US) spiritual or religious songs. [SE *mellow*, i.e. their quality]

mellowspeak n. [1970s+] (US) bland, ameliorative, unaggressive, euphemistic language. [MELLOW adj. (6) + sfx. -*speak*]

mellow yellow n.[1] [1950s–60s] (US Black) a Mulatto girl or woman. [MELLOW adj. (4) + YELLOW (GIRL)]

mellow yellow n.[2] [1960s] (drugs) 1 a variety of LSD. 2 dried banana skins, which, according to contemporary rumour, could be smoked. ['*Mellow Yellow*' (1967) a song by hippie folk-singer Donovan + MELLOW adj. (6)]

mellow yellow/yellow mellow n.[3] [1980s+] (S.Afr. township) a CASSPIR armoured truck, used to maintain order in the townships. [the colour of the vehicles, thence the proprietary name of a yellow-coloured soft drink, ult. f. the song, see MELLOW YELLOW n.[2]]

melo n. [late 19C+] a melodrama on stage or screen. [abbr.]

melon n.[1] (Aus./N.Z./US Black) 1 [20C] the human head; thus *do one's melon*, to lose one's temper, to become over-excited. 2 [1930s+] a fool (cf. MELONHEAD).

melon n.[2] [1930s+] (US) a windfall or unexpected profit. [financial jargon *cut a melon*, to announce an extra dividend]

melonhead n. [1930s+] (Aus./US) a fool. [MELON n.[1] (2) + sfx. -HEAD (1)]

melons n. [1950s+] the female breasts, esp. when large (cf. APPLES n.[1]).

melt n.[1] [mid-19C] (US) one's self (cf. HIDE n.[1]). [metonymy of SE *melt*, the spleen]

melt n.[2] [20C] (Ulster) the tongue, usu. in phr. *break one's melt*, to infuriate one beyond reason; *keep in your melt*, hold your tongue; *knock in one's melt*, to drive one mad. [OE *milt*, spleen; the tongue is spleen-shaped]

melt v. 1 [late 17C+] to spend money, esp. on drink. 2 [mid-19C+] to come to orgasm. 3 [mid–late 19C] to cash a cheque or break a note. 4 [late 19C–1930s] (Aus./N.Z.) to spend one season's pay on one extended binge. 5 [1940s–70s] (US campus) to delight, thrill or attract someone.

melt! *excl.* [1960s] (US) as imper., leave! get lost!

melted adj. [20C] 1 drunk (cf. LUBRICATED). 2 having expended all one's money on drink. [MELT v. (1)]

melted butter n.[1] [19C] semen (cf. BABY GRAVY).

melted butter n.[2] [1950s–70s] (US Black) an attractive woman, esp. a Mulatto. [her 'yellow' skin tone]

melted out adj. [1940s] (US Black) without money and thus desperate. [MELT v.]

melting moments n. 1 [19C] two fat people having sexual intercourse. 2 [late 19C] ardent, intense passion.

melting pot n. [19C] the vagina. [it 'softens' the penis after ejaculation]

melt one's grease, to phr. [mid-19C–1920s] to work very hard.

Melton hot day n. [late 19C] (sporting) a very hot day. [coined as a pun on SE *melting*, and spec. for 3 June 1885, an excessively hot day (as were those that followed) and one on which the horse *Melton* won the Derby]

melvin/marvin/uncle melvin n. 1 [1950s+] (US) a dull, tedious, socially inept and otherwise distasteful person (cf. IRVING) 2 [1980s+] a condition in which clothing gets stuck between the buttocks; thus *give someone a melvin*, to tug someone's underwear up suddenly and roughly (cf. WEDGIE).

[image of *Melvin* as a 'nerdy' proper name; (2) is seen as a typical problem for (1)]

melvin adj. [1950s+] old-fashioned. [MELVIN n. (1)]

melvin v. [1980s+] (US campus) to tug someone's underwear up suddenly and roughly with the aim of lifting them off the ground. [MELVIN n. (2)]

Melvyn Bragg n. [1990s] 1 sexual intercourse. 2 a promiscuous woman. [rhy. sl. *Melvyn Bragg* = (1) SHAG n.[1] (1); (2) SLAG n.[1] (6); ult. UK broadcaster and author *Melvyn Bragg* (b.1939)]

mem n.[1] [19C] a *mem*orandum (cf. MEMO). [abbr.]

mem, the n.[2] [late 19C+] the wife, the mistress of the household. [Anglo-Ind. use *memsahib*, a European married woman, or one who apes her style]

member n.[1] [18C+] the penis (cf. DEAREST MEMBER). [prior use is SE, Lat. *membrum virile*, 'the virile member', i.e. the penis]

member n.[2] 1 [mid-19C–1920s] a fellow, a chap; usu. with adj. e.g. *hot member*. 2 [1960s+] (US Black) a fellow Black person (cf. BLOOD n.[5]). [SE phr. *member of the community*]

member for barkshire n. [late 18C] one who is suffering from a harsh, persistent cough. [pun on SE *bark/Berkshire*]

member for cockshire n. [mid-19C] the penis (cf. DEAREST MEMBER). [puns on SE *member*/MEMBER n.[1] and *Cock*(shire)/COCK n.[2] (1)]

member for horncastle n. [late 18C–early 19C] a cuckold. [punning on SE *member*/MEMBER n.[1] + HORN n.[2]]

member mug n. [late 17C–early 19C] a chamberpot. [MEMBER n.[1] + SE *mug*, a drinking vessel]

member of the catch club n. [late 18C–early 19C] a bailiff or bailiff's assistant. [they *catch* villains]

memo n. [late 19C+] a *memo*randum (cf. MEM n.[1]). [abbr.]

memory box n. [1990s] (Aus.) the mind.

Memphis dominoes n. [1940s–70s] (US) dice.

menace n. [1930s+] an unpleasant, irritating person. [esp. used of children, thus the comic character Dennis the *Menace*, star of the *Beano*]

menavelings see MANAVILINS.

mench see MENSH.

mend v. [late 19C] to improve on.

mended adj. [late 19C] bandaged.

mendic adj. [1920s+] (Aus.) sick, ill. [? SE *mendicant*, a beggar (who may often look or be ill)]

men in suits n. [1980s+] senior managers, usu. those in finance and administration rather than in creative posts, often abbr. to *the suits*.

meno n. [1920s+] the *meno*pause. [abbr.]

meno adj. [1920s+] *meno*pausal. [abbr.]

mensch/mensh n. [1950s+] a 'real man', the implication being of character and integrity rather than sexual or physical prowess. [Yid. *mensch*, Ger. *Mensch*, a person]

mensh/mench v. [1930s+] to *men*tion; usu. in phr. *don't mensh*, don't mention it. [abbr.]

mental n. [1910s+] an insane, deranged person, a mental patient. [abbr. SE *mental case*]

mental adj. [1920s+] 1 insane, crazy, out of one's mind; thus *go mental*, to become insane, to have a mental breakdown or outburst. 2 a general intensifier meaning wonderful, bizarre, terrifying, according to context (cf. CRAZY adj.[1]; MAD adj.[2]).

mental giant n. [1980s+] (US campus) a fool, an idiot.

mental hernia n. [1970s] (US) a mental breakdown.

mental job n. [1920s+] one who is or potentially might be insane. [SE *mental* + JOB n.[6] (1)]

mental midget n. [1960s+] (US) a stupid person.

mentioned in despatches, to be phr. [1950s] to have one's name appear in a newspaper, a parish magazine, or any form of public 'notice-board'. [joc. var. on milit. use]

mentisental *adj.* [late 19C] sentimental. [deliberate mispron./ corruption]

meow *n.* [1990s] (US, Brooklyn) an expedition with the aim of causing trouble or shoplifting. [ety. unknown; link to TOM CAT *v.*]

mephepha *see* MAPHEPHA.

Merc *n.*[1] [1960s+] a *Merc*edes Benz. [abbr.]

merc *n.*[2] [1960s+] a professional *merc*enary soldier. [abbr.]

Mercedes *n.* [1970s] (US Black) an elegant woman with good looks and an attractive figure. [the car of the same name and status]

mercer's book *n.* [late 16C–early 17C] debt; thus *in the mercer's book*, the state of being in debt. [SE *mercer*, a dealer in luxury textiles + SE *book*. Any Elizabethan gallant worth his name was in debt to his clothier]

merchandise *n.* [1930s+] (drugs) drugs.

merchant *n.* [late 19C+] a man, a fellow, esp. as an adept of a particular interest, usu. in a variety of qualifying combs., e.g. BLAG-MERCHANT; BULL MERCHANT; CAPER MERCHANT; CON-MER-CHANT; FEATHER-MERCHANT; GUTTER-MERCHANT; HOIST-MERCHANT; HOP-MERCHANT; JUMP-UP MERCHANT; LAY-DOWN MERCHANT; LEATHER-MERCHANT; LUSH MERCHANT; MEAT-MERCHANT; PETTICOAT MERCHANT; PINTLE-MERCHANT; PLEASURE-MERCHANT; READER MERCHANT; SKIN-MERCHANT; SMOCK MERCHANT; SPEED MERCHANT; TIMBER-MERCHANT; TURKEY MERCHANT; WOOD MERCHANT (cf. ARTIST *n.*[2]).

merchant banker *n.* [1980s+] **1** a masturbator. **2** a general term of abuse (cf. BARCLAY'S; OIL TANKER). [rhy. sl. *merchant banker* = WANKER]

merchant of eel-skins *n.* [mid-16C–late 17C] one who only poses as a merchant. [? his slipperiness, the unlikeliness of their supposed commodity]

merciful hour! *excl.* [1990s] (Irish) a mild excl. or oath.

merck/merk *n.* [1960s+] (drugs) cocaine. [the *Merck* pharmaceutical company]

mercy! *excl.* [14C+] a general oath (esp. popular in the 1950s–60s camp gay world, with its overtones of a classic 'Southern belle').

mercy/messy buckets *phr.* [1930s+] (Aus./US) thank you. [intentional malapropism of Fr. *merci beaucoup*, thank you very much]

mercy buttercups *phr.* [1980s+] (US campus) thank you. [for ety. *see* MERCY BUCKETS]

mercy fuck *n.* [1960s+] (US) an act of sexual intercourse engaged in out of pity (cf. CHARITY FUCK). [SE *mercy* + FUCK *n.*[1]]

mercy mary! *excl.* [1950s+] (gay) an excl. of surprise.

mercy seat *n.* [1940s+] (US) a special pew reserved during a Black church revival for those who wish to be 'saved' and thus receive heavenly mercy (cf. MOANER'S BENCH).

merde! *excl.* [1920s+] a coarse excl., lit. *shit*.[SE *merd*, a piece of excrement, ult. Fr. *merde*, shit and Lat. *merda*, dung]

mere *adj.* [1930s+] foolish, absurd. [phr. *merely ridiculous*]

mere animal *n.* [late 17C–early 18C] a foolish, silly person.

mere/poor/remote circumstance *n.* [mid–late 19C] (US) a person or thing of little or no importance.

mere hen-cackle *phr.* [20C] (N.Z.) a trifle.

merk *see* MERCK.

merkin *n.* [mid-17C–early 18C] the female genitals. [Early Mod. E *malkin*, a mop, thus the false pubic hair as worn by actors and prostitutes, now SE]

mermaid *n.* [16C] a prostitute. [the mythical fish-women (based on the Greek sirens) reputed to lure sailors to their doom]

mero chingón, el *n.* [1950s–60s] (US teen gang) the leader. [Sp. sl., lit. the 'biggest fucker']

merry *adj.* [late 19C+] used in many expressions, e.g. *merry hell*, as an elaboration (cf. MERRY AS …).

merry and bright *n.* [20C] a light, usu. in pl. [rhy. sl.]

merry-arsed Christian *n.* [19C] a prostitute. [*merry-arsed*, cheerful + joc. reversal of CHRISTIAN *n.*[1]]

merry as … *phr.* a number of phrs. meaning 'very cheerful', e.g. *merry as …* [late 14C–early 17C] *a magpie*, [mid–late 16C] *three chips*, [mid-16C–late 17C] *a Greek*, [mid-16C+] *a cricket*, [mid-16C+] *a grig*, [early 17C–late 19C] *mice in malt*, [mid-late 17C] *he that has nought to lose*, [mid–late 17C] *the maids*, [mid-17C–mid-18C] *beggars*, [mid-19C+] *a cuckoo*, [mid-19C+] *wedding bells*.

merry-begotten *n.* [late 18C–early 19C] a bastard. [i.e. conceived when the parents were *merry*]

merry bit/legs *n.* [19C] a prostitute (cf. MERRY-ARSED CHRISTIAN).

merry-bout *n.* [late 18C] sexual intercourse.

merry dancers *n.* [18C] the Northern Lights.

merry-go-down *n.* [16C] a variety of strong ale.

merry-go-round *n.*[1] [late 19C+] £1 sterling. [rhy. sl.]

merry-go-round *n.*[2] **1** [1920s+] (orig. US) an evasion (cf. RUN-AROUND *n.*[2]). **2** [1970s+] (US Black) one who is attempting to deceive or swindle another person.

merry-go-round *v.* [20C] (US Und.) of a prisoner, to clear all administrative and bureaucratic procedures before being discharged from prison at the end of a sentence.

merry-go-up *n.* [early–mid-19C] snuff. [? its effects after 'going up' the nose]

merry grig *n.* [18C] a close companion. [SE *merry* + *grig*, something of below average size]

merryheart *n.* [20C] a sweetheart. [rhy. sl.]

merry legs *see* MERRY BIT.

merrymaker *n.* [19C] the penis (cf. MASTER OF CEREMONIES).

merry men *n.* [late 19C+] followers, subordinates. [SE *merry men*, the followers of a knight or an outlaw chieftain (esp. the mythical Robin Hood)]

merry-merry *n.* [1900s–20s] (US) a chorus line. [i.e. their usual cheeriness]

merry old soul *n.* [20C] **1** coal. **2** a hole. **3** the anus. [rhy. sl.]

merry snob *n.* [early 18C] a pleasant companion. [SE *merry* + generic use of SNOB *n.* (1)]

merry widow *n.*[1] [1900s–10s] Veuve Cliquot champagne (cf. WIDOW *n.*[2]).

merry widow *n.*[2] [1920s–30s] (US) a condom. [a popular brand of condoms]

merzky *adj.* [1990s] (US teen) dirty or nasty. [? echoic of a 'myeugh' snort of disgust or Fr. *merde* + 'Slavic' sfx. *-ski*]

mesc/mezc *n.* [1960s+] (orig. US drugs) *mesc*aline. [abbr.]

mescal *n.* [1960s] (drugs) *mescal*ine. [abbr., note Mex. *mescal*, a drink made from the fermented juice of the agave plant]

meserole *see* MEZZROLL.

meshuga/mashugga/meshuger/meshugga/meshuggah/ meshuggener/mishugge *n.* [late 19C+] a crazy person, an obsessive, an eccentric. [Yid. *mushuge*, crazy, ult. f. Heb. *shagag*, to wander, to go astray]

meshuga / mashugga / meshugenah / meshugener / me-shuger / meshuga / meshuggah / meshuggener / mi-shugge *adj.* [late 19C+] crazy, insane, eccentric. [MESHUGA *n.*]

meshugaas *see* MISHEGAAS.

meshugenah/meshugener *see* MESHUGA *adj.*

meshuger / meshugga / meshuggah / meshuggener *see* MESHUGA *n.*, *adj.*

Mesopotamia *n.* [mid-19C] Belgravia (cf. ASIA MINOR *n.*[1]). [SE *Mesopotamia*, the land between the rivers Tigris and Euphrates, lit. 'between the rivers', although, much earlier, the Westbourne River once meandered through Belgravia. The implication is less geographical than racist; the Belgravia area was seen as the home of newly rich Jews. Oxford University jargon use is geographical, referring to that area of Oxford between the rivers Cherwell and Isis]

mess n.[1] **1** [20C] excrement, usu. canine or feline; thus *make a mess*, to excrete on a carpet, floor or similar unsuitable place. **2** [1930s+] (US Black) nonsense, rubbish (cf. BULLSHIT n.; CRAP n.[3]). [orig. dial.]

mess n.[2] **1** [1900s–50s] (US) a large quantity. **2** [1950s+] (US Black) stuff in general. **3** [1990s] (US) the daylights, the stuffing. [SE *mess*, a sufficient quantity to make a dish]

mess n.[3] [1930s–60s] (US Black) something good or praiseworthy, if slightly confusing or disturbing. [SE *mess*, a state of confusion or muddle]

mess n.[4] [1930s+] (orig. US) an objectionable, ineffectual or stupid person.

mess n.[5] [1990s] semen.

mess v. **1** [18C] to have sexual intercourse, esp. adulterously. **2** [late 19C+] to interfere, disturb (cf. MESS ABOUT; MESS WITH). **3** [1910s–70s] (US) to fight (cf. MUSS v.).

mess! excl. [1910s–20s] a euph. excl. for SHIT!

mess about/around v. [late 19C+] **1** to swindle, to 'play fast and loose' with. **2** to handle roughly, to irritate, to annoy. **3** to indulge in varying degrees of sexual intimacy. **4** to waste time, to wander off the subject, to distract someone's attention. [(4) epitomized in Kenneth Williams's catchphrase *Stop messing about!* used in various Kenneth Horne BBC radio comedy shows and in the UK *Carry On* ... films (1950s–80s)]

mess-around n. [1940s+] (W.I.) a cake made of flour that must be stirred for a long time.

messed adj. [1950s+] extremely intoxicated by a drug or drink (cf. MESSED UP).

messed up adj. **1** [1910s+] ruined in any sense, physically, emotionally or mentally. **2** [1950s+] (orig. US) extremely intoxicated by a drug or drink, one of a number of terms that equate extreme drunkenness with suffering violence. Many of such terms can also apply to the effects of drugs (for a list of synons. cf. BASTED). **3** [1980s+] (US Black) troubled, suffering bad luck, wrong.

messen n. [20C] (Ulster) a contemptible person. [Scot. *messen*, a small dog; thus synon. with SE *cur*]

messenger n. [late 19C] (N.Z.) a false die, used by a cheat. [it passes the cheat a 'message']

messer n. **1** [1910s+] one who indulges in a number of sexual relationships. **2** [1910s+] an 'amateur prostitute', one who while not actively swapping sex for cash, will take 'presents' from her admirers. **3** [1930s] (US Und.) a 'strong-arm man', a 'bouncer'. **4** [1930s+] one who makes a mess, a bungler. **5** [1930s+] (Irish) an extremely incapable or irresponsible person. [MESS ABOUT]

Messjohn see MAS JOHN.

mess/mess with one's mind, to phr. [1950s+] (orig. US Black) to disturb and harm one emotionally. [MESS WITH + SE *mind*]

messorole see MEZZROLL.

mess over v. [1960s+] (US Black) to harm, to mistreat, to annoy (cf. MESS ABOUT). [ext. of MESS v. (2)]

mess-up n. **1** [20C] a blunder, a botch. **2** [1940s+] (US) a person with problems. **3** [1940s+] (US) a troublemaker. [MESS UP v.]

mess up v. **1** [1910s+] (US) to make a mistake, to get into trouble, to fail. **2** [1910s+] (US) to ruin. **3** [1910s+] (orig. US) to beat up, to assault (cf. MESS ABOUT; MESS WITH). **4** [1930s+] to ridicule. **5** [1970s+] (US) to play around, usu. in a sexual manner (cf. MESS ABOUT).

mess up someone's game/action/play/style, to phr. [1970s–80s] (US Black) to interfere in someone else's attempt at seduction. [MESS UP + GAME n.[4] (5)]

mess with v. [late 19C+] (US) **1** to use. **2** to become involved

with. **3** to harass, to annoy, to interfere with. **4** to laugh at, to ridicule (cf. MESS ABOUT; MESS UP).

mess with moby, to phr. [1990s] to masturbate. [MESS WITH + pun on DICK n.[5] (1)/*Moby* Dick, Herman Melville's fictional whale (1851)]

mess with nature, to phr. [1970s–80s] (US Black) **1** to lose one's potency, esp. through excess use of narcotics or alcohol (cf. NO NATURE). **2** to interfere with a couple who are poised to have sexual intercourse. [MESS WITH + NATURE n. (2)]

mess with one's mind see MESS ONE'S MIND.

messy adj.[1] [1920s+] immoral, unethical.

messy adj.[2] [1930s–60s] (US Black) good, first-rate. [MESS n.[3]]

messy attic n. [1950s] (US Black) hair in need of dressing. [SE *messy* + ATTIC]

messy buckets see MERCY BUCKETS.

Met n. **1** [late 19C] the *Met*ropolitan Music Hall. **2** [late 19C+] the *Met*ropolitan Police, serving London. **3** [late 19C+] the *Met*ropolitan Railway, part of the London Underground system. **4** [late 19C+] (US) the *Met*ropolitan Opera House, New York. **5** [1940s+] the *Met*eorological Office, responsible for weather forecasting, usu. as the *Met Office*; thus *Met man*, a weather forecaster. [abbr.]

metal n.[1] [mid-19C] (Anglo-Ind.) sweets. [ety. unknown; ? an Indian language]

metal n.[2] [20C] money. [abbr. *precious metal*]

metalhead n. [1980s+] (orig. US teen) a fan of heavy metal music (cf. DEADHEAD n.[1]). [SE (*heavy*) *metal* + sfx. -HEAD (2)]

metal mouth n. [1970s+] (US campus) a person with orthodontic braces (cf. LASER LIPS).

metal/mettle to the back phr. [late 16C–mid-18C] very brave, utterly dependable. [SE *mettle*, courage, spirit]

mete adj. [20C] (W.I.) meddlesome, interfering. [Sp. *meterse*, to interfere in, to meddle]

meter n. [1940s+] (US Black) a quarter, 25¢. [the coin then required to operate a gas *meter*]

meter thief n. [1960s+] (Und.) a term of contempt for a petty villain. [their targets never rise above gas meters, parking meters etc]

meth n.[1] see METHS.

meth n.[2] [1960s+] (drugs) **1** *meth*edrine **2** *meth*amphetamine. [abbr.]

meth freak n. [1960s–70s] (US drugs) a regular user of methamphetamine (cf. METH-HEAD). [METH n.[2] + sfx. -FREAK]

meth-head n. [1960s+] (drugs) a regular user of methamphetamine (cf. METH FREAK). [METH n.[2] + sfx. -HEAD (2)]

meth monster n. [1960s] (US drugs) a person who has a violent reaction to methamphetamine. [METH n.[2] + SE *monster*]

metho/methy n.[1] [1930s+] (Aus.) **1** *meth*ylated spirits, beloved by extreme alcoholics (cf. METHS). **2** a drinker of *meth*ylated spirits; ext. as *metho fiend*. [abbr.]

metho n.[2] [1940s+] (Aus.) a *Meth*odist (cf. BAPPO). [abbr. + sfx. -O]

Methodist adj. (US) used as synon. for 'puritan'; thus [1930s–40s] *Methodist feet*, religious objections to dancing, [1940s+] *Methodist measure*, a short measure of alcohol. [the supposed levity of dancing and Methodist teetotalitarianism]

Methody n. [mid-19C] (Irish) a Methodist.

meths/meth n. [1930s+] methylated spirits, usu. as drunk by alcoholic tramps or *meth*(*s*)-*drinkers* (cf. METHO n.[1]).

methy see METHO n.[1].

me-too n. [1930s+] (orig. US) one who slavishly copies the behaviour of another. [ME TOO!]

me-too v. [1940s+] to follow suit, to join in (slavishly); thus *me-tooing*, following suit, 'climbing on a bandwagon'. [ME TOO!]

me too! excl. [mid-19C+] a phr. signifying one's agreement or one's willingness or desire to share an opinion, experience or object.

met-pot n. [20C] (W.I.) a large pot used for cooking for parties, celebrations or any occasions requiring many servings. [dial. *met*, a gathering, a dance, a fair]

metrop n. [late 19C+] a *metropo*lis. [abbr.]

mettle n. [late 18C–early 19C] semen (cf. FETCH METTLE). ['the mettle of generation', SE *mettle*, spirit, pluck]

mettle to the back *see* METAL TO THE BACK.

metzel n. [19C] (US) a German-born immigrant. [Ger. *Metzelsuppe*, metzel soup, made with sausage]

Mex n. **1** [mid-19C+] (US) a *Mex*ican. **2** [mid-19C+] (US) the *Mex*ican/Spanish language. **3** [late 19C–1950s] (US) *Mex*ico City. **4** [1910s] (US) *Mex*ican money. **5** [1970s+] (US drugs) *Mex*ican drugs. [abbr.; note late 19C–1940s US forces use *Mex*, any form of foreign currency, esp. that of the Philippine Islands]

Mexicali revenge n. [1970s] (US) diarrhoea, as contracted by travellers in foreign countries (cf. APPLE-BLOSSOM TWO-STEP). [the Mexican town of *Mexicali*]

Mexican n. [19C] (Aus.) a Victorian as seen from New South Wales, or a native of New South Wales or Victoria viewed from Queensland. [such people come from 'south of the border/Down Mexico way']

Mexican adj. [20C] used in a variety of combs. to imply cheapness, inadequacy, stupidity, mediocrity and a dependence on donkeys. The stereotype of Mexicans in the US is uniformly negative (cf. IRISH adj.).

Mexican athlete n.[1] [1910s+] (US) a person who exaggerates. [he 'shoots the bull']

Mexican athlete n.[2] [1940s–50s] (US) an unsuccessful candidate for a college or school sports team.

Mexican bankroll n. [1940s–70s] (US Und.) a banknote of high denomination rolled around a large number of notes of small denomination (cf. CALIFORNIA BANKROLL).

Mexican Bogner's n. [1950s+] (US) jeans worn as ski pants. [*Bogner's*, a fashionable brand of choice in ski-wear]

Mexican breakfast n. [1940s+] (US, Texas) a cigarette and a glass of water, i.e. nothing nourishing at all (cf. AIR PIE AND A WALK AROUND).

Mexican brown/tar n. (US drugs) **1** [1960s+] high-strength marijuana (cf. MEXICAN GREEN). **2** [1970s+] heroin, usu. weak, inferior. [SE *Mexico*, i.e. the country of origin + its 'reputation' in the relevant drugs]

Mexican Buick n. [1950s+] (US) a Chevrolet (cf. MEXICAN MASERATI). [the respective status of the cars]

Mexican bush n. [1940s] (US drugs) an inferior variety of marijuana. [MEXICAN adj. + BUSH n.[6]]

Mexican carriage n. [1950s+] (US) a donkey (cf. ARIZONA NIGHTINGALE). [stereotyping]

Mexican carwash n. [1950s+] (US) washing the car by leaving it out in the rain.

Mexican cashmere n. [1950s+] (US) a sweatshirt.

Mexican chrome n. [1950s+] (US) **1** aluminium paint used to simulate real (and more expensive) chrome on a car. **2** any form of silver paint.

Mexican cigarette n. [1950s+] (gay) a poorly made marijuana cigarette.

Mexican commercial n. [1940s] (US drugs) average strength Mexican marijuana.

Mexican credit card *see* HARLEM CREDIT CARD.

Mexican dragline n. [1960s+] (US) a shovel or spade.

Mexican filling station n. [1950s+] (US) a hose used to siphon petrol from another car into one's own (cf. MEXICAN CREDIT CARD).

Mexican foxtrot n. [1950s+] (US) diarrhoea, dysentery (cf. APPLE-BLOSSOM TWO-STEP).

Mexican green n. [1960s+] (drugs) a weak grade and type of marijuana (cf. MEXICAN BROWN).

Mexican hairless n. [1960s+] an old, hairless tennis ball. [pun on SE *Mexican hairless*, a breed of dog]

Mexican happening n. [1960s+] (US) something that never happens. [racial stereotyping, Mexicans supposedly put everything off until *mañana*]

Mexican horse n. [1970s+] (drugs) heroin. [MEXICAN + HORSE n.[12]]

Mexican jeep n. [1940s+] (US) a donkey (cf. ARIZONA NIGHTINGALE).

Mexican jelly bean n. [1950s+] (US) a Chevrolet that has been lowered in the rear and fitted with a Venetian blind in the rear window. [the car bounces up and down on its special suspension]

Mexican jumping beans n. [1970s] **1** (drugs, gay) amphetamines (cf. A n.[2]). **2** (drugs) barbiturates, esp. Seconal, made in Mexico.

Mexican lawnmower n. [1960s+] (US) a hand-held tool used to trim hedges and grass.

Mexican lightning n. [1970s] (US) tequila (cf. MEXICAN MILK). [MEXICAN + LIGHTNING n.[1] (2)]

Mexican Maserati n. [1950s+] (US) a Mercury (cf. MEXICAN BUICK).

Mexican milk n. [1970s] (US) tequila (cf. MEXICAN LIGHTNING).

Mexican motor mount n. [1950s+] inner tubing used as a shock absorber, rather than the purpose-built material.

Mexican mud n. [1980s+] (US drugs) heroin (cf. MEXICAN BROWN).

Mexican muffler n. [1950s+] (US) a homemade silencer made from a tin can stuffed with steel wool that is then attached to the car's exhaust pipe. [SAmE *muffler*, a silencer]

Mexican mushroom n. [1960s+] (drugs) psilocybin, psilocin. [the psilocybe *mushroom* grows in Mexico]

Mexican nightmare n. [1960s+] (gay) gaudy ceramic crockery, typical of that sold to tourists in Mexico (cf. MEXICAN SHLOCK; TAMALE).

Mexican nose guard n. [1950s+] (US) an athletic support or jockstrap.

Mexican oats n. [1950s+] (US) nonsense, rubbish. [euph. for BULLSHIT n.]

Mexican overdrive n. [1950s+] (US) coasting or freewheeling in order to save petrol (cf. JEWISH OVERDRIVE).

Mexican promotion/raise n. [1950s+] (US) a better job but one that brings no increase in salary.

Mexican quarter-horse n. [1960s+] (US) a mule (cf. ARIZONA NIGHTINGALE).

Mexican raise *see* MEXICAN PROMOTION.

Mexican red n. [1960s+] (drugs) **1** a barbiturate (cf. REDS n.[3]). **2** a potent variety of Mexican marijuana (cf. MEXICAN BROWN; MEXICAN GREEN).

Mexican rig n. [1960s+] (US) anything that has been poorly constructed.

Mexican schlock n. [1960s+] (gay) any art in poor taste, typically that sold to tourists in Mexico (cf. MEXICAN NIGHTMARE). [MEXICAN adj. + SCHLOCK n. (1)]

Mexican seabag n. [1930s] (US) a newspaper or paper bag in which poor sailors carry their belongings.

Mexican stand-off n. **1** [late 19C+] (orig. US) a situation in which two parties are at a deadlock, with neither party willing to back down from a stated position and neither party having a superior edge; the result is that both parties give in and walk off (cf. NIGGERS' DUEL). **2** [20C] (US) a partial victory or defeat, but one that still fails to provide a decisive outcome. **3** [20C] a round in poker when no one is willing to open the betting or no one wins the pot. **4** [20C] a head-on collision between two trains. **5** [1920s–30s] (US) execution by firing squad.

Mexican straight n. [20C] any 5 cards and a knife in poker. [poker jargon *straight*, a run of 5 cards in sequence + the negative stereotyping of the knife-wielding *Mexican*]

Mexican tar see MEXICAN BROWN.

Mexican threads n. [1950s–60s] (US) a stripped bolt that has been forced into a hole to cut new threads.

Mexican time n. [1960s+] (US) poor timekeeping, unpunctuality (cf. AFRICAN PEOPLE'S TIME).

Mexican toothache n. [1960s+] diarrhoea, often contracted on a foreign holiday (cf. APPLE-BLOSSOM TWO-STEP).

Mexican two-step n. [1950s+] diarrhoea (cf. APPLE-BLOSSOM TWO-STEP).

Mexican valve-job n. [1950s–60s] (US) flushing the carburettor of a running engine with kerosene.

Mexican window-shade n. [1950s–60s] Venetian blinds in the back window of a car.

mezc see MESC.

mezz/mighty mezz n. [1930s–70s] (US Black) marijuana. [the jazz musician and marijuana-dealer *Milton 'Mezz' Mezzrow* (1899–1972)]

mezz adj. [1930s–70s] (US Black) honest, dependable. [the positive reputation of *'Mezz' Mezzrow* (see MEZZ n.)]

mezzroll/meserole/messorole/mezz's roll n. [1940s–70s] (drugs) a large, generously filled marijuana cigarette. [MEZZ n. + SE *roll*]

m.f. n. [20C] euph. for MOTHERFUCKER. [abbr.]

m.f. adj. [20C] euph. for MOTHERFUCKING adj. [abbr.]

m.f.u.t.u. phr. [1940s] (US) a term of abuse, *motherfuck you too* (cf. SNAFU phr.). [abbr., orig. WW2 milit., inscribed on B-17 bombers with a cartoon of General Hideki Tojo (1885–1948) getting 'the finger']

m.f.w.i.c. phr. [1970s+] (orig. US milit.) a term of abuse, *motherfucker who's/what's in charge*. [abbr.]

m.g.a. phr. [1970s+] (Aus.) *Mediterranean gut-ache*, an 'illness' supposedly contracted by Greek, Yugoslav and similar 'Mediterranean' immigrants to Aus., seen as innately lazier than their Anglo-Saxon counterparts (cf. MEDITERRANEAN BACK). [abbr.]

mi. adj. [late 18C+] (esp. public school) *minor*, i.e. younger, esp. as used to differentiate brothers, e.g. *Marchbank mi* (cf. MA.). [abbr.]

miaow! miaow! excl. [1920s+] used by a third party when overhearing a pair of speakers engaged in malicious gossip. [such a conversation is SE *catty*]

mic/mike n.[1] [1960s+] (drugs) one *mic*rogram (one millionth of a gram), the basic measurement of LSD. An average dose of LSD is approx. 250 mics. [abbr.]

mic n.[2] [1960s+] a *mic*rophone (cf. MIKE n.[2]).

mic-a-mic n. [late 19C+] (N.Z.) scrub. [? Maori *ukuiki*, scrub]

mice n. [1950s] (Aus.) the girls who accompany the Aus. variety of Teddy Boy (cf. BODGIE; WIDGIE).

michael n.[1] [1910s–30s] (US) a hip flask. [? the 'Irish' name *Michael* and thus stereotype of Irish drinkers]

michael n.[2] [1930s] (Aus.) the vagina (cf. BERKELEY HUNT). [play on *Michael Hunt*, i.e. CUNT n.[1] (1); esp. used in joc. phr. [1930s+] 'Has anyone seen Mike Hunt?']

michael n.[3] [1940s–50s] (US) a 'knock-out drop', as placed in a drink. [abbr. MICKEY FINN]

Michael Caine n. [20C] (lit. + fig.) a pain. [rhy. sl.; ult. the actor *Michael Caine* (b.1933)]

Michelin/Michelin tyre n. [1950s+] (W.I.) **1** a bulla cake. **2** a dumpling. **3** a fat person. [the tyre makers and their 'Michelin man' logo]

Michigan roll/bankroll/stake/Michigan n. [1910s–70s] (US) a fake bankroll, a note of a high denomination around a

large number of notes of smaller denomination (cf. CALIFORNIA BANKROLL).

miching malicho/mallecho/minchin malacho n. [early 17C–late 19C] mischief. [? SE *mitching*, pilfering, skulking, truant-playing, pretending poverty + Sp. *malhecho*, misdeed. The first citation is in Shakespeare, *Hamlet* (1600), III.ii: 'Marry this is *Miching Malicho*, that meanes Mischeefe']

mick n.[1] **1** [mid-19C+] (orig. US) an Irish person (cf. PADDY n.[1]). **2** [mid-19C+] (US) an Englishman. **3** [1920s+] (Aus.) a Roman Catholic. **4** [1930s] a labourer on the roads. **5** [1940s+] (US) a potato. [*Michael*, a common Irish (and by stereotype Catholic, labouring and potato-eating) name]

mick n.[2] [20C] (Aus.) in two-up, the 'tail' of a coin; thus *mick*, to spin the coins so that they come up tails.

mick n.[3] [1930s+] (Aus.) the vagina. [abbr. MICHAEL n.[2]; MICKEY n.[9]]

mick n.[4] [1960s+] (US campus) anything easy, esp. an academic class or test. [MICKEY MOUSE adj.[1] (3)]

mick adj. [late 19C+] (US) Irish. [MICK n.[1] (1)]

mick doolan/doolin/do see MICKEY DOOLAN.

mickey n.[1] **1** [mid-19C+] (US) an Irish person (cf. MIKEY). **2** [1930s+] (US) a potato, esp. a roasted sweet potato. **3** [1940s–60s] (US prison) a fellow inmate. [fig. uses of MICK n.[1], stereotyping of the Irish as criminal and potato-eating]

mickey/micky n.[2] [late 19C+] (Aus.) a wild bullock. [? the stereotyped 'wild Irishman']

mickey n.[3] [late 19C+] (tramp) a casual ward. [rhy. sl. *mickey = mike* = SPIKE n.[1] (1)]

mickey n.[4] [20C] (Irish) the penis. [joc. use of proper name]

mickey n.[5] [1910s+] (mainly Can.) a small bottle of wine or spirits (cf. YUKON MICKEY). [MICHAEL n.[1]]

mickey n.[6] [1930s+] (US) a knockout drug, usu. administered via an alcoholic drink. [abbr. MICKEY FINN]

mickey/micky n.[7] [1940s+] a potato (cf. MICK n.[1]).

mickey n.[8] [1940s–50s] (US) a second-rate, commercial band playing uninspired music. [abbr. MICKEY MOUSE adj.[1] band]

mickey n.[9] [1960s+] (Aus.) the vagina. [MICHAEL n.[2]]

mickey/micky adj.[1] [late 19C] sick (cf. BOB, HARRY AND DICK; TOM AND DICK). [rhy. sl.]

mickey adj.[2] [1950s+] (US) something second-rate, corny. [abbr. MICKEY MOUSE adj.[1]]

mickey/micky/mick doolan/doolin/do n. [20C] (N.Z.) **1** an Irish immigrant. **2** a Roman Catholic. [generic Irish name]

mickey d's/dee's rainbow steakhouse n. [1970s+] (US Black/campus) a McDonald's hamburger restaurant. [initial letters of *McDonald/Mickey D*]

mickey finished adj. [1950s] (US) absolutely drunk. [pun on MICKEY FINN]

mickey finn/flynn n. **1** [late 19C+] (orig. US) a knock-out drug, poss. chloral hydrate, mixed into an unsuspecting victim's drink (cf. SLIP A MICKEY). **2** [1990s] (US drugs) any form of depressant. [the saloon-keeper *Mickey Finn*, who ran Chicago's Lone Star and Palm Saloons *c*.1896–1906. He, in turn, had supposedly picked up the recipe from voodoo operators in New Orleans]

Mickey Mouse n.[1] [20C] **1** a house. **2** a Liverpudlian. [rhy. sl.; (2) = SCOUSE n.[2]; ult. Disney's *Mickey Mouse* (see adj.[1])]

Mickey Mouse n.[2] [1930s–40s] (US) the vagina; thus *Mickey Mouse is kaput*, sex is impossible because of menstruation (cf. TITMOUSE). [ext. of MICKEY n.[9]; ult. Disney's *Mickey Mouse* (see adj.[1])]

Mickey Mouse n.[3] **1** [1930s–60s] (US Black) a White person. **2** [1940s–70s] (US) a small, silly or inconsequential person. **3** [1940s+] (US Black) commercialized music, esp. uninspired jazz music. **4** [1950s+] (US) a trivial, petty or unnecessary activity. **5** [1980s+] (US) foolish or nonsensical talk. [MICKEY MOUSE adj.[1]]

Mickey Mouse n.[4] [1940s+] (US) **1** a black and white police patrol car. **2** a police officer. [Disney's *Mickey Mouse* (*see* adj.[1]) is black and white]

Mickey Mouse n.[5] [1950s+] (US) a watch. [a line of watches manufactured in 1930s with a picture of *Mickey Mouse* (*see* adj.[1]) on the face]

Mickey Mouse n.[6] [1960s] (drugs) a variety of LSD. Squares of blotting-paper overprinted with a picture of *Mickey Mouse* as the Sorcerer's Apprentice, from the film *Fantasia* (1940), are impregnated with a drop of the drug. [Disney's *Mickey Mouse* (*see* adj.[1])]

Mickey Mouse adj.[1] **1** [1930s+] (orig. US) second-rate, badly made, artificial; thus (US Black) *Mickey Mouse music*, commercialized jazz or pop music. **2** [1950s+] (orig. US) silly, puerile, contemptible. **3** [1950s+] (US campus) easy, facile. **4** [1950s+] small. [*Mickey Mouse*, Walt Disney's anodyne, albeit hugely successful, cartoon creation, created in 1928]

Mickey Mouse adj.[2] [1930s+] (Aus.) excellent, wonderful, the best. [rhy. sl. = GROUSE adj.; ult. *see* MICKEY MOUSE adj.[1]]

Mickey Mouse, to phr. [1960s+] (US) to fool around, to botch; often as *Mickey Mouse around*, *Mickey Mouse it*. [MICKEY MOUSE adj.[1]]

Mickey-Mouse book-keeping phr. [1970s+] (Aus.) 'creative accountancy', in order to avoid paying taxes. [MICKEY MOUSE adj.[1] + SE *book-keeping*]

Mickey Mouse boots n. [1950s+] (orig. US milit.) orig. heavy, insulated boots, now any large boots or shoes. [reminiscent of *Mickey Mouse's* (*see* adj.[1]) footwear]

Mickey Mouse habit n. [1980s] (drugs) a limited addiction to or occasional use of heroin. [MICKEY MOUSE adj.[1] + HABIT]

Mickey Mouse in the house, and Donald Duck don't give a fuck! phr. [1990s] (US Black) a phr. used to encourage party guests to move to a new and more abandoned level of self-indulgence. [ult. Disney characters]

Mickey-Mouse money phr. [1970s+] any unfamiliar currency, incl. the UK's decimal coins in the immediate aftermath of their introduction. [MICKEY MOUSE adj.[1] + SE *money*]

mickey-muncher n. [1980s+] (Aus.) a man who performs cunnilingus. [MICKEY n.[9] + SE *muncher*]

Mickey Rooney n. [20C] an eccentric, a mad person. [rhy. sl. *Mickey Rooney* = LOONY n.; ult. film star *Mickey Rooney* (b.1920)]

mickey's n. [1970s] (drugs) a tranquillizer, a depressant. [? MICKEY FINN]

mickey T n. [1990s] (US Black) a woman who pursues powerful and/or wealthy men only. [ety. unknown; ? anecdotal]

Mick O'Dwyer n. [late 19C+] a fire (cf. ANNA MARIA). [rhy. sl.]

mickser n. [1950s+] an Irishman who has emigrated to the UK. [MICK n.[1] (1)]

micky n. see MICKEY n.[2], n.[7].

micky adj. see MICKEY adj.[1].

micky/mike bliss n. [20C] an act of urination (cf. COUSIN SIS; JOHNNY BLISS; RATTLE AND HISS; SNAKE'S HISS). [rhy. sl. *micky bliss* = PISS n. (1)]

micky doolan/doolin/do see MICKEY DOOLAN.

Micky Spillane n. [1950s+] (Aus.) a game. [rhy. sl.; ult. popular novelist *Mickey Spillane* (b.1918)]

micro-beer n. [1990s] (US campus) a 200ml beer. [i.e. smaller than a usual measure]

micro-chip n. [20C] a Japanese person. [rhy. sl. *micro-chip* = NIP n.[5] (1) + ref. to Japanese technological expertise]

microdot n. [1970s] (drugs) a small dose of LSD, usu. as placed on squares of blotting-paper (cf. DOTS n.[2]).

midday n. [1920s–30s] a snack of bread and cheese. [when tramps leave the casual ward in the morning they receive a portion of bread and cheese for the midday meal]

midden n. [19C+] (Scot.) a filthy slattern. [SE *midden*, a dunghill, manure-heap, refuse-heap]

middle n. [1950s–70s] a middle-class person. [abbr.]

middle v. [mid-19C] to make a fool of, to cheat. [SE *middle*, to put in the middle, in this context, of an illicit scheme]

middlebrow n. [1920s+] a person of average intellectual attainments or conventional taste (cf. BROADBROW; HIGHBROW; LOWBROW).

middle cut n. [1970s] (US Black) the vagina (cf. AXIS).

middle finger n.[1] see MIDDLE LEG.

middle finger n.[2] [1960s+] a prostitute's trick to ensure that each client arrives at a speedy orgasm so that she can maximize her nightly earning potential.

middle kingdom n. [19C] the vagina (cf. AXIS). [a pun on SE *Middle Kingdom*, in ancient Egypt, the 11th and 12th dynasties (22nd–18th C BC), doubtless a back-handed tribute to the Victorian fascination with things Egyptian]

middle leg/finger n. [late 19C+] the penis (cf. BEST LEG OF THREE).

middle name n. [20C] (orig. US) something one likes or identifies with strongly; esp. in phr. *... is my middle name*.

middle piece/pie n. [mid-19C–1900s] the stomach (cf. MIDDLE STOREY).

Middlesex clown n. [mid-17C–early 19C] an inhabitant or native of the county of Middlesex.

Middlesex mongrel n. [18C] an inhabitant or native of the county of Middlesex.

middle storey n. [late 17C–late 18C] the stomach (cf. MIDDLE PIECE).

middling adj. [mid-19C+] moderately good, mediocre, second-rate.

middling adv. **1** [early 18C–late 19C] moderately, fairly, tolerably. **2** [19C] fairly well; esp. when used as the answer to a question regarding one's health, and as such it can also mean not very well; thus *middlingish*.

middy n. [1940s+] (Aus.) a measure of beer, approx. 285ml (10fl oz), or the glass that holds it. [SE *middle*; the measure is 'middle sized']

midge-net n. [mid-19C–1900s] a woman's veil (cf. LOUSE-TRAP n.[1]). [SE *midge*, a gnat]

midge's knee-buckle n. [20C] (Ulster) something infinitesimally small. [SE *midge*, a gnat]

midjic see MEJOGE.

midlands n. [19C] the vagina (cf. AXIS).

midnight n.[1] **1** [mid-19C+] (US) a Black person (cf. DARKIE). **2** [1950s–70s] (US Black) a particularly dark-complexioned Black person.

midnight n.[2] [1910s–50s] (US) the point 12 in craps. [? link to the DOZENS]

midnight adj. [mid-19C+] (US) in racial contexts, Black. [MIDNIGHT n.[1]]

midnight cowboy n. [1960s–70s] (US) a male prostitute. [film title *Midnight Cowboy* (1969)]

midnight lace n. [1980s+] (US gay) a Black man's penis. [MIDNIGHT adj. + LACE n.[1]]

midnight oil n. [1940–50s] (drugs) opium. [play on phr. *burning the midnight oil*]

midnight queen n. [1960s+] (US gay) a White homosexual man who prefers Black partners. [MIDNIGHT n.[1] + QUEEN n.[1]]

midnight the cat n. [1950s–60s] (US Black) an especially dark-complexioned Black person. [MIDNIGHT n.[1] (2) + CAT n.[9] (3)]

midshipman's watch and chain n. [late 18C–early 19C] a sheep's heart and pluck (the liver and lungs).

midway n. **1** [late 19C+] (US) the main street or streets of a town or city. **2** [1930s+] (US Black) a hallway or corridor. [carnival/fairground jargon *the Midway*, the central avenue along which the major shows and amusements are situated. The term originated in 1893, when the Chicago Exposition featured the *Midway* Plaisance]

midzer *see* MADZA.

mierda *n.* [1990s] excrement. [Sp. *mierda*, SHIT n.¹ (1)]

miering *n.* [1960s–70s] (S.Afr. township) money. [ety. unknown; ? Afk.]

miesli *see* MISLAIN v.¹.

miff *n.* [early 17C+] a tantrum, a petty quarrel, a tiff; thus *miffed*, irritated, annoyed, *miffiness*, the propensity to take offence at the slightest justification. [an expression of disgust, i.e. 'Mmmpphh!']

miffed *adj.* [early 19C+] annoyed. [MIFF]

miffy *n.* [18C–19C] the Devil. [? Fr. *maufé*, the Devil]

mifky-pifky/moofky-poofky/moofty-poofty *n.* [1980s+] (US) silly behaviour, esp. romantic or sexual (cf. HANKY-PANKY). [ety. unknown]

mifty *adj.* [late 17C–early 18C] apt to take offence for minimal reason. [MIFF]

miggle/miggles *n.* [1940s–50s] (US drugs) marijuana (cf. MUGGLES n.²). [? MEG n.³]

mighty *adv.* [mid-19C+] greatly, exceedingly, very, esp. in ironic use.

mighty!/mighty me! *excl.* [mid-19C+] (Scot.) a general excl.

mighty-come a-tooting/a-right/a-shouting/shouting/whistling *phr.* [20C] (US) quite right, usu. preceded by *you're...* . [MIGHTY adv. + SE]

mighty dome *n.* [1930s–40s] (US Black) the US Congress building or any similar large, institutional edifice.

mighty joe young *n.* [1960s+] (drugs) **1** a depressant. **2** an extremely heavy narcotics addiction (cf. MONKEY ON ONE'S BACK). [the film *Mighty Joe Young* (1949)]

mighty me! *see* MIGHTY!

mighty mezz *see* MEZZ n.

mighty mouth *n.* (camp gay) **1** [1950s–60s] a fellator. **2** [1950s+] a gossip or one who boasts.

mighty quinn *n.* [1970s] (drugs) LSD. [the Bob Dylan song 'The Mighty Quinn' (1966), esp. the line 'You ain't seen nothin' like the Mighty Quinn']

mike *n.¹* **1** [mid-19C–1900s] a labourer, a hod-carrier, esp. when Irish. **2** [1940s–50s] (Aus.) a cup of tea. [abbr. *Michael*, the stereotypical Irish forename]

mike *n.²* **1** [1920s+] a *mic*rophone (cf. MIC n.²). **2** [1930s–60s] (US) a *mic*roscope. [abbr.]

mike *n.³ see* MIC n.¹.

mike *v.* **1** [early 19C–1950s] to loiter, to 'hang about'; thus *do/have a mike*, to loiter, to waste time. **2** [1900s–30s] to steal, to make off with. [MOOCH v.¹, but Hotten (1860) notes racial stereotyping (*Mike* is a generic term for an Irishman and Irish labourers were seen as congenitally idle)]

mike bliss *see* MICKY BLISS.

miker *n.* **1** [late 19C+] a loafer, a scrounger. **2** [1920s–30s] a truant. [MIKE v. or Gloucestershire dial.]

mikes *n.* [1940s] (US Black) ears. [SE *microphones*]

mikey *n.* [mid-19C+] (US) an Irish person. [var. on MICKEY n.¹ (1)]

miking *n.* [mid-19C+] loitering, hanging around. [MIKE v.]

milch-cow *n.* [late 18C–early 19C] **1** one who is easily tricked out of money or property. **2** (prison) a prisoner who is generous in bribing warders. [SE *milch-cow*, a cow 'in milk' + used fig. as an easy source of money]

mild and meek *n.* [20C] (Aus.) the cheek. [rhy. sl.]

mild bloater *n.* [mid-19C–1900s] a second-rate dandy, 'weak young men who keep bull-dogs, and dress in a "loud" stable style, from a belief that it is very becoming...' (Hotten, 1867).

mildewed *adj.* **1** [late 19C–1910s] miserable-looking. **2** [1910s–20s] pitted with smallpox.

mildreds *n.* [1990s] a pair of large and pendulous breasts, usu. on an older woman. [a generic use of proper name]

mileage *n.* [1960s+] **1** (orig. US) experience of life. **2** a criminal record.

mile-eater *n.* [20C] a fast driver or traveller.

mile end *n.* [20C] a friend. [rhy. sl.]

mile high club *n.* [1970s+] (orig. US) a notional 'club' of those who have enjoyed sex in an aeroplane. This has now been joined by the *mile-deep club*, those who have had sex while travelling through the Channel Tunnel between UK and France.

miler/myla *n.* [mid-19C] a donkey, an ass. [Rom. *meila*, a mule, ? ult. Lat. *mulus*]

-miler *sfx.* [mid-19C] a lengthy walk, always comb. with a specific number, e.g. *ten-miler*.

miles away, to be *phr.* [1950s+] to be day-dreaming, lost in thought.

milestone *n.* [early 19C] a country bumpkin. [they stand at the side of the road]

milestone inspector *n.* [1920s–30s] (tramp) a professional tramp (cf. INSPECTOR OF CITY BUILDINGS; INSPECTOR OF PAVEMENTS; MANHOLE INSPECTOR; MILESTONE-MONGER).

milestone-monger *n.* [mid-19C–1920s] (tramp) a professional tramp (cf. MILESTONE INSPECTOR).

milihelen/miliherm *n.* [1960s–70s] (US campus) an imaginary unit of measurement to calculate female/male beauty. [pun on *Helen* of Troy whose face 'launched a thousand ships', in *Doctor Faustus* (1604) by Christopher Marlowe, or on the Greek god *Hermes*]

milikers *n.* [late 19C] the militia. [joking mispron.]

militant *adj.* [1990s] (Black) aggressive, energetic, purposive.

military ceremony/wedding *n.* [1910s+] (US) a wedding that is forced on the groom through his girlfriend's (soon to be bride's) pregnancy (cf. SHOTGUN WEDDING).

milk *n.¹* [mid-17C+] semen.

milk *n.²* **1** [mid-19C+] (US) bourbon or beer. **2** [1990s] methylated spirits mixed with water and drunk by down-and-out alcoholics. [(2) the resulting white 'milky' colour]

milk *n.³* [late 19C–1920s] a weakling. [abbr. SE *milksop*]

milk *n.⁴* [late 19C+] a milkman.

milk *v.¹* **1** [mid-19C–1900s] to defraud, to extract money from. **2** [1940s–50s] (Aus.) to siphon petrol from a car (whether legally or not). [subseq. use of (1) is SE]

milk *v.²* [late 19C+] to add milk to tea or coffee.

milk *v.³* [late 19C+] **1** to masturbate someone else. **2** to masturbate; used in phrs. (cf. MILK THE LIZARD). [note MILK n.¹]

milk a duck, to *phr.* [1930s–40s] (US) to attempt the impossible (cf. MILK THE PIGEON).

milk and honey route *n.* [1910s–30s] (US tramp) a rail route that is renowned for good hand-outs, esp. one passing through Mormon parts of Utah.

milk-and-water *adj.* [late 18C+] weak, diluted, adulterated, e.g. *milk-and-water socialism*.

milk and water! *excl.* [late 18C–early 19C] a toast, further defined as 'Both ends of the busk!' [the ref. is to the female breasts and vagina which give, respectively milk and urine; a SE *busk* is a corset, or the wood, steel or whalebone that stiffens it]

milk bar *n.¹* [1950s+] (Aus.) a corner shop.

milk bar *n.²* [1950s+] the female breasts (cf. CREAM JUGS).

milk bar cowboy *n.* [1950s+] **1** a person, esp. a motorcyclist, who frequents milkbars. **2** a general term of abuse, usu. aimed at the young (cf. DRUGSTORE COWBOY).

milk bottle/can *n.* [late 19C] a baby.

milk bottles *n.* [1930s+] (orig. Aus.) the female breasts (cf. CREAM JUGS). [their primary, non-sexual function as dispensers of milk to a baby]

milk can *see* MILK BOTTLE.

milken *see* MILL-KEN.

milker *n.*[1] [late 19C] one who intercepts telegrams addressed to others. [MILK v.[1] (1)]

milker *n.*[2] [late 19C–1900s] the vagina (cf. MAN'S MILK). [it 'milks' the penis of semen]

milker *n.*[3] [late 19C+] a masturbator. [MILK v.[3]]

milkers *n.* [20C] the female breasts (cf. CREAM JUGS).

milker's calf *n.* [late 19C] (Aus.) a petted, favourite child, a 'mother's boy'. [SE *milker's calf*, a calf that is still with its mother]

milk factories *n.* [1940s–70s] (US) the female breasts (cf. CREAM JUGS).

milkie/milky *n.* [late 19C+] **1** a milkman. **2** milk.

milking pail *n.* [late 19C] the vagina (cf. MILKER n.[2]; MILK JUG n.[1]).

milk in the coconut *phr.* [mid-19C+] (orig. US) a puzzling fact or circumstance, a crux, esp. in phr. *that accounts for the milk ... .*

milk jug/pan *n.*[1] [late 18C–1900s] the vagina. [MILK n.[1] + SE *jug/pan*]

milk jug *n.*[2] [1920s+] (Aus.) a fool, a simpleton (cf. CUNT n.[2]). [rhy. sl. *milk-jug* = MUG n.[5] (1)]

milk jugs *see* JUGS n.[1].

milkman *n.* [1990s] **1** a person who masturbates frequently. **2** the penis. [MILK v.[3]]

milkman's horse *adj.* [late 19C+] cross, annoyed, irritated. [rhy. sl., Cockney pron. 'crorss']

milko *n.* **1** [20C] (orig. Aus.) a milkman. **2** [1940s] (Aus.) a cow-hand. [SE *milk* + sfx. -o]

milk one's dick, to *phr.* [20C] to masturbate. [MILK v.[3] (2) + DICK n.[5] (1)]

milk one's doodle, to *phr.* [late 19C+] to masturbate. [MILK v.[3] (2) + DOODLE n.[2]]

milk oneself *v.* [late 19C+] to masturbate. [MILK v.[3]]

milk pan *see* MILK JUG n.[1].

milkround *n.* **1** [1940s+] (orig. milit.) a round trip, stopping at a regular list of places, addresses etc. **2** [1970s+] the annual graduate recruitment tour, in which firms send representatives on a trip around universities.

milkshake *n.* [1980s+] (N.Z.) a mix of bicarbonate of soda, used illegally in the hope of enhancing a racehorse's performance. [resemblance]

milk shakes *n.* [1910s–70s] (US) the female breasts (cf. CREAM JUGS).

milk shop/milk walk *n.* [19C] the female breasts (cf. CREAM JUGS).

milk the chicken *see* CHOKE THE CHICKEN.

milk the lizard/maggot/moose, to *phr.* [late 19C+] to masturbate (cf. LIZARD n.[3]).

milk the pigeon, to *phr.* [late 18C–early 19C] to attempt an impossible task (cf. MILK A DUCK).

milk walk *see* MILK SHOP.

milk-woman *n.*[1] [19C+] (Scot.) a wet-nurse; thus *green milk-woman*, one who has only recently given birth.

milk-woman *n.*[2] [late 19C–1900s] a female masturbator. [MILK v.[3] (2) + SE *woman*]

milky *n. see* MILKIE n.

milky *adj.*[1] [mid-19C] (Und.) white; thus *milky duds*, white clothes; *milky ones*, white linen rags.

milky *adj.*[2] [1930s+] cowardly. [SE *milksop*]

milky tats *n.* [mid-19C] white rags. [MILKY adj.[1] + TATS n.[2]]

milky way/way to bliss *n.* [18C] the female breasts (cf. CREAM JUGS).

mill *n.*[1] **1** [early 17C–early 19C] a chisel. **2** [17C] a housebreaker (cf. MILL-KEN). [SE *mill*, covering a variety of engines and tools]

mill *n.*[2] [late 18C–early 19C] the vagina (cf. GRINDSTONE).

mill *n.*[3] **1** [early–mid-19C] a fight. **2** [19C–1930s] a prize-fight, a brawl, a fist-fight. [MILL v.[1] (1)]

mill *n.*[4] **1** [mid–late 19C] a tread*mill*. **2** [mid-19C–1950s] a prison. **3** [mid-19C+] a prison guardhouse. [(1) abbr. SE; (2) and (3) ext. that use]

mill *n.*[5] [1910s–40s] (US) a typewriter. [it 'grinds out' the words]

mill *n.*[6] [1910s+] (US) an engine of an aircraft or 'souped up' car; thus *turn the mill*, start the engine. [Fr. *moulin*, a mill, thus WW1 Fr. sl. *moulin à café*, 'coffee-grinder', i.e. a machine gun, operated by a crank handle]

mill *n.*[7] **1** [1940s+] (US) a *mill*ion, usu. dollars. **2** [1960s+] a *mill*imetre, esp. in the diameter of a tube or gun barrel. [abbr.]

mill *v.*[1] **1** [16C–19C] to thrash, to fight, to overcome. **2** [16C–19C] to smash, to break open, to spoil. **3** [early 17C–early 19C] (Und.) to steal, to rob, to break open; thus [late 18C] *mill a go*, to succeed in a robbery or theft, [mid-18C–late 19C] *mill a quod*, to break out of prison. **4** [late 17C–mid-19C] to kill, to murder. [SE *mill*, to grind down, to break into small parts]

mill *v.*[2] [mid-19C] to sentence to the treadmill, to imprison. [MILL n.[4] (1)]

mill a ken, to *phr.* [mid-16C–mid-19C] (Und.) to rob a house. [MILL v.[1] (3) + KEN n.[1]]

mill-clapper *n.* [late 17C–20C] a woman's tongue. [SE *mill-clapper*, an instrument which by striking the hopper causes the corn to be shaken into the mill-stones]

mill doll/dolly *n.* [mid-18C–mid-19C] a prison, orig. the Bridewell in Bridge Street, Blackfriars, London. [MILL n.[4]; ? + SE *Doll*, a woman's name, thus a woman and a play on *bride*]

mill doll/dolly *v.* [mid-18C–mid-19C] to beat hemp in prison. [MILL DOLL n.]

miller *n.*[1] **1** [mid-17C–mid-19C] a housebreaker, a thief. **2** [late 17C–early 19C] a killer, a murderer. **3** [early 19C] a vicious, intractable horse. **4** [19C] a boxer. [MILL v.[1]]

miller *n.*[2] [early 19C–1920s] **1** a joke, esp. an old 'chestnut'. **2** a joke-book. [JOE MILLER]

miller *n.*[3] [1940s+] (Aus.) a cicada. [the grinding of its legs]

miller's daughter *n.* [late 19C+] water (cf. FISHERMAN'S DAUGHTER). [rhy. sl.]

miller's eye *n.* [mid-19C–1920s] a lump of flour in a loaf.

Miller time *n.* [20C] (US) a period of relaxation, the end of the working day. [the advertisements for *Miller Lite Beer*, which promote the end of the day as *Miller time*]

millia murder! *see* MELIA MURDER!

milliner's shop *n.* [19C] the vagina (cf. DOLLYMOP).

milling *n.* **1** [mid-16C–early 19C] robbing, stealing. **2** [early 19C] boxing for money, prize-fighting. **3** [early 19C] fighting with the fists. **4** [early 19C] of a horse, kicking. **5** [early 19C] a beating, a thrashing. [MILL v.[1]]

milling-cove *n.* [early 19C] a prize-fighter. [MILL v.[1] + COVE]

million *n.* [late 19C+] a sure bet. [abbr. MILLION TO A BIT OF DIRT]

million-dollar *adj.* [late 19C+] (US) splendid, of great value.

million-dollar wound *n.* [1940s+] (US milit.) any wound that guarantees the victim a passage out of a war zone and back to the USA. [equivalent to UK *blighty one* (see BLIGHTY) in WW1]

million to a bit of dirt *phr.* [late 19C] a very sure bet.

mill-ken/milken *n.* [late 17C–19C] a housebreaker. [MILL A KEN]

mill lay *n.* [late 17C–early 19C] breaking and entering for the purpose of robbery. [MILL n.[1] (2) + LAY n.[4] (2)]

mill one's glaze, to *phr.* [18C–early 19C] to knock out one's eye. [MILL v.[1] + GLASIERS]

milltag/milltug/milltwig/miltog *n.* [mid–late 19C] a shirt. [Shelta *melthog*, a shirt]

mill the glaze, to *phr.* [late 17C–18C] (Und.) to break a window as a means of entering a house. [MILL v.[1] (3) + GLAZE]

mill town/village *n.* [1960s] (US) the poor area of a town or city. [the housing built by mill-owners to house their workers]

milltug/milltwig *see* MILLTAG.

mill village *see* MILL TOWN.

milly *n.* [20C] a shirt. [abbr. MILLTAG]

milly *adj.* [1990s] (Black) aggressive, pugnacious; thus *get milly*, to become aggressive. [abbr. MILITANT]

miln up *v.* [1940s–50s] (prison) to lock into a cell (cf. CHUBB). [*Milne*, a well-known firm of locksmiths]

milquetoast *see* CASPER MILQUETOAST.

milt *n.* [19C] semen (cf. ROE). [SE *milt*, the roe of the male fish]

milt market/shop *n.* [19C] the vagina. [MILT + SE *market/shop*]

miltog *see* MILLTAG.

milton *n.* [mid-19C] an oyster. [? pun on Gray's *Elegy written in a Country Churchyard* (1751) 'mute inglorious Miltons']

miltonian *n.* [mid–late 19C] a policeman. [ety. unknown]

milt shop *see* MILT MARKET.

milvad *n.* [mid-19C] a blow. [Scot.]

milvader *v.* [mid-19C] to beat, to assault. [MILVAD]

Milwaukee cider/special/water *n.* [1950s–60s] (US) beer. [the city's many breweries]

Milwaukee goitre *n.* [1930s+] (US) a beer belly (cf. GERMAN GOITRE). [a ref. to, *inter alia*, 'Schlitz, the beer that made Milwaukee famous', as did the many beers brewed for the predominantly Ger. immigrant population]

Milwaukee special/water *see* MILWAUKEE CIDER.

mimis *see* MEEMIES.

min *v.* [mid-19C] to steal. [ety. unknown; ? abbr. SE *mind*, to look after]

mince *v.* [1980s+] (N.Z.) to work as a prostitute on several different boats in a single night; used by SHIPGIRLS.

mince about *v.* [1980s+] (N.Z.) to loiter, to 'hang about'.

minces/mince pies *n.* [mid-19C+] the eyes. [rhy. sl.]

minchin malacho *see* MICHING MALICHO.

mind *v.* (Und.) **1** [1920s+] to protect, to act as a bodyguard. **2** [1950s+] to bribe regularly.

mind!/mind you! *excl.* [early 19C+] 'make sure you *mind*', 'bear (something said) in *mind*'. [abbr.]

min dae *phr.* [1960s+] (S.Afr.) used as a greeting in the S.Afr. army by national servicemen who have forty or fewer days to serve (cf. WAKE-UP n.[3]). [Afk. *min dae*, few days]

mind-bender / -expander / -explorer / -opener / -spacer / -tripper *n.* [1960s+] **1** a psychedelic or psychotropic drug (cf. MIND-BLOW; MIND DETERGENT). **2** anything that, through the difficulty of its solution or comprehension, fig. 'bends the mind'. **3** a user of hallucinogens. [SE *mind* + *bend/expand/explore/open*/SPACE OUT/TRIP v.[1]]

mind-bending *adj.* [1960s+] amazing, fantastic, remarkable, orig. in the context of hallucinogenic drug use.

mind-blow/-blower *n.* [1960s+] **1** something that is astonishing, remarkable. **2** a psychedelic drug (cf. MIND-BENDER; MIND DETERGENT). [MIND-BLOWING]

mind-blowing *adj.* [1960s+] astounding, amazing, remarkable, orig. in the context of hallucinogenic drug use. [BLOW ONE'S MIND]

mind candy *n.* [1970s+] (US) anything light and intellectually undemanding.

mind detergent *n.* [1960s+] **1** a psychedelic or psychotropic drug. **2** anything that, through the difficulty of its solution or comprehension, fig. 'bends the mind' (cf. MIND-BENDER; MIND-BLOW).

minder *n.* **1** [1920s+] a criminal's bodyguard, a 'strong-arm man', someone who guards stolen property. **2** [1980s+]

extended to a variety of non-criminal milieux, e.g. *governmental minders, journalistic minders.*

mind-expander/-explorer *see* MIND-BENDER.

mindfuck *n.* **1** [1960s] a fantasy copulation. **2** [1960s+] (orig. US) an emotionally overwhelming experience, usu. through drugs. **3** [1960s+] (US campus) one who delights in manipulating others. **4** [1970s+] a psychotic individual. **5** [1970s+] deception, bafflement, confusion. [SE *mind* + FUCK n.[1]]

mindfuck *v.* [1960s+] (orig. US) to deceive, to tease, esp. while the victim is under the influence of drugs and thus less emotionally stable (cf. HEADFUCK). [SE *mind* + FUCK v.[1]]

mindfucked *adj.* [1980s+] (US campus) drunk, under the influence of drugs. [MINDFUCK v.]

mindfucker *n.* [1960s+] (orig. US) a person or event that is totally confusing or amazing. [MINDFUCK v.]

mindfucking *adj.* [1960s+] (orig. US) baffling, confusing, amazing. [MINDFUCK v.]

mind game *n.* [1960s+] (orig. US) psychological trickery and manipulation, usu. hostile or negative in intent (cf. HEAD GAME).

mind like a sink/sewer *phr.* [1930s+] an imagination that invariably sees a smutty meaning or double-entendre in any statement.

mind mice at the crossroads, to *phr.* [20C] (Irish) **1** to do anything undemanding and simple. **2** to undertake a task requiring deviousness and patience.

mind one's book, to *phr.* [early 18C] of a schoolchild, to work hard.

mind one's own business, to *phr.* [1990s] to masturbate.

mind one's own pigeon, to *phr.* [20C] (N.Z.) to mind one's own business. [corruption of SE *pidgin*, concern, affair]

mind one's ps and qs, to *phr.* **1** [late 18C–early 19C] to have an eye for the main chance. **2** [20C] to behave oneself, to be careful, to be polite (cf. MIND ONE'S STOPS). [? SE *please* and *thank-you*, shorthand for the basic manners taught to infants]

mind one's step *see* WATCH ONE'S STEP.

mind one's stops, to *phr.* [mid-19C+] to watch one's manners, to behave properly (in front of one's 'elders and betters'); thus [mid-19C] *mind your stops!* be careful! (cf. MIND ONE'S PS AND QS). [*mind your full-stops*, said when teaching a child to read, 20C use mainly W.I.]

mind-opener *see* MIND-BENDER.

mind out! *excl.* [late 19C+] be on your guard, watch out.

mind-spacer *see* MIND-BENDER.

mind the fort *see* HOLD THE FORT.

mind the grease *phr.* [late 19C] let me pass, please. [the speaker wishes to 'slip past']

mind the paint *phr.* [late 19C] a phr. used to refer to a passing woman who is considered to be wearing too much make-up. [the sign left by painters to indicate wet paint]

mind the step! *excl.* [late 19C] look out!, be careful! [a teasing phr. used to someone who appears somewhat drunk (there is no actual step)]

mind the store, to *phr.* [1920s+] (US) to take care of someone or something.

mind-tripper *n.*[1] *see* MIND-BENDER.

mind-tripper *n.*[2] [1960s+] (US campus/teen) someone seen as eccentric, odd, abnormal (cf. MIND-BENDER). [SE *mind* + TRIPPER n.]

mind you! *see* MIND!

mind your backs! *excl.* [20C] out of the way! [earlier railway use, coined by porters pushing heavy and thus injurious barrows through the crowds]

mind your eye! *excl.* [mid-19C+] be careful! look out!

mind your own fish *phr.* [20C] (Aus.) mind your own business.

mine! *excl.* [1980s+] (US campus) my fault.

mine/my arse on a bandbox *phr.* [late 18C–early 19C] a phr. used when something offered is inadequate for the purposes required, meaning 'that won't do' (cf. MY ARSE! excl.¹). [ARSE n.¹ (1) + SE *bandbox*, a light cardboard box used to contain millinery etc, which would not make a stable seat]

mine-jobber *n.* [late 19C] a financial fraud. ['When English copper mining became comparatively valueless by reason the import of ... ore as ballast, all the rascals on change floated mine companies, which had not a chance of success' (Ware)]

mine of pleasure *n.* [mid-19C] the vagina.

ming *n.* [1980s] a marijuana cigarette made of discarded butts. [MING v. or, given the unpleasant taste, ? ref. to SF character *Ming the Merciless* in the series *Flash Gordon* (from 1936)]

ming *v.* [1970s] (Scot.) to stink (cf. MINGER). [Scot.]

minge *n.* [20C] **1** the vagina. **2** women in general. [Suffolk dial., ult. synon. Rom. *mingra*, note East Anglian *minge*, to drizzle]

minge bag *n.* **1** [1970s+] an unpleasant or disliked woman. **2** [1990s] a miser. [MINGE + BAG n.³]

minger *n.* [1970s+] one who lit. or fig. smells, a 'stinker'. [MING v.]

minge winker *n.* [1990s] a striptease artiste. [MINGE n. (1) + SE *winker*]

mingles *n.* [1970s+] (US) single and unrelated people who share ownership of a home, usu. for economic benefit. [SE *mingle + singles*, a bureaucratic coinage, defined as 'mingling for fun, economy or companionship']

mingo *n.* [late 18C–mid-19C] (US campus) a chamberpot. [? MING v.]

mingo *v.* [late 18C–mid-19C] (US campus) to urinate. [MINGO n.]

mingra *n.* [20C] (market traders) a policeman. [? *minch*, to prowl around, to move stealthily]

mingy *adj.¹* [late 19C+] mean, tight-fisted, miserly (cf. MINGE BAG). [? SE *mean/mangy + stingy*]

mingy *adj.²* [late 19C+] deceitful. [dial. *minch*, to move stealthily]

mini *n.* [1960s+] a miniskirt. [orig. created as *the* fashion statement of the 'swinging Sixties', more recently resurgent in the 1980s]

minibennie *n.* [1970s] (US drugs) **1** benzedrine. **2** amphetamine (cf. A n.²).

Minié rifle *n.* [mid-19C] (US) cheap strong bourbon. [the power of its effect; ult. SE *Minié rifle*, named after inventor Claude Étienne *Minié* (1804–79), which fired a 'Minié' (or minnie) ball]

mini-mini/minny-minny *n.* [1950s+] (W.I.) small spots that one sees in front of one's eyes, either as a result of a blow to the head, or from the mild hallucinations that may accompany the smoking of 'ganja'. [Lat. *minimus*, smallest, but note Twi *mini-mīnā*, a small, stinging fly + Hausa *míni*, smallness]

minister's coat *n.* [1930s+] (Irish) a Garda (police) greatcoat. [coined after a Tipperary woman claimed she had been seduced when a policeman persuaded her to 'lie down on the Minister's coat']

minister's/parson's face/head/snout *n.* [mid-19C–1950s] (US) a boiled or roasted hog's head with the eyes and jowls removed. [anti-clericalism]

mink *n.* **1** [late 19C; 1960s+] (US Black) a pretty, sexy young woman (cf. FOX n.⁴). **2** [20C] (US) the vagina (cf. BADGER n.⁷). **3** [1900s–70s] (US) a lecher or scoundrel.

mink and manure belt *n.* [1980s+] (S.Afr.) **1** the affluent rural areas that lie between Pretoria and Johannesburg. **2** affluent suburbs, typified by wealth and a love of horses, when found outside any city. Their inhabitants can be Black or White (cf. GIN AND JAG BELT).

Minnesota thirteen *n.* [1920s+] (US) an illegal brand of bourbon. [? the name of the corn used]

Minnie *n.* [1920s+] (US) *Minn*eapolis, Minnesota. [abbr.]

minnie five fingers *n.* [1920s] (US) the hand, as used in male masturbation (cf. MISS FIST).

Minnie Mouse *n.* [1940s+] (Aus.) the house (cf. MICKEY MOUSE n.¹). [rhy. sl.; ult. the Disney character]

minnow *n.* [1970s+] (US campus) a 340ml (12fl oz) bottle or can of beer. [SE *minnow*, the fish; i.e. small bottle/can]

minnow-muncher *n.* [1960s+] (US) a Roman Catholic (cf. MACKEREL-SNAPPER).

minny-minny *see* MINI-MINI.

minor *n.* [1990s] (Black) an unimportant matter.

minor clergy *n.* [late 18C–late 19C] young chimney-sweeps. [? the blackness of their sooty clothes]

minor-league *adj.* [1940s+] (orig. US) small-scale, modest (cf. MAJOR-LEAGUE). [baseball imagery]

minstrel *n.* [1960s–70s] (drugs) Durophet. [the drug's black and white capsules; thus a pun on the popular *Black and White Minstrel Show* (from 1960)]

mint *n.¹* (Und.) **1** [16C–mid-19C] a piece of money. **2** [mid-17C–early 18C] gold. [8C SE *mint*, money. The term was wholly sl. by 16C, although *the Mint*, as a place, remained SE]

mint *n.²* [1950s+] (US gay) effeminacy; usu. in phr. a *hint of mint*, a trace of homosexual tendencies (cf. MINTY n.). [numerous advertisements promoting products with 'a hint of mint']

mint *adj.* [1990s] (US teen) a general term of thorough approval. [SE *mint*, unblemished]

mint drop *n.* [early–mid-19C] (US) a coin; thus in pl. *mint drops*, money (cf. MINT SAUCE). [the synon. sweet, a sugarplum flavoured with peppermint + pun on MINT n.¹]

mintee *see* MINTY n.

mint gold/money, to *phr.* [mid-19C+] to make a good deal of money, to profit (cf. COIN).

mint hog *n.* [early 19C] an Irish shilling. [? MINT n.¹ + image of the hog as a source of income (cf. GENTLEMAN WHO PAYS THE RENT)]

mintie *n.¹* *see* MINTY n.

mintie *n.²* [1930s+] (Aus.) comfort, solace; thus *without a mintie*, penniless. [the advertising slogan of *Minties*, a peppermint-flavoured sweet, 'It's moments like these you need Minties']

mint leaf *n.¹* [1940s+] (US) a banknote, money (cf. MINT DROP). [the colour of dollar bills]

mint leaf/weed *n.²* [1970s] (drugs) mint or poss. parsley leaves impregnated with phencyclidine (PCP) for smoking.

mint money *see* MINT GOLD.

mint sauce *n.* [mid-19C] money (cf. MINT DROPS). [laboured pun on SE *mint + source*]

mint weed *see* MINT LEAF n.².

minty/mintee/mintie *n.* [1910s–70s] (US gay) **1** an effeminate male homosexual. **2** a masculine lesbian. [MINT n.²]

minty *adj.* [1950s–60s] (camp gay) fading, losing one's attractiveness, said of an ageing effeminate male homosexual. [? MINTY n.]

minus *adj.* [early 19C] lacking, bereft of.

mioota! *excl.* [1990s] (US teen) see you later. [? Sp./Ital. *minuta*, one minute]

mira *n.* [20C] (drugs) opium. [abbr. SE *miraculous* or ? Sp. *mira!* look]

miraculous *adj.* [19C] (Scot.) drunk (cf. ABOUT RIGHT adj.¹).

miraculous cairn *n.* [19C] the vagina (cf. BEAUTY SPOT n.¹).

miraculous pitcher/pitcher that holds water with the mouth downwards *n.* [late 18C–mid-19C] the vagina (cf. PIPKIN; PITCHER n.²).

mirthquake *n.* [1940s–60s] (US) anything amusing. [SE *mirth + earthquake*]

mis/miss n. [late 19C+] a miscarriage. [abbr.]

mis adj. [late 19C+] miserable. [abbr.]

misbehave n. [20C] (Aus.) a shave. [rhy. sl.]

mischief n. [late 16C+] euph. for 'the devil'; thus play the mischief/mischief with, what/how the mischief ... ? go to the mischief, like the mischief.

misdeal n. [late 19C] (US) a mistake. [card imagery]

miserable n. [mid–late 19C] weak tea. [? play on the def. of tea as that which 'cheers but does not inebriate'; being weak, it fails to cheer the drinker]

miserable adj. [mid-19C+] (Aus.) tight-fisted, grasping, mean. [pun on SE miserable/miser]

miserables, the n. [late 19C–1920s] a hangover.

misery n.[1] [late 18C+] a depressing person; thus [late 19C+] be a (right old) misery, to be a depressing person, to act in a self-pitying manner, [late 19C+] (long, thin) streak of misery, a very thin, mournful and lugubrious person.

misery n.[2] **1** [early–late 19C] gin (cf. MOTHER'S RUIN). **2** [1930s–50s] (US) bad coffee. [its effects]

misery bowl n. [late 19C] a bowl used for vomiting by sufferers of sea-sickness.

misery-moany n. [1940s+] (Irish) a whinger, a complainer.

misfortune n. [19C] an illegitimate child; thus have/meet with a misfortune, to have an illegitimate child.

mish n.[1] [late 17C–mid-19C] a shirt (cf. CAMESA; COMMISSION; SHIMMY n.[1]; SMISH). [Ital. camisa, a shirt]

mish n.[2] [1930s–40s] a missionary. [abbr.]

mishegaas/meshugaas/mishegoss n. [late 19C] nonsense, obsession, tomfoolery. [Yid.]

mish-mash n. [1950s–60s] an inadequate, confused person, esp. a woman who is undergoing emotional problems.

mish-topper n. [late 17C–early 19C] **1** an overcoat. **2** a petticoat. [MISH n.[1]+ SE topper, lit. 'shirt topper']

mishugge see MESHUGA.

mislain/miesli/misle/misli v.[1] [early 18C+] to rain. [Shelta]

mislain v.[2] [late 19C+] to go (cf. MIZZLE). [? Shelta]

misle/misli see MISLAIN v.[1].

misplaced eyebrow n. [1910s–20s] (US) a moustache.

Miss n.[1] [1950s+] (gay) a title prefixed to a name to imply that the subject's homosexuality is known or obvious. The pfx. was a staple of pre-Gay Liberation Front camp usage, e.g. Miss Ugly (cf. MISS THING; MISS PEACH).

Miss/Mr/Mrs/Ms n.[2] [1950s+] (US campus) a title used in comb. with a n. to express the subject's primary characteristic, e.g. Miss Grind, a very hard worker.

miss n.[1] [late 17C–early 19C] a prostitute, 'a Whore of Quality' (BE). [a heavily ironic use of SE]

miss n.[2] see MIS n.

miss v.[1] [late 19C] (US) to be unlucky.

miss v.[2] [1950s+] (drugs) to inject a drug. [joc. reversal of HIT v.[2] (2)]

Miss Adams see SWEET FANNY ADAMS.

Miss Amy n. [1960s+] (US Black) a young White woman (cf. MISS ANN).

Miss Ann/Anne/Annie n. [1920s+] (US Black) a White woman considered to be hostile or patronizing to Blacks (cf. ANN).

Miss/Mrs Astor n. [1960s+] (US) **1** a woman who overdresses. **2** usu. mocking, an elite 'social leader' of a community (cf. ASTORBILT; MISS LIZZIE TISH). [the wealthy Astor family, once social arbiters of New York]

miss a trick, to phr. [1920s+] (orig. US) to fail to see what is going on, to be ignorant of circumstances, usu. in neg. never miss a trick, to be highly aware. [card imagery]

Miss Brown n. [late 18C] the vagina (cf. BROWN MADAM). [joc./euph. use of proper name]

Miss Carrie n. [1960s] (drugs) a quantity of drugs carried on one's person. [pun on carry/Carrie]

Miss Cubba n. [20C] an effeminate man (cf. CUBBA n.). [in W. African cultures Cuba, the day-name of a woman born on a Wednesday]

Miss Emma n. [1930s+] (drugs) morphine. [the letter M]

Miss Emma Jones n. [1950s+] an addiction to morphine. [MISS EMMA + JONES n.[1]]

Miss Fist n. [20C] the hand, in the context of masturbation (cf. CONVERSE WITH HARRY PALM; FIVE-FINGER MARY; FIVE-FINGERED WIDOW; FOUR SISTERS ON THUMB STREET; LADY FIVE FINGERS; MARY FIST; MINNIE FIVE FINGERS; MR PALMER AND HIS FIVE SONS; MRS PALM AND HER FIVE DAUGHTERS; MOTHER FIST AND HER FIVE DAUGHTERS; ROSY PALM AND HER FIVE SISTERS).

Miss Fitch n. [20C] an unpleasant woman. [rhy. sl. Miss Fitch = BITCH n.[1] (1)]

Miss Flash n. [1950s–60s] (camp gay) a user of amphetamines or Benzedrine. [FLASH n.[7]]

Miss Horner n. [19C] the female genitals. [play on HORN n.[2] (2)]

missile n. [1980s+] (drugs) phencyclidine (cf. ACE n.[3]). [its 'explosive' effects]

missile basing n. [1980s+] (drugs) a mixture of liquid crack cocaine and phencyclidine. [MISSILE + BASING adj.]

missing n. [mid-19C] courtship. [SE miss, a young woman + sfx. -ing]

missing link n. [20C] (US) a stupid person.

mission n. [1980s+] (drugs) **1** a search for drugs, esp. for cocaine (cf. INTERPLANETARY MISSION). **2** a binge on crack cocaine (cf. BEAM ME UP, SCOTTY!). [the specific allusion is to the introduction to episodes of the TV series Star Trek (from 1966)]

missionary man n. [1980s+] (US campus) an uninspired lover. [SE missionary position, considered the least adventurous of all the positions of love-making]

mission squawker n. [1920s] (US tramp) a mission evangelist.

mission stiff n. [late 19C+] (US) **1** a missionary worker. **2** a convert. **3** a tramp or vagrant who frequents charitable missions, looking for hand-outs, food and shelter, esp. one who pretends conversion (cf. BINDLE STIFF; BLANKET STIFF). [SE mission + STIFF n.[2] (3)]

missis n. [mid-19C+] the mistress of the household. [SE Mrs]

Mississippi marbles n. [1920s–50s] (US) dice, or the game of craps.

Mississippi mule n. [1960s] (US) illicitly distilled, 'bootleg' bourbon. [its 'kick']

Miss Jane n. [1950s] (W.I.) an effeminate man (cf. MISS CUBBA; MISS MOLLY; MISS NANCY).

Miss Lashey n. [1950s] (W.I.) a male gossip (cf. CHAT-CHAT). [LASHER n.[2], but while this man also chases women, it is for gossip rather than for seduction, thus the effeminate Miss]

Miss Laycock n. [late 18C–early 19C] **1** the vagina. **2** a prostitute. [pun on LAY v.[1] + COCK n.[2] (1)]

Miss Lillian n. [1960s–70s] (US Black) a White girl or woman of any age, but usu. an older woman.

Miss Lizzie Tish/Tizzie Lish n. [1960s+] (US) **1** a woman who overdresses. **2** usu. mocking, an élite 'social leader' of a community (cf. MISS ASTOR). [? anecdotal or a joc. use of a generic proper name]

Miss Molly/molly/molly-boy n. [early 18C–1920s] an effeminate or homosexual man; thus Miss Mollyism, effeminacy (cf. MISS JANE). [generic use of female name; note US regional dial. cut up molly, to act in an extravagant, frolicsome manner]

Miss Morph n. [1960s] (drugs) morphine (cf. MISS EMMA).

Miss Nancy n. [early 19C–1920s] an effeminate man, presumably a homosexual; thus Miss-Nancyfied, Miss Nancyish, effeminate, *Miss-Nancyism*, effeminacy (cf. MISS JANE). [generic use of female name; NANCY n.² is a later concept]

Miss One *see* MISS THING.

miss one's figure, to *phr.* [late 19C] to miss a chance.

miss one's guess, to *phr.* [20C] (orig. US) to make a mistake, to err.

miss one's tip, to *phr.* [mid–late 19C] (orig. circus) to fail in one's aim or objective.

Missouri bankroll *n.* [1930s] (US) a roll or wad of blank paper, cut to the same size as dollar bills, surrounded by a few real notes of high denomination (cf. CALIFORNIA BANKROLL). [the image of *Missouri* as a poverty-stricken state + SE *bankroll*. The term was coined by the Industrial Workers of the World (IWW or 'Wobblies'), who designed this form of 'bankroll' to foil the thieves who preyed on newly paid-off workers. A worker would create such a roll, flash it in public and inevitably face being beaten and robbed. He would, however, be rescued by sympathetic Wobblies, hitherto hidden, who would pounce on the thieves and give *them* the beating]

Missouri featherbed *n.* [late 19C] (US, mainly West.) a straw mattress.

Missouri hummingbird/nightingale *n.* [1910s–20s] (US) a mule (cf. ARIZONA NIGHTINGALE).

Miss Peach *n.* [1950s–60s] (camp gay) an informer. [MISS n.¹ + PEACH v.]

Miss Piggy *n.* [1970s+] a fat, often melodramatic person. [the character in *The Muppets*, the TV puppet series (1976–80)]

Miss Right *see* MR RIGHT.

Miss Taylor *n.* [early–mid-19C] a strong Spanish liquor. [Sp. *mistela*]

miss the boat, to *phr.* **1** [late 19C+] to be late. **2** [late 19C+] to lose an opportunity, to forfeit a chance (cf. MISS THE BUS). **3** [1960s] of a woman, to miss a menstrual period.

miss the bus, to *phr.* [late 19C+] to lose an opportunity, to forfeit a chance (cf. MISS THE BOAT).

miss the cushion, to *phr.* [early 16C–late 17C] to miss one's mark, to fail.

Miss Thing/Miss One *n.* [1950s+] **1** (orig. US gay) a greeting to a fellow homosexual man. **2** (US Black) a woman who is seen as arrogant and unpleasant.

Miss Tizzie Lish *see* MISS LIZZIE TISH.

Missus *n.* [mid-19C+] (Aus.) the traditional title of the wife of the owner or manager of a sheep station. [SE *missus*, Mrs]

Miss/Mrs Van-/van-Neck *n.* [late 18C–early 19C] a woman with large breasts (cf. BUSHEL-BUBBY). [joc. use of supposed proper name]

Miss Xylophone *n.* [1950s–60s] (camp gay) a notably thin person. [MISS n.¹ + SE *xylophone* (the individual's ribs protrude like the metal bars of the instrument)]

missy *n.* [late 17C+] a young girl, esp. as characterized by servants and sometimes derog.; thus (Anglo-Ind.) *missy-baba*, a young lady.

mist *n.* (drugs) **1** [1970s+] phencyclidine (cf. ACE n.³). **2** [1980s+] smoke created by a crack cocaine pipe.

mistake *n.* [1950s+] an unplanned pregnancy and the child that follows (cf. ACCIDENT n.¹).

Mr *see* MISS n.².

mister *n.* [1920s+] (US) a form of address to a man whose proper name one does not know (cf. SISTER n.¹).

Mr Arnold *see* ARNOLD.

Mr Astorbilt *see* ASTORBILT.

Mr Average *n.* [1960s+] the average member of the public (cf. JOE PUBLIC).

Mr Big *n.* [1930s+] (orig. US) an important, influential person, esp. a 'criminal mastermind'.

Mr Blue *n.* [1960s] (drugs) hydromorphone, the basis of the

synthetic opiate Dilaudid. [? a blue elixir of morphine sulphate]

Mr Boozington *see* BOOZINGTON.

Mr Chad *see* CHAD.

Mr Chant *n.* [1920s–30s] an aunt. [rhy. sl.]

Mr/Mister Charlie/Charley *n.* [1920s+] (US Black) any White man (cf. BOSS CHARLIE). [SE *Mr* + generic 'White' name *Charlie*]

Mr Clean *n.*¹ [1960s+] (US) an obsessively neat and prudish man. [the character '*Mr Clean*' in advertisements for a brand of household cleaner of the same name, first marketed in late 1950s]

Mr Clean *n.*² [1970s+] (orig. US) someone who makes a point of portraying themselves (sincerely or otherwise) as free of corruption; esp. in politics, business, sport or other forms of public life in which a proclaimed moral stance is useful; ext. as *Miss Clean*, *Mrs Clean*.

Mr Cool *see* JOE COOL.

Mr Cracker *n.* [1950s+] (US Black) a White person (cf. MR CHARLIE). [SE *Mr* + CRACKER n.⁴]

Mr Double Tripes *n.* [late 18C–early 19C] an exceptionally fat man (cf. TRIPE AND TRILLIBUBS). [TRIPE]

Mr Do-you-wrong *n.* [1970s] (US Black) a man who mistreats women.

Mr Ed *n.* [1970s+] (US teen) **1** an unimpeachable inside source. **2** a trusted sidekick. [proper name *Ed McMahon*, a regular on US TV's *Johnny Carson Show* (1955–6)]

Mr Eddie *n.* [1900s–30s] (US Black) a White man (cf. MR CHARLIE). [generic use]

Mr Fat *see* FAT n.¹.

Mr Firstnighter *n.* [1930s+] a sophisticated, upper-class person, or one who poses as such. [US radio show *Mr Firstnighter* of 1930s, featuring a white-tie-and-tails star]

Mister/Mr Five by Five *n.* [1940s] (US) a very short, fat man (cf. FIVE BY FIVE). [title of a 1942 pop song by Don Raye and Gene de Paul]

Mr Fixit *n.* [1950s+] **1** a general facilitator. **2** a DIY expert. [a series of short religious films in 1950s (from US?) featured '*Mr Fixit*', a carpenter who combined the mending of furniture with delivering pious homilies to the attendant children]

Mister Franklin *n.* [20C] euph. for MOTHERFUCKER. [initial letters]

Mr/Mrs Fuzzgug *n.* [1930s+] (Aus.) generic for everyman or everywoman. [ety. unknown; ? FISGIG; i.e. humanity's propensity to laugh at each other's failings]

Mr Grim *n.* [late 18C; 1940s+] death.

Mr Gub *n.* [1960s+] (Aus. Aborigine) the White man (cf. MR CHARLIE). [abbr. *gubba*, a low class White person]

Mister/Mr Happy *n.* [1980s+] (US) the penis.

Mr Happy Helmet *n.* [1990s] the penis.

Mister Harding *n.* [20C] (W.I.) a hard task-master, a strict superior. [SE *hard*]

Mister Hawkins *see* HAWKINS n.³.

Mr Hickenbothom *n.* [late 18C–19C] any nameless object (cf. THINGUMABOB).

Mr Hopkins/Hopkins *n.* [late 18C–19C] a lame or limping person; thus *don't hurry, Mr Hopkins*, meaning in US 'hurry up', and in UK 'don't bother to go too fast' (cf. HOPPING GILES). [pun on SE *hop*]

Mr Horner *n.* [19C] a promiscuous man. [pun on SE *whore*]

Mr Hyde *n.* [20C] an unpleasant, untrustworthy person. [rhy. sl. *Mr Hyde* = SNIDE adj.]

Mr Knap is concerned *phr.*¹ [early 19C] (Und.) this is a matter involving theft. [KNAP v.]

Mr Knap is concerned/has been there *phr.*² [early 19C] of a woman, pregnant. [KNAPPED]

Mr Lo *see* LO.

Mr Mason *n.* [1990s] (US campus) particularly strong marijuana. [var. on BENNY MASON]

mister-me-friend/-man *n.* [1970s+] (Irish) a person, an acquaintance.

Mr Mention *n.* [1980s+] (W.I./UK Black teen) a person known as a popular figure or as a successful womanizer.

Mr Milquetoast *see* CASPAR MILQUETOAST.

Mr Moto *n.* [1930s–70s] (US) a Japanese or Asian man (cf. MOTO n.¹). [the fictional Jap. detective created by novelist J.P. Marquand (1893–1960)]

Mr Muggins *n.* [late 19C+] (Aus.) oneself, esp. in the context of behaving like a gullible fool. [MUGGINS n.¹ (2)]

Mister Mutch *n.* [20C] (Aus.) the crutch, the groin. [rhy. sl.]

Mr Nash is concerned *phr.* [early 19C] used of someone who is absent, having run off. [NASH v.]

Mr Nawpost *n.* [late 17C–late 18C] a fool, a simpleton. [one who, if hungry enough, would 'gnaw a post']

Mr Nice-Guy *n.* [1960s+] a pleasant, amenable person, although that status carries a certain conditionality; thus *no more Mr Nice Guy*, also used ironically.

Mr Palmer and his five sons *n.* [1950s+] (gay) the hand, used for masturbation (cf. MISS FIST; MRS PALM AND HER FIVE DAUGHTERS).

Mr Palmer is concerned *n.* [early 19C] the matter involves bribery. [PALM v.]

Mr Patel/Patel's *n.* [1980s+] the local corner newspaper/sweet shop or small grocery. [*Patel*, the most common Ind. surname in the UK and one borne by many of the Ugandan Asians who arrived in the early 1970s and began taking over such shops]

Mr Peanut *n.* [1960s] (US Black) a White man. [? Black scientist George Washington Carver (1864–1943) who worked with *peanuts* + the image of *peanuts* as a 'typical' Black food]

Mr Peaslin *n.* [19C] the penis. [? SE *pizzle*, an animal's penis, esp. a bull's penis]

Mr Prunella *n.* [late 18C–early 19C] a parson. [SE *prunella*, a strong textile, orig. silk, commonly used for gowns worn by clergymen, barristers and graduates]

Mr Pullen is concerned *phr.* [early 19C] an arrest has been made. [PULL IN]

Mr Quarto *see* QUARTO.

Mr/Miss Right *n.* [mid-19C+] the ideal lover, husband, wife, boy- or girlfriend for anyone so searching (cf. LORD RIGHT).

Mr Roper *n.* [mid-17C–mid-18C] the hangman (cf. ROPER n.¹). [his primary tool]

Mister Sin *n.* [1970s–80s] (US Black, Los Angeles) a member of the vice squad.

Mr/Mister Speaker *n.* **1** [mid–late 19C] (US) a revolver, a pistol. **2** [1940s] (US Black) a pistol, a handgun. [its noise + the political office of the *Speaker*, who 'lays down the law' in the US House of Representatives or the British Parliament]

Mr T *n.* [1950s+] (W.I. Rasta) the boss. [ety. unknown; ? anecdotal]

Mr Ten Per Cent *n.* [1920s+] (orig. US) **1** an agent, usu. in show business, who takes 10% (at least) of their client's earnings. **2** a middleman, esp. between interest groups and politicians, who arranges 'favours' and directs influence for some cut of the subsequent profits.

Mr Thingstable *n.* [late 18C–early 19C] 'Mr Constable, a ludicrous affectation of delicacy in the avoiding the pronunciation of the first syllable in the title of that officer, which in sound has some similarity to an indecent MONOSYLLABLE' (Grose 1785).

Mister Thomas *see* MISTER TOM.

Mister Three Balls *n.* [1940s–50s] **1** a pawnbroker. **2** a Jew. [var. on THREE BALLS]

Mister Tom/Thomas *n.* [1960s+] (US Black) a subservient Black person fitting willingly into the stereotyped and inferior image refined by generations of White supremacy. [var. on UNCLE TOM n. (1)]

Mr Twenty-six *n.* [1960s–70s] (drugs) a 26-gauge hypodermic syringe.

Mr Warner *n.* [1960s–70s] (drugs) a marijuana smoker. [MARY WARNER]

Mister/Mr Whiskers *n.* [1930s–60s] (US) the Government, or a government law enforcement agency (cf. UNCLE WHISKERS). [the trad. picture of a bearded 'Uncle Sam']

Mr Wiggins *n.* [early 19C] a fool, a simpleton.

Mr Wigsby/wigsby/wigster *n.* [late 18C–early 19C] a man wearing a wig.

Mister Wind *n.* [1930s+] (US Black) chilly winter winds, esp. as experienced in northern cities (cf. HAWK n.³).

Mr Wood *n.* [1930s+] a policeman's truncheon (cf. BILLY n.¹).

Mr Zip-Zip *n.* [1910s–40s] (US) a barber. [title of a 1917 pop song]

Mrs *n.*¹ [1910s+] a wife, esp. as *the Mrs*. The husband's surname is omitted, e.g. *Here is Mr Smith, Mrs is out shopping.*

Mrs *n.*² *see* MISS n.².

M.r.s. *see* M.R.S. DEGREE.

Mrs Astor *see* MISS ASTOR.

Mrs Astor's pet horse/billy goat/cow/pet cow/plush horse *n.* [1920s+] (US) **1** an over-made-up or overdressed person. **2** an arrogant, haughty person (cf. ASTORPERIOUS). [var. on ASTOR'S PET HORSE]

Mrs Chant's *n.* [1920s] a lavatory; thus *visit Mrs Chant's.* [rhy. sl. *Mrs Chant's* = MY AUNT'S. Mrs Ormiston *Chant* (1848–1923) was a well-known moralist]

M.r.s. Degree/M.r.s. *n.* [1970s+] (US campus) **1** a woman who goes to college mainly to find a husband. **2** a woman who gets married while a student. [abbr. and pun on US 'Master of Science'/Mrs; pron. 'missus']

Mrs Ducket/Duckett *n.* [20C] a bucket. [rhy. sl.]

Mrs Ducket!/Duckett! *excl.* [20C] euph. for FUCK IT!

Mrs Evans *n.* [late 18C] a female cat. [a witch of that name, who was supposedly wont to turn herself into a cat]

Mrs Fuzzgug *see* MR FUZZGUG.

Mrs Gafoops *n.* [1930s+] (Aus.) any otherwise unspecified or unnamed woman. [nonsense word]

Mrs Goff *n.* [early–mid-19C] (US campus) a woman. [ety. unknown; ? anecdotal]

Mrs Greenfields *n.* [20C] (tramp) sleeping in the open air; thus *Mrs Ashpits*, sleeping near a lime-kiln (cf. SIT UNDER DR GREENFIELDS). [imaginary landladies]

Mrs Harris and Mrs Gamp *n.* [mid-19C] the *Morning Herald* and the *Standard* newspapers. [from the two characters, one 'real' and one imaginary, in Charles Dickens's *Martin Chuzzlewit* (1843–4). *Mrs Gamp*, a nurse, constantly quoted the fantastical *Mrs Harris* as the witness and supporter of her every opinion, 'and thus afforded a parallel to the two newspapers, which appealed to each other as independent authorities, being all the while the production of the same editorial staff' (Hotten, 1867)]

Mrs Jones/Jones's house *n.* [mid-19C] the lavatory; thus *visit Mrs Jones*, to use the lavatory (cf. MOTHER JONES; NEIGHBOUR JONES).

Mrs Kelly wouldn't let young Edward play with you *phr.* [1920s+] (Aus.) a phr. addressed to a very dirty or badly behaved child. [the *Kellys* in question are the bushranger *Ned* (1854–80) and his mother]

Mrs Lo *see* LO.

Mrs Lukey Props *n.* [19C] **1** a tramp's female companion. **2** a brothel-keeper. [? an actual person]

Mrs Mopp *n.*[1] [1940s+] a cleaner. [the character *Mrs Mopp* created by Tommy Handley (1892–1949) for the radio comedy series *ITMA* (*It's That Man Again*, from 1939). Her catchphrase was 'Shall I do you now, sir?']

Mrs Mopp *n.*[2] [1940s+] a shop. [rhy. sl.; *see* MRS MOPP *n.*[1]]

Mrs More *n.* [20C] the floor (cf. RORY O'MOORE). [rhy. sl.]

Mrs Murphy *n.* [1960s+] the lavatory (cf. MRS JONES).

Mrs Palm/Palmer and her five daughters *n.* [1950s+] the hand, as used for masturbation (cf. MISS FIST).

Mrs Philip's/Phillip's purse/ware *n.* [late 18C] a condom (cf. BISHOP *n.*[3]). ['These machines were long prepared and sold by a matron of the name of *Phillips*, at the Green Canister, in Half-moon Street, in the Strand. That good lady, having acquired a fortune, retired from business, but learning that the town was not well served by her successors, she, out of a patriotic zeal for the public welfare, returned to her occupation; out of which she gave notice by divers hand-bills, in circulation in the year 1776' (Grose 1796). Whether she was related to Mrs Phillips, that brothel-keeper who, in the mid-19C, ran a house at 11 Upper Belgrave Place, is alas unknown]

Mistress/Mrs Princum-Prancum *n.* [late 17C–mid-19C] a woman who is preoccupied by turning herself out neatly, and thus by the mind-set that is presumed to go with such obsessions. [PRINK]

Mrs Suds *n.* [1910s–20s] a washerwoman.

Mrs Van-/van-Neck *see* MISS VAN-NECK.

Mrs White *n.* [1900s–50s] a drug dealer, presumably in white powders, i.e. narcotics (cf. OLD LADY WHITE).

Mrs White is out of jail *phr.* [1960s+] (US) a warning to a woman that her slip is showing (cf. CHARLIE'S DEAD).

misty *adj.* [1950s+] (US) tearful. [mid–late 19C literary SE]

mit a ... *phr.* [1950s+] (Aus.) sceptically, 'with a grain of salt'. [deliberately 'German' pron. of SE *with a*]

mitching *n.* [late 19C+] (Can.) playing truant (cf. MIKE *v.*).

mite/mitey *n.*[1] [late 18C–19C] a cheesemonger. [SE *mite*, a tiny insect found in cheese]

mite *n.*[2] **1** [mid-19C+] a particle, a tiny piece. **2** [late 19C+] a whit or jot, a bit.

mitey *see* MITE *n.*[1].

mitt *n.* **1** [19C] (US) usu. in pl., a glove. **2** [late 19C–1960s] (US) a hand of cards. **3** [late 19C+] (US) usu. in pl., the hand (cf. FIN *n.*[1]). **4** [1980s] (US Und.) a roll of money. [abbr. SE *mitten*]

mitt *v.* **1** [1900s–20s] (US) to punch. **2** [1900s–50s] (US) to shake hands, or to press something into someone's hand. **3** [1910s–50s] (US Und.) to handcuff, to arrest. [MITT *n.*]

mitt camp/joint *n.* [1940s–50s] a palmist's or fortune-teller's establishment, tent etc. [MITT *n.* + SE *camp*/JOINT *n.*[3] (3)]

mitten *n.* **1** [19C+] the hand, esp. the fist (cf. FIN *n.*[1]; MITT *n.*). **2** [mid-19C+] (US) a rejection or dismissal; usu. as *give/get mitten* (cf. MITTIMUS). **3** [late 19C] a handcuff (usu. in pl.). **4** [late 19C] a boxing glove.

mitten *v.* [mid–late 19C] (US) to seize or grab; usu. as *mitten onto*.

mittflop *v.* [1940s] (US) (orig. milit.) to ingratiate oneself by doing favours; thus *mittflopper* (cf. MITTGLOM). [MITT *n.* (3) + SE *flop*]

mittglom *v.* [1910s–30s] (US) (orig. milit.) to ingratiate oneself by doing favours. [MITT *n.* (3) + GLOM *v.*]

mittimus *n.* [late 16C–mid-19C] a dismissal from an office or job; thus [mid-19C] *get one's mittimus*, to be dismissed, to be killed. [Lat. *mittimus*, we send. The word is used in legal Lat. as the first word of an arrest warrant and thus of the writ itself]

mitting *n.* [mid–late 19C] a shirt. [ety. unknown]

mitt joint *n.*[1] [1910s–30s] (US) a crooked gambling establishment. [MITT *n.* (3) + JOINT *n.*[3] (3)]

mitt joint *n.*[2] *see* MITT CAMP.

mitt man *n.* **1** [late 19C–1950s] (US Black) a religious charlatan who use his flock's credulity to make himself a sumptuous income. **2** [1960s] (US Und.) a confidence man. [? the white MITTs (gloves) such 'preachers' often affected, or the putting out of his MITT *n.* (3) for the suckers' money]

mitt pounding *n.* [1940s] (US Black) applause, clapping. [MITT *n.* (3) + SE *pound*]

mitt-pusher *n.* [1910s–20s] (US) a boxer. [MITT *n.* (3) + SE *pusher*]

mitt-reader *n.* [1920s+] (US) a fortune-teller, a palmist. [MITT *n.* (3) + SE *reader*]

mivey/mivy *n.* [late 19C] a landlady (cf. MIVVY *n.*[2]).

mivvy *n.*[1] [late 19C–1910s] a marble. [? pron.]

mivvy *n.*[2] **1** [late 19C] a contemptuous term for a woman. **2** [late 19C–1920s] the landlady of a lodging-house. [? ironic abbr. SE *marvel* or Cockney pron. of 'mother' as *muvva*]

mivvy *n.*[3] [1900s–50s] an expert, an adept. [? SE *marvel*]

mivy *see* MIVEY.

mix *n.*[1] **1** [mid-19C+] (US) a fight, a brawl. **2** [late 19C–1900s] a muddle, a mess.

mix *n.*[2] **1** [1970s+] (S.Afr.) methylated spirits, as drunk by alcoholics (cf. VLAM). **2** [1980s+] (Aus. drugs) a combination of cannabis and other herbs, usu. tobacco.

mix *n.*[3] [1980s+] (US Black) **1** a difficult situation. **2** the memory.

mix *v.*[1] [mid-19C+] (US) to fight (cf. MIX IN; MIX IT). [MIX *n.*[1] (1)]

mix *v.*[2] [1970s] to inject a drug, usu. heroin. [the *mix* of blood and heroin in solution that forms the injection]

mix and muddle *n.* [20C] a cuddle. [rhy. sl.]

mixed *adj.* [mid–late 19C] **1** confused, at a loss. **2** drunk (cf. ADDLED). [note *mix one's drinks*, to mix 'the grape and the grain' (and to suffer the subsequent hangover)]

mixed-ale oration *n.* [1900s] a poor political oration, typified by its illiterate use of the language; thus *mixed-ale philosopher*, a drunken know-it-all. [the assumption is that the speaker is drunk or may as well be so]

mix'em *see* MIXUM.

mixer *n.*[1] [1910s+] (US) a social gathering designed to introduce people to one another.

mixer *n.*[2] [1930s+] a trouble-maker, a gossip, usu. deliberately malicious, one who 'stirs things up'. [MIX *v.*[1]]

mix giblets *see* JOIN GIBLETS.

mix in *v.* [20C] to initiate or join a fight. [MIX *v.*[1]]

mix it/it up *v.* [late 19C+] (US) to fight, to foster trouble. [MIX *v.*[1]]

mix it up *v.*[1] [early 19C+] 'to agree secretly how the parties shall make up a tale, or colour a transaction in order to cheat or deceive another party, as in case of a justice-hearing, of a law-suit, or a cross in a boxing-match for money' (Jon Bee).

mix it up *v.*[2] *see* MIX IT.

mixmaster *n.* [1950s–80s] (US) a helicopter. [*Mixmaster*, a brand of kitchen appliances, orig. [1940s] used for a propeller-driven bomber]

mix-metal *n.* [late 18C–early 19C] a silversmith. [a silversmith's function]

mixologist *n.* [mid-19C+] (orig. US) a bartender, esp. as a mixer of cocktails; thus *mixology*, mixing cocktails. [SE *mix* + sfx. *-ologist*]

mixum/mix'em *n.* [early 17C–early 18C] an apothecary. [the mixing of medicines]

mix-up *n.* [mid-19C–1930s] a fist-fight. [now SE]

mixy *adj.* [1920s+] sociable, good at mixing.

mizzard *n.* [early 17C–late 19C] the face, the mouth. [MAZARD *n.* (3)]

mizzle *v.* [late 18C–late 19C; 1970s] to leave, to go quickly, to escape; also as *do a mizzle* (cf. NEEDY MIZZLER); thus excl. *mizzle!* go away! be off! [? Shelta *misli*, to go, note naut. jargon *mizzle one's dick*, to miss one's passage]

mizzled *adj.* [late 16C–late 19C] drunk. [? SE *mizmaze*, a state of confusion]

mizzler *n.*[1] *see* RUM MIZZLER.

mizzler *n.*[2] [1940s] a whinger, a complainer. [SE *mizzle*, to complain, to whimper]

Mizzoo *n.* [late 19C–1950s] (US) the Missouri River, Missouri.

m.j. *n.* [1960s+] (orig. US drugs) marijuana. [MARY JANE n.[2]]

mjieta *n.* [1960s+] (S.Afr.) a township playboy. [Zulu *umjita*, an urbanized man]

m.l.a. *n.* [1990s] (US campus) passionate kissing. [abbr. massive *l*ip *a*ction]

mlungu *n.* [1980s+] (S.Afr. Black) used mockingly, a White person (cf. HONKIE). [Nguni *umlungu*, a White man. The term was coined in early 19C, ? f. Xhosa/Zulu *lunga*, to be correct or good, to be in good order. The ironic/mocking use developed much more recently]

m.m.s *n.* [1970s] (drugs) the hunger that follows smoking marijuana; i.e. marijuana munchies. [abbr.; SE *marijuana* + MUNCHIE n. (2)]

m.o. *n.*[1] [1950s+] (Und.) the distinguishing working style of a criminal or gang. [abbr. Lat. *modus operandi*, the way of working]

m.o. *n.*[2] *see* MO n.[5].

Mo *n.*[1] [mid–late 19C] the *Mo*gul Music Hall, later the Middlesex. [abbr.; the *Mogul*, near Drury Lane was established in 1850, according to Ware on the site of 'a public garden there ... kept by some wonderful Indian']

mo *n.*[2] **1** [late 19C+] a moment, a second (cf. HALF A MO phr.). **2** [1910s–50s] (US) a month. [abbr.]

mo *n.*[3] **1** [late 19C+] (Aus./N.Z.) a *mo*ustache. **2** [late 19C+] (Aus.) the female genital area, esp. the pubic area. [abbr.; (2) is pun on (1)]

mo *n.*[4] [1960s+] (US campus) a homosexual. [abbr. HOMO n.[2]]

mo/m.o. *n.*[5] [1970s] (drugs) marijuana. [initial letter, ? abbr. MOHASKY n.]

Mo *n.*[6] [1990s] (US Black teen) the Fillmore area of San Francisco. [abbr. Black pron. of *Fillmo'*]

mo *v.* [1980s+] (US) to act towards someone in a manner that is perceived as being homosexual. [MO n.[4]]

moab *n.* [mid–late 19C] a turban-shaped hat, worn by women. [joc. ref. to Ps. 60:8, 'Moab is my washpot']

Moabite *n.* [late 17C–early 19C] a bailiff (cf. PHILISTINES). [SE *Moabite*, an enemy of the biblical Israelites and occas. used in 16C–17C as a pej. nickname for Roman Catholics]

moan *n.* [1910s+] (orig. milit.) a grievance, a complaint. [MOAN v.]

moan *v.* [1910s+] to complain.

moan and wail *n.* [1940s] a gaol. [rhy. sl.]

moaner *n.* [1920s+] (orig. US) a complainer, a whinger, a pessimist. [MOAN v.]

moaner's bench *n.* [late 19C+] (US Black) a special pew reserved during a Black church revival for those who wish to be 'saved'. Under the direct eye of the preacher and other church dignitaries, they moan and groan, confess their sins and hope to be 'visited by the Spirit'; thus *moaner*, one who makes a public repentance (cf. AMEN BENCH). [Black English pron. of SE *mourner's bench*]

mob *n.*[1] **1** [late 17C–mid-18C] the rabble, the city proletariat (cf. MOBILITY). **2** [late 18C+] (orig. US) a criminal gang. **3** [mid-19C+] a companion or group of associates; thus *mobbed up/up with*, living, travelling or working alongside. **4** [late 19C] (orig. Aus.) a gang of ruffians or thugs. [SE post-1750; abbr. *mobile vulgus*, the fickle crowd, *mob* was a term cited by Swift in 1712 as one of those that should be purged from the language. Surprisingly Johnson, whose *Dictionary* (1755) eschewed (*inter alia*) *dumfound*, *ignoramus* and *touchy* allowed it. *Mob* is an abbr. of MOBILITY as NOB n.[3] is of *nobility*]

mob *n.*[2] [late 18C–early 19C] a prostitute. [var. on MAB n.[1]]

Mob, the *n.*[3] [1920s+] (US) the US Mafia.

Mob *adj.* [1920s+] (US) Mafia-related.

mob *v.* [1990s] (US Black) to go, to travel. [MOBILIZE v.[2]]

mobbed out *adj.* [20C] very full, crammed. [SE *mob*]

mobbed up *adj.* [1970s+] (US Und.) connected with or run by organized crime. [MOB n.[3]]

Mob City *see* MOB TOWN.

mob-handed *adj.* [1970s+] accompanied by a large gang. [MOB n.[1] (2) + sfx. -HANDED]

mo-bike *n.* [1920s+] a *mo*tor*bike*. [abbr.]

mobile *n.* [late 17C] the rabble (cf. MOB n.[1]). [Lat. *mobile vulgus*]

mobility *n.* [late 17C–mid-19C] the populace, the masses. [for ety. *see* MOB n.[1]; Swift allowed *mobility*, while Johnson condemned it as 'cant', i.e. unacceptably common]

mobilize/mopelize *v.*[1] [1910s–70s] (US, esp. New York City) of street gangs, to beat up, to vanquish. [SE *mob* but note *mopel*, to abort]

mobilize *v.*[2] [1990s] (US Black) to drive a car.

mobilized dandruff *see* GALLOPING DANDRUFF.

moboton *n.* [20C] (W.I.) a great many, a large amount. [? SE *mob* + *marathon*]

mobsman *n.* [mid-19C–1960s] (Und.) anyone who use manual dexterity for theft, a category that includes both pickpockets and shoplifters (cf. BUZZER n.[1]; PROP-NAILER; THIMBLE-RIGGER; WIRE n.[2]). [a member of the elite ranks of pickpockets, the SWELL MOB]

mobs of *phr.* [late 19C+] (Aus.) a great many, a large number, a sizeable quantity. [MOB n.[1] (4)]

mobster *n.* [1910s+] (orig. US) **1** a gangster. **2** a member of the US Mafia. [MOB n.[3] + sfx. -STER]

Mob Town/City *n.* [19C] (US) Baltimore, Maryland. [MOB n.[1] (2), suggested by its 'lawless' reputation]

mob up *v.* [1920s–30s] (US Und.) to join a gang. [SE *mob*]

moby *n.* [1990s] a *mo*bile telephone. [abbr.]

moby *adj.* [1960s+] (US campus) enormous. [the fictional whale *Moby-Dick*, created by novelist Herman Melville (1819–91)]

moby dick *n.* [late-19C+] **1** prison. **2** the penis. [rhy. sl. (1) = NICK n.[7] (2) = PRICK n.; ult. the novel *Moby Dick* (1850) by Herman Melville]

moby dick *adj.* [20C] ill, sick. [rhy. sl.]

moccasined *adj.* [mid-19C] (US) drunk. [abbr. phr. *bitten by the moccasin* (*snake*)]

moccasins *n.* [late 19C+] (US) any kind of footwear; also used fig. as (*walk a mile*) *in my moccasins*, to experience my life.

moccasin telegraph *n.* [20C] (US) the informal way in which news moves between Native American communities (cf. BUSH TELEGRAPH). [note synon. Alaskan local use *mukluk telegraph*]

moch *n.* [20C] (US) a Jew. [abbr. MOCKIE]

mocha *adj.* [1940s+] (US) racially Black, African-American. [SE *mocha*, a variety of coffee]

mocha and java, to *phr.* [late 19C] to get on, to be friendly. [the brandnames of coffee, thus the image of chatting over a cup of coffee]

mocho *n.* [late 19C–1920s] mocha coffee.

mock *n.*[1] [20C] (Aus.) a halfpenny. [? MAG n.[1]]

mock *n.*[2] [1920s+] (US) a Jew. [abbr. MOCKIE]

mock *n.*[3] [1950s+] (mainly teaching/juv.) usu. in pl., a mock examination (usu. preceding major state examinations, e.g. GCSE, A-levels).

mocka *see* MOCKER.

mock-duck/-goose *n.* [mid–late 19C] a piece of pork from which the 'crackling' has been removed, baked with a stuffing of sage and onions (cf. CLARE MARKET DUCK).

mocker/mocka *n.* [1940s+] (Aus./N.Z.) clothing, esp. a woman's dress; thus *mockered up*, dressed up in one's best, possibly flashy garments. [according to E.P., *mockered up* is 'low. late C. 19–20', but neither he nor the *OED* nor *AND* offers a possible citation; link to Yid. *macha*, a big man, a 'big shot']

mockered *adj.* [mid-19C+] of a face, pitted, full of holes (the result of smallpox). [Rom. *mockodo, mookeedo*, dirty, filthy]

mockered up like a pox doctor's clerk *see* DONE UP LIKE A POX DOCTOR'S CLERK.

mockey *see* MOCKIE.

mock-goose *see* MOCK-DUCK.

mockie/mockey/mocky/mouchey/mouchy *n.* [1920s+] (US) a Jew (cf. MOCK n.²). [proper name *Moses*, but cf. SMOUS. *DARE* suggests Yid. *makeh*, a boil or sore, but why?]

mock litany men *n.* [late 19C] (Irish) beggars who make their demands in a sing-song or versifying manner. [such beggars are reminiscent of the origins of the CANTING CREW]

mock out *v.* [1960s+] (US campus) to tease. [SE *mock*]

mocktail *n.* [1980s+] (US) a non-alcoholic drink. [SE *mock* + (*cock*)*tail*]

mocky *see* MOCKIE.

mocs *n.* [20C] (US) slip-on shoes. [abbr. SE *moccasins*]

mod *n.¹* [1940s+] often in pl., *mod*ification. [abbr.]

mod *n.²* [1960s+] a member of a teenage cult orig. *c.*1961, who wore specifically distinguishing clothes, rode motor scooters and fought their main rivals, the motorcycle-riding, leather-clad 'rockers'. [abbr. SE *modernist*]

mod *adj.* [1960s+] fashionable, up-to-date. [SE *modern*]

mod *v.* [1950s] to *mod*ify. [abbr.]

modams *n.* [1970s] (drugs) marijuana. [ety. unknown]

mod. cons. *n.* [1930s+] modern conveniences. [a play on estate agent advertising *all mod. cons.*]

mode *adj.* [1980s+] (US/UK) fashionable, modern. [MOD adj.]

mode *v. see* MOULD.

Model, the *n.¹* [mid-19C–1900s] Pentonville prison, Caledonian Road, London. [Pentonville was opened in 1842 and designed as a *model* prison on the 'separate system', i.e. continuous solitary confinement irrespective of one's crime. Such solitude (pioneered in the Haviland Eastern Penitentiary in Philadelphia) led to a huge increase in mental illness among inmates; whether it promoted rehabilitation is less likely]

model *n.²* [late 19C] (Scot.) a model lodging-house.

modelling *n.* [1990s] (S.Afr.) the parading of an offender naked through a township as a form of punishment.

models *n.* [late 19C] purpose-built 'model' housing.

Model T *adj.* [1930s–60s] (US) out-of-date, cheap. [the inexpensive Ford *Model T* motorcar, last manufactured in 1927]

modest quencher *n.* [mid-19C] a glass of gin and water.

modesty *n.* [1910s+] (Aus.) a baby's 'pilch', a triangular flannel wrapper worn over the nappy.

mo dicker *n.* [1960s+] (US) synon. for MOTHERFUCKER. [*mo*, abbr. SE *mother* + DICK n.⁵ (1)]

modicum *n.* **1** [early 17C] something that is eaten to make oneself thirsty. **2** [late 17C–mid-19C] the vagina (cf. BIT n.³; PIECE n.¹). [as well as the comestibles, the vagina is something one can EAT v.³]

modock *n.* [1930s–60s] (US) one who becomes an aviator for the social prestige or publicity. ['a flashy chap who goes around wearing helmet and goggles, and more than likely, leather boots and riding breeches, too, and talking about the big things he is going to do for aviation' (Allen & Lyman, *Wonder Book of the Air*, 1936); ety. unknown. Supposedly a mythical bird, which 'flies backwards to keep the sun out of its eyes', but other than an aviators' joke, this has no validity as an ety.]

mods and rockers *n.* [1960s] the female breasts. [rhy. sl. *mods and rockers* = KNOCKERS n.² (2)]

mod squad *n.* [1970s] plain-clothes police, usu. young and dressed in the prevailing teenage and early 20s fashions, who look for crime in colleges and local youth centres. [MOD adj. + SE *squad*]

mod to the bone *phr.* [1960s+] (US Black) very fashionably dressed (cf. CLEAN TO THE BONE phr.). [MOD adj. + TO THE BONE]

moegie/imoogie *adj.* [1960s+] (S.Afr.) foolish, stupid. [MOEGOE]

moegoe *n.* [1960s+] (S.Afr.) a lazy lout, a country bumpkin, a gullible person. [Afk.]

moer *v.* [1960s+] (S.Afr.) to thrash, to beat up, to kill. [? MOER! or Afk. *moor*, murder]

moer! *excl.* [1940s+] (S.Afr.) an abusive term of address or an obscene excl. of fury or disgust; esp. in excls. *jou moer!, your moer!*, your mother! (cf. MOTHERFUCKER). [Du. *moder*, mother, thus fig. 'your mother's womb']

moey/mooe/mooey *n.* **1** [mid-19C–1950s] the mouth. **2** [late 19C] the vagina. **3** [late 19C+] (Aus.) a moustache. [Rom. *mooï*, the mouth]

moff/moph *n.* [20C] a hermaphrodite. [note farming jargon *moff*, a dual-purpose farm wagon]

moffie *n.* [1950s+] (S.Afr.) **1** a homosexual; thus *koffie-moffie*, an airline steward (lit. 'coffee-queen'). **2** a transvestite (cf. MOFFRY). [? Du. sl. *mofrodiet*, a hermaphrodite; note UK naut. jargon *mophy*, 'a delicate well-groomed youth' (*DSUE* 8)]

moffry *n.* [20C] (W.I.) **1** a her*maph*rodite (cf. MOFFIE). **2** a weak, effeminate man. [abbr.; (2) is fig. use of (1)]

mofo/mo-fo *n.* [20C] synon. for MOTHERFUCKER. [abbr.]

mofo/mo-fo *adj.* [20C] synon. for MOTHERFUCKING adj. [abbr.]

mofuck *n.* [20C] synon. for MOTHERFUCKER. [abbr.]

mog *n.¹* [mid-19C] a lie; thus *no mogue*, no lie. [? Fr. *se moquer de*, to jeer, to deride]

mog *n.²* [1920s–50s] **1** a cat (cf. MOGGIE n.¹). **2** a fur, a tippet, a fur coat.

mog *v.* [late 19C–1950s] (US) to amble, to trudge along slowly. [ety. unknown]

mogadored *adj.* [1930s+] beaten, defeated, confused. [rhy. sl. *mogadored* = FLOORED adj. (2), ? ult. Irish *magadh*, to mock, to jeer, to laugh at, ? Rom. *mokardi/mokodo*, tainted]

mogg *see* MOG v.

moggie/moggy *n.¹* **1** [early 18C–late 19C] an untidily dressed woman, a slattern. **2** [1910s+] a cat. [? proper name *Maggie* or dial. *moggie*, a calf]

moggie *n.²* [1980s+] (drugs) Mogadon, a mild sleeping pill.

moggy *see* MOGGIE n.¹.

mohair *n.* [late 18C] a civilian, as named by a soldier. [a civilian's mohair-covered buttons, a soldier had the unadorned brass]

mohair knickers *n.* [1990s] an extremely hairy vagina.

mohasky/mohasty/mohoska/mosky *n.* [1930s+] (drugs) marijuana. [ety. unknown; play on SE, thus cf. MARIHOOCHIE]

mohasky/mohasty/mohoska/mosky *adj.* [1930s+] (drugs) intoxicated by marijuana. [MOHASKY n.]

mohican *n.* [mid-19C] 'A Mohican, in Cadonian phraseology, is a tremendously heavy man, who rides five or six miles [in an omnibus] for sixpence' (*Tait's Magazine*, May 1848). [*cadonian*, i.e. of a cad or bus-conductor]

mohoska see MOHASKY.

moi prn. [1970s+] me, used ironically or sarcastically, pointing fun at one's pretensions, 'attitude' etc, e.g. *Pretentious, moi? sarcastic, moi?* (with the unspoken coda, 'damn right I am!'). [Fr. *moi*, me]

moisten the chaffer, to phr. [mid-19C] to take a drink. [SE *moisten* + CHAFFER n. (1)]

moisten/moist the clay, to phr. [early–mid-19C] (US) to take a drink, to quench one's thirst (cf. MOISTEN THE CHAFFER). [SE *moisten* + *clay*, the human flesh]

moist round the edges phr. [1900s–20s] slightly drunk.

moist the clay see MOISTEN THE CLAY.

mojo n.[1] **1** [1920s+] (orig. US Black) spirituality, magic, thus power and influence (cf. MOJO AND THE SAY-SO). **2** [1970s] (US Black) a kind of dance. [? Gullah *moco*, witchcraft, magic, Fula *moco'o*, medicine man.]

mojo n.[2] [1930s+] (US drugs) any narcotic drug, esp. morphine. [ext. of MOJO n.[1] (1)]

mojo v. (orig. US) **1** [1930s] to fool, to deceive. **2** [1960s+] to jinx, to charm. **3** [1990s] to go, to leave. [MOJO n.[1] (1)]

mojo and the say-so phr. [1920s+] (orig. US Black) qualities giving one power and influence over others. [MOJO n.[1] + SAY-SO]

moke n.[1] (US) **1** [mid-19C–1920s] a Black person, any dark-skinned foreigner. **2** [mid–late 19C] a White person wearing 'blackface' and performing in a 'minstrel show'. **3** [late 19C–1910s] a foolish, tedious person (cf. MOOK). **4** [1960s] a Hawaiian, esp. a young, thuggish man. [? Sp. *mocha*, dark-skinned; ult. Sp. *café de Moca* (an Arabian port on the Red Sea), but note SMOKE n.[4]]

moke n.[2] **1** [mid-19C–1910s] a fool. **2** [mid-19C+] a donkey, an ass. **3** [late 19C–1920s] (Aus.) a horse, often an second-rate one. [? Devon/Hampshire dial. *mokus*, a donkey. E.P. suggests Rom. *moxio*, a donkey, or *Moke*, the dimin. of the proper name *Margaret*, on the pattern of MOG n.[2] (1)/MOGGIE n.[1] (2), also f. *Margaret*, a cat]

mokes n. [1980s+] (US) a silly fellow (cf. MOKE n.[2]).

moko n. [mid-19C] 'a name given by sportsmen to pheasants killed by mistake in partridge shooting during September, before the pheasant shooting comes in. They pull out their tails and roundly assert they are no pheasants at all, but mokos' (Hotten, 1860).

mokus n. (US) **1** [1920s–50s] a depressed state, the blues. **2** [1950s–70s] a very intoxicated state. [? PUT THE MOCKERS ON]

mokus adj. [1950s–70s] (US) drunk but wanting another drink. [MOKUS n. (2)]

mola n.[1] [20C] a male homosexual. [? var. on NOLA]

mola n.[2] see MOOLA.

molared see MOLO.

mole n.[1] [late 19C–1910s] **1** the penis (cf. MOLE-CATCHER; MOLEST THE MOLE; MOULDIWORP; MOUSE n.[2]). **2** a male homosexual. [the animal and the penis 'burrow in'; (2) is from (1)]

mole n.[2] [20C] (US prison) someone who escapes by digging their way out of prison (cf. TUNNEL RAT).

mole n.[3] [1950s+] (Aus./N.Z.) a woman, esp. a promiscuous one. [? MOLLY or MOLL n. (1)]

mole n.[4] [1970s+] **1** a deep cover agent, who is put in place many years before they can be of use but on the assumption that they will gradually gain greater access to the centres of power and become increasingly useful and damaging as time passes. **2** anyone within an organization or in a position of trust who betrays confidential information. [*mole* is the perfect example of the blurring of fact and fiction. While Sir Francis Bacon uses it first in his *History of the Reign of King Henry VII* (1622) and the *OED* offers earlier uses, albeit not

exactly synon., in 1925 and 1960, it has otherwise been popularized via the fictional world of John Le Carré, notably in *Tinker, Tailor, Soldier, Spy* (1974). In a BBC TV interview Le Carré claimed that *mole* was a genuine KGB term, but it was the televising of *Tinker, Tailor* ... plus the revelations of the 'Fourth Man' (Anthony Blunt) in October 1979 that took *mole* out of fiction and put it into the headlines for good]

mole n.[5] [1990s] (US teen) a really big number. Its opposite is *negative mole*. [SE *mole*, 6.02×10^{23}]

mole-catcher n. [late 19C–1910s] the vagina. [MOLE n.[1] (1) + SE *catcher*]

moles n. [late 19C+] (Aus.) moleskin trousers. [SE *moleskin*, a strong, soft, fine-piled cotton fustian, the surface of which is 'shaved' before dyeing]

moleskin squatter n. [late 19C–1940s] (N.Z.) 'a working man who has come to own a small sheep run.' (*OED*). [his moleskin trousers]

molest the mole, to phr. [1980s+] to masturbate. [SE *molest* + MOLE n.[1] (1)]

moley n. [1950s] a potato, its surface jagged with the edges of safety razor blades. [it 'burrows into' the victim's flesh]

moll n. **1** [late 16C+] a woman, usu. a promiscuous one. **2** [17C+] a prostitute. **3** [early 19C+] a girlfriend; esp. in *gangster's moll*, a gangster's female companion. **4** [1920s–40s] (US) an effeminate male homosexual. [dimin. of proper name *Mary*, reinforced by the early 17C criminal *Moll Cut-purse*, immortalized in Middleton & Dekker's play *The Roaring Girl* (1611). (2) now survives only in Aus. use]

moll v. **1** [late 19C] to go around with women. **2** [late 19C] of a man, to act effeminately; thus *molling*, accompanying women, acting effeminately. **3** [1950s] (US) to work as a prostitute. [MOLL n.]

moll blood n. [late 18C–early 19C] the gallows. [Scot. nick-name]

moll buzzer n. **1** [mid-19C+] (Und./police) a pickpocket or a beggar who specializes in women as victims; thus *moll-buzzing*, purse- or bag-snatching. **2** [late 19C–1930s] (US Und.) a female thief, pickpocket or beggar. [MOLL n. (1) + BUZZER n.[1]]

molled/molled up adj.[1] [mid-19C] sleeping with a woman other than one's wife. [MOLL n.]

molled adj.[2] [mid-19C] followed by a woman. [MOLL n.]

molled adj.[3] see MOLO.

molled up see MOLLED adj.[1].

moll hook n. [late 19C–1910s] a female pickpocket. [MOLL n. (1) + HOOK n.[2]]

moll house n. [18C] a brothel (cf. ACCOMMODATION HOUSE). [MOLL n. (2) + SE *house*/HOUSE n.[1]]

moll-hunter n. [late 19C] a womanizer. [MOLL n. (1) + SE *hunter*]

mollies n. [1970s] (US drugs) amphetamines or sleep-retarding pills (cf. A n.[2]; BLACK MOLLY). [play on SE *black molly*, a species of tropical fish, which the black pills may be seen as resembling]

mollisher n. [early–mid-19C] **1** a woman. **2** a slattern (cf. MOLLY n.[1]). **3** a thief's mistress. [MOLL n., ? link to Rom. *monishi*, a woman]

mollock v. [1930s+] to cavort, to have a good time, to have sexual intercourse. [? dial. *marlock*, to frolic, to gambol + *rollick*, coined by Stella Gibbons in *Cold Comfort Farm* (1932)]

Moll Peatley's/Pratley's gig/jig n. [late 18C–early 19C] sexual intercourse, 'a rogering bout' (Grose 1796). [? the name of a well-known contemporary prostitute + GIG n.[2]/SE *jig*]

mollsack n. [mid-19C] a market basket. [MOLL n. (1) + SE *sack*, lit. 'woman sack']

moll/molly shop *n.* [20C] a brothel (cf. BUTTOCKING SHOP; MEAT-FANCIER'S). [MOLL n. (2) + SHOP n.[1] (1)]

Moll's three misfortunes *phr.* [late 18C] 'broke the [chamber-] pot, bes[hi]t the bed and cut her a[r]se' (Grose 1796). [the phr., while appearing in the British Library edn., was not transferred into any of the published versions of the *Classical Dictionary of the Vulgar Tongue*]

Moll Thompson's mark *n.* [late 18C–mid-19C] used to describe an empty bottle (cf. MAKING MS AND TS). [the sign *M.T.* inscribed on empty packages]

moll-tooler *n.* [mid-19C] a female pickpocket. [MOLL n. (1) + TOOLER]

moll-wire *n.* [late 19C–1930s] a pickpocket who specializes in robbing female victims. [MOLL n. (1) + WIRE n.[2]]

molly *n.*[1] **1** [early 18C–1900s] a male homosexual, an effeminate man (cf. AGNES; MISS MOLLY; MOLL n.). **2** [early 18C–1900s] a prostitute (cf. MOLL n.). **3** [20C] (Irish) a girl. [the proper name]

molly *n.*[2] *see* MISS MOLLY.

molly *n.*[3] *see* MOLLY MALONE.

molly *n.*[4] [1940s+] (US) a female mule.

molly *adj.* [1960s–70s] (Aus.) drunk. [rhy. sl. *molly the monk*]

molly *v.* [mid-18C] to sodomize, to bugger; thus *mollying*, very keen on buggery. [MOLLY n.[1] (1)]

Molly Bán/Bawn *n.* [20C] (Irish) confusion, worry; thus *the times of Molly Bán*, a riotous good time. [used as (?coined by) the title of a popular ballad by Samuel Lover (1797–1868)]

Molly-boy *see* MISS MOLLY.

mollycoddle *n.* [mid-19C+] a weakling, a mother's darling. [MOLLY n.[1] (1) + SE *coddle*]

mollycoddle *v.* [mid-19C+] to pamper, to pet, to indulge a weak person in their weaknesses. [MOLLYCODDLE n.]

molly-dodger *n.* [1920s] (US) euph. for MOTHERFUCKER (cf. GRANNY-DODGER).

molly-dooker/-hander *n.* [1920s+] (Aus.) a left-handed person; thus *molly-dook(ed)*, left-handed. [? MOLLY n.[1] (1) + DUKE n.[3], with derog. sense that an effeminate man, like a left-handed person, would be clumsy or ? MAULEY]

mollyfock *n.* [20C] euph. for MOTHERFUCK.

mollyfocking/mollyfogging *adj.* [20C] euph. for MOTHER-FUCKING adj.

mollygrubs *see* MULLIGRUBS.

molly-hander *see* MOLLY-DOOKER.

mollyhead *n.* [1900s] a fool, a simpleton. [MOLLY n.[1] (1) + sfx. -HEAD (1)]

molly-hogan *n.* [1940s+] (US) anything puzzling or complicated. [logging jargon *molly-hogan*, a wire loop used as a temporary link connecting two cables]

mollyhouse *n.* [early 18C–late 19C] a male homosexual brothel. [MOLLY n.[1] (1) + SE *house*/HOUSE n.[1]]

molly maguire *n.* [20C] (Aus.) a fire. [rhy. sl.]

molly malone/molly *n.* [20C] the telephone. [rhy. sl.]

molly-mop *n.* [early 19C] an effeminate man. [MOLLY n.[1] (1) + DOLLYMOP]

Molly O'Morgan *n.* [late 19C+] an organ. [rhy. sl.]

mollypuff/mullipuff *n.* [early 17C–early 18C] a weakling, used as a general term of contempt. [dial. *mullipuff*, the fungus *Lycoperdon Bovista*, a puff-ball, note F&H suggest an alternative meaning, 'a gambler's decoy' but E.P. dismisses this as an error]

molly's hole *n.* [19C] the vagina (cf. BLACK HOLE n.[1]). [MOLL n. + HOLE n.[1] (2)]

molly shop *see* MOLL SHOP.

molo/molared/molled/mowlow *adj.* [20C] (Aus.) drunk (cf. MOLLY adj.). [? SE *molly*, a meeting of ships' captains, possibly for drinking]

molocher/moloker *n.* [mid–late 19C] a renovated hat, ironed and greased back to something resembling its original condition. [? SE *lacquered*]

molrower *n.* [mid–late 19C] a womanizer. [MOLROWING]

molrowing *n.* [mid–late 19C] **1** going out on a (whoring) spree. **2** caterwauling, making a noise. [MOLL n. + SE *row*, a noise (the woman's amatory groans are compared to the screeching of mating cats)]

mom *n.* [1950s+] **1** the equivalent of the UK *mum*, used here as a generic term for the typical American matriarchal mother; thus *mom-bashing*, *mom cult*, *mom culture*, *mom-like*. **2** (US gay) a passive partner in a lesbian relationship. **3** (US gay) a feminine lesbian.

mom and pop store *n.* [1950s+] a small corner store stocking just the bare essentials (cf. MA AND PA STORE).

mom-dad-buddy-and-sis *n.* [1950s+] shorthand for the clichéd American nuclear family.

mome *n.* [mid-16C–early 18C] a fool, a simpleton. [? Fr. *mome*, a little child or an innocent, or *mum*, dumb]

momma *n.* [20C] (US Black) a term of address to any woman.

momma's game *n.* [1950s–70s] (US Black) a name-calling ritual that depends heavily on mutually abusing the participants' mothers (cf. DOZENS).

mommux/mommux up *v.* [mid-19C–1900s] (US) to confuse, to bewilder, to confound. [? FLUMMOX v.[1] (1)]

mommy up *v.* [1980s+] (US campus) to love, to hug, to comfort. [SAmE *mommy*, mother]

momo/mo-mo *n.* [1950s+] (US) a stupid person. [abbr. SE *mo(ron)* + redup.]

mompara *n.* (S.Afr.) **1** [late 19C+] of Black workers, a novice, a greenhorn. **2** [1940s+] a fool, an idiot, also used as a term of affection. [Fanakalo *mompara*, a fool, waste matter]

mompyns/munpins *n.* [mid-15C] the teeth. [lit. 'mouth-pins']

moms *n.* [20C] (US Black) one's mother.

momser/momza/momzer *see* MAMZER.

mon/mun *n.*[1] [late 19C–1970s] (US) money. [abbr.]

mon *n.*[2] [1970s+] (orig. US campus) as used in address, man. [imitation of W.I. pron.]

monacker *see* MONNIKER.

monaghan *n.* [late 17C–mid-18C] (Irish) a fool, a clown. [proper name, presumably of a specific individual]

monaker *n.*[1] *see* MONNIKER.

monaker *n.*[2] *see* MONARCH n.[2].

Mona Lisa *n.* [20C] a freezer. [rhy. sl.]

monarch *n.*[1] *see* MONNIKER.

monarch/monaker *n.*[2] [mid-19C] **1** a sovereign. **2** £1 (cf. NED n.[1]; NEDDY n.[2]; NOB n.[1]; PORTRAIT n.[1]). [the *monarch*'s head on the coin]

monarcher *see* MONNIKER.

Monday comes before Sunday/Saturday is longer than Sunday/Sunday below Monday/Tuesday is longer than Monday *phr.* [1960s+] (US) phrs. used to tell a woman that her slip is showing (cf. CHARLIE'S DEAD).

Monday morning quarterback *n.* [1930s+] (US) a person who criticizes with the benefit of hindsight. [amateur criticism of the week's football matches played on Sundays]

Monday morning quarterback, to *phr.* [1930s+] (US) to criticize with the benefit of hindsight. [for ety. *see* MONDAY MORNING QUARTERBACK n.]

Monday mouse *n.* [late 19C] a black eye, resulting from a Saturday or Sunday night (drunken) fight. [SE *Monday* + *mouse*]

mondo *adj.* [1980s+] considerable, substantial, huge. [Ital. *mondo*, the world (cf. -CITY), first popularized by the Italian cult film *Mondo Cane* (1961) and, like COWABUNGA!, DUDE and other Californian teen/surfer slang, *mondo* gained a new lease of life with the *Teenage Mutant Ninja Turtles* craze of the late 1980s]

mondo *adv.* [1960s+] (US teen/campus) completely, absolutely, very, exceedingly (cf. DEF). [for ety. *see* MONDO adj.]

mondo- *pfx.* [1960s+] (US) used to describe a bizarre, surprising or anarchic view of the topic under consideration, with the implication of salaciousness or (kitschy) bad taste, usu. combined with a real or cod Italian n., e.g. *mondo trasho, mondo wierdo, mondo bizarro.* [MONDO adj.]

monekeer *see* MONNIKER.

monet *n.* [1990s] (US teen) something that (lit. and fig.) looks good from afar but appears less appealing in close-up. [a critical view of the work of the Fr. artist Claude *Monet* (1840–1926)]

money *n.*[1] [late 18C+] **1** esp. of girls, the vagina (cf. BANK n.[1]). **2** of boys, the anus. [the commercial potential of the organs]

money *n.*[2] [mid-19C] *money's* worth. [abbr.]

money *n.*[3] [1960s+] (US) in general, the critical element or aspect, used fig., e.g. *that's where the money is* (cf. ON THE MONEY).

money/money dog/grip *n.*[4] [1980s+] (US Black) **1** one's best friend. **2** a general form of address to any man (cf. MONEY adj.). [the centrality and importance of cash]

money *adj.* (orig. US) **1** [1930s+] used prenominally to denote success, proficiency, ability to win or to fulfil high expectations; e.g. *money star*, a famous film star; *money jockey*, a jockey who wins often; *money card*, the card that completes a winning hand in poker; *money shot*, a close up shot of orgasm in a pornographic film; *money quote*, a quote of a sensational exposure in a news story. **2** [1990s] used with a n. with the same meaning, e.g. *You're money*; *That's really money!*

moneybag lord *n.* [late 19C] an ennobled millionaire or successful businessman. [MONEYBAG(S) + SE *lord*]

moneybags *n.* [early 19C+] **1** a lover of money. **2** a wealthy person; often as *Mr Moneybags* (cf. GOTROCKS).

money blanket *see* HORSE BLANKET n.[2].

moneybox *n.* [19C] the vagina (cf. BANK n.[1]; MONEY MACHINE; MONEY-MAKER; MONEY-SPINNER). [its commercial potential]

money bugs *n.* [late 19C] (US) millionaires. [SE *money* + BUG n.[1]]

money-cuffee *n.* [late 19C] (W.I.) a foolish spendthrift. [SE *money* + CUFFEE]

money dog *see* MONEY n.[4].

money-dropper *n.* [late 18C–19C] a rogue who specializes in dropping something supposedly valuable which will be found by a potential victim who is then either lured into a game or, in the case of the (invariably fake) 'valuable', persuaded to buy it (cf. SWEETENER).

money for jam *n.* [1910s+] (orig. milit.) anything, incl. money, that is gained for a minimal amount of effort, and is available for purely pleasurable expenditure (cf. MONEY FOR OLD ROPE).

money for old rope *phr.* [1930s+] (orig. milit.) something for nothing (cf. MONEY FOR JAM).

money/labour gone in Maxwell Pond *phr.* [20C] (W.I.) used to describe money or effort that has been wasted or 'thrown away'. [proper name of the *Maxwell* (Sugar) Estate in Barbados. No actual pond, however, has ever been traced]

money grip *see* MONEY n.[4].

money machine *n.* [1960s–70s] (US) the vagina (cf. BANK n.[1]; MONEYBOX). [its commercial potential]

money-maker *n.* **1** [late 19C+] the vagina (cf. BANK n.[1]; MONEYBOX). **2** [1960s+] (US) the female buttocks. [commercial potential]

money-puker *n.* [1990s] (US) an automatic teller machine. [SE *money* + SE *puke*, to vomit]

money shot *see* MEAT SHOT.

money's mammy *n.* [1930s–40s] (US Black) a very rich person (cf. GRANDMA CHANGE). [fig. a 'member of money's family']

money-spinner *n.* [19C] the vagina (cf. BANK n.[1]; MONEYBOX). [its commercial potential]

money talks – bullshit walks *phr.* [1950s+] a dismissive phr. aimed at a person.

money to burn *phr.* [late 19C+] spare cash available for spontaneous excess.

mong *n.*[1] (Aus.) **1** [20C] a dog, not necessarily of mixed breed. **2** [1930s+] a general term of abuse (cf. MONGREL n.[2]). [SE *mongrel*]

mong *n.*[2] [1980s+] a general term of opprobrium. The overriding implication is that of stupidity (cf. MALCO; SPASTIC; SPAS n.); thus *mongie, mongy*, stupid, dull. [abbr. SE *mongol*]

monged *adj.* [1980s+] intoxicated by a drug, usu. MDMA (cf. ECSTASY). [MONG n.[2]]

mongee *n.* [1910s–30s] (US tramp) food. [Fr. *manger*, to eat]

-monger *sfx.* [late 17C; 1970s+] an enthusiast or knowledgeable person. [SE *monger*, a dealer, a trafficker]

mong-mong *n.* [20C] (W.I./Gren.) a poor White. [pron. of Carib.E. *Mount St Moritz Bajan*, a poor White one of whose ancestors moved to the Grenadan estate of St Moritz *c.*1870s, working as a market gardener]

mongo *n.* **1** [1970s+] (US) an idiot. **2** [1980s+] (US, NY) any discarded object that is retrieved. **3** [1980s+] (US, New York) a scrap-metal scavenger. [? MONG n.[2], but *Mongo* is a trad. name for a shambling idiot, often the servant of a 'mad professor' in films etc; however, that too may be rooted in SE *mongol*]

mongo *adj.* [1980s+] (US teen) considerable, substantial, huge (cf. MONDO adj.). [? HUMONGOUS]

Mongolian *n.* [mid-19C–1910s] (Aus.) a Chinese immigrant to Australia.

mongolito *n.* [1980s+] (US campus) a term of endearment. [cod Sp. 'little mongol']

mongoose *n.* [1950s] (W.I.) an albino. [the animal, which has a light-brown coat and reddish eyes]

mongoose gang *n.* [1950s+] (W.I./orig. Gren.) a group of thugs working for a politician and acting as a form of private army/secret police. [1950s campaign to eradicate the mongoose in Grenada; those who claimed a bounty for killing the creatures had to produce a tail and became known as the '*mongoose gang*']

mongrel *n.*[1] (Und.) **1** [16C] an accomplice who helps in a confidence trickster's pose as a poor scholar (cf. FALCONER). **2** [late 17C–early 19C] a hanger-on among confidence tricksters, a sponger.

mongrel *n.*[2] [20C] (Aus./N.Z.) a general term of abuse; i.e. *you bloody mongrel* (cf. MONG n.[1]). [despite the synon. of *mongrel* and *half-breed*, there appears to be no racial implication]

monica/moniker *see* MONNIKER.

monish *n.* [early–mid-19C] (US) money. [imitation of Anglo-Yid. speech]

monk *n.*[1] **1** [mid-19C] a general term of contempt. **2** [late 19C–1930s] (US) a Chinese person. **3** [1920s–40s] (US Und.) a Supreme Court judge. [? abbr. SE *monkey*]

monk *n.*[2] [mid-19C+] (orig. US) a *monk*ey. [abbr.]

monk *n.*[3] [mid-19C+] (orig. US) a sickly parrot. [the bowed head of the ill bird]

monk *v.*[1] [late 19C–1950s] **1** to trifle with, to fool around. **2** to neck. [MONKEY v.]

monk *v.*[2] [1980s] (US) to spend time alone, voluntarily or (as during a jail sentence) not. [the image of an anchorite]

monkery/monkry *n.* (tramp) **1** [late 18C+] the countryside. **2** [mid-19C] as *the monkery*, the world of tramps and vagrants. **3** [mid-19C+] going on the tramp; thus *on the monkery*, living as a tramp. **4** [late 19C–1900s] a specific district in which tramps or beggars work. [SE *monkery*, the contemplative, peaceful, monastic life]

monkey *n.*[1] **1** [17C–mid-19C] a scamp, a rascal. **2** [late 17C+] a general insult, esp. when used since mid-19C by Whites of Blacks. **3** [20C] (US Black) a White person. **4** [20C] (US Black) a West Indian (cf. MONKEY-CHASER n.[1]). **5** [1900s–40s] (US) a Chinese person. **6** [1920s–60s] (US Und.) a victim of a swindler, a dupe. **7** [1930s–40s] (US Und.) a prohibition agent. **8** [1940s–50s] (US) a Japanese person. [(1) now SE]

monkey, the *n.*[2] [19C] fooling around, 'messing about' (cf. MONKEY BUSINESS).

monkey *n.*[3] [early 19C] (Und.) a padlock. [ety. unknown; but note SE *monkey*, 'applied to various machines and implements' (*OED*)]

monkey *n.*[4] [early 19C+] £500, $500. [ety. unknown]

monkey *n.*[5] [mid-19C] a flask, esp. as used to carry liquor on hunting expeditions. [? backform f. SUCK THE MONKEY]

monkey *n.*[6] [mid-19C] ill temper, tetchiness (cf. HAVE A MONKEY ON ONE'S BACK phr.[1]). [ety. unknown; ? play on SE *monkey-wrench*/a *wrench* of pain]

monkey *n.*[7] [mid-19C–1940s] (Aus.) a sheep (cf. MONKEY-DODGER).

monkey *n.*[8] [late 19C] a small bustle. [? the image of a baby monkey clinging to its mother's back]

monkey *n.*[9] **1** [late 19C] as used by artisans or manual labourers, a clerk. **2** [1920s] (US) a chorus-girl. **3** [1930s–40s] (US) one who washes dishes in a restaurant, café etc.

monkey *n.*[10] **1** [late 19C+] (Aus./US) the vagina. **2** [1980s+] (US campus) the penis. [? punning abbr. MONKEY BUSINESS]

monkey *n.*[11] [20C] (US) a person who acts as, works as, or is responsible for something, used in combs. e.g. *bridge monkey*, a bridge builder (cf. GREASE MONKEY).

monkey *n.*[12] **1** [1920s–30s] (US) a taxi-dancer, a dance-hall hostess who charges 10 cents a dance to all-comers; thus *monkey hop*, the taxi-dance. **2** [1980s+] (US campus) 'the other woman', 'the other man', i.e. the woman or man with whom one's supposedly faithful partner is having an affair. [such a person 'climbs all over' their partner]

monkey *n.*[13] [1920s–40s] (US Black) the leader of a band or orchestra. [the on-stage cavorting or their MONKEY SUIT]

monkey *n.*[14] (drugs) **1** [1930s+] any form of narcotics addiction, usu. of heroin, morphine. **2** [1960s–70s] morphine. **3** [1970s] (US Black) a drug addict. **4** [1980s+] a cigarette made from cocaine paste and tobacco. [abbr. HAVE A MONKEY ON ONE'S BACK phr.[2]]

monkey/monkey around *v.* [late 19C+] (orig. US) to fool around, to tamper, to fiddle, usu. in a destructive clumsy manner. [supposed characteristics of the animal]

monkey and parrot time *phr.* [late 19C] (US) an unhappy marriage, in which the two partners fight continually (cf. CAT AND DOG LIFE; PARROT AND MONKEY TIME).

monkey around *see* MONKEY v.

monkey-assed *adj.* [1980s+] (US) damned. [semi-euph.; SE *monkey* + ARSE n.[1]]

monkeyback *n.* [1920s] (US Black) a man who dresses in formal dinner wear, a dude (cf. MONKEY CLOTHES; MONKEY SUIT).

monkey bait *n.* [1950s+] (drugs) free samples of addictive drugs. [MONKEY n.[14] + SE *bait*, the logical development is to HAVE A MONKEY ON ONE'S BACK phr.[2]]

monkey barge *n.* [late 19C–1900s] a horse-drawn canal barge. [? coined by late 29C music-hall singer Gus Elen]

monkey bite *n.* [1940s+] (US) a love-bite.

monkey blanket *see* HORSE BLANKET n.[1].

monkey board *n.* [mid–late 19C] the step on a bus on which the conductor stands.

monkey brand *n.* [1910s–30s] someone who has an ugly face. [a once-celebrated advertisement for Lever Bros. in which a monkey was pictured gazing at itself in a frying-pan]

monkey/monkey-doodle business *n.* [late 19C+] (orig. US) dubious, underhand or crooked practices.

monkey cage *n.* [20C] (US Und.) a prison cell.

monkey-catcher *n.* [mid-19C–1940s] (W.I.) a shrewd, intelligent individual. [the assumed cunningness of monkeys; those who can catch them must be doubly intelligent]

monkey-chaser *n.*[1] [1920s–30s] (US) a man who frequents taxi-dances. [MONKEY n.[12] + SE *chaser*]

monkey-chaser *n.*[2] [1920s+] (US Black) a West Indian. [racist stereotyping]

monkey-chaser *n.*[3] [1950s] (US) a cocktail composed of gin and ice, with a little sugar and a trace of water.

monkey clothes *n.* [1900s–30s] (US) men's dress or evening wear (cf. MONKEY SUIT).

monkey dick *n.* (US) **1** [1960s+] a frankfurter sausage. **2** [1980s+] a contemptible person. [SE *monkey* + DICK n.[5]]

monkey-dodger *n.* [1910s] a sheep-station hand; thus *monkey-dodging*, mustering sheep. [MONKEY n.[7] + SE *dodge*, to avoid]

monkey-doodle business *see* MONKEY BUSINESS.

monkey drill *n.* [1950s] (drugs) a hypodermic syringe. [MONKEY n.[14] + SE *drill*]

monkey dust *n.* [1970s+] (drugs) phencyclidine (cf. ACE n.[3]; ANGEL DUST). [SE *monkey* + DUST n.[6] (3)]

monkey-face *n.* [1930s–60s] (W.I.) **1** a grimace. **2** a stupid, ugly person (cf. MONKEY JESUS).

monkey fart/shit *n.* [20C] (W.I.) utter rubbish, absolute nonsense. [SE *monkey* + FART n./SHIT n.[4]]

monkey farting *n.* [20C] (orig. Can.) playing around, 'messing about', wasting time (cf. MONKEY n.[2]; MONKEY BUSINESS).

monkey farting *adj.* [20C] (orig. Can.) time-wasting, pointless.

monkey house *n.* [1950s–60s] (US) a psychiatric institution. [MONKEY n.[1] (2) + SE *house*]

monkey iron *n.* [1950s] (W.I.) a sweetmeat made of coconut boiled with sugar (cf. IRON CUNNY). [it is very tough to chew]

monkey jacket *n.* [mid–late 19C] (US) a man's dress jacket (cf. MONKEY SUIT).

monkey Jesus *n.* [1940s] (W.I.) a very ugly person (cf. MONKEY-FACE).

monkey jumps *n.* [1950s] (drugs) the staggering and twitching of one who is addicted to narcotics. [MONKEY n.[14] + SE *jumps*]

monkey man *n.*[1] [1920s–60s] (US Black) **1** a weak man, usu. one dominated by his wife or girlfriend. **2** rarely, a West Indian immigrant.

monkey man *n.*[2] [1950s] (N.Z.) one who provides a mortgage.

monkey meat *n.* [1950s] (drugs) a heavily intoxicated drug user. [MONKEY n.[14]]

monkey medicine *n.* [1950s] (drugs) morphine. [MONKEY n.[14] (2) + SE *medicine*]

monkey money *n.* [1910s–30s] (US) any foreign currency. [MONKEY n.[1] (2) + SE *money*]

monkey-monk *n.* [1910s+] (US) a superior or important person, whether in fact or through pretension. [HIGH MUCKY-MUCK]

monkey nuts *n.* [20C] (US prison) prison-cooked meatballs.

monkey on a gridiron *n.* [late 19C–1910s] a cyclist. [SE *monkey*/MONKEY n.[1] + GRIDIRON n.[3] (2)]

monkey on a stick *n*. [late 19C–1910s] a thin person who has abrupt, jerky movements. [the child's toy]

monkey on one's back *phr*. **1** [mid–late 19C] anger or a bad temper. **2** [1930s+] (US drugs) drug addiction, esp. to heroin. [image of the clutching animal]

monkey parade *n*. [late 19C–1910s] the evening promenading up and down a main thoroughfare by (Cockney) young people in search of flirtation. [SE *monkey*/MONKEY n.¹ + *parade*]

monkey piss *n*. [1920s–70s] (US) weak beer (cf. MONKEY SWILL). [SE *monkey* + PISS n.]

monkey rum *n*. [1930s–70s] (US) West Indian rum. [MONKEY n.¹ (4) + SE *rum*]

monkey's *n*. [late 19C+] (orig. US) a damn; thus *I don't care a monkey's fuck, I don't give a monkey's ass* etc.

monkey's allowance *n*. [late 18C–mid-19C] a minimum of payment and a maximum of harsh treatment. [MONKEY n.¹ (2) + SE *allowance*]

monkey's ass *n*. [1970s] (US) used in an excl. or mild oath; as in *I'll be a monkey's ass!* (cf. MONKEY'S UNCLE). [SE *monkey* + ASS n.]

monkey's cousin *n*. [1940s+] (bingo) the number 12. [rhy. sl. *monkey's cousin* = a dozen]

monkey see monkey do *phr*. [1920s+] a phr. used to warn someone to stop what they are doing since a bystander, usu. an impressionable child, might be looking and subsequently imitating.

monkey shine/monkey shines *n*. [early 19C–1960s] (US) tricks or antics. [SE *monkey* + SHINES]

monkey shit *see* MONKEY FART.

monkey's money *n*. **1** [mid-17C–late 18C] payment in kind. **2** [late 17C–18C] empty compliments and meaningless courtesies (cf. SPANISH COIN; SPANISH MONEY).

monkey spank *n*. [1990s] a general term of abuse (cf. WANKER). [SPANK ONE'S MONKEY]

monkey spanker *n*. [1990s] a masturbator. [rhy. sl. *monkey-spanker* = WANKER]

monkey's tail *n*.¹ [early–mid-19C] (orig. naut.) a short crowbar. [resemblance]

monkey's tail *n*.² [20C] usu. in pl., a nail. [rhy. sl.]

monkey suit *n*. [late 19C+] (orig. US) **1** a uniform or overalls. **2** a formal dress suit, evening dress. [? the image of a dark-furred monkey with a light chest; or one looks like a MONKEY n.¹ (2)]

monkey's uncle *n*. [1920s–70s] (US) used in an excl. or mild oath; as in *I'll be a monkey's uncle, I'm very surprised* (cf. MONKEY'S ASS).

monkey's wedding *n*. [1940s+] (S.Afr.) a situation of alternating or simultaneous sunshine and rain (cf. DEVIL IS BEATING HIS WIFE …). [fig. use of *monkey's wedding* (*breakfast*), a presumably chaotic occasion (used as such in parts of US), ? ult. synon. Port. *casamento de rapôsa*, a vixen's wedding]

monkey swill *n*. [1920s–30s] (US) cheap liquor, strong liquor (cf. MONKEY PISS). [the illicit liquor manufactured during US Prohibition]

monkey tie *n*. [1940s] (S.Afr.) an especially gaudy tie. [SE *monkey*/MONKEY n.¹ (2) + SE *tie*]

monkey tranquillizer *n*. [1970s+] (drugs) phencyclidine (cf. ACE n.³).

monkey trap *n*. [1930s+] something decorative worn by women to make themselves attractive to men. [MONKEY n.¹ (2) + SE *trap*]

monkey tricks *n*. **1** [late 19C+] (unwanted) sexual advances. **2** [1920s+] any action considered irritating. [neg. image of the animal + MONKEY n.¹ (2)]

monkey ward *n*. [1910s+] (US) the Montgomery Ward Inc. mail-order company catalogue; thus *monkey ward cowboy*, a

would-be cowboy, who has the clothes but is otherwise spurious (cf. MAIL-ORDER COWBOY). [US regional use *Monkey Ward*, the Montgomery Ward (mail-order) catalogue]

monkey work *n*. [late 19C–1960s] (US) trickery, mischief (cf. MONKEY BUSINESS).

monkry *see* MONKERY.

monniker/monacker/monaker/monarch/monarcher/monekeer/monica/moniker *n*. [19C] (orig. tramp) name, signature; thus [mid–late 19C] *tip someone one's monnicker*, to tell someone one's name. [? *monogram* or Ling. Fr.; E.P. suggests fig. use of SE *monarch*, a king, who like a name rules a person's life]

mono *adj*. **1** [1950s+] *mono*phonic. **2** [1970s+] *mono*chrome. [abbr.]

monochrome *adj*. [1990s] (US teen) boring.

monocular eyeglass *n*. [mid–late 19C] the anus (cf. BACK EYE; BLIND EYE; DEADEYE n.¹; ROUNDEYE).

monolithic *adj*. [1960s–70s] highly intoxicated by a drug. [pun on STONED adj. (2)]

monos *n*. [1980s+] (drugs) a cigarette made from cocaine paste and tobacco. [ety. unknown; ? Sp.]

monosyllable/venerable monosyllable *n*. [18C–19C] the vagina. [i.e. CUNT n.¹ (1)]

monotony *n*. [1970s+] (US campus) one's single, steady girlfriend. [pun on *monogamy*, and its tedium]

mons meg *n*. [19C] the vagina. [a play on *Mons Meg*, a 15C cannon kept at Edinburgh Castle; presumably a coarse ref. to its gaping mouth + poss. play on *mons veneris*]

monster *n*. **1** [1950s–70s] (US) a large and formidable car or plane. **2** [1960s+] (US) an outstanding person, thing, achievement or success. **3** [1970s+] (US drugs) amphetamines (cf. A n.²; METH MONSTER). **4** [1970s+] (drugs) any exceptionally powerful drug. **5** [1980s+] (prison) a sexual offender, a child-molester etc (cf. BEAST n.⁵; NONCE; RULE 43).

monster *adj*. **1** [1960s+] (US) great in size, quantity, significance or achievement. **2** [1990s] (US Black) excellent, first-rate, the very best.

monster *v*. [1960s+] (orig. Aus.) **1** to attack (verbally rather than physically), to pressurize. **2** to harass a woman in the hopes of seduction. [note 1990s journ. use, to subject to intense media scrutiny]

-monster *sfx*. [1980s+] (US campus) used with a relevant n. to denote a person's primary characteristic or passion, e.g. *party-monster, munchie-monster.*

monstro/monstrous *adj*. [1960s+] (US) enormous, outstanding.

monstrous *adj*.¹ [early 18C–mid-19C; 1960s] a general intensifier, e.g. *monstrous fatigue*. [20C use is US]

monstrous *adj*.² *see* MONSTRO.

monstrous *adv*. [early 18C–mid-19C; 1960s] a general intensifier, e.g. *monstrous bad*. [20C use is US]

monte/monte-man/monty *n*.¹ [late 19C–1900s] (Aus.) a racecourse tipster. [MONTE n.² (4)]

monte *n*.² **1** [late 19C+] (Und./gambling) the three-card trick, 'find the lady'. **2** [late 19C+] (Aus.) an absolute certainty (cf. MONTY n.²). **3** [1930s] (Aus.) a lie. [abbr. THREE-CARD MONTE]

monte *n*.³ *see* MONTY n.²

monte *n*.⁴ [1970s] **1** marijuana. **2** good quality marijuana from Mexico (cf. MONTEZUMA GOLD). [(1) Sp. *monte*, a bush, thus a pun]

monte-man *see* MONTE n.¹.

monterey jack *n*. [1990s] a particularly pungent form of smegma. [SAmE *monterey jack*, a variety of strong cheese]

montezuma gold *n*. [1970s] (US drugs) good quality marijuana from Mexico (cf. MONTE n.³). [for ety. *see* MONTEZUMA'S REVENGE]

montezumas *n*. [20C] bloomers. [rhy. sl.]

Montezuma's revenge *n.* [1960s+] (orig. US) food poisoning, esp. with diarrhoea, suffered by tourists in Mexico (cf. APPLE-BLOSSOM TWO-STEP). [named after the last Aztec emperor, *Montezuma II* (*c.*1470–1520)]

monthlies *n.* [late 19C+] the menstrual period (cf. MONTHLY BILL).

monthly bill/dues *n.* [20C] (US) menstruation (cf. MONTHLIES).

month of Sundays *phr.* [late 19C+] a very long time.

Monto *n.* [late 19C–1910s] (Anglo-Irish) the run-down, lowlife area surrounding Montgomery Street, Dublin.

montra *n.* [early 19C] (Und.) a watch. [Fr. *montre*, a watch]

monty *n.*¹ *see* MONTE *n.*¹.

monty *n.*² [late 19C+] (Aus.) a certainty, a 'sure thing'. [MONTE *n.*² (2)]

monty/monte *n.*³ [late 19C+] everything, all that there is, 'the lot'; esp. in phr. *the full monty.* [ety. unknown; the success of the 1997 film *The Full Monty* hugely popularized the phr. and the variety of etys for *monty/monte* were proposed, although none has been accepted as the last word; they range from *monte*, a Sp. and Hisp.Am game of chance, played with a pack of 45 cards, the tailor's *montague* Burton, i.e. a full 3-piece suit; the 'full English breakfast' purportedly enjoyed by Field Marshall *Montgomery*, during WWII; the gambling town of *Monte* Carlo, in which the *full monte* would equate with 'breaking the bank' and several more]

moo *n.*¹ [late 19C+] a woman, esp. a foolish one; often as *silly old moo* (cf. BITCH *n.*¹; COW *n.*¹; MARE). [abbr. MOO-COW]

moo *n.*² (US) **1** [1910s–20s] a beefsteak. **2** [1940s+] milk or cream. [products of the MOO-COW]

moo *n.*³ [1930s–50s] (US) money. [abbr. MOOLA]

mooca/moocah *n.* [1920s+] (drugs) marijuana (cf. MOOTA; MU). [initial letters]

mooch *n.*¹ [mid-19C] a street thief who specializes in snatching (drunken) men's jewellery (cf. BUG-HUNTER *n.*²).

mooch *n.*² **1** [mid-19C+] a sponger, a borrower. **2** [mid-19C+] an idler, a loafer. **3** [mid-19C+] a general term of abuse. **4** [1920s+] (US gambling) a gullible or naïve person. **5** [1940s–50s] (drugs) a drug addict; thus *on the mooch*, addicted to drugs; also *mooch joint*, a bar where one can buy drugs; *mooch pusher*, a drug dealer. [15C SE *mooch*, to act the miser, to pretend to poverty + dial. *mooch*, to play truant]

mooch *n.*³ [late 19C–1900s] (US) a departure or dismissal. [MOOCH *v.*¹ (3)]

mooch *n.*⁴ [1940s–50s] (US drugs) a drug, usu. heroin. [MOOCH *n.*² (5)]

mooch *v.*¹ **1** [mid-19C+] to loaf around. **2** [mid–late 19C] to pilfer, to steal. **3** [mid-19C+] to walk, to go, to amble along. **4** [mid-19C–1970s] to beg, to sponge, to cadge. **5** [late 19C+] (tramp) to live as a tramp. **6** [20C] (Ulster) to play truant, esp. in *on/go on the mooch.* [? OF *muchier*, to hide or skulk]

mooch *v.*² [1960s+] (US) to kiss. [SMOOCH *v.*¹]

moocher *n.* **1** [mid-19C+] a beggar (cf. MOOK). **2** [mid-19C+] a loafer, a loiterer. **3** [1940s–50s] (drugs) a drug addict. [MOOCH *n.*²]

Moocheries *see* MUCKERIES.

moocher's mile *phr.* [1930s–40s] the stretch of Piccadilly (in London) that runs east across the Circus and on to Leicester Square. [MOOCHER *n.* + SE *mile*]

mooch the stem, to *phr.* [20C] (US) to beg in a city's main street. [MOOCH *v.*¹ (4) + (MAIN) STEM]

moo-cow *n.* [early 19C+] (juv.) a cow (cf. BAA-LAMB *n.*¹).

moody *n.* **1** [1930s+] complaints, ill temper, depression. **2** [1930s+] deceit, lies, verbal trickery. **3** [1930s+] gentle persuasion, 'blarney'. **4** [1960s+] a fit of 'the sulks'; thus *pull/throw a/the moody*, to sulk. [(2) rhy. sl. *Moody & Sankey* = HANKY-PANKY; ult. the US evangelists Dwight Lyman *Moody* (1837–99) and Ivo David *Sankey* (1840–1908)]

moody *adj.* [1940s+] illicit, untrustworthy, false.

mooer *n.* [early 19C–1900s] a cow. [SE *moo* + sfx. *-er*]

mooe/mooey *see* MOEY.

mooey-mooey *n.* [mid-19C–1950s] romantic behaviour, flirting. [? SE *moue*, a pout]

moofky-poofky/moofty-poofty *see* MIFKY-PIFKY.

mooi *adj.* [early 19C+] (S.Afr.) a general term of approval meaning pleasant, pretty good, nice. [Du. *mooi*, pretty. Note milit. jargon *mooi-moois*, full dress or 'step-out' uniform (lit. 'pretty-pretties')]

moojin *n.* [20C] (W.I.) a fool, a simpleton. [? MOOCH *n.*²]

moo juice *n.* [1930s+] (orig. US Black) milk. [MOO(-COW) + SE *juice*]

mook *n.* [1930s+] (US) a general term of abuse (cf. MOOCH *n.*²).

moola/moolah/mola/mulla *n.* [1930s+] (orig. US) money. [ety. unknown]

moolie *n.* [1960s] (US) **1** a country person. **2** a Black person. [? SE *muleskinner*]

moo-moo *n.* [20C] (W.I.) **1** an extremely shy person, too nervous to speak out. **2** a fool, a simpleton. [? Twi *e-mumu*, a person who is deaf and dumb]

moon *n.*¹ [mid-18C+] the buttocks, the anus, the rectum; thus *full moon*, the bared buttocks (cf. MOON *v.*²). [resemblance]

moon *n.*² **1** [early 19C–1930s] a month's imprisonment, or multiples thereof, e.g. *nine moon.* **2** [mid-19C+] a month. **3** [late 19C] (US tramp) a night.

moon *n.*³ [late 19C] (US) a large, round biscuit.

moon/moony *n.*⁴ [1920s+] (US) illicitly distilled liquor. [abbr. MOONSHINE *n.* (2)]

moon *n.*⁵ [1960s+] (drugs) a piece of peyote cactus, eaten for the mescaline it contains. [? its half-moon shape]

moon/moon about/along/around *v.*¹ [mid-19C+] to wander around (wretchedly) lost in thought, esp. when a victim of unrequited passion.

moon *v.*² **1** [late 19C–1930s] (US) to have anal intercourse with. **2** [1950s+] to drop one's trousers and underpants and present one's bare buttocks to onlookers, often performed through a car window (cf. DROP TROU; SHOOT THE MOON).

moon about/along/around *see* MOON *v.*¹.

moon-ass *n.* [20C] (US) an infatuated person who pines for an unattainable love-object. [MOON *v.*¹ + ARSE *n.*¹]

moon away *v.* [late 19C+] to lounge, to loiter, to waste time. [MOON *v.*¹]

moon cricket *n.* [20C] (US) a Black person. [ety. unknown; ? a cricket that emerges at night will appear to be black]

moon-curser *n.* [late 17C–early 19C] a link-boy who either robs those for whom he provides a light, or who guides his charges towards some villainous confederates who do the job for him. [dial. *moon-curser*, a ship-wrecker. Urban *moon-cursers* specialized in working the area near Lincoln's Inn Fields in London]

mooner *n.*¹ [mid-19C+] one who moves or looks listlessly or aimlessly, as if moonstruck. [MOON *v.*¹]

mooner *n.*² [1950s] (US Und.) a pathological lawbreaker. [presumably f. the effect of the moon on the mind, or due to the effects of a full moon, during which time the crime rate supposedly increases]

mooner *v.* [mid-19C+] to go around in a moonstruck or listless manner. [MOON *v.*¹]

mooney *see* MOONY *adj.*

moon-eyed *adj.* [18C+] (US) drunk. [the drunkard's seeing double, and thus two moons]

moon-eyed hen *n.* [late 18C–early 19C] 'a squinting wench' (Grose). [SE *moon-eyed*, squinting, orig. used of horses]

mooney's apron *n.* [20C] (Ulster) in cards, the 10 of clubs.

moon-face *n.* [late 19C+] (US) an Asian person; thus *moon-faced*, having Japanese or Asian features.

moon-glow *n.* [1950s] (W.I.) a light-brown complexion.

Moonie *n.* [1970s+] (orig. US) a member of the Unification Church (the Holy Spirit Association for the Unification of World Christianity). [its founder the Rev. Sun Myung *Moon* (b.1920). Founded in 1954 in Korea and now a world-wide religious/political movement, the Church is generally seen, other than by its adherents, as a right-wing, brain-washing cult]

moon juice *n.* [1970s] (US drugs) cough syrup laced with amphetamine.

moonlight *n.* [19C] smuggled spirits. [var. on MOONSHINE n.]

moonlight *v.* **1** [late 19C+] (Und.) to engage in criminal activity at night (cf. MOONLIGHTER) **2** [1950s+] (orig. US) to work at two jobs in order to boost one's income. The second job is usu. night work, and the other employer may not know about it (cf. SUNDOWN adj.).

moonlighter *n.* **1** [late 19C–1930s] (Und.) a thief or burglar who operates at night. **2** [20C] one who escapes paying the rent by leaving a house late at night (cf. MOONLIGHT FLIT). **3** [1920s–40s] a smuggler of illicitly distilled liquor (cf. MOONSHINE n.). **4** [1950s+] one who takes a second job, un-declared for tax purposes. **5** [1970s+] (US Black) a prostitute (cf. EVENING STAR). [all operate by SE *moonlight*]

moonlight flit *n.* [early 19C+] the removal of one's household goods, and with them oneself, late at night in order to escape paying one's rent. [abbr. 18C *make a moonlight flitting*]

moonlight flitting *n.* [early 18C–early 19C] leaving a house late at night to avoid paying rent. [earlier version of MOONLIGHT FLIT]

moonlighting *n.* [1950s+] taking a second, usu. late-night, job in addition to one's daily employment. [MOONLIGHT v. (2)]

moonlight-pon-tick *n.* [1940s+] (W.I.) a gas lamp. [lit. 'moonlight on a stick']

moonlight wanderer *n.* [early 19C] a tenant who cheats the landlord by leaving lodgings late at night, usu. with their household possessions (cf. MOONLIGHT FLIT).

moonman/moon's man *n.* [16C–early 19C] a gypsy. ['A moon-man signifies in English a madman ... But these moon-men ... are neither absolutely mad, nor yet perfectly in their wits. Their name they borrow from the moon, because, as the moon is never in one shape two nights together, but wanders up and down Heaven like an antic, so these changeable-stuff-companions never tarry one day in a place ... .' Dekker (1608); this discussion of England's gypsies is the first ever to be printed]

moon pie *n.* [1970s+] (US) anal intercourse (cf. FUR PIE; HAIR PIE). [MOON n.¹ + fig. use of PIE n.² (1)]

moon-raker *n.* [late 18C–early 19C] **1** a smuggler. **2** a native of Wiltshire. ['It is said that some men of that county, seeing the reflection of the moon in a pond, endeavoured to pull it out with a rake' (Grose 1796). However, the *OED* notes, 'in Wiltshire a more complimentary turn is given to the story: the men were caught raking a pond for kegs of smuggled brandy, and put off the revenue men by pretending folly']

moon rock *n.* [1980s+] (drugs) a mixture of crack cocaine and heroin.

moonshi *n.* [mid-19C] (Anglo-Ind.) a sage, a wise man, a teacher. [Hind. *munshi*, a writer or secretary. The term was first used by the English to describe those who taught them Hindustani]

moonshine *n.* **1** [mid–late 17C] nonsense, a trifle, nothing at all; also as *bag of moonshine*, *moonshine in the mustard pot*. **2** [18C+] illicitly distilled or contraband liquor (cf. BOILO; MOONLIGHT; SHINE n.¹). **3** [20C] adulterated liquor. [the nocturnal activities of the distillers or smugglers who would explain away their boxes and barrels as 'mere moonshine'. *Moonshine* had different meanings according to the county,

in Sussex and Kent it referred to white brandy, in Yorks. to gin]

moonshine *v.* [late 19C+] (US) to distil illicit liquor, usu. bourbon. [MOONSHINE n.]

moonshine darlin' *n.* [1950s] (W.I.) a party to which anyone can come as long as they contribute food or drink. It is held outdoors under the light of the moon.

moon-shooter *n.* [late 19C] one who absconds with their possessions but without paying the rent (cf. MOONLIGHT FLIT).

moon's man *see* MOONMAN.

moontan *n.* [1940s+] (US) sexual activity at night, out-of-doors. [pun on SE *suntan*]

moontan *v.* [1940s+] (US) to indulge in sexual activity at night, out-of-doors. [MOONTAN n.]

moony *n.¹* [mid-19C] a fool (cf. LOONY n.; MOONER n.²). [MOONY adj.]

moony *n.²* *see* MOON n.⁴.

moony/mooney *adj.* **1** [mid-19C–1920s] drunk (cf. ADDLED). **2** [20C] sentimentally romantic. [the supposed effect of the (full) moon on one's brain]

moony cove *n.* [late 19C] an eccentric person. [MOONY adj. + COVE]

Moor, the *n.* [20C] (Und.) Dart*moor* prison in west Devon. [abbr.]

Moorgate rattler *n.* [late 19C] (East London) a dandified person. [play on dial. *Morgan rattler*, a reckless fighter, anyone or anything exceptional or MORGAN RATTLER. Moorgate is an area in the City of London]

moose *n.¹* **1** [1940s+] (US) a little sister or young girl. **2** [1950s–80s] (US) a young Japanese or Korean woman, esp. the wife or mistress of a serviceman stationed in Japan or Korea. [Jap. *musume*, daughter, girl]

moose/bull-moose/regular moose *n.²* [20C] (Can.) **1** a large, powerful, poss. clumsy man. **2** an object that is large and difficult to handle.

moose *n.³* [1990s] an unattractive woman.

moose-face *n.* [mid-19C–1940s] (US) an ugly person (cf. MOOSE n.³).

moose fuck! *see* MOOSE SHIT!

moose-fucker *n.* [1990s] a derog. term for a resident of Canada. [SE *moose* + FUCK v.¹]

moose milk *n.* [1920s+] (Can.) some form of home-brewed alcohol concocted on the Yukon, e.g. milk and rum mixed.

moose shit!/fuck! *excl.* [1960s+] (US) used as an oath.

moosey *n.* [1920s–50s] (US) the vagina. [? dial. *moosie/mosey*, soft, over-ripe; or covered with soft hair]

moosh *see* MUSH n.³, n.⁵, n.⁶.

mooshay *n.* [20C] (W.I.) a poor White, a descendant of the original Fr. settlers on St Kitts (cf. FRENCHIE n.²). [Fr. *monsieur*]

mooshe-/mushe-man *n.* [1940s+] (W.I.) a confidence trick-ster, a hoaxer. [MUSHE + SE *man*; the poor image of Middle Eastern immigrants]

moota/mootah/mooter/mootie/mootos/muta *n.* [1930s+] (drugs) marijuana. [Sp. *mota*, a clod of turf, a handful of earth, thus the link to GRASS n.⁴. Note also weaving jargon *mota*, an imperfection or tangle in wool or cotton, thus the link to a 'tangled' mind (cf. GREEFO; MOOCA; MU)]

mop *n.¹* **1** [19C+] the hair of the head. **2** [1950s–60s] (US Black) hair that has been straightened.

mop *n.²* [mid-19C–1910s] **1** a drinking bout, a drunken spree. **2** a drunk. [SE *mop up* (liquor)]

Mop *n.³* [1920s–30s] (US tramp) the Missouri Pacific Railroad. [abbr.]

mop *v.* [late 19C–1970s] usu. in passive, to defeat. **2** [1970s+] (US gay) to steal, esp. to shoplift. [SE *mop up*]

mop! *excl.* [1940s+] (orig. US) a word used to indicate a sudden occurrence, e.g. *I'm doing this, then mop! I'm doing* that. [jazz use *mop*, the last beat at the end of a jazz number with a cadence of triplets]

mop and bucket! *excl.* [20C] an excl. of annoyance or pain. [rhy. sl.], euph. for FUCK IT!]

mop down *v.* [20C] to empty a glass (cf. MOP UP).

mope *n.*[1] **1** [mid-16C+] a dim-witted, dreamy or miserable person. **2** [mid-16C+] (Irish) a general term of contempt. [SE *mope* v.]

mope *n.*[2] [1910s–70s] (US prison) a stealthy departure; usu. as *cop a mope*, to make an escape. [MOPE v.]

mope *v.* **1** [late 19C–1930s] (US) to walk or move slowly. **2** [late 19C–1970s] to desert or escape.

mopelize *see* MOBILIZE v.[1].

mopery *n.* [20C] (US Und./police) **1** stupidity or ineptitude. **2** a trivial or minor offence, often used ironically, as in a charge of *mopery and dopery*. [SE *mope*]

mopes *n.* [19C–1950s] a feeling of unhappiness; thus *in the mopes*, feeling miserable, 'down in the dumps' [SE *mope*, subseq. use is SE]

mopey as a wet hen *phr.* [20C] (Aus./N.Z.) miserable, gloomy.

moph *see* MOFF.

mopoke/morepork *n.* [mid-19C+] (Aus.) a fool. [SE *mope hawk* or *mopoke*, the tawny frogmouth, a species of owl. Its song sounds like 'more pork, more pork']

moppery *n.* [early–mid-19C] the head. [MOP n.[1] (1)]

moppy *adj.* [early 19C–1940s] drunk. [MOP UP]

mops and brooms/all mops and brooms *phr.* [19C+] drunk. [? the old mop fairs, annual fairs held in the UK West Country, at which servants put themselves up for hire; a young woman would carry a *mop* or *broom* to indicate the job she desired. Such fairs were accompanied by much drinking]

mopsey *see* MOPSY.

mop-squeezer *n.* **1** [late 18C–early 19C] a maidservant. **2** [1940s–60s] (US) a queen in poker. [(2) joc. use of (1)]

mopstick *n.* **1** [late 19C] a fool (cf. DICKHEAD; DIPSTICK). **2** [late 19C–1910s; 1980s] one who loafs around a cheap saloon and cleans up the place in return for drinks. [SE *mopstick*, a mop-handle]

mopsy/mopsey *n.* [late 17C–19C] a homely woman, usu. used affectionately (cf. BUNTY). [SE *mopsy*, a general term of endearment, ult. *mop*, abbr. *moppet*, an affectionate term for a baby]

mop the floor/earth/ground with, to *phr.* [late 19C+] to beat, to thrash, to surpass completely (cf. MOP UP THE FLOOR WITH).

mop up *v.* **1** [18C+] to eat greedily, to drink, to empty one's glass; thus *mopped up*, drunk. **2** [mid-19C] to absorb, to appropriate, to defeat or win. **3** [20C] (orig. milit.) to carry out conclusively, esp. of a gangland or military shooting.

mop up the floor with, to *phr.* [late 19C–1920s] (US) to beat soundly, to thrash (cf. MOP THE FLOOR WITH).

mopus *n.* [late 17C–19C] **1** a halfpenny. **2** a farthing. **3** money in general. [? surname of Sir Giles (according to B.E.) *Mompesson*, a notoriously corrupt merchant of the reign of King James I).

moragrifa/mor a grifa *n.* [1960s–70s] (drugs) marijuana. [? Sp.; ult. GREEFO]

moral *n.* [mid-19C+] (mainly Aus.) a certainty; usu. in *it's a moral ... .* [SE *moral certainty*]

moral Cremorne *n.* [late 19C] (society) the Fisheries Exhibition of 1883. [this otherwise staid exhibition was nonetheless illuminated in the evenings, bringing to mind the original *Cremorne*, the notably immoral Chelsea 'pleasure garden']

more *n.* [1980s] (drugs) phencyclidine (cf. ACE n.[3]). [ety. unknown]

more arse than Jessie *see* HAVE MORE ARSE THAN JESSIE.

more ass than a toilet seat *phr.* [1940s+] (orig. US) conspicuous sexual prowess; usu. as *he gets ...* (cf. MORE PRICKS THAN A SECOND-HAND DARTBOARD).

more butt than ashtrays *phr.* [1990s] (US Black) conspicuous sexual prowess; usu. in *he gets ...* (cf. MORE ASS THAN A TOILET SEAT). [pun on BUTT n.[1]/BUTT n.[2]]

more curtains! *excl.* [1910s–40s] (Cockney) a joc. excl. used by women to tease anyone passing by in an evening dress.

more front than Brighton beach *see* HAVE MORE FRONT THAN BRIGHTON BEACH.

more front than Foy and Gibson's *see* HAVE MORE FRONT THAN MYERS.

more front than Harrods *see* HAVE MORE FRONT THAN HARRODS.

more front than Myers *see* HAVE MORE FRONT THAN MYERS.

more hair on your chest! *phr.* [20C] (Aus.) a general excl. of approval, acclamation, 'good for you', 'well done' etc. [a cliché of masculinity]

moreish/morish *adj.* [early 18C–early 19C] making one desire some more.

more kicks than ha'pence *phr.* [19C] used to describe any situation that yields more trouble than it is worth. [SE in 20C]

more like *phr.* [20C] nearer (a specified number or quantity).

moreno *n.* [1980s+] (US) a Black person. [Sp. *moreno*, dark-skinned]

more often than not *see* AS OFTEN AS NOT.

more or less *n.* [20C] a dress. [rhy. sl.]

morepork *see* MOPOKE.

more power to your elbow! *excl.* [late 19C+] a generally encouraging excl. [the augmented elbow would doubtless be used for bending (cf. BEND ONE'S ELBOW)]

more pricks than a second-hand dartboard *phr.* [1940s+] used of a promiscuous woman; usu. *she's had more pricks ...* (cf. MORE ASS THAN A TOILET SEAT).

more R than F *phr.* [mid-19C–1900s] of a servant, *more rogue than fool*. [abbr.]

more than seven *phr.* [late 19C] aware, knowledgeable, alert, 'on the ball'. [? the role of seven as a magical number]

more than you can shake a stick at *phr.* [early 19C+] (orig. US) beyond number, impossible to count.

more than you could poke a stick at *phr.* [20C] (Aus.) a very large amount.

more time *phr.* [1950s+] (W.I. Rasta) see you later.

Moreton/Moreton bay *n.* [1950s+] (Aus.) an informer. [rhy. sl. *Moreton Bay fig* = FIZGIG n.[2], f. the species of fig that grows at *Moreton Bay*, sited at the mouth of the Brisbane River, Queensland and orig. named Morton by its discoverer Captain Cook, after James Douglas, Earl of Morton FRS (1702–68). Between 1824–39 Moreton Bay was the name of the penal settlement there, and the name of the whole area before Queensland was officially separated from New South Wales in 1859]

more war! *excl.* [late 19C] (Cockney) used to comment on a street fight. [the war in question was the contemporary Spanish-American war of 1898]

more wrinkles than inches *phr.* [20C] (orig. RN) very cold. [the ref. is to the penis, which shrinks when chilly]

morf/morph *n.* (drugs) **1** [1910s] a *morph*ine user. **2** [1910s+] *morph*ine. [abbr.]

morgan rattler *n.* [1900s] a weighted stick used as a weapon, with a knob of lead at one or both ends, often used by garrotters. [earlier use in dial. but ety. unknown; ? anecdotal. Unlike the rigid policeman's truncheon, it was made of a flexible material]

morgue *n.* [late 19C] (US) a particularly unappealing bar or saloon (cf. DEAD HOUSE). [the quality of the liquor on offer.

Such drinks, often adulterated with chemicals to increase their potency, could damage the brain or even kill the drinker]

moriarty n. [20C] a party. [rhy. sl.]

morish see MOREISH.

mork n. [late 19C–1900s] a policeman (cf. MUSKRA). [Rom. *mooshkeroo*, a constable]

morley see MAULEY.

Mormon n. [19C] (US) a promiscuous man. [the polygamy performed by 19C Mormons]

Mormon candy/currency n. [1930s–40s] (US) carrots. [the sect's innate Puritanism]

Mormon poison n. [1980s] (US) coffee. [the Mormon prohibition of any beverages containing caffeine]

Mormon rain/rainstorm n. [1930s+] (US) a dust storm (cf. ARIZONA CLOUDBURST). [the climate of Utah, the home of Mormonism]

morning n. [1960s+] a *morning* newspaper (cf. DAILY n.[1]; EVENING). [abbr.]

morning after/morning after the night before phr. [late 19C+] the state of being hungover after an excess of alcohol.

morning drop n. [19C] **1** the gallows. **2** a hanging. [pun on SE *drop*, a popular form of medicine + *drop*, the fall through the gallows' trapdoor]

morning glory n. **1** [1900s–30s] (US) something which or someone who fails to maintain an early promise, esp. in sporting contexts. **2** [1970s+] (Aus.) sexual intercourse before one gets up in the morning (cf. AFTERNOON DELIGHT). [puns on SE *morning glory*, the plant *Ipomoea purpurea*]

morning mick n. [20C] (Ulster Protestants) the *Irish News*, published in Belfast with a definite Catholic/nationalist slant. [SE *morning* + MICK n.[1]]

morning pride see PRIDE OF THE MORNING.

morning sneak n. [late 18C–early 19C] (Und.) one who specializes in thieving early in the morning (cf. EVENING SNEAK; UPRIGHT SNEAK). [SE *morning* + SNEAK n.[1]]

morning wake-up n. [1980s+] (drugs) the first blast of crack cocaine from the pipe. [SE *morning* + WAKEUP n.[2] (1)]

morning wood n. [1990s] (US) an erection of the penis first thing in the morning (cf. PRIDE OF THE MORNING). [SE *morning* + WOOD n.[2]]

morocco man n. [late 18C–mid-19C] 'Morocco Men, who go about from house to house among their former customers, and attend in the back parlours of Public Houses, where they are met by customers who make insurances' (Patrick Colquhoun, *A Treatise on the Police of the Metropolis*, 1796).

moron n. [1920s+] (orig. US) a stupid or slow-witted person, a fool. [SE *moron* (f. Gk. *moros*, stupid), defined in 1910 by the American Association for the Study of the Feeble-minded as an adult person having a mental age of between 8 and 12]

morotgara n. [1970s] (drugs) heroin. [ety. unknown]

morph see MORF.

morphed adj. [1990s] having passed out from an excess of drugs. [MORF]

morphodite/morphodyte/morphodyke n. [18C+] **1** a hermaphrodite. **2** a male homosexual. [popular mispron. of SE *hermaphrodite*]

morris/morrice v. **1** [early 18C–mid-19C] to dance. **2** [late 18C–early 19C] to be hanged (cf. CUT A CAPER UPON NOTHING; DANCE v.[2]). **3** [late 18C–late 19C] to leave; esp. as *morris off*, *do a morris*. **4** [early 19C] to move quickly. [the movements of the *Morris* dance]

morris minor n. [20C] a black eye. [rhy. sl. *morris minor* = SHINER n.[1] (4)]

Morrison time n. [1940s] double summer time. [the instigator of this short-lived system, Herbert *Morrison* (1888–1965), Minister for Home Security during WW2]

mort n. [mid-16C–late 19C] a woman, esp. a prostitute (cf. AUTEM-MORT; CANTING CREW; MOT n.). [ety. unknown; note SE *mort*, a salmon in its third year, i.e. the popular equation of women with FISH n.[4]]

mortal adj. **1** [early 17C–19C] a general intensifier, e.g. *all my mortal days*. **2** [early 18C–late 19C] extreme, great. **3** [19C] long and tedious.

mortal/mortally adv. [mid-18C–mid-19C] extremely, excessively, e.g. *mortal cold*, *mortal drunk*.

mortal combat n. [1980s+] (drugs) high potency heroin.

mortaller n. [20C] (Irish) a mortal sin, as set down by Roman Catholicism.

mortallious adj. [19C] very drunk. [MORTAL adj. + sfx. *-ious*]

mortal lock n. [1940s+] (US) (orig. gambling) a certainty, a cinch, esp. of a racehorse, a race or a winning hand in cards. [MORTAL adj. (2) + LOCK n.[2] (1)]

mortally see MORTAL adv.

mortar n. [mid-19C] the vagina (cf. PESTLE n.).

mortar and trowel n. [late 19C–1900s] a towel. [rhy. sl.]

mortgage alley / flat / heights / hill / hollow / knob / lane / manor / mesa / row n. [1960s+] (US) the prosperous part of a town or city.

mortgage deed n. [mid-19C] a pawnbroker's ticket.

mortgage flat/heights/hill/hollow/knob/lane/manor/ mesa/row see MORTGAGE ALLEY.

morton n. [1950s+] (Aus.) a busybody. [rhy. sl. *Morton bay fig* = GIG n.[1]]

mort wap-apace n. [16C–early 19C] (Und.) an experienced prostitute or sexually active woman. [MORT + WAP v. and SE *apace* according to B.E.; but Dekker (1612), the source of much of B.E., suggests that the phr. was a one-off, noting that 'there was an abram, who called his mort Madam Wapapace']

m.o.s. n. [1980s+] (US campus) member of the opposite sex. [abbr.]

moschkener see MOSKENEER.

Moscow n. [1910s–50s] (Aus.) a pawnshop; thus *in Moscow*, *gone to Moscow*, in pawn; *Moscow ticket*, a pawn ticket. [MOSKENEER v.]

mose n.[1] [mid-19C] (US) the generic name for a typical 'Bowery b'hoy', a proletarian New Yorker who might work as a fireman but whose main occupation was running with a gang, mixing street thuggery with life as a political mercenary (cf. 'ARRY; LIZE). [the name, if not the type, was originated by Edward Judson (1823–86), a political fixer and bullyboy, who wrote a number of blood-and-thunder burlesques featuring Mose, Lize and their friend Sykesy. Under the pseudonym 'Ned Buntline', Judson went on to create virtually single-handedly the myths of what would become known as the 'Wild West']

mose n.[2] [1940s–70s] (US Black) a Black man who is subservient to Whites. [proper name *Moses*, a stereotypically 'Black' name]

Moses! excl. [mid-19C+] a general excl. of surprise, excitement, alarm etc.

mosey v. [early 19C+] (orig. US) **1** to leave, to wander off; esp. as *mosey about/along/around/off/over*. **2** to go fast, to make haste. [? Sp. *vamos*, let's go, thus US *vamoose*, go away]

mosh/mosh game n.[1] [1920s–30s] (Aus.) any form of illegal gambling. [ety. unknown]

mosh/moshing n.[2] [1980s+] (US) a form of dance, violent and aggressive in manner, involving flinging the limbs wildly, jumping up and down and crashing into other dancers (cf. POGO v.); thus *mosher*, a mosh dancer; *mosh pit*, the area in a club or rock arena where such dancing takes place. [? SE *mash*]

mosh v.[1] **1** [late 19C–1900s] to leave a restaurant without paying one's bill; thus *the mosh*, the practice of committing this fraud. **2** [1920s] to pawn. [MOOCH v.[1]]

mosh v.[2] [1980s+] to dance in a violent and aggressive manner, jumping up and down, crashing into other dancers, waving one's arms etc (cf. POGO v.). [MOSH n.[2]]

mosh game *see* MOSH n.[1].

moshing *see* MOSH n.[2].

moshkeneer *see* MOSKENEER.

mosk v. [1900s] to pawn, esp. at a profit. [abbr. MOSKENEER v.]

moskeneer / moschkener / moshkeneer / moskeener / moskuiner n. [late 19C] a pawner, esp. one who pawns articles for more than they are worth, for a living. [MOSKENEER v.]

moskeneer / moschkener / moshkeneer / moskeener / moskuiner v. [late 19C] to pawn, esp. to pawn for more than an article is actually worth. [Heb. *mashkon*, a pledge, whence *mishken*, to pawn]

mosker n. [late 19C–1900s] a swindler who specializes in defrauding pawnbrokers. [MOSKENEER v.]

mosking/mossing n. [20C] placing things in pawn. [MOSKENEER v.]

moskuiner *see* MOSKENEER.

mosky *see* MOHASKY.

mosquito bites n. [1970s+] (US campus) small breasts.

mosquitos n. [1940–50s] (drugs) cocaine; thus *mosquito bit*, addicted to cocaine. [? the marks left by the hypodermic rather than a ref. to the actual drug]

moss n.[1] **1** [late 18C–early 19C] lead. **2** [19C+] the female pubic hair. **3** [1920s–70s] (US) hair, esp. of the head. **4** [1940s–60s] (US Black) black hair (cf. RIGHTEOUS MOSS). [(1) 'grows on the top' of buildings.

moss n.[2] [mid–late 19C] money. [? pvb. 'a rolling stone – ? a tramp – gathers no moss']

moss-/mossy-back n.[1] (US) [mid-19C] someone who hid themselves to avoid conscription during the US Civil War. [these men were willing to hide until moss grew on their backs]

moss-/mossy-back n.[2] (US) [late 19C+] a diehard conservative (cf. SHELL-BACK). [like some great, lumbering beast, he/she moves so slowly that moss could grow on their back]

Moss Bross n. [1920–70s] *Moss Brothers* of Covent Garden, the UK's leading hirers of dress clothes.

moss dog n. [1910s] a miser. [image of a dog gripping hold of its MOSS n.[2]]

mossie/mozzy n. [1940s+] (Aus.) a mosquito.

mossing *see* MOSKING.

moss-jumper n. [mid-18C–mid-19C] a peasant, a countryman (cf. APPLE-KNOCKER n.[2]). [a peasant's supposed primary preoccupation]

mossoo n. [late 19C] a Frenchman (cf. MOUNSEER). [deliberate mispron. of Fr. *monsieur*, mister, sir]

moss rose n. [19C] the female pubic hair (cf. BEAUTY SPOT n.[1]; MOSS n.[1]; MOSSY BANK; MOSSY CELL; MOSSY COTTAGE; MOSSY DOUGHNUT; MOSSY FACE).

mossy adj.[1] **1** [late 16C–early 17C] stupid, dull. **2** [1900s–40s] (US) very conservative or reactionary; old-fashioned, old. [the image of slow growth or movement]

mossy adj.[2] [20C] of a person, hirsute. [MOSS n.[1] (3)]

mossy-back *see* MOSS-BACK.

mossy bank n. [19C+] the female pubic hair (cf. MOSS ROSE). [MOSS n.[1] (2) + SE *bank*]

mossy cell n. [19C+] the female pubic hair (cf. MOSS ROSE). [MOSS n.[1] (2) + SE *cell*]

mossy cottage n. [1990s] the vagina (cf. MOSS ROSE). [literary euph.]

mossy doughnut n. [1940s] (US) the vagina (cf. APPLE n.[10]; MOSS ROSE).

mossy face n. [late 18C–early 19C] the female pubic hair. [MOSS n.[1](2) + SE *face*]

most, the adv. [1950s–60s] (orig. US) the best, the most exciting, the finest.

mostest adj. [late 19C+] (orig. US) the very best, superlative; thus the popular description of Ella Maxwell (1883–1963), 'the hostess with the mostest'.

mot/mott/mat n. [late 18C+] (orig. UK/US/Irish) **1** a woman, a wife (cf. MORT). **2** a prostitute. **3** a public or lodging-house landlady. [most likely Du. *mot*, a woman, although a bid has been made for Fr. *amourette*, girlfriend]

mot v. [19C] to go out pursuing women. [MOT n.]

mota/moto n. [1930s+] (US drugs) marijuana (cf. MOOTA). [Sp. sl. *mota*, dust]

mot-cart n. **1** [mid-19C] a brougham or similar vehicle owned by a kept woman or well-off prostitute. **2** [late 19C] a mattress. [MOT n. + SE *cart*]

mot-case n. [mid-19C–1910s] a brothel (cf. MOT-HOUSE). [MOT n. + CASA]

mote v. **1** [1920s–40s] to drive a car. **2** [1920s–40s] (Aus.) to move quickly. **3** [1930s+] (Aus.) to walk. [abbr. SE *motor*]

motel hell n. [1970+] (US teen) any situation or place that is considered appalling or unacceptable – a job, a place to stay, a relationship etc.

moth n. [late 19C–1930s] a prostitute.

mothball n. [1940s–50s] (US Black/campus) an irritating person. [? their mind and speech flits around like a moth]

mother n.[1] **1** [late 17C–1910s] a madam, a bawd, a procuress (cf. MOTHER DAMNABLE; MOTHER KNAB-CONEY; MOTHER MIDNIGHT; MOTHER OF ALL THE MAIDS). **2** [late 19C+] one's wife. **3** [1930s+] (US Black) an effeminate man. **4** [1940s+] (US gay) a homosexual who introduces another into the gay world (cf. DAUGHTER). **5** [1940s+] (US gay) a term used by an effeminate gay man to refer to himself, e.g. *Your mother…*.

mother n.[2] [20C] synon. for MOTHERFUCKER. [abbr.]

mother n.[3] [1920s+] the self-proclaimed name of a female owner of a pet, esp. a dog; thus *Come to mother, baby*.

mother n.[4] *see* MA n.[3].

mother/mutha n.[5] [1960s+] (drugs) **1** marijuana (cf. MOOTA). **2** a dealer. [? MOTA or abbr. MOTHERFUCKER or the role of drug as a comforter, i.e. a *mother*]

mother n.[6] [1990s] the ultimate example of something, the extreme version of something (cf. GRAND-DADDY). [mockery of the hyperbolic use of the phr. *mother of all battles* by the Iraqi dictator Saddam Hussein (b.1937) to describe the Gulf War, 1991]

mother adj. [20C] synon. for MOTHERFUCKING adj. [abbr.]

mother/mum, to be phr. [1950s+] to serve portions of food and drink, esp. to pour out cups of tea; thus the invitation *will you be mother?*, will you serve/pour (cf. DO THE HONOURS).

mother and daughter n. [mid–late 19C] water. [rhy. sl.]

Mother Brown n. [20C] town, usu. the West End of London. [rhy. sl.]

Mother Bunch n. [early 17C] water. [joc. use of the name of a noted late-16C ale-wife]

Mother Carey's chicken n. [mid-18C–19C] (orig. US) a stormy petrel. [ext. of the synon. 18C naut. *Mother Carey's goose*]

Mother Carey's chickens n. [early–mid-19C] two people who are sharing living quarters and the payment for them. [? play on SE *stormy petrel* (see MOTHER CAREY'S CHICKEN), one who enjoys controversy or actively promotes it, i.e. the potential squabblings of such housemates]

Mother Cornelius' tub n. [16C] the sweating tub used in the cure of venereal disease (cf. POWDERING TUB). [a presumed actual *Mother Cornelius*, whether a nurse or a procuress]

mother damnable n. [late 17C–18C] a procuress, a madam (cf. MOTHER n.[1]).

mother dog! excl. [1950s+] a general excl., euph. for MOTHER-FUCKER!

motheree/motheren n. [20C] euph. for MOTHERFUCKER.

motheren adj., adv. [20C] euph. for MOTHERFUCKING adj.

motherer n. [late 19C+] (Aus.) a shepherd. [SE mother, to look after]

mother-feryer n. [20C] euph. for MOTHERFUCKER.

Mother Fist and her five daughters/Mother Five Fingers n. [20C] the hand, in the context of masturbation (cf. MISS FIST).

mother-flicker n. [20C] euph. for MOTHERFUCKER.

mother-flunker n. [20C] euph. for MOTHERFUCKER.

mother-flunking adj. [20C] euph. for MOTHERFUCKING adj.

mother-fouler n. [20C] euph. for MOTHERFUCKER.

mother-fouling adj. [20C] euph. for MOTHERFUCKING adj.

motherfuck n. [1960s+] (orig. US) **1** a supreme insult, an expletive (cf. MOTHERFUCKER). **2** a damn, as in I don't give a motherfuck. **3** [1960s+] (orig. US) the hell, e.g. get the motherfuck out.

motherfuck v. [1960s+] (orig. US) a general curse, usu. in imper., e.g. motherfuck the pigs!

motherfuck adv. [1960s+] (US) used as a general intensifier, e.g. don't you motherfuck forget it! [abbr. MOTHERFUCKING adv.]

motherfuck! excl. [1960s+] (orig. US) a general excl. of surprise, rage etc. [MOTHERFUCK n.]

motherfucker n. **1** [1910s+] (orig. US Black/White) a supreme insult, an expletive based on the incest taboo, prob. the ultimate in obscenities. **2** [1940s+] (orig. US) anything one dislikes, an infuriating or surprising state of affairs. **3** [1950s+] (US Black) used with a wide variety of meanings, from good to bad, often as a Black-to-Black term of affection or a compliment, e.g. Jimi Hendrix was a bad motherfucker on guitar; also simply meaning 'thing'. Frequently abbr. to mother (cf. BUGGER n.[1]; MOTHER n.[2]). **4** [1960s+] a damn, e.g. I don't give a motherfucker. **5** [1960s+] an indefinite standard of comparison, e.g. crazy as a motherfucker. **6** [1970s] a large or outstanding example.

motherfucker! excl. [1960s+] (orig. US) a general excl. of surprise, rage etc. [MOTHERFUCKER n.]

motherfucking adj. [1930s+] a general intensifier, also used as an infix, to accentuate or denigrate the word thus altered, e.g. emanci-motherfucking-pation (cf. BUGGERING). [MOTHER-FUCKER n.]

motherfucking adv. [1930s+] a general intensifier, e.g. Start motherfucking talking. [MOTHERFUCKING adj.]

motherfucking-A adj. **1** [1940s+] excellent, superb, the best. **2** [1950s+] goddamned, damned (cf. FUCKING adj.). [ext. of FUCKING-A adj.]

motherfucking-A adv. **1** [1940s+] (orig. US) very little, as good as nothing, e.g. I don't know motherfucking-A about it. **2** [1960s+] generally used for emphasis, absolutely, very well, very much, utterly, completely (cf. FUCKING WELL). [ext. of FUCKING-A adv.]

motherfucking-A! excl. [1970s+] an excl. used to denote astonishment, dismay; acceptance, praise, recognition. [ext. of FUCKING-A!]

mother-fuyer n. [20C] euph. for MOTHERFUCKER.

Mother Ga-ga n. [1950s+] (gay) a fussy, gossipy, interfering older homosexual. [MOTHER n.[1] + GAGA n.[1]]

mother-/father-grabber n. [20C] euph. for MOTHERFUCKER.

mother-/father-grabbing adj. [20C] euph. for MOTHER-FUCKING adj.

motherhead n. [1970s+] (US) euph. for MOTHERFUCKER.

mother-hubba/-hubbard n. [20C] euph. for MOTHERFUCKER.

mother hubbard n. [late 19C+] a cupboard. [rhy. sl.; ult. nursery rhyme Old Mother Hubbard]

mother-hugger n. [20C] euph. for MOTHERFUCKER.

mother-hugging adj. [20C] euph. for MOTHERFUCKING adj.

mother-humper n. [20C] euph. for MOTHERFUCKER.

mother-humping adj. [20C] euph. for MOTHERFUCKING adj.

mothering adj. [20C] euph. for MOTHERFUCKING adj.

mother-in-law n.[1] [late 19C+] a drink composed of equal proportions of old (stout) and bitter.

mother-in-law/mother-in-law exterminator/mother-in-law's hell fire/tongue n.[2] [1980s+] (S.Afr. Ind.) proprietary names for the hottest forms of chile-based hot sauces or curry powders (masalas).

mother-in-law's bit n. [late 18C] a very small portion. [the stereotypically low position of a mother-in-law in the household]

mother-in-law's hell fire/tongue see MOTHER-IN-LAW n.[2].

mother-jiver n. [20C] euph. for MOTHERFUCKER. [SE mother + JIVE v.[1] (1)]

mother-jiving adj. [20C] euph. for MOTHERFUCKING adj. [MOTHER-JIVER]

Mother Jones n. [1930s+] (US) an outdoor privy (cf. MRS JONES). [the US labour leader Mary Harris (1830–1930), also known as Mother Jones]

mother-jumper n. [20C] euph. for MOTHERFUCKER. [SE mother + JUMP v.[1] (1)]

mother-jumping adj. [20C] euph. for MOTHERFUCKING adj. [MOTHER-JUMPER]

Mother Kelly n. [20C] **1** jelly. **2** telly, i.e. television. [rhy. sl.]

Mother Knab-/Nab-Cony n. [early 18C] a madam, a bawd. [SE mother + NAB v.[1] + CONY n.[1], lit. 'Mother Snatch-Sucker']

motherless adj., adv. [late 19C+] (Aus.) a general intensifier, esp. as motherless broke, completely bereft of funds.

motherlove n. [1950s+] a homosexual man having sex with a heterosexual woman.

motherlover n. [20C] euph. for MOTHERFUCKER.

motherloving adj. [20C] euph. for MOTHERFUCKING adj.

Mother Machree n. [20C] (Aus.) tea. [rhy. sl.; ult. Irish mo chroí, my heart. Best known as the title of Rida Johnson Young's 19C ballad]

Mother Machree-ish adj. [20C] (Irish) mawkish, lachrymose, banal. [for ety. see MOTHER MACHREE; the sentimentality of the song]

Mother Midnight n. [late 17C–18C] **1** a bawd, a madam (cf. MOTHER n.[1]). **2** a midwife.

Mother Nab-Cony see MOTHER KNAB-CONY.

mother-naked adj. [late 19C+] (US) absolutely naked. [i.e. as one was when one left the womb]

mother nature n.[1] [20C] (US) menstruation.

mother nature n.[2] [1960s+] (drugs) marijuana.

mother nature's own tobacco n. [1970s+] (drugs) marijuana (cf. GOD'S OWN MEDICINE).

mother of all masons n. [19C] the vagina. [a dig at the Freemasons, for no discernible reason]

mother of all saints n. [late 18C–early 19C] the vagina (cf. MOTHER OF ALL SOULS; MOTHER OF ST PATRICK; MOTHER OF ST PAUL). [a blasphemous joke]

mother of all souls n. [late 18C] the vagina (cf. MOTHER OF ALL SAINTS). [a blasphemous joke]

mother of all the maids n. [late 18C–early 19C] a prostitute.

mother of pearl n. [20C] a girl. [rhy. sl.]

mother of St Patrick n. [18C] the vagina (cf. MOTHER OF ALL SAINTS). [a blasphemous joke]

mother of St Paul n. [early 19C] the vagina (cf. MOTHER OF ALL SAINTS). [a blasphemous joke]

mother of that was a whisker phr. [mid–late 19C] a retort to an utterly implausible story. [? phr. it has whiskers on it]

mother of the maids *n.* [late 18C–mid-19C] a madam, a brothel-keeper.

motheroo *n.* [20C] euph. for MOTHERFUCKER.

Mother Parker *n.* [1950s–60s] (gay) a tough, older homosexual.

mother-raper *n.* [20C] synon. for MOTHERFUCKER.

mother-raping *adj.* [20C] synon. for MOTHERFUCKING *adj.*

mother-rubba/-rubber *n.* [20C] euph. for MOTHERFUCKER.

mothers, the *n.* [1940s–60s] (US Black) the ritualistic name-calling based on insulting one's rival's mother (cf. DOZENS).

mother's *see* MOTHER'S RUIN.

mother's blessing *n.* [19C] laudanum. [a mix of brandy and tincture of opium, often used to keep children quiet]

mother's day *n.* [1960s+] (US Black) the day when welfare cheques arrive from the government.

mother's day pimp *n.* [1990s] (US Black) a man who lives off women, esp. by taking their weekly welfare cheques. [MOTHER'S DAY + PIMP *n.*[1] (1)]

mother's friend *n.* [19C] a quinine pessary, an elementary form of contraceptive, whose inefficiency gave it a parallel name, the *midwife's friend*.

mother's joy *n.* [1900s] (Aus.) a boy. [rhy. sl.]

mother's little helper *n.* [1960s–70s] (drugs) the tranquillizer Miltown. [Rolling Stones' song 'Mother's Little Helper' (1966)]

mother's milk *n.* **1** [early 19C+] gin. **2** [mid-19C] brandy. **3** [1960s] Guinness stout.

mother's pride *n.* [20C] a bride. [rhy. sl.]

mother's ruin/mother's *n.* [1930s+] gin (cf. AUNTIE'S RUIN; BLUE RUIN). [rhy. sl.]

mother-sucker *n.* [20C] euph. for MOTHERFUCKER.

mother superior *n.* [1950s–70s] (camp gay) **1** an older, experienced and open homosexual. **2** a police sergeant.

mot-house *n.* [mid–late 19C] a brothel (cf. ACCOMMODATION HOUSE; MOT-CASE). [MOT *n.* (2) + SE *house*/HOUSE *n.*[1]]

motion lotion *n.* **1** [1970s] (US) alcohol. **2** [1970s+] (US) gasoline, petrol.

motivate *v.* **1** [1950s–60s] (US Black) to move. **2** [1950s–60s] (US Black) to force oneself to do something that one dislikes. **3** [1970s] (US campus) to move around in a group, socializing. **4** [1980s+] (US campus) to leave. [play on SE *motivate* + MOTORVATE]

Moto *n.*[1] [1930s–70s] (US) a Japanese or Asian man. [abbr. MR MOTO].

moto *n.*[2] *see* MOTA.

moto *n.*[3] [1990s] (US campus) a tedious, irritating, boring person. [abbr. *master of the obvious*]

motor *n.*[1] **1** [late 19C] a *motor*car. **2** [1940s+] (US) a motorcycle. [abbr.]

motor *n.*[2] [late 19C] a fast, hard-living man-about-town. [SE *motor*, to drive]

motor *v.* **1** [1970s+] to go well. **2** [1980s+] (US campus) to move quickly, to leave.

Motor City *n.* [1950s+] (US) Detroit, Michigan (cf. MOTOWN).

motor/motorcycle cop *n.* [1910s+] (US) a motorcycle policeman. [SE *motorcycle* + COP *n.*[1] (1)]

motorcycle *n.*[1] [1930s+] (US) euph. for MOTHERFUCKER; usu. as *bad motorcycle*.

motorcycle *n.*[2] [1950s] (US Black) a woman (who can supposedly be 'ridden') (cf. BIKE).

motorcycle bull *n.* [1930s+] (US) a motorcycle policeman. [SE *motorcycle* + BULL *n.*[10]]

motorcycle cop *see* MOTOR COP.

motor-flicker *n.* [20C] euph. for MOTHERFUCKER.

motorhead *n.* (US) **1** [1970s+] an idiot. **2** [1970s+] a car or motorcycle enthusiast.

motorhuckle *n.* [1980s+] (US) a motorcycle. [joc. mispron.]

motor in reverse gear, to *phr.* [1990s] of a woman, to have anal intercourse.

motormouth *n.* [1960s+] (orig. US) **1** a chatterer, a gossip. **2** the mouth of such a person (cf. BLABBERMOUTH; GATEMOUTH; SACK MOUTH).

motormouth *v.* [1960s+] (orig. US) to talk ceaselessly. [MOTORMOUTH *n.*]

motor scooter *n.* [1960s+] (US) a euph. for MOTHERFUCKER.

motorvate *v.* [1970s+] (US campus) to leave (cf. STIMULATE). [? nonce-word *motor-vate*, coined for Chuck Berry's song 'Maybelline' (1955)]

motorway madness *n.* [1970s+] irresponsible, reckless driving on a motorway, esp. in bad and thus dangerous weather (cf. ROAD RAGE).

Motown *n.* [1970s+] (US) Detroit, Michigan (cf. MOTOR CITY).

motser/motsa/motza/motzer *n.* [1930s+] (Aus.) **1** money, esp. as gambling winnings or as a large sum (cf. BREAD *n.*[1]). **2** a 'certainty', which will guarantee such a win. [Yid. *matze*, the unleavened bread eaten at Passover. In traditional form this resembles an outsize round biscuit, and thus an enormous coin]

mott *n.* *see* MOT *n.*

mott *v.* [1920s+] (Aus.) to stare at fixedly. [ety. unknown; ? SE *mott*/*mete*, to ascertain the dimensions and/or quantity of]

mottab/mottob *n.* [mid-19C] the bottom. [backsl.]

mott-carpet/-fleece/motte-fleece *n.* [19C] the female pubic hair. [MOT *n.* (1) + SE *carpet*]

motter *n.* [late 19C] a name coined for the very first motorcar to be seen in the UK. It was driven through London on the day of the Lord Mayor's Show, 1896.

mott-fleece *see* MOTT-CARPET.

motting *n.* [19C] pursuing women, esp. prostitutes. [MOT *n.*]

motto *adj.* [1920s] (tramp) drunk. [Rom.]

mottob *see* MOTTAB.

motza *see* MOTSER.

motzer *n.*[1] [late 19C–1900s] (US) a Jew. [Heb. *matze*, unleavened bread, trad. eaten at the Jewish festival of Passover]

motzer *n.*[2] *see* MOTSER.

mouchet *n.* [early 18C–early 19C] a synthetic beauty mark affixed to a woman's face. [Fr. *mouche*, a fly]

mouchey/mouchy *see* MOCKIE.

mould/mode *v.* [1980s+] (US campus) to embarrass, to humiliate. [SE *mould*, the growth that appears on rotting vegetable matter]

moulded *adj.* [1990s] (US Black) old. [SE *mould*, a form of fungus that grows on rotting food + SE *old*]

mouldies *n.* [late 19C] old clothes.

mouldiworp *n.* [1990s] the penis (cf. MOLE *n.*[1]). [dial. *mouldiwarp*, a mole, lit. 'earth-digger'/'earth-thrower']

mouldy *adj.* **1** [mid-19C] grey-haired (cf. MOULDY-PATE). **2** [mid-19C+] boring, gloomy, sick. **3** [late-19C+] useless, second-rate, out-of-date. **4** [20C] very drunk.

mouldy fig *n.* [1930s+] (orig. US) a very boring or old-fashioned person, esp. as applied by modern jazz fans to their antitheses, the fans of traditional New Orleans jazz.

mouldy grub *n.* [mid-19C] a travelling showman; thus *mouldy grubbing*, performing in the open air. [play on SE *mulligrubs*]

mouldy one/'un *n.* [mid–late 19C] a copper coin (cf. MOULIES). [the colour]

mouldy pate *n.* [mid–late 19C] a servant wearing a grey powdered wig.

mouldy 'un *see* MOULDY ONE.

moulenjam *see* MULENYAM.

mouli *v.* [1980s+] (Aus. drugs) to chop cannabis in a parsley grinder. [brandname *Moulinex*, ult. Fr. *mouli-légumes*, a food processor]

moulies *n.* [late 19C] copper coins (cf. MOULDY ONE). [the colour]

moulonjam *see* MULENYAM.

moult the mouldies, to *phr.* [late 19C] to change one's clothes. [SE *moult* + MOULDIES]

mounseer/mounsear *n.* [late 18C–19C] a Frenchman (cf. MOSSOO). [Fr. *monsieur*]

Mount, the *n.*[1] **1** [early 18C–late 19C] London Bridge. **2** [20C] (Can.) Montreal. [one approached the Bridge up a short incline]

mount *n.*[2] **1** [mid-19C] a wife, a mistress. **2** [mid–late 19C] anything one rides, esp. a dangerous and uncontrollable horse. **3** [1970s+] (US Black) a promiscuous woman, who is 'ridden' (cf. BIKE; RIDE n.[3]).

mount *v.*[1] [late 18C] to provide for, to look after. [SE *mount*, to raise up, to exalt]

mount *v.*[2] **1** [late 18C–mid-19C] to perjure oneself for money. **2** [1960s+] (US Black) to brag, to boast, to attack verbally. [? SE *mount*, to ascend the stage, to make an appearance as a performer]

mount *v.*[3] [19C+] to have sexual intercourse with; also as *do a mount*. [SE before this, and remains so when used of animals]

mount a corporal and four, to *phr.* [late 18C–early 19C] to masturbate. [MOUNT v.[3], 'the thumb is the corporal, the four fingers the privates' (Grose 1785)]

mountain canary *n.* [1910s+] (US, mainly West.) a donkey (cf. ARIZONA NIGHTINGALE). [joc. ref. to its braying]

mountain climber *n.* [1970s] (US campus) a feeling of intoxication produced by drugs. [play on HIGH adj.[1]]

mountain devil *n.* [20C] (Aus.) a native of Tasmania. [the nickname for the thorn-devil (*Moloch horridus*), a Tasmanian lizard]

mountain dew *n.* [early 19C+] **1** whisky, 'advertised as from the Highlands' (Hotten, 1860) (cf. CREAM OF THE VALLEY). **2** contraband whisky. [coined in Scotland and exported to the US, the term is equally popular in W.I. use]

mountain goat *n.* [20C] (US prison) any form of prison meat (cf. BULL n.[7]; MOUNTAIN LAMB).

mountain guinea *n.* [1960s+] (US/Ital.) used by southern Italians, a northern Italian. [SE *mountain* + GUINEA n.[1] (1)]

mountain lamb *n.* [20C] (US) salt pork (cf. ADIRONDACK STEAK).

mountain oyster *n.* [late 19C+] (US) a sheep's or hog's testicle as food, supposed to be a powerful aphrodisiac.

mountain passes *n.* [1900s–50s] spectacles. [rhy. sl. *mountain passes* = glasses]

mountain-pecker *n.* [mid-19C] a sheep's head (cf. BLOODY JEMMY; JEMMY n.[2]).

mountains *n.* [1970s+] (US Black) large, noticeable female breasts.

mountains of Mourne *n.* [20C] an erection. [rhy. sl. *mountains of Mourne* = HORN n.[1] (2)]

mountain wop *n.* [1960s+] (US) a derog. term for an Italian (cf. MOUNTAIN GUINEA). [SE *mountain* + WOP n.]

mounteer *n.* [early 18C] a hat. [Sp. *montera*, a hunter's cap having a spherical crown and a flap capable of being drawn over the ears, ult. f. *montero*, a hunter]

mounter *n.* [early–late-19C] one who swears false oaths. [MOUNT v.[2] (1)]

mount-faulcon *n.* [late 16C–early 17C] the vagina. [lit. 'mount falcon'; coined by lexicographer John Florio (*c*.1553–*c*.1625)]

mount for *v.* [early 19C] to back up someone in their claims, to provide someone with an alibi (cf. BONNET FOR). [ext. of MOUNT v.[2]]

mount/ride one's high horse, to *phr.* [late 18C+] to act in an arrogant, superior manner; thus *get down off one's high horse*, to 'come down to earth'.

Mount Pleasant *n.* [mid-19C] the vagina (cf. BEAUTY SPOT n.[1]). [pun on proper name/MOUNT v.[3] (1)]

Mount St Moritz Bajan *n.* [20C] (W.I./Gren.) a poor White (cf. MONG-MONG).

mount the ass, to *phr.* [late 18C–mid-19C] to become bankrupt. [old Fr. custom of exhibiting a bankrupt riding backwards on a donkey]

mount the cart, to *phr.* [18C] to be hanged. [before the drop, prisoners stood on a cart with the rope around their neck; the cart was then driven away, leaving the victim to suffocate. This was not automatically an instant process, and friends would often haul sharply on the victim's legs to speed matters up]

mount the ladder, to *phr.* [16C–mid-19C] to be hanged (cf. CLIMB THREE TREES WITH A LADDER). [the ladder onto the gallows]

mount the red rag/flag, to *phr.* [19C] to blush.

mourner's bench *n.* [1900s–30s] (US) the court bench on which prisoners sit awaiting trial.

mourning bands *n.* [late 19C] dirty finger-nails. [SE *mourning band*, a strip of black cloth or crape worn round the sleeve of a coat or round a hat as a sign of bereavement]

mourning coach horse *n.* [late 19C] (middle-class) 'a tall, solemn woman, dressed in black and many inky feathers' (Ware).

mourning shirt *n.* [mid-17C] a flannel shirt. [such a shirt needs less regular washing, ref. to the custom of wearing the same clothes through the immediate period of mourning]

mouse *n.*[1] **1** [late 16C–late 18C] a woman, esp. when applied to a prostitute arrested for brawling in the street. **2** [19C] (US Black) one's wife; thus *mousetrap*, marriage. **3** [late 19C+] a mistress. **4** [1910s–60s] (US) a woman. **5** [1930s] (US Und.) an effeminate male homosexual (cf. MOUSER n.[5]). **6** [1950s–60s] a small, very feminine girl who invites being cuddled. **7** [1970s] (US) a child. [there is no discernible link between (1) and (4)]

mouse *n.*[2] [19C] the penis (cf. MOLE n.[1]). [its moving down dark, narrow passageways. Note dial. *mouldiwarp*]

mouse *n.*[3] [19C] a man who does not consummate his marriage on the wedding night. [? f. phr. 'are you a man or a mouse?']

mouse *n.*[4] [mid-19C+] (US) a black eye. [supposed resemblance]

mouse *n.*[5] **1** [late 19C–1900s] a barrister, a solicitor. **2** [late 19C+] (Und.) an informer. [play on RAT n.[3]]

mouse *n.*[6] [1940s] (US Black) a pocket. [ety. unknown; ? abbr. SE *mouse-hole*]

mouse *v.*[1] [late 17C] to hit in the face. [? SE *mouse*, to handle roughly, as a cat does a mouse]

mouse *v.*[2] [1940s–50s] (US Und.) to inform on (cf. RAT v.[1]). [MOUSE n.[5] (2)]

mouse *v.*[3] [1940s+] (US campus) to engage in sexual activity. [MOUSE n.[2]]

mouse *v.*[4] [1970s] (US) to blackmail; thus *the mouse*, extortion. [? ext. of MOUSE n.[4]]

mouse! *excl.* [19C] be quiet! [phr. *quiet as a mouse*]

mousebrain *n.* [1970s+] (US) a fool (cf. BAKEBRAIN). [SE *mouse* + sfx. *-brain*]

mousehole *n.* [19C] the vagina (cf. BLACK HOLE n.[1]; MOUSE n.[2]).

mouse-hunt/-hunter *n.* [late 16C–mid-17C] a womanizer, a wencher. [MOUSE n.[1] + SE *hunter*]

mouse out *v.* [1990s] (US Black) to back down, to give up (cf. CHICKEN OUT). [the timorousness of the mouse]

mouser *n.*[1] [19C+] a cat o'-nine tails (cf. CAT n.[2]).

mouser *n.*[2] [early 19C–1900s] **1** the vagina (cf. MOUSE n.[2];

MOUSETRAP n.²). **2** a fellatrix, esp. one who nibbles rather than sucks the penis.

mouser n.³ [mid-19C+] a black eye (cf. MOUSE n.⁴). [supposed resemblance]

mouser n.⁴ [mid-19C] a detective (cf. MOUSE n.⁵). [like a cat playing with a mouse, they 'watch' criminals]

mouser n.⁵ [1910s–30s] (US) a homosexual (cf. MOUSE n.¹).

mouser n.⁶ [1930s–40s] (US) a moustache. [supposed resemblance]

mousetrap n.¹ [late 19C] a sovereign. [the fanciful similarity of the crown and shield (pictured on the reverse) to a set mousetrap]

mousetrap n.² [late 19C+] **1** the vagina (cf. MOUSE n.²; MOUSER n.²). **2** the mouth (cf. POTATO-TRAP; RAT-TRAP n.²).

mousetrap v. [1960s] (US) to fool or mislead by false promises, to entice, to cajole.

mousse up v. [1980s+] (US campus) usu. of a man, to use a foamy hair-care preparation.

moustache/mustache n. (US) **1** [late 19C+] a man with a moustache (cf. MOUSTACHE PETE). **2** [1930s] oral copulation, cunnilingus (cf. MOUSTACHE RIDE).

moustache/mustache Pete n. [20C] **1** an original Italian immigrant to New York, typified by his heavy moustache. **2** an original member of the US Mafia (cf. OLD MOUSTACHE).

moustache/mustache ride n. [1970s+] (US) an act of cunnilingus. [MOUSTACHE n. (2) + RIDE n.³]

moutagram/moutaphone n. [1940s] (W.I.) a source of gossip and false news. [SE mouth + telegram/telephone]

mout-a-massy n. [1940s–50s] (W.I.) a gossip, a chatterbox. [lit. 'mouth have mercy']

moutaphone see MOUTAGRAM.

mouth n.¹ **1** [late 17C–mid-19C; 1960s+] a noisy, talkative, boorish person. **2** [late 17C–mid-19C] a fool, a dupe; thus [early–mid-19C] rank mouth, an especially impudent person, you are a mouth and you will die a lip, general phr. of abuse/dismissal. **3** [late 19C+] cheek, impudence (cf. MOUTH OFF). **4** [1940s–60s] (US) a lawyer (cf. MOUTHPIECE).

mouth n.² [late 19C+] the dry, foul-tasting mouth that follows a night's excesses (cf. BACK n.²); thus have a mouth on one, to be desperate for alcohol.

mouth v. **1** [mid-19C] (US campus) to bluff a recitation. **2** [1960s+] to insult, to criticize, to speak insolently (cf. MOUTH OFF).

mout-hab-nuttin-fe-do n. [20C] (W.I.) a chatterbox, a malicious gossip. [lit. 'mouth has nothing (better) to do']

mouth almighty n. [mid-19C] a noisy, talkative, loud-mouthed person (cf. MOUTH n.¹).

mouthamassy/mouthamassy Liza n. [20C] (W.I.) a chatterbox (cf. MOUTHAR; MOUTI-MOUTI). [? Twi mmasa-mmasa, confused words, or f. phr. 'mouth have mercy!']

mouthar n. [20C] (W.I.) a chatterbox, one who cannot be trusted to keep secrets (cf. MOUTHAMASSY; MOUTI-MOUTI). [? SE mouth]

mouth bet n. [late 19C] (US gambling) a verbal promise of a bet.

mouth-breather n. [1980s+] a stupid person, esp. a particularly stupid thug. [such individuals are presumed to be breathing heavily]

mouth-breathing adj. [1980s+] **1** stupid. **2** thuggish. [MOUTH-BREATHER]

mouth fuck n. [mid-19C] an act of fellatio. [SE mouth + FUCK n.¹]

mouth fuck v. [1970s+] to fellate. [MOUTH FUCK]

mouthful n. [late 18C; 1910s+] a truthful, striking or confessional comment or speech.

mouth half-cocked n. [late 17C–early 19C] a person who gapes stupidly at anything and everything. [SE mouth + fig.

use of half-cocked, of a pistol that has the cock drawn back]

mouth harp n. [20C] (US) a mouth organ (cf. HARP n.²). [on model of SE jew's harp]

mouth like a lorry-driver's crutch/nun's minge see MOUTH LIKE THE INSIDE OF AN ARAB'S UNDERPANTS.

mouth like the bottom of a cocky's cage phr. [1960s+] (Aus.) a mouth that is unpleasantly furred, the result of excessive drinking (cf. MOUTH LIKE THE INSIDE OF AN ARAB'S UNDERPANTS). [SE cockatoo]

mouth like the inside of an Arab's underpants/like a lorry-driver's crutch/nun's minge phr. [1960s+] the furred tongue and disgusting taste that can accompany a hangover.

mouth music n. [1970s] the practice of cunnilingus.

mouth-o! excl. [1980s+] (US campus) this tastes wonderful! [SE mouth + orgasm]

mouth-off n. [1950s+] (orig. US) a braggart, a boaster, a chatterer. [MOUTH OFF v.]

mouth off v. [1950s+] (orig. US) to boast, to brag, to speak impudently. [ext. of MOUTH v. (2)]

mouth open story jump out phr. [20C] (W.I.) all will be revealed.

mouth organ n. [late 19C–1920s] (US) **1** a spokesman (cf. MOUTHPIECE). **2** the tongue. [puns]

mouth pie n. [late 19C] feminine scolding, nagging.

mouthpiece n. **1** [19C+] a spokesman. **2** [19C+] a lawyer, in the UK a solicitor, in the US an attorney (cf. LIP n.¹; TONGUE n.; WARBLER n.). **3** [1900s–20s] (US) an informer. **4** [1910s–50s] (US) the mouth. **5** [1990s] (US Black) gold caps on one's front teeth. [(1) orig. SE]

mouth runs like parch benny/like sick nigger take salts phr. [20C] (W.I.) a phr. used of an incessant irritating chatterer. [Carib.E. parch = SE parched + benny, a form of sesame-based cooking oil, used in making sweets]

mouth sugar n. [20C] (US Black) a kiss (cf. SUGAR n.³).

mouth thankless n. [early–mid-19C] the vagina. [lit. euph. coined by Sir Walter Scott (1771–1832)]

mouth that cannot bite n. [late 17C–early 18C] the vagina. [lit. euph. coined by Thomas D'Urfey (1653–1723)]

mouth that says no words n. [18C] the vagina.

mouthwash n.¹ [20C] food. [rhy. sl. mouthwash = NOSH n. (2)]

mouthwash n.² **1** [1930s+] a drink of alcohol. **2** [1960s+] (US prison) prison coffee (cf. FLIT n.¹; SPOW)

mouth-worker n. **1** [1950s+] (drugs) one who takes drugs orally. **2** [1960s+] (gay) a fellator.

mouthy adj. [1930s+] boastful, cocky.

mouti-mouti/mowti-mowti n. [1940s–50s] (W.I.) a gossip, a chatterbox (cf. MOUTHAMASSY; MOUTHAR).

mouton n. [19C] 'a spy quartered with an accused person with a view to obtaining incriminating evidence' (OED). [Fr. mouton, a sheep. The Fr. sl. means the same]

move n. **1** [early 19C+] a trick, a scheme, a stratagem. **2** [1980s] (US) the right thing, the proper way, 'what's happening'. **3** [1960s+] (orig. US) a sexual advance.

move v.¹ **1** [late 19C+] to leave. **2** [1930s+] (US) to sell off or to dispose of merchandise, incl. contraband, drugs and stolen property. **3** [1950s+] (orig. US) to dance or play music energetically or with a strong rhythm. **4** [1950s+] (orig. US) to move fast, to be exciting or dynamic.

move v.² [20C] (Irish) **1** to pick up a member of the opposite sex. **2** to get on with very well. [SE move, to stir, to excite]

moveables n. [late 17C–early 19C] (Und.) swords, watches, jewellery and other objects that can be stolen, won at gambling or otherwise taken away from their owner.

movement *n.* [1920s–60s] (US) the provocative swaying of a woman's hips, usu. used in comparison with clocks or watches, e.g. *She's got a movement like a Swiss watch*.

move off *v.* [mid–late 18C] to die (cf. GO OFF v.¹).

move on *v.* [1970s+] (US Black/campus) to hit, to assault, usu. with a weapon.

move/shift one's ass, to *phr.* [20C] (orig. US) to hurry up, to get a move on.

move out *v.* [1920s] (N.Z.) to expand, to bloom.

mover *n.* [1950s+] **1** an ambitious and successful person, both socially and with the opposite sex. **2** someone who moves themself or others physically and emotionally.

moves, the *n.*¹ [1910s+] (US) a film, a movie.

moves *n.*² [1960s+] **1** (orig. US) knowledge, ability, 'smarts'; esp. in phrs. *have all the moves*, *got all the moves*. **2** (US) schemes used for seduction; esp. in phr. *put the moves on*.

move to *v.* [1900s–10s] to bow to.

move to the blind, to *phr.* [late 19C] to leave one's rented premises without paying the rent, to do a 'moonlight flit'. [? SE *blind spot* (of the landlord)]

move with *v.* [1950s+] to associate with, to spend time with.

move/shift your carcass! *excl.* [1920s+] move! get out of the way!

movie *n.* [1960s+] (US) a sequence of events that are unpleasant or boring, esp. in phr. *I don't like this movie*, I am not happy or comfortable.

movies *n.*¹ [20C] diarrhoea. [a coarse pun]

movies *n.*² [1970s] (US Und.) prison. [ironic ref. to the austerity of the prison]

moving dunghill *n.* [late 18C] a notably filthy man or woman.

mow *n.* [mid-16C–18C] the act of copulation. [MOW v.¹]

mow *v.*¹ [mid-16C–18C] to have sexual intercourse. [Scot./ northern dial. *mow*, to copulate, and note MOULDIWORP]

mow/on *v.*² [1980s+] (US campus) to eat heartily, to gorge oneself.

mower *n.* [late 17C–early 19C] (Und.) a cow. [its *moo*-ing]

mow-heater *n.* [late 17C–early 19C] (Und.) a drover. [the drover's habit of sleeping on hay mows, ? + drover's 'heating up' of the MOWER'S behinds as he uses his stick to guide them through gates, down lanes etc]

mowlow *see* MOLO.

mow on *see* MOW v.².

mowrowsky *see* MARROWSKYING.

mow the brigalo suckers, to *phr.* [1990s] (Aus.) to shave one's beard (cf. MOW THE LAWN). [*brigalow*, a form of acacia, found in New South Wales and Queensland. Its rapid growth can render large areas of land unusable]

mow the grass, to *phr.* [1960s+] (drugs) to smoke marijuana. [pun + GRASS n.⁴]

mow the lawn, to *phr.* **1** [1930s–40s] (US Black) to cut one's hair. **2** [1950s+] to shave with an electric razor (cf. MOW THE BRIGAOL SUCKERS).

mowti-mowti *see* MOUTI-MOUTI.

moxie *n.*¹ [20C] (W.I.) an untidy and thus unattractive young woman. [dial. *mawks*, a slattern, an unkempt woman]

moxie *n.*² **1** [1930s+] courage, impudence, ability. **2** [1960s–70s] (US Black) an impudent upstart. [from the tradename of a once-popular US soft drink *Moxie*, developed *c*.1880 and patented 1924; it possibly contained *moxie*, or wintergreen; ult. Algonquin root *maski*-, medicine]

m.o.y. *phr.* [1980s+] my place or yours? [abbr.]

moyo *n.* [1980s+] (US) a Black person. [Sp.]

moz/mozz *v.* [1940s+] (Aus.) to interrupt, to hinder. [SE *muzzle*]

mozart and liszt *see* BRAHMS AND LISZT.

mozz *see* MOZ.

mozzle *n.* [late 19C+] luck. [MAZEL]

mozzle *v.* [1920s+] (Aus.) **1** to hinder, to interrupt (cf. MOZ). **2** to put a jinx on (cf. PUT THE MOZ ON).

mozzle and brocha *n.* [20C] a door-to-door salesman. [rhy. sl. *mozzle and brocha* = ON THE KNOCKER phr.¹, ult. Yid. *mazel*, good luck + *brocha*, a blessing]

mozzy *see* MOSSIE.

m.p. *n.* [mid-19C] (US) a policeman. [? abbr. *Metropolitan Police*]

mpata *n.* [1980s+] (S.Afr. Und.) a new inmate, a fool, one who has not yet learned how to cope with prison conditions (cf. FISH n.⁵). [Zulu *mpatha*, a greenhorn]

m.r.a. *n.* [1980s+] (US campus) unsociable behaviour. [abbr. major *r*eeb *a*ction]

Ms *see* MISS n.².

m.s. *n.* [1960s] (drugs) morphine. [abbr. *m*orphine *s*ulphate]

mshoza *n.* [1980s+] (S.Afr.) the female companion of a township dandy (cf. PANTSULA). [? SE *shows*, thus showy, well-dressed, good-looking]

m.t. *n.* [mid-19C+] an empty bottle. [pron./abbr. of *empty*]

m.t.f. *n.* [1980s+] (society) an overly amorous young man. [abbr. *m*ust *t*ouch *f*lesh]

M25 *n.* [1980s+] (drugs) MDMA (cf. ECSTASY). [the initial letters + the UK's *M25* motorway, an orbital route round London, which played a major part in the siting of the early ecstasy-fuelled raves]

mu *n.* [1930s–70s] (drugs) marijuana. [abbr. MOOCA]

m.u. *n.* [1960s–70s] (drugs) a *m*arijuana *u*ser. [abbr.]

mubble-fubbles *n.* [late 16C–mid-17C] a mental depression. [joc. uses of SE *mumble* + *fumble*]

much! *excl.* [late 16C; mid-19C+] certainly not! (cf. NOT MUCH!; TOO MUCH!).

much goo about nothing *phr.* [1990s] masturbation. [play on Shakespeare's *Much Ado About Nothing* (1600)]

much love *n.* [1990s] (US Black) popularity, respect (cf. MUCH PROPS).

mucho *n.* [1940s+] (orig. US) a great deal. [MUCHO adj.]

mucho *adj.* [1940s+] (orig. US) a lot of, many. [synon. Sp.]

mucho *adv.* [1940s+] (orig. US) exceedingly. [MUCHO adj.]

much of a … *phr.* [mid–late 19C] a phr. used in negative contexts to mean 'not to any great degree', 'not very important', 'not much'.

much of a muchness *phr.* [early 18C+] very similar, of no discernible difference, unworthy of special notice.

much props *phr.* [1990s] (US Black/teen) respect for others (cf. MUCH LOVE). [SE *much* + PROPS n.²]

much-travelled highway *n.* [19C] a large and loose vagina.

muck *n.*¹ [late 17C+] money (cf. CRAP n.¹; DUST n.¹). [the guilty equation of money and dirt]

muck *n.*² [late 19C–1930s] a heavy fall. [abbr. MUCKER n.¹]

muck *n.*³ [late 19C+] a general term covering anything or anyone seen as disgusting, worthless or abhorrent.

muck *n.*⁴ [1900s–50s] (US) an important or self-important person. [MUCK-A-MUCK n. (2)]

muck *n.*⁵ [1920s+] euph. for FUCK in its various forms.

muck *n.*⁶ [1990s] semen, esp. in phr. *spill one's muck*. [SE *muck*, anything filthy, dirty, esp. when part liquid; untraceable prior to 1990s but note JIT ONE'S MUCK]

muck *v.*¹ **1** [mid-19C] to beat, to surpass, to ruin financially. **2** [late 19C] to fail at (cf. MAKE A MUCK OF; MUCK UP). **3** [late 19C+] to make a mess of; esp. as *muck about*, *muck up*.

muck *v.*² [1920s+] euph. for FUCK in its various forms.

muck about *v.* **1** [mid-19C+] to pretend, to act half-heartedly, to play about. **2** [mid-19C+] to irritate, to tease. **3** [1930s+] to fondle intimately.

muck-a-muck/muckety-muck *n.* (US) **1** [mid-19C–1920s] food, drink. **2** [mid-19C+] an important or self-important person; esp. as *high muck-a-muck*, *big muck-a-muck* (cf. HIGH MUCKY-MUCK). [Chinook jargon *muckamuck*, food]

muck and halfpenny afters *n.* [late 19C] (middle-class) a pretentious, unpleasant dinner 'spotted at the corners with custard powder preparations, and half dozens of stewed prunes, etc, etc' (Ware).

muck and truck *n.* [late 19C] miscellaneous articles of trade. [SE *muck* + *truck*, worthless items for trade]

muck-arse/muck-arse about/around *v.* [20C] to 'mess about', esp. in a sexual context.

muck-cheap *adj.* [late 19C+] very cheap, 'dirt-cheap'.

muckcook *v.* [late 19C–1900s] to laugh behind someone's back. [? SE *cook*, to concoct + fig. use *muck*, dirt; thus cf. DISH THE DIRT]

mucked/mucked out *adj.* [early 19C–1900s] penniless. [stable imagery]

muckender/mucketer/muckinder *n.* [late 18C–early 19C] a swab. [SE *muckender*, a handkerchief or napkin, ult. Fr. *mouchoir*, Sp. *mocador*]

mucker *n.*[1] [mid-19C+] a heavy fall; thus *come a mucker*, *go a mucker*, to come to grief, to ruin oneself. [SE *muck*, into which one falls]

mucker *n.*[2] **1** [late 19C–1910s] (US) a street urchin or youth who does not go to college. **2** [late 19C–1930s] a fanatic, a hypocrite. **3** [late 19C–1930s] a rough, coarse person. [SE *muck*, dirt]

mucker *n.*[3] [late 19C+] an unpleasant person. [var. on FUCKER n. (4)]

mucker *n.*[4] [1940s+] a companion, a friend. [MUCK (IN)]

mucker *v.* **1** [mid-19C] to come to grief, to fail. **2** [mid-19C–1920s] to cause problems for someone. **3** [mid-19C+] to fall, to 'take a tumble'. **4** [1920s] to squander, to waste. [MUCKER n.[1]]

Muckeries/Moocheries *n.* [late 19C] the Inventions Exhibition, held in South Kensington in 1885 (cf. COLINDERIES). [SE *muck about*; a pej. ref. to the inventors]

mucker-upper *n.* [1940s] a bungler. [MUCK UP]

mucket *n.* [1950s–60s] (US) a hairpiece or toupee. [? var. on SE *merkin*, a pubic wig]

mucketer *see* MUCKENDER.

muckety-muck *see* MUCK-A-MUCK.

muck-forks *n.* [mid-19C] the fingers.

muckheap *n.* [mid-19C–1900s] a lazy, filthy person.

muckhill *n.* [late 17C–early 18C] a pile of money (cf. CRAP n.[1]; DUST n.[1]); thus *have a good muckhill at one's doorstep*, to be well-off. [MUCK n.[1]]

muckhole *n.* [1960s+] a filthy, unappetizing place or room.

muckibus *adj.* [mid-18C–mid-19C] tipsy, slightly drunk (cf. ADDLED). [SE *muck* + cod Lat. sfx. *-ibus*]

muck in *v.* [1930s+] to join in, to lend a hand, esp. in a dirty or unpleasant task (cf. MUCK IT).

muckinder *see* MUCKENDER.

mucking *adj.* [late 19C] repellent, filthy.

muckings *n.* [late 19C] a mess, rubbish.

mucking-togs *n.* [mid-19C–1910s] a mackintosh. [joc. mispron., but note MUCKING + TOGS (1)]

muck it *v.* [1920s] (US) to work at a menial task, lit. 'to get one's hands dirty' (cf. MUCK IN).

muckle *n.* [mid-late 19C] (US) muscle. [joc. mispron.]

muck out *v.* [mid-19C] (gambling) to take all one's opponents' money (cf. MUCK SNIPE). [SE *muck out*, to clean out]

muckrag *n.* [19C] a handkerchief (cf. MUCKENDER; SNOTRAG).

muck-shoveller *n.* [1940s] (Aus.) a tin-miner. [the dirtiness of the job]

mucksnipe *n.* [mid-19C] a gambler (or anyone else) who has lost all their money (cf. MUCK OUT).

muckspout *n.* [early 19C–1910s] one who uses a good deal of obscene language or has a 'smutty' mentality.

muckstick *n.* [1920s] (US) a shovel; thus *muckstick artist*, a labourer.

mucksuck *v.* [1960s+] (US) to act in a disgusting manner.

mucksucker *n.* [1960s+] (US) one who acts in a disgusting manner. [MUCKSUCK]

muck-suckle *n.* [mid-late 19C] a filthy woman.

muck-sweat *n.* [early 19C+] perspiration, esp. induced through fear or panic; thus *be in a muck-sweat*, to be terrified, to be flustered.

muckty-muck *n.*[1] [1950s+] (US Black) an important person, or one who poses as such. [HIGH MUCKY-MUCK]

muckty-muck *n.*[2] [1950s+] (US Black) **1** nonsense, rubbish, lies. **2** aimless, aggressive talk. [MUCK n.[3]]

muck-up *n.* [1930s+] **1** a blunder, an error, a confusion. **2** a mixture, a mess (cf. FUCK-UP). [MUCK UP]

muck up *v.* **1** [late 19C+] make a mess (of), to spoil or ruin. **2** [late 19C+] to fail, to go wrong. **3** [1910s+] (Aus.) to play the fool (cf. MUCK ABOUT).

muck-worm *n.* **1** [late 16C–mid-18C] a person of the lowest origin. **2** [late 16C–early 19C] a miserly person, a 'money-grubber'. **3** [mid-17C–mid-18C] one who is mentally or morally degraded. **4** [mid-late 19C] a street urchin (cf. MUCKER n.[2]). [SE *muck-worm*, a worm that lives in mud; the sl. is synon. for 'money-grubber']

mucky-muck/-mucky *see* HIGH MUCKY-MUCK.

mucky pup *n.* [20C] **1** (Aus.) a promiscuous person. **2** a dirty person, esp. a child.

mucosa de rosa *n.* [1950s–60s] (camp gay) one who spits. [SE *mucus* + fake Ital. sfx. *-a* + assonance of *rosa*; thus an inference of 'pinkness', i.e. effeminate homosexuality]

mud *n.*[1] [18C–19C] a fool (cf. HIS NAME IS MUD).

mud *n.*[2] [late 19C+] (orig. US) thick, strong coffee.

mud *n.*[3] (drugs) **1** [1910s+] unprocessed opium. **2** [1920s+] opium, esp. second-rate; ext. as *coolie mud*, *green mud*. **3** [1950s+] methadone. **4** [1970s+] the residue of heroin or morphine processing. [the colour (and consistency); note abbr. *foreign mud*, trans. of Chinese name for opium]

mud *n.*[4] [1930s–70s] (US) cheap plaster figurines. [their supposed resemblance to a child's mud pies]

mud and blood *n.* [20C] a drink of 'mild and bitter'. [initial letters + the colours]

mud and ooze *n.* [20C] (Aus.) booze. [rhy. sl.]

mud-bud *n.* [1980s+] (drugs) homegrown marijuana. [SE *mud* + BUD n.[3]]

mudcat *n.* (US) **1** [mid-19C–1940s] a stupid or contemptible person. **2** [late 19C+] a Mississippian. [Mississippi is known as the *Mudcat* State]

mudcrusher *n.* [1970s] (US Black) an extreme form of bully whose aim is to crush everyone into the ground.

mudder *n.* [1940s+] (US) a horse or human runner who is at their best on a muddy course or track.

mudding-face *n.* [late 19C–1910s] a fool, a weakling. [MUD n.[1] + play on SE *pudding-face*]

muddle *n.* [1910s–20s] a state of slight drunkenness. [MUDDLED]

muddle *v.* [19C] to have sexual intercourse (cf. BANG v.[1]).

muddled *adj.* [late 17C+] drunk (cf. ADDLED).

muddle-head *n.* [19C] a fool, a simpleton. [SE *muddle* + sfx. -HEAD (1)]

muddle on *v.* [late 17C–18C] to carry on drinking despite one's gradually increasing drunkenness (cf. MUDDLED).

muddy fuck *n.* [1950s–60s] (gay) anal intercourse with a partner whose anus has not been properly cleaned. [SE *muddy* + FUCK n.[1]]

muddy funster *n.* [20C] a euph. for MOTHERFUCKER. [initial letters]

muddy trench *adj.* [1910s+] French. [rhy. sl.]

muddy waters *n.* [1970s+] (US Black) the loss of a man's erection before or during sex. [ety. unknown; ? the softness of mud]

mud-fat *adj.* [1920s+] (Aus.) very fat. [the thickness and density of mud]

mud flap *n.* [20C] (US) a derog. term for a Black person. [the colour of mud]

mud flaps *n.* [1950s+] (US Black) noticeably large feet.

mud for one's turtle *phr.* [1980s+] (US) from a man's point of view, sexual intercourse.

mudfuck *n.* [20C] synon. for MOTHERFUCK *n.*

mudfucker *n.* [20C] synon. for MOTHERFUCKER.

mudge *n.* [late 19C] a low-crowned circular hat worn by women. [ety. unknown; ? link to MUSH *n.*²]

mudger *n.* [early 19C] a weakling, a 'milksop'. [? dial. *nudge*, to crush or bruise]

mud-head *n.* **1** [late 18C–1950s] a fool; thus *mud-headed*, stupid. **2** [mid-19C+] (US) a native of Tennessee (cf. BUCKSHINE; WHELP). **3** [20C] (W.I.) a native of Guyana, the majority of whom live in the muddy coastal areas of the country. [SE *mud* + sfx. -HEAD (1)]

mud honey *n.* [late 19C–1910s] street slush (cf. HONEY *n.*⁵).

mud hook *n.* (US) **1** [early 19C+] an anchor. **2** [mid-19C+] a foot, a heavy shoe or boot; also as *mud-hopper/-masher/-splasher/-splitter/-squasher*. **3** [1920s+] a finger or hand.

Mud Island *n.* [late 19C] Southend, the popular Cockney resort, which is sited at the seaward end of the Thames estuary.

mud-kicker *n.* [1930s+] (orig. US) a prostitute, esp. later, a second-rate prostitute, one who fails, either through laziness or lack of appeal, to make enough money for her pimp (cf. MUD-STOMPER). [race-track jargon *mud-kicker*, a slow racehorse that gets stuck in the mud; however, the US pimp Iceberg Slim (1987) uses the word positively]

Mudland *n.* [20C] (W.I.) Guyana. [MUD-HEAD (3)]

mudlark *n.* **1** [late 18C–1920s] a hog. **2** [late 18C+] a waterside thief, who pick up packages thrown to them by a ship's crew-member. **3** [early 19C] a duck. **4** [mid-19C] one who scavenges items from the Thames mud. **5** [mid-19C] one who steals copper from the bottom of ships moored in the Thames. **6** [mid-19C] a sewerman. **7** [mid-19C] a street child, a 'gutter urchin'. **8** [20C] (Aus.) a resident or native of Victoria, Australia. **9** [20C] (Aus.) a racehorse that enjoys muddy going.

mud-packer *n.* [20C] (US) a homosexual man. [var. on FUDGE-PACKER]

mud pads *n.* [1910s–20s] the feet.

mud pies *n.* [20C] (Aus.) the eyes. [rhy. sl.]

mud pipes *n.* [mid-19C–1940s] thick boots, gumboots (cf. PIPES *n.*²; MUD SCOWS).

mud-plunging *n.* [mid-19C–1900s] (tramp) walking through muddy streets and lanes in the hope of securing hand-outs; thus *mud-plunger*, one who does this.

mud pup *n.* [1950s+] an agricultural student, esp. when gaining work experience on a farm.

mud puppy *n.* [1980s+] (US campus) an ugly woman (cf. DOG *n.*⁵).

mud-pusher *n.* [late 19C] a street sweeper.

Mud-salad Market *n.* [late 19C] Covent Garden Market.

mud scows *n.* [early 19C–1910s] (US) **1** large, cheap shoes (cf. MUD PIPES). **2** feet. [SE *mud* + *scow*, a large flat-bottomed boat]

mud show *n.* **1** [late 19C–1900s] (society) an agricultural show or any similar outdoor event. **2** [1930s] (US) an old-fashioned circus; thus *mud-showman*, one who runs or works at such a circus.

mud's in your eye *n.* [late 19C–1940s] a tie. [rhy. sl., playing on the popular toast, *here's mud in your eye!*]

mud-slinging *n.* [late 19C+] slandering, talking maliciously behind someone's back; thus *mud-slinger*, one who does this.

mud snake *n.* [1990s] (US) the penis (cf. MUD FOR ONE'S TURTLE).

mud-stomper *n.* [1960s+] (US Black) a second-rate, impoverished prostitute (cf. MUD-KICKER). [SE *mud* + STOMP *v.*, the image is one of a woman who has to struggle her way through deep, clinging mud (fig. as well as actual?) to make ends meet]

mud student *n.* [mid-19C] an agricultural student (cf. MUD PUP).

mud turtle *n.* [late 19C–1930s] (US) a contemptible person.

muff *n.*¹ **1** [late 17C+] the vagina (cf. BADGER *n.*⁷). **2** [late 17C+] the pubic hair. **3** [1910s+] (US) a woman. **4** [1940s–50s] (US) a beard, a toupee. **5** [1970s+] (US) sexual intercourse. [its supposed resemblance; (5) is fig. ext. of (1)]

muff *n.*² **1** [mid–late 19C] (orig. sporting) an incompetent, one who is awkward or stupid. **2** [late 19C] a blunder, an error; esp. in phr. [late 19C] *make a muff of oneself*, to act in an incompetent, foolish manner. [MUFF *v.*¹]

muff *n.*³ [19C–1910s] a fool, albeit an amiable one (cf. MOUTH *n.*¹). [like the SE *muff*, the fool is SOFT *adj.* in the head, but note MUFF *n.*¹ (1) and the use of CUNT *n.*¹ (1) and other terms for the vagina as synons. for a fool]

muff *v.*¹ **1** [early 19C] (orig. sporting) to die. **2** [mid-19C+] (orig. sporting) to make a blunder, to make a mess. **3** [late 19C] to fail an examination. [ety. unknown; ? image of keeping one's hands in a SE *muff* rather than using them properly]

muff *v.*² [1960s+] (US) to perform cunnilingus. [abbr. MUFF-DIVE]

muff-dive/-nosh *v.* [1940s+] (orig. US) to perform cunnilingus (cf. DIVE A MUFF). [MUFF *n.*¹ (1) + SE *dive*/NOSH *v.* (2)]

muff-diver *n.* (US) **1** [1930s+] one who performs cunnilingus (cf. MUFFER). **2** [1940s+] a contemptible person; thus *muff-diving*, despicable. [MUFF-DIVE]

muffed *adj.* [late 19C+] spoilt, bungled, failed. [MUFF *v.*¹]

muffer *n.* [1960s+] (US) a lesbian; i.e. a woman who performs cunnilingus. [MUFF-(DIVE)]

muffin *n.*¹ [mid-19C; 1980s+] **1** a fool. **2** an incompetent, one who is awkward (cf. MUFF *n.*²). **3** [1980s+] (US campus) an admirable person. [? play on FLAT *n.*²; the muffin is a small *flat* cake or link to MUFF *n.*²/*n.*³]

muffin *n.*² **1** [mid-19C–1900s] (Can.) a female companion who accompanies a bachelor on his round of social amusements. **2** [mid-19C–1930s] (US) a male chaperone (cf. WALKER *n.*²). [ety. unknown; ? ext. of MUFFIN *n.*¹ (1)]

muffin/muffin-cap *n.*³ [late 19C–1900s] a 'pill-box' hat or cap. [resemblance]

muffin *n.*⁴ **1** [1950s+] the vagina (cf. APPLE *n.*¹⁰). **2** [1950s–60s] (US) a girl. [ext. of MUFF *n.*¹]

muffin baker *n.* [mid-19C] a Quaker. [rhy. sl.]

muffin-cap *see* MUFFIN *n.*³.

muffin-face/-countenance *n.* [mid-18C–early 19C] **1** a hairless face. **2** an expressionless face. **3** a miserable, depressed face; thus *muffin-faced*, expressionless. [supposed resemblance]

muffin-fight *see* MUFFIN-WORRY.

muffing *n.* [mid-19C+] **1** clumsiness, clumsy failure. **2** bungling, blundering. [MUFF *v.*¹ (2)]

muffing *adj.* [mid-19C+] bungling, blundering. [MUFF *v.*¹ (2)]

muffin-head *n.* [late 19C] a fool. [SE *muffin* + sfx. -HEAD (1)]

muffin-puncher *n.* [late 19C] a baker of muffins.

muffins *n.* [1960s+] (US gay) the buttocks.

muffin-walloper *n.* [late 19C] a gossipy woman who enjoys dissecting her friends and acquaintances over a cup of tea and a muffin (cf. MUFFIN-WORRY). [SE *muffin* + joc. use of WALLOPER n.[1] (1)]

muffin-worry/-fight *n.* [mid-19C] an old ladies' tea-party (cf. BUNFIGHT).

muffish *adj.* [mid-19C] foolish; thus *muffishness*, the state of being a bungler; *muffism*, foolishness. [MUFF n.[3]]

muffling-cheat *n.* [16C–early 19C] a napkin. [SE *muffle* + CHEAT n.]

muff-nosh *see* MUFF-DIVE.

muf fuh *n.* [20C] synon. for MOTHERFUCK n. [pron.]

muffy *n.*[1] [20C] (Aus.) a frill-necked lizard. [the frill or 'muff' around its neck]

muffy *n.*[2] [1980s+] (US campus) a young woman who has the look of a typical sorority member, with bleached blonde hair, an alice band, heavy make-up and conventional clothes. [proper name *Muffy*, the stereotypical name of such young women]

mufti *n.* [19C] a military man's off-duty clothes. [SE post-1900. Orig. Ind. army slang, according to *Hobson-Jobson* f. the *Mufti*, a religious leader and expounder of Islamic law; thus the word 'was perhaps originally applied to the attire of dressing-gown, smoking-cap, and slippers, which was like the Oriental dress of the Mufti, who was familiar in Europe from his appearance in Molière's *Bourgeois Gentilhomme*'. Note the Fr. equivalent, *en Pekin*, Peking-style]

mufugly *adj.* [1980s+] (US campus) extremely ugly. [MOTHER-FUCKING adj. + SE *ugly*]

mug *n.*[1] **1** [18C+] the human face. **2** [19C] the mouth. **3** [early 19C–1900s] a grimace. **4** [late 19C+] a picture of a person, esp. in police records (cf. MUG BOOK). [? 18C use of drinking mugs made in the shape of grotesque human faces]

mug *n.*[2] **1** [mid-19C] an examination. **2** [late 19C] a schoolchild or student who works hard. [MUG UP v.[2]]

mug *n.*[3] [mid-19C–1950s] (US) a chamberpot. [abbr. MEMBER MUG]

mug *n.*[4] **1** [mid-19C+] (US) a thug, a violent person, a crude loutish person. **2** [1980s+] (US Black) euph. for MOTHER-FUCKER. [ext. of MUG n.[1]; (2) is ext. of (1)]

mug *n.*[5] **1** [mid-19C+] a fool, a dupe, orig. the victim of a corrupt card-game; thus *mug's game*, a pointless exercise appealing only to fools; *mug-hunter*, one who beats and robs drunken men as they make their way home; *mug punter*, a foolish, inexpert bettor. **2** [1900s–30s] (US) a policeman. **3** [1930s] anyone not directly involved in the underworld, thus, *de facto*, a gullible fool, a (potential) victim. [SE *mug*, i.e. one into whom one can 'pour' any nonsense]

mug/mogg *v.*[1] **1** [early 18C–mid-19C] to refuse food. **2** [mid-18C+] to pout, to grow sullen, to grimace. **3** [mid-19C+] to make a face, to make people laugh by one's antics and grimaces. [MUG n.[1]]

mug *v.*[2] **1** [19C] to fight, to punch. **2** [19C] to chastise. **3** [early 19C+] to rob, to assault, usu. in the street and often with violence; orig. to garrotte; thus *mugger*, one who carries out such assaults; *the mug*, a chokehold (cf. PUT THE MUG ON). [MUG n.[4] (1)]

mug *v.*[3] [early 19C–1960s] to bribe, usu. by plying with liquor. [SE *mug*, a container for liquids]

mug/mug up *v.*[4] **1** [early 19C+] (UK/Aus./US campus) to kiss, to cuddle, to neck. **2** [1950s–60s] (US Black) to have sexual intercourse with. [MUG n.[1]; (1) *mug up* is later usage]

mug *v.*[5] [mid-19C+] to study hard, esp. for a test or examination, to 'swot'; thus *mugging*, hard studying (cf. MUG UP v.[2]). [? image of pouring the knowledge into one's MUG n.[1]]

mug *v.*[6] **1** [late 19C+] (police) to take identification pictures for prison/court use; thus *mug room*, a room in which such pictures are taken or stored. **2** [1900s–20s] (US Und.) to arrest, esp. for purposes of identification. [MUG n.[1] (4)]

mug *v.*[7] [late 19C] to huddle together in a confined space. [? dial. *muggle*, a mess, a confusion, a disorder]

mug *v.*[8] [late 19C+] (usu. Can.) to eat heartily, to have a good meal (cf. MUG UP v.[3]). [? MUG n.[1] (1)]

mug aleck *n.* [1930s+] (Aus.) an unpleasantly conceited, smug person (cf. CLEVER DICK). [MUG n.[5] + (SMART) ALECK]

mug behind five, to *phr.* [1930s–40s] (US Black) to speak with one's hand shielding one's lips. [MUG v.[1]]

mug book *n.* **1** [20C] (US police) a book of pictures used to help police in keeping records of known criminals (cf. MUG LIST). **2** [1930s+] a reference book used for casting purposes in theatre, TV and films, containing pictures of actual and aspirant stars. [MUG n.[1] (4) + SE *book*]

mug cop/copper *see* MUG JOHN.

mugfaker *n.* [1930s–50s] a street photographer. [MUG n.[1] (1) + FAKER]

mugger *n.*[1] [early 19C] a blow in the mouth. [MUG n.[1] (2)]

mugger *n.*[2] [mid-19C+] a street robber, orig. a garrotter. [MUG v.[2] (3)]

mugger *n.*[3] [late 19C] one who studies hard. [MUG v.[5]]

mugger *n.*[4] [1940s–60s] euph. for BUGGER n.[1], itself a euph. for FUCKER (cf. MUCKER n.[3]).

mugget *n.* [1970s] (US) an artificial vulva for male mastur-bation. [var. on MUCKET]

muggie *see* MUGGLES n.[2].

muggill *n.* [late 16C–early 17C] (Und.) a beadle. [ety. un-known; ? anecdotal f. a beadle named *McGill*]

mugging *n.*[1] [early 19C+] **1** a beating. **2** garrotting. **3** the act of street robbery and assault. [MUG v.[2] (3) has been the general use since 1960s]

mugging *n.*[2] [mid-19C+] learning, working hard, memorizing. [MUG v.[5]]

mugging *n.*[3] [mid-19C+] making faces. [MUG v.[1] (3)]

mugging *n.*[4] [late 19C–1910s] (US) taking photographs of people. [MUG v.[6]]

mugging *n.*[5] [1920s+] (US) kissing, love-making. [MUG v.[4]]

mugging up *n.* [1900s–40s] (US Black) sexual intercourse. [MUG v.[4]]

muggins *n.*[1] **1** [mid-19C] a kind of card-game. **2** [mid-19C+] a fool, a simpleton; thus [late 19C] *talk muggins*, to talk nonsense (cf. BILLY MUGGINS). **3** [late 19C–1900s] a local poli-tician, e.g. a councillor or mayor. [MUG n.[5]]

muggins *n.*[2] **1** [mid-19C] (US) a bottle of bourbon. **2** [1930s] (US prison) food. [MUG v.[8]]

muggins here *phr.* [mid-19C+] a ruefully pej. self-descrip-tion, esp. when recounting a story against oneself in which one has been duped or fooled. [MUGGINS n.[1] (2)]

mugglehead *n.* [1920s–70s] (US drugs) a marijuana smoker. [MUGGLES n.[2] + sfx. -HEAD (2)]

muggler *n.* [1930s] (drugs) a smoker of marijuana. [MUGGLES n.[2] (1)]

muggles *n.*[1] [mid–late 18C] restlessness. [dial. *muggle*, to move restlessly]

muggles/muggie *n.*[2] [1920s–70s] (orig. US drugs) **1** a cigar-ette with marijuana (occas. hashish) substituted for some of the tobacco and packed back inside it; thus *muggled up*, intoxicated by marijuana, *muggle-smoker*, a marijuana user. **2** a smoker of marijuana.

muggy *adj.* [mid-19C] drunk (cf. ADDLED). [SE *muggy*, damp, close]

mughouse *n.* [early 18C] a cheap tavern. [SE *mug* + *house*]

mug-hunter *n.*[1] *see* POT-HUNTER n.[2].

mug-hunter *n.*[2] [late 19C] one who tours the streets late at night in search of drunken men who can be robbed. [MUG n.[5] (3) + SE *hunter*]

mug in and mug out, to be *phr.* [mid-19C] to dawdle, to prevaricate, to fail to make up one's mind. [dial. *muggle*, to live haphazardly, to muddle along]

mug john/mug cop/copper *n.* [1930s–50s] (Aus.) a policeman. [MUG n.⁵ (2) + JOHN n.¹/COPPER n.³ (1)]

mug lair *n.* [1940s+] (Aus.) a contemptuous description, i.e. a stupid, gullible, flashy show-off. [MUG n.⁵ + LAIR n.]

mug list *n.* [1960s+] (Aus.) a book of suspects' pictures kept by the police for identification purposes (cf. MUG BOOK). [MUG n.¹ (4) + SE *list*]

mug oneself *v.* [late 19C–1900s] to make oneself comfortable. [MUG v.² or v.⁴]

mug-punter *n.* [mid-19C+] a sucker in any game of chance or at a racecourse (cf. TOM TUG n.¹). [MUG n.⁵ (3) + PUNTER n.¹]

mugs away! *excl.* [20C] an excl. used in darts matches when the winners of the previous game tell the losers to start the next contest. [joc. use of MUG n.⁵]

mug's game *n.* [1910s+] a foolish endeavour, a pointless effort. [MUG n.⁵ + SE *game*]

mug-shoot *v.* [1930s+] (orig. US) to take a picture of a prisoner for identification; thus *mug shot*, an identification picture (now SE); *mug-shooter*, a police photographer. [MUG n.¹ (4) + SE *shoot*]

mugster *n.* [late 19C] (school) a hard worker. [MUG v.⁵]

mug's ticker *n.* [1970s+] (Und.) a piece of worthless jewellery or a fake Swiss watch. [MUG n.⁵ + TICKER n.²]

mug-trap *n.* [late 19C] a con-man, one who tricks gullible victims. [MUG n.⁵ (3) + SE *trap*]

mug-up *n.* [1910s–60s] a snack, a meal, a drink. [MUG v.⁸]

mug up *v.¹ see* MUG v.⁴.

mug up *v.²* [mid-19C+] to learn, to memorize, esp. a specific lesson for a specific test or examination (cf. MUG v.⁵). [orig. theatrical use, 'paint one's mug', i.e. face, as part of performing a role]

mug up *v.³* [1910s–60s] to drink or eat a snack, a meal. [MUG v.⁸]

mug up *v.⁴* [1950s+] (US Black) to put on one's hat, to leave. [MUG n.¹ (1)]

mugwump *n.* **1** [early 19C+] (orig. US) a person in authority, a self-important person. **2** [early 19C+] (orig. US) an obnoxious person. **3** [mid-19C] an impotent man. **4** [late 19C+] (orig. US) in political terms, one whose vote may go either way and is thus untrustworthy. [SE *mugwump*, 'one who holds more or less aloof from party-politics, professing disinterested and superior views. In 1884, spec. applied to Republicans who refused to support the nominee of their party for president. Also, a person who withdraws his support from any group or organization' (*OED*) and in (3) from sex]

muhfuh/muh-fuh *n.* [20C] synon. for MOTHERFUCK. [US Black pron.]

muhfuhkuh *n.* [20C] synon. for MOTHERFUCKER. [US Black pron.]

mujer *n.* **1** [1970s+] (drugs) cocaine (cf. GIRL n.³). **2** [1990s] (US Black teen) an attractive Puerto Rican/Latino woman or girl (cf. BUTTER PECAN). [Sp. *mujer*, wife]

mul/muller *n.* [1940s+] (Irish) a fool, a useless object. [MULL n.¹ (2)]

muldoon *n.¹* [19C] (US) a policeman. [a typical Irish name; US police were stereotypically Irishmen]

muldoon *n.²* [late 19C] (US) the truth, the real thing. [abbr. 'the solid *Muldoon*', popularized by 'Muldoon the Solid Man', a vaudeville song by Harrigan and Hart (1874)]

mule *n.¹* [20C] any small motor-powered vehicle. [now SE; the use of mules as beasts of burden]

mule *n.²* **1** [1920s+] (US) homemade bourbon made from grain alcohol. **2** [1950s] (US drugs) marijuana soaked in bourbon. [the alcohol 'kicks like a *mule*']

mule *n.³* **1** [1920s+] (US prison) a smuggler, usu. a visitor or prison warder. **2** [1930s+] (drugs) a carrier of drugs, typically across international borders, and in many cases an otherwise 'innocent' person who has no other contact with the drugs trade.

mule *n.⁴* [1940s+] (US) the penis; thus *lope one's mule, water one's mule*, to urinate.

mule *n.⁵* [1950s+] **1** an unattractive woman. **2** an impotent man. **3** (W.I.) an infertile woman, who therefore suffers from *mule-belly*.

mule *v.* [1950s+] (US Und./police) to act as a courier of contraband, esp. illicit drugs. [MULE n.³ (2)]

mule breakfast *n.* [1920s–40s] (US) a straw hat.

mule-mouth *n.* [1970s] (US Black) one who works regularly as a police informer.

mulenyam/moulenjam/moulonjam *n.* [1960s+] (US/Ital.) a Black person. [Ital. *melenzana*, an aubergine, which is a deep purple in colour]

mule shit! *excl.* [1920s+] (US) a mild oath, used to express disbelief or surprise. [var. on BULLSHIT!]

mule-skinner *n.* **1** [late 19C–1930s] (US) a mule-driver. **2** [1980s+] (drugs) one who organizes, pays and supervises a drug courier or MULE n.³ (2). [the lit. or fig. application of the whip]

mule-whacker *n.* [late 19C–1920s] (US) a mule-driver (cf. MULE-SKINNER). [SE *mule* + WHACK v.¹ (1)]

muley-grubs *see* MULLIGRUBS.

mulga *n.* [19C+] (Aus.) an uninhabited, sparsely populated or inhospitable region; thus *mulga madness*, mental decay that can overtake those spending long periods alone in such regions; *mulga scrubbers*, stock that have run wild and deteriorated in condition. [SAusE *mulga*, one of various plants of the genus *Acacia* found in the dry inland of Australia; thus the dry inland itself. The Aus. term comes from Yuwaalaraay *malga*]

mulga wire *n.* [late 19C+] **1** a 'bush telegraph', the 'grapevine'. **2** a rumour, a lie. [MULGA + SE *wire*, a telegram]

mull *n.¹* **1** [19C] a mess; usu. in phr. *make a mull of*, make a mess of. **2** [mid–late 19C] a simpleton, a clumsy person. [? SE *mull*, to grind, to pulverize or SE *muddle*]

mull/mulligatawney *n.²* [early–mid-19C] (Anglo-Ind.) a member of the Imperial Civil Service belonging to the Madras presidency. [abbr. SE *mulligatawny*, a highly seasoned soup, a speciality of Madras]

mull *v.¹* (orig. US) **1** [mid-19C] to work steadily without accomplishing much. **2** [late 19C+] to think about, to cogitate upon, to work over in one's mind. [SE *mull*, to grind, to pulverize]

mull *v.²* [1980s+] (Aus. drugs) to chop and mix cannabis finely for consumption. [SE *mull*, but note MOULI]

mulla *see* MOOLAH.

mullahed *adj.* [1950s+] (prison) beaten severely. [ety. unknown]

mullarkey *see* MALARKEY.

mulled/mulled up *adj.* [1920s–70s] drunk (cf. ALED UP). [abbr. SE *mulled* (*ale*) or *muddled*]

muller *n.¹* [mid-19C–1900s] **1** a hat that has had its shape altered. **2** a type of flat-topped felt hat. [Franz *Muller* (d.1864), the first person ever to commit a murder on the railway, whose attempt to flee justice was augmented by his taking his victim's hat, a topper, and cutting an inch off it. Such short hats were briefly fashionable, under the murderer's name]

muller *n.² see* MUL.

muller *n.³* [1980s+] (Aus. drugs) one who chops and mixes the cannabis. [MULL v.²]

mullet *n.* [1950s+] (US) a fool (cf. LIKE A STUNNED MULLET). [abbr. MULLETHEAD]

mullethead n. [mid-19C+] (US) a fool, thus *mullet-headed*, stupid. [the freshwater fish the *mullet* has a notably large head]

mulligan n.[1] **1** [late 19C–1940s] (US) an Irish person. **2** [1930s+] (US prison) a prison guard. [*Mulligan*, a typical Irish name. Early prison guards, like early policemen, were often Irish]

mulligan n.[2] *see* MULLIGAN STEW.

mulligan n.[3] [1940s–60s] (US Black) a tramp. [backform. of MULLIGAN STEW, the consumers of which were mainly vagrants]

mulligan n.[4] [1990s] (US) an unexpected second chance. [golf jargon *mulligan*, a free shot that is not counted on the score-card]

mulligan car n. [20C] (US) a restaurant car on a railway. [MULLIGAN (STEW) + SE *car*]

mulligan joint n. [20C] (US) a cheap restaurant. [MULLIGAN (STEW) + JOINT n.[3] (3)]

mulligan mixer n. [20C] (US, West.) a cook. [MULLIGAN (STEW) + SE *mixer*]

mulligans n. [1940s–50s] (Aus.) playing cards. [ety. unknown]

mulligan stew/mulligan n. [20] (orig. US tramp) a stew made of whatever meats and vegetables are available. [either proper name *Mulligan*, the name of an otherwise forgotten cook, or *Mulligan* as a generic for Irish and thus an Irish stew; note army jargon *mulligan battery*, the cook wagon]

mulligatawney *see* MULL n.[2].

mulligrubs/mollygrubs/muley-grubs n. **1** [17C+] colic, diarrhoea. **2** [late 18C+] a feeling of unease, not an illness that can be diagnosed, but a general sense of not being fully well (cf. BLUES n.[1]; BOTS). [*OED*: 'a grotesque arbitrary formation'; ? SE *mull*, to grind, to pulverize + *grub*, an insect; note US regional uses: (1) stomach pains, diarrhoea; (2) menstruation]

Mullingar/Munster heifer n. [mid-19C] (Irish) a woman with thick ankles; thus *beef to the heels/knees, like a Mullingar heifer*. The phr. is occas. used of men, to describe them as brawny, stalwart. [the supposed characteristic of *Mullingar/Munster* women]

mullion n. [1950s] (US Black) an unattractive woman or ugly person. [? SE *melungeon*, a member of a racially mixed group of people – half Black, half Native American – centred in the Appalachians, ult. Fr. *mélange*, mixture]

mullipuff *see* MOLLYPUFF.

mullock n. (Aus.) **1** [mid-19C+] rubbish, a worthless object. **2** [late 19C+] an ignorant and generally useless person (cf. BORAK). [dial. *mullock*, rubbish]

mullyfogging adj. [20C] synon. for MOTHERFUCKING adj.

multa *see* MULTY.

multa bona fakement n. [early 19C] (Polari) a well-executed confidence trick. [MULTY + BONA adj. + FAKEMENT]

multee kertever/multicattivo adj. [mid-19C] very bad (cf. MULTY). [Ital./Ling. Fr. *molto cattivo*, very bad]

multi *see* MULTY.

multicattivo *see* MULTEE KERTEVER.

multicoloured yawn n. [1960s+] (orig. Aus.) the act of vomiting (cf. TECHNICOLOUR YAWN). [the multicoloured effluvia so produced]

multi-culti adj. [1980s+] (US) *multi-cult*ural. [abbr.]

multie *see* MULTY.

multiple sadness! excl. [1980s+] (US campus) a general excl. of regret, that's really terrible! oh no! I'm so sorry.

multitask v. [1990s] (US teen) to do more than one thing at a time. [computer jargon]

multy/multa/multi/multie adj. [late 19C–1910s] (orig. Ling. Fr./Polari) of people and things, bad, unpleasant (cf. MULTEE KERTEVER). [Ital. *multo*, many; later use mainly Aus.]

mulvather v. [late 19C] (Irish) to confuse. [Sp. *malvader*, to knock down, to stun]

mum n.[1] [mid-16C–late 19C] a refusal to speak, silence. [late 14C SE *mum*, an inarticulate sound made through the closed lips. Such a sound indicates an unwillingness to speak out loud]

mum n.[2] [20C] a chrysanthe*mum*. [abbr.]

mum n.[3] [1970s] (Und.) one's mistress of many years or one's wife, but not one's actual mother.

mum adj. [late 18C+] silent, quiet. [MUM n.[1]]

mum phr. *see* MOTHER phr.

mum and dad adj. [20C] (Aus.) mad. [rhy. sl.]

mum and daddo n. [20C] (Aus.) a shadow. [rhy. sl.]

mumble and mutter n. [20C] butter. [rhy. sl.]

mumble-a-/mumble-sparrow n. [late 18C–early 19C] a game practised at country fairs. A cock-sparrow, with wings clipped, is placed inside an upturned hat, and a man with his arms tied behind his back attempts to bite off its head.

mumble-crust n. [mid-16C–early 17C] a toothless person. [SE *mumble*, to chew softly, as with toothless gums]

mumble-matins n. [mid-16C–early 17C] a priest.

mumble-peg n. [late 19C] **1** the vagina. **2** the female pubic hair. [SE *mumble-the-peg*; *mumblety-peg*, a game in which each player in turn throws a knife from a series of positions, continuing until they fail to make the blade stick in the ground]

mumblers n. [1990s] women's skintight bicycle shorts. [i.e. one 'can see the lips moving', but one can't understand a word they're saying]

mumble-sparrow *see* MUMBLE-A-SPARROW.

mumbly pegs n. [1920s–40s] (US) the legs (cf. SCOTCH PEGS). [rhy. sl.]

mumbo-jumbo n. [late 19C+] meaningless nonsense. [SE *mumbo-jumbo*, 'an object of unintelligent veneration' (*OED*), ult. *Mama Dyumbo*, the protective spirit of the Khassonkee tribe of Senegal]

mum-figure n. [1950s–60s] a mother-figure.

mum-glass n. [late 17C–20C] the Monument, a 95m (311ft) column erected in 1671–7 in memory of the Great Fire of London (1666) at the junction of what is now Monument Street and Fish Street Hill. [SE *mum-glass*, a glass used for the drinking of *mum* beer, a type of beer originating in Brunswick in Germany and imported into the UK in the 17C–18C. The Monument presumably resembles such a glass]

mummer n. **1** [late 18C–early 19C] the mouth. **2** [mid-19C+] an actor. [SE *mummer*, one who mutters and murmurs and thus an actor in a dumb-show]

mummery and millinery n. [20C] religious ritualism. [the elaborate rituals and costumes of the High Church and of Roman Catholicism]

mummery-cove n. [mid–late 19C] an actor. [SE *mummery*, over-acting + COVE]

mummick v. [late 19C] (US) to handle or feel an object or person. [? dial. *mammock*, to break into pieces, crumble, tear]

mummy v. [1970s] (US Black) to beat a person to death, thus making them into an Egyptian-style mummified corpse.

mummyhead n. [1990s] (US Black gang) a fool. [SE *mummy*, a wrapped, embalmed corpse, orig. Egyptian + sfx. -HEAD (1)]

mummy pussy n. [1970s+] (US Black) a woman who does not respond during sexual intercourse. [SE *mummy*, an embalmed corpse + PUSSY n.[1]]

mump n. [early 18C] a beggar, a scrounger. [MUMPER n. (1)]

mump v. **1** [mid-17C–mid-18C] to cheat (out of). **2** [late 17C+] to beg, to visit a house in the course of one's travels as a beggar. **3** [late 17C] to obtain by begging. **4** [early–mid-18C] to disappoint. **5** [mid-19C] to talk seriously. [? Du. *mompen*, to cheat, dial. *mump*, to mutter, to speak indistinctly]

mumper *n.* **1** [late 17C+] a genteel beggar, a scrounger, 'a Gentiler sort of Beggars, for they scorn to beg for food, but money and cloaths' (Head, 1673). **2** [20C] a tramp. **3** [1950s+] a half-breed gypsy, a 'second-rate' gypsy, i.e. one who has no van. [MUMP v.]

mumper *v.* [20C] (US Black) to travel around, to partner someone on their travels. [MUMP v.]

mumper's brass *n.* [early 18C] money. [MUMPER n. + BRASS n.[1]]

mumper's hall *n.* [late 17C–early 19C] a low-class ale-house, frequented by beggars, who will be 'very Merry, Drunk and Frolicksome' (B.E.). [MUMPER n. + ironic use of SE *hall*]

mumping *n.* [late 17C+] begging. [note police jargon *mumping*, of a policeman, accepting cheap or free goods and services from friendly tradespeople]

mumpins *n.* [late 17C] alms. [MUMP n.; MUMPER n.]

mumps, the *n.* [late 19C] low spirits, 'the sulks'. [dial. *mump*, to complain, to speak querulously]

mums *n.* [late 18C–late 19C] the mouth, the jaws, the face, the lips. [var. on MUNS]

mum's the word *excl.* [early 18C+] be quiet, say nothing about this (cf. SNUG'S THE WORD). [MUM adj.]

mumsy *adj.* [1960s+] motherly, usu. with pej. implications, over-fussy, nagging, respectable. [SE *mum*]

mum-tip *n.* [early 19C] a bribe to ensure one's silence, 'hush-money'. [KEEP MUM]

mum your dubber! *excl.* [late 18C] be quiet! shut up! [MUM n.[1] + DUBBER n.[2]]

mun/mund/munn/munne *n.*[1] **1** [14C–late 19C] the face or mouth. **2** [late 17C] a member of a band of London street thugs. [northern dial.]

mun *n.*[2] *see* MON n.[1].

munch *n.* [1990s] (US teen) a snack. [abbr. MUNCHIES]

munch *v.*[1] **1** [late 19C–1920s] to eat enthusiastically. **2** [1970s+] (US campus) to eat (cf. MUNCH OUT). **3** [1970s+] to perform oral sex (cf. MUNCHER BOY; MUNCH THE CARPET).

munch *v.*[2] [1970s+] **1** to make a blunder, to perform badly. **2** to crash, as from a surfboard or a vehicle.

muncher boy *n.* [1960s+] (US) a fellator. [MUNCH v.[1] (3) + SE *boy*]

munchie/munchies *n.* [1950s+] (orig. US) **1** a snack, snacks or small meal. **2** the craving for food, often sweet or in an otherwise unlikely combination of flavours, that afflicts smokers of hashish or marijuana (cf. CHUCKS n.[1]). **3** a snack eaten to assuage this craving.

Munching House *n.*[1] [late 19C] the Mansion House, London. [SE *munch*, a pun on the aldermanic and corporation dinners that are held there]

munching house *n.*[2] [1910s–20s] a cheap restaurant or café.

munchkin *n.* **1** [1950s+] a child, a small person (cf. MUPPET). **2** [1980s+] (US) a menial employee or inconsequential person. [the *Munchkins*, diminutive characters who featured in the book by L. Frank Baum, *The Wizard of Oz* (publ. 1900, filmed 1939)]

munch-out *n.* [1970s+] (US campus) a large meal. [MUNCH OUT v.]

munch out *v.* [1970s+] (US campus) to eat voraciously, esp. as a result of smoking cannabis.

munch-present *n.* [late 16C–early 17C] one who takes bribes. [he fig. 'eats' the money]

munch/chew the carpet, to *phr.* [1980s+] (US) to perform cunnilingus.

mundane *n.*[1] [late 19C] a fashionable person. [Fr. *mondaine*, a sophisticate]

mundane *n.*[2] [1990s] (US) a boring, unimaginative person. [SE *mundane*, tedious, everyday]

mund *see* MUN n.[1].

munds *see* MUNS.

mung *n.*[1] [20C] a brief glance, a search. [fig. use of MUNG v.]

mung *n.*[2] [1980s+] (US campus) filth or dirt of any kind. [note computer jargon *mung*, to destroy maliciously, to ruin]

mung *adj.* [mid–late 19C] (US) untrue, false, usu. in journ. context. [SE/dial. *mong*, a mixture, a confusion]

mung *v.* [19C] (tramp) to beg. [Rom. *mang*, to beg]

munga *see* MUNGER.

mungaree/mungare/munjari/munjary *n.* [mid-19C–1940s] **1** food. **2** (tramp) begging. [Ital. *mangiare*, to eat. 20C use Aus.]

mungarly *n.* [mid-19C] food (cf. MUNGARLY-CASA; MUNGAS; MUNGEE; MUNGER). [Polari, thence Ital. *mangiare*, Fr. *manger*, to eat. Note Grose, *Provincial Glossary* (1787) *mung*, food for chickens]

mungarly-casa *n.* [mid-19C] a baker's shop. [MUNGARLY + CASA]

mungas/munja *n.* [1910s+] (N.Z.) food, a meal, esp. lunch (cf. MUNGAREE). [Ital. *mangiare*, to eat]

mungee *n.* [20C] (orig. naut.) food. [Fr. *manger*, to eat]

munger/munga *n.* [20C] (Aus./N.Z.) **1** food. **2** a smoke taken during a rest period. [MUNGARLY]

munging *n.* [mid-19C] begging. [dial. *munge*, to whine in low tones]

mungo *n.*[1] [mid–late 18C] ? a person of position, a swell. [def. is queried in *OED*, as also is label 'slang']

mungo *n.*[2] [1990s] (Aus.) a fan of Rugby League (cf. RAH RAH n.). [? SE *mungo*, a tough material, made from recycled rags, ? used for old rugby shirts]

muni/muny *n.* **1** [1930s+] (US tramp) a *muni*cipal lodging house. **2** [1970s+] (US) a *muni*cipal bond. [abbr.]

munja *see* MUNGAS.

munjari/munjary *see* MUNGAREE.

munjay *n.* [1940s] (W.I.) a large dumpling. [Fr. *manger*, to eat]

munn/munne *see* MUN n.[1].

munns *see* MUNS.

munnu *n.* [1940s] (W.I.) romance. [? MUUNA, but ? Fr. *mon amour*, my love]

munpins *see* MOMPYNS.

muns/munns/munds *n.* [17C–19C] the mouth, the jaws, the face, the lips (cf. MUN n.[1]). [dial. *mun*, the face; thus mid-19C street cry 'One a penny, two a penny, hot cross buns,/Butter them and sugar them and put them in your muns']

Munster heifer *see* MULLINGAR HEIFER.

Munster plums *n.* [late 18C–early 19C] potatoes (cf. IRISH APPLE). [proper name of the Irish county *Munster* and thus a synon. of the stereotype IRISH adj.]

munt/muntu *n.* [1930s+] (S.Afr.) a Black person (cf. AF n.[2]). [Bantu *umuntu*, sing. of *abantu*, a person, Black person, servant]

munta *n.* [1990s] an ugly, promiscuous woman. [? MOUNT n.[2]]

munter *n.* [mid-17C] a watch (cf. MONTRA). [Fr. *montre*, a watch]

muntu *see* MUNT.

muny *see* MUNI.

muogh *n.* [18C+] (tramp) a pig. [Shelta]

muppet *n.* [1970s+] **1** a child, a small person (cf. MUNCHKIN). **2** an unattractive person, possibly one who is mentally retarded. [the puppets created by Jim Henson and featured on TV's *Muppet Show* during the 1970s]

mur/myrrh *n.* [mid-19C] rum. [backsl.]

murch *n.* [1990s] a portly woman. [ety. unknown]

murdelize *v.* [1950s+] (US teen) to trounce, to drub. [? play on fig. use of SE *murder*]

murder *n.* **1** [mid-19C+] something unbearable, extremely difficult or infuriating. **2** [1920s+] (US) an excellent or marvellous person or thing. **3** [1970s+] (US campus) anything considered very difficult.

murder *v.* **1** [1920s–40s] (US) to exasperate, to infuriate, e.g. *that just murders me*. **2** [1950s+] (orig. US) to defeat totally or conclusively, esp. at a game or sport. **3** [1950s+] (orig. US) to consume greedily and enthusiastically, e.g. *I could murder a roast duck noodle soup.*

murder! *excl.* [late 18C–1910s] used to express annoyance, pain or surprise.

murderation *n.* [20C] (W.I.) a severe beating, esp. of a woman or child. [ext. of SE *murder*]

murder 8 *n.* [1980s+] (drugs) fentanyl (cf. APACHE n.[2]). [? play on MURDER ONE]

murderer's row *n.* [mid-19C–1910s] (US police) cells for condemned murderers.

murder house *n.* [1960s+] (N.Z., juv.) a school dental clinic.

murder-mouth *v.* [1970s] **1** (US Black) to talk insincerely, to lie, esp. when pursuing sex (cf. TALK TRASH). **2** to make threats that one couldn't or wouldn't ever back up with action.

murder one *n.* [1950s+] (US drugs) heroin and cocaine. [US legal jargon *murder one*, first degree or premeditated murder]

murder ones *n.* [1980s+] (US Black) dark glasses (cf. LOCS n.[2]). [for ety. see MURDER ONE; the wearing of dark glasses is equated with a murderous image]

murder rap *n.* [1920s+] (orig. US) a charge of murder. [SE *murder* + RAP n.[3]]

murder the bishop *see* BANG THE BISHOP.

murerk *n.* [mid-19C] (tramp) the mistress of the house. [? corruption of BURERK].

murk *n.* [1930s–80s] (US) coffee. [its consistency]

murkarker/murkauker *n.* [mid-19C] (London) a monkey. [proper name *Jacky Macauco*, a celebrated fighting monkey to be seen facing off against a variety of canine opponents at the Westminster Pit, *c*.1835. He beat all comers until vanquished by a pit bull. Note Port. *macaco*, a macaque monkey]

murky *n.* [20C] (Aus.) an Aborigine (cf. DARKIE; DINGE n.).

murph *n.*[1] [mid-18C–mid-19C] sleep. [*Morpheus*, the Greek god of sleep]

murph *n.*[2] [late 19C+] a potato. [abbr. MURPHY n.[1]]

Murphia *n.* [1990s] the expatriate Irish people living in the UK, esp. those who have prospered. [*Murph*(y), a common Irish surname + SE (*Maf*)*ia*]

murphies *n.* [mid-19C+] potatoes. [the stereotypical Irish diet (*Murphy* is a common Irish name)]

murphy *n.*[1] [early 19C+] a potato (cf. SPUD n.[1]). [the common Irish surname and the assumption that potatoes are the supreme Irish staple]

Murphy *n.*[2] **1** [late 19C–1930s] (US) an Irish person. **2** [1960s] (US) a police officer. [*Murphy*, a common Irish surname]

murphy/murphy game, the *n.*[3] [1950s+] (orig. US Und.) of a prostitute, luring a client either to a room or a deserted alley, hallway etc and then, instead of having sex, the client is beaten and robbed by a male accomplice, who may just strike, but may also pose as an aggrieved father, lover, brother etc; thus *murphy man*, a man who specializes in this fraud (cf. BADGER n.[4]). [? orig. practitioners promised the victim a meeting with 'a lovely woman called Mrs Murphy'. The *murphy* can be extended to drug 'deals' and other illicit commerce]

murphy *n.*[4] [1970s+] (US) a swindle in general. [ext. of MURPHY n.[3]]

murphy *n.*[5] [1990s] (US campus) a condition of having one's underwear caught between the buttocks; thus *have a murphy* (cf. MELVIN n.; WEDGIE). [? stereotyping of an Irish person as foolish or risible]

murphy *v.* [1960s+] (US Und.) to swindle by promising some variety of illegal pleasure, usu. sex, then taking the money and failing to deliver the promised 'goods'. [MURPHY n.[3]]

murphy game *see* MURPHY n.[3].

murphy land *n.* [mid-19C–1940s] (US) Ireland (cf. PADDY-LAND).

Murphy's countenance/face *n.* [early 19C] a pig's face. [stereotyped relationship between the Irish (*Murphy* being a typical Irish surname) and the pig]

Murphy's law *n.* [1950s+] a 'natural law' derived from human observation, stating that 'if anything can go wrong – it will' (cf. SOD'S LAW). [other laws attributed to *Murphy* include 'Nothing is ever as simple as it seems', 'Everything takes longer than you expect', 'Nature always sides with the hidden flaw'. For a comprehensive list, *see* Paul Dickson, *The Official Rules* (1978). According to the astronaut John Glenn (b.1921), *Murphy* himself ' was a fictitious character who appeared in a series of educational cartoons put out by the US Navy ... a careless, all-thumbs mechanic who was prone to make such mistakes as installing a propeller backwards' (*Into Orbit*, 1962)]

Murrumbidgee jam *n.* [1940s+] (Aus.) brown sugar moistened with cold tea and spread on a damper. [proper name *Murrumbidgee*, a river in southern New South Wales]

Murrumbidgee waler/whaler *n.* [mid-19C–1930s] (Aus.) an itinerant tramp whose 'beat' focuses on the rivers of New South Wales; thus *Murrumbidgee whaling*, tramping; also as *Darling waler*; *Murray waler*. [*Murrumbidgee* + WALER]

muscadoodle *n.* [1950s+] (US) muscatel wine.

muscateer *n.* [1930s+] (Aus.) a drinker of cheap muscat wine. [pun on SE *musketeer*]

muscle *n.*[1] **1** [late 19C+] pressure, threats or coercion. **2** [1930s+] (orig. US) strength, courage. **3** [1930s+] a thug, esp. as a group of thugs hired to intimidate by using violence. **4** [1930s+] political influence, power, usu. based on threats or intimidation. [MUSCLE v.]

muscle *n.*[2] [1960s+] (US) the penis. [abbr. LOVE MUSCLE]

muscle *adj.* [1930s+] (US) physically violent. [MUSCLE v.]

muscle *v.* **1** [1920s–30s] (US) to bluff. **2** [1930s+] (orig. US) to put pressure on, to beat up. **3** [1960s+] (US) to move by using physical force.

musclebound between the ears *phr.* [1910s–40s] (US) very stupid.

muscle car *n.* [1960s+] (orig. US) a motor vehicle that is specially modified to give high power and speed (cf. HOT-ROD n.).

muscle fuck *n.* [1970s] (US) **1** the rubbing of the penis between a woman's breasts (cf. FRENCH FUCK). **2** sexual intercourse in which the woman uses her vaginal muscles to intensify the experience.

musclehead *n.* [1920s+] (US) a stupid if brawny man (cf. MEATHEAD). [SE *muscle* + sfx. -HEAD (1)]

muscle in *v.* [1920s+] (orig. US) to force an entrance, to use violence to gain something one desires. [MUSCLE v.]

muscleman *n.* [1920s+] (orig. US) **1** a thug, usu. as employed by a gangster for purposes of intimidation. **2** a man with an outstanding physique.

muscle shirt *n.* [1970s+] (US) a T-shirt with very short sleeves or no sleeves, thus displaying the wearer's physique.

mush *n.*[1] **1** [late 18C] (US Und.) a thief's girlfriend. **2** [mid-19C+] sentimental nonsense. [SE *mush*, anything soft and pulpy]

mush *n.*[2] [early 19C] (Und.) an umbrella (cf. MUSH-FAKER).

mush/moosh *n.*[3] [mid-19C+] (orig. US) the face. [orig. boxing; it rhymes with 'push' and was something that was 'pushed' by a blow]

mush *n.*[4] [1930s+] **1** (US) a fool. **2** a man, a 'chap'; thus as a term of greeting, e.g. *Oi! Mush!* [? Rom. *moosh*, a man]

mush/moosh *n.*[5] [1940s+] (Aus.) prison food.

mush/moosh *n.*[6] [1960s] a *moustache*. [abbr.]

mush *v.*[1] [1900s–30s] (US) to go, to leave. [dog sledders' *mush*, to cross snow on a dog sled; ult. Fr. *marchez/marchons*, march, let's march!]

mush *v.*[2] **1** [1920s–70s] (US) to kiss and cuddle, also as *mush it up*. **2** [1940s] (US Black) to kiss. [MUSH n.[1]]

mushbrain *n.* [1980s+] (US) **1** stupidity. **2** a dolt (cf. BAKE-BRAIN). [SE *mush* + sfx. *-brain*]

mushe *n.* [1940s+] (W.I.) a Syrian or a Chinese. [Fr. *monsieur*, a term of address; Syria had been under Fr. control, and thus its expatriates might speak the language, but why *Chinese*, perhaps on basis of all foreigners being generically 'French']

mushed-up *adj.* [1920s–30s] well-dressed. [? the implication that one who is dressed well is *de facto* 'soft']

mushe-man *see* MOOSHE-MAN.

musher *n.* [late 19C] (US) an itinerant umbrella maker (cf. MUSH-FAKER).

mush-/mushroom-faker/-toper/-topper *n.* [mid-19C] one who advertises themselves as a mender of umbrellas, or pedlar, but may well use this respectable job as a cover for more fraudulent pursuits (cf. SPUNK-FAKER). [MUSHROOM n.[3] (1) + FAKER]

mush, gush and lush *n.* [late 19C] favourable criticisms that are written in return for cash or food and drink. [MUSH n.[1] (2) + SE *gush* + LUSH n.[1]]

mush-head *n.* [late 19C+] (orig. US) a fool; thus *mush-headed*, stupid. [SE *mush*, anything soft and pulpy + sfx. -HEAD (1)]

mushie *n.* **1** [1930s+] (Aus.) a mushroom. **2** [1960s+] (drugs) usu. in pl., psilocybin, 'magic mushrooms'.

mushmouth *n.* [1930s+] (US) **1** indistinct speech. **2** a person who mumbles. [SE *mush*]

mush-rigger *n.* [1910s] (US) an itinerant umbrella-mender (cf. MUSH-FAKER).

mushroom *n.*[1] **1** [late 18C–early 19C] a *nouveau riche* individual or an *arriviste* family. **2** [1970s+] (orig. Irish) a person who is lied to or kept uninformed. **3** [1980s+] (US) a person who is unwittingly caught in crossfire between criminals. [(1) and (3) the propensity of the fungus to 'spring up overnight'; and (2) to grow in the dark]

mushroom *n.*[2] [19C] the vagina (cf. CABBAGE n.[7]).

mushroom *n.*[3] **1** [mid-19C] an umbrella. **2** [mid-19C–1900s] a low-crowned circular hat, esp. a lady's straw hat with a down-curving brim. **3** [late 19C] a tavern clock. [the supposed resemblances]

mushroom-faker *see* MUSH-FAKER.

mushrooms *n.* [1960s+] (drugs) psilocybin/psilocin, 'magic mushrooms'.

mush-toper/-topper *see* MUSH-FAKER.

mush worker *n.* [1920s–70s] (US Und./police) a woman or a prostitute who obtains money from men by playing on their sympathy, giving them a 'sob story'. [MUSH n.[1] (2) + SE *worker*]

mushy *adj.*[1] [late 19C+] romantic, sentimental. [MUSH n.[1] (2)]

mushy *adj.*[2] [1970s+] (S.Afr.) nice, pleasant. [Zulu *mu* + *hle*, good for one; orig. Zimbabwean use]

music *n.*[1] [late 17C–early 19C] (Und.) a term used among highwaymen to signify that an individual is a friend and must not be hindered on their journey; usu. in phr. *the music's paid*. ['the Watch-word among High-way-men, to let the Company they were to Rob, alone, in return to some Courtesy' (B.E.)]

music *n.*[2] [late 18C–early 19C] (Irish) the 'tail' of a coin. [the 'tail' or reverse side of an Irish halfpenny or farthing bore the image of a harp]

music *n.*[3] **1** [mid-19C+] (US) amusement, fun, lively speech. **2** [mid-19C+] (US) gunfire. **3** [late 19C–1950s] talking, esp. complaints or nagging. **4** [late 19C–1970s] trouble (cf. FACE THE MUSIC).

musical *adj.* [late 19C] used of a horse that suffers from respiratory problems (cf. PIPER n.[1]; ROARER n.[2]).

musical fruit *n.* [1910s+] any fruit or vegetables, esp. beans or Jerusalem artichokes, that produce flatulence.

music box *n.* [mid-19C–1940s] a piano.

Music City/Town *n.* [1970s+] (US) Nashville, Tennessee. [the city's association with country music]

music-duffing *n.* [1910s–20s] reconditioning musical instruments. [SE *music* + DUFF v.[1] (2)]

Music Town *see* MUSIC CITY.

musk *n.* [1960s+] (drugs) psilocybin/psilocin, a 'magic mushroom'. [var. on SE *mushroom*]

musket *n.* [1930s–70s] (US) the penis.

muski/musky *n.* [1960s+] (US) muscatel, thus any cheap wine.

muskin *n.* [mid-18C] an eccentric. ['Those who … call a man a cabbage, … an odd fish, and an unaccountable *muskin*, should never come into company without an interpreter.' Johnson in *The Connoisseur* (1756), in a blast against sl.; James Joyce reiterated the phr. in the *OED*'s only other citation, in *Ulysses* (1922)]

muskra *n.* [late 19C–1900s] a policeman (cf. MORK). [Rom. *mooshkeroo*, a constable]

musk-rat *n.* [19C+] (US) a resident of the state of Delaware (cf. BLUE HEN'S CHICKEN n.[2]).

musky *see* MUSKI.

muslin *n.* [early 19C–1920s] a young woman, usu. as a *bit/piece/bundle of muslin* (cf. BIT OF SKIRT; BIT OF STUFF). [metonymy]

muso *n.* [1960s+] a *musician*, usu. in a rock'n'roll band. [abbr.]

muss *n.* [mid-late 19C] (US) a fight, a dispute, a commotion (cf. ON THE MUSS). [dial.]

muss *v.* [mid-19C–1920s] **1** (US) to pick a fight. **2** to have sexual intercourse (cf. BANG v.[1]). [SE *muss*, to rumple, to untidy]

muss up *v.* [1920s] (US) to treat roughly. [ext. of MUSS v. (1)]

must *n.* [1930s+] something that is essential, mandatory, obligatory.

musta/muster *n.* [mid-19C] (Anglo-Ind.) a pattern or design, whether of a coat, a palace or something in between. [Port. *mostra*, a pattern, that which shows]

mustache *see* MOUSTACHE.

mustache Pete *see* MOUSTACHE PETE.

mustache ride *see* MOUSTACHE RIDE.

mustang *n.* [1970s] (US Black) an independent woman who is 'hard to ride'. [SE *mustang*, note US milit. jargon *mustang*, an officer who has been commissioned from the ranks]

mustard *n.*[1] **1** [1900s–60s] (US) spirit, zest, courage, esp. in adversity. **2** [1920s+] one who is keen or the best, outstanding, excellent at a task or occupation (cf. HOT STUFF n.[2]); thus *mustard at/on*, very good at. **3** [1920s+] a woman who is sexually enthusiastic. [fig. uses of the 'hotness' of SE *mustard*, (3) note the comment, in T.R.G. Lyell, *Slang, Phrase & Idiom* (1931) 'It must never be used of the female sex']

mustard *n.*[2] [1930s] (US) an Asian person (cf. MUSTARD SEED). [their light brown complexion]

mustard-and-cress *n.* [19C] the pubic hair (cf. BROCCOLI; MUSTARD POT n.[2]).

mustard plaster *n.* [late 19C] a miserable young man. [coined in a music-hall comic song, written by E.L. Blanchard (1820–89) and premiered at Drury Lane]

mustard pot *n.*[1] [19C] a carriage with a light yellow body. [the stress is on the colour rather than the shape]

mustard pot *n.*[2] [late 19C+] the vagina (cf. MUSTARD-AND-CRESS). [rhy. sl. *mustard pot* = TWAT]

mustard pot *n.*[3] [1930s] (US prison) a passive homosexual, a pedicant. [the stress is on the *pot*, but note MUSTARD POT n.²/n.⁴]

mustard pot *n.*⁴ [1940s–50s] (US) the anus (cf. MUSTARD ROAD).

mustard road *n.* [1970s+] (US) the anus; thus *go up the mustard road*, to sodomize (cf. MUSTARD POT).

mustard seed *n.* [1920s] (US Black) a light-skinned Black person (cf. MUSTARD n.²).

mustee *n.* [20C] (W.I./Bdos., Guyn.) the offspring of a White and a mulatto parent. [Sp. *mestizo*, a half-caste]

muster *see* MUSTA.

must have swallowed the dictionary *phr.* [1930s+] a phr. used of a person who habitually prefers longer to shorter words.

mustify *v.* [mid-19C] to render musty or mouldy.

must-I-holler *n.* [1980s+] (US Black) the vagina. [ety. unknown; lit. 'do I have to shout'; ? rhy. sl. on SE *collar*]

mustn't-mention-'ems *n.* [mid-19C] trousers (cf. DON'T-NAME-'EMS; UNMENTIONABLES).

muta *see* MOOTA.

mutant *n.* [1980s+] (US campus) a social outcast.

mutcher *n.* [mid–late 19C] a thief who steals from drunks. [var. on MOOCHER n. (1)]

mute *n.* [1970s] (gay) the vagina (cf. MOUTH THAT SAYS NO WORDS).

mute as a maggot *phr.* [1920s] absolutely silent.

mute as mumchance/mumchance who was hanged for saying nothing *phr.* [late 18C–early 19C] a phr. used to refer to an acquaintance who seems silent and miserable. [the 16C–17C game of *mumchance*, resembling hazard, was played in silence. Note dial. *mumchance*, *mumpchance*, one who is stolidly, stupidly silent]

mutha *see* MOTHER n.⁵.

mutie *n.* [1980s+] an adept, typically of skateboarding. [SE *mutant*, the image is of a fan so involved that they have abandoned some of their human characteristics to their obsession]

mutilee *n.* [1980s+] (US campus) an incapacitated, immobile person. [SE *mutilated* or Fr. *mutilée*]

mutt *n.*¹ [late 19C+] (US) a fool, a bungler, an ignoramus. [MUTTONHEAD]

mutt *n.*² **1** [late 19C+] (orig. US) a dog, usu. a mongrel. **2** [1970s+] an unattractive person of the opposite sex (cf. DOG n.⁵). [? affectionate use of MUTT n.¹]

mutt and jeff *n.* **1** [1910s] (orig. US) a pair of stupid, bungling men. **2** [1930s] foolish conversation. **3** [1940s] the King George V Silver medal Jubilee and the Edward VIII Coronation medals or ribbons or the 1918 Victory and Overseas medals or ribbons, which are invariably worn together. [MUTT n.¹ + JEFF n., popularized by the US cartoon characters, orig. by H.C. 'Bud' Fischer in the 1930s]

mutt and jeff *adj.* [1930s+] deaf. [rhy. sl.]

mutt and jeff, to *phr.* [1960s+] (US police/Und.) of police interrogators, to take the parts of the 'good/sympathetic' and 'bad/potentially violent' officers when attempting to gain information from a suspect. Such 'roles' are assumed only for the situation in hand. [MUTT AND JEFF n.]

mutter and stutter *n.* [20C] butter. [rhy. sl.]

mutt-eye/-eyes *n.* [1940s+] (Aus.) corn (as a food). [ety. unknown; ? Aboriginal language]

mutthead *n.* [1940s] (US) a stupid or contemptible person. [MUTT n.¹ + sfx. -HEAD (1)]

mutton *n.*¹ **1** [16C] the vagina; thus [19C] *in her mutton*, having sexual intercourse with a woman (cf. BACON SANDWICH). **2** [late 16C] the penis (cf. BACON n.¹). **3** [late 17C] sexual intercourse, sexual pleasure.

mutton *n.*² [early 16C+] **1** a promiscuous woman. **2** a prostitute (cf. HAWK ONE'S MUTTON; LACED MUTTON; MUTTON-

MONGER). [*OED* suggests 'food for lust', but the image is more simple, an old sheep as opposed to a young lamb]

mutton *n.*³ **1** [late 18C–late 19C] (US) one's person, self, body or flesh (cf. BACON n.¹.). **2** [late 19C–1940s] (orig. US) one's preference, one's liking.

mutton *n.*⁴ [1960s+] (US) cowardice. [the timorousness of sheep]

mutton bayonet *n.* [1990s] the penis (cf. BACON BAZOOKA).

mutton-bird/-eater *n.* [late 19C+] (Aus.) a native of northern Tasmania. [SE *mutton-bird*, an edible species of Puffin, found on the Bass Strait (between Tasmania and the mainland)]

Muttonburg *see* MUTTONTOWN.

mutton-chopper *n.* [late 19C] 'mutton-chop' whiskers.

mutton-chops *n.* [mid-19C] a sheep's head. [the similarity of fleece to mutton-chop whiskers, and pun on SE *mutton chops*. Note milit. jargon *the Mutton Chops* or *Mutton Lancers*, the Royal West Surreys, whose emblem is a lamb and flag]

mutton-cove *n.*¹ **1** [19C] a woman dressing younger than her years (cf. MUTTON DRESSED AS LAMB). **2** [mid–late 19C] a womanizer. [MUTTON n.² + COVE]

mutton-cove *n.*² [mid-19C] the Coventry St end of Windmill St, London, once well-known for its prostitutes. [MUTTON n.² + SE *cove*, abbr. *Coventry*]

mutton-dagger *n.* [1960s+] the penis (cf. BACON BAZOOKA). [MUTTON n.¹ (2) + SE *dagger*]

mutton dressed as lamb/dressed lamb-fashion *n.* [late 19C+] a woman who dresses younger than her years (cf. MUTTON-COVE n.¹).

mutton dummies *n.* [20C] (Ulster) plimsolls, trainers. [ety. unknown; ? *mutton cloth*, a type of cloth used to wrap meat + DUMMY n.¹ (1); i.e. their relative silence, compared to the noise of leather soled shoes]

muttoner *n.* [late 17C–early 19C] a womanizer, a promiscuous man (cf. MUTTON-COVE n.¹; MUTTON-MONGER n.¹.).

mutton-eye *n.* [20C] a nickname applied to one who has a squint. [? resemblance to a sheep's eye]

mutton-fed *adj.* [1910s–20s] large, fat and well fed.

mutton-fist/-hand *n.* [mid-19C] anyone who has large, coarse red hands.

mutton gun *n.* [1940s–50s] (Aus.) the penis (cf. BACON BAZOOKA).

mutton-hand *see* MUTTON-FIST.

mutton-head *n.* [mid-18C+] a fool; thus *mutton-dead*, stupid (cf. BEEF-BRAIN).

mutton in long coats *n.* [late 17C–19C] women (cf. LEG OF MUTTON IN A SILK STOCKING). [MUTTON n.²]

Muttonjerk *see* MUTTONTOWN.

mutton-monger *n.*¹ [early 16C–early 18C] a promiscuous man. [MUTTON n.² + SE *monger*, ult. Lat. *mango*, a dealer or trafficker]

mutton-monger *n.*² **1** [mid–late 17C] a sheep-stealer. **2** [mid-late 17C] a notable eater of mutton. [SE *mutton* + *monger*, ult. Lat. *mango*, a dealer or trafficker]

mutton musket *n.* [1990s] the penis (cf. BACON BAZOOKA).

muttonous *adj.* [late 19C–1900s] slow, tedious, monotonous. [joc. mispron.]

mutton-pies *n.* [19C] the eyes. [rhy. sl.]

muttonpuncher *n.* [1930s] (US, mainly West) a sheep-herder. [play on SAmE *cowpuncher*]

mutton-shunter *n.* [late 19C] a policeman, esp. in his role of harrying street prostitutes. [MUTTON n.² + SE *shunter*]

Muttontown/Muttonburg/Muttonjerk/Muttonville *n.* [1950s+] (US) a small, out-of-the-way town or settlement.

mutton-tugger *n.* [late 16C–early 17C] a pimp (cf. TUG MUTTON). [MUTTON n.² + SE *tug*]

Muttonville *see* MUTTONTOWN.

mutton walk *n.* [mid-19C] **1** the saloon at the Drury Lane Theatre, Covent Garden; often as *the Mutton Walk*. **2** any street where one finds prostitutes, esp. the junction of Coventry Street and Windmill Street in the West End of London (cf. MUTTON-COVE n.²). [MUTTON n.² + SE *walk*]

mutt's nuts *n.* [1990s] anything excellent, admirable, first-rate. [MUTT n.² + NUTS n.¹; var. on DOG'S BALLOCKS]

mutt up *v.* [1930s–40s] (US Und.) to keep a guard dog. [MUTT n.²]

muuna *n.* [1950s] (W.I.) the female genitals. [? link to MOON n.¹]

mux *n.* [mid-19C–1910s] (US) a muddle or a botched job. [orig. unknown. Note 17C N. Eng. *mux*, a sharp, pointed tool for boring holes etc]

mux *v.* [19C] (US) to muddle or to botch. [MUX n.]

muz/muzz *n.* [late 18C?–late 19C] one who works hard at their books (cf. MUG v.⁵). [Westminster School jargon *muz*, to study intently]

muz/muzz *v.¹* [late 18C] to loiter aimlessly, to 'hang about'. [? SE *muss*, to rumple, to untidy]

muz/muzz *v.²* [late 18C–late 19C] to render 'muzzy', to bemuse with drink. [dial. *muzzle*, to drink to excess, to make drunk]

muzz *see* MUZ.

muzzed *adj.* [late 18C–late 19C] tipsy, befuddled by drink. [MUZ v.²]

muzzle *n.¹* **1** [15C+] the face, the nose or the mouth. **2** [late 17C–early 19C] a beard. [(1) orig. SE; (2) '(usually) long and nasty' (B.E.)]

muzzle *n.²* *see* MAZEL.

muzzle *n.³* [1950s–70s] (drugs) heroin. [ety. unknown, ? SE *muzzle*, to silence, a ref. to the immediate effects of an injection, rendering the user comatose]

muzzle *v.¹* **1** [late 17C–early 18C] to kiss and fondle. **2** [late 17C–early 18C] to molest. **3** [mid–late 19C] to fight, to thrash. **4** [mid–late 19C] to hit in the face. **5** [mid–late 19C] to throttle, to garrotte (cf. MUG v.²). **6** [mid–late 19C] (orig. US) to obtain, to take, to steal. **7** [1940s+] (US) to kiss and fondle in a rough manner. [SE *muzzle*, to put a muzzle on; to restrain (usu. speech)]

muzzle *v.²* [mid–late 19C] to drink heavily. [dial. *muzzle*, to drink to excess]

muzzle-chops *n.* [17C] nickname for a man with a prominent nose and mouth. [SE *muzzle*, the front part of an animal's head + SE *chops*, the jaw]

muzzler *n.¹* **1** [early–mid-19C] a blow to the mouth or face. **2** [mid-19C] (US) a strong-arm robber. **3** [20C] (US) a contemptible person. [MUZZLE v.¹]

muzzler *n.²* [19C] a drink. [MUZZLE v.²]

muzzler *n.³* [1920s–50s] (US esp. prison) a homosexual, spec. a fellator. [SE *muzzle*, the mouth]

muzzling cheat *n.* [late 17C] a napkin. [SE *muzzle* + CHEAT n. (1)]

muzzy *adj.* **1** [early 18C–late 19C] blurred, indistinct. **2** [early 18C–early 19C] of weather, dull, gloomy, overcast. **3** [mid-18C–late 19C] of people, vague, befuddled, confused. **4** [mid-18C+] drunk (cf. ADDLED). [SE *bemused* or dial. *mosey*, befuddled with drink]

myall *n.* [1980s+] one who is out of their usual environment. [Abor. *miall*; *myall*, an Aborigine who has had little or no contact with Whites; a stranger]

my arse!/ass! *excl.¹* [late 19C+] a general excl. of disdain, dismissal, arrogant contempt, e.g. *Are you frightened? Frightened, my arse!*

my arse!/ass!/asshole! *excl.²* [1970s+] (US) don't try to fool me! you should be so lucky! I wasn't born yesterday! etc.

my arse for! *see* MY ARSE TO!

my arse is dragging *phr.* [1910s+] (orig. US) I am totally exhausted.

my arse on! *see* MY ARSE TO!

my arse on a bandbox *see* MINE ARSE ON A BANDBOX.

my arse/ass to/for/on ...! *excl.* [late 17C+] a general excl. of contempt or dismissal (cf. BALLS TO; THE HELL WITH).

my ass! *see* MY ARSE!

my asshole! *see* MY ARSE! excl.².

my ass to/for/on ...! *see* MY ARSE TO ... !

my aunt/my Aunt Jones *n.* [mid-19C] the water closet, the lavatory; thus *visit my aunt*, to go to the lavatory (cf. MY AUNT'S).

my aunt! *excl.* [late 19C+] a mild excl.

my Aunt Fanny! *excl.* [late 19C+] a mild excl.

my Aunt Jones *see* MY AUNT.

my aunt's *n.* [mid-19C–1900s] the lavatory (cf. MRS CHANT'S; MY AUNT). [euph.]

my bad *phr.* [1990s] (US teen) 'my fault', 'sorry'.

my balls! *excl.* [1930s–40s] (US) an excl. of refusal, rejection.

my belly thinks my throat is/has been cut *phr.* [mid-19C+] I am very hungry.

my bet is ... *phr.* [1950s+] in my opinion ... , what I think ... .

my biff *phr.* [1990s] (US teen) a phr. used to admit responsibility for a very bad situation. [general use of BIFF v.¹ (6)]

my blood! *excl.* [1920s+] (Aus.) a general expression of agreement (cf. BLOOD OATH!).

my body's captain *n.* [19C] the penis. [literary euph. coined by the US author Walt Whitman (1819–92)]

my cabbage-tree! *excl.* [mid–late 19C] (Aus.) a mild excl., synon. with MY HAT! [*cabbage-tree hat*, a hat made of woven cabbage-tree or cabbage-palm leaves]

my colonial oath! *excl.* [mid-19C+] (Aus./N.Z.) a mild excl. (cf. MY OATH!).

my cousin the weaver *phr.* [late 17C–mid-18C] a pej. form of address (cf. MY DIRTY COUSIN).

my cow! *excl.* [1960s] (US) a general excl.

my cripes! *excl.* [1910s+] a mild oath and general excl. [CRIPES!]

my dick! *excl.* [1970s+] (US) an excl. of disdain, disbelief (cf. MY FOOT!). [DICK n.⁵ (1)]

my dirty cousin *phr.* [late 17C–mid-18C] a pej. form of address (cf. MY COUSIN THE WEAVER).

my eye! *excl.* [mid-18C+] a dismissive excl., nonsense! rubbish! (cf. ALL MY EYE AND BETTY MARTIN).

my eyes! *excl.* [mid-19C+] a general excl.

my feet are staying *phr.* [1980s+] (US campus) a farewell. [a play on the Ger. *auf Wiedersehen*, goodbye]

my friend *n.* [20C] (Ulster) menstruation. [euph.]

my foot! *excl.* [1920s+] an excl. used to imply one's contemptuous rejection of the previous speaker's assertion, sometimes as *your foot!* (cf. MY ARSE! excl.¹).

my gate's shut *phr.* [1920s+] (Aus.) I'll say no more, sometimes as *his/her gate's shut*, he'll/she'll say no more.

my gawd *n.* [late 19C] a sword. [rhy. sl.]

my gentleman/lady *n.* [mid-19C+] he, she (cf. HER LADYSHIP; MY LORD).

my goodness *n.* [1940s–50s] a drink of Guinness stout. [the advertising slogan, 'My goodness, my Guinness']

my goody! *excl.* [late 19C] my goodness!

my gosh! *excl.* [1920s+] a general excl., euph. for *my God!*

my granny!/on your granny! *excl.* [1910s+] rubbish! nonsense!

my great guts are ready to eat my little ones *phr.* [late 18C–19C] I am very hungry (cf. MY GUTS BEGIN TO THINK MY THROAT'S CUT; MY GUTS CHIME TWELVE).

my gun *n.* [1980s+] (US Black) one's best friend.

my guts begin to think my throat's cut *phr.* [late 18C+] I am very hungry (cf. MY GREAT GUTS ARE READY TO EAT MY LITTLE ONES).

my guts chime twelve/cry cupboard/curse my teeth *phr.* [late 18C–19C] I am very hungry (cf. MY GREAT GUTS ARE READY TO EAT MY LITTLE ONES).

my hat! *excl.* [late 16C] a general excl.

my hat to a halfpenny! *excl.* [late 16C] a general excl.

my holy/sacred/sainted aunt! *excl.* [late 19C+] a mild excl. [use post-WW2 is ironic or historical]

my king oath! *excl.* [1910s+] (Aus.) a mild excl. (cf. MY OATH!). [euph. for 'my FUCKING oath!']

myla *see* MILER *n.*

my lady *see* MY GENTLEMAN.

my land! *excl.* [mid-19C+] (Can.) a mild oath.

my left foot!/knacker!/tit! *excl.* [1920s+] an excl. used to imply one's contemptuous rejection of the previous speaker's assertion (cf. MY ARSE!; MY FOOT!).

my lord *n.* [mid-19C] a mocking nickname given to a hunchback.

my man! *excl.* [1930s+] (orig. US Black) a term of endearment and address between two men (cf. MAIN MAN *n.*[1]).

my mother's away *n.* [late 19C–1900s] (Aus.) the other day. [rhy. sl.]

my myrtle *n.* [early 19C] (Cockney) my friend. [SE *myrtle*, a sweet-scented plant, used in perfumery and sacred to Venus]

my nabs *n.* [late 18C–late 19C] myself. [as opposed to YOUR NIBS or HIS NABS]

my name is Haines/Hanes *phr.* [mid-19C] (US) a phr. used on leaving a place or party suddenly (cf. HAINES!). [an encounter between President Thomas Jefferson (1743–1826) and one *Haines* or *Hanes*, a fanatical opponent. Haines, not knowing the identity of his companion, vilified Jefferson in extreme tones as the two men rode side-by-side near Jefferson's home in Virginia. When they arrived at Jefferson's home, the president, affronted but still courteous, invited Haines in. Only then did Haines ask his putative host for his name: 'Thomas Jefferson'. 'Well, my name is Haines,' replied his opponent, before riding promptly away]

my name is Twyford *phr.* [late 17C–early 18C] I know absolutely nothing about it. [proper name of Josiah *Twyford* (1640–1729), whose secret process for glazing provided the basis for his creation of a successful firm of sanitary potters; presumably his response to those who wished to elicit his secret]

my name is Walker *phr.* [mid-19C–1950s] I'm leaving, I'm off. [pun on *Walker*/SE *walker*]

my nigger/nigga *n.* [1980s+] (US Black) **1** a major influence, a role-model, a close friend. **2** a general term of address. [NIGGER *n.*/NIGGA]

my oath! *excl.* [late 19C+] (Aus./N.Z.) a mild excl. (cf. MY COLONIAL OATH!).

m.y.o.b. *phr.* [20C] (US) mind your own business; also extended to *p.m.y.o.b.*, please ... . [abbr.]

my old geezer *phr.* [1910s–20s] one's wife, often as *the old geezer*. [joc. use of GEEZER *n.*[1] (1)]

my old guv'ner *n.* [1960s+] my father.

my part! *excl.* [1920s+] an excl. of disassociation, don't blame me, I don't care, it's not my problem.

my patience! *excl.* [mid-late 19C] an excl. of surprise.

my people *n.* [1950s+] **1** (US Black) one's fellow gang members. **2** any fellow members of a group or minority, usu. used ironically.

my pippin! *excl.* [mid-19C] a term of affectionate address. [PIPPIN]

my pleasure *phr.* [1950s+] a polite response to an offer of thanks, the equivalent of the Ital. *prego* or SAmE *you're welcome*.

my Prussian blue *phr.* [mid-19C] a term of endearment. [SE *Prussian blue*, a colour; Dickensian use as synon. for SE *true blue*]

Myrna Loy *n.* [1930s–40s] a saveloy. [rhy. sl.; ult. film star *Myrna Loy* (1905–93)]

myrrh *see* MUR.

myrtle *n.* [20C] (Aus.) sexual intercourse. [ety. unknown; link to MUDDLE *v.*]

my sacred/sainted aunt! *see* MY HOLY AUNT!

my skull's afly! *excl.* [19C] I know what's happening, I'm well awake! [FLY *adj.*[1]]

mystall crikey! *excl.* [20C] (Aus.) joc. reverse of CHRIST ALMIGHTY!

myst all critey! *excl.* [20C] (Aus.) joc. reverse of CHRIST ALMIGHTY!

my stars! *excl.* [17C] a mild oath (cf. IN MY STARS!).

my stars and garters! *excl.* [mid-late 19C] a general excl. of astonishment or shock. [joc. ref. to orders of merit that are worn by those entitled]

mysteries *see* BAGS OF MYSTERY.

mystery/mystery meat *n.*[1] [late 19C+] (US) low-grade meat as used in sausages, hash, hamburgers etc.

mystery *n.*[2] [1930s+] **1** an unknown young woman, often one recently arrived in London from the provinces. **2** a young prostitute.

mystery *see* BAGS OF MYSTERY.

mystery meat *see* MYSTERY *n.*[1].

mystery punter *n.* [1950s+] any man who prefers his sex and/or relationships with young, naïve women or young prostitutes; thus *mystery mad*, very keen on sex with young women. [MYSTERY *n.*[2] + PUNTER *n.*[1]]

myth *n.* [1950s+] an untrue or popular tale, a rumour.

my troubles! *excl.* [late 19C+] (Aus.) a dismissive excl., 'don't worry about me', 'I don't care' (cf. MY WORRIES!).

my tulip! *excl.* [mid-late 19C] my fine fellow, my good man. [? the tulipomania of 1840s]

my uncle *n.* [mid-18C+] a pawnbroker (cf. UNCLE *n.*[1]).

my uncle's *n.* **1** [mid-18C+] a pawnbroker (cf. MY UNCLE). **2** [late 18C–early 19C] a privy; thus euph. phr. *go and see uncle*, to visit the privy (cf. MY AUNT'S).

my unconverted friend *n.* [mid-late 19C] (US) a revolver, a pistol.

my very word! *excl.* [1940s+] (Aus.) an excl. of surprise. [an intensified version of MY WORD!]

my wig!/wigs! *excl.* [late 19C] a mild excl. of surprise, irritation etc (cf. DASH!).

my word *n.* [20C] a piece of excrement. [rhy. sl. *my word* = TURD *n.* (1)]

my word! *excl.* [mid-19C+] a mild excl. of surprise (cf. MY VERY WORD!).

my worries! *excl.* [1950s+] (Aus.) a dismissive excl. 'don't worry about me', 'I don't care' (cf. MY TROUBLES!).

myxie/myxo/myxy *n.* [1950s+] the disease *myxo*matosis, introduced deliberately in the 1950s to kill off rabbits. [abbr.]

N

N *n.*[1] [1970s] (US) a Black person. [abbr. NIGGER n.]

N *n.*[2] [1980s] (drugs) **1** narcotics. **2** a painkiller, Darvocet-*N*. [abbr.]

N! *excl.* [1980s+] (US campus) no! [abbr.]

'n' *conj.*[1] [mid-19C+] abbr. of SE *than*, e.g. *That boy's madder 'n' ever.*

'n' *conj.*[2] [mid-19C+] abbr. of SE *and*, e.g. *rock 'n' roll.*

naai *n.* (S.Afr.) a prostitute. [NAAI v.]

naai *v.* (S.Afr.) to have sexual intercourse. [Du. *naaien*, to have carnal knowledge of]

naar *adj.* (S.Afr.). **1** [late 19C+] unpleasant, nauseating. **2** [1960s+] sick, queasy. [synon. Afk.]

naar *v.* [1980s+] (S.Afr.) to stink, to smell foul. [Afk. *naar*, nauseated, nauseating]

naartjie *n.* [1970s+] (S.Afr.) a fool, an idiot; thus *Naartjie Republic*, a banana republic (cf. NANA n.). [S.Afr.Du. *naartjie*, a variety of tangerine or mandarin orange; ? f. Tamil *narattai*, citrus]

nab/nabe *n.*[1] **1** [mid-16C–18C] (Und.) the head (cf. NOB n.[1]). **2** [early 17C] the head of a stick. **3** [late 17C–mid-18C] a hat (cf. NAB CHEAT). **4** [late 17C–mid-18C] a coxcomb, a fop. **5** [early 19C] an important person (cf. NOB n.[3]). [ety. unknown; ? link to dial. *nab*, a projecting lump of rock, a promontory]

nab *n.*[2] [early 19C+] a policeman (cf. NABMAN). [NAB v.[1] (2); 1950s+ use mainly US]

nab/nib *v.*[1] **1** [mid-17C+] to snatch, to steal, to seize. **2** [late 17C+] to catch or capture a person unawares, to apprehend and arrest. **3** [mid-18C+] to catch someone out, esp. if cheating. **4** [early 19C+] (US) to obtain for oneself, to grab. **5** [20C] (tramp) to steal a ride on a train. [ety. unknown, but cf. NAP v.[1]]

nab *v.*[2] [early 18C] to cheat with dice (cf. COG v.[1]). [var. on NAP v.[2]]

nab-all *n.* [early 17C] a fool. [? var. on SE *nab-all*, a miser, an unpleasant person; lit. 'snatch-all']

nabber *n.* **1** [early 19C] a bailiff, a constable. **2** [mid-19C–1960s] (US) a police officer. **3** [late 19C] a thief. [NAB v.[1]]

nabbing cheat *n.* [early 18C–mid-19C] the gallows. [NAB v.[1] + CHEAT n.]

nab cheat *n.* [16C] (Und.) a hat, a cap. [NAB n.[1] (3) + CHEAT n.]

nab chete *n.* [late 18C–early 19C] a hat. [NAB n.[1] (3) + CHEAT n.]

nabe *n.*[1] *see* NAB n.[1].

nabe/nabes *n.*[2] [1930s+] (US) **1** a *neigh*bourhood. **2** a local (*neigh*bourhood) cinema or bar; usu. as *nabes*. [abbr.]

nab/nob girder *n.* [late 17C–mid-19C] (Und.) a bridle. [NAB n.[1] + SE *gird*]

nab it on the dial, to *phr.* [mid–late 19C] to take a blow on the face. [NAB v.[1] + DIAL]

nabman *n.* [early 19C] a policeman (cf. NAB n.[2]).

nab the stoop *see* KNAP THE STOOP.

nabob *n.* [mid–late 19C] a capitalist. [Urdu *nawwab*; ult.

Arabic *na'ib*/Port. *nababo*, deputy governor, thus transferred to a merchant who has made his fortune trading in/with India; the sl. use has no India-specific connotations]

nab one's/the bib, to *phr.* [mid-19C] to weep, esp. for effect, i.e. to get one's way, to put across one's point (cf. NAP ONE'S BIB). [NAB v.[1] + BIB]

nabs/knabs *n.* [late 18C–late 19C] oneself, myself (cf. NIBS). [northern dial.]

nab the bib *see* NAB ONE'S BIB.

nab/nap the regulars, to *phr.* [mid–late 19C] (Und.) to take one's usual share of a robbery's proceeds.

nab the rust, to *phr.* [late 18C–early 19C] **1** to be ill-tempered, sullen (cf. RIDE RUSTY). **2** to be punished. [NAB v.[1] + SE *rusty*, refractory (of horses)]

nab the snow, to *phr.* [late 18C–early 19C] (Und.) to steal linen that has been put out to bleach or dry (cf. LULLY PRIGGER; SNOW-DROPPING). [NAB v.[1] + SNOW n.[1]]

nab the stifles/stifler, to *phr.* [19C–1900s] to be hanged. [NAB v.[1] + SE *stifle*, the condition of being choked]

nab the teize/tease/teaze, to *phr.* [late 18C–early 19C] to be whipped as punishment privately (but still in prison). [NAB v.[1] + TEASE v.[1]; whipping were often public]

nace *see* NASE.

nacked *adj.* [20C] (Aus.) annoyed. [var. on NARKED]

nackers *n.* [mid-19C+] the testicles (cf. KNACKERS). [dial.]

nada *n.* [1910s+] (US) nothing. [synon. Sp.]

nadbag *n.* [1990s] the scrotum. [NADS n. (1) + BAG n.[1] (2)]

nadger *n.* [late 19C+] (Ulster) **1** a young boy. **2** a sulky, bad-tempered person.

nadgers *n.* [1950s+] **1** testicles. **2** a general nonsense word, much used in the 1950s on BBC Radio's *Goon Show*. [abbr. GONADS; the Goon use is technically a nonce-word, but the connection to (1) seems very likely]

nads *n.* **1** [1960s+] (orig. US) the testicles. **2** [1970s+] (US) courage (cf. BALLS n.[1]). **3** [1980s+] (US campus) something great or exciting (cf. TITS). [abbr. GONADS]

nael *see* NALE.

naf/naff *n.*[1] [mid-19C] **1** the buttocks. **2** the vagina. [? abbr. backsl. FANNY; but note Scot. *nyaph*, the female genitals]

naf/naff *n.*[2] [1940s+] nothing. [coined in prostitute use]

naf *n.*[3] [1960s+] (S.Afr.) a fool, a weakling, an ineffectual person. [NAF n.[2]]

naff *n.* *see* NAF n.[1], n.[2].

naff *adj.*[1] [1960s+] in poor taste, unappealing, unfashionable, bad. [? north. dial. *naffhead, naffin, naffy*, a simpleton; a blockhead; an idiot or *niffy-naffy*, inconsequential, stupid or Scot. *nyaff*, a term of contempt for any unpleasant or objectionable person]

naff *adj.*[2] [1980s+] (gay) *n*ot *a*vailable *f*or *f*ucking/*f*un (cf. RIBENA ON TOAST).

naffing *adj.* [1950s+] a general intensifier. [euph. for FUCKING adj.]

naff off! *excl.* [1950s+] go away! [euph. for FUCK OFF!]

naff omee *n.* [mid-19C–1960s] a homosexual. [NAFF adj.[1] + OMEE, lit. an 'unappealing man']

naff up *v.* [1980s+] to make a mess, to blunder. [euph. for FUCK UP v.[2]]

nafka *see* NOFFKA.

nag *n.*[1] **1** [late 16C–early 17C] a term of abuse. **2** [late 16C; mid-19C] a woman. **3** [19C] an ageing prostitute. **4** [1960s+] (US) of a prostitute, one who takes her time over making her daily money from her clients. **5** [1980s] (US) a queen in cards. [fig. uses of SE *nag*, a saddle horse]

nag *n.*[2] [late 17C–mid-18C] the penis; thus *tether one's nag on*, to have sexual intercourse, *water one's nag*, to urinate. [? KNACKERS]

nag *n.*[3] [late 18C] a leg. [pun on SE *shanks' pony/mare*, going on foot]

nagah *n.* [1950s+] (W.I. Rasta) a derog. name for a Black person. [NIGGER n.]

nag-drag *n.* [mid-19C–1900s] a three-month period of imprisonment (cf. CARPET n.[2]). [DRAG n.[3]]

naggers *n.* [1990s] inflamed testicles. [NADGERS n. (1) + SE *nag*, to irritate]

naggie/naggy *n.* [19C–1900s] the vagina. [NAG n.[1] (2) + dimin. *-ie*; note SE *naggie*, a pony, which can be 'ridden']

naggle *v.* [mid-19C–1900s] to toss one's head in a stiff and affected manner. [SE *naggle*, to quarrel]

naggy *see* NAGGIE.

nago *n.* [1940s+] (W.I.) a very stupid, ugly or notably dark-complexioned person. [*Nago*, a person born in Nago, a Yoruba-speaker; many such people were transported from Africa as slaves]

nags *n.* [late 17C–mid-18C] **1** the testicles. **2** the penis (cf. NAG n.[2]). [? KNACKERS]

nah! *excl.* [1920s+] (US) no! [pron.]

nail/dead nail/nailing rascal/nails *n.*[1] [early 19C] a shrewd, imposing criminal, 'a person of an over-reaching, imposing disposition' (Vaux). [NAIL v.]

nail *n.*[2] [1910s–70s] (US) a venereal infection. [its stabbing pains]

nail *n.*[3] (drugs) **1** [1910s+] a cigarette (cf. COFFIN NAIL n.[2]). **2** [1930s+] (US) a hypodermic syringe (cf. SPIKE n.[3]). **3** [1970s+] a marijuana cigarette. [? ref. to NAIL IN ONE'S COFFIN]

nail *n.*[4] [1960s+] (US Black) a man. [the opp. of HAMMA]

nail *n.*[5] [1990s] (US campus) a well-built male, esp. a sportsman. [abbr. *nice ass* in Levi's]

nail *v.* **1** [mid-18C+] (orig. Und.) to get hold of, to secure, to apprehend and arrest. **2** [mid-18C+] to steal. **3** [mid-18C+] to catch one out. **4** [late 18C+] to punch, to hit hard or squarely. **5** [early 19C–1900s] to cheat, to overcharge, to get the better of. **6** [early 19C+] to shoot someone, to kill someone. **7** [late 19C+] to corner or defeat, esp. an opponent. **8** [1900s–40s] (US) to identify, to recognize. **9** [1950s+] (US) to seduce, to have sexual intercourse with (cf. BANG v.[1]). **10.** [1960s+] to charge with a debt. **11.** [1980s+] to do something well, to master something. [the image in all is of putting a nail through, or nailing down]

nail a goss, to *phr.* [late 19C] (Und.) to steal a hat. [NAIL v. + GOSS n.]

nail a rattler, to *phr.* [late 19C–1930s] (US tramp) to steal a ride on a moving train. [NAIL v. + RATTLER n.[1]]

nail a strike, to *phr.* [late 19C] (Und.) to steal a watch. [NAIL v. + STRIKE n.[2]]

nail bender *n.* [1920s–40s] (US) a carpenter, a blacksmith.

nail biter *n.* [1970s+] (US) an anxiety-provoking situation, esp. a close contest.

nail can *n.* [late 19C–1940s] (Aus.) a top hat (cf. NAIL KEG). [the shape of the cylindrical hat]

nailed *adj.* [late 19C+] (orig. US drugs) arrested. **2** [1980s+] (US campus) drunk (cf. NAILED UP). [NAIL v. (1), (4)]

nailed up *adj.* [mid-19C] (US) drunk (cf. NAILED). [NAIL v. (4), (7)]

nail 'em and jail 'em *n.* [1970s+] (US Black) the police (cf. NAILERS). [NAIL v.]

nailer *n.*[1] [19C] a general term of excellence, applied to people, animals or objects.

nailer *n.*[2] **1** [mid-19C] a policeman. **2** [late 19C–1920s] an extortionist. [lit. + fig. uses of NAIL v.]

nailer, the *n.*[3] [late 19C+] (Anglo-Irish) the knave or jack in a pack of cards (cf. BOY WITH THE BOOTS.). [NAIL v. (7); its use as a trump or wildcard in certain games]

nailers *n.* [1960s] (US Black) the police (cf. NAIL 'EM AND JAIL 'EM). [NAIL v.]

nail groper *n.* [mid-19C] one who scours the streets in search of old nails and similar saleable pieces of discarded metal.

nailhead *n.*[1] [1930s–40s] (US) a fool. [backform. of NAIL-HEADED]

nailhead *n.*[2] [1970s] (US Black) an unattractive woman, esp. one with short, nappy hair (cf. B.B. HEAD). [her tightly curled hair supposedly resembles a collection of SE *nail heads*]

nailheaded *adj.* [1930s–40s] (US) stupid. [the hardness of a SE *nail head*]

nailing *n.* [early 19C] **1** catching (out). **2** beating up. [NAIL v.]

nailing *adj.* [mid–late 19C] first-rate, excellent, splendid. [NAILER n.[1]]

nailing rascal *see* NAIL n.[1].

nail in one's coffin *n.* **1** [early 18C+] a stage in one's decline, usu. in phr. *put another nail in one's coffin* or *that's another ...*. **2** [early–mid-19C] a drink of liquor. **3** [mid-19C+] anything seen as potentially harmful, however pleasurable in the short term.

nail Jell-O to a tree, to *phr.* [1980s+] (US campus) to do the impossible.

nail keg *n.* [mid-19C] (US) a top hat (cf. NAIL CAN).

nailrod/nail-rod *n.* (Aus./N.Z.) **1** [late 19C–1910s] a stick of 'Two Seas' tobacco. **2** [late 19C–1920s] any dark tobacco. [resemblance to SE *nailrod*, a rod of metal from which nails are cut]

nails *n. see* NAIL n.[1].

nails! *excl.* [16C] an oath (cf. 'SNAILS!; ZOUNDS!). [abbr. SE *God's nails!*, spec. the nails used to crucify Christ]

nails and screws *n.* [20C] (Aus.) news. [rhy. sl.]

nail someone's hide/ass to the wall/barn door, to *phr.* [late 19C+] **1** (orig. US) to punish severely. **2** to beat up comprehensively.

nail someone to the cross/mast, to *phr.* [late 19C–1950s] (orig. US) to punish, to defeat in a decisive act, to castigate.

nail two wames together, to *phr.* [18C] to have sexual intercourse (cf. JOIN GIBLETS; JOIN PAUNCHES; RUB OFFAL). [Scot. *wame*, the belly]

nair *n.* [late 19C] rain. [backsl.]

naked *adj.* [20C] (US Black) without a gun, without possessions or money, generally at a disadvantage. [fig. uses of SE; note 14C SE *naked*, without armour or weapons]

naked! *excl.* [1970s+] (US campus) a general excl. of affirmation, often as a direct response to a previous statement.

naked as a jaybird *phr.* [20C] (US) stark naked (cf. JAYBIRD adj.[2]).

naked city *n.* [1960s+] (US) the poor area of a town (cf. HUNGRY HILL). [note film title *The Naked City* (1948)]

naked dance *n.* [1940s–50s] (US Black) a sexually provocative dance.

naked jazz *n.* [1940s–50s] basic, raunchy jazz music.

naked pretzel *n.* [1990s] (US campus) sexual intercourse. [supposed resemblance to a SE *pretzel*, a crisp biscuit, baked in the form of a knot]

nale/nael *adj.* [mid-19C] lean. [backsl.]

nalga de angel/angelical *n.* [1970s] (US drugs) marijuana. [Sp., lit. 'angel's ass']

nallion *n.* [20C] (Ulster) a lump, a bump. [ety. unknown]

nam *n.*[1] [mid–late 19C] **1** a man. **2** a policeman (cf. NAMESCLOP). [backsl.]

Nam *n.*[2] [1960s+] (US) (orig. milit.) Viet*nam*. [abbr.]

namas *see* NAMMOUS.

nam black/shit/weed *n.* [1960s–70s] (drugs) a variety of marijuana, very dark green and notably potent, grown in Vietnam. [NAM *n.*[2] + BLACK *n.*[1] (5)/SHIT *n.*[5]/WEED *n.*[1] (4)]

namby-pamby *n.* [18C] a weakling, an affected sentimentalist. [SE after 1800; the nickname given to the versifier Ambrose Phillips (1674–1749) by his enemies Henry Carey (author himself of *Sally in Our Alley*) and Alexander Pope, who deplored such lines as *Dimply damsel, sweetly smiling ...* ('To Miss Margaret Pultney, daughter of Daniel Pultney Esq, in *The Nursery*, 27 April 1727')]

namby-pamby *adj.* [18C] effeminate, insipid, childish. [NAMBY-PAMBY *n.*]

name it not/nameless, the *n.* [19C] the vagina (cf. DOWN BELOW).

name of that tune *phr.* [1980s+] (US) the facts, the reality. [the TV quiz show *Name That Tune*; the 'name' is the answer and thus 'reality']

name of the game *n.* [1940s+] the most important aspect of a situation, whatever matters most, the end, the finish. [? the practice of naming the card game when claiming a winning hand]

namesclop *n.* [mid-19C] a policeman (cf. NAM *n.*[1]). [backsl.]

name/nominate your poison *phr.* [mid-19C+] (orig. US joc.) an invitation to a fellow drinker to make a choice of drink at a party or in a bar (cf. POISON *n.*[1]; WHAT'S YOUR POISON?).

name yours! *excl.* [late 19C+] choose your drink (cf. NAME YOUR POISON; GIVE IT A NAME).

nammas *see* NAMMOUS.

nammo/namo/namow/nemmo *n.* [mid-19C+] a woman (cf. NAM *n.*[1]). [backsl.]

nammous/namas/nammas/nammus/nommus *v.* [mid–late 19C] to leave, to run off, to slip away quietly. [? Sp. *vamos*, let's go, but cf. NAMUS!]

namo/namow *see* NAMMO.

nam shit/weed *see* NAM BLACK.

namus/namous *n.* [mid-19C] someone, esp. as warning *namus!*, someone (is coming)! [backsl.]

nan *n.*[1] [18C] a serving maid. [the proper name or abbr. SE *nanny*]

nan *n.*[2] [mid-19C+] a grandmother; grandmother. [childish mispron.]

nan? *excl.* [mid-18C] what did you say? [SE *anan*, I beg your pardon! What did you say?]

nana *n.* (orig. Aus.) **1** [late 19C+] a ba*nana*. **2** [1940s+] the head. **3** [1940s+] a fool, an idiot, an incompetent, esp. as a *right nana*. [abbr. SE *banana*, a soft (punning on SOFT *adj.*) fruit]

nana/nana-ish *adj.* [late 19C] as used in London's 'gentleman's clubs', outrageous, indecent. [Emile Zola's supposedly indecent novel *Nana* (1880)]

nana cut *n.* [1940s+] (Aus.) a haircut in which the back of the head is closely shaved. [NANA *n.* (2); the hair is cut close to the skull]

nan boy *n.* [late 17C–late 19C] an effeminate or homosexual male (cf. AGNES; MISS JANE; MISS NANCY; NANCY *n.*[2]). [the girl's name *Nan*, then synon. with a serving-maid]

nance *n.* [20C] an effeminate man, a homosexual (cf. NANCY BOY). [NANCY *n.*[2]]

nance *v.* [1960s+] (US) to act or speak in an effeminate or homosexual manner. [NANCE *n.*]

nancified *adj.* [1910s+] effeminate, acting in a homosexual manner. [NANCY *n.*[2]]

nancifully *adv.* [1910s+] effeminately. [NANCY *n.*[2]]

nancy *n.*[1] [early 19C] the buttocks, the posterior; thus the dismissive phr. *ask my nancy.* [? joc. use of proper name]

nancy *n.*[2] [late 19C+] (orig. US) **1** an effeminate or weak-willed person. **2** an effeminate male homosexual (cf. AGNES; MISS NANCY; NAN BOY; NANCE; NANCY BOY; NELLIE *n.*[1]; PANSY). [the female name, but note NANCY *n.*[1]]

nancyball *n.* [1950s+] (Irish) an aniseed ball. [mispron.]

nancy boy *n.* [1950s+] **1** an effeminate man. **2** a homosexual (cf. NAN BOY; NANCY *n.*[2]; NANCE).

Nancy Dawson *n.* [late 19C] an effeminate youth, a homosexual. [NANCY *n.*[2] + proper name *Nancy Dawson*, a legendary 18C prostitute, about whom a sailor's hornpipe was written]

nancy lee *n.* [mid-19C–1930s] **1** a flea. **2** tea (cf. ROSIE LEA). [rhy. sl.]

nancy omey *n.* [late 19C+] (Polari) an effeminate man. [NANCY *n.*[2] + OMEE *n.* (1)]

nancy tales *n.* [late 19C] humbug, nonsense (cf. BR'ER NANCY). [Tshi *ananse*, spider; thus *anansesem*, spider-story; a folk- or fairy-tale found in the Gold Coast and the West Indies]

nan nan *n.* [late 19C] (Aus.) **1** a straw hat. **2** a dandy. **3** one of a gang of youths who sported straw hats as their 'colours'. [? NANCY *n.*[2]]

nanny/nannie *n.*[1] [late 17C–early 19C] a prostitute. [generic use of female proper name]

nanny *n.*[2] [late 18C] (Und.) the head. [ety. unknown]

nanny *n.*[3] [late 19C] a ba*nana* (cf. NANA; TOMMY RABBIT). [abbr.]

nanny *n.*[4] [1940s+] (US) an effeminate man. [NANCY *n.*[2]]

nanny *n.*[5] [1950s+] (S.Afr.) a Black woman, also as a term of address. [SE *nanny*, a nursemaid]

nanny/nanny goat *n.*[6] [1960s+] the totalizator. [rhy. sl. *nanny goat* = TOTE]

nanny goat *n.*[1] [mid–late 19C] an anecdote. [mispron.]

nanny goat *n.*[2] [20C] **1** a coat. **2** a boat. [rhy. sl.]

nanny goat *see* NANNY *n.*[6].

nanny goating *n.* [20C] courting. [rhy. sl., albeit imperfect rhyme]

nanny-goat sweat *n.* [1950s] (US) rough or inferior liquor.

nanny house *n.* [late 17C–early 19C] a brothel (cf. ACCOMMODATION HOUSE). [NANNY *n.*[1] + HOUSE *n.*[1] (1)]

nanny shop *n.* [mid-19C] a brothel (cf. BUTTOCKING SHOP; NANNY HOUSE). [NANNY *n.*[1] + SHOP *n.*[1]]

nanoo *n.* [1960s+] (drugs) heroin. [ety. unknown]

nantee/nanti/nantois/nantoisette/nanty *n.* [mid-19C+] nothing, none, esp. as synon. for phr. *I have none.* [Ling. Fr. *nantee*, none or not; ult. Ital. *niente*, nothing]

nantee/nanti/nanty narking *n.* [early–mid-19C] great fun. [NANTEE + NARK *v.*[1] (3); lit. 'nothing irritating']

nantee!/nanti!/nanty! *excl.* [mid-19C+] Stop! [NANTEE *n.*]

nantee palaver!/parlaree! *excl.* [mid-19C+] shut up! be quiet! [NANTEE + PALAVER *n.*]

nanti *see* NANTEE.

nanti pile in the carpet *phr.* [1980s+] (Polari) bald. [NANTEE *n.* + joc. imagery]

nanti pots in the cupboard *phr.* [1980s+] (Polari) toothless. [NANTEE *n.* + joc imagery]

nanto *n.* [late 19C–1910s] (Aus.) a horse. [? Aborigine language]

nantois/nantoisette *see* NANTEE *n.*

nants *n.* [1950s] nothing. [NANTEE *n.*]

nanty *see* NANTEE.

nanty crackling *n.* [late 19C–1920s] (Polari) the vagina. [NANTEE n. + CRACKLING]

nanty handbag *n.* [1990s] (gay) no money. [NANTEE n. + metonymic use of SE *handbag*]

nanty narking *see* NANTEE NARKING.

nanty worster *n.* [late 19C] (Polari) something that is 'no worse'. [NANTEE n. + SE *worst*]

nantz *n.* [late 17C–mid-19C] brandy (cf. COLD NANTZ; COOL NANTZ). [proper name *Nantes* in France, a centre of cognac production]

nap *n.*[1] [late 17C–18C] a hat. [NAB n.[1]]

nap *n.*[2] [late 17C–early 18C] a dose of venereal disease. [? fig. use of NAP v.[1]; the sufferer has been 'seized' by the disease]

nap *n.*[3] [late 17C–early 18C] an instance of cheating while playing dice. [NAB v.[2]]

nap *n.*[4] [late 17C–late 18C] a sheep, only in phr. *napper of naps*, a sheep stealer. [note *knapper's poll*]

nap *n.*[5] [18C] an arrest. [NAB v.[1]]

nap *n.*[6] [late 18C–19C] strong ale (cf. NAPPY n.). [Scot. *nap*, strong beer]

nap *n.*[7] [late 19C] a moustache, of which the two points form a long line that 'cuts' the face. [abbr. proper name *Napoleon III*, whose visit to London in 1855 made the style fashionable]

nap *n.*[8] [late 19C+] (Aus.) **1** a sleeping bag. **2** blankets or some other covering used by a sleeper in the open-air, a pack (as used in Northern Territory). [SE *nap*, (woollen) cloth that has a nap surface on it or SE *knapsack*; but note SE *nap*, a short sleep]

nap/nap selection *n.*[9] [late 19C+] **1** a tip on the winning chances of a greyhound or horse. **2** the horse or greyhound so tipped. **3** a bet on such a horse or greyhound. [GO NAP]

nap *n.*[10] [1900s–60s] (US Black) a Black person. [SE *nappy*, i.e. tight, curly hair]

Nap *n.*[11] *see* NAP TOWN.

nap *n.*[12] [1940s+] (N.Z.) a *nappy* or diaper. [abbr.]

nap *v.*[1] **1** [mid-16C–mid-19C] to seize, to catch, to lay hold of (a person or thing). **2** [mid-17C–early 19C] to suffer punishment (cf. NAP THE TEIZE). **3** [mid-17C–mid-19C] to steal (cf. NAB v.[1]). **4** [late 17C–mid-18C] to take into custody. [NAB v. or related to Swedish/Norwegian *nappa* or Danish *nappe*, to snatch, snap]

nap *v.*[2] [mid-17C–early 18C] to cheat at dice. [ext. of NAP v.[1]]

nap *v.*[3] [mid-19C] to break, to hit with a hammer. [dial. *knap*]

nap and double *n.* [1930s] trouble. [rhy. sl.]

naph *adj.* [mid-19C+] (Polari) bad. [var. on NAFF adj.[1]]

naphead *see* NAPPY HEAD.

nap it *v.* [mid-17C–early 19C] to receive severe punishment, esp. in a boxing-match. [ext. of NAP v.[1] (2)]

nap it at the nask, to *phr.* [late 17C–early 18C] to receive a judicial flogging at Bridewell. [NAP IT + NASK]

napkin ring *n.* [1980s+] (gay) a penis ring.

napkin snatching *n.* [early 19C] stealing handkerchiefs.

Naples canker *n.* [16C] syphilis (cf. FRENCH CROWN). [racial stereotyping]

Napoleon *n.* [1930s–40s] (US Black) a madman, an eccentric. [the clichéd image of the mad believing that they are Napoleon or some other world figure]

nap on *v.*[1] [late 17C–early 19C] to attack, to strike at. [ext. of NAP v.[1]]

nap on *v.*[2] [late 17C–mid-18C] to attempt to play a cheating trick on. [ext. of NAP v.[2]]

nap one's bib, to *phr.* [late 18C–mid-19C] **1** to cry. **2** to push one's point across, whether through melodramatic tears or other means (cf. NAB ONE'S BIB). [NAP v.[1] + BIB]

napoo *adj.* [1910s–40s] finished, ended. [Fr. *il n'y a plus*, there is no more]

nap or nothing *n.* [late 19C] (club) a bet of 'all or nothing'. [GO NAP]

napper *n.*[1] **1** [mid-17C–18C] a thief, usu. in *napper of naps*, a sheep stealer (cf. NAP n.[4]). **2** [18C] a false witness. [NAP v.[1]]

napper *n.*[2] **1** [late 17C–18C] a hat. **2** [early 18C+] the head. **3** [late 19C–1920s] the mouth. [? NAB n.[1] (1)]

napper *n.*[3] [late 19C] (Ulster) anything large or outstanding of its type. [Yorks. dial. *nap*, expert]

napper *n.*[4] [1990s] (drugs) a sleeping pill (cf. SLEEPER n.[2]). [SE *nap*, a short sleep]

nappers' nulls/nolls *n.* [early 18C] sheep's heads, as food. [NAP n.[4] + NOLL]

napper tandy *n.* (Aus.) a shandy (beer and lemonade). [rhy. sl.]

nappy/nappy ale *n.* [late 17C–18C] drink in general, esp. strong ale. [NAP n.[6]; it goes to one's head]

nappy *adj.* **1** [mid–late 19C] ill-tempered, obdurate. **2** [1980s+] (US teen) disgusting. [horseriding use *nappy*, used of a badly-behaved horse]

nappy ale *see* NAPPY n.

nappy-ass *adj.* [1990s] (US Black teen) referring to one who has nappy hair. [SE *nappy*, of hair, tightly curled + sfx. -ASS]

nappy-black *adj.* [1960s] (US Black) very dark-skinned, with African features. [SE *nappy*, of hair, tightly curled + *black*]

nappy dugout *n.* [1990s] (US Black) the female genitals. [baseball imagery; the dugout where Black players, i.e. those with nappy hair which is typically Black, wait to bat]

nappy head/naphead *n.* [1930s+] (US Black) **1** someone with kinky hair. **2** an unsophisticated Black person (cf. NAP n.[9]). [SE *nappy*, of hair, tightly curled; (2) is ext. of (1) in an era when fashionable Blacks straightened their hair]

nappy valley *n.* [1970s+] (N.Z.) a dormitory suburb, mainly populated by families with young babies. [SE *nappy* + play on *Happy Valley*]

naps *n.* [late 19C–1950s] (US Black) kinky hair. [abbr. SE *nappy*, of hair, tightly curled]

nap selection *see* NAP n.[9].

nap the regulars *see* NAB THE REGULARS.

nap the stoop *see* KNAP THE STOOP.

nap the teize, to *phr.* [late 17C–18C] for a prisoner to be flogged as a punishment while in prison, rather than in public (cf. NAB THE TEIZE). [NAP v.[1] (2) + TEASE v.[1]]

nap the winder, to *phr.* **1** [early 19C] to be transported for life. **2** [mid-19C] to be hanged. **3** [mid-19C–1930s] to receive an unpleasant shock. [NAP v.[1] + WINDER n.[1]]

nap the winding post, to *phr.* [mid-19C] to be transported. [var. on NAP THE WINDER]

Nap Town/Nap *n.* [1920s+] (US) Indianapolis, Indiana. [abbr.]

narangy *n.* [late 19C–1900s] (Aus.) a dandy, a 'swell'. [Dharak *narang*, little; applied to those with authority who rank immediately lower than a station manager]

narc *n.* [1950s+] (US) **1** narcotics. **2** a narcotics agent. **3** any informer. [abbr. SE *narcotics*; but for (3) note NARK n. (1)]

narco *n.* [1950s+] (US) **1** a narcotics officer. **2** the narcotics department of a police station. **3** (drugs) narcotics. **4** (drugs) a drug addict or drug dealer. [abbr.]

narc one over, to *phr.* [1950s+] to betray a drug dealer or user to the narcotics police. [NARC]

narco squad *n.* [1950s+] (US drugs/Und.) the narcotics squad. [abbr.]

nard *n.* [1960s] (US) an obnoxious person. [var. on NERD but note NARDS]

nards *n.* **1** [1960s] (US) genitals. **2** [1990s] (US) the female breasts. [(1) ? GONADS]

narikin *n.* [1910s–20s] a nouveau riche. [synon. Jap.]

nark n. **1** [mid-19C+] a police informer (cf. GRASS n.⁵; KNARK). **2** [mid-19C+] a policeman. **3** [mid-19C+] (mainly Aus./N.Z.) an irritating person, a spoilsport. **4** [20C] spite, rancour, umbrage. **5** [1920s+] any annoying or disagreeable situation. **6** [1970s+] (US teen) a tattletale, a telltale. [Rom. *nak*, nose; (3) to (6) fig. uses of (1)]

nark v.¹ **1** [mid-19C] to watch, to survey. **2** [mid-19C+] to inform to the police (cf. GRASS v.²). **3** [late 19C+] (mainly Aus./N.Z.) to annoy, to irritate. [NARK n.; US use of (2) is 1960s+]

nark v.² [late 19C+] to stop, to terminate, to desist; esp. in excl. *nark it!*, shut up!, stop it!; phr. [1910s+] (Aus.) *I'll nark you*, I'll ruin your plan.

narked adj. [late 19C+] annoyed. [NARK v.¹ (3)]

narker n. [1930s+] an informer. [NARK v.¹ (2)]

narkie adj. [20C] (Aus.) short-tempered (cf. NARKED). [NARK v.¹ (3)]

narking dues n. [late 19C] an arrest made on the evidence of an informer. [NARK n. (1)]

nark the titter! excl. [late 19C] look at that woman! [NARK v.¹ + TITTER]

narky adj. [late 19C+] irascible, bad-tempered, sarcastic. [NARK v.¹ (3)]

nar-nar adj. [1910s–30s] (Aus.) of a man, over-dressed, often effeminately so. [? NANA adj.]

nar nar goon n. [20C] (Aus.) a generic name for any small, insignificant, out of the way place (cf. BEE-LUTHER-HATCHEE). [*Nar Nar Goon*, a small town southeast of Melbourne]

narp n. [mid-19C+] a shirt. [Scot.]

narrative n. [late 19C] (middle class) a dog's tail. [pun on SE *narrative*, a tale]

narrow adj. [mid-18C] never a, not a, not one. [? SE *nary*, no, not (a)]

narrish adj. [late 19C] (society) thrifty, mean. [SE *narrow*]

narrow-assed adj. [1910s–60s] (US) slim, skinny. [SE *narrow* + ASS]

narrowback n. [1930s+] **1** (US) an Irish person, esp. a second-generation immigrant. **2** (US) a Protestant. **3** (Irish) an immigrant who returns from the US to live in Ireland. [? their stereotyped physique or Ulster dial. *narrow*, mean, miserly]

narrow in the shoulder phr. [1910s–20s] lacking a sense of humour. [the hunched shoulders of a miserable person]

narrow lane n. [mid-16C] the throat.

narsum n. [late 17C] (Irish) the buttocks, the behind. [ARSE n.¹ (1)]

nasal adv. [1980s+] (US campus) no; thus *nasal on that*, forget it, no chance. [pun on *na(sal)/nay*]

nase/nace adj. [mid-16C] (Und.) drunken, intoxicated (cf. NAZIE). [ety. 'obscure' (*OED*) but B&L suggest Ger. *nass*, wet; given the trad. association of red noses and drunkards there might be a link to obs. 14C SE *nase*, nose]

nase/nazy nab n. [late 17C–early 19C] **1** a red nose. **2** a drunkard. [NASE adj./NAZIE + NEB n.¹ (3)]

nash n. [1950s+] (W.I. Rasta) the female genitalia. [Carib.E. *nash*, soft, effeminate; ult. Eng. dial. *nesh*, juicy, succulent, tender]

nash v. [19C] to leave, to rush off (cf. MR NASH IS CONCERNED). [Rom. *nash, nasher*, to run]

nash gab n. [19C] a cheeky person (cf. RUN AT THE MOUTH). [Rom. *nash*, to run + GAB n.]

nasho n. [1960s–70s] (Aus.) **1** national service. **2** a national serviceman. [abbr. *national* + sfx. -O; Aus. national service was discontinued in 1972]

Nashville n. [1970s] (US Black) any unsophisticated, suburban, middle-American town or person. [*Nashville*, Tennessee, with its links to country music as the epitome of middle-American values]

nask/naskin n. [late 17C–early 19C] a prison, (spec. in London, the *Old Nask*, the City Bridewell, the *New Nask*, the Clerkenwell prison and *Tuttle Nask*, in Tothill Fields).

Nassau nigger n. [1940s+] (US) a Black person from the Bahamas or Jamaica. [*Nassau*, the capital of the Bahamas + NIGGER n.]

nasties n. **1** [20C] (US Black) sexual desire, lust (cf. NASTY n.¹). **2** [1960s+] (US) any unpleasant, disgusting, threatening or scary things or persons. **3** [1980s] (drugs) drugs, of any variety.

nastiness n. [1950s] (W.I.) homosexuality or bestiality (cf. RUDENESS n.). [euph.]

nasty n.¹ **1** [mid-19C] the vagina (cf. JACK NASTY FACE). **2** [1960s–70s] sexual intercourse; thus *do the nasty*, to have sexual intercourse (cf. NAUGHTY n.). [an acknowledgment, if not an agreement, with the Western ambivalence as regards sexuality]

nasty n.² [1980s+] anything unpleasant, varying as to context.

nasty adj. [mid-19C] (orig. US) **1** first-class, exciting, particularly enjoyable. **2** attractive, sexy (cf. AWFUL adj.). [on bad = good model]

nasty adv. [1990s] (US teen) extremely (whether pleasant or unpleasant), e.g. *nasty cool*, very cool indeed.

nasty bit/piece of work n. [1920s+] an unpleasant person.

nastygram n. [1980s+] (US, orig. milit.) an unpleasant note or letter or a communication that brings bad news. [SE *nasty* + *(tele)gram*]

nastyman n. **1** [mid–late 19C] the member of the garrotting team who actually does the choking (cf. BACKSTALL). **2** [1950s–60s] (US Black) a sexual pervert.

nasty-mouthed adj. [20C] (W.I.) foul-mouthed, given to using obscene language.

nasty piece of work see NASTY BIT OF WORK.

nasty up v. [20C] (W.I.) to make a mess of, to dirty.

nat n. [late 19C+] (Ulster) a small person. [? SE *gnat*]

Natal fever n. [20C] (S.Afr.) a sense of laziness and resultant inactivity, attributed to the hot climate of Natal.

Natal rum n. [late 19C] (S.Afr.) rough, strong brandy, distilled in Natal (cf. CAPE SMOKE).

natarnal/netarnal adj. [20C] (Irish) used to express disgust (cf. TARNAL). [pron. SE *eternal*, infinite, in the sense of wearisome, tedious, loathsome]

natch adv. [1940s+] (orig. US) naturally. [abbr.]

natchie n.¹ [1930s–40s] (gambling) a winning combination, esp. in craps. [abbr. NATURAL n.⁴ (1)]

natchie n.² see NATURAL n.⁶.

natch trips n. [1960s] (drugs) a variety of quasi-drug experiences gained from smoking such natural substances as nutmeg, banana, mace etc. [SE *natural* + TRIP n.³ (1)]

nathan n. [1990s] (US Black teen) nothing. [? pron. of SE]

-nation sfx. [20C] (W.I.) a general sfx. used widely to define, usu. derog., various sub-groups in the Caribbean; thus *buck nation*, the Amerindian people of Guyana; *Chinee nation*, Chinese people; *coolie nation*, East Indians; *high nation*, a high caste East Indian; *low nation*, a low caste East Indian; used alone as *nation*, a disreputable or unpleasant person (cf. NO-NATION). [? trans. of Hind. *jaat*, class, kind, race]

'nation adj. [late 18C–late 19C] very much, exceedingly. [abbr. DAMNATION!]

National, the n. **1** [1940s] *National* Assistance. **2** [1940s+] the Grand *National* Steeplechase, at Aintree racecourse. [abbr.]

national exhibition n. [mid-19C] an execution at the Old Bailey. [coined by playwright and *Punch* contributor Douglas Jerrold (1803–57), punning on the Great Exhibition of 1851; public execution continued in the UK until 1868]

national front n. [20C] a general term of abuse. [rhy. sl. *National Front* = CUNT n.²]

national hunt n. [20C] audacity, cheek. [rhy. sl. *National Hunt* = FRONT n.¹ (1)]

national/great national indoor game n. [late 19C+] (Aus.) sexual intercourse. [note the *great Australian game* is two-up]

native n. [late 18C] (Irish) illicitly distilled whisky, poteen. [? abbr. *native brew*]

native cavalry n. [early–mid-19C] unbroken horses, used by country people, as opposed to those ridden by townsmen.

Nat King Cole n. [20C] **1** the dole. **2** a mole (on the skin). **3** a bread roll. [rhy. sl. US singer Nat King Cole (1919–65)]

natomy/nattermy n. [19C] a small, thin and/or deformed person (cf. ATOMY; OTTOMY). [abbr. SE *anatomy*]

natter n. [1940s+] a chat, a light conversation. [NATTER v.]

natter v. [1940s+] to chat, to gossip. [? dial. *gnatter*, to grumble, to 'rattle on' or *natter*, to nag; note services sl. *natter party*, a conference which leads nowhere; *natter can*, one who talks too much]

nattermy see NATOMY.

nattum n. [20C] (Aus.) sexual intercourse. [? *get at 'em*]

natty/natty congo/dread n. [1950s+] (W.I. Rasta) **1** dreadlocks. **2** a person with dreadlocks. [SE *natural* + the Congo/DREAD]

natty adj. **1** [late 18C] well-dressed, smart. **2** [late 18C–mid-19C] neat, spruce. **3** [mid–late 19C] adept with the hands, skilful. [all SE by late 19C]

natty congo/dread see NATTY n.

natty lad n. [late 18C–early 19C] a young thief or pickpocket. [NATTY (3) + SE *lad*]

natural n.¹ **1** [mid-16C–19C] a prostitute. **2** [late 17C+] an idiot, a fool because untutored, unsophisticated; often the potential victim of a confidence trick. **3** [late 18C–early 19C] an illegitimate child. [the images are of a 'state of nature']

natural n.² **1** [late 18C+] (orig. US) one who is naturally suited to a job or skill; one who is naturally talented. **2** [1920s+] (US) something certain to succeed, a winner. [now SE]

natural n.³ **1** [late 19C+] one's life. **2** [1930s] (US) a life sentence. [it lasts 'all one's *natural* life']

natural n.⁴ [1930s–40s] **1** (gambling) a winning combination, esp. in craps. **2** (US prison) a 7-year sentence (suggested by a throw of 7 in craps). [abbr. SE *natural winner*]

natural n.⁵ [1930s+] (US Black) one's self. [abbr. SE *natural-born self*]

natural/natchie n.⁶ [1960s+] (US Black) a bushy hairstyle, in which one's hair is allowed to grow naturally, rather than being subjected to straightening or similar styling (cf. AFRO n.²).

natural-born adj. [1910s+] (US Black) by nature, as if born to.

natural-born man n. [1930s+] (US Black) a 'real' (i.e. heterosexual) man, a good lover, an honest, unpretentious person. [the premise is that a 'natural' person is not hidebound by social conditioning etc]

natural draft n. [20C] (Ulster) someone or something identical, the 'living image'. [SE *natural* + *draft*, a plan or sketch]

natural pick/pick n. [1960s–70s] (US Black) a large comb used spec. for tidying an AFRO n.² or 'natural' hairstyle. [NATURAL n.⁶ + SE *pick*, a pointed tool, here a comb]

natural woman n. [1930s+] (US Black) the female version of NATURAL-BORN MAN.

nature n. **1** [19C] euph. for the vagina. **2** [1970s+] (US Black) one's libido, one's sex-drive (cf. LOT OF NATURE).

nature boy n. [1940s+] (US) a naïve or unsophisticated young man.

nature calls phr. [20C] a euph. excuse used when one wishes to visit the lavatory.

nature hike n. [1980s+] (US drugs) a long walk with no particular destination, enjoyed while intoxicated by a drug.

nature's call n. [20C] the desire to urinate.

nature's duty n. [19C] sexual intercourse.

nature's founts n. [19C] the female breasts. [literary euph.]

nature's privy seal n. [19C] the hymen; also as *Dame Nature's ...* (cf. NATURE). [pun]

nature's scythe n. [19C] the penis.

nature's treasury n. [19C] the vagina (cf. BEAUTY SPOT n.¹).

nature's tufted treasure n. [19C] the vagina (cf. BEAUTY SPOT n.¹). [joc./euph. use of SE]

natwas n. [1930s+] nothing (cf. NANTEE n.; NANTS). [ety. unknown; ? pron. of SE *not was*, i.e. nothing; or link to Ital. *niente*, nothing]

naughties n. [1950s+] sexual liaisons, intercourse (cf. NASTY n.¹).

Naughton and Gold adj. [20C] cold. [rhy. sl.; ult. Charlie Naughton (1887–1976) and Jimmy Gold (1886–1967), music-hall stars and members of the Crazy Gang (1935–62)]

naughty n. **1** [mid-19C–1900s] the vagina. **2** [1950s+] (mainly Aus./N.Z.) sexual intercourse, esp. in phr. *do the naughty*, *go naughty*, to have sex (cf. NASTY n.¹). **3** [1970s+] an injury; thus *do oneself a naughty*, to injure oneself.

naughty adj. **1** [mid-19C–1900s] flashy, vulgarly over-dressed. **2** [1960s+] (Und.) criminal, violent, corrupt.

naughty bits n. [1970s+] the genitals, of either sex. [this quite deliberate euph. was coined *c.*1969 by the Monty Python's Flying Circus comedy team]

naughty dickey-bird/pack n. [19C] a prostitute. [NAUGHTY adj. (1) + ext. of BIRD n.⁵/SE *pack* (cf. BAGGAGE n.²)]

nauky/knackety/knacky/knawky/nawky adj. [late 19C+] (Ulster) cunning, resourceful. [Scot. *knaw*; ult. SE *know*]

naus n. [1950s+] an unpleasant person. [pron. as abbr. of SE *naus(eating)* and commonly used with a derog. implication, but in fact rhy. sl. *Noah's* = Noah's Ark = NARK n. (3)]

nause n. [1950s+] the problem, the difficulty, the annoying thing. [abbr. SE *nauseating*]

nause v. [1950s+] to cause problems, to annoy, to ruin a plan. [NAUSE n.]

nauseous adj. [late 18C–early 19C; 1980s+] unpleasant, distasteful; thus joc. *nauseous toad*, an affectionate term of address. [20C is mainly US campus/teen]

nausie n. [1950s+] (Aus.) a recently arrived immigrant. [SE *new* + AUSSIE]

nautch/nautchery/nautch house/nautch joint n. [late 19C–1940s] (US) a brothel. [Urdu/Hind. *nāch*, dancing, usu. as an exhibition of Indian dancing, thus a *nautch girl*, a dancing girl; the image of the 'exotic' East led inevitably to assumptions of sexual license + HOUSE n.¹ (1)/JOINT n.³ (3)]

nautch broad n. [1940s] (US) a prostitute working in a brothel. [NAUTCH + BROAD n.² (1)]

nautchery see NAUTCH.

nautch house see NAUTCH.

nautch joint see NAUTCH.

nautical miles/nauticals n. [20C] haemorrhoids. [rhy. sl. *nautical miles* = piles]

Navajo time n. [20C] (US) unpunctuality (cf. AFRICAN PEOPLE'S TIME). [racist stereotyping]

naval engagement n. [1940s+] (orig. milit.) sexual intercourse. [pun on SE *naval/navel*]

navigator of the windward passage n. [1990s] a sodomite, a male homosexual. [play on SE]

navigators n. [mid-19C] potatoes; thus *navigator scot*, potatoes all hot. [rhy. sl.; the connection with the predominantly Irish *navigators* (cf. NAVVY n.¹), builders of Victorian Britain's railways and canals, whose stereotype consumed many potatoes, may or may not be coincidental]

navvy n.¹ [early–mid-19C] **1** a labourer working on the railways, canals and roads of Victorian Britain. **2** any unskilled labourer. [SE f. 1860; abbr. 18C *navigator*, a labourer excavating canals, later any earthwork]

Navvy/navvy *n.*[2] [1910s+] (US, mainly southwest) a Navaho or a Navaho pony. [abbr.]

navvy's piano *n.* [1920s+] a pneumatic drill.

navvy's prayer-book *n.* [late 19C–1900s] a shovel. [NAVVY + SE *prayer-book;* the 'prayerful' posture the shoveller has to adopt]

navy *n.* [1900s–60s] a cigar or cigarette end left burning on the pavement. [*Navy* Cut, a brand of tobacco]

navy fish *n.* [1930s+] a beard worn in the RN manner (cf. MAN OF WAR).

Navy Office, the *n.* [early–mid-19C] the Fleet Prison. [pun on *fleet/Fleet;* the prison name refers to the Fleet River, itself f. OE *fléot,* a tidal inlet; thus note *Commander of the Fleet,* the governor]

nawky *see* NAUKY.

naybo!/nayboo!/nayo! *excl.* [1940s+] (US Black) used to express disagreement (cf. NEIGHBO POPS). [? SE *nay, no* + BO n.[1]]

nay-nay *adj.* [20C] (W.I.) insignificant, worthless. [Scot./Irish *nig-nay,* a trifle, a plaything; but note Igbo *neni,* to disregard, to despise]

nay nays *n.* [1950s+] the female breasts. [NINNIES]

nayo! *see* NAYBO!

Nazarene foretop *n.* [late 18C–early 19C] an ornamental wig made in imitation of Christ's head of hair, as represented by painters. [SE *Nazarene,* a synon. for Christ + *foretop,* the lock of hair (whether real or in a wig) that covers the crown of the head]

nazie/nazy *n.* [late 17C–mid-19C] drunk (cf. NAZIE COVE; NAZIE MORT). [for ety. *see* NASE]

nazie cove/mort *n.* [late 17C–19C] a drunken man (*cove*) or woman (*mort*). [NAZIE + COVE/MORT]

Nazi spy *n.* [1940s+] (Aus.) a meat pie. [rhy. sl.]

nazold *n.* [early 17C] a silly, vain or weak-minded person. [SE *nazzard,* an insignificant or feeble person]

nazy *see* NAZIE.

nazy nab *see* NASE NAB.

nazz *n.* [1990s] (US teen) a fool.

nazzy *adj.* [mid-19C] drunk. [NAZIE]

n.b. *adj.*[1] [1900s–10s] penniless, impoverished. [*not* a *bean* + pun on SE *N.B., nota bene,* i.e. beware of such a pauper]

n.b. *adj.*[2] [1970s+] (society) a note appended to names of potential male escorts by debutantes or their mothers to indicate that they were not socially acceptable. [abbr. *no* background]

n.b.d. *phr.* [1980s+] (US campus) a general expression of nonchalance. [abbr. *no big deal*]

n.b.g. *phr.* [20C] *no bloody good.* [abbr.]

n.c. *n.* [1980s+] (US campus) a boorish person (cf. N.C.A.A.). [abbr. *no class*]

n.c. *phr.* [mid-19C–1900s] (US) enough said, it is possible to infer all the facts from what has already been stated (cf. N.S.). [abbr. NUF CED; 'a certain theatrical manager spells [the words], it is said, in this style' (Hotten, 1867)]

n.c.a.a. *n.* [1980s+] (US campus) a boorish person (cf. N.C. n.). [abbr. *no class* at all + a jibe at the sporting *NCAA,* National Collegiate Athletic Assoc.; pron. 'NC double-A']

n.c.d. *see* NO CAN DO.

n.d. *n.* [late 19C] (society) a woman who is attempting to appear younger than she is. [the bibliographical annotation *n.d., no date*]

Neapolitan favour *n.* [16C] syphilis (cf. FRENCH CROWN). [contemporary stereotyping of Italians as pox-ridden]

near/nearbone *n.* [1930s+] (Ulster) a miser.

near and far *n.* [late 19C–1920s] a public house bar. [rhy. sl.]

near as a toucher *phr.* [early 19C+] very nearly, almost;

as near as possible to actually doing/achieving something; the synon. *within a toucher* appears to be a solecism of P.G. Wodehouse (1881–1975)]

near as dammit *phr.* [late 19C+] very near indeed. [abbr. phr. 'near as dammit is to swearing']

near/like as fourpence to a groat *phr.* [mid-16C–late 18C] virtually indistinguishable. [SE *groat,* a fourpenny coin]

near as makes no difference *phr.* [1930s+] virtually the same, almost indistinguishable.

near as no matter *phr.* [late 19C+] very near.

nearbone *see* NEAR.

neardy *n.* [mid-19C] a boss, a master, an overseer. [northern dial. *near,* grasping, covetous]

nearer my God to thee *n.* [1930s–40s] (US Black) straight, silky hair, seen as a badge of Whiteness. [ironic use, the *God* in question being White and the subject's aspirations disapproved of by more politically motivated Black peers]

nearer the bone the sweeter the meat, the *phr.* [1930s] a phr. used of a notably thin woman. [pvb.]

near go *n.* [mid-19C] a near thing a 'close shave'. [SE *near* + GO n.[3]]

nearly lose one's eyesight, to *phr.* [mid-19C+] to gain an unexpected and voyeuristically intimate sight of a member of the opposite sex (cf. FLASH n.[4]).

near-sighted *adj.* [1920s+] (gay) uncircumcised, esp. of an uncircumcised penis with its tip protruding slightly above the foreskin (cf. BLIND adj.[3]).

near the knuckle *phr.* [late 19C+] at the very limit of decency, often as *it's a bit near the knuckle.*

near the mark *phr.* [1950s+] somewhat corrupt, not wholly honest. [SE *mark,* the limit]

neat *adj.* **1** [early 19C] in ironic use, rare, fine, delightful. **2** [1930s+] (orig./mainly US) a term of general approval, pleasant, satisfactory, attractive.

neat as a band-box/new pin *phr.* [early 19C–1900s] first-rate, excellent (cf. NEAT AS NINEPENCE; NEAT AS WAX).

neat as a bee's toe *phr.* [20C] (Ulster) very neat.

neat as ninepence *phr.* [17C] first-rate, excellent (cf. NEAT AS A BAND-BOX). [? SE *ninepins,* which must be arranged properly before a game begins]

neat as wax *phr.* [mid-19C–1900s] first-rate, excellent (cf. NEAT AS A BAND-BOX).

neatnik *n.* [1950s+] (US) someone devoted to neatness and order. [SE *neat* + sfx. -NIK]

neato! *excl.* [1950s+] (US teen) a general excl. of approbation, congratulation.

neato jet! *excl.* [1990s] (US teen) extremely excellent, absolutely wonderful. [ext. of NEATO!]

neb *n.*[1] **1** [late 17C–early 19C] the mouth. **2** [late 17C–early 19C] the face. **3** [late 19C+] (Ulster) the nose. [SE *neb,* a bird's beak; the term dates back to the *Ancren Riwle,* a devotional work composed *c.*1225]

neb *n.*[2] [1920s–40s] (US) a nobody. [abbr. NEBBISH]

neb *n.*[3] *see* NEBBIE.

neb *v.* [late 19C+] (Ulster) to interfere, to 'poke one's nose in'. [NEB n.[1] (3)]

nebbich *see* NEBBISH.

nebbie/neb *n.* [1950s+] *Nemb*utal, a barbiturate (cf. NEMBIE). [abbr.]

nebbish/nebbich/nebich *n.* [late 19C+] a harmless eccentric, a born loser, a nobody. [synon. Yid. *nebech*]

nebby *adj.*[1] [late 19C+] (Ulster) **1** nosy, inquisitive. **2** cheeky. [NEB n.[1] (3)]

nebby *adj.*[2] [1990s] (US) very unsophisticated. [NEBBISH]

nebich *see* NEBBISH.

nebo *n.* [1960s] (Aus.) a drunkard. [abbr. SE *inebriated* + sfx. -O]

nebuary/nebruary morning *n.* [20C] (W.I.) never. [SE *ne(ver)* + *(Fe)bruary*]

nebuchadnezzar *n.*[1] [19C] the penis; thus *take Nebuchadnezzar out to grass* of a man, to have sexual intercourse. [*Nebuchadnezzar* II, (*c.*630–*c.*562 BC) King of Babylon; play on GREENS *n.*[2] and the King's madness, during which period he ate grass]

nebuchadnezzar *n.*[2] **1** [mid-19C] (Aus.) a salad. **2** [mid-19C–1900s] a vegetarian. [SE *greens* + *see* NEBUCHADNEZZAR *n.*[2]]

necessaries *n.* **1** [17C] the lavatory. **2** [20C] the genitals. [euph.]

necessary *n.* **1** [early 17C–mid-19C] an outhouse, a privy (cf. NECESSARY HOUSE). **2** [late 18C–early 19C] a bedfellow, usu. a female one. **3** [late 19C+] money (cf. NEEDFUL). [all plays on the supposed necessity of such items; post mid-19C use of (1) is US]

necessary house *n.* [early 17C–mid-19C] an outhouse, a privy (cf. NECESSARY).

neck *n.*[1] [late 19C+] audacity, daring (cf. BROW); thus *stick one's neck out*, to chance one's luck. [abbr. BRASS NECK]

neck *n.*[2] [1940s+] (US campus) **1** the act of kissing and cuddling. **2** one with whom one kisses and cuddles (cf. NECKER). [NECK *v.*[4]]

neck *n.*[3] [1960s+] (US) a poor farmer, usu. Southern and presumably racist and unsophisticated. [abbr. REDNECK *n.*[1] (1)]

neck *v.*[1] [16C+] to swallow, either alcohol or (latterly) drugs (cf. NECK OIL).

neck *v.*[2] **1** [mid-19C–1900s] (US Und.) to seize by the neck. **2** [mid-19C–1900s] (US) to apprehend and arrest. **3** [1940s+] (Aus.) to kill oneself by hanging. **4** [1940s+] (Aus.) to garrotte.

neck *v.*[3] [1910s–30s] (US) to stare. [abbr. RUBBERNECK *v.*[1]]

neck *v.*[4] [1920s+] (orig. US) to pursue sexual pleasure that stops short of intercourse; usu. teen use and practice; thus *necking* (cf. SNOG). [orig. UK dial. *neck*, to court; i.e. to put one's arm around someone's neck]

neck and crop *adv.* [19C] bodily, completely, altogether. [i.e. the entire throat area; SE f. 1890]

neck and heels *adv.* [late 19C] impetuously, spontaneously. [? one commits every part of the body]

neck and neck *adv.* [mid–late 19C] on equal terms. [SE post-1890; horse-racing jargon]

neck basting *n.* [late 19C–1900s] drinking. [SE *neck* + *baste*, to moisten, usu. in culinary context]

neckbreak/neck-break it *v.* [1950s+] (US Black) to move fast.

neck cloth/squeezer *n.* [early–mid-19C] a hangman's rope (cf. NECKLACE *n.*; NECKTIE *n.*; SCRAG SQUEEZER; SQUEEZER).

necker *n.* [1920s+] (US) one who engages in NECKING *n.*[1] (cf. NECK *n.*[2]). [NECK *v.*[4]]

necking *n.*[1] [1960s+] kissing and cuddling. [NECK *v.*[4]]

necking *n.*[2] [1960s] (Aus.) a means of pickpocketing whereby the thief puts one arm around his victim's neck and the other into his pocket. [NECK *n.*[2] (1)]

neckinger *n.* [mid-19C] a cravat (cf. MUCKENDER). [it goes round the SE *neck*]

neck it *v.* [mid–late 19C] to stand, to exhibit moral courage. [NECK *n.*[1]]

neck job *n.* [1990s] strangulation. [SE *neck* + JOB *n.*[5]]

necklace *n.* **1** [17C] the neck. **2** [mid-17C–1960s] a hangman's noose (cf. NECK CLOTH). **3** [1940s+] (Aus.) a garrotter. **4** [1980s+] (S.Afr.) a petrol-soaked tyre, placed around a victim's neck and then set on fire.

necklace *v.* [1980s+] (orig. S.Afr.) to murder by placing a petrol-soaked tyre around a victim's neck and setting it alight. [NECKLACE *n.* (4)]

necklaced *adj.* [1970s] (US Black) extremely sophisticated, worldly. ['laced by the neck']

necklace/necktie artist *n.* [1940s+] (Aus.) a garrotter. [NECKLACE *n.* (2)/NECKTIE *n.* (1) + ARTIST *n.*[2]]

neck oil *n.* [mid-19C+] alcohol, usu. beer. [SE *neck* + *oil* + note NECK *v.*[1]]

neck or nothing *phr.* [late 17C–mid-19C] desperately, 'come what may'. [? the imagery of horseracing or of capital punishment]

neck squeezer *see* NECK CLOTH.

neck stamper *n.* [late 17C–early 19C] a tavern pot-boy. [? he 'stamps' around carrying bottle by the 'neck']

neck stretcher *n.* [1930s–40s] (US) a garrotter (cf. NECKLACE ARTIST).

neck sugar *n.* [20C] (US Black) a kiss (cf. SUGAR *n.*[3]).

necktie *n.* [19C] **1** the hangman's noose. **2** the gallows (cf. NECK CLOTH).

necktie *v.* [mid-19C+] (US) to hang, to lynch. [NECKTIE PARTY]

necktie artist *see* NECKLACE ARTIST.

necktie party/frolic/sociable/social *n.* [mid-19C+] (US) a hanging, usu. an illicit, impromptu lynching. [NECKTIE *n.*]

neck-to-knees *n.* [1910s–40s] (Aus.) an old fashioned bathing costume which completely covered that area of the body. [the wearing of such costumes was actually commanded by law in a number of popular resorts, starting with those in New South Wales, under an act of 1902]

neck twister *n.* [mid-19C] (US) a form of cocktail. [its effect]

neck verse *n.* [late 18C–early 19C] a Latin verse recited as a means of escaping the gallows. [anyone claiming benefit of clergy, and thus exemption from the gallows, was obliged to read in Lat. the first verse of Ps. 60; the aim was to weed out false clergymen]

neck warmer *n.* [1940s+] (Aus.) a nightdress. [its being pushed up to the neck during sexual intercourse]

neckweed *n.* [mid-16C–early 19C] **1** hemp, the basic constituent of the rope used for the gallows. **2** the hangman's rope itself.

nectar *n.* **1** [19C] a drink. **2** [1980s+] (US campus) alcohol. **3** [1980s +] (US campus) anything exceptionally wonderful. [SE *nectar*, popularly, albeit incorrectly known as the food of the gods (which is in fact *ambrosia*); note use of *amber nectar* in adverts for Foster's (Aus.) lager]

nec ultra *n.* [late 19C] (society) the West End of London, thus the fashionable world. [Lat. *nec ultra*, and not beyond; the line beyond which one might not go was Temple Bar, the line between the West End and the City]

ned *n.*[1] **1** [mid-18C–mid-19C] a guinea (cf. MONARCH *n.*[2]); thus *half-ned*, half a guinea. **2** [mid-19C–1920s] (US) a $10 gold piece; thus *half-a-ned*, a $5 gold piece. [ety. unknown; ? joc. use of proper name on pattern of JEMMY O'GOBLIN]

Ned *n.*[2] [mid-19C–1960s] (US) the Devil, usu. constructed with 'raise', e.g. *raising merry Ned*, causing a commotion, trouble (cf. NICK *n.*[1]; OLD NED *n.*[1]). [generic use of proper name]

ned *n.*[3] **1** [mid-19C–1960s] (US) salt pork or bacon, usu. constructed with *old*. **2** [mid–late 19C] (US) a soldier, whose diet is mainly pork. **3** [1960s] (US Black) a Black person who curries favour with White society (cf. UNCLE TOM *n.*). [orig. Ozark use *ned*, boar and thus generic for any pig; (3) ? the image of such a figure being effectively a PIG *n.*[1] (1)]

ned *n.*[4] [1910s+] (orig. Aus.) the head (cf. NEDDYVAUL). [? rhy. sl.]

ned *n.*[5] [1950s–70s] a hooligan, a thug, a petty criminal. [equation with the SE *Teddy Boy*, or 'Edwardian', i.e. another nickname for *Edward*]

nedash *n.* [early 19C] nothing. [Rom. *nastis*, I cannot]

neddies, the *n.* [20C] (Aus.) the sport of horse-racing. [NEDDY *n.*[1] (3)]

neddy *n.*[1] **1** [17C–1960s] a donkey (cf. BALDWIN). **2** [early 19C+] a fool, a simpleton. **3** [late 19C+] (Aus.) a horse, esp. a race-horse.

neddy *n.*[2] [mid-18C–mid-19C] a guinea. [ext. NED n.[1] (1)]

neddy *n.*[3] [mid–late 19C] (Und.) a cosh, blackjack or life-preserver. [abbr. KENNEDY]

neddy *n.*[4] [mid-19C+] (Irish) a good deal, a considerable amount. [ety. unknown]

neddy *n.*[5] [late 19C] the tucker-bag carried by an itinerant tramp (cf. SWAGMAN n.[2]). [? play on use of MATILDA for the swag itself, to which it is tied; it dangles 'from her apron-strings' (*AND*)]

neddyvaul *n.* [late 19C] a chief, a leader, a commander. [Cockney pron. of *ned of all*, a pun on NED n.[4]; i.e. the head of all]

ned fool *n.* [late 16C–early 17C] a noisy fool, a simpleton. [generic use of proper name *Ned* + SE *fool*]

Ned Kelly *n.*[1] **1** [20C] (Aus.) an unscrupulous businessman; thus *Kelly gang*, an unethical business, a tax-grabbing government. **2** [1930s+] (Aus.) a poker machine. [like *Ned Kelly*, a bushranger (1855–80), they are all robbers]

Ned Kelly *n.*[2] **1** [1920s+] (Aus.) the stomach. **2** [1970s] the television. [rhy. sl. *Ned Kelly* = (1) belly, (2) telly; ult. bush-ranger Ned Kelly (1855–80)]

Ned Kelly *n.*[3] [1920s+] (Aus.) a 'blood-and-thunder' romance. [the dramatic adventures of bushranger *Ned Kelly* (1855–80)]

Ned Kelly *v.* **1** [1900s] to bushrange. **2** [1950s] to kill a bird or any other game unsportingly. [NED KELLY n.[3]]

ned skinner *n.* [late 19C] dinner. [rhy. sl.]

ned stokes *n.* [mid-19C] the 4 of spades. [ety. unknown; ? anecdotal]

neecee princess *n.* [late 19C–1920s] (society) a *nouveau riche* young woman. [London postal district *E*ast *C*entral, the City, as a centre of commerce, however rewarding, supposedly beyond the social pale]

need a foghorn, to *phr.* [1980s] (US campus/teen) to be utterly confused or lost (cf. FOGGY).

needful *n.* **1** [late 18C–1900s] money (cf. BALLAST n.[1]; COLE; CORKS n.[1]; FEATHERS n.[1]; NECESSARY; WHEREWITH). **2** [mid-late 19C] (US) whisky. [the necessity of money or money to life]

needing a reef taken in *phr.* [19C] (orig. naut.) drunk (cf. AFLOAT).

needle *n.*[1] [mid-17C–mid-18C; 1930s–60s] the penis (cf. NEEDLE WOMAN; NEEDLEWORK; SEW). [later usage US]

needle/rank needle *n.*[2] [late 18C–early 19C] a cheat, a card-sharp. [like a *needle*, he is very 'sharp'/SE *rank*, extreme]

needle *n.*[3] [mid-19C+] (orig. tailoring jargon) resentment, bitterness, irritation; thus *get the needle*, to become annoyed.

needle *n.*[4] [1930s–60s] (US) repetitious nagging and complaining. [image of a phonograph needle going round and round]

needle *n.*[5] [1930s+] (drugs) **1** a hypodermic, a syringe; thus *on the needle*, addicted. **2** a narcotic's addict (cf. HYPE n.[2]).

needle *n.*[6] [1970s] a knife.

needle *v.*[1] **1** [early 19C] to haggle, esp. if one takes advantage of the other person. **2** [late 19C+] to annoy, to tease maliciously. **3** [late 19C+] (Irish) to scrounge. [NEEDLE n.[3]]

needle *v.*[2] [1920s–30s] (US) to add alcohol or ether to a non-alcoholic beer or drink, usu. by injection through the cork (cf. NEEDLE BEER). [NEEDLE n.[5]]

needle *v.*[3] [1950s–60s] (US) to apply maximum power or acceleration to a vehicle or plane. [thus moving the speedo-meter *needle*]

needle and cotton *adj.* [20C] rotten. [rhy. sl.]

needle and pin *n.* [1930s+] gin. [rhy. sl.]

needle and pin *adj.* [1930s+] thin. [rhy. sl.]

needle and thread *n.* [mid-19C–1930s] bread. [rhy. sl.]

needle artist/fiend/jabber/pumper *n.* [1920s+] (US drugs) an intravenous drug addict (cf. NEEDLE FREAK). [the use of a hypodermic syringe + ARTIST n.[2]]

needle/needled beer *n.* [1920s–30s] (US) beer that has been strengthened by pure alcohol or ether. [NEEDLE v.[2]]

needlecase *n.* [19C] the vagina (cf. COCK-HOLDER; PIN-CASE). [NEEDLE n.[1] + SE *case*]

needled beer *see* NEEDLE BEER.

needle dick *n.* [1960s+] (US) **1** a particularly small penis. **2** the man who has one. [SE *needle* + DICK n.[5] (1)]

needle dodger *n.* [mid-19C–1920s] a dressmaker (cf. NEEDLE JERKER; NEEDLE PUSHER).

needle fiend *see* NEEDLE ARTIST.

needle freak *n.* **1** [1960s–70s] (US drugs) an intravenous drug user who is as stimulated by the act of injection as by the action of the drug. **2** [1970s+] a prostitute's sadistic client who derives pleasure from hiring a woman with large breasts and paying her for every needle she permits him to stick into her flesh. [NEEDLE n.[5]/SE *needle* + sfx. -FREAK]

needle jabber *see* NEEDLE ARTIST.

needle jerker *n.* [19C] a tailor (cf. NEEDLE DODGER).

needle man/needleman *n.* **1** [1920s–50s] (drugs) a drug addict. **2** [1960s+] (US) a doctor. [NEEDLE n.[5]; the use of a hypo-dermic syringe]

needlenosed *adj.* [1940s–70s] (US) having a pointed nose; thus *needlenose*, one who has such a nose. [occas. but not invariably, used of Jews]

needle park *n.* [1960s+] (drugs) a variety of locations in New York City, small oases of grass in the larger world of streets and buildings, frequented by heroin users. [orig. the traffic island at Broadway and 74th Street; the term was popularized by James Mill's 1966 book *The Panic in Needle Park*]

needle point/pointer *n.* [late 17C–early 19C] a card-sharp or dice cheat. [like a *needle*, he is 'sharp']

needle pumper *see* NEEDLE ARTIST.

needle puncher/queen *n.* [1960s+] (US) a doctor or nurse.

needle pusher *n.* **1** [1920s–30s] (US drugs) an addict who injects narcotics (cf. NEEDLE ARTIST). **2** [1920s–40s] (US) a tailor (cf. NEEDLE DODGER). **3** [1960s+] (US) a doctor or nurse (cf. NEEDLE PUNCHER).

needle queen *see* NEEDLE PUNCHER.

needles *n.* **1** [1900s] the shaking that accompanies with-drawal from heavy cocaine usage. **2** [1920s–30s] (US) the nerves, the jitters. **3** [1950s] the immediate sensation, equivalent to an electric shock, that follows an injection of a drug (cf. RUSH n.[2]). [one's reactions equate with those of one who has been jabbed with a needle]

needles and pins *n.* [late 19C] a warning against marriage. [the rhyme 'Pins and needles – needles and pins/When a man marries his trouble begins']

needless mark-up *n.* [1990s] (US) a Neiman-Marcus depart-ment store. [pun on name and the prices of its luxury goods]

needle woman *n.* [19C] a prostitute (cf. SKAINSMATE). [NEEDLE n.[1] + SE *woman*]

needlework *n.* [19C] sexual intercourse (cf. DO A BIT OF LADIES' TAILORING; DO A BIT OF TAILORING). [NEEDLE n.[1] + SE *work*]

need like a hole in the head, to *phr.* [1940s+] not to need at all. [trans. of Yid. *ich darf es vi a loch in kop*]

needmore *n.* [1960s+] (US) a poor, usu. Black, section of town. [the people *need more*]

need something yesterday *see* WANT SOMETHING YESTERDAY.

needy *n.* [mid-19C] a tramp, a vagrant.

needy mizzler *n.* [early–mid-19C] **1** a shabby beggar. **2** a tramp who leaves without paying for his lodging. [NEEDY + MIZZLE]

neeger *see* NIGGER.

neergs *n.* [mid-19C] greens, green vegetables (cf. SNEERG). [backsl.]

neetewif *see* NETEWIF.

neetewif gens *n.* [mid-19C] 15 shillings (75p). [backsl.]

neetexis *see* NETEXIS.

neetexis/netexis gens *n.* [mid-19C] 16 shillings (80p). [backsl.]

neetrith gens *n.* [mid– 19C] 13 shillings (65p). [backsl.]

neetrouf *see* NETROUF.

neetrouf gens *n.* [mid-19C] 14 shillings (70p). [backsl.]

Nefertiti flat top *n.* [1990s] (US Black) a popular hairstyle. [Egyptian Queen *Nefertiti* (*fl.*1372–1350BC), subject of a celebrated limestone bust in which her hair resembles a modern FLAT TOP]

neg!/negs!/negat! *excl.* [1960s+] (US, orig. milit.) no! [abbr. SE *negative*]

negaholic *n.* [1980s+] (US) a pessimist. [SE *nega*(*tive*) + (*alco*)*holic*]

negat! *see* NEG!

negative *adv.* [1940s+] no. [orig. in radio messages]

negative perspiration! *excl.* [1970s+] (US) no problem! [play on NO SWEAT!]

negatory/negatrix/negatron *adv.* [1950s+] (US, orig. milit.) no, negative. [SE *negative*]

nego *n.* [1950s–70s] (US campus) a student with a negative or objectionable attitude. [SE *negative* or Lat. *nego*, I deny]

negotiate a new contract, to *phr.* [1990s] to masturbate.

negs! *see* NEG!

neighborhood friendly *n.* [1970s+] (US) a well-known local shop, a neighbourhood shop.

neighbour *adj.* [20C] (Ulster) all right, satisfactory. [the pos. image of SE]

neighbour jones *n.* [1930s–40s] (US) an outdoor privy. [var. on MRS JONES]

neither buff nor bum *phr.* [mid-19C–1930s] neither one thing nor the other. [var. on synon. Scot. phr. (*say*) *neither buff nor stye*]

neither one's arse nor one's elbow *phr.* [1910s] (Irish) neither one thing nor another.

Nell Gwyn *n.* [20C] gin. [rhy. sl. Nell Gwyn (1650–87), mistress of Charles II]

nellie/nelly *n.*[1] **1** [1910s+] an overtly homosexual, effeminate man (cf. AGNES). **2** [1970s+] (US campus) a lesbian (cf. MARGE n.[2]). [the female name, but note NELLIE DUFF; Puxley suggests rhy. sl. *nellie dean* = QUEEN n.[1]]

nellie *n.*[2] [1930s] (US) a scraggy cow or other animal fit only for the lower end of the canned meat market. [joc. use of proper name]

nellie *adj.* [1960s+] **1** very effeminate. **2** a general term of disparagement. [NELLIE n.[1]]

nellie/nelly deans *n.* [20C] vegetables, i.e. greens. [rhy. sl.; ? popular song 'Nellie Dean']

nellie/nelly duff *n.* [20C] **1** one's breath. **2** a male homosexual. [rhy. sl. *nellie duff* = (1) PUFF n.[2], (2) PUFF n.[3]]

nelly/nelly bligh *n.*[1] [1910s+] **1** (Aus.) a meat pie (cf. DOG'S EYE). **2** the trousers' fly. **3** an eye, usu. in pl. *nelly blighs*. **4** a tie. **5** a fly. **6** a lie. [rhy. sl.]

nelly *n.*[2] *see* NELLIE n.[1].

nelly/nelly's death *n.* [1940s–50s] (Aus.) cheap wine. [generic use of fem. name; its effects]

nelly deans *see* NELLIE DEANS.

nelly kelly *n.* [20C] (Aus.) the belly (cf. NED KELLY n.[3]). [rhy. sl.]

Nelson/Nelson Riddle *n.* (Aus.) an act of urination. [rhy. sl. *Nelson Riddle* = PIDDLE n.; ult. US composer/arranger *Nelson Riddle* (1921–85)]

nelson eddies *n.* [20C] money, cash. [rhy. sl. *nelson eddies* = READIES; ult. US singer/actor *Nelson Eddy* (1901–67)]

Nelson Eddy *adv.* [20C] ready. [rhy. sl.; US singer/actor *Nelson Eddy* (1901–67)]

Nelson Riddle *see* NELSON.

nelson huntaway *n.* [1940s] (N.Z.) a stone rolled down a hillside to move stock below instead of sending a dog out. [? anecdotal]

nembie *n.* [1950s+] (drugs) *Nemb*utal, a barbiturate (cf. NEBBIE). [abbr.]

nemish *n.* [1960s–70s] (drugs) *Nem*butal, a barbiturate (cf. NEMBIE). [abbr.]

nemmind/nemmine *phr.* [1910s+] (mainly US) popular mispron. of SE *never mind.*

nemmo *see* NAMMO.

nennen *n.* [20C] (W.I.) backside, buttocks. [? NAY-NAY or redup. of Twi *ne*, to defecate]

neo maxi zoom dweebie *n.* [1980s+] (US) an inconsequential or obnoxious person. [ext. of DWEEB; popularized by 1985 film *The Breakfast Club*]

Nep/Nepalese *n.* [1960s+] (drugs) *Nepalese* hashish. [abbr.]

nepsha and kaiah *phr.* [20C] (W.I./Bdos) everybody one can think of, a large, undifferentiated crowd (cf. HABRA, DABRA AND THE CREW). [joc. use of proper names, but specific ety. unknown; ? Biblical]

nerd/nurd *n.* **1** [1950s+] (orig. US) an unpleasant, insignificant or dull person. **2** [1970s+] (campus/teen) anyone outside a peer group and who thus fails to fit in with 'the gang', esp. a studious individual who eschews drink, drugs and similar teen pleasures; thus [1960s+] *adj. nerdy, nurdy*, socially inept, over-scholarly. [? euph. for TURD or infl. by 'Mortimer Snerd' a dummy used by US ventriloquist Edgar Bergen (1903–78), or f. line in *If I Ran a Zoo* (1950) by the children's author Dr Seuss (Theodore Seuss Geisel, 1904–91): 'And then, just to show them,/I'll sail to Ka-Troo/And Bring Back an It-Kutch, a Preep and a Proo,/a Nerkle, a Nerd, and a Seersucker, too!']

nerd pack *n.* [1980s+] (US) a plastic, sectioned liner for the breast pocket that keeps pens from soiling the cloth. [NERD + SE *pack*]

nerdy/nurdy *adj.* [1950s+] (orig. US) used of any form of speech or behaviour that is judged to be socially unacceptable by the speaker(s). [NERD n.]

nerf *v.* [1950s+] (US) (orig. drag-racing) to bump another vehicle slightly with one's own car. [? SE *nerve*, i.e. one has to have strong nerves to perform the manoeuvre]

nerf- *pfx.* [1980s+] (US) used to express stupidity e.g. *nerfbrained*, stupid. [brandname of foam-rubber toys]

nerk *n.* [1950s+] a fool, a yob, generally unappetizing, unacceptable person (cf. NERD). [? var. on BERK]

nerts *n.* **1** [1930s] (US) the testicles. **2** [1990s] (US) nothing. [var. on NUTS n.[2] (1)]

nerts!/nertz! *excl.* [1920s+] (US) nonsense! (cf. BALLS!; NUTS!). [NERTS n.]

nerve *n.* **1** [mid-18C–mid-19C] a dashing man-about-town. **2** [late 19C+] audacity, impudence, cheek, esp. in phr. *have a nerve, have the nerve to.*

nerver *n.*[1] [late 19C–1920s] a bracing drink, a 'pick-me-up'. [it strengthens one's nerves]

nerver *n.*[2] [1900s–30s] (US) a gate-crasher. [they 'have a nerve' to appear uninvited]

nervo and knox *n.* **1** [1940s+] socks. **2** [1970s+] venereal disease, esp. syphilis (cf. BAND IN THE BOX). **3** [1970s+] television. [rhy. sl. *nervo and knox* = (2) POX; (3) the BOX n.[4] (4); ult. Jimmy *Nervo* (1890–1975) and Teddy *Knox* (1896–1974), music-hall comedians and members of the Crazy Gang (1935–62)]

nervous *adj.* [1920s–60s] (US, orig. jazz) great, thrilling.

nervous-jervis *adj.* [1970s] (US campus) extremely nervous. [assonance]

nervous nellie/nelly *n.* [1920s+] (US) a fearful, foolish and timid person. [orig. used of Frank B. Kellogg, Secretary of State (1925–29)]

nervous pudding/salad *n.* [1930s–40s] (US) a dish made with gelatine or aspic. [it shakes]

nervous wreck *n.* [late 19C+] one who is (actually or fig.) suffering from disorder of the nerves.

nervy *adj.* **1** [late 19C+] nervous, scared, cowardly. **2** [late 19C+] (orig. US) daring, audacious, pushing one's luck.

Nescaff/Nes *n.* [1960s+] joc. mispron./abbr. of Nescafé, a popular brand of instant coffee.

nest *n.*[1] [late 18C; 1920s+] the vagina (cf. ARBOUR). [later usage US]

nest *n.*[2] [1960s+] (US) the women who make up a pimp's collection of prostitutes (cf. STABLE).

nest *v.* [1910s+] (US) to squat.

nestcock *see* NESTLECOCK.

nester *n.* [late 19C+] (US West) a squatter, a homesteader, a farmer, a small rancher; thus *Nestersville*, a small, out-of-the-way settlement. [SE *nest*/NEST v.]

nest of sparrows flying out of one's backside *see* FLOCK OF SPARROWS FLYING OUT OF ONE'S BACKSIDE.

nest in the bush *n.* [late 17C] the vagina (cf. NEST n.[1]).

nestlecock/nestcock *n.* [19C] a prostitute. [SE *nestle* + COCK n.[2] (1)]

net *n.* [mid-19C+] the number 10. [backsl.]

net *v.* [early 19C+] to use, to acquire.

netarnal *see* NATARNAL.

netenin *n.* [mid-19C] 19 (cf. NETENIN GENS). [backsl.]

netenin gens *n.* [mid-19C] 19 shillings (95p). [backsl.]

netewif/neetewif *n.* [mid-19C] 15. [backsl.]

netexis/neetexis *n.* [mid-19C] 16. [backsl.]

netexis gens *see* NEETEXIS GENS.

net gen *see* GEN NET.

netheg/net-heg *n.* [mid-19C] 18. [backsl.]

nether beard *n.* [mid-19C] the pubic hair (cf. BEARD n.[1]; LOWER WIG; NETHER EYEBROW). [SE *nether*, lower]

nether end *n.* [19C] the vagina (cf. NETHER EYE; NETHER LIPS). [SE *nether*, lower]

nether eye *n.* [19C] the vagina (cf. NETHER END). [SE *nether*, lower]

nether eyebrow/lashes/whiskers *n.* [19C] the pubic hair (cf. LOWER WIG; NETHER BEARD). [SE *nether*, lower]

Netherlands *n.* [18C] **1** the vagina (cf. LOW COUNTRIES; LOW-LANDS). **2** the buttocks.

nether lashes *see* NETHER EYEBROW.

nether lips *n.* [19C] the vagina (cf. NETHER END). [SE *nether*, lower]

nethers *n.* [mid–late 19C] lodging-house charges. [NETHERSKEN]

nethersken *n.* [mid–late 19C] a cheap lodging house, frequented by beggars, criminals and the very poor. [SE *nether*, used in names of places to mean lower, low + KEN n.[1]]

nether whiskers *see* NETHER EYEBROW.

netnevis *n.* [mid-19C] the number 17. [backsl.]

netnevis gens *n.* [mid-19C] 17 shillings (85p). [backsl.]

netrouf/neetrouf *n.* [mid-19C] the number 14. [backsl.]

netter *n.* [1930s+] a player of lawn tennis. [the SE *net* that is an integral part of the game]

net-heg gens *n.* [mid-19C] 18 shillings (90p). [backsl.]

nettle bed *n.* [early 18C–mid-19C] the vagina (cf. BEAUTY SPOT n.[1]; CABBAGE n.[7]; PARSLEY BED).

nettled *adj.* [late 18C+] annoyed, irritated. [SE *nettle*, to sting]

netty *v.* [1940s] (W.I.) to be funny. [? NUTTY]

net-yeneps *n.* [mid-19C] 10 pence. [backsl.]

neuck *n. see* NYUCK.

neuk *v.* (S.Afr.) **1** [1910s+] to beat up. **2** [1980s+] to interfere, to mess with. [Du. *neuken*, to knock]

neuro *n.* [1970s+] an eccentric, a *neuro*tic. [abbr.]

neuro *adj.* [1970s+] eccentric, *neuro*tic. [abbr.]

neutral *adj.* [1920s] (US) stupid (cf. NEWT).

nevele/nevel *n.* [mid-19C] the number 11. [backsl.]

nevele gens *n.* [mid-19C] 11 shillings (55p). [backsl.]

nevele yeneps *see* LEVEN YENNEPS.

never a dull moment *phr.* [1930s+] a phr. used to indicate the constant variety coming with an experience; also used in ironic sense.

never again *n.* [20C] beer. [rhy. sl. *never again* = Ben (Truman), a beer brewed in East London]

never again *phr.* [late 19C+] a phr. used to emphasize one's refusal never to undergo an experience again.

never been kissed/had it *n.* [1940s+] (bingo) the number 17. [the supposed sexual innocence of a 17-year-old girl]

never better *n.* [20C] (Aus.) a letter. [rhy. sl.]

never fear *n.* [mid-19C] a pint of beer. [rhy. sl.]

never fear *phr.* [mid-19C+] don't worry, there's no chance of that.

never had it *see* NEVER BEEN KISSED.

never happen *phr.* [20C] used to dismiss any idea that the speaker cannot support.

never hachi *phr.* [1950s+] (US) (it will) never happen. [play on SE *never* + mispron.]

never mind *phr.* [early 19C+] don't worry.

never-never/never-never country/land, the *n.* [mid-19C+] (Aus./N.Z.) the deep, deserted interior of Australia. [coined *c*.1830, the name gained wide popularity with the book *We of the Never-Never* (1908) by Mrs Aeneas Gunn; despite the logic of the English term, it may in fact come from Comderoi *nievah vahs*, unoccupied land, although this equally may be pure coincidence; on either count it precedes J.M. Barrie's coinage in *Peter Pan* (1904) by more than half a century]

never-never land/peter pan's never-never land *n.* [late 19C+] the hire purchase system, esp. as *on the never-never*, buying on hire purchase (cf. ON THE DRIP). [one never finishes paying for one's purchase]

never-out *n.* [19C] the vagina. [it is inside the body]

never-ready morning *n.* [20C] (W.I.) never. [var. on NEBUARY MORNING]

never-see-come-see *n.* [20C] (W.I.) **1** an unsophisticated person, seeing the sophisticated world for the first time. **2** anyone showing off their new status or possessions. [ext. of SE]

never squedge *n.* [late 19C] 'a poor, pulseless, passionless youth' (Ware). [? SE *never* + dial. *squedge*, to squeeze, thus one who never gets to 'squeeze' a woman]

never stand still *n.* [19C] a prison treadmill. [its continual movement]

neversweat *n.* **1** [19C+] a lazy person, an idler, one whose job requires little effort. **2** [1970s] (Aus.) a council worker. [20C use of (1) is US; note naut. jargon *do a never*, to shirk, to idle]

never touch it *n.* [late 19C–1900s] (Aus.) a teetotaller. ['it' being alcohol]

never trust me! *excl.* [late 16C+] a general excl. calling for faith from the listener; i.e. 'never trust me again if I break this promise.'

never wag *n.* [late 18C–19C] the Fleet prison, London (cf. MAN OF WAR). [SE *never* + WAG v.[2]]

never was/waser/wozzer *n.* [late 19C+] (US) one who never rose above mediocrity, a has-been (cf. WAS-BIRD). ['he *never was* any good']

neves/nevis *n.* **1** [mid-19C+] the number 7. **2** [late 19C+] (prison) a 7-year sentence. [backsl.]

nevis gens *n.* [mid-19C] 7 shillings (35p). [backsl.]

nevis stretch n. [mid-19C] a 7-year sentence (cf. NEVES). [backsl.]

nevis yeneps n. [mid-19C] 7 pence. [backsl.]

nevvy n. [mid-19C–1950s] a nephew. [abbr.; post mid-19C use mainly UK public schools]

new adj. **1** [late 19C–1910s] (US) cheeky, insolent. **2** [late 19C; 1990s] (US) naïve and gullible.

new acid n. [1970s] (drugs) phencyclidine (cf. ACE n.[3]). [SE *new* + ACID n.[3]]

newbie n. [20C] a new member, a recruit, a novice. [? SE *new boy*]

new bran adj. (W.I./UK Black teen) brand new. [inversion]

new chum n. [mid–late 19C] (Aus./N.Z.) **1** (Und.) a prisoner just arrived in gaol, on the hulks or in Aus. or N.Z. **2** a newly arrived immigrant (cf. NEW HAND; NEWIE). **3** a novice, an inexperienced person. [SE *new* + CHUM n.[1]/n.[2]]

new-chum adj. [mid-19C+] (Aus./N.Z.) inexpert, raw. [NEW CHUM]

new-chum gold n. [mid-19C+] (Aus.) iron pyrites, 'fool's gold'. [a newly arrived 'digger' might be fooled into thinking he had discovered the real metal]

new cock n. [late 19C–1950s] (prison) a new inmate (cf. NEW FISH). [SE *new* + COCK n.[5]]

New College n. [late 17C–early 19C] the Royal Exchange, London. [? its function as one of the sites where, traditionally, a new sovereign is proclaimed]

New Cut warrior n. [late 19C] an inhabitant of the New Cut, in South London, a tough area where fighting was an everyday and unremarked pastime.

new deal n. [mid-19C+] (orig. US) a fresh start. [poker imagery]

New Delhi n. [20C] the stomach, the belly. [rhy. sl.]

new/next double six n. [1940s–70s] (US Black) the New Year. [*double six* = 12 (months)]

Newf/Newfie n. **1** [19C+] (orig. Can.) a *Newf*oundlander. **2** [1940s+] (US) *Newf*oundland. **3** [1980s+] (US) a *Newf*oundland dog (cf. DACHS). [abbr.; *Newfies* are the 'Irish' or 'Poles' of Canada, rural, isolated and thus considered backward and stupid]

new fish n. [1930s+] (US prison) a new inmate. [SE *new* + FISH n.[5]]

Newgate n. [late 16C–mid-19C] any prison. [the first *Newgate* prison was built near the New Gate in the old City Wall in the 12C, possibly earlier. A gaol stood on the site until the last one was demolished to make way for the Old Bailey in 1902. The original prison was rebuilt by Richard 'Dick' Whittington; this one was burned down during the Great Fire (1666) and rebuilt again in 1672 (it included a statue of Whittington plus cat in its ornamentation). This in its turn was demolished and again rebuilt in 1770–8. This version was destroyed during the Gordon Riots of 1780, and a final *Newgate* was put up in 1783. Public hangings took place in the street outside until 1868]

Newgate bird n. [early 17C–19C] a prisoner, esp. a sharper (cf. NEWGATE NIGHTINGALE). [NEWGATE + BIRD n.[3] (1)]

Newgate collar/frill/fringe n. [19C] a collar-like beard worn under the chin (cf. COBBLER'S KNOT). [its being fancifully reminiscent of the hangman's noose (cf. HEMPEN COLLAR)]

Newgate gaol n. [20C] a tale, esp. of the 'hard-luck' variety. [rhy. sl.]

Newgate hornpipe n. [early 19C] a hanging. [hangings were conducted outside Newgate prison; the victim would DANCE v.[2] as they choked to death]

Newgate knocker n. [mid-19C] a lock of hair shaped like the figure 6 and twisted from the temple back towards the ear (cf. AGGERAWATOR). [joc. use of SE ? + implication that those who sported such a style tended to criminality]

Newgate nightingale n. [16C] a novice criminal (cf. NEWGATE BIRD). [*Newgate*, i.e. the prison in which he is destined to end up + play on BIRD n.[2] (1)]

Newgate ring n. [mid-19C] a moustache and beard, but no side-whiskers (cf. COBBLER'S KNOT). [for ety. *see* NEWGATE KNOCKER]

Newgate saint/Newgate saint canonized at the Old Bailey n. [18C] a prisoner under sentence of death.

Newgate solicitor n. [late 18C–early 19C] a second-rate lawyer who hangs around Newgate prison in the hope of picking up work.

new hand n. [late 19C–1910s] (Aus.) a newly arrived immigrant (cf. NEW CHUM).

new hat n. [late 19C] a sovereign. [? the cost]

newie n. **1** [mid-19C–1950s] (US campus) a new student, a newcomer. **2** [20C] (Aus.) a new immigrant (cf. NEW CHUM). **3** [20C] (Aus.) anything new or hitherto unknown.

newington butts/newingtons n. [20C] the stomach. [rhy. sl. *newington butts* = GUTS n.[1] (1)]

new iniquity n. [mid–late 19C] (Aus.) an immigrant. [play on OLD IDENTITY n. (2)]

new jack/jill n. [1980s+] **1** a newcomer or novice, esp. to the fast life of the ghetto streets. **2** a sophisticate, someone who has succeeded in the ghetto culture; the female equivalent is *new jill*. [NEW JACK adj.]

new jack adj. [1980s+] (US Black) **1** superficial, flashy, meretricious; thus *New Jack City*, Detroit, New York City or any other city with a thriving ghetto lifestyle (cf. JACK n.[5]). **2** in tune with the contemporary young Black culture. [SE *new* + JACK n.[16]]

new jack swing n. [1980s+] (US drugs) a mixture of heroin and morphine. [NEW JACK adj. + SWING n.[4]]

New Jerusalem n. [mid-19C] Belgravia (cf. ASIA MINOR n.[1]). [the wealthy Jews who bought houses there]

new jill see NEW JACK.

newk n. [1970s+] (US campus) a newcomer, a novice. [orig. milit.]

newky n. [1970s+] Newcastle Brown Ale. [orig. Newcastle only, but gradually adopted throughout the UK]

newlicks see NOOLUCKS.

new light n. [late 18C–early 19C] a Methodist. [16C SE *new light*, novel religious views or doctrines; the term covered a variety of 18C Protestant sects in the UK and US]

new magic n. [1970s+] (drugs) phencyclidine (cf. ACE n.[3]). [its 'magical' effects]

Newman's n. [mid–late 19C] Newgate prison (cf. NUMANS). [SE *New(gate)* + sfx. -MANS]

Newman's college n. [early–mid-19C] Newgate prison (cf. AKERMAN'S HOTEL; CITY COLLEGE). [NEWMAN'S]

Newman's hotel/tea-gardens n. [early–mid-19C] Newgate prison (cf. AKERMAN'S HOTEL). [NEWMANS]

Newman's lift n. [early–mid-19C] the gallows. [NEWMAN'S]

Newman's tea-gardens see NEWMAN'S HOTEL.

Newmarket Heath commissioner n. [early–mid-19C] a highwayman. [*Newmarket Heath* was a popular site for highway robbery]

new meat n. **1** [20C] (US prison) a new inmate (cf. NEW FISH). **2** [1960s] (US campus) a freshman. [SE *new* + MEAT n. (6)]

new nayga/nigger n. [1940s] (W.I.) a parvenu, a nouveau riche (cf. NEVER-SEE-COME-SEE; OLD NIGGER). [fig. use of sl.]

new pair of boots phr. [late 19C] (middle class) a whole new situation.

New River Head n. [late 17C–early 18C] tears. [the *New River Head*, a group of reservoirs at Clerkenwell, North London]

news bug n. [1950s] (W.I.) a gossip. [dial. *news-bug*, a wood-boring beetle, the appearance of which is supposed to portend coming news]

news butcher *n.* [late 19C+] (US) a seller of newspapers, sweets etc on a train.

news hawk/newshound *n.* **1** [1910s+] (orig. US) a newspaper reporter. **2** [1950s–70s] (US) a newspaper seller. [SE *news* + sfx. -HOUND]

news hen *n.* [1940s–70s] (US) a female journalist. [SE *news* + HEN n.]

newshound *see* NEWS HAWK.

newsie *n.* **1** [mid-19C+] (US) a seller of newspapers in the street; orig. boys and girls only, the term spread, as did the job, to include adults. **2** [1950s+] (US) a news broadcaster or journalist. [abbr. SE *newsboy*]

News of the Screws *n.* [20C] nickname for the *News of the World* (a Sunday paper in the UK). [assonance + SCREW n.¹ (2), punning on its propensity for sex stories]

news of the world *n.* [1930s] a long, but ephemeral letter from a woman. [play on the newspaper title]

newspaper *n.* [1920s–30s] (US Und.) 30 days in prison. [the time it supposedly takes an illiterate to read one]

Newstralian *n.* [1950s] (Aus.) a New Australian, i.e. any immigrant, usu. from continental Europe, whose first language is not English.

newt *n.* [1920s+] (US campus) a stupid, unsophisticated or socially inadequate person (cf. NEUTRAL). [SE *neuter* or *neutral*]

newted *adj.* [1970s+] drunk. [PISSED AS A NEWT]

new thinger *n.* [1960s] (orig. US) devotee of the *new thing*, an experimental form of jazz, which dispensed with the normal harmonic and rhythmic framework, popular in the 1960s.

Newtown pippin *n.* [late 19C–1900s] a cigar. [its fragrance; ult. *Newtown*, Long Island, US, where the *Newton pippin* apple comes from]

newt party *n.* [1920s–30s] a drinking party. [PISSED AS A NEWT]

New York *v.* [1950s] (W.I.) to retch, to vomit. [the supposed similarity between the sound of *york* and that of retching]

New York City silver/white *n.* [1970s+] (drugs) an imaginary brand of marijuana, silver/white because its seeds was grown in darkness, after being flushed away into the sewer system (cf. MANHATTAN SILVER).

New Yorkers *n.* [1980s+] (drugs) MDMA (cf. ECSTASY).

New York minute *n.* [1950s+] (US) an instant. [the city's non-stop energy]

New York nippers *n.* [20C] kippers. [rhy. sl.]

New York tube steak *n.* [late 19C+] (orig. US) a spiced, heated sausage or frankfurter, served on a split roll and garnished, traditionally, with 'rags and paint' (sauerkraut and mustard) (cf. HOT DOG n.¹).

New Zealand death *n.* [mid-19C] (N.Z.) drowning. [its contemporary common-ness]

New Zealand mutton *n.* [late 19C] (N.Z.) pork.

newzie *n.* [1940s] (N.Z.) a *New Z*ealander. [abbr.]

next cab off the rank *see* FIRST CAB OFF THE RANK.

next double six *see* NEW DOUBLE SIX.

next parish to America *n.* [late 19C] (Irish) the island of Arran, the island furthest into the Atlantic from the west coast of Ireland.

next time you make a pie will you give me a piece? *phr.* [late 19C–1910s] (Can.) a sexual double entendre aimed at a woman by an amorous man. [PIE n.² + PIECE n.¹ (2)]

next/next to *adj.* **1** [late 19C+] (US) aware, knowledgeable, informed, sophisticated. **2** [late 19C+] (US) close, friendly (cf. GET NEXT TO).

next thing to the Judgement Day *n.* [19C] (US) an extremely shocking situation.

next to *see* NEXT.

next topic, please *phr.* [1990s] (US teen) used to indicate that the speaker has become boring and a change of subject is requested. [? catchphrase of a TV quiz show]

nexus *n.* [1990s] (drugs) 2C-B, a hallucinogen similar to LSD but without some of its more extreme side effects; most potent when used in conjunction with MDMA (cf. EVE n.²; SYNERGY; VENUS). [one of a large number of psychoactive substances first isolated by the American libertarian pharmacologist Dr Alexander Shulgin, including DOM, STP, DOB, DOI and MDMA (cf. ECSTASY)]

n.f. *n.* [late 19C] *no fool*. [abbr.]

n.f.g. *phr.* [1970s+] (US) *no fucking good*. [abbr.]

n.f.w.! *excl.* [1970s+] (US) *no fucking way!* [abbr.]

n.g. *n.* [late 19C] (US) something bad or inferior. [abbr. *no good*]

n.g. *adj.* (US) **1** [mid–late 19C] *no go*, unsuccessful. **2** [late 19C+] *no good*. [abbr.]

n.g.b. *n.* [1980s+] (US campus) a pleasant person, but not one with whom one wishes to have a sexual relationship. [abbr. *nice guy but*]

n.h. *see* NORFOLK HOWARD.

n.h.b. *n.* [1980s+] (drugs) the butt end of a cannabis cigarette. [abbr. *nasty hot bit*]

Niagara Falls/Niagaras *n.* [1960s+] **1** the testicles. **2** rubbish, nonsense. [rhy. sl. *Niagara Falls* = BALLS n.¹; n.²]

nias *n.* [19C] a simpleton, a fool. [NIZZIE]

nib *n.¹* [late 18C–mid-19C] the mouth or face. [SE *nib*, the beak or bill of a bird]

nib *n.²* **1** [early–mid-19C] a gentleman; thus *nibsome*, gentlemanly; *half-nibs*, one who apes a gentleman (cf. HIS NIBS). **2** [late 19C–1900s] a smartly dressed young man. [var. on NOB n.²]

nib *v.* *see* NAB v.¹.

nibbed *adj.* [mid-19C] arrested. [NAB v.¹]

nibble *n.* **1** [early–mid-19C] a petty thief (cf. NIBBLER; NIBBLING CULL). **2** [1960s+] a non-committal enquiry.

nibble *v.¹* [early–mid-19C] to pilfer, to work as a petty thief. [NIBBLE n.; such a thief cannot take a real 'bite' at a major crime]

nibble *v.²* **1** [mid-19C] to catch. **2** [late 19C+] to assess a possible purchase. **3** [1980s+] (US campus) to have a mild argument.

nibble/do a nibble *v.³* [mid-19C] to have sexual intercourse (cf. RELISH v.; TASTE v.).

nibbler *n.* [early–mid-19C] a petty thief. [NIBBLE n.]

nibbling *adj.* [1980s+] (US campus) of weather, chilly, slightly cold.

nibbling cull *n.* [19C] a petty thief. [NIBBLE v.¹ + CULL n.¹]

nib cove *n.* [early–mid-19C] a gentleman. [NIB n.² (1) + COVE]

nibhead *n.* [mid-19C–1920s] a fool, a grotesque. [printers' jargon *nib*, a fool + sfx. -HEAD (1)]

niblike *adj.* [mid-19C] smart, fashionable. [NIB n.²]

nibs *n.* [early 19C+] **1** oneself. **2** an important, esp. a self-important person (cf. HIS NIBS; NABS). **3** a shabby, genteel person, 'with no means but high pretensions' (Hotten 1859). [NIB n.²]

nibshit *n.¹* [1940s] (US) nil, nothing (cf. JACKSHIT). [? Eng. dial. *nib*, a very small amount + SHIT n.²]

nibshit *n.²* [1960s+] (US) a nosey, inquisitive person. [NIB n.¹ + SHIT n.²]

nibshit *v.* [1960s+] to meddle, to interfere. [NIBSHIT n.²]

nibso *n.* [late 19C–1910s] oneself. [NIBS n. (1)]

n.i.c. *phr.* [1930s+] (US Black) a sarcastic ref. to any Black authority figure (cf. HEAD NIGGER IN CHARGE). [abbr. *nigger in charge*]

Nic *n.* [1930s+] (US) *Nic*aragua. [abbr.]

nice *adv.* [1950s+] (US Black) feeling well, happy, at one with the world, esp. as a result of taking drugs.

nice and *adv.* [mid-19C+] very, usu. in ironical sense.

nice and easy *n.* [1980s+] (drugs) heroin. [its soothing effects]

nice as a nanne/nanny/nun's hen *phr.* [mid-16C] very affected, very fastidious. [obs. use of SE *nice*, fastidious, dainty, difficult to please]

nice as nasty *phr.* [late 19C] extremely objectionable, but phrased as euphemistically as possible.

nice as ninepence *adj.* [mid-19C] safe, satisfactory, comfortable, secure (cf. RIGHT AS …).

nice as pie *phr.* [mid-19C+] (orig. US) very well-behaved, highly amenable; also as *good as pie*, *sweet as pie*.

nice bit *n.* [1930s–50s] (US Und.) a long prison sentence, i.e. 10 years or more. [SE *nice* + BIT n.⁷]

nice car *n.* [1980s+] (US campus) a good-looking man or woman.

nice drop/drop of *n.* [1930s] a fine example of, a tasty bit of (cf. LOVELY DROP).

nice enough *n.* [20C] a male homosexual. [rhy. sl. *nice enough* = PUFF n.³]

nice girl *n.* [1960s] (US) used ironically by men, a sexually permissive woman.

nice going *phr.* [1920s+] (orig. US) a phr. of approval, congratulation.

nice joint *n.* [late 19C] an attractive, if over-made up and over-dressed young woman (cf. CRACKLING). [SE *nice* + *joint*, a piece of MEAT]

nice kettle of fish *phr.* [18C+] an awkward state of things, an unsatisfactory situation.

nice/nice little place you've got here *phr.* [1940s+] an ironic phr. implying that the place in question is either not *nice* or by no means *little*. [coined by the comedian Tommy Handley (1892–1949) performing at Windsor castle in 1942]

nicely, thank you *phr.* **1** [1920s–50s] drunk **2** [1960s+] (Irish) *nicely*, drunk. [response to the question, 'how are you feeling/doing?']

nice name to go to bed with *phr.* [late 19C] an ugly name.

nice nellie *n.* [1930s–70s] (US) a respectable woman, also used ironically. [SE *nice* + *Nelly*, a generic term for a respectable woman]

nice nellie *v.* [1930s–70s] (US) to act in a respectable manner, often excessively and interferingly so. [NICE NELLIE n.]

nice-nellyism *n.* [1930s+] (US) prudishness, excessive gentility, puritanical behaviour or attitudes. [NICE NELLIE n.]

nice one *n.*¹ [late 19C+] a fit or suitable person, usu. in sarcastic or neg. context, e.g. *he's a nice one to be telling me…*

nice one *n.*² [1960s+] a success, esp. referring to a robbery or a large payment.

nice one! *excl.* [1960s+] a general excl. of approval or admiration referring either to an action or to the report of something already carried out.

nice one, Cyril! *phr.* [1960s+] **1** a general term of approval. **2** a squirrel. [football chant created to praise *Cyril* Knowles, a Tottenham Hotspur player; (2) rhy. sl.]

nice pair of eyes *n.* [1960s+] a euph. for attractive breasts, usu. in phr. *she's got a … .*

nice place to live out of *phr.* [late 19C] a phr. used to imply that an area is too squalid, unfashionable or otherwise unappealing to live in.

nice raspberry *phr.* [late 19C] (US) a sarcastic phr. implying that the other person lacks any sweetness. [ironic use of SE]

nicest brawl since Kelsey's wake *phr.* [20C] a joking ref. to a fight, presumably enjoyed by its participants. [for ety. *see* TIGHT AS KELSEY'S NUTS]

nice thin job! *phr.* [late 19C] (orig. US) used when accusing someone of having slipped out of keeping a promise.

nice-up *v.* [20C] (W.I.) to ingratiate oneself with, to play the toady. [ext. use of SE *nice* adj.]

nice work – if you can get it *phr.* [1940s+] implying fairly open jealousy of the previous speaker. [often lit. referring to a job/occupation/activity, but not invariably so]

nicey-nice *adj.* [1930s+] (US) affected, prissy. [SE *nice*, fastidious, dainty, hard to please]

niche cock *n.* [late 18C–late 19C] the vagina (cf. COCK ALLEY). [SE *niche* + COCK n.² (1)]

nichils in a bag/in nine holes/nooks/pokes *n.* [late 16C] nothing at all. [Lat. *nihil*, nothing]

Nicholls *n.* [late 19C] (society) a full riding habit. [*Nicholls* of Regent Street, London, generally acknowledged as a superlative maker of such equipment]

nicht *see* NISHT AKA.

Nick *n.*¹ [mid-17C–1910s] the Devil (cf. NED n.²; OLD NICK). [abbr. of proper name *Nicholas*, but no specific reason; ? link to NICK v.¹ (2), i.e. the Devil snatches his victims]

nick *n.*² **1** [late 17C–mid-18C] the winning throw at dice. **2** [late 18C] as *the nick*, the proper thing, the fashionable thing, the best of health. [SE *the nick/very nick*, the critical moment]

nick *n.*³ **1** [18C–late 19C] the vagina (cf. NOTCH n.¹). **2** [late 19C] the cleft of the buttocks. [SE *nick*, a notch, a groove, a slit]

nick *n.*⁴ [19C] a short measure. [the *nick* or bump in the bottom of a tankard]

nick *n.*⁵ [early 19C+] a hybrid, usu. an animal. [SE *nick*, an instance of cross-breeding]

nick *n.*⁶ (US) **1** [mid-19C+] a *nick*el coin. **2** [1960s+] $5 or $5 worth, as in a gambling chip. [abbr. SE *nickel*, a 5-cent piece]

nick *n.*⁷ [late 19C+] (orig. Aus.) **1** a prison. **2** a police station, esp. its cells. [milit. use *nick*, the guard-room]

nick *n.*⁸ [1900s–50s] (US) the proceeds of a crime, a haul. [NICK v.¹ (4)]

nick *n.*⁹ [1980s] (US) a *nick*name. [abbr.]

nick *v.*¹ **1** [16C–19C] to win at cards by cheating. **2** [17C] to catch, take unawares, to nab, to nail. **3** [early 17C+] to apprehend, to arrest. **4** [17C+] (Und.) to rob, to steal; thus *on the nick*, going stealing. **5** [late 17C+] to cheat, to swindle. **6** [late 19C–1950s] (US) to demand, to beg. [ety. unknown; ? SE *nick*, to catch, to seize, to take advantage of an opportunity]

nick *v.*² [18C] of a man, to have sexual intercourse. [SE *nick*, to cut a notch in; note NICK n.³]

nick *v.*³ [late 19C+] (orig. Aus.) to slip away, to leave on the spur of the moment, often as *nick away*, *nick down/down to*, *nick off* etc. [ety. unknown; ? link to SE *nick of time*]

nick *v.*⁴ [1910s–50s] (US) to shoot. [SE *nick*, to cut into or through]

nick and froth *n.* [early 17C–late 18C] a false measure in a pot of beer; thus *nick and froth victualler*, a landlord. [a dent in the bottom of the pot and an excess of frothy head on top]

nick and go *n.* [20C] (Ulster) a 'narrow squeak', a 'close shave'. [SE *nick*, a slit or notch + *go*]

nick away! *excl.* [late 19C+] (Aus.) go away! clear off! [NICK v.³]

nicked *adj.*¹ **1** [early 17C+] arrested. **2** [1940s+] (prison) put on report to the governor for an infringement of prison rules. [NICK v.¹ (3)]

nicked *adj.*² [20C] (Aus.) a euph. for FUCKED adj., i.e. *go and get nicked!* [? NICK v.²]

nickel *n.*¹ **1** [1940s+] (US) a $5 bill (cf. DIME n.¹). **2** [1960s+] (US prison) a 5-year prison sentence (cf. FIN n.⁴; HANDFUL n.²; POUND n.²). **3** [1960s+] (US drugs) a $5 packet of marijuana, heroin or cocaine (cf. NICKEL BAG). **4** [1970s+] (US) the number five. **5** [1970s+] (US) $500, esp. in gambling. [SE *nickel*, a 5-cent coin]

nickel *n.*² [1980s+] (US) a dent in the bodywork of a motorcar. [ext. of SE *nickel*]

nickel *adj.* [1930s+] (US) second-rate, inferior (cf. NICKEL-AND-DIME adj.). [the low value of the coin]

nickel and dime *n.* [1930s+] (US) time. [rhy. sl.]

nickel-and-dime *adj.* [1940s+] (US) petty, small-time, insignificant. [the low value of the coin]

nickel-and-dime *v.* **1** [1930s+] (US) to carry on a small, cash-starved business; to act in a petty manner, to beg, to manage with little money, oft. as to *nickel-and-dime it.* **2** [1950s+] (US) to treat others meanly and miserly, thus to be petty and irksome, to eat away at. [SE *nickel* + *dime*, i.e. the low value of the coins]

nickel-and-dimer *n.* [1960s+] (US) a contemptible or insignificant person. [NICKEL-AND-DIME adj.]

nickel bag *n.* [1960s+] (drugs) $5 worth of drugs, the quantity varies as to the drug, more marijuana, less heroin. [NICKEL n.¹ + BAG n.⁸]

nickel deck *n.* [1960s+] (drugs) $5 worth of heroin. [NICKEL n.¹ (1) + DECK n.³]

nickel-dime *adj.* [1960s+] small-time, petty, insignificant, esp. of a business or a deal (cf. NICKEL-AND-DIME adj.).

nickel dump *n.* [20C] (US) a cheap cinema, charging only a nickel or 5 cents admission. [SE *nickel* + DUMP n.³; derog. synon. of SE *nickelodeon*]

nickel grabber *n.* [1940s] (US) a streetcar conductor (cf. NICKEL SNATCHER). [the price of a ride at the time]

nickel hop *n.* [1910s–50s] (US) a taxi-dance; thus *nickel-hopper,* a taxi-dancer. [SE *nickel,* 5 cents + HOP n.¹; although the women worked for 10 cents or 'a dime a dance' they split this half and half with the management, thus leaving themselves a nickel]

nickelnose *n.* [1970s+] (US) a Jewish person. [? var. on NEEDLENOSED + stereotypical ref. to money]

nickel note *n.* [20C] (US) a $5 bill (cf. NICKEL n.¹).

nickel nurser *n.* [1910s–70s] (US) a miser; thus *nickel-nursing,* miserly (cf. NICKEL SQUEEZER). [lit. one who 'has a passion for seeing that his nickels don't stray' (Maines & Grant, *The Wise-Crack Dictionary,* 1926)]

nickelonians *n.* [1980s+] (drugs) crack addicts. [addicts of the NICKEL (BAG)]

nickel plate *n.* [late 19C] (US) a fraud, a deception (cf. GERMAN SILVER). [the use of *nickel plate* to counterfeit silver]

nickel-plated *adj.* [late 19C+] (US) first-class, thorough. [paradoxically opp. to NICKEL PLATE; ? var. on SE *gold-plated*]

nickel shot *n.* [1990s] (US Black teen) a 5-storey public housing building in the Fillmore area of San Francisco. [SE *nickel* + SHOT n.²]

nickel slick *adj.* [1990s] (US Black) petty, insignificant, esp. in the context of attempting to do something beyond one's abilities (and thus failing in the effort). [NICKEL adj. + SLICK n.¹; the low value of the coin undermines the slickness]

nickel snatcher *n.* [1910s–50s] (US) a streetcar conductor (cf. NICKEL GRABBER).

nickel squeezer *n.* [1920s–30s] (US) a mean, miserly person (cf. NICKEL-NURSER).

nicker *n.* [1910s+] £1; thus [1980s+] *nicker bit,* the pound coin. [ety. unknown]

nicker bits *n.* [20C] diarrhoea. [rhy. sl.; *nicker bits* = the SHITS]

nickery *n.* [late 17C–early 18C] a *nick*name. [abbr.]

nickie cakes! *excl.* [20C] (Ulster) easy! (cf. WEE BUNS!). [Scot. *nickit bake,* a small biscuit with indentations on the top]

nickin/nikin/nikey *n.* [late 17C–early 18C] a fool, a simpleton. [fig. use of NICK n.²]

nickin/nikin/nikey *adj.* [late 17C–early 18C] foolish, simple. [NICKIN n.]

nick in the notch *n.* [19C] the vagina (cf. ARBOUR; NOTCH n.¹).

nick it *v.* [late 17C+] to win, usu. by good fortune or cheating. [NICK v.¹ (1)]

nick me! *excl.* [mid-18C] a mild oath. [NICK v.²; thus euph. for FUCK ME!, although it predates the latter]

nick-nack *n.*¹ [mid-19C] the vagina (cf. DOWN BELOW; KNICK-KNACK n.¹). [SE *nick-nack,* a curious or pleasing trifle]

nick-nack/nic-nac/knick-knack *n.*² [1960s+] (US) a male homosexual, esp. a promiscuous one. [? SE *nick-nack/knick-knack,* a trinket]

nick-nacks *n.* [18C–19C] the testicles (cf. KNACKERS). [SE *nick-nack,* a trunket, a trifle]

nick-ninny *n.* [late 17C– early 19C] a fool, 'a meer Cod's head' (*B.E.*) [? abbr. NICKIN + SE *ninny*]

nick off *v.* [late 19C+] (orig. Aus.) to leave, to depart, to go from one place to another. [NICK v.³]

nick-pot *n.* [17C–18C] **1** a publican. **2** a false measure in a pot of beer (cf. NICK AND FROTH). [the placing of a *nick* or dent in the bottom of the pot]

nicks *n.* [late 19C] stolen goods. [NICK v.¹ (4)]

nick the pin, to *phr.* [mid-17C–early 18C] to drink fairly, i.e. not taking more than one's share of the tankard (which was marked by pins).

nickum *n.* [late 17C–early 18C] **1** a card sharp or dice fraud. **2** a cheating landlord (although the aspersion can extend to any dishonest retailer). [NICK v.¹]

nickumpoop *see* NINCOMPOOP.

nic-nac *see* NICK-NACK n.².

Nicodemus *n.* **1** [late 17C] a religious fanatic. **2** [1940s] (W.I.) a late-night visitor. [the name of *Nicodemus,* the Jewish ruler who came to Jesus by night (John 3:1 etc)]

niebla *n.* [1980s] (drugs) phencyclidine (cf. ACE n.³). [Sp. *niebla,* mist]

niegor *see* NIGGER.

nieve *n.* [1970s] (drugs) white powdered drugs, i.e. heroin or cocaine. [Sp. *nieve,* snow]

niff *n.* [20C] an unpleasant smell, a stink. [? SE *sniff*]

niff *v.* [1920s+] to smell unpleasantly, to stink. [NIFF n.]

niffkins bridge *n.* [1990s] the perineum. [NIFF n. + dimin. sfx. *-kins* + SE *bridge*]

niffy *adj.* [20C] smelly, malodorous. [NIFF n.]

niffy-naffy fellow *n.* [late 18C–early 19C] a trifler, an unimportant person. [Yorks. dial. *niff-/niffy-naffy,* trifling]

niftik *adj.* [1910s–30s] (US) stylish, neat. [NIFTY adj.¹ (1) + 'European/Slav' sfx. *-ik*]

nifty/bit of nifty *n.*¹ [late 19C+] **1** sexual intercourse. **2** an attractive woman. [NIFTY adj.¹ (1)]

nifty *n.*² (US) [1910s–50s] a joke, a funny story, a clever plan. [NIFTY adj.¹]

nifty *adj.*¹ **1** [mid-19C+] neat, smart. **2** [late 19C+] (orig. US) clever, skilful, agile. **3** [1900s–30s] (US) cheeky, insolent, disrespectful of authority (cf. BIT SWIFT). [ety. unknown; according to US author Bret Harte, quoted in *OED,* abbr. *magnificat*; E.P. dismisses this as 'a joke' and suggests SE *magnificent*]

nifty *adj.*². [late 19C+] (US) of winds, unpredictable. [ext. on NIFTY adj.¹ (3)]

nifty!/nifty beans!/nifty keen! *excl.* [1970s+] (US teen) terrific!, splendid!, wonderful! [NIFTY adj.¹ (1)]

nifty piece *n.* [1920s+] (US) an attractive woman. [NIFTY adj.¹ (1) + PIECE n.¹]

nig *n.*¹ [late 17C–early 19C] (Und.) the clippings from doctored gold coins (cf. CURLE). [? Essex dial. *nig,* a piece or SE *nick*]

nig *n.*² [early 19C+] a Black person. [abbr. NIGGER n.]

nig *n.*³ [mid-19C] gin. [backsl.]

nig *v.*¹ [late 17C–early 18C] to clip money. [? Essex dial. *nig,* a piece]

nig *v.*² [mid-18C] to arrest. [NICK v.¹ (3)]

nig *v.*³ [18C] to have sexual intercourse. [abbr. NIGGLE]

nig *v.*⁴ [early 19C–1950s] (US) to renege on one's debts. [abbr. NIGGER n.; racist stereotyping]

niger *see* NIGGER n.

Nigerian *n.* [1960s+] (gay) a Black man. [generic use of specific nationality]

Nigerian lager *n.* [1970s+] Guinness stout (cf. AFRICAN LAGER). [its blackness]

nigette *n.* [1990s] (US) a Black woman or girl. [NIG(GA) + sfx. -*ette*]

nigga *n.* [1980s+] (US Black) a Black person (cf. WIGGA). [NIGGER; the sp. is exclusive to the world of GANGSTA RAP where the SE sfx. -*er* is transposed to -*a*, a foreshortening that is regularly found in Black sl. as a means of intensifying a term; (cf. PLAYA)]

niggah *see* NIGGER.

niggamation *n.* [19C] (US Black) the speeding up of automobile production lines, on which the bulk of the workers are African Americans, which gets more cars built but does not require the company to pay any more wages. [NIGGER + SE (*auto*)*mation*]

nigger/neeger/niegor/niger/niggah/niggar/niggur *n.* 1 [late 16C+] a derog. term for a Black person, a Negro slave, by extension any non-White; but, [1970s+] (US Black) in a reverse racism, taking pride in such epithets, used by radical Blacks of each other. 2 [mid-18C+] (US) a general derog. term applicable to anyone regardless of race/skin colour, used by Blacks as well as Whites. 3 [mid-19C+] any dark-skinned foreign person. 4 [mid-19C+] (US) a fellow human being, of any race or skin colour. 5 [20C] (US) anger, annoyance (cf. GET ONE'S NIGGER UP). 6 [1950s+] (US Black) a close male or female friend, companion, boyfriend or husband, usu. constructed with possessive pronoun, as in *my* (*main*) *nigger*, my (best) friend. 7 [1970s+] (US Black) a non-Black person who is considered to act in a very pos. manner in relation to Black culture or who identifies strongly with it. [ult. Lat. *niger*, Black in colour, thence Early Mod. Eng. (later dial.) *niger*; thus advocated by Lighter, although the *OED* and E.P. prefer Sp. *negro*, Black. *Nigger* has been used in a variety of combs. since 19C; both *Webster III* and the *OED* list a number of these, usu. referring to birds, animals and crops, without comment – the assumption being that, for better or worse, they are an accepted (if local) usage; while they are also based on stereotypes, it is more that of colour than of racist assumptions. Those combs. listed here, usu. unlisted in the standard dictionaries, may well have been colloq. in the 19C, but by their intrinsic hostility are, *de facto*, sl. Otherwise, *nigger* implies the usual derog. stereotypes as allotted to Blacks: poverty, laziness, stupidity, lasciviousness, a propensity to mindless hedonism and violence]

nigger *adj.* [20C] (US) a derog. phr. indicating something or someone associated with Black culture; thus as derog., contemptible, odd, inferior. [NIGGER *n.*]

nigger/nigger around *v.* [late 19C+] (US) to do menial work, to mess around.

nigger and halitosis *n.* [1940s–50s] (US) liver and onions. [NIGGER *adj.*, i.e. the brown colour of liver + the effect of (raw) onions on the breath]

nigger around *see* NIGGER *v.*

nigger babies *n.* [mid-19C] (US) cannon-balls. [coined by Confederate General Hardee (1815–73) during the siege of Charleston; the cannon from which the missiles were fired were known as *swamp angels*]

nigger baby *n.* [late 19C–1960s] (US) a small liquorice or chocolate sweet or candy shaped like a baby.

nigger bait *n.* [1950s–60s] an excess of chrome accessories on an automobile (cf. JIGABOO JOY SHOP).

nigger ball *n.* [1960s+] (S.Afr.) a large, round, black aniseed flavoured sweet, which gradually changes as one sucks away successive layers. [NIGGER *adj.* + SE *ball*, i.e. the colour and shape]

nigger/nigger's bankroll *n.* [1920s–70s] (US) a roll of $1 bills or a wad of small denomination notes inside one larger denomination note (cf. CHICAGO BANKROLL; MICHIGAN ROLL). [NIGGER *adj.* + SE *bankroll*; thus neg. stereotyping]

nigger box *n.* [1950s+] (US Black) television (cf. WOG BOX). [NIGGER *adj.* + BOX *n.*[4] (4); neg. stereotyping]

nigger catcher *n.* [mid-19C] (US) a small slotted flap on a saddle. [captured runaway slaves were roped to this flap and thus forced to run home alongside their master on his horse]

nigger chaser *n.*[1] [late 19C+] (US) a firework that once lit leaps around along the ground. [in UK, a *jumping jack*]

nigger chaser *n.*[2] *see* NIGGER SHOOTER.

nigger day *n.* [1930s+] (US) Saturday (cf. NIGGER DAYTIME). [the one day of rest permitted to slaves]

nigger daytime *n.* [1930s+] (US) night time. [the time at which Black slaves were allowed their rest]

nigger driving *n.* [mid-19C+] 1 (orig. US Black) the working of Blacks to exhaustion by White bosses. 2 any boss-employee relationship characterized by poor treatment.

nigger drunk *adj.* [1940s–60s] (US) very drunk.

nigger fishing *n.* [1940s–60s] (US) leisurely fishing for catfish or carp. [the implication is of the lazy Black fisherman]

nigger fixings *n.* [1960s] a second-rate job of work.

nigger flicker *n.* [1950s–70s] (US Black) a weapon, usu. a small knife or a razor blade with one side heavily taped to preserve the user's fingers.

nigger flipper *n.* [mid-19C–1930s] (US) a slingshot. [used by White boys, the targets were usu. Blacks]

nigger fronts *n.* [1970s+] (US Black) extreme stylishness in dress. [NIGGER *adj.* + FRONTS]

nigger gallery *see* NIGGER HEAVEN.

nigger gin *n.* [1900s–30s] (US) inferior or synthetic gin.

nigger golf *n.* [1910s] (US) the game of craps (cf. ABYSSINIAN POLO).

niggergram/nigger-mouth *n.* [20C] (W.I.) a stupid rumour, demeaning gossip. [NIGGER + (*tele*)*gram* + sfx -*mouth*]

nigger ham *n.* [1940s–60s] (US) a water melon. [both are pink]

niggerhead *n.*[1] [mid–late 19C] (US) pro-Black civil rights agitators.

niggerhead *n.*[2] 1 [mid-19C+] (US) any outcrop of dark, rough, rounded or lumpy rock, stones or boulders. 2 [mid-19C+] any clump or hummock of thick vegetation, swamp grass, ferns, grass etc. 3 [late 19C–1960s] (US) a dark raincloud. 4 [20C] peaks of coral that jut above the surface of the sea; also as *negro-head*. 5 [1930s–60s] (US Und.) a type of round wall safe. [all fig. uses of NIGGER *adj.* + SE *head*]

nigger-head *adj.* [1950s+] (W.I.) a Black person's naturally kinky hair (cf. BAD HAIR).

niggerhead rum *n.* [19C–1910s] (US) a strong, dark type of tobacco. 2 [1920s–30s] (US) strong, dark rum.

nigger heads *n.* [20C] (US prison) prison-cooked prunes (cf. PRUNE *n.*[2]).

nigger heaven/gallery *n.* (US) 1 [mid-19C–1970s] the top gallery of a theatre (cf. BUZZARD ROOST *n.*[2]). 2 [1920s–60s] a Black neighbourhood (cf. NIGGER HILL). [(1) this gallery was the only one that Black theatregoers could afford]

nigger hill *see* NIGGERTOWN.

nigger in a blanket *n.* [1930s–40s] (US) a pudding made with dark fruits rolled inside pastry.

nigger in charge *n.* [1930s+] (US Black) a sarcastic ref. to any Black authority figure. [for ety. *see* HEAD NIGGER IN CHARGE]

nigger in the woodpile/fence/woodshed *n.* 1 [mid-19C+] (orig. US) a hidden snag or drawback. 2 [1950s+] (US) a suspected or unacknowledged Black relative or ancestor.

niggerish *adj.* [early 19C+] 1 lazy, couldn't-care-less. 2 selfish. [NIGGER *n.*]

nigger it v. [20C] (US) to live in poverty. [the social situation of many US Blacks]

niggeritis n. [20C] (W.I.) the urge to lie down and take a nap after a heavy meal.

niggerize v. [1970s+] (US) to be politically marginalized, i.e. to be rendered 'Black' and *de facto* unimportant.

nigger jigger see NIGGER STICKER.

nigger joint n. [20C] (US) a cheap bar, saloon or restaurant (cf. SHINE BOX). [NIGGER adj. + JOINT n.³ (3)]

nigger juke/jook n. [mid-19C–1940s] (US) a cheap bar, saloon or restaurant (cf. NIGGER JOINT). [NIGGER adj. + JUKE n.]

nigger kickers/stompers n. [1960s+] (US) large boots.

nigger killer n.¹ [late 19C] (US) a yam. [the supposed results of over-eating them]

nigger killer n.² **1** [1940s–70s] a slingshot (cf. NIGGER SHOOTER). **2** [1940s–70s] a revolver. **3** [1960s] a large pocket-knife (cf. NIGGER STICKER).

nigger knocker n. [1960s+] (US) a stick or club for use esp. against Blacks.

nigger knots n. [20C] (W.I.) thick, tough Black hair. [used as an insult between Black people]

niggerlip v. [1940s+] to moisten the end of a cigarette while smoking it.

niggerlipping n. [1950s+] (orig. US) wetting the end of a cigarette while smoking it.

nigger liquor n. [1920s+] (US) any form of bad liquor, esp. when illicitly distilled. [such liquor is 'only good for a nigger']

nigger logic n. [20C] (US) any form of reasoning considered erroneous, over-simplistic, based in fantasy, i.e. totally illogical. [NIGGER adj. + SE *logic*; the stereotype is of the Black person as child-like and simple]

niggerlover n. [mid-19C+] (orig. US) a term of abuse, usu. aimed at a White who fails to display the supposedly necessary loathing of Blacks.

nigger-loving adj. [late 19C+] (US) used of any White person showing favour to Black people. [NIGGER-LOVER]

nigger luck n. [mid-19C–1960s] (US) **1** good luck. **2** bad luck, which one must make the best of, come what may.

nigger mess n. [1990s] (US Black) problems within the Black community, which should be solved within that group.

nigger mouth see NIGGERGRAM.

nigger move n. [1990s] (US Black teen) any action that can be perceived as ignorant, inconsiderate or rude.

nigger navel n. [1920s–60s] (US) a black-eyed Susan plant (*Thunbergia alata*). [the black centre of the yellow flower]

nigger news n. [mid-19C] (US) gossip.

nigger night n. [1920s+] (US Black) Saturday night.

niggerology n. [1950s–60s] (US) a derog. term for Black studies course at college or school. [NIGGER n. + sfx. -ology]

nigger out v. **1** [mid-19C–1940s] to exhaust land by using it constantly without fertilization. **2** [late 19C+] (US) to back out, renege on. [stereotype of Blacks as poor farmers]

nigger pancake n. [1960s] (US) a lump of manure (cf. ALLEY APPLE n.²).

nigger pot n. [1900s–60s] (US, mainly south) illicitly distilled whisky.

nigger-rich adj. [1930s+] (US) deeply in debt but loaded down with glossy, flashy status symbols, car, jewellery etc.

nigger rig n. [1960s+] (US) **1** a bodged job, a piece of do-it-yourself assembly. **2** a home-made skateboard ramp.

nigger rig v. [1960s+] (US) to perform second-rate, sloppy work.

nigger rigged adj. [1960s+] (US) characterized by bad workmanship (cf. AFRICAN ENGINEERING).

nigger row n. [late 19C] (US) the Black area of a town or city (cf. COON BOTTOM).

nigger's bankroll see NIGGER BANKROLL.

niggers' duel n. [late 19C] (US) an argument, a set-to in which no blows are actually struck (cf. MEXICAN STAND-OFF).

nigger shooter/chaser n. [late 19C+] (US) a slingshot (cf. NIGGER KILLER n.²).

nigger's lips n. [1970s–80s] potato chips. [rhy. sl.]

nigger spit n. [late 19C] (US) the lumps in Demerara sugar.

nigger steak n. [1930s+] (US Black) beef liver. [it is especially dark]

nigger stick n. [1960s+] (US) an oversized baton, used by policemen and prison officers.

nigger sticker/jigger n. [1960s+] a large pocket-knife (cf. NIGGER KILLER n.²).

nigger stompers see NIGGER KICKERS.

nigger talk n. [mid-19C] (US) chatter, irresponsible gossip.

nigger toes n. (US) **1** [mid-19C] a type of potato. **2** [late 19C+] Brazil nuts, walnuts.

niggertown/niggerville/nigger hill n. [mid-19C+] (US) a Black neighbourhood (cf. BEAN TOWN n.²; COON BOTTOM). [note W.I. dial. *negro-town*, a community of runaway slaves or *maroons* who would use them as bases for raids on plantations]

nigger up v. [1950s+] (US) to decorate in a vulgar manner.

niggerville see NIGGERTOWN.

nigger war n. [mid–late 19C] (US, South) the US Civil War (1861–5).

niggerwool swamp n. [1930s] (US) a generic term for an area predominantly occupied by Blacks.

nigger work n. [1930s+] (US Black) menial work, ill-performed work.

nigger yard n. [20C] (W.I.) any notably rough area in the slums. [Carib.E, *negro-yard*, that area on a plantation where the slaves were quartered]

nigging n. [late 17C–18C] clipping coins (cf. NIGGLER n.²). [NIG v.¹]

niggle v. [16C] to have sexual intercourse. [the physical activity]

niggled adj. [1950s+] annoyed, irritated, tetchy.

niggler n.¹ [17C–late 18C] **1** a prostitute. **2** a promiscuous man. [NIGGLE]

niggler n.² [late 17C–early 19C] a clipper of coins. [NIG v.¹]

niggling n. [late 17C–early 19C] sexual intercourse. [NIGGLE]

niggling adj. [1950s+] irritatingly petty, intrinsically unimportant but time and energy consuming.

niggly adj. [1950s+] ill-tempered, obsessed with irrelevancies and petty problems.

niggur see NIGGER.

nigh enough n. [1920s–30s] a gay male prostitute. [rhy. sl. *nigh enough* = PUFF n.³]

night and day n. [mid-19C] a play. [rhy. sl.]

night and day adj. [20C] gray, grey. [rhy. sl.]

night and day v. [mid-19C] to see a play. [rhy. sl.]

nightbird n. [mid-19C+] a prostitute (cf. EVENING STAR; NIGHTCAP n.¹). [she 'flies at night']

nightcap n.¹ **1** [early 17C] a bully who specializes in finding victims at night (cf. HUFFCAP). **2** [19C] a thief who prefers to work at night (cf. NIGHTHAWK n.; NIGHT HUNTER; NIGHT WALKER). **3** [19C] a prostitute (cf. NIGHTBIRD; NIGHTHAWK n.; NIGHT POACHER; NIGHT SHADE; NIGHT TRADER; NIGHT WALKER).

nightcap n.² **1** [early 19C+] a final drink before bed, or before the bars shut. **2** [1930s+] (US) the final race or contest of a day's sports, esp. the second game in a baseball 'double-header' (cf. NIGHT SNAP).

nightcap n.³ [1970s] (US Black) a small skull-cap worn by many black men.

night clothes n. [20C] (US Und.) dark, close-fitting clothes used when committing a burglary at night.

nightclub *v.* [1970s+] to go out at night for enjoyment at clubs (cf. CLUB v.²).

night crawler *n.* [1950s+] (US) someone who socializes or works late at night.

night exercises *n.* [1990s] masturbation.

night fighter *n.* **1** [1940s+] (US) a Black person. **2** [1970s] (US campus) a young woman who looks better by night than in daylight.

night-fossick/-fossicker *see* FOSSICK.

night glass *n.* [1940s] (W.I.) a euph. for a chamberpot.

night hack *n.* [1920s–30s] (US Und.) a night watchman. [SE *night* + HACK n.³ (1)]

nighthawk *n.* **1** [mid-19C+] (US) a worker on a night shift. **2** [19C+] anyone who likes to stay up late, usu. for a nefarious reason. **3** [late 19C+] (US) a taxi that plys for trade at night (cf. NIGHT OWL; OWL n.). **4** [20C] (Aus./US) a thief, esp. one who works at night (cf. NIGHTCAP n.¹). **5** [20C] (Aus.) a prostitute (cf. EVENING STAR; NIGHTCAP n.¹).

nighthawk *v.* [late 19C+] (US) to work or socialize at night. [NIGHTHAWK n.]

night hunter *n.* [19C] a thief who prefers to work at night (cf. NIGHTCAP n.¹).

nightie *n.* [1980s+] (US campus) a very bad situation, esp. one over which one has no control. [abbr. SE *nightmare*]

nightingale *n.* **1** [19C] a prostitute (cf. EVENING STAR). **2** [19C–1910s] (US) a singer. **3** [20C] (Und.) an informer (cf. CANARY n.⁷).

night magistrate *n.* [late 17C–early 18C] a constable.

nightman *n.* [late 17C–18C] a collector of nightsoil, i.e. the contents of cesspools, removed at night (cf. GOLD-FINDER).

nightmare *n.* [1980s+] (US campus) an ugly, unattractive person.

night on the city *phr.* [1970s] (US) a night in prison. [the city pays for one's time in prison]

night on the rainbow *phr.* [1940s] (drugs) a night spent under the influence of drugs.

night owl *n.* **1** [mid-19C+] (US) a taxi that plys for trade at night (cf. NIGHTHAWK n.; OWL n.). **2** [late 19C+] late customers of cafés and restaurants (cf. OWL n.).

night physic/work *n.* [late 16C–early 18C] sexual intercourse.

night poacher *n.* [19C] a prostitute (cf. EVENING STAR; NIGHTCAP n.¹).

night shade *n.* [19C] a prostitute (cf. EVENING STAR; NIGHTCAP n.¹).

night snap *n.* [19C] (US) the final race or contest of a day's sports, esp. the second game in a baseball 'double-header' (cf. NIGHTCAP n.²). [ety. unknown]

night's a pup/night's only a pup, the *phr.* [1910s+] (Aus.) it is still early, 'the night is young'; thus occas. *the day's/day's only a pup.*

night starvation *n.* [1940s] sexual frustration. [play on SE, esp. as used in an advertisement of the period]

night stick *n.*¹ [1910s+] (US) the penis (cf. BILLY n.²; COPPER-STICK; TRUNCHEON). [the police practice of carrying a large club on night patrol]

night stick *n.*² [1950s+] (US Black) anyone who lives their life in clubs and bars and generally indulges themself as a 'night person'.

night trader *n.* [19C] a prostitute (cf. EVENING STAR; NIGHTCAP n.¹).

night walker *n.* [late 17C–19C] **1** a prostitute (cf. EVENING STAR; NIGHTCAP n.¹). **2** a bellman or town crier. **3** a thief or rogue (cf. NIGHTCAP n.¹).

night work *see* NIGHT PHYSIC.

nigit *n.* [late 17C–18C] a fool, an idiot (cf. NIGMENOG). [play on SE *an eejit, an idiot*]

nigmenog/nimenog *n.* [late 17C–18C] a fool, an idiot (cf. NIGIT). [? link to dial. *nigmanies*, a trifle]

nig-nog *n.*¹ [1950s–60s] (orig. railway) **1** a novice, an unskilled person. **2** a fool, a simpleton. [*The Times* (30 November 1967) claims the term was used 'long before coloured immigrants appeared...' but the greater likelihood is that the stereotype of the incompetent Black labourer was the real origin, although note NIGMENOG + Scot. *nig-nag*, a worthless, useless thing]

nig-nog *n.*² [1950s+] any non-White, whether Black, Asian or Oriental. [abbr. NIGGER n. + redup.]

-nik *sfx.* [20C] (orig. US) used to denote the involvement or association of a person or thing with the thing or quality described. [it blends the Rus./Yid. sfx. -*nik*; the sfx. had been used for some time but it was hugely popularized by contemporary fascination with the first Sputnik space craft, launched 1957; the orig. such term was *beatnik*, coined derisively by columnist Herb Caen of the *San Francisco Chronicle*]

nikey/nikin *see* NICKIN.

nikkety-boo *adj.* [1940s+] (N.Z.) naked.

nil *n.* [mid-19C] half; thus half-profits.

nil carborundum illegitimi *see* ILLEGITIMIS NON CARBORUNDUM.

nim/nym/nimmer *n.* [early 17C–late 19C] a thief. [NIM v.]

nim/nym *v.* [early 17C–late 19C] (Und.) to steal; thus *nimming*, theft. [9C–16C SE *nim*, to take from]

nim a/speak to a tatler, to *phr.* [mid-19C] to steal a watch. [NIM v. + TATLER]

nimbies *n.* [1960s] (US drugs) Nembutal.

nimble-hipped *adj.* [19C] an enthusiastic lover, used of either sex.

nimbles *n.* [early 17C] the fingers.

nimby *adj.* [1970s+] (orig. US) used of something that is unwanted, esp. new buildings or charitable services in a middle-class locality. [abbr. *not in my back yard*]

nimenog *see* NIGMENOG.

nimgimmer *n.* [late 17C–early 18C] a surgeon or physician, esp. a specialist in venereal diseases. [ety. unknown]

nimmer *see* NIM v.

nimpy *adj.* [1990s] pert, fresh, young and budding. [? SE *nymph*]

nimrod *n.*¹ [19C] the penis (cf. HUNTER n.¹). [biblical proper name *Nimrod*, the 'mighty hunter' of Gen., with an additional punning nod towards ROD n.¹]

nimrod *n.*² [1930s+] (US campus) a socially inept person, someone not attuned to the group norms. [popularized by 1940s Warner Bros. cartoon character Elmer Fludd (a rabbit-hunter), called 'poor little Nimrod' by Bugs Bunny]

nimshi *n.* [mid-19C–1950s] (US) a fool. [? dial. *nimshie*, a flighty girl]

nimshod *n.* [late 19C] a cat. [? Nimrod 'a mighty hunter' or NIM n. + Rom. *shosho*, a rabbit]

nimwad *n.* [1980s+] (US) a fool. [pun on NIMROD n.² + sfx. -WAD]

nina *n.*¹ [1980s+] (US Black) a handgun (cf. NINER). [the 9mm barrel]

nina *n.*² [1990s] (US Black) a teenage girl. [Sp. *niña*, a young girl]

nina with her hair down / nina from Carolina / Argentina / nina ross / nina ross the stable hoss / nina, nina, ocean liner *n.* [1910s+] (US gambling) the point of 9 in craps dice.

nincom/nincum *n.* [19C] (US) a fool. [abbr. NINCOMPOOP]

nincompoop / nincumpoop / nickumpoop *n.* [late 17C+] **1** a fool, a simpleton. **2** 'one who never saw his wife's [CUNT n.¹ (1)]' (Grose 1785).

nincum *see* NINCOM.

nincum noodle *n.* [early 19C] a penniless fool. [NINCOMPOOP + NOODLE n.¹; punning on a SE *noodle* with *no income*]

nincumpoop *see* NINCOMPOOP.

nine *n.* **1** [1910s+] (Aus.) a 9-gallon (41-litre) keg of beer (cf. EIGHTEEN). **2** [1990s] (US) a 9mm pistol (cf. NINA n.¹; NINER).

nine-acre smile *n.* [1930s+] (Can.) a very broad grin.

nine-bob note *n.* [1960s+] anyone or anything fake, spurious, esp. in phr. *bent/queer as a nine-bob note* (cf. NINE-DOLLAR BILL). [the *nine-bob* or nine-shilling note never existed]

nine corns *n.* [mid-19C] a pipeful of tobacco. [Lincolnshire/Salop. dial.]

nine-day blues *n.* [20C] the incubation period for gonorrhoea after the initial sexual contact.

nine-dollar bill *n.* [1960s+] (US) a homosexual; thus *three times as queer as a three-dollar note* (cf. NINE-BOB NOTE). [there is no *nine-dollar bill*]

nine-eight/98 *n.* [1990s] (US) a 98 Oldsmobile. A very limited make of Oldsmobile, usually considered to be the company's best model of car, in any given year and thus a real status symbol.

nine-inch knocker *n.* [20C] the penis (cf. FOUR-ELEVEN-FORTY-FOUR).

nine-mile nuts *n.* [late 19C] anything sustaining, whether to eat or drink. [orig. contemp. Jap. pidgin; f. the supposedly nutritive properties of chestnuts]

9/9 millimetre *n.* [1990s] a 9mm pistol.

911 *n.* [1990s] an emergency. [US telephone code for emergencies, the equivalent of the UK 999]

ninepence *n.* [late 19C+] the vagina, usu. juv. use (cf. HA'PENNY).

ninepennyworth *n.* [1940s–50s] a 9-month prison sentence (cf. SIXPENNYWORTH).

ninepins *n.* [late 19C] the body. [it can be easily knocked over]

niner *n.* **1** [late 19C] a convict serving a 9-year sentence. **2** [1930s+] (Aus.) a woman in her ninth month of pregnancy. **3** [1980s+] a Tech Nine automatic gun (cf. NINA n.¹; NINE).

nine shillings *n.* [late 18C–mid-19C] cool, audacity, calm. [joc. mispron. of SE *nonchalance*]

nine-tail bruiser *n.* [18C–19C] the cat-o'-nine-tails (cf. CAT n.²).

nineteen canteen *adv.* [1940s+] (S.Afr.) a very long time ago. [assonance]

nineteener *n.* [late 19C] (Aus./N.Z.) an untrustworthy, unpleasant person. [? one who talks 'nineteen to the dozen' or the cribbage score of 19, an impossibility to achieve]

nineteenth hole *n.* [20C] the bar at a golf club; esp. used by golfers but understood more widely. [a golf course has 18 holes]

nine-to-five *n.* [1960s+] (orig. US) a regular, routine, uninspiring job. [the hours most usually worked]

nine-to-fiver *n.* [1960s+] (orig. US) an office worker (cf. DINNER PAILER). [NINE-TO-FIVE]

ninety days *n.* [20C] (US gambling) in craps, the point of 9. [ref. to SE *90 days*, the standard sentence for petty crime]

ninety-day wonder *n.* [1950s+] (US) an inexperienced employee or one employed for temporary work. [orig. milit., a junior officer who has completed the 90-day officer training programme]

ninety/90 dog *n.* [late 19C–1900s] a pug. [the curled tail, which resembles the number 9]

ninety-nine *n.* [1940s–70s] (Aus.) anal intercourse. [a play on the usu. SIXTY-NINE]

ninety-six *n.* [1920s–50s] (US gay) homosexual anal intercourse. [for ety. *see* NINETY-NINE]

ninety-three *n.* [1940s–50s] (Aus.) anal intercourse. [for ety. *see* NINETY-NINE]

nine ways from breakfast *phr.* [1970s+] in all sorts of ways (cf. SIX WAYS FOR SUNDAY).

nine winks *n.* [mid-19C] a very brief nap. [var. on FORTY WINKS]

ning-nong/-nang *n.* [early 19C+] (Aus./N.Z.) a stupid, foolish person (cf. NIG-NOG n.¹). [note horse-copers jargon *ning-nang*, a worthless thoroughbred]

ninnies *n.* [20C] (orig. US) the female breasts (cf. NAY NAYS; NINNY JUGS). [SE *ninny*, a child]

ninny *n.*¹ [late 16C–18C] a 'canting, whining beggar' (B.E.). [SE *ninny*, a fool; ? ult. SE *innocent*]

ninny *n.*² [1990s] (US) a Black person. [abbr. SE *pickaninny*]

ninnified *adj.* [1930s] foolish. [SE *ninny*, a fool]

ninny broth *n.* [early 18C] coffee. [SE *ninny* + *broth*; i.e. 'real men' drink beer or wine]

ninnyhammer *n.* [late 16C–1910s] a fool, a simpleton. [? NINNY n.¹ or SE *ninny*, a fool + dial. *hammer*, a clumsy person or v. to stammer]

ninny jugs *n.* [1970s] (US) the female breasts (cf. CREAM JUGS). [NINNIES + SE *jug*]

ninth/tenth part of a man *n.* [18C] a tailor. [pvb. 'nine tailors make a man']

nip *n.*¹ [late 16C–early 19C] a cutpurse. [NIP v.¹ (1)]

nip *n.*² [mid-18C+] a small, usu. alcoholic, drink. [abbr. SE *nipperkin*, a small vessel, holding about half a pint (190ml), thus the amount of liquor contained in such a vessel]

nip *n.*³ [early 19C] 'Passengers who are taken up on stage coaches by the collusion of the guard and coachman, without the knowledge of the proprietors, are called nips' (De Quincey, *King of Hayti*, 1823). [? dial. *nip*, a good bargainer, 'just honest and no more']

nip *n.*⁴ [1930s] (Aus.) one who responds favourably to cadgers, a 'soft touch' (cf. PUT THE NIPS IN). [NIP v.¹ (7)]

Nip *n.*⁵ (orig. US) **1** [1940s+] a Japanese person. **2** [1940s+] the Japanese language. **3** [1990s] any East Asian person. [abbr. SE *Nipponese*, ult. Jap. *ni(chi)* the sun + *pon, hon*, source]

nip *v.*¹ **1** [mid-16C–1900s] (Und.) to cut a purse or pick a pocket. **2** [mid-16C–1930s] (Und.) to arrest. **3** [mid-16C+] to steal, to snatch, to shoplift. **4** [mid–late 19C] (US) to shoot someone. **5** [late 19C+] (US) to defeat. **6** [1910s–20s] of a man, to have sexual intercourse. **7** [1910s–20s] (Aus.) to borrow, to cadge, to wheedle (money) out of. **8** [1920s–40s] (US) to cheat, to take advantage of. [SE *nip*, to cut, to snip]

nip *v.*² [early 19C+] to move quickly, esp. in combs. *nip away*, *nip in*, *nip off*, *nip out*.

nip *v.*³ [1960s+] (S.Afr.) to be scared, terrified; thus intensifier *nip straws*. [? the fig. tightening of the sphincter muscles]

nip a bung, to *phr.* [mid-16C–18C] (Und.) to cut a purse. [NIP v.¹ (1) + BUNG n.¹ (1)]

nipcheese *n.* **1** [late 18C–late 19C] a ship's purser. **2** [late 18C–late 19C] a mean, miserly person. [NIP v.¹ (3) + SE *cheese*]; lit. 'one who steals the cheese']

nip it *v.* [1980s+] (US campus) to stop something. [abbr. SE phr. *nip (it) in the bud*]

nipitate/nippitato *n.* [18C] strong drink in general. [NIP n.²]

nip joint *n.* [1950s–60s] (US) an illegal drinking establishment where drink is sold in *nips* or small (orig. half-pint) measures (cf. HIT HOUSE). [NIP n.² + JOINT n.³ (3)]

nip louse *n.* [mid-19C–1920s] a tailor (cf. NIP SHRED). [SE *nip*, to pinch + *louse*; his removal of lice from the seams of clothes]

nip lug *n.* [19C] (Scot.) a teacher. [SE *nip*, to pinch + LUG n.¹ (1)]

nipper *n.*¹ **1** [late 16C–17C; late 19C] a thief or swindler. **2** [late 18C–early 19C] (Und.) a cutpurse or pickpocket (cf. BUNG-NIPPER). **3** [mid–late 19C] (US) a policeman. [NIP v.¹; later usage of (1) US]

nipper *n.*[2] [mid–late 19C] (US) a small drink. [ext. of NIP n.[2]]

nipper *n.*[3] **1** [mid-19C+] a small child. **2** [mid-19C+] a coster-monger's boy. [NIP v.[2]; children 'nip around']

nipper *n.*[4] [late 19C+] (Aus.) a prawn. [SE nip, to pinch]

nipper *v.* [early 19C] to arrest. [NIP v.[1] (2)]

nippers *n.*[1] **1** [early–mid-19C] (US) fingers or hands. **2** [early 19C–1950s] handcuffs. **3** [late 19C–1920s] a policeman. [NIP v.[1]; 20C use mainly US]

nippers *n.*[2] [late 19C] pince-nez. [their 'nipping' the bridge of the nose to gain a purchase on the face]

nipping Christian *n.* [early–mid-19C] a cut-purse. [NIP v.[1] (1) + joc. generic use of CHRISTIAN n.]

nipping jig *n.* [19C] (US) **1** a gallows. **2** a hanging. [SE nip, to pinch + jig, a dance]

nippitato *see* NIPITATE.

nipple *n.* [1950s] (W.I.) a small finger-shaped dumpling.

nipps *see* NIPS n.[1].

nippy *n.*[1] [mid-19C] the penis. [? PEE n.[1]]

nippy *n.*[2] [1930s–50s] a waitress. [NIP v.[2]; the original *nippies*, waitresses at Lyons Corner Houses, whose name was trade-marked by the firm and came from their speed]

nippy *adj.*[1] [late 19C+] sharp, lively, active. [NIP v.[2]]

nippy *adj.*[2] [late 19C+] of weather, chilly. [SE nip, to pinch; i.e. at one's skin]

nippy with the weight *phr.* [1920s–30s] of a shopkeeper, giving short weight or grudgingly giving the proper weight. [NIPPY adj.[1]; his skill in committing this piece of fraud]

nips/nipps *n.*[1] [late 17C–early 18C] (Und.) shears used to clip coins. [SE nip, to cut, to snip]

nips *n.*[2] [1970s+] (US) a woman's *nipples*; thus a *nip tease*, a woman wearing a shirt without a bra. [abbr.]

nip/nyp shop *n.* [late 18C–early 19C] the Peacock Tavern in Gray's Inn Lane, London, where Burton ale was sold in *nips* or half-pint measures (cf. NIP JOINT). [NIP n.[2] + SE shop]

nip shred *n.* [mid-17C–mid-18C] a tailor (cf. NIP LOUSE). [SE nip, to pinch + shred]

nire *n.* [mid-19C] rain. [backsl.]

nisey *see* NIZZIE.

nisht aka/nicht *n.* [20C] nothing. [synon. Yid.]

nisty *adj.* [1980s+] (US campus) very unattractive. [? SE nasty]

nit *n.*[1] [late 16C+] a fool; thus *nitty*, foolish (cf. NITWIT). [SE nit, a louse; the implication is perhaps more of its insignificance than of its verminous qualities]

nit *n.*[2] [late 17C–18C] 'Wine that is brisk, [i.e. agreeable to the taste] and pour'd quick into a Glass' (B.E.).

nit *v.* [late 19C+] (Aus.) to escape, to decamp, to hurry away. [? NICK v.[3]]

nit! *excl.*[1] [late 19C–1910s] (Aus.) a term used to indicate that someone is coming and that one must stop what one is doing and run away. [NIT v.]

nit! *excl.*[2] [late 19C–1940s] (US) used as an emphatic *no*, also added to pos. assertions to give a neg. meaning e.g. 'I should say nit!' [var. on SE *not*]

niterie/nitery *n.* [1930s] (orig. US) a night-club. [subseq. use is SE]

nit keeper *n.* [1930s+] (Aus.) one who keeps watch while a companion performs some form of illegal activity (cf. KEEP NIT). [NIT! excl.[1] + SE keeper]

nit-nit! *excl.* [1930s–50s] shut up! (cf. NITTO). [NIX v.]

nitraph *n.* [mid-19C] a farthing. [backsl.]

nitro *n.* [20C] (orig. US) *nitro*glycerine, as used in blowing up safes. [abbr.]

nitro *adj.* [1980s+] (US) excellent, wonderful (cf. DYNAMITE). [fig. use of NITRO n.]

nits and lice *n.* [20C] a price, esp. in gambling. [rhy. sl.]

nit-shit *adj.* [1960s+] (US) second-rate, insignificant, trivial (cf. CHICKENSHIT adj.). [SE nit, a louse + SHIT adj.]

nitski! *excl.* [1900s–20s] (US) an emphatic 'no!' (cf. NIT! excl.[2]).

nit squeezer *n.* [late 18C] a hairdresser. [SE nit, a louse; lit. 'nit-squeezer']

nitto *v.* [1950s–60s] (Und.) to stop; thus *nitto!*, stop it! [NIT-NIT!]

nitty *n.* [1970s+] (US) the essentials, the fundamentals. [abbr. NITTY-GRITTY n.]

nitty/knitty *adj.* [early 18C] a general epithet of abuse. [lit. 'suffering from nits']

nitty-gritty *n.* [1950s+] (orig. US Black) the basics, the essentials, the grass roots. [ety. unknown; redup. of SE gritty, composed of minute particles]

nitty-gritty *adj.* [1960s+] (orig. US Black) fundamental, basic. [NITTY-GRITTY n.]

nitwit *n.* [1910s+] (orig. US) a fool. [SE nit, a louse + wit]

nix *n.* **1** [late 18C–1950s] nobody, no one. **2** [1980s+] (drugs) a stranger among the group. [colloq. Du./Ger. nix; ult. nichts, nothing]

nix *adj.* **1** [late 18C+] no, none, negligible. **2** [mid-19C–1950s] (US) worthless or damaged. [NIX n. (1)]

nix *adv.* [late 18C+] no, not possibly, certainly not (cf. NIXEY). [NIX adj.]

nix *v.* **1** [20C] (US) to forbid, to veto, to reject, to cancel or eliminate. **2** [1990s] (US) to ruin or spoil. [NIX n. (1)]

nix! *excl.* [mid-19C+] **1** a warning of someone's approach. **2** (orig. US) an emphatic 'no!', 'stop that (at once)!' [Ger. nichts, nothing]

nix come arouse/cum rouse/come erous/comarous *phr.* [mid-19C+] (US) never, no, it doesn't matter. [Ger. nichts kommt heraus, nothing will come of this]

nix deberr! *excl.* [early 19C] (Cockney) no, my friend. [NIX! (2) + deberr, a perversion of Rus. tovarich, a friend]

nixer *n.* [1960s+] (Irish) work undertaken in one's free time, as part of the 'black economy'. [NIX v.]

nixey!/nixie! *excl.* [late 19C–1910s] (US) no, certainly not (cf. NIX!).

nixies *n.* [1930s] women's knickers. [abbr.]

nix mungarlee *phr.* (Ling. Fr./Polari) nothing to eat, no food. [NIX adj. + MUNGARLY]

nix my doll/dolly *phr.* [late 18C–mid-19C] never mind, it doesn't matter. [thus the sl. verse: 'In the box of a stone jug I was born,/Of a hempen widow and a kid forlorn;/And my noble father, as I have heard say,/Was a famous merchant of capers gay;/Nix my dolly, pals, fake away!'; written by William Ainsworth as 'Jenny Junipers' chant in *Rookwood* 1834; he claimed it as the 'first flash song' but was some 300 years late. Farmer (1896) cites Copland's *Rhymes of the Canting Crew c.1536*]

nix on *phr.* [1900s–50s] (US) enough of, no more of. [NIX adv.]

Nixon *n.* [1960s] (drugs) inferior marijuana sold fraudulently as being of high quality. [US President Richard M. *Nixon* (1913–94), a notably corrupt figure, latterly best known for his role in the Watergate Affair]

nix on it *phr.* [1940s+] (Aus.) no more of that, stop it. [NIX v.]

nix out/out on *v.* [20C] (orig. US Black) to throw away, to get rid of a person. [NIX v.]

niyabinghi *n.* [1950s+] (W.I. Rasta) **1** a society of Rastafarian 'warriors', dedicated to the overthrow of White rule. **2** a large Rastafarian meeting and spiritual gathering. **3** a variety of drumming. [a supposed Ethiopian word *niyabinghi*, 'death to the White man'; orig. adopted by a group, led by Hailie Selassie, who resisted colonial domination in Ethiopia and the Congo]

niyabinghi *adj.* [1950s+] (W.I. Rasta) used of orthodox, tradi-tional Rastafarians. [NIYABINGHI n.]

niyaman *n.* [1950s+] (W.I. Rasta) a Rastafarian. [NIYA(BINGHI) adj. + SE *man*]

nizzie/nizy/nisey *n.* [late 17C–mid-19C] a fool, a dunce. [? 13C SE *nice*, foolish, senseless; ? ult. Lat. *nescius*, ignorant]

nizzie/nizy/nisey *adj.* [late 17C–mid-19C] foolish, dull. [NIZZIE n.]

n.n. *n.* [late 19C] (society) a husband. [abbr. *necessary nuisance*]

N.O. *n.* (US) *New Orleans.* [abbr.]

no-account *adj.* [19C+] (US Black) a general pej., worthless, insignificant, undependable, untrustworthy, criminal. [abbr. SE *of no account*]

no-account nigger *n.* [early 19C+] (US Black) a Black who rejects the second-class role offered by the dominant White society (cf. BAD-ASS NIGGER; DOG NIGGER). [NO-ACCOUNT adj. + NIGGER n.]

noah's *n.* [1960s+] a police informer (cf. NAUS; NOAH'S ARK n.²). [rhy. sl. *Noah's ark* = NARK n.]

Noah's ark *n.*¹ [mid-19C] a long, closely buttoned overcoat, fashionable *c.*1860. [coined by *Punch*, the term supposedly reflected the similarity of the coat to those worn by Noah and his children in toy *Noah's arks*]

Noah's ark *n.*² 1 [late 19C] a lark, a game. 2 [late 19C] a lark (the bird). 3 [late 19C+] a park. 4 [late 19C+] an informer (cf. NOAH'S). 5 [1940s+] (Aus.) a shark. [rhy. sl.; (4) *Noah's ark* = NARK n.]

no arse! *excl.* [20C] (W.I.) a general intensifier, like hell! [fig. use of ARSE n.¹]

nob *n.*¹ 1 [late 17C+] the head. 2 [early 19C] a blow on the head. 3 [mid-19C] a sovereign (cf. MONARCH n.²). [(3) the royal head on the coin]

nob *n.*² [mid–late 18C] the game of prick-the-garter, a form of swindling game, in which one pricked a belt with a large needle; presumably betting on the odds of hitting a given target. [ety. unknown]

nob *n.*³ [mid-18C+] a nobleman, a gentleman; thus *nobbish*, aristocratic; *nobbily*, aristocratically; [early–mid-19C] *nobs' houses*, the Houses of Parliament, divided into *upper nobs' house*, the Lords, *lower nobs' house*, the Commons; [mid-19C] *nob in the fur trade*, a judge. [? abbr. SE *nobility* or *nobleman*, but 18C Scot. use suggests an alternative – if unknown – ety.; according to Jon Bee (1823), 'the swell ... makes a show of his finery ... the nob, relying upon intrinsic worth, or bona fide property, or intellectual ability, is clad in plain-ness']

nob *n.*⁴ 1 [early 19C+] the penis (cf. KNOB n.¹). 2 [1970s+] a socially inept person. [? SE *knob*]

nob *n.*⁵ [mid-19C] in cribbage, the knave of trumps. [? dial. *nob*, an interloper]

nob *v.*¹ [early 19C] to hit on the head. [NOB n.¹ (1)]

nob *v.*² [early 19C+] of a man, to have sexual intercourse. [NOB n.⁴ (1)]

nob *v.*³ [mid–late 19C] 1 to collect money. 2 to make a collection after a sporting contest, a performance etc. [NOB n.¹ (3)]

nob-a-nob *adj.* [mid–late 19C] intimate, close, friendly. [NOB n.¹]

nobba/nobber *n.* [mid-19C] 9; thus *nobba saltee*, ninepence. [Ital. *nove*, 9; 'introduced by the "organ-grinders" from Italy' (Hotten, 1867)]

nobber *n.*¹ [early 19C] 1 a blow on the head. 2 a boxer skilled at delivering such blows. [NOB n.¹ (1)]

nobber *n.*² [late 19C] a collector of money. [NOB n.¹ (3)]

nobber *n.*³ [20C] (Irish) one who is having sexual intercourse. [NOB v.²]

nobbing *n.*¹ [mid-19C+] collecting money, 'passing the hat round'; thus *nobbings*, a collection of money, esp. money tossed into a boxing ring after an amateur or boys' fight. [NOB v.³]

nobbing *n.*² [20C] sexual intercourse. [NOB v.²]

nobble *v.*¹ 1 [mid-19C+] to strike. 2 [late 19C] to hit on the head (cf. NOBBLER n.¹). [NOB n.¹ (1)]

nobble *v.*² 1 [mid-19C] to use illicit methods to obtain a person's help. 2 [mid-19C] to steal, to take illicitly. 3 [mid-19C] to cheat, to over-reach. 4 [mid–late 19C] to swindle, to influence or to corrupt. 5 [mid-19C+] (racing) to interfere with a horse in order to spoil its chance of victory; thus [1960s+] *jury nobbling*, the interference with the impartiality of a jury (through threats or bribes) either by a defendant or their friends. 6 [mid-19C+] to ruin anything deliberately; esp. to impede a rival; to discover (a plot). 7 [mid-19C+] to kidnap. 8 [mid-19C+] to get hold of, to seize, to catch. 9 [1990s] (US) to obtain for oneself undeservedly. [ety. unknown; ? NAB v.¹]

nobbler *n.*¹ [mid-19C] (orig. boxing jargon) a knock-out blow. 2 [late 19C] a blow on the head. [NOB v.¹]

nobbler *n.*² 1 [mid-19C] a man who runs a game of 'find-the-lady' or THREE-CARD MONTE. 2 [mid-19C] a card cheat. 3 [mid-19C] a card-sharp's accomplice. 4 [mid-19C+] one who lames, drugs or otherwise tampers with horses. [NOBBLE v.²; note northern dial. a low, cunning lawyer]

nobbler/nobler *n.*³ [mid-19C+] (Aus.) a small measure of spirits; thus *nobblerize*, to drink spirits, usu. as part of a group. [fig. use of NOBBLE v.²; it 'gets hold of you']

nobby *adj.* 1 [late 18C+] showy, extravagant; thus *nobbily*, vulgarly, showily. 2 [late 18C+] extremely smart or elegant, aristocratic, also *knobby*. 3 [mid-19C–1900s] as *the nobby*, the smart thing. 4 [late 19C] (US) wonderful, also *knobby*. [NOB n.³]

nobby halls *n.* [20C] the testicles. [rhy. sl. *Nobby Halls* = BALLS n.¹ (1); orig. the mono-testicled 'hero' of a music-hall song]

Nobby Stiles *n.* [1990s] haemorrhoids, piles. [rhy. sl.; ult. UK soccer star *Nobby Stiles*]

no beg-pardons *phr.* [20C] (Aus.) no apologies. [SE apology *I beg your pardon*]

no better than he/she should be *phr.* [late 19C+] admitting that the person in question is simply human, warts and all; often used of a woman who is considered promiscuous.

no-beyond jammer *n.* [late 19C–1900s] an extremely attractive woman. [JAM n.³]

nob girder *see* NAB GIRDER.

nob hill *n.* [early 19C+] (orig. US) the most socially exclusive and/or richest area of a town or city (cf. HOB'S KNOB). [NOB n.³ + SE *hill*; note New York's *Nob Hill*, a row of fine houses built *c.*1815 near Bowling Green and *Nob's Hill*, an area of San Francisco colonized by wealthy veterans of the California Gold Rush]

no big deal/biggie *phr.* [1960s+] (US teen) don't worry, it's all right etc. [SE *no* + BIG DEAL n./BIGGIE n. (1)]

nob it *v.* [early 19C] (Und.) to succeed without working in the respectable world. [NOB n.³]

no bitch! *excl.* [1980s+] (US campus) in choosing seats in a car, 'I won't ride in the middle of the back seat.' [RIDE BITCH]

nob jockey *n.* [1990s] a homosexual male. [NOB n.⁴ (1) + JOCKEY n.²]

noble *n.* [1930s+] (US) 1 a man hired as a guard to protect strike-breakers. 2 the boss of a gang of such guards.

noble *adj.*¹ [1900s–20s] (US Black) good, excellent.

noble *adj.*² [1960s–70s] (US prison) used of an inmate considered to be reliable, trustworthy, courageous and generally admirable.

nobler *see* NOBBLER n.³.

noble weed *n.* [1960s] (drugs) marijuana.

nobody home/home upstairs *phr.* [20C] (orig. US) used of someone who is dull of stupid (cf. LIGHTS ON BUT THERE'S NOBODY HOME).

nobody's fool *n.* [19C+] an intelligent, aware person.

no bon *phr.* [1910s–20s] no good. [pidgin Fr. *no* + *bon*, good; coined during WW1]

no bottle *phr.*[1] [mid-19C] impossible, not allowed, out of the question (cf. NO DICE; NO SOAP). [the refusal of further drinks by a bar-tender]

no bottle *phr.*[2] [20C] **1** lacking quality or style. **2** cowardly. [rhy. sl. *no bottle and glass* = (1) no class; (2) no ARSE n.[3]]

nob pitcher *n.* [early 19C] (Und.) a sharp or confidence man who specializes in finding his victims at fairs, races and similar open-air events. [NOB n.[3] ? + NOBBLE v.[2]]

no-brainer *n.* [1970s+] (US) **1** anything that requires no intellectual effort. **2** an easy decision. **3** a foolish person or thing.

no-brand/no-name/no name-brand cigarette *n.* [1970s+] (drugs) a marijuana cigarette. [one rolls such cigarettes oneself; there is no commercial packaging]

no bread and butter of mine *phr.* [late 18C–early 19C] no business of mine.

nobrow *adj.* [1990s] (US) vulgar, tasteless. [pun on LOWBROW adj.]

nobs *n.*[1] [mid-16C] a term of affection used of a woman. [? her figure. i.e. 'knobs' or curves]

nobs *n.*[2] [late 19C–1950s] (US) an important person (cf. NIBS). [NOB n.[3]]

nob scoffer *n.* [1990s] one who offers homosexual fellatio. [NOB n.[4] (1) + SCOFF v.]

nobscratch *n.* [1990s] a general term of abuse. [NOB n.[4] (2) + SE *scratch*; the implication is of pubic lice]

nobsey *n.* [mid-16C] a mistress. [NOBS n.[1]]

nobstick *n.* [mid-19C] a strike-breaker (cf. KNOBSTICK; SNOB-STICK). [SE *knobstick*, a club with a rounded head, used by strike-breakers as a weapon]

nob stilton *n.* [1990s] **1** smegma. **2** a term of general derision/abuse. [play on COCK-CHEESE; (2) is fig. use of (1)]

nob thatch *n.* [mid-19C] human hair. [NOB n.[1] (1) + SE *thatch*]

nob-thatcher *n.* [late 18C–mid-19C] a wig-maker (cf. SKULL-THATCHER). [NOB n.[1] (1) + SE *thatcher*]

no burner of navigable rivers *phr.* [late 18C] a phr. used to describe an unexceptional person, one who will make no mark on the world. [play on SET THE THAMES ON FIRE]

no butter will stick on his bread *phr.* [late 18C+] a phr. used to describe one who has consistently bad luck in whatever they try to achieve.

no can do/n.c.d. *phr.* [20C] (orig. US) it is impossible (usu. with apologetic overtones).

no cash/money, no Swiss *phr.* [20C] no help without payment in advance. [the traditional role of the *Swiss* as mercenary soldiers]

no chance *phr.* [20C] a general term of dismissal or negation, no hope or possibility whatsoever.

no chicken *n.* [early 18C+] a name given to someone, often a woman, who is no longer young. [CHICKEN n.[4] (1)]

no/not much chop *phr.* [19C] (Aus.) no class, second-rate; thus *not much chop*, of no great value (cf. FIRST CHOP). [Hind. *chhaap*, a print, and thus a seal, notably that which is placed on first-rate merchandise]

no Christmas box *see* NO HIDE.

nochy *n.* [mid-19C+] (Ling. Fr./Polari) night. [Ital. *notte*/Sp. *noche*, night]

nock *n.* **1** [late 16C] the vagina. **2** [late 18C] the anus (cf. NOCK-ANDRO). [SE *notch* or *see* NOCKANDRO]

nock *v.* [late 16C–late 18C] to have sexual intercourse. [NOCK n.]

nockandro *n.* [17C–mid-18C] the buttocks. [Early Mod.E *nock*, the cleft of the buttocks]

nocky *n.* [late 17C–19C] a fool, a simpleton. [Suffolk dial.; ? f. the fool's *knock*ing on or knuckling on his forehead]

nocky boy *n.* [late 18C–early 19C] a dullard, a simpleton. [NOCKY + SE *boy*]

no class *adj.* [late 19C+] styleless, socially inept, unable to fulfil the group norms.

no cool *n.* [1980s+] (US campus) northern California (cf. SO COOL). [joc. use of sl. + ref. to the status of that part of the state]

no/not much cop *phr.* [late 19C+] of no or little value or use, worthless.

noctress *n.* [19C] a prostitute (cf. EVENING STAR). [SE pfx. *noct-* + fem sfx. *-tress*]

nocturne *n.* [late 19C–1910s] a prostitute (cf. EVENING STAR). [joc. use of painting jargon *nocturne*, a night-piece]

nod *n.* **1** [1930s–40s] (US Black) a sleep (cf. COP A NOD). **2** [1930s+] (orig. US drugs) the drug-induced stupor or semi-sleep that follows an injection of heroin.

nod/nod off/out *v.* [1950s+] to become temporarily comatose following the immediate effects of an injection of heroin or any other opiate drug. [NOD n. (2)]

no danger *phr.* [1970s+] a general phr. of affirmation, no problem, absolutely, truthfully.

nod/nodge cock *n.* [19C] a fool, a simpleton (cf. NODDY n.[1]). [the foolish nodding of their head]

noddipol/noddy pate *n.* [18C] a simpleton, a fool. [NODDY n.[1] + SE *poll/pate*, head]

noddle *n.* [mid-16C+] **1** the head. **2** used fig. to denote the head as a seat (or not) of intelligence; thus *use your noddle*, use your head, act sensibly. [15C SE *noddle*, the back of the head]

noddle case *n.* [18C] a wig. [NODDLE + SE *case*]

noddle-thatcher *n.* [18C] a wig-maker (cf. NOB-THATCHER). [NODDLE + SE *thatcher*]

noddy *n.*[1] [early 16C–late 19C] a fool, a simpleton (cf. NOD COCK; STRUT-NODDY). [the foolish wagging of his head]

noddy *n.*[2] [mid-19C] (Irish) a one-horse conveyance; thus *noddy-boy*, the driver. [its 'nodding' from side-to-side]

noddy *n.*[3] [1950s+] a weakling. [the children's character *Noddy*, created by author Enid Blyton (1897–1968)]

noddy head *n.* [mid-19C–1900s] a fool; thus *noddy-headed*, drunk (cf. NODDIPOL). [NODDY n.[1] + SE *head*]

noddy pate *see* NODDIPOL.

nodge cock *see* NOD COCK.

no dice *phr.* [1930s+] (orig. US) impossible, out of the question, on no account (cf. NO BOTTLE; NO SOAP). [the refusal of a gambling-house proprietor to allow a player to start or continue playing]

no diggety! *excl.* [1990s] (US teen) a general excl. implying 'without question!' [? var. on HOT DIGGETY]

nod is as good as a wink to a blind horse, a *phr.* [early 19C+] used of a subtle, but undoubtedly comprehensible hint.

nod off *see* NOD v.

no doubt! *excl.* [1980s+] (US campus) a general expression of agreement. [emphatic var. on SE]

nod out *see* NOD v.

no down! *excl.* [early 19C] carry on! don't stop! (cf. FAKE AWAY!).

nod the nut, to *phr.* [1930s+] (Aus.) to plead guilty (cf. BOW THE CRUMPET; DUCK THE SCONE). [SE *nod* + NUT n.[3] (1); the defendant acknowledges his guilt with a nod when asked 'How do you plead']

no dust on *phr.* [late 19C] (US) up to the minute, highly fashionable. [the image of dust gathering on a conservative or old-fashioned person]

no earthly *n.* [late 19C] no hope whatsoever, no possible chance. [abbr. SE *no earthly chance*]

no end/end of *phr.* **1** [early 17C+] a vast quantity or number. **2** [late 19C+] to a great extent, very much.

no eyes *phr.* [1940s+] I'm not interested. [neg. of HAVE EYES FOR]

no fear! *excl.* [mid-19C+] (orig. N.Z.) absolutely not! not a chance!

noffka/nafka *n.* [20C] a prostitute. [synon. Yid.]

no flies!/flies about! *excl.* [mid–late 19C] (Aus.) no problem! no fuss! no doubt about it!

no flies on *phr.* [19C+] as in *no flies on me/her* etc., implying the smartness and imperviousness to trickery of the speaker or subject (cf. FLY adj.¹). [? cattle that were so active that no fly could settle on them]

no freak *n.* [1970s] a client who wishes a prostitute to simulate the role of a rape victim, screaming 'No!' and 'struggling' before he overpowers her. [SE *no* + FREAK n. (4)]

nog *n.* [1960s+] (Aus.) a Vietnamese, orig. a North Vietnamese or Viet Cong soldier (cf. NOGGY). [abbr. NIG-NOG n.²]

noggin *n.¹* [19C+] the head. [? SE *noggin*, a small drinking vessel, a mug; orig. US, but migrated to the UK in mid-19C]

noggin *n.²* [1940s] (W.I.) a farthing (post-1969 value 1¼ cents). [? NOGGIN n.¹, i.e. the head engraved on one side of the coin or SE *noggin*, a quarter (or less) of a pint]

noggy *n.* [1950s+] (Aus.) an Asian, esp. an Asian immigrant to Australia. [abbr. NIG-NOG n.²]

no giggle *adj.* [1930s+] unpleasant (cf. NO JOKE).

no goat's toe *phr.* [20C] (Ulster) used of one who is sensible, 'nobody's fool'.

no-good *n.* [late 19C+] an unappealing, unpleasant, untrustworthy person (cf. NO-GOODER).

no-good *adj.* [20C] (US) a general term of abuse, unpleasant, untrustworthy, dishonest etc.

no-goodnik *n.* [1930s+] a general pej., an unpleasant or unreliable person (cf. ALLRIGHTNIK). [NO GOOD + -NIK]

no-gooder *n.* [1920s+] (US) a bad person, a good-for-nothing (cf. NO-GOOD n.).

no good to gundy *phr.* [20C] (Aus.) no good at all, definitely bad; thus *good enough for gundy*, reasonably good, acceptable, not too bad. [ety. unknown; ? the Welsh dial. *gundy*, to steal, thus 'not worth stealing'; a relict of the great flood of 1852 that devastated *Gundagai*; a comment by an Aborigine, one *Gundy*, when rejecting a proffered drink of whisky; a rebuttal of a temperance preacher, attempting to force his views on the populace of Gundagai]

no great *adv.* [mid–late 19C] (US) not very much, not particularly, e.g. *I don't care no great*.

no great guns *phr.* [early 19C+] nothing exceptional, nothing very important. [GREAT GUNS adv.]

no great scratch *phr.* [mid-19C] (orig. US) not much use, of no great importance. [i.e. it makes little impression]

no great shakes *phr.* [mid-19C+] (US) not very good. [GREAT SHAKES!]

no great things *phr.* [19C] of little or no importance (cf. NO GREAT SHAKES).

no hide, no Christmas box *phr.* [1930s+] (Aus.) no hope of that, not a chance. [HIDE n.³]

no hide off one's back *phr.* [1920s+] a phr. implying one's contemptuous lack of interest, 'I don't care', 'It doesn't bother me'. [var. on NO SKIN OFF ONE'S NOSE]

no holds barred *phr.* [1940s+] (orig. US) anything goes (cf. RAFFERTY'S RULES). [wrestling imagery]

no-hoper *n.* [1940s+] **1** (orig. Aus.) a useless or incompetent person, one from whom no good can be expected. **2** (Aus.) a recidivist. [horse-racing jargon *no-hoper*, an outsider, a horse that has no hope of winning]

no-hoping *adj.* [1920s+] (Aus.) of a person, hopeless, useless. [NO-HOPER]

noiding *n.* [1980s+] para*noia*. [abbr.]

noise *n.¹* **1** [late 19C+] (US) chatter, gossip, empty, foolish talk. **2** [1900s–30s] a self-important person. **3** [1940s+] (US) information, the know.

noise *n.²* [20C] (W.I.) serious trouble, usu. in phr. *be in noise*. [the lit. or fig. SE *noise* that follows]

noise *n.³* [1940s–70s] (drugs) heroin. [? play on SE *nose*]

noise/noise off *v.* [1930s+] (US Black) to boast, to brag, to indulge in foolish talk.

noisola *n.* [1930s–40s] (US Black) a jukebox, a record-player. [SE *noise* + sfx. -OLA; on model of *pianola*, the jukebox's predecessor]

no joke *phr.* [early 19C+] taking all matters as seriously as possible when dealing with a certain subject, i.e. this is not a joking or laughing matter.

no Jonas trip played on me *phr.* [1950s–60s] (US Black) no one is going to take me for a fool. [ety. unknown; ? anecdotal]

no joy! *excl.* [1940s+] an excl. of despair, disappointment, bad luck etc (cf. ANY JOY?).

nokes *n.* [late 17C–18C] a fool, a dullard. [*John-a-Nokes* was, with Tom-a-Stiles, the precursor of John Doe and Richard Roe as the legal jargon providing names for otherwise anonymous plaintiffs and defendants]

no kidding!/kid! *excl.* [mid-19C+] (US) used interrog. or emphatically, i.e. 'Are you serious?' or 'I'm absolutely serious'. [KID v.]

no knock *n.* [1960s+] (US police) a clause in US drug laws that permits police to enter premises without knocking first and thus ensure surprise and probable arrests.

nol *adj.* [mid-19C] long. [backsl.]

nola *n.* [1930s–60s] (US) a homosexual male (cf. AGNES). [the female name]

noli me tangere *n.* [17C–19C] (Scot.) venereal disease. [Lat. *noli me tangere*, don't touch me]

noll *n.* [18C] the head, esp. in comb. *drunken noll*. [OE *hnoll*, the crown of the head]

nolle pros/pross, to *phr.* [late 19C+] (orig. US) to abandon a trial because the plaintiff or prosecutor has given up the suit, usually because there is insufficient hard evidence, a key witness has backed down etc. [legal Lat. *nolle prosequi*, 'to be unwilling to pursue']

no load *n.* [1920s+] (US) a lazy, unenthusiastic or pessimistic person. [they 'carry no weight']

no-man *n.* [1950s+] (orig. US) one who habitually says no, one who will disagree as a matter of policy, rather than on the basis of any rational thought (cf. YES-MAN).

no matter how you slice it/whichever way you slice it *phr.* [1930s+] (US) however you look at or assess it. [abbr. remark by US politician Al Smith in 1936: 'No matter how thin you slice it, it's still BALONEY n.¹']

no mercy *phr.* [1910s] (Aus.) a phr. written on the back of a pay cheque and handed to a publican when a man wanted to spend his entire season's wages in a single binge. [joc. use SE]

nominate your poison *see* NAME YOUR POISON.

nommus *see* NAMMOUS.

nommus! *excl.* [mid-19C+] a warning cry on sighting a policeman. [backsl. *nommus* = someone]

no money, no Swiss *see* NO CASH, NO SWISS.

no more chance than a cat in hell without claws *phr.* [late 18C–mid-19C] absolutely no chance at all (cf. NOT A CAT IN HELL'S CHANCE).

no more chance than a snowball in hell *phr.* [late 19C+] absolutely no chance at all.

no more than ninepence in the shilling *phr.* [late 19C+] referring to one considered a simpleton, a fool (cf. NOT ALL THERE). [a shilling (5p) had 12 pence]

no more use than/as good as a headache/a sick headache *phr.* [1910s+] absolutely useless.

no muss, no fuss *phr.* [1940s+] (US) no problems, either practically or emotionally.

non *n.* [1970s] (US Black) a physically unco-ordinated person; a poor athlete. [? SE *non-performer*]

no-name/no-name brand cigarette *see* NO-BRAND CIGARETTE.

no names, no pack-drill *phr.* [1920s+] **1** if no one is named (as a perpetrator) no one can be punished. **2** a contentious subject is closed and no one should attempt to re-open it. [milit. *pack-drill*, a form of field punishment whereby a defaulter was forced to walk up and down in full marching order, with rifle, bayonet, ammunition, knapsack and overcoat]

no-nation *n.* [20C] (W.I.) a usu. dark-skinned person of more than two racial mixtures. [SE *no* + sfx. -NATION]

no nature *adj.* [1970s+] (US Black) used to describe one who has a low sex drive (cf. LOT OF NATURE). [NATURE *n.* (2)]

non-biologicals *n.* [1990s] (gay) the non-birth parent of a child, i.e. where one of the partners is the biological parent by a previous relationship or alternative means and the other is not.

nonce *n.* [1970s+] sexual offender, spec. of young children (cf. BEAST *n.*[5]). [? dial. *nonce*, a good-for-nothing, thus image of a 'nothing', a 'non-person'; the *Police Review* (18 May 1984) suggests orig. in NANCY BOY]

non-com *n.* [mid-19C+] a *non-com*missioned officer in the army. [abbr.]

non compos *adj.* [late 19C+] **1** eccentric, crazy. **2** drunk, ext. as *non compos poo-poo* (cf. ADDLED). [Lat. *non compos mentis*, not of sound mind]

non-con *n.* [late 17C–early 19C] a religious dissenter, typically a non-conformist or Presbyterian. [abbr. SE *non-conformist*]

nondy/nondi *adj.* [20C] inferior, second-rate. [SE *nondescript*]

no neck *n.* [1950s+] (Black) a weakling, a coward. [boxing jargon *no neck*, one who cannot take a punch; ult. NECK *n.*[1]]

none of John Whoball's/Whoaball's children *phr.* [late 17C–18C] a phr. used to describe one who is no fool. [supposed proper name *John* + WHOABALL]

none of the hasting sort, to be *phr.* [mid-16C–late 18C] to be a tardy, slow person. [SE *hasten*, to go quickly; Grose (1785) suggests a pun on the *Hastings pea*, the first pea of the season]

none of your beeswax *phr.* [20C] (US) none of your business. [play on SE *beeswax/business*]

none of your funeral *phr.* [19C] (US) none of your business, not your concern.

non est *adj.* [mid-19C–1950s] non-existent, absent. [Lat. *non est*, it is not]

nonesuch *see* NONSUCH.

nong *n.* [1940s+] (Aus.) an idiot, a fool, a general derog. description (cf. NING-NONG). [Lat. n*on compos*]

non me *n.* [early 19C] a lie (cf. O BERGAMI!). [the trial of Queen Caroline, *c*.1820, when the Italian witnesses universally replied to counsel *No me ricordo*, I do not remember]

nonny no *n.* [16C] **1** the vagina. **2** sex in general. [SE *nonny no*, the refrain of a song, thus a trifle, a nothing]

no-no *n.* [1940s+] an impossibility, something forbidden. [SE *no* + redup.]

no nothing *n.* [mid-19C+] nothing at all, nothing whatsoever. [rather than cancel itself out, the double-negative emphasizes the phr.]

non-schlock *adj.* [1980s+] (US campus) avant-garde. [SE *non* + SCHLOCK]

nonsense *n.* **1** [late 18C–early 19C] 'melting butter in a wig'

(Grose 1796). **2** [early–mid-19C] money. **3** [1930s+] a fiasco, a farce. [presumably (1) is Grose's own joke def.]

non-skid *n.* [1920s] a Jew (cf. FRONT-WHEEL SKID) [rhy. sl. *non-skid* = YID *n.*[1]]

nonsuch/nonesuch *n.* **1** [18C–19C] the vagina. **2** [late 19C] as *Mr Nonsuch*, a conceited person. [SE *nonesuch*, an unmatched, unrivalled thing]

non-toucher *n.* [1980s+] (drugs) a smoker of crack cocaine who recoils from physical contact while experiencing the drug's effects (cf. TOUCHER *n.*[1]).

no odds *phr.* [mid-17C+] no concern, no matter; usu. as *it makes no odds* (*to me*) or as excl. *no odds!* no matter!

noodge *see* NUDGE *n.*

noodle *n.*[1] [19C+] **1** the human head. **2** used fig. to denote intelligence, the mind (cf. NODDLE). [ety. unknown; (2) is fig. use of (1)]

noodle *n.*[2] [1970s+] (US Black) the penis. [its resemblance, when flaccid, to a cooked noodle]

noodle *v.*[1] [early 19C] to fool, to trick. [SE *noodle*, a fool]

noodle *v.*[2] [1930s+] (US) to tune a musical instrument, to warm up or improvise musically. [? SE *doodle*]

noodle *v.*[3] [1930s+] (US) **1** to think, to brainstorm. **2** usu. constructed as *noodle out/up*, to mull something over, to work something out. [NOODLE *n.*[1] (2)]

noodlehead/noodlebrain *n.* [1910s+] (US) a dull, stupid person. [SE *noodle*, a fool + sfx. -HEAD (1)]

noodnik *see* NUDNIK.

no offence *phr.* [mid-19C+] 'please do not take offence (from what I have said)'.

noogie *v.* [1960s+] (US) to rub one's knuckles hard across one's victim's skull (cf. DRY SHAVE *v.*[2]; DUTCH RUB). [? corruption of SE *knuckle*]

noogies *n.* [1980s] (US) the testicles. [ety. unknown]

no oil painting *n.* [late 19C+] an unattractive person (cf. NO VAN DYCK).

nook *n.* [1910s–30s] a penny. [ety. unknown]

nookie/nooky/nucky *n.* (orig. US) **1** [1920s+] sexual intercourse. **2** [1960s+] the vagina. **3** [1960s+] a woman seen as no more than an object of possible seduction. [? NUG *v.* or Du. sl. *neuken*, to fuck]

nookie *adj.* [1910s–30s] (N.Z.) tiny, little; thus a nickname for a small boy or short person. [? Maori *noke*, small]

nookie bookie *n.* [1940s+] (US) a pimp or a madam. [NOOKIE *n.* + SE *book*, to reserve, to set aside]

nookie house *n.* [1980s] (US) a brothel (cf. ACCOMMODATION HOUSE). [NOOKIE *n.* + HOUSE *n.*[1]]

nooky *see* NOOKIE *n.*

noolucks/newlicks *n.* [mid-19C] an imaginary person. [a nonce-word, ety. unknown]

noom *n.* [mid-19C] the moon. [backsl.]

nooner *n.* **1** [1940s+] a midday alcoholic drink. **2** [1970s+] sexual intercourse, often adulterous, enjoyed around lunchtime (cf. AFTERNOON DELIGHT). [SE *noon*]

noose *v.* [late 17C–early 19C] to hang.

noosed/noozed *adj.* **1** [17C–mid-19C] married. **2** [late 17C–early 19C] hanged. [fig. and lit. uses of NOOSE *v.*]

nope *n.* [early 18C–early 19C] a blow to the head. [15C northern dial. *nawp*, *noup*, *nope*, a blow; ult. a supposed Scandinavian *v. nawpe*, to strike down]

nope! *excl.* [late 19C+] (US) no!

no picnic *n.* [mid-19C+] an unpleasant situation, a formidable task, usu. in response to another speaker, *It was no picnic, I can tell you*. [ironic understatement]

no place *n.* [1930s+] (orig. US) nowhere.

no problem *phr.* [1960s+] (orig. US) don't worry, it's all right.

no probs *phr.* [1980s+] *no problems*. [abbr.]

no rats *n.* [late 19C] a Scotsman. ['it being supposed that a Scot is always associated with bagpipes, and that no rat can bear the neighbourhood of that musical instrument' (Ware)]

no rest for the wicked *phr.* [late 19C+] said of or by someone who, while in no way wicked, is kept very busy; said with pride rather than rancour. [Isa. 48:22: 'There is no peace, saith the Lord, unto the wicked']

no return ticket *phr.* [late 19C] said of one who is seen to be showing signs of madness. [phr. 'He's going to Hanwell and *no return ticket*', the Hanwell Asylum (founded 1831 to the west of London), an 'enlightened asylum' which held about 2000 patients in 1900]

Norfolk capon *see* YARMOUTH CAPON.

Norfolk dumpling/turkey *n.* [late 17C+; early 19C+] a native of Norfolk (cf. YARMOUTH BLOATER n.¹). [the food rather than any particular rotundity of the Norfolk people, although the one can lead to the other]

Norfolk howard/n.h. *n.* [19C] a bedbug. [in cruel memoriam of one Joseph (or Joshua) Bug who, in 1862, changed his name to *Norfolk Howard*, despite popular derision at what was seen as affectation. *The Times* came to his aid, publishing a list of other risible/unpleasant names. Among them were 'Asse, Beaste, Belly, Boots, Cripple, Cheese, Clodd, Dunce, Fatt, Frogge, Hagg, Humpe, Jelly, Kneebone, Lazy, Mudd, Honeybum, Piddle, Paswater, Pisse, Pricksmall, Quicklove, Rottengoose, Swette, Sheartlifte, Silly, Apittle, Teate and Vittels']

Norfolk turkey *see* NORFOLK DUMPLING.

norgies/norgs *see* NORKS.

no risk *phr.* [1920s+] (Aus.) **1** no chance (of). **2** no doubt (about).

norks/norgs/norgies/norkers *n.* [1950s+] (Aus.) the breasts (cf. BORDEN'S; CREAM JUGS). [the *Norco* Co-operative Ltd, butter manufacturer of NSW, featured a cow's udder on its labels]

Nor' Loch trout *n.* [late 18C–early 19C] (Scot.) a piece of mutton. [the *Nor' Loch* abattoir]

norm *n.¹* [1970s+] (Aus.) a generic term used to describe the average Aus. male, beer-drinking, television watching, overweight and inactive (cf. ALF). [the character, created by Victoria's Minister for Sport, Brian Dixon, was launched as part of a 'get fit' campaign in 1975]

norm/normal *n.²* [1980s+] (US campus) a dull conventional person.

norma jean nicotine *n.* [1950s–60s] (camp gay) a smoker. [real name of Marilyn Monroe, *Norma Jean* Baker (1926–62) + SE *nicotine*]

normal *n.¹* [1950s–60s] (gay) a heterosexual male. [usu. with ironic overtones]

normal *n.²* *see* NORM n.².

normans *n.* [1960s+] (mainly rock music) tea. [*Norman's* café, Leicester, very popular among musicians]

normanton cocktail *n.* [1950s–60s] (Aus.) an Aboriginal woman and two blankets. [pun on GIN n.¹/SE *gin*]

no Robin Hood *phr.* [1910s+] (orig. milit.) no good. [rhy. sl.]

Norski *n.* [20C] (Aus.) a person of Norwegian origin. [Scandinavian *Norsk*, Norse + sfx. *-ski*]

north *adj.¹* [mid-19C] clever, cunning; esp. in phr. *he's too far north for me*. [stereotype of northerners, esp. Yorkshiremen, as grasping, cheating and cunning]

north *adj.²* [1980s+] (US) increasing in value, improving. [the image of going 'upwards']

Northallerton *n.* [late 18C–late 19C] a spur. [the quality of spurs made in *Northallerton*, Yorks.]

north and south *n.* [mid-19C+] mouth. [rhy. sl.]

north castle *n.* [late 19C] Holloway prison (cf. HOLLOWAY CASTLE). [its position in north London and the 'castellated' architecture of its original gateway]

North Country compliment *n.* [late 19C] a gift that is neither desired by the recipient nor of any value to him or to the donor. [neg. stereotyping of the north of England]

north end of a southbound horse/mule *phr.* [1960s+] (US) a general term of abuse, used joc. as in *you look like the north end ...* . [play on HORSE'S ARSE]

northern lights *n.* [1990s] a variety of marijuana cultivated under artificial conditions for maximum strength (cf. AURORA BOREALIS; PURPLE HAZE; SKUNK n.²). [SE *Northern lights*, the Aurora Borealis]

Northern Territory champagne *n.* [1970s] (Aus.) methylated spirits mixed with health salts, which give a fizzy head. [drunk by many Aborigines in the *Northern Territory*]

northpaw *n.* [1960s+] (US) a right-handed person (cf. SOUTHPAW). [the term is essentially artificial and rarely used]

north pole *n.* [20C] the anus. [rhy. sl. *North Pole* = ARSEHOLE n.]

north sydney *n.* [20C] (Aus.) the kidney. [rhy. sl.]

Northumberland/Lord Northumberland's arms *n.* [late 17C–late 18C] a black eye. [the red and black spectacle-like badge that is the basis of the Percy, i.e. Lord Northumberland's, arms]

Norway neckcloth *n.* [late 18C–early 19C] the pillory (cf. WOODEN PARENTHESIS; WOODEN RUFF). [it was often made from Norway fir]

Norwegian *n.* [1950s] (W.I.) an albino (cf. FRECKLE-NATURE). [their pale complexion and blond hair]

Norwegian steam *n.* [1940s+] (US) manpower. [image of large, muscular Norwegian immigrants]

norwich *phr.* [1940s+] (k)*nickers off ready when I come home*; an amorous acronym, usually found on the back of envelopes of love letters (orig. by soldiers) (cf. BOLTOP). [abbr.]

norwicher *n.* [mid-19C] more than one's fair share; esp. one who drinks more than half of a shared tankard before passing it on. [ety unknown; E.P. suggests stereotyping, as in the rhyme 'Essex stiles, Kentish miles, Norfolk wiles, many men beguiles']

no salt in a herring *phr.* [mid–late 19C] no use to anyone.

nose *n.¹* **1** [late 18C+] (later use is US prison) a police spy, an informer; thus *nose on*, to inform (against). **2** [mid-19C–1930s] a detective.

nose *n.²* [20C] a win by a narrow margin, esp. in horseracing.

nose *n.³* [1960s+] (drugs) heroin or cocaine. [one can inhale them through the *nose*]

nose *v.¹* [mid-17C–early 18C] to make a fool of, to fool, to dupe, to sneer at. [? SE phr. *lead by the nose*]

nose *v.²* **1** [late 18C–early 19C] to bully. **2** [late 19C–1900s] to hit on the nose.

nose *v.³* (Und.) **1** [early 19C] to pry into someone else's proceedings. **2** [19C+] to inform against, esp. in phr. *nose upon*.

nose *v.⁴* [1960s+] (US) to curry favour. [abbr. BROWN NOSE v.]

nose and chin *n.* **1** [mid-19C] a penny. **2** [late 19C] gin. **3** [20C] a win (on a wager). [rhy. sl. (1) *nose and chin* = WIN n.]

nose around *v.* [mid-19C+] to search, to look over, to survey. [NOSE v.³]

nosebag *n.* **1** [mid-19C–1910s] a holiday-maker who takes their own food with them; thus *the nosebag crowd* are such holiday-makers as a group. **2** [mid-19C–1910s] a veil. **3** [late 19C] a handbag. **4** [late 19C–1900s] a hospitable hotel or lodging-house. **5** [late 19C–1920s] (Aus.) a bag in which an itinerant or SWAGMAN n.² carries his provisions. **6** [late 19C+] a bag of food, a lunch box (cf. PUT ON THE NOSEBAG). **7** [1910s–40s] a gasmask.

nose-bagger *n.* [mid-19C] a day-tripper to the seaside who takes their own provisions and thus makes no useful contribution to the local economy. [NOSEBAG n. (1)]

nosebleed *adj.* [1970s+] (US) very high up, esp. of seats in sports stadiums. [also used fig.; the nosebleed's that can accompany oxygen deprivation]

nose burner *n.* [1960s–70s] (drugs) the butt of a marijuana cigarette (cf. NOSE WARMER).

nose candy *n.* [1920s+] (orig. US) cocaine, occas. heroin (cf. CANDY n.²). [SE *nose* + *candy*/CANDY n.² (3)]

nosecone *n.* [1980s+] (drugs) a large cannabis cigarette rolled with a rosebud-shaped twist of paper on the end.

nose cough *n.* [late 19C] stretorous breathing caused by a blocked nose.

nosedive *n.*¹ [1910s+] (Aus.) a grab at, a snatch towards.

nosedive *n.*² **1** [1930s–70s] (US tramp) a false show of religious belief or action to gain handouts from a religious mission (cf. NOSEDIVER). **2** [1930s+] (US) a loss of emotional or physical control, a fainting spell or a fall.

nosedive *v.* [1930s–70s] (US tramp) to make a false show of religious belief or action to gain handouts from a religious mission. [NOSEDIVE n.²]

nosediver *n.* [1930s–70s] (US tramp) a vagrant who frequents charitable missions, looking for handouts (cf. MISSION STIFF). [NOSEDIVE v.]

nose drops *n.* [1960s+] (drugs) liquefied heroin, methadone. [NOSE n.³ + SE *drops*]

nose 'em *n.* [mid-19C] tobacco. [NOSEY-MY-KNACKER]

no-see-um *n.* [mid-19C+] (US) a tiny biting fly, a midge. [lit. 'no see them']

nose flute *n.* [1950s] (US) a loud, snorting noise produced through the nose and used to imply derision.

nosegent *n.* [16C–18C] a nun. [? Fr. *à genou*, kneeling]

nose habit *n.* [1910s+] (drugs) taking narcotic drugs by sniffing them through the nose rather than by injection. [NOSE n.³ + HABIT]

nose hit *n.* [1970s] (drugs) a puff of a marijuana cigarette taken through the nose rather than the lips. [SE *nose* + HIT n.⁴ (4)]

nose job *n.*¹ [1950s+] a rhinoplasty, cosmetic plastic surgery on one's nose. [SE *nose* + JOB n.⁵]

nose job *n.*² [1960s–70s] (US Black) a sexual obsession with some object of desire. [(HAVE ONE'S) NOSE (OPEN) + JOB n.⁵]

nose-my *see* NOSEY-MY-KNACKER.

nosenheimer *n.* [1970s+] (US) an important person or one who poses as such. [they have their 'nose in the air' + abbr. (WIS)ENHEIMER]

nose paint *n.* [late 19C–1940s] (US) alcohol. [it turns the nose red]

nose picker *n.* [1960s+] (US) a child or person with offensive habits.

nose powder/stuff *n.* [1930s+] (drugs) heroin, cocaine.

noser *n.* [mid-19C+] **1** a bloody nose. **2** a blow on the nose. **3** (US Und.) an informer (cf. NOSE n.¹).

nose rag *n.* [early 19C] a handkerchief (cf. NOSE WIPE n.).

nose stuff *see* NOSE POWDER.

nose to light candles at *n.* [late 16C–early 17C] a drunkard's red and 'fiery' nose.

nose trouble *n.* [1960s–70s] (US) a propensity for interfering. [NOSE v.³ (1)]

nose upon *v.* [early 19C] to inform against, esp. to one's own benefit. [NOSE v.³ (2)]

nose warmer *n.* [late 19C] a short pipe (cf. NOSE BURNER).

nose wipe *n.* [early 19C+] a handkerchief (cf. NOSE RAG; NOSE WIPER).

nose wipe *v.* [early 17C–mid-18C] to cheat, to deceive.

nose wiper *n.* [late 19C+] a handkerchief (cf. NOSE WIPE n.).

nosey *adj.* [late 19C+] inquisitive, esp. when used as a pej. (cf. NOSEY PARKER). [NOSE v.³ (1)]

nosey bob *n.* [late 19C–1930s] (Aus.) **1** a hangman. **2** an inquisitive person, a 'nosey parker'. [R.R. Howard (*c.*1836–1906) the New South Wales hangman from *c.*1874–1904; he earned his nickname from a facial disfigurement]

nosey-my-knacker *n.* [mid-19C] tobacco; thus abbr. *nose-my*, baccy. [rhy. sl.]

nosey o'grady *n.* [1970s+] (Can.) an inquisitive person. [NOSEY + generic use of proper name]

nosey parker *n.* [20C] an inquisitive person; thus *nosey-parkering*, inquisitive; *nosey-park*, to be inquisitive; *nosey-parkerdom*, *nosey-parkerism*, *nosey-parkery*, the display of inquisitive behaviour, the exercise of intrusive questioning; *nosey-parkerishness*, a tendency to inquisitiveness. [the *OED* suggests a blend of *nosey* + *parker*, a rabbit; E.P. prefers the peeping Toms and eavesdroppers who frequented the Great Exhibition (1851); *Brewer* suggests the earlier clergyman Matthew Parker (1504–75), archbishop of Canterbury, known for his detailed inquisitions]

nosh *n.* **1** [1910s+] a delicatessen. **2** [1950s+] food, esp. a snack. [NOSH v.; (1) has a single citation (1917) in Lighter; all other refs. to *nosh* in dictionaries are 1950s+]

nosh *v.* **1** [1950s+] to snack, to eat between meals. **2** [1960s+] to practise fellatio. [Yid. *nosh*, to snack and Ger. *naschen*, to nibble, to eat surreptitiously; mainly US but note *The Nosh Bar*, a long-lived delicatessen/café in Great Windmill Street, Soho, London; (2) is pun on (1)]

nosher *n.* [20C] one who snacks or eats between meals. [NOSH v.]

noshery *n.* [1940s+] (orig. US) a snack-bar. [NOSH n. + sfx. *-ery*, or Yid. *nasherei*, snacks]

no shit! *excl.* [late 19C+] **1** an excl. of (usu.) ironic surprise; 'you don't say!' 'goodness me!'. **2** an excl. of affirmation, I mean it, this is the truth. [SE *no* + SHIT n.¹/(BULL)SHIT!]

no shit, Sherlock! *excl.* [1970s+] (orig. US) ext. of NO SHIT! [*Sherlock* is a pun on HOLMES!, which itself puns on HOMES; plus ironic use of the fictional detective *Sherlock* Holmes]

no-shit *adj.* [1970s+] (US) genuine. [abbr. *no* BULLSHIT n.]

no-shitter *n.* [1970s+] (US) an emphatically true statement. [NO-SHIT adj.]

no-show *n.* **1** [1940s+] (orig. US) a failure to keep an appointment. **2** a person who unexpectedly fails to appear. **3** [1960s+] (US) a person who is paid for a non-existent job.

nosh-up *n.* [1950s+] a feast. [NOSH n.]

no sir!/nossir! *excl.* [late 18C+] an emphatic rejection.

no siree bob!/bobtail! *excl.* [mid-19C+] (orig. US) an excl. of absolute denial. [NO SIR! + *-ee* + BOB n.²]

no skin off one's ass *phr.* [1920s+] (orig. US) no problem, no worries (cf. NO SKIN OFF ONE'S NOSE).

no skin/sweat off one's balls *phr.* [1930s+] (orig. US) of no importance; thus *not give the sweat off one's balls*, not to care at all.

no skin off one's nose/ear *phr.* [1920s+] a phr. implying one's contemptuous lack of interest; 'I don't care', 'it doesn't bother me'.

no slouch *n.* [late 18C+] something or someone good, acceptable, enterprising, energetic.

no soap *phr.* [1920s+] (orig. US) nothing doing, not a chance, no hope of that (cf. NO DICE). [SE *no* + SOAP n.² or f. rhy. sl. *bar of soap* = DOPE n.³ (2)]

no sooner calved than licked *phr.* [20C] (Irish) dealt with immediately. [farming imagery]

nosper *n.* [late 19C–1900s] **1** a person. **2** a stranger. [backsl.]

nosrap *n.* [mid-19C] a parson. [backsl.]

no strings *phr.* [20C] no conditions or obligations.

no stuff *phr.* [1940s–60s] (US Black) no fooling, no lies, absolutely honest and sincere. [STUFF n.¹]

no such animal *phr.* [1920s+] a phr. used to deny a previous statement, esp. when declaratory and controversial.

no sweat! *excl.* [1950s+] (orig. US) no problem; don't worry; it's all right (cf. SWEAT n.[2]). [i.e. there is no need to make an effort that might produce sweat]

no sweat off one's balls *see* NO SKIN OFF ONE'S BALLS.

not! *excl.* [late 19C+] (orig. US) used at the end of a declaratory sentence to reverse everything that has gone before, e.g. *the Home Secretary is a liberal, tolerant and sophisticated person – not!* (cf. OVER THE LEFT SHOULDER). [coined at Princeton University in the 1890s, internationally popularized via the film *Wayne's World* (1992)]

not a bad drop *phr.* [1940s+] (orig. Aus.) an enjoyable, flavoursome alcoholic drink. [DROP n.[2]]

not a bean *n.* [early 19C+] nothing at all, esp. of money. [BEAN n.[1]]

not a bit of it! *excl.* [late 19C+] no, you're absolutely wrong!

not able to hit the ground with his hat *phr.* [20C] (US) **1** used of a complete incompetent. **2** used of one who is extremely drunk.

not about *prep.* [1950s+] (orig. US) not intending (to do something).

not a brass razoo *n.* [20C] (Aus./N.Z.) absolutely penniless. [RAZOO]

not a bugger *phr.* [1930s+] not at all, in no way. esp. in phr. *not give a bugger*, not to care at all. [BUGGER n.[1] (3)]

not a cat in hell's chance *phr.* [1930s+] no chance at all (cf. NO MORE CHANCE THAN A CAT IN HELL WITHOUT CLAWS).

not a circumstance *phr.* [mid-19C–1900s] (US) nothing in comparison with.

not a fair pop *phr.* [1920s+] (N.Z.) unfair, not a fair chance. [POP n.[3]]

not a feather to fly with *phr.* [late 19C–1900s] ruined, penniless.

not a ghost of a chance *phr.* [mid-19C+] no chance whatsoever.

not a glimmer *phr.* [1920s] no idea whatsoever. [abbr. *not a glimmer of an idea*]

not a hope in hell *phr.* [1910s+] no chance whatsoever.

no talent *n.* [1960s+] (US) a useless person.

not all/what it's cracked up to be *phr.* [1910s+] well below expectations. [CRACK UP v.[1]]

not all lavender *phr.* [late 19C–1900s] by no means enjoyable, not very much fun.

not all/quite there *phr.* [mid-19C+] eccentric, insane, crazy. [the root phr. of many synons., all commenting adversely on the subject's intelligence, e.g. BUTTON SHORT; COUPLE OF CHIPS SHORT OF A FISH DINNER; COUPLE OF TINNIES SHORT OF A SLAB; FEW BRICKS SHORT OF A LOAD; FEW PENCE SHORT IN THE SHILLING; FEW SNAGS SHORT OF A BARBIE; FIVE ANNAS SHORT OF THE RUPEE; HAVE A FEW OF ONE'S PAGES STUCK TOGETHER; HAVE A TILE LOOSE; HAVE ONLY FIFTY CARDS IN ONE'S DECK; LIFT DOESN'T REACH THE TOP FLOOR; LOST A BUTTON; NO MORE THAN NINEPENCE IN THE SHILLING; NOT HAVE ALL ONE'S BUTTONS; NOT HAVING BOTH OARS IN THE WATER; NOT PLAYING WITH A FULL DECK; NOT QUITE; NOT THE FULL DOLLAR; NOT THE FULL QUID; ONE BRICK SHORT OF A LOAD; ONE SANDWICH SHORT OF THE PICNIC; ONE SAUSAGE SHORT OF A B.B.Q.; ONE SHINGLE SHORT; ONLY 80 PENCE IN THE POUND; ONLY ONE AND NINEPENCE IN THE FLORIN; PLAY WITH 44 CARDS IN THE DECK; ROW WITH ONE OAR; SHINGLE SHORT; SHORT OF A SHEET; TENPENCE SHORT OF THE FULL QUID; TENPENCE TO THE SHILLING; THERE'S A KANGAROO LOOSE IN THE TOP PADDOCK; THREE BRICKS SHY OF A LOAD; TWO BRICKS SHORT OF THE LOAD; TWO PENCE SHORT OF A BOB; TWO SANDWICHES SHORT OF A PICNIC; TWO WAFERS SHORT OF A COMMUNION]

not an earthly *phr.* [mid-18C+] no chance at all, absolutely impossible. [abbr. SE *not an earthly chance*]

not a patch on *phr.* [mid-19C+] impossible to compare with, nowhere near.

not a pretty sight *phr.* [1980s+] used, ironically, of something that is actually quite unpleasant to see.

not a sausage *n.* [1930s+] absolutely nothing. [SAUSAGE AND MASH]

not a sixpence to scratch one's arse with *phr.* [mid-19C+] absolutely impoverished.

not a sou/sous *n.* [late 18C–early 19C] not a penny, nothing at all. [Fr. *sou*, a coin of very low value (one twentieth of a livre, later five centimes) generally trans. as 'a penny']

not a squeak *phr.* [1970s+] not a sound.

not a word of the pudding! *excl.* [late 17C–early 18C] keep quiet about it, say absolutely nothing about it. [ety. unknown]

not backward in coming forward *phr.* [19C+] brash, direct and to the point (cf. ACCIDENTALLY ON PURPOSE).

not bad/half bad/half so bad/so bad *phr.* [late 18C+] not as bad as might have been feared, quite good.

not bad! *excl.* [1940s+] (US) excellent.

not bat an eyelid, to *phr.* [20C] (orig. US) to show no emotion, to remain imperturbable.

not be able to hit a bull in the ass, to *phr.* [20C] (US) to be clumsy or inept, esp. to be a poor marksman, other combs. include *... with a bass fiddle, ... with a handful of peas, ... with a handful of tapioca, ... with a shovel.*

not be as stupid as one looks, to *phr.* [20C] to possess more intelligence than one has been given credit for.

not behind the door when *... see* BEHIND THE DOOR WHEN *... .*

not bloody likely! *excl.* [1910s+] an emphatic neg. (cf. NOT PYGMALION LIKELY!).

not born yesterday *phr.* [late 19C+] aware, sophisticated, 'on the ball'.

not built that way *phr.* [late 19C+] (orig. US) not like that, not of such a type.

not by a dog's tail *phr.* [20C] (US) not by a long way, in no way.

not by a long jump *phr.* [late 19C–1920s] not by a very long distance.

not care/give a ... , to *phr.* a number of phr. all stating one's absolute lack of interest in the topic; e.g. [late 16C–late 17C] *... a louse;* [early 17C] *... a pin;* [early 18C] *... a farthing;* [mid-18C] *... three damns;* [early 19C] *... a rap;* [early 19C] *... a dump;* [early 19C] *... a sou(s);* [early 19C] *... a fig;* [mid-19C+] *... a tinker's surse/cuss;* [mid-19C+] *... a hoot/two hoots (in hell);* [20C] *... a button;* [20C] *... a brass farthing;* [20C] *... a chip;* [20C] *... a cent;* [20C] *... two tin fucks;* [20C] *... a fuck.*

not care/give a brass button, to *phr.* [20C] to not care at all.

not care/give a fiddlestick, to *phr.* [early 19C+] to not care at all (cf. FIDDLESTICK'S END).

not care/give a fig for, to *phr.* [late 16C+] to not care anything about. [fig. use of SE; but intensified by FIG n.[1] + euph. for FUCK n.[2]]

not care/give a fouter/footer, to *phr.* [early 17C–late 19C] to not care at all (cf. NOT GIVE A FUCK). [Fr. sl. *foutre*, to FUCK v.[1]]

not care/give a hang, to *phr.* [20C] to not care at all.

not care/give a Pall Mall, to *phr.* [late 19C] euph. for to NOT GIVE A DAMN. [rhy. sl. *Pall Mall* = gal = girl; the ref. is to W.T. Steed's series on London prostitution, 'The Maiden Tribute of Modern Babylon' (pub. 1885); the 'gals' were presumably seen as 'damned']

not care/give a raas/rass, to *phr.* [20C] (W.I.) to not care at all (cf. NOT GIVE A FUCK; NOT GIVE A SHIT). [RAAS]

not care/give a toss, to *phr.* [late 19C+] not to care one way or another. [the random outcome of tossing a coin, although later 20C use often equates *toss* with TOSS OFF v.[1], i.e. masturbation]

not care/give a whoop, to *phr.* [20C] (US) to not care at all.

not care/give beans, to *phr.* [mid-19C+] (US) to not care at all. [the image of a bean as an insignificant object]

not care whether school keeps or not, to *phr.* [mid-19C+] (US) to not care at all.

notch *n.*[1] **1** [18C–mid-19C] the vagina. **2** [1910s+] (US) a prostitute or sexually promiscuous woman.

notch *n.*[2] [1990s] (W.I./UK Black teen) a high or top ranking villain. [NOTCH adj.]

notch *adj.* [1980s+] (Black) first-rate, excellent. [TOPNOTCH]

notch house *n.* [1910s–70s] (US) a brothel (cf. ACCOMMODATION HOUSE). [NOTCH n.[1] + HOUSE n.[1]]

notch moll *n.* [1920s] (US Und.) a prostitute. [NOTCH n.[1] + MOLL n. (2)]

not do a tap/tap of work *phr.* [late 19C–1950s] to be absolutely idle. [the image of tapping with a hammer or similar too; cf. SE *stroke of work*]

not done *adj.* [late 19C+] unacceptable (cf. BAD FORM).

note/notes *n.*[1] **1** [mid-19C–1940s] (orig. Aus.) a one pound note, usu. in pl. **2** [1970s+] (US) a cash payment; thus *bad notes*, a bribe.

note *n.*[2] [late 19C] (US) a joke. [? it 'strikes a chord' in the hearer]

no-tell hotel/motel *n.* [1970s+] (US) a cheap hotel which rents out its rooms by the hour to prostitutes and their clients or to illicit lovers (cf. FAST-SHEET HOTEL). [the discretion of the staff]

not enough sense to pour piss out of a boot *phr.* [20C] (US) a phr. used of one who is very stupid.

notergal wash *n.* [late 19C] no wash at all. [? *Nightingale wash*, 'Miss [Florence] Nightingale ... had the misfortune to incur the lower public satire for stating that a person could keep himself clean on a pint of washing water per day' (Ware)]

notes *see* NOTE n.[1].

note shaver *n.* [early 19C–1900s] (US) a promoter of bogus financial companies, a usurer; thus *note-shaving*, making an excessive profit on the discounting of notes. [SE *note* + *shave*]

not even *phr.* [1980s+] (US campus) not at all, in no way.

not even wrapped up *phr.* [18C–19C] put honestly, crudely, with no attempt at censorship or hypocrisy.

not everybody's money *phr.* [1920s–30s] not to everyone's taste.

not exactly one of the world's workers *phr.* [1930s+] a phr. used to indicate the laziness of someone. [ironic]

not fear for dog to hear *phr.* [20C] (W.I.) used of unacceptable/obscene language.

not for all the tea in China *phr.* [late 19C+] (orig. Aus.) on no account, no chance whatsoever.

not for a pension *phr.* [late 19C–1920s] under no circumstances, lit. not for any amount of money.

not for Joe/Joseph *phr.* [mid-19C–1920s] by no means, not on any account. [ety. unknown; ? anecdotal]

not for this child *phr.* [late 19C–1910s] not for me. [CHILD]

not fucking likely! *excl.* [20C] an emphatic neg. (cf. NOT BLOODY LIKELY!).

not get anywhere *see* GET NOWHERE.

not get much change out of, to *phr.* [mid-19C+] to get no return result or satisfaction from; to fail to get the better of (someone).

not give a ... *see* NOT CARE A ...

not give a brass button *see* NOT CARE A BRASS BUTTON.

not give a damn, to *phr.* [18C+] to not care at all. [ostensibly from the curse DAMN (cf. TINKER'S CURSE). Grose (1785), F&H and E.P. all note *dam*, a small, almost valueless Indian coin]

not give a fiddler's fuck, to *phr.* [1930s+] (orig. US) to not care at all.

not give a fiddlestick *see* NOT CARE A FIDDLESTICK.

not give a fig *see* NOT CARE A FIG.

not give a fouter/footer *see* NOT CARE A FOUTER.

not give a fuck/flying fuck, to *phr.* [1940s+] (orig. US) to not care at all.

not give a hang *see* NOT CARE A HANG.

not give a hoot, to *phr.* [mid-19C+] to not care at all. [HOOT n.[2] (2)]

not give a monkey's, to *phr.* [1960s+] to not care at all. [the missing word is FUCK n.[2] or TOSS n.[1]]

not give a Pall Mall *see* NOT CARE A PALL MALL.

not give a raas/rass *see* NOT CARE A RAAS.

not give a rap/rap for, to *phr.* [mid-19C+] to not care at all. [RAP n.[2]]

not give a shit, to *phr.* [20C] to not care at all. [SHIT n.[4]]

not give a sod, to *phr.* [1960s+] to not care at all. [SOD n.[1] (4)]

not give a toss *see* NOT CARE A TOSS.

not give a tuppenny damn/dump/fuck, to *phr.* [late 19C+] to not care at all. [for ety. *see* NOT GIVE A DAMN]

not give a whoop *see* NOT CARE A WHOOP.

not give beans *see* NOT CARE BEANS.

not give much away, to *phr.* [late 19C+] to be cautious, to yield few or no advantages.

not give rotten apples, to *phr.* [1950s] (US) to not care at all.

not give the play, to *phr.* [1980s+] (US Black) to ignore, to reject. [GIVE SOMEONE SOME PLAY]

not go much on, to *phr.* [1920s+] to not be very keen on.

not go to bed with one's boots on, to *phr.* [1950s+] of a man, to have sexual intercourse without a condom.

not half! *excl.* [early 19C+] certainly! really! absolutely! (cf. ABOUT HALF). [i.e. not by half measures, but completely]

not half a one *phr.* [late 19C+] a card, a character, usu. in phr. *you ain't half a one!* (cf. ONE n.[4]).

no thanks! *excl.* [late 19C–1900s] don't think you can fool or trick me.

not have a clue, to *phr.* [1920s+] to have absolutely not the slightest idea.

not have a dog's chance, to *phr.* [late 19C+] to have no chance whatsoever.

not have a halfpenny to jingle on a tombstone, to *phr.* [1900s–20s] to be very poor.

not have all one's buttons, to *phr.* [mid–late 19C] to be not very intelligent, slightly eccentric, odd (cf. BUTTONS n.[1]; NOT ALL THERE).

not have/without a pot to pee/piss in, to *phr.* [20C] to be very poor. [PEE v.; PISS v.[1]]

not have a prayer, to *phr.* [1940s+] (orig. US) to have no chance whatsoever. [i.e. not even prayer will help]

not have a sixpence to scratch one's arse with, to *phr.* [mid-19C+] to be very poor.

not have enough sense to eat peas out of a bottle, to *phr.* [20C] (US) to be very stupid.

not have rounded Cape Turk, to *phr.* [1910s–20s] to regard women as no more than sex objects. [the stereotypes of Turkish sexuality]

not have the brains of a chocolate fish, to *phr.* [1980s] (N.Z. campus) to be very stupid.

not have the brains they were born with, to *phr.* [20C] to be notably stupid.

not have the faintest, to *phr.* [1960s+] to be absolutely ignorant, to not know.

not have the grass of a hen, to *phr.* [20C] (Irish) to be considered stupid.

not having/taking any *phr.* [1910s+] wanting no part in something, rejecting a suggestion or an overture of friendship, refusing to tolerate a situation.

not having both oars in the water *phr.* [20C] not very intelligent, slightly eccentric, odd (cf. NOT ALL THERE; ROW WITH ONE OAR).

not having two halfpennies to rub together *phr.* [20C] very poor.

nothing *adj.* [1950s+] (US) insipid, dull.

nothing! *excl.* [late 19C+] (orig. US) not at all, in no respect, e.g. '*It just slipped out.*' '*Slipped, nothing. You couldn't resist telling ... .*'

nothing but *adj.* [20C] exactly, none other than.

nothing doing *phr.* [early 19C+] absolutely not, not a hope, not a chance (cf. NO DICE; NO SOAP).

nothing happening *phr.* [1940s–50s] (US) used as a response to the greeting WHAT'S HAPPENING? and meaning things are normal (cf. NOTHING SHAKING).

nothing in it *see* NOT MUCH IN IT.

nothing shaking *phr.* [1940s–50s] (US) used as a response to the greeting WHAT'S SHAKING? and meaning things are normal (cf. NOTHING HAPPENING).

nothing to make a song and dance about *phr.* [late 19C+] nothing to worry about.

nothing to the bear but his curly hair *phr.* [1930s–40s] (US Black) a phr. implying that a noisy, bragging aggressive person is in fact all show and cowardice.

nothing to write/wire home about *phr.* [1910s+] (orig. milit.) insignificant, unexciting (despite rumours to the contrary).

notice box *n.* [1980s+] (Irish) one who is keen to attract attention; thus *Miss Notice Box*, a 'forward' woman.

notice to quit *n.* [early–mid-19C] intimations of one's imminent death.

no Tich! *excl.* [mid-19C] (society) don't be dull! that's boring! (cf. PAS DE LAFARGE). [the near-inevitability, at a certain time, of dinner-table conversations centred on the *Tichborne Claimant* case, in which Arthur Orton (1834–98) claimed in 1866 to be Roger Charles Tichborne (1829–54), the heir to an English baronetcy, who was lost at sea. Orton was finally discredited and imprisoned in 1874]

not if I can help it *phr.* [mid-19C+] a phr. used to imply one's unwillingness to back (and thus desire to impede) a project or proposal.

notion *n.* [late 19C+] (Irish) amorous inclinations, usu. in phr. *have a notion of*, to be sexually attracted by. [SE *notion*, an inclination, disposition or desire]

not ... in a hurry *phr.* [late 18C+] not very soon, e.g. *she won't be doing that again in a hurry.*

not in it *phr.* [19C+] (orig. sporting jargon) an absolute failure, lacking any chance. [i.e. fig. *not in* the contest]

not in the same street with *phr.* [late 19C+] utterly unequal to, not to be compared with.

not in these boots *phr.* [late 19C] certainly not, not a chance, 'you must be joking!' (cf. NOT IN THESE TROUSERS).

not in these trousers *phr.* [1920s–30s] absolutely not, under no circumstances (cf. NOT IN THESE BOOTS).

not just a pretty face *phr.* [1950s+] **1** used of a woman who wishes to assert her abilities. **2** used ironically of anyone who has done something worthy of praise.

not know A from izzard, to *phr.* [1910s+] (US) to be wholly ignorant (cf. NOT KNOW B FROM A BATTLEDORE; NOT KNOW B FROM A BULL'S FOOT). [SE *A* + *izzard*, obs. name for the letter Z]

not know apples from oranges, to *phr.* [20C] to be stupid (cf. KNOW HOW MANY BEANS MAKE FIVE; NOT KNOW WHETHER IT'S PANCAKE TUESDAY OR HALF-PAST BREAKFAST TIME).

not know beans, to *phr.* [early–mid-19C] (orig. US) to be ignorant, often ext. as *not know beans when the bag is open, not know butter/apple butter from a bull's foot, – from barley, – from buttons, – from peas.* [the image of a bean as an insignificant object]

not know bee/beef from a bull's foot, to *phr.* [20C] (US) to be absolutely ignorant of the topic in hand. [modern var. of NOT KNOW B FROM A BULL'S FOOT]

not know B from a battledore/broomstick, to *phr.* [mid-16C+] to be completely illiterate (cf. NOT KNOW A FROM IZZARD). [SE *battledore-book*, a basic reading primer, setting out the alphabet etc]

not know B from a bull's foot, to *phr.* [16C] to be ignorant (cf. NOT KNOW BEE FROM A BULL'S FOOT).

not know catnip, to *phr.* [20C] (US) to lack common sense.

not know enough to come in out of the rain, to *phr.* [mid-19C+] to be exceptionally stupid.

not know enough to pee down wind, to *phr.* [1920s+] (Can.) to be a fool.

not know if one's arsehole is bored or punched, to *phr.* [20C] to be an absolute fool. [? engineering use]

not know if one's arse was on fire, to *phr.* [1940s+] (orig. N.Z.) to be very stupid.

not know if someone is Agnes or Angus, to *phr.* [20C] a phr. used after swimming, to describe a man whose genitals have shrunk dramatically on contact with the cold water (cf. NOT KNOW IF SOMEONE IS ARTHUR OR MARTHA). [technically known as the *cremasteric reflex*, f. the *cremaster* or muscle of the spermatic cord, on which the testicles are suspended]

not know if someone is Arthur or Martha, to *phr.* [20C] **1** a phr. used to describe a man who is still ambivalent about his own sexuality. **2** a phr. used after swimming, to describe a man whose genitals have shrunk dramatically on contact with the cold water (cf. NOT KNOW IF ONE IS AGNES OR ANGUS).

not know nothing about nothing, to *phr.* [1940s+] (orig. US) to be absolutely innocent and ignorant, usu. used in self-defence against accusations of bad behaviour or criminality.

not know one's ankle from one's elbow, to *phr.* [20C] to be particularly stupid (cf. NOT KNOW ONE'S ARSE FROM ONE'S ELBOW).

not know one's arse/ass from one's elbow, to *phr.* [1930s+] to be ignorant, to be stupid.

not know one's arse/ass from a hole in the ground, to *phr.* [20C] to be particularly stupid.

not know one's arse/ass from a hot rock/third base, to *phr.* [1930s+] to be particularly stupid.

not know one's arsehole/asshole from one's elbow, to *phr.* [20C] to be particularly stupid (cf. NOT KNOW ONE'S ASS FROM ONE'S ELBOW).

not know whether it's Pancake Tuesday or half-past breakfast time, to *phr.* [1940s+] to be totally ignorant, utterly confused.

not know shit from Shinola, to *phr.* [20C] (US) **1** to not have any idea about a topic. **2** to be particularly wrong in an opinion. [SHIT n.[1] + *Shinola*, a black shoe-polish]

not know someone from ... , to *phr.* in various phrs., many of which are listed below, to proclaim one's ignorance of a person or their face, e.g. [mid-18C+] *... from Adam*; [late 19C+] (Aus.) *...from a crow.*

not know someone from a bar of soap, to *phr.* [1910s+] (Aus.) to have an absolute lack of acquaintance with a person mentioned or seen.

not know someone from a hole in the ground, to *phr.* [20C] (orig. US) a general phr. implying ignorance of a person; vars. include *... a hole in the fence, ... a hole in the road, ... a hole in a tree* (cf. NOT KNOW ONE'S ASS FROM A HOLE IN THE GROUND).

not know something from a bag of beets/meal/potatoes, to *phr.* [20C] (US) a general term of incomprehension; one of many synons. all initiated by *not know...* and including *... ass from a hole in the ground* and *... chicken shit from chicken salad*, in addition to those listed here.

not know something from a bale of hay/bale of crap, to *phr.* [20C] (US) to be completely ignorant (cf. NOT KNOW SOMETHING FROM A BAG OF BEETS).

not know whether it's Pitt Street or Christmas, to *phr.* [1950s] (Aus.) to be very ignorant and confused (cf. NOT KNOW WHETHER IT'S THURSDAY OR ANTHONY HORDERN'S; NOT KNOW WHETHER IT'S TUESDAY OR BOURKE STREET). [*Pitt Street*, the financial centre of Sydney]

not know whether it's Thursday or Anthony Hordern's, to *phr.* [20C] (Aus.) to be totally ignorant (cf. NOT KNOW WHETHER IT'S PITT STREET OR CHRISTMAS.) [proper name *Anthony Hordern's*, in its heyday a major Sydney department store]

not know whether it's Tuesday or Bourke Street, to *phr.* [1950s] (Aus.) to be very ignorant, to be confused (cf. NOT KNOW WHETHER IT'S PITT STREET OR CHRISTMAS.

not know whether one is coming or going, to *phr.* [1920s+] to be utterly confused, lost, disorientated.

not know whether to shit or go blind, to *phr.* [1950s+] (US) to be utterly stupid, to be totally confused.

not know which side one's arse hangs, to *phr.* [20C] to show complete indecision or bewilderment. [fig. use of ARSE n.[1]]

not know which way one is playing, to *phr.* [1920s+] to be impetuous.

not know who's which from when's what, to *phr.* [late 19C] to be extremely stupid.

not likely *phr.* [late 19C+] a phr. implying absolute reluctance, 'in no way will I do that'.

not lost for it *phr.* [1940s+] quite aware of what is going on. [SE *lost*]

not make a Federal case out of it *see* NOT MAKE IT A FEDERAL CASE.

not make a fiddler's fuck, to *phr.* [20C] to not matter in the slightest.

not make head or/nor tail, to *phr.* [early 18C+] to fail to understand, to find incomprehensible.

not make it a Federal case/a Federal case out of it, to *phr.* [1940s+] (orig. US) to not make a minor problem into a major one. [the greater importance of Federal over state prosecutions]

not much *phr.* [late 19C+] **1** far from it, not likely. **2** in ironic use, very much, very likely.

not much chop *see* NO CHOP.

not much cop *see* NO COP.

not much frocks *n.* [late 19C–1900s] socks. [rhy. sl.]

not much/nothing in it *phr.* (orig. racing) a phr. meaning there's no ascertainable difference, they are virtually the same.

not much you wouldn't *phr.* [1940s+] a phr. used to reject the previous speaker's protestations, meaning don't fool me, you certainly would. [ext. of NOT MUCH]

not my cup of tea *phr.* [1930s+] not to my taste.

not nominated *phr.* [1930s+] (Aus.) without any chance of success. [horseracing jargon]

not on *adj.* [1930s+] socially unacceptable, impossible (cf. BAD FORM). [? milit. use, when a proposed operation was 'not on' through unforeseen circumstances]

not on borrowing terms *phr.* [late 19C] (US) unfriendly, esp. a neighbour.

not one's scene *phr.* [1950s+] (orig. US) **1** an unpleasant or unacceptable situation. **2** anything not to one's taste. [SCENE]

not on the same bus *phr.* [1990s] (US teen) used of the one person in a group who fails properly to fit in.

not on your ambrotype *phr.* [late 19C] a general term of derision and dismissal (cf. NOT ON YOUR TINTYPE). [SE *ambrotype*, a photograph on glass, in which the lights are produced by the silver, with the shades by a dark background showing through]

not on your arse!/ass! *phr.* [1960s] no way at all, on no account (cf. NOT ON YOUR LIFE!).

not on your life! *phr.* [late 19C+] no way at all, totally impossible.

not on your nannie!/nanny! *phr.* [1950s+] (Anglo-Irish.) no chance! not a hope! [? var. on NOT ON YOUR NELLIE!]

not on your natural! *phr.* [20C] absolutely not! [abbr. SE *natural life*, thus var. on NOT ON YOUR LIFE!]

not on your nellie!/nelly! *phr.* [1940s+] not a chance! absolutely impossible! (cf. NOT ON YOUR LIFE!). [rhy. sl. *not on your Nellie Duff* = PUFF n.[2] (1)]

not on your tintype *phr.* [late 19C+] (orig. US) a general term of derision and dismissal (cf. NOT ON YOUR AMBROTYPE).

no touch to *phr.* [mid-19C] (US) unable to approach, nowhere near.

not out *adj.* [1930s+] still alive, usu. comb. with a person's age, e.g. *99 not out/and not out*. [cricket imagery]

not pick/unpick one's teeth, to *phr.* [20C] (W.I.) to make no comment, to stay absolutely silent, to say nothing.

not playing with a full deck *phr.* [1960s+] (orig. US) not very intelligent, slightly eccentric, odd (cf. NOT ALL THERE).

not plump currant *phr.* [late 18C–early 19C] out of sorts. [a plump currant would be fig. 'happy']

not put it past someone, to *phr.* [mid-19C+] to expect or assume something (usu. neg.) to be within the capabilities of someone, e.g. *I wouldn't put it past the Home Secretary to bring back hanging.*

not Pygmalion likely! *excl.* [1910s+] a euph. for NOT BLOODY LIKELY! [the George Bernard Shaw play *Pygmalion* (1913), in which the Cockney flowergirl Eliza Doolittle shocked audiences with her then taboo excl. 'Not bloody likely!']

not seem to, to *adj.* [1920s+] (Aus.) mentally deficient, i.e. 'not quite (all) there' (cf. NOT ALL THERE).

not quite-ish *adj.* [1920s+] not very well.

not quite quite *phr.* [1920s+] (society) not wholly acceptable. [neg. ext. of QUITE]

not quite there *see* NOT ALL THERE.

not quite the thing *phr.* [20C] not exactly acceptable.

not ready for people *adj.* [1970s+] (US Black) one who acts stupidly, childishly, who calls attention to their own idiocies.

not say turkey/pea-turkey, to *phr.* [1900s] (US) to say nothing, to stay silent.

not seem to, to *phr.* [late 19C+] **1** to be unable to manage e.g. *I just can't seem to get on with my work.* **2** to fail to comprehend a situation, e.g. *I just don't seem to see it, what exactly is the point?*

not since Julius Caesar was a pup *phr.* [20C] for a very long time. [PUP n.[1]]

not so as you'd notice *phr.* [1930s+] not to a noticeable degree.

not so bad *see* NOT BAD.

not so cold *phr.* [late 19C] (US) rather good (cf. NOT SO DUSTY).

not so dumb *phr.* [1950s+] not as stupid as one might appear. [DUMB adj.]

not so dusty *phr.* [mid-19C+] surprisingly good, not as bad as expected or advertised (cf. ROUGH AND CRUSTY). [17C SE *dusty*, worthless, distasteful; ult. *dust*, rubbish, garbage]

not so hot *phr.* [1920s+] (orig. US) a general neg. phr., not very good, unattractive, displeasing etc. [HOT adj.[1] (7)]

not so much lip!/less of your lip! *phr.* [mid-19C+] don't be so cheeky! [LIP n.[1] (1)]

not stand a bar of, to *phr.* [1930s+] (Aus.) to detest, to reject, to be intolerant of.

not taking any *see* NOT HAVING ANY.

not that I know of *phr.* [mid-18C+] not so far as I know, not to my knowledge.

not that you know of *phr.* [mid-18C] a phr. used to reject or deny the previous speaker's assumption.

not the foggiest *phr.* [1960s+] (orig. US) not the first idea, no clue whatsoever. use. as *I haven't the foggiest*, in answer to a query. [SE *foggy*, unclear, indistinct]

not the full dollar *phr.* [1970s+] (Aus.) not very intelligent, slightly eccentric, odd (cf. NOT ALL THERE).

not/not quite the full quid *phr.* [1940s+] (Aus./N.Z.) not very intelligent, slightly eccentric, odd (cf. NOT ALL THERE). [QUID]

not the half of it *phr.* [1930s+] a phr. implying that there is much more to come, to be recounted.

not the length of a street *phr.* [late 19C] by no great distance, not very far.

not the only onion in the stew *phr.* [1930s+] not alone, not the only person who is equally qualified. [coined by and exclusive to P.G. Wodehouse, in *Right Ho, Jeeves* (1934), although here he substituted 'hash' for stew (for US readers)]

not the only pebble on the beach *phr.* [late 19C+] used of someone who, whatever they may believe, is not unique (esp. in the context of love affairs).

not the ticket *phr.* [20C] physically or more usu. mentally 'below par'. [TICKET n.^{1} (1)]

not three skips of a louse *phr.* [mid-17C–early 19C] absolutely worthless.

not timbered up to one's weight *phr.* [mid-19C–1900s] not one's preferred style.

Nottingham goodnight *n.* [1950s] the loud slamming of doors and saying of *Goodnight* by a courting couple; this supposedly reassures the listening parents, and the couple, neither of whom has left, then retire to the sofa. [*Nottingham* can presumably be replaced by any large city]

not to be sneezed at *phr.* [early 19C+] not to be spurned, over-looked.

not today, baker *phr.* [late 19C] a phr. used to reject un-welcome advances (cf. NOT TONIGHT, JOSEPHINE). [the note left to tell the *baker*, in the days of daily deliveries, that one did not need bread]

not tonight, Josephine *phr.* [late 19C+] a general term of refusal, esp. of sex (cf. NOT TODAY, BAKER). [allegedly first pleaded by the Emperor Napoleon to his wife *Josephine*]

not too nice *phr.* [late 19C–1900s] euph. term for not nice at all.

not take a blind bit of notice, to *phr.* [20C] to have no interest whatsoever, not to care at all. [BLIND adj.^{2}]

not to worry! *excl.* [1950s+] do not worry!

nottub *n.* [late 19C] a button. [backsl.]

not up *adj.* [1930s+] (Aus.) second-rate. [*not up to standard*]

not up to Dick *phr.* [late 19C] unwell, sick and wretched. [UP TO DICK]

not up to much *phr.* [mid-19C+] relatively worthless, gener-ally inferior.

not what it's cracked up to be *see* NOT ALL IT'S CRACKED UP TO BE.

not while pussy's a cat *phr.* [20C] (Ulster) never.

not worth a ... *phr.* a variety of phr. meaning worthless, useless. Other than those listed individually, [13C] ... *a herring*, [13C–14C] ... *a sloe*, [13C–15C] ... *a needle*, [late 13C–mid-14C] ... *a nut*, [late 13C–16C] ... *a haw*, [late 13C+] ... *a fly*, [late 13C+] ... *a straw*, [14C] ... *a cress*, [14C–15C] ... *a cherry*, [14C–16C] ... *a gooseberry*, [14C–16C] ... *a pear*, [14C–mid-17C] ... *a leek/two leeks*, [14C+] ... *a button*, [mid-14C+] ... *a rush/bulrush/two rushes*, [late 14C–mid-15C] ... *an ivy leaf*, [late 14C–16C] ... *a gnat*, [late 14C–mid-16C] ... *a hen*, [late 14C–early 17C] ... *a pea/pease*, [late 14C+] ... *a louse*, [15C–17C] ... *a flea*, [15C–19C] ... *an egg*, [mid-15C–early 16C] ... *a rotten apple*, [16C] ... *a haddock*, [16C] ... *an onion*, [16C–early 19C] ... *a groat*, [mid-16C] ... *a pin*, [mid-16C–late 17C] ... *a point/blue point*, [17C] ... *a chip*, [17C] ... *shoe-buckles*, [17C+] ... *a farthing*, [early 17C] ... *a hair*, [mid-17C–early 18C] ... *three halfpence*, [late 17C] ... *a dodkin/dotkin/doit*, [late 17C] ... *a fig*, [19C] ... *a curse*, [19C+] ... *a bean*, [19C+] ... *a fart*, [mid-19C+] ... *a jigger*, [mid-19C+] ... *a tinker's curse*, [late 19C+] ... *a cobbler's curse*, [20C] (Aus.) ... *a cracker*, [20C] (Aus.) ... *a cupful of cold water*, [1950s+] ... *a monkey's* (*fuck*), [1970s+] ... *a wank*.

not worth a bucket of warm spit *phr.* [1930s+] (US) worth-less.

not worth a bumper *phr.* [1940s+] (Aus.) worthless, useless. [BUMPER n.^{3}]

not worth a cracker *phr.* [1950s+] (Aus.) worthless, useless (cf. RAZOO). [CRACKER n.^{8}]

not worth a cronebane *phr.* [late 18C–early 19C] (Irish) worthless. [SE *cronebane*, a copper token worth one half-penny, circulated by the Associated Irish mines, Cronebane, Co. Wicklow]

not worth a crumpet *phr.* [1940s–60s] (Aus.) worthless, use-less.

not worth a dam/damn/twopenny dam/twopenny damn *phr.* [20C] (orig. US) a neg. phr. used to imply uselessness or incompetence, e.g. *He can't fight worth a damn.* [the orig. ety. is based on the *dam*, a low value Indian coin, but the widely assumed link is to the oath DAMN; the inclusion of 'twopenny' was apparently popularized by the Duke of Wellington (1769–1852)]

not worth a/worse than a fart/two-bob fart in a bottle *phr.* [1970s+] (N.Z.) worthless.

not worth a fart in a noisemaker *phr.* [1960s+] worthless, useless.

not worth a fuck *phr.* [20C] absolutely worthless. [FUCK n.^{2}]

not worth a hill/row of beans *phr.* [mid-19C+] worthless, useless.

not worth a jigger *phr.* [mid-19C] worthless, useless. [SE *jigger*, any unnamed small object]

not worth a light *phr.* [20C] worthless, useless.

not worth a pinch of coonshit *phr.* [20C] (Can.) worthless, useless. [SE *racoon* + SHIT n.^{1} (1)]

not worth a pisshole in the snow *phr.* [1960s+] worthless, useless.

not worth a plugged nickel *phr.* [20C] (US) valueless.

not worth a rap *phr.* [early 19C] worthless, useless. [for ety. *see* RAP n.^{2}]

not worth a row of beans *see* NOT WORTH A HILL OF BEANS.

not worth a tiger tank *phr.* [1970s] worthless, useless. [rhy. sl. *tiger tank* = WANK n.; ult. the advertising slogan for Esso petrol *put a tiger in your tank*, thus oblique link to PUT LEAD IN ONE'S PENCIL]

not worth a turd *phr.* [early 18C+] worthless, useless. [TURD n.]

not worth a twopenny dam/damn *see* NOT WORTH A DAM.

not worth diddley-/diddly-/doodley-/doodly-shit *phr.* [1950s+] (US) worthless, useless. [DIDDLEY-SHIT]

not worth dogshit *phr.* [1960s+] worthless, useless.

not worth doodley-/doodly-shit *see* NOT WORTH DIDDLEY-SHIT.

no two ways about it *phr.* [early 19C+] (orig. US) there can be no doubt.

not wrapped too tight *phr.* [1970s+] (US) unstable, eccen-tric. [the image is of a parcel 'coming apart at the seams']

nought and carry one *n.* [20C] (Irish) a lame person. [var. on SE *dot and go one*]

nouns! *see* CAT'S NOUNS!

nous *n.* [mid-18C–late 19C] instinct or common sense, as opposed to actual learning. [20C use is SE; Gk. *nous*, knowledge, perception]

nous v. [mid-18C–late 19C to understand or learn. [NOUS n.]

no-user n. [1980s+] (Irish) a failure, a 'loser' (cf. NO-HOPER). [SE no use + sfx. -er]

no van dyke n. [20C] an unattractive person (cf. NO OIL PAINT- ING). [the Flemish portraitist Sir Anthony Van Dyck (1599–1641)]

novelty n. [18C] the vagina.

Novy n. [late 19C+] a native of Nova Scotia. [abbr.]

now adj. [1960s+] (US) up-to-date, very fashionable.

— now (and) — later phr. [1960s+] used in various phr. implying that someone can act (usu. pleasurably) now and take responsibility, usu. in the form of payment, in due course. [the locus classicus is the film Live Now, Pay Later (1962), satirizing the 'hire-purchase' boom of the late 1950s– early 1960s; its screenwriter Jack Trevor Storey publ. a novel of the same name in 1963]

now and never phr. [late 19C] clever. [rhy. sl.]

no way! excl. [1960s+] (orig. US) **1** absolutely not; you must be joking! you can't fool me! **2** used in rejoinder to a story that, however bizarre, is true; 'Surely not!' 'Really, that's amazing!'. The usu. affirmative reply is Way!

no way to run a railroad phr. [1960s+] (US) used to indicate that the current situation is utterly unsatisfactory (cf. NO WAY TO RUN A WHELK STALL).

no way to run a whelk stall phr. [1970s+] used to indicate that the current situation is utterly unsatisfactory (cf. NO WAY TO RUN A RAILROAD).

nowhere n. [1930s+] (orig. US) an undesirable, tedious per- son, place, event or idea.

nowhere adj.[1] **1** [mid-18C+] hopelessly beaten, esp. in a race. **2** [1920s+] (orig. US) utterly confused, very mixed up.

nowhere adj.[2] [mid-19C+] (US) **1** useless, pointless, stupid. **2** destitute, at a loss, finished.

nowhere city n. [1960s+] a situation or person who/which is seen as irrelevant, pointless, of no use at all. [SE nowhere + sfx. -CITY]

nowherian/nowhereian n. [1960s] (W.I.) anyone deemed unrespectable; a layabout, an unkempt-looking person who is characterized as a tramp. [Carib.E. nowherian, one who has no religious affiliation]

no/no more wire hangers! phr. [1980s+] (US campus) don't make me do this, don't torture me like this; a melodramatic plea synon. with 'No, no, anything but that!' [a cynical ref. to the book Mommie Dearest (1978), in which film star Joan Crawford's use of the coat hanger as a whip is detailed]

now I've seen everything phr. [1950s+] that's the absolute limit, you cannot be serious, I don't believe you/this etc.

no worries/worries mate phr. [1970s+] (Aus.) a common phr. of assurance; usu. ext. by she'll be all right.

now someone tells me! phr. [1950s+] a phr. implying that the information in question has been imparted only when it is too late.

now we shall be shan't phr. [late 19C] a phr. meaning 'that's all right'. [a jocular play on NOW WE SHAN'T BE LONG]

now we shan't be long phr. [late 19C] a phr. to imply, 'well, that's all right'. [the travellers' remark as they near the journey's end]

now you're shouting phr. [late 19C] (US) now you're saying something meaningful or relevant (cf. COOK WITH GAS). [em- phatic var. on NOW YOU'RE TALKING]

now you're talking phr. [mid-19C+] a phr. stating that the speaker is (finally) dealing with pertinent topics or talking to some purpose.

n.o.y.b. phr. [1910s+] (US) none of your business. [abbr.]

no you don't phr. [late 19C+] a phr. of admonition, under- pinning one's efforts to deny someone the chance to do something (negative) that they desire.

nozzle n. **1** [mid-18C+] the nose or a nostril. **2** [1990s] (US) the penis.

nozzler n. [early 19C] a blow on the nose. [NOZZLE n. (1)]

n.q.o.c.d. phr. [1980s] (US campus/society) used of one who is deemed socially unacceptable (cf. N.S.I.T; N.T.O.; N.T.S.; P.L.U.). [abbr. not quite our class, dear]

n.s. phr. [mid-19C] (US) enough said, it is possible to infer all the facts from what has already been stated (cf. N.C. phr.; NUF CED). [abbr. NUFF said]

n's n. [1990s] (US Black) money. [? SE notes]

n.s.i.t. phr. [1950s+] (society) a note attached to the name of a prospective male escort by a debutante or her mother (cf. N.Q.O.C.D.). [abbr. not suitable in taxis]

n.s.s. phr. [1980s+] (US campus) retort to a stupid question or statement. [abbr. NO SHIT, SHERLOCK]

n.t.o. phr. [1990s] (US campus) a date who does not come up to expectations (cf. N.Q.O.C.D.). [abbr. not the one]

n.t.s. n. [1970s+] (US campus) an attractive man that makes a woman's heart beat so fast that her name tag shakes (cf. N.Q.O.C.D.). [abbr. name tag shaker]

nub n.[1] **1** [late 17C–early 18C] the gallows. **2** [late 17C–early 19C] the neck. [ety unknown; ? SE nub, a protuberance]

nub n.[2] [late 17C–early 19C] **1** sexual intercourse, also nub- bing. **2** a husband. [? dial. nub, to jog, to shake]

nub n.[3] [1940s+] (US) an ugly or repulsive person. [SE nub, a lump]

nub v. [late 17C–early 19C] to hang (cf. NUBBING). [NUB n.[1]]

nubbed adj. [early 19C] hanged. [NUB n.[1]]

nubbies n. [late 19C+] (Aus.) the female breasts (cf. BUBBIES). [SE nub, a lump]

nubbin n. [1930s+] (US Black) the penis. [play on SE nubbin, the remains of something that has been worn away, e.g. a pencil; ult. a dwarfed or imperfect ear of maize]

nubbing n. [late 17C–19C] hanging. [NUB v.]

nubbing cheat n. [late 17C–19C] the gallows (cf. NUB n.[1]). [NUB v. + CHEAT n.; lit. 'the hanging thing']

nubbing cove n. [late 17C–19C] the hangman. [NUB v. + COVE]

nubbing ken n. [late 17C–19C] the Sessions house. [NUB v. + KEN n.[1]; lit. 'the hanging house'; one's trial there might well lead to the gallows]

nubbin-head n. [1930s+] (US Black) a fool, a simpleton. [NUBBIN + sfx. -HEAD (1)]

nubian n. [1970s] (US campus) a socially unacceptable per- son, used for Whites and Blacks despite obvious racist base. [SE nubian, a member of a North African people living near what is now Egypt]

nubs n. [1960s+] (drugs) peyote. [? the 'worn-down' appear- ance of peyote buttons]

nucker n. [1990s] (US Black) a fool. [? KNUCKLEHEAD]

nucky see NOOKIE n.

nuclear adj. [1980s+] (US) enraged (cf. GO BALLISTIC).

nuddikin n. [mid-19C] the head. [NOODLE n.[1] + KEN n.[1]]

nuddy adj. [1940s+] naked, undressed; usu. in phr. in the nuddy. [SE nude; a coy euph. used by those who find any sexual ref. embarrassing]

nudge/noodge/nudzh n. [1960s+] (US) a nag, a pest.

nudge v. [17C] of a man, to have sexual intercourse (cf. BANG v.[1]).

nudge, nudge, wink, wink, know what I mean, say no more phr. [1960s+] used, heavy-handedly, to make a sexual or otherwise dubious innuendo, usu. abbr. to nudge, nudge, wink, wink. [popularized by Eric Idle in Monty Python's Flying Circus, BBC-2 TV c.1969; Idle was dressed as a SPIV and was making heavily sexual innuendoes]

nudger n. **1** [1960s] the penis. **2** [1990s] (US) a male homo- sexual. [NUDGE v.]

nudie *n.* (orig. US) **1** [1930s+] a striptease show or burlesque. **2** [1940s+] a nude performer, a photo of a nude model; thus in combs. e.g. [1960s+] *nudie pic*, an 'adult' cinema or film, *nudie book*, an 'adult' or 'men's' magazine.

nudnik/noodnik *n.* [1920s+] (US) a pest, a fool, an insignificant person. [synon. Yid.; ? ult. Rus. *nudna*]

nudzh *see* NUDGE *n.*

Nueva York *n.* [1950s+] New York. [some ref. to the large Hispanic population, but on the whole, merely an affectation]

nuf ced *phr.* [late 19C+] (orig. US) enough said, it is possible to infer all the facts from what has already been stated (cf. N.S.). [the mis-sp. only works, of course, when printed]

nuff *adj.* [1980s+] (orig. W.I.) enough, esp. in phr. *nuff respect*, a general phr. of approval/admiration. [mis-sp.]

nuffness *n.* [1980s+] (W.I.) showiness, ostentation, vulgarity, precocity. [NUFF + sfx. *-ness*]

nug *n.* **1** [late 17C–19C] a term of affection, e.g. *my dear nug*. **2** [1940s+] (orig. Aus.) an attractive young woman. [NUG v.]

nug *v.* [late 17C–19C] **1** to fondle, to indulge in sexual foreplay. **2** to have sexual intercourse; thus *nugging*, sexual intercourse, *nugging cove*, a womanizer. [NUDGE v. ? + dial. *nug*, to jog with the elbow, to strike]

nugget *n.[1]* [mid-19C+] (Aus.) **1** a small, compact, stocky animal or person. **2** a runt.

nugget *n.[2]* [1980s+] (US campus) a fool, an idiot. [SE *nugget*, a lump; thus synon. with BONEHEAD *n.[1]*; LUNKHEAD and similar terms that equate hardness (of head) with stupidity]

nugget *v.* [1960s+] (N.Z.) a male 'game' in which a victim's trousers and underpants are removed and his genitals blackened with *Nugget* black shoe polish]

nuggets *n.[1]* [late 19C] money. [SE *gold nugget*]

nuggets *n.[2]* **1** [1970s] (drugs) amphetamine (cf. A *n.[2]*). **2** [1980s+] cocaine crystals. **3** [1980s+] crack cocaine. **4** [1980s+] high strength, hydroponically grown cannabis. [SE *nugget*, a lump]

nuggety *adj.* [mid-19C+] (Aus.) chunky, squat, thickset. [the shape of a gold *nugget*]

nuggie *v.* [1940s+] (US) to knuckle someone's head. [NOOGIE]

nuggies *n.* [1970s+] (US) a woman's breasts. [? NUBBIES]

nugging dress *n.* [late 17C–19C] an old-fashioned style of dress. [NUG v. + SE *dress*]

nugging house/ken *n.* [late 17C–18C; mid-18C–early 19C] a brothel (cf. ACCOMMODATION HOUSE). [NUG v. + HOUSE *n.[1]*/KEN *n.[1]*]

nugs *n.[1]* [1980s+] (US drugs) high quality, dense, small hydroponically grown marijuana. [abbr. NUGGETS *n.[2]* (4)]

nugs *n.[2]* [1990s] (US) a woman's breasts. [abbr. NUGGIES]

nuh?/nuh true? *excl.* [1980s+] (W.I./UK Black teen) a general interrog., i.e. 'Isn't that so?'

nuke *n.[1]* **1** [1950s+] a *nuclear* bomb (cf. NUKE v.[1]). **2** [1960s+] (US) a *nuclear* power station. [abbr.]

nuke *n.[2]* [1980s+] (US drugs) marijuana which has been adulterated with especially dangerous and/or toxic substances. [fig. use of NUKE *n.[1]*]

nuke *v.[1]* [1950s+] to launch and explode a *nuclear* bomb (cf. NUKE *n.[1]*). [abbr.]

nuke *v.[2]* **1** [1960s+] (orig. US) to punish severely, to destroy completely, to ruin. **2** [1980s+] (US campus) of food, to warm up, to burn; thus *nuker*, a microwave oven. **3** [1980s+] of hair, to blow dry excessively. **4** [1990s] (US) to electrocute (cf. FRY). [fig./joc. uses of NUKE *v.[1]*]

nuke and puke *n.* [1990s] (US campus) a microwaveable meal. [NUKE *v.[2]* (2) + SE *puke*]

nuking *n.* [1990s] (US teen) smelling of perfume. [play on NUKE *v.[1]*]

nuke oneself *v.* [1980s+] (US campus) to go to the tanning salon. [fig. use of NUKE *v.[2]* (2)]

null *v.* [late 18C–mid-19C] to beat. [? SE *annul*]

nulling cove *n.* [early 19C] a prize-fighter. [NULL]

nully *n.* [1970s] a fool, a stupid person. [? Scot. *nullion*, a stupid fellow or SE *null*, devoid of character and personality]

numans *n.* [17C] **1** Newgate prison. **2** Newgate Market. [corruption of *New* + sfx. -MAN; (2) a general market, which burned down in the Great Fire (1666)]

numb *adj.* **1** [1910s–50s] (US) blind drunk. **2** [1950s–70s] (US) stupid (cf. NUMBHEAD).

number *n.[1]* **1** [late 19C+] (orig. US) a person, usu. a young woman, usu. in a sexual context. **2** [1950s+] (US gay) a casual partner picked up from the street, bar or baths. **3** [1970s+] (US) a romantically involved couple. [undertones of abbr. HOT NUMBER]

number *n.[2]* [late 19C+] an item of clothing, e.g. a *dainty pink number*.

number *n.[3]* **1** [20C] in general, a thing, place or situation, defined by context. **2** [20C] a performance; a scene, a display of excessive emotion. **3** [1910s+] a job or task, esp. in phr. *cushy number/little number*, an easy job. **4** [1940s+] a person. **5** [1970s+] a style, a way of living, a pose, e.g. *the ageing rocker number*.

number *n.[4]* [20C] a bedroom in a hotel or boarding house. [the *number* on its door]

number *n.[5]* [1960s+] (drugs) a marijuana or hashish cigarette. [ext. NUMBER *n.[3]* (1)]

number-chaser *n.* [1930s] (US) an accountant (cf. NUMBER-CRUNCHER).

number-cruncher *n.* [1970s+] (US) **1** an accountant or statistician (cf. NUMBER-CHASER). **2** a person lacking creativity or imagination. [computer jargon *number-cruncher*, a large, sometimes slow machine which is used for calculations that would defeat, by quantity rather than complexity, mere human efforts]

number-cruncher course *n.* [1970s+] (US campus) any course that involves a large amount of maths. [NUMBER-CRUNCHER]

number eight hat *n.* [1940s+] an intellectual. [the link of a large brain – requiring a large hat size – to a large intellect]

number 4/number 8 *n.* [1950s] (drugs) a brand of heroin. [H is the eighth letter of the alphabet; ? D, for *dilaudid*, a synthetic opiate, is the fourth]

number 9 *n.* [early–mid-19C] the Fleet prison, situated at 9 Fleet Market, London (cf. MAN OF WAR).

number nip *n.* [19C] the vagina (cf. CATCH 'EM ALIVE-O). [? SE *number*, a thing + *nip*; i.e. the image of the vagina as 'biting' the male]

number one *n.[1]* [18C+] oneself, one's own interests (cf. LOOK AFTER NUMBER ONE; TAKE CARE OF NUMBER ONE).

number one *n.[2]* **1** [mid-19C+] the best, the finest quality (cf. A-NUMBER-ONE; NUMBER TEN *n.[2]*). **2** [mid-19C+] (orig. US) one's best friend or lover.

number one/ones *n.[3]* [20C] **1** the act of urination. **2** a chamberpot (cf. NUMBER TWO *n.[2]*). [juv. euph.]

number one *n.[4]* [20C] (S.Afr. Black) refined, white mealie meal. [spec. use of NUMBER ONE *n.[2]* (1)]

number one *n.[5]* [1950s+] (US Und.) first degree (i.e. premeditated) murder.

number one *adj.* [mid-19C+] (orig. US) first-rate, excellent. [widely popularized after its importation by veterans of the Korean (1950–3) and Vietnam (1964–75) Wars]

number ones *see* NUMBER ONE *n.[3]*.

number one thousand *adj.* [1970s+] (US) very bad (cf. NUMBER TEN *n.[2]*). [pidgin, imported by veterans of the Vietnam War]

numbers, the *n.* [late 19C+] (US gambling) popular form of street gambling that involves predicting a combination of the winning numbers at a racetrack, esp. widespread in US Black community; thus *numbers racket*, laying odds and betting on numbers; *numbers-man*, one who runs a numbers lottery; *numbers runner*, one who takes the money from individual bettors to the office where the 'racket' is run, and thus the one who delivers any payouts (cf. POLICY). [the SE *numbers* upon which one bets]

number six/6 *n.*[1] [early–mid-19C] (US) Thomson's Compound Tincture of Myrrh and Capsicum, a popular household remedy. [it was regularly listed as the sixth medicine in the firm's catalogue]

number six *n.*[2] [mid-19C] a lock of hair shaped like the figure 6 and twisted from the temple back towards the ear (cf. KNOCKERS; NEWGATE COLLAR; NEWGATE RING).

number ten/tens *n.*[1] [late 19C–1930s; 1970s] (US) a shoe or foot. [ref. to shoe size]

number ten/sixty nine *n.*[2] [1950s+] (orig. US milit.) the worst (cf. NUMBER ONE n.[2]; NUMBER ONE THOUSAND; NUMBER TEN THOU). [pidgin, imported by veterans of the wars in Korea (1950–53) and Vietnam (1964–75)]

number ten thou *adj.* [1980s+] (US) extremely bad, dire, the very worst. [for ety. *see* NUMBER TEN n.[2]]

number the waves, to *phr.* [late 18C–mid-19C] to waste time. [SE *number*, to count]

number 13 *n.* [1950s] (drugs) morphine. [M is the thirteenth letter of the alphabet]

number three *n.*[1] [20C] masturbation, whether by oneself, a partner, or as 'executive relief' i.e. from a 'masseuse' or prostitute. [on model of NUMBER ONES; NUMBER TWO n.[2], although in adult use]

number 3 *n.*[2] [1950s] (drugs) cocaine. [C is the third letter of the alphabet]

number two/twos *n.*[1] **1** [1930s+] (juv.) defecation. **2** [1990s] (US Black) anything considered bad, unpleasant, underhand or deceptive. [euph.; (2) may be fig. use of (1) but may also link to NUMBER ONE n.[2] (1)]

number two *n.*[2] [1950s] (W.I.) a large round dumpling. [it is indented around its circumference to facilitate splitting it in half, but note NUMBER TWO n.[2] (1)]

number two *n.*[3] [1950s+] (orig. milit.) second-in-command, second in rank.

number twos *see* NUMBER TWO n.[2].

numb hand *n.* [early–mid-19C] an inexpert or clumsy person.

numbhead *n.* [mid-19C–1950s] (US) a fool; thus *numb-headed*, stupid (cf. NUMBNUTS; NUMBY). [SE *numb* + sfx. -HEAD (1)]

numbnuts *n.* [1940s+] (US) an idiot, a fool (cf. DUMBNUTS; NUMBHEAD; NUMBY). [SE *numb* + NUTS n.[2] (1)]

numby *n.* [1940s+] (US) a fool, a simpleton. [abbr. NUMBHEAD]

numero uno *adj.* **1** [1940s+] the best, whether of objects or persons. **2** [1950s+] (US) an important person, the boss. [Sp. *numero uno*, number one]

numerous *adj.* [mid-late 19C] (US) superior, notable.

numms *n.* [late 17C–late 18C] a false, detachable collar, to be worn over a dirty shirt. [ety. unknown; ? link to SE *nominal*]

nummy *adj.* [1980s+] (US campus) delicious, mouthwatering. [baby-talk]

num-nums *n.* [1980s+] (US) a woman's breasts (cf. NUNGER). [echoic of sucking]

nun *n.* **1** [early 19C] a prostitute (cf. ABBESS). **2** [1980s+] a prude, a woman who is uninterested in sex.

nun with a price on her head *n.* [1990s] (Irish) a £5 note. [its design]

nungers *n.* [1960s] (Aus.) the female breasts (cf. NUM-NUMS). [echoic of sucking]

nunky *n.* [1920s–30s] **1** a pawnbroker. **2** a Jew, esp. when a

money-lender. [late 16C–mid-18C SE *nuncle*, an uncle; cf. UNCLE n.[1] (1)]

nunnery *n.* [late 16C–early 19C] a brothel (cf. CONVENT). [NUN n.[1]]

nunquam *n.* [mid-16C–early 17C] (Und.) a dawdling messenger. [Lat. *numquam*, never]

nunyare *n.* [mid-19C] (Polari) food, a meal. [Ital. *mangiare*, to eat]

nuppence *n.* [late 19C+] no money, also. used fig. in phr. *not worth nuppence*. [SE *no pence*]

nuprin *n.* [1990s] (US campus) an Asian. [ety. unknown; ? the painkiller]

nurd *see* NERD.

nurds *n.* [1950s–60s] (US) the testes (cf. NADS). [play on GONADS]

nurdy *see* NERDY.

Nuremberg egg *n.* [16C–early 18C] a watch. [an egg-shaped watch, made in Nuremberg]

nurembergs *n.* [1940s+] haemorrhoids. [rhy. sl. *Nuremberg trials* = SE *piles*]

nurse *v.* **1** [late 18C–19C] to cheat or swindle. **2** [mid-19C] for one omnibus to follow a rival closely so as to poach its passengers.

nursery *n.* [19C] the vagina (cf. BABY CHUTE). [its role in procreation]

nurse the hoe handle, to *phr.* [late 19C] (US) to act lazily. [the idler leaning on his hoe, rather than wielding it]

nut *n.*[1] [early–mid-19C] an action that is intended to give pleasure. [the pleasant flavour of a *nut*]

nut *n.*[2] **1** [mid-19C–1940s] a person, a fellow. **2** [late 19C] (Aus.) a thug, a bully, a hoodlum (cf. HARD NUT). **3** [late 19C+] a daredevil. [ext. use of NUT n.[3], often constrained by an unspoken 'tough']

nut *n.*[3] **1** [mid-19C+] the head (cf. BEAN n.[4]). **2** [late 19C–1950s] brains, intelligence; thus *use your nut*, use your sense.

nut *n.*[4] [late 19C–1920s] a drink (cf. OFF ONE'S NUT). [ety. unknown; ? the pleasurable aspects of liquor and nuts]

nut *n.*[5] [late 19C+] (Aus.) a horse that is hard to break in. [abbr. HARD NUT]

nut *n.*[6] [20C] (orig. US) an insane person; thus *nut doctor*, any form of mental health specialist, *nut house*, psychiatric institution; *nut case*, a lunatic (cf. OFF ONE'S NUT).

nut *n.*[7] **1** [20C] (US) (orig. entertainment) the initial outlay, overheads, expenses; the break-even sum, as in a theatre production or film, after which profit starts. **2** [20C] (US) any required sum. **3** [1920s+] (US Und.) protection money paid to corrupt policemen. **4** [1970s] (US) a fund used for bribery and other illegal activities, esp. by police. [SE *nut*, as being the heart of the fruit; such money is at the heart of a project, a relationship etc]

nut *n.*[8] [1900s–20s] a dandy, esp. a second-rate one. [KNUT]

nut *n.*[9] [1910s+] (orig. US) a fan or enthusiast, usu. in defining comb., e.g. *cricket nut, computer nut*; thus *be a nut at, to be a* expert in. [NUTS adj.[2] (1)]

nut/nuts *n.*[10] [1960s+] (US) the basic facts, the core (cf. NITTY-GRITTY). [abbr. NUTS AND BOLTS n.]

nut *n.*[11] **1** [1960s+] an orgasm; thus *bust one's nut, get one's nut*, to come to orgasm. **2** sexual intercourse, esp. in phr. *get a nut*, to have sex. **3** [1990s] (US) semen. [ext. use of NUTS n.[2] (1)]

nut *v.*[1] [19C] (orig. Und.) **1** to curry favour, to toady to. **2** to stare at. [NUT n.[1]; i.e. one (1) offers or (2) receives something pleasant]

nut *v.*[2] [1910s–60s] (US) to castrate, also used fig. [NUTS n.[2] (1)]

nut *v.*[3] [1910s+] to think; thus *nut out*, to work out, to analyse. [NUT n.[3]]

nut *v.*[4] [1930s+] to butt one's opponent in the face, usu. the bridge of his nose, using one's own forehead. [NUT n.[3] (1)]

nut *v.*[5] [1960s] (US) to renege. [NUT n.[7]]

nutball *n.* [1970s+] (US) an idiot. [NUT n.[6] + (SCREW)BALL n.]

nutbar/nutbasket/nutbucket *n.* [1970s+] (US) a lunatic (cf. NUTCAKE). [NUT n.[6] + joc. uses of SE *bar/basket/bucket*]

nutbox/nutbin *n.* [1960s+] (US) a psychiatric institution. [NUT n.[6] + joc. uses of SE *box/bin*]

nutbucket *see* NUTBAR.

nutburger *n.* [1980s+] (US) a lunatic (cf. NUTCAKE). [NUT n.[6] + SE (*ham*)*burger*]

nutbuster *n.* (US) **1** [1940s+] a mechanic or machinist. **2** [1970s+] an insoluble difficulty, the last straw (cf. BALL-BUSTER). [NUTS n.[2] (1) + *buster*]

nutcake *n.* [1960s+] (US) a fool, a lunatic, an eccentric (cf. DATE n.[1]; NUTTER). [NUT n.[6] + SE *cake*]

nutcase *n.* [1940s+] an eccentric, an odd person, a lunatic (cf. DATE n.[1]; NUTS adj.). [NUT n.[6] + SE (*mental*) *case*]

nut college *n.* [late 19C–1960s] (US) a lunatic asylum/psychiatric institution (cf. NUT-HOUSE, BRAIN COLLEGE). [NUT n.[6] + SE *college*]

nutcracker/nutcrackers *n.*[1] [16C–early 19C] the pillory. [despite logical links, both NUT n.[3], head and NUTS n.[2], testicles post-date this usage]

nutcracker *n.*[2] **1** [mid-19C–1950s] (orig. US) a blow to the head. **2** [late 19C–1900s] the head. [NUT n.[3] (1)]

nutcracker/nutcruncher/nutcrusher *n.*[3] (US) **1** [1940s+] something difficult, impossible or dangerous. **2** [1970s+] a martinet (cf. BALL-BREAKER). [NUTS n.[2] (1) + SE *cracker*]

nutcracker *n.*[4] [1950s+] (US) a psychiatrist. [NUT n.[6] + SE *cracker*]

nutcrackers *n.*[1] [late 19C–1900s] the fists. [NUT n.[3] + SE *cracker*]

nutcrackers *n.*[2] [late 19C–1900s] a hooked nose and a prominent chin (à la Mr Punch). [resemblance]

nutcrackers *n.*[3] [late 19C–1900s] the teeth. [one of their functions]

nutcruncher/nutcrusher *see* NUTCRACKER n.[3].

nutcut/nutcutting/nutgut *n.* [1960s+] (US) the fundamental basics, usu. of a ruthless nature, dirty work. [NUTS n.[2] (1); the implication is of castration]

nut-cut *adj.* [mid-19C] (Anglo-Ind.) roguish, mischievous. [NUT n.[3]]

nutcutter *n.* [1960s+] (US) something difficult, impossible or dangerous (cf. NUTCRACKER n.[3]). [NUTS n.[2] (1)]

nutcutting *see* NUTCUT n.

nut doctor *n.* [1930s+] (US) a psychiatrist. [NUT n.[6] + SE *doctor*]

nut ducker *n.* [1990s] (Aus.) one who deliberately ignores a friend in the street. [NUT n.[1] + SE *duck*]

nut factory *n.* [late 19C+] (US) a psychiatric institution (cf. NUT FOUNDRY). [NUT n.[6] + SE *factory*]

nut farm *n.* [1940s–70s] (US) a psychiatric institution (cf. CRAZY FARM). [NUT n.[6] + SE *farm*]

nut foundry *n.* [1930s–40s] (US) a psychiatric institution. [NUT n.[6] + SE *foundry*]

nutgut *see* NUTCUT.

nut hatch *n.* [1940s+] (? orig. US) a psychiatric institution (cf. BOOBY-HATCH; NUT FARM). [NUT n.[6] ? + proper name COLNEY HATCH, a celebrated North London asylum]

nuthead *n.* [20C] (orig. US) a fool, a simpleton. [NUT n.[6] + sfx. -HEAD (1)]

nut house *n.* **1** [20C] (orig. US) a psychiatric institution. **2** [1930s–70s] (US) a chaotic place or situation, a madhouse. [NUT n.[6] + SE *house*]

nut hut *v.* [1990s] to place in a psychiatric institution. [NUT n.[6] + SE *hut*]

nut it out *v.* [1900s–20s] (Aus.) to think it over. [NUT n.[3]]

nut job *n.* [1960s+] (US) a lunatic or very eccentric person (cf. NUT CASE). [NUT n.[6] + JOB n.[5]]

nutmeg/nutmeg maker *n.* [early–late 19C] (US) a White New Englander. [SE *wooden nutmeg*, anything false or fraudulent, a fraud, a cheat, a deception. New Englanders have the image of being deceitful, esp. as businessmen. Note the Nutmeg State, Connecticut, where wooden nutmegs are supposedly manufactured for export]

nutmegs *n.* [late 17C–early 19C] the testicles (cf. NUTS n.[2]).

nut 'n' berry *n.* [1990s] (US campus) someone who identifies with the concerns and styles of the 1960s. [the preference for vegetarianism associated with hippies and early conservationists]

nut on *v.* (US) **1** [20C] to attack physically (cf. NUT v.[4]). **2** [1960s–70s] to ignore. [NUT n.[3] (1)]

nut out *v.* [1960s+] (US Black) to go mad, whether literally or metaphorically. [NUT n.[6]]

nut-rock *adj.* [1920s–30s] bald. [NUT n.[3]; i.e. their 'nut' is as bare as a rock]

nut role *n.* [1960s+] (US Black) a pretence of insanity or stupidity, usu. to avoid something, as in *I'll play the nut role*. [NUT n.[6] + SE *role*]

nut roll *n.*[1] [1940s+] (US Black) an eccentric or mad person. [NUT n.[6] + pun on the sweet]

nut roll *n.*[2] [1990s] a large wad of money. [pun on SE *roll* (of cash) and *Nut Roll*, a popular sweet]

nuts *n.*[1] **1** [17C–1920s] anything agreeable, satisfactory, usu. as *nuts for* or *nuts to*. **2** [1910s+] (US) *the nuts*, the best, the superlative. **3** [1920s+] (US) *the nuts*, a strategic advantage, esp. in gambling, as in a winning hand in cards. [NUT n.[1]]

nuts *n.*[2] **1** [mid-19C+] the testicles (cf. NERTS n.). **2** [20C] (US Black) the clitoris (cf. COCK n.[2]). **3** [1970s+] (US) manly courage (cf. BALLS n.[1]). [SE *nut*, i.e. the shape; E.P. suggests SE *nut*, the head of the penis]

nuts, the *n.*[3] [1910s–70s] (US) something bad or objectionable. [NUTS!]

nuts *n.*[4] *see* NUT n.[10].

nuts *adj.* **1** [late 18C+] fond of, fascinated by, orig. usu. constructed with *upon/on* (cf. NUTS ABOUT; NUTS ON; NUTS UPON). 20C usage usu. constructed with *over/about*, thus influenced by 'crazy about'. **2** [mid-19C+] insane, mad, crazy (cf. NUT-CASE).

nuts! *excl.* [20C] (orig. US) a mild excl., nonsense! rubbish! not a chance! (cf. BALLS!; NERTS!).

nuts about *adj.* [1910s+] obsessed with, usu. in the context of love (cf. NUTS ON; NUTS UPON). [NUTS adj. (1)]

nuts about *v.* *see* NUTS AROUND.

nutsack *n.* [1970s+] (US) the scrotum. [NUTS n.[2] (1) + SE *sack*]

nuts and bolts *n.* [1960s+] the basics of a situation, the fundamental issues; thus *nuts and bolts man*, an uncomplicated 'hands-on' type of person (cf. BRASS TACKS).

nuts-and-bolts *adj.* [1920s–40s] (US) crazy, insane. [ext. of NUTS adj. (2)]

nuts and sluts *n.* [1970s+] (US campus) a course in abnormal psychology. [NUT n.[6] + SE *slut*]

nuts around/about *v.* (US) **1** [1930s–40s] to wander around aimlessly. **2** [1940s–60s] to mess about, to fool around. [NUTS adj. (2)]

nutso *n.* [1960s+] (orig. US) a stupid, unstable or eccentric person. [NUTS adj. (2)]

nutso *adj.* [1960s+] (orig. US) stupid, unstable, eccentric (cf. NUTTY). [NUTSO n.]

nuts on *adj.* [mid–late 19C] obsessed with, in love with (cf. NUTS ABOUT; NUTS UPON). [NUTS adj. (1)]

nuts on *phr.* *see* NUTS TO phr.[2].

nuts to *phr.*[1] [mid-19C+] a source of pleasure or delight for someone (cf. NUT n.[1]). [17C–18C SE]

nuts to/on *phr.*[2] [1910s+] (US) a retort to express rejection, derision etc, to hell with. [NUTS n.[2] (1)]

nuts upon *adj.* [late 18C+] obsessed with, in love with; thus *nuts upon oneself*, extremely pleased with one's own actions. [NUTS adj. (1)]

nutsy *adj.* [1910s+] (orig. US) mad, insane, eccentric, occas. used as a nickname. [NUTS adj. (2)]

nutted *adj.* [mid-19C] fooled by the claims of one who poses as being an obsessive admirer. [NUT v.[1]]

nutten-chops *see* WIND-PIES.

nutter *n.* [1950s+] a lunatic, an eccentric (cf. HEADCASE). [NUT n.[6]]

nutter butter *n.* [1990s] (US campus) someone who is unaware or inattentive. [NUTTER + redup.; note brandname *Nutter Butter*, a form of peanut filled biscuit]

nuttery *n.* [1910s–50s] (US) a mental hospital. [NUT n.[6]]

nutting *adj.* [1930s+] using the top of one's head to butt an opponent during a fight; such a blow can often end the fight instantly (cf. HEADING). [NUT v.[4]]

nutty *adj.*[1] 1 [early–mid-19C] smart, spruce. 2 [late 19C] piquant, spicy.

nutty *adj.*[2] [late 19C+] (orig. US) crazy, eccentric, esp. in punning phr. *nutty as a fruit cake*. [NUTS adj. (2)]

nutty *adj.*[3] [1950s+] (US Black) excellent, first-rate. [the person/object in question makes the speaker go NUTS adj. (2)]

nutty about/for *adj.* [1910s+] (orig. US) fond of, keen on. [NUTS adj. (1)]

nutty/nutty upon *adj.* [early–mid-19C] amorous, fond of. [NUTS adj. (1)]

nut up *v.* [1970s+] to lose one's temper completely, to go berserk. [NUT n.[6]]

nux *n.*[1] [mid-19C] (Und.) the object in question; the 'game'. [northern dial; ? ult. Lat. *nux*, a nut]

nux *n.*[2] [20C] (US prison) prison-cooked tea. [abbr. medical Lat. *nux vomica*, the fruit from which strychnine is produced]

nyaams *n.* [1950s+] (W.I.) foolishness, nonsense, esp. as an excl. [fig./ext. use of NYAM v., i.e. one who thinks of nothing but eating; thus cf. W.I. *coco-head*, a fool, itself the fig. use of *coco-head*, the rhizome of the coco-plant]

nyafflin' *n.* [20C] (Ulster) eating nosily with an open mouth. [onomat.; note Beds. dial. *nyaffle*, to eat in a hasty, gluttonous manner]

nyaams head *n.* [1950s] (W.I.) an absolute fool. [NYAAMS + sfx. -HEAD (1)]

nyam *n.* [late 18C+] (W.I.) food. [NYAM v.]

nyam *v.* [late 18C+] (W.I.) to eat. [*yam*, used orig. in many African languages fort he tuber; several African languages (Wolof, Fula, Hausa, Twi etc) also have similar words meaning to eat]

nyam dog *n.* [1940s] (W.I.) a Chinese person. [NYAM v. + SE *dog*; the Chinese predilection for cooking dog]

nyami nyami *n.* [1940s] (W.I.) a greedy, omnivorous person. [NYAM v.]

nyams/nyamps *n.* [20C] (W.I.) a weakling, a useless idiot. [? Twi *nyamma*, small or NYAM n., in context of being 'a vegetable']

nyanga/yanga *n.* [20C] (W.I.) ostentation, esp. in one's dress. [Mende *nyanga*, showing off]

nyetsi *adj.* [1990s] (US teen) no good, useless, worthless. [Tswana *nyetsi*, useless]

nyiff nyaff *n.* [20C] 1 a trifling thing. 2 a short person. [ety. unknown]

nyiff-nyaff *v.* [20C] to potter about. [NYIFF NYAFF n.]

nying'i-nying'i *adj.* [1950s+] (W.I. Rasta) nagging, whining. [? fig. use of NYANGA]

nylon *n.* [1960s+] (S.Afr.) a police van. [its mesh-covered sides]

nylon road *n.* [1950s+] (W.I.) a good, smooth road, better than the average island road.

nym *see* NIM.

nymph *n.* 1 [mid-17C+] (euph.) a prostitute. 2 [1910s+] a *nympho*maniac, an allegedly sexually insatiable woman (cf. NYMPHO). [SE *nymph*, a semi-divine being, imagined as a beautiful maiden inhabiting the sea, rivers, fountains, hills, woods or trees, thence a young and beautiful woman; (2) abbr.]

nymphette *n.* [1980s+] (US gay) an attractive gay youngster. [SE *nymphette*, a sexually alluring pubescent girl]

nympho *n.* [1910s+] (orig. US) a *nympho*maniac, an allegedly sexually insatiable woman; thus *nympho, nymphy,* sexually insatiable. [abbr.]

nymph of darkness *n.* [18C] a prostitute (cf. EVENING STAR; NYMPH OF DELIGHT; NYMPH OF THE PAVE).

nymph of delight *n.* [early 18C] a prostitute (cf. NYMPH OF DARKNESS).

nymph of the pave *n.* [19C] a prostitute, a street-walker (cf. NYMPH OF DARKNESS; PAVEMENT PRINCESS; PRINCESS OF THE PAVEMENT; SIDEWALK SUSIE). [NYMPH + SE *pave(ment)*]

nyp shop *see* NIP SHOP.

nyuck/neuck *n.* [20C] (Ulster) an unimportant person. [? fig. use of SE *nook*]

O

O *n*. **1** [1930s] (US drugs) an *o*unce of a narcotic. **2** [1930s+] (drugs) *o*pium. **3** [1980s+] (Aus. drugs) an *o*unce of cannabis. [abbr.]

-o *sfx*. [20C] used variously to create **1** shortened forms, e.g. AGGRO; AMMO; BEANO; COMBO. **2** nouns, e.g. BOYO; BUCKO; KIDDO. **3** adjectives, e.g. CHEAPO. **4** (mainly Aus.) added to a variety of nouns (often occupational) to create sl. forms, e.g. ARVO; BERKO; BOMBO; COMMO; COMPO; DERO; ETHNO; GARBO; JOLLO; JOURNO; LESO; METHO; MILKO; NASHO; PISSO; PLONKO; PREGO; PROSSO; RABBIT-O; REFFO; RELLO; SAMBO; SANGO; SANNO; SECKO; SHEEPO; SUSSO; SYPHO; TROPPO). **5** nouns from adj., e.g. PINKO; WEIRDO. **6** as a meaningless ending, e.g. BILLY-O; CHEERIO. [(4) ? f. the *-o* sfx. in street cries such as *milko!* or in the familiarization of names, e.g. *Johno*]

o.a. *n*. [1970s] an overdose of Methedrine. [abbr. OVERAMP]

oafo *n*. [1950s–60s] a ruffian, an oaf. [SE *oaf* + *sfx*. -O]

oak *n*.[1] **1** [16C] (Und.) in a team of confidence tricksters, the one who keeps a watch (cf. HIGH LAWYER). **2** [late 17C–mid-19C] a rich man, a man of substance. [playing on the tree's 'oaken' qualities]

oak *n*.[2] [late 19C] a joke. [rhy. sl.]

oak and ash *n*. [20C] cash. [rhy. sl.]

oaken cudgel/towel *n*. [late 18C–early 19C] a cudgel; thus *towelling*, a thrashing, a beating, and *rub down with an oaken cudgel/towel*, to thrash, to beat (cf. LEAD TOWEL; OAK TOWEL).

Oakie *n*.[1] *see* OKIE n.[1].

oakie *n*.[2] *see* OKIE n.[2].

Oakley *n*. [1920s–60s] (US) a free pass, orig. to a circus, but latterly to the theatre. [abbr. ANNIE OAKLEY]

oak towel *n*. [late 18C–1930s] a policeman's truncheon (cf. OAKEN CUDGEL).

Oaktown *n*. [1970s+] (US Black) Oakland, California.

o.a.o. *n*. [1920s+] (orig. US) one's steady girlfriend. [abbr. one and only]

oary-eyed *see* ORY-EYED.

oat *n*.[1] [mid-19C] an atom, the tiniest amount; thus *have not an oat*, to be penniless. [? SE *iota*]

oat *n*.[2] [mid-19C+] two. [backsl.]

oat burner/consumer/destroyer/grinder/muncher *n*. [1940s+] (Can./US) a horse.

oater *n*. [1940s+] (orig. US) a Western film. [abbr. OAT OPERA]

oat grinder *see* OAT BURNER.

oatmeal *n*. [early 17C] an urban rowdy, usu. in a gang. [SE phr. *sow one's wild oats*. Note 'No trace of this odd appellation has yet been found except that the author of a ludicrous pamphlet has taken the name of Oliver Oat-meale' (*Nares Gloss.*, 1822)]

oat muncher *see* OAT BURNER.

oat opera *n*. [1930s–40s] (orig. US) a Western film (cf. OATER). [the horses and the oats they eat]

oats *n*.[1] [1920s+] sexual satisfaction; thus *get one's oats*, to have sexual intercourse. [SE phr. *feel one's oats*, *sow one's wild oats*]

oats *n*.[2] [1990s] (drugs) cocaine (cf. BARLEY n.[2]).

oats and barley *n*. [mid-19C] a watchman. [rhy. sl.; presumably CHARLEY n.[1] (1)]

oats and chaff *n*. [mid-19C–1930s] a footpath. [rhy. sl.]

oatsmobile *n*. [1910s+] (US) a horse (cf. OAT BURNER). [joc. blend of SE *oats* + (*auto*)*mobile*]

oat-stealer *n*. [mid-19C] an ostler. [pun + derog. ref. to the stereotypically corrupt ostler]

O.B. *n*.[1] [late 19C] (Und.) the *O*ld *B*ailey in London, which is the Central Criminal Court of England. [abbr.]

O.B. *n*.[2] *see* OBIE.

ob *n*. [1980s+] (US campus) *ob*vious. [abbr.]

Obadiah *n*.[1] [18C–mid-19C] a Quaker. [the popularity of that name among the sect]

obadiah *n*.[2] [20C] a fire. [rhy. sl.]

o.b.c. *n*. [1960s+] (US prison) an *o*ld, *b*rutal *c*onvict, who uses experience and power to take advantage of younger, newer inmates. [abbr.]

o begga me! *see* O BERGAMI!

o-be-joyful/oh-be-joyful/oh-be-cheerful *n*. [early 19C+] **1** rum. **2** (US) liquor in general. **3** (US) wine. [orig. naut. jargon]

o-be-joyful house/works *n*. [19C] a public house (cf. TAKE IN SOME O-BE-JOYFUL). [O-BE-JOYFUL + SE *house*]

obelisk *n*. [19C] the penis. [SE *obelisk*, a tapering shaft of stone]

O Bergami!/o begga me! *excl*. [mid–late 19C] used to imply that the person so addressed is a liar (cf. NON ME). [one *Bergami*, a notably mendacious witness in the trial of Queen Caroline in 1820]

obey *see* OBIE.

obfuscated *adj*. [mid-19C] drunk (cf. ADDLED).

obfusticated *adj*. [mid-19C–1960s] (US) bewildered, confused, excited. [ext. of OBFUSCATED]

obie/O.B./obey *n*. [1920s–80s] (US Und.) a post office. [ety. unknown]

obies *n*. [1970s+] (S.Afr. student) sherry. [pron. of O.B.'S, trade-name *Old Brown* sherry]

object *n*. [19C] a person or thing that appears ridiculous or pitiable. [SE *object of pity*, *object of mirth*]

oblige *v*. **1** [19C] to have sexual intercourse (cf. PLEASE; SOLACE). **2** [late 19C] to perform in public, e.g. to *oblige with a song*. **3** [1930s+] a genteel euph. for to work as a charwoman or cleaner. [the implication of all is of offering a favour]

obliterated *adj*. [1980s+] extremely intoxicated by a drug or alcohol (cf. BASTED).

obno/obnoc *n*. [1970s+] (US campus) a crude, obnoxious person. [OBNO adj.]

obno *adj*. [1970s+] (US campus) *obno*xious. [abbr., SE *obnoxious*, pron. 'obeknow']

obnoc *see* OBNO n.

oboe *n.* [1990s] the penis (cf. FLUTE n.²).

O'Brien's dog *n.* [20C] (Irish) one who is all things to all people (cf. BILLY HARRAN'S DOG). [he goes 'a little way with everyone'; presumably a lost anecdote]

O.B.'s *n.* [1980s+] (S.Afr.) Old Brown sherry (cf. OBIES). [abbr.]

obs *n.* **1** [1910s–20s] *obs*ervations. **2** [1970s] a look-out, usu. in phr. *keep obs*, to keep a look-out. [abbr.]

obscure *adj.* [1980s+] (US campus) strange, bizarre, weird.

obsocky *adj.* [20C] (W.I.) **1** of objects (esp. clothes), ill-fitting, misshapen. **2** of people, ungainly, overweight. **3** of events, absurd, ridiculous. [? Yoruba *obo*, monkey + *so*, to break wind + *ki*, to greet; thus cf. MONKEY FART]

obsquatulate *see* ABSQUATULATE.

obstriperous *see* OBSTROPOLOUS.

obstroculous *adj.* [1930s] (Aus.) obstreperous (cf. OBSTROPOLOUS).

obstropolous/obstriperous/obstroperous *adj.* [late 18C+] a corruption of SE *obstreperous* (cf. ABSTROPELOUS; STROPPY).

obvious *adj.* [late 19C] (society) fat, overweight. [one cannot avoid seeing the person]

obviously severe *adj.* [late 19C] (society) extremely rude. [euph.]

o.c. *n.* [1990s] (US Black teen) public housing projects in the Fillmore district of San Francisco. [abbr. *out of control*]

occabot *n.* [mid-19C] tobacco. [backsl.]

occasional *n.* [late 19C+] (orig. US) a part-time worker or employee (cf. CASUAL n.¹).

occifer *see* OSSIFER.

occupant *n.* [16C] a brothel prostitute. [she works in an OCCUPYING HOUSE]

occupy *v.* [early 16C–late 18C] of a man, to have sexual intercourse. [*occupy* is one of those synonyms for copulation listed in John Florio's *Worlde of Wordes* (1598): 'Fottere, to iape, to sard, to fucke, to swive, to occupy.' Like many taboo terms it moved from SE (it is used 10 times in the *Authorized Version*) once it had been perceived as vulgar. Shakespeare notes this in *Henry IV part II* (1597), 'A captaine? Gods light these villaines wil make the word as odious as the word occupy, which was an excellent good worde before it was ill sorted']

occupying house *n.* [16C] a brothel (cf. ACCOMMODATION HOUSE). [OCCUPY + HOUSE n.¹ (1)]

ocean hell *n.* [mid-19C] (Aus.) the penal establishment sited on Norfolk Island for particularly recalcitrant convicts.

ocean liner *n.* [20C] (Aus.) a girl, a girlfriend [rhy. sl. *ocean liner* = CLINER]

ocean pearl *n.* [late 19C+] a girl, a girlfriend (cf. IVORY PEARL). [rhy. sl.]

ocean rambler *n.* [20C] a herring.

ocean wave *n.* [1920s–30s] a shave. [rhy. sl.]

O cheese and crust! *excl.* [late 19C] euph. for *O Jesus Christ!*

ochive/oschive *n.* [early 18C–early 19C] a bone-handled knife. [*ochive* Rom. *o chiv*, the knife, *oschive* ? Lat. *os*, a bone + CHIVE]

ochorboc *n.* [late 19C] beer. [Ital. *bocca*, mouth; popularized by Italian organ-grinders]

ochre *n.* [mid–late 19C] money, gold (cf. DELOG; GELT; GILT; GINGERBREAD; GOLD; GOREE; OLD MR GORY; REDGE; RED 'UN; RIDGE). [SE *ochre*, a pale brownish yellow]

ock *n.*¹ [1970s+] (Aus.) a boorish, loutish, unsophisticated, ultra-nationalist Australian. [OCKER (2)]

ock *n.*² [1980s+] (US campus) a friend, an intimate.

ocker *n.* (Aus.) **1** [1910s+] a nickname for anyone called Oscar. **2** [1970s+] a boorish, loutish, unsophisticated, ultra-nationalist Australian, whose rise, and celebration, coincided with Gough Whitlam's Labour government (1972–5). **3** [1970s+] anyone seen as boorishly nationalist (cf. ALF).

4 [1970s+] Australian English; thus *ocker*, to behave like an ocker, *ockerization*, vulgarization, *ockerized*, vulgarized, *ockerdom*, the world of the ocker. [the character *Ocker* originally portrayed by actor Ron Frazer (1924–83) in the TV series *The Mavis Bramston Show* (1965–8)]

ockerina *n.* [1970s+] (Aus.) a female OCKER. [pun on the musical instrument, an *ocarina*]

ockerism *n.* [1970s+] (Aus.) boorish behaviour, oafish, self-satisfaction. [OCKER]

ock it! *excl.* [1970s+] (US campus) stop it! [? mispron.]

ocky *n.* [1960s+] (Aus.) an octopus. [abbr.]

O cricum jiminy! *excl.* [late 19C] euph. for *O Christ Jesus!*

O cry! *excl.* [late 19C] euph. for *O Christ!*

octane *n.* [1990s] (US) **1** verve, zest. **2** (drugs) phencyclidine laced with gasoline.

octo *n.* [1910s] (Aus.) an *octo*pus. [abbr.]

October *n.* [mid-19C] blood (cf. CLARET). [SE *October ale*, a strong beer brewed in October]

octopus *n.* [1930s+] (US) a man who proves more sexually enthusiastic, thus keen to fondle, than his girlfriend or date might wish.

o.d. *n.* [1950s+] (drugs) **1** an *o*ver*d*ose. **2** one who has taken an *o*ver*d*ose. [O.D. v.]

o.d. *v.* [1950s+] **1** to *o*ver*d*ose (fatally or otherwise) on a given drug. **2** to act excessively, without restraint, to be greedy. [abbr.]

od! *excl.* [late 16C+] l. a general euph., oath, meaning God and usually found in a variety of combinations, e.g. '*od's blood, body, bones, death, feet, flesh, foot, life, mercy, truth, vengeance, blessed will, wounds* etc. Also with dimins. and perversions of words, as '*od's bob, bobs, bodikins, bud* (= blood), *fish, 'odslid, odd's lifelings, odsnigs, odsnouns, odsoons* (= wounds), *od's-pittikins, pittkins, pitlikins* (pity), *od's wucks, odzooks* (= hooks), -*zookers* (-*swookers*), *od zounds* (= wounds), '*od's haricots, kilderkins, od's my life* (cf. ADAD!).

oday *n.* [1920s–80s] (US) money. [pig Lat. *oday* = DOUGH]

odd *n.* [1930s–50s] a policeman; thus *odd-lot*, a police car. [ety. unknown]

odd *adj.* [late 19C–1940s] homosexual. [euph.]

-odd *sfx.* [mid-19C+] of age or number, approximately, slightly more than a stated number, e.g. *thirty-odd* (cf. -SOMETHING).

odd as Dick's hatband *see* QUEER AS DICK'S HATBAND.

oddball *n.* [1940s+] (orig. US) an eccentric, unusual person (cf. SCREWBALL n.). [SE *odd* + fig. use of *ball*]

oddball *adj.* [1950s+] peculiar (cf. MADBALL). [ODDBALL n.]

odd bod *n.* [1940s+] (orig. milit.) **1** an odd man out. **2** any non specific person. [SE *odd body*]

odd-come short *phr.* [mid-19C] one of the these days, sooner or later. [var. on ODD-COME-SHORTLYS]

odd-come-shortlys *phr.* [late 18C–early 19C] one of the these days, sooner or later, usu. as *I'll do it one of these odd-come-shortlys.*

odd fish *n.* [18C+] an eccentric person (cf. QUEER FISH). [SE *odd* + FISH n.¹]

oddish *adj.* [late 19C–1900s] drunk (cf. ADDLED).

odd kick in one's gallop *n.* [late 18C–early 19C] a whim, a fancy, an eccentricity. [equestrian imagery]

odds *n.* see ODS.

odds *v.* [1950s+] **1** to risk, to take a chance. **2** to avoid, to 'get out of'. [SE *odds*, as used in betting]

odds and sods *n.* [1930s+] (orig. milit.) odds and ends, but used of both objects and people. [the orig. WW1 milit. use defined as '"details" attached to Battalion Headquarters for miscellaneous offices, batmen, sanitary men, professional footballers and boxers on nominal duties etc' *Brophy & Partridge* (1930)]

odds, bods and sods n. [1940s+] (Aus.) people at random. [ext. of ODDS AND SODS]

odds-on adj. [late 19C+] favourite, most likely. [betting use]

oddy n. [1900s–10s] (Aus.) a halfpenny. [the 'odd halfpenny' in a sum of money or a price]

O'Donnell's gallon n. [20C] (Irish) a full glass or tankard of alcohol. [generic/anecdotal use of *O'Donnell* + *gallon*, a container for liquids]

od/odd rot/rabbit/rat it! excl. [mid-18C–late 19C] a mild oath, lit. *God rot it!* [euph.]

ods/odds n. [17C–late 19C] (US) a mild euph. for *God's*.

odsbobs! excl. [early 17C–early 19C] a general oath, lit. *God's babes.*

odsbodikins! excl. [18C] a general oath, lit. *God's little body.*

'od's fish! excl. [17C] a general oath, one of many ways of euphemizing God (cf. GADZOOKS!; ODSBODIKINS!; ZOUNDS!). [*God's flesh*, with overtones of the miracle of the loaves and fishes]

odsflesh! excl. [17C] a mild euph. excl., lit. *God's flesh* (cf. GADZOOKS!; ODSBODIKINS!; ZOUNDS!).

odso! excl. [17C] God's oath (cf. ADAD!).

o.d.v./O.D.V. n. [mid-19C–1920s] brandy. [pun on pron. of Fr. *eau-de-vie*]

o.e. n. [1980s+] (US Black) Old English malt liquor. [abbr.]

oedipus rex n. [1970s] sex. [rhy. sl.]

oes adj. [20C] (S.Afr.) seedy, run down, 'under the weather'. [Afk. *oes*, feeble]

of a certain age phr. [mid-18C+] a euph. description of a middle-aged or older person, usu. a woman.

of a dizzy age phr. [late 19C–1900s] (society) ageing. ['Makes the spectator giddy to think of the victim's years' (Ware)]

ofaginzy n. [1940s–50s] (US Black) a White person. [? OFAY adj. + GINZO]

ofay/oofay n. [20C] (US) a usu. derog. term for a White person. [ety. unknown. Links to Fr. *au fait*, aware, have been dismissed, and doubts are also cast on Yoruba *ofe*, 'a charm that lets one jump so high as to disappear', thus trouble (the cause of such vanishing), thus a White man (the essence of trouble)]

ofay/oofay adj. [late 19C+] (US) White (cf. FAY). [OFAY n.]

off n.[1] [mid-19C+] the start. [sporting jargon *off*, the start of any race, esp. that of horses or dogs]

off n.[2] [1960s+] (S.Afr.) free time. [abbr. SE *day/time off*]

off adj.[1] [late 19C+] **1** unfashionable. **2** of food, unavailable on a menu (cf. ON adj.[3]). **3** feeling unwell. **4** stale. **5** aloof, withdrawn.

off adj.[2] [1960s+] happy, elated, enjoying the positive effects of drugs or drink.

off v.[1] **1** [late 19C+] to leave, to go off. **2** [20C] to get rid of, to reject, to dismiss. **3** [1920s–30s] to die. [abbr. SE *make off, send off, go off*]

off v.[2] **1** [1950s+] (orig. US Black) to kill or murder. **2** [1960s+] (orig. US) of a man, to have sexual intercourse. **3** [1960s+] (US Und.) to rob, usu. with violence. **4** [1970s] (US police) to apprehend and arrest someone. **5** [1970s+] (US Black) to beat someone up. [abbr. relevant uses of KNOCK OFF v.[4], v.[5]]

off adv. [late 17C+] to the point of orgasm; in phr. JERK OFF v.[1]; SUCK OFF; TOSS OFF v.[1] etc; for a list of synons. *see* BEAT OFF.

off prep. [1960s+] (orig. US) by means of, e.g. *Sarah was grooving off Belle and Sebastian.*

off and on phr. [mid-19C+] indecisive, variable.

off at the head phr. [mid-19C+] eccentric, mad (cf. OFF ONE'S HEAD).

off beam/the beam adv. [1940s+] (US) wholly incorrect, often intensified as *way off beam*. [orig. air force use, referring to radio beams that guide aircraft]

off-beat n. [1940s] something unconventional or unusual. [OFF-BEAT adj.]

off-beat adj. [1930s+] (orig. US) unconventional, out of the ordinary, later usage also as wrong or mistaken. [orig. jazz use]

off-brand n. **1** [20C] (US) a Black person (cf. GENERIC). **2** [1990s] (US Black gang) a rival gangster. [SE *off-brand*, not a mainstream or *brand*name product]

off-brand adj. [1960s+] (US) **1** odd, peculiar, inferior. **2** of a child, illegitimate.

off-brand cigarette n. [1970s+] (drugs) a marijuana cigarette (cf. NO-BRAND CIGARETTE).

off-breed n. [1960s+] (US) a person or animal of mixed or indeterminate ancestry, a mongrel.

off-chump adj. [late 19C] lacking appetite, off one's food. [SE *chump*, the thick end of a loin of mutton]

off-colour adj. **1** [1950s+] in poor taste, usu. of smutty humour. **2** [1970s] (US Und.) homosexual. [SE *off-colour*, unwell]

offensive n. [1990s] a weapon.

offer n. [early 19C–1920s] an opportunity.

offer out v. [1980s+] (Black) to work as a pimp. [what one offers is the girl]

offer someone out v. [late 19C+] (Aus.) to challenge someone to a fight.

office n.[1] [late 17C+] the place one works; 'His Office, any Man's ordinary Haunt, or Plying-place, be it Tavern, Alehouse, Gaming-house' (B.E.). [this use has been sustained into 20C, found outside the SE business context in a wide range of occupations, from pimping to commercial flying, in all of which the speaker terms their place of work, whether the street or an aircraft cockpit, the *office*]

office n.[2] [early 18C–1960s] a toilet, a privy. [abbr. HOUSE OF OFFICE]

office n.[3] **1** [early 19C+] a hint, a warning, a 'tip-off', usu. in phr. *give one the office*. **2** [20C] (US prison) a signal. [SE *office*, a duty to another, a service, i.e. the look-out's duty is to give a warning]

office v. [early 19C–1960s] (esp. Und.) to warn, to tip off. [OFFICE n.[3]]

office piano n. [1940s+] (US) a typewriter (cf. DESK PIANO).

officerette n. [20C] (US) a policewoman (cf. COPESS).

officers of the 52nds n. [late 19C] (Irish) young men who attend church regularly every Sunday. [there are 52 Sundays each year]

officer-toed adj. [20C] (Ulster) with one's toes turned out. [the stance of police officers on parade]

office sneak n. [mid-19C] one who steals from an office or business. [SE *office* + SNEAK n.[1]]

office worker n. [20C] a shirker. [rhy. sl.]

offie/offy n. [1950s+] an off-licence. [orig. a counter in a public house over which alcohol could be sold for consumption off the premises. The off-licence proper declined during the 1970s–80s but the term is still used for wine merchants and similar stores]

off in left field *see* OUT IN LEFT FIELD.

offish adj. [mid-19C+] reserved, distant, aloof; thus *offishness*, reserve, coolness. [OFF adj.[1] (5)]

off it phr.[1] *see* OFF ONE'S HEAD.

off it phr.[2] *see* OFF THE WALL.

off like a bride's nightie phr. [1960s+] (Aus.) leaving extremely fast, very speedily (cf. OFF LIKE A BUCKET OF PRAWNS IN THE HOT SUN; OFF LIKE A LAMPLIGHTER).

off like a bucket of prawns in the hot sun phr. [1960s+] (Aus.) leaving very quickly (cf. OFF LIKE A BRIDE'S NIGHTIE).

off like a lamplighter phr. [mid-19C–1910s] leaving very quickly (cf. OFF LIKE A BRIDE'S NIGHTIE).

off nicely adj. [19C] tipsy, drunk (cf. ABOUT RIGHT adj.[1]).

off of prep. [early 18C+] from, e.g. *she'd steal off of anyone.*

off one's ass *phr.* [1980s+] (US campus) to a very great extent, extremely.

off one's base *phr.* (US) **1** [late 19C+] insane, crazy, confused, muddled, mistaken (cf. OFF ONE'S BEAN; OFF ONE'S BLOCK; OFF ONE'S CAKE; OFF ONE'S CHUMP; OFF ONE'S DIP; OFF ONE'S DOT; OFF ONE'S HEAD; OFF ONE'S KADOOVA; OFF ONE'S KAZIP; OFF ONE'S NANA; OFF ONE'S NOB; OFF ONE'S NUT; OFF ONE'S ONION; OFF ONE'S PANNICAN; OFF ONE'S ROCKER; OFF ONE'S ROCKET; OFF ONE'S SAUCER *phr.*[2]; OFF ONE'S TOP; OFF ONE'S TOP TRAVERSE; OFF ONE'S TROLLEY). **2** [1930s+] acting in an anti-social or otherwise unacceptable manner, 'out of line', 'out of order'. [baseball jargon]

off one's bean *phr.* **1** [20C] insane, eccentric (cf. OFF ONE'S BASE). **2** drunk. [BEAN n.[4]]

off one's block *phr.* [1920s+] (orig. milit.) **1** angry. **2** insane (cf. OFF ONE'S BASE). [BLOCK n.[1] (2)]

off one's box *see* OUT OF ONE'S BOX.

off one's cake *phr.* [20C] crazy, insane (cf. CAKE n.[1]; OFF ONE'S BASE).

off one's chump/chomp *phr.* [late 19C+] mad, eccentric (cf. off one's base). [CHUMP n.[1]]

off one's dip *phr.* [1900s–20s] mad, eccentric (cf. DIP n.[8]; LOSE ONE'S DIP; OFF ONE'S BASE). [SE *dip*, a sauce]

off one's dot/dotty *phr.* [late 19C] mad, eccentric (cf. OFF ONE'S BASE). [DOTTY]

off one's face *phr.* [1960s+] under the influence of drink or drugs (cf. OUT OF ONE'S FACE).

off one's feed *phr.* [mid-19C+] depressed, miserable, nervous. [horse stable jargon]

off one's gourd *see* OUT OF ONE'S GOURD.

off one's head/off it *phr.* **1** [mid-19C+] insane, out of one's mind (cf. OFF ONE'S BASE). **2** [1960s+] (drugs) intoxicated by a drug.

off one's kadoova *phr.* [late 19C+] (Aus.) crazy, eccentric, mentally unstable (cf. OFF ONE'S BASE). [? KADI, thus fig. head]

off one's kazip *phr.* [1900s–30s] (US) insane, eccentric (cf. OFF ONE'S BASE). [ety. unknown]

off one's nana *phr.* [1940s+] eccentric, mad (cf. OFF ONE'S BASE). [NANA n. (2)]

off one's nob *phr.* [1950s+] eccentric, insane (cf. OFF ONE'S BASE). [NOB n.[1] (1)]

off one's nut *phr.* [mid-19C+] **1** drunk (cf. ADDLED). **2** mad (cf. OFF ONE'S BASE). **3** infatuated, very enthusiastic. [NUT n.[1]]

off one's oats *phr.* [late 19C+] feeling unwell, esp. if this diminishes one's appetite. [equine imagery]

off one's onion *phr.* [late 19C+] crazy (cf. OFF ONE'S BASE). [ONION n.[1] (2)]

off one's own bat *phr.* [late 19C] by oneself, without help. [cricketing imagery, SE in 20C]

off one's pannican/pannikin *phr.* [late 19C–1930s] (Aus.) eccentric, crazy (cf. OFF ONE'S BASE). [PANNIKIN]

off one's peck *phr.* [18C–19C] hungry, without anything to eat (cf. TAKE A HOLIDAY AT PECKHAM). [PECK n.[1] (1)]

off one's rocker *phr.* [late 19C+] crazy (cf. OFF ONE'S BASE). [SE *rocker*, a rocking-chair]

off one's rocket *phr.* [1910s–50s] crazy (cf. OFF ONE'S BASE).

off one's saucer *phr.*[1] [mid-19C–1900s] (Aus.) disinclined, dispirited, 'out of sorts'. [the image of a pet refusing its food]

off one's saucer *phr.*[2] [20C] (Aus.) mad, eccentric (cf. OFF ONE'S BASE). [the image is of a spinning 'flying saucer']

off one's top *phr.* [mid-19C+] mad, eccentric (cf. OFF ONE'S BASE). [SE *top*, a child's spinning toy]

off one's top traverse *phr.* [20C] (Aus.) mad, eccentric (cf. OFF ONE'S BASE).

off one's trolley *phr.* [late 19C+] crazy, eccentric (cf. OFF ONE'S BASE; TROLLEYED). [SE *trolley-car*, a electric-powered coach running along metal tracks set into the roadway. The Manhattan trolleys, which were not allowed overhead cables (as were those in Brooklyn) after so many came down in the hurricane of 1888, picked up their supply from an electrified third rail and so if the car became derailed, its power was lost]

off-ox *n.* [mid-19C+] (US) a stubborn or headstrong person (cf. ADAM'S OFF-OX; GABE'S OFF-OX; GOD'S OFF-OX). [lit. the 'offside' ox of a pair, presumably linked to such characteristics]

offside *adj.* (Aus./N.Z.) **1** [1910s–30s] in poor taste, socially unacceptable. **2** as *offside with*, out of favour, in bad odour with (cf. OFF adj.[1]). [sporting imagery]

off-sider *n.* [mid-19C+] (Aus./N.Z.) an assistant, helper. [SE *off-sider*, an animal positioned on the off-side of a team]

off the arm *phr.* [1940s+] (US) spontaneously.

off the beam *see* OFF BEAM.

off the block *phr.* [20C] (US) local, used of a neighbour, a peer, always implying membership of the working class. [lit. one who lives on the same block or street]

off the bus *see* ON THE BUS.

off the chain *phr.* [1940s] (Aus.) free, unrestrained or unrestricted. [the image of a chained convict]

off the cob *phr.* [1930s–50s] (US) **1** unfashionable, out of style. **2** backwards. **3** poor. [SE *corncob*, thus the implication of rustic poverty]

off the cuff *phr.* [1930s+] (orig. US) impromptu, spontaneous action or speech. [the practice of writing jokes or information on one's cuffs to aid a performer's memory]

off the fly *phr.* [mid–late 19C] retired, esp. from a life of hedonistic amusement. [FLY adj.]

off the graph *phr.* [1940s+] beyond calculation.

off the hinge *phr.* [mid-19C] unemployed. [OFF THE HINGES]

off the hinges *phr.* [17C–18C] physically indisposed, mentally confused. [play on SE *unhinged*]

off the hook *phr.*[1] **1** [mid-19C+] out of trouble, freed of an difficult situation. **2** [1920s+] (Aus.) of a married man, out for a night with male friends only.

off the hook *phr.*[2] [20C] (US) in ill health, in a bad temper, nervous. [OFF THE HOOKS]

off the hook *phr.*[3] [1990s] (US teen) used of something so good as to transcend description. [telephonic imagery]

off the hooks *phr.*[1] **1** [early 17C–late 19C] ill-tempered, peevish. **2** [17C–late 19C] crazy, eccentric. [var. ON OFF THE HINGES]

off the hooks *phr.*[2] [late 17C] to excess. [? imagery of being unfettered]

off the hooks *phr.*[3] [mid-19C] at once. [synon. with SE *off the peg*, i.e. instantly available]

off the hooks *phr.*[4] [19C] dead; thus *drop/go off the hooks*, to die. [the ancient practice of exposing the head and limbs of executed traitors in public places around a city]

off the horn *phr.* [mid-19C] of a piece of meat, very tough.

off the nail *phr.* [early 19C] tipsy, slightly drunk. [phr. *go off at the nail*, to behave strangely]

off the runway *phr.* [1990s] (US campus) used of a very thin girl. [the imagery of the catwalk or *runway* down which ultra-thin supermodels parade]

off the spot *phr.* [late 19C] uncertain, lacking in awareness. [reverse of ON THE SPOT]

off the stones *phr.* [mid-19C+] outside London. [reverse of ON THE STONES]

off the top *phr.*[1] [1970s+] taken first, esp. when sharing out money, legally or otherwise, e.g. expenses come *off the top*.

off the top *phr.*[2] [1990s] (US) from the beginning, immediately. [musical imagery, one reads a score from the top]

off the top of one's head *phr.* [1960s+] spontaneously, extempore, with no factual backing.

off the track *phr.* [20C] behaving badly, making mistakes (cf. OUT OF ORDER).

off the wall/off it *phr.* [1950s+] (orig. US) **1** difficult, obstreperous, strange. **2** bizarre, peculiar. **3** spontaneously. [? the skewed bouncing of a ball thrown against a wall]

off-time *adj.* [1930s+] (US) badly timed, at the wrong time, therefore unacceptable.

off-time jive *n.* [1930s–40s] (US Black) a weak excuse. [OFF-TIME adj. + JIVE n.¹ (1)]

off with *v.* [late 19C+] to take off at once, e.g. *off with you*, 'get going', 'go away'.

offy *see* OFFIE.

of one's asshole *see* OUT THE ASSHOLE.

of sorts *adj.* [20C] undistinguished, second-rate, barely adequate.

ofter *n.* [late 19C] (sporting) a regular attender, usu. at the races, the music-hall etc. [SE *often*]

of the best *phr.* [20C] **1** used with a number to refer to amounts of money, e.g. *10 of the best*, £10. **2** a beating, the number of strokes is specified, e.g. *six of the best*. **3** an admirable person, usu. as *one of the best*.

og/ogg *n.* [1930s–40s] (Aus./N.Z.) a shilling. [HOG n.¹ (1)]

o.g. *n.¹* [late 19C–1970s] (US Black) a woman, esp. one's mother or wife. [abbr. *old girl*]

o.g. *n.²* (US Black) **1** [1970s+] a street-smart guy, a leading member of a gang (cf. GANGSTA n; GHETTO STAR). **2** [1990s] a close male friend. **3** [1990s] a veteran of the streets. [abbr. *original gangster*. The term allegedly appeared with the formation of the Original Gangster Crips, a breakaway group of Los Angeles' West Side Crips. Both gangs were sub-groups or SETS of the larger gang, the Crips. One theory suggests that only proven killers qualify as true *o.g.*s]

o.g.b. *n.* [1990s] (US Black gang) *original ghetto blood* (cf. G n.⁷). [O.G. + BLOOD n.⁵]

ogg *see* OG.

'oggins *see* HOGGINS.

ogle. *n.* **1** [late 17C+] usu. in pl., an eye. **2** [early 18C+] an amorous glance, a frankly sexual stare. [Ital. *occhio, eye*]

ogle *v.* **1** [late 17C–late 18C] to look at invitingly, amorously (cf. OGLES). **2** [mid-19C] (Und.) to examine, to appraise or look over. [(1) SE by 19C]

ogle-fakes *n.* [1980s+] (Polari) false eyelashes [OGLE n. (1) + FAKE n.¹]

ogler *n.* **1** [early 19C] an eye. **2** [late 19C] a punch in the eye. [OGLE n. (1)]

ogles *n.* [late 17C–mid-19C] the eyes (cf. QUEER OGLES; RUM OGLES). [Low Ger. *oegen*, to look at, thence Ger. *Šugeln*, to ogle, to leer, giving the SE v. *ogle*, although this too entered the language as cant before being appropriated by SE]

ogotaspuotas *n.* [late 19C] nonsense, rubbish. [a slogan carried on a flag waved during a pro-Cretan demonstration by the radicals, held in Hyde Park on 7 March 1897. The word was promptly transliterated as 'Oh go to spew!']

ogoy *n.* [1977] (drugs) heroin. [ety unknown; ? Sp.]

oh-be-cheerful/oh-be-joyful *see* O-BE-JOYFUL.

oh boy! *excl.* [1910s+] (orig. US) a general excl.

O. Henry *see* JOHN T. HENRY.

oh mamma! *excl.* [late 19C+] (US) an excl. of wonder.

oh my dear *n.* [mid-19C+] beer. [rhy. sl.]

oh my God *phr.* [20C] bald. [rhy. sl., Cockney pron.]

oh my leg! *excl.* [early 19C] a teasing remark, aimed at anyone recently freed from prison. [the ref. is to the leg-irons one wears there]

-oholic *sfx.* [1960s+] (orig. US) widely used suffix based on the obsessive nature of an alcoholic; thus *chocoholic*, one who cannot stop consuming chocolate, *bookoholic*, an obsessive reader etc (cf. -AHOLIC, which it poss. predates).

oh shit! *excl.* [1920s+] (orig. US) a general excl. of surprise with undertones of dismay (cf. SHIT!).

oh smack! *excl.* [1990s] (US teen) a reaction to something astonishing.

oh swallow yourself! *excl.* [late 19C] an excl. of dismissal, go to hell!

oh, tell your mother ninepence *phr.* [1910s+] used to escape from answering a question that otherwise would have required a degree of serious consideration.

O-H-ten *n.* [20C] (US) Ohio. [abbr.]

Oh Willie, Willie *phr.* [late 19C–1910s] gentle, teasing reproof aimed at one who, while not perhaps lying, is 'telling a tale'. [? a line in a popular song, play or story]

oh Winifred! *excl.* [late 19C] an excl. of disbelief. [joc. use of proper name]

oh-zee *see* O.Z.

oi! *excl.* [1960s+] a general excl. of address, synon. with earlier *hoy!*, come here! pay attention! etc. [note the brief 1980s *Oi music*, geared to the sensibilities of a SKINHEAD/football fan audience and featuring such bands as Sham 69 and Cockney Rejects. Such music mutated into the racist/nationalist songs of Europe's hardcore right-wing music business]

oick *see* OIK.

-oid *sfx.* [1970s+] (orig. US) used in a nominal or adjectival form to express a brainless or automatic quality, e.g. *zomboid*. [abbr. SE *android*]

oik/oick *n.* [1920s+] an unpleasant youth. [orig. school use, a working man, then an unpopular pupil or any member of a rival school]

oil *n.¹* **1** [late 19C–1970s] graft, bribery, and the money for paying it (cf. GREASE n.¹; JUICE n.¹). **2** [late 19C+] (Aus./N.Z.) information, which *oils* the wheels of communication. **3** [1900s–20s] (US Und.) nitroglycerin (cf. GREASE n.³). **4** [1910s–60s] (US) flattery, sweet talk (cf. GREASE n.¹; OIL MERCHANT).

oil *n.²* **1** [1910s+] (Aus./US Black) alcohol, esp. wine. **2** [1940s–70s] (US) coffee. **3** [1960s+] (drugs) hashish oil or purified hashish. **4** [1980s+] (drugs) heroin. **5** [1980s+] (drugs) phencyclidine (cf. ACE n.³).

oil *v.¹* [1920s+] to move quietly, stealthily or in an underhand, surreptitious manner, also in combs. with various adv. *around, in, out, through*.

oil *v.²* [1940s–60s] (US Black) to beat, to whip (cf. HAZEL OIL; OIL OF GLADNESS).

oil *v.³* [1980s+] to inject oneself with a drug, usu. heroin. [OIL n.² (4)]

oil-burner *n.¹* **1** [1920s–40s] (US) a tobacco chewer. **2** [1930s+] a vehicle which, through a malfunctioning or dirty engine, uses up a disproportionate quantity of oil. [US Navy *oil*, chewing tobacco]

oil-burner/oil-burner habit *n.²* [1930s+] (US drugs) an extremely heavy level of heroin addiction (cf. BURNING-DOWN HABIT). [OIL n.² (4) + HABIT n. + play on SE]

oil-butt *n.* [mid-19C+] a black whale. [SE *oil* + BUTT n.¹ (1); its potential for processing for whale oil]

oil can *n.* [1920s–30s] (US) a useless person, a good-for-nothing. [OIL n.² (1)]

oiled/oiled up *adj.* [mid-18C+] (orig. US) drunk. [OIL n.² (1)]

oiled behind *n.* [1930s–40s] (US Black) the buttocks, after a beating (cf. OILED HEAD). [OIL v.²]

oiled head *n.* [1930–40s] (US Black) a head that has been beaten, usu. by the police (cf. OILED BEHIND). [OIL v.²]

oiler *n.¹* **1** [late 19C] an oil well. **2** [late 19C+] (orig. US) an oilskin or oilcloth coat and/or trousers.

oiler *n.²* [1900s–60s] (US) a Mexican. [var. on GREASER n.¹]

oiler *n.³* [1910s; 1990s] a heavy drinker. [OIL n.² (1)]

oiler *n.⁴* [1930s–40s] (US Black) one who regularly involves themself in fights. [OIL v.²]

oil in *v.* [1920s+] **1** to enter. **2** to interfere. [OIL v.¹]

oil it *v.* [20C] (US campus) to stay up late studying. [SE phr. *burn the midnight oil*]

oil merchant *n.* [1930s–50s] (US) a flatterer or a swindler. [OIL n.[1] (4) + MERCHANT]

oil of angels *n.* [17C] money used for bribery, also as *angel's oil*. [OIL n.[1] + SE *angel*, 'an old English gold coin, called more fully at first the angel-noble, being originally a new issue of the Noble, having as its device the archangel Michael standing upon, and piercing the dragon' (*OED*). Initially worth 6s 8d, it was worth 10s when last minted under Charles I]

oil of barley *n.* [late 17C–19C] strong ale (cf. BARLEY BROTH; JOHN BARLEYCORN). [OIL n.[2] (1)]

oil off *v.* [1920s+] to escape one's responsibility, to escape from an onerous duty or similar situation (cf. OIL OUT).

oil of gladness *n.* [late 18C–early 19C] a beating, often in phr. *I will anoint you with the oil of gladness, I will beat you* (cf. HAZEL OIL; OIL OF BIRCH). [this *oil of*... usage is very common in Jamaican herbalism and religious cults, some refer to religious beliefs, others to the wishes that are invested in the oil itself. Terms include *oil of Calvary; oil of Virgin Mary; oil of power; oil of dead-man; oil of kill-him-dead; oil of bound-to-win*]

oil of hazel *see* HAZEL OIL.

oil of joy *n.* [1910s–30s] (US) alcohol. [OIL n.[2] (1)]

oil of palms *see* PALM OIL.

oil of strap'em/strappem *see* STRAP-OIL.

oil out of *v.* [1920s+] **1** to escape one's responsibility, to escape from an onerous duty or similar situation. **2** to slide away as if well-lubricated. [OIL v.[1]]

oil slick *n.* [20C] a Spaniard. [rhy. sl. *oil slick* = SPICK]

oil someone's wheels, to *phr.* [1990s] to take care of, be responsible for, look after.

oil tanker *n.* [20C] a general term of abuse (cf. MERCHANT BANKER). [rhy. sl. *oil tanker* = WANKER]

oil the fist *see* OIL THE HAND.

oil the glove, to *phr.* [1990s] to masturbate.

oil the hand/fist, to *phr.* [early–mid-17C] to bribe (cf. OIL n.[1]).

oil the knocker, to *phr.* [mid-19C–1910s] to tip or bribe a doorman or porter.

oil the tonsils, to *phr.* [20C] to have a drink (cf. MOISTEN THE CHAFFER; MOISTEN THE CLAY; SOAK THE CHAFFER).

oil up *v.*[1] [late 19C+] (Aus.) to have a drink. [OIL n.[2] (1)]

oil up *v.*[2] [late 19C+] (Aus.) to impart information. [OIL n.[1] (2)]

oily *n.*[1] [20C] a cigarette. [rhy. sl. *oily rag* = FAG n.[4]]

oily *n.*[2] [1950s+] (prison) a solicitor's clerk, sometimes a solicitor. [both visit their imprisoned clients to 'clean up' their pre-trial problems]

oingo boingo! *excl.* [1990s] (S.Afr./US teen) an exclamation of surprise. [nonsense words, echoic of surprise]

oink *n.* [1960s+] (orig. US Black) a police officer. [*oink*, onomat. for a pig's grunt, var. on PIG n.[3] (1)]

oinker *n.* [1980s+] (US) **1** a glutton. **2** an ugly young woman. **3** a policeman. [*oink*, onomat. for a pig's grunt, plays on PIG n.[1] (1); n.[1] (3); n.[3] (1)]

oink out *v.* [1980s+] (US) to overeat. [*oink*, onomat. for a pig's grunt, var. on PIG OUT]

oint-jay *n.* [1930s] (drugs) a marijuana cigarette. [pig Latin for JOINT n.[4] (2)]

ointment *n.*[1] [15C–17C] money. [its use in 'soothing' life's problems]

ointment *n.*[2] **1** [late 18C–late 19C] semen. **2** [mid-19C] butter.

o.j. *n.*[1] [1940s+] (orig. US) orange juice. [abbr.]

o.j. *n.*[2] [1960s+] (US drugs, orig. milit.) marijuana laced with opium. [*opium* + JOINT n.[4] (2)]

o.j. *n.*[3] [1980s] (US Black) a large car, typically a Ford or Lincoln. [proper name *O.J.* Simpson (b.1947), the former

football hero turned film star who advertised such cars for Hertz *c.*1980, prior to his 1997 murder trial]

OK/okay/okey *adj.* (orig. US) **1** [mid-19C+] good, fine, satisfactory, occas. splendid. **2** [mid-19C+] safe, unharmed. **3** [mid-19C+] of a person, good, decent e.g. *an OK guy*. **4** [mid-19C+] up to date, fashionable e.g. *it's the OK thing to do*. **5** [1970s+] constructed with 'with' or 'about', comfortable, at ease with. [OK!]

OK *v.* [late 19C+] (orig. US) to pass, to approve, to 'give the go-ahead'. [OK!]

OK! *excl.* [mid-19C+] (orig. US) the best-known statement of agreement, all is fine, everything is in order, I agree, go ahead etc; also used interrog. *OK?*, do you agree?. [corrupted abbr. of SE *all correct,* via its pron. as 'orl korrect'. It dates from 1839 in the US; Hotten (1864) has it (correctly etymologized) without ref. to US origins. The term was used in the election campaign of US president Martin Van Buren in 1840, when it conveniently suited his nickname 'Old Kinderhook', which came from the town of his birth Kinderhook, New York. It was further popularized by the OK Club, founded in 1840, whose members were Democrats who backed Van Buren. According to one popular story (since largely discredited) the first use of 'oll korrect' (still spelt in full) came during the campaign of the Whig Presidential candidate William Henry Harrison when a local handyman in Urbana, Ohio, was commissioned to paint a supportive banner; unfortunately he was illiterate and his slogan read 'The People is Oll Korrect'. *OK* has been the source of wide-ranging, if unproven speculation; it includes: the railway freight agent who signed bills of lading *OK* – after his name *O*badiah *K*elley; an Indian chief known as *O*led *K*eokuck whose friends abbreviated his name to OK and often said 'OK – he's all right'; *Aux K*ayes – a Haitian port from where the best rum came; the initials used by the multi-millionaire John Jacob Astor to sign bills presented to him for credit; an invention by US telegraphers to accompany NM meaning 'no more' and GA meaning 'go ahead'; the British word *hoackey* or *horkey* (as *hockey* in *EDD*) meaning the last load brought from the fields and the beginning of rustic celebrations. More ideas included the Choctaw *okeh* meaning 'it is'; the French *au quai* ('on the quay' and thus either referring to goods ready for transportation, or the quays on which French soldiers met US girls in the War of Independence in 1776); the Finnish word *oikea* meaning correct; the *O*rrins-*K*endall company which put its initials on its boxes of high quality crackers which were eaten widely during the US Civil War and known to soldiers as *OK*s; the House of Lords where at one time certain bills had to be signed and initialed by Lords *O*nslow and *K*ilbracken; the initials 'H.G.' – pronounced 'hah gay' which were used by Scandinavian sailors and came from Anglo-Saxon *hofgor* meaning seaworthy; the Greek *omega chai*, a magical incantation against fleas; the signature of the Prussian General Schliesen who initialed all official documents *O*berst *K*ommandant or OK; the Scottish 'och aye' and the 18C French form of *oui* (meaning yes) which was pronounced *o qu oui*. *Major* (1994) claims a root in a variety of West African languages, e.g. Djabo *o-ke*, Wolof *waw ke*, Dogno *o-kay*, Mandingo *o-key* and Fula West *eeyi-kay*. He adds that '"Oh ki" was being used by Blacks in the South by the 1770s and in Jamaica at least twenty years before the evidence of "okay" in the speech of New England.' However *Cassidy* (1967) fails to support the Jamaica ref., nor does *Lighter* (1997) offer any US cit. prior to 1839]

okapi/ou kappie *n.* [1970s+] (S.Afr.) a single-bladed knife with a pattern of three stars on the handle (cf. THREE STAR). [the tradename, itself based on the *okapi*, a rare mammal of the *Giraffidae* family]

okay see OK adj.

oke n. [1960s+] (S.Afr.) **1** a fellow, a chap (cf. BLOKE). **2** a friend. **3** a general term of address (cf. OU). [abbr. Afk. outjie, little chap]

oke adj. [1920s–50s] (orig. US) all right. [OK n.]

okely-dokely! see OKEY-DOKE!

okey see OK adj.

okey-doke/okey-dokey/okey-pokey n. (US Black) **1** [1930s–50s] White values and opinions. **2** [1930s+] a swindle, a confidence trick. **3** [1960s+] stupidity, foolish talk. [OK; the image of going along with, i.e. saying 'OK', to whatever a listener wishes to hear]

okey-doke/okey-dokey/okey-pokey v. [1990s] (US Black) to swindle. [OKEY-DOKE n.]

okey-doke!/okely-dokely!/okey-dokey!/okey-dokey artichokey!/okey-pokey!/okle-dokle! excl. [1930s+] (orig. US) all vars. of OK!

Okie/Oakie/Oakey n.[1] **1** [1910s+] (US) a derog. term for a migrant worker, orig. from Oklahoma, forced off his land during the Great Depression during the 1930s (cf. ARKY). **2** [1970s+] (S.Afr.) a vagrant, a tramp. [abbr. Oklahoma; (2) is loan f. US use]

okie/oakie/oukie n.[2] [1970s+] (S.Afr.) **1** a form of address to a young boy. **2** an affectionate or slightly patronizing form of address to an adult (cf. OKE; OU). [abbr. Afk. outjie, little chap]

Okker see OSCAR n.[2].

Oklahoma credit card n. [1960s+] (US) a siphon tube for stealing gasoline (cf. ARKANSAS CREDIT CARD). [the image of the poor migrant, forced to steal fuel]

Oklahoma rain n. [1910s+] (US) a dust storm (cf. ARIZONA CLOUDBURST).

okle-dokle! see OKEY-DOKE!

okole n. [1930s+] (US) the buttocks or rear of anything. [Hawaiian okole, the buttocks]

okra n. [1920s–50s] (US) the penis. [resemblance]

okra and prunes n. [1980s] (US) the male genitals (cf. MEAT AND TWO VEG). [coined by Gore Vidal (b.1925) for his novel Duluth (1983)]

OK sign n. [1960s–70s] (US) a hand sign made of a circle with thumb and forefinger, and other fingers upright, to indicate approval, good quality or excellence. [OK!; ? orig. a visual symbol used, or popularized by 1947 Penzoil motor oil advertisement and, subseq., in used car outlets; 1980s+ SE]

-ola sfx. [1910s+] (US) combined with a noun and used as an intensifier of that noun (cf. BOFFOLA; CASHOLA; CRACKOLA; CREEPOLA; DRUGOLA; FAGOLA; GAYOLA; HARMOLA; HOPOLA; LURKOLA; NOISOLA; PAYOLA; SCHNOZZOLA; STACKOLA; STUDOLA). [the original use is in pianola (1901), although in that context it worked as a diminutive. It was greatly popularized in the payola scandals that were unearthed in the US pop music industry during the late 1950s, although payola itself had been a recognized part of the business for 20 years.]

old n. **1** [mid-19C–1900s] as the old, a master, a boss. **2** [late 19C–1900s] money, esp. in the phr. a bit of the old.

old adj.[1] [mid-15C+] great, plentiful, excessive, usu. in comb. with good, great, high etc., e.g. high old time, great old fellow.

old adj.[2] [early 18C+] clever, cunning e.g. come the old soldier.

old adj.[3] **1** [late 18C–early 19C] (Und.) ugly. **2** [mid-19C+] (US) tiresome, usu. constructed with get, e.g. too much of a good thing gets old. [? OLD NICK, OLD BOY and similar devil-related terms; the Devil is assumed to be ugly]

old ... adj. other than those listed below, there are a number of terms for the Devil, all late 17C+, prefaced by 'old', e.g. boots, boy, chap, child, dad, Davy, fellow, hangie, hooky, Mahoun, man, Sanners/Sanny/Saunders, Scrat/Scratchem, Smith, smoke, scooty, soss, thief (cf. OLD BENDY).

old adam n. [19C+] the penis (cf. ADAM'S ARSENAL; OLD BLIND

BOB; OLD BOY n.[1]; OLD FELLOW; OLD HORNIE; OLD HORNINGTON; OLD MAN n.[1]; OLD ROOT; OLD ROWLEY; OLD SOLDIER n.[2]; OLD THING n.[2]). [SE old Adam, original sin]

old-age pension n. [1940+] (bingo) the number 65. [the age of male retirement]

old amber n. [1960s] (Aus.) beer. [AMBER FLUID]

old and bitter n. [1920s–30s] a mother-in-law. [a pun on beer]

old as the itch phr. [18C] very old. [ITCH n.]

old bads/broke n. [1950s] (W.I.) old clothes. [SE old + Shetland dial. bad, an article of clothing/SE broke or dial. brock, rubbish, refuse, remnants]

Old Bailey underwriter n. [early–mid-19C] a small-scale forger. [a pun on SE underwriter + ref. to his probable destination]

old bastard n. [20C] a man, often used as a term of affection.

old bat n. [18C+] an unattractive old woman. [BAT n.[3] (2)]

old bean n. [1910s+] a term of address, usu. to a man. [joc. use of SE bean, but ? SE being]

old beeswing n. [late 19C] a genial drinker. [SE beeswing, the crust that forms on vintage port]

old bendy/blazes n. [18C] the Devil (cf. OLD BILLY; OLD BOY n.[2]; OLD CLOOTIE; OLD DRIVER; OLD GENTLEMAN; OLD GENTLEMAN IN BLACK; OLD GOOSEBERRY; OLD HACK; OLD HAIRY TOE; OLD HARRINGTON; OLD HARRY; OLD HORNIE; OLD MR GRIM; OLD NED; OLD NICK; OLD ONE; OLD POKER; OLD RIP; OLD ROGER; OLD RUFFIAN; OLD SAM; OLD SCRATCH; OLD SPLITFOOT; OLD TOAST; OLD TOOT).

old betsey see BETSY.

old biddy n. **1** [late-18C+] an old woman. **2** [mid-19C+] (US) a maidservant, usu. Irish. [Biddy, a nickname for the popular Irish name Bridget]

Old Bill n. [1950s+] **1** the police; thus Bill from the Hill, officers serving at Notting Hill police station in London W11. **2** the police force as an institution. **3** a police station. [milit. old Bill, a veteran, ult. Old Bill, the character created by the WW1 cartoonist Bruce Bairnsfeather (1888–1959)]

old billy n. [late 19C] the Devil, usu. in the phr. like old billy, very hard, very energetically (cf. LIKE BILLY-O; OLD BENDY).

old bird n. [mid-19C+] a person who has become knowing through experience, esp. an experienced thief; thus wily/cunning old bird. [SE old + BIRD n.[2] (1)]

old black joes n. [20C] (Aus.) the toes [rhy. sl.]

old blazes see OLD BENDY.

old blind bob n. [18C] the penis (cf. OLD ADAM).

old bogey n. [early–mid-19C] the devil. [SE old + BOGEY n.[1]]

old boiler n. [1920s+] an old and unattractive woman. [ext. of BOILER n.[3] (1)]

old boots phr. [mid-19C] used as an intensifier implying speed, promptness, e.g. as old boots, like old boots.

old boy n.[1] **1** [18C] a man. **2** [19C+] an old or older man, esp. as the old boy, one's father. **3** [1940s+] (US) the penis (cf. OLD ADAM).

old boy, the n.[2] (US) **1** [late 18C+] the Devil (cf. OLD BENDY). **2** [mid-19C] 'daylights', stuffing, e.g. I'll knock the Old Boy out of him.

old broke see OLD BADS.

old brown windsor n. [1920s+] (Aus.) the anus. [play on Brown Windsor soup]

old buba n. [1950s] (W.I.) an old person who acts younger than their age. [SE old + dial. buba, a dry leaf, of cabbage, coconut or any plant]

old bubble see BUBBLE n.[5].

old buck n. [early 19C–1900s] (orig. US) a general term of address. [BUCK n.[1] (1)]

old chap n. [late 19C+] a man. [SE old + CHAP n. (1)]

old cheese n. [1990s] (Aus.) one's mother. [affectionate nickname]

old china plate/china *n.* [late 19C+] an old friend. [CHINA n.²]

old chocker *n.* [mid-19C+] an old fellow. [? joc. use of SE *chock full*]

old clo *adj.* [mid–late 19C] worn out, exhausted, out-of-date etc. [the street cry *old clo!*, old clothes]

old clootie/cloots *n.* [mid-18C–mid-19C] (Scot.) the Devil (cf. OLD BENDY). [dial. *cloot*, a cloven leaf]

old cock/cocker *n.* [18C+] a man, esp. as a term of affectionate address. [COCK n.³, underpinned by COCK n.⁵]

old cockalorum *n.* [late 19C–1900s] a man, esp. as a term of affectionate address. [ext. of OLD COCK]

old cocker *n.*¹ *see* OLD COCK.

old cocker *n.*² [20C] (orig. US) an old man, usu. a disreputable one. [Yid. *alte cacka*, old man]

old coon *n.* [mid–late 19C] (US) a shrewd individual. [SE *old + (ra)coon*]

old coot *n.* [late 18C+] a foolish or cantankerous old person.

old crow *n.* [20C] a generally misogynistic ref. to an old woman.

old curiosity *n.* [late 19C–1930s] one's wife.

old dampa *n.* [20C] (W.I.) old clothes (cf. OLD BADS). [ety. unknown]

Old Dart *n.* [late 19C+] (Aus./N.Z.) England. [? SE *old dirt*, cf. OLD SOD]

old dear *n.* [1950s+] an old woman.

old dig *n.* [1940s+] (Aus./N.Z.) a veteran soldier. [DIG n.³]

old ding *n.* [19C] the vagina. [? SE *ding*, to hit, to knock]

old dog *n.*¹ **1** [late 18C+] a man, usu. with overtones of admiration for his less than conventional lifestyle. **2** [1960s+] (US Black) an expert in a given field. [affectionate use of SE *dog*]

old dog, the *n.*² [1930s–50s] (US) syphilis. [? the disease 'bites' the sufferer]

old dog at common prayer *n.* [late 17C–18C] a mediocre clergyman who could read the prayers, but had no skill at preaching.

old dog at it *n.* [late 17C–late 19C] an expert in a given sphere of activity. [OLD DOG n.¹ (2)]

old dog for the hard road *phr.* [20C] (Irish) a phr. meaning the best person for a tough job is a veteran.

old donah *n.* [19C+] one's mother (cf. DONAH). [Polari *donah*, ult. Ital. *donna*, a woman]

Old Doss, the *n.* [19C] the Bridewell prison, sited on the banks of the Fleet River. [DOSS n.¹; the prison, on the site of Henry VIII's palace of Bridewell flourished 1556–1855; there were also Bridewell prisons at Clerkenwell and Westminster and several hundreds in major towns]

old driver *n.* [late 18C–19C] the Devil (cf. OLD BENDY).

old dutch *n.* [late 19C+] one's wife. [rhy. sl. *Duchess of Fife* = wife or *old dutch plate* = mate]

old Ear-ie *n.* [20C] listening in, eavesdropping (cf. ON THE ERIE).

old ebenezer *n.* [late 19C] (US) a grizzly bear. [? anecdotal]

old egg *n.* [20C] a man, esp. as a term of affectionate address. [SE *old + EGG n.¹*]

old enough to know better *phr.* [20C] implying that someone who has just committed some blunder should not have done so.

old ewe dressed as lamb *n.* [late 18C] an old woman dressed like a young one (cf. MUTTON DRESSED AS LAMB).

old-fashioned *adj.*¹ [mid-19C+] of sexual intercourse, performed in the conventional manner, the missionary position.

old-fashioned *adj.*² [1930s] (Irish) precocious, forward.

old-fashioned look *n.* [1930s+] a disapproving glance.

old fellow *n.* **1** [early 19C+] a man. **2** [early 19C+] the penis (cf. OLD ADAM). **3** [20C] (Irish) one's father, usu. written as *oulfella*, to emphasize the Dublin pron.

old flame *n.* [mid-19C+] a former lover. [Fr. *flamme*, a sweetheart (lit. flame), much used in 17C romantic fiction]

old flint *n.* [mid-19C] a miser. [SKINFLINT]

old flower *n.* [20C] (Irish) an affectionate term of address esp. as *my old flower.*

old floorer *n.* [mid-19C–1920s] a fig. name for death. [he 'knocks you down']

old fowl *n.* [20C] (W.I.) an ageing, unattractive and probably over-dressed woman (cf. OLD HEN).

old frizzle *n.* [18C–late 19C] **1** in cards, the ace of spades. **2** the vagina (cf. ACE OF SPADES). [SE *frizzle*, crisp, curly hair; the shape of the spade could resemble a beard; (2) is ref. to pubic hair]

old fruit/tin of fruit *n.* [1920s+] a general term of affectionate address (cf. OLD PIP).

old gal/girl *n.* [late 19C+] **1** one's wife or regular female companion (cf. OLD LADY; OLD WOMAN). **2** a general term of address to a woman or a female dog or horse.

old gang *n.* [late 19C] a group or clique of friends or colleagues.

old geezer *see* MY OLD GEEZER.

old gentleman *n.* **1** [early 19C–1900s] in gambling, a card that is slightly longer than the rest of the pack and thus identifiable by cheats. **2** [mid-19C] the Devil (cf. OLD BENDY). [abbr. OLD GENTLEMAN IN BLACK]

old gentleman in black *n.* [mid–late 17C] the Devil (cf. GENTLEMAN IN BLACK).

old gentleman's bed-posts/four-poster *n.* [mid-19C] the four of clubs, considered an unlucky card. [OLD GENTLEMAN, var. on DEVIL'S BEDPOSTS]

old girl, the *n.*¹ [late 18C] an old woman (cf. GRANNY n.¹).

old girl *n.*² *see* OLD GAL.

old glory *n.* [late 19C–1940s] (US Black) anything seen as unfashionable, out of date. [SE *Old Glory*, nickname for the US flag. The implication is of the stylessness of traditional White values]

old gooseberry *n.* [late 18C–late 19C] **1** the Devil (cf. OLD BENDY). **2** anyone who puts an end to a riot or disturbance whether by threats or actual force (cf. LIKE OLD GOOSEBERRY; PLAY OLD GOOSEBERRY).

old gown *n.* [mid-19C] smuggled tea. [ety. unknown; the label placed on the tea-chest for the purpose of deception]

old grabem pudden *n.* [late 19C] an old woman, whether one's wife or mother. [rhy. sl.; seen as possessing a sweet tooth, i.e. she 'grabs the pudding']

old hack *n.* [late 19C] the Devil (cf. OLD BENDY). [var. on OLD HARRY n. (2)]

old hairy toe *n.* [1930s] the Devil (cf. OLD BENDY). [var. on OLD HARRY n. (2); but note the Devil's depiction as half-goat]

old hand *n.* [late 18C+] an expert (cf. OLD DOG AT IT).

old hannah *n.* [1930s] (US Black) the sun.

old harrington *n.* [late 18C–early 19C] the Devil (cf. OLD BENDY). [ext. of OLD HARRY n. (2)]

Old Harry *n.* **1** [late 17C–19C] a form of unspecified adulterant used in wine; 'a Composition used by Vintners, when they bedevil their Wines' (B.E.). **2** [late 17C+] the Devil; thus *play old Harry with, give old Harry*, to play the Devil with, to make mischief, to tease or scold (cf. BY THE LORD HARRY; OLD BENDY). [*give old Harry* is still current in W.I. use]

old hat *n.* [late 17C–late 19C] the vagina (cf. OLD LING; TILE). ['because frequently felt' (Grose 1796)]

old hat *adj.* [1910s+] out-of-date, old-fashioned.

old haymaker *see* HAYMAKER n.¹.

old head *n.* (US) **1** [late 19C+] an old-timer, an old person. **2** [1950s+] (drugs) a long-time marijuana smoker. [fig. use of SE, boosted in (2) by HEAD n.¹⁰]

old hen *n.* [20C] a woman (cf. OLD FOWL). [HEN n. (3)]

old hickory *n.* [1960s] (US) a $20 bill (cf. ABRAHAM LINCOLN). [it carries the picture of President Andrew 'Old Hickory' Jackson (1767–1845)]

old hige *n.* [1940s+] (W.I.) a nagging old woman. [SE *hag* + dial. *old hige*, an old witch]

old hook, the *n.* [19C] (US) a fellow, a chap.

old hornie/horney *n.* **1** [18C+] the Devil (cf. OLD BENDY). **2** [20C] the penis (cf. OLD ADAM). [the devil's traditional horns + HORN n.²]

old hornington *n.* [19C] the penis (cf. OLD ADAM). [HORN n.²]

old horse/hoss *n.*¹ (orig. US) **1** [19C] a man. **2** [19C+] a term of address by one man to another.

old horse *n.*² [mid-19C] salt beef (cf. JUNK n.¹).

Old Horse *n.*³ *see* HORSE n.⁶.

old hoss *see* OLD HORSE n.¹.

old huddle/huddle and twang *n.* [mid-16C–mid-17C] a miser. [he 'huddles' around his money; the use of *twang*, usu. a prostitute (*see* TWANG n.¹), has no obvious explanation]

old identity *n.* [late 19C+] **1** a person, usu. an eccentric, a 'character'. **2** (Aus./N.Z.) anyone who has lived in the same place for a long time, a regular resident (cf. NEW INIQUITY).

oldie *n.* **1** [late 19C; 1970s+] (usu. teen or youth) the old, esp. those over 40, or at least those who fail to share or appreciate the nuances and delights of the current version of the rebellious youth culture (cf. DUSTY n.²; GERI; OLDSTER; WRINKLY). **2** [1920s+] anything old, esp. an old joke, saying, record or song.

oldie but goodie *n.* [1930s+] (US) something or someone that is old or no longer fashionable or chic but still beloved by its owner/wearer/user, esp. an old song (cf. GOLDEN OLDIE). [OLDIE + GOODIE]

oldies *n.* [1970s+] one's parents. [OLDIE]

old/up in the tooth *phr.* [mid-19C] aged, esp. of old women. [the use of a horse's teeth to ascertain its age, the older a horse, the more faded the distinguishing marks in their teeth]

old iron and brass *n.* [20C] grass. [rhy. sl.]

old Jack Lang *n.* [1960s+] (Aus.) rhyming slang. [rhy. sl.; ? anecdotal]

old Jamaica rum *n.* [20C] the sun. [rhy. sl.]

old joe *n.* [1910s+] (US) syphilis. [orig. US Navy]

old King Cole *n.* [1920s+] the dole (cf. NAT KING COLE). [rhy. sl.]

old lad *n.* [16C+] a man, esp. as an affectionate term of address.

old lady *n.* **1** [late 18C+] mother. **2** [mid-19C+] (orig. US) a wife (actual or common-law). **3** [late 19C] the vagina. **4** [1910s+] (orig. US) a girlfriend or regular partner. **5** [1920s–50s] (US campus) of the same sex, a roommate. **6** [1930s+] (US prison) a passive partner in a homosexual relationship, male or female.

old lady five fingers *see* LADY FIVE FINGERS.

old lady of Westmoreland Street *n.* [mid-19C–1940s] (Irish) the *Irish Times*. [its address in Dublin]

old lady white *n.* **1** [1900s–50s] a drug dealer, presumably in white powders, i.e. narcotics (cf. MRS WHITE). **2** [1940s–50s] any powdered drug, e.g. cocaine, heroin.

old lag *n.* [19C+] an habitual prisoner, a recidivist, orig. a returnee from transportation to Australia. [SE *old* + LAG n.². Although the original *lag* was destined for the penal colonies of Australia, the *old lag* can have served his time in any prison]

old ling *n.* [19C] the vagina (cf. OLD HAT). [ext. of LING]

old mackinaw! *see* HOLY MACKINAW!

old madge *n.*¹ [mid-17C–mid-18C] a cudgel. [note late 19C SE *madge*, a leaden hammer covered thickly with stout woollen cloth, used in solder plating]

old madge *n.*² [20C] (drugs) cocaine. [ety. unknown]

old maid *n.* [1940s–80s] (US) a kernel of popcorn that has failed to pop.

old man *n.*¹ **1** [late 18C+] a woman's lover or husband (cf. OLD LADY). **2** [19C+] a father. **3** [late 19C+] the penis (cf. OLD ADAM). **4** [1950s+] (US) a pimp. **5** [1960s+] (US) a boyfriend or lover, incl. a homosexual one.

old man, the *n.*² **1** [mid-19C+] (orig. US) the man in charge, the boss. **2** [late 19C+] (US Und.) a police chief, judge, prison warden or the head of a criminal gang. **3** [1900s–50s] (US) God (cf. OLD BOY).

old man *adj.* [mid-19C+] (Aus./N.Z.) large, important, of lengthy duration etc, e.g. an *old man kangaroo*, an *old man sand storm*.

old man!/son!/sport! *excl.* [19C+] a general greeting given to a man (usu. one whom one knows).

old man has his Sunday clothes on, the *phr.* [19C] a phr. used of the penis, when erect. [OLD MAN n.¹ (3), freshly laundered Sunday clothes were stiff with starch]

old man Mose *n.* [1940s] (US Black) **1** time. **2** death. [abbr. *Moses*; biblical imagery, via spirituals/hymns]

old man's milk *n.* [mid-19C] whisky (cf. MOTHER'S MILK).

old mick *adj.* [late 19C+] sick. [rhy. sl.]

old Mr Gory *n.* [late 17C–early 19C] gold (cf. GOREE). [*Fort Goree*, on the Gold Coast]

Old Mr Grim *n.* [late 18C–19C] **1** the Devil (cf. OLD BENDY). **2** death.

Old Mo, the *n.* [late 19C–1900s] the Middlesex Music Hall. [abbr.]

old moody *n.* [1930s+] a cunning trick, a fraud; thus *pull the old moody.*

old mother hubbard *n.* [late 19C] an unbelievable story, a fantasy. [the fairy-tale character]

old mother slipper-slopper *n.* [1910s–20s] a little old woman. [a nursery rhyme]

old moustache *n.* [late 19C] a vigorous old man with a grey moustache (cf. MOUSTACHE PETE).

Old Muddy *n.* [mid-19C+] (US) the Mississippi or Missouri rivers (cf. BIG MUDDY).

old nag *n.* [1910s–20s] a cigarette. [rhy. sl. *old nag* = FAG n.⁴ (1)]

Old Nassau *n.* [mid-19C+] (US campus) Princeton University. [Nassau Hall]

Old Ned *n.*¹ [mid-19C+] (US) the Devil; thus *raise Old Ned*, to cause a commotion, to cause trouble (cf. OLD BENDY).

old ned *n.*² [mid-19C+] (US Black) salt pork or bacon. [orig. regional use]

old net *n.* [1950s] (W.I.) ragged work-clothes. [both are torn and are mainly made up of holes]

Old Nick/Nicker/Nickie Ben *n.* **1** [mid-17C+] the Devil (cf. NICK n.¹; OLD BENDER). **2** [late 19C+] (Anglo-Irish) the knave or jack in a pack of cards (cf. BOY WITH THE BOOTS).

old nigger *n.* [1950s] (W.I.) a disreputable, down-at-heel person (cf. NEW NAYGA). [NIGGER n.]

Old Nog *n.* [early 18C] beer. [a specific brandname]

Old Oak *n.* [20C] London. [rhy. sl. *old oak* = the SMOKE]

Old October *n.* [early 18C] beer. [a specific brandname]

old oil *n.* [1910s–60s] (US) flattery, insincere charm (cf. BANANA OIL). [OIL n.¹ (4)]

Old One, the *n.* [late 18C+] the Devil (cf. OLD BENDER).

old one-two, the *n.*¹ [19C+] a knock-out blow, either lit. or fig. [boxing use]

old one-two, the *n.*² **1** [late 19C] masturbation. **2** [20C] sexual intercourse. [the rhythmic movements]

old oyster *n.* [late 19C–1920s] a general term of address, esp. to a reserved, uncommunicative person.

old party *n.* [mid-19C+] an old man.

old pip *n.* [1930s] a general term of affectionate address (cf. OLD FRUIT).

old poker/poger *n.* [late 18C] the Devil (cf. OLD BENDY).

old pot *n.* [late 19C+] (usu. Aus.) an old man, esp. one's father. [rhy. sl. *old pot and pan* = SE *old man*]

Old Prob/Probabilities *n.* [1950s] (US) the chief of the weather bureau.

old put *n.* [late 19C] a pretentious old gentleman. [SE *old* + PUT n.¹]

old rale/ral *n.* [late 19C–1960s] (US) syphilis. [? dial. *rail*, to stagger, to reel. The development of the disease gradually impairs mobility]

old ram *n.* [late 19C+] an old or middle-aged man who still pursues women. [RAM n.¹ (2)]

old raspberry *n.* [1910s–20s] one who has a notably red nose, presumably a drunkard.

old red socks *n.* [20C] (Ulster) the pope. [the identification of Catholicism with red; e.g. the 'the scarlet woman of Rome']

Old Reekie *n.* [late 18C+] the old town and subseq. the whole town of Edinburgh (cf. SMOKE n.). [the smoke and smog that often covered it]

old rip *n.* [20C] the Devil; thus (US) *madder than old rip*, extremely angry (cf. OLD BENDY).

old robin *n.* [late 18C–early 19C] an experienced person. [generic use of proper name]

old roger *n.* **1** [late 17C–18C] the Devil (cf. OLD BENDY). **2** [18C] the pirates' flag the *Jolly Roger*. [popular use of SE *roger* as nickname for a bull]

old root *n.* [19C] the penis (cf. IRISH ROOT; MAN ROOT; OLD ADAM; ROOT; STALK; TAIL). [ext. of ROOT n.¹ (1)]

old rope *n.* [1940s] (orig. RN) very strong, rank tobacco.

old rowley/slimey *n.* [18C] the penis (cf. OLD ADAM). [*rowley*, alternative sp. for SE *rolly*, thus the shape/SE *slimey*, of the semen it ejaculates]

old ruffian *n.* [late 17C–19C] the Devil (cf. OLD BENDY). [ext. of RUFFIN]

Old Ruffin *see* RUFFIN.

olds *n.*¹ [late 19C+] old people, parents (cf. YOUNGS).

Olds *n.*² [1930s+] (US) an *Olds*mobile car. [abbr.]

old salt *n.* [mid-19C+] a veteran sailor. [orig. naut. jargon]

old sam *n.* [1930s] (US Black) the Devil (cf. OLD BENDY).

old saw *n.* [late 19C–1940s] (US Black) one's wife. [? her nagging *saws* away at a man]

old school *adj.* [1980s+] (US Black) **1** in rap music use, used of anything pertaining to the early days of the musical style, esp. the work of such performers as Grandmaster Flash or Afrika Bambaataa. **2** used of anything typical of the fashions, music and general styles of the 1960s–70s. **3** a senior, respected individual; their 'school' is prob. that 'of life' rather than any given college.

old scratch *n.* [mid-18C+] the Devil (cf. OLD BENDY). [mid-19C+ use is US only]

old shoes *n.* [late 19C] rum. [? joking ref. to a strong smell]

old six *n.* [mid–late 19C] old ale priced at sixpence per quart.

old slimey *see* OLD ROWLEY.

Old Slop *n.* [mid-19C] *The Times* newspaper. [Fr. *salope*, a tart; applied to the newspaper when, *c.*1840–50, it was seen as abandoning its role as the impartial 'thunderer' and currying favour wherever it could]

old smokey *n.* [1920s–60s] (US prison) the electric chair (cf. OLD SPARKY).

old soak *n.* [early 19C+] a drunkard. [SOAK n.]

old soaker *n.* [late 18C–early 19C] a drunkard (cf. SOAK n.).

old socks/stockings *n.* [late 19C+] (US) a term of address to a man.

old soldier *n.*¹ **1** [early 18C] an experienced, but somewhat cunning man (cf. COME THE OLD SOLDIER). **2** [mid-19C+] a simpleton, a naïve. [contrasting images of SE]

old soldier *n.*² (US) **1** [mid-19C+] the stub of a cigar or cigarette. **2** [late 19C+] an empty bottle (cf. DEAD adj.²; DEAD SOLDIER). **3** [1970s] (US) the penis (cf. OLD ADAM).

old son! *see* OLD MAN!

old sparky *n.* [1970s+] (US prison) the electric chair (cf. OLD SMOKY).

old splendid *n.* [late 19C] (US) a very admirable person.

old splitfoot *n.* [late 17C–19C] the Devil (cf. OLD BENDY).

old sport! *see* OLD MAN!

old stager *n.* [mid-16C+] an experienced person (cf. OLD HAND). [? OFr. *éstagier*, inhabitant or church Lat. *stagiarius*, an aged monk who was lodged permanently in the infirmary. Equally feasible is *stage-coach*, in this context one who is a regular traveller upon them]

Old Start, the *n.* [20C] the Old Bailey. [START n.¹, i.e. Newgate prison on the site of which the Old Bailey was erected]

oldster *n.* [mid-19C+] (orig. and still mainly US) an old person (cf. OLDIE). [on model of SE *youngster*]

old steve *n.* [1930s–50s] (drugs) heroin. [ety. unknown; ? a well-known dealer]

old stick-in-the-mud *n.* [early 19C+] a conservative, a dedicated traditionalist.

old stockings *see* OLD SOCKS.

old strike-a-light *n.* [late 19C] one's father. [his cry of *strike a light!* when asked for yet another 'loan']

old stripes/stripes *n.* [late 19C–1900s] a tiger.

old sweat *n.* [1910s+] (orig. milit.) any veteran. [? the *sweat* of battle and thus of one's labours. The British philologist Ernest Weekley has suggested, in *Xenophobia* (1932), that it may have originated during the Thirty Years' War as the German *alter Schweele*, old Swede, but its first appearance *c.*1919 militates against the theory]

old-talk *n.* [20C] (W.I.) chatter, gossip, rhetoric, empty boasting (cf. GAFF n.²).

old thing *n.*¹ [mid–late 19C] (Aus.) a meal of salt beef and damper.

old thing *n.*² **1** [mid-19C+] the vagina. **2** [1970s+] the penis (cf. OLD ADAM). [euph.]

old thing *n.*³ [20C] a person, often as a term of address or as *funny old thing* etc.

old timer *n.* [19C] a veteran. [SE from 1900]

old toast *n.*¹ [late 17C–early 18C] the Devil (cf. OLD BENDY). [the heat of hell, in which sinners are *toasted*]

old toast *n.*² [late 17C–early 18C] **1** a drunkard. **2** a lively old man. [their drinking of SE *toasts*]

old tom *n.* [early 19C–1930s] gin (cf. CAT'S WATER). [according to Brewer, the proper name of *Thomas Norris*, who was employed at Hodges' distillery and who opened a gin palace in Great Russell Street, Covent Garden. The drink in which he specialized was concocted by another Hodges' employee, Thomas Chamberlain, who christened his brand in honour of Mr Norris]

old toot *n.* [19C] the Devil (cf. OLD BENDY).

old top *n.* [late 19C–1920s] a general form of address to a man one knows.

old trot *n.* [late 17C+] **1** a fellow, a chap. **2** an old woman. **3** a dubious story, esp. as *a load of old trot*.

old trout *n.* [late 19C+] an older person, usu. a woman and usu. used as a pej. [TROUT n.²]

old whiskers *n.* [late 19C] a working man with long, unkempt, greying whiskers, usu. shouted out by impudent children.

old wigsby *n.* [late 19C] (middle class) a crotchety, narrow-minded, elderly man, a dedicated opponent of any form of 'progress' or modernity. [such a man would still be likely to sport a wig, seen as an 18C affectation]

old wives' paternoster *n.* [late 16C–early 17C] grumbling, nagging. [SE *paternoster*, the Lord's Prayer]

old woman *n.* **1** [late 18C+] a wife, a regular female partner (cf. OLD LADY). **2** [late 18C+] the vagina. **3** [mid-19C+] one's mother (cf. OLD MAN). [reverse of OLD MAN *n.*[1] (1), (3) and (2)]

Ole-Mas *n.* [20C] (W.I.) a shambles, chaos, confusion; thus *turn Old-Mas*, to collapse into confusion. [Carib.E. *Ole-Mas*, the masquerade festival that opens Carnival]

olive oil *phr.* [late 19C–1970s] (*orig. music-hall*) goodbye (cf. AU RESERVOIR). [mispron. of Fr. *au revoir*, goodbye]

oliver *n.*[1] [mid-18C–1920s] the moon; thus (Und.) *oliver is in town*, the moon is full, and thus the nights are too light for stealing safely, *oliver's up*, the moon has risen, *oliver whiddles*, the moon is shining. [? the 'O' shape]

oliver *n.*[2] **1** [late 19C] a fist. **2** [late 19C] (Aus.) the wrist. **3** [1970s] a deliberately incorrect entry in a ledger, usu. bookmaker use (cf. TWIST *v.*[3]). [rhy. sl. *Oliver Twist*; (3) is the use of the *fist* to write]

oliver *n.*[3] *see* OLLIE.

oliver *v.* [mid-19C] to understand, usu. in phr. *do you oliver?*, do you understand? [rhy. sl. *Oliver Cromwell* (pron. 'crummle') = TUMBLE *v.*[2]]

oliver's skull *n.* [late 17C–late 19C] a chamberpot. [originating in the Restoration's hatred of the Commonwealth's Lord Protector, *Oliver* Cromwell]

oliver's summons *n.* [19C] (Irish) an idle person who is forced to work for lack of any alternative means of making money. [anecdote of one *Oliver*, a Limerick landlord, who impounded the goods of those who worked for him until the job was properly done]

ollapod *n.* [mid-19C] a country apothecary. [SE *olla podrida*, a hotchpotch, a mixture. The ref. is to the hodgepodge of herbs etc that they use in their homemade cures]

'oller, boys, 'oller *n.* [late 19C+] a collar. [rhy. sl.]

olli compolli *n.* [late 18C–early 19C] (Und.) 'the name of one of the principle rogues of the canting crew' (Grose 1785). [? Sp. *olla*, a jar, and thus a dish containing a great variety of ingredients, a hotchpotch; thus, suggests E.P., 'the Jack-of-all-trades'. He is mentioned in Dekker's *O per se O* (1612) where the name is cited as a nickname, indicating that he is the chief of a given order of rogues, rather than a designation as such]

ollie/oliver *n.* [1930s–50s] a uniformed policeman. [comedian *Oliver* Hardy (1892–1957), who occasionally played one]

olly *n.* **1** [1960s+] marijuana. **2** [1980s] amphetamines (cf. A *n.*[2]). [rhy. sl. *Oliver Reed* = (1) WEED *n.*[1] (4); (2) SPEED *n.*[2], ult. actor UK *Oliver* Reed (b.1938)]

olly, olly! *excl.* [20C] (Cockney) a general excl. of greeting [? *hello, hello!*]

-ology *n.* [early 19C+] an abstract, a theory, an '-ism'.

olympic pool *n.*[1] [20C] the vagina.

olympic pool *n.*[2] [1950s+] (Aus.) an outdoor cinema. [? where one does the 'breaststroke']

Omahog *n.* [late 19C–1960s] (US) a resident of Omaha, Nebraska.

O'Malley *n.* [1990s] a policeman. [use of Irish surname O'Malley as a generic]

o.m.c.d. *phr.* [1960s+] (gay) *out of my class, darling.* [abbr.]

o.m.d. *n.* [late 19C] (US) a pretty, but empty-headed girl, often a member of the chorus line (cf. BIMBO; DUMB DORA) [abbr. *old men's darlings*]

omee/omer/omey/homee/homey *n.* [mid-19C+] **1** a man. **2** a master, a boss. **3** a landlord. [Polari, Ital. *uomo*, a man]

omee-polone/-paloney *n.* [late 19C+] (Ling. Fr./Polari) a male homosexual (cf. HESH). [OMEE + POLONE]

omer/omey *see* OMEE.

omnibus *n.* [mid–late 19C] a prostitute (cf. BARRACK HACK). [anyone can buy a 'ride']

omnium gatherum *n.* [16C] a mixed gathering of people or things. [mock-Latin]

omnium gatherum *adv.* [mid-17C] chaotically, confusedly. [OMNIUM GATHERUM *n.*]

omo *phr.* [1960s+] a signal used by a part-time or amateur prostitute, denoted by the placing of a packet of the washing-powder *Omo* in one's window, indicating that the husband is away at sea and the woman is therefore available for sex. [abbr. *old man out*]

om-tiddly-om-pom *n.* [1910s–30s] a lavatory. [? euph.]

on *adj.*[1] **1** [early 19C+] involved in a wager; thus [1930s+] *you're on*, your bet has been taken. **2** [late 19C+] (orig. US) in favour of, or willing to take part in, something, e.g. *I'm on*, I agree with that, *you're on*, accepting a challenge or a bet.

on *adj.*[2] [late 19C+] tipsy, slightly drunk.

on *adj.*[3] **1** [late 19C–1920s] (US) fully comprehending or well aware of. **2** [1930s+] (Aus.) alert, keeping one's eye on someone. **3** [1940s–50s] (US Black) sophisticated, informed, at an advantage.

on *adj.*[4] [1930s+] feasible, possible. [billiards use]

on *adj.*[5] [1940s+] available on a menu (cf. OFF *adj.*[1]).

on *adj.*[6] [1950s+] (US) being the focus of attention, performing, needing to impress. [entertainment industry, as if *on stage.*]

on *adv.* [mid-19C+] no. [backsl.]

on *prep.*[1] [mid-19C+] to the disadvantage or detriment of someone, so as to affect or disturb, e.g. *pass out on*, *have a joke on*.

on *prep.*[2] [mid-19C+] synon. for SE *at*, e.g. *on weekends*.

on *prep.*[3] [late 19C+] debited to, paid for by, e.g. *lunch is on me*.

on *prep.*[4] [1920s+] playing a given musical instrument, e.g. *on rhythm guitar, Keith Richards.*

on *prep.*[5] [1930s+] (US drugs) **1** using a given drug, e.g. *on acid*, *on smack*. **2** to be addicted to a narcotic.

on a bat *phr.* [mid-19C+] (orig. US) drunk, on a drinking binge. [BAT *n.*[2] (2)]

on a bender/bend *phr.* **1** [mid-19C+] on a drinking spree; thus [late 19C] *go on the considerable bend*, *have a bend*, to go out on a drunken spree. **2** [1970s+] bingeing on drugs. [BENDER *n.*[1] (1)]

on a brannigan *phr.* [late 19C+] (US) very drunk. [BRANNIGAN *n.* (1)]

on a brave *phr.* [mid–late 19C] (US) suddenly and temporarily courageous. [SE *brave*]

on a bust *phr.* [20C] drinking heavily. [BUST *n.*[3]]

on a ay yo trip *phr.* [1980s+] (W.I./UK Black teen) used of one who is forever demanding attention, making themself conspicuous. [the cry of *Ay! Yo!* + TRIP *n.*[3] (2)]

on account of *see* ACCOUNT OF.

on a dead one *phr.* [late 19C–1910s] **1** betting on a horse that has no chance. **2** making any pointless effort.

on a downer *phr.* [1960s+] (orig. US) in a depressed state. [DOWNER *n.*]

on a good wicket *phr.* [1910s+] (Aus.) party to a profitable deal, in an advantageous situation (cf. STICKY WICKET). [cricketing imagery]

on a hiding to nothing *phr.* [late 19C+] with absolutely no chance, esp. in a sporting contest.

on a jag *phr.* **1** [late 17C+] out on a spree, orig. used of drinking and later ext. to drugs. **2** [1950s+] (orig. US) elated. [JAG *n.*[1]]

on a kick *phr.* [1940s+] (orig. US) **1** having a good time. **2** enthusiastic about. [KICK *n.*[1] (2)]

on a merry pin *phr.* [late 18C] tipsy. [? the pins that once marked off levels in a tankard]

on a mission *phr.* [1990s] **1** (US Black gang) searching for, in pursuit of, performing any gang-related activity, esp. killing members of a rival gang or simply penetrating their territory. **2** (drugs) looking for drugs.

onan's olympics *n.* [19C] masturbation. [the biblical *Onan* who 'cast his seed upon the ground' (Gen. 38:9)]

on a pension *phr.* [1970s+] (Und.) used of a policeman receiving regular bribes.

on appro *adv.* [mid-19C+] on approval. [abbr.]

on a promise *phr.* [1970s+] (Und.) awaiting a promised event, a bribe, a tip-off etc.

on a roll *phr.* [1970s+] (orig. US gambling) on a winning streak, enjoying a period of success, whether lit. or fig. [ROLL n.⁴]

on a shoestring *phr.* [20C] living, working, travelling etc with a very small budget (cf. SHOESTRING).

on a skate *phr.* [20C] drinking heavily. [orig. RN *skate*, to go in search of liquor and/or women; ult. fig. use of SE]

on a/the sneak tip *phr.* [1980s+] (US) clandestinely, surreptitiously, deceitfully. [SE *sneak* + TIP n.⁸]

on at *adv.* [20C] critical of, nagging, telling off. [abbr. GOING ON AT]

on a tight leash *phr.* [1950s+] **1** deeply infatuated. **2** kept under extreme control.

on a tipple *phr.* [late 18C+] very drunk. [TIPPLE n.]

on a toot *phr.* [late 18C+] (orig. US) out on a spree, esp. one that involves heavy consumption of alcohol (and latterly of drugs). [SE *toot*, a copious draught of alcohol, the act of drinking it]

on a trip *phr.* [1960s+] (drugs) **1** under the influence of drugs. **2** disorientated, seemingly 'in another world'. [TRIP n.³]

on board *adv.* [19C+] referring to drink that has been consumed (cf. BALLAST ON BOARD). [naut. imagery]

once *n.*¹ [late 19C] vigour, energy, cheek. [SE *on!*, advance, go forward]

once *n.*² *see* ONCE-OVER.

once *n.*³ [1930s+] a £1 note. [abbr. ONCER n.³]

once a week *n.* [20C] **1** cheek. **2** a magistrate. [rhy. sl., (2) *once a week* = BEAK n.¹]

once-a-week man *n.* [late 19C] a debtor, one who goes out only once a week. [debtors could not be arrested on a Sunday, so for the rest of the week they hid indoors]

once in a blue moon *phr.* [mid-19C+] extremely rarely (cf. BLUE MOON n.¹).

once in a month of Sundays *phr.* [early 19C+] extremely rarely.

once-over/once *n.* (orig. US) **1** [1910s+] a quick glance of appraisal; thus *give the once-over*, to look over, to assess. **2** [1930s+] a quick treatment or superficial job, such as a quick clean-up.

once over lightly *phr.* [1940s+] (US) superficially. [housepainting imagery]

oncer *n.*¹ **1** [late 19C–1910s] a person who only goes to church once on Sunday; thus *twicer*, one who goes to both matins and evensong. **2** [1920s+] (Aus.) anything that happens only once. **3** [1960s+] (gay) a homosexual who never repeats a sexual encounter with any one partner but continues to seek new people.

oncer *n.*² [20C] impudence [rhy. sl., *once a week* = CHEEK n.]

oncer *n.*³ [1930s+] a £1 note.

onces *n.* [late 19C] wages. [they come once a week]

once too often *phr.* [1920s+] of a thing said or done once more than necessary or acceptable, usu. implying unpleasant repercussions.

on clover *adj.* [late 18C+] (Aus.) in comfort (cf. IN CLOVER).

oncus/ongkus/onkiss/onkus *adj.*¹ [1910s+] (Aus./N.Z.) **1** of people, upset, out of sorts, disagreeable. **2** of machinery, out of order. **3** of food or drink, stale. [ety. unknown; ? link to HONK v.¹]

oncus/ongkus *adj.*² [1910s+] (Aus./N.Z.) good, profitable, pleasant. [Baker (1941) sees this as primary use, and adj.¹ as 'occasional'; *AND* cites only adj.²; *DNZE* only adj.¹]

on deck *adj.* (US) **1** [late 19C] on the schedule. **2** [late 19C–1900s] alive. **3** [late 19C+] available, prepared. [naut. imagery]

on doog *adj.* [mid-19C] no good. [backsl.]

one *n.*¹ [mid-16C–mid-19C] oneself, one's own interest (cf. NUMBER ONE n.¹).

one *n.*² [mid-19C+] (orig. US) **1** a blow with the fist; thus *lay one on*. **2** a punishment, a beating e.g. *I'll give you one.*

one *n.*³ [late 19C+] a drink, usu. in the phr. *come and have one*, join me for a drink (cf. ONE FOR THE ROAD; QUICK ONE).

one *n.*⁴ [late 19C+] **1** an eccentric or amusing person (cf. AREN'T YOU THE ONE!; YOU ARE A ONE!). **2** one who stands out in some way, either for impudence, expertise etc, esp. as *a one for*.

one *n.*⁵ [1920s+] an anecdote, an amusing story, a joke, e.g. *have you heard the one about ... ?* (cf. GOOD ONE n.²).

one *n.*⁶ [1930s–60s] a male homosexual (cf. ONE OF THOSE; ONE OF US; SO adj.). [? old US Army joke, Sergeant, counting off, 'Are you one?' Soldier, 'Yeth, are you one too?']

one *n.*⁷ [1940s+] (orig. US) nothing, not a single one, usu. with qualifying negative, e.g. *He won't get dime one out of me* etc.

one *n.*⁸ [1970s+] (US Black) abbr. for one big lie.

one, the *n.*⁹ [1970s+] cannabis oil, THC.

one *adj.* [early 19C+] used with a noun to emphasize a comment, e.g. *one serious boy*, *one angry young man*, esp. as abbr./euph. for *one hell of a* (cf. ONE OF 'EM).

o.n.e. *phr.* [1980s+] of sex, one night's experience. [abbr.]

on e *phr.* [1990s] (US Black) lacking, usu. but not invariably money (cf. ON FULL). [*on empty*]

one a cat couldn't scratch *phr.* [1960s+] (US) used of an especially hard penile erection.

one alone *n.* [20C] (Aus.) a moan. [rhy. sl.]

one-a-man *n.* [1950s] (W.I.) a large, round dumpling, using a pound of flour (cf. MAN DUMPLING). [one of these dumplings will satisfy a man's appetite]

one and a peppermint-drop *n.* [late 19C–1900s] a person with only one eye.

one and eight *n.* [20C] a plate. [rhy. sl.]

one and elevenpence three farden *n.* [late 19C+] a garden. [rhy. sl.]

one and half *n.* [20C] a scarf. [rhy. sl.]

one-and-one *n.* [1950s+] (Irish) a portion of fish and chips. [? early Italian immigrant chip-shop owners, whose lack of English meant that one signalled with one finger for chips and added another for fish]

one and one *phr.* [1980s+] (drugs) to inhale cocaine. [ONE-ON-ONE n.]

one and t'other *n.* **1** [late 19C+] a brother. **2** [20C] a mother. [rhy. sl.]

one and two *n.* [1990s] (rap music) the two turntables used by a DJ.

one another *n.* **1** [late 19C+] a brother. **2** [20C] a mother (cf. ONE AND T'OTHER). [rhy. sl.]

one arm *n.* [1950s–70s] (US) an establishment or operation run by one person (cf. ONE-ARM JOINT).

one-armed bandit *n.* [1930s+] (orig. US) a fruit machine, a coin-operated gaming machine, originally operated by a single lever (cf. BANDIT n.¹).

one-arm joint *n.* [late 19C–1970s] (US) a fast-food café. [SE *one arm* + JOINT n.³ (3), such a café provided food one could eat with one hand]

one away! *excl.* [1940s+] (prison) the cry of alarm from prison officers that signified an escape.

one-bagger *n.* [1980s+] (US campus) a very ugly person (cf. DOUBLE-BAGGER; TWO-BAGGER). [such an individual is so ugly one would need to put a bag over their head before having sex]

one bill *n.* [1970s+] $100 (cf. BILL n.⁵).

one bite *n.* [late 19C] (coster) a sour, small apple that is good for a single bite, after which it gets thrown away.

one-box tissue n. [1980s+] (drugs) 1oz (28g) of crack cocaine. [ety. unknown; ? play on SE blow/BLOW n.[8] (2)]

one brick short of a load phr. [20C] slightly insane, eccentric (cf. NOT ALL THERE).

one-cheek squeek n. [1990s] an instance of breaking wind.

one-drink house n. [late 19C] a public house where only one drink is allowed in a given period. The customer must then go out and come back before being eligible for another.

187/one-eight-seven n. [1980s+] a homicide. [the California penal code for homicide. Codes vary from state to state, e.g. the Oregon homicide code is 163]

187/one-eight-seven v. [1980s+] to murder; thus gang slogan used by the Crips of Los Angeles B187, 'we kill Bloods'. [187 n.]

one-eighty n. [1950s+] (US, orig. milit.) a complete reversal of plans, thoughts, action. [a 180-degree turn]

one-ended furrow n. [19C] the vagina (cf. AGREEABLE RUTS OF LIFE).

one-eyed adj.[1] **1** [early–mid-19C] (US) crooked, dishonest. **2** [late 19C+] (orig. US) inferior, inadequate, unimportant (cf. ONE-HORSE).

one-eyed adj.[2] [1960s+] (US) in poker, used of a king or jack, esp. as wild cards. [the design of the face depicted in profile on cards]

one-eyed adj.[3] [1960s+] (orig. US/Aus.) used in a variety of combs. as the penis; other than those listed here, one-eyed bob, one-eyed guardsman, one-eyed pants python, one-eyed rocket, one-eyed trouser worm, one-eyed wonder worm.

one-eyed boy with his shirtsleeves rolled up n. [1960s+] a circumcised penis.

one-eyed brother n. [1990s] (US Black) the penis. [SE one-eyed + BROTHER n.]

one-eyed cyclops n. [1990s] the penis. [since all Cyclops are one-eyed (the word means 'one-eyed' in Greek) this is, of course, tautological]

one-eyed monster n. [1960s] (US) **1** the penis (cf. SLAY THE ONE-EYED MONSTER). **2** a television set.

one-eyed scribe n. **1** [mid–late 19C] (US) a revolver, a pistol (cf. BLACK-EYED SUSAN). **2** [1970s] (US Black) a monumental liar, an insignificant person, poss. because they cannot be trusted to tell the truth.

one-eyed stag n. [late 18C] the penis.

one-eyed trouser-snake n. [1960s+] (orig. Aus.) the penis.

one-eyed yankee n. [1990s] (US Black teen) 1 a fool. 2 a one-eyed person.

one-eye zipper fish n. [1990s] the penis.

one-eye target practice n. [1990s] masturbation. [ONE-EYED adj.[3]]

one fat lady n. [1950s+] (bingo) the number 8. [resemblance to her opulent curves]

one-fifty-one n. [1980s+] (drugs) crack cocaine. [ety. unknown; ? Calif. or NY penal code number]

one-finger exercise n. [1920s+] manual stimulation of the vagina or clitoris. [pun]

one-finger salute n. [1960s+] (US) an obscene gesture of contempt. [ext. of FINGER n.[3]]

one-foot meat n. [1950s] (W.I.) an edible fungus. [the stem of the 'meaty' fungus]

one for n. [late 19C+] a person who is interested in or proficient at a specified thing.

one for his nob n. [20C] a shilling (5p). [rhy. sl., one for his nob = BOB n.[3] (1)]

one for the bitumen n. [1940s+] (Aus.) a last drink, before starting a journey or leaving (cf. ONE FOR THE DITCH; ONE FOR THE ROAD; SAME AGAIN; SWING OF THE DOOR). [the bitumen, a tarred road, esp. the road from Darwin to Alice Springs]

one for the book n. [1910s+] (US) anything noteworthy, remarkable or incredible, something worthy of long-term record. [the record book]

one for the ditch n. [1960s+] (US) a final drink, but, rather than the traditional ONE FOR THE ROAD, this variation acknowledges the perils of drunken driving.

one for the road n. [20C] a final drink before departure (cf. ONE FOR THE BITUMEN; SWING OF THE DOOR). [virtually SE by 1950]

one good woman n. [1970s+] (US Black) the ideal soulmate, considerate, sympathetic and prob. sexy too.

one-gun salute n. [1990s] masturbation. [GUN n.[2] (1)]

one-hand magazine n. [1960s+] a pornographic magazine, used as an aid to masturbation (cf. STROKE BOOK).

one-hitter/one-hit bowl n. [1970s+] (drugs) a marijuana pipe that contains just enough for a single inhalation. [SE one + HIT n.[4] (3) (+ BOWL)]

one-holer n. [20C] an outside lavatory or privy with one seat only.

one-horse adj. [mid-19C+] (US) insignificant, petty, esp. as in one-horse town, a small town of no importance (cf. ONE-EYED adj.[1]). [18C SE one-horse, drawn or worked, by a single horse]

one hundred per cent phr.[1] [20C] talking without artifice, being absolutely honest.

one hundred per cent phr.[2] [20C] feeling very well, cheerful, high-spirited etc.

one in ten n. [late 18C–early 19C] a parson. [the tithes paid over by the parishioners]

one in the bush is better than two in the hand phr. [1920s+] (Aus.) one instance of proper intercourse is always better than any amount of masturbation. [pun on trad. pvb.]

one in the eye phr. [20C] a sharp response, an unpleasant experience, an insult, esp. as that's one in the eye for…. [the one is a blow]

one-legged race n. [1970s] masturbation (cf. MIDDLE LEG; THIRD LEG).

one-leg trouser n. [late 19C] a style of skirt, tight and straight, popular in the 1890s. [resemblance]

one love phr. [1950s+] (W.I. Rasta) a parting phrase, an expression of unity

one-lunger n. (US) **1** [20C] a single-cylinder vehicle, usu. a motorcycle. **2** [1940s+] any small set-up or device.

one-man band n. [1930s+] one who takes all responsibilities on themself, sometimes with slightly pej. undertones, i.e. they are not really capable of being successful.

one-man show n. [1990s] masturbation.

onener n. [mid–late 19C] a heavy blow (cf. ONE OVER THE GASH). [? SE one and a, i.e. ext. of GIVE SOMEONE ONE]

one-nighter n. (US) **1** [1930s+] of a musician, band or show, a single performance in one place only. **2** [1960s+] an affair or sexual relationship of one night's duration (cf. ONE NIGHT STAND).

one night stand n. **1** [late 19C+] (US) a small rural town. **2** [1930s+] an affair that lasts only a single night, thus a person with whom one has such a relationship. [entertainment jargon one night stand, the giving of only one performance in a specific venue before moving on]

one of 'em n. [mid-19C] (US) a remarkable or admirable person.

one off the wrist n. [1970s+] the act of masturbation.

one of King John's men n. [late 18C–early 19C] a small person, often as one of King John's men, eight score to the hundred.

one of livery n. [late 17C] a cuckold. [livery companies, military or city bands distinguished by their uniforms and badges, in the cuckold's case the 'badge' he 'wears' is that of the HORNS]

one of my cousins n. [late 17C–early 19C] a prostitute (cf. ONE OF US). [euph. used presumably when the man accidentally meets a friend and has to make an introduction]

one of Pharaoh's lean kine phr. **1** [late 16C] a very thin person. **2** [late 19C–1920s] looking as if 'he'd run away from the bone-house' or 'as if he were walking about to save funeral expenses' (F&H). [SE *lean kine*, thin cattle]

one of the faithful n. **1** [17C] a drunkard. **2** [late 18C] a tailor who gives long credit. [SE *one of the faithful*, a member of a religious sect]

one of the knights, to be phr. [1970s] (gay) to have syphilis. [the disease attacks one's 'sword']

one of them n.[1] [mid-18C+] a prostitute (cf. ONE OF MY COUSINS; ONE OF US). [euph.]

one of them n.[2] [late 19C] a shilling (5p). [ety. unknown; ? ONE OF THEM n.[1] i.e. the cost of a cheap prostitute]

one of these fine days/mornings you'll wake up and find yourself dead phr. [20C] addressed to a very dozy, dull person.

one of those n. [late 19C] a male homosexual (cf. ONE OF THEM n.[1]). [euph.]

one of/just one of those things phr. [1930s+] (orig. US) something one cannot understand or explain, something over which one has no control and can do nothing about.

one of us n. **1** [late 18C–early 19C] a prostitute (cf. ONE OF THEM n.[1]). **2** [1930s+] a male homosexual (cf. ONE OF THOSE).

one-on-one n. [1980s+] (drugs) **1** cocaine. **2** a dose of one tablet of Talwin (a painkiller) + one tablet of Pyribenzamine (an antihistamine). [(1) refers to one LINE n.[4] (4) of cocaine for one nostril]

one-on-one adj. [1960s+] (orig. US) person-to-person, intimate or confrontational, e.g. a fight (cf. HEAD-TO-HEAD).

one-on-one house n. [1980s+] (drugs) a place where cocaine and heroin can be purchased. [ONE-ON-ONE n. + SE *house*]

one out adj. [1940s+] (Aus.) alone; thus *two-out*, with a single accomplice or helper, *ten out*, in a team or gang of 10 etc (cf. -HANDED).

one-out fight n. [1920s+] (Aus. teen) a fight between the two champions of a pair of rival teen gangs. [one person comes *out* of the group]

one out of the bag n. [1930s+] (Aus.) an unexpected piece of good luck or pleasant event.

one over the eight phr. [1920s+] (orig. milit.) drunk. [the *eight* being pints, a supposed 'safe' amount of beer.

one over the gash n. [mid–late 19C] a heavy blow, esp. to the face (cf. ONENER). [GASH n.[2]]

one percenter n. [1950s+] an outlaw bike rider. [the supposed 1% of motorcycle users who refuse to abide by the rules and the law]

one-piece overcoat n. [1950s+] a condom (cf. CAPE).

one-pot/two-pot/middy/pint/schooner screamer n. [1950s+] (Aus.) one who cannot hold their liquor without becoming obstreperously drunk; *one-* or *two-pot* refer to the need for only one or two drinks before they lose all control; *middy*, *pint* and *schooner* refer to glass sizes and denote the (small) amount of alcohol required for this effect.

oner/one-er n.[1] **1** [mid-19C] a remarkable or outstanding person or event. **2** [mid-19C] a knock-out blow (cf. ONENER). **3** [1950s+] (Aus.) an amusing or eccentric person.

oner/one-er n.[2] **1** [late 19C–1900s] a shilling (5p). **2** [late 19C+] £1. **3** [1950s+] £100 (cf. ONCER n.[3]).

ones and twos n. [1920s+] (Aus./US) shoes [rhy. sl.]

one sandwich short of the picnic phr. [1960s+] a phr. used of someone who is not very intelligent, slightly eccentric, odd (cf. NOT ALL THERE; TWO SANDWICHES SHORT OF A PICNIC).

one's arse/ass, to be phr. [1940s+] (orig. US) to cause one trouble, to lead to inevitable punishment, e.g. *Do that and it's your ass*. [i.e. one's ARSE n.[1] will get 'kicked']

one's arse/ass is grass phr. [1950s+] (orig. US) one is in severe trouble (cf. ONE'S ASS IS MUD). [ARSE n.[1] (1) + onomat. redup.]

one's arse/ass makes buttons phr. [mid-16C–early 19C] one is terrified. [ARSE n.[1] (1) + SE *buttons*, dung (usu. of animals) the image one's involuntarily soiling one's trousers through fear]

one sausage short of a B.B.Q. phr. [1990s] (US teen) a phr. used of someone who is not very intelligent, slightly eccentric, odd (cf. NOT ALL THERE).

one's ass is mud phr. [1930s+] (US) one is in danger, one's reputation has been destroyed (cf. ONE'S ARSE IS GRASS). [ARSE n.[1] (3) + SE *mud*]

one's ass sucks buttermilk/wind phr. [1950s+] (US) **1** one is absolutely terrified. **2** one is talking (hysterical) nonsense, esp. as a threat, *your ass will suck wind when/unless ...* [ARSE n.[1] (3)]

one's bread is not done phr. [20C] (US) used of one who is considered mentally deficient. [play on HALF-BAKED]

one's chalk is up phr. [late 19C] one's credit at a public house is exhausted. [SE *chalk up*, to put on account]

oneself, be/feel v. [mid-19C+] to feel 'right', usu. in the neg. e.g. *I'm not feeling myself today*.

one's head to a turnip phr. [late 17C–late 18C] a fantasy bet (cf. ALL THE WORLD TO A CHINA ORANGE).

one shingle short phr. [20C] of someone who is not very intelligent, slightly eccentric, odd (cf. NOT ALL THERE).

one-shot credit phr. [1960s+] (drugs) for the dealer to allow a client to default on a payment once only, any further defaults will be met with violence. [SE *one-shot*, a single occurrence + SE *credit*]

one's measure phr. [mid–late 19C] the right person for the circumstances.

one's milk boiled over phr. [mid–late 18C] used of a careless, over-enthusiastic person.

one's name is Dennis phr. [mid–late 19C] (US) one has no chance, one is finished, 'done for'.

one's nose is always brown phr. [1930s+] a dedicated sycophant.

one-spot n. [late 19C+] (US) a $1 bill. [SE *spot*, the pip on a playing card]

one's race is run phr. [20C] used of one who is dead.

one's skin is cracking phr. [1950s–60s] (Aus.) desperate for a drink of alcohol. [play on SE *parched*, dried out, thirsty]

one's thing n. [1960s+] one's personal stance, one's lifestyle, philosophy etc, esp. in the phr. *do one's own thing*.

one-stick drum improvisation n. [20C] masturbation. [STICK n.[1]]

one's ticket n. [1920s+] someone or something that is what one wants or appealing. [TICKET n.[1]]

one's tongue is well hung phr. [mid-18C] one is articulate.

one's trumpeter is dead phr. [late 18C–early 19C] said of a braggart, a self-advertiser. ['He is therefore forced to sound his own trumpet' (Grose, 1796)]

one thin dime n. [1920s] (US) the least amount of money (cf. THIN ONE). [the dime (10 cents) is the thinnest coin, as well as the smallest]

one thing, the n. [20C] (Irish) sexual intercourse. [abbr. *the one thing men desire*]

one-time n. [1990s] (US Black) a police officer or the police as an institution. [ety. unknown; ? warning 'I'll tell you just one more time…']

one time! excl. [1990s] (US Black) exactly! you're quite right! indeed!

one to meet n. [1940s+] (orig. Und.) an appointment.

one-two *n.* [1930s+] (US) a speedy exit, a quick departure. [? boxing jargon *one-two*, two quick punches or jabs]

one-two checker *n.* [1990s] (rap music) a cautious person, one who assesses a given situation. [traditional *one-two, one-two* used to check a microphone or PA system]

one-two, one-two! *excl.* [late 19C+] hurry up! get a move on! [orig. milit., the cadence of marching]

one-two-three *adv.* [20C] at once, immediately, speedily. [phr. *one, two, three go!*]

one/marble upon your taw *phr.* [early 19C] a promise of retribution uttered by one who feels wronged. [marble playing, *taw*, the marble with which one shoots, or the line from which one shoots]

one way *n.* [1960s] (drugs) LSD. [play on SE *one way trip*/TRIP n.³ (1)]

one-way *adj.* **1** [1920s–40s] (US) honest, e.g. a *one-way guy*, an honest man; thus a *two-way guy*, a crook. **2** [1940s+] (US) narrow- or close-minded. **3** [1960s] (US gay) heterosexual.

one-way pockets *n.* [1920s–60s] a miser's pockets. [money enters but never leaves]

one-way ride *n.* [1940s–50s] (US Und.) a gangland murder. [the victim is driven away by his killers but only they will return]

one with t'other *n.* [late 18C–late 19C] an act of sexual intercourse.

on fire *adj.¹* [1970s+] (US campus) having just made a glaring social error (cf. FLAMER). [the person 'goes down in flames']

on fire *adj.²* [1980s+] doing very well, typically of a rock band, a sportsperson or some similar achiever (cf. ON A ROLL).

on flake *adj.* [1970s–80s] (US Black) passed out, unconscious. [FLAKE OUT]

on for a tater/tatur *phr.* [late 19C–1900s] obsessed, fascinated, usu. used of a man who is desperate to talk to a woman he is attempting to pick up. [Fr. *tête à tête*, an intimate conversation]

on for one's greens *phr.* [mid-19C+] of women, sexually eager. [GREENS n.²]

on for young and old *phr.* [1940s+] (Aus.) a complete disorder, utter chaos, a free-for-all.

on full *adj.* [1990s] (US Black) well supplied with a given commodity, usu. (but not always) money (cf. ON E). [car fuel gauge imagery]

ongkus *see* ONCUS.

on good pastures *phr.* [1990s] (Aus.) of a baby, well fed, contented.

on heat *phr.* [late 19C+] of a woman, sexually excited. [SE *on heat*, usu. applied to female animals, esp. bitches]

on high ropes *phr.* [late 17C–mid-19C] elated, disdainful or enraged.

on ice *phr.¹* (orig. US) **1** [mid-19C+] in reserve. **2** [late 19C+] out of the way. **3** [1920s+] dead. **4** [1930s+] in prison. **5** [1930s+] in hiding, esp. from the police.

on ice *phr.²* (US) **1** [1910s–40s] certain, definite, a foregone conclusion, esp. of a sporting contest. **2** [1920s+] to the greatest extent, to the limit. [it is 'frozen']

onicker *n.* [late 19C] a prostitute. [her price, one NICKER]

onion *n.¹* **1** [early–mid-19C] (Und.) a watch-seal; thus *bunch of onions*, a number of seals worn on one ring (cf. TURNIP n.¹). **2** [mid-19C+] the head (cf. BEAN n.⁴). **3** [1920s–50s] (US Und.) a watch or clock (cf. TURNIP n.¹). [resemblance]

onion *n.²* **1** [1900s–40s] (US) an idiot. **2** [1930s–40s] (US Und.) of a crime, a failure. [? he/it 'stinks']

onion *n.³* [1930s–50s] (US) $1. [play on CABBAGE n.⁵; KALE; POTATOES, ETC]

onion *n.⁴* [1960s+] (Aus.) a girl who has sex with two or more men in a single session. [pron. 'on-i-on', i.e. 'on and on']

onion *n.⁵* [1980s+] (US drugs) 28g (1oz) of marijuana. [ety. unknown]

onion act *n.* [1960s+] (US Black) an unacceptable, offensive act or situation. [? like an onion, it reduces one to tears + the use of onions to create fake 'tears']

onionhead *n.¹* [1910s–50s] (US) a stupid person. [SE *onion* + sfx. -HEAD (1)]

onionhead *n.²* (US) **1** [1930s–70s] a bald-headed person. **2** [1990s] a close, shaved haircut. [resemblance to a smooth, peeled onion]

onion skin *n.* [1960s+] (US gay) a long foreskin.

onish *adj.* [20C] late, usu. in the phr. *it's getting onish*. [SE *on* + sfx. -*ish*]

on it *adj.¹* **1** [1930s+] (Aus.) indulging (possibly to a noticeable excess) in drugs or drink. **2** [1950s+] (US) addicted, whether to a drug or to a person or experience.

on it *adj.²* [mid-19C+] (US) ready, prepared, capable of, skilled in, in control; thus (US Black) to be *on it like a hornet*.

on jack *adv.* [1950s–60s] having one's penis erect. [JACK n.⁸ (1)]

on jankers *adv.* [1910s+] in prison or undergoing some form of punitive discipline. [orig. milit. *jankers*, punishment for defaulters; ety. unknown]

onka/onkaparinga *n.* [1960s+] (Aus.) a finger. [rhy. sl., ult. *Onkaparinga*, the brandname of a make of woollen blanket]

onkiss *see* ONCUS.

onkus *see* ONCUS.

onky *adj.* [1920s+] (Aus.) stinking, stale. [ONCUS adj.¹ + HONK v.¹]

only, the *adj.* [1990s] (US teen) the best, the ultimate. [abbr. SE phr. *the one and only*]

only 80 pence in the pound *phr.* [20C] of someone who is not very intelligent, slightly eccentric, odd (cf. NOT ALL THERE).

only huckleberry on the bush *phr.* [20C] (US) of something or someone unique or special, esp. of a self-opinionated person, *He thinks he's the ...* .

only one and ninepence in the florin/two shillings/two bob *phr.* [1910–70s] of someone who is not very intelligent, slightly eccentric, odd (cf. NOT ALL THERE).

only think *phr.* [mid–late 19C] a general excl., 'can you imagine ...'.

on my liberty! *excl.* [20C] a general oath, 'on my honour!'

on my life! *excl.* [20C] an affirmation of absolute truth in the face of an audience's scepticism. [esp. as a cliché phrase forced on every stage Jew]

on my sammy say-so *phr.* [18C] on my word of honour. [assonant ext. of SE *say-so*]

on my skin *phr.* [20C] (US Und.) a phr. that implies absolute honesty. [the primary importance of one's skin colour in prison]

on offer *adj.* [1940s] liable to problems.

on old toes *phr.* [mid-15C] in old age.

on one! *excl.* [20C] (Aus.) listen to one!

on one's ace *phr.* [20C] (Aus./N.Z./S.Afr.) on one's own. [SE *ace*, the highest playing card, equivalent to 'one']

on one's ass *phr.* [1910s+] (US) facing serious problems, esp. financial ones, occasionally extended to *on the balls of one's ass*. [fig. use of ARSE n.¹]

on one's back *phr.* [late 19C+] penniless, impoverished.

on one's beam-ends *phr.* [early 19C+] (orig. US) in financial difficulties. [naut. *beam ends*, the ends of a ship's lateral beams, if these touch the water, the ship is on the verge of capsizing]

on one's bones *phr.* [1900s–30s] nearly destitute (cf. ON ONE'S RIBS).

on one's ear *phr.¹* [late 19C] (US) in disgrace. [the image of a mother grabbing her errant child by their ear and hauls them from the room, shop or street]

on one's ear phr.[2] [1930s–50s] (US) easily, with little effort, usu. in phr. (one) could do that on one's ear. [var. on DO IT STANDING ON ONE'S HEAD]

on one's high horse phr. [late 18C+] arrogant, acting in a superior manner.

on one's j phr. [1990s] (US Black) alert. [abbr. ON ONE'S JOB]

on one's Jack phr. [1930s+] by oneself, alone. [abbr. ON ONE'S JACK JONES]

on one's Jack Jones/Malone phr. [20C] on one's own. [rhy. sl.]

on one's job phr. [1950s+] (US Black) alert, in control; successful at a given task.

on one's keeping phr. [late 19C+] (Irish) in hiding, i.e. 'keeping oneself out of sight'.

on one's knees phr. [1920s+] absolutely exhausted.

on one's last legs phr. [late 16C+] in extremis, in great and seemingly irrefutable distress.

on one's lonely phr. [1910s–30s] by oneself.

on one's nickel phr. [1990s] (US) at one's own expense.

on one's own bat phr. [mid-19C] on one's own account. [var. ON OFF ONE'S OWN BAT]

on one's own hook phr. [mid-19C–1950s] looking after oneself, taking responsibility for one's own life.

on one's ownio/owny-o phr. [20C] by oneself. [cod Italian]

on one's ownsome phr. [1920s+] by oneself.

on one's owny-o see ON ONE'S OWNIO.

on one's Pat phr. [20C] (Aus.) by oneself (cf. ON ONE'S JACK; ON ONE'S TOD). [rhy. sl. Pat Malone = alone]

on one's promotion phr. [mid-19C] behaving in way that indicates that not only is marriage on one's mind, but feasible as well.

on one's puff phr. [20C] on one's own. [? PUFF n.[2] (2) or rhy. sl.]

on one's tibby drop phr. [mid-19C] unawares. [TIBBY DROP, i.e. one is caught 'on the hop']

on one's tod phr. [20C] alone. [rhy. sl. Tod Sloan = alone; ult. the US jockey James Forman 'Tod' Sloan (1874–1933)]

on one's uppers phr. [late 19C+] in great poverty, without any money; thus walk on one's uppers, to be very poor. [the uppers of one's shoes, the soles having long since worn away]

on over-ride phr. [1990s] (US Black) acting quietly, keeping a 'low profile'. [computer imagery, by-passing a computing function by over-riding an application's command]

on paper adj. [20C] (US prison) on parole. [one's 'ticket-of-leave']

on plush adv. [1930s–40s] in luxury. [SE plush, a type of cloth, softer than velvet, used for expensive garments]

on point adj. [1990s] alert, sharp, aware. [milit. point, the lead man of a patrol]

on sentry adj. [late 19C–1910s] drunk.

on someone's ass, to be phr. [1940s+] (US) to pester, to harass, to annoy. [fig. use of ARSE n.[1]]

on someone's barrow phr. [1950s] giving trouble.

on someone's case, to be phr. [1950s+] (orig. US) to harass verbally, to persecute, to pursue. [CASE n.[8]]

on someone's dick phr. [1980s+] (US Black) **1** keen on, supporting (cf. WATCH SOMEONE'S BACK). **2** oppressing, nagging, harassing. [fig. uses of DICK n.[5] (1)]

on someone's duster phr. [20C] harassing, persecuting someone.

on someone's ear phr. [mid-19C+] (US) angry, furious, in an uproar. [the sound 'lands' on the victim's ear]

on someone's ginger phr. [1960s+] (Aus.) on someone's tail. [rhy. sl. ginger ale = tail]

on someone's hammer phr. (Aus.) **1** [1920s+] very close behind. **2** [1940s+] hounding, pestering. [rhy. sl. hammer and tack = back]

on someone's jock strap phr. [1980s+] (US) pursuing, esp. of a woman sexually harassing a man. [JOCK n.[2] (1)]

on someone's tail/hot on someone's tail, to be phr. [20C] to be following, pursuing. [HOT adj.[1] + TAIL n.[1] (3)]

on someone's wavelength phr. [1960s+] to understand, to be aware of another's position or ideas.

on someone's wheel phr. [1940s+] (Aus.) close behind, in pursuit; putting pressure on someone to do something. [cycling imagery]

on song adj. [1960s+] working well, in prime condition. [one is 'in tune']

on speakers/speaks adv. [1920s+] (society) on speaking terms.

on spec adv. [early 19C+] at a risk, without making a firm decision. [SE on + speculation]

on swole adj. [1990s] (US Black teen) relaxed and free of stress (cf. IN EFFECT MODE). [ety. unknown]

on T/time phr. [1990s] (US Black) at the emotionally or psychologically apposite moment (rather than the chronologically prompt one).

on tap adj. [20C] available in unlimited quantities. [the flow of a beer or water from a tap]

on the abram/abraham suit phr. [19C] working as a writer of begging letters, the pursuit of many small-time 19C confidence tricksters (cf. ABRAM WORK). [ABRAM adj. + SE suit, a petition]

on the anxious bench phr. [19C] (US) worried, nervous. [ecclesiastical jargon anxious bench/seat, a seat at the front of the church, near the pulpit, where those particularly concerned about their spiritual status – and willing to admit it – would sit at revival meetings]

on the arfy-darfy phr. [1960s] wandering the roads as a hobo. [? a nonce-coinage by Nelson Algren (1909–81). ? SE artful dodger]

on the arm phr. [1920s+] (US) for free, on credit. [? the writing of notes on one's cuff]

on the avenue phr. [1990s] (US Black) **1** lit. in the street. **2** in general use, from a mass point of view.

on the back burner phr. [1960s+] deferred, pending, put off. [a stove's back burners are not as hot and thus cook more slowly than the front ones]

on the back of one's arse phr. [late 19C+] (Aus.) penniless, impoverished (cf. ON ONE'S ASS phr.; ON ONE'S BACK). [ARSE n.[1]]

on the ball phr. [1910s+] (orig. US) aware, alert, capable. [baseball jargon put something on the ball, to pitch with extra speed or with a deceptive motion]

on the bash phr.[1] [1910s+] (Aus./N.Z.) drinking, usu. to excess. [BASH v.[2] (2)]

on the bash phr.[2] [1930s+] working the streets as a prostitute (cf. BATTER v.). [BASH v.[2] (1)]

on the bat phr.[1] [early 19C+] out for a drunken, sexy, brawling time. [BAT n.[2] (2)]; note Carew has on the battu, from battu, wear and tear]

on the bat/batter phr.[2] [late 19C+] working as a prostitute. [BAT n.[1]]

on the batter phr. (US) [1940s] living as a beggar.

on the battle phr. [20C] (Aus.) working as a prostitute (cf. ON THE BAT phr.[2]). [BATTLE v.]

on the beach phr. [late 19C+] (US) out of work, impoverished (cf. BEACHED adj.[1]). [naval jargon on the beach, discharged from the navy, thus unemployed]

on the beam phr. [1940s+] (orig. US) right on course, heading in the right direction; thus on the beam in short-cut plays. [orig. air force, referring to radio beams that guide aircraft]

on the beat phr. [late 19C–1900s] (US) engaged in a swindle. [BEAT n.[2] (3)]

on the beefment *phr.* [late 19C] (Und.) on the look-out (cf. BEEF!).

on the beer *phr.* [late 19C+] drinking.

on the bend *phr.*[1] [19C+] living riotously, out on a spree. [BENDER n.[1]]

on the bend *phr.*[2] [mid-19C–1910s] crooked, criminal, underhand (cf. BENT adj.).

on the billiard slum *phr.* [early 19C–1910s] (Aus.) working as a confidence trickster; thus *give it them on the billiard slum*, *go on the billiard slum*, to hoax, to defraud. [SE *billiards*, with the image of a ball bouncing at various angles + SLUM, orig. Und.]

on the bing *phr.* [20C] (US) energetic, enthusiastic (cf. ON THE BALL). [SE *bing*, echoic of the noise of something hitting a solid surface and rebounding]

on the blanket *phr.* [1970s+] (prison) of prisoners making a protest against conditions by refusing to wear clothes, refusing to slop out and wrapping their naked bodies in blankets. [orig. applied to members of the IRA in the Maze Prison in Belfast who thus signified their protest against being treated as common rather than political prisoners. The term was extended to any prisoner making a similar protest, political or otherwise]

on the blind *phr.* [20C] (Aus.) at risk, on chance, without any prior information.

on the blink *phr.* [late 19C+] (orig. US) malfunctioning, working badly. [the blinking of electric lights that signalled a 'short' or similar malfunction]

on the blob *phr.*[1] [mid-19C] by word of mouth. [BLAB v.]

on the blob *phr.*[2] [1990s] (US) menstruating. [the *blobs* of blood]

on the block *phr.* [1940s+] (US) **1** in business. **2** working as a street prostitute.

on the bones of one's arse *phr.* (N.Z.) very poor, impoverished. [SE *bone* + ARSE n.[1]; i.e. one's thinness]

on the book *phr.* [20C] on credit. [the debt has been written down]

on the books *phr.* [20C] (US) good for credit.

on the booze *phr.* [mid-19C+] drinking heavily. [BOOZE n.]

on the bottle *phr.*[1] [20C] drinking heavily.

on the bottle *phr.*[2] [20C] **1** working as a male prostitute. **2** (US) working in any form of prostitution. [rhy. sl. bottle and glass = ARSE n.[1]]

on the bottle *phr.*[3] [20C] working as a pickpocket. [rhy. sl. BOTTLE AND GLASS, thus the rear or ARSE trouser pocket, which is vulnerable to theft]

on the bounce *phr.* [1910s+] on the spur of the moment, spontaneously. [the idea 'bounces' into one's brain]

on the bow *see* ON THE ELBOW.

on the box *phr.* [20C] (Irish) having sexual intercourse. [BOX n.[6] + ref. to a SE *box* mattress]

on the box-seat, to be *phr.* [1950s+] (N.Z.) to be in an advantageous or dominant position, to be 'sitting pretty'. [coaching imagery]

on/in the breeze *phr.* [late 19C–1970s] of current news or information.

on the bricks *phr.* [1930s+] (US) **1** on the street after being released from prison. **2** (drugs) walking the streets searching for drugs. **3** working as a street prostitute.

on the bugle *phr.* [1940s] (Aus.) smelly, both lit., i.e. no longer edible and fig. i.e. dishonest, dubious. [BUGLE n.[1]]

on the bum *phr.*[1] [US] **1** [late 19C+] travelling as a tramp or beggar. **2** [1900s] penniless. [BUM n.[3] (1)]

on the bum *phr.*[2] **1** [late 19C+] broken, out of order (cf. ON THE FRITZ). **2** [20C] feeling slightly unwell. [BUM adj.]

on the business *see* ON THE GAME.

on/off the bus *phr.* [1960s+] **1** used of one who is or is not part of a group. **2** sharing the joint consciousness; thus *off the bus*, abandoning the group and its beliefs and ethos. [coined c.1965 by novelist and psychedelic guru Ken Kesey (b.1935), whose 'Merry Pranksters', drove across America on a bus, named Furthur (sic), from San Francisco to Millbrook, New York, where Kesey's opposite number, Timothy Leary (1920–96) held court]

on the button *phr.*[1] [20C] right on target, usu. of a blow. [BUTTON n.[3] (3)]

on the button *phr.*[2] [20C] up to the minute, fully aware. [SE *button*, as used to set machinery, weapons etc in motion]

on the C and B *phr.* [mid-19C+] cadging. [rhy. sl. *C and B* = COAT AND BADGE]

on the cannon *phr.* [1910s+] working as a pickpocket. [CANNON n.[2]]

on the cards *phr.* [mid-19C] feasible, highly possible; thus the antithetic [early–mid-19C] *out of the cards*, very unlikely, impossible. [a fortune-teller's 'reading' of the cards, usu. a tarot pack; later use SE]

on the carpet *phr.*[1] [late 19C] (orig. US) facing a reprimand, scolding or punishment; thus *dance on the carpet*, to await and receive such a dressing down, the image is of a fidgety, nervous person. [the carpet that stands before one's superior's desk]

on the carpet *phr.*[2] [late 19C+] (US) of someone who is eager to marry, esp. widow or widower. [? receiving potential husbands/wives in a room – the parlour? – with a carpet]

on the case *phr.* [1950s+] (orig. US) whether in one's personal or professional life, working or acting efficiently, controlling a situation, 'taking care of business'.

on the cat *phr.* [1960s] (US Black) staying out at night. [CAT v.[2]]

on the charlie *phr.* [1910s+] living as a tramp. [army jargon *charlie*, a pack. Despite the stereotypical *Charlie* Chaplin (1889–1977) 'little tramp' figure, this use slightly predates his appearance]

on the cheap *phr.* [mid-19C+] economically.

on the cheese *phr.* [late 19C–1900s] (US) unsatisfactory, in a bad way. [? CHEESE n.[3] (1)]

on the chopping block *phr.* [1920s+] in a very disadvantageous position, facing serious problems.

on the ceiling *phr.* [1960s] (US) very excited (cf. UP IN THE AIR). [one is FLYING]

on the coat *phr.* [1940s] (Aus.) out of favour. [the gesture of fingering someone's lapel in a vaguely minatory manner]

on the con *phr.* [20C] working as a *con*fidence trickster. [abbr.]

on the corn *phr.* (Aus. prison) serving time in prison (cf. PORRIDGE n.[1]). [the hominy diet therein]

on the croak *phr.* [late 19C] (US) on the verge of death, dying. [CROAK v.[1]]

on the crook *phr.* [15C–mid-19C] working as a professional criminal.

on the cross *phr.* [early 19C+] **1** obtained surreptitiously, illegally. **2** working as a professional criminal. [CROSS n.]

on the cross-cut *phr.* [1900s] (N.Z.) angry with, arguing with. [sawmill imagery]

on the cuff *phr.*[1] [1920s+] (orig. US) **1** on account, on credit. **2** for free; thus *to put the cuff*, to give credit, to ask for credit. [the practice of pencilling debts in shops or bars on a celluloid *cuff*]

on the cuff *phr.*[2] [1940s+] (N.Z.) excessive, usu. as *a bit on the cuff*. [? rhy. sl. *on the cuff* = SE *rough*]

on the cull list *phr.* [19C] (US) of a woman, unmarried and worried about it (cf. ON THE SHELF). [SE *cull list*, a list of those animals that are due to be culled]

on the cushions *phr.* [20C] (US Und.) travelling in a passenger coach as opposed to a freight wagon.

on the dead *phr.* [late 19C–1920s] (US) in earnest, sincerely, straightforward, honest. [abbr. ON THE DEAD LEVEL]

on the dead level *phr.* [late 19C+] in earnest, sincerely, straightforward, honest. [ext. of ON THE LEVEL]

on the deck *phr.* [1920s+] bankrupt, without funds [milit. use *on the deck*, at ground level]

on the dink *phr.* [1900s–10s] in trouble, facing problems. [? var. of ON THE BLINK]

on the d.l. *phr.* [1990s] (US Black) depressed, out of sorts. [abbr. *down low*]

on the dodge *phr.* [20C] **1** involved in something illegal or underhand. **2** hiding from or avoiding the authorities. [SE *dodge*, to act in a dubious, untrustworthy manner]

on the dog list *phr.* [1920s+] (Aus.) barred from drinking. [DOG n.[10]]

on the dot *phr.* [20C] with perfect timing. [the *dot* of the letter 'i'. Note 18C SE *to the dot*, exactly, precisely.]

on the double *phr.* [20C] fast. [milit. *double-time*, 150 paces to the minute, double slow time]

on the downbeat *phr.* [1940s] (US Black) depressed, falling on hard times, losing popularity. [jazz imagery]

on the d.q. *phr.* [late 19C] (US) quietly, surreptitiously, privately (cf. ON THE Q.T.). [abbr. *dead* quiet]

on the drink *phr.* [mid–late 19C] drinking excessively, on a drinking spree.

on the drip *phr.* [1950s+] bought on hire purchase (cf. ON THE NEVER-NEVER).

on the earhole *phr.* [1910s+] (Und.) on the scrounge (cf. ON THE EARIE). [one is talking into a victim's *earhole*]

on the earie *phr.* [1910s+] (Und.) on the scrounge. [var. on ON THE EARHOLE]

on the Erie!/Earie! *excl.* [20C] (US prison) be quiet, someone is listening! [SE *ear*]

on the edge *phr.* [1970s+] (US campus) nervous, neurotic.

on the eightball *phr.* [1990s] (US Black) alert, aware. [pool imagery]

on the elbow/bow *phr.* [1970s+] on the scrounge. [the scrounger nudges or tugs one's elbow]

on the fanteague *phr.* [late 19C] out for a spree, 'on the razzle'. [dial. *fanteague*, a fuss, a lark, a state of excitement]

on the fence *phr.* [1960s+] (gay) turning to heterosexuality (cf. LOSE ONE'S GENDER).

on the flip side *phr.* [1960s+] on the other side, on the reverse, 'on the other hand'. [record industry jargon]

on the floor *phr.*[1] [20C] poor. [rhy. sl.]

on the floor *phr.*[2] [20C] drunk. [where one has collapsed]

on the flutter *phr.*[1] [19C] sexually sophisticated. [FLUTTER n.[1]]

on the flutter *phr.*[2] [mid-19C] out on a spree [FLUTTER n.[3] (1)]

on the fly *phr.*[1] **1** [19C] getting one's living by theft or some other form of crime. **2** [mid-19C] begging by following passers-by and asking for cash, rather than standing in one place. [FLY n.[2]]

on the fly *phr.*[2] **1** [19C] out on a spree. **2** [1970s+] (US Black) living in an expensive, fashionable, self-indulgent manner (cf. LIVING LARGE). [FLY adj.]

on the fly *phr.*[3] [1910s–20s] cunningly, clandestinely, cleverly. [FLY n.[2]]

on the fritz *phr.* [20C] **1** drunk. **2** of machinery, broken down, not working (cf. KAPUT) [? German proper name *Fritz* and thus propagandist dislike of all things German, or *fritz* as onomat. for the sparking of a faulty wire or connection]

on the furilla *phr.* [1990s] (US Black) acting honestly, honourably. [ety. unknown; ? Sp.]

on the game/business *phr.* **1** [late 17C+] involved in prostitution. **2** [mid-19C] working as a thief.

on the gate *phr.* [1920s+] on the danger list in a hospital. [the keeping of a list of dangerously ill patients at the hospital gates, their relatives were permitted extra visits]

on the gee *phr.* [1920s] annoyed. [GEE UP v.]

on the gimme *phr.* [1980s+] (US) willing and keen to be bribed. [*gimme*, i.e. give me]

on the go *phr.* **1** [late 17C] on the verge of destruction. **2** [early 18C–mid-19C] in a state of decline. **3** [19C+] active lively. **4** [early 19C] slightly drunk, tipsy.

on the gridiron *phr.* [late 16C+] under pressure.

on the grin *phr.* [late 18C–early 19C] grinning (cf. ON THE HIGH GRIN).

on the grind *phr.*[1] [late 19C+] involved in hard, demanding work. [GRIND n.[2]]

on the grind *phr.*[2] [late 19C+] having sexual intercourse. [GRIND n.[3]]

on the grog/juice *phr.* [1950s+] very drunk. [GROG; JUICE; the phr. can be adapted to any term meaning drunk]

on the ground *phr.* [20C] (US prison) on the streets, free.

on the hank *phr.* [late 19C] looking for booty. [SE *hank*, a coil or loop, usu. of rope or thread; thus something to which it is attached]

on the hawks *phr.* [1960s+] (US) on the look out. [a *hawk* eye]

on the high fly *phr.* [mid-19C] working as a beggar, a cadger or a begging-letter writer. [HIGH FLYER]

on the high grin *phr.* [early 18C] grinning (cf. ON THE GRIN).

on the hill *phr.* [1950s+] (US) pregnant. [the shape of one's stomach]

on the hip *phr.*[1] [16C+] near defeat. [knocked down, one's *hip* rests on the ground]

on the hip *phr.*[2] [16C+] in a position of control. [? lying relaxed on one's *hip*]

on the hip *phr.*[3] [1910s] of alcohol, in one's *hip* flask. [abbr.]

on the hip *phr.*[4] [1920s+] (drugs) using narcotics, whether opium, heroin or, latterly, crack cocaine. [opium smokers rested on one *hip* as they smoked their pipe]

on the hog train *phr.* [late 19C+] (US) **1** living as a tramp. **2** out of order, chaotic. **3** in bad condition. [neg. image of hogs in a sty]

on the hoof *phr.* [1980s+] passing by, casual. [SE *on the hoof*, on the move]

on the hook *phr.*[1] [mid–late 19C] (US) engaging in theft. [HOOKER n.[1]]

on the hook *phr.*[2] [1900s–40s] (US) playing truant. [PLAY HOOKEY]

on the hook *phr.*[3] [1950s–60s] (drugs) addicted to a drug. [HOOKED adj.[2]]

on the hook *phr.*[4] [1950s–70s] (US) in debt. [one is 'hooked' to the creditor]

on the hop *phr.*[1] [mid-19C–1950s] busy, active, enjoying oneself. [HOP n.[1]]

on the hop *phr.*[2] [20C] running away, escaping, on the run. [HOP v. (1)]

on the hops *phr.* [1920s–40s] drinking.

on the hot *phr.* [1930s–40s] (US Und.) on the run. [HOT adj.[2]]

on the house *phr.* [late 19C+] (orig. US) free, a gift of the management, publican etc.

on the hummer *phr.* [20C] (US) **1** of machinery, out of order. **2** of a person, feeling unwell. **3** at a disadvantage. [ety. unknown; ? the sound of malfunctioning machinery, ext. to the human context]

on the hunks *phr.* [late 19C+] (US) taking equal shares. [HUNKS adj.]

on the hurry up *phr.*[1] [late 19C–1940s] (US) **1** making a romantic proposition. **2** begging.

on the hurry up *phr.*[2] [1970s+] at great speed, in a hurry.

on the hush *phr.* [1980s+] quietly, surreptitiously, secretly.

on the hustle *phr.* [1940s+] (US) living as a confidence trickster, a swindler. [HUSTLE n.]

on the improve *phr.* [1920s+] (Aus.) improving.

on the in, to be *v.* [1920s+] (orig. US) to be an insider, to have inside information. [IN n.]

on the Indian list *phr.* [20C] (Can.) being an habitual drunkard. [racist stereotyping]

on the jack, to be *phr.* [19C] to beat or scold severely (cf. LAY ON THE JACK).

on the Jersey side *phr.* [1940s+] on the wrong side. [usu. jazz sl., New York (esp. Manhattan) is the 'right side']

on the jig *phr.* [late 19C] moving in a fidgety manner. [SE *jig*]

on the job *phr.* [19C+] a euph. for engaged in sexual activity. [JOB v.[1] (1)]

on the juice *see* ON THE GROG.

on the jump *phr.* [1900s] restless (cf. KEEP ON THE JUMP).

on the key-vee *phr.* [mid-19C] alert, on one's guard. [SE *on the qui-vive*]

on the knocker/knock *phr.*[1] [1930s+] **1** (Und.) touring houses, ostensibly to buy or sell goods, but specifically to trick or bully people into selling heirlooms, antiques etc for minimal prices. **2** working as a door-to-door salesman. [one *knocks* at the door]

on the knocker *phr.*[2] [1930s+] on credit. [KNOCK v.[1] (7)]

on the knocker *phr.*[3] [1930s+] (Aus.) at once, on demand, esp. of cash payments. [the creditor is knocking at the door]

on the lam *phr.* [1920s+] (US Und.) on the run from prison; thus *take it on the lam*, to escape, to run off. [LAM n.[1]]

on the lang *phr.* [20C] (Irish) playing truant. [? dial. *on the lang*, yearning, wanting]

on the lay *phr.* [18C–1900s] involved in some form of illegal activity. [LAY n.[4] (2)]

on the level *phr.* [late 19C+] (orig. US) honest, straightforward.

on the line *phr.* [20C] at stake. [gambling use]

on the loose *phr.* **1** [mid-19C–1940s] working as a prostitute. **2** [20C] (Aus.) on a drinking spree. [SE euph. *loose woman*]

on the low *phr.* [1950s] (W.I.) on the floor, usu. referring to one's bed.

on the low gag *phr.* [mid-19C] extremely poor, reduced to the lowest level of beggary.

on the lug *phr.* [20C] begging for a loan. [LUG n.[2] (2)]

on the mace *phr.* [late 19C] on credit. [MACE n.]

on the mag *phr.* [late 19C] working as a confidence trickster. [MAG v. (4)]

on the make *phr.*[1] [mid-19C+] charging excessively high prices. [MAKE v.[1]]

on the make *phr.*[2] (orig. US) **1** [mid-19C+] looking to benefit oneself, ambitious, keen to do whatever will be most useful for one's own advancement or profit. **2** [mid-19C+] engaged in theft or swindling. **3** [1920s+] seeking sexual activity. [MAKE v.[3]]

on the mallet *phr.* [mid-19C] of goods taken on trust. [they are *knocked down/out*]

on the market *phr.* [late 19C+] of a girl, available for marriage.

on the marry *phr.* [late 19C] (US) looking for someone to marry.

on the mat *phr.* [late 19C+] **1** on trial. **2** facing a reprimand and/or punishment. [the small *mat* on which an accused soldier stood in the orderly room]

on the money *phr.* [1940s+] (orig. US) excellent, perfect, just right. [betting imagery]

on the mooch *phr.* [mid-19C–1960s] living as a professional beggar. [MOOCH v.[1]]

on the mop *phr.* [19C+] drunk (cf. MOPS AND BROOMS). [MOP n.[2]]

on the muddle *phr.* [1910s–20s] on a spree. [MUDDLE n.]

on the mump *phr.* [early 18C] begging for one's living. [MUMP v. (2)]

on the Murray cod *phr.* [20C] (Aus.) in gambling, betting on credit. [rhy. sl. *on the Murray cod* = ON THE NOD]

on the muscle *phr.*[1] (US) **1** [mid-19C+] quarrelsome, ready or poised to fight. **2** [1940s+] (US) using a threat of violence. **3** [1950s+] working as protection for a top gangster. **4** [1960s+] nervous, edgy. [MUSCLE n.[1] (1)]

on the muscle *phr.*[2] [1900s–10s] (Can.) behaving honestly. [MUSCLE n.[1] (2)]

on the muss *phr.* [mid-19C–1920s] (US) looking for a fight, acting provocatively. [MUSS n.]

on the nail *phr.* **1** [late 16C+] exactly, immediately, as required (usu. as regards payments). **2** [late 19C+] under discussion. **3** [late 19C+] pertinent, relevant. [? Fr. *sur l'ongle*, precisely, exactly (Du. *op den nagel* and Ger. *auf den nagel* have the same sense). Links to various pillars, such as in Bristol (*see EDD* IV 221 ii) or Limerick, on which sea captains paid their wages, or to shopkeepers 'having a square-headed large nail driven through the counter' (on which payment was placed, according to Ware) must be discounted]

on the natch *phr.* [1950s+] (drugs) not using any drugs or other stimulants. [SE *natural*]

on the needle *phr.* [1940s+] (drugs) using narcotic drugs. [NEEDLE n.[5] (1)]

on the nest *phr.* [20C] (US) pregnant.

on the never-never *phr.* [late 19C+] bought on hire purchase (cf. ON THE DRIP). [NEVER-NEVER]

on the nod *phr.*[1] **1** [late 19C+] on credit. **2** [20C] without argument, typically of Parliamentary or local government business which 'goes through' or 'passes on the nod'. [the shop-owner *nods* their assent to one's request]

on the nod *phr.*[2] [1930s+] (drugs) succumbing to a sleepy stupor after taking an injection of heroin. [NOD n. (2)]

on the nose *phr.*[1] [19C] (betting) a wager on the winning horse, e.g. £5 *on the nose*.

on the nose *phr.*[2] [mid-19C] (Und.) on the watch, on the look out. [NOSE n.[1]]

on the nose *phr.*[3] [late 19C] (US) exactly.

on the nose *phr.*[4] [1940s+] (Aus./N.Z.) unpleasant, lit. smelly, and thus offensive morally or aesthetically as well to the nostrils.

on the nut *phr.* [20C] (US) in debt (cf. IN THE HOLE; OUT IN THE WATER). [NUT n.[7] (2)]

on the ooze *phr.* [1920s+] drunk. [rhy. sl. *ooze* = BOOZE n.]

on the other bus *phr.* [1990s] a phr. used of someone who is a homosexual.

on the outer *phr.* [1920s+] (Aus.) unpopular, out of favour, penniless or destitute (cf. OUTERS adj.). [SE *outer*, the part of a racecourse outside the enclosure]

on the outs *phr.* **1** [early 19C+] out of luck, money, favour, popularity etc. **2** [early 19C+] (US) arguing or angry with someone. **3** [1950s+] (US prison) out of prison.

on the pad *phr.* [19C+] living as a tramp. [PAD n.[1] (1)]

on the picaro/picaroon *phr.* [mid-19C] looking for fun, for adventure, for a means of obtaining easy money. [Sp. *picaro*, a rogue, a cheat, a vagabond]

on the pig's back *phr.* [late 19C] (Irish) in luck. [trans. of Erse *ar mhuin na muice*, referring to an amulet shaped like a pig, supposedly a source of good luck]

on the pineapple *phr.* [20C] on parish relief, on national assistance. [punning on the Dole *Pineapple* Company of Hawaii]

on the pipe *phr.* (drugs) **1** [1920s–30s] using opium on a regular basis. **2** [1980s+] using crack cocaine on a regular basis.

on the piss *phr.* [20C] out drinking, usu. with friends (cf. GO ON THE PISS). [PISS n. (3)]

on the plastic *phr.* [1970s+] (Und.) using stolen credit cards for a variety of frauds and swindles.

on the plate *phr.* [20C] used of one who is seen as stuck-up and 'hoity-toity'. [those who request for their fish and chips to be placed on a plate, rather than in the usual paper wrapping]

on the pop of *phr.* [late 19C+] (Anglo-Irish.) on the verge of. [? POP n.³]

on the pot *phr.* **1** [early 19C+] in the lavatory. **2** [mid-19C] in trouble, annoyed.

on the pounce *phr.* [late 19C] (orig. Irish) preparing to spring, ready to attack. [coined by E. Harrington MP, who was suspended from the House of Commons on 13 September 1887, and told the Speaker: 'You, Mr Speaker, have been on the pounce for me since I rose']

on the prod *phr.* [20C] (US) on the attack, on the offensive. [SE *prod*, to poke at]

on the Q.T. *phr.* [late 19C+] surreptitiously, on the quiet, also ext. as *on the strict Q.T.* [Q.T.]

on the queer *phr.* [20C] acting dishonestly. [QUEER adj.¹ (1)]

on the quiet *phr.* [mid-19C+] surreptitiously, clandestinely.

on the rag *phr.* [1930s+] **1** menstruating. **2** irritated, testy, bad-tempered. [RAG n.⁹; (2) is from (1)]

on the ragged edge *phr.* [late 19C] (orig. US) deserted, abandoned.

on the ramp *phr.* **1** [early 19C] working as a swindler. **2** [1910s–20s] out on a spree. [RAMP n.²]

on the ran-dan *phr.* [mid-18C+] on a spree (cf. ON THE RAN-TAN). [SE *ran-dan*, a spree, lit. 'random (behaviour)']

on the randy *phr.* [mid–late 19C] on a spree. [RANTAN]

on the ran-tan *phr.* [early 18C–mid-19C] out on a spree, drunk (cf. ON THE RAN-DAN). [RAN-TAN]

on the rap *phr.* [late 19C] out on a spree, slightly drunk. [? SE *rap*, to hit, to knock]

on the raw *phr.* [1920s+] (Aus.) living rough.

on the razzle *phr.* [20C] indulging in a series of parties, binges and general self-indulgent excesses. [RAZZLE-DAZZLE]

on the real *phr.* [1990s] (US Black teen) honestly, sincerely, truthfully.

on the rebound *phr.* [20C] a ref. to a relationship that is initiated less through attraction than to exorcise one that has recently collapsed; thus *catch on the rebound*, for a third party to start such a relationship with the recently jilted person.

on the receiving end *phr.* [1930s+] bearing the brunt, suffering (often unfairly).

on the reraw/ree-raw *phr.* [mid-19C] tipsy, drunk (cf. RAN-TAN).

on the ribs *phr.* [1930s+] short of money. [poverty has emptied one's stomach + one's skin thus rests *on the ribs*]

on the right/wrong side of *phr.* [mid-17C+] of age, younger than/older than a specified age, e.g. *the wrong side of fifty*.

on the rocks *phr.* [1940s+] with ice-cubes or cracked ice. [ROCKS n.¹ (3)]

on the rory *phr.* [1970s+] penniless. [fig. use of RORY O'MORE]

on the run *phr.* [early 19C+] in the process of escaping from justice or the authorities. [a development of the earlier 17C *to the run*]

on the sauce *phr.* [1940s+] (orig. US) drinking heavily and consistently. [SAUCE n.¹ (3)]

on the scoop *phr.* **1** [mid–late 19C] on a spree, on a round of dissipation. **2** [1900s–10s] (Aus.) drunk. [SCOOPED adj.²]

on/up on the scoot *phr.* [1910s+] (Aus./N.Z.) on a drunken spree. [SCOOT v.]

on the scuttle *phr.* [late 18C–1920s] out drinking and/or whoring. [SCUTTLE v. (1)]

on the shady side *phr.* [19C] older than (cf. WRONG SIDE).

on the shelf *phr.* **1** [19C] transported. **2** [mid-19C] in pawn (cf. LAID UP IN LAVENDER). **3** [mid-19C+] put on one side for unspecified future use. **4** [mid-19C+] of a woman, unmarried and worried about it, feeling that she has been 'put to one side'. **5** [late 19C] dead. **6** [20C] (US Und.) in solitary confinement.

on the short end *phr.* [20C] lit. or fig. at the unfavourable end of the odds; thus in a 20–1 bet the 1 is the short end.

on the shove *phr.* [late 19C–1930s] on the move.

on the sick *phr.* [1970s+] receiving sickness benefit.

on the side *phr.* [20C] in secret, esp. in the phr. *a bit on the side*, a clandestine lover.

on the skids *phr.* [1920s+] on a social and economic decline. [SE *skid* + SKID ROW]

on the skite *phr.* [20C] (Irish) engaged in serious drinking. [Scot. *scit*, a slight shower]

on the slate *phr.* [late 19C+] on credit. [the practice of writing public house debts on a slate]

on the sleeve *phr.* [1950s+] using narcotics. [the rolling up of a sleeve before the injection]

on the sneak *phr.* [1970s+] surreptitiously, on the sly.

on the sneak tip *see* ON A SNEAK TIP.

on the spend *phr.* [late 19C+] spending money. [earlier use is SE]

on the spot *phr.* **1** [late 19C] alert, aware. **2** [1950s+] (US Und.) marked for death, facing assassination.

on the square *phr.* **1** [mid-19C+] living an honest, law-abiding and tedious life. **2** [1940s+] (Aus.) conducting a regular monogamous relationship. [SQUARE adj. ? + Masonic jargon]

on the squeeze *phr.* [1990s] (Aus.) of a policeman or other official, taking bribes. [SQUEEZE v.¹ (2)]

on the stem *phr.* [20C] (US tramp) walking the main street of a town, begging for subsistence. [MAIN STEM]

on the stick *phr.*¹ [20C] efficient, aware, in control; thus *get on the stick*, to get down to work (cf. ON THE BALL). [the gear-stick of a car or joystick of an aircraft, both of which exert control]

on the stick *phr.*² [1940s+] (orig. Aus.) pregnant (cf. UP THE POLE phr.²; UP THE STICK phr.²).

on the stones *phr.* **1** [mid-19C+] in London (cf. OFF THE STONES). **2** [20C] homeless. **3** [20C] in the open air, usu. referring to a fight, often with sidebets and between local champions, arranged outside the normal boxing world. **4** [20C] selling goods laid out on the pavement rather than on a stall.

on the straight *phr.* [late 19C–1900s] behaving respectably and honestly. [abbr. SE *on the straight and narrow*]

on the straight ticket *phr.* [1920s] in a respectable manner. [fig. use of STRAIGHT ticket + SE *ticket*, a political platform]

on the strap *phr.* [1910s+] (Aus.) impoverished. [STRAPPED adj.¹]

on the street/streets *phr.*¹ **1** [mid-19C+] homeless. **2** [1930s+] (orig. US) out of prison, in public life, the opposite of BEHIND THE WALLS (cf. STREET n.²). **3** [1980s+] unemployed.

on the street *phr.*² [1940s+] (drugs) existing as a regular drug user, buying and consuming drugs on a daily basis and thus living the majority of one's life in the streets.

on the streets *see* ON THE STREET phr.¹.

on the strength *phr.* [1990s] (US Black) used to underline the importance and seriousness of the subject under discussion. [SE *strong*, important, vital]

on the stuff *phr.* [1920s+] (drugs) using a narcotic drug, esp. heroin. [STUFF n.⁵]

on the stun *phr.* [1920s+] (Aus.) drinking heavily. [SE *stun*, to knock out]

on the take *phr.* [20C] of an official, typically a politician or policeman, who accepts bribes. [TAKE n.¹ (1)]

on the tap *phr.* [20C] attempting to beg money. [TAP SOMEONE FOR]

on the tapis *phr.* [late 19C] rumoured. [Fr. *sur le tapis*, lit. 'on the table cloth'; thus fig. under discussion or consideration]

on the tiddley *phr.* [mid-19C+] drunk, or nearly so. [TIDDLEY n.]

on the tiger *phr.* [1910s+] (Aus.) out on a serious drinking-bout. [TIGER n.[8]]

on the tiles *phr.* [mid-19C+] out all night having a riotous good time, usu. in *a night on the tiles*. [the nocturnal exploits of cats]

on the tin/wrist *phr.* [20C] (US police) free, gratis [those gifts and favours – free meals, drinks – obtained by showing one's official badge]

on the top line *phr.* [1950s+] (orig. naut.) in the highest state of perfection or readiness.

on the town *phr.* **1** [late 18C–early 19C] working as a prostitute (cf. GO ON THE TOWN). **2** [early 19C] living as a professional criminal. **3** [early 19C] living as a sophisticate, a man of the world.

on the trot *phr.* [late 19C+] hiding away from the police to avoid an arrest, usu. by leaving one's home, town etc. [TROT v. (1)]

on the turf *phr.* [late 19C] working as a prostitute. [TURF n.[2]]

on the twirl *phr.* [1930s] working as a professional thief. [TWIRL n.[1]]

on the under *phr.* [1990s] (US Black) secretly, surreptitiously.

on the up and up *phr.* [1940s+] (orig. US) in an increasingly favourable, lucky, pleasant situation (cf. UPPISH).

on the verandah *phr.* [1980s+] (N.Z.) marginal, peripheral. [i.e. not in the house proper]

on the wagon/water-wagon *phr.* [20C] voluntarily stopping drinking alcohol. [WATER-WAGON]

on the wallaby *phr.* [mid-19C+] (Aus.) **1** on the move. **2** impoverished. [WALLABY n.]

on the water-wagon *see* ON THE WAGON.

on the way *phr.* **1** [late 16C+] pregnant. **2** [late 19C+] of a child, conceived but not yet born.

on the way out *phr.* [1930s+] due for retirement.

on the whine *phr.* [20C] whinging, whining.

on the whiz *phr.* [1920s+] working as a pickpocket. [WHIZ n.[4]]

on the wire *phr.* [20C] generally known, going the rounds of gossip and rumour (cf. BUSH TELEGRAPH). [SE *wire*, a telegraph/telephone system. Note Papua New Guinea Tok Pisin *wialis*, a gossip, a matchmaker a psychic, f. wireless]

on the wrist *see* ON THE TIN.

on the wrong side of *see* ON THE RIGHT SIDE OF.

on the wrong side of the blanket *phr.* [18C] illegitimate. [the implication being that the conception of such a child does not take place beneath the marital bedclothes]

on the wrong side of the hedge/door when brains were given out *phr.* [19C; 20C] a phr. used of a notably stupid person.

on the wrong tram *phr.* [1950s+] (Aus.) pursuing a futile, unproductive course of action.

on tick *phr.* [mid-17C+] on credit. [the tick against one's name made on a slate or list]

on time! *excl.* [20C] a general expression of approval.

on time *see* ON T.

onto *adj.* [mid-19C+] aware of, esp. of someone's supposedly secret or underhand plans.

on top of, to be *phr.* [1980s+] to have sexual intercourse.

on top of one's game *phr.* [1970s+] (orig. US Black) in control of the situation, succeeding, surviving (cf. AHEAD OF THE GAME). [GAME n.[4] (5) + sporting imagery]

on top of one's head *phr.* [20C] (US) anxious, worried.

on velvet *adj.* [late 18C+] secure, cheerful, enjoying a life without problems.

on wires *adj.* [late 19C+] nervous (cf. WIRED adj.[1]).

on with *adj.* (Aus.) having a relationship with (cf. FULL ON adj.[2]).

on you! *excl.* [1920s+] (Aus.) hello!

on your bike! *excl.* [1960s+] go away, be off with you.

on your granny! *see* MY GRANNY!

onyx *n.* [1990s] (US Black teen) an Afro-American. [SE *onyx*, a black, hard stone]

o.o. *n.* [1910s–40s] (US) a brief glance, a visual assessment (cf. DOUBLE-O n.[2]). [ONCE-OVER]

o.o.c. *adj.* [1980s+] (US campus) drunk, high on drugs, acting crazy. [abbr. *out of control*]

ooch/ootch *v.* [1930s+] (US) usu. constructed with *over*, to slide or scoot along, to move up on a seat or bench (cf. HUTCH UP). [Yorks. dial. *hutch*, to huddle together, to move closer]

oochie *n.* [1980s+] (US campus) a charming, adorable person. [? baby-talk *coochie-coo*]

oodle *n.* [1940s] (Aus./N.Z.) money. [OODLES]

oodles/oodlins *n.* [mid-19C+] (orig. US) a large amount, a great quantity (cf. DEAD OODLES; SCADOODLES). [ety. unknown, though suggestions include a shortening of *the whole boodle* (E.P.), a *huddle* or close-packed group (Webster), which presumes that the var. *oodlins* comes from *huddling*, pressing together in a group. Cohen (1985) rejects these: such *huddle/huddling* refer mainly to animals, *oodles/oddlins* to people, and suggests a simple abbr. of *scadoodles/scadoodlin*']

oodnagalahbi *n.* [1960s+] (Aus.) an imaginary, out-of-the-way, 'uncivilized' place (cf. BULLAMAKANKA). [*Ooodna(datta)*, a small town in Western Australia + GALAH]

oo-er! *excl.* [20C] (mainly juv.) an excl. of surprise, amazement, distaste etc.

oof/ooftish/uff *n.* [late 19C] money; thus *oofy*, wealthy, *oofless*, poor. [Ger. *auf tische*, on the table. The term originated *c*.1850 and, according to the *Sporting Times* 'the aristocracy of Houndsditch, being in the habit of refusing to play cards, unless the money were "on the table"']

oofay *see* OFAY.

oof-bird *n.* [late 19C] a source of money, one who can supply money. [OOF + SE *bird*/BIRD n.[3]]

oofterpa *n.* [1940s] a male homosexual. [pig Latin form of POOFTER]

ooftish *see* OOF.

oofus *n.* [1930s–60s] (US Black) a fool, a simpleton. [? DOOFUS + SE *oaf*]

ooga-booga land *n.* [1980s+] all-purpose term for any unspecified African state. [the racist imagery of chanting Africans]

oogie *n.* [1970s+] (southern US campus) a derog. ref. to Black students. [abbr. BOOGIE n.[2]]

oogle *v.* [1940s+] (US) to stare at, to ogle; thus *oogley*, worth staring at. [OGLE v.]

ooh, gravity! *excl.* [1990s] (US teen) what you say when someone falls down.

ooh-la-la *n.* [1920s+] **1** French sexuality, which, in Anglo-Saxon eyes, is 'spicy' and 'naughty'. **2** a girl, usu. French, who possesses those qualities. [Fr. excl. *ooh-la-la!*]

oojah / ooja-ka-piv / oojah-capiff / ooja-ka-pivi / ooja-ka-pivvy / oojah capivvy / oojiboo *n.* [1910s+] a term used when one cannot find the correct description for an object (cf. THINGUMIBOB; WHATCHMACALLIT). [note [1940s] milit. use *oojah, sauce, custard*]

oojah-cum-spiff *n.* [1920s–30s] all right, as required, in order. [OOJAH + SPIFF adj.]

oojiboo *see* OOJAH.

ook *n.* [1960s+] anything unpleasant, esp. something slimy and/or viscous (cf. YUK). [the sound of disgust that indicates the discovery of such a thing]

ook *v.* [1990s] (US campus) to vomit. [onomat.]

ookey *adj.* [1950s] (US) dangerous, difficult. [ety. unknown]

ooky *adj.* [1960s+] (US) disgusting, esp. sticky, slimy (cf. ICKY; YUKKY). [OOK n.]

oolfoo *n.* [late 19C] a fool. [backsl.]

oomph *n.* [1930s+] (orig. US) enthusiasm, vitality, energy, esp. as sex appeal. [imitative]

oomphy *adj.* [1950s+] (US) lively, energetic or sexy. [OOMPH]

oonchook *n.* [1930s+] (Irish/Newfoundland) one who acts stupidly, a simpleton. [Gael. *òinnseach*, a foolish woman, a clown. The orig. Newf. use refers to a man who dresses as a woman in a mummer's parade]

oons! *excl.* [late 16C–late 19C] euph. oath, *God's wounds* (cf. ZOUNDS).

oont *n.* **1** [mid-19C+] (Aus./Ind.) a camel. **2** [1920s+] a person, a fellow. [Hind. and Urdu *unt*, a camel]

oontz out *v.* [1940s] (US) to crowd out. [dial. *hootch/hutch*, to crowd, sit huddled together]

oonu *prn.* [1980s+] (W.I./UK Black teen) you, you all, y'all. [abbr. SE *you now*]

oony *n.* [20C] (Aus.) sea-sickness. [? cries of 'oh my stomach!']

oopizootics/ooperzootics *n.* [late 19C+] a fit of eccentricity, craziness. [? SE the disease *epizootic*, a plague among cattle]

oops! *excl.* [1930s+] an excl. used on dropping something, tripping over, bumping into someone or something, making a mistake etc.

oops-a-daisy! *see* UPSADAISY!

oopsie doodles! *excl.* [1990s] (US teen) a general excl., usu. on making a mistake, tripping up etc.

oorie/oorey/oory *adj.* [20C] (Ulster) hungover. [Scot. *oorie*, sickly-looking, weakly]

ooroo *see* HOOROO.

oory *see* OORIE.

007 *n.* [1980s+] (US) a large folding knife with a wooden handle. [the brandname; presumably a ref. to 'James Bond *007*']

oosh *v.* [1960s+] to remove, to send away, to eject. [? SE *usher* or HOOSH v.]

oot *n.* [1920s+] (Aus.) money. [? LOOT]

ootch *see* OOCH.

ootchimagootchi/ouchimagooga *n.* [1940s–70s] (US) love-making. [var. on HOOTCHY-KOOTCHY]

ootz *v.* [1940s+] (US) to cheat or trick. [? link to CHUTZPAH]

oo-wop *n.* [1990s] (US) a gun. [? echoic of noise of firing]

ooze *v.* **1** [1920s+] to leave. **2** [1920s–50s] (US) to walk, either casually or furtively. **3** [1930s–40s] (US Black) to walk the streets in search of sexual conquest. [SE *ooze*, to slide and slither around + in (3) CRUISE v.]

oozing scabs *n.* [1980s+] (US campus) any form of venereal disease.

oozlum-bird *n.* [late 19C+] a fantastic bird, absolutely unknown to nature. ['(It) flies round in ever-decreasing circles until it disappears up its own arsehole in a puff of blue smoke' P. Cave, *Dirtiest Picture Postcard* (1974)]

o.p. *n.* [20C] (drugs) opium. [abbr.]

o.p. *phr.*[1] [late 19C+] (US) other people's things, usu. money or alcohol (cf. O.P.M., O.P.P., O.P.S.). [abbr.]

o.p. *phr.*[2] [1960s+] (Can. prison) restricted, off privilege. [abbr.]

op *n.*[1] [late 19C] (society) the *opera*. [abbr.]

op *n.*[2] [1920s+] a surgical *operation*. [abbr.]

op *n.*[3] (US) **1** [1920s+] a private investigator. **2** [1930s+] an operator of any kind, e.g. a telephone operator. [abbr. SE *operative*; thus Dashiell Hammett's (1894–1961) fictional detective the 'Continental Op']

op *v.* [1950s] (US) to manage oneself, to function or to accomplish something. [abbr. SE *operate*]

o.p.'s *n.* [1930s–60s] (US Black) other people's, usu. in ref. to an unspoken commodity, e.g. cigarettes, alcohol or clothes.

o.p.b. *n.*[1] [late 19C] (Aus.) a cheap cigar (cf. BUMPER n.[3]). [abbr. old picked bumpers]

o.p.b. *n.*[2] [1930s–50s] (US Black) a hypothetical brand of cigarette; used by one who rarely purchases their own. [abbr. other people's brand]

op die kop *phr.* [1960s+] (S.Afr.) precisely, on time, 'on the dot'. [Afk. *op die kop*, on the head]

ope *n.* [1920s+] (drugs) *opium*. [abbr.]

open *adj.*[1] [1950s+] (US Black) sexually excited, obsessed. [abbr. HAVE ONE'S NOSE OPEN]

open *adj.*[2] [1970s] (US) *open*-minded. [abbr.]

open a can of worms, to *phr.* [1950s+] (orig. US) to unearth and display a situation that is bound to lead to trouble or to added and unwanted complexity (cf. CAN OF WORMS).

open a keg of nails, to *phr.* [1930s] (US) to get drunk on corn whisky.

open an/one's eye, to *phr.* [mid-19C] to have a drink (? the first of the day). [EYE OPENER n.[2] (1)]

open-arse *n.*[1] [11C–late 19C] a medlar. [the fruit's large open disk between the persistent calyx-lobes. 'A fruit ... of which it is more truly than delicately said, that it is never ripe til it is as rotten as a t—d, and then it is not worth a f—t-t' (Grose 1785)]

open-arse *n.*[2] [late 17C–19C] a prostitute (cf. SPLIT-ARSE MECH-ANIC). [a coarse ref. to her stock-in-trade]

open charms/C *n.* [19C] the vagina.

opener *n.* [1930s–40s] (US) a jemmy (cf. CAN OPENER).

openers *n.* (US) [20C] aperient pills or medicines, used to cure constipation. [17–18C SE]

open game *n.* [1960s+] (US) a prostitute with no specific affiliation to one pimp.

open go *see* FAIR GO.

open one's budget, to *phr.* [mid-16C–mid-19C] to speak freely, to speak one's mind. [SE *budget*, a wallet, a bag]

open one's business, to *phr.* [early 18C] of a woman, to make oneself available for sexual intercourse.

open one's eye *see* OPEN AN EYE.

open one's face, to *phr.* [19C+] (US) to speak, esp. to speak rudely (cf. SHUT ONE'S FACE).

open one's head, to *phr.* [mid-late 19C] (US) to open one's mouth, to speak (cf. SHUT ONE'S HEAD).

open one's mouth wide, to *phr.* [late 19C+] to drive a hard bargain, to ask for an excessive price; thus to *open one's mouth too wide*, to ask for more than one can afford.

open one's pipes, to *phr.* [17C+] to sing.

open one's purse, to *phr.* [1990s] (gay) to break wind.

open out *v.* [1900s–20s] to accelerate. [i.e. to open out the throttle of an engine]

open packy *v.* [1940s] (W.I.) to reveal one's innermost thoughts. [SE *open* + PACKY]

open slather *n.* [1910s+] (Aus.) a situation with no restrictions or limits to one's wishes. [SE *open* + UK dial./SAmE *slather*, to squander, to use in large quantities]

open swinging *n.* [1970s+] a partner-swapping party in which all-comers – married or single – are welcome and all end up in the same bed. [SE *open* + SWINGING n.[2]]

open the ball, to *phr.* [mid-late 19C] to start things off, esp. to start a fight.

open the bomb-bay doors, to *phr.* [1990s] to defecate in an urgent manner.

open the door *n.* [1940s+] (bingo) the number 44. [rhy. sl.]

open to *v.* [late 19C–1900s] to confess, to admit.

open up v. [mid-19C+] of a woman, to have sexual intercourse (cf. DO A SPREAD).

opera cape n. [1960s+] (US gay) a long foreskin.

operator n. **1** [early 19C+] a thief or swindler. **2** [late 19C+] (orig. US) a person who pursues success, often ruthlessly or manipulatively (cf. SMOOTH ARTICLE). **3** [1940s+] a successful seducer of women. **4** [1960s+] a major criminal. **5** [1960s+] the controller of a gambling game.

o per se o n. [early 17C] (Und.) a crier. [Lat.]

o.p.h. adv. [late 19C] off, on one's way. [joc. mis-sp. of SE off]

o.p.m. phr. [20C] other people's money, the ideal commodity for a risky investment (cf. O.P. phr.²). [orig. US Und. and used by confidence tricksters of various types, it was a staple of City or Wall Street jargon by the 1980s]

O Pollaky! excl. [late 19C] nonsense! rubbish! don't make such a fuss! [proper name of Ignatius 'Paddington' Pollaky, a celebrated contemporary private detective, with an office on Paddington Green, whose exploits, and surname, entered the common language; W.S. Gilbert also found room for him in a lyric, 'the keen penetration of Paddington Pollaky' (Patience, 1881). That said, note the euph. for coarser excl. oh bollocks!]

o.p.p. n. [1970s+] (drugs) phencyclidine (cf. ACE n.³). [ety. unknown]

o.p.p. phr. [1990s] (US Black/campus) **1** other people's property, usu. their wife, husband or partner, esp. in the context of their being 'off limits' to new sexual approaches. **2** other people's pussy, the wives and girlfriends of other men (cf. O.P.M.). [abbr.]

oppo n. [1930s+] one's opposite number, best friend. [abbr.]

opposite n. [late 19C–1930s] a public house saloon bar, which is opposite, whether actually or fig., the public bar.

Oprah v. [1990s] (US Black) to question aggressively and persistently. [entertainer Oprah Winfrey whose TV show Oprah features a range of outrageously intimate human interest stories, usu. dependent on her eliciting otherwise intimate confessions from her guests]

ops v. [20C] (S.Afr., usu. juv.) to swap. [? SE opposed/opposite; i.e. one gives the item to one's opposite number]

opsh n. [late 19C–1910s] something that is optional. [abbr./pron.]

o.p.t. n. [20C] other people's tobacco, always popular among poverty-stricken smokers. [abbr.]

optical illusions n. [1960s+] (drugs) LSD. [one of its effects]

optics n. [17C+] the eyes. [SE until late 19C]

or conj. [1930s+] 'an emphatic repetition of a rhetorical question' (OED), e.g. Has that dame got a swell voice or has she?

oracle n.¹ [18C] a watch. [it 'tells', i.e. predicts, the time]

oracle n.² [late 18C–late 19C] the vagina (cf. DUMB ORACLE; HAIRY ORACLE). [the initial 'O' + the 'o' shape; the 'mouth piece of the deity']

-orama/-rama sfx. [1960s+] (orig. US teen) used to indicate a considerable size, quality or expanse, e.g. babe-orama, a very attractive woman (or man) or a large number of attractive women (or men), fun-orama, a great deal of enjoyment. [Gk. orama, a view and orig. used as the second syllable of panorama, diorama, cosmorama, and other London shows created for mass entertainment during the early 19C. This association with large-scale entertainment has persisted in its modern, sl. use]

orange n.¹ [late 17C] the vagina (cf. APPLE n.¹⁰). [? its suckability + ref. to Charles II's mistress the former orange-girl Nell Gwyn (c.1650–87)]

orange n.² [1960s+] (drugs) a variety of LSD, in orange-coloured capsules, usu. in combs., e.g. orange barrels, orange cubes, orange haze, orange micro, orange Owsley, orange sunshine, orange wedges.

orange banana n. [1980s+] (US campus) a flaring effect produced by breaking wind next to a lit match.

orange crystal n. [1970s+] (drugs) phencyclidine (cf. ACE n.³). [the colour of the drug]

orange pip n. [20C] a Japanese person. [rhy. sl. orange pip = NIP]

oranges n. [1960s+] (drugs) amphetamine (cf. A n.²). [the colour of the pills]

orange sunshine n. [1960s+] (drugs) a variety of LSD that was packaged in bright orange pills (cf. A n.³).

orangutan n. [20C] (US) a derog. term for a Black person (cf. APE n. (1); BLACK APE).

oration n. [mid-19C] a disturbance, a commotion, a noise.

orb v. [1970s+] (US teen) to stare at, to look over (cf. EYEBALL).

orbit n. [1980s+] (drugs) MDMA (cf. ECSTASY). [ORBITAL + play on the drug's sending one into orbit]

orbit v. [1980s+] to engage in oral sex; thus orbiter, one who does this (cf. AROUND THE WORLD).

orbital/orbital rave n. [1980s+] a large party often held quasi-illegally, fuelled by MDMA and featuring house music. [a ref. to the holding of many such parties near the M25 motorway that encircles London]

orbs/velvet orbs n. [1960s] (US gay) the testicles (cf. BALLS n.¹). [the shape; and the 'feel']

orchard n. [19C] the vagina (cf. GET JACK IN THE ORCHARD).

orchestra n. [20C] **1** the male genitals. **2** the testicles (cf. ORCHESTRA STALLS).

orchestra stalls n. [20C] the testicles. [rhy. sl. orchestra stalls = BALLS n.¹ (1) + link between Gk. orchis, the testicles and orchestra, although SE orchestra is f. Gk. orchestra, the space on which the chorus danced]

orchestration n. [1940s] (US Black) an overcoat. [music jargon orchestration, which 'wraps around' the individual scores]

orchids and turnips n. [1910s–20s] important and commonplace people.

orchids to you! excl. [1930s–50s] go to hell!, i.e. a euph. for BALLS n.¹ to you! [a pun on SE orchidectomy, castration, lit. Gk. 'testicle cutting']

order of the day n. [late 18C+] (orig. political) the status quo, the current way of doing things. [SE order of the day, in a legislative body, that business set down for debate on a given day]

order of the hempen riband n. [mid-17C–mid-18C] a judicial hanging, esp. at Tyburn. [play on SE hemp, from which the rope is made]

order of the push n. [20C] dismissal from one's job (cf. GET THE PUSH). [PUSH n.⁴]

order of the rag n. [early 18C–1900s] the military life. [rag = flag]

order-racket n. [early 19C] (Und.) obtaining goods by ordering them from a shopkeeper, whose bill will never be paid (cf. LONG FIRM). [SE order + RACKET n.¹ (1)]

ordinary n.¹ **1** [late 19C–1900s] one's wife. **2** [1970s] (US Black) one's regular female companion.

ordinary, the n.² [1970s+] what is customary or usual.

ordinary adj. [mid-19C+] physically plain, commonplace, unattractive.

Oregon boot n. [1900s–40s] (US prison) a heavy lead collar or shackle fitted around a prisoner's ankle. [its original use in Oregon prisons]

or else phr. [mid-19C+] a phr. used to threaten dire consequences, i.e. or else you will get into trouble, or else I will do something unpleasant.

Oreo/Oreo cookie n. **1** [1960s+] (US Black) a derog. description of a fellow Black whose opinions, attitudes and goals are taken from White society; thus Oreolized (cf. APPLE n.¹¹).

2 [1990s] (gay) sex between two Black men and a White man. [proper name *Oreo Cookie*, a popular US biscuit, which is black on the outside, with a white filling]

Oreo queen *n.* [1960s+] (US gay) a Black homosexual who engages in sexual activity with White men. [OREO + QUEEN n.[1]]

-orexia *sfx.* [1980s+] (US campus) a sfx. based on SE *anorexia* (compulsive, excessive dieting) combined with a given noun to mean too much, excessive, e.g. *talkorexia*, ceaseless talking.

orey-eyed *see* ORY-EYED.

org *n.* [1930s+] an *organization.* [abbr.]

organ *n.* [late 18C–mid-19C] a pipe; thus *cock one's organ*, to smoke a pipe. [pun on SE *pipe-organ*]

organ-grinder *n.* [1910s] an Italian immigrant. [their common profession]

organic *adj.* [1970s] (US campus) fashionable. [acknowledgement of 'green' politics]

organize *v.* **1** [1940s+] (orig. milit.) to steal, to loot (cf. ACQUIRE). **2** [1950s+] to arrange at short notice, to 'fix up'.

organized *adj.* [1940s+] (orig. milit.) acquired illicitly, by underhand methods.

organize the family jewels, to *phr.* [1990s] to masturbate. [pun on SE *organize* + FAMILY JEWELS]

organ-pipe *n.* [mid-19C–1920s] the windpipe, the throat, the voice.

orie-eyed *see* ORY-EYED.

orifice *n.* [1970s+] an office. [conscious mispron.]

original *n.* [1960s+] (Black) a fellow Black person; thus *all-originals party*, a party for Blacks only.

original loser *n.* [1950s–60s] (US) a man or woman without talent. Occasionally more fully expressed as *She/he is the original Major Bowes Amateur Hour loser*.

originals *n.* [1950s+] the Levi jeans and jacket (with sleeves cut off) worn at the initiation ceremonies of outlaw bikers clubs. Liberally soiled and 'worn in', the rider wears them until they fall to pieces.

orinoko/oronoko *n.*[1] [late 17C–early 18C] tobacco. [? Aphra Behn's play *Oroonoko* or *The Royal Slave* (1688)]

orinoko *n.*[2] [mid-19C–1920s] **1** cocoa. **2** a poker. [? rhy. sl. (2) pron. 'orinoker']

o'river! *excl.* [1990s] (US campus) a farewell (cf. AU RESERVOIR). [play on Fr. *au revoir*, goodbye]

ork *n.* [1930s+] (orig. US) an orchestra, usu. a jazz or dance band. [abbr.]

orlando *n.* [1990s] (US Black, mainly East Coast) a rural Black person, esp. one who does not keep up with the 'gangsta' styles of music or clothing. [? Orlando, Florida]

or my prick's a bloater *phr.* [1940s+] a phr. used to imply the absolute impossibility or unlikeliness of what has just been said, suggested etc.

ornary/ornery *adj.* **1** [early 19C+] (US) commonplace, of poor quality. **2** [early 19C+] (US) coarse, unpleasant. **3** [early 19C+] low, mean, cantankerous. **4** [late 19C] illiterate. [SE *ordinary*; A.W. Read has suggested its origins were as a coarse synon. for *lewd*, which was described in 1869 as a 'shocking' word that should 'never pass the lips of anyone' quoted in *Maledicta* 12, p.40]

ornithorhynchus *n.* [late 19C] a creditor. [SE *ornithorhynchus*, a duck-billed platypus, i.e. the punning 'beast with a bill']

oronoko *see* ORINOKO n.[1].

-oroonie *see* -EROONIE.

or out goes the gas! *excl.* [late 19C–1900s] a general threat, aimed at bringing a situation or a conversation to an abrupt end.

o.r.p.h. *adj.* [1900s–60s] beneath consideration; thus excl. *off you go!* [pron. of *off* as 'orf']

orphan *n.* [1930s–60s] (US) a discontinued model of a motor vehicle, a rundown, dilapidated motorcar; thus *orphaned*, discontinued.

orphan collar *n.* [late 19C–1900s] (orig. US) a loose collar that does not match one's shirt.

orry-eyed *see* ORY-EYED.

or something *phr.* [early 19C+] used to indicate a vague or unspecified alternative.

ort *n.* [1950s+] (Aus.) the anus, the backside. [ety. unknown, ? dial. *orts*, odds and ends]

or three *phr.* [1930s+] a more emphatic use of the usu. *or two*, more.

or what *phr.* [mid-18C+] a meaningless ending to a question which serves as emphasis but has no actual answer, e.g. *Have you supposed me dead or what?*

or whatever *phr.* [1940s+] a general phr. used to end a sentence and imply that other than the noun actually used, some other synon. might be equally applicable.

or what-have-you *phr.* [1940s+] a general phr. that declines to specify the details of what has already been cited, e.g. *any fruit will do, apples, oranges or what-have-you.*

ory-eyed/oary-eyed/orey-eyed/orie-eyed/orry-eyed *adj.* [late 19C+] (US) **1** very drunk, or looking as if one were. **2** very angry. [SE *awry* + *eyed*, but note Scot. *oorie*, of persons and things, dismal, gloomy, 'having a debauched or dissipated look']

o.s. *adj.* [20C] (Aus.) abroad, anywhere other than Australia. [abbr. *over-seas*]

Oscar *n.*[1] **1** [late 19C–1900s] a male homosexual; thus *oscar*, to sodomize; *Oscar-Wildeing*, homosexuality; *oscarize*, to be a homosexual. **2** [1900s–50s] (US) a stupid or unpleasant man. [the playwright and epigrammatist *Oscar* Wilde (1854–1901), imprisoned for his homosexuality; (2) stereotypes (1)]

Oscar/Oscar Nash/Okker *n.*[2] [1910s+] (Aus./N.Z.) money. [rhy. sl. *Oscar Asche* = cash, ult. actor Oscar Asche (1871–1936)]

oscar *n.*[3] [1930s+] (US Black) the penis (cf. ABRAHAM). [unknown; ? play on *Oscar* Wilde + the 'wild' activity of sex]

oscar *v.* [1920s–30s] (US) to move quickly. [ety. unknown; ? corruption of SE *scurry*]

oscar hock *n.* [1920s–60s] (US) a sock. [rhy. sl.]

Oscar Nash *see* OSCAR n.[2].

oschive *see* OCHIVE.

oscillate the oscar meyer, to *phr.* [1990s] (US) to masturbate (cf. ACCOST THE OSCAR MEYER). [*Oscar Meyer*, brandname for a popular US sausage]

O. Smith *n.* [mid-19C] a cavernous, sinister laugh, esp. as phr. *what an O. Smith.* [the actor *O. Smith* who always played the villainous 'heavy' in music-hall]

osmosis amoebas! *excl.* [1980s+] (US campus) a farewell. [a play on the more common *adios amigos*]

osnaburg *n.* [1950s] (W.I.) **1** rough, ill-cut clothes. **2** first-rate clothes, the product of the best tailoring. [proper name *Osnabrück* (in later Eng. corruptly *Osnaburg*), a town and district in north Germany noted for its manufacture of linen, thus a kind of coarse linen originally made in Osnabrück. In W.I. it was orig. used for the garments issued to slaves and later prisoners]

O soldiers! *excl.* [late 19C] a general excl., presumably euph. for something more coarse, e.g. 'oh shit!'

Ossi *n.* [1990s] an occupant of the former East Germany (cf. WESSI). [Ger. sl., ult. *Ostdeutsche*, East German]

ossifer/occifer *n.* [early 19C+] a joking, slightly offensive ref. to a police officer. [deliberate mispron.]

ossified *adj.* [20C] highly intoxicated on alcohol or a given drug. [pun on STONED]

ostrich *n.* [1950s+] a very inquisitive woman. [her 'long neck' stretched towards other people's business]

ostrobogulous *adj.* [20C] bizarre, unusual, interesting. [coined by the writer Victor B. Neuburg (1883–1940). It can be 'translated' in a variety of ways, e.g. 'mischievous but gorgeous' (of children) or 'indecent or pornographic' (words or pictures). Neuberg's own ety. mixed 'full of (Lat. *ulus*) rich (Greek, *ostro*) dirt (schoolboy, *bog*)']

o.t. *phr.* [late 19C] it is hot. [play on London pron. of *'ot*]

otamy *n.* [late 19C] a surgical operation. [SE *anatomy*]

o.t. & e. *phr.* (society) over-tired and emotional, usu. describing a fractious child. [abbr.]

otay! *excl.* [1990s] (US teen) fine, good, I agree. [var. on OK!]

o.t.d. *adj.* [1980s+] (US) gone, departed. [abbr. *out the door*]

other, the *n.* [1920s+] sexual intercourse, esp. in the phr. *a bit of the other*, usu. hetero- but sometimes homosexual.

other half *n.* [1920s+] (orig. naut.) a second drink, a drink bought in return for another (cf. ONE FOR THE BITUMEN; SAME AGAIN). [the *half* is presumed to be a half-pint]

other man *n.* [1930s–40s] (US Black) a White person, esp. the owner of a neighbourhood store in a Black area.

other side *n.* **1** [late 19C–1920s] either America or Britain, depending on which side of the Atlantic one is; thus *this side*. **2** [late 19C+] (N.Z.) Australia, i.e. the other side of the Tasman Sea.

otis *adj.* [1980s+] (US campus) drunk. [ety. unknown; ? ref. to song title 'Miss Otis Requests']

o.t.l. *phr.* [1950s–70s] (US campus) not in touch with reality, inattentive, unaware. [abbr. OUT TO LUNCH]

o.t.r. *phr.* [1960s+] (US campus) menstruating, so irritable, in a bad mood, tetchy. [abbr. ON THE RAG]

o.t.t. *see* OVER THE TOP.

otter *n.*[1] [late 17C–early 18C] a sailor.

otter *n.*[2] [mid-19C] (Ling. Fr./Polari) **1** the number 8. **2** 8 pence. [Ital. *otto*, 8]

Otto *n.* [20C] a derog. name for a German, with an implication of stolidity. [a popular Ger. name]

ottomized *adj.* [late 18C–early 19C] dissected, subjected to a post-mortem (cf. OTTOMY). [SE *anatomized*]

ottomy *n.* [late 18C–early 19C] a skeleton (cf. ATOMY; OTTOMIZED). [SE *anatomy*]

ou *n.* (S.Afr.) **1** [mid-19C+] a form of address, often in combs *ou china, ou maat, ou pellie*, old mate, old pal. **2** [1940s+] a fellow, a chap. **3** [1970s+] (township) a friend. [Afk. *ou*, a fellow + Du. *ouwe*, old man]

Oubaas *n.* [1900s–50s] (S.Afr.) a nickname for the Roeland Street prison, Cape Town. [Afk. *ou*, old + *baas*, boss, governor]

ouchimagooga *see* OOTCHIMAGOOTCHI.

ou-di-du-dat *n.* [1950s] (W.I.) an East Indian. [lit. 'how does he do that?', ? a question frequently asked by these individuals]

ought *n.* [mid-19C+] zero, nothing, esp. as the number 0. The modern *noughts and crosses* was *oughts and crosses* c.1850. [SE *nought*, i.e. 'an ought']

oui-oui *n.* [1940s] (US/N.Z.) a derog. term for a French person. [Fr. *oui*, yes]

ou kappie *see* OKAPI.

oulap *n.* [1940s] (S.Afr.) a penny (cf. RAG n.[1]). [Afk. *ou*, old + *lap*, rag, thus a valueless old rag]

ould thing, the *n.* [mid-19C] Shelta, or tinker's jargon (cf. BOG LATIN).

ouman *n.* [1970s+] (S.Afr.) **1** a veteran, an 'old hand'. **2** an experienced soldier. **3** a national serviceman who has completed 6 or more months of his enlistment or who has completed his entire time. [Afk. *ou*, old + SE *man*]

ounce *n.* [early 18C–early 19C] a silver coin. [the valuation of silver at 5s an ounce]

ounce man *n.* [1960s+] (US drugs) a small-time drug dealer. [SE *ounce* + MAN n.[3] (3)]

ounce of baccy/ouncer *n.* [20C] an Asian immigrant, esp. the owner of a corner shop. [rhy. sl. *ounce of baccy* = PAKI]

ounds *see* ZOUNDS.

oupa juice *n.* [1990s] (S.Afr.) liquor. [Afk. *oupa*, an old Afrikaans man + JUICE n.[3]]

our food don't cook/ain't cooked in same pot/rice don't cook in same pot *phr.* [20C] (W.I.) used when one wishes to indicate a social difference between oneself and another person (usu. when the others are seen as inferior or even unacceptable).

our friend with the talking brooch *n.* [1980s+] (gay) a policeman. [his walkie-talkie radio, clipped to the front of his uniform]

Our Lady in the straw! *excl.* [17C] a common excl. [the ref. is to Christ's birth, when his mother Mary was supposedly forced to give birth in a manger]

our Miss Brooks *n.* [1950s–60s] (camp gay) a teacher. [the name of a TV character]

our survey said ... *phr.* [1990s] (US teen) used to indicate approval/disapproval or confirmation/denial. [in class, a teacher asks, 'What do you think of that?', the pupil responds, 'Our survey said ... YES!!!!' (to imply approval), 'Our survey said ... NO!!!' (disapproval), 'Our survey said ... ding!' (a bell sound, for yes), 'Our survey said ... ouourgh!' (a buzzer sound, for no)]

oussie *adj.* [20C] (Ulster) over-inquisitive. [ety. unknown]

out *n.*[1] [mid-18C–late 19C] an outing, an excursion, a holiday. [one goes *out*]

out *n.*[2] [mid-19C] an outside passenger on a coach.

out *n.*[3] [mid-19C+] a dram measure of gin or a dram glass; thus *three-out*, a glass holding a third of a measure of a liquor. [? it is poured *out*]

out *n.*[4] [late 19C] a defect, a blemish, a disadvantage.

out *n.*[5] [late 19C–1900s] a loss.

out *n.*[6] (orig. US) **1** [20C] an excuse. **2** [1910s+] a means of escape, avoidance. [one is let *out*]

out *adj.*[1] [17C; 1930s+] unfashionable. [*out* of the current style]

out *adj.*[2] [mid-19C–1900s] having a tendency to lose.

out *adj.*[3] **1** [late 19C] dead. **2** [late 19C] tipsy. **3** [late 19C+] (orig. US) knocked out, unconscious.

out *adj.*[4] [late 19C] recently released from prison.

out *adj.*[5] [1920s–40s] of a couple, *walking out* together.

out *adj.*[6] [1920s+] (orig. US) **1** banned, prohibited. **2** unfeasible, undesirable, usu. in phr. *that's out*, I won't accept that.

out *adj.*[7] [1960s+] in debt, poor. [abbr. *out of pocket*]

out *adj.*[8] [1960s+] (gay) openly homosexual. [OUT v.[4]]

out *v.*[1] [mid–late 19C] to go out, esp. on an excursion. [OUT n.[1]]

out *v.*[2] **1** [late 19C] to kill. **2** [late 19C–1920s] to knock out, to disable. **3** [late 19C+] to dismiss from a job, to discharge. **4** [20C] (Aus.) to throw out of a meeting.

out *v.*[3] [20C] to talk. [? imper. *out with it!*]

out *v.*[4] **1** [1980s+] to expose someone as a homosexual against their will. **2** [1990s] to reveal negative information about an individual, group or organization. [the victim is pushed *out of the closet*. A tactic pioneered by the New York gay magazine *Outweek* and usu. in the form *outing*; thus the converse 'inning', the deliberate masking of homosexuality when a celebrity is known to be gay but the gay/lesbian community finds them (or more likely their politics) so reprehensible that it denies the fact]

out *adv.* [mid-19C–1900s] (US) in existence, e.g. *he is the craziest person out*.

-out *sfx.* [1950s+] (orig. US) completely, e.g. *clapped-out*, *drugged-out*, *stressed-out*.

out and out *n.* [20C] (US Black) a totally unacceptable person. [OUT-AND-OUT adj. (1)]

out-and-out *adj.* **1** [early 19C+] complete, thorough-going, unqualified. **2** [mid-19C+] excellent, first-rate.

out and outer *n.* **1** [early 19C+] one who is seen as reaching extremes of behaviour, both good and bad and defined according to context. **2** [mid-19C–1920s] a notable lie. **3** [late 19C+] (US) a brawl, a fistfight. [OUT-AND-OUT adj. (1); (1) SE after 1880]

outasite/outasight/outen sight *adj.* [late 19C+] excellent, wonderful, top quality. [OUT OF SIGHT phr.² (2)]

out at elbows *phr.* [early 17C–late 19C] in reduced circumstances, poor (cf. OUT AT HEELS). [the state of one's clothes]

out at heels *phr.* [early 17C–mid-18C] run-down, in poor circumstances (cf. OUT AT ELBOWS). [the state of one's clothes]

out box *n.* [1990s] (US Black) the start, the beginning. [OUT OF THE BOX or office jargon *out box*, a box into which out-going mail is placed]

outdoor library *n.* [1930s+] (US) an outdoor privy. [the use of newspapers etc as lavatory paper]

outed *adj.* [20C] **1** (orig. Aus.) killed, dead. **2** (orig. Aus.) dismissed from employment. **3** (orig. US) revealed as a homosexual. [OUT v.², v.⁴]

outen sight *see* OUTASITE.

outer limits *n.* [1980s+] (drugs) a mixture of crack cocaine and LSD. [the TV SF series, *The Outer Limits*]

outers *n.¹* [1910s+] (Und.) a means of escape (cf. ON THE OUTERS). [OUT n.⁶ (2)]

outers *n.²* [1970s+] (S.Afr.) anywhere a vagrant, homeless person finds to sleep, such as a cardboard box, doorway etc. [SE *outdoors*]

outers *adj.* [1970s+] unacceptable, distasteful. [OUT OF ORDER]

outfit *n.¹* [mid-19C+] a person or their possessions, a travelling party or a party in charge of herds of cattle, an organization, a business, an object or device. ['to cross the plains, or go to the mountains, every one must get an outfit; and having outfitted, you become yourself an outfit' J. F. Meline *Two Thousand Miles on Horseback* (1867)]

outfit *n.²* (US drugs) **1** [late 19C+] equipment for the preparation and smoking of opium. **2** [1950s+] the equipment (needle, spoon, cotton etc) used for narcotic injection (cf. BIZ n.²; FIT n.¹).

Outfit, the *n.³* [1920s+] (US Und.) a criminal organization, esp. the Italian gangs in US prisons (cf. MOB n.³).

outfit *n.⁴* [1940s–50s] (prison) whatever is needed for attempting a given escape.

outfit *n.⁵* [1970s+] (US campus) anyone seen as odd or eccentric, who fails to fit in. [SE *out* + *fit*]

out for a pelter *phr.* [late 19C–1900s] in a very bad temper. [dial. *pelter*, a bad temper]

out for the count *phr.* [late 19C+] ruined, defeated, exhausted, asleep. [boxing imagery]

out front *see* UP FRONT.

outhouse *n.* [20C] (US prison) a 'half-way house' or hostel, in which newly released prisoners or parolees can learn to re-acclimatize themselves to the 'real' world. [OUT adj.⁴ + SE *house*]

outie *n.¹* [1970s] (S.Afr.) a vagrant, a tramp (cf. OUTERS n.²). [SE *outdoors*]

outie *n.²* [1970s+] a protruding navel (cf. INNIE).

outing dues *n.* [late 19C–1900s] execution for murder. [OUT v.² (1) + SE *dues*, one's deserts]

out/off in left field *phr.* (US) **1** [1930s+] peculiar, eccentric, in poor taste. **2** [1940s+] out of touch, 'far away'. **3** [1950s+] not fully conscious, unaware. [baseball imagery]

out in one's christening *phr.* [late 19C] mistaken, in error. [SE *out*, miscalculated + *christen*, to name]

out in the water *phr.* [20C] (US) in debt (cf. IN THE HOLE; ON THE NUT).

out it *v.* [late 19C] to go out for an excursion. [OUT v.¹]

outjie *n.* [1950s+] (S.Afr.) little fellow, used either of a child or derog. of an adult. [OU + dimin. sfx. *-tjie*]

outlaw *n.* **1** [late 19C–1960s] (US) a wild and unmanageable horse. **2** [1930s+] (US Black) a prostitute without a regular pimp, or any independent prostitute. **3** [1950s+] (US) a person who flouts conventional practices and regulations (cf. OUTLAW STRIKE).

outlaw *adj.* [1920s+] (W.I.) wild, barbarous, crude.

outlaw *v.* [1930s+] of a prostitute, to operate independently of a pimp.

outlaw strike *n.* [1950s] (US) an unofficial strike. [OUTLAW n. (3) + SE *strike*]

out like a light *phr.* [1930s+] collapsing – through a blow, drink, drugs, exhaustion – instantly.

out-mouthed *adj.* [20C] (Ulster) having protruding teeth.

out of all ho *phr.* [late 14C–early 18C] beyond any limit. [*ho!*, an excl. to attract attention]

out of all nick *phr.* [late 16C–early 17C] beyond count. [? NICK v.¹]

out of collar *phr.* [mid-19C] unemployed, esp. of servants. [var. on SE *out of harness*]

out of commission *phr.* [late 19C+] not working. [orig. of people, now generally of objects, typically automobiles]

out of control *phr.* [1980s+] (US campus) **1** of inanimate as well as animate objects, extreme, excessive, extremely good. **2** of people, drunk, intoxicated.

out of curl *phr.* [mid-19C–1910s] ill at ease, out of sorts. [the image is of hair]

out of flash *n.* [early 19C] a show-off, 'a person who affects any particular habit, as swearing, dressing ... taking snuff ..., merely to be taken notice of, is said to do it "out of flash"' (Vaux). [FLASH n.¹ (1)]

out of here *phr.* [1970s+] having left, esp. to leave suddenly; thus *I'm out of here!* a phr. of farewell (cf. AUDI).

out of it *phr.¹* **1** [late 19C+] (orig. US) excluded from one's usual participation in something. **2** [1940s+] (orig. US) out of touch, behind the times, not au fait with current affairs and interests. **3** [1950s+] (orig. US Black) unfashionable.

out of it *phr.²* (orig. US) **1** [1950s+] unable to function adequately because of one's intoxication by drugs or alcohol. **2** [1960s+] tired, exhausted, ill. ['it' is one' head]

out of left field *phr.* [20C] peculiar, eccentric, in poor taste. [baseball imagery]

out of line *phr.* [1930s+] (orig. US) breaking rules, unacceptable, out of the ordinary. [SE *line*, a style of activity, a discipline]

out of mothballs *phr.* [1940s+] (orig. US milit.) brought back into circulation, esp. of something that has been set aside for a long time (cf. IN MOTHBALLS).

out of one's asshole *see* OUT THE ASSHOLE.

out of one's boots *phr.* [mid–late 19C] (US) comprehensively, convincingly, totally. [one has been 'blown' or 'knocked' out of one's boots]

out of one's/off one's box *phr.* [20C] unstable, mad, insane (cf. OUT OF ONE'S TREE).

out of one's brain *phr.* [1960s+] intoxicated with drugs.

out of one's capsule *phr.* [1960s] (US) insane, eccentric.

out of one's face *phr.* [1970s+] under the influence of drink or drugs (cf. OFF ONE'S FACE).

out of one's gears *phr.* [late 17C–early 18C] unsettled, out of sorts. [GEAR n.¹ (1)]

out of/off one's gourd *phr.* [1960s+] **1** extremely affected by a given drug, usu. cannabis or a hallucinogen. **2** crazy, insane. [GOURD n.²]

out of one's head *phr.* [1950s+] (orig. US) **1** experiencing the effects of a drug (cf. OUT OF IT *phr.*²). **2** utterly miserable. **3** eccentric, insane. **4** desperate, highly emotional.

out of one's jockstrap *phr.* [1970s+] (US) very frightened, utterly confused.

out of one's mind *phr.* [1960s+] **1** intoxicated, either through drink or, later, drugs. **2** crazy (cf. OUT OF ONE'S GOURD).

out of one's misery *phr.* [early 19C+] dead.

out of one's nut *phr.* [late 19C+] **1** intoxicated, either through drink or, later, drugs. **2** crazy (cf. OUT OF ONE'S MIND). [NUT n.³]

out of one's skull *phr.* [1960s+] **1** extremely bored. **2** intoxicated, either through drink or, later, drugs. **3** crazy (cf. OUT OF ONE'S HEAD).

out of one's/the road *phr.* [mid-17C+] out of the way, remote, of no concern, not central to one's aims, beliefs or argument.

out of one's tiny mind *phr.* [1960s+] mentally unbalanced, unstable.

out of one's tree *phr.* [1960s+] crazy, insane (cf. OUT OF ONE'S SKULL). [the sufferer has fig. fallen out of a tree]

out of order *phr.* [1970s+] of events, behaviour or people, unacceptable, excessive, in bad taste.

out of pocket *phr.* [1940s–70s] (US Black) **1** acting in an unacceptable, tasteless manner (cf. OUT OF ORDER). **2** referring to a bad situation, bad news. [pool jargon, an *out of pocket* shot causes a player to miss a turn]

out of sight *phr.*¹ (US) **1** [mid-19C+] utterly, thoroughly. **2** [late 19C–1900s] extremely well.

out of sight *phr.*² **1** [late 19C] (US) unattainable. **2** [late 19C+] (orig. US) excellent, first rate, exceptional; thus ext. as *clean out of sight* (cf. FAR OUT; OUTASITE). **3** [1920s+] (US) extraordinary, esp. bad, insane or deranged.

out of sorts *phr.* [19C] dispirited, miserable. [SE f. early 17C–18C. Note printers jargon *out of sorts*, out of certain fonts of type]

out of state *phr.* [1970s+] (US campus) excellent, first-rate. [pun on OUT OF SIGHT *phr.*² (2)]

out of synch *phr.* [1970s+] fig. out of tune with (cf. IN SYNCH). [film use, sound is out of synchronization]

out of the ark *phr.* [20C] very old, out of date, unfashionable. [the biblical *Noah's Ark*]

out of the bag *phr.* [1950s+] (Aus.) surprising.

out of the blue *phr.* [20C] surprising, quite unsuspected. [a 'bolt from the blue sky']

out of the box *phr.* [1920s+] (Aus.) exceptional, well above average (cf. HAPPY AS A BOX OF BIRDS).

out of the car *phr.* [20C] (US Und.) on bad terms. [reverse of IN THE CAR]

out of the loop *phr.* [1990s] (US teen) not in on a secret, or don't know what's going on. [orig. political jargon, the *loop* of people who have access to a given piece of information]

out of the parlour and into the kitchen *phr.* [late 16C–early 17C] from bad to worse.

out of the picture *phr.* [1940s+] irrelevant, unimportant.

out of there *phr.* [1950s+] (US) having left, esp. having left suddenly (cf. OUT OF HERE).

out of the spoon *phr.* [20C] (drugs) not using drugs (cf. IN THE SPOON). [SPOON n.²]

out of the straight *phr.* [late 19C+] dishonest, illegal, illicit. [STRAIGHT AND NARROW]

out of the tail of the eye *phr.* [late 19C+] (Irish) watching furtively.

out of the wood *phr.* [late 19C+] (orig. US) out of difficulties, often in phr. *not out of the wood yet*, still having problems.

out of this world *phr.* [1920s+] fantastic, amazing, wonderful etc.

out of town *phr.* **1** [early 19C] in prison for debt. **2** [1940s–60s] (US) crazy. **3** [1960s] (US Black) unacceptable, unfashionable. [all have the image of not being completely present]

out of twig *phr.* [early–mid-19C] (Und.) **1** disguised in order to evade arrest. **2** wearing shabby clothes, reduced to that state through poverty. **3** of a stolen article, altered to make the article unrecognizable. [TWIG v.]

out of whack *phr.* [20C] off-centre, out of true, out of order, feeling unwell. [WHACK n.²; i.e. a fig. unfair share of direction, health etc]

out of whole cloth/cut out of the whole cloth *phr.* [mid–late 19C] (US) used of a statement that is a blatant lie.

out on a dike *phr.* [mid-19C] (US) going out in one's best clothes. [DIKED DOWN]

out on a limb *phr.* [late 19C+] (orig. US) in a difficult situation, in trouble. [SE *limb*, a tree branch]

out on its own like a country shit-house *phr.* [1910s+] (N.Z.) unique, unrivalled.

out on one's ear *phr.* [1920s+] ejected unceremoniously, thrown out.

out on one's own *phr.* [20C] of a person or object, excellent, admirable, unrivalled.

out on the nick *phr.* [late 19C+] out thieving. [NICK v.¹ (4)]

outpost *n.* [1980s+] (US campus) someone who is out of touch with reality, a daydreamer.

out-psych *v.* [1970s+] (US) to confuse, manipulate or brainwash someone by psychological means.

outrageous *adj.* [1950s+] (US) excellent, worthy of admiration. [on bad = good pattern]

outrun the constable, to *phr.* [late 17C–mid-19C] **1** to spend more than one can afford. **2** to go too far, whether physically or figuratively. **3** to change the subject.

outside *adj.* [late 19C–1950s] (US Black) illegitimate; thus (W.I.) *outside daughter/son*, *outside kid*, an illegitimate child, *outside man*, a woman's lover, *outside woman*, a man's lover (cf. ON THE WRONG SIDE OF THE BLANKET). [i.e. *outside* the primary relationships or the (fig.) house]

outside *adv.*¹ [mid-19C+] (orig. US) other than, excepting, beyond the number of; thus *at the outside*, at the limit, to the fullest extent.

outside *adv.*² [late 19C+] out of prison, out of the services.

outside! *excl.* [20C] a challenge. [abbr. *come outside and fight!*]

outside child *n.* [20C] (US, mainly southern Black) an illegitimate child (cf. OUTSIDE MAN). [OUTSIDE adj.]

outside edge *n.* [20C] the absolute limit.

outside Eliza!/Liza! *excl.* [late 19C–1900s] go away! be off!, esp. used to a woman considered drunk. [the barman requesting the eponymous Eliza to stop drinking and leave the public house. According to Ware, it derives from the evidence given in a specific court case]

outside job *n.* [1920s+] a crime committed in a house etc by a person not connected or associated with the household or building concerned. [SE *outside* + JOB n.³]

outside Liza! *see* OUTSIDE ELIZA!

outside man *n.* [1920s+] **1** (orig. US) one involved in any of various special roles in a confidence trick or robbery. **2** (US, mainly Black) a married woman's lover; thus *outside woman*, a married man's lover (cf. OUTSIDE CHILD). [OUTSIDE adj.]

outside of a horse *phr.* [late 19C+] on horseback.

outsider *n.* **1** [late 19C+] a person who is considered socially inferior, esp. as *rank outsider*, a complete and utter inferior. **2** [1900s–20s] (Irish) a mentally deficient person. **3** [1980s+] (US) an act of sexual intercourse performed out of doors.

outside the ropes *phr.* [mid-19C] without knowledge of a matter, in the position of an outsider (cf. OUT OF THE LOOP). [boxing imagery]

outslick *v.* [1940s+] (US Black) to outwit, outsmart. [SLICK *v.*]

out someone's light, to *phr.* [20C] (W.I.) to cripple or maim someone, to put out of action.

out the/of one's asshole *phr.* [1960s+] (US) blatantly, excessively, no good, reprehensible. [i.e. fig. excrement]

out the monk *phr.* [1940s+] (N.Z.) unconscious, asleep, often the result of drunkenness. [ety. unknown; ? rhy. sl. *out the monk* = drunk]

out the pocket *phr.* [1990s] (US Black gang) using a gun.

outtie 5000 *see* AUDI 5000.

out to breakfast *phr.* [1990s] (orig. US) **1** crazy, eccentric, weird. **2** intoxicated by drink or drugs. [var. on OUT TO LUNCH]

out to grass *phr.* [late 19C+] retired. [usu. of a horse]

out to it *phr.* [1940s+] (Aus.) extremely drunk, unconscious (cf. OUT OF IT *phr.*[2]).

out to lunch *phr.* [1950s+] (orig. US campus) **1** crazy, eccentric, weird. **2** intoxicated by drink or drugs (cf. OUT TO BREAKFAST). **3** in a daze, stupid, naïve. [image of not being 'all there']

out to pasture *phr.* [20C] (US Und.) serving time in prison. [animals put out to pasture have 'retired' from everyday productive life]

out with *adj.* [late 19C+] on bad terms with, quarrelling, disenchanted with, opposed to. [ON THE OUTS *phr.* (1)]

out with *v.* **1** [early 19C+] to produce, to reveal, to bring out. **2** [late 19C+] to speak out, esp. to say something that has been hitherto held back or concealed; thus [late 19C+] *out with it!* speak! stop keeping quiet or restraining yourself.

oven *n.* **1** [late 17C–1910s] the vagina (cf. KITCHEN). **2** [late 18C–mid-19C] a large mouth (cf. DUTCH OVEN). **3** [1940s+] the womb (cf. BUN IN THE OVEN; HAVE ONE IN THE OVEN).

oven-dodger *n.* [1980s] a derog. term for a Jew. [the implication that those who escaped the crematorium ovens of Auschwitz and other Nazi death camps were somehow doing it deceitfully]

over *adj.* [1990s] (US) out-of-date (cf. HISTORY).

over *v.*[1] [20C] (Ulster) to survive. [abbr. SE *get over*]

over, be *v.*[2] [1980s+] (US campus) to dislike intensely.

over! *see* OVER THE LEFT SHOULDER!

over a barrel *phr.* [1930s+] (orig. US) in another's power, at a great disadvantage; thus *to have over a barrel*, to dominate, to control. [men due to be whipped were tied down *over a barrel*]

overamp *v.* [1960s+] (drugs) to overdose on cocaine or amphetamine. [SE *over* + AMP *n.* (1) and/or abbr. SE *amphetamine*]

overamped *adj.* [1980s+] (US) overwrought, over-excited. [OVERAMP]

over-and-under *n.* [1980s+] (drugs) a combination of a stimulant and a depressant drug. [i.e. an UPPER *n.*[2] and a DOWNER *n.*[4]]

overboard *adj.* [1940s+] (orig. US) over-enthusiastic, very keen.

over boots/shoes *phr.* [16C] totally, recklessly committed. [? water pouring over the top of one's footwear]

overcharged *adj.* [1930s–40s] (US) overdosed on narcotics. [ext. of CHARGED]

overcoat *n.* (US) **1** [1910s–40s] a pie crust. **2** [1920s–70s] a condom. **3** [1940s] a parachute.

overcoat maker *n.* [20C] an undertaker (cf. WOODEN OVERCOAT). [rhy. sl.]

over-do *n.* [1920s] (W.I.) showing off, ostentation.

overdraw one's badger, to *phr.* [mid-19C] to overdraw one's bank account. [pun on SE *badger-drawing*, badger-baiting]

overdue *adj.* [1960s+] of a woman, not having had a menstrual period at the expected time (cf. LATE).

over-easy *adj.* [20C] (US) of fried eggs, turned over in the pan (cf. SUNNY SIDE UP).

over-eye *v.* [late 19C] to watch, to survey. [SE *run one's eyes over*]

over goes the show! *excl.* [late 19C] an excl. of dismay when faced by a sudden disaster.

overheat one's flues, to *phr.* [late 19C] to get drunk.

overjolt *n.* [1950s+] (US drugs) a drug overdose. [SE *over* + JOLT *n.*[1] (1)]

overlander *n.* [late 19C+] (Aus.) **1** a tramp (cf. SUNDOWNER). **2** a large mosquito (cf. SCOTCH GREYS). [SE *overlander*, one who herds cattle from one Aus. state to another]

overland trout *n.* [1900s–50s] (US) bacon.

over my dead body *phr.* [20C] a phr. of absolute negation, in no possible way, ever.

over-'omer *n.* [20C] (Can.) an English person whose conversation centres on the better life to be found in the UK. [lit. 'over there where I have my home']

over-ripe fruit *n.* [1950s–60s] (gay) an ageing male homosexual. [SE *over-ripe* + FRUIT *n.*[2] (2)]

overs *n.* [1970s+] (Und.) proceeds of a theft that can, if not carefully disposed of, become vulnerable themselves to further theft, poss. by one of the gang. [SE *over*, an extra, a remainder]

overseas *adj.* [1930s] drunk (cf. AFLOAT). [modern var. on HALF SEAS OVER]

overseen *adj.* [17C–18C] tipsy.

overseer of the new pavement *n.* [late 18C–early 19C] a man standing in a pillory. [the positioning of the pillory above the passers-by]

over shoes *see* OVER BOOTS.

overshot *adj.* [early 17C+] tipsy, drunk.

overtaken *adj.* [early 18C–mid-19C] drunk.

over the bay *phr.* [late 18C–late 19C] (US) drunk (cf. AFLOAT).

over the bender *phr.* [late 19C] a phr. implying that the previous statement is untrue. [BENDER; 'it is historical in common English that a declaration made over the elbow as distinct from not over it need not be held sacred. Probably from early Christian if not pagan times. The bender is always the left elbow ...' (Ware). Note also the Victorian custom of 'over the left', i.e. pointing with one's right thumb over one's left shoulder, implying disbelief]

over the edge *phr.* [20C] to excess (cf. OVER THE TOP).

over the fence *phr.* [1910s+] (Aus./N.Z.) extreme, beyond the bounds of taste (cf. BEYOND THE RABBIT-PROOF FENCE; OVER THE EDGE; OVER THE TOP).

over the hill *phr.* [20C] **1** free, escaped, esp. of an escaped prisoner or a soldier who has deserted etc. **2** worn out, useless, too old.

over the hill ho *n.* [20C] (US Black) an ageing, worn out prostitute (cf. FLAKY HO; SUMMERTIME HO; WEEKEND HO). [OVER THE HILL + HO *n.*[1]]

over the hump *phr.* [1910s+] (orig. use) over the worst, past the midpoint of a job or experience, usu. an unpleasant one.

over the left shoulder!/over! *excl.* [late 17C+] a general term of disbelief, absolutely not, impossible etc (cf. OVER THE BENDER). [the term is often accentuated by gesturing over the left shoulder with the thumb. Note the superstitious throwing of spilled salt over one's left shoulder, thus one takes such dubious information 'with a pinch of salt']

over the lid *phr.* [1980s+] to excess, beyond the bounds of possibility (cf. OVER THE TOP).

over the mark *phr.* [19C] (Can.) tipsy (cf. OVER THE PLIMSOLL). [a notional 'mark' that denotes a limit to 'safe' drinking]

over the moon *adj.* [1970s+] extremely cheerful, delighted, esp. as a clichéd response attributed to sportspeople, particularly professional football players, when interviewed about a successful game or competition (cf. SICK AS A PARROT). [E.P. adds a single mid-19C citation, in a private letter]

over the plimsoll *phr.* [1920s+] (N.Z.) drunk (cf. OVER THE MARK). [the SE *plimsoll line*, marking the limit of loading a ship]

over-the-shoulder-boulder-holder *see* BOULDER-HOLDER.

over the stile *phr.* [mid–late 19C] committed for trial. [rhy. sl.]

over the top/o.t.t. *phr.* [1980s+] **1** beyond the usual bounds of taste, behaviour, credibility etc. **2** very drunk.

over the wall *phr.* [1930s+] escaped from prison.

o.v.o. *phr.* [late 19C] [unknown; *Ware*, who cites it offers no definition, bar attributing it to 'Lower Class, Hist.', stating, 'Quite inexplicable. No solution ever obtained from the initiates'; 'Perhaps it's just as well' added E.P.]

ow *n.* [late 19C–1930s] (US drugs) the bowl of an opium pipe. [? abbr. + o n. (2)]

o waggernery! *excl.* [late 19C] o agony! [proper name Richard *Wagner* (1813–83), the ridicule of whose music provided much popular amusement during 1890s]

Owen Nares *n.* [20C] chairs. [rhy. sl., UK actor *Owen Nares* (c.1888–1943)]

owie *n.* [1990s] **1** (US) a bruise or minor injury. **2** (US Black) any jewellery that requires the piercing of one's flesh, usu. an earlobe. [the excl. *ow!* on having one's flesh pierced]

owl *n.* **1** [19C] a prostitute who works nights only (cf. EVENING STAR). **2** [1900s–40s] (Aus./US) a thief, esp. one who works at night. **3** [1910s+] the late-night customers of cafés and restaurants.

owl *adj.* [mid-19C+] (orig. US) working, operating or open at night, e.g. *owl shift*, the night shift.

owl-dung *see* OWL-SHIT.

owler *n.* [late 17C–late 19C] one who smuggles wool or sheep from England to France. [in an attempt to curtail smuggling the transportation of wool by night was forbidden in 1674, therefore those who still carried on the illicit trade were known as *owlers*, because, like the bird, they worked at night]

owl-/owly-eyed *adj.* [1900s–60s] (US) very drunk.

owl-feathers *see* OWL-SHIT.

owl-gal *n.* [1940s] (W.I.) a promiscuous girl (cf. OWL n.). [like the owl she's 'out all night']

owlhead/owl's head *n.* [1920s–60s] (US) a short, heavy revolver with a feature enabling it to double as a knuckle duster. [? a brandname]

owlhoot/owlhooter *n.* [1940s+] (US) a contemptible person, esp. a fugitive or outlaw. [? US West *hear the owl hoot*, to travel by night]

owl-shit/-dung/-feathers/-milk *n.* [mid-19C+] (US) excrement, usu. constructed with 'sour', used fig., shit; also in euph. forms (cf. SLICK AS OWL SHIT). [SE *owl* + SHIT n.[1] (1)/SE *dung/feathers/milk*]

owly-eyed *see* OWL-EYED.

own the corn *see* ACKNOWLEDGE THE CORN

own up *v.* [mid-19C+] to confess.

Owsley/Owsley's acid *n.* [1960s–70s] (drugs) LSD. [Augustus

Owsley Stanley III, the best known of all LSD chemists. His 'own-brand' drugs were considered the very best]

owt *n.* [mid-19C] two. [backsl.]

owt gens *n.* [mid-19C] two shillings. [backsl.]

owt yeneps *n.* [mid-19C] two pence. [backsl.]

Oxford *n.* [1940s] (US Black) a particularly dark-skinned person. [brandname of *Oxford* shoe polish]

Oxford scholar *n.* **1** [late 19C+] a crown, 5s (25p); thus *half an Oxford*, two shillings and sixpence (cf. HALF-OXFORD). **2** [1900s] a collar. [rhy. sl.; **1** *Oxford scholar* = DOLLAR]

oxo *n.* [late 19C–1900s] zero, nothing. [maths notation 0×0]

oxo *adj.* [1980s+] (Irish) satisfactory, acceptable, good, esp. in the phr. *the job's oxo*, everything is fine. [var. on OK]

Oxo cube *n.* [20C] the London Underground. [rhy. sl. *Oxo cube* = the tube]

o.y.o. *n.* [1980s+] (N.Z.) a self-contained flat, one of a block, that can be purchased freehold. [abbr. *own your own*]

oyster *n.*[1] **1** [late 17C+] the vagina (cf. BEARDED CLAM). **2** [late 17C+] a girl, a young woman. [one of many terms that equate the vagina with fish; *see* BEARDED CLAM for a full list; (2) fig. use of (1)]

oyster *n.*[2] **1** [late 17C+] semen. **2** [late 18C+] a gob of phlegm. [resemblance]

oyster *n.*[3] [late 19C–1910s] profit, advantage [the *oyster*'s beard, supposedly reminiscent of that of a prophet, thus pun on SE *profit*]

oyster *n.*[4] (US) **1** [late 19C–1950s] a close-mouthed person. **2** [1940s–70s] an odd or stupid person. [the bivalve's 'closed mouthed']

oyster *n.*[5] [1910s–50s] a pearl; thus *real oysters*, genuine pearls.

oyster *v.* [1960s–70s] to shut up, to be quiet (cf. CLAM UP).

oyster-catcher *n.* [late 19C] the vagina (cf. BEARDED CLAM; OYSTER n.[1]). [OYSTER n.[1] (3)]

oyster-faced *adj.* [late 19C–1910s] unshaven. [the oyster's beard]

oysterics *n.* [1900s] (middle class) hysterics. [a pun on the SE, intensified by the worries generated after bad oysters allegedly created a typhoid epidemic c.1900]

oyster months *n.* [late 19C] those months containing an 'r', which in Britain are traditionally those in which it is safe to eat oysters.

o.z./oh-zee *n.* [1930s+] (drugs) an ounce (28g) of a drug. [1*oz*; pron.]

Oz *n.*[1] [20C] Australia (cf. OZZIE). [pron. of *Aus(tralia*) + pun on *The Wonderful Wizard of Oz* (1900)]

oz *n.*[2] [1980s] (drugs) amyl nitrite (cf. AIMIES n.[2]). [it sends you to the land of *Oz*]

ozone *n.*[1] [1900s] **1** [1900s–20s] air. **2** [1920s–40s] a dismissal. [(2) is ext. of GET THE AIR/GIVE THE AIR]

ozone *n.*[2] [1970s+] (drugs) phencyclidine (cf. ACE n.[3]). [ety. unknown]

ozoned *adj.* [1970s+] (US) intoxicated by drugs. [SE *ozone*; i.e. one is HIGH adj.[1]]

ozoner *n.* [1940s+] (US) a drive-in cinema. [SE *ozone*, fresh air]

ozone ranger *n.* [1970s] (US campus) someone who is out of touch with reality. [their 'head is in the clouds']

Ozzie *n.*[1] [1910s+] an Australian. [OZ n.[1]]

ozzie *n.*[2] [1980s+] (Aus. drugs) 1oz (28g) of marijuana.

P

p *n.*[1] [1920s–30s] a *p*once, a *p*imp. [abbr.]

p *n.*[2] *see* PEA.

p *n.*[3] [1980s+] (drugs) **1** *p*eyote. **2** *p*hencyclidine (cf. ACE *n.*[3]). [abbr.]

p *n.*[4] [1990s] (US Black) **1** the vagina. **2** women in general. [abbr. PUSSY *n.*[1] (1),(2)]

p *adj.* [1980s+] *p*ure, unadulterated, esp. of drugs. [abbr.]

p.a. *n.*[1] [1920s–30s] one's father. [PA *n.*[1]]

p.a. *n.*[2] [1930s+] a *p*ublic *a*ddress system. [abbr.]

pa *n.*[1] [early 19C+] (mainly juv.) one's father; thus *pa-in-law*, father-in-law. [SE *papa*]

pa *n.*[2] [late 19C] the *p*arish relieving officer, who distributed money to the poor. [abbr.]

p.a.b.a.c.a.b. *phr.* [1980s+] (US drugs) an exhortation to smoke cannabis. [abbr. *p*ack *a* BOWL *a*nd *c*atch *a* BUZZ *n.*[5] (3)]

pac *n.* [mid-19C] a cap. [backsl.]

pace *v.* [1970s] (US Black) to live a fast, exciting and varied life.

pacer *n.* [late 19C] (US) anything or anyone that goes at a great pace.

pachuco *n.* [1940s+] (US) a Mexican-American, esp. a young man who joins a street gang (cf. BATO; CHOLO). [Mex. Sp. *pachuco*, flashily dressed, vulgar]

Pacific slope *n.* [late 19C] (N.Z.) the countries of the Pacific Rim, esp. as considered places of refuge for wanted criminals; thus *do the Pacific slope*, to flee N.Z. when accused of a crime in order to find refuge in one of the countries of the Pacific Rim. [pun on SE *Pacific slope*, the edge of the Pacific Ocean/ SLOPE *v.*[2]]

pack *n.*[1] [mid–late 19C] a night lodging for the very poor. [? PACK *v.*[1]]

pack *n.*[2] *see* PACKER *n.*[1].

pack *n.*[3] [20C] (US Black) a White person. [abbr. PECKERWOOD]

pack *n.*[4] [1950s+] (drugs) **1** a packet of heroin. **2** a packet of pills. **3** a packet of marijuana.

pack *adj.* [1960s+] (Irish) friendly. [Scot.]

pack *v.*[1] [late 19C+] to live as a tramp, travelling the country. [the SE *pack* that is carried]

pack *v.*[2] [late 19C+] (US) **1** to carry. **2** to carry a gun (cf. PACK A ROD; PACK HEAT).

pack *v.*[3] [1920s+] (Aus.) to surpass, to beat, to be more enjoyable than something. [? SE *send packing*]

pack *v.*[4] [1980s+] (US campus) of male homosexuals, to have anal sex (cf. PACK MUD; PACK PEANUT BUTTER).

pack *v.*[5] [1980s+] (Aus. drugs) to fill a cigarette with marijuana; thus *packer*, one who makes marijuana cigarettes.

package *n.*[1] [20C] (US prison) a positive report on a prisoner. [the package of papers on which it is written]

package *n.*[2] **1** [1940s+] an attractive and usu. small, neat woman (cf. BAGGAGE *n.*[2]). **2** [1980s+] (US) the vagina.

pack a punch, to *phr.* [1920s+] (orig. US) to be capable of delivering a disabling, strong punch.

pack a rod, to *phr.* [1920s+] (US) to carry a gun (cf. PACK HEAT). [PACK *v.*[2] + ROD *n.*[1] (2)]

pack chitlins *v.* [1990s] (US Black) of a man, to be unable to maintain an erection during intercourse (cf. PACKER'S CLUB). [PACK *v.*[2] (1) + SE *chitlins*, pig's intestines (which are *de facto* soft)]

pack 'em/them *v.* [1950s+] (Aus.) to be frightened. [image of holding back fear-induced diarrhoea]

packer/pack *n.*[1] [late 19C–1940s] (Aus.) a *pack*horse. [abbr.]

packer *n.*[2] [1980s+] (US) a homosexual, esp. one who performs anal intercourse. [abbr. FUDGE-PACKER]

packer *n.*[3] [1980s+] (drugs) a thin stick, typically a chopstick, used to pack a cocaine pipe (cf. PUSHER *n.*[4]).

packer's club *n.* [1990s] (US Black) a generic term for men who are unable to maintain an erection during intercourse. [PACK CHITLINS]

packet *n.*[1] [late 16C–late 19C] a false report; thus *sell one a packet*, to hoax, to deceive, to lie (cf. GALLEY-PACKET). [SE *packet*, a bundle of letters; thus lit. a 'packet of lies']

packet *n.*[2] [1910s+] (orig. milit.) **1** a bullet or missile. **2** trouble, esp. in phr. *cop a packet*, to get into trouble.

packet *n.*[3] [1920s+] a large sum of money, esp. in phr. *make/ win a packet* (cf. BUNDLE *n.*[2]).

packet *n.*[4] [1960s+] (gay) the genitals, male or female (cf. BASKET *n.*[1]; BOX *n.*[6]).

packet, the *n.*[5] [1980s+] everything, the lot.

packet/parcel from Paris *phr.* [20C] (Aus./N.Z.) a baby. [? clichéd identification of France with sex, though not usu. with procreative intercourse]

packets *n.* [mid-19C] lies (cf. PACKETS!; SELL SOMEONE A PACKET). [abbr. SE *packet of lies*]

packets! *excl.* [mid-19C] a general expression of disbelief. [PACKETS]

pack guts to a barrel *see* CARRY GUTS TO A BARREL.

pack heat *v.* [1920s+] (US) to carry a gun. [PACK *v.*[2] + HEAT *n.*[3]]

packie *n.* [20C] (N.Z.) one who transports supplies by pack animal. [abbr. N.Z.E. *pack*man]

pack in *v.* [1940s+] to stop, to cease to function, to give up, to die.

packing *n.*[1] [late 19C+] food, esp. of poor quality; thus *packing-ken*, a café or restaurant.

packing *n.*[2] **1** [late 19C+] (US) carrying a gun. **2** [1990s] (US Black) having a large penis. [PACK *v.*[2]]

packing *n.*[3] **1** [1980s+] (US) performing anal intercourse (cf. PACK PEANUT BUTTER). **2** [1990s] (US Black) of a man, having sexual intercourse. [SE *pack in*, to fill]

packing death *phr.* [1950s+] (Aus.) terrified, frightened. [PACK 'EM]

packing it *phr.* [1990s] making a large amount of money. [PACKET *n.*[3]]

pack it in *v.* [1920s+] to stop doing something, usu. as a command (cf. PACK THE GAME IN). [SE *pack*, to put away]

pack mud v. [1970s+] (gay) to have anal intercourse (cf. PACK PEANUT BUTTER).

pack of jacks n. [mid-19C] (US) a pack of cards.

pack of poo tickets n. [1990s] (Aus.) a lavatory roll. [punning on POO n.¹/LIKE A PAKAPOO TICKET]

pack of rockets n. [1940s–50s] (drugs) a packet of marijuana cigarettes.

pack one's coozie, to phr. [1960s] (drugs) to conceal drugs in the vagina. [SE *pack* + COOZE (1)]

pack one's keyster, to phr. [1960s] (drugs) to conceal drugs in the anus or vagina. [SE *pack* + KEISTER n. (4)]

pack one's nose, to phr. [1980s+] (drugs) to snort cocaine.

pack one's palm, to phr. [1990s] to masturbate.

pack peanut butter, to phr. [1970s+] (US) to engage in anal intercourse. [the colour of the spread]

pack rat n. [20C] (US) **1** an obsessive hoarder. **2** a hotel bell-boy. [SE *pack rat*, the US bushy-tailed woodrat, known for its collecting of objects]

pack the banner see CARRY THE BANNER.

pack the game in, to phr. [1920s+] to stop doing something (cf. PACK IT IN).

pack them see PACK 'EM.

pack the trail, to phr. [late 19C+] (Aus.) to journey along a trail, on foot or horseback. [SE *pack*, a rucksack]

pack up v. [1910s+] (orig. milit.) **1** to tire, to abandon one's efforts. **2** of a person, to die. **3** of machinery, or of anything that works mechanically, e.g. the human heart, to stop working.

pack up one's alls/awls and be gone, to phr. [mid-17C–1900s] to leave for good. [SE *alls*, everything, or *awls*, tools]

pack up one's pipes see PUT UP ONE'S PIPES.

packy n. [1940s+] (W.I.) the skull, the head (cf. OPEN PACKY). [dial. *packy*, the calabash fruit, which resembles the human head]

pad n.¹ **1** [mid-16C–mid-19C] (Und.) the road (cf. HIGH PAD; LOW PAD). **2** [mid-16C–mid-19C] (Und.) highway robbery (cf. ON THE PAD). **3** [mid-16C–mid-19C] (Und.) a highway robber (cf. GENTLEMAN OF THE PAD; KNIGHT OF THE PAD; SQUIRE OF THE PAD). **4** [early 17C–19C] an easy-paced horse. **5** [mid-19C] a walk. [Du. *pad*, and OHG *pfad*, the cant equivalent of the SE *path*]

pad n.² **1** [18C+] a bed. **2** [1930s+] a place, house or apartment, e.g. a prostitute's room (cf. CRASH-PAD; CRIB n.³) **3** [1930s+] (US Und.) a cell (cf. DEN n.²; HOUSE n.¹). **4** [1930s–60s] a padded cell. [SE *pad*, a mattress; best known in 20C in drug context, it was orig. used for the bed or couch on which an opium smoker could recline. It was then applied to an opium den, and after that was a beatnik term for a place where one could smoke cannabis]

pad n.³ [late 18C+] an Irishman. [abbr. PADDY n.¹]

pad n.⁴ [1940s+] (Aus.) a large amount, a great deal (cf. BUNDLE n.²). [SE *pad*, a bundle]

pad n.⁵ [1960s+] (US) **1** an establishment that pays bribes to the local police. **2** the regular bribes paid to members of a US police department; thus *on the pad*, eligible to receive such bribes. [SE *pad* (of paper), on which the payments are listed]

pad v.¹ [early 17C+] to travel as a tramp or vagrant. [PAD n.¹ (1)]

pad v.² [mid-17C–mid-19C] to work as a highway robber on foot or on horseback. [PAD n.¹ (2), (3)]

pad v.³ [1950s–70s] (US Black) to live somewhere. [PAD n.² (2)]

pad a bill, to phr. [1960s+] fraudulently to add items to a bill or to an expense account statement in order to obtain money that one is not actually owed.

pad borrower n. [late 18C–early 19C] a horse thief. [PAD n.¹ (4) + ironic use of SE *borrow* (cf. LIBERATE)]

padded adj. [1950s+] (drugs) concealing drugs or other contraband on one's body for international smuggling.

padder n. [16C] **1** a highwayman (cf. HIGH PAD). **2** a beggar (cf.

PAD n.¹). [Rowlands differentiates between the types of high-way thief: 'Such as robbe on horse-backe were called high lawyers, and those who robbed on foote ... called Padders']

padders n. [19C] the feet. [PAD n.¹ (1)/SE *pad*, to walk]

padding n.¹ **1** highway robbery. **2** working as a highway robber. [PAD n.¹ (2), (3)]

padding n.² [early 18C] talk, conversation. [ety. unknown; ? PAD n.¹ (1); i.e. conversation that accompanies walking]

padding crib n. [19C] **1** (Und.) a lodging house (cf. PADDING KEN). **2** (US Und.) a place to hide or to rest. [PAD n.² + CRIB n.³ (1)]

padding ken n. [mid-19C] (Und.) a lodging house frequented primarily by vagrants or thieves. [PAD n.² + KEN n.¹]

Paddington fair/fair day n. [late 17C–early 19C] the hanging day, the day of execution (cf. DANCE THE PADDINGTON FRISK; PADDINGTON SPECTACLES). [Tyburn, the site of London's main 18C gallows, was in the then village of *Paddington*. The phr. is also a grim pun on the actual Paddington Fair]

Paddington spectacles n. [late 18C–early 19C] the hood that is pulled over the condemned man's head before the hanging (cf. PADDINGTON FAIR).

paddist n. [late 17C–late 18C] (Scot.) a highwayman. [PAD n.¹ (3)]

paddle n. [mid-19C+] **1** the hand. **2** the fingers.

paddle v.¹ [mid-19C] to run away, to leave. [SE *paddle*, to walk with short, uncertain steps, to toddle]

paddle v.² [late 19C] to drink strong liquor. [? SE *paddle*, to walk in shallow water]

paddlefoot n. [1940s+] (US) an infantryman. [he 'paddles about']

paddler n.¹ [late 19C–1930s] a paddleboat. [abbr.]

paddler n.² [1940s+] (Aus.) a policeman (cf. WALLOPER n.¹). [SE *paddle*, to beat, implying violence]

paddle the pickle, to phr. [1990s] to masturbate. [SE *paddle*, to beat with a paddle]

Paddo n. [1940s+] (Aus.) the suburb of *Padd*ington, Sydney. [abbr. + sfx. -O (4)]

pad down/out v. [1930s+] (US) to go to bed, to sleep (cf. SACK OUT). [PAD n.²]

paddy/Paddy n.¹ **1** [late 18C+] an Irishman (cf. MICK n.¹). **2** [20C] (US) a bricklayer. **3** [20C] (Aus.) a Chinese person. **4** [1940s+] (US Black) a White man, though not always Irish. **5** [1940s+] (US Black) a policeman. [all race-related usages are derog.; common Irish name, *Patrick*; the occupations are those considered to be stereotypically Irish. (3) uses *Paddy* as generic for any foreigner]

paddy n.² [late 19C] a hobby, a fad, a pastime. [pun on PAD n.¹ (4) = horse, i.e. a hobby horse]

paddy n.³ [late 19C+] a tantrum, a fit of temper. [the supposed irritability of an Irishman (see PADDY n.¹)]

paddy n.⁴ [late 19C+] (Aus.) a smacking, usu. of a child. [SE *paddle*]

paddy n.⁵ [1940s–50s] (prison) a padded cell for mentally disturbed prisoners. [PAD n.² (4)]

paddy and mick adj. [20C] stupid. [rhy. sl. *paddy and mick* = THICK adj.¹; stereotyping of Irish names]

paddy/paddy's funeral n. [20C] any boisterous occasion, not necessarily a wake (cf. IRISH WAKE).

paddy/paddy's land n. [mid-19C] Ireland (cf. MURPHY LAND). [PADDY n.¹ (1) + SE *land*]

Paddy McGinty's goat n. [1950s+] (N.Z.) everyone, 'Tom, Dick and Harry'.

paddy quick n. [mid-late 19C] **1** a stick. **2** a kick. [rhy. sl.]

paddy quick adj. [mid-19C] stupid. [rhy. sl.; *Paddy Quick* = THICK adj.¹]

paddy-row n. [early 19C–1910s] a fight that entails more verbal than physical aggression. [PADDY n.³ + SE *row*]

paddy's apple n. [1920s+] (N.Z.) a potato. [PADDY n.¹ (1) + SE *apple*]

paddy's eyewater n. [20C] (Irish) illicitly distilled whisky, poteen. [PADDY n.¹ (1) + *eyewater*]

paddy's funeral see PADDY FUNERAL.

Paddy's Goose n. [mid-19C] the White Swan public house in High Street, Shadwell, the best known seaman's pub in mid-19C London. [? its Irish landlord. One landlord had a sinister reputation: 'During the Crimean War he recruited for the navy with conspicuous success, "in a small steamer with a band of music and flags", but did not long remain on good terms with authority' (Chesney)]

paddy's land see PADDY LAND.

paddy's lantern n. [1930s+] the moon. [PADDY n.¹ (1) + SE *lantern*; ? a ref. to the lack of electricity in rural Ireland]

paddy's market n. (Aus.) **1** [late 19C] the weekly market for cheap or secondhand goods held in the late 19C near Haymarket Square in Melbourne. **2** [20C] any kind of cheap market. [PADDY n.¹ (1) + SE *market*; note WW2 milit. use, the market in Cairo where Australian troops sold illegally manufactured goods, black market commodities etc.]

paddy's toothache see IRISH TOOTHACHE.

paddy's watch see PADDYWHACK ALMANAC.

paddy wagon n. [1920s+] (orig. US) the vehicle in which arrested people are transported to the local police station or prison. [? abbr. SE *padlock*, or PADDY n.¹ (1), with the implication that most US police would be Irish]

paddy ward's pig n. [mid-18C–mid-19C] a lazy person, one who is relaxing. [anecdotal]

paddywax n. [1910s–20s] a severe beating. [var. on PADDY-WHACK n.²; but note PADDY n.¹ + WAX v.¹ (1)].

paddywhack n.¹ **1** [late 18C–early 19C] a large, brawny Irishman. **2** [late 19C+] (Irish) stage or 'professional' Irishism, e.g. much use of 'Sure an' beggorrah, sorr ...'. [PADDY n.¹ (1) + WHACK n.¹]

paddywhack n.² **1** [late 19C+] a severe beating. **2** [late 19C] a rage, a passionate outburst of temper. [PADDY n.³ + WHACK n.¹]

paddywhack n.³ see PADDYWHACK ALMANAC.

paddywhack v. [late 19C+] to beat severely. [PADDYWHACK n.² (1)]

paddywhack almanac/paddy's watch/paddywhack n. [late 19C] an unlicensed almanac. [PADDYWHACK n.¹ (1); such an almanac 'comes the PADDY n.¹ over', i.e. confuses its user]

padhouse n. [1930s–40s] (US Black) one's house, one's home. [PAD n.² (2)]

pad it v. [early 17C–late 19C] to travel on foot, to walk, esp. as a vagrant or person seeking work (cf. PAD v.¹).

padlock n. [1960s–70s] the penis. [rhy. sl. *padlock* = COCK n.²(1)]

pad money n. [1900s–20s] (US) money for a night's lodging or for admission into an opium den. [PAD n.² (2)]

pad of cold cream n. [1940s] (US Black/South) an ice-cream parlour. [PAD n.² (2)]

pad of dry scarfs n. [1940s] (US Black/South) a grocery store (cf. PAD OF WET SCARFS). [PAD n.² (2) + SCARF n.]

pad of galloping snapshots n. [1940s] (US Black/South) a cinema. [PAD n.² (2)]

pad of stiffs n. [1940s] (US Black) a funeral parlour. [PAD n.² (2) + STIFF n.³ (1)]

pad of stitches n. [1940s–70s] (US Black) a hospital. [PAD n.² (2) + SE (*surgical*) *stitches*]

pad of togs-in-the-rough n. [1940s] (US Black/South) a tailor's shop. [PAD n.² (2) + TOGS (1) + SE *in the rough*, unfinished]

pad of wet scarfs n. [1940s] (US Black/South) a restaurant (cf. PAD OF DRY SCARFS). [PAD n.² (2) + SCARF]

pad out see PAD DOWN.

padre n. [mid-19C+] a (milit.) chaplain. [Sp. *padre*, father, thus a priest]

pad room n. [1930s–50s] (drugs) a room in which drug users can gather and use their drugs. [PAD n.² (2)]

pads n.¹ [1940s–50s] (prison) a padded cell (cf. PADDY n.⁵). [abbr. SE *padded cell*]

pads n.² [1940s–50s] (US) car licence plates. [affixed to the front and back, they 'pad' the car]

pad the bricks see HIT THE BRICKS.

pad the hoof, to phr. [18C+] to walk, to travel on foot; thus *hoof-padder*, a pedestrian (cf. BANG THE HOOF). [PAD v.¹ + HOOF n.]

pad the wall, to phr. [1930s] to lean one's chair against the wall of a bar, restaurant, club etc.

paff! excl. [mid-19C–1920s] an excl. of contemptuous dismissal.

pag n. [20C] (Ulster) a useless individual. [Ulster dial. *paughle*, a fat, lazy person]

pagnol see PAYOL.

paid adj. [mid-17C] drunk. [obs. SE *paid*, satisfied, content]

paik v. [20C] (Ulster) to beat up, to thrash. [Scot. + northern UK dial. *paik*, to beat]

pail n. [1940s] (US Black) the stomach.

pain/pain in the neck n.¹ [20C] a cheque. [rhy. sl.]

pain n.² [1930s+] anything or anyone considered unpleasant, typically a task one does not wish to perform, a bore, often ext. as *pain in the arm/back/balls/bum/penis* etc.

painful adj. [1980s+] (US campus) bad.

pain in the ass/arse/p.i.t.a. n. [1960s+] an annoying person; thus *give someone a pain in the ass*, to irritate someone.

pain in the neck n.¹ see PAIN n.¹.

pain in the neck n.² [1930s+] an annoying person, a euph. for PAIN IN THE ASS.

paint n. [1940s+] (Aus.) cheap red wine (cf. PINKIE n.³).

paint v.¹ [mid-19C] to drink.

paint v.² [1980s+] (US gay) to have a bowel movement during anal intercourse.

paint-brush baronet n. [late 19C] (society) an ennobled artist.

painted mischief n. [late 19C] playing cards. [the neg. image of card-playing]

painted peeper/peepers n. [19C] a black eye, a pair of black eyes (cf. PEEPERS IN MOURNING). [SE *painted* + PEEPERS n. (1)]

painter stainers n. [late 19C] (society) artists. [a remark made by the Lord Mayor at the Royal Academy banquet of 1883, when he referred to the ancient company of *Painter Stainers*, suggesting that it was the predecessor of the Royal Academy]

painting the cat phr. [1990s] (US teen) a response used when asked a completely obvious question about what one is doing.

paint remover n. [20C] (orig. US) **1** cheap, strong whisky. **2** strong, bitter coffee.

paint someone's eye for them, to phr. [late 19C] to give someone a black eye (cf. PAINTED PEEPER).

paint the ceiling, to phr. [1990s] to masturbate (cf. CREATE AN ARCH). [for those who ejaculate upwards]

paint the pickle, to phr. [1990s] to masturbate.

paint the town pink, to phr. [1900s–20s] (orig. US) to go on a spree. [play on PAINT THE TOWN RED]

paint the town red, to phr. [late 19C+] (orig. US) to go on a spree (cf. PAINT THE TOWN PINK). [? the excesses of the Marquis of Waterford and a bunch of aristocratic vandals who on the night of 5–6 April 1837 literally painted Waterford red, daubing the buildings with paint]

paipsey adj. [20C] (W.I.) insipid, weak, unattractive. [? UK dial. *papes*, a flour and water gruel, also a foolish youth; ult. SE *pap*, soft or semi-liquid food for infants or invalids]

pair *n.* [1940s+] the female breasts.

pair, to be a *v.* [1910s+] an often joking accusation, to be as bad as each other, usu. in phr. *you/they are a pair.*

pair of bastards on a raft *phr.* [1910s] (N.Z.) two poached eggs on toast.

pair of compasses *n.* [late 19C] the human legs, esp. when accentuated by the tight trousers fashionable *c.*1880.

pair of footprints *n.* [1930s+] (Aus.) a pipe-wrench. [when opened they are wide at the end and narrow in the middle, like a footprint]

pair off with *v.* [mid-19C] to marry.

pair of hands *n.* [mid-17C] a man. [metonymy]

pair of lawn sleeves *n.* [mid-19C] a bishop. [metonymy, i.e. a bishop's vestments]

pair of pants *see* PANTS *n.*².

pair of tongs *n.* [late 19C–1900s] a very thin person.

pair of wheels *n.* [early 17C] a two-wheeled vehicle.

pair of wings *n.* [late 18C–early 19C] (Und.) a pair of oars.

pair o' round-mys *n.* [late 19C] a pair of trousers. [rhy. sl. *round my houses* = trousers]

paisa/piesa/pisa *n.* [1940s–50s] (W.I.) money. [Hind. *paisa*, the lowest denomination of coin, 100 to the rupee]

paisan *n.* [20C] an Italian, usu. used by fellow members of that race in an affectionate and congratulatory manner (cf. LANDS-MAN). [Ital. *paisan*, a peasant]

Pak *n.* [1950s+] **1** *Pak*istan. **2** a derog. term for a *Pak*istani (cf. PAKI). [abbr.]

pakalolo *n.* [1980s+] (US drugs) marijuana. [Hawaiian]

paki/pakki *n.* [1960s+] a derog. term for any British Asian or East African Asian immigrant (cf. PAK). [abbr. *Pak*istani]

paki-basher *n.* [1960s+] a racist who beats up Asians (cf. FAG-BASHER). [PAKI + SE *basher*]

paki-bashing *n.* [1960s+] racially motivated attacks on the UK Asian community, usu. by White youths (cf. QUEER-BASHING). [PAKI + SE *bashing*]

paki pox *n.* [1960s] a derog. term for smallpox. [its supposed prevalence, in racist eyes, among the era's Pakistani (in fact more likely Bangladeshi or East African Indian) immigrants]

Pakistani black *n.* [1960s+] (drugs) hashish from Pakistan. [it is a blackish-brown colour]

pakki *see* PAKI.

pal *n.* [late 17C+] a friend, an accomplice. [Rom. *pal*, a brother]

palace of pleasure *n.* [19C] the vagina (cf. GENTLEMAN'S PLEASURE-GARDEN).

palam-pam *see* PAM-PALAM.

palampo *n.* [mid-19C] (Anglo-Ind.) a quilt, a bedspread. [? proper name *Palanpore*, an Indian town renowned for its manufacture of chintz counterpanes]

palari *see* PARLYAREE.

palarie *n. see* PARLYAREE.

palarie *v.* [mid-19C] (tramp/circus) to talk, to speak (cf. PARLYAREE). [Ital. *parlare*, to talk]

palatic/parlatic *adj.* [late 19C+] drunk (cf. ADDLED). [PARA-LYTIC; 20C use is mainly Irish]

palava *n.* [1970s] (W.I.) an argument, a row (cf. PLABA). [PAL-AVER *n.*]

palaver *n.* **1** [early 18C+] (orig. Ling. Fr./Polari) chat, talk, conversation. **2** [early 18C+] wearisome, idle talk. **3** [19C] (Scot.) a fussy, ostentatious person, usu. as *old palaver.* **4** [late 19C–1950s] business, concern, goings-on; thus *none of your palaver*, no business of yours. [Port. *palabra*, speech, talk. The term was used by Port. traders on the West Coast of Africa, where it was picked up by British sailors, incorporated into their jargon and thence to mainstream sl.]

palaver *v.* [early 18C+] (orig. Ling. Fr./Polari) **1** to talk, to converse; thus *what a palaver*, what a fuss. **2** to ask (someone) for something, to beg from, to wheedle out of. [PALAVER *n.*]

palaver to someone for *v.* [mid-19C] to beg for, to demand. [PALAVER *v.*]

pale *n.* **1** [mid-19C] brandy. **2** [1900s–40s] (US Black) a White person.

paled/paled out *adv.* [1960s+] (Can. teen) intoxicated by drink or drugs. [one's complexion]

paleface *n.* [1940s+] (orig. US Black) a White person (cf. BLANCO). [SE *paleface*, supposedly used by Native Americans to describe White settlers, but rarely found other than in fiction]

paleface nigger *n.* [1940s+] (US Black) a highly unpopular White person, whose skin does not save them from the opprobrium usu. heaped on Blacks. [PALEFACE + NIGGER *n.*]

Palestine in London *n.* [early–mid-19C] St Giles, Bloomsbury, mainly occupied by the poor Irish and a well-known criminal slum (cf. HOLY LAND).

palette *n.* [late 18C–mid-19C] the hand.

palimony *n.* [1970s+] compensation claimed by a deserted partner after a couple who are not married, but have lived together for some time, split up, usu. the province only of the rich and/or famous. [PAL + SE *alimony*]

palone/paloney *see* POLONE.

pall *v.*¹ [mid-19C] to stop, to cease; thus *pall that!*, stop that!; *you pall me*, you confound me. [orig. naut. jargon *pawl*, a short bar that locks the windlass or capstan and stops it from unwinding]

pall *v.*² [mid–late 19C] to detect (cf. PAWL). [ety. unknown; ? link to SE *paw*, to handle]

palled *adj.* [mid-19C] not daring to say any more. [SE *ap-palled*]

palled-in *adv.* [late 19C+] of a man, living with a woman. [PAL]

palliard *n.* **1** [late 15C–late 18C] a professional beggar (cf. CANTING CREW). **2** [mid-19C] (US) a beggar-woman who uses a child, either her own or one borrowed for the purpose, to excite the pity of passers-by (this pity often increased by the child's piteous cries, created by judicious pinches and prods). [Fr. *paille*, straw, upon which the beggars slept as they wandered the country, taking nightly refuge in barns or outhouses. The antithesis of the UPRIGHT MAN, palliards adorned themselves with faked but still convincingly hideous sores and wounds. Their clothes were invariably ragged, and their patched cloaks almost a badge of office. The term emerged *c.*1484, alongside its SE definition, 'a low or dissolute knave; a lewd fellow, a lecher, a debauchee' (*OED*)]

palliasse *n.* [19C] a prostitute. [SE *palliasse*, a straw bed or mattress]

pall mall *n.* [late 19C–1900s] a woman. [rhy. sl. in Cockney pron. *Pall Mall* = *gal* = girl]

pally *n.* [1920s+] a dance-hall. [*Palais de Dance*]

pally *adj.* [1910s+] friendly, affectionate (cf. CHUMMY *adj.*). [PAL]

palm *v.* [19C+] to pass over money as a bribe; thus *palmed*, used of one who has been bribed.

palmer *n.* **1** [late 17C–late 19C] a cheat who palms cards, dice etc. **2** [mid-19C] a shoplifter. **3** [mid-19C] a beggar who visits shops and claims to be collecting halfpence engraved with a harp, offering the shopkeeper thirteen pence for a shilling's worth and persuading them to empty all their coppers on the counter. While they search the pile, the palmer hides as many coins as possible. [SE *palm*, to conceal in the palm of one's hand; (2) also puns on SE *palmer*, an itinerant monk, bound by vows of eternal poverty]

palmer house *v.* [1930s–40s] (US Black) to walk flat-footed; thus *palmer houses*, flat feet. [the walking done by the hard-working waiters of Chicago's *Palmer House* Hotel]

palming *n.* [mid-19C] (Und.) the robbery of a shop by a pair of thieves, one engaging the shopkeeper in banter, the other committing the robbery. [PALMER *n.*³]

palming-racket *n.* [early 19C] (Und.) the concealing of money in one's palm. [SE *palm*, to conceal in one's palm]

palmistry *n.* [1910s–20s] bribery (cf. PALM OIL). [PALM v.]

palm oil/soap *n.* [mid-19C] money, usu. in the form of a bribe (cf. GOLDEN GREASE). [used to 'grease the palm']

palm-presser *n.* [20C] a politician who attempts to curry favour and win votes by shaking hands with anyone they meet (cf. FLESH-PRESSER).

palm soap *see* PALM OIL.

palooka *n.* [1920s+] **1** a boxer, usually one who is both large and stupid. **2** a large and stupid person. [coined by Jack Conway (d.1928) of *Variety* magazine, and given wide currency by Ham Fisher's comic strip 'Joe Palooka' (launched 1930)]

palsy *n.* [1930s+] (US) a friend, esp. as form of address. [ext. of PAL]

palsy-walsy *adj.* [1930s+] overly friendly. [PAL + redup.]

pam *n.* [late 17C–18C] **1** the knave of clubs. **2** a popular card-game. [Fr. *pamphile*, a card-game in which the knave of clubs is the highest card, trumping all opposition; ult. Gk. *pamphilos*, beloved of all. The Fr. game was imported to Scot., where *pamphie* and *pawnie* were popular alternatives, both meaning knave of clubs, and to England, where *pam* became the term of choice]

Pam and her five sisters *n.* [1990s] the hand as an agency of masturbation. [pun on *Pam*/*palm*]

pam-palam/palam-pam *n.* [1970s+] (W.I.) fuss, confusion, disorder. [Twi *pam*, the report of a gun; *pam-pam*, to drive away]

pam-pam *n.* [1940s] (W.I.) **1** a flogging. **2** an argument, a fuss, a noisy disorder. [echoic; but note Twi *pam*, to chase away, and *pam-pam*, to persecute, to drive away]

pamper *v.* [20C] (W.I./Bdos.) to feel the sting of a lashing. [? W.I. *pam-palam*, a child's term, used to register their amusement of another child's punishment]

Pamper pirate/sniffer *n.* [20C] (US Und.) a child molester. [*Pampers*, brandname of a line of disposable nappies or diapers + SE *pirate*/*sniffer*]

pampoen *n.* [1940s+] (S.Afr.) a fool (sometimes used affectionately) (cf. NANA n.). [Cape Du. *pampoen*, pumpkin]

pampootie *n.* [1900s] (Irish) a slipper. [Irish *pamúpta*, a basic leather shoe, but note Fr. *pantouffle*, a slipper]

pan, the *n.*[1] [18C] a bed. [ety. unknown; E.P. suggests Rom. *pan*, to shut, to fasten, but note SE *pane*, a counterpane, or architectural *pan*, a wooden framework]

pan *n.*[2] [mid-late 19C] the workhouse, esp. the St Pancras workhouse (cf. LUMP n. (3); SPINNIKEN). [abbr. St *Pan*cras]

pan, the *n.*[3] [20C] (Ulster) a frying pan of food, a fry-up.

pan *n.*[4] [1920s+] the human face. [BRAINPAN]

pan *v.*[1] [late 19C] (US/Colonial) to catch. [SE *pan*, to sieve silt for gold]

pan *v.*[2] **1** [1910s+] (orig. US) to criticize severely, to denigrate (cf. PANNING). **2** [1940s+] to hit in the face. [the blow is lit. or fig. given with a SE *pan*]

pan *v.*[3] [1950s+] (US) to survey, to look around. [film jargon, to move the camera in an arc, ult. abbr. SE *panorama*]

Panama cut/gold/red *n.* [1960s+] (drugs) a variety of marijuana, grown in Panama.

panarly *see* PARLYAREE.

panatella *n.* [1930s–60s] (drugs) **1** high-grade marijuana, esp. that imported from South or Central America. **2** a large marijuana cigarette, resembling a cigar. [Am. Sp. *panatella*, a long slender cigar tapering at the sealed end]

panatrope *n.* [1910s–30s] a hermaphrodite. [Gk. *panatrope*, turning in every direction]

pancake *n.*[1] **1** [19C+] the vagina (cf. APPLE n.[10]). **2** [1930s+] (US) an attractive young woman (cf. BANANA n.[2]).

pancake *n.*[2] [late 19C–1940s] (US Black) a Black person viewed as overly friendly towards, or imitative of Whites (cf. UNCLE TOM n.). [SE *pancake*, cooked brown on the outside but still white within]

pancake *n.*[3] [1950s] (gay) a masculine lesbian who permits herself to take the passive role. [she is 'flipped' from TOP n.[3] to BOTTOM n.[4]]

pancake *v.* [1980s+] (US Black/teen) to lower the body of an automobile. [making it 'flat as a pancake']

pancakes! *excl.* [1910s–20s] used in phr. to convey one's derision for what has just been said, e.g. *She's a pretty girl. Pretty, pancakes!* (cf. BOLLOCKS!; MY FOOT!).

pancakes and syrup *n.* [1950s+] (drugs) a combination of glutetimide and codeine cough syrup.

pancake turner *n.* [1940s+] (US) a disk jockey. [joc. equation of a pancake with a record]

pancridge parson *n.* [early 17C–late 18C] a general term of contempt. [corruption of St *Pancras*, London, where the clergy were presumably held in low esteem]

pancrocked *adj.* [20C] (Ulster) exhausted. [ety. unknown; ? link to CROCKED]

panda/panda car *n.* [1960s–70s] a type of police patrol car painted black and white and thus supposedly reminiscent of the markings of the giant panda.

p and q *n.* [20C] (US Und.) solitary confinement. [abbr. *peace and* quiet]

pane *see* WINDOWPANE n.[2].

panel *n.* [19C] a prostitute (cf. PANEL CRIB). [PARNEL]

panel *v.* [20C] to attack, to beat up. [SE *panel-beat*]

panel-beater *see* BODY-BASHER.

panel crib/den/house *n.* [19C] a brothel, esp. one which specializes in robbing the clients (cf. BADGER-CRIB; HOOK HOUSE). [PANEL GAME + CRIB n.[3] (2); such brothels were supplied with false panels that permitted access to the prostitute's room so that the client could be robbed or beaten up]

panel dodger *see* PANEL THIEF.

panel game *n.* [mid-19C] (US Und.) the robbing of a prostitute's client by stealing his possessions while he is having sex (cf. BADGER n.[4]). [for ety. *see* PANEL CRIB]

panel house *see* PANEL CRIB.

panel joint *n.* [19C] a brothel that features mirrors on ceilings, two-way mirrors in walls etc. [the false SE *panels*]

panel thief/dodger *n.* [mid–late 19C] (US) a thief, usu. the accomplice of a prostitute, who takes advantage of her client's preoccupation to rob him, using a special panel to enter her room (cf. BADGER n.[4]). [PANEL GAME + SE *thief*/*dodger*]

panem *see* PANNAM.

pan for white gold, to *phr.* [1990s] to masturbate.

pang *v.* [20C] (Ulster) to cram full. [Scot.]

pangonadalot *n.* [1970s] (drugs) heroin. [ety. unknown]

panhandle *n.*[1] [mid-19C+] (US) the act of begging; thus the *panhandle beat*, the world of beggary; *work the panhandle*, to beg. [SE *pan*, into which the charitable donor placed money, or the goldfields, where hopefuls panned for gold, washing earth and rocks in perforated 'pans']

panhandle *n.*[2] [1990s] **1** an erect penis. **2** a fool, an unpleasant person (cf. DICKHEAD). [resemblance; (2) is fig. use of (1)]

panhandle *v.* [20C] (US) to beg. [PANHANDLE n.[1]]

panhandler *n.* [19C+] (US) a professional beggar. [PANHANDLE v.]

pan-head *n.* [1940s] (W.I.) a district constable (cf. PAN KIBBA). [the resemblance of their badge to a pan-lid]

pania *n.* [20C] (W.I./Belize) a Belizian of Spanish descent (cf. PANYA). [*Spania*rd; such individuals are seen as setting themselves aside from mainstream Belize society and culture]

panic *n.* [1930s+] (drugs) a period when drugs are hard to purchase; thus *panic man*, a dealer or a drug addict who is desperate for supplies.

panic button *n.* [1950s+] any form of switch or button that summons emergency aid, shuts down malfunctioning machinery etc; thus [1960s+] *hit the panic button*, to panic, to summon aid (lit. or fig.).

panicked out *adj.* [1970s+] (US) in a complete panic.

panicky *adj.* [1940s] (US Black) extremely elated, ecstatically happy, highly excited.

panic party *n.* [1940s+] (Aus.) any sudden move. [WW1 naut. use *panic party*, the apparent abandoning of a decoy or Q-ship by its crew with the attention of luring a submarine to the surface. If the submarine did surface, it would be attacked by those members of the crew who had remained hidden on board]

panic stations *n.* [1960s+] a crisis, a drama. [orig. naval use and punning on 'action stations'. Note also milit. *panic party*, a rush move]

pan kibba *n.* [1940s] (W.I.) a district constable (cf. PAN-HEAD). [SE *pan cover*]

pannam / panem / pannum / pennam *n.* [16C–mid-19C] (Und.) bread; thus [mid-19C] *pannam-fencer*, a street pastry-seller. [Lat. *panis*/Fr. *pain*, bread]

pannam bound *v.* [mid-19C] to stop the issue of rations to a prisoner. [PANNAM + SE *bound*]

pannam-struck *adj.* [mid-19C] (Und.) very hungry. [PANNAM + SE *struck*]

panney/panny *n.*[1] [mid-18C–mid-19C] the highway. [ety. unknown; ? Rom.]

panney/panny *n.*[2] [late 18C–early 19C] (Und.) **1** a house. **2** a burglary; thus *do a panny*, rob a house. [? SE *butler's pantry*, the repository of the silverware and similar valuables]

panney-/panny-lay *n.* [early 19C–1910s] burglary, housebreaking. [PANNEY n.[2] + LAY n.[4] (2)]

pannikin *n.* [late 19C–1930s] (Aus.) the head. [SE *pannikin*, a small iron drinking vessel]

pannikin boss/panno *n.* [late 19C+] (Aus.) a minor official, a 'jack-in-office'. [SE *pannikin*, a small drinking vessel + SE *boss* or abbr. *pannikin* + sfx. -O; the image is of one who was allowed to serve water to a gang of convicts]

panning *n.* [1930s+] a very harsh review (cf. PAN v.[2]).

panno *see* PANNIKIN BOSS.

pannum *see* PANNAM.

panny *n.*[1] *see* PANNEY n.[1].

panny *n.*[2] *see* PANNEY n.[2].

panny *n.*[3] [late 19C] a fight between two or more women. [PANEL v. ? + link to the women who work in a PANEL CRIB]

panny-lay *see* PANNEY-LAY.

pannyman *n.* [19C] a housebreaker, a burglar. [PANNEY n.[2] (2) + SE sfx. -*man*]

panorama *n.* [late 19C] a lover. [corruption of SE *paramour*]

pan out *v.* **1** [mid-19C+] (orig. US) to work out, to result in. **2** [late 19C] (Aus./US) to hand over (money). [SE *pan*, to sieve silt for gold]

pansy *n.* [20C] an effeminate homosexual man (cf. BUTTERCUP).

pansy up *v.* [1930s–70s] of a man, to titivate oneself in an effeminate manner. [PANSY]

panter *n.* [late 18C–early 19C] **1** a hart or male deer. **2** the human heart. [the line 'As pants the hart for cooling streams/ When heated in the chase' (Nahum Tate and Nicholas Brady, *New Version of the Psalms*, 1696); ult. f. Ps. 42:1, 'As the hart panteth after the water brooks so panteth my soul after thee, O God'. The pun indicates, as does B.E., that (2) is the general use. However, Grose (1785) cites 'the animal' and adds 'the human heart, which temporarily pants in times of danger' only in 1796]

panters *n.* [late 19C–1900s] the female breasts (cf. LUNGS n.[2]). [their motion when breathing]

panther piss / milk / purge / sweat / panther *n.* [1930s+] strong home-brewed or cheap liquor, usu. gin.

panties *n.* **1** [mid-19C] pantaloons. **2** [20C] (US prison) the underwear worn by a prison homosexual.

pantile/pantiler *n.*[1] [18C] a religious dissenter; thus *pantile-house*, *pantile-shop*, a dissenters' meeting house. [SE *pantile*, a roofing tile; the meeting houses of rural dissenters were often roofed with pantiles]

pantile *n.*[2] [mid-19C] **1** a hat. **2** a hard biscuit, sometimes with jam spread on it. [SE *pantile*, a tile in an ogee shape, often used as a roofing tile]

pantile *adj.* [18C] dissenting. [PANTILE n.[1]]

pantile park *n.* [late 19C] London, as seen from a high window. [SE *pantile*, a roofing tile + SE *park*]

pantiler *see* PANTILE n.[1].

pantry *n.* [20C] (US) the stomach (cf. BREADBASKET).

pantry politics *n.* [late 19C] (society) servants' talk.

pants *n.*[1] **1** [mid-19C] pantaloons (cf. PANTIES). **2** [mid-19C+] (US) trousers.

pants/pair of pants *n.*[2] [1930s–40s] (US Black) a man. [metonymy]

pants *n.*[3] [1990s] nonsense, rubbish. [var. on KNICKERS!]

pants *v.* [1960s+] (mainly juv.) to remove someone's trousers whether they like it or not (cf. DE-BAG). [PANTS n.[1] (2)]

pants! *excl.* [1990s] nonsense! rubbish! [PANTS n.[3]]

pants and vest *n.* [20C] best (bitter beer). [rhy. sl.]

pants man *n.* [1960s+] (Aus.) a womanizer.

pants rabbit *n.* [1910s+] (US) a body louse (cf. SEAM SQUIRREL).

pantsula *n.* [1970s+] (S.Afr.) a township dandy whose life is dedicated to the purchase of expensive, fashionable clothes (cf. TSOTSI). [? S. Sotho *patsola*, to split open (referring to links with violent crime) or S. Sotho *pasola*, to slap, to strike sharply (with a whip) (referring to elements of typical dance styles]

pantyman *n.* [20C] (W.I.) an effeminate man, a homosexual. [the image of his wearing women's *panties*]

pantywaist *n.* [1930s+] (orig. US) a weak, effeminate man. [the image of his wearing women's *panties*]

panya *adj.* [1940s+] (W.I.) Spanish (cf. PANIA). [mispron. of *Spanish*]

pap *n.* [late 19C+] *paper* money. [abbr.; orig. UK but by mid-20C Aus. only]

pap *adj.* [1910s+] (S.Afr.) of persons or objects, weak, feeble. [Afk. *pap*, soft]

papa *n.* **1** [20C] (US Black) an affectionate name used by a woman to her husband, lover or pimp. **2** [1950s+] a masculine lesbian. **3** [1950s+] an older homosexual man. [SE *papa*, father]

papa!/poopa!/pupa! *excl.* [1960s+] (W.I.) **1** a general expression of surprise and approval. **2** an emphasis placed at the end of a sentence, the equivalent of SE *sir!*, esp. in excl. *no, sir!* [? Twi *papa*, very well, very much]

papa-tree-top-tall *n.* [1930s–40s] (US Black) an extremely tall man.

papbroek *n.* [1930s+] (S.Afr.) a coward, a weakling. [Afk. *pap*, soft + *broek*, trousers, breeches]

paper *n.*[1] **1** [late 18C+] free passes of admission to a theatre or other entertainment. **2** [late 18C+] the people who use these passes. **3** [late 19C–1920s] (US) marked cards. **4** [late 19C–1940s] (US) posters or similar publicity material. **5** [20C] any form of money order, IOU or financial document other than actual cash. **6** [20C] (US) a forged or useless cheque (cf. WALLPAPER). **7** [1950s+] a cigarette-paper. **8** [1990s] (US Black) money, usu. notes (cf. PAPES).

paper *n.*[2] [1950s+] (US drugs) **1** a measure of heroin, contained in a folded square of paper; the most common is the *quarter paper*, $25 worth of a narcotic (cf. BINDLE; FOLD n.). **2** a drug prescription.

paper *v.* **1** [mid-19C+] to boost an audience by giving out free passes to a show or entertainment; thus *papered*, filled by means of free passes. **2** [1920s+] (US) to pass bad cheques or any other form of fraudulent money-related document (cf. LAY v.⁴). [PAPER n.¹]

paper acid *n.* [1960s+] (drugs) LSD, esp. when dropped onto a square of blotting-paper, or when combined with another drug (cf. BLOTTER n.²).

paper bag *n.* [1960s+] (drugs) a container for drugs. [ext. of PAPER n.²]

paper bag *v.* [20C] to nag. [rhy. sl.]

paper belly *n.* [20C] (US) a non-drinker.

paper blunts *n.* [1980s+] (drugs) marijuana within a paper casing. [PAPER n.² + BLUNT n.²]

paper boy *n.* [1960s] (drugs) a heroin peddler. [PAPER n.²]

paper-chewing *n.* [1930s] bureaucracy.

paper-collar bushman *n.* [mid-late 19C] (N.Z.) a bush-boss who prefers supervising to any hard work. [for ety. *see* PAPER-COLLARED SWELL]

paper-collared swell *n.* [mid-late 19C] (N.Z.) a clerk, a 'white-collar worker'. [SE *paper collar*, as worn by clerks pretending to superior elegance + SWELL n.]

paper doll *n.* [1960s+] a promiscuous, sexually available woman. [rhy. sl. *paper doll* = MOLL n.]

paper doll *v.* [1960s–70s] (US) to play truant; thus phr. *make like a paper doll and cut*, go away. [pun on SE *cut out*/CUT OUT v.²]

paperer *n.* [late 19C] one who issues or receives free passes to a theatre or other entertainment. [PAPER n.¹]

paper-fake *v.* [mid-19C] to sell ballads on the street. [PAPER n.¹ + FAKE n.¹ (3)]

paper fiend *n.* [1940s–50s] (drugs) one who sucks the amphetamine-impregnated strips from an amphetamine inhaler. [PAPER n.² + FIEND n.²]

paper hanger *n.* [1910s+] (US Und.) one who habitually passes bad cheques; thus *paper-hanging*, passing dud cheques. [PAPER n.¹ (6) + pun]

paper maker *n.* [mid-19C] **1** a gatherer of rags and other saleable rubbish from the streets and gutters. **2** a beggar who poses as an agent of a paper-mill and is thus given cast-off rags, which are then sold for profit.

paper man *n.* [mid-19C] (Aus.) a convict holding a ticket of leave. [PAPERS n.² (2)]

paper marriage *n.* [late 19C] a society wedding. [the banknotes employed in funding it; there may be an added implication of *paper*, spurious, i.e. the marriage is for social convenience rather than love]

paper minister *n.* [mid-19C] (Scot.) a minister who reads rather than first learns their sermons.

paper mushrooms *n.* [1980s+] (drugs) LSD, esp. that which has been dropped onto blotting-paper. [the hallucinogenic qualities of certain mushrooms]

paper pusher *n.* [20C] a bureaucrat or clerk of the lowliest rank, the implication being that they never write on, only push around, paper (cf. PAPER STAINER).

papers *n.¹* [20C] (drugs) cigarette papers, esp. when used for rolling marijuana cigarettes.

papers *n.²* **1** [1940s+] (US Black) a marriage certificate and allied documents (cf. HAVE PAPERS ON). **2** [1950s+] (US prison) documents that deal with a prisoner's parole application.

paper skull/scull *n.* [late 18C–early 19C] a fool; thus *paper-skulled/-sculled*, foolish, simple. [lit. 'one with a paper-thin skull']

paper stainer *n.* [mid-late 19C] a clerk (cf. PAPER PUSHER). [SE *paper-stainer*, an author]

paper trunk and twine lock *n.* [late 19C] (US) the least possible amount of luggage, i.e. 'a bundle wrapped in paper and tied with string'.

paper worker *n.* [mid-19C] a street-seller of broadsides (cf. CHANTER). [PAPER n.¹ (4)]

paper yabber *n.* [20C] (Aus.) a letter. [SE *paper* + YABBER n.]

papes *n.* [1990s] (orig. US Black) money. [SE *paper*]

pap feeder *n.* [mid-19C] a spoon (cf. FEEDER n.¹). [SE *pap*, liquefied food given to babies and invalids]

paphian *n.* [19C] a prostitute. [*Paphos*, the city in south-western Cyprus, where it is claimed that Aphrodite, goddess of love, was born]

papiyot *n.* [20C] (W.I.) a weakling, a frail person, a useless opponent in a game. [Fr. *papillon*, a butterfly]

pappy *n.* [mid-18C–late 19C] (juv.) father, papa.

pappy guy *n.* [1920s] (US tramp) an old man. [PAPPY + GUY n.²]

pappy show *n. see* POPPY SHOW n.².

pappy-show *adj. see* POPPY SHOW adj.

pappy show *v. see* POPPY SHOW v.

para *n.* [1960s+] (Aus.) a *para*plegic (cf. SPASTIC). [abbr.]

para *adj.* [1980s+] *para*noid (cf. PARRO). [abbr.]

parable *n.* [late 19C] (US) a long, dreary, egotistical statement.

parachute *n.¹* [mid-19C] a parasol.

parachute *n.²* [1980s+] (drugs) a mixture of crack plus heroin or phencyclidine. [the 'slowness' of the heroin or phencyclidine reduces the 'speed' of the crack]

paracki *n.* [1950s+] (drugs) paraldehyde.

paradise *n.¹* [mid-19C] the upper gallery of a theatre, the 'gods' (cf. ETHIOPIAN PARADISE; NIGGER HEAVEN). [Fr. sl. *paradis*, the gods]

paradise/paradise white *n.²* [1980s+] (drugs) cocaine. [its effects]

paradise strokes *n.* [20C] for a man, the immediately pre-orgasmic thrusts of sexual intercourse.

paradise white *see* PARADISE n.

paraffin *n.* [20C] (S.Afr.) gin. [rhy. sl.]

paraffin lamp *n.* [20C] a tramp. [rhy. sl.]

parakeet *n.* [1960s] (US) a Puerto Rican. [their stereotyped noisiness and love of bright colours]

parallel parking *n.* [1980s+] (US preppie/campus) sexual intercourse.

paralysed *adj.* [1970s+] drunk (cf. ADDLED).

paralytic *adj.* [1910s+] (orig. Aus.) extremely drunk, to the point of passing out cold (cf. ADDLED).

param/parum *n.* [16C] milk. [var. on YARRUM]

parangles *n.* [1940s] (W.I.) bustle and confusion, trouble and worry, any bothersome, complicated situation. [UK dial. *peramble*, a rigmarole, ult. SE *preamble*. Legal papers, wills and similar material tend to begin with a summary preamble before moving to the detailed clauses]

paranoid *adj.* [1960s] frightened, worried, disturbed. [all non-clinical uses originated in 1960s hippie era, often occasioned by an excess of drug use; ult. SE *paranoia*, 'functional psychosis characterized by delusions of grandeur and persecution, but without intellectual deterioration' (C. Rycroft, *A Critical Dictionary of Psychoanalysis*, 1968)]

par-banging *n.* [late 19C] tramping the streets. [? Fr. *pavé*, the pavement + BANG v.¹ (1)]

parcel *n.* **1** [mid-19C+] (US) a small group, amount or collection. **2** [late 19C–1920s] a substantial sum of money, esp. when won or lost in gambling. **3** [late 19C] a British woman sold into a foreign brothel. **4** [20C] (Ulster) a difficult, troublesome person. **5** [1910s] (Aus. tramp) a rolled blanket which contains one's possessions.

parcel from Paris *see* PACKET FROM PARIS.

parcel post n. [1930s–50s] (Aus.) used in the Northern Territory to describe a person who is newly arrived and thus inexperienced. [? the image of an unwrapped parcel]

parchment dab n. [early 18C] a writ. [SE *parchment* + *dab*, a mark]

pard/pardner n. [late 19C+] (US) partner. [a classic 'Wild West' term, its 20C use is exclusively fictional, mainly in films]

pardon! excl. [late 19C+] excuse me. [abbr. SE *I beg your pardon*]

pardoner n. [16C] (Und.) a mendicant beggar posing as a seller of indulgences (cf. AURIUM). [SE *pardoner*, a person licensed to sell papal pardons or indulgences]

pardon me for breathing!/living! excl. [1940s+] an ironic or sarcastic excl. after one has been criticized for some minor error.

pardon my French phr. [1950s+] a 'genteel' euph., excuse my swearing (cf. EXCUSE MY FRENCH). [FRENCH adj. (1)]

Pare see PARRY.

parental units/units n. [1980s+] (US campus) parents (cf. RENTAL UNITS). [originating in the 'Coneheads' sketches on the TV show *Saturday Night Live*]

par for the course phr. [1940s+] as expected, predictable, nothing special. [golfing use]

parfum de corsage n. [1920s–30s] a euph. for the mixed odour of cosmetics and sweat that accrues to a woman participating energetically at a dance or ball. [Fr., lit. 'the perfume of (one's) corsage']

parings n. [late 17C–18C] the clippings of money (cf. CURLE).

Paris brothers n. [1950s–60s] (gay) homosexuals, esp. twins. [play on stereotyped views of French sexuality]

Paris bun n. [20C] a Protestant. [ety. unknown]

parish bull/prig n. [mid-19C] (Und.) a parson (cf. TOWN BULL). [SE *parish* + *bull*/PRIG n.¹]

parisheen n. [late 19C–1910s] (Irish) a child brought up by the parish. [SE *parish* + Irish dimin. sfx. -*een*]

parish lantern n. [mid-19C] the moon.

parish pick-axe n. [late 19C] a prominent nose.

parish prig see PARISH BULL.

parish rig n. [late 19C] (orig. naut.) **1** a badly-rigged ship. **2** an ill-dressed man. [SE *parish-rigged*, cheaply rigged; (2) is fig. use of (1)]

parish soldier n. [late 18C–mid-19C] a militia-man. [the hiring of substitutes by the parish in which the originally chosen militia-men lived]

parish stallion n. [late 19C] a parson (cf. PARISH BULL).

park n. [early–mid-19C] a prison.

park v.¹ [1950s+] (US) of a teenage couple, to park in a secluded spot for petting and, perhaps, sex.

park v.² [1960s–70s] (Ling. Fr./Polari) to ask, to speak, to beg (cf. PARKER v.²). [Ital. *parlare*, to speak]

park a custard, to phr. [1970s+] (society) to vomit.

park a darkie, to phr. [1990s] to defecate. [var. on CHOKE A DARKIE]

park a leopard/tiger, to phr. [1990s] to vomit. [the 'spotted' nature of the material that is vomited up]

park ape n. [1930s–40s] (US Black) an extremely unattractive and very dark-skinned person. [? ref. to apes in Central Park Zoo, New York City]

park a tiger see PARK A LEOPARD.

parker n. [late 19C] a well-dressed man, a dandy. [his strolling in the fashionable London parks]

parker v.¹ [late 19C+] (Ling. Fr./Polari) to pay; thus [late 19C] *parker from/with dinarly*, to pay one's debts. [Ital. *partire*, to pay out]

parker v.² [late 19C+] (Ling. Fr./Polari) to ask, to speak, to beg. [Ital. *parlare*, to speak]

parkering ninty n. [late 19C] wages. [PARKER v.¹ + NANTEE]

parkers n. [1960s+] (Aus.) parking lights.

parking n. [1950s+] (US) of a teenage couple, using the boy's car parked in a discreet spot for petting and possible intercourse. [PARK v.¹]

parking lot n. [1960s–70s] (US teen) the vagina. [play on PARK v.¹]

parking-meter bandit n. [1970s+] a petty thief (cf. BANDIT n.¹; INTERNATIONAL MILK THIEF).

parking place n. [20C] the buttocks. [one 'parks' them on a seat]

park one's fudge, to phr. [1990s] to defecate. [FUDGE n.²]

park-palings/-railings n. **1** [early–mid-19C] the teeth. **2** [late 19C] a neck of mutton. [SE *park* + *palings*, a fence/railings]

park the pink cadillac, to phr. [1990s] to have sexual intercourse.

Parktown prawn n. [1980s+] (S.Afr.) the king cricket (*Libanasidus vittatus*). [*Parktown*, an upper-class Johannesburg suburb + SE *prawn*; the cricket, which grows to 7cm (2¾in), can seem to resemble an outsize prawn]

parky adj. [late 19C+] chilly. [Midland dial, ult. ? SE *perky*, sharp]

park your carcass / arse / fanny / frame / stern phr. [20C] (orig. US) an invitation to sit down. [SE *park* + *carcass*/ARSE n.¹/FANNY n.¹ (3)/FRAME n.² (1)/STERN; note US radio comedian Harry Einstein (1904–58) used the pseudonym 'Parkyakarkus']

park yourself in/take a pew phr. [late 19C+] an invitation to sit down. [SE *park* + PEW]

park your stern see PARK YOUR CARCASE.

parlary see PARLYAREE.

parlatic see PALATIC.

parlay n. [1980s+] (drugs) crack. [ety. unknown; ? its role as a money-making commodity, improving the dealer's life]

parlay v. **1** [late 19C+] (orig. US) to improve one's position, esp. by taking what one already has, material or otherwise, and using it as the basis of one's next move. **2** [1990s] (US Black) to calm down, to relax. [Ital. *paroli*, a cast at dice, which was taken up by faro and other card-players to mean to leave one's winnings on the table and then to stake double the sum already staked]

parlaying n. [1990s] (US Black) partying, enjoying oneself. [PARLAY v. (2)]

parleyvoo n. **1** [mid-18C+] the French language. **2** [early 19C+] a French person. [PARLEYVOO v. (1)]

parleyvoo adj. **1** [early 19C+] French. **2** [late 19C+] foreign. [PARLEYVOO v. (1)]

parleyvoo v. [mid-18C+] **1** to speak a foreign language, esp. to speak French. **2** to chatter meaninglessly. [Fr. *parlez-vous?*, do you speak?]

parliament/parliament house n. [late 19C] a privy. [one's 'sitting' there ? + pun on Cromwell's *Rump Parliament* (1648–53)]

parliamentary adj. [1900s–20s] (Irish) respectable, esp. in phr. *the parliamentary side of one's arse*.

parliamentary whisky n. [late 18C–late 19C] (Irish) whisky on which duty has been paid, as opposed to contraband or home-distilled.

parliament house see PARLIAMENT.

parlor girl n. [mid-19C–1900s] (US) a prostitute who works in a sophisticated, up-market brothel (cf. PARLOR HOUSE).

parlor house n. [mid-19C–1900s] (US) a high-class brothel, situated in what appears to be a fashionably furnished middle-class house, and run by a complaisant 'aunt' whose bevy of attractive 'nieces' gather in the front parlour to meet, and make themselves available to visitors. Cheaper brothels had little more than bedrooms in which one had sex (cf. ACCOMMODATION HOUSE).

parlor lizard

parlor lizard ... 895 ... **party**

parlor lizard/snake *n.* [1910s+] (US) a poor or miserly man who would rather court a woman in her own house than take her out on the town (cf. LOUNGE LIZARD).

parlour *n.* [19C] the vagina; thus *let out one's parlour and lie backwards*, to work as a prostitute (cf. FORE-ROOM; FRONT PARLOUR).

parlour-jumper *n.* [late 19C] (Und.) a thief who robs private rooms or houses; thus *parlour-jumping*, practising such a form of robbery (cf. BACK-JUMPER).

parlour pink *n.* [1920s+] a socialist whose activism is limited by the confines of their dinner table and does not extend on to the streets, let alone the barricades (cf. BOLLINGER BOLSHEVIK). [SE *parlour* + PINK n.[4]; an earlier form was *parlour Bolshevik*]

parlous *n.* [late 17C–18C] a notably shrewd individual. [SE *parlous*, dangerously cunning, mischievous, capable of causing harm]

parlyaree / palari / palarie / panarly / parlary / polari *n.* [17C+] theatrical slang (cf. PALARIE v.). [Ital. *parlare*, to speak. It was evolved, according to E.P. (*Slang Yesterday and Today*, 1933), because 'until about the end of the eighteenth century, actors were so despised that, in self-protection, they had certain words that, properly, should be described as cant and were actually known as Parlyaree'. He also notes that rather than a whole language, it was a 'glossary, a vocabulary'. Relatively few terms remain, and their last great showcase was BBC Radio's 1950s comedy series 'Round the Horne', in which the camp duo Julian and Sandy, ostensibly a pair of actors, still conversed in a variety of Parlyaree terms. It is still, however, extant in gay use. Its Ital. roots are best seen in the numbers one to ten, *una, duey, trey, quater, chinker, sey, setter, otto, nobber, dacha*]

parm! *excl.* [1940s+] an abbr. of SE *pardon me!*

parnel *n.* [late 17C–18C] a prostitute who works in a brothel rather than walking the streets (cf. TENDER PARNEL). [SE *parnel*, a priest's concubine or mistress, a harlot, a wanton young woman]

Parnell shout *n.* [1910s–40s] (N.Z.) shared payment for food or drinks. [*Parnell*, a rundown suburb of Auckland + SHOUT n.[1]]

parney *n.* **1** [mid-19C] (Anglo-Ind.) a shower of rain. **2** [mid-19C] water. **3** [20C] (Ling. Fr./Polari) tears (in the eyes). [Rom. *pani*, water, ult. f. Hind. *pani*, water]

Parra *n.* [1970s+] (Aus.) an inhabitant of the western suburbs of Sydney (cf. WESTIE). [abbr. *Parramatta*, New South Wales, one of those suburbs]

parro *adj.* [1980s+] *para*noid. [abbr.]

parrot and monkey/parrotty time *n.* [late 19C] (US) an unhappy marriage, in which the two partners fight continually (cf. CAT AND DOG LIFE; MONKEY AND PARROT TIME).

Parry/Pare *n.* [1980s+] (N.Z. Und) the *Pare*moremo high security prison; thus *Parry Blues*, the blue prison uniform. [abbr.]

parsley *n.[1]* [mid-19C] the female pubic hair (cf. BROCCOLI). [? resemblance]

parsley *n.[2]* [1900s–10s] nonsense, rubbish (cf. ALFALFA n.). [? the insignificance of the herb]

parsley *n.[3]* [1970s] (drugs) **1** marijuana. **2** phencyclidine (cf. ACE n.[3]). [the use of parsley as a base for smoking phencyclidine]

parsley bed *n.* [early 18C–mid-19C] the vagina (cf. BEAUTY SPOT n.[1]; CABBAGE n.[7]; PARSLEY n.[1]). [esp. as the answer to the question 'where do babies come from'; traditionally the *parsley bed* brings girls, while boys come from the less appealing nettle bed or from beneath the gooseberry bush]

parson *n.* [late 18C–early 19C] a signpost, esp. a finger-post (cf. BISHOP n.[4]). [the parson supposedly 'sets people in the right way' (Grose, 1785)]

parsoned *adj.* [late 19C] married.

parson palmer *n.* [late 18C–early 19C] anyone who stops the communal glass circulating by talking before passing it on (cf. REMEMBER PARSON MALHAM!). [a real-life, if forgotten, clergyman]

parson's barn *n.* [late 18C] a place that is 'never so full but there is still room for more' (Grose, 1796).

parson's collar *n.* [1940s+] the froth on top of a glass of beer.

parson's face *see* MINISTER'S FACE.

parson's mousetrap *n.* [late 17C–early 19C] marriage. [the role played by a clergyman in solemnizing the wedding ceremony]

parson's nose *n.* [mid-19C+] the rump of a chicken, duck, goose or other poultry (cf. POPE'S NOSE). [the noun varies as to one's religion]

parson's week *n.* [late 18C+] Monday to Saturday, esp. a holiday that lasts from Monday to Saturday. [irrespective of other duties, the clergyman's trad. 'working day' is Sunday]

parson's wife *n.* [1920s+] (Aus.) gin, esp. Vicker's Gin. [pun on *Vickers/vicar's* + GIN n.[1]/SE *gin*]

parson trulliber *n.* [mid-19C] a rude, vulgar country clergyman. [SE *parson* + ? TROLLOBUBS]

part *v.* [mid-19C] to give up, to hand over, to restore (usu. of money) (cf. PART UP). [SE *part with*]

partake of His/Her Majesty's hospitality, to *phr.* [late 19C] to spend time in prison. [joc. var. on SE *at His/Her Majesty's pleasure*]

part brass rags, to *phr.* [late 19C+] to part on bad terms. [naval custom of two sailors, when on good terms, sharing their cleaning rags]

parter *n.* [mid-19C] a generous person, one who pays up without complaint. [PART]

partial/partial to *adj.[1]* [late 17C–late 19C] fond of, esp. food or drink.

partial *adj.[2]* [late 18C] inclining more to one side than another; crooked.

Partick Thistle *n.* [20C] a whistle. [rhy. sl.; the Scot. football team]

particular *n.* [19C–1900s] one's special choice, e.g. *a glass of my particular*.

particular *adv.* [late 19C] especially, very much.

particulars *n.* [1970s+] (US prison) any member of the authorities who has an immediate effect on a prisoner's life: a warder, the sentencing judge, the parole board etc.

partlet *n.* [15C] a hen. [Fr. and briefly English proper name *Pertelote*; thus the popular synon. *Dame Partlet*]

partner *n.* [19C] the penis.

part of India *n.* [early–mid-17C] the female genitals (cf. ANTIPODES). [the shape of the pubic triangle is reminiscent of the sub-continent]

part of the furniture *n.* [1910s+] anything or anyone so familiar as to make no more impression than a familiar piece of furniture. [cf. SE *wallpaper*, of a person or thing, unobtrusive].

part one's head with a towel, to *phr.* [late 19C] (US) to be bald.

partridge *n.* [17C–19C] a prostitute (cf. CANARY n.[2]).

parts of shame *n.* [19C] the vagina. [trans. of Lat. *pudendum*, lit. 'that which is shameful']

part someone's hair, to *phr.* [late 19C+] (US) **1** to shoot at someone, to kill someone. **2** to hit someone on the head.

part that goes over the fence last *n.* [late 19C] (US) the buttocks. [euph.]

part the red sea, to *phr.* [1990s] of a woman, to masturbate.

part up *v.* [late 19C–1950s] (Aus.) to pay money. [ext. of PART]

party *n.[1]* [mid-18C+] man; still found in *old party*, and the basis of such legal terms as *the guilty party*, and *being a party to*. [obs. SE *party*, a person]

party n.² [1930s+] **1** any form of sex act, usu. provided by a prostitute; often used in a prostitute's question, *What kind of party would you like?*, what speciality would you prefer? **2** a sexual encounter involving two or more women and one man.

party v. [1960s+] **1** to enjoy oneself. **2** to have sex. **3** to partake in an orgy. **4** to drink or take drugs.

party animal n. [1980s+] anyone notably devoted to going out and having a good time.

party boy n. [1960s+] (US) a male homosexual prostitute (cf. PARTY GIRL). [PARTY n.²]

party favors n. [1980s+] (US campus) drugs.

party foul v. [1980s+] (US campus) to behave in a socially unacceptable manner at a party, esp. to vomit or spill alcohol; also as excl. *party foul!*, that was a blunder! how embarrassing!

party girl n. [1920s–60s] a promiscuous young woman, not necessarily a prostitute, a 'good-time girl' (cf. PARTY BOY).

party hat n. **1** [1970s+] (US) the flashing light on top of a police car. **2** [1980s+] (orig. US campus) a condom.

party hearty v. [1980s+] (US teen) to have a good time at a party.

party hop v. [1980s+] (orig. US) to move from one party to the next and so on during the course of a single evening and night.

party on! excl. [1980s+] (US teen) a general excl. of approval, either party-orientated, meaning 'enjoy yourself!' 'have a good time!' or, more broadly based, meaning 'good job!'. [popularized by the film *Wayne's World* (1992)]

party pooper/poop n. [1950s+] (orig. US) a spoilsport, one who sabotages the pleasures and enjoyments of their companions, whether at a party or other amusement. [SE *party* + POOP v.³]

party tits n. [1990s] artificially enlarged breasts, esp. as adopted by young and famous women, which are then displayed at social and other occasions. [SE *party* + TIT n.¹ (1)]

parum see PARAM.

pas de Lafarge phr. [mid-19C] (society) don't be dull, that's boring (cf. NO TICH!). [lit. 'no Lafarge (talk)'; the French case of the alleged poisoner Madame *Lafarge*; the frequency of dinner-party conversations about the case led to it becoming a synon. for tedium]

pas de problème phr. [1980s+] that's fine, no matter. [Fr. *pas de problème*, no problem]

pasear n. [mid-19C–1940s] (US) a walk or stroll, often used fig. to describe something more substantial (a trek across mountains) or portentous (a journey to prison). [Sp. *pasear*, to walk. The term is used of the traditional evening promenade in Sp. or S. American towns]

pash n. [1920s+] an infatuation, usu. between junior and senior pupils of girls' schools. [SE *passion*]

pash on v. [1950s+] (Aus.) to indulge in heavy petting or even intercourse. [PASH n.]

pash show n. [1950s+] (Aus.) **1** a film that includes candid sex scenes. **2** enthusiastic love-making. [SE *passion* + *show*]

pas op!/passop! excl. [early 19C+] (S.Afr.) be careful! look out! [Afk. *oppassen*, to be on guard]

pass v.¹ [1930s+] **1** of a Jew, to pretend to be a Christian. **2** of a homosexual, to appear heterosexual to those one encounters. **3** of a light-skinned Black person, to pose as White.

pass v.² [1940s+] to ignore, to have no interest in, esp. in phr. *I'll pass*, as a response to an offer or suggestion. [card-playing imagery]

pass a compliment, to phr. [late 19C–1900s] to give a tip.

pass a/the remark, to phr. [late 19C+] to make a (usu. disparaging or sarcastic) comment.

pass around the arm, to phr. [late 19C] (US) to spank a child.

pass a sham saint, to phr. [early 18C] to play the hypocrite.

pass-bank n. [late 17C–early 19C] a gaming round.

passenger n.¹ [mid-19C+] one who, while nominally one of a group, team, crew etc, takes no active or useful part in the general efforts.

passenger n.² [late 19C+] (US) a passenger train.

passenger on the Cape Ann stage, to be a phr. [mid-19C] (US campus) to be drunk. [ety. unknown; ? anecdotal]

passer n. [1920s–50s] one who passes counterfeit money.

pass for grass, to phr. [20C] (W.I./Guyn.) to be treated disrespectfully, to be someone who does not matter. [the 'invisibility' of grass]

pass/pass muster in a crowd, to phr. [early 18C–mid-19C] to blend in with a group, to be an average, inconspicuous person.

pass in one's checks, to phr. [mid-19C+] (orig. US) to die (cf. CASH IN ONE'S CHECKS). [gambling imagery]

pass in one's chips, to phr. [late 19C+] (orig. US) to die (cf. CASH IN ONE'S CHECKS). [gambling imagery]

pass in one's dinner pail see HAND IN ONE'S DINNER PAIL.

pass in one's marble/marbles, to phr. [1900s–50s] (Aus.) to die.

pass in the pot adj. [late 19C–1900s] randy, amorous. [rhy. sl. *pass in the pot* = HOT adj.¹(1)]

passion flaps n. [1990s] the labia.

passion/love gap n. [1950s+] (S.Afr.) the space between the front teeth; such spaces are created by the extraction of up to 4 teeth.

passion-killers n. [1940s+] (orig. milit.) any article of women's underwear deemed to reduce the chances of (male) exploration.

passion pit n.¹ [19C] the vagina (cf. BLACK HOLE n.¹).

passion pit n.² [1930s+] (US) a drive-in cinema. [the petting and/or sex encouraged within]

passion stick n. [1950s] (Aus.) the penis.

passion wagon n. [1950s+] any vehicle, often a van, in which teenage boys hope to seduce young women (cf. FUCK TRUCK; SHAG-WAGON). [note 1940s+ milit. use, the truck taking men for a day's, or part of a day's, leave, into a town or place of entertainment]

passive bucket n. [1920s] a quiescent listener. [no matter what 'garbage' is poured into it, this bucket remains a willing receptacle]

pass math v. [1990s] (US) to masturbate. [? play on US *math*, mathematics/*masturbate*]

pass muster in a crowd see PASS IN A CROWD.

pass oneself v. [20C] (Ulster) to behave as expected. [? abbr. SE *surpass*]

pass one's mouth on, to phr. [20C] (W.I.) to slander, to speak rudely about. [var. on SE *pass an opinion/a remark*]

pass one's persimmon, to phr. [early 19C] to be beyond one's capabilities or knowledge. [ext. of HUCKLEBERRY ABOVE ONE'S PERSIMMON]

passop! see PAS OP!

pass out v. **1** [late 19C] to die. **2** [1900s] (Aus.) to knock out (cf. PASS SOMEONE ONE). **3** [1970s+] to fall asleep.

pass out cold, to phr. [1940s] to faint.

passremarkable adj. [1980s+] (Irish) **1** worthy of comment. **2** prone to making tactless remarks. [SE *pass a remark*, to comment]

pass someone a jolt, to phr. [1910s] (Aus.) to hit someone with a short, sharp blow.

pass someone one, to phr. [1900s–10s] (Aus.) to punch or hit someone.

pass the bottle of smoke, to *phr.* [mid-19C] to accept conventional untruths, to tell white lies. [one is conscious of the vagueness/insubstantiality of such speech]

pass the buck, to *phr.* **1** [19C+] (orig. US) to shift responsibility onto another; thus *buck-passer*, one who will not take responsibility on themselves; *buck-passing*, avoiding one's responsibilities. **2** [20C] to die. **3** [1900s–40s] (US) to chatter, to tell tales. [abbr. SE *buckhorn knife*; in mid-19C games of poker it was the custom to place an object, typically a knife, in front of the person who was to deal. When this person had dealt, the knife was passed onto the next player.

pass the pikes, to *phr.* [late 17C–18C] to be out of danger. [SE *turnpike*, a toll gate; villains who had passed this barrier might presume themselves free of effective pursuit]

pass the remark *see* PASS A REMARK.

pass the time of day, to *phr.* [mid-19C+] to exchange compliments or small talk with someone one meets before going on one's way.

pass through the fire, to *phr.* [19C] to catch venereal disease (cf. BURN V.[1]; SCALD V.[1]).

pasta/paste *n.* [1980s+] (drugs) coca paste, the basis of cocaine. [Sp. *pasta*, paste]

past dying of her first child, to be *phr.* [mid–late 17C] of a woman, to have given birth to an illegitimate child.

paste/population paste *n.*[1] [1980s+] semen. [resemblance]

paste *n.*[2] *see* PASTA.

paste *v.* [mid-19C+] to hit hard. [var. on BASTE]

paste away/away at *v.* [late 19C+] to keep on hitting someone. [PASTE V.]

pasteboard *n.* **1** [mid–late 19C] a visiting card; thus *pasteboard*, to leave one's card, often ext. as [mid-19C] *leave one's pasteboard*, [mid-19C] *lodge one's pasteboard*, [late 19C] *shoot one's pasteboard*, [1900s] *drop one's pasteboard*. **2** [mid-late 19C] a playing card. **3** [mid-19C–1900s] a railway ticket. [SE *pasteboard*, a thin card made of pasting together three or more sheets of paper]

pasted *adj.* [1950s+] (US) intoxicated by drink or drugs. [PASTE V.]

paste-horn *n.* [19C] the nose (cf. BUGLE N.[1]). [SE *pastehorn*, a cow's horn used to hold paste]

paste it to your hat *see* PIN IT TO YOUR HAT.

past gorgeous *adj.* [1990s] (US) extremely attractive.

pasties *n.* [1980s+] (US drugs) dryness in the mouth after smoking cannabis. [? PASTED or Sp. *pasto*, marijuana; lit. 'a pasture']

pasting *n.* [mid-19C+] a violent assault, a beating up. [PASTE V.]

past it *adv.* [mid-19C+] **1** of animate and inanimate objects, too old or worn-out to be of use (cf. PAST ONE'S SELL-BY DATE). **2** dead.

past one's sell-by date *phr.* [1980s+] out of date, over the hill, 'past it'.

pastry *n.* [late 19C–1930s] a generic term for pretty young women (cf. BANANA N.[2]).

pat *n.*[1] **1** [early 19C+] an Irishman. **2** [1930s–40s] (Aus.) a Chinese person (cf. PADDY N.[1]). [var. on PADDY N.[1]; the two, while of differing backgrounds, were both immigrants]

pat *n.*[2] [1960s] (drugs) marijuana. [? misspelling of POT N.[9]]

patacca *n.* [1970s] worthless rubbish, esp. fake jewellery, watches etc. [Ital. *patacca*, worthless]

Patagonian pasodoble *n.* [1990s] diarrhoea, esp. that contracted on holiday (cf. APPLE-BLOSSOM TWO-STEP).

pata-kyat *n.* [1940s] (W.I.) a thief. [dial. *pata*, a kitchen shelf + *kyat*, cat]

pat and mick *n.* [late 19C+] the penis (cf. MAD MICK; STORMY DICK). [rhy. sl. *pat and mick* = DICK N.[5] (1) or PRICK (2)]

pat and mick *v.* [20C] (Aus.) **1** to lick. **2** to beat with the fists. [rhy. sl. *pat and mick* = LICK V.]

pat and mike *n.* [late 19C+] a bicycle. [rhy. sl. *Pat and Mike* = SE *bike*]

pata-pata/phata-phata *n.* [1970s] (S.Afr. township) sexual intercourse. [Xhosa/Zulu *phatha*, to touch, to feel; thence the popular dance *pata-pata*, a highly suggestive dance characterized by the way in which pairs of dancers touch each other]

Pat Cash *v.* [1990s] to urinate. [rhy. sl. *Pat Cash* = SLASH N.[4]; ult. Aus. tennis star Pat Cash (b.1965)]

patch *n.*[1] **1** [mid-16C–late 17C] a fool, a jester. **2** [19C+] an ill-natured or bad-tempered person, esp. a child (cf. CROSS-PATCH). [? Ital. *pazzo*, a fool, a jester, a madman (which was its orig. SE use mid-16C–mid-17C), or *Patch*, nickname of Sexton, Cardinal Wolsey's jester *c.*1520]

patch *n.*[2] [19C] **1** the pubic hair. **2** the vagina.

patch *n.*[3] [1950s+] (orig. US) any form of insignia as worn by criminal or youth gangs, e.g. the Hell's Angels, US prison gangs, N.Z. street gangs etc.

patch *v.* [1960s+] (Can. prison) to arrange for bribes to be paid, deals to be made etc (cf. FIX V.[1]).

patch needle and burn thread, to *phr.* [20C] (W.I.) to waste one's time in an irritating manner.

patch up *v.* [1970s+] (N.Z.) to become a full gang member. [one is awarded a PATCH N.[3]]

patchy *adj.* [mid-19C] cross, bad-tempered. [PATCH N.[1] (2)]

patent coat *n.* [mid-19C] a coat with the pockets on the inside, making it harder to pick. [? its patented design]

patent-digester *n.* [mid-19C] brandy. [its supposedly beneficial effects on the digestion; ? corruption of *Papin's digester*, a vessel designed for dissolving bones etc]

pater *n.* [early 18C–1900s] (school) one's father, esp. as *the pater* (cf. MATER). [Lat. *pater*, father]

pater cove *n.* [late 17C–mid-19C] (Und.) a priest, a wandering beggar posing as a priest; the 15th rank of the underworld (cf. CANTING CREW). [for ety. *see* PATRICO]

patess *n.* [early–mid-19C] an Irishwoman. [PAT N.[1] (1) + SE fem. sfx *-ess*]

pathetic *adj.* [1930s+] **1** of people, absurd, ridiculous. **2** of actions, weak, useless. [SE *pathetic*, exciting a feeling of pity, sympathy]

patico *n.* [1980s+] (drugs) crack. [Sp.]

patience on a monument *n.* [late 19C+] a long-suffering, patient person.

Patland *n.* [19C] Ireland; thus *Patlander*, an Irishman. [PAT N.[1] (1), generic for an Irishman + SE *land*]

pat malone/pat maloney *adv.* [20C] (Aus.) alone (cf. TOD SLOAN). [rhy. sl.]

pato *n.* [1960s+] a male homosexual. [Sp. *pato*, a duck; i.e. he 'ducks' down for sex]

patoot *see* PATOOTIE N.[2].

patootie *n.*[1] [1920s+] (US) an attractive young woman. [? SE *potato*, esp. *sweet potato*]

patootie/patoot *n.*[2] [1920s+] (US) the buttocks. [ext. of PATOOTIE N.[1]]

pat out *v.* [1920s] to speak openly, honestly. [SE *pat*, appositely, directly to the point]

patriarch co/patriarke co *n.* [16C] (Und.) a fake priest, specializing in performing illegal marriage ceremonies (cf. PATRICO). [poss. punning on SE *patriarch* (although *see also* PATRICO for ety.) + *co* = COVE (1)]

patrico/patring-cove/pattering-cove *n.* **1** [mid-16C–mid-17C] (Und.) a priest, or a wandering beggar posing as one; the 15th rank of the underworld (cf. CANTING CREW; JARKMAN; PATER COVE). **2** [17C–19C] any legitimate clergyman. [either Lat. *pater*, father, or PATTER V. + *co*, abbr. COVE (1): 'strolling priests that Marry under a Hedge without a Gospel or Common-prayer Book, the Couple standing on each side a Dead Beast, are bid to live together till Death them do's Part, so shaking Hands, the Wedding is ended' (B.E.)]

patrico's kinchin *n.* [16C] (Und.) a pig. [PATRICO + KINCHIN, lit. 'the (fake) priest's child']

patri-cove *n.* [early 18C] (Und.) a priest, or a wandering beggar posing as one; the 15th rank of the underworld. [var. on PATRICO]

patring-cove *see* PATRICO.

pat someone down *v.* [20C] to submit someone to a body search.

patsy *n.* [20C] a fool, a dupe. [the popular Irish name *Patrick* and thus an example of a racial stereotype, in this case the supposed stupidity of the Irish]

patsy *adj.* [1930s–50s] (US) satisfactory, all right. [ety. unknown; ? lost rhy. sl.]

patten-ken *n.* [1910s–20s] (Und.) a lodging house frequented primarily by vagrants or thieves. [var. on PADDING KEN; ? + underpinning by SE *patten*, the sort of shoe worn by the poor]

patter *n.* [mid–late 19C] **1** any form of speech or speechifying, e.g. a street seller's sales talk, a judge's summing up. **2** talk considered as empty chatter. [PATTER v.]

patter *v.* **1** [early 15C–early 19C] to talk rapidly, fluently or glibly, to chatter, to prattle. **2** [early–mid-19C] to put on trial. **3** [early–mid-19C] to talk the cant of thieves, beggars etc. **4** [early 19C+] (Und.) to talk, to speak. **5** [mid-19C] to speechify as a cheapjack does in extolling wares, or a conjurer while performing tricks. [SE *patter*, to mumble one's prayers at speed and without note of their meaning; ult. the *Paternoster*, 'Our Father']

patter-cove *n.* [late 19C] (Und.) a fake priest, specializing in performing illegal marriage ceremonies (cf. PATRICO). [PATTER v. + COVE (1)]

patter-crib *n.* [mid-19C] a criminal public or lodging house. [PATTER n. + CRIB n.³ (1)]

patterer *n.* [19C] a street seller who specializes in last dying speeches, true confessions and similarly melodramas. [PATTER v.; self-proclaimed, according to Mayhew as 'the aristocracy of the street sellers']

pattering *n.* [late 17C–1920s] overly 'smart' or irritatingly vague responses made by a servant. [PATTER v.]

pattering-cove *see* PATRICO.

pattern *n.* [mid-19C] mispron. of SE *patent*.

pattern *adj.* [late 19C] (Irish) excellent, first-rate, brilliant. [abbr. SE *pattern fair*, mispron. of *patron fair*, ult. *patron saint's fair*]

patter the flash, to *phr.* [early–mid-19C] **1** to talk slang or underworld cant. **2** to talk. [PATTER v. + FLASH n.¹]

pattie *n.* [1970s+] a first class degree (cf. RAGING n.; RICHARD n.³). [rhy. sl. *Pattie Hearst* = first; ult. *Pattie Hearst* (b.1954), US heiress-cum-urban terrorist]

pattin' leather *adv.* [1930s+] (US Black) being out of work. [one walks the streets (on shoe-leather) in search of employment]

patty *n.* [1940s+] (US Black) a derog. term for a White man. [PADDY n.¹ (4)]

patu *n.* [late 19C+] (W.I.) an ugly or foolish person. [dial. *patu*, used of an owl or a nightjar; the bird's mouth gapes hugely – out of proportion to its relatively small beak]

patu-eye *n.* [1950s] (W.I.) an albino (cf. FRECKLE-NATURE). [PATU + SE *eye*]

patzer/potzer *n.* [1940s+] an inferior chess-player. [? Ger. *patzen* to bungle, but note derog. PUTZ]

pauca! *excl.* [late 16C–early 17C] quiet! be quiet! [Lat. *pauca verba*, few words]

Paul Henry *see* JOHN T. HENRY.

paulie *n.* [late 19C–1900s] during the Boer war, a derog. term for a pro-Boer. [*Paul* Kruger (1825–1904), the Boer leader + pun on SE *poor lies*]

paul pry *n.* [early 19C+] (orig. US) an inquisitive person; thus *paul pry*, to be unashamedly inquisitive; *paul pryism*, the behaviour of such a person. [popular US song, composed *c*.1820]

Paul Revere *phr.* [1980s+] (US campus) a farewell, goodbye. [play on Fr. *au revoir*/US revolutionary hero *Paul Revere* (1735–1818)]

paul's work *n.* [early 17C] a badly done job, a mess. [SE *poor work* or ref. to a *Paul's man*, anyone who frequented St Paul's Cathedral, London, for gossip, confidence trickery etc]

paunch *v.* [17C] to eat. [Scot. *paunch*, to swallow greedily]

paup along *v.* [late 19C–1910s] to subsist. [SE *pauper*]

paut *v.* [20C] (Ulster) to walk around in stockinged feet. [Scot. *paut*, to move in a leisurely manner]

Pav/P.V. *n.¹* [mid-19C] the *Pa*vilion Theatre, London. [abbr.]

pav *n.²* [1960s+] (Aus./N.Z.) a *pav*lova, Australia's 'national dessert', a large, soft-centred meringue topped with whipped cream and passion-fruit. [abbr.; named/created for the ballerina Anna *Pa*vlova (1885–1931)]

pave *v.* [late 19C–1930s] (school) to add marginal or interlinear translations to a classical text. [the image is of paving, i.e. smoothing the 'road' of Latin and Greek study]

paved *adj.* [1990s] (US campus) drunk. [? one has collapsed on the pavement]

pavee *n.* [20C] (Irish) an itinerant Jewish pedlar. [? their walking the pavements]

pavement pizza *n.* [1980s+] (Aus.) a pile of vomit.

pavement pounder *n.* [1940s–50s] (orig. US) a policeman.

pavement princess/pretty *n.* [20C] (US) a prostitute (cf. NYMPH OF THE PAVE; PRINCESS n.²).

paviour's/pavior's workshop *n.* [late 18C–late 19C] the street. [SE *paviour*, a layer of paving stones]

paw *n.* **1** [late 17C+] the human hand, usu. in pl. (cf. FIN n.¹). **2** [early 18C+] handwriting, esp. a signature. [SE *paw*, used only of animals]

paw *adj.* [mid-17C–early 18C] improper, naughty, obscene. [? excl. *pah!*, nasty! horrible!]

paw *v.* [20C] to fondle sexually (esp. when the recipient is unwilling). [PAW n. (1)]

paw-case *n.* [mid-19C] a glove. [PAW n. (1) + SE *case*]

pawked up *adj.* [late 19C] (sporting) poor quality, usu. of horses or dogs. [Scot. *pawk*, a trick]

pawky *adj.* [20C] (Ulster) easy-going, lazy. [dial. *pawk*, a cheeky individual; *pawky*, artful, sly, shrewd is SE]

pawl *v.* [early–mid-19C] **1** to bring to a standstill, to stop, to bring up short. **2** to detect. [PALL v.¹]

pawn *n.* [mid-19C] a *pawn*broker. [abbr.]

pawn *v.* [late 17C–early 18C] to leave an inn or tavern, forcing one's companion to pay the bill.

paw-paw *adj.* [late 18C] naughty, improper; thus *paw-pawness*, naughtiness, impropriety. [PAW n. (1)]

paw-paw tricks *n.* **1** [late 18C–19C] any form of naughty trick. **2** [19C] masturbation. [PAW-PAW; orig. used by nurses to children]

paws off! *excl.* [20C] get your hands off! leave it alone! [PAW n. (1)]

paws off, Pompey *phr.* [early 19C–1930s] hands off! leave me alone! [coined *c*.1803 without the comma, as *paws off Pompey* and used as an anti-Napoleonic phr., meaning 'keep your hands off Pompey' (a nickname either for Lord Nelson (1758–1805) or the naval town of Portsmouth). By the 1830s the comma had been introduced and the phr. was generally used by women wishing to restrain an admirer's wandering hands]

pax *n.* [20C] (US) a passenger. [abbr.]

pax! *excl.* [mid-19C+] (juv.) a cry used to call a truce in a (fighting) game; thus *pax*, a friend; to *be good pax*, to be good friends. [Lat. *pax*, peace]

pax on it!/one! *excl.* [mid-17C–mid-18C] confound it! the hell with it! [Lat. *pax*, peace; i.e. enough! leave it in peace!]

pay *v.*[1] [mid-18C–late 19C] to beat, to punish; thus *pay over face and eyes, as the cat did to the monkey*, to give someone a serious beating about the head.

pay *v.*[2] [mid-19C] (Anglo-Chinese) to deliver.

pay a call, to *phr.* [1950s+] to visit the lavatory. [SE *call of nature*]

payaka *adj.* [1950s+] (W.I. Rasta) heathen. [? link to PAYOL]

payaso/payass *n.* [20C] (W.I.) fooling around, buffoonery. [Port. *palhaço* or Sp. *payaso*, jester, clown]

pay as Paul paid the Ephesians, to *phr.* [mid-19C] to beat severely; the full saying is *pay as Paul paid the Ephesians over the face and eyes and all the damned jaws*.

payass *see* PAYASO.

pay away *v.* [mid-19C] to continue, to go on with, esp. of a story that is being told. [naut. jargon *pay away*, to let rope run out of a vessel]

payback/paybacks *n.* [1930s+] (US) revenge, retaliation. [SE *pay back*]

payday stakes *n.* [1960s] (gambling) betting on credit, against the guarantee of one's forthcoming wages.

paydirt *n.* [1950s+] (orig. US) success, profit (cf. HIT PAYDIRT). [gold-mining imagery]

pay for one's whistle, to *phr.* [late 19C–1910s] to pay over the odds for something one desires. [the whistle of emphasis that acknowledges one's interest]

pay into *v.* [late 19C] to attack, to lay into. [ext. of PAY *v.*[1]]

pay me rent *n.* [20C] (Aus.) a tent. [rhy. sl.]

pay no mind, to *phr.* [1910s+] (US) to ignore.

payoff *n.* 1 [1910s–40s] (US Und.) a confidence trick whereby the victim is encouraged to wager a large sum of money, having been lured into the trick when a smaller wager, also suggested by the trickster, seems to have paid off satisfactorily. 2 [1920s+] (orig. US) the end result, the outcome, the conclusion (whether positive or negative). 3 [1930s] (Und.) the division of criminal spoils. 4 [1930s+] (US Und.) a bribe. 5 [1940s] (US Black) a generous person. 6 [1950s+] a final payment for services rendered. 7 [1950s+] the denouement of a book, film or play. 8 [1950s+] one's deserts.

payoff man *n.* [1930s] (US Und.) 1 a confidence trickster. 2 the cashier for a criminal gang. [PAYOFF (1), (3) + SE *man*]

payoff queen *n.* [1950s–60s] (gay) a homosexual who prefers to pay for sex. [PAYOFF (6) + QUEEN *n.*[1]]

pay-off Wednesday *n.* [mid-19C] the Wednesday before Advent (cf. CRIB-CRUST MONDAY; STIR-UP SUNDAY; TUG-BUTTON TUESDAY).

payol/pagnol *n.* [20C] 1 (W.I., Trin.) a mixed-race person who retains traces of Spanish ancestry and culture (cf. COCOA PAYOL). 2 (W.I., Gren.) a Spanish-speaking person, esp. a Venezuelan. [Sp. *español*. The word is equated with NIGGER *n.* or COOLIE *n.*[1] in terms of offensiveness. Payols thus call themselves 'Spanish' or, in Sp. *venezolanos*]

payola *n.* [1930s+] (orig. US) the practice (ostensibly illegal and generally denied by its practitioners) of bribing (with cash or kind) those with access to the public to tout a product (cf. LURKOLA). [SE *pay* + sfx. -OLA; esp. common in the record business where disc jockeys are offered massive inducements to push a certain record or artist. Major scandals in the US *c.*1959 supposedly ended payola, but some believe that the practice persists]

pay one's dues, to *phr.* [1940s+] (orig. US) to undergo usu. undesirable experiences before one attains a desirable goal.

pay one's/the shot, to *phr.* [18C+] to pay one's share. [SE *pay* + SHOT *n.*[1]; prior use is SE]

pay one's water bill, to *phr.* [1970s] (US Black) to urinate.

pay on the stump, to *phr.* [late 19C] to hand over, esp. of money (cf. STUMP UP). [the placing of the money on a *stump* or some equivalent]

pay out *v.* [mid-19C+] to take revenge upon, to give (someone) their deserts, to punch.

pay out the slack of one's gammon, to *phr.* [late 19C] to recount too many anecdotes. [GAMMON *n.*[1] (3)]

pay school *n.* [1980s+] (US Black) a private school that charges for tuition.

pay someone's coat, to *phr.* [19C] to thrash, to beat severely (cf. BASTE SOMEONE'S COAT).

pay someone their rent, to *phr.* [14C–late 15C] to punish someone.

pay the bearer, to *phr.* [late 19C+] to bounce a cheque. [the screed promising to 'pay the bearer' on a sterling note]

pay the earth, to *phr.* [1920s+] to pay excessively. [SE *pay* + EARTH *n.*[2]]

pay the freight, to *phr.* [1950s+] (US) to pay, to bear the expense (cf. PICK UP THE TAB).

pay the shot *see* PAY ONE'S SHOT.

pay through the nose, to *phr.* [mid-19C+] to pay exorbitantly. [fig. use of SE; ? origin in the Nose tax, levied by the Danes upon the Irish during the 9C. Those who refused to pay had their noses split]

pay with a hook, to *phr.* [late 19C] (Aus.) to steal. [SE *pay* + HOOK *n.*[2]]

paz *n.* [1980s] (drugs) phencyclidine (cf. ACE *n.*[3]). [Sp. *paz*, peace]

pazzer *n.* [1990s] (teen) a parent. [abbr. + 'Oxford' sfx. -*er*]

p.c. *n.* 1 [late 19C] (society) the poor classes. 2 [20C] (society) a *postcard*. 3 [1940s–50s] (Und.) a *previous conviction*. 4 [1970s+] politically correct, ideologically pure. 5 [1990s] (US teen) a *private conversation*. 6 [1990s] (drugs) a *piece of crack*. 7 [1990s] (drugs) *part commission*, in a drug deal. [abbr.]

PCP/PCPA/PCE *n.* [1960s+] (drugs) phencyclidine (cf. ACE *n.*[3]). [abbr. peace pill]

p.d. *n.* [1930s+] an embarrassing situation; thus *caught p.d.*, caught in an embarrassing situation. [abbr. pants *down*]

p.'d *adj.* [1970s+] (US) angry (cf. PEED OFF; PISSED; P.O. ; P.O.'ED). [PISSED OFF]

p.d.a. *n.* [1980s] (US preppie) kissing and cuddling in public. [abbr. public *display of affection*]

p.d.k. *n.* [1980s+] (US campus) someone who is out of fashion. [abbr. polyester double-knit, the epitome of unfashionable tailoring]

p-dope *n.* [1980s+] (drugs) 20–30% pure heroin. [pure + DOPE *n.*[1] (17)]

p.d.q. *phr.* [late 19C] pretty damn quick. [abbr.]

P.E. *n.* [late 19C+] (S.Afr.) Port Elizabeth. [abbr.]

pe *adj.* [1990s] (US teen) first-rate, wonderful. [? abbr. pretty excellent or abbr. DOPE *adj.*]

pea/p *n.* [1960s+] (Aus.) 1 the ideal, the perfect choice, the favourite. 2 someone in a favourable position. [horse-racing *pea*, the favourite]

pea and thimble *n.* [1910s+] (Aus.) a version of the three-card trick; thus *pea and thimble man*, one who conducts the game (cf. FIND THE LADY; THIMBLE-RIG).

peabrain/peahead *n.* [20C] (orig. US) a fool, a simpleton (cf. BAKEBRAIN). [SE *pea* + sfx. -*brain*/-HEAD (1)]

peace *n.* [1970s+] (drugs) 1 STP. 2 LSD. 3 phencyclidine (cf. ACE *n.*[3]; PAZ).

peace! *excl.* [1960s+] (orig. US) farewell, goodbye. [much loved by hippies; in ironic or historical use since]

peace and quiet n. [20C] a diet. [rhy. sl.]

peacemaker n.¹ **1** [mid-19C+] (US) a pistol or revolver. **2** [1950s] (W.I.) a male lover. **3** [1970s] (US Black) the penis (cf. GUN n.²; HOGLEG). [? the nickname of the Wild West's legendary Colt .45 revolver, or, just possibly in (3), from the ironic nickname accorded the nuclear arsenal's MX missile]

peacemaker/peaceman n.² [1950s] (W.I.) a policeman (cf. PEACEMAKER n.¹).

peace out!/up! excl. [1990s] (US teen) goodbye (cf. PEACE!).

peace person n. [1990s] (US campus) someone who identifies with the concerns and the style of the 1960s. [the 'love and peace' era]

peace pills n. [1970s+] (US drugs) **1** a mixture of LSD and methedrine. **2** phencyclidine (cf. ACE n.³; PEACE n.).

peace tablets n. [1970s+] (US drugs) LSD. [the association of LSD with 'love and peace']

peace up! see PEACE OUT!

peace weed n. [1970s+] (drugs) phencyclidine (cf. ACE n.³; PEACE n.). [SE peace + weed/WEED n.¹ (4)]

peach n.¹ **1** [mid-18C+] a pretty young woman (cf. BANANA n.²). **2** [mid-19C+] someone or something of exceptional worth, quality or desirability.

peach n.² [mid–late 19C] a detective, esp. as employed by a stage-coach or omnibus company to check receipts. [PEACH v.]

peach v. [late 18C+] to betray, to inform against. [SE impeach]

peacherino n. [20C] (US) something of exceptional worth, quality or desirability. [ext. of PEACH n.¹ (2) + sfx. -ERINO (see -ERINE)]

peaches n.¹ [1960s+] (drugs) dexedrine. [the colour of the capsules]

peaches n.² [1980s+] (US gay) the buttocks. [resemblance]

peach-fuzz n. [1950s–60s] (gay) an attractive teenager (cf. PEACH n.¹).

peaching n. [mid-15C–mid-19C] informing upon someone. [PEACH v.]

peach-perch n. [1930s] a motorcycle pillion. [PEACH n.¹ (1) + SE perch]

peachy adj. [1920s+] wonderful, excellent, delightful. [PEACH n.¹ (2)]

peachy-keen adj. [1960s+] (US) **1** excellent, first-rate. **2** (ironically) not good enough to warrant enthusiasm but adequate. [PEACH n.¹ (2) + KEEN]

peacock v.¹ [late 19C] **1** (Anglo-Ind.) to promenade up and down in one's best clothes. **2** to pay morning calls. [the bird's characteristic display]

peacock v.² [late 19C] (Aus.) **1** to buy up the best sections of land, thus making the adjoining territory worthless. **2** to outwit. [the speculator 'picks out the eyes' of the land]

peacock horse n. [late 19C] a horse that pulls a hearse. [such horses are bedecked in mourning black, and step in a very ceremonial way]

pea-dodger n. [1930s] (Aus.) a bowler hat (cf. EGG-BOILER). [ety. unknown]

peahead see PEABRAIN.

peak n.¹ [19C] the human nose.

peak n.² [1960s] (drugs) the central two hours or so of an LSD trip when the hallucinogen is at its most powerful.

peak v. [1960s+] to reach the limit of a particular experience.

peaked adj. [mid–late 19C] looking ill (cf. PEAKY). [one's features are brought into sharper, 'peaked' definition by illness]

peaked-cap n. [1920s] a police inspector. [the uniform]

peaking n. [1920s+] (Aus.) nagging, whinging, making a fuss over a minor injury. [SE peak, to mope about]

peaky/peeky adj. [mid-19C+] feeble, weak. [SE peak, to look sickly]

peamey/peamy n. [mid-19C] a pea-seller. [SE pea-merchant]

peanut n.¹ [1960s+] (drugs) a barbiturate. [the shape of the pill]

peanut n.² [1960s] (US Black) a White man. [abbr. MR PEANUT]

peanut alley/row n. [1940s+] (Aus./US) the front row of the stalls in a cinema (cf. BUZZARD ROOST n.²).

peanut buffer n. [1990s] a male homosexual (cf. PACK PEANUT BUTTER). [SE buff, to polish]

peanut butter n. [1970s+] (drugs) **1** phencyclidine mixed with peanut butter. **2** heroin, in the brown treacly form that it takes when heated preparatory to being smoked.

peanut gallery n. **1** [late 19C+] the top gallery, the 'gods' in a theatre (cf. BUZZARD ROOST n.²). **2** [late 19C+] ignorant, vociferous spectators. **3** [1940s+] (Aus./US) the front row of the stalls in a cinema. [the consumption of peanuts by the occupants of these seats]

peanut-packer n. [1950s+] (US) a male homosexual (cf. BUM-PUNCHER). [PACK PEANUT BUTTER]

peanut politics n. [mid–late 19C] (US) underhand, clandestine politicking, aimed at the securing of minor personal gains; thus peanut politician, one who indulges in such tactics. [PEANUTS + SE politics]

peanut roaster n. [1940s] (US) **1** a small locomotive. **2** an old or ramshackle automobile. [joc. resemblance]

peanut row see PEANUT ALLEY.

peanuts n. [1930s+] (orig. US) anyone or anything insignificant, petty, esp. money, wages.

pear n. [late 19C] King Louis Philippe of France. [the shape of the head of Louis Philippe (1773–1850). The term was coined by the French satirist Charles Phillipon in 1831, in the magazine La Caricature. As well as meaning 'pear', la poire is Fr. sl. for 'fathead']

pear and quince n. [20C] (Aus.) a prince. [rhy. sl.]

pea-rigger n. [19C] a 'find-the-lady' man, betting against the likelihood of a player calling correctly as to under which thimble a pea will be found (cf. THIMBLE-RIGGER). [SE pea + RIG v.¹ (2)]

pearl n.¹ [1980s+] (drugs) cocaine. [its whiteness]

pearl n.² [1980s+] (US gay) a drop of semen (cf. PEARL NECKLACE). [resemblance and colour]

pearl adj. [1980s+] (Aus.) first-rate, excellent. [on pattern of DIAMOND]

pearl dive v. [1960s+] (US) to perform cunnilingus. [the clitoris is the 'pearl']

pearl diver n. [20C] (US) a dishwasher in a hotel or restaurant; thus pearl-diving, washing up (cf. DIVE FOR PEARLS).

pearlies n. **1** [mid-19C+] pearl buttons, esp. found on a costermonger's clothes. **2** [mid-19C+] costermongers as a class. **3** [late 19C+] the teeth.

pearl necklace n. [1990s] **1** fellatio. **2** drops of semen ejaculated onto a partner's neck after fellatio. [in (1) the woman's teeth are the 'pearls' and the man's penis is the 'neck']

pearls n. [1960s+] (drugs) amyl nitrite (cf. AIMIES n.²). [the resemblance of amyl nitrite capsules to pearls]

pearly gate n. [20C] a plate. [rhy. sl.]

pearly gates n. [1980s+] (drugs) LSD. [the image of LSD giving visions of heaven, i.e. the 'pearly gates']

pearly king n. [20C] the anus. [rhy. sl. pearly king = RING n.¹ (2)]

pearly passion potion n. [1990s] semen (cf. PEARL n.²).

pear-making n. [19C] (Und.) enrolling in a regiment, taking the offered bounty and then deserting. The process can be repeated several times. [dial. pear, appear, i.e. one makes appearances, but does not stay]

peasant n. [1940s+] a general term of abuse, implying stupidity, boorishness, a lack of sophistication. [16C–17C SE use had derog. overtones, initially used for 'the subjects of France']

pease pudding hot n. [20C] nasal mucus. [rhy. sl. *pease pudding hot* = SNOT n. (1)]

peashooter n. [20C] (orig. US) a small, low-powered firearm.

peas in the pot adj. [late 19C+] hot. [rhy. sl.]

peasoup/peasouper n. (US) **1** [19C+] a French-born immigrant. **2** [1940s+] a French-Canadian; thus *talk peasoup*, to talk in French-Canadian patois (cf. JEAN POTAGE). [the stereotyping of pea soup as a French-Canadian staple]

peasouper n.[1] *see* PEASOUP.

peasouper n.[2] [mid-19C+] a very dense fog. [orig. the pollution-based London fogs, but since the Clean Air legislation of 1950s, any exceptionally impenetrable fog]

peasouper n.[3] [mid-19C–1900s] (Aus.) a newly arrived British immigrant. [PEASOUPER n.[2]]

peasouper n.[4] [late 19C] (N.Z.) a teetotaller. [? their preferred diet]

peat-reek n. [early–mid-19C] (Scot.) illicitly distilled whisky. [the flavour of peat smoke that permeates the liquor]

peb n. [1900s–50s] (Aus.) a youthful gangster. [abbr. PEBBLE]

pebble n. [early 19C+] (orig. boxing jargon, but Aus. thereafter) anyone seen as hard to deal with, e.g. a youthful ruffian (cf. LARRIKIN); thus *game as a pebble*, ready for anything, up to any challenge. [the hardness of the SE *pebble*]

pebble-beached adj. **1** [late 19C] penniless, destitute (cf. STONY). **2** [1930s] dazed, absent-minded. [image of a castaway on such a beach]

pebbles n.[1] [19C] the testicles (cf. ROCKS n.[3]). [play on STONE n.[1] (1)]

pebbles n.[2] [1980s+] (drugs) crack. [play on ROCKS n.[4]]

pec n. [1960s+] a *pec*toral muscle, the development of which is popular among body-builders; usu. in pl. [abbr.]

peck n.[1] **1** [mid-16C–late 19C; 1940s–50s] (orig. Und.) food (cf. PECK ALLEY; PECK AND PERCH; PECK AND TIPPLE). **2** [late 19C–1900s] a business, a concern. [SE *peck*, to eat (of a bird); 20C use is US Black. The concepts of food and business are closely allied here]

peck n.[2] [19C] money. [Lat. *pecunia*, money]

peck n.[3] [late 19C+] a perfunctory kiss. [a 'peck on the cheek']

peck n.[4] [1930s+] (US Black) a White person. [abbr. PECKERWOOD]

peck v.[1] [mid-16C–late 19C; 1970s+] (Und.) to eat. [20C use is US Black]

peck v.[2] [late 19C] to trip, to stumble, usu. of a horse. [dial.]

peckage/peckadge/peckidge n. [late 17C–mid-19C] food, esp. scraps. [PECK n.[1] (1)]

peck alley n. [mid-19C] the throat. [PECK n.[1] + SE *alley*]

peck and booze *see* PECK AND TIPPLE.

peck and perch n. [early 19C] board and lodging. [PECK n.[1] (1) + fig. use of SE *perch*]

peck and tipple/booze n. [early–mid-18C] meat and drink. [PECK n.[1] (1)+ TIPPLE n./BOUSE n.]

pecker n.[1] [mid-19C] **1** an eater. **2** the appetite. [PECK v.[1]]

pecker n.[2] **1** [mid-19C+] courage (cf. KEEP ONE'S PECKER UP). **2** [late 19C+] (orig. US) the penis. [SE *pecker*, that which pecks, i.e. a beak, a bill]

pecker n.[3] [1930s–50s] (US Black) a White man. [abbr. PECKERWOOD]

pecker cheese n. [1990s] (US) smegma. [PECKER n.[2] (2) + CHEESE n.[2]]

peckerhead n. [1950s+] (US) an objectionable, aggressive person. [PECKER n.[2] (2) + sfx. -HEAD (1)]

pecker snot n. [1990s] (US) semen (cf. COCK SNOT). [PECKER n.[2] (2) + SNOT n.[4]]

pecker tracks n. [1990s] (US) sperm left on a sheet or other similar object after masturbation. [PECKER n.[2] (2) + SE *tracks*]

peckerwood n. [1920s+] (orig. US Black) a White person, usu. a Southerner (cf. APPLE-KNOCKER n.[2]). [the red *woodpecker*, symbol of Whites, rather than the black crow, symbol of Blacks]

Peckham/Peckham Rye n. [1920s+] a tie. [rhy. sl.]

peckidge *see* PECKAGE.

peckie *see* PEKKIE.

pecking and necking n. [1970s] (US Black) foreplay, kissing and cuddling. [SE *peck*, to nibble at + NECK v.[4]]

peckings n. [1940s–50s] (US Black) food. [PECK n.[1] (1)]

peckish adj. [late 18C–19C] hungry. [PECK n.[1] (1); 20C use is SE]

pecks n. [1940s–50s] (drug and street gang) food. [PECK n.[1] (1)]

peck's bad boy n. [late 19C+] (US) a mischievous child. [the name of a fictional character created by George Wilbur *Peck* (1840–1916)]

pecnoster n. [late 19C] the penis. [PECKER n.[2] (2) + pun on SE *paternoster*, our father]

peculiar n. **1** [early 17C] a wife. **2** [late 17C–19C] a mistress. [SE *peculiar*, private]

peculiar adj. [late 19C+] deranged, eccentric. [euph.]

ped n. [late 19C+] a *ped*estrian. [abbr.; 20C use mainly US]

pedal v. [1930s+] (Aus.) to send a message over the radio. [the pedalling of the generator]

pedal music n. [late 19C] (US) stamping one's feet.

pedal one's dogs, to phr. [1920s+] (US) to leave, to go away, esp. as excl. *pedal your dogs!* [SE *pedal* + DOGS n.[4]]

pedal-pusher n. [1930s] (US) a cyclist, esp. a racing cyclist.

peddle one's arse, to phr. [20C] to work as a (usu. male) prostitute (cf. ASS PEDDLER). [SE *peddle*, to sell + ARSE n.[1] (1)]

peddle one's hips, to phr. [1920s–40s] to work as a prostitute.

peddle one's papers, to phr. [20C] (US) to go about one's business.

peddle out v. [20C] (US) to sell one's possessions, esp. to a second-hand store.

peddle pussy v. [1960s+] to work as a prostitute. [SE *peddle*, to sell + PUSSY n.[1] (1)]

peddler/pedlar n. **1** [late 19C] (US) a seller of counterfeit money. **2** [20C] a male prostitute (cf. ASS PEDDLER). **3** [1920s+] a drug seller.

peddler's French *see* PEDLAR'S FRENCH.

pedestals n. [early 18C] the feet.

pedigree n. [1910s+] (US prison) a criminal record (cf. JACKET n.[2]; RAP SHEET); thus *pedigreed*, having a criminal record.

Pedigree Chum n.[1] [20C] semen. [rhy. sl. *Pedigree Chum* (a make of dogfood) = COME n.[1] (2)]

Pedigree Chum n.[2] [1980s+] a 'deb's delight', an eligible young man. [pun on SE *Pedigree Chum*, a make of dogfood]

pedlar *see* PEDDLER.

pedlar's/peddler's French n. **1** [14C–late 19C] cant, criminal slang (cf. GREEK n.[2]; HEBREW). **2** [late 17C–early 19C] any incomprehensible language. [the image is of alien foreignness rather than of France itself]

pedlar's pack n. [1970s+] dismissal from one's job. [rhy. sl. *pedlar's pack* = SACK n.[3]]

pedo n. [1960s+] (US) a waste of time. [Sp. *pedo*, a fart]

pedro n. [1940s–50s] (US) any Spanish-speaking person. [Sp. name *Pedro*, Peter]

pee n.[1] **1** [20C] an act of urination. **2** [1960s+] urine. [PEE v.]

pee n.[2] [1970s] (drugs) pure heroin (cf. SHIT n.[5]).

pee v. [20C] to urinate. [abbr./euph. PISS v.[1]]

pee between two heels, to phr. [1950s–60s] (US Black) a phr. used when referring to a woman, or to female qualities, e.g. *the finest bitch that ever peed between two heels*. [the position of a woman when urinating]

peeble v. [20C] (Irish) to whistle out of tune. [Scot.; note Yorks. dial. *peeagle*, to do something badly]

peedie n. [20C] (Ulster) a small boy's penis (cf. PEENIE).

peed off *adj.* [1970s+] (US) angry, irritated (cf. P.'D). [euph. for PISSED OFF]

pee-eye *see* P.I.

pee it off *v.* [1920s] (US) to waste, to squander (cf. PISS AWAY).

peek-a-boo *n.* **1** [late 19C+] a translucent or transparent garment, usu. a blouse. **2** [1950s+] (Aus.) a garment made of *broderie anglaise* (open-work embroidery). [one is able to peek at the flesh behind the garment]

peekers *n.* [1940s] (US Black) the eyes.

peek freak *n.* [1950s+] a homosexual voyeur who watches two other men during sex. [SE *peek*, to glance at]

peeko *n.* [1910s–40s] a brief glance around. [SE *peek*]

peek show *n.* [20C] a live sex show. [SE *peek* + *show*]

peek through one's liquor, to *phr.* [1930s–40s] (US Black) to pose as sober when one is in fact drunk.

peeky *see* PEAKY.

peel *n.* [1920s+] (Aus.) a policeman. [abbr. PEELER n.¹]

peel *v.* **1** [late 18C+] to strip off one's clothes. **2** [1990s] (US teen) to go beyond the first page of a web site. [both imply the peeling of layers, whether of clothes or web pages]

peel a fine green banana, to *phr.* [1940s] (US Black) to seduce an attractive, light-skinned woman. [BANANA n.² (2)]

peel caps *v.* [1990s] (US Black/teen) to attack violently. [lit. 'to peel the flesh from someone's skull']

peel down *v.* [20C] to remove one's clothes. [ext. of PEEL v. (1)]

peeled *adj.* [19C] naked. [PEEL v. (1)]

peeled egg *n.* [20C] (Ulster) anything easy or simple.

peeler *n.*¹ [mid-19C+] a policeman (cf. BOBBY; BOBBY PEELER). [proper name Sir Robert *Peel* (1788–1850), founder of the Metropolitan Police. The term is now obsolete except in Northern Ireland]

peeler *n.*² [20C] (US) a striptease or burlesque artist. [PEEL v. (1)]

peel garlic/peele garlic *see* PILGARLIC.

peel-head *adj.* [1920s+] (W.I.) bald, esp. as a description of certain species of chickens or vultures.

peel it *v.* [mid-19C] (US) to run at full speed. [var. on SE *peel off*]

peel off *v.* [1940s–60s] (US Black) to remove one of the large bills which has been wrapped round a roll of singles, ensuring that no one sees that the roll is in fact worth less than appears.

peel off a mass, to *phr.* [1990s] (W.I./UK Black teen) to hand out money.

peel one's best end, to *phr.* [late 19C–1910s] to enter a woman's vagina. [the sliding back of the foreskin]

peel some chillis, to *phr.* [1990s] to masturbate (cf. PEEL THE BANANA).

peel the banana, to *phr.* [1990s] to masturbate (cf. ADJUST THE BOWL OF FRUIT; PEEL THE CARROT; PEEL SOME CHILLIS). [SE *peel* + BANANA n.² (1)]

peel the carrot, to *phr.* [1990s] to masturbate (cf. PEEL THE BANANA).

peel the patch off the weak point, to *phr.* [late 19C] (US) to attack a person at their most vulnerable point.

peely-wally *adj.* [20C] (Ulster) sickly-looking, wan. [Scot.]

peenie *n.* [20C] (juv.) the penis (cf. PEEDIE; WEENIE n.¹). [dimin. of SE *penis*]

p.e.e.p. *n.* [20C] the vagina. [abbr. perfectly elegant eating PUSSY n.¹ (1)]

peep *n.*¹ [1930s+] (orig. US) a word, esp. one of complaint; thus *not a peep*, not a sound. [SE *peep*, a shrill noise]

peep *n.*² [1970s+] (drugs) phencyclidine (cf. ACE n.³). [pron. of the two 'P's in PCP]

peep *v.*¹ [late 17C–18C] (Und.) to sleep. [rhy. with SE *sleep*]

peep *v.*² [1990s] (US Black) **1** to discover something that was meant to be kept secret. **2** to put someone or something under surveillance; to watch.

pee-pee *n.*¹ [1920s+] (usu. juv.) urination. [euph. for PISS n.]

pee-pee *n.*² [1920s+] (usu. juv.) the penis. [SE *penis*]

pee-pee lover *n.* [1970s+] (gay) one who prefers the youngest boys for sex. [PEE-PEE n.² + SE *lover*]

peeper *n.* **1** [late 17C–late 19C] a looking-glass. **2** [late 19C+] a policeman. **3** [1940s] a private investigator, with implications of voyeurism. **4** [1940s+] a Peeping Tom, a voyeur (cf. PEEP FREAK).

peepers *n.* **1** [late 17C+] the eyes. **2** [20C] (US) sunglasses. [SE *peep*, to look at]

peepers in mourning *n.* [19C] a pair of black eyes (cf. PAINTED PEEPER). [PEEPERS (1) + IN MOURNING (2)]

peep freak *n.* [1960s+] (US) a voyeur. [SE *peep* + FREAK n.]

peeping *adj.* [late 17C–early 18C] drowsy, nodding. [one's eyes keep opening and shutting]

peep-o!/-oh! *excl.* [19C+] (juv.) used by a child (or parents) when playing a game of hiding.

peeps *n.* [1980s+] (US Black/campus) **1** parents. **2** friends, people in general. [SE *people*]

peeps dig the range, to *phr.* [1930s–40s] (US Black) to look around one's immediate environs. [PEEPS + DIG v.⁶ + RANGE n.]

peep someone's hole-card, to *phr.* [1950s+] (US prison/Black) to work out a person's hidden attitudes and emotions (cf. SHOW ONE'S CARDS; SHOW ONE'S HOLE-CARD). [poker use *hole-card*, a card kept face down on the table]

peep things out, to *phr.* [1990s] (US Black) to see what is going on. [PEEP v.²]

peepy *adj.* [late 17C–mid-19C] (Und.) sleepy. [PEEP v.¹]

peer *v.* [late 18C–mid-19C] to act cautiously.

peer queer *n.* [1960s+] (gay) a gay voyeur (cf. PEEK FREAK). [SE *peer* + QUEER n. (4)]

peery *adj.* **1** [late 17C+] sly. **2** [late 17C–mid-19C] shy, fearful. **3** [late 17C–mid-19C] suspicious. **4** [early 19C+] inquisitive. [SE *peer*, to look around suspiciously]

peeties *n.* [late 19C+] (US gambling) loaded dice. [REPEATERS n.²]

peety *adj.* [late 19C] cheerful. [? SE *pert*]

pee-warmer *see* PISS-WARMER.

pee-wee/peewee *n.* **1** [19C] the penis, usu. of a small boy. **2** [mid-19C+] a small marble. **3** [1900s–50s] (drugs) a very thin marijuana cigarette. **4** [1910s] (Aus.) a bowler hat. **5** [1960s] a nickname for any noticeably small person. **6** [1980s+] (US drugs) crack cocaine, esp. $5 worth of crack (i.e. very little). [orig. dial. *pee-wee*, diminutive, tiny]

pee-wee *v.* [late 19C+] (juv.) to urinate. [PEE v. + WEE n.]

pee-willy *n.* [1920s+] (Can.) an effeminate man. [? PEE-WEE n. (1) + WILLIE]

peg *n.*¹ [late 18C–early 19C] a blow, esp. a straight-armed jab; thus *peg in the daylight*, a blow in the eye; *peg in the victualling office*, a blow in the stomach; *peg in the haltering place*, a blow under the ear (cf. PEG IT INTO).

peg *n.*² [mid-19C+] (orig. Anglo-Ind.) a drink, esp. of brandy and soda. [? each drink was seen as 'a peg [nail] in one's coffin'; but note 17C SE *peg*, 'one of a set of pins fixed at intervals in a drinking vessel as marks to measure the quantity which each drinker was to drink' (*OED*)]

peg *n.*³ [mid-19C+] a shilling (5p). [Scot. *peg*, one shilling; mainly Aus. use after 19C]

peg *n.*⁴ [mid-19C] a wooden leg. [abbr. SE *pegleg*]

peg *n.*⁵ [1980s+] (drugs) heroin. [ety. unknown; ? link to opium jargon or PEG n.²]

peg *v.*¹ [late 17C+] to throw (at), to pitch (at); thus [20C] (Aus.) *peg a gooly*, to throw a stone. [SE *peg*, to target or aim at with a peg]

peg *v.*² [early 19C] to drive, esp. a cab. [? pun on SE *peg*, to drive in a peg]

peg *v.*³ [mid-19C] **1** to run, to move fast. **2** to have sexual intercourse, usu. as *peg up/down* (cf. BANG *v.*¹). [orig. UK northern dial. but note PEG n.⁴]

peg *v.*⁴ [mid–late 19C] (Aus.) to starve; thus *pegging for*, desperate for. [? one has *put the peg* into one's stomach, i.e. blocked it off; ? var. on SE *beg*]

peg *v.*⁵ [late 19C] to drink. [PEG n.²]

peg *v.*⁶ [1920s+] (orig. US) to recognize, to work out, to analyse (cf. HAVE SOMEONE PEGGED).

peg along *v.* [mid-19C+] to persist. [var. on PEG AWAY]

peg away/off *v.*¹ [19C] to move off quickly. [ext. of PEG *v.*³ (1)]

peg away *v.*² [early 19C+] to work hard and energetically for a long period; often in form *peg away at*. [the hammering in of tent pegs]

peg-boy *n.* [1970s] a male homosexual prostitute (cf. PEG-HOUSE n.²).

pegged *adj.* [20C] (Ulster) angry. [? fig. use of PEG *v.*¹]

pegged off *adv.* [1920s+] under surveillance. [PEG *v.*⁶]

pegged out *adj.* **1** [mid-19C+] dead (cf. PEG OUT). **2** [late 19C] notorious, infamous. [cribbage use, *pegged out*, finished]

pegger *n.* [late 19C] a regular or heavy drinker, a person who 'constantly stimulates themselves by means of brandy and soda-water' (Hotten, 1873). [PEG n.²]

peggy *n.*¹ **1** [mid-19C–1920s] a thin poker used to facilitate the raking out of fireplaces. **2** [late 19C+] a tooth (cf. TOOTHY-PEGS). **3** [20C] a wooden leg, a peg-leg (cf. PEG n.⁴). **4** [20C] a one-legged person. [fig. uses of SE *peg*]

peggy *n.*² [1970s+] (Aus.) an unskilled worker who makes tea, sweeps up and takes on similar undemanding tasks. [naut. jargon *peggy*, a ship's mess-steward or menial; ult. *peg-leg*, a one-legged man who was often given such duties]

peggy's leg *n.* [20C] (Irish juv.) a type of boiled sweet. [dial. *peggy*, an implement for stirring washing; presumably a supposed resemblance]

peg-house *n.*¹ [1920s–30s] a public house. [PEG n.² + SE *house*]

peg-house *n.*² [1940s+] a male brothel (cf. ACCOMMODATION HOUSE). [the East Indian equivalents where the boys allegedly sat on wooden pegs to maintain a well-distended anus]

peg it into *v.* [mid–late 19C] to hit. [ext. of PEG *v.*¹]

peg-legger *n.*¹ [1930s–40s] a one-legged man. [SE *peg-leg*, one who has a wooden leg]

peg-legger *n.*² [1930s–40s] a beggar. [rhy. sl.]

peglegs *n.* [20C] (US) tapered trousers. [PEGS n.²]

pego *n.* [late 17C–late 19C] the penis. [? Gk. *pege*, spring or fountain; this 'classical' aspect made the term especially popular in 19C pornography]

peg off see PEG AWAY *v.*¹.

peg out *v.* [mid-19C+] **1** to die (cf. PEGGED OUT). **2** to be financially ruined. **3** to lose one's energy, esp. during a strenuous exercise or sport. [cribbage use ? + the image of taking down a tent]

peg puff *n.* [19C] an older woman dressed younger than her years (cf. MUTTON DRESSED AS LAMB). [? generic use of *Peg*, Margaret + *puffed up*]

pegs *n.*¹ [mid-19C+] the legs. [abbr. SCOTCH PEGS]

pegs *n.*² [1930s–60s] (US Black) trousers that taper sharply. [mid-19C *peg-top trousers*, very wide in the hips and correspondingly narrow at the ankles]

peg too low, a *phr.* [late 19C–1910s] tipsy. [PEG n.²]

pekkie/peckie/pek *n.* [1960s+] (S.Afr.) a Black person. [? Zulu *umpheki*, a cook]

pekoe *n.* [1950s] (drugs) top-quality opium. [SE *pekoe*, a superior variety of Chinese tea]

pelfry *n.* [16C] (Und.) the booty gained by those who pick

locks. [SE *pelf*, stolen property; *pelf* and *pelfry* are both SE in 14–15C]

pelican *n.* [mid-19C+] (US) a native of Louisiana. [the pelican on the state flag]

pelile *adj.* [20C] (S.Afr.) exhausted, absolutely finished. [Nguni *ukuphela*, to finish]

pellets *n.* [1960s–70s] (drugs) capsules of LSD.

pellicle *n.* [1950s] (drugs) high-quality opium. [? Lat. *pellis*, the skin. The ref. is to the slashing of the skin of the poppy-heads to release opium]

pellie *n.* [1950s+] (S.Afr., mainly Western Cape) a friend, a pal; thus *ou pellie*, old friend; *pellie blou*, a 'real pal', a 'bosom-buddy' (the *blou* means blue, as in 'true blue'). [PAL]

pelt *n.*¹ [late 16C–late 18C] a temper, a rage. [SE *pelt*, to attack (verbally or physically)]

pelt *n.*² [17C+] **1** the human skin; thus *in one's pelt*, naked. **2** a human being.

pelter *n.*¹ [late 18C+] a drenching downpour. [SE *pelt*, to beat violently]

pelter *n.*² [mid-19C–1930s] a horse, esp. a slow, old one. [ironic use of SE *pelt* (*along*) or 16C *pelter*, a paltry or peddling person]

pelter *n.*³ [late 19C] **1** something that goes fast, incl. a horse; thus *in a pelter*, in a hurry. **2** anything conspicuously large. [SE *pelt*, to move rapidly]

pelt your skin! *excl.* [20C] (W.I.) be off! go away! [SE *pelt*, to move fast]

pen *n.*¹ **1** [late 16C–1900s] the penis. **2** [mid-19C–1900s] the vagina. [resemblance]

Pen, the *n.*² [19C] Edinburgh prison (cf. TEN n.¹). [abbr. SE *penitentiary*]

pen *n.*³ [early 19C+] a penitentiary. [abbr.; 20C use mainly US]

pen *n.*⁴ [mid-19C+] a stink. [rhy. sl. *pen and ink* = stink]

pen *n.*⁵ [late 19C–1900s] (Aus.) a threepenny piece. [ety. unknown]

penance *n.* [mid-19C+] (US) an inhabitant of Pennsylvania. [pun on *Pennsylvania* and the religiosity of its citizens]

penance board *n.* [late 18C–early 19C] the pillory.

pen and ink *n.* **1** [mid-19C+] a stink. **2** [1960s] (Aus./N.Z.) a drink. [rhy. sl.]

pen and ink *v.* [late 19C+] **1** to stink. **2** to cause problems, to complain, to 'kick up a stink'. [rhy. sl.]

pen and inker *n.* [1940s+] a suspicious person, esp. a possible informer. [rhy. sl. *pen and inker* = STINKER n.¹ (1)]

Penang lawyer *n.* [mid-19C+] a walking stick made from the stem of a dwarf palm (*Licuala acutifolia*) found in Malaya and Singapore (cf. TIPPERARY LAWYER). [? the use of such sticks in settling disputes at Penang; or Malay *pinang líyar*, wild areca, or *pinang láyor*, fire-dried areca]

pencil *n.* [1930s+] the penis, usu. that of a small boy; thus [1940s] *pencil and tassel*, a small boy's penis and testes (cf. BLACK PENCIL; PEN n.¹). [resemblance]

pencil dick *n.* [1980s+] (US) a general term of abuse, the implication being that the person in question has a small penis. [SE *pencil* + DICK n.⁵ (1)]

pencil geek *n.* [1970s+] (US campus) anyone who works more devotedly than their peers see fit. [SE *pencil* + GEEK n.¹ (6)]

penciller *n.* **1** [mid–late 19C] a bookmaker's clerk. **2** [late 19C+] (Aus.) a bookmaker or their clerk. **3** [late 19C] (US) a journalist (cf. PENCIL-PUSHER). [SE *pencil*]

pencil, open, lost and found *phr.* [late 19C] £10. [rhy. sl.]

pencil-/pen-pusher *n.* **1** [late 19C+] (orig. US) a clerk, a white-collar worker; thus *push a pencil/pen*, to perform office work. **2** [1980s] a journalist (cf. PENCILLER).

pencil-squeezer *n.* [1970s+] a masturbator. [PENCIL + SE *squeezer*]

pen-driver *n*. [late 19C] a clerk. [var. on PENCIL-PUSHER]

pendulum *n*. [19C] the penis (cf. CRANK n.⁵). [it 'swings']

penelope/penelopes *n*. [1990s] (US) a policeman, the police. [initial letters]

penguin *n*. [20C] (US) (mainly juv.) a nun. [her traditional black and white habit]

penguin suit *n*. [1960s] a dinner jacket. [the black jacket and trousers and accompanying white shirt resemble a penguin's markings]

Peninsular *n*.¹ [19C] a veteran of the *Peninsular* War (1808–14). [abbr.]

peninsular *n*.² **1** [mid-19C] a female pickpocket. **2** [1950s+] a very inquisitive woman. [? play on SE *peninsular*, a project-ing strip of land; i.e. she sticks out a finger either for thieving or for emphasis]

penis wrinkle *n*. [1980s+] (US campus) an unpleasant, un-sophisticated man.

penitentials *n*. [mid-18C–mid-19C] mourning garments. [SE *penitential robe*, a robe worn by a public penitent + *peniten-tials*, the signs and behaviour of a penitent]

penitentiary agent *n*. [1950s+] (US Und.) a lawyer who seems to be working more for the courts and police than for the defence of their client.

penitentiary despatcher *n*. [1960s+] (US Und.) a public defender. [the supposed failing of these court-appointed law-yers, whose caseload is often said to be too heavy for them to put forward an adequate defence, and whose clients thus end up in the penitentiary]

penitentiary highball *n*. [1930s] (US prison) home-brewed prison alcohol, based on strained shellac and milk. [SE *peni-tentiary* + HIGHBALL n.]

penitentiary/pen shot *n*. [1930s–40s] (US drugs/prison) an injection achieved by using a rudimentary 'needle', in fact a pin and a medicine dropper. The pin is pushed into the vein and the dropper, filled with a solution of heroin and water, pushed over it. [SE *penitentiary* + PEN n.³/SHOT n.⁵ (2)]

penman *n*. **1** [mid-19C+] (Und.) a forger of counterfeit notes (cf. SCRATCHER n.²). **2** [20C] (US) a student who signs their parent's name to excuse notes.

pennam *see* PANNUM.

pennif *n*. [mid–late 19C] **1** a £5 note (cf. FINNIP). **2** any bank-note. [backsl.]

penn'orth of bread *n*. [20C] the head. [rhy. sl.]

penn'orth of chalk *n*. [late 19C+] a walk (cf. BALL OF CHALK n.). [rhy. sl.]

penn'orth o' treacle *n*. [late 19C] a pretty woman (cf. JAM n.³).

penn'orth o' treason *n*. [late 19C] an anonymous but presumably scandalous Sunday paper: 'a notorious penny Sunday London paper which attacks every party and has no policy of its own' (Ware).

Pennsylvania salve *n*. [20C] (US tramp) apple butter. [SE *Pennsylvania* + SALVE n. (2)]

penny *n*.¹ **1** [mid-19C+] (Can./US) one cent. **2** [1940s–60s] (US) one dollar.

penny *n*.² [20C] (US teen) a policeman. [pun on COPPER n.²/COPPER n.³ (1)]

penny-a-liar *n*. [late 19C] a hack journalist. [pun on PENNY-A-LINER]

penny-a-liner *n*. [mid-19C+] a freelance literary or journal-istic hack. [the rate of pay offered to such writers]

penny-a-mile *n*. **1** [late 19C–1920s] a hat. **2** [late 19C–1920s] the head. **3** [20C] a smile. [rhy. sl. ; for (1) *penny-a-mile* = TILE]

penny ante *adj*. [mid-19C+] (orig. US) insignificant, un-important. [poker jargon; an *ante* is a deposit that entitles a player to join a round of play; thus an ante of only one penny is *de facto* insignificant]

penny a/the pound *n*. [late 19C+] the ground. [rhy. sl.]

penny awful/horrible *n*. [late 19C–1910s] a sensationally written 'true crime' story, sold for one penny. [var. on PENNY DREADFUL]

penny banger *n*. [20C] a mistake, a blunder. [rhy. sl. *penny banger* = CLANGER (1)]

penny black *n*. [20C] the back. [rhy. sl.; the *penny black*, the UK's first postage stamp, issued 1840]

penny-boy *n*. **1** [late 19C–1910s] 'a boy who haunted the cattle markets on the chance of driving beasts to the slaughter-house' (F&H). **2** [late 19C–1910s] a term of mild contempt. **3** [20C] (Ulster) anyone seen as being at the beck and call of someone else. [such a boy would presumably be tipped a penny]

penny brown *n*. [20C] (Aus.) a town. [rhy. sl.]

penny bun *n*. [20C] **1** one. **2** the sun. **3** a son. [rhy. sl.]

penny-buster *n*. [mid-19C–1900s] a small loaf (cf. PENNY STARVER). [it 'busts' one's stomach or appetite]

penny-catcher *n*. [1940s] (W.I.) one who is willing to work for derisory pay.

penny death-traps *n*. [late 19C] glass paraffin lamps. Made cheaply in Germany, they broke easily and caused a number of deaths.

penny dreadful *n*. [mid–late 19C] a sensationally written 'true crime' story, sold for one penny (cf. DREADFUL; PENNY AWFUL).

penny gaff *n*. [mid–late 19C] a cheap theatre or music-hall. [SE *penny* + GAFF n.¹ (2)]

penny gush *n*. [late 19C] the effusive journalese found in penny newspapers, the late 19C tabloids. [SE *penny* + GUSH n.²]

penny hang *n*. [19C–1930s] (orig. naval) a cellar or basement which features ropes strung from side to side on which drunken or exhausted clients, orig. sailors, drape themselves for a fitful sleep. In the morning one end of the rope is untied and the sleepers are dumped on the floor.

penny hop *n*. [mid-19C] a cheap dance; thus *twopenny hop*; *shilling hop*. [SE *penny* + HOP n.¹]

penny horrible *see* PENNY AWFUL.

penny lattice-house *n*. [18C–early 19C] a poor alehouse. [RED LATTICE]

pennyline *n*. [1960s+] (S.Afr. Black) a cheap prostitute (cf. TICKEY-LINE). [? ext. of PENNY-A-LINER]

penny loaf *n*. [late 19C] (Und.) a coward. [one who would rather live on a penny loaf than make a greater effort and steal beef]

penny locket *n*. [late 19C] a pocket (cf. LUCY LOCKET). [rhy. sl.]

penny numbers *n*. [1950s+] very small, insignificant num-bers.

penny pick *n*. [mid-19C] a cheap cigar. [SE *penny* + PICK n.¹]

penny-pinching *adj*. [20C] mean, avaricious; thus [1930s+] *penny-pincher*; [1960s+] *penny-pinch*.

penny pots *n*. [mid-19C–1920s] pimples found on a heavy drinker's face.

penny puzzle *n*. [late 19C] a sausage (cf. BAGS OF MYSTERY). [its dubious ingredients are 'never found out']

penny rush *n*. [1910s–20s] (Irish) cheap children's matinées at the cinema; thus [reflective of changing prices] [1930s–40s] *twopenny rush*; [1950s] *fourpenny rush*; [1950s–60s] *six-penny rush*.

penny starver *n*. [late 19C] the cheapest brand of cigars, three for twopence.

penny stinker *n*. [late 19C–1930s] a cheap cigar (cf. GUINEA STINKER).

penny swag *n*. [mid-19C] a seller of penny lots. [SE *penny* + SWAG n.¹]

penny the pound *see* PENNY A POUND.

penny toff *n*. [late 19C] a lower-class dandy who can only imitate the richer, genuine article. [SE *penny* + TOFF]

pennyweighter *n*. [late 19C–1950s] (US) **1** one who steals jewellery or precious stones or metals, esp. by entering a shop, asking to inspect the stock and, using an adhesive substance on their hands, picking up certain items; thus *penny-weighting*, performing this variety of theft. **2** one who steals by substituting paste gems for the real ones. [SE *pennyweight*, a measure used to state the fineness of silver]

penny-white *adj*. [late 17C–early 18C] usu. of a woman, rich but unattractive. [lit. 'one who has been rendered *white*, i.e. beautiful, by her possession of (silver) pennies']

penocha *n*. [1960s+] (US Black/Sp.) the vagina. [synon. Sp. sl.]

pen-pusher *see* PENCIL-PUSHER.

pen shot *see* PENITENTIARY SHOT.

pension-book crowd *n*. [1950s–60s] (gay) older male homosexuals, considered as a group.

pensioner/pensioner to the petticoat *n*. [18C–19C] a pimp (cf. CUNT-PENSIONER; SMOCK PENSIONER).

penthouse-nab *n*. [late 17C–early 19C] a large, high hat. [SE *penthouse*, a smaller building (often with a sloping roof) attached to the main structure + NAB n.[1] (3)]

penwiper *n*. **1** [19C] the vagina. **2** [1900s–40s] a handkerchief.

pen yen/pin yen *n*. [1910s+] (drugs) opium. [Chinese *nga pun-yin*, opium]

peola *n*. [1940s+] (US Black) a light-skinned Black woman. [Bantu *peula*, skin]

people *n*.[1] **1** [mid-19C–1930s] one's relatives, one's family; usu. qualified as *my people*, *her people* etc. **2** [1920s–50s] (orig. US) a person, an individual, e.g. *Sarah is good people*.

people *n*.[2] (US Black/drugs) **1** [1950s–60s] narcotics agents. **2** [1960s+] as *the people*, high-level drug dealers.

people-in-law *n*. [late 19C+] one's married partner's family. [PEOPLE n.[1] (1) + SE sfx. *-in-law*]

people's bank *n*. [20C] (Irish) a pawnbroker's shop.

peoria *n*. [20C] (US) a thin, meagre soup. [mispron. of Fr. *purée* + derog. ref. to the city of Peoria]

pep *n*.[1] [1910s+] (orig. US) energy, enthusiasm, spirit. [? abbr. PEPPER n.]

pep *n*.[2] [1970s+] (drugs) phencyclidine (cf. ACE n.[3]).

pep-'em-ups *n*. [1960s+] (drugs) amphetamine (cf. A n.[2]). [their effects]

pepper *n*. [20C] zest, vitality (cf. PEP n.[1]).

pepper *v*. [mid-19C–1920s] to tease, to deceive. [SE *throw pepper in one's eyes*]

pepper alley *n*. [early 19C] a state of being beaten up. [an actual London street + SE *pepper*, to beat severely]

pepper and salt *n*. [1960s–70s] (US Black) Black and White people running together in the street, presumably in the civil rights, anti-Vietnam and other demonstrations of the era.

pepper belly *n*. [20C] (US) a derog. term for a Mexican. [the stereotyped Mexican love of hot food]

pepper-castor/-caster *n*. [late 19C] (US) a revolver. [? resemblance]

peppered *adj*. [late 17C–18C] **1** badly hurt. **2** very badly infected with venereal disease. [SE *pepper*, to pelt with shot or missiles]

peppered off *adj*. [late 17C–18C] very badly infected with venereal disease (cf. PEPPER-PROOF). [SE *peppered*, pelted with shot, sprinkled with pepper; the general implication is of small, hot wounds]

pepper 'em up *v*. [1970s+] (US Black) **1** to prepare for something. **2** to get drunk or intoxicated on drugs. **3** to work out in a gym. **4** to fight and possibly injure one's assailant. [all imply some preparatory 'seasoning']

pepper-fly *n*. [1950s] (W.I.) an irascible, quick-tempered

person. [dial. *pepper-fly*, a sand-fly, which can give a painful sting]

pepper gut *n*. [20C] (US) a Mexican-American. [SE (*chili*) *pepper*, a main constituent of Mexican cooking]

pepper into *v*. [late 19C] to perform vigorously, to 'go at' hard. [ext. of SE *pepper*]

pepper-kissing *n*. [1970s+] (US Black) attempting to put the best face on bad news. [euph. for ARSE-KISSING]

pepper-kissing *adj*. [1970s+] (US Black) a neg. intensifier meaning no good, useless etc. [euph. for MOTHERFUCKING adj.]

peppermint flavour *n*. [1960s] a favour. [rhy. sl.]

peppermint rocks/peppermints *n*. [20C] socks (cf. ALMOND ROCKS). [rhy. sl.]

peppermint swirl *n*. [1970s–80s] LSD, esp. when combined with another drug. [? the name of a sweet]

pepper-proof *adj*. [late 17C–18C] (temporarily) free of venereal disease. [PEPPERED OFF]

pepper-upper *n*. [1930s] a stimulant, usu. alcoholic (cf. PEP-'EM-UPS). [PEP UP]

pep pill *n*. [1940s+] (drugs) an amphetamine (cf. A n.[2]). [PEP n.[1]]

peppy *adj*. [1910s+] (orig. US) cheerful, enthusiastic. [PEP n.[1]]

Pepsi *n*. [1960s–70s] (Can.) a modern, young French-Canadian (as opposed to their older forbears). [their drinking of *Pepsi-Cola*, rather than more potent 'men's drinks']

Pepsi/Pepsi-Cola habit *n*. [1980s+] (drugs) a limited or occasional use of drugs. [*Pepsi-Cola*, a soft rather than alcoholic drink + HABIT]

pepst *adj*. [16C] drunk. [ety. unknown]

pep-talk *n*. [1920s+] any kind of talk, esp. an inspirational lecture, designed to improve the listener's morale. [PEP n.[1] + SE *talk*]

pep up *v*. [1920s+] (orig. US) to cheer up, to inspire, to exhort. [PEP n.[1]]

perc/perk *n*. [1930s–50s] (US) (orig. cowboy, then tramp) *perc*olated coffee, as opposed to that boiled up in a pan. **2** a coffee *perc*olator. [abbr.]

perc *v*. *see* PERCOLATE v.[1], v.[2].

perceive what's what *see* WHAT'S WHAT.

percentage *n*. [mid-19C+] (US) advantage, use, 'point', e.g. *what's the percentage*.

perch *n*.[1] [early 19C] death. [ext. of DROP OFF THE PERCH]

perch *n*.[2] [mid-19C] a bed; thus *off to perch*, going to bed.

perch *n*.[3] [1970s+] **1** (Aus.) a glass of beer. **2** (US campus) a pint of liquor (cf. BASS; BREAM). [SE *perch*, a common freshwater fish]

perch *v*.[1] [late 19C] to die. [PERCH n.[1]]

perch *v*.[2] [20C] (US) to kiss. [the image of a pair of lovebirds perched on a branch]

percher *n*.[1] [early 18C] a dying person. [PERCH v.[1]]

percher *n*.[2] [1960s+] (Und.) **1** a gullible victim for a swindle or con-game. **2** a simple arrest. [the victim is 'perched' in innocent vulnerability]

percolate/perc/perk *v*.[1] [1920s+] **1** (US) to run smoothly, esp. of an engine. **2** to penetrate the mind.

percolate/perc/perk *v*.[2] [1930s–40s] (US) to stroll, to wander around. [misuse of SE *perambulate*]

percolating *n*. [1930s–40s] (US Black) walking around looking for sexual conquests. [PERCOLATE]

percolator *n*. [1930s–40s] (US Black) a party held so that the host can collect money from their guests so as to pay the rent. [? the money *percolates* through from the guests to the host]

percy *n*.[1] [mid–late 19C] (US) a small amount of drugs, for personal use only (cf. PERSY). [abbr. SE *personal*]

percy/percy-boy/percy-pants *n*.[2] [20C] (US) an effeminate man, a weakling. [the 'effeminate' image of the proper name]

percy *n*.[3] [1960s+] the penis (cf. ABRAHAM). [joc. use of proper name, based on initial letters]

percy-boy/-pants *see* PERCY n.².

Percy Thrower *n.* [20C] the telephone. [rhy. sl. *Percy Thrower* = BLOWER n.²; ult. UK gardening expert Percy Thrower (1913–88)]

peremptory *adj.* [late 16C] absolute, thorough, complete.

peremptory *adv.* [late 16C] absolutely, entirely.

perfect *adj.* **1** [early 17C+] utter, complete, total, e.g. 'a perfect idiot'. **2** [1910s+] wonderful, ideal, delightful.

perfect high *n.* [1980s+] (drugs) heroin. [SE *perfect* + HIGH n.]

perfect/real lady *n.* [late 19C] **1** (US) a drunken woman (cf. LADY FROM THE GROUND UP). **2** a prostitute.

perfecto! *excl.* [1980s+] wonderful! excellent! perfect! [cod Sp.]

perforate *v.* [late 19C+] of a man, to have sexual intercourse with, esp. to take a woman's virginity (cf. BANG v.¹).

perform *v.¹* **1** [late 19C+] (Aus.) to display extreme anger or bad temper, to swear loudly, to make a great fuss. **2** [1940s–50s] (Und.) to commit a crime.

perform *v.²* [late 19C+] to have sexual intercourse (cf. DO v.²; HAVE v.¹).

perform a bottom-wetter *see* DO A BOTTOM-WETTER.

performance *n.* [1930s+] a display of (uncontrolled) emotion, a tantrum, a 'scene'.

perform a self-test, to *phr.* [1980s+] to masturbate. [computer imagery]

performer *n.¹* [late 19C–1900s] a philanderer, a promiscuous man. [PERFORM v.²]

performer *n.²* [1930s+] (orig. naut.) one who makes a fuss or a good deal of noise. [PERFORM v.¹]

perform on *v.* [19C] **1** of a man, to have sexual intercourse. **2** to cheat, to deceive.

perfume *v.* [1940s] (US Black) to put the best possible face on otherwise unpalatable facts.

perfumed talk *n.* [late 19C] (US) obscenities, bad language.

perico *n.* [1980s+] (drugs) cocaine. [Sp. *perico*, Pete]

periin *n.* [1940s] (W.I.) an albino (cf. FRECKLE-NATURE). [? SE *peering*; albinos stereotypically suffer from poor eyesight]

period *n.* [1930s+] (US) that is that, there is no more to be said. [SAmE *period* = SE *full stop*]

period hitter *n.* [1960s] (drugs) an occasional drug user. [SE *period* + HIT n.⁴]

periodical *n.* [late 19C–1900s] (US) a drinking bout. [? one does it *periodically*]

period, point blank *phr.* [1930s+] (US) absolutely, utterly, without question. [ext. of PERIOD]

periphery *n.* [1910s–20s] a pot-belly. [play on SE *periphery*, a circumference]

perish *v.¹* [late 19C] (mainly Aus.) to attack, to punish, to kill.

perish *v.²* [late 19C+] (Aus.) **1** to suffer a state of virtual starvation; thus *do a perish*, to starve, to go without food. **2** to be homeless, to sleep out at night.

perisher *n.¹* **1** [late 19C–1920s] a short coat (cf. ARSEHOLE-PERISHER). **2** [20C] a spell or day of very cold weather. [one 'perishes' of the cold]

perisher *n.²* [late 19C+] a person, often in a derog. sense, and often, as *little perisher*, applied to a child.

perishing *adj.* [mid-19C+] a general intensifier, e.g. *perishing cold*, *perishing hard*.

perish me pink! *excl.* [20C] a general excl. of surprise, shock, amazement (cf. STRIKE ME PINK!).

periwinkle *n.* **1** [late 18C–early 19C] a peruke or wig. **2** [mid-19C–1900s] the vagina (cf. BEARDED CLAM).

perk *n.¹* [late 19C+] a bonus, esp. that which comes with a job, usu. in pl.; thus *perker*, one who looks for such extras. [SE *perquisite*]

perk/purko *n.²* [1910s] (Aus.) beer. [? PERKINS]

perk *n.³* *see* PERC.

perk *n.⁴* [1960s] (Aus.) an act of vomiting; thus *perk/perk up*, to vomit, usu. after excessive drinking. [echoic or PERKINS]

perk *v.* *see* PERCOLATE v.¹, v.².

perked *adj.* [late 19C] (Aus./N.Z.) drunk. [PERKINS]

perkin *n.* [late 18C–mid-19C] weak cider; the washings from a cider barrel. [? SE *perry*, a drink made from pears + dimin. sfx. *-kin*]

perking *n.* [late 17C–early 18C] 'any pert, forward, silly fellow' (B.E.). [PERK UP]

perkins *n.* [mid-19C] beer. [abbr. BARCLAY PERKINS]

perkmeister *n.* [1990s] (US) an official, typically in a company or in government, who can offers favours, jobs etc. [PERK n.¹ + sfx. -MEISTER]

perks *n.* [1970s] (drugs) tablets of *Percodan*, a painkiller. [abbr.]

perk up *v.* [mid-17C+] to cheer up, to improve one's spirits; thus [20C] (orig. US) *perker-upper*, one who cheers people up. [SE *perk*, to thrust oneself forward, to act in brisk or jaunty manner]

perky *adj.* [mid-19C+] jolly, cheerful. [PERK UP]

perma- *pfx.* [1980s] (US campus) a pfx. indicating permanence, continuity.

permanent pug *n.* [late 19C] a man employed by a public house to keep order or eject troublesome customers. [orig. journalistic jargon *permanent pug*, a man employed to stand at a newspaper office to head off any complainers; ult. PUG n.⁴]

perm one's poodle, to *phr.* [1990s] of a woman, to masturbate (cf. PET THE POODLE). [the curls of the pubic hair and those of the dog]

pernicated dude *n.* [late 19C–1910s] (Can.) a swaggering dandy. [? SE *pernickety*]

perp *n.* [1980s+] **1** (US) a *perp*etrator, an accused criminal. **2** (US Black) one who is pretending or faking (cf. PERPETRATE). **3** (US drugs) fake crack made of candle wax and baking soda. [abbr. SE *perpetrator*, (3) is an ext. of (2)]

perpendicular *n.* **1** [mid–late 19C] sexual intercourse in which the partners are standing up. **2** [late 19C] a meal taken standing up, a party at which the guests stand rather than sit in a formal 'placement'.

perpetrate *v.* **1** [mid-19C+] to do anything which the speaker pretends to find shocking or otherwise disgraceful. **2** [1980s+] (US Black teen/campus) to pretend to be something that one is not. [SE *perpetrate*, to perform (usu. a crime or other reprehensible act)]

perpetrator *n.* [1980s+] (US campus) one who pretends to greater attainments, social position or popularity than they actually have (cf. WANNABE). [PERPETRATE (2)]

perpetual staircase *n.* [late 19C–1900s] the prison treadmill (cf. EVERLASTING STAIRCASE).

Perry Como *n.* [1950s] a homosexual. [rhy. sl. *Perry Como* = HOMO n.² (1); ult. singer Perry Como (b.1912)]

persnickety *adj.* [20C] (US) over-fastidious, petty. [var. on SE *pernickety*]

personal *n.* [1960s] a close friend.

persp *n.* [1920s+] *persp*iration. [abbr.; all uses appear in the works of P.G. Wodehouse (1881–1975)]

persuader *n.* **1** [late 18C–early 19C] a spur (cf. TORMENTORS). **2** [mid-19C+] a weapon, usu. a pistol or revolver, which persuades victims to its wielder's point of view (cf. CONVINCER).

persuasion *n.* [mid-19C+] nationality, gender, type, e.g. *of the Hebrew persuasion*, *of the female persuasion*.

persy *n.* [1980s+] (US drugs) one's own supply of drugs. [abbr. SE *personal*]

pertish *adj.* [mid-18C–early 19C] tipsy, quite drunk. [SE *pert*]

per usual *see* AS PER USUAL.

Peruvian *n.*[1] [late 19C–1900s] (S.Afr.) **1** a Jew, esp. an East European Jew who retains their accent, mannerisms and general culture. **2** a fellow Jew who fails to meet the community's ethical and moral standards. [? pun on initials of the *Polish and Russian Union*, an organization that facilitated the immigration of Jews from Russia and Eastern Europe]

Peruvian/Peruvian flake/Peruvian lady *n.*[2] [1980s+] (drugs) cocaine. [its origin]

Peru window *n.* [1960s+] (Aus.) a two-way mirror in a bedroom, through which voyeurs can observe a couple having sex. [? SE *peer through*]

perv/perve *n.* [1940s+] (orig. Aus.) **1** one who is categorized as a sexual pervert, esp. a child-molester. **2** pornography. **3** a voyeur. **4** a male homosexual. [abbr. SE *pervert*]

perv/perve *adj.* [1940s+] pornographic, e.g. *perv film*, *perv book*, *perv show*, a strip show. [PERV n.]

perv/perve *v.* [1940s] (orig. Aus./N.Z.) **1** to behave in a sexually perverted manner, esp. used of child-molesters. **2** to stare at, to watch, usu. in a prurient manner. [PERV n.]

perv/perve about *v.* [1940s+] (orig. Aus.) to search for potential sexual conquests. [the use of PERV v. here is facetious rather than an actual ref. to any sexual eccentricity]

perve *see* PERV n., adj., v.

perve about *see* PERV ABOUT.

perv/perve on *v.* [1940s+] (Aus.) **1** to act in a sexually perverted manner. **2** to indulge in voyeurism. [PERV v.]

pervin' *adj.* [1990s] (US Black teen) intoxicated, drunk. [? fig. use of PERV v.]

pervo *n.* [1940s+] (Aus.) a pervert. [PERV n. + sfx. -O]

pervy *adj.* [1940s+] (orig. Aus.) sexually perverted. [PERV n.]

pesh *n.* [20C] (W.I.) money (cf. PAISA). [Sp. *peso*, a coin of low denomination or Fr. *pièce*, a coin]

pesky *adj.* [mid-18C+] (US) annoying, irritating. [? SE *pesty*, plague-ridden, or Irish *peasgach*, rough, rugged]

peso *n.* [19C] (US) a dollar. [Mex. Sp. *peso*, a coin approx. equivalent to $1]

pest *v.* [1930s+] (Aus.) to *pester*. [abbr.]

pestilence *adj.* [early–mid-17C] unpleasant, unappealing, 'plaguey'.

pest it!/it all! *excl.* [late 19C] a general excl. of annoyance or irritation.

pestle *n.* **1** [early 17C] a constable's staff. **2** [19C] the penis (cf. BAT n.[7]).

pestle *v.* [late 19C–1900s] of a man, to have sexual intercourse. [PESTLE n. (2)]

pestlehead *n.* [19C] a fool. [SE *pestle* + sfx. -HEAD (1)]

pestle of pork *n.* [late 19C–1900s] the leg. [SE *pestle*, the leg of certain animals used for food, esp. the ham or haunch of the pig]

petal *n.* [1970s+] a general term of address.

pete/pete-box *n.*[1] [1910s–50s] a safe (cf. PETER n.[3]).

pete *n.*[2] *see* PETER n.[5].

pete *n.*[3] [1930s–40s] (US) nitroglycerine, used to open safes. [PETER v.[2]]

pete-box *see* PETE n.[1].

peted *adj.* [mid-19C+] (Can.) exhausted. [PETER OUT]

pete-man *n.* [1910s–30s] a safecracker (cf. PETERMAN n.[2]). [PETER n.[3] (2) + sfx. -man]

peter *n.*[1] [early–mid-17C] a form of Spanish wine. [abbr. PETER SEE ME]

peter *n.*[2] [late 17C–mid-18C] (Und.) a variety of loaded dice, used for cheating. [? SE *petard*, upon which the loser is 'hoist']

peter *n.*[3] **1** [late 17C–1930s] a trunk, a bundle or parcel of any kind. **2** [mid-19C+] a safe or cash-box, a cash register, a till. **3** [late 19C+] a cell, whether in gaol, a police station or elsewhere, thus also a prison. **4** [late 19C+] (Aus.) a punishment cell. **5** [late 19C–1950s] (Aus.) a witness box; thus *mount the peter*, enter the witness box. [? fig. use of proper name *Peter*, based on its ety., Gk. *petros*, a stone]

peter *n.*[4] [late 19C+] the penis, esp. of a young boy (cf. ABRAHAM). [joc. use of proper name + initial letters]

peter/peter drop/pete *n.*[5] [1920–60s+] a knockout drug (cf. MICKEY n.[6]). [PETER v.[3]; the drug is derived from nitroglycerine]

peter *v.*[1] [early 19C] to stop, to cease. [? PETER OUT but it appears to be earlier. ? Fr. *peter*, to explode weakly]

peter *v.*[2] [1920s+] to blow open a safe with nitroglycerine. [PETER n.[3] (2)]

peter *v.*[3] [1920s–60s] (US) to use knockout drops on a victim. [PETER n.[5]]

peter and lee *n.* [1990s] a cup of tea. [rhy. sl.; ult. singing duo Lennie *Peters* (1939–92) and Dianne *Lee* (b.1950)]

peter-beater *n.* [1980s+] (US) a masturbator. [PETER n.[4]]

peter-boatman *n.* [late 18C–mid-19C] a thief who operates on the river. [PETER n.[3] (1)]

peter-claiming *n.* [late 19C] stealing unguarded parcels and bags from railway stations; thus *peter-claimer*, the thief who does this. [PETER n.[3] (1) + CLAIM v.[1] (1)]

peter-cutter *n.* [mid-19C] an implement used to break into safes. [PETER n.[3] (2)]

peter-drag *n.* [19C] the stealing of boxes, parcels, bags etc., esp. f. carriages. [PETER n.[3] (1) + DRAG n.[2]]

peter drop *see* PETER n.[5].

peter-eater *n.* [1980s+] (US) a fellator, a fellatrix. [PETER n.[4] + EAT v.[3]]

peterer *n.* [mid–late 19C] a thief who specializes in stealing goods from the back of vans and carts (cf. PETERMAN n.[2]; VAN DRAGGER).

peter funk *n.* [early 19C] (US) a fraudulent salesman, often operating in the guise of an auctioneer, who augments the appeal of their third-rate merchandise by intimating that it had in some way been acquired illegally. [a generic proper name, orig. Ger./Du.]

peter grievous/grievance *n.* [late 18C–1930s] a whiner, a complainer, a whinging child.

peter gunner *n.* [17C–late 19C] a poor shot; thus [19C] *Peter Gunner who will kill all the birds that died last summer*. [a supposed name but note *peter*, saltpeter (used in bullets)]

peter-hunting *n.* [19C] (Und.) the stealing of baggage and boxes (cf. PETER LAY). [PETER n.[3] (1) + SE *hunting*]

peter jay *n.* [1980s+] (US Black/Los Angeles) a policeman. [ety. unknown]

peter lay *n.* [late 18C–early 19C] (Und.) the stealing of baggage and boxes (cf. BITER OF PETERS). [PETER n.[3] (1) + LAY n.[4] (2)]

peter lug *n.* [late 17C–early 19C] (Und.) a dawdling drinker, usu. as in phr. *who is peter lug*, whose glass is still undrunk. [generic use of *Peter* + SE *lug*, anything heavy or clumsy]

peterman *n.*[1] [late 17C–early 18C] one who poaches fish from the River Thames. [SE *peterman*, a fisherman, ult. after the apostle Simon Peter, a fisherman]

peterman *n.*[2] **1** [mid-19C] a thief who specializes in stealing goods from the back of vans and carts (cf. PETERER). **2** [late 19C+] a safecracker. [PETER n.[3] (1), (3)]

peterman *n.*[3] [late 19C–1900s] one who uses knockout drops to facilitate a robbery. [PETER n.[5]]

peter-meter *n.* [1980s+] (US) a notional means of measuring the size of a penis. [PETER n.[4] + SE *meter*. Coined by *Screw* magazine in the late 1960s, when it was used as part of reviews to assess the degree to which a pornographic film or book was arousing]

peter out *v.* [mid-19C+] to give out, to fade away. [orig. US mining jargon, but note PETER v.[1]]

peter pan *n.*[1] [20C] a van. [rhy. sl.]

peter pan *n.*[2] [1970s+] (drugs) phencyclidine (cf. ACE n.[3]).

Peter Pan's Never-Never Land *see* NEVER-NEVER LAND.

peter player *n.* **1** [mid–late 19C] (US) one who uses knockout drops to facilitate a robbery (cf. PETERMAN n.[3]). [PETER n.[5]]

peter-popping *n.* [1950s–60s] blowing open safes with gelignite or nitroglycerine. [PETER n.[3] (2) + SE *pop*, to burst]

peter puffer *n.* [20C] (US) one who performs oral sex. [PETER n.[4] + SE *puff*, to blow]

peter-ringer *n.* [mid-19C] a stealer of carpet-bags. [PETER n.[3] (1) + RINGER n.[2]]

peter school *n.* [1900s–30s] (Aus./N.Z.) a gambling den. [*DNZE* claims 'unknown'; ? PETER n.[3] (2), i.e. the casino's cash-box]

peter-screwing *n.* [mid-19C+] breaking open safes. [PETER n.[3] (2) + SCREW v.[2]]

peter see me *n.* [early–mid-17C] a Spanish wine, properly named *Pedro Ximenes* (cf. PETER n.[1]). [*peter* = *Pedro*, a famous grape + Cardinal *Ximenes* (1436–1517)]

peter that! *excl.* [19C] shut up! be quiet! [PETER v.[1] or PETER n.[3], with image of 'locking up' the noise]

pete tong *adj.* [1980s] wrong. [rhy. sl.; ult. UK dance DJ/mixer *Pete Tong*]

peth *n.* [1980s+] (drugs) depressant. [abbr. SE *pethidine*]

pet-napper *n.* [20C] (US) one who kidnaps pets. [SE *pet* + NAP v.[1] (1)]

peto *n.* [late 19C] (society) please turn over, i.e. the abbr. *p.t.o.*

pet one's pussycat, to *phr.* [1980s+] of a woman, to masturbate. [SE *pet* + PUSSY n.[1] (1)]

Petricelli *n.* [1980s+] (US Black) a high fashion suit. [brand-name of a popular tailors]

petrified *adj.* **1** [1900s+] very drunk (cf. ADDLED). **2** [1950s] under the influence of a drug. [pun on STONED]

petro *adj.* [1980s+] (US) terrified, fearful, paranoid; thus *petrolyze*, to render paranoid. [P.R.Sp. *petro*, scared]

petrol-head *n.* [1980s] (Aus.) a devotee of motor-racing.

petrols *n.* [1970s] (Aus.) trousers. [rhy. sl. *petrol bowsers*]

petronel *n.* [17C] a braggart, a blusterer, a bully. [SE *petronel*, a kind of large pistol or carbine, used in the 16C and early 17C]

petter *n.* [1930s–40s] (US) one who enjoys indulging in sexual fondling and caresses. [SE *pet*, to fondle]

pet the lizard, to *phr.* [1970s+] to masturbate. [SE *pet* + LIZARD n.[3]]

pet the poodle, to *phr.* [1960s+] of a woman, to masturbate (cf. PERM ONE'S POODLE).

petticoat *n.* [mid-19C] a woman (cf. APRON n.[1]). [metonymy]

petticoat government *n.* [late 17C+] a domestic relationship in which the wife dominates her husband.

petticoat hold *n.* [late 18C–early 19C] a husband's interest in his wife's estate, limited to his lifetime only (cf. APRON-STRING HOLD). [generic use of PETTICOAT + SE *hold*, freehold, tenure]

Petticoat Lane *n.* [20C] a pain. [rhy. sl.; *Petticoat Lane*, the East London street market]

petticoat merchant *n.* [19C+] a pimp. [PETTICOAT + MERCHANT]

petticoat pensioner *n.* [late 16C–early 19C] a kept man.

pettifogger *n.* [16C+] a second-rate lawyer, condemned by their inadequacies to dealing only in minor cases. [SE *petty* + *fogger*. The proper name *Fugger*, the great Augsburg banking family of the 15C and 16C, which appears (usually with the 'u' changed to an 'o') in a number of European languages meaning initially a merchant, usurer or monopolist and subsequently an avaricious rich man, a cheap huckster, and anyone who uses corrupt methods for personal gain. The term persists today. Du. *fokker*, Walloon *foukeur* etc are all contemptuous designations for a person of great wealth. Thus the *petty-* or *pettifogger* was one whose methods emulated those of the great merchants but at the lowest level]

pettitoes *n.* [early 18C] the feet.

petty *n.* [1910s+] a *petticoat*. [abbr.]

pettyfogging *adj.* [1940s+] (W.I.) insignificant, silly, small. [PETTIFOGGER]

petty house *n.* [19C] the lavatory (cf. LITTLE HOUSE). [lit. 'small house']

pew *n.* [late 19C+] a seat.

pewter *n.* [mid-late 19C] **1** money, esp. silver. **2** a pewter drinking pot, esp. as given as a prize.

peysle/picell/pisel *v.* [20C] (Ulster) to work lazily, half-heartedly. [Scot. *peist*, to work feebly]

pez *n.* [1940s–50s] (US Black) facial hair, the hair on one's head. [ety. unknown]

pfat *adj.* [1990s] (US Black) very wise, sophisticated. [ext. of PHAT adj.[2]]

pfotz *n.* [20C] the vagina (cf. FUTY; FUTZ). [? euph. for FUCK n.[1]]

pfft *adj.* [1930s–50s] (orig. US) finished, terminated, over. [GO PFFT]

pfui! *see* PHOOEY!

p-funk *n.* [1980s+] (drugs) **1** heroin. **2** a mixture of crack and phencyclidine. [initial letter *p* + FUNK n.[3]; ult. the 1970s musical style *P-funk*, pioneered by George Clinton]

p.g. *n.*[1] [1910s+] a paying guest. [abbr.]

p.g. *n.*[2] [1930s–60s] (drugs) paragoric. [abbr.; a cough medicine based on opium linctus, which heroin addicts use when no stronger drugs are available]

P.G. tips *n.* [20C] the lips. [rhy. sl.; a popular brand of tea]

p.h. *n.* [1960s] (drugs) purple *h*earts, amphetamine pills (cf. A n.[2]). [abbr.]

p.h.a. *n.* [1990s] the penis. [abbr. *p*urple-*h*eaded *a*venger]

phallic thimble *n.* [1920s–30s] a sheath pessary. [play on *phallic symbol*]

phar lap *n.* (Aus.) **1** [1930s+] a very slow person. **2** [1950s] a wild dog, with its hair burnt off, trussed up and cooked in the ashes. [proper name *Phar Lap*, flash of lightning, Australia's most famous racehorse, fl. 1930s]

phar lap gallop *n.* [1930s–40s] (Aus.) a foxtrot. [*Phar Lap* + SE *gallop*]

pharaoh *n.*[1] [late 17C–18C] a particularly strong malt beer (cf. HUM CAP). [abbr. the brandname *Old Pharaoh*; ? the power attributed to the Egyptian kings]

pharaoh *n.*[2] [19C–1920s] (US Black) a young woman. [Kanuri (an African lang. of N.E. Nigeria) *fero*, a girl]

phase out *v.* [1980s+] (US campus) to become unaware, as if asleep.

phat *adj.*[1] [1960s+] (US Black/campus) used to describe an attractive woman. [*p*hysically *a*ttractive or *p*retty *h*ips *a*nd *t*highs]

phat *adj.*[2] [1990s] (orig. US Black) **1** rich. **2** a general term of approval, admiration (cf. DEF). [deliberately skewed sp. of SE *fat*]

phata-phata *see* PATA-PATA.

phat pocket *n.* [1990s] (US Black) a wealthy person. [PHAT adj.[2] + SE *pocket*]

phat tape *see* FAT TAPE.

pheasant *n.* **1** [late 17C–early 19C] a promiscuous woman (cf. CANARY n.[2]). **2** [late 19C] a herring (cf. BILLINGSGATE PHEASANT). [note naut. jargon *Spithead pheasant*, a bloater or kipper]

pheasant plucker *n.* [1970s+] reverse of 'pleasant fucker', and always used ironically to attack the person so named.

pheasantry *n.* [19C–1900s] a brothel. [PHEASANT n. (1)]

pheeze *see* FEEZE n.[1], n.[2], v.

phennies *n.* [1960s+] (drugs) phenobarbitol, a depressant.

pheno/phenos *n.* [1960s–70s] phenobarbital, phenobarbitone (a soporific drug best known by the US tradename Luminol). [abbr.]

phenom n. [late 19C] (US) an outstanding person or thing, a prodigy. [abbr. SE *phenomenon*]

phenomenon n. [mid-19C] an exceptional person, a prodigy. [thus Dickens's 'infant phenomenon – Miss Ninetta Crummles' in *Nicholas Nickleby* (1838)]

Philadelphia bankroll see CALIFORNIA BANKROLL.

Philadelphia lawyer n. [mid-19C] (US) a shrewd or unscrupulous lawyer, an expert in exploiting the minutiae of the law (cf. YANKEE v.). [the stereotyped characteristics of the city]

philander v. [mid-19C–1900s] 'to ramble on incoherently, to write discursively and weakly' (Hotten, 1874). [play on SE]

philharmonic n. [20C] tonic water. [rhy. sl.]

philip and cheyney/philip, hob and cheyney n. [mid-late 16C] generic for average people, the mass (cf. HABRA, DABRA AND THE CREW). [the contemporary commonness of these names]

philiper/philliper n. [mid-19C] a thief's accomplice. [? dial. *philip*, a sparrow]

philip, hob and cheyney see PHILIP AND CHEYNEY.

philistines n. [late 17C–19C] 1 bailiffs (cf. MOABITE). 2 a group of drunkards. [Judg. 16:20, 'The Philistines be upon thee, Samson']

Phillie see PHILLY.

phillies n. [1990s] (US) a rolling paper (cf. BLUNT n.[2]).

philliper see PHILIPER.

Philly/Phillie n. 1 [late 19C+] (US) *Phil*adelphia. 2 [1980s+] (US Black/drugs) a marijuana cigarette made of buds rolled in a tobacco leaf taken from the wrapper of a *Phillies* Blunt cigar (cf. BLUNT n.[2]). [abbr.]

Philly bankroll see CALIFORNIA BANKROLL.

Phil McBee n. [mid-19C–1930s] a flea. [rhy. sl.]

phil the fluter n. [20C] a gun. [rhy. sl. *phil the fluter* = SHOOTER n.[1] (1)]

phiz/phyz/phyzog n. [late 17C+] the face. [abbr. SE *physiognomy*; UK use obs. by late 19C, but revived by US Blacks in mid-20C]

phizgig n.[1] [19C] an old woman dressed younger than her years. [SE *fizgig*, a frivolous woman]

phizgig n.[2] see FIZGIG n.[2].

phizzer see FIZZER n.[4].

phlegm-cutter n. [1960s+] the first drink of the day, usu. that taken by an alcoholic soon after waking up (cf. ALLEVIATOR).

phlizz n. [1920s] a failure. [FLOP n.[4] (1) + FIZZLE n.[2]]

phoby n. [mid-19C] 1 a dread or horror of water. 2 madness. [abbr. SE *hydrophobia*]

phoebe n. [1930s+] (gambling) the point of 5 in craps dice.

phoenix men n. [late 18C–early 19C] firemen employed directly by the Phoenix Insurance Office.

phoenix nest n. [19C] the vagina (cf. BIRD'S NEST). [? it makes the penis 'rise again']

phone booth baby n. [1960s–70s] (US Black) a child whose paternity is uncertain. [the image is of the mother giving birth in a phone booth or leaving the newborn child inside one]

phone freak n. [1970s+] a client who arranges to phone up a prostitute and listen while she runs through a pornographic monologue and he masturbates. [SE *phone* + sfx. -FREAK]

phone ho n. [1990s] (US Black) a woman, not necessarily a working prostitute, who offers 'telephone sex' to credit-card paying clients. [SE *phone* + HO n.[1] (1)]

phones n. [1910s+] head*phones*. [abbr.]

phoney n.[1] 1 [late 19C+] an insincere, untrustworthy, 'fake' person. 2 [1960s+] (gay) a mean or cheap client for a gay prostitute. [PHONEY adj.]

phoney n.[2] [1980s+] (US campus) a crank telephone call. [abbr. SE *telephone*]

phoney adj. [late 19C+] (orig. US) fake, counterfeit, insincere;

thus *phoney as a three-dollar bill* (cf. BENT AS A NINE BOB NOTE). [? FAWNEY or (*Major*, 1994) Mandingo *foni*, false]

phoney/phony v. [1940s+] (US) to counterfeit, to falsify, to make up. [PHONEY adj.]

phoney baloney life n. [20C] (US Und.) a sentence of 25 years to life (cf. ALL DAY FROM A QUARTER). [PHONEY adj. + BALONEY n.[1] + SE *life* (sentence); i.e. a 'fake' life sentence]

phoney jazz n. [1950s] (US Black) nonsense, insincere talk, deliberate lies. [PHONEY adj. + JAZZ n.[2]]

phonus balonus n. [1920s+] (US) rubbish, nonsense. [PHONEY adj. + BALONEY n.[1]]

phony see PHONEY v.

phooey!/pfui!/fooey!/fooy! excl. [1930s+] (orig. US) an excl. of disdain or dismissal, rubbish! nonsense!; thus ext. as *phooey on that!* [synon. Ger. *pfui*]

phos/phoss/foss n. 1 [early 19C] *phos*phorus, used by burglars for illumination; thus *ding the phos*, throw away the bottle of phosphorus. 2 [late 19C] *phos*phorus necrosis (cf. PHOSSY JAW). [abbr.]

phossy/fossy jaw n. [late 19C] *phos*phorus necrosis, the occupational disease of match-makers. [abbr.]

photo finish n. [20C] (a pint of) Guinness (stout). [rhy. sl.]

photog/fotog n. [1910s+] (orig. US) a *photog*rapher. [abbr.]

phreak v. [1970s+] (US) to use a variety of special equipment ('black boxes', 'blue boxes') to obtain free calls from the telephone system. [play on FREAK v.]

phrynne n. [19C] a prostitute. [*Phrynne*, a 4C BC courtesan]

phukk n. [1990s] a euph. sp. of FUCK, thus *muthaphukka*, MOTHERFUCKER.

phungky adj. [1990s] (US) cool (cf. FUNKY adj.[3]).

phuza/poosa/pusa/puza n. [20C] (S.Afr. township) liquor; thus *phuza-face*, a face bearing the marks of prolonged heavy drinking; *phuza-joint*, a bar; *phuza-buddy*, a drinking companion; *phuza-cabin*, a shebeen. [Xhosa/Zulu *phuza*, a drink, a sip]

phuza/poosa/pusa/puza v. [20C] (S.Afr. township) to drink. [PHUZA n.]

phuzawise adv. [20C] (S.Afr. township) as regards (the consumption of) liquor. [PHUZA n. + SE sfx. -*wise*]

phy n. [1970s] (drugs) *phy*ceptone, methadone. [abbr.; both forms of synthetic heroin]

physic n. [late 17C–early 18C] sexual intercourse. [play on SE *physic*, medicine]

physic v. [early 19C] to punish, either physically or through depriving of money. [SE *physic*, to give a dose of medicine]

physical n. [1990s] 1 a thug, a strong-arm man. 2 one's body. [in (1) the *physical* damage inflicted]

physical jerks n. [1910s+] physical or gymnastic exercises.

physicals n. [mid-19C] physical powers.

physical torture n. [20C] physical training.

physic-bottle n. [late 19C] a doctor. [lit. a 'medicine bottle']

physics for poets n. [1970s+] (US campus) a course in basic physics for arts specialists.

physio n. [1960s+] 1 a *physio*therapist. 2 *physio*therapy. [abbr.]

phyz/phyzog see PHIZ.

p.i./pee-eye n. [20C] (US Black) a *pi*mp. [abbr.]

pi adj. [mid-19C+] (orig. juv.) pious, always in a derog. sense of self-righteous, unctuous, poss. hypocritical.

pianist in a brothel see PIANO-PLAYER IN A BROTHEL.

piano n.[1] [1910s–40s] (US Black) spare ribs; thus *piano on a platter*, barbecued ribs on a plate. [supposed resemblance to piano keys]

piano n.[2] [1930s+] a cash register. [abbr. JEWISH PIANO n. (2)]

piano v.[1] [late 19C] (society) to stay in the background, to act unobtrusively. [Ital. *piano*, softly, used as direction in musical scores]

piano v.[2] [1980s+] (drugs) to search on hands and knees for any small pieces of crack cocaine that may have fallen to the floor. [? one hands are tapping at the floor in the hope of feeling a tiny piece]

pianoforte legs n. [1910s–20s] a bishop's legs when clad in gaiters. [the days when a piano's legs were covered so as to avoid offending Victorian proprieties]

piano-player/pianist in a brothel n. [1970s+] (Aus.) one who is involved in a situation, but adamantly refuses to take any responsibility for it.

p.i.b. n. [1990s] (US campus) a brooding, gloomy adolescent who wears dark clothes and listens to gloomy alternative music (cf. GOTH). [abbr. people in black]

pic n.[1] [mid-19C] (orig. US) a person or thing seen as small, mean, insignificant. [abbr. PICAYUNE n.]

Pic, the n.[2] **1** [mid–late 19C] the *Pic*cadilly Saloon. **2** [1920s–30s] the *Pic*cadilly Restaurant and Grill Room (cf. BAZE). [abbr.]

pic n.[3] **1** [late 19C+] a *pic*ture (cf. PICCY). **2** [20C] a film. [abbr.]

pic/piccolo n.[4] [1930s–40s] (US Black) a jukebox, a record-player. [SE *piccolo pianoforte*, a small piano]

picaro n. [early 18C–early 19C] a rogue; thus *on the picaro*, looking for easy opportunities for money-making (cf. ON THE MAKE phr.[2]). [Sp. *picarón*, a rogue]

picayune n. [early 19C+] (orig. US) a person or thing seen as small, mean, insignificant. [SAmE *picayune*, used in Louisiana, Florida etc for the Spanish half-real, value 6½ cents or 3 pence; later the US 5-cent piece or other coin of small value]

picayune adj. [early 19C+] paltry, small, insignificant. [PICAYUNE n.]

piccadill see TYBURN PICCADILL.

piccadilly adj. [20C] silly. [rhy. sl.; *Piccadilly*, area in central London]

Piccadilly bushman n. [1920s–40s] (Aus.) a wealthy Australian who has left their native land for London.

Piccadilly crawl n. [late 19C] an affected style of walking adopted by society during the 1880s.

Piccadilly daisy n. [1900s–50s] a prostitute. [before the Street Offences Act 1959, which took prostitutes off the streets; note WW2 army *Piccadilly commando*, a prostitute]

Piccadilly fringe n. [late 19C] a popular women's hairstyle in which the hair is cut short into a fringe and curled over the forehead. [the style allegedly orig. in Paris *c.*1870]

Piccadilly percy n. [1970s] mercy. [rhy. sl.]

Piccadilly weepers n. [mid–late 19C] long side whiskers, worn without a beard and temporarily fashionable (cf. DUNDREARY; WEEPER n.[1])

Piccadilly window n. [late 19C–1900s] a monocle. [affected by the fashionable men promenading in *Piccadilly*]

piccaninny/pickaninny n. [late 18C+] (orig. W.I.) a Black child, occasionally any Black person. [adopted in W.I. f. Sp./Port. *pequeño*, small or Port. *pequenino*, tiny. The term was seen, since used mainly of children, as neutral, but is now generally seen as patronizing and thus derog.]

piccaninny adj. [mid-19C–1930s] (Aus.) tiny; thus *piccaninny daylight*, the moments just before dawn. [PICCANINNY n.]

piccaninny kaya/piccaninny kia/p.k. n. [1960s+] (S.Afr.) an outdoor privy (cf. KLEINHUISIE). [PICCANINNY adj. + Nguni *kia*, house]

piccolo see PIC n.[4].

piccolo and flute n. [20C] a suit (cf. WHISTLE AND FLUTE). [rhy. sl.]

piccolo-player n. [1950s] a fellator or fellatrix (cf. CLARINET-PLAYER).

piccolos and flutes n. [1930s+] boots. [rhy. sl.]

piccy n. [late 19C+] a picture (cf. PIC n.[3]).

picell see PEYSLE.

picey adj. [late 19C+] mean. [Hind. *pice/pais*, a small East Indian copper coin equal in value to one-fourth of an anna]

pick n.[1] [late 19C] a third-rate cigar (cf. PENNY PICK). [abbr. SE *pickwick*; the type of cigar smoked by the character Mr Pickwick in Charles Dickens's *Pickwick Papers* (1836)]

pick n.[2] **1** [late 19C] a tooth*pick*. **2** [20C] (Und.) a *pick*pocket. **3** [20C] an ice *pick*. [abbr.]

pick n.[3] [20C] (Anglo-Irish) a quick-tempered person. [PICK ON]

pick n.[4] see NATURAL PICK.

pick adj. [early 19C] best. [SE *pick*, to choose]

pick v.[1] [late 18C–late 19C] to eat. [SE *pick*, to eat daintily]

pick v.[2] [1920s+] (Aus.) to guess. [SE *pick out*]

pick v.[3] [1950s+] (Aus.) to victimize. [PICK ON]

pick a berry, to phr. [20C] (US) to rob a clothes-line (cf. GOOSEBERRY LAY).

pick a bone with, to phr. [mid-19C+] **1** to argue with (cf. HAVE A CROW TO PICK). **2** to share a meal with. [the SE *bone* is (1) fig. + (2) lit.]

pick a crow with, to phr. [19C+] (US) to pick a quarrel with someone (cf. PICK A BONE WITH).

pick a daisy, to phr. [mid-19C+] to defecate in the open air (cf. PICK THE DAISIES).

pick a lime, to phr. [1970s+] (orig. W.I.) to sit around and relax with friends or family; thus *liming*, hanging around, chatting (cf. LIME v.). [? LIMEY n. (2), i.e. the groups of US sailors who frequented the Trinidad red-light areas during WW2]

pick and choose n.[1] [20C] alcohol, liquor. [rhy. sl. *pick and choose* = BOUSE n.]

pick and choose n.[2] [1920s] (W.I.) fastidiousness, esp. if taken to irritating extremes.

pick-and-choose adj. [1950s] (W.I.) hard to satisfy, pernickety. [PICK AND CHOOSE n.[2]]

pick and cut, to phr. [late 16C] to work as a cut-purse. [one *picks* up or holds the purse, then *cuts* it]

pick-and-dab n. [19C+] (Ulster/Scot.) a meal of potatoes flavoured with salt. [one *picks* up a potato and *dabs* it in the salt]

pick a needle without eye, to phr. [20C] (W.I.) of a young woman, to give oneself in marriage to a man whom one knows will be of no use as a sexual partner.

pickaninny see PICCANINNY.

pick at v. [1910s+] (Aus.) to irritate, to nag at, to annoy.

pick-axe n. [late 19C] (S.Afr.) a drink composed of whisky or rough brandy, Pontac (a sweet red dessert wine) and ginger-beer. [its effects]

pick cherries v. [1900s–30s] (US Black) to play the double bass or a guitar. [ety. unknown; ? the use of cherrywood in making the instruments]

picked before one was ripe phr. [1920s+] (Aus.) used of someone physically small or emotionally immature.

picked-hatch/pick-hatch/pickthatch/picthatch n. [17C] a brothel, orig. one situated either in Turnmill Street, a notorious 'red-light' district, or between Old Street and Goswell Road in Clerkenwell, London. [SE *picked*, spiked + *hatch*, a half door, designed to prevent unauthorized entrance.

pick 'em up and lay 'em down, to phr. [20C] (US) **1** to walk, to march. **2** to dance. ['em (them) are the feet]

picker n. [mid-19C] a hand (cf. FEELER n.[2]).

pickers n. [1940s] (US Black) the hands (cf. PICKER).

pickers and stealers n. [17C+] the hands (cf. FEELER n.[2]). [16C catechism, 'To keep my hands from picking and stealing']

picker-up n.[1] see ROPER n.[2].

picker-up n.[2] [late 19C] (Und.) a prostitute.

pickethatch/pickthatch vestal n. [late 18C–early 19C] a prostitute (cf. COVENT GARDEN NUN). [PICKED-HATCH + joc. use of SE *vestal* (*virgin*)]

pick fares v. [20C] (W.I./Bdos.) to work as a prostitute. [she gives her clients a 'ride']

pick-hatch see PICKED-HATCH.

picking n. [1990s] (drugs) searching on hands and knees for any small pieces of crack cocaine that may have fallen to the floor (cf. PIANO v.[2]).

picking up the vibrations phr. [1970s] (gay) watching other men perform a sex show, all-male voyeurism. [hippie use, when pleasures were more cerebral]

pickle n.[1] **1** [late 18C–late 19C] a difficult, troublesome person, often a child but by no means invariably; 'an arch, waggish fellow' (Grose, 1785). **2** [early–mid-19C] a wild, undisciplined young man. **3** [mid-19C+] a predicament, a difficult situation. **4** [1950s+] a woman of a sour, unpleasant disposition.

pickle n.[2] [late 19C+] (Ulster) a very small quantity. [Scot. pickle, a grain of corn, a hailstone]

pickle n.[3] [20C] (orig. US) the penis.

pickle v. **1** [19C] to tease, to hoax, to deceive. **2** [20C] (US) to spoil, to wreck.

pickle and pork/pickled pork n. [1940s–50s] (Aus.) a walk. [rhy. sl.]

pickled adj.[1] [mid-17C+] drunk; intensified as pickled to the gills (cf. ALED UP).

pickled adj.[2] [late 17C–18C] waggish, roguish. [PICKLE n.[1] (1)]

pickled pork n.[1] [late 19C–1930s] talk, conversation. [rhy. sl.]

pickled pork n.[2] see PICKLE AND PORK.

pickle-herring n. [late 19C] an amusing companion, a 'wag'. [ext. of PICKLE n.[1] (1)]

pickle-jar n. [mid-19C–1900s] a coachman with a yellow uniform. [the yellow colour of some pickles]

pickle kisser n. [1990s] a male homosexual. [PICKLE n.[3] + SE kisser]

pickle me bloody agates!/pickle me daisy!/pickle me tit! excl. [1960s+] (N.Z.) a general excl. of surprise or disbelief. [SE pickle + AGATES/SE daisy/TIT n.[1] (1)]

picklepuss n. [20C] (US) a sour-faced individual. [SE pickle, a sour gherkin + PUSS n.[3]]

pickles n.[1] [19C] a corpse. [medical student jargon, pickles, a corpse used for dissection]

pickles/dead pickles n.[2] [mid–late 19C] nonsense, rubbish. [PICKLE n.[1] (3)]

pickles! excl. [mid-19C] a general excl. of disbelief, nonsense! rubbish!

pickling tub see POWDERING TUB.

pickling tubs n. [mid-19C] high or Wellington boots.

picklock n. [17C] the penis. [note LOCK n.[2] (3)]

pick man n. [1960s+] (Can. prison) one who picks locks.

pick meat for dead goats, to phr. [20C] (W.I.) to waste one's time on fruitless tasks.

pick-me-up n. **1** [mid-19C+] any form of drink that relieves the physical and mental state of the imbiber, esp. used for those concoctions advertised as curing hangovers (cf. ALLEVIATOR). **2** [late 19C+] a person or circumstance that has a similar effect. **3** [1940s+] (S.Afr.) a police van, a black maria.

pick-mouth n. [mid–late 19C] (W.I.) one who sets out to pick a quarrel.

pickney n. [20C] (W.I.) a young child. [PICCANINNY n.]

pick of the basket/bunch n. [mid–late 19C] the best, the choicest on offer. [SE in 20C]

pick on v. [20C] **1** to pick a quarrel with. **2** to attack verbally, to victimize.

pick one's teeth to/with, to phr. [20C] (W.I.) to gossip with.

pick-penny n. [18C] a card-sharp. [SE pick-penny, one who greedily collects or steals money]

pick straws see DRAW STRAWS.

pickthatch see PICKED-HATCH.

pickthatch vestal see PICKETHATCH VESTAL.

pick the bones out of that! excl. [1950s+] a phr. of dismissal, retaliation, challenge, now see what you can do with that!

pick the daisies, to phr. [19C] a euph. excuse used when one wishes to absent oneself to visit the lavatory (cf. PICK A DAISY).

pick the eyes out of, to phr. [mid-19C+] (Aus.) to get the best bits for oneself (cf. PEACOCK v.[2]). [orig. referring specifically to a system whereby a squatter chose the best bits of a tract of land (a 'run') so as to render the remainder useless to a rival]

pick them v. [1940s+] to choose one's partner(s) in relationships (amatory or otherwise); often in ironic form as you can pick/certainly pick them, you do/do know how to pick them, i.e. they were a foolish choice.

pick-up n.[1] **1** [mid-19C] a confidence trick in which a prostitute lures a client to a room or deserted place, where, instead of having sex, the client is robbed by a male accomplice (cf. MURPHY n.[3]). **2** [mid-19C+] a casual sex partner, met and seduced without previous introduction. **3** [20C] robbery, theft; thus at the pick-up, working as a professional thief. **4** [1940s+] an arrest but no subsequent criminal charge; thus (S.Afr.) pick-up van, a police van.

pick-up n.[2] [1930s+] (drugs) a dose or injection of narcotics (cf. PICK-ME-UP).

pick up v.[1] **1** [late 18C–1920s] to rob, to steal. **2** [early 19C+] (Und.) to accost or enter into conversation with the intention of practising a hoax or confidence trick on someone. **3** [early 19C+] to accost for possible sex; also pick up a cull. **4** [mid-19C] to cheat, to deceive. **5** [mid-19C] (Und.) to rob by deception. **6** [mid-19C–1920s] to find fault with, to criticize. **7** [mid-19C+] to arrest.

pick up v.[2] [mid-19C+] (US) **1** to tidy or clean up, to put in order. **2** to resume where one has left off. **3** to stimulate, to invigorate.

pick up v.[3] [1930s–40s] (US Black) to put together a meal from assorted leftovers and scraps.

pick up v.[4] [1930s–50s] (US Black) **1** to do, to act, to perform. **2** to notice. **3** to set in motion, to start.

pick up v.[5] [1950s] to use narcotics. [PICK-UP n.[2]]

pick up a flat, to phr. [19C] of a prostitute, to meet a client. [PICK UP v.[1] (3) + FLATTIE n.[1]]

pick up a nail, to phr. [20C] (W.I.) to contract venereal disease. [the way in which venereal disease can lead to a sharp pain in the penis when urinating]

pick up fag-ends, to phr. [1910s+] to listen in to other people's conversations and attempt to comment upon them or join in, esp. as don't pick up fag-ends. [SE pick up + fig. use of FAG END n.[2]]

pick-up man n. **1** [1920s] a thief, esp. of luggage. **2** [1940s–60s] (US) one who collects money wagered with bookmakers.

pick up on v. [mid-19C+] (orig. US) to notice, to understand.

pick up one's crumbs, to phr. [mid-19C] **1** to recover from an illness, esp. to begin eating after a period of fasting. **2** to begin enjoying improved circumstances.

pick up one's foot see MAKE FOOT.

pick up one's marbles, to phr. [1920s–50s] (US) to quit, to leave, usu. indignantly. [the image is of a petulant child]

pick up sticks n. [20C] the number 6. [rhy. sl.]

pick up the bill/check, to phr. [1940s+] (orig. US) to pay a bill, usu. in a restaurant. The implication is one of treating one's fellow eaters (cf. PICK UP THE TAB).

pick up the soap for, to phr. [1960s–70s] (gay) to permit oneself to be sodomized. [the posture necessarily adopted for both activities]

pick up the tab, to phr. [1950s+] (orig. US) **1** to pay a bill, usu. in a restaurant; the implication is one of treating one's fellow eaters (cf. PAY THE FREIGHT; PICK UP THE BILL). **2** to take responsibility, to accept the consequences.

pick up yourself! excl. [20C] (W.I.) get up and get out! (cf. HICE YOURSELF!).

picky head see PICKY-PICKY HEAD.

picky-picky adj. [1950s] (W.I. Rasta) **1** finicky or choosy, esp. in eating. **2** used of uncombed hair just starting to turn into dreadlocks. [SE picky + redup.]

picky-picky head/picky head n. [1960s] (W.I.) very short hair growing close to the scalp in small balls of fluff (cf. BLACK-PEPPER BRAIN).

picnic n. [late 19C+] **1** any simple, pleasurable experience; thus (UK/Aus.) no picnic, an understated description of an unpleasant experience. **2** (Aus.) an unpleasant, tricky experience. [(2) ironic use of (1)]

picthatch see PICKED-HATCH.

picture n.[1] [early 19C+] anything or anyone considered very beautiful, e.g. you look a picture, she looks a picture, a picture of good health.

picture n.[2] [1940s+] (orig. milit.) a situation.

picture of Abe n. [1950s–60s] (US) a $5 bill (cf. ABRAHAM LINCOLN).

picture of ill-luck n. [late 18C–19C] 9 pence. [the ill luck comes since 9d is not the whole shilling]

piddle n. **1** [late 19C+] urine. **2** [late 19C+] an act of urination. **3** [1910s] nonsense. [PIDDLE v.]

piddle v. **1** [late 18C+] to urinate. **2** [late 19C+] to rain, with an implication of drizzle rather than heavy rain. [mid-16C piddle, to trifle, to work or act in a petty or insignificant way. The ext. to urination began as a childish expression, ? implying the insignificant amount of urine produced. The compounds piddle away, piddle around thus refer back to the 16C use, even if the assumption is of the later one (cf. PISS ABOUT; PISS AWAY)]

piddle about/around see PISS ABOUT.

piddle away v. [1940s+] to waste (cf. PISS AWAY). [PIDDLE v. but note one 1760 use, 'A house where she used to piddle away her leisure hours' (Charles Johnstone, Chrysal)]

piddling adj. [late 17C+] small, insignificant, irrelevant. [SE piddle, to trifle]

piddly adj. [1940s+] insignificant. [SE piddle, to trifle]

pie n.[1] **1** [mid-19C+] (orig. US) a treat, a bribe, something highly desirable. **2** [1910s] political or other patronage or favours. [the image is of cutting up or distributing the 'pie' among supporters]

pie n.[2] [late 19C+] (orig. US) anything easy or simple; often as easy as pie, good as pie, sweet as pie.

pie n.[3] **1** [1950s+] (US) the vagina (cf. APPLE n.[10]; HAIR PIE). **2** [1970s+] (US campus) an attractive, sexually desirable woman (cf. BANANA n.[2]).

pie adj. [20C] (Aus.) small-time, insignificant, second-rate (cf. PIE-EATER).

pie adv. [1940s] (N.Z.) good at, expert in (cf. HALF-PIE). [Maori pai, good]

pie and liquor n. [20C] a vicar. [rhy. sl.]

pie and mash n. [1970s+] **1** money. **2** urination. [rhy. sl. pie and mash = cash/SLASH n.[4]]

pie and one n. [20C] **1** a son. **2** the sun. [rhy. sl.]

piebald n. [late 19C+] (Aus.) a half-caste.

piebald v. [late 19C] to give a black eye; thus piebald eye, a black eye.

piebald mucker sheeny n. [late 19C] a dirty, old Jew. [SE piebald + MUCKER n.[2] (3) + SHEENY n.[1]]

piebald pony n. [1920s+] (Aus.) a half-caste White/Aboriginal child.

pie-biter see PIE-EATER.

pie-can n. [1910s–20s] a fool, a simpleton.

pie-card n. (US) **1** [1900s–20s] a ticket that entitles one to a meal. **2** [1920s–60s] one who begs for a meal. **3** [1920s–60s] a union-card, esp. when used as a credential for begging. **4** [1920s–60s] the holder of a union-card.

piece n.[1] **1** [late 18C+] a woman, esp. when appraised sexually (cf. ACTION PIECE n.[1]; PIECE OF ASS). **2** [1910s+] an act of sexual intercourse. [coined 14C; SE until 18C]

piece n.[2] [19C+] (Irish/Scot.) **1** a piece of bread and butter. **2** a sandwich, a worker's packed lunch; thus piece-plate, a sandwich plate; piece-time, lunchtime.

piece, the n.[3] [late 19C–1930s] the crux of the matter, the affair, the current situation.

piece n.[4] [1930s+] (orig. US) **1** a gun (cf. ACTION PIECE n.[2]). **2** the penis (cf. GUN n.[2]). [SE use late 16C–mid-19C, then sl.]

piece n.[5] **1** [1930s+] (drugs) a quantity of heroin, cocaine or morphine, approx. 28g (1oz). **2** [1980s+] a container for drugs.

piece n.[6] [1980s+] (US campus) a hairdo. [abbr. SE hairpiece]

piece n.[7] [1980s+] something undesirable. [PIECE OF SHIT]

piece n.[8] [1980s+] (orig. US) a major work of graffiti, typically as displayed on a New York City subway train. [abbr. SE masterpiece]

piece v. [1990s] (US teen) to snack. [SE piece of food]

piece/hunk of ass/arse/butt n. **1** [1910s+] a woman, not used as derog. but invariably from a sexual point of view and usu. dismissive. **2** [1910s+] heterosexual sexual intercourse. **3** [1930s+] hetero- or homosexual anal intercourse. [SE piece/ PIECE n.[1] + ARSE n.[1] (cf. PIECE OF FLESH; PIECE OF GOODS; PIECE OF SKIRT; PIECE OF TAIL)]

piece of cake n. [1930s+] anything seen as simple, easily achieved, no bother (cf. APPLE SAUCE n.[4]).

piece of chickenshit n. [1980s+] (US campus) a coward, a weakling. [CHICKENSHIT n. (1)]

piece of entire n. [mid–late 19C] an admirable person. [they are 'entirely' excellent]

piece off v. [1930s+] (US) to bribe, to pay off, to give out a 'piece' of cash.

piece of flesh/skin n. [20C] (W.I.) an attractive woman (cf. PIECE n.[1]; PIECE OF ARSE).

piece of goods n. **1** [mid-19C+] a flighty young woman who has 'abandoned the proprieties' (Ware) (cf. LOOSE BIT OF GOODS). **2** [late 19C+] a person.

piece of magnolia n. [1960s+] (Can.) **1** a sexually available woman (cf. PIECE OF ARSE). **2** sexual intercourse.

piece of meat n. [20C] anyone regarded as no more than a physical object, esp. in a sexual context.

piece of muslin n. [late 19C–1900s] a woman, usu. in sexual context (cf. BIT OF MUSLIN). [her dress]

piece of mutton n. [late 17C–early 19C] a woman, seen as a sex object (cf. BIT OF MUTTON). [MUTTON n.[2]]

piece of one's ass n. [1950s+] (US) a beating, a thrashing, a punishment. [ARSE n.[1] (1)]

piece of piss n. [1940s+] (orig. RAF) anything seen as supremely easy. [PISS n.]

piece of pudding n. [late 19C] **1** an example of good luck. **2** a welcome change in circumstances.

piece of resistance n. [1930s+] (Aus.) constipation. [a pun on Fr. pièce de résistance, the supreme example, esp. the best dish in a meal]

piece of seven n. [1970s] (US Black) any one of the 7 days of the week.

piece/pile of shit n. [1930s+] (orig. US) anything unpleasant, disgusting, of poor quality, e.g. a disliked person, a piece of gross hypocrisy etc. [fig. use of SHIT n.[1] (1)]

piece of skin see PIECE OF FLESH.

piece of skirt *n.* [17C+] a woman, seen as a sex object (cf. PIECE OF ARSE; PIECE OF MUSLIN; PIECE OF MUTTON). [metonymy]

piece of strange *n.* [1950s+] an unknown woman, usu. in a sexual context. [SE *piece* + STRANGE]

piece of stuff *n.* [1950s–60s] **1** (drugs) narcotic drugs, irrespective of quantity. **2** [1950s–60s] (drugs) 1oz (28g) of cocaine. [SE *piece*/PIECE n.⁵ + STUFF n.⁵]

piece of tail *n.* [1940s+] (US) a woman, a girl, not used derog. but invariably from a sexual point of view and usu. dismissive (cf. PIECE OF ARSE). [SE *piece*/PIECE n.¹ + TAIL n.¹ (2)]

piece of the action *n.* [1950s+] (orig. US) a share in what is going on, usu. monetary, criminal or gambling. [ACTION n. (3)]

piece of thick *n.* [late 19C] a cake of pressed tobacco.

piece of trade *n.* [late 17C+] a prostitute. [TRADE n. (1)]

piece of work *n.* **1** [19C] a fuss, a 'to-do'. **2** [1920s+] a person; usu. as *a nasty piece of work*, an unpleasant person.

pieces *n.*¹ [mid-19C–1900s] money. [? SE *pieces of eight*]

pieces *n.*² [1970s+] (US Black) clothes (cf. LEATHER PIECE). [? SE *piece of goods*]

pieces of eight *n.* [20C] weight. [rhy. sl.]

piece up *v.* **1** [20C] (US Und.) to divide up the spoils of a robbery. **2** [1950s+] (drugs) to divide a large amount of a drug into smaller, saleable pieces (cf. PIECE n.⁵).

piedras *n.* [1980s+] (drugs) crack cocaine. [Sp. *piedras*, rocks]

pie-eater/-biter *n.* [1940s+] (Aus. prison) **1** a small-time criminal (cf. CRUNCHER n.¹). **2** a fool, a simpleton. **3** an insignificant person. [some criminals who were forced into the army during WW2 promptly deserted. They consequently subsisted, having no legitimate source of an identity card and thus food coupons, on the free meat pies provided by military canteens. However, *Simes* notes that there was 'an earlier cluster of pejorative terms related to *pie*' (e.g. [1910s] *meat-pie bookie*, a small-time bookmaker) and that while this ety. is correct in context, it merely amplified an earlier use]

pie-eyed *adj.* [20C] **1** drunk. **2** astonished, amazed. [one's eyes are popping out of one's face]

pie-face *n.*¹ [1920s+] a person with a round or blank face, a stupid person.

pie-face *n.*² [1980s] (Aus.) an Asian. [the cuts in a pie-crust that supposedly resemble slanted Asian eyes]

pie hole *n.* [1990s] (US teen) the mouth. [var. on CAKEHOLE]

pie in the sky *n.* [1910s+] (orig. US) fantasies, fond hopes and illusions. [the line 'There'll be pie in the sky when you die', in the song 'The Preacher and the Slave' (1911) penned by Joe Hill, leader of the Industrial Workers of the World, a prototype US union]

pieman *n.* [mid-19C+] **1** the game of pitch and toss. **2** the player who shouts out in pitch and toss. [the old pieman's cry 'Hot pies, toss or buy! Toss or buy!']

pie out *v.* [1970s] (US campus) to become drunk. [PIE-EYED]

piepiejoller/pippiejoller *n.* [1970s+] (S.Afr.) an adolescent. [Afk. sl. *piepie*, a penis + JOL n. (4) + sfx. *-er*, lit. 'one who has fun with his penis']

pie-pusher *n.* [late 19C] a street pie seller.

piercer *n.* [mid-18C–mid-19C] a penetrating, keen glance.

pierce the hogshead, to *phr.* [17C] to have sexual intercourse, esp. to deflower a virgin.

pies *n.* [1940s] (US Black) the eyes (cf. MINCE S; PUDDINGS AND PIES).

piesa *see* PAISA.

pie shop *n.* [mid–late 19C] a dog. [the popular belief that when in 1842 one Blauchard opened a pie shop in London, he used dead dogs as meat]

pie wagon *n.* [late 19C+] (US) a police van, used to transport villains.

piffed/piffled *adj.* [20C] (US) drunk. [? echoic of one's drunken spluttering]

piffer *n.* [late 19C+] 'A member of the Punjab Frontier Force. [a military unit raised in 1849 and employed esp. to police the North-West Frontier of India during British rule] or of one of the regiments that succeeded it' (*OED*). P.F.F.]

piffin bridge *n.* [1990s] the perineum on a man. [ety. unknown; ? link to Lancashire dial. *piff*, a puff of wind]

piffle *n.* [late 19C+] nonsense, rubbish, esp. as a dismissive excl.; thus *piffler*, one who talks nonsense; *piffling*, nonsensical, insignificant. [PIFFLE v.]

piffle *v.* [mid-19C+] to talk or act in a trifling or ineffective way (cf. FAFF v.). [? echoic; the image is of someone talking feebly]

piffled *see* PIFFED.

pifflicated *adj.* [1900s–30s] drunk. [PIFFLE v. + SPIFLICATE]

pig *n.*¹ **1** [mid-16C+] a general insult, esp. to one who is fat, ugly and/or greedy. **2** [20C] (US horse-racing) a slow or otherwise useless horse, not to be betted on. **3** [20C] a fat, unattractive woman. **4** [1930s+] (Can.) a prostitute. **5** [1960s+] (US campus) a woman considered to be drunken, promiscuous and sexually available. [stereotypically negative views of the pig]

pig *n.*² [late 17C–1900s] sixpence (2.5p) (cf. GRUNTER n.²). [it is smaller than a HOG n.¹ (1); though note HOG n.¹ (2)]

pig *n.*³ **1** [early 19C+] a policeman; thus *pigs*, the police as a group (cf. BACON n.³). **2** [mid-19C–1910s] an informer. **3** [1960s+] any conventional person, member of the Establishment or authorities. [*Egan's Grose* (1823) suggests that a pig's rooting for food is the image behind the TRAPS who root up the haunts of the PRIGS n.¹]

pig *n.*⁴ [20C] a venereal ulcer.

pig *n.*⁵ **1** [20C] (US) an inferior racehorse. **2** [1950s+] (US) a discontinued model of motorcar, a run-down, dilapidated motorcar, a car that looks good but has a small, low-powered engine. **3** [1950s+] (US Black) a Cadillac (cf. HOG n.²). **4** [1950s+] (US) a large motorcycle, esp. a Harley-Davidson (cf. HOG n.²).

pig *n.*⁶ [1970s+] anything considered difficult or exhausting to achieve (cf. SWINE).

pig *v. see* PIG OUT.

pig and roast *n.* [20C] toast. [rhy. sl.]

Pig and Tinder-box *n.* [mid-19C] the Elephant and Castle tavern in south London.

pi-gas *see* PI-JAW.

pig brother *n.* [1960s+] (US Black) any Black who informs against their own people to the (White) police. [PIG n.³ + BROTHER n.]

pig dog *n.* [1980s+] (US campus) someone who eats a lot. [PIG n.¹ + DOG n.⁵ (6)]

pig-eater *n.* [19C] a general term of affection.

pigeon *n.*¹ [16C+] a young woman.

pigeon *n.*² **1** [late 16C+] (Und.) a sucker, a victim; thus the *pigeon drop*, a confidence trick that involves dropping a wallet where a victim can find it or a scheme in which the con-man tells the victim that they have found a large sum of money and, if the victim will advance some money as a show of good faith, they can have a share in the 'windfall' (cf. HAWK n.¹). **2** [18C–early 19C] 'Pigeons – sharpers who, during the drawing of the lottery, wait ready mounted, near Guildhall, and as soon as the first two or three numbers are drawn, which they receive from a confederate, ride, i.e. 'fly', with them to some distant insurance office where there is another of the gang, commonly a decent looking woman to her he secretly gives the numbers, which she insures for a considerable sum' (*Sporting Magazine* XVIII, 1801).

pigeon *n.*³ [mid-19C+] (orig. US) an informer. [abbr. STOOL-PIGEON n.¹]

pigeon v. [late 17C–early 18C] to trick, to hoax, to deceive. [PIGEON n.¹]

pigeon-cracking n. [mid-19C] stealing lead from the roofs of buildings (cf. BLUEY-CRACKING). [BLUE-PIGEON + CRACK v.⁵]

pigeon dropping n. [1940s] (US Und.) playing any form of confidence trick (cf. PLUCK A PIGEON). [PIGEON n.¹]

pigeonhole n. 1 [late 16C–late 17C] (Und.) the stocks. 2 [late 19C–1900s] the vagina (cf. BLACK HOLE n.¹). [SE pigeonhole, a small hole or recess]

pigeon on v. [20C] (Aus.) to drop something on (someone) from above.

pigeon pair n. [late 19C] a family whose children are a boy and a girl. [the pigeon's brood is usu. one male, one female]

pigeon's milk n. [mid-19C] the subject of a fool's errand which apprentices are sent on, traditionally on 1 April.

pigeon-'tomach n. [20C] (W.I.) a woman with larger than average breasts. [play on SE pigeon-chested]

pig-fucker n. [1930s+] (US) a worthless, very unpleasant person; thus pig-fucking, worthless, disgusting. [SE pig + FUCKER n.]

pigger/pigmouth n. [20C] (US Black) a very fat woman. [PIG n.¹]

piggery n. [20C] a room that is rarely cleaned or tidied but which is very much the private concern of its occupant.

pigging adj. [20C] an intensifier; euph. for FUCKING adj.

piggot see PIGOT.

piggy bank n. [20C] masturbation (cf. BARCLAY'S). [rhy. sl. piggy bank = WANK n.]

piggy in the middle see PIG IN THE MIDDLE n.².

pig hash see PIGSWILL.

pighead n. [late 19C+] a stubborn, uncompromising person. [SE pig + sfx. -HEAD (1)]

pig heaven n.¹ [1960s+] (US Black) a police station. [PIG n.³ (1) + SE heaven]

pig heaven n.² [1960s+] a fantasy paradise that would delight the gross rather than the fastidious.

pig-ignorant adj. [20C] extremely stupid.

pig in v. 1 [early 18C+] to share a home, usu. as pig in with (cf. PIG TOGETHER). 2 [20C] to gorge oneself, often as exhortation pig in! (cf. PIG OUT).

pig in the middle n.¹ [20C] an act of urination. [rhy. sl. pig in the middle = PIDDLE n.]

pig/piggy in the middle n.² [1960s+] someone caught between two warring parties. [the children's game]

pig-iron n. 1 [1920s] cheap, unpleasant alcohol. 2 [1920s] alcohol in general. 3 [1980s+] (Irish) fun, devilment, amusement; usu. as for the pig-iron, for the fun of it. [joc. use of SE; all refer to the low value of pig-iron]

Pig Island n. [20C] (Aus./N.Z.) New Zealand; thus Pig Islander, New Zealander. [the introduction of pigs to New Zealand by Captain Cook]

pig it v. [late 19C+] to live in squalor, albeit unworried by that squalor. [PIG n.¹ (1). Note SE pig, to live in squalor together]

pig jump v. [late 19C–1940s] (Aus.) of a horse, to jump with all four legs in the air at once.

pig killer n. [1970s+] (drugs) phencyclidine (cf. ACE n.³). [play on HOG n.⁸]

pig meat n.¹ [late 19C–1940s] (US Black) 1 a promiscuous woman. 2 a young woman. 3 a prostitute. [PIG n.¹ + MEAT]

pig meat n.² [20C] a failure, a loser. [boxing jargon; the image is of one who is overweight and wallows around in the ring]

pig months n. [late 19C] the 8 months in which there is a 'r'. [these months are considered the safest for eating pork, known to decay in the hotter summer season]

pigmouth see PIGGER.

pigot/piggot n. [late 19C] a flagrant lie; usu. as piggotted,

cheated, fooled. [proper name of Richard Pigott (c.1828–89), the forger of the Parnell papers]

pig/pork out v. 1 [mid-19C] to die. 2 [1970s+] to overeat massively, ext. as pig out on (a food or drink) (cf. MAC OUT; PIG IN). 3 [1970s+] to overindulge in anything. [PIG n.¹]

pig party n. [1960s] an orgy, a gang-rape. [PIG n.¹ (5) + SE party]

pigpen n. [20C] (US) any dirty, unpleasant place.

pig room n. [1980s+] (US gay) an orgy room. [PIG n.¹ (5) or PIG OUT (3)]

pig-root v. [1910s] (Aus.) to ride. [SE pig-root, for a horse to buck violently with its hind legs]

p.i.g.s. n. [1960s+] (US) Poles, Italians, Greeks and Slavs (cf. WASP n.²). [abbr.]

pigs see PIG'S EAR n.¹.

pigs! excl. [20C] (mainly Aus.) a general expression of disgust, contempt, negation etc; often as pigs to you!

pig's arse n. [20C] (Aus.) a glass. [rhy. sl.]

pig's arse!/ass!/bum!/ear! excl. [1910s+] a contemptuous excl. [ARSE n.¹/BUM n.²/SE ear]

pig's back n. [20C] luxury, indolence, security; usu. as on the pig's back, living very comfortably, securely (cf. SHEEP'S BACK). [primary use is Aus./N.Z.]

pig's bastard n. [1930s+] a term of abuse, a very unpleasant person.

pig's breakfast see DOG'S DINNER.

pig's bum n. [20C] (Aus.) a glass. [euph. for a SE pig's ARSE]

pig's Christmas parcel! excl. [1960s+] (N.Z.) a general excl. of annoyance. [rhy. sl.; pig's Christmas parcel = pig's ARSE-HOLE]

pig sconce n. [mid-17C–late 19C] a stubborn fool, a 'pig-headed' person. [SE pig + sconce, the head]

pig's ear/pigs n.¹ [late 19C+] beer. [rhy. sl.]

pig's ear n.² [1940s+] a mess, chaos; usu. as make a pig's ear of... [? euph. for SE pig's ARSE]

pig's ear! see PIG'S ARSE!

pig's eye n. [mid-19C] in cards, the ace of diamonds; thus [1930s–40s] (Can.) the pig's eye, something excellent, outstanding, first-rate.

pig's fry n. [late 19C+] a tie. [rhy. sl.]

pig's fry v. [1930s+] to try. [rhy. sl.]

pigshit n. [1950s+] nonsense, rubbish (cf. BULLSHIT n.; HORSE-SHIT n.); also as excl. pigshit!, rubbish!

pig-sick adj. [20C] furious, enraged; thus pig-sick of, infuriated by, incapable of tolerating.

pigskin artist n. [1940s] (Aus.) a jockey. [the material used for saddles + ARTIST n.²]

pigsnyes n. [late 18C] a coarse term of endearment used to a woman. [SE pig's eyes, small eyes; ? the implication is of a pig, greedy, in this case, for sex]

pig's orphan n. [1930s+] a very unpleasant person. [euph. for PIG'S BASTARD]

pigsticker n. 1 [late 19C+] any form of sharpened, stabbing weapon, e.g. a lance, a bayonet, a large knife etc (cf. TOAD-STICKER). 2 [late 19C–1940s] a pig-butcher.

pigsticking n. [1920s+] (Can.) sodomy.

pigsty n. [1960s] a police station (cf. PIG HEAVEN n.¹). [PIG n.³ (1) + play on SE]

pigstyle adv. [20C] (US Black) living in filthy circumstances.

pig sweat n. [20C] (US) 1 beer. 2 inferior 'rotgut' bourbon.

pig's whisper n. [mid-19C] 1 a nearly inaudible whisper, a grunt. 2 a very short space of time; usu. as in a pig's whisper (cf. PIG'S WHISTLE). [note SE cockstride, a very short space of time; lit. 'the length of a cock's pace']

pig's whistle n. [mid-19C] a very short time (cf. PIG'S WHISPER).

pigswill/pig hash n. [20C] nonsense, rubbish; thus excl. pigswill!, rubbish! (cf. HOGWASH).

pigtail *n.*¹ [late 18C–mid-19C] a roll of coarse tobacco. [resemblance]

pigtail *n.*² [early–mid-19C] an old man. [a ref. to the fact that some old men still wore their hair in a pigtail, an 18C affectation]

pigtail *n.*³ [early–mid-19C] (Aus.) a Chinese immigrant to Australia. [the wearing of pigtails by the Chinese]

pigtail *n.*⁴ [20C] the penis.

pigtail *adj.* [19C] **1** wearing a pigtail. **2** Chinese, e.g. *pigtail brigade*, *pigtail land*, *pigtail party* (cf. PIGTAIL *n.*³).

pigtail alley/town *n.* [late 19C] (US) Chinatown in New York City, centred on Mott Street (cf. BEAN TOWN *n.*²). [SE *pigtail + alley/town*]

pig together *v.* [late 18C+] to lie together. [the proximity resembles pigs in a sty]

pig wagon *n.* [1990s] a police van. [PIG *n.*³ (1) + SE *wagon*]

pig widgeon/widgin *n.* [late 18C–early 19C] a fool, a simpleton (cf. WIDGEON). [*pig* is used as an intensifier. The word presumably comes f. SE *pigwidgen*, *pig-widgeon*, described in *OED* as 'of obscure origin and meaning', although it is either a proper name, as used of a constable by sl. collector Robert Greene (1558–92) or that of a 'fairy knight' as suggested by the writer Michael Drayton (1563–1631)]

pi-jaw/-gas *n.* [late 19C–1940s] an earnest, moralizing lecture, esp. as delivered by parents or teachers. [PI + JAW/GAS *n.*¹ (1)]

pik *n.* [1970s] (S.Afr.) **1** an affectionate or contemptuous term for a small person, a child, a small object. **2** a nickname for a small or large person. [abbr. PIKKIE]

pike *n.*¹ [mid-18C–19C] **1** a toll-gate. **2** the toll paid on one; thus *pike-keeper*, *pike-man*, one who takes the tolls; *bilk a pike*, cheat the toll-gate keeper. **3** [mid-19C+] a road, a highway. [abbr. SE *turnpike*, initially a toll-gate, thence the 'high road']

pike *n.*² [19C] the penis (cf. BAYONET).

pike *v.* [mid-17C–1920s] to leave, to run off quickly; often as *pike it*, *pike off*. **2** [late 17C–1920s] (Und.) to die. **3** [late 19C+] (US) to hold back, to shirk, to act cautiously (cf. PIKER). [fig. uses of SE *turnpike*]

piked off *adv.* [late 17C+] safely escaped. [PIKE *v.* (1)]

pike on the been/bene, to *phr.* [mid–late 17C] to run away at top speed. [PIKE *v.* (1) + BENE]

pike out *v.* [1990s] (Aus.) to leave a party early. [PIKE *v.*]

piker *n.* **1** [19C] a vagrant, a tramp, a gipsy (cf. PIKEY). **2** [late 19C+] (orig. US) a mean, grasping person, one who will not take the least risk, esp. to help others. **3** [late 19C+] (US) a small-time gambler. **4** [1930s+] (Aus.) a confidence trickster. **5** [1940s+] (orig. US) a lazy person. **6** [1940s+] (Aus.) an unpleasant, unpopular person. **7** [1990s] (Aus.) a bore, a 'party pooper'. [PIKE *v.*; lit. 'one who walks the turnpikes'. All forms f. fig. uses of (1); note N.Z. agricultural *piker*, a wild bull]

piker joint *n.* [late 19C+] (US) a casino or gambling house specializing in the small-time gambler. [PIKER (3) + JOINT *n.*³ (3)]

pikestaff *n.* [late 18C–1900s] the penis.

pikey *n.* [mid-19C+] a vagrant (cf. PIKER). [Kentish dial.; ult. PIKE *n.*¹]

piking *n.* [late 19C+] (orig. US) cheating, using sharp practices. [PIKE *v.*]

pikkie *n.* [1940s+] (S.Afr.) **1** used either affectionately or contemptuously of a small person, a child, a small object. **2** a nickname for a small or large person. [Afk. *pikkie*, a little fellow]

pil *see* PILLETIJIE.

pilch *n.* [1930s–40s] (US Black) one's residence, a house, a home, an apartment. [? 11C–16C SE *pilch*, an outer garment, a wrapper]

pilcher *n.* [early–mid-17C] a general term of abuse. [? 'one who wears a pilch or leathern jerkin or doublet' or 'one who pilches, a thief' (*OED*); ult. SE *pilchard*]

pile *n.* [mid-19C+] a large amount, usu. of money; thus *make a/one's pile*, to become rich; *go a/one's pile/whole pile*, to bet heavily, to the extent of one's purse (cf. BUNDLE *n.*²).

pile *v.* [1970s+] (US Black/campus) to have sexual intercourse. [one 'makes a heap']

pile-driver *n.* **1** [19C] the penis (cf. ARSE-OPENER). **2** [1960s–70s] a male homosexual. [play on SE *piledriver* + in (2) SE *piles*]

pile into/onto *v.* [late 19C+] (orig. US) to attack physically, to crash into, to get to work on.

pile it on *see* PILE ON THE AGONY.

pile of bricks *n.* [1940s] (US Black) a building.

pile of shit *see* PIECE OF SHIT.

pile on/put on lugs, to *phr.* [late 19C–1900s] (US) to put on airs, to act affectedly. [LUG *n.*³ (1)]

pile on the agony/it on, to *phr.* [mid-19C+] to embellish an already painful or disturbing factual or fictional statement with more and more (poss. specious) details.

pile onto *see* PILE INTO.

piles *n.* [1980s+] (drugs) crack. [? play on ROCKS *n.*⁴]

pile up/up at *v.* [late 19C+] (US) to end up (at), esp. of an evening out.

pile up some Zs, to *phr.* [1960s+] (US teen) to get some sleep (cf. BAG ZS). [SE *pile up* + z *n.*¹]

pile up the rocks, to *phr.* [mid-19C+] to amass a great deal of money.

pilgarlic/peele garlic/peel garlic/pilgarlick *n.* [17C–late 19C] an outcast; often as *poor pilgarlick*, poor me. [SE *peel garlic*, a peeled, thus smooth, garlic clove, and thence a bald-headed man; seen presumably as an outcast]

pilgrim *n.*¹ [mid-19C] (Can./N.Z./US) an early immigrant from Britain to New Zealand (cf. SHAGROON).

pilgrim/advertising pilgrim *n.*² [1960s] (US gay) a well-dressed, attractive heterosexual, unaware of the reaction he gains from watching gay men.

pilgrim/pilgrim's salve *n.* [late 17C–early 19C] human excrement. [16C SE *pilgrim's salve*, an ointment, made mainly of swine's grease and isinglass]

pilgrim's staff *n.* [18C] the penis.

pill *n.*¹ **1** [early 17C+] a cannon-ball or bullet, a bomb; thus [1950s] *big pill*, the atomic bomb. **2** [mid-19C+] (orig. US) any form of ball, esp. a basketball.

pill/pills *n.*² [mid-19C–1920s] (orig. milit.) a doctor, a surgeon.

pill *n.*³ **1** [mid-19C+] an unpleasant person, a weakling, a bore. **2** [late 19C] anything unpleasant, suffering, punishment. The term is 'endless in application' (Ware). [the image of *pill* as something innately unpleasant]

pill *n.*⁴ **1** [late 19C] a drink. **2** [1910s–60s] a cigarette. **3** [1960s+] (S.Afr. drugs) a marijuana cigarette. [? they all 'cure' one's ills]

pill *n.*⁵ [1960s+] (drugs) a generic term for any form of barbiturate or amphetamine drug capsule.

pill *v.* [mid–late 19C] **1** to blackball. **2** to fail a candidate in an examination (cf. PIP *v.*¹). [PILL *n.*¹ (2)]

pill and poll, to *phr.* [mid-19C] (Und.) to cheat one's accomplice or partner in crime. [SE *pillage + poll*, to plunder, to despoil]

pillar and post *n.* [20C] a ghost. [rhy. sl.]

pillars *n.* [1930s] (US Black) the human legs.

pill-box *n.*¹ [mid–late 19C] a small carriage. [milit. jargon *pill*, a doctor; such carriages were typically used by doctors]

pill-box *n.*² **1** [mid–late 19C] a pulpit. **2** [late 19C–1900s] a soldier's hat. **3** [late 19C+] a small brimless hat. [joc. use of SE *pill-box* for anything small, circular and box-like]

pill-box n.[3] [mid–late 19C] (US) a revolver, a pistol. [PILL n.[1] (1) + SE box]

pillcock see PILLICOCK.

pill cooker n. [1920s] (drugs) an opium smoker. [SE pill, the ball of opium that is prepared for each pipe + cooker]

pill driver n. [mid-19C] a travelling apothecary.

pilled up adj. [1960s+] (drugs) under the influence of amphetamines or barbiturates. [PILL n.[5]]

pilletijie/pil n. [1960s+] (S.Afr. drugs) a marijuana cigarette (cf. PILL n.[4]). [lit. 'a little pill']

pill-grinder n. [20C] a pharmacist (cf. PILL-ROLLER).

pill-head n. [1960s+] (drugs) a regular user of amphetamine or barbiturate drugs. [PILL n.[5] + sfx. -HEAD (2)]

pillicock/pillcock/pillock n. 1 [early 14C–early 18C] the penis. 2 [late 16C–mid-17C] a term of affection for a young boy. [north. dial.; ult. Norwegian dial. pill, the penis + COCK n.[2] (1)]

pilling n. [1980s+] (drugs) experiencing the effect of some form of pill, e.g. an amphetamine or barbiturate (cf. SPEEDING; TRIPPING n.[1]). [PILL n.[5]]

pillionaire n. [1930s] a motorcycle passenger, usu. a woman. [SE pillion + pun on millionaire]

pillion pussy n. [1950s] (N.Z.) a young woman who accompanies a motorbike-riding young social outlaw. [SE pillion + PUSSY n.[1] (2)]

pillock n.[1] see PILLICOCK.

pillock n.[2] [1960s+] 1 a fool, a simpleton (cf. DICKHEAD). 2 a general term of abuse. [dial. pillock, the penis]

pillocks n. [late 19C+] nonsense; thus talk pillocks, to talk nonsense; thus pillocky, stupid, nonsensical. [PILLS n.[3] + BALLOCKS n.[2] (2)]

pillory n. [late 17C–18C] a baker. [? the placing of bakers who were caught giving false measure in the pillory. The baker's profession was often synon. with trickery and fraud]

pill out v. [1950s+] to accelerate sharply in a vehicle from a standing start and thus leave traces of rubber tyres on the tarmac. [SE peel, to leave]

pillow n. [late 19C] (US) a boxing glove. [its padding]

pillow-biter n. [1960s+] (orig. Aus.) a homosexual (cf. MATTRESS-MUNCHER). [the supposed agonies of anal intercourse]

pillow-mate n. [19C] a prostitute.

pillow pigeons n. [1940s] (US Black) bedbugs.

pillow-puncher n. [20C] (US) a chambermaid. [her making of beds]

pill-pad n. [late 19C+] an opium den, a place where opium users can gather to smoke. [SE pill, a pellet of opium + PAD n.[2] (2)]

pill-pate n. [16C] a friar. [14C–17C SE pill, to shave + pate, head; f. the tonsure adopted by friars]

pill-peddler n. [20C] a doctor.

pill-popper n. [1930s+] (drugs) a regular user of any drugs in pill form. [PILL n.[5] + POP v.[6] (2)]

pill-popping n. [1930s+] (drugs) 1 taking pills. 2 addicted to pills. [PILL n.[5] + POP v.[6] (2)]

pill-pusher n. [late 19C+] a doctor.

pill-roller n. [20C] 1 a doctor. 2 a pharmacist.

pills n.[1] see PILL n.[2].

pills n.[2] [late 19C–1900s] billiards. [PILL n.[1] (2)]

pills n.[3] [late 19C+] the testicles (cf. BALLS n.[1]). [joc. use of PILL n.[1] (2)]

pill-shooter n. [1920s–30s] a doctor.

pilot n. 1 [early–mid-19C] a watchman. 2 [20C] (US) a jockey.

pilot cove n. [20C] (Aus.) a clergyman. [SKYPILOT + COVE n. (1)]

pilot of the chocolate runway n. [1990s] a male homosexual (cf. HITCHHIKER ON THE HERSHEY HIGHWAY). [SE pilot + CHOCOLATE RUNWAY]

pi-man n. [20C] a pious, earnest person. [SE pious + man, but ? pun on pieman]

pimgenet/pimginnit n. [late 17C– early 18C] a prominent, red pimple. [? SE pomegranate, a fruit that might be seen as being covered in 'pimples'. Halliwell (1847) cites the 'old saying': 'Nine pimgenets make a pock royal']

pimp n.[1] 1 [17C] a procurer. 2 [18C] a small piece of wood used for lighting fires. 3 [1940s] (US Black) a male prostitute. [? Fr. pimpreneau, a scoundrel; pimpant, alluring or seducing in outward appearance or dress; or pimpesouée, a pretentious woman. The term began life as sl. but entered SE c.1660]

pimp n.[2] 1 [late 19C+] (Aus./N.Z./S.Afr.) an informer (cf. IMPIMPI). 2 [20C] (Aus.) a sneak, a tell-tale. [fig use of PIMP n.[1] (1)]

pimp/pimp dust n.[3] [1970s] (drugs) cocaine. [PIMP n.[1] (1) + SE dust, based on the assumption that this is the pimp's drug of choice]

pimp adj. [1940s+] (US Black) stylish, expensive. [PIMP n.[1] (1); the enviable status of the pimp in Black street culture]

pimp v.[1] [1940s+] (Aus./N.Z.) to tell tales; to inform on someone. [PIMP n.[2] (2)]

pimp v.[2] [1980s+] (US campus) to dress up. [PIMP n.[1] (1), alluding to the pimp's flashiness]

pimp crazy adj. [1950s–70s] (US) of a prostitute who goes from one sadistic, abusing pimp to another, apparently unable to break the habit. [PIMP n.[1] (1) + SE crazy]

pimp dust see PIMP n.[3].

pimped down/out adv. [1960s] (US Black) fashionably or smartly dressed. [PIMP n.[1] (1) + SE down/out]

pimp fronts n. [1950s+] (US Black) a particular style of dress associated with pimps. [PIMP n.[1] (1) + FRONT n.[2] (3)]

pimping n. [1970s+] (US campus) doing well. [PIMP adj.]

pimping adj. [1970s+] (US campus) well-dressed. [PIMP adj.]

pimpish adj. [1970s+] (US teen) stylishly dressed. [PIMP adj.]

pimple n.[1] [late 17C–early 18C] a boon companion. [ety. unknown; ? link to PIMP n.[1] (1)]

pimple n.[2] 1 [early 19C–1940s] the head. 2 [late 19C+] a baby's penis.

pimple and blotch n. [20C] Scotch (whisky). [rhy. sl.]

pimple and wart n. [late 19C–1950s] a quart. [rhy. sl.]

pimple cover n. [19C] a hat. [PIMPLE n.[2] (1)]

pimple in a bent n. [late 16C–mid-17C] something infinitesimally small. [SE pimple + bent, a grass-stalk]

pimply n. [1970s+] an acned youth. [SE pimple]

pimpmobile n. [1960s+] a flashy, ostentatious car, potentially the choice of a pimp, but not restricted to such drivers (cf. PIMP RIDE; SPIVMOBILE). [PIMP n.[1] (1) + (auto)mobile]

pimp on v. [1940s] (US Black) to take advantage of.

pimp one's pipe, to phr. [1980s+] (drugs) to lend or rent one's crack pipe.

pimp post/rest n. [1970s+] the armrest between driver and passenger in a car.

pimp ride n. [1970s+] (US Black) an expensive car, suitable for a pimp (cf. PIMPMOBILE). [PIMP n.[1] (1) + RIDE n.[2]]

pimps see PIMPSY.

pimp shades/tints n. [1960s+] a style of dark glasses affected by pimps. [PIMP n.[1] (1) + SHADES n.[2]/TINTS]

pimp slap n. [1970s+] (US Black) an open-handed slap across the face. [PIMP n.[1] (1) + SE slap]

pimp socks n. [1950s–70s] (US Black) ultra-thin nylon socks, usu. with a pattern of vertical stripes. [PIMP n.[1] (1) + SE socks]

pimp stick n.[1] 1 [1920s–50s] (Can./US) a cigarette. 2 [1950s+] (Can./US drugs) a marijuana cigarette. [PIMP n.[1] (1) + STICK n.[11] (2)]

pimp stick n.[2] [1930s–60s] (US Black) two wire coat hangers twisted together to make an improvised and vicious whip. [PIMP n.[1] (1) + SE stick]

pimp stride/strut/walk *n.* [1920s–70s] (US Black) a strutting style of walking, intended to emphasize one's pride, independence and masculinity (cf. AKIMBO v.). [PIMP n.[1] (1) + SE *stride/strut/walk*]

pimp's turban *n.* [1920s–30s] (US) a derby hat. [PIMP n.[1] (1) + SE *turban*]

pimpsy/pimps *adj.* [1980s] far too easy, utterly simple. [dial. *pimpy*, paltry, mean, small]

pimp talk *n.* [1950s–60s] (US Black) the 'line' used by a pimp when attempting to persuade a new young woman to join his group of prostitutes. [PIMP n.[1] (1) + SE *talk*]

pimp tints *see* PIMP SHADES.

pimp walk *see* PIMP STRIDE.

pimp whisk/whiskin/whisking *n.* [late 17C–early 19C] **1** a mean-spirited, bigoted man. **2** a first-rate pimp. [PIMP n.[1] (1) + WHISK; although *whisk* (as in (2)) usu. means the derog. *whipper-snapper*]

pin *n.*[1] **1** [late 17C+] the penis (cf. PIN-CASE). **2** [1960s+] (drugs) a very thin marijuana cigarette. **3** [1970s+] (drugs) a hypodermic syringe (or a makeshift alternative), used for injecting narcotic drugs.

pin *n.*[2] [1980s+] a drug dealer. [? abbr. SE *kingpin*]

pin *v.*[1] [mid-18C–1900s] **1** to seize, to catch, to arrest. **2** to snatch, to steal.

pin *v.*[2] [late 19C–1930s] to pawn clothes. [? SE *pawn*]

pin *v.*[3] [20C] of a man, to have sexual intercourse. [? SE *pin down*, but note PIN n.[1] (1)]

pin *v.*[4] **1** [1920s+] (Aus.) to target someone for one's (often amatory) attentions. **2** [1930s–60s] to mark down visually, to notice. **3** [1950s+] (US campus) to state one's commitment to a person of the opposite sex by giving them one's fraternity pin.

pin *v.*[5] [1930s–40s] (Aus.) to cause trouble for, to 'do down'. [? wrestling imagery]

pin a can on *see* GET A CAN ON.

pin back one's ears, to *phr.* **1** [1920s+] to shock, to surprise. **2** [1940s+] (orig. US) to defeat, to punish verbally or physically, to reprimand. **3** [1950s+] to give one's full attention, esp. as *pin your ears back!* (cf. PIN BACK ONE'S LUGHOLES).

pin back one's lugholes, to *phr.* [1940s+] to give one's full attention (cf. PIN BACK ONE'S EARS). [LUGHOLE]

pin basket *n.* [late 18C–mid-19C] the youngest child. [SE *pin-basket*, a large ornamented pin-cushion with pins of varying lengths arranged to resemble a basket; such a pin-cushion was traditionally given to a mother after the birth of a child]

pin-case *n.* [19C] the vagina (cf. COCK-HOLDER). [PIN n.[1] + SE *case* + play on SE]

pinch *n.*[1] **1** [mid-18C+] a theft, an act of stealing or plagiarism. **2** [late 19C+] (orig. US) an arrest.

pinch *n.*[2] [late 19C–1900s] a certainty, something easily achieved.

pinch *n.*[3] [1970s+] (drugs) a small amount of marijuana, enough for perhaps two cigarettes.

pinch *v.* **1** [late 17C+] to steal. **2** [19C] to pass counterfeit money in exchange for goods. **3** [early 19C+] to arrest. [orig. Und., mainstream sl. from mid-19C]

pinch a loaf, to *phr.* [1990s] (US) to defecate (cf. PINCH ONE OFF).

pinch and padlock man *n.* [19C] a policeman. [PINCH n.[1] (2) + SE *padlock*]

pinch-back/-belly *n.* [17C–early 19C] a miser (cf. PINCH-COMMONS; PINCH-FART; PINCH-FIST; PINCH-GUT; PINCH-PENNY; PINCH-PLUM). [they *pinch* someone else's *back* by refusing to pay them enough to buy enough clothes]

pinch-bottom *n.* [19C] **1** a prostitute (cf. PINCH-PRICK). **2** a pimp (cf. PINCH-BUTTOCK; PINCH-CUNT).

pinch-buttock *n.* [19C] a pimp (cf. PINCH-BOTTOM; PINCH CUNT).

pinch-commons/-crust *n.* [17C–early 19C] a miser (cf. PINCH-BACK). [PINCH v. + SE *commons*, provisions that are provided in common for a group/*crust*]

pinch-cunt *n.* [19C] a pimp (cf. PINCH-BOTTOM). [PINCH v. + CUNT n.[1]]

pincher *n.*[1] **1** [late 18C–early 19C] a rogue specializing in short-changing. **2** [19C] a policeman. **3** [19C+] a shoplifter. [PINCH v.]

pincher *n.*[2] [late 19C+] the 'traditional' nickname of anyone surnamed Martin. [Admiral Sir William Martin (1696?–1756), who had a reputation for 'pinching' seamen for petty offences. Note the title of William Golding's novel *Pincher Martin* (1960)]

pinchers *n.* [1920s–50s] (US Black) shoes. [their tightness]

pinch-fart *n.* [late 16C–early 17C] a miser (cf. PINCH-BACK). [PINCH v. + FART n.]

pinch-fist *n.* [late 16C–1900s] a miser (cf. PINCH-BACK). [PINCH v. + SE *fist*]

pinch for *v.* [late 17C+] to rob a person of. [PINCH v.]

pinch-gloak *n.* [19C] a petty thief who specializes in stealing small articles from jewellers. [PINCH v. + GLOAK]

pinch-gut *n.* [mid-17C+] a miser (cf. PINCH-BACK). [their constant desire to 'tighten their belt']

pinch-gut vengeance *n.* [19C] very thin beer (cf. WHIP BELLY).

pinch hit *n.* [1970s] (drugs) one who is hired to inject an addict too ill to do it themselves. [for ety. *see* PINCH HIT v.]

pinch hit *v.* [1930s+] to act as a substitute, esp. in an emergency. [baseball jargon *pinch-hit*, to substitute for a batter, esp. at a crucial point in the game]

pinching lay *n.* [late 18C–early 19C] a variety of petty crimes involving cash, passing counterfeit money, stealing from shops, giving short change (cf. AT THE PINCH). [PINCH v. + LAY n.[3]]

pinch it off! *excl.* [1920s+] (Aus.) hurry up! [fig. use of PINCH ONE OFF]

pinch one off *v.* [1990s] (US) to defecate. ['one' is a piece of excrement; the phr. reflects the basic meaning of TURD, something that is 'torn off' from the body]

pinch on the parson's side, to *phr.* [late 18C–early 19C] to cheat a parson of their tithes.

pinch-penny *n.* [15C–mid-18C] a miser (cf. PINCH-BACK). [PINCH v. + SE *penny*]

pinch-plum *n.* [late 19C] a miser (cf. PINCH-BACK). [PINCH v. + SE *plum*]

pinch-prick *n.* [19C] a prostitute (cf. PINCH-BOTTOM). [PINCH v. + PRICK n. (1)]

pinch the cat, to *phr.* [late 19C+] of a man, to fondle one's genitals through one's trouser pocket.

pinch-wife *n.* [late 19C–1900s] a mean, boorish husband, who does not trust his wife.

pin-cushion *n.* [19C] the vagina (cf. PIN-CASE). [PIN n.[1] + SE *cushion* + play on SE]

pineapple *n.*[1] **1** [1910s] the vagina (cf. APPLE n.[10]). [? male fear/fascination with vagina: 'prickly' on the outside, sweet within]

pineapple/pineapple bomb *n.*[2] [1910s+] a bomb, a grenade. [the shape]

pineapple *n.*[3] [1930s+] unemployment benefit, the 'dole'. [the Dole *Pineapple* company]

pineapple *n.*[4] [1960s–70s] a male homosexual. [play on FRUIT n.[2]]

pineapple bomb *see* PINEAPPLE n.[2].

pineapple chunk *n.* **1** [20C] departure, escape. **2** [1990s] (Scot.) semen. [rhy. sl.; *pineapple chunk* = (1) BUNK v.[1]; (2) SPUNK n.]

pineapple cut *n.* [20C] (Aus.) a rough haircut, leaving the hair shaggy and irregular.

pineapple princess/queen n. [1960s+] (gay) a person from Hawaii. [SE *pineapple*, Hawaii's state fruit + SE *princess/ queen* n.¹]

pine-box parole/release n. [20C] (US prison) an inmate's death in prison (cf. BACK-DOOR PAROLE). [the *pine box* is a coffin]

pineapple queen see PINEAPPLE PRINCESS.

pine-box release see PINE-BOX PAROLE.

pine drape/overcoat n. [mid-19C–1940s] (US) a coffin (cf. DEAL SUIT). [SE *pine*, pinewood + DRAPE n./SE *overcoat*]

pine-top n. [mid-19C–1940s] (US) cheap or illicitly distilled bourbon. [? the wood used in its barrels]

ping n.¹ [1980s+] (N.Z. drugs) an injection of a narcotic drug. [SE *ping*, echoic of a sudden high-pitched noise]

ping n.² [1980s+] (N.Z.) a derog. name for an Asian person. [*Ping* as a 'typical' Chinese name]

ping v.¹ [early–mid-19C] (sporting) to speak in a quick, singing, high voice. [the pinging noise of a musket]

ping v.² [1980s+] (N.Z. drugs) to inject narcotics. [PING n.¹]

pinga n. [1960s+] (US) the penis. [Sp.]

ping-in-wing/-in-the-wing/ping-wing v. [1940s–50s] (drugs) to inject a drug. [SE *ping*, onomat. for a sharp, sudden sound, thus here for the injection + WING n.¹ (2)]

pin gon n. [late 19C+] (drugs) opium. [ety. unknown; ? Chinese]

ping-pong n.¹ [20C] (W.I./Bdos.) a passport-sized photograph of one's face. [not a 'real' photo; see PING-PONG v.]

ping-pong n.² [1940s–50s] (drugs) Pantopon, a synthetic opiate. [play on brandname]

ping-pong v. [1940s+] (W.I.) to play at something, not to take one's commitments seriously. [the image of *ping-pong* or table-tennis as not being a 'serious' sport]

ping-wing see PING-IN-WING.

pinhead n.¹ (US drugs) **1** [late 19C–1930s] a small pill of opium, costing 25 cents (cf. HIGH HAT). **2** [1920s–40s] one who injects narcotics (cf. PIN-JABBER). **3** [1960s] an amphetamine user. **4** [1960s+] a very thin marijuana cigarette (cf. PIN n.¹).

pinhead n.² [1940s+] **1** a stupid person. **2** a person with a small head.

pin/paste it to your hat phr. [late 19C–1910s] (US) don't forget.

pin-jabber n. [1920s+] (drugs) a drug user who injects their preferred drug (cf. PINHEAD n.¹).

pin joint n. [1970s] (drugs) a very thin marijuana cigarette (cf. PIN n.¹). [SE *pin* + JOINT n.⁴ (2)]

pink n.¹ [early 19C] a fashionable, well-dressed person. [SE *in the pink*]

Pink/Pinkerton/Pinkie n.² [mid-19C+] (US) a member of Pinkerton's Detective Agency; thus *the Pinks*, the Agency as a whole (cf. FED). [abbr.]

pink n.³ [late 19C+] (US Black) a White person; thus [1960s+] *pink boy*, a White man of any age. [the actual skin colour of a White person]

pink n.⁴ [1920s+] (orig. US) one whose politics are left of centre, but who is certainly not a communist (sometimes with an implication of insincerity) (cf. BOLLINGER BOLSHEVIK; RED n.³).

pink n.⁵ **1** [1950s] (W.I.) a prostitute. **2** [1970s+] the open vagina, esp. as in pornography. [PINK adj.² (2)]

pink adj.¹ [early 19C] (US) fashionable, exclusive. [16C SE]

pink adj.² **1** [late 19C–1940s] violent, extreme, absolute, esp. as (*not*) *a pink thing*. **2** [late 19C+] slightly indecent, violent or vulgar, mildly 'blue'.

pink adj.³ [20C] homosexual (cf. LAVENDER). [use predates Gay Liberation days]

pink blotters n. [1980s+] (drugs) a variety of LSD sold on pink blotting-paper. [BLOTTER n.²]

pink bus n. [1990s] the penis.

pink champagne n. [1990s] (drugs) a mixture of cocaine and heroin (cf. SPEEDBALL n.¹).

pink chaser n. [late 19C+] (US Black) a Black person who pursues the company and friendship of Whites. [PINK n.³ + SE *chaser*]

pink elephants n. [1930s+] the supposed fantasy creatures that traditionally appear to those in the throes of delirium tremens (cf. PINK SPIDERS).

Pinkerton see PINK n.².

pink-eye n.¹ **1** [late 19C+] (Aus./Can.) the cheapest red wine, methyl alcohol (cf. PINKIE n.³). **2** [20C] (Aus.) a regular drinker of methylated spirits or 'pinkie'. **3** [1920s+] (Aus./Can.) a drinking bout. **4** [1950s] (US) cheap, rotgut bourbon (cf. RED-EYE n.¹).

pink-eye n.² [20C] (US) the vagina.

pink flamingoes n. [1990s] (drugs) a variety of MDMA (cf. ECSTASY). [the pills are coloured pink]

pink floyd n. [1970s] (US campus) something immensely enjoyable. [*Pink Floyd*, Britain's leading 'psychedelic' rock band in 1960s+]

Pinkie n.¹ see PINK n.².

pinkie n.² **1** [late 19C+] a very light coloured Black person (cf. PINKTOE). **2** [1960s+] (US Black) a White person (cf. PINK n.³).

pinkie/pinky n.³ (Aus.) **1** [late 19C+] cheap red wine; thus *pinky-shop*, a store specializing in such wine; *pinkyite*, a drinker of such wine (cf. SCARLET RUNNER; PINK-EYE n.¹). **2** [20C] methylated spirits mixed with cheap red wine or Condy's crystals (cf. CONDY).

pinkie n.⁴ [1970s] (Aus.) a communist (cf. PINK n.⁴; PINKO n.).

pinkies n. [19C] the fingers. [Scot. dial.]

pinkindindies n. [mid–late 18C] (Irish) a gang of dissolute, rich young men who cut off the bottom few inches of their scabbards and prod or 'pink' with their exposed sword point those whom they encounter and with whom they can start an argument. [lit. 'a turkey-cock given to pinking with a rapier']

pink ink n. [20C] (US) a romance novel. [SE *pink*, i.e. romantic + *ink*]

pink lady n. [1950s+] (drugs) a barbiturate, usu. Seconal/ Darvon. [the colour of the capsules]

pinkler n. [late 19C+] (teen) the penis. [its colour]

pink lint adj. [20C] penniless, very poor. [rhy. sl. *pink lint* = SKINT]

pinko n. [1930s+] (orig. US) a communist, socialist or even mildly liberal sympathizer (depending on the speaker's viewpoint) (cf. RED n.³). [PINK n.⁴]

pinko adj.¹ [1920s–40s] (Aus.) drunk, esp. on methylated spirits. [PINK-EYE n.¹]

pinko adj.² [1950s+] left-wing. [PINK n.⁴]

pink oboe n. [1990s] the penis (cf. FLUTE n.²).

pink owsley/panther/robot n. [1960s+] (drugs) LSD. [SE *pink* + OWSLEY/SE *panther/robot*; ? the colour of the capsules + play on *Pink Panther* films (1964–78)]

pink pimp suit n. [1960s] (US Black) a baby's cot. [like a pimp, the baby is still freeloading, not on women but on its parents]

pink robot see PINK OWSLEY.

pinks n. [1970s] (S.Afr. drugs) Wellconal tablets, a form of synthetic heroin. [the colour]

pink slip n. [1910s+] **1** a notice of dismissal. **2** a brush-off, a rejection. [(1) the *pink* paper on which they are written/ printed; (2) is fig. use of (1)]

pink spiders n. [19C] delirium tremens (cf. PINK ELEPHANTS).

pink steel n. [1990s] the erect penis.

pink studs n. [1980s+] (drugs) MDMA (cf. ECSTASY). [colour of the pills]

pinktea n. **1** [1920s+] (US/Can.) a very formal or exclusive tea party. **2** [1950s+] (gay) an upper-class homosexual, able to stand aloof from the pleasures and problems of their less insulated peers. [the orig. *Pink Tea* was held in 1886 by the US Women's Christian Temperance Union; men wore pink ties and women pink caps]

pinktoe/pinktoes/pinky *n.* [late 19C+] (US Black) **1** a light-skinned Black woman (cf. PINKIE n.²). **2** a Black man's White girlfriend (cf. PUNK n.¹).

Pink 'Un *n.* **1** [late 19C–1900s] the *Sporting Times*. **2** [late 19C–1900s] a reporter or writer for the *Sporting Times* (esp. such 'stars' as Arthur Binstead, nicknamed 'The Pitcher', William Farn Goldberg, 'The Shifter', and Nathaniel Newnham-Davies, 'The Dwarf of Blood'). **3** [1910s+] the *Financial Times*. [the colour of the newsprint, and, in the case of the *Sporting Times*, to distinguish it from the *Sportsman's Guide to the Turf* (cf. BROWN 'UN)]

pink velvet sausage wallet *n.* [1990s] the vagina.

pink wedge/witches *n.* [1960s+] (drugs) varieties of LSD in pink capsules.

pink whoogie *n.* [20C] (US) a derog. term for a White person. [PINK n.³ + WHOOGIE]

pink widow *n.* [1990s] (US gay) an HIV-negative man who forms a relationship with an HIV-positive man on the understanding that he will become his partner's sole heir. [PINK adj.³ + SE *widow*; such 'widows' are known to move from one relationship to the next as funeral follows funeral]

pink wine *n.* [late 19C–1900s] (orig. milit.) champagne. [? the desire to pretend one were drinking something else/cheaper]

pink witches *see* PINK WEDGE.

pinky *n.¹* [early 19C+] the little finger; thus [20C] (US) *pinkycrooker*, an affected person, a poseur. [Scot.]

pinky *n.²* *see* PINKTOE.

pinky *n.³* *see* PINKIE n.³.

pinky *n.⁴* [1960s+] a passive lesbian (cf. FEMME). [the image of SE *pink* as a 'feminine' colour]

pinky and perky *n.* [1950s] a turkey. [rhy. sl.; ult. *Pinky and Perky*, popular characters from children's TV]

pin money *n.* **1** [late 17C+] small sums of money allotted to a woman for housekeeping. **2** [late 17C+] the money earned by a woman at a part-time job (cf. EGG MONEY). **3** [late 19C+] money gained by a woman for amateur, part-time prostitution. [(1), (2) lit. *money* to buy *pins*; (3) has the same image of small, insignificant earnings]

pinna *see* PINNY.

pinnace *n.* [17C] a prostitute (cf. FRIGATE). [SE *pinnace*, a light vessel in attendance upon a larger one]

pinnacles *n.* [late 19C] spectacles, glasses. [mispron. of BARN-ACLES]

pinned *adj.* **1** [1950s+] (drugs) used of eyes in which the pupils are reduced, irrespective of the light available, to pinpricks. **2** [1980s+] (US campus, drugs) under the influence of cocaine. [in both the effect of the drugs is to shrink the pupils]

pinner *n.¹* *see* PINNY.

pinner/pinroll *n.²* [1960s+] (drugs) a very small marijuana cigarette. [PIN n.¹ (2) + ROLL v.⁴/ROLL-UP n.]

pinner *n.³* [1980s+] (US campus) a thin person.

pinner *adj.* [1980s+] (US campus) thin. [PINNER n.³]

pinner-up *n.* [mid-late 19C] a street-seller of printed songs and ballads, which are pinned up at their pitch. [PIN UP]

pinnie *n.* [1990s] (N.Z.) a *pin*ball machine. [abbr.]

pinny/pinna/pinner *n.* [mid-19C+] a *pina*fore. [abbr.]

pin on *v.* [1970s+] to accuse, to lay the blame on someone. [SE *pin on*, to attach]

pin one on someone *v.* [20C] (US) to hit someone, to punch someone.

pin-pannierly fellow *n.* [17C] a conspicuously grasping miser. [? one who keeps all their pins in a *pannier*, a basket, or pins a pannier to their clothes]

pinroll *see* PINNER n.².

pins *n.* [mid-19C+] legs (rarely in sing.).

pins and needles *n.* [20C] beetles. [rhy. sl.]

pin shot *n.* [1920s–50s] (drugs) an injection of a narcotic using a rudimentary 'syringe' made of a pin or needle and an eye-dropper. [SE *pin* + SHOT n.⁵ (2)]

pint *n.* [1950s] (W.I.) a 6-month prison sentence. [i.e. half a QUART n.²]

pinta *n.¹* [1950s+] a pint of milk, milk in general. [SE *pint of …* . A late 1950s+ advertising campaign called on people to 'Drinka pinta milka-day']

pinta, la *n.²* [1960s+] (US) prison. [Sp.]

pin the basket, to *phr.* [mid-late 17C] to bring to a conclusion, to settle (cf. PIN BASKET). [the *pin* or peg that secured the basket-lid]

pin the rap on, to *phr.* [1930s+] to impute a crime (to a criminal) (whether or not they are actually implicated) (cf. HANG THE RAP ON). [SE *pin* + RAP n.³]

pintle *n.* **1** [early 18C–19C] the penis. **2** [20C] (Ulster) a small, irritating person (cf. PRICK). [OE *pintel*, the penis]

pintle-bit/-maid *n.* [19C–1900s] a mistress (cf. PINTLE-MERCHANT). [PINTLE (1) + BIT n.³/SE *maid*]

pintle-blossom *n.* [18C–1900s] a bubo, the result of syphilis (cf. GROG BLOSSOM; PINTLE-FEVER). [PINTLE (1) + joc. use of SE *blossom*]

pintle-case *n.* [19C] the vagina (cf. COCK-HOLDER). [PINTLE (1) + SE *case*]

pintle-de-pantledy *adj.* [mid-17C–early 19C] frightened, scared. [ety. unknown; ? echoic of nervous fidgeting]

pintle-fancier/-ranger *n.* [early 19C–1900s] a promiscuous woman. [PINTLE (1) + SE *fancier*/RANGER (2)]

pintle-fever *n.* [19C–1900s] any form of venereal disease (cf. PINTLE-BLOSSOM). [PINTLE (1) + SE *fever*]

pintle-keek *n.* [19C–1900s] a sexually inviting look, a leer. [PINTLE (1) + Scot. *keek*, a glance]

pintle-maid *see* PINTLE-BIT.

pintle-merchant/-monger *n.* [late 18C–1900s] a prostitute (cf. PINTLE-BIT). [PINTLE (1) + MERCHANT/sfx. -MONGER]

pintle-ranger *see* PINTLE-FANCIER.

pintle-smith/-tagger *n.* [late 18C–1900s] a surgeon. [PINTLE (1) + sfx. -SMITH/SE *tag*, to stitch together]

pinto *n.* [1960s+] (US) a former convict. [PINTA n.²]

pint of mahogany *n.* [late 19C] a mug of coffee. [the colour]

pint peddler *n.* [1930s] (US) a petty bootlegger who carries a number of pints of liquor about their person. Their sales pitch is usu. a pool room.

pint-pot *n.* **1** [late 16C] a beer-seller. **2** [late 19C+] (Aus.) a tin can, holding a pint, which is used for boiling water.

pin up *v.* [mid-late 19C] to sell the sheet music of popular songs in the street.

pinurt pots *n.* [mid-19C] turnip tops. [backsl.]

pin yen *see* PEN YEN.

pioneer of nature *n.* [19C] the penis (cf. NATURE'S SCYTHE).

piong *n.* [20C] (W.I.) an enthusiast, esp. for a food or game. [16C Fr. *pion*, excessive drinking, thus modern Fr. sl. *pion*, a hard drinker]

p.i.p. *n.* [20C] (W.I.) a toady, a sycophant. [abbr. party *in* power]

pip *n.¹* [late 19C+] ill humour or poor health; usu. as *get the pip*, *give one the pip*. [SE *pip*, 'a disease of poultry and other birds, characterized by the secretion of a thick mucus in the mouth and throat, often with the formation of a white scale on the tip of the tongue' (*OED*)]

pip *n.²* [late 19C] (orig. US) the very best, the finest example. [abbr. PIPPIN (4)]

pip *n.³* [1950s+] (US teen) a pimple, a spot. [SE *pip*, a blemish, a mark]

pip *v.*[1] [late 19C+] **1** to blackball. **2** to defeat, to beat. **3** to hit with a shot. **4** to fail (a candidate) in an examination (cf. PILL *v.*). [? fig. uses of SE *pip*, a spot on a die, card or domino, reinforced by PIP AT THE POST]

pip/pip out *v.*[2] [1910s–20s] to die. [gambling imagery]

pip *v.*[3] [1970s] to give birth. [the *pip* of a fruit]

pip at the post, to *phr.* [1920s+] **1** to do something before someone else has had the chance. **2** to beat by a narrow margin at the last moment. [PIP *v.*[1]]

pipe *n.*[1] [17C] a voice. [SE *pipe*, the voice, as used in singing]

pipe *n.*[2] [late 18C–late 19C] 'A spell of travelling between two rest-periods at each of which a pipe is smoked; the distance covered or the time taken, in such a spell; also, the distance covered while smoking a pipeful of tobacco' (*OED*). [best-known in Sherlock Holmes' 'three-pipe' problems, although his 'travelling' was usually in the head]

pipe *n.*[3] (drugs) **1** [late 19C+] an opium pipe. **2** [1950s] an opium addict. **3** [1960s+] a marijuana pipe. **4** [1960s+] a marijuana smoker. **5** [1960s+] a vein into which a drug can be injected. **6** [1960s+] (S.Afr.) enough marijuana to fill a pipe **7** [1980s+] a pipe for smoking base cocaine or crack.

pipe *n.*[4] [late 19C+] a glance, a look (at). [PIPE *v.*[2] (2)]

pipe *n.*[5] [20C] (US) a telephone.

pipe *n.*[6] [20C] any form of clubbing weapon. [SE *lead pipe*]

pipe *n.*[7] [20C] (US) anything that is easily accomplished; thus (campus) *pipe course*, an easy academic course. [abbr. LEAD-PIPE CINCH]

pipe *n.*[8] [1960s+] **1** the penis (cf. LAY SOME PIPE). **2** the vagina.

pipe *v.*[1] [mid-19C] (US) to smoke a pipe.

pipe *v.*[2] [mid-19C+] **1** orig. of a detective, to follow, to pursue. **2** to look over, to inspect. [? SE *peep*]

pipe *v.*[3] **1** [late 18C–late 19C] to weep (cf. PIPE ONE'S EYE). **2** [late 19C+] to talk, esp. as *pipe up*, to start talking, to interrupt. [SE *pipe*, to play a pipe]

pipe *v.*[4] [1960s+] (drugs) to mix drugs with other substances. [? they are smoked together in a *pipe*]

pipe and drum *n.* [20C] the buttocks. [rhy. sl. *pipe and drum* = BUM *n.*[2]]

piped *adj.*[1] [1910s–50s] (US) drunk. [SE *pipe*, a large barrel]

piped *adj.*[2] [1940s+] under the influence of drugs. [PIPE *n.*[3]]

pipe down *v.* [late 19C+] to talk more quietly; often as *pipe down!*, shut up! [naut. *pipe-down*, the call on the bosun's pipe signifying 'lights out']

pipe-fiend *n.* [1910s–30s] (US) a regular opium user. [PIPE *n.*[3] (1) + FIEND *n.*[2] (1)]

pipe-head *n.* [1980s+] (drugs) a regular user of crack. [PIPE *n.*[3] (7) + sfx. -HEAD (2)]

pipe in an ivy-leaf, to *phr.* [14C–17C] to waste time, esp. when appearing to be busy. [? the piping god Pan, associated with nature]

pipe-man *n.* [1980s+] a seller of crack. [PIPE *n.*[3] (7) + SE sfx. -*man*]

pipe off *v.* [1910s–20s] to 'pump' a person for information.

pipe one's eye, to *phr.* [late 18C–late 19C] (orig. naut.) to cry, to weep.

pipe-opener *n.* **1** [mid–late 19C] exercise taken to clear the lungs or throat. **2** [1930s+] anything exploratory, e.g. a trial run, a rehearsal.

piper *n.*[1] [late 18C–early 19C] a broken-down horse (cf. ROARER *n.*[2]). [? SE *pipes*, the lungs and the wheezing noise they make]

piper *n.*[2] [mid-19C–1900s] a spy, esp. one employed on an omnibus. [PIPE *v.*[2]]

piper *n.*[3] [1990s] (drugs) a smoker of crack cocaine. [PIPE *n.*[3] (7)]

piper fou *adj.* [late 18C–19C] very drunk (cf. BITCH-FOU; GREETIN' FOU; PISSING FOU; ROARING FOU). [SE *piper* + FOU *adj.*[1]]

pipero *n.* [1980s+] (drugs) a smoker of base cocaine or crack. [Sp. 'a pipe-er']

piper's cheeks *n.* [late 16C–late 17C] fat or swollen cheeks.

piper's news *n.* [19C] (Scot.) stale news. [? the piper traditionally receives the news last]

piper's wife *n.* [18C] (Scot.) a prostitute. [derog. stereotyping]

pipes *n.*[1] **1** [16C+] the voice. **2** [1930s] (US Black) the lungs, esp. of a singer.

pipes *n.*[2] [early 19C] top boots (cf. MUD PIPES). [? the tubular shape, or cleaning with pipe-clay]

pipe smoker *n.* [1990s] a gay man. [PIPE *n.*[8] (1)]

pipe the stem, to *phr.* [20C] (US) to beg in a city's main street (cf. MOOCH THE STEM). [PIPE *v.*[2] + STEM *n.*[2]]

pipe up *v.* [19C+] to speak more audibly. [PIPE *v.*[3] (2)]

pipieri *n.* [mid-19C+] (W.I.) an aggressive person. [dial. *pipieri*, the tyrant flycatcher, a small fighting bird]

piping *n.*[1] [late 18C–late 19C] crying. [PIPE *v.*[3] (1)]

piping *n.*[2] [1980s+] smoking crack cocaine. [PIPE *n.*[3] (7)]

pipkin *n.* [mid-19C] **1** the stomach. **2** the head. **3** the female genitals (cf. CRACK A PIPKIN). [SE *pipkin*, a small, earthenware pot]

pip off *v.* [1930s] to die. [the radio 'pips' that signal a time-check]

pip out *see* PIP *v.*[2].

pipped *adj.*[1] [1910s+] annoyed, irritated. [GET THE PIP]

pipped *adj.*[2] [1920s+] beaten. [abbr. PIP AT THE POST]

pipperoo *n.* [1940s+] (orig. US) something excellent, remarkably good. [PIP *n.*[2] + sfx. -EROO]

pippiejoller *see* PIEPIEJOLLER.

pippin *n.* **1** [mid-17C–late 19C] a term of approval or congratulation, applied to a person. **2** [late 17C–late 18C] a pej. term of address or description. **3** [late 19C] a loved one. **4** [late 19C+] a perfect example of whatever is under discussion; usu. as *it's a pippin*. [SE *pippin*, the name of various types of apple]

pippin-squire *n.* [mid–late 17C] a pimp (cf. APPLE MONGER; SQUIRE OF THE BODY; SQUIRE OF THE PLACKET). [play on APPLE SQUIRE; i.e. SE *pippin*, used in the names of various types of apple]

pip-pip! *excl.* **1** [late 19C] a street cry, often launched at passing cyclists (still a novelty in late 19C). **2** [late 19C+] goodbye! hello! [the noise of the cyclist's horn]

pippish *adj.* [1910s+] irritated, out of sorts. [GET THE PIP]

pippy *adj.* [1940s+] (Aus.) irritated, out of sorts. [GET THE PIP]

pippy-poo *adj.* [20C] (US) extremely small, tiny.

pipsqueak *n.* [1910s+] **1** an insignificant person. **2** (Aus.) a parasite, a toady. [SE *pip*, a shrill, sudden noise + *squeak*]

pip the pumpkin, to *phr.* [1990s] to masturbate.

pipy *adj.* [mid-19C] tearful, prone to tears. [PIPE *v.*[3] (1)]

pirate *n.* [1920s+] (Aus.) a man who wanders around looking for a casual pick-up; thus *on the pirate*, looking for a casual pick-up.

pirate *v.* [1920s+] (Aus.) to pick up in the hope of seduction. [PIRATE *n.*]

pirate's dream *n.* [1980s+] (US campus) a flat-chested woman (cf. CARPENTER'S DREAM). [she has a 'sunken chest']

pisa *see* PAISA.

pisel *see* PEYSLE.

pish *v.* [20C] (Ulster) to rain heavily. [PISS *v.*[1]]

pishery-pashery *n.* [late 16C–early 17C] nonsense, rubbish. [SE *pish!*, nonsense! rubbish!]

piskey/pisky *adj.* [mid–late 19C (Scot.) E*pisco*palian. [abbr.]

pi-squash *n.* [1910s–20s] (mainly teen) a prayer meeting. [SE *pi*(*ous*) + *squash*(*ed together*)]

piss *n.* **1** [early 19C+] urine, an act of urination. **2** [1910s+] any sort of weak drink, whether alcoholic or non-alcoholic. **3** [1920s+] beer. [PISS *v.*[1]]

piss v.[1] [mid-18C+] to urinate. [? echoic; prior use of the word is SE and medieval in origin]

piss v.[2] [20C] (orig. US) to complain, to whinge (cf. PISS AND MOAN).

piss!, a excl. [late 17C] a general excl. of disgust or annoyance. [PISS n.]

piss- pfx. [1940s+] (orig. US) a general derog. intensifier.

-piss sfx. [1940s+] a general intensifier, usu. used to modify the accompanying adj. in an ironic or deprecating sense, esp. of drinks, e.g. cat-piss, rat-piss.

pissabed n. [mid-17C+] **1** a bed-wetter. **2** a general derisive epithet. [PISS v.[1]]

piss/piddle about/around v. **1** [20C] to waste time, to act in a pointless manner. **2** [1950s+] to annoy, to waste someone's time (cf. ARSE ABOUT). **3** [1950s+] to deceive, to play tricks upon. [fig use of PISS v.[1]/PIDDLE v. (1)]

piss all over see PISS ON.

piss and moan, to phr. [20C] (orig. US) to complain, to whinge.

piss and punk n. [20C] (US Und.) bread and water (cf. ANGEL CAKE AND WINE). [PISS n. (2) + PUNK n.[2]]

piss and vinegar n. [1940s+] (orig. US) energy, enthusiasm, cheekiness. [fig. use of PISS n. (1) + SE vinegar]

piss and wind n. [1920s+] **1** empty talk. **2** one who is full of pompous braggadocio.

pissant n. [1940s+] an insignificant person, a 'nobody'; thus [1930s+] (Aus.) drunk as a pissant, very drunk; [1940s+] game as a pissant, very brave. [SE pissant, an ant]

pissant/pissant around v. [1940s+] (Aus.) to mess around (cf. PISS ABOUT). [PISSANT n.]

piss around see PISS ABOUT.

piss-arse see PISSY-ARSE.

piss-arse around v. [1920s+] (orig. milit.) to mess about (cf. PISS ABOUT). [PISS v.[1] + ARSE n.[1]]

piss artist n. [1940s+] **1** a regular drunk. **2** a general term of abuse. [PISS n. (3) + ARTIST n.[2]]

piss-ass see PISSY-ARSE.

piss away v. [20C] to waste. [fig. use of PISS v.[1]]

piss-awful adj. [1970s+] very bad, very unpleasant. [PISS n. (1)]

piss backwards v. [late 19C–1900s] to defecate.

piss-ball around v. [1920s+] to mess about, to idle (cf. PISS ABOUT).

piss blood v. **1** [late 19C+] to work extremely hard (cf. SWEAT BLOOD). **2** [1960s+] to worry excessively, to make a great fuss. [fig. use of PISS v.[1] + SE blood]

piss bones/children/hard v. [late 19C–1900s] to go into labour, to give birth.

piss broken glass, to phr. [1960s+] to have venereal disease, esp. gonorrhoea (cf. PISS PINS AND NEEDLES). [PISS v.[1]; the pain experienced when urinating during a bout of VD]

piss-burned adj. [late 18C–early 19C] discoloured, esp. of a grey wig which has turned yellow.

piss children see PISS BONES.

piss-cutter n. [1940s+] (US) **1** a generally obnoxious person. **2** an admirable person. [? the sharpness, whether seen as pos. or neg.]

piss down/up someone's back, to phr. [late 18C–19C] to flatter someone.

piss-easy adj. [1980s+] (N.Z.) very easy. [PISS n. (1)]

pissed adj.[1] [20C] drunk; thus half-pissed, tipsy. [PISS n. (3)]

pissed adj.[2] [1970s+] (US) annoyed (cf. P.'D). [abbr. PISSED OFF]

pissed as a ... for expressions other than those listed below see DRUNK AS A ... .

pissed as a chook phr. [1960s+] (N.Z.) very drunk (cf. SILLY AS A CHOOK). [PISSED adj.[1] + CHOOK n.]

pissed as a fart phr. [20C] very drunk. [PISSED adj.[1] + fig. use of FART n. (1)]

pissed as a newt phr. [20C] very drunk.

pissed as a parrot phr. [1990s] (Aus.) extremely drunk.

pissed as arseholes phr. [1960s+] extremely drunk. [PISSED adj.[1] + fig. use of ARSEHOLE n. (1)]

pissed off adj. [1940s+] (orig. US) furious, very annoyed (cf. P.'D).

pissed out adj. [1960s+] (US) exhausted, finished.

pissed to the ears phr. [1950s+] extremely drunk.

pissed to the gills phr. [1970s+] (US) very inebriated.

pissed up adj. [1970s+] very drunk.

piss elegant n. [1950s+] a pretentious, ostentatious, self-obsessed male homosexual. [PISS-ELEGANT adj.]

piss-elegant adj. [1950s+] extremely elegant (usu. used ironically or deprecatingly).

pisser n.[1] **1** [late 19C+] a urinal. **2** [20C] the penis. **3** [20C] the vagina. **4** [20C] (N.Z.) a woman. **5** [1920s+] a day on which it rains heavily and continuously. **6** [1930s] an electric pylon. [PISS n. (1)/v.[1]; (6) f. phallic imagery]

pisser n.[2] [1940s+] (US) **1** an extraordinary person or thing. **2** a difficult or distasteful event or task, an unpleasant person. **3** a bloke, a chap, esp. one who is tough and purposeful. **4** something or someone considered hilariously funny (cf. PISS ONESELF). [PISS v.[1], used here in the sense of 'that which makes one (fig.) piss']

piss-factory n. [late 19C–1900s] a public house. [mix of PISS n. (3)/PISS v.[1]]

piss flaps/flappers n. [20C] the labia (cf. FLAPS). [PISS n. (1) + SE flaps/flappers]

piss hard see PISS BONES.

piss-head n.[1] [20C] an obnoxious person (cf. SHITHEAD). [PISS n. (1) + sfx. -HEAD (1)]

piss-head n.[2] [20C] a heavy drinker (cf. ACID-HEAD; SMACK-HEAD). [PISS n. (3) + sfx. -HEAD (2)]

pisshole n. [1930s+] **1** a urinal, a lavatory. **2** any very dirty house, room or place. [PISS n. (1) + SE hole]

pisshole adj. [1950s+] second-rate, inferior (cf. BUMHOLE adj.). [PISSHOLE n.]

pisshole bandit n. [1960s+] **1** a minor criminal (cf. BANDIT n.[1]). **2** a male homosexual who solicits in lavatories. [PISSHOLE n. + BANDIT n.[1]]

pisshouse n. [20C] a lavatory. [PISS n. (1) + SE house]

piss in a quill, to phr. [mid-18C] to agree on a plan. [PISS v.[1]; the narrowness of the quill and the need to bend the flow of urine to achieve the feat]

pissing adj. [20C] a general adj. of abuse, based on a sl. term for a bodily function or part (cf. BUGGERING). [PISS v.[1]]

pissing contest n. [1970s+] (mainly US) any form of competition in which the participants are motivated more by the need to assert their superiority than by any desire to attain an accurate or positive conclusion. [fig. use of PISS v.[1] + SE contest; the image of two small boys urinating against a wall, each attempting to aim the flow of urine higher]

pissing fou adj. [19C] very drunk (cf. PIPER FOU). [PISS v.[1] + FOU adj.[1]; the idea of urinating through drunkenness]

pissing-/pissy-tail adj. [20C] (W.I.) **1** esp. of a young person, disrespectful, bumptious. **2** officious but impoverished and socially unimportant (cf. JOBSWORTH). [PISS v.[1] + TAIL n.[1] (3); the image is of a toddler still wetting itself]

pissing time n. [20C] (Irish) a very short time. [PISS v.[1]; i.e. long enough to urinate]

pissing while n. [mid-16C–late 17C] a short time. [PISS v.[1]; i.e. long enough to urinate]

piss in someone's pocket, to phr. [1940s+] (Aus.) to curry favour, to be extremely close to someone, to ingratiate oneself.

piss in the hand n. [1970s+] (N.Z.) anything considered very easy. [PISS n.]

piss in the wind n. [20C] a waste of time. [PISS n. (1)]

piss it v. [1970s+] to succeed with no difficulty whatsoever, to win very easily. [fig. use of PISS v.[1]]

piss it up the wall, to phr. [20C] to waste money (cf. PISS MONEY AGAINST THE WALL). [PISS v.[1]; the idea of 'wasting' a drink – and therefore money – by urinating afterwards]

piss-kitchen n. [18C] a kitchen maid. [PISS v.[1] + SE kitchen; i.e. where she (fig.) urinates]

piss-maker n. [late 18C–early 19C] a heavy drinker. [PISS n. (1); the results of alcohol consumption]

piss money against the wall, to phr. [late 18C–early 19C] to waste money on drink (cf. PISS IT UP THE WALL). [PISS v.[1]; the cost of a drink lost through urinating afterwards]

pisso n. [1940s+] (Aus.) a drunkard. [PISS(ED) adj.[1] + sfx. -O]

piss off v. [1930s+] **1** to annoy; thus piss-off, a state of anger. **2** to leave, esp. as piss off!, go away (cf. FUCK OFF!). [PISS v.[1]]

piss-off pal n. [1990s] (US Black teen) an intimate in whom one confides when very angry, such a friend being valued not for advice, but for their willingness to take the speaker's side. [PISS OFF + SE pal]

pissoir n. [1980s+] (US campus) the lavatory. [Fr.]

piss on/all over v. [1950s+] to treat contemptuously. [fig. use of PISS v.[1]]

piss on a nettle, to phr. [mid-16C–late 18C] to be annoyed, uneasy, tetchy. [fig. use of PISS v.[1]]

piss oneself v. [1960s+] **1** to be utterly terrified. **2** to laugh uproariously. [fig. use of PISS v.[1]]

piss one's pants, to phr. [1960s+] to be utterly terrified. [fig. use of PISS v.[1]]

piss one's tallow, to phr. [17C–19C] to sweat. [SE piss one's grease/tallow, said of a deer becoming lean in rutting-time]

piss on ice, to phr. [20C] (US) **1** to visit an upmarket restaurant. **2** to live well. [PISS v.[1]; the blocks of ice placed in the urinals to keep down the smell and ensure a continual flush of water]

piss on someone's parade, to phr. [1970s+] (orig. US) to shatter illusions, to ruin an otherwise satisfactory situation. [fig. use of PISS v.[1]]

piss or get off the pot! excl. [1940s+] (orig. US) either make a decision or let someone else do it (cf. SHIT OR GET OFF THE POT!). [PISS v.[1]]

piss out of a dozen holes, to phr. [late 19C+] of a man, to be infected with syphilis. [PISS v.[1]; i.e. the rotting of one's penis]

piss-parade v. [1970s+] (W.I.) to shatter illusions, to ruin an otherwise satisfactory situation. [PISS ON SOMEONE'S PARADE]

piss-/pee-warmer n. [20C] (Can.) a general term of extreme approval. [PISS n. (1)/PEE n.]

piss pins and needles, to v. [late 18C–early 19C] to have venereal disease, esp. gonorrhoea (cf. PISS BROKEN GLASS). [PISS v.[1]; pain during urination can be one of the symptoms of venereal disease]

piss pipe n. [1990s] the male urinary tract. [PISS n. (1) + SE pipe]

piss-poor adj. **1** [1920s+] totally lacking in finances. **2** [1940s+] third-rate, incompetent, useless. [PISS n. + SE poor]

piss poor bag o' shite n. [1990s] something without merit. [PISS-POOR + SHITE n.]

pisspot n. **1** [mid-18C+] a chamberpot; thus [late 18C] Piss Pot Hall, 'a house [? a tavern] at Clapton, near Hackney [in northeast London] built by a potter chiefly out of the profits of chamberpots, in the bottom of which the portrait of Dr Sacheverell preacher was depicted' (Grose 1796) (cf. TWISS). **2** [late 19C–1900s] an unpleasant person. **3** [1920s+] a drunkard (cf. ALECAN). [PISS n. (1) + SE pot. Dr Henry Sacheverell (c.1674–1724) was a High Church and high Tory cleric, who preached two sermons in 1709 that resulted in his impeachment on charges of seditious libel. He was condemned, but

received so light a punishment as to claim victory. His supporters were as vehement as the unknown potter. The Rector of Whitechapel commissioned an altarpiece in which the figure of Judas Iscariot was represented by that of the Dean of Peterborough, one of the Doctor's most virulent critics. (2) and (3) are fig. uses of (1)]

pisspot juggler n. [20C] (Can.) a chambermaid. [PISSPOT n. (1)+ SE juggler]

piss prophet n. [early 17C–early 19C] a physician who makes all their diagnoses on the basis of inspecting the patient's urine. [PISS n. (1) + SE prophet]

piss-proud adj. [1920s+] of a man, having an erection on waking (cf. P.P. adj.).

piss pure cream, to phr. [late 19C] to have gonorrhoea. [PISS v. (1); the discharge that accompanies the sickness]

piss-quick n. [mid-19C] gin mixed with marmalade topped up with boiling water. [PISS v.[1] + SE quick; its resemblance to urine or ? its micturative effect]

piss-rotten adj. [1940s] appalling, unpleasant, distasteful (cf. PISS-POOR). [PISS n. (1) + SE rotten]

piss rusty water, to phr. [1990s] to have very severe diarrhoea. [PISS v.[1]; i.e. the colour]

piss-take n. [1940s+] a tease, a hoax, a practical joke. [TAKE THE PISS]

piss-tank n. [20C] a drunkard (cf. PISSPOT). [PISS n. (3) + SE tank]

piss test n. [20C] (drugs) a urine analysis, carried out to check for drug use. [PISS n. (1) + SE test]

piss through v. [1910s+] to do something with no difficulty (cf. PISS IT). [fig. use of PISS v.[1]]

piss-ugly adj. [20C] (orig. US) very ugly. [PISS- pfx. + SE ugly]

piss-up n. [1950s+] a drunken party (cf. BEER-UP). [PISS n.]

piss up a storm, to phr.[1] [20C] (US) to complain strongly, to make a major fuss. [fig. use of PISS v.[1]]

piss up a storm, to phr.[2] [1990s] (US) to urinate for a relatively long time. [PISS v.[1]]

piss up someone's back see PISS DOWN SOMEONE'S BACK.

piss-warm adj. [late 19C+] tepid, lukewarm in an unpleasant way. [PISS n. (1)]

piss where one cannot whistle, to phr. [late 18C–early 19C] to be hanged. [PISS v.[1]; the loss of bowel control that results from being hanged]

pissy adj.[1] **1** [20C] drunken. **2** [1950s+] weak, ineffectual, trifling. [fig. uses of PISS n. (1)]

pissy adj.[2] [1950s+] cocky, arrogant. [used of one who annoys their fellows (cf. PISS OFF)]

pissy-arse/-ass/piss-arse/-ass adj. [1920s+] insignificant, useless. [PISSY adj.[1] (1) + ARSE n.[1] (3)/ sfx. -ASS]

pissy-arsed adj. [20C] likely to get extremely drunk. [PISSY-ARSE]

pissy-ass see PISSY-ARSE.

pissy pal n. [late 19C+] **1** an acquaintance picked up in a public house or a friend whom one only sees in the pub. **2** a close friend. [PISS n. (1), (3) + PAL n.; the pair drink and visit the urinals together]

pissy-tail see PISSING-TAIL.

pistakle/pistarckle n. [20C] (W.I.) **1** a foolish confusion. **2** a confused, foolish person, one who makes a fool of themselves in public. [? PISS ABOUT + SE spectacle]

pistol n. **1** [late 16C+] the penis (cf. GUN n.[2]). **2** [20C] (US) anything or anyone seen as remarkable, exemplary etc. [thus Shakespeare's double pun 'Pistol's cock is up' (Henry V, 1599); (2) underpinned by phr. 'hot as a pistol']

pistol pete n. [20C] (US) a zealous and effective lover. [PISTOL n. (1) + generic use of proper name]

pistols n. [1940s] (US Black) the trousers of a ZOOT-SUIT. [they 'shoot forward']

pistol-shot *n.* [mid-19C–1910s] a drink, a shot of liquor.

piston *n.* [20C] the penis.

pit *n.*[1] [late 17C–18C] (Und.) the common grave, beneath the gallows, in which those who fail to pay a burial fee of 6s 8d are buried after their remains have been cut down.

pit *n.*[2] **1** [early–mid-19C] a breast pocket; thus (Und.) *pit-man*, a wallet carried in that pocket; *pit-worker*, a pickpocket who specializes in robbing inside pockets. **2** [early 19C+] the vagina (cf. BLACK HOLE n.[1]). **3** [late 19C+] (Und.) a wallet. **4** [1960s] (drugs) the place on the inside of the elbow that is often used for injections. **5** [1960s+] usu. in pl., the armpit, with an implication of body odour.

pit *n.*[3] **1** [1920s+] a bed. **2** [1940s+] a real mess, esp. a room that is untidy.

pit *n.*[4] [1970s+] (drugs) phencyclidine (cf. ACE n.[3]). [initial letter]

p.i.t.a. *see* PAIN IN THE ASS.

pitch *n.*[1] **1** [mid-19C+] sales talk, esp. when inflated. **2** [late 19C] a conversation, a chat. **3** [1940s+] (orig. US) any plan that should benefit its maker, a scheme, esp. a piece of trickery or deceit. **4** [1940s+] (US) a situation. **5** [1970s] the line of talk used by a swindler. [fig. uses of SE *pitch*, to throw]

pitch *n.*[2] [late 19C–1900s] a nap, a short sleep. [PITCH v.[1]]

pitch *n.*[3] [20C] (Aus.) a camp. [SE *pitch camp*; although Mayhew apostrophises it; *pitch*, 'a spot in a street or other public place at which a stall for the sale or display of something is pitched or set up, or at which a street performer, a bookmaker, etc stations himself' (*OED*) has been SE since late 17C]

pitch *n.*[4] [1970s+] (US campus) an unattractive, unpleasant, promiscuous woman. [PIG n.[1] (3) + BITCH n.[1] (1)]

pitch *v.*[1] [late 18C–mid-19C] to sit down for a rest. [SE *pitch* (a tent)]

pitch *v.*[2] **1** [mid-19C+] to tell a tale, to speak persuasively. **2** [1940s–50s] (drugs) to sell drugs (cf. SLANG v.[3]). [fig. use of SE *pitch*, to throw]

pitch *v.*[3] [1960s+] (gay) to be the active partner in anal sex or in sado-masochism (cf. CATCH v.[6]). [baseball imagery; ult. fig. use of SE *pitch*, to throw]

pitch a ball, to *phr.* [1940s] (US Black) **1** to host an exciting, entertaining party. **2** to enjoy oneself at a party. [SE *pitch* + BALL n.[6]]

pitch a bitch, to *phr.* [1930s+] (US Black) to complain, to fight, to cause a disturbance. [SE *pitch*, to throw + BITCH n.[3]]

pitch a boogie-woogie, to *phr.* [1920s+] (US Black) to make a fuss. [SE *pitch*, to throw + fig. use of BOOGIE-WOOGIE]

pitch a fork, to *phr.* [mid–late 19C] to tell a story, esp. a sad or romantic one. [note Arthur Binstead (1861–1914), a late 19C sporting journalist and *bon viveur*, whose fund of stories, retailed to cronies as well as the readers of *The Sporting Times* (cf. PINK 'UN), gave him the nickname *Tale-Pitcher*, usu. abbr. to *Pitcher*]

pitch and fill *n.* [mid-19C] Bill, thus William. [rhy. sl.]

pitch and pay, to *phr.* [15C–mid-19C] to pay promptly.

pitch and toss *n.* [1940s+] the boss. [rhy. sl.]

pitch a tale, to *phr.* [mid-19C+] to recount a story (cf. PITCH A FORK).

pitch a tent/a tent in one's shorts, to *phr.* [1990s] (orig. US) to get an erection.

pitcher *n.*[1] [late 17C–18C] a prison, esp. Newgate in London (cf. STONE JUG n.[1]). [SE *pitcher*, a jug, thus play on JUG n.[1] (1)]

pitcher *n.*[2] [late 17C–1900s] the vagina (cf. MIRACULOUS PITCHER; PIPKIN). [SE *pitcher*, a jug]

pitcher *n.*[3] **1** [late 19C+] a street vendor. **2** [20C] a member of a three-card monte team. **3** [1980s] (drugs) a drug dealer, esp. when working on the street and actually handing over the drugs to the buyer. [SE *pitch*, the place in the street where such an individual works]

pitcher *n.*[4] [20C] (Aus.) a chatterbox. [PITCH A TALE]

pitcher *n.*[5] [1960s+] (gay) **1** the male partner in heterosexual intercourse. **2** the dominant partner in male homosexual intercourse (cf. CATCHER n.[2]). [PITCH v.[3]]

pitcher-bawd *n.* [late 17C–18C] a worn-out or semi-retired prostitute who runs errands in a tavern, either bringing drinks or providing customers with her more alluring peers. [SE *pitcher* + *bawd*]

pitch-fingers *n.* [19C] a thief. [SE *pitch*, a sticky substance used, *inter alia*, for sealing ships' timbers + *fingers*]

pitch fly *n.* [1970s] someone who takes over another's street-selling position without permission. [SE *pitch*, a street seller's site + fig. use of *fly*, an insect which has settled on one's spot]

pitch fog *v.* [1940s] (US Black) to make a scene.

pitch-in *n.* [late 19C] (Scot.) a railway collision.

pitch in *v.* [mid-19C+] **1** to set to work, to join in. **2** to start eating; often as request *pitch in!*

pitching and catching *n.* [1960s+] the two opposed and complementary sides of any form of physical sex, esp. sado-masochism, bondage and discipline or coprophilia. [baseball imagery]

pitch in lemons! *excl.* [mid–late 19C] a cry of encouragement (cf. GO IN LEMONS). [LEMONS adv.]

pitch into *v.* [mid-19C+] to fight, esp. to commence a fight (cf. GET STUCK IN).

pitch it high/hot *see* PITCH IT STRONG.

pitch it mild, to *phr.* [late 19C+] to talk without exaggeration (cf. PITCH IT STRONG). [PITCH v.[2] (1)]

pitch it strong/high/hot/warm, to *phr.* [mid-19C+] to speak forcefully, to state a case with feeling or enthusiasm, to exaggerate (cf. PITCH IT MILD). [PITCH v.[2] (1)]

pitch-kettled *adj.* [mid-18C–mid-19C] utterly puzzled, nonplussed. [? the image of black pitch being poured over a person, obscuring their vision]

pitchman *n.* [mid-19C+] one who entices customers to a street-seller's pitch (cf. BARKER n.[1]). [SE *pitch*, a street-seller's site + sfx. *-man*]

pitch on *v.* [20C] (Aus.) to nag, to attack verbally, to tell off. [PITCH v.[2]]

pitch over the perch, to *phr.* [late 16C–17C] to die (cf. DROP OFF ONE'S PERCH). [SE *pitch over*, to fall over]

pitch the cuffer, to *phr.* [late 19C–1900s] to tell exaggerated stories, esp. as a confidence trickster (cf. PITCH THE TALE). [PITCH v.[2] (1) + SE *cuffer*, a yarn or story; ult. *cuff*, to discuss, to tell a story]

pitch the dirt, to *phr.* [1950s] (US) to gossip, to slander. [PITCH v.[2] (1) + DIRT n.[1] (2), (3)]

pitch the nob *see* PRICK THE GARTER.

pitch the tale, to *phr.* [mid-19C+] to tell exaggerated stories, esp. as a confidence trickster (cf. PITCH THE CUFFER). [fig. use of SE *pitch*, to toss, to throw + *tale*]

pitch the woo, to *phr.* [1940s+] (Aus./US) to utter affectionate pleasantries. [PITCH v.[2] (1) + SE *woo*]

pitchy-man *see* DOLLY-MAN.

pitchy-patchy *n.* [1940s] (W.I.) **1** ragged old work-clothes. **2** one who is wearing them. [SE *patch* + redup.]

pit city *n.* [1960s+] a wretched, depressing situation (cf. PITS n.[1]). [PIT n.[3] (2) + sfx. -CITY]

pit hole/mouth/of darkness *n.*[1] [19C] the vagina. [neg. characterization]

pit-hole *n.*[2] [late 19C] a grave.

pit mouth/pit of darkness *see* PIT HOLE n.[1].

pit-pat's the way! *excl.* [late 19C] carry on! don't stop! [SE *pit-pat*, patteringly, making a repeated sound]

pits, the *n.*[1] [1950s+] (orig. US) **1** the depths of despair (cf. PIT CITY). **2** a situation or an object which is or a person who is totally undesirable.

pits, the *n.*[2] (US campus) body odour. [abbr. SE *armpits*]

pit stop *n.* [1960s+] (orig. US) a stop on a car journey for passengers to relieve themselves.

Pittsburgh feathers *n.* [1930s] (US tramp) coal, as slept on in a freight train. [coal that is being transported to the steel mills of Pittsburgh]

Pitt's picture *n.* [late 18C–early 19C] a bricked up window. [in order to help finance the war against the American colonists, Prime Minister William *Pitt* (1759–1806) increased the tax on windows, charging householders for each one they owned. This was generally disliked and the poor and mean preferred to brick up windows rather than pay the tax]

Pitt Street farmer *n.* [1970s+] (Aus.) a business person who owns or shares a farm from which they take annual profits but which they rarely visit; earlier versions include [1920s] *Pitt Street stockman*, [1920s–60s] *Pitt Street bushman*, [1930s] *Pitt Street drover* (cf. COLLINS STREET FARMER). [*Pitt Street*, the financial centre of Sydney]

pitty *adj.* [1970s+] (US campus) messy, untidy, disgusting. [PIT *n.*[3] (2)]

pitzu *n.* [1980s+] (drugs) impure morphine base. [? Sp.]

pix *n.* [1920s+] (orig. US) *pic*tures, whether still or motion. [abbr./pron.]

pixie *n.*[1] [late 19C] a homosexual man. [var. on FAIRY *n.*[2]]

pixie *n.*[2] [1930s–40s] (Aus.) **1** a slender beer glass, with an 'hour-glass' shape. **2** the drink served in such a glass (cf. LADY'S WAIST). [SE *pixie*, an elf or fairy; used fig. to reflect the size of the glass]

pixie *n.*[3] [1950s+] (US Black) **1** a short hairstyle for women. **2** straightened hair on a man. [SE *pixie*, a sprite; the haircut supposedly resembles illustrations of such figures]

pixies *n.* [1980s+] (drugs) amphetamine (cf. A *n.*[2]). [? the drug 'picks one up']

pixie stick *n.* [1960s+] (US gay) any phallic object carried by a cruising gay man, e.g. a cigarette holder, a rolled umbrella (on a dry day), a long-stemmed rose. [play on FAIRY'S WAND]

pixillated/pixilated/pixolated *adj.* **1** [mid-19C+] confused. **2** [1930s+] drunk. [SE *pixie*, a sprite, thus lit. 'one who has been taken over by pixies']

piz/pizz *n.* [late 18C] a fashionable man-about-town. [var. on PUZ]

pizz/pizicato *adj.* [1930s] tipsy. [euph. for PISSED *adj.*[1]]

pizza face *n.* [1980s+] (US teen) one who suffers from a severe case of acne.

pizza toppings *n.* [1980s+] (drugs) psilocybin/psilocin 'magic' mushrooms.

pizzazz *n.* [1930s+] (orig. US) **1** style, glamour, ostentation (cf. BIZZAZ). **2** energy, zest. [ety. unknown. but note RAZZLE *n.*; RAZZMATAZZ]

pizzle *n.* [1960s] (Aus.) the penis. [SE *pizzle*, a bull's penis; thus *pizzle guard*, a fictitious object in search of which young drovers are sent, only to be told 'I've only got a left-handed one']

pizzle *v.* [18C–19C] of a man, to have sexual intercourse. [SE *pizzle*, a bull's penis]

p.j.'s *n.* **1** [1920s–30s] *p*hysical *j*erks. **2** [1960s+] *pyj*amas. [abbr.]

p.k. *see* PICCANINNY KAYA.

plaasjapie *n.* [1950s+] (S.Afr.) a country bumpkin. [Afk. *plaas*, farm + JAAP]

plaba/ploba *n.* [1950s] (W.I.) an argument. [Carib.E. *plaba*, a stew, but note PALAVER *n.* (4)]

placa *n.* [1960s+] (US) one's 'street' or gang name. [Sp.]

place, the *n.*[1] [20C] the vagina (cf. DOWN BELOW). [euph.]

place *n.*[2] [1900s–50s] a lavatory (cf. PLACE WHERE ONE COUGHS). [euph.]

placebo *n.* [mid-14C–early 17C] a toady or sycophant (cf. AT THE SCHOOL OF PLACEBO). [Lat. *placebo*, I shall please; popularized as the name commonly given to Vespers in the Office for the Dead, from the first word of the first antiphon (*Placebo Domino in regione vivorum*, Ps. cxiv. 9)]

place of convenience/resort *n.* [17C] the lavatory. [euph.]

place of sixpenny sinfulness *n.* [19C] a suburban brothel. [costing less than its West End of London equivalent]

placer *n.* [1960s+] a middle-man who places stolen goods with a purchaser (cf. FENCE *n.*[1]).

place where one coughs *n.* [1920s+] euph. for the lavatory. [the shy person's coughing, hoping to disguise the sound of urination]

plack *n.* **1** [late 17C–early 19C] (Irish) anything of small value. **2** [20C] (Ulster) a mouthful. [SE *plack*, either a small 15C–16C Flemish coin or contemporary Scot. coin, worth 4d]

placket *n.* [17C] **1** the vagina (cf. ARBOUR). **2** a woman considered only as a sex object. [SE *placket*, the slit at the top of an apron or petticoat, facilitating dressing and undressing]

placket-box *n.* [17C] the vagina (cf. ARBOUR). [PLACKET + SE *box*]

placket-lady *n.* [17C] a prostitute. [PLACKET + SE *lady*]

placket-racket *n.* [17C] the penis. [PLACKET + SE *racket*, an implement for hitting balls]

placket-stung *adj.* [mid–late 17C] suffering from a venereal disease. [PLACKET + SE *stung*]

placky/plakky *adj.* [1970s+] *plas*tic; esp. in *placky bag*, a polythene carrier bag (cf. PLAZZY; POLY *adj.*). [abbr.]

plague *n.* [early–mid-19C] anything considered a nuisance, an irritation.

plaguey/plaguy *adj.* [early 17C–late 19C] 'confounded', excessive, exceeding, very great; also as adv. [euph. for BLOODY *adj.*]

plaguily *adv.* [late 16C–early 19C] irritatingly, annoyingly, to a great extent.

plaguy *see* PLAGUEY.

plain *n.* [1980s+] (Irish) Guinness stout, seen as the basic Irish drink.

plain and gravy *n.* [late 19C–1900s] the Royal Navy (cf. SOUP AND GRAVY). [rhy. sl.]

plain and jam *n.* [1900s–20s] a tram. [rhy. sl.]

plain as … *phr.* extremely obvious; e.g. in phr. [16C+] *plain as a packstaff/pikestaff*, [mid-16C–mid-18C] *… a pack-saddle*, [17C+] *… a pipe-stem*, [late 17C+] *… the nose on your face*, [mid-19C] *… Salisbury*.

plain people *n.* [19C] (US Black) White people. [a deliberate play on the SE White term, *coloured people*]

plain-/plains-turkey *n.* [1930s–50s] (Aus.) a tramp, a vagrant (cf. SCRUB-TURKEY). [SE *plains-turkey*, the Australian bustard, *Ardeotis australis*]

plain vanilla *see* VANILLA *adj.*

plaister/plaster of warm guts *n.* [late 18C–early 19C] sexual intercourse. ['one warm belly clapped to another: a receipt frequently prescribed for different disorders' (Grose 1785)]

plak *v.* [1960s+] (S.Afr.) **1** to stick on, to slap on, to glue on. **2** to plaster, to paint. [Du. *plakken*, to glue]

plakkies *n.* [1960s+] (S.Afr.) thongs, flip-flops. [PLAK; they 'stick' to one's feet]

plakky *see* PLACKY.

planet *n.* [mid-19C] (Und.) a candle. [it gives off light]

plank *n.* [1950s+] (Irish) a cache of money. [? PLANK *v.*[1] or the planks beneath which it is hidden, or the wooden box in which it is kept]

plank *v.*[1] [early 19C+] to pay money down, to lay out money, esp. when done without quibbling (cf. PLANK DOWN).

plank *v.*[2] **1** [late 19C] to place, to put, to deposit, to plant. **2** [1960s+] to have sexual intercourse (cf. BANG *v.*[1]). [fig. uses of SE *plank*, to lay a floor, thus in (2) added pun on *lay*/LAY v.¹ (1)]

plank down/up v. [mid-19C+] to pay money down, to lay out money, esp. when done without quibbling. [PLANK v.¹]

planker n. [20C] (US) a steak. [the 'slab' of meat]

plank in/the knife in v. [late 19C] to stab deeply. [PLANK v.² (1)]

plank up see PLANK DOWN.

plant n. **1** [late 17C+] (Und.) a hiding place for stolen goods. **2** [early–mid-19C] a detective, a spy, a decoy, esp. one who works under cover in a criminal gang. **3** [mid-19C] a swindle, a fraudulent trick. **4** [mid-19C+] a site where a street-seller is established. **5** [1920s+] (orig. US) someone who has been deliberately placed in an environment, typically an audience, where they respond (ostensibly as one more punter) to a call for 'volunteers' from the stage. **6** [1920s+] (drugs) a hiding place for drugs. [PLANT v.¹]

plant v.¹ **1** [17C+] to hide (cf. SPRING A PLANT). **2** [18C–19C] to post a spy or detective. **3** [early 19C] to abandon, to leave. **4** [mid-19C] to mark out a potential victim for robbery. **5** [mid-19C] to swindle, to deceive. **6** [mid-19C+] (orig. US) to bury a body (cf. PLANTING). **7** [mid–late 19C] to 'salt' a gold-field in the hope of attracting investors. **8** [1960s+] (Und.) of the police, to hide evidence in the clothes, home or car of a suspected person in order to ensure they have something with which to charge their victim. [(1) is mainly Aus. from mid-19C+]

plant v.² [early 19C+] (Irish) to hit; thus *plant*, a blow. [boxing jargon]

plantain leaf n. [1940s+] (W.I.) a £1 note (cf. ALFALFA n.). [like the note, it is green]

plant a man, to phr. [18C–19C] usu. of a man, to have sexual intercourse. [the ejaculation of 'seed']

planter n.¹ [mid–late 19C] (Anglo-Ind.) a bad-tempered horse. [? it plants its feet and refuses to obey the rider]

planter n.² [late 19C+] (Aus.) one who steals and then hides cattle. [PLANT v. (1)]

planter n.³ [late 19C+] (Ulster) an outsider. [the 'plantation' of Ulster in 17C–18C by English and Scot. settlers]

planter's medicine n. [mid-19C] (W.I.) a flogging. [administered every Monday to slaves who complained of ulcers and went to the plantation hospital. The punishment was meted out until the ulcers healed]

plant home v. [late 19C–1900s] in an argument, to make a telling point. [PLANT v.²]

planting n. **1** [late 18C+] (Aus.) the hiding of stolen items, esp. horses, and then 'discovering' them as soon as a reward is offered. **2** [20C] (US) a funeral. [PLANT v.¹ (1), (6)]

plants n. [17C–18C] the feet.

plant show n. [late 19C] (US) a 'black and white' minstrel show. [ety. unknown]

plant the whids and stow them, to phr. [mid-17C–mid-19C] (Und.) to talk carefully, to guard one's tongue. [PLANT v. + WHID n. + STOW v. (1)]

plant upon v. [early 19C] (Und.) **1** to survey a person suspected of being a criminal. **2** deliberately to place something valuable in someone's way, in the hope that they will steal it and thus lay themselves open to arrest. [PLANT v.¹]

plant you now, dig you later phr. [1930s–60s] (US Black) goodbye for now, and see you later. [pun on SE *dig*/DIG v.⁶]

plarry n. [20C] (Ulster) an unappealing mess of food. [Scot. *plorie*, a piece of ground that has been trodden into mud; ult. SE *plough*]

plaster n.¹ **1** [mid-19C+] (US) a banknote (cf. BALM OF GILEAD). **2** [1920s+] (Can.) a mortgage; thus *plaster*, to pay money towards a mortgage. **3** [1930s+] (Aus.) a bill, an account. [the rectangular shape + its efficacy in 'curing' financial ills]

plaster n.² [late 19C] an outsize collar. [resemblance, though E.P. suggests Fr. *plastron*, a stiff shirt-front. The style was popularized by the Duke of Clarence (1864–92)]

plaster n.³ [20C] **1** (US) a follower, a 'tail'. **2** (Irish) an unpleasant person. **3** (Irish) an encumbrance, a burden. **4** (Irish) one's wife. [they all 'stick to you like a plaster']

plaster v. **1** [1910s+] to hit (cf. PASTE). **2** [1970s+] (US Black) to flatter. **3** [1970s+] (US Black) to shoot someone.

plastered adj. [1910s+] (orig. milit.) drunk (cf. BASTED). [joc. use of PLASTER v. (1)]

plasterer's trowel and seringapatam/seringapatam n. [late 19C] a fowl and ham. [rhy. sl.; *Seringapatam*, apparently used purely for assonance, was the former capital of the Indian state of Mysore]

plaster of warm guts see PLAISTER OF WARM GUTS.

plastic n. [1970s+] any form of credit card; thus (US) *work plastic*, to obtain goods using a stolen credit card. [the *plastic* construction of such cards]

plastic adj. [1960s+] synthetic, false, insincere.

plastic cow n. [1980s] (US campus) non-dairy creamer. [SE *plastic* + COW n.⁴ (1)]

plastic job n. [1980s+] (orig. US) plastic surgery. [SE *plastic* (*surgery*) + JOB n.⁵]

plastic out v. [1970s] (US campus) to assume temporarily an artificial mode of behaviour or personality. [PLASTIC adj.]

plastic paddies n. [1980s+] the children of first-generation Irish immigrants to the UK. [PLASTIC adj. + PADDY n.¹ (1)]

plat n. [1920s+] (Aus.) a fool, an 'easy mark' (cf. FLATIE n.¹). [Fr. *plat*, flat]

plate n.¹ [1930s+] (US) a gramophone record. [resemblance]

plate n.² [1950s+] an act of oral sex, usu. fellatio. [PLATE v.]

plate v. [1950s+] to fellate. [rhy. sl. *plate of ham* = GAM v.¹]

plate it v. [late 19C–1900s] to walk. [PLATES]

plate of meat n. [mid-19C] the street. [rhy. sl.]

plate of straight n. [1950s] (W.I.) a dish of boiled bananas. [? SE *straight*, no trimmings]

plate-rack n. [late 19C+] a horse. [rhy. sl. *plate-rack* = SE *hack*, a horse for everyday riding]

plates/plates of meat n. [late 19C+] the feet. [rhy. sl.]

plates and dishes n. [20C] kisses. [rhy. sl.]

plates of meat see PLATES.

plating n. [1960s+] oral sex, fellatio, cunnilingus. [PLATE v.]

platinum adj. [1950s–60s] having a big heart, generous (cf. DIAMOND).

plato n. [1960s+] (US) a fight, a problem, an argument. [Mex. Sp.]

platsak adj. [1950s+] (S.Afr.) out of funds, impoverished. [Du. *plat*, flat + *sak*, pocket]

platter n.¹ [mid-19C] broken crockery. [? SE *plates* + *clatter*]

platter n.² [1940s–60s] (orig. US Black) a gramophone record. [resemblance]

platter-faced adj. [late 17C–early 19C] plain, broad-faced.

platters/platters of meat n. [1920s] the feet (cf. PLATES).

plausy/plauzy adj. [1920s] (Anglo-Irish) smooth-tongued, overly polite, apparently weak. [SE *plausible*]

play n.¹ [20C] (US Black) any form of action, plan or scheme (cf. GAME n.⁴).

play n.² [20C] (US Black) a form of greeting that involves the slapping of palms. [note 9C–14C SE *play*, to clap the hands]

play n.³ [1920s+] (orig. US) a show of interest, patronage, publicity; thus *to give* (*it/one*) *a play*, to try out, to give a chance.

play n.⁴ [1960s+] (US Black) money, objects of value, investments. [SE *play*, to gamble]

play v.¹ [late 16C–early 17C] to finish, to 'toss off'.

play v.² **1** [late 19C] (Aus.) to mock, to make fun of, to tease. **2** [late 19C+] (orig. Aus./US Black) to trick, to deceive.

3 [1960s+] (US Black) to be involved in an affair outside one's primary relationship.

play v.[3] [1930s+] (orig. US) to cooperate, to comply, to accept, to tolerate; usu. as neg. *I don't play that, that doesn't play.*

play/play at ... [18C–19C] a phr. used in various combs. as synons. for having sexual intercourse; *see* below or at individual nouns for more detail; e.g. *play at brangle, ... bouncy-bouncy, ... buttock, ... cock in cover, ... mumble-peg, ... prick the garter, ... pully-hauly, ... put in all, ... stable my naggie, ... thread the needle, ... tops and bottoms, ... top sawyer, ... where the Jack takes Ace.*

playa n. [1980s+] (US Black) anyone who uses wit, charm, intelligence to gain objectives, whether honestly or (more usu.) dishonestly. [PLAYER n.[1] (1); the sp. *playa* appeared during 1980s, as part of the general sp. changes used by GANGSTA rappers]

play about v. [20C] to waste money.

play a-cross/across v. [early 19C] (Und.) to lose deliberately, so as to lure one's victim deeper into the game (cf. PLAY BOOTY).

play a flute solo/a flute solo on one's meat whistle, to phr. [19C+] to masturbate (cf. MAKE A SOLO FLIGHT; PLAY A LITTLE FIVE-ON-ONE; PLAY AN ORGAN SOLO; PLAY A ONE-STRINGED GUITAR; PLAY A SOLO ON ONE'S MEAT WHISTLE; PLAY A TUNE ON THE ONE-HOLED FLUTE).

play a game at loll-tongue, to phr. [late 18C–early 19C] to have one's saliva checked for traces of syphilis.

play a good stick, to phr. [mid-18C–mid-19C] of a fiddler, to perform competently.

play a harp, to phr. [1920s+] (orig. US) to be dead. [the stereotyped image of angels]

play a little five-on-one, to phr. [20C] to masturbate (cf. PLAY A FLUTE SOLO). [*five* fingers, one penis or vagina]

play a lone hand, to phr. [19C+] (orig. US) to act independently. [poker imagery]

play along v. **1** [1920s+] (orig. US) to agree, to cooperate. **2** [1960s+] to deceive gradually, to 'take for a ride'.

play an organ solo, to phr. [1990s] to masturbate (cf. PLAY A FLUTE SOLO). [pun]

play another tune, to phr. [19C+] to alter one's opinions, to reverse one's stated position.

play a one-stringed guitar, to phr. [1990s] to masturbate (cf. PLAY A FLUTE SOLO).

playa hater *see* PLAYER HATER.

play/play with a placebo, to phr. [mid-14C–late 17C] to be a toady or sycophant (cf. AT THE SCHOOL OF PLACEBO). [PLACEBO]

play around v. [1920s+] (orig. US) to have a number of affairs, lovers, entanglements.

play a solo on one's meat whistle, to phr. [1990s] to masturbate (cf. ACCOST THE OSCAR MEYER; MAKE A SOLO FLIGHT).

play at Adam and Eve, to phr. [19C] to have sexual intercourse (cf. ADAMIZE).

play at all fours, to phr. [19C] to have sexual intercourse.

play at belly-to-belly, to phr. [19C] to have sexual intercourse.

play at bo-peep, to phr. [late 18C] **1** to live alternately hidden and then appearing in public. **2** to keep watch, to lie hidden. [SE *bo-peep*, a nursery game in which one amuses a child by hiding (usu. the face), revealing, then repeating the process]

play at buttock and leave her, to phr. [late 17C–mid-18C] to have sexual intercourse.

play at cherry pit, to phr. [20C] to have sexual intercourse. [SE *cherry pit*, the chewy stone]

play at/play fathers and mothers/dads and mums/ mummies and daddies, to phr. [1940s+] to have sexual intercourse. [the adult version of children's sex games, the main one being playing doctors and nurses]

play at handie dandie, to phr. [16C] (Scot.) to have sexual intercourse. [Scot./SE *handie-dandy*, a children's game based on the rapid moving of an object from one hand to another, then back]

play at handies *see* PLAY HANDIES.

play at hide-and-seek, to phr. [late 18C–19C] to go into hiding in order to avoid arrest, one's creditors etc.

play at hooper's hide, to phr. [20C] to have sexual intercourse. [SE *hooper's hide*, hide-and-seek]

play at hot cockles, to phr. [18C–19C] to caress and stimulate the female genitals. [SE + COCKLES]

play at houghmagandie, to phr. [16C] to have sexual intercourse. [SE/Scot. *hough* = hock = back of the knee + Scot. *canty*, cheerful, active]

play at/play itch-buttocks, to phr. [late 16C–19C] to have sexual intercourse (cf. ITCH).

play at level-coil *see* PLAY LEVEL-COIL.

play at lift-leg, to phr. [early 18C–mid-19C] to have sexual intercourse (cf. LIFT-LEG).

play at mummies and daddies *see* PLAY AT FATHERS AND MOTHERS.

play at pully-hawly *see* HAVE A GAME AT PULLY-HAWLY.

play at push-pin/-pike, to phr. [17C–18C] to have sexual intercourse. [pun on children's game, in which each player pushes or fillips their pin with the object of crossing that of another player]

play at put-pin, to phr. [mid-16C–mid-18C] to have sexual intercourse. [PLAY AT PUSH-PIN]

play at rantum-scantum, to phr. [late 18C–early 19C] to have sexual intercourse. [SE *rantum-scantum*, chaos, a disorderly situation]

play at stink-finger *see* PLAY STINK-FINGER.

play at two-handed put *see* PLAY TWO-HANDED PUT.

play a tune on the one-holed flute, to phr. [19C+] to masturbate (cf. FLUTE n.[2]; PLAY A FLUTE SOLO).

play at up-tails all, to phr. [late 17C–early 18C] of a man, to have sexual intercourse. [SE *uptails-all*, the name of a song; ult. SE *up* + TAIL n.[1] (1), (2)]

play away v. [1970s+] to philander, to commit adultery. [sporting imagery]

play-away n. [1970s+] (society) a weekend staying in the country. [? sporting imagery]

play baby v. [20C] (US) to act in a childish, infantile manner.

play bad v. [20C] (W.I.) **1** of a child, to behave badly, rudely. **2** of an adult, to put on a show of defiance.

play bad-mind v. [20C] (W.I.) to act in a spiteful, malicious way. [SE *play* + BAD-MIND]

play ball/play ball with v. [1930s+] to cooperate. [one 'plays a game' with]

play big v. [20C] (W.I.) to pretend to be more worthy, powerful, important, wealthy etc than one is.

play billy with, to phr. [late 19C–1930s] to tease, to 'mess one about'. [? BILLY BARLOW n.[1] or fig. use of Scot. *billy-blind*, blind man's buff]

play booty v. [early 16C–early 19C] to cheat in cards or dice, usu. in conspiracy with a confederate. The result of such play is either to gang up on a third party, and share the resulting profits or 'booty', or deliberately to play to lose (cf. PLAY A-CROSS; PLAY THE WHOLE GAME).

playboy n. [late 19C–1900s] (Irish) a fun-loving rascal.

play brother n. [late 19C+] (US Black) an extremely close friend, one who resembles a brother; thus also *play cousin, play mother, play sister.*

play buggery with, to phr. [late 19C+] to play havoc with (cf. BUGGER ABOUT).

play cagey-cannon v. [1960s] (Irish) to act cautiously. [SE *cagey*; ety. of *cannon* unknown]

play camels v. [late 19C] (Anglo-Ind.) to drink excessively, to get drunk. [the animal's large capacity for liquid]

play catch-up v. [20C] (US) to recover from a set-back, to make good a disadvantage.

play chaneys v. [late 19C] (Aus.) to exert influence; thus *play at chaneys*, to bribe. [? SE *Chinese*, so far as the racial stereotype is concerned, the Chinese person is 'not straight']

play cheap v. [1940s–60s] (US Black) to take seriously; often as *don't play someone cheap*, make sure someone is not underrated.

play checkers v. [1960s+] (US gay) to move from seat to seat in a cinema in search of a receptive sex partner. [the movements in checkers (UK draughts)]

play chick/chicken/chickie v. [1940s+] (US) to maintain a look-out during the carrying out of a crime (cf. KEEP CHICK). [CHICK n.³/CHICKEN n.²]

play chicken v.¹ [1950s] to indulge in dangerous games. [the loser is a CHICKEN n.²]

play chicken v.² [1970s+] (US Black) to intrude on another (man's) sexual advances. [fig. use of CHICKEN n.² (3), i.e. the intruder 'dares' his rival]

play chickie see PLAY CHICK.

play chopsticks v. [1960s+] (gay) to indulge in mutual masturbation. [joc. use of 'Chopsticks', a basic piece learnt by a novice piano-player]

play close v. [1980s+] (US Black) to become intimate with, esp. with the aim of using one's supposed friend for one's own purposes.

play cock in cover, to phr. [19C] to have sexual intercourse. [pun on SE *play cock*, to display oneself/COCK n.² (1)]

play cocum v. [late 19C] to act in an artful, cunning manner. [COCUM]

play coddem v. [late 19C] to tease, to trick. [COD n. + SE *them*]

play consumption v. [late 19C] (US) to malinger, to fake an illness. [SE *consumption*, tuberculosis]

play couple your navels, to phr. [18C] to have sexual intercourse (cf. WRIGGLE NAVELS).

play crimp/crimp v. [late 17C–late-18C] to cheat, to act criminally, esp. to bet openly on one side and then to cheat in favour of the other, on which one has bet surreptitiously. [SE *crimp*, one who entraps seamen into service, often by violence. Such activities were banned subsequent to the Merchant Shipping Act (1854)]

play cuddle my cuddie, to phr. [19C] to have sexual intercourse. [SE *cuddle* + dial. *cuddy*, a woman]

play dads and mums see PLAY AT FATHERS AND MOTHERS.

play diddle-diddle v. [16C] to play tricks, to importune. [pun on SE *diddle-diddle*, a fiddle/SE *to fiddle*]

play dirt v. [late 19C] (US) to deceive.

play dirty v. [1910s+] (orig. US) to behave reprehensibly, to cheat.

play dolly up, dolly down, dolly sick, to phr. [20C] to masturbate.

play down on v. [1900s] to take a mean or unfair advantage of.

play ducks and drakes with/make ducks and drakes of, to phr. [16C+] to squander one's fortune, to spend money unwisely. [SE *ducks and drakes*, a game based on the tossing of flat stones across a pond; thus in a financial context one is idly tossing away one's money. Mainly US in 20C]

played adj.¹ [late 19C] (US) exhausted, worn-out, finished. [abbr. SE *played out*]

played adj.² [1990s] (US Black) **1** insulted. **2** cheated on by one's girlfriend or boyfriend. [? PLAY v.²]

player n. **1** [1950s+] (orig. US Black) anyone who uses intelligence, wit, brains to gain objectives, whether a businessman, politician etc or criminal (cf. BALLER; PLAYA). **2** [1950s+] (orig. US Black) a man who uses his wit and charm to obtain money and other favours from wealthy White women. **3** [1950s+] (orig. US Black) a pimp. **4** [1950s+] (orig. US Black) a man who is a gambler by nature, who makes friends easily, and never gives up trying. **5** [1980s+] (US campus) a promiscuous person.

player n.² [1960s+] (N.Z.) a woman who is seen as enthusiastic about sex. [SE *play*/PLAY AROUND]

player/playa hater/hata n. [1990s] (US Black) one who resents the achievements and extravagant lifestyle of a ghetto success, whether gained legally or otherwise. [PLAYER n.¹/ PLAYA + SE *hater* or 'gangsta' sp. *hata*]

play fathers and mothers see PLAY AT FATHERS AND MOTHERS.

play favourites v. [20C] (orig. US) to show favouritism.

play fiddly-fuck v. [1960s] (US) to play around. [SE *fiddle* + FUCK (AROUND) v.²]

play footsie/footy/fotie v. [1940s+] **1** to nudge someone's foot with one's own, out of sight of companions, as a possible prelude to further intimacy (cf. FOOTSIE-FOOTSIE). **2** to indulge in the cautious sounding out of any relationship, economic, political etc.

play for a sucker, to phr. [late 19C+] (US) to deceive a gullible victim. [SUCKER n.¹ (1)]

play for blood, to phr. [1990s] (US Black) to play seriously, whether the game is sporting, electronic or figurative.

play for keeps, to phr. [mid-19C+] **1** to commit oneself permanently. **2** to commit oneself in absolute earnest. [FOR KEEPS]

play funny buggers see PLAY SILLY BUGGERS.

play games v. [20C] to manipulate, to manoeuvre, to act in a deceptive, dishonest manner.

play gooseberry v. [mid-19C+] (teen) for an unwanted third party to hang around a couple who would prefer to be left alone (cf. DO GOOSEBERRY). [GOOSEBERRY n.²]

play grab-ass v. [1950s+] (US) to make physical advances towards someone. [SE *grab* + ARSE n.¹]

play/play at handies v. [1910s+] (Aus.) of a pair of lovers, to hold hands.

play hardball/hardball it/play rough v. [1970s+] (orig. US) to act ruthlessly and single-mindedly in pursuit of a goal; thus *hardballer*, one who is ruthless and aggressive. [baseball imagery]

play hard to get, to phr. [1920s+] usu. of a woman, to resist sexual advances, though not necessarily to reject them altogether.

play hell with v. [20C] **1** to give someone a hard time. **2** to damage (an object, a plan etc).

play hey gammer cook, to phr. [18C] to have sexual intercourse. [? dial. *gammocks*, wild play]

play hide the salami/wienie, to phr. [1950s+] (US) to have sexual intercourse. [SE *salami*/WEENIE n.¹]

play hob v. [early 19C] (orig. US) to cause as much trouble as one can (cf. RAISE CAIN). [SE *Hob*, a mischievous sprite]

play hookey/hooky v. [mid-19C+] (US) to play truant from school (cf. BUNK OFF; HOOKY n.¹; HOOK JACK). [SE *play* + ? Du. *hoekje* (*spelen*) to play hide-and-seek]

play hoop-snake with v. [1960s–70s] (gay) **1** for two men to indulge in mutual fellation. **2** to indulge in homosexual SIXTY-NINE.

play horse with v. **1** [late 19C] (US campus) to ridicule, to tease. **2** [late 19C–1910s] to indulge in horseplay. [HORSE n.⁵]

playhouse n. [20C] (US Und.) a prison known for its liberal regime (cf. DISNEYLAND).

play house v. [1950s+] (US) to cohabit.

play huggy-bear v. [1950s+] (US) to kiss and cuddle.

play in and in, to phr. [17C] to have sexual intercourse.

play in and out, to phr. [19C] to have sexual intercourse.

play in a one-man show, to phr. [1990s] to masturbate.

play in Peoria, to *phr.* [20C] to succeed in rural, provincial areas. [*Peoria*, Illinois, as a emblematic stop on theatrical/ vaudeville tours]

playing out of the pocket *phr.* (US Black) **1** cheating or tricking. **2** letting something happen without noticing it. [OUT OF POCKET]

playing too close *phr.* [1960s+] (US prison) becoming over-familiar and invading the privacy of a fellow inmate.

play in someone's family *see* PLAY IN THE FAMILY.

play in someone else's yard, to *phr.* [1950s–60s] (US Black) to have an adulterous affair.

play in the/someone's family, to *phr.* [1920s–30s] (US Black) to indulge in a bout of ritualized name-calling, based on insulting each other's mother (cf. DOZENS).

play Irish whist, to *phr.* [20C] to have sexual intercourse (cf. IRISH TOOTHACHE).

play it by ear, to *phr.* [1940s+] to act in an *ad hoc*, spontaneous manner. [a musician who has no score as a guide]

play itch-buttocks *see* PLAY AT ITCH-BUTTOCKS.

play it close to one's chest, to *phr.* [1950s+] to act in a reserved, secretive manner. [card-playing imagery: the player holds their cards close to their body in order to stop any opponent seeing them]

play it cool *v.* [1940s+] (orig. US Black) to act in an uninterested or disinterested manner, to control every emotion (cf. TAKE IT COOL). [SE *play* + COOL adj.³]

play it off *v.* [late 16C–mid-17C] to bring something to an end.

play it on the throat, to *phr.* [20C] of a man, to have sexual intercourse. [ety. unknown]

play it straight *v.* [1960s+] (orig. theatre) to behave in an honest manner, to resist embellishing one's actions with artifice. [the warning used to actors not to overact]

play kissyface/kissy-kissy/kissy-poo *v.* [1970s+] (US campus) to kiss and cuddle. [KISSYFACE]

play least in sight, to *phr.* [late 18C–early 19C] to hide, to keep out of the way.

play/play at level-coil, to *phr.* [early 17C–early 18C] to have sexual intercourse. [SE *level-coil*, any form of rough game, spec. that once played at Christmas (an embryo form of musical chairs) in which each player is in turn driven from their seat and replaced by another; Fr. (*faire*) *lever la cul* (*à quelqu'un*), to make someone raise their buttocks, properly 'arse'; also found in Ital. as *levaculo*]

play lighthouses *v.* [20C] of a man, to have an erection while in the bath.

play low *v.* [late 19C] (US) to act meanly.

play man on *v.* [20C] (US Black) to intimidate, to bully.

play mummies and daddies *see* PLAY AT FATHERS AND MOTHERS.

play musical beds, to *phr.* [1960s+] **1** to swap partners for sexual experimentation. **2** of a number of people sharing the same living quarters (a house, a hotel etc), to commit adultery. [SE *musical chairs*, a children's party game]

play night baseball, to *phr.* [1960s+] to have sexual intercourse.

play off *v.* [late 16C–early 17C] to finish a drink, to toss off a glass.

playoffs *n.* [1930s–40s] (US Black) patrons. [? one *plays* one *off* against another]

play old gooseberry, to *phr.* [late 18C–late 19C] 'to play the devil', 'play the deuce'. [OLD GOOSEBERRY]

play on *v.* [1960s+] (US Black) to cheat on, to cuckold. [PLAY v.² (3)]

play one's ace, to *phr.* [1990s] of a woman, to have sex with a man. [SE *play* + (RED) ACE]

play one's cards right, to *phr.* [20C] to behave sensibly, to act in one's best interests.

play oneself *v.* [1980s+] (US Black) to delude oneself as to one's success, sexuality, character etc, to aggrandize oneself. [PLAY v.² (1)]

play oneself off *v.* [18C–19C] to masturbate.

play on Front Street, to *phr.* [1960s+] (US) to act openly, to abandon any pretences. [FRONT STREET n. (2)]

play on velvet, to *phr.* [mid-19C+] to gamble with one's winnings. [SE *play* + ON VELVET]

play out *v.* [1980s+] **1** (orig. US Black) to wear out, to lose usefulness, interest, value. **2** (US campus) to use so much that it will eventually fade out.

play owings *v.* [late 19C] (sporting) to live on credit.

play past *v.* [1960s] (US Black) **1** to circumvent obstacles, mental as well as physical. **2** to lose an opportunity.

play patty-fingers *v.* [1950s+] (Irish) to touch hands in the holy water font. [SE *pat* + *finger*]

play pickle-me-tickle-me *v.* [mid-17C–early 18C] to have sexual intercourse.

play-play *n.* [1940s+] (S.Afr.) a pretence, insincerity.

play-play *adj.* [1940s+] (S.Afr.) fake, make-believe. [PLAY-PLAY n.]

play-play *v.* [1940s+] (S.Afr.) to pretend. [PLAY-PLAY n.]

play penny pool, to *phr.* [20C] (US) **1** to deal with trivial matters. **2** to act in a trivial manner. [betting the lowest sums on a game of pool]

play pocket billiards/pinball, to *phr.* [1940s+] **1** to play with one's genitals through a trouser pocket (cf. POCKET BILLIARDS). **2** to masturbate.

play pooh sticks, to *phr.* [1990s] to have anal sex. [pun on SE *pooh sticks*, a game played in the children's book by A.A. Milne, *Winnie-the-Pooh* (1926)/POO n.¹ + STICK n.¹]

play possum *v.* [early 19C+] (orig. US/Aus.) **1** to pretend to be ill or even dead (cf. ACT POSSUM; COME POSSUM OVER). **2** to dissemble. [SE *play* + POSSUM; i.e. the habits of the animal]

play puck *v.* [1980s+] (Irish) to cause confusion. [PUCK n.¹]

play pussy and get fucked, to *phr.* [1990s] (US Black) to act weakly and to suffer as a result. [PUSSY n.¹ (3) + FUCK v.² (1)]

play ring a rosie, to *phr.* [20C] (US) to fool about, to make great effort with no result. [*ring a ring o'roses*, a children's game]

play rough *see* PLAY HARDBALL.

play second fiddle, to *phr.* [mid-19C+] to take a secondary, subsidiary role; thus (less common) *play first fiddle*, to play a leading role, *play third fiddle*, to act as a third party (cf. SECOND FIDDLE). [orchestra use]

play silly/funny buggers, to *phr.* [1960s+] to act uncooperatively, to mess around, to cause a deliberate nuisance. [var. on BUGGER ABOUT]

play smash *v.* [mid-19C–1910s] (US) **1** to come to grief. **2** to cause trouble for, to 'play hell with'. [SE *smash*, to break]

play solitaire *v.* [1990s] to masturbate.

play someone any of one's parts, to *phr.* [late 19C] to play a mean or unpleasant trick on someone. [theatrical imagery]

play someone for a Chinaman, to *phr.* [late 19C] (US) to treat someone like a fool. [racial stereotyping of the Chinese]

play someone too close, to *phr.* [1980s+] (US Black) to involve oneself too intimately and without invitation in another person's life.

play something off *v.* [1990s] (US Black) to avoid confrontation, whether verbal or physical, by diverting attention onto a new and less problematical topic.

play staff *see* RIDE STAFF.

play sticky *v.* [1920s+] to be mean with one's money, esp. if it has only recently arrived. [it 'sticks' to one's fingers]

play/play at stink-finger, to *phr.* [late 19C+] usu. of a man, to stimulate the female genitals (cf. FINGER FUCK v.). [STINK-FINGER]

play stinky pinky, to *phr.* [20C] of a woman, to masturbate. [SE *stinky* + *pinky*, the little finger]

play stuff *v.* [1970s+] (US Black) to deceive by a smart line of verbal patter. [STUFF n.¹ (1)]

play tag with the pink torpedo, to *phr.* [1990s] to masturbate.

play that on your aunt Emma's piano! *excl.* [1970s] deal with that, whether you like it or not (cf. PUT THAT IN YOUR PIPE AND SMOKE IT!).

play that shit, to *phr.* [1950s+] (US Black) to act in a particular way; usu. in neg. as *I don't play that shit*, I don't do that. [SHIT n.³]

play the ... act *see* DO THE ... ACT.

play the bear, to *phr.* [16C–17C] to act roughly or coarsely, to act rudely; thus [19C] *play the bear with*, to inflict great damage upon.

play the beaver, to *phr.* [1990s] of a woman, to masturbate. [BEAVER n.⁴]

play the charley wag, to *phr.* [mid–late 19C] to play truant. [var. on PLAY THE WAG]

play the chill, to *phr.* [1930s+] to ignore, to avoid, to act coldly towards (cf. DO COLD WITH). [CHILL n.¹]

play the con, to *phr.* [1950s+] to pretend, to attempt to swindle or deceive. [CON n.³]

play/shoot the dozens, to *phr.* [20C] (US Black) **1** to compete in ritualized mutual insults. **2** to take advantage of, to deceive (cf. DO A NUMBER phr.¹). [DOZENS]

play the dozens with one's uncle's cousin, to *phr.* [1940s] (US Black) to go about things in quite the wrong way, to make a mess of things. [DOZENS]

play the duck, to *phr.*¹ [17C] to behave in a cowardly manner. [SE *duck*, to lower one's head]

play the duck, to *phr.*² [20C] to avoid. [DUCK OUT]

play the field, to *phr.* [1930s+] to enjoy a variety of lovers. [betting imagery; one bets on several horses instead of concentrating on one]

play the first game ever played, to *phr.* [19C] to have sexual intercourse.

play the flute, to *phr.*¹ [20C] (US gay) to perform fellatio (cf. BLOW ONE'S PIPE; BLOW THE SKIN FLUTE; PLAY THE SKIN FLUTE). [FLUTE n.² (1)]

play the flute, to *phr.*² [1980s+] (drugs) to smoke crack cocaine. [the equation of the crack pipe with a flute]

play the fox, to *phr.* [late 19C] to cheat, to sham, to dissemble. [FOX n.¹]

play the gallery, to *phr.* [late 19C] to applaud. [theatrical imagery]

play the game, to *phr.* [late 19C+] to act in an honourable, 'sporting' manner. [modern use is often ironic]

play the giddy goat, to *phr.* [late-19C+] to act foolishly, impetuously (cf. ACT THE ANGORA).

play the goat, to *phr.* **1** [18C] to copulate energetically. **2** [late 19C–1900s] to lead a degenerate, dissipated life. [goatish characteristics]

play the harp, to *phr.*¹ [20C] (Anglo-Irish) to wander drunkenly, tapping the railings as one passes. [the supposed similarity of the railings to harp-strings]

play the harp, to *phr.*² [20C] to die. [the harp-playing angels of heaven]

play the heel, to *phr.* [1910s+] (US) to act unpleasantly, to be mean or cruel. [HEEL n. (2)]

play/go on the hop, to *phr.* [1950s–60s] to play truant from school. [HOP THE WAG]

play the iggie, to *phr.* [1960s+] (US) to ignore. [abbr.]

play the jack, to *phr.* **1** [mid-16C–late 17C] to act the villain. **2** [19C] to play the fool. [JACK n.¹⁴]

play the male organ, to *phr.* [19C] to masturbate (cf. PLAY A FLUTE SOLO).

play the mouth organ, to *phr.* [1960s] (drugs) to smoke heroin with a rolled-up matchbook cover substituted for the usual roll of tinfoil, which is used to suck up the heated, smoking heroin (cf. CHASING THE DRAGON).

play the nanny-goat, to *phr.* [20C] to play the fool. [var. on PLAY THE GIDDY GOAT]

play the nod, to *phr.* [1930s–40s] (drugs) to doze off as a result of injecting a narcotic drug. [NOD n.]

play the nut role, to *phr.* [1960s+] (US Black) **1** to pose as a shambling incompetent in order to swindle or otherwise trick a possible victim. **2** to pretend to madness. [NUT ROLE]

play the organ, to *phr.* [20C] (Aus.) to have sexual intercourse. [pun on SE]

play the part of the strong man, to *phr.* [late 18C–early 19C] to be whipped at the cart's tail (cf. SHOVE THE TUMBLER).

play the percentages, to *phr.* [1960s+] to act in a cautious manner, the opposite of GOING FOR BROKE. [gambling use]

play the pink oboe, to *phr.* [1990s] to fellate. [PINK OBOE]

play the Scotch fiddle, to *phr.* [18C–19C] 'to work the index finger of the right hand like a fiddlestick between the index and middle finger of the left. This provokes a Scotchman in the highest degree, it implying that he is afflicted with the itch' (Hotten 1864) (cf. SCOTCH FIDDLE).

play the skin flute, to *phr.* [20C] **1** to masturbate. **2** to fellate. [SKIN FLUTE]

play the sober Indian, to *phr.* [20C] (US) to resist joining in a drinking session. [racist stereotyping]

play the tom, to *phr.* [late 19C+] (US Black) to pretend to a fawning stupidity, in order to fool a gullible or self-important White person. [TOM n.¹¹]

play the traveller *see* TIP THE TRAVELLER.

play the wag, to *phr.* **1** [mid-19C–1900s] to play truant (cf. HOP THE WAG). **2** [1910s–20s] to be amusing or mischievous, to play the fool. [SE *wag*, a mischievous boy; ult. ? SE *waghalter*, one likely to end up 'wagging a halter', i.e. being hanged]

play the whale, to *phr.* [1960s–70s] (Aus.) to vomit. [? the biblical story of Jonah, who was vomited up by a whale]

play the whole game, to *phr.* [late 18C–early 19C] to play at cards or dice with the intention of losing (cf. PLAY BOOTY). [? one has to play to one's utmost – the whole extent of one's game – to ensure defeat; presumably the context is of a cheat aiming to ensnare a victim, for whom this will be their only success]

play three to one/three one and sure to lose, to *phr.* [18C–20C] of a man, to have sexual intercourse (cf. ENGAGE IN THREE TO ONE). [*three*, the penis and testes, and *one*, the vagina; what the man is *sure to lose* is semen]

play tiddlywinks *v.* [20C] to have sexual intercourse.

play tonsil hockey/tennis, to *phr.* [1980s+] (US campus) to kiss deeply (cf. FRENCH KISS).

play too close *v.* [20C] (US prison) **1** to invade someone's privacy. **2** to tease or intimidate someone.

play tricks *v.* [late 19C–1900s] to become pregnant.

play tug-o-war with the cyclops, to *phr.* [1990s] to masturbate. [ONE-EYED CYCLOPS]

play/play at two-handed put, to *phr.* [18C–early 19C] to have sexual intercourse. [pun on *put* = Fr. *putain*, prostitute]

play up *v.* [late 19C+] **1** of a wound or disease, to cause discomfort, e.g. *my bad arm's playing me up today*. **2** of machinery, to malfunction. **3** of people or animals, to irritate, to 'mess around'.

play up old gooseberry with, to *phr.* [mid-19C] to deal with in a peremptory manner, to shut (someone) up. [OLD GOOSEBERRY]

play upon the prick, to *phr.* [16C] (Und.) to mark cards with pinpricks. [play on SE]

play up to *v.* [early 19C+] to indulge, to humour. [SE *play*, to act]

play-White *n.* [1950s+] (S.Afr.) one who attempts to 'pass' as White (cf. WINDOW MEN).

play with a placebo *see* PLAY A PLACEBO.

play with 44 cards to the deck, to *phr.* [1960s+] to be mentally deficient, to be stupid (cf. NOT ALL THERE). [a full deck has 52 playing cards]

play with oneself *v.* [1920s+] to masturbate.

play with one's stuff out the window, to *phr.* [1900s–40s] (US Black) **1** to act with caution, esp. to act carefully when conducting a love affair. **2** to play cards without risk of losing. [? image of one who, planning an escape, has already placed their possessions outside the house]

play with the little man in the boat, to *phr.* [20C] of a woman, to masturbate. [BOY IN THE BOAT + LITTLE MAN *n.* (2)]

play with your willy wanker, to *phr.* [1990s] to masturbate. [WILLIE *n.*[1] + WANKER, but clearly also a pun on the character *Willy Wonka* in Roald Dahl's children's book, *Charlie and the Chocolate Factory* (1964)]

play whupass *v.* [20C] (US) to play or fight roughly. [WHIP SOMEONE'S ARSE]

play wriggle your navels *see* WRIGGLE NAVELS.

play Yankee with *see* COME YANKEE OVER.

plazzy *adj.* [1960s+] plastic (cf. PLACKY). [abbr.]

plead *v.* [1950s+] (Und.) to plead guilty. [abbr. SE *plead guilty*]

pleader *n.* [1910s–20s] a person, a fellow, a 'bloke'. [? euph. for BLEEDER *n.*[3]]

plead the baby act, to *phr.* [mid-19C+] (US) to attempt to mitigate unpleasant circumstances by pleading one's innocence or inexperience.

plead the fifth, to *phr.* [1950s+] (US) to avoid committing oneself, to refuse to take an action or make a statement. [the Fifth Amendment (1791) to the US Constitution states that no person 'shall be compelled in any criminal case to be a witness against himself']

pleasant *adj.* [mid-19C] drunk, tipsy.

please *v.* [19C] to have sexual intercourse with (cf. OBLIGE; SOLACE).

pleased as a dog with two cocks/choppers/tails *phr.* [late 19C+] very pleased, delighted. [COCK *n.*[2]/CHOPPER *n.*[3]/SE *tail*]

please I want the cook-girl *n.* [late 19C] a youth who hangs around outside a large London house. [his typical phr. when accosted as to what he is doing]

please mother open the door *phr.* [late 19C] a phr. used to express one's admiration of a passing woman.

please oneself *v.* [late 16C+] to indulge one's own wishes, to have one's own way, esp. as *please yourself*, do what you want (even if no one else agrees).

please one's pisser, to *phr.* [20C] to masturbate. [PISSER *n.*[1] (2)]

please the pope, to *phr.* [1990s] to masturbate (cf. BANG THE BISHOP). [the Catholic rejection of contraception]

pleasure *v.* [19C] to have sexual intercourse with.

pleasure and pain *n.* [20C] rain. [rhy. sl.]

pleasure-baulker *n.* [early–mid-19C] a petticoat. [SE *pleasure* + *baulk*, to hinder; the garment inhibits easy access to the vagina]

pleasure boat/ground/place *n.* [19C] the vagina (cf. GENTLE-MAN'S PLEASURE-GARDEN).

pleasure garden padlock *n.* [17C–early 19C] a menstrual cloth or towel (cf. GARDEN PADLOCK).

pleasure ground *see* PLEASURE BOAT.

pleasure hound *n.* [mid-19C] (US) a man-about-town, a *bon*

viveur (cf. BROADWAY JOE; CHIPPY-CHASER; DUDE *n.*; HOG IN TOGS; MASHER *n.*). [SE *pleasure* + sfx. -HOUND]

pleasure-lady *n.* [19C] a prostitute.

pleasure-merchant *n.* [19C] a prostitute (cf. PLEASURE-LADY).

pleasure place *see* PLEASURE BOAT.

pleasuring *n.* [early 19C+] going out for pleasure; thus *pleasured*, delighted, pleased.

pleb/plebbie/plebby *adj.* [1970s] *pleb*ian. [abbr.]

pledge *n.* [late 19C+] (US) a student who has promised to join a fraternity or sorority.

plenish *v.* [20C] to furnish a house. [SE *replenish*; ult. Fr. *plenir*, to fill]

plenty *adv.* [mid-19C+] (US) abundantly, very much.

plenty of guts, but no bowels *phr.* [late 18C–mid-19C] a phr. used of one who is tough and ruthless but lacks compassion.

pleuro/pleura/ploorer *n.* [mid-19C+] (Aus.) contagious bovine *pleuro*-pneumonia, a disease of cattle. [abbr.]

plex *v.* **1** [1960s+] (US prison) to get psychologically prepared to start a gang fight (cf. FLEX *v.*[1]). **2** [1990s] (US) to show disrespect, to slander (cf. DIS *v.*). [ety. unknown; ? (2) SE *perplex*]

plier/plyer *n.* **1** [late 18C–mid-19C] (Und.) a crutch. **2** [mid-late 19C] a hand. **3** [late 18C–early 19C] a tradesman. [SE *ply one's way*; *ply one's trade*]

pliers *n.* [1950s] (W.I.) a small, finger-shaped dumpling. [because of its toughness, it would need a pair of pliers to break it]

pling *v.* [20C] (tramp) to beg. [? abbr. SE *pleading*]

plink *n.* [1910s+] (Aus.) cheap or second-rate wine (cf. PLINKITY-PLONK). [PLONK *n.* + PINK EYE *n.*[1] (1)]

plinker *n.* [1980s+] (US) **1** an airgun. **2** a cheap, low-calibre weapon (cf. SATURDAY NIGHT SPECIAL). **3** one who owns and uses such weapons. [the 'plinking' noise it makes]

plinkity plonk *n.* [1910s+] (Aus.) white wine; cheap and second-rate wine (cf. PLINK; PLONK *n.*). [rhy. sl. *plinkity plonk* = *vin blanc*, white wine; orig. WW1 milit.]

ploba *see* PLABA.

plocker/plugher *n.* [20C] (Ulster) **1** a clearing of the throat. **2** a smoky atmosphere. [Irish *plúch*, to choke; *plúchadh*, asthma]

plod *n.*[1] (Aus.) **1** [1920s+] a story, a piece of information. **2** [1940s+] a work sheet giving information about the ground worked by a miner; thus *pitch the plod*, for miners to gossip as they come off and on shift. **3** [1940s+] a specific piece of ground worked by a miner. [Cornish dial. *plod*, a short story, a lying tale; (3) is what is accounted for in (2)]

plod *n.*[2] [1970s+] a policeman. [children's story character *PC Plod*, created by Enid Blyton (1897–1968) in her *Noddy* books]

ploll-cat *n.* [late 19C] a prostitute. [corruption of SE *pole-cat*]

plongkas/pluncas *n.* [1940s] (W.I.) **1** a heavy cake or dumpling. **2** a heavy shoe. [echoic *plonk*, the noise it makes hitting a plate or the floor]

plonk *n.* [1910s+] cheap or second-rate wine; thus (Aus.) *plonk bar*, a wine bar; *plonk-dot*, a heavy drinker of wine; *plonk-up*, a cheap wine party; *plonked-up*, drunk. [? mispron. of Fr. *vin blanc*, white wine, picked up by Anglophone soldiers during WWI; the brandname 'Plonque' was merchandized in the early 1970s]

plonk *v.* **1** [20C] to have sexual intercourse (cf. BANG *v.*[1]). **2** [1940s+] to put down (cf. PLONK ONESELF DOWN).

plonker *n.* **1** [mid-19C+] anything large or substantial. **2** [1960s+] the penis. **3** [1960s+] a general term of abuse (cf. DICKHEAD). [fig. use of SE *plonk*, to hit or strike with a plonking noise; widely popularized by the 1980s BBC TV series *Only Fools and Horses*]

plonkers *n.* [1920s+] the feet. [one 'plonks them down']

plonko *n.* [1960s+] (Aus.) one who is addicted to cheap wine. [PLONK n. + sfx. -O]

plonk oneself down *v.* [1940s+] to sit down, often as an invitation, e.g. *please, plonk yourself down*, please, sit down. [PLONK v. (2)]

ploorer *see* PLEURO.

plootered *adj.* [1920s+] (Scot.) drunk (cf. BLOOTERED). [*plouter*, to wade through water or mud]

plot *n.* [1960s+] the place where street-sellers or confidence tricksters operate, e.g. the street, an alley or a doorway.

plot up *v.*[1] [1960s+] (Und.) of a gang or group, to seek out and establish territory, e.g. in a soccer stadium, club, crowded place etc. [SE *plot* (of land)]

plot up *v.*[2] [1960s+] to plan, to conspire. [SE *plot*, to plan, to scheme]

plotzed *adj.* [20C] drunk (cf. BLASTED adj.[2]). [Yid. *plotzen*/Ger. *platzen*, burst, split]

plough *v.*[1] [mid–late 19C] to reject a candidate as not reaching the pass standard in an examination (cf. PLOUGHED).

plough/plow *v.*[2] [1950s+] (US) to have sexual intercourse (cf. TILL v.).

ploughed/plowed *adj.* [mid-19C+] drunk. [? Oxford University jargon *ploughed*, rejected in an examination]

plough into *v.* [1910s–20s] to begin eating enthusiastically.

ploughshare *n.* [19C] the penis (cf. PLOUGH v.[2]).

plough/plow the back forty *phr.*[1] [1950s–60s] (US) to waste time. [SE *plough* + BACK FORTY]

plough/plow the back forty, to *phr.*[2] [1950s+] to have sexual intercourse. [PLOUGH v.[3] + BACK FORTY]

plough the deep, to *phr.* [mid-19C] to go to sleep. [rhy. sl.]

plover *n.* **1** [early–mid-17C] a victim, a dupe (cf. PIGEON n.[2]). **2** [17C] a promiscuous woman, a prostitute (cf. CANARY n.[2]). [fig. uses of the bird's name]

plow *see* PLOUGH v.[2].

plowed *see* PLOUGHED.

plow jockey *n.* [19C] (US) a farmer, a rustic (cf. PUMP JOCKEY). [SAmE *plow* = SE *plough* + JOCKEY n.[2]]

plow the back forty, to *see* PLOUGH THE BACK FORTY.

plowter *v.* [19C] to have sexual intercourse. [northern dial. *plowter*, to splash about in mire or water]

p.l.u. *phr.* [1980s+] (society) *people like us* (cf. N.Q.O.C.D.). [abbr.]

pluck *n.*[1] [late 18C–1900s] courage (cf. HEART n.). [SE *pluck*, the intestines of an animal that are plucked out during its cleaning. The term began as early boxing jargon, then moved into sl. Despite its apparent neutrality, the term was not used by women before the 1860s]

pluck *n.*[2] [20C] (Aus.) a stone. [? one *plucks* it from the ground]

pluck *n.*[3] [1960s+] (US Black) wine, esp. cheap wine. [? SE *pluck*, to harvest grapes]

pluck *n.*[4] [1960s+] (US Black) an attractive woman. [she is 'plucked' from the bunch; or ? ref. to fig. use of SE *pluck*, offal, i.e. the vagina]

pluck *v.* **1** [late 19C] to rob. **2** [1940s] (US) to cashier or retire a military officer. **3** [1960s+] (US Black) to have sexual intercourse. **4** [1970s+] (US Black) to choose one's woman.

pluck a crow with, to *phr.* [late 18C–early 19C] to settle a dispute, usu. after engaging in a difficult and antagonistic discussion.

pluck a pigeon, to *phr.* [late 18C] to fleece a sucker. [PIGEON n.[2] (1) + pun]

pluck a rose, to *phr.* [17C+] to visit the lavatory. [euph.]

pluck'd 'un *n.* [mid-19C] a brave person, a 'stout fellow'. [PLUCKY]

plucked *adj.* [1960s+] (US Black) enjoying a feeling of mental and physical contentment following sexual intercourse. [PLUCK v. (4) or euph. for FUCK v.[1]]

pluck one's chicken, to *phr.* [1990s] to masturbate.

pluck Sir Onion, to *phr.* [late 17C–18C] to knock on the tavern door (cf. PLUCK THE RIBAND). [? the round 'onion-shape' of a tavern knocker]

pluck the riband, to *phr.* [late 17C–18C] to ring the bell at a tavern (cf. PLUCK SIR ONION). [SE *pluck* + *riband*, ribbon, thus presumably the tavern bell-pull]

pluck-up fair *n.* [late 16C–mid-17C] 'a general scramble for booty or spoil' (*OED*). [SE *pluck up*, to gather, to grab]

plucky *adj.* [mid-19C+] brave, courageous. [PLUCK n.[1]]

pluff *n.* [late 19C] a shot of a musket or fowling-piece; also as excl. *pluff!* [SE *pluff*, a puff of smoke, as from an explosion]

pluffer *n.* [early–mid-19C] a gun. [PLUFF + sfx. -er]

plug *n.*[1] [late 18C–late 19C] a blow, a punch.

plug *n.*[2] [early 19C] **1** a draught of beer. **2** wine, esp. cheap wine (cf. PLUCK n.[3]). [? play on SE *plug*, i.e. it 'fills a gap']

plug *n.*[3] [mid–late 19C] a top-hat. [abbr. PLUG-HAT n. (1)]

plug *n.*[4] [mid–late 19C] a translation, a 'crib'. [? it 'plugs up' the gaps in one's knowledge]

plug *n.*[5] **1** [mid-19C+] (US) a worn-out old horse. **2** [mid-19C+] (US) an incompetent or undistinguished person. **3** [mid-19C+] (US) a damaged or malfunctioning object. **4** [mid-19C+] (US) a fellow, a person, a chap. **5** [late 19C+] (Can.) an unpleasant person. [Du. *plug*, a worn-out horse]

plug *n.*[6] [mid-19C+] (Aus./N.Z.) a sturdy horse, standing about 15 hands high, that does the work required. [PLUG v.[2]]

plug *n.*[7] [late 19C] (US) **1** a silver dollar. **2** a counterfeit coin. [ext. use of SE *plug*, a small piece of solid material used to stop up a hole]

plug *n.*[8] [20C] an advertisement, a puff, esp. when filtered through a TV or radio programme. [PLUG v.[2]]

plug *v.*[1] **1** [late 18C+] to have sexual intercourse (cf. BANG v.[1]). **2** [mid-19C+] to strike, either with the fist or with a missile. **3** [1960s+] (gay) to perform anal intercourse.

plug/plug along/at/away/on *v.*[2] [mid-19C+] to persist, to struggle hard against whatever odds (cf. PLUGGER n.[2]).

plug *v.*[3] [late 19C] (US) to experience problems, to get into trouble. [SAmE *plug*, to hinder another person's plans]

plug along/at/away *see* PLUG v.[2].

plug for *v.* [1920s+] to act in support of, to make favourable statements about. [PLUG n.[8]]

plugged in *adv.* [1970s+] abreast of the times, fashionable (cf. SWITCHED ON). [electrical imagery]

plugger *n.*[1] [mid-19C+] a person who shoots, a killer. [PLUG v.[1] (2)]

plugger *n.*[2] [late 19C] (US/Aus.) one who does not give up. [PLUG v.[2]]

pluggy *adj.* [early–mid-19C] short and stumpy. [SE *plug*, a cake of tobacco]

plug-hat *n.* **1** [mid–late 19C] a top hat, a silk hat. **2** [1930s–40s] (Aus.) a bowler hat. [the head supposedly fits the hat like a plug]

plugher *see* PLOCKER.

plug-holed *adj.* [1940s+] ruined, beyond repair, useless. [such objects have 'gone down the plug-hole']

plug in both ways, to *phr.* [1970s+] to be bisexual. [electrical imagery]

plug in the neon, to *phr.* [1960s+] (US gay) to inhale amyl nitrite at the moment of orgasm. [the drug 'brightens up' one's senses]

plugola *n.* [1950s+] (orig. US) an illicit payment or favour given for mentioning a commercial product in a non-commercial context. [PLUG n.[8] + sfx. -OLA]

plug on *see* PLUG v.[2].

plug-tail n. [late 18C–mid-19C] the penis (cf. ARSE-OPENER). [SE plug + TAIL n.[1] (1)]

plug the mug, to phr. [1940s] (US Black) to be quiet, to stop talking. [SE plug + MUG n.[1] (2)]

plug-ugly n. [mid-19C+] (orig. US) a thug, a violent person. [proper name *Plug-Uglies*, a New York (and Baltimore) street gang of the period. The origin of the name is debatable. One suggestion is that they were named after the large PLUG HAT n. (1), stuffed with paper, that each member wore for protection from the clubs of such opponents as the Dead Rabbits or the Bowery Boys. Alternatively f. UGLY PLUG, or, as a correspondent of *The Times* (4 November 1876), writing of the Baltimore variety, suggested, 'it was derived from a short spike fastened in the toe of their boots, with which they kicked their opponents in a dense crowd, or, as they elegantly expressed it, "plugged them ugly"']

pluke n. [20C] **1** a spot, a pimple, a boil. **2** a general term of abuse. [Scot. dial. *plook, pluke*, a pimple, a spot; (2) is fig. use of (1)]

plukey-faced adj. [2C] a general term of abuse, lit. 'spotty, acne-faced'. [PLUKE]

plum/plumb n. [late 17C–19C] **1** a fortune of £100,000, usu. as a legacy or as the possession of an heiress. **2** a fortune. **3** a rich man (cf. WEDGE n.[1]). [SE *plumb*, a lump of lead]

plum/plumb adv. [late 16C+] a general intensifier, completely, entirely, absolutely, quite, e.g. *plumb loco*, totally mad. [SE *plum-ripe*. Despite citations in 16C and 18C, the main use, developed since mid-19C, is US, esp. in such clichés as *plumb loco*, utterly crazy]

plumb n.[1] see PLUM.

plumb n.[2] [1970s] (US Black) a very serious error. [PLUM adv.]

plumb v. [mid-19C–1900s] to fool, to deceive. [? SE *plumb someone's depths*]

plumb adv. see PLUM adv.

plumb a track, to phr. [mid–late 19C] (US) to trace or follow a road or path. [SE *plumb*, to sound out]

plumber n. [1970s+] (US Black) a man with a frequent and varied sex life. [PLUMBING n. (4)]

plumber's toolbag n. [1990s] the vagina. [pun on TOOL n. (4) + BAG n.[1] (3)]

plumbing n. **1** [1930s–50s] (US) a trumpet, trombone, or similar wind instrument. **2** [1950s+] a lavatory. **3** [1950s] fillings in teeth. **4** [1960s+] (orig. US) the excretory tract, the urinary system, the genitals.

plume of feathers n. [late 16C–17C] a trivial, trifling person (cf. JACK WITH THE FEATHER). [the insubstantiality of feathers]

plum job n. [20C] an excellent job.

plummy adj. **1** [mid–late 19C] good, excellent. **2** [mid–late 19C] round, sleek, fat, jolly. **3** [mid-19C+] of a voice, affected or upper-class. [SE *plum*]

plummy adv. [mid–late 19C] nicely, satisfactorily, pleasantly. [PLUM]

plummy-voiced adj. [mid-19C+] having an affected or upper-class voice (cf. PLUM IN THE MOUTH). [PLUMMY adj. (3) + SE *voiced*]

plump n. [mid-18C–early 19C] a blow; thus *a plump in the bread-basket*, a blow to the stomach; *a plump in the peepers*, a blow to the eyes (cf. PLUMPER n.[1]).

plump v. [late 18C–mid-19C] to hit, to shoot. [PLUMP n.]

plump currant n. [late 18C] used of one who is in good health, usu. as neg. i.e. *Charles is not the plump currant*.

plumper n.[1] **1** [late 18C–late 19C] a heavy blow. **2** [early 19C] a major lie. **3** [late 19C] an unusually large version of its type. [PLUMP n.]

plumper n.[2] [late 18C–late 19C] **1** a single vote at an election. **2** a heavy bet. [SE *plump for*, to commit wholeheartedly]

plumpies n. [1990s] large female breasts. [SE *plump*]

plumping adj. [20C] unusually or surprisingly large. [PLUMPER n.[1] (3)]

plump in the pocket adv. [late 17C–mid-19C] satisfactorily well-off.

plump-pate n. [19C] a fool. [var. on FAT-HEAD]

plump someone up to, to phr. [1910s–20s] to tell someone something secretly. [they are 'plumped up' with the information]

plum pud n. [20C] (Aus.) good. [rhy. sl.]

plum-pudding/-pudding dog n. [mid–late 19C] a variety of the dog Dalmatian, with notable dark spots.

plums n. [20C] the testicles (cf. APRICOTS). [resemblance]

plum tree n. **1** [17C] the vagina; thus *plum tree shaker*, the penis (cf. APPLE n.[10]). **2** [20C] (US) the spoils of political office; thus *shake the plum-tree*, to extract graft from one's office.

pluncas see PLONGKAS.

plunge v.[1] [mid–late 19C] to spend money or bet recklessly, to speculate heavily, to run into debt.

plunge v.[2] [1990s] to kill, to murder. [? the plunging of a knife]

plunger n.[1] [mid–late 19C] a reckless gambler. [PLUNGE v.[1]; they 'plunge' deep into the game; but note milit. jargon *plunger*, a cavalryman]

plunger n.[2] [1930s+] the penis (cf. PLUMBER; PLUMBER'S TOOLBAG).

plunger n.[3] [1940s] (US Black/Harlem) a bathtub.

plunk n. **1** [mid-18C–mid-19C] a large sum, a fortune. **2** [early 19C–1920s] (US) a dollar. [ety. unknown; *OED* states 'from plunk v.' but PLUNK n. was 40 years old when the v. was coined]

plunk v.[1] [20C] (Ulster) to fail an examination (cf. FLUNK v.).

plunk v.[2] [1910s+] (orig. Aus.) **1** to hit someone. **2** to shoot. [echoic of the sound of a blow]

plunk a baby, to phr. [20C] (Aus./N.Z.) to have a baby; thus *get plunked*, to be pregnant. [the Royal New Zealand *Plunket* Society, founded 1907, the N.Z. version of the UK Royal Society for the Protection of Women and Children; ult. Lady *Plunket*, wife of the then governor of N.Z.]

plunk down v. [late 19C+] (orig. US) to wager. [money is 'plunked' on the table]

plunk one's twanger, to phr. [1990s] to masturbate. [PLUNK v.[2] + TWANGER n. (2)]

plurry adj. [20C] (Aus./N.Z.) synon. for BLOODY adj. [Maori mispron.]

plus adj. [1950s+] used with a noun to indicate a better-than-average version.

plus conj. [1960s+] (orig. US) in addition, e.g. *I was cold; plus I had no money.*

plush n. [19C] female pubic hair. [PLUSH adj.]

plush/plushy adj. [1920s+] luxurious, expensive, stylish (cf. RIDE PLUSH). [see PLUSH n.; first *OED* cit. is 1927, but it is prob. earlier]

plushery n. [20C] (orig. US) a luxurious hotel, expensive restaurant, smart nightclub etc. [PLUSH adj.]

plushy see PLUSH adj.

plute n. [mid–late 19C] (US/Aus.) the very rich, the social elite; thus *plutish*, elitist. [abbr. SE *plutocrat*]

plyer see PLIER.

Plym n. **1** [1910s] an inhabitant of *Plym*outh. **2** [1950s+] a member of the religious cult, the *Plym*outh Brethren. [abbr.]

Plymouth Argyll n. [20C] a file. [rhy. sl.; name of a soccer team]

Plymouth blade/cloak n. [17C–18C] a cudgel. [the violence of the naval town]

ply the acid see PUT THE ACID ON.

ply the toby, to phr. [19C] to practise highway robbery (cf. HIGH-TOBY-MAN). [TOBY n.]

p.m. *n.* [late 19C+] the afternoon (cf. A.M.). [colloq. version of SE *p.m.*, *post meridiem*, used in chronological notation]

p-maker *n.* [mid-19C–1900s] the vagina. [abbr. PISS-*maker*]

p.m.s. *v.* [1990s] (US campus) of a woman, to feel irritable, anxious. [abbr. *pre-m*enstrual *s*yndrome, or *p*utting up with *m*en's *s*hit]

p.m.s. monster *n.* [1980s+] (US campus) a menstruating woman. [abbr. *pre-m*enstrual *s*yndrome]

pneumonia blouse *n.* [1910s] a transparent blouse of muslin and lace with next to no collar and thus, for some puritan contemporaries, a shockingly low neckline. [orig. introduced in late 19C as a garment to be worn by sufferers from the disease]

p.o. *n.* [1950s+] (US) a parole officer. [abbr.]

p.o. *adj.* [1970s+] (orig. US) angry (cf. P.'D). [abbr. PISSED OFF]

po *n.* [late 19C+] the lavatory (cf. AFTER YOU WITH THE PO, JANE). [abbr. SE *chamberpot* + Fr. pron. of *pot de chambre*]

poach *see* POOCH.

poached egg *n.* [1940s] (Aus.) a yellow 'sleeping policeman' placed in the centre of intersections.

po'chaise/po'chay/pochay *n.* [19C] a travelling carriage seating two or four, with the coachman or postilion riding one of the horses. [abbr. SE *post-chaise*]

pocket billiards *n.* [1910s+] playing with one's genitals through a trouser pocket (cf. PLAY POCKET BILLIARDS; POCKET PINBALL; POCKET POOL).

pocket-book *n.* [1950s] (W.I.) a large, flat, fried dumpling. [resemblance]

pocket cabbage/lettuce *n.* [1920s+] (US) money. [SE *pocket* + CABBAGE *n.*[8] (1)/LETTUCE *n.*[1]]

pocketful of rocks *n.* [mid-19C+] (US) a large amount of money. [SE *pocketful* + ROCK *n.*[1] (1)]

pocket lettuce *see* POCKET CABBAGE.

pocket pinball *n.* [1930s+] (orig. US) playing with one's genitals through a trouser pocket (cf. POCKET BILLIARDS; POCKET POOL).

pocket pistol *n.* [mid-19C] a dram flask, a hip-flask. [it gives one a 'shot in the arm']

pocket pool *n.* [1950s+] playing with one's genitals through a trouser pocket; thus *play pocket pool*, to masturbate (cf. POCKET BILLIARDS).

pocket rocket *n.* [1980s+] (drugs) marijuana. [it gets you 'high']

pocket roll *n.* [1960s+] (US Black) a roll of paper money kept in the pocket.

pockets to let *phr.* [19C] out of money, impoverished.

pocket the rocket, to *phr.* [1990s] to masturbate.

pocket-thunder *n.* [19C] the breaking of wind.

pock-/poke-pudding/pock-pud *n.* [early 18C–late 19C] (Scot.) an Englishman. [Scot. *poke-pudding*, a bag-pudding, thus a glutton]

pocky *adj.* [late 16C–late 17C] a general term of abuse, lit. 'syphilitic'. [SE *pocky*, covered in syphilitic sores]

pocky-nosed *adj.* [16C] a general term of abuse. [SE *pocky* + *nosed*, lit. 'a nose covered in syphilitic sores']

pod *n.*[1] [18C–19C] a pillow, a bed. [resemblance]

pod *n.*[2] [late 19C–1910s] a large stomach. [dial. *pod*, a large stomach]

pod *n.*[3] [1950s+] (US drugs) marijuana. [POT *n.*[9]]

pod *v.* [late 19C+] to give birth; thus *in pod*, *podding*, pregnant.

podding *n.* [19C] toddling. [PODS]

poddy *n.* [late 19C–1950s] (Aus.) a bottle of alcohol. [? dial. *poddinger*, an earthenware pot, orig. used for porridge]

poddy *adj.*[1] [mid-19C] corpulent, obese. [dial. *pod*, a large stomach]

poddy *adj.*[2] [1900s–10s] drunk. [PODDY *n.*]

poddy calf *n.* [20C] (Aus.) half-a-crown, 2s 6d (12½p). [rhy. sl.]

poddy dodger *n.* [1910s–50s] (Aus.) one who steals unbranded cattle, a cattle rustler. [SAusE *poddy*, an unbranded calf + *dodge*, to steal (cattle)]

podge *n.* [mid-19C+] **1** a short, fat person, esp. a chubby child. **2** a short, stout, thick-set animal. **3** excess weight, fat. [dial. *pudge*, anything or anyone short and thick; also used as a nickname]

podger *n.* [late 19C] (Irish) a cudgel. [dial. *podger*, a short person]

podgy *adj.* [18C–mid-19C] drunk. [Ital. *poco acqua*, a little water, or Rom. *pogado*, crooked, thus the way one walks, or POGGLE *n.*]

pod people *n.* [1970s+] stupid or robotic people; thus *podspeak*, meaningless talk. [film *Invasion of the Body-Snatchers* (1956, 1978), in which aliens spawn as humans]

pods *n.* [19C] children's legs. [dial. *pod*, a child's foot]

podunk *n.* [mid-19C+] (US) a generic term for a small town. [Algonquin *podunk*, a marshy meadow, used esp. by a small tribe of Indians formerly inhabiting an area around the Podunk river in Hartford County, Connecticut. When the word was used (on the grounds of its amusing sound) in a series of letters featuring the supposed small town of Podunk, published in the US in 1846, it gained a greater currency and took on the meaning it has retained ever since. A secondary ety. notes the 'po-dunk' croak of a bullfrog, *podunker* in dial.; thus such towns are out where the bullfrogs can croak undisturbed]

p.o.'ed *adj.* [1970s+] (US teen) very annoyed (cf. P.'D). [abbr. PISSED OFF]

poegaai/poeg-eyed *adj.* [1940s+] (S.Afr.) **1** drunk. **2** exhausted. [Du. *pooien*, to tipple + sfx. -*eyed*]

poep *n.* [1960s+] (S.Afr.) **1** breaking wind. **2** faeces. **3** a fool. [Afk. *poep*, a fart]

poep *adj.* [1960s+] (S.Afr.) bad, unpleasant. [POEP *n.*]

poephol *n.* [1960s+] (S.Afr.) a general term of abuse, fool, idiot (cf. ARSEHOLE *n.*). [Afk. *poep-hol*, arsehole]

poep-scared *adj.* [1960s+] (S.Afr.) terrified, lit. 'shit-scared'. [Afk. *poepbang*, dead scared]

poes *n.* [1960s+] (S.Afr.) **1** the vagina (cf. PUSS *n.*[1]; PUSSY *n.*[1]). **2** a general term of abuse (cf. CUNT *n.*[2]). [synon. Afk. sl.]

poet's day *n.* [1970s+] Friday (cf. T.G.I.F.). [abbr. *p*iss *o*ff *e*arly, *t*omorrow's *S*aturday]

po-faced *adj.* [1930s+] arrogant, stand-offish, humourless. [? PO or SE *poh*! + sfx. -*faced*]

p. off! *excl.* [1960s+] go away! [abbr. PISS OFF!]

poge *see* POGUE.

poge-hunter *n.* [late 19C] a purse-snatcher or pickpocket who specializes in taking purses. [POGUE *n.*[1]]

pogey *n.* [late 19C+] (US Und.) **1** a workhouse. **2** a house of correction, a prison. **3** a prison cell (cf. POKEY *n.*[1]). [ety. unknown; ? fig. extension of Fr. *poche*, a pocket]

pogey *adj.* [20C] (Ling. Fr./Polari) small. [Ital. *poco*, little]

pogey/pogy acqua *excl.* [early 19C] make the drink strong! [Ital.; lit. *poco acqua*, little water]

poggle/puggle/puggly *n.* [late 19C–1900s] a fool, an eccentric; thus [20C] *poggled*, mad, drunk, crazy, *pogglekhana*, a picnic, lit. a 'fool's dinner'. [Hind. *pagal*, a madman]

poggle/puggle pawnee *n.* [19C] rum. [POGGLE + Hind. *pani*, water, thus lit. 'crazy water']

poggler *n.*[1] [20C] a pocket. [? POKE *n.*[2] (1)]

poggler *n.*[2] [20C] a male homosexual. [POGUE *n.*[2]]

pogo *n.* [1970s+] (Aus.) the penis. [rhy. sl. *pogo stick* = PRICK *n.* (2)]

pogo *v.* [1970s+] to perform a rough form of dance, orig. by fans of *punk rock* and involving much jumping up and down, flailing of the arms etc (cf. MOSH *v.*[2]). [SE *pogo stick*]

pogram *n.* [mid-19C] a dissenter. [proper name *Pogram*, a well-known dissenting preacher of the time]

pogue/poge *n.*[1] [early 19C+] (Und.) a purse, a wallet, a pocket (cf. POGGLER n.[1]). [? POKE n.[2] (1) or 9C *pough*, a bag, a sack]

pogue/poge *n.*[2] **1** [20C] (gay) a young boy. **2** [1980s+] (US gay) the passive partner in anal intercourse. [Ital. *poco*, small]

pogy *adj.* [late 18C–early 19C] drunk (cf. POGGLE; PUGGY-DRUNK). [? Rom. *pogado*, crooked]

pogy acqua! *see* POGEY ACQUA!

poindexter *n.* [1980s] (US teen) an intellectual, bookish person. [play on POINTED-HEAD]

Point, the *n.*[1] [early 19C+] (US) West *Point*, properly the United States Military Academy at West Point, New York. [abbr.]

point *n.*[2] [1910s+] (US) anyone standing guard or leading the way. [milit. jargon *point*, the man standing at the head of a patrol; ult. ranching jargon *point*, the front of a herd]

point *n.*[3] **1** [1930s+] (drugs) a hypodermic syringe. **2** [1960s–70s] (gay) any form of writing implement.

Point, the *n.*[4] [1990s] (US Black teen) Hunter's *Point*, San Francisco. [abbr.]

point *v.* (Aus.) **1** [mid-19C–1900s] to take unfair advantage of. **2** [20C] to waste time, to malinger. [SE *score points*]

pointed-/pointy-head/pointhead *n.* [1960s+] (US) **1** a fool. **2** an intellectual. [both terms are derog. and suggest that an excess or an absence of brain lead to a 'pointed' head]

pointer *n.*[1] (Aus./N.Z.) **1** [mid-19C+] an idler, a loafer, a malingerer. **2** [mid–late 19C] a confidence trickster, a cardsharp. **3** [late 19C+] one who takes an unfair advantage, esp. by trickery. [POINT v. (2), (1)]

pointer *n.*[2] **1** [late 19C+] the penis. **2** [1930s] (W.I.) a knife.

pointer *n.*[3] [late 19C+] (orig. US) a hint, a suggestion.

pointhead *see* POINTED-HEAD.

point percy at the porcelain, to *phr.* [1960s+] to urinate. [PERCY n.[3] + SE *porcelain*, i.e. the lavatory bowl]

point the bone, to *phr.* [1940s+] (Aus.) to betray a friend and leave them in the lurch; thus *bone-pointer*, *bone-pointing*. [Aborigine practice of pointing a bone (the 'death bone') at one whose death is desired]

pointy *adj.* [1900s] pithy, terse. [SE *to the point*]

pointy-head *see* POINTED-HEAD.

pointy-head *adj.* [1970s+] (US) intellectual, cultured. [POINTED-HEAD n. (2)]

poison *n.*[1] [19C+] an ironic term for drink in general; thus [1910s+] (Aus.) *poison-shop*, a public house (cf. NAME YOUR POISON).

poison *n.*[2] [20C] an unpleasant person, best to be avoided.

poison *n.*[3] [1950s+] (drugs) **1** heroin, esp. in its pure state. **2** fentanyl (cf. APACHE n.[2]).

poison *adj.* [1960s+] (S.Afr.) excellent, admirable, first-rate. [on bad = good model]

poison dwarf *n.* [1970s+] a very unpleasant person.

poisoned *adj.* [late 17C–early 19C; 20C] pregnant. [the swelling that often follows actual poisoning; 20C use is US Black]

poisoner *n.* [20C] (Aus./N.Z.) a cook, esp. one serving a team of sheep shearers; thus *poison*, to cook.

poisonous *adj.* [20C] very unpleasant.

poison-pate *n.* [late 17C–mid-19C] a redhead; thus *poison-pated*, red-haired. [SE *red* being a symbolically 'dangerous' colour + *pate*]

poison people *n.* [1950s–60s] (US Black) heroin addicts, taken as a group. [POISON n.[3] (1)]

poke *n.*[1] **1** [late 18C+] a blow; thus [20C] *take a poke at*, attack, aim a blow at. **2** [late 19C+] sexual intercourse (cf. BASH n.[2]). **3** [1960s+] usu. of cars or motorcycles, speed, horsepower.

poke *n.*[2] **1** [mid-19C+] (US) a wallet. **2** [mid-19C–1900s] stolen property. **3** [late 19C+] a bag of food handed out to a beggar

(cf. POKE-OUT). **4** [1920s+] a roll of banknotes, money in general. **5** [1940s+] (Irish) a cone-shaped bag, esp. for sweets or chips, or an ice-cream cornet; thus *poke man*, an icecream seller; *poke van*, an icecream van. [SE *poke*, a bag; ult. Fr. *poche*, pocket]

poke *n.*[3] [late 19C+] a promiscuous woman seen as a partner in sexual intercourse; often as *good poke*, *lousy poke* (cf. SCREW n.[1]). [POKE v. (2)]

poke *n.*[4] [1900s–20s] (US) a shirt collar. [abbr. ? SE *poke bonnet*, which had a projecting rim]

poke *n.*[5] [1940s+] (drugs) a puff on a marijuana cigarette (cf. TOKE n.[3]). [play on SE *poke*/HIT n.[4] (4)]

poke *v.* **1** [early 19C] to protrude, to stick out. **2** [mid-19C+] of a man, to have hetero- or homosexual intercourse (cf. BANG v.[1]). **3** [20C] (orig. US) to hit, to strike.

poke along *v.* [late 18C+] to walk slowly.

poke a smipe, to *phr.* [mid-19C] to smoke a pipe. [joc. reversal]

poke bogey/bogey at *v.* [late 19C–1900s] to trick, to fool, to deceive. [SE *poke* + *bogus*]

poke borak/poke the borak *v.* [mid-19C+] (Aus./N.Z.) to make or poke fun. [SE *poke* + BORAK]

poked *adj.* [1970s+] (N.Z.) exhausted. [POKE v. (2); thus euph. for FUCKED]

poked up *adj.* [late 19C] (US) embarrassed. [SE *poke*; the image is of a poked fire, in which the flames, i.e. blushes, roar up]

poke-/poking-hole *n.* [late 19C+] the vagina. [POKE v. (2) + SE *hole*]

poke mullock *v.* [20C] (Aus.) to mock, to tease, to deride. [SE *poke* + *mullock*, nonsense, rubbish (orig. mining refuse)]

poke one's mouth off, to *phr.* [1970s+] (US Black) to lose one's temper (cf. SHOOT ONE'S MOUTH OFF).

poke one's pussy, to *phr.* [1960s+] of a woman, to masturbate. [POKE v. (2) + PUSSY n.]

poke-out *n.* [1950s–60s] (US) **1** food cooked outdoors. **2** a gathering to eat such food. **3** a long trek that involves eating outdoors. [POKE n.[2] (3)]

poke-pudding *see* POCK-PUDDING.

poker *n.*[1] **1** [17C–18C] a sword (cf. PORKER n.[1]). **2** [early 19C] the penis. **3** [20C] (US Und.) a single-barrelled shotgun.

poker *n.*[2] [mid-19C] a womanizer, a 'sexual athlete'. [POKE v. (2)]

poker-breaker *n.* [19C–1900s] one's wife. [POKER n.[1] (2) or SE *poker* + SE *breaker*]

pokerino *n.* [20C] (US) **1** any form of paltry, trivial game. **2** any trivial business or transaction. [SE *pokerino*, a game of poker for very low stakes]

poker talk *n.* [19C] **1** exaggerated talk, boasting, bragging. **2** fireside chat. [CHANT THE POKER]

poke-shakings *n.* [20C] **1** the last pig in a litter. **2** the last child of a family. [POKE n.[2] (1) + SE *shaking*; the image of turning out one's wallet]

poke someone under the fifth rib, to *phr.* [late 19C] **1** to hit, to punch. **2** to amaze, to dumbfound.

poke the borak *see* POKE BORAK.

poke the pucker, to *phr.* [1990s] of a woman, to masturbate. [SE *poke* + *pucker*, a fold, i.e. the vagina]

pokey *n.*[1] [late 19C+] **1** a prison, usu. small and local. **2** a prison cell. [? POGUE n.[1] or the 'poky' conditions]

pokey *n.*[2] [20C] (orig. W.I. teen) the vagina. [POKE v. (2)]

pokey *n.*[3] *see* POKIE.

pokie/pokey *n.* [1960s+] (Aus.) an electronic *poker* machine, used in casinos; also as *pokie bandit* (cf. ONE-ARMED BANDIT). [abbr.]

poking *n.* [1960s+] sexual intercourse. [POKE v. (2)]

poking-hole *see* POKE-HOLE.

pol *n.*[1] [1930s+] (US) a *pol*itician. [abbr.]

pol *n.*[2] [1940s+] (prison) a talkative person, a chatterer or gossip. [abbr. *polly parrot*]

pol! *excl.* [late 16C–early 17C] a general excl. [abbr. *by Pollux*, one of the twins of the Gemini constellation]

Polack *n.* [20C] **1** a Pole. **2** (mainly Jewish) a Jew whose family come from Poland (cf. LITVAK).

Polack town *n.* [20C] (US) the Polish community within an urban area (cf. BEAN TOWN n.[2]). [POLACK n. (1) + SE *town*]

polari *see* PARLYAREE.

polboron/pulboron *n.* [1970s] (drugs) heroin. [Sp. *polboron*, 'big powder']

pole *n.* [19C+] the penis.

pole *v.*[1] [19C+] usu. of a man, to perform sexual intercourse. [POLE n.]

pole/pole on *v.*[2] [20C] **1** (Aus./N.Z.) to take advantage of someone, to impose or sponge off. **2** (Aus.) to steal; thus *poled*, stolen. [bullock-driving use; *polers*, the pair of bullocks nearest the wagon's pole, seen as most likely to 'take things easy']

pole-axe *n.* [mid-19C] a policeman. [mispron. ? + allusion to police violence]

polecat *n.* [1950s+] (US Black) a dirty, untrustworthy woman (cf. LIONESS). [SE *polecat*, a notoriously aggressive animal, or POLE n. + CAT n.[1] (3), i.e. a masculine woman]

pole-/prick-climber *n.* [19C] a prostitute. [POLE n./PRICK n. (2) + SE *climber*]

pole hole *n.* [1970s+] the vagina. [POLE n. + SE *hole*]

pole pleaser *n.* [20C] (US) a homosexual man. [POLE n. + SE *pleaser*]

poler *n.*[1] [1900s–10s] (US campus) a very diligent student. [? they are climbing the 'greasy pole']

poler *n.*[2] [1930s–50s] (Aus.) a cadger, a sponger, one who shirks work. [POLE v.[2]]

pole on *see* POLE v.[2]

poles apart/removed *adj.* [1910s+] extremely different, irreconcilable. [the global SE *poles*]

pole-work *n.*[1] [mid-19C+] tedious, lengthy work. [dial. *pole-work*, a tedious business]

pole-work *n.*[2] [mid-19C+] sexual intercourse. [POLE n. + SE *work*]

poley *adj.* [mid–late 19C] (Aus. Und.) wanted by the police. [colloq. *poley*, one-horned (of cattle) or broken (of a utensil's handle), thus a pun on CROPPIE, a convict who has lost their 'horns', i.e. hair]

police *n.* [mid-19C+] (Scot./US) a *police*man. [abbr.]

police clothes *n.* [1980s+] (Irish) free second-hand clothes distributed to the poor by the police.

policeman *n.* **1** [mid-19C] a bluebottle fly (cf. BLUEBOTTLE). **2** [mid-19C] 'among the dangerous classes, a man who is unworthy of confidence, a sneak or mean fellow' (Hotten 1874). **3** [early–mid 20C] an informer. [neg. views of the police]

policeman's helmet *n.* [1930s+] the glans penis (cf. BOBBY'S HELMET; GERMAN HELMET). [resemblance to UK *police helmets*]

police-nippers *n.* [mid-19C–1900s] handcuffs, leg-irons.

policy *n.* [mid-19C+] (US) a popular form of street gambling that involves predicting a combination of the winning numbers at a racetrack (cf. NUMBERS). [SE *policy certificate*; the original game may date to early 18C UK, although it is now US and esp. widespread in the Black community]

polish *v.* [mid-19C–1900s] to beat, to thrash.

polish ... [1980s+] used in combs. to mean to masturbate, e.g. *polish Charlie Brown, ... one's antlers, ... one's sword, ... percy, ... the lighthouse, ... the penguin, ... the pole, ... the rocket, ... the sword, ... the viper.*

polish a bone, to *phr.* [late 18C–early 19C] to eat a meal.

Polish airlines *n.* [1960s] (gay) walking (cf. ITALIAN AIRLINES). [racial stereotyping]

polish and gloss, to *phr.* [20C] to masturbate. [rhy. sl. *polish and gloss* = TOSS v.[1]]

Polish handball *n.* [1960s] (gay) dried nasal mucus. [racial stereotyping; the image of the peasant picking their nose]

polish off *v.* **1** [mid-19C+] to complete, esp. of a meal or a job of work (cf. POLISH A BONE). **2** [1910s–20s] to kill clandestinely.

polish one's arse on the top sheet, to *phr.* [20C] of a man, to have sexual intercourse. [ARSE n.[1]; presumably in the missionary position]

polish the apple/apples, to *phr.* [20C] (prison) to curry favour, to act the sycophant. [APPLE-POLISHER]

polish the king's iron with one's eyebrow, to *phr.* [late 18C– mid-19C] to look through one's prison bars; thus [20C] (Aus.) *polisher*, a gaolbird.

polish the knob, to *phr.* [20C] (US) to perform oral sex. [SE *polish* + KNOB n.[1] (1)]

polish the old German helmet, to *phr.* [20C] (US) to perform oral sex. [SE *polish* + GERMAN HELMET]

polite as a basket of chips *phr.* [1940s–60s] (US) very courteous (cf. GRIN LIKE A BASKET OF CHIPS). [SE *chips* (of wood); note Shropshire dial. saying, *smile like a basket of chips*]

political *adj.* [20C] (US Und.) concerning prison gang life and activities. [the racial politics that underpins US prison gangs]

political tats *n.* [20C] (US Und.) specialized tattoos that refer to one's membership of a gang. [POLITICAL + TAT n.[4]]

politician *n.* [20C] **1** a flatterer, a clever talker. **2** (US prison) one who gains good jobs and maximum privileges. [both uses take a dim view of the SE use]

politico *n.* [20C] one involved in *politic*s, both conventional and 'alternative' activists. [abbr.]

poll *n.*[1] [late 18C–early 19C] a wig. [SE *poll*, the head]

poll *n.*[2] [mid-19C] a prostitute, a loose woman. [the proper name *Polly*]

poll *v.* **1** [16C] (Und.) to rob, by trickery rather than violence. **2** [16C] (Und.) to cheat one's accomplice in crime (cf. PILL AND POLL). **3** [late 19C–1900s] to ignore, to snub. [fig. uses of SE *poll*, to cut, to shear, more usu. of the hair]

poll axe *n.* [19C] the penis (cf. ARSE-OPENER). [pun on SE *poleaxe*/POLL n.[2]]

polled off *adj.* [20C] drunk. [GET ON THE POLE]

polled up *adv.* [mid-19C] living 'in sin' with a woman. [POLL n.[2]]

poller *n.* [late 17C–mid-18C] a pistol. [SE *poller*, plunderer, extortionist]

polling *n.* [16C] robbery. [POLL v. (1) + SE *pillage*]

polling and pilling *n.* [16C] robbery. [POLL v. (1) + SE *pillage*]

pollock *v.* [mid–late 18C] (Irish) to trick, to hoax, to defraud. [? racist allusion to a Pole; i.e. POLACK]

poll off *v.* [late 19C] to get drunk. [GET ON THE POLE]

pollone *see* POLONE.

poll parrot *n.* [mid-19C+] a talkative, gossipy woman.

pollrumptious/polrumptious *adj.* [mid-19C+] unruly, restless, uproarious, obstreperous. [Kentish dial.; ult. ? SE *poll*, a head + *rambunctious* or *rumbustious*]

poll talk *n.* [mid–late 17C] (Irish) slander, tale-telling. [ME *poll*, the nape of the neck, i.e. one is 'talking through the back of one's neck']

poll up *v.* [mid–late 19C] to court, to live with without being married. [? POLL n.[2]]

polluted *adj.* **1** [1910s+] extremely drunk (cf. ADDLED). **2** [1960s+] (drugs) intoxicated by a drug. [joc. use of SE; ? the state of one's bloodstream]

polly *n.*[1] [19C] a mistress, a prostitute who lives with a man (cf. POLL n.[2]; POLL UP). [*Polly*, nickname for *Mary* = MOLL n.]

polly n.[2] [1940s+] (Aus./US) a *politician*; thus *pollies*, politicians. [abbr.]

polly flinder n. [late 19C+] **1** a window. **2** a cinder. [rhy. sl. both with Cockney pron.; ult. the nursery rhyme, 'Little Polly Flinders sat among the cinders']

polly parrot n. [20C] a carrot. [rhy. sl.]

polone/palone/paloney/pollone n. [1930s+] (Ling. Fr./ Polari) **1** a young woman. **2** an effeminate man (cf. CHICK n.[3]; OMEE). [Ital. *pollone*, chick]

polony n. [mid-19C] a sausage, a salami. [Ital. *Bologna* sausage]

polrumptious see POLLRUMPTIOUS.

polter/poulter/powter v. [late 19C+] (Ulster) **1** to work carelessly. **2** to potter about. [synon. Scot. *pouter/powter*]

polvo n. [1970s+] (drugs) **1** heroin. **2** phencyclidine (cf. ACE n.[3]). [Sp. *polvo*, powder, dust]

polvo blanco n. [1970s+] (drugs) cocaine. [Sp. *polvo blanco*, white powder]

polvo de angel n. [1970s+] (drugs) phencyclidine (cf. ACE n.[3]; ANGEL DUST). [Sp. *polvo de angel*, angel powder]

polvo do estrellas n. [1970s+] (drugs) phencyclidine (cf. ACE n.[3]). [Sp. *polvo do estrellas*, powder of the stars]

poly n. [mid-19C+] a *poly*technic (cf. POLYTECH). [abbr.]

poly adj.[1] [1970s+] *poly*thene, esp. in *poly bag*, a polythene bag, usu. the carrier bags available in shops and supermarkets (cf. PLACKY; PLAZZY). [abbr.]

poly adj.[2] [1990s] (gay) *poly*gamous, open to or preferring to have two or more partners at once. [abbr.]

polyester n. [1990s] (US campus) something out of style or fashion; thus *polyester princess*, a woman who dresses in out-of-date fashions (cf. PLASTIC adj.; P.Q.).

polyphemus n. [19C] the penis (cf. ONE-EYED BROTHER; ONE-EYED CYCLOPS; ONE-EYED TROUSER-SNAKE). [from Homer's *Odyssey*, where *Polyphemus* is a Cyclops, distinguished by his single eye]

polytech n. [1910s+] a *polytech*nic (cf. POLY n.). [abbr.]

pom n.[1] [20C] a *Pom*eranian dog (cf. DACHS). [abbr.]

pom n.[2] see POMMIE.

pomegranate/pommygranate/pommygrant n. [1910s–20s] (Aus.) an immigrant from Britain (cf. JIMMY GRANT; POMMIE). [play on the similarity of the sound of *pomegranate* and *immigrant*]

Pomgolia n. [1970s+] (N.Z.) Britain. [POMMIE + play on *Mongolia*]

pommie/pom/pommy n. [1910s+] (Aus.) an English person, usu. an immigrant; thus [1910s+] *pommyland*, Britain. [abbr. POMEGRANATE]

pommie-/pommy-bashing n. [1970s+] (N.Z.) verbal abuse of British immigrants (occas. affectionate). [POMMIE + BASH v.[2] (3)]

pommygranate/pommygrant see POMEGRANATE.

pommy's breakfast n. [1990s] (Aus.) a cup of tea and a cigarette (cf. AIR PIE AND A WALK AROUND). [POMMIE + SE *breakfast*]

pomp n. [1990s] (US campus) someone who acts as if they are better than others. [abbr. SE *pompous*]

pomp v. [20C] (S.Afr.) to have sexual intercourse (cf. PUMP v.[3]). [Afk. *pomp*, to pump]

Pompey n. [late 19C+] (orig. naut.) Portsmouth; also used in expressions such as *Pompey Royal*, a Hampshire-brewed beer. [abbr.]

Pompey's pillar to a stick of sealing-wax phr. [early–mid-19C] long odds (cf. ALL THE WORLD TO A CHINA ORANGE).

pompey whore n. [1900s–40s] (bingo) the number 24. [rhy. sl.]

pompkin see PUMPKIN n.[1].

Pompkinshire see PUMPKINSHIRE.

pom-pom n. [1970s+] (US Und.) a pump-action shotgun. [milit. *pom-pom*, a quick-firing gun]

poms n. [1930s–490s] (Irish) dancing shoes. [ety. unknown; ? their shine resembled hair greased with pomade]

ponce n. **1** [late 19C+] one who lives off the earnings of one or more prostitutes (cf. PONT). **2** [1930s+] a derog. epithet for any man. [OED suggests SE *pounce*. Hancock notes Fr. argot *pont* (*d'Avignon*) or *pontonnière*, a prostitute (who works from the arches of a bridge) or PUNK n.[1]. Note that many 'ponce' usages show the very different status of such a man in the UK compared with the US pimp; note OED suggests def. 'a male homosexual' but none of the cits. seem to reflect this]

ponce v. [1930s+] **1** to work as a pimp or ponce. **2** to sponge (although with no implication of 'immoral earnings'). [PONCE n.]

ponce about/around v. [1960s+] to wander aimlessly, to live as a good-for-nothing. [PONCE n.]

ponce off/on v. [1930s+] **1** to live off immoral earnings. **2** to scrounge (money) from someone. [PONCE v.]

ponce up v. [1920s+] (orig. milit.) to decorate (an object), to dress up (a person) (cf. TART UP). [fig. use of PONCE n.; the term implies some ostentation and flashiness]

poncey see PONCY.

ponch n. [1980s+] (US campus) a term of address for a man. [? the character nicknamed *Ponch* in the 1980s TV police show *C.H.I.P.S.*]

poncy/poncey adj. [1960s+] affected, ostentatiously 'artistic', poss. homosexual. [PONCE n.; however there is no actual link to a pimp or procurer]

pond n. [early 19C+] the Atlantic Ocean (cf. BIG POND; HERRING POND).

pondlife adj. [1990s] a term used to describe someone seen as unintelligent, simple.

pond scum see SHOWER SCUM.

pone n. [1920s–40s] (US Black) a roll of fat on the neck. [? SE *pone*, bread baked from maize flower; the lump of flesh resembles a loaf]

pong n.[1] [mid-19C–1900s] beer. [abbr. PONGELO]

pong n.[2] [20C] (Aus.) **1** a Chinese person. **2** a Japanese person. [the *ong* sound in Chinese speech]

pong n.[3] [1910s+] (orig. Aus.) a smell. [ety. unknown; ? ext. of SE *pong*, the sound of a blow; usu. reserved for use in mass-market children's comics or by society speakers who retain much juvenile vocabulary from school]

pong v.[1] [mid-19C–1900s] to drink. [PONG n.[1]]

pong v.[2] [1920s+] to stink, to smell bad; thus *pongy*, vile-smelling. [PONG n.[3]]

ponge see PONGELO.

pongello n. [mid-19C–1900s] (Aus.) a dice game which determines which of the players pays for the next round of drinks. [PONGELO]

pongelo/pongelow/ponge/ponjello n. [mid-19C–1900s] beer, esp. pale ale or half-and-half. [ety. unknown; given origins of the word in the Indian Army there may be a link to the Tamil festival of Pongol, the festival of the new rice]

pongo n. **1** [1940s+] (Aus./N.Z.) a British person. **2** [1940s+] (Aus./N.Z.) a marine, a soldier. **3** [1960s–70s] a Black person. **4** an African. [Angola or Loango *mpongo*, a large anthropoid ape, the chimpanzee or gorilla; this 17C use was in late 18C transferred to the orang-utan of Borneo and Sumatra]

ponjello see PONGELO.

ponk n. [20C] (mainly N.Z.) a stench (cf. PONG n.[3]). [Baker (1941) suggests that the word in N.Z. context is a mix of PONG n.[3] + Maori *puhonga*, stinking]

'pon my life n. [late 19C] a wife. [rhy. sl.]

'pon my sivvy/sivy/sivey see UPON MY SIVVY.

'pon my soul! see BLESS MY SOUL!

pont *n.* [late 19C] one who lives off the earnings of one or more prostitutes. [PONCE n.]

ponte *n.* [mid–late 19C] (Ling. Fr./Polari) £1 sterling. [Ital. *pondo*, a weight]

Pontius Pilate *n.* [late 18C–early 19C] a pawnbroker. [his venality]

pontoon *n.* [1950s+] (prison) a 21-month sentence. [card use, the game of *pontoon* or '21']

pony *n.*[1] [18C–mid-19C] a bailiff, esp. one who accompanies a debtor on a day out from prison.

pony *n.*[2] **1** [late 18C+] £25. **2** [early–mid-19C] money in general. **3** [late 19C+] a double-headed coin. **4** [1910s] (N.Z.) a £5 note; £5. [? relatively small sums, as a pony is a small horse]

pony *n.*[3] [early 19C+] (US campus) a literal translation of a classical text, a 'crib' (cf. ANIMAL n.[3]; HORSE n.[7]). ['So called, it may be, from the fleetness and ease with which a skilful rider is enabled to pass over places which to a common plodder present many obstacles' (Hall, 1856)]

pony *n.*[4] **1** [mid-19C+] (orig. US) a small glass of beer; thus (W.I.) *pony-glass*, a small glass, with a capacity of approx. 6ml (2fl oz). **2** [1900s–50s] (US) a (small) dancer or chorus girl. [fig. use of SE *pony* in its sense of a small horse]

pony *n.*[5] [late 19C+] an act of defecation. [rhy. sl. *pony and trap* = CRAP n.[3] (3)]

pony *n.*[6] [20C] (US) a race-horse; thus *the ponies*, horse-racing.

pony *n.*[7] [1960s+] a prostitute. [she is 'ridden']

pony *n.*[8] [1980s+] (drugs) crack cocaine. [ety. unknown; ? one 'rides' the drug]

pony *v.*[1] [late 19C+] to defecate. [PONY n.[5]]

pony *v.*[2] [1990s] (US teen) to understand. [? PONY n.[3]]

pony in white *n.* [1940s–50s] (Und.) 25s (£1.25) in silver coins. [PONY n.[2]+ WHITE adj.[1]]

ponytail *n.* [1960s–70s] (S.Afr.) the girlfriend of an urban gangster (cf. SHEILA n.). [her distinctive hairstyle]

pony up *v.* [early 19C+] (orig. US) to pay one's debts or one's dues. [PONY n.[2]]

poo/pooh *n.*[1] [1950s+] (usu. children) excrement (cf. POOEY; POO-POO n.). [SE *poo!* excl. announcing an unpleasant smell or expressing disbelief]

poo *n.*[2] [1980s] (US preppie) champagne. [abbr. SHAMPOO]

poo/pooh *v.* [1950s+] (juv.) to defecate (cf. POO-POO v.[2]). [POO n.[1]]

pooch *n.*[1] [1920s+] a dog; thus *pooch-flop*, dog excrement. [? Ger. *Putzi*, a popular name for a lap-dog]

pooch *n.*[2] [1960s+] (gambling) a loser. [POOCH n.[1], i.e. an underdog]

pooch, the *n.*[3] [1990s] (US teen) a Greyhound bus (cf. DOG n.[23]).

pooch/poach *v.* [1920s+] (Irish) to poke around, to laze about. [SE *poke*]

pood *n.*[1] [1910s+] (Aus.) an effeminate young man. [abbr. SE *poodle*, seen as an 'effeminate' species of dog]

pood/poodle/poodle-dink *n.*[2] [1920s–50s] (US) the penis. [? PUD n.[2]]

poodle *n.*[1] **1** [late 19C–1900s] any breed of dog. **2** [1900s–10s] a sausage.

poodle *n.*[2] *see* POOD n.[2].

poodle *n.*[3] [1970s+] (US Black) a sexy or sophisticated woman (cf. FOX n.[4]). [the image of the over-groomed pedigree French poodle]

poodle *v.* [1930s+] to move or travel in a leisurely manner; often as *poodle around, poodle down, poodle off*. [the image of the strolling dog]

poodle-dink *see* POOD n.[2].

poodle-faker *n.* [20C] (orig. milit.) **1** one who cultivates women's society, esp. for social advancement. **2** a womanizer, a 'ladies' man'. [the role of a *poodle* as a fashionable pet]

poodler *n.* [1950s–60s] a small motor vehicle. [POODLE v.]

pooey/poohy *adj.* [1930s+] (Aus.) used of anything unpleasant, smelly; thus excl. *pooey!* that's rubbish, that's disgusting (cf. POO n.[1]). [SE *poo(h)!* an excl. of disgust]

poof/pouffe *n.* [early 19C+] a homosexual (cf. POOVE). [? 'camp' cries of 'pooh!' or 'poof!'. *Poof* is supposedly the synon. of *puff*, an effeminate or homosexual man. F&H, however, introduced this idea only in their 1902 revision (assigned as 'tramps' use but with no citation), while *poof* has been traced to an Old Bailey case of 1833]

poof *v.*[1] [1970s] (US campus) to kiss. [SE *puff*]

poof *v.*[2] [1990s] (US campus) to leave. [? to vanish in a 'puff of smoke']

poof about *v.* [20C] to act in an ostentatiously homosexual manner. [POOF n.]

poofdah *see* POOFTER.

poof-rorting/-wroughting *n.* [1930s–40s] beating and robbing male prostitutes (cf. POOFTER-RORTER; QUEER-BASHER). [POOF n. + RORT v.]

poofter/poofdah/poofta *n.* [late 19C+] (orig. Aus.) **1** a homosexual man (cf. POOF n.). **2** an effeminate-looking but not necessarily gay man, often a derog. term of address. **3** anyone considered to have 'unmanly' interests, e.g. art, reading. [POOF n.; note WW2 RN jargon *poofter*, a flashy civilian suit, supposedly indicative of homosexual tastes]

poofter-basher *n.* [1970s+] (Aus.) one who beats up homosexuals (cf. POOFT-RORTING).

poofter-rorter *n.* [1940s+] (Aus.) **1** a procurer for male homosexuals. **2** one who beats up homosexuals (cf. POOFTER-BASHER). [POOFTER + RORT v.]

poof-wroughting *see* POOF-RORTING.

poofy *adj.*[1] [1940s+] (juv.) smelly. [SE excl. *poof!*, what an unpleasant smell!]

poofy *adj.*[2] [1960s+] effeminate, pertaining to homosexuality. [POOF n.]

poogie *n.* [20C] (US Und.) prison. [POKEY n.[1]]

pooh *n. see* POO n.[1].

pooh *v. see* POO v.

pooh-bah *n.* [late 19C+] an important person. [Gilbert and Sullivan's Savoy opera, *The Mikado* (1885) in which 'Ko-Ko' is 'Lord High Executioner of Titipu' and 'Poo-Bah' is 'Lord High Everything Else']

pooh chute *n.* [1990s] the rectum. [POO n.[1] + SE *chute*]

poo-head *n.* [1980s+] (US campus) an irritating person. [POO n.[1] + sfx. -HEAD (1); euph. for SHIT-HEAD]

poohed/poohed out *adj.* [1930s+] (US) exhausted, tired out. [var. on POOPED]

pooh-pooh *see* POO-POO.

poohy *see* POOEY.

pooja/puja *n.* [mid-19C] (Anglo-Ind.) prayers. [Hind. *puja*, worship]

pool *v.* [1910s+] (Aus.) to involve someone in, to implicate, to inform against. [? the image of tossing someone into a swimming pool]

poole *n.* [late 19C] (society) perfectly cut and tailored clothing. [proper name of *Poole*, a leading Savile Row tailor]

pooley/poolie *n.* [1930s+] (Irish) urination; usu. as *do pooley*, to urinate. [SE *pool* (of liquid)]

pool shark *n.* [20C] (US) an expert pool player, esp. one who makes money by winning at pool. [SE *pool* + SHARK n.]

poon *n.*[1] [1920s+] **1** the vagina. **2** a nubile girl. **3** sexual intercourse. **4** a woman or women in general when seen purely in a sexual context. [abbr. POONTANG]

poon *n.*[2] **1** [1940s+] (Aus.) one who lives alone in the outback. **2** a simpleton, a fool, a useless person (cf. NONG). [ety. unknown; note Northamptonshire dial. *pun*, a slow, dreamy, inactive person]

poon v. [1940s+] (Aus.) to dress up in a showy manner. [ety. unknown; ? link to POONTANG]

poona n. [mid-19C] (Ling. Fr./Polari) a sovereign, £1 sterling. [SE *pound*]

poona n. (Ling. Fr./Polari) £1 sterling. [PONTE]

poonce/punce n. **1** [late 19C+] the vagina. **2** [1930s+] (Aus.) a procurer (cf. PONCE n.). **3** [1930s–50s] (Aus.) a catamite. [Yid. *punse*, the vagina]

pooned up adj. [1940s+] (Aus.) usu. of youths looking to pick up women, flashily dressed. [POON v.]

poontang n. [1920s+] **1** the vagina. **2** a nubile woman. **3** sexual intercourse; thus *on a poontang trip*, obsessed with seducing women. **4** a woman or women in general, when seen purely in a sexual context. [? Fr. *putain*, a prostitute]

poonts n. [late 19C] the female breasts. [? SE *font* or *fountain*]

poop n.[1] **1** [early 17C] the 'dickey' or rear seat of a coach. **2** [18C+] the buttocks. [SE *poop*, the stern or highest stern deck of a boat]

poop n.[2] **1** [mid-18C+] excrement. **2** [1930s+] the act of breaking wind. **3** [1940s+] (orig. US) rubbish, tripe, nonsense. [SE *poop*, echoic of the report of a gun and thus the sound of defecation]

poop n.[3] [20C] a fool. [? abbr. NINCOMPOOP]

poop n.[4] [1930s+] (orig. US) news, information, gossip (cf. HOT POOP). [OED suggests ety. unknown, but ? fig. use of POOP n.[2] (cf. SHIT n.[3])]

poop v.[1] [16C] of a man, to have sexual intercourse. [? SE *poop*, to deceive, to cheat]

poop v.[2] **1** [early 18C+] to break wind. **2** [late 19C+] to defecate. **3** [1930s] to shoot someone. [SE *poop*, onomat. for the report of a gun]

poop v.[3] [1930s+] (orig. US) **1** to tire, to exhaust. **2** to malfunction. [ety. unknown]

poopa! *see* PAPA!

poo-packer n. [1990s] a male homosexual. [POO n.[1] +SE *packer*]

poopbutt/pootbutt n. [1960s+] (US Black) **1** a lazy person (cf. DRAG-ASS). **2** an uninformed, unsophisticated, immature person. [POOP n.[2]/POOT n.[2] + BUTT n.[1] (1)]

poop-catchers *see* SHIT-CATCHERS.

poop-chute n. [20C] the anus (cf. DIRT CHUTE). [POOP n.[2] + SE *chute*]

pooped adj. [1930s+] (orig. US) exhausted, tired out. [POOP v.[3]]

pooper n. [1950s+] **1** the posterior, the buttocks (cf. POOP-CHUTE) **2** the penis. [POOP n.[1]]

poo percolator n. [1990s] a male homosexual. [POO n.[1] + SE *percolator*]

pooper-scooper n. [1970s+] (orig. US) a small scoop used by fastidious dog owners to remove traces of a dog's excreta from urban pavements or even parks. [POOP n.[2] (1) + SE *scoop*]

poophead n. [1970s+] (US campus) a fool, a dullard (cf. SHIT-HEAD). [POOP n.[2] (1) + sfx. -HEAD (1)]

poopie-plops n. [1950s+] (juv.) excrement. [ext. of POOP n.[1] (3)]

poop-noddy n. [16C] sexual intercourse. [POOP n.[1] (2) + SE *nod*, to bob up and down]

poo-poo/pooh-pooh n. [1960s+] excrement. [POO n.[1] + redup.]

poo-poo/pooh-pooh v.[1] [20C] to deride, to dismiss. [SE *poo!* + redup.]

poo-poo/pooh-pooh v.[2] [1960s+] to defecate (cf. POO v.). [POO-POO n.]

poop out v. [1940s] (US Black) **1** to fail. **2** to have a breakdown. [POOP v.[3]]

poop sheet n. [1930s+] (US campus) any form of information posted on a noticeboard or distributed to students. [POOP n.[4] + SE *sheet*]

poop stick n. [1930s] an unpleasant person. [POOP n.[2] + SE *stick*]

poo pusher n. [1990s] a male homosexual. [POO n.[1] + SE *pusher*]

poor as a Connaught man phr. [late 19C] (Irish) extremely poor. [local stereotyping]

poor as a drover's dog phr. [1940s+] (Aus.) very poor.

poor as a rat phr. [early 18C+] extremely poor.

poor as Job's turkey/cat/mouse phr. [mid-19C+] (orig. US) extremely poor. [the biblical *Job*, regarded as the personification of poverty]

poor as paddy murphy's pig phr. [late 19C+] (US) very poor. [neg. stereotyping of Irish immigrants]

poor-ass adj. [20C] (US) wretched, lousy, unpleasant. [SE *poor* + sfx. -ASS]

poor blind Nell phr. [20C] (Aus.) a sarcastic phr. used to describe a woman who has been seduced and abandoned. [the saying 'And did he marry poor blind Nell?' 'Did he ... fucking hell!']

poor boy n. [1960s] (US Black) an unemployment cheque.

poor boy it, to phr. [20C] (US) to be extremely poor, to be severely deprived.

poor circumstance *see* MERE CIRCUMSTANCE.

poor creatures n. [early 19C] potatoes. [mispron. + ref. to their role as poverty food]

poor-great adj. [20C] (W.I.) proud but impoverished, unwilling to take charity however much it might be needed.

poor knight of Windsor n. [early 19C] the blade-bone of a shoulder of mutton (cf. POOR-MAN-OF-MUTTON). [a play on 'Sir Loin', i.e. a sirloin steak]

poorly adj. [mid-18C] unwell.

poorly time n. [late 19C] the menstrual period. [euph.]

poor-man-of-mutton n. [early 19C] the remains of a shoulder of mutton, usu. the blade bone, broiled (cf. POOR KNIGHT OF WINDSOR).

poor man's blessing n. [19C] the vagina. [sex, if nothing else, is free]

poor man's cocaine n. [1980s+] (drugs) **1** methylamphetamine. **2** isobutyl nitrite. [similar effects for less expenditure]

poor man's diggings n. [1940s] (Aus.) alluvial gold deposits, which can be mined far more easily than reef-gold that requires capital to develop.

poor man's goose n. [19C] baked liver with sage and onions.

poor man's oyster n. [late 19C] a mussel.

poor man's piano n. [mid-19C+] (Can.) a meal of dried beans. [the wind-inducing, 'musical' effect it has on one's stomach]

poor man's pot n. [1950s+] (drugs) any form of inhalant. [POT n.[9]]

poor man's treacle n. **1** [17C] garlic. **2** [19C] onions. [not so sweet, but flavoursome]

poor-me-one n. [20C] (W.I.) a miserable looking person, desperate for sympathy.

poor-me-one adj. [20C] (W.I.) miserable-looking.

poor mouth v. [20C] to belittle, oneself or others; thus (Irish) *make/play the poor mouth*, to complain, to slander (cf. BADMOUTH v.; PUT A POOR MOUTH ON).

poor relation n. [20C] the station. [rhy. sl.]

poor robin n. [mid-17C–mid-18C] an almanac. [the title *Poor Robin's Almanac* (1661), sometimes attributed to the poet Robert Herrick (1591–1674)]

poosa *see* PHUZA.

pooshie *see* PUSHIE.

poo-stabber n. [1990s] a male homosexual (cf. SHIT-STABBER). [POO n.[1] + SE *stabber*]

poot n.[1] [late 19C] a shilling (5p). [Hind. *poot*, a shilling, coined by East London's many Indian beggars]

poot *n.*[2] **1** [20C] a fart. **2** [1950s+] (US, usu. juv.) soft excrement (cf. POOP *n.*[2]; POO-POO *n.*). **3** [1950s+] (US) an unpleasant person. [onomat.]

poot *v.* [20C] (US) to break wind. [POOT *n.*[2] (1)]

poot about/around *v.* [1930s+] to dawdle, to mess around (cf. FART ABOUT). [fig. use of POOT *v.*]

pootbutt *see* POOPBUTT.

pootenanny *n.* [1990s] (US Black) the vagina. [PUNAANY + HOOTENANNY]

poove *n.* [1960s+] a homosexual. [POOF; PUFF *n.*[3]]

poove/poove about/around *v.* [1960s] to act in an ostentatiously homosexual manner. [POOVE *n.*]

poozle *n.*[1] [late 19C+] the vagina (cf. CAT *n.*[10]). [? PUSSY *n.*[1] (1)]

poozle *v.* [1970s+] (N.Z.) to scavenge for collectible objects. [ety. unknown]

pop *n.*[1] [18C–1950s] a pistol. [onomat.]

pop *n.*[2] [early 19C+] **1** (usu. juv.) a fizzy drink. **2** champagne. [the pop of a cork]

pop *n.*[3] [mid–late 19C] the act of pawning; thus *in pop*, in pawn. [POP *v.*[2]]

pop *n.*[4] **1** [mid-19C+] an orgasm, usu. male. **2** [1960s+] a single instance of sexual intercourse. [SE *pop*, the firing of a gun]

pop, a *n.*[5] [late 19C+] a time, a go, a turn etc, usu. in phrs. including a sum of money, e.g. *20 bucks a pop*.

pop *n.*[6] [late 19C+] **1** a try, an attempt; thus *first pop*, the first try, the first time. **2** a hit at. [SE *pop*, the sound of an explosion, thus fig. an instant]

pop/pops *n.*[7] [1920s+] one's father. [SE *papa*]

pop *n.*[8] [1930s+] (drugs) an injection of a narcotic drug.

pop *n.*[9] [1960s+] (US) a *popsicle* (the UK 'ice lolly'). [abbr.]

pop *v.*[1] **1** [early 18C–mid-19C] to fire a gun. **2** [1950s+] (orig. US) to hit, to punch. **3** [1950s–70s] (US) to seduce, to have sexual intercourse. **4** [1950s+] (US) to deflower (cf. POP A CHERRY). **5** [1950s+] (US) to make pregnant. **6** [1950s+] to arrest, to catch. **7** [1960s+] (US campus) to initiate someone into drug use. [(2) to (7) fig. uses of (1)]

pop *v.*[2] [mid-19C+] to pawn (cf. POP SHOP). [SE *pop in*]

pop *v.*[3] **1** [1940s+] (W.I.) to tell, to reveal, to gossip. **2** [1950s+] (US Black) to lie, to cheat, to manipulate (cf. GET OVER *v.*[1]).

pop *v.*[4] [1950s+] (orig. US Black) **1** to live well. **2** to feel elated, extremely pleased, enthusiastic. [one is 'exploding' with bonhomie]

pop *v.*[5] [1950s+] (US Black) to steal; thus *pop a car*, to steal an automobile. [? the SE *popping* open that prefaces theft]

pop *v.*[6] (drugs) **1** [1950s+] to inject a drug; thus *skin pop*, to inject under the skin rather than into a vein. **2** [1960s+] to swallow a pill. **3** [1960s+] (US campus) to take amphetamines specifically for staying up and working all night. **4** [1970s+] to inhale cocaine.

pop/pop for *v.*[7] [1950s–60s] to pay for.

pop a cap, to *phr.* [1950s+] to fire a weapon (cf. BUST A CAP). [SE *pop*, to make an explosion + CAP *n.*[3]]

pop a/someone's cherry, to *phr.* [1950s+] to deflower a girl or woman. [SE *pop*, to explode/POPV.[1] (4) + CHERRY *n.*[1] (1)]

pop a gut, to *phr.* **1** [late 17C+] to work very hard (cf. BUST A GUT). **2** [late 19C+] to laugh uproariously. **3** [1940s+] to be furious. [SE *pop*, to explode + *gut*]

pop a nut, to *phr.* [1960s+] to masturbate. [SE *pop* + NUT *n.*[11]]

pop a roll, to *phr.* [1970s+] (drugs) to swallow a number of pills at one go. [POP *v.*[6] + ROLL *n.*[3]]

pop a tuck, to *phr.* [1970s] to lose one's temper, to display one's emotions. [SE *pop* + *tuck*; ? the image of bursting a seam in rage]

pop a wad/a wad by hand, to *phr.* [20C] to masturbate. [SE *pop* + WAD *n.*[3]]

popcorn *n.*[1] [20C] an erection. [rhy. sl. *popcorn* = HORN *n.*[2]]

popcorn *n.*[2] [1950s] one with a legitimate job, rather than a

criminal or a confidence man. [? the banality of the foodstuff ? + CORNY]

popcorn *adj.* [1950s+] (US Black) foolish, slow-witted, lightweight, second string (cf. PEANUTS). [POPCORN *n.*[2]]

popcorn pimp *n.* [1950s+] (US Black) **1** a small-time, ineffectual pimp. **2** a man who claims to be, but is not, a pimp. [POPCORN *adj.* + SE *pimp*]

pop off the hooks, to *phr.* **1** [mid-18C+] to die (cf. DROP OFF THE HOOK). **2** [1930s+] (US) to exit, to vanish. [SE *pop*, to move]

pope/pope of Rome *n.* [mid-19C+] home. [rhy. sl.]

pope *v.* [20C] (W.I.) to get in without paying, to 'crash' a party. [? obs. SE *poop*, to deceive, cheat; ult. ? Du. *poep*, a clown]

popehead *n.* [1990s] (Ulster) a Roman Catholic. [SE *pope* + sfx. -HEAD (3)]

pope of Rome *see* POPE *n.*

poperin/poperine pear *n.* [late 16C] the penis. [*Poperinghe*, in west Flanders. The word comes in Shakespeare's *Romeo and Juliet* (1594), that repository of so much innuendo. 'O Romeo, that she were/An open et-caetera/Thou a poperin pear!' says Mercutio. The term may even, as E.P. suggests in *Shakespeare's Bawdy* (1947), pun on 'pop her in']

pope's eye *n.* [mid-19C+] the lymphatic gland surrounded with fat, found in a leg of mutton. [earlier use is SE]

pope's nose *n.* [late 18C+] the rump of a chicken or turkey (cf. BISHOP'S NOSE; PARSON'S NOSE). [usu. in Protestant use]

pope's telephone number *n.* [20C] Vat 69 whisky. [pun on *Vatican*; from an era that mixed letters and numbers in big city numbering]

popeye *n.*[1] [1930s+] (US) spinach. [*Popeye*, the film cartoon character produced by Max Fleischer in 250+ shorts between 1933 and 1950. Among his idiosyncrasies was a love of spinach, from which he gained superhuman strength]

popeye *n.*[2] [1940s+] the pope. [for ety. *see* POPEYE *n.*[1]]

popeyed *adj.* [20C] **1** drunk. **2** regrettable, bad. [SE *pop-eyed*, with bulging eyes; (2) is fig. use of (1)]

popeye the sailor *n.* [20C] a tailor. [rhy. sl.]

pop for *see* POP *v.*[7].

pop goes the weasel *n.* [20C] diesel. [rhy. sl.]

pop goes the weasel *phr.* [mid-19C+] a non-specific catchphrase originating among Londoners *c.*1870. [E.P., echoing Ware, suggested an 'erotic' ety., but the writer Claud Cockburn put forward an alternative: *pop*, pawn, and *weasel*, a flat-iron; such a household item could be pawned to help the beneficiary continue to go 'in and out the *Eagle*' (a well-known City Road public house), as the rhyme has it]

pop it in *v.* [late 19C+] to enter a woman, to have sexual intercourse. [POP *v.*[1] (3)]

pop it on *v.* [late 19C+] **1** to ask for more, esp. when raising a commodity's price. **2** to make a bet. [SE *pop on*, to place on]

pop junk *v.* [1940s+] (US) to gossip. [POP *v.*[3] + JUNK *n.*[2] (4)]

popla/poplar *n.* [1970s+] (S.Afr. township) beer. [ety. unknown]

poplars/poplers/poppelars *n.* [16C–early 19C] (Und.) porridge. [SE *pap*, infant food]

po-po *n.* [1990s] (US Black) the police. [abbr. + redup.]

pop-off *n.*[1] [mid-19C] (US) a death, a killing. [POP *v.*[1]]

pop-off *n.*[2] [1930s+] (US) a brash or boastful statement. [POP OFF *v.*[2]]

pop-off *n.*[3] [1940s+] (W.I.) the proceeds of some form of illegal deal or racket, a reduction in price, e.g. on stolen goods.

pop off *v.*[1] [18C+] **1** to die. **2** to depart. [SE *pop*, to move]

pop off/off at *v.*[2] [1930s+] **1** to criticize. **2** to brag, to boast. **3** to talk in an aggressive, threatening manner. [SE *pop*, to explode sharply]

pop one's cake, to *phr.* [1920s] (US) to vomit (cf. POP ONE'S COOKIES). [SE *pop*, to explode]

pop one's cap, to *phr.* [1950s] (US Black) to feel depressed, to suffer pain. [SE *pop* + CAP n.[5]]

pop one's clogs/nuts/rocks, to *phr.* [1970s+] to die. [POP v.[2] + SE *clogs*/NUTS n.[2] (1)/ROCKS n.[3] (1)]

pop one's cookies, to *phr.* [1930s+] (US) to vomit (cf. BLOW ONE'S COOKIES phr.[1]; POP ONE'S CAKE). [SE *pop*, to explode + COOKIES n.[2]]

pop one's cork, to *phr.* [1960s+] **1** to surrender sexually, to come to orgasm. **2** to lose one's temper, to lose patience (cf. BLOW ONE'S CORK). **3** to masturbate.

pop one's nuts, to *phr.*[1] [1920s+] (orig. US) to achieve male orgasm. [SE *pop*, to explode + NUTS n.[2] (1)]

pop one's nuts *phr.*[2] *see* POP ONE'S CLOGS.

pop one's peter, to *phr.* [1990s] to masturbate. [SE *pop*, to explode + PETER n.[4]]

pop one's rocks *see* POP ONE'S CLOGS.

poppa *n.* [late 19C+] (orig. US) a father. [SE *papa*]

poppa large *n.* [1990s] (US Black teen/East coast) an important, influential figure. [POPPA + LARGE adj.]

poppa-stoppa *n.* [1930s–40s] (US Black) **1** a man. **2** an older man who still possesses his faculties and strength. [POPPA + SE *stop*, i.e. his ability to 'stop' an opponent]

popped *adj.* **1** [1960s+] arrested. **2** [1980s] (US campus) in a difficult situation. [POP v.[1] (6)]

poppelars *see* POPLARS.

popper *n.*[1] [mid-18C–mid-19C; 1940s] a pistol, a gun. [ext. of POP v.[1] (1); 20C use is US Black]

popper *n.*[2] (drugs) [1960s] **1** an intravenous drug user. **2** an injection. [ext. of POP v.[6]]

popper *n.*[3] [1960s+] (drugs) amyl or (iso)butyl nitrite (cf. AIMIES n.[2]). [SE *pop*, to explode; i.e. the necessity of breaking open the ampoule that contains the drug]

poppers *n.* [1940s] (US Black) the fingers. [? one 'pops' them in time to music]

popping *n.* [1940s] (US Black) spending money recklessly and enthusiastically. [POP v.[4]]

pop-pop *n. see* POPPY n.[3].

pop-pop *phr.* [1990s] (US Black teen) the noise of a gun being fired (cf. BUCK-BUCK!). [echoic]

poppy *n.*[1] [1930s+] (drugs) **1** opium. **2** heroin. [prior 17C–19C use was literary SE, e.g. Shakespeare's 'Not Poppy, nor Mandragora' in *Othello* (1604)]

poppy *n.*[2] [1940s+] money. [? POP v.[2]]

poppy/pop-pop *n.*[3] [1940s+] (Irish) a hole in one's sock or stocking (cf. POTATO n.[3]). [? one's flesh 'pops out']

poppycock *n.* [mid-19C+] nonsense, rubbish (cf. POOP n.[2]). [Du. *pappekak*, soft faeces; thus orig. euph. for excreta]

poppy show *n.*[1] [late 19C; 1950s+] an inadvertent display of one's underclothes, orig. those made of red or brown flannel. [SE *poppy* + *show*; 1950s+ use is N.Z.]

poppy/pappy/puppy show *n.*[2] **1** [late 19C+] (W.I.) foolishness, showing off. **2** [late 19C+] (W.I.) one who makes a stupid exhibition of themselves. [SE *puppet show*]

poppy-/pappy-/puppy-show *adj.* [late 19C+] (W.I.) foolish, ridiculous. [POPPY SHOW n.[2]]

poppy/pappy/puppy show *v.* [late 19C+] (W.I.) to make a fool of someone. [POPPY SHOW n.[2]]

pop quiz/pop test/shotgun quiz *n.* [20C] (US campus) a surprise test. [it 'pops up' or 'explodes']

pops *n.*[1] [mid-19C] pocket-pistols (cf. POPPER n.[1]). [the explosive noise]

pops *n.*[2] *see* POP n.[7].

pops *n.*[3] [1920s+] (orig. US Black) a term of address between men. [POP n.[8]]

pop shit *v.* [20C] to boast, to talk nonsense. [POP OFF v.[2] + SHIT n.[3]]

pop shop *n.* [late 18C+] a pawnbroker's shop. [POP v.[2] + SE *shop*]

pop shot *n.* [early 19C] irritating trifles. [? SE *pot-shot*, a random shot]

popsicle *n.* [1980s+] (US gay) the penis. [SAmE *popsicle* = SE *lollipop*]

popsicle stand *n.* [1980s+] (US campus) one's current location.

popsie/popsy *n.* [mid-19C+] a woman, usu. one who is young and attractive. [SE *pop*/*poppet*, a term of endearment for a woman + sfx. *-sy*, as in Betsy, Topsy etc]

popskull *n.* [mid-19C+] (US) illicitly distilled whisky (cf. CRACKSKULL; FOXHEAD). [SE *pop*, to explode + *skull*]

pop someone off, to *phr.* (orig. US) **1** [mid-19C+] to murder someone, to kill someone. **2** [1950s+] to bring someone to orgasm (cf. POP n.[4]). [lit. + fig. uses of POP v.[1]]

pop someone's cherry *see* POP A CHERRY.

pop someone's cookies, to *phr.* [1970s+] to give one's partner an orgasm.

pop someone's nuts, to *phr.* [1950s+] to give someone an orgasm. [SE *pop*, to explode + NUTS n.[2] (1)]

pop style *v.* [1950s+] (W.I.) of a woman, to walk in a provocative manner or to act stylishly.

popsy *see* POPSIE.

popsy-wopsy *n.* [late 19C] 'a smiling, doll-like attractive girl' (Ware). [POPSIE + redup.]

pop test *see* POP QUIZ.

pop the question, to *phr.* [early 19C+] to propose marriage (cf. FIRE THE QUESTION). [SE *pop the question*, to question abruptly]

pop tops *v.* [1980s+] (US campus) to drink beer. [SE *pop*, to explode + *top* (of a beer can)]

popular *adj.* [mid–late 19C] (US) **1** conceited. **2** good, e.g. *a popular pie.*

population paste *see* PASTE n.[1].

pop visit *n.* [late 19C] (society) a brief visit. [one 'just pops in' for a moment]

pop wine *n.* [20C] (US) sweet wine with a low alcohol content. [POP n.[2] + SE *wine*]

porangi *adj.* [late 19C+] (N.Z.) mad, insane. [Maori]

porch climber *n.* [1900s–20s] (US) a burglar (cf. SECOND-STOREY MAN).

porch monkey *n.* [1970s+] (US) a derog. term for a Black person. [SE *porch* + MONKEY n.[1] (4); the stereotyped image of Black laziness, i.e. sitting on the porch]

pork *n.*[1] [18C–1900s] a generic term for a woman or women viewed as sex objects (cf. MUTTON n.[2]).

pork *n.*[2] [late 19C+] (US) Federal funds obtained for particular areas or individuals on the basis of political patronage. [PORK BARREL]

pork *n.*[3] [1950s+] a fool. [? PIG n.[1]]

pork *v.* [1970s+] of a man, to have sexual intercourse. [he uses his PORK SWORD]

pork and bean *n.* [1960s+] (Aus.) a male homosexual. [rhy. sl. *pork and bean* = QUEEN n.[1]]

pork barrel *n.* [late 19C+] (US) a political 'slush' fund. [? the use of large barrels of salt pork for the feeding of slaves]

pork chop *n.*[1] [20C] a policeman. [rhy. sl. *pork chop* = COP n.[1] (1)]

pork chop *n.*[2] [1970s+] (US) a Black person who, despite supposed advances in equality, is willing to accept an inferior position to that of Whites. [the stereotypical linkage of pork chops and Blacks]

pork-chopper *n.* [1940s+] a full-time union official, 'a political appointee, union official, or relative or friend of a politician, union officer, or the like, who receives payment for little or no work; one who is put on a payroll as a favor or as a return for past services' (*DAS*, 1960).

porker *n.*[1] [late 17C–mid-18C] a sword. [? POKER n.[1] (1), but cf. PIGSTICKER]

porker *n.*[2] [late 18C+] a Jew (cf. PORKY n.[1]). [the Jewish laws of *kashrut*, which forbid the consumption of pig flesh]

porker *n.*[3] [late 19C+] a fat person. [SE *porker*, a pig, when raised for its meat]

porker *n.*[4] [1970s] a policeman. [var. on PIG n.[3]]

pork fritz *see* FRITZ n.[2].

Porkopolis *n.* (US) **1** [19C] Cincinnati. **2** [20C] Chicago. [both centres of the meat trade]

pork out *see* PIG OUT.

pork-pie/-pie hat *n.* **1** [mid-19C] a style of fashionable women's hat. **2** [late 19C] a fashionable 'toreador'-style hat. **3** [1920s+] a style of men's hat. [resemblance]

pork sword *n.* [1960s+] the penis (cf. BACON BAZOOKA).

porkwah, babycakes *phr.* [1990s] (US Black teen) **1** I think I'm falling in love with you. **2** you are very physically attractive, and I want to have sex with you. [Fr. *pourquoi*, why + PORK v. + BABYCAKES]

porky *n.*[1] [late 19C] **1** a pork-butcher. **2** a Jew (cf. PORKER n.[2]). [their respective relations with pork]

porky *n.*[2] [20C] **1** a lie. **2** an eye. [rhy. sl. *porky pie*]

porky *adj.* [mid-19C+] obese.

porky pig *adj.* [20C] big, esp. in sense of generous. [rhy. sl.]

porn/porno *n.* [1940s+] *porn*ography; thus *porn flicks*, 'blue' films; *porn shop*, an 'adult' bookshop specializing in pornography. [abbr.]

porny *adj.* [1940s+] *porn*ographic, though usu. only mildly so. [abbr.]

pornzine *n.* [1970s+] a *porn*ographic maga*zine*. [abbr.]

Porra *n.* [1970s+] (S.Afr.) a derog. term for a person of Portuguese descent. [? mispron. of Portuguese or Port. *porra!*, a coarse excl.]

porridge *n.*[1] [1940s+] imprisonment. [the staple morning diet of such establishments in the UK + pun on STIR n.[1]/SE *stir*]

porridge *n.*[2] [1990s] (Irish) a confusion, e.g. a traffic jam. [SE *porride*, a hotch potch]

porridge *v.* [1960s] to imprison. [PORRIDGE n.[1]]

porridge bowl *n.* [mid-19C–1900s] the stomach.

porridge gun *n.* [1990s] the penis. [the supposed similarity of semen to porridge]

porridge hole *n.* [late 19C] (Scot.) the mouth (cf. BACON HOLE).

Porsche *n.* [1970s+] (US Black) a woman whose body is small, rounded, compact and stylish. [resemblance to *Porsche* cars]

port *n.* [20C] (Aus.) *port*manteau. [abbr.]

portable pocket rocket *n.* [1990s] the penis (cf. HEAT-SEEKING MISSILE).

Portagee/Portugee colonial/chic *n.* [20C] (US) cheap furniture, touted as ultra fashionable and peddled mainly to gullible recent immigrants; also as *immigrant chic*. [racial stereotyping]

Portagee/Portugee lawnmower *n.* [20C] a goat used to keep the grass down. [racial stereotyping]

Portagee/Portugee lift *n.* [late 19C+] one who carries less than their share of a load. [orig. used on US docks]

Portagee overdrive *n.* [20C] (US) freewheeling down hills to save petrol (cf. JEWISH OVERDRIVE). [the stereotyped poverty of Portuguese immigrants]

port and brandy *adj.* [20C] randy. [rhy. sl.]

portcullis *n.* [17C] a halfpenny. [the SE *portcullis* engraved on one side of the silver coin]

porter's knot *n.* [late 19C] a large bob worn by women on the back of the head. [SE *porter's knot*, a kind of double shoulderpad, with a loop passing round the forehead, used by London market-porters for carrying their burdens]

porter-without-froth *n.* [1950s] (W.I.) a layabout, a ne'er-do-well. [SE *porter*, a dark beer, so called from its being preferred by market porters. Porter, e.g. Guinness, should have a head or 'froth' if poured properly]

porthole *n.* [17C] **1** the anus. **2** the vagina.

Port Melbourne Pier *see* MELBOURNE PIER.

portrait *n.*[1] [mid-19C] a sovereign (cf. MONARCH n.[2]). [the monarch's face on the coin]

portrait *n.*[2] [1900s] (US Black) one's face.

portrait of Madison *n.* [1940s+] (US) a $5000 bill (cf. ABRAHAM LINCOLN; PORTRAIT n.[1]). [the face of *James Madison* (1751–1836), 4th President of the US, is printed on $5000 bills]

portsammy/sammy *n.* [20C] (N.Z.) a portmanteau, a travelling bag. [joc. mispron.]

port-sider *n.* [20C] (US) a left-hander (cf. SOUTHPAW n.). [naut. imagery; *port*, the left-hand side of the boat]

Portugee colonial/chic *see* PORTAGEE COLONIAL.

Portugee lawnmower *see* PORTAGEE LAWNMOWER.

Portugee lift *see* PORTAGEE LIFT.

Portuguese parliament *n.* [late 19C+] a meeting at which everyone gathers but no one listens to anyone else. [neg. stereotyping; orig. naval jargon]

Portuguese pump *n.* [1950s] masturbation.

Portuguese time *n.* [1970s] any time later than that appointed for an appointment (cf. AFRICAN PEOPLE'S TIME). [neg. stereotyping]

pos/poss/pozz *adj.* [early 18C–mid-19C] *pos*itive. [abbr.]

posa *n.* [mid-19C] (Anglo-Chinese) a treasurer, as employed by Anglo-Chinese merchants. [mispron. of SE *purser*]

pose off *v.* [1950s] (W.I.) to strike an exaggerated pose.

poser *n.* [1970s+] someone who pretends to be other than what they actually are. [SE *pose*]

posey *adj.* [1990s] (US campus) pretentious. [SE *pose*]

posh *n.*[1] [mid-19C–1900s] a dandy. [despite the links in sense, the n. and adj. uses come apparently from different origins. E.P. suggests link to POSH n.[2], while *OED* suggests a completely discrete word]

posh *n.*[2] [mid-19C] a coin or money, usu. a halfpenny. [Rom. *posh*, a half]

posh *n.*[3] [1990s] (drugs) cocaine. [POSH adj.; i.e. the drug's image]

posh *adj.* [20C] (orig. milit.) smart, pertaining to the upper classes. [ety. unknown. The *OED*, like most modern authorities, rejects the traditional 'port out, starboard home' derivation. E.P. and J.P. Mayer (in Cohen, 1985) opt for a contraction of *polished*, well turned out, smart, sophisticated. The novelist P.G. Wodehouse uses *push* in 1903, which *OED* sees as a synon., but this may be linked to PUSH n.[2] (4), a clique]

posh/posh up *v.* [1910s+] of a person, to smarten one's clothes, house etc (cf. DOLL UP; TART UP). [POSH adj.]

posh horri *n.* [mid-19C] a halfpenny. [POSH n.[2] + Rom. *horri*, penny]

posh korona *n.* [mid-19C] half-a-crown, 2s 6d (12½p). [POSH n.[2] + Rom. *korona*, crown]

posh up *see* POSH v.

posh wank *n.* [1990s] an act of masturbation while wearing a condom. [POSH adj. + WANK n.]

posie *n.* [20C] (W.I.) a chamberpot. [ext. of PO]

posish *n.* [mid-19C+] (orig. US) *posi*tion. [abbr.]

positive *adj.* [19C+] absolute, undeniable, certain.

positively *adv.* [late 18C+] yes indeed, absolutely.

poss *n.* [1940s+] (Aus.) a fool, esp. a trickster's victim (cf. POSSUM n.).

poss *adj. see* POS.

posse *n.* [1980s+] **1** (orig. US Black) a teenage gang (cf. CREW). **2** (US campus) one's own circle of friends. **3** (orig. US Black) oneself, as described in the third person, e.g. *the posse can't did this*, I am unhappy. [SE *posse*, an armed band recruited to pursue law-breakers]

posse/posse down *v.* [1980s+] (orig. US Black) to move in a gang or group. [POSSE n.]

posse mobilitatis *n.* [late 18C–mid-19C] the mob. [play on Lat. *posse comitatus*, force of the county, a band of citizens summoned by the sheriff to deal with outbreaks of rioting and similar disorder]

possesh *n.* [1930s] a homosexual teenage boy who is used for sex by the tramp whom he accompanies everywhere. [abbr. SE *possession*]

possession *n.* [1960s+] (drugs) possession of (rather than dealing in) drugs.

posse up *v.* [1980s+] (US Black/teen) of a gang, to move together as a group. [POSSE n.]

possible *n.* [early 19C] a coin (cf. NEEDFUL). [i.e. it makes things possible]

possibles *n.* [early–mid-19C] **1** necessities, supplies. **2** money.

possible sack *n.* [late 19C+] (orig. US) **1** a bag for personal belongings. **2** a bag containing items that can be taken to the pawnbroker.

possie *n.* [20C] (Aus.) a position, usu. an advantageous one. [abbr.]

possle *n.* [late 19C] an earnest advocate of a course or opinion. [abbr. SE *apostle*]

posso-de-luxe/possodeluxe *n.* [1930s+] (Aus.) an extremely rich fool, esp. when used as a confidence trickster's victim. [POSSUM n. (5)]

possum *n.* **1** [mid-19C] (US) a friend. **2** [late 19C] (US) a coward. **3** [late 19C+] (Aus.) a person (used either affectionately or derog.). **4** [20C] (Aus.) a fraudulent substitution. **5** [1900s] (US) a Black person. **6** [1930s+] (Aus.) a fool, esp. a trickster's victim; sometimes intensified as *possodeluxe*. **7** [1940s+] (Aus.) a thief. [one of the animal's characteristics is feigning death when threatened]

possum belly *n.* [19C] 'a baggy, dried cowhide fastened horizontally beneath the wagon box and used for carrying a reserve of fuel' (P.A. Rollins, *Gone Haywire*, 1939). [thus used for similar arrangements on livestock and circus wagons]

possum-eater *n.* [1940s–50s] (Aus.) a peasant, a country bumpkin; thus *possum-eating*, countrified. [their supposed diet]

possum-guts *n.* **1** [mid–late 19C] (Aus.) a general term of abuse (cf. WIMP-GUTS). **2** [1950s–60s] (Aus.) a coward; thus *possum-gutted*, cowardly. [reflecting low opinion of the animal]

post *n.* [1900s–30s] (US) a *post*-graduate. [abbr.]

post *v.*[1] [late 18C+] to lay down or stake money, esp. to put up bail; thus [late 18C] *post the cole*; [late 18C] *post the neddies*; [early 19C] *post the pony*; [mid-19C] *post the tin*. [SE *post*, a trading station, or Ital. *posta*, a stake + COLE/NEDDY n.[2]/PONY n.[2]/TIN n.[1]]

post *v.*[2] [early–mid-19C] (orig. US) to inform; thus *keep one posted*, keep one up to date (cf. POST UP). [? *posting* accounts in a ledger or nailing announcements to a post]

post *v.*[3] [1960s+] (Aus.) to abandon, to 'leave in the lurch'. [SE *post*, to hurry]

post a flyer, to *phr.* [1960s+] (gay) to advertise one's sexual availability.

postage stamp *n.*[1] [mid–late 19C] any tavern or hotel named the 'Queen's Head'. [the head of Queen Victoria (1819–1901) also adorned contemporary stamps]

postage stamp *n.*[2] [20C] (US) a bar. [rhy. sl. = RAMP n.[3]]

postal *n.* [late 19C–1900s] (US) a postcard. [abbr. SAmE *postal card*]

postal *adj.* [1990s] (US) crazy, psychotic. [contemporary news stories of deranged US postal workers who shoot people and then commit suicide]

post a letter, to *phr.* [20C] to defecate.

post-and-rail *n.*[1] [late 19C–1940s] (Aus.) a wooden match. [the resemblance to a *post-and-rail* fence]

post-and-rail *n.*[2] [1940s] (Aus.) a lie, a (fairy) tale. [rhy. sl. *post-and-rail* = *fairy tale* (see FAIRY STORY)]

post-and-rail tea *n.* [mid-19C+] (Aus.) poor quality tea, with particles of stalk and other impurities floating on its surface; such impurities may have been deliberately added to bulk out a grocer's measure. [the idea of chunks of wood floating in it]

post-chay/-shay *n.* [late 18C] a post-chaise or travelling carriage.

posted *adj.*[1] [mid-19C+] (orig. US) aware, in the know, shrewd. [POST v.[2]]

posted *adj.*[2] [1960s+] (Aus.) abandoned.

posteriors/posterior *n.* [early 17C+] the buttocks, the behind. [20C use usu. in sing.]

postern gate *n.* [late 19C] (US) that part of a pair of trousers that fits over the buttocks. [SE *postern*, a backdoor or gate]

postgrad *n.* [1950s+] a *postgrad*uate. [abbr.]

post-horn *n.* [19C] the nose (cf. BUGLE n.[1]).

postie *n.* [1950s+] (Aus.) a postman. [abbr.]

postilion *v.* [19C+] to insert and manipulate a finger in the anus of a sexual partner as a means of sexual excitement. [SE *postilion*, a swift messenger; thus the practice makes one 'COME v.[1] faster']

postilion of the gospel *n.* [late 18C–early 19C] a parson who rushes through the service.

postman *n.* [1990s] a homosexual who plays the active role in anal intercourse (cf. LETTERBOX).

postman's knock *n.* [20C] a clock. [rhy. sl.]

postman's sister *n.* [late 19C] a secret informant (cf. JINKS THE BARBER). [the implication is that her brother can somehow read the mail – perhaps the postcards – and gossips about its contents]

postmaster-general *n.* [late 18C] the prime minister. [their patronage of official posts]

post nointer *n.* [late 18C–mid-19C] a house painter. [he 'anoints' the door posts]

post-op *adj.* [1970s+] *post-op*erative, having recently undergone an operation. [abbr.]

post-shay *see* POST-CHAY.

post toasties *n.* [1950s–70s] (US camp gay) the mailman. [brandname of a US breakfast cereal]

post up *v.* [mid–late 19C] (US) to supply with the latest information, to learn the latest news; usu. as passive *posted up*, informed. [POST v.[2]]

pot *n.*[1] *see* POT HAT.

pot *n.*[2] [19C+] **1** a large sum of money. **2** the favourite in a horse-race, upon whom 'pots of money' have been wagered.

pot *n.*[3] [19C+] a prize, esp. a cup given to a sporting victor. [SE *pot*]

pot *n.*[4] [mid-19C] the top. [backsl.]

pot *n.*[5] [mid-19C] sixpence. [the contemporary price of a quart pot of HALF-AND-HALF n.[1]]

pot *n.*[6] **1** [late 19C–1900s] an important person. **2** [20C] (US) an unattractive woman. **3** [20C] (US) an obnoxious person. [abbr. BIG POT; later use is SE]

pot *n.*[7] [20C] an enlarged stomach, usu. developed through excessive drinking (cf. BEER GUT). [abbr. SE *pot belly*; ult. a *pot* of ale]

pot n.[8] [1910s+] (Aus.) in Queensland, a 10 oz (285 ml) beer glass.

pot n.[9] [1930s+] (drugs) marijuana, hashish; thus *pot party*, a gathering of people to smoke marijuana. [Mexican Sp. *potiguaya*, marijuana leaves]

pot n.[10] [1940s–60s] (US) a carburettor. [resemblance]

pot v.[1] [19C] to outdo, to outwit, to deceive. [16C–17C SE]

pot v.[2] **1** [mid-19C+] to shoot, esp. food for eating; thus SE *pot-shot*. **2** [20C] (Aus.) to throw a stone. **3** [20C] (US) to hit, to strike. [the food goes in the SE *pot*]

pot v.[3] [1910s+] (Aus./N.Z.) to inform against, to hand over for trial (cf. PUT ONE'S POT ON). [to put in the fig. SE *pot*]

pot v.[4] [1940s+] to train (a child) to use a chamberpot.

-pot *sfx.* [20C] a person; usu. found in combs., e.g. BARMPOT; BIG POT; CRANKPOT; FUSSPOT; SEXPOT. [SE *pot*, container. In such combs. the person is seen as a container for a characteristic]

pot and pan n. [20C] a man. [rhy. sl.]

potash n. [1940s] (Irish) a stew. [Fr. *potage*, soup]

potash and perlmutter n. [1910s–50s] butter. [rhy. sl.; ult. a play by Montague Glass, first performed 1914]

potato n.[1] [mid-18C–mid-19C] a general insult; e.g. *he's a rotten potato*.

potato, the n.[2] [19C] the right thing, the apposite thing; usu. as *quite the potato*; thus negative, *not quite the potato* (cf. CLEAN POTATO n.[1]).

potato n.[3] [late 19C+] a large hole in a sock or stocking through which the flesh shows (cf. POPPY n.[3]; SPUD n.[1]). [? the shape + the dirt that accrues to the bare flesh]

potato n.[4] [20C] (US) **1** the head. **2** a dollar. **3** a football. [the shape]

potato n.[5] [1950s] (Can.) a native of New Brunswick. [the province grows many potatoes; the implication is one of rural stolidness and stupidity]

potato/potato peeler n.[6] [1950s+] (Aus.) a woman, a girlfriend. [rhy. sl. *potato peeler* = SHEILA]

potato n.[7] [1980s+] (drugs) LSD. [ety. unknown; ? the vegetative state it produces in users]

potato v. [1980s+] (US campus) to lie around doing nothing (cf. COUCH POTATO; VEG).

potato-box n. [late 18C] the mouth (cf. POTATO-TRAP).

potato chips n. [1980s+] (drugs) crack cocaine cut with benzocaine. [ety. unknown]

potato-eater n. [late 19C+] (US) an Irishman. [racial stereotyping]

potatoes n. [1930s+] (US) money (cf. ALFALFA. [on pattern of CABBAGE n.[8], KALE etc; although potatoes are not green]

potatoes in the mould phr. [20C] cold (cf. TATERS). [rhy. sl.]

potato-finger n. [17C] **1** a long, thick finger. **2** the penis. **3** a dildo. [the shape + the supposed aphrodisiac quality of the sweet potato]

potato-fingered Irishman n. [20C] a clumsy person. [the alleged predilection of the Irish for potatoes]

potato-head n. [20C] (US) a fool, a simpleton. [SE *potato* + sfx. -HEAD (1)]

potato jack n. [20C] (US prison) illicit liquor distilled from potatoes. [SE *potato* + JACK n.[21]]

potato jaw n. [late 18C] the mouth. [its use in consuming the vegetable]

potato peeler see POTATO n.[6].

potato-pillin' n. [1930s] a shilling. [rhy. sl.]

potato queen n. [1980s+] (US gay) an oriental gay man who prefers Western partners. [? the SE *potato* as a quintessential Western food + QUEEN n.[1]]

potato-trap n. [late 18C–late 19C] the mouth (cf. POTATO-BOX).

pot-boiler n. [mid-19C+] a literary or similar work created purely for the money. [it keeps the creator's 'pot boiling']

pot burst phr. [20C] (W.I.) a phr. used of a friendship to indicate that it has come to an end. [the pot breaks under the relationship's stress]

potch n. [20C] a slap, a smack, usu. given to a child. [Yid./Ger. *Patsch*, a smack, a splash]

potch v. [20C] to slap, to smack, usu. a child. [POTCH n.]

potchky/potchkie/potskie v. [20C] (US) to mess about. [fig. use of POTCH v.]

pot convert n. [late 18C–early 19C] a convert to Roman Catholicism who is won over by the free provision of food and drink. [SE *pot*, a container for food or drink]

poted see POTTED adj.[2].

pot-faker n. [mid-19C] a hawker of crockery, a cheap-jack. [SE *pot* + FAKER n. (2)]

pot-guts n. [18C+] a fat person.

pot-gutted adj. [20C] (Aus.) pot-bellied. [POT-GUTS]

pot hat/pot n. **1** [late 18C–late 19C] a bowler hat. **2** [19C] a low-crowned hat, as opposed to the more common top hat of the period.

pothead n.[1] [mid-19C] a fool; thus *potheaded*, stupid. [SE *pot* + sfx. -HEAD (1)]

pothead n.[2] [1960s+] (drugs) a smoker of marijuana or hashish. [POT n.[9] + sfx. -HEAD (2)]

pothooks and hangers n. [19C] shorthand (cf. HOOKS AND CROOKS). [SE *pothooks and hangers*, the curved strokes used in writing, which supposedly resemble the hooks and hangers found in a kitchen]

pot-house n. [late 19C] a small, unpretentious tavern or public house. [SE *pot* + *house*]

pot-hunter n.[1] [16C] a confidence trickster, one of a team but posing as an independent person, often drunk, who befriends a potential victim and lures them into a swindle (cf. BARNARD). [SE *pot*, a tankard, i.e. the pose as a drunkard + *hunter*]

pot-/mug-hunter n.[2] **1** [late 18C–19C] one who pursues a sport for glory rather than pleasure. **2** [20C] (US) a scavenger. [POT n.[2] + SE *hunter*]

pot-lick v. [1960s] to toady to, to curry favour (cf. ARSE-LICK).

pot-licker n. [20C] (W.I.) a mongrel, kept as a watchdog and allowed to forage for its food (cf. SALMON-TOT RETRIEVER).

pot liquor n. [1950s] (drugs) a drink derived from brewing marijuana leaves and stalks. [POT n.[9] + play on SE *pot liquor*, the liquid derived from boiling greens]

pot o'/of bliss n. [late 19C] a handsome, good-looking woman (cf. QUARTERN OF BLISS).

pot of all n. [late 19C–1910s] a supreme hero (cf. BIG POT). [POT n.[6] (1)]

pot of beer n. [late 19C] amongst teetotallers, a bottle of ginger beer.

pot of bliss see POT O' BLISS.

pot of glue n. [20C] **1** a Jew (cf. BOX OF GLUE). **2** a queue. [rhy. sl.]

pot of honey n. [late 19C+] money (cf. BEES AND HONEY). [rhy. sl.]

pot of O n. [mid–late 19C] a glass or tankard of beer. [rhy. sl., *pot of* OH MY DEAR = beer]

pot on v. [late 19C] to be keen on, to enthuse about. [fig. use of billiards SE *pot*, to sink a ball]

pot out v. [1960s] (drugs) to smoke marijuana. [POT n.[9]]

pot pork for, to phr. [20C] (W.I.) **1** of a young woman, to cook special meals for the object of one's affections. **2** to get a husband through deliberate scheming.

pots n. [1980s+] (Polari) the teeth.

pots adj. [1920s–30s] insane, eccentric; usu. as *to be pots*. [POTTY adj.]

pots and dishes n. [1970s] wishes. [rhy. sl.]

pot-shot adj. [early 17C–mid-19C] drunk (cf. POTSICK). [one has been fig. *shot* by drinking a *pot* of beer]

potsick *adj.* [19C] drunk (cf. CUP-SHOT; POT-SHOT).

potskie *see* POTCHKY.

pot-slinger *n.* [20C] (US) a cook.

potsy *n.* [20C] (US) a police badge, an identification card. [the tin (used for *pots*) that is allegedly made into badges]

pottage *n.* [17C] the Book of Common Prayer. [the ref. is to Esau, who sold his birthright for 'a mess of pottage']

potted/potted out *adj.*[1] **1** [mid–late 19C] confined. **2** [mid–late 19C] dead and buried. **3** [late 19C] snubbed, suppressed. [gardening imagery]

potted/poted *adj.*[2] [1920s+] (US) drunk (cf. CANNED adj.[2]; JARRED adj.[1]; TANKED). [SE *pot*, a container for drink]

potted *adj.*[3] [1960s+] (drugs) intoxicated by marijuana. [POT n.[9]]

potted out *see* POTTED adj.[1].

potten bush *n.* [1950s] (drugs) hashish. [SE *potted*, confined in a small space + BUSH n.[6]]

potter-carrier *n.* [mid-18C–early 19C] an apothecary. [mispron.]

pot the white, to *phr.* [1930s+] of a man, to have sexual intercourse. [billiards/snooker use, in which potting the white is a 'foul stroke']

pottie/potty *n.* [19C+] a chamberpot. [abbr.]

potting *n.* [late 19C–1900s] shooting. [POT v.[2]]

potty *n.*[1] *see* POTTIE.

potty *n.*[2] [late 19C] a tinker. [SE *pot*, which they mend]

potty *adj.* **1** [mid-19C+] usu. of a plan or scheme, dubious, indifferent. **2** [mid-19C+] insignificant, feeble. **3** [late 19C+] easy to manage, simple. **4** [20C] crazy, eccentric; thus *potty about*, madly in love with, obsessed by (cf. POTS adj.). [SE *pot*, a tankard, thus lit. 'drunken']

potty house *n.* [late 19C+] a lunatic asylum. [POTTY adj. + SE *house*]

pot-valiant *adj.* [late 17C–18C] exhibiting the bravado that comes from imbibing alcoholic drink. [play on SE]

pot-walloper *n.* **1** [mid–late 19C+] a scullion, a kitchen servant. **2** [late 19C] a heavy drinker. [a pun on SE *pot-walloper*, lit. 'the boiler of a pot'. 'The term applied in some English boroughs, before the Reform Act of 1832, to a man qualified for a parliamentary vote as a householder (i.e. tenant of a house or distinct part of one) as distinguished from one who was merely a member or inmate of a householder's family; the test of which was his having a separate fire-place, on which his own pot was boiled or food cooked for himself and his family' (*OED*). 20C use is Irish]

pot-wrestler *n.* [19C] a scullion, a kitchen-hand. [SE *pot* + *wrestler*]

potz *see* PUTZ.

potzer *see* PATZER.

pouch *n.*[1] [late 19C–1900s] a present of money. [SE *pouch*, which contains it]

pouch *n.*[2] [1940s–50s] (Aus.) **1** the vagina. **2** women considered purely as sex objects. [(2) is fig. use of (1)]

pouch *v.* **1** [mid-19C] to give a gift of money. **2** [late 19C] to eat. **3** [1920s] to steal, to grab. [SE *pouch*, to place in a bag]

pouffe *see* POOF.

poulain *n.* [late 18C–early 19C] a venereal bubo. [synon. Fr., which also means the penis]

poule *n.* [1920s+] a prostitute; thus *poule-de-luxe*, a high-class prostitute, a courtesan. [adoption of Fr. sl. *poule*, a prostitute (lit. 'a chicken')]

poult *n.* [mid-18C–late 19C] a child, a youth. [Scot. *poult*, anything young, e.g. a bird]

poulter *see* POLTER.

poulterer *n.* [19C] a thief who specializes in removing the contents of letters. [the image is of a poulterer gutting chickens]

poultice *n.* **1** [late 19C] (society) a high stiff collar, which resembles a medical poultice. **2** [late 19C] (society) a fat woman. **3** [20C] (Ulster) an unpleasantly persistent person (cf. PLASTER n.[3]). **4** [1930s–50s] a mortgage. **5** [1950s–70s] a bribe, a large sum of money.

poultice over the peeper *n.* [late 19C] a blow on the eye. [SE *poultice* + PEEPER(s) n. (1)]

poultry *n.* [19C] women in general (cf. CHICK n.[4]). [play on CHICKEN n.[4]]

pounce *v.* [1950s] (gay) to take the active role in homosexual anal intercourse.

pounce-shicer *n.* [19C] a pimp (cf. POUNCEY). [PONCE n. + SHICER]

pouncey *n.* [19C] a pimp (cf. POUNCE-SHICER). [PONCE n.]

pound *n.*[1] [late 19C+] the human head. [rhy. sl., *pound of lead* = head]

pound *n.*[2] [1930s–60s] **1** (US) money, esp. $1 or $5. **2** (US Und.) a 5-year sentence (cf. FIN n.[4]; HANDFUL n.[2]; NICKEL n.[1]; POUND NOTE n.[2]). [an era when the *pound* sterling equalled $5]

pound *v.*[1] [early 19C] to place a bet that one is sure one will win (cf. POUNDABLE). [the cockfighting practice of offering £10 to 5s, a very extravagant bet which was known as *pounding a cock*. If no one took it the match was automatically off]

pound *v.*[2] [1970s+] **1** (US Black/campus) to drink beer quickly (cf. HAMMER v.[1]; POWER). **2** (US Black) of a man, to perform sex vigorously (cf. BANG v.[1]).

poundable *adj.* [19C] certain, definite, inevitable, esp. as regards the result of a wager. [POUND v.[1]]

poundcake *n.* [1930s+] (US) an attractive woman (cf. BANANA n.[2]).

pounded *adj.* [early–mid-19C] caught out in some form of (? homosexual) impropriety. [SE *pound*, an enclosure where animals are kept]

pounder *n.* [1930s–60s] (US Black) a policeman (cf. BEAT POUNDER)

pounders *n.* [17C] the testicles. [? their knocking together]

pounding match *n.* [early 19C] a boxing match, a fight.

pound it *v.* [19C] to bet, esp. on what is considered a virtual 'sure thing'. [POUND v.[1]]

pound note *n.*[1] [20C] a coat. [rhy. sl.]

pound note *n.*[2] [1930s–40s] (US) $5. [the contemporary exchange rate of $5 = £1]

pound-note geezer *n.* [1950s+] (orig. Aus.) a rich man. [SE *pound note* + GEEZER n.[1] (1)]

pound-noteish *adj.* [1930s–60s] pompous, affected. [seen as characteristics of the rich]

pound off *v.* [1980s+] (US gay) to masturbate (cf. BEAT OFF; WHACK OFF).

pound o'/of lead *n.* [late 19C–1900s] the head. [rhy. sl.]

pound one's ear, to *phr.* [late 19C–1940s] (US) to sleep. [tramps attempting to sleep in the boxcars of US railroads as they bumped over the rails]

pound one's flounder, to *phr.* [1990s] to masturbate. [assonance]

pound one's meat, to *phr.* [1950s+] to masturbate (cf. ACCOST THE OSCAR MEYER). [MEAT n. (2)]

pound one's peenie, to *phr.* [1960s] to masturbate. [abbr. SE *penis*]

pound one's pork, to *phr.* [1960s] to masturbate (cf. ACCOST THE OSCAR MEYER). [PORK SWORD]

pound one's pud, to *phr.* [1960s] to masturbate. [PUD n.[2] (1)]

poundrel *n.* [17C] the head. [SE *poundrel*, scales]

pound salt up your ass! *excl.* [20C] (US) euph. for GO TO HELL!

pounds and pence *n.* [20C] sense. [rhy. sl.]

pound someone's name, to *phr.* [20C] (W.I.) to denigrate someone, to criticize someone behind their back.

pound-text n. [late 18C–late 19C] a parson. [his thumping of the Bible]

pound the bald-headed moose, to phr. [1990s] to masturbate.

pound the beat, to phr. [1960s+] (Aus.) to walk the streets as a prostitute. [on the model of the police use]

pound the books, to phr. [20C] (US campus) to study hard.

pound the bricks see HIT THE BRICK.

pound the pavement, to phr. [1950s–60s] **1** (US) to walk the streets in search of a job. **2** (US drugs) to search for drugs, which can often require hours of walking.

pound the pelican, to phr. [1990s] to masturbate (cf. PROMPT ONE'S PORPOISE).

pound to an olive phr. [late 19C] a sure bet (cf. ALL THE WORLD TO A CHINA ORANGE). [Ware calls this a Jewish term, 'resulting out of the Hebrews' love of olives']

pour it on, to phr. [1930s+] (orig. US) **1** to make a great effort. **2** to flatter outrageously (cf. POUR ON THE OIL).

pour-man n. [1940s] (US Black) a bartender. [pun]

pour money down the drain/the rat-hole, to phr. [1920s+] to waste money. [fig. use of SE + DOWN THE DRAIN/SE *rat-hole*]

pour on the coal, to phr. [1920s] (US) of a person or a vehicle, to accelerate. [railroad use]

pour on the oil, to phr. [late 19C+] to flatter, to talk glibly but insincerely (cf. APPLY THE OIL). [OIL n.[1]]

pour the pork, to phr. [1950s+] (orig. US) of a man, to have sexual intercourse. [PORK SWORD]

pout n. [18C] a mistress (cf. POUTER). [SE *pullet*, a young hen]

pouter n. [19C] the vagina (cf. DIDDLEY-POUT). [i.e. 'that which pouts']

poverty n. [early–mid-18C] gin. [its effect and/or its drinkers]

poverty-basket n. [mid-19C] a wicker cradle.

poverty-truck n. [1920s] (W.I.) ? a small hand-cart. [no absolute def. is available (*see* Cassidy & LaPage)]

pow n.[1] [20C] (US) *pow*er. [abbr.]

pow n.[2] [20C] (Ulster) a bald head. [SE *poll*]

powder n. [1910s+] (drugs) any form of powdered drug, e.g. heroin, cocaine, amphetamine (cf. POLVO).

powder v.[1] [mid-17C–mid-18C] to run off (cf. TAKE A POWDER). [the explosive qualities of powder]

powder v.[2] [20C] (US) to hit very hard. [fig. to reduce to powder]

powder away v. [1920s] to do morally admirable but ultimately pointless activities. [the sprinkling of powder]

powder diamonds see POWDERED DIAMONDS.

powdered chalk n. [late 19C+] a walk; thus *take a powdered chalk*, to take a walk. [rhy. sl.]

powdered diamonds n. [1950s–70s] (US drugs) cocaine (cf. POWDER n.). [its cost and the sparkle of high quality cocaine]

powdering/pickling tub n. [late 16C–18C] **1** the sweating tub used for the cure of venereal disease (cf. MOTHER CORNELIUS' TUB). **2** the hospital for sexual diseases, near Kingsland, London. [SE *powdering/pickling tub*, the tub in which the flesh of dead animals was pickled or 'powdered']

powder one's hair, to phr. [18C] to get drunk. [euph.]

powder one's nose, to phr. [1970s+] (drugs) to take cocaine. [pun]

powder puff n. [1920s+] **1** an effeminate male homosexual (cf. POOF n.). **2** a cautious fighter. [the term was notoriously used to attack the silent film god Rudolph Valentino (1895–1926)]

powderpuff adj. [1960s] (US) of a woman, pampered.

power n. **1** [mid-19C+] a good deal, a large number. **2** [mid-19C+] the penis. **3** [late 19C–1930s] (US Black) money.

power adj. [1980s+] (US campus) extreme.

power v. [1980s+] (US campus) to drink beer quickly (cf. HAMMER v.[4]; POUND v.[2]). [SE *power*, to move with speed or force]

power adv. [1980s+] (US campus) extremely.

poweration n. [mid-19C–1900s] a large amount, much.

power dance see BLACK POWER DANCE.

powerful adj. **1** [early–mid-19C] great in quantity or number. **2** [20C] (W.I.) of objects and people, attractive, beautiful.

powerful adv. [early 19C+] (orig. US) in a great degree, very, exceedingly. [POWERFUL adj. (1)]

powerhouse n. [1910s+] a strong, important, energetic and influential person.

power on/through v. [1980s+] (US campus) to do well, to succeed. [SE *power*, to move with speed or force]

power puller n. [1980s+] (drugs) a rubber piece attached to a crack pipe to facilitate smoking. [SE *power* + *pull*, a puff on a pipe]

power through see POWER ON.

power tool n. [1960s+] (US campus) a very diligent student. [SE *power*, supreme, outstanding + TOOL n. (9)]

power trip n. [1960s+] (orig. US) a show of personal power, esp. if blatant; thus *power trip*, to flaunt one's ego and importance. [SE *power* + TRIP n.[3] (2)]

powter see POLTER.

pow-wow v. [mid-19C+] (orig. US) to chat, to converse with, to talk to. [Algonkin (Narragansett) *pow'waw* or *po'wah*, a priest, a medicine man; thus the ceremonies over which such figures officiated and thus any gathering or conference]

pox n.[1] [16C+] **1** syphilis. **2** any venereal disease. [the SE *pocks* or eruptive pustules on the skin that are a sign of syphilis]

pox n.[2] [1940s–50s] (drugs) opium. [? abbr. YEN POK]

pox v. [mid-18C+] to infect with syphilis. [POX n.[1]]

pox!, a excl. [late 16C+] a general excl. of annoyance, irritation (cf. POX ON!; WHAT A POX!). [POX n.[1]]

pox doctor n. [1930s+] a doctor specializing in venereal diseases. [POX n.[1]]

poxed/poxed-up adj. [late 17C+] venereally diseased, esp. suffering from syphilis; also used figuratively. [POX n.[1]]

pox on! excl. [16C+] a general oath (cf. POX!; WHAT A POX!). [POX n.[1]]

pox take you! excl. [late 16C+] a general oath of dismissal. [POX n.[1]]

poxy adj. [1920s+] unpleasant, dirty, disgusting. [POX n.[1]]

pozz see POS.

pozzie n. [1990s] (Aus.) **1** a *posi*tion. **2** a seat. [abbr.; (2) is from (1)]

p.p. n. [late 19C] a pickpocket. [abbr.]

p.p. adj. [1920s+] of a man, having an erection on waking. [abbr. PISS-PROUD]

p.p. phr.[1] [late 19C–1910s] a warning from one woman to another that her petticoat is peeping, i.e. that her petticoat or slip is visible (cf. S.S. phr.[1]).

p.p. phr.[2] [1990s] (US Black) used dismissively to designate unimportant problems, usu. because they worry someone else rather than oneself. [abbr. *personal* problems]

p.p.c. n. [late 19C] (society) a curt, barely polite farewell; thus *p.p.c.*, to fall out, to quarrel, to 'cut' (cf. P.P.M.). [abbr. Fr. *pour prendre congé*, to take leave, written on a visiting card]

p.p.d. n. [1980s+] (US campus) an attractive person of the opposite sex. [abbr. *possible/potential prom date*]

p.p.m. phr. [late 19C] (society) goodbye, as inscribed on visiting cards (cf. P.P.C.). [abbr. Fr. *pour p'tit moment*, for a little while]

p.q. n. [1980s+] (US campus) someone who is out of date (cf. POLYESTER). [abbr. *polyester queen*]

p.r. n.[1] [19C] the prize ring, a generic term for the world of prize-fighting and pugilism. [abbr.]

p.r. *n.*[2] [1960s+] (US) a *P*uerto *R*ican. [abbr.]

p.r. *n.*[3] [1960s+] (drugs) marijuana. [abbr. *P*anama *R*ed]

practicable *adj.* [early 19C] easily manipulable, gullible. [SE *practicable*, capable of being used]

practical *n.* [early 19C] a practical joke.

practical politician *n.* [late 19C+] a saloon-bar orator.

practise the Heimlich maneuver/manoeuvre, to *phr.* [1990s] to masturbate. [SE *Heimlich maneuver/manoeuvre*, a first-aid technique used to dislodge objects trapped in someone's throat]

practitioner *n.* [mid-19C] a thief. [euph.]

prad *n.* [18C+] a horse; thus *pradback*, horseback; *prad-cove*, a horse-dealer; *prad-holder*, a bridle; *prad-napper*, a horse-thief (cf. PRAD LAY; PRAD-NAPPING). [Du. *paard*, a horse; ult. Lat. *paraveredus*, which gives the SE *palfrey*, a riding horse as opposed to a war-horse. 20C use is Aus./N.Z. only]

prad lay *n.* [late 18C] the stealing of bags from behind horses. [PRAD + LAY n.[4]]

prad-napping *n.* [mid-19C] horse-stealing. [PRAD + NAP v.[1] (3)]

prag *n.* [late 16C] (Und.) a thief. [var. on PRIG n.[1]]

prairie oyster *n.* [late 19C] (orig. US) 'an egg broken into a cup without smashing the yolk, the toast [a shot of liquor] poured in on the top of it, and the whole taken at a swallow' J.T. Keane, *On Blue-Water* (1883); generally, but not invariably taken as a hangover cure (cf. KALAHARI OYSTERS).

pram *n.* [late 19C] a milkman's hand-cart. [abbr. SE *perambulator*]

pram! pram! *phr.* [1980s+] (W.I./UK Black teen) a sound made by mouth, simulating gun shots fired in appreciation of something, such as a dance-hall song etc (cf. BOOYAKA!). [echoic]

prancer *n.* **1** [16C–mid-19C] (Und.) a horse. **2** [late 17C–18C] a highwayman. **3** [19C–mid-19C] a horse thief. **4** [mid-19C] a cavalry officer. [SE *prancer*, a mettlesome, spirited horse]

prancer's nab/nob/poll *n.* [late 17C–18C] (Und.) a horse's head seal, when used for counterfeiting documents. [PRANCER + NAB n.[1]/NOB n.[1]/SE *poll*, head]

prang *adj.* [1990s] (Black) extremely intoxicated, esp. by crack cocaine. [? PRANG v.]

prang *v.* [1940s+] **1** to crash one's car (cf. SHUNT). **2** to break, e.g. an arm, a leg. **3** to have sexual intercourse. [orig. WW2 RAF use]

prank *v.* [late 16C] to work as a prostitute. [SE *prank*, to play tricks]

pranker *n.* [late 17C] (Und.) a horse. [PRANCER]

prannet *n.* [1970s] a fool, an idiot. [PRANNIE]

prannie/pranny *n.* [late 19C+] **1** the vagina. **2** a general term of contempt. [? Scot. *pran/prann*, to squeeze, to crush; (2) is fig. use of (1)]

pra-pra *adj.* [20C] (W.I.) cheating, mixed up. [PRA-PRA v.]

pra-pra *v.* [20C] (W.I.) to snatch, to steal. [Twi *pra*, to carry away]

prat/pratte *n.* **1** [16C+] a buttock, the buttocks. **2** [late 17C–19C] a tinder-box. **3** [19C+] the vagina. **4** [20C] a young woman. **5** [1910s+] (US) a hip pocket; thus *prat-digger*, a pick-pocket; *prat frisk*, the theft of a wallet from a hip pocket; *prat-kick*, a hip pocket; *prat leather*, a wallet kept in the hip pocket; *prat poke*, a wallet stolen from the hip pocket. **6** [1960s+] a fool, an idiot (cf. ARSE n.[1]; ARSEHOLE n.; CUNT n.[2]; PRICK). [? echoic of the buttocks hitting a hard surface; (2)–(6) are fig. uses]

prat *v.*[1] **1** [16C+] to beat. **2** [late 19C] to go. [Rom. *praster*, to run]

prat *v.*[2] [1910s+] (Aus.) to talk to someone. [abbr. SE *prattle*]

prat *v.*[3] [1930s–50s] (US Black) of a woman, to play sexually hard to get, to tease physically. [PRAT n.[3]]

prat about/around *v.* [1960s+] to act foolishly, to act in an irritating manner. [PRAT n. (6)]

prater *n.* [19C] **1** the mouth. **2** an itinerant, bogus preacher. [SE *prate*, chatter]

prate-roast *n.* [late 17C–19C] a talkative boy. [SE *prate*, chatter]

pratfall *n.* [1950s+] **1** (orig. US) a humiliating defeat, a sudden failure. **2** a danger, a pitfall. [PRAT n. (1) + SE *fall*; orig. theatre jargon *pratfall*, a fall onto the buttocks, usu. as part of a slapstick routine]

prat for/pratt for *v.* [20C] (gay) to indulge, actively or passively, in anal intercourse. [PRAT n. (1)]

pratie/praty *n.* [late 18CC+] (Anglo-Irish) a potato.

prat in *v.* [20C] (Aus.) to push oneself forward, to barge in; also as *prat oneself in*; *prat one's frame in* (cf. BUTT IN). [PRAT n. (1) + FRAME n.[2]]

prating cheat *n.* [mid-16C–mid-19C] the tongue (cf. PRATTLING-CHEAT). [SE *prate*, to talk, to chatter + CHEAT n.]

pratte *see* PRAT n.

pratt for *see* PRAT FOR.

pratting-ken *n.* [mid–late 19C] a cheap lodging house. [PRAT n. (1) + KEN n.[1], i.e. a place one can rest one's buttocks]

prattle-box *n.* [early 18C] a chatterer, a gossip.

prattle-broth/scandal-broth/scandal-water *n.* [late 18C–early 19C] tea (cf. CHATTER-BROTH). [the stereotypical chattering women supposed to gather around a tea-table]

prattler *n.* [19C] the mouth (cf. PRATTLE-BOX; PRATTLING-CHEAT). [SE *prate*]

prattling-box *n.* [late 18C–mid-19C] a pulpit (cf. PRATTLE-BOX).

prattling-cheat *n.* [16C] (Und.) a tongue. [SE *prattle* + CHEAT n.]

prattling parlour *n.* [mid-19C] a private apartment.

praty *see* PRATIE.

prawn *n.* [late 19C+] (Aus.) a fool. [the image of the SE *prawn* as a 'humorous' or 'stupid' fish]

prawn cocktail offensive *n.* [1960s+] the after-dinner-speaking circuit; esp. as followed by political hopefuls. [the poor quality of the food (almost always including the prawn cocktail, a perennial middle English favourite) on offer]

prawnhead *n.* [1960s+] (Aus.) a fool, a simpleton (cf. BLOCK-HEAD n.[1]). [PRAWN + sfx. -HEAD (1)]

prawn-headed mullet *n.* [1930s+] (Aus.) a fool. [ext. of PRAWN/PRAWNHEAD]

prawnie/prawny *n.* [1920s+] (Aus.) a fisher or seller of prawns.

prayer-bones *n.* [late 19C–1940s] (US Black) the knees. [one's genuflection]

prayer book *n.* **1** [mid–late 19C] (US) a pack of rolling papers (cf. BIBLE n.[3]). **2** [late 19C] *Ruff's Guide to the Turf*, the racing man's 'Bible'.

prayer-book parade *n.* [late 19C–1910s] a promenade taken after Sunday church service.

prayer-dukes/-handles *n.* [1920s–40s] (US Black) the hands (cf. PRAYER-BONES). [SE *prayer* + DUKE n.[3]/SE *handle*; they are clasped in prayer]

pray to the porcelain god *see* KISS THE PORCELAIN GOD.

pray TV *n.* [1980s+] (orig. US) religious broadcasting, esp. TV evangelism, which uses its broadcasts to gather donations from the faithful. [SE *pray* + *TV* + pun on 'pay TV']

pray with one's knees upwards, to *phr.* [late 18C–early 19C] of a woman, to have sexual intercourse. [the 'missionary position']

preach *n.* [early 16C–mid-19C] an act of preaching, a sermon, esp. a tediously moralizing one (cf. PI-JAW). [abbr. SE *preacher*]

preach at Tyburn cross, to *phr.* [late 16C–18C] to be hanged (cf. FETCH A TYBURN STRETCH; MAKE A TYBURN SHOW). [TYBURN, the site of the main Middlesex gallows]

preachify *v.* [late 18C+] to preach a dull, moralizing sermon; thus *preachification*, preaching in this way; *preachifying*, moralizing.

preaching-shop *n.* [mid–late 19C] a church, a chapel.

preach on Tower Hill, to *phr.* [16C] to be hanged. [ironic use of SE *preach*, referring, perhaps, to the criminal's last words on the scaffold + *Tower Hill*, the site of many London executions]

preach someone's funeral, to *phr.* [20C] (US) to tell someone off, to reprimand someone.

preachy *adj.* [early 19C+] tediously moralizing.

preachy-preachy *adj.* [late 19C] tediously moralizing. [PREACHY + redup.]

precheck *n.* [1960s+] an inspection of a client's penis made by a prostitute before intercourse.

precious *adj.* **1** [early 18C+] over-fastidious, over-refined. **2** [early 18C+] arrogant. **3** [mid-18C+] very, exceedingly, e.g. *precious few*, *precious little*. **4** [mid-18C+] awful, terrible, disastrous, e.g. *a precious mess*. [for (1) cf. orig. SE use of *nice*]

precious coals! *excl.* [late 16C–early 17C] a general expletive. [? var. on *God's precious blood/body*]

precious juice *n.* [1980s+] (US campus) any alcoholic drink.

preciously *adv.* [mid–late 19C] very greatly, exceedingly, extremely.

predator *n.* [1980s+] (drugs) a variety of heroin (cf. TERMINATOR). [the film *Predator* (1987)]

pre-dawn vertical insertion *n.* [1980s] (US campus) sexual intercourse that takes place in the early morning. [a satirical ref. to the description of the invasion of Grenada given by the government of President Ronald Reagan (1983)]

predido/prendida *adj.* [1960s+] (US) eager, keen. [Sp.]

preem *n.* [1930s+] (orig. US) a theatrical or cinematic *premi*ère; thus *preem*, to have a première, a first night. [abbr.]

preemie/preemy/premie *n.* [1920s+] (US) a *prem*ature baby. [abbr.]

preesh! *excl.* [1980s+] (US campus) an expression of approval. [abbr. SE *appreciation*]

preeze *v.* [mid–late19C] to make ineffectual, straining efforts to urinate or defecate. [northern dial.]

prefab *n.* [1940s+] a *prefab*ricated house. [abbr.]

preg *adj.* [1940s+] (orig. US Black) *preg*nant (cf. PREGGERS; PREGGY; PREGO adj.). [abbr.]

preggers *adj.* [1920s+] pregnant. [abbr. SE *pregnant* + 'Oxford' sfx. *-ers*]

preggo *see* PREGO adj.

preggy *adj.* [1920s+] pregnant (cf. PREG).

pregnant *adj.* [1980s+] (US drugs) referring to a marijuana cigarette that is rolled incorrectly, usually with a bulge of cannabis in the middle.

prego *n.* [1950s+] (US) a pregnant teenager. [abbr. SE *pregnant*]

prego/preggo *adj.* [1920s+] (Aus.) pregnant (cf. PREG).

preheat the oven, to *phr.* [1990s] of a woman, to masturbate.

preke/preky *n.* [1940s+] (W.I.) **1** a fool, a gullible person. **2** a low-class prostitute. **3** a good-for-nothing, an ill-kempt, dirty, slovenly man. [Sp. *pereque*, an intolerable person]

premie *see* PREEMIE.

premises *n.* [19C] **1** a brothel. **2** the vagina. [euph.]

premium blend *n.* [1990s] an attractive couple enjoying sexual intercourse. [play on 'premium blend' tea, coffee etc; ? ref. to the Nescafé Gold Blend advertising campaign of 1990s, focused on the relationship of two such individuals]

premiums *n.* [20C] (US prison) brandname, commercially produced cigarettes (cf. G n.⁵; GIS n.²).

prems *n.* [late 19C] *prem*ises, buildings. [abbr.]

premune *n.* [mid-17C] a difficulty, a scrape, a predicament. [SE *praemunire*, 'A writ by which the sheriff is charged to summon a person accused, originally, of prosecuting in a foreign court a suit cognizable by the law of England, and later, of asserting or maintaining papal jurisdiction in England, thus denying the ecclesiastical supremacy of the sovereign' (*OED*)]

prendida *see* PREDIDO.

preppie *n.* [1980s] (US campus) one who attends one of the major US 'prep' schools (St Paul's, Choate, Groton, Miss Porter's, Dana Hall etc), the equivalent of UK public (i.e. private) schools. The graduates of such schools are the children of the US establishment and share similar codes, styles, language and society (cf. HOORAY HENRY).

pre-pre *v.* [1960s] (W.I.) to suffer from diarrhoea. [dial. *pre-pre*, to lose control, to become hysterical]

pres *n.*¹ *see* PREXY.

pres/prez *n.*² [1920s+] a *pres*ent, a gift. [abbr.]

presbo *n.* [1960s+] (Aus.) a *Presb*yterian (cf. BAPPO). [abbr. SE + sfx. -O]

presbyteress *n.* [mid-18C–mid-19C] a procuress, a brothel-keeper (cf. ABBESS).

prescott *see* CHARLIE PRESCOTT.

prescription *n.* [1980s+] (drugs) a marijuana cigarette. [? 'just what the doctor ordered']

prescriptions *n.* [1970s+] (drugs) any drug that comes primarily in pill form, barbiturates, amphetamines etc; thus *prescription reds*, Seconal (cf. REDS n.³). [the SE *prescription* that is issued for it]

presenterer *n.* [mid-19C] a prostitute. [she presents herself for trade]

presents *n.* [late 19C+] white spots on one's fingernails, supposedly auguring good luck. [play on synon. SE *gift*]

presh *adj.* [1980s+] (US campus) favourable, enjoyable. [abbr. SE *precious*]

press *n.* [1980s+] (drugs) cocaine, crack cocaine. [ety. unknown]

press and scratch *n.* [19C] a safety-match. [rhy. sl.]

press button *n.* [20C] (Aus.) a Presbyterian (cf. PRESSED BEEF). [joc. mispron.; usu. Catholic use]

pressed *adj.* [1960s+] (US Black) very well dressed. [the state of one's clothes]

pressed beef *n.* [1950s+] a Presbyterian (cf. PRESS BUTTON). [joc. mispron.; usu. Catholic use]

pressed to the max *adj.* [1980s+] very well dressed, very smart. [PRESSED + TO THE MAX]

press ham *v.* [1950s+] (college) to press a bare buttock against a window in order to shock passers-by (cf. MOON v.²).

pressie *n.*¹ [1950s+] (Aus.) a *Presb*yterian. [abbr.]

pressie *n.*² [1970s+] a gift, a *pres*ent (cf. PRES n.²; PREZZIE). [abbr.]

press one's hair, to *phr.* [1960s–70s] (US Black) to straighten one's hair.

press on regardless, to *phr.* [1940s+] (orig. milit.) to persevere irrespective of any problem.

press someone's button, to *phr.* [1960s] to annoy someone, to irritate someone.

press the bricks, to *phr.* [20C] (US) **1** to stand around in the street, loafing and gossiping. **2** to walk the streets in search of work (cf. BEAT THE BRICKS). [SE *press* + BRICKS]

press the button, to *phr.* [1930s+] to set an event or a chain of circumstances in motion.

press the flesh, to *phr.* [1920s+] (orig. US) usu. of a politician on a campaign tour to meet the electors, to shake hands; thus *press-the-flesh*, ingratiating, insincere, oleaginous.

press the panic button, to *phr.* [1960s+] (orig. Aus.) to panic.

pretender to the throne *n.* [1950s–60s] (US gay) **1** a heterosexual who poses as gay for the purposes of avoiding the draft. **2** a vice squad policeman who poses as gay to entrap genuine homosexuals. [pun on SE + THRONE]

pretendica/pretendo *n.* [1980s+] (drugs) (? low quality or fake) marijuana. [Sp.; i.e. it 'pretends' to be good]

preterite *n.* [late 19C] (society) an old person, but esp. a woman. [SE *preterite*, pertaining to former times]

pretties *n.* [1960s+] innocent, hitherto untouched young sex objects, either male or female (cf. CHICKEN n.⁴). [PRETTY n.]

prettify *v.* [mid-19C+] to make pretty, esp. in a 'cheap and cheerful' manner; thus *prettification*, the act of prettifying.

pretty *n.* [1930s+] **1** a pretty woman. **2** (gay) a young, inexperienced homosexual man.

pretty *adj.* **1** [mid-19C+] rather, considerably, e.g. *pretty awful*; *pretty much*. **2** [1980s+] (US campus) a general neg., ridiculous, unpleasant, problematical.

pretty as paint *phr.* [1920s] extremely attractive.

pretty-behaved *adj.* [late 18C+] well-behaved, well-mannered.

pretty-boy *n.* [20C] an effeminate-looking young man, though not necessarily a homosexual.

pretty-boy clip *n.* [late 19C] a hairstyle for men in which the hair is brushed straight forward over the forehead and cut in a straight line from ear to ear.

pretty horse breaker *n.* [mid-19C] a high-class prostitute (cf. LIGHT HORSE). [the way such women showed themselves off in a horse and trap, mixing with society as it too paraded in Hyde Park in London and similar places. Their riding costume was often known as ABANDONED HABITS]

pretty kettle of fish *phr.* [18C+] an awkward state of things, an unsatisfactory situation.

pretty please *phr.* [1950s+] an intensified form of 'please'; thus an exaggerated, even self-abasing, form of request; esp. as *pretty please, with sugar on it*.

pretty police *n.* [20C] a policeman or police squad specializing in the entrapment of gay men.

pretty-spoken *adj.* [early 19C+] well-spoken.

pretty steep *adj.* **1** [mid-19C+] (orig. US) rather expensive. **2** [late 19C] (US) threatening. [PRETTY adj. (1) + STEEP]

pretty up *v.* [1950s+] (Aus.) to disfigure. [ironic reverse of SE]

pretzel *n.* [1930s–40s] (US jazz) a French horn; thus *pretzel bender*, a French horn player. [the shape]

prevert *n.* [1960s+] a pervert. [deliberate mispron. of SE]

previous *n.* [1930s+] previous convictions (cf. FORM n.⁵; JACKET n.²; PEDIGREE; RAP SHEET).

previous *adj.* **1** [late 19C–1900s] (orig. US) arriving or occurring too soon, hasty, premature. **2** [1920s+] (US) usu. of clothing, tight, snug. **3** [1970s+] forward, cheeky; often as *that's a bit previous* (cf. OUT OF ORDER).

previousness *n.* [late 19C] (US) anything seen as coming too soon, too hastily or too prematurely (cf. PREVIOUS adj.).

prexy/prex/pres *n.* [early 19C+] (orig. US college) the *President* (of a college, a corporation or firm and of America). [mispron.]

prey *n.* [late 17C–early 19C] money. [i.e. what one 'preys upon']

prez *n.*¹ (US) **1** [late 19C+] president. **2** [1950s+] (US Black) an important, influential individual. [tenor saxophonist Lester Young (1909–59) was so nicknamed by Billie Holiday]

prez *n.*² *see* PRES n.².

prezzie *n.* [1960s+] (orig. Aus.) a present (cf. PRES n.²; PRESSIE n.²). [abbr.]

price of one *phr.* [20C] (Irish) all one is worth, one's due desserts, one's fate; esp. as *the price of me*.

priceless *adj.* [20C] very amusing, witty, droll.

pricey *see* PRICY.

price of a pint *n.* [late 19C] any sum less than sixpence. [contemporary values]

price of greens *n.* [mid–late 19C] the cost of hiring a prostitute. [GREENS n.²]

price of meat *n.* [19C+] a prostitute's tariff. [MEAT n. (1)]

price of one's hat isn't the measure of one's brain, the *phr.* [19C–1940s] (US Black) one's material possessions have no bearing on one's intelligence and wisdom.

prick *n.* **1** [mid-16C–late 17C] a woman's term of endearment for a man. **2** [late 16C+] the penis (cf. NEEDLE n.¹; WIMBLE). **3** [17C–18C] a pimple, a spot. **4** [1920s+] (orig. US) an idiot, a fool, an incompetent (cf. ARSEHOLE n.; DICKHEAD). [SE *prick*, a pointed weapon or implement. Although the *OED*, with its first citation in 1592, labels it unequivocally as 'coarse slang', E.P. suggests that *prick* was SE before becoming taboo *c.*1700. The *OED*'s citation – 'The pissing Boye lift up his pricke' ('R.D.', *Hypnerotomachia*) – may appear coarse to modern ears, but it should be noted that *piss*, certainly, was still SE at the time. In 1540, *prick* denoted 'a pert, forward, saucy boy or youth; a conceited young fellow', thus (1). The term is defined as 'humorous or contemptuous', but not indecent; it might have referred simply to the lad's 'sharpness'. That said, given that the synon. alongside which it appears is *princock* (lit. 'prime cock'), a sexual interpretation is possible]

prick-chinking *n.* [18C] having sexual intercourse. [PRICK n. (2) + CHINK n.²]

prick-climber *see* POLE-CLIMBER.

prick-ear/-ears *n.* [mid–late 17C] a Roundhead, a Parliamentarian, 'a Crop, whose Ears are longer than his Hair' (B.E.). [the Roundheads and Puritans were typified by their tight-fitting black skullcaps, which sat above the ears]

prick-eared *adj.* [mid-17C–18C] crop-headed. [PRICK-EAR]

prick-ears *see* PRICK-EAR.

prickhead *n.* [20C] a fool, a simpleton (cf. DICKHEAD). [PRICK n. (2) + sfx. -HEAD (1)]

prick-holder/-purse/-scourer/-skinner *n.* [19C] the vagina (cf. CATCH 'EM ALIVE-O). [PRICK n. (2) + SE]

prickish *see* PRICKY.

prick-lick *v.* [1980s+] (US) to perform fellatio. [PRICK n. (2) + SE *lick*]

prick-louse/-the-louse *n.* [early 16C–early 19C] a tailor; thus *prick a louse*, to work as a tailor. [SE *prick*, i.e. the needlework + the lice that accrued to clothing]

pricknic *n.* [1980s+] (US gay) fellatio. [PRICK n. (2) + pun on SE *picnic*]

prick peddler *see* DICK PEDDLER.

prick-pride *n.* [20C] an erect penis. [PRICK n. (2) + SE *pride*]

prick-purse/-scourer/-skinner *see* PRICK-HOLDER.

prick sucker *n.* [late 19C+] one who sucks the penis, whether male or female. [PRICK n. (2) + SE *sucker*]

pricktease *n.* [1950s+] a woman (or man in a homosexual context) who appears to be offering unrestrained sexual favours but stops short of intercourse, leaving the male partner frustrated. [PRICKTEASE v.]

pricktease *v.* [1950s+] to lead on sexually but to stop short of intercourse. [PRICK n. (2) + SE *tease*]

prickteaser *n.* [1950s+] a woman who allows some physical intimacies but who, no matter how daring, will always stop short of intercourse (cf. COCKCHAFER). [PRICKTEASE v.]

prick the belt *n.* [late 16C] a gambling and cheating game, in which a belt is folded and held out to the punter, who bets that by pricking with a pin they can hit the place where the material is folded (cf. FIND THE LADY).

prick the garter/pitch the nob n. [mid-19C] a gambling and cheating game, in which a garter is folded and held out to the punter, who bets that by pricking with a pin they can hit the place where the material is folded; almost inevitably they fail and lose their money (cf. FIND THE LADY; THIMBLE-RIG). [Shakespeare (1564–1616) mentions earlier versions, known as PRICK THE BELT and FAST AND LOOSE]

prick-the-louse see PRICK-LOUSE.

pricky/prickish adj. [1960s+] (US) obnoxious. [PRICK n. (4)]

pricy/pricey adj. [1910s+] (orig. Aus./N.Z.) expensive.

pride and joy n.[1] [1930s–40s] (Aus./US) a boy. [rhy. sl.]

pride and joy n.[2] [1930s–40s] (Aus./US) the penis.

pride-and-pockets n. [late 19C–1910s] a half-pay officer. [lots of pride, empty pockets]

pride of the morning/morning pride n. [late 19C] an early morning erection, more due to the need to urinate than actual sexual desire (cf. PISS-PROUD).

priest n. [1950s+] (US) a celibate. [the status of Roman Catholic clerics]

priest-linked adj. [late 17C–early 19C] married.

priest of the blue bag n. [mid-19C] a barrister. [the traditional colour of the bag in which they carry their gown and wig]

priest's share n. [late 19C–1900s] (Irish) one's soul.

prig/prigg/prigger/prigman n.[1] [16C–19C] (Und.) a thief, esp. a mendicant villain who specializes in stealing clothes from hedgerows where they are left to dry, or poultry from the farmyard (cf. PRAG). **2** [16C–19C] a ne'er-do-well who, accompanied by his woman, wanders the country, mixing villainy and legitimate work, pursuing neither, it appears, with particular enthusiasm (sometimes known as the DRUNKEN TINKER). **3** [late 17C–early 19C] a dandy, a fop. **4** [late 17C–mid-19C] a cheat. [either Lat. pregare, to pray, or SE prig = prick = sting = rob or cheat. SE prig, meaning a carping know-all, may have similar roots, but may be based on the divine Richard Baxter (1615–91), who in 1684 associated it with the initial letters of proud ignorance]

prig n.[2] [late 16C–mid-19C] a horse. [? it is 'pricked' with spurs]

prig v.[1] **1** [mid-16C–19C] (Und.) to steal. **2** [early 18C–1900s] to cheat, to swindle. [? SE prick, to skewer]

prig v.[2] [late 16C–mid-19C] to ride. [SE prick, to urge a horse forward]

prig v.[3] [late 17C–18C] to have sexual intercourse. [PRICK n. (2)]

prig and buzz n. [late 18C] pick-pocketing. [PRIG n.[1] + BUZZ n.[1] (1)]

prig-beard n. [late 16C–early 17C] a degenerate, a seducer (cf. FRIG-BEARD). [PRIG v.[1] + SE beard; BEARD n.[1] (1) is too late, although uncited usage may well have existed]

prigg n.[1] see PRIG n.[1].

prigg n.[2] [1940s–50s] (Aus.) a busybody. [rhy. sl. Wally Prigg = GIG n.[11]]

prigger n.[1] see PRIG n.[1].

prigger n.[2] [17C] **1** a highwayman. **2** a thief; thus priggery, priggism, theft. [PRIG n.[1]]

prigger n.[3] [early 19C] a fornicator, a womanizer. [PRIG v.[3]]

prigger of cacklers/the cacklers n. [late 17C–18C] (Und.) a chicken stealer. [PRIGGER n.[2] (2) + CACKLING-CHEAT]

prigger of prancers/prauncers n. [16C] (Und.) a horse-thief (cf. CANTING CREW). [PRIGGER n.[2] (2) + PRANCER]

prigger of the cacklers see PRIGGER OF CACKLERS.

prigging n.[1] **1** [mid-16C–late 17C] horse-stealing; thus prigging law/lay, horse-stealing as a criminal profession. **2** [late 18C–mid-19C] pilfering, small-time thieving. [PRIG v.[1]]

prigging n.[2] [late 16C–18C] riding. [PRIG v.[2]]

prigging n.[3] [late 16C–18C] having sexual intercourse (cf. RIDE v.[1]). [PRIG v.[3]]

priggish adj. [late 17C–early 18C] thievish. [PRIG n.[1]]

priggling adj. [1930s+] pregnant. [IN PIG + PREGGERS]

prigman see PRIG n.[1].

prig-napper n.[1] [late 17C–early 19C] a thief-taker. [PRIG n.[1] + NAP v.[1] (1)/(2)/(4)]

prig-napper n.[2] [late 17C–18C] (Und.) a horse-thief. [PRIG n.[2] + NAP v.[1] (3)]

prigstar n. [late 17C–18C] **1** a rival in love. **2** a thief. **3** a general pej. (cf. PRIGSTER). [ext. of PRIG n.[1]]

prigster n. **1** [16C–19C] (Und.) a thief. **2** [late 17C–mid-18C] a general pej. **3** [late 17C–mid-18C] a rival in love (cf. PRIGSTAR). [ext. of PRIG n.[1]]

prim n. [late 17C–early 19C] 'a silly, empty, starcht fellow' (B.E.).

prima donna n. [mid-19C] **1** the second rank of superior prostitutes, immediately below that of kept mistresses. **2** one who behaves in a self-important or temperamental manner. [Ital. prima donna, the first or principal female singer in an opera]

prime adj. [mid-17C–late 19C] excellent, first-rate.

prime adv. [19C] sexually excited. [SE primed, prepared, orig. of a gun]

prime cut n. [1970s+] the vagina (cf. BACON SANDWICH). [SE prime cut, a superior cut of meat]

primed adj. [1950s+] **1** prepared, ready. **2** drunk (cf. ABOUT RIGHT adj.[1]). **3** intoxicated by drugs. [SE prime, to prepare a gun for firing; all imply a readiness to 'explode into action']

prime flat n. [early 19C] (Und.) an extremely susceptible person, the ideal victim for a confidence trickster. [PRIME adj. + FLAT n.[2]]

primely adv. [mid-18C–late 19C] excellently, very well.

prime oneself v. [19C] to become drunk.

prime plant n. [mid-19C] (Und.) a potential victim, as assessed by a villain. [PRIME adj. + PLANT v.[1] (4)]

prime someone's/one's pump, to phr. [1950s+] **1** to excite sexually. **2** to masturbate.

prime twig n. [mid-19C] high spirits, good order. [PRIME adj. + TWIG n.[1] (1)]

primitive adj. [late 19C] of a drink, unadulterated, undiluted.

primo n. (drugs) **1** [1970s+] any top quality drug. **2** [1980s+] a marijuana cigarette laced with cocaine and heroin. [the intensified effects]

primo adj. [1960s+] first-rate, excellent; usu. referring to the quality of a drug. [Sp. primo, first]

prinado n. [17C] a card-sharp. [? Sp. prenada, pregnant (as cited in the OED) is hard to justify. E.P. opts for primada, first and thus most skilful, but the feminine '-a' ending makes this link unlikely]

prince n. **1** [1910s+] a general term of approval, an admirable or generous person. **2** [1970s–80s] (US Black) a charismatic man.

Prince Albert n. [1990s] body piercing performed on the penis, usu. a small bolt through the glans. [? Victoria's consort, Prince Albert (1819–61) was pierced]

prince alberts/alfreds see ALBERTS.

prince prig n. [late 17C–early 19C] **1** a leading thief, esp. one who acts as a receiver for the robberies of colleagues. **2** the King of the Gypsies. [SE prince + PRIG n.[1]]

prince's points n. [late 19C] (society) whist played for a shilling a point. [Edward, Prince of Wales (1841–1910), a whist devotee, suggested that the best players were not invariably the richest, and suggested a limit of a shilling per point, thus making it possible for poorer, if more talented players, to join him. The habit became highly fashionable for a while]

princess n.[1] [1960s+] a general form of (affectionate) address to a woman.

princess n.[2] [1960s] **1** a prostitute (cf. PAVEMENT PRINCESS). **2** (gay) an effeminate and relatively youthful male homosexual (cf. QUEEN n.[1]).

princess of the pavement n. [mid-19C] a prostitute (cf. NYMPH OF THE PAVE).

Princeton rub/style/first-year n. [1950s+] (US gay) body-to-body rubbing (cf. COLLEGIATE FUCKING). [a practice attributed to freshmen at Princeton University]

princock/princox n. **1** [16C] a dandified, conceited young man. **2** [late 16C–mid-19C] the vagina. [? SE prime cock (as suggested by John Florio in 1598) or Lat. praecox, early, precocious]

princod n. [late 18C–early 19C] a plump man or woman. [Scot. preencod, a pincushion]

princox see PRINCOCK.

princum-prancum see PRINKUM-PRANKUM.

prink v. [mid-16C–late 19C] to dress up, to spruce oneself up; thus prinked, spruced up, dressed in one's best clothes; prinking, sprucing oneself up. [SE prank, to dress oneself up in a bright or showy manner; ult. Du. pronk, show, finery, ornament]

prinker n. [mid-19C] one who takes infinite care in dressing. [PRINK]

prinkum-prankum/princum-prancum n. [late 16C–early 17C] a trick, a game, a prank. [redup. of SE princome, a prank, ult. SE prank]

printed character n. [mid-19C–1920s] a pawn ticket.

Printing House Square phr. [late 19C] powerful, overpowering, crushing. [Printing House Square, the office of the Times newspaper in its days as 'the Thunderer' and Britain's newspaper of record]

print mittens n. [1960s+] (US Und.) gloves worn to avoid leaving fingerprints.

prior n. [1960s+] a prior conviction, a criminal record; often in pl. priors.

prison wolf n. [1960s+] (Can. prison) a prisoner who prefers women when free, but turns to men when imprisoned. [SE prison + WOLF n.[1]]

prison-yard queen n. [1980s+] (US Und.) a prison homosexual. [SE prison-yard + QUEEN n.[1]]

priss n. [late 19C+] a weakling. [PRISSY adj.]

prissy n. [1940s–60s] (camp gay) a Black homosexual (cf. BUTTERFLY n.[2]). [Prissy, the Black maid in the book/film Gone With The Wind (1936/1939)]

prissy adj. [late 19C+] over-particular, prim, prudish, esp. in a supposedly effeminate way; thus prissy-pants, one who has such a character, esp. when old. [? SE prim + sissy]

prittle-prattle n. [early 18C] idle chatter, gossip. [redup. of SE prattle]

private dick n. [20C] (orig. US) a private detective. [SE private + DICK n.[6] (1)]

privateer n. [late 19C–1910s] an amateur, part-time prostitute. [SE privateer, a volunteer soldier, a guerrilla]

private eye n. [1930s+] (orig. US) a private detective (cf. EYE n.[1]). [the orig. eye was that displayed as a badge of the Pinkerton's National Detective Agency (founded 1852)]

private Idaho n. [1990s] (US campus) one's own little world. [the title of the film My Own Private Idaho (1991)]

private property n. [20C] the genitals (cf. PRIVATES).

privates n. [late 18C+] the male genitals (cf. PRIVATE PROPERTY). [abbr. of euph. SE private parts]

privy paradise n. [19C] the vagina (cf. GENTLEMAN'S PLEASURE-GARDEN).

privy-queen n. [1960s+] (gay) a homosexual who seeks sex in or around public lavatories. [SE privy + QUEEN n.[1]]

prize adj. [20C] absolute, complete, utter. [i.e. worthy of a SE prize]

prize faggots n. [late 19C] large female breasts. [in culinary terms a 'prize' faggot implies a larger than average specimen]

pro n.[1] **1** [mid-19C+] a professional, an expert in a field; esp. as the pro, the professional employed by a golf club. **2** [1930s+] a prostitute (cf. WORKING GIRL). [abbr.; note (2) is abbr. professional woman, not prostitute]

pro n.[2] [1940s–50s] (US) a condom. [abbr. SE prophylactic]

pro v. [1940s–60s] (N.Z.) to take out a prohibition order against a heavy drinker. [abbr.]

prob n. [1990s] (US) a problem. [abbr.]

probably adv. [1980s+] (US campus) probably not.

proboscis n. [mid-17C+] the human nose. [joc. use of SE, coined to describe an elephant's trunk]

process n. [1930s+] (US Black) straightened hair. [the process of straightening]

processed mind n. [1960s] (US Black) a Black mind that appears to prefer seeing things from a White perspective. [fig. use of PROCESS + SE mind]

process-pusher n. [late 19C] a lawyer's clerk. [SE process, a legal writ or SUMMONS; note artists' jargon process-server, a photogravure printer]

Prod n.[1] [1940s+] a Protestant, esp. in Northern Ireland; ext. as Proddywoddy/Proddywhoddy; Proddy dog (cf. TAIG). [abbr.]

prod n.[2] [late 19C+] **1** the penis. **2** the act of sexual intercourse (cf. BASH n.[2]). [SE prod, a pointed implement]

prod v. [late 19C+] usu. of a man, to engage in sexual intercourse (cf. BANG v.[1]). [SE prod, to push at]

Proddo n. [20C] (Aus.) a Protestant. [abbr.; Catholic use]

proddy/proddy dog n. [1950s+] (usu. Anglo-Irish) a Protestant, as used by Roman Catholics (cf. TAIG). [abbr.]

proddyhopper n. [20C] (N.Z.) a derog. term (mainly juv.) for a Protestant.

produce v. [1970s] to produce good results, to 'come up with'.

producer n. [1990s] a summons to produce one's driving licence and car insurance at a police station, following an infringement of traffic laws.

product n. [1970s+] (drugs) a quantity of a drug, usu. as described by a dealer.

prof n. [mid-19C+] (orig. US) a professor. [abbr.]

professional woman n. [1950s+] a euph. term for a prostitute (cf. WORKING GIRL).

professor n. **1** [1900s–30s] (US) a pianist in a bar, cabaret or brothel. **2** anyone considered particularly clever or even educated (cf. TEACH n.). [stereotyped identification of piano-playing with 'long-hair music']

profile v. [1960s+] (US Black/teen) to show off, to act in an exhibitionistic manner; thus profiling for the fans, showing off for an audience.

prog n.[1] [mid-17C–late 19C] (Und.) food, esp. supplies that have been secreted away for later use, e.g. on a journey; thus rum prog, high-quality food. [PROG v.; note Carib.E. prag, to beg for, to forage]

prog n.[2] [1920s; 1970s+] a radio or TV programme, e.g. the J.Y. prog, the Jimmy Young programme. [abbr.]

Prog n.[3] [1960s+] (S.Afr.) a member of the Progressive Party (1959–75) and its successors the Progressive Reform Party (1975–7), Progressive Federal Party (1977–89) and the Democratic Party (from 1989). [abbr.]

prog v. [mid-17C–1900s] to poke about for food or to scavenge; thus on the prog, scavenging. [PROG n.[1]]

progger n. [1900s] (Irish) a scavenger. [PROG v.]

progging n. **1** [17C] foraging. **2** [17C+] begging. [PROG n.[1]]

progging day n. [late 19C] (W.I.) market day. [PROG n.[1]]

program n. [1990s] (orig. US Black) **1** any form of verbal plan or stratagem whereby one can deal with circumstances, one's preferred way of conducting one's life. **2** the established routine of an institution.

program v. [1960s+] (US prison) to follow the prison rules in the hope of gaining time off for good behaviour.

project gold n. [1990s] (US Black) very large gold earrings. [the sort of jewellery preferred by those who live in SAmE *housing projects*]

prole n. [1920s+] a member of the working or underclass; thus *prole*, typical of such individuals. [abbr. SE *proletarian*]

prole v. [late 17C–18C] to wander around in search of seducible women. [SE *prowl*]

prom n. [late 19C+] (US) a dance, usu. at a school or college; thus *prom queen*, the most outstanding young woman at the dance. [abbr. SE *promenade*]

prom date n. [1980s+] (US campus) an unattractive person of the opposite sex. [PROM + DATE n.³; the implication being that no one fashionable or sophisticated would attend such a dance]

prominence n. [19C] an important or prominent person.

promiscuous adj. **1** [mid–late 19C] casual, carelessly irregular. **2** [late 19C] a general descriptive term denoting derision and contempt. [SE *promiscuous*, part of a mixed company]

promiscuously adv. **1** [early 17C] unceremoniously, promptly. **2** [early–mid-19C] casually, incidentally.

promises, promises phr. [1970s+] a sarcastic phr. of dismissal, used when someone else has made what seems an extravagant promise (whether positive or threatening).

promo n. [1960s+] *promo*tion, publicity, public relations etc. [abbr.]

promoss n. [late 19C–1900s] (Aus.) **1** to talk nonsense. **2** to play the fool. [ety. unknown]

promote v. **1** [20C] (US Und./tramp) to survive by theft, begging or persuasion. **2** [1930s–40s] (Aus./US) to borrow, to exploit someone else for one's own advantage.

promoted adj. [late 19C] dead. [coined at the funeral of Mrs Booth, wife of General William Booth (1829–1912), the founder of the Salvation Army]

promoted pimp n. [1970s+] (US Black) **1** a pimp who gives advice to other pimps or to their prostitutes. **2** a method of getting money; i.e. the way a pimp would set about using his brains/mouth to get funds.

promoter n. [late 19C–1910s] a confidence trickster.

prompt one's porpoise, to phr. [20C] to masturbate (cf. ACCOST THE OSCAR MEYER; FIGHT ONE'S TURKEY; GALLOP ONE'S ANTELOPE; LIZARD n.³; POUND THE PELICAN; PUFF THE ONE-EYED DRAGON; PUMP THE MONKEY; PUMP THE PYTHON; SIPHON THE PYTHON; STROKE THE DOG; TAKE ONE'S SNAKE FOR A GALLOP; TEASE ONE'S CRABS; TEASE THE WEASEL; WHACK THE ONE-EYED WORM; WALK THE DOG).

prong/pronger n. [1960s+] **1** penis. **2** an erection.

prong v. [1940s+] **1** to seduce, to have sexual intercourse. **2** (US Black) to enjoy oneself. [PRONG n.]

pronger see PRONG n.

prong-on n. [1960s+] an erection. [PRONG n.]

pronk n. [1950s] a fool, an idiot. [? PRAT n. (6) + PONCE n. + WANK n.]

pronto adv. [20C] immediately, at once. [Sp.]

prop n.¹ **1** [late 18C–late 19C; 1950s–60s] the leg. **2** [late 18C–late 19C] the arm, esp. when extended to strike a blow (cf. PROPS n.¹). **3** [mid-19C] a blow, esp. an upper-cut. [20C use of (1) is US Black]

prop n.² [mid-19C] the gallows. [it 'holds one up']

prop n.³ **1** [mid–late 19C] a gold scarf- or tie-pin. **2** [mid–late 19C] a diamond or other valuable piece of jewellery (cf. PROP-GETTER; PROP-MAN; PROP-NAILER). **3** [20C] a woman's brooch. [Du. *proppe*, a brooch, a skewer]

prop n.⁴ [1950s–60s] (US Und.) a suggestion, made by the police, that one turns informer in return for a lighter sentence or reduction in charges; thus *shoot someone a prop*, to make such a suggestion. [abbr. SE *proposition*]

prop v.¹ [mid–late 19C] to hit, to knock down. [PROP n.¹ (2)]

prop v.² [1940s+] (Aus./N.Z.) to stop, to come to a halt. [PROP n.¹ + SE *prop oneself up*]

propeller head n. [1990s] a fool. [the SAmE *propeller beanie*, a small hat, like a skullcap, with a propeller fixed to the top, worn by children]

proper adj. [19C+] **1** correct, first-rate, often used ironically. **2** a general intensifier, e.g. *a proper idiot*. [SE 14C–17C]

proper adv. [late 19C+] properly, correctly (cf. SPEAK PROPER; TALK PROPER).

proper article n. [1910s+] (N.Z.) exactly what is required, the perfect thing. [PROPER adj. + SE *article*]

proper bit of frock n. [late 19C] an attractive, well-dressed woman. [PROPER adj. + SE *frock*]

proper charlie see RIGHT CHARLIE.

proper crowd n. [1920s+] (Aus.) one's intimates, one's best friends. [PROPER adj. + SE *crowd*]

proper do n. [1910s+] an important celebration, 'with all the trimmings'. [PROPER adj. + DO n.³]

proper little madam see LITTLE MADAM.

properly adv. [late 19C] thoroughly, perfectly, completely, very.

propers n.¹ [late 19C] ? sexual intercourse. ['Meaning refused – but thoroughly comprehended by the coster[monger] classes. Erotic', Ware; ? abbr. of a *proper seeing-to*]

propers n.² see PROPS n.².

prop-getter n. [1900s–30s] **1** a stealer of diamond and other brooches. **2** a pickpocket in general. [PROP n.³]

Prophet n.¹ [late 18C–early 19C] a nickname for the Cock Tavern at Temple Bar. [a crowing cock 'prophesies' the coming dawn]

prophet n.² [mid–late 19C] a racing tipster.

prop-man n. [1930s] (US) a thief specializing in small pieces of personal jewellery (cf. PROP-GETTER; PROP-NAILER). [PROP n.³ + sfx. *-man*]

prop-nailer n. [mid–late 19C] a thief who steal scarf- or tie-pins, brooches and similar small pieces of jewellery. [PROP n.³ + NAIL v. (2)]

proposition cheat n. [20C] a ruthless card-sharp who never gives victims even the slightest chance of winning, but takes 100% of the pots.

props n.¹ **1** [late 18C–19C] the arms. **2** [late 18C–19C] crutches. **3** [1940–70s] (US Black) a woman's legs, esp. if attractive.

props/propers n.² [1980s+] (US Black) **1** any form of support, e.g. weapons, friends, influence. **2** respect, admiration (cf. GIVE PROPS).

prop up v. [1970s] (Und.) **1** to make a proposition. **2** to arrange, to suggest, to fabricate a story. [SE *proposition*]

propvol adj. [1970s+] (S.Afr.) full to bursting. [Afk. *propvol*, stuffed]

pros/pross n. [mid–late 19C] **1** a prostitute. **2** a sponger, a cadger; thus *on the pross*, sponging. [abbr. (1) SE *prostitute*; (2) PROSSER]

prose n. **1** [late 17C–late 19C] a dull, boring person. **2** [early–mid-19C] a chat, a gossip, a talk.

prose v. **1** [late 18C–late 19C] to write or talk in a long-winded, tedious manner. **2** [19C] to gossip, to chat. [PROSE n.]

prospect n. [1950s+] **1** (orig. US) a recruit to an outlaw motorcycle gang before any initiation rites. **2** (gay) a potential client for a street prostitute.

pross n. see PROS.

pross v. [mid–late 19C] to sponge on one's acquaintances, to cadge, usu. drinks or money.

pross about v. [late 19C–1900s] to hang around, to mooch about. [PROSS v.]

prosser n. [mid–late 19C] an idler or sponger. [note the celebrated *Prossers' Avenue* in London's Gaiety Theatre, the theatre bar where the more raffish elements of society were wont to promenade; also the P.G. Wodehouse (1881–1975) character *Oofy Prosser*, lit. 'rich sponger'. The Royal Poinciana Hotel in Palm Beach, Florida, had its 'Hypocrites' Alley', so-called for its population of self-proclaimed teetotallers, on holiday from their northern homes and from their pledge of abstinence]

prossie/prosso/prossy/prozzy n. [1930s+] (orig. Aus.) a *prosti*tute (cf. PROSTIE). [abbr.]

prostie/prosty n. [1930s+] (US) a *prosti*tute (cf. PROSSIE). [abbr.]

Prot n. [early 18C+] a *Prot*estant (cf. PROD n.¹). [abbr.]

protected adj. [1910s+] (Aus./N.Z.) lucky, fortunate. [? the protection is that of the gods]

protection n. [1950s+] (US Black) a condom.

Protestant herring, a n. [mid-19C+] (Irish) **1** a bad, stale herring. **2** any form of stale or unpleasant food. **3** anything second-rate, inferior.

proud adj. [late 17C–19C] sexually aroused, 'delirious of Copulation' (B.E.). [a man's penis, which 'stands erect'; ? underpinned in 19C by SE *proud*, slightly raised or project-ing]

prough/pruck/prugh n. [20C] (Ulster) anything gained for free, a perquisite, esp. when illicitly come by. [Scot. *pruch*, a perquisite; ult. PROG v.]

provender n. [16C–early 19C] (Und.) **1** the victim of highway robbery. **2** the money that is stolen in such a robbery. [SE *provender*, provisions, food]

proverbial adj. [1960s+] archetypal, typical, e.g. *the proverbial lovelorn lad.*

provide one's chump see GET ONE'S CHUMP.

provider n. [1950s+] (gambling) one who habitually loses when playing and thus provides their fellow players with regular wins.

Provie/Provvie n. [1970s+] a member of the *Provi*sional IRA (cf. PROVO). [abbr.]

provincial n. [mid-17C] a procuress, a brothel-keeper (cf. ABBESS). [SE *provincial*, the chief of a religious order in a dis-trict or province]

Provo n. [1970s+] a member of the *Provi*sional IRA (cf. PROVIE). [abbr.]

Provvie see PROVIE.

provvy n. [1950s] an Ap*prov*ed School, used to detain offenders still too young to enter an adult prison. [abbr.]

prowl v. **1** [late 17C–18C] to wander around in search of sedu-cible women (cf. PROLE v.). **2** [1910s+] to inspect the site of a possible robbery before carrying out the robbery. **3** [1930s–40s] (US) to search a person, to frisk someone.

prowl car n. [1930s+] (US) a police car that patrols the streets.

prowler n. [19C] **1** a petty thief. **2** (US) a housebreaker.

prozzy see PROSSIE.

Pru, the n. [1920s+] the *Pru*dential Assurance Company; esp. in phr. *the man from the Pru*, a representative of the company who calls at private houses to collect insurance premiums. [abbr.]

pruck see PROUGH.

prugge n. [17C] a street-walker. [PRIG v.³; despite apparent chronological disparity]

prugh see PROUGH.

prune n.¹ **1** [late 19C] a disagreeable, odd or irritable person. **2** [1940s+] a simpleton, a fool. [note WW2 RAF jargon *P.O.* (Pilot Officer) *Prune*, the personification of stupidity and in-competence. The character was created by Squadron Leader Anthony Armstrong and the artist 'Raff' (L.A.C. W. Hooper) to teach pupils and other flying personnel how things should not be done]

prune n.² [1920s–50s] (US) a Black person's head. [supposed resemblance]

prune adj. [1960s+] of women, unattractive, prudish.

pruneface n. [20C] (US) a plain or miserable-looking person.

prune-juice n.¹ [19C] hard liquor (cf. PRUNO).

prune-juice n.² [1950s–60s] (US) nonsense. [? PRUNE-JUICE n.¹; i.e. its effects on the stomach; thus euph. for BULLSHIT n.]

prune-picker n. [1910s–20s] (US) a Californian. [the preval-ence of the crop]

prune-pusher n. [1950s–60s] (gay) a male homosexual. [his predilection for anal intercourse]

prunes n. [20C] (US) a Black person. [the colour]

prune the fifth limb, to phr. [19C] to masturbate (cf. THIRD LEG).

pruno n. [1960s+] (US prison) illegally distilled liquor. [made from fermented prunes]

prussian guard n. [1940s+] a card. [rhy. sl.]

p.'s n. [1980s+] (US campus) parents. [abbr.]

p.s. n.¹ [1910s–20s] penal servitude. [abbr.]

p.s. n.² [20C] (US Und.) **1** protective *s*egregation. **2** those who seek protective segregation: punks and snivellers (cf. PUNK n.¹).

psalm-singer n. [1910s] (US) an informer, a prison trusty.

psalm-singing muzzler n. [20C] (US Und.) a religious person (cf. JESUS STIFF). [SE *psalm-singing* + MUZZLE n.¹ (1)]

psalm-smiter n. [mid-19C] a non-conformist, a street preacher (cf. BRISKET-BEATER). [their thumping of their text]

p's and q's n. [late 19C–1900s] shoes. [rhy. sl.]

pseud n. [1960s+] a *pseud*o-intellectual; a derog. description, often of quite genuine, if pretentious, intellectuals, who offend their perhaps less academic critics. [abbr.]

pseudie tudie n. [1950s+] an architectural style popular in the UK Home Counties, featuring fake beams and the other appurtenances of (Hollywood-style) Elizabethan and Tudor England. [SE *pseudo* + *Tudor*]

pseudo- pfx. [1980s+] (US campus) phoney, imitation.

psych n. [20C] **1** (US campus) *psych*iatry, as a course. **2** (US) a *psych*iatrist. [abbr.]

psych v. **1** [1920s] to *psych*oanalyse. **2** [1960s+] (orig. US) to manipulate or control another person's mind. [abbr.]

psych!/psyche!/sike! excl. [1970s+] (US campus/teen) fooled you! just kidding! [abbr. PSYCH OUT]

psyched/psyched up adj. [1960s+] (US teen) extremely excited; a more extreme version is *psyched to death* (cf. PSYCH UP). [SE *psychology*, i.e. psychologically prepared]

psychedelic to the bone phr. [1970s+] (US Black drugs) extremely intoxicated by a drug, but not necessarily an hallucinogen. [fig. use of SE *psychedelic* + TO THE BONE]

psyched up see PSYCHED.

psych-jockey n. [1950s+] (US) one who hosts a radio/TV programme or phone-in on emotional and sexual problems. [SE *psychology/psychiatry* + JOCKEY n.² (2)]

psycho n. (orig. US) **1** [1920s] *psycho*analysis. **2** [1940s+] a *psycho*path. **3** [1940s+] a strange or eccentric person. [abbr.]

psycho adj. [1980s+] (US teen) weird, eccentric, bizarre. [abbr. SE *psychotic*]

psycho v. [1930s–40s] (Aus.) **1** to work out a person's inten-tions. **2** to examine someone as to their general state of mind. [SE *psychoanalyse*]

psychobabble n. [1970s+] (orig. US) the jargon of the New Age and the New Therapy, esp. when used by lay people to aggrandize (discussions of) their own condition. [coined by R.D. Rosen in his book *Psychobabble* (1977)]

psycho hose beast n. [1980s] (US campus/teen) a very attractive, sexy, hopefully promiscuous girl. [PSYCHO adj. + HOSE n.² + SE *beast*]

psychological adj. [1950s] mentally disturbed or defective.

psych out v. [1970s+] **1** to astonish, to amaze. **2** to frighten or at least perturb someone else by playing on their inner fear (cf. PSYCH!) **3** to lose emotional control. [SE *psychologize*]

psych up v. [1960s+] to put oneself or another person into a confident, aggressive etc frame of mind as preparation for dealing with a situation. [SE *psychologize*]

p.t. n. [1950s+] (orig. US) **1** a woman (or man in a homosexual context) who appears to be offering unrestrained sexual favours but stops short of intercourse, leaving the male partner frustrated. **2** an attractive, desirable woman. [abbr. PRICKTEASE n.]

p.t.a. phr. [1970s+] (US Black) *pussy, tits and armpits*, all of which allegedly smell.

P-town n. [1970s+] (US) *P*hiladelphia. [abbr.]

p.u.! excl. [20C] an excl. expressing impatience, contemptuous distaste or disregard. [SE *poo!*]

pub n. [mid-19C+] a *pub*lic house. [abbr.]

pub-crawl n. [late 19C+] a gradual progress from public house to public house, with the participants becoming gradually more drunk as they go along (cf. BEER-CRAWL; GIN-CRAWL). [PUB + SE *crawl*]

pubehead n. [1980s+] (US teen) a person with short, curly hair. [PUBES + SE *head*]

pubes n. [1950s+] the *pub*ic hair. [abbr.; orig. SE but colloq. by 20C]

pubickers n. [1990s] (Irish) the pubic hair.

pub it v. [late 19C+] to frequent a public house. [PUB]

public n. **1** [early 18C+] a *public* house. **2** [1950s+] a *public* bar. [abbr.]

Publican, the n. [late 19C] General William Booth, founder of the Salvation Army. [in 1883 Booth (1829–1912) purchased two former public houses, the Grecian Theatre and the Tavern in the City Road]

public convenience n. [20C] a prostitute. [pun]

public ledger n. [late 18C–early 19C] a prostitute. ['Like that paper, she is open to all parties' (Grose 1796). The newspaper *The Public Ledger* was founded in 1760]

public man n. [19C] a bankrupt. [? the publication of his name in the newspapers]

public patterer n. [mid-19C] a confidence trickster who poses as a dissenting preacher, thus attracting a crowd who can be robbed by the 'preacher's' confederates. [SE *public* + PATTERER]

published adj. [1990s] (US campus) very ugly. [play on BOOKED adj.²]

pub pet n. [1980s+] (N.Z.) a two-litre plastic beer flagon or the beer it contains.

pub-stiff n. [1940s] (N.Z.) a look-out or sentinel acting on behalf of a licensee selling alcoholic drinks after the legal closing time. [PUB + STIFF n.⁴]

puck n.¹ [1970s+] a sudden commotion, a disturbance (cf. PLAY PUCK). [Irish *poc*, a short, sudden blow, esp. of a hurling ball]

puck n.² [1970s+] (US campus) anyone deemed socially unacceptable. [? PUCKEY or euph. for FUCK n.⁵]

puck-chaser/-pusher n. [late 19C+] (orig. US) an ice-hockey player. [also Can. 1920s+]

pucker n. [mid-18C+] a state of fear or excitement, a fuss, a panic. [ext. of SE use; 19C+ use is Irish/US]

pucker v. [mid–late 19C] to speak incomprehensibly. [SE *pucker*, to draw the lips tightly together]

pucker-assed adj. [20C] (US) timid, fearful. [fig. use of SE *pucker* + sfx. -ASSED]

puckeroo/pukaroo adj. [mid-19C+] (N.Z.) useless, broken; thus *to puckeroo*, to ruin. [Maori *pakaru*, broken]

puckerow/pukkaroo v. [mid–late 19C] (Anglo-Ind.) to seize. [imper. of Hind. *pakro*, to seize]

pucker up v. [mid-19C] to get into a bad temper, to become tense. [orig. facial expression]

pucker-water n. [late 18C–early 19C] water mixed with alum or a similar astringent, used to tighten the vaginal muscles by those who wish to counterfeit virginity.

puckey/pucky n. [1950s+] excrement. [? similarity to SE *puck*, a disk of hard rubber, used in hockey or POO n.¹]

puck-pusher see PUCK-CHASER.

pucky see PUCKEY.

pud n.¹ [1910s+] a *pud*ding. [abbr.]

pud n.² [1930s+] (US teen/campus) **1** the penis. **2** a fool, an idiot (cf. DICKHEAD). [abbr. PUDDING n.¹ (2)]

pud n.³ [1930s+] (US teen/campus) an easy job, an easy course at college; thus *pud course*, an easy course. [abbr. PUDDING n.²]

pud v. [mid–late 19C] to greet affectionately. [SE *pud*, a child's hand; ult. SE *pad*]

pudden v.¹ [late 17C+] to treat to or supply with pudding.

pudden v.² [mid-19C] to drug a dog in order to silence it during the carrying out of a burglary. [PUDDING n.¹ (5)]

pudding n.¹ **1** [late 17C+] sexual intercourse. **2** [late 17C+] the penis (cf. PUD n.²; PULL ONE'S PUD). **3** [late 17C+] semen. **4** [18C] the stomach (cf. PUDDING-HOUSE). **5** [19C] meat, usu. liver, that has been impregnated with drugs or poison, used by a thief to silence a house dog (cf. PUDDEN v.²). **6** [1930s+] an unborn child, a foetus (cf. HAVE A BUN IN THE OVEN; IN THE PUDDING CLUB; PUDDING IN THE OVEN). [SE *pudding*, guts, entrails]

pudding n.² [late 19C+] (US) anything easily accomplished (cf. PUD n.³). [PIE n.²]

pudding about the heels phr. [late 19C–1900s] having thick ankles.

pudding and gravy n. [1940s+] the Royal Navy. [rhy. sl.]

pudding-belly n. [late 18C–1900s] a fat person; thus *pudding-bellied*, fat-stomached.

pudding club n. [20C] the state of pregnancy, usu. in phrs. e.g. *put in the pudding club* (cf. IN THE PUDDING CLUB).

pudding-head n. [late 18C+] a fool, a simpleton. [SE *pudding* + sfx. -HEAD (1)]

pudding-house n. [late 16C+] the stomach.

pudding in the oven phr. [1940s+] pregnant (cf. HAVE A BUN IN THE OVEN). [PUDDING n.¹ (6)]

pudding-ken n. [19C] a cook-shop (cf. PUDDING-SNAMMER). [SE *pudding* + KEN n.¹]

puddings and pies n. [mid-19C] the eyes. [rhy. sl.]

pudding-sleeves n. [late 18C–early 19C] a parson (cf. MR PRUNELLA). [the voluminous sleeves of their vestments]

pudding-snammer/snammer n. **1** [19C–1900s] a cook-shop (cf. PUDDING-KEN). **2** [mid-19C] one who robs a cook-shop. [SE *pudding* + SNAM]

puddle n.¹ [late 19C–1910s] the vagina (cf. DAMP n.). [its dampness when excited]

puddle n.² [late 19C+] a mess, a muddle. [SE in 16C–17C]

puddle n.³ **1** [late 19C+] the sea, esp. the Atlantic Ocean; thus *this/the other side of the puddle*, the UK or the US (cf. BIG DITCH; POND). **2** [1960s+] a small pool of urine; thus *make a puddle*, of a child or animal, to urinate.

puddle n.⁴ [1980s+] (drugs) a large dose of liquid LSD.

puddled adj. [1930s] eccentric, insane. [PUDDLE n.²]

puddlejumper n. (US) **1** [1930s] a buggy. **2** [1940s+] any form of small, speedy transport, e.g. a fast small car, a light aeroplane or lightweight truck (cf. CANDY WAGON).

pudenany see PUNAANY.

puderhead n. [1980s+] (US campus) a disappointment, a person who fails to come up to one's expectations. [? PUD n.² + SE *head*]

pudge n. [early 19C] a short squat person, occasionally a thing (cf. PODGE n.). [orig. dial.]

pudpuller n. [1950s+] (US) a masturbator. [PUD n.² (1) + SE *puller*]

pudsey/pudsy n. **1** [17C] the hand. **2** [late 18C+] (teen) a foot. **3** [late 18C+] a term of affection for a child. [? Du. *poot*, a paw]

pud wrestling n. [1950s+] (US) masturbation. [PUD n.² (1) + SE *wrestling*]

Puerto Rican Pendleton n. [1960s] (US) an old work shirt. [derog. ref. to the poverty of Puerto Rican labourers, for whom an expensive Pendleton shirt would be an impossible dream]

puff n.¹ [early-mid-18C] a house player in a gambling house, one who decoys victims into a crooked game. [SE *puff*, to praise to excess and for one's own interest]

puff n.² **1** [early-mid-19C] wind, breath. **2** [1920s+] life, esp. as in *my puff, on my puff*. [SE *puff*, breath, thus breath of life]

puff n.³ [20C] a male homosexual. [var. on POOF n.]

puff n.⁴ (drugs) **1** [1940s-50s] an opium user. **2** [1980s+] cannabis. [SE *puff*, an emission of smoke]

puff v.¹ [late 19C+] to break wind. [SE *puff*, to discharge a puff of air]

puff v.² [1980s+] (drugs) to smoke cannabis. [PUFF n.⁴ (2)]

puff and dart n. [late 19C-1930s] a start; thus *make a puff and dart*, to begin, to make a start. [rhy. sl.]

puff and drag n. [20C] a cigarette. [rhy. sl. *puff and drag* = FAG n.⁴]

puff artist n. [20C] (US) one who flatters or praises insincerely, esp. in the commercial world. [SE *puff*, to praise excessively + ARTIST n.²]

puffed air n. [1940s] (US Black) no food; thus *I'm eating puffed air*, I'm hungry. [play on the cereal *Puffed Wheat*]

puffer n. (drugs) **1** [1970s+] an opium smoker. **2** [1980s+] a smoker of crack cocaine. [SE *puff*, to smoke tobacco]

puff guts n. [late 18C-1900s] a fat man. [SE *puff*, a swelling + *guts*]

puffless adj. [late 19C] out of breath. [SE *puff*, breath]

puff lye v. [1990s] (US Black drugs) to smoke marijuana. [ety. unknown; ? SE *puff* + LA n.]

puffoon see BAFOON.

puff-puff n. [late 19C+] (juv.) a steam engine.

puff the dragon/magic dragon, to phr. [1960s-70s] (drugs) to smoke marijuana. [play on the song title *Puff, the Magic Dragon* (1963)]

puff the one-eyed dragon, to phr. [1960s+] to masturbate (cf. ONE-EYED TROUSER-SNAKE; PROMPT ONE'S PORPOISE). [play on the song title *Puff, the Magic Dragon* (1963)]

puffy n. [1980s] (drugs) phencyclidine (cf. ACE n.³). [one 'puffs' it]

puffy adj. [20C] (US) adulatory. [SE *puff*, to extol]

pug n.¹ [late 16C-early 17C] a bargee; thus *western pugs*, those who navigate barges down the Thames to London. [? SE *pug*, to pull, to tug]

pug n.² **1** [mid-16C-early 17C] a pet name for an animal, usu. a dog or monkey; and also for a person, usu. a woman or child. **2** [19C] a fox. [? SE *pug*, a demon, an imp]

pug n.³ [late 16C-early 18C] **1** a prostitute or courtesan. **2** an unpleasant woman, esp. one who is regarded as sexually immoral (cf. PUGNASTY). [PUNK n.¹; but note PUG n.² (1)]

pug n.⁴ [mid-19C+] **1** a prize-fighter, a boxer, esp. one who relies more on savagery than skill. **2** a thug, a hoodlum. [abbr. SE *pugilist*]

pug n.⁵ [mid-late 19C] an upper servant in a great house; thus *pug's hole/parlour*, the housekeeper's room in such a house. [fig. use of PUG n.² (1), i.e. their role as the master's 'pet']

pug n.⁶ [20C] (US Black) a homosexual. [? PUNK n.¹]

pug n.⁷ [1900s-40s] (Aus.) a lift on a horse (cf. DINK n.⁴).

pug v.¹ [20C] to hide, to secrete. [? Northants. dial. *pug*, to crush]

pug v.² [1930s-40s] (US) to fight as a professional boxer. [PUG n.⁴]

pug drink n. [late 18C-early 19C] watered-down cider. [dial. *pug*, the pulp of apples that have been pressed for cider, presumably used in its making]

puggard n. [early 17C] (Und.) a thief. [SE *pug*, to pull, to tug, thus to steal from + sfx. -*ard*]

puggle see POGGLE.

puggle pawnee see POGGLE PAWNEE.

puggly see POGGLE.

puggy n.¹ **1** [late 17C-early 18C] a term of affection used to women or children. **2** [mid-19C] (Scot.) a monkey. **3** [mid-19C] a fox. [PUG n.²]

puggy n.² [mid-19C+] a hoodlum. [PUG n.⁴]

puggy-drunk adj. [late 19C+] very drunk. [? POGY/POGGLE + pun on PUG n.² (2, thus on FOXED]

pugified adj. [late 18C-mid-19C] snub-nosed. [PUG n.² (2)]

pug-nancy n. [early 18C] a prostitute. [PUG n.³ (1) + SE *nasty* or variation on PUGNASTY]

pugnasty n. [late 17C-18C] an unpleasant woman, esp. one who is cast as sexually immoral. [PUG n.³ (2) + SE *nasty*]

puja see POOJA.

pukaroo see PUCKEROO.

puke n.¹ [mid-19C+] (US) **1** an obnoxious person or thing, a pest. **2** a college freshman. **3** a person from Missouri. [apparently but not definitely linked to late 17C+ SE *puke*, vomit (ety. unknown), although it may be an abbr. of unrecorded *spuke*. This would lead logically to the Indo-European root *spu-, speu-*, which certainly lies behind OE and OHG *spiwan*, to spew, spit, and Lat. *spuere*. An alternative ety. is at PUKE n.²]

puke n.² [late 19C+] (Ulster) a supercilious person, a picky eater, an unhealthy-looking, poor person. [Irish *pioc*, to pick at food]

pukey see PUKY.

puke-in n. [1960s] a meeting or public occasion at which participants express their strong, usu. antagonistic, feelings about a topic. [SE *puke* + model of BE-IN]

pukka adj. [late 18C+] genuine, correct, honest. [Hind. *pakka*, substantial]

pukkaroo see PUCKEROW.

puku n. [20C] (N.Z.) the stomach. [Maori]

puky/pukey adj. [1960s+] disgusting, 'sick-making'. [SE *puke*, to vomit]

pulboron see POLBORON.

pull n.¹ **1** [early 19C] an ulterior motive, a hidden agenda. **2** [early 19C+] influence, advantage (cf. CLOUT n.⁵). **3** [mid-19C] a trick, a fraud, a knack. **4** [late 19C] an anxious or worrying moment that 'tugs at one's heartstrings'.

pull n.² **1** [1950s+] an arrest (cf. TUG n.⁴). **2** [1960s+] an object of sexual conquest, one who can be seduced. [PULL v.¹ (2), (3)]

pull v.¹ **1** [early-mid-19C] to pilfer, to steal. **2** [early 19C+] to arrest, to stop and search on the street. **3** [1960s+] to pick up for sexual purposes, to seduce.

pull v.² **1** [20C] to act in a way that is calculated to shock, amuse or, deceive, e.g. *pull a gag, pull some dirty stuff, pull a stunt* (cf. PULL A FAST ONE). **2** [1920s+] (orig. US) used with a proper name to mean imitate, act in the manner of, esp. when the proper name is almost synon. with a certain type of extreme or easily identifiable behaviour, e.g. *pull a Daniel Boone*, to act drunkenly; *pull a Lindbergh*, to act in a heroic manner.

pull v.³ **1** [20C] (US campus) to earn a grade in an examination. **2** [1930s] to earn a wage (cf. PULL DOWN).

pull v.⁴ [1950s] (US) to leave, to go away. [SE *pull out*, to leave]

pull a boner/bone, to phr. [1910s+] (US) to make a mistake, to blunder. [PULL v.² (1) + BONER n.²]

pull a book, to phr. [1960s] (US campus) to study hard.

pull about v. **1** [19C] esp. of a man abusing or harassing a woman, to handle roughly or unceremoniously. **2** [early–mid-19C] to masturbate.

pull a cluck, to phr. [late 19C–1910s] to die. [PULL v.² (1) + SE *cluck*, a guttural sound; ? the death-rattle]

pull a clue out of the clue bag! phr. [1980s+] (US campus) use your brains! act sensibly! think about it!

pull a croak see DO A CROAK.

pull a disappearing act, to phr. [1950s+] (US) of a spouse or lover, to run off without warning and without leaving any message. [PULL v.² (1)]

pull/do a fade out, to phr. [1910s–60s] (US) to vanish, to escape, to depart. [PULL v.² (1) + FADE OUT]

pull a fast one/a line, to phr. [1920s+] **1** (milit.) to malinger. **2** to get away with something, usu. a slightly nefarious scheme (cf. BIT SWIFT).

pull a Ferris Bueller, to phr. [1980s+] (US campus) to cut class, to take time away from studies. [PULL v.² (2) + film *Ferris Bueller's Day Off* (1986)]

pull a gag, to phr. [1920s+] (US) to play a trick (cf. PULL A TRICK). [PULL v.² (1) + GAG n.]

pull/do a Hank Snow, to phr. [1960s+] (US) to leave, to move on. [PULL v.² (2)/SE *do* + song 'I'm Moving On' by Country and Western star *Hank Snow* (b.1914)]

pull/do a Houdini, to phr. [20C] (US) to escape, to vanish suddenly. [PULL v.² (2)/SE *do* + escapologist Harry *Houdini* (1874–1926)]

pull a house over one's head see PULL AN OLD HOUSE ON ONE'S HEAD.

pull a jap, to phr. [1940s+] (US) to take by surprise, to ambush. [PULL v.² (2) + JAP n.²; stereotype Japanese duplicity]

pull a job, to phr. [1910s+] (orig. US) to carry out a robbery or other criminal act. [PULL v.² (1) + JOB n.³]

pull a johnson, to phr. [1990s] (US teen) to execute a U-turn in the middle of the street, usu. as a last-minute decision. It is illegal in most states. [PULL v.² (1) + the shape of the 'J' in Johnson]

pull a jones, to phr. [1990s] (US teen) constantly to scrounge from one's friends; thus *Mr/Mrs Jones*, one who scrounges constantly. [PULL v.² (1) + generic *Jones*]

pull a kite, to phr. [late 19C] to make a face, to grimace. [? dial. *kite-nipped*, suffering from stomach cramps]

pull a line see PULL A FAST ONE.

pull a longbow see DRAW A LONGBOW.

pull a long face, to phr. [early 19C+] to look miserable, serious or worried.

pull a McGuyver, to phr. [1990s] (US campus) to do something mechanically very clever. [PULL v.² (2) + 1980s TV detective show *McGuyver*]

pull an act, to phr. [1930s+] to put on a show with the intention of deceiving or defrauding someone. [PULL v.² (1) + SE *act*]

pull an all-nighter, to phr. [1980s+] (US campus) to stay up all night working. [PULL v.² (1) + ALL-NIGHTER n. (4)]

pull an el-foldo, to phr. [1950s+] (US) to collapse, to give in. [FOLD v.¹]

pull an old house on one's head/a house over one's head, to phr. [early 17C–mid-19C] to get oneself into trouble (cf. BRING AN OLD HOUSE ON ONE'S HOUSE).

pull a number, to phr. [1970s+] (orig. US) to trick, to deceive (cf. DO A NUMBER). [NUMBER n.³]

pull a pee-wee, to phr. [1990s] (US teen) to make a fool of oneself or say something stupid. [PULL v.² (2) + the entertainer *Pee-Wee* Herman (b.1952), who poses as a foolish, child-like figure]

pull a pop, to phr. [late 19C] (US) to fire a gun. [PULL v.² (1) + SE *pop*, the sound of a gunshot]

pull a punk one, to phr. [1910s] (US) to tell a bad (unfunny/ dirty) joke. [PULL v.² (1) + PUNK adj.]

pull a quick park, to phr. [1970s+] (US Black) to make a quick pick-up of a sexual partner. [PULL v.² (1) + PARK v.¹]

pull a rabbit, to phr. [1960s] to perform an abortion.

pull a Rommel, to phr. [1940s] (US Black) to turn back, to reverse direction (physically or fig.). [the about-turn made by Nazi General Erwin *Rommel* (1891–1944) as he began to face defeat in the North African desert]

pull a Ronnie, to phr. [1980s] (US campus) to do something stupid. [PULL v.² (2) + a negative view of the intelligence of former US president *Ronald* Reagan (b.1911)]

pull a Rudolph Hess, to phr. [1940s] (US Black) to vanish. [PULL v.² (2) + *Rudolph Hess* (1894–1987), Hitler's one-time secretary, who flew to Britain in 1941, apparently on a peace mission, and spent the remainder of his life in prison]

pull a stroke, to phr. [1960s+] to attempt and/or get away with anything outrageous or daring. [PULL v.² (1) + SE *stroke*. *Stroke* may be used here in the sense of 'a vigorous attempt to gain or do something'. A suggested link with rowing strokes seems implausible]

pull a train, to phr. [1940s+] **1** to be the victim of a gangrape. **2** to participate in a gangrape. **3** of a woman, to have sex voluntarily with a number of partners in quick succession. [the woman is the 'engine', her assailants/partners are the 'rolling-stock']

pull a trick, to phr. [1930s+] to play a trick (cf. PULL A GAG). [PULL v.² (1) + SE *trick*]

pull a will, to phr. [1980s+] (drugs) to vomit after excessive drug consumption. [ety. unknown; ? proper name *William*, thus orig. anecdotal]

pull-back n. [mid-19C] a check, something that acts to hinder one's efforts.

pull bacon v. [mid-19C+] to thumb one's nose. [SE *pull* + (LONG) BACON]

pull bull v. [20C] (W.I.) to run an illegal, unlicensed taxi service, to use one's own car as an unlicensed taxi. [fig. use of BULL n.¹²; i.e. their illicit service is 'nonsense']

pull caps v. [mid-18C] of women, to fight, to squabble, esp. over a man. [they tear at each other's headgear]

pull-down n. [late 19C] a style of moustache with long extensions to the sides that became fashionable c.1870–90. [one pulls on its ends]

pull down v. [1910s+] to earn money, e.g. *I pulled down £500*.

pull down someone's ear, to phr. [late 19C] to extract money from someone.

pull down the blind! excl. [late 19C] an excl. used to an overly amorous couple whose activities are embarrassing those around them.

pull down the shutter n. [late 19C] butter. [rhy. sl.]

pull down the shutters, to phr. [mid-19C–1900s] to become bankrupt. [one's last act before abandoning one's business]

pull down your basque! excl. [late 19C] (US) an excl. used to a young woman seen as acting with less than proper decorum, behave yourself! [SE *basque*, a corset-like garment]

pull down your vest! excl. [late 19C] (US) an excl. used to a young man, behave yourself! [US *vest*, waistcoat]

pull dude n. [1980s+] (US Black) an informer. [PULL v.¹ (2) + DUDE n.]

pulled/pulled up adv. [mid-19C] arrested and taken before a magistrate. [PULL v.¹ (2)]

pulled in *adv.* [mid-19C+] arrested. [PULL v.[1] (2)]

pulled up *see* PULLED.

puller *n.*[1] [1930s] (US) a smuggler. [they 'pull in' contraband]

puller *n.*[2] [1950s] (US drugs) a marijuana smoker. [SE *pull*, to puff on a pipe or cigarette]

puller-in *n.* [mid-19C–1900s] (US) an employee of a saloon or similar place of recreation and entertainment whose task is to lure passers-by in from the street (cf. CHUCKER-OUT).

pullers *n.* [1980s+] (drugs) users of crack cocaine who pull at parts of their bodies excessively.

pullet *n.* [16C] (Und.) a young woman who accompanies a RUFFLER, i.e. a vagrant posing as a discharged soldier as a disguise for robbery.

pullet-squeezer *n.* [mid–late 19C] a woman who prefers younger partners.

pulley *n.* [mid-19C] a thief's accomplice, usu. a female one. [Fr. *poulet*, chicken]

pulleys *n.* [1940s] (US Black) suspenders, braces.

pull foot *v.* [late 18C+] (US/W.I.) to run away. [W.I. only after 1920s]

pull for *v.* [20C] to support, to back up.

pull-guts *n.* [early 18C] a fishmonger. [their 'evisceration' of the fish]

pull hemp *v.* [mid-19C–1950s] (US) **1** to be hanged (cf. STRETCH HEMP). **2** to kill oneself by hanging. [the *hemp* used to make the noose]

pull in *v.* [early 19C+] (orig. Und.) to arrest. [PULL v.[1] (2)]

pulling party *n.* [1970s] (US) group masturbation (cf. CIRCLE JERK). [PULL (ONE'S PUD) + SE *party*]

pull in one's ear, to *phr.* [1910s–30s] (US) to mind one's own business.

pull in one's ears, to *phr.* [20C] (US) to act cautiously, to minimize one's aggression. [var. on SE phr. *pull in one's horns*]

pull in one's neck, to *phr.* [1920s+] (US) to mind one's own business. [the image of a tortoise]

pull in the pieces, to *phr.* [mid-19C–1920s] to make a good wage (cf. PULL DOWN). [the *pieces* are pieces of money]

pull it *v.* [early 19C] to run off as fast as one can.

pull no punches, to *phr.* [1930s+] to speak or act openly, candidly. [boxing imagery]

pull off *v.*[1] [late 19C] (US) to steal. [PULL v.[1] (1)]

pull off *v.*[2] [late 19C+] to achieve, to succeed. [sporting imagery]

pull off *v.*[3] [1960s+] to masturbate, oneself or another person (cf. BEAT OFF).

pull on *v.*[1] [20C] (Aus.) to marry a woman.

pull on *v.*[2] **1** [1920s+] (Aus.) to deal with, to test, to tackle. **2** [20C] (Can./US) to adopt something as an excuse. [the image of trying on a garment]

pull oneself over *v.* [late 19C] to eat.

pull/take one's finger out/remove one's digit, to *phr.* [1940s+] (orig. Aus.) to get on with something, to stop malingering and commit oneself to positive action; esp. as command *pull your finger out.* [it is withdrawn, presumably, from the anus]

pull one's freight, to *phr.* [1900s–20s] (US) to rush off, to leave in a hurry.

pull one's joint, to *phr.* [1930s+] **1** to masturbate (cf. ACCOST THE OSCAR MEYER). **2** to whine, to complain. [JOINT n.[5] (1)]

pull one's load, to *phr.* [late 19C+] (Can.) to make one's best effort.

pull one's plonker, to *phr.* [1910s+] to masturbate. [PLONKER n. (2)]

pull one's pocket, to *phr.* [20C] (W.I.) to pay with difficulty. [one must pull out the pocket's lining to find the necessary coins]

pull one's pud/pudding, to *phr.* [1920s+] (orig. US) to masturbate. [PUDDING n.[1] (2)]

pull one's punches, to *phr.* [1930s+] to restrain oneself, esp. in conversation or speech. [boxing imagery]

pull one's socks up/pull up one's socks, to *phr.* [late 19C+] to make greater efforts, to improve one's performance.

pull one's/the stops out, to *phr.* [1950s+] to make a real effort. [the stops are those of an organ]

pull one's weight, to *phr.* [late 19C+] to take one's fair share of a job of work, manual or otherwise. [rowing imagery]

pull one's wire, to *phr.* [1970s+] to masturbate.

pull on peter, to *phr.* [late 19C+] to masturbate. [PETER n.[4]]

pullout *n.* [1990s] (Black) any item that can be stolen and carried away, e.g. car stereos, jewellery, computer games etc. [one pulls it out of the car, house etc]

pull out *v.* [mid-19C] **1** to extend oneself, to make a great effort. **2** to exaggerate.

pull out, the dogs are pissing on your swag *phr.* [1970s] (Aus.) a phr. used to advise someone who finds themselves in a no-win position that the only sensible course of action is retreat.

pull over the coals *see* HAUL OVER THE COALS.

pull rank/stripes *v.*[1] [20C] (orig. US) to use one's status within a hierarchy to impose one's will on one's inferiors, irrespective of the justice of one's position. [milit. *rank* or the *stripes* that go with rank]

pull rank *v.*[2] [20C] to masturbate. [rhy. sl. *pull rank* = WANK v.]

pull shit *v.* [1990s] (US Black) to do something devious, underhand, treacherous. [PULL v.[2] (1) + SHIT n.[4]]

pull shoe strings, to *phr.* [1930s–40s] (US Black) to exert influence, esp. surreptitiously. [ext. of PULL STRINGS]

pull someone's card, to *phr.* [1980s+] to attack, to beat up, to kill.

pull someone's chain, to *phr.* [1920s+] to annoy someone, to agitate.

pull someone's coat, to *phr.* **1** [20C] (orig. US Black) to draw attention, to point out, to nag. **2** [1940s+] to arrest (cf. FEEL SOMEONE'S COLLAR).

pull someone's cock, to *phr.* [1930s] (US) to tease, to deceive, to hoax (cf. PULL SOMEONE'S LEG; PULL SOMEONE'S PISSER; PULL SOMEONE'S TIT). [SE *pull* + COCK n.[2] (1)]

pull someone's cover/covers, to *phr.* [1950s–70s] (US Black) to reveal some hidden characteristic or activities, usu. in another in but occas. in oneself; also as *blow someone's cover.* [the image of pulling back the bedclothes]

pull someone's jacket, to *phr.* [1950s+] to arrest (cf. FEEL SOMEONE'S COLLAR).

pull someone's/give someone the leg, to *phr.* **1** [early 19C+] to tease (cf. PULL SOMEONE'S COCK). **2** [late 19C] (US campus) to curry favour with, to act the toady. **3** [late 19C+] (US) to ask for a loan of money.

pull someone's pisser, to *phr.* [1960s+] to tease (cf. PULL SOMEONE'S COCK). [PISSER n.[1] (2)]

pull someone's tit, to *phr.* [1910s+] (Aus.) to tease (cf. PULL SOMEONE'S COCK). [SE *pull* + TIT n.[1] (1)]

pull something out of one's ass, to *phr.* [1970s+] (US) to invent or produce something, apparently 'by magic'. [ARSE n.[1] (1)]

pull something out of the bag, to *phr.* [1920s+] to come up with something special or surprising, something held in reserve.

pull strings *v.* [20C] to exert influence, esp. behind the scenes (cf. PULL SHOE STRINGS; PULL THE STRING phr.[1]; PULL WIRES). [puppet imagery]

pull stripes *see* PULL RANK v.[1].

pull the ... act *see* DO THE ... ACT.

pull the bacon, to *phr.* [1990s] of a man, to have sexual intercourse. [PULL v.¹ (3) + BACON n.¹]

pull the bung out, to *phr.* [1900s] (US) to deflate someone's ego.

pull the chain, to *phr.*¹ [20C] (US) to masturbate.

pull the chain, to *phr.*² [1930s+] (orig. US) to bring to a conclusion, to make a decisive move to end a period of uncertainty.

pull the chain! *excl.* [1920s] (US) shut up! stop talking (rubbish)!

pull the chain on, to *phr.* [20C] (US) to murder, to kill.

pull the coat, to *phr.* [1970s] (Aus.) to make little effort. [the image is of being held back by a hand pulling one's coat]

pull the cord, to *phr.* [late 19C] (Anglo-Irish) to court. [? the cord of one's 'heart-strings']

pull the cork, to *phr.* [1930s] (US) to get busy, to hurry up.

pull the covers off, to *phr.* [1950s+] (US prison) to expose a fellow prisoner's sexual preferences.

pull the devil by the tail, to *phr.*¹ [late 18C] to fall into rapid financial ruin; to be very impoverished. [? one is willing to ask even the Devil for help]

pull the devil by the tail, to *phr.*² [late 18C] to take a very great risk. [the 'courage' required for such an action]

pull the other one!/pull the other one, it's got bells on it! *phr.* [1960s+] a derisive rebuttal of an improbable statement.

pull the pin, to *phr.* [1960s+] (US) to resign, to quit, to be fired from a job. [the pulling of the connecting pin between two railroad wagons]

pull the plug, to *phr.* [20C] to commit suicide. [electrical imagery]

pull the plug on, to *phr.* [20C] to terminate, to bring to an end, usu. abruptly. [electrical imagery]

pull the rug from under/out from under, to *phr.* [1940s+] (orig. US) to discomfit by a sudden withdrawal of presumed support.

pull the stops out *see* PULL ONE'S STOPS OUT.

pull the string, to *phr.*¹ [late 19C] **1** to exert influence. **2** to succeed, to do well. [puppet imagery]

pull the string/the string of the shower-bath, to *phr.*² [1920s–30s] to cause something to be released or made common knowledge, to reveal something previously hidden.

pull the weight, to *phr.* [1910s+] (Aus.) to deal with a sudden financial problem.

pull the wrong pig/sow by the ear *see* GET THE WRONG PIG BY THE EAR.

pull-through *n.* [1970s] a Jew. [rhy. sl.]

pull time *v.* [mid-19C+] (US prison) to be sentenced to a term of imprisonment.

pull to a set, to *phr.* [1970s+] (US Black) to attend a party. [SET n.³]

pull up *v.*¹ [18C] to work as a highwayman; thus *pull up a jack,* to stop a coach in order to rob it.

pull up/pull up stakes *v.*² [19C+] (US) to leave.

pull up one's boot, to *phr.* [late 19C] (costermonger) to prosper, to make money (cf. MAKE UP ONE'S LEG). [the adoption of smart boots as a sign of affluence]

pull up one's socks *see* PULL ONE'S SOCKS UP.

pull up stakes *see* PULL UP v.².

pull wires *v.* [1950s] [20C] to exert influence, esp. behind the scenes (cf. PULL STRINGS).

pully *n.* [1930s+] a *pull*over or sweater. [abbr.]

pull your head in! *excl.* [1940s+] (Aus.) an excl. of annoyance, mind your own business! don't interfere! [the action of the tortoise]

pulp *n.* [1920s] nonsense, extreme sentimentality.

pulpit *n.* [19C] the vagina (cf. VESTRY).

pulpit-banger / -cackler / -cuffer / -drubber / -drummer / -smiter/-thumper *n.* [late 17C+] a ranting parson. [their thumping of the Bible]

pulver *n.* [1980s+] (drugs) amphetamines (cf. A n.²). [Sp. *polvo,* powder]

pummeled *adj.* [1990s] (US campus) drunk.

pummel the love truncheon, to *phr.* [1990s] to masturbate. [LOVE TRUNCHEON]

pummel the priest, to *phr.* [1990s] to masturbate (cf. BANG THE BISHOP).

pump *n.*¹ **1** [18C–late 19C] the penis. **2** [1970s+] a promiscuous woman.

pump *n.*² **1** [mid-19C–1900s] a pompous fool (cf. FART n.). **2** [late 19C+] (Scot.) a breaking of wind.

pump *n.*³ [late 19C–1900s] (Scot.) a public house. [its beer pumps]

pump *n.*⁴ [20C] the heart.

pump *n.*⁵ [1970s+] a gun, esp. a *pump*-action shotgun. [abbr.]

pump *v.*¹ [late 17C+] to ask questions, esp. in 20C to interrogate in a police station; thus *your pump is good but your sucker is dry,* your questions are good, but I have nothing to offer.

pump *v.*² [late 17C–mid-18C] to duck under the *pump,* as a punishment.

pump *v.*³ **1** [18C] to urinate. **2** [mid-19C] to weep. [SE *pump,* to raise up water]

pump *v.*⁴ **1** [18C+] to have sexual intercourse. **2** [1950s+] (US teen) to excite sexually (cf. PRIME ONE'S PUMP). [SE *pump,* to move vigorously up and down]

pump *v.*⁵ [1950s+] (US teen) to ride pillion on a motorcycle or scooter. [ety. unknown; ? PUMP v.³; coarse imagery of the passenger sodomizing/having rear-entry intercourse with the driver]

pump *v.*⁶ [1980s+] (drugs) to sell crack cocaine. [one 'pumps' it out]

pump *v.*⁷ [1990s] (US Black) to play music loudly. [one 'pumps up the volume']

pumpage *n.* [1960s–70s] sexual intercourse. [PUMP v.³ + sfx. -AGE; but possibly a nonce-word coined for the novel *King's Road* (1971) by Mariella Novotny]

pump a gusher, to *phr.* [1990s] to masturbate.

pump bilge *v.* [20C] (US) **1** to urinate. **2** to vomit (cf. PUMP SHIP). [SE *pump the bilges,* to pump out the water that has collected inside the bottom of a ship]

pump cream *v.* [1990s] to masturbate. [CREAM n.¹ (1)]

pump dale *n.* [17C] the vagina (cf. DAMP n.). [SE *pump,* one of several equations of water production and the vagina + SE *dale*]

pumped nuts *n.* [20C] (US) temporary courage. [SE *pump up* + NUTS n.² (1)]

pumped up *adj.* [20C] (US) full of oneself, excited.

pumper *n.*¹ [late 19C] anything exhausting, e.g. a running race. [PUMP n.⁴; one's pounding heart]

pumper *n.*² [1910s–20s] a very boring questioner. [PUMP v.¹]

pumpernickel *n.* [20C] a Black prostitute, especially a mulatto. [SE *pumpernickel,* dark wholemeal rye bread]

pump gas at the self-service island, to *phr.* [1990s] to masturbate.

pump-handle *n.* [18C–late 19C] the penis (cf. PUMP n.¹).

pump-handle *v.* [mid–late 19C] to shake hands vigorously, as if wielding a pump-handle; thus *pump-handler,* a handshake of this nature.

pumping *n.* [1980s+] (drugs) selling crack cocaine. [PUMP v.⁶]

pump/push/throw iron *v.* [1970s+] (orig. US) to work out with weights, to practise bodybuilding.

pump jockey *n.* [1930s+] (US) a petrol pump attendant (cf. COW JOCKEY; LOX JOCK; PLOW JOCKEY). [SE *pump* + JOCKEY n.² (2)]

pumpkin/pompkin n.[1] [late 18C–early 19C] a native of Boston, Massachusetts (cf. PUMPKINSHIRE). [the popularity of the *pumpkin* as a crop and a foodstuff]

pumpkin n.[2] **1** [19C] the head (cf. BEAN n.[4]). **2** [1940s] (US Black) the sun, the moon. [the shape]

pumpkin/punkin n.[3] [mid-19C+] (US) an important person or object; esp. as *some pumpkins/punkins*.

pumpkin-face n. [late 19C] (US) a round, expressionless face.

pumpkin head n. [1970s] **1** a person with an abnormally large head. **2** a fool. [SE *pumpkin* + SE *head*/sfx. -HEAD (1)]

pumpkin-roller n. [20C] (US) a rustic, a farmer.

pumpkin-seed/skin n. [19C–1920s] (US Black) a light-coloured person.

Pumpkinshire/Pompkinshire n. [late 18C] Boston, Massachusetts. [PUMPKIN n.[1]]

pump off v. [1950s+] to masturbate (cf. BEAT OFF). [PUMP v.[3]]

pump oneself up v. [20C] (orig. US) to exert or arouse oneself, to prepare oneself mentally for a challenge (cf. PSYCH UP).

pump one's pickle, to phr. [20C] to masturbate (cf. JERK ONE'S GHERKIN).

pump-pump n. [1990s] (US Black teen) an imitation of the sound of gunfire (cf. BUCK-BUCK!). [echoic]

pumps n. [19C] the eyes. [they *pump* out tears]

pump ship v. [late 18C+] **1** to urinate. **2** to vomit. [naut. jargon *pump ship*, to pump the ship dry of water]

pump-sucker n. [late 19C–1920s] a teetotaller. [they fig. 'suck' the water-*pump*]

pump the monkey, to phr. [1990s] to masturbate (cf. PROMPT ONE'S PORPOISE).

pump the python, to phr. [1990s] to masturbate (cf. PROMPT ONE'S PORPOISE).

pump the stump, to phr. [1940s] (US Black) to shake hands.

pump-thunder n. [19C] a braggart, a boaster. [PUMP n.[2] + SE *thunder*]

pump-thunder v. [late 19C–1900s] to bluster. [PUMP-THUNDER n.]

pum-pum n.[1] [late 18C–late 19C] a fiddler. [the 'pum-pum, pum-pum' of the tunes]

pum-pum n.[2] [1980s+] (W.I.) the vagina (cf. PUNAANY); thus *pum-pum-pum*, a fool (cf. CUNT n.[1]). [? Krio *pumbe*, the female vulva]

pump up v. [1980s+] **1** (US campus) to make livelier, to fill with energy. **2** to exaggerate.

punaany/pudenany n. [1980s+] (W.I./UK Black teen) **1** the female genitals (cf. PUM-PUM n.[2]). **2** sexual intercourse. [ety. unknown; ? link to PUM-PUM n.[2]; also note PUNDU]

punce see POONCE.

punch n. [1970s+] (US campus) a promiscuous woman (cf. PUNCHABLE). [PUNCH v. (2)]

punch v. [late 18C–19C] **1** to deflower (cf. PUNCHABLE). **2** [1970s+] (US campus) to engage in sexual intercourse (cf. BANG v.[1]).

punchable adj. [early 18C–early 19C] a woman considered ripe for seduction; thus *punchable nun*, a prostitute. [PUNCH v. (1)]

punch and judy n. [late 19C–1910s] lemonade. [ety. unknown; ? a brandname]

punch and judy adj. [20C] sulky, moody. [rhy. sl.]

punchboard n. [1950s+] (US campus) a promiscuous woman (cf. PUNCH n.; PUNCHABLE). [pun on SE *punchboard*/PUNCH v. (2)]

punch clod n. [late 19C–1900s] a peasant, a farm labourer (cf. CLODHOPPER).

punch hell out of see BEAT HELL OUT OF.

punch house n. **1** [late 17C–mid-19C] a brothel, or a tavern that doubles as such (cf. ACCOMMODATION HOUSE). **2** [1920s–40s] (US Black) a spontaneous get-together, a party. **3** [1970s] (US Black) a party frequented by pimps and their women, usu. an orgy. [orig. the provision of alcoholic *punch* at such establishments but underpinned by PUNCH v., esp. in (2), (3)]

punch in v. [1920s+] to arrive at work (cf. PUNCH THE CLOCK).

punching bag n. [1930s+] one who is constantly beaten up, e.g. an abused woman. [boxing jargon *punching bag*, a fighter who has no real abilities and is useful only as the recipient of a fortunate opponent's punches]

punch in the mouth n. [1960s] cunnilingus. [pun on SE *punch*/PUNCH v. (2)]

punch it v.[1] [late 18C–early 19C] (Und.) **1** to run away, to escape (cf. BEAT IT). **2** to walk. [one's feet 'punch' the street]

punch it v.[2] [early–mid-19C] to drink punch.

punch-out n. [1960s+] (US) a fight. [PUNCH OUT v.]

punch out v.[1] [1920s+] **1** to leave work (cf. PUNCH THE CLOCK).

punch out v.[2] [1960s+] (US) to beat up, to assault with the fists.

punch-out artist n. [1960s+] (US) anyone who enjoys and is expert in beating up their opponents with their fists. [SE *punch* + ARTIST n.[2]]

punch out someone's lights see PUT OUT SOMEONE'S LIGHTS.

punch the bag, to phr. [1900s–20s] (US) **1** to gossip, to chatter. **2** to complain; thus *bag-puncher*, a gossip, a whinger; *bag-punching*, gossiping, complaining. [boxing imagery]

punch the breeze, to phr. [late 19C+] (US) to leave (cf. HIT THE BREEEZE).

punch the clock, to phr. [1920s+] **1** to 'clock on' or 'clock off' for work (cf. PUNCH IN; PUNCH OUT v.[1]). **2** to be employed, to go to work. [SE *punch* + (*time*)*clock*]

punch the clown, to phr. [1990s] to masturbate.

punch the hell out of see BEAT HELL OUT OF.

punch-up n. [1940s+] a fight, usu. in the street, a pub etc (cf. SWEAR-UP; SWINE-UP).

punchy adj. [1930s+] disorientated, eccentric, out of control. [boxing jargon *punch drunk*, a boxer who has taken too many punches and is becoming eccentric.

punda/pundah n. [1980s+] (S.Afr.) women, seen collectively as sex objects (cf. POONTANG; PUSSY n.[1]; TAIL n.[3]). [PUNDU]

pundu n. [1970s+] (S.Afr.) **1** the buttocks, the posterior. **2** the vagina (cf. PUNDA). [Xhosa *impundu*, buttocks]

punish v. **1** [early 19C] to hurt badly in a boxing match or a fight. **2** [early 19C] to make inroads into, esp. a stock of food or wine. **3** [mid-19C+] to attack, esp. in sports. **4** [1960s+] to play a musical instrument badly, thus 'abusing' it.

punisher n. **1** [early 19C] a demanding, laborious task. **2** [early–mid-19C] a heavy hitter; thus *punishing*, hard-hitting. **3** [1950s+] a long-winded bore (cf. PUNISH ONE'S LUGS).

punishment n. **1** [early 19C+] physical or emotional pain, damage or loss. **2** [1960s+] (gay) taking an extra-large penis either in the mouth or the anus.

punish one's lugs, to phr. [1950s+] (Aus.) to chatter on incessantly. [SE *punish* + LUG n.[1] (1)]

punish percy in the palm/the harlequin/the penguin, to phr. [1990s] to masturbate.

punish the pope, to phr. [1990s] to masturbate (cf. BANG THE BISHOP).

punk/punque n.[1] **1** [late 16C–1900s] a young female prostitute. **2** [20C] (Ling. Fr./Polari) a male prostitute. **3** [20C] (US prison) a young inmate used for sex by older, stronger peers. **4** [1910s+] (US) a young criminal or street gang member. **5** [1920s+] (US) a tramp's younger companion (cf. GONSEL). **6** [1930s+] a youngster, a child. **7** [1950s+] (US/W.I.) a coward, a weakling. **8** [1950s+] (US) a male homosexual. [? SE *punch*, to pierce and linked to PUNCH v. (1); note Sp. *punto*, *puto*, a male prostitute]

punk *n.*[2] [19C+] (US) bread (cf. PISS AND PUNK; PUNK AND PLASTER). [ety. unknown]

punk *n.*[3] [mid-19C+] nonsense, rubbish. [? US *punk*, rotten wood or a fungus growing on it]

Punk *n.*[4] [1970s+] a mid-1970s youth cult, started in the UK, spread to the US by such apostles as the Sex Pistols (*fl.*1975–8) and Malcolm McLaren (b.1946). Where the hippies had been bourgeois, *punks* were proletarian, complaining not against a consumer society but against their exclusion from its delights; they specialized in bizarre hair styles (mohican, multicoloured), ripped clothes and safety pins, through flesh as well as fabric; thus *punk rock*, the music; *punk rocker*, a fan of punk; *punkette*, a female fan; *punkish, punkoid*, characteristic of a punk fan. [PUNK *n.*[1] (4), (6); as with similar movements, e.g. ROCK 'N' ROLL, *punk*, while technically sl., has become effectively SE]

punk *adj.* (US) **1** [late 19C+] second-rate, inferior, distasteful, worthless, unimportant. **2** [1950s+] weak, effeminate. [PUNK *n.*[1]]

punk *v.* [1970s+] to engage in anal intercourse. [PUNK *n.*[1] (2), (3)]

punkah one's face, to *phr.* [late 19C] (Anglo-Ind.) to fan one's face. [Hind. *panka*, a fan, esp. the large fixed fans, essentially a sheet stretched across a hinged frame and operated by a servant, designed to keep whole rooms cool]

punk and plaster *n.* [late 19C+] (US) bread and butter. [PUNK *n.*[2] + joc. use of SE *plaster*]

punk-ass *adj.* [1970s+] (US) of a person, useless, second-rate, worthless. [PUNK *n.*[1] + sfx. -ASS]

punkawn *n.* [20C] (Irish) a talkative, self-assertive person. [Irish *poncán*, an American, esp. a Yankee]

punk day *n.* [1930s+] (US) a day on which children have free admission to a museum, cinema etc. [PUNK *n.*[1] (6)]

punker *n.*[1] [18C] one who pursues prostitutes. [PUNK *n.*[1] (1)]

punker *n.*[2] [1970s+] (US) a fan of punk rock music. [PUNK *n.*[4]]

punkin *see* PUMPKIN *n.*[3].

punkish *adj.* [18C] showy, flashy. [PUNK *n.*[1] (1)]

punk out *v.* [1920s+] (US) **1** to display cowardice. **2** to make someone into an acquiescent weakling. [PUNK *n.*[1]]

punk pills *n.* [1960s–70s] (drugs) any form of tranquillizer. [PUNK *n.*[1] (7) + SE *pills*; their creation of artificial courage]

punk's run *n.* [1980s+] (US prison) the protective custody unit for those whose lives would be at risk if they were kept with the prison population as a whole. [PUNK *n.*[1] (3) + pun on SE *chicken run*]

punque *see* PUNK *n.*[1] (1).

punse *n.* [late 19C+] the vagina. [Yid.]

punt *v.*[1] [mid-19C+] **1** to gamble, to wager (cf. PUNTER *n.*[1]). **2** to sell, to promote. [ety. unknown; orig. SE use in certain card-games, to bet against the bank; note also faro jargon, *punt*, a point]

punt *v.*[2] [1970s+] (US campus) to give up, esp. one's work. [US football imagery; the team that fails to score within 4 downs is forced to punt the ball to the opposition]

punt around *v.* [1940s+] to try one's luck, esp. when looking for a person. [PUNT *v.*[1]]

punter *n.*[1] **1** [early 18C+] a gambler, on cards, dice, horses, dogs etc. **2** [20C] (N.Z.) a pickpocket's assistant. **3** [1930s+] the victim of a confidence trickster's schemes. **4** [1950s+] generic for a member of the general public, particularly when in the role of customer, esp. of a prostitute, a casino and other slightly 'shady' enterprises. [? Sp. *ponto*, a point, or *ponte*, the player against the bank]

punter *n.*[2] [1930s+] a large beer mug. [pun on 'a big MUG' *n.*[5] (1)]

punting-shop *n.* [18C–mid-19C] a casino, a gambling house. [PUNT *v.*[1] + SHOP *n.*[1] (2)]

punt off *v.* [1970s+] (US campus) to forget, to put to the back of one's mind. [PUNT *v.*[2]]

pup *n.*[1] **1** [late 19C+] a youthful, inexperienced person; esp. as *young pup* (cf. DOG *n.*[16]) **2** [1950s+] (US) a 4-wheeled trailer drawn by a tractor, lorry or other road vehicle. [(2) is reverse anthropomorphism]

pup *n.*[2] [20C] (US) a spiced, heated sausage, served on a split roll. [play on HOT DOG *n.*[1]]

pup *v.* [mid-19C+] to experience childbirth. [reverse anthropomorphism]

pupa! *see* PAPA.

pupa-lick/pupperlick *n.* [late 19C+] (W.I.) a somersault. [Carib.E. *pupa*, father + LICK *v.* (1); the image is of being turned over the father's knees, buttocks in the air, for a spanking]

puppet-head *n.* [1960s+] (US teen) a gullible, conventional person, esp. one who permits hearsay to 'pull their strings' in matters of current taste. [SE *puppet* + sfx. -HEAD (1)]

puppied *adj.* [1980s+] so relaxed one wants to engage in gentle physical contact with another person. [puppies snuggling together]

puppies/pups *n.*[1] [1910s+] the feet. [play on DOG *n.*[14]; thus the brandname *Hush Puppies*, supposed to comfort one's feet]

puppies, the *n.*[2] [1940s+] (Aus.) racing greyhounds (cf. DOGS *n.*[2]; YAPPIES).

puppies *n.*[3] [1990s] the female breasts. [their 'snuggling' together]

puppy *n.*[1] [mid-19C] a blind man. [the blindness of new-born puppies]

puppy *n.*[2] **1** [1930s+] (US Black) a half-pint bottle of fortified wine. **2** [1980s+] (US Black) a small penis. **3** [1980s+] (US campus) an otherwise unspecified and nameless object. **4** [1990s] (US) a handgun. [SE *puppy*; i.e. implying small-ness]

puppy/puppy dog *n.*[3] [1960s+] **1** a love-sick young man. **2** a sexually inexperienced man (cf. DOG *n.*[16]). [PUP *n.*[1] (1)]

puppy boy *n.* [1990s] (US teen) a young man who is deeply in love. [PUPPY *n.*[3] (1)]

puppy dog *see* PUPPY *n.*[3].

puppy-foot/-dog foot *n.* [20C] in cards, any of the club suit, esp. the ace. [the similarity to a small paw-print]

puppy-match *n.* [late17C–mid-18C] a trap, a snare.

puppy show *n. see* POPPY SHOW *n.*[2].

puppy-show *adj. see* POPPY SHOW adj.

puppy show *v. see* POPPY SHOW v.

puppy's mamma *n.* [late 18C] a euph. for BITCH *n.*[4] (cf. DOGGESS).

pups *see* PUPPIES *n.*[1].

purby *n.* [late 19C] (society) the Pre-Raphaelite Brotherhood. [*P.R.B.*, the initials by which the group of artists centred on Holman Hunt (1827–1910), J.E. Millais (1829–96) and D.G. Rossetti (1828–82) was popularly known]

pure *n.*[1] [17C–early 19C] a mistress, a prostitute (cf. PUREST PURE). [ironic use of SE]

pure *n.*[2] [1950s–60s] (drugs) **1** the best heroin. **2** top quality drugs.

pure *adj.*[1] [late 17C–late 19C] fine, jolly, splendid, esp. when ironic.

pure *adj.*[2] [20C] simple. [SE phr. *pure and simple*]

pure *adv.* [mid-18C+] a general intensifier; purely, absolutely, completely.

pure guava *phr.* [1990s] (US teen) that's a good decision, let's do it. [the excellence of the fruit]

pure love *n.* [1970s] (drugs) LSD. [LSD's image as a creator of 'love and peace']

purely *adv.* [late 17C–mid-19C] excellently, nicely, satisfactorily.

pure merino *n.* [early 19C+] 'an early immigrant to Australia with no convict origins; a member of a leading family in Australian society; a person of fine breeding or good character' (*OED*). [*Merino sheep*, a variety of sheep with especially fine wool, introduced from Spain to England in the late 18C and used for the improvement of the fleece-bearing sheep of Britain and the colonies. *AND* notes 'one who finds in this a basis for social pretension']

pure merino *adj*. [early 19C+] first-class, well-bred, excellent. [PURE MERINO n.]

pure nast! *phr*. [1990s] (US teen) really disgusting. [PURE adv. + SE *nast*(*y*)]

pure pipe *v*. [1980s+] (drugs) to smoke cannabis, without additional tobacco, in a small pipe.

pure/clear quill *n*. [1950s+] (US) something that is excellent or flawless. [? a perfect SE *quill* or feather]

pure silk *n*. [1960s] (US Black) a male homosexual. [an image of softness and smoothness]

purest pure *n*. [late 17C–early 19C] the highest class of prostitute, a courtesan. [ext. of PURE n.¹]

purge *n*. [19C+] any form of alcoholic liquor. [SE *purge*, an aperient; 20C use is only N.Z.]

purger *n*. [mid-19C–1910s] **1** a teetotaller. **2** a general pej. [neg. image of teetotallers]

puritan *n*. [17C] an ironic term for a prostitute.

purko *see* PERK n.².

purl *n*.¹ [late 17C–1900s] beer warmed nearly to boiling, mixed with gin or wormwood (the basis of absinthe), sugar and ginger; a later version substituted gin for the wormwood (cf. DOG-NOSE). Both were considered suitable for a morning pick-me-up; thus *purl-royal*, a glass of Canary wine with a dash of wormwood (cf. EARLY PURL). [? link to SE *purl*, a rill or whirl of water]

purl *n*.² [mid-19C] **1** a heavy fall. **2** the acting of whirling or pitching head-first or head-over-heels. [PURL v.]

purl *v*. [mid–late 19C] to turn upside down, to overturn, to upset, to turn a somersault. [SE *purl*, often of a top, to spin round and round; an earlier version was *pirl*]

purler *n*. **1** [mid-19C+] a crash, an accidental fall (cf. CROPPER). **2** [mid-19C+] a knock-out blow. **3** [1940s+] (Aus./N.Z.) something of outstanding excellence or perfection. [PURL v.; (3) is fig. use of (2)]

purple *n*. (drugs) **1** [1960s+] amphetamine (cf. A n.²; PURPLE HEARTS). **2** [1960s+] LSD. **3** [1980s+] ketamine (cf. K n.⁴). [the colour of the pills]

purple *adj*. [late 19C–1900s] splendid, regal. [the image of purple as a 'royal' colour]

purple and mauve *n*. (Aus.) the stove. [rhy. sl.]

purple barrels/dragons/flats/microdots/owsky/wedges *n*. [1960s] (drugs) LSD. [SE *purple* + BARRELS/SE *dragons*, i.e. the stamp on the pill/FLAT BLUES/MICRODOTS/OWSLEY/WEDGE; i.e. the colour of the capsules]

purple bob *n*. [1940s] **1** a man who is kept by a homosexual. **2** one who sponges off homosexuals (cf. RED BOB). [SE *purple* as a code word for homosexuality (cf. LAVENDER) ? + generic use of proper name. In neither case need the man himself be gay]

purple death *n*. [1940s+] cheap Italian wine (cf. DAGO RED). [its colour and possible effect; mainly N.Z. use]

purple dragons *see* PURPLE BARRELS.

purple flats *see* PURPLE BARRELS.

purple haze *n*. (drugs) **1** [1960s] LSD. **2** [1990s] a strong variety of cannabis. [the Jimi Hendrix song title (1967)]

purple-headed custard chucker/love truncheon/monster/warrior/womb broom/womb ferret/womb spoon *n*. [1970s+] the penis.

purple hearts *n*. [1960s] (drugs) **1** amphetamines (cf. A n.²; BLUES n.²). **2** (rarely) barbiturates. [the colour of the pills]

purple microdots/owsky *see* PURPLE BARRELS.

purple para *n*. [1960s+] (Aus.) cheap, unpleasant port wine. [SE *purple* + *paraffin*]

purple rain *n*. [1980s+] (drugs) phencyclidine (cf. ACE n.³). [the 1983 film by rock star Prince]

purple ridgeback *n*. [1990s] the penis.

purple wedges *see* PURPLE BARRELS.

purse *n*. **1** [late 17C–18C] the scrotum. **2** [late 17C+] the vagina (cf. BANK n.¹). [(2) is underpinned by the commercial potential of the vagina]

purse *v*. [late 16C–early 17C] to steal purses.

purse-bouncer *n*. [1900s] a swindler.

purse-catcher *n*. [early 17C] a pickpocket.

purse-emptier *n*. [early 17C–late 19C] **1** a swindler. **2** a high-wayman.

purse-finder *n*. [19C] a prostitute. [the 'purse' is both the SE *money-bag* and PURSE n. (1)]

purse-lifter *n*. [1900s] a pickpocket.

purse-milking *n*. [early 17C] swindling, robbery. [note MILK v.¹]

purse-net *n*. [late 16C–early 19C] **1** a small purse. **2** a person who is sold goods at vastly inflated prices and on credit and who ends up owing many times the original sum (cf. RABBIT SUCKER). [PURSE-NETS]

purse-nets *n*. [late 16C–mid-19C] goods sold to a gullible young person at vastly inflated prices and on credit. [SE *purse-net*, a bag-shaped net, the mouth of which can be drawn together with cords; used esp. for catching rabbits, also used as a fishing net]

purse-proud *adj*. [late 17C–18C] lecherous, amorous. [PURSE n. (1) + PROUD]

purse-snatcher *n*. [1900s] a pickpocket.

pursie *adj*. [1950s–60s] (Aus.) well-off, 'in funds' (cf. BROKIE). [SE *purse*]

purting glumpot *n*. [mid-19C] a sulky, miserable person. [dial. *purt*, to sulk, to pout + SE *glum* + sfx. *-pot*, a person]

pusa *see* PHUZA.

pus-bag *n*. [20C] (US) a contemptible person (cf. SCUMBAG).

pus-/pustle-gut *n*. [20C] **1** a fat stomach (cf. PUZZLEGUT). **2** one who has a fat stomach. [SE *pus/pustle* = *pustule* + *gut*]

push *n*.¹ [18C+] sexual intercourse; thus *do a push*, to have sexual intercourse. [the thrusting movements of the man, but note PUSH IN THE TRUCK]

push *n*.² **1** [18C–early 19C] a crowd, a 'press' of people. **2** [mid–late 19C] (Aus.) a criminal gang; thus *upper-ten push*, upper-class criminals and prisoners. **3** [mid-19C] a robbery, a swindle. **4** [late 19C+] (US/Aus.) a crowd, thence a clique, a set, among the most celebrated of which was the *Sydney Push*, or Sydney University Libertarian Society of the early 1960s; thus *pushite*, a member of a gang or 'crowd'. **5** [1900s–40s] (US) a street fight between gangs.

push *n*.³ [mid–late 19C] money. [? fig. use of SE, i.e. it lets one 'push forward' in life]

push, the *n*.⁴ [late 19C+] dismissal from a job; usu. as *get/give the push*, to be dismissed, to dismiss, occasionally to throw out of a place, e.g. a public house.

push *n*.⁵ [20C] (Irish) **1** help, encouragement. **2** a problem, a difficult situation. [SE *push*; (1) used pos., (2) used neg.]

push *v*.¹ [18C+] to have sexual intercourse. [PUSH n.¹]

push *v*.² [1920s+] to leave (cf. PUSH ALONG; PUSH OFF v.²).

push *v*.³ [1930s+] to approach a certain age; usu. as *pushing*, e.g. *pushing 50*, nearly 50 years old.

push *v*.⁴ [1930s+] (orig. US) **1** to sell, to promote, to advertise. **2** (drugs) to sell drugs. **3** to distribute counterfeit money. **4** to smuggle.

push/push across *v*.⁵ [1930s+] (US) to kill, to murder.

push v.[6] [1970s] (US Black) to drive a car. [one pushes the accelerator]

push across see PUSH v.[5].

push along v. [1920s+] to leave (cf. PUSH v.[2]; PUSH OFF v.[2]).

push-bike n. [20C] a pedal cycle, as opposed to a motorcycle; thus *push-bike*, to ride a bicycle.

push clouds v. [1920s] (US) to be dead. [one's ascent to heaven]

pushed adj.[1] [mid-19C–1900s] drunk. [one of many words associating physical violence with drunkenness]

pushed adj.[2] [1930s+] lacking, bereft, in need of, e.g. *pushed for cash, pushed for time*.

pushed out of shape phr. [1970s] (US campus) upset, angry.

pusher n.[1] [late 19C–1940s] a young woman, esp. a prostitute; thus *square pusher*, a respectable young woman. [PUSH v.[1]]

pusher n.[2] [1930s+] **1** (drugs) one who sells drugs. **2** (US) a distributor of counterfeit money. [PUSH v.[4] (2), (3)]

pusher n.[3] [1950s+] (Aus.) a pushchair.

pusher n.[4] [1980s+] (drugs) **1** a thin stick, typically a chopstick, used to pack a cocaine pipe (cf. PACKER n.[3]). **2** a metal hanger or umbrella rod used to scrape residue in crack stems.

push fire v. [20C] (W.I.) to urge others into a fight, with no intention of participating oneself. [one 'fans the flames']

push-foot n. [1920s–40s] (W.I.) a Ford Model T automobile (cf. SHOVE-AND-LET-GO). [on this car low gear was engaged by pressing a foot-pedal]

pushie/pooshie n. [1960s+] (Ulster) **1** an over-sensitive person. **2** a coward. [PUSSY n.[1] (3)]

push-in n. [1940s+] (orig. US) a certainty. [image of an unlocked door; one need only push it open]

pushing school n. [late 17C–19C] a brothel (cf. ACADEMY). [PUSH v.[1] + SE *school*. Note SE *pushing school*, a fencing school, linking to the various sl. uses of DAGGER n.[1] and other synons. meaning the penis]

push-in job n. [1980s+] a mugging that takes place on the victim's doorstep. [SE *push-in* + JOB n.[3]]

push in the bush n. [1920s+] sexual intercourse. [PUSH n.[1] + BUSH n.[4]]

push in the truck n. [1930s] sexual intercourse. [rhy. sl. *push in the truck* = FUCK n.[1]]

push iron see PUMP IRON.

push it v. [1960s+] to approach a limit, often in one's conduct; esp. as *don't push it*, don't go too far (or you will face the consequences).

push money n. [1930s+] (US) commission paid to a salesperson on each item sold (cf. SPIFF n.). [PUSH v.[4] (1) + SE *money*]

push off v.[1] [20C] to start, esp. to start a game. [SE *push off*, to push a boat off from its mooring]

push off v.[2] [1920s+] to leave; esp. as [1940s+] *push off!* go away. [ext. of PUSH v.[2]]

push one's bib in see STICK ONE'S BIB IN.

push one's face, to phr. [mid-19C+] to obtain credit through deceit or bravado. [variant on RUN ONE'S FACE FOR]

push one's own barrow, to phr. [1910s+] (Aus.) **1** to brag. **2** to look out for one's own interests first.

push-out n. [1970s+] (US) a student expelled from school for unsatisfactory performance. [a play on SE *dropout*, i.e. implying such students are forced, rather than volunteer, to leave]

pushover n. **1** [late 19C+] (orig. US) one who is easily overcome, convinced or imposed upon. **2** [late 19C+] (orig. US) a situation that presents no difficulties or problems. **3** [1920s+] one, esp. a woman, who is easily seduced.

push ponies v. [1960s+] of a pimp, to promote prostitutes. [PUSH v.[4] (1) + PONY n.[7]]

push-push n. [20C] (US) sexual intercourse. [PUSH n.[1] + redup.]

push shit up hill, to phr. [1980s+] to work, talk etc, unsuccessfully, against the odds.

push shorts v. [1930s] (drugs) **1** to sell in small amounts. **2** to sell short measure. [PUSH v.[4] (2)]

push someone's/the right buttons, to phr. [1920s+; 1970s+] to manipulate someone emotionally.

push someone's face in, to phr. [1920s+] to hit someone in the face.

push someone's key, to phr. [20C] (US) to irritate someone, to tease someone.

push the boat out, to phr. [1930s+] **1** to spend heavily, usu. on pleasure, eating, drinking etc, often treating others. **2** to exaggerate.

push the knot, to phr. [20C] (Aus.) to live as a tramp. [KNOT n.[1]]

push the panic button, to phr. [1960s+] (orig. US) to panic, to become hysterical.

push the right buttons see PUSH SOMEONE'S BUTTONS.

push up daisies/the daisies/kick up daisies, to phr. [1910s+] to die; thus *pushing daisies/up the daisies*, dead (cf. TURN ONE'S TOES UP; UNDER THE DAISIES).

push-up man n. [1910s–30s] (Aus.) a pickpocket's accomplice who pushes up the arm of the victim to facilitate access to their wallet; thus *push-up mob*, a gang of pickpockets specializing in this; *at the push-up*, working as a pickpocket.

push up on v. [1990s] (US Black) **1** to make romantic moves towards someone, usu. in the hope of seduction. **2** to frighten, to intimidate.

push up the daisies see PUSH UP DAISIES.

pushy adj. [1930s+] (orig. US) unpleasantly forward or self-assertive, aggressive.

puss n.[1] **1** [17C+] the vagina (cf. CAT n.[10]). **2** [1970s+] the 'female' of a lesbian couple. [SE *puss*; the association of women and cats]

puss n.[2] [early 19C+] a hare. [dial.]

puss n.[3] [late 19C+] **1** a face. **2** (Irish) a sulky look. [Irish *pus*, the mouth, a sulky expression]

puss n.[4] (W.I.) **1** [1940s] rubber-soled canvas shoes. **2** [1950s] a thief. [SE *puss*, a cat; i.e. one walks as quietly as a cat]

puss n.[5] [1950s] (W.I.) an albino (cf. FRECKLE-NATURE). [abbr. PUSS-EYE]

puss-boots n. [1940s] (W.I.) rubber-soled canvas shoes. [the quietness of one's steps in such shoes, ? + ref. to the folktale 'Puss-in-Boots']

pussbucket n. [1950s+] (orig. US) a general derog. term. [the use of *puss*, i.e. pus, may offer a link to other derog. terms relating to venereal diseases]

pussery n. (W.I.) **1** [1940s] trickery. **2** [1950s] theft. [PUSS n.[4]]

puss-eye n. [1950s] (W.I.) an albino (cf. FRECKLE-NATURE). [? SE *pus* + *eye*; the stereotype of short-sighted albinos]

puss gentleman n. [1960s+] (US Black) a weak man. [PUSSY adj.]

puss-in n. [20C] (W.I.) a young woman. [var. on PUSSY n.[1] (2)]

puss-pelmet see PUSSY-PELMET.

puss Sunday n. [20C] (Irish) the first Sunday in Lent. [PUSS n.[3] (2). Women who had not married before Lent had to wait until Easter, hence the idea of going around in a sulk]

pussums n. [1920s+] a general term of endearment. [SE *puss* + DIDDUMS]

pussy n.[1] **1** [mid-19C+] the vagina (cf. BADGER n.[7]; CAT n.[10]). **2** [20C] women in general, with an implication of their being sexually available. **3** [20C] a coward, with an implication of homosexuality. [SE *pussy*, an affectionate name for a cat]

pussy *n.*[2] **1** [20C] (Aus.) a rabbit (cf. PUSS *n.*[2]). **2** [1900s–40s] the cat-o'-nine-tails (cf. CAT *n.*[2]). [SE *pussy*, a cat]

pussy *n.*[3] [1930s+] a fur garment; thus *pussy-hoisting*, stealing furs; *pussy mob*, a gang of fur thieves. [SE *pussy*, a cat]

pussy *adj.* [20C] (orig. US) scared, cowardly. [PUSSY *n.*[1] (3)]

pussy *v.* [1910s+] (Aus.) to move (in) quietly or unobtrusively. [SE *pussy*, i.e. like a cat]

pussy-ass *adj.* [1970s+] (US) cowardly, weak. [PUSSY *adj.* + sfx. -ASS]

pussy bandit *n.* [1950s+] (US) a man who is obsessed with sex and seduction. [PUSSY *n.*[1] (1) + BANDIT *n.*[1]]

pussyboy *n.* [1950s] a passive male homosexual, a catamite (cf. FUCKBOY). [PUSSY *n.*[1] (3) + SE *boy*]

pussy butterfly *n.* [1970s] (US) an inter/intra-uterine contraceptive device. [PUSSY *n.*[1] (1) + SE *butterfly*, i.e. the shape]

pussycat *n.* **1** [19C+] (US Black) the vagina (cf. PUSSY *n.*[1]). **2** [1950s+] a weak or at least amiable and passive person.

pussycats *n.* [mid-19C] Puseyites, followers of the mid-19C Tractarian movement in the Church of England. [proper name of Dr E.B. *Pusey* (1800–82), professor of Hebrew at Oxford University, Canon of Christ Church and influential member of the Tractarian movement (so-called because of its publication of a series of pamphlets, *Tracts for the Times*, which criticized the current state of the Church of England). The movement was also popularly known as the Oxford Movement]

pussyclot *n.* [1960s+] (W.I./US Black) a general pej., a coward, an informer (cf. BLOOD CLAAT; RAASCLAT; SMEERLAP). [PUSSY *n.*[1] (1) + SE *clot(h)*]

pussy fodder *n.* [1990s] the penis. [PUSSY *n.*[1] (1) + fig. use of SE *fodder*]

pussyfoot/pussyfoot around *v.* [1920s+] to compromise, to act in a cowardly or weak manner. [the animal's cautious movements]

pussy game *n.* [1960s+] (US) the world of prostitution. [PUSSY *n.*[1] (1) + GAME *n.*[4]]

pussy hair *n.* [1970s+] the female pubic hair. [PUSSY *n.*[1] (1) + SE *hair*]

pussy-hound *n.* [1950s+] a man who is obsessed with the pursuit of sex (cf. COCK-HOUND). [PUSSY *n.*[1] (1) + sfx. -HOUND]

pussy in a can *n.* [1960s+] (US prison) sardines sold in a can at a prison commissary. [PUSSY *n.*[1] (1) + SE *can*; the derog. association of the smell of the vagina with the smell of fish]

pussy-/puss-pelmet *n.* [1960s–70s] a very short miniskirt. [PUSSY *n.*[1] (1) + SE *pelmet*]

pussy posse *n.* [1960s+] (US police) the Vice Squad, esp. those members who deal with prostitutes. [PUSSY *n.*[1] (1) + fig. use of SE *posse*]

pussy-struck *adj.* [20C] obsessed by sex (cf. CUNT-STRUCK). [PUSSY *n.*[1] (1) + SE *struck*, fascinated]

pussy tickler *n.* [1940s–50s] (US Black) a moustache. [PUSSY *n.*[1] (1) + SE *tickler*]

pussy whip *v.* [1950s+] (orig. US) of a woman, to dominate one's husband or partner. [backform. of PUSSY-WHIPPED]

pussy-whipped *adj.* [1950s+] **1** (orig. US) dominated by a woman, esp. a wife or girlfriend. **2** (US campus) besotted with, infatuated by. [PUSSY *n.*[1] (2) + fig. use of SE *whip*]

pussy willow *n.* [20C] a pillow. [rhy. sl.]

pustle-gut *see* PUS-GUT.

put *n.*[1] **1** [17C–early 19C] a peasant, a countryman (cf. COUNTRY PUT). **2** [early–mid-19C] a general term of derision. [ety. unknown]

put *n.*[2] [19C] a prostitute. [Fr. *putain*, a prostitute]

put *v.* [mid–late 19C] (US) to make off, to be off, to 'clear out'.

puta *n.* [1950s+] (US Sp.) **1** a prostitute. **2** a very promiscuous woman. [synon. Sp.]

put a baby on, to *phr.* [1990s] (US Black) **1** of a woman, to have a child without the father's knowledge and/or agreement. **2** to claim a man as one's child's father, even though he is not.

put a barracuda on, to *phr.* [1980s+] (US) to treat roughly. [the viciousness of the fish]

put a bit in it/a piece of wood in it/the wood in the hole, to *phr.* [20C] to shut the door; usu. as imper.

put a bit of pudding on *see* PUT PUDDING ON.

put a blossom on it for, to *phr.* [1950s] (Aus.) to commit pederasty. [ety. unknown; ? ref. to the freshness of a SE *blossom* + IT *n.*[1] (2)]

put a bone in someone's hood, to *phr.* [mid–late 16C] to cuckold someone. [BONE *n.*[6]; ext. of SE phr. *put a bone in someone's hood*, to break or cut off someone's head]

put a boy on *phr.* [1940s+] (Aus.) a male sexual boast, usu. in response to a question such as 'Getting any?' 'I'm so busy I've had to ...' (cf. CLIMBING TREES TO GET AWAY FROM IT).

put a bug in someone's ear, to *phr.* [1900s–30s] (US) to confide a secret to someone. [BUG *n.*[7]]

put a bung in it! *excl.* [20C] shut the door!

put a churl upon a gentleman, to *phr.* **1** [late 16C–early 19C] to drink malt whisky after drinking wine (cf. PUT THE BEGGAR ON THE GENTLEMAN). **2** [late 17C–18C] to drink ale immediately after drinking wine. [the supposed links of social class and drinking habits]

put a cork in it! *excl.* [1980s+] (US) shut up! be quiet!

put a crimp into, to *phr.* [late 19C+] (US) to thwart, to block, to impair, to interfere with (cf. APPLY A CRIMP).

put across a beauty, to *phr.* [1910s+] (N.Z.) to do something smart or clever.

put a curl in one's hair *see* PUT ONE'S HAIR IN A CURL.

put a dent in one's hip, to *phr.* [1970s+] (US Black) to cost an appreciable amount of cash. [one's wallet is carried on one's hip]

put a down on, to *phr.* [early 19C] to inform against someone. [DOWN *n.*[1]]

put a few back/down, to *phr.* [20C] to have a few drinks.

put a finger in one's eye, to *phr.* [late 18C] to weep. [the implication is of forced, and thus insincere, tears]

put a foot in someone's ass, to *phr.* [1940s+] (US Black) to treat someone unkindly, to beat someone physically. [ARSE *n.*[1]]

put/hang a hat on someone, to *phr.* [1970s+] (US Black) **1** to dislike someone intensely. **2** to single someone out for revenge.

put a hurting on, to *phr.* [1970s+] (US Black) to cause deliberate harm to someone.

put a jerk in it, to *phr.* [1910s+] to act vigorously, smartly or quickly.

put a lid on, to *phr.* [20C] (orig. US) to suppress, e.g. facts, emotions, noise; thus imper. *put a lid on it!* be quiet! stop talking!

put all one's cards on the table *see* PUT ONE'S CARDS ON THE TABLE.

put a move/the moves on, to *phr.* [1960s+] (orig. US) usu. of a man, to make advances to wards the opposite sex. [MOVE *n.*]

put a name up, to *phr.* [1950s+] (Und.) to inform against someone, often to save one's own skin.

put and take *n.*[1] [1920s+] sexual intercourse. [the 'backwards-and-forwards' movement of intercourse]

put and take *n.*[2] [1920s+] a cake. [rhy. sl.]

put a new face/head on, to *phr.* [mid-19C–1920s] (US) **1** punch or assault another, to disfigure in a fight. **2** to defeat, to overcome. **3** to silence, to shut up another.

put another nail in one's coffin, to *phr.* [19C] to get drunk.

[pun on the sealing of a coffin + the pegs that once marked off alcoholic measures in a tankard]

put another record on! *excl.* [1960s+] an excl. used in the hope of silencing a nagging or critical person.

put a notice on, to *phr.* [1960s+] (Und.) to arrange to have someone murdered (cf. CONTRACT).

put a piece of wood in it *see* PUT A BIT IN IT.

put a poor mouth on, to *phr.* [late 19C] (Irish) to complain, to whinge. [POOR MOUTH]

put a ring around, to *phr.* [1950s+] (N.Z.) to be sure of, to be certain of. [image of *ringing* important dates on a calendar]

put a sham upon, to *phr.* [early 18C] to trick, to hoax, to defraud.

put a sock in it, to *phr.* [1910s+] to stop talking, to be quiet; esp. as *put a sock in it!* [the sock gags the mouth]

put a steam on the table, to *phr.* [late 19C] to make enough money to buy a piece of meat for Sunday lunch. [the meat would be boiled rather than roasted]

put a streak into it, to *phr.* [20C] (Anglo-Irish.) to hurry up, to 'get a move on'; esp. as excl. *put a streak into it!* [STREAK n.[1]]

put a tin ear on, to *phr.* [1920s] (US) to batter the head and ears, giving the victim a 'cauliflower' ear.

put a tooth in it, to *phr.* [130s+] to come straight to the point; also in neg., *not put a tooth in it* (cf. BITE THE BULLET). [one starts 'chewing' immediately]

put-away n.[1] [late 19C–1900s] one's appetite. [PUT AWAY v.[3]]

put-away n.[2] [late 19C–1900s] imprisonment. [PUT AWAY v.[2]]

put away v.[1] [late 16C+] to kill, to murder.

put away v.[2] **1** [mid-19C+] to imprison. **2** [late 19C+] (Und.) to inform against and thus be instrumental in having imprisoned. **3** [late 19C–1920s] to pawn. **4** [1930s+] to put in a lunatic asylum or old people's home.

put away v.[3] [late 19C+] to eat, esp. a large amount.

put away/away proper v.[4] [late 19C+] to bury, to give a funeral to.

put away v.[5] [20C] (orig. US) **1** to defeat an opponent. **2** to impress greatly.

put away proper *see* PUT AWAY.

put back v. [1970s] to eat, esp. a large amount (cf. KNOCK BACK v.[2]; PUT AWAY v.[3]).

put balls/hair on v. [1950s+] to make more emphatic, more effective. [BALLS n.[1] (3)/HAIR n.[5]]

put beans up one's nose, to *phr.* [20C] (US) to do something stupid despite having been warned not to (cf. HAVE BEANS UP ONE'S NOSE).

put-down n. [1940s+] a verbal attack, criticism, condemnation. [PUT DOWN v.[2]]

put down v.[1] [late 19C] to eat (cf. PUT AWAY v.[3]; PUT BACK).

put down v.[2] [1940s+] to deride, to slander, to attack verbally, to tease (cf. DOWN v.[1]).

put down v.[3] [1940s+] to act, to do, to say.

put down v.[4] [1950s+] (US) to reject, to give up. [SE *put down*, to set down]

put down a routine, to *phr.* [1950s+] (US) to hoax or otherwise persuade someone with a clever story. [PUT DOWN v.[3] + show business *routine*, a regularly performed sketch, song, dance etc]

put down roots, to *phr.* [1920s+] to settle down in a locality or occupation.

put down some hair, to *phr.* [late 19C; 1960s+] to have sexual intercourse. [HAIR n.[3] (2); 20C use is US]

put down south, to *phr.* [mid-19C] to pocket (money), to save. [SOUTH adj.]

put foot v. [1980s+] (S.Afr.) to drive fast. [abbr. of 'put one's foot on the accelerator']

put four quarters on the spit, to *phr.* [18C] to have sexual intercourse. [cooking imagery; the *quarters* are the couple's legs]

put fowl to mind corn, to *phr.* [20C] (W.I.) to make a very foolish decision, to trust someone unwisely. [a chicken, of course, would eat the corn]

put France on, to *phr.* [20C] (W.I.) to scold severely, to give a tongue-lashing to. [FRANCE]

put hair on *see* PUT BALLS ON.

put hair on one's chest, to *phr.* [20C] to cheer up to strengthen; esp. in context of offering a drink, e.g. *that'll put hair on your chest.*

pu the elop adv. [20C] pregnant. [backsl. UP THE POLE phr.[2]]

put her there *see* PUT IT THERE.

put-in n. [mid–late 19C] (US) one's turn to speak, one's affair. [poker imagery]

put in v.[1] [mid-19C+] of time, to expend, to serve, usu. referring to a job.

put in v.[2] [1920s+] (Aus.) to get someone into trouble, esp. to inform on (to the police). [abbr. *put in trouble*]

put in chancery, to *phr.* [19C+] to have absolute control over an opponent, to dominate completely (cf. IN CHANCERY). [boxing jargon *put in chancery*, to pin one's opponent's head beneath the crook of one arm, thus immobilizing them and making it easy for one to hit their face at will; ult. f. the supposed inflexibility of the Court of Chancery, and the financial 'damage' incurred there by plaintiffs]

put ink in one's pen, to *phr.* [1910s+] to cheer up, to strengthen, esp. in a sexual context (cf. PUT LEAD IN ONE'S PENCIL).

put in lay-away, to *phr.* [1960s] (US Black) to postpone, to put 'on hold'.

put in one's best licks, to *phr.* [mid-19C+] (US) to work as hard and well as one can. [SE *lick*, a blow]

put in one's motto, to *phr.* [late 19C] to interfere in a conversation, esp. to thrust forward one's own point of view.

put in one's oar/put one's oar in, to *phr.* [early 18C+] to meddle, to interfere in another's concerns (cf. SHOVE ONE'S OAR IN). [the last and surviving variation on 16C *have an oar in every man's boat/barge* and *put one's oar in another man's boat*]

put in one's papers, to *phr.* [20C] **1** (US campus) to apply for admission. **2** (US) to resign.

put in one's spoke, to *phr.* [late 16C–early 17C] to interfere (cf. PUT IN ONE'S OAR).

put in one's two cents, to *phr.* [1940s+] (US) to make a contribution, usu. gratuitous and/or malicious, to an argument or conversation.

put in the acid, to *phr.* [1970s+] (Und.) to inform against. [var. on COME THE ACID WITH]

put in the bucket/garden/hole/well, to *phr.* [early 19C] (Und.) to deceive, to cheat, to swindle, to ruin; esp. to rob an accomplice of their share of a robbery. [BUCKET v.[1] (1)/SE *garden/hole/well*; the image is of hiding away the partner's share]

put in the gee, to *phr.* [1920s+] to deceive, to 'tell the tale'. [GEE n.[3] (2)]

put in the hole *see* PUT IN THE BUCKET.

put in the leather, to *phr.* [1940s+] to kick. [i.e. the use of leather shoes]

put in the nips *see* PUT THE NIPS IN.

put in the peg, to *phr.* [late 19C–1920s] **1** (Aus.) to stop doing something, esp. to stop drinking (cf. PUT IN THE PIN). **2** to cut off one's credit. [the pins or pegs that once divided a large tankard]

put in the pin, to *phr.* [mid–late 19C] to stop drinking during a session, or to give up drinking completely. [PUT IN THE PEG]

put in the poison, to *phr.* [20C] to slander, to malign a person's character, esp. in court.

put in the red, to *phr.* [1920s+] to bankrupt. [the writing of debit accounts in red]

put in the slipper, to *phr.* [1940s+] (Aus., orig. prison) to give a kicking (cf. PUT THE BOOT IN).

put in the stings, to *phr.* [1910s+] (Aus.) to demand a loan or a gift. [STING v.]

put in the well *see* PUT IN THE BUCKET.

put in work, to *phr.* [1990s] (US Black gang) to get busy, esp. in the performance of any dangerous and/or illegal act. e.g. theft or murder. [an ironic allusion to the SE, but ? an oblique tribute to the line in Quentin Tarantino's film hit *Reservoir Dogs* (1993), 'Let's go to work']

put in wrong with, to *phr.* [1930s+] (orig. US) to denigrate, to ruin someone's reputation.

put it about *v.* [1970s+] **1** to work as a prostitute. **2** to indulge in a wide-ranging sex life.

put it/one across *v.* [1910s+] (orig. US) to cheat or confuse someone.

put it all over *v.* [late 19C+] (US) to excel, to outdo. [ext. of PUT ONE OVER ON]

put it all together, to *phr.* [1960s+] to consolidate one's position, to work out one's life satisfactorily.

put it around *v.* [1970s] to circulate information.

put it in and break it, to *phr.* [20C] of a man, to have sexual intercourse. [the erect penis 'breaks' after orgasm]

put it in cruise mode/overdrive, to *phr.* [1980s+] (US campus) to seek a partner for romance or sex. [automobile imagery]

put it in the wind, to *phr.* [1970s+] (US Black) to leave.

put it in your brain *see* PUT IT ON A BULLET.

put it in your ear! *excl.* [1930s+] a general dismissive excl. (cf. STICK IT IN YOUR EAR!).

put it on *v.* **1** [20C] to overcharge. **2** [20C] to show off. **3** [1920s+] (Aus.) to make a suggestion, to propose.

put it on a bullet/in your brain *phr.* [1990s] (US Black teen) remember that, don't forget.

put it on/on someone *v.* **1** [late 19C] to extort money, with or without menaces (cf. PUT THE BITE ON). **2** [late 19C–1940s] to charge to someone else's account.

put it on the line *see* LAY IT ON THE LINE *phr.*²

put it on the street, to *phr.* [1950s+] (orig. US) to make gossip, information etc available for general consumption (cf. STREET TALK).

put it over *v.* [1910s+] (orig. US) to cheat or confuse someone (cf. PUT IT ACROSS).

put it/her there! *excl.* [late 19C+] shake hands!; esp. in the context of sealing a deal or affirming a friendship. ['there' being the speaker's outstretched hand and 'it'/'her' being the hand of the person spoken to]

put it to *v.* [20C] (US) to have sexual intercourse with.

put it up *v.* [1990s] of a man, to have sexual intercourse. ['it' being the penis]

put it up! *excl.* [mid-19C] stop it! be quiet!

put it up to *v.* [1990s] (Irish) to attack physically. ['it' being a fist or boot]

put it where the monkeys shove their nuts *phr.* [20C] a phr. of coarse dismissal, i.e. shove it up your arse!

put lead in one's pencil, to *phr.* [1940s+] (orig. Aus.) to cheer one up, to strengthen, esp. in a sexual context; thus *this will put lead in your pencil*, used to accompany the offer of a drink, food or even drug – any of which is cited as a presumed adjunct to potency.

put legs on someone, to *phr.* [late 19C–1930s] to make someone hurry up.

put manners on, to *phr.* [1980s+] (Irish) to discipline, to force into line (cf. HEAVY MANNERS).

put next to *v.* [20C] (US) to introduce, to direct towards.

puto *n.* [1950s+] **1** a male homosexual. **2** a male prostitute. **3** the penis. **4** a general derog. term (cf. DICKHEAD; DORK n.²; PRICK). [masc. version of Sp. *puta*, a prostitute]

put off *v.* [1900s+] to disconcert.

put-on *n.*¹ [mid-19C+] a joke, a hoax. [PUT ON v.¹]

put-on *n.*² [late 19C] an old female beggar who specializes in putting on a look that makes her look as pitiful as possible.

put-on *adj.* [late 19C+] (US) affected, pretentious.

put on *v.*¹ [mid-19C+] to tease, to joke with, to deceive for one's own gain. [the image is of adding things in excess of the actual facts]

put on *v.*² [20C] (Ulster) to get dressed. [abbr. *put on one's clothes*]

put on *v.*³ [1930s+] to eat, e.g. *put on the chicken pie*. [abbr. PUT ON THE FEEDBAG]

put on a boss, to *phr.* [late 19C] to affect a squint in order to make oneself look more threatening. [BOSS-EYED]

put on a bridge, to *phr.* [1970s+] (Aus.) of a woman, to flaunt oneself. [BRIDGE n.¹ (1)]

put on a cigar, to *phr.* [late 19C] to smoke a cigar in order to make oneself seem smarter than one is. [a cigar was seen as more genteel than the working-class pipe]

put on a crosstown bus, to *phr.* [1960s] (US Black) to mislead deliberately.

put on a crumb act, to *phr.* [1950s] (Aus.) to impose on another person. [CRUMB n.¹ (2)]

put on a face, to *phr.* [19C+] to change one's expression.

put on/get a gut, to *phr.* [1920s+] usu. of a man, to put on weight.

put on an act, to *phr.* [1930s+] to show off, to talk for display, to behave insincerely.

put on a queue, to *phr.* [1960s] (Aus.) of a woman, to permit sex with multiple partners in the same session (cf. PULL A TRAIN).

put-on artist *n.* [late 19C+] (US) a hoaxer, a tease. [PUT ON v.¹ + ARTIST n.²]

put on a slab, to *phr.* [20C] (US prison) to fight in private to settle a score (cf. TAKE IT IN THE BLIND).

put on a smoke, to *phr.* [late 19C–1900s] to light a pipe or cigarette.

put on beef, to *phr.* [mid-19C+] to put on weight. [BEEF n.¹ (4)]

put on dog, to *phr.* [mid-19C+] (orig. US) **1** to do something energetically, noisily. **2** to show off, to put on airs (cf. CARRY DOG). [DOG n.⁶]

put one across *see* PUT IT ACROSS.

put one back *v.* [20C] to cost; often as *how much did that put you back?* (cf. SET ONE BACK).

put one on *v.* [1930s+] (orig. Aus.) to hit (cf. BUNG ONE ON; STICK ONE ON). [the *one* is a blow]

put/slip one over on *v.* [late 19C+] (orig. US) to cheat, to deceive. [ext. of PUT ON v.¹; *one* is a trick, a hoax]

put one's ass on the line, to *phr.* [20C] (US) to put oneself into a position of responsibility, to take risks. [ARSE n.¹ (1)]

put one's balls in a knot, to *phr.* [1930s+] (Aus.) to discomfit, to embarrass, to irritate. [BALLS n.¹ (1)]

put one's best side towards London, to *phr.* [late 19C] to make the best of things. [the practice of country people putting on their best clothes for their visits to the capital]

put one's bib in *see* STICK ONE'S BIB IN.

put one's bones up, to *phr.* [late 19C] to get ready to fight. [abbr. SE *knuckle-bones*]

put one's business on front street/the street/put on front street, to *phr.* [1960s+] (US Black) to make indiscreet disclosures about another person. [FRONT STREET]

put one's cards/all one's cards on the table, to *phr.* [20C] to be absolutely open, candid, honest. [poker imagery]

put one's checks in the rack, to *phr.* [1930s+] (US) to die (cf. CASH IN ONE'S CHECKS). [gambling imagery]

put one's cue in the rack, to *phr.* [1980s+] **1** to retire. **2** to die. [billiards/snooker imagery]

put one's ears out, to *phr.* [1990s] to listen for news, to gather information.

put oneself about *v.* [1970s+] to lead an active social or sexual life.

put oneself out of twig *see* PUT SOMEONE OUT OF TWIG.

put oneself outside something, to *phr.* [late 19C] to eat; the food is usu. specified.

put one's eye on, to *phr.* [20C] (W.I.) to become obsessed with at first sight and thus to desire to possess immediately (cf. EYES CATCH FIRE).

put one's face on/put on one's face, to *phr.* [1950s+] usu. of women, to put on make-up. [the term has also gained male currency among gay men and male teenagers who enjoy make-up]

put one's fist to, to *phr.* [mid-19C] to sign (cf. MAULEY).

put one's flags out, to *phr.* [20C] to have a menstrual period (cf. FLY THE RED FLAG; HAVE THE FLAG OUT).

put one's foot down, to *phr.* [1930s+] to insist, to be adamant. [a pettish stamp of the foot]

put one's foot in it, to *phr.* [late 18C+] to make an error. ['it' = the dirt, 'the shit']

put one's foot in one's hand *see* MAKE FOOT.

put one's foot in one's mouth, to *phr.* [20C] to make an embarrassing verbal mistake, discomfiting oneself as well as the hearer.

put one's foot in someone's ass, to *phr.* [1950s+] (US) to attack someone physically. [ARSE n.¹]

put one's foot on the floor, to *phr.* [1920s+] to accelerate a motorcar. [the pressing down of the accelerator pedal]

put one's foot up, to *phr.* [1920s–30s] (US Black) to make one's presence felt in an arrogant, threatening manner (cf. PLAY THE DOZENS). [the tradition among Black communities, when two people were quarrelling, for the injured party to appear at their enemy's home, put a foot up on the porch or jam it in the front door, and curse the opposing family and their forebears]

put one's guts into it, to *phr.* [late 19C+] to make one's best effort.

put one's hair in/into a curl/put a curl in one's hair, to *phr.* [mid-19C–1910s] to make oneself feel extremely healthy or fit (cf. PUT HAIR ON ONE'S CHEST).

put one's hand down, to *phr.* [20C] to pay, to stand one's turn.

put one's hand in an empty corn-jar, to *phr.* [20C] (W.I.) to marry a poor woman.

put one's hand up, to *phr.* [1950s+] to confess. [classroom practice]

put one's hat up *see* PUT UP ONE'S HAT.

put one's head on the block, to *phr.* [1960s+] to declare oneself openly, to take a risk or a stand that may be dangerous.

put one's money where one's mouth is, to *phr.* [1940s+] (orig. US) **1** to back one's opinions with wagered money. **2** to back one's boasting with suitable action.

put one's mouth in one's pocket, to *phr.* [20C] (W.I.) to be forced to make a heavy payment after losing a libel suit.

put one's mouth on, to *phr.* [20C] (W.I.) to denigrate, to slander (cf. BADMOUTH v.; POOR MOUTH).

put one's nose in the manger *see* HAVE ONE'S NOSE IN THE MANGER.

put one's oar in *see* PUT IN ONE'S OAR.

put/set one's own house in order, to *phr.* [late 19C+] to set one's affairs in order.

put one's pot on, to *phr.* [1910s–50s] (Aus./N.Z.) to inform against, to tell tales, to destroy the prospects of. [POT v.³]

put one's shirt on, to *phr.* [late 19C+] (gambling) to bet heavily.

put one's skates on *see* GET ONE'S SKATES ON.

put one's snout in the trough *see* GET ONE'S SNOUT IN THE TROUGH

put one's stuff down, to *phr.* [1970s+] (US Black) to disparage, to ridicule. [PUT DOWN v.² + STUFF n.¹]

put one's thumbs up, to *phr.* [20C] to be cheerful. [the Roman amphitheatre, where life and death were decided on the position of the patrician thumb. It is generally accepted that the Romans actually signified death with an extended thumb (pointing either upwards or outwards, depending on source), but authorities argue as to the exact position of the thumb when signifying life. The relevant Lat., *police compressio*, means the thumb was held 'close', which is taken to mean that the other fingers were closed around it. Whatever the truth, the modern phr., seeing a fig. use of 'down' as a neg., has reversed the actual gesture]

put one's time in, to *phr.* [late 19C+] to spend time, to occupy one's time.

put one's tongue in someone's purse, to *phr.* [mid-16C–early 17C] to silence someone, to keep someone quiet.

put one's trademark on someone *see* DRAW ONE'S TRADEMARK ON SOMEONE.

put one together *v.* [1940s+] (Und.) to plan a crime.

put on front street *see* PUT ONE'S BUSINESS ON FRONT STREET.

put on hold, to *phr.* [1960s+] to delay, to postpone, to defer (cf. PUT ON THE BACK BURNER). [telephone etiquette]

put on ice, to *phr.* **1** [late 19C+] to put aside (a project or idea), for later development or use. **2** [1930s+] (orig. US) to hide away, to keep out of the limelight until required, e.g. a witness, the 'star' of a newspaper exclusive etc. **3** [1930s+] (orig. US) to maintain a distant, minimally emotional relationship (cf. PLAY THE CHILL). **4** [1940s] to kill, to murder. [ON ICE phr.¹]

put on jam, to *phr.* [late 19C+] (Aus.) to put on airs.

put on lugs *see* PILE ON LUGS.

put on one's face *see* PUT ONE'S FACE ON.

put on one's frills, to *phr.* [late 19C] (orig. US) **1** to swagger. **2** to become very amorous.

put on one's own pot, to *phr.* [20C] (W.I.) to take care of oneself; thus *not put on the pot for, not make one's pot bubble*, to refuse to help someone.

put on one's travelling shoes, to *phr.* [late 18C+] (US Black) **1** to die. **2** to leave.

put on pot, to *phr.* [mid-19C–1900s] **1** to exaggerate. **2** to overcharge. [ext. use of BIG POT]

put on someone's ear, to *phr.* [late 19C] to set on, to attack. [the victim is knocked down, 'on their ear']

put on the bag *see* PUT ON THE FEEDBAG.

put on the bib, to *phr.* [1930s] (US) to eat (cf. PUT ON THE FEEDBAG).

put on the bounce, to *phr.* [1930s+] (Aus.) to accost, esp. in pursuit of a loan. [BOUNCE v.¹ (4)]

put on the chill, to *phr.* (US) to snub, to ignore (cf. COLD SHOULDER). [CHILL n.¹]

put on the clothes-line, to *phr.* [20C] (US) to make one's family affairs a matter for public knowledge and discussion (cf. AIR ONE'S DIRTY LINEN). [the practice of stringing clothes-lines between tenement blocks and thus displaying one's washing and underclothes to all and sundry]

put on the feedbag/bag, to *phr.* [1920s+] to eat (cf. PUT ON THE BIB; PUT ON THE NOSEBAG).

put on the floor, to *phr.* [20C] (US) to please enormously. [? they fall to the floor with delight]

put on the fluence *see* PUT THE FLUENCE ON.

put on the fritz *see* PUT THE FRITZ ON.

put on the front burner, to *phr.* [1970s+] to make into a priority (cf. ON THE BACK BURNER).

put on the gee, to *phr.* [1920s+] to boast, to brag, to 'swank about'. [GEE n.³ (2)]

put on the guiver, to *phr.* [late 19C+] (Und.) to affect an upper-class accent. [GUIVER adj., a working class dandy; ult. Heb. pride]

put on the high dick, to *phr.* [20C] (US) to dress in one's best clothes, to put on airs. [SE *up to dick*, up to standard, as required]

put on the kitz, to *phr.* [1930s] to put on one's best clothes. [ety. unknown; KIT n.⁵ is too late; ? link to Yid. or Ger.]

put on the long finger, to *phr.* [20C] (Irish) to postpone indefinitely. [one pushes it as far away as one can]

put on the nosebag, to *phr.* [mid-19C+] to eat (cf. PUT ON THE FEEDBAG).

put on the pot, to *phr.* [late 19C–1900s] to put on airs. [POT n.⁶]

put on the ritz, to *phr.* [1920s+] (orig. US) to make a display of wealth or luxury, to dress stylishly. [César *Ritz* (1850–1918), Swiss hotelier and the hotels he founded. Popularized by Irving Berlin's song 'Putting on the Ritz' (1929): 'If you're blue and you don't know what to do/Why don't you go where Harlem sits/Puttin' on the Ritz']

put on the screw, to *phr.* [mid-19C] to set a limit on someone's credit. [SE *screw*, that which tightens]

put on the skid, to *phr.* [late 19C] to speak or act cautiously. [SE *skid*, a block used to retard a wheel]

put on the spot, to *phr.* [1920s+] (orig. US) **1** to place in a difficult or disadvantageous position. **2** to arrange to have someone killed.

put on the stake, to *phr.* [20C] (US Und.) to blackmail. [the stake as an instrument of torture]

put on White folks, to *phr.* [19C+] (US Black) to act and speak in a manner White people wish to see and hear from Blacks.

put out *v.*¹ [1930s+] to murder. [? abbr. SE *put out of one's misery*]

put out *v.*² [1940s+] (US) to offer oneself for sex. [SE *put out*, to display]

put out *adv.* [late 19C+] murdered, killed. [SE *put out*, to extinguish]

put out of sight, to *phr.* [late 19C] to eat (cf. GET OUTSIDE).

put out one's fins, to *phr.* [15C] to get into action, to make a start. [image of a fish]

put out one's hand, to *phr.* [1950s+] to go through a drunk's pockets looking for cash and/or valuables.

put/punch out someone's lights, to *phr.* [mid-19C+] **1** to kill, to murder (cf. BLOW OUT SOMEONE'S LAMP). **2** to knock unconscious. [fig. use of SE *daylights*. The orig. use may have referred to one's eyes and/or one's intestines, i.e. 'liver and lights', but the 'electrical' imagery has long since superseded this]

put out the miller's eye, to *phr.* [17C–19C] (orig. Scot.) to put too much water in one's liquor or into one's dough mixture (cf. DROWN THE MILLER; PUT OUT THE MILLER'S THUMB).

put out the miller's thumb, to *phr.* [18C] (orig. Scot.) to put too much water in one's liquor or into one's dough mixture (cf. DROWN THE MILLER; PUT OUT THE MILLER'S EYE).

put out to grass, to *phr.*¹ [late 16C–early 17C] to send out to work as a prostitute.

put out to grass/pasture, to *phr.*² [20C] to send into retirement. [animal imagery]

put over *v.* [mid-19C] to knock over with a gunshot.

put paid to, to *phr.* [1910s+] to bring (someone's hopes,

aspirations, efforts) to an end, to dispose of, to terminate. [SE *pay off*]

put pudding/a bit of pudding on, to *phr.* [20C] (Aus.) to put on weight.

putrid *adj.*¹ [early 17C+] a general neg. intensifier. [SE *putrid*, rotten, stinking]

putrid *adj.*² [20C] drunk (cf. ADDLED). [SE *putrid*, rotten, stinking]

put roach on one's bread, to *phr.* [20C] (W.I.) to be sexually unfaithful, to cuckold. [SE *cockroach*]

put sand in someone's Vaseline, to *phr.* [1970s+] to ruin someone else's pleasure or endeavours. [SE *sand* is gritty; cosmetic product *Vaseline* is a smooth cream]

putsch *n.* [1930s+] a sudden vigorous effort or campaign. [SE *putsch*, a revolutionary attempt, ult. Swiss Ger. *Putsch*, a knock or thrust]

put shit on, to *phr.* [1990s] (US Black) **1** to take advantage. **2** to trick, to deceive. [SHIT n.⁴]

put snow in one's game, to *phr.* [1960s+] (US Black) to ensnare a White person for financial gain. [SNOW n.⁴ (4) + GAME n.⁴ (5)]

put some beef into it, to *phr.* [20C] to make a physical effort; often as excl. *put some beef into it!* [BEEF n.¹ (4)]

put someone away *v.* [1950s+] (orig. US) **1** to knock out, to win a fight. **2** of an entertainer, to score a resounding success with one's audience. [PUT AWAY v.⁵]

put someone crook with, to *phr.* [1930s+] (Aus/N.Z.) to lower someone's standing, to get someone into trouble. [CROOK adj.]

put someone down *v.* [early 19C] to convey information to someone, to explain, to make someone aware; thus (Und.) *put a swell down*, to alert one's target (typically the target of a pickpocket) that one is about to rob them.

put someone down the track, to *phr.* [1910s+] to dismiss someone from a job.

put someone flash to, to *phr.* [early 19C] to put someone on their guard, to warn someone, to pass on information. [FLASH adj.⁴]

put someone in/in with *v.* [1920s+] (Aus.) **1** to inform against. **2** to ruin someone's reputation, to talk maliciously behind someone's back. ['one' is the report or the person thus 'put in' prison]

put someone in a bag, to *phr.* [17C] to gain an advantage over someone.

put someone in a sling, to *phr.* [1950s+] (US) to cause someone extreme trouble, whether actually physically damaging or not.

put someone in with *see* PUT SOMEONE IN.

put someone off their stroke, to *phr.* [1910s+] to disconcert someone, to disturb someone. [fig. use of golfing imagery]

put someone off the walk, to *phr.* [late 19C–1930s] (Anglo-Irish) to murder.

put someone on the block/the corner, to *phr.* [1950s+] (US) of a pimp, to launch a woman into a career as a prostitute.

put someone on the heavy jacket, to *phr.* [1980s+] (N.Z.) to ostracize.

put someone on to *v.* [late 19C+] (orig. US) to introduce a topic, to point out, esp. to point out a chance of possible social or financial gain etc.

put someone onto someone, to *phr.* [20C] to introduce someone, to give access to someone.

put someone out of business, to *phr.* [20C] to halt someone's activity and/or efforts, usu. through injury, destruction of their premises etc.

put someone/oneself out of twig, to *phr.* [early 19C] to remove someone/oneself from the understanding of what is going on. [TWIG v.²]

put someone over the door, to phr. [late 18C–mid-19C] to throw someone out into the street.

put someone's back up, to phr. [late 18C+] to annoy someone, to irritate someone. [the risen hairs on a cat's back that denote, inter alia, aggression]

put someone's dick in the dirt see KNOCK SOMEONE'S DICK IN THE DIRT.

put someone's lights out see PUT OUT SOMEONE'S LIGHTS.

put someone's monkey up, to phr. [mid-19C] to annoy someone, to infuriate someone (cf. HAVE ONE'S MONKEY UP).

put someone's nose out of joint, to phr. [late 18C+] to discomfit someone, to embarrass someone, to irritate someone.

put someone's pot on, to phr. [late 19C+] (Aus./N.Z.) 1 to tell tales, to inform against, to destroy the hopes of. 2 to catch someone out in wrong-doing. [i.e. putting a pot or saucepan on their hopes or activities]

put someone's tits in a tangle, to phr. [1930s+] (Aus.) to discomfit, to embarrass, to irritate someone (cf. CATCH ONE'S BALLS IN A WRINGER; PUT ONE'S BALLS IN A KNOT).

put someone up to, to phr. [19C+] to make someone aware of, to inform someone of, to persuade or incite someone, esp. to do something underhand or nefarious.

put some slobber on the knobber, to phr. [20C] (US) to perform oral sex (cf. KNOBBER). [SE slobber + KNOB n.[1] (1)]

put some stuff on, to phr. [1940s–50s] (US Black) to trick, to cheat, to deceive. [STUFF n.[1]]

put something down v. [1970s+] (US Black) to stop what one is doing.

put stuffing into, to phr. [1930s+] to strengthen someone's morale or resolution.

putter-up n. [early 19C–1920s] (Und.) one who plans a robbery or tips off thieves as to where a robbery might profitably be committed, e.g. a servant in a great house, a bank clerk etc. [SE put up (a plan)]

put that in your pipe and smoke it! excl. [early 19C+] an excl. meaning deal with that, whether you like it or not.

put the acid/squeaks in, to phr. [1910s] to inform on, to tell tales about, to poison another's mind against.

put the acid on/ply/try the acid, to phr. [20C] 1 to test out a person or a statement. 2 to put a stop to. 3 (Aus.) to exert pressure on a person for a loan, a favour, sexual compliance etc. [supposedly orig. used by gold assayers who tested 'real' gold with acid]

put/keep the anchors on, to phr. [1970s+] to slow down intercourse so as to delay one's orgasm. [ANCHORS]

put the arm on, to phr. [1930s+] (US) 1 (Und.) to attack from behind by choking the victim with one's forearm before robbing them. 2 to pressurize with threats of violence, to extort 'protection' payments, to beg for money, to blackmail (cf. ARM n.[2]). 3 to reveal scandalous facts about someone. [synon. with TWIST SOMEONE'S ARM]

put the bag on, to phr.[1] [20C] (orig. Aus.) to halt, to interfere with, to bring to a standstill. [SE bag; the image of covering something up, ? a caged bird]

put the bag on, to phr.[2] [20C] (Ulster) to start out as a beggar. [a beggar's bag]

put the bag on, to phr.[3] [1930s+] (US) to enjoy a raucous drinking bout or party. [BAG n.[6]]

put the bag on, to phr.[4] [1980s] (N.Z.) to breathalyse. [the polythene bag that is part of the breathalysing kit]

put the bee on, to phr.[1] [1910s–30s] 1 to air one's obsession. 2 of a woman, to pursue a man with the intention of marriage. [SE phr. have a bee in one's bonnet]

put the bee on, to phr.[2] [1910s–40s] (US) to quash, to bring to an end, to ruin. [initial letter of 'bag' in PUT THE BAG ON phr.[1]]

put the bee on, to phr.[3] 1 [1910s+] (US) to extort, to blackmail, to pressurize, esp. for a loan (cf. STING v.). 2 [1920s–30s] (US) to swindle, to hoax, to victimize. [initial letter of 'bite' in PUT THE BITE ON]

put the beggar on the gentleman, to phr. [mid–late 19C] to drink beer after spirits (cf. PUT A CHURL UPON A GENTLEMAN).

put the bite on, to phr. 1 [1910s+] (orig. Aus.) to extort, to blackmail, to force someone to do something they would rather avoid. 2 [1910s+] to ask for a loan or for the repayment of a debt. 3 [1960s] (US) to put the blame on (cf. PUT THE BEE ON phr.[3]). [BITE n.[2] (5)]

put the bit on, to phr. [1950s] (Aus.) to extort, to blackmail, to force someone to do something they would rather avoid (cf. PUT THE BITE ON). [SE bit, the mouthpiece of a horse's bridle, used to restrain the animal]

put the black on, to phr. [20C] to blackmail. [abbr.]

put the blast on, to phr. (US) 1 [1920s+] to attack verbally, to criticize severely. 2 [1940s–50s] to shoot dead.

put the bleed on, to phr. [1960s] to extort from. [BLEED v.[1] (1)]

put the blind on, to phr. [20C] (Irish) to curse someone. [BLIND v.[2]]

put the blink on, to phr. [late 19C] (US) to cause problems for. [the victim blinks nervously]

put the block on, to phr. [20C] to interfere with, to stop. [SE block, to impede]

put the blocks on, to phr. 1 [late 19C+] to give someone a hard time. 2 [1940s–50s] (prison) to tighten up regulations that have become temporarily lax. [SE block, to impede]

put the blocks to, to phr. [late 19C+] (US) of a man, to have sexual intercourse (cf. BLOCK v.[3]). [SE block, a lump of wood, i.e. the penis]

put the boogaloo on, to phr. [1970s] to annoy, to cause trouble (for). [fig. use of BOOGALOO v.]

put the boot in, to phr. [1910s+] (orig. Aus.) to kick someone during a fight; thus in with the boot, no holds barred (cf. SINK THE BOOT IN).

put the boot on, to phr. [1940s] (Irish) to bring to a close. [one puts on one's boots before leaving the house]

put the boots to see GIVE THE BOOTS TO.

put the breeze up see GET THE BREEZE UP.

put the bubble in, to phr. [1920s+] (Und.) to inform. [BUBBLE n.[4]]

put the bug on, to phr. [mid-19C–1920s] (US) to tease, to play tricks on. [BUG n.[8]]

put the bull on, to phr. [1960s+] (US) to pressurize, to act aggressively towards. [the animal's characteristics]

put the bush in the gap! excl. [20C] (Irish) shut the door! (cf. PUT A BIT IN IT)

put the change on, to phr. [late 17C–late 19C] to mislead. [one has 'changed' the truth for lies]

put the chill/shake on, to phr. [20C] (US prison) to intimidate.

put the clamps on, to phr. [20C] (US) to steal. [i.e. one SE clamps hold of the stolen item]

put the claws on, to phr. [20C] (US Und.) 1 to arrest. 2 to inform on.

put the clip on, to phr. [1920s+] (US) to overcharge, to defraud. [CLIP v.[2] (3)]

put the collar on, to phr. [mid-19C] (US) to arrest. [COLLAR n.[2]]

put the comether on, to phr. [mid-19C+] (Anglo-Irish) to coax, to wheedle, to impress. [SE come hither]

put the cosh on, to phr. [1950s+] to pressurize, to compel (cf. UNDER THE COSH).

put the cross on, to phr. [20C] to mark for death. [a cross placed, lit. or fig., against the victim's name]

put the devil into hell, to *phr.* [18C] to have sexual intercourse (cf. HELL). [a euph. coined by Boccaccio in a ribald story in the *Decameron* (1358), in which a hermit seduces a virgin by persuading her of the necessity of letting him 'put the devil into hell']

put the double on, to *phr.* [1920s] to double-cross. [abbr.]

put the drags on, to *phr.* [1910s+] (Aus.) to ask someone for a loan. [SE *drag*, in the sense of dragging on someone's sleeve; + poss. link to DRAG n.[11]]

put the eye on, to *phr.* [20C] (US) 1 to look at seductively. 2 to examine, to stare at.

put the fangs into, to *phr.* [20C] (Aus.) 1 to pressurize, to blackmail. 2 to demand a loan. [var. on PUT THE BITE ON]

put the finger on, to *phr.* [1920s+] 1 to betray, to inform against. 2 to identify a target or possible victim. [FINGER n.[2]]

put the fixments on, to *phr.* [19C+] to take revenge on (cf. FIX v.[1]). [dial. *fixment*, a dilemma]

put the flimp on, to *phr.* [mid-19C–1900s] to rob on the highway, to rob and garrotte. [FLIMP]

put the fluence on/put on the fluence, to *phr.* 1 [late 19C] to influence through mental, rather than physical, pressure. 2 [1910s+] (orig. Aus./N.Z.) to persuade. 3 [1910s+] (orig. Aus./N.Z.) to hypnotize. [FLUENCE]

put the freeze on, to *phr.* [1970s+] (US) 1 to stop. 2 to reject, to snub.

put the frighteners on, to *phr.* [1960s+] (Und.) to menace, to blackmail, to threaten with violence. [FRIGHTENERS]

put the fritz on/put on the fritz, to *phr.* [20C] to spoil, to render out of order, to put a stop to. [ON THE FRITZ]

put the gas on, to *phr.* [1900s] (Aus.) 1 to test out a person or a statement. 2 to put a stop to. 3 to exert pressure on a person for a loan, a favour, sexual compliance etc (cf. PUT THE ACID ON).

put the gloves on someone, to *phr.* [late 19C] (Scot.) to improve someone's standing and circumstances. [wearing gloves is a sign of gentility]

put the hammer down, to *phr.* [1970s+] to drive fast, esp. used by truck-drivers. [HAMMER n.[1] (3)]

put the hammer on, to *phr.* (US) 1 [1940s+] to take decisive action. 2 [1960s+] to demand money. 3 [1980s+] to attack verbally, to slander.

put the hard word on, to *phr.* [1910s+] (orig. Aus./N.Z.) to make demands (esp. financial or sexual) of someone.

put the heart on, to *phr.* [1920s+] (Irish) to terrify. [i.e. one's 'heart misses a bit']

put the heat on, to *phr.* [1960s+] to pressurize, to threaten.

put the horns on, to *phr.* [1940s+] (US) to jinx. [fig. use of HORNS; its usual use as adultery can also be said to jinx the victim]

put the hurt on, to *phr.* [1960s+] (orig. US) to hurt deliberately, to assault physically and/or emotionally.

put the icing on the cake, to *phr.* [20C] to add the finishing touches to a plan, a scheme etc.

put the ig on, to *phr.* [1960s+] (US Black) to snub, to 'cut', to ignore. [abbr. SE *ignore*]

put the Indian sign on, to *phr.* [20C] (US) to place a curse on someone, to jinx or 'hex'. [the belief that Native Americans have the power of cursing. Note also SE *Indian sign*, a smoke-signal]

put the kibosh on, to *phr.* [mid-19C+] to spoil, to ruin. [KIBOSH v.]

put the knock on, to *phr.* [late 19C+] to disparage, to criticize. [ext. of KNOCK v.[1] (4)]

put the leather in, to *phr.* [1940s+] to kick someone during a fight. [one's leather footwear]

put the leg-rope on, to *phr.* [20C] (Aus.) to curb a person who is acting in a hysterical or very bad-tempered manner. [SE *leg-rope*, a rope used to tether or control an animal]

put the lid on, to *phr.*[1] [1920s+] (Aus.) to shut a bar at the legal closing time.

put the lid on, to *phr.*[2] [1920s+] (orig. US) 1 to cover up, to hide, esp. news that is offensive or embarrassing to an establishment. 2 to clamp down on corruption, esp. that of an urban administration.

put the lug on, to *phr.*[1] [1920s+] (US) 1 to demand money with menaces, to extort, to blackmail. 2 [1970s+] (US Black) to criticize harshly. [LUG n.[1]]

put the lug on, to *phr.*[2] [1930s–40s] (US) to beat up, to use violence against. [LUG n.[2]]

put the maginnis/macginnis/mcginnis on, to *phr.* [1900s–40s] (Aus.) to put in a position from which there is no escape, to pressurize; thus *crooked maginnis*, an unfair form of control, e.g. (moral) blackmail. [SE *mcginnis*, a wrestling hold]

put the make on, to *phr.* [1950s+] (US) to make sexual advances. [MAKE n.[3] (2)]

put the mockers/mocker/mocks on, to *phr.* [1910s+] to jinx, to put a curse on, to frustrate someone's plans. [? Yid. *makkes*, ult. Heb. *makot*, plagues, blows, (evil) visitations. The phr was possibly orig. used in Aus., but given the ety., there may be a link to 19C London market traders]

put the moves on see PUT A MOVE ON.

put the moz/mozz on, to *phr.* [1920s+] (Aus.) to inconvenience, to jinx. [PUT THE MOCKERS ON; ? *moz* a mis-reading of MAZEL]

put the mug on, to *phr.* [mid-19C–1940s] to throttle (cf. MUG v.[2]).

put them up! *excl.* [mid-19C+] get ready to fight. ['them' are the fists or arms]

put the muscle on, to *phr.* [1940s+] (US Und.) to coerce, to threaten with violence (cf. PUT THE ARM ON).

put the nadgers on, to *phr.* [1950s+] to jinx, to cause trouble for, to 'hex'. [NADGERS]

put the nark on, to *phr.* [20C] to put off, to ruin (a plan), to discourage. [NARK n.]

put the nips in/put in the nips, to *phr.* [1930s+] (Aus./N.Z.) to cadge from. [NIP n.[4]]

put the nix on, to *phr.* [1940s] (US) to negate, to make unavailable. [NIX v.]

put the oliver on, to *phr.* [late 19C] to do something illegally. [play on *Oliver Twist*/SE *twist*, to cheat]

put the pedal to the metal, to *phr.* [1970s+] (orig. US) to accelerate a car.

put the pot on, to *phr.* [mid-19C] 1 to overcharge. 2 to exaggerate. [POT n.[2]]

put the scream out, to *phr.* [1960s+] (Und.) to put out an alert for a person. [SCREAM n.[1]]

put the screws on, to *phr.* [20C] to pressurize. [SE *thumbscrew*]

put the shake on see PUT THE CHILL ON.

put the shit up, to *phr.* [1940s+] to terrify. [SHIT n.[1]]

put the shoe on the left foot, to *phr.* [1970s+] (US Black) to put blame where it does not belong (cf. PUT THE SHOE ON THE RIGHT FOOT).

put the shoe on the right foot, to *phr.* [1950s+] (US Black) to place blame where it duly belongs (cf. PUT THE SHOE ON THE LEFT FOOT).

put the shuck on, to *phr.* [1970s+] (US) to trick, to deceive, to fool verbally. [SHUCK v.]

put the skids to/under, to *phr.* [1910s+] (orig. US) 1 to sack someone from a job. 2 to make someone hurry up, usu. in doing their work. 3 to hasten someone's downfall.

put the sleeve on, to *phr.* [1930s] to arrest. [the police officer grabs the villain's sleeve]

put the slinkers in for, to *phr.* [1950s–60s] to tell malicious tales about. [? SE *slink*, to act in a sly manner]

put the slug on, to *phr.* [1940s+] (US) **1** to beat up. **2** to criticize harshly. [SLUG v.²]

put the smack down, to *phr.* [20C] to hit, to assault. [SMACK n.² (1)]

put the smother on, to *phr.* [1900s] (Aus.) to censor, to suppress. [SE *smother*]

put the snatch on, to *phr.* [1930s+] (US) to kidnap, to seize, to take over. [SNATCH n.²]

put the squeaks in *see* PUT THE ACID IN.

put the squeal on, to *phr.* [1980s+] to betray, to inform against. [SQUEAL v.]

put the squeeze on, to *phr.* [1940s+] (orig. US) to pressurize, esp. for money. [but note 18C use of SE *squeeze* to mean the same thing]

put the stunners on, to *phr.* [mid-19C] to astonish, to amaze, to surprise (cf. FRIGHTENERS).

put the tin hat on, to *phr.* [1930s] (Irish) to finish off for good.

put the touch on, to *phr.* [mid-9C+] to attempt to borrow money. [TOUCH n.¹]

put the whisper on, to *phr.* [1960s–70s] to inform against. [WHISPER n.¹ (2)]

put the windows in, to *phr.* [late 19C+] to smash windows.

put the wind up, to *phr.* [1920s+] to worry, to frighten.

put the wood in the hole *see* PUT A BIT IN IT.

put the wood to, to *phr.* [20C] (US) to punish, to coerce by threats. [? image of hitting with a wooden club]

put this reckoning up to the Dover wagoner *phr.* [early–mid-19C] put this (usu. tavern bill) on credit. [a pun on the contemporary Dover wagoner, one *Owen*, i.e. 'owing']

put through a/the wringer, to *phr.* [1940s+] (orig. US) to pressurize, to subject to severe interrogation.

put through changes, to *phr.* [1960s+] (orig. US Black) to alter another person's mental or emotional state, opinions or attitudes (cf. GO THROUGH CHANGES). [CHANGES]

put through the hoop, to *phr.* [20C] (orig. milit.) to make suffer, to punish, to reprimand, to interrogate.

put through the mill, to *phr.* [early 19C+] to subject to an arduous or harsh situation or experience.

put through the wringer *see* PUT THROUGH A WRINGER.

put to bed, to *phr.* [20C] (US) to murder. [ironic euph.]

put to bed with a mattock/with a mattock and tucked up with a spade *phr.* [18C–early 19C] dead and buried. [SE *mattock* and *spade*, tools for digging graves]

put to bed with a pickaxe and shovel *phr.* [19C] dead and buried.

put to bed with a shovel/spade *phr.* [late 18C–19C] dead and buried.

puttock *n.* [16C] **1** an unpleasant person. **2** a prostitute. [SE *puttock*, a kite or buzzard, hence the human version of a 'bird of prey']

put to find *v.* [late 19C–1900s] to imprison. [i.e. where one can always be found]

put to the pin of the collar, to *phr.* [19C+] to put in very great difficulties, to be stretched to very limit. [20C use is Irish; saddlery imagery]

putt-putt *n.* (orig. US) **1** [20C] a small vehicle or motor-boat. **2** [1920s] (Und.) a machine-gun. [the sound of its mechanism]

putty *n.* [mid–late 19C] (mainly US) money. [i.e. it 'fills in the cracks']

putty *adj.* [1910s–20s] stupid, foolish. [play on putty's flexible consistency and on SOFT adj.; note dial. *putty-brain*, a fool]

putty-head *n.* [1910s+] (US) a fool. [SE *putty* + sfx. -HEAD (1)]

putty in one's hands, to be *phr.* [1920s+] to be ineffectually malleable to another's whims or wishes.

putty medal *n.* [late 19C] a fig. award given to someone who has botched a job or in some other way failed to do what is required. [a proper medal would be made of metal]

putty pusher *n.* [1990s] a homosexual man. [image of anal intercourse]

put under the jail, to *phr.* [1970s+] (US Black) to imprison in the severest conditions. [the punishment cells are often under the main prison]

put under the screw, to *phr.* [mid-19C] to coerce, to compel, to force. [PUT THE SCREWS ON]

put under the sod, to *phr.* [late 19C+] to kill, to murder. [SE *sod*, a lump of earth]

put/see under the table, to *phr.* [1920s+] to make insensibly drunk.

put up *v.*¹ [mid-19C] (N.Z. Und.) to hold up and rob.

put up *v.*² [late 19C] **1** to plan in advance, esp. a crime or some form of deception. **2** to pay out money in advance, esp. on a bet or for the purchase of drugs.

put up a black, to *phr.* [1940s+] (orig. RN) to make a mistake. [? the two black balls hauled to the mast of Royal Navy ships when a ship was out of control; but note the general neg. imagery of SE *black*]

put up a drink, to *phr.* [late 19C–1930s] (Aus.) to buy a drink on credit.

put up affair *see* PUT UP JOB.

put up a fight, to *phr.* [1910s+] to make an effort, whether in a lit. or fig. fight.

put up a job/job on, to *phr.* [late 19C+] (US) to trick, to deceive (someone). [JOB n.³]

put up a stall, to *phr.* [late 19C+] to act in a deceptive, misleading manner. [STALL n.²]

put up job/affair *n.* [early 19C+] a pre-arranged, and usu. criminal or at least deceptive, plan. [PUT UP v.² + JOB n.³. Mainly *put up job* from late 19C+]

put up one's forks, to *phr.* [late 19C] to ready oneself for a fight (cf. PUT ONE'S BONES UP). [FORKS]

put up one's hat/put one's hat up, to *phr.* [late 19C] to pay court to; thus *put your hat up there*, make yourself at home. [the image is of the lover looking forward to joining the family]

put up/pack up one's pipes, to *phr.* [16C] **1** to stop talking. **2** to cease from an action. [PIPES n.¹ (1)]

put up one's shovel, to *phr.* [late 19C–1900s] to stop work for the day.

put up or shut up! *excl.* [late 19C+] (orig. US) a challenge; back your big talk with a genuine commitment (cf. PUT YOUR MONEY WHERE YOUR MOUTH IS!). [gambling imagery]

put up the ropes, to *phr.* [late 19C] to acquaint with correct information, to 'put in the picture'. [naut. imagery]

put up the shutters against, to *phr.* [1920s–30s] to blacklist, to bar.

put wise *v.* [20C] (orig. US) to explain, to pass on information (cf. WISE UP).

put work in *v.* [1980s+] (US gang) to take part in an attack on a rival gang.

put years on someone, to *phr.* [20C] to make someone wretched, worried, tired etc.

put Yorkshire on *see* COME YORKSHIRE OVER.

put your head in a bag! *excl.* [late 19C+] be quiet! shut up! (cf. BAG YOUR FACE!).

put your money where your mouth is! *excl.* [1940s+] a challenge; back your big talk with a genuine commitment (cf. PUT UP OR SHUT UP!). [gambling imagery]

putz/potz *n.* [1930s+] **1** the penis. **2** an idiot, a fool, a simpleton (cf. DICKHEAD; SCHMUCK; YUTZ). [Yid. *putz*, the penis]

putz around *v.* [1930s+] to act like a fool, to mess around. [PUTZ + SE *around*]

puz/puzz *n.* [mid–late 18C] a young man about town. [ety. unknown]

puza *see* PHUZA.

puzz *see* PUZ.

puzzle *n.* [16C] a prostitute. [Fr. *pucelle*, a virgin]

puzzle-cause *n.* [late 18C–early 19C] an ignorant, incompetent lawyer (cf. PUZZLE-COVE; PUZZLE-TEXT). [SE *puzzle* + *cause*, a legal suit]

puzzle-cove *n.* [mid–late 19C] a lawyer (cf. PUZZLE-CAUSE). [SE *puzzle* + COVE]

puzzlegut *n.* [1900s–40s] (US Black) an exceptionally large stomach. [var. on PUSTLE-GUT]

puzzle-palace *n.* [1950s+] (US) a place where decisions are made, e.g. the White House; thus *five-sided puzzle-palace*, the Pentagon, HQ of the US armed forces.

puzzle-text *n.* [late 18C–early 19C] a clergyman (cf. PUZZLE-CAUSE). [SE *puzzle* + *text*]

puzzling stick *n.* [early 19C] a triangle to which a criminal is tied to receive a judicial whipping. [the criminal fig. 'puzzles' the crimes while being punished]

P.V. *n.*[1] *see* PAV n.[1].

p.v. *n.*[2] [1960s+] (US prison) *parole violator*. [abbr.]

p.w. abney *n.* [late 19C] a style of hat fashionable 1896–1900, featuring three black, upright ostrich feathers, reminiscent of the three feathers of the Prince of Wales' crest. [*Prince of Wales Abney Cemetery*. Abney Park Cemetery, Stoke Newington, was founded in 1840 as London's main nonconformist burying ground]

p.w.t. *n.* [1990s] (US) the poor White population of the southern states of the US. [abbr. SE *poor* + WHITE TRASH]

pyah/pyaa-pyaa *adj.* [mid-19C+] (W.I.) weak, inadequate, useless. [SE *pariah* or Fante *piapia*, to constrain]

pyaka *adj.* [1950s+] (W.I. Rasta) tricky or dishonest. [Carib.E. *pyaka-pyaka*, messy, dirty; ult. unknown Afr. language's *poto-poto*, muddy]

p.y.c. *phr.* [20C] (Aus.) *pay your cash*. [abbr.]

pygostole *n.* [mid-19C] a short coat worn by Tractarians (cf. M.B. COAT). [Greek lit. 'rump-stole']

pyjams/pyjies *n.* [1920s+] *pyjamas*. [abbr.]

py korry! *excl.* [1930s+] (N.Z.) by golly! [mispron.]

pyramids *n.* [20C] (US) very thick-soled shoes. [the shape]

Pyrmont Yank *n.* [1950s+] (Aus.) a relatively unsophisticated person who attempts to emulate the supposed greater sophistication of an American (cf. WOOLLOOMOOLOO YANK). [proper name *Pyrmont*, a suburb + YANK n.]

pyu *v.* [1950s+] (W.I. Rasta) of a running sore etc, to drip or ooze. [SPEW V.]

Q

Q n.[1] [20C] (US Und.) San Quentin Prison, California. [abbr.]

Q n.[2] **1** [1930s] (US) a quart of liquor. **2** [1980s+] (drugs) a quarter ounce (7g) of a drug, usu. cannabis. [abbr.]

Q n.[3] [1940s–50s] (US Black) barbecued ribs. [abbr.]

Q n.[4] [1970s] (drugs) methaqualone. [the brandname Quaalude]

Q.E. v. [1950s+] (prison) to turn Queen's Evidence, thus to inform. [abbr. Queen's Evidence]

q.p. n. [1980s+] (US drugs) a quarter pound of cannabis. [abbr.]

q.p. phr. [1990s] (US teen) how embarrassing. [Sp. que pena, how embarrassing]

q.q. n. [1950s] (W.I.) a quarter-quart (of rum). [abbr.]

q.s. n. [early 19C+] any difficult situation. [abbr. QUEER STREET]

quack n.[1] **1** [mid-17C+] an incompetent medical charlatan. **2** [20C] (orig. Aus./N.Z.) a doctor, irrespective of their abilities. [abbr. of SE quacksalver, one who 'quacks' mendaciously about the quality of their medicines and salves]

quack/quacker n.[2] [late 19C+] a duck.

quack n.[3] [20C] (US Black) a homosexual. [? he 'ducks down' for sex]

quack v. [1990s] to break wind noisily.

quacker see QUACK n.[2].

quacking cheat n. [16C–early 19C] (Und.) a drake or duck. [SE quack + CHEAT n. (1)]

quacktail n. [1960s–70s] (S.Afr.) the girlfriend of a township gangster (cf. SHEILA). [her hairstyle, either a ponytail or a DUCK'S ARSE]

quaco n. [1940s+] (W.I.) an unsophisticated, ignorant person, a countrified person. [Twi kwacu, a boy who is born on a Wednesday]

quad n.[1] [late 18C+] a prison (cf. QUOD). [abbr. SE quadrangle]

quad n.[2] **1** [mid-19C] a horse. **2** [late-19C] a quadricycle. [pfx. quad-, four, i.e. legs, wheels]

quad n.[3] [1970s] (drugs) methaqualone. [abbr. Quaalude, a brandname]

quad n.[4] [1970s+] (US campus) a very clumsy person (cf. SPASTIC; SPAS n.). [SE quadriplegic]

quadro n. [1970s] quadraphony. [abbr.]

quadro adj. [1970s] quadrophonic. [abbr.]

quaedam n. [17C–18C] a prostitute (cf. ONE OF THOSE). [Lat. quaedam, one of those]

quaegemes n. [early 18C–early 19C] an illegitimate child. [Lat. quaegemes, of what marriage?]

quail n. [late 17C+] **1** a prostitute (cf. CANARY n.[2]). **2** a young woman (cf. CHICK n.[3]). [SE quail, a supposedly amorous bird]

quailer n. [20C] (Aus.) a stone. [ety. unknown; ? link to dial. quail, to frighten]

quail pipe n. **1** [late 17C–18C] the throat. **2** [late 17C–19C] a woman's tongue, esp. as the seducer of foolish men. [SE quail pipe, a pipe or whistle that imitates the notes of the female quail and lures birds into a net]

quaint n. [16C–late 19C] the vagina (cf. COYNTE; QUEYNTE; QUIFF n.[2]; QUIM; QUIMSBY; QUONIAM). [CUNT n.[1] (1)]

'quake n. [late 19C+] an earthquake. [abbr.]

quake breach/buttock n. [late 16C–early 17C] a coward. [lit. 'fear-anus', 'fear-buttock']

quaker n. [18C–19C] a hard, and possibly lengthy piece of excreta. [it is long and thin, hard and 'wears brown']

Quaker oat/oats n. [20C] a coat. [rhy. sl.]

Quaker's bargain n. [late 18C–early 19C] a 'take it or leave it' bargain. [YEA AND NAY MAN]

Quaker's burying ground n. [18C–19C] a lavatory. [QUAKER]

quaking cheat n. [mid-16C–mid-19C] **1** a sheep. **2** a calf. [SE quake, to tremble + CHEAT n. (1)]

Quaky Isles n. [20C] (Aus.) New Zealand. ['QUAKE, i.e. the islands' earthquakes]

qualified adj.[1] [late 19C+] euph. for damned. [play on SE qualified, modified, i.e. the word is modified by the expletive]

qualified adj.[2] [1950s+] (US Black) of a prostitute, experienced.

qualify v. [late 19C] to have sexual intercourse. [? 18C qualify on, to submit, but note QUALIFIED adj.[1]]

qualify in the testicular time trial, to phr. [1990s] to masturbate.

quality, the n. [mid-19C+] the upper classes, 'society'.

quality Joe/folks n. [1950s] (US drugs) a non-addict. [QUALITY n. + JOE PUBLIC/SE folks]

quality toss n. [1910s–20s] (Irish) attributes and style of the upper classes. [QUALITY n. + SE toss, a heap]

qually n. [late 17C–mid-18C] cloudy, sour wine. [? SE cloudy or squally]

quamin/quarmin n. [1940s+] (W.I.) an unsophisticated, ignorant person, a countrified person (cf. QUACO). [Twi kwamé, a boy who is born on a Saturday]

quandary n. [mid-16C–late 18C] a dilemma, state of extreme uncertainty. [SE f. 1800; ? f. Fr. qu'en dirai-je, what shall I say of it?, but the pron. militates against this; 'possibly a corruption of some term of scholastic Latin' (OED)]

quandong n. (Aus.) **1** [1930s+] a country bumpkin. **2** [1930s+] a disreputable figure, living on their wits. **3** [1970s+] a young woman who accepts any amount of gifts but still refuses to cede her sexual favours. [SE quandong, a fruit which is soft on the outside but hard inside]

quanger n. [1960s+] (Aus. teen) a quince. [initial letters]

quantum n. [mid-19C] a drink. [Lat. quantum, enough]

quantum suff. phr. [19C] enough. [medical Lat., used for prescriptions quantum sufficit, 'as much as suffices']

quare adj. [20C] (Irish) **1** good, excellent, very; also as general intensifier. **2** odd, eccentric, 'queer', thus quare fella/fellow, an eccentric, an unusual person. [Irish pron. of SE queer]

quare harp/hawk n. [20C] (Irish) an odd person. [QUARE adj.

(2) + ? HARP n.[1] (2) or fig. use of the *harp* as a symbolic Irish artefact, thus person/SE *hawk*]

quare man m'da! *excl.* [20C] (Ulster) a general excl. of disbelief. [lit. 'odd man, my father']

quare place *n.* [1960s+] (Irish) hell. [fig. use of QUARE adj. (2) + SE *place*]

quare stuff, the *n.* [1960s+] (Irish) illicitly distilled whisky, poteen. [QUARE adj. (1) + SE *stuff*]

quarmin *see* QUAMIN.

quarrel picker *n.* [late 17C–18C] a glazier. [pun on SE *quarrel*, a small, usu. diamond-shaped pane of glass, used for lattice-windows, ult. Fr. *carreau*, pane + SE *picker*]

quarrel with one's bread and butter, to *phr.* [late 18C] to act against one's own best interests. [image of SE *bread and butter* as an essential necessity of life]

quarrom/quarrome/quarroms/quarromes/quarron *n.* [mid-16C–mid-19C] (Und.) a body. [Ital. *carogna* or Fr. *charogne*, flesh]

quarry *n.* [18C] the vagina (cf. BLACK HOLE n.[1]). [SE *quarry*, a pit ? + *quarry*, that which is hunted]

quarry/rockpile cure *n.* [1950s–60s] (US drugs) a 'cure' for drug addiction that involves being imprisoned and working in the rock quarry.

quart *n.*[1] [late 19C–1900s] (Aus.) a quart pot, used for drinking; thus *quart-pot tea*, tea, made in the open air and in a quart.

quart *n.*[2] [1950s] (W.I.) a one-year prison sentence (cf. PINT).

quarter *n.*[1] **1** [mid-19C] 5 shillings (25p). **2** [late 19C–1900s] (Und.) a three-month's prison sentence. **3** [20C] (US Und.) a 25-year prison sentence (cf. 25 BOFFOS). **4** [20C] £25.

quarter *n.*[2] [1930s+] (drugs) a ¼ ounce (7g) or $25 worth of drugs.

quarter bag *n.* [1960s+] (drugs) $25 worth of marijuana. [SE *quarter* + BAG n.[8]]

quartereen *n.* [mid-19C] a farthing. [? Ital. *quattrino*; a farthing was ¼ of a penny]

quarter flash and three parts stupid *phr.* [early 19C] a fool who claims to have a small degree of fashionable worldliness. [FLASH n.[6]]

quarter moon *n.* [1970s] (drugs) hashish. [on model of HALF-MOON n.[2]]

quartern o'Bry *n.* [late 19C] a ¼ pint of gin. [rhy. sl. BRIAN O'FLYNN = gin]

quartern of bliss *n.* [late 19C] a short, attractive woman (cf. POT O'BLISS).

quartern o'finger *n.* [late 19C] a measure of rum. [SE *quartern* + rhy. sl. *finger and thumb* = rum]

quarter piece *n.* [1930s–50s] (US drugs) a ¼ ounce (7g) of drugs. [SE *quarter* + PIECE n.[5](1)]

quarter-pound of bird's eye *n.* [late 19C] a ¼ ounce (7g) of tobacco. [SE *bird's-eye*, a variety of tobacco in which the ribs of the leaves are cut together with the fibre]

quarter to two *n.* [20C] a Jew (cf. BOX OF GLUE). [rhy. sl.]

quart mania *n.* [19C] a hangover, delirium tremens.

Quarto/Mr Quarto *n.* [18C] a bookseller. [SE *quarto*, a paper size]

quartz *n.* [1980s+] (drugs) smokeable methamphetamine. [resemblance]

quas *n.* [1970s] (drugs) methaqualone. [abbr. *Qua*alude, brandname]

quashiba *n.* [1940s+] (W.I.) a foolish, uncultivated woman (cf. QUASHIE). [Twi *akwasiba*, a girl born on a Sunday]

quashie *n.* [1940s+] (W.I.) a country bumpkin, a peasant, a stupid person (cf. QUASHIBA) [Twi *kwasi*, a boy born on a Sunday]

quasimodo *n.* [20C] soda. [rhy. sl.; Cockney pron.]

quat *n.* [early 17C] a derog. term used for a young man. [SE *quat*, a pimple]

quaterer *n.* [mid–late 19C] (Polari) the number 4. [Ital. *quatro*, 4]

quattie *n.* [mid-19C+] (W.I.) 1½d (post-1969 value 1.25 cents). [? a *quarter* of 6d]

quaver *n.* [mid-19C–1950s] a musician. [SE *quaver*, a note, equal in length to half a crotchet or one-eighth of a semibreve]

quaw/quawy *n.* [mid-19C+] (W.I.) **1** a stupid, ugly person, a peasant or bumpkin. **2** an albino (cf. FRECKLE-NATURE). [Twi *kwaw*, a boy who is born on a Thursday]

quean *n.* **1** [late 16C–19C] a strumpet, a prostitute. **2** [late 19C+] a (passive) homosexual (cf. QUEANIE; QUEEN n.[1]). [11C SE *quean*, woman (with no pej. aspect)]

queanie *n.* [1920s+] a homosexual. [ext. of QUEAN (2)]

queanie/queany *adj.* [1920s+] (Aus.) effeminate. [QUEANIE n.]

quean/queen up *v.* [1920s+] (Aus.) to dress carefully, though not invariably effeminately so, usu. in phr. *all queaned up*. [QUEAN n. (2)/QUEEN n.[1]]

queany *see* QUEANIE adj.

queeb *n.* [1960s] (US teen) any small problem, esp. mechanical. [ety. unknown; ? SE *quibble* n.]

queef *n.* [1990s] (US) unpleasantly smelling gas excreted through the vagina. [QUIFF n.[2] (1) ? + SE *whiff*]

queen *n.*[1] [late 19C+] an effeminate (older) homosexual male. Popular culture offers a number of variations based on words and phrases including *queen*, e.g. *Queen for a day*; *Queen Mother*; *Queen of All the Fairies*; the variety of homosexual tastes is often denoted by a comb. of adj. + *queen*, e.g. LEATHER QUEEN; RICE QUEEN; RUBBER QUEEN (cf. QUEAN). [16C SE *quean*, a woman, esp. a promiscuous woman or prostitute; this spelling is still occasionally used to distinguish it f. SE use]

queen *n.*[2] **1** [20C] (US) a pretty girl, a beauty. **2** [1940s+] (S.Afr.) a woman who runs an illicit township bar or shebeen. **3** [1980s+] (US campus) used with a suitable n. or v. to denote the best of a type; the female equivalent of KING n.[2].

-queen *sfx.* [1980s+] (US campus) a combining form indicating a female enthusiast.

Queen Anne's fan/anne's fan *n.* [early 18C–mid-19C] thumbing one's nose (cf. SIGHT n.[1]). [the spread fingers resemble a fan]

Queen Ann's lace *n.* [1980s+] (drugs) marijuana. [SE *Queen Ann's lace*, the popular name for various umbelliferous plants with clusters of white flowers, e.g. (US) the wild carrot, (UK) cow parsley]

queen bee *n.* [1950s–60s] (camp gay) a woman who likes to surround herself with young men, who may or may not be gay (cf. FAG-HAG n.[1]). [play on SE; QUEEN n.[1] + SE *bee* but ? abbr. *bitch*]

Queen Bess *n.* [mid-19C] in cards, the queen of clubs. ['perhaps because that queen [Elizabeth I], history says, was of a swarthy complexion' (Hotten, 1867)]

queenie *n.* [late 19C] an affectionate nickname used of 'a fat woman trying to walk young' (Ware). [the line 'Queenie, come back, sweet', from the 1884 Drury Lane pantomime in which it was addressed to 'Mr H. Campbell, one of the heaviest men on the stage, and then playing "Eliza" a cook' (Ware)]

Queen Mary *n.* [1980s+] (US gay) an obese gay man. [QUEEN n.[1] + MARY n.[2]]

queen of holes *n.* [19C] the vagina (cf. BLACK HOLE n.[1]).

queen of Scotch *n.* [1970s] (US gay) an alcoholic gay man. [pun on *Mary Queen of Scots*]

queen of the Nile *n.* [1990s] (US Black) a self-deceiving woman. [pun on SE *denial*]

queen of the south *n.* [20C] the mouth. [rhy. sl.; a Scot. soccer team]

queen pin *n.* [1960s+] the female equivalent of KINGPIN, i.e. a woman who heads an institution or arranges an event.

queen's bad bargain *see* HER MAJESTY'S BAD BARGAIN.

queen's gold medal *n.* [late 19C–1900s] a shilling (5p). [the monarch's head on the coin]

queen's head *n.* [mid–late 19C] a postage stamp. [the monarch's head on the stamp]

Queensland salute *see* BARCOO SALUTE.

Queen's Park Ranger/Rangers *n.* [1960s+] a stranger or strangers. [rhy. sl.; the West London football club]

queen's pictures *n.* [19C] money. [the pictures of the reigning monarch, in this case Queen Victoria, on one side of the coin]

Queen's Row *n.* [1950s+] (US gay) the Public Gardens, Boston, Massachusetts. [QUEEN n.¹ ? + ref. to 1941 film *King's Row*, starring Ronald Reagan]

queen's stick *n.* [late 19C–1900s] a stately, noble person. [? various offices of state such as 'Black Rod']

queen's tears *n.* [1940s+] (S.Afr. Zulu) alcohol, usu. gin. [? ref. to the tears Queen Victoria supposedly shed after the defeat at Isandhlwana]

Queen Street cocky/farmer *n.* [1980s+] (N.Z.) a businessman who owns a farm as an investment. [*Queen Street*, the business/financial centre of Auckland + COCKY n.² (1)]

Queen Street yank *n.* [1950s] (N.Z.) a New Zealander who apes American styles etc (cf. WOOLLOOMOOLOO YANK). [*Queen Street*, the business/financial centre of Auckland + YANK n.]

queen's weather *n.* [mid-19C–1900s] excellent, sunny weather. [Queen Victoria (r.1837–1901), so it was claimed, always enjoyed good weather to accompany her public appearances]

queen's woman *n.* [mid-19C] 'a prostitute who received medical attention under the terms of the Contagious Diseases Acts of the 1860s' (*OED*).

queen up *see* QUEAN UP.

queen ween *n.* [1990s] (US campus) someone who backs out of a commitment. [QUEEN n.¹ + WIENIE n. (2)]

queer *n.* **1** [late 18C–1900s] a hoax, a confidence trick. **2** [19C] counterfeit money. **3** [late 19C] a look (on one's face). **4** [1920s+] a male homosexual. **5** [1920s+] (Aus.) a fool, a simpleton.

queer *adj.*¹ **1** [16C–19C] (Und.) an all-purpose neg., the antonym of RUM adj. **2** [1920s+] homosexual. [Ger. *quer*, oblique, skewed; the line between SE *queer*, strange, odd or peculiar, and the Und. use is both semantically and chronologically slim; the SE slightly predates (at least in printed citations) the cant, but as the *OED* remarks, some examples of the one may in fact equally well serve for the other. Only the context gives any real clue, the most obvious of which occur in such undeniably Und. combs. as QUEER CUFFIN; QUEER COLE etc. The use as a pej. description of homosexuals does not emerge until *c.*1925]

queer *adj.*² [late 18C+] ill, out of sorts; esp. in phr. *feel queer, look queer*. [the potential for double-entendre has rendered the term, and its combs., almost obs., at least in 'PC' circles]

queer *v.* **1** [late 18C–mid-19C] to quiz or ridicule, to puzzle. **2** [late 18C+] of a person, to spoil the reputation of, to spoil someone's efforts or opportunities. **3** [early 19C+] to spoil, to put out of order. **4** [mid–late 19C] to impose on, to swindle, to cheat; thus *queer a flat*, to hoodwink a gullible victim (cf. QUEER SOMEONE'S PITCH). [SE *queer*, odd]

queer about/around the gills *see* BLUE ABOUT THE GILLS.

queeralities *n.* [20C] (Ulster) eccentricities, peculiarities. [QUEER adj.¹ (1)]

queer as a clockwork orange *phr.* [1950s+] **1** extremely odd. **2** ostentatiously homosexual.

queer as a nine-bob note *phr.* [20C] unusual, particularly

suspicious; the phrase survives the demise of the currency (cf. QUEER AS A THREE-DOLLAR BILL). [such a 'nine-shilling' note does not exist]

queer as a three-dollar bill *phr.* [20C] (US) **1** extremely odd. **2** ostentatiously homosexual (cf. QUEER AS A NINE-BOB NOTE). [such a bill does not exist]

queer/odd as Dick's hatband *phr.* **1** [18C+] odd, eccentric (cf. DICK'S HATBAND). **2** [18C+] referring to something comical. **3** [18C+] referring to something one cannot recognize or identify; thus *I would know him from Dick's hatband*. **4** [late 18C] out of sorts, dispirited, 'under the weather'. [the proper name *Dick*, some long-dead eccentric figure + SE *hatband*, a band or narrow ribbon that runs around a hat just above the rim; the dial. phr. is, *as queer as Dick's hatband that went nine times round and wouldn't meet*]

queer bail *n.* [late 18C–1900s] fraudulent bail (cf. JEW BAIL). [QUEER adj.¹ (1) + SE *bail*]

queerbait *n.* [1950s+] an effeminate young boy who attracts, or is supposed to attract older male homosexuals (cf. JAILBAIT n.¹). [QUEER n. (4) + SE *bait*]

queer-basher *n.* [1960s+] one who specializes in beating up (and usually robbing) male homosexuals; thus *queer-bashing*, beating up (and robbing) male homosexuals (cf. FAG-BASHER). [QUEER n. (4) + SE *basher*]

queer-bashing *n.* [1960s+] the beating up (and usu. robbing) of male homosexuals (cf. GAY-BASHING). [QUEER-BASHER]

queer beer *n.* [1970s] (US) 'near bear', beer with a low alcohol content. [QUEER adj.¹ (1) + SE *beer*]

queer belch *n.* [mid-19C] sour beer. [QUEER adj.¹ (1) + BELCH n.¹]

queer bird *n.* **1** [16C–18C] (Und.) a mendicant villain who, recently released from prison, returns to robbery, specializing in stealing horses (cf. PRIGGER OF PRANCERS; QUEER COVE). **2** [mid–late 19C] an odd, eccentric person. [QUEER adj.¹ (1) + BIRD n.²; by 18C the term referred to any unreformed villain]

queer bit *n.* [late 18C–late 19C] counterfeit money (cf. QUEER COLE). [QUEER adj.¹ (1) + BIT n.¹ (1)]

queer bitch *n.* [early 19C] 'an odd out of the way fellow' (Grose 1785). [QUEER adj.¹ (1) + BITCH n.¹ (11); despite appearances, there is no hint of homosexuality]

queer bit-maker *n.* [late 18C–late 19C] (Und.) a coiner, a counterfeiter (cf. BIT-MAKER). [QUEER BIT + SE *maker*]

queer bluffer *n.* [late 17C–early 19C] a 'sneaking, sharping, Cut-throat Ale-house or Inn-keeper' (B.E.). [QUEER adj.¹ (1) + BLUFFER n.¹]

queer booze *n.* [mid-16C–mid-19C] sour or inferior beer, 'small and naughtye drynke' (Harman). [QUEER adj.¹ (1) + BOUSE n.]

queer bub *n.* [17C–18C] second-rate or sour beer. [QUEER adj.¹ (1) + BUB n.²]

queer bung *n.* [late 17C–18C] (Und.) an empty purse (viewed as an object of robbery). [QUEER adj.¹ (1) + BUNG n.¹ (1)]

queer card *n.* [mid-19C–1940s] an odd, eccentric person (cf. QUEER FELLOW). [QUEER adj.¹ (1) + CARD n.³ (1)]

queer clout *n.* [late 17C–18C] (Und.) a cheap, probably cotton handkerchief that as such is not worth stealing. [QUEER adj.¹ (1) + CLOUT n.¹]

queer cole *n.* [late 17C–18C] (Und.) counterfeit money; thus *queer cole fencer*, the distributor of counterfeit money; *queer cole maker*, a counterfeiter (cf. QUEER BIT; QUEER MONEY; QUEER PAPER; QUEER SCREENS; QUEER SOFT). [QUEER adj.¹ (1) + COLE]

queer cove *n.* [late 16C–mid-19C] (Und.) a villain. [QUEER adj.¹ (1) + COVE n. (1)]

queer cramp-ring *see* CRAMP-RING.

queer cuffin/cuffen *n.* **1** [16C–18C] (Und.) a Justice of the Peace. **2** [late 17C–18C] a peasant. [QUEER adj.¹ (1) + either CUFF n.¹, a miserly old man, or a simple corruption of COVE n. (1)]

queer cull n. [late 17C–18C] **1** a foolish dandy, a fop. **2** a poor, ill-dressed person. [QUEER adj.[1] (1) + CULL n.[1] (4)]

queer customer/merchant n. [19C+] an odd or eccentric person (cf. QUEER FISH; UGLY CUSTOMER). [QUEER adj.[1] (1) + CUSTOMER/MERCHANT]

queer degen n. [late 17C–mid-19C] (Und.) a brass, iron or steel-hilted sword, with no special ornamentation (cf. RUM DEGEN). [QUEER adj.[1] (1) + DEGEN n. (1)]

queer detail n. [1950s+] (US) that branch of the Vice Squad specializing in homosexual crime (cf. PUSSY POSSE). [QUEER n. (4) + SE detail]

queer diver n. [late 17C–early 19C] (Und.) a bungling, incompetent pickpocket. [QUEER adj.[1] (1) + DIVER n. (2)]

queer doxy n. [late 17C–mid-18C] a slatternly woman. [QUEER adj.[1] (1) + DOXY n.(2)]

queer drawers n. [late 17C–18C] (Und.) yarn, coarse worsted, ordinary or old stockings. [QUEER adj.[1] (1) + SE drawers]

queer duke n. [late 17C–18C] **1** an impoverished gentleman. **2** a lean, half-starved person. [QUEER adj.[1] (1) + DUKE n.[1]]

queered adj. [early–mid-19C] tipsy. [QUEER adj.[2]]

queer 'em/queer'm/queerum n. [early 19C] the gallows. [QUEER v. (3)]

queer-faced adj. [1980s+] a general pej.; lit. 'looking like a homosexual'. [QUEER n. (4) + sfx. -faced]

queer fellow n. [early 18C+] an odd, eccentric person (cf. QUEER CARD). [QUEER adj.[1] (1) + SE fellow]

queer fish n. [19C+] an odd or eccentric person (cf. QUEER CARD; QUEER CUSTOMER). [QUEER adj.[1] (1) + FISH n.[1]]

queer for adj. [1950s+] obsessed with, sexually or otherwise (cf. HARD-ON). [the origin is QUEER adj.[1] (2), but there need be no actual homosexuality involved]

queer fun n. [late 17C–18C] (Und.) a cheat or trick that does not work out as intended. [QUEER adj.[1] (1) + SE fun]

queer-gammed adj. [late 18C] lame, crippled. [QUEER adj.[1] (1) + GAM n.[1] (1)]

queer gill n. [19C] a shabby fellow (cf. QUEER FISH). [QUEER adj.[1] (1) + GILL n.[1]]

queer in the attic phr. [19C] mad and drunk. [QUEER adj.[2] + ATTIC]

queer in the garret phr. [mid–late 19C] eccentric, mad. [QUEER adj.[2] + GARRET n. (1)]

queer ken n. (Und.) **1** [mid-16C–early 19C] a prison. **2** [late 17C–18C] a house not worth robbing. [QUEER adj.[1] (1) + KEN n.[1]]

queer ken hall n. [early 17C] a prison. [QUEER KEN n. (1)+ SE hall]

queer kicks n. [late 17C–early 19C] (Und.) old, worn-out trousers. [QUEER adj.[1] (1) + KICKS n.[1]]

queerly adv. [late 17C–early 18C] (Und.) in a criminal manner. [QUEER adj.[1] (1)]

queer'm see QUEER 'EM.

queer merchant see QUEER CUSTOMER.

queer money n. [19C] (Und.) counterfeit money (cf. QUEER COLE). [QUEER adj.[1] (1) + SE money]

queer mort n. [late 17C–19C] 'a dirty Drab, a jilting Wench, a Pockey jade' (B.E.). [QUEER adj.[1] (1) + MORT]

queer nab n. [late 17C–early 19C] a cheap, shabby hat, thus one that is not worth stealing; 'a felt, Carolina, Cloth or ord'nary Hat, not worth whipping off a man's head' (B.E.) (cf. CAPTAIN QUEER-NABS). [QUEER adj.[1] (1) + NAB n.[1] (3)]

queer ogles n. [late 17C–mid-19C] (Und.) cross eyes, thus queer-ogled, squinting. [QUEER adj.[1] (1) + OGLES]

queer on adj. [1940s+] (orig. Aus.) homosexually attracted towards. [QUEER adj.[1] (2)]

queer on v. [19C] to treat cruelly. [QUEER v. (2)]

queer paper n. [late 18C–late 19C] counterfeit paper money (cf. QUEER BIT; QUEER COLE). [QUEER adj.[1] (1) + SE paper]

queer peeper n. [late 17C–early 18C] a badly made, thus distorting mirror. [QUEER adj.[1] (1) + PEEPER n. (1)]

queer peepers n. [18C–19C] (Und.) squinting or short-sighted eyes. [QUEER adj.[1] (1) + PEEPERS n. (1)]

queer place n. **1** [1920s–30s] prison. **2** [1940s–50s] a lavatory. [QUEER adj.[1] (1), with poss. implication of (2) + SE place]

queer plunger n. [18C] a confidence trickster who plunges into water and is saved from 'drowning'. Conveniently pre-assembled 'rescuers' then claim money for saving the person. [QUEER adj.[1] (1) + SE plunger, a diver]

queer prancer n. [late 17C–18C] (Und.) **1** a cowardly horse stealer. **2** an ageing prostitute. **3** a second-rate horse. [QUEER adj.[1] (1) + PRANCER n. (1)]

queer put n. [early–mid-19C] an odd simple person. [QUEER adj.[1] (1) + PUT n.[1]]

queer rolling n. [1960s+] the beating up (and robbery) of homosexual men (cf. QUEER-BASHING). [QUEER n. (4) + ROLL v.[1]]

queer rooster n. [late 18C–late 19C] a police spy who poses as one of a band of thieves. [QUEER adj.[1] (1) + SE rooster]

queer rums n. [early 19C] confusing talk. [QUEER adj.[1] (1) + RUM adj. (1), lit. 'bad good things']

queer screens n. [early 19C] (Und.) forged banknotes (cf. QUEER COLE). [QUEER adj.[1] (1) + SCREEN n.[1]]

queer shover n. [late 19C] (Und.) a passer of counterfeit money. [QUEER n.[1] (1) + SE shove]

queer soft n. [mid-19C] counterfeit money (cf. QUEER BIT; QUEER COLE). [QUEER adj.[1] (1) + SOFT MONEY]

queer someone's/the act, to phr. [1960s] (US) to interfere, to spoil someone's plans (cf. CRAB SOMEONE'S ACT). [QUEER v. (2) + SE act]

queer someone's pitch, to phr. [mid-19C+] to spoil someone else's efforts, usu. deliberately. [QUEER v. + SE pitch, a stall; music-hall use, where it dealt with one actor stealing a scene from the others, and in turn from street patterers, whose open-air pitch would be queered by an over officious policeman]

queer start n. [19C] a strange affair, an odd situation. [QUEER adj.[1] (1) + START n.[2]]

queer stick n. [19C+] an odd person, an eccentric. [QUEER adj.[1] (1) + STICK n.[7]]

Queer Street n. [early 19C+] any difficult situation. [QUEER adj.[1] (1) + SE street]

queer the act see QUEER SOMEONE'S ACT.

queer the game, to phr. [19C] to cause trouble for someone (cf. QUEER SOMEONE'S PITCH). [QUEER v. + GAME n.[3], n.[4]]

queer the stifler, to phr. [mid-19C] to escape the gallows (cf. NAB THE STIFLES). [QUEER v. + STIFLER n. (1)]

queer topping n. [late 17C–18C] (Und.) a second-rate or worn-out wig. [QUEER adj.[1] (1) + SE topping]

queerum see QUEER 'EM.

queer up n. [1950s+] male homosexual intercourse. [QUEER n. (4)]

queer wedge n. **1** [late 18C–early 19C] a large belt buckle. **2** [19C] adulterated gold or silver. [QUEER adj.[1] (1) + WEDGE n.[1]]

queery adj. [mid-19C] shaky. [QUEER adj.[2]]

quencher n. [mid-19C] a drink (cf. ALLEVIATOR). [SE quench]

que pasa? phr. [1980s+] (US campus) a greeting. [Mexican Sp. que pasa?, what's happening?]

querier n. [mid-19C] a chimney sweep who goes from house to house offering their services (cf. KNULLER). [they query householders]

queynte n. [16C] the vagina (cf. QUAINT). [CUNT n.[1] (1)]

quick n. [1950s+] (US Black) instantly available money.

quick adj. [late 19C] (society) well-dressed and clever.

quick adv. [20C] quickly.

quick and dirty n. [1960s] (orig. US) a cheap café. [the standard of the service, the hygiene and the food]

quick and dirty *adj.* [1970s+] used of any kind of instant remedy, poss. not the best one for long-term dependence (cf. QUICK FIX).

quick fix *n.* [1960s+] any kind of instant remedy, poss. not the best one for long-term dependence; thus *quick-fix*, of a solution, instant, if not wholly dependable.

quickie/quicky *n.* [1940s+] **1** a spontaneous and brief act of sexual intercourse. **2** a quick drink. **3** a quick, 'dirty' story, retailed at the end of a party or drinking session. [SE *quick*]

quick one *n.* **1** [20C] a spontaneous and brief act of sexual intercourse (cf. QUICKIE). **2** [1910s+] a quick drink of alcohol (cf. QUICKIE). **3** [1910s+] an act of urination.

quick on the draw/trigger *phr.* [20C] bright, intelligent (cf. SLOW ON THE DRAW). [gunfighting imagery]

quick quid *n.* [1920s+] (Aus.) money that is earned quickly and, poss., illicitly (cf. FAST BUCK ARTIST). [SE *quick* + QUID *n.*]

quicksilver *n.* [1970s–80s] (drugs) **1** LSD when combined with another drug. **2** isobutyl nitrite.

quick starts *n.* [1970s+] (US campus) rubber soled sneakers; popular for those who need to make a speedy exit.

quick step *n.* [mid-19C] (US) diarrhoea (cf. APPLE-BLOSSOM TWO-STEP; AZTEC TWO-STEP; AZTEC HOP; BOOT-HILL TWO-STEP; CRAB-APPLE TWO-STEP; GREEN-APPLE QUICKSTEP; MEXICAN TWO-STEP).

quick sticks! *excl.* [20C] (Aus.) hurry up! [IN QUICK STICKS]

quicksville *adv.* [1950s] (US) fast, quickly. [SE *quick* + sfx. -VILLE]

quick tempered *adj.* [19C] drunk (cf. TIRED AND EMOTIONAL). [euph.]

quicktime *adv.* [1990s] (Black) quickly, immediately.

quick worker *see* FAST WORKER.

quicky *see* QUICKIE.

quicumque/quicunque vult *n.* [late 18C] a prostitute (cf. ATHANASIAN WENCH). [Lat. *quicumque vult*, whomsoever wants; ? ref. in *quicunque* to CUNT *n.*[1] (1)]

quid *n.* **1** [late 17C–late 18C] a guinea. **2** [late 17C+] a pound sterling (cf. BALLAST *n.*[1]; COLE; CORKS *n.*[1]; NEEDFUL). **3** [19C] the vagina. [? Lat. *quid*, what (one needs)]

quid box *n.* [late 18C–mid-19C] a snuff box. [SE *quid*, something, usu. tobacco, that can be held in the mouth and chewed + *box*]

quid fishing *n.* [late 19C] (Und.) first-class, expert thieving. [QUID + SE *fish*]

quidlet *n.* [1900s–10s] one pound sterling. [QUID + dimin. *-let*]

quids *n.* [late 18C+] money. [QUID]

quids in *phr.* [1910s+] doing well. [QUIDS; the image of making a successful bet and the money thus gained]

quid to a bloater *n.* [late 19C–1900s] a certain bet, esp. in phr. *it's a quid to a bloater* (cf. OR MY PRICK'S A BLOATER). [lit. 'a sovereign to a herring']

quien *n.* [mid-19C–1900s] a dog. [Fr. *chien*, or a Fr. dial.]

quiet as a wasp in one's nose *phr.* [late 17C] restless, nervy, tense.

quiet mouse *n.* [mid-19C] a prostitute who works in a brothel rather than on the streets. [SE *quiet* + MOUSE *n.*[1] (1)]

quiet the trouser snake, to *phr.* [1990s] to masturbate. [SE *quiet* + ONE-EYED TROUSER-SNAKE]

Quiet Village *n.* [1980s+] (US Black, Los Angeles) Venice, California.

quiff *n.*[1] [late 19C+] **1** a smart trick or clever dodge, esp. one that makes a task easier. **2** (Anglo-Ind.) an idea, fancy, movement or suggestion. [ety. unknown]

quiff *n.*[2] [20C] **1** the vagina (cf. QUAINT). **2** females, esp. sexually available ones. [QUIFF *v.*[1]]

quiff *v.*[1] [early 18C–19C] to have sexual intercourse. [on pattern of QUEYNTE etc, thus ult. CUNT *n.*[1] (1)]

quiff *v.*[2] [late 19C] **1** to come up with a cunning dodge or trick. **2** to go or do well, to get along pleasantly. [QUIFF *n.*[1]]

quiff the bladder, to *phr.* [late 19C] to compensate for one's baldness. [QUIFF *v.*[2] (1) + *bladder*, an inflated balloon, mimicked by a bald head]

qui-hi/-hai/-hy *n.* (Anglo-Ind.) **1** [mid-19C] an English resident of Calcutta. **2** [mid-19C+] as *old qui-hi*, a former colonial administrator or Ind. Army soldier. [Urdu *koi hai*, is anyone there?, the usual summons to a servant; note E.F. Benson's ex-Indian Army Major Flint, in the *Lucia* stories, whose catchphrase this is]

quill *n.*[1] [1920s–30s] (US) first-rate whisky, the genuine thing as opposed to the 'bathtub' or 'rotgut' versions producing during Prohibition. [PURE QUILL]

quill *n.*[2] [1950s–70s] (drugs) **1** methamphetamine. **2** heroin. **3** cocaine. **4** a folded over matchbook cover that hides a narcotic drug. **5** anything, e.g. a dollar bill, rolled up to make a 'straw' through which to sniff a powdered narcotic. [(4) and (5) are ext. of SE; drug use ety. unknown other than in their relationship to the implements]

quiller *n.* [mid-19C] a toady, a parasite. [one who 'sucks up' (through a *quill*, the precursor of the modern straw)]

quilt *n.* [20C] (Irish) **1** a petulant, pedantic, pernickety man. **2** a timid, effeminate man. **3** a fool, someone who acts against their own interests. [ety. unknown; ? the making of quilts is a quintessentially female occupation]

quilt *v.*[1] [mid-19C+] (Aus./Irish) to thrash, to beat, to flog. [Scot./Cumberland dial.]

quilt *v.*[2] [20C] (Irish) to run away. [ety. unknown; ? fig. use of QUILT *v.*[1]]

quim *n.* **1** [early 18C+] the vagina (cf. QUAINT). **2** [1930s+] a woman, women collectively (cf. CUNT *n.*[1]; PUSSY *n.*[1]). [? play on Celtic *cwm*, a valley; ult. CUNT *n.*[1]]

quim *adj.* [20C] (Ulster) **1** prim, affectedly 'nice'. **2** moving easily, precisely. [Scot. *queem*, pleasant]

quim *v.* [early 18C+] to have sexual intercourse. [QUIM *n.* (1)]

quim bush *n.* [late 18C+] the female pubic hair. [QUIM *n.* (1) + BUSH *n.*[4] (1)]

quimfill *adj.* [1990s] having one's penis fully embedded in the vagina. [QUIM *n.* (1) + SE *fill*]

quimling *n.* [1990s] manipulation of a woman's body in an attempt to produce orgasm, generally regarded as genital manipulation by the tongue, but not limited to such. [QUIM *n.* (1)]

quim nuts *n.* [1990s] (US) notably large and pendant labia. [QUIM *n.* (1) + NUTS *n.*[2] (1)]

quimp *n.* [1970s] (US campus) a socially inept person. [? QUEER *n.* + WIMP *n.*[2]]

quimsby *n.* [early 18C+] the vagina (cf. QUAINT). [ext. of QUIM *n.* (1)]

quimstake/quimwedge *n.* [17C] the penis (cf. ARSE-OPENER). [QUIM *n.* (1) + SE *stake/wedge*]

quim-sticker *n.* [19C] a womanizer (cf. BEARD-JAMMER). [QUIM *n.* (1) + SE *sticker*]

quimwedge *see* QUIMSTAKE.

quim whiskers/wig *n.* [19C] the female pubic hair. [QUIM *n.* (1) + SE *whiskers/wig*]

quin *n.* [1950s–60s] a derisive term for any woman who is an easy pick-up. [QUIM *n.* (2)]

quince *n.* [1930s+] (Aus.) **1** a weakling, a fool. **2** a homosexual, esp. one who can be both active and passive. [puns on SE *quince*, a SOFT *adj.* fruit]

quinine *n.* [20C] (US gambling) the point of 9 in craps dice. [play on SE *nine*]

quinkydink *n.* [1990s] (US teen) a coincidence (cf. COINKIDINK). [deliberate mispron.]

quips *n.* [1950s+] (W.I. Rasta) a tiny piece or amount. [? SE *quip*, an odd or whimsical trifle]

quire bird *n.* [late 18C–early 19C] (Und.) a mendicant villain who, recently released from prison, returns to robbery, specializing in stealing horses (cf. PRIGGER OF PRANCERS; QUEER COVE). [QUEER BIRD n. (1)]

quirk *n.* [20C] (Ulster) an untrustworthy individual. [synon. Scot. *quirk*]

quirker *n.* [1900s–10s] anything considered slightly odd, whether animate or otherwise. [SE *quirk*, a trick or peculiarity in action or behaviour + sfx. *-er*]

quirley/quirly *n.* [1930s+] (Aus./US) a hand-rolled cigarette. [SE *quirl*, to twist, to twirl]

quisby *n.* [mid-19C] an idler; thus *doing quisby*, not working, idling; *quisby*, bankrupt, impoverished. [ext. of QUIZ n.¹]

quit *v.* [1970s+] (orig. US Black) to die. [abbr. QUIT IT]

quitam/qui tam *n.* [early–mid-19C] a solicitor who takes an informer's fee for their prosecution of the case. [Lat. *qui tam*, to whom so much]

quite *adj.* [1920s+] (society) socially acceptable, *comme il faut*, usu. in neg. use. [abbr. SE '*quite* the thing']

quite! *excl.* [late 19C+] an expression of agreement, absolutely, indeed; sometimes expanded as *quite so.*

quite/that's another/a different pair of shoes/boots *phr.* [mid-19C] quite/that is a different matter.

quite a stranger *phr.* [20C] a phr. used to address an intimate whom one has not seen for some time.

quite a while *phr.* [20C] a long time.

quite something *phr.* [1950s+] a deliberately understated expression of approval or praise (cf. FEW!).

quite the gay drunkard, to be *phr.* [late 19C] to be slightly drunk.

quite too *adj.* [late 19C–1900s] (society) a general intensifier, e.g. *quite too amusing.*

quit it *v.* [1940s–50s] (US Black) to die.

quitsest *n.* [late 16C–early 17C] a release, a discharge. [Lat. *quietus est*, it is discharged, thus modern SE *quits*]

quitter *n.* [1960s+] (drugs) one who has abandoned drug use. [SE *quit*]

quit the scene, to *phr.* [1950s] (US Black) to die. [SE *quit* + SCENE n. (4)]

quiver *n.* [19C] the vagina. [the lit. translation of Lat. *vagina*]

quiver and shake *n.* [20C] (Aus.) a steak. [rhy. sl.]

quiz *n.*¹ [late 18C–mid-19C] an eccentric person, thus an odd-looking thing. [? Lat. *quis*? who?]

quiz *n.*² [mid-19C] a monocle. [abbr. SE *quizzing-glass*]

quiz *v.* [late 19C] to watch, to spy on. [SE *quiz*, to interrogate, to find out]

quizzy *adj.* [mid-1950s] (Aus.) inquisitive. [abbr.]

quockerwodger *n.* [mid-19C] a politician acting in accordance with the instructions of an influential third party, rather than properly representing their constituents. [SE *quockerwodger*, a wooden puppet which can be made to 'dance' by pulling its strings]

quod *n.* [late 17C+] prison (cf. QUAD n.¹). [abbr. SE *quadrangle*; the original was Newgate, but the term became general]

quod *v.* **1** [late 17C+] to imprison. **2** [late 19C] to serve a prison sentence. [QUOD n.]

quod cove *n.* [early 19C] (Und.) the governor of a prison. [QUOD n. + COVE n. (1)]

quodded *adj.* [late 17C+] imprisoned. [QUOD v.]

quodding dues are concerned *phr.* [early 19C] (Und.) it is a matter that will involve imprisonment. [QUOD v.]

quoit *n.* [1940s+] (Aus.) the anus, the buttocks; thus *go for one's quoit(s)*, to hurry. [it is 'round with a hole in it']

quoit *v.* [16C] (Und.) to use any form of illicit sleight of hand, spec. to make a surreptitious change of a crooked dice for a legitimate one (or vice versa) during a game (cf. COG v.¹). [SE *quoit*, to play at quoits; perhaps the dice cheat used a slightly spinning throw (as in quoits) to achieve the manoeuvre]

quoniam *n.* [late 14C–early 18C] the vagina (cf. QUAINT). [Lat. *quoniam*, whereas, or one of the CUNT n.¹ (1)/QUEYNTE group]

quot *n.* [late 17C–early 18C] a man who meddles in 'women's work' around the house. [var. on COTQUEAN]

quota *n.* [late 17C–18C] (Und.) a share of plunder.

quoz *n.* [late 18C–early 19C] an absurd person. [var. on QUIZ n.¹]

qwasha *n.* [1980s+] (S.Afr. township) a homemade gun, made from piping, springs and rubber tubing. [Zulu ideophone for a crunching noise; in this context echoic of the sound of the explosive click that is made when the gun is fired]

R

r.a. *see* RED ARSE.

ra, the *n.* [1980s+] (Ulster) the provisional I*R*A. [abbr.]

raany/ranny *n.* [20C] (Ulster) an emaciated, stunted or delicate looking person. [Irish *ranaí*, thin]

raasclat *n.* [1940s+] (W.I./Jam.) an extreme derog. term (cf. BUMBO-CLAAT; PUSSY-CLOT; SMEERLAP). [lit. *arse/ass cloth*, i.e. a sanitary towel]

raas!/rass! *excl.* [18C+] (W.I.) an all-purpose abusive term. [? f. phr. *your arse* or Du. *raas*, to rage, to rave; one of the most taboo words in the W.I., it has been banned from public use in the majority of islands]

raatid/rahtid *adj.* [1910s+] (W.I.) furious, very angry. [? SE *wrath/wrathed*; used as euph. for RAAS]

raatid!/rahtid! *excl.* [1940s+] an excl. implying great anger, surprise. [RAATID *adj.*]

rabbi *n.* [1950s+] (US) (orig. police) an influential sponsor or patron.

rabbit *n.*[1] [late 18C–mid-19C] a newborn baby. [an affectionate nickname, but ? ref. to one Mary Tofts (*c.*1701–63) who, in 1726, allegedly (but fraudulently) 'gave birth' to a litter of rabbits]

rabbit *n.*[2] [late 19C+] a coat made of, or lined with, rabbit fur.

rabbit *n.*[3] [late 19C+] (Aus.) a bottle of beer; thus *run the rabbit*, to bring home beer from the off-licence or liquor store. [? late 17C *rabbit*, a wooden drinking vessel]

rabbit *n.*[4] [1900s–50s] a smuggled or stolen article. [naut. jargon *rabbit*, an article made by a sailor at sea as a gift to a friend or girlfriend]

rabbit *n.*[5] **1** [20C] a poor player, esp. in golf or tennis. **2** [1940s+] (Aus.) a simpleton, a victim. **3** [1940s+] (S.Afr.) a male homosexual (cf. BUNNY BOY). **4** [1960s+] a client who ejaculates quickly and thus leaves the prostitute free to carry on her trade. **5** [1970s+] (US Black) a White person. [the animal's perceived characteristics]

rabbit *n.*[6] [1940s+] a talk, a conversation. [rhy. sl. *rabbit-and-pork* = talk]

rabbit *v.*[1] [20C] to scrounge. [RABBIT *n.*[4]; but note NZ use (post 1950) which comes from the image of a *rabbit* attacking the tops of root crops]

rabbit *v.*[2] [1930s+] to leave quickly, to run away.

rabbit *v.*[3] [1940s+] to talk; thus *rabbit on*, to chatter, to grumble, to complain. [rhy sl. *rabbit and pork* = talk]

rabbit *v.*[4] [1990s] (US teen) to work at a job. [the rabbits' supposedly endless copulations, or mis-reading of RABBIT (ON) *v.*[3]]

rabbit catcher *n.* [late 18C–early 19C] a midwife. [RABBIT *n.*[1] + SE *catcher*]

rabbit ears *n.* [1950s+] (orig. US) a V-shaped television antenna.

rabbit fever *n.* [20C] (US Und.) **1** the compelling desire to run off whenever things get difficult (cf. RABBIT *v.*[2]). **2** the compulsion to attempt escapes from any form of imprisonment. [rabbits 'run']

rabbit/rabbit's food *n.* [20C] vegetables or salad greens considered unfit for consumption, esp. by a carnivore (cf. BUNNY CHOW; HOG FEED).

rabbit foot *n.*[1] [late 19C–1930s] (US Black) **1** attention. **2** good luck. [the trad. wearing of a rabbit's foot as a good-luck charm]

rabbit foot *n.*[2] [20C] (US) an escaped convict (cf. RABBIT *v.*[2]; RABBIT FEVER). [rabbits 'run']

rabbit hutch *n.* [20C] **1** the crotch. **2** a crutch. [rhy. sl.]

rabbit killer *n.* [1940s+] (Aus.) a chopping blow to the back of a neck. [the blow used by farmers etc to dispatch rabbits]

rabbit-o *n.* [20C] (Aus.) an itinerant seller of rabbits as food. [the cry, but note Aus. sfx -O; thus rugby jargon *The Rabbit-Os*, the South Sydney Rugby Club, whose fortunes suffered so much in the 1930s Depression that its officials were reduced to raffling and selling rabbits]

rabbit pie *n.* [19C] a prostitute; thus *rabbit-pie shifter*, a policeman. [LIVE RABBIT]

rabbitry *n.* [1930s] **1** in a sport, poor players considered collectively. **2** poor play. [RABBIT *n.*[5] (1)]

rabbit's food *see* RABBIT FOOD.

rabbit skin *n.* (US campus) a college diploma or degree. [the fur tippet worn by graduating students]

rabbit's paw *n.* [1930s+] talk, conversation (cf. RABBIT *n.*[6]). [rhy. sl. *rabbit's paw* = JAW *n.* (1)]

rabbit sucker *n.* [early 17C–mid-19C] **1** (Und.) a confidence trickster who would gull rich young men into running up huge bills, then dun them for their debts (cf. FERRET *n.*[1]; PURSE-NETS). **2** a pawnbroker. [SE *rabbit-sucker*, a very young rabbit]

rabbit tooth *n.* [early 19C] a buck or protruding tooth, usu. in pl. [supposed resemblance]

rabbo *n.* [late 19C–1930s] a *rabb*it; *rabb*its as a group, thus *rabbo!* the street-cry of a seller of rabbits. [abbr.]

rabshackle/rabshakle *n.* [18C] a ne'er-do-well, a wastrel. [? SE *ramshackle*]

racan *n.* [20C] (Irish) a lanky, raw-boned person. [Irish *racán*, a rake]

race *n.*[1] [late 19C] a bet on a horse-race.

race *n.*[2] [20C] (Ulster) a short visit or journey. [16C SE *race*, a journey]

racehorse *n.* [1950s–60s] (Aus./N.Z.) **1** a very thin roll-up cigarette. **2** a thin pack. [SE *racehorse*, used to mean sleek and lean]

racehorse charlie *n.* [1930s–50s] (drugs) any powdered drug, esp. heroin. [var. on HORSE *n.*[12]; though note CHARLIE *n.*[7]]

race man *n.* [1930s] (US) a Black person, esp. one who advocates Black civil rights. [i.e. one who is conscious of their SE *race*]

race/whiz off *v.* [1960s+] (Aus.) to seduce, to go off with a woman in the hope of achieving seduction.

race one's motor, to *phr.* [1940s–50s] (US) to become over-excited.

rachel v. [late 19C] to rejuvenate. [the contemporary sham 'cosmetician' Madame *Rachel*, who operated a 'beautiful for ever' scam]

racial adj. [1940s] (W.I.) generous, open-handed. [i.e. characteristic of the Black race]

rack n.[1] [1910s+] (Irish) **1** coarse hair. **2** a comb (cf. RACK PICK). [Irish *raca*, a comb]

rack n.[2] [1950s+] (orig. US milit.) a bed.

rack n.[3] [1960s+] (US) the female breasts, esp. when large and firm. [note RACKS OF MEAT]

rack n.[4] [1970s+] (US Black) a card holding bubble-packed birth control pills.

rack v. [1950s+] (US) **1** to sleep, thus *racked out*, asleep. **2** to seduce a woman, to make love. [RACK n.[2]]

rackaback n. [late 18C] a man on horseback with a woman behind him riding side-saddle. [for Grose's explanation, *see* GORMAGON]

rackabone *see* RACK OF BONES.

rack attack n. [1970s+] (US campus) a sudden onset of sleepiness. [RACK n.[2] + SE *attack*]

racked adj. [1970s+] tired out, exhausted. [RACK n.[2]]

racked adv. [1950s+] (US) for certain (cf. TAPED). [i.e. put away on]

rackerbone *see* RACK OF BONES.

racket n.[1] **1** [early 19C+] any form of deception, criminal trickery, hoaxing (cf. LETTER-RACKET; ORDER-RACKET). **2** [20C] (US) *the rackets*, organized crime. **3** [20C] (US) an easy job or situation, esp. a sinecure.

racket n.[2] [late 19C–1900s] (US) an organized dance, held in a dance-hall and frequented by lower-class young people (cf. BLOWOUT n.[1]). [SE *racket*, a noise, a disturbance]

racketeer n. [1920s+] (US) a member of an organized crime syndicate, a criminal. [RACKET n.[1]]

racket jacket n. [1930s–40s] (US Black) a ZOOT SUIT. [SE *racket*, a noise + *jacket*; in visual terms it 'makes a noise']

racket man n. [mid-19C] a thief. [RACKET n.[1] + SE *man*]

rackety adj. [mid–late 19C] insalubrious. [RACKET n.[1] ? + pun on SE *rackety*, noisy]

rack monster n. [1970s+] (US campus) sleepiness, exhaustion. [RACK n.[2] + SE *monster*]

rack of bones/rackabone/rackerbone/rack-o'-bones n. [early 19C–1940s] (US) a skeleton, an emaciated person or animal.

rack off v. [19C] to urinate. [wine trade jargon *rack off*, to draw off liquor from the lees]

rack off! excl. [1970s+] (Aus.) go away! be off! [SE *rack*, to move, to travel]

rack one's soul-case *see* BURST OUT ONE'S SOUL-CASE.

rack out v. [1970s+] (US) to fall asleep, to go to bed. [RACK n.[2]]

rack pick n. [1960s+] (US Black) a comb designed specifically for use on a NATURAL n.[6] or an AFRO n.[2] hairstyle (cf. NATURAL PICK). [SE *rack*, i.e. the widely spaced teeth resemble objects hanging from a rack + *pick*, a pronged instrument]

racks/racks of meat n. [20C] the female breasts. [rhy. sl. *racks of meat = teat/*TIT n.[1] (1)]

rack up v.[1] [20C] (US) to damage, to wreck. [SE *rack*, to strain, to stretch]

rack up v.[2] [1950s+] (US) to accumulate, to register or to achieve. [the *racking up* of pool balls before a game]

raclan n. [mid-19C] (tramp) a married woman. [Rom. *rakli*, a girl]

rad n.[1] [1960s+] a radical. [abbr.]

rad n.[2] [1990s] (Black) a policeman. [ety. unknown; ? link to Scot. *rad*, to regulate]

rad adj. [1980s+] (orig. US teen) a general intensifier; extreme, excessive, very much, excellent, the best (cf. DEF). [SE use of *radical* as 'basic, essential, from the roots' and eschewing political overtones; like a number of other terms, the word moved from surfer jargon, to 'Valley Girls' use and thence, via the *Teenage Mutant Ninja Turtles* craze, to general use]

rada n. [1960s–70s] (US Black) a Cadillac Eldo*rado*. [abbr.]

raddie n. **1** [20C] an Italian living in London, orig. spec. in Clerkenwell. **2** [1930s+] a radical. [(1) ? image of Italians as anarchistic]

raddle v. [late 19C] (Aus.) to swindle. [northern UK dial. *raddle*, to twist, to beat]

raddled adj. [late 17C] drunk.

raddle someone's toe, to phr. [late 19C] (Aus.) to request someone to buy a round of drinks. [shearing jargon *raddle*, to mark a sheep as imperfectly shorn]

radge n. [20C] a psychotic. [northern dial., ult. SE *rage*]

radge/radgy adj. [20C] mad, furious, insane. [RADGE n.]

radical n. [mid-19C] roasted corn (cf. HUNT'S BREAKFAST POWDER). [so called from its being the favourite breakfast of the *radical* Henry 'Orator' Hunt (1773–1835)]

radio adj. [1970s+] insane, mad. [rhy. sl. *radio rental* = MENTAL adj.]

radio! excl. [1960s+] (US prison) be quiet! stop that! [the two-way radios carried by guards; the term initially used to warn of an approaching *radio* or guard, widened into a general imper.]

radio ham n. [1910s+] **1** a student or amateur telegraphist. **2** a radio amateur, i.e. one who makes a hobby of picking up and transmitting radio messages. [SE *radio* + HAM n.[3]]

radishes! excl. [1970s+] (US campus) a general excl. of disgust and annoyance.

rado n. [1970s+] (US Black) a Cadillac Eldo*rado* (cf. L.D.; RADA). [abbr.]

r.a.f. adj. [1990s] used of a very unattractive woman (cf. WING COMMANDER). [abbr. rough *as fuck*]

rafe/ralph n. [mid-19C] a pawnbroker's ticket. [? Suffolk dial. *rafe/ralph*, a fool]

Raff, the n. [1940s+] The Royal Air Force. [never used by actual servicemen]

Rafferty's rules n. [1920s+] (Aus./N.Z.) no rules whatsoever, anything goes. [despite use of capital 'R', which implies a proper name, the term comes f. mispron. of SE *refractory*]

raffle ticket n. [20C] a mistake. [rhy. sl. *raffle ticket* = RICKET]

raffle coffin n. [19C] a ruffian, a villain. [SE *rifle-coffin*, a resurrectionist or grave-robber]

raft n.[1] [early 19C+] (US) a large number.

raft n.[2] [20C] (Ulster) a tall, thin person. [synon. Norwegian dial. *raft*]

rag n.[1] **1** [late 16C–18C] a farthing. **2** [early–mid-19C] money in general. [(1) play on a valueless SE *rag*; (2) if fig. use of (1)]

rag n.[2] [early 18C+] a newspaper. [derog. ref. to its worthlessness, but note the use of *rags* in paper-making]

rag n.[3] [early–mid-19C] a banknote. [the use of rags in paper making]

rag n.[4] **1** [early 19C+] the tongue. **2** [late 19C] abuse, teasing, talk; usu. as *ragging*. [RED RAG n.[1]]

rag n.[5] **1** [mid-19C] a pocket handkerchief. **2** [mid-19C+] (orig. US) an article of clothing, esp. a dress.

rag n.[6] [mid-19C+] abbr. *Rag and Famish*, the Army and Navy Club, London. ['The familiar name of the *Rag*, by which it is generally known, was invented by Captain William Duff, of the 23rd Fusiliers. Coming in to supper late one night, the refreshment obtainable appeared so meagre that he nick-named the club the *Rag and Famish*' (Nevill & Jerningham, *Piccadilly to Pall Mall*, 1908)]

rag n.[7] [late 19C] **1** (US) a girlfriend, a female companion. **2** (Aus.) a promiscuous woman. [ety. unknown; ? derog. use of SE or link to RAGS n.[2]]

rag *n.*[8] **1** [20C] (US) a playing card. **2** [1930s–40s] (N.Z.) a low playing card in a suit.

rag *n.*[9] [1940s+] a sanitary towel; thus *ride the rag*, to be menstruating. [abbr. JAM RAG]

rag *n.*[10] [1970s+] (US campus/teen) an unpleasant person. [abbr. WET RAG, but ? ult. 16C–19C SE *rag*, a derog. description of a person, a 'rag of a man']

rag *n.*[11] [1990s] (US Black) a gang member. [the bandanna or DO-RAG bearing the gang colours]

rag *v.*[1] **1** [mid-18C+] to scold, to talk severely to. **2** [early 19C+] to annoy, to tease (esp. in context of school or university). **3** [late 19C] to argue over a topic, to wrangle. **4** [1900s–10s] to question closely, to interrogate. **5** [1950s+] (US Black) to criticize, to mock (cf. DIS v.). [RAG n.[4]; ? abbr. BULLYRAG]

rag *v.*[2] [mid-19C] to share, esp. to divide up the proceeds of a crime; thus *go rags*, to share out. [? SE *rag*, to tear in pieces]

rag *v.*[3] [late 19C–1910s] (US) to play or dance to ragtime music. [abbr. SE *ragtime*]

ragamofi/ragamorfi *n.* [1950s] (W.I.) ragged clothes (cf. RAGA-RAGA). [SE *ragamuffin*]

ragamuffin/ragga/raggamuffin *n.* [1980s+] **1** (Black) a hooligan, a lout (cf. RUDE BOY). **2** (US Black) an unaffected, down-to-earth person. **3** (W.I./UK Black) a lover of modern dance-hall reggae. [SE *ragamuffin*, orig. the name of a demon, latterly a ragged, dirty, disreputable man or boy; like a number of teen terms, this pej. is used as a term of approval]

ragamuffin tip *n.* [1990s] (US Black) a down-to-earth situation. [RAGAMUFFIN + TIP n.[8]]

rag and bone *n.* [20C] the lavatory. [rhy. sl. *rag and bone* = THRONE]

rag-and-bone shop *n.* **1** [late 19C] a filthy, untidy room. **2** [1910s–20s] a decrepit old woman. [SE *rag-and-bone-shop*, a junk shop]

raga-raga/ragga-ragga *adj.* [1940s+] (W.I.) ragged, worn-out, usu. of clothes. [SE *rags, ragged*]

rag baby *n.* [20C] (US Black) a poor, ill-clothed woman, who is nonetheless attractive.

rag bag *n.*[1] [mid-19C+] a miscellaneous collection of anything.

rag bag/doll *n.*[2] [late 19C+] a sloppily-dressed woman, a slattern. [play on SE, but not BAG n.[3] (1)/DOLL n.[1] (1)]

rag box/shop *n.*[1] [late 19C] the mouth. [RAG n.[4] (1) + SE *box/shop*]

rag box *n.*[2] [1970s+] (US Black) the vagina. [fig. use of RAG BOX n.[1]]

rag carrier *n.* [late 18C] an ensign, charged with carrying the flag. [SE *rag*, a flag + *carrier*]

rag chewing *n.* [late 19C+] (US) talking, esp. chatting. [CHEW THE RAG]

rag doll *see* RAG BAG n.[2].

rage *n.* [1970s+] (Aus./N.Z.) **1** a noisy, exciting party. **2** a good time.

rage *v.* [1970s+] (Aus./N.Z./US campus) **1** to have a great time. **2** to look fashionable. **3** to have sexual intercourse.

rager *n.* [1970s+] (Aus./N.Z./US campus) **1** a particularly good party. **2** a person known for wild behaviour. [RAGE v.]

ragga/raggamuffin *see* RAGAMUFFIN.

ragga-ragga *see* RAGA-RAGA.

ragga-arse *see* RAGGED-ARSE.

ragged *adj.* **1** [late 19C] of person or object, second-rate, inferior. **2** [late 19C] of an era, unfortunate, ill-fated. **3** [1950s+] (orig. Aus.) nervy, out of sorts, 'under the weather'.

ragged/ragg/raggedy-arse/-arsed *adj.* [late 19C+] **1** of clothes, tattered. **2** of people, disreputable, seedy, run-down. [SE *ragged* + sfx. -ARSED]

ragged down/ragged down heavy *adv.* [1950s+] (US Black) exceptionally well-dressed (cf. SILKED). [RAGS n.[2] + HEAVY adj.[2] (3)]

ragged out *adj.* [1980s] (US teen) appa [RAG n.[9] + SE *ragged*]

ragged to the bone *see* CLEAN TO THE BON

raggedy android *n.* [1950s–60s] (camp g and thus impoverished male prostitute. *Ann*, a children's doll + SE *android*]

raggedy-arse/-arsed *see* RAGGED-ARSE.

raggedy-ass ride *n.* [1990s] (US Black) an (of motor vehicle that has become run down [RAGGED-ARSE + RIDE n.[2]]

ragger *see* RAG TOP.

rag gorger/gorgy *n.* [early 19C] a wealthy SPLAWDGER. [RAG n.[1] (2) + Rom. *gorgio*, a (non-gy)

raggy *adj.* [late 19C–1900s] irritated. [RAG v.[1] (2)]

rag-head *n.*[1] (US) **1** [20C] a gypsy. **2** [1920s+] an Arab of the Middle East (cf. TOWELHEAD). [the cloth that each as a head-covering]

rag-head *n.*[2] (US Black) **1** [1900s–60s] one who wears a scar or bandanna tied round the head. **2** [1980s+] anyone who is not absolutely up to date with current information, gossip, style etc. [the bandanna or DO-RAG worn by old ladies and latterly gang members]

rag/cot house *n.* [1920s–30s] (US) a cheap rooming house or 'hotel', esp. in a town based on an oil-drilling camp. [the canvas sides or roofs that such buildings often had]

raging *n.* [1980s+] a first class degree (cf. PATTIE). [rhy. sl. *raging thirst* = first]

raging *adj.* **1** [late 19C+] a general intensifier, esp. in phr. *raging favourite*, a 'hot' favourite in racing. **2** [1980s+] (US campus/teen) of a party, of a drug, wild, fantastic, very enjoyable. [SE *rage*/RAGE v. (1)]

rag-mannered *adj.* [late 19C–1900s] aggressively uncouth, very badly mannered. [SE *rag* adj., a general derog. term]

ragmop *n.* [1940s–50s] (US Black) an unkempt, messy person. [SE *ragged* + MOP n.[1]]

rag on *v.* [1980s+] (US teen) to nag, to criticize (cf. RIP ON). [RAG v.[1]]

rag out *v.*[1] [mid-19C; 1950s–70s] (US) to dress up, to wear one's best clothes (cf. RAGGED DOWN). [RAGS n.[2]; 20C use is mainly Black]

rag out *v.*[2] [late 19C–1900s] to act in a cowardly manner. [? SE *rag* adj., a general derog. term]

rag out *v.*[3] [1970s] (US campus) to become tired. [? RACK OUT]

rags *n.*[1] [early–mid-19C] paper money. [RAG n.[1] (2)]

rags *n.*[2] **1** [mid-19C+] (orig. US) clothes. **2** [mid-19C+] (US Black) stylish, fashionable clothes. **3** [20C] (US Und.) clothing and insignia that indicate one's membership of a (prison) gang (cf. COLOURS).

rags and bones *n.* [1970s] (US Black) the corpse of a poor person.

rags and jags *n.* [mid-19C–1900s] tattered clothing. [SE *rag* + *jag*, a shred of cloth, a rag]

rag shop *n.*[1] [mid-19C] a bank; thus *rag-shop boss*, a banker, *rag-shop cove*, a banker, a cashier. [RAG n.[1]/n.[3] + SHOP n.[1] (2)]

rag shop *n.*[2] *see* RAG BOX n.[1].

rag splawdger/splawger *n.* [mid–late 19C] a wealthy man (cf. RAG GORGER). [RAG n.[1] (2) + SPLODGER n.[2]]

rag stabber *n.* [late 19C–1920s] a tailor. [RAG n.[5] (2) + SE *stabber*; his 'weapon' is a needle]

ragster *n.* [19C] a thug, a bully. [RAG v.[1] + sfx. -STER]

rag stick *n.* [late 19C] an umbrella, esp. one that is not rolled up. [SE *rag*, a piece of cloth + *stick*]

rag tacker *n.* **1** [mid-19C] a coach trimmer. **2** [mid-19C–1910s] a dressmaker. [SE *rag*/RAG n.[5] (2) + SE *tacker*]

rag, tag and bobtail/tag, rag and bobtail *n.* **1** [mid-17C–late 18C] the rabble, the masses. **2** [early 19C] everyone, the whole lot. [later uses are SE]

adj. [late 19C] tattered, raggedy.

dj. **1** [1900s] jolly, merry. **2** [1910s+] ragged; inferior, ...ly; disreputable. **3** [1910s+] higgledy-piggledy, out of ...haotic. [SE *ragtime*, a style of music popular late 19C ...e precursor of jazz; an essentially Black music it was ...matically suspicious and the adj. (2) is correspondingly ...tive]

...ime girl *n.* [1900s–20s] **1** a girlfriend. **2** a prostitute. [the ...bivalent status of *ragtime* music]

...g top/ragger *n.* [1950s+] (US) **1** a car with a 'convertible' ...soft top. **2** a truck that has an open back, which, when loaded, is covered with a tarpaulin.

rag trade *n.* **1** [mid-19C] the purchasing of counterfeit bank-notes and the subsequent passing them off to innocent victims. **2** [mid-19C+] the garment industry. [SE *rag*/RAG n.⁵ (2) + *trade*]

rag water *n.* [late 18C–early 19C] spirits, esp. gin. [the effect of over-indulgence, 'these liquors seldom failing to reduce those that drink them to rags' (Grose 1796)]

ragweed *n.* [1960s+] (drugs) **1** inferior quality marijuana. **2** heroin. [SE *rag* + WEED n.¹ (4)]

rag week *n.* [1980s+] the menstrual period (cf. ON THE RAG). [RAG n.⁹ + punning link to university *rag weeks*]

rah-rah *n.*¹ [1940s] (US Black) clothes fashionable among students in Black colleges. [*rah! rah!* the stereotypical college yell]

rah-rah *n.*² [1980s+] (Aus.) a fan of Rugby Union (cf. MUNGO n.²). [implying the educated, middle-class image of rugby union, i.e. the *rah-rah* accents of the fans]

rah-rah *adj.* [1910s+] (US) enthusiastic, excited, esp. in the context of college students cheering a team; thus *rah-rah boy, rah-rah girl*, over-excited students. [used slightly disparagingly, as are other refs. to US college students, e.g. JOE COLLEGE]

rahtid *see* RAATID.

rahtid! *see* RAATID!

rahzo *see* RARZO.

rahzoo *see* RAZOO.

raid the ice box, to *phr.* [1970s+] to have intercourse with a corpse.

raifield *v.* [1950s–60s] (US Black) to steal without concealment or regard for the consequence, to break the law in a contemptuous manner. [? dial. *raffle*, an idle vagabond]

rail *n.* [1980s+] (US drugs) a thin line of a powdered narcotic (cf. LINE n.⁴).

railbird *n.* (gambling) **1** [late 19C+] a racetrack fan who stands next to the rails to get as near as possible to the racing. **2** [1940s+] a fan or spectator who crowds round the rails that surround a big game in a casino.

railings *n.* **1** [mid-19C–1910s] the ribs. **2** [1910s–30s] the teeth. [resemblance]

railroad *n.*¹ [19C] (US) rough whisky. [? as drunk by railroad workers and tramps]

railroad *n.*² [late 19C+] any arrest and allied criminal proceeding that ignores the facts, evidence, truth etc and concentrates on the speedy conviction, the guilt or innocence of the victim notwithstanding. [RAILROAD v. (2) + image of the direct line from arrest to conviction, i.e. that of railroad tracks]

railroad *v.* **1** [mid-19C] (US) to enforce a mild punishment by dragging the victim up and down along the floor until the seat of their trousers is worn through. **2** [late 19C+] (US) to arrest, try and convict without allowing the person concerned due process of law; to imprison on trumped up charges and faked evidence; to accelerate the legal process in order to ensure – through inadequate defence, legal knowledge etc – that a person will be found guilty and sentenced, even though

their trial is ostensibly 'fair'. **3** [1970s+] (US campus) to use influence in the pursuit of personal interests.

railroad bible *n.* [late 19C] (US) a pack of cards. [note Wink Martindale's country/pop hit 'Deck of Cards' (1959) in which the cards are reinterpreted along religious lines]

railroader *n.* [1970s+] (drugs) a drug addict. [RAILROAD TRACKS n.²]

railroad stiff *n.* [1920s+] (US tramp) a tramp who travels free by rail. [SE *railroad* + STIFF n.³ (3)]

railroad tracks *n.*¹ [1950s+] (US) braces on the teeth. [resemblance]

railroad tracks *n.*² [1970s+] (drugs) the scars that accompany repeated injections of narcotics into one's veins. [SE *railroad* + TRACKS]

railroad weed *n.* [1970s] (drugs) marijuana. [SE *railroad* + WEED n.¹ (4); ? it grows at the side of the tracks]

railroad whisky *n.* [1970s+] (US Black) cheap wine. [Santa Fe wine, based on the name of a US railroad]

rain *n.* [late 19C–1950s] (US Black) hard times, material suffering. [they 'fall' on one]

rain *v.* [late 19C–1950s] (US Black) to complain, esp. about one's hard, impoverished situation.

rain and pour, to *phr.* [20C] to snore. [rhy. sl.]

rainbow *n.*¹ [18C] a golden guinea. [it sparkles in the sun]

rainbow *n.*² [early 19C] a large, discoloured bruise, gained through boxing. [its colourfulness]

rainbow *n.*³ **1** [early 19C] a footman, abbr. [late 18C] *knight of the rainbow*, a footman in livery. **2** [early 19C] a pattern book. **3** [early–mid-19C] a mistress. **4** [mid-19C] a young man about town. **5** [1950s] (W.I.) a tall, thin person. [its shape or colourfulness, usu. in context of clothes]

rainbow kiss *n.* [1990s] (US) a passionate kiss, which follows an orgasm reached through reciprocal oral sex between a man and a menstruating woman, and thus involves mixing the semen and vaginal secretions/blood in the mouth. [SE *rainbow* + *kiss*]

rainbow necker *n.* [1990s] a person who has oral sex with a women while she is menstruating. [SE *rainbow* + NECK v.⁴]

rainbow queen *n.* [1980s+] **1** (US Black/gay) anyone who is involved in a Black/White sexual relationship. **2** (US gay) a gay man who prefers inter-racial sex and/or relationships. [SE *rainbow* (*coalition*), a campaign involving a variety of races + QUEEN n.¹]

rainbows *n.* [1960s+] (drugs) any form of pill (usu. the barbiturates Amytal and Seconal which have red-and-blue capsules) in a coloured jacket.

rain bullock sterks, to *phr.* [20C] to rain very hard. [Scot. *stirk*, a steer]

rain cats and dogs, to *phr.* [early 18C+] to rain heavily; thus vars. [19C] *rain cats and dogs and pitchforks and shovels*; *rain chicken coops*; *rain darning needles*; [1900s–20s] *rain trams and omnibuses*.

raincoat *n.* [1950s+] a contraceptive sheath.

rain curtain-rods *see* COME DOWN STAIR-RODS.

raindance *n.* [20C] (US) an impressive political function or reception. [SE *raindance*, a dance performed by a tribal group in the hope of summoning rain]

rain like a cow/a bull pissing on a flat rock, to *phr.* [1940s+] (US) to rain heavily.

rain duke Georges/like a drunken dog, to *phr.* [1930s+] (N.Z.) to rain heavily.

rainmaker *n.* [20C] (US) an extremely successful member of a firm, often a lawyer, who commands high fees and is thus a lucrative asset to their employer.

rain napper *n.* [late 19C] an umbrella. [SE *rain* + NAP v.¹ (1)]

rain on *v.* [1920s+] **1** to kill. **2** to make suffer, to beat up, to lose one's temper with.

rain on someone's parade *see* PISS ON SOMEONE'S PARADE.

rain pitchforks and nigger babies, to *phr.* [1930s–60s] (US) to rain very heavily.

rain stair-rods *see* COME DOWN STAIR-RODS.

rainy day money *n.* [1960s+] funds set aside to deal with unforeseen difficulties.

rainy days *n.* [20C] (US Black) hard times.

rainy day woman *n.* [1960s] (drugs) marijuana. [ety. unknown; popularized and poss. coined by Bob Dylan in the song 'Rainy Day Women Nos. 12 and 35' (1966)]

raise *n.*[1] **1** [late 19C+] a rise in salary or wages. **2** [1910s+] (W.I.) a tip or monetary contribution, whether given voluntarily or extorted. **3** [1950s+] (W.I.) an opportunity to pick up some money, legal or otherwise. **4** [1950s+] (Black) robbery. [(2), (3), (4) fig. uses of (1)]

raise *n.*[2] [1950s–60s; 1980s+] (US Black/campus) one's parents. [SE *raise*, to rear]

raise, the *n.*[3] [1950s–70s] (US Black) the police (cf. FUZZ n.[1]). [? they raise the alarm/a hue and cry]

raise *v.*[1] **1** [mid-19C+] to obtain, to get hold of. **2** [mid-19C+] to put up bail for. **3** [1940s+] (W.I.) to get hold of some money (legally or otherwise). [RAISE n.[1]/SE *raise money*]

raise *v.*[2] [mid-19C+] (US) **1** to go, to leave. **2** to escape, to get out of, to be released from prison. [SE *raise up/rise up*, to get up]

raise a cloud, to *phr.* [mid-19C] to smoke a pipe of tobacco (cf. BLOW A CLOUD).

raise a kite, to *phr.* [1940s] (W.I.) to grumble, to make a fuss.

raise ants' nest, to *phr.* [20C] (W.I.) to make trouble, to foster an argument. [the effect on ants when one breaks open their nest]

raise arse upwards *see* RISE ARSE UPWARDS.

raise Cain *v.* [mid-19C+] (orig. US) to cause as much trouble as one can. [Adam's wicked son, *Cain*, here used as synon. for HELL]

raise hell/merry hell, to *phr.* [late 18C+] (orig. US) **1** to cause a good deal of trouble deliberately. **2** to celebrate rowdily. **3** to castigate; sometimes intensified as *raise merry hell and put a shingle under it* (cf. RAISE CAIN; RAISE HOB). [a popular ety. credits the phrase to a slogan, *Kansas should raise less corn and more hell*, attributed. c.1896 to Mrs Mary Ellen Lease (1853–1933) but there is no solid proof and the early coinage seems infinitely more likely]

raise Hob, to *phr.* [20C] (US) to cause as much trouble as one can (cf. RAISE CAIN; RAISE HELL). [SE *raise* + SE *Hob*, the Devil]

raise merry hell *see* RAISE HELL.

raise mountain *n.* [18C] a braggart. [who boasts that he can *raise mountains*]

raise-my-thoughts *n.* [1900s] (W.I.) a drink of rum (cf. SEARCH-MY-HEART). [its effects]

raise Ned *v.* [mid-19C+] to cause a disturbance, to make trouble (cf. RAISE HELL; RAISE HOB). [SE *raise* + NED n.[2]]

raise sand *v.* [late 19C+] (US) **1** to cause a stir, a commotion. **2** to fight. **3** to complain. **4** to stop. [image of kicking sand in someone's face or blowing up a sand storm]

raise the colour, to *phr.* [mid–late 19C] (Aus.) to discover gold. [the *colour* being gold]

raise the decibel level, to *phr.* [1920s+] (US) to intensify something, to make it more conspicuous.

raise the elbow, to *phr.* [early 19C+] to drink, usu. to excess (cf. BEND ONE'S ELBOW; LIFT ONE'S LITTLE FINGER).

raise the roof, to *phr.* [mid-19C+] to cause an uproar, to make a great noise.

raise the wind, to *phr.* [late 18C–early 19C] to obtain money, to obtain a loan (cf. FLY A KITE).

raise up *v.* (US Black) **1** [1970s+] to leave a place. **2** [1970s+] (US prison) to be given leave or parole to leave a prison. **3** [1990s] (teen) to get out of the way.

raisin bag *n.* [1990s] (Can.) the scrotum. [play on NUTSACK]

raj *n.* [1940s+] (W.I.) a villain, a trickster. [? SE *rogue* or RADGE n.]

Rajah, the *n.*[1] [late 19C] the Mogul, a well-known centre of entertainment on Drury Lane, London.

rajah *n.*[2] [1940s+] (N.Z.) an erection.

rake *n.*[1] [mid-19C+] a comb, thus *bug-rake, garden-rake*.

rake *n.*[2] [1950s] (W.I.) **1** a hunch. **2** any form of trickiness, e.g. a duplicitous answer that hides the true situation. [SE *rake*, an implement used for smoothing over soil]

rake *n.*[3] [1950s] (W.I.) a piece of gossip. [SE *rake up*, a fabrication, a concoction]

rake *n.*[4] [1980s+] (Irish) a large number. [Irish *reic*, lavish spending]

rake *v.* [20C] of a man, to have sexual intercourse (cf. BANG v.[1]).

raked *adj.* [1980s+] (US campus) **1** humiliated. **2** emotionally or intellectually exhausted. **3** having suffered an horrific experience. **4** having lost in a competition. [all SE phr. *raked over the coals*]

rake down *v.* [mid-19C+] (orig. US) to win money at gambling, esp. cards. [? the croupier's *rake* at a casino]

rake/shake down the persimmons, to *phr.* [mid-19C] to succeed, to win, to make a profit.

rake it in *v.* [mid-19C+] to make a great deal of money. [RAKE DOWN]

rake jakes *n.* [18C] a villain. [lit. 'clean out the privy', play on SE *rake-kennel*, a scavenger]

rake-off *n.* [late 19C+] (orig. US) a commission, esp. on some form of illegal deal. [the croupier's *rake* in a casino]

rake on *v.* [1980s+] (US campus) to humiliate, to criticize.

rake one's cage out, to *phr.* [1990s] to visit the lavatory. [the cleaning of a bird-cage]

rake-out *n.* [late 19C–1900s] a pipeful of tobacco. [SE *rake out*, to clean out, e.g. a boiler, a grate]

rake out *v.* [late 19C] of a man, to have sexual intercourse. [ext. of RAKE v.]

raker *n.*[1] [mid-19C] **1** a heavy bet. **2** a very fast pace. [SE *rake*, a 'fast' man-about-town]

raker *n.*[2] [late 19C] a comb (cf. BUG RAKE).

rake up the coals, to *phr.* [20C] (US) to snore. [i.e. the noise so caused]

raleigh bike *n.* [20C] a lesbian. [rhy. sl. *raleigh bike* = DYKE]

rally *v.* [1970s+] (US campus) to have a good time; to act utterly madly, drunkenly, obstreperously. [? SAmE *pep rally*]

ralph *n.*[1] *see* RAFE.

ralph *n.*[2] [1950s–60s] (camp gay) an effeminate, timid or plain and undistinguished man. [stereotyping of *Ralph* as a 'sissy' name]

ralph/rolf *v.* [1970s+] (US campus) to vomit (cf. BUICK). [echoic]

ralph lynn *n.* [1920s–40s] gin (cf. VERA LYNN). [rhy. sl.; ult. UK actor *Ralph Lynn* (1882–1964), best-known in the Ben Travers farces of 1920s]

ralph spooner *n.* [late 17C–19C] a fool (cf. RAFE). [Suffolk dial.]

ram *n.*[1] **1** [late 19C+] an act of sexual intercourse. **2** [1930s+] a virile and/or promiscuous man (cf. STUD n.[1]). [animal imagery]

ram *n.*[2] [1940s+] (Aus.) a trickster's confederate who encourages the public to lose their money in a con-game (cf. AMSTER). [RAMP v. (1) + image of the animal's horns, pushing at the victim]

ram *n.*[3] [1980s+] (drugs) alkyl nitrites. [ety. unknown]

ram *adj.* [1980s+] (Black) full. [SE *ram*, to force]

ram *v.*[1] [late 19C+] to have sexual intercourse (cf. TUP *v.*). [RAM *n.*[1] (1)]

ram *v.*[2] [1940s+] (Aus.) to work as a confidence trickster's accomplice (cf. AMSTER). [RAM *n.*[2]]

ram! *excl.* [1930s+] damn!; thus *rammed*, damned. [orig. Irish/Kent dial.]

rama *n.* [1960s–70s] (drugs) marijuana. [Sp. *rama*, a branch]

-rama *see* -ORAMA.

ram and dam/damn *n.* [mid–late 19C] a muzzle-loading gun. [one *rams* in the charge and *damns* the target]

ramasammy *see* RAMSAMMY.

ramatracks *n.* [20C] (Ulster) purposeless wandering. [? SE *ramble* + *track*; Share suggests 'nonce-wd.' but note Shetland Islands dial. *rammatrack*, a rabble]

ramble *v.* [early 17C–early 18C] to go out looking for sex.

rambler *n.* [early 17C–early 18C] a person who goes out looking for sex. [RAMBLE *v.*]

rambling *adj.* [1920s+] (US tramp) fast, e.g. a *rambling freight*.

rambo *n.* [1980s] (drugs) heroin. [the macho *Rambo* films of the 1980s]

ram cat/cove *n.* [mid–late 19C] a man wearing furs. [SE *ram-cat*, a tomcat + COVE]

ramfeezled *adj.* [late 19C] exhausted. [Scot.]

ram it!/ram it up your arse/ass! *excl.* [1930s+] (orig. US) an excl. of dismissal, 'go to hell!' [ARSE *n.*[1]]

ram jam *v.* [late 19C+] to stuff with food; thus *ram-jam full*, absolutely stuffed.

ramjollock *v.* [19C] to give the cards a thorough shuffle. [Salop. dial.]

rammaged *adj.* [18C] drunk. [SE *ramage*, wildness, high spirits]

rammer *n.* **1** [late 18C–19C] the arm. **2** [19C+] the penis (cf. PILE-DRIVER; RAMROD).

rammies *n.* [1910s–60s] (Aus./S.Afr.) **1** trousers. **2** knickers. [Malay *rami*, a Chinese and East Indian plant of the nettle family (*Boehmeria nivea*); thus the fine fibre of this plant, extensively employed in weaving]

ramming *adj.* [early 19C] forcible, 'go-ahead'.

rammish/rammy *adj.* [late 18C–early 19C] of either sex, sexually enthusiastic. [RAM *n.*[1] (2)]

rammy rousers *n.* [20C] (Aus.) trousers. [rhy. sl. + link to RAMMIES]

ramp *n.*[1] [17C–19C] a high-spirited, independent woman, usu. synon. with a prostitute; thus *ramping*, high-spirited, promiscuous. [SE *rampant*, exhibiting fierceness or high spirits]

ramp *n.*[2] **1** [early 19C] robbery with violence. **2** [mid-19C] a racecourse swindler, also *ramper*, *rampsman*. **3** [late 19C+] any form of swindle or fraud. [RAMP *v.*[1]]

ramp *n.*[3] [1930s] a public house or its bar. [the long wooden bar]

ramp *v.* **1** [19C; 1990s] to swindle. **2** [19C; 1990s] to rob with violence; thus *done for a ramp*, convicted of a violent crime. **3** [19C] to force someone to pay their debts. **4** [1910s+] (Aus.) to search a prisoner and/or their cell. [20C use is UK Black; SE *ramp*, to act in a threatening manner]

rampacious *adj.* [1910s–20s] crazy, eccentric. [SE *rampageous*, violent; unruly; boisterous]

rampager *n.* [19C] a tramp, a vagabond.

ramped *adj.* [1990s] (US campus) drunk. [SE *ramage*; high spirits or *rampage*, a state of boisterous excitement]

ramper *n.* [late 19C] **1** a street thug, a hooligan. **2** a racehorse swindler (cf. RAMP *n.*[2]). [RAMP *v.*]

ramping *adj.* [late 19C] rampant, extreme.

ramps *n.* [1910s–20s] a faked-up argument or similar commotion intended to disguise a swindle or confidence trick. [RAMP *n.*[2] (2)]

rampsman *n.* [mid-19C+] a robber with violence (cf. RAMP *n.*[2]; RAMPER). [SE *rampant*, acting in a violent or threatening manner]

ram raid *n.* [1990s] a method of stealing from shops that have erected blinds, shutters, bars etc whereby the thief steals a car, then drives at high speed into the shop-front, smashing its way through any defences; the car is filled with loot, then driven away; thus *ram-raid*, to steal in this manner; *ram-raider*, one who carries out such thefts. [SE *ram* + *raid*]

ramrod *n.* [19C] the penis.

rams *n.* [20C] delirium tremens. [ety. unknown]

ramsammy/ramasammy *n.* [late 19C+] (orig. Indian Army) **1** a generic name for any Hindu, esp. Indian coolies. **2** a commotion, a riotous party. **3** a fight, a family quarrel. [Hind. *Ramaswami*, Lord Rama]

ramscootrify *v.* [20C] (Ulster) **1** to defeat verbally. **2** to beat up. [Scot. *ramscooter*, to induce panic]

ramsgate sands *n.* [20C] the hands. [rhy. sl.]

ram-shackled *adj.* [1990s] subjected to anal intercourse, usually by a person with a large penis. [pun on SE *ram-shackled*/RAM *n.*[1] + SE *shackle*]

ram's horn *n.* [1910s–20s] someone who speaks very loudly.

ram skin *n.* [19C] (Anglo-Irish) a bailiff. [their willingness to take any and all possessions, even a *ram skin* mat]

ram something down someone's craw, to *phr.* [20C] (W.I.) to repeat ad nauseam in the hope of forcing someone to agree or do what you want. [SE *ram* + CRAW *n.*]

ram the ham, to *phr.* [1990s] to masturbate (cf. ACCOST THE OSCAR MEYER).

ranch *v.* [1990s] (US) to ejaculate. [? RAUNCH *v.*]

ranchy *adj.* [early 19C+] (US) dirty, disgusting, indecent (cf. RAUNCHY). [? *OED* suggests var. on *raunchy*, but impossible given cited chronology; ref. to a SE *ranch* and the conditions associated with it]

rancid *adj.* [1980s+] (US teen) ugly, unattractive.

randal's man *n.* [mid-19C] a silk handkerchief with a green base and white spots (cf. BILLY *n.*[4]). [its being favoured by the contemporary boxer Jack *Randal*]

randem/random tandem *n.* [mid–late 19C] three horses driven in tandem.

r. & i. *phr.* [1980s+] (US campus) extremely exciting or enjoyable. [abbr. *radical* and *intense*]

randle *n.* [late 18C–19C] a set of nonsense verses that a schoolchild was forced to recite, to the accompaniment of pinching, hair-pulling and similar juvenile tortures, if they were caught breaking wind in public; thus *randling*, punishing a child in this way; *randle*, to punish with a randle. [the verses varied as to area. In Cumberland: 'The offender is seized by the ear or by the back hair, whilst the following is repeated "Rannel me! Rannel me! Grey goose egg/Let every man lift up a leg./By the hee (high) by the low, by the buttocks of a crow; Fish, cock or hen." If "cock" was the reply then the other said, "Hit him a good knock" and did so. If "fish" was the answer, the other said, "Spit in his face". (*EDD*)]

Randolph Scott *n.* [20C] a spot. [rhy. sl.; ult. film star *Randolph Scott* (1903–87)]

random *n.* [1980s+] (US campus) a stranger; someone who does not fit in.

random *adj.* [1980s+] (US campus) **1** ordinary, run-of-the-mill. **2** eccentric, bizarre, odd.

random Joe/person *n.* [1980s+] (US campus) an unspecified person. [RANDOM *adj.* (1) + JOE *n.*[7]/SE *person*]

random tandem *see* RANDEM TANDEM.

r and r *n.* [1990s] rape and robbery (cf. JUNIOR JUMPER). [abbr. + play on US milit. *r and r*, rest and recreation]

randy *adj.* [late 18C+] **1** violent, emotional. **2** sexually aroused, eager. [Scot. *randy*, wanton, lustful]

randy dandy *n.* [19C] a prostitute. [RANTAN/RANDY + redup.]

randyvoo *n.* [late 19C] noise, arguments. [milit. jargon *randyvoo*, a tavern frequented by recruiting sergeants; ult. Fr. *rendezvous*, meeting (place)]

ranfla *n.* [1960s+] (US) a car that has been lowered and otherwise customized for teen use (cf. LOWRIDER n.²). [Sp.]

rangatang/ranggatan/rango *n.* [20C] (W.I.) a belligerent, aggressive, coarse person. [SE *orang-utang*]

range *n.* [20C] (US Und.) the open area outside a row of cells (cf. ALLEY n.³).

range *v.* **1** [late 17C–early 19C] (of a man) to live promiscuously. **2** [19C] to work as a prostitute. [SE *range*, to wander around or RANGER]

ranger *n.* **1** [17C–18C] the penis. **2** [17C–18C] a prostitute. **3** [late 19C–1900s] (Aus.) a bushranger. [SE *ranger*, a wanderer]

ranggatan *see* RANGATANG.

ranging *adj.* [17C–18C] of a man, pursuing women, philandering. [RANGE v. (1)]

Rangitoto yank/yankee *n.* [1960s+] (N.Z.) a derog. term for an Aucklander. [*Rangitoto*, an island in Auckland harbour + *yank*; i.e. the supposedly Americanized city]

rango *see* RANGATANG.

rangoon *n.*¹ [20C] a prune. [rhy. sl.]

rangoon *n.*² [1960s] (drugs) marijuana grown wild. [ety. unknown; ? wild marijuana is common in *Rangoon*]

Rangoon runs *n.* [1940s+] diarrhoea, esp. contracted on foreign holidays (cf. APPLE-BLOSSOM TWO-STEP). [proper name *Rangoon* + RUNS]

rank *adj.*¹ **1** [late 18C+] second-rate, inferior, disgusting. **2** [20C] (W.I.) foul-smelling. **3** [20C] (W.I.) impertinent, extremely cheeky. [ext. uses of SE *rank*, (1) rotten (usu. of meat); (2) rancid, strong-smelling; (3) grossly coarse or indecent]

rank *adj.*² [1950s+] (Black) excellent, first-rate, admirable. [SE *rank*, stout, strong]

rank *v.*¹ **1** [mid-19C] to cheat. **2** [1920s–50s] (US) to betray **3** [1920s–50s] (US) to catch in the act of committing a crime. [SE *rankle* or dial. *rank*, to lead a dissipated life]

rank *v.*² [1950s+] (Black) to admire, to respect. [SE *rank*, to assign a rank, in this case high]

rank/rank on/rank out *v.*³ [1960s+] (US street gang) **1** to insult, often by ritual insults directed at the other person's mother. **2** to harass, annoy (cf. DOZENS). [SE *rank*, to assign a rank, in this case low and thus to put someone 'in their place']

rank and smell *n.* [late 19C] a common person. [a pun on SE *rank*, (high) class and *swell*]

ranked *adj.* [1990s] (US campus) drunk. [? RANK adj.¹ (1)]

ranker *n.* [mid-19C] an absolute idiot. [abbr. SE *rank* + DUFFER n.⁴]

ranking *n.*¹ [1950s+] (US Black) insulting, usu. one's family and esp. one's mother. [RANK v.³]

ranking *n.*² *see* RANKS.

rank needle *see* NEEDLE n.².

rank on *see* RANK v.³.

rank out *v.*¹ *see* RANK v.³.

rank out *v.*² [1980s+] (US Black) to beg for help, to surrender to pressure, to behave badly or weakly. [RANK v.³ + *out*, i.e. to abandon one's aggressive posture (on model of COP OUT etc)]

rank rider *n.* [16C–18C] (Und.) a highwayman. [SE *rank rider*, a reckless rider, ult. Danish *rank*, upright, erect and thence proud, headstrong]

ranks/ranking *n.* [1980s+] (W.I./UK Black teen) a highly regarded (and revered) person; thus *ranks/ranking*, admirable, excellent. [RANK v.²]

rank someone's style/game/action/play, to *phr.* [1970s+] (US Black) to obstruct deliberately another's sexual advances (cf. COCK BLOCK). [RANK v.³ + SE *style*/GAME n.⁴ (5)/ACTION n. (1)/PLAY n.¹]

ranky dank *n.* [1960s–70s] (US Black) an unsophisticated, unworldly person. [? RINKY-DINK adj. + RANK adj.¹ (1)]

ranny *see* RAANY.

rannygazoo *n.* [late 19C+] nonsense; irrelevant, irritating activity. [ety. unknown; ? links to ? dial. *ranny*, rash, giddy + Fr. sl. *gazouiller*, to sing, to speak]

rant *n.* [19C] (cf. RANTAN; RANTY TANTY). [Scot./dial. *rant*, boisterous merry-making]

rant *v.* [late 19C] to take by violence. [RAMP v.]

rantallion *n.* [late 18C–early 19C] 'one whose scrotum is relaxed so as to be longer than his penis' (Grose 1785).

rantan *n.* **1** [mid-17C–mid-19C] a loud, banging noise. **2** [mid-19C] a drinking bout, a spree, a riot. [echoic, but note SE *randan*, riotous behaviour]

rantipole/rantipoll *n.* [19C] **1** a prostitute. **2** a 'madcap', a boisterous woman. **3** sexual intercourse with the woman taking the superior position; thus *ride a rantipole*, to have intercourse in this position (cf. RIDE A ST GEORGE). [SE *rantipole*, a wild, abandoned woman]

rantum scantum *n.* **1** [mid-18C–early 19C] sexual intercourse; thus *play at rantum cantum*, to have sexual intercourse (cf. RANTIPOLE). **2** [19C] a noisy argument. [redup. of SE *rant*, to lead a dissolute life, to be merry]

ranty tanty *n.* [18C] a prostitute (cf. RANDY DANDY). [? RANDY adj. (2) + redup.]

rap *n.*¹ [18C] the theft of a purse. [fig use of SE *rap*, a blow, a stroke]

rap *n.*² [late 18C–early 19C] **1** (Irish) a counterfeit halfpenny, seen in 1700–50 (cf. NOT GIVE A RAP). **2** a halfpenny. **3** money in general. [Ger. penny engraved with an eagle that had been drawn so crudely that it was known as a *Rabe*, a raven. The coin was presumably introduced to Ireland by Ger. mercenaries]

rap *n.*³ **1** [late 18C+] (orig. US) a rebuke, the blame, esp. in phr. *take the rap*. **2** [1910s–20s] (US) an identification. **3** [1920s+] (US) an official complaint or reprimand. **4** [1920s+] (US) a jail sentence. **5** [1920s+] (US) an arrest (cf. BUM RAP). **6** [1930s+] (Aus.) congratulations, a commendation, praise. [SE *rap*, a blow, a tap (on the shoulder)]

rap *n.*⁴ [1940s+] (orig. US Black) **1** a 'line' used for seduction or picking up members of the opposite sex. **2** speech or conversation, esp. the spontaneous wise-cracking repartee of street life. [RAP v.⁴; (2) adopted in 1960s by the hippies]

rap *n.*⁵ [1970s+] a style of music with singing or chanting of the lyrics against a heavy bass line, usually produced by a drum machine or synthesizer (cf. HIP-HOP n.). [while the terms are often used interchangeably, *rap* gives more emphasis to the words, while hip-hop often features a more elaborate, even dominant backing track]

rap *v.*¹ [late 17C–late 18C] to swap, to exchange, to barter. [? SE *rap*, to seize or snatch]

rap *v.*² **1** [early 18C] to swear (evidence) against someone. **2** [late 18C–early 19C] to swear a false oath. **3** [late 18C–early 19C] to curse. **4** [20C] (US) to charge; to prosecute, to arrest with a view to prosecution. [SE *rap*, to hit]

rap *v.*³ [late 19C] (Aus.) to knock out, to kill. [SE *rap*, to knock]

rap *v.*⁴ (orig. US Black) **1** [1920s+] to talk, to converse; thus [1960s+] *rap session*, an intense conversation; by ext., in new therapy use, an encounter group. **2** [1960s+] to indulge in repartee, street-talk. **3** [1960s+] to have any form of impromptu dialogue. [SE *rap*, to hit; note synon. Yorks. dial.]

rap/wrap/rap up/wrap up *v.*⁵ [1950s+] (Aus.) to praise, esp. to praise to excess. [RAP n.³ (6)]

rap *v.*⁶ [1960s+] (orig. US Black) to sing or chant a rap song. [RAP n.⁵]

rap attack n. [1980s+] (US Black) extended, emotional, aggressive talk. [RAP v.⁴ + SE *attack*]

rap club/studio n. [1970s] (US) an ostensible club that supposedly provides conversation but actually doubles as a brothel (cf. RAP PARLOR). [RAP v.⁴]

rape n. [mid-19C] a pear. [backsl.]

rape v. (US campus) **1** [1970s] to abuse. **2** [1980s] to diminish the effects of. **3** [1990s] to misuse, to steal. **4** [1990s] to defeat. [weak uses of SE]

rape-o n. [20C] (US Und.) a rapist (cf. STRANGE-O).

rape someone's buzz, to phr. [1980s+] (US campus) to put a damper on someone's pleasure. [SE *rape* + BUZZ n.⁵]

rape wagon n. [1960s+] (US) a flashy car belonging to a pimp (cf. PIMPMOBILE).

rap group n. [1960–70s] (US) a discussion or encounter group. [RAP v.⁴ + SE *group*]

rapid! excl. [1980s+] (Irish) a general term of approval, excellent! wonderful!

rapless adj. [late 19C–1900s] penniless. [RAP n.²]

rap on the real, to phr. [1980s+] (US Black) to speak sincerely, honestly. [RAP v.⁴ + ON THE REAL]

rap over the knuckles n. [late 19C+] a scolding or reprimand.

rap parlor n. [1970s+] (US) a euph. for a massage parlour, itself a cover for a store-front organization behind which, while legitimate massage may be available, men pay for a variety of sexual services from 'relief' or 'executive' massage (masturbation) to full intercourse. [RAP n.⁴]

rapped adj. **1** [late 19C] killed. **2** [late 19C–1920s] financially ruined. [SE *rap*, to hit]

rapper n.¹ [late 17C–mid-19C] a major lie (cf. THUMPER n.³; WHOPPER). [SE *rap*, a blow]

rapper n.² **1** [mid-18C–mid-19C] a professional perjurer. **2** [mid-18C–1900s] (US) a plaintiff, a prosecutor. [RAP v.²]

rapper n.³ [1960s+] (US) a chatterer, a talker. [RAP v.⁴]

rapper n.⁴ [1970s+] (orig. US Black) a practitioner or devotee of RAP n.⁵ music.

rappie n. [1920s+] (US prison) a confederate. [both men have faced or would face the same charge or RAP n.²; they would also talk or RAP v.⁴ together when plotting]

rapping n.¹ [mid-18C–mid-19C] perjury. [RAP v.²]

rapping n.² (orig. US Black) **1** [1960s+] talking. **2** [1980s+] performing RAP n.⁵ music. [RAP v.⁴/v.⁶]

rapping adj. [mid-19C] enormous, huge (cf. RAPPER n.¹). [SE *rap*, a blow]

rap sheet n. [1950s+] (US) a criminal record (cf. FORM n.⁵; JACKET n.²; PEDIGREE; PREVIOUS n.). [RAP n.³]

rap studio see RAP CLUB.

rapt adj. [1960s+] (Aus.) overjoyed with, carried away, delighted. [SE *enraptured*]

raptavist n. [1980s+] (US Black) a politically active rap artist. [RAP n.⁵ + SE *activist*]

rap up see RAP v.⁵.

Raquel Welch n. [20C] a belch. [rhy. sl.; ult. film star *Raquel Welch* (b.1940)]

rare adj. **1** [mid-17C–late 19C] a general term of approval, splendid, excellent, fine, also in ironic, neg. use. **2** [mid–late 19C] also as *rare and*, an intensifier of a noun, e.g. *a rare passion*, *rare and hungry*.

rare v. [1950s–70s] to inhale narcotics. [the injected drug must first be 'cooked']

rare as rocking horse manure, as phr. [1940s+] (Aus.) a phr. used of anything extremely rare.

rarefied adj. [late 19C–1900s] tamed, subdued, docile. [proper name *Rarey*, a horse-tamer; the term, usu. with a capital 'R', was also applied to horses]

raring to go phr. [20C] very keen on commencing. [SE *rear* (up)]

rarzo/rahzo n. [late 19C+] a red-nosed man. [its *raspberry* tones]

rascal n. [late 18C–early 19C] a man without genitals. [SE *rascal*, a young or inferior deer, whose antlers have yet to grow properly; Grose (1785) also suggests Ital. *rascaglione*, a eunuch]

rash n. [1970s+] (teen) an overly enthusiastic boy. [he 'gets all over you' like a rash]

rasher n. [1990s] (Irish) sexual intercourse; thus ext. as *rub of a rasher*. [ety. unknown; ? SE *rash* which results from rubbing]

rasher and a doorstep n. [late 19C] a rasher of bacon and a thick slice of bread. [SE *rasher* + DOORSTEP]

rasher and bubble n. [1970s] in darts, a 'double'. [rhy. sl.]

Rasherhouse n. [1990s] (Irish) the Mountjoy women's prison. [RASHER n. + SE *house*]

rasher of bacon n. [mid-18C] a fiery drink (cf. GLIM n.²). [ety. unknown]

rasher of wind n. [mid–late 19C] a very thin person.

rasher wagon n. [mid–late 19C] a frying pan. [it cooks SE *rashers* of bacon]

rashing n. [1970s] (US Black) an assault, violence. [SE *thrashing* + *harassing*]

rasp n. **1** [late 19C–1900s] the vagina (cf. CATCH 'EM ALIVE-O). **2** [1940s–50s] a shave. [SE *rasp*, a file, that which rubs]

rasp v. [late 19C–1900s] to have sexual intercourse (cf. BANG v.¹). [SE *rasp*, to rub against]

raspberries! excl. [1920s] (US) an excl. used to express disbelief or defiance. [RASPBERRY n.¹]

raspberry n.¹ [late 19C+] a coarse, dismissive, jeering noise (cf. BIG RAZZOO). [rhy. sl. *raspberry tart* = fart, the noise of which this resembles]

raspberry n.² [1960s] (drugs) an abscessed injection site. [its resemblance to the fruit]

raspberry n.³ [1970s+] **1** a nipple. **2** a disabled person (cf. STRAWBERRY n.³). [rhy. sl.; (2) *raspberry ripple* = cripple]

raspberry n.⁴ [1980s+] (drugs) a woman who trades sex for crack cocaine or money to buy the drug. [? pun on abbr. *raspberry tart*, i.e. TART n. (2)]

Raspberry-landers n. [20C] (Aus.) Tasmanians. [? the raspberry is a common plant there]

raspberry tart n. **1** [late 19C+] the heart. **2** [1950s+] a fart. [rhy. sl.]

rasper n. **1** [mid-19C+] a person or thing of an unpleasant character. **2** [mid-19C+] anything remarkable or extraordinary. **3** [20C] a very noisy breaking of wind. [SE *rasp*, to rub roughly]

raspin n. [early 19C] a prison (cf. REESBIN). [? Scot. *rasp-house*, ult. Du. *rasphuis*, house of correction in which prisoners were employed in rasping wood]

rasping gang n. [mid-19C] toughs and thieves who attend prize-fights. [SE *rasp* or RASPIN + SE *gang*]

raspy/rasty adj. [1970s+] **1** (US Black) unattractive, unkempt. **2** (US teen) excellent, wonderful (by bad = good syndrome). [SE *rasp*, to grate upon, to irritate]

rass n. [1940s+] (W.I.) **1** the buttocks (vulgar rather than anatomical). **2** nonsense, rubbish. **3** a great fool, an absolute idiot. [ARSE n.¹ or elision of *your arse*]

rass! excl. see RAAS!

rass to you! excl. [20C] (W.I.) go to hell! [RASS]

rasta weed n. [1960s+] (drugs) marijuana. [SE *Rasta* + WEED n.¹ (4); the role of marijuana as a Rastafarian sacrament]

Rastus n. [mid-19C+] a derog. term for a Black man. [popular mid-19C slave name *Erastus*; depending on context, as much patronizing as actively derog.]

rasty see RASPY.

rat *n.*[1] [17C–late 18C] a clergyman. ['Rats. Of these there are the following kinds, a black rat and a grey rat, a py-rat and a cu-rat' (Grose 1796)]

rat *n.*[2] [late 17C–18C] a drunken person who has been arrested and taken to the cells. [? phr. DRUNK AS A RAT]

rat *n.*[3] **1** [early 19C+] an unpleasant person. **2** [early 19C+] an informer. **3** [late 19C+] (Aus.) a street urchin. **4** [late 19C+] (Aus.) a wharf labourer. **5** [20C] a person, esp. an enthusiast (cf. GYM RAT; SPUNK RAT).

rat *n.*[4] **1** [late 19C] (US) a hair-pad with tapering ends used as the base of the elaborate pompadour hairstyles affected by women in the late 19C. **2** [1930s] (US Black) a wig. **3** [1990s] the pubic hair. **4** [1990s] the vagina. [? the rat's fur and, in (1), its tail]

rat *n.*[5] [20C] (W.I.) the lowest rank of prostitute. [SE but ? Fr. *rat*, a young woman, esp. a young ballet dancer between the ages of 7–14; cited as a young whore in Balzac, *A Harlot High and Low* (1839–47)]

rat *n.*[6] [1940s+] (US) a near-derelict but just driveable second-hand car.

rat *v.*[1] **1** [early 19C+] to betray one's own party or cause. **2** [early 19C+] to change sides. **3** [1910s+] (orig. US) to inform on, to betray. [RAT *n.*[3] (2)]

rat *v.*[2] [late 19C+] (Aus./N.Z.) to steal, to ransack, esp. as *ratted*, (of people) robbed or (of objects) stolen. [note mining jargon *ratter*, one who steals one's finds]

rat!/rat it!/rat me! *excl.* [late 17C–late 19C] a general excl. (cf. DRAT!). [SE *rot*]

-rat *sfx.* [1980s+] (US) constructed with a noun to indicate someone's habit or particular preference e.g. *arcade rat*, *gym rat*.

rat and mouse *n.* **1** [late 19C+] a house. **2** [20C] fig. a louse, an unpleasant person. [rhy. sl.]

rat around *v.* [20C] (US) to loaf about, to idle.

rat-arsed *adj.* [1980s+] drunk. [SE *rat* + ARSED]

rat arse/ass *n.* [1950s+] (orig. US) a general term of abuse. [SE *rat* + ARSE *n.*[1]]

rat back clip *n.* [late 19C] a short haircut. [the supposed similarity to a rat's fur]

ratbag *n.* [late 19C+] (Aus./N.Z.) a general term of abuse, a rogue, an eccentric; thus *ratbaggery*, acting in such a manner.

rat bastard *n.* [1950s+] (orig. US) a general term of abuse.

rat castle *n.* [early 18C] a prison, esp. the Poultry Counter, a prison in London (cf. RATTA CASTLE). [its population of vermin]

ratcatcher's daughter *n.* [20C] water, as drunk rather than sailed or swum in (cf. FISHERMAN'S DAUGHTER). [rhy. sl.]

rat/rat trap cheese *n.* [1930s+] (US) the American equivalent of 'mousetrap', i.e. an undistinguished cheese considered worth placing only in rat or mousetraps.

ratchet mouth/jaw *v.* [1950s+] to talk nonsense, to talk for the sake of hearing oneself talk; thus *ratchet mouth/rachet jaw*, a chatterer. [SE *ratchet*, a notched wheel used in a machine + *mouth/jaw*]

rate *v.* [1970s+] **1** to assess positively, optimistically. **2** to deserve or merit, to be highly regarded.

ratepayers' hotel *n.* [1920s–30s] (tramp) a workhouse. [paid for by the ratepayers]

rat face *n.* [20C] (US) a contemptible person, esp. if treacherous or cunning.

rat fink/r.f. *n.* [1960s+] an unpleasant person, with overtones of working as an informer. [SE *rat*/RAT *n.*[3] (2) + FINK *n.* (3)]

rat fink *v.* [1980s+] (US campus) to play a practical joke on. [RAT FINK *n.*]

rat fuck *n.*[1] (US) **1** [1920s+] a general term of personal abuse. **2** [1970s+] a damn, e.g. *who gives a rat fuck.* **3** [1970s+] (US campus) a term of approval (on bad = good pattern). [SE *rat* + FUCK *n.*[5]; the rat is stereotyped as a 'bad' animal]

rat fuck *n.*[2] [1950s+] (orig. campus) a prank, a practical joke. [note political jargon *rat fuck*, to sabotage an opponents' campaign by whatever means (usu. illegal) necessary; the original *rat fuckers* learned their trade in college politics and were later recruited to Richard Nixon's national campaign team; it was their techniques that would lead to Watergate]

rat fuck *v.*[1] (US) **1** [1960s+] to blunder, to make a (stupid) mistake. **2** [1960s+] to outwit, to trick. **3** [1980s+] (campus) to break off a relationship.

rat fuck *v.*[2] [1970s+] (US) to have a good time. [i.e. fig. to 'fuck like a rat']

rat fucker *n.*[1] [1950s–60s] (US campus) a home-made tool, which approximates a car's starting-handle. [SE *rat* + FUCKER *n.* (6)]

rat fucker *n.*[2] [1960s+] a general term of dislike.

rat fucking/kissing *n.* [1920s+] (US) any form of destructive, negative activity, esp. on campus or in the forces. [RAT FUCK *v.*[1]; SE *kiss* is euph.]

rather! *excl.* [mid-19C–1930s] a general term of agreement, indeed! I agree! very much so! (cf. FEW!). [later uses are historical or satirical]

rather of the ratherest *phr.* [late 18C–19C] applied to anything seen as either slightly too much or slightly too little.

rathole *n.* **1** [early 19C+] (US) a dirty or unpleasant place or room. **2** [1940s] (US Black) a pocket.

rathole *v.* [1930s] (US) **1** to palm money during a gambling game. **2** to hide away, to save up money, to hoard.

rathouse *n.* [1920s+] (Aus.) a psychiatric institution (cf. RATS IN THE ATTIC). [IN THE RATS]

rations *n.* [1930s–40s] (drugs) **1** a dose or injection of drugs. **2** a cache of drugs.

rat it! *see* RAT!

rat kissing *see* RAT FUCKING.

rat me! *see* RAT!

rat muncher *n.* [1980s+] a general term of abuse (cf. RAT FUCKER *n.*[2]). [i.e. one who eats rats]

rat off/off on *v.* [1930s+] (US) to betray, to inform against. [RAT *v.*[1] (3)]

rat on *v.* [1930s+] to betray. [RAT *v.*[1] (3)]

rat one's hair, to *phr.* [1950s] to backcomb one's hair in order to create the once popular 'beehive' style. [RATTY *adj.*[1] (1)]

rat out *v.*[1] [20C] (W.I.) of a woman, to work as a prostitute. [RAT *n.*[5]]

rat out *v.*[2] [1930s+] (W.I.) to act like a rat, to abandon one's responsibilities or friends. [RAT *v.*[1]]

rat pack *n.*[1] [1950s] (US) a juvenile gang. [best known of such gangs are Hollywood's Holmby Hills Rat Pack whose members included not juveniles but such stars as Humphrey Bogart and its successor, the *Rat Pack*, led by Frank Sinatra, Dean Martin et al. (which group had formerly been known as *The Clan*]

rat/wolf pack *n.*[2] [1960s+] (US prison) a group that has assembled for the purpose of administering a beating.

rat pack *v.* [1960s+] (US prison) to attack in a group. [RAT PACK *n.*[2]]

rat patrol *n.* [1970s+] (US Black) a police patrol in the ghetto. [RAT *n.*[3] (1), (2); Los Angeles use]

rat prick *n.* [1940s+] a general term of abuse. [SE *rat* + PRICK *n.* (4)]

rat race *n.* [1930s–40s] (US) a dance.

rat run *n.* [20C] any narrow passageway, back alley or relatively unknown short cut.

rats, the *n.* [mid–late 19C] a hangover, delirium tremens (cf. RAT-ARSED). [GET RATS]

rats! *excl.* [late 19C+] (orig. US) a general excl. of disgust or disbelief.

rats and mice *n.* **1** [1930s] a game of dice. **2** [1970s+] rice. [rhy. sl.]

rat's arse/ass *n.* [20C] a general pej. implying anything bad or insignificant, small or trivial e.g. *not worth a rat's ass.* [SE *rat* + ARSE n.[1]]

rat's asshole *n.* [1950s+] (US) a contemptible person. [SE *rat* + ASSHOLE]

rat shagger *n.* [1980s+] a general term of abuse. [SE *rat* + SHAGGER n.[1] (2)]

rat's head *n.* [20C] a dullard, a fool.

ratshit/r.s. *n.* [1970s+] (orig. US) a very unpleasant person. [RATSHIT adj.]

ratshit *adj.* [1970s+] (orig. Aus.) unpleasant, disgusting, annoying (cf. APESHIT). [SE *rat* + SHIT n.[1]]

ratshit! *excl.* [1970s+] a general excl. of annoyance or distaste. [RATSHIT adj.]

rats in the attic/garret/loft/upper storey *phr.* [20C] insane, mad (cf. ATTIC; RATHOUSE). [var. on HAVE BATS IN THE BELFRY]

rat someone out *v.* [1930s+] to betray, to inform against. [RAT v.[1] (3)]

rat's tail *n.* [early 18C] a pig-tail, as fashionable as a man's hairstyle.

ratta *n.* [1940s–50s] (W.I.) a bulging bicep. [dial. *ratta*, a rat, thus the supposed resemblance to a large rat]

ratta castle *n.* [1940s–50s] (W.I.) a rundown old house filled with idling inhabitants (cf. RAT CASTLE). [dial. *ratta*, a rat; ? link to the Anancy folktale in which Rat lives in a castle]

rattat *n.* [mid-19C] a potato (cf. RATTAT). [backsl. = 'tater' = potato]

ratted *adj.* [1980s+] (society) drunk. [RAT-ARSED]

ratter *n.[1]* [1910s] (Aus./N.Z.) a general term of abuse. [var. on RATBAG]

ratter *n.[2]* [1930s+] (US) an informer. [RAT v.[1]]

rattle *n.* **1** [early 18C] a dispute, a quarrel. **2** [late 18C–early 19C] a coach (cf. RATTLER n.[1]). **3** [late 19C–1920s] money, cash.

rattle/rattle along/away/off *v.[1]* [late 17C+] to leave, to move off, usu. quickly and noisily.

rattle *v.[2]* **1** [mid-19C+] to unnerve, to frighten. **2** [mid-19C+] to have sexual intercourse. **3** [20C] (Ulster) to work energetically. **4** [1910s–20s] to hit someone, thus *rattle the ivories*, to hit someone in the teeth.

rattle along *see* RATTLE v.[1].

rattle and clank *n.* [20C] a bank. [rhy. sl.]

rattle and hiss *n.* [20C] an act of urination (cf. COUSIN SIS; JOHNNY BLISS; MICKY BLISS; SNAKE'S HISS). [rhy. sl. *rattle and hiss* = PISS n.]

rattle and pad *n.* [late 18C–early 19C] a coach and horses. [RATTLER n.[1] (1) + PAD n.[1] (4)]

rattle away *see* RATTLE v.[1].

rattle bag/bladder/brain/cap/head/pate/skull *n.* [19C+] a gossip.

rattle-belly-pop *n.* [late 19C] (US) whisky and lemonade. ['changed, when speaking to the more elegant sex, to "rattle-blank-pop"' (Ware)]

rattle bladder *see* RATTLE BAG.

rattle bollocks *n.* [18C] the vagina (cf. CATCH 'EM ALIVE-O).

rattle box *n.* [1940s] a machinegun.

rattle brain *see* RATTLE BAG.

rattle can *n.* [20C] (Ulster) a noisy child.

rattle cap *n.[1]* *see* RATTLE BAG.

rattle cap *n.[2]* [mid-19C] a promiscuous man. [SE *rattle*/RATTLE v.[1] (2); the *cap* is that of his partner]

rattle cap *n.[3]* [mid-19C] a volatile, emotionally unstable person. [RATTLE v.[2] (1) + SE *cap*]

rattled *adj.* [late 19C+] **1** drunk. **2** anxious, unnerved.

rattle head *see* RATTLE BAG.

rattle one's beads, to *phr.* [1950s+] to complain; usu. gay use.

rattle one's dags, to *phr.* [1960s+] (Aus.) to hurry up, to get a move on. [SE *rattle* + DAGS n.[2]]

rattle pate *see* RATTLE BAG.

rattler *n.[1]* **1** [early 17C–19C] a coach. **2** [early 19C–1900s] a cab. **3** [mid-19C] in phr. *the rattlers*, the railway. **4** [late 19C–1900s] (US) a passenger train. **5** [late 19C–1950s] (US) the Manhattan elevated railway, cable cars or streetcars. **6** [late 19C+] the London underground railway. **7** [1920s] a bicycle.

rattler *n.[2]* [1920s] **1** an amorous man. **2** a promiscuous woman. [RATTLE v.[2] (2)]

rattlers *n.* [19C] the teeth.

rattles, the *n.* **1** [late 18C+] the croup. **2** [19C] the death-rattle. [abbr. SE *death-rattle*]

rattle skull *see* RATTLE BAG.

rattlesnake canyon *n.* [20C] the vagina (cf. CANYON; RATTLE BOLLOCKS).

rattlesnakes *n.* [20C] delirium tremens. [rhy. sl.; *rattlesnakes* = the SHAKES n. (1)]

rattle someone off *v.* [late 18C–early 19C] to scold, to tell off.

rattle someone's cage, to *phr.* [1970s+] to annoy, to irritate.

rattle someone's chain, to *phr.* [1960s+] (orig. US) to annoy, to distract forcefully, to taunt. [var. on JERK SOMEONE'S CHAIN]

rattle the bottle, to *phr.* [1950s+] (US) to masturbate.

rattle the can, to *phr.* [1940s] (US) to beg in the street.

rattletrap *n.* [1810s] **1** the mouth. **2** a gossip, a chatterer (cf. RATTLE BAG). [SE *rattle* + TRAP n.[3]]

rattling-cove *n.* [late 17C–18C] (Und.) a coachman. [RATTLER n.[1] (1) + COVE]

rattling mumper *n.* [late 17C–19C] (Und.) a beggar who specializes in approaching those who ride in coaches. [RATTLER n.[1] (1) + MUMPER n.]

rat track whisky *n.* [1920s] (drugs) very strong whisky.

rat trap *n.[1]* [mid-19C+] a shabby or ramshackle building or dwelling.

rat trap *n.[2]* [1920s+] the mouth (cf. POTATO-TRAP; RATTLETRAP).

rat trap *n.[3]* [1940s+] a Japanese person. [rhy. sl.; *rat trap* = JAP n.[2]]

rat trap cheese *see* RAT CHEESE.

ratty *adj.[1]* **1** [mid-19C+] (orig. US) rundown, ramshackle, unkempt. **2** [20C] irritated, annoyed, obstreperous. **3** [1930s] (US) drunk. [neg. imagery of the animal]

ratty *adj.[2]* [20C] (Aus./N.Z.) mad, eccentric; thus *ratty on/over*, infatuated with. [RATS IN THE ATTIC]

raunch *n.* [1960s+] (US) **1** vulgarity, grubbiness. **2** obscenity, pornography. [backform. of RAUNCHY]

raunch *v.* [1960s+] (US) to have sexual intercourse. [backform. of RAUNCHY]

raunch out *v.* [1970s] (US campus) to offend by making sexual remarks or using offensive language. [backform. of RAUNCHY]

raunchy/ronchie *adj.* **1** [1930s+] (orig. US) sordid, sloppy, contemptible, excessive, seedy (cf. RANCHY). **2** [1960s+] (orig. US) suggestive, sexually provocative, smutty, salacious. **3** [1960s+] (US teen) inferior, cheap (cf. CRUMMY adj.[2]). **4** [1960s+] (US campus) ill, unwell. **5** [1960s+] (US) drunk. [ety. unknown; E.P. suggests SE *rancid* or fig. use of dial. *raunch*, of vegetables, uncooked, i.e. 'raw']

raus mit 'em! *excl.* [20C] (US) get out! away with you! [Ger. *heraus mit ihm!* out with him!]

raughty *see* RORTY.

rave *n.[1]* **1** [20C] a sudden display of enthusiasm, a 'craze'. **2** [1910s–40s] an obsession with someone or something (cf. PASH n.). **3** [1920s+] (orig. US) an extremely favourable review of a show, film, book etc. **4** [1920s+] (orig. US) any strong, usu. favourable opinion. **5** [1950s+] the person or object who excites such emotions.

rave/rave-up n.² [1960s+] in the early 1960s, a party; the term was revived in the 1980s, with much the same meaning, although the parties concerned were often held in clubs or, in the case of the much-vilified ACID HOUSE PARTIES, in disused warehouses, hangars etc.

rave v.¹ [late 19C+] to praise enthusiastically.

rave v.² **1** [1960s+] to go out in search of a good time. **2** [1980s+] to attend a club or larger gathering to listen to music and, almost invariably, to take MDMA (cf. ECSTASY). [RAVE n.²]

rave-up see RAVE n.².

raven n. [late 19C] a small portion of bread and cheese. [the Biblical story of ravens taking small portions of food to the prophet Elisha]

raver n. **1** [1950s+] anyone devoted to having an energetically good time with variations of 'dope, sex and rock 'n' roll' as to individual taste and situation; esp. in *right little raver*, a hedonistic woman who is also presumed to be sexually available. **2** [1960s+] someone who goes to a party. [RAVE v.²]

ravers adj. [1930s+] insane, mad; thus intensified as *stark ravers*. [SE *raving* + 'Oxford' sfx. *-ers*]

ravilliac n. [late 17C–18C] an assassin. [François *Ravaillac*, the assassin in 1610 of King Henri IV of France]

raving adj. [late 19C] utmost, excellent, very much. [SE *raving*, insane, crazed]

raw n. [1980s+] (drugs) crack cocaine that has not been adulterated or 'cut'. [SE *raw*, a natural, unadorned and undiluted state]

raw adj.¹ **1** [mid-19C+] inexperienced, unsophisticated (cf. JOHNNY RAW). **2** [1940s+] naked (cf. IN THE RAW). **3** [1940s+] harsh, inhospitable (cf. RAW DEAL). **4** [1990s] (US) used of sexual intercourse without a condom (cf. BAREBACK). [SE *raw*, in a natural, unadorned and undiluted state]

raw adj.² [1990s] (US Black/teen) **1** excellent, powerful, impressive. **2** honest, candid, unadorned. [SE *raw*, in a natural, unadorned and undiluted state]

raw and ripe n. [20C] a tobacco pipe. [rhy. sl.]

rawlpindi adj. [1940s–50s] of the weather, windy. [rhy. sl.]

raw chaw n. [1940s+] (W.I.) an uncouth, ill-mannered person. [SE *raw* + *chaw* (*chew*), to chew coarsely]

raw deal n. [1910s+] (orig. US) unfair, harsh treatment, particularly poor luck; usu. from the point of view of the victim (cf. FAIR DEAL). [RAW adj.¹ (3) + DEAL n.² (3)]

raw dogg n.¹ [1990s] the use of obscenity in a situation where such language would usually be outlawed. [RAW adj.² + GANGSTA sp. of SE *dog*]

raw dogg n.² [1990s] (US Black teen) sexual intercourse without a condom. [RAW adj.¹ + DOG OUT]

rawhide n. [19C+] (US) a cowboy. [metonymy; i.e. his *rawhide* whip]

raw jaw v. [20C] (US Und.) to ignore, to refuse to speak to. [SE *raw* + JAW v.¹ (1)]

raw jaws n. [1980s+] (US gay) someone who is still a novice as a fellator (cf. IRON JAWS).

rawk n. [1990s] (US teen) the currently fashionable pron. of *rock* (music).

raw lobster n. [early 19C] a policeman (cf. BOIL ONE'S LOBSTER; LOBSTER n.¹; UNBOILED LOBSTER). [the blue uniform, which resembles an unboiled or raw lobster]

raw meat n. **1** [late 18C+] the penis. **2** [19C+] a prostitute caught *in flagrante*. **3** [late 19C–1900s] a woman who partakes, naked, in sex shows. [SE *raw* + MEAT n.]

raw prawn n. [1940s+] (Aus.) **1** an unfair action or circumstance, anything far-fetched; thus *come the raw prawn*, to act resentfully or unpleasantly; to be rude. **2** someone who is easy to deceive, a dupe. [the foodstuff and the concept are both 'hard to swallow']

raw recruit n. [late 19C] a shot of undiluted spirits.

raws n. [late 19C] the fists. [one's bare skin]

rawskin n. [1940s+] (Aus.) an inexperienced criminal (cf. CLEANSKIN). [RAW adj.¹ (1)]

raw sole n. [1950s+] (US Black) a virgin Black woman (cf. FISH n.⁴). [SE *raw* + pun on *sole*/SOUL n.²]

raw tea n. [1920s+] 'black' tea without milk or sugar.

raw 'uns n. [early 19C] the fists, esp. as used in a fight.

rax/rax up v. [1940s+] (W.I.) to abuse. [? RAZZ v.²]

ray n. [mid-19C] one shilling and sixpence. [? obs. SE *ray*, a small piece of gold or gold-leaf]

rays n. [1960s+] (US) sunshine, usu. in phr. *catch some rays*, to get a suntan.

razed adj. [1980s+] (drugs) under the influence of drugs.

razmataz see RAZZMATAZZ.

razmataz! see RAZZMATAZZ!

razoo/rahzoo n. [20C] (orig. N.Z., then Aus./N.Z.) a small amount of money; usu. in phr. *not a brass razoo*, absolutely penniless. [*AND* says 'unknown origin'; E.P. suggests Maori *rahu*]

razor n.¹ [20C] a notably 'sharp' person.

razor n.² [1960s+] a Black person. [rhy. sl. *razor blade* = SPADE]

razor v.¹ [19C] (US Und.) to share out loot. [i.e. to 'cut up']

razor v.² [1980s+] (Irish) to be spoiling for a fight. [one is feeling 'sharp'; note Westminster School jargon *razor*, 'a defiant, quarrelsome or bad-tempered person' (Ware)]

razor ridge n. [early 18C] shaving. [SE *razor* + sfx. *-age*]

razz, the n. [1930s+] (US) mocking insults, rude noises (cf. BIG RAZZOO). [abbr. RASPBERRY]

razz v.¹ see RAZZLE.

razz v.² [1930s+] (orig. US) to tease, to heckle, to barrack (cf. RAX). [RASPBERRY n.¹]

razzing n. [1930s+] (orig. US) a scolding, a telling off. [RAZZ v.²]

razzle n. [20C] a spree, a good time. [abbr. RAZZLE-DAZZLE n. (3)]

razzle/razz v. [20C] (Aus.) to steal. [? SE *rustle*]

razzle-dazzle n. [late 19C+] (US) **1** confusion, chaos, often deliberately engineered to 'blind' the onlooker. **2** extravagant publicity, entertainment, pleasure, celebration (cf. ON THE RAZZLE). [ety. unknown; redup. of SE *dazzle* + ? link to fig. use of Yorks. dial. *razzle*, to scorch, to burn]

razzle-dazzle adj. [late 19C+] (US) spectacular, dazzling. [RAZZLE-DAZZLE n.]

razzle-dazzle v. **1** [late 19C+] (US) to dazzle, to deceive. **2** [1970s] (US Black) to hang around, to loiter. **3** [1970s] (US Black) to pretend something has happened or is happening when in fact nothing is. [RAZZLE-DAZZLE n.]

razzle-dazzler n. [late 19C] a very brightly patterned sock. [RAZZLE-DAZZLE n.]

razzmatazz/razmataz n. [late 19C+] **1** (orig. US) anything old-fashioned, corny, out-of-date. **2** (orig. US) a garish, meretricious display, an event or occasion surrounded by such excesses. **3** (US) a slick deception (cf. RAZZLE-DAZZLE n.). [jazz use *razzmatazz*, a variety of old-fashioned, traditional jazz; ult. echoic of the brassy, syncopated music]

razzmatazz!/razmataz! excl. [late 19C+] (US) an excl. of delight or pleasure. [RAZZMATAZZ n.]

razzo n. [late 19C–1930s] a nose. [var. on RARZO]

r.b. see RUGGER BUGGER.

reach n. [1980s+] (US campus) someone who is out of touch with reality. [? they are *reaching* for the stars]

reach v. **1** [20C] (US) to bribe (cf. GET TO v.). **2** [1970s] (US Black) to help.

reach-me-down adj. **1** [late 19C+] (US) inferior, shoddy (cf. HAND-ME-DOWNS). **2** [1910s–20s] thrown together, improvised. [SE *reach-me-down*, a ready-made new or second-hand garment, often trousers; ult. any garment that is hung up on display and must be 'reached down']

read v.[1] [1960s+] to understand. [SE *read one's mind*]

read v.[2] [1980s+] (US Black/campus) to reprimand. [READ THE RIOT ACT but note READ UP]

read and write n. [mid-19C] a flight, an escape. [rhy. sl.]

read and write, to phr. [mid-19C] to fight. [rhy. sl.]

read braille v. [1960s+] (US gay) to grope someone's genitals through their clothing. [SE *braille*, the written language of the blind which is accessed by touch]

read 'em/them and weep n. [20C] (US) some unwelcome or distressing news or information, the truth; often as an imper., either delivered on retailing bad news or as a confirmation of the speaker's superiority. [gambling jargon, to acknowledge/announce a winning hand]

reader n. **1** [17C–19C] (Und.) a wallet or pocket-book (cf. READER HUNTER; READER MERCHANT). **2** [mid-19C–1950s] a newspaper. **3** [mid-19C+] (Und.) a 'wanted' poster. **4** [late 19C+] a marked card; thus [late 19C+] (gambling) *readers*, a crooked deck of cards that a cheat can read from the backs. **5** [1920s+] (US Und.) a warrant for arrest. **6** [1920s+] (US Und.) a small-time thief who follows postmen or delivery men to their destination, having sneaked a look at the label, then claims to be the official recipient (cf. SLOW WALKER). **7** [1940s–50s] (prison) any form of reading matter, books, magazines, comics etc. **8** [1980s+] (drugs) a drug prescription.

reader hunter n. [early 19C] (Und.) a pickpocket specializing in stealing wallets and pocket-books (cf. DUMMY-HUNTER). [READER n. (1) + SE *hunter*]

reader merchant n. [late 18C+] a pickpocket specializing in the theft of wallets and pocket-books. [READER n. (1) + MERCHANT]

readers n. [1920s+] spectacles.

readies n. [1930s+] cash, rather than cheques etc. [READY n.[1]/abbr. SE *ready money*]

read my lips phr. [1980s+] used to convey that one is thinking something insulting or obscene but choosing not to speak it. [play on the use of the phr. in a campaign speech by ex-President George Bush in which he told the media, *read my lips, no more taxes*]

read of tripe n. [mid-19C] transportation for life. [rhy. sl.; SE *read*, the stomach of an animal (from which comes *tripe*) + the '*tripe*' that is *read* out in court]

read one's beads, to phr. [1950s+] (gay) to chastise, to berate, to attack someone verbally. [ref. to SE *rosary beads*]

read one's plate, to phr. [20C] (US) **1** to say grace before a meal. **2** to eat in silence.

read someone's shirt, to phr. [1910s–30s] (orig. milit.) to check the seams of someone's shirt for lice.

read the maker's name see LOOK AT THE MAKER'S NAME.

read them and weep see READ 'EM AND WEEP.

read the riot act, to phr. [20C] to tell off severely and threateningly. [the practice, before its repeal in 1973 but effectively abandoned in 19C, of reading the Riot Act (1715) to unruly crowds before attacking with police or troops if they refused to calm or disperse]

read the tea leaves, to phr. [1960s] (drugs) to smoke marijuana. [TEA n.[2] (1)]

read up v. [20C] (Irish) to tell off, to reprimand; ext. as *read from a height*. [the practice in Catholic churches of the priest reading out a list of alleged moral or financial defaulters]

ready n.[1] [late 17C–mid-19C] cash in hand, usu. as *the ready* (cf. READIES; READY GELT). [abbr. *ready money*]

ready n.[2] [late 19C+] (Aus.) a swindle (cf. READY-UP n.; WORK A READY). [SE *ready*, to prepare, in this case the victim]

ready adj. **1** [1930s+] (US Black) aware, sophisticated, prepared to deal with the real world. **2** [1930s+] (US Black) (esp. of musicians) excellent, first-rate, mature, fully competent. **3** [1980s+] (W.I./UK Black teen) sexually attractive.

ready v. **1** [late 19C–1900s] to bribe. **2** [late 19C+] to contrive, to manipulate, to 'wangle'. **3** [1910s+] to drug someone so as to knock them out. [SE *ready*, to prepare]

ready-come-at n. [20C] (Irish) any form of skimpy woman's garment.

ready eye v. [late 19C+] (Und.) to plan, to scheme.

ready-eyed adj. [late 19C+] fully aware of a situation in all its ramifications, both obvious and hidden. [READY EYE v.]

ready for Freddie phr. [1950s–70s] (US) ready and eager. [redup.]

ready for the fox farm phr. [20C] (US) of an animal or a human, old, broken-down, at death's door. [the practice of feeding horsemeat to foxes that are being raised for their fur]

ready gelt/gilt n. [mid-19C] cash in hand. [var. on READY n.[1] + GELT/GILT n.[3]]

ready john n. [late 19C] (US) money (cf. JOHN DAVIES). [READY n.[1] + JOHN n.[5]]

ready-made n. [1940s–50s] (N.Z.) a factory-made cigarette.

ready rhino n. [late 17C+] money. [READY n.[1] + RHINO]

ready rock n. [1980s+] (drugs) crack cocaine; ext. to cocaine and heroin. [READY(WASH) + ROCK n.[4]]

ready the rosser/rozzer, to phr. [late 19C+] to bribe the police. [READY v. (2) + ROZZER n.[1]]

ready to leap nine hedges phr. [late 17C–late 18C] absolutely ready.

ready to spit phr. [20C] on the verge of orgasm. [SE *ready* + SPIT v.[1]]

ready-up n. [1920s–60s] (Aus.) a conspiracy or swindle; a fake. [READY UP v.]

ready up v. (Aus.) **1** [late 19C–1930s] to manipulate events or a person so as to achieve an improper or illegal end, usu. a fraud or swindle. **2** [1910s+] to find or hand over some money. **3** [1910s+] to hand on information, to 'put one in the picture'.

readywash n. [1980s+] (drugs) crack cocaine (cf. WASH v.[3]). [the process of chemical purification that is used when making the drug]

real, the n. [19C+] the genuine article, esp. in phr. *what's the real?*, what's going on? what's the meaning? [abbr. REAL THING]

real adj. [1950s+] used by a succession of teen generations as an all-embracing term of approbation.

real adv. [late 19C+] (US) very, e.g. *real bad, real soon*.

real Alie/Ally Daley, the phr. [1910s] (Irish) the real thing, the ultimate example. [*Alice Daley* (*fl.* early 19C), a noted producer of butter]

real A.V. n. [1920s–30s] (US) pre-Prohibition liquor, thus 'pure' liquor. [*ante*-Volstead Act]

real babe n. [1990s] (US teen) an admirable, attractive person of the opposite (or preferred) sex. [REAL adj. + BABE n.[1] (3)]

real deal n. [1970s+] (orig. US Black) the end result, the final assessment, the absolute truth (cf. BOTTOM LINE). [SE *real* + DEAL n.[2]]

real deal adj. [1970s+] (orig. US Black) genuine, trustworthy. [REAL DEAL n.]

real estate n. [20C] (US) dirt, esp. on the hands and face.

real George, the n. [1940s–50s] (US teen) the best, the ideal. [GEORGE adj. (2)]

real grit n. [1970s] (US Black) the absolute truth, the essential facts. [var. on NITTY GRITTY]

real jam n. [mid-19C] of objects or people, the best, the superlative (cf. TRUE MARMALADE). [sporting jargon]

real Kate n. [late 19C] a kindly older woman. [one Kate, a well-known and well-loved stall holder at Clare Market; whence the phr. spread]

real lady see PERFECT LADY.

real live adj. [late 19C+] a joking intensifier, e.g. *a real live supermodel, a real live nuclear physicist*, and tending to emphasize the near supernatural image of such creatures.

real McCoy/McKay *n.* [late 19C+] (orig. US) the genuine article, the 'real thing'. [the fighting name of Norman Selby 'Kid' McCoy (1873–1940), welterweight champion (1898–1900) and sometime strike-breaker or 'scab-herder' for the Ford Motor Co. Ironically, Selby was not in fact the *real McCoy*, this was another, slightly older welterweight, Peter *McCoy*, who toured with John L Sullivan c.1885 and who killed himself after a bad loss. Alternative etys. include the *real Macao*, a high-grade brand of Far Eastern heroin, much sought after by users; Joseph *McCoy*, the founder of Abilene, the first 'cow-town' of the West; a Prohibition era rum-runner Bill *McCoy*, this a development of the earlier (c.1908) clear *McCoy*, first-rate whisky and presumably named for a contemporary bartender; Und. use of the *McCoy*, commercially produced nitroglycerine, preferred by professionals for blowing open safes, rather than the home-made SOUP n.² adapted from dynamite; a late-19C Irish ballad; the African-American scientist and inventor Eligah *McCoy*, whose inventions were well known throughout the African American community]

real man *n.* [1960s+] (US prison) a prisoner well respected by his peers (cf. MENSCH n.).

real money *n.* **1** [1910s+] (orig. US) a large amount of money. **2** [1970s+] the currency to which one is used; thus *what is that in real money?*, used when a sum is mentioned in a strange or foreign denomination.

real raspberry jam *n.* [late 19C] an extremely attractive woman. [var. on BIT OF RASPBERRY]

real root *n.* [1900s–20s] the optimum way, the ideal thing. [? SE *root of the matter*]

real scorcher *n.* [late 19C] a very attractive young woman, but also a chaste one. [she gets one HOT adj.¹]

real stuff *n.* [1950s+] (Irish) illicitly distilled whisky (cf. REAL THING).

real thing, the *n.* [19C+] **1** the genuine article. **2** the highest quality Scotch whisky.

real woman *n.* [1970s+] (US Black) a heterosexual woman (cf. NATURAL WOMAN).

ream *adj.* [mid-19C] good; thus *ream bloak*, a good man. [var. on RUM adj. (1)]

ream *v.*¹ (US) **1** [1910s+] to cheat, to swindle. **2** [1950s+] to scold, to reprimand. [SE *ream*, to stretch, to tear in pieces]

ream *v.*² [1950s+] (US gay) to have anal sex with. [var. on RIM v.², but note SE *ream*, to enlarge or widen a hole]

ream *v.*³ [1980s+] (US campus) to treat unfairly. [fig. use of REAM v.² + poss. pun, i.e. 'to go behind one's back']

reamer *n.* [1970s+] the penis (cf. BAT n.⁷). [SE *ream*, to enlarge a hole/REAM v.²]

reaming *n.* [1970s+] a telling-off, a scolding. [REAM v.¹ (2)]

ream job *n.* [1970s] the licking and sucking of the anus, orig. gay use. [RIM v.² + JOB n.⁵]

ream out *v.* [1940s+] to scold, to reprimand. [ext. of REAM v.¹ (2)]

ream penny *n.* [17C] a tithe. [? *Rome-penny*, although such tithes no longer went there]

rear *n.*¹ [late 18C+] the buttocks.

rear/rears *n.*² [20C] (orig. campus) a lavatory; thus *do/have a rear*, to defecate (cf. BACK n.¹). [the position in the rear of a college or REAR n.¹]

rear end *n.* [1930s+] (orig. US) the backside or buttocks.

rear end *v.* [1970s+] of a vehicle, to run into the back of another.

rear-ender *n.* [1970s+] a crash in which one vehicle hits the back of that in front. [REAR END v.]

rearer *n.*¹ [late 17C] a battledore. [SE *rear*, to rise up]

rearer *n.*² [early 19C] a vehicle turned upside down after sliding into a ditch etc. [the horses have *reared* up]

rears *see* REAR n.².

rear seat gunner *n.* [1990s] a male homosexual. [the image of sodomy]

rear up *v.* [1910s–20s] to become very angry; thus *rear-up*, an argument.

rearview *n.* [1980s] (US Black/campus) the buttocks, the posterior.

reat *see* REET.

Reb/Rebel *n.* [mid-19C+] (US) a White Southerner. [the Confederate, i.e. Southern 'rebellion' that triggered the US Civil War (1861–5)]

rebop *n.* [1940s–60s] (US) nonsense (cf. ALL THAT JAZZ). [SE *rebop*, an echoic nonsense syllable used by jazz musicians]

rec *n.* [1920s+] *rec*reation, usu. in combs. e.g. *rec room, rec hall*. [abbr.]

recap *v.* [1940s+] (orig. US) *recap*itulate. [abbr.]

recce *n.* [1940s+] *recce*nnaissance; orig. milit. use, now a general term for making a preliminary exploration, assessment etc. [abbr.]

recce *v.* [1940s+] to look around, to explore. [RECCE v.]

receipt of custom *n.* [late 18C] the vagina. [for ety. *see* CUSTOM HOUSE]

receive a notice to quit, to *phr.* [early–mid-19C] to be informed of one's imminent death.

receive one's marching orders *see* GET ONE'S MARCHING ORDERS.

receiver *n.* [20C] a passive male homosexual (cf. CATCHER n.²). [baseball terminology]

receiver general *n.* [early 19C] a prostitute. [pun; i.e. she 'receives' such lovers as pay their money]

receive the canvas *see* GET THE CANVAS.

Recent Incision, the *n.* [mid-19C] the New Cut, SE1. [running from Waterloo Road to Great Charlotte Street, the New Cut was one of the busiest and most notorious Victorian street markets, as well known for its pickpockets and con-men as for the wide range of goods on sale]

recently struck it *n.* [late 19C] (US) a nouveau riche. [he has 'recently struck' gold']

reckless eyeballing *n.* [20C] (US) shameless ogling of the opposite sex (cf. EYEFUCK).

reckon *v.* **1** [16C+] to consider, to think, to suppose, to be of the opinion. **2** [1950s+] to esteem, to value, usu. as neg., *I don't reckon that lot*. **3** [1950s+] to know, to be aware of. [ext. use of SE *reckon*, to count, to ascertain; (1) mainly US since mid-19C]

reckon! *excl.* [late 19C+] (Aus.) a general excl. of affirmation, you bet! absolutely! [RECKON v. (1)]

reckon oneself *v.* [1940s+] to think a great deal of oneself, to be arrogant. [RECKON v. (2)]

reckon/reckon up one's ream pennies, to *phr.* [mid–late 17C] to confess one's errors or sins. [SE *reckon*, calculate + REAM PENNY]

recluse *n.* [1960s+] (US prison) someone who has been inside a prison for five years or more without hearing from anyone in the free world.

recorder's nose *n.* [mid-19C+] the rump of a chicken, duck, goose or other poultry (cf. PARSON'S NOSE). [unlike the usual refs. to clergyman, this phr. depends on the Recorder, a legal official appointed by the Mayor and aldermen of London as the guardian of the City's customs and of their own legal proceedings; thus ? an underlying ref. to ALDERMAN n.¹ (1)]

record hop *n.* [1960s] (US) a dance at which the music is supplied by gramophone records. [SE *record* + HOP n.¹]

record jockey *n.* [1940s] (US) the predecessor of the disc jockey. [SE *record* + JOCKEY n.² (2)]

recoup *v.* [1970s+] (US Und./Black) to start off fresh and determined on one's release from prison, undeterred by a few years' absence from the world. [SE *recoup* (one's losses)]

recruit v.[1] [late 18C–early 19C] to obtain a new supply of money. [RECRUITS]

recruit v.[2] [1980s+] (US Black) of a man, to go out looking for an available woman.

recruiting services n. [early 19C] highway robbery. [RECRUITS + play on SE]

recruits n. [late 17C–early 19C] (Und.) money; thus the punning phr. *raise the recruits*, to obtain money (cf. RECRUITING SERVICES).

rectal/rectum ranger n. [1990s] a male homosexual.

rector n. [late 19C–1920s] **1** the bottom half of a sliced teacake, which received the most butter (cf. CURATE). **2** a poker kept only for show. [(1) the *rector* was given (and expected) the best part of the cake; (2) such a poker was brought out when the rector was visiting]

rector of the females n. [17C] the penis. [SE *rector*, ruler ? + pun on *erection*]

rectum ranger see RECTAL RANGER.

recycle n. [1980s+] (drugs) LSD. [ety. unknown; ? it 'recycles' one's mind]

red n.[1] **1** [17C–1900s] (Und.) gold (cf. RED STUFF). **2** [19C] a smoked herring (cf. DUTCH RED). **3** [1910s–20s] a sovereign. **4** [1960s+] (US/Texas) chilli. [the colour]

red n.[2] [18C–19C] a soldier (cf. BIT OF RED). [abbr. SE *redcoat*]

red n.[3] [1920s+] a Bolshevik, a Communist, a socialist or anyone considered to have left-wing leanings (cf. PINKO n.). [RED adj.[4]]

red adj.[1] [17C+] golden, made of gold. [RED n.[1] (1)]

red adj.[2] [20C] (US) used of a poor, bigoted White Southerner (cf. NECK n.[3]). [abbr. REDNECK n.[1] (1)]

red/red-skin adj.[3] [20C] (W.I.) used of any skin colour from brown to near-White, but not pure Black.

red adj.[4] [1920s+] communist, socialist, left-wing (cf. PINK adj.[3]). [*red* has been synonymous with communism since its birth in 1848 and has been thus used as a synon. adj.; its mass and thus slangier use came after the Russian Revolution of 1917; a handy right-wing insult, it is often used of anything that frightens a conservative speaker]

red adj.[5] [1950s+] [W.I. Rasta] extremely intoxicated by marijuana. [one's eyes become *red*]

red ace/c. n. [mid–late 19C] **1** the vagina. **2** the female pubic hair (cf. RUFUS n.[1]). [SE *red* + ACE (OF SPADES)/abbr. CUNT n.[1]]

red and blue n. [1960s–70s] (drugs) Tuinal, a barbiturate. [the colour of the pills]

red 'Arry n. [1930s–60s] (Aus.) a £10 note. [the colour ? + the signature on the note]

red arse/ass/r.a. n. [1960s+] bad temper, irritation; thus *red-arsed/-assed*, furious.

redball n. [1930s] (US) a fast freight train (cf. MANIFEST). [on early railroads such trains mounted a red ball on the engine as a signal calling for priority]

red band n. [1950s+] (US prison) a trusty, i.e. a prisoner given special privileges. [the *red band* around the arm that denotes privileged status]

red beard n. [early 17C] a watchman, a constable, poss. a young man. [the implied youthfulness, thus energy of a *red beard*, as opposed to the 'white hair' of an older man]

red biddy n. [1910s+] **1** the cheapest red wine, beloved of down-and-outs (cf. DAGO RED). **2** methylated spirits, as a drink, often mixed with red wine. [SE *red* + fig. use of *Biddy*, nickname for Bridget]

red birds n. [1950s+] (drugs) a barbiturate, esp. Seconal (secobarbital). [the colour of the pills]

red, black and green n. [1960s+] (US Black) a generic term for Africa and African-ness. [the colours that are predominant on many African flags + deliberate ref. to the synon. generic for America, the 'red, white and blue']

red blanket n. [late 19C] (Aus.) tinned meat. [the otherwise unmarked red-painted tins in which it was sold]

red bob n. [1940s+] (Aus.) a pimp (cf. PURPLE BOB). [play on RED SHILLING]

redbone n. [mid-19C–1970s] (US Black) a pale skinned Black person, esp. one who has native American blood. [Fr. *os rouge* (lit. 'red bone'), one who has native American blood]

red bread n. [1960s] (drugs) money obtained by blood donation. [SE *red*, the blood + BREAD n.[1] (2)]

redbreast see ROBIN REDBREAST.

red bullets n. [1970s] (drugs) Seconal, a barbiturate. [the colour of the pills]

red c. see RED ACE.

red cap n.[1] [1910s+] the penis.

redcap n.[2] [1910s+] (orig. milit.) a military policeman (cf. SNOWDROP n.). [the uniform]

red caps n. [1980s+] (drugs) crack cocaine. [the *red-capped* vial in which the drug is sold]

red carpet n. [1990s] a used sanitary towel.

red cent n. [19C+] (US) a trivial amount of money, usu. in phr. *not a/one red cent*, absolutely nothing. [the copper colour of a cent]

red centre n. [20C] (Aus.) the central areas of Australia. [the predominantly *red* soil]

red chenke see RED LEG.

red chicken n. [1960s+] (drugs) Chinese heroin. [RED adj.[3] + pun on CHICKEN n.[4] (1), punning on GIRL n.[3]]

red clock n. [late 19C] a gold watch. [RED adj.[1] + SE *clock*]

red cross n. [1920s–50s] (drugs) morphine (cf. WHITE CROSS). [? the packaging]

red death n. [20C] (US prison) prison-cooked barbecue beef or pork.

red deener see RED SHILLING.

red devil n. [1980s+] (drugs) phencyclidine (cf. ACE n.[3]). [ety. unknown; ? its neg. image]

red devils n. [1970s+] (drugs) any form of barbiturate available in a red capsule, e.g. Seconal. [the colour of the capsules]

redding n. [mid–late 19C] a gold watch. [var. pron. of RED 'UN n.[1] (2)]

red dirt adj. [1950s+] (US drugs) of marijuana, growing in the wild. [SE *red* + SAmE *dirt*, earth]

red disturbance n. [mid–late 19C] (US) whisky. [the colour and the effects]

red dog n. [mid–late 18C] (Anglo-Ind.) prickly heat, or *Lichen tropicus*, an inflammatory disorder of the sweat glands (cf. BLACK DOG n.[2]). [SE *red*, the colour of the inflammation + fig. use of SE *dog* to mean a feeling of being 'out of sorts', i.e. 'dogged' by illness]

red dog/knight on a white horse n. [1970s+] (US Black) a woman having her menstrual period.

red duster n. [1910s+] the Red Ensign, the flag of the (British) Mercantile Marine.

reddy n. [20C] an Italian living in London. [var. of RADDIE, but note Ital. *red* wine]

red eagle n. [1980s+] (drugs) heroin. [packaging]

red eel n. [late 19C] a general term of derision.

red-eye n.[1] [early 19C+] (US) strong, poor quality whisky (cf. CHAIN LIGHTNING; WHITE EYE). [the after-effects on the hung-over drinker]

red-eye n.[2] **1** [1920s–60s] (US) tomato ketchup. **2** [1970s+] (Can.) a drink made from mixing beer and tomato juice. [the colour + play on RED-EYE n.[1]]

red-eye n.[3] [1950s+] the anus. [SE *red* + ROUNDEYE n. (1)]

red-eye n.[4] [1960s] (orig. US) any air flight that deprives the traveller of proper sleep, due to take-off times, arrival times or differences in time zones. [abbr. SE *red-eye special*]

red-eye n.[5] [1980s+] (US Black) a long, hard, aggressive stare.

red-eye n.[6] [1980s+] (US drugs) the telltale redness of the eyes when smoking cannabis.

red-eye adj. [1980s+] (W.I./UK Black teen) jealous, envious. [one's *eyes* supposedly *redden*, although the usu. colour of envy is green]

red fed n. [1920s+] (N.Z.) a left-winger, an agitator, a militant. [RED adj.[4] + abbr. SNZE *Federation of Labour*]

redfern n. [late 19C] (society) a perfectly cut lady's coat or jacket. [the makers, *Redfern* of Maddox Street, London, re- nowned for their tailoring]

red flannel n. [19C] the tongue.

red fustian n. [late 17C–early 19C] **1** port or claret. **2** porter (cf. WHITE FUSTIAN). [SE *red* + *fustian*, a coarse cloth; thus note the contrast with 'smooth' SATIN, denoting gin]

redge n. [late 17C–19C] gold, thus money (cf. DELOG; GELT; GILT n.[3]; GINGERBREAD n.[2]; GOLD n.[1]; GOREE; OCHRE; OLD MR GORY; RED 'UN n.[1]). [var. on RIDGE]

red grate see RED LATTICE.

red gravy n. [1940s] (US Black) blood.

red head n. [1950s+] (US prison) a match.

red herring n. [mid-19C] a soldier (cf. SOLDIER n.[1]). [play on LOBSTER n.[1] (1)]

red horse n. [mid-19C+] (US) corned beef.

red hot n.[1] [late 19C+] (US) a frankfurter, a hot dog. [its flavour and temperature]

red hot n.[2] [1970s+] (US Black) a highly aggressive, volatile person.

red-hot adj.[1] [late 19C+] (Aus.) unfair, unreasonable.

red-hot adj.[2] [1900s–30s] (US) erotic, sexy, provocative. [ext. of HOT adj.[1]]

red hot mama/mamma see HOT MAMA.

red-hot poker n. [late 19C+] the penis. [HOT adj.[1] (1) + POKER n.[1] (2)]

red hots n. [1950s+] (Aus.) **1** trotting races. **2** dysentery. [rhy. sl., *red hots* = (1) TROTS n.[3], (2) TROTS n.[1]]

red-hot treat n. [late 19C] a very dangerous person.

red ink n.[1] [1910s+] (US) **1** cheap red wine. **2** tomato ketchup.

red ink n.[2] [1920s+] (orig. US) **1** the debit side of an account. **2** (US) a financial loss. [in pre-computing days debts were written in *red*, credits in black]

red-ink joint n. [20C] (US) a cheap Italian restaurant. [RED INK n.[1] (1) + JOINT n.[3] (3)]

red jackets n. [1960s–70s] (drugs) Seconal, a barbiturate. [packaging]

red kettle see RED TOY.

red knight on a white horse see RED DOG ON A WHITE HORSE.

red lamp n. [late 19C] a brothel. [such a lamp hung outside]

Redland n. [1940s+] Communist Russia, the USSR. [RED adj.[4] + SE *land*]

red lane n. **1** [late 18C+] the throat. **2** [20C] the vagina (cf. ALLEY n.[1]).

red lattice/grate n. [16C] **1** an inn. **2** a brothel. [a *red lattice* or grate was a popular tavern sign and thence, if the tavern was thus inclined, could also indicate a brothel; at one time an actual *Red Lattice* inn stood at Butcher's Row, off the Strand]

red lead n. [1920s+] **1** (US) jelly; (UK) jam. **2** (US) tomato ketchup. **3** (Irish) luncheon meat.

red leg/chenke/shanks n. [20C] (W.I./Bdos.) a poor White. [SE *red* + *leg/chenke/shank*; i.e. their skin tone; *chenke* is pron. of *shank*]

red-letter man n. [late 17C–18C] a Roman Catholic. [SE *red letter day*, a saint's day or church festival indicated in the calendar by *red letters*]

red light n. [late 19C–1930s] a supervisor, a manager (cf. BIG BLOKE n.[1]). [the use of a *red light* as a warning signal]

red light v. [1930s+] (US) **1** to kill someone by pushing them from a moving train. **2** to throw someone out of a car or other vehicle and force them to walk home, often over a great dis- tance (cf. SHELL ROAD). [the red rear-lights of the train or car recede into the distance]

red lighter n. [20C] (US) a prostitute. [SE *red-light district*, the brothel area of a town or city]

red liner n. [mid-19C] an officer of the Mendicity Society, a mid-Victorian society devoted to the suppression of street beggars. [when a boy was caught begging his name was noted down, with a *red line* drawn beneath it]

red lion lane n. [mid-19C] the throat. [ext. of RED LANE + play on the London street name]

red lizzie n. [1930s] cheap red wine (cf. DAGO RED). [var. on RED BIDDY n. (1)]

red lobsters n. [mid-19C] the Metropolitan Police. [SE *red* + LOBSTER n.[1]; many were ex-soldiers]

red lot n. [late 19C] a gold watch and chain. [RED adj.[1] + SE *lot*]

red mare/steer n. [late 19C] (Aus.) a bush fire.

red mary n. [20C] (US Black) a menstrual period (cf. BLOODY MARY).

redneck n.[1] **1** [early 19C+] (orig. US) a derog. term for a coun- try dweller, a peasant, esp. a southern US poor farmer who is stupid and racist; strictly *rednecks* came from swampy areas while *hill-billies*, their peers, came from the mountains. **2** [20C] (Irish) a yokel. [their sunburn; orig. a Presbyterian, then transferred to all poor Whites; (2) borrows f. (1)]

redneck n.[2] [early 19C+] **1** an Irish immigrant. **2** a Roman Catholic. [Lancashire dial.]

redneck n.[3] [20C] (S.Afr.) an English immigrant. [Boer War era *redneck*, a British soldier, f. his uniform and the sunburn]

red-necked adj. [20C] (US) angry. [one's neck blushes with emotion]

redneck foreplay n. [1960s+] the complete absence of any preliminary physical contact. [REDNECK n.[1] + SE *foreplay*]

red ned n. [1950s+] (Aus./N.Z.) cheap red wine (cf. DAGO RED). ['masculine' var. on RED BIDDY n. (1)]

red nigger n. [20C] (W.I.) a person both of whose parents are of mixed-African/White descent. [RED adj.[3] + NIGGER n.]

red nugget n. [1920s] (US) an illicit saloon. [ety. unknown; ? the name of a specific saloon]

red paint n. [1920s+] (US) tomato ketchup.

red pants n. [20C] irritation, bad temper.

red penny see RED SHILLING.

red peppers! excl. [late 19C] (US) a euph. form of swearing. [one feels so HOT adj.[1] (2)]

red rag n.[1] [late 17C–late 19C] the tongue; thus *too much red rag*, speaking too long and too loud, *give the red rag a holiday*, be quiet, stop talking (cf. RAG n.[4]; RED FLANNEL). [its colour and its 'flapping']

red rag n.[2] [20C] a menstrual cloth or sanitary towel (cf. HAVE THE RAG ON; RAG n.[9]).

red-ragger n. [1910s+] (Aus.) a left-winger, a socialist. [the red flag, the symbol of the revolutionary left]

redraw n. [late 19C] a warder. [backsl.]

red ribbon n. [early 19C–1900s] brandy (cf. BLUE RIBBON; WHITE RIBBON). [RED adj.[1] + RIBBON n.[3] (2)]

red rock n. [1980s+] (drugs) **1** methadone. **2** heroin. [? its packaging]

red rogue n. [early 17C] a gold coin. [RED adj.[1] + SE *rogue*]

red ruin n. [1930s] (US) any form of strong liquor. [SE *red* + *ruin*; play on BLUE RUIN ? + ref. to the red-brown colour of brandy/whisky]

red rum adj. [1970s+] dumb. [rhy. sl.; ult. the triple Grand National winning horse *Red Rum*]

reds n.[1] [late 19C] blushes. [the colour of one's cheeks]

reds n.[2] [1920s+] communists, socialists, any form of left- winger. [RED adj.[4]]

reds n.[3] [1960s+] barbiturates (cf. APPLE n.[7]; BLUES n.[2]). [the colour of the capsules]

red sail-yard docker n. [late 18C–early 19C] a criminal dealer who specialized in goods and stores stolen from the Royal Navy's dockyards. [? the identification of such goods with a red mark]

red sea n. [late 18C+] the throat (cf. RED LANE).

red seal n. [1980s+] (drugs) a variety of cannabis resin. [a brand of cannabis stamped with a red seal]

red seam n. [1910s+] (W.I.) a police officer. [the red seam that runs up the uniform trousers]

Red Sea pedestrian n. [20C] (Aus.) a Jew. [the exploits of the Hebrews during their Exodus from Egypt, among them the crossing of the temporarily dried up Red Sea with divine assistance]

Red Sea's out, the phr. [20C] menstruation, usu. used by men.

redshank n.[1] **1** [16C] (Und.) a duck. **2** [18C] a turkey. [dial., usu. as redshank gull (Totanus calidris) of the snipe family (Scolopacidae)]

redshank n.[2] **1** [18C] a derog. term for a Scottish Highlander. **2** [mid-19C–1910s] a woman wearing no stockings. [the kilted Highlander's or the woman's bare legs, thus coloured through exposure to the elements]

red shanks see RED LEG.

red shilling/deener/penny n. [1940s+] (Aus.) a pimp. [ety. unknown; ? fig. use of SE red, i.e. scarlet meaning sinful + SE shilling/DEENER/PENNY n.[1]]

red shirt n. [mid-19C] a back that has been scarred by a judicial flogging. [the colour of the blood and subseq. the scars]

redshirted adj. [1990s] (US campus) jilted. [college sports jargon redshirt, an athlete taking a year off from playing sport to extend their eligibility as a 'student']

red-skin see RED adj.[3].

red snapper n. [20C] (US) the vagina (cf. BEARDED CLAM; SNAP-PER n.[7]). [play on the fish name + ref. to the mythical vagina dentata]

red steer n.[1] see RED MARE.

red steer n.[2] [1940s] (US) beer. [rhy. sl.]

red stuff n. [1970s] (Und.) gold; esp. jewellery (cf. RED LOT). [RED adj.[1] (1) + SE stuff]

red tape n. **1** [late 18C–early 19C] brandy (cf. BIT OF TAPE). **2** [19C] red wine. [SE red + TAPE n.]

red tapers n. [1960s+] bureaucrats, civil servants. [SE red tape, bureaucratic obfuscation]

red tide n. [1990s] (US) the menstrual flow.

red toy/kettle n. [late 19C] a gold watch. [RED adj.[1] + TOY n.[2]/ KETTLE n.[2] (2)]

reduced/starved to the last buckle-hole of one's belt phr. [late 19C] extremely hungry, virtually dying from starvation.

red 'un n.[1] [late 19C–1900s] **1** a gold coin, a sovereign. **2** a gold watch. [RED adj.[1] + SE one/'un]

red 'un n.[2] [1930s] a match with a red tip. [SE red + one/'un]

red-up adj. [1990s] (W.I.) intoxicated by marijuana (cf. BLACK-UP). [one's red eyes]

red, white and blue n. [1970s] a shoe. [rhy. sl.]

red wings n. [1950s+] cunnilingus with a menstruating woman. [orig. Hell's Angels, where those who achieved this were awarded a patch in the shape of a pair of red wings]

redwop n. [late 19C] powder. [backsl.]

reeb n.[1] [mid-19C+] beer. [backsl.]

reeb n.[2] [1980s+] (US campus) a socially inept person, an outsider. [? var. on DWEEB]

reed horn n. [1940s] (US) a saxophone.

reef v. **1** [late 19C–1950s] (orig. pickpocket jargon) to steal money; thus (US/Aus. Und.) reef a leather, to steal a wallet

by pulling out the lining of the pocket that contains it. **2** [1960s–70s] (gay) to fondle someone's genitals. [SE reef, to roll up and secure all or part of a sail]

reefer n.[1] [1920s+] (drugs) **1** marijuana. **2** a marijuana cigarette, esp. [1980s] a large and slender version. **3** someone who smokes marijuana. [abbr. GREEFO]

reefer n.[2] [1930s–40s] (Und.) **1** a pickpocket. **2** a pickpocket's accomplice. [REEF v. (1)]

reefer man n. [1920s+] (drugs) a marijuana seller (cf. DOPE-MAN). [REEFER n.[1] + SE man]

reefer weed n. [1950s] marijuana. [REEFER n.[1] + WEED n.[1] (4)]

reef it off in lumps, to phr. [1920s+] (Aus.) to obtain large sums of money. [REEF v. (1)]

reeking adj. [20C] drunk (cf. ADDLED).

reeler n.[1] [late 19C] a policeman. [PEELER n.[1]; + ? an implication that the officers were reeling drunk]

reeler n.[2] [1930s–50s] (US) a spree, a drunken carouse; thus cop a reeler, to get drunk. [SE reel]

reeling n. [late 19C] a feeling. [rhy. sl.]

reeling and rocking n. [1950s–60s] a stocking. [rhy. sl.]

reel in the biscuit, to phr. [1970s+] (US campus) to seduce a woman successfully. [SE reel in + BISCUIT n.[2]]

reels of cotton adj. [1970s] rotten. [rhy. sl.]

re-entry n. [1960s+] returning to the 'normal' world after a period spent taking drugs, esp. a hallucinogen. [spaceflight jargon re-entry, a space vehicle returning to the pull of Earth gravity]

reesbin n. [mid-19C] (tramp) a prison. [Shelta]

reesch adj. [1980s+] (US campus) disgusting, unpleasant. [SE retch, or echoic]

reestie n. [1990s] (US) an unpleasant odour, object or person. [? Scot. reest, to smoke (fish)]

reet/reat/reet and compleat adj. [1930s+] (orig. US Black) ideal, perfect, excellent, quintessential. [mispron. SE right]

reet pleat n. [1930s–40s] (US Black) a sharply pleated ZOOT SUIT. [mispron. of SE right + the large pleats that distinguish the suit trouser]

ref n. **1** [late 19C+] a referee. **2** [20C] a reference (for a job etc). [abbr.]

reffo/refo n. [1930s+] (Aus.) a derog. term for any European (esp. Italian, Greek, Yugoslav) immigrant to Australia (cf. REFUJEW). [abbr. refugee]

refresh n. [late 19C] an alcoholic drink. [abbr. SE refreshment]

refresher n. [mid-19C] an alcoholic drink (cf. ALLEVIATOR). [it refreshes the consumer]

refujew n. [1930s–40s] (US) a Jewish refugee from Germany or Central Europe (cf. JEW CHUM; REFFO).

reg n. [1960s] (drugs) regular strength marijuana. [abbr.]

regent n. [mid-19C] half a sovereign. [pun]

rege-rege n. [1950s+] (W.I.) **1** rags, ragged old clothes (cf. RAGA-RAGA). **2** a quarrel. [Yoruba rege-rege, rough, in a rough manner or Hausa rega, to shake]

reggie and ronnie n. [20C] a condom. [rhy. sl.; reggie and ronnie = JOHNNIE n.[11]; ult. UK gangsters Reggie Kray (b.1933) and his brother Ronnie (1933–95); they offered 'protection']

reggin n. [1950s+] (US prison) a Black person. [despite origin in backsl. NIGGER n., there are no racist overtones]

reggo/rego n. [1960s+] (Aus.) motor vehicle registration. [abbr. SE registration + sfx. -O]

reg grundys/reggys/reginalds n. [1980s] (Aus.) underwear. [rhy. sl. reg grundys = UNDIES]

Reginald Denny n. [1940s–50s] a penny. [rhy. sl.; the British film actor Reginald Denny (1891–1967)]

reginalds see REG GRUNDYS.

register n. [late 19C] the human face. [it registers the emotion]

register v. [1960s+] (drugs) to drop blood in an eyedropper while injecting a vein.

regjegs *n.* [1940s] (W.I.) rags, old clothes (cf. REGE-REGE). [? SE *rags + jags*, rags, tatters]

regmaker *n.* [1950s+] (S.Afr.) a drink taken in the hope of curing a hangover, the 'hair of the dog'. [Du. *recht*, right + SE *maker*; the word is also used as the title of the house magazine of the S.Afr. Alcoholics Anonymous and for a brand of caffeine tablets, supposed to cure hangovers]

rego *see* REGGO.

regs *n.* [1950s+] regulations. [abbr.]

regular *n.* [mid-19C+] one's usual or habitual drink or order in a pub, bar etc (cf. USUAL n.).

regular *adj.* **1** [early 19C+] thorough, complete, absolute, perfect. **2** [1920s+] (US) dependable, trustworthy, honest.

regular crow *n.* [1910s–20s] a big success. [SE *regular* + CROW n.[4]]

regular fellow *see* REGULAR GUY.

regular flat fish *see* FLAT FISH.

regular guy/fellow *n.* [1920s+] (US) a thoroughly good person; in the speaker's opinion their peer, intellectually, in sense of humour, opinions, politics etc.

regular Hell *n.* [1900s–40s] (US) an out-of-the-way place (cf. GINNY GALL).

regular Indian *n.* [20C] (Can.) an habitual drunkard. [racist stereotyping]

regular joe *n.* [20C] a conventional, conservative person (cf. JOE PUBLIC). [SE *regular* + JOE n.[7]]

regularly *adv.* [late 18C–late 19C] thoroughly, completely.

regular moose *see* MOOSE n.[2].

regular oner *n.* [late 19C] an incorrigible rogue, 'one who is past praying for' (Ware); by no means invariably derog. but often implying a sneaking admiration.

regular p *n.* [1980s+] (drugs) crack cocaine. [ety. unknown]

regulars *n.* [mid-19C] a share of criminal booty; thus *go regulars*, to share profits (cf. NAB THE REGULARS).

regulator *n.* [18C] the vagina. [? it stops men getting 'overheated']

rehab *n.* [1940s+] **1** rehabilitation, from drug or alcohol abuse **2** the ward or hospital in which *reha*bilitation takes place. **3** the state of being *reha*bilitated. [abbr.]

rehoboam *n.* [mid-19C] a shovel hat. [the name of *Rehoboam*, son of Solomon, King of Judah (1 Kgs. chapters 12–14)]

reimburse *v.* [1970s] (US Black) to lose one's life for the refusal or inability to pay off a debt or favour.

reindeer dust *n.* [1940s–50s] (drugs) any powdered narcotic. [pun on SNOW n.[2]]

relation *n.* [mid–late 19C] a pawnbroker. [play on UNCLE n.[1]]

relic *n.* [mid-19C+] an old person; thus *relics*, parents.

relief *n.* [20C] (US prison) anything sent in to a prisoner from the outside world (cf. BOODLE n.[1]; SCORE n.[3]).

reliefer *n.* [1930s–40s] (US Black) someone who exists on welfare relief.

reliever *n.* **1** [mid-19C] a coat that is kept in a variety of public places, that can be lent to anyone who does not possess one. **2** [20C] (Irish) slippers. [the garments or footwear *relieve* suffering]

relieving officer *n.* [late 19C] one's father. [SE *relieving officer*, an officer appointed by a parish or union to administer relief to the poor]

religious *adj.* [late 18C–early 19C] of a horse, one that is always on its knees. [pun]

religo *n.* [1940s] (N.Z.) one who objects to war on *religious* grounds. [abbr.]

Relish, the *n.* [late 18C–early 19C] the Cheshire Cheese tavern, in Wine Office Court, off Fleet Street; frequented by such figures as Johnson, Garrick and later Dickens. [also known as *The House*, according to Weinreb and Hibbert]

relish *v.* [early–mid-19C] to have sexual intercourse (cf. NIBBLE v.[3]).

rellie/rello *n.* [20C] (orig. Aus.) a family *rel*ative. [abbr.]

reltney *n.* [20C] (US) the penis. [ety. unknown]

remedy *n.* [18C] a sovereign. [pun on SE phr. *sovereign remedy*]

remedy critch *n.* [late 18C–early 19C] a chamberpot. [SE *remedy*, ease + *critch*, an earthenware vessel; ult. *cratch*, a stable hayrack and thus a *crèche*; the term is used as such in early descriptions of Christ's birth]

remember Parson Malham!/Mallum!/Meldrum! *excl.* [late 16C–18C] drink up! finish your glass! (cf. PARSON PALMER). [? the proper name of a once celebrated toping cleric; presumably, since B.E. adds 'Norfolk', from that county]

r.e.m.f. *n.* [1960s+] (orig. US milit.) rear echelon motherfuckers; used by combat troops and brought into civilian life by veterans. [abbr.]

remish *n.* [1950s] of a prison sentence, *remis*sion. [abbr.]

remit *n.* [late 19C–1900s] a small sum of money. [abbr. SE *remittance*]

remo *n.* [1980s+] (US campus) a fool, an incompetent. [? SE *remo*dial + sfx. -O]

remote circumstance *see* MERE CIRCUMSTANCE.

remove one's digit *see* PULL ONE'S FINGER OUT.

renchild *n.* [1940s] children; used in an attempt to hide sensitive topics from the young, thus phr. *not in front of the renchild*. [syllable reverse]

renee *n.* [1980s] a girlfriend. [the popular working-class name]

renk *adj.* [1950s+] (W.I. Rasta) out of order, impudent, as in a rank-imposter; thus *yu too renk!* your behaviour is unacceptable. [RANK adj.[1] (3)]

reno *n.* [20C] (Can.) a *reno*vated house or property. [abbr.]

rent *n.*[1] **1** [late 18C–mid-19C] loot, booty. **2** [late 19C–1930s] money. **3** [1920s–50s] blackmail.

rent *n.*[2] [1930s+] a male homosexual prostitute. [abbr. RENT BOY]

rent *v.* [late 19C+] to obtain money either by criminal means or by offering homosexual favours.

rent-a- *pfx.* [1960s+] (orig. US) a general pfx. used to demean whatever noun it is attached to by implying a monetary rather than emotional basis for its existence, e.g. *rent-a-crowd*, *rent-a-mob*, a group of demonstrators who, it is inferred, will turn up purely to demonstrate, irrespective of the actual event; thence in general use e.g. *rent-a-nigger*, a Black private security guard, seen as protecting White interests against Black individuals; *rent-a pig*, *rent-a-cop*, a security guard. [a play on the care-hire firm *Rentacar*, a US proprietary name, dating from 1921]

rental units/rents *n.* [1970s] (US campus) parents. [abbr. PARENTAL UNITS]

rent boy *n.* [1960s+] a young male homosexual prostitute. [he is for hire]

rent collector *n.* [late 18C–early 19C] a highwayman, esp. one who prefers cash to jewels etc.

rent/rents coming in *phr.* [early 17C–mid-18C] rundown, ragged, dilapidated. [pun on economic *rent/rent*, a tear or rip]

renter *n.* [late 19C+] a young male homosexual prostitute (cf. RENT n.[2]; RENT BOY). [he is for hire]

renting *n.* [1950s+] obtaining money either by criminal means (blackmail) or by offering homosexual favours. [RENT v.]

rent party *n.* [1930s+] (orig. US Black) a party where the guests buy their refreshments to help pay the rent (cf. JUMP n.[4]).

rents *see* RENTAL UNITS.

rents coming in *see* RENT COMING IN.

rep *n.*[1] **1** [late 18C] something worthless. **2** [late 18C–mid-19C] a man or woman who has a (usu. bad) reputation. [abbr. SE *reprobate*, underpinned by *reputation*]

rep *n.*[2] **1** [late 18C+] *rep*utation. **2** [1950s+] (orig. US teen) a member's standing and status in a street gang. [abbr. SE *reputation*]

rep *n.*[3] [late 19C+] a commercial traveller, a sales *rep*resentative. [abbr.]

rep *n.*[4] [1920s+] *rep*ertory theatre. [abbr.]

repap *n.* [mid-19C+] paper. [backsl.]

repat *n.* [1940s+] a *repat*riate; thus *repat*, to *repat*riate. [abbr.]

repeat *v.* [late 19C+] a genteel euph. for belching or farting. [the food is 'repeating' itself]

repeaters *n.*[1] [20C] (Aus.) belching after rich or 'windy' food. [REPEAT]

repeaters *n.*[2] [20C] (US gambling) loaded dice. [they keep coming up with the same numbers]

repentance curl *n.* [mid–late 19C] (society) a woman's hairstyle, pioneered by the Princess of Wales (later Queen Alexandra; 1844–1925), in which a single lock of the backhair was brought forward over the left shoulder and allowed to hang over the left breast (cf. ZARNDRER). [? the lock of hair hanging over the heart signified *repentance*]

repent pad *n.* [1940s–70s] (US Black) a bachelor's apartment. [SE *repent* + PAD *n.*[2] (2); a woman who visits may 'repent of her sins' later]

repo *n.* [1960s+] (US) a car which is *repos*sessed for non-payment of instalments. [abbr.]

repo man *n.* [1960s+] (US) a *repos*session man, one who is employed by finance companies to repossess goods on which the owner is defaulting as to his payments. [abbr. + SE *man*]

reposer *n.* [late 19C] a nightcap, a final drink of the night. [SE *repose*, rest, sleep]

repository *n.* [late 18C–early 19C] a lock-up, a prison.

reppock *n.* [mid-19C+] a policeman (cf. ESCLOP). [backsl. COP-PER *n.*[3] (1)]

represent *v.* [1990s] (US Black) to act positively, to perform as required, to do (something) well, to behave authentically.

reptiles *n.* [1970s] (US Black) shoes. [the skins used for many popular styles]

republic of letters *n.* [early 19C] the post office. [pun on SE *republic of letters*, the world of literature]

res *n.* [1980s+] (drugs) an oily deposit left in a pipe after smoking crack cocaine. [abbr. SE *residue*]

rescue station *n.* [1970s+] (US Black) a liquor store. [ironic var. on SE *rescue mission*, a centre for alcoholics and other down-and-outs]

residenter *n.* [1950s+] (Irish) **1** an old inhabitant. **2** a fixture. [SE *resident*]

resinated *adj.* [1980s+] (US drugs) of a cannabis pipe or other smoking apparatus, clogged with resin.

resin scraping *n.* [1980s+] (US drugs) scraping out and then smoking the resin that has accumulated in a cannabis pipe.

Resistance, the *n.* [1930s] an area of West Hampstead colonized by a large proportion of German refugees. [ironic ref. to SE]

reso *n.* [1950s+] (Aus.) a residential boarding house. [abbr. SE *residential* + sfx. -O]

respeck *see* RISPECK.

respeck due *see* RISPECK DUE.

respect *see* RISPECK.

respect due *see* RISPECK DUE.

rest *n.*[1] [late 19C–1940s] (Aus.) a year's imprisonment.

rest *n.*[2] [1910s–20s] a *rest*aurant. [abbr.]

rest *v.* [late 19C] to ar*rest*. [abbr.; prior use from mid-15C is SE]

rest and be thankful *n.* [19C] for a man, the vagina.

rest 'em up area/place *n.* [1970s] (US) a highway rest area.

rest one's jaw, to *phr.* [20C] (US) to cease talking, to be quiet.

rest powder *n.* [1930s–40s] (US) snuff. [? one uses it when *resting* from work]

result *n.* [1950s+] (orig. Und.) a successful outcome to an endeavour, a sporting victory; an arrest for policemen, a lucrative robbery for villains etc.

resurrection-cove *n.* [late 18C–early 19C] a body snatcher, who robbed (usu. fresh) graves to sell the corpses to a surgeon for dissection. [SE *resurrection* + COVE]

resurrection jarvey *n.* [mid-19C] a driver of a night hackney carriage. [SE *resurrection* + JARVEY *n.* (1); a play on SE *resurrection man*, a grave-robber who also works at night]

resurrection pie *n.* [mid–late 19C] any dish made from yesterday's left-overs which have thus 'risen from the dead'; thus *resurrection bolly*, a beefsteak pudding.

reswort *n.* [mid-19C] trousers. [backsl.]

ret *n.* [1960s–70s] (US) a ciga*ret*te. [abbr.]

retard *n.* [1970s+] (orig. US) a mentally retarded person, whether actually or fig.

retired to stud *phr.* [1940s+] (Aus.) used of a woman who has abandoned social life for marriage.

retool *v.* [1940s+] (US) to make changes for the better, esp. in one's behaviour and attitude.

retread *n.* [1940s+] **1** anything or anyone old that has been given a new lease of life, esp. someone who has been retrained for a new job. **2** someone who has recently been divorced. **3** (Aus.) a retired schoolteacher who is still teaching. [SE *retread*, a tyre that has been reprocessed, with a new tread, to extend its practical life; note 1940s Aus. milit. jargon *retread*, a WW1 soldier who re-enlists for WW2]

retread *v.* [1960s] to retrain a person or give them a new job. [RETREAD *n.*]

retreat from Moscow *n.* [1940s] the exodus from England to Ireland by the better off that followed the Labour party landslide of 1945, with its imposition of higher taxes, the extension of rationing and the onset of 'Austerity'. [ironic ref. to Napoleon's *retreat from Moscow* in 1812]

retriever *see* VERSER.

retsio *n.* [mid-19C] an oyster. [backsl.]

rettes *n.* [1970s–80s] (US preppie) ciga*rettes*. [abbr.]

return to sender *phr.* [1990s] (US Black teen) **1** take it back, I don't want it. **2** what you just said or did was unpleasant or unacceptable.

reuben *n.* [19C] (US) a country bumpkin, a farmer (cf. ALVIN). [the 'rustic' proper name]

re-up *v.* (US) **1** [1960s+] (orig. milit.) to re-enlist, to join up again. **2** [1980s+] (drugs) to replenish one's stocks of a drug.

rev *n.* [1940s+] a term of address to any clergyman. [abbr. SE *Reverend*]

rev *v.* [1970s+] (society) to improve, to gee up. [SE *rev up*]

revelation *n.* [19C] (US) a drink of liquor. [pun on 'outpouring of the spirit']

reverend/right reverend *n.* [early 17C+] a clergyman.

Reverend Ronald Knox *n.* [1950s] syphilis (cf. BAND IN THE BOX). [rhy. sl. *Reverend Ronald Knox* = POX *n.*[1]; ult. the Catholic clergyman *Ronald Knox* (1888–1957)]

reverse *v.* [late 17C–18C] (Und.) to turn someone upside down and shake them until the money falls out of their pockets (cf. HOIST *v.*[1]).

reverse gears *v.* [1980s+] (US teen) to vomit.

rev-head *n.* [1970s–80s] (Aus.) a young man dedicated to driving fast as well as drinking heavily and getting sex whenever possible (cf. BOY RACER). [SE *rev up* + sfx. -HEAD (2)]

review of the black cuirassiers *n.* [late 18C] a gathering of black-garbed clergymen (cf. CROW FAIR).

reviver *n.* [mid-19C] a stimulating drink (cf. ALLEVIATOR; CORPSE-REVIVER).

revlis *n.* [mid-19C] silver. [backsl.]

revo, the *n.* [1960s–70s] the *Revo*lution; that unspecified explosion that stands as a grail for radicals everywhere. [orig. serious the term now tends to be ironic or historic]

revolving-door *adj.* [1980s+] (US) rapid or of short duration e.g. *revolving-door policies, presidents* etc.

revved/revved up *adj.* [1960s+] excited, tensed up, emotionally intense. [SE *rev up*]

rewired *adj.* [1970s] (drugs) of an addict, returning to drug use after abstention. [electrical imagery]

rez *n.* [1980s+] (US drugs) cannabis *res*in. [abbr./pron.]

r.f. *n.*[1] [1920s] a general term of personal abuse. [abbr. RAT FUCK n.[1] (1)/RATFUCKER n.[2]]

r.f. *n.*[2] *see* ROYAL FUCKING.

r.f. *n.*[3] *see* RAT FINK n.

r.f.d. dopehead/gowster/junker *n.* [1930s] (US drugs) a drug addict who travels between small towns, hoping to persuade sympathetic or naïve doctors to write narcotics prescriptions. [abbr. *R*ural *F*ree *D*elivery + DOPEHEAD n.[1]/GOWSTER/JUNKER n.[1]]

r.f.d. queen *n.* [1970s] (US) a homosexual living in a rural area, outside the main gay world. [abbr. *R*ural *F*ree *D*elivery + QUEEN n.[1]]

r.g. *see* ARGEE.

rhine *n.* [1980s+] (drugs) her*oin*. [abbr.]

rhino/rino/ryno *n.* [17C+] money; thus [19C] *rhino-fat*, wealthy. [ety. unknown; one suggestion, that it refers to the rhinoceros, then a fabulous creature 'worth its weight in gold', implies a certain lexicographical desperation; the term moved f. Und. to general sl., in mid-19C]

rhinocerical *adj.* [late 17C–early 19C] well-off, wealthy. [RHINO]

rhode *n.* [1940s] (US Black) one's best friend (cf. RUNNING PARTNER). [? ROAD DOG]

Rhodes scholar *n.* [20C] (Aus.) **1** a derog. description of someone who the speaker feels is trying to set themselves above the mass. **2** a non-derisive phr. of thanks for a favour done, *you're a Rhodes scholar, mate*. [the *scholarships* established by Cecil *Rhodes* (1853–1902), sending students born and educated in the colonies (incl. the US) to Oxford University]

Rhodie *n.* [1980s+] (S.Afr.) a White southern Rhodesian who emigrated to South Africa (and Australia) when the country became Zimbabwe in 1980 and Black rule was instituted. [abbr. *Rhodesia*]

rhodo *n.* [1920s+] a *rhodo*dendron (cf. CHRYSANTH). [abbr.]

rhoid *n.* [1970s] (US Black) anyone or anything that makes one's life less easily manageable (cf. PAIN IN THE ASS). [abbr. SE *haemorrhoid*]

rhubarb *n.*[1] [late 19C+] the genitals, of either sex; thus the coarse query, *How's your rhubarb, Missus?* [20C use is US]

rhubarb *n.*[2] [20C] an advance on one's wages. [rhy. sl. *rhubarb* = SUB n.[2] (4); (Cockney pron. 'rubub')]

rhubarb *n.*[3] **1** [1940s+] (US) an argument, a noisy dispute, esp. one that takes place on the field of play at a sporting event. **2** [1960s+] nonsense, rubbish (cf. APPLE SAUCE n.[2]). [a mix of uses, e.g. theatrical, the actors' traditional muttering of *Rhubarb* to provide background in crowd scenes; and sporting, baseball fans' term to describe a disturbance. The term was popularized *c*.1943 by the US baseball commentator 'Red' Barber, whose memoirs were entitled *Rhubarb in the Catbird Seat* (1968); for detail *see* Cohen 4: 52–55]

rhubarb and custards *n.* [1990s] (drugs) capsules of MDMA (cf. ECSTASY). [the colour of the pills; note cricket jargon, *rhubarb and custard*, the MCC tie, again f. the colour]

rhubarb pill *n.* [late 19C] **1** a bill. **2** a hill. [rhy. sl.; (1) puns on both requiring a 'giving out']

rhubarbs, the *n.* [20C] (US) the suburbs, the provinces. [play on SE *rhubarbs/suburbs* + pun on STICKS n.[3]]

rhygin *see* RYGIN.

rhyme *v.* [1950s+] (W.I.) to tell funny stories, to joke; thus *rhymer*, a teller of jokes or amusing tales.

rhyme slinger *n.* [mid–late 19C] a poet.

rhythm *n.*[1] [1960s–70s] (drugs) amphetamine (cf. A n.[2]). [play on BLUES n.[2] (2)]

rhythm *n.*[2] [1990s] (US Black) sexual advances.

'ria *n.* [late 19C] the generic name for a costermonger's woman, often a coster herself (cf. 'ARRY). [abbr. proper name *Maria*]

riah *n.* [mid-19C+] (orig. Ling. Fr./Polari) hair; thus *riah-zshumpah*, a hairdresser. [backsl. but note Sp. *raya*, a parting in the hair]

rial *n.* [1940s+] (W.I.) a half-caste, the offspring of an East Indian woman and a Black man; usu. combs. e.g. *Chiney-rial*, *Indian-rial* (cf. ROYAL n.[2]). [SE *rial*, a coin of low value]

Rialto *n.* [mid-19C–late 19C] (US) the centre of New York's theatrical life; spec. the south side of Union Square, on 14th Street. [proper name *Rialto*, that quarter of Venice in which the Exchange was situated, thus the centre of commercial life; actors presumably picked up the ref. from Shakespeare's use of the name in *The Merchant of Venice* (1596); like the STROLL n., the *Rialto* moved, as did the activities it denoted. In 1890 it meant the stretch of Broadway between Union and Madison Squares, in 1905 it centred on Herald Square, by 1910, during theatrical Broadway's heyday it meant the stretch between 34th and 47th Streets, centring on Times Square; its last gasp was the blocks along W. 42nd Street]

rib *n.*[1] [1930s+] (US) a joke, a trick. [RIB v. (4)]

rib *n.*[2] [1960s] (US Black) a woman. [the Biblical story of the first woman, Eve, woman being created from Adam's *rib*]

rib *v.* **1** [18C] to hit someone in the ribs. **2** [1920s–30s] (US) to discredit, to incriminate. **3** [1920s–30s] (US) to annoy or threaten, to pressurize (someone). **4** [1930s+] (US) to tease, to make fun of. **5** [1930s+] (Aus.) to swindle, to cheat. [one lit. or fig. 'tickles' or pokes the *ribs*]

ribband *see* RIBBIN.

rib baste *v.* [late 16C–late 17C] to thrash, to beat up (cf. RIB BENDER; RIB ROAST).

ribbed-up *adj.* [1910s–30s] (Aus.) financially secure. [one's full wallet, sitting next to one's ribs]

rib bender *n.* [early 19C] a blow to the ribs (cf. RIB BASTE). [boxing jargon]

ribbin/ribband/ribbon *n.* [late 17C–mid-19C] money; thus *the ribbin runs thick, the ribbin runs thin*, implying the availability or otherwise of cash. [? SE *ribbon*; the image is of the richness of ribbon-bedecked packages]

ribbing *n.* [1930s+] the act of teasing. [RIB v. (4)]

ribbon *n.*[1] [late 17C–early 18C] a bell-pull.

ribbon *n.*[2] *see* RIBBIN.

ribbon *n.*[3] [18C–mid-19C] **1** gin (cf. BLUE RIBBON; TAPE). **2** spirits in general. [SATIN and like it implying the smoothness of good gin]

ribbon and curl *n.* [20C] a little girl. [rhy. sl.]

ribbon clerk *n.* **1** [1920s–50s] (US) a small-time trader, esp. in the stock market. **2** [1960s+] (US gay) a gay man who has a desk job.

ribby *adj.*[1] [1930s+] short of money. [ON THE RIBS]

ribby *adj.*[2] [1930s+] second-rate, poor quality, dirty, run-down. [fig. the 'ribs are showing']

rib cushions *n.* [1990s] large female breasts.

ribena *n.* [1990s] a menstruating woman. [brandname *Ribena*, a blackcurrant drink]

ribena on toast *phr.* [1980s+] (gay) used of one who is unavailable for sex (cf. NAFF adj.²). [ety. unknown; ? the impossibility/unlikeliness of such a dish; differing sexualities preclude a link to RIBENA n.]

rib joint n.¹ [1940s+] (US) **1** a brothel. **2** any form of sex show which permits the customers to watch, but definitely not to touch. [SE *rib* + JOINT n.³ (3)]

rib joint n.² [1940s+] (US) a restaurant featuring spare ribs. [SE (*spare*) *rib* + JOINT n.³ (3)]

rib roast *v.* [late 17C–18C] to thrash, to beat up (cf. RIB BASTE). [pun]

rib roaster n. [late 17C–18C] a blow to the ribs (cf. RIB BENDER). [RIB ROAST]

ribs n. [late 19C–1900s] a fat person. [ironic use of SE; they are unlikely to be visible]

rib shirt n. [late 19C] a false shirt-front, covering only the ribs and chest, worn over an otherwise dirty garment.

ribston/ribstone n. [late 19C] a general term of affection, admiration (cf. PIPPIN). [the *Ribston pippin*, a dessert apple originally introduced from Normandy *c.*1707]

rib tickle/tickle someone's ribs *v.* [mid-19C+] to thrash, to beat.

rib tickler n. [19C] a thrashing, a beating. [RIB TICKLE]

ribuck *see* RYEBUCK.

ribuck! *see* RYEBUCK!

rice *v.* [20C] (W.I.) to maintain financially, to look after, to feed; thus *rice at* (one), to be supported as a servant, a kept woman etc. [the role of SE *rice* as a staple]

rice and beaner n. [1990s] (US campus) someone who identifies with the styles and concerns of the 1960s. [the popular staple macrobiotic diet of the era]

rice bags n. [late 19C–1900s] trousers.

rice-belly n.¹ [20C] (W.I.) **1** a stomach swollen from malnutrition and eating only rice. **2** a child who has such a stomach (cf. BANG-BELLY).

rice-belly n.² [20C] (US) (derog.) a Chinese person (cf. RICE-EATER). [racist stereotyping]

rice-burner n. [1980s] (US campus) a Japanese manufactured motorcycle. [racist stereotyping]

rice Christian n. [late 19C–1930s] (society) an inhabitant of a rice-growing country who volunteered for conversion less through religious fervour and more through a desire to gain food from gullible missionaries. [the use continued in the Far East to 1960s]

rice crispies/krispies n. [1970s] (drugs) amyl nitrite (cf. AIMIES n.²). [the cereal's slogan, 'Snap, crackle and pop']

rice dog n. [20C] (W.I.) a mongrel, fed on scraps (mainly rice) and useless as a watchdog.

rice don't cook in same pot *see* OUR FOOD DON'T COOK.

rice-eater n. [1990s] (Aus.) a derog. term for a Chinese person (cf. RICE-BELLY n.²). [racist stereotyping]

rice krispies *see* RICE CRISPIES.

rice man n. [1930s+] (US Black) an Oriental (cf. RICER). [racist stereotyping]

rice paddy Hattie n. [1980s+] (US gay) an Oriental gay man (cf. RICE QUEEN). [stereotyped link between *rice* and the East + joc./assonant use of the female name, a nickname for Harriet]

rice queen n. [1960s–70s] (camp gay) someone who favours Asian partners (cf. RICE PADDY HATTIE). [SE *rice* + QUEEN n.¹]

ricer n. [1930s+] a derog. term for an Asian person (cf. RICE MAN). [SE *rice*, the predominant Oriental staple]

rice rocket n. [1990s] (US Black) a Japanese-made four-wheel drive Jeep clone, e.g. a Shogun. [racist stereotyping]

rich *adj.* [mid-19C+] surprising, highly unlikely; usu. *that's rich*.

Richard n.¹ *see* RICHARD SNARY.

Richard/Richard the Third n.² **1** [late 19C+] a piece of excrement (cf. HENRY III). **2** [20C] a word. **3** [1920s+] booing, barracking. **4** [1940s+] a young woman, a girlfriend. **5** [1980s+] a third class degree (cf. GEORGE THE THIRD). [rhy. sl. *Richard the Third* = (1) TURD n.; (3) BIRD n.⁸; (4) BIRD n.⁵]

Richardanary *see* RICHARD SNARY.

Richard Burton n. [20C] a curtain. [rhy. sl.; ult. actor *Richard Burton* (1925–84)]

richard snary/richard/richardanary n. [late 18C–19C] a dictionary. [play on abbr. *dick*; 'A country lad, having been reproved for calling persons by their christian names, being sent by his master to borrow a dictionary, thought to show his breeding by asking for a *Richard Snary*' (Grose 1796)]

Richard the Third *see* RICHARD n.².

rich as crazes *phr.* [late 19C] (Anglo-Irish) extremely rich. [Irish pron. of phr. *rich as Croesus*]

rich as mud *phr.* [early 19C] (US) very rich.

rich friend n. [early 19C] a prostitute's keeper; i.e. a wealthy man rather than a pimp. [euph.]

rich one n. [late 19C] a wealthy wife. [the term was used by upmarket prostitutes with ref. to the wives that their clients dared not leave altogether]

ricing n. [late 19C] (middle-class) throwing rice over the departing bride and groom. [the belief, originating in the East, that rice, itself a quick grower, promoted marital fertility]

rick n. [1950s+] an error, a mistake. [? RICKET or bookmakers' jargon *rick*, a spurious bet]

rick and dick *phr.* [1960s] stupid. [rhy. sl. *rick and dick* = THICK adj.¹]

rickaticks n. [20C] (W.I.) a very bad temper; thus *get in one's rickaticks*, to lose one's temper and stay furious for some time. [UK dial. *rickmatick*, a (rowdy) affair]

ricket n. [1950s–60s] a mistake, a blunder. [ety. unknown; link to the disease SE *rickets*]

rickety kate n. [20C] (Aus.) a gate [rhy. sl.]

ricky-tick/-tick-tock/-ticky *adj.* [1930s+] **1** (orig. US) old-fashioned, predictable, monotonous. **2** (US) cheap and shabby. [jazz use *ricky-tick*, old fashioned jazz]

ricockulous *adj.* [1970s] (US Black) ludicrous, absurd, worthy of verbal denigration. [SE *ridiculous* ? + COCK n.⁴ (2)]

riddle-me-ree n. [20C] an act of urination. [rhy. sl. *riddle-me-ree* = PEE n.¹ (1)]

ride n.¹ [late 17C] (Scot.) a golden coin issued by James VI. [it carried the image of a man on horseback]

ride n.² [1930s+] (US) an automobile. [metonymy]

ride n.³ [1930s+] **1** sexual intercourse. **2** (orig. Irish) a woman when regarded as a partner in intercourse. **3** (Irish) an attractive man. [RIDE v.¹]

ride n.⁴ [1960s+] (US prison) a companion, a fellow gang-member. [a member of the same group or CAR n.]

ride n.⁵ [1960s+] treatment, a way of dealing with someone, esp. in phr. *(give) an easy/rough ride*.

ride n.⁶ [1980s] (US drugs) a state of intoxication. [play on TRIP n.³ (1)]

ride v.¹ [late 18C+] of a man, to have sexual intercourse. [prior use SE]

ride v.² [late 19C] (US campus) to use a translation in an examination or when preparing classwork (cf. HORSE n.⁷; PONY n.³). [pun]

ride v.³ [20C] (US Und.) to move from a local gaol to prison proper (cf. CATCH THE CHAIN; SHIP).

ride v.⁴ [1910s+] to annoy, to irritate. [one is 'on one's back']

ride a blind piece, to *phr.* [1960s] (gay) to fellate an uncircumcized penis. [play on SE *ride* + BLIND adj.³ + PIECE n.⁴ (2)]

ride a cotton horse/a white horse, to *phr.* [20C] to be menstruating. [*white cotton* sanitary towels]

ride a jock, to *phr.* [1980s+] (US campus) of a woman, to attempt to get to know a man of her own peer group with the intentions of ultimately having a relationship with that person because of his personality, not his material possessions. [SE *ride* + JOCK n.²]

ride a rampage, to *phr.* [late 19C–1900s] (US) to rush about in a reckless or riotous manner.

ride a St George, to *phr.* [19C] to have sexual intercourse with the woman on top of the man (cf. DRAGON UPON ST GEORGE; ST GEORGE A-HORSEBACK). [illustrations of a mounted St George slaying the Dragon]

ride a white horse *see* RIDE A COTTON HORSE.

ride backwards up Holborn Hill *see* WALK BACKWARDS UP HOLBORN.

ride bareback, to *phr.* [1950s+] to have sexual intercourse without a condom. [RIDE v.¹ + BAREBACK]

ride Bayard of ten toes, to *phr.* [late 16C–18C] to walk. [proper name *Bayard*, a horse that featured in various medieval romances; the name itself comes from Fr. *bayard*, bay-coloured]

ride bitch/punk/pussy, to *phr.* [1970s+] (US Black/teen) to ride in the middle of the back seat (cf. SIT BITCH). [SE *ride* + BITCH n.¹/PUNK n.¹/PUSSY n.¹, i.e. the supposed 'woman's seat']

ride by/go in the marrowbone/Marylebone stage, to *phr.* [early 19C] to walk. [*Marylebone* is simply a mispron. of SE *marrowbone*, itself metonymic for the legs]

ride down *v.* [20C] (US prison) to attack in a group (cf. RAT PACK V.; TAKE OVER THE HURDLES). [image of a 'Wild West' posse]

ride down on *v.* [1990s] (US Black gang) **1** to drive into a rival gang's territory in order to confront or attack its members. **2** to track someone down in one's vehicle. [image of a 'Wild West' posse]

ride down to the ground, to *phr.* [1950s+] (US Black) to attack verbally, to criticize heavily. [image of a 'Wild West' posse]

ride grub *v.* [late 18C–late 19C] to be bad-tempered or sulky. [SE *grub*, an unpleasant person]

ride herd on, to *phr.* [late 19C+] (US) to control or manage someone or something. [cowboy imagery]

ride in another man's boots, to *phr.* [late18C–19C] to marry another man's ex-wife, or to start keeping his former mistress.

ride in old shoes, to *phr.* [late 19C–1900s] to marry or take on another man's former mistress.

ride like a town bike, to *phr.* [1920s+] (Aus.) to copulate with great vigour. [RIDE v.¹ + TOWN BIKE]

rideman *n.* [1920s–40s] (US) someone who operates a ride at a fair or amusement park.

ride one's high horse *see* MOUNT ONE'S HIGH HORSE.

ride one's low horse, to *phr.* [1930s+] to act as a drunken fool.

ride out *v.* **1** [early 17C–late 18C] to be a highwayman. **2** [1950s] (teen) to leave.

ride plush *v.* [late 19C+] (orig. US) to travel by rail without paying. [SE *ride* + PLUSH adj.]

ride post for a pudding, to *phr.* [18C–19C] to make a great deal of effort for a minor cause. [abbr. SE *posthaste*, very fast]

ride punk/pussy *see* RIDE BITCH.

rider *n.*¹ [18C+] an overly amorous man.

rider *n.*² [late 18C–early 19C] someone who receives part of the salary for a job through an agreement with the job's actual appointee or with their patron; the rider is said to be 'quartered' on the job's possessor and a single possessor may have several riders in tow. [SE *rider*, one who rides + legal jargon, an additional clause tacked on to a document after its first drafting]

ride rusty *v.* [late 18C–mid-19C] to be ill-tempered or sullen (cf. NAB THE RUST). [SE *ride* + *rusty*, refractory (of horses)]

ride shank's mare/pony, to *phr.* [mid-18C+] to walk. [SE *ride* + SHANK'S PONY]

ride/sit shotgun *v.* [1950s+] **1** (orig. US) to sit in the seat next to the driver in a car (cf. RIDE BITCH). **2** (US) to act as a security guard, esp. on a vehicle. [stage-coach era use of a shotgun-wielding assistant who sat next to the coachman and protected him against marauding Indians, bandits etc]

ride someone bug hunting, to *phr.* [19C] (US) to punish, esp. to whip or beat. [ety. unknown]

ride/play staff *v.* [1960s+] (S.Afr.) to cling to the outside, or stand on the roof, of a moving train, having boarded it while in motion (cf. STAFFRIDER). [Zulu sl. *ukubamb' istuff*, to board a moving train, ult. ? f. *staff*, the pole in the doorway of railway carriage, which is grasped by those jumping aboard when the train is already moving]

ride the baloney pony, to *phr.* [1990s] (US) of a woman, to have sexual intercourse astride the man. [SE *ride* + BALONEY n.²]

ride the beef, to *phr.* [20C] (US Und.) to take the blame. [SE *ride* (*out*) + BEEF n.²]

ride the black donkey, to *phr.* [mid-19C] to be in a bad temper.

ride the blinds, to *phr.* [20C] (US tramp) to ride in the closed baggage compartment of a train.

ride the bolt, to *phr.* [1950s] (US) to be executed in the electric chair. [SE *bolt*, an electric shock]

ride the buick, to *phr.* [1960s+] (US) to vomit. [ext. of BUICK]

ride the bull, to *phr.* [1990s] to masturbate.

ride the corner horse, to *phr.* [1960s] (US Black) to hang around on street corners.

ride the cushions, to *phr.* [1910s+] (US tramp) to ride in a passenger car rather than in a boxcar. [the upholstered seats]

ride the deck, to *phr.* [1960s+] (US prison) to perform anal intercourse. [RIDE v.¹ + fig. use of DECK n.⁴]

ride the dolphin, to *phr.* [1920s+] to masturbate. [var. on FLOG THE DOLPHIN]

ride the Erie, to *phr.* [1940s] (US) to eavesdrop. [ON THE ERIE + play on the *Erie* railroad]

ride the E-train, to *phr.* [1990s] (US campus) to feel the effects of the drug MDMA (cf. ECSTASY). [play on the New York subway *E-train*/E]

ride the forehorse, to *phr.* [late 17C–mid-19C] to arrive early. [SE *forehorse*, the leader of a team]

ride the goat, to *phr.* [late 19C–1910s] (US) to be initiated into a secret society. [the fantasy that initiate Masons have to ride a live goat]

ride the gravy train/boat, to *phr.* [20C] (US) to enjoy a comfortable life (cf. GRAVY-RIDER). [GRAVY TRAIN]

ride the great white knuckler, to *phr.* [1990s] to masturbate. [play on SE *white-knuckle ride*, a terrifying fairground rollercoaster]

ride the gridiron, to *phr.* [19C] to travel by an East Indiaman. [the bumpy journey]

ride the gun, to *phr.* [1970s+] (US teen) to ride in the front passenger seat of a car. [RIDE SHOTGUN n. (1)]

ride the handcar, to *phr.* [1940s+] (US) to masturbate. [from the up-and-down movement of a handle with which one drives the vehicle]

ride the hobby horse, to *phr.* [1980s+] (US campus) to have sexual intercourse. [it is unlikely that the ref. to HOBBY-HORSE n.¹ is more than coincidental]

ride the horse foaled by/of an acorn, to *phr.* [mid-17C–mid-19C] to be hanged. [HORSE FOALED BY AN ACORN]

ride the lightning, to *phr.* [1930s–60s] (US) to be executed in the electric chair.

ride the mainline, to *phr.* [1950s] (drugs) **1** to inject narcotics. **2** to be a narcotics addict. [SE *ride* + MAINLINE n.]

ride the odno, to *phr.* [late 19C–1920s] to travel by train without paying a fare. [backsl. *odno* = nod, thus 'on the nod']

ride the pine, to *phr.* [1980s+] (US campus) to sit on the bench during an athletic event, esp. when one wants desperately to play. [the pine bench]

ride the planks, to *phr.* [1950s+] (Aus.) to go surfing. [surf jargon *plank*, a surfboard]

ride the poppy train, to *phr.* [1950s–60s] (drugs) to smoke opium.

ride the porcelain bus/Honda, to *phr.* [1960s+] (US campus) **1** to vomit. **2** to have diarrhoea (cf. DRIVE THE PORCELAIN BUS). [i.e. the porcelain lavatory bowl]

ride the rag, to *phr.* [1940s+] (US Black) to have a menstrual period. [RAG n.⁹]

ride the rap, to *phr.* [1980s+] (US) to accept the consequences of one's crimes, such as arrest and imprisonment, and deal with them as well as possible. [SE *ride (out)* + RAP n.³]

ride the riggen/riggin/rigging, to *phr.* [late 19C–1900s] to be very physically intimate. [dial. *rigging*, the backbone; note Scot. *riggin*, a tall, ungainly woman]

ride the rods, to *phr.* [20C] (US tramp) to ride on the steel bars beneath a freight car.

ride the silver steed, to *phr.* [20C] to be subjected to a cure of bismuth subcarbonate and neoarsphenamine for venereal disease; injections of the drugs continue weekly over a period of years. [the silver hypodermic]

ride the toby, to *phr.* [mid-19C] to practise highway robbery (cf. HIGH-TOBY-MAN). [SE *ride* + TOBY n.²]

ride the wagon, to *phr.* [1970s] (US Black) to enjoy a pleasant experience on a drug. [the image of lying on a hay-laden wagon as it moves through the fields]

ride the waterslide, to *phr.* [1990s] of a woman, to masturbate. [the vaginal secretions]

ride the wild mare, to *phr.* [late 16C–mid-17C] **1** to ride on a see-saw. **2** to live a riotous, wild life.

ride to Romford/Rumford, to *phr.* [late 18C–early 19C] **1** to get a new pair of breeches or to get a new bottom put in an old pair. **2** to be blunt, properly, *you may ride to Romford on this knife.* [proper name *Romford*, Essex, esteemed for the quality of its leather breeches]

ride tough *v.* [1970s+] (US Black) **1** to be intoxicated by a drug. **2** to be riding in a noteworthy car.

ride up a gumtree, to *phr.* [1910s+] (Aus.) to fall off one's horse (cf. GO UP A TREE).

ride with *v.* [1960s+] (US prison) **1** to side with (in a fight). **2** to be friends with. [fig. use of SE, but note CAR n.]

ridge *n.* [late 17C–mid-19C; 1940s+] gold, thus money, a guinea (cf. REDGE). [the term vanished in the UK during the 19C but reappeared in Aus. in the mid-20C]

ridge *adj.* [1930s+] (Aus.) valuable, good. [RIDGE n.]

ridge cully *n.* [late 17C–early 19C] a goldsmith. [RIDGE n. + CULLY n. (2)]

ridge montra *n.* [19C] (Und.) a gold watch. [RIDGE n. + MONTRA]

ridgerunner *n.* [1930s+] **1** (US) a southern mountain farmer, a hill-billy (cf. APPLE-KNOCKER n.²). **2** (US Black) any White person. [orig. f. Arkansas only]

ridgie-didgie/ridgie-didge/ridgy-dig/ridgy-dite/rigi-dig *adj.* [1950s+] (Aus.) genuine, honest. [RIDGE adj. + redup.]

ridic *adj.* [1980s+] (US campus) *ridic*ulous. [abbr.]

ridiculous *adj.* [1950s+] outstanding, excellent.

ridiculous *adv.* [mid-19C+] a general intensifier, very much, outstandingly, excellently.

riding *n.* [1920s–30s] (orig. US) annoying, irritating, teasing. [RIDE v.⁴]

riding a thorn *phr.* [1950s] (drugs) injecting narcotics. [i.e. the needle]

riding the wave *phr.* [1920s–30s] (drugs) under the influence of drugs. [surfing imagery]

riding the white horse *phr.* [1950s] (drugs) using heroin. [HORSE n.¹²]

riding the witch's broom *phr.* [1950s] (drugs) using heroin.

riff *n.¹* [20C] (US) a dismissal, a dismissal note or a demotion. [? jazz use *riff*, a simple musical phrase; i.e. one is 'drummed out' of a job]

riff *n.²* [1960s+] (US Black) **1** familiar or habitual words. **2** one's personal style. [jazz use *riff*, a simple musical phrase repeated over and over]

riff *v.¹* [20C] (US) to dismiss an employee. [RIFF n.¹]

riff *v.²* (orig. US Black) **1** [1960s+] to chatter, to talk. **2** [1980s+] (US) to complain. **3** [1990s] to inform on. **4** [1990s] to offend. [RIFF n.²]

riff-raff *n.* [20C] a Welsh person. [rhy. sl. *riff-raff* = TAFF n.]

riffs and rills *n.* [1940s] (US Black) ideas, plans. [RIFF n.² + SE *rill*, to sing with liquid notes]

rifle *v.* [17C] to have sexual intercourse (cf. CAULK; CLICKET; COVER v.; MOUNT v.³; SERVICE; TREAD; TUP v.). [SE *rifle*, of a hawk, to tread the hen]

rifleman *n.* [1940s+] a womanizer, a philanderer (cf. SHARP-SHOOTER). [? RIFLE + sfx. *-man* or play on SE]

rifler *see* TOLLER.

rifle range *n.¹* [20C] change. [rhy. sl.]

rifle range *n.²* [1960s] (drugs) **1** a house, apartment or room in which addicts gather to inject drugs (cf. BASING GALLERY). **2** a detoxification ward. [play on SHOOT v.⁵]

rig *n.¹* [late 16C–late 19C] a wanton, promiscuous woman (cf. RIG MUTTON; RIGSBY). [? SE *rig*, to play the wanton, to romp about; ult. ety. unknown]

rig *n.²* [late 18C–early 19C] **1** ridicule, mockery. **2** a dodge, a confidence trick (cf. RACKET n.¹). **3** a prank or game. [? dial.]

rig *n.³* **1** [mid-19C+] one's clothing, one's style of dress. **2** [1960s+] the male genitals (cf. DONKEY-RIGGED; GEAR n.²; TACKLE n.¹). [naut. imagery]

rig *n.⁴* [1930s+] (orig. US) a truck. [early 19C SE *rig*, a horse and its vehicle; ult. the 'rigging' or harness]

rig *n.⁵* [1960s–70s] (drugs) the equipment needed to inject narcotics (cf. BIZ n.⁴).

rig *v.¹* **1** [19C] to play tricks on, to fool. **2** [mid-19C+] to manipulate illegally (cf. SATCHEL v.). [RIG n.²]

rig *v.²* [19C+] to clothe; thus *rigged out*, dressed (up). [RIG n.³ (1)]

rig a jig, to *phr.* [1970s] (US Black) **1** of a pimp, to set up a potential customer with a woman. **2** of a confidence man, to set up a victim for deception. [SE *rig (up)* + JIG n.¹/JIG n.³]

rig city/rigville *n.* [1940s–50s] (US Black) hard times, unemployment, any materially impoverished situation. [RIG(OR MORTIS) + sfx. -CITY/-VILLE]

rigger *n.* [1940s] (Aus./N.Z.) a quart bottle of beer, esp. a quart of draught beer in a square-faced gin bottle. [? SE *square-rigger*]

rigging *n.* [17C–20C] (Und.) clothes; thus *rum rigging*, fashionable, expensive clothes. [RIG OUT + naut. *rigging*, the various ropes that are used on a sailing ship]

right *adj.¹* [mid-17C+] sane, mentally balanced; usu. in neg. to mean insane, e.g. *not right*, and usu. in combs., e.g. *right in the wits*, *right in the head*. **2** [mid-19C+] (Und.) reliable, trustworthy (from the criminal's point of view). **3** [20C] (Aus.) safe.

right *adj.²* [late 19C+] used for emphasizing how good or bad someone or something is, e.g. *a right bastard*, *a right good 'un*.

right!/yeah, right! *excl.* [1980s+] a dismissive, sarcastic phr. 'sure, I (don't) believe you'.

right arm! *excl.* [1970s] (US campus) a parody of the 1960s slogan RIGHT ON!

right as ... *phr.* [15C+] a phr. meaning safe, satisfactory, comfortable, secure, e.g. [15C–early 17C] ... *a line*, [early 17C] ... *a gun*, [late 17C–mid-19C] ... *my leg*, [early 19C] ... *my glove*, [mid-19C] ... *ninepence*, [mid-19C] ... *a trivet*, [late 19C+] ... *rain*, [late 19C] ... *the bank*, [late 19C–1900s] ... *nails*. [1900s] ... *a fiddle*, [1900s] ... *anything*.

right as a bank *phr.* [1940s–50s] (N.Z.) perfectly satisfactory, perfectly happy.

right as a ram's horn *phr.* [14C–late 17C] crooked. [the twisted shape of a ram's horn]

right/proper charlie *n.* [1960s+] a fool, a simpleton. [? the pathetic 'little tramp' stereotype created by film star *Charlie* Chaplin (1889–1977) or US milit. *charlie*, a soldier who cannot understand orders and so makes foolish mistakes]

right copper *n.* [1960s+] a corrupt policeman. [RIGHT adj.[1] (2) + COPPER n.[3] (1)]

right croaker *n.* [1920s+] (US) a doctor who is willing to write prescriptions for narcotic drugs, patch up wounded villains and perform other illegal services. [RIGHT adj.[1] (2) + CROAKER n.[3] (1)]

right down *adv.* [mid-19C–1910s] a general intensifier: completely, utterly, absolutely.

right down one's alley *see* RIGHT UP ONE'S ALLEY.

right enough! *excl.* [late 19C+] indeed! certainly!

righteous *adj.* [1930s+] (orig. US Black) **1** honest, trustworthy, honourable. **2** of things, esp. drugs, excellent, first-rate. **3** attractive, beautiful. **4** ideologically pure.

righteous bush *n.* [1940s] (drugs) marijuana. [RIGHTEOUS + BUSH n.[6]]

righteous grass *see* RIGHTEOUS MOSS.

righteous jones *n.* [1950s+] (drugs) a severe drug addiction. [RIGHTEOUS + JONES n.[1] (1)]

righteous moss/grass *n.* [1930s–50s] (US Black) White people's hair. [RIGHTEOUS + MOSS n.[1]/GRASS n.[3] (1)]

righteous nod *n.* [1940s] (US Black) a good night's sleep. [RIGHTEOUS + NOD n. (2)]

righteous rags *n.* [1930s–50s] (US Black) expensive, well-cut, fashionable clothes. [RIGHTEOUS + RAGS n.[2]]

righteous riff *n.* [1940s] (US Black) good conversation, inspiring, intelligent talk. [RIGHTEOUS + RIFF n.[2]]

righteous yellow *n.* [1920s–40s] (US Black) an attractive, light-skinned young woman. [RIGHTEOUS + YELLOW adj.[3]]

right from the giddyap *phr.* [1970s+] (orig. US) right from the start, the beginning. [the image is of starting a horse with a cry of *Giddyap!*]

right guy *n.* [1960s+] (US prison) a popular prisoner, respected by his peers (cf. REAL MAN). [RIGHT adj.[1] (2) + GUY n.[2] (1)]

right-handed *adj.* [20C] (US) heterosexual (cf. LEFT-HANDED). [trad. distrust of left-handedness]

right-ho! *see* RIGHTO!

right into one's barrel *phr.* [20C] (Aus.) absolutely what one wants.

rightio!/righty-ho!/righty-o! *excl.* [1920s+] an excl. of affirmation. [var. on RIGHTO!]

right joint *n.* [20C] (US Und.) **1** a safe criminal haunt or establishment. **2** a prison, esp. one considered to treat prisoners fairly. [RIGHT adj.[1] (2) + JOINT n.[3] (3)]

right money *see* SMART MONEY.

righto!/right-ho!/right-oh! *excl.* [late 19C+] certainly!

right/hot off the bat *phr.* [20C] (orig. US) at once, immediately, from the outset. [baseball imagery]

right off the reel *phr.* [late 19C] (US) immediately, at once.

right-oh! *see* RIGHTO!

right oil *n.* [1920s+] (Aus.) the honest truth, true facts. [RIGHT adj.[1] (3) + OIL n.[1] (2)]

right on! *excl.* [1950s+] excellent, perfect, exactly right; orig. Black use but taken up by White hippies, radicals etc (cf. STRAIGHT AHEAD!). [abbr. earlier *right on T/right on time*; the later use implied movement/progress rather than chronology]

right one *n.* [20C] (Ulster) an unpredictable person. [RIGHT adj.[2]]

right reverend *see* REVEREND.

right screw *n.* [late 19C+] a corrupt prison warder (cf. RIGHT TWIRL). [RIGHT adj.[1] (2) + SCREW n.[2] (2)]

right sort *n.[1]* [early 19C] an alcoholic drink, esp. gin. [play on SE]

right sort *n.[2]* [20C] a promiscuous woman. [RIGHT adj.[1] + SORT n. (2)]

right stuff *n.* [1920s+] any alcoholic drink, esp. in phr. *a drop of the right stuff*.

right twirl *n.* [late 19C] a corrupt prison warder (cf. RIGHT SCREW). [RIGHT adj.[1] (2) + TWIRL n. (2)]

right up/down one's alley *phr.* [1920s+] (orig. US) absolutely as one wishes, specifically to one's taste.

right up one's barrel *phr.* [1940s+] (Aus.) absolutely perfect, completely to one's taste. [fitting snugly into a gun barrel]

right up one's barrow *see* INTO ONE'S BARROW.

right up there *phr.* [20C] (US) in the running, in a winning position, at the forefront of things.

righty-ho!/righty-o! *see* RIGHTIO!

right you are! *excl.* [mid-19C+] a general excl. of agreement.

rigid *adj.* [1960s+] drunk and passed out.

rigi-dig *see* RIDGIE-DIDGIE.

rigmarole *n.* [1990s] (US Black teen) a woman who plays whatever games are necessary to obtain the material or sexual things she wants. [SE *rigmarole*, a succession of incoherent statements; an unconnected or rambling discourse; a long-winded harangue of little meaning or importance]

rigmatick *n.* [20C] (US) a complicated procedure, a rigmarole. [UK dial. *rickmatick*, a rowdy affair]

rigmo *n.* [1960s–70s] the stiffening of the body that follows death. [abbr. *rigor mortis*]

rig mutton *n.* [mid–late 16C] a wanton, promiscuous woman (cf. RIGSBY). [RIG n.[1] + MUTTON n.[2]]

rigol *n.* [17C–18C] the vagina (cf. AGREEABLE RUTS OF LIFE). [SE *rigol*, a watercourse or furrow, ult. Fr. *rigole*, water-course, gutter, furrow, drill, groove]

rigor mortis *n.* [1940s–50s] (US Black) hard times, unemployment, any materially impoverished situation.

rig-out/rig-up *n.* [early 19C+] a suit of clothes, an outfit. [RIG n.[3]]

rig sale *n.* [late 19C] a false sale, a mock auction. [RIG n.[2] + SE *sale*]

rigsby *n.* [mid-16C–late 17C] a wanton, promiscuous woman (cf. RIG MUTTON). [RIG n.[1]]

rig-up *n.[1]* *see* RIG-OUT.

rig-up *n.[2]* [1990s] (US Black) an unpleasant, intolerable situation. [RIG n.[2] (3)]

rigville *see* RIG CITY.

rile *v.* [mid-19C+] (orig. US) to annoy, to irritate, thus *riled*, irritated, *riling*, annoying. [SE *roil*, to stir up, thus to annoy, to vex]

riley *n.* [1960s+] (Irish) a life of pleasure, success. [abbr. LIFE OF RILEY]

rileyed *adj.* [late 19C] (US) drunk (cf. LIFE OF RILEY). [typical Irish surname *Riley* (plus *Reilly* and *O'Reilly*) and thus the stereotyping of the Irish as drunkards; the spec. source is the stage production of *The Mulligan's Silver Wedding* 'a low life comedy' in Feb. 1881, in which was featured a song 'John Riley's Always Dry' which listed the eponymous Riley's prodigious drinking]

rim *v.*[1] [1940s+] (US) **1** to cheat, to swindle. **2** to cause failure, to ruin someone's chances, esp. by deception. [SE *ream*, to enlarge, to scrape out]

rim *v.*[2] [1950s+] to stimulate the anus with the lips and tongue (cf. REAM v.[2]). [SE *ream*, to stretch, to scrape out]

rimadona *n.* [1960s] (gay) a sodomite, a male homosexual. [puns on SE *primadonna*/RIM v.[2]]

rimble-ramble *n.* [late 17C] nonsense, thus *rimble-ramble*, nonsensical, absurd.

rim job *n.* [1950s+] an act of anilingus. [RIM v.[2] + JOB n.[5]]

rimmer *n.* [1990s] someone who stimulates another's anus with their tongue. [RIM v.[2] + sfx. *-er*]

rim queen *n.* [1950s+] a homosexual who enjoys anilingus. [RIM v.[2] + QUEEN n.[1]]

rim slide *n.* [1960s+] (US prison) a silent but foul-smelling fart. [the fart *slides* from the *rim* of the anus]

rince/rinse *n.* [19C] a drink, thus *rince*/*rinse*, to drink (cf. GARGLE n.).

rinctum/rinktum *n.* [20C] (US Black) the rectum (cf. SPIZZERINCTUM).

rind *n.*[1] [20C] cheek, impudence, effrontery. [play on CRUST n.[1]]

rind *n.*[2] [1940s] (US Black) the human skin.

ring *n.*[1] **1** [16C–18C] the vagina (cf. BLACK HOLE n.[1]; BLACK RING; HAIRY RING; HANS CARVEL'S RING). **2** [late 19C+] the anus, the buttocks; thus *ring-snatcher*, a sodomite, *ring-snatching*, sodomy (cf. RINGPIECE). **3** [1980s+] (US Black) anal intercourse. [the shapes]

ring *n.*[2] [late 16C–early 19C] (Und.) **1** the money that is stolen by a highwayman. **2** money that is procured by begging. [? SE *ring*, thus an object worth money, or the ringing noise the cash makes as it is thrown from the coach/into the begging bowl]

ring *n.*[3] [1940s] (Aus.) the site of a two-up game. [boxing imagery]

ring *v.*[1] **1** [early 19C+] to change, to alter; thus *ringing castors*, changing hats, typically by going to some public place, stealing an expensive hat from where it has been deposited and leaving a cheap one. **2** [late 19C+] to cheat. **3** [late 19C+] (US) to illegally substitute a horse for another in a horse-race. **4** [1950s+] to alter a car for the purposes of using it as a getaway vehicle, hold-up van etc, or for reselling it to an unsuspecting customer (cf. CAR-RINGING). [fig. use of abbr. SE phr. *ring the changes*]

ring *v.*[2] [late 19C+] (Aus.) to be the most successful shearer in a shed. [RINGER n.[1] (1); ult. SE *ring the bell*, to win a victory]

ring a bell, to *phr.* [1930s+] to remind one of something, to jog one's memory.

ring-a-ding/ring-a-ding-ding *adj.* [1950s–60s] **1** a term of approval for a beautiful woman. **2** perfect, ideal (cf. RING ONE'S CHIMES). [the image of celebratory bell-ringing]

ring a peal/ring a peal in a man's ears, to *phr.* [late 18C–early 19C] to scold, usu. of a wife scolding her husband.

ring around the rosy *n.* [1960s+] (US gay) an orgy (cf. DAISY CHAIN). [the children's game]

ringbarked *adj.* [1980s+] (N.Z.) circumcised (cf. SKIN BOY). [SE *ringbark*, to kill a tree by removing a ring of bark from the trunk]

ring bells/ring any bells with someone, to *phr.* [1930s+] to appeal to, to impress, to carry any weight with, usu. in neg. [the fairground sideshow in which one's strength is determined by hitting a spring hard enough to ring a bell]

ringbolt *v.* [1980s+] (N.Z.) to obtain a free ship voyage by posing as a crew member.

ringburner *n.* [1970s+] (society) diarrhoea, or very painful defecation. [RING n.[1] (2) + SE *burner*]

ring changes, to *phr.* [20C] (US) to try out new ways, to make changes. [bell-ringing imagery]

ring-dang-do *n.* [1950s+] **1** (Aus.) a spree, a party. **2** (US) a complicated affair, a rigmarole.

ring-ding *n.*[1] (W.I.) **1** [1900s] hilarity, lively entertainment. **2** [1940s] a quarrel.

ring-ding *n.*[2] [1970s+] (US) a fool, a second-rate person, a no-hoper. [? a punch-drunk boxer who has 'bells ringing' in his head]

ring dropper *see* RING FALLER.

ring dropping *n.* **1** [16C–19C] a swindle whereby some valuable object is dropped in the road, where it is found by a potential victim. This leads to an encounter, after which the victim is either lured into a fixed game or, in the case of the (fake) valuable, persuaded to buy it, claiming that while they should share the profits, he, the con-man, will sell his share and let the victim have the whole benefit (cf. DROPPER n.[4]; DROP-COVE; GOLD-DROPPER; MONEY-DROPPER). **2** [late 19C] a term of scorn, 'equivalent to "tell your grandmother to suck eggs"' (Ware); so common had (1) become that anyone could spot a ring-dropper.

ringer *n.*[1] (Aus.) **1** [late 19C] the fastest and best shearer in a shed. **2** [late 19C–1900s] anything outstanding or superlative of its kind. **3** [1910s+] an expert. [RING v.[2]]

ringer *n.*[2] (orig. US) **1** [late 19C+] a fake, someone posing as a person they are not; esp. a pool or bowling hustler who pretends not to be an expert. **2** [late 19C+] a horse or dog substituted either for a better or a worse animal for the purposes of those betting either for or against it. **3** [late 19C+] someone who illegally substitutes a horse or animal in a race. **4** [1960s+] a second-hand car made up to look better than it is. **5** [1960s+] someone who specializes in stealing then improving second-hand cars for sale in the UK or Europe. **6** [1960s+] a false registration plate attached to a stolen motor vehicle; thus the thief who uses one. [RING v.[1]]

ringer *n.*[3] [1980s+] (drugs) a strong puff of crack cocaine. [it 'rings one's bells']

ringerangeroo *n.* [1930s+] (US) the vagina. [nonce-word, but ? ref. to RING n.[1] (1)]

ring faller/dropper *n.* [16C–19C] a con-man who plays a trick of dropping a fake valuable object in the road and offering to let their victim buy it so they can have all the supposed profit. [RING DROPPING]

ring her bell, to *phr.* **1** [1910s+] to produce (female) orgasm during intercourse. **2** [1930s+] to make pregnant.

ringie *n.* [1940s+] (Aus./N.Z.) the keeper of the RING n.[3] in a game of two-up (a gambling game played by tossing two coins, bets being laid on the showing of two heads or two tails).

ring-in *n.* [1920s+] **1** (Aus./N.Z. Und.) anything that has been fraudulently substituted for something else, typically a race-horse or dog. **2** (Aus.) a stacked deck of cards. [RING v.[1]]

ring in *v.* [early 19C+] to substitute fraudulently, e.g. one race-horse for another (cf. RINGER n.[2]). [RING v.[1]]

ring it *v.* [20C] (Aus.) to act in a cowardly way (cf. PLAY POSSUM). [RINGTAIL n.[2] (1)]

ring it on *v.* [1910s+] (orig. Aus./N.Z.) to outwit, to fool. [RING v.[1]]

ring master *n.* [1990s] a male homosexual. [RING n.[1] (2) + SE *master*]

ring/wring neck *n.* [20C] (W.I./Guyn.) a tough, brawling person, esp. a woman. [SE *wring a neck*]

ring off! *excl.* [1900s–20s] be quiet! shut up! [telephony]

ring off the hook, to *phr.* [20C] (orig. US) for the phone to ring incessantly.

ring one's chimes, to *phr.* [1970s+] (orig. US) **1** to excite one's attention, to enthuse (cf. RING SOMEONE'S BELL phr.[1]). **2** to have an orgasm (cf. RING HER BELL; RING SOMEONE'S BELL phr.[2]).

ring one's dong, to phr. [1990s] to masturbate. [SE ring + DONG n.[2]]

ring one's own bell, to phr. [mid–late 19C] (US) to boast, to brag (cf. BLOW ONE'S OWN TRUMPET).

ring one's tail, to phr. [20C] (Aus.) to surrender, to give in, in a game. [RINGTAIL n.[2] (1)]

ringpiece n. [late 19C+] the anus; thus [1990s] ringpiece licker, an anilinguist. [RING n.[1] (2)]

ring pigger n. [mid–late 16C] a drunkard. [ety. unknown]

ring raider n. [1990s] a male homosexual, a sodomite. [RING n.[1] (2) + SE raider]

ringsend uppercut n. [20C] (Irish, Dublin) a kick in the testicles. [Ringsend, an area of Dublin]

ringside n. [1930s+] (orig. US) the tables nearest to the stage in a nightclub or similar establishment. [boxing imagery]

ring snatcher n. [20C] a sodomite; thus ring-snatching, sodomy. [RING n.[1] (2) + SE snatcher]

ring someone's bell, to phr.[1] [1960s+] **1** (orig. US) to concuss, esp. in US football use when this may well follow a clash of helmets. **2** (US) to attract sexually, e.g. She really rings my bell.

ring someone's bell/chimes phr.[2] [1970s+] (orig. US) to give one's partner an orgasm (cf. RING ONE'S CHIMES).

ringtail n.[1] [20C] the anus. [RING n.[1] (2) + TAIL n.[1] (3)]

ringtail n.[2] **1** [1920s+] (Aus.) a coward. **2** [1940s+] (US) an irritable, unpleasant person. **3** [1940s+] (US) a tramp (who is seen as inevitably ill-tempered). [SAusE ringtail, a possum, known for 'playing dead' when threatened]

ringtailed snorter n. [early 19C] (US) an impressive person. [a fantasy creature]

ring the bell, to phr. [1900s–60s] to carry off the prize; to be the best of a lot. [the 'try-your-strength' machine found at a traditional fairground]

ring the bell on, to phr. [late 19C] (US) to dismiss, to declare useless. [boxing imagery]

ring the changes, to phr. (Und.) **1** [early 19C+] to defraud, to deceive, esp. by passing counterfeit money or substituting a worse article for a better one (cf. RING v.[1]). **2** [late 19C+] to adopt a series of variant disguises with the intention of confusing, thus ringer, one who practices this form of deception.

ring-ting n. [1940s] (W.I.) the genuine article, the real thing. [? the ring of a glass that indicates it is pure crystal]

ringworm n. [1920s–50s] (US) a boxing fan. [pun on the boxing ring]

ringy adj. [1930s+] (US) ill-tempered, tetchy. [RINGTAIL n.[2] (2)]

rinktum see RINCTUM.

rinky dink n.[1] [20C] pink. [rhy. sl.]

rinky dink n.[2] [1910s+] (US) a swindle, a deception. [ety. unknown]

rinky-dink/-dinky adj. [1910s+] (US) **1** cheap, second-rate. **2** outdated, unfashionable. [ety. unknown; OED suggests link to jazz use ricky-tick, old-fashioned, monotonous rhythms]

rinky-dink joint n. [1930s–50s] (US Black) a cheap tavern or inn. [RINKY-DINK adj. + JOINT n.[3] (3)]

rinky-dinky see RINKY-DINK adj.

rino see RHINO.

rinse see RINCE.

rinse pitcher n. [mid-16C] a drunkard. [lit. one who drinks even the rinsings of a barrel or tankard]

riot n. **1** [20C] a great success. **2** [20C] an extremely enjoyable and amusing, if somewhat rowdy, occasion or performance. **3** [1950s+] (US) a 'riot' sale, i.e. one in which the prices are more than usually low.

riot season n. [1960s–70s] (US Black) the summer. [the urban riots of 1966, following which Black civil rights leader Martin Luther King (1929–68) coined the term 'long hot summer']

rip n.[1] **1** [late 18C–early 19C] an exhausted, worn-out horse. **2** [late 18C–1950s] a worthless person, a rake; usu. used of a (young) man, but occas. of a woman. [? SE rebrobate]

rip n.[2] [mid-19C] (US) a quick rush. [SE rip, a tear; the pun on TEAR v. is coincidental]

rip n.[3] [20C] (US) **1** a try, an attempt. **2** (US) a pleasure, a joy. [ext. of RIP n.[2]]

rip n.[4] [1970s+] (US campus) a fraud, a cheat, a disappointment. [abbr. RIP-OFF n.]

rip v.[1] [20C] (US) to steal (cf. RIP OFF v.).

rip v.[2] [20C] to do very well, to be successful. [SE rip, to move fast]

rip v.[3] [1940s+] (Aus.) to annoy intensely; thus wouldn't it rip you, wouldn't it drive you mad? [SE rip, to tear]

rip and run, to phr. [1900s–70s] (US Black) to move restlessly, to act in an aimless but frenzied manner. [SE rip, to move fast + run]

rip and tear, to phr. [20C] to swear. [rhy. sl.]

rip ass v. [1950s+] (US) to speed, to go fast. [var. on TEAR ASS v.]

ripcord n. [1960s+] the small loop attached to the back of some men's shirts (cf. FAG TAG; FRUIT LOOP n.[1]).

ripe adj.[1] [early 19C–1920s] drunk (cf. ADDLED).

ripe adj.[2] **1** [1930s+] excessive, in poor taste, beyond the bounds of acceptability, e.g. phr. a bit ripe, ripe old time. **2** [1940s+] thoroughgoing, complete, esp. in phr. (you) ripe bastard.

ripe adj.[3] [1940s+] (W.I.) old, esp. too old to work.

ripe adj.[4] [1960s] angry, irritated.

ripe banana n. [1950s] (W.I.) a derog. term for an albino (cf. FRECKLE-NATURE). [their colour]

ripe fruit n. [1980s+] (US gay) someone who is just discovering their homosexuality. [pun on fruit/FRUIT n.[2] (2)]

rip hell out of, to phr. [20C] (orig. Aus.) **1** to defeat comprehensively. **2** to tell off, to reprimand.

rip her guts down, to phr. [1970s+] (US Black) to copulate aggressively, sadistically, but with implication that both partners achieve mutual satisfaction (cf. RIP OFF v.).

rip into v.[1] [late 19C+] **1** to start a fight. **2** [1910s+] to criticize harshly (cf. TEAR INTO).

rip into/rip it into v.[2] [1940s+] (Aus.) to scold, to tell off.

rip joint n. [1970s+] (US campus) any store that charges exorbitant prices to students. [RIP n.[4] + JOINT n.[3] (3)]

rip me! excl. [mid-19C–1900s] a general excl. of anger, surprise.

rip-off n. [1960s+] (orig. US) **1** a fraud, a cheat, a disappointment. **2** something stolen or plagiarized. [RIP OFF v.]

rip off v. (orig. US) **1** [1950s+] (US Black) to have sexual intercourse. **2** [1960s+] to steal. **3** [1970s+] to cheat, to defraud, esp. in drug deals. **4** [1970s+] to kill, to assassinate. **5** [1970s+] to beat up, to attack physically. **6** [1970s+] to satirize. **7** [1970s+] to copy, to plagiarize. **8** [1970s+] to exploit financially. **9** [1970s+] (orig. US Black) to rape (cf. RIP HER GUTS DOWN). [SE rip off, to tear off]

rip off a piece, to phr. [1950s+] (US) to seduce, to have sexual intercourse. [RIP OFF v. (2) + PIECE n.[1] (2)]

rip-off artist/merchant n. [1970s+] **1** a thief. **2** a prostitute who specializes in robbing her clients and as such is more thief than purveyor of commercial sex. **3** any form of cheat, emotional as well as material. [RIP OFF v. + ARTIST n.[2]/-MERCHANT]

rip on v. [1980s+] **1** (US campus) to criticize, to nag (cf. RAG ON). **2** (US Black) to harass, to insult. [SE rip, to tear open]

ripped adj.[1] [20C] having one's trouser fly open. [the gaping fly could seem like a rip in the cloth]

ripped adj.[2] [1970s+] (orig. US) **1** extremely intoxicated by drink, drugs or a mixture (cf. RIPPED TO THE TITS). **2** unhappy. **3** very unattractive. [SE ripped, torn]

ripped *adj.*[3] [1980s+] (US campus) well-built, muscled. [var. on CUT adj.[3]]

ripped off *adj.* [1970s+] **1** of people, exploited, stolen from. **2** of objects, stolen. [RIP OFF v. (1)]

ripped out of one's gourd *phr.* [1980s+] (US campus) drunk. [RIPPED adj.[2] (1) + GOURD n.[2]]

ripped to the tits/gills *phr.* [1970s+] (orig. US) very intoxicated by drink, drugs or a combination. [RIPPED adj.[2] (1) + TITS n.[2] (1)/SE *gills*]

ripper *n.*[1] **1** [mid-19C] a first-rate man, an excellent article. **2** [mid-19C] an attractive young woman. **3** [mid–late 19C] a very great lie. [SE *rip*, to tear open, i.e. all uses 'tear open' the usual standards]

ripper *n.*[2] [late 19C] a person who behaves badly. [RIP n.[1] (2)]

ripper *n.*[3] [late 19C+] a murderer who specializes in mutilation, often for sexual purposes. [late 19C criminal Jack the *Ripper*, thus christened by the contemporary press]

ripper *n.*[4] [late 19C+] (US Und.) a tool used in the opening of a safe (cf. CAN OPENER). [SE *rip*]

ripper *n.*[5] [1970s+] a cheat, someone who steals or raises prices beyond reason (cf. RIP-OFF ARTIST) . [RIP v.[1]]

ripper *adj.* [mid-19C+] (Aus.) excellent wonderful, perfect, first-class (cf. BONZER). [RIPPER n.[1]; 20C use mainly Aus.]

ripper! *excl.* [1960s+] (Aus.) a general excl. of approval, admiration, pleasure. [RIPPER adj.]

rippers *n.* [1960s–70s] (drugs) amphetamine (cf. A n.[2]). [RIPPED adj.[2] (1)]

ripping *adj.* **1** [mid-19C+] excellent, first-rate, wonderful. **2** [1990s] (US campus) excellent, worthy of admiration. [(2) is a joc. use of the old UK term, long abandoned to ridicule in the UK]

ripping slum *n.* [late 19C] a successful trick or hoax. [RIPPING + SLUM n.[1] (4)]

ripple *n.* [20C] (US) a try, an attempt. [? one fig. 'ripples' the surface]

rip rap *v.* [1930s+] to borrow money, thus *the rip-rap*, the act of obtaining such a loan. [rhy. sl. *rip-rap* = TAP SOMEONE FOR]

rip shit *v.* [1980s+] to have a party, to act energetically, to make a disturbance (cf. TEAR UP). [SE *rip* + SHIT n.[10]]

rip, shit or bust *phr.* [1940s+] (N.Z.) used of a situation in which one forges on, irrespective of the consequences. [ext. of SHIT OR BUST]

rip shit out of, to *phr.* [1980s+] (orig. US) to assault physically. [ext. of RIP SHIT]

ripskated *adj.* [1990s] (US campus) drunk. [ety. unknown]

rip snorter *n.* **1** [mid-19C+] (orig. US) a remarkable or wonderful person or thing of which the speaker approves. **2** [1940s+] a very loud breaking of wind. [SE *rip* + SNORTER n.[2] (1)]

rip the rug, to *phr.* [1970s] (US campus) to dance. [var. on CUT THE RUG]

rip van winkle, to *phr.* [20C] to urinate. [rhy. sl. *rip van winkle* = TINKLE v.]

rise *n.*[1] **1** [mid-19C] a commotion, a noise. **2** [mid-19C+] a response, esp. a fit of anger, thus *get a rise out of*, to cause to respond, to spur to anger.

rise *n.*[2] [1940s+] an erection; thus *get/have a rise*, to get an erection; *give a rise*, of a woman, to give a man an erection.

rise *v.*[1] [mid-19C+] to bring up, to raise. [orig. Yorks. dial.]

rise *v.*[2] [mid-19C+] **1** to listen credulously. **2** to become foolishly annoyed (by what one hears). [angling imagery, the fish *rising* to the bait]

rise and shine *n.* [20C] wine. [rhy. sl.]

rise and shine! *excl.* [20C] a joc. wake-up call; sometimes preceded by 'wakey-wakey!' (cf. HANDS OFF COCKS)

rise a plant, to *phr.* [early 19C] (Und.) of a thief, to unearth some loot from where you or another thief have hidden it. [SE *rise* + PLANT n. (1)]

rise/raise arse upwards, to *phr.* [late 17C–late 18C] to be lucky. [getting up from a fall in this manner was believed to be lucky]

rise to the occasion, to *phr.* [1920s+] to have an erection when required.

rising blowback *n.* [1980s+] (US drugs) exhaling cannabis smoke into someone else's mouth, then moving from a crouching position and slowly standing up for an increased sensation. [SE *rising* + BLOWBACK]

rising damp *n.* [20C] cramp. [rhy. sl.]

risk it for a biscuit, to *phr.* [1980s+] (Irish) to take a chance, esp. in a sexual context.

risky *adj.* [late 19C] (society) clandestinely adulterous.

rispeck/respeck/respect *v.* [1980s+] (W.I./UK Black teen) to hold someone or something in high esteem.

rispeck/respeck/respect due *phr.* [1980s+] (W.I./UK Black teen) a phr. used to accord the subject the respect they have earned on the basis of earlier positive or praiseworthy actions.

rissole *n.* [1970s+] (Aus.) the anus. [joc. mispron. of ARSEHOLE n. (1)]

risy *adj.* [1930s] impudent, cheeky. [SE *take a rise out of*]

rit *n.*[1] [late 19C–1900s] a ritualistic clergyman. [abbr.]

rit *n.*[2] [1970s+] (drugs) a tablet of *Rit*alin (cf. RITIES). [abbr.]

rita *n.* [1940s–50s] (S.Afr. camp gay) a male prostitute. [gay icon Hollywood star *Rita* Hayworth (1918–87)]

rith *n.* [1910s–20s] three. [backsl.]

rities *n.* [1980s+] (drugs) *Rit*alin (methylphenidate hydrochloride, a central nervous system stimulant related to amphetamine). [abbr.]

ritz *n.* [20C] glamour, elegance, wealth, sophistication; thus phr. *in the ritz*, living well; *this ain't the Ritz*, don't expect anything special (cf. PUT ON THE RITZ). [the chain of hotels established by César *Ritz* (1850–1918), esp. the *Ritz-Carlton* in New York City]

ritzy *adj.* [1920s+] **1** smart, chic, fashionable. **2** pretentious, posturing, esp. in phr. *don't get ritzy with me.* **3** wealthy, affluent. [RITZ + sfx. *-y*]

riv/rivie *n.* [1970s+] (US Black) a Buick *Riv*iera. [abbr.]

riverina *n.* [1920s–60s] (Aus.) one shilling. [rhy. sl. *riverina* = DEANER]

River Lea *n.* **1** [mid-19C] tea (cf. ROSIE LEA). **2** [1900s] the sea. [rhy. sl.]

River Murry *n.* [20C] (Aus.) a curry. [rhy. sl.]

River Nile *n.* [20C] a smile. [rhy. sl.]

River Ouse/Ooze *n.* [1930s+] alcoholic drink. [rhy. sl. *River Ouse* = BOOZE n.]

river rat *n.* [19C] a thief who specializes in stripping the corpses of those who drowned in London's River Thames.

River Tyne *n.* [20C] wine. [rhy. sl.]

riveted *adj.* **1** [late 17C–mid-18C] married. **2** [1970s+] (society) fascinated by; thus *riveting*, absolutely fascinating.

rivets/rivits *n.* [mid-19C–1930s] money. [fig. use of SE on pattern of BRADS; HORSE NAILS]

rivie see RIV.

riz *adj.* [1970s+] (Irish) annoyed. [SE *rise*]

roach *n.*[1] **1** [1930s+] (US) a pej. term for a policeman. **2** [1930s+] (US) an inferior racehorse. **3** [1970s+] (US campus) an unattractive woman. [joc. uses of SE *cockroach*]

roach *n.*[2] [1930s+] (drugs) the unsmoked portion of a marijuana or hashish cigarette. [SE *cockroach*]

roach and dace *n.* [20C] the face (cf. CHEVY CHASE). [rhy. sl.]

roach bender *n.* [1930s] (drugs) a marijuana smoker. [ROACH n.[2] + SE *bend*; i.e. the grasping of the very last portion of the cigarette]

roach clip/holder *n.* [1960s+] (drugs) a small spring clip or pair of tweezers used to hold the last fragments of a marijuana cigarette, which is otherwise too hot to hold in one's fingers. [ROACH n.² + SE *clip/holder*]

roach hotel n. [1980s+] (US drugs) a collection of cannabis cigarette stubs that can be recycled. [ROACH n.² + pun on US *Roach Motel*, a patented cockroach trap]

roach killers n. [1960s] men's highly pointed shoes. [abbr. COCKROACH KILLERS]

road n. [late 16C–early 17C] **1** the vagina (cf. ALLEY n.¹). **2** a prostitute.

road apple n. [1930s+] (US) horse manure, as deposited in the road (cf. ALLEY APPLE n.²).

road brew/roadies/road sauce n. [1970s+] (US campus) beer. [SE *road* + BREW n.¹ (3)/dimin. sfx. *-ies*/SAUCE n.¹ (3)]

road dog/roadie n. [1980s+] (US Black) an extremely intimate friend (cf. DOG n.²⁴; RUNNING PARTNER). [SE *road* + DOG n.⁹]

road dope n. [1980s+] (drugs) amphetamines (cf. A n.²). [the drug's use during long-distance driving]

roader n. [late 19C] (East End) a young man who disports himself on the Mile End Road, London, in his finest clothes, usu. with his woman, on a Sunday (cf. WHITECHAPEL ONER). [abbr. Mile End *Road*]

roadie n.¹ **1** [1960s+] a member of a rock band's support unit who sets up and dismantles stage, equipment etc. **2** [1980s+] (N.Z.) one employed in road maintenance. [(1) they go 'on the road' with the band or (2) they lit. work on it]

roadie n.² *see* ROAD DOG.

roadies *see* ROAD BREW.

road kid n. [1900s–30s] (US) a young tramp.

roadkill n. (orig. US) [1970s+] **1** any form of creature (usu. small animals or birds) killed by a vehicle on the roads and used for food. **2** a person or object that is considered absolutely useless, i.e. 'dead meat'.

road less travelled n. [1990s] the female anus as a hosting place for a penis.

road making/road up for repairs phr. [mid–late 19C] used of a woman who is menstruating.

road man n. [1920s–50s] (US) an itinerant thief.

road people n. [1960s+] (US) young people who live and travel about in vans (the equivalent of UK travellers).

road queen n. [1980s+] (US gay) a gay hitch-hiker, looking for sex with those who pick him up. [SE *road* + QUEEN n.¹]

road rage n. [1990s] the blind fury that overtakes a driver, who in other circumstances may well be a reasonable individual, when trapped in a traffic jam or similar hindrance to driving (cf. MOTORWAY MADNESS). [the convenience of the phr. for media use made it SE almost immediately]

road rash n. [1970s+] (orig. US) cuts, scratches and grazes that come with falling off a skateboard.

road roller n. [1900s–30s] (N.Z.) an unsophisticated country person, a bushman.

road sauce *see* ROAD BREW.

road stake n. [20C] (US tramp) money. [SE *road* + *stake*, a bet, a wager]

road starver n. [late 19C] (tramp) a long coat made without pockets. [the pockets would be used to hold food for a journey]

roadster n. [late 19C+] (Aus.) a tramp, someone who has no fixed abode.

road to a christening/to heaven n. [19C] the vagina (cf. ALLEY n.¹). [ext. of ROAD n. (1)]

road up for repairs *see* ROAD MAKING.

Roadwatch accent *see* DART ACCENT.

road whore n. [1980s+] (US campus) a promiscuous woman.

road work n. [1920s–50s] (US) crimes committed by an itinerant thief. [SE *road* + WORK n. (1)]

roaf n. [mid-19C+] 4; thus *roaf yenneps*, 4 shillings (20p). [backsl.]

roak v. [1970s] (US Black) to beat savagely about the head. [? abbr. CROAK v.¹]

roar v. [16C] to riot (cf. ROARER n.¹; ROARING BOY).

roaration *see* RORATION.

roaratorios and uproars n. [late 18C–early 19C] oratorios and operas.

roaratorious *see* RORTORIOUS.

roarer n.¹ [16C–17C] a riotous hooligan, a roisterer. [SE *roar*, to riot, to behave in a boisterous manner]

roarer n.² [late 18C–early 19C] a broken-down horse (cf. HIGH BLOWER). [the sound of its breathing]

roarer n.³ [19C] (US) something superlatively good.

roaring adj. **1** [mid-19C] boisterous, exuberant. **2** [1920s+] a general intensifier, extreme, uncompromising. [SE *roar*, to riot, to behave in a boisterous manner]

roaring boy/blade/girl/lad/ruffian n. [early–mid-17C] a riotous hooligan, a roisterer (cf. ROARER n.¹). [ROAR v. + SE *boy/ blade/SE girl/lad/ruffian*]

Roaring Forties/Forties n. [1920s–40s] (US) Broadway, New York City, in the area immediately around Times Square, spec. 40th Street to 49th Street. [joc. use of naut. jargon *Roaring Forties*, exceptionally rough seas that occur between latitudes 40° and 50° south, where strong westerly winds blow; formerly also applied to the part of the Atlantic Ocean between latitudes 40° and 50° north]

roaring fou adj. [19C] extremely drunk, lit. roaring drunk (cf. BITCH-FOU). [SE *roaring* + FOU adj.¹]

roaring girl *see* ROARING BOY.

roaring horn/jack n. [late 19C] (Aus.) an erection, esp. one that feels very demanding. [ROARING adj. + HORN n.² (2)/JACK n.⁸ (1)]

roaring horsetails n. [20C] (Aus.) Aurora Australis. [rhy. sl.]

roaring jack *see* ROARING HORN.

roaring lad *see* ROARING BOY.

roaring rain n. [20C] (Aus.) a train. [rhy. sl.]

roaring ruffian *see* ROARING BOY.

roar like a town bull, to phr. [late 18C–mid-19C] to make a good deal of noise.

roart *see* RORT n.

roar up v. **1** [late 19C] to talk loudly, to abuse. **2** [1910s+] (Aus.) to scold, to tell off, to reprimand.

roast n. [1950s+] (W.I.) a second job, kept secret and thus part of the 'black economy'. [ROAST COCO]

roast v. **1** [late 17C–early 18C] to arrest. **2** [late 17C+] to jeer, ridicule or banter; to criticize aggressively. [? play on *roast*, 'a roast', or as v. to give the subject 'a hot time'; according to Hotten, 1867 one can only be *roasted* by 'the whole company', when the teasing comes from one person only, it is *quizzing*]

roast a stone, to phr. [early 16C–early 17C] to waste time. [the impossibility of improving the 'dish']

roast a time, to phr. [20C] (W.I.) to enjoy oneself thoroughly.

roast beef n. [20C] teeth. [rhy. sl.; Cockney pron. 'teef']

roast coco, to phr. [1950s] (W.I.) to plot, to scheme, to bide one's time (cf. ROAST; ROAST PLANTAIN FOR SOMEONE). [the habit of roasting coco-yams as the conclusion of the meal; thus fig. waiting for something desirable]

roasted duck n. [1930s] sexual intercourse (cf. RUSSIAN DUCK). [rhy. sl. *roasted duck* = FUCK n.¹; unmentioned by E.P. or Franklyn, this may be a nonce-word, invented by Isherwood and Auden in their play *The Dog beneath the Skin* (1935), *O how I cried when Alice died/ The day we were to have wed!/ We never had our Roasted Duck/ And now she's a Loaf of Bread*]

roaster n. [late 19C+] a very hot day (cf. SCORCHER).

roastie *see* ROAST POTATO.

roasting jack n. [19C] the vagina (cf. KITCHEN). [pun on SE/ JACK n.⁸ (2)]

roast-meat clothes n. [late 17C–18C] one's best clothes (cf. CRY ROAST MEAT). [the meat in question being the 'Sunday roast' and the clothes one's 'Sunday best' outfit; note naval jargon *roast-beef dress*, full uniform]

roast plantain for someone, to phr. [1920s+] (W.I.) **1** to get ready to benefit from someone else's misfortune. **2** to plot actively to bring about this downfall (cf. ROAST; ROAST COCO).

roast pork n.[1] **1** [1910s+] a talk. **2** [1940s] a table fork. [rhy. sl.]

roast pork n.[2] [1940s] (W.I.) a variety of cactus whose leaves resemble chunks of meat; such leaves can be roasted for medicinal use.

roast potato/roastie n. [20C] a waiter. [rhy. sl.]

roast snow in a furnace, to phr. [19C+] to attempt the impossible.

rob v. [1980s+] (US campus) to silence with a witty remark or rejoinder. [one's victim is 'robbed' of speech]

rob blind v. [1950s+] to rob without restraint (cf. STEAL BLIND). [SE *rob* + BLIND adj.[2] (1)]

robbo n. [late 19C–1900s] (Aus.) a cab. [the late 19C Sydney cabbie Four Bob *Robbo* who specialized in undercutting his rivals]

rob-davy/roberdavy/rob-o'-davy n. [18C] metheglin or spiced mead. [Welsh *meddyglyn*, a combination of *meddyg*, healing or medicinal and *llyn*, liquor. *Davy* was presumably a ref. to the Welsh name *Dafyyd*, anglicized as *Taffy*]

roberdsmen/roberts men n. [late 17C–18C] (Und.) 'the third (old) rank of the CANTING CREW', outlaw thieves who act, according to B.E., like real-life Robin Hoods. [early 14C SE *Roberdsmen*, a type of marauding vagabond]

robert/roberto n. [late 19C] a policeman. [elaboration of BOBBY n. (1)]

Roberta Flack n. [1970s] (Aus.) the bed; thus *hit the Roberta*, to go to bed. [rhy. sl. *Roberta Flack* = SACK n.[2]; ult. disco diva *Roberta Flack* (b.1937)]

robert dinero n. [1990s] (US teen) money. [pun on DINERO/ film star *Robert de Niro* (b.1943)]

robert e. n. [20C] **1** a knee. **2** urination. [rhy. sl.; (2) *Robert E. Lee* = PEE n.[1]; Confederate general *Robert E. Lee* (1807–70)]

roberto see ROBERT.

roberts men see ROBERDSMEN.

robertson and moffatt n. [1940s+] (Aus.) a profit. [rhy. sl.]

robin n.[1] [mid–late 19C+] the penis (cf. JOHN THOMAS; PERCY n.[3]; PETER n.[4]; ROGER n.[4]; SIR MARTIN WAGSTAFFE). [20C use is US; note *robin* is the pet name for a servant's penis in the late 19C pornographic classic *The Modern Eveline* (the heroine's brother is named *Percy*)]

robin n.[2] [late 19C] a child beggar, 'standing about like a starving robin' (Ware). [a philanthropic clergyman, the Rev. Charles Bullock, organized a series of 'Robin dinners', at which he fed thousands of such unfortunate children]

robin n.[3] [late 19C–1910s] a penny. [ety. unknown]

robin hog n. [early 18C] a constable (cf. BACON n.[3]). [ety. unknown; ? simply derog. since the PIG n.[3] is not coined until early 19C]

Robin Hood n. [late 19C] an audacious lie. [the 'tale' of *Robin Hood*]

Robin Hood adj. [late 19C+] good. [rhy. sl.]

robin hoods n. [20C] **1** (material) goods. **2** woods. [rhy. sl.]

Robin Hood's bargain n. [18C] a very good bargain. [var. on ROBIN HOOD'S PENNYWORTH]

Robin Hood's choice n. [17C] no choice whatsoever, 'hobson's choice'. [an anecdote about the semi-fictional outlaw *Robin Hood*]

Robin Hood's pennyworth n. [17C] a very good bargain (cf. ROBIN HOOD'S BARGAIN). ['it takes from the rich and gives to the poor']

robin redbreast/redbreast n. [mid–late 19C] a Bow Street

runner. [Charles Dickens, letter (18 April 1862): 'The Bow Street runners ... had no other uniform than a blue dress-coat, brass buttons ... and a bright red cloth waistcoat. The waistcoat was indispensable and the slang name for them was "red-breasts" in consequence']

robin ruddock see RUDDOCK.

robin's eye n. [mid-19C–1900s] a sore, an ulcer, a scab. [resemblance]

Robinson and Cleaver n. [20C] a fever. [rhy. sl.; ult. the defunct London department store]

Robinson Crusoe v. [late 19C–1940s] to do so, often as imper. [rhy. sl.]

rob my pal n. [20C] a woman (cf. BOB MY PAL). [rhy. sl. *rob my pal* = gal, i.e. girl]

robocop n. [1980s] (US) a policeman, esp. one who is known to be brutal or racist. [film *Robocop* (1987), in which the hero is a half-man/half-robot policeman]

rob-o'davy see ROB-DAVY.

robot n. [1950s+] (W.I.) a privately owned vehicle, used to provide public transport when the usual drivers of such transport are on strike.

Rob Roy n. [mid-19C–1920s] a boy. [rhy. sl.; ult. Scots hero *Rob Roy* McGregor (d.1734)]

rob the barber, to phr. [late 19C] to wear one's hair long and uncut.

rob the cradle, to phr. [1940s+] (orig. US) to have a relationship with someone much younger than oneself (cf. CRADLE-SNATCHER).

rob the knob, to phr. [1990s] to masturbate. [KNOB n.[1] (1)]

rob the ruffian n. [19C] the vagina (cf. CATCH 'EM ALIVE-O). [SE *rob* + BELLY RUFFIAN]

robustious adj. [mid-18C–late 19C] violent, boisterous, noisy, strongly self-assertive, pompous. [SE mid-16C–mid-18C, thereafter condemned by Dr Johnson as 'low']

roby douglas n. [late 18C] the posterior. ['with one eye and a stinking breath' (Grose 1785); presumably f. a real person]

roca n. [1980s+] (drugs) crack cocaine. [Sp. *roca*, a rock]

roche n. [1990s] (drugs) Rohypnol, better known as the 'date-rape' drug, as it is allegedly given to people to knock them out and facilitate their rape. [the manufacturer, *Roche*]

Rochester portion n. [late 17C–early 19C] the vagina, lit. 'two torn smocks and what Nature gave' (B.E.) (cf. IRISH FORTUNE). [orig. use is in a Kentish pvb.]

rock n.[1] **1** [mid-19C+] (US) $1. **2** [1960s+] (US prison) one carton of prison cigarettes, the equivalent of $1 in a barter economy.

rock n.[2] **1** [20C] a diamond. **2** [20C] a man who is sturdy and solid both emotionally, physically and in his character.

Rock, the n.[3] [1930s–60s] Alcatraz Federal prison on Alcatraz Island, California. [the rocky islet in San Francisco Bay on which it is built]

rock n.[4] **1** [1960s+] cocaine. **2** [1980s+] crack cocaine. [the small chunks found in powdered cocaine or in which crack cocaine is sold]

rock n.[5] [1960s+] (US prison) a cellblock. [the stone walls]

rock n.[6] [1970s+] (S.Afr.) an Afrikaner. [abbr. ROCK SPIDER]

rock adj. [1980s+] excellent, outstanding. [i.e. it knocks one off-balance]

rock v.[1] **1** [19C] (mainly US) to throw rocks or stones at. **2** [1980s+] (US campus) to fight with, to beat up.

rock v.[2] [late 19C+] to talk (cf. ROCKER v.). [Rom. *roker*, to talk]

rock v.[3] [20C] (orig. US Black) **1** to have sexual intercourse. **2** of music, to make one move in a rhythmical manner. [like JAZZ v.[1] the roots of rock music stem directly from sexual imagery, thus the 1922 song title 'My man rocks me (with one steady roll)'; for further details on sexual imagery of rock/ blues see Cohen V pp.127 ff]

rock v.[4] [20C] to get drunk. [one's unsteadiness]

rock a beat, to phr. [1990s] (US) to play music. [ROCK v.[3] (2) + SE beat]

rock along v. [20C] (orig. US) to go on with life in one's usual manner.

rockalow/rock-a-low n. [mid-19C] an overcoat. [Fr. roquelaure, an overcoat]

rock and lurch n. [20C] (Aus.) a church (cf. IN THE LURCH; LEAN AND LURCH; LEFT IN THE LURCH). [rhy. sl.]

rock and roll n. [20C] the dole. [rhy. sl.]

rock and roll v. [1990s] to have sexual intercourse. [rhy. sl. rock and roll = GET ONE'S HOLE]

rock ape n. [1970s+] (Aus.) **1** a derog. term for a Black person. **2** anyone viewed with disfavour, e.g. a teenager.

rock attack n. [1980s+] (drugs) a desire for crack cocaine. [ROCK n.[4] (2) + SE attack]

rock candy n. [1940s] (US Black) diamonds. [resemblance]

rockchopper n. [1940s–50s] (Aus.) a derog. term for a Roman Catholic. [used by Protestants as a derog. ref. to the original Irish immigrants, who were mainly convicts and, as such, condemned to hard labour]

rock crank n. [1980s+] (drugs) methylamphetamine. [SE rock + CRANK n.[3] (2)]

rock crusher n. [20C] (US) a convict. [hard labour in the rock quarry]

rocked adj. **1** [early 19C] forgetful, esp. used of an ex-prisoner whose mental state has been affected by their punishment, whether prison or transportation. **2** [1980s+] (US campus) drunk. [i.e. they have 'rocks in the head']

rocked in a stone kitchen phr. [late 18C–early 19C] foolish, stupid. [someone who has been thus rocked will have had their brain injured]

rocker/rokker v. **1** [mid-19C+] to speak, esp. to speak tramps' jargon (cf. ROCK v.[2]; VOKER). **2** [20C] to understand. [Rom. roker, to talk]

rockers n.[1] [1960s+] a youth cult whose members wear leather, ride powerful motorcycles and fight their ritual rivals, the 'Mods'; latterly the hard-core rockers developed into a UK version of the US Hell's Angels.

rockers n.[2] [1970s+] (W.I. Rasta) reggae music, esp. the latest sound.

rocket n.[1] [1940s+] (orig. milit.) a severe reprimand or telling off; thus get a rocket, give a rocket.

rocket n.[2] [1980s+] (drugs) a marijuana cigarette. [one 'blasts' off]

rocket v.[1] [1940s+] (orig. milit.) to scold severely, to reprimand. [ROCKET n.[1]]

rocket v.[2] [1990s] (drugs) to suddenly become extremely intoxicated when smoking cannabis. [ROCKET n.[2]]

rocket caps n. [1980s+] (drugs) the dome-shaped caps on crack cocaine vials. [resemblance]

rocket fuel n. [1970s] (drugs) phencyclidine (cf. ACE n.[3]).

rocket rattling n. [1960s] using one's force of nuclear weapons to threaten other countries. [SE sabre rattling]

rockets n. **1** [1970s+] (US Black) bullets. **2** [1990s] breasts (cf. ARTILLERY n.[3]). [the shape]

rocket scientist n. [1990s] (US campus) someone who is stupid. [ironic use of SE]

rocket ship n. [1970s] (drugs) a hypodermic syringe and needle. [resemblance]

rockette n. [1980s+] (drugs) a woman who uses crack cocaine. [ROCK n.[3] + fem. sfx. -ette + ref. to the Rockettes, the chorus line at Radio City Music Hall, NYC]

rockhead n. [20C] (US) a stupid person. [SE rock + sfx. -HEAD (1)]

rock hound n. [1920s+] (orig. US) **1** a geologist. **2** an amateur mineralogist. [SE rock + sfx. -HOUND]

rock house n. [1980s+] (drugs) a place where crack cocaine is sold and smoked. [ROCK n.[4] (2) + SE house]

rock in v. [20C] (Aus.) to intensify, to accelerate, esp. in phr. rock it in! hurry up! make it snappy!

rockin' n. [20C] (US prison) a prison riot (cf. BINGO n.[2]; KICK-UP). [SE rock, to shake]

rockin' adj. [1990s] (US teen) a general term of approval. [fig. use of ROCK v.[3]]

rockiness n. [late 19C] **1** drunkenness (cf. WALK ON ROCKY SOCKS). **2** insanity, madness. [SE rock, to shake; thus the images are of instability]

rocking chair n. [1940s] (US Black) sexual intercourse, esp. as used metaphorically in blues lyrics.

rocking horse n. [20C] **1** sauce (condiment). **2** sauce (cheek). [rhy. sl.]

rocking-horse manure n. [1950s+] (orig. Aus.) something extremely hard, if not impossible to find.

rock in/over/up v. [1970s+] (S.Afr.) to arrive without prior announcement or appointment, to 'roll up'. [SE rock, to stagger]

rock it in v. [1940s] (Aus.) to boast. [one is throwing verbal 'rocks']

rock 'n' roll n. [20C] **1** a hole. **2** the dole. [rhy. sl.]

rock 'n' roll v. [1990s] (US Black) to leave. [one 'dances' off]

rock of ages/rocks n. [1930s+] wages. [rhy. sl.]

rock on v. [1960s+] (US) to enjoy oneself, esp. by playing or dancing to rock music (cf. ROCK OUT v.[1]).

rock one's world, to phr. [1980s+] (US campus) to have sexual intercourse. [the now clichéd description of lovemaking – 'make the earth move' – from Ernest Hemingway's For Whom the Bell Tolls (1940)]

rock out v.[1] [1960s+] **1** (US) to enjoy oneself, esp. by playing or dancing to rock music. **2** (US Black) to collapse, to be exhausted.

rock out v.[2] [1980s+] (drugs) to collapse through an excessive consumption of crack cocaine. [ROCK n.[4] (2)]

rock out! excl. [1960s+] keep enjoying yourself! have a great time!

rock over see ROCK IN.

rockpile n. **1** [late 19C+] a heap of stones. **2** [late 19C+] (US prison) the prison quarry, in allusion to the convict's task of breaking stones. **3** [1940s] (US Black) any tall building; thus topside of the rockpile, the top flat, the penthouse. [note naut. use rockpile, a ship on which the work is especially demanding]

rockpile cure see QUARRY CURE.

rocks n.[1] **1** [20C] the teeth. **2** [1920s+] precious stones, jewels, esp. diamonds. **3** [1940s+] (orig. US) ice-cubes. [resemblance]

rocks n.[2] see ROCK OF AGES.

rocks n.[3] [1940s+] **1** the testicles (cf. AGATES). **2** courage, bravery. [play on STONES n.[1] (1)]

rocks n.[4] (drugs) **1** [1960+] a form of crystallized, smokeable heroin (cf. CHINESE ROCKS). **2** [1970s+] cocaine (cf. ROCK n.[4]). **3** [1980s+] crack cocaine (cf. ROCK n.[4]). [resemblance]

rocks and boulders n. [late 19C–1920s] the shoulders. [rhy. sl.]

rock scorpion n. [mid–late 19C] (orig. milit.) a civilian inhabitant of Gibraltar (cf. ROCK SPIDER).

rocks for jocks n. [1960s+] (US campus) an undergraduate course in 'introductory geology'. [SE rock + JOCK n.[2] (3)]

rocks in the head n. [20C] (US) stupidity.

rocks of hell n. [1980s+] (drugs) crack cocaine. [? ironic; ROCK n.[4] (2)]

rock spider/spider n. **1** [1930s+] (Aus.) a thief who robs courting couples in parks or at the seaside when their attention is elsewhere. **2** [1950s+] (S.Afr.) an Afrikaner (cf. ROCK SCORPION).

rock star *n.* [1980s+] (drugs) a smoker of crack cocaine, esp. a woman who trades sex for crack cocaine or money to buy crack cocaine. [ROCK *n.*⁴ (2) + play on SE]

rock the boat, to *phr.* [1910s+] (orig. US) to cause (unnecessary) trouble, to disturb the status quo, often in neg. imper. *don't rock the boat.*

rock up *see* ROCK IN.

rocky/Rocky III *n.* [1990s] (drugs) crack cocaine. [ROCK *n.*⁴ (2) + play on the *Rocky* films of 1980s]

rocky *adj.* (orig. US) **1** [late 19C+] difficult, problematical. **2** [20C] drunk. **3** [1920s] penniless, impoverished. **4** [1920s+] unwell, 'off-colour'. [SE *rock*, to sway]

Rocky Mountain canary *n.* [20C] a donkey, an ass (cf. ARIZONA NIGHTINGALE). [the noise of its braying, the antithesis of that of a mellifluous bird]

rocky road *n.* [20C] (US) the anus. [? an ice-cream variety, which features *chocolate*, punning on CHOCOLATE adj. (2)]

Rocky III *see* ROCKY *n.*

rod *n.*¹ [20C] **1** the penis, erect penis (cf. GUN *n.*²). **2** [1920s+] (US) a gun, a pistol. [the shape]

rod *n.*² [1900–60s] (US) **1** the draw-*rod* of a railway carriage or truck, usu. in pl.; thus *ride the rods*, to travel the railroads as a vagrant. **2** a freight train. [abbr.]

rod *n.*³ [1930s+] an overcoat. [ety. unknown; ? link to ROCK-ALOW]

rod *n.*⁴ [1940s+] (US) a car modified for speed. [abbr. HOT-ROD *n.* (1)]

rod *v.* **1** [late 19C+] of a man, to have sexual intercourse. **2** [1920s+] to arm oneself with a gun. [ROD *n.*¹]

rodda *n.* [1960s] (US Black) a Cadillac. [? ROD *n.*⁴]

rodded *adj.* [1920s+] carrying a gun. [ROD *n.*¹ (2)]

roddy *n.* [mid-19C] a *rhodo*dendron. [abbr.]

rodeo *n.* [1990s] (US Black teen) a style of sexual intercourse, the woman 'rides' on top (cf. RIDE A ST GEORGE). [RODEO V.]

rodeo *v.* [1990s] (US) of a man, to sodomize a woman, while pulling her hair and slapping her buttocks. [the image of a rodeo bronco-rider]

rodge *n.* [1970s] (US campus) a fact, anything that's true. [airforce jargon, *roger* = message received and understood]

rod in pickle/lye/piss *n.* [late 17C–19C] **1** a punishment in prospect. **2** any agent of revenge or aggression that has been put aside for use at the right time. [from the toughening of rods by marinating them in lye]

rodman *n.* [1920s+] (US) a gunman. [ROD *n.*¹ (2) + sfx. -*man*]

rodney *n.* [mid-19C+] (Irish) a fool. [dial. *rodney*, an idler, a loafer, a fool]

Rodney King *n.* [1990s] (US Black) an arrest, esp. one involving brutality; thus *pull a Rodney King*, to initiate police brutality. [*Rodney King*, a Black man, was severely beaten by the police during his arrest. A videotape of the beating led to the trial of the officers involved and, after their controversial acquittal, the Los Angeles riots of 1992]

Rods *n.* [1970s+] (society) Har*rods* (cf. FRED'S). [abbr.]

rod up *v.*¹ [1920s+] (US Und.) to arm oneself with a gun. [ROD *n.*¹ (2)]

rod up *v.*² [1970s] (US) to convert a car by giving it a very powerful engine to make it go fast (cf. HOT-ROD *n.*; ROD *n.*⁴).

rod walloper *n.* [1950s+] (orig. Aus.) a masturbator. [ROD *n.*¹ (1) + SE *walloper*]

rody *see* RUDE BOY.

roe *n.* [mid-19C–1900s] semen (cf. MILT).

rofe *n.* [1840s–50s] (prison) a 4-year sentence. [backsl.]

rofefil/rouf-efil *n.* [mid-19C] a life sentence. [backsl.; lit. 'for life']

roger/roger of the buttery *n.*¹ [16C] a goose or gander (cf. TIB OF THE BUTTERY). [the proper name]

roger *n.*² [16C] a wandering beggar who pretended to be a poor

scholar from Oxford or Cambridge (cf. AURIUM). [despite the 'e' the g was pronounced hard, thus ? corruption of SE *rogue*]

roger *n.*³ [late 17C–early 19C] a suitcase. [? dial. *roger*, the paunch of a pig]

roger *n.*⁴ **1** [late 17C+] the penis (cf. ABRAHAM). **2** [mid-18C–late 19C] a ram. [SE *roger*, a bull]

roger *v.* [early 18C+] to have sexual intercourse, to seduce; also as *do a roger*. [ROGER *n.*⁴ (1)]

roger gough *n.* [late 19C+] (Aus.) scrub, brushwood. [? Gen. *Roger Gough*, victor of Sobraon and Ferozeshah or f. long-lost Native Australian word]

rogering *n.* [early 18C+] sexual intercourse. [ROGER V.]

rogering iron *n.* [18C–19C] the penis. [ROGER *n.*⁴ (1) + SE *iron*]

roger of the buttery *see* ROGER *n.*¹.

roger ramjet *n.* [1990s] a homosexual. [the children's TV cartoon character, but note ROGER *n.*⁴ (1) + SE *ram*, to force]

rogers *n.* [late 19C] (society) a ghastly face. [? the pirate 'skull-and-crossbones', the Jolly *Roger* or Samuel *Rogers* (1763–1865), who combined banking with poetry and apparently, while not chronologically old, had a notably aged face]

roger the lodger *n.* [1920s+] a lodger who seduces his landlady, or the wife of his landlord. [rhyme, but also pun on ROGER *n.*⁴ (1)]

roglan *n.* [late 19C] a four-wheeled vehicle. [Shelta]

rogue *n.*¹ [16C] (Und.) a professional villain, 'neither as stout or hardy as the upright-man' (Harman) (cf. ARCH-ROGUE; CANTING CREW; ROGUING JOE; WILD ROGUE). [the term is an original cant coinage and refers to a specific order of villain, the Fourth Order of Canters; its absorption into SE, meaning a general-purpose rascal, ran in parallel, albeit slightly later by some 20 years]

rogue *n.*² [1960s+] (US Black) a ladies' man, a sexually active man. [SE *rogue male*]

rogue *v.* **1** [mid-16C–mid-17C] (Und.) to live as a professional beggar; thus *roguing*, living in this way, *roguishness*, being a rogue. **2** [1980s+] (US campus) to steal. [ROGUE *n.*¹]

rogue and pullet *n.* [mid-19C+] (Und.) a man and woman working together as a criminal team. [ROGUE *n.*¹ + PULLET]

rogue and villain *n.* [mid-19C] a shilling. [rhy. sl.]

rogue in grain *n.* [late 17C–early 19C] **1** a very great rogue. **2** a corn-chandler. [stereotyping]

rogue in spirit *n.* [late 18C–mid-19C] a distiller or brandy merchant. [pun]

rogue's walk *n.* [late 19C] (society) a stroll along Piccadilly from the Circus to Bond Street. [ROGUE *n.*¹ + SE *walk*; a ref. to the deviousness that created the fortunes of many of the strollers]

rogue with one ear *n.* [late 17C–early 18C] a chamberpot. [the 'ear' is the handle]

roguing Joe/Tom *n.* [1950s] (W.I.) **1** a wandering scrounger or pilferer (cf. ROGUE *n.*¹). **2** the bag into which such a person places their finds. [mid-16C–mid-17C SE *rogue*, to wander as a rogue or vagrant]

roid rage *n.* [1980s+] (drugs) aggressive behaviour caused by excessive steroid use. [abbr. SE *steroid* + play on ROAD RAGE]

roi nègre, le *n.* [1960s+] (Can.) the Anglophone élite who dominate Canadian politics and society. [Fr. *roi nègre*, the Black king; the term was coined by French-Canadian editor and campaigner André Laurendeau; the implication is that the élite resemble the British in Africa, who backed a local ruler so long as he pursed what were ultimately policies that they dictated]

roister/royster *n.* [mid-16C–late 18C] a swaggering, blustering bully, a noisy reveller. [Fr. *rustre*, a ruffian, a royster, a hackster, a swaggerer; ult. Lat. *rusticus*, a peasant]

roker/rooker *n.* [late 19C+] (S.Afr.) a marijuana smoker. [Du. *roken*, to smoke]

rokker *see* ROCKER.

rolf *see* RALPH V.

rolie *n.* [1980s+] (N.Z. drugs) a *Roly*pnol. [abbr.]

roll *n.*[1] [mid-19C+] a bank*roll* (cf. ROLL JACK RICE COULDN'T JUMP OVER). [abbr.]

roll *n.*[2] [1940s+] (orig. US) sexual intercourse. [abbr. ROLL IN THE HAY n. (1)]

roll *n.*[3] **1** [1960s] (US drugs) a roll of benzedrine tablets. **2** [1970s+] (US Black) a month's supply of contraceptive pills.

roll *n.*[4] [1970s+] a spell of good fortune, a winning streak, whether lit. or fig. [SE *roll*, the roll of a dice]

roll *n.*[5] [1980s+] (US campus) a very funny person. [ROLL v.[6]]

roll *v.*[1] [late 19C+] to rob; usu. a drunk or any helpless person; thus *roll a stiff*, *roll a lush*. [one *rolls* the victim over]

roll *v.*[2] **1** [20C] (US Black) to survive, to live, to conduct oneself. **2** [1930s+] (US) to start moving. **3** [1940s] (US Black) to drive a car. **4** [1980s+] (US campus) to leave. **5** [1990s] (US Black) to walk.

roll *v.*[3] [1920s+] (US Black) to have sexual intercourse. [orig. meaning work, it was extended in blues songs to mean intercourse, i.e. the physical effort involved]

roll *v.*[4] [1960s+] (drugs) to roll a marijuana cigarette.

roll *v.*[5] [1960s+] (US) to prosper, to do well, to succeed. [ON A ROLL]

roll *v.*[6] [1980s+] **1** to laugh hysterically. **2** to make someone laugh. [abbr. ROLLING IN THE AISLES]

roll a number, to *phr.* [1960s+] (drugs) to prepare a marijuana cigarette. [ROLL v.[4] + NUMBER n.[5]]

roll big enough to choke a bullock *see* ROLL JACK RICE COULDN'T JUMP OVER.

roll 'em! *excl.* [1950s+] (US prison) open the cell doors! [cell doors slide open and shut and their movement is controlled by a central locking system]

roller *n.*[1] **1** [late 19C–1940s] someone who rolls opium into smokeable pellets. **2** [1920s–40s] a drug user or addict. **3** [1930s] a tobacco cigarette. **4** [1960s] (drugs) a vein that rolls as one attempts to insert a needle. **5** [1990s] (drugs) a drug seller, thus *rolling*; dealing drugs.

roller *n.*[2] [20C] (US Black) someone who keeps moving continuously. [ROLL v.[2]]

roller *n.*[3] **1** [1910s+] (US) a pickpocket who specializes in stealing from drunks (cf. LUSH-WORKER). **2** [1960s+] (US Black) a policeman, esp. one who specializes in stopping and searching people on the street. **3** [1960s+] (US prison) a prison guard. [ROLL v.[1]]

Roller *n.*[4] [1950s+] a *Rolls* Royce car. [abbr.]

roller *n.*[5] [1950s+] (US) a police car. [ROLL v.[2]]

rollers *n.* [early 19C] a nightly patrol, on both horse and foot, that covered London in the hope of preventing robberies. **2** [1950s+] (US Black) the police. [? SE *patrol*]

rollerskate *n.* **1** [1960s] a small, light wagon. **2** [1970s+] (US) a small foreign-made car.

rollick *v.* [1920s+] **1** to tell off, to reprimand; thus *a good rollicking*. **2** to make a fuss, to complain loudly. [rhy. sl. *rollick* = BOLLOCK v.]

rollicks! *see* ROLLOCKS!

rollie *n.* [1940s] (US prison) a hand-rolled cigarette (cf. ROLL-UP)

rollies *n.* [1930s+] the testicles. [abbr. ROLLOCKS]

roll in/up *v.* [mid-19C+] **1** (orig. Aus.) to arrive, to come home. **2** (US) to go to bed (cf. ROLL OUT).

rolling *n.*[1] [? mid-16C+] robbery. [E.P. and the *OED* both have vb. *roll*, to rob, esp. of a drunk, as 19C; but Copland (1536) offers 'Taverners that keep bawdry and polling/Marring wine with brewing and *rolling*', thus poss. earlier, though equally poss. it means simply rolling the barrels and over-fermenting the wine]

rolling *n.*[2] [1980s+] (drugs) MDMA (cf. ECSTASY). [ety. unknown]

rolling *n.*[3] [1980s+] (US Black teen) **1** driving around very slowly. **2** being associated either with an individual or a larger group. [ROLL v.[2]]

rolling *adj.*[1] [late 18C–late 19C] clever, sophisticated.

rolling *adj.*[2] [20C] rolling with money, very well off, or abundantly supplied with anything. [abbr. SE phr. *rolling in money*]

rolling *adj.*[3] [20C] very drunk. [SE *roll*, to tumble]

rolling billow *n.* [late 19C+] a pillow. [rhy. sl.]

rolling deep *n.* [20C] (Aus.) sleep. [rhy. sl.]

rolling in the aisles *phr.* [1940s+] very much amused, reduced to near-hysterical laughter (cf. LAY THEM IN THE AISLES). [orig. theatrical use referring to a comedian's success]

rolling Joe *n.* [mid–late 19C] a smart, fashionable person (cf. ROLLING KIDDY). [ROLLING adj.[1] + JOE n.[7]]

rolling kiddy *n.* [early–mid-19C] (Und.) a dandified thief. [ROLLING adj.[1] + KIDDY n.[1] (2)]

rolling-pin *n.* [mid–late 19C] the penis (cf. BAT n.[7]).

rolling refinery *n.* [1970s] (US) a truck that hauls petrol/gasoline or oil.

roll in one's ivory/ivories, to *phr.* [mid-18C–late 19C] to kiss. [IVORY n.[1] (1); sing. use until mid-19C]

roll/tumble in the hay *n.* [1940s+] (orig. US) **1** sexual intercourse, with the implication of spontaneity, adultery or the open air (cf. HAVE A ROLL IN THE HAY). **2** a person viewed as a possible sexual partner.

roll into *v.* [late 19C] (Aus.) to attack.

roll Jack Rice couldn't jump over/roll big enough to choke a bullock/roll that would choke an anteater *n.* [1940s–70s] (Aus.) a large quantity of money. [proper name of *Jack Rice*, Aus. champion hurdler]

roll me/roll me in the dirt *n.* [20C] a shirt. [rhy. sl.]

roll me in the gutter *n.* [20C] (Aus.) butter. [rhy. sl.]

roll me in the kennel *n.* [early–mid-18C] gin. [the drunken toper will sleep anywhere]

rollocking *n.* [1930s+] a scolding, a reprimand. [euph. of BOLLOCKING).

rollocks *n.* [20C] the testicles (cf. JIMMY ROLLOCKS; TOMMY ROLLOCKS). [euph of BALLOCKS n.[1]]

rollocks!/rollicks! *excl.* [1960s+] nonsense, rubbish. [euph. for BALLS!; BOLLOCKS!]

roll on! *excl.* [1950s+] **1** a general excl. of dismissal, resignation, amazement, surprise etc, often intensified as *fucking roll on!* (cf. STROLL ON!). **2** used to introduce a variety of wishes, usu. referring to escaping the environment that one is in, e.g. *roll on payday*, *roll on Friday* etc.

roll one's bones, to *phr.* [20C] (US) to get into action, to move oneself.

roll one's hoop, to *phr.* [late 19C–1920s] to do well, to succeed.

roll one's marbles, to *phr.* [1950s] (US) to masturbate. [SE *roll* + MARBLES n.[3]]

roll one's own, to *phr.* [1930s+] (Aus.) to do it oneself, on one's own terms. [hand-rolling cigarettes]

roll one's pannikin into another shed, to *phr.* [late 19C–1900s] (Aus.) to go looking for a new job.

roll one up *v.* [1960s+] to prepare a marijuana cigarette.

roll out *v.* **1** [late 19C+] to get out of bed, to get up. **2** [1970s] (US campus) to leave, to depart.

roll out the red carpet, to *phr.* [1930s+] to give someone a grand welcome. [the *red carpet* ceremonially laid for visiting dignitaries]

rollover *n.* [20C] (US prison) the last night of a prison sentence (cf. WAKE-UP n.[3]). [one wakes up, rolls out of bed, and the sentence is over]

roll over v. [20C] **1** to give up, to acquiesce, to surrender. **2** in phr. *roll over on*, to betray, to inform against. [the way in which a dog *rolls over* on its back to indicate surrender]

rolls n. [19C] a baker. [their product]

Rolls-can-hardly/canardly n. [1950s+] (orig. Aus.) a run-down old car. [it *rolls* down the hills but *can hardly* get up them + ref. to the antithetical *Rolls* Royce; note the letter once sent to the manufacturers of Rolls Royces by Sir W.S. Gilbert (1836–1911): 'your car rolls but it will not royce']

roll someone up v. [1980s+] to beat someone up.

rolls royce n. [20C] the voice. [rhy. sl.]

roll sets on see RUN SETS ON.

roll that would choke an anteater see ROLL JACK RICE COULDN'T JUMP OVER.

roll the bars, to phr. [20C] (US prison) to open a row of cell doors using a remote mechanism that opens every door simultaneously (cf. SLAM THE SLATS).

roll the bones, to phr. [1920s+] (US) to play at dice. [BONES n.¹ (1)]

roll the dough, to phr. [1990s] to masturbate.

roll the log, to phr. [1930s] (drugs) to smoke opium.

roll them bones! phr. [1920s+] (gambling) a phr. meaning, throw those dice! [used with consciousness of slight archaism and only in the context of a crap game]

roll them in the aisles see LAY THEM IN THE AISLES.

roll-up n. **1** [1940s+] (orig. prison) a handmade cigarette of papers and tobacco. **2** [1980s+] (N.Z.) an illicit smoke.

roll up v.¹ see ROLL IN.

roll up v.² **1** [mid-19C+] (orig. US) to congregate, to assemble. **2** [mid-19C+] (orig. US) to arrive, to appear. **3** [1910s+] to die.

roll up v.³ **1** [late 19C+] (Aus.) to pack one's belongings before leaving. **2** [20C] (US Und.) of an inmate, to leave the prison, whether temporarily (for a court appearance) or permanently (after completing a sentence or moving to a new prison). [(1) the rolling up of one's pack; (2) the old practice of rolling up one's mattress on every occasion of leaving one's cell]

roll up the sidewalk, to phr. [mid-19C] (US) of shops and entertainments in towns or cities, to close down at nightfall.

roll with v. [1960s+] (US Black) to associate with. [ROLL v.²]

roll with the punches, to phr. [1950s+] (orig. US) to take events as they come and not to be unbalanced by problems. [boxing imagery]

roll your own, to phr. **1** [1970s] (US Black) an invitation to make yourself at home, do whatever you fancy. **2** [1990s] to masturbate. [image of rolling one's own cigarettes]

roly-poly n.¹ [early 19C] a game known as 'un-deux-cinq'. [? the same game as that noted by Johnson (1755): 'a sort of game, in which, when a ball rolls into a certain place, it wins']

roly-poly n.² [19C] the penis (cf. BAT n.⁷). [play on PUDDING n.¹ (2) ? + SE *roly-poly*, stout, podgy]

Roman adj. [1950s+] in the world of (gay) sex, used to describe group sex. [Rome is identified with orgies, thanks to popular fantasies of the 'decline and fall' of Rome]

Roman candle n.¹ [20C] a sandal. [rhy. sl.]

Roman candle n.² [1940s+] **1** a Roman Catholic. **2** an Italian. **3** (gay) an Italian-American's penis.

romance boy n. [1950s] (W.I.) a young man who chases women.

Roman collar n. [1960s+] (Irish) a generous head on a glass of stout. [SE *Roman collar*, a priest's collar]

Roman culture n. [1960s+] orgies, group sex (cf. AMERICAN CULTURE). [ROMAN]

Roman engagement n. [1960s+] (gay) anal intercourse with a virgin woman.

Roman fall n. [mid-19C] a way of walking in which the shoulders are thrust back, thus creating a droop backwards

(cf. ALEXANDRA LIMP). [officers of the Fr. Empire were forced to adopt this unnatural posture because of the tightness of their uniforms]

Roman fountains n. [1960s+] (gay) urinals. [play on ROMAN CULTURE]

Roman historian n. [1960s+] (gay) an enthusiast of orgies. [ROMAN]

Roman night n. [1960s+] (gay) an orgy. [ROMAN]

Roman roulette n. [1960s] contraception using no other system than the notoriously hit-and-miss 'rhythm method' as ordained by conservative popes (cf. VATICAN ROULETTE).

Romany rye n. [mid-19C] a non-gypsy gentleman who associates with gypsies. [Rom. *rai*, a gentleman; best-known through George Borrow's book *Romany Rye* (1857)]

romboyle/rumboyle n. [16C–early 18C] the watch (an early form of policing). [ety. unknown]

romboyle/rumboyle v. [16C–early 18C] **1** to seek out by hue and cry. **2** to arrest on a warrant; thus *romboyled*, wanted by the watch (cf. RUMBLE v.²). [ety. unknown]

rombustical see RUMBUSTIOUS.

rome see RUM adj.

rome bouse n. [mid-16C–19C] good drink, esp. good wine (cf. RUM BOOZE). [RUM adj. (1) + BOUSE n.]

Rome-cove n. [16C] (Und.) a leading beggar, whether through strength or intelligence (cf. RUM-COVE). [RUM adj. + COVE; lit. a 'good man']

rome mort see RUM MORT.

Rome pad n. [16C] (Und.) the highway. [RUM adj. + PAD n.¹ (1)]

Rome runner n. [14C–15C] anyone, usu. a clergyman, who makes frequent journeys to Rome in hope of spiritual stimulation.

Rome-ville/-vyle/Rum ville/Rumville n. [16C–18C] (Und.) London. [RUM adj. + SE *vill*, village]

Romford lion n. [17C] a calf (cf. JERUSALEM PONY). [joc. ref. to *Romford*, Essex, then a market town]

romp n. [1950s–60s] (US) a fight between street gangs. [ROMP v. (1)]

romp v. **1** [1950s–60s] (US) of street gangs, to fight. **2** [1980s+] (US campus) to have sexual intercourse. [note the coincidental UK tabloid press use of *romp*, a sexual entanglement, e.g. 'three-in-a-bed romp']

romper room n. [1980s+] (US campus) a place to get rowdy.

romp home/in v. [20C] (orig. racing) to win easily.

romp it v. [1970s+] (US campus) to accelerate in a car.

rompworthy adj. [1930s+] of a woman, ripe for sexual conquest. [ROMP v. (2) + sfx. *-worthy*]

ronchie see RAUNCHY.

roni n. [1990s] (US Black teen) a sweet woman. [cod Ital. *tenderoni*]

ronk n. [late 19C+] (mainly northern) a stink. [dial. *ronk/rank*, over-ripe]

ronnie biggs n. [20C] lodgings. [rhy. sl. *ronnie biggs* = DIGS n.¹; ult. *Ronald Biggs* (b.1929), one of the Great Train Robbers of 1963]

ronson n.¹ [1950s] a pimp. [rhy. sl. *rons(on)* = PONCE n. (1)]

ronson n.² [1990s] the anus; thus dismissive excl. *up your ronson!* [rhy. sl. *ronson lighter* = SHITTER n.¹ (1)]

roo n.¹ [mid-19C–1900s] a rake. [Fr. *roue*]

roo n.² [late 19C+] (Aus.) a kanga*roo*. [abbr.]

roof n. **1** [mid-19C–1940s] a hat; thus *drop one's roof*, to lose one's hat. **2** [late 19C] the human head.

roof v. [1940s+] (Aus.) to kick or punch. [? SE *rough* or phr. *knock him through the roof*]

roof caves in see ROOF FALLS IN.

roofer n.¹ **1** [19C+] (orig. US) a hat (cf. CHIMNEY; PANTILE n.²). **2** [1910s–20s] a third-rate, rundown theatre. [SE *roof*; Aus. use in 20C]

roofer/hospitable roofer n.[2] [1910s+] a 'thank-you letter' (cf. COLLINS). [the thanks are for the SE *roof* (over one's head) + 'Oxford' sfx. *-er*]

roof falls/caves in, the phr. [mid-19C+] a disaster occurs, everything possible goes wrong (at once).

roofie n. [1970s+] (S.Afr.) a junior National Serviceman, part of the latest intake. [? Afk. *roof*, scab]

roofies/roples/ruffles n. [1990s] (drugs) Rohypnol; a strong sedative. [the drug, which causes users to appear drunk, is allegedly popular as a new form of knock-out drop, prob. used to facilitate a number of rapes]

roof it v. [1950s+] (US) to have sex on the roof of a New York apartment building.

roogodoo n. [20C] (W.I.) a commotion, a noisy uproar. [? SE *ruckus*]

roogodung/rukadung adj. [20C] (W.I.) tumble-down, dilapidated. [? ROOGODOO + SE *down*]

rooibaard n. [1980s+] (S.Afr. drugs) very strong marijuana, with tiny red hairs. [Afk. *rooibaard*, red beard]

rooinek n. [late 19C+] (S.Afr.) an Englishman. [Afk. *rooinek*, redneck; the effect of the sun]

rook n.[1] **1** [late 16C+] a cheat or swindler (cf. HAWK n.[1]). **2** [late 19C+] a swindle. [the allegedly larcenous character of the bird]

rook n.[2] [early–mid-19C] (Und.) a small crow bar. [pun; a reverse of nature, where the rook is larger than the crow]

rook n.[3] [mid-19C] a clergyman. [the black clothes or, according to Hotten (1867) f. the nursery rhyme *Who Killed Cock Robin?*, 'I, says the Rook,/With my little book,/I'll be the parson']

rook v. [late 19C+] to cheat, to swindle, to steal. [ROOK n.[1] (2)]

rook and diath n. [1990s] in body-piercing, two rings set in the inner ear. [ety. unknown]

rooker see ROKER.

rookery n. **1** [mid-18C] a gambling den. **2** [late 18C–mid-19C] a criminal slum 'inhabited by dirty Irish and thieves' (Hotten, 1867); the best known was the *St Giles Rookery* (now occupied by the Centre Point tower) in central London (cf. PALESTINE IN LONDON). **3** [early 19C] a brothel. **4** [early 19C–1940s] a row, disturbance. [note milit. jargon *rookery*, that part of the barracks occupied by the subalterns]

rookery nook n. [1920s+] a book. [rhy. sl.]

rookie n. [late 19C+] a novice, a beginner, a new recruit; esp. in milit., police, sports use. [? SE *recruit* or children's use *rookie*, a look-out, if one considers that a look-out would have the least active and thus newest/youngest member of a gang; note *crow-boy*, a look-out, used in Southwark in the late 19C and derived f. the rural term for the boy who scared birds away from growing crops]

rookus juice n. [1920s–50s] (US) liquor. [SE *ruckus*, a commotion + JUICE n.[3]]

rooky adj. [mid–late 19C] rascally, roguish. [ROOK n.[1] (1)]

room see RUM adj.

room cuttle n. [16C] (Und.) a sword (cf. CUTTLE-BUNG). [RUM adj. + SE *cuttle*, a knife; ult. OF *coutel*]

roomer n. [late 19C+] (orig. US) a lodger.

roomie n. [1910s+] (US) a *room*-mate, one who shares an apartment or other dwelling. [abbr.]

rooms n. [1990s] (US campus) a *room*-mate. [on pattern of HOMES]

room to rent n. [1980s] (US teen) a stupid person. [their brain is 'vacant']

roosevelt see F.D.R.

roosher n. [late 19C–1900s] a policeman. [ROZZER n.[1]]

Rooshian/Roosian see RUSSIAN n.[1].

roost n. **1** [mid-19C] a bed (cf. PERCH n.[2]). **2** [1940s–50s] (US Black) one's home, one's house.

roost v.[1] [19C] to sit down. [SE *perch*]

roost/roost over v.[2] [late 19C–1920s] **1** to cheat, to trick. **2** to tease, to mock. [ROAST v. (2)]

rooster n.[1] **1** [mid-19C–1900s] the vagina (cf. COCK n.[2]). **2** [19C+] the penis (cf. COCK n.[2]). **3** [1950s–70s] (US Black) a sexually active man. [all f. the farmyard bird]

rooster n.[2] [1980s+] (drugs) crack cocaine. [? its packaging; ? devel. from next]

rooster brand n. [late 19C–1930s] (US drugs) ashes from smoked opium, sold for recycling by poor but desperate users. [ety. unknown; ? packaging]

roostered adj. [mid-19C–1900s] (US) drunk (cf. COCKED). [parody on taboo use of even SE *cock*; the fear of which had allegedly brought about the late 18C coinage (in the puritan US) of SE *rooster*]

rooster time n. [1960s+] (US teen) the early morning, cock's crow.

roosting ken n. [late 19C] a lodging house. [SE *roosting* + KEN n.[1]]

roost lay n. [early 19C] poultry-stealing. [SE *roost* + LAY n.[4] (2)]

root n.[1] **1** [mid-19C+] the penis. **2** [late 19C+] an erection, thus phr. *get/have the root*, to get an erection. **3** [1950s+] (orig. Aus.) the person with whom one has intercourse, usu. the woman (cf. FUCK n.[4]). **4** [1950s+] (Aus.) the act of sexual intercourse (cf. BASH n.[2]).

root n.[2] [late 19C–1900s] money. [the '*root* of all evil']

root n.[3] **1** [1900s–30s] a cigarette. **2** [1950s+] (drugs) marijuana. [? SE *cheroot*]

root v.[1] [late 19C–1940s] to kick a ball or a person. [? SE *up-root*]

root/root for v.[2] [late 19C+] (US) to cheer and urge on. [ety. unknown; Cohen II 67–8 suggests *root* = SE *dig*, and thus an image of cheering and stamping so hard that one 'digs a hole' in the grandstand]

root v.[3] **1** [1940s+] (Aus.) to outwit, to baffle, to exhaust, to utterly confound (someone); thus excl. *get rooted!*, go to hell!; *root my old boot!*, I don't believe you, I am very surprised. **2** [1950s+] (Aus.) to have sexual intercourse; thus *root/shag like a rattlesnake*, to have very vigorous sex; also used as euph. for FUCK v.[1] in a variety of similarly negative uses, e.g. *get rooted, wouldn't it root you* (cf. BANG v.[1]). [despite chronology of available citations, (1) seems definitely a fig. use of (2) (cf. synon. uses of FUCK v.[1]) and must, therefore be earlier]

root about/around v. [mid-19C+] to rummage, to search through.

rooted adj. [1940s+] (Aus.) exhausted, crippled, out of action (cf. FUCKED). [ROOT v.[3] (1)]

rooter n.[1] [mid-19C] a form of pony-tail, worn by men. [the hair appeared to be throwing out a root]

rooter n.[2] [mid-19C–1910s] **1** anything considered excellent, first-class. **2** anything extreme, violent, highly aggressive. [SE *root*, meaning the basis, the ultimate]

rooter n.[3] [late 19C+] (US) a sports fan, esp. a baseball fan (cf. CRANK n.[2]). [ROOT v.[2]]

rooter n.[4] [1950s+] anyone seen as being keen on sex. [ROOT v.[3] (2)]

root-faced adj. [20C] humourless, sanctimonious, censorious. [a face carved into the hard twists of a tree root]

root for see ROOT v.[2].

root, hog or die, to phr. [early 19C+] to work extremely hard, or face inevitable failure.

rooti/rooty n. [19C] (Anglo-Ind.) bread. [Hind. *roti*, a flat, unleavened bread]

rootiepoot/rootypoot n. [1960s+] (US Black) an uninformed, unsophisticated person. [var. on POOPBUTT]

rootie-poot adj. [1960s+] (US Black) inferior, superficial. [ROOTIEPOOT n.]

rootin'-tootin' see ROOTING-TOOTING.

rooting n.[1] [late 19C+] (US) cheering, encouraging, supporting one's sports team. [ROOT v.[2]]

rooting n.[2] [1920s+] (mainly Aus.) the act of copulation. [ROOT v.[3] (2)]

rooting-tooting/rootin'-tootin' adj. [mid-19C+] (orig. US) noisy, boisterous, rip-roaring. [SE *root around* + *toot*]

rootle v. [mid-19C–1920s] to have sexual intercourse, thus phr. [late 19C–1920s] *do a rootle*. [SE *rootle*, to rummage about]

root my boot! excl. [1960s] (Aus.) a general expression of exasperation (cf. FUCK MY OLD BOOTS!). [ROOT v.[3] (2)]

root-on n. [1990s] an erection. [ext. of ROOT n.[1] (2); on the pattern of HARD-ON]

roots n.[1] [mid-19C] (costermonger) plants and flowers.

roots n.[2] [20C] (Aus.) boots. [abbr. DAISY ROOTS]

roots/rootsy adj. [1950s+] (orig. W.I. then US/UK Black) authentic, culturally sound (by Rastafarian standards); thus *roots people*, those who feel they belong in Africa, rather than in the W.I. or the Black diaspora.

roots! excl. [1950s+] (W.I./Rasta) used as a greeting to a fellow Rastafarian.

rooty n. see ROOTI.

rooty adj. [20C] (US) sexually aroused (cf. HORNY adj.). [ROOT n.[1] (1)]

rootypoot see ROOTIEPOOT.

ropable/ropeable adj. [mid-19C+] (Aus./N.Z) in a very bad temper, infuriated (cf. FIT TO BE TIED). [the image of an enraged horse or bull]

rope n.[1] [1930s+] (US) a cigar, esp. a foul-smelling one.

rope n.[2] [1940s+] (drugs) marijuana. [? the use of hemp in rope-making]

rope n.[3] [1940s+] (drugs) a vein. [resemblance]

ropeable see ROPABLE.

rope in v. 1 [early 19C+] (US) to swindle or cheat. 2 [late 19C–1900s] to involve, to include. 3 [late 19C–1900s] as *rope in the pieces*, to make money. 4 [1920s+] to arrest. [all images of roping cattle; subseq. use of (2) is SE]

roper, the n.[1] [mid-17C–mid-18C] the hangman; also [early 19C] as abbr. *roper* (cf. MR ROPER). [his primary tool]

roper/roper in/runner/picker-up n.[2] [mid-19C] (US) an employee of a dance-hall or gambling house whose task was to entice passers-by into the establishment; some ropers worked from hotel lobbies, where they paid the clerk a fee to introduce them to wealthy or gullible tourists (cf. STEERER n.[1]). [SE *rope in*, to lure, to decoy, to attract]

roper's news phr. [mid-17C–mid-18C] no news at all. [? anecdotal, or ref. to ROPER n.[1]; any news he offered would be of no use to his victim]

rope the goat/pony, to phr. [1990s] to masturbate.

rope the pope, to phr. [1990s] to masturbate (cf. BANG THE BISHOP).

rope walk n. [19C] the Old Bailey. [London's major court; one might *walk* thence to the gallows]

ropey adj. [1940s+] (orig. RAF) second-rate, inadequate, mediocre, rundown etc. [? RAF use, an obsolete aircraft, overburdened with a variety of ropes]

roples see ROOFIES.

ropper n. [19C] a scarf. [Scot. *roppin*, to wrap + SE *wropper*]

roration/roaration n. [late 18C] a speech given in a 'loud, unmusical voice' (Grose, 1785). [SE *roar* + *oration*]

rorf v. [1950s+] (S.Afr.) to indulge in horseplay. [ety. unknown]

roritorious see RORTORIOUS.

roro n. [20C] (W.I.) slander, malicious gossip; thus *put one in roro*, to slander, to cause trouble for. [? Fr. *ronron*, whirring, buzzing]

rort/roart/wrought n. (Aus./N.Z.) 1 [1920s+] any form of trick or deception, usu. qualified by a relevant noun, e.g. 'New Labour election rort'. 2 [1920s+] anything exceptionally good. 3 [1930s+] a crowd, a wild, noisy party. 4 [1970s+] an act of sexual intercourse. 5 [1970s+] a woman seen as a sex object. [RORT v.]

rort v. (Aus./N.Z.) 1 [1910s+] to deceive, to defraud, to hoax. 2 [1930s+] as *rort at*, to shout, to complain loudly, to shout abuse. 3 [1930s+] to call the odds at a race-meeting. 4 [1940s+] to have sexual intercourse. 5 [1950s+] to go out on a spree. 6 [1980s+] to manipulate ballots or any form of record; thus *rorted*, rigged. [? RORTY]

rorter n.[1] [1920s+] something exceptionally good. [RORT n. (2)]

rorter n.[2] 1 [1920s+] (Aus.) a professional fraudster or confidence trickster. 2 [1980s+] someone who engages in a form of fraudulent manipulation. [RORT v. (1)]

rorting n. 1 [1910s+] confidence trickery. 2 [1920s+] any form of 'sharp practice'. [RORT v. (1)]

rortorious/roaratorious/roritorious adj. [early–mid-19C] happily, triumphantly noisy. [RORATION]

rorty/raughty adj. [late 19C+] 1 fine, splendid, jolly. 2 boisterous, rowdy, noisy. 3 of drinks, intoxicating. 4 of behaviour, speech etc, coarse, earthy, crudely comic. [? Yid., *rorität*, anything choice or f. rhy. sl. *rorty* = naughty]

rorty bloke/dasher/toff n. [late 19C] a good fellow, an engaging companion, a fashionable upper-class gentleman. [RORTY adj. (1) + BLOKE/DASHER/TOFF; the *bloke* is seen (according to Ware) as a superior being to the *toff* (? because the *toff* had pretensions, while the *bloke* was down to earth)]

rortyness n. [late 19C] energy, vitality. [RORTY]

rorty toff see RORTY BLOKE.

rory/Rory O'Moore n. 1 [mid-19C+] the floor. 2 [late 19C+] a door. 3 [late 19C+] a prostitute. [rhy. sl.]

rosa n. [1980s+] (drugs) amphetamine (cf. A n.[2]; ROSES n.[2]). [Sp. *rosa*, red]

rosa marie n. [1930s] (US drugs) marijuana. [play on MARY JANE n.[2]]

roscoe/john roscoe n. [late 19C+] (US) a handgun. [? anecdotal]

rose n.[1] [18C+] the vagina, esp. of a virgin; thus *pluck a rose*, to deflower (cf. BEAUTY SPOT n.[1]). [literary euph.]

rose n.[2] [mid-19C] an orange. [? the pleasant smell]

rose among the thorns n. [1960s–70s] (US) a good-looking prostitute in a group of less attractive women.

rosebud n. 1 [late 19C+] the mouth. 2 [1950s–60s] (drugs) a distended, inflamed rectum after passing a painful stool, the result of extended opium or heroin use. 3 [1950s–60s] (US gay) the anus. [resemblance]

rosebuds n. [late 19C+] potatoes. [rhy. sl. *rosebuds* + SPUDS n.[1] (1)]

rose-coloured adj. [1920s] a euph. synon. for BLOODY.

roseleaf v. [mid-19C+] to perform anilingus. [? synon. Fr. *faire feuille de rose*, 'to do the rose-leaf'; note ROSEBUD (3)]

rosella n. [late 19C] (Aus.) a European, working stripped to the waist; the resulting sunburn initially pinkened the complexion.

rose mane n. [1980s+] (drugs) marijuana. [? SE *resin*]

Rosemary Lane to a rag shop phr. [19C] the longest possible odds, an absolute certainty (cf. ALL THE WORLD TO A CHINA ORANGE). [var. on LOMBARD STREET TO A BRUMMAGEM SIXPENCE]

roses n.[1] [mid-19C–1920s] the menstrual period (cf. FLOWERS).

roses n.[2] [1980s+] (drugs) amphetamine (cf. A n.[2]; ROSA). [play on REDS n.[3]]

roses red n. [20C] (Aus.) a bed. [rhy. sl.]

rosewood n. [1920s–50s] (US Black) a policeman's nightstick. [the wood from which it is made]

rosie lea/rosy lee *n.* [1920s+] (orig. milit.) **1** tea (cf. BETTY LEA; DICKY LEE; GYPSIE LEE; HAY LEE; JENNIE LEE; NANCY LEE). **2** a flea. [rhy. sl.]

rosie/rosy loader/loder *n.*[1] [20C] a whisky and soda (cf. MAJOR LODER). [rhy. sl.]

rosin *n.* **1** [mid-18C] liquor (cf. ROSINER). **2** [mid-19C] beer or other drink given to the musicians who entertain at a dance or party; thus *rosin*, to supply the musicians with drink. **3** [mid-19C] a fiddler, a violinist, also *rosin-the-bow*. [? SE *rosin*, a sticky material that is smeared on a violin string or bow, to facilitate its playing; fiddlers were assumed to be drinkers; or Irish *raisín*, a snack]

rosin-drunk *adj.* [20C] drunk. [? ROSIN or the rosy pinkness of the drunkard's cheeks and nose]

rosiner/rosner/rozner *n.* [20C] (Aus./Irish) any form of stiff drink, a pick-me-up. [Irish 20C; Aus. 1930s+; ROSIN n.(1) + sfx. -*er*]

rosin heel *n.* [19C] (US) a native of Florida (cf. BOGUE n.[1]). [ety. unknown; ? play on TARHEEL]

rosner *see* ROSINER.

rosy, the *n.* **1** [mid-19C] (red) wine. **2** [1930s+] tea (cf. ROSIE LEA).

rosy *adj.* [20C] drunk, tipsy. [one's pink face]

rosy lee *see* ROSIE LEA.

rosy loader/loder *see* ROSIE LOADER.

rosy palm and her five sisters/five little sisters *n.* [20C] the hand, as used in masturbation (cf. MISS FIST).

rot *n.* [mid-19C+] rubbish, nonsense; esp. in *talk rot*, to talk nonsense.

rot *v.* **1** [late 19C] to talk nonsense. **2** [late 19C–1930s] to tease heavily, to abuse, to denigrate. **3** [20C] to spoil, to interfere with, to ruin. **4** [1960s+] (US teen) to deride, to condemn e.g. *that rots* (cf. STINK v.; SUCK v.[2]). [ROT n.]

rot! *excl.*[1] [late 16C–late 19C] a general excl. of irritation, disbelief, dismissal, usu. in phr. *rot it! rot 'em! rot on!*

rot! *excl.*[2] [mid-19C+] nonsense! rubbish!

rot about *v.* [late 19C–1920s] (society) to laze around, to idle, to fool around. [ROT n.]

rotan *n.* [early 18C] (? Und.) a wheeled vehicle, esp. a cart. [? Lat. *rota*, a wheel]

rotary/rotary ho! *excl.* [1960s] (Aus.) fine! OK! (cf. RIGHTO!). [pun on SE *rotary hoe*]

rotgut *n.* **1** [late 16C+] cheap or inferior beer. **2** [19C+] (US) cheap whisky (cf. ARGEE). [its effects]

Rothschild *n.* [early 19C+] a very rich man (cf. VANDERBILT). [proper name of the Jewish banking family of *Rothschild*, the English branch of which was founded by Mayer Amschel *Rothschild* (1744–1812) of Frankfurt]

rotic *adj.* [1990s] (US campus) *romantic*, without the 'man' and thus used in a non-sexual context. [abbr. SE *romantic*, lit. without the 'man']

roti ou *n.* [1970s+] (S.Afr.) a Hindi speaker. [Hind. *roti*, bread (in the form of a chapatti) + OU]

rotten *adj.* **1** [late 19C+] in a very poor state, of a very bad quality, quite worthless. **2** [late 19C+] a general intensifier, e.g. *rotten luck, rotten bastard* etc. **3** [1930s+] (Aus.) very drunk; thus *get rotten*, to become very drunk (cf. ADDLED).

rotten apple *v.* [late 19C] (US) of an audience, to boo, hiss and generally give the actors a hard time. [the throwing of rotten fruit]

rotten guts *n.* [1910s–20s] a person who has bad breath.

rotten orange *n.* [late 17C] a pej. term for a follower of King William III (r.1688–1702). [pun on SE *rotten*, stale/*rotten*, unpleasant; William had been Prince of *Orange* before ascending the English throne]

rotten row *n.* **1** [late 19C] a bow. **2** [20C] a blow. [rhy. sl.; *Rotten Row* is a riding track, used by 19C fashionable society,

around Hyde Park; promenading on horseback 'in the Row' was a daily necessity for the smart]

rotten sheep *n.* [late 19C] **1** an unpleasant person. **2** (Irish) a traitor to the Fenian cause.

rotter *n.*[1] [late 19C+] a 'bad lot', a socially unacceptable person. [ROT n.]

rotter *n.*[2] [1930s+] (Aus.) an expert. [in sceptical eyes a talker of ROT n.]

rot the socks off, to *phr.* [1960s] to defeat comprehensively (cf. KNOCK THE SOCKS OFF).

rottie *n.* [1980s+] a Rottweiler dog (cf. DACHS). [abbr.]

rotto *n.* [late 19C] bad or second-rate liquor. [SE *rotten*]

rotto *adj.* [1920s] (Anglo-Irish) **1** drunk. **2** rotten, e.g. *rotto with money* (cf. LOUSY adj.[1]; STINKING adj.[2]). [ROTTEN]

rouf *n.* [mid-19C+] 4, 4 pence; thus 4 shillings, £4, £400, a 4-year prison term etc. [backsl.]

rouf-efil *see* ROFEFIL.

rouf gens *n.* [mid-19C] 4 shillings. [backsl.]

rouf yeneps *n.* [mid-19C] 4 pence. [backsl.]

rouge route *n.* [late 17C] London's 'red light district'. [Fr. *rouge route*, a red road]

rough *n.* [1940s+] **1** rough cider. **2** draught bitter beer.

rough *adj.*[1] [mid–late 19C] of foodstuffs, coarse, stale, 'off', decaying.

rough *adj.*[2] **1** [1940s+] unfair, unreasonable. **2** [1960s+] (US Black/campus) excellent, admirable, very good (cf. AWFUL adj.). **3** [1980s+] a general pej. [(2) on bad = good model]

rough and crusty *phr.* [1940s] (W.I.) pretty well, not so bad, in answer to the question 'How are you?' (cf. NOT SO DUSTY).

rough and ready/tumble *n.* [mid-19C] the vagina (cf. CATCH 'EM ALIVE-O).

rough around the edges *phr.* [20C] (orig. US) of people or objects, unfinished, crude or imperfect.

rough as a badger's arse/behind *phr.* [late 19C+] bristly, straggly, coarse.

rough as a bag/bags *phr.* [20C] (Aus./N.Z.) uncouth, illmannered. [abbr. SE *sandbag*]

rough as a cob *phr.* [1940s+] (US) very rough. [the use of corn *cobs* as toilet paper in country districts]

rough as a dog's breakfast *see* ROUGH AS A PIG'S BREAKFAST.

rough as a goat's knees *phr.* [20C] very rough.

rough as a pig's/dog's breakfast *phr.* [20C] (Aus./N.Z.) uncouth, ill-mannered (cf. ROUGH AS A BAG).

rough as a soojee bag *phr.* [mid-19C] (N.Z.) very rough. [Hind. *suji*, a flour based on Indian wheat, thus the bag that held it]

rough as bags *see* ROUGH AS A BAG.

rough as guts *phr.* [20C] (Aus./N.Z.) **1** lacking in refinement. **2** a phr. of admiration, praising the 'rough diamond' who may be vulgar but remains tough and ingenious and ultimately successful.

rough as old guts *phr.* [1940s+] of objects, very rough.

rough-ass *adj.* [20C] (US) crude, coarse.

rough as sacks *phr.* [1940s+] (N.Z.) very rough (cf. ROUGH AS A BAG).

rough bananas *n.* [1950s] (US) something that is very hard to achieve (cf. ROUGH END OF THE PINEAPPLE).

rough-dried hair *n.* [1930s–40s] (US Black) very kinky hair. [as opposed to blow-dried hair and thus neatened or even straightened]

rough end of the pineapple *n.* [1960s+] (Aus.) hostile or unfair treatment (cf. FUZZY END OF THE LOLLIPOP; ROUGH BANANAS).

roughey *see* ROUGHIE.

rough fam/fammy *n.* [early 19C] (Und.) a waistcoat pocket. [SE *rough* + FAM n.[1]; ? f. one's putting one's thumbs into the waistcoat pockets and the rubbing this entails]

rough-guts n. [1940s+] (N.Z.) a hooligan, an uncouth person [SE rough + guts]

roughhouse n. [late 19C+] (orig. US) 1 boisterous behaviour, usu. harmless. 2 physical violence.

roughhouse v. 1 [late 19C+] (orig. US) to fight, to beat up. 2 [late 19C+] (orig. US) to behave in a rowdy, boisterous manner. 3 [1960s+] (US) to enjoy the sleazier aspects of sex; to be a devotee of sado-masochism.

roughie/roughey/roughy n. (Aus./N.Z.) 1 [20C] any person or animal considered tough and intractable. 2 [1910s+] a fraud, a deception, esp. in phr. put a roughie over, to cheat. 3 [1910s+] in horse and dog racing, an outsider. 4 [1910s+] an implausible story. 5 [1910s] an unqualified or incompetent worker. [ROUGH adj.²]

rough it v. [mid-19C+] to live deprived of life's material comforts; not simply to be poor, but to volunteer oneself, as in camping, the forces etc, for such hardy existence.

rough malkin n. [late 17C–18C] the vagina (cf. CAT n.¹⁰). [SE rough + MALKIN]

roughneck n. [mid-19C+] (orig. US) 1 a thug, a hoodlum, a fighter. 2 a labourer on an oil rig.

roughneck adj. 1 [1980s+] a general pej. 2 [1990s] excellent, admirable, very good. [(2) on bad = good model (cf. BAD adj.; WICKED)]

rough-o n. [19C] the vagina (cf. CATCH 'EM ALIVE-O).

rough on adj. [mid-19C+] difficult for, unpleasant for, hard on.

rough on rats n. [late 19C] (Aus.) bad luck. [proper name Rough on Rats, a proprietary rat and vermin poison]

rough riding n. [20C] having unprotected sex (cf. BAREBACK).

rough spin n. [1920s–40s] (Aus.) 1 bad luck. 2 unfair treatment. [ROUGH adj.² + SPIN n.²; two-up imagery]

rough stuff n. 1 [1910s+] (orig. Aus.) physical violence. 2 [1960s+] (drugs) marijuana that contains a lot of unsmokeable debris.

rough trade n. [1930s+] (gay) a violent sexual partner; often a man who is, or poses as, a construction worker, serviceman, truck driver, motorcyclist etc, with appropriate costumes, often of leather.

rough trot n. [1960s] (Aus.) a period of bad luck. [SE rough + TROT n.² (5)]

rough-up n. [late 19C+] a street-fight, a violent fracas.

rough up v. [late 19C+] (US) to beat up, to injure, esp. to intimidate.

rough up the suspect, to phr. [1990s] to masturbate.

roughy see ROUGHIE.

roulie n. [1990s] (drugs) a cigarette made from a mix of marijuana and crack cocaine (cf. FIFTY-ONE). [ety. unknown; ? link to ROLLIE]

round see ROUNDS n.¹

round v.¹ [mid-19C] 1 to elicit information from someone by trickery. 2 to obtain information about someone by questioning a third party. [abbr. GET ROUND]

round/round on v.² [mid-19C+] 1 to inform against, to betray. 2 to become an informer. [SE round on, to turn against, to attack]

round adv. [1920s+] (of time) approximately, nearly, e.g. round nine o'clock.

round and square adv. [late 19C–1900s] everywhere. [rhy. sl.]

roundball n. [1970s+] (US Black) basketball (as opposed to football, played with an oval ball).

roundem n. [mid-19C–1900s] 1 a button. 2 the head. [ext. of SE round]

rounder n.¹ 1 [early 19C–1900s] (US) a pimp, a procurer. 2 [early 19C–1900s] (US) a rich, fashionable man-about-town, a playboy. [SE do the rounds/know one's way around]

rounder n.² [late 19C] a tight, short jacket.

rounder n.³ [late 19C+] (US Und.) an informer. [SE round on, to turn against]

rounder n.⁴ 1 [20C] (US Und.) a member of a prison gang, esp. of an Italian gang. 2 [1960s+] (Can. prison) anyone familiar with the underworld. [one who has 'been around']

rounders n. [20C] (W.I.) confusion, trouble. [events have fig. 'turned around' on the sufferer + the image of the running in a game of SE rounders]

roundeye n. 1 [1950s+] the anus (cf. DEAD-EYE DICK). 2 [1960s+] a White person, as opposed to an East Asian person (cf. SLANT n.³). [(2) metonymy]

round file n. [1970s+] (orig. US) a wastepaper basket.

roundhead n.¹ [late 19C+] (US) an immigrant from northern Europe, esp. a Swede. [? physiognomy]

roundhead n.² [20C] (usu. teen) 1 a circumcised penis. 2 the boy or man who has a circumcised penis (cf. CAVALIER; CLIPPED adj.²).

roundhead n.³ [1970s+] (drugs) any drug contained in a capsule with curved ends.

roundheel/roundheeler/roundheels n. [1920s+] (US) 1 an inferior prize-fighter. 2 a promiscuous woman. [both of them fall over easily; the image is of pivoting on the rounded heel]

roundheeled adj. [1920s+] (US) 1 easily defeated. 2 of a woman, promiscuous. [ROUNDHEEL]

roundhouse n. [1920s+] a blow delivered with a wide sweep of the arm.

roundhouse v.¹ [1920s+] to hit someone with a wide sweep of the arm. [ROUNDHOUSE n.]

roundhouse v.² [1960s+] (US) of a prostitute, to lick, suck and otherwise stimulate every orifice and erogenous zone her client has to offer (cf. AROUND THE WORLD).

roundie n. [1940s+] (N.Z.) a factory-made cigarette.

round me/the houses n. [mid-19C+] trousers (cf. TERRACE). [rhy. sl.]

round mouth n. [early 19C] the anus. [abbr. BROTHER ROUND MOUTH]

round mys n. [late 19C–1900s] trousers. [abbr. ROUND ME HOUSES]

round o n. [17C] a great lie. [the oh! of disbelief it elicits]

round on see ROUND v.².

round pussy n. [20C] (US) the anus (cf. ROUNDEYE). [SE round + PUSSY n.¹]

round robin n. 1 [mid-16C–17C] the host (in communion). 2 [mid-18C+] a complainant, a petitioner. 3 [late 19C] a swindle. [SE round robin, a document, typically a complaint or petition, in which the signatories place their names in a circle, thus hiding any form of hierarchy]

rounds/round n.¹ [mid-19C] shirt collars. [abbr. all rounds, all rounders, trade names of fashionable collars]

rounds n.² [late 19C] trousers. [abbr. ROUND ME HOUSES]

round shaving n. [late 19C–1920s] a telling-off, a scolding.

rounds of the kitchen n. [20C] (Ulster) a thrashing. [the victim is beaten up and down the room]

round the bend phr. [1920s+] eccentric, crazy, insane; ext. as [1950s+] round the bend – and back again; [1950s+] round the bend – and halfway down the straight (cf. AROUND THE BEND; HARPIC).

round the corner phr.¹ 1 [mid-19C+] of a person or place, nearby; thus euph. used by those going for a drink, I'm just going round the corner... 2 [1910s+] of an upcoming event, imminent.

round the corner, to phr.² [1960s+] to be 'one up' on one's peers whether through honest methods or otherwise. [one has already 'gone on ahead']

round the horn phr. [20C] (US Und.) detained on a minor criminal charge but suspected of a more serious crime. [ety. unknown]

round the houses *see* ROUND ME HOUSES.

round the johnny/johnny horner *phr.* [1900s] round the corner, i.e. at a public house. [JOHNNIE N.⁷/JOHNNY HORNER]

round the twist *phr.* [1960s+] mad, eccentric, insane. [var. on ROUND THE BEND]

round the world for threepence/fourpence/ninepence *phr.* [1980s+] (N.Z.) drinking methylated spirits. [the effects and cheap price]

round up *v.* [1920s+] (orig. US) to assemble, to get together.

rouse *n.* [17C] a large glass. [? SE *carouse*, or Ger. *rausch*, intoxication, drunken fit]

rouse/roust/rouse on *v.* [late 19C+] (Aus.) to scold, to berate; thus *get roused on*, to be scolded. [Scot. *roust*, to roar, bellow]

rouser *n.*¹ [19C] a womanizer. [? SE *arouse*]

rouser *n.*² [19C] the first drink of the day, used as a 'pick-me-up' (cf. ALLEVIATOR).

rouser *n.*³ [1970s+] (drugs) any type of amphetamine or stimulant drug which 'gets one up' (cf. A N.²).

rouse on *see* ROUSE.

rouse the possum *see* STIR THE POSSUM.

rousie *n.* [20C] (Aus.) a general hand on a rural property. [SE *rouseabout*]

roust *n.*¹ [late 16C–early 17C] sexual intercourse. [ROUST V.¹]

roust *n.*² [20C] (orig. US Und.) an arrest. [ROUST V.³ (3)]

roust *v.*¹ [late 16C–early 17C] to have sexual intercourse. [SE *roust*, to roar, to bellow]

roust *v.*² *see* ROUSE V.

roust *v.*³ (US) **1** [1900s] (Und.) to jostle, as in picking a pocket. **2** [1930s+] to raid an establishment. **3** [1930s+] to arrest. **4** [1970s+] (Black) to harass, esp. of the police. **5** [1970s+] (campus) to tease, to harass. [SE *roust*, to stir, to wake up, to arouse]

rout *v.* [1970s] (US campus) to engage in sexual intercourse. [SE *rout*, to poke about]

router *n.* [19C] (Scot.) a cow, thus *router-putters*, hooves. [dial. *rout*, to low (as cattle)]

routine *n.* [1920s+] (US) an evasive or contrived response. [show business jargon *routine*, a carefully rehearsed act]

Rover *n.* [late 19C] (US) an inhabitant of Colorado. [ety. unknown]

Row, the *n.*¹ **1** [early 17C] Goldsmith's Row. **2** [19C] Rotten Row. **3** [mid-19C] Paternoster Row, EC4 the centre of London publishing. **4** [mid-19C] Booksellers Row, euph. for Holywell St, WC., the contemporary pornography centre.

row *n.*² [mid-18C+] a disturbance, a noisy quarrel; thus *what's the row?*, what's all the noise about?; *hold your row*, be quiet. [virtually SE today, *row* began as sl. and is cited as 'a very low expression' in Todd's revision of Johnson's *Dictionary* (1818)]

row *n.*³ [1980s+] (US drugs) a small quantity of a narcotic, esp. cocaine. [var. on LINE N.⁴]

row *v.* **1** [late 18C] to rouse up by making a noise. **2** [late 18C–mid-19C] to attack or assail a person in a rough manner. **3** [early 19C] to criticize sharply or severely. **4** [19C+] to scold a person angrily or severely, to take sharply to task. **5** [late 19C+] to make a row or disturbance, to quarrel noisily or heatedly. [ROW N.²]

row back from *v.* [1970s+] to avoid trouble.

row-de-dow *n.* [mid-late 19C] an argument, a row, a set-to. [ext. of ROW N.²]

rowdy *n.* [mid-19C] money, one of those words implying the efforts involved in obtaining money (cf. BUSTLE N.¹; SCRAMBLE N.¹; SCRATCH N.²). [note Thackeray's fictitious bankers, *Rowdy and Stump*, a firm who can also be found in Cuthbert Bede's *Adventures of Mr Verdant Green* (1853)]

rowdy-dow *adj.* [mid-19C] socially unacceptable, vulgar, noisy, rough. [redup. of SE *rowdy*, rough, disorderly]

rower *n.* [1980s+] (prison) an argument. [ROW N.²]

row in *v.* (Und.) **1** [late 19C+] to allow someone to join a scheme, a conspiracy. **2** [1960s+] to implicate a suspect in a crime; thus *row out*, to exonerate a suspect from a crime.

row in the boat/row in the same boat, to *phr.* [late 18C+] to join, to take shares with.

rowl *n.* [19C] money. [? SE *royal*, i.e. the portraits of monarchs found on coins and notes]

row oneself onto *v.* [1940s+] to associate oneself with a group.

row someone up Salt River, to *phr.* [early 19C–1940s] (US) to defeat (a political opponent); to overcome, send to oblivion (cf. ROW UP SALT RIVER). [? *Salt River roarer*, a backwards, unsophisticated country dweller (poss. from Kentucky, where there is an actual Salt River)]

row up *v.* [late 19C] to wake up someone roughly and noisily. [ROW N.²]

row up Salt River, to *phr.* [early 19C–1940s] (US) to become drunk, i.e. to send oneself 'to oblivion' (cf. ROW SOMEONE UP SALT RIVER). [? *Salt River roarer*, a backwards, unsophisticated country dweller (poss. from Kentucky, where there is an actual Salt River)]

row with one oar, to *phr.* [20C] (US) to be irrational or stupid (cf. NOT ALL THERE; NOT HAVING BOTH OARS IN THE WATER).

rox/roxanne *n.* [1980s+] (drugs) **1** cocaine. **2** crack cocaine. [ROCKS N.⁴]

roy *n.* [1960s–70s] (Aus.) a chic, sophisticated, 'trendy' Australian (cf. ALF; OCKER). [a stereotypically 'smart' name]

royal *n.*¹ [late 18C+] a member of a royal family.

royal *n.*² [20C] **1** (W.I./Jam.) any Black person from a race other than West Indian (cf. RIAL). **2** (W.I.) a mixed Black/Chinese person. **3** (US Black) a West Indian. [? fig. use of Sp. *real*, a coin of very low value and considered inferior to UK sterling; such individuals have low social status; the US use is prob. ignorant of such overtones]

royal *n.*³ [20C] (W.I./Trin.) the buttocks. [for ety. *see* ROYAL N.²; in this case the physical 'lowness' of the buttocks]

royal/boss's royal *n.*⁴ [1930s–60s] (N.Z.) a management stooge.

royal *adj.* [1950s+] (orig. US) a general intensifier, often used before so-called taboo terms, e.g. *a royal screwing*, *a royal shafting* (cf. ROYALLY). [SE *royal*, pertaining to a royal family]

royal alberts *n.* [mid-late 19C] (Aus.) **1** strips of cloth (usu. calico and rubbed with suet to cut down possible chafing) used as a substitute for socks, usu. by tramps. **2** rough, lace-up boots (cf. ALBERTS). [joc. ref. to Prince *Albert* (1819–61), consort of Queen Victoria; the use came from the myth that before his marriage, Albert was so poor that he was forced to use *toerags* instead of proper socks]

royal blues *n.* [1970s] (drugs) LSD. [the pills are blue]

royal bob *n.* [18C] gin (cf. ROYAL POVERTY). [ety. unknown]

royal boozer *n.* [mid-19C–1930s] a heavy drinker. [ROYAL adj. + BOOZER N. (2)]

royal docks *n.* [20C] venereal disease. [rhy. sl. *royal docks* = POX N.¹]

royal fucking/r.f. *n.* [1950s+] (US) harsh or very bad treatment. [ROYAL adj. + FUCKING N.]

royalie/royaly *n.* [1900s–20s] (Aus.) an effeminate young man, a homosexual. [play on QUEAN N. (2)/QUEEN N.¹]

royally *adv.* [mid-19C+] extremely, very, e.g. *royally drunk*.

royal mail *n.* [20C] (mainly Und.) bail. [rhy. sl.]

royal navy *n.* [20C] gravy. [rhy. sl.]

royal order, the *n.* [1920s+] (Aus.) dismissal from one's job. [abbr. *royal order of the sack*]

royal poverty *n.* [mid-late 18C] gin. [gin may be drunk when one is 'feeling right royal' but it will lead to poverty]

royal repose *n.* [mid-late 19C] the Queen's Bench prison.

royal scamp *n.* [late 18C–early 19C] a highwayman who specializes in robbing rich victims and in causing them no physical harm (cf. SCAMP n.). [the highwayman more of romantic fiction rather than of the recorded type]

royal shaft/shafting *n.* [1950s+] an act of extreme harshness or unfairness, as meted out on oneself or to another person.

royalty *n.* [1980s+] (drugs) cocaine. [its superior ranking in the hierarchy of drugs]

royaly *see* ROYALIE.

roy rodgers *n.* [20C] second-rate builders. [rhy. sl. *roy rogers* = *bodgers*; ult. film cowboy *Roy Rogers* (1912–98)]

royster *see* ROISTER.

roz *n.* [1980s+] (drugs) crack cocaine. [ROCKS n.⁴]

rozner *see* ROSINER.

rozzer *n.*¹ [late 19C+] policeman (cf. ROOSHER). [? Rom. *roozlo*, strong or *roast*, a villain]

rozzer *n.*² [1970s] (US Black) a rubber contraceptive with small protrusions for extra stimulation of the vagina. [? SE *arouser/rouser*]

r.s. *see* RATSHIT n.

r/s *phr.* [1970s+] used in sex contact advertisements, rough stuff, i.e. sadomasochism, urolagnia, piercing and rubber-wear. [abbr.]

R2 *n.* [1990s] (drugs) Rohypnol (cf. ROOFIES). [initial letter; ? ref. to robot *R2-D2* in *Star Wars* films]

rub *n.*¹ [late 17C–early 19C] a round or rubber of a card-game, usu. whist. [abbr. SE *rubber*]

rub *n.*² [late 18C–early 19C] an impediment. [bowls jargon *rub*, an obstacle hindering the ball's smooth progress across the green]

rub *n.*³ **1** [1920s+] (US) a dance, typified by the overt sexuality and physical proximity of the partners (cf. BELLY RUB; RUB JOINT; TOUGH DANCING). **2** [1950s] (W.I.) a dance or dancing party (cf. RUB-UP n.²).

rub/rub to *v.*¹ [late 17C–early 18C] (Und.) to carry off to gaol, to imprison. [SE *rub*, to go]

rub *v.*² **1** [1920s+] (US) to steal, to burglarize. **2** [1970s] (US Black) to criticize.

rub-a-dub/rub-a-dub-a-dub-dub/ruddity dub *n.*¹ [late 19C+] **1** a pub or public house. **2** a nightclub or social club. **3** a 'sub' or advance on wages. [rhy. sl.]

rub-a-dub *n.*² [1950s] (US) sexual intercourse; esp. quick and spontaneous. [SE *rub-a-dub*, the beat of a drum]

rubacrock/rubbacrock *n.* [19C] a dirty, lazy woman. [dial.]

rubbed *adj.* [20C] murdered, killed. [RUB OUT v. (1)]

rubbed down with the Book, to be *phr.* [late 19C] to take an oath on the Bible.

rubbed off *adj.* [late 17C–18C] (Und.) bankrupt and thus run away. [SE *rub*, to run away]

rubbed out *adj.* **1** [mid-19C] dead. **2** [20C] murdered. [the 19C use has no implication of foul play, one has simply been erased from the 'Book of Life']

rubbedy/rubberdy/rubbidy/rubbity/rubby/rupperty *n.* [late 19C+] (Aus.) a public house. [RUB-A-DUB n.¹ (1)]

rub belly *n.* [18C–19C] sexual intercourse.

rubber *n.*¹ **1** [16C] (Und.) a member of a team of confidence tricksters who works as a back-up to those running the fraud; if the victim realizes they are being tricked, the rubber swiftly causes a disturbance, usually by picking a fight with the earn-est bystander, thus allowing their confederates to grab the stakes and run. **2** [early 17C–mid-19C] any form of deception or trick. [? SE *rub* (*up against*); ? link to the sporting use, coined in the 16C, meaning a match, adopted in the 17C as a quarrel or fight]

rubber/India rubber *n.*² [mid-19C+] (US) a rubber overshoe or galosh.

rubber *n.*³ [20C] (US Und.) a professional killer. [RUB OUT v. (1)]

rubber *n.*⁴ [1940s–50s] (US Black) a car. [its tyres]

rubber *n.*⁵ [1940s+] (orig. US) a contraceptive sheath (cf. RUB-BER JOHNNY). [the thin rubber from which such sheaths are made]

rubber *v.* (US) **1** [late 19C+] to look around, to gaze at. **2** [1920s–50s] to eavesdrop on someone else's conversation (feasible in the era of party line telephones). [RUBBERNECK n.]

rubber boot *n.* [1970s+] a contraceptive sheath. [ext. of RUB-BER n.⁵]

rubber cheque/kite *n.* [1920s+] a cheque that is not hon-oured by the writer's bank. [SE *rubber* + *cheque/*KITE n.² (3); it 'bounces']

rubber-chicken circuit *n.* [1950s+] (US) the after-dinner-speaking circuit; esp. as followed by political hopefuls. [the poor quality of the food (almost always chicken) on offer]

Rubber City *n.* [1970s] (US) Akron, Ohio. [tyre-making, its primary industry]

rubber dick *v.* [1970s+] to fool, to con, to hoax. [SE *rubber* + DICK n.⁵ (1) = a dildo, i.e. a fake penis]

rubber dollies *n.* [1970s+] (Irish) plimsolls, gymshoes, trainers. [dial. *dollies*, rags]

rubber drink *n.* [20C] (US) a drink which causes vomiting. [it 'bounces back']

rubber duck *n.*¹ [20C] sexual intercourse. [rhy. sl. *rubber duck* = FUCK n.¹]

rubber duck/rubber duckie *n.*² [1980s+] (Aus./S.Afr./US) a small, inflatable rubber boat. [Aus./US prefer the sfx. *-ie*]

rubberdy *see* RUBBEDY.

rubber heel *n.* [1940s+] **1** (US) a private detective (cf. GUM-SHOE n.). **2** someone who spies on their fellow employees; thus *rubber heel boy*, *rubber heel inquiry*, *rubber-heel mob*. [note police jargon *rubber heels*, (1) the Special Branch, (2) the internal investigations department of Scotland Yard, policing the police]

rubber johnny *n.* [1950s+] a contraceptive sheath. [RUBBER n.⁵ + JOHNNIE n.¹¹]

rubber kite *see* RUBBER CHEQUE.

rubber knackers *n.* [20C] a cheeky fellow. [SE *rubber* + KNACKERS; ? they keep 'bouncing back']

rubberneck/rubbernecker *n.* [late 19C+] (orig. US) **1** a tourist, esp. to New York City (cf. BOING-BOING). **2** a very in-quisitive, curious person. [RUBBERNECK v.¹]

rubberneck *v.*¹ [late 19C+] to act as an obvious tourist (cf. BOING-BOING). [visitors to New York City craning their necks to view the high buildings]

rubberneck *v.*² [1970s] (US Black) to masturbate, to self-fellate (if one is acrobatically capable). [joc. use of RUBBERNECK v.¹ + SE *rub*]

rubbernecker *see* RUBBERNECK n.

rubber pill *n.* [1950s] (drugs) a condom or the finger of a rubber glove used to store or transport narcotics.

rubber queen *n.* [1960s+] (orig. gay) a rubber fetishist. [SE *rubber* + QUEEN n.¹]

rubber tramp *v.* [1920s] (US) to live as a vagrant. [? image of bouncing from place to place + pun on SE *rubber-stamp*]

rubberneck wagon *n.* [late 19C+] (US) a sightseeing bus. [RUBBERNECK (1) + SE *wagon*]

rubber sock *n.* [20C] (US tramp) a timid person. [? the limp-ness of such a supposed garment]

rubbidy *see* RUBBEDY.

rubbin' one's nubbin *phr.* [20C] masturbating.

rubbish *n.* **1** [mid-19C] money (cf. DUST n.¹). **2** [1940s+] (S.Afr.) an unpleasant person.

rubbish *adj.* [1970s+] inferior, second-rate.

rubbish *v.* [1950s+] (orig. Aus.) **1** to attack verbally, to slander. **2** to treat badly, with disrespect. [i.e. to talk *rubbish* about, to treat like *rubbish*]

rubbity n.[1] *see* RUBBEDY.

rubbity n.[2] *see* RUB-A-DUB n.[1]

rubblehead n. [20C] a fool, an idiot, an incompetent. [SE *rubble* + sfx. -HEAD (1)]

rubby n. *see* RUBBEDY.

rubby-dub/rubby-dubby n. **1** [20C] cheap alcohol, or some substance, e.g. paint-thinner, bay-rum, that can substitute. **2** [1920s+] (Can./US) a drinker of such liquids. [? RUB-A-DUB n.[1] and/or joc. ref. to SE *rubbing alcohol*]

rub down v. **1** [late 19C–1920s] to scold, to reprimand. **2** [late 19C+] (orig. US) to search a person's clothes and body, either for security reasons or as a preliminary to picking their pocket. [RUB v.[2]]

rub down with an oaken cudgel/towel, to phr. [late 18C–early 19C] to thrash, to beat. [SE *rub down* + OAKEN CUDGEL]

rube n.[1] [late 19C+] (US) **1** a rustic, a farmer (cf. ALVIN). **2** a fool, an unsophisticated person (cf. HEY RUBE!). [the 'rustic' name *Reuben*]

rube n.[2] [1920s+] (Aus.) something seen as exceptional, first-rate etc. [? ironic view of RUBE n.[1]]

Rube Goldberg n. [1910s+] a very complicated thing, machine or arrangement. [the intricate machine drawings of cartoonist *Rube Goldberg* (1888–1970)]

rub elbows/rub elbows with, to phr. [20C] (US) to mix and mingle with people in a social or public context.

rub fat into the sow's arse, to phr. [20C] (Irish) to 'gild the lily'. [joc. use of sl. imagery]

rubies n. [1940s] (US Black) the lips, esp. large or full lips. [? a full-lipped film-star (cf. RUBY n.)]

rubigo n. [16C] (Scot.) the penis. [? Lat. *ruber*, red]

rub in v. [mid-19C+] to emphasize, often with malicious pleasure; thus [late 19C] (Und.) *rub it in well*, to give (true or false) evidence that will certainly lead to a conviction.

rub it up the wrong way, to phr. [1990s] to masturbate. [ext. of RUB UP v.[1] (1)]

rub joint n. [1910s–40s] a low dance-hall, which features dances such as the *lovers' two-step*, the *bunny hug* and the *turkey trot*, all of which permit much more physical intimacy than those on offer at more staid establishments (cf. BELLY RUB; TOUGH DANCING). [RUB n.[3] + JOINT n.[3] (3)]

rub-off n. [19C+] **1** masturbation. **2** sexual intercourse. [RUB OFF v.]

rub off v. [19C] **1** to masturbate (cf. BEAT OFF). **2** to have sexual intercourse (cf. RUB UP v.).

rub offal v. [1990s] to have sexual intercourse (cf. JOIN GIBLETS).

rub out v. **1** [mid-19C+] (orig. US) to murder, to assassinate, to kill. **2** [20C] (Aus.) to debar, to ban (a person). **3** [1920s+] (Aus.) to reject an idea or a suggestion.

rub parlor n. [1960s+] (US) a massage parlour.

rub the rod, to phr. [20C] to masturbate. [SE *rub* + ROD n.[1] (1)]

rub to *see* RUB v.[1]

rub-up n.[1] **1** [mid-17C; 19C+] an act of sexual intercourse. **2** [19C+] stimulating another's genitals. **3** [19C+] masturbation. [RUB UP v.[1]]

rub-up n.[2] [1950s] (W.I.) a dance or dancing party. [RUB n.[3] (2)]

rub up v.[1] **1** [mid-17C; 19C+] to stimulate the penis to erection using the hands. **2** [19C+] to stimulate the vagina. **3** [19C+] to masturbate. [the apparent gap between uses of (1) is prob. due to the lack of printed citations]

rub up v.[2] [late 17C+] to revise, to refresh one's memory. [the image of cleaning something tarnished]

rub up the wrong way, to phr. [mid-19C+] to annoy, to infuriate. [stroking a cat against the 'grain' of its fur]

ruby n. [1950s–60s] (camp gay) a man with large, prominent lips. [? filmstar *Ruby* Keeler (1909–93)]

ruby-dazzler n. [1940s+] (Aus./N.Z.) something exceptional. [var. on BOBBY-DAZZLER]

rubyfruit n. [1960s+] the female genitals. [the colour and supposed appearance; best known as title of novel *Rubyfruit Jungle* (1973) by Rita Mae Brown (b.1944)]

Ruby Murray n. [1970s+] a curry. [rhy. sl.; the popular singer *Ruby Murray* (1935–96)]

ruby note n. [1920s] a 10-shilling note. [the colour]

ruby red n. [1900s] the head. [rhy. sl.]

ruby rose n. [20C] the nose. [rhy. sl.]

ruca n. [1950s–60s] (US teen gang) a female gang-member. [Sp. *ruca*, old lady]

ruck n.[1] **1** [late 19C] (US) nonsense, rubbish. **2** [1920s] a cigarette end. [SE *ruck*, the general run of things, the undistinguished crowd]

ruck n.[2] [1950s+] an argument, a fight, esp. a gang fight; thus *rucker*, a fighter. [? SE *ruckus*]

ruck v.[1] **1** [late 19C–1930s] to get angry with. **2** [late 19C+] to lay information against, to inform on. **3** [20C] to scold, to tell off. [? SE *ruck*, to disturb, orig. clothes and thence tempers]

ruck v.[2] **1** [1950s+] to involve oneself in a gang fight. **2** [1960s–70s] to masturbate. [RUCK n.[2]]

ruck and row n. [20C] an unpleasant woman. [rhy. sl. *ruck and row* = COW n.[1] (1)]

rucker n. [1950s+] an arguer, a combative person. [RUCK v.[2]]

ruckerky adj. [late 19C] (society) choice, rare. [deliberate mispron. of synon. Fr. *recherché*]

rucking n. [1950s+] a severe reprimand. [RUCK v.[1] (3)]

ruck on v. **1** [late 19C] to betray, to abandon one's loyalty to, to go back on. **2** [1930s] to quarrel with. [RUCK v.[1]]

ruction/ructions n. [early 19C+] disturbances, riots; disorderly disputes or quarrels; with implications of unpleasant consequences. [? SE *insurrection*; note the Irish Insurrection of 1798, known locally as the *ruction*]

ructious adj. [early 19C+] (US) turbulent, harrowing. [RUCTION]

rudder n. **1** [19C] the penis (cf. STERNPOST). **2** [20C] an animal's, usu. a dog's tail.

ruddity dub *see* RUB-A-DUB n.[1]

ruddock/robin ruddock n. [mid-16C–early 17C] a gold coin; in pl. money, often extended as [early 17C] *red ruddock, golden ruddock*. [SE *ruddock*, a robin redbreast, i.e. the 'red' colour of the golden money]

ruddy adj. [1910s+] a general intensifier, a euph. synon. for BLOODY.

rude adj.[1] [1950s+] sexual (cf. IN THE RUDE). [euph.]

rude adj.[2] [1980s+] (US campus) **1** excellent, admirable. **2** unfair, distasteful, offensive, generally poor, flagrantly bad.

rude!/rudeness! excl. [1980s+] (US campus) how rude! (cf. HOW RUDENESS!).

rude boy/rude bwoy/rudie/rody n. (orig. W.I.) **1** [1960s+] 'a young, Black Jamaican male who is an aggressive social dropout; he may be a ghetto type, a gang type or one who adopts some Rastafarian cultist habits' (Allsopp). **2** [1960s+] someone who poses as such a 'drop-out' but is in fact more middle-class. **3** [1970s+] young people, of any colour, who like W.I. music, typically blue-beat, rock-steady and ska; the term was revived in the early 1980s for fans of Two-Tone music (itself reviving the old blue-beat, etc). [ext. use + W.I. pron. of SE *rude boy*]

rude gal/girl n. [1960s+] (W.I./UK Black teen) the female equivalent of the RUDE BOY.

rudeness n. [20C] (W.I.) sexual intercourse; thus *do rudeness*, to have sex.

rudeness! *see* RUDE!

rude parts n. [1970s+] the genitals, both male or female (in the latter case extended to breasts also) (cf. NAUGHTY BITS). [euph.]

rudesby *n.* [19C] an unpleasant, boorish person. [SE *rude* + sfx. *-by*]

rudie *see* RUDE BOY.

rudolph *n.* [1990s] a red-nose, gained through drinking (cf. BARDOLPH). [the Christmas song 'Rudolph, the red-nosed reindeer']

ruff *n.* [1940s] (US Black) 25 cents, a quarter. [ety. unknown]

ruffelar/ruffeler *see* RUFFLER.

ruffer *n.* [late 19C] a rough person, a thug.

ruffian *n.*[1] [late 17C–18C] a justice of the peace.

ruffian *n.*[2] [late 17C–18C] an assassin, a murderous thug.

ruffian cly thee!, the *excl.* [16C] (Und.) an excl. meaning 'the Devil take thee'. [RUFFIN + CLY]

Ruffian's Hall *see* RUFFIN'S HALL.

Ruffin, the/Old Ruffin *n.* [mid-16C–early 19C] the Devil (cf. OLD RUFFIAN). [SE *ruffian*, rogue + 13C SE *Ruffin*, the name of a specific demon]

Ruffin's/Ruffian's Hall *n.* [late 16C–late 17C] that area of London, now Smithfield, where trials of skill were held amongst 'ordinary, Ruffianly people, with Sword and Buckler' (T. Blount, *Glossographia*, 1674), thus phr. [mid-17C–mid-19C] *he is only fit for Ruffian's Hall*, used of an overdressed apprentice.

rufflar *see* RUFFLER.

ruffle *n.*[1] [1950s+] (gay) the passive partner in a lesbian relationship. [? RUFUS *n.*[1]]

ruffle *n.*[2] [1970s] (US Black) a fight.

ruffler/ruffelar/ruffeler/rufflar/ruffleer/rufler *n.* [16C–early 19C] (Und.) a villain, of the 'first rank of canters', who posed as a discharged soldier (and might indeed have been one, though equally likely might have been a former servant), but actually worked as an itinerant robber (cf. CANTING CREW). [SE *ruffle it*, to swagger; it is linked to the idea of a bird ruffling up its feathers]

ruffles *n.*[1] [late 18C–mid-19C] (Und.) handcuffs. [? ironic use of SE *ruff*]

ruffles *n.*[2] *see* ROOFIES.

ruffmans *n.* (Und.) **1** [16C–mid-19C] the woods or bushes (cf. CRACKMANS). **2** [17C] the eaves of a house. [SE *rough* (as in ground) + sfx. *-MAN*]

ruff neck *n.* [1980s+] (W.I./UK Black teen) a rebellious person; a bohemian; a person with a couldn't-care-less attitude. [deliberate mis-sp. of ROUGHNECK *n.*]

ruff peck *n.* [16C–early 18C] (Und.) bacon. [SE *rough* + PECK *n.*[1] (1); lit. 'rough food']

rufler *see* RUFFLER.

rufus *n.*[1] **1** [19C] the female genitals (cf. RED ACE). **2** [1950s] a red-head. [Lat. *rufus*, red]

rufus *n.*[2] [1900s–50s] (US) a country person, a peasant (cf. RUBE *n.*[1]). [the 'rustic' name]

rug/rughead *n.*[1] [20C] (US) a Black person. [the texture of Black hair]

rug *n.*[2] [1940s–60s] (Aus.) a £1 note. [? RAG *n.*[3]]

rug *n.*[3] [1940s+] (orig. US) a wig, a toupee, a hairpiece, esp. in show business. [it lies on/covers one's bald patch]

rug ape *n.* [1970s+] (US) a small child (cf. CARPET RAT; RUG RAT).

rug beat *n.* [1920s–50s] (US Black) a noisy, festive party where the dancing 'beats the rug'.

rugby team *n.* [1940s+] (bingo) the number 15. [the 15 members of a rugby team]

rug cut *see* CUT THE RUG.

rug cutter *n.* [1920s–50s] (US Black) a good and energetic dancer. [CUT THE RUG]

rugged *adj.* [1940s+] of activity, tough, difficult.

rugged up *adj.* [1990s] (Aus.) wearing warm clothes. [SE *rug*]

rugger *n.* [late 19C+] rugby football, usu. Rugby Union. [SE *rugby* + 'Oxford' sfx. *-er*]

rugger bugger/r.b. *n.* [1950s+] a dedicatedly masculine man, whose lack of sensitivity is more than compensated for by his enthusiasm for all forms of sport. [RUGGER + BUGGER *n.*[1] (1)]

ruggins/ruggins's *n.* [early–mid-19C] in bed (cf. AT RUG). [one is under the SE *rug*]

ruggsy/warry *adj.* [1980s+] (orig. milit.) used of a consciously 'macho' image, featuring torn T-shirts, faded fatigues, large boots and larger muscles. [SE *rugged/war*]

ruggy *adj.* [mid-19C] fusty, frowsy. [the warmth and cosiness of being wrapped in a *rug*]

rughead *see* RUG *n.*[1].

rug joint *n.* [late 19C] (US) an elegant, expensive restaurant, patronized by the wealthy (cf. SAWDUST JOINT). [SE *rug*, a carpet + JOINT *n.*[3] (3); such restaurants were as distinguished by the splendours of their interior decoration as by their menus]

rug-muncher *see* CARPET-MUNCHER *n.*[2].

rug rat *n.* [1970s+] a small child who is still crawling on the carpet (cf. ANKLE-BITER *n.*[2]; RUG APE).

rug's the word *phr.* [early 18C] everything is fine, all is safe; thus [late 19C–1900s] *ruggy*, safe. [? the security of a *rug*]

rug up *v.* [1990s] (Aus.) to dress warmly.

rugy *n.* [1970s+] (US Black) unattractive; ill-tempered. [? elision of *rude guy*]

ruin *n.* [19C] cheap, inferior gin (cf. BLUE RUIN; MOTHER'S RUIN).

ruin *v.* [1950s+] (gay) to deliberately exaggerate one's effeminacy as a shock tactic.

ruin and spoil *n.* [20C] oil. [rhy. sl.]

ruined *adj.* [1960s+] (orig. US Black) **1** beaten, injured. **2** drunk, under the influence of drugs (cf. SMASHED; WASTED *adj.*).

rukadung *see* ROOGODUNG.

rulable *adj.* [late 19C] (US) permissible. [it 'falls within the rules']

rule 43 *n.* [1950s+] (prison) voluntary solitary confinement for the sake of a prisoner's safety; child molesters, rapists etc choose this in preference to the natural justice of their peers.

rule of three *n.* **1** [18C] the male genitals. **2** [19C] sexual intercourse. [SE *rule* + *three*, i.e. the penis and testicles]

Rules *n.* [1940s+] (Aus.) Australian *Rules* Football. [abbr.]

—rules/rules OK *phr.* [1970s] the text of a graffitto proclaiming the excellence of a star, a local gang etc, e.g. *Eric rules OK*.

rum *n.*[1] [mid-18C] (Irish) an impoverished rural clergyman. [ety. unknown; ? RUM *adj.*[2]]

rum *n.*[2] [1950s–60s] (US Black) **1** a fool, a dupe, a victim. **2** a drunkard. [abbr. RUMMY *n.*[1]]

rum/room *adj.* **1** [mid-16C–early 19C] (Und.) excellent, first-rate. **2** [late 18C+] odd, peculiar, strange, thus [early 19C] *rummily*, oddly, *rumminess*, eccentricity, *rummish*, strange, odd. [most probably from SE *Rome* (and indeed could be spelled 'rome' until the 18C), which, as a city, meant glory and grandeur. Other origins include the Romany *rom*, a male gypsy, or the Turkish *Röm*, a gypsy, many of whom passed through the Ottoman Empire. Reversing the process, the Latin *Roma* (Rome) is cognate with the Teutonic root *hruod* (fame) (as found in the names Roger and Roderick) which appears in the German *Ruhm* (fame). Since early 18C (as first noted in the *New Canting Dictionary* 1725) *rum* has reversed its meaning, now defined as odd, eccentric or suspect. As such it can be seen as the ancestor of the bad = good constructions, e.g. WICKED, NASTY *adj.*[1] and BAD *adj.* itself, now so common]

rumba *n.* (US) [1930s] **1** a spree, a celebration, a party. **2** a fight, esp. a gang fight (cf. RUMBLE *n.*[2]).

rum bag *n.* [20C] (US) a drunk.

rum beck/beak *n.* [early 17C– early 19C] (Und.) a justice of the peace. [RUM *adj.* (1) + BECK *n.*/BEAK *n.*[1] (1)]

rum bite n. **1** [late 17C–early 19C] (Und.) a clever trick, a cunning ploy. **2** [early 19C] a clever fraud or confidence trickster. [RUM adj. (1) + BITE n.^{2}]

rumble n.^{1} **1** [1910s+] a tip-off, an alarm (during the course of a crime). **2** [1960s+] (US) a rumour. [ROMBOYLE v.]

rumble n.^{2} **1** [1930s+] (US) a street gang fight. **2** [1940s+] a fight. **3** [1980s+] (US drugs) a police drug raid (cf. ROUST n.^{2}). [RUMBLE v.^{1}]

rumble v.^{1} **1** [early–mid-19C] to handle roughly, to rule out without any discussion **2** [1950s+] (drugs) to be searched by the police. **3** [1950s+] to hit, to fight. **4** [1950s+] (US) to steal, esp. from an aeroplane.

rumble v.^{2} [late 19C+] to discover, to find out, to unmask. [ROMBOYLE v.]

rum-bleating cheat n. [late 17C–early 19C] (Und.) a very fat wether or castrated ram. [RUM adj. (1) + BLEATING CHEAT]

rumbler n. [mid-19C] **1** a hackney carriage. **2** a 4-wheeled cab; thus *rumbler's flunkey*, a footman who runs for cabs in return for tips (cf. BOUNDER n.^{1}; RATTLER n.^{1}).

rumble-tumble n. [early 19C] a stage-coach (cf. RUMBLER). [note Anglo-Indian use *rumble-tumble*, scrambled eggs]

rum blowen/blower n. [late 17C–18C] (Und.) a good-looking woman, esp. an attractive mistress or kept woman. [RUM adj. (1) + BLOWEN/BLOWER n.^{1} (1)]

rum bluffer n. [late 17C–early 19C] (Und.) an honest, jovial, accommodating alehouse-keeper or publican (cf. QUEER BLUFFER). [RUM adj. (1) + BLUFFER n.^{1}]

rumbo/rumbo-ken n.^{1} [early 18C] a prison. [? ironic use of RUM adj. (1) + KEN n.^{1}]

rumbo n.^{2} [mid-18C–late 19C] a mixture of rum, water and sugar. [SE *rum*]

rumbo n.^{3} [late 19C] a sufficiency, a plenitude. [Sp. *rumbo*, liberality, generosity]

rumbo adj. [late 19C] **1** plentiful, sufficient. **2** elegant, fashionable. [RUMBO n.^{3}]

rumbo! excl. [late 19C] (middle class) an excl. of congratulation, i.e. *splendid! excellent!* used (exclusively) by two men. [Sp. *carambo* and ? adopted f. gypsy use]

rum bob n. [late 17C–early 19C] (Und.) **1** a smart young apprentice. **2** a sharp, fly trick. **3** a neat, short wig. [RUM adj. (1) + lit./fig. uses of BOB n.^{2}]

rumbo-ken n.^{1} see RUMBO n.^{1}.

rumbo-ken n.^{2} [early 18C–mid-19C] a pawnshop. [RUMBO n.^{3} + KEN n.^{1}]

rum booze/bouse/bouze/buse/buze n. [mid-16C–19C] good drink, esp. good wine (cf. BENE BOUSE). [RUM adj. (1) + BOUSE n.]

rum-boozing welts n. [mid-17C–19C] (Und.) bunches of grapes. [RUM BOOZE + SE *welt*, a ridge or raised portion]

rum bouse/bouze see RUM BOOZE.

rumboyle see ROMBOYLE.

rum bub n. [late 17C–early 18C] excellent liquor. [RUM adj. (1) + BUB n.^{2}]

rum bubber n. [late 17C–18C] a thief who specializes in stealing silver tankards from taverns. [RUM adj. (1) + BUBBER n.^{1} (3)]

rum buffer n. [18C–early 19C] (Und.) a valuable and attractive dog. [RUM adj. (1) + BUFE]

rum bughar n. [late 17C–19C] (Und.) a valuable and attractive dog (cf. RUM BUFFER). [RUM adj. (1) + BUFE/BUGHER]

rum-bump n. [1950s] (W.I.) **1** the adam's apple. **2** a swelling in the throat supposedly caused by excessive rum drinking.

rum-bumper n. [1950s] (W.I.) a rum drunkard (cf. ALECAN; BUMPER n.^{1}; RUM-BUMP).

rumbumtious/rumbumptious adj. [late 18C–early 19C] **1** obstreperous (cf. RUMBUSTIOUS). **2** haughty. [vars. on SE *rambunctious*]

rum bung n. [late 17C–early 19C] (Und.) a full purse. [RUM adj. (1) + BUNG n.^{1} (1)]

rum buse see RUM BOOZE.

rumbusticate v. [late 19C–1900s] of a man, to have sexual intercourse. [RUMBUSTIOUS + sfx. *-ate*, e.g. in SPIFLICATE]

rumbusticator n. [late 19C–1900s] a rich man. [RUMBUSTIOUS]

rumbustious/rumbustical/rombustical adj. [late 18C–late 19C] boisterous, noisy, unruly, turbulent.

rum buze see RUM BOOZE.

rum chant n. [late 17C–early 19C] (Und.) a song. [RUM adj. (1) + CHANT n. (1)]

rum clank n. [18C] (Und.) a gold or silver cup or tankard. [RUM adj. (1) + CLANK n.]

rum clout n. [late 17C–mid-19C] (Und.) a handkerchief made of silk or other high-quality material (cf. QUEER CLOUT). [RUM adj. (1) + CLOUT n.^{1} (1)]

rum co see RUM COE.

rum cod n. [late 17C–18C] a friend. [RUM adj. (1) + COD n.^{3}]

rum coe/co n. [late 17C–early 19C] a smart lad (cf. RUM COVE). [RUM adj. (1) + COVE]

rum cole/gelt/ghelt/gilt n. [late 17C–early 19C] (Und.) **1** new money. **2** 'Medals, curiously Coyn'd' (B.E.), presumably counterfeit (cf. QUEER COLE). [RUM adj. (1) + COLE/GELT/GILT n.^{3}]

rum-cove n. **1** [late 17C–18C] a successful villain. **2** [mid-19C+] an odd or eccentric character. [RUM adj. (1), (2) + COVE]

rum cull/cully n. **1** [late 17C–mid-19C] (Und.) a gullible, rich fool, open to fraud, especially at the hands of his mistress. **2** [mid–late 19C] an intimate friend. [RUM adj. (1) + CULL n.^{1}/CULLY n.]

rum cuttle n. [early 17C] a sword. [RUM adj. (1) + CUTTLE n.]

rum dab n. [late 17C–early 18C] (Und.) a very successful sharper, pickpocket and thief. [RUM adj. (1) + DAB n.^{1}]

rumdadum n. [1910s–20s] the buttocks. [? rhy. sl. *rumdadum* = BUM n.^{2}]

rum degen/tilter/tol n. [late 17C–early 19C] (Und.) a sword with a silver hilt or a hilt or blade inlaid with silver (cf. QUEER DEGEN). [RUM adj. (1) + DEGEN n. (1)/TILTER/TOL n.^{1}]

rum dell see RUM DOXY.

rum diver n. [late 17C–early 19C] (Und.) an accomplished pickpocket (cf. RUM FILE; QUEER DIVER). [RUM adj. (1) + DIVER n. (2)]

rum doxy/dell n. [late 17C–early 19C] (Und.) a beautiful woman. [RUM adj. (1) + DOXY n. (2)/DELL n.]

rum drawers n. [late 17C–18C] (Und.) stockings made of silk or some similar quality material. [RUM adj. (1) + DRAWERS]

rum dropper n. **1** [late 17C–early 19C] (Und.) a vintner. **2** [early 18C] a landlord. [SE *rum* + DROPPER n.^{2}]

rum dubber n. [late 17C–18C] (Und.) an expert pick-lock (cf. GILT DUBBER). [RUM adj. (1) + DUBBER n.^{1}]

rum duchess n. [late 17C–mid-18C] (Und.) a jolly, buxom woman (cf. RUM DUKE). [RUM adj. (1) + DUCHESS n.^{1}]

rum duke n. (Und.) **1** [late 17C–early 19C] an odd, eccentric, showy man (cf. RUM DUCHESS). **2** [late 17C–19C] a tough villain who is sent by a bankrupted individual to guard their possessions, while they leave home and take refuge from arrest in a criminal rookery. [RUM adj. (1) + DUKE n.^{1}]

rum-dum n. [1930s+] (US) a heavy drinker. [SE *rum* + redup.]

rum fam/fem n. [mid–late 19C] (Und.) a diamond ring. [RUM adj. (1) + FAMBLE n. (2)]

rum file n. [late 17C–early 19C] (Und.) an expert pickpocket (cf. RUM DIVER). [RUM adj. (1) + FILE n. (1)]

rum fun n. [late 17C–18C] (Und.) a clever trick, a cunning fraud. [RUM adj. (1) + FUN n.^{1}]

rum gagger n. [late 18C–19C] (Und.) a confidence trickster who raises money on the basis of telling fraudulent tales of supposed suffering at sea, at the hands of the pirates of the Barbary Coast and so on (cf. DRY-LAND SAILOR). [RUM adj. (1) + GAGGER n.^{1}]

rum gelt/ghelt see RUM COLE.

rum gill *n.* [early–mid-19C] (Und.) **1** a clever thief. **2** a good-looking man. [RUM adj. (1) + GILL n.[1]]

rum gilt *see* RUM COLE.

rum glimmer/glymmar *n.* [late 17C–early 19C] (Und.) the head of the link-boys, who were employed to carry a link to light passengers along the street. [RUM adj. (1) + GLIMMER n. (1)]

rumgumption *n.* [mid-19C] knowledge, ability; thus *rumgumptious*, knowing, positive, blunt, pert. [note Scot. *rumblegumption*, common sense]

rum gutlers *n.* [late 17C–18C] (Und.) **1** Canary wine. **2** good eating. [? RUM adj. (1) + SE *guzzle*]

rumhead *n.* [late 19C+] a drunkard, esp. a rum-drinker. [SE *rum* + sfx. -HEAD (2)]

rum hopper *n.* [late 17C–18C] (Und.) someone who draws ale or wine at a tavern. [RUM adj. (1) + SE *hopper*, one who moves quickly and efficiently, who 'hops to it']

rum hound *n.* [1910s–50s] a heavy drinker (cf. BOOZE HOUND). [SE *rum* + sfx. -HOUND]

rum Johnny *n.* [19C] (Anglo-Ind.) an Indian wharf labourer. [? SE *rum*/RUM adj. (2) + JOHNNIE n.[2] (1)]

rum ken *n.* [early–mid-19C] (Und.) a well-known criminal public house or brothel. [RUM adj. (1) + KEN n.[1]]

rum kicks *n.* [late 17C–early 19C] (Und.) breeches that have been adorned with silver or gold embroidery. [RUM adj. (1) + KICKS n.[1]]

rum kiddy *n.* [late 18C–early 19C] (Und.) a popular, successful young thief. [RUM adj. (1) + KIDDY n.[1] (2)]

rumly *adv.* **1** [late 17C–late 18C] bravely, honestly, excellently. **2** [early 19C+] oddly, eccentrically. [RUM adj. (1), (2)]

rummage *v.* [19C] of a man, to have sexual intercourse (cf. BANG v.[1]).

rummarian *see* RUMMER.

rum maund/mawnd/maunder *n.* [late 17C–18C] (Und.) a beggar who poses as more stupid than they really are to encourage donations. [RUM adj. (2) + MAUND n.]

rummer/rummarian *n.* [1940s] (W.I.) a rum drunkard (cf. RUM BUMPER). [SE *rum*]

rummie *see* RUMMY n.[1], n.[2].

rum mizzler/mizzler *n.* [mid-19C] (Und.) someone who is clever at escaping difficult situations, whether physically or through words. [RUM adj. (1) + MIZZLE]

rum/rome mort *n.* (Und.) **1** [mid-16C–early 19C] a queen. **2** [late 17C–early 19C] a great lady. [RUM adj. (1) + MORT; (1) was orig. coined for Elizabeth I]

rummy/rummie *n.*[1] [mid-19C+] (US) a drunkard. [SE *rum*]

rummy/rummie *n.*[2] [1910s+] a fool, a dupe. [RUM adj. (2)]

rummy *adj.* [20C] odd, peculiar, bizarre. [RUM adj. (2)]

rum nab *n.* [late 17C–18C] (Und.) a well-made, fashionable hat, a beaver hat. [RUM adj. (1) + NAB n.[1] (3)]

rum nantz *n.* [late 17C–early 19C] (Und.) the best quality French brandy. [RUM adj. (1) + NANTZ]

rum ned *n.* [late 17C–18C] (Und.) a very foolish man. [RUM adj. (1) + NEDDY n.[1] (2)]

rum ogles *n.* [late 17C–mid-19C] (Und.) bright, clear eyes. [RUM adj. (1) + OGLES]

rum one/'un *n.* **1** [early 19C+] anything considered odd or eccentric, whether animate, inanimate or theoretical. **2** [mid-19C] an admirable fellow. [RUM adj. (2, 1)]

rumor/rumour *n.* [1970s+] (orig. US teen) anything considered dead, finished or currently irrelevant. [ext. use of SE]

rump *n.* [19C] a prostitute. [SE *rump*, the buttocks]

rump *v.* **1** [late 18C–early 19C] to turn one's back on. **2** [19C] to flog. **3** [19C+] to copulate. [SE *rump*, the buttocks]

rum pad *n.* [late 17C–early 19C] (Und.) **1** the highway. **2** a highwayman (cf. RUM PADDER). [RUM adj. (1) + PAD n.[1] (1), (3)]

rum padder *n.* [late 17C–early 19C] (Und.) a highwayman (cf. RUM PAD). [RUM adj. (1) + PADDER n. (1)]

rump and a dozen *n.* [late 18C–early 19C] an Irish wager, a rump of beef and a dozen of claret (cf. BUTTOCK AND TRIMMINGS).

rump-and-kidney men *n.* [late 17C–early 19C] fiddlers who play for weddings, feasts, fairs and similar festivities. [their payment in kind, they were given the leftovers]

rump and stump *phr.* [late 19C] completely, totally. [Yorks. dial.]

rum peck *n.* [mid-16C–18C] (Und.) good food. [RUM adj. (1) + PECK n.[1] (1)]

rumped *adj.* [early 19C] flogged, whipped. [RUMP v. (2)]

rum peeper *n.* [late 17C–18C] (Und.) a silver mounted looking glass (cf. QUEER PEEPER). [RUM adj. (1) + PEEPER n. (1)]

rumper *n.* [19C] **1** a prostitute. **2** a pimp. [RUMP v. (3)]

rum phiz/phyz *n.* [late 18C] an odd-looking face. [RUM adj. (2) + PHIZ]

rumpkin/rumpskin *n.* [1970s+] (US Black) a fool. [RUM adj. (2) + SE *bumpkin*]

rumplety-thump *adj.* [20C] (Ulster) muddled, untidy. [echoic of the noise of objects being tossed to the floor]

rumpo *n.* [1950s+] sexual intercourse. [RUMP v. (3)]

rumpot *n.* [1930s+] a drunkard (cf. ALECAN).

rum prancer *n.* [late 17C–early 19C] (Und.) a beautiful, well-made horse (cf. QUEER PRANCER). [RUM adj. (1) + PRANCER n. (1)]

rump ranger *n.* [1950s+] a male homosexual.

rumpscuttle *n.* [16C] a tomboy. [SE *rump* + *scuttle*]

rump shaker *n.* [1990s] (US) an act of sexual intercourse.

rumpskin *see* RUMPKIN.

rump-splitter/split-rump *n.* **1** [19C] the penis (cf. ARSE-OPENER). **2** [19C–1900s] a lecher, a womanizer (cf. BEARD-JAMMER).

rump-sprung *adj.* [1930s] (US) of a dress, stretched out of shape over the buttocks through the wear and tear of bending.

rumption *n.* [early 19C] an uproar, a disturbance. [? RUMPUS n. (1) + SE *eruption*]

rumpty/rumpty dooler *n.* [1940s] (Aus./N.Z.) **1** anything excellent, first-rate. **2** something broken down, unattractive, disreputable. **3** a fuss, an uproar. [ext. of RUMPTY adj.]

rumpty *adj.* [1910s+] (Aus.) excellent, first-rate. [RUMTITUM]

rumpty dooler *see* RUMPTY n.

rumpty-foo *adj.* [mid-19C] thrown together, amateurish. [echoic]

rumptyvump *n.* [1980s+] (US campus) a course in radio-television-motion pictures. [? echoic of melodramatic film music]

rumpus *n.* **1** [mid-18C–late 19C] an uproar, a disturbance; also used without the article. **2** [early–mid-19C] a masquerade. [? Gk. *rombos*, a spinning top, thus a commotion or disturbance; E.P. suggests SE *rumble*, the noise of an upset stomach; *rumpus* SE by 20C]

rump work *n.* [late 19C–1900s] sexual intercourse.

rumpy-/humpy-pumpy *n.* [1970s+] sexual intercourse. [SE *rump* + HUMP v.[1]/PUMP v.[4]]

rum quids/quidds *n.* [late 17C–early 19C] (Und.) a good haul of cash. [RUM adj. (1) + QUIDS]

rum ruff peck *n.* [late 17C–18C] (Und.) Westphalia ham. [RUM adj. (1) + RUFF PECK; Westphalia ham was considered to be of the best quality]

rum slim *n.* [mid-19C] rum punch. [SE *rum* + var. on SAmE *sling*, a form of cocktail; ? ult. SLING n.[1] (1)]

rum snitch *n.* [late 17C–early 19C] (Und.) a hard blow on one's nose. [RUM adj. (1) + SNITCH n.[1] (1)]

rum squeeze *n.* [late 17C–18C] (Und.) a good measure of drink distributed among the fiddlers at a wedding or similar event. [RUM adj. (1) + SE *squeeze*, a few drops squeezed out]

rum strum *n.*[1] [late 17C–early 19C] a long wig. [RUM adj. (1) + STRUM n.[1]]

rum strum *n.*[2] [late 17C–early 19C] a pretty young strumpet. [RUM adj. (1) + STRUM n.[2]]

rum talking *phr.* [20C] (W.I.) used of one's state of drunkenness, as an excuse for talking nonsense or being rude (cf. APPLETON TALKING).

rum tilter *see* RUM DEGEN.

rumtitum/rum-ti-tum *adj.* [early 19C+] in excellent condition, usu. of a bull or a pimp; intensified [mid-19C] as *rum ti tum with the chill off*.

rum tol *see* RUM DEGEN.

rum Tom Pat *n.* [late 18C–mid-19C] (Und.) a clergyman. [RUM adj. (1) + TOM PAT n. (1)]

rum topping *n.* [late 17C–early 19C] (Und.) a first-rate or brand-new wig (cf. QUEER TOPPING). [RUM adj. (1) + SE *topping*]

rum touch *n.* [early 19C] an odd, eccentric person; a strange affair. [RUM adj. (2) + SE *touch*, with the implication of someone against whom one brushes up]

rum 'un *see* RUM ONE.

Rum ville/Rumville *see* ROME-VILLE.

rum wipe/wiper *n.* [19C] (Und.) a handkerchief made of silk or other high-quality material (cf. QUEER CLOUT/RUM CLOUT). [RUM adj. (1) + WIPE n.[2]/WIPER n.[1]]

rumy *n.* [mid-19C] a good woman. [Rom. *romeni*, a wife, a bride]

run *n.*[1] [20C] (US Und.) the walkway that runs the length of a line of cells (cf. RANGE n.).

run *n.*[2] [1950s+] amongst outlaw motorcyclists, a full-scale club outing involving all the members of a given chapter or gang and devoted to maximum excess in all possible areas of activity.

run *n.*[3] [1950s+] (drugs) the immediate and intense feeling that follows the injection of heroin into a vein (cf. RUSH n.[2]).

run *v.*[1] [mid-19C] to understand, to comprehend.

run *v.*[2] [mid-late 19C] (Aus./US) to harass verbally, to tease; thus *running*, teasing, scolding.

run *v.*[3] [20C] (drugs) to be an habitual drug user.

run *v.*[4] [1900s–30s] to report or hand over (someone) to the police. [RUN IN v.]

run *v.*[5] [1900s–40s] (Aus.) to cover the expenses of. [SE *run to*, to cover, to extend sufficiently, usu. of money]

run *v.*[6] [1910s] to go out with one's boyfriend or girlfriend on a regular basis.

run *v.*[7] [1960s+] to suffer from diarrhoea (cf. RUNS). [one *runs* to the lavatory]

run *v.*[8] [1980s+] (US teen) to play basketball.

run *v.*[9] [1980s+] (US campus) to play a song over and over again to the point of getting tired of hearing it.

run a banker, to *phr.* [late 19C+] (Aus.) to be intense; usu. of emotions or feelings. [SE *banker*, a river with its water level with or over-running its banks]

runabout *n.* [1970s] (US Black) the facts of a situation. [var. on RUN DOWN v.[2] (1)]

run about after someone's arse, to *phr.* [late 19C+] to toady to, to act as a parasite. [fig. use of sl. phr.]

run a buck, to *phr.* [late 18C–early 19C] (Anglo-Irish) to register an invalid vote. [ety. unknown]

run a crimp, to *phr.* [early–mid-18C] to set up a crooked horse-race (cf. PLAY CRIMP). [CRIMP n.]

run a double train, to *phr.* [1940s+] (US Black) for two men to penetrate a woman simultaneously by the vagina and the anus (cf. MAKE A SANDWICH). [var. on PULL A TRAIN]

run a drag on, to *phr.* [1980s+] (US Black) to deceive, to trick, to hoax. [DRAG v.[9] (2)]

run a game on/run game on, to *phr.* [1940s+] (US Black) to bamboozle, to deceive, to seduce, to confuse, to obtain money by trickery. [GAME n.[5] (3)]

run a gorilla game, to *phr.* [1960s–70s] (US Black) to strong-arm, to use aggression to trick a victim. [GORILLA n.[1] (1)]

run a jack, to *phr.* [1960s] (US Black) to grab a man's shirt and pull it over his head, before robbing him. [JACK n.[22]]

run a line *see* SHOOT A LINE.

run a make, to *phr.* (US police) to identify a suspect. [MAKE n.[4]]

run a mile, to *phr.* [1940s+] to run off because of fear or instincts of self-preservation, esp. in the context of men escaping what they see as predatory women.

run a rag/run a rag on, to *phr.* [1990s] (US Black gang) to play a confidence trick on, to deceive. [RAG n.[3]/v.[1]]

run a railroad, to *phr.* [1960s] (drugs) to be addicted to narcotics. [RAILROAD TRACKS n.[2]]

run-around/-round *n.*[1] [mid-19C+] (US) a suppurative inflammatory sore or swelling in a finger or thumb.

run-around *n.*[2] [1950s+] (orig. US) a short trip, an excursion.

run around in circles *see* GO AROUND IN CIRCLES.

run around like a cut cat, to *phr.* [1950s] (Aus.) to be very angry (cf. MAD AS A CUT SNAKE). [SE *cut*, castrated]

run a scare/run a scare into, to *phr.* [mid–late 19C] (US) to terrify, to threaten (cf. PUT THE FRIGHTENERS ON).

run a skirt, to *phr.* [20C] to keep a mistress. [SKIRT n.]

run as swift as a pudding would creep, to *phr.* [early 17C] to go very slowly.

run a tight ship, to *phr.* [20C] to keep full control of a situation, to be an efficient organizer or leader. [naut. imagery]

run a train, to *phr.* [1950s+] (orig. US) to gangrape (cf. PULL A TRAIN). [the victim is the 'engine'; the attackers the 'passengers']

run/run off at the mouth/jaw/jibs, to *phr.* [1940s+] (US) to talk to excess and to the irritation of one's audience. [RUN OFF v.[2] + SE *jaw*/JIB n.[1] (2)]

run away and play marbles! *excl.* [late 19C+] an excl. of contemptuous, patronizing dismissal.

run away and play trains!/with yourself! *excl.* [20C] an excl. of contemptuous, patronizing dismissal.

runcible *adj.* [1920s–30s] of women, sexually attractive. [play on Edward Lear's nonsense word, coined in 1871 to describe a spoon with three broad prongs, thus ? pun on SPOON v.[1]]

run dirty/nasty *v.* [20C] to behave badly.

rundown/run-down *n.* [1940s+] (orig. US) a summary, a brief list of the most important facts or points on which to act. [RUN DOWN v.[2] (1)]

run down *v.*[1] [20C] (W.I.) to seduce someone, to persuade them to become one's lover.

run down *v.*[2] [1940s+] **1** to rehearse, to practice, to explain. **2** to denigrate someone, to slander someone.

run down game, to *phr.* [1960s+] (US Black) of a pimp, to explain the principles of the pimping business, both from experienced pimps to novices and from the pimp to his prostitutes, telling them the tricks of their trade. [RUN DOWN v.[2] (1) + GAME n.[5] (2)]

run down one's best game, to *phr.* [1960s+] (US Black) to make one's best, cleverest and most skilful efforts. [RUN DOWN v.[2] (1) + GAME n.[4] (2)]

run down some lines, to *phr.* [1950s+] (US Black) **1** to make conversation. **2** to attempt seduction by smooth talking. [RUN DOWN v.[1] + LINE n.[1] (3)]

rung *adj.* [1950s+] of cars, supplied with false plates, documents etc for use in a robbery (cf. RINGER n.[2]). [RING v.[1] (4)]

run game on *see* RUN A GAME ON.

run goods *n.* [late 18C–early 19C] a woman's virginity (cf. CUSTOM HOUSE GOODS; CUSTOMS OFFICER; EVE'S CUSTOM HOUSE; RECEIPT OF CUSTOM). [SE *run*, to smuggle; smuggled goods 'have never been entered' (in the customs' ledger)]

rung up *adj.* [20C] (US) emotionally disturbed.

run home on one's ear phr. [late 19C] (US) utterly crushed, comprehensively defeated (cf. OUT ON ONE'S EAR).

run-in n.[1] [20C] an argument, a controversy, a fight.

run-in n.[2] [1950s–60s] a place to which stolen goods are delivered and where they are subsequently hidden.

run in v. [early–mid-19C+] to arrest, to run in to prison.

run into money, to phr. [1930s+] (orig. US) to amount to a considerable sum, to cost a considerable amount.

run into the ground, to phr. [late 19C+] to persist in an action or in speech to the extent that all meaning and importance is lost; from driving a car or riding a horse until it collapses. [orig. cowboy use]

run it down v. [1960s+] (mainly US Black) to explain, to point out facts. [ext. of RUN DOWN v.[2] (1)]

run it fine see CUT IT FINE.

run it/something up the flagpole/flagpole and see if anyone salutes, to phr. [1960s+] (US) to test a reaction to a new idea or concept, usu. as let's run it up … .

run like a hairy goat, to phr. (N.Z.) **1** [1950s+] of a racehorse, to run very badly; occas. to run fast. **2** [1960s+] of a motor vehicle, to run badly. [HAIRY GOAT]

run mouth n. [20C] (W.I./Gren.) a gossip, a rumour-monger.

run nasty see RUN DIRTY.

runner n.[1] (Und.) **1** [late 17C–late 18C] a sneak thief, esp. one who specializes in entering houses and taking furs, cloaks and coats (cf. BUDGE n.[1]). **2** [late 19C] a dog-stealer. **3** [1930s+] someone engaged in conveying prohibited goods (such as drugs, liquor) secretly.

runner n.[2] see ROPER n.[2].

runner n.[3] [late 19C] a wave of the hand. [? one waves as one runs off]

runner n.[4] **1** [1930s+] a bookmaker's clerk or assistant. **2** [1980s+] (drugs) a drug dealer's assistant, who ferries drugs from seller to buyer.

runner n.[5] [1960s+] (Und.) **1** an act of evasion or escape; usu. in phr. do a runner. **2** someone who is on the run from the police.

runner and rider n. [20C] cider. [rhy. sl.]

runners n.[1] [late 17C] crooked dice that will always produce a high number (cf. HIGH MEN). [they will 'run' in the direction one desires]

runners n.[2] [1950s+] (Aus./Irish) track shoes, training shoes.

running n. [1980s+] (drugs) MDMA (cf. ECSTASY). [ety. unknown]

running adj. [1980s+] (US Black) busy.

running a levant see LEVANTING.

running buddy see RUNNING PARTNER.

running down n. [1940s+] assessing, going through. [RUN DOWN v.[2] (1)]

running horse/nag n. [late 18C–mid-19C] a venereal discharge (cf. RUNNING RANGE). [SE running, oozing + HORSE n.[4]/ NAG n.[2]]

running out of one's head/ears phr. [20C] (US) referring to something that one possesses in full measure or to excess.

running partner/buddy n. [1930s+] (US Black) a close friend with whom one pursues most of one's daily activities.

running patterer/stationer n. [late 17C–mid-19C] a streethawker of books, pamphlets, ballads and similar printed material. [SE running + PATTERER/SE stationer]

running range n. [1920s–50s] (US Black) the discharge from the penis or vagina that accompanies gonorrhoea (cf. RUNNING HORSE).

runnings n. [1980s+] (UK Black) what is going on, the situation 'the score', a plan. [RUNDOWN n.]

running stationer see RUNNING PATTERER.

running with adj. [1930s+] (orig. US Black) allied to, in partnership with, on the same side as.

run-off n. [1960s] urination. [RUN OFF v.[1]]

run off v.[1] [19C] to urinate. [SE run off, of liquid, to let flow away]

run off v.[2] [mid-19C+] (US) to talk excessively, to talk rubbish. [SE run off, of water, to flow away]

run off a batch by hand, to phr. [1990s] to masturbate.

run off at the lip see GO OFF AT THE LIP.

run off at the mouth see RUN AT THE MOUTH.

run off of v. [1970s+] (US Black) to be sustained by something, esp. a drug. [SE run, to function]

run off one's legs phr. [late 17C–mid-18C] bankrupt.

run on v. [late 19C] to run up an account.

run one on, to v. [20C] to arrest. [var. on RUN IN]

run one's chops out, to phr. [1960s] (US Black) to talk, to complain. [CHOPS]

run/go on one's face/shape for, to phr. [mid-19C+] (orig. US) to obtain credit. [SE run, to enter into a race, i.e. to bet one's face or shape, i.e. body, as the agent of obtaining credit]

run one's hand up the flagpole, to phr. [20C] to masturbate (cf. VARNISH ONE'S POLE). [ironic use of SE]

run one's head, to phr. [1970s+] (US) to talk at length or out of turn. [var. on RUN ONE'S MOUTH]

run/fly one's mouth, to phr. [1930s+] (orig. US/W.I.) to gossip, to tell tales (cf. RUN OFF v.[2]). [one's mouth runs like an engine]

run one's rig upon, to phr. [late 18C–early 19C] to ridicule. [RIG n.[2]]

run one's shape for see RUN ONE'S FACE FOR.

run one way and look another, to phr. [1970s+] (US Black) to act in a duplicitous manner, to cheat deliberately.

run on pattens, to phr. [mid-16C–early 17C] to talk very fast and volubly. [the click-clack noise of wooden pattens]

run on tick, to phr. [late 17C+] to set up a line of credit, to get into debt. [TICK n.[2]]

run out at v. [1920s+] (Aus.) of a bill, to amount to.

run out of gas, to phr. [1920s+] (US) to lose impetus, to weary, to fail.

run out of road, to phr. [1960s+] of a motorcar or its driver, to fail to negotiate a curve properly and to skid off the road rather than turn the corner; thus also in fig. use.

run out of steam, to phr. [1960s+] to lose energy and impetus, to fail.

run out on v. **1** [late 19C–1910s] to embellish a story. **2** [20C] to abandon, to leave suddenly.

run-out powder n. [1920s+] (US) an escape, a speedy departure (cf. SNIFF A POWDER). [a fig. SE powder that inspires speed or POWDER v.[1]]

run over v. [mid-19C+] to treat contemptuously, to victimize.

run over shoes, to be phr. [late 16C–early 17C] to be in serious debt, to get oneself into serious debt. [i.e. the poor state of repair of one's shoes]

run rings around, to phr. [late 19C+] (orig. Aus.) to beat comprehensively, to make someone look foolish.

run-round see RUN-AROUND.

runs, the n. [1960s+] diarrhoea (cf. BACK-DOOR TROT; COWS'S COURANT; TROTS n.[1]). [the diarrhoea runs from one's body; one runs to the lavatory]

run scared v. [20C] (US) to show signs of fear and panic, to flee.

run/roll/throw sets on, to phr. [1970s+] (US Black) to hit with combination left and right punches (cf. ONE-TWO). [a set of punches]

run someone ragged, to phr. [1920s+] (orig. US) to exhaust or wear out someone.

run something fine see CUT IT FINE.

run something up the flagpole see RUN IT UP THE FLAGPOLE.

run straight v. [late 19C] (society) to remain faithful to one's husband. [horse-racing imagery]

runt n. [early 18C+] a contemptible person. [weak use of SE *runt*, the smallest of a litter]

run taper v. [mid–late 19C] of money, to run short. [SE *run* + *taper*, to grow thinner]

run the bar, to phr. [1940s] to buy drinks for everyone in a bar.

run the cutter, to phr. [1900s–10s] (Aus.) to buy beer in bulk, to be brought home and drunk there. [Scot. *cutter*, a small whisky bottle, but note phr. *run the cutter*, to smuggle liquor ashore, avoiding the customs' cutter]

run the rabbit, to phr. [1910s+] **1** to bring home liquor from a public house. **2** to obtain liquor illegally.

run the rule over, to phr. **1** [mid-19C] of a pickpocket, to check all a person's pockets. **2** [1910s+] to give someone a medical examination. **3** [1940s+] of police, to interrogate a suspect.

run the show, to phr. [1930s+] to take charge, to direct operations or activities.

run the street/streets, to phr. [1930s+] (US Black) to spend one's time in self-indulgence, partying, drinking and enjoying the freedoms of a non-domestic life.

run thin v. [late 19C–1920s] to extract oneself from a deal. [dial.]

run through the mill, to phr. [20C] to subject to a difficult and arduous experience (cf. PUT THROUGH THE MILL).

run through the nose with a cushion, to phr. [late 17C–early 18C] to attack playfully.

run to v. [mid-19C] **1** to understand. **2** to be able to afford, usu. in neg. [(2) is SE in 20C]

run to seed phr. **1** [mid-19C] pregnant. **2** [mid-19C+] run down, seedy.

run up a score, to phr. [mid-19C] to buy on credit, esp. at a public house. [? the old *scoring* of one's debts on some form of tally]

run up on, to be phr. [1990s] (US Black gang) to be ambushed.

run up side o' one's head, to phr. [1950s+] (US Black) to beat up.

run up the walls see CLIMB THE WALLS.

run with v. [late 19C+] (orig. US Black) to associate with, to be friends with (cf. RUNNING PARTNER).

run with the ball, to phr. [1960s+] to take on a problem and tackle it on one's own initiative, rather than passing the buck. [sporting imagery]

run with the big dogs, to phr. [1980s+] (US campus) to do anything anyone else can.

rupert n. [1970s+] (orig. milit.) a generic name for any young male aristocrat (cf. ALGIE). [the stereotypical 'classiness' of the name]

rupert bears n. [1980s+] (business) shares. [rhy. sl.]

rupperty see RUBBEDY.

rupture a gut see BUST A GUT.

ruptured duck n. [1940s+] (US milit.) the lapel pin or pocket insignia worn by an honourably discharged US serviceman; thus the honourable discharge itself (cf. SCREAMING EAGLE).

ruquita de aquella n. [1960s+] (US) an exceptionally attractive, sexy woman. [Sp.]

rush n.[1] **1** [early 19C] (Und.) robbery with violence; if *the rush*, then usu. of a single item, e.g. a cloak hanging outside a shop; if *a rush*, an assault by a number of men on a house with the intent of robbing the owners of their money and valuables. **2** [mid–late 19C] a swindle (cf. RAMP n.[2]).

rush n.[2] (drugs) **1** [1950s+] the immediate and intense feeling that follows the injection of heroin into a vein. **2** [1970s+] isobutyl nitrite, which produces an instant effect.

rush v. **1** [late 18C–early 19C] (Und.) to rob; 'A number of villains assemble at the door of a house, and as soon as opened rush in, bind the family, and plunder the house' (*Gentleman's Magazine* LV 1785). **2** [mid-19C+] (US campus/W.I.) to make a pass at, to make sexual advances towards. **3** [late 19C+] to cheat, to overcharge, the victim is not given time to think. **4** [late 19C+] (Aus.) to stampede. **5** [1920s+] to show intense interest in something or someone. **6** [1920s+] (US campus) to pay court to a student with the hope of having them join a fraternity. **7** [1920s+] (US campus) to confront. **8** [1920s+] (US campus) to obtain, to go and get. **9** [1980s+] (US campus) to gang up on a particular person. **10** [1990s] (US Black) to jump on someone, to beat someone up.

rush act, the n. [20C] (US) a seduction of a woman. [RUSH v.[1] (2)]

rush around in circles see GO AROUND IN CIRCLES.

rush buckler n. [19C] a thug, a bully. [SE *rush*, to force violently + *buckler*, a shield]

rush/rushed job n. [20C] spontaneous, fast sexual intercourse.

rushed off one's feet phr. [1930s+] extremely busy.

rusher n.[1] [late 18C–mid-19C] **1** a thief, as in 'Thieves who knock at the doors of great houses in London, in summer time, when the families are gone out of town, and on the door being opened by a woman, rush in and rob the house' (Grose 1785). **2** a housebreaker who specializes in breaking into secluded houses.

rusher n.[2] [19C+] (US) a boy or girl who is sent to the saloon to bring back beer either for their parents or for working men who could not leave the job (cf. LUSH TROTTER). [SE *rush*, i.e. 'rush down to the pub and ...']

rusher n.[3] [late 19C] (US) a 'go-ahead', fashionable person. [ext. use of SE]

rushing business n. [late 19C] (Und.) robbery through confidence tricks and hoaxes. [RUSH v.[1] (3)]

rushlight n.[1] [mid-18C] a fiery drink (cf. GLIM n.[2]).

rushlight n.[2] [late 19C] a very thin person. [SE *rushlight*, something insignificant or of little account; a glimmer]

rush of blood to the crutch phr. [1930s+] a sudden feeling of lust. [play on SE *rush of blood to the head*]

rush of brains to the feet/head n. [1930s+] a sudden 'bright idea'. [play on SE *rush of blood to the head*]

rush snappers n. [1970s+] (drugs) isobutyl nitrite. [RUSH n.[2] (2) + SNAPPERS n.[2]]

rush the can see CHASE THE CAN.

rush the growler/can/duck, to phr. [19C+] (US) to buy beer from a tavern and bring it home for drinking there; also as *work the growler*. [16C SE *rush*, to carry rapidly + GROWLER n.[3]/SE *can*/DUCK n.[8]]

rush the kip, to phr. [1900s–10s] (N.Z.) to make a precipitate, over-hasty decision. [SE *rush* + *kip*, the small flat piece of wood used to toss the pennies into the air, in the game two-up]

rush up the frills/petticoats, to phr. [mid–late 19C] to have sexual intercourse while virtually fully clothed.

russell harty n. [20C] a party. [rhy. sl.; ult. TV personality *Russell Harty* (1934–88)]

Russian/Rooshian/Roosian n.[1] [early 19C+] (Aus.) a wild horse, wild cattle. [? pun on *rush around*]

Russian n.[2] [1930s–50s] (US Black) a newly arrived southern Black who has moved to the north. [pun on *rush-in*; many Blacks moved north during WW2 to work in war-related manufacturing industries]

Russian n.[3] [1940s+] (S.Afr.) **1** any of the gangs from the south townships in South Soto known for their violence and terror from 1940s. **2** any south Sotans. [neg. image of Russia during the Cold War]

Russian coffeehouse *n.* [early 19C] the Brown Bear public house in Bow Street, Covent Garden, a popular haunt for both thieves and thief-takers. [the bear is a 'Russian' animal]

Russian duck *n.* **1** [1910s–20s] dirt. **2** [1970s] sexual intercourse (cf. ROASTED DUCK). [rhy. sl. (1) = SE *muck*; (2) = FUCK *n.*[1]]

Russian high *n.* [1950s–60s] (gay) simultaneous fellatio and anal intercourse. [? assumptions of Russian sexual preferences]

Russian law *n.* [mid-17C] a punishment of one hundred blows on the shins. [a traditional Russian punishment]

Russian salad party *n.* [1950s–60s] (gay) an orgy in which all participants are covered in baby oil. [SE *Russian salad*, a mix of chopped or shredded vegetables and mayonnaise]

Russian sickles *n.* [1960s+] (drugs) LSD. [the imprint of the hammer and sickle on the pill]

Russian Turk *n.* [mid-19C–1900s] work. [rhy. sl.]

Russki *n.* [1910s+] a derog. term for a Russian. [orig. WW1 milit.]

rust *n.* **1** [mid-19C] money. **2** [late 19C–1920s] old metal.

rust *v.* [late 19C–1920s] to collect and sell old metal.

rust bowl/belt *n.* [1980s+] (US) the declining industrial areas, esp of the Middle West.

rust bucket *n.* **1** [1940s+] (US) a rusty old ship. **2** [1960s+] (Aus./N.Z.) a car that is noticeably and dangerously rusty.

rusted in *adj.* [late 19C] (US) settled down.

rustiness *n.* [mid-19C–1900s] irritability, bad temper.

rustle *n.*[1] [late 19C] (US) bustle, hustle. [SE *rustle*, that which rustles, e.g. a leaf]

rustle *n.*[2] [late 19C] (US) a robbery. [SE *rustler*, a cattle robber]

rustle *n.*[3] [20C] (US Black) an orphan, esp. one whose parents are unknown (cf. DROP *n.*[3]). [SE *rustle*, to act quickly, to hurry about; such a child is the product of a quick, brief relationship]

rustle *v.* [mid–late 19C] (US) to rush around, to bustle about; thus ext. as (US) *rustle one's bustle*.

rustle up *v.* [mid–late 19C] (orig. US) to obtain or (of food) put together very quickly and without prior preparation. [SE *rustle*, to move with a rustling sound]

rustling *n.* [late 19C] (US) energetic, bustling activity; thus *rustling*, bustling, energetic, active. [RUSTLE *v.*]

rusty *n.*[1] [mid–late 19C] an informer. [? CUT UP RUSTY]

rusty *n.*[2] [20C] a nickname for anyone with red or auburn hair. [the colour]

rusty *adj.*[1] [late 18C+] exhausted, out of practice. [SE *rusty*, covered in rust through lack of use, but ? cognate with SE *reasty*, rancid (of meat)]

rusty *adj.*[2] [mid-19C] ill-tempered, anti-social. [one who lacks the 'polish' to make a successful path in the world]

rusty *adj.*[3] [late 19C+] (Aus.) lecherous, amorous. [? Somerset dial. *rusty*, gross, obscene]

rusty bucket *n.* [1990s] ginger female pubic hair. [play on SE; RUSTY *n.*[2]]

rusty bullet wound/sheriff's badge/washer *n.* [1990s] the anus. [supposed resemblance]

rusty-dusty *n.* [1930s–50s] (US) the buttocks, esp. with the implication that someone has been sitting around doing nothing; thus they are *rusty* and *dusty* from lack of movement.

rusty gun *n.* [1960s+] (US) a veteran policeman. [his weapon has rusted in its holster]

rustyguts/rusty-guts *n.* [late 17C–early 19C] a surly, unpleasant old man. [SE *rustic*, countrified, rough, boorish + SE *guts*, the intestines, used fig. as a man]

rusty sheriff's badge/rusty washer *see* RUSTY BULLET WOUND.

rutabaga *n.* [20C] (US) a dollar (cf. CABBAGE *n.*[8]; KALE; LETTUCE *n.*[1]; SPINACH *n.*[1]). [SAmE *rutabaga* = SE *swede*]

ruth buzzy *n.* [1960s–70s] (US Black) a plain-looking woman. [proper name *Ruth Buzzi* (b.1936), the actress best known for her work on *Rowan & Martin's Laugh-In* (1967–73)]

ruttat *n.* [late 19C] a potato (cf. RATTAT). [backsl. *ruttat = tatur* = potato]

ruttat pusher *n.* [late 19C] the owner of a potato-cart. [RUTTAT + SE *pusher*]

rutter *n.* [late 16C] (Und.) one of a team of four swindlers; their task was to stand at the door and keep watch (cf. RUBBER *n.*[1]). [? SE *router*, a lawless person, a robber, a ruffian]

rux *v.* [late 19C] to scold, to reprimand. [? RUCK *v.*[1] (3) or dial. *rux*, to shake up]

r.w.v. *n.* [1940s–50s] (Und.) robbery with violence. [abbr.]

ryache *n.* [mid-19C+] a chair. [backsl.]

rybeck *n.* [mid-19C] a share. [? Yid.]

rybuck *see* RYEBUCK.

rybuck! *see* RYEBUCK!

ryder *n.* [late 19C–1900s] a cloak. [? Rom. *ruder*, to clothe]

rydim *n.* [1940s] (W.I.) the buttocks. [SE *rhythm*, i.e. that of the moving buttocks]

ryebuck!/ribuck!/rybuck! *n.* [late 19C–1960s] (Aus.) something good, worthwhile, the 'real thing'. [RYEBUCK *adj.*]

ryebuck/ribuck/rybuck *adj.* [late 19C–1960s] (Aus.) good, excellent, first-rate. [ety. unknown; ? Ger. *Reibach*, var. of *rebbach*, profit, ult. synon. Yid./Heb. *revach*]

ryebuck/ribuck/rybuck *excl.* [late 19C–1960s] (Aus.) a general expression of agreement or approval. [RYEBUCK *adj.*]

rye mort/mush *n.* [1900s–30s] a lady, a gentleman. [Rom. *rei*, a gentleman + MORT/MUSH *n.*[4] (2)]

rygin/rhygin *adj.* [1940s] (W.I.) **1** angry. **2** vigorous, lively, spirited. **3** first-class, extremely able. [SE *rage* + RAG *v.*[1]; the locus classicus is the epon. *Rygin*, the name adopted by the RUDE BOY hero of the film *The Harder They Come* (1972)]

ryno *see* RHINO.

S

S *n.* [1980s+] (US drugs) hashish. [abbr.]

's *abbr.*[1] [16C–18C] an abbr. of 'God's', as found in a number of oaths (cf. 'ADS; 'SBLOOD!; 'SBODY!; 'SBORES!; 'SDEATH!; 'SDEYNES!; 'SDIGGERS!; 'SFLESH!; 'SFOOT!; 'SHEART!; 'SLID!; 'SLIDIKINS!; 'SLIFE!; 'SLIGHT!; 'SNAILS!; 'SNIGGERS!; 'SNOWNS!; 'SPRECIOUS!; 'STREWTH!; 'SWILL!; 'SWORBOTE!; 'SWOUNDS!).

's *abbr.*[2] [1930s+] does, e.g. *what's he know?* [abbr.]

s.a. *n.* [1920s–30s] *s*ex *a*ppeal. [abbr.]

saali *adj.* [1940s+] (W.I.) attractive, well-dressed. [SE *salty*]

s.a.b. *n.* [1980s+] (US campus) *s*ocial *a*irhead *b*itch. [abbr.]

sab *n.* [1950s] (W.I.) a haircut in which the back of the hair is rounded rather than tapered. [the film star *Sabu* (Dastagir) (1924–63), 'the Elephant Boy', whose hair was thus cut]

sabana *n.* [20C] (Hisp.Am.) a White person. [Sp.]

Sabba-/Sabber-day *n.* [late 18C–mid-19C] (US) Sunday, i.e. *Sabbath*-day.

sabbe/sabby/sabe *see* SAVVY *n.*

Sabber-day *see* SABBA-DAY.

sable maria *n.* [late 19C–1910s] a police or prison van (cf. BLACK ANNIE). [SE *sable*, black; i.e. var. on BLACK MARIA *n.*[1]]

s.a.b.u. *phr.* [1940s] (orig. US milit.) a complete disaster. [abbr. *s*elf-*a*djusting *a*rmy *b*alls-*u*p]

sac *see* ZAC.

sachem *n.* [late 19C+] (US) a political leader, orig. one of the leaders of New York's Tammany Society. [Algonquian *sachem*, a supreme chief]

sack *n.*[1] **1** [late 17C] the vagina. **2** [late 17C–early 19C] a pocket; thus *dive into a sack*, to pick a pocket.

sack *n.*[2] [early 19C+] a bed; thus *sack time*, the time one spends in bed (cf. BAG *n.*[9]). [RN use *sack*, a hammock]

sack, the *n.*[3] [mid-19C+] dismissal from one's job. [note both Fr. 'On luy a donné son sac, hee hath his pasport giuen him (said of a seruant whom his master hath put away)' (Cotgrave, 1611) + Du. *iemand den zak geven*, to give someone the sack, *den zak krijgen*, to get the sack]

sack *n.*[4] [1960s+] (US Black) an overcoat, a jacket. [mid-19C SE *sack*, a loose-fitting coat]

sack *n.*[5] [1980s+] (US Black/campus) a second-rate athlete. [? SAD SACK OF SHIT]

sack *n.*[6] [1980s+] (drugs) heroin. [the packet in which it is sold]

sack *v.*[1] [19C] **1** to put in one's pocket. **2** to steal, to take possession of, to pocket. [SACK *n.*[1] (2)]

sack *v.*[2] **1** [mid-19C+] to dismiss from a job. **2** [1980s+] (US campus) to end a relationship, esp. in an abrupt, brutal manner. [SACK *n.*[3]]

sack artist *n.* [1940s+] (US) a chronic idler. [SACK *n.*[2] + ARTIST *n.*]

sack-chaser *n.* [1990s] (US Black) a woman (but not a prostitute) who pursues men, bartering her sexual favours for his financial status (cf. DIGGER *n.*[5]). [SACK *n.*[1] (2), as a wallet + SE *chaser*]

sack down *v.* [1950s+] to go to bed, to sleep (cf. SACK OUT). [SACK *n.*[2]]

sack drill *n.* [1940s] (orig. US milit.) sleep, time spent in bed (cf. SACK DUTY). [SACK *n.*[2] + SE *drill*]

sack duty *n.* [1940s–60s] (orig. US milit.) sleep, time spent in bed (cf. SACK DRILL). [SACK *n.*[2] + SE *duty*]

sacked out *adj.* [1940s+] fast asleep. [SACK OUT]

sack 'em up man *n.* [mid-19C] a resurrectionist or grave-robber. [the corpse is placed in a *sack* before its delivery to a hospital]

sack in *v.* [1940s+] (US) **1** to go to bed, to sleep (cf. SACK OUT). **2** to lie in, to stay in bed. [SACK *n.*[2]]

sacking *n.* [late 16C–early 17C] working as a prostitute. [SACKING LAW]

sacking law *n.* [16C–early 17C] (Und.) the occupation of a prostitute (cf. CHEATING LAW). [SE *sack*, to plunder, to lay waste. The object of such 'sacking' is the client]

sack it up *v.* [1970s–80s] (US Black) to terminate, to bring to a conclusion. [SE *sack*]

sack lunch *n.* [1960s+] cunnilingus (cf. BOX LUNCH). [SACK *n.*[1] (1) + SE *lunch*]

sack mouth *n.* [1980s+] (US Black) a chatterer, a gossip.

sack o' nuts *n.* [1970s] (US Black) the scrotum (cf. NUTSACK). [SE *sack* + NUTS *n.*[2] (1)]

sack out *v.* [1940s+] to fall asleep, to go to bed. [SACK *n.*[2]]

sack rat *n.* [1940s+] (US) a chronic idler (cf. SACK ARTIST). [SACK *n.*[2] + SE *rat*]

sack-shaker *n.* [late 19C–1930s] (US Black) a cotton-picker. [the sacks that were filled with cotton]

sack time *n.* [1940s+] (orig. US milit.) time spent in bed, time to go to bed. [SACK *n.*[2] + SE *time*]

sackwah *n.* [1970s] (Black) anywhere that drinking, generally illicit, takes place. [ety. unknown; ? Fr. *ce quoi*, that which, thus a euph.]

sacrament *n.* [1960s–70s] (drugs) LSD (cf. A *n.*[3]). [the placing of the pill or the blotter on the tongue, reminiscent of a Communion wafer]

sacred mushroom *n.* [1960s+] (drugs) psilocybin.

sad *n.* [18C–mid-19C] a degenerate person.

sad *adj.* **1** [17C–mid-19C] usu. of a place, mischievous, troublesome, corrupt. **2** [1990s] (teen) a general term of abuse, esp. for someone who is unfashionable by current teen standards. [note paradoxically that the earliest use of *sad*, *c.*1000, is wholly positive, meaning satisfied or sated and thence settled, firmly established in purpose or condition, steadfast, valiant, orderly, trustworthy etc. The neg. connotation emerges only in the mid-14C; the positive use is found in W.I. (1920s–50s) where *sad* = excellent, first-class]

sad and sorry *n.* [20C] a lorry. [rhy. sl.]

sad apple *n.* [20C] (US) **1** a contemptible person. **2** a pessimist.

sad-ass *n.* [1960s+] (US gay) a sadist. [deliberate mispron.; thus ref. to ARSE *n.*[1]]

sad-ass/-assed *adj.* [1960s+] (US) depressing. [SE *sad* + sfx. -ASS]

sad cattle *n.* [late 17C–early 18C] prostitutes, viewed as a group.

saddity/seddity/sidity/siditty *n.* [1960s+] (US Black) a stuck-up, conceited, snobbish person. [SADDITY adj.]

saddity/seddity/sidity/siditty *adj.* [1960s+] (US Black) **1** arrogant, haughty, snobbish, conceited. **2** elegant, high-class, sophisticated. [SIDE n.[1]]

saddle *n.*[1] [late 17C–early 19C] the vagina (cf. OMNIBUS; RIDE v.[1]; TOWN BIKE).

saddle *n.*[2] [mid–late 19C] a loaf. [? resemblance]

saddleback *n.* [mid–late 19C] a louse. [its shape]

saddle bags *n.* **1** [1960s+] the excess flesh around a portly stomach that may be seen in a kinder light by those who appreciate the Rubenesque figure (cf. BAGELS; LOVE HANDLES). **2** [1990s] the labia majora.

saddle blanket *see* HORSE BLANKET n.[2]

saddle-leather *n.* [mid–late 19C] the skin of the buttocks.

saddle one's nose, to *phr.* [late 18C–mid-19C] to wear spectacles.

saddler *n.* [late 19C] (US) a saddle-horse.

saddle-sick *adj.* [late 18C–early 19C] tired or injured through excessive riding.

saddle the spit, to *phr.* [late 18C–early 19C] to host a dinner or supper. [SE *saddle a spit*, to put meat upon a spit]

saddle-tramp *n.* [20C] (US) a cowboy who moves from ranch to ranch, dependent for survival on local hospitality.

saddle up *v.* [1980s+] to engage in mutual fellatio and cunnilingus.

saddling paddock *n.* [mid–late 19C] (Aus.) **1** the bar of the Theatre Royal, Melbourne, generally accepted as a place to pick up prostitutes. **2** any place of assignation (cf. FILLY; RIDE v.[1]).

sad dog *n.* [early 18C–early 19C] a wicked, debauched fellow (cf. SAD MAN). [SAD adj. (1) + SE *dog*, a general term of abuse]

sadie and maisie *n.* [1960s+] sado-*m*asochism (cf. S AND M; SLAVES AND MASTERS). [euph.]

sad man *n.* **1** [18C] a mischievous, dissipated individual. **2** [1980s+] (teen) a general pej. for a person who fails to fit the norms of a group.

sado-maso *n.* [1970s] (US) a *sado-m*asochist. [abbr.]

sado-maso *adj.* [1970s] (US) sado-masochistic. [SADO-MASO n.]

sad sack *n.* [1920s+] (orig. US campus) a miserable, depressed (and depressing) person, usu. thus singled out in an institution, such as prison or the army. [abbr. SAD SACK OF SHIT, and thus the eponymous cartoon, created by George Baker (1915–75) in the US Army's *Yank* magazine]

sad sack of shit *n.* [1920s+] (orig. US) a miserable, pessimistic, morale-lowering person. [SE *sad* + *sack* + SHIT n.[1] (1)]

sad vulgar *n.* [late 19C] (society) a common, vulgar person.

safe *n.* [late 19C+] (US) a condom (cf. FRENCH SAFE). [SE *safety*]

safe *adj.* [1980s] used in sex contact advertisements, the man advertising has had a vasectomy.

safe! *excl.* [1980s+] an all-purpose term of approval used by teenagers (cf. DEF).

safe and sound *n.* [20C] the ground. [rhy. sl.]

safe as ... *phr.* a variety of phr. meaning extremely safe, e.g. [early–mid-17C] *... a mouse in a mill*, [mid-17C–mid-18C] *... a crow/sow in a gutter*, [mid–late 17C] *... a mouse in a malt-heap*, [late 17C] *... a mouse in a cheese*, [late 18C–early 19C] *... the bank*, [mid-19C–1910s] *... coons*, [mid-19C–1920s] *... the bellows*, [mid-19C+] *... houses*, [late 19C] *... a church*, [late 19C+] *... anything*.

safe as a thief in a mill *phr.* [early 17C–late 18C] a phr. meaning not safe at all.

safe as Kelsey *phr.* [1910s+] extremely safe, absolutely secure. [for ety. *see* TIGHT AS KELSEY'S NUTS]

safe card *n.* [mid-19C–1920s] a trustworthy person. [SE *safe* + CARD n.[3]]

safety *n.* (US Black) **1** [1940s–50s] a bed. **2** [1950s] a condom (cf. SAFE n.).

saffers/saffron *n.* [1990s] a person who is very intoxicated by a drug. [? the yellowish complexion]

saga/sagger *adj.* [1950s] (W.I.) fashionable, showy, garish, over-dressed; thus *saga-boy*, *saga girl*, young people who adopt a particular style of dressing, e.g. tight-waisted jackets and peg-top trousers. [SE *swagger*]

sagebrusher *n.* [1920s] (US) a Western cowboy film (cf. HORSE OPERA).

sage hen *n.* [late 19C] (US) an inhabitant of Nevada. [? the state's abundance of prairie fowl]

sagger *see* SAGA.

sagging deuce *n.* [1990s] (US Black) a lowered Cadillac automobile. [SE *sagging* + DEUCE 25]

sago *n.* [1950s+] (Aus.) a Pacific Islander. [the food]

Sahara *n.* [1940s] (S.Afr.) a very tall, thin person. [? they look as if they have walked across the *Sahara* desert]

sail/sail about *v.* [late 17C–early 18C] to saunter.

sail close to the wind, to *phr.* [mid-19C+] to take risks, esp. with a set of rules and regulations. [naut. imagery]

sail in/into *v.* [mid-19C+] (orig. US) **1** to attack, physically or verbally. **2** to launch oneself headlong on a course of action. **3** to arrive, to enter, esp. in a slow and measured manner.

sail on another board, to *phr.* [16C–early 17C] to alter one's behaviour.

sailor's champagne *n.* [late 19C] beer.

sailor's farewell *n.* [late 19C+] any form of goodbye that is essentially a curse (cf. BEGGAR'S BENISON).

sailor's joy *n.* [20C] masturbation. [note SE *sailor's pleasure*, overhauling his sea-chest]

sailors on the sea *n.* [20C] tea. [rhy. sl.]

sails *n.* [1940s] (US Black) the human ears. [resemblance]

saint *n.* [mid-19C+] a long-suffering, altruistic person.

St Alban's clean shave *n.* [late 19C] a clergyman's beardless face, typical of the High Church.

saint and sinner *n.* [late 19C+] dinner. [rhy. sl.]

St Brew *n.* [1940s–50s] (US Black) St Louis, Missouri. [? the beer production of Missouri or play on jazz classic 'St Louis Blues']

St Geoffrey's day *phr.* [late 18C] never. [there is/was no St Geoffrey]

St George a-horseback *n.* [17C–18C] sexual intercourse in which the woman takes the superior position. [for ety. *see* RIDE A ST GEORGE]

St Giles's carpet *n.* [late 19C] (London) a sprinkling of sand on the street. [coined in the parish of *St Giles*, which included the criminal slums of Seven Dials]

St Giles's Greek *n.* [early 17C–19C] slang, cant (cf. HEBREW; PEDLAR'S FRENCH). [proper name *St Giles*, the central London criminal 'rookery', destroyed when New Oxford Street was cut through the slums in 1847 + GREEK n.[2]]

St Grotlesex *n.* [1980s] (US) a portmanteau description of the East coast preparatory schools *St* Marks, *St* Paul's, *Grot*on and Midd*lesex*.

St Hugh's bones *n.* **1** [early 17C–18C] shoemaker's tools. **2** [mid-19C] dice. [given that the trad. patron saints of shoemakers are St Crispin and St Crispinian, the link to (1) is not obvious; whether the Hugh in question was St Hugh (*c.*1140–1200) or Hugh of Lincoln (d.1255), supposedly murdered in a race libel against the city's Jews, is unknown]

St Johnstone's tippet *n.* [early 19C] the noose (cf. TYBURN TIPPET). [? a hanging judge or prison governor]

St John's Wood dona n. [late 19C] an up-market prostitute or kept woman (cf. ST JOHN'S WOOD VESTAL). [*St John's Wood*, the home of many courtesans + DONA]

St John's Wood vestal n. [19C] a prostitute. [*St John's Wood* + play on SE *vestal virgin*]

St Louis blues n. [20C] (Aus.) shoes. [rhy. sl.]

St Louis flats n. [1900s–30s] (US Black) flat, moccasin-like shoes with a design on the toe, a style of shoe popular among jazz musicians and gamblers.

St Lubbock n. [late 19C] a drunken riot; thus *feast of St Lubbock*, *St Lubbock's day*, a bank holiday. [the invention of the August and other bank holidays by Sir John *Lubbock*, 1st Baron Avebury (1834–1913), in 1871]

St Luke's bird n. [late 18C–mid-19C] an ox. [pictures of St Luke always feature him with an ox]

St Margret's ale n. [17C] water (cf. ADAM'S ALE). [ety. unknown]

St Martin's/Martin's/St Martin's le Grand n. [mid-19C–1940s] the hand. [rhy. sl.; *St Martin's le Grand* was a monastery and college founded *c*.1050. Its bells rang the nightly curfew, and prisoners on their way from Newgate to Tyburn regularly passed it; those who managed to escape were able to claim sanctuary within its walls – thieves and coiners were accepted, Jews and traitors were barred. It was suppressed in 1540, and its only memory is a street name]

St Martin's lace/rings/stuff/ware n. [early 17C] respectively, fake gold lace, imitation gold rings and counterfeit goods of any sort; thus *Martin chain*, an imitation gold chain. [16C SE *St Martin's*, 'the parish of St Martin-le-Grand, London, formerly celebrated as the resort of dealers in imitation jewellery' (*OED*)]

St Monday n. [late 18C–mid-19C] a day off; thus *keep St Monday*, take a day off work. [the workman's incapacity following a weekend's drinking. The phr. mocks the trad. SE *saint's day*, a religious holiday]

St Nicholas's clergyman/clerk n. [late 16C] a highwayman. [? mis-reading of OLD NICK; i.e. the Devil]

St Patrick n. [mid-17C–mid-19C] the very best whisky. [DRINK AT ST PATRICK'S WELL]

St Peter n. [19C] the penis. [he 'keeps the keys of Paradise']

St Peter's sons n. [late 18C] petty thieves, who take anything they can lay their hands on (cf. ANGLER; FIDLAM-BEN; HOOKER n.¹). [proper name *St Peter*, 'the greatest fisherman' and disciple of Christ; such thieves 'having every finger a fish-hook' (Grose, 1796)]

St Tibb's/Tib's eve n. [late 18C–1900s] never. [defined as 'when Adam was an oakum-boy in Chatham dockyard' (Hotten, 1867)]

St Vitus's dance n. [20C] (Aus.) the pants. [rhy. sl.]

sakes!/sakes alive! excl. [mid-19C+] (US) a mild oath. [i.e. *for Lord's/God's sake!*]

sal n.¹ [18C] a form of treatment for syphilis; thus *in a high sal*, undergoing such a treatment. [abbr. SE *salivation*]

Sal/Sally n.² [1910s+] (US/UK) the *Sal*vation Army (cf. SALLY ANN). [abbr.]

sal n.³ *see* SALTING.

salad n. [1980s+] (US drugs) a mixture of different varieties of cannabis.

salad basket n. [1960s] a police van (cf. BLACK ANNIE). [trans. of Fr. sl. *panier à salade*, lit. 'salad basket'. So called from the iron grating or trellis that covered the rear of the original 'baskets', horse-drawn carts in which prisoners were transported]

salad oil n. [1910s–20s] hair oil.

salamander n. [mid-19C] a fire-eating juggler. [SE *salamander*, a mythical lizard-like animal, once thought to be capable of living in fire]

salami slapper n. [1990s] **1** a masturbator. **2** a general pej. term.

salamon/salmon/solomon n. [late 17C–18C] (Und.) the Mass, usu. as in the beggars' oath *by salamon!* by the Mass! (cf. SOLOMON; UPON MY SAM!). [? Fr. *serment*, a sermon (*OED*), or cant term for an altar (Harman)]

salbe n. [1960s–70s] (US Black) King Solomon wine, a cheap, sweet wine, available only in Black communities. [? Sp.]

salesman's dog n. [late 17C–mid-18C] a shop tout. [pun on BARKER n.¹ (3)]

sal hatch n. [late 19C] an umbrella. ['origin quite obscure – but probably salacious' (Ware). However, ? SE *sal hatch*, a dirty wench, via the fictional embodiment of umbrella users, Charles Dickens's Mrs Sarah Gamp in *Martin Chuzzlewit* (1843–4)]

salisbury n.¹ [17C] a gallon pot of wine with a tap (cf. SHAFTES-BURY). [ety. unknown]

salisbury n.² [late 19C] a polite evasion, a 'white lie'. [the alleged characteristic of British Prime Minister, Lord *Salisbury* (1830–1903)]

Salisbury Crag n. [1980s] (drugs) heroin. [rhy. sl. *Salisbury Crag* = SCAG n.²]

sallenger's/sallinger's dance/round phr. [17C–early 18C] sexual intercourse (cf. DANCE SALLENGER'S ROUND). [*Sallenger*, St Leger. 'St Leger's Round' was a popular ballad *c*.1600]

Sallies, the n. [1910s+] (Aus.) the *Sal*vation Army. [abbr.]

sallinger's dance/round *see* SALLENGER'S DANCE.

Sally n.¹ *see* SAL n.².

sally n.² [1980s+] (US campus) a person who is punctilious to an absurd, near-certifiable degree. [film *When Harry Met Sally* (1989)]

Sally Ann/Army n. [1920s+] the *Sal*vation *Army* (cf. SALVO). [abbr.]

Sally B. n. [late 19C] (US) a tall, thin woman. [abbr.; a ref. to the actress *Sarah Bernhardt* (1844–1923)]

Sally bash n. [1970s+] the *Sal*vation Army. [abbr. + SE *bash*]

Sally Lunn n. [late 19C+] a round, flat bun made with sweet yeast dough, usu. served hot. [proper name of the bun's inventor. 'The bun ... called the Sally Lunn, originated with a young woman of that name in Bath, about thirty years ago. She first cried them ... Dalmer, a respectable baker and musician, noticed her, bought her business, and made a song ... in behalf of Sally Lunn' (William Home, *Every-day Book*, 1827)]

salmagundy n. [late 18C–early 19C] a cook. [the dish]

salmon *see* SALAMON.

salmon and trout n. **1** [mid-19C+] tobacco, esp. prison use. **2** [mid-19C+] the mouth (cf. SALMON TROUT). **3** [20C] the nose (cf. I SUPPOSE). **4** [20C] stout beer (cf. IN-AND-OUT n.²). **5** [1930s] a bookmaker's tout. **6** [1930s+] gout. [rhy. sl.; (1) *salmon and trout* = SNOUT n.²; (3) = SE *snout*]

salmon canyon n. [1990s] the female genitals (cf. BEARDED CLAM; FISH n.⁴). [equation of the female genitals with SE *fish*]

salmon-tot retriever n. [20C] (W.I.) a mongrel, kept as a watch-dog and allowed to forage for its food. [Carib.E. *salmon-tot*, a salmon-tin + mockery of the pedigree *retriever* breed]

salmon trout n. [mid-19C] the mouth (cf. SALMON AND TROUT).

saloman *see* SOLOMON.

salomon *see* SALAMON.

saloon-bar cowboy n. [20C] a man who specializes in picking up women who, like him, can be found frequenting the saloon bars of public houses (cf. CORNER BOY).

saloon smasher n. [1900s] (US) one who wrecks saloons as a protest against the supposed 'evils of alcohol'. [the best known was the US temperance campaigner Carrie Nation (1846–1911)]

salop *n.* [20C] (W.I.) a dirty, grubby person, esp. a woman or child. [Fr. *salope*, a slut, a prostitute]

sal slappers *n.* [late 19C] (coster) a prostitute or promiscuous woman. [SE *Sal*, abbr. *Sarah* + SLAPPER]

salt *n.*[1] [mid-17C–early 18C] sexual intercourse. [SE *salt*, lecherous]

salt *n.*[2] [mid-19C+] a veteran sailor. [abbr. OLD SALT]

salt *n.*[3] [1960s–70s] (drugs) heroin. [resemblance]

salt *n.*[4] [1990s] (US Black) trouble, annoyance, difficulties; thus *get salt*, to be thwarted, to encounter misfortune (cf. SALT adj.[5]). [the image of oversalting one's food]

salt *adj.*[1] [early 18C–late 19C] costly, expensive, esp. over-expensive. [the 'salting' of mines, thus the padding of bills]

salt *adj.*[2] [mid-19C] of high rank, of great wealth. [? SE phr. *above the salt*]

salt *adj.*[3] [late 19C+] very drunk (cf. SALT!). [later use W.I. ? rhy. sl. SALT JUNK = drunk. Allsopp prefers pun on PICKLED adj.[1]]

salt *adj.*[4] [1950s+] (W.I. Rasta) impoverished, empty-handed, low on funds or food. [? the bitterness of the condiment]

salt *adj.*[5] [1990s] (W.I.) unlucky, ill-starred, in a bad state. [SALT n.[4]]

salt *v.*[1] [late 16C–early 17C] (student) to initiate new students by a variety of rituals, esp. making them drink salt water or swallow dry salt.

salt *v.*[2] [mid-19C+] (orig. US) to 'improve' the apparent quality of a mine by planting specimens of the ore it supposedly yields; also used fig.

salt! *excl.* [late 19C] used to indicate that someone is drunk. [SALT adj.[3]]

salt and pepper *n.*[1] [1940s–50s] (drugs) marijuana, esp. of poor quality. [ety. unknown]

salt and pepper *n.*[2] [1950s+] (US Black) **1** an inter-racial couple. **2** friends of different races. **3** a police team, usu. operating from a squad car, that consists of one Black and one White policeman. **4** a black and white squad car.

salt-and-pepper *adj.* [1950s+] (US) **1** of a person, mixed-race. **2** of a place, frequented by both Blacks and Whites, e.g. *salt-and-pepper neighbourhood*. [SALT AND PEPPER n.[2]]

salt-and-pepper queens *n.* [1970s+] (gay) a mixed-race gay couple. [SALT-AND-PEPPER + QUEEN n.[1]]

salt as Lot's wife's backbone *phr.* [late 19C] extremely salty. [the biblical story of Sodom and Gomorrah and the turning of Lot's wife into a pillar of salt (Gen. 19:26)]

salt away *v.* [mid-19C+] to store, to put away (cf. SALT DOWN v.[1]).

salt-box *n.* [mid-19C] the condemned cell at Newgate prison. [? the salt tears shed within it]

salt-cellar *n.*[1] [19C] the vagina. [SE *salt*, lecherous]

salt-cellar *n.*[2] [late 19C] the cavity above a woman's collar-bone. **2** [1950s+] (nursery) the navel.

salt down *v.*[1] [mid–late 19C] to put by, to store away (cf. SALT AWAY).

salt down *v.*[2] [1900s–10s] (US) to tell off, to reprimand. [SALTY]

salted *adj.*[1] [18C] drunk (cf. ALED UP). [? play on PICKLED adj.[1]]

salted *adj.*[2] [mid–late 19C] experienced. [SE *salted*, of a horse, having survived a disease]

saltee *n.* [mid-19C] (Ling. Fr./Polari) one penny; thus *oney saltee*, one penny, *dooe saltee*, twopence, *tray saltee*, threepence, *quarterer saltee*, fourpence, *chinker saltee*, five-pence, *say saltee*, sixpence, *setter saltee* or *say oney saltee*, sevenpence, *otter saltee* or *say dooe saltee*, eightpence, *nobba saltee* or *say tray saltee*, ninepence, *dacha saltee* or *say quarterer saltee*, tenpence, *dacha oney saltee* or *say chinker saltee*, elevenpence, *oney beong*, one shilling, *beong say saltee*, one shilling and sixpence (cf. BEONG). [Ital. *soldi*, pl. of *soldo*, one-twentieth of a lira. Combs. are based on Ital.

numbers one to ten, *uno, due, tre, quattro, cinque, sei, sette, otto, nove, dieci*]

salt eel *n.* [early 17C–1940s] a rope's end, used for flogging; thus *have salt eel/a salt eel for supper*, to be flogged.

salt horse *n.* [19C] salt beef (cf. OLD HORSE n.[2]).

saltie *n.* [1950s+] (Aus.) a *salt*-water crocodile. [abbr.]

salting/sal *n.* [1950s+] (W.I. Rasta) the vagina. [fig. use of Carib.E. *salting*, i.e. 'salt thing, or *salt food*, dishes cooked with salt fish or meat]

salt it for someone *v.* [1910s–20s] to make problems for someone.

salt junk *adj.* [late 19C–1900s] drunk. [rhy. sl.]

salts *n.* **1** [mid-18C–mid-19C] smelling *salts*. **2** [mid-18C–late 19C] Epsom *salts* (magnesium sulphate). [abbr.]

salts and senna *n.* [mid–late 19C] a doctor. [their common prescriptions]

salt someone's game, to *phr.* [1990s] (US Black) to interfere in another person's planned seduction (cf. BURRITO ON SOMEONE'S NOSE; SALT UP). [SE *salt* + GAME n.[4] (5)]

salt the books, to *phr.* [late 19C+] to improve the state of a firm's accounts by judicious, if illicit, alterations to the figures. [SALT v.[2]]

salt up *v.* [1980s+] (US campus) to cause trouble for, to place in a difficult or embarrassing situation (cf. SALT SOMEONE'S GAME). [? the image of 'adding flavour' to the situation]

salt water *n.* **1** [late 17C–early 18C] urine. **2** [mid-19C] a sailor (cf. SALT n.[2]).

salt-water negro *n.* [early 19C] (W.I.) an African-born Black person, so called by the Creoles, who were born in the West Indies (cf. GUINEA BIRD). [note *salt-water Creole*, a Black person born during the voyage from Africa; to be a full Creole it is necessary to be born on the islands]

salty *adj.* (US) **1** [1930s+] irritated, annoyed, feeling sour (cf. JUMP SALTY). **2** [1970s+] tough, aggressive, used of a veteran of a particular environment, e.g. a prison. **3** [1970s+] (teen) a general pej., unpleasant, uncouth, crude. [? US navy jargon *salty*, tough, aggressive]

salty bananas *n.* [20C] (Aus.) sultanas. [rhy. sl.]

salty dog *n.* [1970s] (US Black) one who uses an excess of obscene language. [SALTY (2)]

salty yogurt slinger *n.* [1990s] the penis.

salubrious *adj.* [19C] drunk (cf. ABOUT RIGHT adj.[1]). [SE *salubrious*, conducive to good health]

salute the sailor, to *phr.* [1990s] to masturbate.

salvage *v.* [1910s+] (Aus./US) to steal, to pilfer (cf. ACQUIRE).

salvation *n.* [late 19C–1910s] a station. [rhy. sl.]

Salvation Army *adj.* [late 19C] **1** crazy, eccentric. **2** drunk. [rhy. sl. *Salvation Army* = BARMY]

salvation juggins *n.* [late 19C] a member of the Salvation Army; also *salvation rotter, salvation soul-sneaker*. [SE *salvation* + JUGGINS/ROTTER n.[1]/SE *soul-sneaker*; all these negative nicknames came from many people's dislike of the Army's heavy-handed religiosity, esp. its attacks on drinking and similar pleasures, which undermined its charitable reputation]

salve *n.* **1** [mid-19C–1900s] praise, flattery; thus (US) *spread the salve*, to talk in a conciliatory, soothing manner; [mid-19C] *salve over*, to persuade by smooth speech. **2** [20C] (US tramp) butter (cf. PENNSYLVANIA SALVE). **3** [20C] (US) a bribe (cf. PALM OIL). **4** [20C] (US) money esp. as a reward for something difficult.

salve *v.* [20C] (US) to pay, usu. a bribe or reward. [SALVE n.]

salve-eater *n.* [late 19C+] (US) an immigrant from northern Europe, esp. a Swede. [derog. ref. to national habits; ? anecdotal]

Salvo *n.* [late 19C+] (Aus.) the *Salv*ation Army or one of its members (cf. SAL n.[2]; SALLY ANN). [abbr. + sfx. -O]

sam *n.*[1] [mid-19C] a fool, a simpleton. [abbr. SAMMY n.[3]]

sam *n.*[2] [1940s–50s] (US Black) a Black man who willingly conforms to White stereotyping (cf. TOM n.[11]). [*Old Black Sam* or SAMBO n.[1]]

sam *n.*[3] [1950s–60s] a generic used when the proper name has been forgotten, esp. of women.

sam *n.*[4] [1950s–60s] (camp gay) the embodiment of the male side of one's personality (cf. JANE n.[2]).

sam *n.*[5] [1980s+] (drugs) a Federal narcotics agent. [UNCLE SAM n.[1]]

sam *v.*[1] [late 19C] to pay for a drink. [abbr. STAND SAM]

sam *v.*[2] [1960s–70s] to cheat, to deceive. [? SAMMY n.[2]]

sam and dave *n.* [1980s] the police, when working in a team of two. [soul singers *Sam Moore* (b.1935) and *Dave Prater* (1937–88)].

sambie *see* SAMBO n.[2].

sambo *n.*[1] **1** [18C+] a derog. term for a Black man. **2** [1950s+] (W.I. Rasta) the colour between brown and black, someone who is a cross between a mulatto (brown) and a full Black. [Sp. *zambo*, used to describe those of mixed Negro and Indian or European blood. The word also describes a breed of yellow monkey. The US use, which emerged during the era of slavery, may have a different root; the Foulah *sambo*, uncle or Hausa *sambo*, second son, or name of the spirit. The suggestion by F&H of a third root, an African tribe, the Samboses (for whom they claim an appearance in a text of 1558) has no validity. *Sambo* began as a neutral term, but as slavery fell into increasing disrepute, so did its terminology. The word was widely popularized by Helen Bannerman's best-selling children's book *The Story of Little Black Sambo* (1923), but the term, and that book, have long since been considered unacceptable]

sambo/sambie *n.*[2] [1970s+] (Aus.) a sandwich (cf. SAMMO; SANGER; SANGO; SARMIE; SARNIE). [abbr.]

sambo backra *n.* [1950s] (W.I.) a person of mixed race, usu. three-quarters Black. [SAMBO n.[1] + BACKRA]

same again *n.* **1** [1930s] the third drink of a session (cf. BINDER n.[2]; FINAL; ONE FOR THE BITUMEN; OTHER HALF; SWING OF THE DOOR). **2** [1930s+] a general response to an offer of another drink, usu. in a public house setting.

same but different *phr.* [1940s+] (US) essentially the same, but nevertheless differing in subtleties.

same difference/diff *n.* [1940s+] exactly the same thing, no difference at all.

same lick at the same pop *phr.* [late 19C] (US Black) two different things happening simultaneously. [SE *lick*, a hit + POP n.[6]]

same man with his knee bent *phr.* [20C] (Irish) said of something or someone virtually identical to another object or person.

same o.b. *n.* [late 19C] one shilling (5p), esp. in the context of the charge for most contemporary places of entertainment. [SE *same old* + BOB n.[3]]

same old/ol' same old/ol' *phr.* [1930s+] (orig. US Black) a general expression to imply that nothing has changed in one's life, used in response to a question as to one's current health or feelings.

same old three and four/3 and 4 *n.* [late 19C] a weekly wage, 6 days at 3 shillings and 4 pence a day gives £1 for a 6-day week.

same ol' same ol' *see* SAME OLD SAME OLD.

same shit, different day *phr.* [20C] (orig. US Black) life goes on as normal, with no surprises, good or bad (cf. SAME OLD SAME OLD). [SHIT n.[3]]

samey *adj.* [1920s+] boring, tedious, undistinguished. [SE *same*]

samfai/samfi *see* SAMFIE v.

samfie/samfie man *n.* [20C] (W.I.) a confidence trickster; thus *samfieism*, deceit, trickery. [dial. *samfai*, an obeah-man, one who has magical powers, ult. ? Twi *asumanfo*, a magician, a sorcerer]

samfie/samfai/samfi *v.* [1970s+] (W.I./UK Black teen) to trick, to 'lead down the garden path'. [SAMFIE n.]

samfie man *see* SAMFIE n.

s.a.m.f.u. *phr.* [1940s+] (orig. milit.) self-adjusting military fuck-up (cf. S.N.A.F.U. phr.). [abbr.]

Sam Henry *see* JOHN T. HENRY.

Sam Hill! *excl.* [early 19C+] (orig. US) euph. for *hell* and as such often found as *what the Sam Hill!*

sammo *n.* [1950s] (Aus.) a sandwich (cf. SAMBO n.[2]).

sammy *n.*[1] [18C–1930s] (Ind. Army) the Hindu god Siva. [SE *Swami*]

sammy *n.*[2] **1** [19C–1940s] (S.Afr.) a generic name for any Hindu, esp. Indian people living in South Africa. **2** [1910s] an Indian fruit pedlar. [abbr. RAMSAMMY]

sammy/sammy soft *n.*[3] [early 19C–1930s] a fool (cf. SAM n.[1]).

sammy *n.*[4] *see* PORTSAMMY.

sammy *n.*[5] [1910s] (US) a US soldier during WW1. [UNCLE SAM n.[1]]

sammy *adj.*[1] [early 19C–1930s] foolish, dull. [SAMMY n.[3]]

sammy *adj.*[2] [1990s] (US teen) generous. [ety. unknown]

sammy soft *see* SAMMY n.[3].

samosa *n.* [1990s] (US teen) money. [ety. unknown]

sample *v.* **1** [19C] to caress or fondle a woman sexually. **2** [mid-19C] to drink.

sampler *n.* [19C] the vagina (cf. NEEDLEWORK). [SE *sampler*, a piece of embroidery, which is worked with a NEEDLE n.[1]]

sample room *n.* [mid–late 19C] (US) a bar, often as attached to a grocery, in which one can purchase liquor by the glass. ['Sometimes the bar is at the side, screened off, and genteelly disguised under the name of "sample room". You enter ostensibly to purchase cherries, and immediately "put yourself outside" a "tot" of Bourbon' (G.A. Sala, *My Diary in America*, 1865)]

sample the secret sauce, to *phr.* [1990s] to masturbate.

sampson *see* SAMSON.

samshoo *n.* [mid-19C] (Anglo-Chinese) a fiery liquor, distilled from rice or sorghum. [Chinese pidgin *samshoo, sam shu*; ult. ? *san shao*, thrice distilled, but this is a popular rather than a scholarly ety.]

samson/sampson *n.* [mid-19C] a drink combining brandy, cider, sugar and water. [the biblical strongman *Samson*; ? it gives one strength]

samurai sword *n.* [1980s+] (US gay) the penis of a Japanese gay man (cf. BAYONET; EGG ROLL n.[2]).

san *n.* [20C] a *sanitarium*, esp. at a boarding school. [abbr.]

-san *sfx.* [1990s] (US campus) a sfx. that conveys familiarity. [Jap. honorific; abbr. of formal *sana*, Mr/Mrs etc]

sancho *n.* [1980s+] (US prison) the new boyfriend/lover who takes one's place while one is incarcerated (cf. JODIE). [generic use of proper name]

sancocho *v.* [1980s+] (drugs) to steal. [Sp.]

sanctification *n.* [1970s] blackmail, esp. by secret services or foreign diplomats. [SANCTIFY]

sanctify *v.* [1970s] to blackmail someone, esp. for the purposes of extracting political favours. [SE *sanctify*, to render holy, to set apart as sacred]

sand *n.* **1** [early 19C+] sugar, now mainly US prison or short-order jargon; thus *Joe with cow and sand*, a cup of coffee with milk and sugar. **2** [late 19C] (US) money. **3** [late 19C–1910s] bread. **4** [late 19C] (US) courage, firmness of purpose, determination; thus *have sand in one's craw*, to act courageously (cf. GRIT n.[1]). [fig. uses of SE. Despite the BREAD n.[1] (2)/money link, (2) and (3) have no connection; (2)

refers to money not as a 'staff of life' but as dirt (cf. DUST n.[1])]

sand and canvas, to *phr.* [1910s–30s] (orig. naut.) to clean thoroughly. [the use of such materials for cleaning the decks]

sandbag *v.*[1] **1** [late 19C+] (orig. US) to ambush, to take by surprise. **2** [20C] (US) to intimidate (cf. BULLDOSE v.). [i.e. to hit with a SE *sandbag*]

sandbag *v.*[2] (US) **1** [20C] to feign weakness in order to mislead an opponent. **2** [1940s+] (poker) to resist raising the bet immediately in the hope of making a larger raise later on. [the use in war of SE *sandbags* as a protective wall from which one can then emerge]

sandbeef *n.* [late 19C–1920s] a sandwich. [mispron. by Italian snack-bar owners]

sand-grope *v.* [late 19C] (Aus.) to bungle. [SE *sand-grope*, to walk in soft sand]

sand-groper *n.* [late 19C+] (Aus.) an inhabitant of Western Australia; thus *sand-groper land*, Western Australia. [SE *sand-grope*, to walk through soft sand. Western Australia encompasses a large area of sandy desert]

sand-hog *n.* [1920s+] a caisson worker, working under compressed air, digging and laying the foundations of bridges etc (cf. GROUND-HOG n.[2]).

sandiness *n.* [late 19C] (US) the quality of having courage or 'guts'. [SAND n. (4)]

s and m/S&M *n.* [1960s+] **1** *sado-m*asochism (cf. SADIE AND MAISIE). **2** a *sado-m*asochist. [abbr.]

sandman *n.* [1910s+] (Aus.) a footpad, a mugger. [they 'sand-bag' their victim]

sand nigger *n.* [1980s+] (US) a derog. term for an Arab or any other native of the Middle East (except Israelis). [SE *sand* + NIGGER n.[1]]

sandoz *n.* [1960s+] (drugs) LSD (cf. A n.[3]). [the discovery of the drug by Dr Albert Hofmann at *Sandoz* Pharmaceuticals, Switzerland]

sandpaper suit *n.* [1940s] (N.Z.) a school cadet uniform. [the roughness of the material]

sandra bullocks *n.* [1990s] itching, uncomfortable testicles. [the film star *Sandra Bullock* (b.1966); play on *sweaty bollocks*]

sand scratcher *n.* [20C] (US) a derog. term for Syrian, an Indian (from India) (cf. CAMEL CHASER).

sand the banister/wood, to *phr.* [1990s] to masturbate.

sandwich *n.*[1] [mid–late 19C] a sandwich man, carrying a pair of advertising boards around the streets (cf. TOAD IN THE HOLE). ['the doleful broken-down men employed at one shilling a day to carry pairs of advertisement boards, tabard-fashion, one on the unambitious chest, the other on the broken back' (Ware)]

sandwich *n.*[2] [1960s+] a sexual threesome, involving any permutation of the sexes.

sandwich *n.*[3] [1980s+] (drugs) two layers of cocaine with a layer of heroin in the middle.

sandwich *v.* [1950s] (W.I.) to kiss (cf. TONGUE SUSHI).

sandwich lane *n.* [1970s+] (US) the middle lane of a three-lane highway (cf. GRANNY LANE). [one is sandwiched between the fast and slow lanes]

sandwich man *n.* [1970s+] (US Black) a man having sex with two women at the same time. [SANDWICH n.[2] + SE *man*]

sand wood *see* SAND THE BANISTER.

Sandy *n.* [late 18C+] a generic name for any Scot. [common Scot. name *Alexander*]

Sandy Bay peach *n.* [20C] (S.Afr.) a nectarine, as termed by street vendors. [the name of a popular nudist beach; the nectarine lacks the peach's furry 'coat']

Sandy Macnab *n.* **1** [1910s+] a crab, a body louse, usu. in pl. **2** [1920s+] (Aus.) a scab. **3** [1940s+] a taxi-cab. [rhy. sl.]

Sandy Powell *n.* [1940s–50s] **1** a trowel. **2** a towel. [rhy. sl.; the northern radio/music-hall comedian Albert '*Sandy*' *Powell* (1898–1982)]

sane/sein *n.* [1940s+] (Aus.) 10, in a variety of contexts, e.g. a 10-shilling note, a 10-year prison sentence, 10 ounces of tobacco. [Ger. *zehn*, 10]

san fairy ann *phr.* [1910s+] (orig. milit.) no matter, forget it. [synon. Fr. *ça ne fait rien*]

san fairy ann! *excl.* [1910s+] (orig. milit.) a general excl. of negation, e.g. I don't care! the hell with you! [SAN FAIRY ANN]

sang *n.* [mid-19C+] (US) gin*seng.* [abbr.]

sangaree *n.* [early–mid-19C+] a drinking bout. [SE *sangaree*, spiced wine, diluted with water; ult. Sp. *sangria*]

sanger *n.* [1940s+] (Aus./Irish) a sandwich (cf. SAMBO n.[2]).

sango *n.* [1960s+] (Aus.) a sandwich (cf. SAMBO n.[2]).

sangster *n.* [late 19C] an umbrella. [one *Sangster*, who patented a lightweight umbrella]

sanguinary *adj.* [late 19C–1940s] euph. for BLOODY.

sanguinary doubles *n.* [mid-19C] the Piccadilly Saloon, at 222 Piccadilly, London. [play on BLOODY adj.; ? the site of much bloodshed]

sanguinary james *n.* [early 19C–1910s] an uncooked sheep's head. [play on BLOODY JEMMY]

San Juan Hill *n.* [1900s–20s] (US) an area of New York City with a predominantly Black population, covering those blocks between 10th and 11th Avenues, between 59th Street and the low 60s. [the Battle of San Juan Hill (1898) in which many Black troops were involved]

sankey *n.* [1920s–50s] (W.I.) a hymn. [Ira David *Sankey* (1840–1908), who, with his partner Dwight Lyman Moody (1837–99), was the best known evangelist of the mid-19C]

sank work *n.* [mid-19C] the making of soldiers' clothes. [? Fr. *sang* (thus Norman *sanc*), blood, referring either to the scarlet uniform or the blood-letting that comes with soldiering]

san lo *n.* [late 19C–1930s] (US drugs) cheap, refined opium residue (cf. ROOSTER BRAND). [Chinese or fake Chinese]

s.a.n. man *phr.* [1970s+] (US prison) someone who is dangerous and violent, a stop *at* nothing *man*. [abbr.]

sanno *n.* [1930s+] (Aus.) a *san*itary carter or inspector. [abbr. + sfx. -O]

sanny *n.* [1940s+] a *san*itary towel. [abbr.]

sanpaku *adj.* [1960s+] out of touch, out of balance, physically and spiritually. [Zen use *sanpaku*, visibility of the white of the eye below the iris as well as (as usual) on either side; ult. Jap. *san*, three + *haku*, white]

San Quentin briefcase *n.* [1970s] (US) a large, portable tape-recorder-cum-radio (cf. GHETTOBLASTER). [*San Quentin* prison, California; the suggestion that those who carry such pieces of equipment are, *de facto*, criminals; accentuated by the racist stereotyping of the original users, young Black men]

San Quentin quail *n.* [20C] (US) a girl still under the age of consent who sleeps with an older man. [proper name of *San Quentin* prison + QUAIL; having sex with such a girl is likely to result in being imprisoned for statutory rape]

Santa Claus *n.* (US) **1** [20C] a generous benefactor. **2** [1970s+] (Black) a vulgar, gaudy and tasteless dresser (cf. CAUTION SIGN). [the popular image of the Christmas figure as both generous and gaudy]

Santa Claus hijack *n.* [1990s] (US campus) a mugging or other street robbery in which the victim and perpetrator are equally poor.

Santa Marta gold/red *n.* [1970s+] (drugs) a potent brand of marijuana from Colombia.

santar *n.* [16C] (Und.) that member of a team of parcel thieves who actually removes the stolen goods and takes them to a hide-out (cf. LIFTING LAW). [SE *sanctuary*]

san toys *n.* [1930s] villains, criminals. [rhy. sl. *san toys* = BOYS n.[1]; ult. *San Toy*, brandname of a small cigar]

sao *n.* [1960s+] (US) a repulsive, obnoxious person. [orig. US milit. in Vietnam]

sap *n.*[1] [late 18C–19C] (school) a hard worker. [Lat. *sapiens*, wise]

sap *n.*[2] [early 19C+] a fool, a dupe (cf. SAPSKULL). [SE *sap*, the vital juice of a plant; the image is of one who is thus 'green']

sap *n.*[3] [late 19C+] (US) a small club, orig. of wood, latterly a small leather 'bag' filled with sand, lead shot or similar material. [SE *sapling*, from which the weapons were orig. made]

sap *v.*[1] [late 18C–19C] (school) to work overly hard. [SAP n.[1]]

sap *v.*[2] [late 19C+] to attack using a blackjack. [SAP n.[3]]

s.a.p.f.u. *phr.* [1940s+] (milit.) surpassing all previous fuck-ups (cf. S.N.A.F.U. phr.). [abbr.]

sap-happy *adj.* [20C] (US) drunk. [SE *sap*, juice + sfx. *-happy* + pun on SLAP-HAPPY adj.]

sap-head *n.* [early 18C–late 19C] a fool (cf. SAP n.[2]; SAP-PATE; SAPSKULL). [SE *sap* + sfx. -HEAD (1)]

sapient *n.* [16C] (Und.) a travelling quack (cf. AURIUM). [SE *sapient*; ult. Lat. *sapiens*, wise man]

sap one's woody, to *phr.* [1990s] to masturbate. [SE *sap*, to drain + WOODIE n.[3]]

sap-pate *n.* [early 18C] a fool (cf. SAP n.[2]; SAP-HEAD; SAPSKULL). [SE *sap* + SE *pate*]

sapper *n.* [mid–late 19C] a man-about-town, a 'gay dog'. [a line sung by the Parisian music-hall star Theresa, who visited London *c.*1866, 'Rien est sacré pour un s–s–sapeur!', although note Fr. cant *sapeur*, a judge]

sapphire *n.* [1940s–60s] (US Black) an unpopular woman. [? she makes one BLUE adj.[1] (like the jewel); or f. the character Sapphire in the radio (later TV) show *Amos 'n' Andy* (late 1920s–50s), a portrait, as stereotyped as the rest of the cast, of a complaining, emasculating, unpleasant Black woman. Note the use of the name as the pseudonymous author of the 1996 novel *Push*, a story of poverty and abuse in the ghetto]

sappho *n.* [1950s+] a lesbian; thus *sapphic*, code-word for female homosexuality. [proper name *Sappho* (*c.*600BC), the poetess of the island of Lesbos]

sappho daddy-o *n.* [1950s] (US gay) a heterosexual man who socializes extensively with lesbians. [SAPPHO + DADDY-O n. (1)]

sappiness *n.* [20C] (US) stupidity. [SAPPY]

sappy *adj.* **1** [late 17C+] foolish, stupid. **2** [mid-19C+] (US) sentimental and mawkish. [SE *sap/*SAP n.[2]]

sapskull *n.* [18C] a fool. [SE *sap*, juice, liquid + *skull*; thus one who is 'soft in the head']

sap the tlas *phr.* [late 19C–1900s] a phr. used to urge a fellow drinker to pass the bottle. [backsl. lit. 'pass the salt']

Sarah Soo *n.* [1920s+] a Jew (cf. BOX OF GLUE). [rhy. sl.]

sarajevo! *excl.* [1980s+] (US campus) a farewell. ['see you later']

sard *v.* [16C–17C] to copulate. [10C when the *Lindisfarne Gospel* used it in its translation of Matt. 5:27, 'Ye have heard that it was said by them of old time, Thou shalt not commit adultery'. By the 17C it was the basis of a Nottingham proverb, 'Go teach your Grandma to sard', but vanished soon afterwards. It is one of Florio's synons. for Ital. *fottere*]

sardine box *n.*[1] [late 19C] a prison or police van (cf. BLACK ANNIE). [the close-packing of the prisoners]

sardine box/tin *n.*[2] [late 19C+] (Aus.) any extremely small dwelling.

sardine tin *n.* [1960s] a mini-car.

sarey gamp *n.* [mid-19C] an outsize umbrella used by stallholders; thus *gamp(ish)*, of an umbrella, bulging. [Charles Dickens's character *Sarah Gamp* in *Martin Chuzzlewit* (1843–4)]

sarge *n.* [mid-19C+] *serge*ant. [abbr.]

sargentlemanly *adv.* [late 19C] sarcastic allusion to one who is acting 'so gentlemanly'.

sargent's pie *n.* [1940s–50s] (Aus.) an eye. [rhy. sl.; a popular brand of meat pie, sold in Sydney]

sark *n.* [1980s+] (N.Z.) a sanitary towel. [? Scot. *sark*, a woman's undergarment]

Sarken News *n.* [late 19C] the *Clerkenwell News*, a major local paper of the period.

sarky *adj.* [1910s+] (usu. teen) *sarc*astic, ill-tempered. [abbr.]

sarm *n.* [1940s+] the physical likeness of, the image. [? SE *same*, but E.P. cites a correspondent who suggests Cantonese *san* (pron. 'sarm') meaning the number 3 in fan-tan; this is the 'safest' number on which one can bet]

sarmie/sarmy *n.* [1960s+] (S.Afr.) a sandwich (cf. SAMBO n.[2]). [abbr.]

sarnie *n.* [1960s+] a sandwich (cf. SAMBO n.[2]). [abbr.]

sarse/sarpidilly *n.* [1910s+] (Aus.) *sars*parilla, the dried root of *Smilax officinalis*, at one time used as a tonic. [abbr.]

sarvo *n.* [1940s+] (Aus./N.Z.) this afternoon. [abbr. SE *this* + ARVO]

sasfras *see* SASSAFRAS.

sashay *v.* [early 19C+] (US) **1** to walk or travel in a casual manner. **2** to wander, to saunter. **3** to strut, to parade, to walk in an ostentatious or provocative manner. [Fr. *chassé*, a gliding step in dancing]

sass *n.* [early 19C+] (US) cheek, impertinence. [SAUCE n.[2]]

sass *v.* [early 19C+] (US) to answer back, to cheek. [SASS n.]

sassafras/sasfras/sassfras *n.* [1940s–50s] (drugs) marijuana. [SE *sassafras* tree, the leaves of which are also used for *sassafras* TEA n.[2]]

sassiger/sassinger *n.* [late 19C+] a sausage. [mispron.]

sassy *adj.* [early 19C+] (US) cheeky, spirited, back-talking. [SE *saucy*]

sassy box *n.* [1970s] (US Black) **1** a saucy young woman (cf. SAUCY BOX). **2** the vagina. [SASSY + BOX n.[6]]

sata/satta *v.* [1950s+] (W.I. Rasta) to rejoice, to meditate, to give thanks and praise; thus *go satta*, to claim how spiritual one is.

satan's scent *n.* [1980s] (drugs) any inhalant.

satch *n.*[1] [1900s–40s] (US) **1** (Black) a notably large mouth; thus a person with a large mouth (cf. SATCHEL-MOUTH). **2** a talkative person. [abbr. SE *satchel*]

satch *n.*[2] [1930s–50s] (drugs) papers, letters, cards, clothing etc, saturated with drug solution (used to smuggle drugs into prisons or hospitals). [SE *saturate*]

satch *n.*[3] [1940s–50s] (US Black) a jacket. [? SACK n.[4]]

satch cotton *n.* [1960s] (drugs) fabric used to filter a solution of narcotics before injection; the cotton may be boiled later and the drug residue used. [SATCH n.[2] + COTTON n.[1]]

satchel *n.* [19C] the anus or buttocks (cf. KEISTER n.).

satchel *v.* [20C] (US) to pre-arrange the outcome of a contest, race or fight (cf. FIX v.[1]; RIG v.[1]). [SE 'in the bag']

satchel-arsed *adj.* [19C] a general term of abuse, often ext. to *satchel-arsed fellow, ... son of a whore*. [SE *satchel* + ARSE n.[1]]

satchel-mouth *n.* [1900s–40s] (US Black) anyone with a large mouth. [note the jazz musician Louis 'Satchmo' (*Satchel-Mouth*) Armstrong (1900–72)]

satellite *v.* [1980s] to hang around. [satellites circling a planet]

sate-poll *n.* [late 19C] a fool. [SE *sate*, to fill + *poll*, head; ? a head that is filled with nonsense]

satin *n.* **1** [mid-19C–1930s] gin (cf. RIBBON n.[3]; TAPE; WHITE n.[1]; WHITE SATIN). **2** [1970s+] (US Black) Italian Swiss Colony Silver *Satin* wine. [its supposed smoothness]

satin and silk *n.* [20C] milk. [rhy. sl.]

sativa *n.* [1970s] (drugs) cannabis. [abbr. botanical name *Cannabis sativa*]

satta see SATA.

sat-upon *adj.* [late 19C+] depressed, miserable.

saturated *adj.* [late 19C–1930s; 1980s+] very drunk (cf. LUBRICATED). [metaphorical, but also a lit. description of the bloodstream; its 1980s resurgence emerged in US campuses]

Saturday is longer than Sunday see MONDAY COMES BEFORE SUNDAY.

Saturday middles *n.* [late 19C] (society) the articles on the left-middle pages of the newspaper the *Saturday Review*.

Saturday night palsy/paralysis *n.* [1920s+] (US) the temporary paralysis of the arm, esp. a weakness in the wrist, after it has rested on a hard edge for a long time, as during sleep following a bout of drinking.

Saturday night pistol *n.* [1920s–30s] (US) a small handgun (cf. SATURDAY NIGHT SPECIAL).

Saturday night security *n.* [1940s+] (Aus.) a regular boyfriend.

Saturday night soldier *n.* [1910s+] **1** a member of the British Territorial Army (cf. SATURDAY SOLDIER). **2** (US) a member of the National Guard or militia. [they parade on weekends]

Saturday night special *n.* [1960s+] (US) a small handgun, often used in the many fracas that occur over Saturday night in big US cities (cf. SATURDAY NIGHT PISTOL).

Saturday pie *n.* [late 19C] pastry, esp. when covering the week's collected left-overs.

Saturday soldier *n.* [late 19C] a milit. volunteer (cf. SATURDAY NIGHT SOLDIER).

Saturday-to-Monday *n.* [1900s–10s] a mistress whom one sees only at weekends.

satyr *n.* [early 18C] (Und.) a professional horse thief. [SE *satyr*, a mythological Greek woodland demon, usu. pictured with the ears and tail of a horse. 'Men living wild in the Fields, that keep their Holds and Dwellings in the Country and forsaken Places, stealing Horses, Kine, Sheep, and all other sort of Cattle' (A. Smith, *Lives of the Highwaymen*, 1714)]

sauce *n.*[1] **1** [late 18C–early 19C] a venereal disease. **2** [1910s] (US) petrol, gasoline. **3** [1940s+] (orig. US) alcohol, (rarely) drugs.

sauce *n.*[2] [early 19C+] cheek, impudence. [? SE *saucy*, impudent + *sauce*, something that adds piquancy to a word, thought or action]

sauce *v.* [19C] to have sex. [the bodily fluids involved]

saucebox *n.*[1] [late 16C–19C] an impudent person. [SAUCE *n.*[2] + SE *box*]

saucebox *n.*[2] [mid-19C+] the mouth.

sauced *adj.* [1940s+] (orig. US) drunk (cf. LUBRICATED). [SAUCE *n.*[1] (3)]

sauce-hound *n.* [1940s+] (US) a drunkard, an alcoholic (cf. BOOZE HOUND). [SAUCE *n.*[1] (3) + sfx. -HOUND]

saucepan lid *n.* **1** [late 19C] money, esp. in pl. **2** [late 19C+] a tease. **3** [1950s+] a Jew. **4** [1960s+] a child. [rhy. sl.; (1) = QUID; (2) = KID *v.*; (3) = YID *n.*[1]; (4) = KID *n.*[1]]

saucer *n.* [mid-19C] an eye. [SE phr. *eyes like/as big as saucers*, coined 14C]

saucered and blowed *phr.* [20C] (US) prepared and ready. [the image of pouring hot tea into a saucer and blowing on it]

saucy box *n.* [18C] an impudent person (cf. SASSY BOX). [SE *saucy* + *box*]

saucy jack *n.* [mid-16C–late 18C] a cheeky, impudent man. [SE *saucy* + JACK *n.*[5]]

sauerkraut *n.* [mid–late 19C] (US) a derog. term for a German (cf. KRAUT); thus [1910s] *sauerkraut-eater*. [the popular German dish]

sausage *n.*[1] [19C+] the penis (cf. BACON *n.*[1]).

sausage *n.*[2] [late 19C–1920s] a German. [the stereotypical German partiality to sausages]

sausage *n.*[3] [20C] an ineffectual, easily imposed-upon person, esp. in teasing phr. *silly sausage/old sausage*.

sausage *n.*[4] [20C] (US) a prize-fighter, esp. one with a swollen bruised face.

sausage *n.*[5] [1940s+] a bitch 'on heat'. [pun on 'hot dog']

sausage *v.* [1920s+] to cash (a cheque) . [rhy. sl. SAUSAGE AND MASH *n.* (1) = cash]

sausage a goose's, to *phr.* [1920s] to cash a cheque. [SAUSAGE *v.* + rhy. sl. *goose's neck* = cheque]

sausage and mash *n.* **1** [late 19C+] cash (cf. NOT A SAUSAGE). **2** [1950s] a smash, a crash. [rhy. sl.]

sausage dog *n.* [1930s+] a dachshund (cf. DACHS). [its German origins and its roughly tubular shape]

sausage-eater *n.* [1910s] a German. [SAUSAGE *n.*[2]]

sausage jockey *n.* [1990s] (US) a male homosexual. [SAUSAGE *n.*[1] + JOCKEY *n.*[2]]

sausage roll *n.* **1** [1920s+] the dole. **2** [1940s+] a Pole. **3** [1960s+] (Aus.) a goal. [rhy. sl.]

sausages *n.* **1** [mid-19C] fetters; thus *string of sausages*, a chain. **2** [mid–late 19C] side-whiskers. [resemblance]

sausage sandwich *n.* [1990s] intercourse between the breasts. [SAUSAGE *n.*[1] + SE *sandwich*]

sausage smuggler *n.* [1990s] a male homosexual. [SAUSAGE *n.*[1] + SE *smuggler*]

sausage toad *n.* [late 19C+] a sausage 'toad-in-the-hole'. [the orig. *toad-in-the-hole* was made of meat baked in batter; most modern versions are based on sausages]

sausage wrapper *n.* [late 19C–1910s] (Aus.) a newspaper.

sausie/sossie *n.* [1990s] (N.Z.) a *sausage*. [abbr.]

sav *n.* [1940s–70s] (Aus.) a *saveloy*. [abbr.]

savage *n.* [20C] (US) a keen young police officer eager to make arrests.

savage *adj.* [early 19C+] extremely annoyed, furious. [weak use of SE]

save a life, to *phr.* [late 19C] to take a drink, to give a timely drink.

save-alls *n.* [late 18C–mid-19C] (Anglo-Irish) 'boys running about gentlemen's houses in Ireland, who are fed on broken meats that would otherwise be wasted.' (Grose, 1785). [SE *save-all*, 'a kind of candlestick used by our frugal forefathers to burn snuffs and ends of candles' (Grose, 1785)]

saved by the bell *phr.* [20C] (US) rescued or relieved at the last minute. [boxing imagery]

save it! *excl.* [1970s+] (US) be quiet! shut up!

saveloy *n.* [20C] a boy. [rhy. sl.]

Saveloy Square *n.* [late 19C] Duke Place, Aldgate. [as a centre of the East End Jewish community, no pork sausages, only beef *saveloys* were to be found there]

save one's bacon, to *phr.* [17C+] to escape safely from a place or situation. [SE *save* + BACON *n.*[1] (1)]

save one's gizzard, to *phr.* [late 19C] (US) to save oneself.

save one's groats, to *phr.* [late 18C–19C] to succeed, to do well. [university custom, those taking their finals deposit 9 groats with an academic officer; if they pass with honours the groats are returned]

saver *n.* [late 19C+] a hedging bet. [the gambler hopes to 'save' their money, which may be lost on the other, main bet]

save-reverence see SIR-REVERENCE.

save them all for Lisa *phr.* [late 19C] used of a young man who will neither swear nor fight. [the assumption is that this public probity is overturned when in private; there he berates and even beats his girlfriend]

savey see SAVVY *n.*

saving chin *n.* [late 18C–mid-19C] a protruding chin. [it supposedly catches the food that drops from the mouth when its owner is eating badly]

savoury rissole *n.* [20C] **1** a lavatory. **2** anywhere dirty or unpleasant. [rhy. sl. *savoury rissole* = PISSHOLE n.]

savvy/sabbe/sabby/sabe/savey/savvey/scavey *ŋ.* [late 18C+] understanding, intelligence, awareness. [SAVVY v.]

savvy *v.* [late 18C+] to understand, to be aware of; thus *savvy,* intelligent, aware. [Fr. *savoir*, to know, to understand]

saw *n.*[1] (US) **1** [mid-19C+] a *saw*-handled pistol. **2** [mid-19C+] $10. [abbr.; (2) SAWBUCK]

saw *n.*[2] (US Black) **1** [1900s–50s] an unpleasant, mean person. **2** [1970s] the owner of a cheap rooming house. [? their 'rough/sharp edges']

saw/saw off a chunk/length/piece, to *phr.* [1960s+] to have sexual intercourse (cf. KNOCK OFF A PIECE; TEAR OFF A PIECE).

saw away *v.* [early 19C] to talk incessantly, to chatter on.

sawbones *n.* [mid-19C+] a doctor, a surgeon.

sawbuck/sawski *n.* **1** [mid-19C+] (US) $10 (cf. DOUBLE SAWBUCK). **2** [1920s+] a 10-year prison sentence (cf. DIME n.[1]). [SE *sawbuck*, an X-shaped sawhorse; the X of the sawhorse is equated with the Roman numeral *X*, 10 + BUCK n.[2]/joc. use of 'Slavic' sfx. *-ski*]

sawder *n.* [mid-19C] flattery, nonsense, empty words. [SE *(soft) solder*, a pliable form of solder, made of tin and lead]

sawder *v.* [mid-19C] to flatter. [SAWDER n.]

sawdust *n.*[1] [late 19C] flattery, insincerity. [? SAWDER n.]

sawdust *n.*[2] [20C] **1** (US Und.) dynamite. **2** (US campus) sugar.

sawdust game *n.* [late 19C–1930s] (US) a confidence trick based on the passing of bad banknotes. [? SAWDUST n.[1]]

sawdust joint/parlour *n.* [late 19C] a down-market restaurant or bar (cf. RUG JOINT). [SE *sawdust* + JOINT n.[3]/SE *parlour*; such places lacked smart interiors and their plank floorboards were covered only by sawdust]

sawed off *n.* [late 19C+] (US) **1** a sawn-off shotgun (cf. SAWN OFF). **2** a short person.

saw gourds *v.* [mid-19C+] (orig. US) to snore loudly.

saw-handle *n.* [late 19C] (US) a saw-handled pistol.

sawn *n.* [1950s+] (Aus.) a simpleton. [abbr. SAWNEY n.[1] (1)]

sawney *n.*[1] **1** [late 17C–mid-19C] a fool (cf. YAWNEY). **2** [mid-19C] a clumsy person, a thug (cf. SONKRY). [SE *zany*, a fool a laughing stock]

sawney *n.*[2] [early 18C–mid-19C] a Scotsman. [proper name *Sawney*, SANDY, thus Alexander]

sawney *n.*[3] [mid–late 19C] bacon. [? SE *sawn*, i.e. the 'sawing off' of bacon into rashers, or the cannibalistic *Sawney* Beane (*fl.*15C), who killed people, smoked their corpses and ate them]

sawney *v.* [mid-19C] to work as a pimp or procurer. [SE *sawney*, to soft soap, to cajole, to wheedle]

sawney-hunter *n.* [mid-19C] one who steals bacon or cheese from grocers' shops. [SAWNEY n.[3]]

sawneying *n.* [mid-19C] pimping. [SAWNEY v.]

sawn off *n.* [1910s+] a *sawn-off* shotgun (cf. SAWED OFF). [abbr.]

sawn-off *adj.* [1930s+] short. [the presumption being that a short person was once taller than they are now]

saw-off *n.* [1910s+] (Can.) a tie, a draw.

saw off a chunk *see* SAW A CHUNK.

sawski *see* SAWBUCK.

saw them off *v.* [1930s–40s] to snore (cf. SAW GOURDS).

saw wood *v.*[1] [late 19C–1930s] (US) to carry on as normal, to get on with one's work, to keep to oneself. [the mundane act of sawing wood]

saw wood *v.*[2] [20C] (US) to snore (cf. CHOP WOOD; SAW GOURDS; SAW THEM OFF). [the noise produced]

saw your timber! *excl.* [mid-19C] go away! be off! (cf. AMPUTATE ONE'S MAHOGANY).

sax *n.* **1** [1910s+] a *saxophone*. **2** [1920–70s] (Aus.) *six*pence. [abbr.; (2) is mispron.]

saxa *n.* [1920s+] (Aus.) a *sax*ophone. [abbr.]

Saxon shilling *n.* [1910s+] (Irish) the payment of one shilling (5p) made to Irish volunteers to the British Army. [abbr. SE *Anglo-Saxon*]

say/sei/sey *n.* [mid-19C+] (Ling. Fr./Polari) the number 6. [Ital. *sei,* 6]

say *adv.* [mid-19C] yes. [backsl.]

say! *excl.* [late 19C+] (US) listen! wait a minute!

say a mouthful, to *phr.* (orig. US) **1** [late 19C+] to say something important and true. **2** [1960s+] (gay) to reprove a fellow homosexual in detail and at great length.

say an ape's paternoster, to *phr.* [early 17C] to chatter with cold. [the chattering of one's teeth, presumably reminiscent of an ape 'praying']

say away! *excl.* [mid-19C+] an invitation for the speaker to carry on talking, to come to the point, to say exactly what they want to say (cf. AWAY adv.).

say calf-rope *see* HOLLER CALF-ROPE.

say/tell howdy to, to *phr.* [mid-19C+] (orig. US) to say hello to someone. [SE *how d'you do?*]

say neither buff nor baff, to *phr.* [late 15C–17C] to say nothing. [both ? echoic of a dog's bark]

say no more *see* NUDGE, NUDGE, WINK, WINK.

say nothing *v.* [1950s–60s] (US Black) to talk trivially (cf. SAY SOMETHING).

say one's piece, to *phr.* [1910s+] to make oneself heard, to say what one has decided to say, esp. for moral reasons (cf. SPEAK A PIECE).

say one's prayers backwards, to *phr.* [early 18C–early 19C] to blaspheme. [the supposed rituals of 'black magic', in which this was done]

say-so *n.* [late 18C+] the power of decision.

say soldi *n.* [late 19C] 6 shillings (30p). [Ital. *sei soldi* or Polari SAY + SALTEE n.]

say something *v.* [1950s–60s] (US Black) to make an important statement, to say something profound (cf. SAY NOTHING).

says which? *phr.* [20C] (US) a derisive, rhetorical question, e.g. what did I hear you say? (cf. SAY WHAT?).

says/sez you! *excl.* [late 17C+] a general excl. of contempt and disbelief, dismissing as beneath argument the previous speaker's words.

say uncle *v.* [1920s+] (US) to surrender, to give up, usu. in a children's fighting game. [ety. unknown; ? lit. use of SE *uncle*]

say what?/which? *phr.* [19C+] (US) an expression of mock disbelief, e.g. what did you say? are you telling the truth?

say when *phr.* [late 19C+] formula used when pouring someone else a drink, i.e. say when you want me to stop pouring.

say which? *see* SAY WHAT?

s.b.d. *n.* [1960s+] the breaking of wind silently and with a foul smell. [abbr. *s*ilent *b*ut *d*eadly]

'sblood!/'sblud!/'sbud!/'slud!/'zblood/'zbud! *excl.* [17C] a euph. oath, lit. 'God's blood' (cf. 's abbr.[1]).

'sbody! *excl.* [17C] a euph. oath, lit 'God's body' (cf. 's abbr.[1]; GOD'S BODIKINS!).

'sbores! *excl.* [mid-17C] an oath, lit. 'God's bores!' (cf. 's abbr.[1]; ZOUNDS!). [SE *bore*, a hole or puncture inflicted by penetration; thus the wounds inflicted on the crucified Christ]

sbud! *see* 'SBLOOD!

s.c. *n.* [1990s] (US Black teen) *S*outh-*C*entral Los Angeles. [abbr.]

scab *n.* **1** [late 16C+] an unpleasant person. **2** [17C] a prostitute (cf. DIRTY LEG). **3** [17C–18C] a sheriff's officer, a constable.

4 [late 18C+] a strike-breaker (cf. BLACKLEG n.²). **5** [1960s+] (US Black) an unattractive woman.

scab v. **1** [early 19C+] to break a strike. **2** [early 19C–1920s] to brand a company or fellow worker as a strike-breaker. [SCAB n. (4)]

scabbado n. [17C] syphilis. [a 'Spanished' version of SE scab, syphilis]

scabbard n. [19C] the vagina. [a trans. of Lat. and euph. for SE vagina]

scabbed adj. [1960s] (drugs) cheated in a deal. [SCAB v.]

scabbery n. [1910s–60s] (Aus.) the betrayal of one's fellow workers, the breaking of a strike. [SCAB v.]

scabby n. [1910s+] (Aus.) a non-union worker. [SCAB n. (4)]

scabby adj.¹ [mid-19C] of a person, unpleasant, contemptible, generally distasteful. [SE scab, a variety of skin diseases, incl. syphilis, which is the most likely ref. in a sl. context]

scabby adj.² [late 19C+] (Aus.) non-union. [SCAB n. (4)]

scabby-neck n. [mid-19C] a native of Denmark. [orig. naut. use]

scabby sheep n. [mid-19C] 'a person who has been in questionable society, or under unholy influence, and become tainted' (Hotten, 1864). [SE scabby sheep, a sheep that has a diseased mouth; thus a moral leper, a corrupt person; sheep also puns on the popular religious use of the word]

scad n. [19C] (US) $1 (cf. SCADS).

scadger n. [mid–late 19C] a general term of abuse, a mean, contemptible person, someone who always wants a loan. [SE cadger + ? Cornish scadgan, a tramp]

scadoodle v. [mid-19C] to run off, to leave in a hurry. [SKEDADDLE v. + SCOOT v.]

scads/scadoodles n. [19C+] large quantities (cf. SCAD). [ety. unknown]

scaffle n. [1980s+] (drugs) phencyclidine (cf. ACE n.³). [var. on SCUFFLE n.²]

scaffold pole n. [late 19C] a chipped potato. [joc. resemblance]

scag/skag n.¹ [1910s–20s] (US) a cigarette, a cigar, a cigarette butt. [? elision of SE cigar(ette)]

scag/skag n.² **1** [1960s+] (drugs) heroin. **2** [1960s] hard liquor. [ety. unknown; note Smitherman: 'low-grade heroin that has been diluted']

scagged/skagged adj. [1960s+] (drugs) addicted to heroin. [SCAG n.² (1)]

scag/skag hag n. [1960s+] (gay) one who enjoys associating with heroin addicts (cf. FAG HAG). [SCAG n.² (1) + SE hag]

scag/skag jones n. [1960s+] (US drugs) a heroin addiction. [SCAG n.² (1) + JONES n.¹]

scag/skag town n. [1960s+] (drugs) an area of a city or town where addicts live and heroin is easily available. [SCAG n.² (1) + SE town]

scald n. [20C] (Irish) tea. [Irish scal, hot tea]

scald adj. [17C] suffering from venereal disease (cf. BURN v.¹; PASS THROUGH THE FIRE). [obs. 16C dial. scald, scabbed, afflicted with the 'scall' (any scaly or scabby disease of the skin, esp. of the scalp; dry scall was psoriasis, humid or moist scall was eczema)]

scald v.¹ [17C–late 19C] to infect with venereal disease. [SCALD adj.]

scald v.² [20C] (Irish) to reprimand, to scold. [Irish scall, to scald; thus fig. to grieve bitterly]

scalded adj. [19C] suffering from venereal disease. [ext. of SCALD adj.]

scalder n.¹ [17C] venereal disease. [SCALD adj.]

scalder n.² [late 19C] tea. [SE scald, to burn]

scaldrum/scoldrum n. [mid-19C] (Und.) a beggar, esp. one who poses as the victim of a disfiguring accident (cf. SCALDRUM DODGE). [SE scald, burn]

scaldrum dodge n. [mid-19C–1900s] (Und.) the practice of deliberately burning the body with a mixture of acids and gunpowder in order to simulate scars and wounds that should soften the hearts of those from whom one begs. [SCALDRUM + DODGE n.]

scaldy n. [20C] (Irish) a bald-headed person. [ON scalle, a bald head; Irish scalltán, a fledgling]

scale n.¹ [late 19C–1920s] (US) money. [SE scale, a thin piece of metal, used in scale-armour]

scale n.² [1960s+] (US prison) a louse. [SE scale, a form of skin disease]

scale v.¹ [early 16C+] of a man, to enter a woman and commence intercourse. [SE scale, to climb; thus synon. with MOUNT v.³]

scale v.² [late 19C] to impress, to astonish. [? SE phr. scale the heights]

scale v.³ (Aus./N.Z./S.Afr.) **1** [1910s+] to steal, to defraud; thus scale a train/tram, to board and ride without paying. **2** [1910s–20s] to leave surreptitiously or speedily, esp. as scale off. [SE scale, to strip the scales from]

scale-backed 'un n. [1910s–20s] a louse (cf. SCALE n.²). [lit. 'scale-backed one']

scaler n. **1** [20C] (Aus./N.Z.) a fraud, anyone who betrays a financial trust. **2** [1920s+] one who rides illegally for free on public transport; thus scaling, riding for free on buses etc. [SCALE v.³]

scallawag see SCALLYWAG.

scalloped potatoes n. [1960s] (US gay) sunburned testicles.

scally adj. [1980s+] a hooligan youth. [abbr. SCALLYWAG n.¹; coined in Liverpool, where it is tinged with a degree of admiration]

scallywag/scallawag n.¹ (orig. US) **1** [mid-19C+] a ne'er-do-well, a disreputable person (cf. SCALLY). **2** [mid–late 19C] a political intriguer, a corrupt politician; thus scallywaggery, scallywagism, roguery, political opportunism, scallywagging, acting in a corrupt manner. **3** [mid–late 19C] (US) a White Southerner willing to accept the terms of Reconstruction after the US Civil War (1861–5). **4** [1990s] (US) the penis. [? link to Scot. scurryvaig, a vagabond or scalrag, a raggedly dressed person, ? ult. Lat. scurra vagas, a wandering fool]

scallywag/scallawag n.² [mid-19C] undersized or ill-conditioned cattle. [ext. use of SCALLYWAG n.¹]

scalp v.¹ [mid-19C+] to tout tickets (orig. to theatres) at above face value price (cf. SCALPER). [orig. Stock Exchange use, to buy shares very cheap, then sell below the prevailing price; theatre scalpers look for greater profits]

scalp v.² [1970s] (US Black) to perform cunnilingus.

scalp v.³ [1990s] (N.Z.) to capture the insignia or PATCH n.³ of a rival gang-member. [SE scalp, to remove the enemy's scalp as a trophy]

scalper n. (orig. US) **1** [mid-19C+] a ticket tout. **2** [late 19C] one who buys the unused portions of long-distance railroad tickets in order to sell them at a profit. **3** [late 19C+] 'any human being of merciless tendencies, especially in his financial dealings' (Ware). **4** [1950s+] (gambling) a person who bets in such a way that they never lose. [SCALP v.¹]

scalping n. [mid-19C+] (orig. US) working as a ticket tout. [SCALP v.¹]

scalp ticket n. [1940s] (Aus.) the unused half of a return ticket. [SCALP v.¹]

scaly n. [1910s+] (Aus.) a crocodile.

scaly adj.¹ [late 18C–mid-19C] **1** shabby. **2** sick, run down. **3** mean, miserly. [SE scaly, suffering from a skin disease, typically ringworm]

scaly adj.² [1980s+] (S.Afr.) of a person, unpleasant. [SCALE v.³]

scaly bloke n. [1930s] (N.Z.) a thin man. [SCALY adj.¹ + BLOKE]

scaly fish *n.* [late 18C] 'an honest, rough, blunt sailor' (Grose, 1796).

scam *n.* [1960s+] **1** a plan, a scheme. **2** a large-scale plan to smuggle and distribute illegal drugs. **3** (US) information (cf. LOW-DOWN). [? SE *scheme*]

scam *v.* **1** [1960s+] to carry out any form of scheme, usu. dubious or illegal; thus *scam in*, to gain entry to a concert, performance etc without paying for a ticket. **2** [1960s+] to defraud, to trick. **3** [1980s+] (US campus) to go in search of the opposite sex with no interest other than in short-term amusement; thus *scam on*, to flirt. [SCAM n.]

scamander *v.* [mid-19C] of persons, to wander about, to take a devious or winding course. [the classical river *Scamander*, ult. SE *meander*; note Yorks. dial. *skimaundering*, hanging or hovering about]

scamhead *n.* [1980s+] a trickster, anyone who can get 'something for nothing', someone who is cunning but not necessarily criminal. [SCAM n. + sfx. -HEAD (1)]

scammer *n.* [1980s+] **1** a confidence trickster. **2** (US campus) a flirt. [SCAM n.]

scammered *adj.*[1] [mid-19C] drunk (cf. BASTED).

scammered *adj.*[2] [1960s+] (US prison) homosexual. [? fig. use of SCAM n., the image of deception]

scamp *n.* **1** [late 18C–early 19C] a highwayman (cf. ROYAL SCAMP). **2** [late 18C–early 19C] highway robbery; thus *on the scamp*, working as a highwayman. **3** [mid-19C] a cheat, a swindler; thus *scamp*, to give short measure. [Scot. *scamp*, to wander, to shirk; note late 16C *scampant*, a burlesque 'coat-of-arms', modelled on SE *rampant* and illustrating 'a roge in his ragges' (cit. in *OED*)]

scamp/scamp on the panney *v.* [mid-18C–19C] to work as a highwayman on the highroad. [SCAMP n./SE *scamper*, to go hastily from place to place + PANNEY n.[1]]

scamper *v.* [late 17C–mid-18C] to run, to run off. [SE since early 19C]

scamperer *n.* [early 18C–mid-19C] a street thug. [SCAMP n.]

scamp-foot *n.* [late 18C–early 19C] a foot-pad (cf. ROYAL SCAMP). [SCAMP n. + SE *foot*]

scampi belt *n.* [1960s+] the middle-class commuter villages around London where, in the late 1950s–early 1960s, it was considered fashionable to eat scampi. [by the 1980s scampi was reserved for the 'basket meal' trade, and such areas should perhaps be renamed the 'fresh pasta belt' or 'sun-dried tomato belt']

scamping *adj.* [early–mid-19C] dishonest. [SCAMP v.]

scampsman *n.* [late 18C–mid-19C] a highwayman. [SCAMP n.]

Scand/Scan *n.* [1930s+] a *Scand*inavian. [abbr.]

Scandahoovian/Scandanoovian *n.* [late 19C+] (US) a Scandinavian person. [joc. mispron.]

Scandahoovian/Scandanoovian *adj.* [late 19C+] (US) Scandinavian. [SCANDAHOOVIAN n.]

scandal-broth *see* PRATTLE-BROTH.

scandalous *n.* [late 17C–early 19C] a wig. [? joc. use of SE]

scandalous *adj.* [1990s] excellent, first-rate. [on bad = good pattern]

scandal-proof *adj.* [late 17C–18C] applied to a professional thief 'harden'd or past Shame' (B.E.).

scandal-water *see* PRATTLE-BROTH.

Scandie/Scandy *n.* [late 19C+] (orig. N.Z.) a *Scand*inavian. [abbr.]

scank *see* SKANK n.[1].

scankie *see* SKANKY adj.

scanmag *n.* [19C] chatter, gossip, scandal; thus *scanmag*, to chatter, to gossip. [legal jargon *scandalum magnum*, the 'scandal of magnates', coined in a statute of King Richard II (*2 Ric. II* stat. 1 c. 5), which forbade anyone from publishing a malicious report against any person holding a position of dignity]

scan on *v.* [1960s–70s] (US Black) to watch closely, to look closely, esp. at something one intends stealing. [SE *scan*]

scanties *n.* [1920s+] (orig. US) women's (brief) lingerie. [SE *scant* + *panties*]

scapa *v.* [1960s+] to go, esp. to run off. [abbr. SCAPA FLOW]

Scapa Flow *v.* [1910s+] to go, esp. to run off (cf. SCARPER). [rhy. sl.]

scapali *see* SCARPER.

scapper *v.* [1960s+] (Irish) to go, to run off. [SCAPA FLOW]

Scarborough warning/surprise *n.* [mid-16C–late 19C] a warning that is given too late to be of use. [the theory, offered by Fuller (*Worthies of England*, 1662) and others that the phr. stems from the seizure in 1577 of Scarborough castle is undermined by the *OED's* first use, in Heywood's *Proverbs*, 1546]

scarce as hen's teeth *phr.* [mid-19C+] (orig. US) very scarce; thus (W.I.) *when cock get/make teeth*, never.

scarce-o-fat *n.* [1950s] (W.I.) a nickname for a thin person. [SCARCE-O-FAT adj.]

scarce-o-fat *adj.* [1950s] (W.I.) thin.

scare, the *n.* [1930s] (US Und.) extortion using menaces (cf. FRIGHTENERS).

scared fartless *adj.* [1930s+] (Can.) extremely frightened. [semi-euph. for SCARED SHITLESS]

scared shitless *adj.* [1930s+] extremely frightened. [SHIT n.[1] (1)]

scared spitless/witless *adj.* [1970s+] absolutely terrified. [euph. for SCARED SHITLESS]

scaredy-cat *n.* [1910s+] (juv.) anyone who is, or appears to be, frightened (cf. FRAIDY-CAT).

scarehead *n.* [20C] (US) a sensational newspaper headline (cf. SCREAMER n.[1]; SCREAM SHEET).

scare party *n.* [1940s–50s] (US Black) a Halloween party. [the ghost motif]

scare rigid *v.* [1970s+] to terrify.

scare seven bells out of *see* KNOCK SEVEN BELLS OUT OF.

scare shitless *v.* [1930s+] to terrify (cf. SCARED SHITLESS; SCARED SPITLESS). [ext. of SCARE THE SHIT OUT OF]

scare spitless/witless *v.* [1970s+] euph. for SCARE SHITLESS.

scare stiff *v.* [1910s+] to terrify; thus *scared stiff*, utterly terrified. [one is unable to move through terror]

scare the bejazus out of, to *phr.* [mid-19C+] to terrify completely and utterly. [BEJAZUS!]

scare the daylights out of *phr.*[1] *see* BEAT THE DAYLIGHTS OUT OF.

scare the daylights out of, to *phr.*[2] [late 19C+] to terrify (cf. FRIGHTEN THE DAYLIGHTS OUT OF). [SE *scare* + DAYLIGHTS]

scare the dookey out of, to *phr.* [1960s+] (US) to terrify (cf. SCARE THE SHIT OUT OF). [DOOKEY]

scare the lights/liver and lights out of, to *phr.* [late 19C] to terrify (cf. SCARE THE DAYLIGHTS OUT OF phr.[2]).

scare/frighten the pants off, to *phr.* [1930s+] to terrify.

scare the shit/living shit out of, to *phr.* [late 19C+] to terrify (cf. SCARE SHITLESS; SCARE THE DOOKEY OUT OF). [SHIT n.[1]; the image of defecating with fright]

scare up *v.* [mid-19C+] (US) to obtain, usu. with some difficulty and poss. by threatening the supplier. [SE *scare up*, to frighten game out of cover]

scare witless *see* SCARE SHITLESS.

scarf *n.* [1930s+] (US) food. [SCOFF v.]

scarf/scorf *v.* [1960s+] (orig. US) **1** to eat, esp. to gobble up, to eat aggressively. **2** (campus) to throw away, to abandon. **3** to pilfer (cf. SWIPE v.[2]). [SCOFF v.]

scarfer *n.* [1980s+] a football supporter. [the scarf that is worn]

scarf out v. [1960s+] (US) to over-eat (cf. PIG OUT). [ext. of SCARF v.]

scarlet n. [mid-19C] an upper-class ruffian. [a synon. for BLOOD n.[1]]

scarlet adj. [1980s+] (Irish/Dublin) highly embarrassed. [red with embarrassment]

scarlet fever n. [mid-19C] a partiality for soldiers (cf. JUNGLE FEVER). [the scarlet uniform]

scarlet horse n. [late 18C–early 19C] a hired or hack horse. [pun on SE hired/high-red]

scarlet runner n. **1** [mid-19C] a Bow Street runner. **2** [mid–late 19C] a footman. **3** [late 19C–1900s] a soldier. **4** [1940s+] (Aus.) cheap red wine (cf. PINKIE n.[3]). [the colour of their uniforms or of the wine]

Scarlet-town n. [mid-19C] Reading. [pun on pron. of Reading as 'red-ing']

scarp v. [1910s+] (Aus.) to escape, to run off. [SCARPER]

scarper/scapali/scarpy v. [mid-19C+] (orig. Ling. Fr./Polari) to escape, to run off (cf. SCAPA FLOW). [Ital. scappare, to escape, to get away]

scars see WHORE SCARS.

scarve n. [late 19C–1900s] (Polari) a ring. [in the Polari vocab. but lacking the usual Ital. root; E.P. suggests adaptation of SE scarf-ring]

scarver v. [late 19C–1900s] (Aus.) to escape, to run off. [SCARPER]

scat n.[1] [20C] an itinerant, a tramp. [? SCATTER!]

scat n.[2] [1960s+] scatology, defecation for sexual purposes. [abbr.; SE is properly 'filthy writing']

scat/scate n.[3] [1970s+] (drugs) heroin. [var. on SCAG n.[2] (1)]

scat n.[4] [1970s+] (US Black) the vagina (cf. SCATE n.[1]).

scat v. [mid–late 19C] to leave, to go away. [SE scat! be off!]

scate n.[1] [17C] **1** the vagina. **2** a prostitute. [SE scat, a skate; thus ref. to equation of the vagina with fish]

scate n.[2] see SCAT n.[3].

scatman n. [1990s] a male homosexual. [SCAT n.[2] + sfx. -man]

scats see SCATTY.

scatter n.[1] [19C] urine (cf. SCATTERS).

scatter/scatter joint n.[2] [1930s–40s] (US) a bar, saloon, nightclub or speakeasy where one can purchase alcoholic drinks. [? SE scatter one's money + JOINT n.[3] (3)]

scatter! excl. [20C] go away!

scatter joint see SCATTER n.[2].

scatterling n. [19C] a tramp (cf. SCAT n.[1]).

scatters n. [19C] diarrhoea (cf. SCATTER n.[1]).

scatting n. [1960s+] the sexual practice of defecating on one's partner's face. [SCAT n.[2]]

scatty/scats adj. [1910s+] incapable of logical thought or speech, feather-brained, eccentric. [SE scatter-brained]

scavenge v. [1940s+] (Aus.) to pilfer (cf. ACQUIRE).

scavenger's daughter see SKEFFINGTON'S DAUGHTER.

scavey see SAVVY n.

scene n. **1** [1930s+] (orig. US Black) choice, preference (cf. BAG n.[6]). **2** [1940s+] a place, esp. a party. **3** [1940s+] (drugs) the drug-taking environment. **4** [1960s+] any situation. **5** [1970s+] (gay) a lengthy, paid-for sexual encounter (cf. QUICKIE).

scene on v. [1970s+] (US Black) **1** to belittle. **2** to attempt to gain an advantage over someone by out-talking them.

scene queen n. [1980s+] (gay) one who frequents the world of bars, restaurants and streets equated with the gay lifestyle. [SCENE n. (2) + QUEEN n.[1]]

scenery n. [1960s+] (US gay) **1** sexually attractive individuals in a particular environment, e.g. the baths or a club; thus have lots of scenery, to be filled with sexually available men. **2** anyone in whom one is interested but who is of a different sexual orientation. [play on SE + SCENE n. (5)]

scenic route n. [1990s] (orig. US) the long way around.

scent-bottle n. [late 19C] a lavatory.

scent-box n. [early 19C] the nose.

sceptre n. [19C] the penis (cf. BAT n.[7]). [joc. resemblance]

sces n. [1980s+] (US drugs) cannabis. [pron. 'sess'; SENSIMILLIA]

scew see SKEW n.[1].

scharn n. [20C] excrement. [dial. scharn, cowdung]

sched n. [1950s+] a schedule. [abbr.]

scheisse n. [1980s+] (US campus) stuff (cf. SHIT n.[6]). [Ger. Scheisse, shit]

scheisse! excl. [1980s+] (US campus) a euph. for SHIT! (cf. SHEE-IT!; SHEESH!; SHEET!; SHERBERT!; SHOOT! excl.[1]; SUGAR!). [for ety. see SCHEISSE n.]

scheisspot n. [1960s+] a general term of abuse (cf. SHITBAG). [Ger. Scheisse, shit + SE pot]

scheisty see SHYSTY.

scheitl n. [1980s+] a wig. [Yid. sheitl, the wig trad. worn by orthodox Jewish women subsequent to their marriage]

scheme v. **1** [1930s+] (Irish) to play truant. **2** [1970s+] (S.Afr.) to think, to 'reckon'.

scheme-on n. [1980s+] an opening line used when chatting someone up. [SCHEME ON v.]

scheme on v. [1950s+] (US Black) to make designs on.

schemie n. [20C] a person who lives on a Scot. scheme or council estate.

schfatzer n. [1930s+] an old or elderly man, often as a pej. term. [Ger. Schwatzer, a chatterbox, a bore]

schicer/sheister n. [1970s+] a cheat, spec. one who refuses to pay a debt (cf. SHICER). [? fig. use of Ger. Scheisse, shit or SHYSTER]

schickery adj. [mid-19C] shabby, bad. [SHICER]

schickery adv. [mid-19C] shabbily, badly. [SCHICKERY adj.]

schism-shop n. [late 18C–early 19C] a nonconformist meeting house. [the theological schisms debated there]

schitz/schiz/skitz/skiz n. [1920s+] (orig. US) an eccentric, a mad person (cf. SCHIZO n.).

schitzi/schizo/schizy/schizzy adj. [1940s+] eccentric, insane, disoriented. [SE schizophrenic, having schizophrenia, 'a mental disorder ... characterized by a breakdown in the relation between thoughts, feelings and actions, usu. with a withdrawal from social activity and the occurrence of delusions and hallucinations' (OED)]

schiz n. see SCHITZ.

schizo n. [1940s+] (orig. US) an eccentric, a mad person. [abbr. SE schizophrenic]

schizo adj. see SCHITZI.

schiz/schizz out v. [1920s+] (orig. US) to go mad, to exhibit the signs of insanity. [SCHIZO n.]

schizy see SCHITZI.

schizzed adj. [1950s+] drunk (cf. ADDLED). [SE schizophrenic]

schizz out see SCHIZ OUT v.

schizzy see SCHITZI.

schlang see SCHLONG.

schleinter see SLANTER.

schlemazel/schlemasel/shlemozzle n. [late 19C+] a fool, esp. an unfortunate, an incompetent (cf. SCHLEMIEL). [west Yid. schlimm Masel, bad luck]

schlemiel/schlemihl/shlemiel n. [late 19C+] a fool, a clumsy person, a misfit, a gullible person etc. [Yid. schlemiel, a bungler, a simpleton; ? the proper name Shelumiel, cited in Num. 25:8, as meeting an unfortunate end. He is generally equated with Zimri, whose fornication with a pagan, as recounted in the Talmud, led to his being killed in flagrante delicto by Phinehas. The details of the execution were suppressed by pious Jewish historians, but when schlemiel entered Yid. it meant anyone in 'an unfortunate (if unspecified) predicament' and thence, by phonetic confusion

with Western Yid. *schlimm Masel*, a luckless fellow (cf.
SCHLEMAZEL) it took on the 20C popular meaning]

schlemozzle *n.* [late 19C+] noise, uproar, excitement (cf.
SHEMOZZLE n.). [Yid.]

schlemozzle *v. see* SHEMOZZLE v.

schlent *n.* [1920s+] an imposter. [abbr. *schlenter* (*see*
SLANTER)]

schlent *v.* [1920s+] to double-cross, to hoax, to be evasive.
[SCHLENT n.]

schlenter *n. see* SLANTER.

schlenter/slenter/slinter *adj.* [late 19C+] (Aus./S.Afr.)
counterfeit, spurious, fake; thus (mining jargon) *schlenter*, a
fake diamond sold as the real thing (cf. SLANTER). [Du. *slenter*,
a trick]

schlenter *v.* [1970s+] (S.Afr.) to obtain by underhand means;
thus *schlenterer*, a devious, untrustworthy person. [SCHLENTER
adj.]

schlep *n.*[1] [1930s+] (orig. US) a general term of abuse (cf. SLOB
n.[1]). [Yid. *schlep*]

schlep *n.*[2] [1950s+] a long and unappealing distance. [SCHLEP
v. (2)]

schlep *v.* [1950s+] **1** to carry an inconvenient weight for an
equally inconvenient distance. **2** to travel further than one
might prefer. [Yid. *schlep*, Ger. *shleppen*, to drag]

schlepper *n.* [1930s+] **1** (orig. US) an insignificant person, a
second-rater. **2** (US) a miserly person who wants something
for nothing. [Yid. *schlep*]

schleppy *adj.* [1930s+] (US) awkward, clumsy, stupid (cf.
KLUTZY). [SCHLEP n.[1]]

schliver *n.* [19C] a clasp-knife. [CHIV]

schlock/shlock *n.* **1** [20C] cheap, inferior merchandise,
anything defective or in poor taste, e.g. a *schlock movie*.
2 [1920s–30s] (drugs) narcotics, usu. heroin. [Ger. *Schlag*, a
blow; thus merchandise that has been 'knocked about']

schlock joint *see* SCHLOCK SHOP.

schlockmeister *n.* [1980s+] (US) a successful seller of cheap,
meretricious goods. [SCHLOCK n. (1) + sfx. -MEISTER]

schlock shop/joint *n.* [1910s+] a store selling flashy but
cheap clothes. [SCHLOCK n. (1) + SE *shop*/JOINT n.[3]]

schlocky *adj.* [20C] in poor taste, vulgar, second-rate.
[SCHLOCK n. (1)]

schloep/shloep/schloop/shloop *n.* [1960s+] (S.Afr.) a
sycophant, a toady; thus *schloep*, to ingratiate oneself, *schloe-*
py, ingratiating. [? SCHLUB or onomat. for sucking 'slurping'
noise]

schlog/slog it on *v.* [1930s+] (Aus.) to raise a price extortionately; thus *get schlogged/slogged*, to be charged an
excessive price. [? Ger. *auf den Preis schlagen*, 'clap the price
on', or SCHLOCK n. (1)]

schlong/schlang/schlontz/shlang/shlong/shlontz *n.*
[1930s+] the penis. [Yid. *schlang*, snake]

schloomp/schlump/shloomp/shlump *n.* [1960s+] (US) a
stupid person. [Ger. *Schlumpe*, a slovenly woman]

schloomp/shalump around *v.* [1960s+] (US) to loaf about.
[SCHLOOMP n.; ? underpinned by SE *slump*]

schloop *see* SCHLOEP.

schlub/shlub/shlubbo/zhlob/zhlub *n.* [1950s+] **1** a fool, a
moron. **2** a coarse bumpkin. [Yid. *schlub*, ult. Slavic *zhlob*, a
coarse fellow]

schlub *v.* [1980s+] (US campus) to fight. [SCHLUB n.]

schlubette *n.* [1950s+] a stupid young woman. [SCHLUB n. +
fem. sfx. -*ette*]

schlump *see* SCHLOOMP.

schmaltz/schmalz/shmaltz *n.* [1930s+] **1** anything
mawkish, over-emotional, esp. in show business use. **2** (US)
any viscid substance. [fig. + lit. uses of Yid. *schmaltz*,
(animal) fat]

schmaltzy/schmalzy/shmaltzy *adj.* [1930s+] sentimental,
mawkish. [SCHMALTZ]

schmatte/schmattah/schmatteh/shmatte/shmotte *n.*
[20C] (US) a shabby or unfashionable garment (cf. SCHMUT-
TER).

schmear *n.*[1] *see* SCHMEER n.[1].

schmear/schmeer/shmear *n.*[2] [1950s+] (US) a slander, a
slur. [mispron. of SE *smear*]

schmear *v. see* SCHMEER v.

schmeck/shmeck/shmee *n.* [1960s+] (drugs) **1** heroin (cf.
SMACK n.[5]). **2** cocaine. **3** a taste. [Yid./Ger. *schmecken*, a taste]

schmecker *n.* [1960s+] (drugs) a heroin user. [SCHMECK]

schmeer/schmear/shmear *n.*[1] [1950s+] (US) **1** a daub or
spread of butter, cream cheese etc; thus fig. **2** a bribe (cf.
GREASE SOMEONE'S PALM; PALM OIL). **3** a situation, a circumstance, usu. *the whole schmeer*, the entire package, the complete deal. [despite ety. of v., authorities claim that *whole*
schmeer is not Yid.; N. Süsskind (Cohen, 1991) suggests Ger.
Schmiere, a small, insignificant and third-rate piece of art or
performance. Trans. to the artist or theatre company that
produces it, and thence to the company, its props, and
everything it possesses; thus *whole schmeer* = WHOLE KIT AND
CABOODLE = everything; note Rosten (1968), who includes v.
but does not mention n.]

schmeer *n.*[2] *see* SCHMEAR n.[2].

schmeer/schmear/shmear *v.* [1950s+] **1** to bribe. **2** to
flatter and cajole someone. **3** to treat someone roughly (cf.
CLOBBER v.; CREAM v.[1]). [Yid. *schmir*, to apply ointment, to
lubricate]

schmegegge/schmegeggy/shmegeggy *n.* [20C] **1** an unpleasant, petty person. **2** an inept, incompetent person. **3** a
sycophant, a toady. **4** nonsense. [US Yid.]

schmegma *n.* [1990s] (US campus) any slimy substance. [a
'Yiddishizing' of SE *smegma*]

schmendrick/shmendrick *n.* [1940s+] a contemptible,
foolish or immature person, an upstart, a 'sucker'. [the name
of a character in an operetta by Abraham Goldfaden (1840–
1908); cited as Yid. by Rosten (1968) but no further/previous
ety. given]

schmiel/schmielage *n.* [1980s+] (US campus) a woman (cf.
SCHLEMIEL).

schmiel on *v.* [1980s+] (US campus) to act pleasantly in order
to pick up a woman.

schmock *see* SCHMUCK.

schmo/schmoe/shmo/shmoe *n.* [1940s+] (orig. US) a fool.
[*schmo* is not a Yid. word *per se*, but was invented as a
deliberate euph. for the taboo SCHMUCK]

schmoo *n.* [1990s] (US teen) an unpleasant but not wholly
unbearable day. [ety. unknown]

schmoose *n.* [19C] an itinerant Jewish pedlar. [SMOUS n.]

schmooze/shmooze *n.* [1950s+] a chat, a long and intimate
conversation. [Heb. *schmuos*, things heard]

schmooze/shmooze *v.* [1950s+] to flatter, to butter up (cf.
SCHMOOZER). [SCHMOOZE n.]

schmoozefest *n.* [1980s+] any gathering devoted to mutual (if
momentary and insincere) congratulation. [SCHMOOZE v. + sfx.
-FEST]

schmoozer/shmooser *n.* [20C] a flatterer. [SCHMOOZE v.]

schmuck/schmock/shmuck *n.* [20C] **1** the penis. **2** a fool,
an unpleasant person (cf. DICKHEAD; PUTZ). [Yid. *schmuck*, the
penis; ult. Ger. *Schmuck*, an ornament]

schmutter *n.* [1950s+] clothes (cf. SCHMATTE). [Yid. *shmatte*,
rags, ult. Polish *szmata*, a piece of cloth, a rag]

schmutz *n.* [1950s+] filth, dirt. [synon. Ger.]

schnack *n.* [1990s] (US campus) affection. [cod. Yid. sp. of SE
snack, i.e. 'I like you so much I could eat you']

schneider *v.* [1940s+] (US) **1** to win a game before an opponent has scored. **2** to defeat decisively, to trounce. [Ger. *Schneider*, a butcher]

schnicky-schnacky *n.* [1990s] (US campus) a public display of affection. [redup. of SCHNACK]

schnifter *see* SNIFTER *n.*[1].

schnitzel *n.* [1950s+] the penis (cf. BACON *n.*[1]). [Ger. *Schnitzel*, a veal cutlet]

schnockered *see* SNOCKERED.

schnoink *n.* [1960s+] used by a non-Jew, a derog. term for a Jew (cf. SHONK). [a deliberately faked 'Yiddish' word]

schnook *n.* [1940s+] a fool, a naïve or ineffectual person, esp. a victim. [US Yid.; there is no orig., i.e. European Yid., equivalent]

schnorrer *n.* [20C] **1** a beggar, esp. one who lives by his wits. **2** a cheat, a mean person. **3** a tramp, a drifter. **4** a compulsive bargain-hunter, a haggler. [Yid. *schnorrer*, a beggar, itself Ger. sl. *schnurren*, to go out begging, and poss. related to *schnarchen*, to snore, a ref. to the beggar's supposed 'whining']

schnozzle/schnoz/schnozz *n.* [1950s+] the nose. [Ger. *Schnauze*, a snout]

schnozzola *n.* [1950s+] the nose. [ext. of SCHNOZZLE]

schoful *see* SHOFUL.

school *n.*[1] **1** [early 19C+] a group of gamblers gathered for a game (cf. SCHOOL *v.*[1]). **2** [mid–late 19C] a gang of beggars or thieves (usu. pickpockets) working as a team.

school *n.*[2] [late 19C–1920s] prison (cf. SCHOOLING *n.*[2]). [SE *school of crime*]

school *n.*[3] [1990s] any specific era in the history of HIP-HOP/RAP *n.*[5] music; usu. as *Old School* and *New School*. [the exact division between the two remains a source of much debate among fans]

school *v.*[1] [1930s+] to gamble in a group. [SCHOOL *n.*[1] (1)]

school *v.*[2] [1940s+] (orig. US Black) to explain a situation or a plan to someone else, to teach.

schoolbook chump *n.* [1970s+] (US Black) one who is academic, but not very sophisticated or worldly-wise (cf. EDUCATED FOOL).

schoolboy *n.* **1** [1960s–70s] (drugs) cocaine, codeine, cough syrup, anything seen (by heroin users) as a drug for 'beginners'. **2** [1970s+] (US Black) a neophyte in the street life, an apprentice criminal.

schoolboy scotch *n.* [1970s+] (US Black) cheap wine.

school-butter *n.* [late 17C–19C] a whipping (cf. BUTTER *v.*).

schoolcraft *n.* [1980s+] (drugs) crack cocaine. [? its popularity among teenagers]

schoolie *n.* **1** [late 19C+] (Aus.) a *school*teacher. **2** [1950s+] a *school*girl. [abbr.]

schooling *n.*[1] [mid-19C] a criminal gambling party. [SCHOOL *n.*[1] (1)]

schooling *n.*[2] [late 19C] a term of confinement in a reformatory. [SCHOOL *n.*[2]]

schoolman *n.* [early–mid-19C] a fellow member of a gang. [SCHOOL *n.*[1] + SE *man*]

schoolmarm/schoolmarm tree *n.* [1930s+] (US) a tree with a forked trunk. [the schoolteacher's gesticulating hands]

school of hard knocks *n.* [20C] (orig. US) a hard life, seen as a means of education (cf. UNIVERSITY OF LIFE).

schooly *n.* [1980s+] (US Black) **1** anyone who wishes to go to school and further their education. **2** a naïve, unsophisticated person, a conformist.

schooner screamer *see* ONE-POT SCREAMER.

schpritz *n.* [1950s+] (US) a small bit, a dose. [Yid. *schpritz*, a squirt]

schpritz/shpritz *v.* [1950s+] (US) to attack, to slander. [Yid. *schpritz*, to spray]

schroff/shroff *n.* [mid-19C] (Anglo-Ind.) **1** a banker, a treasurer. **2** an official who specializes in sorting good coin

from counterfeit; thus *shroff*, to check the validity of coins, *shroffing-school*, the office in which one is taught the skill. **3** a confidential clerk. [Anglo-Indian *saraf*, a banker or money-changer, ult. f. Arab. *saraf*, to exchange]

schtarka/shtarka/shtarker *n.* **1** a strong, brave man, an important person (esp. used ironically). **2** a thug, a hoodlum. [Yid.]

schtick/shtik/shtick *n.* (orig. US). [1950s+] *n.* **1** an act, a performance. **2** a personal habit or trait. **3** a device or gadget. [show business jargon *shtick*, one's stage speciality, one's act, esp. of a comedian's monologue; ult. Ger. *Stück*, a piece]

schtoonk/schtunk/shtoonk/shtunk *n.* [1950s+] (US) a detestable person. [Ger. *Stunk*, a scandal, a 'stink']

schtup/shtup *n.* [1950s+] sexual intercourse; thus *shtupper*, a woman who is willing to have sex. [SCHTUP *v.*]

schtup/shtup/stup *v.* [1950s+] to have sexual intercourse. [Yid.; ult. Ger. *stupsen*, to push]

schvantz *see* SCHWANTZ.

schvartze/schvartzer/schvartzeh *see* SCHWARTZE.

schvonce/schvonch *see* SHVANTZ.

schvug/schvugie *n.* [1940s+] (US) a Black person. [SCHWARTZE + BOOGIE *n.*[2]]

schwag *n.* [1980s+] (US drugs) inferior quality cannabis.

schwantz / schvantz / schvonce / schvontz / schwanz / shvantz / shvonce / shvuntz *n.* [20C] (US) the penis. [Yid. *schwantz*, the tail]

schwartze / schvartze/schvartzeh / chvartzer / schwartzer/shvartze / shvartzer / swartzer *n.* **1** [20C] a Black person. **2** [1960s+] (US gay) one who prefers Black partners. [Ger. *schwartz*, black]

schwassle-box *see* SWATCHEL-BOX.

science, the *n.*[1] [mid-19C+] boxing or fencing, esp. the former; also known as *the sweet science*.

science *n.*[2] **1** [1950s+] (W.I. Rasta) obeah, witchcraft. **2** [1980s+] (US Black) wisdom, skill (cf. DROP SCIENCE).

scientific *n.* [mid–late 19C] a man of science.

scientist *n.* [1950s+] (W.I. Rasta) an occult practitioner. [SCIENCE *n.*[2]]

sci-fi *n.* [1950s+] (orig. US) *sci*ence *fi*ction. [abbr.]

scillion *see* SKILLION.

scissor bill *n.* [1910s+] (US) **1** a foolish, incompetent, gossipy or objectionable person. **2** a wealthy or privileged person. **3** (tramp) a railroad detective or police officer (cf. SCISSORS BULL).

scissors *n.* [1970s] (drugs) marijuana. [ety. unknown]

scissors! *excl.* [mid–late 19C] a mild excl. [? euph. for SHIT!]

scissors bull *n.* [1910s+] (US tramp) a railroad police officer or detective. [var. on SCISSOR BILL + BULL *n.*[10] (1)]

sclerry *n.* [1990s] a sufferer from sclerosis of the liver, a terminal alcoholic.

scobe *n.* [1940s] (US Black) a Black person. [? dial. *scob*, a dark hole]

scode *n.* [1980s+] (N.Z. drugs) the butt end of a marijuana cigarette that is unwrapped and recycled.

scoff *n.* [mid-19C+] food (cf. SCARF *n.*). [SCOFF *v.*]

scoff *v.* **1** [mid-19C+] to eat, to gobble up. **2** [late 19C+] to grab. **3** [1950s+] (US teen) to steal, to pilfer (cf. SWIPE *v.*[2]). [Scot. *scaff*, to beg or ask for (food etc) in a mean or contemptible manner, but note S.Afr. *scoff*, food, a meal, f. Du. *schoft*, a quarter of a day, thus each of the day's four meals]

scoff fishheads/fishheads and scramble the gills, to *phr.* [1940s–50s] (US Black) to have a difficult time, to encounter problems. [fig. use of SCOFF *v.*]

scoffings *n.* [late 19C+] (US tramp) food. [SCOFF *n.*]

scoldrum *see* SCALDRUM.

scold's cure *n.* [19C] a funeral, a coffin; thus *nap the scold's* *cure*, to be placed in one's coffin. [the misogynistic concept that only death would silence a nagging woman]

scollogue *v.* [mid–late 19C] to live in a debauched, degenerate manner. [? link to SCALLYWAG n.[1]]

scolopendra *n.* [mid-17C] a prostitute. [SE *scolopendra*, a centipede or millipede, orig. 'a fabulous sea-fish which feeling himselfe taken with a hooke casteth out his bowels vntill hee hath vnloosed the hooke and then swalloweth them vp againe' (Bullokar, *English Expositour*, 1616)]

sconce *n.* **1** [mid-16C–early 19C] the head. **2** [mid-16C–early 19C] judgement, sense. **3** [late 16C] a person (whose head it is). [either SE *sconce*, a lantern or *sconce*, a fort or earthwork]

sconce off/sconce the reckoning *v.* [mid-18C–late 19C] to cut down the size of a bill. [orig. univ. jargon *sconce*, to mulct, to fine, usu. a tankard of ale or similar forfeit]

sconce one's diet, to *phr.* [late 19C] to eat less, to diet. [for ety. *see* SCONCE OFF]

sconce the reckoning *see* SCONCE OFF.

scone *n.*[1] [1920s+] (Aus.) a policeman, a detective (cf. HOT SCONE).

scone *n.*[2] [1940s+] (Aus./N.Z.) the head; thus *do one's/the scone* (with), to lose one's temper (with), *scone-doer*, an over-emotional person, *scone-doing*, a lost of control..

scone *v.* [1940s–50s] (Aus./N.Z.) to hit someone on the head. [SCONE n.[2]]

scone-hot *adv.* [1920s+] (Aus.) an intensive, either pos. or neg.; e.g. *go scone-hot at*, to attack aggressively.

scoob *n.* [1980s+] (Aus. drugs) cannabis. [abbr. SCOOBY-DOO n. (1)]

scoob *v.* [1980s+] (US campus) to eat, usu. to eat snacks. [TV cartoon character *Scooby-Doo*]

scoobied/skoobied *adj.* [20C] **1** beaten up, defeated. **2** under the influence of drink or drugs. **3** confused. [SCOOBY]

scoobie snax *n.* [1980s+] (US drugs) food eaten when suffering the hunger-pangs promoted by smoking cannabis. [SCOOBY-DOO + SE *snacks*]

scooby/skooby *v.* [20C] **1** to defeat, to trounce, to outwit (cf. SCUPPER v.). **2** to confuse. [? journalist jargon *scoop*, to outwit a rival, esp. in printing 'their' story first + ? link to the cartoon character *Scooby-Doo*, a singularly stupid dog]

scooby-doo *n.* [1990s] **1** (US Black/teen) a large cannabis cigarette (cf. BLUNT n.[2]). **2** (US campus) someone who eats a lot and never gains weight. [the cartoon character *Scooby-Doo*]

scooch *n.* [1990s] (Irish) a lift in a car. [? nonce-word *scootch up*, move over]

scood! *excl.* [1990s] (US campus) an elision of the SE *it's good*; thus *scoodnuff*, it's good enough.

scoop *n.*[1] **1** [late 19C+] an advantage, a lucky result in one's business or similar dealings. **2** [1970s+] (US teen/campus) important, fresh information (cf. POOP n.[4]). [journalist jargon *scoop*, an exclusive or (as yet) unrivalled story]

scoop *n.*[2] [1980s+] (Irish) a drink.

scoop *v.* [1960s+] (US) to arrest (cf. LIFT v.[1]).

scooped *adj.*[1] [19C] drunk. [ON THE SCOOP]

scooped *adj.*[2] [late 19C] (US) swindled. [the money is 'scooped' from one's pocket]

scoop in/up *v.* [mid-19C+] **1** (orig. US) to have a stroke of luck, a 'lucky break', usu. in business (cf. SCOOP THE POOL). **2** to gather in large quantities (esp. to the exclusion of others).

scoop on *v.* [1980s+] (US campus) to pick up, to make advances to.

scoop the pool/kitty, to *phr.* [1910s+] to make a major profit. [poker imagery]

scoop up *see* SCOOP IN.

scoot *n.*[1] [mid-18C–1900s] an escape. [SCOOT v.]

scoot *n.*[2] [20C] (Ulster) diarrhoea; thus a general term of abuse (cf. RUNS). [euph. of SHIT n.[1]]

scoot *n.*[3] [1950s–60s] a motorcycle or motorcar.

scoot/scoot off *v.* **1** [mid-18C–1900s] to run away, to flee. **2** [mid-19C+] (US) of a person or object, to slide. [mid-18C–early 19C naut. jargon *scout*, to run off swiftly]

scooter *n.*[1] [19C] one who leaves quickly, an escapee. [SCOOT v.]

scooter *n.*[2] [1930s–40s] an automobile, esp. [1930s] a car used for the smuggling of rum.

scoots *n.*[1] [20C] (US campus) diarrhoea (cf. RUNS). [ext. of SCOOT n.[2]]

scoots *n.*[2] [1940s–50s] dollars. [ety. unknown]

scope *n.* [1960s+] the erect penis. [abbr. SE *telescope*]

scope/scope on/scope out *v.* [1970s+] (US Black/campus) **1** to look over, to stare at, to investigate. **2** to stare at someone intently, usu. with sexual interest. **3** to look in various public places for a partner for romance or sex. [abbr. SE *telescope*]

scope a vic, to *phr.* [1970s+] (US Und.) to look for a suitable person to mug or rob. [SCOPE v. + abbr. SE *victim*]

scope on/scope out *see* SCOPE V.

scorch *n.* [1940s+] (US Black) best quality, top-rank goods. [SCORCHER (5)]

scorch *v.* [20C] (US) to go or move very fast.

scorcher *n.* **1** [mid–late 19C] a severe reprimand, a telling-off. **2** [mid-19C+] a very hot day (cf. ROASTER). **3** [late 19C+] an attractive and sexually voracious woman. **4** [late 19C–1900s] one who cycles or motors with above average speed or energy. **5** [1940s+] anything sensational, esp. when seen as risqué or 'naughty'.

scorching *adj.* [late 19C+] astounding, sensational, licentious, risqué (cf. HOT adj.[1]). [SCORCHER]

score *n.*[1] [late 19C+] 20, in a variety of contexts, e.g. 20 years' prison, a 20-ounce packet of tobacco, $20, £20 etc. [SE *score*, a group of 20; ult. the counting of sheep in 20s, each of which was 'scored' on some form of tally, e.g. by cutting notches in a stick]

score *n.*[2] **1** [1900s] a successfully made point in an argument; thus (US campus) *the score*, the crux or bottom line. **2** [1940s+] the situation, the facts, what is going on; usu. as in *know the score*, to be aware, *what's the score?* what's going on?

score *n.*[3] **1** [20C] (US Und.) anything sent in to a prisoner from the outside world (cf. BOODLE n.[1]; RELIEF). **2** [1930s+] (Und.) the profits from a robbery, fraud or similar criminal act. **3** [1930s+] (US Und.) a planned killing. **4** [1930s+] (orig. US Und.) a success or coup in criminal activity or gambling. [SCORE v.[2]]

score *n.*[4] [1960s+] **1** (orig. US) a male or female prostitute's client. **2** (US) a potential partner for sex. [SCORE v.[1] (2)]

score *v.*[1] **1** [late 19C+] to succeed, to do well. **2** [1950s+] (orig. US) to seduce, to have sexual intercourse (cf. SCORE BETWEEN THE POSTS). **3** [1970s+] (US campus) to obtain something desirable, usually sex.

score *v.*[2] **1** [1910s+] to commit a robbery, to make a dishonest gain, to filch something from a counter or stall. **2** [1930s+] to buy drugs. [SE *score*, to win, to gain a victory]

score between the posts, to *phr.* [1970s+] (Aus.) to have sexual intercourse, to seduce a woman. [SCORE v.[1] + football imagery]

score-card *n.* [1930s] (US) a menu.

score off *v.* [late 19C+] to make a point at another's expense.

score ten *v.* [1980s] (Aus.) to seduce, to have sexual intercourse. [SE *score* + ? TEN n.[4]]

score yoks *v.* [1940s+] (US) to make people laugh. [SE *score* + YOKS]

scorf *v.*[1] [20C] (US prison) to eat prison food (cf. CHUCK v.[4]; GRAZE v.; JUG UP). [var. on SCARF v.]

scorf *v.*[2] *see* SCARF V.

scorpion *n.* [1980s+] (drugs) cocaine. [it has a 'sting']

scot *n.* [early 19C–1910s] **1** an ill-tempered person, esp. one who is susceptible to teasing. **2** a bad temper, a fit of irritation. [stereotyping; but ? note Jon Bee: 'the small Scots oxen coming to their doom with little resignation to fate']

Scotch *adj.* [19C+] mean. [racial stereotyping]

Scotch/Welsh bait *n.* [late 18C–mid-19C] a rest taken as one walks along. [SE *Scotch/Welsh* + *bait*, a snack]

Scotch bum *n.* [early 17C] a form of dress-bustle. [SE *Scotch* + BUM n.[2]]

Scotch by absorption *phr.* [1930s+] describing one who likes Scotch whisky.

Scotch casement *n.* [late 18C–mid-19C] the pillory. [neg. stereotyping; SE *casement*, a window frame]

Scotch chocolate *n.* [late 18C–mid-19C] brimstone (sulphur) and milk.

Scotch coffee *n.* [mid-19C] hot water flavoured with burned biscuit. [orig. naut. jargon]

Scotch convoy *n.* [20C] (Ulster) a walk home with a visitor, who then comes back with you.

Scotch eggs *n.* [mid-19C+] the legs (cf. SCOTCH PEGS). [rhy. sl.]

scotches *n.* [mid-19C+] the legs. [abbr. SCOTCH PEGS]

Scotch/Welsh fiddle *n.* [18C–19C] venereal disease (cf. PLAY THE SCOTCH FIDDLE).

Scotch/Scots greys/grays *n.* **1** [late 18C–mid-19C] lice; thus *headquarters of the Scots greys*, a lousy head, *the Scots greys are in full march by the crown office*, lice are crawling on one's head (cf. LIGHT INFANTRY; LIGHT TROOPS). **2** [late 19C] (Aus.) large mosquitoes (cf. OVERLANDER). [Hotten (1860), partly eschewing Johnson's prejudice, notes that 'our northern neighbours are calumniously reported, from their living on oatmeal, to be particularly liable to cutaneous eruptions and parasites']

Scotch hobby *n.* [late 17C–late 18C] a small, stunted Scot. horse. [SE *Scotch* + *hobby*, a small or middle-sized horse]

Scotchie/Scotchy *n.*[1] [mid-19C+] a Scot.

scotchie/scotty *n.*[2] [late 19C–1930s] a leg. [abbr. SCOTCH PEGS]

Scotch lick *n.* [20C] (Irish) a poorly done cleaning job. [stereotyping; SE *Scotch* + *lick*, a hit, a dab]

Scotchman *n.* [mid–late 19C] (S.Afr.) a florin (a two-shilling/ 10p piece). [the story that a Scottish immigrant to S.Afr. fooled his Black employees by giving them florins (worth 2s) but calling the coins half-crowns (worth 2s 6d/12½p)]

Scotchmen *n.* [late 19C] lice. [SCOTCH GREYS]

Scotch mist *n.* [1940s+] anything insubstantial, mythical, esp. used sarcastically when one wants to imply that the other speaker has failed to grasp the point or, lit., perceive something that is clear and obvious.

Scotch ordinary *n.* [late 18C–early 19C] a lavatory. [SE *Scotch* + *ordinary*, an eating house]

Scotch pegs *n.* **1** [mid-19C+] the legs (cf. SCOTCH EGGS). **2** [20C] eggs. [rhy. sl.]

Scotch pint *n.* [early–mid-19C] a bottle holding two quarts (4 pints/2.3 litres).

Scotch polo *n.* [20C] (US) golf.

Scotch screw *n.* [20C] a nocturnal emission. [SE *Scotch* + SCREW n.[1]; the stereotypical Scot is too mean to ejaculate into a vagina]

Scotch shout *see* YANKEE SHOUT.

Scotch/Scottish warming-pan *n.* **1** [mid-17C–late 18C] a complaisant young woman. **2** [19C] the breaking of wind.

Scotchy *see* SCOTCHIE n.[1].

scotia! *excl.* [1970s] (US Black) all right, fine (cf. OK!).

Scotland Yard *n.* [1970s] (US Black) a plain-clothes police officer. [? New *Scotland Yard*, the headquarters of the Metropolitan Police in London]

Scots greys *see* SCOTCH GREYS.

Scotsman's cinema *n.* [1930s–40s] Piccadilly Circus or, properly, its neon lights, which can be viewed as a free spectacle. [the stereotypical meanness of the Scot]

Scotsman's grandstand/stand *n.* [1970s+] **1** a grandstand erected on private property overlooking a sports arena in which seats are available cheaply. **2** a vantage point that allows people to watch an event, usu. sporting, for free. [neg. stereotyping]

Scotsman's half-crown *n.* [1940s–70s] (N.Z.) a two-shilling (10p) coin (cf. SCOTCHMAN). [neg. stereotyping; a proper SE *half-crown* was worth 2s 6d (12½p)]

Scotsman's shout *n.* [1940s+] (N.Z.) a round of drinks in which everyone pays for their own. [neg. stereotyping + SHOUT n.[1]]

Scots warming-pan *n.* [19C] the breaking of wind (cf. SCOTCH WARMING-PAN).

scott *n.* [1960s] (drugs) heroin. [? SCAT n.[3]]

Scottish *adj.* [19C] irritable, easily annoyed. [neg. stereotyping]

Scottish warming-pan *see* SCOTCH WARMING-PAN.

scotty *n.*[1] *see* SCOTCHIE.

Scotty *n.*[2] [1970s+] (drugs) **1** cocaine. **2** crack cocaine (cf. BEAM ME UP, SCOTTY!). [the character Scotty, in the TV series *Star Trek* (from 1966), 'makes one's engines run']

scotty *adj.* [mid-19C+] (Aus.) tetchy, irritable. [racial stereotyping; note Vaux (1812): '*Scot*, a person of irritable temper, who is easily put in a passion']

scour *v.*[1] [mid-15C–early 18C] **1** to wear fetters. **2** to sit in the stocks. [SE *scour*, to rub]

scour/scowre *v.*[2] **1** [late 16C–mid-18C] to run away. **2** [17C–19C] of a man, to have sexual intercourse (cf. BANG v.[1]). **3** [mid-17C–mid-18C] to roam about at night uproariously, breaking windows, beating the watch and molesting wayfarers. [SE *scour*, to move around hastily and energetically]

scourer/scowrer *n.* [17C–18C] a dissolute young man who roams the streets, usually as one of a gang, beating up passers-by, breaking windows, attacking the watch and generally acting in a hooligan manner (cf. HAWCUBITE). [SCOUR v.[2]; the term was used as the title of the play by Thomas Shadwell, *The Scowrers* (1691) 'an excellent but coarse comedy, which gives an interesting picture of the times' (*DNB*)]

scouring *n.* [early 18C] imprisonment (cf. SCOUR THE CRAMP-RINGS; SCOUR THE DARBIES). [SCOUR v.[1]]

scours *n.* [1910s–20s] a purge. [SE *scours*, diarrhoea]

scour the cramp-rings, to *phr.* [mid-15C–mid-19C] to wear chains or fetters (cf. SCOURING). [SCOUR v.[1]]

scour the darbies, to *phr.* [late 17C–mid-19C] to wear chains or handcuffs (cf. SCOURING). [SCOUR v.[1]]

scouse *n.*[1] [1900s–10s] (US) cheap, tasteless food, esp. a thin stew. [abbr. LOBSCOUSE]

Scouse *n.*[2] **1** [1940s+] a Liverpudlian. **2** [1960s+] the dialect spoken in Liverpool; thus *Scouse*, Liverpudlian, typical of Liverpool, esp. as *Scouse accent*. [LOBSCOUSE]

Scouser *n.* [20C] a Liverpudlian; thus *Scousers*, a collective name for Liverpudlians. [SCOUSE]

scout *n.*[1] **1** [17C–18C] a mean person. **2** [late 19C] (Anglo-Irish) a bold, forward young woman. **3** [1950s+] (W.I. Rasta) a person of inferior status. [late 14C–19C ? SE *scout*, a term of contempt]

scout *n.*[2] [late 17C–early 19C] **1** a member of the watch. **2** a pocket watch. [orig. milit. use; (2) puns on (1)]

scout *n.*[3] [1910s–70s] a person, esp. as *good scout*, an admirable person. [the popular image of the Boy Scouts]

scout-cull *n.* [early 18C] a watchman. [SCOUT n.[2] (1) + CULL n.[1]]

scout ken *n.* [early 19C] a watch-house. [SCOUT n.[2] (1) + KEN n.[1]]

scowbanker/skowbanker/skullbanker *n.* [mid-19C] (orig. Aus.) a rogue, a rascal, one who loiters around in the hope of hand-outs, which will save him from earning a living; thus *scowbanking*, loafing, idling (cf. COASTER). [dial., lit. one who scours or wanders the banks; E.P. and *OED* offer alt. etys. but the *EDD* ety., cited here, seems obvious]

Scowegian *n.* [1920s+] (Aus./Can./US) a Scandinavian.

scowre *see* SCOUR v.².

scowrer *see* SCOURER.

scrag *n.*¹ **1** [18C] the hangman's noose. **2** [18C] the gallows. **3** [mid–late 19C] the neck.

scrag *n.*² [1940s+] (US campus) an unattractive woman. [? SE *scrag-end*, the worst part of anything, itself ult. SCRAG n.¹ (3)]

scrag *v.* **1** [mid-18C–mid-19C] to hang (on the gallows). **2** [early 19C+] to do harm, to beat up, to kill. **3** [mid-19C+] to throttle, to choke, to garrotte. **4** [1930s+] (US) to have sexual intercourse (cf. SCROG). [SCRAG n.¹]

scrag a lay, to *phr.* [late 18C–early 19C] to steal clothes that have been laid out on a hedge to dry (cf. TAKE A SHEET OFF A HEDGE). [SCRAG n.¹ + SE *lay*, to place upon]

scrag-boy *n.* [late 18C–1900s] a hangman. [SCRAG n.¹]

scrag 'em fair *n.* [18C] an execution by hanging (cf. PADDINGTON FAIR; TUCK-'EM FAIR). [SCRAG n.¹]

scragged *adj.* [mid-18C–19C] **1** hanged. **2** dead. [SCRAG v.]

scragger *n.* [late 19C] a hangman. [SCRAG v.]

scragging *n.* **1** [mid-19C] a hanging. **2** [mid-19C+] a beating. [SCRAG v.]

scragging post *n.* [19C] the gallows (cf. SCRAG SQUEEZER). [SCRAGGING (1) + SE *post*]

scragg's hotel *n.* [late 19C] (tramp) a workhouse. [? a lost proper name]

scraggy *adj.* [20C] (US) unkempt, scrawny. [SE *scrag-end*]

scrag squeezer *n.* [early–late 19C] (Und.) the gallows (cf. NECK CLOTH; SCRAGGING POST). [SCRAG n.¹ + SE *squeezer*]

scram *n.*¹ [1920s+] (US Und.) money, clothing; thus *scram money*, cash reserved for a sudden departure, *scram-bag*, a suitcase packed ready for leaving in a hurry. [SCRAM v.]

scram *n.*² [1940s–50s] (US) a derog. term for a Black person. [? they *scramble* for money or *scram*, i.e. run off]

scram *v.* [1920s+] to escape, to run off. [SE *scramble* or Ger. *schrammen*, to run away]

scramble *n.*¹ [early 19C+] (US) money (cf. BUSTLE n.¹; SCRATCH n.²). [i.e. that which one *scrambles* to obtain]

scramble *n.*² [1950s+] (Aus./N.Z.) pedestrians rushing across a 'buzz crossing' (cf. BARN DANCE).

scramble *n.*³ [1960s–70s] **1** the effect achieved by a balding man who attempts to comb his hair to maximum effect. **2** (US teen) any effort to stretch a thinning resource beyond realistic limits.

scramble *n.*⁴ [1980s+] (drugs) crack cocaine. [? it *scrambles* one's brains]

scramble *v.* [1960s+] (US Black) to make one's money by a variety of schemes, not always legal ones.

scrambled eggs *n.*¹ [20C] the legs (cf. BACON AND EGGS; SCOTCH EGGS). [rhy. sl.]

scrambled eggs *n.*² [1940s+] **1** the gold braid that adorns a senior officer's cap. **2** a senior officer.

scramble for the gills, to *phr.* [20C] to have a bad time, to meet problems. [SE *scramble* + GILL n.²]

scrambler *n.* [1990s] (US drugs) a low-level runner for a drug dealer.

scramboose *v.* [1940s–60s] (US Black) to leave. [SCRAM v. + VAMOOSE]

scrammy *n.* [mid-late 19C] (Aus.) one who has a withered or defective hand or arm; thus *chuck a scrammy*, to pretend to have a withered arm (so as to shirk work). [dial. *scram*, withered]

scramsville *n.* [1950s–60s] desertion, running off. [SCRAM v. + sfx. -VILLE]

scran *n.* **1** [18C] payment for food at an inn. **2** [early 19C+] food, esp. various bits of food, left-overs, 'broken victuals' etc, thrown together for an impromptu meal or a meal taken onto their job by a labourer. [ety. unknown; date of (1) suggests that (2) may, albeit un-cited, have existed somewhat earlier; note RN jargon *scran*, rations]

scran *v.* **1** [mid-18C–mid-19C] to provide with food. **2** [mid-18C–mid-19C] to collect scraps of food to make up a meal; thus *out on the scran*, begging for scraps of food. **3** [19C] (Scot.) to make any sort of random collection. [SCRAN n.]

scran-bag/-pocket *n.* [mid-19C] **1** a beggar's receptacle for the scraps of food they solicit. **2** any form of bag into which bits of food can be placed (cf. KNIGHT OF THE SCRAN-BAG). [SCRAN n. (2) + SE *bag*; note milit. jargon *scran-bag*, a haversack]

scranning *n.* [mid-19C] (Scot.) begging for scraps of food. [SCRAN v.]

scran-pock *n.* [19C] **1** a beggar's wallet, used for picking up whatever bits and pieces might be encountered. **2** a bag used by women who follow an army to gather up and store whatever they plunder from the battlefield dead. [SCRAN n. (2) + POKE n.²]

scran-pocket *see* SCRAN-BAG.

scrap/scrapp *n.*¹ [late 17C–early 19C] a plot, a villainous scheme. [SE *scrape*]

scrap *n.*² **1** [mid-19C+] (orig. boxing) a fight. **2** [late 19C–1920s] a heated argument, a quarrel. [? SE *scrape*]

scrap *n.*³ [late 19C+] a small person, usu. as *a scrap of a …* .

scrap *v.* [early 19C+] **1** to fight, to box. **2** to argue heatedly. [SCRAP n.²]

scrap a lick, to *phr.* [1990s] to have a poor fighting ability. [SCRAP v. + LICK n.¹]

scrape *n.* **1** [early 19C+] a shave. **2** [early 19C+] butter; thus *bread and scrape*, bread and butter, esp. as offered in institutions. **3** [late 19C] short shrift. **4** [20C] (Irish) a sexually complaisant woman. **5** [1960s+] an abortion; thus *scrape clinic*, an abortion clinic, *scrape doctor*, an abortionist.

scrape *v.*¹ [1950s+] (Aus.) to have sexual intercourse (cf. RASP v.).

scrape *v.*² [1970s+] (US Black/teen) to have one's car lowered to such an extent that it scrapes the road and shoots up showers of sparks.

scrape-all *n.* [late 17C–18C] **1** a miser. **2** an unpleasant person. [they *scrape* everything into their own hands/pocket]

scrape and snort, to *phr.* [1980s+] (drugs) to share crack cocaine by scraping off small pieces for inhaling. [SE *scrape* + SNORT v. (1)]

scrape Dixie *v.* [1940s] (US Black) to walk the streets of a Southern city or town in search of work. [SE *scrape* + DIXIE n.¹]

scrape/cut one's horns, to *phr.* [1960s+] (US) **1** of a man, to engage in sexual activity, esp. after a period of abstinence. **2** to masturbate. [SE *scrape/cut* + HORN n.²]

scraper *n.*¹ [late 18C] a barber. **2** [mid-late 19C] a razor. [SCRAPE n. (1)]

scraper/three-cornered scraper *n.*² [late 18C–early 19C] a cocked hat. [its shape]

scraper *n.*³ [late 19C] (society) of a man's beard or moustache, a short (2.5–5cm/1–2in) whisker, slightly curved. [? resemblance to some form of SE *scraper*]

scrape the barrel/bottom of the barrel, to *phr.* [1940s+] **1** to make do with the most mediocre people, objects etc, simply because no others exist. **2** to utilize the very last of one's resources, irrespective of quality.

scrape the kettle, to phr. [late 19C] to attend confession. [? var. on SCRAPE THE BARREL, one's search for confessible sins]

scraping castle n. [mid-19C] a water closet, a lavatory. [one 'scrapes' oneself clean; but note CRAPPING CASTLE]

scrapings n. [1980s+] (N.Z. drugs) resin scraped from a smoking device, e.g. a pipe for cannabis or crack cocaine.

scrap iron n.[1] [1960s+] (US prison) weights, used for exercising and body-building.

scrap iron n.[2] (US) [1940s+] **1** homemade whisky, bad liquor. **2** (prison) a drink made of rubbing alcohol, mothballs and chlorine solution.

scrapp see SCRAP n.[1].

scrappy adj. [late 19C+] pugnacious, aggressive. [SCRAP v.]

scratch n.[1] [mid-19C] any competitor who has no advantage given to him in a handicapped contest; thus also used fig. [SE scratch, the starting line; such competitors must run the full race, play the full distance of the holes etc]

scratch n.[2] **1** [1910s+] money (cf. BUSTLE n.[1]; SCRAMBLE n.[1]). **2** [1910s+] (US) a loan. **3** [1930s+] (US) publicity, a favourable mention in the media. [the image of scratching in the dirt for funds etc]

scratch v.[1] [mid-19C–1900s] (US) to leave at speed. [one's tracks are scratched in the ground]

scratch v.[2] [mid-19C–1930s] (US) to forge banknotes or other documents.

scratch/scratch the gravel v.[3] [late 19C–1940s] (Aus.) to move fast. [the car's rotating wheels]

scratch/scratch off v.[4] [1910s+] (Aus.) to dismiss from a job. [SE scratch, to erase the name of (a person) from a list]

scratch v.[5] [1970s] (US Black) to work. [abbr. SE scratch for (money)]

scratch a beggar's arse, to phr. [mid-18C] to be impoverished. [ARSE n.[1]]

scratch around v. [20C] (orig. US) to search for something, esp. when hard to find.

scratch-crib n. [1940s] (US Black) a cheap hotel or rooming house. [SE scratch + CRIB n.[3]; one scratches at the bites inflicted by bedbugs]

scratch down v. [late 19C] for a woman to tell her husband off in public.

scratched adj. [early 17C] drunk (cf. BASTED).

scratcher n.[1] **1** [19C] (Anglo-Irish) a toe. **2** [early–mid-19C] a hand, usu. in pl.

scratcher n.[2] [mid-19C] (US) a forger, a counterfeiter. [SCRATCH v.[2]]

scratcher n.[3] **1** [late 19C+] a match. **2** [1970s+] (Irish) a lottery scratch-card. [SE scratch; (1) prison use only by 1950s]

scratcher n.[4] [1970s+] (Irish) a bed (cf. SCRATCH-CRIB).

scratch/dig/throw gravel v. [mid-19C+] (US) **1** to work hard. **2** to leave hurriedly. [the image of wheels spinning furrows in the gravel]

scratch house n. [late 19C+] a cheap hotel or lodging house (cf. BUGHOUSE n.). [the scratching caused by bedbugs]

scratchie n. [108s+] (N.Z.) a lottery 'instant' scratch card.

scratching n. [1950s–60s] (US Black) writing.

scratching adj. [1910s+] (Aus.) **1** worried, bemused, in a quandary. **2** struggling for a living. [the image is of a hen]

scratching rake n. [late 19C] a comb (cf. BUG RAKE). [the image is of removing lice]

scratch it v. [1910s–20s] to rush off. [SCRATCH v.[1]]

Scratchland n. [late 18C–early 19C] Scotland (cf. ITCHLAND). [derog. image of Scotland as louse-ridden]

scratch me n. [late 19C] a match. [var. on SCRATCHER n.[3] (1)]

scratch off see SCRATCH v.[4].

scratch platter n. [late 18C–mid-19C] bread soaked in the dressing in which cucumbers have stood (cf. TAILOR'S RAGOUT). [SE scratch, impromptu + platter]

scratch-rash n. [late 19C] scratches on one's face, presumed to be caused by an angry woman.

scratch someone's back, to phr. [mid-late 19C] (orig. Aus.) to do someone a favour, usu. in phr. you scratch my back and I'll scratch yours (cf. CLAW ME AND I'LL CLAW YOU). [SE in 20C]

scratch the gravel see SCRATCH v.[3].

scratch the itch/patch, to phr. [1990s] of a woman, to masturbate.

scraunched/scronched adj. [20C] (US) drunk (cf. BASTED). [? dial. scranched, crushed or SE scrunch]

scream n.[1] **1** [late 19C+] (orig. US) someone or something considered uproariously funny. **2** [1920s] a fuss. **3** [1920s] an urgent message. **4** [1930s+] a complaint, esp. against criminal activities or to the police. **5** [1930s+] the act of informing on or betraying a criminal accomplice.

scream n.[2] [1980s] (US preppie) ice-cream. [abbr./pron.]

scream v. [1920s+] to inform to the police.

scream down some heavy lines see SCREAM SOME HEAVY LINES.

screamer n.[1] **1** [mid-19C+] (orig. US) anything exceptional, in size, attractiveness, wit etc. **2** [mid–late 19C] (orig. US) a thrilling or funny story, a 'screaming' farce. **3** [mid–late 19C] (orig. US) a teller of exaggerated or very funny stories. **4** [late 19C+] an exclamation mark. **5** [late 19C+] a powerful shot in a game, e.g. of cricket, golf, hockey. **6** [20C] (US) a sensational newspaper headline (cf. SCAREHEAD; SCREAM SHEET). **7** [20C] (US) a conspicuous advertisement. **8** [1960s+] (gay) a flagrant homosexual (cf. SCREAMING FAIRY). **9** [1970s+] (US campus) anything exceptionally challenging, difficult, esp. work.

screamer n.[2] [20C] an informer. [SCREAM v.]

screamer n.[3] [1960s+] (US Black) a siren, esp. on a police car.

screamer and creamer n. [1970s+] a sexually enthusiastic woman. [SE scream + CREAM n.[2]]

screaming adj. **1** [mid–late 19C] first-rate, splendid (cf. SCREAMER n.[1]). **2** [20C] (US Black) fantastic, amazing, extreme. [SE scream; note 19C Adelphi Theatre playbills, which advertised a 'screaming farce']

screaming abdabs n. [1930s+] **1** the horrors, utter disgust, abhorrence; usu. as in gives me the screaming abdabs. **2** delirium tremens. [SE screaming + ABDABS]

screaming blue murder phr. [mid-19C+] in a state of hysteria, utterly and completely overwrought or terrified. [SE screaming + BLUE MURDER]

screaming eagle n. [1940s+] (US) a GI discharge button, issued after WW2 (cf. RUPTURED DUCK). [the image engraved on it]

screaming fairy/queen n. [1940s+] an ostentatiously effeminate homosexual man (cf. SCREAMER n.[1]). [SE scream + FAIRY n.[2]/QUEEN n.[1]]

screaming gasser n. [1940s] (US Black) a police car moving at speed and sounding its siren.

screaming meemies/mimis n. [1940s–50s] (US) nerves, paranoia (cf. MEEMIES; SCREAMING ABDABS). [? var. on HEEBIE-JEEBIES]

screaming queen see SCREAMING FAIRY.

scream on v. [1960s–70s] (US Black) **1** to betray a confidence, to inform against, to gossip about. **2** to attack verbally. [SCREAM v.]

scream oneself into fits, to phr. [mid-19C+] to become hysterical.

scream sheet n. [1940s+] (US) a tabloid newspaper. [SCREAMER n.[1] (6) + SHEET n. (1)]

scream/scream down some heavy lines, to phr. [1970s+] (US Black) **1** to impress with one's smart talk. **2** to debate or argue intensely and emotionally. [SE scream + HEAVY adj.[1] + LINE n.[1] (3)]

scream the place down, to *phr.* [1930s+] (orig. Und.) to report a burglary.

screamy *adj.* [late 19C] **1** extreme, exaggerated, undignified. **2** of colour, glaring, violent. [used of something that fig. SE *screams*]

screave *see* SCREEVE n.

screech n.[1] [19C+] (US) cheap, rotgut whisky. [its effect on women]

screech n.[2] [1970s+] (gay) the throat, the mouth.

screechie *v.* [1950s+] (W.I. Rasta) to sneak by. [var. on SE *squeak by*]

screen n.[1] [mid-19C–1920s] a banknote (cf. QUEER SCREENS). [? SCREEVE n. (3)]

screen n.[2] [1960s+] (US Black) a television.

screeve/screave/scrieve/scrive n. **1** [19C] a begging letter (cf. SCREEVER). **2** [19C] a letter. **3** [19C] (Scot.) a banknote. **4** [mid–late 19C] a chalk drawing on the pavement. [? Scot. *scrieve*, to read or write quickly or continuously; or SCREEVE v.]

screeve *v.* **1** [late 18C–late 19C] to write, esp. to write fraudulent documents or letters; thus *screeve a fakement*, to concoct or write a begging letter or any other document aimed to extract money by trickery. **2** [mid-19C] to draw on the pavement with chalk. [Ital. *scrivere*, ult. Lat. *scribere*, to write]

screever n. [mid-19C] **1** a pavement artist, who draws in coloured chalks on the paving stones. **2** a writer of begging letters. **3** a begging letter. [SCREEVE v.]

screigh n. [19C] (Scot.) whisky. [ety. unknown; ? Scot. *screigh*, screech, thus cf. SCREECH n.[1]]

screw n.[1] **1** [early 18C] a prostitute. **2** [1920s+] an act of sexual intercourse (cf. BASH n.[2]). **3** [1920s+] one's partner in intercourse, esp. as a *good screw* or *bad screw*; usu. applied to a woman. **4** [1960s+] a dismissive and pej. ref. to a woman, relegating her to the status of a pure sex object. [SCREW v.[1]]

screw n.[2] **1** [early–mid-19C] (Und.) a skeleton key (cf. SCREWSMAN). **2** [early 19C+] a prison warder. **3** [19C] a robbery achieved with a skeleton key.

screw n.[3] [mid-19C] (US campus) **1** a particularly demanding instructor. **2** the essays and examinations they set. [SE *screw*, to pressurize]

screw n.[4] [mid–late 19C] a miser. [? they *screw down* their money or *screw* it out of creditors]

screw n.[5] [mid–late 19C] an old and/or broken-down horse. [? racing jargon *screw*, to force a horse to the front; thus a horse can be made to gain a better than expected place]

screw n.[6] [mid-19C+] wages, salary. [? the money one can *screw out* of one's employer]

screw n.[7] [late 19C] a pick-me-up, a tonic. [it 'pulls one together']

screw n.[8] [20C] (orig. Aus.) a look, a stare, a gaze, esp. a challenging one; thus (mainly Aus.) *take a screw at*, to look at, to glance.

screw v.[1] **1** [early 18C+] to have sexual intercourse; poss. the most common example of the equation sex = violence (cf. BANG v.[1]). **2** [20C] (orig. US) to cheat, to swindle, to take advantage of, to treat badly or unfairly; esp. as *get screwed*, to be swindled, cheated. **3** [1930s+] (orig. US) to ruin, to pervert, to upset (cf. FUCK v.[2]). **4** [1940s+] used as a synon./euph. for FUCK v. in a variety of senses and parts of speech, e.g. *screw the government! screw you!*

screw v.[2] [early 19C+] to break into, to rob, orig. with a skeleton key. [SCREW n.[2]]

screw v.[3] [1910s+] (orig. Aus.) to stare intently at someone; thus the challenging query *who you screwin'?* as a prelude to a fight. [SCREW n.[8]]

screw v.[4] [1980s+] (W.I./UK Black teen) **1** to crumple up one's

face in annoyance, tightly puckering the lips and features into a vexed look. **2** (UK Black) to complain, to make a fuss.

screw a chat, to *phr.* [late 19C] (Und.) to break into a house. [SCREW v.[2] + CHEAT n.]

screw around *v.* [1930s+] (orig. US) **1** to act in a promiscuous manner (cf. FUCK AROUND). **2** to fiddle with, mess around with, to annoy, to irritate. [SCREW v.[1]]

screwball n. [1930s+] (orig. US) an eccentric, an out-of-the-ordinary person. [baseball use *screwball*, a ball pitched with reverse spin against the natural curve]

screwball *adj.* [1930s+] (orig. US) eccentric, mad, crazy (cf. MADBALL). [SCREWBALL n.]

screw-belly/scribley n. [late 19C] (provincial) sour, weak beer. [SE *screw* + *belly*]

screwboy n. [1950s] one who is victimized by his superiors (cf. FUCKBOY). [SCREW n.[1] + SE *boy*]

screwdriver n.[1] [20C] the penis. [SCREW n.[1] + pun]

screwdriver n.[2] [1940s–50s] (prison) a principal officer who 'drives' his subordinates. [SCREW n.[2] (2) + pun]

screwed *adj.*[1] [mid-19C+] drunk; thus *half-screwed*, tipsy (cf. TIGHT adj.[3]).

screwed *adj.*[2] [20C] in trouble, in great difficulties; ext. as *screwed, blued and tattooed* (cf. FUCKED). [SCREW v.[1] + ? *blewed*, robbed + SE *tattooed*, to be repeatedly struck]

screwed *adj.*[3] [20C] (Aus.) worn out with hard work. [SCREW v.[1] (2)]

screwed up *adj.* **1** [late 19C] in serious financial difficulties. **2** [1960s+] neurotic, very miserable, anxious. [abbr. phr. *screwed up in a corner*]

screwee n. [20C] (US) one's sexual partner. [SCREW v.[1] (1)]

screwer n. [1930s–50s] **1** a thief, a burglar. **2** burglary. [SCREW v.[2]]

screwface n. [1980s+] (W.I./UK Black teen) one whose face is crumpled up in annoyance. [SCREW v.[4]]

screwing n.[1] [early 19C+] house-breaking. [SCREW v.[2]]

screwing n.[2] [20C] **1** sexual intercourse. **2** cheating, fooling, deceiving. **3** punishing. [SCREW v.[1]]

screw it! *excl.* [1970s+] the hell with it! forget it! [SCREW v.[1]; euph. for FUCK IT!]

screw it on *v.* [1960s+] to drive one's car or motorcycle very fast. [SE *screw*, to tighten]

screw-loose n. [late 19C+] (orig. US) **1** a crazy or eccentric person. **2** insanity or eccentricity. [HAVE A SCREW LOOSE]

screwman n. [1930s–50s] a thief, a burglar (cf. SCREWER). [SCREW v.[2] + sfx. *-man*]

screw-off n. [1940s+] (US) an idler, a loafer (cf. FUCK-OFF n.). [fig. use of SCREW v.[1]]

screw off *v.* [20C] (US) to masturbate (cf. BEAT OFF). [SCREW v.[1]]

screw off out *see* SCREW OUT.

screw one's nut, to *phr.* **1** [late 19C] to dodge a blow aimed at one's head. **2** [1900s–20s] (US) to turn around, to leave, to go. [SE *screw* + NUT n.[3]]

screw out/screw off out *v.* [late 19C+] (orig. US) to leave, to depart. [mid-20C uses seem to be euph. for FUCK OFF v., but early ones may be autonomous]

screw over *v.* [20C] to cheat, to swindle, to treat badly or harshly. [ext. of SCREW v.[1] (2)]

screws, the n. [late 19C+] rheumatism. [SE *screw*; the pains it causes]

screwsman n. [19C+] a skilled house-breaker. [SCREW v.[2] + sfx. *-man*]

screws me *phr.* [1970s] (US campus) excuse me. [joc. mispron.]

screw someone out of *v.* [20C] (orig. US) to defraud, to cheat, to deceive. [SCREW v.[1] (2)]

screw the arse off, to *phr.* [1950s+] to indulge in aggressive, vigorous copulation. [SCREW v.[1] + ARSE n.]

screw the dog/pooch, to *phr.* [1960s+] to waste time (cf. FORNICATE THE POODLE; FUCK THE DOG). [SCREW v.¹ + SE *dog/* POOCH n.¹]

screw-up *n.* [1920s+] (orig. US) a failure, an incompetent (cf. FUCK-UP n.). [SCREW UP v.³]

screw up *v.*¹ [late 17C–late 19C] to force someone into concluding a deal. [SE *screw up*, to tighten]

screw up *v.*² [mid-19C] to garrotte. [SE *screw up*, to tighten]

screw up *v.*³ [1920s+] (orig. US) to make a mess, to blunder badly (cf. ARSE UP). [SCREW v.¹]

screwy *adj.*¹ [19C] drunk. [HAVE A SCREW LOOSE; note Tok Pisin (Papua New Guinea pidgin) *waialus*, an unstable, crazy person (f. 'wire loose')]

screwy *adj.*² [mid–late 19C] mean. [SCREW n.⁴]

screwy *adj.*³ [late 19C+] (orig. US) foolish, stupid, insane. [HAVE A SCREW LOOSE]

screw you! *excl.* [20C] (US) an excl. of dismissal, contempt (cf. FUCK YOU!). [SCREW v.¹]

screw your buddy week *see* FRIG YOUR BUDDY WEEK.

scribe *n.* **1** [mid-19C+] (US Black) a letter. **2** [late 19C] a writer. **3** [1920s+] (US) a newspaperman.

scribe *v.* [mid-19C+] to write.

scribley *see* SCREW-BELLY.

scrieve *see* SCREEVE n.

scrilla/scrill *n.* [1990s] (US Black teen) money; thus *gotta get me scrill on*, I must find some cash. [? Sp.]

scrimmage *n.* [late 18C+] a disturbance, a confused, noisy struggle. [? SE *skirmish*]

scrimshank *v.* [late 19C] (orig. milit.) to shirk one's work, to laze around; thus *scrimshanker*, one who acts thus. [ety. unknown; ? link to *scrimshaw*, handicrafts practised by sailors on long voyages, e.g. carving ivory, bone etc. E.P. notes old whaling logs with the comment 'all hands at scrimshanking']

scrip *n.*¹ [20C] (US) a forger. [abbr. SE *script*]

scrip *n.*² [1920s+] (US) $1. [SE *scrip*, a scrap of paper or a certificate of indebtedness, as issued to workers in lieu of actual cash]

scrip *n.*³ [1930s+] (drugs) a prescription (cf. SCRIPT). [abbr.]

scripper/scrippet *n.* [16C] (Und.) the member of a team of highway robbers who keeps a watch (cf. HIGH LAWYER). [? Lat. *scripsit*, he wrote, and poss. referring to written instructions given to this member of the gang]

scrip-scrap *n.* [19C] odds and ends, bits and pieces. [SE *scraps* + redup.]

script *n.* [1930s+] (drugs) a prescription for narcotics. [abbr.]

scrive *see* SCREEVE n.

scroby *n.* [mid–late 19C] a judicial flogging. [? dial. *scrobble*, a quarrel, a problem, a scratching]

scrog *v.* [1980s+] (US campus) to engage in sex. [var. on SCREW v.¹]

scronched *see* SCRAUNCHED.

scrooch *see* SCRUNCH v.

scrooched *adj.* [1920s] (US) drunk (cf. BASTED). [Yorks. dial. *scrooch*, to crouch]

scroodge *see* SCROUGE v.

scroof *v.* [mid-19C–1900s] to sponge off. [? SE *scrounge* + *off*]

scroof *n.* [mid-19C+] a miser. [the miserly Ebenezer *Scrooge*, created by Charles Dickens in *A Christmas Carol* (1843); ult. SCROUGE v.]

scrooge *v. see* SCROUGE v.

scrooge up *v.* [20C] (US) to squeeze, to tighten up (cf. SCROUGE v.).

scroop *v.* [1910s–20s] to rub up against, to pass very closely. [SE *scroop*, to make a scraping noise]

scrope *n.* [18C] a farthing (cf. ARCHER). [proper name of Sir John *Scrope*, secretary of the Treasury from 1724–52]

scrote *n.* [1970s] a general term of abuse. [abbr. SE *scrotum*]

scrote-shrinking *adj.* [1970s] (US Black) very cold. [the effect of the cold on the male genitals, esp. the scrotum]

scrotty *adj.* [1980s+] unpleasant, dirty. [SCROTE + GROTTY]

scroucher/scrousher/scrowcher *n.* [20C] (Aus.) a general derog. term for a person. [? SE *scrounger*; dial. *scringer*, one who pries around looking for trifles or dial. *skreenger*, one who is (neg.) energetic]

scroudge *see* SCROUGE v.

scrouger *n.* [mid-19C] (orig. US) something large or forceful. [SCROUGE n.]

scrouge/scrowge *n.* [mid-18C+] a crowd, a crush. [? 16C SE *scruze*, to squeeze]

scrouge / scroodge / scrooge / scroudge / scrowge / skrowdge *v.* [mid-18C+] **1** to encroach on a person's space, to crowd. **2** to push something out of the way, to squeeze a thing. [SCROUGE n.]

scrounge *v.* [20C] (orig. US) **1** to beg off others, to sponge on. **2** to hunt about, to rummage. **3** to cadge; thus *scrounger*, one who cadges from others, *on the scrounge*, begging, cadging.

scroungy *adj.* [20C] (US) inferior, second-rate, grubby (cf. GRUNGY; SCRUNGY).

scrouperize *v.* [mid-17C–early 18C] to have sexual intercourse. [SE *scroop*, to rub against]

scrousher *n.*¹ (Aus./N.Z.) **1** [mid–late 19C] a worn-out prospector. **2** [20C] a prostitute. [? SE *scrounger*]

scrousher *n.*² *see* SCROUCHER.

scrowcher *see* SCROUCHER.

scrowge *see* SCROUGE.

scrub *n.* **1** [late 17C–early 18C] one who does not pay their share of the tavern bill. **2** [18C+] a low-class prostitute (cf. SCRUBBER n.²; SCRUBBING BRUSH). **3** [20C] (US) a derog. term for a Black person. **4** [20C] (US Black) a fool. **5** [1980s+] (US campus) a general pej. term, a lout, a failure, a dirty or unpleasant person. [SE *scrub*, an insignificant, unattractive person]

scrub *v.*¹ [late 19C+] to work at a menial task, to drudge. [ext. of SE]

scrub *v.*² **1** [1940s+] (orig. US) to cancel, to wipe out, to forget. **2** [1980s+] (US campus) to fail. [milit. use *scrub*, a flight cancellation; *OED* has a single early 19C citation, but then nothing until WW2]

scrubado *see* SCRUBBADO.

scrub along *v.* [mid-19C] to survive with difficulty.

scrubbado/scrubado *n.* [mid-17C–early 18C] 'the itch', venereal disease. [SE *scrub*, 'the itch' + Sp./Port. sfx. *-ado*, thus giving underpinning of racist stereotyping]

scrubber *n.*¹ (Aus./N.Z.) **1** [mid-19C+] a rough, unkempt person. **2** [mid-19C+] one who lives in the scrub or wooded countryside. **3** [late 19C+] a cow or horse that has run wild in the scrub and has deteriorated in condition. **4** [1940s+] an unpleasant weakling. [SE *scrub*, heavily wooded country, whether growing small or large bushes and trees]

scrubber *n.*² [1950s+] **1** a promiscuous woman, usu. young (cf. SLAPPER). **2** (Irish) a common working-class woman, with no sexual implications. [? SE *scrubber*, a charwoman, one who scrubs; orig. sl. use was in jazz community, where it described 'a girl who slept with a jazzman but for her own satisfaction as much as his' (George Melly, *Owning Up*, 1965). ? link to Aus. term, defined as 'a mare that runs wild in the scrub country, copulating indiscriminately with stray stallions' (quote cited in *OED*)]

scrubbing brush *n.* **1** [mid-19C+] the pubic hair (cf. SHAVING BRUSH). **2** [late 19C–1920s] (Aus.) a loaf of bread made from inferior materials.

scrub bull *n.* [1920s+] (Aus.) a solo prospector, living out in the desert and characterized by surliness, taciturnity and general misanthropy (cf. DEATH ADDER). [SAusE *scrub bull*, a bull that was bred in, or escaped into, the wild]

scrub cockie *n.* [20C] (Aus.) a small farmer working tree-covered or otherwise rough land. [SE *scrub* + COCKIE]

scrub-dangler *n.* [late 19C–1910s] (Aus.) a wild bullock.

scrub-dashing *n.* [1940s] (Aus.) riding through bush or scrub in pursuit of strayed cattle or horses.

scrub it *v.* [1940s+] to forget something, to ignore, to let it pass. [SCRUB v.²]

Scrubs, the *n.* [1910s+] (police/Und.) Wormwood *Scrubs* prison, London (cf. VILLE n.²). [abbr.]

scrub the kitchen *see* CLEAN UP THE KITCHEN.

scrub the slate clean, to *phr.* [late 19C+] (US) to cancel or ignore the past and start again.

scrub-turkey *n.* [1950s] (Aus.) an itinerant who moves around the Australian bush (cf. PLAIN-TURKEY).

scrud *n.* [1930s+] (US, orig. milit.) a painful disease, esp. a venereal disease (cf. CRUD n.¹).

scrudge *n.* [18C] a prostitute. [SCROUGE v. (2)]

scruff *n.* [mid-19C+] an unkempt, messy person; thus [1930s+] *scruff-bag*, a down-and-out. [dial. *scruff*, refuse, thus human refuse; ult. SE *scurf*]

scruff *adj.* [mid-19C+] messy, unkempt. [SCRUFF n.]

scruff *v.* **1** [19C] to hang. **2** [mid-19C–1940s] (Aus.) to grab by the scruff of the neck. **3** [mid-19C–1940s] (Aus.) to attack, to manhandle. [dial. *scruff*, the nape of the neck]

scrum/scrummy *n.* [late 19C–1910s] (Aus./N/Z.) a three-penny piece. [rhy. sl. *scrum* = THRUMS]

scrumdolious *adj.* [19C] wonderful, excellent, often but not always of food (cf. SCRUMMY adj.; SCRUMPTIOUS).

scrummy *n.* see SCRUM.

scrummy *adj.* [1910s+] **1** excellent, fine. **2** of food, enjoyable, delicious (cf. SCRUMDOLIOUS). [abbr. SCRUMPTIOUS]

scrump *v.* [1980s+] (US campus) to engage in sex. [? SCRUMPTIOUS]

scrumptious *adj.* [mid-19C+] (orig. US) **1** fastidious, hard to please. **2** first-rate, excellent. **3** stylish, handsome. **4** (mainly teen) delicious, extra-tasty, nearly always of food but occas. of an attractive person. [dial. *scrumptious*, mean, stingy, close-fisted; although the senses seem totally opposed, cf. SE *nice* for a similar shift in meaning from overly fastidious to attractive and appealing]

scrunch *n.* [1920s+] (Aus.) food, esp. sweets (cf. SCRUNCHER). [SE *scrunch*, the noise of crunching]

scrunch/scrooch *v.* [1940s] (US Black) to dance extremely close to someone.

scruncher *n.* [late 19C+] a glutton. [SE *scrunch*, to bite with a crunching noise]

scrunge *n.* [1970s+] (orig. US campus) filth, mess, dirt (cf. GRUNGE n.).

scrungy *adj.* [1970s+] (orig. US campus) filthy, messy, dirty, disgusting (cf. SCROUNGY). [SCRUNGE]

scrunt *v.* [20C] (W.I.) to eke out a living, to suffer great poverty, to be forced into begging. [dial. *scrunt*, to scratch + SE *scrounge*]

scruples *n.* [1980s+] (drugs) crack cocaine. [? dial. *scroop*, to scrape]

scud *n.* [1960s+] (Ulster) **1** a jinx. **2** a smack. **3** a general term of abuse. [Scot. *scud*, a blow]

scud *adj.* [1990s] bad, unpleasant. [SAmE *scut*, tedious work]

scud *v.* [1990s] to partake in the act of copulation. [SE *scud*, to move fast; ? reinforced by the *Scud* missiles used in the Gulf War (1991)]

scuddick/scuddock *n.* [late 18C–mid-19C] a tiny sum of money (cf. SCURRICK). [dial. *scud*, a wisp of straw]

scuffer/scufter *n.* [1960s+] (mainly Liverpool) a policeman; thus *judy scuffer*, a policewoman. [? dial. *scuff*, to strike;

Yorks. dial. *scuff*, 'mean, sordid fellow, the scum of the people' (EDD); or *scurf*, the back of the neck, and thus one who grabs you by it]

scuffle *n.*¹ [late 19C–1950s] (US Black) difficult circumstances, poverty (cf. SCRAMBLE v.). [SCUFFLE v.¹]

scuffle *n.*² [1970s+] (drugs) phencyclidine (cf. ACE n.³; SCAFFLE; SKUFFLE). [ety. unknown]

scuffle *v.*¹ [late 19C+] (US, orig. jazz) **1** to survive with difficulty, to eke out one's bare living, often through unpleasant, degrading methods. **2** [1940s+] (US Black) to collect, raise or obtain money.

scuffle *v.*² [late 19C+] (US, orig. jazz) to dance. [SE *scuffle*, shuffle]

scuffle-hunter *n.* [19C] a dockside pilferer. [they *scuffle around*, hunting for items to steal]

scuffler *n.* [late 19C–1950s] (US Black) one who works hard and honestly for their living. [SCUFFLE v.¹]

scuffle up *v.* [1940s+] (US Black) to collect, raise or obtain money. [ext. of SCUFFLE v.¹ (2)]

scuff up *v.* [20C] (US prison) to fight (cf. JACKPOT v.). [abbr. SE *scuffle*, to struggle confusedly together]

scufter *see* SCUFFER.

scull/skull *n.*¹ [early 18C–mid-19C] the head, principal or master of a university college.

scull/sculler *n.*² [late 18C–early 19C] a one-horse chaise or buggy. [SE *scull*, a light boat rowed by a single oarsman]

scull around *v.* [1920s+] to wander aimlessly.

sculler *see* SCULL n.².

scullery-science *n.* [mid-19C] phrenology. [pun on SE *skull*]

scully *n.* [1980s+] (US campus) an unspecified person. [? SE *scullion*]

scum *n.* [1960s+] (US) semen.

scumbag *n.* [1920s+] **1** a contraceptive sheath. **2** a term of general abuse (cf. DIRTBAG). [SCUM + SE *bag*; but note BAG n.⁶]

scumball *n.* [1980s+] (US) an unpleasant person (cf. SCUM-BAG). [SCUM + sfx. *-ball*]

scumber/scummer *n.* [20C] excrement. [dial. *scumber*, animal dung or sticky, viscous mud]

scumbucket *n.* [1980s+] (US) an unpleasant person. [SCUM + SE *bucket*]

scumhead *n.* [1990s] a general term of abuse (cf. SCUMBAG). [SCUM + sfx. *-HEAD* (1)]

scummer *see* SCUMBER.

scummy *adj.* [1930s+] unpleasant, disgusting. [SE *scum*]

scumsucker *n.* [1960s+] (orig. US) **1** a person who performs fellatio. **2** a derog. term of general abuse; thus *scumsucking* (cf. COCKSUCKER). [SCUM + SE *sucker*]

scunge *n.* **1** [20C] (Ulster) one who is always 'on the make'. **2** [1960s+] (N.Z.) an unpleasant, objectionable person. **3** [1970s+] (N.Z.) dirt, filth, often associated with the body. [Scot. *scunge*, slink around]

scungies *n.* [1970s] (Aus.) men's bikini-style swimming trunks, often worn under surf shorts or 'baggies'. [joc. use of SCUNGY adj.; suck trunks are seen as too sordid for public display]

scungy *adj.* [1960s+] (Aus./N.Z.) filthy, dirty. [SCUNGE or var. on SCRUNGY]

scunner *n.* [late 19C+] (US) extreme dislike, hostility. [Scot. *scunner*, an abomination]

scupper *n.* [1930s+] a prostitute. [? SE *scupper*, a boat's drain through which dirty water can run]

scupper *v.* [1910s+] (orig. milit.) to defeat, to ruin, to put an end to. [? SE *scupper*; see SCUPPER n.]

scurf *n.* [mid–late 19C] **1** an unpleasant person, esp. a miser or skinflint (cf. SCAB n.; SCABBY SHEEP). **2** an employer who pays less than average wages. **3** a worker who accepts less than the average rate (cf. SCAB n.). [SE *scurf*, a general term referring to a variety of skin diseases]

scurf *adj.* [mid–late 19C] of labour, cheap. [SCURF n.]

scurf *v.* [early 19C] to arrest; thus *scurfed*, arrested. [? SE *scruff*, to seize by the nape of the neck]

scurrick *n.* [late 18C–mid-19C] a halfpenny. [SCUDDICK]

scurve *n.* [20C] (US) **1** a contemptible person. **2** (Black) any form of ugliness or shabbiness. [SCURF n. ? + SE *scurvy*]

scut *n.*¹ **1** [late 16C+] the female genitals, the pubic hair (cf. BADGER n.⁷). **2** [early 18C] the buttocks, the posterior. [SE *scut*, a rabbit or hare's tail]

scut *n.*² **1** [late 19C+] a contemptible person. **2** [20C] (US) a novice or new recruit (cf. SCUT WORK). [? dial. *scutter*, diarrhoea or SCOUT n.¹]

scutcher *n.* [1910s+] (Aus.) anything notably large or esp. outstanding. [? SE *scotch*, to kill; thus a 'killer']

scutter *n.*¹ [20C] an unpleasant person. [Scot. *scutter*, a slovenly, untidy worker]

scutter *n.*² [1970s+] (Irish) excrement; thus *scutter*, to defecate. [Irish *sciodar*, diarrhoea]

scuttered *adj.* [1960s+] (Irish) tipsy, drunkenly loquacious. [dial. *scutter*, to expend a great deal of energy in doing nothing constructive + Irish *sciotarálaí*, idle chatter]

scuttle *n.* [1900s] (US) a derog. term for a Black person. [abbr. SE *coalscuttle*]

scuttle *v.* **1** [19C] to deflower a woman. **2** [mid-19C] to stab. [SE *scuttle*, to make a hole in a ship's bottom in order to sink her]

scuttle a ship, to *phr.* [19C] to deflower a woman. [ext. of SCUTTLE v. (1)]

scuttlebutt *n.* [20C] gossip, rumour (cf. FURPHY; SHUTTLEBUTT). [US Navy *scuttlebutt*, a ship's water barrel, around which sailors gathered and gossiped; the term, however, was orig. RN]

scuttle-mouth *n.* [mid-19C] (coster) a small oyster with a deceptively large shell.

scuttler *n.* [mid–late 19C] (Manchester) a young street thug. [Lancashire dial. *scuttle*, a street brawl; ? SE *scuttle*, to run off]

scuttle someone's nob, to *phr.* [mid-19C] to break someone's head. [SE *scuttle* + NOB n.¹ (1)]

scut work *n.* [1950s+] (US) menial or routine work. [? SCUT n.²]

scuzz *n.* [1970s+] **1** (orig. US teen) dirt, mess, any horrible substance. **2** a sexually active, thus by sexist definition, promiscuous, woman (cf. DIRTY LEG). [? SCUMMY + SE *fuzzy*]

scuzz *v.* [1970s+] to make a mess of. [SCUZZ n. (1)]

scuzzbag *n.* [1970s+] (US) **1** (campus) a sexually promiscuous woman. **2** a contemptible person (cf. SLEAZEBAG). [SCUZZ n. + SE *bag*]

scuzz-food *n.* [1970s+] (US) any cheap, greasy or sweet snack foods, e.g. chips, crisps, popcorn (cf. JUNK FOOD). [SCUZZ n. + SE *food*]

scuzzed out *adj.* [1970s+] (US teen) disgusted, nauseated (cf. GROSSED-OUT). [SCUZZ v.]

scuzzy *adj.* [1970s+] **1** unkempt, down at heel, ragged. **2** (US teen) filthy, repellent (cf. GRUNGY). [? SCUMMY + SE *fuzzy*]

s.d. *n.* [1980s+] self-*d*estruction, usu. through excessive use of drugs. [abbr.]

'sdeath!/zdeath! *excl.* [17C] a euph. oath, lit. 'God's death' (cf. 's abbr.¹).

'sdeynes! *excl.* [late 16C–early 17C] a mild, euph. oath, lit. 'by God's dines!', i.e. by God's dignity or honour (cf. 's abbr.¹).

'sdiggers! *excl.* [late 17C] a mild, euph. oath, lit. 'God's diggers!', i.e. God's fingers (cf. 's abbr.¹).

sea-coal *n.* [mid-18C–mid-19C] smuggled spirits. [SE *sea-*

coal, coal that is exposed at low tide or washed up on the coastline]

seacow *n.* [1990s] (gay) a derog. term for a woman with a sailor boyfriend. [SE *sea* + COW n.¹ (1)]

sea-crab *n.* [late 18C] a sailor.

seafood *n.*¹ [1920s] (US Und.) whisky. [? the smuggling of whisky by sea during the Prohibition era, 1920–33]

seafood *n.*² [1930s+] (gay) sailors (cf. DOG FOOD n.³). [i.e. something to EAT v.³]

seafood *n.*³ [1950s+] (US) **1** cunnilingus. **2** a woman as a partner for cunnilingus (cf. SEAFOOD BLANCMANGE). [the association of the vagina with FISH n.⁴; thus cf. BEARDED CLAM]

seafood blancmange *n.* [1990s] the female genitals (cf. BEARDED CLAM). [SEAFOOD n.³]

seafood plate *phr.* [1980s] (US campus) please (cf. AU RESERVOIR). [Fr. *s'il vous plait*, please]

seagull *n.* [1960s] (Aus./N.Z.) a casual wharf labourer. [like the seagull, they hope to pick up 'scraps', in this case, of work]

seal *n.*¹ [mid-17C] the penis. [coined by John Donne (1572–1631)]

seal *n.*² [1920s–30s] (US) a Black woman. [the smoothness of her skin]

seal *v.* [mid-17C] to impregnate a woman. [SEAL n.¹]

seal-a-meal *n.* [1980s+] (drugs) small plastic bags used for the selling of crack cocaine. [brandname]

sealer *n.* [late 17C–early 19C] 'one ready to give bond and judgement for goods or money' (Grose, 1785). [SE *sealer*, one who affixes a seal to a document]

sealing wax *n.* [20C] (Aus.) tax. [rhy. sl.]

seals *n.* [mid-19C] the testicles (cf. SEAL n.¹; WATCH AND SEALS). [which 'seal' a sexual 'bargain']

seam squirrel *n.* [1910s+] (US) a body louse.

sea pie *n.* [19C+] a stew. ['A dish of meat and vegetables, etc, boiled together, with a crust of paste, or in layers between crusts, the number of which denominate it a two or three decker' (Smyth, *Sailor's Word-book*, 1867)]

sea pussy *n.* [1980s+] (US gay) a gay sailor. [SE *sea* + PUSSY n.¹ (3)]

sear/sere *n.* [16C] the female genitals (cf. BLACK HOLE n.¹). [SE *sear*, the touch-hole at which the match sets off the charge in a pistol, but note *tickle/light of the sear*, 'easily made to "go off"', readily yielding to any impulse' (*OED*)]

searcher *n.* [1920s–50s] a penetrating or embarrassing question.

search me! *excl.* [20C] (orig. US) a general assertion of ignorance, I don't know, don't ask me (cf. EXPLORE ME!).

search-my-heart *n.* [1900s] (W.I.) a drink of rum (cf. RAISE-MY-THOUGHTS). [its effects]

sea-rover *n.* [19C] a herring.

Sears Roebuck library *n.* [20C] (US) an outdoor privy. [the common use of old Sears catalogues as lavatory paper]

seaside moths *n.* [late 19C] (middle class) bedbugs. [euph.]

seasoner *n.* [1910s–20s] a fashionably dressed person. [SE *the* (social) *season*]

seat *v.* [1950s+] (Aus.) (orig. prison) to sodomize; thus *seatman*, a sodomite. [SE *seat*, the buttocks]

seat check! *excl.* [1990s] (US teen) an excl. used to claim a position in the front passenger seat of a car. [it overrules SHOTGUN!, another phr. used in this situation]

seat-man *n.* [1950s+] (US gambling) a professional card-dealer.

seat of honour/shame/vengeance *n.* [19C] the posterior, the buttocks.

seat of the pants *n.* [1940s+] (US) instinct, impulse (cf. FLY BY THE SEAT OF ONE'S PANTS).

seat of vengeance *see* SEAT OF HONOUR.

seats *n.* [1940s–50s] the buttocks. [SE *seat*]

sec *n.* **1** [late 19C+] a *sec*ond. **2** [1910s–20s] a *sec*retary. [abbr.]

secco *see* SECKO.

seccy/seggy *n.* [1960s+] (drugs) *Sec*onal. [abbr.]

secko/secco/sekko *n.* [1940s+] (Aus.) a sexual pervert, usu. prison use. [SE *sex* + sfx. -O]

second banana *n.* [1950s+] the second most important person, the second-in-command (cf. TOP BANANA). [show business use *second banana*, a supporting comedian to the star, a 'straight man']

second base *n.* [1930s–50s] (US Black/teen) sexual exploration above a woman's waist (cf. FIRST BASE *n.*). [baseball imagery]

second closet *n.* [1960s+] (gay) the hiding of one's specific sexual preferences and practices, even if the basic fact of homosexuality can be admitted. [CLOSET *n.*]

second fiddle *n.* [mid-19C+] someone or something that is considered less than the best or is not in the top position (cf. PLAY SECOND FIDDLE). [orchestra imagery]

second-hand sue *n.* [1940s–50s] (Aus.) a worn-out prostitute. [SE *second-hand* + assonant use of proper name *Sue*]

second-hand sun *n.* [late 19C] reflected sunlight, as found in many poor homes, deprived in the narrow streets of direct sunlight.

second-hand woman *n.* [late 19C] (Anglo-Ind.) a widow.

second hole from the back of the neck *phr.* [20C] the vagina (cf. BLACK HOLE *n.*[1]).

second liker *n.* [late 19C] a second drink, of the same sort as the first. ['I'll have a second one like that']

second line *v.* [20C] (US) to follow a leader or someone first-rate, with the hope of advancement or promotion.

seconds *n.* **1** [late 18C+] a second helping of food. **2** [20C] (US) coffee brewed from used grounds.

second-storey job *n.* [late 19C+] (US) a break-in, spec. one that involves climbing above ground level (cf. HIGH-WALL JOB).

second-storey man *n.* [late 19C+] (US) a thief who climbs into buildings above the ground floor (cf. PORCH-CLIMBER).

secret service *n.* [1980s+] (Black) illicit sex. [SE *secret* + *service*, usu. of an animal, to copulate]

secrets of the alcove *n.* [late 19C] (society) a wife's influence over her husband, which was not, in late 19C, generally paraded in public.

sectioned *adj.* [1970s+] **1** mandatorily detained in a mental institution under section 3 of the Mental Health Act. **2** used of any one seen as eccentric, though not actually mad.

section eight *n.* [1940s+] (US) **1** spec. section 8 discharge, discharge from the US army on grounds of mental instability. **2** insanity, instability. **3** a crazy, neurotic or eccentric person.

security blanket *n.* [1950s+] (US) something or someone that provides emotional comfort and a sense of safety. [SE *security blanket*, a blanket or piece of cloth carried by young children to soothe and comfort themselves]

seddity *see* SADDITY.

seducer *n.* [1970s+] (US Black) one who supplies the means of making fast, poss. illegal, money.

see *v.*[1] [mid-18C–early 19C] to take care, to do something, usu. combined with another *v.*, e.g. *see that you get*.

see *v.*[2] [19C] to have sexual intercourse (cf. SEEING-TO).

see *v.*[3] [mid-19C+] (orig. US) to understand, to appreciate the veracity of an idea or statement.

see *v.*[4] [late 19C+] (orig. US) **1** to visit a person, esp. a politician, in order to influence them, either legally or, more likely, illegally. **2** (Und.) to pay protection money. **3** (gambling) to equal or raise a bet.

see *adv.* [mid-19C] yes. [backsl.]

see? *excl.* [mid-19C+] do you understand? (cf. SEEN!; YOU KNOW).

see a dog about a man, to *phr.* [1920s+] to urinate (cf. SEE A MAN ABOUT A DOG).

see/have to see a man about a dog, to *phr.* **1** [mid-19C+] a euph. used to disguise one's need or desire to visit the lavatory. **2** [mid-19C+] an excuse to absent oneself from home in order to visit one's mistress or to go out for a drink. **3** [1920s–30s] (US) a coded exit-line implying that one is meeting a bootlegger or going to a speakeasy.

see anything? *phr.* [mid-19C] euph. question to a woman, have you had your period? ['anything' is blood]

see/sit up with a sick friend *phr.* [late 19C+] an excuse used by a married man slipping out to consummate an illicit affair.

see a wolf, to *phr.* [19C] of a woman, to be seduced (cf. SEE THE ELEPHANT).

see candles *see* SEE STARS.

see company *v.* [mid–late 18C] **1** to visit a brothel. **2** to live as a prostitute. [euph.]

seed *n.* [1960s+] (US Black) a child, children. [SE *seed* of one's loins]

seeds *n.* [1960s+] (drugs) **1** marijuana. **2** the butt end of a marijuana cigarette.

seedy/seedy-boy *n.* [mid–late 19C] a derog. term for a Black person. [ironic use of Urdu *sidi*, my lord]

see foot *v.* [20C] (W.I.) to see how fast a person runs away.

see France/your days/your nennen/your skin/your tail *v.* [20C] (W.I.) to endure hardships, esp. in the hope of ultimate success (cf. CATCH FRANCE). [SE *see* + FRANCE/SE *days/* NENNEN/SE *skin*/TAIL *n.*[1]]

see/smell hell *v.* [20C] (W.I.) to find it hard to make enough money to live, to suffer great hardship (cf. CATCH FRANCE).

see how the land lies, to *phr.* [late 18C–early 19C] to check the state of one's tavern bill.

see if I care *phr.* [1940s+] a dismissive phr. indicating one's lack of concern.

see if it fucks, to *phr.* [20C] to see if something works or runs. [FUCK *v.*[1]]

see Indians *v.* [19C] (US) to be drunk. [one's hallucinations]

seeing as/as how *phr.* [late 19C+] given that, in the circumstances.

seeing double *adj.* [19C] drunk (cf. SEE PINK ELEPHANTS).

seeing the devil *phr.* [18C] in a state of drunkenness.

seeing-to *n.* [1970s+] **1** referring to a woman, sexual intercourse. **2** referring to a man, a beating up, violence (cf. ATTEND TO).

seek a clove, to *phr.* [late 19C] (US) to take a drink. [? the use of *cloves* to disguise the smell of drink on the breath]

seek others and lose oneself, to *phr.* [late 16C] to play the fool.

seek-sorrow *n.* [19C] a general term of abuse, esp. of a whining malcontent.

see Mrs Murray, to *phr.* [late 19C+] (Aus.) to visit the lavatory (cf. MRS CHANT'S; MRS JONES). [ult. ref. is to the *Murray* River, Australia's longest river]

seems to me *phr.* [late 19C+] I think, it is my opinion.

seen! *excl.* [1970s+] (orig. W.I.) a general excl. of affirmation (cf. SIGHT?). [although the term is used as a synon. for SE *yes*, the implication is one of bearing witness and thus of a more profound agreement with the speaker]

see ning-ning *v.* [20C] (W.I.) to reel from shock, to suffer a spell of dizziness. [Carib.E. *ning-ning*, dizziness]

see-o *n.* [mid-19C] shoes. [backsl.]

see off *v.* [1910s+] to deal with, to dismiss, to send away, to defeat.

see one's grandmother, to *phr.* [mid-19C–1920s] to have a nightmare.

see pink elephants, to *phr.* [1940s+] to have hallucinations from alcoholism (cf. SEE SNAKES).

seer *n.* [19C] the eye. [lit. 'see-er']

see rats *see* GET RATS.

see red *v.* [20C] to become very angry. [a bull's trad. reaction to a red rag]

see royal *v.* [20C] (W.I.) to find it hard to make enough money to live, to subsist, to suffer great hardship (cf. CATCH FRANCE; CATCH NENNEN). [SE *see* + fig. use of ROYAL n.³]

sees *n.* [late 18C–early 19C] (Und.) the eyes.

see sailor *n.* [late 19C] a beggar who poses as a discharged seaman. [? one *sees* him as a *sailor*]

see-saw *n.* [1970s] (US Black) an up-and-down, uncertain relationship.

see snakes *v.* [late 19C] (US) to have delirium tremens (cf. SEE PINK ELEPHANTS).

see someone coming, to *phr.* [late 19C+] to take advantage of someone.

see someone home, to *phr.* [1920s–30s] to tell someone off, to scold.

see stars/candles/spots *v.* [mid-19C+] 'to have a sensation as of flashes of light, produced by a sudden jarring of the head, as by a direct blow' (*Century Dict.*, 1891). [*candles*, mid-18C–mid-19C; *spots*, mid–late 19C]

see the big animal, to *phr.* [mid-19C] (US) to see the world and to become bored and jaded by doing so (cf. SEE THE ELEPHANT; SEE THE LIONS; SEE THE MONKEY SHOW).

see the breeze, to *phr.* [late 19C] to enjoy the fresh air, usu. on a trip out of the city.

see/hunt/get a look at the elephant, to *phr.* (orig. US) **1** [mid-19C+] to see the world and to become bored and jaded by doing so (cf. SEE THE BIG ANIMAL). **2** [mid-19C+] to seek out excitement, esp. in the context of going slumming in poor and/or dangerous urban areas. **3** [late 19C] to be seduced (cf. SEE A WOLF). [despite US origin, poss. popularized in the UK by the appearance in London in 1867 of the original Jumbo, a major attraction at first but then palling in the face of greater novelties. After many years at London Zoo, Jumbo was sold to Barnum and Bailey's Circus in 1882]

see the king, to *phr.* **1** [late 19C] to be sophisticated, knowing. **2** [1960s+] to have sexual intercourse.

see the light at the end of the tunnel, to *phr.* [late 19C+] to glimpse the end of a long or difficult process or situation, to feel some optimism.

see the lions, to *phr.* [mid-19C+] **1** to see the fashionable 'sights' (cf. LION n.¹). **2** to have some experience of life (cf. SEE THE BIG ANIMAL).

see the monkey show/dance, to *phr.* [mid-19C] (US) to see entertaining things (cf. SEE THE BIG ANIMAL).

see the nose-cheese first, to *phr.* [late 19C–1900s] to make a refusal rudely or contemptuously. [ety. unknown]

see the stars lying upon one's back, to *phr.* [19C] of a woman, to have sexual intercourse.

see the wheels/see what makes the wheels go round, to *phr.* [1920s+] to find out the way in which something (an object or organization) works.

see things *v.* [1920s+] to have hallucinations, usu. in phr. *seeing things*.

see through *v.* [mid-19C] to find it difficult to finish a meal.

see through a brick wall, to *phr.* [19C] to be particularly perceptive, to be intelligent, to be aware, sometimes ext. as *see further through a brick wall than most.*

see through a mill-stone, to *phr.* [19C] to be aware, to understand what is going on.

see through blue glasses, to *phr.* [1930s] to see things from a pessimistic point of view.

see under the table *see* PUT UNDER THE TABLE.

see what makes the wheels go round *see* SEE THE WHEELS GO ROUND.

see what the cat's brought in *see* LOOK WHAT THE CAT'S BROUGHT IN.

see/watch which way the cat jumps, to *phr.* [early 19C+] to wait to see how events turn out before making one's own decision or move.

see with half an eye, to *phr.* [mid-16C–late 18C] to possess shrewdness or native wisdom, to be well aware. [later use is SE]

see ya! *excl.* [1980s+] (US campus) **1** goodbye. **2** a general excl. of dismissal, shut up! leave me alone!

seeyabye! *excl.* [1980s] (US teen) goodbye! [SEE YA! + SE *goodbye*]

see ya later alligator *phr.* [1950s–60s] *See ya later, alligator ... in a while, crocodile*, an all-purpose synon. for 'goodbye', popularized by the 1956 Bill Haley and the Comets pop hit of the same name (written by R.C. Guidry: 'See you lat-er, al-li-ga-tor,/Aft-er 'while, croc-o-dile,/Can't you see you're in my way, now,/Don't you know you cramp my style?'), and by the widely publicized use of the phrase by Princess Margaret (b.1930) (cf. ALLIGATOR!). [according to *DARE* f. ALLIGATOR n.³ (2); given that alligator is essentially (if not invariably) derog., the phr. certainly began as a dismissal, even if its popular use among those who had no idea of its origin rendered it neutral; an alternative response is 'on the Nile, crocodile']

see you! *excl.* [1960s+] goodbye (cf. ABYSSINIA!).

see you anonski *phr.* [1930s–50s] (Aus.) a general phr. of farewell. [SE phr. *see you anon* + 'Slavic' sfx. *-ski*]

see you in court *phr.* [1960s+] used as synon. for goodbye.

see you in the funny papers *phr.* [1920s+] (US) goodbye, see you later.

see you in the soup *phr.* [20C] (Aus.) goodbye, see you around.

see your days/nennen/skin/tail *see* SEE FRANCE.

sef *n.* [1950s+] (US teen) a street gang. [? SE *safe*; i.e. safety in numbers]

seg/seggie *n.*¹ [1960s+] **1** (US) a *seg*regationist. **2** (prison) a *seg*regation unit or cell. [abbr.]

seg *n.*² [1970s+] (US campus) a sequel, a follow-up. [SE *segue* + use of SE *seg* for an episode of a TV series]

seg *n.*³ [1980s] (US campus) a toadying or hypocritical smile. [abbr. SHIT-EATING GRIN]

seg/segue *v.* [1970s+] (US) to go straight from one thing to another, to make a smooth transition. [SE *segue*]

seggie *see* SEG n.¹.

seggy *see* SECCY.

segue *see* SEG v.

sei *see* SAY n.

sei-cordi box *n.* [1940s+] (Polari) a guitar. [lit. '6-cord box']

sein *see* SANE.

sekko *see* SECKO.

seldom seen *n.* [20C] the queen. [rhy. sl.]

self-starter *n.* [1960s+] one who acts, esp. when employed, on their own initiative rather than await instructions or orders (cf. TAKE-CHARGE).

Selina Scott *n.* [20C] a spot. [rhy. sl.; TV personality *Selina Scott*]

sell *n.*¹ [mid–late 19C] **1** a hoax, a trick, a deception. **2** a lying joke. **3** a disappointment. [SELL v.]

$ell *n.*² [1990s] (US Black teen) an act of betrayal. [the $ sign is used to emphasize the lit. or fig. payment involved]

sell *v.* **1** [mid-17C+] to deceive, to swindle, to take in. **2** [early 19C] (Und.) to betray, to inform against.

sell a bargain, to *phr.* [late 16C–18C] to fool, to hoax. [Shakespeare used the term in late 16C. Grose (1796) mentions a specific 'bargain', quoted by Swift, as being popular among

Queen Anne's courtiers: 'A lady would come into a room full of company, apparently in a fright, crying out, "It is white, and follows me!" On any of the company asking, "What?", she sold him the bargain, by saying, "Mine a—ee"']

sell a boy, to phr. [1960s+] (gay) for one man to obtain the services of a boy prostitute at a price and then to offer him to a second man for the actual sex.

sell a dummy, to phr. [1960s+] to deceive, to fool. [rugby jargon *sell a dummy*, to pass the ball so as to deceive one's opponent]

sell a pup, to phr. [1960s+] to deceive, esp. in business or financial transactions; thus the person deceived *buys a pup*. [stock market jargon *pup*, a worthless investment]

sellary n. [16C] a male homosexual prostitute (cf. SPINTRY). [Lat. *sellarius*, one who sits upon a *sella*, a couch, i.e. in a brothel]

sell a woof/wolf ticket, to phr. [1960s+] (US Black) **1** to boast, to brag. **2** to talk nonsense, to lie (cf. TRASH TALK). **3** to threaten, to intimidate (cf. BUY A WOOF TICKET). [WOOF v.[1]]

sell down the river, to phr. [19C+] (orig. US Black) to betray. [the practice of selling an errant slave to a Mississippi sugar-cane plantation. The journey to the plantation, where work was especially hard, meant a trip 'down the river']

sell honey for a halfpenny, to phr. [late 16C–early 17C] to think very badly of someone. [? proverbial]

selling a horse n. [1920s–30s] (N.Z.) a bar game played to determine who buys a round of drinks (cf. SELL THE PONY). [one person thinks of, or writes down, a number under 10; the group starts counting down, and the one who gets the chosen number pays]

sell lemons v. [1950s+] to sell second-rate or fake drugs. [SE *sell* + LEMON n.[1] (5)]

sell one on v. [1920s+] to convince, to persuade, to convey enthusiasm. [SELL v. (1)]

sell oneself v. [1920s+] (US) to attempt to make oneself appealing in the eyes of others.

sell out v.[1] [late 19C+] (orig. US) **1** to betray. **2** to sacrifice one's beliefs and principles for money or position; thus *sell-out*, a person who sells out or an instance of selling out.

sell out v.[2] [20C] (Aus.) to vomit.

sell out v.[3] [1930s–40s] (US Black) to run in terror.

sell out to the Yankees, to phr. [late 19C] (US Black) to leave the South and move to a northern city.

sell someone a packet, to phr. [late 19C] to deceive, to trick (cf. PACKETS n.). [SE phr. *packet of lies*]

sell someone blind, to phr. [late 19C] to deceive, to defraud (cf. DO SOMEONE BLIND).

sell souse v. [17C] to act in a surly manner, to frown. [SE *souse*, a pickling liquid]

sell the pony/lady, to phr. [late 19C] to toss a coin to determine who pays for a round of drinks; thus *buy the pony/lady*, to pay for that round (cf. SELLING A HORSE).

selopas n. [mid-19C] apples. [backsl.]

s'elp me bob!/s'elp my bob!/so help me baub! excl. [19C+] a general phr. of intensification and affirmation. [SE *so help me* + BOB n.[4]]

s'elp me Dash! excl. [1920s] a laboured euph. of *s'elp me God!* (cf. DASH IT!). [SE *dash*, i.e. —]

s'elp me/my greens! excl. [late 19C] a general excl. of intensification and affirmation, i.e. 'may I lose the attributes of masculine vigour if I am diverging from the line of rectitude' (Ware) (cf. S'ELP MY TATER!).

s'elp me never! excl. [late 19C] a general excl. of intensification and affirmation (cf. S'ELP ME BOB!; SWOP ME BOB!).

s'help my bob! see S'ELP ME BOB!

s'help my greens! see S'ELP ME GREENS!

s'elp my tater! excl. [mid-19C] a general oath (cf. S'ELP ME GREENS!).

semen demon n. [20C] (US) a male homosexual.

semi n. **1** [1910s+] a *semi*-detached house. **2** [1940s+] (Aus./US) a *semi*-trailer or articulated truck. [abbr.]

semi adv. [1970s+] partly, to some extent.

seminary n. [19C] the vagina. [pun on SE *semen*]

semolia n. [late 19C–1930s] (US Black) a fool. [? name of a lunatic asylum]

semolina n. [20C] a cleaner, a charwoman. [rhy. sl.]

sempstress n. [19C] a prostitute (cf. NEEDLE WOMAN; SMOCK PIECE).

sen n. [1980s+] (drugs) marijuana. [abbr. SENSEMILLIA]

senal pervitude n. [late 19C] penal servitude. [a weak joke based on reversing the initial letters + a possible pun on 'senile perversity']

send v. [1900s–50s; 1990s] (orig. US) to excite emotionally. [orig. beatnik use, esp. as used of music; near obsolete for a while, but revived in late 1990s]

send along v. [late 19C+] (Aus.) to have someone arrested, to send to prison.

send by/stay for tom/john long the carrier phr. [16C–19C] to postpone, to put off for a long time. [TOM LONG]

send down v. [mid-19C+] to imprison. [either var. on (US) SEND UP THE RIVER or (UK) walking down the steps from the dock (orig. at the Old Bailey) back to the cells]

send down the road/track, to phr. [1950s+] (N.Z.) to dismiss from employment; thus *go/get/be sent down the road/track*, to be dismissed.

sender n.[1] [19C] (orig. boxing jargon) a solid, hard blow. [? it sends the victim spinning]

sender n.[2] [1920s–40s] (US Black) a person (usu. a musician) or thing (usu. a record) who or which is emotionally arousing (cf. SOLID SENDER). [SEND]

send for Gulliver phr. [late 19C] (society) a phr. used to imply that the matter under discussion is not worthy of attention. ['from a cascadescent incident in the first part of Dr Lemuel Gulliver's travels' (Ware); i.e. that in which he urinates on a fire (itself reminiscent of Pepys's first comment on the Great Fire of London: 'Why, a woman could piss it out')]

send for the green van! excl. [1950s] a joc. cry, implying that a person is mad and should be taken away to a psychiatric institution. [an actual or fig. green van]

send her/it down Davey!/Hughie!/Steve! excl. [20C] (Aus./N.Z.) a general appeal to the gods for rain. [*Hughie*, the mythical deity of surfing and as such invoked by surfers who want suitable waves; also used as synon. for God by US loggers of Pacific Northwest/*Davey*, ? St David, the patron saint of Wales, the land of 'leeks'/generic use of proper name *Steve*]

send home in a box, to phr. [19C] to bury.

send in by the servant's entrance, to phr. [1960s+] of a man, to have sexual intercourse from the rear position. [SE *servant's entrance*, usu. in the rear or bottom storey of the house]

send in one's checks, to phr. [mid-19C+] (US) to die (cf. CASH IN ONE'S CHECKS). [gambling imagery]

send it down Davey!/Hughie!/Steve! see SEND HER DOWN DAVEY!

send it in v. [early–mid-19C] to push in, to drive something home.

send mail by Netscape, to phr. [1990s] (US campus) to harass someone sexually. [*Netscape*, a proprietary Web Browser/e-mail software]

send-off n. **1** [19C+] death. **2** [19C+] (US) a funeral. **3** [mid-19C+] some form of celebration to mark a person's departure. [the imagery of starting a race]

send off v. [1950s+] (Aus.) to steal.

send off the blue, to phr. [1970s+] (N.Z.) to start a fight. [BLUE n.[7] (2)]

send on a humbug/humbug trip/merry-go-round, to phr. [1950s+] (US Black) to send on a wild goose chase, a fool's errand.

send one's wife to the devil's arse-peak, to phr. [late 17C] to upbraid one's wife when she starts nagging. [the specific instance of a courtier's wife being sent home to the Peak District, Derbyshire; the *Devil's Arse Peak* is the Peak Cavern]

send out the troops, to phr. [1990s] to ejaculate.

send someone into Cornwall without a boat, to phr. [mid-16C–early 19C] to cuckold (cf. CORNUTED).

send someone to the cleaners see TAKE SOMEONE TO THE CLEANERS.

send someone up the wall see DRIVE SOMEONE UP THE WALL.

send the daylights out of, to phr. [20C] (W.I.) to beat severely, to hit an animal hard enough to kill it. [DAYLIGHTS]

send to Birchen/Birchin/Birching Lane, to phr. [18C] to administer a flogging. [SE *birch* + *Birchin Lane*, London EC3, once known for its ready-made clothes shops, although the name ? f. OE meaning 'lane of the barbers']

send to grass, to phr. [late 19C] (orig. boxing) to knock down. [boxing orig. took place on grass]

send to graze, to phr. [mid-18C] to dismiss. [farming imagery]

send to Long Beach, to phr. [1960s–70s] (Los Angeles drugs) to flush drugs down the lavatory before or during a drugs raid. [? the sewer outlets at Long Beach]

send to the pack, to phr. [1910s–20s] (Aus./N.Z.) to discard, to dismiss.

send to the showers, to phr. [1960s+] (US) to dismiss or reject. [sporting imagery]

send-up n. [1950s+] an instance of teasing, a joke at someone's expense. [SEND UP v.[2]]

send up v.[1] [mid-19C+] (US Und.) to imprison (cf. SEND UP THE RIVER). [abbr. SE *send up* for punishment]

send up v.[2] [1930s+] to mock, to tease, esp. to parody or imitate.

send up the river, to phr. [1930s+] (US Und.) to imprison. [ext. of SEND UP v.[1] + UP THE RIVER]

send up Zs, to phr. [1990s] (US teen) to fall asleep (cf. BAG ZS). [z n.[1]]

Senegambian n. [1900s–40s] (US) a derog. term for an African-American. [SE *Senegambian*, a native or inhabitant of Senegambia, former name of the region surrounding the Senegal and Gambia rivers in West Africa]

seni n. [1970s] (drugs) **1** peyote. **2** mescaline. [ety. unknown]

senior out v. [1970s+] (US teen) to give up the teen lifestyle, to act like an adult (in the rejection of teen excess).

senor-eater n. [1980s+] (US gay) a gay man who prefers Latin or Hispanic partners (cf. BEAN QUEEN). [puns on Sp. *senorita*, miss + *senor*, mister + SE *eater*, i.e. one who indulges in oral sex]

sensation n.[1] [mid-19C] an able, competent person. [weak use of SE]

sensation/slight sensation n.[2] [mid-19C] **1** a taste, a small quantity. **2** 143ml (¼ pint) of gin. **3** (Aus.) a half glass of sherry. [ironic understatement]

sensimillia/sense/sensi n. [1980s+] (W.I./UK Black teen) a variety of extremely potent marijuana; it has no seeds because it is isolated from male pollen during the blooming process; instead, the marijuana plant makes more tetrahydrocannabinol (YHC) , thus intensifying the effects (cf. SCES; SESS; SEZZ; SINSE). [lit. 'seedless']

sensitive plant n. [early–mid-19C] **1** (orig. boxing) the nose. **2** the penis.

sensitive truncheon n. [19C] **1** the nose. **2** the penis.

sent adj.[1] [late 19C] imprisoned. [abbr. of *sent to prison*]

sent adj.[2] [1930s–50s] emotionally overcome, esp. by a jazz solo. [SEND]

sentimental n. [1920s–70s] (Aus.) a cigar or cigarette. [rhy. sl. *sentimental bloke* = SMOKE n.[3]]

sentimental hairpin n. [late 19C] (society) an affected, insignificant woman.

sentinel n. [19C] (Anglo-Irish) a candle used at a wake. [it 'keeps watch']

sent to the skies, to be phr. [late 19C–1910s] to be murdered.

sent up adj. [late 19C+] (orig. US) imprisoned. [SEND UP v.[1]]

separate n. [mid-19C+] (Aus. Und.) solitary confinement in prison.

separate the men from the boys see SORT OUT THE MEN FROM THE BOYS.

seppo see SEPTIC n.

September morn n. [1970s+] an erection (cf. COLLEEN BAWN). [rhy. sl. *September morn* = HORN n.[3]; note *September Morn*, a painting by Paul Chabas of a young woman bathing nude, which was first exhibited at the 1912 Salon in Paris. Censors attempted to ban a reproduction of the picture from public exhibition in the US, a farcical effort, which led to the sale of more than 7 million reproductions – appearing on dolls, statues, umbrella handles, tattoos and many other places – and the assurance that Chabas need never work again]

septic/seppo n. (Aus.) **1** [1960s+] a septic tank. **2** [1970s+] an American. [(2) rhy. sl. *septic tank* = YANK n.]

septic adj. [1910s+] unpleasant, rotten, mean.

sepulchre n. [late 19C] (middle class) a flat cravat that covers the shirt front, effectively hiding that portion that would otherwise appear between the coat and the throat. [SE *sepulchre*, a tomb; it 'buries' a shirt that is no longer clean]

sere see SEAR.

sergeant n. [1950s] a 'masculine' lesbian. [abbr. TOP SERGEANT]

Sergeant Kite/Snap n. [mid–late 19C] a recruiting sergeant. [? SE *kite*, a bird of prey/*snap*, the click of a fig. lock or the order, 'Snap to it!']

sergeant-major n.[1] [20C] (S.Afr.) a zebra. [its stripes]

sergeant-major n.[2] [1920s+] **1** (US) coffee with cream or milk and sugar. **2** strong sweet tea or tea with rum. [the NCO's preferred beverage]

Sergeant Snap see SERGEANT KITE.

sergeant space n. [1980s+] (US campus) someone who is out of touch with reality. [SPACED OUT]

serial speedballing n. [1970s+] (drugs) the practice of sequencing cocaine, cough syrup and heroin over a 1–2 day period. [SE *serial*, continuous in sequence + SPEEDBALL n.[1]]

seringapatam see PLASTERER'S TROWEL AND SERINGAPATAM.

serious adj. **1** [1940s+] (US Black) excellent, first-rate. **2** [1980s+] an all-purpose intensifier, e.g. *serious drinking*.

seriously adv. [1980s+] an all-purpose intensifier, e.g. *seriously rich*.

sernyl n. [1970s+] (drugs) phencyclidine (cf. ACE n.[3]). [brandname *Sernylan*]

serpent/silver serpent n. [1960s–70s] a hypodermic syringe and needle.

serpent socket n. [1990s] the vagina (cf. COCK-HOLDER).

Serpico/Serpico 21 n. (drugs) **1** [1970s+] cocaine. **2** [1980s+] crack cocaine. [the film *Serpico* (1973)]

Serps, the n. [1930s] the *Serpentine*, Hyde Park, London. [abbr.]

servant n. [19C] a womanizer, a promiscuous man. [SE *service*, usu. of an animal, to copulate]

servant's meat see BOY'S MEAT.

serve n. [1960s+] (Aus.) negative criticism, a reprimand. [SERVE v.[2]]

serve *v.*[1] **1** [19C+] to have sexual intercourse (cf. BANG *v.*[1]). **2** [1980s+] (US prison) to assault sexually, to rape. [SE *service*, usu. of an animal, to copulate]

serve *v.*[2] **1** [early 19C] (Und.) to rob. **2** [early 19C] (Und.) to convict and sentence. **3** [early 19C] (Und.) to injure, to wound; thus *serve out and out*, to murder. **4** [1980s+] (US Black teen) to give someone their due deserts.

serve *v.*[3] [late 19C+] to serve a term of imprisonment.

serve *v.*[4] [1980s+] (drugs) to sell narcotics. [SE *serve*, to sell goods in a shop]

serve out *v.* [mid-19C] to revenge oneself upon, to punish, to retaliate. [boxing jargon]

server *n.* [1980s+] (drugs) a dealer in crack cocaine. [SERVE *v.*[4]]

serve right!/serves you right! *excl.* [mid-19C+] an excl. of one's own pleasure at seeing someone else suffer as a result of their foolish or evil actions.

serve someone a ticket, to *phr.* [early 19C] (Anglo-Irish) to hit someone.

serve someone glad, to *phr.* [late 19C–1930s] to give someone their deserts, to 'serve them right'. [orig. northern dial.]

serves you right! *see* SERVE RIGHT!

service lay *n.* [early 18C] (Und.) a method of thieving whereby someone enters a house posing as a servant later to decamp with whatever they can steal. [SE *service* + LAY *n.*[4]]

service of beef *n.* [1990s] sexual intercourse (cf. ACHING FOR A SIDE OF BEEF). [BEEF *n.*[1] (2)]

service station *n.* [1980s+] (US gay) a public lavatory used for sexual assignations.

sese *n.* [1980s+] (W.I./UK Black teen) whisperings, rumours, gossip. [SESE *v.*]

sese *v.* [1980s+] (W.I./UK Black teen) to whisper. [echoic]

sesh *n.* [1980s+] a session of drinking or taking drugs. [abbr. SESSION *n.* (3), (4)]

sess *n.* [20C] (US Black) top grade marijuana. [? SENSIMILLIA]

session *n.* **1** [1910s+] (Aus./US) a disturbance, an argument. **2** [1930s] (US teen) a dance, a party. **3** [1940s+] (orig. Aus.) a period of time devoted to drinking. **4** [1970s+] (drugs) a period of time devoted to drug taking.

sessions *n.* [late 19C] noise, chaos, disturbance, quarrelling. [SE *legal sessions*, events that were rarely known for their quietness]

sessions *v.* [mid-19C] to commit a person to the sessions for trial. [SE *sessions*]

sessions! *excl.* [late 19C–1900s] a general excl. of surprise, astonishment.

set *n.*[1] [early 18C] a scheme considered to be a certainty (cf. DEAD SET *n.*).

set *n.*[2] [1960s+] (US drugs) a dose of two Seconals and one amphetamine. [jazz use *set*, two pieces of music played consecutively before a break]

set *n.*[3] **1** [1960s+] (US Black) wherever the night life takes place. **2** [1960s+] (drugs) a place where drugs are sold. **3** [1960s+] (US Black) a group of friends. **4** [1970s+] (US Black) a discussion (cf. RAP *n.*[4]). **5** [1980s+] (US Black) the neighbourhood. [theatre/film jargon *set*, the backdrop to the action]

set *n.*[4] [1960s+] (Aus.) the female breasts. [abbr. TOP SET]

set *n.*[5] [1980s+] (US gang) a local gang, part of the larger gang but working autonomously in its own neighbourhood or area of influence; e.g. the Crips are the larger gang, but *sets* include Eight Trey Gangsters or ETGs, West Side Crips, Compton Santana Block Crips etc.

set *adj.* [late 19C] conquered, defeated. [? SE *set back*]

set *v.* **1** [late 17C–late 19C] to target a potential victim, to survey before robbing. **2** [1910s+] (Aus.) to attack verbally, to think little of. [? SE *set upon*]

set about *v.* [late 19C–1900s] to attack, often in phr. that specify the weapon, i.e. *set about him with a stick*.

set a fox to keep one's geese, to *phr.* [mid-17C] to confide in an untrustworthy person.

set-down *n.* [early 19C–1940s] (US) a sit-down meal. [regional pron. of SE *sit*]

set horses *v.* [1980s+] (US Black) to get along in a friendly manner. [i.e. fig. hitching one's horses to the same pole]

set in a crack, to *phr.* [late 19C+] (N.Z.) to settle something quickly. [? the speedy crack of a whip]

set it alight! *excl.* [1940s+] (N.Z.) get a move on! hurry up!

set joint *n.* [1920s–30s] any form of gambling device that has been 'set' to ensure that the player will always ultimately lose (cf. FLAT JOINT). [SE *set* + JOINT *n.*[3] (2)]

set-me-up/young set-me-up *n.* [late 19C–1910s] a person/young person who poses as someone more important than they are, usu. pej.

set mouth/mouth on *v.* [1970s+] (US Black) to gossip, to malign.

set of drapes *n.* [1940s] (US Black) a draped suit (cf. ZOOT SUIT).

set of horseshoes *n.* [late 19C] (US) a horse. [metonymy]

set of seven brights *n.* [1930s–40s] (US Black) 7 days, a week.

set of threads *n.* [1930s–50s] (US Black) a suit of fashionable, well-cut clothes. [THREADS]

set of wheels *n.* [1950s+] (orig. US) a car. [metonymy]

set on/something on *v.* [1990s] (US Black) **1** to give, esp. of drugs. **2** to tell, to impose facts upon (cf. LAY ON).

set one on one's ass, to *phr.* [1970s+] (drugs) to render unconscious from excessive drug consumption. [SE *set* + ARSE *n.*[1]]

set one's cap at, to *phr.* [early 19C+] to determine to gain the affections of the object of one's desires. [the cocking of one's headgear at an appealing angle. Orig. used of women, but subsequently applicable to either sex]

set one's child a-crying, to *phr.* [early–mid-19C] for a watchman, to 'spring his rattle', i.e. to sound an alarm. [the watchman's rattle was the predecessor of the policeman's whistle]

set one's own house in order *see* PUT ONE'S OWN HOUSE IN ORDER.

set-out *n.* **1** [19C] a person's horse or horses and carriage. **2** [early 19C] a display of china and plate. **3** [early 19C] a table full of dishes of food. **4** [early 19C] an entertainment, a private party. **5** [mid-19C] a group of people. **6** [mid–late 19C] a person's clothes or way of dressing. **7** [1920s–30s] a disturbance, a fuss.

set over *v.* [1920s–40s] (US Und.) to kill, to murder.

set someone back *v.* [late 19C+] (orig. US) to cost, e.g. *her coat must have set him back a few quid*.

set something alight, to *phr.* [1940s+] (N.Z.) to start, to set something going.

set something on *see* SET ON.

setter *n.*[1] **1** [mid-17C–18C] the member of a criminal gang who keeps watch or entices a victim into a crooked gambling game. **2** [mid-17C–18C] one of a number of officials – 'a Sergean't Yeoman, or Bailiffs' Follower, or Second, and an Excise Officer' (B.E.) – whose job is to ensure that brewers do not defraud the Excise. **3** [mid-17C–late 19C] a police spy or informer. **4** [mid-19C] 'A person employed by the vendor at an auction to run the biddings up' (Hotten, 1860). [SE *setter*, a species of hunting dog]

setter *n.*[2] [mid-19C] (orig. Ling. Fr./Polari) **1** the number 7. **2** 7 pence (cf. SALTEE). [Ital. *sette*, seven]

set the hair *v.* [20C] (US) to surprise, to astonish, to give pause. [farming jargon *set the hair*, to set the hair on end when one is butchering a hog. The carcass is plunged into scalding water, which makes the hair stand on end, thus rendering it simpler to scrape it from the flesh]

set the hare's head to the goose's giblets, to *phr.* [17C] to give as good as one gets, to pay like with like. [the perceived 'equivalence' of the two foodstuffs]

set the Hudson on fire, to *phr.* [late 19C+] (US) to accomplish something remarkable (cf. SET THE THAMES ON FIRE). [the Hudson River, New York City]

set the Thames on fire, to *phr.* [18C+] to accomplish a noteworthy feat (cf. BURN UP THE MILLPOND; SET THE HUDSON ON FIRE). [London's River *Thames*. A similar phr. was used, in 1638, of the River Rhine]

settle *v.* **1** [late 18C+] to knock down, to stun. **2** [mid-19C] to sentence to penal transportation. **3** [late 19C–1950s] to sentence to a term of imprisonment, usu. life. [semi-euph.]

settled/wind-settled *adj.* **1** [mid-19C] sentenced to transportation. **2** [late 19C] imprisoned. [SETTLE v.]

settlement *n.* [late 19C+] (Aus.) a cemetery. [pun]

settle one's coffee, to *phr.* [mid-19C] (US) **1** to deal with someone who has wronged you, to take revenge. **2** to resolve one's difficulties (cf. SETTLE ONE'S HASH).

settle one's hash, to *phr.* [early 19C+] **1** to deal with someone who has wronged you, to take revenge. **2** to resolve one's difficulties. [SETTLE v. (1) + SE *hash*, a mess, a jumble]

settler *n.* **1** [mid-18C] a parting drink, 'one for the road'. **2** [early 19C+] a knock-out blow, esp. in fig. use, i.e. something that brings things to a conclusion. [(1) such a final drink supposedly 'settles' the stomach after an evening's indulgence]

settler's clock *n.* [19C] (Aus.) a kookaburra. [i.e. it wakes one up]

settler's matches *n.* [late 19C] (Aus.) easily lit strips of bark, used to light fires.

settle someone's tater, to *phr.* [1920s] to beat someone up. [SE *settle* + fig. use of TATER n. (1)]

set tripping *n.* [1980s+] (US gang) the attacking of another gang. [SET n.⁵ + TRIP v.²]

set-up *n.¹* **1** [late 19C–1930s] one's carriage, one's deportment. **2** [20C] (US) a place, esp. one's home, office etc.

set-up *n.²* [1920s] (US Und.) a one-day prison sentence. [one 'sets' or sits it out]

set-up *n.³* [1930s+] **1** (US) the ice, mixer and other ingredients provided in unlicensed premises, to which patrons must bring their own alcohol, but in which they can then drink. **2** (US) the makings of a drink, e.g. whisky, ice and a chaser, served in a bar. **3** a place setting in a restaurant.

set-up *n.⁴* [1950s+] **1** a situation planned to put a third party in a position of weakness, poss. to be murdered. **2** any situation, experience, e.g. *what's the set-up over there?* **3** (US Und.) a scheme whereby a criminal is caught red-handed. **4** (US) a person who is easily duped, a 'sucker'. **5** a woman with whom a man has made a date. [SE *set up*, put in place]

set-up *adj.* **1** [mid-19C] conceited, snobbish. **2** [1920s+] (orig. US) pleased, successful or comfortable, usu. as *well set-up*. [SET UP FOR]

set up *v.* [1950s+] to place a potential victim in a position of weakness, esp. a target for murder.

set up for *v.* [mid-16C+] to be well provided with.

set-up man *n.* [1950s+] (US Und.) someone who organizes and plans major robberies, recruits those who carry them out, disposes of the loot etc. [SET-UP n.⁴ + sfx. -*man*]

set up one's ebenezer, to *phr.* [19C+] (US) to make up one's mind (cf. EBENEZER). [Heb. *eben ha-ezer*, the stone of help, the memorial stone set up by Samuel (1 Sam. 7:12); i.e. the enduring solidity of such a memorial]

set up one's pipes, to *phr.* [17C] to yell, to scream. [PIPES n.¹]

set up shop on Goodwin Sands, to *phr.* [mid-16C–mid-18C] to be shipwrecked. [*Goodwin Sands*, a notoriously dangerous area for sailors]

seven *n.* [1960s–70s] (Aus.) a 7-ounce (200ml) glass of beer.

seven and six *see* WAS SHE WORTH IT?

Seven Dials *n.* [1970s+] haemorrhoids (cf. FARMER GILES). [rhy. sl. *Seven Dials* = piles]

Seven Dials raker *n.* [late 19C–1920s] a prostitute whose home is in Seven Dials and who pursues her trade elsewhere; thus she 'never smiles out of the Dials' (Ware).

sevendible *adj.* [mid-19C] (Ulster) severe, harsh, esp. of a beating. [SE *seven double*, 7-fold; thus the severity is fig. multiplied 7-fold]

seven digits *n.* [1970s+] (US Black) a telephone number (in the multiple exchanges of the major cities).

sevener *n.* [mid-19C] (Aus.) a convict sentenced to a 7-year prison sentence. [such convicts were lower in the prison hierarchy than those serving longer terms or life sentences]

seven-forty-seven-B/747–B *n.* [1960s] (New York City drugs) possession of barbiturates. [police code]

seven kinds of hell *phr.* [20C] intense unpleasantness, esp. in phr. *knock/kick seven kinds of hell out of*, to beat severely.

seven pennorth *n.* [mid-19C] **1** a sentence of 7 years' transportation. **2** 7 months in prison. **3** 7 years in prison.

sevens and elevens *phr.* [1910s+] (Can.) a satisfactory situation, esp. in phr. *everything is/will be sevens and elevens*, everything is/will be fine. [craps use, 7 and 11 are the best points to achieve on one's initial throw]

seven-sided animal *n.* [late 18C–late 19C] 'A one-eyed man or woman, each having a right side and a left side, a fore side and a backside, an outside, an inside and a blind side' (Grose, 1796).

seven-sided son of a bitch *n.* [19C] (US) a man or a woman with one eye, having a right side and a left side, a fore side and a backside, an outside, an inside and a blind side (cf. SEVEN-SIDED ANIMAL). [the US definition was presumably taken direct from Grose, above]

seventeener *n.* [20C] (Aus.) a corpse. [ety. unknown]

Seventh Avenue *n.* [20C] (US) the fashion and garment industry (cf. RAG TRADE). [7th or Fashion Avenue, New York, the trad. centre of the clothing industry]

seven-times-seven man *n.* [late 19C] a hypocritical evangelist. [? rhy. sl. *seven-times-seven* = heaven]

seven-twenty-four *see* TWENTY-FOUR-SEVEN.

seventy-five cent word *n.* [late 19C] (US) a polysyllabic word. [one 'pays' for all the syllables]

seventy-'leven *n.* [20C] (US) an indefinite number of anything (cf. FORTY-ELEVEN).

seventy-one *n.* [1940s–50s] (Aus.) anal intercourse. [a play on SIXTY-NINE]

seventy-three/73 *n.* [1940s] (US) goodbye, best wishes. [ety. unknown; ? telegraphese]

seven-up *n.* [1980s+] (drugs) **1** cocaine. **2** crack cocaine. [the brandname of the fizzy and supposedly energizing drink 7–Up]

severe *adj.* [19C] **1** (US) very big or powerful, hard to overcome. **2** excellent, first-rate (cf. SERIOUS).

severely *adv.* [mid-19C] to a great or excessive degree, esp. unwisely (cf. SERIOUSLY).

se voet! *excl.* [1970s+] (S.Afr.) an excl. of dismissal or disbelief, 'my foot!' [Afk. *se voet*, my foot]

sew *v.* **1** [19C] to have sexual intercourse (cf. STITCH v.). **2** [1960s+] (US Black) to masturbate. [the movements of the needle and of the body or hand]

sewed up *adj.* [mid-19C] **1** drunk (cf. BASTED). **2** ill, sick. **3** pregnant. **4** cheated, swindled. **5** orig. of horses only, exhausted. **6** confirmed, unsusceptible to error, esp. of a sporting contest in which the result has already been assured. [SEW UP]

sewer *n.*[1] [late 19C–1900s] the Metropolitan and Metropolitan District Railway. [like a *sewer* it runs beneath the London streets]

sewer *n.*[2] [1940s–60s] (drugs) the median cephalic vein in the arm; thus *go into/hit the sewer*, to inject a narcotic, usu. heroin, into that vein. [play on SHIT *n.*[5]]

sewermouth *n.* [1970s+] (US campus) anyone who regularly uses obscenities or profanities. [the image of such language as 'dirty']

sewer trout *n.* [1950s+] (US prison) any species of fish served at mealtimes.

sew someone's sees, to *phr.* [late 18C] to give someone a black eye (cf. DARKEN SOMEONE'S DAYLIGHTS). [SEES]

sew up *v.* **1** [19C] to impregnate; thus *sewn up*, pregnant (cf. SEWED UP). **2** [early–mid-19C] of a horse, to tire out. **3** [early–mid-19C] to make hopelessly drunk. **4** [early 19C+] of a person, to tire out, to nonplus, to bring to a standstill, to put *hors de combat*. **5** [early 19C+] to outwit, to cheat, to swindle. **6** [20C] (orig. US) to conclude, to possess completely, to finalize, to place under complete control; thus *sewed/sewn up/all sewed/sewn up*, brought to a satisfactory conclusion. **7** [1940s] to bring about the conviction of someone. **8** [1960s+] to surround, to seal off.

sew up someone's stocking, to *phr.* [mid-19C] to put to silence, to strike dumb.

sew with a hot needle, to *phr.* [20C] (US) to act over-hastily, to work fast but poorly. [phr. *sew with a hot needle and burning thread*]

sex *n.* [1930s+] **1** the penis. **2** the vagina.

sex *v.* [1960s+] to have sexual intercourse.

sexboat *n.* [1960s] a very attractive man or (usu.) woman (cf. SEX-BOMB; SEXPOT).

sex-bomb *n.* [1960s+] a very attractive man or (usu.) woman (cf. SEXBOAT).

sex bunny *see* SEX KITTEN.

sexed up *adj.* [20C] sexually excited.

sex fight *n.* [1990s] (US) a sexual game played between two people (of the same or opposite sex) in which each partner tries to make the other reach orgasm first; thus *sex fighter*, a participant in such a game.

sex goddess *n.* [1930s+] (US) a woman, esp. a film star (and latterly rock star), who is viewed as sexually provocative.

sex house *n.* [1990s] (US) anywhere where sex is on sale.

sex in *v.* [1990s] (US Black/teen) to gang rape (cf. DO IN).

sexing-piece *n.* [1920s+] the penis. [SEX *v.*]

sex job *n.* [1930s+] (US) a sexually provocative or available person. [SE *sex* + JOB *n.*[5]]

sex kitten/bunny *n.* [1950s+] a young woman with overt sex-appeal. [coined in the late 1950s for the charms of the young Brigitte Bardot (b.1933)]

sex machine *n.* [1960s+] a sexually virile man, a womanizer (cf. LOVE MACHINE).

sexo/sexoh *n.* (N.Z.) **1** [1940s+] a sexual offender. **2** [1950s+] someone seen as over-sexed or obsessed with sex.

sexocet missile *n.* [1990s] the penis (cf. BAYONET). [SE *sex* + *Exocet*]

sexoh *see* SEXO.

sex on *v.* [1950s+] (Aus.) to indulge in 'heavy petting' or even intercourse (cf. PASH ON).

sexpert *n.* [1960s+] (US) a sex expert, typically a sex therapist.

sexploitation *n.* [1960s+] (US) the commercial exploitation of sex (cf. BLAXPLOITATION).

sexpot *n.* [1950s+] **1** a very attractive man or (usu.) woman (cf. SEXBOAT). **2** one who is obsessed with sex.

sexton blake *n.* [late 19C+] **1** a cake. **2** a fake. [rhy. sl.; the fictional detective created by 'Hal Meredith' (Harry Blyth) in *The Halfpenny Marvel* magazine (1893)]

sex up *v.* [1940s+] to increase the sexual content of, e.g. a film script.

sex wagon *n.* [1960s+] (US) a flashy car owned by a pimp (cf. PIMPMOBILE).

sex with Jesus *phr.* [1980s+] (orig. US) a general phr. of satisfaction, praise, delight, e.g. *that movie – sex with Jesus*.

sexy *adj.* [1960s+] **1** (orig. media) of anything that pulls in audiences, readers etc, thus usu. violence, disaster, scandal etc. **2** (US) of anything very appealing.

sey *see* SAY *n.*

sey-dooe *n.* [mid-19C+] (Ling. Fr./Polari) the number 8. [SAY *n.* + DOOE]

sey-oney *n.* [mid-19C+] (Ling. Fr./Polari) the number 7. [SAY *n.* + SE *one* + sfx. -y]

sey-tray *n.* [mid-19C+] (Ling. Fr./Polari) the number 9 (cf. NOBBA). [SAY *n.* + TRAY *n.*[1]]

sez you! *see* SAYS YOU!

sezz *n.* [1980s+] (drugs) cannabis. [abbr. SENSIMILLIA]

s.f.a. *phr.* [1910s+] absolutely nothing at all (cf. SWEET FANNY ADAMS). [abbr. *sweet fuck all*]

s.f. & t. *phr.* [1990s] sucked, fucked and tattooed. [abbr.]

S.F.C./s.f.c. *n.* [1990s] (US Black teen) San Francisco City or sucka-/sucker-free city. [abbr.; capitals and lower case letters are interchangeable]

'sflesh! *excl.* [18C] a mild oath, lit. 'God's flesh!' (cf. 's abbr.[1]).

'sfoot! *excl.* [17C] a mild oath, lit. 'God's foot!' (cf. 's abbr.[1]).

sfoot *v.* [17C] to have sexual intercourse (cf. FOOT *v.*). [Fr. *foutre*]

shab *n.* [early 17C–mid-19C] an unpleasant, sneaky person (cf. SHABERS). [? SCAB *n.*[1] (1)/SE *scab*, a rascal, a scoundrel or *shabby*]

shab *v.* [mid-18C–mid-19C] to cheat, to deceive, to act in an underhand manner. [SHAB *n.*]

shabba *v.* [1990s] to masturbate. [rhy. sl. *shabba rank* = WANK *v.*; reggae star *Shabba* Ranks (Rextion Gordon; b.1965)]

shabberoon *n.* [late 17C–18C] a shabby, down-at-heel person; also as [18C–19C] *shabaroon* and *shabroon* (cf. SHAB-RAG). [SE *shabby*]

shabby *adj.* [mid-19C+] of weather, unpleasant. [SE *shabby*, 'a word that has crept into conversation and low writing, but ought not to be admitted into the language' (Johnson, 1755); ult. SE *scab*, a disease of sheep]

shabeen *see* CHABEN.

shabers *n.* [1940s] (W.I.) a disreputable person. [? SHAB *n.*]

shab off *v.* [late 17C–mid-18C] **1** to cheat someone, then to dismiss them without apology or explanation. **2** to sneak away. [? SHAB *v.*]

shab-rag *adj.* [mid-18C–mid-19C] shabby, damaged, worn. [dial. *shab-rag*, a mean beggarly person, a ragamuffin]

shabster *n.* [mid–late 19C] an unpleasant, sneaky person. [SHAB *n.* + sfx. -ster]

shabu *n.* [1980s+] (drugs) methylamphetamine (cf. ICE *n.*[5]). [ety. unknown]

shack *n.*[1] [mid-19C] (US) **1** a tramp, a vagrant. **2** any place where tramps congregate. [SE *shake-rag*, a beggar + dial. *shackle-bag*, a lazy loiterer, a vagabond]

shack *n.*[2] **1** [late 19C+] (US) one's home, one's house. **2** [1920s+] a wireless or radio room, as used by radio hams.

shack *v.* **1** [late 19C+] (US) to live alone, to live as a bachelor or single woman. **2** [1960s+] to live with a partner (cf. SHACK UP). [SHACK *n.*[2]]

shack fever *n.* [mid-19C] (US tramp) weariness, fatigue. [SHACK *n.*[1] + SE *fever*]

shackie *n.* [1950s] a White woman living with a Black man (cf. SHACK JOB). [SHACK UP]

shackies! *excl.* [20C] (US) that's mine! I want to do that! I want a share! a child's term used to claim the whole or an equal part of an object; the negative response to the cry is *fen shackies!*, no shares! [SE *share* + ACKIES!]

shack job *n.* [1950s+] **1** the person with whom one lives. **2** a couple or the state of being a couple. [SHACK UP + JOB n.⁵]

shackles *n.* [1910s–20s] the off-cuts from a butcher's preparing of meat for sale.

shackle-up *n.* [1930s–50s] (tramp) a midday meal cooked at the roadside. [SHACKLE UP v.]

shackle up *v.* [1930s–50s] (tramp) to cook a midday meal. [? SHACK n.¹]

shack man/rat *n.* [1940s] (US) an adulterous man. [SHACK UP + SE *man*/RAT n.³]

shack-per-swaw *phr.* [mid-19C] everyone for himself. [Fr. *chacun pour soi*, each for himself]

shack rat *see* SHACK MAN.

shacks! *excl.* [1980s+] (US campus) a mild excl. of surprise, regret, annoyance etc. [var. on SHUCKS!]

shack-stoner *n.* [late 19C–1900s] (Aus./N.Z.) a sixpence (cf. ZAC).

shack up *v.* [1950s+] **1** to live with a sexual partner, to have sex with. **2** (US) to live or reside, usu. temporarily. [SHACK n.²]

shaddup! *excl.* [1950s+] mispron. of SE *shut up!*

shade *n.¹* **1** [mid–late 19C] (US) a derog. term for a Black person. **2** [1920s] (US Und.) a receiver of stolen goods (cf. FENCE n.¹). [SE *shade*, partial darkness]

shade *n.²* [mid-19C+] a minute quantity.

shade *v.¹* [1950s+] (orig. Aus.) to be superior to, albeit by a small margin (cf. FADE v.¹). [SHADE n.²]

shade *v.²* [1980s+] (US Black) to hide, to conceal. [SE *shade*, to protect from the light]

shades *n.¹* [mid–late 19C] a variety of late-night music-halls and bars on or near the Strand, London (cf. DARKIES; DIVE n.¹). [their opening during the 'shady' hours]

shades *n.²* [1940s+] dark glasses, sunglasses.

shad mouth *n.* [1930s–40s] (US) **1** a person with a large upper lip. **2** a derog. term for a Black person. [the fish]

shadow *n.* [late 19C+] (US) a derog. term for a Black person (cf. SHADE n.¹).

shady *adj.* [mid-19C+] (orig. university) **1** uncertain, unreliable. **2** stupid.

shady grove of the evangelist *see* GROVE OF THE EVANGELIST.

shady spring *n.* [mid-19C] the vagina (cf. BEAUTY SPOT n.¹; DAMP n.).

shaft *n.¹* [late 18C+] the penis (cf. SHAFT OF DELIGHT. [20C use mainly US Black; note blaxploitation films of the 1970s, starring private eye 'John Shaft']

shaft *n.²* [1950s+] a woman's body, considered simply as a sexual object. [SHAFT v.]

shaft *n.³* [1950s+] (orig. US) unfair treatment, often as *the shaft*. [SHAFT v.]

shaft *v.* [1950s+] **1** to have sexual intercourse with a woman; thus *shaftable*, of a woman, suitable for and hopefully susceptible to seduction (cf. BANG v.¹). **2** (orig. US) to defeat, to defraud, to harm, to treat unfairly. [SE *shaft*, to shoot with an arrow]

shafted *adj.* [1950s+] **1** treated unfairly, in serious trouble. **2** stood up by one's date. **3** suffering a broken relationship. [SHAFT v.]

shaftesbury *n.* [late 17C–early 19C] a gallon pot full of wine, with a cock (cf. SALISBURY n.¹). [? proper name of the Dorset town]

shafting *n.* [1970s+] **1** sexual intercourse. **2** (US) unfair or cruel treatment. [SHAFT v.]

shaft of delight *n.* [mid-18C] the penis. [ext. of SHAFT n.¹]

shafts *n.* [1930s–40s] (US Black) the human legs.

shag *n.¹* [1930s+] **1** an act of sexual intercourse. **2** (US teen) a party where teenagers experiment sexually. **3** (US teen) a person who is one's date or escort. **4** a person, usu. a woman but in 1990s also a man, seen simply as a sexual object; thus *good shag, lousy shag* (cf. BELT n.¹). [SHAG v.¹]

shag *n.²* [1950s+] (W.I. Rasta) home-cured tobacco, straight from the field. [SE *shag*, strong tobacco, cut into shreds]

shag *n.³* [1960s+] (drugs) heroin (cf. SCAG n.).

shag *adj.¹* [1950s] (US prison) worthless. [? SE *shag*, a rascal, a rogue]

shag *adj.²* [1970s+] (US teen) excellent, wonderful. [SHAG n.¹]

shag *v.¹* **1** [late 18C+] to have sexual intercourse (cf. BANG v.¹). **2** [1980s+] to masturbate. [? SE *shake*]

shag *v.²* (US) **1** [1910s+] to chase. **2** [1930s] (teen) to tease, to harass. **3** [1930s+] to wander around. **4** [1980s+] (Black) to walk slowly, whether through laziness or exhaustion. [Gloucester dial. *shag*, to make off, to traipse around]

shag artist *n.* [1960s+] a womanizer, a sexual athlete. [SHAG n.¹ (1) + ARTIST n.²]

shag ass *v.* [1960s+] (US) **1** to work hard, to move fast, to expend effort and energy. **2** to depart or leave hurriedly (cf. SHAKE ONE'S ARSE). [SE *shake*]

shag-bag *n.* **1** [late 17C+] a worthless, shabby person (cf. SHAKE-BAG). **2** [1930s+] (orig. milit.) a prostitute. **3** [1940s+] (orig. Aus.) a general pej. term for a woman; sexual availability is presumed but not automatic. [SHAG v.¹ (1) + BAG n.³]

shag end *n.* [1970s+] (US) the butt end of a cigarette. [var. on FAG END + SE *shag*, strong tobacco; ? ref. to SHAGGED]

shagged/shagged out *adj.* [1930s+] exhausted. [fig. use of SHAG v.¹]

shagged to a thin whisker *phr.* [1940s–50s] absolutely exhausted. [fig. use of SHAG v.¹]

shagger *n.¹* **1** [20C] one who copulates. **2** [1990s] a nuisance, a disobedient person (cf. FUCKER). [SHAG v.¹ (1)]

shagger *n.²* [1930s] (US) **1** a policeman. **2** a person who shadows or follows someone. [SHAG v.²]

shagger's back *n.* [1950s+] (orig. Aus.) a particularly painful backache. [SHAGGER n.¹ + SE *back*]

shagging-wagon *see* SHAG-WAGON.

shag-nasty *n.* [20C] a general pej. name for any unpopular man. [SHAG v.¹]

shagroon *n.* [mid-19C] (N.Z.) an early settler in Canterbury, New Zealand, from anywhere except Britain, esp. one from Australia (cf. PILGRIM n.¹). [? Irish *seachrán*, wandering]

shags like a rattlesnake *phr.* [1960s+] used of a woman who is presumed to be a sexual enthusiast, usu. in phr. *I'll bet she shags … .* [SHAG v.¹ (1)]

shag-/shagging-wagon *n.* [1960s+] a van or car used primarily for sex (cf. PASSION WAGON). [SHAG n.¹ (1) + SE *wagon*]

shah *n.* [late 19C] (cockney) a 'tremendous swell'. [Pers. *shah*, a king]

shake *n.¹* **1** [16C–1900s] an act of sexual intercourse (cf. SHAG n.¹). **2** [mid–late 19C] a prostitute (cf. SHAG n.¹; SHAKE-BAG). **3** a disreputable man.

shake *n.²* **1** [mid-19C+] (US) a dance. **2** [mid-19C+] a moment, a second, esp. in phr. *a brace of shakes*. **3** [1920s] (US Black) a party at which the guests pay an admission fee to help pay the rent and pay for the refreshments (cf. RENT PARTY). **4** [1950s+] a party.

shake *n.³* [late 19C+] blackmail, extortion. [abbr. SHAKEDOWN. n.²]

shake *n.⁴* [1980s+] (drugs) **1** marijuana, esp. the residue of a bag of cannabis after the smokeable buds are removed. **2** diluted cocaine. [note dial. *shake*, the residue of grain after harvesting]

shake, the *n.⁵* [1980s+] (US campus) an undesirable person.

shake *v.*[1] [16C–1900s] to have sexual intercourse; thus [late 19C+] *shake oneself*, to masturbate (cf. BANG v.[1]; SHAKE HANDS WITH ABRAHAM LINCOLN; SHAKE HANDS WITH THE UNEMPLOYED; SHAKE HANDS WITH THE WIFE'S BEST FRIEND; SHAKE THE BOTTLE; SHAKE THE WEASEL; SHAKE UP).

shake *v.*[2] [early 19C] (Und.) to steal, to run off with (cf. WHAT SHAKES?). [use after mid-19C mainly Aus.]

shake *v.*[3] [mid-19C+] to disturb, to shock.

shake *v.*[4] [20C] (US) to get rid of (cf. SHUKS). [abbr. SE *shake off*]

shake a cloth in the wind, to *phr.* [late 18C–mid-19C] **1** to be hanged in chains. **2** to be slightly drunk (cf. SHEET IN THE WIND; THREE SHEETS IN THE WIND). [(1) refers to one's flapping clothes; (2) orig. naut. jargon]

shake a leg! *excl.* [late 19C+] get on with it! wake up! (both lit. and fig.) (cf. SHAKE IT UP).

shake and shiver *n.* [20C] (Aus.) a river. [rhy. sl.]

shake apart *v.* [1900s–40s] (US Black) to lose emotional control, whether through an excess of happiness or sorrow.

shake a sock, to *phr.* [20C] to urinate (cf. SHAKE HANDS WITH AN OLD FRIEND; SHAKE HANDS WITH THE WIFE'S BEST FRIEND; SHAKE THE DEW OFF THE LILY).

shake a tart, to *phr.* [late 19C+] of a man, to have sexual intercourse. [SHAKE v.[1] + TART]

shake a wicked calf/hoof, to *phr.* [1920s] (US) to dance well. [var. of SE *shake a leg/foot/toe* etc]

shake baby *n.* [1920s] (US Black) a dress that is tight across the hips and has a short, full skirt. [BABY n.[2] (1) is encouraged to 'shake that thing']

shake-bag *n.* [early 18C–late 19C] **1** a prostitute (cf. SHAG-BAG). **2** the vagina.

shake-buckler *n.* [mid-16C–mid-17C] a bully, a thug. [SE *shake* + *buckler*, a sword]

shakedown *n.*[1] [mid-19C+] (US) an impromptu bed, somewhere to sleep, not necessarily a proper bed.

shakedown *n.*[2] **1** [late 19C+] blackmail, extortion; thus *shakedown artist*, *shakedown man*, an extortionist. **2** [1910s+] a search, either of a person or place. **3** [1910s+] (US prison) a search, whether of a cell or of an individual prisoner. [the image of shaking one's clothes (or cell) until money falls out]

shake down *v.* **1** [mid-19C+] to blackmail, to extort. **2** [1980s+] (US Black) to have sex with (cf. SHAKE v.[1]). **3** [1980s+] (US Black) to rape.

shake down the persimmons *see* RAKE DOWN THE PERSIMMONS.

shake-em-up *n.* [1970s+] (US Black) white port and lemon juice. [its effects]

shake five! *excl.* [1950s+] (W.I.) greeting between two men, lit. 'shake my five fingers' (cf. GIVE ME FIVE!).

shakefoot/shake-up *n.* [1940s+] (W.I.) a party or dance, esp. one to which an invitation is not required; thus *shakefoot*, to dance. [Celtic dial. *shake a foot*, to dance]

shake-glim *n.* [mid–late 19C] a begging letter, based on the fantasy that the writer has lost all their possessions through fire (cf. SHAKE-LURK). [SE *shake*, to wave + GLIM n.[1] (3)]

shake hands *v.* [late 19C+] (US) to make use of.

shake hands with Abraham Lincoln, to *phr.* [1990s] to masturbate (cf. ADDRESS CONGRESS; SHAKE v.[1]).

shake hands with an old friend/Mr Right/him/the baby/ the fellow who stood up with me at my wedding *phr.* [1960s+] to urinate (cf. SHAKE A SOCK).

shake hands with the unemployed, to *phr.* [1990s] to masturbate (cf. SHAKE v.[1]).

shake hands with the wife's best friend, to *phr.* [1960s+] **1** to masturbate (cf. SHAKE v.[1]). **2** to urinate (cf. SHAKE A SOCK).

shake it rough, to *phr.* [1940s+] (Can.) to serve a prison sentence 'the hard way', i.e. rebelling, refusing to cooperate with authority, fighting with fellow prisoners etc.

shake it up *v.* [late 19C+] (US) to hurry up (cf. SHAKE A LEG!).

shake-lurk *n.* [mid-19C] a piece of paper, carried by a beggar, which purports (falsely) to give an account of a terrible disaster, usu. a shipwreck, in which the beggar has suffered (cf. SHAKE-GLIM). [SE *shake*, to wave + LURK n.]

shake 'n' bake *n.* [1970s+] (US Black) any form of trickery that ensures that one eludes work and/or responsibilities. [brandname of popular US instant food. Note US milit. jargon *Shake 'n' Bake*, a sergeant who attended NCO school and gained rank after only a short time in uniform. This, in turn, has similar synon., *Ready Whip*, *Nestle's Quick*]

shake/shakings of the bag *n.* [1930s+] (Irish) **1** the runt of the litter. **2** an unappealing person (cf. SHAKE-BAG). [the image of shaking the very last crumbs from a bag]

shake one's arse/ass, to *phr.* [1920s+] (orig. US) to hurry up (cf. GET ONE'S ARSE IN GEAR). [SE *shake* + ARSE n.[1]]

shake one's drawers in someone's face, to *phr.* [1930s] (US Black) of a woman, to make sexual advances.

shake one's elbow, to *phr.* [17C–19C] to play dice. [the shaking of the dice-box; Hotten (1864) adds 'to play at cards', but this must be an error]

shake one's fleas, to *phr.* [late 19C] to beat, to thrash.

shake one's shambles, to *phr.* [late 17C–early 18C] to hurry up, to get started (cf. STIR ONE'S STUMPS).

shake one's skirt, to *phr.* [1980s+] (US campus) of a woman, to go out dancing.

shake one's toe-rag, to *phr.* [late 19C] (tramp) to run away. [SE *shake* + *toe-rag*]

shake one's trotters at Beilby's/Bilby's ball, to *phr.* [late 18C] to be hanged. [for ety. *see* DANCE AT BEILBY'S BALL]

shake out *v.* [1950s+] (W.I. Rasta) to leave without haste, casually.

shaker *n.*[1] [mid-19C] a shirt. [? dial. *shaker*, a worn-out, shabby garment]

shaker *n.*[2] **1** [mid-19C] a beggar who pretends to have fits. **2** [mid-19C] a hand. **3** [late 19C+] (Aus.) a rickety motor vehicle.

shaker *n.*[3] [1980s+] (drugs) a small glass bottle used for heating and 'cooking' crack cocaine.

shakes, the *n.* [late 19C+] **1** delirium tremens, the shaking associated with an alcoholic who has been deprived of sufficient drink to achieve normality. **2** extreme terror, nervousness.

shake someone's tree, to *phr.* [1970s+] to pressurize someone emotionally.

Shakespeare navel *n.* [mid–late 19C] a long-pointed and turned-down collar. [? reminiscent of the classic portrait of the playwright]

shakester/shickster *n.*[1] [mid-19C] **1** a gentile woman. **2** a non-Jewish servant-girl (cf. SHICKSA). **3** a woman. [mispron. of Yid. *shikse*, a gentile female; according to Hotten (1867) a term used by the costers to refer to the women of the class immediately above, i.e. tradesmen's wives/daughters]

shakester *n.*[2] *see* SHICKSA.

shake the bottle, to *phr.* [1990s] to masturbate (cf. SHAKE v.[1]).

shake the bullet, to *phr.* [mid-19C] to threaten with dismissal, but not actually to dismiss. [modification of GET THE BULLET]

shake the cross, to *phr.* [late 19C] to go out thieving. [CROSS n.]

shake/knock the dew off the lily, to *phr.* [1960s+] to urinate (cf. SHAKE A SOCK).

shake the ghost into, to *phr.* [mid-19C–1900s] to terrify.

shake the hoof *see* SLING THE HOOF.

shake the lead out/out of one's arse/ass, to *phr.* [1940s+] (orig. US) to make an effort, to 'get a move on', to stop being lazy (cf. GET THE LEAD OUT!).

shake them on down v. [1930s] (US Black) of a woman, to make oneself available for sex. ['them' presumably refers to her underwear]

shake the money tree, to phr. [20C] (US) to make a large financial profit. [the fantasy of money 'growing on trees']

shake the pagoda-tree, to phr. [mid-19C–1900s] (Anglo-Ind.) to become rich quickly. [SE *pagoda*, a gold (occas. silver) coin, formerly current in southern India, worth about 7 shillings; it had a pagoda engraved on one side]

shake the weasel, to phr. [1990s] to masturbate (cf. SHAKE v.[1]).

shake-up n.[1] [late 19C] an unnerving experience.

shake-up n.[2] [1930s–40s] (US Black) a form of cocktail, made from a variety of liquors, plus wine.

shake-up n.[3] see SHAKEFOOT.

shake up v. [19C] to masturbate.

shakings of the bag see SHAKE OF THE BAG.

Shaky City n. [1960s+] (US trucker) Los Angeles, California (cf. SHAKY ISLES). [frequency of earthquakes on the San Andreas Fault]

shaky do n. [1940s–50s] an unfair, one-sided deal or bargain. [SE *shaky* + *do*]

Shaky Isles n. [1930s+] (Aus.) New Zealand (cf. SHAKY CITY). [the frequency of earthquakes]

shaler n. [early 19C+] (Aus.) a woman (cf. SHEILA).

shall-I n. [1940s] (W.I.) cheap material. [abbr. dial. *shalligo-naked*, 'a thin flimsy garment, cloth of an inferior kind' (EDD)]

shall I put a bit of hair on it? phr. [20C] directed at a work-man who is failing to put something into something else. [the hair in question would be female and pubic]

shallow n. [early 19C] a hat. [its shape]

shallow adj. [mid-19C] naked; thus *do/go on the shallows*, to go around half-naked (for the purpose of begging) (cf. SHALLOW COVE).

shallow cove n. [19C] a wandering beggar, adopting tattered clothing and posing as a madman (cf. ABRAHAM MAN; SHIVERING JAMES). [SHALLOW adj. + COVE]

shallow dodge n. [mid-19C] the practice of dressing in mini-mal rags for the purpose of begging. [SHALLOW adj. + DODGE n.]

shallow mot n. [mid-19C] the female companion of wander-ing beggar (cf. SHALLOW COVE). [SHALLOW adj. + MOT n.]

shallow pate n. [late 18C–early 19C] a fool, a simpleton. [SE *shallow*, lacking depth of mind + *pate*, head]

shallow screever n. [mid–late 19C] a pavement artist. [ext. of SCREEVER n. (1)]

shalump around see SCHLOOMP AROUND.

sham n.[1] [mid-17C–early 18C] **1** a trick, a hoax, a fraud. **2** something intended to impose upon, delude or disappoint. [subsequent use is SE. SE *shame* or *shamed*; thus this anec-dote: 'The word Sham is true Cant of the Newmarket Breed. It is contracted of ashamed. The native Signification is a Town Lady of Diversion, in Country Maid's Cloaths, who to make good her Disguise, pretends to be so sham'd! Thence it became proverbial, when a maimed Lover was laid up, or looked meager, to say he had met with a Sham' (R. North, *Examen*, 1740)]

sham/shammy n.[2] [19C] *cham*pagne (cf. CHAM n.). [abbr.]

sham n.[3] see SHAMUS.

sham v. [19C] to ply with, or treat oneself to, champagne. [SHAM n.[2]]

sham abram/abraham v. **1** [mid-16C–19C] of a beggar, to travel the country posing as a madman. **2** [late 18C–late 19C] to fake illness (cf. ABRAHAM SHAM).

shame n. [mid-18C–late 19C] anything seen as unpleasant, distasteful, objectionable.

shame down v. [1990s] to humiliate.

sham-legger n. [late 18C–1900s] a seller of second-rate goods at very low prices. [SHAM n.[1] + LEGGER n.[1]; *OED* cites *legger* as abbr. of 1920s+ *bootlegger*, but this use predates it]

shammus see SHAMUS.

shammy see SHAM n.[2].

sham on v. [1970s+] (US Black) to cheat, to deceive. [SHAM n.[1]]

shamos see SHAMUS.

shampata n. [20C] (W.I. Rasta) a sandal of wood or tyre rubber. [Sp. *zapato*]

shampoo n. [1950s+] champagne (cf. SHAM n.[2]).

shampoo the rug, to phr. [1990s] to ejaculate onto a pubic mound.

shamrock n. [19C+] (US) **1** a policeman (cf. MULDOON n.[1]; PADDY n.[1]; SHAMUS). **2** a mixed drink, esp. whisky and stout. [the stereotyped link between the Irish and the police and drinking]

shamrock tea n. [20C] (tramp) weak tea. [it has only three leaves in it]

sham saint n. [early 18C] a hypocrite.

shamshite v. [1940s+] (Irish) to skulk. [SE *sham* + SHITE; lit. 'pretending to defecate']

shamus/sham/shammus/shamos/shommus n. [1920s+] (US) **1** a policeman. **2** a detective, esp. a private operative (cf. CHOMUS). **3** a police informer. [*Seamus*, the common Irish name of many policemen; but note Heb./Yid. *shames*, a syna-gogue official]

shan/shand n. [early 19C] counterfeit money (cf. SHEEN n.[1]). [SHAN adj.]

shan adj. [20C] **1** unsteady. **2** bashful, confused. **3** pitiful, shameful. [Scot.]

shand see SHAN n.

shandy n. [20C] a male homosexual. [rhy. sl. *shandy* = *chan-delier* = QUEER n. (4)]

shandygaff n. [late 19C–1930s] (Aus./N.Z.) an uneasy compromise, anything that fails to please either party in a dis-pute; thus *shandygaffy*, prone to compromise. [SE *shandy-gaff*, a drink composed of beer and ginger-beer, both mixed and alcoholically weak]

shaney n. [19C] a rustic simpleton (cf. SHANNY).

shanghai/shang/shangie/shong n.[1] [20C] (Aus./N.Z.) a catapult. [? Scot. *shangie*, a cleft stick]

shanghai n.[2] [20C] a broken-down old vehicle. [? dial. *shandrydan*, a rickety, old-fashioned vehicle]

shanghai v. [1910s+] to kidnap, to abduct. [naut. use *shang-hai*, to press a man into service at the port of *Shanghai*]

shanghai ballast n. [1910s–50s] (N.Z.) rice. [the Chinese city of *Shanghai* + SE *ballast*]

shanghaied adj. [20C] (Aus.) thrown from one's horse. [SHANGHAI n.[1]]

shangie see SHANGHAI n.[1].

shank n.[1] [early 19C+] (US) the end or last part of a period of time, e.g. *the shank of the evening*. [SE *shank*, a shaft or stem]

shank n.[2] (US) **1** [1950s+] a stiletto-like weapon, similar to a screwdriver, used by street gangs. **2** [1970s+] any form of knife. [17C SE *shank*, the tang of a knife or chisel, i.e. the part that is inserted into the handle]

shank v.[1] [late 19C+] to walk. [SHANKS'S PONY]

shank v.[2] [20C] to masturbate. [? rhy. sl. *shank* = WANK v.]

shank v.[3] [1950s+] (US) **1** to stab with a knife. **2** to kick, esp. a ball in sports. [SHANK n.[2]]

Shank End, the n. [late 19C+] (S.Afr.) the Cape Peninsula; thus *Shankender*, an inhabitant of Cape Peninsula. [SE *shank*, a shaft or stem]

shanker n. [late 18C–early 19C; 1940s–50s] a venereal wart. [SE *chancre*, an ulcer arising from venereal disease; 20C use is Aus.]

shanks's pony/mare/nag/naggie *n.* [mid-18C+] walking. [SE *shank*, a leg + *pony/mare/nag/naggie*; note synon. US regional *ride one's mother's colt/granny's colt/mother's pony* etc]

shanny *adj.* [late 19C] crazy, insane (cf. SHANEY). [Suffolk dial. *shanny*, half-witted, crack-brained]

shant/shanty *n.* [mid-19C] **1** a quart pot or a quart of liquor. **2** a drink. **3** beer money. [? Aus./N.Z. *shanty*, a public house, esp. when unlicensed; ult. SE *shanty*, a makeshift dwelling]

shanting *n.* [1910s+] the drinking of alcohol. [SHANT]

shants *n.* [1990s] (US teen) extremely baggy, long shorts. [SE *shorts* + *pants*, i.e. trousers]

shanty *n. see* SHANT.

shanty Irish *n.* [20C] (US) lower-class Irish (cf. LACE-CURTAIN IRISH). [SE *shanty*, a rough cabin, a hut; ult. Irish *sean tí*, an old house]

shap *see* SHAPO.

shape *n.* [17C] a fop, a dandy. [his figure]

shape/shape up/shape up to *v.* [20C] to prepare to fight someone.

shapes *n.*[1] [late 17C–early 18C] **1** an ugly, ill-proportioned man. **2** 'a nice finikin Lass that goes extream tightly laced' (Dyche & Pardon, *A New General English Dictionary*, 1735).

shapes *n.*[2] [1920s–30s] (US) crooked dice with bevelled faces on some sides of the cube, thus causing an irregular roll.

shape up *v.*[1] *see* SHAPE V.

shape up *v.*[2] [1930s+] **1** of a person, to improve one's behaviour, activities, attitude etc. **2** of a situation or person, to develop satisfactorily.

shape up or ship out *phr.* [1950s+] (orig. milit.) either do properly what one is supposed to be doing or simply go away (rather than keep doing it badly). [SHAPE UP V.[2] + SHIP OUT]

shape up to *see* SHAPE V.

shapo/shap/shappeau/shappo *n.* [late 17C–early 19C] a hat. [Fr. *chapeau*, a hat]

share *n.* [1920s+] a sexually available woman; ext. as *a bit of share*. [? her favours have been shared around]

share certificate *n.* [1960s+] (US) a pimp's favourite woman. [she is his 'investment']

share lashes/licks *v.* [20C] (W.I.) **1** to flog a number of people, usu. schoolchildren, at the same time. **2** (orig. political) to trounce one's opposition. [SE *share* (*out*) + SE *lick*]

sharge *v.* [19C] to have sexual intercourse. [? dial. *sharge*, to grind]

shark *n.* **1** [16C+] a confidence trickster. **2** [late 16C–early 18C] a parasite, a hanger-on. **3** [18C] a pickpocket. **4** [late 18C+] a sharp operator, a crooked businessman (cf. LAND-SHARK). **5** [19C] a custom house officer. **6** [late 19C–1920s] (US campus) a very intelligent or hard-working student. **7** [20C] a supplier of private loans at maximum interest (cf. LOAN SHARK). **8** [1990s] (Aus.) a second-hand car salesman.

shark and taties *n.* [1980s+] (N.Z.) fish and chips.

shark-bait/-baiter *n.* [1920s+] (Aus.) a solitary swimmer swimming too far out at sea.

shark biscuit *n.* [1920s+] (Aus.) a novice surfer. [on model of SE *dog biscuit*]

sharking *n.* [1960s+] the practice of a private credit company taking high interest on loans. [SHARK]

sharking *adj.* [20C] (W.I./Nevis) greedy, gluttonous.

shark out *v.* [19C] to run off, to decamp.

sharks, the *n.*[1] [mid–late 19C] the press gang. [ext. of SHARK n. (4)]

sharks *n.*[2] [1970s+] (US Black/teen) a *sharks*kin suit. [abbr.]

shark-shift *n.* [16C] a confidence man. [SHARK n. (1) + SHIFTER n.[1] (1); although in *Every Man out of Humour* (1599) Ben Jonson describes the character Shift as: 'A Thredbare Sharke. One that neuer was Soldior, yet liues vpon lendings. His

profession is skeldring and odling, his Banke Poules, and his Ware-house Pict-hatch']

Sharon/Shaz/Tracey *n.* [1980s+] (middle class) a pej. description of working-class young women whom they regard as overly flashy and socially unacceptable (cf. KEVIN). [archetypal working-class name]

sharp *n.*[1] **1** [late 18C+] a confidence trickster. **2** [mid–late 19C] an expert or connoisseur, a clever person or one who poses as such. [note shop assistants' jargon *Mr Sharp*, a known shop-lifter or fraud]

sharp *n.*[2] [1960s+] (US) a second-hand car in excellent condition (cf. SHARPIE n.[1]). [SHARP adj. (2)]

sharp *adj.* **1** [18C+] intelligent, perceptive. **2** [1920s+] fashionable, good, admirable. **3** [1950s–60s] used of a person who dresses well and with style, e.g. a *sharp dresser*, *sharp threads*.

sharp *v.* [late 17C–late 19C] to trick, to defraud.

sharp and blunt *n.* [20C] the vagina; thus *have a bit of sharp and blunt*, to have sexual intercourse (cf. BERKELEY HUNT). [rhy. sl. *sharp and blunt* = CUNT n.]

sharp as a mosquito's peter *phr.* [1970s+] (US Black) very smartly and fashionably dressed. [pun on SE *sharp*/SHARP adj. + *mosquito* pron. 'moskeeter' for assonance + PETER n.[4]]

sharp as the corner of a round table *phr.* [late 19C] stupid, dull. [i.e. not sharp at all]

sharp end *n.* [1980s+] the challenging, demanding and sometimes unpleasant aspect of an experience.

sharper *n.* [late 17C+] a confidence trickster. [SHARP v.]

sharper's tools *n.* [late 18C–20C] **1** false dice. **2** fools. [SHARPER + SE *tools*; (2) rhy. sl.]

sharpie/sharpy *n.*[1] **1** [late 19C] a cheat, a liar, a confidence trickster (cf. SHARP v.). **2** [1930s+] a slick operator, one who lives and hopes to prosper by their wits. **3** [1930s] (US) a devotee of swing music. **4** [1940s+] (US) a stylish dresser **5** [1970s+] (US) anything in conspicuously good condition, esp. a motorcar (cf. SHARP n.[2]).

sharpie *n.*[2] [1960s–70s] (Aus.) a member of a crop-haired teen cult. [the equivalent of the SKINHEAD]

sharping *n.* [early 19C] swindling and cheating in its various forms. [SHARP v.]

sharping-omee *n.* [mid-19C] a policeman. [SHARP adj. + OMEE]

sharpish *adj.* [late 19C+] sharply, quickly.

sharps *n.* [1980s+] (drugs) needles. [orig. medical jargon *sharps*, needles, scalpels etc]

Sharp's Alley blood worms *n.* [mid–late 19C] beef sausages or black puddings. [proper name *Sharp's Alley*, an abattoir near the Smithfield meat market in London]

sharps and flats *phr.* [19C] confidence tricksters and their victims. [SHARP n.[1] + FLAT n.[2] + pun on musical notation]

sharpshooter *n.* **1** [19C+] a womanizer (cf. RIFLE MAN). **2** [1940s] (US) an expert (cf. SHARP n.[1]). [puns]

sharp's the word and quick's the motion *phr.* [late 18C–20C] said of anyone seen as notably attentive to their own interest.

sharp up *v.* [1950s] (US) to dress oneself up smartly. [SHARP adj. (3)]

sharpy *see* SHARPIE n.[1].

sharry *see* CHARA.

shaster *n.* [1990s] a sudden attack of diarrhoea. [? SHIT n.[1]]

shat *n.* [early 18C] a chatterbox, a gossip, a 'tattler'. [? SE *chat*]

shat/shat-off *adj.* [1940s+] (Aus.) very angry, furious. [past participle of SHIT v.[1]; thus cognate with phr. *it makes me want to shit*]

shat on *adj.* [late 19C+] abused, humiliated. [past participle SHIT ON v.]

shattered *adj.* [1930s+] **1** drunk (cf. BASTED). **2** utterly exhausted (physically or emotionally).

shatting on one's uppers *phr.* [late 19C+] (US) completely out of money. [var. on SHIT v.[1] + SE *uppers*]

shaun spadah *n.* [1920s] a motorcar. [rhy. sl.; the horse *Shaun Spadah*, winner of the 1921 Grand National]

shave *n.*[1] [19C] (US) an excessive discount on a note. [SHAVE A NOTE]

shave *n.*[2] [mid-19C+] a narrow escape, esp. as *close shave*. [SE *shave*, a glancing touch]

shave *n.*[3] [late 19C] a drink. [? excuse given as 'I'm just off out for a shave']

shave *v.* **1** [late 16C–19C] to defraud, to rob, to overcharge; thus intensified as [mid-16C] *shave to the quick*. **2** [late 16C–early 18C] to steal. [SE *shave*; (1) used in this sense as SE in late 14C–early 16C]

shave-and-a-haircut *n.* [20C] (orig. US) a sequence of knocks, tum-ti-ti-tum-tum, often as *shave-and-a-haircut – two bits*, which has an final tum-tum (cf. BARBER'S KNOCK). [the echoic rhythm of the phrase]

shave a note, to *phr.* [19C] (US) to discount a promissory note at a very high rate of interest. [SHAVE v.]

shaved *adj.* [19C] drunk (cf. BASTED). [SHAVE n.[3]]

shaver *n.*[1] [late 16C+] a man. [lit. one who shaves and has thus reached manhood; best known in phr. *young shaver* (usually referring to a younger person); now used ironically]

shaver *n.*[2] [mid-19C] a narrow escape, a 'close shave'. [SHAVE n.[2]]

shaver *n.*[3] [1920s] a *shave-coat*, a man's casual garment resembling a housecoat and worn when shaving (cf. ARSEHOLE-PERISHER).

shavetail *n.* [1960s+] (US) an inexperienced person. [milit. use *shavetail*, an untrained pack animal, identified by a shaven tail; thus a newly commissioned second lieutenant]

shaving *n.* **1** [early 17C–mid-19C] the act of swindling or defrauding. **2** [early–mid-19C] (US) discounting bills or promissory notes at a very high rate of interest (cf. SHAVE A NOTE). [SHAVE v.]

shaving brush *n.* [20C] the pubic hair (cf. SCRUBBING BRUSH).

shaving cream *n.* [1950s] (US) excrement; i.e. a euph. for SHIT n.[1] (1).

shavings *n.* [late 17C–18C] (Und.) the clippings from shaved coins (cf. CURLE).

shaw/shawl *n.* [1910s+] an automobile. [var. on SHORT n.[2] (2)]

shawk *n.* [late 19C] (Anglo-Ind.) a kite (a bird of prey). [elision of milit. nickname *shitehawk*, a ref. to its scavenging habits]

shawl *n.*[1] [late 19C] (middle class) an announcement of one's engagement. [? the putative groom being now allowed the intimacy of placing a shawl round his beloved's shoulders]

shawl *n.*[2] [1900s–20s] a prostitute (cf. SHAWLIE).

shawl *n.*[3] *see* SHAW.

shawlie/shawly *n.* [late 19C–1930s] (Irish) **1** an Irish, usu. Dublin, fisherwoman. **2** any working-class woman wearing a shawl.

shaygets/sheygets *n.* [late 19C+] **1** a young male gentile, as referred to by a Jew. **2** a mischievous rascal, a 'charming devil', whether Jewish or gentile. **3** an arrogant person. **4** an illiterate, one who lacks education, which in traditional-learning-focused Jewish eyes is equated with (1). [Heb. *sheygets*, a rascal]

Shaz *see* SHARON.

shazzam *v.* [20C] to flash dramatically, both lit. (of a light) and lit. (of an idea). [SHAZZAM!]

shazzam! *excl.* [20C] (US) a cry of triumph. [echoic]

she *n.*[1] [late 19C] (society) Queen Victoria. [Ayesha, 'she who must be obeyed' the heroine of H. Rider Haggard's novel *She* (1887), coincidentally the year of the queen's diamond jubilee]

she *n.*[2] **1** [late 19C+] the vagina (cf. IT n.[1]). **2** [1920s+] the penis, esp. in phr. *up she rises*.

she *n.*[3] [1970s+] (drugs) cocaine (cf. GIRL n.[3]).

she *n.*[4] [1990s] (US) the wife (cf. HER n.[2]).

shearer's joy *n.* [late 19C+] (Aus./N.Z.) beer (cf. BULLOCKY'S DELIGHT).

'sheart! *excl.* [late 16C–early 18C] a mild, if blasphemous, oath, lit. 'God's heart' (cf. 's abbr.[1]).

sheba *n.* [1920s] (US) an attractive, fashionable woman (cf. SHEIK n.[1]). [the Queen of *Sheba*]

shebang *n.* [late 19C+] (US) **1** a house, a home, a dwelling place. **2** (Und.) a prison cell. [SE *shebang*, a hut, a dwelling, one's quarters]

shebeen *n.* [late 18C+] an unlicensed drinking place, an illegal, late-night drinking club. [Irish *síbín*, illicit whisky; 20C use usu. linked to S.Afr. townships or to UK W.I. community]

she can sit on my face anyday *phr.* [1940s+] (US) said by a man of a woman by whom he is very sexually aroused.

sheckles *see* SHEKELS.

sheckles! *excl.* [late 19C–1900s] a general excl. [? euph. for SHIT!]

shed *n.*[1] [1920s+] (Aus./N.Z.) a term of general abuse. [elision of SHITHEAD; thus cf. SHAWK; SHOUSE]

shed *n.*[2] [1990s] an unattractive, promiscuous young woman. ['something you put your tools in']

shed *v.* [mid–late 19C] to dispose of, to give away. [weak use of SE]

shed a tear, to *phr.* [mid-19C] **1** to urinate. **2** to take a drink, esp. a quick one (cf. WIPE ONE'S EYE phr.).

shed a tear for Nelson, to *phr.* [mid-19C+] to urinate. [presumably the UK naval hero Horatio, Lord *Nelson* (1758–1805)]

she didn't seem to mind it very much *phr.* [late 19C] an ironic phr.; the real meaning, with ref. to one's girlfriend being jealous, is that she minded it a great deal.

shed one's baby teeth, to *phr.* [19C] (US) to grow up, esp. to become impervious to deception.

sheeba *n.* [1970s+] (US drugs) marijuana. [var. on CHEEB]

shee-it! *excl.* [20C] (US) a joc. imitation of a Southern pron. of SHIT! (cf. SCHEISSE!).

sheela *n.* [late 19C–1910s] (Irish) a man who takes excessive interest in stereotyped 'women's affairs', i.e. housework, gossip, child-rearing. [Irish name *Síle*, but note SHEILA]

sheen *n.*[1] **1** [mid-19C] a counterfeit coin (cf. SHAN). **2** [20C] (Aus.) money. [the SE *sheen* of the coins or Ger. *Schein*, a banknote]

sheen *n.*[2] [1950s–60s] (US Black) a machine, either a car or a motorcycle (cf. 'CHINE).

sheena *n.* [1950s–60s] (camp gay) a Black homosexual man. [the cartoon character, *Sheena, Queen of the Jungle*]

sheeny *n.*[1] [19C] a derog. term for a Jew. [as laid out by Nathan Süsskind (Cohen, 1989), Yid. *shayner Yid*, a pious (lit. 'a beautiful-faced') Jew; the pious, thus old-fashioned and trad. Jew. According to the Talmud such a Jew who has a full beard – beauty in this case being spiritual rather than physical. The phr. was used by assimilated German Jews, who had emigrated to England, as a derog. term, meaning 'an old-fashioned Jew', i.e. in habits, clothing and religion, which mocked their less sophisticated successors, who followed them from Germany and clung on (at least initially) to their old-fashioned ways. The first half of the phrase, which the 'uncultured' Jews pron. *sheena* rather than the more Germanic *schön*, was taken up by gentile Jew-baiters to create *sheeny*]

sheeny *n.*[2] [mid-19C+] a pawnbroker. [racial stereotyping of SHEENY n.[1]]

sheeny *adj.* [late 19C+] **1** of people, deceitful, dubious, fraudulent. **2** of money, counterfeit. [SHEENY n.[1] + reinforced by SE *sheeny*, shiny]

sheep-biter *n.* [late 17C–18C] **1** a butcher. **2** a wretched, miserable person.

sheep cocky *n.* [1940s+] (Aus./N.Z.) a small-scale sheep farmer. [SE *sheep* + COCKIE]

sheep dip *n.* [1960s] **1** (Aus.) coarse tobacco, issued in prisons. **2** (US) inferior whisky.

sheep-dodger *n.* [20C] (Aus.) a sheep hand.

sheep-guts *n.* [19C] a general term of contempt.

sheepish *adj.* [1970s] (US campus) of men, long-haired.

sheepo *n.* [late 19C–1900s] (Aus./N.Z.) a sheep-shearer, spec. one who works in the catching sheds, filling the catching pens. [SE *sheep* + sfx. -o]

sheep's back *n.* [late 19C+] (Aus.) luxury, indolence, security; usu. in phr. *on the sheep's back*, living very comfortably or living securely (cf. PIG'S BACK). [the wealth of sheep farmers]

sheep's head *n.* [late 17C–19C] a fool, esp. a talkative one (cf. BEEF-BRAIN). [saying, 'like a sheep's head, all jaw']

sheep-shearer *n.* [16C–mid-18C] a swindler, a confidence trickster, esp. one who works the JACK IN A BOX confidence trick. [pun on SE *fleece*, to rob]

sheepskin *n.[1]* [mid–late 19C] a college diploma, received on graduation. [such diplomas are trad. made of *sheepskin*-based parchment]

sheepskin *n.[2]* [1990s] (US campus) a condom. [an allegedly superior material for contraceptives]

sheepskin fiddle *n.* [early 19C] a drum; thus *sheepskin fiddler*, a drummer.

sheep-tail *n.* [1970s] (W.I.) **1** a bit of shirt-tail that protrudes through a hole in torn trousers. **2** the person (usu. a boy) who has such a costume.

sheep-wash *n.* [20C] (Aus./N.Z.) poor liquor (cf. HORSE PISS).

sheesh! *excl.* [1950s+] (US) a mild oath; euph. for JESUS! or SHIT! (cf. SCHEISSE!). [? popularized through the *Yogi Bear/Huckleberry Hound* TV cartoons]

sheet *n.* **1** [mid-18C+] a newspaper, a magazine. **2** [1930s+] paper money, e.g. a £1 note, a $1 bill. **3** [1950s+] (US Und.) an official police record (cf. RAP SHEET). [abbr. SE *sheet of paper*. (1) mainly US since 20C]

sheet! *excl.* [20C] euph. for SHIT! (cf. SHEE-IT!).

sheet alley/lane *n.* [mid-19C–1900s] bed; thus *go down sheet alley into Bedfordshire*, to go to bed.

sheet in the wind *phr.* [mid-19C+] half drunk (cf. SHAKE A CLOTH IN THE WIND). [for ety. *see* THREE SHEETS IN THE WIND]

sheet it home to, to *phr.* [1910s–20s] to prove something against someone. [? putting a criminal on a charge sheet i.e. SHEET n.(3); but note date]

sheet lane *see* SHEET ALLEY.

sheet rocking *n.* [1980s+] (drugs) smoking a mixture of crack cocaine and LSD. [SHEETS n. (3) + ROCK n.[4]; play on SE *sheet-rock*, a form of plasterboard]

sheets *n.* **1** [1920s+] cigarette rolling papers. **2** [1930s+] (orig. US) paper money. **3** [1960s+] perforated sheets of LSD-impregnated blotting-paper, which can be torn into 100 separate doses of LSD (cf. A n.[3]). **4** [1970s+] phencyclidine (cf. ACE n.[3]).

she-familiar *n.* [19C] a mistress. [SE *she* + *familiar*, an intimate relation, but note slight overtone of the occult]

Sheffield handicap *n.* [20C] an act of defecation. [rhy. sl. *Sheffield handicap* = CRAP n.[3]]

she-flunkey *n.* [late 19C–1910s] a lady's maid. [SE pfx. *she-*, female + SE *flunkey*]

sheg *v.* (W.I.) **1** [1940s+] to annoy, to provoke. **2** [1950s] to seduce (cf. SHAG v.[1]). [SE *shag*, to shake about]

sheg round *v.* [1940s] (W.I.) to work as a petty criminal. [ext. of SHEG v. (1)]

sheg-up *n.* [1940s] (W.I.) a confidence trickster, whose role is to appear as gullible as the potential victim. [SHEG ROUND]

sheg up *v.* [1950s+] (W.I. Rasta) **1** to be messed up, to be ruined. **2** to bother, as in *all sheg up*, all hot and bothered, or all spoiled, as of work that has been ruined. [SE *shake(n)*]

she-he *n.* [1940s–60s] (US) a lesbian (cf. HESH; SHE-MALE).

she house *n.* [late 18C–mid-19C] a house in which a wife rules her husband (cf. HEN HOUSE n.[1]).

sheik *n.[1]* **1** [1920s] a lady-killer, a romantic lover (cf. SHEBA). **2** [1920s–50s] a fashionably dressed young man (cf. JELLY BEAN n.[1]). [*The Sheik*, a novel by E.M. Hull, pub. 1919 + its film adaptation, released 1921, starring Rudolph Valentino; ult. Arabic *sheikh*, a tribal chieftain, a leader]

sheik *n.[2]* [1980s+] (US Black) a scarf or handkerchief worn by men over their hair, then tied in the back. [? its vaguely Arabic image]

sheik *v.* [1920s] (orig. US) to go out looking for female conquests. [SHEIK n.[1]]

sheikha *n.* [1920s] the female consort of a SHEIK n.[1] (cf. SHEBA). [*Sheikha*, an Arab lady or matron of good family; the chief wife of a *sheikh*]

sheila *n.* **1** [early 19C+] (Aus.) a woman (cf. SHALER). **2** [1960s–70s] (S.Afr.) the girlfriend of an urban gangster (cf. DUCKTAIL; TSOTSI). [proper name *Sheila*, ult. Irish *caille*, a young girl]

sheila-day/sheila's day *n.* [1970s+] (S.Afr. Black) Thursday, the day that most nannies and maids are allowed off work. [*Sheila*, generic name for Black domestic servants]

sheister *see* SCHICER.

sheisty *adj.* [1990s] (US Black/campus) underhand, unethical, untrustworthy, criminal. [SHIT n.[2]/SHICER + FEISTY]

she is/was so innocent she thinks/thought fucking is/was a town in China *phr.* [1940s+] a phr. used of an especially naïve young woman. [pun on *Fukien*, an area in southeast China]

sheive *see* SHIV.

shekel *v.* [1980s+] (US campus) to give, to hand out. [SHEKELS]

shekels/sheckles *n.* [mid-19C+] money; thus *rake in the shekels*, to prosper. [Heb. *shekel*, a Babylonian, hence Heb. monetary unit; ult. Heb. *shāqal*, to weigh]

shelf *n.[1]* [1920s+] (Aus.) the dress circle in a cinema.

shelf *n.[2]* [1920s+] (Aus./N.Z.) a police informer. [? one places things, i.e. information, on it]

shelf *v.* [1920s+] (Aus./N.Z.) to inform to the police. [SHELF n.[2]]

shelfer *n.* [1960s+] (Aus.) a police informer. [ext. of SHELF n.[2]]

she-lion *n.* [late 18C–early 19C] a shilling (5p). [a pun on the pron.]

shell *n.* **1** [19C] the vagina (cf. BEARDED CLAM). **2** (US Und.) a safe. **3** [1910s–20s] a condom.

shell *v.* [1980s+] (N.Z. drugs) to remove painkilling drugs from their capsule before making home-produced narcotics.

shellac *v.* [1930s+] to beat, to thrash, to punish. [SE *shellac*, to coat or varnish with shellac]

shellacked *adj.* [1920s–40s] (US) drunk (cf. BASTED; PLASTERED). [for ety. *see* SHELLAC]

shellacking *n.* [1930s+] a severe beating or defeat. [SHELLAC]

shell-back *n.* [1940s+] an ultra-conservative, slow-witted person (cf. MOSS-BACK n.[2]). [the image of a slow-moving turtle]

she'll be grannies *phr.* [1960s] (Aus.) everything will be all right (cf. APPLES adj.). [*Granny Smith*, a brand of apple; originated in Aus. and named for Maria Ann 'Granny' Smith (d.1870)]

she'll be right *phr.* [1940s+] (Aus.) a phr. used to reject offers of assistance, don't worry, don't fuss, everything will be fine in the end (cf. APPLES adj.; SHE'S RIGHT).

shell game *n.* [late 19C+] a swindling game in which a small object is concealed under a walnut shell or the like, the manipulator then moves the shells round at speed; bets are made on the shell under which the object is found (cf. FIND THE LADY; THIMBLE-RIG).

shellmex *n.* [20C] sex. [rhy. sl.]

shell out *v.* **1** [early 19C+] to hand over, usu. money. **2** [1910s–20s] to take an opponent's money when playing cards or dice. [the removal of a seed from a shell]

shell road *v.* [20C] to throw a person, often a woman who refuses to have sex, out of a vehicle and thus force them to walk home an inconvenient and possibly embarrassing distance (cf. RED LIGHT). [SAmE *shell road*, a back road having a bed or layer of shells]

shells *n.* [16C–early 17C] (Und.) money, esp. as taken from a victim by cut-purses or pickpockets (cf. WAMPUM).

shell-shock *n.* **1** [1910s–50s] cocoa. **2** [1920s–30s] (tramp) tea served in a casual ward or hostel. **3** [1930s–50s] (Aus./N.Z.) a mixed alcoholic drink, usu. very potent, e.g. port and stout.

shell the bean pod, to *phr.* [1990s] to masturbate.

s'help the cat! *see* SWOP ME BOB!

she-male *n.* **1** [late 19C] a woman. **2** [20C] a male homosexual or transvestite (cf. HESH; SHE-HE).

she-man *n.* [20C] a homosexual man (cf. HESH). [play on SE *he-man*]

she-mi-a-play-wid *n.* [1950s] (W.I.) one's female sweetheart. [lit. 'she plays with me']

shemozzle / chemozzle / shimozzel / shlamozzle / shlemozzle *n.* [late 19C+] a fuss, a disturbance (cf. SCHLEMOZZLE n.). [coined in UK and not 'real' Yid.; similar sp. to *shlimazel*, but with no other links]

shemozzle/chemozzle/schlemozzle/shimozzel *v.* [20C] to run off, to decamp. [SHEMOZZLE n.]

shemp the hog, to *phr.* [1990s] to masturbate.

shenanigan / shenanegan / shenangin / shenanickin / shenanigans / shenanikin / shenannegan / shenannigan / shinanegan *n.* [mid-19C+] trickery, skulduggery, machination, intrigue, teasing, 'kidding', nonsense; (usu. pl.) a plot, a trick, a prank, an exhibition of high spirits, a carry-on. [? Erse *sionnach*, (pron. 'shinnuck') hiding, malingering, 'playing the fox'; East Anglian dial. *nannicking*, playing the fool, 'messing about']

she-napper *n.* [late 17C–mid-19C] **1** a madam. **2** a female pimp or procuress. **3** a female thief-taker. [SE *she* + NAP v.[1]]

she-oak *n.* [late 19C] (Aus.) beer. [SE *she-oak*, a tree of the genus *Casuarina*; note Aus. use of *she* for wood to indicate inferior texture, colour etc]

Sheol *n.* [1900s–20s] joc. euph. for SE *hell*, e.g. *sheol to pay*, *this side of sheol*. [Heb. *she'ol*, the underworld, the abode of the dead or departed spirits, translated as 'the pit' or 'hell']

shepherd *v.* **1** [late 19C+] to watch over carefully, to shadow. **2** [late 19C+] (Und. usu. Aus.) to follow someone who is a potential target for robbery or fraud.

shepherd's/shepherd's plaid *adj.* [mid-19C–1910s] bad. [rhy. sl.]

shepherd's bush *n.* [20C] dismissal. [rhy. sl.; *shepherd's bush* = PUSH n.[4]]

shepherd's clock *n.* [late 19C+] (Aus.) a kookaburra or laughing jackass (cf. BUSHMAN'S CLOCK). [its sounds punctuate the day]

shepherd's pie *n.* [20C] the sky. [rhy. sl.]

shepherd's plaid *see* SHEPHERD'S.

sherbert/sherbet *n.*[1] **1** [late 19C] grog or any warm, alcoholic drink, also as *old sherbert*. **2** [20C] (Aus.) any form of alcoholic drink. **3** [1910s+] beer. [Turk. *sherbet* (ult. Arab. *sharbah*, a drink), a cooling drink made of fruit juice and water sweetened, often cooled with snow]

sherbert *n.*[2] [1990s] a taxi-cab. [rhy. sl. *sherbert dab* = cab]

sherbert! *excl.* [20C] euph. for SHIT! (cf. SCHEISSE!).

sherbert dip *n.* [20C] a tip. [rhy. sl.]

sherberty *adj.* [late 19C] drunk. [SHERBERT n.[1]]

sherbet *see* SHERBERT n.[1].

sheriff's ball *n.* [late 18C–mid-19C] a hanging (cf. DANCE AT THE SHERIFF'S BALL).

sheriff's basket/tub *n.* [early–mid-17C] a basket or tub placed outside a prison to receive charitable gifts for the prisoners.

sheriff's bracelets *n.* [late 18C–early 19C] handcuffs (cf. BRACELETS).

sheriff's hotel *n.* [late 18C–early 19C] a prison (cf. AKERMAN'S HOTEL). [SE *sheriff* + HOTEL n.]

sheriff's journeyman *n.* [late 18C–early 19C] the hangman.

sheriff's picture frame *n.* [late 18C–early 19C] the gallows.

sheriff's posts *n.* [late 16C] two painted posts, set up at the sheriff's door, to which proclamations are affixed.

sheriff's tub *see* SHERIFF'S BASKET.

sherk *see* SHIRK.

sherlock *n.* [1980s+] (US campus) a friend. [for ety. *see* SHER-LOCK HOLMES].

Sherlock Holmes *n.* [1960s+] (US Black) the police. [proper name *Sherlock Holmes*, the private consulting detective invented by Sir Arthur Conan Doyle (1859–1930)]

sherm/shermans/sherms *n.* [1980s+] (US Black) phencyclidine (cf. ACE n.[3]; BLUNT n.[2]). [the smoking of *Sherman* cigarettes laced with phencyclidine]

sherman *n.* [1940s+] **1** an American. **2** masturbation (cf. BARCLAY'S). [rhy. sl.; *Sherman tank* = (1) YANK n.; (2) WANK n.]

shermans/sherms *see* SHERM.

sherry *n.*[1] [mid-19C] a *sheriff*. [abbr.]

sherry *n.*[2] [late 19C] cheap beer, sold at fourpence a quart (1.14 litres).

sherry/sherry off *v.* [late 18C–late 19C] to run off. [? SE *sheer off*, to change one's course, to turn]

sherry one's ribs, to *phr.* [late 19C–1900s] (US) to leave in a hurry. [ext. of SHERRY v.]

she's been a good wife to him *phr.* [late 19C] an ironic phr. used of a drunken woman.

she-she *n.* [1950s+] (US) a young woman. [Oriental Pidgin English, but note date of SHE-SHE TALK]

she-she talk *n.* [mid-19C–1920s] (US Black) women's talk.

she's right *phr.* [1950s+] (Aus.) everything is in order (cf. APPLES adj.; SHE'LL BE RIGHT).

she's sweet *phr.* [1940s+] (Aus.) everything is satisfactory (cf. APPLES adj.).

sheviss *n.* [mid–late 19C] a shift, a smock. [? corruption of SE *chemise*]

shevvle *n.* [late 19C] cat's meat. [Fr. *cheval*, horse]

she was so innocent she thought fucking was a town in China *see* SHE IS SO INNOCENT SHE THINKS FUCKING IS A TOWN IN CHINA.

she wouldn't know if someone was up her *phr.* [1910s+] (Aus.) a phr. used of a very stupid young woman. [SE *up*/UP v.[2]]

sheygets *see* SHAYGETS.

shice/shish *adj.* [mid-19C+] useless, worthless. [SHICER]

shice/shish *v.* [mid-19C+] to defraud, to cheat, to betray, to abandon. [SHICER]

shicer/shiser *n.* **1** [mid-19C+] a worthless, idle person (cf. SCHICER). **2** [mid-19C+] nothing, something worthless. **3** [mid-19C+] counterfeit money. **4** [mid-19C+] (Aus.) a worthless or worked-out mine. **5** [20C] a criminal. [Ger. SCHEISSE, excrement, lit. SHIT n.[1]]

shicery *see* SHICKERY adj.[1].

shicker/shick/shikkar/shikker/shikkur *n.* (Aus./N.Z.) **1** [late 19C+] alcohol. **2** [1910s+] a drunkard. [SHICKER adj.]

shicker/shiker/shikker *adj.* [late 19C+] (mainly Aus./N.Z.) drunk; thus *on the shicker*, drinking heavily. [synon. Yid.; ult. Heb. *shikor*, drunk]

shicker *v.* [20C] (Aus./N.Z.) to drink, usu. to drunkenness; thus *shickering*, drinking, *shicker-up*, a drinking bout (cf. SCHICKERED). [synon. Yid.; ult. Heb. *shikor*, drunk]

shicker! *excl.* [1910s–40s] (Aus./N.Z.) a mild oath, e.g. *shicker me grandmother!* [? euph. for SHIT!]

shickered/shikkared/shikkered/shikkured *adj.* [20C] (mainly Aus./N.Z.) drunk (cf. BASTED). [SHICKER n.]

shickerhood *n.* [1920s] (Aus./N.Z.) drunkenness. [SHICKER n.]

shickery/shicery *adj.*[1] [mid–late 19C] **1** bad, fake. **2** shabby, useless. [SHICE adj.; but note dial. *shiggyry*, shaky]

shickery *adj.*[2] [late 19C–1900s] drunk. [SHICKER n. (1)]

shickery *adv.* [mid-19C] shabbily, badly. [SHICE adj.]

shicksa/chickster/shakester/shickse/shickster/shikster *n.* [mid-19C+] (Jewish) **1** a gentile woman. **2** a non-Jewish servant-girl (cf. SHAKESTER n.[1]; SHICKSTER n.[1]). [Yid. *shikse*, a gentile female; ult. Heb. *shequas, a blemish*; while *goy*, a gentile man, or gentiles in general, is a relatively neutral term, *shicksa*, strictly the fem. of SHAYGETS, always carries pej. overtones]

shickster *n.*[1] *see* SHAKESTER n.[1].

shickster *n.*[2] [mid-19C] a promiscuous woman, 'a "gay" lady' (Hotten, 1867).

shickster *n.*[3] *see* SHICKSA.

shickster-crabs *n.* [mid-19C] (tramp) women's shoes. [SHAKE-STER n. (3) + CRABS n.[2]]

shield *n.* [1920s+] (US) a policeman (cf. BADGE n.[2]). [the wearer's shield-shaped badge of office]

shiesty-tricker *n.* [1990s] (US Black/campus) an immoral person, one who gets away with a crime. [SHEISTY + SE *tricker*]

shiever *n.* [1920s] (US Und.) a traitor. [? CHIV n.[1]; thus a 'backstabber']

shif *n.*[1] [mid-19C] fish. [backsl.]

shif *n.*[2] [1970s] (Aus.) the face (cf. CHIV n.[3].)

shife *n.* [1990s] one who purports to be more than they are. [? SHIF-MAN]

shif-man *n.* [1950s] (W.I.) **1** an effeminate man. **2** a ne'er-do-well, a lazy idler. [SE *shift*, the woman's undergarment and/or *shiftless*, lazy; the first suits (1), while the second suits (2)]

shift *v.*[1] **1** [late 19C] to kill, to murder. **2** [late 19C+] to consume, esp. to eat or drink a large amount. **3** [late 19C+] (orig. Aus.) to move fast, to run. [fig. or ext. uses of SE *shift*, to move]

shift *v.*[2] [1990s] (Irish) **1** to pursue women. **2** to deep kiss. **3** to have sexual intercourse. [? SHAFT v.]

shifted *adj.* [1990s] (Black) arrested. [? SHAFTED]

shifter *n.*[1] [16C] (Und.) a trickster, a confidence man. **2** [early 19C] a warning from one thief to another. **3** [20C] (US Und.) a receiver of stolen goods. [SE *shift*, to employ underhand methods, to deceive, also to live by one's wits]

shifter *n.*[2] [late 19C] a drunkard. [SHIFT v.[1] (2)]

shift gears *v.* [1990s] to masturbate.

shift into high gear, to *phr.* [20C] (US) to increase or intensify. [automobile imagery]

shift-monger *n.* [late 19C] a young man-about-town. [SE *shift*, a large, highly starched shirt-front, sported as part of such a person's evening dress + sfx. *-monger*]

shift off *v.* [mid–late 17C] to get rid of the effects of drinking. [SE *shift*, to move]

shift one's ass *see* MOVE ONE'S ASS.

shift one's bob, to *phr.* [mid-18C–late 19C] to leave, to run off. [? naut. *bobstay*, a rope that keeps the bowsprit steady]

shift-round *n.* [1940s+] movement, a changing of one's place.

shift service *see* SHIFT WORK.

shift the weight, to *phr.* [20C] to place the blame on someone else (cf. TAKE THE WEIGHT).

shift work/service *n.* [19C] sexual intercourse.

shift your carcass! *see* MOVE YOUR CARCASS!

shigs *n.* [mid-19C] money, esp. shillings. [? abbr.]

shiker/shikker *see* SHICKER adj.

shikkar *see* SHICKER n.

shikkared *see* SHICKERED.

shikker/shikkur *see* SHICKER n.

shikkered/shikkured *see* SHICKERED.

shikster *see* SHICKSA.

shill *n.*[1] [late 19C+] (US) a police officer's truncheon. [abbr. Irish *shillelagh*, cudgel + links of the Irish and the police]

shill *n.*[2] [1910s+] (gambling) **1** a house player in a casino. **2** a member of the three-card monte team who appears to be another innocent gambler and who lures players into the game. [abbr. *shillaber*, one who publicizes a circus, carnival etc]

shilling dreadful *see* SHILLING SHOCKER.

shilling in/shilling in and the winner shouts *n.* [late 19C–1900s (Aus./N.Z.) a bar-room dice gambling game in which everyone puts one shilling (5p) in a kitty and the winner pays for the round (and possibly makes a small profit). [var. on BOB IN]

shillings and pence *n.* [20C] sense. [rhy. sl.]

shilling shocker/dreadful *n.* [late 19C] a short sensational novel, published at a shilling (5p) (cf. DREADFUL).

shilling sicker *see* SIXPENNY SICKER.

shillings in/to the pound *phr.* [1930s+] used in various combinations/amounts to denote someone who is mentally inadequate, i.e. NOT ALL THERE; e.g. *only ten shillings in the pound, barely six shilling in the pound* ; also as *bob in/to the pound*. [SE *shilling*/BOB n.[3] (1); the full *pound* sterling had 20 shillings]

shilling tabernacle *n.* [late 19C] a Baptist or Methodist tea-meeting, where refreshment was available at a shilling (5p) a head.

shilly-shally *n.* [late 18C–mid-19C] **1** hesitation, vacillation. **2** one who hesitates, an irresolute, undecided person. [SE after 1850; orig. *stand shill I, shall I*; f. *shall I this? shall I that?*]

shilly-shally *v.* [late 18C–mid-19C] to vacillate. [SHILLY-SHALLY n.; SE after 1850]

shim *n.*[1] [20C] a male homosexual. [? SE *shimmy*, to wriggle, or SE *she + him*]

shim *n.*[2] [1950s] (US) a person who does not appreciate rock and roll. [ety. unknown]

shim *n.*[3] [1960s+] a piece of plastic used to open a door (cf. LOID n.). [SE *shim*, a sliver of metal, used to fill the space between parts of machinery that are subject to wear]

shim *v.* [1970s] (US) to open a door or lock with a piece of plastic (cf. LOID v.).

shimmy *n.*[1] [early 19C+] **1** a woman's undergarment, essentially synon. with a petticoat (cf. CHIMMY n.[2]). **2** a man's shirt (cf. SMISH). [abbr. SE *chemise*, a shift or smock; the *OED* suggests that this 'vulgar corruption' was the result of people assuming *chemise* was a pl.]

shimmy/chimmy *n.*[2] [late 19C] the gambling game of *chemin de fer*. [abbr.]

shimozzel *see* SHEMOZZLE.

shim-sham *n.* [1970s+] (US campus) feelings of unease, of nervousness. [? JIM-JAMS n.[1]]

shin *n.* [1960s+] (US prison) any contraband gun or knife. [? CHIV n.[1]]

shin *v.* [mid-19C+] (US) to borrow money. [for ety. *see* BREAK SHINS]

shinanegan *see* SHENANIGAN.

shin battle *n.* [1950s–60s] (street gang) a fake, practice battle. [? one kicks only shins; weapons are not used]

shindig *n.* [1950s+] an altercation, a violent quarrel, a tremendous fuss. [SE *shindig*, a noisy party or festivity + SHINDY]

shindy *n.* [mid-19C] **1** a noise, a disturbance, a commotion; thus *cut shindies*, *kick up a shindy*, to create a disturbance. **2** a fancy for, an affection for. [naut. jargon *shindy*, a form of dance among sailors; ? ult. SE *shinty*, a game, mainly played in Ireland, that resembles a rougher form of hockey]

shindykit *n.* [late 19C–1910s] (Aus.) a business consortium. [SE *syndicate* + SHINDY n. (1)]

shine *n.*[1] [early 19C+] (US) illicitly distilled whisky. [abbr. MOONSHINE n.]

shine *n.*[2] [mid-late 19C] money. [? SHINERS n.[1]]

shine *n.*[3] [mid-late 19C] a noise, a commotion (cf. SHINDY).

shine *n.*[4] [late 19C] (US) a smile. [? one's glinting teeth]

shine *n.*[5] [late 19C+] (US) a derog. term for a Black person. [the reflection of a blue-Black skin. As used in W.I. the term refers to someone with a very dark, smooth complexion and has no derog. connotations]

shine/shyin' *adj.*[1] [20C] (Aus./N.Z.) **1** of objects, excellent, first-rate. **2** of people, likeable.

shine *adj.*[2] [20C] (W.I./US) Black (cf. BROWN POLISH). [SHINE n.[5]]

shine *v.*[1] [late 19C–1900s] to raise money, to display money. [SHINE n.[2]]

shine *v.*[2] [1970s+] (US campus) **1** to play truant, to skip classes. **2** to abandon, to fail (cf. PUNT v.[2]). [SHINE ON]

shine! *excl.* [1980s+] (US campus) impossible! absolutely not! on no account! [euph. SHIT!]

shine box *n.* [1940s–50s] (US) a nightclub featuring entertainment by Black jazz musicians; it may also be patronized by a primarily Black clientele (cf. NIGGER JOINT; SHINE JOINT). [SHINE adj.[2] + BOX n.[1], a`nightclub, Fr. sl. *boîte*, a nightclub (lit. 'a box')]

shine joint *n.* [1940s–50s] (US) **1** an illicit liquor-selling establishment. **2** a nightclub patronized by a primarily Black clientele (cf. SHINE BOX). [SHINE n.[1]/SHINE adj.[2] + JOINT n.[3] (3)]

shine like a diamond/dime in a goat's ass, to *phr.* [1980s+] (US) to shine very brightly. [ARSE n.[1]]

shine like a shilling up a sweep's arse, to *phr.* **1** [1900s–30s] to shine very brightly. **2** [1960s] to be very conspicuous. [ARSE n.[1]]

shine like a shitten barn door, to *phr.* [late 18C–early 19C] to shine brightly. [SE *shitten*, filthied with excrement; the image of wet ordure glistening on a barn door]

shine on *v.* [1950s+] (US Black) to ignore. [euph. SHIT v.[1]]

shine one's pole, to *phr.* [20C] to masturbate (cf. SHINE THE BARREL).

shiner *n.*[1] **1** [19C] a mirror, esp. as used by card-sharps to spy on otherwise hidden hands. **2** [mid-19C] a silk hat. **3** [late 19C+] a diamond, or other jewel, also in pl. **4** [20C] a black eye.

shiner *n.*[2] **1** [early-mid 19C] a clever person. **2** [1930s+] (Aus.) one who wants the limelight, but is unwilling to work towards gaining it.

shiner *n.*[3] [1950s+] a window-cleaner. [their job]

shiners *n.*[1] [mid-18C–late 19C] money, esp. sovereigns (cf. SHINE n.[2]). [the shininess of coins]

shiners *n.*[2] [1990s] (Black) fellatio. [? SHINE ONE'S POLE]

shines *n.* [mid-19C+] (orig. US) **1** tricks (cf. MONKEY SHINE). **2** sexual intercourse. [SE *shine*, a brilliant display]

shine the barrel/helmet/salami, to *phr.* [1990s] to masturbate (cf. SHINE ONE'S POLE). [SE *shine* + *barrel*/HELMET/ *salami*]

shine up to *v.* [20C] (US) to flatter someone, to curry favour

(cf. SUCK UP). [? SHINE n.[4], i.e. one's shining teeth, set in a false smile]

shiney *n.*[1] *see* SHINY.

shiney *n.*[2] [late 19C–1930s] (US) a Black person. [SHINE n.[5]]

shingle short *adj.* [mid-19C+] (Aus.) eccentric, crazy (cf. NOT ALL THERE).

shingle-splitting *n.* [mid-late 19C] (Aus.) escaping one's creditors by vanishing into the countryside. [SAusE *shingle-splitter*, a builder of houses, esp. in the outback]

Shinkin-ap-Morgan *n.* [mid-17C–mid-18C] a generic nickname for any Welshman (cf. TAFFY n.[1]). [a stereotypical Welsh name, lit. 'Jenkins son of Morgan']

Shinner *n.* [1920s+] a member of the Irish nationalist movement Sinn Fein.

shinny *n.* [1930s] (US Black) illegally distilled alcohol (cf. SHINE n.[1]).

shino *n.* [mid-19C–1910s] money. [SHINE n.[2] + RHINO]

shin off *v.* [late 19C] (US) to run away, to abscond (cf. TIN-SHIN-OFF).

shin out *v.* [mid-late 19C] to pay up (one's share, one's debts). [ext. of SHIN v.]

shinplaster *n.* **1** [mid-19C+] (US) a banknote (cf. BALM OF GILEAD). **2** [late 19C–1920s] (Can.) a 21-cent note. **3** [20C] (Aus.) a promissory note. [SE *shinplaster*, a square piece of paper saturated with vinegar etc, used as a plaster for sore legs. Like a number of terms for money, it 'cures one's ills']

shinrapper *n.* [19C] (prison/Und.) the prison treadmill (cf. SHINSCRAPER). [its knocking against the shins of the 'walker']

shinscraper *n.* [mid-late 19C] (prison/Und.) the treadmill (cf. COCKCHAFER). [for ety. *see* SHINRAPPER]

shin stage *n.* [18C] walking, travelling on foot (cf. SHANKS'S PONY). [SE *shin* + *stage-coach*]

shints *n.* [1990s] (US teen) one's possessions. [? corruption of posse*ss*ions]

shiny/shiney, the *n.* [mid-late 19C] money (cf. SHINE n.[2]; SHINERS n.[1]). [glittering coins]

shiny and bright *adj.* [20C] all right. [rhy. sl.]

shiny Bob *n.* [1920s+] (Aus.) one who has a very high opinion of themselves. [SE *shiny* + BOB n.[2]]

shiny-bum *v.* [1940s] (Aus.) to hold down a desk job. [SE *shiny* + BUM n.[2]; one's bottom polishes the seat]

ship *v.* [20C] (US Und.) to move or to be moved from one prison to another (cf. CATCH THE CHAIN).

ship in full sail *n.* [mid-19C] a pot of ale. [rhy. sl.]

ship-moll/shippie *n.* [1960s+] (N.Z.) a prostitute who works on docked ships; a descendant of the 19C Maori *ship-girl*. [SE *ship* + MOLL n. (2)]

ship out *v.* [20C] (orig. milit.) to leave, to depart.

shippie *see* SHIP-MOLL.

ship under sale *n.* [1930s] a story used for begging or for a confidence trick. [rhy. sl. *ship under sale* = tale]

ship-wrecked *adj.* [late 19C–1900s] drunk (cf. BASTED).

shipyards *n.* [20C] (Ulster) large feet or shoes. [joc. ref. to the Cammell-Laird shipyards, Belfast]

shiralee *n.* [late 19C+] (Aus.) a bundle of blankets or personal belongings (cf. SWAG n.[1]). [ety. unknown]

shirk/sherk *n.* [mid-17C–mid-18C] **1** a sponger, a parasite. **2** a cheating gamester. [SHARK n., but cf. 17C SE *shirk*, to practise fraud or trickery, esp. instead of working, to sponge upon others]

shirl *n.* [1970s] (Aus.) the female counterpart of the OCKER (cf. OCKERINA). [the proper name *Shirley*]

shirt collar/shirt and collar *n.* [mid-19C–1930s] 5 shillings (25p) (cf. OXFORD SCHOLAR). [rhy. sl. *shirt collar* = DOLLAR n.[1]]

shirtlifter *n.* [1960s+] (orig. Aus.) a male homosexual. [i.e. before sodomy]

shirtsleeves and shirt-sleeves *phr.* [late 19C] a phr. that distinguishes real work ('shirtsleeves') from idling ('shirt-sleeves'). ['the first are rolled up to the shoulders ... (the second) are fair, white and smooth, and only displayed, as a rule, at the cuff' (Ware)]

shirt-stretcher *n.* [1990s] the female breast.

shirt-tail *adj.* [20C] (US) impoverished, deprived, mean. [one's shirt-tail is (fig.) hanging out]

shirt-tail relation *n.* [20C] (US) a distant relation, a family friend (cf. BUTTONHOLE COUSIN).

shirty *adj.* [mid-19C+] irritable, angry, tetchy. [GET ONE'S SHIRT OUT phr.[1]]

shiser *see* SHICER.

shish *see* SHICE.

shista *n.* [1990s] (US Black) a crooked lawyer. [SHYSTER]

shit *n.*[1] [early 18C+] **1** excrement. **2** an act of defecation. [OE *scite*/MLG *Schite*, dung + OE *scitte*, diarrhoea; SE 14C–late 17C, henceforth sl.]

shit *n.*[2] [late 19C+] a contemptible person; often in combs., e.g. *little shit*, *dumb shit* (cf. ARSEHOLE n.). [prior use SE since early 16C; Florio (1598) includes a *shitten fellow*, which he defines as synon. with *goodman turd*]

shit *n.*[3] [1930s+] (orig. US Black) a general abstract term, a thing, a situation, an opinion or idea, the precise meaning varies as to the context, e.g. *I don't like this shit*, I don't like what's happening, *woofing some crazy shit*, talking nonsense etc.

shit *n.*[4] **1** [1930s+] any inferior, rubbishy, shoddy or pretentious thing. **2** [1930s+] problems, difficulties; thus *hit the shit*, to get into trouble. **3** [1950s+] nothing; thus *not mean shit*, not matter, not mean anything, *not worth shit*, not worth anything (cf. BULLSHIT n.; FUCK-ALL). **4** [1960s+] abuse, offensive and contemptuous treatment, e.g. to *take a lot of shit*, *don't take any shit*.

shit *n.*[5] [1940s+] (drugs) drugs in general, esp. heroin, cannabis. [the 'guilty' image of drug use]

shit *n.*[6] [1950s+] one's possessions, one's actions, one's life; thus *get one's shit together*, to assemble or tidy one's possessions, fig. to work out one's life.

shit, the *n.*[7] [1960s+] (US Black/campus) of things or people, the best, the ideal, the ultimate.

shit, the *n.*[8] [1960s+] (orig. US) a general intensifier, e.g. *who the shit are you? let's get the shit out of here*. [note synon. uses of the stronger FUCK n.[3] and the milder HELL phr.]

shit, the *n.*[9] [1980s+] (US campus) an important person (in their own opinion) (cf. KING SHIT).

shit *n.*[10] [1980s+] (US Und.) any form of weapon.

shit *adj.* [1930s+] (orig. US) applied to any thing or person considered bad, obnoxious, unpleasant, inferior, worthless, e.g. a *shit teacher*. [SHIT n.[1] (1)]

shit *v.*[1] [late 18C+] to defecate. [SHIT n.[1] (1)]

shit *v.*[2] [late 19C] to vomit. [abbr. SHIT THROUGH ONE'S TEETH phr. (1)]

shit *v.*[3] [1930s+] to deceive, to bamboozle, to tell lies, to exaggerate, to respond dramatically, with alarm, fear, anger, e.g. *he'll shit himself when he hears this*. [abbr. BULLSHIT v.]

shit! *excl.* [20C] an excl. of fury, irritation, disappointment. [SHIT n.[1] (1)]

shit a brick/bricks, to *phr.* **1** [late 19C+] to defecate after a lengthy period of constipation. **2** [1950s+] to tremble with extreme fear (cf. HAVE A SHIT HAEMORRHAGE). [SHIT v.[1] + fig. use of SE *brick*/*bricks*]

shit a brick! *excl.* [1950s+] (orig. Aus.) an excl. of extreme surprise, annoyance. [SHIT v.[1]]

shit-all *see* FUCK-ALL.

shit and derision! *excl.* [20C] a general excl. of annoyance. [SHIT n.[1] (1)]

shit and wish *phr.* [20C] (US Black) a general retort to anyone who says 'I wish ...' . [SHIT v.[1]; 18C phr. 'shit in one hand and wish in the other; see which fills up first']

shit ass/arse *n.* [20C] (US) a contemptible person. [SHIT n.[1] (1) + ARSE n.[1]]

shit-ass/-arse *adj.* [20C] (orig. US) very bad. [SHIT ASS n.]

shit-ass/arse *v.* [20C] (US) to behave obnoxiously, unfairly or reprehensibly towards another. [SHIT ASS n.]

shitbag *n.* **1** [late 19C–1910s] the stomach. **2** [late 19C+] (orig. Aus.) a general pej. term, whether of people or things. **3** [1990s] (US Black/teen) a colostomy bag. [SHIT n.[1] (1) + SE *bag*]

shitbird *n.*[1] [1950s+] a general term of abuse (cf. SHIT-FOR-BRAINS; SHITHEAD; SHIT-HEEL). [SHIT n.[1] (1) + BIRD n.[2]]

shitbird *n.*[2] [1950s+] a narcotic drug abuser, a heroin addict. [SHIT n.[5] + BIRD n.[2]]

shit-box *n.* [1990s] the anus. [SHIT n.[1] (1) + SE *box*]

shit bricks *see* SHIT A BRICK.

shit bullets *v.* [20C] to be terrified (cf. SHIT A BRICK; SWEAT BULLETS). [SHIT v.[1] + SE *bullets*]

shit cake baker *n.* [1990s] an absolutely repellent, unappealing person. [SHIT n.[1] (1)]

shitcan *v.* **1** [1950s+] (Aus.) to do someone a wrong. **2** [1970s+] (Aus./US) to stop, to abandon a course of action, to toss away. [SHIT n.[1] (1) + CAN n.[1]]

shit-/poop-catchers *n.* [1930s] (Aus.) knickerbockers. [SHIT n.[1] (1)/POOP n.[2] (1) + SE *catchers*]

shit-chute *n.* [20C] the anus (cf. DIRT CHUTE). [SHIT n.[1] (1) + SE *chute*]

shit comes in piles *phr.* [1990s] (US Black) problems always come at the same time, rather than one by one. [SHIT n.[4] (2)]

shit creek *n.* [1950s+] an unpleasant, problematic situation (cf. UP SHIT CREEK WITHOUT A PADDLE). [fig use of SHIT n.[1] (1) + SE *creek*]

shit detail *n.* [1940s+] (orig. milit.) any unpleasant or dirty task. [SHIT adj. + SE *detail*, a job]

shit-disturber *n.* [20C] a malicious gossip (cf. SHIT-STIRRER). [SHIT n.[4]]

shite *n.* [late 19C+] **1** a derog. form of address. **2** rubbish, nonsense. [var. on SHIT and combs.; before 1990s usu. found in dial. and often put into the mouths of those a writer is attempting to portray as Irish. For no discernible reason it is now often found in place of the more usu. SHIT n.[1] and n.[4]]

shit-eating grin *n.* [1950s+] (orig. US) a smug, self-satisfied smile (cf. SEG n.[3]). [SHIT n.[1] (1)]

shitefire *n.* [17C] a braggart, a boaster. [lit. trans. of CACAFUEGO]

shit, eh! *excl.* [1950s+] (Aus.) an excl. of moderate astonishment or irony. [SHIT!]

shitehawk *n.* [1970s+] a person of little worth (cf. GOBSHITE).

shite-poke *n.* [late 19C+] (Can.) the bittern. [its habit of defecating when frightened]

shiter *n.* [1950s+] **1** the anus (cf. SHITTER). **2** a general term of abuse. [SHIT v.[1]]

shitface *n.*[1] [1960s+] an unpleasant, distasteful person. [SHIT n.[1] (1) + SE *face*]

shitface *n.*[2] [1960s+] a drunken party. [SHITFACED]

shitface *adv.* [1960s+] extremely drunk, usu. *shitface drunk*. [SHITFACED]

shitfaced *adj.* [1960s+] (orig. US) very drunk (cf. FACED adj.[2]). [SHIT n.[1] (1) + SE *faced*]

shitfit *n.* [1990s] (US) an emotional outburst. [SHIT n.[4] + SE *fit*]

shit-for-brains *n.* [1970s+] an all-purpose insult (cf. SHITBIRD n.[1]). [SHIT n.[1] (1) + SE *brains*]

shit green *v.* [1960s+] (US) **1** to be extremely shocked. **2** to be enraged. [SHIT v.[1]]

shit happens *phr.* [1980s+] an all-purpose statement of resignation in the face of life's vicissitudes, i.e. these things happen. [SHIT n.[3]]

shithead *n.* [20C] a derog. term of general abuse (cf. SHITBIRD n.[1]). [SHIT n.[1] (1) + sfx. -HEAD (1)]

shitheap *n.* [20C] a dirty, unpleasant, disgusting place. [SHIT n.[1] (1) + SE *heap*]

shit-heel *n.* [20C] (US) **1** a generally derog. term of abuse (cf. SHITBIRD n.[1]). **2** (Und.) an informer. [SHIT n.[1] (1) + HEEL n. (2)]

shithole *n.* **1** [19C+] a lavatory. **2** [19C+] the anus. **3** [1960s+] a general term of hostility. [SHIT n.[1] (1) + SE *hole*]

shithook *n.* [1960s+] (orig. US campus) **1** a foolish, clumsy person. **2** an unpleasant, aggressive individual. [SHIT n.[1] (1) + SE *hook*; note US milit. use *shithook*, CH-47 'Chinook' helicopter]

shit-hot *adj.* [1910s+] excellent, fashionable. [SHIT n.[1] (1) + SE *hot*]

shit-hot *adv.* [1910s+] extremely, superlatively, especially. [SHIT n.[1] (1) + SE *hot*]

shithouse *n.* **1** [20C] a lavatory. **2** [20C] any dirty, messy, disgusting place. **3** [20C] an unpleasant person (cf. SHIT n.[2]). **4** [1990s] (orig. Aus.) a bad situation. [SHIT n.[1] + SE *house*]

shithouse *adj.* [20C] unpleasant, disgusting, filthy, messy. [SHITHOUSE n.]

shithouse full *n.* [20C] (US) a very large number or amount. [SHITHOUSE + SE *full*]

shit-hunter *n.* [late 19C–1900s] a sodomite. [SHIT n.[1] (1) + SE *hunter*]

shit in high cotton, to *phr.* [1930s+] (US) to live prosperously, to feel happy, to be important; euph. alternatives incl. *fly in high cotton, live in high cotton, travel in high cotton* (cf. FART THROUGH SILK). [SHIT v.[1]; the wealth that comes from a high cotton crop]

shit in high grass, to *phr.* [20C] (W.I.) to aim for or reach a higher social class than that to which one was born. [SHIT v.[1]]

shit in one's own backyard, to *phr.* [1950s+] (orig. US) to do anything that jeopardizes one's life by its proximity to one's personal, social or professional life, e.g. to steal from one's own workplace, to conduct an affair with an in-law. [SHIT v.[1]]

shit in your hat! *excl.* [20C] a general excl. of dismissal (cf. GO SHIT IN YOUR HAT!). [SHIT v.[1]]

shit in your teeth! *excl.* [18C–mid-19C] a general excl. of dismissal (cf. EAT SHIT!). [SHIT v.[1]]

shit it *v.* [1950s+] to be terrified. [abbr. SHIT A BRICK]

shit jacket *n.* [1970s] (US Black) an outside lavatory. [SHIT n.[1] (1) + SE *jacket*]

shitkick *v.* [1990s] (US) to beat up, to kill. [KICK THE SHIT OUT OF]

shitkicker *n.*[1] [20C] a shoe or boot, esp. one used for everyday wear or work (cf. KICKERS). [SHIT n.[1] (1) + SE *kicker*]

shitkicker *n.*[2] [1960s+] **1** (US) a farmer or other country person. **2** (US) a fool, a person of meagre intelligence. **3** (Aus.) an unskilled labourer. **4** (US) a Western film (cf. HORSE OPERA). [for ety. *see* SHITKICKER n.[1]; their trudging through the fields or farmyard]

shitkicking *adj.* [1960s+] (US) rough, crude, rural. [SHIT-KICKER n.[2]]

shitkicking music *n.* [1960s+] (orig. US) music that makes the hearer want to get up and dance, shout, sing, generally have a good, boisterous time. [SHITKICKING + SE *music*]

shitlaw! *excl.* [1980s+] (US campus) a general excl. of annoyance (cf. SHIT!; FUCK!). [? *shit, Lord!*]

shit list/shitlist *n.* [1960s+] a list of people one considers distasteful, untrustworthy and otherwise unacceptable; thus *on my shit list*, very unpopular in my eyes. [SHIT n.[2] + SE *list*]

shit little blue cookies, to *phr.* [20C] to be utterly terrified (cf. SHIT A BRICK). [SHIT v.[1]]

shitload *n.* [1960s+] a great many, a large amount; thus *by the shitload*, in large amounts. [SHIT n.[1] (1) + SE *load*]

shit off *v.* [20C] **1** to annoy, to irritate. **2** to run away. [SHIT v.[1]]

shit on *adj.* [1960s+] humiliated. [SHIT ON v.]

shit on *v.* [late 19C+] to abuse, to humiliate. [fig. use of SHIT v.[1]]

shit on a shingle *n.* [1940s+] (mainly US milit.) minced beef on toast. [SHIT n.[1] (1) + SE *shingle*]

shit on a stick *n.* [1970s+] (US Black) a self-appointed tough guy, more words than action. [SHIT n.[1] (1) + SE *stick*]

shit on a string *n.* [1960s+] something extremely hard or impossible to do. [SHIT n.[1] (1) + SE *string*]

shit oneself *v.* [1960s+] to be terrified. [for ety. *see* SHIT ONE'S PANTS]

shit one's pants, to *phr.* [1960s+] to be terrified. [SHIT v.[1]; i.e. the effect of terror on the sphincter muscle]

shit on from a great height, to *phr.* [1920s+] (orig. RAF) to be extremely unpleasant, to make a great deal of trouble for someone else. [fig. use of SHIT v.[1]]

shit on one's own doorstep/backdoor *phr.* [late 19C+] used of one who foolishly has adulterous affairs within their circle of friends and acquaintances. [fig. use of SHIT v.[1]]

shit on wheels *n.* [1950s+] (orig. US) an important person, a person who thinks that they are important (cf. HOT SHIT n.). [SHIT n.[1] (1)]

shit on you! *excl.* [1960s+] (orig. US) a general term of abuse. [SHIT v.[1]]

shit or bust, to *phr.* [late 19C+] to make a last, absolute gamble (cf. GO FOR BROKE). [SHIT v.[1] + SE *burst*/BUST v.[2] (3)]

shit or get off the pot! *excl.* [1940s+] either make a decision or let someone else do it (cf. FISH OR CUT BAIT; SPIT OR GET OFF THE CUSPIDOR). [SHIT v.[1] + SE (chamber) *pot*]

shit out *v.* [1960s+] to behave as a coward, to run away from danger or confrontation (cf. CRAP OUT v.). [SHIT v.[1]]

shit out of luck *phr.* [20C] (US) at the end of one's good fortune, in serious trouble with no escape. [SHIT n.[1] (1)]

shit-pit *n.* [20C] a lavatory (cf. SHITHOUSE n.). [SHIT n.[1] (1) + SE *pit*]

shitpot *n.* [mid-19C–1910s+] an unpleasant person. [SHIT n.[1] (1) + SE *pot*; despite what should be a logical use of *shitpot*, to mean a commode or potty, none appears to exist]

shitpot *adj.* [1970s+] (Aus.) second-rate, inferior. [SHITPOT n.]

shit-ringer *n.* [1940s+] (Aus.) a stockman. [SHIT n.[1] (1) + SAusE *ringer*, a stockman]

shits, the *n.* [1940s+] **1** diarrhoea (cf. JIMMY BRITTS; TOMTITS). **2** anything objectionable or unpleasant. [SHIT n.[1] (1)]

shitsack *n.* **1** [late 18C+] a general pej., an unpleasant person. **2** [late 18C–mid-19C] a nonconformist. [fig. use of SHIT n.[1] (1) + SE *sack*; (2) the term was euphemized in 19C as *shick-shack* (also *shig-shag*; *sic-sac*; *shuck-shack*; *shiff-shack* etc). Orig. a term of abuse for people who were found not wearing the customary oak-apple or sprig of oak before noon on Royal-oak Day (29 May, commemorating Charles II's hiding in an oak tree). Such people would most likely be nonconformists or Puritans. That day became known in dial. as *Shick-shack Day* and the oak-apple or sprig of oak became known as *shick-shack*. If you wore your oak sprig after noon you became a *shick-shack*, a fool]

shit-scared *adj.* [20C] terrified (cf. POEP-SCARED). [SCARE THE SHIT OUT OF]

shit-shark *n.* [mid–late 19C] a night-soil collector. [SHIT n.[1] (1) + SE *shark*]

shit-shoe/-shod *n.* [late 19C] one who has trodden in excrement. [SHIT n.[1] (1) + SE *shoe*/*shod*]

shit-skin *n.* [20C] a derog. term for a Black person. [SHIT n.[1] (1) + SE *skin*]

shit-stab *v.* [1960s+] to perform sodomy. [back-form. of SHIT-STABBER]

shit-stabber *n.* [1960s+] (orig. gay) **1** the penis (cf. ARSE-OPENER). **2** a male homosexual. [SHIT n.¹ (1) + SE *stabber*]

shitstain *n.* [1990s] (US) a fool. [SHIT n.¹ (1) + SE *stain*]

shit-stick *n.* (US) **1** (prison) a billy-club. **2** the penis, esp. when used for anal intercourse (cf. ARSE-OPENER). **3** a contemptible person. [SHIT n.¹ (1) + SE *stick*]

shit-stirrer *n.* [late 19C+] a malicious gossip (cf. SHIT-DISTURBER). [SHIT n.⁴ + SE *stirrer*]

shit stompers *n.* [1970s+] (US campus) **1** cowboy boots (cf. SHITKICKER n.¹). **2** cowboys (cf. SHITKICKER n.²). [SHIT n.¹ (1) + STOMPERS]

shit-stopper *n.* [1960s+] a prank, a funny scene, an escapade. [SHIT n.¹ (1) + SE *stopper*; the image of an event so dramatic or surprising that it suspends one's normal bodily processes]

shitstorm *n.* [20C] (US) a very confused situation. [SHIT n.¹ (1) + SE *storm*]

shitsure *adv.* [20C] (US) certainly, definitely. [SHIT n.¹ (1) + SE *sure*]

shitten!/shitting! *excl.* [16C] a general excl. of derision. [SE *shitten*, fouled with excrement; thus disgusting]

shitten Saturday *n.* [mid-19C] (mainly school/provincial) Easter Saturday. [mispron. of SE *shut-in Saturday*, referring to the day on which Christ's body was enclosed in his tomb]

shitter *n.¹* [20C] **1** the anus. **2** (US) a lavatory. **3** (Und.) a thief who likes to excrete inside the places he robs.

shitter *n.²* [1910s+] (orig. US) a braggart, a boaster. [abbr. BULLSHITTER]

shitters, the *n.¹* [late 19C+] diarrhoea (cf. SKITTERS; SQUITTERS). [SHIT v.¹]

shitters *n.²* [1940s] (Aus.) cattle. [SHIT v.¹; i.e. the state of the average cowyard]

shit the bed! *excl.* [1990s] an excl. of surprise. [one's shock after having SHIT v.¹ *the bed*]

shit through one's teeth, to *phr.* **1** [late 18C+] to vomit. **2** [20C] to lie blatantly. [SHIT v.¹ + SE *teeth*]

shitting! *see* SHITTEN!

shittle-cum-shaw!/shittle-cum-shite!/shittletidee! *excl.* [late 19C] a general excl. of annoyance. [SE *shittle*, inconstant, fickle, flighty]

shitty *n.* [1960s+] (Aus.) a fit of temper. [SHITTY adj. (5)]

shitty *adj.* **1** [1920s+] unpleasant, disgusting. **2** [1920s+] (US) mean, malicious, nasty. **3** [1920s+] (US) tedious, futile. **4** [1920s+] (US) unwell, ill. **5** [1960s+] (Aus.) bad-tempered. [SHIT n.¹ (1)]

shit weighs heavy *phr.* [late 19C+] (Can.) a phr. used of a braggart. [SHIT n.⁴]

shit where one eats, to *phr.* [20C] (orig. US) to commit a crime in one's own neighbourhood. [SHIT v.¹]

shitwork *n.* [1960s+] unpleasant, unwanted, probably dirty occupations. [SHIT adj. + SE *work*]

shiv/sheive/shive *n.* **1** [early 18C+] a knife. **2** [1930s+] (US tramp) a razor. [CHIV n.¹]

shivaree *n.¹* *see* SHIVOO n.

shivaree *n.²* [1920s+] verbose official talk. [SHIVOO n.; but more likely euph. for SHIT n.⁴ (3)]

shivaree *v.* *see* SHIVOO v.

shivaroo *see* SHIVOO.

shive *see* SHIV.

shiveau *see* SHIVOO.

shivering James/Jemmy *n.* [mid–late 19C] a beggar who parades in rags and tatters in the hope of attracting greater sympathy. [SE *shivering* + generic *James/Jemmy*]

shiver my timbers! *excl.* [late 18C+] a general excl.; given its nautical origin, the phr. is usu. found when a stereotypical 'old salt' needs to be conjured up.

Shivery Isles *n.* [1930s–50s] (Aus.) New Zealand (cf. SHAKY ISLES). [the frequency of earthquakes]

shivoo/shivaree/shivaroo/shiveau *n.* [mid-19C+] (Aus.) a party, a celebration. [Fr. *chez vous*, at your house]

shivoo/shivaree/shivaroo/shiveau *v.* [mid-19C+] (Aus.) to entertain. [SHIVOO n.]

shiznit *n.* [1990s] (US Black) the ultimate, the best. [ext. of SHIT n.⁷]

shlamozzle *see* SHEMOZZLE.

shlang *see* SCHLONG.

shlanter *see* SLANTER.

shlemiel *see* SCHLEMIEL.

shlemozzle *n.¹* *see* SCHLEMAZEL.

shlemozzle *n.²* *see* SHEMOZZLE n.

shlinter *see* SLANTER.

shlock *see* SCHLOCK.

shloep *see* SCHLOEP.

shlong/schlontz *see* SCHLONG.

shloomp *see* SCHLOOMP n.

shloop *see* SCHLOEP.

shlub/shlubbo *see* SCHLUB.

shlump *see* SCHLOOMP n.

shmaltz *see* SCHMALTZ.

shmaltzy *see* SCHMALTZY.

shmatte *see* SCHMATTE.

shmear *n.¹* *see* SCHMEER n.¹.

shmear *n.²* *see* SCHMEAR n.².

shmear *v.* *see* SCHMEER v.

shmeck/shmee *see* SCHMECK.

shmeez *v.* [1980s+] (US drugs) to smoke good cannabis.

shmegeggy *see* SCHMEGEGGE.

shmendrick *see* SCHMENDRICK.

shmo/shmoe *see* SCHMO.

shmooser *see* SCHMOOZER.

shmooze *see* SCHMOOZE.

shmotte *see* SCHMATTE.

shmuck *see* SCHMUCK.

shnide *see* SNIDE adj.

shock a broe/brew *n.* [1980s+] (US campus) an invitation to have a beer. [Hawaiian pidgin *shaka brah*, right on, brother; but note BREW n.¹ (3)]

shock-absorbers *n.* [1950s+] the female breasts.

shocker *n.* [1920s] an appalling person or situation.

shocker! *excl.* [1990s] (US campus) an ironic excl., that's not remotely surprising.

shock house *n.* [late 19C] (US) a tavern, catering mainly to Black people, in which customers would most likely be given some form of knock-out drop in their drink and then robbed.

shocking *adj.* [mid-19C] a general intensifier, e.g. *a shocking bad hat*, a very unpleasant person.

shockingly *adv.* [late 18C–late 19C] a general intensifier.

shocks for jocks *n.* [1960s+] (US campus) a course in introductory engineering (cf. AIDS FOR GRADES). [SE *shocks* + JOCK n.⁵]

shod all round *phr.* **1** [18C–19C] *au fait* with the niceties of married life. **2** [late 18C–early 19C] a phr. used of a parson at a funeral who receives a hat-band, gloves and scarf. [SE *shod*, wearing shoes]

shoddy *adj.* [mid-19C] (US) used of those who either claim a degree of importance to which they have no actual right or of *nouveaux riches*, whose importance is not backed up by breeding or manners; thus *shoddydom*, the world of social climbers, also as *shoddies, shoddyites, shoddy aristocracy, shoddy society*. [SE *shoddy*, woollen yarn obtained by tearing to shreds refuse woollen rags, which, with the addition of some new wool, is made into a kind of cloth; thus, worthless material that is made to appear as if it boasts a higher quality. The term was used of people f. mid-19C. It was underlined after the US Civil War (1861–5), when fortunes were made by the sellers of shoddy, who then attempted to use their money to enter society]

shoddy-doo *n.* [1960s–70s] (US Black) any form of ritual hand-slapping that serves as a greeting or farewell. [? corruption of SE *how do you do*]

shoddy-dropper *n.* [1930s+] a hawker, a pedlar. [post-WW2 use mainly Aus./N.Z.; SE *shoddy* (for ety. *see* SHODDY adj.) + DROPPER n.⁵]

shoe *n.*¹ [20C] (US Und.) a private detective. [abbr. GUMSHOE n.]

shoe *n.*² **1** [1910s–30s] a tyre. **2** [1940s+] (Aus.) a sanitary towel.

shoe *n.*³ [1950s+] **1** (orig. US Black) a smartly dressed person. **2** (US campus) a highly acceptable person. [orig. jazz use; the quality of the subject's footwear]

shoebox *n.* [19C] a prison cell.

shoe-horn *v.* [17C] to cuckold. [? play on HORN n.²]

shoelaces *n.* [20C] (S.Afr. Black) chicken intestines, as used in cooking. [resemblance]

shoe-leather! *excl.* [mid-19C] (Und.) a warning cry uttered by a thief to their confederate on sighting the police. [i.e. get one's *shoe-leather* (shoes) moving]

shoemaker's pride *n.* [19C–20C] creaking shoes or boots. [new leather shoes often creak, thus drawing attention to the maker's handiwork]

shoemaker's stocks *n.* [late 17C–1900s] tight shoes; thus *in the shoemaker's stocks*, wearing tight shoes.

shoe one's mule, to *phr.* [mid-17C–early 18C] to embezzle (cf. SHOE THE HORSE). [? fig. use to which one puts the money]

shoes and sox *n.* [20C] venereal disease. [rhy. sl. *shoes and socks* = POX n.¹]

shoes on the mast *phr.* [late 19C] (orig. naut.) now is the time to 'let your hair down'. [18C naval custom of nailing a shoe to the mast as the ship neared the end of a long journey, it stood as a sign of relaxation of discipline]

shoestring *adj.* [20C] minimally funded, costing very little (cf. ON A SHOESTRING).

shoe the goose, to *phr.* [early 17C] to be drunk. [? the impossibility of such a task, other than to a drink-sodden mind]

shoe the horse, to *phr.* [1910s–20s] to cheat one's employer (cf. SHOE ONE'S MULE).

shoful/schoful/shofel/shovel/show-full *n.* **1** [mid-19C] counterfeit coins, sham jewellery. **2** [mid–late 19C] a humbug, an impostor. **3** [mid-19C–1900s] a low tavern. [Gk. thence Yid. *schofel*, worthless stuff, rubbish; ult. Ger.-Jewish pron. of Heb. *shāphāl*, low]

shofulman *n.* [mid–late 19C] one who passes counterfeit money. [SHOFUL + sfx. *-man*]

shoful-pitcher *n.* [mid-19C] a distributor of counterfeit money; thus *shoful-pitching*, passing counterfeit money (cf. SNIDE PITCHER). [SHOFUL + PITCHER n.³]

shoful-pullet *n.* [mid-19C] a spurious 'virgin' prostitute, whose maidenhead is miraculously renewed for each new client. [SHOFUL + PULLET]

shog *v.* [20C] to amble along. [synon. Yorks. dial.]

sholda than show *phr.* [1990s] (US Black) absolutely positive. [lit. 'surer than sure']

sholl *v.* [mid-19C–1900s] to crush someone's hat over their ears. [ety. unknown; link to SE *shell*, i.e. to turn the hat into a shell for the head]

shommus *see* SHAMUS.

shong *see* SHANGHAI n.¹.

shonk *n.* **1** [19C] a derog. term for a Jew. **2** [20C] the nose. [? SHONNICKER; note RN *shonky*, a miser whose meanness is typified by their like of drinking but unwillingness to stand a round]

shonky *adj.* [1970s+] (Aus./N.Z.) unreliable, dishonest,

'crooked'; thus one who is engaged in irregular or illegal business activities. [SHONK; SHONNICKER]

shonnicker *n.* [mid-19C+] a derog. term for a Jew. [Yid. *shonnicker*, a small trader or pedlar]

shont *n.* [late 19C–1910s] a foreigner. [? SHONK]

sho' 'nuff *adj.* [late 19C+] (US) a general term of approval, genuine, qualified, responsible, trustworthy. [SE *sure enough*]

sho' 'nuff *phr.* [late 19C+] (orig. US Black) yes indeed. [SE *sure enough*]

shoob *v.* [1950s+] (W.I. Rasta) to shove.

shoobie *n.* [20C] (US) a passenger on a day-trip excursion. [the *shoebox* in which they carry their lunch]

shoo-fly *n.* [late 19C+] (US Und.) **1** a plain-clothes police officer on observation duty. **2** an undercover police officer who spies on their colleagues. [song lyric 'Shoo fly! Don't bother me']

shoofty *see* SHUFTIE.

shoo-in *n.* [1930s+] a dead certainty, usu. in political use. [SE *shoo-in*, of a racehorse, an easy winner]

shook *adj.* **1** [19C] robbed, lost by robbery (cf. SHAKE v.²). **2** [early 19C+] forgetful, esp. used of an ex-prisoner whose mental state has been affected by prison or transportation (cf. ROCKED). **3** [late 19C+] (US) highly excited, disturbed, frightened, upset (cf. SHOOK UP).

shook on *adj.* [mid-19C+] (Aus./N.Z.) infatuated with, obsessed with. [SE *shake*, quiver, tremble (in this case with passion)]

shook one *n.* [1990s] a person who is scared, upset, emotionally unstable etc. [SHOOK adj. + SE *one*]

shook up *adj.* [late 19C+] upset, disturbed. [ext. of SHOOK adj.]

shool *n.* [late 19C] a place of worship. [adapted by Londoners from Yid. *shool*, a synagogue]

shool/shoole *v.* [late 18C–mid-19C] **1** to go begging. **2** to skulk around. **3** to impose upon someone. [SE *shoal*, to move as a shoal; thus the meanderings of a shoal of fish or dial. *shool*, to go about begging]

shooler/shoolman/shuler *n.* [mid-19C] a beggar and scrounger, a tramp. [SHOOL v.]

shoomer *n.* [1980s] a fan of acid house music (cf. ACID HOUSE PARTY). [London's *Shoom* club, which was at its most popular *c.*1988]

shoon *n.* [late 19C–1900s] a fool. [ety. unknown]

shoop *v.* [1990s] (US Black) to have sexual intercourse. [? echoic]

shooper *see* SHUPER.

shoo-shoo *v.* [19C–1940s] (US Black) to whisper; thus *shoo!*, be quiet. [SE *ssh*, quiet, be quiet]

Shoot, the *n.* [1900s] **1** Walworth Road station, London. **2** Walthamstow, London. [SE *rubbish-shoot*, both areas were associated with the poor or with menial workers]

shoot/shoot dead *v.*¹ [late 19C] (Aus.) to dismiss from a job.

shoot *v.*² [late 19C+] to leave, esp. as imper. [abbr. SHOOT OFF v.¹]

shoot *v.*³ [late 19C+] **1** of a man, to have sexual intercourse (cf. BANG v.¹; SHOOT IN THE BUSH; SHOOT IN THE TAIL). **2** to ejaculate. [the equation of sex and violence]

shoot *v.*⁴ [1900s–10s] (Aus.) to give, to pay for.

shoot *v.*⁵ [1910s+] to hurry someone along, to send someone quickly to a place.

shoot *v.*⁶ [1910s+] (drugs) to inject a narcotic, usu. in comb. with the drug, e.g. *shoot smack*, inject heroin, *shoot coke*, inject cocaine (cf. SHOOT UP v.²).

shoot! *excl.*¹ [20C] an excl. of annoyance or surprise. [euph. for SHIT!]

shoot! *excl.*² [1910s+] (US) go on! go ahead! get on with it! esp. as regards telling a story, delivering a piece of gossip etc (cf. SHOOT v.⁵).

shoot a/the bishop, to *phr.* [late 19C–1910s] to have a nocturnal emission, a 'wet dream' (cf. BANG THE BISHOP).

shoot a blank, to *phr.* [1950s–60s] (US) to fail, to have no luck.

shoot a bone *see* FLAG A BONE.

shoot a card, to *phr.* [1900s–20s] to leave a visiting card.

shoot a cat, to *phr.* [1980s+] (society) to vomit. [ext. of CAT v.[1]]

shoot a dud *see* SHOOT BLANKS v.[1].

shoot a good shot, to *phr.* [1970s+] (US Black) to defeat someone in a verbal contest, e.g. DOZENS.

shoot a hook, to *phr.* [mid-19C+] (US) to truant from school. [PLAY HOOKEY]

shoot/run a line, to *phr.* [1940s+] to concoct a smooth patter with the specific aim of seduction (cf. SPILL A LINE). [SE *shoot* + LINE n.[1] (3)]

shoot a lion, to *phr.* [19C] to urinate (cf. KILL A SNAKE).

shoot/make an eyeball, to *phr.* [1970s] (US) to look at, to see.

shoot a paper-bolt, to *phr.* [1910s–20s] to circulate a false or dubious rumour.

shoot back *v.* [1970s+] (orig. US) to respond, to riposte.

shoot balls *v.* [20C] (W.I.) to talk nonsense (cf. SHOOT BULL; SHOOT SHIT). [BALLS n.[2]]

shoot between/betwixt wind and water, to *phr.* [late 17C–1900s] **1** of a man, to have sexual intercourse. **2** to infect with venereal disease. [for ety. *see* SHOT BETWEEN WIND AND WATER]

shoot blanks/a dud, to *v.*[1] [1970s+] (US Black) to engage in idle conversation, to use words that have no 'target'.

shoot blanks *v.*[2] [1980s+] of a man, to fail to achieve an erection, to be impotent (cf. FIRE A BLANK).

shoot bull *v.* [20C] (W.I.) to talk nonsense (cf. SHOOT BALLS). [BULLSHIT n.]

shoot dead *see* SHOOT v.[1].

shoot down/down in flames *v.* [1930s+] **1** to reject an invitation to dance or go for a date. **2** to humiliate, to ridicule. **3** to reject a line of argument, to overrule an opinion.

shoot-'em-up *n.* [1950s+] (orig. US Black) a Hollywood Western film. [the predominant on-screen activity]

shooter *n.*[1] **1** [early 19C+] (Und.) a gun, a revolver. **2** [20C] (gambling) the player currently throwing the dice in a game of craps.

shooter *n.*[2] [1970s+] (US) a measure of spirits, esp. whisky. [SHOT n.[5] (1)]

shooter's hill *n.* [19C] the vagina (cf. ALLEY n.[1]; TAKE A TURN ON SHOOTER'S HILL). [play on the proper name, but note SHOOT v.[3]]

shoot-flier *n.* [late 19C–1930s] (Und.) a thief who specializes in snatching wallets, watches and similar small items. [SHOOT-FLY]

shoot-fly *n.* [late 19C–1930s] (Und.) the robbery of watches, wallets and similar small personal items.

shoot for *v.* [1960s+] to aim for, to target, often as *shooting for*, e.g. *he's got 50 runs and now he's shooting for a century.*

shoot for the moon, to *phr.* [1990s] to masturbate (cf. SHOOT ONE'S SQUIRT; SHOOT SKEET; SHOOT TADPOLES).

shoot for the sky, to *phr.* [20C] (gambling) to bet one's entire funds against one's opponent's entire funds.

shoot from the hip, to *phr.* [1950s+] to attack a problem head-on, to be a tough, purposeful performer. [Western film imagery]

shoot gravy *v.* [1950s+] (drugs) for a narcotics addict to reinject the blood that has been drawn into the syringe and there mixed with the heroin solution. [SHOOT v.[6] + GRAVY n.[3] (2)]

shoot hoop/some hoop *v.* [1950s+] (US Black/campus) to play basketball.

shooting/shooting up *n.*[1] [1950s+] (drugs) injecting a narcotic drug. [SHOOT UP v.[2]]

shooting *n.*[2] [1960s–70s] (US Black) aggressive, provocative talk, often leading to a fight.

shooting gallery/gallery *n.* [1950s+] (drugs) a place, often an apartment or an abandoned building, used by a number of heroin addicts to take the drug (cf. BASING GALLERY). [pun on SE, the fairground sideshow]

shooting iron *n.* **1** [late 18C+] a pistol or gun. **2** [19C] (US) the penis (cf. GUN n.[2]).

shooting stick *n.* [19C] **1** the penis (cf. GUN n.[2]). **2** a gun. [play on SE + (1) SHOOT v.[3] + STICK n.[1]; (2) STICK n.[3]]

shoot in my boot! *excl.* [1990s] (Can.) an expression of great joy. [? SHOOT v.[3] (2) + redup.]

shoot in the bush, to *phr.* [1950s+] to have sexual intercourse. [SHOOT v.[3] + BUSH n.[4] (1)]

shoot in the eye, to *phr.* [late 19C] to do someone a bad turn.

shoot in the stubble, to *phr.* [18C–19C] to have sexual intercourse; thus *shoot over the stubble*, to ejaculate prematurely, and outside the vagina (cf. TAKE A TURN IN THE STUBBLE). [SHOOT v.[3] + STUBBLE]

shoot in the tail, to *phr.* [mid-19C+] to have anal intercourse. [SHOOT v.[3] + TAIL n.[1] (3)]

shoot into the brown, to *phr.* [late 19C–1910s] (orig. milit.) to fail. [in rifle practice the outermost part of the target, denoting a 'miss', is brown; but note shooting jargon *into the brown*, an indiscriminate blast into the heart of a covey of passing birds. By extension this was used by sporting officers of firing into a large group of advancing (brown-uniformed) troops]

shoot jokes/jokes on *v.* [1970s+] (US Black) to belittle, to tease aggressively (cf. SHOOT ON).

shoot London Bridge, to *phr.* [early 18C] to have sexual intercourse. [? a nonce usage in Ned Ward (1700), punningly describing a 'buttocking brimstone' who could 'show you how the Watermen shoot London Bridge or how the lawyers go to Westminster']

shoot off *v.*[1] [late 19C+] to leave quickly. [ext. of SHOOT v.[2]]

shoot off *v.*[2] [1960s+] to ejaculate. [ext. of SHOOT v.[3] (2)]

shoot off at the mouth, to *phr.* [mid-19C+] (US) to boast, to brag.

shoot off one's face, to *phr.* [late 19C+] (US) to talk effusively (cf. SHOOT ONE'S MOUTH OFF).

shoot on *v.* [1970s+] (US Black) to mock, to tease, to discredit (cf. SHOOT JOKES).

shoot one's best mack, to *phr.* [1970s+] (US Black) to make an all-out effort at seduction by one's persuasive conversation. [SE *shoot* + MACK n.[1]; MACKING]

shoot one's bolt, to *phr.* [20C] to give everything one has, to be incapable of further effort.

shoot one's cookies, to *phr.* [1970s+] (US campus) to vomit. [SE *shoot* + COOKIES n.[2]]

shoot one's cuff, to *phr.* [late 19C] to dress up as smartly as one can and generally present oneself in the most positive way possible. [the 'shooting' of the cuffs – making them project fashionably beyond the jacket sleeves – that is indulged in by the well-dressed]

shoot oneself in the foot, to *phr.* [20C] (orig. US) to blunder so that one harms oneself or exposes oneself to further hardship.

shoot one's face, to *phr.* [20C] (US) to make a fuss (cf. SHOOT ONE'S MOUTH OFF).

shoot one's grandmother/granny, to *phr.* **1** [mid-19C] to announce as news something that is long since well known (cf. TEACH ONE'S GRANDMOTHER TO SUCK EGGS). **2** [mid-19C+] to make a mistake, to be disappointed.

shoot one's linen, to *phr.* [late 19C] to shoot one's cuffs.

shoot one's load, to *phr.* [1920s+] to ejaculate (cf. BLOW ONE'S LOAD). [LOAD n.[4] (2)]

shoot one's milt, to *phr.* [mid-19C–1910s] to ejaculate (cf. SHOOT ONE'S ROE). [SE *milt*, seed]

shoot one's mouth off/off one's mouth, to *phr.* [mid-19C+] (orig. US) **1** to talk, esp. in a loud or boastful way. **2** to betray secrets.

shoot one's roe, to *phr.* [mid-19C–1900s] to ejaculate (cf. SHOOT ONE'S MILT). [SE *roe*, seed]

shoot one's squirt, to *phr.* [1990s] to masturbate (cf. SHOOT FOR THE MOON).

shoot one's star, to *phr.*[1] [late 19C–1900s] to die.

shoot one's star, to *phr.*[2] [1970s] (US Black) **1** to perform anal intercourse. **2** to arrest a homosexual. [SE *star*, its shape supposedly resembling the anus]

shoot one's wad, to *phr.*[1] [1920s+] (orig. US) to ejaculate. [SHOOT v.[3] (2) + WAD n.[3]]

shoot one's wad, to *phr.*[2] [1920s+] **1** (orig. US) to spend all one's money. **2** (orig. US) to exhaust oneself. **3** (US) to commit or bet everything one has, to say all one has to say. [WAD n.[1]]

shoot-out *n.* [1960s+] **1** a gun battle. **2** a decisive confrontation.

shoot out one's marbles, to *phr.* [1970s] (US Black) to go crazy (cf. LOSE ONE'S MARBLES).

shoot over *v.* [20C] to go quickly to a place.

shoot shit *v.* [20C] to talk nonsense (cf. SHOOT BALLS). [SE *shoot* + SHIT n.[4]]

shoot skeet *v.* [1990s] to masturbate (cf. SHOOT FOR THE MOON).

shoot skin *v.* [1950s+] (drugs) to miss the vein when one is injecting heroin or another narcotic. [SHOOT v.[6] + SE *skin*]

shoot some hoop *see* SHOOT HOOP.

shoot straight/straight from the shoulder *v.* [20C] to talk openly or candidly.

shoot tadpoles/the tadpoles *v.* [20C] to masturbate (cf. SHOOT FOR THE MOON). [SHOOT v.[3] (2) + the tadpole-like shape of sperm]

shoot that! *excl.* [late 19C–1900s] be quiet! shut up!

shoot that hat! *excl.* [mid-19C] (US) a mild oath (cf. SHOOT! excl.[1]).

shoot the agate, to *phr.* [20C] (US Black) to walk jauntily with one's thumbs extended. [the extension of the thumb when playing marbles]

shoot the beaver, to *phr.* [1960s+] **1** of a man, to look under a woman's skirt in the hope of seeing pubic hair or her vagina (cf. SHOOT THE SQUIRREL). **2** of a woman, to display one's genitals, usu. while otherwise dressed. [SE *shoot* + BEAVER n.[4]]

shoot the bishop *see* SHOOT A BISHOP.

shoot the bone *see* FLAG A BONE.

shoot the boots off, to *phr.* [20C] (Ulster) to wipe out, lit. or fig.

shoot the breeze, to *phr.*[1] [1940s+] (orig. US) to gossip, to talk idly (cf. BACK THE BREEZE).

shoot the breeze, to *phr.*[2] [1960s+] (drugs) to inhale nitrous oxide.

shoot the bull, to *phr.* [1930s+] to gossip, to chat (cf. SHOOT THE SHIT). [SE *shoot* + BULLSHIT n.]

shoot the cat, to *phr.* [late 18C+] to vomit (cf. CAT v.[1]; JERK THE CAT; WHIP THE CAT phr.[1]).

shoot the chimney, to *phr.* [late 19C] (US) to be quiet, to stop talking. [*shoot*, to discard, to get rid of + ? SE *chimney* to mean throat]

shoot the crow, to *phr.* [19C] (Scot.) to leave. [ety. unknown; earlier, pre-1930s, use implied departure without paying, but that meaning appears to have fallen away]

shoot the dozens *see* PLAY THE DOZENS.

shoot the gift, to *phr.* [1990s] (US Black) to gossip, to talk idly (cf. SHOOT THE SHIT). [SE *shoot* + GIFT OF THE GAB]

shoot the gulf, to *phr.* [mid-17C–mid-18C] to succeed in a very hard task, to achieve the impossible. [? according to Daniel Defoe, *A Voyage Round the World*, 1725: 'Such a mighty and valuable thing also was the passing this strait [the Straits of Magellan] that Sir Francis Drake's going through it gave birth to that famous old wives' saying viz., that Sir Francis Drake shot the gulf; ... as if there had been but one gulf in the world']

shoot/drag the gut, to *phr.* [1960s+] (US teen) to drive up and down the main street. [SE *shoot*/DRAG v.[11] + GUT n.[4]]

shoot the lights, to *phr.* [1950s+] of a motorist, to accelerate away from traffic lights before they have properly changed from red or amber to green. [model of SE *shoot the rapids*]

shoot the lights out, to *phr.* [20C] (US) to excel, to perform outstandingly.

shoot the marbles from all sides of the ring, to *phr.* [1930s–40s] (US Black) to be in a very dangerous situation.

shoot/bolt the moon, to *phr.* [mid-19C+] to abscond from a house or flat, taking one's furniture and possessions but avoiding payment of any outstanding rent, utility bills etc (cf. SHOVE THE MOON).

shoot the pill/peel, to *phr.* [1980s+] (US campus) to shoot baskets, to play a pick-up game of basketball. [SE *shoot* + PILL n.[1] (2)]

shoot the regular, to *phr.* [1970s+] (US Black) to chatter on in the usual, predictable manner. [SHIT n.[3] is unspoken]

shoot the shit, to *phr.* [1930s+] to gossip, to chat (cf. SHOOT THE BULL). [SE *shoot* + BULLSHIT n.]

shoot the squirrel, to *phr.* [1970s+] (US campus) to catch a glimpse of a woman's panties or pubic hair (cf. SHOOT THE BEAVER). [SE *shoot* + SQUIRREL n.[5] (1)]

shoot the tadpoles *see* SHOOT TADPOLES.

shoot the thrill, to *phr.* [1970s] (US Black) to lead a promiscuous and varied sex life.

shoot the works, to *phr.* [1920s+] (US) to commit oneself absolutely, to make every effort no matter what the cost (cf. GO FOR BROKE).

shoot through *v.* [1940s+] (Aus./N.Z.) to leave, to exit quickly.

shoot/go through like a Bondi tram, to *phr.* [1940s+] (Aus.) to leave very quickly, to run off. [SHOOT THROUGH + *Bondi tram*, a tram running through a suburb in Sydney]

shoot through the grease, to *phr.* [1950s–60s] (US Black) to let down, to betray, to deceive, to victimize.

shoot to kill, to *phr.* [20C] to aim ruthlessly for a goal without reservation or compromise.

shoot up *v.*[1] [late 19C+] (orig. US) to rampage around firing weapons, to destroy a place with gunfire.

shoot up *v.*[2] [1920s+] (drugs) to take narcotic drugs by injection. [ext. of SHOOT v.[6]]

shoot white *v.* [late 19C] to ejaculate. [SHOOT v.[3] (2) + the colour of semen]

shoot with the long bow, to *phr.* [mid-19C] to tell lies, to exaggerate (cf. THROW THE HATCHET).

shop *n.*[1] **1** [late 17C–early 18C] a prison (cf. TOIL SHOP). **2** [late 18C+] a place of business, any place where one pursues one's occupation (cf. OFFICE n.[1]). **3** [early–mid-19C] a public house.

shop *n.*[2] [mid–late 19C] the mouth (cf. SHUT YOUR SHOP!).

Shop, the *n.*[3] **1** [late 19C+] the Royal Military Academy, Woolwich. **2** [1960s+] (Aus.) Melbourne University (cf. FARM n.[5]).

shop *n.*[4] [1960s+] an act of shopping.

shop *v.*[1] **1** [mid-17C+] to imprison. **2** [early 19C+] to inform on and thus cause to be imprisoned. [SHOP n.[1] (1)]

shop *v.*[2] [mid-19C] to dismiss, esp. to dismiss a shop assistant.

shop around *v.* [1960s+] to have a number of sexual relationships before choosing one that will serve for marriage or a longer term. [SE *shop around*, to search out the best bargain]

shop-bouncer *n.* [mid–late 19C] a thief who steals from shops while distracting the merchant's attention with argumentative bargaining; thus *shop-bouncing*, shoplifting. [SE *shop* + BOUNCER n.[1] (5)]

shop-door *n.* [late 19C+] the fly buttons; thus warning *your shop-door is open*, your flies are undone.

shop-dropper *n.* [1940s–50s] (Aus.) one who delivers goods, liquor etc from a market or store to retailers.

shopkeeper *n.* [mid-17C–mid-18C] an item that cannot be sold (cf. STOREKEEPER). [pun; i.e. such an item has been in the shop as long as its owner]

shoplift *n.* [late 17C] a shoplifter, one who steals goods from shops while pretending to be a legitimate customer. [SE f. 1700]

shop-lobber *n.* [mid-19C] a dandified shop assistant (cf. SHOP-MASHER). [SE *shop* + LOB v.[1]]

shop-masher *n.* [late 19C–1900s] a dandified shop assistant (cf. SHOP-LOBBER). [SE *shop* + MASHER n.]

shop-pad *n.* [18C] a shoplifter. [SE *shop* + PAD n.[1]]

shopped *adj.* **1** [late 16C–early 19C] imprisoned. **2** [early 19C+] betrayed, informed on (cf. GRASS v.[2]). [SHOP v.[1]]

shopper *n.* [1920s–50s] an informer. [SHOP v.[1]]

shoppie/shoppy *n.* **1** [1910s–30s] a female *shop* assistant. **2** [20C] (Aus.) a *shop*lifter. [abbr.]

shopping *n.*[1] [20C] (US Und.) **1** shoplifting. **2** looking for something to steal.

shopping *n.*[2] [1930s+] an act of betrayal, of informing. [SHOP v.[1]]

shopping and fucking *adj.* [20C] used of a type of block-busting novel, developed during the materialist 1980s, in which the normal ingredient of a certain type of bestseller – 'procrastinated rape' (V.S. Pritchett) – is boosted by regular excursions into the world's up-market shopping malls in search of lovingly delineated designer-labelled garments and other consumables. When bowdlerized the term is found as *sex and shopping*.

shoppy *see* SHOPPIE.

shop teeth *n.* [20C] (Irish) false teeth, dentures.

shore dinner *n.* [1980s+] (US gay) a sailor who allows himself to be fellated while on shore leave. [play on SE *dinner*/EAT v.[3]]

Shoreditch fury *n.* [19C] an aggressive woman. [*Shoreditch*, a notably tough area of East London]

short *n.*[1] [mid-19C+] **1** neat gin. **2** any form of undiluted spirits. [? the shortness of the measure compared with that of beer]

short *n.*[2] [1910s+] **1** a street car. **2** an automobile. [the comparatively short distance a street car or automobile would travel compared to a railway train]

short *n.*[3] [1930s–40s] (US) a *short*-barrelled revolver (cf. LONG n.[1]). [abbr.]

short *n.*[4] [1970s] (US Black) a cigarette butt.

short *n.*[5] [1980s+] (drugs) a measure of drugs, esp. crack cocaine, that is sold at a reduced price.

short *n.*[6] [1980s+] a child. [the size relative to an adult]

short *adj.*[1] [mid-19C] of banknotes, in large denominations (cf. LONG adj.[2]). [orig. cashiers' jargon, large denominations mean fewer notes, which take a *shorter* time to count]

short *adj.*[2] [20C] (Aus.) eccentric, insane. [abbr. SHINGLE SHORT]

short *adj.*[3] [1960s+] **1** (US prison) used to describe a prisoner with only a few weeks or days of a sentence to serve (cf. LONG adj.[4]). **2** (US milit.) near the end of a term of duty, spec. the 12-month tours of Vietnam (cf. WAKE-UP n.[3]).

short *adj.*[4] [1960s+] (US) insufficient, esp. of money; thus *short bread*, not enough cash.

short *v.* [1960s–70s] (US drugs) to inhale a narcotic. [error for SNORT v.]

short and curly, to *phr.* [1990s] to beat up. [HAVE BY THE SHORT AND CURLIES]

short arm *n.* [20C] the penis (cf. ARM n.[4]; BEST LEG OF THREE).

short-arm bandit *n.*[1] [20C] a rapist (cf. SHORT-ARM HEISTER). [SHORT ARM + BANDIT n.[1]]

short-arm bandit *n.*[2] [1960s–70s] (gay) a male homosexual. [SHORT-ARM INSPECTION, inspection of the genitals + ARSE BANDIT]

short-arm heister *n.* [20C] (US Und.) a rapist (cf. SHORT-ARM BANDIT n.[1]). [SHORT ARM + HEISTER]

short-arm inspection *n.* [1910s+] (orig. milit.) medical inspection of the genitals. [SHORT ARM + SE *inspection*]

short-arse/-ass *n.* [1940s+] a small person, an insignificant person; thus *short-arsed*, small. [note 18C SE *short-arse*, a stumpy, short person]

short bit *n.* [mid-19C–1950s] (US) 10 cents, in contrast to 12½ or 15 cents, a LONG BIT n.[2]. [BIT n.[1]]

short con *n.* [1930s+] (US Und.) any variety of confidence trick that can be performed spontaneously and on the spot, with no elaborate props, preparation etc (cf. SHORT STUFF). [abbr. SE *short* (*time*) + *con*(*fidence trick*)]

short dog *n.* [1960s+] (US Black) a small bottle of cheap wine (cf. SHORT NECK). [SE *short* + DOG n.[11]]

short end *n.* [mid-19C+] (US) the losing end, the bad side of a deal or situation. [abbr. SHORT END OF THE STICK]

short-end money *n.* [20C] (gambling) money bet on the possibility of a team or individual (esp. in boxing) losing a contest (cf. ON THE SHORT END).

short end of the stick *phr.* [mid-19C+] (orig. US) unfair treatment, deliberately engineered bad luck.

shortening *n.* [mid-19C] the practice of clipping coins as a profession (cf. SHORTER).

shorter *n.* [mid-19C] a clipper of coins (cf. SHORTENING).

short eyes *n.* [1960s+] (US prison) a child molester (cf. BEAST n.[5]). [for ety. *see* SHUT EYES]

short fuse *n.* [1960s+] (orig. US) a short temper.

short-heeled wench/short heels *n.* [late 18C–early 19C] a promiscuous woman (cf. LITTLE MISS ROUNDHEELS). [her 'short heels' mean that she is constantly falling on her back]

short heist *n.* [20C] (US Und.) petty theft. [SE *short* (*time*) + HEIST n.]

shorthorn *n.* [late 19C–1940s] (US, mainly west) **1** a north-erner. **2** a newcomer, an innocent (cf. LONGHORN). [agricultural imagery]

short-length *n.* [mid-19C] (Scot.) a glass of brandy.

short-limbered *adj.* [late 19C–1900s] short-tempered. [SE *short* + *limber*. 'The detachable fore part of a gun-carriage, consisting of two wheels and an axle, a pole for the horses, and a frame which holds one or two ammunition-chests. It is attached to the trail of the gun-carriage proper by a hook' (*OED*)]

short line *n.* [1940s–50s] (US) very little money (cf. SHORTS n.[1]). [gambling jargon; i.e. a *short line* of credit]

short-money game *n.* [1960s] (US Und.) the money that a pimp can make from a prostitute who works for him for only a short period (cf. SHORT-STOP MONEY).

short-mouthed *adj.* [1900s] (W.I.) verbally agile, good at snappy repartee.

short nail *n.* [1960s–70s] (US Black) a Black woman with short, kinky hair. [SE *short* + NAILHEAD n.[2]]

short neck *n.* [1930s–40s] (US) a 285ml (½ pint) bottle of wine (cf. SHORT DOG).

short of a sheet *phr.* [20C] used of someone who is not very intelligent (cf. NOT ALL THERE).

short reply in the plural, a *phr.* [20C] euph. synon. for BALLS!

shorts, the n.[1] [20C] (US) lack of money (cf. SHORT LINE).

shorts n.[2] [1970s] the last few puffs of a discarded cigarette (cf. SHORT n.[4]).

short sheet v. [20C] (US) to mistreat, to trick someone. [SAmE *shortsheet*, the UK 'apple-pie bed']

short/long soup n. [1920s+] (Aus.) soup with either short or long noodles in it.

short stop n. **1** [1950s–60s] (US Black) a temporary arrangement, a short period of time. **2** [1960s–70s] a fool, a dupe, a coward. [baseball imagery]

short stop v. [1970s] (US Black) **1** to abruptly stop someone from moving or carrying on with what they are doing. **2** (US) to take food as it is being passed to someone else at a meal. [SE *stop short*]

short-stop money n. [1950s–70s] (US Und.) money that a pimp can make from exploiting a woman on welfare (cf. SHORT-MONEY GAME).

short strokes n. [20C] the final stage of sexual intercourse, immediately preceding male orgasm; thus *be on the short strokes*, of a man, to be approaching orgasm (cf. LONG STROKES; PARADISE STROKES; VINEGAR STROKES).

short stuff n. [20C] (US Und.) a quick and spontaneous con trick, thought up on the spur of the moment and workable only while the target is on hand (cf. SHORT CON).

short time n. **1** [late 19C+] of a prostitute, the time spent with one client before taking on a new one, rather than spending a whole night with the same man. **2** [20C] (prison) a short sentence, a short part of one's sentence left to run. **3** [20C] (milit.) a short-service commission, a short period of enlistment. **4** [1930s+] of a prostitute's client, a short visit, giving time for a single bout of sexual intercourse (cf. HURRY-WHORE).

short-time girl n. [late 19C+] a basic, cheap prostitute who satisfies her client's immediate need and then looks for her next customer. [SHORT TIME n. (4) + SE *girl*]

short-timer n. **1** [20C] (US) one who has only a short period left of his service in the military (cf. SHORT adj.[3]). **2** [1910s] one who is serving a short prison sentence. **3** [1920s+] one who frequents a prostitute for a brief visit, involving a single act of intercourse (cf. ALL-NIGHTER).

short-timers n. [1920s+] a couple who rent a room for an hour in order to have adulterous sex.

short trill n. [1940s] (US Black) a short walk. [? obs. SE *trill*, to trundle, to whirl]

short 'un n. **1** [18C+] a short person. **2** [late 19C] 285ml (½ pint) of coffee. [SE *short one*]

short-weight adj. [20C] mentally defective, stupid.

shorty n. **1** [20C] a young person. **2** [1990s] (orig. US Black) a woman, a girlfriend. [SE *shorty*, a person of short stature]

shot n.[1] [late 18C] money, esp. an amount that is due to be paid or one's share of it (cf. WHOLE BANG SHOOT).

shot n.[2] [early 19C+] **1** an opportunity, a chance, an attempt. **2** anything that has a reasonable chance of success, usu. preceded by a qualifying figure indicating the odds against, e.g. *ten to one shot* (cf. BAD SHOT; LONG SHOT). **3** (US) one's preference, style or choice. [SE *shoot* (at a target)]

shot n.[3] [mid-19C] a corpse that has been disinterred by body-snatchers for the purpose of selling it to a medical school.

shot n.[4] [mid-19C+] (US) a sneering remark, aimed at another person with the express purpose of wounding them (cf. HAVE A SHOT AT phr.[2]).

shot n.[5] **1** [mid-19C+] a measure of liquor; usu. with the drink specified, e.g. *a shot of rum*. **2** [late 1920s+] an injection of a narcotic drug.

shot n.[6] [20C] (US) an ejaculation. [SHOOT v.[3] (2)]

shot n.[7] [1910s] (Aus.) baking powder. [? SE *shot*, the lead shot contained in a shotgun cartridge]

shot n.[8] [1910s–20s] a very hard cake. [SE *shot*, a cannonball]

shot n.[9] [1920s] anything very hard to understand or believe.

shot n.[10] [1960s–70s] (US Black) a professional pickpocket.

shot adj. **1** [mid-19C+] (US/Aus./N.Z.) drunk (cf. BASTED). **2** [1920s+] (US) of a thing, worn out or beyond repair. **3** [1930s+] (orig. Aus.) of a person, exhausted or in bad shape.

shot v. [late 19C] to give a horse a dose of small shot, which makes it appear sound-winded.

shot between/betwixt wind and water phr. [late 17C–19C] infected with venereal disease (cf. BETWEEN THE TWO WS). [naut jargon *betwixt wind and water*, that part of a ship's side that is sometimes above water and sometimes submerged, in which part a shot is particularly dangerous]

shot-clog n. [mid–late 19C] a fool who is tolerated only because of their willingness to pay their share for drinks. [SHOT n.[5] (1) + SE *clog*]

shot down adj. [1960s+] **1** (drugs) under the influence of drugs. **2** (US campus) miserable, useless, distasteful.

shot full of holes phr. [1910s+] (Aus./N.Z.) drunk (cf. BASTED). [ext. of SHOT adj.]

shot-ging n. [1920s+] (Aus.) a catapult (cf. SHANGHAI n.[1]).

shotgun n.[1] [20C] (US) a matchmaker, a marriage broker. [play on SHOTGUN WEDDING]

shotgun n.[2] [1960s+] (US drugs) a type of pipe used for smoking marijuana.

shotgun v. [1960s+] **1** to drink a full can of beer in a single swallow, esp. when a hole has been poked through the bottom. **2** (drugs) to blow cannabis smoke into someone else's mouth by reversing the cigarette inside one's own mouth and blowing; the other person places their open lips near the stream of smoke and inhales for as long as they can; thus *shot-gunning*, the act of doing this (cf. GIVE A BLOW).

shotgun! excl. [1980s+] (US teen) when choosing seats in a car, 'I want to ride in the front seat next to the driver!' (cf. NO BITCH!; SEAT CHECK!). [abbr. RIDE SHOTGUN]

shotgun marriage see SHOTGUN WEDDING.

shotgun mike n. [1960s+] a directional microphone.

shotgun mixture n. [20C] a pharmaceutical mixture.

shotgun quizz see POP QUIZ.

shotgun seat n. [1980s+] the seat next to that of the driver in a car. [for ety. *see* RIDE SHOTGUN]

shotgun wedding/marriage n. [1920s+] (orig. US) a wedding that is forced on the groom through his girlfriend's (soon to be bride's) pregnancy. [the image of the aggrieved father holding a shotgun to the reluctant groom's back]

shot in v. [1940s+] (Aus.) to be imprisoned. [SE *shoot in*, to throw in]

shot in one's locker phr. [late 18C+] sufficient in reserve, e.g. money. [naval imagery]

shot in the arm/ass n. [1920s+] (orig. US) anything (verbal, physical, stimulant) that cheers one up, energizes one etc. [lit. an injection]

shot in the dark n. [late 19C+] a wild guess, a random try.

shot in the eye n. [late 19C+] an ill-turn. [SHOOT IN THE EYE]

shot in the neck phr. [early–mid-19C] (US) drunk (cf. BASTED).

shot in the tail phr. [20C] pregnant. [SHOOT v.[3]/SE *shot* + TAIL n.[1] (2)]

shot-locker n. [20C] (US) the vagina. [into which the man can SHOOT v.[3]]

shot on the swings n. [1940s+] (Scot.) sexual intercourse. [ety. unknown; ? the movements of the two bodies]

shotten herring n. [17C] an emaciated, worthless and generally good-for-nothing person. [Du. *schoten haringh*, a fish, esp. a herring that has spawned. Such herrings are 'empty' of their spawn. In a human context, therefore, it also means fig. 'empty']

shotten soul n. [17C] an emaciated, worthless and generally good-for-nothing person (cf. SHOTTEN HERRING). [lit. an 'empty soul']

shot through adj. [1930s] in a state of complete collapse, exhaustion (cf. SHOT TO HELL).

shottie v. [1980s+] (N.Z. drugs) to inhale a puff of a marijuana cigarette through a large funnel and then drop from a standing position to a crouch when the lungs are filled to capacity, to force more smoke into the lungs. [abbr. SE *shotgun*]

shot to hell/pieces phr. [1920s+] in a state of utter collapse.

shotty n. [1990s] (US Black) a *shot*gun. [abbr.]

shot-up adj.[1] [1910s+] (drugs) under the influence of narcotic drugs. [SHOOT v.[6]]

shot-up adj.[2] [1930s+] (US) **1** of a person, severely wounded. **2** of an object, e.g. a car, damaged by shooting. [SE *shot*]

shoulder v. **1** [early 19C] of a stage-coachman, to take on (and charge) extra passengers, without informing the coach company; thus *shoulder-stick*, a passenger who takes advantage of such corruption. **2** [mid-19C] of a servant, to cheat or embezzle from their master. [ety. unknown]

shoulder boulders n. [1990s] large female breasts.

shoulder-clapper n. [17C–early 19C] a bailiff (cf. CLAP ON THE SHOULDER; SHOULDER-DAB; SHOULDER-KNOT; SHOULDER-TAPPER). [the physical action that accompanies an arrest for debt]

shoulder-dab n. [late 19C] a bailiff (cf. SHOULDER-CLAPPER). [their 'dabbing' or tapping their target on the shoulder]

shoulder-hitter/-striker n. [mid-19C] (US) a bully, a ruffian. [lit. 'one who hits from the shoulder']

shoulder-knot n. [mid-19C] a bailiff (cf. SHOULDER-CLAPPER). [their taking their victim by the shoulder]

shoulder-sham n. [late 17C–early 19C] (Und.) a partner to a pickpocket. [SE *shoulder* + SHAM n.[1]]

shoulder-striker see SHOULDER-HITTER.

shoulder-tapper n. [late 18C–early 19C] a bailiff (cf. SHOULDER-CLAPPER). [their taking their victim by the shoulder]

shoulder walnut v. [mid-19C] to enlist as a soldier. [the walnut wood from which gun stocks are made]

shouse/shoush/sh'touse n. [1940s+] (Aus.) a lavatory. [elision of SHITHOUSE n.]

shout n.[1] [mid-19C+] (orig. Aus./N.Z.) **1** one's turn to order a round of drinks; thus *your shout, my shout, go on the shout, stand shout.* **2** a round of drinks. [SHOUT v.[1]]

shout n.[2] [late 19C+] (US Black) a party, esp. a RENT PARTY. [its noisiness]

shout/shout out n.[3] [1980s+] as used on pirate radio stations, esp. 1990s stations playing jungle music, a greeting, an acknowledgement to a named listener or group of listeners.

shout v.[1] **1** [mid-19C+] (Aus./N.Z.) to buy a round of drinks. **2** [late 19C+] to treat. [one shouts to the publican for drink]

shout v.[2] [late 19C] (US) of things, to be undeniably important.

shout v.[3] [late 19C+] (US Black) to cry out or 'speak in tongues', usu. in church, as the apparent result of being possessed by spirits.

shout and holler n. [20C] a collar. [rhy. sl.]

shouted adj. [20C] (Aus./N.Z.) used of a drink that is paid for by someone other than the drinker. [SHOUT v.[1]]

shouter n.[1] [mid-19C] (Aus./N.Z.) one who stands a round of drinks. [SHOUT v.[1]]

shouter n.[2] (US) **1** [late 19C–1920s] a gospel or blues/gospel singer. **2** [late 19C–1920s] a Black church. **3** [20C] a soapbox or street-corner orator. **4** [1920s] (US Und.) a criminal's girl-friend. [SE *shouter*, a loud or voluble speaker]

shout for murder see HOLLER FOR MURDER.

shout oneself hoarse, to phr. **1** [late 19C+] to buy a round of drinks for the whole bar. **2** [late 19C–1900s] to get drunk.

[SHOUT v.[1] ? + pun on the actual shouting – to attract attention to one's generosity and as a result of one's drunkenness]

shout out see SHOUT n.[3].

shout the odds, to phr. [1910s+] to talk loudly, to boast.

shout-up n. [1960s+] a noisy argument.

shout up v. [1930s] to shout at by way of warning.

shov n. [late 19C] (Und.) a knife. [CHIV n.[1] + SE *shove*, one 'shoves it in' to the victim]

shove n.[1] **1** [early 18C+] sexual intercourse; thus *give her a shove*, to have sexual intercourse with a woman. **2** [late 19C] energy, high spirits, self-glorification, hollow talk.

shove, the n.[2] [late 19C] dismissal from one's employment.

shove v.[1] **1** [late 17C+] to have sexual intercourse. **2** [mid-19C+] (US) to pass counterfeit money. **3** [20C] (US Und.) to kill.

shove v.[2] [20C] to put, to place.

shove v.[3] [1910s+] to stop, to forget, usu. in phr. *you can shove that* or imper. *shove it!* [abbr. SHOVE IT UP YOUR ARSE!]

shove along v. [1900s–20s] to move quietly.

shove-and-let-go n. [1920s–40s] (W.I.) a Model T Ford (cf. PUSH-FOOT). [on this car low gear was engaged by pressing a foot-pedal]

shove a trunk, to phr. [late 18C–late 19C] to interfere where one has not been asked or invited (cf. SHOVE ONE'S NOSE IN). [SE *shove* + TRUNK n.[1]]

shove for v. [late 19C] to move towards, to go to.

shove in v. [late 19C] to pawn. [one 'shoves' the pawned item across the pawnbroker's counter]

shove in the eye n. [late 19C+] a punch in the face.

shove in the mouth n. [mid-19C] a glass of spirits.

shove it! excl. [1940s+] (orig. Aus.) a general excl. of dismissal and rudeness. [abbr. SHOVE IT UP YOUR ARSE!]

shove/stick it up your arse/ass! excl. [1970s+] an excl. of contempt, dismissal. [SE *shove* + ARSE n.[1]]

shove/stick it up your nose! excl. [1920s+] (orig. US) a general excl. of dismissal. [euph. precursor of SHOVE IT UP YOUR NOSE!]

shovel n. see SHOFUL.

shovel v. [1920s–50s] (S.Afr.) to hand over, to pass.

shovel and broom n. [1920s–50s] (Aus./US) room. [rhy. sl.]

shovel and pick n. [20C] **1** a prison. **2** an Irishman. [rhy. sl. *shovel and pick*; (1) = NICK n.[7] (1); (2) = MICK n.[1]]

shovel and spade n. [20C] a blade, a knife. [rhy. sl.]

shovel and tank n. [20C] a bank. [rhy. sl.]

shovel city n. [1970s] (US teen) anything one really appreciates and enjoys. [pun on SE *shovel*/DIG v.[6]]

shovel guts v. [1960s+] (US) to perform menial, distasteful tasks.

shovelhead n. [20C] (US) an idiot. [SE *shovel* + –HEAD (1)]

shovel of malt n. [early 19C] a pot of porter. [SE *malt*, the main constituent of the drink]

shovel shit v. [1930s+] to talk nonsense, esp. in an attempt to defraud or deceive someone (cf. BULLSHIT v.). [SE *shovel* + SHIT n.[1] (1)]

shovel shit against the tide, to phr. [1930s+] to make one's best efforts, despite overwhelming odds. [SHIT n.[1] (1)]

shovel the shit, to phr. [20C] to gossip, esp. maliciously (cf. SHIT-STIRRER). [SE *shovel* + SHIT n.[1] (1)]

shove off v. [late 19C+] to leave, to go away, usu. as imper. [naut. jargon to push a boat away from the side of another one or off the harbour wall before setting out]

shove one's nose in, to phr. [late 19C+] to interfere (cf. SHOVE A TRUNK).

shove one's oar in, to phr. [late 19C+] to interfere where one is not wanted (cf. PUT IN ONE'S OAR).

shover/shover of the queer n.[1] [mid–late 19C] a passer of counterfeit money. [SHOVE v.[1] (2) + QUEER n. (2)]

shover/shuffer n.[2] [20C] a chauffeur. [mispron.]

shover of the queer see SHOVER n.[1].

shove shit uphill, to phr. [1960s+] to sodomize. [SE shove + SHIT n.[1] (1)]

shove-straight n. [18C] the penis.

shove the moon, to phr. [late 18C] to abscond from a house or flat, taking one's furniture and possessions, but paying no bills (cf. SHOOT THE MOON). [such exits are usu. nocturnal]

shove the queer, to phr. [mid-19C–1910s] to pass counterfeit money (cf. SHOVER n.[1]). [SHOVE v.[1] (2) + QUEER n. (1)]

shove the tumbler, to phr. [late 17C–18C] (Und.) to be whipped at the cart's tail (cf. HAVE AIR AND EXERCISE). [SE shove + TUMBLER n.[2]; the image is one of pushing the cart forward as one strains beneath the blows]

shove under v. [20C] (Aus.) to kill, usu. in passive, i.e. to be shoved under, to be killed. [i.e. to push under the ground]

shovin' and pushin' adj. [1970s] (US Black) trying as hard as possible to succeed.

show n.[1] **1** [late 18C+] (orig. US) a matter, an event, an affair; thus good show, bad show, poor show. **2** [mid-19C+] (Aus./ US) a chance, an opportunity; thus give him a show, give him a chance. **3** [late 19C+] (orig. milit.) a battle, a military engagement, a war; thus big show, a major campaign, a war. **4** [1900s] (orig. US) a group of people. [SE show, a display]

show n.[2] [1940s+] (Aus.) a sanitary towel. [the blood thereon]

show/show up v.[1] [19C] to appear in society. [SE show, display (rather than 'appear')]

show v.[2] [late 19C] to exhibit oneself for money.

show v.[3] [late 19C+] (US) to appear, to arrive. [abbr. SE show up]

show v.[4] [1930s+] of a woman, to be obviously pregnant; thus showing, pregnant.

show a clean pair of heels/legs, to phr. [late 19C+] to leave at speed.

show/hang out a/the flag of distress, to phr. [20C] to have one's shirt out.

show a leg! excl. [1910s+] a wake-up call. [orig. used in institutions to ensure that the leg was masculine and not, illicitly, female]

show a lick, to phr. [mid-19C–1960s] of a horse, to move fast. [LICK n.[1] (5)]

show an Abyssinian medal, to phr. [late 19C] of a man, to have a fly-button undone, to have one's penis sticking inadvertently through one's flies. [the Abyssinian War 1893–6]

show and prove, to phr. [1990s] (US Black) to demonstrate.

show and tell n. [1950s+] (US) an elaborate exhibit intended to impress, persuade or inform. [play on juv. show-and-tell periods at school]

show a point to, to phr. [late 19C+] (N.Z.) to swindle, to act dishonourably towards.

showbiz n. [1940s+] (orig. US) show business, the entertainment industry; thus that's showbiz, that's how things are (and there's nothing you can do about it).

showboat n. [1970s] a flashy car. [for ety. see SHOWBOAT v.]

showboat v. [1970s] (orig. US) to show off, esp. by parading oneself in front of an audience. [SE showboat, a river steamer on which entertainments are given]

show case v. [1990s] (US Black) to commit a fraud. [ety. unknown; ? the image of one who shows a case of samples]

showcase nigger n. [1960s–70s] (US Black) a token Black employee, hired to parade the liberal racial attitudes of a White-owned organization. [SE showcase, a display cabinet + NIGGER n.]

showdown n. [late 19C+] **1** (US) a confrontation. **2** (gambling) a poker game in which cards are dealt face up.

show drink v. [late 19C] (US) to be tipsy, to be drunk.

shower n.[1] [late 19C+] (Aus.) a dust-storm, usu. prefaced by a local name, e.g. Cobar shower, Darling shower.

shower n.[2] **1** [1930s+] an unimpressive group of people. **2** [1940s+] a term of abuse aimed at a single person. [abbr. SE shower of + SHIT n.[1] (1)]

shower bath n. [20C] 10 shillings (50p); thus (sporting) showers to a shilling, odds of 10:1. [rhy. sl., Cockney pron. of shower bath, 'shahr barf' = half]

shower of rain n. [20C] (Aus.) a train. [rhy. sl.]

shower/pond scum n. [1980s+] (US campus) a highly unpleasant person (cf. BATHTUB SCUM).

shower spank v. [1980s+] (US teen) to masturbate in the shower (cf. SPANK v.[2]).

show-full see SHOFUL.

showhouse n. [20C] (gay) a brothel, a place where homosexuals can meet openly (sex is usually performed off the premises) (cf. ACCOMMODATION HOUSE).

showie/showy n. [1950s+] (Aus.) a display handkerchief, worn in one's top jacket pocket. [abbr.; it is worn for 'show']

showing next week's washing phr. [20C] a phr. used to warn a man that their fly is open or a woman that her slip is showing.

show it v. [20C] to become obviously drunk.

show-leg day n. **1** [late 19C] a very windy day. **2** [1920s] a very muddy day (cf. SHULLEG-DAY). [in both cases the leg is female]

show more roots than Kunta Kinte, to phr. [1970s] (US Black) of a woman with dyed hair, to need to have it re-dyed. [a pun on the hero of Roots (1976), the best-selling novel by Alex Haley]

show one's ass, to phr. [1950s+] (US Black) to appear foolish.

show one's cards/hole-card, to phr. [20C] (orig. US) to reveal oneself, usu. to a greater extent than desired (cf. PEEP SOMEONE'S HOLE-CARD). [poker imagery; the hole-card is that held face-down at the table]

show one's color, to phr. [1950s–60s] (US Black) to act in a stereotyped way, to behave in the way Whites expect Blacks to behave. [ironic reversal of SE show one's colours, to declare one's own standpoint, to act proudly despite any opposition]

show one's hole-card see SHOW ONE'S CARDS.

show one's paces, to phr. [late 19C+] to display one's abilities. [horse-riding imagery]

show one's shape, to phr. [18C–19C] to make an appearance, to come into view. [SE shape, one's figure]

show one's shapes, to phr. **1** [late 17C–early 18C] to turn around, to march off. **2** [late 18C] to take off one's clothes, esp. preparatory to a judicial flogging. [SE shape, one's figure]

show out v. **1** [late 19C+] (US Black) to show off, to flaunt oneself. **2** [1950s] to lead on, to deceive.

show pony n. [1960s+] (Aus.) one who cares more for appearance than performance. [SE show pony, one that looks good in shows but may be less useful in practical life]

show shapes v. **1** [mid-19C] to play pranks, to act in a flighty manner. **2** [1960s+] to dance, esp. at a discotheque.

show someone what for, to phr. [late 19C+] to show someone who is in charge, to make someone take notice.

show someone where the bear shit in the buckwheat, to phr. [19C] (US) to let someone know what's what, to tell someone off; also as … where the bear came out of the mountains, … how the bear came out of the buckwheat. [SHIT v.[1]]

show stopper n. [1950s–60s] (camp gay) a particularly attractive young man.

show the elephant, to phr. [mid–late 19C] (US) to show someone the sights, esp. of the town-dweller thus regaling their 'country cousins'. [var. on SEE THE ELEPHANT]

show the flag, to phr. [1910s+] to attend, apparently reluctantly, any official function. [imperial imagery]

show the flag of distress *see* SHOW A FLAG OF DISTRESS.

show the ropes, to *phr.* [1940s+] to explain, esp. to explain the details of a task or operation. [naut.]

show the white rag/the white feather, to *phr.* [early 19C+] to surrender or act in a cowardly manner. [a *white feather* in a game-bird's tail is a mark of inferior breeding; note earlier synon. *find a white feather in one's tail, mount the white feather*]

showtime *v.* [1990s] (US Black) to show off, to flaunt oneself.

show tunes *n.* [1960s+] (US gay) noises made during intercourse or fellatio. [SE *show tunes*, the songs performed in a musical]

show-up *n.* [1920s+] (US) an identification parade.

show up *see* SHOW v.¹.

show what's what *see* WHAT'S WHAT.

showy *see* SHOWIE.

shpilkes *n.* [20C] (US) anxiety, nervousness. [Yid.]

shpritz *see* SCHPRITZ v.

shrap/shrape *n.* [16C] (Und.) wine used to weaken the will of a confidence trickster's victim. [SE *shrape*, bait of chaff or seed laid for birds; hence a snare]

shrapnel/shrap *n.* [1910s+] (N.Z.) copper coins, small change. [SE *shrapnel*, shell or bomb fragments]

shred *n.* [late 16C–early 18C] a tailor. [the shreds of cloth he discards]

shred *v.* [1980s+] (US campus) to overcome, to conquer.

shredded *adj.* [1980s+] (US teen) drunk (cf. BASTED).

shreddies *n.* [1960s] men's underwear. [the ref. is to its often-ragged state + pun on popular breakfast cereal]

shreds and patches *n.* [late 18C–late 19C] a tailor. [metonymy]

shred the tube, to *phr.* [1980s] (US teen) to go surfing. [SE *shred* + surf jargon *tube*, the top part of the wave, where it starts to curl over, forming a tube]

shrewd-head *n.* [20C] (Aus./N.Z.) a cunning person. [SE *shrewd* + sfx. -HEAD (1)]

shrewdy *n.* [20C] (Aus./N.Z.) a shrewd person, one who lives on their wits.

shriek/shriek-mark *n.*¹ [mid-19C+] an exclamation mark (cf. SCREAMER n.¹).

shriek *n.*² [1920s+] **1** [late 19C+] something seen as very funny (cf. SCREAM n.¹). **2** an excl. of alarm, annoyance or similar emotion.

shriek-mark *see* SHRIEK n.¹.

shrimp *n.*¹ [15C+] a small, weak, insignificant person.

shrimp *n.*² [mid-17C] a prostitute. [the association of prostitution/women with FISH n.⁴ (cf. BEARDED CLAM)]

shrimper *n.* [1960s+] a foot fetishist. [toes are supposed to resemble pink shrimps]

shrimping *n.* [1960s+] toe-sucking. [for ety. *see* SHRIMPER]

shrink *n.*¹ [1960s+] (orig. US) a psychoanalyst, a psychiatrist etc (cf. HEAD-CANDLER; TRICK CYCLIST). [abbr. SE *head-shrinker*]

shrink *n.*² [1970s] (US campus) a young woman's tight-fitting sweater.

shrink someone's head, to *phr.* [1950s+] (orig. US) to psychoanalyse someone. [SE *head-shrinker*]

shrinksville *n.* [1950s+] (orig. US) a state of mind that makes it advisable for a person so afflicted to consult a psychoanalyst. [SHRINK n.¹ + sfx. -VILLE]

shroff *see* SCHROFF.

shroom dog *n.* [1980s+] (US campus) someone who uses hallucinogens. [SHROOMS + DOG n.⁹]

shrooms *n.* [1980s+] psilocybin mushrooms, used as a recreational hallucinogenic drug. [abbr. SE *mushrooms*]

shrubbery *n.* [19C] the pubic hair (cf. BUSH n.⁴).

shtarka/shtarker *see* SCHTARKA.

shtik/shtick *see* SCHTICK.

shtoonk *see* SCHTOONK.

sh'touse *see* SHOUSE.

shtum *adj.* [20C] quiet, silent, dumb. [synon. Yid.]

shtunk *see* SCHTOONK.

shtup *see* SCHTUP.

shuck *n.* [mid-19C+] **1** (US, esp. Black) a hoax, a lie, a deceit (cf. SHUCK AND JIVE n.). **2** (US Black) a theft, a fraud. [SE *shuck*, a husk; thus fig. nonsense, deception]

shuck *v.* [mid-19C+] (US, esp. Black) to defraud, to tease, to lie. [SHUCK n.]

shuck and jive *n.* [late 19C+] (US, esp. Black) deception, play-acting, obfuscation. [SHUCK n. + JIVE n.¹ (1)]

shuck and jive, to *phr.* [late 19C+] (US, esp. Black) **1** to act deceptively, to confuse. **2** to make a promise one has no intention of keeping. [SHUCK AND JIVE n.]

shuck down *v.* [20C] (US) to strip off one's clothes, to undress. [SE *shuck*, to pod, to strip husks]

shuck drop *v.* [1940s] (US Black) to take advantage of a victim or fool. [SHUCK n. + DROP n.²]

shucking and jiving *n.* [1960s+] (US Black) fooling, playing around. [SHUCK AND JIVE phr.]

shucks *n.* [mid-19C] (US) the paper money issued by the Confederate States during the US Civil War (cf. BLUE-BACKS). [SE *shuck*, shells of peas, husks of corn and similar refuse; thus implying the worthlessness of the Confederate currency]

shucks! *excl.* [mid-19C+] (orig. US) a mild excl. of surprise, regret, annoyance etc. [SE *not worth shucks*, worthless, useless]

shuck the corn, to *phr.* [20C] to masturbate.

shuffer *see* SHOVER n.².

shuffle *n.* [1900s–60s] (US Black) a Black man deliberately playing dumb and acting out the White man's stereotyped view of their race; thus *shuffle*, to play this part. [the shuffling walk, along with shiny smiles and 'natural rhythm' are major parts of this image]

shuffle *v.* [1950s] (US street gang) to have a fist-fight.

shuffled out of the deck *phr.* [20C] dead. [card-playing imagery]

shuffle off *v.* [1920s+] to die. [orig. in *Hamlet* (1602) III.i.67: 'When we have shuffel'd [*sic*] off this mortall coile']

shuffler *n.*¹ [mid-17C] one who cadges drinks. [their shuffling, hesitant demeanour]

shuffler *n.*² [20C] (US Und.) a confidence trickster. [their ability, lit. or fig., to 'shuffle one's deck', i.e. either to perform as a card-sharp or to render the victim confused]

shuffle the deck, to *phr.* [1990s] to masturbate.

shuftie/shoofty/shufty *n.* [1940s+] a brief glance, a quick look. [Arabic *sufti*, have you seen?]

shug/sug *n.* **1** [mid-19C+] (US Black) an affectionate name for a woman. **2** [1920s+] (Aus.) money (cf. SUGAR n.¹). [abbr. SE *sugar*]

shuks *v.* [1950s] (W.I.) to hurt someone's feelings. [SHAKE v.⁴ or SE *shuck* (*off*), but note excl. of disappointment, SHUCKS!]

shuler *see* SHOOLER.

shulleg-day *n.* [late 19C] a wet day (cf. SHOW-LEG DAY). [on such days ladies are forced to raise their long skirts and thus 'show a leg', or at least an ankle]

shundicknick *n.* [late 19C–1930s] a pimp, a ponce. [Yid.]

shunt *n.* [1970s+] a car crash. [orig. racing driver jargon]

shunter *n.* [1990s] a male homosexual. [? play on his 'coupling up' or cf. PULL A TRAIN]

shunter's pole *n.* [20C] the penis. [railway jargon *shunter's pole*, a rod used to facilitate the coupling and uncoupling of goods wagons and engines]

shunt off *v.* [20C] (Aus.) **1** to get rid of a thing. **2** to dismiss a person.

shuper/shooper *n.* [20C] (US) a large beer glass. [ety. unknown; ? link to SE *super*]

shurk *n.* [late 17C–18C] a pickpocket. [SE *shirk*]

shut *n.*[1] [late 18C] a *shut*ter. [abbr.]

shut *n.*[2] [1930s] (Scot.) a trick, a deception. [phr. 'Now, just shut your eyes ...']

shuteye *n.* [late 19C+] sleep, rest.

shut eyes *n.* [1960s+] (US police) a sexual offender (cf. BEAST *n.*[5]; SHORT EYES). [their suggestion, 'Now just shut your eyes ...']

shut it! *excl.* [late 19C+] be quiet! shut up! (cf. SHUT ONE'S HEAD; SHUT ONE'S PAN; SHUT ONE'S TRAP; SHUT YOUR BEAK!; SHUT YOUR CAN!; SHUT YOUR GOBBLE!; SHUT YOUR RAG-BOX!; SHUT YOUR SHOP!). ['it' is the mouth]

shut one's arse/ass, to *phr.* [1950s+] to be quiet, esp. in imper. *shut your ass!* [SE *shut* + ARSE *n.*[1]]

shut one's face, to *phr.* [19C+] to be quiet, esp. as imper. *shut your face!*

shut one's gob, to *phr.* [17C+] to be quiet, esp. in imper. *shut your gob!* [SE *shut* + GOB *n.*[1]]

shut one's head/neck, to *phr.* [19C+] (US) to be quiet, usu. as imper. *shut your head! shut your neck!* (cf. OPEN ONE'S HEAD; SHUT IT!). [dial. *head*, face]

shut one's light off, to *phr.* [1920s+] to commit suicide.

shut one's pan, to *phr.* [mid-19C] to be quiet, esp. as imper. *shut your pan!* (cf. SHUT IT!). [SE *shut* + PAN *n.*[4]]

shut one's trap, to *phr.* [late 18C+] to be quiet, usu. as imper. *shut your trap!* (cf. SHUT IT!). [SE *shut* + TRAP *n.*[1]]

shut someone down *v.* [1950s+] (US) **1** to beat a rival in a drag race. **2** to gain a victory in any competition.

shutter-bug *n.* [1940s+] (orig. US) a photographer. [SE *shutter* + BUG *n.*[5]]

shutter clicker *n.* [1940s] (US Black) a cinema projectionist.

shuttered *adj.*[1] [late 19C] in a state of total ignominy. [SE *shutter*, which one pulls down over one's shame]

shuttered *adj.*[2] [late 19C] taken away on a shutter, esp. of drunkards (cf. BARROWED).

shutter-racket worker *n.* [19C] a thief who specializes in boring through a shutter, removing a pane of glass and reaching through for anything to steal. [SE *shutter* + RACKET *n.*[1]]

shutters *n.* [1940s] (US Black) **1** the eyes. **2** the eyelids.

shut the books, to *phr.* [mid-19C–1920s] to shut down one's business.

shuttlebutt *n.* [1970s+] (US campus) a fat woman, esp. referring to the buttocks. [SE *shuttle*, i.e. its movement backwards and forwards + BUTT *n.*[1] (1); play on SCUTTLEBUTT]

shut up *v.* [mid-19C] to bring to an end.

shut up! *excl.* **1** [mid-19C+] be quiet! stop talking! **2** [1960s+] a general excl. of disbelief, you can't fool me! forget it! don't make me laugh!

shut up one's garret, to *phr.* [late 19C] to be quiet, to stop talking. [GARRET *n.* (4)]

shut up shop, to *phr.* [mid-19C–1940s] to stop talking.

shut up someone's shop, to *phr.* [late 19C–1900s] to kill someone, to murder someone.

shut your beak! *excl.* [20C] (W.I.) shut up! be quiet! (cf. SHUT IT!).

shut your can! *excl.* [1910s] (US) shut up! be quiet! (cf. SHUT IT!). [CAN *n.*[4] (3)]

shut your gobble! *excl.* [late 19C] shut up! be quiet! (cf. SHUT IT!).

shut your rag-box! *excl.* [late 19C] shut up! be quiet! (cf. SHUT IT!). [RAG-BOX *n.*[1]]

shut your shop! *excl.* [mid-late 19C] be quiet! (cf. SHUT IT!). [SE *shut* + SHOP *n.*[2]]

shuvly-cowss/-kouse *n.* [late 19C] a public house. [the term

was popularized when a 'half-witted girl used it ... in a police court' (Ware)]

shvantz *see* SCHWANTZ.

shvartze/shvartzer *see* SCHWARTZE.

shvonce/shvuntz *see* SCHWANTZ.

shy *n.*[1] **1** [late 18C–late 19C] a quick, jerking or careless throw, as of a stone etc. **2** [mid-19C] an attempt to damage by sarcasm or verbal attack. **3** [mid-late 19C] an attempt, a 'go'. [ety. unknown; *OED* suggests link to SE *shy cock*, a cowardly cock and thus person, but the logic is hard to comprehend – unless one had to throw the cock at its opponent]

shy *n.*[2] *see* SHYLOCK *n.*

shy *adj.*[1] **1** [mid-19C] doubtful in amount or quality. **2** [mid-19C–1900s] disreputable, of dubious character. [orig. gambling]

shy *adj.*[2] [late 19C+] (orig. US) short of, esp. short of money.

shy *v. see* SHYLOCK *v.*

shy-cock *n.* [late 18C–early 19C] one who hides from the bailiff. [SE *shy-cock*, a fighting cock that will not fight; but ? pun on *Shylock*, one who does not wish to let go of their money]

shyin' *see* SHINE *adj.*[1].

shylock/shy *n.* [20C] one who supplies private loans (cf. LOAN SHARK). [the money-lender in Shakespeare's *Merchant of Venice* (1600)]

shylock/shy *v.* [20C] to lend money at extortionate rates of interest. [SHYLOCK *n.*]

shypoo *n.* [1900s–60s] (Aus./N.Z.) **1** second-rate liquor. **2** the place that sells such liquor; also *shypoo house/joint/shanty/ shop*. [SHYPOO *adj.*]

shypoo *adj.* [20C] (Aus./N.Z.) second-rate, inferior. [ety. unknown; ? 'bastard Chinese' (cit. in *AND*) for 'soft drink'; ? Canton. *sai po*, a small shop]

shyster *n.* **1** [mid-19C+] (orig. US) a crooked lawyer (cf. SHICER). **2** [1910s] (Aus.) a worthless mine (esp. as used in a fraud). [Ger. *Scheisser*, shitter or Du. *scheidsman* or *schieds-reichter*, an arbitrator, an umpire. Alternatively, f. a New York lawyer named *Scheuster* (pron. *shyster*), whose courtroom antics so infuriated Justice Osborne of the city's Essex Market Court that he began talking of 'scheuster' practices]

shysty/scheisty *adj.* [mid-19C+] (US) tight-fisted. [SHYSTER]

Siberia *n.* [1960s+] (US prison) the solitary confinement cells. [*Siberia*, centre of the Russian *gulag*]

sice *n.* [mid-17C–mid-19C] sixpence (cf. SYEBUCK). [14C SE *sice*, the 6 on a die]

sices *n.* [mid-19C] in dice-playing, a throw of 6. [14C SE *sice*]

sick *n.* [1930s+] (drugs) the illness that accompanies withdrawal from drug addiction (cf. SICK *adj.*[2]).

sick *adj.*[1] **1** [mid-19C+] annoyed, worried, disgusted. **2** [1950s+] (US) mentally disturbed, psychopathic, esp. in a sadistic way (cf. SICKO). **3** [1950s+] (US) morbid, depraved, e.g. a sick sense of humour.

sick *adj.*[2] [1930s+] (drugs) suffering from withdrawal symptoms when addicted to narcotics, esp. heroin (cf. SICK *n.*).

sick *adj.*[3] [1980s+] (US campus) **1** a general pej., of poor quality, unfashionable, unappealing, stupid, weak, bizarre. **2** excellent, first-rate. [(2) on the bad = good pattern]

sick and wrong *phr.* [1980s+] (US campus) a general pej., absolutely impossible, unthinkable, totally disgusting; also used ironically. [ext. of SICK *adj.*[3]]

sick as a cat *phr.* [mid–late 19C] very sick (cf. SICK AS A CUSHION; SICK AS A DOG; SICK AS A HORSE; SICK AS A PARROT; SICK AS A RAT).

sick as a cushion *phr.* [late 17C–late 18C] very sick (cf. SICK AS A CAT).

sick as a dog *phr.* [late 17C+] very sick; thus ext. (Aus.) *sick as a blackfellow's dog* (cf. SICK AS A CAT).

sick as a horse *phr.* [late 18C–early 19C] extremely ill (cf. SICK AS A CAT). [a horse cannot vomit, so such sickness has no immediate relief]

sick as a parrot *phr.* [1970s+] extremely depressed, usu. mentally rather than physically distressed (cf. OVER THE MOON; SICK AS A CAT). [the term became widespread as the clichéd response attributed to many sportsmen, esp. soccer players and managers, after a loss or defeat. Note 17C *melancholy as a parrot,* quoted by E.P.]

sick as a rat *phr.* [19C+] very sick (cf. SICK AS A CAT).

sick-ass *adj.* [20C] (US) unpleasant, crazy. [SICK adj.[1] + sfx. -ASS]

sickener/sickner *n.* [mid-19C+] anything depressing, disappointing, frustrating (cf. CHOKER n.[2]).

sickie *n.*[1] [1950s+] (Aus.) a day's sick leave; thus *chuck a sickie,* to take the day off sick when one is perfectly healthy. [SE *sick leave*]

sickie *n.*[2] [1960s+] (orig. US) anyone considered to be 'sick in the head', insane, crazy. [SICK adj.[1]]

sick in fourteen languages *phr.* [late 19C] (US) very sick.

sickner see SICKENER.

sicko/sicksicksick *n.* [1950s+] a mentally unstable person, with overtones of sexual perversion. [SICK adj.[1]]

sick on see SIC ON.

sickrel *n.* [late 17C–early 18C] a puny, weak, sickly person. [SE *sick* + sfx. *-rel*]

sickroom *adj.* [20C] (US) repellent, unpleasant.

sicksicksick see SICKO.

sick wine *n.* [19C] wine that has soured or 'gone off'.

sic/sick on *v.* [mid-19C+] to set on, to have someone attack a third party, to set someone on another person. [SE *sick on,* to set a dog on]

siddi *n.* [1960s+] (drugs) marijuana. [? Arab. *sayyidi,* my lord]

side *n.*[1] [late 19C+] pretentiousness, swagger, conceit; thus *put on side,* to give oneself airs. [? play on billiards jargon *side,* spin or dial. *side,* proud; post-1940s use tends to be consciously archaic]

side *n.*[2] [1930s–80s] (US Black) a gramophone record.

side *n.*[3] [1960s] (US Black) the Black area of town; the original was Chicago's *South Side.* [also used (in London) as *West Side, South Side,* meaning Shepherd's Bush or Brixton – somewhat romanticized analogies with areas of US cities]

side *n.*[4] [1960s+] (US Black) a woman. [ideally she is on or at one's *side* in all circumstances]

sidebar *adj.* [1950s+] (US) supplementary. [journalistic jargon *sidebar,* a story that is supplementary to the main piece]

sideboard *n.* 1 [mid-late 19C] a stand-up collar. 2 [late 19C+] side-whiskers.

side-door Pullman *n.* [late 19C–1920s] (US tramp) a freight car. [the side-opening doors of the freight wagon. The real Pullman is a luxury passenger coach]

sidedywry *adj.* [late 18C–early 19C] crooked. [SE *side* + *awry*]

side-hill halibut *n.* [20C] (US) deer that has been illegally shot by poachers (cf. CAMP MEAT).

sidekick *n.*[1] [20C] (Aus./US) an assistant, a partner, an accomplice. [abbr. SIDE-KICKER]

sidekick *n.*[2] [1910s–50s] (US Und.) a side pocket. [SE *side* + KICK n.[4]]

sidekick *n.*[3] [1950s+] a 'throwaway', passing criticism.

side-kicker *n.* [late 19C–1930s] (Aus./US) an assistant, a partner, an accomplice (cf. SIDEKICK n.[1]).

side-levers *n.* [1920s+] sideburns, side-whiskers (cf. BUGGER'S GRIPS; SIDELILACS; SIDE-WINGS; SIDIES).

sidelilacs *n.* [late 19C–1910s] (US) sideburns, side-whiskers (cf. LILACS).

side-partner *n.* [late 19C–1920s] (US) an accomplice, an assistant (cf. SIDEKICK n.[1]).

side-pocket *n.* [late 18C–1900s] used in a variety of phr. implying a lack of need, e.g. *as much need of a wife as a dog of a side-pocket,* of a worn-out old man, *want as much as a toad/dog wants a side-pocket,* does not want (need) at all.

side-pork *n.* [1950s] (W.I.) an albino (cf. FRECKLE-NATURE). [the similarity in colour of the meat and the human skin-tone]

sides *n.* [1920s–40s] (US Black) padding used by women to enlarge the appearance of the hips.

side-scrapers *n.* [late 19C] (middle class) short sideburns, fashionable 1879–82.

side-sim *n.* [17C] a fool, a simpleton. [SE *side* + abbr. *simpleton* or abbr. *Simon* as in late 16C *Sim subtle,* a cunning fellow]

sideswipe *n.* [early 19C] an insinuation, a 'snide' remark (cf. SIDEKICK n.[3]).

sidetrack *v.* [late 19C+] (US Und.) to arrest.

side up with *v.* [late 19C–1900s] to compete with, to compare with.

sidewalk snail *n.* [1940s–50s] (US) a policeman (cf. PAVEMENT POUNDER).

sidewalk superintendent *n.* [1950s+] (US) 1 any unofficial critic or observer. 2 a pedestrian who watches from the sidelines of a construction site.

sidewalk surfing *n.* [1970s+] (US) skate-boarding; thus *sidewalk surfer,* a skate-boarder.

sidewalk susie *n.* [mid-19C] a prostitute (cf. NYMPH OF THE PAVE).

sideways *n.* [1960s+] (N.Z. prison) suicide. [euph.; weak rhy. sl.]

sideways! *excl.* [1990s] (US Black) a general excl. of departure, I'm off! goodbye! see you later!

side-wheeler *n.* [20C] (US) a left-handed person.

sidewinder *n.* [mid-19C+] (US) 1 a wide-reaching blow with the fist. 2 a thug, esp. a gangster's bodyguard (cf. SIDEKICK n.[1]).

side-wings *n.* [late 19C–1900s] sideburns, side-whiskers (cf. SIDE-LEVERS).

sidey *adj.* [late 19C–1900s] conceited. [SIDE n.[1] + -*y*]

sidies *n.* [1960s] *side*burns (cf. SIDE-LEVERS). [abbr.]

siding *n.* [1980s+] (US Black/Los Angeles) leaning to the side in an exaggeratedly relaxed manner while driving.

sidity/siditty see SADDITY.

siege *n.* 1 [15C] a privy. 2 [16C] excrement. [Lat. *sedem,* a seat]

sieg heil *phr.* [1970s] (US campus) affirmative response to 'How are you?' [Ger. Nazi salute]

siff see SYPH.

sift *v.* [mid–late 19C] to steal small coins. [such that would pass through a sieve]

sifton's pets *n.* [1900s] (Can.) east European immigrants, esp. Galicians and Ruthenians. [Sir Clifford *Sifton* (1861–1910), then Canadian Minister of the Interior]

sig see SIGNIFY.

sigging *n.* [1940s] (US Black) competing in rounds of ritualized mockery (cf. DOZENS). [SIGNIFY]

sight *n.*[1] [late 17C–mid-19C] a gesture of derision, made by placing the thumb on the tip of one's nose and spreading out the fingers like a fan; thus *double sight,* the same gesture, intensified by joining the tip of the little finger to the thumb of the other hand, which in turn has its fingers extended fanwise (cf. MAKE A LONG NOSE; PULL BACON; TAKE A GRINDER).

sight *n.*[2] [mid-18C–late 19C] a large number, a great deal.

sight *n.*[3] [early 19C+] a good deal, a large amount, usu. in phr. *a sight more.*

sight *n.*[4] [mid-19C+] 1 anything that gives rise to horrified, amused or disgusted glances. 2 a shocking, repulsive or ridiculous spectacle, esp. used of people who see themselves or others improperly or inelegantly dressed.

sight *v.* [1910s+] (Aus.) 1 to tolerate, to put up with. 2 to observe, to see.

sight? *excl.* [1950s+] (W.I. Rasta) do you understand? (cf. SEEN!).

sight a pebbly beach *see* LAND ON A PEBBLY BEACH.

sightball *n.* [1980s+] (drugs) crack cocaine. [ety. unknown]

sight delight *n.* [1980s+] (US campus) a good-looking man.

sight for sore eyes *n.* [early 19C+] a welcome appearance, often used as an affectionate greeting, *you're a sight for sore eyes.*

sightseers *n.* [1960s+] (Und.) the crowd that gathers round illicit street traders or gamblers (cf. HEDGE n.).

sigmunds *n.* [1990s] haemorrhoids (cf. EMMAS). [rhy. sl. *sigmund freuds*; ult. *Sigmund Freud* (1856–1939)]

signboard *n.* [late 19C–1900s] the human face.

signification *n.* [20C] (US Black) negative or hostile talk, criticism, ritualized abuse (cf. DOZENS). [SIGNIFY]

signifier *n.* [1960s+] (US Black) one who boasts or makes insulting remarks. [SIGNIFY]

signify/sig *v.* (US Black) **1** [20C] to cause trouble, to stir things up, often purely for fun, whatever the actual results. **2** [20C] a ritual game of testing a rival's emotional strength by insulting their relatives (cf. DOZENS). **3** [1930s+] to boast or to pretend to a greater sophistication than one actually possesses. **4** [1930s+] to recite one of a variety of purpose-written 'tales', usu. recounting the exploits of some mythical gangster-cum-sexual athlete.

signifying *n.* [1950s+] (US Black) boasting, insinuating. [SIGNIFY v.]

sign of a house/tenements to let *phr.* [late 18C–late 19C] [mid-19C+] a widow's weeds. [ext. of APARTMENT TO LET]

sign of the five shillings *n.* [late 18C] any public house called the Crown; thus the *sign of the 10 shillings*, the Two Crowns, *15 shillings*, the Three Crowns. [SE *5 shillings* (25p), the value of the obsolete crown piece]

sign one's last check, to *phr.* [20C] (US) to die (cf. CASH ONE'S LAST CHECK). [banking imagery]

sigoggling *see* SKYGODLIN.

Sigourney Weaver *n.* [1990s] the female genitals, esp. the pubic hair. [rhy. sl. *Sigourney Weaver* = BEAVER n.⁴; ult. film star Sigourney Weaver (b.1949)]

sigster *n.* [mid-19C] a nap, a short sleep (cf. ZIZZ n.²).

sike! *see* PSYCH!

sil *adj.* [1960s+] of a lesbian, involved in an affair. [abbr. SE *silly about*]

silence *v.* **1** [late 18C+] to stun, to knock down. **2** [19C+] to kill.

silencer *n.* [19C+] a stunning blow.

silence-yelper *n.* [late 19C] (Und.) a courtroom usher. [their main task, the frequent orders of 'Silence in court!']

silent *adj.* [early 18C] murdered.

silent beard *n.* [19C] the pubic hair. [development of 18C BEARD n.¹]

silent beef *n.* [1960s+] (US Und.) a note attached to an individual's police record stating that they have been suspected (but not charged due to lack of proof) of committing a crime; the note requests that they be punished to the maximum extent for such lesser charges that can be brought. [SE *silent* + BEEF n.²]

silent but deadly/violent *n.* [1990s] a silent, but very smelly, breaking of wind (cf. S.B.D.).

silent city *n.* [1970s] (US Black) a graveyard.

silent cop *n.* [1930s+] (Aus.) a yellow 'sleeping policeman' placed in the centre of road intersections (cf. POACHED EGG).

silent flute *n.* [19C+] the penis (cf. FLUTE n.²).

silent night *n.* [20C] light (ale). [rhy. sl.]

Silicon Valley *n.* [1980s+] Santa Clara County, California, home of the USA's microchip technology industry. [the use of silicon in microchip manufacturing]

silk *n.*¹ [early 19C+] a Queen's Counsel. [the material of their gowns, rather than the cotton of a junior barrister's]

silk/silk broad *n.*² [1930s–50s] (US Black) a White woman. [the texture of her hair + BROAD n.²]

silk and satin *n.*¹ [1970s+] (US Black) an attractive White or light-skinned woman. [ext. of SILK n.²]

silk and satin *n.*² [1970s+] (drugs) any combination of amphetamines and barbiturates or tranquillizers.

silk broad *see* SILK n.².

silked *adj.* [1980s+] (US Black) dressed up (cf. RAGGED DOWN HEAVY).

silked to the bone *phr.* [1930s+] (US Black) dressed in the height of fashion (cf. CLEAN TO THE BONE phr.). [SILKED + TO THE BONE]

silks *n.* [1950s] (US Black) expensive clothing, poss. actually made of silk. [SE early 16C–19C]

silk-snatcher *n.* (Und.) **1** [18C] a thief who specializes in stealing cloaks by twitching them from the wearer's back. **2** [late 18C–early 19C] a thief who grabs the bonnets and hats from pedestrians.

silk stocking *n.* [1950s–70s] (US Black) a rich person. [metonymy]

silk stockings *n.* [late 18C–late 19C] (US) the social élite; thus *Silk Stocking District*, the Upper East Side of Manhattan (cf. FANCY PANTS n.). [such stockings, as opposed to the more usual cotton stockings, were a luxury item until the invention of nylon c.1935]

silkworm *n.* [early–mid-18C] a woman who tours clothes shops and examines the goods but never buys.

sillikin *n.* [mid-19C–1910s] a fool, a simpleton. [SE *silly* + dimin. sfx. -*kin*]

silly *n.*¹ [mid-19C+] a foolish person.

silly *n.*² [1970s] (N.Z. juv.) an erection. [? it makes one 'feel silly']

silly *v.* [mid-late 19C] to stun, i.e. to render silly or 'insensible'.

silly as a bag *phr.* [1930s+] (Aus./N.Z.) extremely silly (cf. SILLY AS A CHOOK; SILLY AS A CUT SNAKE; SILLY AS A HATFUL OF ARSEHOLES; SILLY AS A HATFUL OF WORMS; SILLY AS A TWO-BOB WATCH; SILLY AS A WHEEL).

silly as a chook *phr.* [1940s+] (Aus./N.Z.) extremely silly (cf. SILLY AS A BAG).

silly as a cut snake *phr.* [1930s+] (Aus./N.Z.) extremely silly (cf. MAD AS A CUT SNAKE; SILLY AS A BAG).

silly as a hatful of arseholes *phr.* [1940s–50s] (Aus.) extremely silly (cf. SILLY AS A BAG; UGLY AS A HATFUL OF ARSEHOLES). [ARSEHOLE n.]

silly as a hatful of worms *phr.* [1950s+] (orig. Aus.) euph. for SILLY AS A HATFUL OF ARSEHOLES (cf. SILLY AS A BAG).

silly as a two-bob/Woolworth's watch *phr.* [1950s+] (Aus.) very silly indeed (cf. SILLY AS A BAG).

silly as a wheel *phr.* [1950s+] (Aus.) extremely foolish (cf. SILLY AS A BAG).

silly as a Woolworth's watch *see* SILLY AS A TWO-BOB WATCH.

silly billy *n.* [late 19C+] a fool, a simpleton. [SE *silly billy*, a clown's stooge]

silly cow *n.* [1910s+] a derog. ref. to a woman, irrespective of her actual character. [SE *silly* + COW n.¹ (1)]

silly house *n.* [1960s] (US) a psychiatric institution.

silly moo *n.* [late 19C] a stupid woman. [this softened version of SILLY COW enjoyed a nationwide revival in the UK in the late 1960s with the success of the TV sitcom *Till Death Us Do Part*, in which it was used by Alf Garnett (played by Warren Mitchell) as a knee-jerk description of his put-upon wife]

sillypop *n.* [late 19C] a fool, esp. a foolish, flighty woman.

silly putty *n.* [1980s+] (drugs) psilocybin/psilocin. [joc. use of proprietary name of the children's toy]

silly season *n.* [20C] (Aus.) the Christmas holidays. [note journalists' jargon *silly season*, the summer holiday period, esp. August, when no real news is supposed to happen]

silly syrup *n.* [1950s+] sodium pentathol, the so-called 'truth drug', which is used to augment lie detector tests.

silly willy *n.* [17C–18C] a fool, a simpleton (cf. SILLY BILLY).

silver *n.* [1980s+] (N.Z. drugs) aluminium foil, used for smoking heroin.

silver beggar/lurker *n.*[1] [mid-19C] a beggar who claims to have suffered in some disaster or other, e.g. a fire or shipwreck, and asks for money in order to rebuild their life; such pleas are accompanied by a variety of documents, supposedly 'proving' the legitimacy of their claims.

silver beggar *n.*[2] [mid-19C] a counterfeit banknote or forged document.

silver cooper *n.* [19C] a kidnapper. [naut. jargon, the press gang, who 'cooped up' men for a payment of silver coins]

silver hell *n.* [mid-19C] a low-class casino. [SE *silver*, fig. inferior to gold + HELL n.[2]]

silver jeff *n.* [1950s] (US) a quarter or a nickel coin. [the image of Thomas *Jefferson* on the nickel, ? presumably confused with that of George Washington on the quarter]

silver-laced *adj.* [19C] suffering from an infestation of lice. [SE *silver-laced*, silver-threaded]

silver lurker *see* SILVER BEGGAR n.[1].

silver pearl *n.* [1990s] (drugs) a type of marijuana. [? the silveriness of this particular strain]

silver pheasant *n.* [1920s] a beautiful upper-class woman.

silver plate *phr.* [1910s–20s; 1990s] please (cf. AU RESERVOIR). [Fr. *s'il vous plait*; revived in campus use]

silver serpent *see* SERPENT.

silver spoon *n.* [1940s+] (Aus.) **1** the moon. **2** a pimp. [rhy. sl.; (2) *silver spoon* = HOON]

silvertail *n.* [late 19C–1950s] (orig. Aus.) **1** a wealthy or upper-class person (cf. COPPERTAIL). **2** one who puts on 'airs and graces', a social climber. **3** (prison) a better class prisoner. [SE *silver* + TAIL n.[1]]

silver-wig *n.* [1920s] a grey-haired man. [SE *silver* + *wig*/WIG n.[1] (1)]

silver wing *n.* [1950s] (US) a 50-cent piece. [the engraving of eagle's wings on the coin]

silvery moon *n.* **1** [1950s+] a derog. term for a Black person. **2** [1970s+] (Aus.) a pimp (cf. SILVER SPOON). [rhy. sl. *silvery moon* = (1) COON n. (3); (2) HOON]

simkin/simpkin *n.*[1] [late 17C–late 18C] a fool, a simpleton (cf. SIDE-SIM). [proper name *Simon*, presumably SIMPLE SIMON n.[1]; note 19C theatrical jargon *Simkin* or *Simpkin*, the fool in (usu. comic) ballets]

simkin/simpkin *n.*[2] [mid-19C–1920s] (Anglo-Ind.) champagne. [Ind. pron.]

simmer *v.* [1990s] to calm down.

simmon *n.* [late 18C+] per*simmon*, esp. in *simmon beer*. [abbr.]

simoleon *n.* [late 19C+] (US) $1. [? SIMON N. (2) + SE *Napoleon*, a Fr. coin worth 20 francs]

simoleons *n.* [late 19C+] (US) money. [SIMOLEON]

simon *n.* **1** [late 17C–18C] a sixpence. **2** [late 19C+] (US) $1 (cf. SIMOLEON). [for ety. *see* TANNER]

simón! *excl.* [1960s+] (US) yes. [Sp.]

simon legree *n.* [late 19C] (US Black) a cruel overseer or employer. [the character *Simon Legree*, the stereotypically evil slave-master, in the novel *Uncle Tom's Cabin* (1852) by Harriet Beecher Stowe]

simon pure *n.* [mid-19C] **1** the genuine article, the real thing. **2** the best quality whisky. [proper name of a Quaker character in *A Bold Stroke for a Wife* (1717) by Susannah Centlivre; he is impersonated by another character during Act V]

simon soon gone *n.* [mid–late 16C] a lazy servant; 'He, that

when his Mayster hath any thing to do, he will hide him out of the way' (Awdeley).

simp *n.* [20C] (orig. US) a fool, a *simpleton*. [abbr.]

simper like a frumety-kettle/furmity-kettle, to *phr.* [late 17C; 18C–19C] to smile, to look cheerful. [SE *frumenty*, a dish made of hulled wheat boiled in milk and seasoned with cinnamon, sugar etc]

simpkin *see* SIMKIN.

simple pimp *n.* [1950s–70s] (US Black) one who barely manages as a pimp and has no hope of transcending that level of employment within the criminal hierarchy.

simpler *n.* [late 16C–early 17C] **1** (Und.) the dupe or victim of a confidence trickster. **2** a simpleton, a fool. [SE *simple*]

simple simon *n.*[1] **1** [late 18C+] a fool, a simpleton. **2** [1950s] (drugs) a non-addict. [the nursery rhyme]

simple simon *n.*[2] **1** [1920s+] a diamond, usu. a diamond ring. **2** [1960s] (drugs) psilocybin/psilocin. [rhy. sl.]

simply throwing up buckets *phr.* [late 19C–1900s] (Aus.) emotionally distraught, very annoyed, very disappointed. [THROW UP v.[1]]

simpson *n.* [late 19C] **1** water used in adulterating milk. **2** adulterated milk. **3** a milkman. [one *Simpson*, a dairyman who *c*.1868 was prosecuted for watering down his milk supply]

sinbad the sailor *n.* [late 19C+] a tailor. [rhy. sl.]

sin bin *n.*[1] [1950s+] (orig. US) **1** (sports) an enclosure where errant players, e.g. in ice hockey, have to sit for a predetermined period of time. **2** (education) a school to which otherwise uneducable pupils, whose activities have disrupted their original school, are sent as a last resort.

sin bin *n.*[2] [1980s] (Aus.) a van or car used primarily for sex (cf. PASSION WAGON; SHAG-WAGON).

sin-buster *n.* [1930s] (US) a clergyman (cf. SIN-SHIFTER).

since … *phr.* various phr. all meaning a very long time, e.g. [late 19C–1900s] (Can.) … *the battle of Crecy*, [20C] … *Caesar was a pup*, [20C] … *Jesus Christ played half-back for Jerusalem*, [20C] … *Nellie had her operation*, [20C] (orig. RAF) … *Pontius was a Pilate/pilot*, [20C] … *Willie died*, [1900s] … *George Washington was a 'lance jack'*, [1900s–40s] (N.Z.) … *God called the chickens home*, [1900s–40s] (N.Z.) … *the Lord had the measles*, [1920s+] … *Christ was a corporal*, [1940s+] (N.Z.) … *Dick Seddon died/was a boy*, [1960s+] (N.Z.) … *was a cowboy*.

since Adam named the animals/was a yearling *phr.* [mid-19C+] a very long time ago (cf. WHEN ADAM WAS AN OAKUM BOY IN BROOKLYN NAVY YARD).

since Hector/Heck was a pup *phr.* [19C+] (US) for a very long time.

since hell and gone *phr.* [1920s] (US) since before anyone can remember, from time immemorial.

since the hog/hogs ate grandma/my brother/my little sister *phr.* [20C] (US) a very long time.

since time *n.* [1930s] (US Black) for a very long time. [abbr. *since time began*]

since when? *phr.* [20C] a question that casts doubt on the accuracy of the previous statement.

Sin City *n.* [1970s+] (orig. US) any city seen as a centre of vice and corruption, esp. Las Vegas, Nevada.

sinful *adj.* [1920s+] excessive, far too much.

sing *v.* [17C+] **1** to make a confession to the authorities. **2** to inform against, to betray (cf. CHIRP v.; SING OUT). [proverbial phr. 'he that sings once, weeps all his life after']

sing a placebo *see* SING PLACEBO.

Singapore tummy *n.* [20C] the diarrhoea that often afflicts travellers in foreign countries (cf. APPLE-BLOSSOM TWO-STEP).

singed cat *n.* [1910s] (US) a plain-clothes 'undercover' police officer. [the US saying 'a singed cat is better than he looks']

singer *n*. [1930s–60s] (US Und.) an informer (cf. CANARY n.[8]; STOOL-PIGEON n.[1]). [SING v.]

singing *n*. [1930s+] the act of informing. [SING v.]

single *n*. [1930s+] (US) **1** a $1 bill. **2** a person, esp. a criminal, who works or lives alone.

single *v*. [1930s–40s] (US) to work as a criminal by oneself. [SINGLE n. (2)]

single broth *n*. [18C] small beer.

single dingles *n*. [1990s] masturbation.

single fish *n*. [1990s] an act of urination.

single-jack *n*. [20C] (US tramp) a one-legged, one-armed or one-eyed beggar. [SE *single* + JACK n.[5]]

single-o *n*. [1910s–60s] **1** (US Und.) a criminal who works alone and the crimes they commit; thus *single-o*, solo, working alone. **2** (US) an unmarried person. [SINGLE n. (2) + sfx. -O]

single peeper *n*. [late 18C–early 19C] a one-eyed person. [SE *single* + PEEPERS n.]

single-pennif *n*. **1** [mid–late 19C] a £5 note. **2** [20C] £1. [FINNIF]

singleton/single ten *n*.[1] [late 17C–early 19C] a very foolish person. [? SE *single*, simple or as an elision of a *single ten*; the 10 in cards ranks one below the knave, 'he' must therefore be a fool]

singleton *n*.[2] [late 18C–early 19C] a corkscrew. [*Singleton*, a Dublin corkscrew maker, who lived 'in a place called Hell ... his screws are famous for their excellent temper' (Grose)]

singleton *n*.[3] [1990s] an unmarried person. [coined by Helen Fielding in *Bridget Jones's Diary* (1996)]

sing like a canary, to *phr*. [1950s+] (Und.) to make a full confession to the police (cf. CANARY n.[8]; SING v.).

sing o-be-joyful/oh-be-easy, to *phr*. [late 18C–early 19C] to pretend to satisfaction when one wants, in fact, to complain but dare not.

sing on *v*. [20C] (W.I.) to gossip about. [Carib.E. *sing on*, to sing a song or hymn with the intention of using its lyrics to mock a third party]

sing one's song, to *phr*. [20C] to make a remark, whether complimentary or otherwise.

sing out *v*. [early–mid 19C] of a villain, on being arrested, to betray one's accomplices. [ext. SING v. + naut. jargon *sing out*, to call out]

sing out beef, to *phr*. [early–mid 19C] to cry 'stop thief!' [SE *sing out* + (HOT) BEEF]

sing placebo/a placebo *v*. [mid-14C–late 17C] to be a toady or sycophant. [PLACEBO]

sing small *v*. [mid-18C–late 19C] to modify one's speech, esp. when it had previously been arrogant and boastful.

sings more like a whore's bird than a canary bird *phr*. [late 18C–early 19C] said of one who has a strong, manly voice. [WHORE'S BIRD]

sing the black psalm, to *phr*. [late 18C] usu. of children, to weep.

sing the blues, to *phr*. [1910s+] to complain, to whinge. [BLUES n.[1]]

sing the hallelujah chorus, to *phr*. [20C] (US prison) to be released from prison.

sing with rosie, to *phr*. [1990s] to masturbate (cf. CONVERSE WITH HARRY PALM). [ROSY PALM AND HER FIVE LITTLE SISTERS]

Sinjin's Wood *n*. [late 19C] St John's Wood. [the affectedly smart pron. of *St John's* + deliberate puns on the 'sin' and 'gin' available in St John's Wood, then an area of London notorious for its kept women and prostitutes]

sink *n*. [mid-19C–1910s] a drunkard (cf. SEWER n.[2]).

sink *v*. [1910s+] (orig. Aus.) to drink alcohol, e.g. *sink the amber*, to drink beer.

sinker *n*.[1] [mid-19C] a counterfeit coin. [it fails to 'keep a man afloat']

sinker *n*.[2] [late 19C+] (US) any form of doughy cake, esp. a doughnut; thus *sinkers and suds*, doughnuts and coffee. [habit of dunking a doughnut into one's coffee]

sinker *n*.[3] **1** [late 19C–1900s] (US) $1. **2** [1930s] (tramp) a shilling (5p).

sinkers *n*. [mid-19C] counterfeit money. [SINKER n.[1]]

sink her *v*. [20C] of a man, to have sexual intercourse (cf. SINK THE SOLDIER).

sink-hole *n*. [mid–late 19C] the throat.

sinks *n*. [mid-19C] in dice-playing, a throw of 5. [Fr. *cinq*, 5]

sink the black, to *phr*. [1990s] to drink stout. [snooker imagery + ref. to the colour of stout]

sink the boot in, to *phr*. [1910s+] (Aus.) to give a kicking. [var. on PUT THE BOOT IN]

sink the Dutch! *excl*. [1910s+] a general excl. of distaste (cf. BEAT THE DUTCH).

sink the guttie, to *phr*. [1980s+] (Irish) to drive very fast. [GUTTIES; thus to push one's plimsoll-clad foot down on the accelerator]

sink the sausage, to *phr*. [1980s+] of a man, to have sexual intercourse (cf. HIDE THE SALAMI).

sink the soldier, to *phr*. [20C] of a man, to have sexual intercourse.

sink tokes *n*. [1980s+] (US drugs) a gravity pipe, made from 2-litre (3½-pint) bottle and pipe bowl.

sinner *n*.[1] [mid-19C–1920s] a publican. [Luke 18:13 'And the publican, standing afar off, would not lift up so much as his eyes unto heaven, but smote upon his breast, saying, God be merciful to me a sinner']

sinner *n*.[2] [late 19C+] an affectionate term for an otherwise unnamed man; usu. prefaced by 'old'.

sinny *n*. [1990s] (US teen) films, cinema. [abbr. SE *cinema*]

sinse *n*. [1980s+] (drugs) cannabis. [abbr. SENSIMILLIA]

sin-shifter *n*. [1910s+] any form of clergyman (cf. SIN-BUSTER). [? pun on SE *scene-shifter*]

sip *n*. [mid-19C–1900s] a kiss. [a bee 'sipping' nectar from a flower]

sip *v*. [1900s] to urinate. [backsl. *sip* = PISS v.[1]]

sip at the fuzzy cup, to *phr*. [1970s+] (US Black) to perform cunnilingus.

siphon/syphon off the tank, to *phr*. [1990s] to masturbate.

siphon/syphon the python, to *phr*. [1960s+] **1** (Aus.) to urinate. **2** (US) to have sex (cf. POUR THE PORK).

sipper *n*. [late 19C] gravy. [SE *sibber-sauce*, ? ult. Lat. *cibarius*, pertaining to food]

si quis *n*. [mid-19C] a candidate for holy orders. [the notification of the candidacy begins *si quis ...*, if anyone ...]

Sir *n*. [1950s+] a schoolmaster.

Sir Andrew's/Sir Tristram's knot *n*. [16C] the hangman's noose. [? notorious hanging judges]

Sir Anthony Blunt *n*. [1980s] a highly objectionable person. [rhy. sl. *Sir Anthony Blunt* = CUNT n.[1]; ult. UK art historian and traitor Anthony Blunt (1907–83)]

Sir Berkeley *n*. [1930s] **1** the vagina (cf. BERKELEY HUNT). **2** sexual intercourse. [rhy. sl. *Sir Berkeley Hunt* = CUNT n.[1]]

Sir Cloudesley *n*. [late 17C–18C] a hot drink of small beer mixed with brandy, plus lemon juice, spices and sugar (cf. FLIP n.[1]). [orig. a naval speciality, proper name *Sir Cloudesley* Shovel (1650–1707), a notable British admirable who was knighted for his suppression of piracy]

Sir Courtly Nice *n*. [late 17C–18C] a foolish, foppish dandy.

siretch/sirretch *n*. [mid-19C] cherries. [backsl.]

Sir Garnet *adv*. [late 19C] all in order, everything as it should be. [for ety. *see* ALL SIR GARNET]

Sir Harry *n*. **1** [mid-19C] a close-stool, a commode (cf. SIR JOHN). **2** [1920s] constipation. [euph.]

Sir James Cotter's salad *n.* [late 18C] hemp. [for ety. *see* COTTERELL'S SALAD]

Sir John *n.* **1** [late 17C–18C] a country parson. **2** [early 19C] a close-stool, an enclosed chamberpot (cf. SIR HARRY). **3** [late 19C] the penis.

Sir Martin Wagstaffe *n.* [mid-17C] the penis. [play on SE *wag* + *staff*]

Sir Oliver *n.* [early 19C] the moon. [ext. of OLIVER n.[1]]

Sir Posthumous Hobby *n.* [late 17C–early 19C] an obsessive dandy. [a pun on SE *hobby*: 'one that Draws on his Breeches with a Shoeing-horn; also a Fellow that is Nice and Whimsical in the set of his Cloaths' B.E.]

Sir Quibble-Queer *n.* [late 17C–mid-18C] a trifling fool.

sirretch *see* SIRETCH.

sir-/save-reverence *n.* [16C–19C] faeces, excrement. [14C formal phrase meaning 'begging your pardon'. By the late 16C it had taken on this euph. secondary meaning and is the basis of the 20C euph. to 'excuse oneself' and the schoolchild's cry of 'Can I be excused?' Thus: '*reverence*, an ancient custom which obliges any person easing himself near the highway or foot-path, on the word *reverence* being given to him by a passenger, to take off his hat with his teeth, and without moving from his station to throw it over his head, by which it frequently falls into the excrement ...' (Grose, 1796)]

Sir Sydney *n.* [early–mid-19C] a clasp-knife. [ety. unknown]

Sir Timothy *n.* [late 17C–18C] a very generous man. [? anecdotal]

Sir Tristram's knot *see* SIR ANDREW'S KNOT.

Sir Walter Scott *n.* [mid-19C] a pot, usu. of beer. [rhy. sl.; ult. Scot. novelist *Sir Walter Scott* (1771–1832)]

sis/siss *n.* **1** [mid-17C+] a sister. **2** [late 19C+] (orig. US) an effeminate boy or man. **3** [late 19C+] (US) a young woman. [abbr. SISSIE]

sis!/cess! *excl.* [mid-19C+] (S.Afr.) an excl. of disgust, contempt, disappointment, dismay. [Du.]

siserary/siserara *n.* [late 18C–mid-19C] **1** a severe reprimand. **2** a hard blow. [popular corruption of a writ of *certiorari*: 'A writ, issuing from a superior court, upon the complaint of a party that he has not received justice in an inferior court, or cannot have an impartial trial, by which the records of the cause are called up for trial in the superior court' (*OED*)]

siss *see* SIS.

sissie/cissie/cissy/sissy *n.* [late 19C+] **1** a weakling. **2** an effeminate homosexual man. [SE *sissy*, a coward; ult. *sis*, *sissy*, a sister]

sissy/sissified *adj.* [late 19C+] (orig. US) weak or effeminate. [SISSIE]

sissy-bar *n.* [1960s+] a metal loop fixed behind the seat of a cycle or motorcycle. [SISSIE n.; i.e. the perceived cowardice of one who holds onto the loop]

sissy pants *n.* **1** a weakling. **2** an effeminate homosexual man. [ext. of SISSIE; on model of SMARTIEPANTS]

sissy soft sucker/soft sucker *n.* [1980s+] (US Black) a weak, effeminate man (though not necessarily a homosexual). [SISSY adj. + SE *soft* + SUCKER n.[1]]

sister *n.*[1] **1** [1920s+] (US) a term of address to any woman whose proper name one does not know (cf. MISTER). **2** [1940s–60s] (gay) the platonic gay buddy of another gay man; similarly used by lesbians. **3** [1960s+] (orig. US) a feminist.

sister *n.*[2] [1940s+] (US Black) a Black woman, esp. as *the sisters*. [abbr. SOUL SISTER]

sister-act *n.* [1960s+] **1** a homosexual couple. **2** a homosexual man having sex with a heterosexual woman.

sister girl *n.* [1980s+] (US campus) a term of address among female friends.

sister-in-law *n.* [1940s+] (US Black) any woman working for a pimp other than his favourite or TOP WOMAN.

sister of the Charterhouse *phr.* [early–mid-16C] a vociferous woman, esp. when arguing with her husband. [the ref. is to the silent monks of the Charterhouse, who would be unable to answer back]

sisters *n.* [1950s–60s] (camp gay) the police, when working in pairs.

sit a woman, to *phr.* [1950s+] (US Black) to entertain a woman. [trans. use of SE *sit*, to sit someone down]

sit beside her *n.* [20C] a spider. [rhy. sl.]

sit bitch *v.* [1970s+] (US Black/teen) to ride in the middle of the back seat (cf. RIDE BITCH). [SE *ride* + BITCH n.[1]; i.e. the supposed 'woman's seat']

sit chilly *see* LAY CHILLY.

sit down *n.* [1910s–30s] (US tramp) a free sit-down meal.

sit down *v.*[1] [20C] (Aus.) to settle in a place, to take up a piece of land.

sit down *v.*[2] [1960s+] (US teen) to make a telling, lasting impression, to have a major effect.

sit down like Miss Priss/Miss Queensie, to *phr.* [20C] (W.I.) to sit around while others are working (cf. COCK TEN). [the names of fig. lazy women]

sit-down money *n.* [1970s+] (Aus.) unemployment benefit. [SE *sit-down*, a rest + *money*]

sit-down-upons *n.* [mid-19C] trousers (cf. SIT-IN-'EMS; SIT-UPONS).

sit eggs *v.* [1970s] (US Black) to overstay one's welcome. [the image of a hen awaiting her chicks]

sit fat *v.* [20C] (US) to be successful and powerful (cf. FAT CAT; SIT IN THE CATBIRD SEAT; SITTING PRETTY). [FAT adj.[1]]

sith-nom *n.* [mid-19C] a month. [backsl.]

sit-in-'ems *n.* [late 19C] trousers (cf. SIT-DOWN-UPONS).

sit in the catbird seat, to *phr.* [1940s+] (US) to be in an advantageous position (cf. SIT FAT). [CATBIRD SEAT]

sit in the garden with the gate unlocked, to *phr.* [late 19C–1900s] **1** to conceive an illegitimate child. **2** to catch a cold.

sit in the hot seat, to *phr.* [20C] (US) to suffer execution by the electric chair (cf. TAKE THE HOT SQUAT). [HOT SEAT]

sit in tight boots, to *phr.* [mid-19C] to feel uncomfortable when talking to a superior.

sit like a monkey on a gridiron, to *phr.* [late 19C–1920s] of a horse-rider, to sit badly on a horse.

sit like a toad on a chopping-block, to *phr.* [late 18C–late 19C] to sit badly on a horse.

sit-me-down *n.* [1920s+] the buttocks (cf. SITTING ROOM; SIT-UPON).

sit on/upon *v.* [mid-19C+] **1** to rebuke, to snub. **2** to suppress, to keep quiet.

sit on a bag of fleas, to *phr.* [mid–late 19C] to be uncomfortable, to keep shifting in one's seat.

sit on a beast, to *phr.* [1970s+] (US Black teen/Los Angeles) to ride in a car that has been mechanically lifted and appears higher off the ground than normal models (cf. SIT ON A DAGO). [SE *beast*, a monster, i.e. the height of the car]

sit on a dago, to *phr.* [1970s+] (US Black teen/Los Angeles) to ride in a car that has been mechanically lowered and thus appears lower off the ground than normal models (cf. SIT ON A BEAST). [fig. use of DAGO n.; i.e. a style preferred by Hispanics]

sit on it and rotate! *excl.* [1960s+] (US) a general excl. of abuse suggesting that a hard and painful object be thrust into the subject's anus.

sit on it, Potsie *phr.* [1990s] (US Black teen) a general phr. of dismissal or mockery. [*Potsie* Weber, a character in the 1970s *Happy Days* TV show; the names of other characters can be substituted]

sit on one's ass, to *phr.* [20C] (US) to be idle when one has responsibilities to carry out. [ARSE n.¹]

sit on one's hands, to *phr.* [1920s+] (orig. theatre) to withhold one's applause, to withhold one's approval or commitment.

sit on one's stuff, to *phr.* [1970s] (US Black) to work as a prostitute. [STUFF n.⁴]

sit on someone's face, to *phr.* [1960s+] for a woman, to position her vagina directly above her partner's mouth, either literally sitting or squatting above their face, in order to facilitate cunnilingus.

sit on the penniless bench, to *phr.* [early 17C+] to be impoverished.

sit on the throne, to *phr.* [1920s+] to use a lavatory. [THRONE]

sit on tight, to *phr.* [1990s] (US Black) to stay where one is, esp. to stand firm and unruffled in the face of adversity (cf. SIT TIGHT).

sit on top of the world, to *phr.* [1930s+] (orig. US) to be absolutely secure, satisfied, happy etc, often as *sitting ...* (cf. SITTING PRETTY).

sit pad *see* STAND PAD.

sit shotgun *see* RIDE SHOTGUN.

sitter *n.¹* [late 19C+] an easy target, both in shooting and in metaphor.

sitter *n.²* [1940s+] (Aus., mainly Sydney) a regular and heavy drinker in a bar or public house. [they do nothing but sit and drink]

sitters *n.* [1930s–40s] (US) **1** homeless men and women, employed by taverns to sit near the fire and shiver in an obvious way so that kind-hearted patrons would buy them drinks (thus profiting the tavern). **2** women who frequent taverns or nightclubs and who get a percentage on the drinks they induce male patrons to buy.

sit there/stand around with one's finger/thumb up one's ass, to *phr.* [20C] (US) to be passive, unresponsive, idle and useless. [ARSE n.¹]

sit tight *v.* **1** [mid-18C] to apply oneself closely to something. **2** [late 19C+] to stay where one is, esp. to stand firm and unruffled in the face of adversity (cf. SIT ON TIGHT).

sitting duck *n.* [1940s+] (orig. milit.) an easy target, someone or something vulnerable and defenceless, both lit. and fig. [hunting imagery]

sitting next to/by/with Nelly *phr.* [1950s+] on-the-job learning, by watching an experienced older worker.

sitting-pad *n.* [mid-19C] (Und.) the cross-legged position adopted by beggars positioning themselves on the pavement. [SE *sit* + PAD n.¹]

sitting pretty *adj.* [1920s+] secure, safe, enjoying an easy life, esp. as to material things (cf. SIT FAT).

sitting room *n.* [late 19C–1900s] the buttocks (cf. SIT-ME-DOWN).

situation *n.* [1960s+] (S.Afr. Black) a member of the Black middle class, a Black 'white-collar' worker and regarded as a social climber. [SE *situation*, a job]

sit under Dr Greenfields, to *phr.* [20C] (tramp) to sleep in the open air (cf. MRS GREENFIELDS). [one is listening to an imaginary sermon or lecture]

sit up and beg, to *phr.* [late 19C+] of the penis, to become erect.

sit up and take notice, to *phr.* [late 19C+] (orig. US) to take an interest in something.

sit up like jacky, to *phr.* [1940s+] (N.Z.) to sit up straight and confident. [SE *sit up* + JACKY JACKY]

sit-upon *n.* [mid-19C] the buttocks (cf. SIT-ME-DOWN).

sit-upons *n.* [mid-19C] trousers. [abbr. SIT-DOWN-UPONS]

sit up with a sick friend *see* SEE A SICK FRIEND.

siwash *n.* [20C] (US) any small, archetypal college. [cowboy jargon *siwash outfit*, a second-rate ranch]

siwash *v.* [late 19C+] (US) to ban someone from buying alcohol. [*Siwash*, a Native American of the northwest Pacific Coast. The term, ult. Fr. *sauvage*, savage, became a generic pej.; drunkenness was seen as one of many endemic vices]

siwashed *adj.* [19C] (US cowboy) 'blackballed', i.e. used of a ranch that was barred from sending cowboys to the general round-up or to work on other ranches. [fig. use of SIWASH v.; such exclusions were often made when ranchers were seen as being over-friendly to known cattle-rustlers]

siwash side *n.* [late 19C+] (US) **1** anything done ineptly or clumsily. **2** the right-hand side of a horse. **3** the left-hand side of a cow. [*Siwash*, pej. for a Native American, who mounted horses from the right-hand side, and wrestled down cows from the left; Whites preferred the left and right sides respectively]

six *n.¹* [mid-19C–1920s] a 6-month prison sentence.

six *n.²* [1940s] (US Black) a grave (cf. DEEP SIX n.). [SIX FEET UNDER]

six-and-eight *n.¹* [1930s+] honest. [rhy. sl. *six and eight* = straight]

six-and-eight *n.²* [1960s+] an emotional 'state'. [rhy. sl.]

six-and-eightpence *n.* **1** [late 17C–18C] the accepted fee demanded for the removal of a felon from the gallows and for their burial in sacred ground (cf. PIT n.¹). **2** [mid-18C–1900s] a country solicitor, whose basic fee usually came to this amount.

six-and-four *n.* [1960s+] (drugs) heroin that has been adulterated and weakened by mixing one part pure heroin to 6 or 4 parts sugar.

six-and-tips *n.* [late 18C–early 19C] whisky and small beer. [SIXES]

six-bit *adj.* [mid-19C+] (US) cheap, worth 75 cents, e.g. *a six-bit sandwich*. [SIX BITS]

six bits *n.* [mid-19C+] (US) 75 cents.

six-cornered oath *n.* [late 19C] (US) a complex and many-worded oath.

sixer *n.¹* **1** [mid-19C] a sixth term of imprisonment of whatever length. **2** [mid-19C+] a 6-month prison sentence, 6 months' hard labour (cf. TWELVER). **3** [late 19C] a 6-ounce (170g) loaf. **4** [1920s+] (school) a punishment of 6 strokes of the cane. **5** [1980s+] (US campus) a 6-pack of beer.

sixer *n.²* *see* SHICKSA.

sixes *n.* [late 18C–early 19C] small beer. [its trad. price of 6 shillings (30p) per barrel]

six feet above contradiction *phr.* [late 19C] (US) absolutely certain, totally arrogant, impervious to any argument.

six feet and itches *n.* [late 19C] over 6 foot (1.8m) tall. [common 19C abbr. of SE *inches* as *ichs*]

six feet under *phr.* [1930s+] (orig. US) dead and buried (cf. UNDER THE SOD).

six-foot bungalow *n.* [20C] a coffin (cf. DEEP SIX).

six foot/blooming foot of tripe *phr.* [late 19C] a large policeman (cf. BLOOMING SIX FOOT OF TRIPE). [pun on SE *tripe*, intestines/TRIPE n.²]

six-foot subway *n.* [1940s] (US Black) a grave (cf. DEEP SIX).

six man *n.* [1960s+] (Can. prison) a look-out. [ety. unknown]

six-monthser *n.* [late 19C] a severe magistrate, who, whenever they can, gives the longest sentence, 6 months, that the law allows.

six months' hard *phr.* [20C] (bingo) a card. [rhy. sl.]

six months in front and nine behind *phr.* [1930s–40s] (US Black) obese. [the resemblance of one's stomach and buttocks to the swelling stomach of a pregnant woman]

six o'clock swill *n.* [1930s+] (Aus./N.Z.) the rushed orders of drinks that, between 1916 and 1955 (before a change in the laws), took place in pubs in New South Wales and parts of N.Z. before 'last orders'. [SE *six o'clock* + SWILL v.]

six of everything *phr.* [late 19C] respectable. [used by working families to describe a woman about to be married; her trousseau has 6 sets of everything necessary]

six-pack *n.*[1] [1990s] (orig. US Black) a tight, flat stomach. [the ripples resemble beer cans]

six-pack *n.*[2] [1990s] (Ulster) a paramilitary punishment involving shots to the knees, ankles and hands.

sixpenny *adj.* [late 16C–mid-17C] second-rate, cheap, worthless.

sixpenny rush *n.* [1950s–60s] (Irish) cheap admission to children's matinées at the cinema.

sixpenny/shilling sicker *n.* [20C] a seaside pleasure-boat. [it may make holiday-making 'landlubbers' sick; note local *sixpenny sick*, the Portsmouth to Gosport ferry]

sixpennyworth *n.* [1940s–50s] a 6-month prison sentence (cf. NINEPENNYWORTH).

six pounder *n.* [late 18C–early 19C] a maid. [her annual wages were for many years set at £6]

sixteen-year-old after shave *n.* [1970s] (US Black) very cheap and nasty wine.

six to four *see* TWO BY FOUR.

sixty-eight *n.* [1970s+] fellatio, i.e. 'you suck me and I'll owe you one'. [play on SIXTY-NINE]

sixty-four/64 *n.* [1990s] (US) **1** a 64-ounce (1.9-litre) bottle of malt liquor (cf. FORTY-DOG). **2** a 1964 Chevrolet Impala.

sixty-nine/soixante-neuf *n.* [late 19C+] mutual oral-genital stimulation. [synon. Fr. *soixante-neuf*; the numerals 69 supposedly mimic the head-to-tail bodily positions]

sixty-per-cent *n.* [mid–late 19C] a money-lender, a usurer, a bill-discounter. [the exorbitant rate of interest]

sixty-six *n.* [1940s–50s] (Aus.) anal intercourse. [play on SIXTY-NINE]

sixty-two *n.* [1980s+] (drugs) two half-ounces of crack cocaine. [ety. unknown]

six-up! *excl.* [1980s+] a warning shout to alert drug-users or illicit street vendors to the presence of the police or security guards; the drugs or merchandise should be hidden or even thrown away to prevent problems in a search. [DEEP SIX v.]

six ways for Sunday *phr.* [mid-19C+] askew, at an angle; thus *look six/two/nine ways for Sunday*, to squint badly (cf. NINE WAYS FROM BREAKFAST). [ety. unknown]

size *n.*[1] [19C] a half-pint (285ml). [16C *size*, the portion of bread and beer allowed to undergraduates in Cambridge colleges

size *n.*[2] [mid-19C] a jelly. [? play on SE *shape*, a jelly mould]

size/size up *v.* [late 19C+] (US) to estimate, to assess, to get to know about.

size queen *n.* [1950s+] (gay) one who is obsessed by the size of the penis of a potential partner. [SE *size* + QUEEN n.[1]]

size up *see* SIZE v.

sizzle *n.* [1930s–60s] (US Black) narcotics, when carried on the person. [play on HOT adj.[2]]

sizzle *v.* [1930s–60s] (US Black) to be exceptionally prone to arrest, esp. when holding drugs or acting in an outrageous manner (cf. HOT adj.[2]).

sizzler *n.* **1** [20C] (US) any exciting thing or person. **2** [1900s] (US) a very hot day. **3** [1950s–70s] something salacious, risqué, e.g. a book.

sizzle seat *n.* [20C] (US prison) the electric chair (cf. HOT CHAIR).

skaam *n.* [1970s+] (S.Afr.) shame. [synon. Afk.]

skaam *adj.* [1970s+] (S.Afr.) shy, embarrassed. [SKAAM n.]

skaap *n.* [1920s+] (S.Afr.) a country bumpkin, a fool. [Afk. *skaap*, a sheep]

skag *n.*[1] *see* SCAG n.[1].

skag *n.*[2] [1920s+] (US Black) an unattractive, slutty-looking woman; thus *skaggy*, ugly, sluttish (cf. SKANK n.[1]). [term revived in 1990s by campus use]

skag *n.*[3] *see* SCAG n.[2].

skagged *see* SCAGGED.

skag hag *see* SCAG HAG.

skag jones *see* SCAG JONES.

skag town *see* SCAG TOWN.

skainsmate *n.* [late 16C] a prostitute. [ety. unknown. Used in *Romeo and Juliet* (1594–5): 'Scurvie knave I am none of his flurt-gils I am none of his skaines mates.' The context seems to indicate a prostitute. ? dial. *skain*, a dagger; thus fig. a penis or *skein* of thread or wool, and thus relates to the 'sewing' imagery of intercourse (cf. NEEDLE WOMAN)]

skamas *n.* [1930s–40s] (US drugs) opium. [ety. unknown; ? Yid.]

skank *n.*[1] [1970s+] (orig. US Black) **1** an unattractive, easily available girl. **2** (US) a prostitute. **3** dirt, filth, malevolence. [? backform. of SKANKER n.[2]]

skank *n.*[2] [1980s+] (W.I./UK Black teen) a confidence trick, a fraudulent scheme. [SKANK v.[1]]

skank *v.*[1] [1960s+] (W.I.) **1** to steal and run away. **2** to loaf around. **3** to use deception to get one's way. [according to Allsopp, perhaps orig. echoic and poss. 'associated with motorbike getaways']

skank *v.*[2] [1970s+] (orig. W.I.) to dance in a style associated with dub or reggae music. [ext. of SKANK v.[1]; Allsopp suggests the dance style is 'derived from the kind of hip-swinging dancing which is both typical of people of generally low social status and reminiscent of the waist movements of a motorcyclist speeding in and out of other traffic']

skanker *n.*[1] [1970s+] (W.I.) an untrustworthy, dissolute person. [SKANK v.[1]]

skanker *n.*[2] [1980s+] (US campus) an unattractive girl. [ext. of SKANK n.[1]]

skanky *n.* [1980s+] (drugs) a dirty, clogged marijuana pipe. [SKANKY adj. (1)]

skanky/scankie *adj.* [1970s+] (US Black) **1** dirty, second-rate, unattractive, cheap-looking, ugly. **2** of a woman, attractive, sexy. [SKANK n.[1]; (2) on *bad* = *good* principle]

skanky box *n.* [1980s+] (US) an unpleasant, dirty (physically and ethically) woman. [SKANK n.[1] + BOX n.[6]]

skate *n.* **1** [late 19C+] (US) an inferior horse. **2** [late 19C+] a mean or contemptible person (cf. CHEAPSKATE n.). **3** [1970s+] (S.Afr.) 'a disreputable White male (from a working-class background) whose behaviour is uncouth, hedonistic, and irresponsible' (*DSAE*). [fig. use, but for (3) note Afk. *skuit*, excreta]

skate *adj.* [1970s+] (US campus) easy, simple, esp. of work or a course. [one can SE *skate* it]

skate *v.* **1** [1910s+] to rush off, to leave at speed. **2** [1930s+] (orig. US Black) to get away with anything, to shirk one's responsibilities, esp. to avoid paying one's debts.

skate rat *n.* [1980s+] (US teen) a fanatical skate-boarder.

skates-lurk *n.* [mid-19C] (Und.) the practice of posing as a sailor for the purposes of begging. [? SE *skate*, the fish + LURK n. (1). Beale in Partridge (1984) suggests that this might 'just poss[ibly]' be the origin of SKATE n.[1] (2)]

skating *adj.* [1950s+] intoxicated with drugs or drink.

skating rink/flies' skating rink *n.* [1910s+] a bald head.

sked *n.* [1920s+] (US) a schedule. [abbr.; note US pron. 'skedule']

skedaddle *n.* [late 19C+] a rush, a hurry.

skedaddle/skidoodle *v.* [mid-19C+] (orig. US) **1** of people, to rush off, to scamper, to escape. **2** of animals, to stampede. [orig. US milit. jargon *skedaddle*, to flee the battlefield, to retreat quickly; thence 'civilian' uses. Webster (1867) suggests

Scand. roots, but *OED* and other authorities reject this. The term may have existed in Eng. dial./Scot. (meaning to scatter, to spill, as of a pail of milk, a bucket of potatoes) slightly earlier than its US use, but that seems merely coincident. Hotten adds a ref. to 'very fair Greek, the root being that of "skedannumi" to disperse, to "retire tumultuously" ... it was probably set afloat by some professor at Harvard'. A number of other commentators – incl. Cohen (1985), Flexner and Bartlett – agree. Other theories include a link to the Irish *scegadol*, scattered, which has been disproved, but there may still be one to a variety of other Gaelic words, e.g. *scead*, fright, *sgadarlach*, anything scattered or dispersed, *scaoll*, fright, panic. Cohen, in an extensive analysis (Cohen, 1985, pp.29–63), suggests Scot. *skiddle*, to scatter + ? comb. *jabble*, to scatter. Thus the earlier use must be accepted and the Scot./northern 'spill/scatter' transfers to the US 'flee' through the image of blood and corpses being thus 'spilled and scattered' on the battlefield before the flight of a demoralized army]

skee *n.*[1] [late 19C+] (US, then Aus./N.Z.) whisky. [abbr./pron.]

skee *n.*[2] [1920s–50s] (drugs) opium. [? SKEE *n.*[1] or SKAMAS]

skeef *adj.* [1960s+] (S.Afr.) crooked, off-beat. [Afk. *scheef*, askew]

skeeger *see* SKEEZA.

skee joint *n.* [late 19C] (US) a bar or saloon (cf. ALKY JOINT). [SKEE *n.*[1] + JOINT *n.*[3] (3)]

skeet *v.* [20C] (US Black) to have sexual intercourse. [? SE *skeet-shooting*]

skeeter *n.* [19C] (Aus./US) a mosquito. [abbr. + Aus./N.Z. pron.]

skeeve *v.* [1990s] (US) to disgust, to repel; thus *skeeve*, a disgusting person. [? Ital. *schifoso*, disgusting]

skeeza/skeeger/skeezer *n.* [1980s+] **1** (US Black) a woman who trades sex for status or free drugs; her chosen partners are often drug dealers or performers (cf. BAND RAT; GROUPIE). **2** (US campus) a person, usu. female, who attempts to have a relationship with a member of the opposite sex only for their material possessions, in order to make an impression on other people. [SKEEZE]

skeeze *v.* [1980s+] (US Black) **1** to have sexual intercourse (cf. SKEEZA). **2** to have an orgy. [? SAmE *skeezicks*, a 'mean, contemptible fellow' (Bartlett); ? ult. Cornish *skeese*, to frisk about + *skicer*, a lamb that kills itself through excess activity]

skeezer *see* SKEEZA.

skeffington's/scavenger's daughter *n.* [mid-late 16C] an instrument of torture, consisting of a broad iron hoop, which was locked around the prisoner's body, compressing it unnaturally to such an extent that the victim was effectively squeezed to death. [its inventor, Sir William *Skeffington*, Lieutenant of the Tower of London *c.*1530–40]

skeggy *adj.* [20C] unpleasant, disgusting, the implication is of rotting or faecal matter. [echoic; the sense is of a cry of disgust]

skein of thread *n.* [late 19C–1930s] a loaf of bread. [rhy. sl.]

skelder *v.* [late 16C–early 17C] **1** to work as a professional beggar, esp. to pose as a wounded or discharged soldier. **2** to swindle, to defraud; thus *skeldering*, begging, swindling (cf. SKELL). [Du. *skellum*, a rogue, a villain, a pestilence]

skeleton army *n.* [late 19C] street-fighters. [the *Skeleton Army* flourished briefly as an opposition force to the Salvation Army, a more physically militant organization *c.*1880s than subsequently]

skell *n.* [1950s+] (US) a villain, a rogue, esp. a vagrant who lives on the streets. [SKELDER]

skelm *adj.* [20C] (S.Afr. Und.) fake, counterfeit. [SKELM *v.*]

skelm *v.* [20C] (S.Afr. Und.) to do something in an underhand

way. [Afk. *skelm*, a villain, a rascal; note obs. SE *skelm* a rascal, itself f. Du. *schelm*, a rascal]

skelter *n.* [late 19C–1910s] a scamper, a rush. [SE *helter-skelter*]

skeng *n.* [1970s] (W.I.) a ghetto weapon, e.g. a gun, a ratchet-knife. [? Carib.E. *skengay*, a form of music in which the guitar sounds are seen as mimicking those of gunfire]

skerrick *n.* **1** [early 19C] a halfpenny. **2** [mid-19C+] (Aus./N.Z.) a small amount, a small fragment, the slightest bit. [dial. *skewick*, an atom, a fragment]

sketch *n.*[1] [late 19C] a very small quantity, a single drop. [SE *sketch*, an outline]

sketch *n.*[2] [1910s–30s] a ridiculous or amusing person or sight; thus *hot sketch*, a comical or colourful person.

sketch *n.*[3] [1980s+] (US campus) **1** one who feels confused, unstable, odd. **2** a close call, a narrow escape.

sketch *adj.* [1980s+] (US campus) risky, dangerous. [SKETCHED OUT]

sketch *v.* [1980s+] (US campus) to feel unstable or confused. [SKETCH *n.*[3]]

sketched *adj.* [1980s+] (US campus) bad, bizarre, weird. [SKETCHED OUT]

sketched out *adj.* [1980s+] (US campus) suffering paranoia due to the effects of hallucinogenic drugs; thus *sketching*, coming down from a drug-induced high. [SKETCHY (2)]

sketchy *adj.* **1** [late 19C+] flimsy, insubstantial, vague. **2** [1980s+] (US campus) confused, unstable, strange, unsettling.

skew/scew *n.*[1] [mid-16C–mid-18C] a cup or dish. [Lat. *scutella*, a dish]

skew *n.*[2] [mid-19C] weeks. [backsl.]

skewer *n.* **1** [mid-19C] a sword. **2** [late 19C–1920s] a pen.

skew-fisted *adj.* [late 17C–early 18C] awkward, ungainly. [SE *askew*]

skewgee *n.* [20C] a squint. [SKEWGEE *adj.*]

skewgee *adj.* [late 19C+] squinting, crooked. [SE *askew*]

skewings *n.* [mid-19C] **1** extras, bonuses. **2** money, esp. for nothing (cf. BLUE PIGEON; BUNCE *n.*). [SE *skew*, to escape; i.e. money that has 'escaped' from the regular accounts]

skew-the-dew *n.* [late 19C] a splay-footed person. [SKEW-THE-DEW *adj.*]

skew-the-dew *adj.* [late 19C] splay-footed. [SE *skew*, to take an oblique course + *dew*; i.e. the way one's feet point outwards when walking]

skewvow *adj.* [late 18C–early 19C] askew, out of true, crooked. [var. on SKEW-WHIFF]

skew-whiff *adj.* **1** [mid-18C+] crooked, out of true, aslant. **2** [20C] drunk (cf. SQUIFFY). [SE *askew*]

skezag *n.* [1960s+] (drugs) heroin. [SCAG *n.*[3], with pig Latin insertion of -*ez*]

ski *n.*[1] [1950s] (Aus.) a taxi. ? weak why. sl.]

ski *n.*[2] [1980s+] (US drugs) cocaine. [play on SNOW *n.*[2]]

-ski *sfx.* [1980s+] (US campus) a sfx. added to names to indicate stupidity. [? implication of the supposed stupidity of eastern European immigrants]

skibby/skippy *n.* (US) **1** [1920s+] a derog. term for a Japanese person. **2** [1950s] an Oriental prostitute. [Jap. *sukibei*, randy or lecherous. The word had also meant a courtesan, and the sense was extended to mean 'loose' or 'unchaste'. In US mouths it tended to refer to a female domestic servant, but the seeming synonymity of the term *skivvy*, also a maid of all work, may in fact be coincidental]

ski bum *n.* [1960s+] (orig. US) a skiing enthusiast who takes a job as an instructor at a skiing resort. [SE *ski* + BUM *n.*[3] (6)]

ski bunny *n.* [1960s+] (US) a woman who frequents ski resorts to solicit rather than to ski. [SE *ski* + BUNNY *n.*[2]]

skid *n.*[1] *see* SKIV.

skid *n.*[2] [1970s] (drugs) heroin, usu. heavily diluted; thus *skid bag*, a bag of inferior heroin. [var. on GREASY BAG]

skid *v.* **1** [1900s–20s] to leave, to go (cf. SKIDOO). **2** [1920s+] (US) to blunder, to make a mistake, to decline.

skid artist *n.* [1960s+] (Und.) an expert driver of a get-away car, used on robberies. [the speedily driven car *skids* around corners + ARTIST *n.*[2]]

skid bag *n.* [1970s] (US drugs) a bag in which heroin is transported and/or sold (cf. GREASY BAG). [SKID *n.*[2] + BAG *n.*[8]]

skid-bid *n.* [1980s+] (US prison) a term in prison or in juvenile detention. [SE *skid*, i.e. off the 'straight and narrow' + BIT *n.*[7]]

skiddoo *v. see* SKIDOO *v.*

skiddoo! *see* SKIDOO!

skid grease *n.* [1920s+] (US) butter.

skidlid *n.* [1950s+] a crash helmet. [SE *skid* + LID *n.*[1]]

skid marks *n.* [1930s+] faecal stains on one's underwear.

skidoo/skiddoo *v.* [late 19C+] (US) to leave quickly, to run off. [? SKEDADDLE or SCADOODLE or SE *skid*; alt. ? link to SKID ROW/ON THE SKIDS]

skidoo!/skiddoo! *excl.* [late 19C+] a general term of abuse, scram! go away! [SKIDOO *v.*]

skidoodle *see* SKEDADDLE *v.*

skid-pipe plumber *n.* [1990s] a male homosexual.

skid row *n.* [1920s+] the centre, in any town or city, for down-and-outs, alcoholics, tramps and other poor or homeless individuals. [late 19C logging jargon *skid road*, a grassed track over which logs were hauled towards the river that would float them down to the sawmill; *c.*1915 the term was extended into sl. to mean that part of a town where loggers spent their free time or lived when they were out of work. It was the latter meaning, with its added implication of a man, rather than a log, who was 'skidding downhill' economically that dominated usage by the 1930s, when *skid road* became *skid row*, once more with an overtone, the use of *row* to denote the concentration of certain businesses or occupations in certain urban streets, e.g. Hollywood's *Poverty Row*, the area where the cheaper studios congregated]

skidsville *n.* [1920s+] (US) a state of poverty. [ON THE SKIDS + sfx. -VILLE]

skied *adj.*[1] [1980s+] (drugs) extremely intoxicated by a drug. [pun on SE *sky*/HIGH]

skied *adj.*[2] [1980s+] (US campus) ready for anything. [play on PSYCHED]

skiet *v.* (S.Afr.) **1** [1950s+] to gamble with dice. **2** [1970s+] to tell lies, to deceive (cf. SHOOT A LINE). [Afk. *skiet*, to shoot. (2) Afk. *spek skiet*, 'shoot bacon', to tell lies or *kaart skiet*, to shoot a line]

skiets *n.* [20C] (S.Afr.) diarrhoea (cf. SHITS). [Afk. *skyt*, to defecate]

skiet und donder *phr.* [1960s+] (S.Afr.) a melodrama, an action film or book; also ext. as *skop, skiet and donder*, lit. 'kick, shoot and thunder' (cf. SKOP *n.*[1]; THUD AND BLUNDER). [Afk. *skiet und donder*, shoot and thunder; thus blood and thunder]

skiff *n.* [late 19C–1900s] a leg. [? Dorset dial. *skife*, to kick up one's heels]

skiffle *n.* [1930s–40s] (US Black) a party at which the guests pay a subscription to cover refreshments and to help the host out with the rent (cf. RENT PARTY). [SE *scuffle* via dial. *skiffle*; music at such parties was provided by non-professional musicians; thus the *skiffle groups* (who were paid but performed on essentially homemade instruments) of the 1950s]

skiffling and shuffling *n.* [1940s] (US Black) any form of frenetic activity. [SKIFFLE and SE *shuffle*]

skilagolee/skilligalee/skilligolee *n.* [mid-19C+] **1** (prison,

workhouse) thin, un-nourishing broth, gruel. **2** a small coin of minimal value, usu. in phr. *not worth a skilagolee*; thus *skilagolee*, worthless. [ext. of SKILLY]

skilamalink *adj.* [late 19C] secret, under cover. [ety. unknown]

skillet *n.* [1920s–50s] (US Black) a Black person. [SE *skillet*, a cast-iron (black) frying pan]

skillet blonde *n.* [1920s–30s] (US Black) a Black woman wearing a blonde wig. [SKILLET + SE *blonde*]

skilligareen *n.* [1910s–20s] a very thin person. [ext. of SKILAGOLEE; the link being the thinness]

skilligolee *see* SKILAGOLEE.

skillion/scillion *n.* [20C] (US) a very large and indefinite number. [pattern of SE *trillion* etc]

skilly *n.* [mid-19C+] **1** (prison/workhouse) gruel, broth (cf. CLODS AND STICKINGS; SMIGGINS). **2** any weak beverage, e.g. tea or coffee. [abbr. SKILAGOLEE]

skilly and toke *phr.* [mid-late 19C] anything mild or insipid. [prison use *skilly and toke*, thin gruel and dry bread; ult. SKILLY + TOKE *n.*[1]]

skim/skim money *n.* [1960s+] (orig. US) **1** that percentage of the takings at a casino that is not declared in the accounts and thus illicitly withheld from taxation. **2** any money that is stolen from an operation (e.g. numbers, gambling, racecourse betting) by a lower echelon employee and not declared to those who control that operation. [SKIM *v.*]

skim *v.* [1960s+] (orig. US) **1** to conceal some part of one's earnings in order to avoid paying tax on them. **2** of an employee, to hold back a proportion of the profits from one's job (usu. in some form of gambling), thus stealing from one's employer.

skimish/skimmish *n.* [20C] (usu. tramp) beer, alcohol; thus *skimisher/skimmisher*, a heavy drinker; *skimished/skimmished*, drunk. [Shelta *skimis*, to drink, *skimisk*, drunk]

skimmer *n.*[1] [early 19C+] (US) a broad-brimmed boater with a very low crown, esp. when made of straw (cf. FLYER *n.*[5]). [SE *skimmer hat*, so called from the potential of skimming it like a frisbee]

skimmer *n.*[2] [1970s] (US) a financial criminal who withholds money from their firm's profits. [SKIM *v.*]

skimming *n.* [1960s+] stealing from the till, taking money 'off the top', esp. as found in casinos, strip clubs and other places where a degree of criminality is already endemic. [SKIM *v.*]

skimmish *see* SKIMISH.

skim money *see* SKIM *n.*

skin *n.*[1] [early–mid-19C] a purse, a pocketbook, a wallet; thus *queer skin*, an empty wallet. [the leather of which it is made]

skin *n.*[2] [mid-19C] a sovereign. [? SKIN *n.*[1]]

skin *n.*[3] [late 19C+] **1** a person, e.g. in phr. *a decent old skin*. **2** (US) oneself, one's life. [metonymy]

skin/skins *n.*[4] [20C] (orig. naut.) a derog. generic for women. [ext. of SKIN *n.*[3]]

skin *n.*[5] [1920s–30s] (US Black) a drum (cf. SKIN-BEATER). [abbr. SE *drumskin*]

skin *n.*[6] [1920s–40s] (US/Aus.) a horse, a mule.

skin *n.*[7] [1930s+] (US) $1 (cf. FROG *n.*[5]). [abbr. FROGSKIN]

skin *n.*[8] [1930s+] (US Black) the hand as in a handshake (cf. GIVE SOME SKIN; SLAP FIVE).

skin *n.*[9] *see* SKINPOP *n.*

skin/skins *n.*[10] [1950s–70s] a tyre.

skin *n.*[11] [1960s+] a cigarette paper, esp. those used for rolling, usu. in pl. (cf. SKIN UP *v.*[3]). [it provides a *skin* for the tobacco (and cannabis)]

skin *n.*[12] [1970s+] a *skin*head. [abbr.]

skin *n.*[13] [1990s] (US Black) a condom.

skin *adj.*[1] [late 19C] (US campus) unfair. [SKIN v.[1]]

skin *adj.*[2] [1950s+] (US) featuring nudity (cf. SKIN FLICK; SKIN GAME n.[2]; SKIN HOUSE n.[2]; SKIN MAG).

skin *v.*[1] **1** [early 19C+] to take all a person's money in a gambling game. **2** [early 19C+] to cheat or defraud someone of their money or other possessions. **3** [mid-19C] to drop in price or value. **4** [mid-19C+] (US) to beat, to overcome completely. **5** [late 19C] to steal from.

skin *v.*[2] [mid-19C] (US campus) to copy, to cheat in an examination. [? ext. of SKIN v.[1] (2)]

skin *v.*[3] [mid-19C–1920s] (US) to abscond, to run off; thus *skin through*, to slip through, to pass through narrowly.

skin *v.*[4] [late 19C] (US) to glance at, to examine. [one fig. 'removes their skin']

skin *v.*[5] see SKINPOP v.

skin-a-guts *n.* [1910s–20s] a very thin person. [SE *skin-and-bones*]

skin alive *v.* [late 19C+] (orig. US) to thrash.

skin a louse, to *phr.* [20C] (Irish) to be extremely mean and covetous (cf. HE WOULD SKIN A TURD).

skin-and-blister *n.* [1920s+] a sister. [rhy. sl.]

skin-and-grief *n.* [late 19C] a very thin person (cf. SKIN-A-GUTS).

skin and grin, to *phr.* **1** [1950s+] (W.I.) to laugh foolishly or ingratiatingly, to pretend to be friendly; thus *skinning and grinning*, laughing foolishly, pretending to be friendly. **2** [1990s] (US Black) to act in an openly friendly, happy manner. [GIVE SOME SKIN + SE *grin*]

skin a razor, to *phr.* [late 19C–1900s] to drive a very hard bargain (cf. HE WOULD SKIN A TURD).

skin-beater *n.* [1930s–50s] a drummer. [SKIN n.[5] + SE *beater*]

skin boy *n.* [1980s] (N.Z.) an uncircumcised male (cf. RING-BARKED). [abbr. SE *foreskin*]

skin catch fire/fire for, to *phr.* [20C] (W.I.) to become obsessed with someone at first sight and thus to desire to possess them immediately (cf. EYES CATCH FIRE).

skincoat *n.* [16C] the vagina (cf. LEATHER n.[2]).

skinder/skinner *n.* [1970s+] (S.Afr.) gossip, slander; thus *skinderbek*, a scandalmonger (lit. 'scandal-mouth') (cf. SKINNY n.[1]). [Afk. *skinder*, to slander, to gossip, to tattle]

skin-disease *n.* [late 19C–1910s] fourpenny ale. [? its deleterious effects or its (relatively) high cost, which will SKIN v.[1] the purchaser]

skin-diver *n.* [20C] a male homosexual. [his supposed appetite for fellatio]

skin flick *n.* [1960s+] a pornographic film (cf. SKIN GAME n.[2]; SKIN MAG). [SKIN adj.[2] + FLICKS]

skinflint *n.* [late 18C+] a mean person. [obs. SE phr. *skin a flint*, to be very mean or greedy]

skin flute *n.* [19C+] the penis (cf. FLUTE n.[2]).

skin frisk *n.* [20C] (US prison) a skin search. [SE *skin* + FRISK v.[2]]

skin game *n.*[1] [mid-19C+] **1** (US) any form of gambling that is designed to fleece the uninitiated. **2** (US Black) a card-game, spec. tonk or coon can. [SKIN v.[1] + SE *game*]

skin game *n.*[2] [1960s+] the pornography trade (cf. SKIN FLICK). [SKIN adj.[2] + *game*, occupation, trade]

skinhead *n.* **1** [1950s+] (orig. US) a bald person. **2** [1960s+] a member of a teen youth cult whose main identifying features are bald heads, large 'bother' boots, turned-up jeans and braces and who provide much of the 'heavy' element of the modern neo-Nazi movements.

skin house *n.*[1] [mid-19C–1900s] (US) a gambling establishment. [SKIN v.[1] + SE *house*]

skin house *n.*[2] [1970s+] (US) an establishment providing pornographic entertainment. [SKIN adj.[2] + *house*]

skin mag/magazine *n.* [1960s+] a pornographic magazine

(cf. ONE-HAND MAGAZINE; SKIN FLICK; STROKE BOOK). [SKIN adj.[2] + SE *magazine*]

skin me! *excl.* [1950s+] (US Black) a form of greeting involving ritual palm slapping. [imper. form of GIVE SOME SKIN]

skin-merchant *n.* [late 18C–mid-19C] a military recruiting officer. [ironic use of SE]

skinned *adj.* **1** [1900s–20s] comprehensively beaten, utterly defeated. **2** [1930s+] deprived of one's money, esp. after gambling unsuccessfully. [SE *skin*/SKIN v.[1]]

skinned mush *n.* [mid-19C] (US) a cane. [SE *skinned* + MUSH n.[2]]

skinned rabbit *n.* [late 19C–1910s] a very thin person. [resemblance]

skinner *n.*[1] [mid-19C] a thief, usu. a woman, who waylays young children and strips them of their clothes, which she then sells. [SE *skin*]

skinner *n.*[2] **1** [mid-19C] a bet that brings large profits to the bookmakers. **2** [mid–late 19C] one who defrauds another of their money. **3** [late 19C+] (Aus.) a horse that wins despite very long odds. **4** [20C] (Aus.) any form of racing coup. **5** [1940s+] (N.Z.) a person who is out of money or an object that is useless or used up (cf. SKINNED). [SKIN v.[1]]

skinner *n.*[3] [late 19C+] (Can.) a horse-driver. [abbr. SE *mule-skinner*]

skinner *n.*[4] [20C] (US Und.) a rapist. [SE *skin*]

skinner *n.*[5] [1920s+] (Aus.) an appointment that one has deliberately avoided. [? phr. 'by the skin of one's teeth']

skinner *n.*[6] see SKINDER.

skinners *n.* [late 19C] mental torture. [one's mind, rather than one's body is 'flayed alive']

skinning *n.*[1] [1920s+] (US) a beating, whether physical or verbal. [SE *skin*/SKIN v.[1] (3)]

skinning *n.*[2] [1970s+] the injecting of a narcotic into the skin but not into a vein (cf. SKINPOP n.).

skinny *n.*[1] [1940s+] **1** information, often as *inside skinny*. **2** the truth. [? play on SE *skin*, i.e. 'the naked truth', 'the bare facts']

skinny *n.*[2] [1940s] (Aus.) a woman. [SKIN n.[4]]

skinny as a broom *n.* [20C] a bridegroom (cf. FAT AND WIDE). [rhy. sl.]

skinny dip *v.* [1960+] (orig. US) to bathe in the nude.

skinny down *v.* [20C] (US) to reduce something to a minimum. [SE *skinny down*, to lose weight]

skinny Lizzie *n.* [20C] a thin woman.

skin off your nose *phr.* [1920s–50s] (orig. naut.) a popular toast, often ext. as *here's to the skin off your nose* (cf. NO SKIN OFF ONE'S NOSE).

skin of the creature *n.* [mid-19C+] (Anglo-Irish) a bottle of whisky. [SE *skin* + CREATURE n.[1]]

skin one's eels, to *phr.* [mid–late 19C] to mind one's own business.

skin one's teeth, to *phr.* [20C] (W.I.) to smile falsely, although one feels furious or embittered, to laugh cynically (cf. GIVE SKIN-TEETH). [the amount of gum revealed by such a broad, empty smile]

skin out *v.* [late 19C] (US) to produce, to show.

skinpop/skin *n.* [1950s+] (drugs) an injection into the flesh rather than directly into a vein. [SKINPOP v.]

skinpop/skin *v.* [1950s+] (drugs) to inject a narcotic beneath the skin rather than directly into a vein; the effect of such an injection is less immediate and somewhat weaker; thus *skin-popper*, one who injects heroin in this way and is, supposedly, a less habituated user (cf. MAINLINE v.). [SE *skin* + POP v.[6] (1)]

skin queen *n.* [1960s+] (US gay) a male homosexual who views his partners as no more than sex objects, a gay sexist. [SE *skin* + QUEEN n.[1]]

skins *n.*[1] [late 18C] a tanner. [their job]

skins n.[2] see SKIN n.[4].

skins n.[3] [1920s+] a set of drums. [SKIN n.[5]]

skins n.[4] see SKIN n.[10].

skins n.[5] [1990s] (US Black) **1** fried pork rinds. **2** shoes made from exotic animal skins, e.g. alligator or lizard.

skin-search n. [1930s+] **1** a search in which the subject is stripped naked and searched, usu. for narcotics or, in prison, concealed weapons. **2** a person who suffers such a search.

skint adj. [late 19C+] without money, out of funds, sometimes intensified as skint stony (cf. BROKE). [SE skinned]

skin teeth n. [1970s+] (W.I.) a false smile.

skin teeth/'kin teet' v. [1970s+] (W.I./UK Black teen) **1** to have a laugh or a joke with someone or at something, to mess around. **2** to bare one's teeth, to smile broadly.

skin the cat, to phr. [19C+] to have sexual intercourse (cf. SKIN THE PIZZLE). [SE skin + CAT n.[4] (2)]

skin the goose, to phr. [1970s] (US) to masturbate.

skin-the-lamb n.[1] [mid-19C] the card-game lansquenet, sometimes as lamb skin-it. [pun on pron.]

skin-the-lamb n.[2] (US Black) **1** [late 19C–1940s] a fraud, a cheat. **2** [1920s–60s] an adulterous man. [SKIN THE LAMB]

skin the lamb, to phr. [mid–late 19C] **1** to swindle, to hoax, to blackmail. **2** to fix a horse-race. [SKIN v.[1]; a play on SE fleece]

skin the live rabbit, to phr. **1** [19C] to have sexual intercourse. **2** [late 19C–1900s] of a man, to peel back one's foreskin. [SE skin + LIVE RABBIT]

skin-the-pizzle n. [mid-19C–1900s] the vagina (cf. CATCH 'EM ALIVE-O). [SKIN THE PIZZLE phr.]

skin the pizzle, to phr. [mid-19C–1900s] to have sexual intercourse (cf. SKIN THE CAT). [SE skin + PIZZLE n.]

skintights n. [20C] sausages.

skin up v.[1] [20C] (W.I.) **1** to overturn. **2** of a woman, to expose oneself, esp. one's buttocks, in an indecent manner, also as skin up one's clothes/dress/oneself. [SE skin]

skin up/up with v.[2] [1950s+] (W.I.) to laugh foolishly and ingratiatingly (cf. SKIN AND GRIN).

skin up v.[3] [1960s+] (drugs) to roll a cannabis-filled cigarette. [SKIN n.[11]]

skin up one's face/lip/mouth/nose, to phr. [1950s+] (W.I.) to make a grimace of displeasure, scorn or disapproval. [SKIN UP v.[2]]

skin up with see SKIN UP v.[2].

skin worker n. [20C] (US Und.) a shoplifter, usu. of furs. [SE skin, a fur]

skin your eye phr. [mid–late 19C] (US) a phr. of warning, watch out, keep your eyes open. [var. on KEEP ONE'S EYE PEELED]

skip n.[1] [early 18C+] the captain. [abbr. SKIPPER n.[2]]

skip n.[2] [late 19C–1900s] (Anglo-Irish) a dance (cf. HOP n.[1]).

skip n.[3] [1910s+] (US) an absconder, esp. one who leaves without paying their debts. [SKIP v.]

skip v. [early 19C+] to leave, to escape, to run off. [SE 15C–early 19C]

skip and jump n. [20C] the heart. [rhy. sl. skip and jump = PUMP n.[4]]

skip it! excl.[1] [1930s+] (orig. US) forget it! don't bother! etc. [SE skip, to miss out]

skip it! excl.[2] [1950s+] (orig. US) go away! leave! [SKIP v.]

skip-jack n. **1** [16C–18C] a conceited fop or dandy. **2** [17C] a horse-trader's boy, who puts the horses through their paces. **3** [17C] a jockey. [SE skip + SE jack, generic for a man]

skip-kennel n. [late 17C–mid-19C] a footman. [he skips or jumps over the kennel or gutter]

skip on v. [1980s+] (US campus) to go away, to leave. [ext. of SKIP v.]

skip out/out on v. [late 19C+] (orig. US) to desert, to abandon, to run off. [ext. of SKIP v.]

skipper n.[1] **1** [16C+] a shelter for tramps and other homeless people. **2** [late 16C–19C] a barn. **3** [mid-19C] one who sleeps in hedges and outhouses (cf. SKIPPERING). [Welsh ysgubor, a barn]

skipper n.[2] **1** [19C] the devil. **2** [1920s+] a boss, a manager, a police sergeant etc. **3** [1920s+] a general mode of address. [SE skipper, a ship's captain]

skipper n.[3] [late 19C] one who is retreating or leaving. [SKIP v.]

skipper n.[4] [1990s] a promiscuous young woman. [SE skip, i.e. from bed to bed, from partner to partner]

skipper/skipper it v. [late 16C+] to sleep rough. [SKIPPER n.[1]]

skipper-bird n. [mid-19C] one who sleeps in a barn, a tramp, a vagrant. [SKIPPER n.[1] (3) + BIRD n.[2]]

skippering n. [mid-19C+] sleeping in derelict, empty houses. [SKIPPER v.]

skipper it see SKIPPER v.

skippy n.[1] see SKIBBY.

skippy n.[2] [1930s–40s] (US Black) an effeminate homosexual man. [SE skip, to jump around]

skippy n.[3] [1980s] (Aus.) a White child (cf. JOEY n.[11]). [the TV series Skippy, the Bush Kangaroo]

skips n. [1980s] (US teen) tennis shoes.

skip tracer n. [1950s+] (US) an investigator who tracks down those who default on hotel and other bills. [SKIP n.[3] + SE tracer]

skirmish v. [mid-19C–1900s] (US) to look around in search of something.

skirt n. [late 19C+] **1** a woman, usu. an attractive woman. **2** a generic term for women as a group (cf. APRON n.[1]). [metonymy]

skirt-chaser n. [1940s+] (orig. US) a Don Juan, a habitual and dedicated ladies' man.

skirt duty n. [1920s] **1** of a woman, the practice of acting in a way designed to attract men. **2** of a man, associating with women.

skirt-foist n. [mid–late 17C] a female cheat. [SE skirt + FOIST n.[1]]

skirt-hunting n. [late 19C+] the activity of looking for female companionship, whether amateur or professional.

skirt patrol n. [1940s] (US) the activity of wandering around looking for female companionship.

skis n. [1940s–60s] (US Black) very large shoes.

skit n. [1920s] a large number, a crowd, often in pl., i.e. skits of. [ety. unknown; ? link to SCADS]

skit v.[1] [late 18C–early 19C] to wheedle. [SE skit, to caper or leap around]

skit v.[2] [1950s+] (S.Afr.) to steal, to 'pinch'. [Afk. skut, to impound]

skite n. (Aus./N.Z.) **1** [mid-19C+] boasting, bragging. **2** [late 19C+] a braggart, a boaster. [SKITE v.]

skite v. [mid-19C+] (Aus./N.Z.) to boast or brag; thus skite up, to extol, to praise, nothing to skite about, nothing to make a fuss about. [abbr. BLATHERSKITE]

skiter n. [late 19C+] (Aus./N.Z.) an incessant talker. [SKITE v.]

skite-the-gutter n. [20C] (Ulster) an unimportant person. [OE skite, to defecate]

skitey adj. [20C] (Aus./N.Z.) boastful. [SKITE v.]

ski the pink run, to phr. [1990s] of a man, to have fast and vigorous sexual intercourse.

skiting n. [mid-19C+] (Aus./N.Z.) boasting, bragging. [SKITE v.]

ski-trip n. [1970s+] (US drugs) a dose of cocaine. [play on SNOW n.[2] + TRIP n.[3]]

skits n. [1960s] (US Black) clothes. [? link to Scot. skit, a piece of ostentation]

skitter n. [1900s–20s] a person. [? SE skit, to act skittishly]

skitters, the n. [1930s+] diarrhoea. [dial. skitter; ult. OE scitte, diarrhoea]

skittle/skittle out/over v. [late 19C+] (orig. Aus.) to knock down, to kill.

skittles n. [mid-19C–1900s] nonsense, rubbish; also used as excl. *skittles!*, rubbish! [i.e. one can 'knock it down' easily; note chess jargon *skittles*, chess played without serious application]

skitz see SCHITZ.

skitzing n. [1990s] (US Black teen) acting in a bizarre or eccentric manner. [SE *schizophrenia*]

skiv/skid n. [mid-19C] a sovereign. [ety. unknown; 'fashionable slang' (Hotten, 1859)]

skive n. [1910s+] an evasion, a way of getting out of one's responsibilities (cf. DOSS n.[2]). [SKIVE v.]

skive/skive off v. [1910s+] (orig. milit.) to neglect one's duties or work. [? dial. *skive*, to move quickly or Fr. *esquiver*, to dodge, to slink away]

skiver n. [1910s+] a 'lazybones', a shirker. [SKIVE v.]

skivvies n. [1930s+] (US) **1** men's underwear, esp. underpants. **2** a vest, esp. in the form of a *skivvy shirt*. **3** a pair of light slippers. [ety. unknown; (3) ? link to SKIVVY n.[1], i.e. typical Japanese footwear]

skivvy n.[1] [late 19C] a derog. term for a Japanese person. [presumably a var. on SKIBBY n. (1), although citations put dates at variance]

skivvy n.[2] [20C] a maid of all work. [? SLAVEY; *see also* ety. for SKIBBY]

skiz see SCHITZ.

skollie see SKOLLY.

skolliwoll n. [1990s] (US teen) school.

skolly/skollie n. [1930s+] (S.Afr.) a street thug, a hoodlum, usu. a member of a gang. [? Du. *schoelje*, a scavenger, but note *skorriemorrie*, a rascal, riffraff, ult. Yid. *soyrerumoyre*, a rogue, a hoodlum; *DSAE* suggests SE *scullery boy*, 'a very low form of humanity']

skoobied see SCOOBIED.

skooby see SCOOBY.

skoofer/skoofus/skroofus/skrufer n. [1970s+] (US Black/drugs) a marijuana cigarette. [ety. unknown; ? link to SKUIF]

skookum adj. [late 19C+] (Can., mainly west coast) satisfactory, OK. [Chinook jargon *skookum*, strong]

skookum house n. [1900s–40s] (Can., mainly west coast) a prison, often preceded by *strong*. [SKOOKUM + SE *house*]

skroofus see SKOOFER.

skop n.[1] (S.Afr.) **1** [1920s+] a kick. **2** [1960s+] a good time, a dance, a party; thus *skop, skiet en donder*, lit. 'kick, shoot and thunder', any rough and tough activity, an action film (cf. SKIET UND DONDER). **3** [1980s+] a thrill, a kick (from a drink or drug). [Afk. *skop*, a kick]

skop n.[2] see SMILEY n.[1].

skop v. [1960s+] (S.Afr.) **1** to enjoy oneself, to 'party'; thus *skop lawaai*, to have a rowdy, noisy good time. **2** to kick something or someone; thus *skop it*, to die (cf. KICK OFF; KICK IT; KICK THE BUCKET). [SKOP n.[1]]

skosh n. [1940s+] (orig. US milit.) a little bit. [Jap. *sukoshi*]

skowbanker see SCOWBANKER.

skraal adj. [1970s+] (S.Afr.) **1** thin, scrawny. **2** hungry. [Afk. *skraal*, thin, flimsy]

skrik n. [late 19C+] (S.Afr.) a fright, a tremor of fear. [Du. *schrik*, a fright]

skrik v. [late 19C+] (S.Afr.) to be terrified. [SKRIK n.]

skroofus see SKOOFER.

skrowdge see SCROUGE v.

skrufer see SKOOFER.

skrungy adj. [1960s+] unappealing, unappetizing, disgusting. [echoic; var. on GRUNGY]

skuffle n. [1970s] (drugs) phencyclidine (cf. ACE n.[3]). [var. on SCUFFLE n.[2]]

skuif/skuifie/skyf/skyfie n. [1970s+] (S.Afr.) **1** a cigarette. **2** a marijuana cigarette (cf. DRAW n.[4]; SKOOFER). [Afk. *skuif*, a draw, a puff]

skulk v. [1970s] (US campus) to steal.

skulker n. [late 18C–early 19C] one who hides themselves to avoid labour. [Scand. *skulka*, to lurk, *skolka* to play truant; orig. milit. jargon *skulker*, a soldier who shirks his duties by hiding away; SE from mid-19C]

skull n.[1] see SCULL n.[1].

skull n.[2] [20C] (W.I./Trin.) a trick, an act of deception; thus *pull a skull on*, to deceive. [? SE *skulk*]

skull, a n.[3] [1920s–50s] each person, per person, in phr. denoting price, *so much a skull*.

skull n.[4] [1940s] (US Black) a star, an outstanding performer. [i.e. what is within the skull: brains, talent, ability]

skull n.[5] [1970s+] (orig. US Black) **1** fellatio. **2** cunnilingus (cf. HEAD n.[8]).

skull v.[1] [1940s+] (US/Aus.) to hit someone on the head.

skull v.[2] [1970s+] (orig. US Black) to perform oral sex (cf. HEAD n.[8]; WHIP SOME SKULL ON). [SKULL n.[5]]

skull v.[3] [1980s+] (Aus./N.Z.) to down a large container of beer in one go. [SE *skull*, into which it is poured + *skol!* a toast]

skull and crossbones n. [1970s] (US Black) **1** poison. **2** anyone who is 'poison', esp. one who disrupts one's plans. [the acknowledged sign for 'poison']

skullbanker see SCOWBANKER.

skull-buggery n. [1990s] fellatio. [SE *skull* + *buggery*; note SKULL n.[5]]

skull-buster n. **1** [1920s+] (US) anything seen as especially intellectually challenging, esp. a hard college course. **2** [1930s+] (US Black) a policeman (cf. KNOCKO; SLAPMAN; STICKMAN n.[4]; WALLOPER n.[1]). [SE *skull* + BUST v.[1] (1)]

skulldrag n. [1950s–60s] (US Black) any activity that taxes the mind or emotions. [SE *skull* + DRAG n.[15]]

skull drag v. [mid-19C+] (Aus.) to haul along, to drag by force. [note late 19C N.Z. gang, the *Skulldraggers*]

skull drive v. [late 19C–1920s] (Aus.) to work as a schoolteacher. [i.e. to drive knowledge into reluctant skulls]

skulled adj. [1960s+] **1** intoxicated by a drug or by an excess of alcohol. **2** insane, crazy. [OUT OF ONE'S SKULL]

skull fuck n. [1990s] (US) fellatio. [SE *skull* + FUCK n.[1]; note SKULL n.[5]]

skull job n. [1950s+] oral sex, whether fellatio or cunnilingus. [SE *skull*/SKULL n.[5] + JOB n.[5]]

skullneck v. [20C] to decapitate. [one removes the skull from the neck]

skull note v. [1950s–60s] (US Black) to memorize.

skull pussy n. [1980s+] (US gay) a fellator. [SE *skull*/SKULL n.[5] + PUSSY n.[1]]

skull session n. [1950s+] (US) a discussion, a conference.

skull-thatcher n. **1** [late 18C–late 19C] a wig-maker. **2** [mid-19C] a maker of straw bonnets (cf. NOB-THATCHER).

skunk n.[1] [mid-19C+] a very unpleasant, contemptible person, although sometimes used jokingly (cf. STINKER n.[1]). [the animal's poor image]

skunk/skunkweed n.[2] [20C] an exceptionally strong variety of marijuana (often grown in the user's home) with up to 30% tetrahydrocannibonol (THC) content, thus intensifying the effects from the merely stimulating to those of such hallucinogens as LSD; thus *superskunk*, an even stronger variety. [play on SE *skunk*, an animal with a particularly strong smell]

skunk v. [mid-19C+] (US/W.I., sport) to beat decisively.

skunked adj.[1] [20C] very drunk (cf. BASTED). [phr. *drunk as a skunk*]

skunked adj.[2] [1990s] deceived, tricked. [SKUNK SOMEONE OUT OF]

skunk someone out of *v.* [mid-19C+] (US campus) to cheat someone out of something. [the animal's supposed characteristics]

skunkweed *see* SKUNK n.².

skutcher *n.* [1930s+] (Aus./N.Z.) anything or anyone considered excellent, attractive etc (cf. SNOZZLER). [ety. unknown]

sky *n.*¹ [mid-19C] a foreigner, an outsider, a disagreeable person, an enemy. [orig. Westminster School jargon *ski*, a non-Westminster; f. *Vesci*, the trad. enemies of the Romans, i.e. Westminsters]

sky/sky rocket *n.*² [late 19C+] a pocket. [rhy. sl.]

sky *n.*³ [1920s+] (Aus.) an Italian. [rhy. sl. *sky* = EYETIE]

sky *n.*⁴ [1930s–40s] (US Black) a policeman (cf. BLUE n.³). [the blue uniform]

sky *n.*⁵ [1950s+] (Aus.) whi*sky* (cf. SKEE n.¹). [abbr.]

sky *v.*¹ **1** [early 19C+] to toss into the air (cf. SKY A COPPER). **2** [late 19C–1900s] to spend all one's funds, esp. in a carefree, spendthrift manner. [SE *sky*]

sky *v.*² [1940s+] (orig. US milit.) to leave (cf. SKY OFF).

sky *v.*³ [1960s+] (drugs) to become intoxicated by a drug. [play on HIGH adj.¹]

sky a copper, to *phr.* [19C] **1** to toss into the air. **2** to make a noise, to make a nuisance of oneself. [SKY v.¹ + COPPER n.²]

sky bear *n.* [1970s] (US) a helicopter-mounted policeman. [SE *sky* + BEAR n.⁸]

sky blue *n.*¹ **1** [late 18C–mid-19C] gin, esp. second-rate gin (cf. BLUE RIBBON). **2** [mid-19C–1900s] 'London milk, much diluted with water, or from which the cream has been too closely skimmed' (Hotten, 1860). **3** [mid-19C] (N.Z.) a milkman or a nickname for a milkman. **4** [1900s–10s] vegetable soup.

sky blue *n.*² **1** [19C] (Can.) an officer of the Hudson's Bay Company, usu. in pl. **2** [20C] (S.Afr.) a long-term prisoner. [their blue uniforms]

sky cap *n.* [1950s+] (US) a porter at an air terminal. [model of *red cap*, a railroad porter]

sky-clad *adj.* [20C] of a self-appointed 'witch', naked. [their mystic communion with nature, which ideally obviates the need for earthly clothes]

sky-diver *n.* [20C] £5, i.e. a fiver. [rhy. sl.]

skyf *see* SKUIF.

skyfarmer *n.* **1** [mid-18C–early 19C] (Und.) a criminal beggar who tours the country posing as a gentleman farmer fallen on hard times, backed by suitably impressive, if counterfeit, papers. **2** [19C] (Anglo-Irish) a farmer with very little, if any, land. ['the isle of Sky(e), or some other remote place ... or else from their farms being *in nubibus*, "in the clouds"' (Grose, 1785)]

skyfie *see* SKUIF.

skygodlin/sigoggling *adj.* [mid-19C+] (US) askew, slanted. [? SE *sky* + GOGGLE v.; i.e. one who, instead of looking straight ahead, looks upwards]

skyhacking *n.* [1920s+] (Aus.) slandering, talking behind someone's back. [CHI-IKE n.]

sky high *v.* [late 19C] to tell off, to scold. [BLOW SKY HIGH]

sky hoot *v.*¹ [late 19C–1920s] to run off, to move fast. [SCOOT v.]

sky hoot *v.*² [late 19C–1920s] (US) to rise, to increase. [SE *sky* + *hoot*, i.e. *blow (sky high)*]

sky-juice *n.* [20C] rainwater.

sky-lantern *n.* [mid-19C] the moon.

skylark *n.* [20C] a park. [rhy. sl.]

skylark *v.* [1950s+] to park (a vehicle). [rhy. sl.]

skylarker *n.* [18C] a thief who doubles as a journeyman bricklayer. [using the legitimate job to facilitate the villainy, he gets up early – 'with the lark' – to spy out vulnerable houses]

skylight *n.* [19C] a small space between the top of one's glass and the level of the drink within it (cf. DAYLIGHT n.¹).

sky-lodging *n.* [late 19C–1920s] a garret (cf. SKY-PARLOUR).

sky off *v.* [1970s+] (US Black) to depart, to exit. [ext. of SKY v.²]

sky-parlour *n.* [late 18C–mid-19C] a garret (cf. SKY-LODGING).

sky-piece *n.* [1930s–40s] (US Black) any form of headgear.

skypilot *n.* [late 19C+] a priest, a prison chaplain. [he guides one to heaven]

sky-pocket *n.* [1940s] (US Black) an inside pocket. [? rhy. sl.]

sky rocket *n.*¹ [late 19C–1940s] (US) a form of college cheer, rounded off with a cry of *sis-boom-bah!*, supposedly that of an ascending and exploding rocket.

sky rocket *n.*² *see* SKY n.².

sky rug *n.* [1940s+] (US) a wig or toupee. [SKY-PIECE + RUG n.³]

sky-scraper *n.*¹ [early 19C] a tall horse. [the horse *Skyscraper*, sired by Highflyer, which won the Epsom Derby in 1789]

sky-scraper *n.*² [mid-19C] **1** a notably tall person. **2** a rider on a 'penny-farthing' cycle. **3** a tall hat or bonnet. **4** the penis. [18C naut. jargon *sky-scraper*, a triangular sky-sail, the highest sail on a boat. Such sails were also known as *moon-rakers*. The orig. US use of the term to mean a tall building, began life as sl. (c.1888; cited as such in Maitland's *American Slang Dictionary*, 1891) but had entered the mainstream by 1920]

sky the wipe, to *phr.* [1910s+] (Aus.) to surrender (cf. THROW IN THE TOWEL). [orig. boxing jargon; SKY v.¹ + WIPE n.²]

sky-topper *n.* [late 19C–1920s] someone or something very high.

slaat *n.* [20C] (S.Afr.) a blow. [synon. Du.]

slaat *v.* [20C] (S.Afr.) to hit, to beat up. [SLAAT n.]

slab *n.*¹ **1** [early 19C–1900s] a milestone. **2** [1930s+] (US Black) a bed. **3** [1940s] bread, a sandwich. **4** [1960s+] (Aus.) a case of 24 bottles or tins of beer. **5** [1970s+] (US Black) $1.

slab *n.*² [mid–late 19C] a bricklayer's boy. [he works on the mixing slab]

slab *n.*³ [1980s+] (drugs) weak or impure crack cocaine. [? SE (*mortuary) slab*, i.e. it is 'dead']

slabba-slabba *adj.* [20C] (W.I. Rasta) big and fat, slobby, droopy. [dial. *slabby*, sloppy + redup.]

slabbed and slid *adj.* [1940s–50s] (prison) dead and gone, or certainly long since departed from the prison and thus the immediate knowledge or interest of those left behind. [SE (*mortuary) slab + slid*]

slabber *n.* [late 18C–early 19C] a filthy, slobbering person. [Du. *slabberen*, muddy ground + SE *slobber*, to dribble saliva]

slabberdegullion/slubberdegullion *n.* [early 17C–1900s] a filthy, slobbering fellow. [Du. *overslubberen*, to wade through mud + SLABBER]

slabbering bib *n.* [late 18C–mid-19C] a neckband as worn by a lawyer or parson. [SE *slobber*, to dribble + *bib*]

slabbing *n.* [1970s+] sexual intercourse with a corpse; thus *slab boy*, a necrophiliac. [the corpse is laid out on a mortuary *slab*]

slab city *n.* [1950s+] (US) the morgue. [SE *slab*, the stone on which a corpse is laid in a mortuary + sfx. -CITY]

slabdab *n.* [early 18C] a glover. [? SE *slap* + *dab*, i.e. actions involved in making gloves]

slabs *n.* [20C] the testicles. [backsl. BALLS n.¹]

slack *n.* **1** [19C] impertinence, cheek. **2** [mid-19C] a spell of inactivity, idleness. **3** [mid-19C+] the seat of the trousers. **4** [1950s] a prostitute (cf. SLAG n.¹). **5** [1950s] (W.I.) a slovenly person. **6** [1950s+] (W.I.) a promiscuous woman. **7** [1960s+] freedom, relief of pressure; thus *give some slack*, to let someone relax, to stop pressurizing. [SE *slack*, that which hangs loose]

slack *adj.* **1** [1970s] (US campus) of work or performance, below standard. **2** [1990s] (US teen) or a person, either unmotivated or just plain lazy, intensified as *slack daddy*.

slack/slack off v. [late 19C+] to urinate. [the relaxation of one's bladder]

slack and slim phr. [late 19C] slender and elegant.

slacken your glib! excl. [late 19C] shut up! be quiet! [SE slacken + GLIB n. (2)]

slacker n. 1 [late 19C+] one who shirks work or avoids exertion etc. 2 [1990s] (orig. US) a member of the generation in their 20s who, for whatever reason, perhaps cynicism or indolence, sees no point in joining the social mainstream. [SE slack]

slack-jaw n. [early 19C] cheek or impudence. [ext. of SLACK n. + SE jaw/JAW n.]

slackness n. (W.I.) 1 [1950s+] vulgarity. 2 [1980s] lewd, vulgar lyrics used in popular songs (cf. BADNESS). [SLACK n. (5), (6)]

slack off see SLACK v.

slag n.[1] 1 [18C+] a worthless or insignificant person, frequently used as a term of contempt, e.g. you slag! 2 [1930s+] a coward. 3 [1940s+] a rough or brutal person. 4 [1940s+] any objectionable or contemptible person. 5 [1950s+] a vagrant, a petty criminal; thus [1950s–60s] the slag, such persons collectively. 6 [1950s+] a prostitute, a promiscuous woman, a slattern. [18C slag, a coward, f. slack-mettled]

slag n.[2] [mid-19C–1900s] (Und.) a gold or silver chain; thus nip the slag, to cut a watch chain. [SLANG n.[2]]

slag v.[1] [1960s+] (Aus.) to spit. [dial. slag, to smear]

slag/slag off v.[2] [1970s+] to criticize, to slander, to attack verbally. [SLAG n.[1]; i.e. to call a SLAG n.[1], or whatever kind]

slag about v. [1970s] to wander about aimlessly. [SLAG n.[1] (5)]

slagger n. [late 19C] one who keeps a brothel. [? SE slacker or spec. use of SLAG n.[1] (6)]

slagging/slagging off n. [1970s+] criticizing, attacking verbally. [SLAG v.[2]]

slaggy adj. 1 [1940s+] dirty, unpleasant, offensive. 2 [1970s+] promiscuous, immoral. [SLAG n.[1]]

slag off see SLAG v.[2].

slake v. [19C] to kiss. [SE slake one's thirst]

slake the bacon, to phr. [1990s] to masturbate (cf. ACCOST THE OSCAR MEYER). [assonance, but note BACON n.[1] (3)]

slam n.[1] (US) 1 [late 19C+] an insult. 2 [1930s+] a violent blow given to a ball.

slam n.[2] [1960s+] (orig. US) a prison. [abbr. SLAMMER n.[2]]

slam n.[3] see SLAM DANCE n.

slam v.[1] 1 [19C] to talk, to boast (cf. SLUM v.[1]). 2 [late 19C+] (US) to insult, to criticize harshly; thus slamming contest, a fight in which the contestants criticize each other verbally. 3 [20C] (orig. US) to beat up, to hurt badly. 4 [1980s+] (US Black/campus/W.I./UK Black teen) of a man, to have sexual intercourse (cf. BANG v.[1]). 5 [1980s+] (US Black/campus) to drink fast, usu. beer; thus slam a forty, to drink a 40-ounce (1.2-litre) bottle of beer (cf. HAMMER v.[4]).

slam v.[2] [late 19C] (US) to hurry off. [? the slamming of a door behind one or the slamming of one's feet on the ground]

slam v.[3] [1960s+] (drugs) to use heroin regularly (cf. BANG v.[4]).

slam v.[4] see SLAM DANCE v.

slambam adv. [1940s+] (W.I.) at once, immediately. [echoic]

slam-bang n. [1920s] (US) a vicious prize-fight. [SE slam-bang, rough, aggressive]

slam-/slap-bang adj. [1930s+] (orig. US) 1 exciting, first-rate, excellent. 2 vigorous, energetic. [echoic]

slam-/slap-bang adv. [1930s+] energetically, vigorously. [SLAM-BANG adj.]

slam dance/slam/slamming n. [1970s+] a particular energetic style of dance that involves physical collision with other dancers (cf. MOSH n.[2]). [SE slam + dance; usu. associated with the audiences of PUNK or THRASH n.[2] music]

slam dance/slam v. [1970s+] (US) to perform a slam dance; thus slam dancer, one who dances in this way. [SLAM DANCE n.]

slam-dunk v. [1980s+] (US Black) to make an aggressive, powerful move. [basketball jargon slam-dunk, to slam the ball down through the basket, jumping high and using both hands]

slamkin/slammerkin/slammocks n. [late 18C–early 19C] a slovenly woman. [note the slovenly Mrs Slammekin in John Gay's Beggar's Opera (1727), although the name reflected the sl. rather than creating it]

slam me! excl. [mid-17C–late 18C] euph. for damn me!

slammed adj. [1980s+] (US campus) drunk (cf. BASTED). [SLAM v.[1] (5)]

slammer n.[1] [late 19C–1900s] anything or anyone exceptional. [SE slam, to hit with a bang]

slammer n.[2] 1 [1930s+] prison. 2 [1940s–60s] (US Black) a door. [the slamming shut of (cell) doors]

slammer n.[3] [1980s+] an energetic dancer (cf. SLAM DANCE n.).

slammerkin see SLAMKIN.

slamming n.[1] see SLAM DANCE n.

slamming n.[2] [1980s+] (US Black) fighting, either with fists or knives; thus slamming and jamming, of the Guardian Angels group, raiding a crack house or similar establishment to smash it up, rough up the patrons and take away the drugs. [SLAM v.[1] (3)]

slamming adj. [late 19C–1900s; 1980s+] a general intensifier, overwhelming, extraordinary, the best, the most fashionable, attractive etc; thus synon. slamminest. [SE slam, to hit; later use is US Black]

slamming partner n. [1990s] (US Black) the person with whom one has sex in a purely sex-based relationship. [SLAM v.[1] (4)]

slammocks see SLAMKIN.

slam off v. [20C] to die.

slam-piece n. [1990s] (US campus) a sexual partner. [SLAM v.[1] (4) + PIECE n.[1]]

slam pit n. [1980s+] that part of a nightclub dedicated to slam dancers (cf. MOSH n.[2]).

slams n. [1930s+] (US prison) cell doors (cf. SLAMMER n.[2]). [the sound they make when shut]

slam-slam v. [mid-19C–1900s] (Anglo-Ind.) to salute. [Urdu salaam, to salute, to compliment]

slam the clam, to phr. [1960s+] of a woman, to masturbate. [SE slam + (BEARDED) CLAM]

slam the ham/salami/salmon, to phr. [1950s+] of a man, to masturbate (cf. ACCOST THE OSCAR MEYER). [SE slam + ham/salami/salmon]

slam the hammer/spam/wapper, to phr. [1990s] of a man, to masturbate (cf. ACCOST THE OSCAR MEYER). [SE slam + HAMMER n./spam/wapper]

slam the salami/salmon see SLAM THE HAM.

slam the spam see SLAM THE HAMMER.

slam the slats, to phr. [20C] (US Und.) to close a row of cell doors using a remote mechanism that closes every door simultaneously (cf. ROLL THE BARS). [SE slam + slat, a bar]

slam the wapper see SLAM THE HAMMER.

slamtrash n. [19C] a general insult, an unpleasant, disgusting person (cf. SLAMKIN). [dial. slam, an ill-shaped person + SE trash]

slang n.[1] 1 [mid-18C–mid-19C] illiterate, 'low' language. 2 [mid-18C–mid-19C] cant, i.e. the jargon of criminals (cf. FLASH n.[1]). 3 [mid–late 18C] nonsense, rubbish. 4 [late 18C] a line of work, an occupation; thus on/upon the slang, involved in one's own profession or job. 5 [early–mid-19C] a set of counterfeit scales, as used by cheating costermongers, counterfeit measures; thus the slang quart, a measure with a false bottom that actually holds only 1½ pints (855ml), the *slang pint*, ¾ pint (428ml) etc, *work slang*, to use such weights and measures. **6** [mid-19C] a hawker's licence; thus *out on the slang*, working as an itinerant hawker. **7** [mid-19C] a travelling show. **8** [mid-19C] a single performance or 'house' in a travelling show. [ety. debatable. Of the various theories the most likely is SE *sling*, to throw; thus fig. 'thrown' language, underpinned by cognates in Nor. *slenja-keten*, sling the jaw etc. (2) to (8) all fig. uses of (1)]

slang *n.*[2] **1** [19C] a watch-chain. **2** [early 19C] any form of chains or fetters used to secure a prisoner. [Ger. *Schlange*, a chain, watch-chain or Du. *slang*, a snake]

slang *v.*[1] **1** [late 18C] to exhibit at a fair. **2** [early–mid-19C] to cheat, to swindle, to defraud. **3** [mid-19C+] to abuse. [SLANG *n.*[1]]

slang *v.*[2] [early–mid-19C] to chain up, to place in fetters. [SLANG *n.*[2]]

slang *v.*[3] [1980s+] (orig. US Black) to sell drugs. [SE *sling*/SLING *v.*[6]]

slang and pitcher shop *n.* [late 19C–1900s] **1** a cheapjack's shop. **2** the stock it holds. [SLANG *n.*[1] (6) + PITCHER *n.*[3] (1)]

slang-boy/boy of the slang *n.* [late 18C] one who can speak underworld cant. [SLANG *n.*[1] (2)]

slang cove/cull *n.* [mid–late 19C] a showman. [SLANG *v.*[1] (7) + COVE/CULL *n.*[1] (4)]

slang-dipper *n.* [20C] one who gilds ordinary metal chains and attempts to pass them off as 'gold'; thus *slang-dropper*, the person who actually does the 'trade', usu. by dropping a chain in the street, picking it up as the victim is passing, then asking them to suggest how much it might be worth; they then get the dupe to buy it, assuring them that they themselves are losing by the deal. [SLANG *n.*[2] + SE *dip*]

slanged *adj.* [early 19C] chained up, fettered. [SLANG *v.*[2]]

slanging-match *n.* [late 19C+] a vituperative argument. [SLANG *v.*[1]]

slang it *v.* [mid–late 19C] to use false weights and measures. [SLANG *v.*[1] (5)]

slangs *n.* [mid-18C–mid-19C] cant, i.e. the jargon of criminals. [SLANG *n.*[1] (2)]

slang the mauleys, to *phr.* [late 18C–late 19C] to shake hands. [SE *sling* + MAULEY]

slangy *adj.* [mid-19C] flashy, vulgar, whether in speech or appearance. [SLANG *n.*[1] (1)]

slant *n.*[1] **1** [mid–late 19C] an opportunity to push forward a plan or stratagem. **2** [late 19C–1920s] (Aus.) a plan or scheme specifically designed to ensure a favourable result. [naut. jargon *slant*, a favourable wind]

slant *n.*[2] [1910s–30s] (US) a glance, a brief look. [i.e. 'out of the corner of one's eye']

slant/slant-eye *n.*[3] [1950s+] a derog. term for an Oriental person (cf. ROUNDEYE; SLIT *n.*[2]). [the shape of Oriental eyes]

slanter/schleinter/schlenter/shlanter/shlinter/slinter *n.* [mid-19C+] (Aus./S.Afr.) a fraudulent trick; thus *work a slanter*, to defraud, to hoax, to play a confidence trick on (cf. SCHLENTER *adj.*). [Du. *slenter*, knavery, a trick]

slanters *n.* [1940s] (US Black) the eyes. [despite SLANT *n.*[3], there is no ref. to Asian eyes]

slant-eye *see* SLANT *n.*[3].

slantindicular/slantingdicular *adj.* [mid-19C] (orig. US) oblique, awry. [a play on SE *perpendicular*]

slaoc *n.* [mid-19C] coals. [backsl.]

slap *n.*[1] **1** [late 18C–early 19C] (mainly Anglo-Irish) booty, the proceeds of a robbery, 'swag'. **2** [20C] (Irish) a large amount, a quantity. [SE *slap*, a blow]

slap *n.*[2] [mid-19C+] make-up, esp. in theatre use. [one SE *slaps* it on]

slap *adj.*[1] [mid-19C] first-rate, excellent. [SLAP-UP]

slap *adj.*[2] [1960s+] (S.Afr.) **1** weak, feeble; thus intensified

as *slapgat*, lit. weak-arsed. **2** sloppy, slovenly. [Afk. *slap*, feeble]

slap/slap along *v.* [early 19C; 1990s] to move or walk quickly. [one's shoes SE *slap* the ground; 20C use is UK Black]

slap *adv.* **1** [late 17C+] quickly, unexpectedly, suddenly. **2** [mid-19C+] exactly, perfectly, e.g. *slap in the middle*. [SE *slap*, the sound of a sharp blow]

slap along *see* SLAP *v.*

slap and tickle *n.*[1] [20C] a pickle. [rhy. sl.]

slap and tickle *n.*[2] [1920s+] playful kissing and cuddling.

slap-bang/slap-bang-shop *n.*[1] [late 18C–mid-19C] a small eating-house or restaurant where one pays on receipt of the food, rather than eating then receiving a bill. ['a petty cook's shop where there is no credit given, but what is had must be paid down with the ready slap-bang, i.e. immediately. This is a common appellation for a night cellar frequented by thieves, and sometimes for a stage coach or caravan' (Grose, 1796)]

slap-bang *n.*[2] [mid-19C] a form of alcoholic drink. [used by Benjamin Disraeli in *Sybil* (1863) as 'the Mowbray slap-bang', but otherwise unspecified. Presumably it was tossed off in a single gulp, guaranteed to 'hit the spot' or, like the *tequila slammers* of the 1990s, the glass was knocked against the table before taking a drink]

slap-bang *see* SLAM-BANG.

slap-bang-shop *see* SLAP-BANG *n.*[1].

slap-dab *adv.* [late 19C+] directly, straight at, immediately (cf. SLAM-BANG *adv.*) [echoic]

slap-dash *adv.* [mid-19C+] suddenly, violently. [UK usage became SE in 18C, and the term is taken up by Aus. speakers; the adj. meaning careless, undisciplined is SE]

slap/lay/slip five *v.* [1910s+] (US) to indulge in a mutual hand-slapping ritual used by Blacks (and some Whites) for greeting, emphasis, congratulation etc (cf. GIVE FIVE; GIVE ME FIVE; GIVE SOME SKIN).

slap-happy *n.* [1940s] (US Black) a devotee of swing music. [the use of the jazz jargon *slap bass*]

slap-happy *adj.* [1930s+] cheery, slightly eccentric (cf. PUNCHY). [SE *slap* + *happy*; orig. boxing use, someone whose brain has suffered from an excess of fighting]

slap-head *n.* [1980s+] a bald person.

slap high fives with Yul Brynner, to *phr.* [1980s+] to masturbate (cf. BALD-HEADED HERMIT; CHOKE KOJAK). [SLAP FIVE + the bald Hollywood star *Yul Brynner* (1915–85)]

slap into *adv.* [early 19C+] used with verbs of collision or impact, directly, straight at, e.g. *ran slap into the wall*.

slap it *v.* [20C] to masturbate.

slapman *n.* [1920s+] (US Und.) a policeman (cf. SKULL-BUSTER). [SE *slap*; i.e. his violent treatment of suspects]

slap of the tongue *n.* [late 19C] (Anglo-Irish) a reprimand, a scolding, a sharp retort. [play on SE *slip of the tongue*]

slap pappy *v.* [1990s] to masturbate.

slapped with an ugly stick *phr.* [1960s–70s] (US) unattractive (cf. BEAT WITH AN UGLY STICK *phr.*[1]).

slapper *n.* [1970s+] **1** a promiscuous woman (cf. SCRUBBER *n.*[2]). **2** a prostitute. [? Yid. *schlepper*, a unkempt, untidy person or the 'slapping on' of make-up]

slappie *n.* [1990s] (US) a fool, a simpleton, a madman. [SLAP-HEAD]

slapping/slapping the plank *n.* [1930s+] (US Black) exchanging ritualized slaps of greeting, congratulation etc. [var. on SLAP FIVE]

slapping *adj.* [20C] first-rate, excellent (cf. SLAMMING *adj.*).

slappy *n.* [1990s] (orig. US) a trim, attractive young woman. [? misunderstanding of SLAPPER]

slap queen *n.* [1950s–60s] (gay) a male homosexual given to the heavy use of make-up. [SLAP *n.*[2] + QUEEN *n.*[1]]

slapsie maxie *n.* [1930s+] (Aus./N.Z.) a taxi. [rhy. sl.; US boxer *Slapsie Maxie* Rosenbloom]

slap skins *v.* [1990s] (orig. US Black) to have sexual intercourse.

slap tar *see* BEAT TAR.

slap the pavement, to *phr.* [20C] (US Black) to walk around (cf. BEAT TAR).

slap the salami, to *phr.* [1990s] to masturbate (cf. ACCOST THE OSCAR MEYER).

slap-up *adj.* [early 19C+] fashionable, first-rate, of superior quality.

slash *n.*[1] [19C] an outside pocket. [SE *slash*, a slit in a garment that is designed to reveal the colour of the lining]

slash *n.*[2] [20C] (US) the vagina (cf. ARBOUR).

slash *n.*[3] [1930s–50s] an alcoholic drink. [E.P. suggests est. of SLASH *n.*[4], on model of PISS-UP]

slash *n.*[4] [1930s+] urination. [? SE *slash*, a thin, sloping line, i.e. that of urine; or echoic of the urine hitting the lavatory water]

slash *v.* [1970s] (US Black) to demolish someone verbally, with a rapier-like wit.

slasher *n.* **1** [mid-16C–19C] a violent thug, a bully. **2** [19C] anyone or anything seen as exceptional, whether positively or otherwise. **3** [1900s] (Aus.) a general term of praise, an excellent fellow; thus [1940s+] *slasheroo*, an intensified form. [note the comedian Sid Field's 1940s SPIV character *Slasher* Green, whose name may have equally referred to the contemporary 'razor gangs' of Soho and the racetrack]

slashers *n.* [1960s] the testicles. [? misunderstanding of SLASH *n.*[4]]

slashing *adj.* [19C] excellent, wonderful, the best (cf. SLAMMING *adj.*; SLAPPING *adj.*). [SLASHER *n.* (2)]

slashing *adv.* [late 19C] excellently, wonderfully, exceptionally. [SLASHING *adj.*]

slash job *n.* [20C] (US prison) slashing one's own wrists in a suicide attempt. [SE *slash* + JOB *n.*[5]]

slat *n.*[1] **1** [late 17C–18C] half-a-crown, 2s 6d (12½p) (cf. LOONSLATE). **2** [1950s–60s] (US Black) $1. [SLATE *n.*[2]; the term was used by market traders in the 20C until decimalization made the half-crown obsolete]

slat *n.*[2] **1** [late 17C–18C] a sheet (cf. SLATE *n.*[1]). **2** [20C] (US) a ski.

slat *n.*[3] [1940s–50s] (US Black) used as a term of quantity, esp. in the context of the length of a prison sentence. [? Irish *slat*, a rod or measuring stick]

slate *n.*[1] [16C–early 19C] a bedsheet. [SE *slate*]

slate *n.*[2] [late 17C–early 19C] (Und.) half-a-crown, 2s 6d (12½p). [ety. unknown]

slate *n.*[3] [late 19C] an argument, a quarrel. [SLATE *v.*[2]]

slate *v.*[1] [19C] to knock a man's hat over his eyes (cf. BONNET *v.*). [SE *slate*, a roof-covering]

slate *v.*[2] [mid-19C] **1** (orig. Irish) to thrash or beat up. **2** to criticize severely. **3** to abuse. [Scot. *slate*, to attack with a dog, to drive away with abuse; ? Irish *slat mara*, ult. *slad-mhara*, murder and robbery]

slate *v.*[3] **1** [late 19C–1900s] to bet heavily against a boxer, a racehorse etc. **2** [late 19C+] (orig. milit.) to assign to a job. [SE *slate*, to set down in writing]

slated *adj.* [late 19C] dead. [hospital practice of writing the names of those currently likely to die on a *slate*]

slater's pan *n.* [late 18C–early 19C] the prison at Kingston, Jamaica. [proper name *Slater*, the deputy provost-marshal in Grose's era; given the heat of the West Indies, prisoners were presumably 'cooked' in the 'pan']

slather/slathers *n.* [mid-19C+] (US) a large amount, e.g. *a whole slather of pretty women*, *slathers of fresh fruit*. [SE *slather*, to squander]

slather *v.* [1910s+] to defeat utterly, to thrash, to criticize harshly. [SE *slather*, to spread, or smear liberally]

slathered *adj.* [1920s+] (Aus.) tipsy, slightly drunk. [? SLATHER *v.* or dial. *slather*, to spill, to slobber]

slathers *see* SLATHER *n.*

slather-up *n.* [1910s–50s] (N.Z.) a fight, a brawl. [SLATHER *v.*]

slats *n.*[1] [late 19C+] (orig. US) the ribs. [resemblance]

slats *n.*[2] [20C] (US prison) the steel mesh that covers the front of a prison cell.

slaughter *n.*[1] [1950s+] (Und.) an immediate dumping ground for recently stolen property, before it is shared out or hidden more permanently and securely. [abbr. SLAUGHTERHOUSE *n.*[1] (2)]

slaughter *n.*[2] [1990s] man*slaughter*. [abbr.]

slaughter *v.* [20C] to defeat completely.

slaughtered *adj.* **1** [late 19C] heavily overworked, 'sweated'. **2** [1980s+] (US campus) drunk (cf. BASTED).

slaughterer *n.* [mid-19C] a dealer who buys from small makers at extremely low prices. [such one-sided deals *slaughter* the sellers]

slaughterhouse *n.*[1] **1** [early 19C] a crooked gambling house or casino. **2** [mid–late 19C] a shop where goods are bought from small makers at very low prices. **3** [late 19C] a factory paying very low wages. **4** [1920s+] a cheap brothel. [in all cases, the buyer or customer is fig. *slaughtered*]

slaughterhouse *n.*[2] [late 19C] (Und.) the Surrey Sessions House.

slaughterhouse *n.*[3] [1970s] (US Black) anywhere a couple can indulge in sexual intercourse. [play on KILLING FLOOR]

slave *n.* [1930s+] (US Black/campus) work, any form of job.

slave market *n.* (US) **1** [mid-19C+] an office, a café or any other meeting place where unemployed actors seek work. **2** [1910s+] cheap employment agencies, offering menial jobs for poor wages.

slaves and masters *n.* [1960s+] (US) sadists and masochists (cf. SADIE AND MAISIE).

slave tip *n.* [1940s] (US Black) information regarding a possible job. [SLAVE *n.* + SE *tip*]

slavey *n.* [early 19C+] a servant, whether male or female; thus [1920s] *slavey market*, an employment agency for servants.

slaving gloak *n.* [late 19C] a servant. [SE *slaving* + GLOAK]

slawminyeux *n.* [mid-19C] a Dutchman. [? Du. *ja mynheer*, yes sir]

slay *v.* **1** [20C] to reduce to complete hysterical laughter, to amaze, to impress, to shock (cf. KILL *v.*[2]). **2** [1950s+] (gay) to gossip maliciously behind a third party's back.

slay the one-eyed monster, to *phr.* [1980s+] to masturbate (cf. ONE-EYED MONSTER).

sleath *n.* [1980s+] (US drugs) a cannabis cigarette. [ety. unknown; ? var. on SLEEF]

sleaze *n.* **1** [1960s+] (US) anything considered disgusting, shabby or offensive. **2** [1960s+] an unappealing, seedy person. **3** [1980s+] (US campus) a sexually promiscuous woman (cf. DIRTY LEG). [backform. SLEAZY]

sleaze *v.* [1960s+] to move in a repellent or seedy manner.

sleazebag/sleazeball *n.* [1980s+] a distasteful person, with overtones of dirtiness and criminality. [SLEAZE *n.* + sfx. *-ball*]

sleazebucket *adj.* [1960s+] (US) revolting, disgusting. [SLEAZE *n.* + SE *bucket*]

sleazemonger *n.* [1960s+] (US) a producer or seller of inferior, trashy or pornographic entertainment. [SLEAZE *n.* + sfx. -MONGER]

sleazo/sleazoid *n.* [1980s+] (US campus) **1** a disgusting, obnoxious person. **2** a sexually promiscuous woman. [SLEAZE *n.*]

sleazy/sleazo/sleazoid/sleezy *adj.* [1940s+] **1** of a person, unpleasant, poss. criminal, generally distasteful. **2** of a thing, dirty, rundown, decayed. [SE *sleazy*, of textile fabrics or materials, thin or flimsy; ult. *sleazy*, of ropes or yarn, rough from projecting fibres]

sled *n.* [20C] (US) an automobile.

sledge *n.* [1970s+] (Und.) **1** a sledgehammer. **2** one who carries a sledgehammer for use in a bank robbery, an assault or other violent crime.

sleef *n.* [1990s] (drugs) a cigarette that mixes marijuana and crack cocaine (cf. FIFTY-ONE). [ety. unknown; ? SE *sleeve*]

sleek and slum/sleek and slum shop *n.* [early 19C] a public house frequented by 'single men and their wives' (Jon Bee), i.e. prostitutes and their male clients. [SE *sleek*, i.e. a well-dressed, 'smooth' man + SLUM *n.*[1] (4), i.e. the tricks the woman might play or SLUM *n.*[2] (1)]

sleek lady *n.* [1960s–70s] (US Black) an extremely attractive woman.

sleek wife *n.* [19C] a handkerchief. [? rhy. sl.]

sleep *n.* [1910s+] (UK/US/Aus.) a short term in prison (cf. SLEEPING TIME). [the UK/US versions are somewhat longer, about 12 months, than the Aus., which is 3 months]

sleep around *v.* [1920s+] (orig. US) to be sexually promiscuous.

sleep at Mrs Green's/with Mrs Green, to *phr.* [1920s–30s] (N.Z. tramp) to sleep in the open air (cf. STAR HOTEL).

sleep-drunk *adj.* [late 19C] drowsy.

sleeper *n.*[1] [late 19C+] any product that gains acceptance and success only slowly.

sleeper *n.*[2] [1960s+] (drugs) **1** any form of barbiturate sleeping pill. **2** heroin.

sleeper *n.*[3] [1970s] (US campus) a lazy, useless person.

sleep in a tent, to *phr.* [1990s] (US) to have a large penis. [one's erection 'tents' the sheet]

sleep in chapters, to *phr.* [1960s] (drugs) to experience broken, fragmentary sleep during withdrawal from heroin.

sleeping dictionary *n.* [1920s+] a foreign woman with whom a man has a sexual relationship and from whom he learns her language.

sleeping Jesus *n.* [1960s+] (US Black) **1** a dull, tedious person. **2** a person who is comatose due to the influence of heroin. [pun on CREEPING JESUS]

sleeping time *n.* [20C] (US Und.) a short prison sentence (cf. SLEEP; WINO TIME). [SE *sleeping* + TIME *n.*[1]; one could sleep it away]

sleepless hat *n.* [mid-19C–1900s] a hat on which the nap has worn off (cf. WIDE-AWAKE *n.*). [pun on *nap*]

sleep like a cow, to *phr.* [late 18C] to sleep like a married man, i.e. with one's back to one's wife. [Grose (1785) defines it as 'i.e. with a **** [CUNT *n.*[1]] at one's a—see' and quotes a contemporary rhyme: 'All you that in your beds do lie/ Turn to your wives, and occupy [have sex],/And when that you have done your best,/Turn a-se to a-se, and take your rest']

sleep on *v.* [1990s] (US Black) **1** to ignore. **2** to be unaware or unprepared but otherwise awake. **3** to attack, to criticize negatively (cf. SLEPT ON).

sleep on bones, to *phr.* [19C–1910s] of a child, to fall asleep on one's nurse's lap.

sleep upon the queer roost/dorse, to *phr.* [late 18C] to live together as man and wife. [SE *sleep* + QUEER *adj.* + DOSS *n.*; the arrangement is queer because it is fraudulent]

sleepville *adj.* [late 19C+] (US) sleepy. [SE *sleep* + sfx. -VILLE]

sleepwalker *n.* [20C] (Aus.) a sneak-thief.

sleep white *v.* [1960s–70s] (US Black) to sleep with a White person.

sleep with *v.* [late 19C+] to have sexual intercourse with (cf. STAY WITH *v.*[2]). [euph.]

sleep with Mrs Green *see* SLEEP AT MRS GREEN'S.

sleep with the fishes, to *phr.* [1950s+] to have been

drowned, whether accidentally or as a form of homicide. [invariably associated with the US Mafia thanks to Mario Puzo's book *The Godfather* (1969)]

sleepy *adj.* [late 18C–early 19C] old, worn-out (cf. WIDE-AWAKE *adj.*). [punning remark 'the cloth of your coat must be extremely sleepy, for it has not had a nap this long time' (Grose, 1796)]

Sleepy Hollow *n.* **1** [mid-19C+] (N.Z.) Nelson, New Zealand. **2** [1940s+] (S.Afr.) Pietermaritzburg. **3** [1980s+] any quiet provincial place. [SE *Sleepy Hollow*, a name given to a place with a soporific atmosphere, esp. as title of Washington Irving's story 'The Legend of Sleepy Hollow' (1820)]

sleepytime girl *n.* [1950s+] (US) a promiscuous woman, a man's mistress. [SAmE *sleepytime*, bedtime]

sleestak *n.* [1980s+] (US campus) an unappealing, sexually promiscuous woman. [creature in the 1980s TV series *Land of the Lost*]

sleet *n.* [1980s+] (drugs) crack cocaine. [play on SE *sleet*/SNOW *n.*[2]]

sleeve *n.* [1990s] (US campus) **1** the vagina. **2** a generic for any woman.

sleeve button *n.* [20C] a long drink. [? SLEEVER]

sleever *n.* **1** [late 19C+] (mainly Aus./N.Z.) a beer glass holding 369ml (13fl oz). **2** [20C] (N.Z.) a drinking straw. [abbr. LONG-SLEEVER]

sleezy *see* SLEAZY.

sleighride *v.* [1900s–50s] (US drugs) to take cocaine; thus *sleighrider*, a cocaine user, *on a sleighride*, on a cocaine binge. [play on SNOW *n.*]

slenter *see* SCHLENTER *adj.*

slept on *adj.* [1990s] (US Black) attacked, criticized negatively (cf. SLEEP ON).

slew/slue *v.* [late 19C+] (Aus.) to defeat, to 'do for', to 'settle'. [dial. *slew*, to twist around]

slewed *adj.* **1** [mid-19C+] drunk, off-balance. **2** [mid-19C+] confused, baffled. **3** [late 19C+] (Aus.) lost, esp. in the bush. [dial. *slew*, to twist around, then naut. jargon; note also SLEW *v.*]

slewfoot *n.* [20C] (US) **1** a shambling or clumsy person. **2** a police officer (cf. FLATFOOT *n.*[2]).

slice *n.*[1] **1** [mid-18C+] the vagina (cf. PRIME CUT). **2** [mid-18C+] a generic for women; thus *take a slice*, to have an affair with a married woman. **3** [1980s] an attractive woman. [the equation of women with food, reinforced in (2) by pvb. 'a slice off a cut loaf is never missed']

slice *n.*[2] [1940s–60s] (Aus.) a £1 note. [? a single 'slice' of a wad of notes]

slice *n.*[3] [1980s+] (US campus) a friend, an intimate. [abbr. HOME SLICE]

slice and dice *n.* [1950s+] (US) a horror film. [the fate of the victims]

sliced *adj.* [1980s+] (US gay) circumcised.

slice of bread/the bread *n.* [1970s+] (US Black) a tale, a story, a piece of information.

slice off the legs *n.* [1960s+] (Irish) sexual intercourse (cf. SLICE *n.*[1]).

slice of ham *n.* [20C] fellatio. [rhy. sl. *slice of ham* = GAM *n.*[4]]

slice of knuckle pie *n.* [1960s] a punch in the face (cf. KNUCKLE SANDWICH).

slice/spice of life *n.* [20C] the vagina (cf. ARBOUR).

slice of toast *n.* [20C] a ghost. [rhy. sl.]

slice one's chops, to *phr.* [1940s] (US Black) to talk. [SE *slice* + CHOPS]

slicer *n.* [1960s–80s] (US Black) a knife.

slick *n.*[1] [mid-19C+] (orig. US Black) **1** a smart, charming, fashionable, sophisticated person. **2** a swindler, a hoaxer. [SE *slick*, smooth, plausible, glib]

slick *n.*[2] [1980s+] (drugs) methcathinone (cf. BATHTUB SPEED). [ety. unknown; ? its effects]

slick *v.* **1** [mid-19C+] to swindle, to hoax, to cheat. **2** [mid-19C] to get something finished with or disposed of. [SE *slick*]

slick-a-dee *n.* [mid-19C] a pocket-book. [SE *slick* + DEE n.[1]]

slick as owl shit *phr.* [1940s+] (US) very smooth, very slick. [SHIT n.[1] (1)]

slick-boy *n.* [1990s] (US Black) a confidence trickster, a cheat, a liar (cf. SLICKSTER). [SE *slick* + *boy*]

slick chick *n.* [1930s+] (US Black) a smart, attractive young woman. [SE *slick* + CHICK n.[4]]

slick-'em-plenty *n.* [1970s] (US Black) **1** a derog. term for a Jew. **2** a pawnbroker. **3** a smooth-talking confidence trickster. [racial stereotyping both as to ethics and occupation]

slicker *n.* [20C] **1** (orig. US) a dandy, a smart dresser (cf. CITY SLICKER; SLICK n.[1]). **2** (US) a cunning or dishonest businessman, a shrewd and predatory lawyer, a confidence trickster (cf. SLICKSTER). [SE *slick*]

slickies *n.* [1990s] (US campus) members of a sorority. [their 'slick' appearance]

slick one's stick, to *phr.* [1990s] to masturbate. [SE *slick*, to polish + STICK n.[1]]

slicks, the *n.* [1920s+] (US) glossy, expensive, middle-class magazines (cf. GLOSSY). [SE *slick*, i.e. high-quality, glossy paper]

slick shit *n.* [1950s+] (orig. US Black) any clever stratagem that gets one what is desired. [SE *slick* + SHIT n.[3]]

slickster *n.* [mid-19C+] (US Black) a cheat, a smooth talker, a hustler (cf. SLICKER). [SLICK v. (1)]

slickum *n.* [20C] (US) hair oil. [SE *slick*, to polish]

slick up *v.* [mid-19C–1900s] (US) to tidy, to make neat. [SE *slick*]

'slid! *excl.* [17C] euph. oath, lit. 'God's eyelid!' (cf. 's abbr.[1]).

slide *n.*[1] [20C] (drugs) a syringe, used for injecting narcotic drugs. [the sliding plunger that is part of the syringe]

slide *n.*[2] [1930s–60s] (US Black) a trouser pocket. [? SE *side*; or one 'slides' things into it]

slide *n.*[3] [1960s+] (Und.) **1** an establishment where transvestites can solicit conventionally dressed men. **2** (US) the member of the three-card monte team who keeps an eye out for police and warns the rest so that all can *slide off* in time.

slide *n.*[4] [1970s] (US campus) an easy course (cf. SKATE adj.). [one *slides* through it]

slide *v.*[1] [16C] (Und.) to use any form of illicit sleight of hand, spec. to make a surreptitious change of a crooked dice for a legitimate one (or vice versa) during a game (cf. COG v.[1]).

slide *v.*[2] [mid-19C+] to leave.

slide *v.*[3] [1930s–40s] (US Black) to dance. [the use of smooth parquet dance-floors]

slide *v.*[4] **1** [1970s+] to forgive, to pardon. **2** [1970s+] to ignore. **3** [1990s] (US Black) to give credit, esp. in a drug deal. [LET IT SLIDE]

slide *v.*[5] [1980s+] (US campus) to hit someone so hard that they fall to the ground.

slide by *v.* [1950s–60s] (US Black) to drop in uninvited, without previous notice.

slide one's jib, to *phr.* [1930s–40s] (US Black) to talk unrestrainedly. [SE *slide* + JIB n.[1]]

slider *n.* [1910s+] an ice-cream placed between two wafers. [? its potential for sliding out]

slides *n.* [1930s–40s] (US Black) shoes.

slide the shaft, to *phr.* [1990s] to masturbate.

slidewalk *n.* [1940s+] (US Black) a specific style of walking, one foot takes normal paces, the other drags; one hand is tucked into the side, the other is positioned with the wrist pressed to the waist and the elbow sticking out (cf. AKIMBO v.).

'slidikins! *excl.* [late 17C–mid-18C] a mild, blasphemous oath, lit. 'God's little eyelids' (cf. 's abbr.[1]; 'SBODIKINS). ['SLID]

'slife! *excl.* [17C–18C] a mild oath, lit. 'God's life!' (cf. 's abbr.[1]).

'slight! *excl.* [16C] a mild oath, lit. 'God's light!' (cf. 's abbr.[1]).

slightly tightly *adj.* [late 19C] tipsy but not actually drunk. [SE *slightly* + TIGHT adj.]

slight sensation *see* SENSATION n.[2].

slim *n.*[1] [late 18C–mid-19C] rum. [ety. unknown]

slim *n.*[2] [1940s–60s] (US Black) a plain tobacco cigarette, as opposed to a marijuana-filled one. [its dimensions, which tend to be leaner than those of a marijuana cigarette]

slim *n.*[3] [1960s+] (US prison) a police spy. [? their attempts to be unobtrusive; but note SLIM adj.]

slim *adj.* [early 19C+] (S.Afr.) clever, crafty, wily. [Du. *slim*, crafty]

slim-dilly *n.* [1920s+] (Aus.) a young woman. [ety. unknown; ? link to DILLY n.[4]]

slime *n.*[1] [19C+] semen. [its consistency + implication of distaste]

slime *n.*[2] **1** [1940s+] (Aus.) flattery, ingratiation. **2** [1980s+] an extremely unpleasant person (cf. SHOWER SCUM). [note the character Chevy *Slime* in Charles Dickens's *Martin Chuzzlewit* (1843–4)]

slime *n.*[3] [1980s+] (drugs) heroin. [the neg. image of narcotics]

slime *v.* [1940s+] (Aus.) to flatter. [SLIME n.[2] (1)]

slimebag/slimeball *n.* [1960s+] (US) a highly objectionable or offensive person. [SLIME n.[1]/SE *slime* + sfx. *-bag/-ball*]

slimebucket *n.* [1990s] (US campus) a highly objectionable or offensive person. [SLIME n.[1]/SE *slime* + *bucket*]

sling *n.*[1] [late 18C] a draught, a 'pull' at a bottle or glass. [SE *sling*, to throw (back)]

sling *n.*[2] [20C] (US prison) a belt with a sharpened buckle, used as an offensive weapon.

sling/slingback *n.*[3] [1930s+] (Aus.) a bribe, a gift (cf. BUNG n.[1]). [lit. 'a throwback']

sling *v.*[1] **1** [15C+] to speak. **2** [mid-19C] to pass from one person to another. **3** [mid-19C] to give. **4** [mid-late 19C] to do easily. **5** [mid-19C+] to tell, esp. in phr. *sling a yarn*, tell a story. **6** [20C] (Aus.) to abandon, to give up. [SE *sling*, to throw]

sling *v.*[2] [mid-late 19C] to blow one's nose with one's fingers. [abbr. SLING A SNOT]

sling *v.*[3] [mid-19C+] (US) to work as a waiter or waitress, esp. in phr. *sling hash*, to wait at tables, *sling beer*, to work as a bartender (cf. SLINGER n.[2]). [SE *sling*, to throw]

sling *v.*[4] [late 19C] to steal; thus *sling the smash*, to steal tobacco. [SE *sling* or SLANG v.[1] (2)]

sling/sling to *v.*[5] [1940s+] (Aus./N.Z.) to pay a bribe or a commission, esp. on one's winnings at gambling (cf. BUNG v.[2]). [SE *sling*/SLING v.[1] (2), (3)]

sling *v.*[6] [1980s+] (drugs) to sell drugs. [var. on SLANG v.[3]]

sling a book/an article/a piece/a poem, to *phr.* [late 19C+] to write a book, article etc.

sling about *v.* [late 19C+] to loiter, to hang around with particular intent.

sling a cat, to *phr.* [19C] to vomit (cf. JERK THE CAT; SHOOT THE CAT). [SE *sling* + echoic use of *cat*, i.e. the sound of retching]

sling a daddle, to *phr.* [late 19C] to shake hands (cf. TIP A DADDLE). [SE *sling* + DADDLE n.]

sling a foot, to *phr.* [mid-late 19C] to dance.

sling a hat, to *phr.* [mid-19C–1920s] to wave or throw up one's hat to express one's applause.

sling an article/a piece/poem *see* SLING A BOOK.

sling a pot, to *phr.* [late 19C] to drink heavily.

sling a poultice, to *phr.* [1920s+] (Aus.) to offer a bribe. [SE *sling* + POULTICE n. (5)]

sling a slobber, to *phr.* [late 19C] to throw a kiss, to kiss. [SE *sling* + SLOBBER]

sling a snot, to *phr.* [late 19C] to blow one's nose with one's fingers (cf. SLING v.³). [SE *sling* + SNOT n.]

sling a tinkler, to *phr.* [late 19C–1920s] to ring a bell. [SE *sling* + TINKLER n.²]

sling a yarn, to *phr.* [20C] **1** to tell a story. **2** to tell a lie. [SLING v.¹ (5) + SE *yarn*]

slingback *see* SLING n.³.

slinger n.¹ [mid-19C+] (US) a waiter or waitress. [SLING v.³]

slinger n.² [1940s–50s] (Und.) one who passes forged notes. [SLING v.¹ (2)]

slinger n.³ [1990s] (US Und.) a drug dealer (cf. SLANG v.³). [SLING v.⁶]

slingers n.¹ [late 19C+] (orig. milit.) **1** bread or ship's biscuits soaked in tea or coffee. **2** food in general. [? elision of SE *sailing* or SE *sling*, i.e. one 'throws' the food into the liquid]

slingers, the n.² [1940s+] rejection, dismissal. [SE *sling out*]

sling fish v. [1980s+] (US) **1** to have sexual intercourse. **2** to work as a prostitute. [SE *sling* + FISH n.⁴]

sling ink v. [mid-19C+] (orig. US) to write professionally, to work as a journalist (cf. SPOUT INK).

sling it v. **1** [mid-19C+] (US) to talk nonsense, to chatter about trivialities (cf. SLING THE BULL). **2** [1910s+] (Aus.) to leave one's job or one's work. [ext. SLING v.¹ (5)]

sling joints v. [late 19C] (US) to make one's living by physical rather than mental effort.

sling language/words v. [mid-19C–1910s] to talk (cf. SLING A YARN; SLING THE BAT; SLING THE LANGUAGE). [SLING v.¹ (1), (5)]

sling mud v. [20C] (orig. US) to defame, to malign.

slingo n. [1990s] (US teen) any form of slang or inventive, amusing language. [SE *slang* + *lingo*]

sling off/off at v.¹ [20C] (orig. Aus./N.Z.) to mock, to tease, to cheek (cf. THROW OFF v.¹). [SLING v.¹ (1), (5)]

sling off v.² [1920s+] (Aus.) to leave. [SLING ONE'S HOOK phr.¹]

sling one's body, to *phr.* [late 19C] to dance vigorously.

sling one's bunk, to *phr.* [mid-19C–1900s] to leave, to depart. [naut. imagery]

sling/take one's daniel, to *phr.* [mid-19C] (US) to leave (cf. SLING ONE'S HOOK phr.¹). [ety. unknown; ? lost rhy. sl. referring to some form of pack; given occas. synon. *sling one's dannet* ? link to dial. *donnot/dannet*, a good-for-nothing]

sling/take one's hook, to *phr.*¹ [mid-19C+] **1** to leave. **2** to die (cf. COIL ONE'S ROPES). [? the raising of the anchor (*hook*) before departure or the SE *hook* on which a working miner left his day clothes. When he finished his shift he removed his possessions from the hook and left for home]

sling one's hook *phr.*² [late 19C] to pick pockets. [SE *sling* + HOOK n.²]

sling one's jaw, to *phr.* [late 19C+] (US) **1** to speak out of turn. **2** to speak angrily. [lit. 'throw one's jaw']

sling one's jelly, to *phr.* [19C] of a woman, to masturbate. [SE *sling* + JELLY n.¹]

sling one's juice, to *phr.* [19C] of a man, to masturbate. [SE *sling* + JUICE n.² (2)]

sling one's mauley, to *phr.* [19C] to shake hands. [SE *sling* + MAULEY]

sling out v. [1950s+] to eject, to throw out.

sling pussy v. [1960s+] to work as a prostitute. [SE *sling* + PUSSY n.¹]

sling round on the loose, to *phr.* [late 19C] to act in a reckless manner. [SE *slink*]

sling sassy v. [mid-19C+] (US Black) to show sudden contempt or cheekiness. [SE *sling* + SASSY]

sling shot n. [1970s+] (US Black) a sanitary towel. [the shape]

sling someone one in the eye, to *phr.* [late 19C] to punch someone in the eye.

sling someone slang, to *phr.* [late 19C–1920s] to tell someone off aggressively, to scold, to abuse. [SLING v.¹ (5) + SLANG n.¹ (1)]

sling Ss v. [1960s+] (US prison) to stare. [SE *sling* + initial letter of *stare*]

sling the bat, to *phr.* [late 19C–1920s] (orig. milit.) to speak the local (foreign) language. [SLING v.¹ (5) + Hind. *bat*, speech]

sling the billy/pot, to *phr.* [mid-19C+] (Aus.) to make a cup of tea, esp. as an act of hospitality (cf. SWING THE BILLY).

sling the booze, to *phr.* [late 19C] to treat one's companions. [SE *sling* + BOOZE n.]

sling the bull, to *phr.* [mid-19C+] (US) to talk nonsense, to chatter about trivialities. [SE *sling* + BULLSHIT n.]

sling the dirt at, to *phr.* [1930s] (N.Z.) to malign, to slander.

sling the hatchet, to *phr.* **1** [late 18C–1930s] to exaggerate, to tell fantastical tales (cf. THROW THE HATCHET). **2** [mid-19C] to skulk about. **3** [1920s] to run away, to abscond.

sling/fling/shake the hoof, to *phr.* [mid-19C–1920s] (US) to dance.

sling the language/words, to *phr.* [1900s–10s] to swear fluently and creatively (cf. SLING LANGUAGE).

sling the pot *see* SLING THE BILLY.

sling the tip, to *phr.* [mid–late 19C] to warn, to 'tip off'. [SE *sling* + TIP n.⁴]

sling the words *see* SLING THE LANGUAGE.

sling to *see* SLING v.⁵.

sling words *see* SLING LANGUAGE.

sling yourself! *excl.* [late 19C] an excl. urging immediate action, hurry up! get on with it!

sling your tross! *excl.* [late 19C] go away! be off! [SE *sling* + DAB TROS]

slink n. [mid-19C] a general pej. term, a sneak, a skulker, a cheat. [SE *slink*, a premature calf or lamb (thus a human illegitimate child) or *slink*, to creep around]

slink v. [1920s] to abort. [SE *slink*, of animals, to abort]

slinky adj. [late 19C+] sneaky, underhand; thus (teen) *slinky one*, a 'silent but deadly' breaking of wind. [SE *sling*, to creep around]

slinter n. see SLANTER.

slinter adj. see SCHLENTER adj.

slip n.¹ [late 16C] a counterfeit coin. [ety. unknown]

slip n.² [early 19C] the back pocket of a tail-coat. [for *slipping* things into]

slip v. **1** [1920s+] (US) to lose one's competence, to decline. **2** [1980s+] (US Black) to let one's attention waver, to become too casual, to abandon one's vigilance. **3** [1980s+] (drugs) to become somnolent after taking heroin.

slip a fast one/fast one over, to *phr.* [1910s+] to take advantage of someone by trickery, to hoodwink (cf. PULL A FAST ONE; SLIP UP).

slip a joey, to *phr.* [20C] (Aus.) **1** to have a miscarriage. **2** to give birth. [SE *slip*, of animals, to miscarry, to give birth prematurely + *joey*, a young kangaroo]

slip a length into, to *phr.* [late 19C+] (Aus.) of a male homosexual, to have intercourse.

slip a mickey, to *phr.* [late 19C+] (US) to add a sedative, esp. choral hydrate, secretly to a drink. [SE *slip* + MICKEY FINN]

slip five *see* SLAP FIVE.

slip-gibbet n. [late 18C–19C] a thief or pickpocket or one who associates with them (cf. GALLOWS-BIRD). [SE *slip*, to escape + *gibbet*, the gallows]

slip her a crippler/quick crippler, to *phr.* [1940s+] of a man, to have sexual intercourse with a woman.

slip her a length, to *phr.* [1940s+] of a man, to have sexual intercourse with a woman (cf. GIVE HER A LENGTH).

slip in daintie davie/willie wallace, to *phr.* [19C] (Scot.) of a man, to have sexual intercourse.

slip in the gutter *n.* [20C] butter. [rhy. sl.]

slip into *v.* **1** [mid-19C+] to beat; thus *let slip at*, to attack violently. **2** [late 19C] to set about a task enthusiastically. **3** [late 19C+] of a man, to have sexual intercourse. [20C uses only Aus.]

slip in willie wallace *see* SLIP IN DAINTIE DAVIE.

slip it about *v.* [20C] of a woman, to have sexual intercourse.

slip it to her *v.* [1940s+] of a man, to have sexual intercourse with a woman.

slip me five *see* GIVE ME FIVE.

slip of the shoulder *n.* [19C] by a woman, seduction. [her body language]

slip one over on *see* PUT ONE OVER ON.

slip one's braces, to *phr.* [20C] to consent to male gay sex. [preparatory to discarding one's trousers]

slip one's breath, to *phr.* [early 18C] to die (cf. COIL ONE'S ROPES). [naut. imagery]

slip one's cable, to *phr.* [late 18C] to die (cf. COIL ONE'S ROPES). [naut. imagery]

slip one's cog, to *phr.* [1930s] to lose one's emotional sense, to become eccentric, to 'have a screw loose'. [engineering imagery]

slip one's cork, to *phr.* [1960s] (US) to go crazy. [SE *slip*, to let go; the image of a foaming bottle]

slip oneself *v.* [late 19C] to indulge oneself to the full, to take advantage of an opportunity.

slip one's trolley, to *phr.* [1940s+] to lose emotional control, to go mad (cf. OFF ONE'S TROLLEY). [? trolley-bus or tram imagery; i.e. the vehicle 'comes off the rails']

slip one's wind, to *phr.* [early–mid-19C] to die (cf. COIL ONE'S ROPES). [naut. imagery]

slip on one's guava *see* COME ON ONE'S GUAVA.

slipper *v.* [1920s+] (US Und.) to reform and renounce the criminal life. [the SE *slippers* that symbolize a peaceful life]

slippery *n.* [mid-19C] soap. [its essential quality]

slippery-dip *n.*[1] [20C] (Aus.) lip, cheekiness. [rhy. sl. *slippery-dip* = LIP n.[1] (1)]

slippery-dip *n.*[2] [1990s] (Aus.) a children's slide.

slippin' *adj.* [1990s] (US teen) a general adj. of approval. [SE *slipping along nicely*]

slipping *n.* [1990s] (US Black) not paying attention. [SLIP v. (2)]

slipping and sliding *n.* [1980s+] (US Black) sneaking around, acting in a clandestine manner.

slippy *adj.* [late 19C+] agile, nimble, speedy.

slippy tit *n.* [20C] (Ulster) a sly, untrustworthy person. [SLIPPY + TIT n.[1]]

slip-slapping *n.* [1930s+] a mutual hand-slapping ritual used by Blacks (and some Whites) for greeting, emphasis, congratulation etc. [SLAP FIVE]

slip-slop *n.*[1] [18C] kissing. [echoic of the exchange of spittle]

slip-slop *n.*[2] [1960s+] (S.Afr.) a thong sandal. [the noise it makes as one walks]

slip-slops *n.* [18C] **1** any form of soft drink, esp. tea (cf. SLOPS n.[2]). **2** a non-alcoholic drink taken for medicinal purposes. [SE *slip-slop*, any form of sloppy mixture, whether food or drink]

slip something over/over on *v.* [1910s+] to deceive, to take advantage of in a surreptitious manner.

slipstick *n.* [1950s] (US campus) a slide rule.

slip the berries to *see* GIVE THE BERRIES TO.

slip the calf *see* CAST THE CALF.

slip up *v.* [late 19C] (Aus.) to defraud, to swindle (cf. SLIP A FAST ONE).

slit *n.*[1] [mid-17C+] **1** the vagina (cf. ARBOUR; SLOT n.[2]). **2** a derog. term for a woman.

slit *n.*[2] [1940s+] a derog. term for an Asian or Oriental person (cf. SLANT n.[3]). [the shape of the Oriental eye]

slither *n.*[1] [late 19C+] a lodge (e.g. of Freemasonry). [rhy. sl. *slither and dodge* = lodge]

slither/slitherum *n.*[2] [1900s–30s] counterfeit money. [it slithers through one's fingers]

slither *n.*[3] [1910s] a rush, a hurry.

slither *v.* [late 19C+] to hurry away. [later use is Aus.]

slitherum *see* SLITHER n.[2]

slithery *n.* [1930s+] **1** the vagina. **2** women in general (viewed as sex objects). **3** sexual intercourse.

slive-andrew *n.* [18C] a 'lazybones', an idle person. [SE/dial. *slive*, to sneak away + 17C SE *andrew*, a servant]

sloan *v.* [late 19C] to balk, to hinder, to get in the way of. [coined and abandoned in 1899; f. the US jockey Tod *Sloan* (1874–1933), who cut his horse Holocaust across those of his rivals in an attempt to win that year's Derby; Sloan had picked up the trick from the British champion Archer, but the sl. gave him the tribute]

Sloane Ranger *n.* [1970s+] a stereotypical British upper-middle-class young woman, resolutely trad., invariably Conservative-voting and happier with dogs or horses than humans; she may live in London, but her spiritual home remains the country; often abbr. as *Sloane* (cf. HOORAY HENRY). [coined by Peter York and Ann Barr in *Harpers & Queen*, October 1975. It puns on *Sloane* Square, London SW3, home of such women + the TV lawman the Lone *Ranger*]

slob *n.*[1] [mid-19C+] (orig. US) a lazy, dirty, unkempt, good-for-nothing person, usu. a man. [Slavic *zhlub*, a coarse fellow]

slob *n.*[2] [20C] a harmless simpleton, a 'soft', fat fellow. [Irish *slaba*, mud; thus a slovenly person]

slob *v.* [1950s–60s] (US Black) to kiss. [abbr. SE *slobber/* SLOBBER n.]

slob a knob, to *phr.* [1940s+] (US) to perform fellatio. [SE *slob(ber)* + KNOB n.[1]]

slobber *n.* [late 19C–1900s] a kiss (cf. SLING A SLOBBER). [the swapping of spittle]

slobberation *n.* [1910s–20s] sloppy kissing. [SLOBBER]

slobberer *n.* [late 18C] a general insult, spec. a bad farmer. [dial. *slobber*, to work in a slovenly manner]

slobber-slobber *n.* [1950s] (W.I.) a slovenly, unkempt, lazy person (cf. SLOB n.[1]).

slockdologer *see* SOCKDOLAGER.

slog *n.* [late 19C+] work that is definitely hard and possibly unrewarding. [SLOG v. (3)]

slog *v.* [mid-19C+] **1** to hit, to punch. **2** to thrash, to beat. **3** to work hard; thus *slog one's guts out*. [? Yorks. dial./SE *slug*, to hit hard]

slogger *n.* **1** [early 19C+] one who delivers heavy blows, esp. in boxing or cricket. **2** [mid-19C–1950s] a hard, ponderous worker. **3** [late 19C–1900s] a weight attached to a string and used as a weapon. [SLOG v.]

slogging *n.* [mid-19C+] **1** a beating, a thrashing. **2** working hard, esp. as *slogging away/away at*. [SLOG v.]

slog it on *see* SCHLOG IT ON.

slog the log, to *phr.* [1970s+] to masturbate (cf. FLOG THE LOG). [SLOG v. + LOG n.[5]]

slonchways *adj.* [mid-19C] (US) askew (cf. SKYGODLIN). [? SE *slouch*]

sloop of war *n.* [mid-19C] a prostitute. [rhy. sl.]

sloosh *n.* [20C] a quick wash. [echoic]

slop *n.*[1] **1** [early 19C] tea. **2** [20C] (US) food in general. **3** [1940s+] (Aus./N.Z./US) beer. [SE *slop*, watered-down food]

slop *n.*[2] [mid-19C] a policeman. [backsl.]

slop *n.*[3] [mid-19C+] sentimentality, mawkish emotion. [SE *slop*, liquid or semi-liquid food, esp. as served to invalids]

slop *n.*[4] [1940s] (US Black) a saxophone (cf. SLUSH PUMP). [the spittle that collects in it]

slop a bib full, to *phr.* [1920s] (US) to talk excessively. [SE *slop*, to spill or splash]

slop about/around *v.* [20C] **1** to wander around aimlessly. **2** to move in a slovenly manner. [SE *slope*, to move obliquely, underpinned by SLOPPY adj. (1)]

slop and flop *n.* [1920s–30s] (US tramp) food and accommodation, esp. in transient camps, typically those set up by an oil-drilling company. [SLOP n.¹ (2) + FLOP n.⁵]

slop around *see* SLOP ABOUT.

slop at the hog trough, to *phr.* [1930s] (US Black) to perform cunnilingus.

slop back/slop it back *v.* [1920s+] (N.Z.) to drink.

slope/slopehead/slopy *n.* [1940s+] a derog. term for an Oriental person, esp. Vietnamese, Korean (cf. SLANT n.³). [the supposed 'slope' of Oriental eyes]

slope *v.¹* [17C] to sleep. [synon. Du.; Rowlands notes that this replaces Harman's and Dekker's synon. COUCH A HOGSHEAD, which is 'like an Almanac that is out of date']

slope *v.²* (orig. US) **1** [mid-19C+] to leave, to move off. **2** [1900s] to leave one's lodgings without paying. **3** (US Und.) to escape from prison. [SE *let's lope* or *slope*, to move obliquely]

slope *v.³* [1990s] (US Black) to disrespect, to treat badly. [SE *slope*; thus a *sloped* or slanted attitude or reminiscent of a SLOPE n.]

slopehead *see* SLOPE n.

slope off *v.* [mid-19C+] (orig. US) to leave, esp. surreptitiously. [ext. SLOPE v.²]

sloper *n.* [late 19C+] (Aus.) one who leaves without paying off their debts or bills. [dial. *sloper*, a trickster + SLOPE v.²]

sloper's island *n.* [late 19C–1900s] a neighbourhood of weekly tenements (i.e. flats that are rented by the week). [F&H cite 'the artisans' village near Loughborough Junction, originally in the midst of fields; now in the centre of a densely populated neighbourhood'. The possibility that impoverished tenants would SLOPE OFF without paying]

slop-feeder *n.* [early 19C] a teaspoon (cf. SLOP-TUBS). [SLOP n.¹ + SE *feeder*]

slophead *n.* [20C] (Aus./US) a beer drunkard. [SLOP n.¹ (3) + sfx. -HEAD (2)]

slop it back *see* SLOP BACK.

slop joint *n.* [20C] a cheap, unappetizing restaurant. [SLOP n.¹ (2) + JOINT n.³ (3); note US milit. *slop chute*, the barracks/base canteen]

slop-made *adj.* [late 19C] (Aus.) disjointed. [synon. with SE *slop-built*]

slop out *v.* **1** [1950s+] (prison) to empty a chamberpot. **2** [1990s] to masturbate. [SE *slop*, to spill, to pour]

slop-pail *n.* [1920s] a man who does housework.

slopped *adj.* [1920s+] drunk. [SLOP n.¹ (3), underpinned by SE *sloppy*, weak, feeble, waterlogged]

slopping up *n.* [late 19C–1920s] (US tramp) a session of heavy drinking.

sloppy *adj.* **1** [early 19C+] lazy, inefficient, imprecise. **2** [late 19C+] mawkishly sentimental. [SE; ult. *slop*, an act of spilling, the liquid thus spilt]

sloppy joe *n.* (US) **1** [1940s+] a loose, floppy sweater. **2** [1960s+] a multi-decked sandwich (the fillings ooze out when eating it). **3** [1960s+] a type of hamburger in which the meat filling is diluted to a form of sauce. **4** [1960s+] a slovenly, inefficient person.

sloppy joe's *n.* [1940s+] (US) a cheap restaurant or snack bar (cf. GREASY SPOON). [generic use of a supposed cook + SLOPPY JOE]

sloppy seconds *n.* [1960s+] **1** sexual intercourse with a woman who has had another partner/partners immediately previously. **2** the woman who is participating in this sequential sex.

slops *n.¹* [early 16C] wide, baggy breeches or hose. [SE *slop*, an outer garment; dial. the leg(s) of a pair of breeches; ult. ety. unknown]

slops *n.²* **1** [mid-19C] tea, esp. when still in a chest. **2** [20C] any form of badly cooked or ill-tasting food. **3** [1900s–10s] (US tramp) beer. [SE *slop*, watered-down food]

slops and slugs *n.* [1940s] (US Black) coffee and doughnuts (cf. SINKER n.²). [SLOPS n.² (2) + SE *slug*, i.e. the hardness of the doughnut]

slop-tubs *n.* [19C] a tea-service (cf. SLOP-FEEDER). [SLOPS n.² (1) + SE *tub*]

slop up *v.* [late 19C–1920s] to drink heavily, to become drunk. [SLOP n.¹]

slopy *see* SLOPE n.

slorch *n.* [1990s] (US campus) a promiscuous woman. [? SE *slut* + *whore* + *bitch*]

slosh *n.¹* **1** [late 19C+] a drink, alcoholic or otherwise. **2** [1920s+] (Aus.) coffee. **3** [1920s+] mawkish emotionalism. [SE *slosh*, weak, watery, unappetizing drink, ult. *slush*, liquid mud]

slosh *n.²* [1930s+] a hit, a blow. [SLOSH v.¹]

slosh *v.¹* [late 19C+] to hit; thus *slosh the burick, slosh the old gooseberry*, to hit one's wife.

slosh *v.²* [late 19C] to swallow carelessly, to eat heartily. [the consumption of SLOSH n.¹ (1), (2)]

slosh around *v.* **1** [late 19C] (US) to hit out at random. **2** [1910s–20s] to strut about, to swank. [SLOSH v.¹]

sloshed *adj.* [late 19C+] drunk (cf. BASTED). [SLOSH n.¹ (1) + SLOSH v.¹]

slot *n.¹* **1** [late 19C–1950s] (US) an Automat. **2** [1950s+] (orig. US) a slot-machine. [the slot into which one places money. (1) the coin-operated self-service Automats, popularized in New York (although in no other city) by the Horn & Hardart Baking Co.]

slot *n.²* [1940s+] **1** the vagina (cf. ARBOUR; SLIT n.¹). **2** (Aus./N.Z.) a prison cell. [into which one is put]

slot/slot in *v.* [1960s+] (orig. milit.) to choose someone for a task or vacancy. [thus milit. jargon *slot*, to shoot dead]

'slot! *excl.* [1940s+] (Aus.) thank you very much. [abbr. SE *thanks a lot*]

sloth *n.* [1980s+] a very lazy person (cf. SLUG n.⁵).

slot in *see* SLOT v.

slotties *n.* [1980s+] (Polari) **1** money. **2** a handbag. [? one uses it for slot machines]

slouch *n.* **1** [late 19C+] an indifferent, second-rate or inefficient thing, place, person etc. **2** [1970s] (US Black) an eccentric, lazy, unprofessional prostitute (cf. FLAKY HO).

slough *v.* [mid-19C–1930s] to lock up, to put in prison. [SE *slough*, to be swallowed up, ult. *slough*, a piece of soft, muddy ground]

sloughed *adj.* [20C] (US Und.) imprisoned, locked up. [SLOUGH v.]

slour/slour up *v.* [early 19C–late 19C] (Und.) **1** to lock up, to fasten. **2** to button up a garment; thus *sloured hoxter*, a buttoned inside pocket. [ety. unknown]

slousher *n.* [1900s] (N.Z.) a lazy person, usu. in phr. *be no slousher/slousher at.* [SE *slousher*]

slow *adj.* **1** [early–mid-19C] unfashionable. **2** [mid–late 19C+] of places, dull, boring. **3** [mid-19C] of people, dull, lifeless, insipid. **4** [late 19C+] sexually timid (cf. FAST adj.¹).

slow as a wet week *phr.* [late 19C+] very backward, dull, esp. in sexual matters.

slow as Christmas *n.* [19C] a very slow person (cf. SO'S CHRISTMAS). [dialogue: 'I'm coming!' 'So's Christmas']

slow-ass *adj.* [1970s+] (US Black) slow. [SE *slow* + sfx. -ASS]

Slowbart n. [late 19C–1900s] (Aus.) Hobart, the capital city of Tasmania. [the slow pace of its life]

slow boat n. [1960s+] (S.Afr. drugs) a marijuana cigarette. [? the song 'I want to get you on a slow boat to China'; the emphasis is on the supposed exoticism of marijuana, although, given 'China', the link should be to opium]

slow burn n. [1930s+] (orig. US) the gradual development of an intense fury, slowly brought to a peak, rather than simply exploding with rage.

slow con n. [20C] a fraudulent scheme or *con*fidence trick in which the victim is nurtured slowly and carefully towards their downfall (cf. SHORT CON).

slowed adj. [mid-19C] (prison) locked up. [? SLOUR]

slow-em-ups n. [1970s+] (drugs) any form of barbiturate, tranquillizer or sleeping pill. [the effects]

slow one's roll, to phr. [1990s] (US Black) to slow down whatever one is doing. [SE *slow* + ROLL v.² (1)]

slow one's row, to phr. [1940s+] (US Black) to lower one's profile, to keep off the streets, perhaps through fear of police or rival criminal interest. [ploughing imagery or Black pron. of *roll*, thus predating SLOW ONE'S ROLL]

slow on the draw phr. [20C] **1** not very intelligent (cf. QUICK ON THE DRAW). **2** (Irish) reluctant to stand one's round of drinks. [gun-fighting imagery]

slow on the trigger phr. [20C] stupid, dull. [gun-fighting imagery]

slow pay/walk v. [20C] (US) to stall, to put someone off.

slowpoke n. [mid-19C+] (US) a sluggard, a lethargic, lazy person. [SE *slow* + POKE ALONG]

slow track n. [1940s] (US Black) **1** the whoring and high-life centre in a small town or city. **2** the West Coast (cf. FAST TRACK). [the image of the small town or the West Coast being 'slower' than New York]

slow walk see SLOW PAY.

slow walker n. [1960s+] (US Und.) one who follows postmen on their rounds with the intention of stealing the mail they have just delivered.

slubberdegullion see SLABBERDEGULLION.

'sluck! excl. [1910s–30s] a toast, i.e. *here's luck*.

'slud! see 'SBLOOD!

sludgeball n. [1960s+] (US) a slovenly person. [SE *sludge* + sfx *-ball*]

slue see SLEW.

sluff v. [20C] (US) to avoid or shirk one's responsibilities or work. [SE *slough off*]

slug n.¹ **1** [mid-18C] a fiery drink (cf. GLIM n.²). **2** [mid-18C+] a portion or measure of liquor (cf. SHOT n.⁵). [SE *slug*, a roughly formed bullet; thus that which is 'shot']

slug n.² [late 19C–1900s] a disappointment. [SLUG v.²]

slug n.³ [late 19C+] (US) **1** $1. **2** a counterfeit coin. **3** a token. **4** a bullet. [SE *slug*, a piece of lead]

slug n.⁴ [1940s+] (orig. Aus. navy) the penis. [resemblance to the gastropod]

slug n.⁵ [1980s+] a very lazy person (cf. SLOTH). [the slow progress of a SE *slug*]

slug v.¹ [mid-19C+] to drink. [SLUG n.¹]

slug v.² **1** [late 19C+] (orig. Und.) to hit hard. **2** [1940s+] (Aus.) to overcharge (cf. HIT FOR; SCHLOG). [SLOG v.]

slug and snail n. [20C] a (finger)nail. [rhy. sl.]

slugfest n. [1910s+] (US) a rough battle, a hard-hitting contest. [SLUG v.¹ (1) + sfx. -FEST]

slugged adj. [20C] (US) drunk (cf. BASTED). [SLUG v.¹ (1)]

slugger n. **1** [late 19C+] a fighter, professional or otherwise, who relies on brute force rather than skill for their conquests. **2** [1970s] (US campus) a sexual success, a seducer (cf. HITTER n.¹). [SLUG v.² (1)]

sluggers n. [late 19C+] (US) whiskers that extend from the ear

to the chin, typically worn by a stage Irishman. [SLUG v.² (1); such whiskers were orig. a sign of a pugnacious fighter, stereotypically Irish]

slug-nutty adj. [1930s–50s] (US) punch-drunk (cf. SLAP-HAPPY adj.). [SLUG v.² (1) + NUTTY adj.]

sluice n. **1** [17C] the vagina (cf. DAMP n.). **2** [mid-19C–1920s] the mouth. **3** [1950s–70s] sexual intercourse. [SE *sluice*, a channel]

sluice-cunted adj. [mid-19C+] having a large vagina (cf. BUSHEL-CUNTED). [SE *sluice*, a channel, a run off + CUNT n.¹ (1)]

sluice-house n. **1** [mid-19C] a public house, a tavern (cf. SLUICERY). **2** [mid-19C–1920s] the mouth. [SE *sluice*, to wash down + *house*]

sluicery n. [19C] a gin-shop or public house (cf. SLUICE THE GOB). [SE *sluice*, to wash down]

sluice the bolt/ivories, to phr. [late 18C–mid-19C] to drink heartily. [SE *sluice* + BOLT n.¹/IVORY n.¹]

sluice the dominoes, to phr. [mid-19C–20C] to drink heartily. [SE *sluice* + DOMINO n. (1)]

sluice the gob, to phr. [late 18C–1940s] to take a hearty drink (cf. SLUICERY). [SE *sluice* + GOB n.¹]

sluice the ivories see SLUICE THE BOLT.

sluk v. [1970s+] (S.Afr.) to gulp down, to drink. [Afk. *sluk*, to swallow]

sluker n. [late 19C–1900s] a prostitute who works in the City Road, London, itself part of the parish of *St Luke*'s (cf. ANGEL n.¹). [such women were considered socially inferior to those who worked in Islington]

slum n.¹ **1** [19C] nonsensical talk or writing, gammon, blarney. **2** [early 19C] the jargon of gypsies. **3** [early 19C] an insinuation, an innuendo. **4** [early 19C] a trick, a hoax. **5** [mid-19C] a professionally written begging letter; thus *slum-scribbler*, a writer of such documents, letters. **6** [20C] (Und.) a letter written from prison. [SE *slum*, a run-down, poverty-stricken area; thus a generic neg.]

slum n.² **1** [early–mid-19C] (Und.) a room. **2** [mid-19C] a chest or box. [? SE *slumber*]

slum n.³ **1** [20C] the virtually worthless prizes offered at fairs, carnivals etc. **2** [1910s+] cheap or counterfeit jewellery, typically that sold illegally by street vendors. [SLUM n.¹ (4)]

slum v.¹ [mid-19C] **1** to boast. **2** to talk nonsense. **3** to trick or cheat. [SLUM n.¹]

slum v.² [mid-19C+] **1** to saunter about, esp. in poor or 'redlight' areas, possibly with an eye on 'immoral pursuits'. **2** to play the tourist in impoverished areas, looking for 'atmosphere' and 'characters', but secure in the knowledge that one's real life is elsewhere. [SE *slum*]

slum-box n. [1920s] a typical example of slum housing. [SE *slum* + *box*]

slumgudgeon/slumgullion n. [mid–late 19C] 'any cheap, nasty, washy beverage' or foodstuff. (Hotten, 1874). [ety. unknown; ? SE *slum* + Lancashire dial. *gullion*, a worthless wretch]

slumguzzle v. [1900s–10s] (orig. US) to trick, to cheat. [SLUM n.¹ (1), (4) + GUZZLE v.]

slum hustler n. [1920s+] (Und.) one who sells cheap jewellery, pretending to the gullible buyer that it is stolen property (cf. DUDDER; DUFFER n.¹). [SLUM n.³ + HUSTLER]

slummery n. [mid-19C] a form of gibberish or ziph (a language invented at Winchester). [originated at Winchester College, it substitutes 'wa' for the first of two initial consonants and inserts 'p' or 'g', making 'breeches' into wareechepes; a simpler version ignores the 'wa' substitution, e.g. 'shagall wege gogo' = 'shall we go', while Jon Bee (1823) offers another version, i.e. 'Willus youvus givibus glasso ginibus' = 'will you give [me] a glass of gin']

slumming *n.* [19C] the practice of passing counterfeit money. [SLUM n.^{3}]

slummock/slummuck *v.* [1910s–20s] to clean carelessly or half-heartedly. [SE *slummocky*, slovenly]

slummy *n.* [late 19C–1930s] **1** a servant girl. **2** an ill-dressed, unattractive woman. **3** a slum-dweller. [SE *slum*]

slumopolis *n.* [late 19C] the London slums. [on the model of COTTONOPOLIS]

slums and bums *n.* [1970s+] (US campus) a course in urban local government. [SE *slum* + BUM n.^{3} (1)]

slum the gorger, to *phr.* [mid-19C] **1** to cheat on the sly, to be an *eye servant*, i.e. a servant who works hard only when the master's or mistress's eye is on them. **2** to hide, to pass to a confederate. [SLUM v.^{1} (3) + GORGER n.^{1}]

slung *adj.* [20C] (Aus.) thrown from one's horse. [SE *get slung off*, to be thrown]

slup *see* SLURP *n.*

slur *v.* [mid-17C–mid-18C] to cheat at dice; *spec.* to slide a dice out of the dice-box without actually letting it roll. [? Low Ger. *slurrn*, to drag the feet]

slurb *n.* [20C] (US) the dormitory suburbs of a big city, mass-produced, featureless, sprawling and aesthetically null. [SE *slum* + suburb]

slush *n.^{1}* [mid-19C+] (US) blatant sentimentality. [SE *slush*, watery, melted snow]

slush *n.^{2}* [20C] **1** (tramp) the tea or coffee available in lodging houses. **2** any form of sloppy food, e.g. a thin stew. [RN jargon *slush*, the refuse fat from boiled meat, the selling of which was a perk accorded the SLUSHY or ship's cook]

slush *n.^{3}* [1920s–30s] (Und.) forged, counterfeit money. [for ety. see SLUSH n.^{2}]

slush *v.* **1** [late 19C] (Aus.) to work as a cook's assistant. **2** [late 19C–1910s] (Anglo-Irish) to work extremely hard. [SLUSHY]

slush-bucket *n.* [late 18C–mid-19C] an ill-mannered eater. [RN jargon *slush*, refuse fat + SE *bucket*]

slusher *n.^{1}* *see* SLUSHY.

slusher *n.^{2}* [1910s–20s] a printer and distributor of counterfeit notes. [SLUSH n.^{3}]

slusher *n.^{3}* [1990s] (Black) a promiscuous woman. [? she is constantly damp with desire]

slush fund *n.* [late 19C+] an emergency fund for unforeseen expenditure, esp. that which may be illegal or extra-legal; such funds came into prominence during the Watergate Affair of 1972–4. [fig. use of RN jargon *slush*, refuse fat, the sale of which was a cook's perk]

slush pump *n.* [1930s–50s] (US) a trombone (cf. SLOP n.^{4}). [the spittle that collects while playing it]

slushy/slusher *n.* **1** [mid-19C+] a cook. **2** [mid-19C+] (Aus./N.Z.) a cook's assistant, esp. for a shearing gang. **3** [mid-19C+] any unskilled assistant. **4** [1920s–30s] (Aus.) a fat lamp, a wick placed in a dish of fat. [SLUSH n.^{2}; orig. naut. jargon *slushy*, a ship's cook, who collected and sold refuse fat or *slush*]

slut/slut-lamp *n.^{1}* [late 19C–1930s] (US, West.) an improvised lamp made of a twist of rag in a container of grease. [play on BITCH n.^{2}]

slut *n.^{2}* [1980s+] (US campus) **1** an affectionate term of address among women. **2** an habitué; usu. in combs. (cf. BUTT SLUT).

slut hut *n.* [1980s+] (US gay) **1** a gay brothel. **2** anywhere that gay men congregate for sex. ['homosexualizing' of SE *slut*, usu. applied to women + *hut*]

slut-lamp *see* SLUT n.^{1}.

slut-puppy *n.* [1980s+] **1** a derog. term for a lesbian (cf. BUTT SLUT). **2** (US campus) a promiscuous woman. [SE *slut* + play on DOG n.^{4} (6)]

sly *adj.* [early 19C+] (Aus.) illicit, illegal. [SE *sly*, secretive, underhand]

sly-bag *n.* [1930s+] (Aus.) a cunning person.

slyboots *n.* [late 17C+] a cunning, deceptive person, usu. with overtones of affection rather than an expression of outright disapproval.

sly-grog/-house *n.* [19C] (Aus./N.Z.) liquor sold without a license, often through a sly-grog shop; thus *sly-groggery*, an illicit saloon or liquor store, *sly-grogger*, *sly-grogster*, an illicit liquor seller, *sly-grogging*, selling liquor illegally. [SLY + GROG n.]

sly, slick and wicked *n.* [1920s+] (US Black) an individual who plans to be caught out in a small act of deceit, which exposé will facilitate plans for a larger confidence trick.

smaak *v.* [1960s+] (S.Afr.) to like, to enjoy, to 'fancy' someone. [synon. Afk.]

smabble *v.* **1** [early 18C] to knock down, to plunder. **2** [19C+] to have sexual intercourse with. [echoic or var. on SNABBLE]

smabbled *adj.* [late 18C–mid-19C] killed in battle. [SMABBLE v.]

smack *n.^{1}* [mid-19C+] a liking for. [SE *smack*, enjoyment, appreciation]

smack *n.^{2}* [late 19C+] **1** (US) a blow, a slap. **2** a try, a 'go'; thus *have a smack at*, to have a go at (cf. SHOT n.^{2}).

smack *n.^{3}* (US Black) **1** [1900s–40s] a kiss (cf. SMACKER n.^{1}). **2** [1950s–60s] sexual intercourse. [SE 17C–early 19C]

smack *n.^{4}* [1930s+] (US Und.) the use of a specially doctored coin for heads-or-tails gambling. [the trickster's smacking his hand on the coin as he catches it]

smack *n.^{5}* [1940s+] (drugs) **1** heroin. **2** adulterated cocaine. [Yid. *schmeck*, to hit]

smack *n.^{6}* [1960s+] (US Black/teen) **1** flirtatious talk. **2** nonsense. [SE *smack*, to hit]

smack *n.^{7}* [1980s+] (US campus) an overly hard-working student. [? they are constantly smacking their head in concentration]

smack *v.^{1}* **1** [late 18C–early 19C] to kiss. **2** [1990s] (US Black gang) to act sycophantically, to toady (cf. KISS ARSE v.). [echoic of the sound of kissing]

smack *v.^{2}* [1990s] (US Black) to criticize someone behind their back. [SE *smack*, to hit]

smack a blue, to *phr.* [1930s+] (Aus.) to get into trouble. [SE *smack* + BLUE n.^{7}]

smack calf-skin/the calf-skin *v.* [late 18C–late 19C] (Und.) to kiss the Bible when taking an oath. [SMACK v.^{1} + the SE *calf-skin* cover]

smack-dab *adv.* [late 19C+] (US) exactly, precisely. [echoic]

smack down *v.* [late 19C+] (US) **1** to hit hard, esp. to hit in the face. **2** to tell off, to reprimand, to put in one's place.

smacked-out *adj.* [1930s+] (drugs) under the influence of heroin (cf. AMPED-OUT). [SMACK n.^{5}]

smacker *n.^{1}* [late 19C+] a kiss (cf. SMACK n.^{3}). [the sound]

smacker *n.^{2}* [1930s+] (Aus.) a boy, a young man. [on pattern of CRACKER n.^{10}]

smackeroos *n.* [1980s+] dollars or pounds sterling. [ext. SMACKERS]

smackers *n.* [1920s+] (orig. US) dollars or pounds sterling (cf. BANGER n.^{6}).

smack freak *n.* [1970s+] (drugs) a heroin addict. [SMACK n.^{5} + sfx. -FREAK]

smack-head *n.* [20C] (drugs) heroin addict (cf. ACID-HEAD). [SMACK n.^{5} + sfx. -HEAD (2)]

smacking-cove *n.* [late 17C–early 19C] a coachman. [SE *smack*, i.e. his whipping of the horses + COVE]

smack in the eye *n.^{1}* [late 19C+] a rebuff, a rejection, a severe and surprising disappointment.

smack in the eye *n.^{2}* [20C] a pie. [rhy. sl.]

smacko *n.* [1940s] (US Black) **1** a street person. **2** a thug. **3** an unemployed person. [SE *smack*, a blow; thus one who either hits or, lit. or fig., is likely to be hit]

smack off v. [1990s] to masturbate (cf. BEAT OFF).

smack on adv. [20C] accurately, right in the middle of.

smack smooth adj. [mid–late 19C] absolutely level, perfectly smooth.

smack the calf-skin see SMACK CALF-SKIN.

smack-up n. (Aus./N.Z.) **1** [1900s–10s] a fight. **2** [1950s] (juv.) a caning at school. [SE *smack*]

smack up v. [1910s+] to attack physically; thus *smacked up*, bested in a fight. [SMACK-UP]

small and early n. [late 19C] (society) an informal dance (as opposed to a full-scale ball), to which few guests are invited and which starts early and ends before midnight.

small apples adj. [late 19C] (US) unimportant, of no matter (cf. SMALL POTATOES).

small beer adj. [early 17C+] inferior, worthless, second-rate; thus [19C] phr. *think small beer of*, to have a low opinion of. [SE *small beer*, thin, inferior beer]

small bore adj. [20C] (US) trivial, insignificant. [SE *small bore*, a small calibre gun barrel]

small bread n. [1940s–50s] (US Black) anything insignificant, esp. a small amount of money. [SE *small* + BREAD n.¹ (2)]

small change n. [1970s+] (US) an insignificant, weak person. [monetary imagery]

small cheque n. [late 19C] a dram; thus to *knock down a cheque*, to spend all one's money on alcohol.

smallest room n. [1930s+] euph. for the lavatory in a private house.

small fortune n. [1910s+] (orig. US) a very large sum of money, esp. when paid out for some commodity. [understatement]

small gang v. [mid–late 19C] to rob in the street. [? the 'gang' requires only one or two people]

small meat n. [1960s+] (US gay) a small penis (cf. BACON n.¹). [SE *small* + MEAT n. (2)]

small nickel n. [20C] (US gambling) a bet of $500 (cf. BIG NICKEL). [SE *small* + NICKEL n.¹ (5)]

small pipe n. [1940s–50s] (US) an alto saxophone.

small potatoes adj. [early 19C+] (orig. US) insignificant, of little worth, irrelevant, ext. as *small potatoes and few in a/the hill* (cf. SMALL APPLES).

small print n. [20C] (orig. US) the disadvantageous details of any situation. [SE *small print*, conditions stipulated in a legally binding document written in such small print that they are easily overlooked at the time of signing]

small timber n. [mid–19C] matches.

small time n. [20C] a mediocrity, a failure, the second-rate, the unprofitable (cf. BIG TIME n.¹). [theatre jargon *small time*, a vaudeville circuit for second-rate acts]

small-time joint n. [1970s+] (S.Afr.) the lowest class of shebeen; thus *big-time joint*, a superior shebeen. [SMALL TIME + JOINT n.³ (3)]

smarm n. [1930s+] an unctuous bearing, flattering or toadying behaviour (cf. SMARM v.). [SE *smalm*, to smooth down with some form of greasy substance]

smarm v. [1930s+] to toady, to ingratiate. [SMARM n.]

smarmy adj. [1930s+] **1** unctuous, ingratiating. **2** of a voice, sonorous, rich (cf. PLUMMY adj.). **3** smug and self-righteous. [SMARM n.]

smart alec/aleck n. [mid-19C+] (orig. US) an unpleasantly conceited, smug person (cf. ALEC; CLEVER DICK). [proper name *Alec* Hoag, a celebrated New York City thief of 1840s, who, with his wife Melinda and his accomplice French Jack, specialized in the PANEL GAME; for a detailed account of Hoag and his career, see Cohen (1985)]

smart apple n. [20C] (US) a bright, intelligent person.

smart-arse/-ass n. [1930s+] (orig. Aus.) one who sees

themselves as cleverer than they really are (cf. WISE-ASS n.). [SE *smart* + ARSE n.¹]

smart as a carrot new scraped phr. [late 18C–mid-19C] smartly dressed.

smart as be-damned phr. [1920s–30s] very well dressed.

smart-ass see SMART-ARSE.

smart as threepence phr. [late 19C] very well dressed.

smart cookie n. [1920s+] (orig. US) a bright, opportunistic person. [SE *smart* + COOKIE n.³]

smarten up v. [late 19C+] to explain, to pass on information (cf. WISE UP).

smart guy see WISE GUY.

smartiepants/smartipants n. **1** [1940s+] (orig. US) a general term of light-hearted abuse. **2** [1940s–50s] (US Black) a young man at the outset of his sexual career (cf. SMARTY-BOOTS).

smart/right money n. [1920s+] (US) **1** spec. the way in which experienced gamblers bet. **2** good sense. [note milit. jargon *smart money*, compensation for injuries received in service]

smart mouth v. [1960s+] **1** to attack verbally, to slander (cf. BADMOUTH v.). **2** to be cheeky, to tease.

smarts n. [1970s+] (orig. US) wit, intelligence.

smart stuff n. [1940s–50s] (US Black) deceitful, underhand activity.

smarty n. **1** [mid-19C+] (orig. US) one who is 'too smart to work' and lives by their wits (prob. illegally). **2** [1930s] a fashionable person.

smarty-boots/-pants n. [1940s+] (orig. US) **1** a general term of light-hearted abuse. **2** [1940s–50s] (US Black) a young man at the outset of his sexual career (cf. SMARTIEPANTS).

smash n.¹ [18C] mashed turnips. [note 1960s+ *Smash*, brand-name for instant mashed potatoes]

smash n.² **1** [18C] iced brandy and water. **2** [1950s+] (US Black) wine.

smash n.³ [late 18C–1900s] counterfeit money. [? it smashes the hopes of those who use it]

smash n.⁴ [19C] (prison) tobacco. [ext. of SMASH n.³, i.e. its role as prison currency]

smash n.⁵ [mid-19C] (US) **1** a failure, a disaster. **2** a great success, a 'smash hit' (cf. BOMB n.¹).

smash n.⁶ [mid-19C+] cash. [rhy. sl.]

smash n.⁷ **1** [late 19C] a heavy blow. **2** [1910s+] (Aus.) a violent, frightening man, usu. one who is drunk.

smash v.¹ **1** [late 17C–early 19C] (Und.) to kick downstairs. **2** [mid-19C] to fail financially, to be ruined, to become bankrupt (cf. ALL TO SMASH).

smash v.² [mid-19C] to pass counterfeit money. [SMASH n.³]

smash v.³ [early 19C+] to give change for a note. [SE *smash*, to break]

smash v.⁴ [1990s] to paint a piece of graffito on a wall or similar surface.

smash and grab n. [20C] a cab. [rhy. sl.]

smash and grab, to phr. [1990s] (US Black) to kill or beat someone up, and then rob them. [ext. of SE *smash and grab*, to break in and steal]

smashed adj. **1** [1940s+] very drunk (cf. BASTED). **2** [1960s+] intoxicated with a drug, esp. cannabis or LSD. **3** [1960s+] very tired.

smashed-up adj. [mid–late 19C] impoverished, broke. [SMASH v.²]

smasher n.¹ (Und.) **1** [late 18C+] one who passes counterfeit money. **2** [1920s–30s] a receiver of stolen goods. [SMASH v.³]

smasher n.² **1** [late 18C+] anything exceptionally large or excellent. **2** [early 19C–1950s] a crushing remark, a highly neg. review. **3** [late 19C–1910s] a hard blow. **4** [1940s+] a pretty woman.

smash-feeder n. **1** [mid-19C] a silver spoon. **2** [mid-19C–1900s] a Britannia-metal spoon, made from a metal resembling silver but in fact an alloy of tin and regulus of antimony. [SMASH n.¹ + SE *feeder*; the best counterfeit coins were made from such spoons]

smash hell through a gridiron, to phr. [late 19C] (US) to be extremely drunk.

smashing n. [1990s] (US Black teen) the activity of exchanging ritual handshakes or slaps (cf. SLAP SKINS). [SE *smash*, to hit]

smashing adj. [1910s+] (usu. teen) wonderful, delightful, excellent. [i.e. it *smashes* all rivals]

smash the teapot, to phr. [late 19C] to abandon one's pledge of abstinence (taken earlier at the urging of the Salvation Army or a similar teetotalist body). [the symbolic rejection of tea as one's sole liquid stimulant]

smatter hauling n. [mid–late 19C] the stealing of handkerchiefs. [SCHMATTE + SE *haul*]

smear n.¹ **1** [late 17C–mid-18C] a house-painter. **2** [early 18C–early 19C] a plasterer. **3** [20C] (Aus.) the corpse of a murdered person. [metonymy]

smear n.² [1940s] (US) a bribe. [abbr. SMEAR-GELT]

smear v. **1** [1930s] to kill, to murder. **2** [1920s+] (orig. US) to knock unconscious, to beat up. **3** [1930s+] (US) to defeat, to trounce. **4** [1930s+] (US) to bribe.

smear and smudge n. [20C] a judge. [rhy. sl.]

smear-gelt n. [late 18C–mid-19C] a bribe. [Yid. *smiergelt*, a bribe, lit. 'money for greasing' (the palm)]

smears n. [1970s] (drugs) LSD (cf. A n.³). [it has been smeared onto paper or tablets]

smeerlap n. [mid-19C+] (S.Afr.) a general term of abuse, a 'bastard', a 'swine' (cf. BLOOD CLAAT). [Du. *smeerlap*, 'grease cloth'; i.e. a cloth used for wiping spillage, stains etc]

smeg n. [1980s+] a dirty, unkempt person. [SMEG!]

smeg! excl. [1980s+] a general excl. of annoyance, surprise; thus *smegging*. [SE *smegma*, penile secretions. Coined as a deliberate euph. for FUCK! by Grant Naylor, scriptwriters of the BBC's *Red Dwarf* science fantasy series, from 1989]

smeggy adj. [1980s+] dirty, unkempt. [SMEG!]

smeghead n. [1980s+] a general term of abuse. [SMEG! + sfx. -HEAD (1)]

smell v.¹ [1960s] (US drugs) to inhale a narcotic drug.

smell v.² [1990s] (US Black) to understand.

smell a mice, to phr. [mid-19C–1910s] (US) to be suspicious. [joc. var. on SMELL A RAT]

smell a rat, to phr. [mid-16C–mid-19C] to be suspicious of people or situations. [SE f. 1850]

smell blood v. [20C] (US) to be aware of one's imminent victory over an opponent or prey.

Smellbourne/Smellbun/Smellburn n. [late 19C–1910s] (Aus.) Melbourne, capital city of Victoria. [coined by *The Bulletin* magazine. The name reflects the city's poor sewage, which was simply dumped into the River Yarra]

smeller n.¹ **1** [17C] (Und.) a garden. **2** [late 19C+] (N.Z.) an unpleasant person (cf. STINKER n.¹). [pos. and neg. uses of SE *smell* v.]

smeller n.² **1** [late 17C–1900s] the nose (cf. SMELLING-CHEAT). **2** [19C] a blow on the nose (cf. NOSER). **3** [late 19C] (US) a spy, a prying person. **4** [late 19C] anything exceptional, esp. very strong, very aggressive etc. [SE *smell* v.; in (4) the 'smell' is fig.]

smeller n.³ [late 19C–1930s] a heavy fall; thus *come a smeller*, to tumble down heavily. [one SE *smells* the ground on hitting it]

smellers n. **1** [late 17C] the nostrils. **2** [18C–early 19C] a cat's whiskers. [SE *smell* v.]

smell garlic v. [late 19C–1920s] to be suspicious of people or

situations (cf. SMELL A RAT). [? underpinned by xenophobia, i.e. the image of garlic as 'funny foreign food']

smell hell v.¹ [mid-19C+] (US) to face danger.

smell hell v.² see SEE HELL.

smelling-cheat/-chete n. [16C–early 19C] **1** a garden, an orchard (cf. SMELLER n.¹). **2** the nose (cf. SMELLER n.²). **3** a nosegay. **4** one who smells. [SE *smell* + CHEAT n.]

smelling of the cork phr. [19C] drunk.

smell like a badger's touch-hole, to phr. [17C–late 19C] to smell very unpleasant.

smell like a ram-goat, to phr. [20C] (W.I.) to smell disgusting, esp. after one has passed out drunk and urinated down one's legs.

smell like a rose, to phr. [20C] (US) to appear pure and innocent.

smell like a whore's garret, to phr. [20C] to smell strongly of cheap perfume, as applicable to a man or a place as to a woman.

smell of broken glass phr. [1900s–30s] a stench of body odour, typically in a sports changing room.

smell one's hat, to phr. [late 19C] to pray into one's hat on reaching one's pew in church.

smell-powder n. [early 19C] a duellist. [the *powder*-powered pistols that are used in duelling]

smell-smock n. [18C] a pimp (cf. APPLE-MONGER). [SE *smell* + SMOCK]

smell trap v. [late 17C–19C] to sense danger. [TRAP n.¹]

smelly adj. [1920s+] dubious, suspicious (cf. FISHY adj.¹).

smell you/smell you later phr. [1990s] (US campus) goodbye.

smell your monkey! excl. [1990s] a general insult, a less injurious version of SMELL YOUR MOTHER!

smell your mother! excl. [1990s] an insult, usu. accompanied by waving the middle finger under the insultee's nose; the implication is of recent sexual foreplay.

smelt n. [17C–19C] a half guinea or 10 shillings (50p). [ety. unknown, but E.P. suggests SE *melt*, to melt down; thus a half guinea is a 'melted down' guinea]

smiddys n. [1990s] the female breasts. [var. on TIT n.¹]

smiflicated see SPIFLICATED.

smifligate see SPIFLICATE.

smifligated see SPIFLICATED.

smiggins n. [mid-19C] (Und.) a poor quality soup served up to convicts, esp. those imprisoned on the hulks (cf. SKILLY). [ety. unknown; ? SE *smidgen*, i.e. the small amount of appetizing meat or vegetables present in the broth]

smile n.¹ [mid-19C+] (orig. US) a drink, usu. of whisky.

smile n.² **1** [1910s–40s] the gap of bare flesh above a stocking. **2** [1950s+] bare flesh appearing between the top of a skirt or pair of trousers and the shirt, blouse etc (cf. BUILDER'S BUM; SMILEY n.²; WORKING-MAN'S SMILE).

smile v. [mid-19C–1930s] (orig. US) to drink, esp. whisky. [SMILE n.¹]

smile and smirk n. [20C] work. [rhy. sl.]

smile like a brewer's horse, to phr. [mid-17C] to look cheerily satisfied or pleased with oneself. [the brewer's horse is supposedly the epitome of contentment]

smiler n.¹ [late 19C] a form of shandygaff, a mixture of beer and ginger beer. [? SMILE v.]

smiler n.² [20C] the face.

smiley/skop n.¹ [1980s+] (drugs) LSD in capsule or tablet form (cf. A n.³). [the 'smiley' face with which some LSD pills are emblazoned, although this image is usu. attached to MDMA]

smiley n.² [1980s+] (US) a man who is showing a slice of flesh above the top of his trousers. [SMILE n.²]

smiley n.³ [1990s] (S.Afr.) a sheep's or goat's head (sometimes split in half), cleaned and grilled or stewed with or without the tongue and brain. [the 'grinning' aspect of the cooked head]

smiling faces *n.* [1970s] (US Black) hypocrites, false friends.

smirk *n.* [late 17C–late 18C] 'A finical [finicky], spruce Fellow' (B.E.). [SE *smirk*, an affected simpering smile]

smish *n.* [early–mid-19C] a shirt (cf. CAMESA). [abbr. COMMISSION]

smit *adj.* [mid–late 19C] in love, obsessed by. [abbr. SE *smitten*]

smitch off *v.* [late 19C–1900s] to run off, to abscond. [ety. unknown; ? SE *mitch*, to shrink from view]

smiter *n.* [late 17C–early 19C] the arm. [SE *smite*, to hit]

smithereens *n.* [mid-19C+] tiny fragments, atoms, esp. in phr. *smashed to smithereens*, *blow/break/knock/split to/into smithereens*, to shatter into fragments, *all to smithereens*, smashed to pieces, often in fig. use. [SMITHERS + Irish dimin. *-een*. Share suggests Irish *smiodar*, a fragment]

smithers *n.* [mid-19C] tiny fragments, atoms (cf. SMITHEREENS). [Lincolnshire dial. *smithers*, fragments, shivers; ult. ? SE *smite*, to smash]

Smithfield bargain *n.* **1** [late 17C–mid-19C] a bargain in which the buyer is cheated (cf. SOLD LIKE A BULLOCK IN SMITHFIELD). **2** [late 18C–mid-19C] a marriage of convenience, based on financial interest. [proper name *Smithfield* market, London's horse and cattle, and later meat market, flourishing on the same site since the 12C]

smit smoke *n.* [1940s] (US Black) a highly intelligent Black person. [? SE *smart* + SMOKE n.⁴]

smoaky *see* SMOKY *adj.*

smock *n.* [17C] an immoral woman, esp. when used as a pfx. (cf. APRON n.¹; SMELL-SMOCK). [SE *smock*, a chemise or shift; thus generically 'womankind']

smock alley *n.* [18C] the vagina (cf. ALLEY n.¹). [SMOCK + SE *alley*]

smockface *n.* [19C] a male homosexual. [SE *smockface*, a pale, smooth or effeminate face; thus one who is so endowed]

smock-faced *adj.* [late 18C–early 19C] attractive. [SE *smock*, a chemise; thus the smooth whiteness of the garment]

smock merchant/tearer *n.* [17C] a pimp (cf. APPLE-MONGER). [SMOCK + sfx. -MERCHANT/SE *tearer*]

smock pensioner *n.* [18C] a pimp, a kept man (cf. APPLE-MONGER; CUNT-PENSIONER; PETTICOAT PENSIONER). [SMOCK + SE *pensioner*]

smock piece/servant *n.* [19C] a prostitute (cf. SMELL-SMOCK). [SMOCK + PIECE n.¹/SE *servant*]

smockster *n.* [17C] a pimp (cf. SMELL-SMOCK). [SMOCK + sfx. *-ster*]

smock tearer *see* SMOCK MERCHANT.

smock toy *n.* [17C] **1** a mistress. **2** a woman's male lover. [SMOCK + SE *toy*]

smogged *adj.* [20C] (US prison) executed in the gas chamber. [SE *smog*, a dense, toxic fog]

smoke *n.*¹ [mid-16C+] myth, illusion, fantasy, esp. when actively promoted as disinformation or lies; thus *all smoke*, nonsense.

Smoke, the *n.*² [mid-19C+] **1** London, as regarded from the provinces, occas. as *Smokes*. **2** (US) any big city. [the pall of pollution that, before the clean air legislation of the 1950s, hung over the industrialized city]

smoke *n.*³ **1** [mid-19C+] anything smokeable, a cigar, a pipe, a cigarette. **2** [1930s+] (drugs) any form of smokeable drug, e.g. marijuana, opium, heroin and, latterly, crack cocaine. **3** [1940s+] a marijuana cigarette.

smoke *n.*⁴ [late 19C+] a derog. term for a Black person (cf. CLOUD n.²; SHADOW; SMOKESTACK; SMOKY n.¹).

smoke *n.*⁵ [1930s+] any cheap, rotgut alcohol, esp. denatured alcohol shaken up with water and drunk by down-and-out alcoholic tramps; thus *smoke bum*, a regular drinker of such alcohol (cf. STEAM n.¹). [the liquid turns cloudy when shaken]

smoke *n.*⁶ [1970s] (US campus) $1. [so small a sum 'goes up in smoke']

smoke *v.*¹ **1** [16C] to be discovered (cf. BOIL). **2** [late 16C+] to discover, to unmask. [SE *smoked out/smoke out*]

smoke *v.*² [17C] to have sexual intercourse. [SE *smoke*, to move or ride at a rapid pace]

smoke *v.*³ [late 17C–early 18C] to ridicule or attack a stranger verbally as soon as they enter the room.

smoke *v.*⁴ [late 17C–18C] to cheat, to deceive. [one blows *smoke* in the victim's eyes]

smoke *v.*⁵ **1** [mid-19C] (teen) to blush. **2** [20C] (US) to get angry.

smoke *v.*⁶ [late 19C–1960s] (Aus.) to make a hasty departure. [SE late 17C–19C; the fig. smoke exuded by one's rapid departure]

smoke *v.*⁷ [20C] (US Und.) to be executed in a gas chamber (cf. SMOGGED).

smoke *v.*⁸ [20C] to perform fellatio. [note Fr. *faire une pipe*, to fellate]

smoke *v.*⁹ (US) **1** [1920s+] to kill, to murder (with a firearm). **2** [1920s+] to beat comprehensively (at sport). **3** [1970s] to throw very fast, usu. of a ball. **4** [1980s+] to beat up. **5** [1990s] (campus) to perform well. [all depend on the imagery of smoke being created by the energy involved in the action; (1) has the added image of smoke coming from the gun]

smoke a bowl, to *phr.* [1960s+] (US) to smoke marijuana, usu. from a pipe. [? imported by veterans of the Vietnam War (1964–75), where pipes, rather than cigarettes, were the preferred means of smoking]

smoke a toke, to *phr.* [1980s+] (US) to smoke marijuana. [SE *smoke* + TOKE n.³; lit. 'smoke a smoke' thus as much f. assonance as accuracy]

smoked out *adj.* [1990s] (US Black gang) heavily intoxicated by a drug, usu. marijuana or crack cocaine. [SMOKE n.³ (2)]

smoke-eater *n.* [1930s+] (US) **1** a heavy smoker. **2** a firefighter.

smoke factory *n.* [1900s–10s] (US) an opium den. [SMOKE n.³ + SE *factory*]

smoke-hound *n.* [1930s+] (US) an alcoholic who drinks rotgut alcohol. [SMOKE n.⁵ + sfx. -HOUND]

smokehouse *see* SMOKER n.¹.

smoke it white/white-pipe, to *phr.* [1960s+] (S.Afr. drugs) to smoke a mixture of marijuana and powdered Mandrax (methaqualone) (cf. WITPYP). [Mandrax capsules are white]

smoke-joint *n.* [1930s] (US) a bar that specializes in selling cheap, second-rate liquor. [SMOKE n.⁵ + JOINT n.³ (3)]

smoke-o/smoke-oh *see* SMOKO.

smoke one *v.* [20C] (drugs) to smoke marijuana.

smoke out *v.* [1970s+] (US Black) **1** to impress, to outdo. **2** to get information from someone.

smoke over *v.* [1930s–40s] (US Black) to stare at, to look at closely.

smoke pad *n.* [1940s–50s] (drugs) anywhere that people can gather to smoke marijuana. [SMOKE n.³ (2) + PAD n.²]

smoke-pole *n.* [1970s+] a firearm (cf. SMOKE-STICK).

smoker/smokehouse *n.*¹ [19C] a chamberpot (cf. SMOKE-SHELL). [the steam that rises from hot urine in cold weather]

smoker *n.*² **1** [mid-19C] (US) a steamship. **2** [1950s+] a motor vehicle that emits stronger than average exhaust fumes.

smoker *n.*³ [mid-19C] (teen) one who blushes. [SMOKE v.⁵ (1)]

smoker *n.*⁴ [late 19C] a hot day (cf. SCORCHER).

smoker *n.*⁵ [1970s] (US campus) something difficult. [it fig. makes the brain *smoke* with effort]

smoker's lung *n.* [1990s] a pot of Marmite. [the similarity of the dark viscous spread and the tobacco residue that accrues in the smoker's lungs]

smoker's tickers *n.* [20C] (Aus.) any variety of dark tobacco.

smokes *n.* [20C] cigarettes.

smoke screen *n.* [1940s] (US Black) underarm deodorant. [its masking of body odour]

smokeshell *n.* [19C] a privy (cf. SMOKER n.¹). [the vapour that rises from hot urine in cold weather]

smoke shop *n.* [1930s+] (US drugs) a place or shop where marijuana is sold, esp. somewhat openly. [SMOKE n.³ (2)]

smokestack *n.* [late 19C+] (US Black) a Black person, esp. when very dark.

smoke-stick *n.* [1900s–40s] a firearm (cf. SMOKE-POLE).

smoke the baldy man/big one/white owl, to *phr.* [1990s] to fellate.

smoke-wagon *n.* [late 19C] (US) a revolver, a pistol (cf. SMOKE-POLE; SMOKE-STICK).

smokey *see* SMOKY n.¹.

smoking *n.*¹ [mid-19C] (teen) blushing. [SMOKE v.⁵ (1)]

smoking *n.*² [1980s+] (drugs) phencyclidine (cf. ACE n.³).

smoking *adj.* **1** [1970s+] (US Black) very urgent, very excited, esp. in a sexual context. **2** [1970s] (US campus) difficult. **3** [1990s] first-rate, excellent (cf. DOPE adj.). **4** [1990s] (US Black) well-dressed, elegant, smart. [orig. jazz use *smoking*, technically skilled]

smoking gun *n.* [1980s+] (drugs) a mixture of heroin and cocaine. [its powerful effects]

smokkel *v.* [1940s+] (S.Afr.) to deal in drugs or in illicit liquor; thus *smokkelhuis*, *smokkie*, an illicit bar or shebeen. [Du. *smokkeln*, to smuggle]

smoko/smoke-o/smoke-oh *n.* [mid-19C+] (Aus./N.Z.) a break for smoking; thus [1920s+] the cup of tea that often accompanies it. [SE *smoke* + sfx. -o]

smoky/smokey *n.*¹ **1** [1930s–40s] (US Black) a Black person; esp. as a generic term for Blackness or a number of Black people gathered together. **2** [1980s+] (N.Z.) a derog. term for a Maori.

Smoky/Smoky Bear *n.*² [1970s+] a traffic policeman, a Highway Patrolman (cf. BEAR n.⁸). [*Smoky the Bear*, a character used in US fire prevention campaigns]

smoky/smoaky *adj.* [late 17C–late 18C] alert, shrewd, suspicious, jealous. [SMOKE v.¹]

Smoky Bear *see* SMOKY n.².

smoky beaver *n.* [1970s] (US) a female motorcycle police officer. [SMOKY n.² + BEAVER n.⁴]

smoky joe *n.* [1990s] human excrement (cf. SMOKER n.¹). [the fumes it exudes]

smoky seat *n.* [20C] (US) the electric chair (cf. OLD SMOKEY). [the smoke that rises from the electrocuted victim]

smoo *n.* [1940s+] (Aus.) the vagina. [SMOOEY]

smooch *n.* [1930s+] a bout of kissing and cuddling. [SMOOCH v.¹]

smooch *v.*¹ [1930s+] (orig. US) to caress amorously, to kiss. [late 16C *smouch*, to kiss]

smooch/smooge *v.*² [1940s] (US) to steal, to pilfer. [? MOOCH v.¹ (2)]

smooch/smooge *v.*³ [1980s+] (US) to murder, to kill (cf. KISS OFF v.). [fig. use of SMOOCH v.¹]

smooching *n.* [1930s+] (orig. US) kissing and cuddling. [SMOOCH v.¹]

smoodge *v.* [20C] (Aus.) to ingratiate oneself, to cuddle up; thus *come the smoodge*, *do a smoodge*. [SCHMOOZE v. or SMOOCH v.¹ or SE *smudge*, to caress]

smoodger *n.* [late 19C+] (Aus.) a toady, a sycophant, a flatterer. [SMOODGE]

smooey *n.* [1940s–70s] (Aus.) sexual intercourse; thus *have a bit of smooey*, to have sexual intercourse (cf. SMOO). [SMOODGE]

smooge *see* SMOOCH v.², v.³.

smoogy *adj.* [1900s–50s] (Aus.) affectionate, ingratiating. [SMOODGE]

smooth *adj.* (orig. US) **1** [late 19C+] clever, skilful, superior or impressive. **2** [1920s+] of manners or dress, elegant, fashionable, suave.

smooth article/smoothie/smooth operator *n.* [late 19C+] a sophisticated, smart person, both mentally and physically.

smother *n.*¹ [1900s] (Aus.) a plan, an undercover stratagem. [SE *smother*, to hide]

smother *n.*² [1930s+] a coat, a wrap. [SE *smother*, to hide, to cover up; it 'smothers' the wearer, but note SCHMATTE]

smother a parrot, to *phr.* [late 19C] to drink off a glass of absinthe in a single gulp. [trans. of Fr. argot *asphyxier un perroquet*, to drink a glass of absinthe]

smouch *see* SMOUS.

smouge *v.* [late 19C] (US) to steal (cf. SMOOCH v.²).

smous/smouch/smouse/smouser/smoutch *n.* **1** [early 18C+] a German Jew. **2** [mid-19C+] (S.Afr.) an itinerant Jewish pedlar. [Du. *smous*/Yid. *schmus*, patter or profit; ult. Heb. *schmuoss*, news or tales]

smous/smouch/smouse/smouth *v.* (S.Afr.) **1** [mid-19C+] to work as an itinerant Jewish pedlar. **2** [mid-19C+] to solicit business, esp. in a demeaning manner. **3** [1970s+] to obtain in an underhand way. **4** [1990s] to search out bargains. [SMOUS n.]

smouse/smouser *see* SMOUS n.

smoush *n.* [1960s] (Aus.) a kiss. [SMOOCH n.]

smoutch *see* SMOUS n.

smouth *see* SMOUS v.

s.m.s. *n.* [1990s] (US campus) fellatio. [abbr. suckle *my* sac]

smuckered *adj.* [1970s] (US campus) drunk (cf. BASTED). [SE *smack*]

smudge *n.* [1940s+] (US) a derog. term for a Black person. [SE *smudge*, a dirty mark]

smug *n.*¹ [early 17C–early 18C] a blacksmith. [? SE *smuggy*, dirty, grimy. The late-20C use of *Smugs* for W.H. Smith, the chain of stationers and booksellers, is probably coincidental – the term refers more to the company's reputation as self-appointed guardians of its customers' morals than for any back-ref. to the name *Smith*]

smug *n.*² [mid-19C] (Anglo-Chinese) *smug*gling. [abbr.]

smug *n.*³ [late 19C] (teen) a hard worker. [SE *smug*, i.e. their self-satisfaction]

smug *adj.* [mid-19C] extremely neat and tidy; thus *smug*, a person who is excessively neat.

smug *v.* **1** [mid-19C] to snatch another's property and run off with it. **2** [mid-19C] to silence, to 'hush up'. **3** [mid–late 19C] to copy, to cheat. **4** [late 19C] to arrest. **5** [20C] (Irish) to engage in homosexual practices. [? SE *smuggle* or dial. *smug*, to hide, to move stealthily]

smugger *n.* [19C] a thug, specializing in snatch-and-grab thefts (cf. SNABBLER; SNAFFLER; SNAGGLER). [SMUG v.]

smuggings! *excl.* [mid-19C] (teen) mine! [the excl. used at the end of a game of marbles or spinning tops when the child who shouted thus first was allowed to keep the toy in question]

smuggle the coal/cole, to *phr.* [late 17C] to pretend that one has no money when it is time to pay a bill at an inn or tavern. [SE *smuggle* + COLE (1)]

smuggling-ken *n.* [late 18C–early 19C] a brothel. [dial. *smuggle*, to smother with hugs and kisses + KEN n.¹]

smug-lay *n.* [early–mid-19C] the selling of virtually worthless goods on the pretext that they are actually smuggled contraband. [SMUG v. + LAY n.⁴]

smug up *v.* [17C] to smarten oneself up. [SE *smug*, neat, well turned-out; *OED* accepts *smug* as SE, but its 17C citations – Greene, Dekker, Middleton, Wycherley – are all colloq, if not sl.]

smurf *v.* [1990s] (US campus) to steal. [? *The Smurfs*, a TV cartoon]

smush *n.* [1930s] (US) the mouth. [MUSH n.³]

smuss *v.* [late 18C–early 19C] to snatch, to seize. [obs. SE]

smut *n.*¹ [late 17C+] pornography, obscenity; thus *smut-peddler*, a seller of pornography. [SE *smut*, a black stain; i.e. the identification of sexuality and 'dirt']

smut *n.*² [early–mid-19C] a copper boiler, a furnace. [its smokiness]

smut-butt *n.* [1970s] (US campus) a derog. term for a Black student (cf. COAL n.²; SMOKE n.⁴). [SE *smut* + BUTT n.¹]

smut-hound *n.* [1920s+] **1** one who is obsessed by the tiniest trace of obscenity, esp. in the arts or media. **2** a censor. [coined by H.L. Mencken (1880–1956) and one of the coinages (along with BIBLE BELTER + BOOBOISIE), of which he was 'vainest' (letter, 2 December 1927)]

snaaks *adj.* [1910s+] (S.Afr.) strange, peculiar, bizarre. [Du. *snaaks*, droll, comical]

snabble *v.* **1** [early 18C] to knock down, to plunder (cf. SMABBLE). **2** [early 18C] to arrest. **3** [late 18C] to kill in battle. **4** [19C+] to have sexual intercourse with (cf. BANG v.¹). [? dial. *snabble*, to eat greedily]

snabbler *n.* [19C] a thug, specializing in snatch-and-grab thefts (cf. SMUGGER). [SNABBLE]

snack *n.*¹ [mid-17C–mid-19C] (Und.) a share of booty. [SE *snack*, a portion, itself linked to *snack*, a snap or bite, esp. of a dog]

snack *n.*² [1940s+] (Aus.) anything simple (cf. SNIP n.²). ['a piece of cake']

snack *n.*³ **1** [1950s–60s] (US Black) the penis. **2** [1990s] a small penis. [its role in oral sex; (2) plays on LUNCHBOX n.³]

snack *v.*¹ [mid-17C–mid-19C] (Und.) to divide up, to hand over a share of the loot (cf. GO SNACKS). [SNACK n.¹]

snack *v.*² [1980s+] (US campus) to kiss passionately; thus *snack bar*, one's boyfriend or girlfriend.

snackpack *n.* [1980s+] (US gay) the male genitalia, when seen in a jockstrap or bikini briefs (cf. LUNCHBOX). [SNACK n.³]

snaffle *n.*¹ [16C–18C] (Und.) a highwayman 'that never alights off a rich farmer or country gentleman, till he have drawn money from him'. [SE *snaffle*, a light bridle + SNAFFLE v.¹]

snaffle *n.*² **1** [mid-19C] talk that no one but the speaker either understands or cares about. **2** [1910s–20s] secret talk. [SE *snaffle*, a horse's bridle-bit; a speaker is similarly restrained; note also ety. at SNAFFLE v.²]

snaffle *v.*¹ [16C–18C] **1** to steal. **2** [mid–late 19C] to arrest. **3** [1990s] to seduce. [SE *snaffle*, to place a bridle-bit on a horse]

snaffle *v.*² [19C] to talk, esp. to talk in a way and on topics that baffle or bore other people. [East Anglian dial. *snaffle*, to talk nonsense; note also ety. at SNAFFLE n.²]

snaffle-biter *n.* [early 18C] a horse-thief. [SE *snaffle* + BITE v.¹ (2)]

snaffler *n.* [late 18C–early 19C] a highwayman; thus *snaffler of prancers*, a horse-thief (cf. SMUGGER). [SNAFFLE v.¹]

snaffling lay *n.* [mid-18C–early 19C] the profession of highway robbery. [SNAFFLE v.¹ + LAY n.³]

s.n.a.f.u. *phr.* [1940s+] (orig. US milit.) a mistake, an error, a situation, often within an institution/organization, that has gone awry; *fouled-up* can provide a euph. substitute. [abbr. situation *normal, all fucked up*; orig. a WW2 milit. catch-phrase, *s.n.a.f.u.* quickly entered mainstream sl. and generated a number of variations, although none has had the same impact (cf. F.I.G.M.O.; F.U.B.A.R.; F.U.B.B.; F.U.B.I.S.; F.U.M.T.U.; G.F.O.; M.F.U.T.U.; S.A.M.F.U.; S.A.P.F.U.; S.U.S.F.U.; T.A.R.F.U.; T.U.I.F.U.)]

s.n.a.f.u. *v.* [1940s+] (orig. US milit.) to mess up, to go wrong, esp. in a complex, elaborate manner (cf. FUCK UP v.). [S.N.A.F.U. phr.]

snag *n.*¹ [20C] (Aus./N.Z.) an adversary worthy of consideration. [SE *snag*, an impediment or obstacle]

snag *n.*² [1910s+] (Aus.) a jagged tooth. [SE *snag*, a jagged or angular projection, a short stump projecting from a tree trunk]

snag *n.*³ [1950s–60s] (US Black) an unattractive or unpleasant woman. [? dial. *snag*, to carp, to nag]

snag *v.* **1** [late 19C+] to grab, to steal. **2** [1920s] (N.Z.) to hunt for bargains, as a means for poor people to survive. **3** [1950s] (street gang) to attack an individual without warning. **4** [1970s–80s] (US Black) to have sexual intercourse. [SE *snag*, to be caught or pierced by a snag or rough projection]

snag-catcher *n.* [late 19C–1910s] a dentist (cf. SNAG n.²). [SE *snag*, a short stump, standing out from a tree trunk + *catcher*]

snagg *n.* [late 18C–early 19C] (Und.) a snail. [Sussex dial. *snag*, a snail]

snaggler *n.* [early 19C+] a thug, specializing in snatch-and-grab thefts (cf. SMUGGER). [dial. *snaggler*, an eel-fisher]

snaggle-tooth *n.* [1900s] a woman with poor, uneven teeth. [SE *snaggle-tooth*, irregular or projecting teeth]

snaggling *n.* [mid-19C] the practice of angling for geese with a hook and line, the bait being a worm or snail. [? dial. *snaggler*, an eel-fisher]

snaggs *n.* [late 18C–early 19C] large teeth. [SE *snag*, a broken or unsightly tooth]

snags *n.* [1940s+] (Aus./N.Z.) sausages; rarely used in sing. [dial. *snag*, a morsel, a snack]

snail *n.* [late 19C] (Aus.) a shepherd, a musterer, one who mends boundary fences (cf. LIZARD n.²).

snailer *n.* [1990s] (Irish) a trail of mucus running down the face. [resemblance to a snail track]

'snails! *excl.* [16C] a mild, if blasphemous, oath (cf. 's abbr.¹). [SE *God's nails* (although the nails in question are those suffered by Christ rather than God)]

snake *n.*¹ (US) **1** [1950s+] (gang) a spy. **2** [1950s+] an unreliable, deceptive person. **3** [1970s] (Black) a homosexual, whether male or female. **4** [1970s] (campus) someone who steals something, particularly someone else's date.

snake *n.*² [1980s+] the penis. [abbr. ONE-EYED TROUSER-SNAKE]

snake *v.*¹ [mid-19C] (US) to beat, to thrash. [the snake-like whip]

snake/snake off *v.*² [1910s+] (orig. Aus.) to slip along, to move stealthily. [the reptile's characteristic]

snake *v.*³ [1970s+] (US campus) **1** to steal. **2** to steal someone else's date. **3** to cheat. [SNAKE n.¹]

snake *v.*⁴ [1980s+] to masturbate. [SNAKE n.²]

snakebite *n.* **1** [1920s+] (US) a strong alcoholic drink, usu. cheap but strong whisky. **2** [1980s+] a 'cocktail' of cider mixed with lager. [its effects]

snakebite remedy *n.* [1950s+] (US) potassium permanganate, washing with which after sexual intercourse is used as a prophylactic against venereal disease.

snake-bitten *adj.* [1920s+] (US) incapacitated. [SNAKEBITE n. (1)]

snake charmer *n.* [1930s] (Aus.) a railway plate-layer (in Western Australia); also *hairy leg* (New South Wales), *woolly nose* (South Australia). [the prevalence of snakes along the track]

snake-eyes *n.*¹ [1910s–30s] (US) tapioca. [resemblance]

snake-eyes *n.*² [1930s+] (gambling) the point of two in craps dice. [i.e. a pair of ones]

snake gully *n.* [1940s+] (Aus.) an imaginary place that is a byword for backwardness and remoteness (cf. WOOP WOOP).

[*Snake Gully* was the location of the long-running radio serial *Dad and Dave*]

snake-headed *adj.* [1900s–40s] (Aus.) testy, irritated. [the neg. image of the reptile]

snake in the grass *n.* [mid-19C+] **1** a looking glass, a mirror. **2** a drinking glass. [rhy. sl., either of which might prove a 'treacherous friend']

snake-juice *n.* [late 19C+] (Aus.) any form of liquor, esp. when cheap and potent; thus *snake-juicer*, a drinker of such liquor (cf. SNAKE POISON).

snake off *see* SNAKE v.².

snake out *v.* [early–mid-19C] (US) to hunt down, to pursue. [the hunting of deadly snakes]

snake poison *n.* [late 19C–1940s] (Aus./US) whisky (cf. SNAKE-JUICE).

snakes *n.* [late 19C] alcoholic hallucinations, delirium tremens. [from the *snakes*, pink elephants and other wonders one supposedly sees]

snake's *see* SNAKE'S HISS.

snakes alive! *excl.* [late 19C+] (US) a mild excl.

snake's hiss/snake's *n.* [20C] (Aus.) **1** an act of urination. **2** a lavatory (cf. SNAKE'S HOUSE). [rhy. sl. *snake's hiss* = PISS n.]

snake's house *n.* [20C] (orig. Aus.) a lavatory. [SNAKE'S HISS]

snakesman *n.* [late 18C–19C] a member of a gang of thieves who is sufficiently small and lithe to enter buildings through any narrow entrance that would otherwise be impassable; once within they unlock a main door through which all can pass (cf. LITTLE SNAKESMAN).

snake-tart *n.* [mid-19C–1900s] eel pie (cf. DOVE-TART). [joc. resemblance]

snakey *see* SNAKY adj.².

snake yarn *n.* [20C] (Aus.) a fantastical tale, a 'tall story'. [lit. or fig. involving snakes]

snaky *adj.*¹ [late 19C+] (orig. US) devious, underhand, cunning. [the Eden biblical story]

snaky/snakey *adj.*² (Aus.) **1** [20C] irritable, tetchy. **2** [1930s+] jealous. [SNAKE-HEADED]

snaky-bony *n.* [1950s] (W.I.) a very thin person; sometimes in comb. with SCARCE-O-FAT.

snaky-bony *adj.* [1950s] (W.I.) very thin. [SNAKY-BONY n.]

snam *v.* [mid-19C–1900s] to steal, to pilfer. [Scot. *snam*, to snap at greedily. 'That kind of theft which consists in picking up anything lying about, and making off with it rapidly' (Hotten, 1874)]

snammer *see* PUDDING-SNAMMER.

snap *n.*¹ [mid-16C–18C] **1** a share, a portion; thus *snap/go snap*, to share half-and-half (cf. SNACK n.¹; SNAPPINGS). **2** a pickpocket, cut-purse or card-sharp, spec. an experienced one who demanded a share of their younger peers' profits (cf. CLOYER). **3** (Und.) a cut-purse's assistant. [SE *snack*, a share or part; synon. with *snatch*, the image is of a grabbed or snatched handful or mouthful]

snap *n.*² **1** [mid-19C+] (orig. US) anything easy, a simple task or achievement (cf. SNIP n.²). **2** [late 19C+] (US campus) an easy course.

snap *n.*³ [1950s+] (drugs) amyl nitrite (cf. AIMIES n.²). [the snapping of the ampoules in which the drug is packaged]

snap *n.*⁴ [1980s+] (US Black) a wisecrack, a witty retort. [SNAP v.²]

snap *v.*¹ [1920s+] to alter one's behaviour quickly; usu. in combs. (cf. SNAP BACK; SNAP INTO; SNAP OUT OF).

snap *v.*² [1960s+] (US Black) **1** to tease. **2** to laugh along with.

snap! *excl.* [1990s] (US teen) an excl. of surprise, apology, esp. after making a mistake or blunder.

snap a cap, to *phr.* [mid-19C–1920s] (US) to fire a shot (cf. BUST A CAP). [SE *snap* + CAP n.³]

snap a snapper, to *phr.* [1940s] (US Black) to light a match. [SE *snap* + SNAPPER n.⁶]

snap assholes *v.* [1950s+] (US) to fight (cf. LOCK ASSHOLES). [ASSHOLE adj.]

snap back *v.* [1940s+] to make a quick recovery from a setback. [SNAP v.¹]

snap into *v.* [1940s+] to involve oneself enthusiastically. [SNAP v.¹]

snap it up *v.* [1910s+] to speed up, to hurry up; often as imper. [SNAP v.¹]

snap one off *v.* [1990s] to masturbate.

snap one's cap, to *phr.* [20C] (US) to lose control, to become insane. [SE *snap* + CAP n.⁵]

snap out of *v.* [1920s+] to make an abrupt and self-willed change in one's attitude, emotions, behaviour etc (usu. from negative to positive), often as imper. *snap out of it!* cheer up, pull yourself together. [SNAP v.¹]

snappage *n.* {early 17C} (Und.) a share in the booty. [SNAP n.¹]

snapped *adj.*¹ [late 17C–18C] arrested, caught. [abbr. SE *snapped up*]

snapped *adj.*² [late 19C] abrupt, sudden, surprising.

snapper *n.*¹ [16C] an assistant or look-out man for a criminal gang or team of fraudsters. [SNAP n.¹]

snapper *n.*² [mid-19C] (N.Z.) a sixpence. [ety. unknown]

snapper *n.*³ (US) **1** [mid-19C+] a caustic remark. **2** [mid-19C+] the point of a story or joke (cf. PUNCHLINE; ZINGER). **3** [1930s+] (gay) the foreskin. [SAmE *snapper*, the cracker on the end of a whip]

snapper *n.*⁴ [1930s–50s] a ticket inspector. [the clipping of tickets]

snapper *n.*⁵ [1940s+] (orig. US) a photographer. [SE *snap*, a photograph]

snapper *n.*⁶ [1940s] (US Black) a match. [one 'snaps' it alight]

snapper *n.*⁷ [1960s+] **1** (US) the vagina (cf. BEARDED CLAM; RED SNAPPER; SNAPPING TURTLE). **2** (US Black) excellent sex. [the image of the vagina as both a FISH n.⁴ + a predator]

snapper *n.*⁸ [1980s+] (Irish) a baby. [abbr. BREADSNAPPER]

snappers *n.*¹ **1** [late 16C–early 19C] pistols. **2** [1920s–50s] false teeth. [their noise]

snappers *n.*² [1960s+] (drugs) amyl nitrite, isobutyl nitrite (cf. AIMIES n.²). [SNAP n.³]

snapping *n.* [late 16C–early 17C] (Und.) a share in the booty (cf. SNAPPAGE). [SNAP n.¹]

snapping *adj.* [1990s] (US Black teen) excellent, wonderful. [the finger-snapping that demonstrates one's approval]

snapping puss *see* SNAPPING TURTLE.

snappings *n.* [late 16C–early 17C] (Und.) goods that are pilfered from stalls or shop windows (cf. SNAP n.¹). [SE *snap up*]

snapping turtle/puss *n.* [20C] the vagina (cf. BEAR n.⁷; BEARDED CLAM).

snapps *n.* [mid-19C] **1** a share, a portion. **2** anything that will serve as a means of making money; thus *looking out for snapps*, waiting for a lucky break or a windfall. [var. on SNAP n.¹]

snappy *adj.*¹ [late 19C+] (orig. US) **1** smart, clever, esp. of language. **2** energetic. **3** neat, elegant. **4** sharply flavoursome.

snappy *adj.*² [late 19C+] (orig. US) irritable, irascible. [SE *snap one's head off*]

snaps *n.*¹ [late 19C+] (US) handcuffs (cf. SNIPS). [they *snap* onto the wrist]

snaps *n.*² [1990s] (US Black teen) money. [the 'snapping' of a dollar bill]

snap someone's dick, to *phr.* [1970s+] (US) to hurry someone up. [SE *snap* + DICK n.⁵]

snap the glaze, to *phr.* [late 18C–early 19C] (Und.) to smash shop windows (cf. SPANK A GLAZE; STAR THE GLAZE). [SE *snap* + GLAZE]

snap the rubber, to *phr.* [1990s] to masturbate.

snap the whip, to phr. [1990s] to masturbate.

snap to/to it v. [1910s+] (US) to get going, to get busy, to hurry up, esp. as imper. snap to it!

snare v. [1910s+] (Aus.) to obtain, to grab, to win.

snarf v. [1960s+] to eat, to drink. [? var. on SCARF v.]

snarky adj. [20C] (US) irritable, touchy. [dial. snark, to fret, to grumble]

snarl/snarl-up n. [1930s+] (orig. US) a traffic jam. [SNARL UP v.]

snarl up v. [1930s+] to confuse, to entangle, to impede.

snatch n.[1] [17C] quick sexual intercourse, esp. with a prostitute. [one 'snatches' the time]

snatch n.[2] [1920s+] (orig. US) a kidnapping.

snatch n.[3] **1** [late 17C+] sexual intercourse, esp. quick or illicit or with a prostitute. **2** [late 19C+] the vagina. **3** [1920s+] a generic word for women. **4** [1990s] (US campus) a notably ugly woman. [Yorks. dial.; ult. SE snatch, to grab]

snatch v. [1930s+] **1** (mainly US) to kidnap. **2** (US Black) to threaten someone by grabbing their lapels and talking menacingly into their face. **3** (US) to steal, esp. to shoplift.

snatch bald v. [1960s] (US) to treat roughly, to manhandle (cf. JERK BALD-HEADED).

snatch bald-headed see JERK BALD-HEADED.

snatch-blatch n. [late 19C–1910s] the vagina. [SNATCH n.[3] (2) ? + dial. blatch, dirt]

snatch-box n. [late 19C] the vagina (cf. SNATCH-BLATCH). [SNATCH n.[3] (2) + SE box/BOX n.[6]]

snatch cly n. [late 18C–early 19C] (Und.) a thief who specializes in stealing from women's pockets. [SE snatch + CLY n.]

snatcher n. **1** [19C] a policeman. **2** [19C] a young and inexperienced pickpocket. **3** [1920s–40s] (US) a kidnapper. [SE snatch/SNATCH v.]

snatch game n. [1920s+] kidnapping. [SNATCH n.[2] + GAME n.[4]]

snatch it see SNATCH ONE'S TIME.

snatch mouse n. [1990s] a tampon. [SNATCH n.[3] (2) + SE mouse; i.e. its string 'tail']

snatch one's time/it/one's bit/one's rent, to phr. [20C] (Aus.) to resign. [i.e. to snatch one's time back for oneself]

snatch play n. [1940s] (US Black) sexual activity. [SNATCH n.[3] + PLAY n.[1]]

snatch-thatch n. [18C] the female pubic hair. [SNATCH n.[3] (1) + THATCH n.]

snatch-up n. [1980s+] (US Black) an arrest.

snavel/snavvel v. [late 18C–1940s] **1** to steal, to pilfer. **2** to catch, to grab hold of. [dial. snavel, to remove slyly; post-19C use mainly Aus.]

snazz n. [1930s+] (US) style, elegance (cf. PIZZAZZ). [backform. of SNAZZY]

snazz up v. [1930s+] (US) to enliven by making something smarter and more attractive. [SNAZZ]

snazzy adj. [1930s+] (orig. Aus.) smart, fashionable, brightly coloured; thus snazzy chassis, an attractive (female) figure. [? SNAPPY adj.[1] + JAZZY]

sneak, the n.[1] [18C+] the act of robbery, esp. sneak-thievery (cf. EVENING SNEAK; MORNING SNEAK).

sneak n.[2] [late 19C+] (mainly teen) one who tells tales on their fellow pupils.

sneak n.[3] [late 19C+] a soft-soled, canvas-topped shoe, often in pl. [abbr. SNEAKER n.[3]]

sneak n.[4] [1940s+] (orig. US) a sneak preview (usu. of a film) to an unsuspecting audience to assess its appeal.

sneak v.[1] **1** [early 19C] to rob. **2** [early 19C] to act in a surreptitious manner, esp. when looking for something to steal. **3** [late 19C–1900s] (US) to slip away quietly.

sneak v.[2] [late 19C+] (teen) to tell tales on one's fellows.

sneak-a-toke n. [1980s+] (US drugs) a hand-held smokeless pipe. [SE sneak + TOKE n.[3]]

sneaker n.[1] [late 17C–mid-18C] a small bowl of punch. [SE sneaker, a small bowl with a lid or cover]

sneaker n.[2] [early–mid-19C] a coward. [SE sneak, a tell-tale]

sneaker n.[3] [late 19C+] (orig. US) a soft-soled, noiseless slipper or shoe, a gym shoe (cf. SNEAK n.[3]). [SE sneak, to move quietly]

sneaking budge n. [late 17C–late 18C] a sneak thief, esp. one who specializes in entering houses and taking furs, cloaks and coats (cf. BUDGE n.[1]).

sneak job n. [1930s+] (US Und.) house-breaking. [SNEAK n.[1] + JOB n.[5]]

sneak play n. [20C] a furtive entrance and exit from a brothel. [baseball imagery or SE sneak + PLAY n.[1]]

sneaksman n. [19C] **1** the lowest order and more contemptible species of thieves who lurk around and grab whatever they can regardless of value. **2** a shoplifter.

sneaky pete n. **1** [1920s+] cheap, rotgut wine. **2** [1970s+] (drugs) marijuana mixed with wine. [the effects 'sneak up' on the consumer]

sneaky pete v. [1940s+] (US) to creep quietly, to move stealthily.

sneck drawer n. [early–mid-19C] a sly, cunning, flattering person (cf. DRAW-LATCH). [Scot. sneck, a latch + SE drawer, one who pulls; lit. one who opens a latch (in order to enter surreptitiously)]

sneck/snick up! excl. [late 16C–early 17C] an excl. of dismissal, the hell with you! [SE sneck, a latch, i.e. draw the latch and get the other side of the door]

sned v. [20C] (Ulster) of a man, to have sexual intercourse. [dial. sned, to prune, to cut off]

sneerg n. [mid-19C] greens, green vegetables (cf. NEERGS). [backsl.]

sneeze n. **1** [19C–1910s] the nose (cf. SNEEZER n.[1]). **2** [1960s+] (US prison) pepper, esp. red pepper (cf. GLITTER).

sneeze v. [early 19C+] to disdain, to regard as of low worth; thus not to be sneezed at, not to be ignored, worthy of value.

sneeze in the cabbage/canyon, to phr. [1960s+] to perform cunnilingus (cf. YODEL IN THE CANYON). [SE sneeze + CABBAGE n.[7]/CANYON]

sneeze it out v. [1970s+] to confess (cf. COUGH UP).

sneeze-/snuff-lurker n. [mid-19C] (Und.) a thief who temporarily blinds a victim by throwing snuff in their face and then robs them as they stagger around blindly; thus give it (one) on the sneeze-/snuff-racket, to attack and rob someone in this way. [SE sneeze + LURK n.]

sneeze machine n. [1970s+] (S.Afr.) an appliance for the dispersal of tear gas and other crowd-breaking irritants carried by army and police vehicles.

sneezer n.[1] **1** [early 18C–mid-19C] a snuff-box. **2** [early 19C] the nose. **3** [early–mid-19C] a measure of alcohol, a dram (cf. SNIFFLER). **4** [mid-19C–1940s] a pocket handkerchief. **5** [1930s] (US) prison.

sneezer n.[2] [19C] something exceptionally good, strong, violent etc. [dial. sneezer, a severe blow]

sneezer to breezer see BREEZER TO SNEEZER.

sneezing coffer n. [early 19C] a snuff-box (cf. SNEEZER n.[1]). [SE sneeze + coffer]

snells n. [mid–late 19C] buttons and other small wares carried by a street-hawker (cf. DUMPS n.[2]). [Scot. snell, sharp ? + Somerset dial. snell, a short stick pointed at both ends]

snelt n. [20C] (Aus./N.Z.) a sneak-thief. [? link to SNAVEL]

snib n. [early 17C–mid-19C] (Scot. Und.) a petty thief. [Scot. snib, to cut into]

snib v. [19C] (Scot.) to have sexual intercourse with a woman. [Scot. snib, to cut into, to snuff a candle]

snibbet n. [20C] sexual intercourse. [SNIB v.]

snibley *n.* [20C] sexual intercourse, often as a *bit of snibley.* [SNIB v.]

snicker *n.* [late 18C–early 19C] a horse suffering from glanders, a contagious disease typified by swellings beneath the jaw and discharge of mucus from the nostrils.

snicket *n.* **1** [1940s] a woman. **2** [1990s] the vagina. **3** [1990s] sexual intercourse, esp. as *a bit of snicket.* [? Yorks. dial. *snicket*, a narrow passage; or Lancashire dial. *snicket*, a forward woman]

snick fadger *n.* [mid–late 19C] a petty thief. [SE *snick*, to cut, snip, clip, nick + FADGE n.[1]]

snickle *v.* [mid–late 19C] (mainly US) to inform against, to betray. [SNEAK v.[2] or SE *snickle*, to ensnare in a noose]

snick up! *see* SNECK UP!

snid/snide *n.* [mid-19C] a sixpence. [? SNIDE n. (1)]

snide *n.* [mid-19C+] **1** (orig. US) spec. counterfeit money; thus *snide lurk*, the passing of counterfeit money, *snide shop*, an agency that organizes the passing of counterfeit money. **2** (S.Afr.) imitation diamonds. [? Ger. *aufschneiden*, to boast, to brag, to show off, or Ger. *schneide*, to cut, i.e. the cutting of fake coins]

snide/shnide *adj.* [mid-19C+] fake, unpleasant, mean. [SNIDE n.]

snide and shine *n.* [late 19C] an East End Jew. [SNIDE adj. + SHEENY n.[1]]

snide pitcher *n.* [mid–late 19C] one who passes bad money; thus *snide pitching*, passing counterfeit money. [SNIDE n. + PITCH v.[2]]

snidesman *n.* [late 19C] a counterfeiter. [SNIDE n. + sfx. *-man*]

snide sparkler *n.* [late 19C] a counterfeit diamond. [SNIDE adj. + SPARKLER n.[1]]

snider *see* SNYDER.

snidey *adj.* **1** [late 19C+] bad, unfavourable. **2** [1950s+] sneering, supercilious. [SNIDE adj.]

snidget *adj.* [1930s+] (Aus. teen) excellent, first-rate. [? SNODGER]

sniff *n.* (drugs) **1** [1920s+] narcotics, esp. cocaine. **2** [1960s+] glue, paint thinner and other chemicals used for intoxication. **3** [1960s+] amyl nitrite, butyl nitrate; thus (US gay) *sniff queen*, a devotee of such drugs (cf. AIMIES n.[2]). [SE *sniff*, i.e. the methods of consumption]

sniff *v.* [1920s+] **1** to drink alcohol. **2** (drugs) to inhale cocaine, glue or any other intoxicating substance.

sniff a powder, to *phr.* [1940s] (US Black) to leave fast, to run away (cf. TAKE A POWDER). [RUN-OUT POWDER]

sniffer *n.* **1** [mid-19C+] the nose. **2** [1920s+] (drugs) a cocaine or heroin user. **3** [1940s+] any device used to sense gas, radiation etc; thus *sniffer dog*, a dog trained to sniff out drugs or explosives. **4** [1960s+] (drugs) one who sniffs glue. **5** [1970s] a prostitute's client who enjoys sniffing her used underwear. **6** [1970s] an investigator from the DHSS/Benefits Agency who checks on the validity of unemployment benefit claims. [SE *sniff*]

sniffler *n.* [late 19C–1930s] (Anglo-Irish) an alcoholic drink, usu. in phr. *will you have a sniffler?* (cf. SNEEZER n.[1]).

sniffles, the *n.* [1900s] (US) a fit of depression. [SE *sniffles*, weeping, tearfulness]

sniffy *adj.* [late 19C+] disdainful, arrogant, ill-tempered (cf. SNIFTY). [the *sniffs* of contempt]

snifter/schnifter *n.[1]* [mid-19C+] an alcoholic drink. [SE *snifter*, a brandy glass, shaped to be warmed by the hands and for the fumes, so intensified, to be sniffed]

snifter *n.[2]* [late 19C+] anyone or anything seen as especially important, large or powerful.

snifter *n.[3]* (drugs) **1** [1920s–50s] a cocaine user. **2** [1930s+] a measure of cocaine, enough for a single inhalation (cf. SNORT n.). [SNIFF v. (2) + play on SNIFTER n.[2]]

snifty *adj.* [late 19C–1940s] (US) haughty, arrogant, disdainful. [var. on SNIFFY]

snig *v.* [late 19C] to steal, to pilfer (cf. SNEAK v.[1]). [Yorks. dial. *snig*, to chop off, to steal]

'sniggers!/'snigs! *excl.* [17C] a general oath, lit. 'God's nigs' (cf. 'S abbr.[1]).

sniggle *n.* [1930s+] (Aus.) **1** a woman seen as a sex object. **2** sexual intercourse. [? SNIGGLE v. or SE *snuggle*]

sniggle *v.* [19C] to wriggle, to creep stealthily. [? dial.]

sniggy *adj.* [20C] penny-pinching, mean. [? Yorks. dial.]

'snigs! *see* 'SNIGGERS!

snilch *v.* [late 17C–early 19C] (Und.) **1** to look at. **2** to spy upon. [ext. of SE *sneck*]

sninny *n.* [1920s+] (Aus.) a young woman. [var. on SKINNY n.[2]]

snip *n.[1]* [late 16C–mid-19C] a tailor; also used as a generic proper name, e.g. *Master Snip, Snip the Tailor* (cf. SNIPES; SNIPS). [SE *snip*, to cut]

snip *n.[2]* **1** [early 18C–early 19C] a swindle, a deception. **2** [late 19C+] anything simple, an easy task (cf. SNAP n.[2]). **3** [1920s+] a bargain. [SE *snip*, a single slice of the scissors]

snip *v.* [early 18C–early 19C] to swindle, to deceive. [SE *snip*, to slice, to cut]

snip a dolly, to *phr.* [1940s] (US Black) to leave, to go away. [ety. unknown]

snip-cabbage/-louse *n.* [18C; 19C] a tailor. [SE *snip* + CABBAGE n.[2]/SE *louse*]

snipcock *n.* [1960s+] a derog. term for a Jew. [SE *snip* + COCK n.[2] (1); i.e. circumcision]

snipe *n.[1]* [mid–late 19C] **1** a lawyer, esp. one that has presented a large bill (cf. WOODCOCK). **2** the inflated bill itself. [SE *snipe*; a pun on the bird's bill]

snipe *n.[2]* [late 19C+] (orig. US tramp) a cigarette or cigar butt; thus *snipe-shooting*, picking up cigar or cigarette ends from the gutter (cf. FAG END). [SE *snipe*, the long-beaked bird or SE *snip*, to cut off; note dial. *snipe*, a mean person]

snipe *n.[3]* [20C] (Ulster) one who has a long nose. [the bird's long beak]

snipe *n.[4]* [1940s+] (Aus.) a small wall poster, a flyer, usu. political. [SE *snipe*, to shoot at]

snipe *v.[1]* [late 19C+] (mainly US) **1** to pick up, to pilfer, to filch. **2** to prospect for gold in old diggings. [? image of the bird foraging with its beak]

snipe *v.[2]* [1970s+] (US Black) to kill. [orig. milit. use]

snipe on *v.* [1970s+] (US Black) to malign, to criticize, to gossip about someone. [var. on synon. SE *snipe at*]

sniper *n.* [1930s+] (Aus.) a non-union wharf worker. [SE *sniper*, i.e. they 'shoot down' available work]

snipes *n.* [early–mid-19C] a pair of scissors (cf. SNIPS). [SE *snip*]

sniping *n.* [late 19C+] (US) prospecting for gold in old, abandoned diggings. [SNIPE v.[1] (2)]

snip-louse *see* SNIP-CABBAGE.

snippety *n.* [late 19C] any form of publication, e.g. *Tit-Bits*, made of material cut (or *snipped*) from others.

snippy *adj.* [mid-19C+] (orig. US) hypercritical, having a tendency to complain over petty problems or cut down other people. [categorized as a 'woman's word' in its orig. citation in Bartlett (1848)]

snips *n.* **1** [mid-19C+] a pair of scissors (cf. SNIPES). **2** [late 19C] handcuffs (cf. SNAPS n.[1]).

sniptious *adj.* [early 19C] (US) neat and elegant. [anything unnecessary has been *snipped* away]

snit *n.* [1930s+] (orig. US) an outbreak of temper, generally a children's term. [? echoic; coined by US writer/diplomat Clare Booth Luce (1903–87)]

snitch *n.[1]* **1** [mid-17C+] the nose. **2** [mid-17C–mid-18C] a blow on the nose. **3** [late 18C+] an informer, initially in phr.

turn snitch (cf. SNITCHER n.[2]). [(3) one fig. 'sticks one's nose in']

snitch n.[2] [1900s–30s] (Aus./N.Z., mainly juv.) any person or thing considered notably excellent, attractive, strong etc (cf. SNITCHER n.[3]).

snitch n.[3] [1940s+] (N.Z.) **1** a grudge. **2** hostility, bad feeling. [ety. unknown; ? link to SNIT]

snitch v. **1** [late 18C+] to inform, to turn King's/Queen's evidence. **2** [late 19C+] to arrest. **3** [1920s+] to steal. [SNITCH n.[1]]

snitch-ass adj. [1980s+] (US Black) untrustworthy, tale-telling. [SNITCH n.[1] + sfx. -ASS]

snitchball n. [20C] (US prison) any game played by those inmates who live in protective segregation. [SNITCH n.[1] (3) + sfx. -ball]

snitchel n. [late 17C–18C] a blow on the nose. [SNITCH n.[1]]

snitchel v. [late 17C–18C] to hit on the nose. [SNITCHEL n.]

snitcher n.[1] [late 18C] a member of a set of fashionable young men or 'bloods'. [? SNITCH n.[1] (1), i.e. their devotion to punching people on the nose]

snitcher n.[2] **1** [mid-19C+] an informant, a tell-tale (cf. SNITCH n.[1]). **2** [mid-19C] (Scot.) handcuffs, esp. strings used in place of handcuffs. **3** [1900s–20s] a detective. **4** [1930s–40s] (US Black) a newspaper reporter or columnist, a writer. [SNITCH n.[1] (3)]

snitcher n.[3] [1900s–30s] (Aus./N.Z.) any person or thing considered notably excellent, attractive, strong etc. [? SNEEZER n.[2]]

snitcher n.[4] [1950s+] (N.Z.) a grudge, a feeling of hostility towards. [ext. of SNITCH n.[3]]

snitcher adj. [1930s+] (Aus./N.Z.) first-rate, excellent, attractive. [SNITCHER n.[3]]

snitching n. **1** [early 19C+] informing. **2** [1930s+] (US) stealing. [SNITCH n.[1], (1), (3)]

snitching-rascal n. [19C] an informer (cf. SNITCHER n.[2]). [SNITCH v. (1) + SE rascal]

snitch-pad n. [1930s–40s] (US Black) a notebook. [SNITCH v. (1) + SE pad]

snitch-rag n. [1940s] a handkerchief. [SNITCH n.[1]]

snitch-sheet n. [1930s–40s] (US Black) a newspaper. [SNITCH v. (1) + SHEET n. (1)]

snitchy adj. [1970s+] (N.Z.) tetchy, ill-tempered. [SNITCH n.[3]]

snite one's snitch, to phr. [late 18C–early 19C] to wipe one's nose. [SE snite, to wipe + SNITCH n.[1] (1)]

snitzy adj. [20C] (US) elegant, smart. [? SNOB + RITZY]

sniv v. [early–mid-19C] to hold one's tongue. [SE snib, to reprove, to reprimand]

sniv! excl. [early 19C] nonsense! humbug! rubbish! (cf. WALKER!). [SNIV v.]

snizzle v. [1910s–20s] to have sexual intercourse. [? dial. sniggle, to wriggle]

snob n. **1** [late 18C–19C] a cobbler, a shoemaker; thus *snobbing*, shoemaking or repairing. **2** [mid-19C] a strike-breaker. **3** [20C] (Aus./N.Z.) the last, most recalcitrant sheep to be sheared (cf. COBBLER n.[1]). [the class-conscious, modern use of SE snob, one who despises their inferiors and/or toadies to those seen as superior, began as Cambridge University jargon c.1793 as a description of a townsman, as opposed to a university member. This may have been based on the orig. sl. use, implying the desire of tradesmen to flatter custom out of the undergraduates. It was widely popularized through the success of William Thackeray's *Book of Snobs* (1848). Ironically, a parallel use (early–mid-19C) means simply an ordinary person, with no pretensions to superiority, and in mid-19C Aus. *snobs* were tradesmen, while *nobs* were the 'gentlemen'. Similarly, in university use *snobocracy*, in SE the world of the influential upper classes, meant the world of

townspeople, as opposed to undergraduates – again the use returns to the orig. sl. meaning]

snob-nob n. [1900s] (N.Z.) the self-appointed rural 'aristocracy'. [SE snob + NOB n.[3]]

snob's duck n. [19C] a leg of mutton stuffed with sage and onions (cf. CLARE MARKET DUCK). [SNOB n. (1) + SE duck]

snobstick n. [mid-19C] a strike-breaker (cf. SCAB v.). [var. on or misreading of SE knobstick, a strike-breaker; ult. knobstick, a knobbed stick or cane]

snob zoning n. [20C] (US) a method of placing restrictions on specific city areas in a deliberate attempt to make it impossible for low-income families, e.g. non-White, non-middle-class families, to purchase homes there. [SE snob + zoning]

snockered/schnockered adj. [1970s+] drunk (cf. BASTED). [? dial. snock, a blow]

snoddy n. [late 19C–1910s] a soldier. [var. on SWADDY]

snodger adj. [20C] (Aus./N.Z.) excellent, first-rate, very good. [ety. unknown; OED suggests link to Scot/dial. snod, smart, neat, comfortable and/or Scot. snog, smooth, neat]

snoek-town n. [late 19C] (S.Afr.) Cape Town. [Du. snoek, the European pike (Esox lucius), in S.Afr. use usu. the snake mackerel (Thyrsites atun) + SE town; Cape Town was once the home of the snoek fishing and processing industry]

snoep adj. [1960s+] (S.Afr.) mean, greedy, selfish, stingy. [Afk. snoep, greedy]

snog v. [1950s+] to enjoy sexual preliminaries, stopping short of intercourse, usu. of teenage experimentation (cf. NECKING n.[1]). [? SE snug; orig. 1930s RAF usage]

snollygoster n. [mid-19C+] (US) a shrewd, unprincipled person, esp. a politician. [? Ger. schnelle Geister, lit. 'wild host', and thus a bird of prey that terrorizes man, or schnelle Geeschte, lit. 'quick spirits', also defined as a monster. According to Safire (1978), it was coined during or near the time of the US Civil War (1861–5). It was defined in a Georgia newspaper as: 'a fellow who wants office, regardless of party, platform or principles, and who, whenever he wins, gets there by the sheer force of monumental, talknophical assummancy. 'There may be a link to the Maryland snallygaster, a mythical monster supposedly part reptile and part bird, designed to terrify ex-slaves out of voting]

snood/snoodge n. **1** [1900s] a dose of a drug. **2** [1980s+] crack cocaine. [ety. unknown; var. on SNORT n. (3)/SE snort]

snoodge see SNOOZE v.

snooker v. **1** [1910s+] to trick, to cheat. **2** [1960s+] (Aus.) to hide. [SE snooker, to impede]

snookered adj. [1910s+] cheated, hoaxed, trapped in a difficult position (cf. BEHIND THE EIGHT BALL). [SNOOKER v.]

snooks n. **1** [mid-19C] 'an imaginary personage often brought forward as the answer to an idle question, or as the perpetrator of a senseless joke' (Hotten, 1860). **2** [1920s+] a term of endearment, either to a child or lover (cf. SNOOKUMS).

snookums n. [1920s+] a term of endearment (cf. DIDDUMS; SNOOKS). [orig. addressed esp. to lap-dogs]

snooky adj. [1910s–50s] (Aus.) critical, fault-finding. [? SE phr. cock a snook, to disdain]

snoop n. [1920s+] (US) a detective. [SNOOP v. (1)]

snoop v. [1920s+] (orig. US) **1** to pry, to interfere, to listen in. **2** to steal. [Du. snoepen, 'to appropriate and consume dainties in a clandestine manner' (OED)]

snoop and pry, to phr. [20C] to cry. [rhy. sl.]

snoot n. **1** [mid-19C+] the nose (cf. NOZZLE; SNITCH n.[1]). **2** [mid-19C+] a snob, an arrogant person who 'sticks their nose in the air'. **3** [1970s] arrogance, superciliousness (cf. SNOOTY). [SE snout]

snoot v. [1950s+] (Aus.) to snub. [backform. of SNOOTY]

snooted see SNOOTERED.

snooter *n.* [1960s+] (drugs) anyone who inhales a narcotic rather than injecting it. [SNOOT n. (1)]

snootered/snooted *adj.* [19C+] drunk (cf. SNOOTFUL). [SNOOT n. (1)]

snootful *n.* [1910s+] (US) an alcoholic drink; thus *have a snootful*, to be drunk (cf. GET A SKINFUL). [SNOOT n. (1)]

snooty *adj.* [1930s+] snobbish, stand-offish, used of one who 'looks down their nose'. [SNOOT n. (1)]

snooze *n.* **1** [late 18C+] a nap, a brief or light sleep. **2** [early–mid-19C] a lodging. **3** [20C] (Aus.) a three-month prison sentence (cf. SLEEP). [? SE *snore + doze*]

snooze/snoodge *v.* [late 18C+] to doze, to sleep for a short time; thus *snooze-case*, a pillow-slip. [SNOOZE n.]

snooze job *n.* [1970s+] anything especially boring. [SNOOZE n. + JOB n.[5]]

snooze ken *see* SNOOZING KEN.

snoozem *n.* [mid–late 19C] a nap. [ext. of SNOOZE n.]

snoozer *n.[1]* [mid–late 19C] a thief who steals from the hotel or house in which they are staying. [SNOOZE n. (2)]

snoozer *n.[2]* **1** [late 19C+] a person, a 'chap', a woman. **2** [20C] (Aus.) a baby. [SNOOZE v. + sfx. *-er*]

snoozing and snoring *phr.* [20C] boring. [rhy. sl.]

snoozing/snooze ken *n.* [early–mid-19C] **1** a brothel. **2** a lodging house. **3** a bedroom, a bed (cf. SNORING KENNEL). [SNOOZE v. + KEN n.[1]]

snoozle *v.* [mid–late 19C] **1** to nestle. **2** to snuggle up to. [? SNOOZE v. + SE *snuggle + nuzzle*]

snoozy *n.* [early 19C] a night constable. [SNOOZE v.]

snoozy *adj.* [late 19C+] sleepy, drowsy. [SNOOZE v.]

snop *n.* [1960s] (drugs) marijuana. [? borrowing f. SNOPSY]

snops *n.* [late 19C] (US) gin. [for ety. *see* SNOPSY]

snopsy *n.* [19C] (US) drunk. [SE *Schnapps*, the drink]

Snor City *n.* [1980s+] (S.Afr.) Pretoria. [Afk. *snor*, a moustache + SE *city*; many male Pretorians supposedly wear moustaches]

snore *n.* **1** [mid-19C–1920s] a sleep. **2** [1960s–70s] (Aus.) a sleeping place, esp. a hostel for tramps and vagrants. **3** [1970s+] a boring person or thing.

snore-off *n.* [1950s–60s] (Aus./N.Z.) a sleep or nap, esp. after a drinking session. [SNORE OFF v.]

snore off *v.* [1920s–60s] (Aus.) to go to sleep. [ext. of SE *snore*]

snorer *n.[1]* [late 19C–1950s] the nose. [SE *snore*]

snorer/snorrer *n.[2]* [20C] **1** a scrounger, a beggar. **2** a difficult customer. [SCHNORRER]

snoresville *see* SNOREVILLE.

snore through/through it *v.* [early 19C] to glide along, to move easily (cf. WALK IT).

snoreville/snoresville *n.* [1960s+] (orig. US) anything or anywhere considered tedious, boring. [SE *snore(s)* + sfx. -VILLE]

snoring kennel *n.* [early 18C] a bedroom (cf. SNOOZING KEN).

snork *n.* (Aus./N.Z.) **1** [1940s+] a baby. **2** [1970s+] a young man, a boy. [SE *snork*, a piglet]

snorker *n.* [1940s+] (Aus.) **1** a sausage (cf. SNAGS). **2** the penis (cf. BACON n.[1]).

snorrer *see* SNORER n.[2].

snort *n.* **1** [late 19C+] (Aus.) a pot of tea. **2** [late 19C+] a gulp of alcohol. **3** [1950s+] (drugs) a dose or measure of a powdered narcotic.

snort *v.* (drugs) **1** [1930s+] to inhale narcotics, usu. cocaine or heroin, through the nostrils. **2** [1960s+] to inhale glue etc.

snorter *n.[1]* **1** [early 19C+] the nose. **2** [early 19C] a blow on the nose. **3** [1970s+] (drugs) one who inhales (rather than injects) narcotics (cf. SNOOTER).

snorter *n.[2]* **1** [mid-19C] anything exceptionally large, strong, violent etc (cf. SNEEZER n.[2]; SNITCHER n.[3]). **2** [mid-19C] (US) 'a dashing, riotous fellow' (Bartlett). **3** [mid–late 19C] a

gale, a stiff breeze. **4** [1920s] (N.Z.) an ill-tempered, tetchy person.

snorter *n.[3]* **1** [late 19C+] a drink of alcohol. **2** [1930s] a drunkard. [SNORT n. (2), (3)]

snorting *adj.* [1920s] a general intensifier, excellent, first-rate, very large etc.

snort out *v.* [1980s+] (US campus) to overeat, to eat voraciously. [SE *snort*; i.e. the noise one makes while eating]

snorts *n.* [1970s] (drugs) phencyclidine (cf. ACE n.[3]). [? play on HOG n.[8]]

snorty *adj.* [late 19C] bad-tempered, disagreeable. [SE *snort*]

snossidge *n.* [late 19C] a sausage. [joc. mispron.]

snot *n.* **1** [18C] nasal mucus. **2** [early 19C+] a pej. term for a person, the usual implication being of their arrogance (cf. SNOTNOSE) or, in the case of women, their promiscuity (cf. DIRTY LEG). **3** [1980s+] (drugs) residue produced from smoking amphetamine. **4** [1980s+] semen (cf. COCK SNOT). [MDu. *snotte*; SE in 15–17C but was generally seen as sl. by 18C; cognate with 14C SE *snite*, to wipe mucus from the nose and thus ult. to SE *snout*]

snot *v.* [early 19C+] (US) to treat disdainfully. [SNOT n. (2)]

snot and tears *phr.* [1960s+] (S.Afr.) misery, wretchedness. [synon. Afk. phr. *snot en trane*]

snot balls *n.* [1980s+] (drugs) rubber cement rolled into balls and burned. [SNOT n. (1) + SE *balls*]

snot-box *n.* [20C] (US) the nose. [SNOT n. (1) + SE *box*]

snotgobbler *n.* [1990s] a general term of derision. [SNOT n. (1) or (4) + SE *gobbler*]

snot horn *n.* [late 18C+] the nose (cf. HORN n.[3]). [SNOT n. (1) + SE *horn*]

snot-locker *n.* [1980s] (US) the vagina. [SNOT n. (4) + SE *locker*]

snotnose *n.* [1940s+] (orig. US) **1** a small child with a running nose, a grubby child. **2** an arrogant, snobbish person (cf. SNOTTY); thus *snotnosed*, arrogant, conceited, snobbish. [SNOT n. (1) + SE *nose*]

snotrag *n.* [late 19C+] a handkerchief. [SNOT n. (1) + SE *rag*]

snotter *n.* **1** [mid-19C] the nose (cf. SNOTTLE-BOX). **2** [mid-19C] a pickpocket who specializes in stealing handkerchiefs (cf. WIPER-DRAWER). **3** [mid-19C] a (dirty, ragged) handkerchief; thus *snotter-hauling*, stealing handkerchiefs. **4** [20C] (Ulster) a dirty, unpleasant person. [SNOT n. (1)]

snottery *adj.* [20C] unpleasant, arrogantly annoyed. [? var. on SNOTTY adj. (1)]

snottinger *n.* [mid-19C] a pocket handkerchief. [SNOT n. (1)]

snottle-box *n.* [19C] the nose (cf. SNOTTER). [SNOT n. (1) + SE *box*]

snotty *adj.* **1** [mid-19C+] superior, snobbish, stuck-up. **2** [1950s+] dirty, paltry, contemptible. [orig. late 17C SE; colloq. by 19C]

snotty-nose *n.* [19C+] **1** a dirty, contemptible, grubby person. **2** an arrogant, snobbish person. [SNOT n. (1), (2); SE until 19C]

snout *n.[1]* [late 18C–early 19C] a hogshead. [play on SE *hogshead*, i.e. a 'pig's nose']

snout *n.[2]* **1** [late 19C+] tobacco; thus (prison) *snout baron*, one who controls the clandestine sale of tobacco, the prison 'currency', *snout day*, the weekly issue of tobacco. **2** [1940s+] a cigarette. [SE *snout*; when tobacco was barred from prisons, a prisoner would mask their smoking by pretending to rub their nose]

snout *n.[3]* [20C] an informer; thus *snouting*, passing on information to the police (cf. NOSE n.[1]; SNITCH n.[1]). [SE *snout*, i.e. one who 'pokes their nose in']

snout *v.[1]* [20C] (Aus./N.Z.) to bear ill-will towards, to treat with disfavour, to rebuff; thus *snouted*, rebuffed, jilted. [SE *snout*; to 'stick one's nose in the air']

snout *v.[2]* [1920s+] to act as a police informer. [SNOUT n.[3]]

snout about/around v. [1960s+] to search. [the image of a pig rooting for food]

snouter n. [1940s–70s] a tobacconist. [SNOUT n.²]

snout-piece n. [17C–19C] the nose, the face. [SE snout]

snouty n. [1930s] (prison) tobacco. [var. on SNOUT n.² (1)]

snouty adj. [mid-19C] overbearing, insolent. [having one's 'snout' or nose in the air]

snow n.¹ [early–mid-19C] (Und.) wet linen (cf. SNOW-DROP-PING). [the colour + it 'falls' on the hedges where it is left to dry]

snow/snowball n.² [1910s+] (orig. US drugs) **1** cocaine. **2** heroin. **3** morphine. **4** amphetamine (cf. A n.²). [the colour and consistency; the usu. ref. is to cocaine]

snow n.³ [1910s–20s] (Aus.) a derog. description of an Italian or another Latin person. [SE snow, a white haircream, similar to Brylcreem, supposedly favoured by such men]

snow n.⁴ **1** [1920s+] money, silver coins, small silver change. **2** [1950s–60s] (US Black) a White woman. **3** [1950s+] any White person. **4** [1960s+] (Aus. school) a blond-haired weakling (cf. SNOW QUEEN). [the colour of the money, hair or skin]

snow n.⁵ [1940s+] (orig. US) smooth talk, bluff, bluster, lies. [abbr. SNOW JOB]

snow/snow under v. [1940s+] (US) to confuse with a deluge of smooth, if insincere, talk (cf. SNOW JOB). [SNOW n.⁵]

snow again phr. [1930s–50s] used to request someone to repeat an ill-heard statement, often ext. as snow again, I didn't catch your drift. [pun]

snow and ice n. [20C] the price. [rhy. sl.]

snowball n.¹ **1** [late 18C–early 19C] a Black person (cf. LILY-WHITE n.¹). **2** [20C] (US Black) a White person. [(1) a humourless 'joke']

snowball n.² see SNOW n.².

snowball n.³ [1990s] semen that has been ejaculated in a partner's mouth and that is then returned, via a passionate kiss. [? SE snowball, a cocktail orig. based on crème de menthe, now on advocaat]

snowballs n. [1990s] (drugs) MDMA (cf. ECSTASY).

snowball's chance in hell, a phr. [1950s+] no possibility at all.

snow bird n.¹ (US) **1** [1900s–30s] an impoverished tramp who enlists in the army as the winter arrives in order to get food and shelter for the next few months, then deserts when the warmer weather returns. **2** [1920s+] (Florida and other southern states) a winter tourist who travels south to avoid the chilly weather. **3** [1920s+] a fan of winter weather and/or winter sports. **4** [1990s] (US gay) a wealthy gay man who moves to Miami, Florida, one of the US's gay capitals, to enjoy sun and sex. [SE snow + BIRD n.²]

snow bird n.² (drugs) **1** [1910s–60s] a cocaine user. **2** [1930s] a woman involved in the cocaine trade. [SNOW n.² + BIRD n.²/BIRD n.⁵]

snow-birding n. [1970s+] (Aus./N.Z.) stealing washing, usu. women's underwear, from clothes-lines (cf. SNOW-DROPPING).

snow-broth n. [late 19C–1910s] cold tea. [SE snow-broth, water produced or obtained by the melting of snow, esp. from natural causes]

snow bunny n. [1950s+] **1** (orig. US) a woman who frequents the ski slopes as much for the sex as for the sport (cf. SKI BUNNY). **2** (US Black) a White woman. [SE snow + BUNNY n.² (2)]

snow cap n. [1980s] (drugs) cocaine sprinkled onto a pipe of marijuana and smoked. [SNOW n.²]

snowcones n. [1980s+] (drugs) cocaine. [SNOW n.²; play on US ice-cream brand]

snowdrop n. [1940s+] **1** a US military policeman. **2** any military policeman (cf. REDCAP n.²). [the distinctive white caps]

snow-drop v. [late 19C+] (Aus.) to steal. [? non-specific use of SNOW-DROPPING]

snow-dropping n. [mid-19C+] (Aus./UK Und.) the stealing of washing, usu. women's underwear, from unguarded clothes-lines; thus snow-dropper/-gatherer one who steals from clothes-lines (cf. SNOW-BIRDING). [SNOW n.¹]

snowed adj. [1920s+] (drugs) under the influence of cocaine; thus punning synons. snowed in, snowed up. [SNOW n.²]

snowed over adj. [1970s+] (US campus) obsessively in love, infatuated. [play on SNOWED UNDER]

snowed under/snowed up adj. [1930s+] (orig. US) over-burdened with work, commitments, responsibilities etc.

snowfall see SNOW JOB.

snowflake n. [1980s+] (drugs) crack cocaine. [SNOW n.² + FLAKE n.³]

snowing n. [mid–late 19C] the stealing of linen from the drying grounds. [abbr. SNOW-DROPPING]

snowing down below! excl. [1930s–40s] (N.Z.) an excl. to a woman that her petticoat is showing.

snow job/snowfall n. [1940s+] (US) an untrue but totally convincing story, a con-man's patter. [SNOW v. + JOB n.⁵]

snowman n. [1960s+] (US) anyone who has a smooth, seductive line of talk. [SNOW v.]

'snowns! excl. [late 16C] a mild oath, lit. God's nouns, i.e. 'God's wounds' (cf. 's abbr.¹; ZOUNDS!).

snow out v. [20C] to lose one's bearings. [the image is of a blizzard]

snow pallets n. [1980s+] (drugs) amphetamine (cf. A n.²). [SNOW n.²]

snow queen/shoveller n. [1970s+] (US Black) a homosexual, whether Black or White, who prefers blond, 'Nordic' partners. [SNOW n.⁴ + QUEEN n.¹]

snow seals n. [1970s+] (drugs) a mix of cocaine and amphetamine. [SNOW n.²]

snow shoveller see SNOW QUEEN.

snow soke n. [1980s+] (drugs) crack cocaine. [SNOW n.²]

snow under see SNOW v.

snow white n. [1980s+] (drugs) cocaine. [SNOW n.²]

snow whites n. [1970s+] tights. [rhy. sl.]

snowy n. [late 19C] linen. [SNOW n.¹]

snozzle/snoz n. [1930s+] the nose. [var. on SCHNOZZLE]

snozzled adj. [1930s+] (US) drunk (cf. SNOOTERED).

snozzler n. [1930s+] (Aus./N.Z.) anything or anyone considered excellent or attractive (cf. SKUTCHER; SNEEZER n.²; SNITCHER n.³).

snubby/snubbie n. [1960s+] (US) a cheap, short-barrelled revolver. [SE snub-nosed]

snub devil n. [late 18C–late 19C] a parson. [SE snub, to reject; i.e. he 'renounces the Devil and all his works']

snubs! excl. [1930s–40s] (mainly teen) used to indicate one's complete contempt for the subject of the excl.; usu. as snubs to him/her. [SE snub; ult. Scand. snubba, to cut short]

snudge n. [late 17C–early 18C] (Und.) a thief who first enters a house, then hides, and emerges when the coast is clear to effect the robbery. [? SNEAK v.¹ + BUDGE n.¹]

snuff n.¹ [late 18C–1930s] the liquor left at the bottom of a glass (cf. HEELTAP). [SE snuff, a candle end]

snuff n.² [1930s+] a murder (cf. SNUFF MOVIE). [SNUFF v.²]

snuff v.¹ [19C] (Und.) to throw snuff into a victim's face, rendering them temporarily blind and thus easier to rob (cf. SNEEZE-LURKER).

snuff v.² [1930s+] to murder, to kill. [SE snuff out]

snuff and butter/butter maiden n. [1920s–40s] (Anglo-Ind.) a derog. term for a Eurasian woman. [her skin colouring]

snuff and snifter phr. [early–mid-19C] energetically, continuously.

snuff-bottle/-box n. [20C] anything astounding, shocking. [fig. use of SNUFF v.²]

snuff-box n. 1 [early–mid-19C] the nose. 2 [1940s] a gas mask.

snuff dipper n. [1970s] (US) a prostitute working from a car. [? play on SE *snuff-dipper*, a snuff-chewer, i.e. a ref. to the provision of oral sex or SNUFF v.², i.e. the possibility of her being killed while working]

snuffer n.¹ [1940s] (US Black) the nose (cf. SNIFFER; SNUFF-BOX; SNUFFERS). [SE *snuff*, to sniff]

snuffer n.² *see* SNUFF MOVIE.

snuffers n. [mid-17C–early 18C] the nostrils. [SNUFFER n.¹]

snuff it v. [mid-19C+] to die. [SE *snuff out*]

snuffle n.¹ [early–mid-19C] the nose.

snuffle n.² [1900s] (N.Z.) pious cant, humbug. [the SE *snuffling* tones of the self-appointed moralist]

snuffle-buster n. [late 19C–1900s] (Aus./N.Z.) a puritan; thus *snuffle-busting*, puritanical. [SNUFFLE n.²]

snuffler n. [early 18C] a degenerate old lecher.

snuffling community n. [early 18C] prostitutes, seen collectively. [ety. unknown; SE *snuffle*, to sniff, to talk through the nose was a characteristic of contemporary prostitutes?]

snuff-lurker *see* SNEEZE-LURKER.

snuff movie/snuffer n. [1960s+] (orig. US) a film, usu. pornographic, that climaxes in the actual death of one of the participants, usu. an actress or, if paedophiliac, a child. [SNUFF v.²]

snuff out v. [mid-19C–1910s] to die.

snuff pepper *see* TAKE PEPPER IN THE NOSE.

snuff someone's candle, to phr. [late 19C] to kill, to murder.

snuff stick n. [1970s] (N.Z.) a cigarette. [SE *snuff-stick*, an implement for dipping snuff]

snuffy adj. [mid-19C] tipsy, drunk.

snug n. 1 [mid-19C+] the bar-parlour of a public house or inn. 2 [20C] (US Und.) a small revolver that can be concealed easily. [SE *snug*, comfortable, cosy]

snug adj. [19C] drunk (cf. ABOUT RIGHT adj.¹). [SE *snug*, comfortable, cosy]

snug v.¹ [19C] to have sexual intercourse with. [SE *snug*, to snuggle]

snug v.² [mid-19C] (US) to steal, to conceal from the proper owner. [SE *snug*, to place neatly]

snug as ... phr. various combs., all meaning extremely comfortable; thus [mid–late 17C] *snug as a pig in pease-straw*, [mid-18C] *snug as a bug in a rug*, [late 19C] *snug as old Pamp*.

snuggies n. [1970s] (US campus) women's underwear. [despite the root in SE *snug*, i.e. cosy, not necessarily of winter thickness]

snuggle-pup n. [1920s–30s] (US teen) one's boyfriend or girlfriend.

snuggy n. [1940s–50s] 1 the female pubic hair. 2 (US) a sexually attractive woman who is looking for sexual liaisons. [SE *snug/snuggle*]

snug's the word! excl. [18C–mid-19C] say nothing about this (cf. MUM'S THE WORD!).

snurge n. 1 [1920s–40s] a Poor Law Institution. 2 [1930s–50s] a generally contemptible person (reputed to sniff women's bicycle seats). 3 [1930s–50s] a tattle-tale, a sycophant. [ety. unknown]

snurge v. [1930s+] (US) to sneak off to avoid work or responsibilities.

snyder/snider n. [late 17C–1900s] a tailor. [Ger. *schneider*, a tailor]

so adj. 1 [19C] drunk. 2 [mid-19C+] menstruating. 3 [late 19C–1950s] homosexual (cf. THAT WAY adj.²). [euph.]

so! excl. [1910s+] used to add emphasis to a statement

contradicting a negative assertion made by the previous speaker, e.g. 'No you didn't,' 'I did – so!'

soak n. [early 19C+] a drunkard, usu. as *old soak* (cf. OLD SOAKER). [SOAK v.¹ (1)]

soak v.¹ 1 [early 18C–mid-19C] to drink heavily; thus [late 19C] *come out of soak*, to get over one's hangover (cf. ABSORB). 2 [19C] to ply with liquor. 3 [1900s] to spend money on drink.

soak v.² [late 19C] to pawn. [one leaves one's possession 'to soak']

soak/soak it to v.³ [late 19C–1930s] (US) to punish, to beat up, to criticize harshly. [var. on SOCK v.¹]

soak v.⁴ [late 19C+] (orig. US) to charge a high price, to tax heavily, to extort money from.

soak v.⁵ [late 19C+] (US) to hit. [var. on SOCK v.¹]

soakapee n. [1940s] (W.I.) an habitual drunkard, an alcoholic. [SE *soak* + PEE n.¹; such drunkards may well foul their clothes]

soaked adj. [mid-18C+] drunk (cf. LUBRICATED). [SOAK v.¹]

soak it/let it soak v. [late 19C+] of a man, to linger before withdrawing one's penis after intercourse.

soak it to *see* SOAK v.³.

soak one's/the clay, to phr. [19C] to drink, to quench one's thirst. [SE *soak* + *clay*, one's body or 'mortal clay']

soak one's/the face, to phr. [19C] to drink, to quench one's thirst.

soak the chaffer, to phr. [19C] to drink, to quench one's thirst (cf. MOISTEN THE CHAFFER; SOAK ONE'S CLAY; SOAK ONE'S FACE). [SE *soak* + CHAFFER]

soak the clay *see* SOAK ONE'S CLAY.

soak the face *see* SOAK ONE'S FACE.

soak the mill, to phr. [late 19C] (US) to drink away one's possessions. [SE *mill*, used as generic for one's property]

so-and-so n. [late 19C+] 1 a euph. for any derog. name, esp. SON OF A BITCH. 2 an unspecified object (cf. THINGUMAJIG).

soap n.¹ [19C] a thick soup.

soap n.² [mid–late 19C] (US) money (cf. NO SOAP).

soap n.³ [mid-19C+] 1 flattery. 2 the act of flattering someone. [abbr. SOFT SOAP n.]

soap n.⁴ [late 19C–1900s] women, esp. promiscuous ones or prostitutes. [abbr. BIT OF SOAP]

soap n.⁵ [1950s+] (Aus.) a fool, a simpleton. [? JOE SOAP]

soap v. [mid-19C+] to flatter. [SOAP n.³]

soap and flannel n. [1910s–40s] the drawing of sickness benefit. [rhy. sl. *soap and flannel* = the panel, those doctors who accepted patients under the National Health Insurance Act (1913)]

soap and lather n. [late 19C+] a father. [rhy. sl.]

soap and water n. [20C] a daughter. [rhy. sl.]

soapbox artist n. [1930s] (N.Z.) a public orator, esp. an extremist or rabble-rouser. [SE *soapbox* + ARTIST n.²]

soap-crawler n. [mid-19C–1900s] a toady. [SOAP n.³ + CRAWLER n.²]

soapdodger n. [20C] a Protestant, as used in Scotland and Northern Ireland. [the supposed dirtiness of those concerned]

soaper n.¹ *see* SOAP OPERA.

soaper n.² *see* SOPOR.

soap-freak n. [1930s+] (US) a fan or devotee of daily television or radio drama series. [SOAP OPERA n. + sfx. -FREAK]

soapie n. [1980s+] (N.Z.) a TV soap opera.

soap lock n. [mid-19C] (US) a hairstyle favoured by the New York gangs of the period. A lock of hair was carefully curled then covered with soap to make it lie flat (cf. AGGERAWATOR).

soap opera/soaper n. [1930s+] (orig. US) a radio or TV drama series, e.g. *The Archers*, *Coronation Street*, which tells the interminable tale of supposedly 'ordinary life' (cf. HORSE OPERA). [the original 1920s radio show, *The Goldbergs*, was sponsored by US soap manufacturer Proctor & Gamble]

soap opera *adj.* [1930s+] (US) typical of family and social life as it is portrayed in the television and radio drama series, e.g. *soap opera mentality*. [SOAP OPERA n.]

soap over *v.* [mid-19C] to humbug. [SOAP v.]

soaps, the *n.* [1940s+] (orig. US) a generic term for radio and television series (cf. SOAP OPERA n.).

soap suds *n.* [18C] hot gin and water, with lemon and lump sugar.

soap the geyser, to *phr.* [1940s+] (N.Z.) to get started, to set off. [the addition of special *soap* to a geyser to improve its spouting]

soapy *adj.* **1** [mid-19C–1910s] ingratiating, unctuous, smoothly insincere. **2** [1920s+] (Aus.) foolish, silly, effeminate. [? originated in the nickname 'Soapy Sam', used of Bishop Wilberforce (1805–73)]

soapy fits *n.* [late 19C] (Und.) a fake fit used to obtain sympathetically donated alms, created by chewing a small piece of soap, thus creating 'foam' at the mouth.

soapy Isaac *see* SUETY ISAAC.

s.o.b. *phr.* **1** [1910s+] a general term of abuse, i.e. *son of a bitch*. **2** [1910s+] silly *old bugger/bastard*. **3** [1920s+] *shit or bust*. [abbr.]

sob *see* SOV.

sob! *excl.* [1980s+] (US campus) a mild oath, euph. for DAMN! HELL! SOD IT! [the speaker is supposedly reduced to tears]

sob act *n.* [1950s+] (US) a pretence of emotion, an appeal to someone's sympathies.

sob brother *n.* [1910s] (US) a sentimental man. [play on SOB SISTER]

sober-water *n.* [mid-19C] soda water. [the pun reflects its use as a partial cure for hangovers]

sob-raiser *n.* [1910s] (US) one who plays on the public's emotion to elicit sympathy for a cause.

sob-reporter *n.* [1920s] (US) a journalist specializing in 'human interest' stories.

sob sister *n.* [1910s+] an advice columnist, usu. a woman (cf. AGONY AUNT).

sob story *n.* [1910s+] a pitiful tale, which may reduce the listener to tears whether it has any basis in truth or is designed merely for felonious purposes.

sob stuff *n.* [1910s+] distressing facts, stories etc, often used to obtain sympathy and poss. money too.

soc/soch/sosh *n.* [20C] (US teen) **1** a social climber. **2** one who behaves in a socially acceptable manner. [abbr. SE *social*]

socdollager *see* SOCKDOLAGER.

Social, the *n.* [1970s+] the local office of the Department of Health and Social Security, from where one gets unemployment and other benefits (cf. LABOUR).

social donut hole *n.* [1980s+] (US campus) a socially inept person. [an 'empty space']

social E *n.* [late 19C] (middle class) a euph. for *social evil*, itself coined in 1857 as a euph. for prostitution.

society *n.* [late 19C] the workhouse.

society high *n.* [1930s+] (drugs) cocaine. [SE *society* + HIGH n.; the identification of cocaine as a 'rich people's drug']

society-maddist *n.* [late 19C] a social climber.

sock *n.*[1] **1** [late 17C–18C] a pocket. **2** [mid-late 19C] credit, esp. as *on sock*, on credit. **3** [1930s–50s] a sock used as a receptacle for money. **4** [1930s–50s] the store of money itself, as in a bag, safe etc. **5** [1970s] a filthy, messy room, i.e. as used by a student, young man etc. [(5) was coined by UK novelist Martin Amis (b.1949) and enjoyed brief popularity]

sock *n.*[2] [late 17C–18C] a farthing or any small coin (cf. RAG n.[1]).

sock *n.*[3] **1** [late 17C+] a blow. **2** [1930s+] (US) a thrill, excitement, a 'kick'. [SOCK v.[1]]

sock *adj.* [20C] excellent, first-rate (cf. BOFF n.[1]; BOFFO adj.; SOCKO). [fig. use of SOCK n.[3]]

sock *v.*[1] [late 17C+] to hit, to punch; thus *sock into*, to assault, to beat, *give someone sock*, to give someone a thrashing.

sock *v.*[2] [mid-late 19C] to obtain credit. [SOCK n.[1]]

sock/sock away/down *v.*[3] [1910s–60s] (Aus.) to drink (alcohol). [SOCK v.[1]]

sock/sock away *v.*[4] [1940s+] (orig. US) to set aside money for savings. [SOCK n.[1]]

sock *adv.* [20C] violently, e.g. *hit him sock in the face*. [SOCK v.[1]]

sock away *see* SOCK v.[3], v.[4].

sockdolager / **slockdologer** / **socdollager** / **sockdologer** / **sogdologer** / **stockdolager** *n.* (orig. US) **1** [early 19C+] a knock-down blow, a heavy blow (cf. SOLLICKER). **2** [mid-19C+] anything exceptional. [SOCK v.[1] + ? Irish *dallacher*, the act of blinding or dazing or UK dial. *dallack*, to dress gaudily. The adj. form, *sockdolagizing*, was among the last words that President Abraham Lincoln heard: it is used in the play *Our American Cousin* in a line that was spoken by the cousin himself (Asa Trenchard) at the very moment when Lincoln's assassin fired the fatal shot]

sock down *see* SOCK v.[3].

socker *n.*[1] **1** [late 18C] a thug, a lout. **2** [late 18C] a simpleton, a fool. **3** [late 19C+] a heavy blow. **4** [1930s+] one who hits powerfully. [SOCK v.[1]]

socker *n.*[2] [1940s+] (US) a teenage girl wearing bobby-socks (cf. BOBBY SOXER).

sockeroo *n.* [20C] (orig. US) something very successful, a hit. [SOCK adj. + sfx. -EROO]

socket *n.* [late 17C–18C] the vagina (cf. BLACK HOLE n.[1]). [unattributable but assumed backform. of SOCKET-MONEY]

socketer *n.* [mid-19C] a blackmailer. [SOCKET-MONEY]

socket-money *n.* **1** [late 17C–mid-19C] a dowry. **2** [early 19C] money paid by a man to his wife to placate her after he has been caught in an adulterous affair. **3** [early 19C] the payment given to a prostitute. **4** [mid-19C] hush-money. [SE *socket*, i.e. the vagina + *money*]

sock frock *n.* [1940s] (US Black) one's best suit. [SOCK adj. + joc./assonant use of SE *frock*]

sockhead *n.* [late 18C] **1** a simpleton, a fool. **2** a thug, a lout (cf. SOCKER n.[1]). [SOCK n.[3] + sfx. -HEAD (1)]

sockie *n.* [late 18C] a thug, a lout (cf. SOCKER n.[1]). [SOCK v.[1]]

sock it to *v.* [1960s] (orig. US Black) **1** to have sexual intercourse. **2** to explain. **3** to shock, to surprise; thus excl. *sock it to me!*, amaze me, surprise me. [fig. use of SOCK v.[1]; *sock it to me!* was popularized on TV's *Rowan & Martin's Laugh-In* (1967–73)]

socko *adj.* [1930s+] (esp. show business) wonderful, excellent (cf. BOFFO adj.). [SOCK n.[3]]

sock the clock, to *phr.* [1930s+] to register on the time clock. [SOCK v.[1] + SE *clock*]

so cool *n.* [1980s+] (US campus) southern California (cf. NO COOL). [COOL adj.[3]; a play on the area's self-image]

so crooked they couldn't lie straight in bed *phr.* [1920s+] (Aus.) used of a very untrustworthy person.

sod *n.*[1] **1** [early 19C+] an unpleasant person. **2** [mid-19C+] a sodomite, a male homosexual. **3** [late 19C+] a general term of address, not necessarily pej. (cf. BASTARD; BUGGER n.[1] etc). **4** [1930s+] anything categorized as difficult or annoying to perform. [abbr. SE *sodomite*, but, except in (2), the sexual ref. is coincidental]

sod *n.*[2] [20C] (Aus.) a wet damper, i.e. a flour and water pancake. [abbr. SE *sodden*]

sod *n.*[3] [1920s+] (US campus) a drunkard. [SOD n.[1] + SE *sot*]

sod *v.* [mid-19C+] to *sodomize*. [abbr.]

soda *n.*[1] [1930s+] (Aus.) something easy to accomplish, a simple task, an easy victim. [? faro jargon *soda*, the top card that is exposed before the start of the game; this card is not counted for betting]

soda *n.*[2] [1980s+] (US drugs) a form of injectable cocaine used in Hispanic communities.

sod about *v.* [1950s+] to mess around, to waste time (cf. ARSE ABOUT). [SOD *n.*[1] (1)]

soda cracker *n.* [1990s] (US campus) a White person. [such *crackers* or (UK) water biscuits are light in colour]

sod-all *n.* [1950s+] absolutely nothing (cf. DAMN-ALL). [fig. use of SOD *n.*[1] (4)]

sod-buster *n.* [1930s+] a peasant, a farmer, an unsophisticated rural person. [SE *sod*, a lump of earth + BUST *v.*[1]]

sodden *adj.* [1930s] drunk (cf. LUBRICATED).

sodding *adj.* [late 19C+] a derog. intensifier. [SOD *n.*[1]]

sodgeries *n.* [late 19C] a military exhibition, held in 1890 at the Chelsea Barracks (cf. COLINDERIES). [mispron. of SE *soldier*]

sod it! *excl.* [late 19C+] a general excl. of exasperation, resignation, annoyance etc (cf. BUGGER IT!; FUCK IT!). [SOD *n.*[1]]

sod off! *excl.* [20C] go away! (cf. BUGGER OFF; FUCK OFF!). [SOD *n.*[1]]

so drunk that he opened his shirt collar to piss *phr.* [19C] extremely drunk.

sod's law *n.* [1970s+] a metaphorical 'law' of human experience, in this case the belief that 'if anything can go wrong in any situation, it will' (cf. MURPHY'S LAW). [SOD *n.*[1] (4)]

so dumb she thinks her bottom is just to sit on *phr.* [late 19C+] used of a very stupid (and naïve) woman. [DUMB *adj.*]

sod widow *n.* [1930s+] an actual widow, whose husband has died (cf. GRASS WIDOW). [the corpse is 'under the sod']

sod you! *excl.* [late 19C+] a general excl. of hostility, dismissal. [SOD *n.*[1]]

sofa spud/yam *n.* [1980s+] (US campus) someone who lies around doing nothing (cf. COUCH POTATO). [SE *sofa* + SPUD *n.*[1]/*yam*]

soft *n.*[1] see SOFT MONEY.

soft *n.*[2] [mid-19C+] **1** a weakling (cf. SOFTY). **2** a male homosexual.

soft *adj.* **1** [late 17C+] stupid, dull, foolish (cf. SOFT IN THE HEAD). **2** [mid-19C+] easy, comfortable, requiring no effort. **3** [late 19C] overly kind, easily imposed upon. **4** [1950s+] (W.I. Rasta) unable to cope, impoverished. **5** [1950s+] (W.I. Rasta) not well done, amateurish. **6** [1980s+] (US campus) weak, timid, not able to defend oneself. **7** [1980s+] (US campus) partially or totally intoxicated by drink or drugs.

soft as a whore-lady's heart *phr.* [late 19C–1910s] very hard-hearted.

soft-ass *adj.* [1970s+] (US) weak, ineffectual. [SE *soft* + sfx. -ASS]

soft as shit and twice as nasty *phr.* [late 19C+] a general pej. phr. used of anyone the speaker dislikes.

soft as silk *n.* [20C] (Aus.) milk. [rhy. sl.]

softball *adj.* [1970s+] (US) trivial, not worthy of consideration.

softballs *n.* [1970s] (drugs) barbiturates.

soft bit/time *n.* [20C] (US Und.) a system of imprisonment whereby an inmate must serve 50% of the sentence before becoming eligible for parole. [SOFT *adj.* (2) + BIT *n.*[7]/TIME *n.*]

soft boy *n.* [1980s+] (Black) a homosexual man.

soft butch *n.* [1960s+] (gay) a 'masculine' lesbian with a soft side and gentle demeanour. [SE *soft* + BUTCH *n.*[3]]

soft clothes *n.* [1950s+] (US) civilian clothes, plain clothes.

soft collar *n.* [1900s] (Aus.) an easy job. [SE *soft*, easy + *collar*, to get hold of, or one's wearing of a *soft collar* at work]

soft cop *n.*[1] [1920s+] (Aus.) anything seen as easy, esp. in phr. *be on a soft cop*, to have it easy (cf. SWEET COP). [SOFT *adj.* (2) + COP *v.*[3]]

soft cop *n.*[2] [1980s+] a gullible, well-meaning person, e.g. a community/social worker whose sympathies can be

exploited. [SE *soft* + COP *n.*[1]; the trad. *soft cop/hard cop* interrogation routine]

softcore *adj.* [1960s+] (orig. US) mild, not extreme. [on model of SE *softcore* pornography, titillating but not legally 'obscene']

soften the cough, to *phr.* [1990s] (Irish) to reduce, to 'take down a peg'.

soften up *v.* [1950s+] to break down someone's resistance. [orig. in milit. use]

soft ha'porth *n.* [20C] a weakling, a simpleton. [SOFT *adj.* + SE *ha'porth*]

softhorn *n.* **1** [19C] a donkey, an ass. **2** [mid-19C] a simpleton, a fool. [a donkey has soft ears rather than horns]

softie see SOFTY.

softing loose *n.* [1990s] taking things easy and not doing anything. [one is living a *soft, loose* life]

soft in the head *phr.* [late 18C+] stupid, possibly insane (cf. FAT IN THE HEAD).

soft is your horn *phr.* [early–mid-19C] you're mistaken, lit. 'you're an ass'. [SOFTHORN]

soft-leg *n.* [1950s–70s] (US Black) a woman, esp. an attractive woman.

soft mark *n.* [late 19C+] a gullible victim (cf. EASY MARK). [SOFT *adj.* (1) + MARK *n.*[2] (1)]

soft-mash/-shoes *n.* [20C] (W.I.) a pair of rubber-soled, canvas sneakers. [SE *soft* + *mash*, to crush/*shoes*]

soft money/soft *n.* **1** [mid-19C] notes, bills, paper money; thus *do some soft*, pass counterfeit notes (cf. CRISP). **2** [mid-19C+] (US) currency that is likely to lose its value.

soft number *n.* [1910s+] (orig. milit.) an easy job. [SOFT *adj.* (2) + NUMBER *n.*[3] (3)]

soft pedal *v.* [20C] to play down, to diminish, to keep a low profile.

soft-roed *adj.* [late 19C–1900s] kind-hearted. [SE *soft roe*, the sperm of a male fish]

soft roll *n.* [1940s–50s] a woman who is easy to seduce. [SOFT *adj.* (2) + ROLL IN THE HAY]

soft sawder/sawder to order *n.* [mid-19C] flattery. [SE *solder*, i.e. something malleable]

soft sawder *v.* [mid-19C] to flatter. [SOFT SAWDER *n.*]

soft-sawderer *n.* [mid–late 19C] a flatterer. [SOFT SAWDER *n.*]

soft snap *n.* [mid–late 19C] (US) an easy, pleasant job, a profitable business or undertaking (cf. SOFT SPOT). [SOFT *adj.* (2) + SNAP *n.*[2]]

soft-shoes see SOFT-MASH.

soft soap *n.* [mid-19C+] (orig. US) **1** flattery. **2** an act of flattering someone.

soft soap *v.* [mid-19C+] (orig. US) to flatter, to charm. [SOFT SOAP *n.*]

soft-soft *adj.* [1950s] (W.I.) gullible, easily taken in. [SOFT *adj.* + redup.]

soft spot *n.* [late 19C+] anything, esp. a job, considered easy and enjoyable, undemanding.

soft sucker see SISSY SOFT SUCKER.

soft swing *n.* [1970s+] a partner-swapping party where the only intercourse is performed by couples who arrived together; non-penetrative sex, however, is enjoyed at random. [SE *soft* + SWING *n.*[3]]

soft tack *n.* [mid-19C] (orig. naut.) bread as opposed to biscuits or *hard tack* (cf. TOMMY *n.*[1]).

soft thing *n.* **1** [mid-19C+] an easily duped simpleton. **2** [late 19C+] an easy job, an easy win etc. [SOFT *adj.* (1), (2)]

soft time see SOFT BIT.

soft tommy *n.* [late 18C–19C] white bread. [SE *soft* + TOMMY *n.*[1]]

soft-top *n.* [1940s] (US Black) a padded stool, esp. as found in a bar.

soft touch n. [1940s+] **1** one who can easily be solicited for money. **2** an easy job or sinecure. [SOFT adj. (1) + TOUCH n.³]

softy/softie n. [mid-19C+] a foolish weakling. [SOFT adj. (1)]

sogdologer see SOCKDOLAGER.

soggies n. [1970s+] (society) breakfast cereal. [a hangover from nursery talk]

soggy biscuit n. [1960s] (orig. Aus.) a masturbation game, popular among schoolboys, whereby the participants masturbate and then ejaculate onto a biscuit; the last to reach orgasm must eat the semen-covered biscuit.

so help me baub see S'ELP ME BOB.

s.o.h.f. phr. [1970s+] (society) *sense of humour failure*. [abbr. Often discerned in someone who fails to appreciate the throwing of bread rolls, baiting of minorities etc]

SoHomosexual n. [1980s+] (US) a style of interior design favoured by the chic loft-dwellers of New York City's *SoHo*. [*SoHo* + (*ho*)*mosexual*]

soiled dove n. [late 19C–1960s] (Aus./US) a prostitute. [literary euph.]

so is/so's your old man! excl. [1910s+] (orig. US) an excl. used as a retort to an insult or slur.

soixante-neuf see SIXTY-NINE.

s.o.l. n. [1930s+] (Aus.) a bad temper. [abbr. *shit on one's liver*]

s.o.l. adj. [1980s+] (US campus) unfortunate, unlucky, in a difficult situation. [abbr. *shit out of luck*]

sol adj. [20C] (US Und.) in *solitary confinement*. [abbr.]

solace v. [19C+] to have sexual intercourse (cf. OBLIGE; PLEASE v.).

sold adj. [mid-19C+] tricked, fooled, successfully persuaded. [SELL v.]

soldier n.¹ [19C] **1** a red herring (cf. RED HERRING). **2** a boiled lobster (cf. LOBSTER n.¹). [they both have a 'red coat']

soldier n.² [1960s+] **1** (US Mafia) a lower echelon member of a Mafia family, the run-of-the-mill gangsters who fight the gang wars. **2** (US Und.) a member of a prison gang. **3** (Black) a member of a teen gang.

soldier v. [mid-19C–1910s] (Aus.) to use an animal (usu. a horse) without its owner's knowledge; thus *soldier*, the animal so used. [the practice of soldiers in commandeering private goods]

solder ants n. [20C] pants. [rhy. sl.]

soldier bold n. [mid-19C–1930s] a (head) cold. [rhy. sl.]

soldier's bite n. [late 19C] a large bite (cf. SOLDIER'S BOTTLE). [large military appetites]

soldiers bold adj. [20C] cold. [rhy. sl.]

soldier's bottle n. [late 17C–early 19C] a very large bottle (cf. SOLDIER'S BITE). [orig. naut. jargon; the presumption being that soldiers either drink excessively or need alcohol to fortify their courage]

soldier's farewell n. **1** [late 19C+] goodbye, good luck and fuck you! (cf. BEGGAR'S BENISON). **2** [1930s+] the weekly maintenance paid by the father of an illegitimate child.

soldier's joy n. [mid-19C–1900s] masturbation (cf. PULL ONE'S PUD; SAILOR'S JOY). [note naut. jargon *soldier's joy*, pease pudding]

soldier's maund/mawnd n. [late 17C–18C] (Und.) a fake wound, assumed by beggars who wish to pose as soldiers returned from the wars (cf. RUM MAUND). [SE *soldier* + MAUND n. (2)]

soldier's pomatum n. [late 18C–mid-19C] a piece of tallow or animal-fat candle. [SE *soldier* + *pomatum*, pomade; thus a sneer at soldiers who cannot afford to dress their hair with anything better than tallow]

soldier's supper n. [late 19C+] **1** nothing. **2** a drink of water and a cigarette or pipe (cf. AIR PIE AND A WALK AROUND). [the soldier's last meal of the day was tea; there was no supper]

soldier's thigh n. [mid–late 19C] an empty pocket. [military poverty]

soldier's wash n. [20C] the washing of one's face with a scoop of water in cupped hands rather than using a flannel. [the privations of the battlefield]

sold like a bullock in Smithfield phr. [early–mid-19C] badly cheated (cf. SMITHFIELD BARGAIN). [SOLD; founded in the 12C, Smithfield remains London's main wholesale meat-market, although live animals have not been brought there since 1855]

sold on adj. [1920s+] convinced, fascinated by (cf. SELL v.).

sold out/up adj. [mid-19C+] bankrupt.

soles n. [1970s] (drugs) hashish. [the smuggling of hashish in the soles of purpose-built shoes]

sole-slogger n. [late 19C] a bootmaker. [SE *sole* + SLOGGER n. (2)]

sol-fa n. [late 18C–early 19C] a parish clerk. [SE *sol-fa man*, a music teacher; thus f. the clerk's leading of the sung responses in church]

solicitor general n. [19C] the penis. [a pun on SE *solicit*]

solid n.¹ [20C] (tramp) the road.

solid n.² [1990s] (US Black) a favour, e.g. *do me this solid*, do me this favour. [SE *solid*, something that has substance, thus something dependable]

solid adj. **1** [early 18C+] full, complete, entire, esp. of time, e.g. *a solid month*. **2** [1910s–60s] (Aus./N.Z.) severe, difficult, unfair, unreasonable. **3** [1920s+] (orig. jazz) trustworthy, dependable, exciting, outstanding. [SE *solid*, thorough, downright, vigorous]

solid! excl. [1920s+] (orig. US) a general excl. of approbation, implying a firm bond, honesty, excellence etc.

solid con n. [20C] (US Und.) a trustworthy fellow criminal or prison inmate. [SOLID adj. (3) + CON n.¹ (6)]

solidement! excl. [1980s+] (US campus) an affirmative response. [Fr. *solidement*, solidly]

solid sender n. [1920s+] (US Black) an admirable person, esp. a jazz or swing musician. [SOLID adj. (3) + SEND v.]

solitaire n. [1940s] (US Black) suicide. [SE *solitaire*, a game played by oneself]

solitary n. [mid-19C+] *solitary confinement* in prison. [abbr.]

solitary as a bastard on Father's Day phr. [20C] (Aus.) extremely lonely.

sollicker n. (Aus.) **1** [late 19C+] something notably large, 'a whopper'. **2** [1940s–50s] a large penis. [? SOCKDOLAGER or dial. *sollock*, impetus, force]

Solly n. [late 19C+] a generic term for any Jew. [the once-popular Jewish given name *Solomon*]

solomon/saloman n. [16C] (Und.) an altar or mass; thus *by the solomon! by the saloman!* by the Mass! (cf. SALAMON). [the biblical king, *Solomon*, or Fr. *serment*, an oath. Rowlands notes that while *solomon/salomon* duly means Mass, 'Many men I have heard take this word Solomon to be the chief commander among the beggars. But to put them out of doubt, this is not he. Marry, there was one Solomon in King Henry the Eighth's time that was a jolly fellow among them, who kept his court most an end at Foxhall (Vauxhall) ... who was successor to Cock Lorel. Of him and his successors much is to be spoken ... but here enough']

Solomon Isaac n. [late 19C–1910s] a Jew (cf. SOLLY).

so long phr. [mid-19C+] (orig. + mainly US) goodbye. [? Heb. *shalom*, peace, and used as a basic word of greeting and farewell or Heb. *selah*, God be with you]

solo player n. [late 18C–early 19C] a poor player, on any instrument, whose musicianship immediately empties a room of listeners and leaves them playing without an audience. [pun on SE use, in this case the soloist performs alone whether they wish it or not]

so lucky if he fell in the river he'd only get dusty *phr.* [20C] used of an exceptionally fortunate person.

soma *n.* [1970s] (drugs) phencyclidine (cf. ACE n.³). [Skrt. *soma*, a drug used in Vedic rituals. Note *Soma*, Aldous Huxley's name for the 'happiness' drug used in his novel *Brave New World* (1932) + SOMA, the Society of Mental Awareness, formed in 1967 to campaign for the legalization of cannabis in the UK]

sombitch *see* SON OF A BITCH.

some *n.* [20C] sexual intercourse, esp. in phr. *give me some* (cf. ANY). [euph.]

some *adj., adv.* [early 19C+] (orig. US) very, great, much.

so mean ... *phr.* [20C] (Aus.) a phr. denoting an individual's meanness, and prefaced by *he/she's so mean he/she wouldn't ... include ... give you a light for your pipe at a bushfire, ... give a dog a drink at his mirage, ... give a shout if a shark bit him, ... give a wave if he owned the ocean, ... give you a fright if he was a ghost, ... give you a shock if he owned the powerhouse, ... give a rat a railway pie, ... spit in your mouth if your throat was on fire, ... give you their cold* and *so mean the still have their lunch money from school.*

so mean one wouldn't give you the time of day *phr.* [mid-19C+] used of a very mean person.

some beans *adj.* [mid-19C] (US) impressive, of some account.

some hope! *excl.* [20C] no hope whatsoever, often ext. as *you've got some hope!*

some kind of *phr.* [20C] (US) very good, special.

some mothers do have 'em *phr.* [1920s+] describing a particularly foolish or absurd person.

someone blew out his/her pilot light *phr.* [1970s+] (US campus) referring to anyone considered somewhat odd, intoxicated on drugs etc (cf. LIGHTS ON BUT THERE'S NOBODY HOME).

someone's ass, to be *phr.* [1990s] (US campus) to cause someone's downfall, to destroy someone. [ARSE n.¹ (4)]

someone's muttons *adj.* [20C] (N.Z.) regarded in a very positive light, favoured. [MUTTON n.³ (2)]

some people! *excl.* [20C] a derisory or critical comment by the speaker on the opinions or more likely the activities of others; the details are unspoken but will be a condemnation of what *some people* are doing.

some pig *n.* [1940s–50s] (US Black) talk, conversation.

some pumpkins/punkins *n.* [mid-19C+] (US) anything or anyone of importance (cf. BIG CHEESE).

some stuff *adj.* [late 19C+] (US) impressive, outstanding. [STUFF n.³]

something *n.¹* [mid-19C+] euph. for the obscenity or oath of the speaker's choice.

something *n.²* [20C] (US) a remarkable thing or person, e.g. *She's really something!*

something *adj.¹* [mid-19C+] a general intensifier, usu. neg., e.g. *something cruel, something dreadful.*

something *adj.²* [late 19C+] euph. for *damn well* or *bloody well,* e.g. *I'll do as I something please ... .*

-something *sfx.* [1980s+] of age, a little more than, in a specified decade, e.g. *thirty-something;* thus used in pl. to categorize a generation, *thirty-somethings, twenty-somethings* (cf. -ODD). [the popular 1980s TV show *Thirty-something*]

something damp *n.* [mid-19C–1900s] a drink.

something else *n.* [mid-19C] a coy euph. for hugs and kisses.

something else! *excl.* [20C] an excl. or description of approval or wonder.

something good *n.* [1900s–30s] a good racing tip.

something in socks *n.* [1910s+] a bachelor, a single man, supposedly what 'every woman wants'.

something in the City *n.* [late 19C] a dubious figure, probably a fraudster or even a burglar. [ironic play on SE]

something like *phr.* [early 18C+] a phr. used to emphasize that the 'something' is 'like' what one desires or intends.

something on the ball *phr.* [1910s+] (US) skill, talent, great ability. [baseball imagery]

something short *n.* [mid-19C] a glass of spirits.

something's rotten in Denmark *phr.* [1950s+] (gay) referring to someone who is presumed to have had a sex-change (cf. COPENHAGEN CAPON; DANISH PASTRY). [*Hamlet* I:iv: 'Something is rotten in the state of Denmark']

something the cat brought in *phr.* [1920s+] a distasteful, prob. dirty or unkempt, object or person.

something to shout about/write home about *phr.* [20C] anything worthy of note, exciting, surprising etc.

sometime *n.* [1960s+] (US prison) one who cannot be depended upon. [? the excuse, 'I'll do it sometime, I'll get round to it sometime'; cf. Sp. *mañana*, lit. tomorrow]

sometimey *adj.* [mid-19C+] (US Black) moody, changeable, inconsistent. [i.e. *sometimes* they are this, *sometimes* that]

sommer *adv.* [20C] (S.Afr.) just, merely, simply, without further fuss, used of an action of which the speaker may have had a few doubts but has decided to go ahead and do it, nonetheless. [Afk.]

somnambulance *n.* [1980s+] (US campus) someone who is funny, likeable, eccentric. [play on SE *somnambulance*, sleep-walking]

son *n.* [1990s] (US Black) a general term of address to a man or boy. [UK use, dating from 10C, is SE]

song and dance *n.¹* [late 19C+] an elaborate excuse or account of a situation aimed at persuading or manipulating the listener.

song and dance *n.²* [1910s–30s] a male homosexual. [rhy. sl. *song and dance* = NANCE n.]

song of the thrush *n.* [mid–late 19C] **1** a brush. **2** a brush-off, a rebuff. [rhy. sl.]

sonk *n.* [1950s–60s] (Aus.) an ungainly, clownish figure. [backform. of SONKEY n.]

sonk *v.* [1950s] (N.Z.) to hit, to thump. [SOCK v.¹]

sonkey/sonky *n.* [mid-19C+] **1** a thug. **2** a foolish, clumsy person. [dial. *sonkie*, a man like a sackful of straw]

sonkey/sonky *adj.* [20C] (Aus.) stupid, foolish. [SONKEY n.]

sonno *n.* [1910s+] (Aus.) a general form of address to a man or boy (cf. SON). [SE *son* + sfx. -O]

son of a bitch / sombitch / son-of-a-bitch / sonofabitch / sonuvabitch / sumbitch *n.* [17C] **1** a derog. general term of abuse. **2** a thing, 'it'; thus *sonofabitching, sonofabitch!* (cf. BUGGER n.¹; FUCKER). [coined *c.*1330 in the form *Biche-sone* and in its current form in Shakespeare's *King Lear* (1605). Like a number of otherwise derog. terms (cf. BASTARD; MOTHERFUCKER), it can be used affectionately and of a woman, albeit rarely, as much as of a man. It can also be used as a general non-specific referent meaning 'thing', e.g. *pass the sonofabitch over here*]

sonofagun *n.* [mid-19C+] euph. for SON OF A BITCH. [SE *son* + GONNOF]

sonofagun! *excl.* [20C] a general excl. [SONOFAGUN n.]

son of a sea-cook *n.* [mid-19C+] a general pej., euph. for SON OF A BITCH.

sonofa/sonova *n.* [1950S+] abbr. of SON OF A BITCH.

son of a sow/sow-gelder *n.* [17C–mid-19C] a general pej., euph. for SON OF A BITCH.

son of prattlement *n.* [early 18C–early 19C] a lawyer.

sonova *see* SONOFA.

sonuvabitch *see* SON OF A BITCH.

sook/sookey/sookie/sooky *n.* [1930s+] (Aus./N.Z.) a coward, a crybaby. [dial. *suck*, a stupid fellow]

sooky *adj.* [1930s+] (Aus./N.Z.) cowardly, weak, sentimental. [SOOK]

sool v. (Aus./N.Z.) **1** [late 19C+] to set a dog on. **2** [late 19C+] of a dog, to worry. **3** [20C] to confuse, to fool; thus *soolin' sod*, a hypocrite. **4** [1930s+] (teen) to run. [? dial. *sowl*, to handle roughly or *sowl into*, to attack fiercely]

sool after v. [1930s+] (Aus./N.Z.) to pursue for sexual purposes. [SOOL]

Sooner n.[1] [late 19C+] (US) an Oklahoman. [SE *sooner than*; used of those who attempted to take over a territory before official permission, the main example was in Oklahoma]

sooner n.[2] **1** [late 19C+] (Aus.) a lazy person, one who would 'sooner' loaf around than work or, in context, fight. **2** [20C] a mongrel or any dog that would 'rather feed than fight'; the same applies to cats. **3** [1920s+] (Aus.) a confidence trickster. **4** [1930s–40s] (US Black) a dirty, unkempt person. **5** [1930s–40s] (US Black) dirty, ragged clothes. [all ref. to something or someone that would 'soon as be/sooner do one thing as another']

sooner n.[3] [20C] (US) an illegitimate child (cf. COME-TOO-SOON). [too soon for the wedding]

soon-man/-woman n. [19C] (US Black) a smart, alert, intelligent man or woman.

sooper-dooper see SUPER-DUPER.

soor n.[1] [mid-19C–1930s] a general pej. term. [Hind. *soor*, a pig; pron. 'sewer' and used famously as such by Nancy Mitford's fictional Uncle Matthew (in *The Pursuit of Love*, 1945 *et al.*), although he confuses matters by spelling it 'sewer']

soor n.[2] [20C] (W.I./Guyn.) a useful piece of confidential information, esp. when passed on to ingratiate or flatter. [? SE *swear*, i.e. 'I swear this is true ...']

soot-bag n. [mid-19C] a reticule or small basket.

soother n. [19C] a drink (cf. ALLEVIATOR). [its positive effects]

sooty n. [1950s+] a derog. term for a Black person (cf. COAL n.[2]; SMOKE n.[4]).

sooty jimmy n. [1980s+] (US Black) a Black penis. [SE *sooty* + JIMMY n.[6]]

sop n. [late 16C+] a fool, a simpleton (cf. SOP-CAN; SOPPY). [abbr. SE *milksop*, a weakling, a spiritless person, lit. a piece of bread soaked in milk]

sop-can n. [1950s+] a simpleton, a weakling (cf. SOPPY). [ext. of SOP]

soper see SOPOR.

soph n. [20C] (US) a *soph*omore. [abbr.]

sophead n. [19C] a fool, a simpleton. [SE *sop* + sfx. -HEAD (2)]

sophisticated lady n. [1970s+] (US Black) cocaine. [play on GIRL n.[3] + the 'smart' image of the drug]

sophisticated scum n. [1950s–60s] (US Black) a city-dweller. [self-deprecating irony]

sopor/soaper/soper n. [1980s+] (drugs) any form of barbiturate drug. [brandname of *Sopor*, a form of methaqualone, but note SE *soporific*]

sopped through adj. [late 19C] soaking wet.

soppie/soppies n. [1960s–70s] (S.Afr.) a cinema tea-room or bio-café, a form of cinema at which one can eat snacks while watching a film. [ety. unknown; ? one can SE *sop up* food or drink]

soppy adj. [1910s+] (teen) vapid, naïve, esp. romantic; thus *soppy date*, a sentimentalist, a romantic (cf. SOUPY). [? joc. use of SE *sopping wet*]

soppy ha'porth n. [1930s+] a fool, often used affectionately (cf. SOFT HA'PORTH).

soppy on adj. [1920s+] obsessed with to a foolish extent. [SOPPY]

sore adj. [mid-19C+] (mainly US) angry, irritated.

sore as a boil phr. [20C] (Aus.) very angry, annoyed. [ext. of SORE]

sore as a snouted sheila phr. [1940s+] (Aus.) extremely

angry, as a woman who has been 'stood up'. [SORE + SNOUT v.[1] + SHEILA]

soreback n. [20C] (US) a native of Virginia (cf. HIT-YOUR-BACK). [the supposed hospitality of Virginians, an attitude that is underlined by their constantly slapping one another's backs in camaraderie]

sore-foot n. [20C] (W.I.) any unsightly, continually bandaged sore, irrespective of its position on the body.

sore hand n. [1980s+] (Ulster) a very thick sandwich of bread and jam. [resemblance to a cut hand]

sore-head n. [mid-19C+] (US) a grumpy, irritable person.

sore leg n. [late 19C] **1** a sausage. **2** plum pudding. [the supposed resemblance]

sore piece n. [20C] (Ulster) a troublesome person. [SE *sore* + *piece*, a person]

sore up v. [1920s+] (US) to annoy, to irritate. [SORE]

sorghum n. [1970s] (S.Afr.) a derog. term for a Black person. [the racist response to the replacement of such offensive terms as 'kaffir beer' or 'kaffir corn' by 'sorghum beer' and 'sorghum corn']

sorority n. [1990s] (US campus) a stereotypical sorority member.

sorrel-top n. [late 19C–1910s] (US) a red-headed person. [the reddish colour of SE *sorrel*]

sorrowful tale n. [mid-19C] **1** a prison. **2** three months in prison. [rhy. sl. *sorrowful tale* = gaol]

sorry and sad adj. [1950s+] bad. [rhy. sl.]

sorry-ass adj. [1990s] (US Black) unfortunate, despicable. [SE *sorry*, worthless + sfx. -ASS]

sort n. **1** [mid-19C+] a person, a type, usu. as *bad sort, good sort*. **2** [1910s+] (orig. Aus.) a woman; very occas. applied also to men.

sort/sort out v. **1** [20C] to tease, to 'pull someone's leg'. **2** [1940s+] (orig. Aus.) to deal with, esp. violently.

sorta see SORT OF.

sorted adj. [1980s+] an all-purpose term of approval, worked out, content, satisfactory, supplied with drugs etc.

sort of/sorta phr. [late 18C+] to an extent, in a way (cf. KIND OF).

sort of thing phr. [1930s+] a phr. used to indicate the vagueness or lack of specificity of the statement that has just been made (cf. LIKE; YOU KNOW). [a form of barely conscious verbal punctuation]

sort out see SORT v.

sort out/separate the men from the boys, to phr. [1960s+] to show which individuals in a group are more able, qualified, sophisticated, mature etc.

sorts n. [1950s] (US gambling) marked cards. [? SE *sorted out* or *special sort*]

sorty adj. [late 19C–1900s] **1** of one kind or sort, similar, alike. **2** consisting of various sorts, mixed.

s.o.s. phr.[1] [1940s+] (US) the same thing as usual. [abbr. same old shit]

s.o.s. phr.[2] [1940s+] (US) chipped beef on toast. [SHIT ON A SHINGLE]

s.o.s. phr.[3] [1990s] (US gang) smash on sight, i.e. a contract to murder. [abbr.]

so's Christmas phr. [1930s+] (orig. US) a dismissive phr., usu. directed at someone who promises, *I'm coming* ... (cf. SLOW AS CHRISTMAS).

sosh see SOC.

so-so adj. **1** [early 19C] drunk. **2** [mid–late 19C] menstruating. [euph.]

so-so adv. [1950s+] (W.I. Rasta) only, solely, unaccompanied. [? SE *solo* + redup.]

soss-brangle n. [late 18C–early 19C] a slatternly woman. [SE *soss*, a sloppy mess of food + *brangle*, a muddle]

sossie *see* SAUSIE.

sossled *see* SOZZLED.

so's your Aunt Tilly/Emma/Fanny *phr.* [1930s+] (US) a phr. of dismissal, rejection, 'no way', 'you must be joking'.

so's your old man *see* SO IS YOUR OLD MAN.

sot *adj.* [20C] (W.I.) stupid, silly, foolish. [Fr. *sotte,* foolish + UK dial. *sot,* a fool]

sothead *n.* [20C] a fool, a simpleton. [dial. *sot,* a fool + sfx. -HEAD (1)]

so thin you can smell shit through him *phr.* [late 19C+] a phr. used of a very slim person. [SHIT n.[1] (1)]

s.o.t.s *n.* [1990s] a Wonderbra, designed to enhance a woman's cleavage. [abbr. strap-on *tits*]

sot-weed *n.* [late 18C–early 19C] tobacco. [SE *sot,* a fool or a drunkard + *weed*; the implication being that only such figures smoked]

soul *n.*[1] [late 17C–mid-18C] a drunkard, esp. on brandy.

soul *n.*[2] [1930s+] (orig. US Black) the essential quality of Black being, unavailable, however much aped and pirated, to anyone who is not Black (and American).

soul *adj.* [1930s+] (orig. US Black) Black, used in a variety of combs. for which *see* below. [SOUL n.[2]]

soul-bolt *n.* [mid-19C–1900s] (US/Aus.) a metaphorical 'bolt' that holds the soul, and thus the person, together, esp. in phr. *knock/shake the soul-bolts out of,* to disturb or worry to a substantial degree, *start my soul-bolts!* (cf. SOUL-CASE).

soul brother *n.* [1930s+] (orig. US Black) a fellow Black man (cf. SOUL SISTER). [SOUL adj. + SE *brother*]

soul-case *n.* **1** [late 18C–early 19C] the body; thus *make a hole in one's soul-case,* to wound. **2** [late 19C+] (US/Aus.) one's spirit, usu. in the context of worry, suffering or oppression; thus *worry/belt/sweat the soul-case out of,* to annoy, to drive, to punish (cf. BURST OUT ONE'S SOUL-CASE; SOUL-BOLT).

soul child *n.* [1970s] (US campus) of Black students, anyone with conspicuous Black pride and identity. [SOUL adj. + SE *child*]

Soul City/Soulville *n.* [1960s] (US) Harlem, New York, the centre of Black America. [SOUL adj. + sfx. -CITY/-VILLE]

soul dancing *n.* [1950s+] (US Black) dancing in accordance with the current dance style favoured in the Black community. [SOUL adj. + SE *dancing*]

soul-doctor *n.* **1** [late 18C–19C] a clergyman (cf. SOUL-DRIVER). **2** [1950s] a psychiatrist.

soul-driver *n.* [late 17C–19C] a clergyman (cf. SOUL-DOCTOR).

soul-faker *n.* [late 19C] a member of the Salvation Army. [SE *soul* + FAKER]

soul food *n.* [1960s+] (US Black) food prepared and preferred by the Black community. [SOUL adj. + SE *food*]

souling *n.* [1950s+] (US Black) doing anything well, esp. when playing jazz.

soul kiss *n.* [1950s+] a deep kiss, involving putting one's tongue into one's partner's mouth; thus *soul kiss,* to kiss in this way (cf. FRENCH KISS).

soul language *n.* [1940s+] (US Black) Black American slang. [SOUL adj. + SE *language*]

soul minority *n.* [1960s–70s] (US Black) African Americans considered collectively. [SOUL adj. + SE *minority*]

soul on *phr.* [1960s–70s] (US Black) do your best, keep your Black identity.

soul patch *n.* [1990s] a single tuft of hair worn beneath the lower lip.

soul power *n.* [1960s–70s] (US Black) the political and cultural influence wielded by the Black community. [SOUL adj. + SE *power*]

soul sauce *n.* [1980s+] (US gay) a Black man's semen. [SOUL adj. + SE *sauce*; *see also* SAUCE v.]

soul-searcher *n.* [1900s–10s] a drink. [one of the effects of drunkenness]

soul session *n.* [1960s–70s] (US Black) a gathering of Black people. [SOUL adj. + SE *session*]

soul shake *n.* [1960s+] (orig. US Black) the ritualized shaking and slapping of hands (cf. DAP n.[1]). [SOUL adj. + SE *shake*]

soul sister *n.* [1930s+] (orig. US Black) a Black woman (cf. SOUL BROTHER). [SOUL adj. + SE *sister*]

soul sounds *n.* [1950s–70s] (US Black) music (cf. SOUNDS). [SOUL adj. + SE *sounds*]

soul talk *n.* [1950s–70s] (US Black) a conversation between two or more Black people. [SOUL adj. + SE *talk*]

Soulville *n.*[1] [1950s] (US Black) **1** the Black area of a city or town. **2** Africa. [SOUL n.[2] + sfx. -VILLE]

Soulville *n.*[2] *see* SOUL CITY.

souly *adj.* [1910s] soulful.

sound *n.*[1] **1** [1940s–50s] (US Black) one's point of view. **2** [1950s] (US street gang) conversation, talk.

sound *n.*[2] [1980s+] (Black) a group of reggae or rap artists (cf. RAP n.[5]).

sound/sound on *adj.*[1] [mid-19C+] (orig. US) **1** knowledgeable about, expert in. **2** dependable, trustworthy, of sober judgement (in the view of the speaker).

sound *adj.*[2] [1990s] (teen) excellent, first-rate, totally satisfactory.

sound *v.*[1] [mid-19C] (Und.) to knock on a door to see if the occupants are at home.

sound *v.*[2] **1** [1940s–50s] (US Black) to inform, to tell. **2** [1950s] (street gang) to tease, to taunt, to joke with. [SOUND n.[1]]

sound boy/man *n.* [1970s+] (W.I./UK Black teen) a sound system operator.

sound egg *n.* [1920s–30s] a 'good chap', a 'decent fellow'. [SE *sound* + EGG n.[1] (1)]

sound man *see* SOUND BOY.

sound off/off about *v.* [1910s+] (orig. US) **1** to boast, to brag. **2** to make a noisy fuss, to become angry about a topic or situation.

sound on *adj. see* SOUND adj.[1].

sound on *v.* (US Black) **1** [1950s–60s] to flirt. **2** [1960s+] to compete in ritualized mutual insults (cf. PLAY THE DOZENS).

sounds *n.* [1950s+] (orig. US) music, spec. records.

sounds and tunes *n.* [1970s] (US campus) songs.

sound system *n.* [1970s+] (orig. W.I./UK Black teen) a huge, high-wattage, mobile disco.

sound the bugle! *excl.* [1940s] (US Black) start playing! start the music!

soup *n.*[1] [mid–late 19C] melted silver plate; thus *soup-shop,* a place where such plate is melted down and disposed of.

soup *n.*[2] **1** [late 19C+] (orig. US Und.) gelignite, nitroglycerine, as used in the blowing open of a safe (cf. SOUP MAN). **2** [20C] (US) gasoline, petrol.

soup *v.* [late 19C+] to cause someone to fail. [IN THE SOUP]

soup and fish *n.* [1910s+] a dinner jacket. [the food one eats when wearing it]

soup and gravy *n.* [20C] the Royal Navy (cf. PLAIN AND GRAVY). [rhy. sl.]

souped *adj.* [late 19C+] (Anglo-Irish) in trouble. [IN THE SOUP]

souped-up *adj.* [1930s+] intensified, accelerated, usu. of a car that has been modified by its owner to exceed the basic factory-created performance; thus (US) *soup job,* anything (orig. a car) that is increased, heightened in value, competence or attractiveness. [SOUP n.[2] or racing use *soup,* anything injected into a horse to alter its speed or temperament]

souper *n.*[1] [mid–late 19C] **1** (orig. Irish) a convert from Roman Catholicism to Protestantism. **2** one who scrounges free soup tickets. **3** a Protestant. [such conversions, however nominal, were often achieved by the appeal of Protestant missionaries handing out free soup, orig. at the time of the great famine of 1845–7]

souper *n.*[2] *see* SUPER *n.*[2].

soup jockey *n.* [1930s+] (US) a waiter or waitress. [SE *soup* + JOCKEY *n.*[2] (2)]

soup man *n.* [1960s] a professional villain who specializes in handling nitroglycerine to blow open safes. [SOUP *n.*[2] + SE *man*]

soup-plate track *n.* [1920s+] (Aus.) a small racecourse.

soup-strainer *n.* [1930s+] a large moustache.

soup up *v.*[1] [1930s+] (orig. of engines) to increase in power, to aggrandize in some manner (cf. SOUPED-UP).

soup up *v.*[2] [1980s+] (US) to stimulate a woman's vagina. [the moisture thus produced]

soupy *adj.*[1] [late 19C] very drunk, usu. to the point of vomiting. [SE *soup*, i.e. the vomit]

soupy *adj.*[2] [1910s+] (teen) vapid, naïve, esp. romantic. [var. on SOPPY]

sour *n.* [19C] counterfeit money, apparently silver but made from pewter.

sour-apple quickstep *n.* [1990s] diarrhoea (cf. APPLE-BLOSSOM TWO-STEP).

sourball/sourbelly *n.* [20C] (US) a grumpy person (cf. SOUR-PUSS).

sourcrout *n.* [mid-19C] (US) a German, a German immigrant (cf. KRAUT). [for ety. *see* SAUERKRAUT]

sour cudgel *n.* [early 17C] a severe thrashing.

sourdough *n.* [late 19C+] (orig. Can.) an experienced prospector in Alaska, the Yukon or the Northwest Territories. [the use of sourdough (fermenting dough, esp. that left over from a previous baking, used as leaven) in the making of bread in mining camps. Allegedly, the need to keep this warm meant that, on cold nights, the miners would sleep with a lump]

sour on *adj.* [late 19C] (Aus./US) hostile towards.

sour on *v.* [mid-19C+] (orig. US) to become hostile towards.

sourplanter *n.* [19C] a distributor of counterfeit money; thus *plant the sour*, to spread around such 'money'. [SOUR + SE *planter*]

sourpuss *n.* [1930s+] (orig. US) a sour-faced person, a grumbler, a killjoy (cf. DRIZZLEPUSS; SOURBALL). [SE *sour* + PUSS *n.*[3]]

souse *n.* [20C] **1** a drunkard (cf. SOAK *n.*). **2** a drinking bout. [SOUSE *v.*]

souse *v.* [20C] to drink heavily, to become drunk. [SE *souse*, to marinate, to soak with water]

souse-crown *n.* [late 17C–18C] a fool. [lit. a 'drunken head']

soused *adj.* [17C+] drunk (cf. ALED UP; LUBRICATED). [SOUSE *v.*]

soused to the gills *phr.* [20C] (US) very drunk (cf. FULL TO THE GILLS; LIT TO THE GILLS). [ext. of SOUSED]

soush *n.* [mid-19C] a house. [backsl.]

South, the *n.* [late 19C–1910s] the *South* London Music Hall. [abbr.]

south *adj.* [19C+] used in var. phr. to mean downwards, e.g. DIP SOUTH; GO DOWN SOUTH; GO SOUTH *v.*[2]; IT'S SNOWING DOWN SOUTH; PUT DOWN SOUTH; SOUTH POLE.

South County Indian *n.* [20C] a Portuguese immigrant to the US. [South County, Rhode Island, such immigrants have congregated]

Southend-on-Sea *n.* [20C] urination. [rhy. sl. *Southend-on-Sea* = PEE *n.*[1]]

Southend pier *n.* [20C] an ear. [rhy. sl.]

southerly buster/burster *n.* [20C] (Aus.) **1** the cool, gusty wind that springs up at the end of a hot day, sometimes accompanied by a shower. **2** a cocktail.

southern can *n.* [1930s–50s] (US Black) the buttocks. [SE *southern* + CAN *n.*[4]]

south of France *n.* [late 19C+] a dance. [rhy. sl.]

south of the border *phr.* [20C] (US) second-rate, a failure. [the *border* between the US and Mexico; thus racist stereotyping]

southpaw *n.* (orig. US baseball) **1** [mid-19C+] the left hand. **2** [late 19C+] a left-hander, esp. in boxing (cf. NORTHPAW). [SOUTH *adj.* + PAW *n.*[1] (1)]

southpaw *adj.* [late 19C+] left-handed. [SOUTHPAW *n.*]

south pole *n.* **1** [19C] the vagina (cf. ANTIPODES). **2** [20C] the anus. [rhy. sl. *south pole* = HOLE *n.*[1] (1), (2)]

south sea/south sea mountain *n.* [early 18C–early 19C] gin, or any other strong liquor. [? the *South Sea Bubble*, a financial scandal of 1727. The effects of gin, like that of the Bubble, are to promote deleterious fantasies]

south Sydney *n.* [20C] (Aus.) a kidney. [rhy. sl.]

soutie *n.* [1940s+] (S.Afr.) an Englishman who retains his colonialist mentality. [abbr. SOUTPIEL]

soutpiel *n.* [1970s+] (S.Afr.) an Englishman, esp. one who has a notably colonialist mentality. [Afk. *sout*, salt + *piel*, penis; thus lit. 'salt-dick', because he has one foot in South Africa, one in England and his penis dangling in the ocean in between. Despite the date, as cited in *DSAE*, it must be assumed that the term is much older, but left unprinted through taboo; thus Namibian synon. *sandpiele*, in this case the penis rests on the burning sands of the Kalahari desert]

souvenir *v.* [1910s+] to steal (cf. ACQUIRE). [orig. WW2 milit. use]

souvenir egg *n.* [late 19C] (US) an old, rotten egg.

sov/sob *n.* [early 19C+] a sovereign, £1 sterling. [abbr.; *sob* is mispron.]

so very human *phr.* [late 19C] (society) a generalized (and ironic) excuse for a variety of failings.

Sovs *n.* [1960s–80s] the *Soviets*, the Russians. [abbr.]

sow *n.*[1] [late 18C+] a fat woman (cf. DRUNK AS DAVID'S SOW).

sow *n.*[2] [1930s–40s] (US Black) any coin, esp. a nickel (5 cents). [on pattern of UK GRUNTER *n.*[2]; HOG *n.*[1]; SOW'S BABY, but no apparent connection]

sow-belly *n.* [mid-19C+] (US) a side of salted pork.

so what? *phr.* [1930s+] widely used term of disinterest or defiance, a rejoinder to the previous speaker's announcement, revelation etc.

so what else is new? *phr.* [1950s+] (US) a dismissive rejoinder. [imitative of Yid. idiom, e.g. 'I'm late with my tax' 'So who needs taxes?'; the comment 'well in that case', 'very well' is assumed]

sow's baby *n.* **1** [late 17C–late 18C] a sucking pig. **2** [mid-19C] sixpence (2½p) or a shilling (5p) (cf. GRUNTER *n.*[2]; PIG *n.*[2]). [i.e. it is smaller than a HOG *n.*[1] (1)]

soy pucks *n.* [20C] (US prison) prison-cooked hamburgers. [resemblance]

sozzle *n.* [20C] human excrement. [? dial. *sossle*, a liquid mess]

sozzle *v.* [1930s–50s] to drink heavily. [backform. of SOZZLED]

sozzled/sossled *adj.* [late 19C+] drunk (cf. BASTED). [SOUSE *v.*]

s.p. *n.* [1950s+] basic information, facts. [orig. racing jargon *starting price*]

spa *adj.* [1980s+] (Irish) crazy, inept, socially unacceptable. [abbr. SPASTIC]

space *v.*[1] [1960s] (US Black) to leave, to depart. [SE *make a space*]

space *v.*[2] *see* SPACE OUT.

space bandit *n.* [1940s+] (US) a press agent. [the unscrupulous manner in which agents gain newspaper space for their clients]

space base/dust *n.* [1980s+] (drugs) a cigar stuffed with a mixture of phencyclidine and crack cocaine (cf. BLUNT *n.*[2]; SPACE CADET). [SPACED OUT + BASE/SE *cadet*/SE *dust* + play on the 1980s sweet Space Dust]

space cadet *n*. **1** [1970s+] (drugs) any heavy user of drugs, esp. cannabis or hallucinogens. who is continually 'flying'. **2** [1970s+] (US) a mad or eccentric person. **3** [1980s+] (drugs) a cigar stuffed with a mixture of phencyclidine and crack cocaine (cf. SPACE BASE). [pun on SE/SPACED OUT]

space-cake *n*. [20C] a cake augmented by hashish or marijuana (cf. HASH-CAKE). [SPACED OUT + SE *cake*]

space case *n*. [1980s+] a crazy person (cf. SPACE CADET). [SPACED OUT + SE *case*]

spaced out/spaced *adj*. [1960s+] **1** intoxicated by a drug, esp. a hallucinogen. **2** generally disorientated, with or without drugs. [the image of 'flying']

space dust *see* SPACE BASE.

space opera *n*. [1970s+] (US) an SF or outer space drama film. [on model of HORSE OPERA; SOAP OPERA]

space out/space *v*. [1960s+] (US) to daydream, to drift off, often under the influence of drugs. [one 'flies' into space]

spacer *n*. [1980s+] (Irish) a streetwise young person. [SPACED OUT; the underlying implication is of their probable drug-taking]

space ship *n*. [1980s+] (drugs) a glass pipe used to smoke crack cocaine. [SPACE OUT + play on SE]

spacey *n*. [1970s+] (drugs) anything that simulates the intoxication of LSD or other hallucinogens

spacey *adj*. [1970s+] (drugs) **1** of an experience or event, generally disorientating, with or without drugs. **2** of a person, disorientated, whether through drug use or not. [SPACED OUT]

spacies *n*. [1980s] (N.Z.) the video/computer game *Space Invaders*. [abbr.]

spacka/spacker *n*. [1990s] a general term of abuse. [abbr. SPASTIC]

spackahead *n*. [1990s] a fool, an eccentric (cf. HONCH-HEAD). [SPASTIC + sfx. -HEAD (1)]

spacker *see* SPACKA.

spacy *adj*. [1960s+] **1** in a daze, out of touch with reality, eccentric. **2** exhibiting characteristics actually or fig. reminiscent of those experienced when taking a hallucinogen. [SPACED OUT]

spade *n*. [1920s+] (orig. US) a Black person, esp. West Indian or African; thus *spadelet*, a Black child. [SE phr. *black as the ace of spades*; *spadelet*, a nonce-word, found only in Colin MacInnes, *Absolute Beginners* (1959); poss. derog. in the US, it is seen as a neutral/affectionate term in the UK]

spadet *n*. [1980s+] (US campus) a student who is preoccupied with studies. [? SPACE CADET (2)]

spadger *n*. **1** [late 19C] a boy. **2** [1990s] (Aus.) the vagina. [dial. *spadger*, a sparrow; (1) thereafter historical use]

spag *n*.[1] [1950s+] (Aus.) a sparrow. [dial. *spadger*]

spag *n*.[2] [1960s+] (society) spaghetti; thus *spag bog*, spaghetti bolognese (usu. in some adulterated British version). [abbr., a retained juv. use]

spag/spaggie *n*.[3] [1960s+] (Aus.) an Italian. [abbr. SE *spaghetti*, a staple Italian food]

spa-gag-me *n*. [20C] (US prison) prison-cooked spaghetti (cf. LEAD PIPE). [abbr. SE *spaghetti* + *gag*, to choke]

spag fag *n*. [1990s] (gay) one who prefers Italian partners. [SPAG n.[2] + FAG n.[5]; play on FAG-HAG n.[2]]

spaggers *n*. [1960s+] spaghetti. [SPAG n.[2] + 'Oxford' sfx. *-er*]

spaggie *see* SPAG n.[3].

spaghetti *n*.[1] [1930s+] (orig. US) an Italian (cf. SPAG n.[3]). [stereotyping]

spaghetti *n*.[2] [1980s+] the collection of wires linking amplifiers, record decks, computer hardware etc.

spaghetti bender *n*. [20C] an Italian (cf. SPAGHETTI n.[1]).

spaghetti corner *n*. [1950s+] (US) an Italian community within an urban area.

spaghetti head *n*. [20C] (US) an Italian (cf. SPAGHETTI BENDER).

spaghetti junction *n*. [1960s] a complex of motorways forming a multi-levelled interchange, esp. the Gravelly Hill interchange between the M1 and M6 outside Birmingham, UK.

spaghetti western *n*. [1970s+] (US) a cowboy film, usu. made in Europe by Italian directors.

spagingy-spagade/spaginzy *n*. [1900s–20s] (US Black) a Black person. [pig Latin for SPADE]

spalpeen *n*. [early 19C+] a rogue, a rascal. [Irish *spailpín*, a low or mean fellow, orig. a casual farm labourer]

spam javelin *n*. [1990s] the penis (cf. BACON BAZOOKA).

spammed up *n*. [1990s] (US teen) a hairstyle that is heavily greased then parted in the centre.

span *n*. [1960s+] (S.Afr., mainly teen) a lot, very much. [fig. use of SAfE *span*, a team of oxen]

span *adj*. [1980s+] (Irish) new. [abbr. SE *spic and span*; ult. ON *spán-nýr*, chip-new]

spang *adv*. [mid-19C+] (orig. US) absolutely, entirely, e.g. *right spang in the middle*. [? SPANK v.[1]]

spangle *n*. [19C] a 7-shilling piece. [SE *spangle*, i.e. its glitter and shininess]

spaniard *n*. [1940s–50s] (Can.) a louse, a flea. [? neg. stereotyping]

Spanish, the *n*.[1] [late 18C–early 19C] cash, ready money.

Spanish *n*.[2] [late 18C–early 19C] sack (cf. ENGLISH n.[3]). [SE *sack*, a type of white wine produced in Spain and the Canary Islands]

Spanish *n*.[3] [mid–late 19C] a *Spanish* onion. [abbr.]

Spanish archer, the *n*. [1980s+] dismissal, rejection (cf. KING OF SPAIN'S TRUMPETER). [pun on cod Spanish *El Bow*; thus cf. ELBOW v.[2]]

Spanish coin *n*. [late 18C–mid-19C] empty compliments and meaningless courtesies (cf. SPANISH MONEY). [stereotyping of the Spanish as impeccably courteous but deeply untrustworthy]

Spanish cure *n*. [20C] treatment of drug addiction by forced, total abstinence. [? as used in Spain]

Spanish faggot *n*. [late 18C–mid-19C] the sun. [the stereotype of the Spanish Inquisition; the sun burns, as did the Inquisition]

Spanish gout/needle *n*. [late 17C–early 19C] venereal disease, syphilis (cf. SPANISH POX). [reflecting the contemporary role of Spain as the national enemy. This was soon replaced by France; cf. FRENCH CROWN etc, although the old term lingered into 19C]

Spanish guitar *n*. [20C] (US) a cigar. [rhy. sl.]

Spanish machete *n*. [late 19C+] (W.I.) a hypocrite (cf. BACK-AND-BELLY n.[2]). [the Spanish machete has a two-edged blade and thus 'cuts both ways']

Spanish main *n*. [20C] a drain. [rhy. sl.]

Spanish money *n*. [late 17C–18C] empty compliments and meaningless courtesies (cf. SPANISH COIN). [stereotyping of the Spanish as impeccably courteous but deeply untrustworthy]

Spanish needle *see* SPANISH GOUT.

Spanish onion *n*. [20C] a bunion. [rhy. sl.]

Spanish padlock *n*. [late 16C–mid-19C] a chastity belt.

Spanish pox *n*. [late 17C–18C] venereal disease, syphilis (cf. SPANISH GOUT). [SE *Spanish* + POX n.[1]]

Spanish rice *n*. [1960s] (gay) lumpy semen.

Spanish supper *n*. [1940s–50s] (US) no supper at all or very little supper (cf. MEXICAN BREAKFAST).

Spanish time *n*. [1990s] (Aus.) unpunctuality (cf. AFRICAN PEOPLE'S TIME). [the Spanish, stereotypically, are reputed to maintain a flexible attitude to appointments]

Spanish trumpeter *n*. [late 18C–mid-19C] a donkey (cf. KING OF SPAIN'S TRUMPETER). [pun on SE *Don Key/donkey*]

Spanish tummy *n*. [1960s+] a form of stomach upset experienced by tourists to Spain (cf. APPLE-BLOSSOM TWO-STEP).

Spanish waiter n. [20C] a potato. [rhy. sl. (Cockney pron. 'potater')]

Spanish walk n. [late 19C] (US) a constrained style of walking assumed, willy-nilly, by those who are being ejected from a bar or saloon (cf. FRENCH WALK). [? the way Spanish pirates supposedly forced their prisoners to walk on tiptoes while they were held by the scruff of the neck, or the tip-toeing gait of flamenco dancers]

Spanish worm n. [late 18C–early 19C] a nail found embedded in a piece of wood that one is sawing. [contemporary dislike of Spain]

spank n.[1] [early 18C–mid-19C] a gold or silver coin. [SPANKER n.[1]]

spank n.[2] **1** [late 18C] a slap with an open hand. **2** [early 19C] the breaking of a shop window before grabbing whatever can be reached.

spank v.[1] **1** [early 18C] to slap. **2** [early 19C] (Und.) to rob a shop by breaking its window and grabbing whatever is within reach. **3** [late 19C–1940s] (N.Z.) to milk a cow. **4** [1960s+] to beat up. **5** [1960s+] to beat comprehensively in a sport or game. [later use of (1) is SE]

spank v.[2] **1** [early–mid-19C] to move smartly, briskly and stylishly, esp. when seated on horseback. **2** [mid-19C] to crack a whip. **3** [mid-19C] to drive a horse stylishly and fast. **4** [1980s+] (US teen) to masturbate in the shower (cf. SHOWER SPANK).

spank v.[3] [20C] in var. combs. meaning, of a man, to masturbate; thus *spank the bishop*, ... *the carrot*, ... *the donkey*, ... *frank*, ... *one's monkey*, ... *one's little boy*, ... *the plank*, ... *the salami*, ... *the tank*, ... *wank.*

spank a/the glaze, to phr. [early 19C] (Und.) to break a shop window, reach in and grab whatever one can reach, having previously tied up the shop door so the shopkeeper cannot pursue (cf. SNAP THE GLAZE). [SPANK v.[1] (2) + GLAZE n.]

spanker n.[1] [late 17C–late 18C] a gold coin. [dial. *spank*, to sparkle]

spanker n.[2] [mid-18C–late 19C] **1** anything exceptional or particularly admirable of its type (cf. BUMPER n.[1]). **2** a fast horse (cf. SPANK v.[2]).

spanker n.[3] [late 18C–late 19C] a hard, resounding slap or blow.

spanker adj. [mid-17C] large, first-class, showy (cf. SPANKING adj.).

spankhead n. [1990s] a general term of abuse (cf. WANKER) [SPANK ONE'S MONKEY]

spanking n. [1960s+] a beating. [SPANK v.[1]]

spanking adj.[1] **1** [late 17C+] large, first-class, showy. **2** [mid-18C–late 19C] of horses, moving fast or vigorously. **3** [early 19C] of people, dashing, lively.

spanking adj.[2] [late 19C+] very, exceedingly; thus *brand spanking new.*

spank the glaze see SPANK A GLAZE.

spanky adj. [late 19C–1930s] smart, esp. when overly so. [SPANKING adj.[1]]

spanners n. [1950s+] (Aus.) a sexually provocative woman. [she 'tightens your NUTS n.[2]']

spar n.[1] [mid-19C] an argument. [SE *spar*, to practise boxing]

spar n.[2] [1960s+] (orig. W.I.) a friend (cf. SPEE). [SE *sparring partner*]

sparagrass see SPARROW-GRASS.

sparaser see SPRARSER.

spare n.[1] [1900s] the fly of a man's trousers. [dial. *spare*, a slit in the front of a garment]

spare n.[2] **1** [1940s] (US Black) a friend. **2** [1960s+] an unattached woman, considered to be open to male sexual advances, esp. as *bit of spare.*

spare adj. **1** [1910s+] idle, useless, superfluous. **2** [1940s+] (orig. milit.) overwrought, distraught.

spare boy n. [1920s+] (Aus. rural) treacle, golden syrup. [ety. unknown; ? the sugar gives one extra energy, the equivalent of an assistant]

spare me/my days! excl. [1910s+] (Aus./N.Z.) a general excl.

spare prick at a wedding phr. [1930s+] anything or anyone considered absolutely useless. [PRICK n. (2)]

sparesie see SPRARSER.

spare the crows! see STONE THE CROWS!

spare tire see SPARE TYRE.

spare tongue n. [1960s] (mainly lesbian) the clitoris.

spare tyre/tire n. **1** [1920s+] the roll of flesh that surrounds an overweight stomach (cf. BAGELS). **2** [1940s+] (US) an unwelcome or irrelevant person, a boring person.

spark v.[1] [19C] (US) to pay court to, to make love to, to play the suitor. [SE *spark*, a beau, lover or suitor]

spark v.[2] [late 19C+] (Aus. Und.) to watch carefully. [? SE *spark*, a beau, i.e. a womanizer, who watches women intently]

spark v.[3] [1950s+] to respond to a stimulus. [electrical imagery]

spark v.[4] [1970s+] (Black) to light a tobacco or cannabis cigarette. [the *spark* of one's lighter flint]

sparkers adj. [1930s+] asleep, exhausted (cf. SPARKO). [SPARK OUT]

spark it up v. [1970s+] (drugs) to smoke marijuana. [SPARK v.[4]]

spark jiver n. [1950s] (US Black) an electric organ. [SE *spark*, i.e. electricity + JIVE v.[1]]

sparkle n. [1930s+] **1** a diamond. **2** (Und.) jewels. [appearances notwithstanding, this use has no link other than homonymic with the mid-15C–late 17C SE *sparkle*, a small ruby or diamond]

sparkle plenty n. [1960s–70s] (drugs) amphetamine (cf. A n.[2]; SPARKLER n.[3]). [*Sparkle Plenty*, a character in the *Dick Tracy* comic strip by Chester Gould (1900–85)]

sparkler n.[1] **1** [mid-18C–mid-19C] a bright or sparkling eye. **2** [early 19C+] jewellery, spec. diamonds.

sparkler n.[2] [early 19C+] a lie. [? it shines out of the rest of one's conversation, but note dial. *spark*, a spot of dirt]

sparkler n.[3] **1** [19C] a drink of liquor. **2** [1970s] (drugs) amphetamine (cf. A n.[2]; SPARKLE PLENTY). [they both help the consumer 'sparkle']

sparkle up v. [mid–late 19C] to hurry up, to 'get on with' things.

sparko adj. [1970s+] asleep, exhausted. [var. on SPARKERS]

spark out v. [1930s+] to fall fast asleep. [electrical imagery]

spark plug n. [1940s+] (US) one who sets events or plans in motion, a facilitator; thus *spark plug*, to initiate, to spur on (cf. LIVE WIRE).

spark-prop n. [late 19C–1920s] (Und.) a diamond pin or tie-pin. [SPARK n. + PROP n.[3]]

sparks n.[1] [late 19C–1930s] diamonds, precious stones in general. [SPARK n.]

sparks n.[2] [1910s+] an electrician, usu. theatrical and film use.

sparrer n. [19C] a boxer or sparring partner. [SE *spar*]

sparring bloke n. [mid–late 19C] a sparring partner. [SE *spar* + BLOKE]

sparrow n.[1] [19C] a prostitute (cf. SPADGER). [FLUTTER n.[1]]

sparrow n.[2] [late 19C] a tip, as given to a dustman or milkman or any regular provider of services to one's door. [note dustman's jargon *sparrow*, anything saleable, e.g. a silver spoon or thimble, found in a dustbin]

sparrow n.[3] [20C] (Aus.) a physically weak individual. [SE *flutter*]

sparrow-brain n. [1930s+] a person of little or no intelligence (cf. BAKEBRAIN).

sparrow-cheater n. [late 19C–1900s] a boy who cleans horse-dung from the streets with a brush and dustpan (cf. SPARROW-STARVER). [the bird's appetite for horse-dung]

sparrow cop n. [late 19C–1960s] (US) a park policeman. [a duty often allotted officers currently out of favour with their superiors]

sparrow-fart n.[1] [late 19C+] dawn (cf. AT SPARROW-CROW; AT SPARROW'S FART).

sparrow-fart n.[2] **1** [1920s+] an unimportant person. **2** [1920s+] (Irish) an irritable child. [its insignificance]

sparrow-grass/sparagrass n. [late 19C+] asparagus. [the word, based on the 16C–18C *sparagus*, was SE mid-17C–mid-19C, but dropped into sl. thereafter]

sparrowhawk v. [1960s+] to pick up homeless youngsters of either sex for sexual exploitation, esp. runaways who have just arrived at rail or bus stations (cf. CHICKEN-HAWK). [the predatory bird]

sparrow-mouth n. [late 17C–1900s] a very large mouth. [the bird's anatomy]

sparrow-starver n. [1950s–60s] (Aus.) a street-cleaner (cf. SPARROW-CHEATER). [*sparrows* peck at garbage]

sparrow tail n. [19C] a tail-coat, as worn as part of full evening dress (cf. SWALLOW TAIL). [the shape of the tails]

sparzer see SPRARSER.

spasm band n. [1900s–20s] (US Black) a spontaneously assembled musical group, playing on homemade instruments (washtubs, washboards etc); the precursors of the SKIFFLE groups of the 1950s. [the jerky, arrhythmical sounds of the makeshift instruments]

spasm chasm n. [1990s] the vagina. [the SE *spasm* is that of orgasm]

spas/spaz n. [1960s+] (student/school) one who is useless, clumsy, incompetent and is thus socially unacceptable. [SE *spastic*, one who suffers from spastic paralysis, i.e. 'a condition in which some muscles undergo tonic spasm (sometimes resulting in abnormal posture) ... so that voluntary movement of the part affected is difficult and poorly coordinated' (*OED*)]

spas/spaz/spas out/spaz out v. [1980s+] to act foolishly, to lose control, to act in an uncoordinated manner – either mentally or physically. [SPAS n.]

spaso n. [1970s+] (Aus.) a spastic, either actual or as a derog. term fig. [SPAS n. + sfx. -O]

spas out see SPAS v.

spastic adj. [1960s+] **1** convulsed with laughter and thus incapable of coherent mental or physical activity. **2** [1960s+] uncoordinated, socially unacceptable. [SE *spastic*, afflicted by spastic paralysis, characterized by sudden muscle spasm; (2) generally considered unacceptable since it is, in effect, a derog. attack on those who suffer this paralysis]

spat n. **1** [early 19C+] (orig. US) a tiff, a dispute, a quarrel. **2** [19C] a smart blow, smack or slap. **3** [late 19C] a sharp, smacking sound. [echoic]

spatter v. [1940s+] to beat up severely.

spawny adj. [20C] lucky. [ety. unknown. ? link to Scot. game *spawnie*, played with buttons, in which one player throws a button, the others attempt to throw theirs nearest to it, and the button that comes within a *spawn* (SE span) is the winner]

spaz see SPAS.

spaza/spaza shop/sphaza/ sphaza shop n. [1980s+] (S.Afr. township) an illicit (thus 'camouflaged') or latterly informal grocery or general store. [Ngwenya *spaza*, camouflaged]

spaz out see SPAS v.

spaz pads n. [1970s+] orthopaedic shoes. [SPAS n. + SE *pads*]

spazwheels n. [1990s] a wheelchair. [SPAZ n. + WHEELS n.[1]]

spaz-wit n. [1980s+] a fool, an idiot. [SPAZ n. + sfx. *-wit*]

spazzy adj. [1960s+] stupid, uncontrolled, bizarre, intense. [SPAZ n.]

speak n. [1920s–30s] (US) an illicit drinking establishment. [abbr. SPEAKEASY]

speak v. (Und.) **1** [late 18C–early 19C] to hold up. **2** [late 18C–early 19C] to arrest. **3** [early 19C] to commit a robbery; thus *rum speak*, an especially lucrative robbery (cf. MAKE A SPEAK).

speak a/one's piece, to phr. [mid-19C+] (orig. US) to make oneself heard, to say what one has decided to say, esp. for moral reasons (cf. SAY ONE'S PIECE).

speak bandog and Bedlam, to phr. [late 16C–early 17C] to fall into a rage, to act like a madman. [BANDOG + SE *Bedlam*, Hospital of St Mary of Bethlehem, London, celebrated as the capital's main lunatic asylum]

speak brown tomorrow, to phr. [late 19C] to get sunburned.

speakeasy n. [late 19C+] (US) an illicit drinking establishment. [SE *speak* + *easy*, speak softly, e.g. the tone of voice in which one addressed the look-out or in which the patrons were urged to talk in case the police were at the door; the *speakeasy* appeared *c*.1890, when it meant an illicit liquor shop or an unlicensed bar. The advent of Prohibition (1920–33) elevated the once-marginal institution into the mainstream of US life]

speaker n. [1930s–40s] (US Black) a gun. [its noise]

speak French v. [20C] to indulge in unconventional sexual play. [FRENCH adj.]

speak holiday v. [late 16C–early 17C] to speak elegant, formal English. [SE *holiday*; thus the image of one's 'best' language]

speak like a book, to phr. [mid-19C+] to appear well-educated and literate (cf. TALK LIKE A BOOK).

speak like a mouse in cheese, to phr. [late 18C–early 19C] to speak quietly or indistinctly.

speako n. [1920s–30s] (US) an illicit drinking establishment. [SPEAKEASY]

speak one's piece see SPEAK A PIECE.

speak/talk pretty v. [late 19C] to speak in an affectionate, friendly manner.

speak proper v. [20C] to talk in Standard English, rather than in colloq., dial. or sl., often as an imper. (cf. PROPER adv.). [abbr. *speak proper English* or, thus ironically, misusing *proper* in place of *properly*]

speak Spanish v. [early–mid-19C] (Aus.) to have money. [the *Spanish dollar*, the basic currency of the early years of the Australian colony, worth 5s (25p); other contemporary coins were the *colonial dollar*, worth 75% of the Spanish one, and the *dump*, worth 25%]

speak/talk on/to the great white telephone, to phr. [1960s+] (orig. US) to vomit (cf. TALK TO RALPH ON THE BIG WHITE TELEPHONE).

speak the same language, to phr. [1930s+] to share the same sentiments.

speak to v. [early 19C] (Und.) to rob. [ext. of SPEAK v.]

speak to a tatler see NIM A TATLER.

speak white v. [1950s+] (Can.) used by English speakers, to speak English (as opposed to French, which is the first language of many Canadians, esp. the Québecois).

speak with v. [18C] to rob (cf. SPEAK v.; SPEAK TO). [ironic euph. Note 20C 'I'll make him an offer he can't refuse', I'll threaten him]

speaky n. [late 19C] the proceeds of a robbery. [SPEAK v.]

spear n.[1] [1900s–40s] (Aus.) dismissal from a job; thus *get the spear*, to be dismissed (cf. SHAFT n.[3]).

spear n.[2] [1980s+] (US drugs) a branch of marijuana, 15–35cm (6–14in) long, weighing several ounces.

spear v. **1** [1900s–40s] (Aus.) to dismiss from a job. **2** [1900s–40s] (Aus.) to throw out of a pub, dance-hall etc. **3** [1910s–40s] (US) to beg, to obtain through begging. **4** [1960s+] (US prison) to arrest.

spear a job, to phr. [20C] (Aus.) to get a job.

spear-carrier n. [1960s+] **1** a proponent, an advocate. **2** an insignificant person. [theatrical jargon *spear-carrier*, an actor with a walk-on and thus minor (non-speaking) role]

spearchucker n. [1960s+] **1** (US) a derog. term for a Black person. **2** (US campus) a college student, a young adult. [the image of the African tribesman as (1) a 'primitive', (2) a young warrior]

spearo n. [1960s–70s] (Aus.) a spear-fisherman.

spear the bearded clam, to phr. [1960s+] (Aus.) to have sexual intercourse with a woman (cf. BANG v.¹). [SE *spear* + BEARDED CLAM]

spear the hairy doughnut, to phr. [1990s] to have sexual intercourse with a woman. [SE *spear* + HAIRY DOUGHNUT]

spec n. [late 18C–late 19C] a business, a commercial enterprise. [SE *speculation*]

spechie n. [1980s+] (W.I./UK Black teen) a gun, particularly a .38 special. [SE *special*]

special n. [1970s+] a prostitute's client who has any particular tastes, costumes, bondage, fetishes etc.

special adj. [early–mid-19C] especially interested or informed.

Special/vitamin K n. [1980s+] **1** (drugs) ketamine (cf. K n.⁴). **2** a heroin-based hallucinogen. [the breakfast cereal *Special K*, supposedly an adjunct to better health]

Special K pinches n. [1980s+] (US campus) bulges of fat around the waist. [the 1980s+ advertisements for *Special K* cereal, which feature such bulges or their lack]

special la coke n. [1980s+] (drugs) ketamine (cf. K n.⁴). [ety. unknown]

specimen n. [mid-19C+] a human being, esp. in pej. use, e.g. a *queer specimen, an odd specimen.*

speck n.¹ [mid-19C] (costermonger) a decaying orange. [it has *specks* of mould]

Speck, the n.² [1930s+] (Aus.) Tasmania (cf. FLY SPECK). [its relatively small (to mainland Aus.) size]

speck n.³ [1970s] (US Black) a Black person. [? abbr. SE *speck of dirt*; if so then used ironically]

speck bum n. [20C] (US tramp) a very decrepit, alcoholic tramp (cf. STUMBLEBUM). [SE *speck*, a contemptible person + BUM n.³]

specked wiper n. [late 17C–late 19C] a coloured handkerchief, presumably with spots. [SE *speckled* + WIPER n.¹]

specker n. [1910s] (Aus.) a financial spec*ulator*. [abbr.]

speckle n. [1950s] (W.I.) an albino (cf. FRECKLE-NATURE). [their complexion]

speckle-belly n. [late 19C] (US) a dissenter, a nonconformist. [? a distinctive style of garment, presumably a waistcoat, sported by such figures, but note also northeastern US dial. *speckle-belly*, a grey duck. Nonconformist clergymen were more likely to dress in muted than colourful tones]

speckled adj. [mid-19C–1900s] mixed, motley.

specks see SPECS.

specky adj. [20C] wearing spectacles.

specs/specks n. [early 19C+] glasses, spec*tacles*. [abbr.]

spectacles-seat n. [late 19C] the nose.

sped n. [1980s+] (US campus) a slow or stupid person (cf. SPAS n.; SPASTIC). [abbr. *special education*]

spee n. [1990s] (Black) a friend (cf. SPAR n.²).

speech n. [mid-late 19C] a horse-racing tip, esp. in phr. *get the speech*, to receive a tip, *give the speech*, to pass on information.

speech v. [1980s+] (Black) to argue.

speeching n. [1980s+] (Black) **1** talking seductively to a woman. **2** talking fluently and well. **3** defeating in an argument. [SE *speech*]

speechless adj. [late 19C] euph. for drunk.

speed n.¹ [1920s] (US) **1** a fast liver, a hedonist. **2** of a man, an affectionate term of address.

speed n.² [1960s+] any amphetamine-based stimulant drug (cf. A n.²). [its effect]

speed v. [1960s+] (drugs) to use amphetamines. [SPEED n.²]

speedball n.¹ **1** [1920s–30s] (US) a glass of wine, strengthened by a shot of spirits. **2** [1930s] (drugs) a dose of a narcotic. **3** [1930s+] (drugs) a mixture of cocaine and heroin, either injected or sniffed by the user (cf. A-BOMB; ATOM BOMB). **4** [1970s] (drugs) amphetamine (cf. A n.²).

speedball n.² [1960s+] (Aus.) a rissole, esp. as cooked for shearers. [? the speed with which it is cooked or passes through the eater's stomach]

speed boat n. [1980s+] (drugs) **1** marijuana. **2** phencyclidine (cf. ACE n.³). **3** crack cocaine.

speed bug n. [1910s–20s] (US) a fan of travelling at high speed. [SE *speed* + BUG n.⁵]

speed bump n. [1970s+] a 'sleeping policeman', i.e. a ramp in the road that jars a moving motor vehicle, forcing motorists to reduce their speed.

speed cop n. [1920s+] (orig. US) a motorcycle-mounted policeman, charged with enforcing speed limits. [SE *speed* + COP n.¹ (1)]

speed for lovers n. [1980s+] (drugs) MDMA (cf. ECSTASY). [SPEED n.²; its aphrodisiac or at least affection-enhancing effects]

speed freak n. [1960s+] **1** (drugs) a user of amphetamines. **2** (US Black) one who enjoys driving or being driven at high speed (cf. SPEED BUG). [SPEED n.²/SE *speed* + sfx. -FREAK]

speed hog n. [1970s] one who consistently ignores speed limits when driving. [SE *speed* + HOG n.³]

speeding n. [1960s+] (drugs) the taking of or experiencing amphetamines or a similar 'go-faster' drug (cf. PILLING; TRIPPING). [SPEED v.]

speed king n. [1910s+] (US) a motor-racing champion.

speed limit n. [1940s+] (bingo) the number 30. [the urban speed limit, 30mph (48kph)]

speed merchant n. [1910s+] (orig. US) one who drives excessively fast. [SE *speed* + sfx. -MERCHANT]

speedo n. [1930s+] a *speedo*meter. [abbr.]

speedrap v. [1960s+] to talk fast, usu. under the influence of amphetamine. [SPEED n.² + RAP v.⁴]

speed shop n. [1950s+] (US) an automobile supplier specializing in the parts for (and sometimes building) modified cars (cf. HOT-ROD n.).

speed the wombats! excl. [1920s+] (Aus.) a general excl. of surprise, alarm, fascination etc (cf. STARVE THE BARDIES!; STARVE THE CROWS!; STARVE THE LIZARDS!; STIFFEN THE LIZARDS!; STONE THE CROWS!).

speed trap n. [1930s+] (S.Afr.) methylated spirits, as drunk by alcoholics and tramps.

speedy adj. [1910s–20s] living a pleasure-seeking, hedonistic life. [play on FAST adj.¹]

speedy Gonzales n. [20C] (US) a person who moves, works or operates very fast. [the old joke about *Speedy Gonzales*, a quick and eager fornicator]

speel v. [mid-19C–1900s] to run away, to decamp. [Scot. *speel*, to clamber]

speeler see SPIELER.

speelken see SPELLKEN.

speel the drum, to phr. [mid-late 19C] to go off with stolen property. [SPEEL + DRUM n.²]

speewa see SPEWAH.

speiler/speler see SPIELER.

spell *n.*[1] [early 19C] a theatre (cf. SPELLKEN). [Ger. *spiel*, to play]

spell *n.*[2] [1940s–50s] a sentence of three months' imprisonment. [SE *spell*, a short time]

spell *v.* [mid-19C] to advertise, to put into print. [SE *spell out*]

spell baker *v.* [mid-19C] (US) to perform a difficult or challenging task. [ety. unknown; ? ironic, since *baker* is easily spelled]

spell for *v.* **1** [mid-19C+] to long for. **2** [20C] (W.I.) to wait for, with the intention of attacking verbally or physically. [SE *spell*, to engage in study or contemplation of something]

spell job *n.* [1980s+] (Ulster) a job of uncertain or indefinite duration. [SE *spell*, a period of time]

spellken/speelken/spiel-ken *n.* **1** [late 18C–early 19C] (Und.) a cockpit. **2** [mid-19C] a theatre (cf. BREAKING UP OF THE SPELL). [Ger. *spiel*, to play + KEN *n.*[1]]

spence *n.* [20C] (W.I.) ejaculated semen. [obs. SE *spend*(*ings*), semen]

spencer *n.* [early–mid-19C] a small glass of gin. [ety. unknown]

spend *n.* [late 19C] semen, ejaculation. [SPEND *v.*]

spend *v.* [mid-17C–late 19C] to have an orgasm, to ejaculate.

spend a penny, to *phr.* [1950s+] to urinate. [the 1d (predecimalization) charge in public lavatories]

spendings *n.* [mid–late 19C] an orgasm, an ejaculation. [SPEND *v.*]

speng *n.* **1** [1980s+] (W.I./UK Black teen) a gun. **2** [1980s+] (W.I./UK Black teen) an urban gangster (cf. RUDE BOY). **3** [1990s] a fool. [? Carib.E. *spengle*, a fighting cock]

sperm burper *n.* [1990s] a male homosexual, usually the one performing fellatio.

sperm-sucker *n.* [19C] the vagina (cf. SUCK AND SWALLOW; VACUUM).

sperm the worm, to *phr.* [1990s] to masturbate.

sperrib *n.* [late 19C] (middle class) a wife. [SE *spare rib*, that bone from which the Bible claimed Eve was created]

spew *n.* [1980s+] (US campus) semen. [SE *spew*, vomit]

spew *v.* **1** [20C] to speak, esp. to confess. **2** [1980s+] (US campus) to ejaculate. **3** [1990s] (US Black) to argue angrily, to let loose a diatribe. [SE *spew*, to vomit]

spewah/speewa *n.* [late 19C+] (Aus.) a fantasy outback station, used as a site for a variety of far-fetched tales; thus the tale itself.

spew alley *n.* **1** [19C] the vagina (cf. ALLEY *n.*[1]). **2** [mid-19C–1900s] the throat. [SE *spew* + *alley*]

spewing *adj.* [1990s] (Aus.) in a furious temper.

spew it out! *excl.* [20C] say your piece! make your point! [SPEW *v.* (1)]

spew one's goo, to *phr.* [1990s] to ejaculate. [SPEW *v.* (2) + GOO *n.*]

spew one's guts, to *phr.* [1930s+] **1** to vomit violently. **2** to make a full confession of crimes (cf. SPILL ONE'S GUTS).

spew one's ring, to *phr.* [1960s+] to be violently sick (cf. BRING ONE'S RING UP). [SE *spew* + RING *n.*[1]]

spewsome *adj.* [1990s] (Aus.) of food, drink or people, disgusting, repellent. [SE *spew* + AWESOME; lit. enough to make one vomit]

spewterer *n.* [mid-17C] a drunkard. [SE *spew*]

sphaza/sphaza shop see SPAZA.

sphinx *n.* [1990s] (US Black teen) a woman who is beautiful from the neck up. [the mythical *Sphinx*, a monster with the head of a woman and body of a lion]

sphukupuk/sphukupuku *n.* [20C] (S.Afr.) a fool, a dunce, a blockhead. [used in Fanagalo, a Zulu/English/Nguni pidgin spoken in the mines; this pidgin, created by Whites, is generally disliked by Black miners]

spic/spick *n.* [1910s+] **1** (US) a derog. term for a Puerto Rican,

a Mexican (but cf. WETBACK). **2** any Spanish language. **3** (US campus) a course in Spanish. [abbr. SPIGGOTY; orig. an Italian, when seen as a mispron. of *spaghetti* or 'no spicka da English']

spic and span *n.* [1950s+] (US Black) a mixed Puerto Rican and Black couple. [play on SE phr. + SPIC + *Span*(*ish*), although both refer only to the Hispanic partner]

spice *n.* [early 19C] (Und.) mugging, footpad robbery (cf. HIGHTOBY SPICE; SPICE GLOAK). [SPICE *v.*[2]]

spice *v.*[1] [late 18C] to adulterate. [ext. of SE]

spice *v.*[2] [early 19C] (Und.) to rob; thus *spice the swell*, to rob the gentleman. [? Ger. *speissen*, to eat or SPEAK *v.*]

spice gloak *n.* [18C] a footpad, a highwayman, a mugger. [SPICE *n.* + GLOAK]

spice island *n.* [early–mid-19C] **1** the anus. **2** a privy. **3** any dirty, stinking place. [pun]

spice of life see SLICE OF LIFE.

spick see SPIC.

spicy *adj.* **1** [19C] smart, spirited. **2** [mid-19C] smart-looking, neat. **3** [late 19C+] sexually provocative. [(3) may have started out as a genuine euph. but invariably carries slightly ludicrous 'dirty old man' overtones]

spicy as all round my hat *phr.* [late 19C] sensational.

spiddock-pot legs *n.* [17C] ungainly legs. [northern dial. *spiddock*, a spigot, and their supposed resemblance to one]

spider *n.*[1] [mid-late 19C] **1** (Aus.) a drink composed of brandy and lemonade, brandy and beer or sherry and lemonade. **2** claret and lemonade. [? it 'creeps up' on the drinker]

spider *n.*[2] [1910s–40s] (Aus.) a light gig or two-wheeled, one-horse carriage.

spider *n.*[3] [1970s] (US campus) a hard worker. [the industrious arachnid]

spider *n.*[4] see ROCK SPIDER.

spider blue *n.* [1980s+] (drugs) heroin. [a brandname based on the packaging]

spider-brusher *n.* [mid-19C] a domestic servant. [their housework]

spider-catcher *n.* **1** [late 17C–early 18C] an extremely thin man (cf. SPIDER-SHANKED). **2** [early–mid-19C] a monkey. [in SE *spider-catcher* is a general, if vague, term of abuse, but refers not to anatomy but propensity]

spider claw *v.* [late 19C] of a man, to play with one's testicles. [the clawing movements of one's hand, reminiscent of a spider's scrabbling legs]

spider-shanked *adj.* [late 18C–early 19C] used to describe a man with very thin legs (cf. SPIDER-CATCHER).

spiel *n.* **1** [late 19C–1900s] (US) a dance, as found in New York dance-halls (cf. SPIELER). **2** [late 19C+] patter, speech, esp. of a salesman or market stall-holder (cf. LINE *n.*[1]). **3** [20C] (Aus.) formal advice, a set of instructions. **4** [20C] a verbose, 'wordy' explanation. **5** [1970s+] a drinking club (cf. SPIELER). [Ger. *spielen*, to play]

spiel *v.*[1] **1** [mid-19C+] to gamble. **2** [late 19C+] to patter, to talk glibly. **3** [1930s+] to 'shoot a line', to tell a tale. [Ger. *spielen*, to play]

spiel *v.*[2] [late 19C–1910s] (Aus.) to gallop. [dial. *speel*, to move fast]

spieler/speeler/speiler/speler *n.* **1** [mid-19C+] a swindler, a fraud, a card-sharp. **2** [late 19C+] an illegal gambling club. **3** [late 19C–1900s] (US) a young, lower-class single woman, esp. as found frequenting dance-halls. **4** [20C] (Aus./US) a plausible, 'sharp' individual. [SPIEL *v.*[1]; (1) briefly US, Matsell includes it in *Vocabulum* (1859)]

spieling *n.* [late 19C+] (Aus./N.Z.) card-sharping, swindling. [SPIEL *v.*[1]]

spiel-ken see SPELLKEN.

spierpon orchestra *n.* [late 19C] (society) the Spiers and Pond Orchestra, whose music accompanied meals at such fashionable restaurants as the Criterion at Piccadilly Circus.

spiff *n.* [mid-19C+] a dandy. [SPIFFY; note drapery jargon *spiff*, a percentage allowed to salesmen when they sell off old or unfashionable stock]

spiff *adj.* [mid-19C] smartly dressed, dandified (cf. OOJAH-CUM-SPIFF). [? echoic of a sharp sound and thus fig. exciting, important, astonishing (cf. SPANG; SPANK n.²)]

spiffed *adj.*¹ [mid-19C] (Scot.) tipsy, slightly drunk (cf. ABOUT RIGHT adj.¹).

spiffed/spiffed out/up *adj.*² [late 19C+] dressed particularly well. [SPIFFY]

spiffing *adj.* [late 19C+] excellent, first-rate (cf. SPIFFY). [? Derby dial. *spiffyn*, work well done or *spiffer*, anything exceptional in quality or size]

spifflicate *see* SPIFLICATE.

spifflicated *see* SPIFLICATED.

spifflicating *see* SPIFLICATING.

spifflication *see* SPIFLICATION.

spiffy *adj.* [mid-19C+] excellent, wonderful, neatly dressed. [SPIFF adj.]

spiflicate/smifligate/spifflicate *v.* **1** [late 18C+] to thrash, to beat, to overcome completely. **2** [late 18C+] to confound, to silence, to dumfound. **3** [early 19C] to betray to the authorities. **4** [late 19C+] to cause pain or unhappiness, in some unspecified manner. [ety. unknown; ? 'fanciful' (*OED*); SE *stifle* + *suffocate* (Hotten, 1864); SE *suffocate* or dial. *smothercate* (Ware); SE *spill* + *stifle*/dial. *stiffle* (E.P.)]

spiflicated/smiflicated/smifligated/spifflicated *adj.* [20C] (orig. US) drunk (cf. BASTED). [SPIFLICATE]

spiflicating/spifflicating *adj.* [late 19C] aggressive, crushing. [SPIFLICATE]

spiflification/spifflication *n.* [mid-19C–1920s] absolute destruction. [SPIFLICATE]

spiggoty *n.* [19C] (US) a Spanish-speaking native of Central or South America (cf. SPIC). [? broken English 'spikka da English']

spigot *n.* [19C] the penis; thus *spigot-sucker*, a fellator or fellatrix. [SE *spigot*, a tap]

spike *n.*¹ **1** [mid-19C+] a lodging house, orig. local authority workhouse or lodging house; thus *spike-ranger*, a tramp who wanders from one such place to another. **2** [1960s+] (Irish) a maternity hospital. [the lack of comfort]

spike *n.*² [late 19C] (US) a shot of alcohol (when added to an otherwise non-alcoholic drink). [SPIKE v.¹]

spike *n.*³ **1** [20C] the erect penis. **2** [1920s] a needle. **3** [1920s+] a hypodermic syringe.

spike *v.*¹ **1** [late 19C+] to add alcohol (clandestinely) to an ostensibly non-alcoholic drink. **2** [1960s+] to dose someone with an hallucinogenic drug (usu. LSD) without their knowing (usu. by putting it into a drink or, occas., food). [such adulteration adds 'sharpness']

spike *v.*² [20C] (US) to reject, to quash, to delete. [? SE *spike a gun*, to immobilize a cannon by driving a spike into the touchhole, or *spike*, a pointed stick for holding papers, bills etc]

spike *v.*³ **1** [20C] to have sexual intercourse. **2** [1920s+] (Aus.) to hit someone hard, to knock someone down. [SE *spike*, to pierce]

spike *v.*⁴ [1920s+] (drugs) to inject a drug with a hypodermic syringe. [SPIKE n.³ (3)]

spike-faggot *n.* [17C] the penis (cf. BAT n.⁷). [SE *spike* + FAGGOT n.¹]

Spike Park *n.* [mid-19C] the Queen's Bench prison; thus *spike park*, the grounds of a prison (cf. AKERMAN'S HOTEL).

spikes *n.* [1980s+] (US campus) shoes, for either sex and of any kind. [the spikes used on running and other sports shoes]

spike team *n.* [mid-19C] (US) a coach drawn by three horses, two abreast and one in the lead (cf. UNICORN). [the lead horse represents the *spike*]

spike up *v.* [1920s+] (US drugs) to inject narcotics. [SPIKE v.⁴]

spiky *adj.* [late 19C+] **1** in religious terms, extremely ritualistic or High Church Anglican. **2** aggressive, harsh, unsympathetic, uncompromising (cf. FLUFFY). [(1) the SE *spike* or spire of a trad. church]

spill *n.*¹ **1** [late 17C–late 18C] a small gift of money. **2** [!late 19C–1910s] a drink. [? SE *spill*, to pour out a small amount]

spill *n.*² [1940s–50s] (US Black) **1** a person of mixed US Black and Puerto Rican blood. **2** a Puerto Rican. **3** a Black person. [ety. unknown; ? SE *spill*, either of blood or semen]

spill *v.*¹ **1** [18C+] to cause to fall. **2** [1980s+] (US campus) to fall.

spill *v.*² [late 19C–1910s] to drink. [SPILL n.¹ (2)]

spill *v.*³ [1910s+] (orig. US) to confess (cf. SPILL ONE'S GUTS). [abbr. SPILL THE BEANS]

spill *v.*⁴ [1950s+] (drugs) to miss the vein when making an injection and thus waste the heroin/water mixture.

spill a line, to *phr.* [20C] to concoct a smooth patter with the specific aim of seduction (cf. SHOOT A LINE). [SE *spill* + LINE n.¹]

spillin' *n.* [1980s+] (US Black) a gunfight in which quantities of bullets are fired and wounds inflicted. [SE *spill blood*]

spill milk against posts *phr.* [late 19C] an extreme condemnation of the behaviour of the person who is the topic of conversation; the presumption is that they are, on top of other crimes, utterly wasteful.

spill one's breakfast, to *phr.* [20C] to vomit.

spill one's guts, to *phr.* [1920s+] (orig. US) **1** to confess one's crimes in full. **2** to lose one's temper.

spill one's nut, to *phr.* [1930s+] to confess, to make an admission. [SE *spill* + NUT n.³ (2)]

spill the beans/works, to *phr.* [1910s+] (orig. US) to confess, to let out a secret, to talk unguardedly.

spin *n.*¹ [late 19C] a poor, unmarried young woman who travels to India in the hope of finding a husband. [abbr. SE *spinster*]

spin *n.*² [1910s+] (Aus./N.Z.) an experience, a piece of luck, whether good or bad. [? a spin of the dice]

spin *n.*³ [1940s–60s] (Aus.) 5 in various contexts, e.g. £5 sterling, 5 ounces weight, a 5-year prison sentence. [SPINNAKER]

spin *n.*⁴ [1970s+] the playing of a gramophone record, esp. on a radio station.

spin *v.*¹ [mid–late 19C] to fail a candidate for a university examination, esp. in passive use, *spun*.

spin *v.*² [1970s+] (Und.) to search, usu. in *spin a drum*, to search a house.

spinach *n.*¹ (US) **1** [late 19C+] a beard. **2** [20C] money (cf. ALFALFA n.).

spinach *n.*² [1920s–40s] (US) rubbish, nonsense (cf. ALFALFA n.). [generally asserted as f. the *New Yorker* cartoon caption (8 December 1928), 'It's broccoli dear.' 'I say it's spinach, and I say the hell with it' but note GAMMON AND PICKLES]

spin a dit, to *phr.* [1940s] (Aus.) (usu. milit.) to tell a story (cf. SPIN A YARN). [SE *spin* + *ditty*]

spin a hen, to *phr.* [1940s] (US Black) to dance with an older woman. [SE *spin* + HEN (1)]

spin at the track with a fool's dime, to *phr.* [1940s] (US Black) to go out dancing with a maid-servant on her night off.

spin a yarn/twist, to *phr.* [early 19C+] (orig. naut.) to tell a story, esp. a long one; thus *yarn-spinner*, a teller of stories. [YARN/SE *twist* + the pun on SE *spin* + *yarn/twist*]

spin crooked spindles *see* MAKE CROOKED SPINDLES.

spindle *n.* [19C] the penis.

spindle-prick! *excl.* [late 19C] a slightly derog. term used to address a lethargic man. [SE *spindle* + PRICK n. (2)]

spinebasher *n.* [1940s+] (Aus.) an idler, a loafer; thus *spine-bashing*, loafing. [SE *spine* + BASH v.; i.e. the hitting of the back against a chair]

spin for *v.* [1930s+] (Aus.) to court a woman. [the game of two-up or fishing imagery]

spin-house *see* SPINNING HOUSE.

spinifex wire *n.* [1930s+] (Aus.) **1** the outback version of the 'bush telegraph' (cf. MULGA WIRE). **2** a rumour. [SE *Spinifex*, 'One or other of a number of coarse grasses ... which grow in dense masses on the sand-hills of the Australian deserts, and are characterized by their sharp-pointed, spiny leaves' (*OED*) + *wire*, a telegraph]

spinnaker *n.* [late 19C–1950s] (Aus.) a £5 note, a $5 bill (cf. SPIN n.[3]). [SE *spinnaker*, a large three-cornered sail carried by racing-yachts]

spinner *n.* [1910s–60s] (Aus.) £50. [SPINNAKER]

spinniken *n.* [mid-19C] a workhouse, esp. the St Giles's work-house. [Du. *spinnhuis*, a women's house of correction; presumably the inmates were forced to spin thread + KEN n.[1]]

spinning *adj.* [late 19C] speedy, quick.

spinning house/spin-house *n.* [19C] a workhouse. [for ety. *see* SPINNIKEN]

spinning jenny *n.* [19C] the vagina (cf. ITCHING JENNY).

spinning jinny *n.* [late 19C–1930s] a roulette table. [naut. *spinning jenny*, a prismatic compass]

spin one's own propellor, to *phr.* [1960s+] (US) to masturbate.

spin one's wheels, to *phr.* (US) **1** [1970s+] to waste time or work fruitlessly. **2** [1990s] (campus) to excite, esp. sexually.

spin out *v.* [1950s+] (orig. US) of a vehicle, to go out of control.

spin round on one's ear *see* GET UP ON ONE'S EAR.

spinsrap *n.* [mid-19C] parsnips. [backsl.]

spinster *n.* [early 17C–early 18C] a prostitute (cf. MAKE CROOKED SPINDLES).

spin street-yarn, to *phr.* [mid-19C–1920s] (orig. US) to wander from house to house, chatting and exchanging gossip.

spin the bat, to *phr.* [late 19C] (Anglo-Ind.) to speak slangily. [SE *spin* + Hind. *bat*, speech, a word]

spin the dope, to *phr.* [1920s+] (Aus.) to tell a good story. [SE *spin* + DOPE n.[3]]

spin the record, to *phr.* [1990s] to masturbate.

spin top in mud, to *phr.* [20C] (W.I.) to waste one's time attempting a frustrating task.

spintry *n.* [16C] a male homosexual prostitute (cf. SELLARY). [? Lat. *spinter*, a bracelet; thus those men who wear them]

spire and steeple *n.* [20C] (Aus.) people. [rhy. sl.]

spirit *n.* [1970s+] (US Black) jazz or blues music.

spiritual flesh-broker *n.* [late 17C–18C] a parson (cf. FLESH BROKER).

spiry *adj.* [early 19C] highly distinguished. [fig. resembling a tall spire]

spit *n.*[1] [mid-17C–late 19C] a sword. [SE *spit*, a sharpened rod used to roast meat]

spit *n.*[2] [18C+] identity, similarity, esp. in familial resemblance; thus *the spit of, the dead spit of, the very spit of*. [earlier phr. 'as like as his father as if he had been spit out of his mouth']

spit *n.*[3] [1940s–50s] a cigarette. [? SPIT AND A DRAG]

spit *v.*[1] [late 18C–late 19C] of a man, to have sexual intercourse (cf. BANG v.[1]; PUT FOUR QUARTERS ON THE SPIT). [SE *spit*, to pierce]

spit/spit cards *v.*[2] [late 18C–1920s] to leave visiting cards on one's social round.

Spitalfields' breakfast *n.* [mid-19C] a tight necktie and a

short pipe, i.e. no breakfast (cf. AIR PIE AND A WALK AROUND). [*Spitalfields*, in the East End of London and, as such, an impoverished area]

Spital whore *n.* [17C] a prostitute. [*Spitalfields*, a tough East End area of London + SE *spital*, a hospital (and origin of the district's name), thus underlining the physical perils of being a prostitute]

spit amber *v.* [late 19C] (US) to spit while chewing tobacco. [the colour of the spittle]

spit and a drag/draw *n.* [late 19C+] (orig. RN) **1** a surreptitious smoke. **2** a cigarette. [? rhy. sl. *spit and a drag* = FAG n.[4], or the result of a badly rolled cigarette, from which one spits out the odd strand of tobacco, while dragging or drawing down the smoke]

spit-and-scratch game *n.* [1910s–20s] a fight, usu. between women.

spitball *n.* [20C] (US) an insult, a jibe. [SE *spitball*, a small saliva-soaked ball of paper]

spitball *v.* [20C] (US) to accuse or taunt. [SPITBALL n.]

spit-bit *n.* [1970s] (US Black) smooth, persuasive talk. [SE *spit* + BIT n.[8]]

spit blood *v.* [1960s+] to be in a furious temper (cf. SPIT CHIPS).

spit cards *see* SPIT v.[2].

spit-cat/-kitten *n.* [late 19C–1910s] a termagant, one who has a very short temper. [cf. SE *spitfire*]

spit chips *v.* [20Cs] (orig. Aus.) **1** to feel extreme thirst. **2** to manifest acute anger or vexation (cf. SPIT BLOOD). [SE *spit* + *chips* of wood]

spit cotton *v.* [early 19C–1940s] (US) **1** to be very thirsty, to have a dry mouth. **2** to be very angry.

spit-fuck *n.* [1960s+] (gay) anal intercourse or penetration of the anus by the fingers or fist where the only lubricant is spit. [SE *spit* + FUCK n.[1]; thus the saying 'If spit doesn't work, it isn't love']

spit it out! *excl.* [20C] speak up! confess! explain yourself!

spit-kitten *see* SPIT-CAT.

spit o' my hand! *excl.* [late 19C–1920s] used to emphasize whatever it is one has said, e.g. *spit o' my hand, you know it's the truth*. [the spitting on one's hand that seals a bargain]

spit one off *v.* [1990s] to masturbate.

spit one's death, to *phr.* [late 19C–1910s] to swear one's honesty (cf. STRIKE ONE'S BREATH). [the practice of spitting to confirm the sincerity of one's oath]

spit one's guts, to *phr.* [1930s] (US) **1** to confess one's crimes in full. **2** to lose one's temper (cf. SPILL ONE'S GUTS).

spit or get off the cuspidor *phr.* [1940s+] (Can.) euph. for SHIT OR GET OFF THE POT.

spit out of the window, to *phr.* [1930s+] (gay) to spit out one's partner's semen after fellatio.

spit out the dummy, to *phr.* [1980s] (Aus.) to lose one's temper badly. [the image of a furious baby]

spit-polish the purple helmet, to *phr.* [1990s] to masturbate. [SE *spit-polish* + HELMET n. (1)]

spit roast *n.* [1990s] a woman who is simultaneously fellating one man while having intercourse, from the rear, with a second.

spit sixpences/white broth *v.* [late 18C–late 19C] to spit out small gobbets of white mucus.

spit tacks *v.* [1970s+] (US) to be irate, furious. [note synon. UK milit. *spit button-sticks*]

spitting at the tongs *phr.* [20C] (Ulster) pregnant. [ety. unknown; ? a folk saying]

spitting on the sidewalk *phr.* [20C] any trivial offence for which one still faces prosecution. [tramp jargon for police harassment, an arrest for no other reason than one is a vagrant]

spit white broth *see* SPIT SIXPENCES.

spitz poodle *n.* [late 19C] (US) a mild degree of drunkenness. [ety. unknown; the variety of dog seems to have no relevance]

spiv *n.* [20C] a flashy, sharp individual who exists on the fringes of real criminality, living by their wits rather than a regular job. [? Rom. *spiv*, sparrow, used by gypsies as a derog. ref. to those who existed by picking up the leavings of their betters, criminal or legitimate; alternative theories include the reverse of *V.I.P.s* or police abbr. *suspected persons and itinerant vagrants*]

spivmobile *n.* [1980s+] an exceptionally ostentatious and flashy car, such as might be driven by a SPIV or their successors (cf. PIMPMOBILE). [SPIV + sfx, -*mobile*]

spizzerinktum *n.* [mid-19C] (US) vigour, zest. [nonce-word, reminiscent of *fizz, pizzazz* etc]

splang *n.* [1970s] (US Black) sharp words; thus *splang*, to curse. [? echoic]

splash *n.*[1] **1** [mid–late 18C] style, dash. **2** [19C] a striking or ostentatious display, appearance or effect, usu. in phr. *cut a splash, make a splash*.

splash *n.*[2] [mid-19C] make-up, cosmetics, esp. *poudre de riz* used to whiten the complexion (cf. SLAP n.[2]).

splash *n.*[3] [1940s] (US Black) any form of water, e.g. a river, a lake, the sea, a bath.

splash *n.*[4] (drugs) **1** [1960s+] liquid amphetamine. **2** [1980s] an injection of methamphetamine and the quasi-orgasmic sensation this brings.

splash *n.*[5] [1980s+] a woman who is the object of gang-rape or a voluntary participant in multiple intercourse. [the bodily fluids thus discharged]

splash *adj.* [mid-19C–1900s] elegant, fashionable, distinguished. [SPLASH n.[1]]

splash *v.*[1] **1** [1910s+] to spend money extravagantly. **2** [1930s+] to masturbate.

splash/splash on *v.*[2] [1990s] (US Black gang) to shoot.

splasher *n.* [1910s+] an extravagant person. [SPLASH v.[1] (1)]

splashing *n.* [late 19C–1900s] garrulous or foolish chatter.

splashing/splashy *adj.* [late 19C–1910s] fine, excellent, first-rate. [SPLASH n.[1]]

splashing *adv.* [late 19C–1910s] wonderfully, excellently, superbly. [SPLASH n.[1]]

splash on *see* SPLASH v.[2].

splash one's/the boots, to *phr.* [20C] to urinate.

splash out/out on *v.* [1930s+] to spend money unrestrainedly.

splash the boots *see* SPLASH ONE'S BOOTS.

splash-up *adj.* [late 19C+] first-rate, excellent (cf. BANG-UP adj.; SLAP-UP).

splashy *see* SPLASHING adj.

splat *n.* [1950s+] the slapping or splashing noise of something that hits a hard surface. [echoic]

splat movie *see* SPLATTER MOVIE.

splatterdash *n.* [late 19C] an uproar. [synon. Yorks. dial.]

splatter face *n.* [late 19C] a broad face. [Northumberland/ Oxon. dial. *splatter-faced*, broad-faced, 'platter-faced']

splatter/splat movie *n.* [1970s+] a genre of ultra-violent films, coined as a name by director George Romero (b.1939), e.g. *The Texas Chainsaw Massacre* (1974), *The Driller Killer* (1979).

splatter one's batter, to *phr.* [1990s] to ejaculate.

splay *n.* [1940s] (drugs) marijuana. [ety. unknown]

spleef *n.* [1980s+] (US drugs) a coned-shaped cigarette with a touch of hash. [SPLIFF]

spleefer *n.* [1990s] (drugs) a cigarette made from a mix of marijuana and crack cocaine (cf. FIFTY-ONE). [SPLIFF + REEFER n.[1]]

splendacious/splendidious/splendidous *adj.* [mid-19C+] splendid, excellent, first-rate (cf. SPLENDIFEROUS). [intensifier of SE *splendid*]

splendiferous *adj.* [mid-19C+] wonderful, perfect (cf. SPLENDACIOUS). [intensifier of SE *splendid*]

spleuchan *n.* [late 18C] the vagina (cf. MONEYBOX; PURSE n.; SPORRAN; TILL n.). [Gael. *spliùchan*, a tobacco pouch, a purse]

splib *n.* [1940s–70s] (US Black) **1** a fellow Black person. **2** 'a liberal Black who looks angry but will not upset the status quo' (*American Speech* XLIX, 1976). [abbr. *slip-de-wib*; ? jazz *splibby*, possessing 'soul']

splibby *n.* [1930s–60s] (US Black) a feeling of well-being. [for ety. *see* SPLIB]

splice *n.* **1** [early 19C–1920s] one's wife. **2** [mid–late 19C] the act or institution of marriage. [SPLICE v.]

splice *v.* [early 18C+] **1** to marry; thus *spliced*, married. **2** to have sexual intercourse. [SE *splice*, to join]

splicer *n.* [1910s–20s] a sailor. [their SE *splicing* of ropes or of 'the mainbrace']

splice the mainbrace, to *phr.* [19C+] (orig. naut.) to drink. [SE *splice* + *mainbrace*, the brace attached to the main-yard of a sailing ship]

splice-toby *n.* [mid–late 19C] the highway, the main road (cf. HIGH-TOBY). [SE *splice*, to join + TOBY n.[2]]

splif/spliff *n.* [1930s+] (orig. W.I., esp. Rasta) a marijuana or hashish cigarette. [SPIFLICATE; i.e. the effects]

splim *n.* [1960s+] (drugs) marijuana. [SPLIF]

splish and splash, to *phr.* [1970s+] (US Black) to debate a topic, to ponder without coming to a decision.

split *n.*[1] **1** [late 19C] a drink composed of two different alcoholic liquors. **2** [late 19C+] a small bottle of mineral water. **3** [late 19C+] a half-bottle of champagne. **4** [1900s] a half-glass of spirits.

split *n.*[2] [late 19C] small change. **2** [1920s–30s] a 10-shilling note (50p), i.e. a *split* pound note.

split *n.*[3] [late 19C] a pimp, a procurer. [he *splits* the woman's earnings with her]

split *n.*[4] [late 19C+] the division of criminal spoils.

split *n.*[5] [late 19C+] **1** an informer. **2** a detective. [SPLIT v.[3]]

split *n.*[6] [20C] (Aus.) a safety match.

split *n.*[7] [1910s+] (Aus./US) **1** the vagina. **2** women, viewed as sex objects. [physiology]

split *v.*[1] **1** [late 18C–mid-19C] to walk or run at great speed. **2** [1950s+] to leave, to depart. [the fig. *split* or 'tear' in a group that such a departure makes]

split *v.*[2] [late 18C+] to have sexual intercourse (cf. BANG v.[1]; SPLIT THE DIFFERENCE).

split *v.*[3] **1** [late 18C+] to betray, to inform against, usu. *split on*. **2** [mid-19C] to disclose, to reveal secrets. [to split or break a confidence]

split *v.*[4] **1** [mid-19C] to quarrel with someone, to break off relations. **2** [1940s+] (orig. US) to divorce.

split *v.*[5] [1910s+] to share out profits or proceeds. [SPLIT n.[3]]

split about *v.* [mid-19C] to inform, to betray, esp. to the police. [ext. of SPLIT v.[3]]

split a gut, to *phr.* **1** [late 17C; 1950s] to vomit. **2** [1950s+] to laugh hysterically (cf. BUST A GUT). **3** [1950s+] to become very angry (cf. BUST A GUT). **4** [1950s+] (US) to exert maximum effort.

split along *v.* [19C] to move fast. [SPLIT v.[1]]

split apricot *n.* [late 17C–19C] the vagina (cf. APPLE n.[10]; SPLIT ARSE; SPLIT FIG; SPLIT KIPPER; SPLIT MUTTON).

split arse *n.* [20C] a woman (cf. SPLIT APRICOT). [SE *split* + ARSE n.[1]]

split-arse *adv.* [1910s–20s] very quickly. [SE *split* + ARSE n.[1]; the movement of one's legs and buttocks]

split-arsed one *n.* [late 19C] a woman, esp. a baby girl. [SPLIT ARSE]

split-arse mechanic *n.* [late 19C] a prostitute. [SPLIT ARSE + SE *mechanic*; note RAF jargon *split-arse merchant*, a reckless, showy or daring airman, *split-arse cap*, the Royal Flying Corps cap, similar to a Glengarry]

split asunder *n.* [mid-19C] a costermonger. [rhy. sl.]

split/spread beaver *n.* [1970s+] the wide-open vagina, esp. as found in hardcore pornography (cf. PINK n.[5]). [SE *split/spread* + BEAVER n.[4]]

split bit *n.* [20C] (US Und.) a sentence of 2–10 years. [SE *split* + BIT n.[7]]

split-cause *n.* [late 17C–18C] a lawyer (cf. SPLITTER).

split crow *n.* [late 18C–early 19C] the sign of the spread eagle. [supposed resemblance]

split fair *v.* [mid–late 19C] to tell the truth. [SPLIT v.[2] + SE *fair*]

split fig *n.* [late 17C–early 19C] **1** a grocer. **2** the vagina (cf. APPLE n.[10]; SPLIT APRICOT).

split kipper *n.* [1990s] the vagina (cf. BEARDED CLAM; SPLIT APRICOT).

split me!/split my windpipe! *excl.* [late 17C–18C] an oath used by contemporary upper-class dandies.

split mutton *n.* **1** [17C–19C] the penis (cf. BACON n.[1]). **2** [18C–1900s] the vagina (cf. BACON SANDWICH; SPLIT APRICOT). **3** [18C–1900s] a derog. generic term for womankind. [SE *split* + MUTTON n.[1]]

split my windpipe! *see* SPLIT ME!

split one's wig, to *phr.* [1950s] (US) to suffer pain, to feel depressed, to be at the end of one's tether (cf. FLIP ONE'S WIG; WIG OUT). [SE *split* + WIG n.[1] (1)]

split out *v.*[1] **1** [1920s+] to quarrel. **2** [1930s] (US) to separate. **3** [1930s+] (US) to part company, to take one's leave. [ext. of SPLIT v.[4]]

split pea *n.* [mid-19C] tea. [rhy. sl.]

split-rump *see* RUMP-SPLITTER.

split-stuff *n.* [late 19C+] (Aus.) women, viewed as sexual objects. [SPLIT n.[7] + STUFF n.[4]]

splitsville *n.* [1960s+] (orig. US) the end of a relationship, a divorce etc. [SPLIT v.[4] + sfx. -VILLE]

splitter/splitter of causes *n.* [late 17C] a lawyer (cf. SPLIT-CAUSE). [the profession's reputation as splitters of legal hairs]

split the blanket, to *phr.* [20C] (US) to divorce.

split the breeze, to *phr.* [1950s+] to depart, to travel, to run fast (cf. BUST THE BREEZE; HIT THE BREEZE).

split the cup, to *phr.* [1970s] (US Black) to deflower a virgin. [SE *split*/SPLIT v.[2] + FUZZY CUP]

split the difference, to *phr.* [1970s] of a man, to have sexual intercourse. [pun]

split the peach, to *phr.* [1990s] to sodomize.

split 'un *n.* [20C] (Aus.) a banknote that has been divided in halves.

split-up *adj.* [late 19C] of humans or horses, long-legged.

split up *v.* [1940s+] (orig. US) to become divorced. [ext. of SPLIT v.[4]]

split-whisker *n.* [1940s+] (Aus.) women, viewed sexually. [SPLIT n.[7] + SE *whisker*]

spliv *n.* [1990s] (US Black) a fellow Black person. [SPLIB]

splivins *n.* [1960s–70s] (drugs) amphetamine (cf. A n.[2]). [ety. unknown]

splodger *n.*[1] [mid-19C] **1** a lout, a rough countryman. **2** a grave-robber. [dial. *splodge*, to wade through mud]

splodger *n.*[2] [mid-19C] an old man. [rhy. sl. *splodger* = codger]

splooge *n.* [1980s+] (US campus) semen (cf. SPEW n.; SPOO; SPOOCH).

splooge *v.* [1980s+] (US campus) to ejaculate. [SPLOOGE n.]

splosh *n.*[1] [late 19C+] money. [? SPLASH v.[1]]

splosh *n.*[2] [1940s–50s] tea. [SE *splosh*, the sound of a liquid falling or having something dropped into it]

splosh it on *v.* [1920s+] to bet heavily, esp. at race-tracks. [ext./var. SPLASH v.[1]]

splutter *n.* [1910s–20s] a scandal. [dial. *splutter*, a fuss, a disturbance]

s.p.o. *n.* [1920s–30s] a cheap restaurant, specializing in sausages, potatoes and onions. [abbr.]

spod *n.* [1980s] (teen) an unpopular schoolchild (cf. GOGGY). [? Scot. *spodlin*, a child who is just learning to walk]

spod *v.* [1990s] to engage in meaningless activities whether or not there is work to do. [ety. unknown]

spodiodi *n.* [1940s+] (orig. US) a mixture of cheap port and generic bar whisky, much loved by jazz musicians and beatniks. [ety. unknown; noted as a song lyric, 'Drink wine spodiodi', in Jack Kerouac, *On the Road* (1957); ? the rhythmic sound of the word is echoic of the mixing of the drinks]

spoffish *adj.* [mid-19C] interfering, meddlesome (cf. SPOFFY). [? SE *officious*]

spoffle *v.* [mid-19C–1910s] to make a fuss, to bustle about. [East Anglian dial. *spuffle*, to fuss or bustle about]

spoffskins *n.* [late 19C–1900s] a prostitute, esp. one who poses as her regular client's 'wife'. [ety. unknown]

spoffy *adj.* [mid-19C] interfering, meddlesome, acting like a busybody (cf. SPOFFISH).

spog/spogh *v.* [mid-19C+] (S.Afr.) to boast, to brag. [Du. *spochen*, to boast]

spoil/spoil a woman's shape *v.*[1] [late 17C–late 19C] to make pregnant.

spoil *v.*[2] [19C] **1** to stop someone else achieving their object. **2** (US) to kill.

spoil a woman's shape *see* SPOIL v.[1]

spoil-bread *n.* [mid-19C–1920s] a baker (cf. SPOIL-BROTH; SPOIL-IRON).

spoil-broth *n.* [mid-19C–1920s] a cook (cf. SPOIL-BREAD).

spoilers *n.* [1940s+] (S.Afr.) a township thug or criminal (cf. TSOTSI). [proper name *Spoilers*, a leading gang in the 1940s, then applied to all such young men, gang members or not; ult. title of a popular film]

spoil-iron *n.* [late 18C–early 19C] a blacksmith (cf. SPOIL-BREAD).

spoil-pudding *n.* [late 18C–early 19C] a parson. [a long-winded parson keeps the congregation in church so long that their cooking spoils]

spoil someone's dough, to *phr.* [late 19C] (US) to sabotage someone's plans.

spoke-box *n.* [19C] the mouth (cf. BOX OF WORRIES). [the 'spokes' are the teeth]

spoken to *adj.* [mid-19C] deceived, tricked. [SPEAK v./SPEAK TO]

spoke to *adj.* **1** [late 18C–early 19C] suffering a great misfortune, beyond help. **2** [early 19C] (Und.) robbed; the type of robbery can be added; thus *spoke to upon the screw/crack/sneak/hoist/buz*. [? SPEAK v. or a message from the deity]

sponditious *adj.* [1980s] excellent. [coined by UK comedian Lenny Henry (b.1958); ? SE *spontaneous* + del*icious*]

spondulics/spondulacks/spondulicks *n.* [mid-19C+] money (cf. WAMPUM). [? Gk. *spondulikos*, the adjectival form of *spondulox*, a type of shell used as early 'money'; or corruption of GREENBACK n.[2]]

sponge *n.*[1] **1** [late 16C+] a heavy drinker. **2** [17C] a dedicated scholar. [their absorption, whether of alcohol or knowledge]

sponge *n.*[2] [1950s] a hollow sponge that is placed inside the mouth of the vagina by a prostitute as protection against disease and accidental pregnancy; thus *sponge*, to use such a sponge; *sponge tricks*, deceiving clients by using a sponge.

sponge *v.* [mid-19C] to surrender. [abbr. THROW IN THE TOWEL]

sponge cake *n.* [late 19C] (US) anything simple, ridiculously easy. [i.e. SOFT adj. (2)]

sponge hair *n.* [1930s–50s] (US Black) hair that resists combing.

sponge it out *v.* [late 19C] (US) to forget something, to wipe something from one's memory.

sponging-/spunging-house *n.* [late 18C–early 19C] a bailiff's lock-up. ['to which persons arrested are taken, till they find bail, or have spent all their money; a house where every species of fraud and extortion is practised, under the protection of the law' (Grose, 1785). The corrupt bailiff's officers 'sponge up' their victims' money]

spons *n.* [mid-19C–1910s] (Aus.) money. [abbr. SPONDULICS]

sponsor *n.* [1970s] (US Black) a man who 'keeps' a woman, in return for sexual favours.

spoo *n.* [1980s+] (US campus) semen; thus *spoo*, to ejaculate. [SPEW n.]

spooch *n.* [1980s+] (US campus) semen; thus *spooch*, to ejaculate (cf. SPEW n.; SPLOOGE; SPOO).

spoof *n.*[1] [late 19C–1900s] a hoax, a confidence trick; thus *spoofer*, one who practises such trickery. [SE *spoof*, a game, involving hoaxing one's rival players, invented by the comedian Arthur Roberts (1852–1933)]

spoof *n.*[2] [1910s+] (Aus.) semen; thus *spoof*, to ejaculate. [? *spit* + *poof!*, onomat. noise of a small explosion]

spoof *adj.* [late 19C+] fake, spurious, sham. [SPOOF n.[1]]

spoof *v.* [late 19C–1920s] to hoax, to fool, to trick. [SPOOF n.[1]]

spooferies *n.* [late 19C] a second-rate sporting club (cf. COLINDERIES). [SPOOFERY. The orig. *Spooferies* seems to have been the Trafalgar Club in Maiden Lane near the Strand, but the term was generic and the card-game *spoof* (in which the appearance of certain cards at the same time is called a 'spoof') was invented at the Adelphi Club]

spoofery *n.* [late 19C] trickery, hoaxing. [SPOOF v.]

spoofie *n.* [1970s] (Aus.) an attractive young woman (cf. FUCKY). [SPOOF n.[2]]

spooge *n.* [1990s] (US) semen (cf. SPEW n.; SPLOOGE; SPOO).

spoogy *adj.* [1990s] (US teen) scary. [? SPOOKY adj.[2]]

spook *n.*[1] **1** [1900s–10s] (drugs) a heroin addict. **2** [1940s+] a derog. term for a Black person (cf. JIGABOO). **3** [1980s+] (S.Afr.) a fright, a scare. [SE *spook*, a ghost]

spook *n.*[2] [1940s+] (US) an intelligence agent, esp. CIA; thus *spookic/spookical, spookish, spookism, spookological, spookology*. [Yale University secret society Skull & Bones, from among whose members were recruited the personnel of the OSS, the WW2 predecessor of the CIA]

spook *v.* [1920s+] (US) **1** to scare, to unnerve. **2** to take fright, to become scared. [SE *spook*]

spooked *adj.* [1920s+] under the influence of a malign spirit. [SE *spook*]

spooky *adj.*[1] **1** [mid-19C+] (orig. US) frightening, eerie, pertaining to the 'spirit world'. **2** [1920s+] (US) nervous, easily frightened, superstitious. [note surfing jargon *spooky*, of a dangerous or frightening wave]

spooky *adj.*[2] [1970s+] (US) pertaining to the world of spies and espionage. [SPOOK n.[2]]

spoon *n.*[1] **1** [late 18C–late 19C] a fool, a simpleton (cf. SPOONY n.). **2** [mid-19C] a foolish, sentimental affection. **3** [mid-19C] the lover who feels such emotions. **4** [mid-19C] a flirt; thus *come the spoon*, to offer sentimental and ridiculous protestations of love, *at spoons with*, sentimentally in love with. [SE *spoon*, which is open and shallow. 'A spoon has been defined to be "a thing that touches a lady's lips without kissing them"' (Hotten, 1867)]

spoon *n.*[2] [1950s+] (drugs) **1** 1.2g (1/16oz) of heroin. **2** enough heroin to provide a single injection. [(1) approx. 1 teaspoonful; (2) the contents of the spoon that is used to heat the drug]

spoon *v.*[1] [mid-19C+] to flirt with, esp. in a foolish or sentimental manner. [SPOON n.[1] (4)]

spoon *v.*[2] [1970s] (US campus) to eat together. [SE *spoon*]

spoon and gravy *n.* [20C] a dinner jacket (cf. SOUP AND FISH).

spoony/spooney *n.* **1** [late 18C] a fool, a simpleton (cf. SPOON n.[1]). **2** [mid-19C] one who is in sentimental love. **3** [mid-19C] an effeminate young man, poss. homosexual. [ext. of SPOON n.[1]]

spoony/spooney *adj.* [mid–late 19C] **1** weak minded, simple. **2** besotted with a member of the opposite sex. [SPOONY n.]

spoons on *adj.* [mid–late 19C] **1** sentimentally in love with. **2** courting; also as *spoons about, spoons with*. [SPOON n.[1] (2)]

spoon the burick, to *phr.* [late 19C] to pay attentions to one's best friend's wife or girlfriend. [SPOON v.[1] + BURICK]

spoorie *n.* [20C] (S.Afr.) a Black artisan. [Afk. *spoor*(weg), railway + sfx. *-ie*; lit. a railway worker, the term is used as generic for all artisans]

spores *n.* (drugs) **1** [1960s] a psilocybe or 'magic' mushroom. **2** [1970s+] phencyclidine (cf. ACE n.[3]).

sporran *n.* [19C] the pubic hair (cf. SPLEUCHAN). [Gael. *sporan*, a purse]

sport *n.*[1] [19C] sexual intercourse. [SPORT v.[2]]

sport *n.*[2] **1** [late 19C] (US) an eccentric. **2** [late 19C+] a playboy, a man-about-town, with the accent on gambling, womanizing and other areas of the 'fast' life (cf. SPORTING LIFE n.[1]). **3** [20C] a male prostitute (cf. SPORTING GOODS). **4** [1920s+] (esp. Aus.) a man; thus a general term of address to a man (cf. OLD SPORT).

sport *v.*[1] **1** [late 17–early 18C] to read an author for amusement (rather than instruction). **2** [early 18C–early 19C] to behave showily or ostentatiously in public. **3** [early 18C–mid-19C] to make a speculative investment in sport or business, to wager, to make a bet. **4** [early–mid-19C] to treat, usu. to food and/or drink. **5** [mid–late 19C] to spend money freely or extravagantly. **6** [1980s+] (US campus) to give. **7** [1980s+] (US Black/campus) to wear stylish clothes. **8** [1980s+] (US Black) to spend money, usu. on a woman (cf. TRICK v.[1]).

sport *v.*[2] [19C] to have sexual intercourse; thus (W.I.) *sporter, sportgirl*, a prostitute (cf. SPORTING LADY). [euph.]

sport a report, to *phr.* [mid–late 19C] to spread information around.

sport a toe, to *phr.* [early–mid-19C] to dance.

sport away money *see* SPORT MONEY.

sport a woody, to *phr.* [1980s+] (US teen) to have an erection. [SE *sport*, to show off + WOODIE]

sport blubber *v.* [late 18C–20C] to expose one's bosom, esp. of a large, coarse woman. [SE *sport* + BLUBBER n.[2]]

sportfuck *v.* [1960s+] to have spontaneous, casual sexual intercourse. [SE *sport* + FUCK v.[1]]

sport-house *n.* [20C] (W.I.) a brothel (cf. ACCOMMODATION HOUSE; SPORTING HOUSE). [SPORT n.[1]]

sportify *v.* [1950s] (W.I.) to make people laugh, to amuse.

sporting *n.* [1960s] (drugs) the inhaling of cocaine. [the indulgence of a modern SPORT n.[2] (2)]

sporting *adj.* [1980s+] (US Black/campus) well-dressed, looking good. [SPORT v.[1] (7)]

sporting chance *n.* [late 19C+] a fair chance, although one that cannot be predicted.

sporting goods *n.* [20C] a male homosexual prostitute (cf. SPORTING LIFE n.[1]). [ext. of SPORT n.[2] (3)]

sporting house *n.* [late 19C–1940s] (US) a brothel (cf. ACCOMMODATION HOUSE). [SPORT n.[1] + SE *house*/HOUSE n.[1]]

sporting lady *n.* [mid-19C] (US) a prostitute, esp. when employed in a brothel. [SPORT n.[1] + SPORTING HOUSE]

sporting life *n.*[1] [20C] the 'good' life, i.e. money, liquor, women, all the desired pleasures of the flesh; the term is particularly popular as a description of the lifestyle of a US pimp. [SPORT v.[1]]

sporting life *n.*[2] [20C] a wife. [rhy. sl.]

sport money/sport away money v. [20C] (W.I.) to spend money freely on a hedonistic lifestyle. [SPORT v.¹]

sport off v. [late 19C] to do something easily. [SPORT v.¹ (5)]

sport one's ivory, to phr. [late 18C] to grin. [SE *sport* + IVORY n.¹]

sports king n. [1930s] (Irish) a noisy, drunken, hedonistic individual. [SPORT v.¹ (2)]

sportsman n. [19C] a womanizer, a promiscuous man. [SPORT n.¹ (2)]

sportsman for liquor n. [late 19C–1900s] a dedicated drinker (but not, in this context, a drunkard).

sportsman's gap/hole n. [19C] the vagina (cf. BLACK HOLE n.¹).

sport the dairy/dairies, to phr. [18C] of a woman, to reveal one's breasts (cf. AIR THE DAIRY). [SE *sport* + DAIRY]

sporty adj. [1980s+] (US campus) attractive, good-looking.

spot n.¹ [late 19C] a cake; thus *spot and scalder*, cake and tea.

spot n.² **1** [late 19C+] a small drink. **2** [20C] a small amount, a little bit, a portion, esp. in combs., e.g. *a spot of bother*, *a spot of trouble*.

spot n.³ **1** [20C] (orig. US) a term of imprisonment, usu. preceded by the number of years (cf. FIVE-SPOT; TEN-SPOT). **2** [1930s–60s] (Aus./N.Z.) £10. **3** [1940s+] (Aus.) £100 or $100. [sfx. -SPOT]

spot n.⁴ [1910s–20s] a detective. [omnibus jargon *spot*, a plainclothes official, employed by the company to oversee drivers and conductors; ult. SE *spot*, to notice]

spot n.⁵ [1930s+] a guess. [SPOT v.²]

spot n.⁶ **1** [1940s+] (orig. US Black) a nightclub. **2** [1940s+] (orig. US Black) an after-hours club. **3** [1970s+] (S.Afr.) an illicit bar, a shebeen. **4** [1990s] (US) an apartment used specifically for the sale of drugs (cf. DOPE HOUSE). [abbr. SE *night spot*]

spot v.¹ **1** [early 18C–mid-19C] to mark or note as a criminal or suspected person. **2** [mid-19C] to inform against.

spot v.² [late 19C] to gamble. [*spotting* winners]

spot v.³ [late 19C–1900s] (S.Afr.) to mock, to jeer at. [synon. Du. *spotten*]

spot v.⁴ [20C] to advance on credit. [? to place a mark or 'spot' on a ledger]

spot v.⁵ [1920s+] (N.Z.) to treat (others or oneself) to a drink. [SPOT n.² (1)]

-spot sfx. [mid-19C+] (US) a denomination of US currency note, e.g. *5-spot*, $5 bill, *10-spot*, $10 bill (cf. ACE-SPOT; SPOT n.³).

spotlight n. [1940s–60s] (US Black) **1** a light-skinned Black woman. **2** an African-American of mixed ancestry.

spot on adv. [1940s+] perfect, exactly right, accurate (cf. BANG ON adv.).

spot on burnt n. [1920s] a poached egg on toast, often in pl. with *pfx. two, three* etc.

spots n. [1980s+] (N.Z. drugs) small pieces of marijuana or hashish heated between two hot knives and inhaled.

spot someone out v. [1970s] (US Black) to ascertain the characteristics, hidden or otherwise, of a person (cf. PEEP SOMEONE'S HOLE-CARD).

spotted adj. [mid-19C] known by the police, under surveillance. [SPOT v.¹]

spotted dick n. [mid-19C+] a suet pudding with currants or raisins (cf. SPOTTED DOG; SPOTTED DONKEY; SPOTTED DUFF; SPOTTED LEOPARD). [20C use is SE]

spotted dick adj. [20C] sick. [rhy. sl.]

spotted dog n. **1** [mid-late 19C] a plum pudding (cf. SPOTTED DICK n.). **2** [20C] a currant loaf. [joc. pron. of SE *spotted dough*, the 'spots' are plums]

spotted donkey n. [19C] a plum pudding (cf. SPOTTED DICK n.).

spotted duff n. [late 19C] a plum pudding (cf. SPOTTED DICK n.). [joc. pron. of SE *spotted dough*]

spotted leopard n. [late 19C] a plum pudding (cf. SPOTTED DICK n.).

spotter n. **1** [mid-19C] a detective. **2** [mid-19C] an informer. **3** [1980s+] (drugs) a look-out. [SPOT v.¹/SE *spot*]

spotters n. [1940s] (US Black) the eyes. [SE *spot*]

spounce/spunks n. [20C] (W.I.) brashness, sauciness, courage, esp. of a young woman. [SPUNK n. (1) + SE *bounce*]

spouse n. [1980s+] (US campus) one's regular boy- or girl-friend.

spout n. [late 19C] a large and ever-open mouth.

spout v.¹ [early–mid-19C+] to pawn (cf. UP THE SPOUT). [the pawnbroker's SE *spout*]

spout v.² [mid-19C+] to talk effusively (cf. SPOUT OFF).

spout Billy v. [19C] to make one's living by reciting portions of Shakespeare in public houses. [SPOUT v.² + William, i.e. *Billy* Shakespeare]

spout ink v. [late 19C–1920s] to write for a living (cf. SLING INK). [SPOUT v.² + SE *ink*]

spout off/on v. [mid-19C+] to gabble on. [ext. of SPOUT v.²]

spow n. [20C] (US prison) prison-made coffee (cf. FLIT n.¹; MOUTHWASH n.²). [? SE *spew*, vomit]

spraff v. [20C] to talk, to chat. [ety. unknown]

sprag n. [early 18C] a fop, a dandy. [SE *sprag*, a sprightly young fellow, ? ult. SE *sprig*]

sprag v. [1910s–30s] (Aus.) **1** to meddle in someone's plans, to thwart. **2** to accost truculently. [SE *sprag*, a piece of wood used to check the revolution of a wheel or roller, usu. by inserting it between two of the spokes; a rod or bar used to prevent a vehicle from running backwards]

sprain one's ankle, to phr. [late 18C+] to be seduced, to be pregnant out of wedlock. [euph.]

sprang adj. [1990s] (Black) extremely intoxicated, esp. by crack cocaine. [var. on PRANG adj.]

sprarser/sparaser/sparesie/sparzer/sprasey/sprasy n. [1900s–70s] a sixpence. [? SPRAT n.¹]

sprat n.¹ [mid-19C] a sixpence. [its diminutive size, like that of the fish]

sprat n.² [late 19C+] an affectionate name used between lovers. [like many such names, it is based on a diminutive]

sprat day n. [mid-late 19C] the Lord Mayor's Day in London. [the arrival of *sprats* in the market at approx. the same time]

sprats n. [late 19C] one's possessions. [ety. unknown; ? fig. use of SPRAT n.¹]

spratz n. [1980s+] (US) semen, esp. at the moment of ejaculation. [Ger. *spritz*, to spray]

spray n. [1990s] (drugs) an inhalant. [the use of aerosol sprays to package inhalants]

spray someone's tonsils, to phr. [1930s+] (gay) to ejaculate in one's fellator's mouth.

spray starch n. [1960s+] (US gay) a fig. substance that keeps heterosexual wrists from drooping. [the theory that every man would be gay given the opportunity]

spray the spectators, to phr. [1990s] to masturbate.

spread n.¹ [late 18C–mid-19C] a saddle. [SE *spread*, a coverlet; the saddle also *spreads* the rider's legs]

spread n.² [early 19C+] a meal, esp. a sumptuous one; sometimes further defined as *morning spread*, breakfast etc. [by 20C the term was mainly facet./archaic, classically found in the children's stories of Enid Blyton (1897–1968)]

spread n.³ **1** [early–mid-19C] butter. **2** [early–mid-19C] jam, marmalade or any similar addition to bread and butter. **3** [mid-19C] an umbrella. **4** [mid-19C] a lady's shawl. **5** [mid-19C+] (US) a newspaper; thus a page, as in coverage of a news article or advertisement in a paper or magazine e.g. a *two-page spread*. **6** [1930s+] the thickening of one's waistline; esp. in *middle-aged spread*, the onset of fat in middle age. [lit. + fig. uses of SE]

spread/spread for *v.* [mid-19C] to have sexual intercourse (cf. BANG v.[1]; DO A SPREAD; SPREAD EAGLE). [the man *spreads* and the woman *spreads for*]

spread a technicolour rainbow, to *phr.* [1970s+] (US campus) to vomit (cf. TECHNICOLOUR YAWN).

spread beaver *see* SPLIT BEAVER.

spread city *n.* [20C] (US) the dormitory suburbs of a big city (cf. SLURB). [the SE *spread* of such real estate developments + sfx. -CITY]

spread eagle *n.* [20C] a position of heterosexual intercourse (cf. SPREAD v.).

spreader *n.* [17C] (Und.) butter. [its properties]

spread for *see* SPREAD v.

spread it thick, to *phr.* **1** [mid-19C+] (US) to exaggerate or elaborate. **2** [1920s] to live well; thus *spread it thin*, to live in poverty. [the spreading of butter and/or jam on bread]

spread one's jenk, to *phr.* [1920s–30s] (US Black) to have a good time, to celebrate, to have sex. [SE *spread* + *jenk*; ety. unknown but note SE (*high*) *jinks* or dial. *jannock*, liberal, hospitable, one who pays their share]

spread the broads, to *phr.* [mid-19C+] to play cards, esp. to cheat or to play a swindling game such as find the lady. [SE *spread* + BROADS, from the fanning out of the cards across the table for the punters to make their choice]

spread the bull, to *phr.* [1930s+] to talk boastfully, if inaccurately, of one's prowess. [SE *spread* + BULLSHIT n.]

'sprecious!/sprecious!/s'pretious! *excl.* [early–mid-17C] a mild oath, lit. 'God's precious' (cf. 's abbr.[1]).

spree *n.*[1] [early 19C+] **1** a hearty, boisterous good time. **2** a prolonged bout of drinking; thus [mid-19C+] *on a spree*, out on a party. [? SE *spray*, a drinking bout, but ? dial. *spreagh/ spreath*, a cattle raid, ult. Gaelic *spréidh*, cattle (E.P.); Hotten (1860) suggests Fr. *ésprit*, spirit or Du. root, as do B&L]

spree *n.*[2] [1940s] (W.I.) a girlfriend (cf. SPREE-BOY; SPREE-CHILD). [? SPREE n.[1]]

spree *v.* [early 19C+] to go out on a party, to take it easy. [SPREE n.[1]]

spree-boy *n.* [1950s] (W.I.) **1** a very well-dressed man, a dandy. **2** one who prefers pursuing pleasure to working hard; thus *spree-girl/-man/-master/-woman*. [SPREE n.[1] + SE *boy*]

spree-child *n.* [1950s] (W.I.) a very well-dressed, stylish woman (cf. SPREE n.[2]). [SPREE n.[1] + SE *child*]

spreeish *adj.* [19C] tipsy, drunk (cf. ABOUT RIGHT adj.[1]). [SPREE n.[1]]

s'pretious! *see* 'SPRECIOUS!

sprig *n.* [early 17C] a show-off. [? SE *sprig*, a young descendant]

spring *n.* [20C] an escape from prison; thus *make a spring*, to escape. [SPRING v.[4]]

spring *v.*[1] **1** [mid-19C] to offer a higher price. **2** [mid-19C–1900s] to pay over a sum of money, to buy a certain amount. **3** [late 19C–1910s] to afford. [SE *spring*, to cause to appear]

spring *v.*[2] [mid-19C] to appear suddenly, e.g. *where did you spring from?*

spring/spring for *v.*[3] [20C] (orig. US/Aus.) to pay for, to treat. [ext. of SPRING v.[1]]

spring *v.*[4] [1930s+] (orig. US) **1** to escape from prison. **2** to get a person out of prison, to have someone released.

spring *v.*[5] [1940s+] (Aus.) to see.

spring a leak *see* TAKE A LEAK.

spring ankle warehouse *n.* **1** [late 18C–early 19C] a prison (cf. ANKLE-SPRING WAREHOUSE; WAREHOUSE n.). **2** [19C] the work-house. [SE *spring*, i.e. sprain an *ankle* + *warehouse*, once confined in such a place, the inmates are unable to run off]

spring a partridge, to *phr.* [late 17C–18C] of a confidence trickster, to entrap a victim and then rob or otherwise defraud them. [sporting jargon *spring a partridge*, for a beater to cause a partridge to rise from cover]

spring a plant, to *phr.* [early–mid-19C] (Und.) to uncover the hiding place another villain uses for their plunder. [SE *spring*, to make something 'spring up' + PLANT]

springbutt *n.* [1960s+] (US) a keen, eager person (cf. EAGER BEAVER). [SE *spring* + BUTT n.[1]]

spring chicken *n.* [1910s+] a young or youthful person, almost always in phr. *he's/she's no spring chicken*.

springer *n.* [20C] (US Und.) a bail bondsman. [SPRING v.[4]]

springer-up *n.* [mid-19C] **1** a cheap tailor, selling off-the-peg clothing. **2** a tailor who pays employees the lowest possible wages. [the clothes 'spring up' without much art]

spring for *see* SPRING v.[3].

spring it/spring on *v.* [1940s+] to reveal a plan, with some element of surprise.

spring like a halfpenny knife *phr.* [late 19C] floppy, lacking tension or resilience. [the weak mechanism of a cheap clasp-knife]

spring on *see* SPRING IT.

springs *n.* [1990s] (US Black) the ability to jump high during a game of basketball (cf. HOPS n.[3]).

spring-sides *n.* [20C] (Aus.) elastic-sided boots.

spring to *v.* [1900s] **1** to afford, to come up with sufficient money for. **2** to achieve, to manage. [SPRING v.[1]]

spring up *v.* [mid-19C] to make cheap, off-the-peg clothes (cf. SPRINGER-UP).

sprinkle *v.*[1] [mid-19C+] to christen. [the application of holy water]

sprinkle *v.*[2] [1990s] (US Black teen) to tell a story, to lay out a situation.

sprite ... a'ite! *excl.* [1900s] (US teen) an excl. used when someone is using too much slang or speaking in a dialect which cannot readily be understood. [the excl. is supposed to mimic the speaker's incomprehensibility]

spritz *n.* [1910s+] (US) **1** carbonated water as a mixer for drinks. **2** a light shower of rain. [Yid. *spritz*, spray]

spritz *v.* [1950s+] **1** (mainly show business) to perform a stage monologue with much impromptu ad libbing, free-associating etc. **2** to air one's feelings, to emote. [Yid. *spritz*, to spray]

spritz *adv.* [1950s+] spontaneously, extempore, ad lib. [SPRITZ v.]

sprog *n.* [1940s+] a child. [18C *sprag*, a lively young fellow; note milit. *sprog*, a recruit]

sprout *n.*[1] [mid–late 19C] (US) a beating; thus *put through a course of sprouts*, to beat, to flog, to subject to intense, harsh discipline. [BUNCH OF SPROUTS]

sprout *n.*[2] [1930s+] (US) a child, a youngster. [SE *sprout*, usu. of vegetation, to grow]

sproutsy *adj.* [1970s+] (US) unconventional, hippie-like. [? the hippie diet of bean *sprouts* etc]

sprout wings *v.* [20C] (US) **1** to become morally superior or chaste. **2** to die. [i.e. one 'joins the angels']

spruce *adj.* [1900s–30s] spurious, fake, esp. in the context of a practical joke (cf. MADAME DE LUCE). [SPRUCE v.]

spruce *v.* [20C] to tell lies, 'stories'. [SE *spruce up*, i.e. the facts, or SPRUIK v.]

spruik *n.* [1910s+] (Aus./N.Z.) a showman's or other sales-man's patter.

spruik *v.* [1910s+] (Aus./N.Z.) to speak in a way that resembles a showman (cf. SPRUIKER). [? Yid. *shpruch*, saying, charm, incantation or Du. *spreken*, to talk]

spruiker *n.* [1910s+] (Aus.) **1** a loud and continual talker. **2** a barker for a fairground or carnival sideshow or a cinema, theatre or similar entertainment, who stands on the street to promote the show and attract an audience. [SPRUIK v.]

sprung *adj.*[1] [19C] drunk. [? one bounces along]

sprung *adj.*[2] [1980s+] (drugs) used of one who has just starting to use drugs. [? SE *sprung up*]

sprung *adj.*[3] [1990s] **1** (US Black gang) mentally unstable. **2** (US teen) sexually obsessed, romantically besotted. [abbr. LIGHTLY SPRUNG]

sprung on *adj.* [1990s] **1** (US Black/campus) romantically infatuated by, having a 'crush on'. **2** (US Black teen) having an erection. [(1) one's hopes etc *spring up*; (2) one's penis *springs up*]

spud *n.*[1] **1** [mid-19C+] a potato. **2** [1940s+] (W.I.) a ripe banana. **3** [1960s+] a hole in a sock (cf. POTATO n.[3]). **4** [1980s+] (N.Z. teen) a general term of abuse. [? SE *spud*, a digging fork with three broad prongs or dial. *spud*, a stumpy thing]

spud *n.*[2] [mid–late 19C] a baby's hand. [SE *pudgy* or dial. *spud*, a short, stumpy person]

spud *v.* [1920s–30s] (US Black) to play cards for low stakes. [? dial. *spud*, to muddle, to be uselessly busy]

spud barber *n.* [1930s+] one who peels potatoes (cf. SPUD-BASHING). [SPUD n.[1] (1) + SE *barber*]

spud-bashing *n.* [1940s+] the activity of peeling potatoes (cf. SPUD BARBER). [SPUD n.[1] (1) + BASH v.[1]; orig. milit. use, when the job was compulsory and part of kitchen fatigues]

spuddy *n.* [mid-19C] **1** a seller of bad potatoes. **2** a seller of hot baked potatoes. [SPUD n.[1] (1)]

spudge around *v.* [1920s] (US) to exert oneself, to apply oneself.

spud-grinder *n.* [1970s] the throat. [SPUD n.[1] (1) + SE *grinder*]

spud islander *n.* [1950s+] a native or inhabitant of Prince Edward Island, Canada. [SPUD n.[1] (1); the high quality of its potatoes]

spudsacked *adj.* [1990s] passed out in a heap. [SPUD n.[1] (1) + SE *sack*]

spudwater *n.* [1990s] thin, watery semen. [SPUD n.[1] (1) + SE *water*]

spuff *n.* [1990s] semen. [echoic of the ejaculation]

spuff up *v.* [1990s] to masturbate (cf. BEAT OFF). [SPUFF n.]

spug *n.* [1920s+] (Aus./N.Z.) a sparrow. [dial. *spadger*, a sparrow]

spume *n.* [1990s] semen.

spun *adj.* **1** [20C] defeated, lost for ideas. **2** [1920s] exhausted, drained of energy.

spunging-house *see* SPONGING-HOUSE.

spunk *n.* **1** [late 18C+] courage, bravery. **2** [late 19C+] semen. **3** [1960s+] (Aus.) someone seen as sexually attractive (cf. SPUNK RAT). [? fig. use of Scot./dial. *spunk*, a spark]

spunk/spunk off *v.* [late 19C+] (US) to ejaculate. [SPUNK n. (2)]

spunk-bound *adj.* [late 19C+] of a man, lethargic, lacking energy. [SPUNK n. (2); ? the belief that sexual inactivity leads to indolence]

spunk bubble *n.* [1970s] (Aus.) an attractive young woman, a nubile teenager. [SPUNK n. (3) + SE *bubble*]

spunk-bucket/-dustbin *n.* [1990s] a promiscuous woman or one who is branded as such (cf. SPUNK-POT). [SPUNK n. (2) + SE *bucket/dustbin*]

spunk-faker *n.* [mid-19C] an ostensible match-seller, whose outwardly respectable, if impoverished profession often hides less reputable, and usu. fraudulent, pursuits (cf. MUSH-FAKER). [dial. *spunk*, a spark, thus a match + FAKER]

spunk-fencer *n.* [mid-19C] a match-seller (cf. TIMBER-MER-CHANT). [dial. *spunk*, spark, tinder; note dial. *spunks*, lucifer matches]

spunk-gullet *n.* [20C] a general term of abuse, lit. a fellator. [SPUNK n. (2) + SE *gullet*]

spunk-head *n.* [1990s] a general term of abuse. [SPUNK n. (2) + sfx. -HEAD (1)]

spunko *adj.* [1980s+] (teen society) an attractive, intelligent and fashionable man. [SPUNK n. (2) + sfx. -O]

spunk off *see* SPUNK v.

spunk-pot *n.* [1990s] the vagina (cf. SPUNK-BUCKET). [SPUNK n. (2) + SE *pot*]

spunk rat *n.* [1980s+] (Aus.) a sexually attractive person. [SPUNK n. (3) + SE *rat*]

spunks *see* SPOUNCE.

spunky *adj.* **1** [late 18C+] courageous, brave, plucky. **2** [1960s+] (Aus.) sexy. [SPUNK n.]

spurge *n.* [1920s+] (Aus.) an effeminate young man. [SE *spurge*, one or other of several species of the genus *Euphorbia*, some of which are considered near weeds; thus a pun on WEEDY]

spurt *n.* [mid–late 19C] a small amount, a small quantity, esp. of alcohol.

spurter *n.* [1990s] a particularly attractive young woman.

spurt one's curd, to *phr.* [1990s] to ejaculate.

sputnik *n.* [1980s+] (drugs) a mixture of Pakistani cannabis and opium. [SE *sputnik*, the Russian spacecraft (lit., 'travelling companion', 'fellow traveller') launched in 1957; it puts you 'into orbit']

sputterbudget *n.* [20C] (US) one who chatters on to excess (cf. FUSSBUDGET; TATTLEBUDGET). [SE *sputter* + *budget*, one who has certain characteristics]

spy *n.* [19C] the eye.

spy the cloven foot, to *phr.* [18C] to see the worst side of a situation, to suspect criminality or fraud. [the proverbial belief that no matter how hard the Devil tries to disguise his true personality, he can never hide his cloven foot]

s.q.p.q. *phr.* [1970s+] (society) a warning note appended to the name of a possible male escort by a debutante or her mother. [abbr. *suspiciously quiet, probably queer*]

squab *n.*[1] [early 18C] a very fat person. [? SE *squab*, a fat cushion or a well-upholstered sofa]

squab *n.*[2] (US) **1** [19C+] a fool, an unsophisticated person, a peasant. **2** [1920s] a young woman (cf. CHICK n.[4]). [SE *squab*, a raw, inexperienced person + later uses as a young, unfledged bird or animal]

squab *v.* [1990s] (US Black) to confront. [? abbr. SE *squabble*]

squabby *adj.* [mid-18C–mid-19C] squat, short and thick. [SQUAB n.[1]]

squab-job *n.* [1910s] a job that suits a young woman. [SQUAB n.[2] (2) + JOB n.[9]]

Squad, the *n.* [1950s+] (Und.) the Flying *Squad* (cf. SWEENEY n.[1]). [abbr.]

squaddie/squaddy *n.* [1940s+] a regular private soldier. [SE *squad*]

squalino *v.* [early 19C] to squeal or squall. [SE *squall*, to scream loudly or discordantly]

squall/squawl *n.* [early 18C] (Und.) a voice. [weak use of SE]

square, the *n.*[1] [mid-19C] (Und.) the laws and customs of the underworld, by which all criminals should abide (cf. CROSS n.).

square *n.*[2] [mid-19C–1960s] (Aus.) gin, a bottle of gin, also as *square cut* (cf. SQUAREFACE; SQUARE GIN). [the shape of the bottle]

square *n.*[3] [late 19C+] (US) a proper or *square* meal. [abbr.]

square *n.*[4] [late 19C] (society) a quadrille or the lancers (a dance that developed from the quadrille in the mid-19C). [such dances involve the forming of squares]

square *n.*[5] **1** [late 19C+] (Aus.) a respectable woman; thus expanded as *square Jane and no nonsense* (cf. HALF-SQUARE). **2** [1940s+] (orig. US) a regular working man or woman (cf. CHUMP n.[2]; DINNER PAILER; WORKING STIFF). **3** [1940s+] (orig. US Black) a naïve person, one who believes in White America's promises, one who has little sexual sophistication. **4** [1950s+] (gay) a heterosexual. [fig. rectilinearity]

square n.[6] [1920s+] (US prison) a factory-made cigarette, whether prison-issue or commercially produced (cf. STRAIGHT n.[2]; TAILOR; TAILOR-MADE; T.M.). [SQUARE adj. (1)]

square adj. **1** [mid-19C+] honest, respectable, upright. **2** [1940s+] (orig. US Black) conventional, conservative, naïve, dull. [prior use SE from 16C]

square v. **1** [mid-19C+] to settle, to put right, spec. to deal with problems, often by using influence, bribes, threats etc; thus *square his nibs*, to pay off a policeman. **2** [late 19C] to murder, to kill. [i.e. to make SQUARE adj. (1)]

square adv. **1** [mid-19C] (US) completely, unreservedly. **2** [mid-late 19C] fairly, honestly, straightforwardly. **3** [mid-19C+] (US) completely, exactly. **4** [late 19C] properly, correctly. [SQUARE adj. (1)]

square affair/bit/piece n. [late 19C–1910s] one's regular girlfriend (cf. SQUARE PUSHER). [SQUARE adj. (1) + SE *affair*/BIT n.[5]/PIECE n.[1]]

square an' all phr. [1910s+] (Aus.) absolutely, honestly, truly. [SQUARE adj. (1)]

square a rap, to phr. [1940s+] to have a criminal charge dropped. [SQUARE v. + RAP n.[3]]

square as a billiard/golf/tennis ball phr. [1940s–50s] (Aus.) anything but honest or 'square', whether morally, sexually or otherwise (cf. BENT AS A NINE-BOB NOTE). [SQUARE adj. (1)]

square-ass adj. [1940s+] (US Black) unsophisticated, naïve, 'straight'. [SQUARE adj. (2) + sfx. -ASS]

square at see SQUARE UP v.[1].

square away v. **1** [mid-19C] to deal with, to settle. **2** [20C] to sort out, to put away. **3** [1920s] to explain, to put in the picture. [milit. jargon *square away*, to put in proper order]

square-bashing n. [1950s+] military drill; thus *square-basher*, a private soldier. [SE *square*, the parade ground + BASH v.[1]]

square bit see SQUARE AFFAIR.

squarebrain n. **1** [20C] a fool (cf. BAKEBRAIN). **2** [1940s–50s] (US Black) a conventional person, a fool, a dullard, with overtones of conservatism. [SQUARE n.[5] (3) + sfx. -*brain*]

square broad n. [1940s–70s] (US Black) any woman who is not a prostitute. [SQUARE adj. (2) + BROAD n.[2]]

square business n. [1950s+] (US Black/prison) honesty, truth; often affixed to a declaratory sentence as a means of emphasizing the speaker's sincerity. [SQUARE adj. (1) + SE *business*]

square cove n. [mid-19C] an honest man. [SQUARE adj. (1) + COVE]

square-crib n. [early 19C] a respectable house (cf. CROSS-CRIB). [SQUARE adj. (1) + CRIB n.[3]]

square deal n. [mid-19C+] (orig. US) honest treatment, a proper business deal, a good bargain etc (cf. FAIR DEAL). [SQUARE adj. (1) + SE *deal*]

square dinkum! see FAIR DINKUM!

squaredom n. [1950s+] (orig. US) the world of the unsophisticated, the unworldly. [SQUARE n.[5] (3)]

square-eyes n. [1960s+] one who watches an excess of TV and thus, supposedly, develops eyes the same shape as the screen.

squareface n. [19C] gin (cf. SQUARE n.[2]). [the shape of the bottle]

square gin n. [late 19C–1900s] (Aus./N.Z.) gin (cf. SQUARE n.[2]). [the shape of the bottle]

square-go n. [20C] a fair fight. [SQUARE adj. (1) + GO n.[3] (5)]

squarehead n.[1] **1** [mid-19C+] an honest person. **2** [1920s+] (Aus.) a timid or conscience-ridden thief. **3** [1930s+] (Aus.) one who has no previous criminal convictions. [SQUARE adj. (1) + sfx. -HEAD (1)]

squarehead n.[2] [20C] **1** a German or one of German origins. **2** (US) a Scandinavian (cf. BOXHEAD). **3** (Can.) an Anglophone Canadian. [SE *square* + *head*; (1), (2) ? the severe 'Prussian' haircuts]

square in a social circle n. [1930s–40s] (US Black) a misfit. [var. on SE *square peg in a round hole*]

square it v. [late 19C] to live or act honestly. [SQUARE n.[5]]

square john n. [1920s+] **1** a respectable member of society (cf. JOHN Q PUBLIC). **2** (US Und.) a prisoner who is not a professional criminal. **3** (drugs) one who eschews drugs. [SQUARE adj. + JOHN n.[1]]

square-john adj. [1940s+] (US) respectable, upright. [SQUARE JOHN]

square mackerel n. [1980s+] (drugs) marijuana. [sea-borne smuggling of marijuana]

square moll n. [mid-19C] an honest woman. [SQUARE adj. (1) + MOLL]

square-off n. [1910s+] (Aus.) an excuse. [SQUARE v. (1)]

square off v.[1] [early 19C+] (US) to prepare for a fight, to adopt an aggressive posture (cf. SQUARE UP v.[1]). [SE *square*]

square off v.[2] [1940s+] (Aus.) **1** to placate or conciliate someone, to apologize. **2** to pay; can be used quite legitimately, but often carries a sense of corruption, bribery etc. [SQUARE v.]

square one n. [1930s+] (US) the starting point, the beginning. [the image of children's board-games, e.g. snakes and ladders]

square one's circle, to phr. [1980s+] (US campus) to have sexual intercourse with someone.

square out v. [1960s+] (US Black) **1** to ridicule, to tease. **2** of two people, to indulge in a series of ritual insults (cf. PLAY THE DOZENS). [SQUARE OFF v.[1]/SQUARE UP v.[1]]

square piece see SQUARE AFFAIR.

square plug n. [1920s+] (US Und.) a prisoner who is not a professional criminal (cf. SQUARE JOHN).

square pusher n. [late 19C–1930s] **1** a boyfriend (cf. SQUARE AFFAIR). **2** a respectable young woman; thus *square-pushing*, courting nursemaids and similar women. [SQUARE adj. (1) + PUSHER n.[1]]

square-rigged adj. [mid-19C] well-dressed, smart, respectable. [naut. jargon]

square rigger n.[1] [20C] a derog., euph. term for a Black person. [rhy. sl. *square rigger* = NIGGER]

square rigger n.[2] (N.Z.) **1** [20C] a square gin bottle, often used to hold beer. **2** [1980s] a half-gallon (2.3 litre) flagon of beer.

square setting n. [1950s–60s] (US Black) a respectable party, without drugs, loud music etc. [SQUARE adj. (2) + SET n.[3]]

square shake n. [1940s+] (US) a fair deal, honest treatment. [SQUARE adj. (1) + SE *handshake*]

square shooter n. [1910s+] (US) an honest, trustworthy person. [SQUARE adj. (1) + SE *shooter*]

squaresville/squareville n. [1950s–70s] (US Black/teen) a conventional and thus boring place, person or event (cf. CUBESVILLE). [SQUARE n.[5] (3) + sfx. -VILLE]

square the beef, to phr. [20C] (orig. US Und.) to repair a difficult or grievous situation. [SQUARE v. + BEEF n.[2]]

square time bob n. [1980s+] (drugs) crack cocaine. [ety. unknown]

square-toes n. [late 18C–early 19C] an old man. [his chosen, old-fashioned style of footwear]

square to the wood phr. [1940s+] (US Black) extremely respectable, conservative, naïve. [intensifier of SQUARE adj. (2)]

square-up n. [1940s] a quarrel, an argument. [SQUARE UP v.[1]]

square up/at v.[1] [mid-19C+] to challenge, usu. preparatory to a fight (cf. SQUARE OFF v.[1]). [the head-on postures of the opponents]

square up v.[2] [mid-19C] to pay off one's debts. [SQUARE v. (1)]

square up *v.*[3] (US Black) **1** [1940s–60s] to leave the underworld, whether of pimping, drug sales and use or general criminality and devote oneself to a conventional lifestyle (cf. TURN SQUARE). **2** [1960s] to betray. [SQUARE adj. (2)]

squareville *see* SQUARESVILLE.

square with *v.* [mid-19C+] to make amends, to make up for, to even up. [SQUARE v. (1)]

squarie/squarey *n.*[1] [1910s+] (Aus.) a young woman, a girlfriend. [SQUARE n.[5] (1)]

squarie/squarey *n.*[2] (Aus.) **1** [1920s+] a timid or conscience-ridden thief. **2** [1930s+] one who has no previous criminal convictions. [abbr. SQUAREHEAD n.[1]]

squash *v.* [20C] **1** to crush verbally (cf. PUT DOWN v.[2]). **2** to argue, to fight. **3** (US) to sort out a problem.

squashed *adj.* [1970s+] very drunk (cf. BASTED).

squashed flies/fly *n.* [late 19C+] biscuits containing currants, Garibaldi biscuits.

squashed tomatoes/sardines *n.* [1950s+] (juv.) **1** a game that involves knocking on a door and then rushing away before the home-owner answers it. **2** a game in which two children rush towards and then run into each other.

squasho *n.* [late 19C+] (US) a derog. term for a Black person. ['the negro's love of melons, pumpkins, squashes etc' (Ware) but more likely QUASHIE]

squash the noggin, to *phr.* [1990s] to indulge in an act of anal intercourse. [SE *squash* + misuse of NOGGIN n.[1]; i.e. the head is that of the penis]

squat *n.*[1] **1** [late 19C–1940s] a seat, a chair. **2** [1970s+] (US) excrement.

squat *n.*[2] [1930s+] (US) nothing, zero. [abbr. DIDDLY-SQUAT]

squat *v.* [1930s+] (US) **1** to sit down. **2** to defecate.

squat hot *v.* [1920s+] (US) to be executed in the electric chair. [HOT SQUAT]

squat on *v.* [late 19C] (US) to oppose.

squat-pad *n.* [1940s] (US Black) a lobby, a lounge. [SQUAT v. (1) + PAD n.[2]]

squattage *n.* [1930s+] (Aus.) a farmer's home and the land they own. [SE *squatter* + sfx. *-age*, implying a sphere of action]

squatter *n.* **1** [20C] the buttocks. **2** [1940s] (US Black) a stool, a chair. **3** [1960s+] (Ulster) a voyeur.

squatter's daughter *n.* [20C] (Aus.) water. [rhy. sl.]

squattez-vous! *excl.* [late 19C+] (teen) sit down! [cod Fr.]

squattocracy *n.* [mid-19C+] (Aus.) the élite of the country's farming magnates, viewed as an Australian aristocracy. [SE *squatter* + sfx. *-ocracy*]

squaver *v.* [20C] (Ulster) to wave one's arms, to direct vehicles (as in parking), to square up to. [SE *quaver*]

squawk *n.* **1** [20C] (US) a complaint. **2** [1940s–50s] (prison) any form of petition, to the governor or to the Home Secretary.

squawk *v.* [late 19C+] (US) **1** to complain. **2** to inform, to betray.

squawk-box *n.* [1940s+] (orig. US) an internal office communication system.

squawl *see* SQUALL.

squeak *n.*[1] **1** [late 17C–mid-19C] an informer, esp. one who turns informer to save themselves after being arrested. **2** [20C] a piece of information passed over to the police. [SQUEAK v.]

squeak *n.*[2] [1980s] a precociously trendy youngster, so termed by their (slightly) elders. [abbr. SE *pipsqueak*]

squeak *v.* [late 17C+] to inform, to confess; thus [20C] *squeak on*, to betray, to inform against, [1930s+] *put the squeak in*, to turn informer, to inform.

squeak beef *v.* [late 17C–early 19C] to cry 'stop thief!' [var. on HOT BEEF!]

squeak box *n.* [1940s–50s] (US Black) a violin.

squeaker *n.*[1] **1** [late 17C–18C] a pot-boy. **2** [late 17C–18C] a

child, esp. an illegitimate child (cf. STIFLE THE SQUEAKER). **3** [late 18C] an organ pipe. **4** [early 19C] a foxhound. **5** [mid-late 19C] a young pig.

squeaker *n.*[2] [late 19C] a heavy blow. [it makes the recipient 'squeak']

squeaker *n.*[3] [late 19C+] an informer. [SQUEAK v.]

squeaker *n.*[4] [1960s+] (US/Can.) a very close contest. [SE *squeak by/through*]

squeakers *n.* [20C] (Aus.) boots, shoes. [SE *squeak*]

squeaky shoe *n.* [20C] a plain-clothes police officer (cf. GUMSHOE n.; ROUNDHEEL).

squeal *n.*[1] **1** [early 19C] an informer. **2** [mid-19C+] (US police) the report of a crime by a member of the public (cf. SQUEAK n.[1]). [SQUEAL v.]

squeal *n.*[2] [late 19C+] bacon. [esp. in short-order cooking use]

squeal/squeal on *v.* [mid-19C+] **1** to inform against one's partners in crime. **2** to report a crime to the police. [late 19C+ use mainly US, but note Edgar Wallace title, *The Squealer* (1927)]

squealer *n.* [mid-19C+] an informer. [SQUEAL v.]

squeal on *see* SQUEAL v.

squeal rule/law *n.* [1960s+] (US) the law requiring parental notification when an underage girl applies for a prescription for contraceptives. [SQUEAL v. + SE *rule*]

squeedunk *n.* [20C] (US) a generic name for a small town. [var. on PODUNK]

squeek *v.* [1980s+] (US campus) to engage in sex. [? play on SE *squeak*]

squeezable *adj.* [1910s–20s] used of one whom it is easy to make speak (and reveal information). [SQUEEZE v.[1]]

squeeze *n.*[1] **1** [late 18C–late 19C] a crowded social gathering (cf. CRUSH n.[1]). **2** [early-mid-19C] an escape; thus *narrow squeeze*, a lucky escape. **3** [late 19C+] a hard bargain. **4** [20C] a difficult situation.

squeeze *n.*[2] **1** [19C] the neck. **2** [mid-19C] the gallows rope. **3** [1920s+] (Aus.) the female waist. **4** [1940s] (US Black) a belt. [i.e. that which squeezes or is squeezed]

squeeze *n.*[3] [19C] a plan, an occupation. [? one 'squeezes' the brain]

squeeze *n.*[4] [mid-19C; 1970s+] silk, and any garment made of it, e.g. a silk tie. [the quality of the fabric that will squeeze into a minuscule space]

squeeze *n.*[5] [late 19C–1940s] (orig. Aus.) an impression of a key made for criminal purposes.

squeeze *n.*[6] [1920s+] (orig. US Black) a close friend (cf. HOME SQUEEZE; MAIN SQUEEZE). [SE *squeeze*, i.e. the physical affection involved]

squeeze *n.*[7] [1970s] **1** (US Black) liquor. **2** (drugs) phencyclidine (cf. ACE n.[3]). [ety. unknown; (1) ? the *squeezing* of grapes]

squeeze *adj.* [1980s+] (US campus) **1** accidental, fortunate. **2** of poor quality, second-rate. [events, objects that *squeeze through*]

squeeze *v.*[1] **1** [early 19C] to bring in trouble, to cause difficulties for. **2** [1940s] (orig. US) to pressurize, to blackmail. **3** [1940s+] (orig. US) to inform, to pass on information.

squeeze/squeeze one's head *v.*[2] [20C] to defecate.

squeeze-box *n.* **1** [late 19C–1900s] a harmonium. **2** [1930s+] an accordion or concertina. [(1) the pressing of feet on the pedals; (2) the pressing together of the two sides of the instrument]

squeeze clout *n.* [late 18C] a neck-cloth. [SQUEEZE n.[2] (1) + SE *clout*]

squeeze crab *n.* [late 18C–mid-19C] a morose man, a diminutive man. [SE *squeeze* + CRAB n.[1] (1)]

squeeze-'em-close *n.* [mid-late 19C] sexual intercourse.

squeeze-eye *n.* [1940s] (W.I.) a derog. term for a Chinese person. [the 'squeezed' shape of the Oriental eye]

squeeze me *phr.* [1990s] (US campus) excuse me. [pron.]

squeeze off/off on *v.* [1980s+] to fire a gun, to fire a gun at someone. [SE *squeeze* the trigger]

squeeze one's head *see* SQUEEZE V.².

squeeze one's/the lemon *phr.* **1** [late 19C+] of a man, to urinate. **2** [1930s+] (orig. US Black) to have sexual intercourse. [note blues use, as a sexual euph.: 'Squeeze my lemon, till the juice runs down my leg']

squeeze-pidgin *n.* [1970s] a bribe. [SE *squeeze* + *pidgin*, language (here of corruption); but note PIGEON n.²]

squeeze play *n.* [1910s+] (US) the application of force or pressure to get what one wants. [SQUEEZE V.¹ + PLAY n.¹ + pun on baseball jargon *squeeze play*, 'a tactic whereby the batter bunts so that a runner at third base can attempt to reach home safely and score' (*OED*)]

squeezer *n.* **1** [mid-19C] the neck. **2** [mid-19C] the gallows (cf. SCRAG SQUEEZER). **3** [1950s] (W.I.) a pair of pince-nez spectacles.

squeeze the cheese, to *phr.* [1990s] to masturbate.

squeeze the lemon *see* SQUEEZE ONE'S LEMON.

squeeze up *v.* [20C] of a man, to enter one's female partner to begin intercourse.

squeeze-wax *n.* [late 17C–early 19C] **1** a surety for a loan. **2** 'a good-natured foolish fellow, ready to become security for another, under hand and seal' (Grose, 1785) (cf. SEALER).

squeezing *adj.* [1970s+] of age, approaching, e.g. *squeezing 50*.

squelch *n.* [1940s+] **1** (orig. US) a devastating argument or retort, a crushing blow. **2** (Aus.) a blunder, a *faux pas* (cf. PUT ONE'S FOOT IN IT).

squelcher *n.* [mid–late 19C] **1** a crushing blow. **2** one who crushes, physically or intellectually. [SE *squelch*]

squelch-gutted *adj.* [late 18C–early 19C] fat-bellied.

squelching *n.* [1950s–60s] (gay) sex without any pretence at affection. [note former punk star Johnny Rotten (John Lydon; b.1957): 'Love is two minutes fifty-nine seconds of squishing noises. It shows your mind isn't clicking right']

squelchy monkey *n.* [1990s] a very wet vagina. [SE *squelchy* + MONKEY n.¹⁰]

squib *n.*¹ [mid-19C] a gun; thus *double-tongued squib*, a double-barrelled gun. [SE *squib*, a small firework]

squib *n.*² [mid-19C] **1** a paintbrush. **2** (coster) a head of asparagus. **3** a form of sweet made from treacle. [resemblance]

squib *n.*³ (Aus.) **1** [20C] a coward, one who backs down. **2** [20C] a weakling, a small person. **3** [1910s+] a plan that fails to work. [SE *damp squib*]

squib/squib it *v.* [1930s+] (Aus.) **1** to evade a responsibility, to shirk a duty, to betray, to let down. **2** to behave in a cowardly manner, to back down, to squirm. [SQUIB n.³ but note UK dial. *squib*, to run away]

squibbed off *adj.* [1930s] (US) shot, murdered. [SQUIB OFF]

squib it *see* SQUIB V.

squib off *v.* [1930s] (US) to murder, to shoot. [SQUIB n.¹]

squib on *v.* [1910s+] (Aus.) to betray. [SQUIB n.³ (1)]

squid/squidjigger *n.*¹ [20C] (Can.) any resident of the Maritime provinces. [fishing jargon *squidjigging*, fishing for squid with a baited hook that one 'jigs' in the hope of luring one's target]

squid *n.*² [1980s+] (US campus) **1** a particularly hard worker. **2** a fool, an incompetent.

squidge *v.* [late 19C+] to squeeze together, esp. of malleable substances. [Isle of Wight dial.]

squidjigger *see* SQUID n.¹.

squiff *n.* [1920s+] (Aus.) a drunkard. [SQUIFFY]

squiff *v.* [19C] to drink. [? SE *quaff*]

squiffed *adj.* [late 19C+] drunk (cf. SQUIFFY). [SQUIFF v.]

squiffer *n.* [late 19C–1910s] a concertina. [? SE *squeezer*]

squiff it *v.* [1940s+] (Aus.) to die. [ext. of SQUIFF OUT or var. on SNUFF IT]

squiff out *v.* [20C] to collapse through drunkenness. [SQUIFF v.]

squiffy *adj.* **1** [mid-19C+] drunk. **2** [1920s+] (Aus.) foolish, silly. **3** [1930s+] (teen) menstruating. **4** [1940s+] askew, unbalanced. [SQUIFF v. ? underpinned by SKEW-WHIFF]

squiffy-eyed *adj.* [late 19C+] drunk. [ext. of SQUIFFY (1)]

squilde *n.* [late 19C] 'a term of street chaff. Word designed from a Christian name and a surname coalesced' (Ware). [the name in question being *Oscar Wilde* (1854–1900), then facing his rapid fall from grace]

squillion *n.* [1950s+] a hypothetical and enormous number, a multiple of many millions (cf. SKILLION).

squinny-eyes *n.* [late 17C–mid-19C] squinting eyes; thus *squinny-eyed*, squinting (cf. SQUINT-A-PIPES; SQUINTERS).

squint-a-pipes *n.* [late 18C–mid-19C] a squinting man or woman (cf. SQUINNY-EYES). ['Said to be born in the middle of the week, and looking both ways for Sunday' (Grose, 1796)]

squinters *n.* [late 19C] squinting eyes (cf. SQUINNY-EYES).

squint like a bag of nails, to *phr.* [late 18C–mid-19C] to squint in a noticeable manner. [the squinter's eyes point in as many directions as nails dropped into a bag]

squire *n.*¹ **1** [late 17C–19C] a general title used ironically in a number of contexts (cf. APPLE SQUIRE; SQUIRE OF ALSATIA; SQUIRE OF THE BODY; SQUIRE OF THE COMPANY; SQUIRE OF THE GIMLET; SQUIRE OF THE PAD; SQUIRE OF THE PETTICOAT; SQUIRE OF THE PLACKET). **2** [late 17C–mid-18C] a fool. [SE *squire*, a title originally used to denote an esquire, a young man of good birth, attendant upon a knight, but by 17C referring mainly to a country gentleman; in (2) a squire is one who is foolish enough to serve another]

squire *n.*² [early 19C+] a general term of address, no particular rank or intimacy indicated (cf. GUV; GUVNOR).

squire of Alsatia *n.* [late 17C–early 19C] **1** a gentleman who has been drawn to the criminal world and there found himself fleeced, robbed and generally rendered destitute by its denizens. **2** an overly generous man (cf. SIR TIMOTHY; STAND SQUIRE). **3** a rich fool (cf. SQUIRE n.¹). [SE *squire* + ALSATIA; best known as the title of Thomas Shadwell's play, first staged in 1688]

squire of the body *n.* [17C] a pimp (cf. APPLE-MONGER; SQUIRE n.¹). [*squire*, mocking the SE *esquire* or the 'country squire' + SE *body*; cf. KNIGHT and its combs.]

squire of the company *n.* [late 18C–early 19C] one who treats the rest of the company (cf. SQUIRE n.¹).

squire of the gimlet *n.* [late 17C–late 18C] a publican, a tapster (cf. SQUIRE n.¹). [SE *gimlet*, used as a corkscrew]

squire of the gusset *see* KNIGHT OF THE GUSSET.

squire of the pad *n.* [18C] a highwayman (cf. SQUIRE n.¹). [PAD n.¹]

squire of the petticoat *n.* [late 17C–18C] a pimp (cf. SQUIRE n.¹; PETTICOAT MERCHANT).

squire of the placket *n.* [17C] a pimp (cf. APPLE-MONGER; SQUIRE n.¹). [SE *squire*, mocking the SE *esquire* or the 'country squire' + PLACKET; cf. KNIGHT and its combs.]

squirish *adj.*¹ [late 17C–early 18C] used of 'One that pretends to Pay all Reckonings, and is not strong enough in the Pocket' (B.E.).

squirish *adj.*² [late 18C–early 19C] foolish. [SQUIRE n.¹ (2)]

squirl *n.* [mid–late 19C] an ornate flourish in one's writing. [? SE *squiggle* + *twirl*]

squirm, the *n.* [1900s–10s] the art nouveau style. [the curves and curlicues that typified it]

squirms, the *n.* [1930s+] a sensation of great embarrassment.

squirrel *n.*[1] [late 18C–early 19C] a prostitute. ['like that animal she covers her back with her tail' (Grose, 1796)]

squirrel *n.*[2] [1920s–30s] (US) illicitly distilled liquor. [? it is 'squirreled away']

squirrel *n.*[3] [1940s+] (US) **1** an eccentric person. **2** a psychoanalyst. [pun on NUTS *adj.*]

squirrel *n.*[4] [1970s] (drugs) a mixture of LSD and some other drug, or of cocaine, marijuana and phencyclidine. [the effects are to make one SQUIRRELY]

squirrel *n.*[5] [1970s] (US campus) **1** the female pubic hair (cf. BEAVER *n.*[4]). **2** a woman. [? coined independently of SQUIRREL *n.*[1]]

squirrel-food *n.* [1940s+] (US) one who is crazy or eccentric. [pun on NUTS *adj.*]

squirrel-kisser *n.* [1990s] (US campus) an environmentalist.

squirrely *adj.* [1970s+] (US campus) eccentric, odd. [play on NUTS *adj.*]

squirrel-shooter *n.* [20C] (US) a farmer, a rustic.

squirt *n.*[1] [mid-19C] **1** a drink. **2** champagne.

squirt *n.*[2] [mid-19C] a doctor, a chemist. [their use of syringes]

squirt *n.*[3] [mid-19C+] (orig. US) **1** a dandy, a fop. **2** a small, insignificant person, often a child.

squirt *n.*[4] [late 19C–1940s] (Aus.) a revolver. [it *squirts* bullets]

squirt *n.*[5] [1920s+] very cheap but still effective beer. [it *squirt'* from the beer-tap]

squirt *n.*[6] **1** [1980s+] (US gay) ejaculation. **2** [1980s+] (US campus) a faecal stain on one's underwear due to liquid emitted when breaking wind or through a badly cleaned anus (cf. HERSHEY SQUIRT). **3** [1990s] an act of urination.

squirt and a squeeze *n.* [mid-19C] sexual intercourse; thus *do a squirt and a squeeze*, to have intercourse (cf. SQUIRT *n.*[6]).

squirter *n.* [late 19C–1930s] a pistol. [ext. of SQUIRT *n.*[4]]

squirt game *n.* [1920s+] drinking the cheapest forms of alcohol for intoxication's sake alone. [SQUIRT *n.*[5]]

squirt 'n' spurt *n.* [1990s] (US) masturbation; thus *play squirt 'n' spurt*, to masturbate.

squirt one off *v.* [1990s] to masturbate.

squirt one's juice, to *phr.* [20C] of a man, to ejaculate. [SE *squirt* + JUICE *n.*[2] (2)]

squish *n.* [1910s] rubbish, nonsense. [? dial. *squish*, a soggy mess]

squish *adj.* [1990s] (US teen) crooked, off-centre. [SQUISH *v.* (1)]

squish *v.* [1950s+] **1** to squash, to squeeze. **2** to make one's way (usu. through ground water of some sort or mud) while making a 'squishing' sound. [echoic]

squishy *adj.* [1950s+] (US) sentimental, mawkish (cf. SCHMALTZY). [fig. use of SQUISH *v.*]

squit *n.* [late 19C+] (esp. teen) a worthless, contemptible person. [SQUIRT *n.*[3]]

squitters, the *n.* [late 19C+] diarrhoea. [SHIT *n.*[1]/ME *scite*; prior use f. 17C is SE]

squivalens *n.* [late 19C–1900s] (Aus.) extras, 'perks'. [? SE *equivalents*]

squiz/squizz *n.* [1910s+] (Aus./N.Z.) a look, a glance; thus *squiz*, to inspect, to peep at surreptitiously. [SE *quiz*, to look at ? + *squint* or Devon dial. *squiz*, to examine critically]

squooshy *adj.* [1950s+] (US) soft and insubstantial. [SE *squishy*]

sres-wort *n.* [mid-19C] trousers. [backsl.]

sret-sio *n.* [mid-19C] oysters (cf. SWRET-SIO). [backsl.]

'sright/'sri *phr.* [1930s+] that's right. [elision]

s.r.o *phr.* [20C] **1** orig. entertainment use, a full house. **2** anything that sells out or is very popular. [abbr. standing room only]

s.s. *n.*[1] [early 19C–1930s] a fool (cf. SOFT *n.*[2]). [abbr. sammy soft (see SAMMY *n.*[3])]

s.s. *n.*[2] [1930s] (drugs) a skin *shot*, i.e. one that does not hit a vein. [abbr.]

s.s. *n.*[3] [1960s+] (US Und.) a suspended *sentence*. [abbr.]

s.s. *phr.*[1] [late 19C–1910s] a warning (from one woman to another) that her 'shimmy's showing', i.e. that her petticoat or slip is visible (cf. P.P. *phr.*[1]).

s/s *phr.*[2] [1970s+] used in contact advertisements, safe *sex*; either condoms are used or the sex is non-penetrative. [abbr.]

s'strue's Bob! *see* STRUESBOB!

s.t. *n.* [1940s+] a sanitary *towel*. [abbr.]

stab *n.*[1] [late 19C+] (orig. US) a try, an attempt; thus *have/ make a stab at*, to try (cf. HAVE A SHOT AT *phr.*[1]).

stab *n.*[2] [1940s+] (Aus.) sexual intercourse. [STAB *v.*]

stab *v.* [late 16C–early 17C] to have sexual intercourse (cf. BANG *v.*[1]). [the image of the penis as a weapon]

stabbed with a Bridport dagger, to be *phr.* [mid-17C–18C] to be hanged. [the best variety of British hemp (used for the noose) was grown near Bridport, Dorset]

stabber *n.* [1980s+] (Irish) the butt end of a cigarette. [SE *stub out*]

stab in the main vein, to *phr.* [1950s+] **1** of a man, to have sexual intercourse. **2** to run away (cf. CUT ONE'S STICK).

stab in the thigh, to *phr.* [19C] to have sexual intercourse (cf. BANG *v.*[1]).

stable *n.* (US) **1** [1930s+] a group of prostitutes working for a pimp (cf. FLOCK; NEST *n.*[2]). **2** [1940s+] any group of people working under one manager. [ext. uses of SE]

stable mind *n.* [late 19C] (society) one that has no other interests than horseflesh and its performance on a racecourse. [play SE *stable* (for horses)/*stable*, balanced]

stab oneself and pass the dagger, to *phr.* [19C] to take a glassful then circulate the bottle.

stach *see* STASH *v.*[1].

stache *n.* [1940s+] (US campus) a mou*stache* (cf. STASH *n.*[3]; TASH). [abbr.]

stack *n.*[1] [late 19C+] (orig. US) a large amount of money.

stack *n.*[2] [1950s–60s] (drugs) a pack of marijuana cigarettes.

stack *n.*[3] [1970s+] (US) a car's exhaust pipe, e.g. *a twin-stacked racer*. [SE *stack*, a chimney or funnel]

stack *v.*[1] [1900s] (US campus) to break up a college room. [one 'stacks' the furniture]

stack/stack on *v.*[2] [1960s+] (Aus.) to contrive, to produce. [SE *stack*, to pile up]

stack *v.*[3] [1990s] (US Black gang) to save money.

stack asses *v.* [1970s] (US) to defeat heavily, to thrash. [SE *stack* + ARSE *n.*[1]]

stacked/stacked up *adj.* **1** [20C] wealthy, sometimes ext. as *well-stacked*. **2** [1930s+] of a woman, well-built, attractive.

stacking *n.*[1] [1970s+] (drugs) taking steroids without a prescription. [one SE *stacks* up muscles]

stacking *n.*[2] [1990s] (US Black teen) making money. [STACK *n.*[1]]

stackola *n.* [1990s] (US Black) a large amount of money, a pile of money. [STACK *n.*[1] + sfx. -OLA]

stack on *see* STACK *v.*[2].

stack on an act, to *phr.* [1920s+] (Aus.) to lose one's temper and deliver a stream of obscenities/oaths (cf. BUNG ON AN ACT).

stack on a turn, to *phr.* [1950s+] (Aus.) to make a fuss. [var. on STACK ON AN ACT]

stack one's drapery, to *phr.* [1920s+] (Aus.) to put one's jacket (and at one time hat) on the ground before starting a fight.

stacks *n.* [late 19C+] (orig. US) a great many, a good deal, a large amount.

stack the deck/cards, to *phr.* [early 19C+] (US) to arrange things in one's favour, usu. dishonestly. [poker imagery]

stack-up *n.* [1950s+] (US) a multiple car crash. [STACK UP *v.*[2]]

stack up v.[1] [late 19C+] to emerge, to develop, to maintain, to appear as it should; also in neg. phr. *that doesn't/don't stack up*, that isn't logical, that fails to reach a standard.

stack up v.[2] [1950s] (US teen) to crash a car.

stack Zs v. [1950s+] (US) to have a sleep, to nap (cf. BAG ZS). [Z n.[1]]

stadge n. [1990s] the vagina, especially that of a fat woman. [? SE *stodge*, something thick and sticky]

stadsjapie n. [1970s+] (S.Afr.) a city-dweller, esp. when ignorant of country ways (cf. PLAASJAPIE). [Afk. *stad*, city + JAAP]

staff breaker/climber n. [19C] the vagina. [STAFF OF LIFE + SE *breaker/climber*]

staff-naked n. [mid-19C] gin (cf. STARK-NAKED n.). [? a misprint of the synon.]

staff of life n. [19C] the penis (cf. STAFF BREAKER). [punning on SE *staff of life*, bread or any other staple]

stafford law n. [late 16C–mid-17C] a beating, often in the context of a punishment. [pun on SE *staff*, a stick]

staffrider n. [1960s+] (S.Afr.) one who clings to the outside (or stands on the roof) of a moving train, having boarded it while it is in motion. [for ety. *see* RIDE STAFF]

staff striker n. [16C–early 18C] (Und.) a beggar who works with a female companion and who might deliberately poison themselves to raise impressive sores (cf. CLAPPERDUDGEON; PALLIARD). [they *strike* their *staff* on the ground as they walk]

stag n.[1] **1** [late 17C–1920s] a large, energetic woman. **2** [late 19C–1910s] (Irish) a cruel, selfish woman.

stag n.[2] **1** [late 18C–early 19C] an informer. **2** [1940s–50s] (US) a detective. [deer supposedly turn on any one of their number that is being hunted; but note Irish *staig*, an informer + UK dial. *stag*, an informer]

stag n.[3] [early–mid-19C] a man who attends courts in order to hire himself out as a defence witness, usu. to provide an alibi for an otherwise guilty defendant. [ety. unknown; ? link to dial. *stag*, an informer]

stag n.[4] [mid-19C] a shilling. [? play on HOG n.[1] (1)]

stag n.[5] **1** [20C] (orig. US) an unaccompanied man at a dance or similar gathering; thus *go stag*, to attend a social event without a female partner. **2** [1910s+] a spell of sentry-duty, i.e. the soldier is alone. [both are unaccompanied men]

stag/stag night n.[6] [20C] **1** any social event from which women are excluded. **2** the trad. uproarious eve-of-wedding party held by the groom and his male cronies (cf. BITCH PARTY; STAG PARTY). [STAG n.[5]]

stag v.[1] **1** [late 18C–late 19C] to find, to observe. **2** [mid-19C] to inform against. [STAG n.[2]]

stag v.[2] **1** [early–mid-19C] to refuse a request for a loan. **2** [mid-19C] to demand money, to cadge. [ext. of STAG v.[1] (1)]

stag v.[3] [20C] (US) for a man, to attend a social function without a female companion. [STAG n.[5]]

stag v.[4] [20C] (Anglo-Irish) to tease, to make fun of, to deride.

stag-dance n. [mid-19C] (US) a men-only dance, usu. performed in bar-rooms or taverns. [STAG n.[5] + SE *dance*]

stage-door johnnie/johnny n. [late 19C+] a man, poss. rich, who hangs around theatre stage doors hoping to meet his female idols. [SE *stage-door* + JOHNNIE n.[2]]

stage fright n. [20C] light (ale). [rhy. sl.]

stag film *see* STAG MOVIE.

stagger n.[1] [mid-19C] a watcher, a look-out. [STAG v.[1]]

stagger n.[2] [late 19C] (US) an effort, a try.

stagger-back n. [1950s] (W.I.) a form of toffee that is so tough that one 'staggers back' as one attempts to chew it (cf. JOHN STAGGER-BACK; TIE-TEETH).

staggering bob n. [19C+] meat declared unfit to eat. [meat trade jargon *bob*, *bobby*, inedible meat, esp. that taken from animals that have died rather than been slaughtered; note

dial. *staggering bob* (*with his yellow pumps*), a new-born calf (with yellow hooves) that is killed for veal]

stagger juice n. [late 19C–1960s] (orig. Aus./N.Z.) alcohol; thus *stagger juicery*, a public house. [SE *stagger* + JUICE n.[3]]

staggers/blind staggers n. [late 19C+] extreme drunkenness. [SE *stagger*]

stag line n. [1920s] (US) a number of unescorted men at a dance, who usu. stand in line eyeing the women. [STAG n.[5]]

stag-month n. [late 19C] the first month that follows childbirth (cf. GANDER MONTH; STAG-WIDOW). [dial. *stag*, a gander; at such a time a man's infidelities were considered acceptable]

stag movie/film n. [1950s+] a pornographic film. [STAG n.[5]]

stag night *see* STAG n.[6].

stag or shag? phr. [1940s+] (orig. US) will you be coming, usu. to a party, alone or with a female companion? [STAG n.[5] + SHAG n.[1]]

stag party n. [mid-19C+] (orig. US) an all-male party, esp. on the night preceding the wedding of one of the men (cf. BEAR PARTY; BITCH PARTY; BUCK PARTY; BULL PARTY; STAG n.[6]). [STAG n.[5]]

stag-widow n. [late 19C] a man who's wife has just given birth (cf. GANDER MONTH; STAG-MONTH). [dial. *stag*, a gander]

stains n. [1980s+] a gauche, inept, socially unacceptable person. [the stains are of semen, produced not by intercourse but masturbation]

stair-dancer n. [1950s+] a thief who steals from buildings, e.g. offices, that have not been properly secured. [SE *stair* + DANCER]

stair-steps/-steppers n. [1920s] a family with children ranged at equal intervals. [their respective heights resemble a flight of stairs]

stairs without a landing n. [19C] a prison treadmill (cf. EVERLASTING STAIRCASE).

stairway to heaven n. [1960s] (US Black) the female thighs.

stake n. **1** [early 19C] the booty gained in a robbery. **2** [early 19C] gambling winnings. **3** [late 19C+] a large sum of money.

stake/stake to v. [mid-19C+] to lend money, to put up funds for someone's enterprise. [STAKE n.]

stake long and deep, to phr. [1970s] (US Black) to invest large sums of cash. [STAKE v.]

stake-man n. [late 19C–1900s] (US) a hobo, a tramp. [the need of a STAKE n. on which to survive]

stake-out n. [1930s+] (orig. US) the surveillance of a suspect by police stationed in clandestine hiding places. [STAKE OUT v.]

stake out v. [1930s+] (orig. US) to conduct a surveillance. [the *staking* up of a goat to attract a tiger]

stakes n. [late 19C+] used fig. to indicate some form of profession or occupation in which there is an implication of challenges that must be overcome, e.g. the *matrimonial stakes*, the *novel-writing stakes*. [racing jargon *stakes*, a race for money, usu. defined by a specific name, e.g. St Leger Stakes]

stake to *see* STAKE V.

stale n.[1] [16C] (Und.) **1** a pickpocket or cut-purse (cf. STALL n.[1]). **2** a thief's or card-sharp's accomplice. [10C SE *stale* and OHG *stala*, theft, stealing]

stale n.[2] [1980s+] (US drugs) the cannabis equivalent of a hangover (cf. STALE DRUNK).

stale-bread adj. [1940s–50s] stale, out of date.

stale drunk adj. [19C] hungover (cf. STALE n.[2]). [SE *stale*]

stale mutton n. [17C] a prostitute. [SE *stale* + MUTTON n.[2]]

stalk n.[1] [late 16C+] the erect penis.

stalk n.[2] [mid-19C] the gallows.

stalk n.[3] [1930s] a tie-pin. [resemblance]

stalk n.[4] [1970s] cheek (cf. NECK n.[1]).

stalk a judy, to phr. [late 19C+] to follow a woman in the hope of sex. [SE *stalk* + JUDY n.[1]]

stalks *n.* [1960s] (US Black) the human legs.

stall *n.*[1] **1** [16C] any form of decoy who works with a criminal gang. **2** [late 16C+] a pickpocket's helper who distracts the attention of the victim whose pocket is being emptied or purse cut. **3** [mid–late 19C] a pretext, which offers an opportunity to steal. **4** [mid-19C+] a pickpocket's assistant who blocks the passage of the intended victim. **5** [1940s+] an act of time-wasting or prevarication, an excuse. [SE *stall*, a decoy bird]

stall/stall off *n.*[2] [early 19C+] any form of evasive story or trick. [STALL OFF v.]

stall *n.*[3] [20C] (Irish) an act of sexual intercourse. [? Irish *stail*, a stallion]

stall *v.*[1] [16C] (Und.) to apprentice or to work with, i.e. 'to stall a beggar to a rogue' (cf. STALL TO THE ROGUE). [SE *stall*, to set in a place, itself the root of *install*]

stall *v.*[2] **1** [16C+] (Und.) to shield a pickpocket (cf. HEDGE). **2** [16C+] (Und.) to jostle and distract one whose pocket is about to be picked. **3** [mid-19C+] to play for time, to make excuses, to delay; thus (US) *quit stalling*, stop wasting time, stop making excuses. **4** [1910s+] (US) to loiter or linger around. [STALL n.[1]]

stall *v.*[3] [mid–late 19C] **1** to spend the night in a room provided by a public house. **2** to walk off. **3** to travel about. [SE *stall*, to live with]

stall-farming *n.* [late 19C] working in a pickpocketing gang. [STALL n.[1] + fig. use of SE *farm*]

stall-fed *adj.* [20C] (Irish) pampered. [synon. dial.; the image is of an indulged horse]

stalling/stalling for a dip *n.* [19C] (Und.) the shielding of a pickpocket by an accomplice. [STALL v.[2] + DIP n.[3]]

stalling-/stuling-ken *n.* [mid-16C–mid-18C] (Und.) a depository for stolen goods, esp. as used by the RUFFLER to hide his booty (cf. SLAUGHTER n.[1]). [SE (*in*)*stall*, to put in place + KEN n.[1]]

stallion *n.* **1** [mid-16C+] a man with greater than average sexual powers (cf. STEED; STUD n.[1]). **2** [late 16C–late 17C] a courtesan, a kept woman. **3** [late 17C–18C] (Und.) a pimp. **4** [late 17C–18C] a heterosexual male prostitute. **5** [1960s+] (US Black) a tall, good-looking woman, poss. highly sexed. [for (3) ? Fr. *estalon*, a decoy, an enticement, or *stale*, the lowest class of prostitute]

stall off *n.*[1] [early–mid-19C] one who gets away with a successful ruse for a friend. [STALL OFF v.]

stall off *n.*[2] *see* STALL n.[2].

stall off *v.* **1** [early–mid-19C] (Und.) of a villain's accomplice, to screen or disguise a robbery. **2** [early–mid-19C] (Und.) to save an accomplice from arrest or disgrace. **3** [late 19C] to impede, to get in the way of, to hinder; thus one who gets away with a successful ruse for a friend has *stalled him off in prime twig*. [ext. of STALL v.[2]]

stall one's mug, to *phr.* [mid-19C] to run off, to leave quickly; esp. as excl. *stall your mug!*, go away! [? STALL OFF v. + MUG n.[1] (1)]

stallsman *n.* [mid-19C] a pickpocket's assistant. [STALL n.[1]]

stall to the rogue/order of rogues, to *phr.* [mid-16C–late 17C] to enlist a beggar as a full member of the underworld; thus *stalling*, the enlistment or 'ordaining' process. [STALL v.[1]]

stall up *v.* [early 19C] (Und.) to surround a person, forcing them to hold their hands in the air while they are stripped of their possessions; thus *staller-up*, one who robs in this way. [STALL v.[2]]

stall-whimper *n.* [late 17C–mid-19C] (Und.) an illegitimate child.

stam flash/flesh *v.* [late 17C–early 19C] (Und.) to talk in thieves' cant. [? Ger. *stimmen*, to make one's voice heard, to sing + FLASH n.[1] (3)]

stamina daddy/mummy *n.* [1980s+] (W.I./UK Black teen) a man or woman known for their powers of sexual endurance.

stammel/strammel *n.* [late 16C–mid-18C] 'a brawny, lusty, strapping Wench' (B.E.). [SE *stammel*, a coarse woollen petticoat]

stammer and stutter *n.* [20C] butter (cf. ROLL ME IN THE GUTTER). [rhy. sl.]

stamp-crab *n.* [late 19C–1900s] one who walks heavily. [SE *stamp* + CRABS n.[2]]

stamp-drawers *n.* [17C–early 19C] stockings. [STAMPS n.[1] + DRAWERS]

stamped paper *n.* [early–mid-19C] a promissory note.

stampers *n.* **1** [mid-16C–early 19C] shoes (cf. STAMPS n.[1]). **2** [late 17C–18C] (Und.) members of a criminal gang who wander about the country in the hope of picking up information about possible robberies (cf. DEUSEAVILLE STAMPERS).

stamping ground *n.*[1] [late 19C] anywhere known as a 'lover's lane'. [the stamping of a stallion in rut]

stamping ground *n.*[2] [20C] one's home territory, one's area of operation (cf. MANOR; TURF n.[1]). [18C SE, a place frequented by animals]

stamp-in-the-ashes *n.* [early 16C] a form of mixed drink, no ingredients are stated.

stamps *n.*[1] **1** [mid-16C–late 18C] (Und.) legs. **2** [early 19C] boots or shoes (cf. STAMPERS). [SE *stamp*]

stamps *n.*[2] [mid–late 19C] (US) money (cf. STAMPED PAPER). [the stamping of money-orders and similar documents]

stanch/stanch out *v.* [1930s–40s] (US Black) to begin. [? SE *start out*]

stand *n.*[1] [late 16C–early 17C] (Und.) a look-out, spec. for a team of lock-pickers (cf. OAK n.[1]).

stand *n.*[2] [mid-19C–1900s] an erection. **2** [late 19C] a prostitute who specializes in fellatio. [abbr. COCKSTAND]

stand *v.* [early 19C+] **1** to give as a present. **2** to bear the company's expenses, to pay for everyone with whom one is eating or drinking. [abbr. SE *stand treat*]

stand ace/ace with *v.* [1990s] (US) to be held in the highest esteem by someone. [SE *stand* + ACE n.[1]]

stand a good fag, to *phr.* [late 18C–mid-19C] **1** to put up a good fight. **2** to resist tiredness, to persevere. [SE *stand*, to bear + FAG n.[1]]

stand around with one's finger up one's ass *see* SIT THERE WITH ONE'S FINGER UP ONE'S ASS.

stand a shout *see* GO ON THE SHOUT.

stand at ease *n.* [late 19C+] (orig. milit.) **1** fleas. **2** cheese. [rhy. sl.]

stand bitch *v.* [late 18C] **1** to make tea. **2** to preside as hostess at a tea party. [SE *stand* + pre-sl. use of *bitch*, woman as a species; thus to perform in a (typically) female role]

stand bluff *v.* [late 17C+] to swear, to be adamant (cf. STAND BUFF). [SE *stand* + BLUFF v.]

stand buff *v.* **1** [late 17C+] to swear, to be adamant (cf. STAND BLUFF). **2** [late 17C–mid-19C] to suffer without complaining, to bear the brunt. [SE *stand* + fig. use of BUFF n.[1]]

stander *n.* [early 17C] a look-out for a criminal gang (cf. OAK n.[1]; STAND n.[1]). [they *stand* and watch]

stander-up *n.* [19C] a street thief who robs drunks under the pretence of helping them up from the gutter into which they have fallen (or been pushed).

stand for *v.* [late 19C+] (orig. US) to tolerate, to put up with.

stand frisk *v.* [19C] to be searched. [SE *stand* + FRISK v.[2] (1)]

stand from under *n.* [20C] thunder. [rhy. sl.]

stand/stay hitched *v.* [20C] (US) to be trustworthy, to keep a secret.

stand-in *n.*[1] [late 19C–1920s] (US) **1** a friendly or profitable arrangement. **2** a corrupt arrangement, a 'put-up job'.

stand-in *n.*[2] [20C] a deputy. [orig. milit.; one who 'stands in line' for you]

stand in *v.*[1] [mid–late 19C] (society) to cost, e.g. *it stands me in £10.* [SE mid-15C–mid-19C]

stand in *v.*[2] [mid-19C–1910s] **1** to go shares with, to join, to be a partner with. **2** to have a friendly or profitable understanding with, to be in league with, to be on good terms with.

standing budge *n.* [late 17C] a thief's accomplice or a lookout (cf. DARKMANS BUDGE). [SE *stand* + BUDGE n.[1]]

standing on the top step *phr.* [1940s–50s] (Und.) a phr. used of a man on trial who is facing the likely prospect of a maximum sentence (cf. UP THE STAIRS).

standing patterer *n.* [mid-19C] a man who takes 'a stand on the curb of a public thoroughfare, and deliver[s] prepared speeches to effect a sale of any articles [he has] to vend' (Hotten, 1859). [SE *stand* + PATTERER]

standing room for one *n.* [19C] the vagina. [STAND n.[2]]

standings *n.* [1950s+] (Irish) a second-hand clothes stall. [? the stallholder *stands* behind it]

standing there like a tit in a trance *see* STAND THERE LIKE A TIT IN A TRANCE.

standing ware *n.* [mid–late 19C] the erect penis. [ext. of STAND n.[2] + SE *ware*]

stand Moses *v.* **1** [late 18C–early 19C] to have another man's illegitimate child fathered upon one's wife; one is obliged by the parish to maintain it. **2** [mid-19C] (US) to act as a surrogate father and, for money, impregnate another man's wife. **3** [mid-19C–1930s] to adopt a child. [biblical myth]

stand mum *v.* [late 19C] to keep quiet. [MUM adj.]

stand-off *n.* [late 19C–1900s] (US) **1** an extension of credit, a postponement of payment. **2** a deadlock, a stalemate. [STAND OFF v.]

stand-off *adj.* [20C] (Aus.) haughty, unfriendly. [abbr. SE *standoffish*]

stand off *v.* [late 19C] (US) **1** to keep at a distance, to repel, to hold at bay. **2** to put off, to evade (a creditor, a questioner).

stand on *v.* [1930s+] to trust, to rely on (cf. STAND ON ME!).

stand one down *v.* [1920s+] (Aus.) to cost. [STAND v.]

stand one's corner, to *phr.* [late 19C+] to take or pay for one's share of anything, to do one's share. [STAND v.]

stand one's hand, to *phr.* [late 19C] to treat the assembled company (cf. STAND SHOT). [STAND v.]

stand on me! *excl.* [1930s+] believe me!

stand on one's head, to *phr.* [20C] (US) to make a great effort.

stand on one's hind leg *see* GET ON ONE'S HIND LEGS.

stand on one's own bottom, to *phr.* [17C–18C] to act in an independent manner. [later use SE; BOTTOM n.[1]]

stand on velvet, to *phr.* [late 19C+] to be in a financially advantageous position, esp. following successful gambling.

stand-out *n.* [1920s+] (US/Can.) one who distinguishes themselves from a crowd; thus *stand-out,* conspicuous, better than average.

stand out like ... *phr.* [20C] a phr. appearing in various combs., meaning to be very obvious, very large, e.g. *chapel hatpegs* (usu. of erect nipples), *cod's ballocks, dog's ballocks, a sore thumb,* (Can.) *a shit-house in the fog.*

stand-over *n.* [1930s–50s] (Aus.) a threat, an act of intimidation. [STAND OVER]

stand over *v.* [1930s+] (Aus.) to demand money with menaces; thus *stand over man/merchant,* a thug, a heavy. [the menacing position the demander adopts]

stand pad/sit pad/stand paddy *v.* [late 18C+; mid-19C–1910s] to beg at the roadside, usu. with a small piece of paper attached to one's jacket, declaring 'I am hungry'. [SE *stand* + PAD. n.[1]]

stand pat *v.* [late 19C+] to stay as one is, to refuse to move (cf. SIT TIGHT). [poker jargon]

stand patter *see* STAND THE PATTER.

stand point *v.* [1960s+] (Can. prison) to be on the alert. [milit. *point,* the lead man of a patrol]

stand sam *v.* [mid-19C+] **1** (orig. US) to pay for, to pick up a bill. **2** to buy a drink or round of drinks (cf. STAND SHOT). [? generic use of proper name *Sam(uel)*; SALAMON; US icon *Uncle Sam,* and the letters 'US' stencilled on US Army knapsacks; he 'pays for all']

stand shot/stand the shot/shot to *v.* [late 19C+] to pay the bill for everyone else. [STAND v. + SHOT n.[1]]

stand someone on their ear, to *phr.* [20C] (US) to knock down, to defeat.

stand squire *v.* [late 18C–mid-19C] to treat the company (cf. SIR TIMOTHY; SQUIRE OF ALSATIA).

stand still for, to *phr.* [1960s+] to tolerate, to permit, to accept.

stand tall *v.* [1960s+] (US) to be proud and confident.

stand the acid, to *phr.* [late 19C] (US) to stand up under pressure, to maintain one's composure.

stand the bears, to *phr.* [early 18C] to suffer (cf. BRING ON THE BEARS).

stand the gaff, to *phr.* [late 19C–1920s] (US) to receive severe treatment, criticism etc; thus *give/take the gaff,* to give or receive such treatment. [SE *gaff,* the steel spur attached to a fighting cock]

stand the grin, to *phr.* [early 19C] to suffer ridicule.

stand the huff, to *phr.* [late 18C–mid-19C] to take responsibility for the bill in the public house. [SE *huff*/HUFF v.[1]; image is of the boastfulness that can underpin the gesture]

stand the patter/patter, to *phr.* [early 19C] to be tried in a court. [PATTER n.]

stand/do the push, to *phr.* [late 19C+] of a woman, to have sexual intercourse.

stand the racket, to *phr.* **1** [early–mid-19C] to take the blame for the crimes of one's confederates. **2** [mid-19C–1920s] to pay the bill, to treat one's companions. [RACKET n.[1]; (2) in a non-criminal use]

stand/standing there like a tit in a trance *phr.* [20C] said of one who is lost in thought, abstracted. [TIT n.[1]]

stand the shot *see* STAND SHOT.

stand there with one's bare face hanging out, to *phr.* [20C] (US) to speak openly, candidly, brazenly.

stand to/stand to attention *n.* [20C] a pension. [rhy. sl.]

stand to attention, to *phr.* [1990s] to have an erection.

stand to one's lick-log, salt or no salt, to *phr.* [mid-19C+] (US) to stand by one's decision come what may; thus *come to the lick-log,* to face up to a tough decision. [SAmE *lick-log,* a notched log (occas. a wooden trough) used to hold salt for livestock]

stand to pan-pudding, to *phr.* [late 17C–early 18C] to stand one's ground, in lit. or fig. use. [SE *pan-pudding,* a heavy pudding made of flour, with small pieces of bacon in it, baked in a pan]

stand-up *n.*[1] **1** [mid-19C] a dance. **2** [mid-19C] a seatless carriage used on the early railways (cf. TUB). **3** [late 19C] a snack taken standing up. **4** [late 19C+] sexual intercourse when both partners are standing up (cf. KNEE-TREMBLER; PERPENDICULAR).

stand-up *n.*[2] [1930s+] (orig. US) the act of 'standing someone up', i.e. breaking an appointment; thus *give the stand-up,* to miss a scheduled meeting, esp. to break a date. [STAND UP v.[3]]

stand-up *n.*[3] [1930s–40s] (US) a police identification parade.

stand-up *adj.* [1940s+] (US Und.) honest, trustworthy, dependable. [STAND UP AND BE COUNTED]

stand up *v.*[1] [mid-19C–1900s] to take shelter from the rain.

stand up *v.*[2] [20C] to have sexual intercourse when both partners are standing.

stand up *v.*[3] [1930s+] (orig. US) to fail to keep an appointment with someone. [i.e. one 'leaves them standing']

stand up *v.*[4] [1950s+] (orig. US) to confess (cf. PUT ONE'S HAND UP). [SE *stand up for*]

stand up *v.*[5] [1950s+] (orig. US) to withstand pressure, esp. police questioning. [SE *stand up to*]

stand up and be counted, to *phr.* [20C] (orig. US) to make one's presence felt, to join in a group action or decision, esp. at a certain risk to oneself.

stand up drinks, to *phr.* [20C] (Aus.) to set out drinks.

stand-up guy *n.* [1950s+] (US) an honest, dependable person, one who 'stands up to be counted'. [STAND UP *v.*[5] + GUY *n.*[2]]

stand up in *v.* [20C] to wear clothes, esp. in phr. *the clothes/only the clothes one stands up in.*

stand upon one's pantables/pantacles/pantaphels/pantapples / pantocles / pantofles / pantopples / pantibles, to *phr.* [late 16C–mid-18C] to stand upon ceremony, to act in a dignified manner. [SE *pantofle* (ult. Fr. *pantoufle*), a slipper, esp. one with a high heel and a built-up sole to make the wearer appear taller and more imposing]

stand-up supper *n.* [late 19C] (society) anything mean or niggardly. [SE *stand-up supper*, a late supper at which those invited ate while on their feet; such a supper was, *de facto*, less grand (and less expensive to cater) than a full-scale sit-down meal]

stand up with *v.* **1** [early 19C] to dance with. **2** [mid-19C–1900s] to act as a bridesmaid or male attendant to the groom.

stangey/stangy *n.*[1] [mid-19C] a tailor. [SE *stang*, a sting or prick; i.e. the needle]

stangey/stangy *n.*[2] [mid-19C] a man who is dominated by his wife. [phr. *ride the stang*, 'to be mounted astride of a pole borne on the shoulders of two men, and carried through the streets for the derision of the spectators' (*OED*). This custom, however, once popular in Scot. and the north, focused on unpopular, rather than specifically wife-dominated people, but the implication is that he has to ride a pole, since he cannot 'ride' his wife]

stank *n.* [1970s+] **1** (US Black) the anus. **2** (US Black) the vagina (cf. STENCH-TRENCH). **3** (US campus) an ugly woman. [SE *stink*]

stank ho *n.* [1970s+] (US campus) an ugly woman. [STANK + HO *n.*[1]]

stanky *adj.* [1970s+] (US) smelly, dirty, unattractive. [STANK]

staph *n.* [1930s+] *staph*ylococcus, a genus of disease-inducing bacteria. [abbr.]

stap me! *excl.* [late 17C–19C] an oath popular among upper-class dandies (cf. STAP MY VITALS!). [SE *stab*]

stap/stop my vitals! *excl.* [late 17C+] an oath popular among upper-class dandies (cf. STAP ME!). [SE *stab*; the first printed use appears in the play *The Relapse, or, Virtue in Danger* (1696) by John Vanbrugh; it is spoken by Lord Foppington, among whose affectations is the consistent pron. of 'o' as 'a']

star *n.*[1] **1** [19C] a conspicuous member of society, who shines out among their peers. **2** [mid-19C] one who is exceptional within their own world. **3** [1950s+] (US Black) a man's favourite woman, a very attractive woman. **4** [1990s] a very unpleasant person, e.g. *what a fucking star!* [the theatrical/film/sports/rock use of *star*, while obviously linked, has been SE since its early 19C coinage]

star, the *n.*[2] [early 19C] (Und.) the practice of cutting a hole in a shop's window, then extracting such items as can be reached.

Star, the *n.*[3] [mid-19C] the Star and Garter public house, in Richmond, south of London.

star *n.*[4] [late 19C+] (prison) a first offender. [abbr. prison jargon *star prisoner*; a star is affixed to their name in the prison records]

star *n.*[5] [1980s+] (drugs) methcathinone (cf. BATHTUB SPEED).

star! *excl.* [1980s+] (W.I./UK Black teen) **1** a term of respect, synon. with SE *sir*. **2** a general term of address, synon. with MAN *n.*[1], e.g. *Wha' apen star?*, What's up man?

starboard light *n.* [1920s] crème de menthe. [like the light, it is green]

starbolic naked *see* STARK BALLOCK NAKED.

starcher *n.* [late 19C–1900s] **1** a starched cravat. **2** a stiff white tie.

starchy *adj.* [mid-19C+] **1** drunk. **2** stiff, unbending, reserved, lacking in social warmth.

stardust *n.* (drugs) **1** [1950s] cocaine. **2** [1970s] phencyclidine (cf. ACE *n.*[3]). [ext. of DUST *n.*[6] (2), (3), underpinned in (1) by the popularity of cocaine among rock and film stars]

stare at the ceiling, to *phr.* [20C] of a woman, to have sexual intercourse, often ext. as *stare at the ceiling over a man's shoulder.*

stare-cat *n.* [20C] (orig. US) an inquisitive neighbour, usu. a woman. [SE *stare* + CAT *n.*[1]]

stare like a dead/stuck pig, to *phr.* [late 17C–early 18C] to gape, to stare at fixedly.

starer *n.* [1900s] a pair of lorgnettes or of eye-glasses with a long handle.

star-fucker *n.* [1960s+] a sycophant, a hanger-on, esp. of celebrities (cf. GROUPIE). [SE *star* + FUCKER]

star-fucking *n.* [1960s+] **1** acting as a toady, a parasite. **2** living as a GROUPIE. [STAR-FUCKER]

star-gazer *n.* **1** [17C–18C] the erect penis. **2** [late 18C–early 19C] a horse that persistently throws its head up (cf. ASTRONOMER). **3** [late 18C–mid-19C] a country prostitute who plies her trade in the open air or under hedges.

star-glazing *n.* [mid–late 19C] removing a pane of glass in order to steal items from a shop display or to break onto a house. [the star-shaped hole in the glass + play on SE *star-gazing*]

star/starlight hotel/starlight boarding house *n.* [1930s+] the open air, esp. in phr. *sleep/doss in the star hotel*, to sleep in the open air (cf. SLEEP AT MRS GREEN'S).

stariben *see* STURRABIN.

staring quarter *n.* [late 18C–early 19C] an ox-cheek. [note dial. *staring-quarter*, a laughing-stock]

stark ballock/bollock/bollux/starbolic naked *phr.* [late 19C+] absolutely naked. [SE *stark* + BOLLOCK NAKED]

starkers *adj.* [1910s+] nude. [SE *stark naked* + 'Oxford' sfx. -ers]

stark-naked *n.* [early–mid-19C] neat, undiluted gin (cf. STRIP-ME-NAKED *n.*[1]). [the neat alcohol comes without 'clothing' + the poverty that results from excessive consumption]

stark-naked *adj.* [mid–late 19C] unadulterated, esp. of drinks. [STARK-NAKED *n.*]

stark, staring bonkers *phr.* [1950s+] absolutely crazy. [ext. of BONKERS]

star lay *n.* [early 19C] robbery by breaking shop or house windows. [STAR *n.*[2] + LAY *n.*[3]]

starlight boarding house/hotel *see* STAR HOTEL.

starn *n.* [late 19C+] the buttocks. [SE *stern*]

star of the line *n.* [1960s+] (US Black) a pimp's favourite prostitute (cf. STAR *n.*[1]).

star-pitch *n.* [late 19C] (tramp) sleeping in the open air. [SE *star* + PITCH *n.*[3]]

starps *n.* [mid-19C] sprats. [backsl.]

starrer *n.* [1950s+] (orig. US) a film that provides a vehicle for a major star.

stars and stripes *n.* [late 19C] Bostonians, esp. the more puritanically religious of them. [their trad. Sunday meal of baked beans (*stars*) and pork belly (*stripes*)]

stars for studs n. [1970s+] (US campus) a course in basic astronomy. [SE *star* + STUD]

star-spangled powder n. [1980s+] (drugs) cocaine. [its crystalline sparkle + play on the *Star-Spangled Banner*, the US national anthem]

Start, the n.[1] [late 18C–early 19C] **1** a prison, esp. Newgate. **2** the Old Bailey. **3** (tramp) London. [? SE *start*, a shock, a surprise; thus the effect of entering prison + a new *start* to one's life, whether good or bad. (3) because London is the starting point for a tramp's journeying round Britain]

start n.[2] [mid-19C] an odd circumstance, a surprise, often as *rum* or *rummy start*. [SE *start*, a shock]

start n.[3] **1** [20C] (Aus.) a job. **2** [1970s+] (S.Afr.) money. [? a lit. or fig. SE *start* on a project, an activity]

start v.[1] [early 19C] to reprimand. [i.e. to make someone *start* or jump with surprise]

start v.[2] [late 19C+] to commence complaining, nagging, being a nuisance etc, usu. in phr. *now, don't you start* (cf. START ON). [SE *start*, to begin; *nagging* etc are assumed]

start a fowl-roost, to phr. [20C] (Aus.) to take on a 'double-barrelled' surname. [ety. unknown]

start a jolly, to phr. [late 19C] to start the applause, for a performer or turn, at a music-hall or theatre. [JOLLY n.[3]]

starter n.[1] [late 17C–18C] (Und.) a question. [SE *start*, to jump in surprise; a question, esp. as to one's clandestine activities, may cause one to do this]

starter n.[2] [19C] **1** a restless person, one who leaves a convivial company. **2** one who cannot stay in the same job for any length of time. [SE *start*, to jump in surprise]

starter n.[3] [late 19C–1920s] a laxative. [its starts one's stomach working]

starter n.[4] [1940s–50s] (Aus.) one who makes a brave attempt. [SE *start*, to begin]

starter n.[5] [1960s+] the first course of a meal (cf. AFTERS).

starters n. [1960s+] initial actions, plans etc; thus *for starters*, to begin with.

star the glaze, to phr. [late 18C–early 19C] (Und.) to break shop windows (cf. SNAP THE GLAZE). [SE *star*, to make a star-shaped crack or hole + GLAZE]

start on/start in/up on v. [late 19C+] (orig. US) to nag, to assail verbally, to attack physically (cf. BEGIN ON; START v.[2]).

start shit v. [1950s+] (US Black) to initiate trouble, to start an argument. [SHIT n.[4]]

start something v. **1** [1910s+] (orig. US) to cause trouble, to start a fight. **2** [1940s+] to get a woman pregnant.

start the ball rolling v. [mid-19C+] to initiate the progress of a situation (cf. KEEP THE BALL ROLLING).

starvation adj., adv. [late 19C+] a neg. intensifier, excessively, extremely; lit. 'productive of starvation', e.g. *starvation cruel*, very cruel.

starved to the last buckle-hole of one's belt see REDUCED TO THE LAST BUCKLE-HOLE OF ONE'S BELT.

starver n. [1930s–50s] (Aus.) a saveloy. [a large sausage, it fills the stomach of a starving person]

starve the bardies! excl. [1940s+] (Western Aus.) a general excl. (cf. SPEED THE WOMBATS!). [SE *bardy*, an edible Australian wood-boring grub (*Bardistus cibarius*) or its larva]

starve the crows! excl. [1910s+] (Aus.) a general excl. (cf. SPEED THE WOMBATS!).

starve the lizards! / mopokes! / ninnies! / rats! / roan bullocks!/snake's head!/wombats! excl. [1910s+] (Aus.) a general excl. (cf. SPEED THE WOMBATS!).

stash n.[1] [20C] (W.I./Guyn.) a woman who dresses flashily; thus *stash*, to dress showily. [? SE *ostentatious*]

stash n.[2] **1** [1920s] (US) money. **2** [1920s+] (orig. US) a hiding place. **3** [1930s+] (drugs) a hiding place for drugs. **4** [1930s+] (drugs) any drug, esp. cannabis. [STASH v.[1]]

stash n.[3] [1940s+] (US) a mous*tache* (cf. STACHE; TASH). [abbr.]

stash/stach v.[1] **1** [late 18C–1900s] (Und.) to stop, to refrain, to give up; esp. in excl. *stash it!*, stop that!; *stash the glim*, douse the light. **2** [late 18C+] to hide, usu., since 1930s, drugs. **3** [1940s+] to stay where one is. **4** [1960s+] to place, whether clandestinely or in view. [18C Und. *stash*, put a stop to + influences f. SE *stop*, *stow*, *squash* + Fr. *cacher*, to hide; orig. cant, the term was dormant during 19C but has been revived, mainly among drug users, since mid-20C]

stash v.[2] [late 19C] to leave.

stash catcher n. [1980s+] (drugs) one who stands outside a window to catch drugs that are thrown out during a police raid. [STASH n.[2] + SE *catcher*]

stashie adj. [20C] (W.I.) smartly or showily dressed. [STASH n.[1]]

stash it v. [mid-19C+] to give up one's bad habits (cf. STASH UP). [fig. use of STASH v.[1]]

stash pad n. [1980s+] (drugs) a room, apartment or house where drugs are stored (cf. SPOT n.[6]). [STASH n.[2] + PAD n.[2]]

stash up v. [20C] to stop doing something instantly, abruptly (cf. STASH IT). [fig. use of STASH v.[1]]

stat n.[1] [1960s+] **1** a photo*stat*, a Xerox copy. **2** (usu. pl.) a *statistic, statistics*. [abbr.]

stat n.[2] [1980s+] (drugs) methcathinone (cf. BATHTUB SPEED). [? medical jargon *stat*, immediately, i.e. the immediacy of its effects]

statch n. [1960s+] (US) statutory rape. [mispron. of SE]

state n. **1** [mid-19C+] a condition of emotional distress or mental agitation. **2** [late 19C+] an unkempt, dirty condition of dress or cleanliness.

state con n. [20C] (US Und.) a prisoner who is seen as overly friendly with the authorities.

state-o n. [1950s+] (US prison) a prisoner's official prison clothing.

state-raised adj. [20C] (US) used of one who has been brought up in institutions.

Stateside n. [1940s+] (US) the USA, as opposed to foreign countries; thus *Stateside*, of or pertaining to the USA.

state tea n. [late 19C] (society) a grand tea party at which the full range of one's best tea service, cutlery and the like can be put on display. [SE *state occasion*, when the nation's finest – be it soldiers or plate – is put on display]

static n. [1920s+] (orig. US) difficulties, aggravation, impudent or argumentative talk. [radio use]

static! excl. [1980s+] a cry of warning, e.g. from a street dealer's look-out at the approach of the police. [STATIC n.]

station-jack n. [mid-19C] (Aus.) a boiled meat pudding, usu. cooked in the bush or at a sheep station. [? link to JACK n.[8]]

statue-lover n. [20C] (US) a Roman Catholic (cf. BEAD-COUNTER). [the multiplicity of religious statues to be found in Catholic churches]

stave-off n. [late 19C] a snack, a light meal. [it *staves off* hunger]

stavin chain n. [1900s–20s] (US Black) a ladies' man, a wanderer. [the mythical hero of the ballad 'Winning Boy Blues' by Jellyroll Morton (1890–1941)]

staving adj. [mid-late 19C] (US) very strong, excessive. [SE *stave*, to go with a rush or dash]

stay n. [early 19C] a cuckold. [? SE *stays*, which the errant wife might also discard for the pleasures of sex]

stay v. [20C] (US) to maintain an erect penis. [abbr. SE *stay hard*, *stay up*]

stay and be hanged! excl. [late 19C] a general excl. of resigned exasperation, oh all right! see if I care! do what you want!

stay-awake n. [1960s+] (drugs) any form of stimulant and amphetamine (cf. WAKE-UP n.[2]).

stay down low, to *phr.* [1970s+] (US Black) to remain inconspicuous, to behave normally.

stay for john long the carrier see SEND BY FOR JOHN LONG THE CARRIER.

stay hitched see STAND HITCHED.

stay-home sauce/soup/tea *n.* [20C] (W.I.) food that supposedly contains 'magic' ingredients that will influence a man to choose a particular woman (cf. BAD-FOOD).

stay in the closet, to *phr.* [1960s+] to continue hiding one's homosexuality. [CLOSET n.]

stay loose! *excl.* [1970s+] goodbye, esp. in communities influenced by California's post-hippie era 'new therapies' (cf. HANG LOOSE!). [LOOSE adj.¹ (2)]

stay on someone's case, to *phr.* [1950s+] to attack, to harass continually and consistently. [ON SOMEONE'S CASE]

stay on the wagon, to *phr.* [20C] (US) to comply with requirements, to act as ordered (cf. GET IN THE BUGGY).

stay put *v.* [mid-19C+] (orig. US) to remain, to stay where one is, to keep steady.

staytape *n.* [late 18C–early 19C] a tailor. [SE *staytape*, material used for binding the edges of fabric]

stay with *v.*¹ **1** [late 19C] (US) of food, to assuage or satisfy one's hunger. **2** [late 19C+] to keep up with, to persist in an endeavour. [SE *stay*, to last]

stay with *v.*² [1940s+] to have sexual intercourse (cf. SLEEP WITH). [euph.]

steady *n.* [late 19C+] (orig. US) a regular girl- or boyfriend.

steady as she goes!/steady on!/steady there! *excl.* [late 19C+] an excl. calling upon one's companions to keep calm or to act carefully.

steady on the case *phr.* [1950s–60s] (US Black) persistent, unremitting.

steady the Buffs! *excl.* [mid-19C+] keep calm, don't lose control etc. [*the Buffs*, orig. the 3rd Foot, a regiment descended from troops raised to fight the Dutch in 1572 and the London trainbands or citizen militia – both of which had buff facings to their uniforms; by 1702 it was known as the Buffs, a name that was continued when it was officially renamed the Royal East Kent Regiment in 1935; the phr. presumably refers to some unspecified military anecdote]

steady there! see STEADY AS SHE GOES!

steak and bull's eyes *n.* [20C] steak-and-kidney pudding.

steak and kidney *n.* [20C] **1** the proper name Sidney. **2** (Aus.) Sydney. [rhy. sl.]

steakdahoyst/steaka-da-oyst *n.* [1910s–20s] (Aus.) an Italian restaurant specializing in *steak* and *oysters* (cf. SURF AND TURF). [the 'Italian' pronunciation]

steak drapes *n.* [1990s] the labia majora (cf. BEEF CURTAINS).

steal *n.* **1** [late 19C] an act of theft. **2** [1940s+] (orig. US) a bargain, esp. in phr. *it's a steal*, often + *at ...* (a sum of money).

steal blind *v.* [1970s+] (US) to rob or cheat to an extreme extent (cf. ROB BLIND).

stealers/ten stealers *n.* [mid-17C] the fingers (cf. PICKERS AND STEALERS).

steal the show/scene/picture, to *phr.* [1930s+] to make oneself the centre of attention. [orig. theatrical/film use]

steam *n.*¹ **1** [1930s+] (Aus./N.Z.) cheap wine laced with methylated spirits, methylated spirits drunk by itself (cf. SMOKE n.⁵). **2** [1950s–60s] (US Black) beer, wine. **3** [1970s] (drugs) phencyclidine (cf. ACE n.³). [it 'gets one's steam up']

steam *n.*² [1960s] (US) **1** problems, difficulties, trouble. **2** blame, sarcasm, intense criticism (cf. HEAT n.⁴).

steam *adj.* [1970s+] old-fashioned (cf. STEAM RADIO). [the obsolete railway *steam* engines, long displaced by diesel]

steam/steam ahead/away *v.*¹ [mid-19C+] to work vigorously, to make great progress.

steam *v.*² [1950s+] (orig. US) **1** to be annoyed, to be angry, to talk aggressively. **2** to make someone amorous (cf. STEAM UP).

steam ahead/away see STEAM v.¹.

steamboated/steamboats *adj.* [1980s+] very drunk. [? STEAMED UP]

steamed up *adj.* [1920s+] **1** tense, annoyed. **2** fighting drunk. **3** sexually excited.

steam-engine *n.* [mid-19C] (Lancashire) a potato pie. [? the steam that emerges from the pierced crust]

steamer *n.*¹ **1** [early 19C] a tobacco pipe. **2** [1950s+] (W.I.) a form of hookah or water-pipe used for smoking marijuana (cf. CHILLAM). [the smoke or SE *steam* produced]

steamer *n.*² [1930s+] a fool, a gullible person. [rhy. sl. *steam tug* = MUG n.⁵]

steamer *n.*³ [1950s–60s] a male homosexual who prefers passive partners. [? STEAM IN]

steam in *v.* [1970s+] to commit oneself completely, esp. in a fight (cf. WADE IN).

steaming *n.*¹ [19C] any form of steamed pudding.

steaming *n.*² [1970s+] the act of mugging, especially when performed *en masse* against a 'captive audience' by a gang on a bus or, more likely, an underground train. [? STEAM IN]

steaming *adj.*¹ [20C] drunk.

steaming *adj.*² [1950s+] a general intensifier with euph. overtones, since usu. in neg. use, e.g. *steaming great prawn*, an absolute, utter fool.

steam-packet *n.* [mid-19C] a jacket. [rhy. sl.]

steam radio *n.* [1950s+] radio. [STEAM adj. + SE *radio*; the implication is that like steam trains, the radio is an old-fashioned, outdated medium compared with television]

steamroller *n.* [20C] a bowler hat. [rhy. sl.]

steam tug *n.* [1930s+] **1** a fool (cf. STEAMER n.²). **2** (Aus.) a pug, i.e. a prize-fighter. **3** (Aus.) a bug. [rhy. sl.]

steam up *v.* [1910s–30s] to stimulate emotionally, to arouse (cf. STEAM v.²).

steamy *adj.* [1960s+] (orig. US) sexually arousing, erotic, salacious (cf. HOT adj.¹). [euph.]

steed *n.* [20C] a sexual expert (cf. STALLION; STUD n.¹). [SE *steed*, a horse, although he does the 'riding']

steel, the *n.*¹ [mid-19C] **1** a prison. **2** a treadmill. [abbr. BASTILLE]

steel *n.*² [1940s–50s] (US Black) whiteness.

steel *n.*³ [1990s] (US Black) a gun. [metonymy]

steel *v.* [20C] (US) to stab. [the *steel* blade of a knife]

steel bar *n.* [late 18C–early 19C] a needle (cf. STEEL BAR FLINGER).

steel bar flinger/driver *n.* [late 18C–early 19C] a tailor. [STEEL BAR]

steel bottom *n.* (W.I.) **1** [1950s] an alcoholic cocktail that mixes gin and wine (cf. STEEL-NOSE). **2** [1970s] a drink of white rum with a beer chaser. [? the need for a SE *steel bottom* in one's stomach to drink such a thing]

steele rudds *n.* [20C] (Aus.) spuds, potatoes. [rhy. sl.]

steel helmet *n.* [1940s] an Anderson air-raid shelter.

steel jockey *n.* [1940s] (Aus.) one who rides a train without paying. [SE *steel*, i.e. the railway + JOCKEY n.²]

steel-nose *n.* [mid-17C] a form of strong drink (cf. STEEL BOTTOM). [? it gives one a red nose that 'glows' like molten steel]

steel-pen *n.* [late 19C] (US) a 'swallow-tail' or tail-coat, worn for formal evening wear (cf. CLAW-HAMMER). [the resemblance of the tail to a pen nib]

steep *adj.* [mid-19C+] (orig. US) over-priced, exorbitant, excessive, exaggerated.

steer *n.* (US) **1** [late 19C+] (Und.) someone who gives directions (cf. STEERER n.¹). **2** [1920s+] facts, a useful piece of information (cf. BUM STEER). [SE *steer*, to direct]

steer v. [late 19C+] (US Und.) to decoy someone into a place, activity or situation (cf. BUM STEER; BUNCO-STEERER).

steerer n.[1] [late 19C+] (US Und.) anyone, e.g. a cab driver, hotel doorman or similar figure, who points a searcher towards the variety of self-indulgence they seek, e.g. sex, drugs, gambling. [STEER v.]

steerer n.[2] [20C] one who makes predictions. [SE steer, to direct]

steer joint n. [1930s+] (orig. US) a nightclub to which patrons are directed by a cab-driver, doorman etc, who is paid by the establishment (cf. CAB JOINT). [SE steer + JOINT n.[3] (3)]

steever's worth of copper n. [late 19C] one penny. [STIVER]

Steffie Graf n. [1990s] a laugh. [rhy. sl.; ult. Ger. tennis player Steffie Graf (b.1969)]

stella dallas n. [1930s–50s] (camp gay) a loser, an unfortunate. [film title Stella Dallas (1937), a celebrated tear-jerker starring Barbara Stanwyck]

stellar adj. [1980s+] excellent, wonderful, 'out of this world'.

stem n.[1] (drugs) 1 [late 19C+] an opium pipe. 2 [1960s] marijuana stems, as unsmokeable debris. 3 [1980s+] a crack cocaine pipe.

stem n.[2] [20C] (US tramp) the main street of a town (cf. WORK THE STEM).

stem, the n.[3] [1920s–30s] (US) the practice of begging.

stem v. (US) 1 [1920s] to grab, to get hold of. 2 [1920s–30s] to beg. [STEM n.[3]]

stemming n. [mid-19C] (US) begging. [MOOCH THE STEM]

stems n. [mid-19C+] the legs, esp. of an attractive woman.

stem-wheeler n. [20C] (US) a homosexual man. [SE stem-wheeler, a truck powered from behind]

stem-winder n. [late 19C+] (US) anything considered excellent, first-rate; thus stem-winding, persuasive, powerful. [the then newly invented stem-winding watch, which, with its rejection of any need for the usual key, was seen as the finest example of state-of-the-art technology. The term currently exists only in US political speech, meaning a rousing speech]

stench-trench n. [20C] 1 the anus (cf. ROBY DOUGLAS; SPICE ISLAND; STANK; WINKER-STINKER). 2 the vagina (cf. STANK).

stencil n. [1970s–80s] (drugs) a long, thin marijuana cigarette. [? play on SE pencil]

steno/stenog n. [20C] (US) a stenographer, a typist. [abbr.]

step n.[1] [late 19C–1900s] a slice of bread (cf. DOORSTEP).

step n.[2] [late 19C+] a step-relation. [abbr.]

step/step it v.[1] 1 [mid-19C+] to leave, to go away, esp. quickly. 2 [mid-19C] to run away, to escape. 3 [1950s+] (US Black) to dance, to run.

step v.[2] [late 19C] to clean doorsteps; thus stepper, one who performs this task, whether for themselves or as a job.

step v.[3] [1960s+] (US Black) to work as a prostitute. [? stepney, a White-slaver's temporary best woman; more simply her 'street-walking']

step fast v. [1960s+] (US Black) to do what is necessary to survive in a harsh world.

stephen/steven n. [early 19C] money; thus Steven's at home, one has money (cf. EVEN STEPHEN). [? STIVER]

stepinfetchit n. [1930s+] (US Black) a subservient Black person, fitting willingly into the stereotyped and inferior image refined by generations of White supremacy. [lit. 'step and fetch it'; nickname of Lincoln Perry (1892–1985), who specialized in playing stereotypical 'dumb nigger' roles for Hollywood; he chose the nickname after a winning race-horse]

step it see STEP v.[1].

stepmother's breath n. [20C] (Ulster) a sudden draught of cold air. [the trad. neg. image of the 'wicked stepmother']

step-off n. [1940s] (US Black) a street curb.

step off/off on v.[1] [20C] (US Black) of a husband, to leave, to desert one's family.

step off v.[2] [1920s] to die (cf. STEP OUT v.[2]).

step off! excl. [1990s] (US Black teen) go away! leave me alone!

step off on see STEP OFF v.[1].

step off the carpet, to phr. [mid-19C] (US) to get married.

step off the curb, to phr. [20C] (US) to die, to fail.

step on v. [1960s+] (drugs) to adulterate narcotics for more profitable sales. [the image of lit. squashing something and thus making it appear larger than it is]

step on it v. [1920s+] (orig. US) to drive faster, esp. as an imper.; also sometimes in fig. use (cf. STEP ON THE GAS).

step on/trip over one's cock, to phr. [1970s+] (orig. US) to get oneself into serious trouble, to make a major blunder (cf. STEP ON ONE'S DICK). [COCK n.[2] (1)]

step on one's dick/prick, to phr. [1950s+] to make a fool of oneself (cf. STEP ON ONE'S COCK). [DICK n.[5] (1)/PRICK n. (1)]

step on someone's meat, to phr. [1970s] (US) to tell someone off, to scold someone.

step/tread on someone's toes, to phr. [mid-19C+] to annoy, to give offence to.

step on the gas, to phr. [1920s+] (orig. US) 1 to accelerate a motorcar. 2 to go faster, esp. in imper.

step out v.[1] [19C+] 1 (US Black) to go to a party, dance or some form of entertainment. 2 (US) to escort or go out with someone socially, usu. as step out with ... .

step out v.[2] [mid-19C–1900s] (US) to die (cf. STEP OFF v.[2]; STEP OFF THE CURB).

step out on v. [20C] (US Black) to cuckold, to commit adultery. [ext. of STEP OUT v.[1]]

stepper n.[1] [mid-late 19C] the treadmill.

stepper n.[2] [late 19C] a door-step cleaner, a 'step-girl'. [STEP v.[2]]

stepper n.[3] [late 19C–1900s] a trotting-horse.

stepper n.[4] [1970s+] (US Black) a prostitute. [STEP v.[4]]

steppers n. [mid-19C] the feet.

stepping n. [1970s+] (US Black) working as a prostitute. [STEP v.[4]]

stepping ken n. [mid-19C] (US) a cheap dance-hall. [SE step, to dance + KEN n.[1]]

stepping on a carpet frog phr. [1990s] breaking wind.

step someone out v. [1970s+] (N.Z.) to challenge someone to a fight. [for ety. see STEP SOMEONE OUT ON THE GREEN]

step someone out on the green, to phr. [1970s] (US Black) to challenge someone to a fight. [the image of 'going outside' to some supposed turf]

step to/up v. [1980s+] (US Black) 1 to challenge. 2 to make sexual advances towards. [SE step towards or step up to]

step up v. [1980s+] (drugs) to move from selling drugs retail to distributing larger quantities wholesale.

-ster sfx. [1970s+] a sfx. implying agency. [ult. ME, where it represents nouns of action; in SE such terms include jokester, trickster, punster etc. Recent sl. uses have adopted the sfx., adding it to a surname or nickname and prefixing that with the, e.g. the US wrestler 'Hulk' Hogan is The Hulkster etc]

sterics n. [mid-late 18C] hysteria. [abbr. SE hysterics]

sterks/sturks n. [1930s+] (Aus.) a fit of anger or exasperation; thus give one the sterks, to aggravate, to irritate. [abbr. SE hysterics]

sterky adj. [1930s+] (Aus.) 1 frightened, terrified. 2 suffering a bout of diarrhoea, engendered by fear. [STERKS, but note stercoraceous, consisting of, containing, or pertaining to faeces]

sterling n. [19C] (Aus.) one born in Britain who has emigrated to Australia (cf. CURRENCY). [play on SE (pound) sterling/sterling, of high quality]

stern *n.* [early 17C+] the buttocks; thus punning phr. [1940s–50s] *stern approach*, buggery (cf. KEEL; POOP n.¹).

stern over appetite *phr.* [1930s+] (Aus.) head over heels. [euph. ARSE OVER APPETITE]

sternpost *n.* [mid–late 19C] the penis (cf. RUDDER).

steve *n.* [20C] (Aus.) a generic term of address to a man (cf. GEORGE n.²; JACK n.³; JOHN n.¹).

steven *see* STEPHEN.

stew *n.¹* [mid-18C+] (US) **1** a drunkard. **2** a drunken carouse. [STEWED adj.¹]

stew *n.²* [19C] a mess, a troublesome situation. [20C use is SE]

stew *n.³* [mid–late 19C] one who studies hard but still learns nothing. [they *stew* in a hot room]

stew/stewie *n.⁴* [1970s+] a *stew*ardess, an air hostess. [abbr.]

stew *v.¹* [mid-19C–1910s] to study hard. [STEW n.³]

stew *v.²* [20C] (W.I.) to abort a pregnancy. [? obs. SE *stew*, to check, to restrain]

Stewart Granger *n.* [1980s] **1** danger. **2** a chance, an opportunity. [rhy. sl.; ult. film actor Stewart Granger (1913–93); (2) is fig. use of danger (cf. NO DANGER)]

stew bum *n.* [1900s–30s] a down-and-out alcoholic, the most deprived of vagrants (cf. FUZZY TAIL). [STEW n.¹ + BUM n.³]

stewed *adj.¹* [mid-18C+] drunk (cf. ALED UP).

stewed *adj.²* [1980s+] (US campus) in trouble. [STEW n.²]

stewed as a prune *adj.* [1920s+] extremely drunk. [STEWED adj.¹]

stewed prune *n.* [20C] a tune. [rhy. sl.]

stewed Quaker *n.* [late 18C–early 19C] (US) burnt rum with a piece of butter, a remedy for a cold. [? its brown colour, the *Quaker* colour; or the use of such a remedy among Quakers]

stewed to the gills/ears/eyeballs/eyebrows *phr.* [1920s+] extremely drunk. [STEWED adj.¹]

stewer *n.* [1900s–40s] (US Black) a malicious, gossiping old woman. [her *stewing* up of gossip, rumours, slander etc]

stewie *n.¹* [1940s] (US Black) a drunkard. [STEWED adj.¹]

stewie *n.²* *see* STEW n.⁴.

stews *n.* [1900s–10s] (orig. US) a group of people crowded together. [SE *students*]

stibber-gibber *n.* [mid-16C] an habitual liar. [Beale (*DSUE*, 1984) suggests a corruption of two typical contemporary names, *Stephen* and *Gilbert*, generic for lying clerks]

stick *n.¹* [17C+] the penis (cf. CREAMSTICK).

stick *n.²* [mid–late 18C] a sermon. [? the 'wooden' delivery of some sermons or the wooden pulpit]

stick *n.³* [late 18C–late 19C] (Und.) a pistol; thus *stow your sticks!* hide your pistols! [abbr. *shooting stick*]

stick *n.⁴* **1** [19C] a shot of spirits, usu. rum or brandy added to coffee or tea; usu. in phr. *with a stick in it*. **2** [1920s] a small glass of beer. **3** [1930s] (US) one who deals in illicit liquor. **4** [1940s] (US Black) a drunkard. [? one *sticks* it in the cup or glass]

stick *n.⁵* [19C+] a piece of furniture; usu. in pl. [i.e. wooden furniture]

stick *n.⁶* [mid-19C] (Und.) a crowbar, a jemmy.

stick *n.⁷* [mid-19C+] an awkward or dull person (cf. STICK-IN-THE-MUD); since 1950s also used affectionately, e.g. *not a bad old stick*. [the image is of being 'wooden' or 'cross-grained']

stick *n.⁸* **1** [late 19C+] a policeman's truncheon. **2** [1940s+] (US) a billiard cue.

stick, the *n.⁹* [late 19C+] venereal disease. [? the *sticky* discharge of gonorrhoea]

stick *n.¹⁰* [20C] **1** a reprimand, a criticism. **2** influence (cf. CLOUT n.⁵). **3** violence.

stick *n.¹¹* [1910s+] a cigarette (cf. CANCER STICK; CONSUMPTION STICK).

stick *n.¹²* [1920s+] (US Und.) a criminal's accomplice who poses as an ordinary person to distract or influence the

victims of an intended crime or swindle. [ext. of STICK n.⁷]

stick *n.¹³* (US gambling) **1** [1920s+] an accomplice who loses deliberately so as to encourage the victim to continue playing (cf. SHILL n.²). **2** [1950s+] a croupier. [the croupier's rake or *stick*]

stick *n.¹⁴* (drugs) **1** [1930s–40s] an opium pipe. **2** [1930s+] a marijuana cigarette; ext. as *stick of tea*, *stick of weed*; thus [1960s–70s] *stick man*, a marijuana smoker.

stick *n.¹⁵* [1930s+] an inquisitive person, one who *sticks their nose in*. [abbr. STICKYBEAK n.]

stick *n.¹⁶* [1960s–70s] (Black) a prostitute. [? she *sticks* around on the street]

Stick, the *n.¹⁷* [1990s] (US Black teen) Candle*stick* Park, in San Francisco, home of the SF 49ers and Giants. [abbr.]

stick *adj.* [mid-19C+] synon. of SE *stark*, as in phr. *stick, staring wild* (cf. STARK, STARING BONKERS).

stick *v.¹* [late 17C+] **1** to cheat or swindle, esp. to overcharge. **2** to take in, to impose upon.

stick *v.²* [19C] of a man, to have sexual intercourse (cf. BANG v.¹).

stick *v.³* [19C] to stymie, to bring to a stop, to render unable to move.

stick *v.⁴* [late 19C] to nonplus; thus *stuck for*, bereft of ideas.

stick *v.⁵* [late 19C+] to tolerate, to put up with.

stick *v.⁶* **1** [1920s+] to stab with a knife. **2** [1940s+] (US) to inject with a hypodermic syringe.

stick *v.⁷* [1920s–40s] (drugs) to supply marijuana; esp. in phr. *are you sticking?* [STICK n.¹⁴ (2)]

stick *v.⁸* [1980s+] (US campus) **1** to hit; thus *stuck*. **2** to have sexual intercourse with; thus *sticked*.

stickability *n.* [1920s+] the ability to endure or preserve. [STICK v.⁵]

stick a bust, to *phr.* [late 19C] (Und.) to commit a burglary. [STICK v.¹ (2) + BUST n.² (1)]

stick and bangers *n.* [late 19C] **1** the penis and testes. **2** a billiard cue and the balls with which one plays. [STICK n.¹; STICK n.⁸ (2) + SE *banger*, that which bangs together]

stick and lift, to *phr.* [late 19C–1920s] to eke out an impoverished life. [the actions of digging]

stick a pin there! *excl.* [early–mid-18C] wait! hold it!

stick a point, to *phr.* [late 19C–1920s] to settle an argument.

stick around *v.* [1910s+] (orig. Can./US) to stay close by.

stick as close as shit to a blanket, to *phr.* [1930s+] to stay very close. [SHIT n.¹ (1)]

stick a tail on, to *phr.* [1960s+] to admire sexually, usu. in phr. *I could stick a tail on that!*

stick-at-it *n.* [1900s] a persistent, dedicated person. [STICK v.⁵]

stick away *v.* [20C] **1** to hide something away. **2** to go into hiding.

stick 'em up! *excl.* [1930s+] put your hands up! a robber's trad. order to their victim to raise their hands above their head. [the first-use date reflects the probable creation of the phr. for the Western film, rather than in the 19C world that such films claimed to portray]

sticker *n.¹* [19C] a commodity that does not find a ready sale. [it SE *sticks* in the shop]

sticker *n.²* **1** [mid–late 19C] a butcher. **2** [late 19C+] a pointed, stabbing weapon, e.g. a knife, rather than one that is used to slash. [SE *stick*, to pierce]

sticker *n.³* [mid-19C] a difficult, surprising, embarrassing or pointed question. [one is *stuck* for a response]

sticker *n.⁴* [mid–late 19C] something that halts someone in their tracks, makes them pause for thought.

sticker *n.⁵* [late 19C–1940s] (US) a thorn, a burr. [it SE *sticks* to one's clothes]

sticker *n.*[6] [1900s] a guest who overstays their welcome (cf. STICK AROUND).

sticker *n.*[7] [1900s–20s] (US) a postage stamp.

sticker-licker *n.* [1980s] (South Aus.) a parking policeman (cf. BLUE MEANIE). [the SE *stickers* they affix to cars]

sticker shock *n.* [1970s+] (US) a shock from learning the price of something. [the price sticker]

sticker-up *n.*[1] [mid-19C–1900s] (Aus.) one who stages hold-ups and robberies. [STICK UP v.[4]]

sticker-up *n.*[2] [mid-19C] a defender, one who *sticks up* for something.

stick-flams *n.* [late 17C–18C] gloves. [SE *stick* + FAM *n.*[1], for which *flams* is probably a misprint; thus lit. 'stick [to] hands']

stick for drinks, to *phr.* [20C] to play and win a toss of the dice to determine who pays for the next round of drinks.

Stickies, the *n.*[1] [1960s+] the Official Irish Republican Army (cf. PROVO). [? the Officials *stick to* trad. IRA policies or they *stick on* their Easter lilies while the Provisionals use pins. Share suggests 'adhesive employed on identity badge']

stickies *n.*[2] [1980s+] (N.Z. drugs) the potent flowering tops of marijuana plants. [play on SE *sticky-buds*]

stickies *n.*[3] [1980s+] dessert wines and liqueurs. [their sweetness]

stick Indian *n.* [mid-19C+] (Can.) a member of the North American Indian peoples inhabiting the forests of British Columbia and the Yukon. [Chinook jargon *stick siwash*, forest Indian, a term used by the Coast Indians for those of the interior in this area]

sticking-plaster *n.* [1910s–20s] a very boring visit, made by an acquaintance (cf. STICKER *n.*[6]). [the visitor *sticks around*]

stickings *n.* [late 19C] butcher's off-cuts laid out on the chopping board, to which they stick.

stick in one's gizzard, to *phr.* [mid-17C–19C] to be unpalatable, to infuriate, to be unacceptable (cf. STICK IN ONE'S THROAT).

stick in one's throat, to *phr.* [20C] to be unpalatable, to infuriate, to be unacceptable (cf. STICK IN ONE'S GIZZARD).

stick-in-the-middle *n.* [1950s] (W.I.) a form of dumpling. [although the dumpling is shaped like a doughnut and might have had a stick pushed through its centre to make the requisite hole, the term more likely refers to the way the heavy dumpling *sticks to* one's stomach]

stick-in-the-mud *n.* [early 18C+] an old-fashioned, conservative person.

stick-in-the-ribs *n.* [19C] a thick soup.

stick it! *excl.* [1940s+] a derog. reply to a question, i.e. 'What shall I do with this?', or in response to an opinion with which one disagrees. [*up your ass* is assumed]

stick it in/on *v.* 1 [late 19C+] to charge extortionately. 2 [20C] (Aus.) to work hard.

stick it into *v.* [20C] (Aus.) to beg for a loan.

stick it in your ear!/up your chimney! *excl.* [1930s+] a general dismissive excl. (cf. PUT IT IN YOUR EAR!; STICK IT!).

stick it on *see* STICK IT IN.

stick it out *v.* [late 17C+] to persist, to tolerate a situation (esp. an unpleasant one). [ext. of STICK v.[5]]

stick it to *v.* [1970s+] (US) 1 to copulate. 2 to tease, to malign, to attack. 3 (US) to assault violently (cf. SOCK IT TO).

stick it up *v.*[1] [mid-19C+] to place on account (cf. STICK UP v.[3]). [i.e. to *stick it* on the running bill]

stick it up *v.*[2] [mid-19C+] to take advantage of, esp. financially. [the image is of *sticking* something sharp *up* the victim]

stick it up to *v.* [mid-19C+] to charge to, to give responsibility to.

stick it up your arse! *see* SHOVE IT UP YOUR ARSE!

stick it up your chimney! *see* STICK IT IN YOUR EAR!

stick it up your cunt! *excl.* [1930s+] (Aus.) a general expression of disdain, dismissal, rejecting the previous speaker's idea, opinion, insult etc. [CUNT *n.*[1]]

stick it up your jumper! *phr.* [1930s+] (usu. teen) rejecting the previous speaker's idea, opinion, insult etc.

stick it up your nose! *see* SHOVE IT UP YOUR NOSE!

stick-jaw *n.* 1 [early 19C+] any sweet food, e.g. a pudding, a sweet, that is hard to chew. 2 [1910s–20s] anything seen as extremely tedious.

stickman *n.*[1] [mid-19C] the member of a pickpocket gang who is handed the stolen goods by the actual pickpocket and who must also try to hinder any attempts to capture their confederate by police or public.

stickman *n.*[2] [20C] a good lover, a potent, experienced man. [STICK *n.*[1]]

stickman *n.*[3] [1930s+] (US) a croupier. [the rake or *stick* with which they collect and distribute chips]

stickman *n.*[4] [1950s–70s] (US Black) a policeman. [STICK *n.*[8] (1)]

stick of chalk *n.* [20C] (Aus.) a walk. [rhy. sl.]

stick of gage/tea *n.* [1930s–50s] a marijuana cigarette. [STICK *n.*[14] (2) + GAGE *n.*[2]/TEA *n.*[2]]

stick of rock *n.* [20C] the penis. [rhy. sl. *stick of rock* = COCK *n.*[2] (1)]

stick of tea *see* STICK OF GAGE.

stick on/on the price *v.* [mid-19C+] to overcharge.

stick one on *v.* [1940s+] to hit (cf. BUNG ONE ON; PUT ONE ON). ['one' is a blow or punch]

stick one out *v.* [1900s–10s] to maintain a position, to persist in one's argument.

stick/push/put one's bib in, to *phr.* [1950s+] (Aus.) to interfere, to intrude; thus the reverse, *keep one's bib out*.

stick one's duck in the mud, to *phr.* [1970s] (US) of a man, to have sexual intercourse.

stick oneself up/up to be *v.* [late 19C] to claim, to make oneself out to be.

stick one's neck out, to *phr.* [1910s+] (orig. US campus) to exceed one's brief, to interfere in affairs in which one is not directly concerned and often, having stuck out one's neck, fig. to have one's head cut off.

stick one's spoon in the wall, to *phr.* [19C] to die.

stick on someone *v.* [20C] (US) to force something on someone, to subject someone to something.

stick on someone like white on rice, to *phr.* [20C] (W.I.) to nag continually, to harass.

stick on the price *see* STICK ON.

stick-out *n.* [1930s+] (US) 1 a horse that seems a certain winner. 2 an outstanding sportsman.

stick-out *adj.* (US) [1940s–50s] superlative, excellent.

stick out *v.*[1] [mid-19C] to be conspicuous. [prior use was SE]

stick out/out for *v.*[2] [1900s] to persist in one's demand.

stick out a mile *see* STICK OUT LIKE A SORE THUMB.

stick out for *see* STICK OUT v.[2].

stick out like a sore thumb/mile, to *phr.* [1930s+] to be very conspicuous or obvious.

stick-picker *n.* [1920s+] (Aus.) a man employed to pick up the remnants after clearing or burning off in the bush (cf. EMU-BOBBER).

sticks *n.*[1] 1 [early–mid-19C] the legs (cf. DRUMSTICKS; TIMBERS). 2 [20C+] (US) a drummer.

sticks *n.*[2] (S.Afr.) 1 [late 19C] an obstinate horse. 2 [20C] an obstinate person. [they both SE *stick in their heels*]

sticks *n.*[3] [20C] (US) the world beyond the big cities, esp. small towns and hamlets. [SE *stick*, as a generic for the world of trees and nature + theatrical jargon *stick*, a town outside the regular touring circuits and far beyond New York City]

sticks and stones n.[1] [mid–late 19C] furniture. [ext. of STICK n.[5]]

sticks and stones n.[2] [20C] bones. [rhy. sl.]

sticksing n. [1970s+] (UK W.I.) the practice of picking pockets. [STICKSMAN]

stick slinger n. [mid-19C] (Aus.) a pimp. [STICK n.[1] + SE *sling*]

sticksman n. [1970s+] (UK W.I.) a pickpocket. [? one *sticks* one's hand in another's pocket]

stick someone for v. [20C] to make someone pay a bill, to charge excessively (cf. STICK IT IN v. (1)]

stick someone with v. [20C] **1** to charge with. **2** to make responsible for usu. unpleasant responsibility or with something unpleasant, e.g. a faulty computer (cf. STICK IT TO).

stick to v. [late 19C+] to remain loyal.

stick-to-it-iveness n. [mid-19C+] persistence, determination.

stick to one's knitting, to phr. [20C] (US) to mind one's own business.

stickum n. [20C] (US) **1** glue, cement. **2** any viscous substance.

stick-up n. **1** [late 19C+] (orig. Aus.) a hold-up, an armed robbery. **2** [1900s–30s] an armed robber. **3** [20C] (Aus.) a hold-up, a delay, a problem.

stick up v.[1] [mid-19C] to hold one's ground in an argument.

stick up v.[2] [mid–late 19C] (Aus./N.Z.) to hinder, to impede, to puzzle, to confuse.

stick up v.[3] [mid-19C+] to place on account (cf. STICK IT UP v.[1]). [the sum is *stuck on* a running account]

stick up v.[4] [mid-19C+] to rob, to hold up. [the shout of 'stick up your hands!']

stick-up artist n. [20C] an armed robber. [STICK-UP + ARTIST n.[2]]

stick up for v. [mid-19C+] to defend, to champion. [STICK UP v.[1]]

stick-up guy n. [20C] an armed robber. [STICK-UP + GUY n.[2]]

stick-ups n. [mid-19C] stiff shirt collars (cf. GILLS).

stick up to v.[1] [mid-19C+] to challenge, to oppose, esp. when one is ostensibly at a disadvantage. [ext. STICK UP v.[1]]

stick up to v.[2] [1900s] (N.Z.) to court, to pursue sexually]

stickville n. [20C] the world beyond the big cities. [STICKS n.[3] + sfx. -VILLE]

stick with it! excl. [1960s+] a general excl. of farewell (cf. HANG IN).

sticky n.[1] **1** [mid-19C] sealing wax. **2** [late 19C+] sticking plaster. **3** [1930s+] sticky tape. **4** [1940s–60s] sticky buns.

sticky n.[2] [1920s+] (Aus.) a look around, a glance. [abbr. STICKY-BEAK]

sticky n.[3] [1980s+] a cannabis cigarette. [one *sticks* two or more cigarette papers together]

sticky adj.[1] [mid-19C+] (US) mawkish, sentimental (cf. SQUISHY; SCHMALTZY). **2** [late 19C+] of weather, muggy. **3** [late 19C+] of a person, awkward, uncooperative, punctilious, prone to cause trouble. **4** [1910s+] of circumstances, awkward, presenting great difficulty, disagreeable because of hardship or danger. **5** [1930s+] of a social function, slow to start, stiff, uncomfortable. **6** [1940s+] unpleasant.

sticky adj.[2] [1940s+] (Aus./N.Z.) inquisitive, curious. [abbr. STICKYBEAK n.]

stickyback n. [1910s] a small photograph with a sticky back that can be gummed into an album.

stickybeak n. [1920s+] (Aus./N.Z.) **1** an inquisitive person, one who *sticks* in their BEAK n.[2]. **2** an inquisitive look; thus *have a sticky*, have a look around.

stickybeak v. [1940s+] (Aus./N.Z.) to pry, to snoop; thus *stickybeaking*, prying, 'poking one's nose in'. [STICKYBEAK n.]

sticky bun n. [20C] a son. [rhy. sl.]

sticky spud gun n. [1990s] the penis. [the ejaculated semen]

sticky toffee n. [1970s] coffee. [rhy. sl.]

sticky wicket n. [1940s+] difficulties, problems (cf. BAT ON A STICKY WICKET). [cricket imagery]

stiff n.[1] [17C+] an erection; thus [1970s+] (US Black) *sport a stiff*, to have an erection (cf. STIFFIE n.[2]).

stiff n.[2] **1** [early 19C–1900s] paper, a document, esp. a promissory note or bill of exchange, a clandestine letter. **2** [mid-19C+] a note or cheque, whether genuine or forged (cf. BIT OF STIFF n.[2]). **3** [mid-19C+] a hawker's licence. **4** [late 19C–1930s] paper money. **5** [late 19C+] (US/Aus./N.Z. Und.) a note, usu. between prisoners or passed illicitly into a prison by a relation etc. **6** [20C] (Aus./N.Z.) a summons from the police.

stiff n.[3] **1** [early 19C+] a corpse. **2** [mid–late 19C] (horse-racing) a useless, losing horse and thus an erroneous, losing wager. **3** [late 19C+] (US) a penniless man, a wastrel, a tramp, a migratory or unskilled worker. **4** [late 19C+] (N.Z./US) a mean, disagreeable, or contemptible person (cf. BIG STIFF). **5** [20C] a drunkard. **6** [1930s+] (US) any failure, a flop. [(1) rigor mortis; (2) to (6) fig. use thereof]

stiff n.[4] [1950s+] an average person, often with a description, e.g. WORKING STIFF. [? fig. use of STIFF n.[3] (1), i.e. one so dull as to be 'half-dead' anyway; or as one who can be 'stiffed' because of their rectitude]

stiff adj.[1] [mid-18C+] (US) very drunk and passed out cold. [SE *stiff*, rigid]

stiff adj.[2] [mid-18C+] strong, usu. of liquor, e.g. *a stiff drink, a stiff one*.

stiff adj.[3] [mid-19C+] (US Und.) forged. [STIFF n.[2]]

stiff adj.[4] [late 19C–1910s] **1** of a competitor, certain to win. **2** of a competition, a certainty.

stiff adj.[5] (Aus./N.Z.) **1** [late 19C+] impoverished; thus *stiff and swagless*, with neither money nor possessions (cf. STIFF AS A CRUTCH). **2** [1910s+] unlucky.

stiff v.[1] [late 19C] to curse, to swear. [? the response, 'I say, that's a bit stiff,' to such an outburst]

stiff v.[2] [1930s+] of a man, to have sexual intercourse. [STIFF n.[1]]

stiff v.[3] [1950s+] (US) **1** to cheat, to swindle, to rob. **2** to fail to tip a waiter, doorman etc. [i.e. to treat as a STIFF n.[3] (1) or STIFF n.[4]]

stiff v.[4] [1970s+] to murder. [STIFF n.[3] (1)]

stiff v.[5] [1970s+] (US) to mistreat, to snub, to push aside. [ext. of STIFF v.[3]]

stiff and jive, to phr. [1930s–50s] (US Black) to show off, to boast (cf. STIFFIN' AND JIVIN'). [jazz use *stiff and jive*, to play flashily but with little genuine skill]

stiff and stout n. [19C] the erect penis (cf. STIFF n.[1]).

stiff-arm v. [1970s+] (US) to mistreat, to snub, to push aside.

stiff-arsed adj. [1930s+] supercilious, arrogant, standoffish. [SE *stiff* + sfx. -ARSED]

stiff as a crutch phr. [late 19C+] (Aus./N.Z.) completely penniless. [ext. of STIFF adj.[5]]

stiff as a poker phr. [late 18C+] very stiff.

stiff/tough bickkies/biccies/bickies phr. [1970s+] (N.Z.) tough luck, hard luck. [SE *tough/stiff* + BIKKIES]

stiff cheddar/cheese/luck n. [1910s+] (N.Z.) bad luck.

stiff-dealer n. [early 19C] a dealer in promissory notes. [STIFF n.[2] (1)]

stiff deity n. [19C] the erect penis.

stiffen v.[1] [late 19C–1900s] to bribe, to corrupt. [1920s+] to swindle, usu. in passive. [STIFF v.[3]]

stiffen v.[2] [late 19C–1900s] to kill, to murder. [STIFF v.[4]]

stiffener n.[1] [mid-19C+] **1** (orig. Aus.) a fortifying alcoholic drink. **2** a knock-out punch.

stiffener n.[2] [20C] a cigarette card. [its use in a soft-sided cigarette pack]

stiffen it, God! excl. [late 19C–1900s] a general excl. [lit. 'let it grow dead and stiff']

stiffen the lizards!/crows!/snakes! *excl.* [1940s+] (Aus.) an excl. of surprise, shock etc (cf. SPEED THE WOMBATS!).

stiff-fencer *n.* [mid-19C] a street-seller of writing paper. [STIFF n.² + FENCER]

stiffie *n.¹* [1980s+] an invitation. [the thick card on which it is printed]

stiffie *n.²* [1980s+] an erection. [STIFF n.¹]

stiffin' and jivin' *phr.* [1930s–50s] (US Black) making unreal, empty conversation (cf. STIFF AND JIVE). [STIFF v.³ + JIVE v.¹ (2)]

stiff in the back *phr.* [late 19C] resolute, determined. [i.e. SE *unbending*]

stiff luck *see* STIFF CHEDDAR.

stiff-rump *n.* [late 17C–19C] a pompous, arrogant person; thus *stiff-rump*, arrogant, pompous (cf. SHOVE IT UP YOUR ARSE!).

stiff the stroll, to *phr.* [1930s–40s] (US Black) to loiter, to hang around on a street corner. [STIFF n.⁴ + STROLL n.]

stiff 'un *n.* [mid-19C+] a corpse. [STIFF n.³]

stiffy *n.* [late 19C–1900s] a corpse (cf. STIFF n.³; STIFF 'UN).

stifle *v.* [early 17C] to slip money surreptitiously into another person's hand. [SE *stifle*, to conceal]

stifler *n.* 1 [early 19C] the gallows. 2 [19C] a dram of spirits. [both 'take one's breath away']

stifle the squeaker, to *phr.* 1 [late 17C–1900s] to murder a child 'and throw it into a House of Office [privy]' (B.E.). 2 [19C–1900s] to procure an abortion. [SE *stifle* + SQUEAKER n.¹ (2)]

stift *n.* [1920s+] (tramp) one who does not work. [synon. Rom.]

still *n.¹* [mid–late 19C] a *still*-born child. [abbr.]

still *n.²* [late 19C] (US) a quiet drunkard. [pun on SE *still*, quiet/*still*, a distillery]

still *v.* [late 18C] to silence, by murdering or knocking out.

still alive and kissing *see* ALL ALIVE AND KISSING.

still and all *phr.* [early 19C+] even so, nevertheless.

still hill *n.* [20C] (US) a cemetery (cf. HILL).

still sow *n.* 1 [late 16C] 'a close, slie lurking knave' (Florio, 1598). 2 [early 18C] a prostitute. [pvb. 'the still sow eats up half the draff', i.e. the quiet pig eats more than its share of fodder]

stilly *n.* [1940s] (W.I.) a faithful lover (cf. STUCKY). [? they are *still there*]

Stilton, the *n.* [late 19C] 1 the best of a type or style, the superlative. 2 an important or influential person, the boss. [play on CHEESE n.¹; CHESHIRE]

stilts *n.* [1940s] (US Black) the human legs.

stimulate *v.* [mid-19C–1910s] to drink alcohol.

sting *n.¹* [late 19C] the penis (cf. PRICK n.).

sting *n.²* [1920s+] (Aus.) 1 strong drink (cf. STINGO n.). 2 methylated spirits. 3 a drug, esp. as given to a racehorse.

sting *n.³* (US Und.) 1 [1930s+] a reasonably large sum of money ($500 average) obtained by some form of deception or trickery. 2 [1930s+] any form of robbery, as a complex fraud planned well in advance. 3 [1970s+] a police undercover operation designed to entrap alleged criminals.

sting *v.* 1 [19C] to demand or beg for something. 2 [early 19C+] to steal, to cheat, both in fact and as merely overcharging.

sting-bum *n.* [late 17C–early 19C] a miser, a mean person. [STING v. + BUM n.³]

stinger *n.¹* [mid-16C+] 'something that stings or smarts, e.g. a sharp blow, or the hand that delivers it; something that causes sharp distress, a pungent speech or crushing argument; a sharp frost.' (*OED*)

stinger *n.²* [mid-19C+] (Aus.) any period of extreme weather, hot or cold. [SE *sting*]

stinger/stringer *n.³* [1970s] (US Black) a hotplate that is run from two wires attached to a light socket. [STING v. (2) or SE *string*, i.e. the wires]

stinger box *n.* [20C] (Aus.) a jellyfish.

sting for *v.* [20C] (orig. US) to extort money from someone by begging or borrowing it in a demanding manner. [ext. of STING v.]

stingo *n.* [late 17C+] very strong ale. [it *stings* the drinker]

stingo *adj.* [late 19C] energetic, spirited, lively. [SE *sting*]

stingtail *n.* [17C] a prostitute (cf. SCOLOPENDRA). [the *sting* in a scorpion's *tail*, in this context venereal disease]

stingy-brim *n.* [1940s–60s] (orig. US Black) a hat with a narrow brim. [lit. a 'mean brim']

stink *n.¹* 1 [early 19C+] a fuss, a furore, esp. in phr. *kick up a stink*, to make a fuss. 2 [late 19C+] a fight. 3 [1970s+] (US Black) the vagina (cf. STANK).

stink *n.²* [1910s+] a contemptible person.

stink *v.* 1 [mid-19C+] to behave offensively, to appear offensive to someone. 2 [1930s+] (orig. US) to be morally inadequate or physically incompetent (cf. STINK TO HIGH HEAVEN).

stinka *see* STINKER n.².

stink bomb *n.* [1950s+] (US) something disgusting or deplorable.

stink-car *n.* [1900s] a motorcar. [pun on STINKER n.¹ (3)]

stinker *n.¹* 1 [17C+] a loathsome, unpleasant person or object (cf. SKUNK n.¹). 2 [early 19C–1950s] a black eye. 3 [early 19C+] anything that emits an offensive smell, orig. aimed at cigars and cigarettes (cf. GUINEA STINKER). 4 [20C] (Aus.) a very hot or humid day (cf. SCORCHER). 5 [1910s+] a strongly-worded letter, a disagreeable review or other communication. 6 [1910s+] anything considered unpleasant because of the difficulty in accomplishing it, e.g. a school essay; thus [1920s+] *come a stinker*, to fall into difficulties (cf. COME A CROPPER). 7 [1990s] a promiscuous woman (cf. SCRUBBER n.²; STOINKER). [(2) 20C use is Aus.; (6) ? phr. a nonce-usage coined by P.G. Wodehouse]

stinker/stinka *n.²* [1970s+] (S.Afr. Black) a passbook. [the wholly negative image it enjoyed in the Black community; such passes were scrapped in 1985]

stinkeroo *n.* [1940s+] (US) something disgusting or deplorable. [STINKER n.¹ (1) + sfx. -EROO]

stink-finger/stinky-finger *n.* [late 19C+] the middle finger. [its use in sexual foreplay]

stinkibus *n.* [18C] bad beer or liquor, esp. when adulterated. [SE *stink*; note smugglers' use, a case of liquor that has been left under the water so long as to be undrinkable]

stinking *adj.¹* 1 [1910s+] as abbr. of *stinking rich*, very well-off. 2 [1920s+] very drunk (cf. ADDLED).

stinking *adj.²* [1940s+] a general neg. intensifier, disgusting, repellent, odious. [prior use from 13C is SE]

stinkingly *adv.* [20C] excessively, extraordinarily.

stinking with *adj.* [1910s+] in possession of a large amount of something, usu. money.

stinkious *n.* [18C] gin. [? a misprint for STINKIBUS]

stinko *n.* 1 [1920s+] (Aus.) wine. 2 [1930s–40s] (US) an alcoholic tramp. [STINKO adj. + in (2) ref. to Sterno or 'canned heat']

stinko *adj.* [1920s+] very drunk (cf. ADDLED).

stink of/with *v.* [late 19C+] (US) to be full of, characterized by, e.g. *stink of success*, *stink with money*.

stink of a ... *phr.* [1970s+] a great deal of, a large amount of (cf. DEVIL OF A ... ; FUCK OF A ... ; HELL OF A ...).

Stinkomalee *n.* [mid-19C] London University. [coined by the Tory wit and writer Theodore Hook (1788–1841) with ref. to contemporary concerns over Trincomalee, to the fact that the university, founded in 1836, allowed in nonconformists (Oxford and Cambridge did not), and to the farms and their animals that formerly occupied the site]

stink on ice, to *phr.* [20C] (US) to be disgusting or deplorable. [ext. of STINK v.]

stinkpot *n.* **1** [mid-19C+] a general term of abuse, aimed usu. at people rather than things. **2** [20C] (Aus.) a small firework. **3** [1950s–70s] (US Black) the vagina (cf. BEARDED CLAM). **4** [1970s+] an engine that emits foul fumes. [(1) esp. refers in N.Z. to a child who wets themselves]

stink to high heaven, to *phr.* [1950s+] (orig. US) to be very disgusting and unpleasant. [ext. of STINK v.]

stinks *n.* [mid-19C] (public school) chemistry, as a subject.

stink up *v.* [1950s+] (US) **1** to soil, to sully. **2** to 'smell' suspicious.

stink weed *n.* [1940s–70s] (drugs) marijuana.

stink with *see* STINK OF.

stinky *adj.* [1940s+] (orig. US) disgusting, nasty.

stinky-finger *see* STINK-FINGER.

stinky-pie rich *adj.* [1900s–20s] (US Black) extremely rich. [var. on STINKING adj.¹ + SE *rich*]

stipe *n.* [mid-19C+] **1** a *stipe*ndiary magistrate. **2** (Aus.) a *stipe*ndiary racing steward. [abbr.]

stir *n.*¹ [mid-19C+] prison (cf. JOE GURR). [abbr. Rom. *sturiben*, a prison, *staripen*, to imprison]

stir *n.*² [late 19C] a crowd. [SE *stir*, movement]

stir *n.*³ **1** [1940s+] (Ulster) a plan, a scheme. **2** [1940s+] (orig. Ulster) fun, enjoyment, a party (cf. CRACK n.⁸). **3** [1970s+] (N.Z.) a bout of troublemaking. [SE *stir*, movement]

stir *v.*¹ [1960s+] **1** to gossip maliciously, to cause trouble deliberately by so doing. **2** (orig. Aus.) to tease, to provoke; thus *for a stir*, for trouble's sake. **3** (Aus.) to cause trouble (other than through gossip etc). [abbr. SE *stir up trouble*]

stir *v.*² [1960s–70s] (US Black) to steal a car, to strip a car of its chrome, parts, radio etc. [SE *stir*, to mix up]

stir-about *n.* [late 19C] **1** porridge. **2** any pudding that requires stirring.

stir-bugs *adj.* [20C] (Can. prison) insane from too long a confinement in prison (cf. STIR-CRAZY). [STIR n.¹ + BUGS adj.]

stir-crazy *adj.* [1930s+] (orig. US) used of a prisoner who has succumbed to prison-induced insanity. [STIR n.¹ + SE *crazy*]

stir it up *v.* [1950s+] of a woman, to masturbate.

Stirling Moss *n.* [20C] a damn, a curse, usu. in phr. *I don't give a stirling*. [rhy. sl. *Stirling Moss* = TOSS n.¹; ult. UK racing driver *Stirling Moss* (b.1929)]

stir one's stew/the batter, to *phr.* [1950s+] to masturbate.

stir one's stumps, to *phr.* [late 16C+] **1** to get a move on (cf. SHAKE ONE'S SHAMBLES). **2** to dance. **3** to do one's duty keenly. [SE *stir* + *stump*, a leg]

stirrer *n.* **1** [1960s+] (Aus.) one who stirs up trouble or discontent, an agitator, a trouble-maker. **2** [1970s+] an unpleasant, malicious gossip. [STIR v.¹]

stirrup *v.* [early–mid-18C] to thrash someone with a shoemaker's stirrup.

stir-shit *n.* [late 19C–1900s] a sodomite, a male homosexual. [SE *stir* + SHIT n.¹ (1)]

stir shit/the shit *v.* [1950s+] to go out of one's way to make trouble, esp. by gossiping or telling tales. [SE *stir* + SHIT n.¹ (1)]

stir shit of *v.* [1940s+] (N.Z.) to criticize harshly, to reprimand severely. [SE *stir* + SHIT n.¹ (1)]

stir the batter *see* STIR ONE'S STEW.

stir the porridge, to *phr.* [1960s+] (orig. Aus.) to have sexual intercourse with a woman immediately after she has had sex with another man, esp. used of the final man in a gang rape (cf. SLOPPY SECONDS).

stir/rouse the possum, to *phr.* [20C] (Aus.) to create a disturbance, to start things moving, to jolt the general apathy (cf. PLAY POSSUM). [the animal's habit of keeping quite still for long periods]

stir the shit *see* STIR SHIT.

stir the stew, to *phr.* [1900s–10s] of a man, to have sexual intercourse.

stir up *v.* [late 19C] to visit without any previous announcement (cf. BEAT UP THE QUARTERS).

stir-up Sunday *n.* [mid-19C] the Sunday before Advent (cf. CRIB-CRUST MONDAY). [the collect for that day begins with the words 'Stir up ...']

stirwise *adj.* [20C] (US Und.) well-adjusted to prison life, capable of sustaining one's existence in prison (cf. CONWISE). [STIR n.¹ + sfx. -WISE]

stitch *n.*¹ [late 17C–early 19C] a tailor. [metonymy]

stitch *n.*² [1980s] (US campus/teen) anything or anyone seen as amusing; intensified as *stitch and a half*. [the physical SE *stitch* that can accompany laughter]

stitch/go on the stitch *v.* **1** [late 18C–mid-19C] to have sexual intercourse (cf. LADIES' TAILOR; NEEDLE n.¹). **2** [1930s+] to beat in a fight or contest. [the in and out SE *stitching* movement of the penis or of the fists]

stitch-back *n.* [late 17C–18C] very strong ale. [? its back-strengthening properties. Note early 17C SE *steelback*, Alicante wine, which was supposed to help back problems]

stitched *adj.*¹ [1920s+] **1** (Aus.) defeated. **2** drunk (cf. BASTED). [SE *stitched up*, i.e. enclosed, confined]

stitched *adj.*² [1950s+] convicted by false police evidence. [abbr. STITCH UP]

stitch-louse *n.* [mid-19C] a tailor.

stitch up *v.* **1** [1950s+] of the police, to ensure a conviction by planting evidence, faking confessions etc. **2** [1970s+] to complete a task to one's complete satisfaction. [sewing up a garment neatly and conclusively]

stiver/stuiver/stuyver *n.* [mid-18C–20C] something of little value. [Du. *stiver*, a low-valued coin, the smallest monetary unit in use at the Cape under the Dutch East India Co., one-twentieth of a florin or gulden, worth a little more than one (old) penny]

stiver-cramped *adj.* [late 18C–mid-19C] impoverished. [STIVER]

stoat *n.* [1990s] the vagina (cf. BADGER n.⁷).

stoater/stoter *n.* **1** [17C–late 18C] a violent blow; thus *tip someone a stoater*, give someone a blow (cf. STOTOR). **2** [20C] a bruise. [Du. *stooter, stooten*, to knock, to push]

stoater/stoter *v.* [17C–late 18C] to hit. [STOATER n.]

stocious/stoshious/stoshus/stotious *adj.*¹ [late 19C+] tight-lipped, discreet. [ety. unknown]

stocious/stoosh/stoshious/stoshus/stotious *adj.*² [20C] (W.I.) **1** well-dressed, stylish, high-class. **2** good-looking. **3** snobbish. [? SE *ostentatious*]

stocious *adj.*³ [1980s+] (Irish) drunken. [? Scot. *stot*, staggering]

stock *n.*¹ [late 18C–early 19C] cheek, often as *good stock*. [abbr. SE *stock of impudence*]

stock *n.*² *see* STOOK n.

stock *v.* [mid-19C] in card-games, to *stack* the cards in a certain way to facilitate cheating.

stockbanger *n.* [1930s] (Aus.) a stockman; thus *stockbanging*, working on a cattle farm.

stockbroker Tudor *n.* [1930s+] fake Tudor architecture, with an emphasis on exposed beams, to be found in the wealthy commuter villages of the Home Counties of England wherein live many brokers (cf. PSEUDIE TUDIE).

stockdolager *see* SOCKDOLAGER.

stock-drawers *n.* [late 17C–early 19C] (Und.) stockings.

stocker *n.* [1970s+] (US) a stock-car racer.

stocking *n.* [late 19C] the practice of arranging cards in a certain manner for cheating purposes. [STOCK v.]

stock-in-trade *n.* [late 19C–1900s] the genitals. [SE *stock-in-trade*, a workman's tools]

stocks and shares *n.* [20C] stairs. [rhy. sl.]

stodge *n.* **1** [mid-19C+] heavy, filling, nutritionless food. **2** [mid-19C+] heavy, demanding but relatively unrewarding work. **3** [mid-19C+] heavy, tedious writing or speech. **4** [late 19C–1940s] food in general. [SE *stodge*, thick, liquid, viscous mud]

stodge *v.* **1** [mid-19C+] to gorge, to eat to excess; thus *stodging*, eating heavily, gorging. **2** [mid-19C+] to work steadily at something tedious. **3** [mid-19C–1920s] to trudge through sticky, clinging mud or slush. [STODGE n.]

stodger *n.* **1** [late 19C–1920s] a glutton. **2** [1900s–20s] a dull, spiritless person; thus *stodgery*, the manner in which such a person behaves. [STODGE v.]

stoepkakker *n.* [1980s+] (S.Afr.) 'a small, fat and old dog of the spoiled rotten variety which has found its sunny spot on the stoep (veranda) and refuses, with miniature fangs at full snarl, to budge for anyone or anything, not even to take care of its bodily functions' (*Cyberbraai*, Internet, 1997). [Afk. *stoep*, porch, veranda + *kakker*, SHITTER]

stoep-sitter *n.* [1930s+] (S.Afr.) a farmer who is not primarily dependent on agriculture for their income (cf. CHEQUE-BOOK FARMER; PITT STREET FARMER). [Afk. *stoep*, veranda + SE *sitter*]

stog *n.* [1990s] (US Black) a cigarette. [STOGIE]

stogie/stogy *n.* (US) **1** [late 19C+] a cigar. **2** [1960s+] (drugs) an over-sized marijuana cigarette. [abbr. *Conestoga*; supposedly smoked by the 'stoga drivers', i.e. the drivers of the Conestoga wagons plying between Wheeling and Pittsburgh, Pennsylvania]

stoinker *n.* [1990s] a malodorous (whether lit. or fig.) and promiscuous woman. [STINKER n.[1] (7)]

stoke *v.* [20C] (W.I.) to humiliate, to treat badly. [? obs. SE *stoke*, to make a thrust at]

stoked/stoked on *adj.* [1960s+] **1** (orig. Aus.) drunk (cf. ABOUT RIGHT adj.[1]). **2** (US campus/teen, esp. California) elated, delighted, thrilled. [SE *stoke*, to build up and stir a furnace]

stoked out *adj.* [1960s–70s] exhausted. [STOKED]

stoke me!/stoke me up! *excl.* [1980s+] (US campus) a general excl. of approval, that's wonderful! I'm so happy! great! [STOKED adj.(2)]

stoke on trent *n.* [1970s+] a male homosexual. [rhy. sl. *stoke on trent* = BENT n.]

stoke the furnace, to *phr.* [1990s] to masturbate.

stoke-up *n.* [mid-19C–1950s] a large, sustaining meal.

stoke up *v.* **1** [late 19C+] to eat. **2** [1980s+] (US campus) to please, to encourage.

stokkies *n.* [20C] (S.Afr. Und.) a prison. [? Afk. *stok*, the stocks]

s.t.o.l. *phr.* [1980s] a one-night or one-evening sexual encounter. [abbr. *short time of love* ? + ref. to milit. abbr. short take-off *and landing*]

stolen a manchet/a roll out of the brewer's basket *phr.* [late 17C–early 19C] tipsy. [SE *manchet*, a small loaf or roll made from the finest wheat flour]

stole on *v.* [1990s] (US Black) to hit with a surprise punch. [? SE *steal a march*]

stoli/stoly *n.* [1970s+] *Stoli*chnaya vodka. [abbr.]

stoll *v.*[1] [mid-19C] (northern Und.) to understand. [SE *stall*, to put in place]

stoll *v.*[2] [late 19C] to drink; thus *stolled*, tipsy. [? Norfolk dial. *stole*, to drink, to swallow]

stoly *see* STOLI.

stomacher *n.* [20C] (teen) a sour apple that may produce a stomach-ache.

stomach habit *n.* [1950s–70s] (drugs) heroin addiction. [SE *stomach* + HABIT n.]

stomach Steinway *n.* [20C] (US) a piano accordion. [SE *stomach*, against which it is held + *Steinway*, a piano]

stomach-worm gnaws, the *phr.* [late 18C–early 19C] a melodramatic way of saying that one is hungry.

stomp *n.* [1950s–70s] (US Black) a shoe. [SAmE *stomp*, to stamp]

stomp/stomp on *v.* **1** [1940s+] (US) to beat up. **2** [1950s+] (Aus. teen) to dance. [SE *stamp*/SAmE *stomp*]

stomp-ass *adj.* [1940s+] (US) violent, aggressive. [STOMP v. + sfx. -ASS]

stomp-down woman *n.* [1960s–70s] (US Black) the hardest working woman in a pimp's 'stable' of prostitutes. [STOMP v.]

stompers/stomps/stumpers *n.* [late 19C+] (US) large, heavy boots, esp. cowboy boots. [SAmE *stomp*, to stamp]

stompie *n.* [1940s+] (S.Afr.) a cigarette butt, a partially smoked cigarette, esp. one stubbed out and kept for relighting later; thus a worthless remnant. [Afk. *stomp*, stump]

stomping *n.* [1950s+] (US) a beating, esp. one in which the victim is kicked or trampled on. [STOMP v. (1)]

stomp-jumper *n.* [19C] (US) a farmer, a peasant (cf. APPLE-KNOCKER n.[2]). [SE *stump* + *jumper*]

stomp on *see* STOMP v.

stomps *see* STOMPERS.

stomp someone's buzz *see* KILL SOMEONE'S BUZZ.

stoms *see* STUMBLERS.

stone *n.*[1] **1** [mid-18C+] a testicle; thus fig. *stones*, courage, bravery (cf. AGATES). **2** [1900s–50s] (US Und.) a diamond (cf. ROCK n.[2]). **3** [1980s+] (drugs) crack cocaine (cf. ROCK n.[4]). [(1) SE mid-12C–early 18C]

stone *n.*[2] [1960s+] a state of drugged intoxication. [STONED]

stone *adj.* [1940s+] (drugs) intoxicated by a drug. [abbr. STONED]

stone *v.* [1950s+] (drugs) to render intoxicated with a drug, usu. marijuana or hashish. [the image of being knocked over with a rock]

stone *adv.* [late 19C+] (orig. Aus./US) absolutely, purely, completely, to the highest degree, e.g. *stone addict*, one who is deeply addicted to a drug, *stone blind*, extremely drunk, *stone bonkers*, absolutely crazy etc (cf. STONE FOX). [i.e. the solidity of a stone]

stone broke/stony-broke *adj.* [late 19C+] penniless, absolutely impoverished. [STONE adv. + BROKE]

stone-cold *n.* [1930s+] (Aus. Und.) a villain who would never betray their fellows whatever the circumstances.

stone-cold fox *n.* [1970s] (US Black) a very attractive woman. [SE *stone-cold* + FOX n.[4]]

stoned/stoned out *adj.* [1940s+] **1** drunk. **2** intoxicated with some form of drug, thus *stoned out of one's brain/gourd/head/mind/skull*, very intoxicated, on drink or, more usu., drugs.

stone doublet *n.* [late 17C–18C] a prison, esp. Newgate prison (cf. IRON DOUBLET; STONE DUMP; STONE HOUSE; STONE JUG n.[1]; STONE TAVERN). [SE *stone* + *doublet*, tight-fitting body armour]

stoned out *see* STONED.

stoned over *adj.* [1980s+] (US drugs) lethargic after smoking cannabis. [STONED]

stoned to the eyes/eyeballs *phr.* [1950s+] (orig. US) very intoxicated from drugs or alcohol. [STONED]

stone dump *n.* [20C] (US Und.) a prison (cf. STONE DOUBLET). [SE *stone* + DUMP n.[3]]

stone end/finish *n.* [1940s+] (Aus.) the absolute end, an intolerable situation. [STONE adv. + SE *end/finish*]

stoneface *n.* [1940s+] a totally unemotional person. [the first (SE) use of the phr. is in Nathaniel Hawthorne's story 'The Great Stone Face' (*National Era*, 16 January 1850), in which it referred to a natural rock formation. The unsmiling silent era comedian Buster Keaton (1898–1966) was the 'Great Stone Face']

stone fence n. [mid–late 19C] (US) **1** ginger-beer and brandy. **2** whisky mixed with cider. **3** neat whisky. [ety. unknown]

stone finish see STONE END.

stone fox n. [1980s+] (US campus) a beautiful woman. [STONE adv. + FOX n.[4]]

stone fruit n. [late 19C–1900s] children. [STONE n.[1] (1) + SE *fruit*; lit. the 'fruit of one's loins']

stone-ginger adj. [1930s+] absolutely certain. [the N.Z. racehorse *Stone Ginger*, known as phenomenally successful; ult. STONE adv. + racing *ginger*, a showy, fast horse]

stone house n. [1930s–60s] a prison (cf. STONE DOUBLET).

stone jug/pitcher n.[1] [late 18C–mid-19C] Newgate prison, the main criminal prison in London (cf. JUG n.[1]; STONE DOUBLET).

stone jug n.[2] [1920s+] a fool, a dupe. [rhy. sl. *stone jug* = MUG n.[4]]

stone me! excl. [1960s+] an excl. of surprise. [SE *stone*, to throw stones at]

stone out v. [1950s+] (drugs) to become over-intoxicated by a drug, usu. marijuana or hashish. [STONED]

stone pitcher see STONE JUG n.[1]

stoner n. [1970s+] a drug user (cf. DOPER n.[2]). [STONED]

stones and bones n. [1970s+] (US campus) a course in prehistory.

stone tavern n. [late 18C–early 19C] a prison (cf. STONE DOUBLET).

stone/spare the crows! excl. [1930s+] (orig. Aus./N.Z.) an excl. of surprise, wonder, alarm (cf. SPEED THE WOMBATS!).

stone to the bone adj. [1950s+] (US Black) said of one who is considered wholly admirable in every respect. [STONE adv. + TO THE BONE]

stonewall v. [late 19C+] (orig. Aus.) to put up barriers, to obfuscate, to prevaricate; thus *stonewall*, a person or thing that obstructs. [the earliest cited use is late 19C cricket jargon, thence to political use and thence to general, but note US General Thomas 'Stonewall' Jackson, nicknamed for the implacable stand he conducted during the US Civil War Battle of Bull Run, 21 July 1861]

stonewall horrors n. [20C] (Anglo-Irish) delirium tremens (cf. CAST-IRON HORRORS).

stoney see STONY.

stonicky n. [1970s] (Und.) a cosh. [naut. *stonicky*, a rope's end, used for punishment]

stonies n. [1970s+] (US) strong sexual desire. [? STONE n.[1] (1)]

stonker n. [1980s+] **1** anything large, or impressive of its type. **2** an erection. [STONKER v.; note the only *OED* citation for (2) (thus poss. a nonce-word), is *Sex with Paula Yates* (1987)]

stonker v. [1910s+] (Aus.) **1** to render useless, to put out of action, to thwart. **2** to kill, to destroy. **3** to defeat, to outwit. [echoic; orig. milit. use]

stonkered adj. [1920s+] (orig. Aus.) **1** drunk; thus *stonkering*, drinking (cf. BASTED). **2** satiated. [STONKER v.]

stonking adj. [1980s+] a general term of approval, enormous, excellent etc, esp. as *stonking great ...* (cf. LICKING adj.). [STONKER n.]

stony/stoney adj. [late 19C+] absolutely penniless (cf. PEBBLE-BEACHED). [abbr. STONE BROKE]

stony blind adj. [1920s–30s] (Aus.) absolutely drunk. [STONE adv. + BLIND DRUNK]

stony-broke see STONE BROKE.

stoob n. [mid-19C] boots. [backsl.]

stooge n. [late 19C+] (orig. US) any despised underling (cf. GOFER). [? SE *student*; orig. show business, a comedian's assistant or 'straight man']

stooge v. [1930s+] (orig. US) to work as an assistant or underling. [STOOGE n.]

stook/stock/stuke n. [mid-19C] a pocket handkerchief; thus

stook-buzzer, stook-hauler, a pickpocket specializing in pocket handkerchiefs. [? Ger. *Stück*, a piece of cloth]

stook v. [20C] (S.Afr.) to stir up trouble. [S.Afr.E. *stook*, to distil spirits]

stooked adj. [mid-19C+] of stolen goods or money, hidden.

stool n. [1930s+] an informer. [abbr. STOOL-PIGEON n.[1]]

stool v. [1910s+] (US) to act as an informer. [abbr. STOOL-PIGEON n.[1]]

stoolie/stooley n. [1920s+] (orig. US) an informer. [abbr. STOOL-PIGEON n.[1]]

stool of ease n. [17C] a privy, a lavatory (cf. CHAPEL OF EASE; CLOSET OF EASE; HOUSE OF EASE).

stool-pigeon n.[1] [mid-19C+] (orig. US) an informer, one who makes a confession implicating others. [SE *stool-pigeon*, a bird that is tied to a stool in order to lure other birds towards the waiting hunter. In this case the 'stool' is that in a police station]

stool-pigeon n.[2] [1980s+] (US gay) one who loiters in men's lavatories in order to offer fellatio. [SE *stool*, excrement or seat + pun on STOOL-PIGEON n.[1]]

stoom v. [late 19C–1920s] (Aus.) to ruin financially, usu. as *stoomed*, ruined. [STUMER n.[1]]

stoomer see STUMER n.[1].

stoop n.[1] see STUPE n.

stoop n.[2] [late 18C–early 19C] the pillory; thus *stooped*, placed in the pillory (cf. STOOP-NAPPER). [the position one adopts while thus confined]

stoop n.[3] [1940s+] (Aus.) a petty thief. [they *stoop* to pick up things]

stoop v.[1] **1** [late 16C] be ensnared by a confidence trickster or a thief. **2** [1970s+] (US Black) to have sexual intercourse (cf. GET DOWN v.[3]).

stoop v.[2] [early 19C] to put someone in the pillory. [STOOP n.[2]]

stooper n.[1] [1900s–10s] (US) one who sits on the stoop of a house and conducts a semi-public life, half-way between the privacy of the home and the total public life of the street corner. [Du. *stoep*, step, the short flight of stairs that leads from street level to the raised, main floor of many New York City houses and tenements]

stooper n.[2] [1930s+] **1** (tramp) a cigarette stub, picked up in the street (cf. B.D.V.). **2** (US) a person who forages for betting tickets on the ground at racetracks. [SE *stoop*, to bend down]

stooping-match n. [early 19C] the placing of a number of people in the pillory at the same time. [STOOP n.[2]]

stoop-napper n. [late 18C–early 19C] a man standing in a pillory. [STOOP n.[2] + NAPPER n.[2]]

stoosh see STOCIOUS adj.[2].

stop n.[1] [mid-19C] a policeman. [he *stops* malefactors]

stop n.[2] [1940s+] (S.Afr. drugs) **1** marijuana. **2** a single pipeful of marijuana or enough to roll a single cigarette. **3** the smallest measure of marijuana sold. [Afk. *stop*, a plug or fill of tobacco]

stop n.[3] [1950s+] (US Und.) a receiver of stolen goods. [play on FENCE n.[1]]

stop v. [20C] (Aus.) in a fight, to knock one's opponent down or knock out.

stop and go n. [20C] a toe. [rhy. sl.]

stop and start n. [20C] the heart. [rhy. sl.]

stop a packet, to phr. [1910s+] to be killed or wounded. [SE *stop* + PACKET n.[2]]

stop a pot/pint, to phr. [1930s] (Aus.) to have a drink (cf. STOP ONE).

stop-gap n. [1910s–20s] the last child born to a family.

stop-hole abbey n. [late 17C–18C] (Und.) the headquarters of the contemporary London underworld. [SE *stophole*, a plug; presumably some large if otherwise abandoned and decaying building, possibly in the criminal zone of ALSATIA, to which easy entrance, i.e. by the authorities, was barred]

stop it out *v.* [mid-19C] to save money for purchase A by economizing on purchase B.

stop moing me! *excl.* [1980s] (US preppie) a demand made of one boy to another who he feels is pushing or jostling him unnecessarily. [SE *stop* + MO v.]

stop my vitals! *see* STAP MY VITALS!

stop off *v.* [late 19C+] (N.Z.) to stop doing something, often as imper.

stop on a dime, to *phr.* [1960s+] (US) to stop quickly and precisely. [the tiny size of the 10-cent coin]

stop one *v.* [1920s–30s] (Aus.) to have a drink (cf. STOP A POT).

stop-out *n.* [20C] one who stays out enjoying themselves longer than the speaker considers respectable.

stopper *n.* [early 19C+] **1** (boxing) a heavy blow. **2** anything that causes events to come to a halt, esp. in phr. *put a stopper on*, to bring to a halt.

stopper *v.* [early 19C–1900s] to stop, to bring to a halt. [STOPPER n.]

stoppers *n.* [1970s] (drugs) depressants, barbiturates. [they SE *stop* one moving]

stopping oyster *see* CHOKING OYSTER.

stoppo *n.* **1** [1930s] a break from work. **2** [1930s+] an escape, a getaway; thus *stoppo driver*, a getaway driver, *stoppo car*, the car in which criminals escape. [SE *stop* + sfx. -O]

stoppo! *excl.* [1930s+] stop what you are doing!

stop someone's blubber, to *phr.* [early 18C] to silence, possibly by murder. [SE *stop* + BLUBBER n.[1]]

stop someone's clock, to *phr.* [1940s+] **1** to defeat heavily. **2** to kill.

stop-the-clock *n.* [20C] (Ulster) a pessimist. [the custom of stopping the clocks following a death in the house]

stop thief *n.* [mid-19C] beef (cf. HOT BEEF!). [rhy. sl.]

stop ticking *v.* [1930s+] to die.

stop trippin' over no luggage! *excl.* [1990s] (US Black teen) an excl. used to calm down one who is making a fuss or worrying to excess.

stop two gaps with one bush, to *phr.* [16C] to accomplish two tasks simultaneously. [later use is SE]

stop work *n.* [1940s+] (bingo) the number 65. [the male retirement age]

stop your andrew makins! *excl.* [20C] (Anglo-Irish) stop fooling! [? var. on ANDRAMARTINS; E.P. notes dial. *andrew*, a clown + SE *merry-Andrew* + SE *making*, i.e. doing]

stop your gab! *excl.* [early 19C–1900s] be quiet! [SE *stop* + GAB n.]

stop your gap! *excl.* [late 19C+] shut up! be quiet! [SE *stop* + GAP n.[1]]

stop your jaw! *see* HOLD YOUR JAW!

storch *n.* [20C] (US) **1** an easy victim (cf. MARK n.[2]; PATSY n.). **2** an ordinary person. [SE *extort/extortion*]

store-bought hair *n.* [1900s–30s] (US Black) a wig, a hairpiece.

stored away *adj.* [20C] (US Und.) in prison (cf. AWAY adv.[1]).

storefront preacher *n.* [20C] (US Black) a local gossip, who 'preaches' only to those who idle away their days outside the general store of some small town.

storekeeper *n.* [late 19C] (US) an article that has remained unsold for so long that it may never leave the shop (cf. SHOPKEEPER).

stork *v.* [1970s] (US campus) to make pregnant. [the myth of storks bringing babies]

storm and strife *n.* [20C] one's wife (cf. TROUBLE AND STRIFE). [rhy. sl.]

storm-buzzard *n.* [1930s–40s] (US Black) a homeless or unemployed person, a beggar.

storm-stick *n.* [1920s+] (Aus.) an umbrella.

stormy dick *n.* [20C] (US) the penis. [rhy. sl. *stormy dick* = PRICK n. (1)]

storrac *n.* [mid-19C] carrots. [backsl.]

story *n.*[1] [late 17C+] (mainly teen) euph. for a lie; thus [mid-18C+] *story-teller*, a liar, *story-telling*, lying. ['a Puritanism that came into fashion with the trade against romances, all novels and stories being considered as dangerous and false' (Hotten, 1867)]

story *n.*[2] [1970s] (US campus) an afternoon television soap opera.

stoshious/stoshus *see* STOCIOUS adj.[1], adj.[2].

stoshy *n.* [1940s–50s] (W.I.) a boyfriend. [? STOCIOUS adj.[2]; but note UK dial. *stoushie*, a stout and healthy child]

stoter *see* STOATER.

stotious *see* STOCIOUS adj.[1], adj.[2].

stotor *n.* [mid-19C] (Und.) a heavy blow, a 'settler'. [for ety. *see* STOATER n.]

stoush/stouch/stoush up *n.* [late 19C+] (Aus./N.Z.) a fight; thus *stoush-artist/-merchant*, an habitual and competent fighter, a bully, *deal out stoush*, *put in the stoush*, to attack violently, to fight enthusiastically, *take stoush*, to take a beating, *the Big Stoush*, WW1. [? UK dial. *stashie*, a quarrel, an uproar]

stoush/stouch/stoush up *v.* [late 19C+] (Aus./N.Z.) to have a fight. [STOUSH n.]

stousher *n.* [20C] (Aus./N.Z.) a fighter; thus *stoushie*, a soldier, *stoushing*, fighting, beating up.

stoush up *see* STOUSH v.

stout *n.* [late 17C–early 18C] strong beer. [the modern use, as a synon. for SE *porter* emerged *c.*1750]

stout across the narrow *phr.* [1900s] fat. [? the *narrow* is one's waist]

stove *n.* [20C] (Ulster) a strong or unpleasant smell, esp. that of drink; thus *stoving*, drunk. [SE *stove*, to fumigate with sulphur]

stove lid *n.* [1900s–30s] a derog. term for a Black person. [the blackening of the utensil]

stove-pipe *n.* **1** [mid–late 19C] a tall hat, a top hat, also as *stove-pipe hat*. **2** [mid-19C+] tight, narrow trousers (cf. DRAIN-PIPES).

stove-up *adj.* [20C] (US) usu. of people, run-down, exhausted, worn-out. [SE *stave*, to smash]

stow *v.* **1** [mid-16C–mid-19C] to stop talking, esp. in phr. *stow it!*, shut up!; *stow that*, that's not true!; *stow your noise*, be quiet! **2** [late 17C+] to stop, to desist. [SE *stow*, to put away, to put on one side]

stowed *adj.* [19C] packed closely, very full. [dial. *stow*, to fill up]

stow faking! *excl.* [mid-19C] stop that! [STOW + FAKE v.[3]]

stow magging!/manging! *excl.* [19C] be quiet! stop talking! (cf. STOW ONE'S MAG). [SE *stow* + MAG v.]

stow one's jabber, to *phr.* [early 19C] to be quiet, to stop talking (cf. STOW ONE'S WHIDS). [SE *stow* + JABBER n.[1]]

stow one's mag, to *phr.* [mid-19C] to be quiet, to stop talking, esp. in imper. *stow your mag!*, shut up! (cf. STOW MAGGING; STOW ONE'S WHIDS). [STOW + MAG v.]

stow one's whids/whidds, to *phr.* [late 17C–18C] (Und.) to be quiet, to stop talking (cf. STUBBLE ONE'S WHIDS). [SE *stow* + WHID v.]

stow you! *excl.* [mid-16C–18C] (Und.) hold your peace! shut up! [SE *stow*, to put away, to store; although 16C SE also has *stow*, to cut off, to crop]

s.t.p. (drugs) **1** [1960s+] a form of hallucinogen. **2** [1980s+] phencyclidine (cf. ACE n.[3]). [(1) abbr. of either *serenity, tranquillity and peace*, or play on *scientifically treated petroleum*, a gasoline additive; (2) is a mistaken use of (1)]

straddle v. [early–mid-18C] to draw lots or throw dice to determine who shall pay a bill.

straight n.¹ **1** [mid-19C–1920s] (US) unadulterated or very strong whisky. **2** [1950s+] (S.Afr. Black) a 750ml (26fl oz) bottle of spirits or beer (cf. HALF-JACK n.⁴). **3** [1960s+] (drugs) a tobacco cigarette.

straight n.² **1** [1940s+] (Und.) someone one can trust, and thus, usu. not at all 'straight' (cf. SQUARE n.¹). **2** [1950s+] a cigarette (cf. JOINT n.⁴). **3** [1950s+] (orig. gay) a heterosexual person. **4** [1960s+] a conventional, respectable person.

straight adj.¹ **1** [early 17C+] of accounts, satisfactorily settled, balanced. **2** [mid-19C+] esp. of language, unadorned, undiluted, expressed in a straightforward manner. **3** [late 19C] of a woman, chaste, of a man, honest. **4** [1940s+] in criminal terms, trustworthy. **5** [1960s] respectable, law-abiding. **6** [1960s] heterosexual.

straight adj.² (drugs) **1** [1950s+] not currently using narcotics. **2** [1950s+] cured of one's withdrawal pains by an injection of heroin. **3** [1960s+] of an addict, having had the first dose of the day. **4** [1970s+] (US campus) under the influence of drugs.

straight adj.³ [1980s+] (orig. US Black) a general intensifier, e.g. *straight chilling*.

straight/strizzy adj.⁴ [1990s] (US teen) cheerful, satisfied.

straight adv. [1940s+] (orig. US) consecutively, in a row.

straight! excl. **1** [1910s+] an excl. of affirmation, honestly! really! **2** [1980s+] (US Black) a general term of agreement.

straight-ahead adj. [1960s+] (US) committed, reliable, e.g. *a straight-ahead guy* (cf. STRAIGHT ARROW).

straight ahead! excl. [1960s] (US Black) an excl. of encouragement, support, affirmation (cf. RIGHT ON!).

straight and narrow, the phr. [1910s+] conventionally moral and law-abiding behaviour; thus *keep on the straight and narrow*, to maintain a regular, law-abiding life. [Matt. 7:14: 'Because strait is the gate, and narrow is the way which leadeth unto life, and few there be that find it.' Note the mid-19C hymn: 'Loving Shepherd, ever near,/Teach Thy lamb Thy voice to hear;/Suffer not my steps to stray/From the straight and narrow way']

straight arrow n. [1950s+] (US) an honest, clean-living, clean-cut, upright, if naïve and unsophisticated person; thus *straight arrow*, respectable, clean-living etc (cf. STRAIGHT-AHEAD).

straight as a dog's hind leg phr. [late 19C] crooked.

straight as a pound of candles phr. [mid-18C] absolutely straight.

straight as they make 'em phr. [late 19C+] absolutely honest and trustworthy – although not always as judged by conventional morals. [STRAIGHT adj.¹ (5)]

straight bit of goods n. [late 19C] a respectable young woman. [STRAIGHT adj.¹ (3) + BIT OF GOODS]

straight bogey/bogy n. [late 19C+] (Und.) a corrupt policeman. [STRAIGHT adj.¹ (4) + BOGEY n.² (2)]

straight-cut adj. **1** [1920s–30s] of a woman, absolutely respectable. **2** [1930s+] honest.

straight drinking n. [late 19C] drinking while upright, i.e. standing at a bar rather than sitting at a table.

straighten v.¹ [late 19C] (Aus.) to defeat, to overcome.

straighten/straighten up v.² [late 19C+] (Und.) to bribe, usu. to bribe a policeman. [i.e. to make STRAIGHT adj.¹ (4)]

straighten v.³ [1910s+] to settle an account or debt. [STRAIGHT adj.¹ (1)]

straighten v.⁴ [1910s+] to settle an argument or a grudge by fighting. [SE *straighten things out*]

straighten v.⁵ [1950s+] (drugs) to give an injection of narcotics to relieve someone's withdrawal symptoms. [i.e. to make STRAIGHT adj.² (2)]

straightener n.¹ [1950s+] an argument that may escalate into an physical fight.

straightener n.² [1950s+] a bribe. [STRAIGHT adj.¹ (4)]

straighten out v. [20C] **1** to teach someone manners, to make them socially acceptable within a context. **2** (US) to give an explanation.

straighten up v.¹ see STRAIGHTEN v.².

straighten up v.² [1900s+] to take up an honest, respectable life. [i.e. to make oneself STRAIGHT adj.¹ (5)]

straighten up and fly right, to phr. [mid-19C+] (US Black) to behave oneself, to mend one's ways and live a sensible, respectable life. [orig. used in folktale, recorded by Joel Chandler Harris in *Short Stories Told After Dark* (1889)]

straight-faced adj. [1940s+] (US) stern, unflinching.

straight from the bog phr. [late 19C+] a derog. term used of an Irish immigrant to the UK.

straight from the horse's mouth phr. [1920s+] (orig. racing jargon) of news, information, absolutely reliable (cf. STRAIGHT FROM THE NOSEBAG).

straight from the nosebag phr. [1910s] of news, information, absolutely reliable (cf. STRAIGHT FROM THE HORSE'S MOUTH).

straight goer n. [late 19C–1950s] (Aus.) an honest, dependable person. [STRAIGHT adj.¹ (3) + GOER]

straight goods n. [late 19C+] (US) the absolute truth. [STRAIGHT adj.¹ (2) + GOODS n.¹]

straight-hair n. (Aus.) **1** [mid-19C] a convict. **2** [late 19C+] a Western Australian. [the convict crop; thus derog. ref. to Western Australia]

straight john n. [20C] (US Und.) a former prisoner who has been released and is now leading a legitimate life. [STRAIGHT adj.¹ (5) + JOHN n.¹]

straight off the turnips phr. [1930s+] (Aus./N.Z.) used of a country bumpkin.

straight oil n. [1910s+] (Aus.) the honest truth, the facts. [STRAIGHT adj.¹ (2) + OIL n.¹ (2)]

straight out of the trees phr. [1950s+] a derog. phr. used of Black immigrants, irrespective of background, to the UK.

straight-peg n. [1980s+] a law-abiding person (cf. STRAIGHT n.²).

straight shit n. [1960s+] **1** the truth. **2** utter lies. [STRAIGHT adj.¹ (2) + SHIT n.³]

straight shooter n. [1920s+] (US) an honest, dependable, trustworthy person.

straight shot n. [1970s+] (US Black) sexual intercourse without contraception (cf. BAREBACK).

straight skinny n. [1950s+] (US) the truth. [STRAIGHT adj.¹ (2) + SKINNY n.¹]

Straights, the n. [17C] a network of alleyways and small courts in an area bounded by St Martin's lane, Half Moon Street and Chandos Street, all in Covent Garden, London; the haunt of pimps, thugs and similar unsavoury characters.

straight tip n. [mid–late 19C] honest advice. [STRAIGHT adj.¹ (2) + TIP n.⁴]

straight trick n. [1960s+] a prostitute's client who requires no 'extras' beyond normal intercourse. [STRAIGHT adj.¹ (2) + TRICK n.⁴ (2)]

straight up adj.¹ [1930s+] a general term of emphasis, implying honesty and genuineness, e.g. *straight up nigger*; thus excl. *straight up!* honestly, really.

straight up adj.² [1970s+] (US) of drinks, served without ice cubes. [ext. of SE *straight*, undiluted]

straight up on a Columbo tip phr. [1990s] (US Black) a dead certainty, inside knowledge. [TV detective *Columbo*, played by Peter Falk in 1971–8 and revived in the 1990s]

straight up six o'clock girl n. [1940s] (US Black) a very thin woman. [the position of the clock's hands]

straight walk-in n. [1920s–30s] a woman who is seen as easy to seduce. [i.e. one needs only walk in and introduce oneself]

straight wire n. [late 19C–1950s] (Aus./N.Z.) the honest truth; also used without an article to emphasize the truth of an assertion. [STRAIGHT adj.¹ (2) + WIRE n.¹]

straight word n. [1990s] (US Black) an accurate statement, acceptable policy.

strain n. [1970s+] (US) gonorrhoea. [? abbr. *a strain of venereal disease*]

strain hard v. [late 17C–18C] to tell a substantial lie. [ext. use of SE]

strain off v. [20C] to urinate.

strain one's greens, to phr. **1** [1900s–30s] of a man, to have sexual intercourse. **2** [1950s+] to urinate (cf. STRAIN THE POTATOES). [SE *strain* + pun on *greens*/GREENS n.²]

strain one's/the milk, to phr. [20C] (US) to strain oneself.

strain some potatoes, to phr. [1990s] to defecate (cf. STRAIN THE POTATOES).

strain the main vein, to phr. [1950s+] to masturbate.

strain the milk see STRAIN ONE'S MILK.

strain the potatoes/spuds/taters, to phr. [1960s+] (Aus.) to urinate (cf. STRAIN ONE'S GREENS; STRAIN SOME POTATOES).

stram, the n. [late 19C–1900s] the profession of street-walking. [? SE *strumpet*, or US *stram*, to walk some distance or dial. *stram*, to bang, to strike (cf. ON THE BAT phr.²) and the widespread equation of sexual intercourse with 'banging' (cf. BANG v.¹)]

strammel see STAMMEL.

strammer n. [mid–late 19C] anything exceptional, whether in size or effect. [fig. use of dial. *stram*, to bang]

strange n. [1950s+] an unknown woman, usu. in a sexual context; thus *a bit of strange* (cf. PIECE OF STRANGE).

strangely weird n. [20C] a beard. [rhy. sl.]

strange-o n. [1950s–60s] an eccentric, a madman (cf. RAPE-O).

stranger n.¹ (usu. tramp) **1** [late 18C–19C] a guinea. **2** [1900s–30s] a sovereign. [to encounter so large a sum is a rare event]

stranger n.² **1** [early 19C+] (orig. US) a term of address to one whose name is unknown. **2** [1930s+] anyone one knows but has not seen for some time; thus *hello stranger*, a greeting to a long-absent friend.

strangioso adj. [1970s+] (US) very weird. [ext. of SE *strange*]

strangle and smother n. [20C] (Aus.) a mother. [rhy. sl.]

strangle-goose n. [late 18C–late 19C] a poulterer.

strangler n. [1920s–30s] a necktie. [? SE + pun on *choker*]

strangle the goose, to phr. [1990s] to masturbate.

strap n.¹ [mid-19C] a barber. [the SE *strop* used to sharpen razors. Note Hugh *Strap*, a barber, in Tobias Smollett's *Roderick Random* (1748)]

strap n.² [mid-19C+] credit; thus *on the strap*, on credit. [? it 'holds one together']

strap n.³ [1950s+] (US campus) a sports enthusiast (cf. JOCK n.²). [abbr. SE *jockstrap*, an athletic support]

strap n.⁴ [1980s+] (US Black) a gun; thus *strap me*, give me a gun. [one 'straps' it to one's waist or into a holster]

strap v.¹ [late 17C–late 18C] to have sexual intercourse (cf. STRAP ON v.; STRAPPING). [the ref. is to a SE *strapping wench*]

strap/strap at v.² [19C–1910s] to work hard; thus *strap to*, to get on with, to buckle down to. [? one applies the fig. strap to one's own back]

strap v.³ [mid–late 19C] to give credit. [STRAP n.²]

strap at see STRAP v.².

strap-oil/oil of strap'em n. [mid-19C] a flogging with a strap. [thus popular April Fool's joke of sending a boy for 'a pennyworth of strap-oil']

strap on n. [1960s+] a dildo, with straps that anchor it to the user's body.

strap on v. [1960s+] to have sexual intercourse (cf. STRAP v.¹). [coarse use of SE]

strapped/strapped for cash adj.¹ [mid-19C+] (orig. US) impoverished, poor. [? the consequent 'tightening of one's belt', usu. a leather strap; or dial. *strap*, to drain dry, esp. of a cow's udder]

strapped adj.² [1980s+] carrying a gun. [STRAP n.⁴]

strapped adj.³ [1990s] wealthy. [? STRAP v.³]

strapped for cash see STRAPPED adj.¹.

strapper n. [mid-19C] a big, strong man, a notably hard worker; thus 19C *strapping-shop*, any workplace where an especially large volume of work is required of the employees. [one who is fig. 'bound together with straps']

strapping n. [late 17C–18C] sexual intercourse. [STRAP v.¹]

straps n.¹ [late 19C] sprats. [joc. mispron.]

straps n.² [1940s] (US Black) suspenders (UK, braces).

straps it to his ankle phr. [1970s+] a description of a man with a supposedly extra-large penis; often used ironically of a sexual braggart.

strap up v. [1910s+] (Aus.) to obtain on credit. [ext. of STRAP v.³]

strat n. [1960s+] a *Strat*ocaster guitar. [abbr.]

straw n.¹ see STRAWING.

straw n.² [1920s+] a person with light blond hair. [abbr. SE *straw blond(e)*]

straw n.³ (drugs) **1** [1940s–50s] an opium pipe. **2** [1960s] marijuana. **3** [1960s] rolling papers.

straw n.⁴ [1960s–70s] (US Black) a hat, although not necessarily a straw hat. [note 19C SE use, a straw hat]

straw basher n. [1900s–40s] a boater, a straw hat. [SE *straw* + BASHER n.²]

strawberries n. (drugs) **1** [1960s] tablets of mescaline. **2** [1970s] amphetamines (cf. A n.²). [the colour of the tablets]

strawberry n.¹ **1** [late 19C] a broken-veined, bloated nose that exhibits signs of its possessor's heavy drinking. **2** [20C] a red nose. [the colour]

strawberry n.² **1** [1920s+] a bruise, esp. a graze or sore that results from friction with the ground. **2** [1980s+] (US teen) a promiscuous woman, esp. one who barters sex for drugs (cf. CRACK HO; RASPBERRY n.⁴). [? the premise of (2) is that the woman spends so much time on her knees (for fellatio) or on her back (for intercourse) that she gets scars]

strawberry/strawberry ripple n.³ [1980s+] a disabled person. [var. on RASPBERRY n.³]

strawberry box n. [1930s–60s] (Aus./N.Z.) a receptacle used for vomit on ships and aeroplanes.

strawberry fields n. [1960s–70s] (drugs) LSD (cf. A n.³). [the Beatles' song 'Strawberry Fields Forever' (1967)]

strawberry ripple see STRAWBERRY n.³.

strawberry tart n. [1960s+] the heart. [rhy. sl.]

straw boss n. [late 19C+] (US) **1** a person who is second-in-command, assistant to the boss. **2** (tramp) the foreman of a work crew. [a threshing crew hierarchy in which the chief deals with the grain, the subordinate with the straw]

strawbug n. [1950s] (school) a strawberry (cf. GOOSEGOG). [joc. mispron.]

straw-cat n. [20C] (US) a migratory worker who is employed at harvest time. [SE *straw* + CAT n.⁹]

straw-chipper n. [early–mid-19C] a barber.

strawer n. [mid-19C] a street-seller of pornography. [STRAWING]

straw fagot n. [19C] a prostitute, a mistress. [SE *straw*, a bed + dial. *faggot*, a woman]

straw hat n. **1** [early 18C] a Billingsgate fish-wife (cf. FLAT-CAP). **2** [1900s–30s] (Aus.) a dandy, a fashionable person; thus *straw hat push*, the social élite. [metonymy]

strawing/straw n. [mid-19C] a form of illicit street-selling by which the buyer purchases a straw, usu. for one penny, and is given, as a 'free gift', a pamphlet (either pornographic or political) or a gold ring, neither of which items, the seller claims, are they allowed to sell.

straw yard *n.*[1] [mid-19C–1900s] a night-shelter or casual ward, occupied by the impoverished street-dwellers. [the straw laid down for bedding]

straw yard *n.*[2] [late 19C–1900s] a man's straw hat. [note naut. jargon *straw-yarder*, a man who frequents the docks but never goes to sea]

stray *n.* [1960s+] (Irish) casual sexual intercourse.

stray piece *n.* [1980s+] (US Black) a casual sexual encounter. [SE *stray* + PIECE n.[1]]

stray tup on the loose *n.* [late 19C] a man on the hunt for sex. [SE *tup*, a ram]

strayway *adj.* [20C] (W.I./Gren.) **1** given to wandering the streets. **2** undisciplined, unsettled. [SE *stray away*]

streak *n.*[1] **1** [mid-19C+] (orig. US) a rapid journey or rapid move. **2** [1970s] (US campus) an exciting time, esp. at a party.

streak *n.*[2] [1940s+] (orig. Aus.) a tall, lean person. [abbr. *long thin streak*]

streak *n.*[3] [1970s+] an act of discarding one's clothes in public, usu. at a sporting occasion, and disporting oneself in front of the crowd. [STREAKER]

streak *v.* **1** [late 18C–late 19C] to run away. **2** [1960s+] to strip in public and run naked in front of the crowd; thus *streaking*, performing this exhibition. [STREAKER]

streaked *adj.* [mid-19C] (US) irritable, irascible, ill-tempered (cf. STREAKY).

streaker *n.* [1970s+] (orig. US) one who runs naked through a public place. [originated on US campuses, where it amounted to the trad. *mooning* (cf. MOON n.), writ much larger, then transferred into a variety of larger arenas, notably the venues of major sporting events around the world]

streaker's defence *n.* [1980s] (Aus.) a verbal defence that consists of no more than the statement that 'it seemed like a good idea at the time'. [STREAKER; during the 'streaking' craze of the late 1970s–early 1980s this was often the excuse offered by those who undertook the feat]

streak of lavender *n.* [1930s] an effeminate man. [LAVENDER]

streak of lightning *n.* [mid-19C] gin. [LIGHTNING n.[1]]

streaky *adj.* **1** [mid-19C] irritable, irascible (cf. STREAKED). **2** [late 19C–1900s] variable in character, unstable, changeable. [one is neither one emotional 'colour' nor another]

streamer *n.* [1920s+] a bad cold. [its effect on one's nose]

streamer issue *n.* [1930s–40s] (US Black) a necktie.

stream's town *n.* [late 18C–early 19C] the vagina (cf. BALLINOCACK; DAMP n.).

Street, The *n.*[1] **1** [19C+] (US) Wall Street. **2** [19C+] (US) Madison Avenue. **3** [20C] Fleet Street, London EC4. **4** [1900s–10s] (US) Broadway. **5** [1930s–40s] (US) 52nd Street, between 5th and 6th Avenues, then the centre of New York jazz clubs. [all but (3) refer to New York City]

street, the *n.*[2] [1940s+] (orig. US Und.) the world of freedom, as opposed to that of prison; thus *on the street*, at liberty, *street time*, time on parole or between prison sentences.

street *n.*[3] [1940s+] (orig. US) the mythical world of 'real life', which exists on the streets, rather than in the protected environments of home, office, family etc; thus adjectivally, *X is truly street ...* .

street *v.* [20C] (drugs) of a prisoner, to send out money so that a confederate can buy and smuggle back in some drugs.

street Arab *n.* [1940s–50s] (US Black) a member of the Black Muslims. [the Muslims' identification with (mainly Arabic) Islam + play on SE *street Arab*, a homeless urchin]

street beef *n.* [20C] (US Und.) crimes committed inside prison by a serving prisoner who is tried in a normal court

rather than facing internal prison discipline; such crimes include murder, escape, sex- or drug-related offences. [STREET n.[2] + BEEF n.[2]]

street buy *n.* [1980s+] (drugs) a purchase of drugs that is carried out on the *street* as opposed to meeting the dealer in either their home or in one's own.

streetcleaner *n.* [1930s–50s] (US Black) **1** a promiscuous woman. **2** a prostitute. [the term underpins the presumed 'dirtiness' of such women]

street cred *n.* [1970s+] acceptability on a mass cultural level. [STREET n.[3] + SE *credibility/credible*. Coined in the rock business and subsequently popular in any industries targeting the young consumer, it is based in the belief that the 'artist' must relate genuinely to the 'people', i.e. the working-class youth of the streets and housing estates and thus, sincerely or otherwise, offer an air of rebellion and informality]

streetified *adj.* [1970s+] (US Black) well-versed with the ways of the urban lifestyle as seen on the inner-city streets (cf. STREET SMART). [STREET n.[3]]

streetman *n.* [20C] a petty criminal who 'works' on the street, usu. as a drug dealer or pickpocket.

street money *n.* [1960s+] (US) money earned on the street, usu. through drug-dealing, pickpocketing or prostitution.

street people *n.* [1960s–70s] a form of hippie, who wears the clothes but espouses more of a trad. begging ethic than that of the 'love and peace' generation.

street-pitcher *n.* [mid-19C] anyone who makes a living from selling articles in the street. [SE *street* + PITCHER n.[3]; i.e. declaiming ballads or songs (with or without accompanying sheet music), selling 'true confessions', posing as a 'nigger minstrel' etc]

street rat *n.* [mid-19C] (US) a street child, usu. the homeless offspring of Irish immigrants (cf. ARAB n.[1]).

streets ahead/better *adj.* [late 19C+] infinitely superior, much better (cf. STREETS BEHIND).

streets behind *phr.* [20C] far inferior (cf. STREETS AHEAD).

streets better *see* STREETS AHEAD.

street smart *adj.* [1970s+] (orig. US) able to survive in the inner city or the ghetto streets, despite a lack of material, bourgeois advantages (cf. STREETIFIED). [STREET n.[3]]

street smarts *n.* [1960s+] instinctive knowledge as opposed to learned knowledge (cf. SUSS). [STREET n.[3] + SMARTS]

street talk *n.* [1940s+] gossip, rumour (cf. PUT IT ON THE STREET). [such information, the product of the *street* culture of petty crime, is considered valueless]

streetwise *adj.* [1960s+] (orig. US) able to survive in the inner city or the ghetto streets despite a lack of material, bourgeois advantages (cf. STREET SMART). [STREET n.[3] + sfx. -WISE]

street-yelp *n.* [late 19C] any street-orientated catchphrase, e.g. BEEN AND GONE AND DONE IT; DOES YOUR MOTHER KNOW YOU'RE OUT?

strel/strell *n.* [late 19C+] (Polari) a banjo; thus *strel/strell-homey*, a banjo-player. [Ital. *strillare*, to shriek]

strength *n.* [20C] (Aus./N.Z.) the facts, the details of a situation, usu. as the *strength of*; thus *get the strength of*, to understand.

strep *n.* **1** [1920s+] *strep*tococcus, a form of bacterium, esp. in comb. *strep throat* (cf. STAPH). **2** [1950s+] *strep*tocmycin, an antibiotic orig. used to combat tuberculosis, but now usu. used in combination with other drugs because of its toxicity. [abbr.]

stress *v.* [1980s+] to panic, to lose control.

stress case *n.* [1980s+] (US campus) a very nervous, tense person (cf. STRESS-MONGER).

stress-monger/-monster *n.* [1980s+] (US campus) a very stressed, nervous person (cf. STRESS CASE). [SE *stress* + sfx. -MONGER/*monster*]

stress out v. [1980s+] **1** to cause someone to become stressed. **2** to become stressful. [ext. of STRESS v.]

stretch n.¹ **1** [early 19C] a yard (3ft/91cm). **2** [mid-19C] a march, a long journey.

stretch n.² [mid-19C+] (Und./prison) a 12-month sentence; thus *two stretch*, two years, *three stretch*, three years etc. [abbr. SE *stretch of time*]

stretch/stretch it v.¹ [late 17C+] to exaggerate, to lie (cf. STRETCHER n.¹). [SE *stretch the truth*]

stretch v.² [mid-19C] to hang, to be hanged. [abbr. SE *stretch one's neck*]

stretch v.³ [late 19C+] to knock down, to kill. [abbr. SE *stretch out on the ground*]

stretch v.⁴ **1** [1930s+] to outstay one's opponent. **2** [1950s+] to extend a person to the limits of their ability.

stretch a pipe, to phr. [late 19C] to cry (cf. TAKE A PIPE). [PIPE ONE'S EYE]

stretched adj.¹ [late 17C–1960s] hanged. [the neck is SE *stretched*]

stretched adj.² [20C] very drunk. [? abbr. SE *stretched out on the floor*]

stretched adj.³ [20C] whipped. [the fabric of one's trousers is SE *stretched* over the tightened buttocks]

stretcher n.¹ [early 17C–mid-19C] a lie. [it SE *stretches* the truth]

stretcher n.² [mid-18C] a large penis (cf. KID STRETCHER). [it SE *stretches* the vagina]

stretcher n.³ [late 19C] (Anglo-Irish) a layer-out of the dead.

stretcher n.⁴ [20C] a long stretch of road, the journey taken upon it. [STRETCH n.¹ (2)]

stretcher n.⁵ [1930s–40s] (US Black) **1** a necktie. **2** a belt.

stretcher case n. [1940s+] a liar. [STRETCHER n.¹]

stretcher-fencer n. [mid-19C] a street-seller of (UK) braces or (US) suspenders.

stretchers n. [mid-19C+] **1** (UK) braces. **2** (US) suspenders (cf. GALLUSES; HANG OVER THE STRETCHER).

stretch hemp/the hemp v. [mid–late 19C] to be hanged (cf. PULL HEMP). [the hempen noose]

stretching n. [late 19C–1900s] helping oneself at table without waiting for a servant to offer the relevant dish.

stretching match n. [mid-19C] a judicial hanging (cf. HEMP PARTY). [STRETCH v.²]

stretch it see STRETCH v.¹.

stretch leather v. [18C–20C] to have sexual intercourse, also as *go leather-stretching* (cf. STRETCHER n.²). [SE *stretch* + LEATHER n.²]

stretch out v. [1950s–60s] (US Black) to live one's life without restraint, to act uninhibitedly. [jazz use *stretch out*, to play to one's limits, with no restraints other than one's stamina and skill]

stretch out tough, to phr. [1950s–60s] (US Black) to prosper, to do well. [ext. of STRETCH OUT]

stretch some jeans, to phr. [1960s+] (US prison, esp. homosexual) to have sexual intercourse. [the removal of one's jeans or trousers]

stretch some meat, to phr. [1980s+] (US) to have sexual intercourse. [MEAT n.]

stretch someone's breeches, to phr. [late 19C] to administer a thrashing; thus *have one's breeches stretched*, to suffer a beating (cf. STRETCHED adj.³). [the bent-over buttocks tighten the cloth that covers them]

stretch someone's neck, to phr. [late 19C+] to hang (cf. STRETCH HEMP).

stretch the blanket, to phr. [late 19C+] (US) to exaggerate.

stretch the fox, to phr. [mid-18C–late 19C] to exaggerate, to 'tell the tale'. [the image of huntsmen exaggerating the day's chase]

stretch the hemp see STRETCH HEMP.

'strewth!/'struth! excl. [late 19C+] a mild, euph. oath; lit. 'God's truth' (cf. 's abbr.¹).

strib n. [20C] (US Und.) a prison warden. [? fig. use of dial. *strib*, to drain]

strictly adv. [1930s+] (orig. US) totally, entirely.

strictly! excl. [1970s+] (US campus) really! honestly! absolutely!

strictly for the birds see FOR THE BIRDS.

strictly from adv. [1930s+] in the style of, derivative of, exactly like.

strictly from hunger phr. [1930s+] **1** driven by dire necessity, usu. financial. **2** emptily, foolishly, to a distressing degree. **3** most unsatisfactorily. [STRICTLY adv.]

stride v. [1970s] (US Black) to perform with great skill.

stride and fade! excl. [1960s] (US Black) do what you have to do, then vanish! [STRIDE + FADE v.²; used as a slogan among inner-city demonstrators]

striders n. [1940s] (US Black) trousers. [var. on STRIDES]

strides n. **1** [late 19C+] (now mainly Aus.) trousers (cf. STRIDERS). **2** [1910s+] (Aus.) knickers, panties. **3** [1940s–50s] (US) shoes.

stride-wide n. [18C] a strong beer. [? its effects]

striding n. [1960s–70s] (US Black) performing any activity very well. [STRIDE]

strife n. [1960s] (Aus.) trouble, disgrace, difficulties, esp. as *in strife*. [weak use of SE]

strike n.¹ [early 18C–1900s] a sovereign. [SE *strike*, to mint a coin]

strike n.² [late 19C–1900s] a watch (cf. NAIL A STRIKE). [SE *strike*, to mark the time]

strike n.³ [1970s+] (US) an arrest and the prison sentence that follows; thus *two strikes*, two terms in prison, *three strikes*, three arrests and the mandatory life sentence that follows in many states. [baseball imagery, *three strikes and you're out*]

strike v.¹ **1** [mid-16C–mid-18C] to steal goods, to rob a person (cf. HIT v.⁷; KNOCK OVER v.¹). **2** [17C] to borrow money. **3** [mid-18C–late 19C] to make a sudden and pressing demand upon someone for a loan etc.

strike/strike it v.² [18C–late 19C] to be. [STRIKE v.¹; 19C use is Aus.]

strike! see STRIKE ME BLIND!; STRIKE ME PINK!

strike a blow for liberty, to phr. [1920s–30s] (US) in Prohibition era, to take a clandestine drink.

strike a bright, to phr. [late 19C] to have a sudden, pleasant thought, to have a piece of good luck. [SE *bright thought*]

strike a jigger, to phr. [mid-19C] (Und.) to pick a lock, to break down a door. [STRIKE v.¹ + JIGGER n.¹]

strike a light! excl. [1930s+] (orig. Aus.) a general excl. of surprise, shock, amazement etc (cf. STRIKE ME BLIND!; STRIKE ME PERP!; STRIKE ME PINK!; STRIKE ME SILLY!).

strike all of a heap, to phr. [early 18C+] to shock.

strike-fire n. [early 18C] gin. [? play on LIGHTNING n.¹]

strike it see STRIKE v.².

strike it lucky see STRIKE LUCKY.

strike it rich, to phr. [mid-19C+] to gain sudden wealth. [orig. used in oil-/goldfields]

strike lucky/it lucky v. [1950s+] to become lucky.

strike-me n. [20C] bread. [rhy. sl. *strike me dead* = bread]

strike me! excl. [20C] a mild excl. [abbr. STRIKE ME BLIND!; STRIKE ME PINK!]

strike me blind!/strike! excl. [early 18C+] a general excl. of surprise, amazement; implies calling on God/the gods to make some concomitant gesture (cf. STRIKE A LIGHT!).

strike-me-blind n. [late 19C] boiled rice and black-strap molasses. [the belief that rice would make one blind; thus naut. jargon *strike-me-blind*, rice]

strike me blue!/bloody horray!/hooray! *excl.* [1910s+] (Aus./N.Z.) a mild oath (cf. STRIKE ME DEAD!).

strike-me-dead *n.* [late 19C+] bread. [rhy. sl.]

strike me dead! *excl.* [late 19C+] a mild oath (cf. STRIKE ME BLUE!).

strike me fat! *excl.* [late 19C+] (Aus./N.Z.) a mild excl.

strike me handsome! *excl.* [1950s–60s] (Aus.) a mild excl.

strike me hooray! *see* STRIKE ME BLUE!

strike me lucky! *excl.* [mid-19C+] a general oath, esp. on the sealing of a bargain by slapping hands together. [UK in 19C, it re-emerged in mid-20C Aus. use]

strike me perp!/perpendicular! *excl.* [late 19C–1900s] a general excl. of surprise, alarm, shock etc (cf. STRIKE A LIGHT!).

strike me pink!/strike! *excl.* [mid-19C+] a mild excl. of surprise, irritation etc (cf. PERISH ME PINK!; STRIKE A LIGHT!).

strike me roan! *excl.* [1910s+] (Aus./N.Z.) a mild excl.

strike me silly! *excl.* [mid-19C] a mild excl. of surprise, irritation etc (cf. STRIKE A LIGHT!).

strike oil *v.* [mid-19C+] (orig. US) to do well, to prosper.

strike one's breath, to *phr.* [late 19C+] (Aus.) to 'cross one's heart and hope to die', as part of an assurance of one's honesty.

strike out *v.* [20C] (US) **1** to fail, esp. in an attempt to seduce a woman. **2** to die (cf. END OF THE BALL-GAME). [baseball jargon *strike out*, for the batter to fail to make legal contact with the ball in four attempts]

strike paydirt *v.* [late 19C] to gain one's objective, often but not invariably financial – for a journalist, for instance, the 'dirt' could be a revelation. [mining use, esp. when mining for gold]

striker *n.*[1] [19C] the penis (cf. BAYONET). [its image as a 'weapon']

striker *n.*[2] [1950s+] a match.

strike that! *excl.* [1970s+] forget I said that! ignore my last statement! [SE *strike*, to erase]

strike the ball under the line, to *phr.* [mid–late 16C] to fail. [royal tennis imagery]

strike the gag, to *phr.* [mid-19C] to stop playing around, to stop joking. [SE *strike*, to desist from + GAG n.]

strike the jackpot *see* HIT THE JACKPOT.

strike the mace, to *phr.* [mid-19C] to persuade a shopkeeper to sell one goods on credit, although one has no intention of ever making that credit good. [MACE n.]

strike the pink match, to *phr.* [1960s+] to masturbate.

striking *adj.* [1950s] (W.I.) a general intensifier. [linked to such excl. as STRIKE ME DEAD!; STRIKE ME PINK! etc]

strill *n.* [late 19C+] (Ling. Fr./Polari) a musical instrument, esp. a portable harmonium or a piano; thus *strill-homey*, a male pianist, *strill-polone*, a female pianist. [Ital. *strillare*, to shriek, to cry out]

string *n.*[1] [mid-19C–1930s] a hoax, a fraud. [STRING v.]

string/string of ponies *n.*[2] [1910s+] (US) a group of prostitutes working for a single pimp (cf. PONY n.[5]; STABLE). [SE *string*, a set or stud of horses]

string *n.*[3] [1950s+] (US) the penis; thus *string and nuggets*, the penis and testicles.

string *v.* **1** [early 19C+] to fool, to deceive, esp. over a drawn-out period of time. **2** [late 19C] (Aus./N.Z.) to encourage, to egg on (cf. STRING ALONG).

string along *v.* (orig. US) **1** [late 19C+] to deceive someone over a period of time (cf. STRING ON). **2** [1950s+] to accompany. [the image of dragging a toy along on the end of a string]

string along with, to *phr.* [1930s+] (orig. US) **1** to accompany. **2** to agree with.

string a mark, to *phr.* [late 19C+] (US Und.) of a confidence trickster, to entrap a victim. [STRING v. + MARK n.[2]]

string and top *n.* [20C] a policeman. [rhy. sl. *string and top* = COP n.[1] (1)]

string bean *n.* **1** [1930s+] a tall, skinny person. **2** [1970s] (US Black) a very thin, long penis (cf. BEAN n.[3]).

string beans *n.* [1970s+] jeans. [rhy. sl.]

string city *n.* [20C] suburban ribbon development (cf. STRIP CITY). [it is 'strung out' along the road]

stringer *n.*[1] [mid-19C] a hoax, a trick. [STRING n.[1]]

stringer *n.*[2] [late 19C–1910s] (N.Z.) a woman who works in a public house or bar encouraging the patrons to drink. [STRING ON]

stringer *n.*[3] [1910s+] (US) a pimp. [STRING n.[2]]

stringer *n.*[4] *see* STINGER n.[3].

stringers *n.* [late 19C] handcuffs.

stringing up *n.* [1920s] a severe telling-off.

string of ponies *see* STRING n.[2].

string on *v.* [late 19C+] (Aus./N.Z.) to deceive (cf. STRING ALONG).

string oneself out *v.* [20C] (US) to be disturbed, upset or worried.

string out *v.* [1960s–70s] (drugs) to use and be addicted to narcotic drugs. [STRUNG OUT]

string up *v.*[1] [late 19C–1910s] to garrotte. [*string up*, to hang is SE]

string up *v.*[2] [1920s+] to keep someone waiting. [ext. of STRING ALONG]

stringybark *n.* [late 19C–1900s] (Aus.) a supposed 'whisky', actually made of turpentine and fuel oil. [for ety. *see* STRINGYBARK adj.]

stringybark *adj.* [mid-19C+] (Aus.) **1** unsophisticated, rural, remote. **2** tough, brave, hardy. [SE *stringybark*, one of many trees, typically the eucalyptus, that has a thick, rough and fibrous bark and is found in the bush of southeast Aus.]

stringybark cockatoo *n.* [20C] (Aus.) a small farmer, often a failed prospector forced to turn to farming in order to survive. [STRINGYBARK adj. + COCKATOO n.[2]]

Strip, the *n.* [1930s+] (US) any main street or central area of a city, esp. Las Vegas.

strip *v.*[1] [late 17C–18C] (Und.) **1** to rob a house, esp. when the thieves empty it of all moveable contents. **2** to rob a person.

strip/strip a load *v.*[2] [1960s+] (US) to unload or empty a lorry or truck.

strip act *n.* [1950s] (US) a striptease show; similarly *strip club*, *strip dancer*, *strip show*.

strip a load *see* STRIP v.[2].

strip a peg, to *phr.* [1900s–20s] to purchase second-hand clothing. [for ety. *see* STRIP A PEG IN PLUNKET STREET]

strip a peg in Plunket Street, to *phr.* [late 18C] (Irish) to dress in second-hand clothes. [*Plunket Street*, the old-clothes market in Dublin]

strip-bush *n.* [mid-19C] one who steals washing from its drying lines. [laundry was orig. laid out on hedges to dry]

strip city *n.* [20C] (US) suburban ribbon development, the shops and houses that grow up alongside a major arterial road (cf. STRING CITY). [SE *strip*, a long, narrow tract of land + sfx. -CITY. A link to [1930s+] *the strip*, the night- and lowlife centre of a city, typically Hollywood's Sunset Strip, would be ironic only]

strip-down *n.* [1950s] (US) an automobile that has been modified to improve its performance.

stripe *n.* **1** [1910s+] a scar, usu. the result of being slashed with an open razor. **2** [1990s] a police patrol car, carrying some form of fluorescent stripe on its sides.

stripe *v.* [1910s+] to slash with a cut-throat razor. [STRIPE n. (1)]

strip-eel *n.* [early 18C] a fishmonger. [one of their jobs]

stripes *n.*[1] *see* OLD STRIPES.

stripes *n.*[2] [late 19C–1940s] (US) a prison uniform; thus *wear the stripes*, to serve a prison sentence.

strip joint *n.* [1940s+] (US) a bar or club that offers striptease shows. [SE *strip* + JOINT *n.*[3] (3)]

strip-me-naked *n.*[1] [mid-18C] a fiery drink, esp. raw gin (cf. GLIM *n.*[2]).

strip-me-naked *n.*[2] [1950s] (W.I.) any form of food made from flour, e.g. biscuits, cake. [? the quantity of the food fills one up and one gets relief by taking off one's clothes, or the expense involved in purchasing the food leaves one 'naked' of cash]

strip me with the wrought end of a wallaby's dong! *excl.* [1990s] (Aus.) a general excl. of surprise, irritation etc.

stripped *adj.* [mid-19C–1900s] of spirits, neat.

stripped to the buff *adj.* [mid-19C+] naked, without one's clothes (cf. IN THE BUFF). [SE *buff*]

stripper *n.*[1] [mid–late 19C] a thief, usu. a woman, who specializes in luring young children into secluded places, where they are stripped of their clothes, which are later sold, and left naked in the street.

stripper *n.*[2] [1930s+] (orig. US) a striptease performer. [abbr. SE *striptease*]

stripping law *n.* [late 16C–early 17C] (Und.) the practice of stripping prisoners of their valuable possessions as carried out by prison staff. [SE *stripping* + LAW *n.*[1]]

strip the table, to *phr.* [late 17C–18C] (Und.) of a gambler, to win everything on the table.

strivers' row *n.* [20C] (US Black) a generic name for well-off Blacks who hope to move up in society by buying large properties, taking out large mortgages etc. [the orig. *Striver's Row* was a development designed by architect Stanford White (1853–1906) on West 138th and 139th Streets. The 130 terraced houses, named King's Model Houses, were completed in 1891 and remained a Whites-only block until 1919. When they did come on the market, Harlem's wealthiest Blacks competed to move in]

strizzy *see* STRAIGHT *adj.*[4].

strobe-light honey *n.* [1990s] (US Black teen) a woman who is attractive at a distance or in poor light, e.g. in a club, but less so in close-up. [SE *strobe-light* + HONEY *n.*[4]]

stroke *n.*[1] [late 18C; 20C] sexual intercourse; thus *take a stroke*, to have sexual intercourse. [20C use is mainly US Black]

stroke *n.*[2] [1960s+] a gesture or action designed to comfort and reassure. [coined by Eric Berne in *Games People Play* (1964): '"stroking" may be employed colloquially to denote any act implying recognition of another's presence']

stroke *v.*[1] [late 18C; 20C] to have sexual intercourse. [20C use is mainly US Black]

stroke/stroke it/off *v.*[2] [1950s+] to masturbate; *stroke* is used in a number of combs. to mean masturbate, e.g. *stroke one's beef*, ... *one's ego*, ... *one's poker*, ... *one's steven*, ... *the bloke*, ... *the dog*, ... *the goat*, ... *the trumpet*.

stroke *v.*[3] [1960s+] (US prison) to curry favour with a more powerful inmate or with the authorities.

stroke above *adj.* [mid-19C–1910s] of higher quality, 'a cut above'. [play on SE *cut*, a stroke with a cane or whip]

stroke book/mag/magazine *n.* [1960s+] a pornographic book or magazine. [STROKE *v.*[2]]

Stroke City *n.* [1960s+] (Ulster) Derry/Londonderry. [SE *stroke*, a solidus + sfx. -CITY; the dual names of the city, claimed respectively by Catholics/Protestants and the futile attempt to rename it 'Londonderry/Derry']

stroked out *adj.* [1960s] exhausted.

stroke house *n.* [1970s] a cinema showing pornographic films. [STROKE *v.*[2]]

stroke it *see* STROKE *v.*[2].

stroke mag/magazine *see* STROKE BOOK.

stroke off *see* STROKE *v.*[2].

stroke one's oar, to *phr.* [1970s] (US) to masturbate.

stroll *n.* **1** [late 19C+] (US Black) the main street, esp. when used as a social centre (cf. CRAWL *n.*). **2** [late 19C+] (US pimp) those streets or blocks on which prostitutes ply their trade. **3** [1930s+] (US) anything requiring only minimal effort, an easy task. [SE *stroll*, to wander along; the original *stroll* was situated between 26th and 63rd Streets on New York's West Side, the mid–late 19C centre of the Black population. During the 1890s the stroll moved to Seventh Avenue between 23rd to 34th Streets and when the focus of Black life moved again, to Harlem (*c.*1920), the stroll moved up-town on Seventh Avenue between 131st and 132nd Streets]

stroller *n.* [1980s+] (S.Afr.) a homeless young street beggar (cf. MALALAPIPE). [Scot. *stroller*, a vagabond; ult. SE *stroll*]

strolling/strowling mort *n.* [17C–early 19C] (Und.) an unmarried female beggar, often accompanied by a child, who claims to be widowed and begs for her and her offspring's keep (cf. STROLL; WALKING MORT). [SE *stroll* + MORT]

stroll on! *excl.* [1950s+] a general excl. of dismissal or disbelief, 'you must be joking!' (cf. ROLL ON!).

strommel *n.* (Und.) **1** [mid-16C–early 19C] straw (cf. STRUMMEL). **2** [mid-16C–early 19C] hair; vars. incl. [17C–18C] *stromell*, [18C] *stramel*, [18C] *strumil*, [18C–19C] *strammel*.

strommel-faker *n.* [late 18C–early 19C] a barber. [STROMMEL *n.* (2) + FAKER *n.*]

strommel-patch *n.* [late 16C–early 17C] a pej. name for a person. [STROMMEL *n.* (1) + SE *patch*]

strong *n.* [1910s+] (Aus.) the truth, the facts, the essential information; thus *what's the strong of it?*, what is the truth? what are the precise facts? (cf. STRENGTH).

strong *adj.* **1** [mid-17C+] extreme, excessive. **2** [mid-19C+] of people, uncompromising, zealous. **3** [1960s+] pornographic, usu. found in advertisements in such magazines.

strong arm *v.* [late 19C+] (orig. US) to rob or otherwise influence someone through threats and potential, rather than actual, violence.

strong-arm man *n.* [20C] a thug, a hoodlum, a gangster. [STRONG ARM + SE *man*]

strong as a drink of water *phr.* [20C] weak, i.e. not strong at all.

strong box *n.* [20C] (prison) a punishment cell.

strongers *n.* [1930s] strong drink. [SE *strong* + 'Oxford' sfx. -*ers*]

stronger than horseradish *phr.* [1900s] (US) very strong.

stronger than pig shit *phr.* [20C] (US) very strong. [SHIT *n.*[1] (1)]

strong-eye *n.* [1900s] (W.I.) covetousness (cf. STRONG-MOUTH; STRONG-PHYSIC *n.*).

strong-eye *adj.* [1900s] (W.I.) **1** covetous, greedy. **2** selfish, domineering. **3** determined. [STRONG-EYE *n.*]

strong it *v.* [1930s+] to act in an aggressive or extreme manner (cf. COME IT *v.*[4]). [i.e. to pose as a SE *strong man*]

strong joint *n.* [1920s+] (US) **1** a crooked or cheating gambling game. **2** a crooked casino or gambling house. [SE *strong* + JOINT *n.*[3] (3)]

strong man *n.* [1920s+] (Aus.) a confidence trickster. [he 'pushes through' one's resistance]

strong-mouth *n.* [mid–late 19C] (W.I.) bullying, browbeating (cf. STRONG-EYE *n.*).

strong-physic *n.* [mid–late 19C] (W.I.) a self-willed person (cf. STRONG-EYE *n.*). [lit. 'strong medicine']

strong-physic *adj.* [mid–late 19C] (W.I.) hot-tempered, irascible. [STRONG-PHYSIC *n.*]

strong suit *n.* [mid-19C+] (orig. US) an advantage or special talent. [card-playing imagery]

strop *n.* [1980s+] (S.Afr.) trouble, 'backchat', obstreperous behaviour. [STROP v.]

strop *v.* [1970s+] to display one's bad temper; thus *strop around*, to wander about in a bad mood. [? backform. of STROPPY]

strop one's beak, to *phr.* [19C] of a man, to have sexual intercourse. [SE *strop*, to sharpen]

stropper *n.* [1960s] (Aus.) one who is testy, irritable, dissatisfied. [STROPPY]

stroppy *adj.* [1950s+] bad-tempered, irritable (cf. ABSTROPELOUS). [mispron. OBSTROPOLOUS, i.e. SE *obstreperous*; note naut. jargon *jack strop*, a know-it-all, a braggart]

strowling mort *see* STROLLING MORT.

struck *adj.* [20C] (W.I.) greedy, gluttonous. [abbr. STRUCK ON]

struck comical *adj.* [late 19C] astonished, amazed. [i.e. one is rendered foolish]

struck on *adj.* [late 19C+] obsessed with, esp. in a sexual sense.

structural engineering *n.* [1950s+] (Aus.) notably large female breasts, apparently (thanks to a foundation garment) defying the laws of gravity (cf. CANTILEVER BUST).

structure *n.* [1950s+] (W.I. Rasta) the body, health.

struesbob!/s'strue's Bob!/'strue as Bob!/struse Bob! *excl.* [1970s+] (S.Afr.) a general excl. of assertion. [lit. *it's true as Bob*, i.e. God]

struggle *n.* [1920s] (US) a party or dance.

struggle and strain *n.* [20C] a railway train. [rhy. sl.]

struggle and strain, to *phr.* [1980s+] to train. [rhy. sl.]

struggle and strainers *n.* [1980s+] trainers. [rhy. sl.]

struggle and strife *n.* [20C] **1** one's wife (cf. TROUBLE AND STRIFE). **2** life. [rhy. sl.]

struggle-buggy *n.* [1920s–40s] (US) a run-down old car, esp. an early model Ford. [it 'struggles along']

struggle valley *n.* [20C] (Aus.) a tramps' encampment. [the SE *struggle* to survive]

struggling *adj.* [1990s] (US teen) used of something that requires improvement.

strum *n.*[1] [late 17C–18C] a wig (cf. RUM STRUM n.[1]). [STROMMEL]

strum *n.*[2] [late 17C–18C] a promiscuous woman, a prostitute. [abbr. SE *strumpet*]

strum *v.* [19C] to have sexual intercourse (cf. PLAY A TUNE ON THE ONE-HOLED FLUTE). [SE *strum*, to play on a stringed instrument]

strum and stroll *n.* [20C] (Aus.) the dole. [rhy. sl.]

strummel *n.* [16C] straw (cf. STROMMEL). [? OF *estramer*, to spread with straw or rushes]

strum the banjo, to *phr.* [1990s] to masturbate (cf. STRUM v.).

strung out *adj.* [1950s+] **1** (drugs) addicted to narcotics. **2** unhappy, depressed. **3** obsessively in love, infatuated with someone. **4** obsessed with a topic or activity.

strunt *n.* [early 17C] the penis. [SE *strunt*, the fleshy part of an animal's tail]

strunz *n.* [1970s+] (US) rubbish. [Ital. *strunz*, rubbish, shit]

struse Bob! *see* STRUESBOB!

strut *n.* [1930s+] (orig. US Black) a party where the guests buy their refreshments to help pay the rent (cf. RENT PARTY). [SE *strut*]

'struth! *see* 'STREWTH!

strut-noddy *n.* [19C] an arrogant fool with no idea of their own stupidity. [SE *strut* + NODDY n.[1]]

strut one's stuff, to *phr.* [1920s+] (orig. US Black) to act proudly, uninhibitedly. [SE *strut* + STUFF]

stub *n.* [late 19C] a short person.

stub *v.* [mid–late 19C] (US) to walk along kicking objects, e.g. stones, cans. [one *stubs* one's toes]

stubbie/stubby *n.* (Aus.) **1** [1950s+] a short, squat beer bottle holding 375ml (13fl oz). **2** [1950s+] a squat milk bottle. **3** [1970s] shorts. [(2) underpinned by brandname *Stubbies*]

stubble *n.* [18C–20C] a woman's pubic hair (cf. BUSH n.[4]; SHOOT IN THE STUBBLE). [SE *stubble*]

stubble it! *excl.* [late 17C–19C] (Und.) hold your tongue! be quiet! [SE *stubble*, to clear the land of stubble, to cut it short]

stubble-jumper *n.* [20C] (Can.) a poor farmer (cf. APPLEKNOCKER n.[2]).

stubble one's whids/whidds, to *phr.* [late 17C–mid-19C] (Und.) to be quiet, to stop talking (cf. STOW ONE'S WHIDS). [STUBBLE IT! + WHID]

stubbs *n.* [19C] nothing. [SE *stub*, the end of a cigar or cigarette]

stubby *see* STUBBIE.

stub-faced *adj.* [late 18C–19C] having one's face pitted with the scars of smallpox. [SE *horse stubs*, horse nails; thus 'the devil run over his face with horse stubs in his shoes' (Grose, 1796)]

stub one's toe, to *phr.* [20C] to menstruate (cf. SPRAIN ONE'S ANKLE). [euph.]

stuck *adj.* [mid-19C] **1** left in an impossible position, deceived, completely mistaken. **2** out of money, impoverished. [fig. uses of SE, but note IN SHTUCK]

stuckadee/stuckedee *n.* [1940s] (W.I.) a faithful lover. [ext. of STUCKY]

stuck by *phr.* [late 19C] deceived, abandoned, 'left in the lurch', esp. by a supposed friend.

stuckedee *see* STUCKADEE.

stuck for *adj.* [1930s+] at a loss, unable to think of, unable to obtain.

stuck in the mud *phr.* [late 19C] confused, abandoned, lost for ideas (cf. STUCK FOR).

stuck on *adj.* [late 19C+] (orig. US) **1** obsessed with, devoted to. **2** in love with (cf. STUCKY).

stuck-up *adj.*[1] [early 19C+] (mainly school) arrogant, snobbish, reserved. [one SE *sticks one's nose in the air*]

stuck-up *adj.*[2] [late 19C] penniless. [STUCK adj. (2)]

stuck with *adj.* [mid-19C+] (orig. US) saddled with, unable to get rid of either a person or an object.

stucky *n.* [1930s–50s] (W.I.) a faithful lover (cf. STILLY). [? STUCK ON]

stud *n.*[1] **1** [1920s+] (US White) a man, not invariably but usu. sexually successful. **2** [1920s+] (US Black) a sophisticated man, but with no sexual connotation. **3** [1920s+] a male prostitute catering to either sex. **4** [1940s+] (US) a masculine lesbian (cf. STUD BROAD). [SE *stud*, a stallion or mare kept for breeding]

stud/stud gin *n.*[2] [1920s+] (Aus.) an Aboriginal woman seen as an object of sexual pleasure for a White man.

stud *n.*[3] [1950s+] (US) a *Stude*baker automobile. [abbr.]

stud *adj.* [1940s+] (US) fine, excellent, outstanding. [STUD n.[1]]

stud *v.* [1920s+] (US) to pursue sexually (cf. HORSE AROUND). [STUD n.[1]]

stud broad *n.* [1940s+] (US) a masculine lesbian. [STUD n.[1] (4) + BROAD n.[2]]

student *n.* [1930s–50s] (drugs) an inexperienced or novice drug-taker.

studette *n.* [1980s+] (US teen) a sexually and socially successful, physically attractive woman. [STUD n.[1] + sfx. *-ette*]

stud gin *see* STUD n.[2].

stud-horse!/-hoss! *excl.* [mid-19C+] (US) a general form of greeting between men.

studio gangsta *n.* [1990s] (US Black teen) one who poses as a GANGSTA n. purely for the purpose of making records; their experience of street life, however, is marginal.

studly *adj.* [1980s+] (US campus) displaying the characteristics of a sexually successful man. [STUD n.¹ (1)]

stud-muffin *n.* [1990s] (orig. US campus) an exceptionally successful and attractive person. [STUD n.¹ (1) + MUFFIN n.¹ (3)]

studola *n.* [1980s+] (US campus) a concentration of sexually successful men. [STUD n.¹ (1) + sfx. -OLA]

stud out *v.* [1980s+] (US campus) to achieve something, to do well; usu. in past tense, referring to a proven success. [fig. use of STUD n.¹ (1)]

stud with many fingers *n.* [1940s] (US Black) the Federal Bureau of Investigation (FBI) and its director, J. Edgar Hoover (1895–1972). [STUD n.¹ (2); the 'fingers' were in a variety of criminal 'pies']

study *n.* [late 19C+] an expression of incredulity, shock, usu. in phr. *You should have seen your face – it was a study!* (cf. PICTURE n.¹). [SE *study*, a portrait]

study *v.* **1** [mid-18C–1900s] to humour, to take note of another person's sensitivities. **2** [1950s+] (gay) to appraise a potential sexual conquest or partner.

study mongrel *n.* [1990s] (US campus) someone who studies hard.

study on *v.* [1930s–50s] (US Black) to consider, to think about; thus *studying*, pondering, thinking.

stuff *n.¹* **1** [mid-19C+] things or activities in general, varying as to context (cf. SHIT n.³). **2** [1920s+] anything that has no proper name, things that one cannot be bothered to describe properly.

stuff *n.²* [mid-19C] money (cf. FOLDING).

stuff, the *n.³* [late 19C+] what one wants, the ideal, usu. in phr. *that's the stuff.*

stuff *n.⁴* [late 19C; 1980s+] a woman, usually attractive and often out, enjoying herself (cf. BIT OF STUFF). [20C use is US Black]

stuff *n.⁵* **1** [1920s] alcohol, esp. bootleg liquor. **2** [1920s+] (drugs) drugs, esp. heroin (cf. BROWN STUFF; ON THE STUFF). [euph.]

stuff *v.¹* [mid-late 19C] **1** to tease, to tell lies, to fool, to hoax. **2** to defeat, to outwit. [SE *stuff*, to fill up]

stuff *v.²* [late 19C] to sit indoors when one could/should be out enjoying the fresh air. [SE *stuffy*]

stuff *v.³* [1950s+] to have sexual intercourse (cf. BANG v.¹). [SE *stuff*, to fill up but essentially euph. for FUCK v.¹]

stuff *v.⁴* [1960s+] to load or pack a freight container.

stuff a fat pig in the arse *see* GREASE A FAT PIG IN THE ARSE.

stuff cuff *n.* [1940s] (US Black) the padded cuff of a draped suit (cf. ZOOT SUIT).

stuffed *adj.¹* [mid-late 19C] put-down, mocked, denigrated. [STUFF v.¹ (1)]

stuffed *adj.²* [1930s+] bothered, concerned, usu. in phr. *can't/won't be stuffed.* [euph. synon. for FUCKED]

stuffed monkey *n.* [late 19C] (East London Jewish) 'a very pleasant close almond biscuit' (Ware).

stuffed rat *n.* [1930s+] (Aus.) a loaded die.

stuffed shirt *n.* [1910s+] (orig. US) a pompous, aristocratic but ineffectual person, a bore (cf. STUFF-JACKET). [i.e. the shirt is there, but there is no one inside it]

stuffer *n.¹* [1970s+] (drugs) a drug addict. [STUFF n.⁵ (2)]

stuffer *n.²* [1970s+] (drugs) a smuggler who hides drugs in the anus or vagina (cf. SWALLOWER). [SE *stuff*]

stuffing *n.¹* [late 19C+] (US) the daylights, as in *beat/knock the stuffing out of.*

stuffing *n.²* [1970s] (US Black) the practice of tricking or conning a victim. [STUFF v.¹]

stuff it! *excl.* [1930s+] a euph. excl. for FUCK IT!

stuff-jacket *n.* [1910s–30s] a pompous, aristocratic but ineffectual person, a bore (cf. STUFFED SHIRT).

stuff one's craw, to *phr.* [20C] (W.I.) to overeat. [ext. use of SE]

stuffy *n.¹* [mid-19C–1900s] a woman. [STUFF n.⁴]

stuffy *n.²* [1950s+] a pompous, arrogant person. [STUFFED SHIRT]

stuffy *adj.¹* **1** [19C] angry, sulky. **2** [late 19C+] pompous, snobbish. [STUFFY n.²]

stuffy *adj.²* [1930s+] (orig. US) wealthy, rich. [STUFF n.²]

stuiver *see* STIVER.

stug *n.* [late 19C–1930s] courage, bravery, staying power. [backsl. GUTS n.²]

stuk *n.* [1940s] (S.Afr.) a (promiscuous) woman (cf. PIECE n.¹; STUKKIE). [Afk. *stuk*, a piece, a part]

stuke *see* STOOK n.

stukkie *n.* [1970s+] (S.Afr.) **1** a woman, esp. when viewed as a sex object (cf. PIECE n.¹; STUK). **2** a girlfriend. [Afk. *stukkie*, a small piece]

stuling-ken *see* STALLING-KEN.

stum *v.* [1970s+] (drugs) to be intoxicated by a drug. [abbr. SE *stumble*]

stuma *see* STUMER n.¹.

stumble *v.* [1940s] **1** (US Black) to suffer serious problems and misfortunes. **2** (US Und.) to be arrested.

stumble and fall, to *phr.* [1940s] (US Black) **1** to suffer serious misfortunes. **2** to be arrested. **3** to be killed. [STUMBLE + FALL v.¹]

stumble at the truckle-/trundle-bed, to *phr.* [mid-17C–mid-18C] to 'mistake' the maid's bed for one's wife's. [*truckle-/trundle-bed*, a low bed running on truckles or castors and often given to a servant]

stumblebum *n.* [1930s] (US) **1** a shambling, useless, foolish person. **2** a drunk, a homeless drifter (cf. SPECK BUM). [SE *stumble* + BUM n.³]

stumble bumble *n.* [1970s+] (drugs) a narcotic drug. [play on STUMBLEBUM]

stumblers/stoms/stums *n.* [1960s] (drugs) barbiturates. [their effects]

stumer/stoomer/stuma *n.¹* **1** [late 19C+] a dud cheque or other fraudulent monetary draft, a counterfeit banknote. **2** [late 19C+] (Aus./N.Z.) a person without money, a defaulter, a bankrupt. **3** [late 19C+] something or someone worthless, useless, a 'flop'. **4** [20C] a fool. **5** [1930s] a state of agitation. **6** [1960s+] a blunder, a mistake. [ety. unknown; ? fig. use of SHTUM]

stumer *n.²* [1910s+] a deaf-mute. [SHTUM]

stumm and crum *adj.* [1960s+] extremely quiet, 'silent as the grave'. [ext. of SHTUM]

stump *n.¹* [19C] a fool. [i.e. one who is short and THICK adj.¹]

stump *n.²* [early–mid-19C] money (cf. STUMPY n.¹).

stump *n.³* [late 19C] (US) a dare, a challenge to do something difficult or dangerous.

stump *n.⁴* [20C] the penis.

stump *v.¹* [early 19C] to pay (cf. STUMP UP). [STUMP n.²]

stump *v.²* [early 19C–1900s] to go on foot, to be off, to leave, esp. as *stump it.* [SE *stump*, to walk clumsily]

stump *v.³* [mid-late 19C] to ruin economically, usu. in pass. *stumped,* ruined. [? SE *stump*, to confuse or to reduce to a fig. *stump* of wood]

stump *v.⁴* [1920s+] (Can.) to challenge to a fight. [? ext. of STUMP v.³]

stump *v.⁵* [1970s] (US Black) to rob or mug a person. [? STOMP v.]

stumped/stumped up *adj.* [mid-19C] ruined, impoverished. [STUMP v.³]

stumper *n.* [1990s] an unattractive woman. [? SE *stump*, something broken off]

stumpers *see* STOMPERS.

stump for *v.* [20C] (US) to actively support someone or something. [SAmE *stump*, to conduct a political campaign; the image is of standing on a *tree stump* to make a speech]

stumping *adj.* [mid-19C] (US) awkward, clumsy (cf. LUMPING). [SE *stump*, to walk clumsily]

stump-jump *v.* [20C] of a woman, to masturbate. [SE *stump* (of wood); i.e. with some form of dildo]

stump-jumper *n.* [19C] (US) a rural person, a yokel, a farmer (cf. APPLE-KNOCKER n.²). [stereotyping]

stump-knocker *n.* [20C] (US) an unprofessional, part-time lay preacher (cf. CHAIRBACKER). [they jump up on a *tree stump* to preach]

stumps *n.* **1** [early 18C] the teeth. **2** [19C+] the legs, esp. in phr. *stir one's stumps*, to move quickly, to start moving. [SE *stump*, something broken off; only the pl. is sl.]

stump the pew, to *phr.* [early–mid-19C] to pay up (cf. STUMP UP). [STUMP v.¹ ? + abbr. PEWTER]

stump up *v.* [mid-19C+] to hand over, esp. of money. [STUMP n.²]

stumpy *n.*¹ [early–mid-19C] money. [STUMP n.²]

stumpy *n.*² [late 19C+] (US) a crippled beggar, esp. one with a leg missing (cf. GIMP n.²; GROPER n.¹). [SE *stump*]

stums *see* STUMBLERS.

stun *n.* [mid-late 19C] nuts. [backsl.]

stun *v.* [mid-19C] (Und.) to cheat, to swindle, esp. in phr. *stun out of*, to defraud.

stung *adj.*¹ [1910s+] (Aus.) persuaded to lend money. [STING v.]

stung *adj.*² [1910s+] (Aus.) drunk. [STING n.²]

stung by a serpent *phr.* [19C] of a woman, pregnant (cf. SERPENT SOCKET).

stung for *adj.* [20C] cheated, esp. as overcharged. [STING v.]

stunlaws *n.* [mid-19C] walnuts. [backsl.]

stunned *adj.* [1910s–30s] (Aus./N.Z.) drunk (cf. BASTED).

stunned on skilly *phr.* [mid-19C] (Und.) sent to prison and thus forced to endure a diet of gruel. [SE *stun*/fig. use of STUN v. + SKILLY]

stunner *n.* **1** [mid-19C] an expert in their own job or profession. **2** [mid-9C+] a first-rate person or object. **3** [mid-19C+] a notably attractive young woman, revived in the late 1980s+ to describe a woman posing as a pin-up for the tabloid press or for softcore pornographic magazines; often spelled *stunna/stunnah*.

stunning *adj.* **1** [mid-19C+] very attractive (cf. STUNNER). **2** [mid-19C+] excellent, first-rate (cf. STUNNING JOE BANKS). **3** [mid-late 19C] clever, knowing.

stunning *adv.* [mid-19C+] excellently, wonderfully. [STUNNING adj. (2)]

stunning joe banks *adj.* [mid-late 19C] excellent to the highest degree. [STUNNING adj. (2) + proper name *Joe Banks*, a contemporary publican-cum-receiver, based in Dyott Street, Seven Dials, London, and later in the Cranbourne Street ROOKERY, who always gave a fair price to the thieves with whom he dealt. Like many receivers, he added to his income by returning, for a price, the stolen goods to their original owners. His neckties, adds Hotten (1860), were as *stunning* as his character and the aristocracy, as well as the underworld, patronized his after-hours drinking club]

stunt *n.* [late 19C+] anything done with the intention of improving or advertising one's image or gaining an advantage over rivals, a gimmick or device for attracting attention. [orig. US campus sports use, 'an act which is striking for the skill, strength, or the like, required to do it; a feat' (*Webster* Supplement, 1900)]

stup *see* SCHTUP.

stupe/stoop *n.* [mid-18C+] a fool, an idiot. [abbr. SE *stupid*]

stupe *adj.* [20C] (US) stupid. [STUPE]

stupe-head *n.* [1950s+] (US) a fool. [STUPE adj. + sfx. -HEAD (1)]

stupid *n.* [early 18C–late 19C] a fool.

stupid *adj.* **1** [late 19C+] drunk. **2** [20C] (W.I.) insignificant, small, contemptible. **3** [1980s+] (US campus) crazy, insane. **4** [1980s+] (US campus) pleasant, popular.

stupid *adv.* **1** [1980s+] (US) extremely, very (cf. CRAZY adv.). **2** [1990s+] (US teen) used of a large quantity of something.

stupid as arseholes *phr.* [1920s+] extremely stupid. [ARSEHOLE n.]

stupidie *n.* [20C] (W.I.) a fool, an idiot. [SE *stupid*]

stupidie *adj.* [20C] (W.I.) stupid, idiotic. [STUPIDIE n.]

stupo *n.* [1920s] (Anglo-Irish) a fool (cf. STUPE). [SE *stu(pid)* + sfx. -o]

sturks *see* STERKS.

sturrabin/stariben *n.* [late 19C] a prison (cf. STIR n.¹). [Rom. *sturiben*, a prison, *staripen*, to imprison]

stute *n.* [20C] a club. [abbr. SE *institution*]

stutter and stammer *n.* [20C] a hammer. [rhy. sl.]

stuyver *see* STIVER.

style *n.* [1950s+] (US Black) anything one needs (fancy clothes, a clever line of patter, a personal style, a mental attitude) for the successful promotion of one's schemes (cf. FRONT n.²).

style/style off *v.* [1950s+] (orig. US Black) to show off, to strut around. [STYLE n.]

-style *sfx.* [1940s+] used in comb. with a noun to create an adv. meaning 'in that manner'.

style off *see* STYLE v.

stylie *n.* [1980s+] a White person wearing trad. Black dreadlocks.

styling *n.* [1980s+] (US campus) doing well, succeeding, academically as well as socially. [STYLE v.]

styling and profiling *phr.* [1980s+] (US Black/campus) posing as a cool, sophisticated individual, and backing that image with smart, fashionable clothes. [STYLE v. + PROFILE v.]

stymied *adj.* [20C] (orig. US) confused, frustrated, in difficulties (cf. BUNKERED). [golfing imagery]

suave/swave *n.* [1980s] (US teen) smooth style, charm. [SE *suave*, soothingly agreeable; ult. Lat. *suavis*, sweet]

sub *n.*¹ [mid-19C–1940s] everything, all, the lot (cf. SUB-CHEESE). [Hind. *sab*, all]

sub *n.*² **1** [mid-19C] a *sub*ject of the monarch. **2** [mid-19C] a *sub*altern. **3** [mid-19C] a *sub*scriber. **4** [mid-19C+] an advance on wages; thus *do a sub*, to borrow money. **5** [mid-19C+] a *sub*stitute. **6** [20C] a *sub*scription. **7** [1910s+] a *sub*marine. [abbr.]

sub *n.*³ [1970s] a general term of abuse, denoting a despised, poverty-stricken or otherwise inadequate person. [SE *sub-human*]

sub *v.* [mid-19C+] to give or get an advance on wages, a loan. [SE *subsistence money*]

subaltern's butter *n.* [late 19C–1920s] (N.Z.) the flesh of an avocado pear. [the officer's preference]

subaltern's luncheon *n.* [late 19C–1900s] a glass of water and the tightening of one's belt.

sub-beau *n.* [late 17C–mid-18C] an aspirant dandy (cf. DEMI-BEAU). [SE *sub*, secondary + *beau*, a dandy]

subby/subbie *n.* [1970s+] (Aus.) a *sub*-contractor. [abbr.]

sub-cheese *n.* [mid-19C+] (mainly Anglo-Ind.) everything, the lot, all there is. [SE *sub*, inferior + CHEESE n.¹]

sub-human *n.* [1980s+] (US campus) a socially unacceptable person; thus *sub-human*, distasteful, gross, stupid (cf. SUB n.³).

sublime *adj.* [late 19C+] audacious. [an ironical use of the SE]

sublime rascal *n.* [mid-19C] a lawyer.

submarine *n.*¹ [1910s–40s] (US) a doughnut (cf. SINKER n.²). [one dips it into one's coffee]

submarine *n.*² **1** [1950s+] (US) a type of large, over-filled sandwich (cf. GRINDER n.[6]). **2** [1980s+] (US campus) a tampon. [resemblance]

sub rosa/under the rose *adj.* [mid-16C+] dubious, suspicious, secretive. [SUB ROSA adv.]

sub rosa *adv.* [mid-16C+] privately, in secret, in strict confidence. [? Ger. *unter der Rose*, under the rose. The rose is a symbol of silence, poss. from its tight petals. 'The Rose of Venus was given ... to Harpocrates, the God of Silence, by Cupid, as a bribe not to "peach" about the Goddess' amours. It was commonly sculptured on the ceilings of banqueting rooms, as a sign that what was said in free conversation there was not ... to be divulged; and about 1526 was placed over the Roman confessionals as an emblem of secrecy' (Hotten, 1867)]

subscribing to the bookies' benefit *phr.* [20C] betting recklessly and thus effectively donating one's money to the bookmakers.

subtle *adj.* [17C] drunk.

subtle as a dead pig *phr.* [late 17C–early 18C] extremely stupid or ignorant.

sub up *v.* [mid-19C+] to hand over money, whether owing or not. [SUB v.]

suburb *adj.* [late 16C–late 17C] used in a variety of phr., all denigrating suburban life and poss. near-SE, *suburb-garden*, a house in which one installs a mistress; *suburb-humour*, unpleasant humour, usu. at another's expense; *suburb justice*, corrupt justice, easily amenable to bribes; *suburb-trade*, prostitution; *suburb tricks*, sexual amusements; *suburb sinner*, a prostitute; *suburban roarer*, a pimp or male 'heavy' in a brothel; *house in the suburbs*, a brothel; *minion of the suburbs*, a male prostitute.

suburban/suburban wench *n.* [late 19C] a prostitute who works in the suburbs rather than the West End of London.

suburb trade *n.* [late 19C] the world of suburban prostitution.

subway alumni *n.* [1940s+] (US) supporters of college sports teams who are not actually *alumni*, i.e. members or former members of the college. [they turn up at the college by *subway*]

subway dealer *n.* [20C] (US Und.) a crooked card-sharp who deals from the bottom of the pack. [SE *subway* as 'underground']

such *adj.* [mid-16C+] 'used as an absolute intensive, the implied clause of comparison being indeterminate and quite lost sight of' (*OED*), e.g. 'such an argument', 'such an awful place'.

such a few/many *phr.* [mid-19C] so few, so many.

such a reason pissed my goose/my goose pissed *phr.* [late 18C–early 19C] used in response to anything the speaker considers foolish or absurd. [PISS v.]

suck *n.[1]* [late 17C–19C] (Und.) wine or strong alcohol (cf. SUCK-CASA). [SE *suck*, a small measure or glass of liquid]

suck *n.[2]* [mid-19C] some form of suckable sweetmeat.

suck *n.[3]* [mid-19C+] **1** (orig. US) a disappointment. **2** (US Black) empty words, nagging, pointless arguments.

suck *n.[4]* **1** [1900s–50s] a parasite, a toady (cf. SUCK UP n.). **2** [1970s+] (Can.) a worthless, contemptible person. [SUCK UP v.]

suck *n.[5]* [1920s+] the act of fellatio. [SUCK v.[2] (1)]

suck *v.[1]* **1** [mid-19C] to pump someone for information. **2** [1950s] (W.I.) to nag (cf. SUCKER n.[6]).

suck *v.[2]* **1** [1920s+] to perform fellatio. **2** [1960s+] to be worthless, contemptible, pointless, objectionable (cf. CHOMP).

suck *v.[3]* [1970s+] (US campus) to be on one's last legs, to be struggling (cf. SUCK WIND). [one *sucks for air*]

suck *v.[4]* [1970s+] (US campus) to make someone into a victim of one's plans, tricks etc. [? backform. f. SUCKER n.[1]]

suck! *excl.* [1980s+] (US campus) a general excl., a euph. for FUCK!

sucka *n.* [1990s] (US Black teen) **1** a foolish, gullible person. **2** a general term of abuse. [deliberate mis-sp. of SUCKER n.[1] (1)]

suck a dog's dick, to *phr.* [1950s+] (orig. US Black) to perform the lowest act of which one is capable.

suck a fatty! *excl.* [1990s] (US) a general excl. of dismissal, aggression. [lit. *go and suck a fat penis!*]

Sucka Free *n.* [1990s] (US Black teen) San Francisco. [SUCKA + SE *free*]

suck/suckle a hoe handle, to *phr.* [20C] (US) to work lazily. [the worker standing still, gazing into space and chewing on the end of their hoe]

suck air *v.* [1970s+] (US) to be fearful. [var. on SUCK WIND]

suck and swallow *n.* [19C] the vagina (cf. CATCH 'EM ALIVE-O). [the image of the vagina as a predator]

suck around/round *v.* [1930s+] (US) to act in a toadying manner. [SUCK UP v.]

suck arse *see* KISS ARSE.

suck-arse/ass *adj.* [1970s+] useless, pointless, unpleasant; all deriving from the need to be obsequious. [SUCK ASS v.]

suck ass *v.[1]* *see* KISS ARSE.

suck ass *v.[2]* [1970s+] (US) to curry favour, to attempt to win over someone. [ARSE n.[1]]

suck-bottle *n.* [mid-17C–mid-18C] a drinker (cf. SUCK-CAN; SUCK-PINT; SUCK-POT; SUCK-SPIGOT).

suck-can *n.* [19C] a drinker (cf. SUCK-BOTTLE). [SUCK n.[1] + SE *can*]

suck-casa *n.* [mid-19C] a public house, a tavern. [SUCK n.[1] + CASA]

suck-crib *n.* [mid–late 19C] a public house, a tavern (cf. SUCK-CASA). [SUCK n.[1] + CRIB n.[3]]

suck-egg *n.* [mid-19C] a foolish person. [17C SE *suck-egg*, a young man]

suck eggs *v.* [20C] **1** (US, esp. South) to be mean and irritable. **2** (US) of a person, to behave in a disgusting manner, to be reprehensible. **3** (US) of a thing or situation, to be appalling or disgusting, to be generally without merit, e.g. *that sucks eggs*.

suck eggs! *excl.* [20C] (US) a general excl. of hostility or dismissal. [abbr. TEACH ONE'S GRANDMOTHER TO SUCK EGGS]

sucker *n.[1]* [early 19C+] (orig. US) **1** the victim of any kind of crooked plan. **2** an innocent, a dupe. **3** a bettor at a casino. [14C *sucker*, an animal before it is weaned, a child at the breast; thus the innocence of both]

sucker *n.[2]* [early 19C+] a sweet, esp. a lollipop; thus [20C] (US) *all-day sucker*, a form of sweet that can (in theory) be sucked for a whole day.

sucker *n.[3]* [mid-19C] (US) a parasite. [SE *sucker*, one who sucks, in this case money and favours]

sucker *n.[4]* [mid-19C+] (US) an inhabitant of Illinois. [? the state fish (*Catostomus commersoni*), the sucker; the sucking of much-needed water from the natural artesian wells; the gullibility of the early settlers in the hands of unscrupulous land speculators]

sucker *n.[5]* [late 19C+] **1** a fellatrix. **2** a lesbian. [SE *suck*; note SUCK v.[2] + COCKSUCKER]

sucker *n.[6]* [1950s] (W.I.) a nagging old woman. [note dial. *old suck*, a blood-sucking demon in the shape of an old woman]

sucker *n.[7]* [1950s+] a generally pej. description. [euph. for FUCKER]

sucker *v.* [1930s+] (orig. US) to cheat, to trick; thus *sucker in*, to ensnare, to entrap. [SUCKER n.[1]]

sucker-bait *n.* [1950s+] young women hired by casinos to appear available and thus lure and distract gamblers. [SUCKER n.[1] (3)+ SE *bait*]

sucker-bashing *n.* [1940s+] (Aus.) cutting down saplings that persist in growing on newly cleared land. [SE *sucker*, a shoot thrown out from the base of a plant]

sucker-punch *n.* [1960s+] a surprise punch. [SUCKER n.¹ + SE *punch*]

sucker-punch *v.* [1960s+] **1** to hit when the victim is not looking or is otherwise unprepared. **2** to fool, to trick. [SUCKER-PUNCH n.]

sucker snow *n.* [1950s+] (drugs) second-rate, over-adulterated cocaine, esp. as sold to gullible consumers. [SUCKER n.¹ + SNOW n.²]

sucker weed *n.* [1950s+] (US Black/drugs) poor-quality marijuana, esp. as sold to gullible consumers. [SUCKER n.¹ + WEED n.¹ (4)]

suck face *v.* [1970s+] (US campus) to kiss (cf. CHEW FACE; SUCK TONSILS).

suck hind tit, to *phr.* [1940s+] (US) **1** to be inferior, to take a secondary role. **2** to curry favour (cf. SUCK ASS).

suck-hole *n.* [1950s+] (Aus./Can.) a toady, a flatterer; thus *suck-holer*, a toady. [SUCK UP v. + ARSEHOLE n.]

suck hole *v.* [1950s+] (Aus./Can.) to toady, to curry favour. [SUCK-HOLE n.]

suck-in *n.* [mid-19C–1900s] a disappointment. [SUCK IN v.]

suck in *v.* [mid-19C–1900s] to deceive, to cheat.

sucking *n.*¹ [1920s+] (orig. US) fellatio. [SUCK v.²/abbr. COCK-SUCKING]

sucking *n.*² [1940s+] sycophancy. [SUCK UP v.]

sucking duppy *n.* [1940s] (W.I.) tuberculosis. [SE *sucking* + dial. *duppy*, a ghost, a malevolent spirit (allegedly of the dead)]

suck it and see! *phr.* [late 19C+] a phr. aimed derisively at someone who has asked what is considered a stupid or impudent question.

suck it easy, to *phr.* [1980s+] (US campus) to relax, to lie around. [the image of lying peacefully sucking on a cool drink]

suck it up *v.* [1980s+] (US campus) to tolerate, to endure, to deal with.

suckle a hoe handle *see* SUCK A HOE HANDLE.

suck my arse!/ass! *see* KISS MY ARSE!

suck-off *n.* [1920s+] (US) a despicable person esp. a toady; thus *suck-off*, repellent, contemptible. [SUCK OFF v.]

suck off *v.* [1920s+] **1** to fellate. **2** to toady to. [ext. of SUCK v.² (1); the *off* (cf. COME OFF v.¹) implies orgasm]

suck one's face, to *phr.* [late 17C–18C] to drink.

suck out of the thumb, to *phr.* [20C] (S.Afr.) to lie, to make up, to fabricate. [equivalent Du. phr. *iets uit zijn duim ziegen*]

suck-pint *n.* [mid-17C–19C] a drinker (cf. SUCK-BOTTLE).

suck-pot *n.* [19C] a drinker (cf. SUCK-BOTTLE).

suck rope *v.* [1960s+] (US) to be worthless, contemptible. [ext. of SUCK v.² (2)]

suck round *see* SUCK AROUND.

sucks!/sucks to you! *excl.* [1910s+] (usu. teen) a disdainful, dismissive excl. [? euph. for FUCK!]

suck salt *v.* [20C] (W.I.) to suffer hardship.

suck-spigot *n.* [late 16C–early 17C] a drinker (cf. SUCK-BOTTLE).

suckster/suckstress *n.* [late 19C–1900s] a fellator, a fellatrix. [SUCKER n.⁵]

sucks to be you *phr.* [1990s] (US campus) an expression of commiseration. [SUCK v.² (2)]

sucks to you! *see* SUCKS!

suck suds *v.* [1940s+] (US) to drink beer. [SE *suck* + SUDS]

suck the monkey, to *phr.* [late 18C–late 19C] **1** to suck liquor through a straw from the ship's barrel which has been bored with a gimlet (cf. TAP THE ADMIRAL). **2** to drink the liquid from a coconut. **3** to drink from the bottle (cf. MONKEY n.⁵).

suck the mop, to *phr.* [mid–late 19C] for one omnibus to lose its passengers to those of a rival firm, which has boxed it in; thus *left sucking the mop*, rendered impotent and beyond hope, to be put at an utter disadvantage. [play on NURSE v. (2); SE *mop*, a baby's dummy]

suck the sugar-stick, to *phr.* [19C] **1** of a woman, to have sexual intercourse. **2** usu. of a woman, to fellate. [SE *suck* + SUGAR-STICK]

suck tonsils *v.* [1990s] (US campus) to kiss passionately (cf. SUCK FACE; SWAB TONSILS).

suck-up *n.* [mid-19C+] one who curries favour with others, a toady, a parasite (cf. BOOTKISSER).

suck up/suck up to *v.* [mid-19C+] to curry favour, to be obsequious, to grovel shamelessly in return for favours, esteem etc (cf. ARSE LICK; BOOTLICK v.).

suck wind *v.* [1970s+] (US) to be on one's last legs, to be struggling. [one fig. gasps for air]

sucky *adj.*¹ [late 17C–18C] tipsy, slightly drunk. [SUCK n.¹]

sucky *adj.*² [1980s+] (US campus) awful, terrible, unpleasant. [SUCK v.² (2)]

sucky-sucky *n.* [20C] fellation (cf. FUCKY-FUCKY). [SUCK OFF + redup.]

suction *n.*¹ [early 19C–1910s] the heavy drinking of alcohol (cf. SUCK ONE'S FACE); thus [mid-19C] *power of suction*, one's drinking capacity, [1900s] *live on suction*, to drink heavily.

suction *n.*² [1950s–70s] (US Black) empty words, nagging, pointless arguments (cf. STATIC). [? fig. use of SE or pun on SUCK WIND]

sudden *adj.* [1940s+] **1** (Aus.) fast, efficient. **2** (orig. Aus.) brutal, ruthless, drastic.

sudden death 1 [mid-19C+] (sporting) in a variety of games (orig. coin-tossing) to decide the victor in a tied contest by giving the judgement to the next individual or team to score; thus [20C] *sudden-death play-off*. **2** [mid-19C] (Anglo-Ind.) a spatch-cocked fowl. **3** [late 19C] a crumpet or bun. **4** [late 19C–1900s] coffee. **5** [late 19C] (US) a strong alcoholic drink. **6** [late 19C] a plain boiled pudding. [in (2) the bird was caught and killed as the putative eater dismounted from his horse and by the time he had washed and dressed was ready for the table]

sudden death on *phr.* [1920s+] (Aus.) **1** expert, skilled at. **2** unnecessarily cruel or harsh towards. [SUDDEN adj. (1), (2)]

suds *n.* [20C] (US teen) beer. [the product's intense soap-suds-like fizziness and (to UK palates) taste. The late 18C phr. *in the suds*, tipsy, is presumably coincidental]

sudser *n.* [1950s+] (US) a soap opera. [SE *soap suds*]

sue *n.* [1980s+] (US campus) a usu. derog. term for a stereotypical sorority member; thus *sue out*, to dress, look and act like a sorority member (cf. SUZI SORORITY). [generic use of the proper name]

sue city *n.* [1960s+] (US) involvement in a court case or similar legal situation. [SE *sue* + sfx. -CITY + pun on *Sioux City*]

suede *n.* [1940s–50s] (Black) a dark-skinned Black person.

suedehead *n.* [1970s] a form of SKINHEAD whose hair was grown slightly longer than the usual absolute bald look and thus presents a slight fuzz, somewhat reminiscent of suede.

suety/soapy Isaac *n.* [1900s–20s] a suet pudding. [? its sallow 'complexion', supposedly reminiscent of a Jew; i.e. the 'Jewish' proper name *Isaac*]

suff *adj.* [late 19C–1910s] (N.Z.) *sufficient*. [abbr.]

suffer *n.* [1940s] (US Black) a lengthy story, tediously recounted. [the listeners 'suffer' through it]

suffer a recovery, to *phr.* [late 19C] (Aus.) to have a hangover. [joc. euph.]

sufferer *n.*¹ [mid–late 19C] a tailor. [? their professional problems, usu. poverty]

sufferer *n.*² [mid–late 19C] a sovereign. [for ety. *see* SUFFERING]

suffering *n.* [1910s] a sovereign. ['Cockney' mispron.]

suffering cats! *excl.* [late 19C+] a euph. for SUFFERING CHRIST!

suffering Christ! *excl.* [late 19C+] a mild, if blasphemous, excl. of surprise or annoyance.

suffer with the shorts, to *phr.* [1940s] (US Black) to be out of cash, to be impoverished. [i.e. *short* of cash]

suffler *n.* [16C] (Und.) that member of a team of confidence tricksters passing off fake gold who poses as a drunk (cf. BARNARD). [? Netherlands High Ger. *suff*, drink]

sug *n.*[1] *see* SHUG.

sug *n.*[2] [20C] (S.Afr.) a moan, a whinge; thus *sug*, to whinge. [Du. *zuchten*, to sigh, to groan]

sugar *n.*[1] [mid-19C+] money. [rhy. sl. *sugar and honey*; Cohen (1989) suggests that on the basis of *honey* = gold, *sugar* = silver as well as the plain generic]

sugar *n.*[2] [late 19C] a grocer. [their stock-in-trade]

sugar *n.*[3] [20C] (US Black) a kiss (cf. DEEP SUGAR; MOUTH SUGAR; NECK SUGAR). [the 'sweetness' thereof]

sugar *n.*[4] [1920s+] (US Black) semen. [double entendre, e.g. Bessie Smith, 'Want Some Sugar in My Bowl']

sugar *n.*[5] [1930s+] (orig. US) a general term of endearment, can be used of and to either sex.

sugar *n.*[6] (drugs) **1** [1950s] heroin; thus [1970s] *sugar people*, rich young heroin addicts (cf. BROWN SUGAR). **2** [1960s] LSD (cf. A n.[3]). **3** [1970s+] cocaine. [note that *sugar people* is also influenced by SUGAR DADDY]

sugar *n.*[7] [1990s] (US Black) homosexuality. [? gay men are so 'sweet']

sugar *v.* [late 19C] to present a fake appearance, to 'cook the books', to pose as something one is not. [SE phr. *sugar the pill*]

sugar! *excl.* **1** [mid-19C] a cry of exultation after a victory, supposedly given as one stands on one leg and waves the other about. **2** [late 19C+] euph. for SHIT! (cf. FUDGE!).

sugar and spice *n.* [20C] ice. [rhy. sl.]

sugar and spice *adj.* [20C] nice. [rhy. sl.]

sugar-bag *n.* [late 19C+] (Aus.) one who accepts bribes. [they are willing to take a SE *sweetener*]

sugar-bag *adj.* [1970s] (Aus./N.Z.) second-rate, cheap, impoverished. [the Depression-era use of *sugar bags* (made of fine sacking) for a variety of makeshift and do-it-yourself tasks]

sugar basin *n.* [19C] the vagina (cf. APPLE n.[10]; SALT-CELLAR n.[1]; SUGAR-STICK).

sugar block *n.* [1980s+] (drugs) crack cocaine. [resemblance]

sugar-candy *adj.* **1** [mid-19C–1920s] brandy. **2** [20C] handy. [rhy. sl.]

sugar cubes/lumps *n.* [1960s+] (drugs) LSD (cf. A n.[3]). [early doses of LSD came on *sugar cubes/lumps*]

sugar daddy/papa/sweet sugar *n.* [late 19C+] (orig. US) an older man who is willing to provide the various material wants of a younger mistress or, if gay, a younger male lover (cf. SUGAR MAMA; SWEET DADDY).

sugared *adj.* [20C] euph. for BUGGERED etc, usu. in phr. *I'll be sugared! I'm sugared!*

sugar hill *n.* (US Black) **1** [1920s–40s] that area of Harlem otherwise known as Coogan's Bluff, between Amsterdam and Edgecombe Avenues, between 138th and 155th Streets. As well as the rich, many Black intellectuals and artists chose to live in the area, known for its grand apartment houses, once the original White population had moved out during the 1920s. **2** [1930s–50s] the brothel and 'red-light' area of the Black part of any southern town. [SUGAR n.[1] + SE *hill*]

sugar lumps *see* SUGAR CUBES.

sugar mama *n.* [1980s+] (US gay) an older gay man providing material support for his younger lover. [feminization of SUGAR DADDY]

sugar-mummy *n.* [1980s+] (S.Afr. township) a wealthy White woman who pays for the companionship of attractive, younger Black men. [on the model of SUGAR DADDY]

sugar on *adj.* [late 19C] in love with, infatuated with (cf. SWEET ON).

sugar papa *see* SUGAR DADDY.

sugar/sweet pimp *n.* [1960s+] a pimp who prefers charm and persuasion to threats and violence when dealing with his women (cf. GORILLA PIMP; SWEET MACK). [SE *sugar* + *pimp*]

sugar report *n.* [1940s+] (US campus) a letter from one's sweetheart. [orig. milit. WW2]

sugar shack *n.* [1960s] (US Black) spare space used for putting up a temporary guest.

sugar-shop *n.* [late 19C] a place where, during an election, voters can expect to receive bribes in return for the promise of their votes. [SUGAR n.[1] + SE *shop*]

sugar-stick *n.* [late 18C–1900s] the penis (cf. LADIES' LOLLIPOP; SUGAR BASIN). [Puxley suggests rhy. sl. on PRICK n. (1), but rhy. sl. tends to be coined later]

sugar tit *n.* [20C] (US) something comforting (cf. SECURITY BLANKET). [SE *sugar* + TIT n.[1] (1); the use of a cloth dipped in sugar water as a way of soothing a baby]

sugar up *v.* [1910s–20s] to flatter, to toady to.

sugar weed *n.* [1960s–70s] (drugs) second-rate, adulterated marijuana (cf. SUCKER WEED). [the marijuana is compressed into a block mixed with sugar or honey]

suicide *n.* **1** [mid-19C] 4 horses driven in a line (cf. HARUM-SCARUM). **2** [1940s+] (Aus.) a punning ref., used by motorists, to the 'side' of a vehicle on which one should not attempt to pass. **3** [1970s+] (Aus.) used in Northern Territory to refer to the rainy season or 'wet', considered unendurable by many people.

suicide blonde *n.* [1930s+] (orig. US) a woman with dyed blonde or peroxide blonde hair (cf. BOTTLE BABY n.[2]). [? she drives men to *suicide*]

suit *n.*[1] [early 18C–mid-19C] a gold watch and seals. [SE *suit*, a full set of clothes]

suit *n.*[2] [mid-18C+] nudity. [abbr. BIRTHDAY SUIT]

suit *n.*[3] [early–mid-19C] a trick, a scheme. [SE *suit*, a pursuit]

suit *n.*[4] [1980s+] **1** a member of management, a businessman, anyone who has to wear a suit for their daily work, as opposed to more casually dressed creative or freelance workers, or those in jobs that in any case have no need for suits. **2** an uncreative, authoritarian person.

suit and cloak *n.* [late 17C–19C] a drink, esp. brandy. [rhy. sl. *suit and cloak* = SOAK n.]

suit/suit one as a saddle fits a sow, to *phr.* [18C] to be utterly unsuitable, to be highly incongruous.

suitcase *n.*[1] [20C] (US) the anus (cf. KEISTER).

suitcase *n.*[2] [1990s] (US teen) one who is neither so boring as to be objectionable nor so fashionable as to be sought-after.

suit down to the ground, to *phr.* [late 19C+] to suit perfectly.

suited down *adj.* [1960s+] (US Black) especially well-dressed.

suit one as a saddle fits a sow *see* SUIT AS A SADDLE FITS A SOW.

suit up *v.* [1990s] to dress oneself in a suit.

suit yourself *phr.* [late 19C+] do what you like, with the implication 'and see if I care'.

sukey *n.* **1** [19C–1950s] a kettle. **2** [19C] a general lower servant girl. **3** [mid-late 19C] a fool. [*Sukey*, a dimin. of proper name *Susan*, but ? Welsh Gypsy *sukar*, to hum, to whisper (cf. BLACK SAL; the immediate root was presumably mid-18C+ nursery rhyme 'Polly put the kettle on']

sukey-tawdry *n.* [mid-19C] a slatternly woman, dressed in a flashy, vulgar style. [SUKEY (2) + SE *tawdry*]

sulph *n.* [1980s+] (drugs) amphetamine *sulph*ate. [abbr.]

sulphate *n.* [1970s+] amphetamine *sulphate*. [abbr.]

sulphur *n.* [late 19C–1900s] pungent, melodramatic talk.

sultry *adj.* [late 19C–1900s] of language, writing or pictures, coarse, obscene, vulgar, 'smutty' (cf. HOT adj.¹).

sumbitch *see* SON OF A BITCH.

sumjao *v.* [19C] (Anglo-Ind.) to warn, to correct, to threaten. [Hind. *samjhana*, to know, warn, correct, usu. with implication of physical coercion]

summer cabbage *n.*¹ [19C] an umbrella. [the spread of its leaves]

summer cabbage *n.*² [19C] sexual intercourse; usu. as *do/ have a bit of* ... (cf. CABBAGE n.⁷). [play on GREENS n.²]

summer-game *n.* [mid–late 19C] (US gambling) playing for amusement, but using another person's money.

summerhead *n.* [late 18C] (Anglo-Ind.) a parasol. [SE *sombrero*]

summertime ho *n.* [1970s+] an occasional prostitute who works, not necessarily in summer, but only when she needs the money or the mood takes her; often incl. high school girls, who turn to whoring in the summer holidays.

summon the genie, to *phr.* [1990s] to masturbate. [one 'rubs the lamp']

sumph *n.* [18C] **1** a stupid fellow, a simpleton. **2** a surly or sullen man; thus *sumphish*, *sumphishly*. [synon. Scot.]

sunbake *v.* [20C] (Aus.) to sunbathe.

sunbeam *n.* [1980s] (Aus.) an item of crockery or cutlery laid out on the table but still unused. [*as bright as a sunbeam*]

sunburned/sunburnt *adj.*¹ [late 17C–early 19C] having too many male children. [pun on SE *son*]

sunburned/sunburnt *adj.*² [early 18C–late 19C] infected with venereal disease. [pun on SE *burned*]

sunburned Irishman *n.* [20C] a derog. term for a Black person. [immigrant Blacks and Irish occupy the same low social position in the UK]

Sun City *n.* [1980s+] (S.Afr.) an ironic nickname for Diepkloof Prison, Gauteng Province. [*Sun City*, the luxury hotel and entertainment complex near Rustenberg, North-West Province]

Sunday *v.* [late 19C] (society) to spend Sunday with a person or persons (cf. CHRISTMAS v.).

Sunday below Monday *see* MONDAY COMES BEFORE SUNDAY.

Sunday best *n.* [20C] a vest (undershirt). [rhy. sl.]

Sunday clothes *n.* [20C] (US) one's best clothes. [abbr. SUNDAY-GO-TO-MEETING CLOTHES]

Sunday face *n.* [19C] the backside. [play on SE *Sunday face*, a sanctimonious expression]

Sundayfied *adj.* [mid–late 19C] fit for a Sunday, i.e. acting in a pious manner, dressed in one's best clothes etc.

Sunday flash togs *n.* [late 19C–1900s] one's best clothes. [SE *Sunday* + FLASH adj.² + TOGS]

Sunday girl *n.* [late 19C] a mistress one sees only at weekends (cf. SUNDAY MAN n.²; WEEKEND HO).

Sunday go-to-meeting *adj.* [18C+] (US) of clothes, the best (cf. GO-TO-MEETING-CLOTHES).

Sunday-go-to-meeting clothes *n.* [mid-19C+] (US) one's best clothes (cf. GO-TO-MEETING-CLOTHES; SUNDAY CLOTHES). [one dresses for church]

Sunday jinal *n.* [1950s] (W.I.) any variety of clergyman or preacher. [SE *Sunday* + dial. *jinal*, a clever person; thus a conman, a crook; ult. pron. of SE *general*]

Sunday man *n.*¹ [late 18C–mid-19C] a criminal who only dares go out on Sunday, when the police are inactive.

Sunday man *n.*² [late 19C] a pimp. [Sunday is the only day he can go out with his woman; the remainder of the time she will be working]

Sunday morn *n.* [20C] an erection. [rhy. sl. *Sunday morn* = HORN n.²]

Sunday out *n.* [mid–late 19C] the one Sunday per month or

fortnight that a servant is allowed off; thus *Sunday-outer*, a servant enjoying this day of leisure.

Sunday promenader *n.* [late 19C] a debtor, one who risks going out on Sundays only (cf. ONCE-A-WEEK MAN).

Sunday punch *n.* [1920s+] (orig. US) **1** a knockout blow. **2** one's best effort. [on the pattern of *Sunday*, therefore best, suit]

Sunday saint *n.* [late 19C+] one whose degenerate weekday behaviour is replaced every Sunday by an air of sanctimonious and ultimately hypocritical piety.

sundodger *n.* [mid-19C] (Aus.) one who loiters around in the hope of hand-outs, which will save them from having to earn a living (cf. SCOWBANKER). [since their likely job would be on a farm, such indolence keeps them out of the sun]

sundown *adj.* [late 19C–1940s] (US) used of one who works outside their normal hours of practice, e.g. lawyers, doctors (cf. MOONLIGHT v.).

sundown *v.* [1920s] (Aus.) to beg someone for food and drink. [SUNDOWNER]

sundowner *n.* **1** [late 19C–1900s] (US) a professional who takes on extra work outside their normal hours of practice. **2** [late 19C+] (Aus./N.Z.) a tramp or vagrant who arrives at a station about sundown under the pretence of seeking work, but really, since work stops at dusk, to obtain food and a night's lodging. **3** [late 19C+] a drink taken at or around sundown. **4** [20C] (Aus.) a lazy sheepdog or cattle-dog.

sunk *adj.* [1920s+] hopeless, finished, no chance. [naut. imagery]

sunnies *n.* [1980s] (Aus./N.Z.) sunglasses. [abbr.]

sunny bank *n.* [late 18C–early 19C] a good fire in winter. [pun on SE *banking*, a fire]

sunny side *n.* [20C] the good, easy, materially satisfying life. [the *sunny side of the street*]

sunny side up *phr.* [late 19C+] (orig. US) of eggs, fried with the yolk-side up (cf. OVER-EASY).

sunny south *n.* [late 19C] the mouth. [rhy. sl.]

sunshine *n.*¹ [1960s–70s] (drugs) a variety of LSD (cf. A n.³). [abbr. ORANGE SUNSHINE; i.e. the orange-coloured pills containing the drug]

sunshine *n.*² [1970s+] a general form of address, e.g. *Oi! sunshine!*

sunspecs *n.* [1970s+] sunglasses. [abbr. + SPECS]

sup/supp *n.* [1920s+] a supplement. **2** [1960s+] a newspaper colour supplement and spelled with double *p*, often as *colour supp.*

's up *phr.* [1980s+] (US Black/campus/teen) a greeting. [contraction of *what's up?*]

super *n.*¹ [mid-19C+] (orig. US) a superintendent, a janitor.

super/souper *n.*² [mid-19C–1900s] (Und.) a watch; thus *super/souper and slang*, a watch and chain (cf. KETTLE n.²; SUPER-SCREWING). [? SE *soup-plate*; i.e. the size and shape of a watch]

super *n.*³ [1970s+] (Aus.) a *super*annuation pension. [abbr.]

super *n.*⁴ [1980s+] (drugs) phencyclidine (cf. ACE n.³).

super *n.*⁵ [1980s+] (Black) a star, an important figure.

super *adj.* [late 19C+] very good or pleasant, first-rate, excellent. [Lat. *super*, above]

super *v.* [1970s+] (Aus.) to dismiss, to superannuate.

super acid *n.* [1980s+] (drugs) ketamine (cf. K n.⁴). [SE pfx. *super-* + ACID n.³]

superbad *see* SUPERFLY.

super bio *n.* [1990s] (drugs) marijuana. [play on washing powder advertising]

super buick *n.* [1990s] (US drugs) a cocktail of heroin and/or cocaine plus various prescription drugs, incl. scopolamine (cf. HOMICIDE). [SE pfx. *super-* + BUICK v.; the effects are unpleasant and poss. nauseating]

super c *n.* [1980s+] (drugs) ketamine (cf. K n.[4]).

supercharge *n.* [1980s+] (drugs) crack cocaine. [its effects]

supercloud *n.* [1980s+] (drugs) crack cocaine. [the clouds of smoke that accompany its use]

supercolossal *adj.* [1930s+] extremely large, outsized; remarkable, stupendous.

supercool *adj.* [1960s+] extremely relaxed, sophisticated. [SE pfx. *super*- + COOL adj.[3]]

super-duper/sooper-dooper *adj.* [1940s+] (teen) excellent, first-rate, wonderful. [SE pfx. *super*- + redup.]

superfatted *adj.* [1920s–40s] very fat.

superfly/superbad *adj.* [1960s–70s] (US Black) of people, situations, drugs etc, excellent, first-rate. [SE pfx. *super*- + FLY adj./BAD adj.]

superglue *n.* [1990s] (US Black) hair gel.

supergrass/superweed *n.*[1] **1** [1960s+] (drugs) especially strong marijuana. **2** [1970s+] phencyclidine (cf. ACE n.[3]). [SE pfx. *super*- + GRASS n.[4]]

supergrass *n.*[2] [1970s+] (Und.) an informer who betrays a large number of important fellow criminals, thus helping solve many hitherto unresolved crimes. [SE pfx. *super*- + GRASS n.[5]]

super-honkie *n.* [1960s] (US Black) an exceptionally authoritarian White person. [SE pfx. *super*- + HONKIE]

super ice *n.* [1980s+] (drugs) smokeable methylamphetamine. [SE pfx. *super*- + ICE n.[5]]

superintendent/supervisor of the pavement *n.* [1950s] (Aus.) anyone, other than those employed at the work, who enjoys standing staring at buildings under construction (cf. INSPECTOR OF PAVEMENTS).

super joint *n.* [1980s+] (drugs) phencyclidine (cf. ACE n.[3]). [SE pfx. *super*- + JOINT n.[4] (2)]

super kools *n.* [1980s+] (drugs) phencyclidine (cf. ACE n.[3]). [SE *super* + *Kools*, a brand of mentholated cigarette]

supermario *n.* [20C] a brand of LSD (cf. A n.[3]). [the Nintendo computer game character]

supermarket conversation *n.* [1990s] (US Black) empty, meaningless chatter. [with no more intrinsic quality than the Muzak played in supermarkets]

supernacular *adj.* [mid-19C] of alcohol, first-rate, excellent. [SUPERNACULUM]

supernaculum/supernagulum *n.* [late 16C–18C] exceptionally good liquor; thus *supernaculum*, to the last drop, to the bottom (cf. MAKE A PEARL ON THE NAIL). [Lat. *supernaculum*, over the nail. The tradition of upending one's emptied glass onto the left thumbnail, thus proving that one had drunk every drop]

supernotch *n.* [1980s+] (Black) a style leader, a charismatic man (cf. SUPERFLY). [SE pfx. *super*- + NOTCH n.[2]]

super-screwing *n.* [mid-19C] (Und.) watch-stealing. [SUPER n.[2] + SCREW v.[2]]

superskunk *n.* [1990s] (drugs) an extremely potent form of marijuana. [SE pfx. *super*- + SKUNK n.[2]]

supersnagative *adj.* [late 19C] (Aus./N.Z.) excellent, wonderful, superb.

supersonic *adj.* [1940s+] (teen) absolutely wonderful.

supersoul *n.* [1970s] (US campus) of Black students, an exceptionally sophisticated individual. [SE pfx. *super*- + SOUL n.]

super-spade *n.* [1940s–60s] (US Black) a Black person who is noticeably self-conscious about their race. [SE pfx. *super*- + SPADE]

superstitious pie *n.* [late 17C–18C] a mince pie or Christmas pie, as made by Puritans or Precisians sometime before Christmas.

super toke *v.* [1980s+] (US drugs) to inhale a cannabis cigarette from both ends. [SE pfx. *super*- + TOKE v.]

supervisor of the pavement *see* SUPERINTENDENT OF THE PAVEMENT.

superweed *see* SUPERGRASS n.[1].

superwhite *n.* [1980s+] (drugs) crack cocaine. [THE COLOUR]

supouch *n.* [late 17C–18C] a hostess or landlady. [? SE *sup*, to drink]

supp *see* SUP.

supped all one's porridge *phr.* [1910s–20s] to have had one's teeth fixed. [one can thus return to solid foods]

suppelar *n.* [mid-19C+] (Ling. Fr./Polari) a hat. [Ital. *suppelettile*, household fittings]

suppose *n.* [mid-19C+] a nose (cf. I SUPPOSE). [rhy. sl.]

surat *n.* [mid-19C] any article of inferior quality, made from a mix of first- and second-rate materials. [textile jargon *surat*, second-rate cotton made from a mix of US (good) cotton and *surat* (bad) cotton]

sure! *adv.* [early 18C+] a general intensive, definitely, absolutely. [coined in the UK, the term moved to the US by the mid-19C, although it returned to the UK in the early 20C]

sure as God made little green apples *phr.* [20C] (US) definitely, for sure.

sure as hell *phr.* [1970s+] without a doubt, certainly.

sure as shit *phr.* [1970s+] (US) **1** used as an affirmation. **2** certainly. [SHIT n.[1] (1)]

sure as you're/I'm a foot high *phr.* [late 19C–1950s] (US) absolutely, without a doubt.

sure card *n.* [late 17C+] a safe plan, a trustworthy person. [SE *sure* + CARD n.[3]; note mid-16C SE *sure card*, an expedient to gain a desired object, a person whose name will help one]

sure cop *n.* [1940s+] (Aus.) an absolute certainty, a 'sure thing', a 'dead cert'. [SE *sure* + COP n.[2]]

sure-enough *adj.* [19C+] (US) definite, absolute, certain.

sure find *n.* [mid-19C] something that will definitely be found where one expects it. [fox-hunting use *sure find*, a place where a 'find' is sure to be made]

sure-fire *adj.* [mid-19C+] (orig. US) certain, definite, unassailable. [the image of an efficient firearm]

sure, I knew you could *phr.* [1980s+] (US campus) sarcastic expression of doubt. [a play on the supportive catchphrase of the US children's TV character Mr Rogers]

sure-ly *adv.* [mid-19C] a general intensive. [the breaking of the word and the emphatic stretching of the 'ly' makes it colloq. and no longer SE]

surely me *phr.* [late 19C] synon. for *to be sure*.

sure pop *n.* [1940s–50s] (US Black) a certainty, an absolute fact. [SE *sure* + POP n.[5]]

sure thing *phr.* [mid-19C+] (US) an affirmation, absolutely, certainly, I agree; thus *sure thing*, an absolute certainty, a guarantee.

surface *v.* **1** [1930s+] to awaken, to get out of bed. **2** [1950s+] (US) to reveal a secret, esp. in media context.

surf and turf *n.* [1970s] (orig. US) a restaurant specializing in seafood and steak (cf. STEAKDAHOYST).

surf bum *n.* [1950s+] (orig. US) a surfing enthusiast who devotes (usu.) their entire existence to pursuing the sport (cf. SKI BUM). [SE *surf* + BUM n.[3] (5)]

surf bunny *n.* [1950s+] (US) a woman who associates with surfers (cf. BEACH BUNNY). [SE *surf* + BUNNY n.[2]]

surfer *n.* [1970s+] (drugs) phencyclidine (cf. ACE n.[3]). [? one *surfs* inner space]

surf-hurdling *n.* [1930–40s] (N.Z.) transporting goods between ship and shore in an open boat.

surfie *n.* [1960s+] (Aus.) a surfer; thus *surfie chick*, a woman who associates with surfers.

surfoholic *n.* [1990s] (US teen) one who is addicted to browsing the Internet. [SE *surf*, to browse the Internet]

surf or die! *excl.* [1980s+] (US campus) ironic use of a popular slogan to belittle those who are obsessed with surfing to the exclusion of any other activity.

sur le tapis *adj.* [mid-19C+] in trouble, facing a reprimand or telling-off. [lit. Fr. ON THE CARPET, but used only in the UK; cf. PAS DE PROBLÈME]

surly-boots *n.* [late 17C+] a surly, morose person. [SE *surly* + sfx. *-boots*]

surprise, surprise! *excl.* [1960s+] ironic or sarcastic rejoinder to a piece of supposedly revelatory information.

Surrey docks *n.* [1970s] venereal disease. [rhy. sl. *Surrey docks* = POX n.[1]]

surround *v.* [1900s] (Aus.) to drink. [? 'get your mouth around that']

surveyor of the highways *n.* [late 18C–early 19C] a drunkard (cf. INSPECTOR OF PAVEMENT). [the drunkard's frequent falling over]

sus/suss *adj.* [1930s+] *sus*picious; thus the *sus laws*, controversial powers that permitted the police to stop and search persons allegedly suspected of a crime and that were considered as racist by the Black and Asian communities. [abbr.]

sus *v.* [1920s+] to *sus*pect. [abbr.]

Susan B. Anthony *n.* [1990s] (US Black teen) a generic name for a conventional White woman. [proper name *Susan B. Anthony* (1820–1906), the 19C US feminist pioneer]

susancide *n.* [late 19C] suicide. [joc. blend of SE *Susan* + *suicide*]

susan saliva *n.* [1950s–70s] (camp gay) a fellator, esp. one who works as a male prostitute. ['he lives by his spits']

s.u.s.f.u. *phr.* [1940s+] (milit.) situation unchanged, still *f*ucked *u*p (cf. S.N.A.F.U. phr.). [abbr.]

sushi taco *n.* [1990s] the labia majora. [mix of popular Japanese (*sushi*, i.e. raw fish) and Mexican (*taco*) dishes]

susie *see* SUSY.

susie sorority *see* SUZI SORORITY.

suspended *n.* [1970s+] a *suspended* sentence. [abbr.]

sus. per coll. *adj.* [late 18C–early 19C] hanged. [Lat. *suspensus per collum*, hanged by the neck; this notation is entered in the prison ledger]

suss *n.* [1970s+] natural intelligence, instinctive knowledge, esp. as used in petty crime or other marginal occupations (cf. STREET SMARTS). [backform. of SUSS OUT]

sussed out *adj.* [1960s+] aware, perceptive. [SUSS OUT]

Sussex bang *n.* [early 19C] (Anglo-Irish) a daredevil. [ety. unknown; ? a lost anecdote]

Sussex weeds *n.* [1910s] oak trees. [the many oak trees growing in the county]

susso *n.* [1930s] (Aus.) **1** state government relief paid to the unemployed, esp. during the 1930s depression. **2** one who is receiving the relief; thus *on the susso*, receiving state benefits. [SE *sustenance* + sfx. *-o*]

suss out *v.* [1960s+] to understand, to work out, to discover. [SE *suspicious*]

sussy *adj.* [1970s+] suspicious, aware. [SUSS OUT]

su-su *n.* [1950s+] (W.I. Rasta) gossip, the sound of whispering. [SUSU v.]

susu *v.* [1950s+] (W.I.) to gossip, to malign. [? echoic or Twi *susuw ka*, to utter a suspicion + SE *sussurate*, to whisper]

susy/susie *n.* [1930s+] sixpence. [rhy. sl. *Susy Anna* = TANNER]

sutler *n.* [late 17C–early 18C] 'He that Pockets up, Gloves, Knives, Handkerchiefs, Snuff and Tobacco-boxes, and all the lesser Moveables' (B.E.). [SE *sutler*, one who sells provisions to soldiers, whether in the garrison or in camp]

suzi/susie/suzie sorority *n.* [1970s] (US campus) a stereotypical sorority member (cf. SUE). [play on proper name]

suzie wang/wong *n.* [1960s] (camp gay) an Oriental homosexual. [the musical/film *The World of Suzie Wong* (1960) + pun on WANG]

suzy *n.* [20C] (US) a $1 coin bearing the portrait of pioneer feminist *Susan B. Anthony* (1820–1906).

swab *n.*[1] [early 18C] an unpleasant person (cf. SCAB n.). [SE *swab*, a washcloth or mop]

swab *n.*[2] **1** [late 18C–mid-19C] the epaulette worn by a naval officer. **2** [late 18C–mid-19C] a naval officer. **3** [20C] (US) a merchant seaman, a sailor in the US Navy (cf. SWAB JOCKEY). [SE *swab*, a washcloth or mop, used to clean the decks]

swabbers *n.* [late 17C–early 19C] in cards, the ace of hearts, the knave of clubs, the ace and deuce of trumps. [? SE *swab*, to mop up. In the variety of whist known as *whisk and swabbers* a player that held these cards was automatically entitled to a share of the pot]

swabbie *see* SWABBY.

swabble/swobble *v.* [1940s] (US Black/Harlem) to eat fast and greedily. [? SE *swill* + *gobble*]

swabby/swabbie *n.* [20C] (US) a sailor (cf. SWADDY). [SWAB n.[2] (3)]

swab jockey *n.* [20C] (US) a merchant seaman, a sailor in the US Navy. [SWAB n.[2] (3) + JOCKEY n.[2]]

swab tonsils/one's tonsils *v.* [1920s+] to kiss (cf. SUCK TONSILS).

swack *n.*[1] [mid-19C] a hoax, a deception (cf. SWACK UP). [SE *swack*, supple, lithe, smart; ult. Flem. *zwak*, nimble + Du. *zwak*, pliant, weak]

swack *n.*[2] [1970s+] (US Black) the penis (cf. ARSE-OPENER). [? dial. *swack*, a blow]

swacked *adj.* [1940s+] very drunk (cf. BASTED). [dial. *swack*, a blow, but note Scot. *swack*, to drink deeply]

swacko *adj.* [1940s+] very drunk (cf. BASTED). [SWACKED]

swack-up *n.* [mid-19C] a lie. [SWACK n.[1]]

swack up *v.* [mid-19C] to deceive, to trick. [SWACK n.[1]]

swad *n.* [late 18C–late 19C] a soldier (cf. SWADDY).

swadder/swaddler *n.* [mid-16C–early 19C] (Und.) a criminal pedlar (cf. CANTING CREW). [SWADDLE. Harman claims they are 'not at all evil, but of an indifferent behaviour' but by 1725 the *New Canting Dict.* condemns them as 'not content to rob and plunder, [but] beat and barbarously abuse, and often murder the Passengers']

swaddle *n.* [late 16C–mid-19C] to beat up, to assault (cf. SWADDER). [SE *swaddle*, to wrap up, to restrict movement]

swaddler *n.*[1] *see* SWADDER.

swaddler *n.*[2] **1** [mid-18C–19C] a Methodist; thus *swaddling*, Methodism. **2** [mid–late 19C] any type of Protestant. [Charles Wesley, *Journal*, 10 September 1747: 'We dined with a gentleman, who explained our name to us. It seems we are beholden to Mr Cennick for it, who abounds in such like expressions as, "I curse and blaspheme all the gods in heaven, but the babe that lay in the manger, the babe that lay in Mary's lap, the babe that lay in swaddling clouts", &c. Hence they nicknamed him, "Swaddler, or Swaddling John"; and the word sticks to us all, not excepting the Clergy.' Hotten (1860) adds that during the sermon, 'an ignorant Romanist, to whom the words of the English Bible were a novelty ... shouted out in derision "A swaddler! a swaddler!", as if the whole story were the preacher's invention']

swaddy/swoddy *n.* [early 18C+] a soldier. [16C dial. *swad*, a country bumpkin]

swad-/swod-gill *n.* [early 18C–early 19C] a soldier (cf. SWADDY). [dial. *swad* + GILL n.[1]]

swadkin *n.* [early 18C–mid-19C] a newly enlisted soldier (cf. SWADDY). [dial. *swad* + dimin. sfx. *-kin*]

swag *n.*[1] **1** [late 17C–early 19C] (Und.) a shop (and its contents) viewed as booty. **2** [late 18C+] (Und.) a thief's booty (esp. linen or clothes as opposed to jewels or plate) or a pedlar's wares. **3** [19C] a lot or plenty of anything. **4** [early 19C+] (Und.) a share in booty. **5** [mid-19C] a trader in such articles, the keeper of a SWAG-SHOP. **6** [mid–late 19C] the trade in small articles (cf. SWAG-SHOP; SWAG-TRADE). **7** [mid-19C+] (Aus./N.Z.) the pack carried by an itinerant or vagrant (cf. SWAGMAN n.²). **8** [20C] (Aus.) a roll of money. **9** [1990s] (US teen) paper money, currency. [14C SE *swag*, a bulgy bag]

swag n.² [1970s+] (US Black) liquor. [? SE *swig* or Scot. *swag*, a deep draught of liquid]

swag adj. [mid–late 19C] worthless. [SWAG n.¹ (6)]

swag v. **1** [mid-19C+] to steal, to take forcibly. **2** [mid-19C+] to drag away, to arrest. **3** [1930s+] to hustle along, to hurry. [SWAG n.¹ (2)]

swag away v. [1950s+] to abduct, to kidnap. [ext. of SWAG v.]

swag-barrow man n. [mid-19C] a costermonger; thus *swag-barrow*, a coster's cart. [SWAG n.¹ (6)]

swag-chovey n. [mid–late 19C] (Und.) a criminal receiver's shop or store; thus *swag-chovey bloke*, a marine store dealer. [SWAG n.¹ (2) + CHOVEY]

swagger n. see SWAGMAN n.².

swagger adj. [late 19C–1920s] (society) smart, fashionable. [SE *swagger*, to flaunt oneself]

swaggering n. [late 19C+] (Aus./N.Z.) living as a tramp, esp. in the outback. [SWAG n.¹ (7)]

swaggery adj. [late 19C] smart, fashionable. [lower-class version of SWAGGER adj.]

swaggie/swaggy n. [20C] (Aus./N.Z.) a vagrant, a tramp. [abbr. SWAGMAN n.²]

swagging n. [mid-19C] (US prison) stealing, spec. stealing state-owned property. [SWAG v.]

swaggy see SWAGGIE.

swag in v. [1910s–20s] to cause one to enter surreptitiously. [SE *swag*, to make someone sway or sag]

swag it v. [1940s] (Aus.) to live as a tramp (cf. SWAGMAN n.²).

swagman n.¹ [mid–late 19C] a man in the SWAG-SHOP trade. [SWAG n.¹ (6)]

swagman/swagger n.² [mid-19C+] (Aus./N.Z.) an itinerant worker, who travels with his pack on his back while looking for employment (cf. BAGMAN n.¹). [SWAG n.¹ (7) + sfx. -*man*]

swag of, a phr. [1930s+] (N.Z.) many, much. [SWAG n.¹ (4)]

swag-shop n. [early–mid-19C] a shop that deals the wholesale of cheap, trashy articles. [SWAG n.¹ (6) + SE *shop*]

swagsman n. **1** [mid-19C] (Und.) one who takes the booty away after a successful burglary. **2** [late 19C–1900s] a receiver of stolen goods. [SWAG n.¹ (2)]

swag-trade n. [mid–late 19C] the trade in small, trivial or second-rate articles. [SWAG n.¹ (6)]

swailer n. [1960s+] (Und.) a cosh. [? dial. *swail*, to swing the arms while walking; thus to swing the cosh]

swain v. [1990s] (US) spontaneously to revoke or take back, as in words or actions.

swak adj. [20C] (S.Afr.) weak, feeble. [Du. *zwak*, feeble]

swalk phr. [20C] sealed with a loving kiss; usually found on the back of envelopes; other versions include *s.w.a.k.*, sealed with a kiss; *s.w.a.n.k.*, sealed with a nice kiss, and *s.w.a.l.c.a.k.w.s.*, sealed with a lick 'cos a kiss won't stick (cf. BOLTOP). [abbr.]

swallow n. **1** [19C] the throat. **2** [mid–late 19C] one's capacity for food. **3** [late 19C] a mouthful. **4** [20C] a puff of a cigarette.

swallow/swallow it v. [1920s+] **1** to accept, esp. a false story that one is told. **2** to abandon life as a professional criminal, to 'go straight'.

swallow a gudgeon, to phr. [late 16C–late 19C] to be duped, fooled (cf. GAPE FOR GUDGEONS). [GUDGEON]

swallow a hare, to phr. [late 17C–early 19C] to become very drunk. [? the drunkard may leap around like the animal; or SE *hair*, which must be washed down the throat]

swallow and sigh n. [20C] a collar and tie. [rhy. sl.]

swallow a sailor, to phr. [late 19C] (port/harbour) to get drunk on rum. [the naval predilection for rum]

swallow a spider, to phr. [mid–late 17C] to become bankrupt. [joc. use of SE; but no obvious reason]

swallow a stake/a stake and cannot bend, to phr. [late 17C–early 18C] to be a very upright, unbending person, both physically and in personality.

swallow a tavern token, to phr. [late 17C–18C] to become drunk. [SE *swallow* + *tavern token*, a token given as part of one's change; it can be used in payment for subsequent drinks]

swallow a watermelon seed, to phr. [20C] (US) to become pregnant. [one's expanding stomach]

swallow bobby v. [mid-19C] (Aus.) to make a false witness. [ety. unknown; ? link to BOBBY n. or dial. *bobby*, neat, smart]

swallower n. [1980s+] (drugs) a drug smuggler who swallows carefully wrapped drugs to take them through customs (cf. STUFFER n.²).

swallow it see SWALLOW v.

swallow one's spit, to phr. [1940s+] (W.I.) to keep quiet, to hold one's tongue.

swallow-pipe n. [20C] (W.I./Bdos.) the throat (cf. QUAIL PIPE).

swallowtail n. [mid–late 19C] a swallow-tailed coat (cf. CLAW-HAMMER).

swallow the apple/olive, to phr. [20C] (US) esp. of sports players, to become tense and unable to perform. [the lump in their throat]

swallow the Bible, to phr. [1930s] (US) to lie. [the use of the Bible when taking oaths]

swallow the dick, to phr. [late 19C+] to use long words. [abbr. *swallow the dictionary*]

swallow the olive see SWALLOW THE APPLE.

swally n. [1950s+] (Scot.) alcohol, a drink. [SE *swallow*]

swamp/swamp down v.¹ [mid-19C–1920s] (Aus.) to drink; thus *swamp a cheque*, to drink away one's entire pay cheque at one sitting. [SE *swamp*, to engulf in water]

swamp v.² [20C] (Aus.) to exchange, to barter. [? SE *swap*]

swamp v.³ [1960s+] (US prison) to arrest. [Scot. *swamped*, arrested]

swamp donkey n. [1990s] a very unattractive woman.

swamp down see SWAMP v.¹.

swamper n. **1** [mid-19C+] (US) an assistant to a driver of horses, mules or bullocks; thus [20C] a truck- or van-driver's assistant. **2** [late 19C+] (Aus.) one who travels on foot but has their pack carried on a wagon. **3** [1920s+] (Aus.) one who obtains a lift. [? logging jargon *swamper*, one who clears a way for the loggers to move through the woods]

swamp one's way/one's way with v. [1950s–60s] (Aus.) to travel, to travel with. [SWAMPER]

swamp-rat n. [20C] (US) a rural Southerner from the southern coastal states.

Swamps, the n. [1990s] (US Black teen) a derog. term for the Sunnydale projects in the southern part of San Francisco.

swan n. [1940s+] (orig. milit.) an apparently aimless wander, a trip made for pleasure or for looking around one's area. [SWAN ABOUT]

swan about/around v. [1940s+] (orig. milit.) to wander blithely and carelessly without a care in the world. [the image of a swan gliding over water]

swank n. **1** [mid-19C–1900s] arrogant, showing-off behaviour. **2** [late 19C] the tricks and stratagems one uses to deceive, one's 'game'. **3** [late 19C] insincere flattery. [SWANK v.]

swank adj. [1910s+] showy, vulgar, arrogant (cf. SWANKY adj.). [SWANK v.]

swank v. **1** [early 19C+] to swagger. **2** [mid-19C+] to boast. **3** [late 19C–1910s] to work hard at school or university.

[? OHG *swanc*, swing the body; orig. use as Midlands dial., then general sl. *c*.1900]

swankey *see* SWANKY n.

swankey swipes *see* SWANKY SWIPES.

swanking *n.* [20C] showing off, acting in an arrogant or vulgar manner. [SWANK v.]

swankpot *n.* [20C] a boaster, a braggart. [SWANK v. + weak use of POT n.⁶]

swanky/swankey *n.*¹ [mid-19C–1900s] table beer, weak beer (cf. SWIPES). [? Essex dial. *swank*, the last portion of liquor/ beer in a glass, enough for a single draught]

swanky/swankey *n.*² [mid–late 19C] an arrogant, showy, vulgar person. [SWANK v.]

swanky *adj.* [late 19C+] **1** smart, sophisticated, chic. **2** conceited, arrogant, vulgar, showy. [SWANK v.]

swanky/swankey swipes *n.* [mid-19C–1910s] weak beer. [SWANKY n.¹ + SWIPES]

swan lake *n.* [20C] a cake. [rhy. sl.]

Swannee River *n.* [20C] the liver, whether human or animal. [rhy. sl.]

Swannee Rivers/Swannees *n.* [20C] (Aus.) the shivers. [rhy. sl.]

swans *n.* [1990s] (drugs) MDMA (cf. DOVE; ECSTASY). [the picture of a *swan* stamped on some MDMA pills]

Swan Stream *n.* [mid-19C] Perth, Australia. [the city is on the Swan River]

swap/swop *n.* [mid-19C+] an act of exchange. [SWAP v.]

swap/swop *v.* **1** [mid-19C+] to exchange. **2** [mid-19C–1900s] to dismiss from a job. **3** [late 19C] (US) to cheat, to take in. **4** [1900s] to change one's clothes. [echoic *swap*, the sound of a slap; thus the slaps exchanged on sealing a bargain. Orig. Irish tinker's/horse-dealer's term, to *swap a bargain*, to strike a deal. Despite these origins, *swap* is now effectively SE]

swap cans *v.* [1960s+] (US prison) to take alternate active/ passive roles in anal intercourse. [SE *swap* + CAN n.⁴]

swapper/swopper *n.*¹ [late 17C–late 19C] one who effects swaps or exchanges. [SWAP v.]

swapper/swopper *n.*² [early 18C–early 19C] something large of its type, e.g. a barefaced lie. [SE *swap/swop*, to hit]

swapping/swopping *n.* [late 17C+] exchanging one thing for another, bartering. [SWAP v.]

swapping/swopping *adj.* [mid-19C+] very big, enormous, huge. [SWAPAPER n.²]

swap slob *v.* [20C] to French kiss (cf. SWAP SPIT). [abbr. SE *swap slobber*]

swap spit *v.* [20C] **1** to perform oral intercourse. **2** to kiss, usu. a French kiss (cf. SWAP SLOB).

swarfed *adj.* [1910s] dirty, soiled. [SE *swarf*, any fine waste produced by a machining operation]

swart varkie *n.* [1970s+] (S.Afr.) a 20-litre (35-pint) black plastic container, used for buying wine in bulk. [Afk. *swart*, black + *varkie*, a piglet; such bulk purchases were banned in July 1982]

swartzer *see* SCHWARTZE.

swash-bucket *n.* [late 19C] a slatternly woman. [SE *swash-bucket*, a receptacle for household rubbish; orig. dial.]

swassle-box *see* SWATCHEL-BOX.

swat *n.*¹ *see* SWOT n.

swat *n.*² [1920s+] (US) a heavy blow; thus *swat*, to hit. [northern dial.; the term had faded in UK before re-appearing in the US, most noticeably in the nickname of the big-hitting 1920s baseball star 'Babe' Ruth (1895–1948), the 'Sultan of Swat']

swat *v. see* SWOT v.

swatched *adj.* [1950s] tipsy. [? Warwickshire dial. *swatched*, of a woman, untidily dressed]

swatchel-/schwassle-/swassle-box *n.* [mid-19C] a Punch

and Judy show, esp. the booth in which it is performed. [showman's jargon *Swatchel*, Mr Punch; ult. *swatchel*, the distorting instrument a puppeteer holds in his mouth in order to produce Punch's characteristic squeaky tones or Ger. *schwätzeln*, usual form of *schwatzen*, to chatter, to tattle]

swatchel-cove *n.* [mid-19C–20C] a Punch and Judy man (cf. SWATCHEL-BOX). [for ety. *see* SWATCHEL-BOX + COVE]

swat flies *v.* [20C] (US tramp) to beg.

swattled *adj.* [19C] drunk (cf. BASTED). [SE *swat*]

swave *see* SUAVE.

swave and blaze *phr.* [1960s+] deliberate mispron. of *suave* and *blasé*.

swear *n.*¹ [late 19C] **1** an oath. **2** an outburst of obscenities. [SE *swear*]

swear *n.*² [late 19C] a harsh noise made by a dog or cat or occas. a bird. [SWEAR v.¹]

swear *v.*¹ [early 19C–1900s] to make a harsh or guttural sound, like a dog or cat.

swear/swear at *v.*² [late 19C] of colours, to clash.

swear and curse/cuss *n.* [20C] a bus. [rhy. sl.]

swear at *see* SWEAR v.².

swear blind *v.* [1960s+] to affirm emphatically and without qualification. [SE *swear* + BLIND adj.²]

swear by *v.* [early 19C+] to accept as the truth, to have complete faith in.

swearing apartment *n.* [late 19C] the street. [the disapproval of swearing, however unlikely this may seem, found inside taverns and public houses]

swear like a cutter, to *phr.* [mid-16C–17C] to swear with great vehemence. [SE *swear* + CUTTER n.¹]

swear off *v.* [late 19C+] to give up, to abandon, to renounce. [? one's oath of self-denial]

swear on a stack of Bibles/of Bibles a mile high, to *phr.* [mid-19C+] (orig. US) to make an elaborate or exaggerated oath, usu. in the face of another's disbelief.

swear pink *v.* [1950s] to make vehement statements. [SE *swear* + PINK adj.²]

swear-up *n.* [20C] an argument heavily punctuated by 'bad language' (cf. PUNCH-UP; SWINE-UP).

sweat *n.*¹ [18C] a form of amusement practised by such street gangs as the Mohocks, who surrounded a victim, pricking him with their swords and thus keeping him 'dancing' until through his exertions he had sweated sufficiently; thus *sweater*, one who practised this urban terrorism.

sweat *n.*² [1920s+] a problem, a worry, a struggle, anything that works up real or fig. sweat (cf. NO SWEAT!). [SWEAT v.²]

sweat *v.*¹ **1** [late 16C] to spend money. **2** [late 18C–early 19C] (Und.) to lighten gold coins by immersing them in acid. **3** [late 18C–early 19C] to pawn. **4** [early–mid-19C] to remove some of the contents of. **5** [mid-19C] to deprive someone of something. **6** [mid-19C–1940s] (Aus.) to borrow (usu. a horse) without its owner's permission. **7** [mid-19C+] to extract money, usu. through menaces or violence (cf. BLEED v.¹). **8** [late 19C] to squander money, whether one's own or someone else's. **9** [late 19C] (Und.) to melt down the solder that holds together an otherwise impenetrable strong-box.

sweat *v.*² **1** [mid-18C+] to put someone, esp. a prisoner, under pressure. **2** [late 18C] (Irish) to deprive of. **3** [1960s+] (orig. US) to worry about, to take trouble over. **4** [1970s+] (US Black) to proposition.

sweat *v.*³ [late 19C+] to work very hard.

sweat/sweat on *v.*⁴ [1920s+] (US) to be near to attaining, to wait for.

sweat a cheque, to *phr.* [late 19C] (Aus./N.Z.) to spend all one's pay on drink.

sweat blood *v.* [1910s+] **1** to work very hard, esp. in phr. *don't sweat it*, don't worry. **2** to be terrified.

sweat-box *n*. **1** [late 19C] a cell for prisoners waiting to appear in a magistrate's court. **2** [late 19C] (US) the upper gallery of a theatre. **3** [late 19C+] a room, usu. in a police station, in which prisoners undergo interrogation. **4** [20C] (orig. US) an oppressively small cell. **5** [1980s+] a prison van, used to transport prisoners from court to prison etc. [note 'The original "sweat box" used during the period following the (US) Civil War … was a cell in close proximity to a stove, in which a scorching fire was built and fed with old bones, pieces of rubber shoes etc, all to make great heat and offensive smells, until the sickened and perspiring inmate of the cell confessed in order to get released' (deposition to the Rep. Nat. Comm. Law Observance & Enforcement, 1931)]

sweat bullets *v*. [1950s+] (US) **1** to worry excessively. **2** to work very hard.

sweat cobs *v*. [1950s+] to perspire very heavily. [SE *sweat* + *cob*, a rounded lump, but cf. HAVE A COB ON]

sweat drink *n*. [1960s+] (Irish) a trad. 'after-work' drink. [one is still sweating from one's labours]

sweat duds *v*. [19C] to pawn one's clothes. [SWEAT v.¹ (3) + DUDS]

sweater *n*. [mid-19C] a hard, demanding job. [SE *sweat*]

sweat hog *n*. [1970s+] (US campus) **1** an exceptionally difficult student, singled out at school or college for special attention. **2** an exceptionally unattractive woman. **3** a sexually promiscuous woman (cf. DIRTY LEG). [SE *sweat* + SE *hog*/HOG n.⁷]

sweat it out *see* SWEAT OUT.

sweat like a bull/a pig, to *phr*. [late 19C+] to perspire profusely.

sweat like a nigger/a nigger at election, to *phr*. [1900s–50s] (US) to sweat profusely. [NIGGER n.]

sweat like a pig *see* SWEAT LIKE A BULL.

sweat on *see* SWEAT v.⁴.

sweat one's guts out, to *phr*. [late 19C+] to work to one's utmost.

sweat one's tail off *see* WORK ONE'S TAIL OFF.

sweat on the top line, to *phr*. [1910s+] (Aus.) to be within a touch of obtaining what one desires. [SWEAT ON + the 'lines' that must be filled in the game of lotto or bingo]

sweat out/sweat it out *v*. [mid-19C+] (orig. US) to endure hardships and difficulties in the hope of achieving solutions or successes in the end.

sweat pads *n*. [1940s+] (Can.) pancakes.

sweat-rag *n*. [mid-19C+] (US) a rag used for wiping the sweat from one's eyes.

sweats *n*. [1930s+] (drugs) the sweating that is one of a heroin addict's withdrawal symptoms; thus *sweat cure*, the sudden and unsupported withdrawal from drugs, *sweat it out*, to withdraw from drug use by sudden and complete abstention.

sweat something out of *v*. [late 19C] (US) to extract information from someone, usu. by intimidation.

sweat the fence, to *phr*. [20C] (US prison) to fantasize about escape. [SWEAT v.² + SE *fence*]

sweaty *adj*. [1910s+] of a task, harsh, demanding; also in fig. use.

sweaty sock *n*. [20C] a Scot. [rhy. sl. *sweaty sock* = JOCK n.¹]

sweaty-toe *n*. [20C] cheese. [the smell]

sweave *v*. [1980s+] (US campus) to *swerve* and *weave* when drunk or drugged.

swede *n*.¹ [20C] (US) a blunderer. [the stereotype of Swedish immigrants as strong but stupid]

swede *n*.² [1920s] the head; thus *crash/crash down the swede*, *set the swede down*, to go to sleep (cf. BEAN n.⁴).

swede *n*.³ [1970s+] an ignorant country person; thus [1950s+] *Swedeland*, the countryside, [late 19C+] *swede talk*, rural talk (cf. CARROT CRUNCHER). [SE *swede* (US rutabaga). The urban

conception of the country's main product, foodstuff etc; thus *Swedey*, Metropolitan Police nickname (punning on SWEENEY n.¹) for Operation Countryman, an investigation into corruption carried out by officers of rural and provincial forces]

swede *adj*. [1960s] rural, unsophisticated. [SWEDE n.³]

swede-basher *n*. [1930s+] a country bumpkin, an unsophisticated peasant. [ext. of SWEDE n.³]

swedge *n*. [20C] (Scot.) a fight. [? SE *swedge*, a type of chisel with a bevelled edge, orig. used for making a groove around a horseshoe and latterly used for various jobs requiring the bend of cold metal]

Swedish *n*. [1960s+] **1** mutual masturbation. **2** the use of rubber garments in sex. [the companionship and the sweating one experiences in a Swedish sauna bath]

Swedish *adj*. [1990s] (US) homosexual. [? misreading of the sex-change operations carried out in Denmark]

Swedish culture *n*. [1960s+] the use of rubber, PVC etc in sex (cf. AMERICAN CULTURE). [SWEDISH n. (2)]

Swedish fiddle *n*. [late 19C+] (US) an accordion. [its popularity among Swedish immigrants]

Swedish headache *n*. [1960s+] (US) intense sexual frustration. [? a problem of Swedish immigrants]

sweedle *v*. [1910s–30s] to trick with flattery, to 'sweet-talk'. [SE *swindle* + *wheedle*]

Sweeney, the *n*.¹ [1930s+] the Flying Squad; thus *sweenies*, members of the Flying Squad. [rhy. sl. *Sweeney Todd*]

sweeney *n*.² [1960s+] a barber. [the fictional *Sweeney Todd*, the 'demon barber' of Fleet Street, who sold 'golophshious' pies made from the flesh of those he had murdered]

sweep *n*. [mid-19C–1900s] an unpleasant person. [SE *chimney sweep* whose job, if not person, is regarded as unpleasant]

sweep one's own doorstep, to *phr*. [20C] (US) to mind one's own business.

sweep's frill *n*. [late 19C] a beard and whiskers that run round the line of the chin, leaving the rest of the face clean-shaven. [such facial hair was typical of a sweep]

sweep's trot *n*. [mid-19C] a high-stepping form of amble, the best way to carry the sweep's load of brushes etc.

sweet *n*. [1970s] (US Black) a male homosexual. [play on SUGAR n.⁷]

sweet *adj*.¹ [early 18C–early 19C] dextrous, expert.

sweet *adj*.² **1** [early 18C–early 19C] gullible. **2** [1930s+] amenable, usu. in phr. *keep someone sweet*, to keep someone well-disposed towards oneself, esp. by complaisance or bribery.

sweet *adj*.³ **1** [late 18C+] a general term of approval, applicable to people, objects, actions and events. **2** [late 19C+] (orig. Aus.) excellent, perfect, simple, correct, in order, also used neg., e.g. a *sweet mess* (cf. HANDSOME!; RIGHT!).

sweet *adj*.⁴ (W.I.) **1** [1940s] tipsy, slightly drunk. **2** [1950s] of a man, fashionably dressed, dandified.

sweet *adj*.⁵ [1950s–70s] effeminate.

sweet *adv*. [20C] without any problems, easily.

sweet air *n*. [1980s+] nitrous oxide.

sweet as a nut *phr*. [late 19C+] (Und.) easy, simple, no problems, delightful, esp. of a robbery or other 'job'.

sweet b.a. *phr*. [1940s+] nothing at all (cf. B.A. phr.; SWEET FANNY ADAMS). [abbr. *sweet bugger all*]

sweetback/sweetback man *n*. [1900s–60s] (US Black) a womanizer, a ladies' man. [his physique, which women like to touch]

sweet bleeding Jesus! *excl*. [20C] a general excl.

sweetbread *n*. [mid–late 17C] a bribe. [SE *sweetbread*, the pancreas, or thymus gland, of an animal, a delicacy]

sweet briar *n*. [17C] the female pubic hair (cf. BUSH n.⁴).

sweetcakes *n*. [1980s+] (US gay) the buttocks.

sweetcheeks *n*. [1980s+] (US gay) the buttocks.

sweet cop n. [1910s+] (Aus.) a pleasant, enviable situation (cf. SOFT COP). [SWEET adj.² + COP n.²]

sweetcorn shiner n. [1990s] a male homosexual. [coarse ref. to sodomy]

sweet daddy n. [20C] (US Black) a lover or any man who provides for a woman (cf. COOL PAPA; DADDY ONE; SUGAR DADDY). [SE sweet + DADDY n. (7)]

sweet damn all phr. [1940s+] nothing whatsoever (cf. SWEET B.A.; SWEET FANNY ADAMS).

sweet dreams n. [1980s+] (drugs) heroin. [the comatose state it induces]

sweeten v.¹ (Und.) 1 [late 16C+] to lure, to decoy, to swindle, to flatter. 2 [18C] to calm a suspicious victim. 3 [18C+] to bribe.

sweeten/sweeten the pot v.² [late 19C+] to make a proposition more alluring. [poker jargon to add money to a pot, to raise the betting]

sweetener/sweetner n.¹ [late 17C–early 19C] (Und.) one who poses as an innocent player in order to ensnare a genuine innocent into playing a game in which he will invariably find himself the defrauded loser.

sweetener/sweetner n.² [late 17C–early 19C] (Und.) a rogue who specializes in dropping something supposedly valuable where it will be found by a potential victim, who is either lured into a game or persuaded to buy the 'valuable', while the con-man claims that although they should, by rights, share the profits, he will sell his share and let the victim have the whole benefit (cf. GOLD-DROPPER).

sweeteners n. [late 19C] (Und.) the lips (cf. FAKE THE SWEETENERS).

sweetening n. [late 17C–mid-19C] a confidence trick based on deliberately dropping a guinea and swindling the dupe who picks it up. [ext. of SWEETENER n.²]

sweeten the pot see SWEETEN v.².

sweet-eye n. [20C] (W.I.) a lustful glance or wink; thus make sweet-eye, to glance in this way, get sweet-eye, for a woman to receive such a glance.

sweet Fanny Adams/Miss Adams phr. [1910s+] absolutely nothing at all (cf. S.F.A.). [euph. for sweet fuck all; the identity of Fanny Adams remains a mystery and is presumably based only on the initial letters]

sweet fucking Jesus! excl. [20C] (US) an expletive with no particular meaning, conveying annoyance and surprise.

sweetheart and bag-pudding n. [17C–early 18C] a woman whom one has made pregnant.

sweetheart contract/deal n. [1950s+] (orig. US) 1 a union-employer contract that favours the company over its employees. 2 a union-employer contract that favours all those negotiating, but not the workers the union supposedly represents.

sweetheart life n. [1950s] (W.I.) the state of living together but not being married.

sweetie n. 1 [1920s+] (orig. US) a boy- or girlfriend. 2 [1920s+] a term of address, not necessarily implying intimacy. 3 [1970s+] used ironically to mean an unpleasant person, e.g. He's a real sweetie. 4 [1970s+] an effeminate homosexual.

sweetie-pie n. [20C] a general term of affection.

sweet Jesus n. [1960s+] (drugs) 1 morphine. 2 heroin. [the addict's 'saviour']

sweet Jesus! excl. [20C] a mild, if blasphemous, oath (cf. SWEET BLEEDING JESUS!; SWEET FUCKING JESUS!).

sweet kid/sweetmeat n. [1960s+] (Can. prison) a younger prisoner who joins up with an older man.

sweet-lips n. [late 19C–1900s] a glutton.

sweet Lucy n. (drugs) 1 [1940s] hashish dissolved into wine.

2 [1960s] marijuana. 3 [1960s] barbiturates dissolved into muscatel wine.

sweet mack n. [1960s+] a pimp who treats his women well (cf. SUGAR PIMP). [SE sweet + MACK n.¹]

sweet mama n. [1950s+] (US Black) a Black man's female lover. [SE sweet + MAMA]

sweetman n. [1960s+] 1 (Und.) a pimp who runs only one prostitute and lives off her earnings alone. 2 (US Black) a male lover. 3 (W.I.) a married woman's lover, to whom she gives money and presents.

sweetmeat n.¹ [mid–late 19C] 1 an underage prostitute. 2 a mistress. [SE sweet + MEAT n. (1)]

sweetmeat n.² see SWEET KID.

sweetmeat n.³ [1980s+] (US gay) the penis (cf. LADIES' LOLLIPOP). [SE sweet + MEAT n. (2) + pun]

sweet Miss Adams see SWEET FANNY ADAMS.

sweet morpheus n. [1970s+] (drugs) morphine. [Morpheus, the Greek god of dreams; the root of morphine]

sweetmouth n. [mid-19C+] (W.I.) 1 a flatterer, a persuasive person. 2 flattery, persuasiveness.

sweetmouth adj. [1950s] (W.I.) greedy, gluttonous.

sweetmouth v. [1940s+] (orig. US Black) to flatter. [SWEET-MOUTH n.]

sweetner see SWEETENER.

sweetness and light n. [20C] (Aus.) whisky.

sweet nothings n. [20C] sentimental trivia, esp. the clichés of seduction.

sweet on adj. [late 17C+] in love with, infatuated by (cf. SUGAR ON).

sweet papa n. [1920s+] (US Black) a man who provides for the material wants of his lover (cf. SUGAR DADDY; SWEET DADDY).

sweet patootie n. [1920s+] a woman, a girlfriend. [SE sweet + PATOOTIE n.¹]

sweetpea n.¹ [19C] 1 whisky. 2 tea. 3 urine. [rhy. sl.; (3) sweet-pea = PEE n.¹. Note (1) E.P. suggests 'the colour of the resulting urine']

sweet pea n.² [1930s] a girl- or boyfriend.

sweet pimp see SUGAR PIMP.

sweet poppa n. [1900s–50s] a male lover (cf. COOL PAPA; DADDY ONE).

sweet potato pie n. [1980s+] (US Black) 1 an attractive young man or woman (cf. BANANA n.²). 2 male or female genitals (cf. CABBAGE n.⁷). 3 a general term of endearment. [the common equation of sex and food]

sweets n. [1960s+] (drugs) amphetamines (cf. A n.²). [resemblance]

sweet stuff n. [1930s–40s] (drugs) 1 heroin. 2 cocaine. [SE sweet + STUFF n.⁵ (2)]

sweet sugar see SUGAR DADDY.

sweet talk v. [1930s+] (orig. US Black) 1 to persuade, to charm, to lull into false confidence. 2 spec. to seduce.

sweet-tooth n. [1960s] (US drugs) a craving for, or addiction to, narcotics (cf. SWEET STUFF).

swell n. [late 18C+] 1 an aristocrat, a sophisticated, stylish, rich person; thus swellism, the world of a 'swell', swellness, being a 'swell' (cf. HEAVY SWELL). 2 the outstanding member of any profession or occupation. [for the connoisseur of such gradations, the swell differed from the older aristocracy in the need and capacity for display; the aristocracy had position but no fashion, the swell had fashion and used it to win position, but his social position might be fractionally less grand. In time he, or at least his children, might attain the absolute social peaks]

swell adj. [early 19C+] (orig. Und.) 1 excellent, wonderful, delightful; thus swell article, anything of high quality, swell crib, a genteel house. 2 showy, ostentatious, usu. as regards dress; thus *swell mollisher*, a very well-dressed woman etc. [SWELL n.; 20C use mainly US]

swell *adv.* [1920s+] (US) very well, excellently, kindly.

swell dona *n.* [late 19C] a lower-class woman affecting airs of grandeur. [SWELL adj. + DONA]

swelled-head *see* SWELLHEAD n.¹.

swell-fencer *n.* [mid-19C] a street-seller of needles. [SWELL n. + FENCER; needles are required for the tailoring that garbs a swell]

swellhead/swelled-head *n.*¹ [mid-19C+] a braggart, a boaster, a show-off. [backform. of SWELL-HEADED]

swellhead *n.*² **1** [late 19C] a drunkard. **2** [1960s+] (US Black) one who has passed out through drug use. [SE *swell* + *head*]

swellhead *n.*³ [20C] conceit, arrogance. [backform. of SWELL-HEADED]

swell-headed *adj.* [early 19C+] arrogant, conceited. [SE *swell* + *head*]

swell hung in chains *n.* [mid-19C] a rich or ostentatious man given to wearing quantities of jewellery. [SWELL n.]

swellish *adj.* [19C] **1** fashionably dressed. **2** gentlemanly. [SWELL n.]

swell mob *n.* [mid-19C] leading pickpockets whose dress reflects their success (as well as facilitating their entry into the wealthy world on which they prey). [SWELL adj. + MOB n.¹]

swell mobsman *n.* [mid–late 19C] a leading pickpocket. [SWELL MOB]

swell-nose *n.* [early 16C–18C] strong beer. [its effects]

swell's lush *n.* [mid–late 19C] (Aus.) champagne. [SWELL n. + LUSH n.¹ (1)]

Swell Street *n.* [mid-19C] the West End of London (cf. LIVE IN SWELL STREET). [SWELL n. + SE *street*]

swell-up *n.* [1980s+] (drugs) crack cocaine. [ety. unknown]

swelp me davy!/taters!/ten me! *see* SWOP ME BOB!

swelter *n.* [late 19C] hot, hard work.

swept *adj.* [1910s+] (N.Z.) totally without money. [it has been *swept away*]

swep'/swept *adj.* [1980s+] (US Black) sexually or emotionally obsessed with. [abbr. SE phr. *swept off one's feet*]

swerve *v.* [1950s+] (Aus.) to practise coitus interruptus. [one 'avoids a child']

swerver *n.* [1990s] (US Black teen) an automobile.

swi *see* SWY.

swift *adj.* **1** [late 19C+] sexually forward. **2** [1970s+] smart, clever, cunning. **3** [1970s+] of a policeman, carrying out any illegal activities, esp. during an arrest.

swiftie/swifty *n.*¹ [1940s+] (Aus./N.Z.) a hoax, a fraud, a deception, esp. in phr. *pull a swiftie*, to deceive (cf. PULL A FAST ONE; ROUGHIE).

swiftie/swifty *n.*² [1940s+] (US) one who moves fast, either physically or mentally.

swiftly flow *v.* [late 19C–1900s] (Aus.) to go. [rhy. sl.]

swift 'un *n.* [1950s+] (Und.) corrupt police procedure when arresting a suspect (cf. BIT SWIFT; SWIFT). [SWIFT adj. (3)]

swifty *see* SWIFTIE.

swig *n.* [mid-16C–mid-17C] a drink. [ety. unknown; ? Nor. *svik*, a tap (Weakley)]

swig *v.* [late 17C+] to drink, to gulp down. [SWIG n.]

swigged *adj.* [mid–late 19C] tipsy. [SWIG v.]

swiggled *adj.* [19C] drunk. [SWIG v.]

swigman *n.* [16C] (Und.) a criminal beggar, posing as a legitimate pedlar (cf. IRISH TOYLE). [? unrecorded early use of SWAG n.¹]

swill *n.* [20C] (orig. US) unpleasant food or drink. [? SE *swill*, kitchen refuse]

swill *v.* [late 18C+] to drink heavily. [SE *swill*, to drink heavily; from 1916 to 1955 New South Wales pubs took 'last orders' at 6 p.m. and the resultant rush of the all-male drinkers was

termed the SIX O'CLOCK SWILL; other states maintained the law for longer]

'swill! *excl.* [early 17C] a mild oath, lit. 'by God's will' (cf. 's abbr.¹).

swilled *adj.* [16C] drunk. [SE *swill*, heavy drinking]

swillery *n.* [1940s+] (Aus.) a hotel with a bar. [SWILL v.]

swill like a tinker, to *phr.* [late 17C–early 19C] to drink to excess. [SE *swill*]

swill tub *n.* [early 18C–early 19C] a drunkard. [SE *swill* + SE *swill tub*, a refuse container]

swim *n.* [mid-19C–1900s] a scheme, a plan; thus *in a good swim*, having a spell of good luck. [SE *swim*, a section of river well stocked with fish]

swim *v.*¹ [early 19C+] to experience a dizzy, giddy feeling, e.g. *one's head is swimming*.

swim *v.*² [20C] (US) to perform well, to succeed.

swim in golden grease/lard/oil, to *phr.* [17C] to be offered and to take an abundance of bribes.

swimmer *n.*¹ [late 17C–18C] (Und.) a counterfeit coin. [? the metal used was light enough to float]

swimmer *n.*² [early 19C] **1** a tender or guard-ship. **2** a thief who escapes a prison sentence by enlisting in the Royal Navy.

swimmer *n.*³ [1920s+] a bathing costume.

swimmers *n.* [1920s+] (Aus.) a bathing costume.

swindle *n.* **1** [19C] tossing to decide who pays for the next round of drinks. **2** [mid–late 19C] a disappointment, something that proves to be a fraud and not what it was advertised as being. **3** [late 19C] a lottery. **4** [late 19C] (US) the cost, the bill, esp. in phr. *what's the swindle?* (cf. DAMAGE).

swindler *n.* [mid-18C–early 19C] (Und.) a trickster, a fraud. [Yid. *schwindeln*, to be giddy, to act thoughtlessly or extravagantly, to swindle. Orig. Und. and supposedly imported to the UK by German Jewish immigrants *c.*1762, it entered SE during the 19C]

swindle sheet *n.* [1920s+] (orig. US) an expense account. [orig. boxing use, the accounts made up by a manager and shown to his fighter. Bitter fighters felt that these were rarely relevant to the actual money involved]

swine *n.* [1930s+] anything considered as difficult or exhausting to achieve (cf. PIG n.⁶).

swine-eater *n.* [1950s+] (US Black Muslim) a White person. [the Muslim prohibition on pig products]

swine-hound *n.* [1910s] a term of abuse. [lit. trans. of Ger. insult *Schweinhund*]

swine-up *n.* [early 19C–1900s] (orig. US) an argument (cf. PUNCH-UP; SWEAR-UP). [pigs are supposedly ill-tempered]

swing, the *n.*¹ [late 18C–mid-19C] the gallows. [SWING v.¹]

swing *n.*² [1910s+] (US) **1** a rest period between two shifts. **2** time-off, leave.

swing/swing party *n.*³ [1970s+] (orig. US) an orgy, esp. when the participants are husband-and-wife swapping couples. [SWING v.⁵]

swing *n.*⁴ [1980s+] (US Black) stimulation, excitement, something that makes things 'go with a swing'.

swing *v.*¹ **1** [mid-16C+] to hang (cf. SWING IN A HALTER). **2** [early 19C] to have someone hanged.

swing/swing over *v.*² [1920s–50s] to turn the starting handle of an automobile.

swing/swing it *v.*³ [1930s+] to cope, to deal with a situation, to make sure that things work out as one desires, often through trickery/deception/manipulation.

swing *v.*⁴ [1950s+] (US) to be a member of a teenage street gang.

swing *v.*⁵ [1960s+] **1** (gay) to achieve the supreme level of well-being and satisfaction. **2** to arrange and participate in husband-and-wife swapping parties (cf. SWING n.³). **3** to carry on an affair with someone. **4** to enjoy an active and varied sex life, to have sexual intercourse. **5** to enjoy oneself, to have a good time. **7** of a party, to go well, to be enjoyable.

swing *v.*[6] [1970s+] (gay) to fellate.

swing a bag, to *phr.* [1920s+] (Aus.) to work as a street-walker (cf. BAG-SWINGER). [the prostitute's inevitable handbag]

swing both ways/either way *phr.* [1960s+] to practise bisexuality. [SWING v.[5]]

swing daddy *n.* [1970s+] (US Black) **1** an attractive, well-dressed man. **2** a male lover. [SWING v.[5] + DADDY (7)]

swingdog *n.* [1990s] (US teen) a fashionable dresser. [SWING v.[5] + DOG n.[9]]

swinge *v.* **1** [early 16C–mid-17C] to drink up, to drink off. **2** [17C] to have sexual intercourse (cf. BANG v.[1]; SWIVE). [SE *swinge*, to beat, to castigate]

swingeing/swinging *adj.* [late 16C+] a general intensifier, very large, very forceful, very powerful. [SE *swinge*, to beat; SE in 20C, typically as *swingeing cuts* in the health budget]

swing either way *see* SWING BOTH WAYS.

swinge off/up *v.* **1** [early 16C–mid-17C] to toss down a drink. **2** [17C–18C] to infect with a bad case of venereal disease. [ext. of SWINGE v.]

swinger *n.*[1] **1** [late 16C–late 19C] anything notably large or forceful of its type. **2** [late 17C–18C] an outrageous lie (cf. WHOPPER). **3** [1920s+] (Aus.) an admirable person.

swinger *n.*[2] [1960s+] (orig. US) **1** one who leads an active and varied sex life. **2** one who participates in husband-and-wife swapping parties. [SWING v.[5] (4), (2)]

swingers *n.* **1** [19C] the testicles. **2** [1920s+] (Aus.) the female breasts, esp. when unsupported but still firm.

swinge someone's jacket *see* TRIM SOMEONE'S JACKET.

swinge up *see* SWINGE OFF.

swing for/for one *phr.* [19C] a general threat. [SWING v.[1]. The implication that the speaker is willing to commit murder to get what they want and thus face the gallows]

swing in a halter, to *phr.* [mid–late 16C] to be hanged. [ext. of SWING v.[1]]

swinging *n.*[1] [late 16C–late 19C] hanging. [SWING v.[1]]

swinging *n.*[2] [1960s+] indulging in husband-and-wife swapping parties (cf. SWINGING adj.[4]). [SWING v.[5] (2)]

swinging *adj.*[1] *see* SWINGEING.

swinging *adj.*[2] [late 18C–19C] a general intensifier, e.g. *swinging fellow*, a very large man, *swinging lie*, an outrageous lie (cf. SWINGER n.[1]).

swinging *adj.*[3] [1950s+] **1** uninhibited, lively, fashionable, esp. in phr. *swinging* London, *swinging '60s*. **2** a general term of approval (cf. DODGY adj.[1]). [SE *swing* + SWING v.[5]]

swinging *adj.*[4] [1960s+] referring to those who participate in husband-and-wife swapping parties or those who enjoy a promiscuous sex life (cf. SWINGING n.[2]). [SWING v.[5] (2)]

swinging! *excl.* [1950s–60s] (orig. US Black) a general term of approval. [the term migrated to UK as the catchphrase of entertainer Norman Vaughan, compere of television's *Saturday Night at the London Palladium*, who alternated the positive *swinging* with the negative DODGY adj.[1]]

swinging dick *n.* [1960s+] (US) a person, usu. in phr. *every swinging dick*. [SE *swinging* + DICK n.[5] (1). Popularized in Tom Wolfe's novel *Bonfire of the Vanities* (1987) where *big swinging dicks* was used to characterize the most successful of Wall Street's financial wheeler-dealers]

swinging on the meat *phr.* [1940s] (US) overly anxious to please.

swinging single/swingle *n.* [1960s+] (US) a sexually promiscuous unmarried person. [SWING v.[5]]

swinging the stick *n.* [mid-19C] robbery with violence (cf. BLUDGEON BUSINESS).

swing it *see* SWING v.[3].

swing it on across *v.* [20C] (mainly Aus./N.Z.) to deceive, to impose on, to do a bad turn. [SWING v.[3]]

swingle *see* SWINGING SINGLE.

swing like sixty, to *phr.* [1960s+] (US teen) to perform at one's peak, to achieve ultimate success or pleasure (cf. GO ALONG LIKE SIXTY). [SWING v.[5] + LIKE SIXTY]

swing low *v.* [1990s] (US Black teen) to have oral sex. [SWING v.[5] + SE *low*]

swing man *n.* [1970s] a drug dealer. [? he makes things go *with a swing*]

swing of the door *n.* [1930s] the seventh drink of a session, supposedly the very last one has before leaving the pub (cf. BINDER n.[2]; FINAL; ONE FOR THE BITUMEN; OTHER HALF; SAME AGAIN).

swing-out *n.* [1950s–60s] (US Black) a violent street fight between rival urban gangs. [SWING v.[4]]

swing over *see* SWING v.[2].

swing party *see* SWING n.[3].

swing-tail *n.* [late 18C–early 19C] a hog (cf. SWISH-TAIL).

swing the bag, to *phr.* [1960s+] (Aus.) of a bookmaker, to take bets at a racetrack. [the bookmaker's money *bag*]

swing the billy/pot, to *phr.* [1920s+] (Aus.) to light a fire under one's billy or cooking pot preparatory to making a cup of tea.

swing the dice, to *phr.* [1990s] (US Black) to accept that much of life is a matter of luck and to live it accordingly.

swing the gate, to *phr.* [1930s+] (Aus.) to work hard, to do well, to win in a contest (cf. DRAG THE CHAIN). [sheep-shearing jargon]

swing the lead, to *phr.* [1910s+] **1** (orig. milit.) to malinger, to avoid one's duties. **2** to brag, to boast. [the image is of a leadsman, taking soundings from a ship, but that job is skilful rather than easy]

swing with *v.*[1] [1960s+] to enjoy, to appreciate. [SWING v.[5]]

swing with *v.*[2] [1960s+] to ally oneself to a group, to agree with a concept.

swinny *adj.* [19C] drunk. [dial. *swinny*, giddy]

swip *n.* [1920s–50s] **1** (US) a groom or stableboy. **2** an objectionable person. **3** objectionable people considered collectively. [? obs. SE *swip*, to hit, to slip away]

swipe *n.*[1] **1** [20C] cheap, inferior, home-brewed alcohol. **2** [1920s–50s] (US) an unpleasant, objectionable person.

swipe *n.*[2] [1950s–70s] (US Black) the penis (cf. ARSE-OPENER). [? SE *swipe*, to hit, or abbr. KIDNEY-WIPER]

swipe *v.*[1] [19C] to drink hastily and copiously (cf. SWIPES).

swipe *v.*[2] [late 19C+] (orig. US) to steal. [SE *swipe*, to strike]

swiper *n.* [mid-19C] a heavy drinker. [SWIPE v.[1]]

swipes *n.* **1** [late 18C–late 19C] weak beer (cf. SWIPEY adj.). **2** [late 18C–late 19C] any beer. **3** [early–mid-19C] a public-house potman. [naut. jargon *swipes*, weak or 'small' beer furnished by the purser; a sailor was allowed 4 quarts (4.5 litres) a day, but the quality was atrocious; ult. SWIPE v.[1]]

swipey *n.* [mid-19C] a brewery drayman. [SWIPES]

swipey *adj.* [late 18C–late 19C] drunk, tipsy (cf. ALED UP). [SWIPES]

swipington/swippington *n.* [20C] (Aus.) a drunkard. [SWIPES + LUSHINGTON]

swips *v.* [1950s] (W.I.) to drink off at a single draught, to 'knock back'. [SWIPE v.[1]]

swish *n.*[1] [1930s] soda water, e.g. *Scotch and swish*.

swish *n.*[2] [1930s+] (orig. US) **1** a homosexual man. **2** his effeminate style. [SWISH v.[2]]

swish *n.*[3] [1980s+] (N.Z. prison) abuse, harassment, heckling. [SE *swish*, echoic of cane used in corporal punishment]

swish *adj.*[1] [20C] fancy, elegant, 'posh'. [? the SE *swishing* of a fashionable woman's dress]

swish *adj.*[2] [1930s+] effeminate. [SWISH v.[2]]

swish v.[1] [mid-19C+] (teen) to cane; thus *swishing*, a caning. [the sound of the cane]

swish v.[2] [1930s+] of a man, to act in an effeminate manner. [SE *swish*, to move with a swish]

swish v.[3] [1980s+] (N.Z. drugs) to distribute or sell drugs, esp. in phr. *swish on luckies*, to distribute or sell LSD or DMA (a designer hallucinogen).

swish! excl. [1920s] a disdainful, ironic excl., is that it? is that all?

Swish Alps n. [1950s–60s] (US gay) a gay area in the Hollywood Hills (cf. BOYSTOWN; JEWISH ALPS). [play on SWISH adj.[2]/*Swiss*]

swished/switched adj. [mid-19C] married. [? fig. use of SWISH v.[1]/SE *switch*, to whip]

swish-tail n. [late 18C–late 19C] a pheasant (cf. SWING-TAIL).

swishy adj. [1940s+] effeminate, exhibiting the supposed characteristics of a male homosexual. [SWISH n.[2]]

Swiss adj. [1970s+] (US teen) neutral, of no specific opinion. [the trad. role of the Swiss in international relations]

Swiss itch n. [1960s] a popular method of drinking tequila, one places a pinch of salt on the back of the hand, licks it off, drinks down a shot of tequila and immediately bites into a segment or a slice of lime. [ety. unknown; ? anecdotal]

swissy adj. [1990s] (US teen) bizarre, fashionable, daring.

switch n.[1] [1930s+] an exchange, esp. when it involves criminal deception. [SE *switch*, to swap]

switch n.[2] [1940s–60s] (US) a *switch*-blade knife. [abbr.]

switch v. [17C] to have sexual intercourse (cf. BANG v.[1]). [SE *switch*, to whip]

switched see SWISHED.

switched off adj. [1960s+] (orig. US) unfashionable, unconventional (cf. SWITCHED ON).

switched on adj. [1960s+] (orig. US) **1** intoxicated by drugs. **2** sexually stimulated. **3** aware, sophisticated, up to the minute (cf. TURNED ON). [SWITCH ON]

switcher n. [20C] (US) one who swaps one thing for another. [SE *switch*]

switcheroo n. [20C] (US) the opposite, the reverse. [SE *switch* + sfx. -EROO]

switch-hitter n. [1950s+] (US) a bisexual. [baseball jargon *switch-hitter*, an ambidextrous batter]

switching n. [mid-late 19C] a marriage. [? fig. use of SE *switch*, to whip]

switch off! excl. [1900s–20s] shut up! be quiet! [electrical imagery]

switch on v. [1960s+] **1** (US drugs) to become intoxicated by drugs. **2** (US) to excite, to arouse sexually. **3** (US) to participate in the latest cultural trends (cf. TURN ON). [electrical imagery]

swive v. [18C] to have sexual intercourse. [OE *swifan*, to move in a course + ON *svifa*, to rove, to ramble, to drift. Coined c.1440, *swive* was SE until c.1700. Like a number of 'obscenities' it is not genuine sl., but was for many years excluded from SE dictionaries as a taboo vulgarism]

swivel! excl. [1990s] (US teen) go away! leave me alone!

swivel-eye n. [mid-19C] a squint.

swivel-eyed adj. [mid-late 18C] squint-eyed.

swivelly adj. [late 19C–20C] drunk (cf. SQUIFFY).

swivet n. [late 19C+] (US) an irritable mood (cf. SNIT n.). [dial. *swivet*, haste, hurry, passion]

swiz/swizz n.[1] [mid-18C–mid-19C] intoxicating liquor. [abbr. SWIZZLE n.]

swiz/swizz n.[2] [late 19C+] (mainly teen) a fraud, a hoax, a disappointment. [SE *swindle*]

swiz/swizz n.[3] [1920s+] (Aus.) an excellent, first-rate thing. [SWISH adj.[1]]

swiz/swizz v. [1930s] (mainly teen) to cheat, to swindle. [SWIZ n.[2]]

swizzle n. [mid-18C–mid-19C] **1** any form of intoxicating liquor. **2** (US) a mix of spruce ('Prussian') beer, rum and sugar.

swizzle v.[1] [mid-late 19C] to drink. [SWIZZLE n.]

swizzle v.[2] [late 19C+] to hoax, to trick. [SWIZ v.]

swizzled/swozzled adj. [mid-19C+] drunk (cf. BASTED). [SWIZZLE v.[1]]

swizzy n. [mid-18C–mid-19C] any form of intoxicating drink. [var. on SWIZZLE n.]

swizzy v. [mid-late 19C] to drink. [var. on SWIZZLE v.[1]]

swob! excl. [1910s–20s] a general excl. of intensification and affirmation. [var. on S'HELP ME BOB!]

swobble see SWABBLE.

swoddy see SWADDY.

swod-gill see SWAD-GILL.

'swolks! see 'SWOUNDS!

Swone one n. [1970s+] (society) Battersea, London SW11. [S.W.-One-One]

swonie see SWOON UNIT.

swoon! excl. [1980s+] (US campus) an excl. of approval used by a woman on seeing an attractive man.

swoon unit/swonie n. [1990s] (US teen) a particularly attractive woman. [SE *swoon*, to faint]

swoony adj. [1930s+] distractingly attractive, delightful. [lit. inducing a *swoon*]

swoop v. **1** [1950s+] (US Black) to move fast, to approach or leave quickly. **2** [1950s+] (US Black) to steal someone else's lover, esp. when the manoeuvre is conducted quickly. **3** [1980s+] (US campus) to make a pass at, to make sexual advances towards. **4** [1980s+] (US campus) to overtake in a car.

swop see SWAP.

swop me bob!/swelp me davy!/swelp me taters!/swelp me ten me!/s'help the cat!/swop me dickey! excl. [late 19C+] a general excl. of intensification and affirmation (cf. S'ELP ME NEVER!). [all vars. on S'ELP ME BOB!]

swopper see SWAPPER.

swopping see SWAPPING.

swoppy adj. [1990s] ignorant or unintelligent, usually of a woman or young man. [ety. unknown]

swop slob v. [1940s] (US Black/campus) to kiss (cf. SWAP SPIT). [abbr. SE *swap slobber*]

'sworbote! excl. [late 16C–early 17C] a mild oath, lit. 'God's forbote (forbode)' (cf. 's abbr.[1]).

sword n. [late 16C–early 17C] the penis (cf. BAYONET).

sworder n. [early 19C] a swordsman.

sword-racket n. [early 19C] a means of making money by enlisting in a regiment, taking the bounty, deserting and moving on to a new regiment. [SE *sword* + RACKET n.[1]]

swordsman n. [1960s+] a male sexual athlete. [SWORD n.]

sword-swallower n. **1** [late 19C+] (orig. Aus.) a fellator or fellatrix. **2** [1940s] (Aus.) one who eats from his knife. [SWORD n.]

sworn at Highgate phr. [late 18C–19C] clever, smart. ['a ridiculous custom formerly prevailed at the public houses in Highgate (then a village north of London), to administer a ludicrous oath to all travellers of the middling rank who stopped there. The party was sworn on a pair of horns, fastened on a stick, the substance of the oath was never to kiss the maid when he could kiss the mistress, never to drink small beer when he could get strong, with many other injunctions of the like kind to all of which was added the saving clause of "unless you like it best"' (Grose, 1785)]

swosh n. [late 19C–1920s] rubbish, nonsense. [HOGWASH]

swot/swat n. [mid-19C+] a hard worker. [SWOT v.]

swot/swat v. [mid-19C+] to work extremely hard, esp. on the eve of examinations or tests; thus *swot up*, to learn intensely. [supposedly via Dr William Wallace, an instructor at the Royal Military College, Sandhurst, whose Scot. pron. turned the word 'sweat' (as in work that is so hard as to make one sweat) into *swot*. The 20C implication is slightly derog. – to work harder than seen as necessary by your peers]

swotter *n.* [1900s–10s] a very hard worker. [SWOT v.]

'swounds!/'swolks! *excl.* [late 16C–early 17C] a mild oath, lit. 'God's wounds' (cf. 's abbr.[1]).

swozzled *see* SWIZZLED.

swret-sio *n.* [mid-19C] oysters (cf. SRET-SIO). [backsl.]

swuft *adj.* [1970s] (US campus) smart, clever, cunning. [var. on SWIFT adj.]

swy/swi *n.* [late 19C+] **1** two, esp. a two-shilling (10p) coin or a two-year prison sentence. **2** the game of two-up, also as *swy-up*, the *swy game*, a game of two-up, *swy school*, a group of persons who have gathered to play two-up. [Ger. *zwei*, two]

swydeaner *n.* [late 19C–1950s] (Aus.) two shillings (10p). [SWY + DEANER]

sycher/zoucher *n.* [late 19C] an objectionable, unpleasant person. [dial. *sycher*, a bad man]

Sydney bird *n.* [mid-late 19C] a convict (cf. SYDNEY DUCK; SYDNEYSIDER). [*Sydney* + BIRD n.[1]]

Sydney blanket *n.* [late 19C+] (Aus.) a rough blanket, used by vagrants and tramps and made of a sack or bag.

Sydney duck *n.* [mid-19C] **1** a convict (cf. SYDNEY BIRD). **2** (US) an Australian who joined the Californian Gold Rush of 1849.

Sydney Harbour *n.* [1940s+] (Aus./US) a barber. [rhy. sl.]

Sydney or the bush *phr.* [20C] (Aus.) all or nothing. [the comparison between making a fast fortune in the big city or eking out a much harder life in the outback]

Sydneysider *n.* (Aus.) **1** [mid–late 19C] a convict (cf. SYDNEY BIRD). **2** [1940s+] a native of New South Wales. [*Sydney*, the state capital]

syebuck *n.* [late 18C–mid-19C] sixpence (cf. SICE).

syff *see* SYPH.

sylvester *n.* [1950s] (US Black) a White man.

sympathy *n.* [20C] sexual caresses. [a pun on 'a fellow feeling']

sympathy generator *n.* [1990s] (US) a child. [the use of children by beggars, charities, religions, cults etc to elicit interest, sympathy and, ultimately, cash]

synagogue *n.* [late 19C] a shed – its use is not specified – standing at that time in the northeast corner of Covent Garden, London. [by late 19C, Covent Garden market was very much a Jewish enterprise]

sync *v.* [1920s+] to *sync*hronize. [abbr.]

synergy *n.* [1990s] (drugs) 2-CB (4-bromo-2,5-dimeth-oxyphenethylamine) (cf. NEXUS).

syntax *n.* [late 18C–early 19C] a schoolmaster. [SE; popularized through *The Tour of Dr Syntax* (1813) by William Combe]

synth *n.* [1970s+] a *synth*esizer. [abbr.]

syph/siff/syff *n.* [late 19C+] *syph*ilis. [abbr.]

sypho *n.* [1910s+] (Aus.) syphilis. [abbr. SE *syphilis* + sfx. -O]

syphon off the tank *see* SIPHON OFF THE TANK.

syphon the python *see* SIPHON THE PYTHON.

syrup *n.* [20C] a wig. [rhy. sl. *syrup of figs* = wig]

system d *v.* [1910s+] to deal with an otherwise problematic situation by taking a short cut, to muddle through. [Fr. argot *Système D*, system D, for *débrouillard*, one who can accomplish anything, albeit unconventionally]

s.y.t. *phr.* [1950s+] (Aus. gay) of a young man or woman (according to context), *sweet young thing*. [abbr.]

T

T *n.*[1] [1950s] (drugs) marijuana. [abbr. TEA n.[2] (1)]

T *n.*[2] **1** [1960s+] (US drugs) a gram of methamphetamine. **2** [1970s] phencyclidine (cf. ACE n.[3] TIC; TAC). **3** [1970s] Tuinal. [abbr.; (2) = PCP which is misreading of THC, i.e. *tetra*hydro*cannabinol*]

t.a. *see* TITS AND ASS.

ta! *excl.* [late 18C+] thank you; thus (S.Afr.) *ta for niks*, thanks for nothing, *ta, hey!* thank you very much! *no ta hey!* absolutely not, thank you very much.

tab *n.*[1] [mid-19C+] the human ear. [dial.]

tab *n.*[2] **1** [late 19C+] (US) the bill, credit, an IOU, used fig. to imply that an action, good or bad, will be paid for later (cf. TAB ACTION). **2** [20C] (US prison) any form of prison documentation, esp. reports on prisoners that are submitted to the parole board. [abbr. SE *table*]

tab *n.*[3] **1** [1900s–10s] an elderly woman. **2** [1910s+] (Aus.) a young woman. [TABBY]

tab *n.*[4] [1910s+] a *tab*loid newspaper. [abbr.]

tab *n.*[5] [1920s+] a cigarette. [dial. *tab*, the pointed end of anything]

tab *n.*[6] [1930s–40s] (US Black) a physical blow.

tab *n.*[7] [1950s+] (drugs) a *tab*let, esp. one containing an hallucinogenic drug. [abbr.]

tab *v.*[1] [20C] (US) to identify, to categorize. [abbr. SE *tabulate*]

tab *v.*[2] [1930s–40s] (US Black) to hit someone. [TAB n.[6]]

tab action/issue *n.* [1930s] (US Black) a line of credit at a bar or any other type of business. [TAB n.[2] (1) + ACTION n.[1]/SE *issue*]

tabankca/tabanka *n.* [20C] (W.I.) love-sickness, sexual obsession. [? Fr. *t'as bon ça*, you are good]

tabankca *adj.* [20C] (W.I.) passionate, obsessed. [TABANKCA n.]

tabbed *adj.* [1970s+] (US Black) well-dressed (cf. TACKED DOWN). [? SE *tab*, a label]

tabbed to the bone *phr.* [1970s+] (US Black) dressed in one's very best, most fashionable clothes (cf. CLEAN TO THE BONE phr.). [TABBED + TO THE BONE]

tabby *n.* **1** [late 18C+] an old lady, usu. as pej. **2** [1910s–50s] a young woman, esp. an attractive one. [SE *tabby cat*, ult. *tabby*, striped or watered silk (orig. produced in the Baghdad suburb of Attabiy), and thus applied to the colouring of the cat; thus theatrical jargon *tabs*, an old woman]

tabby meeting *n.* [late 19C] a meeting of evangelists and their congregations at Exeter Hall, London. [? proper name *Tabitha*, a typically 'religious' name, note TABBY]

tabby party *n.* [19C] a party consisting only of women (cf. BITCH PARTY). [TABBY + SE *party*]

tab issue *see* TAB ACTION.

table-end man *n.* [late 19C+] a man whose sexual desire is so intense that he makes love to his partner over the dining/kitchen table rather than waiting until they reach the bedroom.

table-hop *v.* [1950s+] (orig. US) to circulate among the tables at a restaurant, greeting and chatting with friends and acquaintances.

table pimp *n.* [1990s] (US Black) a child.

tables, the *n.* [late 19C–1930s] a casino, esp. its roulette tables (cf. SPINNING JINNY n.[2]).

table-tapper *n.* [20C] (US) an unprofessional, part-time lay preacher (cf. CHAIRBACKER). [their thumping of the *table* as they preach]

table-topper *n.* [1980s+] a necrophile. [the mortuary *table* or slab]

table zamboni *n.* [1980s+] (US campus) a rag for wiping spills from a table or bar top. [the *Zamboni* machine used to polish the ice at ice hockey games]

tabloid *n.* [1990s] a sub-literate person, a young layabout. [i.e. their choice of newspaper]

tac *n.* [20C] (drugs) phencyclidine (cf. ACE n.[3]). [PCP is a misappropriation of initials *THC*, i.e. tetrahydrocannabinol]

tace is Latin for a candle *phr.* [late 17C–early 19C] be quiet (cf. BRANDY IS LATIN FOR PIG AND GOOSE). [Lat. *tace*, be silent + the snuffing out of a candle]

tach *n.*[1] [mid-19C] a hat. [backsl.]

tach/tacho/tack *n.*[2] [1960s+] a *tach*ometer, an instrument that measures the velocity of machines. [abbr.]

tache *see* TASH.

tack *n.*[1] [mid-19C] anything mouldy or sour, esp. a taste (in food or drink) that is other than one expects. [SE *tack*, an alien, odd or unpleasant flavour; ? ult. Lat. *tactus*, infection]

tack *n.*[2] [mid-19C+] **1** (orig. naut.) food, ship's biscuit. **2** money. [? SE *tackle*]

tack *n.*[3] [mid-19C+] (orig. US) bad taste; thus [1990s] *tack attack*, a rush of bad taste or an experience of bad taste. [ety. unknown, ? link to SE *tack*, a rundown horse, a poor Southern White]

tack *n.*[4] [20C] (Irish) a rancid flavour in food; thus *tacked*, rancid. [orig. dial.; thus dial. phr. *neither tack nor twist*, of meat, flavourless]

tack *n.*[5] **1** [1940s–60s] (US Black) a nickel, 5 cents. **2** [1950s+] (W.I. Rasta) a bullet.

tack *n.*[6] (US Black) **1** [1950s–60s] a fool. **2** [1950s–60s] an unsophisticated person. **3** [1950s–60s] a conservative. **4** [1960s] a clever person. [? SE *tacit*, silent]

tack *n.*[7] *see* TACK n.[2].

tack *v.* [early 18C–early 19C] to join in marriage.

tacked down *adj.* [1960s] (US Black) well-dressed (cf. TABBED). [SE *tack*, to join]

tacker *n.* [1940s+] (Aus.) a small boy. [dial. *tacker*, a child]

tackhead *n.*[1] [20C] (US) an overdressed or excessively stylish person (cf. B.B HEAD). [TACK n.[3] + sfx. -HEAD (1)]

tackhead/tackyhead *n.*[2] [1960s–80s] **1** (US Black) an unattractive woman. **2** (US) a stupid person. **3** (US) a troublemaker. [TACKY adj.[1] (1) + sfx. -HEAD (1); equating ill-kempt or unfashionable hair with an unappetizing person]

tackie *n. see* TACKIE.

tackie *v.* [1990s] (S.Afr.) to drive fast, to accelerate. [S.Afr.E. *fat tackie*, a large tyre, used for racing or beach-driving]

tacking *n.* [late 19C] obtaining what one wants by roundabout means. [nautical jargon *tack*, to make a run or course obliquely against the wind]

tackle *n.*[1] **1** [late 17C–early 18C] a prostitute, a mistress. **2** [late 17C–18C] one's best clothes. **3** [19C+] any clothes (cf. KIT n.[5]). **4** [mid–late 19C] food. **5** [20C] the genitals (cf. ACCOUTRE-MENTS). **6** [1980s+] (Ulster) a showily or bizarrely dressed woman. [SE *tackle*, equipment, appliances etc]

tackle *n.*[2] [late 19C] a watch chain; thus *red tackle*, a gold watch chain; often as *toy and tackle*, a watch and chain.

tackle *n.*[3] [1980s+] (Ulster) **1** a cantankerous, verbally abusive woman. **2** a 'difficult' child (cf. BLADE n.[4]). [SE *tackle*, to handle; here one who is 'hard to tackle']

tackle *v.* **1** [19C] to grip, to lay hold of. **2** [19C] to take in hand, to deal with. **3** [19C] to attack. **4** [mid–late 19C] to enter into a discussion with, to approach or question some subject. **5** [mid-19C+] to grapple with, to attempt to deal with. **6** [mid-19C+] to fall upon (food), to eat. **7** [1950s+] (W.I.) to get to know someone with the specific aim of initiating an affair.

tackleshack *n.* [1990s] underpants. [TACKLE n.[1] (5) + SE *shack*, a hut, a small building]

tack-on *n.* [1900s] **1** the act of tacking something on. **2** something tacked on or added.

tack together *v.* [mid-18C–late 19C] to marry. [ext. of TACK v.]

tacky *adj.*[1] [mid-19C+] (orig. US) **1** unattractive, second-rate. **2** off-putting, in poor taste. **3** untidy, unkempt. [TACK n.[3]]

tacky *adj.*[2] [1950s] (W.I.) **1** tricky, hard to beat, cunning. **2** good, skilled, clever. [SE *tack*, a new or altered course or line of action, endurance, stability, strength]

tackyhead *see* TACKHEAD n.[2].

taco *n.* [1960s+] (US) a derog. term for a Mexican (cf. TIO TACO). [Sp. *taco*, a fried, unleavened cornmeal pancake or tortilla holding a variety of seasoned fillings, a popular Mexican food]

taco-bender *n.* [1960s+] (US) a derog. term for a Mexican, a Chicano (cf. BAGEL-BENDER; BEAN-EATER; TACO-EATER; TACO-HEAD). [TACO + SE *bender*]

taco-eater *n.* [1960s+] (US) a derog. term for a Mexican, a Chicano (cf. BEAN-EATER). [TACO + SE *eater*]

taco-head *n.* [1960s+] (US) a derog. term for a Mexican or a Chicano (cf. BEAN-EATER). [TACO + sfx. -HEAD (3)]

taco town *n.* [1960s+] (US) a derog. term for San Jose, US (cf. BEAN TOWN n.[2]). [TACO + SE *town*, the Mexican population]

tacou *adj.* [20C] (W.I.) foolish, stupid. [ety. unknown]

taco wagon *n.* [1950s–60s] (US) a derog. term for a car with its rear end lowered. [TACO + SE *wagon*, such cars are popular among Mexican youths]

tad *n.* [20C] (US) an Irish Catholic. [abbr. *Thaddeus*, a popular Irish name]

taddler *n.* [1900s] **1** a large sausage. **2** the penis (cf. BACON n.[1]). [? link to TADGER]

tadger/todger *n.* [late 19C+] the penis. [northern UK dial.]

tad-larruping *see* LARRUPING.

tadpole *n.* [late 19C] (US) a native of Mississippi.

tadpole carrier *n.* [1990s] the scrotum. [sperm's resemblance to *tadpoles*]

taepo *see* TAIPO.

taf/taff/taffy *adj.* [mid-19C] fat. [backsl.]

Taff *n.* [19C+] a Welshman. [abbr. TAFFY n.[1]]

taff *adj. see* TAF.

taffee *see* TOFFY n.

Taffy *n.*[1] [late 17C+] a Welshman; thus *Taffy's day*, St David's Day (cf. SAWNEY). [Welsh *Dafydd*, David]

taffy *n.*[2] [late 19C–1900s] (US) insincere and obvious flattery. [SE *taffy*, toffee]

taffy *n.*[3] *see* TOFFY n.

taffy/taffy goat/ram *n.*[4] [1950s] (W.I.) an old person. [? the white ram that is the regimental symbol of the Royal Welch Fusiliers regiment, which has been stationed in Jamaica. This use, lit. an 'old goat', is used respectfully]

taffy *adj. see* TAF.

taffy goat/ram *see* TAFFY n.[4].

taffy-tugger *n.* [1990s] a masturbator. [TUG ONE'S TAFFY]

tag *n.*[1] **1** [mid-19C] a servant, esp. an under-servant who assists another. **2** [1960s+] one who 'tags along' behind another person, esp. for detective or spying purposes. [SE *tag along*]

tag *n.*[2] [mid-19C–late 19C] an actor. [the SE *tag* or 'moral' added to the end of a play]

tag *n.*[3] **1** [1930s+] a vehicle number-plate. **2** [1930s+] (US Und.) an arrest warrant. **3** [1960s] a label commonly given to a person or thing. **4** [1960s+] the 'signature' used by a graffiti artist, spraying their name on walls, subway trains etc. **5** [1960s+] (Black) a name. [SE *tag*, a label]

tag *v.* [1960s+] (orig. US) of graffiti artists, to affix one's name to a picture, a wall etc. [TAG n.[3] (4)]

tag-a-long *n.* [1950s–60s] (Aus.) a girl- or boyfriend.

tag on *v.* [1960s+] **1** to understand. **2** to overhear.

tag, rag and bobtail *see* RAG, TAG AND BOBTAIL.

tag the play with the slammer issue, to *phr.* [1940s] (US Black) to put a troublesome person in prison. [SE *tag* + PLAY n.[1] + SLAMMER n.[2]]

Taig/Teague *n.* [17C+] Roman Catholic, spec. as used by Protestants in Northern Ireland (cf. PROD n.[1]; PRODDY). [Irish name *Tadhg*, usu. rendered as Thaddeus in English]

tail *n.*[1] **1** [late 17C–early 18C] the penis; thus synons. *tail-pike*, *tail-pin*, *tail-tackle*, *tail-trimmer*. **2** [late 17C+] the vagina; thus synons. *tail-gap*, *tail-gate*, *tail-hole*; also *tail-feathers*, pubic hair; *tail-fruit*, children; *tail-juice*, urine; *tail-trading*, prostitution; *tail-wagging*, *tail-work*, sexual intercourse (cf. BADGER n.[7]). **3** [early 18C+] the posterior, the buttocks. **4** [late 18C–mid-19C] a prostitute. **5** [mid-19C+] a woman. **6** [mid-19C+] women viewed collectively and as sex objects; thus [1930s+] a *bit/piece of tail*, an attractive woman. **7** [1950s+] young boys suitable for homosexual relationships. **8** [1960s+] sexual intercourse.

tail *n.*[2] [late 17C–early 19C] (Und.) a sword. [the way it projects beyond the wearer's body]

tail *n.*[3] [18C–late 19C] the train attached to a woman's dress, usu. for formal use only. [coined in 13C, SE to 18C]

tail, the *n.*[4] [mid-19C] stealing from the pocket in the *tail* of a gentleman's coat.

tail *n.*[5] [1910s+] (orig. US) one who carries out a surveillance, esp. when following the target in the street. [TAIL v.[3]]

tail *v.*[1] [late 18C+] to have sexual intercourse with. [TAIL n.[1] (1), (2)]

tail *v.*[2] [mid–late 19C] to run away, to 'turn tail'.

tail *v.*[3] [20C] to follow, to keep under (police) surveillance.

tailbone *n.* [20C] (US) the buttocks. [ext. of TAIL n.[1] (3)]

tail-buzzer *n.* [mid-19C] (Und.) a thief who specializes in the picking of coat pockets. [TAIL n.[1] (3) + BUZZER n.[1]]

taildraft *n.* [20C] (Ulster) an idler, one who holds back. [SE *tail* + *draught/draft*, the act of pulling]

tail-drawer *n.* [late 17C–early 19C] (Und.) a thief who steals gentlemen's swords from their sides. [TAIL n.[2] + SE *drawer*]

tail-end charlie *n.* [1940s+] the person or vehicle that comes last in a queue. [RAF jargon *tail-end charlie*, a tail-gunner, the last aircraft in a flying formation]

tailgate *v.* [1940s+] **1** to drive a car closely (too closely) behind the one in front. **2** (US campus) to watch women passing by. [SAmE *tailgate*, the tailboard of a truck or wagon; (2) is pun on (1) and TAIL n.¹ (3)]

tailgunner *n.* [1980s+] (US) a male homosexual. [TAIL n.¹ (3) + SE *gunner*]

tailist *n.* [19C] a prostitute (cf. TAIL-TRADER; TAIL-WORKER; TENANT IN TAIL). [TAIL n.¹ (2)]

tail it *v.* [1920s+] to die. [SE *tail*, the end]

tail light alley *n.* [1940s+] (Aus.) a Lovers' Lane, used by 'parking' couples. [the SE *tail lights* of the parked car but note pun on TAIL n.¹ (5)]

tail lights *n.* [1960s+] (drugs) LSD. [i.e. the hallucinations produced by the drug]

tail-off *n.* [1970s+] a lowering of demand, a withering away. [TAIL OFF v.]

tail off *v.* [mid-19C+] to run away, to withdraw. [the *tail* of a retreating bird or animal]

tailor *n.* [1920s+] (US prison/Aus.) a factory-made cigarette, whether prison-issue or commercially produced (cf. SQUARE n.⁶). [abbr. TAILOR-MADE]

tailor *v.* [late 19C–1900s] to shoot badly at birds so as to wound rather than actually kill them. [? snobbish dismissal of 'trade' shooters; or one 'cuts them up']

tailor-made *n.* [1920s+] (usu. prison) a factory-produced cigarette (cf. ROLL-UP).

tailor's ragout *n.* [late 18C–early 19C] bread soaked in the dressing in which cucumbers have stood (cf. SCRATCH PLATTER). [? its popularity with tailors; they could not afford a proper meat ragout]

tail out *v.* [late 19C] (US) to run away, to make one's escape (cf. TAIL OFF). [SE *tail*/TAIL n.¹ (3); i.e. one 'moves one's arse']

tail over top/top over tail *phr.* [mid-18C+] head over heels. [TAIL n.¹ (3) + SE *top*]

tails *n.* [20C] a formal *tail*coat; thus *white tie and tails*. [abbr.]

tail tea *n.* [late 19C] (society) an afternoon tea attended by aristocratic ladies who had already been at the day's 'royal drawing room' (Queen Victoria's formal receptions) where trains were a part of formal dress. [TAIL n.³ + SE *tea*. Once Victoria had died, her son Edward VII (r.1901–10) moved the 'drawing rooms' to the evening, a time more congenial to his own lifestyle]

tail timber *n.* [late 19C] lavatory paper. [TAIL n.¹ (3) + SE *timber*]

tail-trader *n.* [19C] a prostitute (cf. TAILIST). [TAIL n.¹ (2) + SE *trader*]

tail water *n.* [18C] urine. [TAIL n.¹ (1), (2) + SE *water*]

tail-worker *n.* [19C] a prostitute (cf. TAILIST). [TAIL n.¹ (2) + SE *worker*]

taima *n.* [1980s+] (drugs) marijuana. [Sp.]

t'aint/taint/taintmeat *n.* [1990s] (US) a woman's perineum, the space between the vagina and the anus. [i.e. *t'aint pussy and t'aint asshole*]

tainted money *n.* [1930s+] money that belongs neither to the speaker nor to anyone else in the group. [i.e. *t'aint mine and t'aint yours*]

taintmeat *see* T'AINT.

taipo/taepo *n.* [mid-19C+] (N.Z.) a vicious horse, often used as the name for a dog. [? Maori]

tait *n.* [late 19C] (church) a moderate clergyman, a follower of Archbishop *Tait* (1811–82), who wished (vainly) to bring the high and low branches of the Anglican communion together.

taj *adj.* [late 19C+] (teen) excellent, wonderful, luscious. [proper name *Taj*Mahal, synon. with fabulous luxury]

take *n.*¹ **1** [late 19C+] money acquired by theft or fraud. **2** [1930s+] (US) a share of money that is deducted for tax or some other form of levy. **3** [1930s+] (US) a portion, an extract, a bit. **4** [1930s+] wages. **5** [1930s+] (US) the entrance money taken at a musical, sporting or gambling event. **6** [1930s+]

(orig. US) bribery; thus *on the take*, receiving regular bribes. **7** [1930s+] (Aus.) a thief, a villain, esp. a cheat at cards. **8** [1930s+] (Aus.) a theft, a robbery.

take *n.*² [1960s+] (US) an opinion, a view, e.g. *what's your take on it?* [abbr. SE *take a stance*]

take *v.*¹ [19C] to become, to fall into a state of, e.g. *take ill*, *take sick*. [note late 17C nonce use *take with child*, to become pregnant]

take *v.*² [mid-19C+] to succeed, to become popular. [SE *take*, of a plant, to start flourishing]

take *v.*³ [late 19C+] to require, to need, e.g. *it would take a genius to ...* .

take *v.*⁴ [20C] to accept, used esp. in neg., e.g. *I'm not taking that*.

take *v.*⁵ **1** [1920s+] to swindle, to cheat, to extort money from. **2** [1920s+] to break in, to rob. **3** [1930s+] to confront, to attack. **4** [1930s+] to overcome, to defeat, to kill. **5** [1930s+] to accept bribery.

take! *excl.* [20C] (Can.) a general excl. of affirmation, all right! that's correct! etc.

take a back seat, to *phr.* [late 19C+] to accept without complaint a subordinate, second-rate position (cf. PLAY SECOND FIDDLE).

take a bashing, to *phr.* [1940s+] (orig. milit.) to suffer heavy losses, to do badly. [BASHING n.²]

take a bath/beating, to *phr.* [1930s+] to lose or suffer badly, esp. in business, sport or gambling (cf. GO TO THE CLEANERS).

take a beating, to *phr.*² [1960s+] to masturbate (cf. BEAT OFF).

take a bit of/lot of/some doing, to *phr.* [1930s+] to require all one's efforts, to be difficult to do.

take a blinder, to *phr.* [mid-19C–1900s] to die. [lit. 'take a blind leap' into the next world]

take a brace, to *phr.* [late 19C+] (US) to pull oneself together, to smarten up. [SE *brace*, used of straps, belts etc that tighten]

take a brodie, to *phr.* [late 19C+] to commit suicide (cf. DO A BRODIE). [Steve *Brodie*, a 23-year-old New York saloon-keeper who on 23 July 1886 allegedly leaped some 41.5m (135ft) from the city's Brooklyn Bridge in order to win a $200 wager. He survived the fall and was scooped out of the East River by a friend in a small boat. He was subsequently charged by the police with attempted suicide. Whether he actually made the jump remains unproven (the witnesses, all of them his friends, claimed that he did, but the general consensus was that a dummy was tossed over the bridge and Brodie, hiding on shore, quickly swam underwater to the point where it had hit the river, in time to be 'rescued'). This scepticism is reflected in theatrical jargon: a *brodie*, a (much touted) flop]

take a Burford bait, to *phr.* [19C] to get drunk. [dial.; ? an anecdote from the Cotswolds town of *Burford*, UK]

take a bye, to *phr.* [20C] (US) to refuse or decline to act or participate in something. [sporting imagery]

take a carrot! *excl.* [mid-19C] an insulting excl., usu. used to women. [the potential of a *carrot* as a dildo. Note naut. jargon *carrots*, go away!]

take a chill/chill pill, to *phr.* [1980s+] (US Black/campus) to relax, to calm down (cf. CHILL OUT). [SE *take* + CHILL v.³]

take a course with, to *phr.* [mid-17C–early 19C] **1** to cause problems for, to interfere with. **2** to follow closely.

take a crap, to *phr.* [late 19C+] to defecate. [CRAP n.³]

take a D, to *phr.* [1920s+] (US) to commit suicide. [a failed actor or actress is believed to have committed suicide by jumping from the letter D of the gigantic letters spelling 'Hollywood' on Mount Lee]

take a dim view, to *phr.* [1930s+] (orig. milit.) to disapprove.

take a dip, to *phr.*¹ [1980s+] (US campus) to chew tobacco. [SE *dip*, a pinch of snuff, thus ext. for chewing tobacco]

take a dip, to *phr.*² [1990s] of a woman, to masturbate.

take a dirt nap, to *phr.* [1990s] (US Black) **1** to be buried. **2** to die. **3** to be knocked out.

take a dive, to *phr.* (US) **1** [1910s+] in boxing, for a fighter deliberately to lose a fight (cf. GO IN THE TANK). **2** [1980s+] to compromise oneself. **3** [1980s+] to fail. [one lit. + fig. *dives* to the canvas]

take a douche, to *phr.* [1980s+] (US teen) to leave hurriedly, esp. as imper. *take a douche!*

take a drop, to *phr.* [late 19C] to run off. [one *drops* out of sight]

take a drop in the eye, to *phr.* [18C] to have a drink. [a *drop* of alcohol]

take a drop to, to *phr.* [late 19C+] to realize, to understand. [play on TUMBLE TO]

take a dump, to *phr.* [1940s+] (orig. US) to defecate, often in sense of incontinence. [DUMP n.⁴]

take a fade *see* DO A FADE.

take a fall, to *phr.* **1** [1920s+] (US Und.) to be arrested, to be imprisoned (cf. FALL GUY; FALL MONEY). **2** [1930s+] (US) to fall in love. **3** [1950s+] to tumble, to slip over.

take/get a fall out of, to *phr.* [late 19C–1910s] (US) **1** to get the better of someone. **2** to involve oneself with something.

take a fashion risk, to *phr.* [1980s+] (US campus) to dress in an unfashionable or outlandish manner (cf. FASHION ARREST; FASHION VICTIM).

take a feather out of, to *phr.* [20C] (Irish) to confuse, to surprise, to astonish. [the pulling out of a *feather* will make a bird jump]

take a flier/flyer, to *phr.* **1** [late 18C] to have quick and spontaneous sexual intercourse with both parties fully or partially dressed. **2** [mid-19C+] to go out on a spree. **3** [late 19C+] (US) to take a chance, to gamble, esp. financially. **4** [20C] (US prison) to escape from prison. **5** [1920s+] to fall heavily. [SE *take a flying leap*]

take a flourish, to *phr.* [late 18C] to have swift and spontaneous sexual intercourse, usu. when both parties are wholly or partially dressed (cf. TAKE A FLIER).

take a flyer *see* TAKE A FLIER.

take a flying fuck/frig/jump/leap *phr.* [1920s+] (orig. US) a derisory, dismissive phr.; also ext. by ... *at a galloping goose!*; ... *at a rolling doughnut!*; ... *at a rubber duck!*; ... *at the moon!*; ... *at yourself!* [*frig* is a euph. for *fuck*]

take a foolish powder, to *phr.* [late 19C–1910s] (US) to act foolishly.

take a fright *n.* [mid-19C] the night. [rhy. sl.]

take a gander, to *phr.* [20C] (orig. US) to look at, to glance at (cf. HAVE A GECKO AT). [the bird's long neck]

take a grinder, to *phr.* [mid-19C] to make a coarse gesture similar to thumbing one's nose and using the other hand to work an imaginary coffee-grinder (cf. SIGHT n.¹). [GRINDER n.¹]

take a hand of *see* MAKE A HAND OF.

take a hike, to *phr.* [1960s+] (orig. US) to leave, esp. as imper. *take a hike!* (cf. HIKE OFF; HIT THE ROAD). [SE *hike*, to walk]

take a hinge at, to *phr.* [1930s] (US) to look at. [the turning of one's head]

take a holiday, to *phr.* **1** [late 19C–1900s] to be dismissed. **2** [1940s+] to 'jump' bail.

take a holiday at Peckham, to *phr.* [18C–mid-19C] to have nothing to eat (cf. OFF ONE'S PECK). [a pun on SE *peck + ham*]

take a hosing, to *phr.* [1920s+] (US) to be cheated or badly treated. [HOSE v.² (3)]

take a jerry/jerry to, to *phr.* [1910s+] (Aus./N.Z.) to investigate and understand something, to work something out. [JERRY v.¹ (2)]

take a lark *see* GO ON A LARK.

take/spring a leak, to *phr.* [1910s+] to urinate. [LEAK n.³]

take a leap at Tyburn, to *phr.* [17C–early 19C] to be hanged. [*Tyburn*, the site of main London gallows]

take a leap in the dark, to *phr.* [17C–early 18C] to be hanged.

take a lend of *see* HAVE A LEND OF.

take a load off one's feet, to *phr.* [1940s+] to sit down and rest, esp. used as invitation.

take a load off one's mind, to *phr.* [1990s] to masturbate. [pun on SE phr. *take a weight of one's mind*/LOAD n.⁴ (2)]

take a lot of doing *see* TAKE A BIT OF DOING.

take a mickey finn, to *phr.* [1920s] (US) to run off, to abscond. [fig. use of MICKEY FINN]

take a Midol! *excl.* [1980s+] (US campus) relax! calm down! [brandname *Midol*, menstrual relief tablets]

take a mope *see* COP A MOPE.

take an airing, to *phr.* [18C] to ride out as a highwayman.

take an application/a test drive, to *phr.* [1960s–70s] (US) to interview a woman as a prospective prostitute.

take and give, to *phr.* [late 19C] to live, esp. as man and wife. [rhy. sl.]

take an oath, to *phr.* [late 19C–1900s] to have a drink.

take a nose-dive, to *phr.* [1920s+] to collapse, to fail utterly. [flying imagery]

take an outing with tom thumb and his four brothers, to *phr.* [20C] to masturbate (cf. CONVERSE WITH HARRY PALM).

take a page from/out of someone's book, to *phr.* [20C] (US) to imitate or emulate someone.

take a pew *see* PARK YOURSELF IN A PEW.

take a picture! *excl.* [1980s+] (US campus) stop staring!

take a piece out of, to *phr.* [1950s+] (Aus.) to scold, to reprimand severely.

take a pill! *excl.* [1990s] (US teen) calm down! (cf. TAKE A CHILL PILL).

take a pipe, to *phr.* [late 19C] to cry (cf. TUNE ONE'S PIPES). [PIPE v.³ (1)]

take a poke at, to *phr.* [1930s+] (orig. US) **1** to assault, to aim a blow at. **2** to have a try, to attempt.

take a pop/pop at, to *phr.* [late 19C+] **1** to make an attempt (at). **2** to hit (someone). [POP n.⁶]

take a potshot at, to *phr.* [mid-19C+] (US) to criticize someone severely.

take a powder, to *phr.* [1930s+] **1** to escape, to run away. **2** to leave without paying one's rent. [abbr. TAKE A RUN-OUT POWDER]

take a pull, to *phr.* [late 19C+] (Aus.) to stop, to desist (cf. GIVE IT A PULL); thus *take a pull on yourself*, stop it.

take a punt, to *phr.*¹ [1940s+] (orig. Aus.) to have a try, to make a bet. [PUNT v.¹]

take a punt/punt at, to *phr.*² [1950s+] to have a look (at). [ext. of TAKE A PUNT phr.¹; the look is speculative]

take a rain check, to *phr.* [1930s+] (orig./mainly US) to defer something until a later, unspecified, time. [sporting use, a check (ticket) issued for future use if a baseball game was cancelled due to rain]

take a red-hot potato! *excl.* [mid-19C] be quiet! shut up! [the effect of a *red-hot potato* in the mouth]

take a run *see* HAVE A RUN.

take a run at someone, to *phr.* [20C] (US) to attempt to capture, assault or seduce someone.

take a run at yourself! *excl.* [20C] (Aus.) a general excl. of dismissal, dislike, i.e. go to hell!

take a running jump! *excl.* [20C] an excl. of dismissal or dislike.

take a running jump/at the moon! *excl.* [1910s+] a general excl. of dismissal (cf. TAKE A FLYING FUCK!).

take a run-out powder, to *phr.* [1920s+] to escape, to run away. [RUN-OUT POWDER]

take a screw at *see* HAVE A SCREW AT.

take a set on *see* HAVE A SET ON.

take a shake break, to *phr.* [1990s] to masturbate.

take a sheet off a hedge, to *phr.* [17C] to steal openly (cf. GOOSEBERRY LAY; SCRAG A LAY). [an era when *sheets* and other laundry were laid on *hedges* to dry]

take a shingle off, to *phr.* [late 19C] (N.Z.) to lose one's temper, i.e. to 'hit the roof']

take a shine to, to *phr.* [early 19C+] (orig. US) to find attractive or appealing. [UK dial. *shiner*, a sweetheart]

take a shit, to *phr.* [20C] to defecate. [SHIT n.¹]

take a shot, to *phr.* [mid-19C+] to try, to make an attempt. [SHOT n.²]

take a sickie, to *phr.* [1930s+] to take a day off, ostensibly through illness, but often for other reasons (cf. THROW A SICKIE). [SICKIE n.¹]

take a sight/double sights, to *phr.* [mid-19C] to place the thumb against the nose and close all the fingers except the little one, which is agitated as a token of derision.

take a slice/slice off the joint, to *phr.* [late 18C+] of a man, to have sexual intercourse (cf. CARVE A SLICE). [CUT A SLICE]

take a snout on someone *see* HAVE A SNOUT ON SOMEONE.

take a spill, to *phr.* [1960s+] (US) to fall in love (cf. TAKE A FALL).

take a squat, to *phr.* [1930s+] to defecate (cf. SQUAT v.).

take a squiz, to *phr.* [20C] (Aus./N.Z.) to take a look. [SE *quiz* ? + *squint*]

take a stink for a nosegay, to *phr.* [late 18C–mid-19C] to make a foolish blunder, to be very gullible. [a *nosegay* smells sweet, a *stink* does not]

take a stone up in the ear, to *phr.* [late 17C–early 18C] of a woman, to fall into an immoral lifestyle. [ety. unknown; ? link to SE *stone*, a testicle; or to the *stoning* of adulteresses in some cultures]

take a stretch, to *phr.* [late 19C+] (Aus.) to exercise, usu. to exercise a horse.

take a swing/swipe/swing at/swipe at, to *phr.* [1920s+] **1** to aim a blow (at), to punch. **2** to criticize. [(2) is fig. use of (1)]

take a test drive *see* TAKE AN APPLICATION.

take a text/text on, to *phr.* [20C] (US Black) to scold a person in a melodramatic way. [US Black church use *take a text*, to announce that day's reading, then to read and analyse it according to a regular, predictable pattern]

take a toss, to *phr.* [1930s] to be attracted to a person, to fall in love with. [thus 'to fall for']

take a turn among her frills/up her petticoats, to *phr.* [19C] to have sexual intercourse.

take a turn among the cabbages/parsley, to *phr.* [19C] to have sexual intercourse.

take a turn in bushey park, to *phr.* [19C] to have sexual intercourse. [pun on proper name *Bushey Park*, Middlesex, UK and BUSH n.⁴]

take a turn in cock alley/lane, to *phr.* [19C] to have sexual intercourse. [pun on a fictitious street COCK n.² (1) + SE *alley/lane*]

take a turn in Cupid's alley/corner and hair court, to *phr.* [19C] to have sexual intercourse. [proper name *Cupid* + SE *alley/corner* + HAIR COURT]

take a turn in love lane and mount pleasant, to *phr.* [19C] to have sexual intercourse. [facetious use of London street names]

take a turn in/through the stubble, to *phr.* [18C–19C] to have sexual intercourse (cf. SHOOT IN THE STUBBLE). [STUBBLE]

take a turn on hair court, to *phr.* [19C] to have sexual intercourse. [joc. ref. to pubic hair]

take a turn on one's back, to *phr.* [19C] to have sexual intercourse. [facetious use of SE *back*]

take a turn on shooter's hill, to *phr.* [1970s] (US Black) to have sexual intercourse. [SHOOT v.³]

take a turn through the stubble *see* TAKE A TURN IN THE STUBBLE.

take a turn up her petticoats *see* TAKE A TURN AMONG HER FRILLS.

take a vegetable breakfast, to *phr.* [18C–19C] to be hanged (cf. HAVE A HEARTY-CHOKE FOR BREAKFAST). [pun on SE *artichoke*, a vegetable + SE *choke*]

take a walk, to *phr.* (orig. US) **1** [mid-19C+] to leave, to be dismissed, esp. as imper. *take a walk!* go away! **2** [1930s+] of a group of workers, to resign.

take a whack at *see* HAVE A WHACK AT.

take beef *v.*¹ [mid-19C] to run away. [CRY BEEF]

take beef *v.*² [1990s] (US Black) to get into arguments, to face criticism. [SE *take* + BEEF n.² (1)]

take bread and salt, to *phr.* [1920s] to swear. [the taking of one's master's *bread and salt* provided a symbolic underpinning of an oath of fealty]

take care of *v.* **1** [late 19C] to arrest. **2** [20C] to kill. **3** [1920s+] to bribe. [euphs.]

take care of business, to *phr.* [1950s+] (US Black, though increasingly widespread) to deal efficiently with matters in hand, also as *t.c.b.*

take care of number one/numero uno, to *phr.* [1960s+] to put oneself first, no matter what the situation (cf. LOOK AFTER NUMBER ONE).

take-charge *n.* [1950s+] an individual, usu. a member of a team, who drives their colleagues forward in their work (cf. SELF-STARTER).

take charge *v.* [late 19C] to go out of control, usu. with disastrous consequences. [usu. of inanimate objects, which run out of human control]

take coals to Newcastle *see* CARRY COALS TO NEWCASTLE.

take double sights *see* TAKE A SIGHT.

take-down *n.* [late 19C–1930s] **1** a swindle, a deception. **2** (Aus.) a deceiver, a swindler, a cheat. [TAKE DOWN v. (3)]

take down *v.* **1** [17C] to abuse. **2** [mid-19C+] to challenge, to overcome (cf. TAKE ONE DOWN A PEG). **3** [late 19C] (Aus.) to cheat, to swindle, to rob.

take down someone's particulars, to *phr.* [1920s+] of a man, to remove a woman's underwear. [pun on stereotyped police activity at the outset of an interrogation]

take down/down through there, to *phr.* [20C] (US prison) to beat up. [the victim is removed to some hidden or subterranean spot]

take five/ten *v.* [1940s+] (US) to take a short break, i.e. a 5-minute or 10-minute break.

take foot *see* MAKE FOOT.

take for a ride/an airing, to *phr.* [1920s+] **1** (Und.) to assassinate, usu. by taking the victim out in a car and killing them at some stage, then dumping the body far from one's base. **2** to deceive, to fool, to trick, usu. for financial gain.

take for a sleighride, to *phr.* [1930s–60s] (US) to mislead, to trick. [var. on TAKE FOR A RIDE phr. (2)]

take French lessons, to *phr.* [20C] to contract venereal disease. [stereotyping]

take gas *v.* [1950s+] (US) to be scolded and abused (cf. GIVE GAS).

take gruel *v.* [late 19C] to die (cf. GIVE SOMEONE THEIR GRUEL). [the giving of gruel to those on or near their deathbed]

take gruel together *v.* [late 19C] to live together as man and wife. [a clergyman who, as reported in *The Referee* of 14 December 1884, offered this euph. to explain his relations with his elderly 'housekeeper']

take heat *v.* [1920s+] (US) to suffer or endure punishment or criticism. [HEAT n.²]

take-in *n.*[1] [late 18C–mid-19C] a hoax, a swindle. [TAKE IN v.[1]]

take-in *n.*[2] [late 19C] a man who escorts a woman in to a formal dinner. [SE *take in to dinner*]

take-in *adj.* [late 18C–mid-19C] deceptive, swindling. [TAKE-IN n.[1]]

take in *v.*[1] [mid-19C+] to hoax, to cheat, to deceive.

take in *v.*[2] [20C] (US) to arrest.

take in a cargo, to *phr.* [early 19C] to get drunk (cf. CARRYING A LOAD; GET A LOAD ON).

take in and do for, to *phr.* [mid-19C] of women, to have sexual intercourse (cf. TAKE IN BEEF). [pun on the same phr. used in lodging house advertisements, 'Single men taken in and done for', note DO v.[2] (4)]

take in beef, to *phr.* [mid-19C] of women, to have sexual intercourse (cf. ACHING FOR A SIDE OF BEEF). [BEEF n.[1] (3)]

take in some o-be-joyful, to *phr.* [19C] to have a drink (cf. O-BE-JOYFUL HOUSE). [O-BE-JOYFUL]

take into the woodshed, to *phr.* [20C] (US) to scold, to punish. [the practice of taking an errant child *into the woodshed* for a thrashing]

take in wood, to *phr.* [mid-19C] (US) to drink, usu. in question *Do you take in wood?*, Will you have a drink? [? the *wooden* barrels that hold liquor]

take it *v.* [1930s+] **1** to suffer adversity and unhappiness without complaint. **2** to surpass others, to beat all rivals (cf. TAKE THE BISCUIT; TAKE THE CAKE).

take it! *excl.* [1930s–40s] (gay) an excl. used by one demanding fellatio.

take it any way, to *phr.* [1930s–40s] (gay) to enjoy fellatio.

take it big/hard, to *phr.* [1930s] (US) to react emotionally, usu. when distressed or angry.

take it cool, to *phr.* [mid-19C+] to relax, to remain undisturbed by events (cf. PLAY IT COOL). [COOL adj.[3]]

take it down a thousand! *excl.* [1980s+] (US campus) relax! calm down! [image of some form of gauge or dial]

take it easy *phr.* **1** [mid-19C+] relax, don't worry. **2** [1970s+] (US) goodbye, see you later. [naut. jargon *take it easy*, to neglect one's duties]

take it easy, greasy *phr.* [1930s–40s] (US Black) a general expression of farewell. [ext. of TAKE IT EASY]

take it fighting, to *phr.* [late 19C] (US) to approach in a courageous manner, to act aggressively.

take it from the top, to *phr.* [1930s+] (US) to start at the beginning. [jazz use, i.e. *the top* of the score]

take it hard *see* TAKE IT BIG.

take it in/up the ass/arse, to *phr.* (orig. US) **1** [20C] to submit to anal intercourse. **2** [1980s+] to be victimized, treated unfairly or harshly. [ARSE n.[1]]

take it in the blind, to *phr.* [20C] (US prison) to fight in private to settle a score (cf. PUT ON A SLAB). [i.e. no one else is aware of the activity]

take it in the ear, to *phr.* [1960s+] (US campus) to be severely criticized.

take it light, to *phr.* [1960s] (US Black) to act in a restrained manner, to resist excess, to go slowly.

take it lying down, to *phr.* **1** [late 19C+] to give in without a fight, to act weakly (cf. TAKE IT FIGHTING). **2** [1950s+] of a woman, to submit, willingly or otherwise, to sexual intercourse.

take it on! *excl.* [1980s+] (US campus) a general excl. of encouragement (cf. GO FOR IT!).

take it on one's toes *see* HAVE IT AWAY ON ONE'S TOES.

take it on the Arthur Duffy, to *phr.* [1900s–50s] (US) to run off, to escape. [proper name *Arthur F. Duffy*, US world record-holder of the 100-yard (100m) dash (1902–5)]

take it on the chin, to *phr.* [1920s+] (orig. US) **1** to suffer hardship and adversity without complaint. **2** to be defeated, to be trounced. [boxing imagery]

take it on the lam, to *phr.* [20C] (US Und.) to run away, to escape (esp. from prison). [LAM n.[1]]

take it out *v.* [1910s+] (Aus.) to serve a prison term rather than pay a fine.

take it out in trade, to *phr.* [1940s+] (Can.) to have sexual intercourse as the 'price' of taking a woman out.

take it out of one, to *phr.* [late 19C+] to tire, to exhaust.

take it out of someone, to *phr.* [mid-19C+] to take revenge on, to get one's satisfaction from.

take it out of that! *excl.* [early–mid-19C] an excl. used to offer a challenge to fight. [the words were trad. accompanied by the patting of one's elbow]

take it out on *v.* [20C] (US) to treat badly, to punish, often an innocent victim.

take it slow *phr.* [1930s–40s] (US Black) goodbye, see you later (cf. TAKE IT EASY).

take it to the hoop, to *phr.* [1980s+] (US Black) to take something to its limit, to do something with maximum commitment. [basketball imagery]

take it to the street, to *phr.* [20C] (US) to take a private conflict or issue into the public arena.

take it up the ass/arse *see* TAKE IT IN THE ASS.

take it up the dirt road, to *phr.* [1950s+] to be sodomized. [DIRT ROAD n.[2]]

take large stock in/of *see* TAKE STOCK IN/OF.

take low *v.* [1980s+] (US Black) to adopt a humble attitude in order to forward one's aims.

take Ludgate *v.* [late 16C–late 17C] to go bankrupt. [*Ludgate Prison*, which specialized in debtors]

take matters into one's own hands, to *phr.* [20C] to masturbate. [pun]

take/travel by Mr Foot's horse, to *phr.* [early 19C] to go on foot.

take my bradlaugh *phr.* [late 19C] take my oath, on my honour; thus *take one's bradlaugh*, to swear an oath. [proper name of Charles *Bradlaugh* (1833–91), the freethinker and reformer who involved himself in the campaign for the Affirmation Act, whereby one might 'affirm' one's oath in court, rather than swear on a Bible]

taken/took bad, to be *phr.* [mid-19C+] to have fallen ill.

take no shit, to *phr.* [1930s+] (orig. US) to brook no arguments, to accept no diversions or irritations, often as imper. [SHIT n.[4]]

take no shorts, to *phr.* [1980s+] (US Black) to refuse to be fooled, cheated or put at a disadvantage. [SE *short change*]

taken short, to be *phr.* [late 19C+] to be forced to make an emergency visit to the lavatory. [the *short* time one has to reach the lavatory, or the *short* steps one takes on one's way]

take-off *n.*[1] [mid-19C+] an imitation, a parody, usu. mocking.

take-off *n.*[2] [1940s+] (US Und.) an armed street robbery or mugging (cf. HOLD-UP n.).

take off *v.*[1] [mid-18C+] to imitate, to mimic, to parody. [ext. of SE *take off*, to draw a likeness of someone]

take off *v.*[2] [1940s+] to leave, also in imper. *take off!* go away! [the sl. use derives immediately from aircraft imagery, but *take off*, to go off, to start off, to run away, has been SE since early 19C]

take off *v.*[3] [1940s+] (US Black/Und.) to rob, to hurt, to kill. [SE *take off*, to remove]

take off *v.*[4] [1950s+] **1** (drugs) to feel the effects of a drug (cf. HIGH n.[1]). **2** (US) to be suddenly successful or very active.

take-off artist *n.* [1940s+] (US Und.) **1** a successful robber, rapist or killer. **2** one who does the job then 'takes off'. [TAKE OFF v.[2], v.[3] + ARTIST n.[2]]

take off corner-pieces, to phr. [late 19C] to beat, usu. one's wife.

take off like a big-assed bird/bat out of hell, to phr. [1940s+] (US) to leave very quickly. [SE + sfx. -ARSED]

take off one's coat, to phr. [late 19C] to challenge someone to a fight. [the preparatory action]

take-on n. [1920s+] (Aus.) a fight, usu. with the fists. [TAKE ON v.³ (1)]

take on v.¹ [mid-19C+] to grieve, usu. in phr. *don't take on so*, don't make such a fuss. [earlier use SE; the image is of 'taking on an emotion']

take on v.² [late 19C] to become popular. [var. on SE *catch on*]

take on v.³ [1910s+] **1** to engage in a fight, to challenge. **2** (US) to become angry. **3** (US police) to stop and search.

take one off the wrist, to phr. [1960s+] to masturbate. [ONE OFF THE WRIST]

take one's best hold, to phr. [1970s+] (US) to prepare oneself emotionally for dealing with a problem. [wrestling imagery]

take one's best shot, to phr. [20C] (orig. US) to do the best one can, to try one's hardest. [SHOT n.², ult. boxing imagery]

take one's change out of, to phr. [early–mid-19C] to take revenge on, esp. in phr. *take your change out of that!* accompanied by a blow or a rude remark.

take one's daniel see SLING ONE'S DANIEL.

take one's degrees, to phr. [mid-19C] to be imprisoned, to serve a sentence. [play on ACADEMY]

take one's drops, to phr. [early 19C] to drink heavily. [SE *drop* (of liquor)]

take oneself in hand, to phr. [1950s+] (orig. naut.) to masturbate (cf. BRING UP BY HAND; HAND-REARED). [pun]

take one's end, to phr. [20C] (Irish) to be convulsed with laughter. [SE *end*, death, i.e. 'to laugh oneself to death']

take one's eye/eyes pass somebody see MAKE ONE'S EYE PASS SOMEBODY.

take one's finger out see PULL ONE'S FINGER OUT.

take one's hair down see LET ONE'S HAIR DOWN.

take one's hat off to, to phr. [mid-19C+] to compliment, to praise.

take one's hook see SLING ONE'S HOOK.

take one's lumps, to phr. [1950s+] (orig. US) to accept and deal with one's problems and setbacks.

take one's meat out of the basket, to phr. [1930s+] (gay) to reveal one's genitals to another man. [MEAT n. (2) + SE *basket/* BASKET n.¹ (2)]

take one's medicine, to phr. **1** [mid–late 19C] to drink. **2** [mid–late 19C] to have sexual intercourse. **3** [late 19C+] to accept a punishment or reprimand, usu. with the implication that it is deserved.

take one's snake for a gallop, to phr. [20C] to masturbate (cf. GALLOP ONE'S ANTELOPE; PROMPT ONE'S PORPOISE).

take one's teeth to, to phr. [late 19C–1910s] to start eating.

take one's toe, to phr. [20C] (Ulster) to affect, to 'get into'.

take one's whack see HAVE ONE'S WHACK.

take on some backs, to phr. [1970s+] (US Black) to have anal intercourse.

take on with v. [1910s–20s] to form an association with (a man or woman).

take-out n. [20C] (US) a percentage of profits (cf. CUT n.⁴).

take out v.¹ [1930s+] (orig. US) to kill, to destroy (a specific target). [abbr. SE *take out of the picture*]

take out v.² [1980s+] (US campus) to engender happiness, to make (someone) laugh. [abbr. SE *take one out of oneself*]

take-out guy n. [1950s+] (US Und.) the man in a crooked card-game who always wins and as such attracts attention away from the real cheat who is manipulating all winning and losing cards (cf. MECHANIC).

take over the hurdles, to phr. [20C] (US prison) to attack in

a group (cf. RAT PACK; RIDE DOWN; WOLF PACK). [horse-racing imagery]

take pepper in the nose/snuff pepper, to phr. [16C–early 18C] to become angry. [SE *pepper* makes one HOT adj.¹ (2)]

take plush, to phr. [1910s–20s] to accept an inferior position or job. [? SE *plush*, generic for a servant]

taker n. [20C] (US) a person who accepts an offer or challenge.

take rattle, to phr. [late 17C–early 18C] to leave at speed. [either RATTLER n.¹ or SE *rattle off*]

taker-up n. [mid-17C–18C] the member of a criminal gang who keeps watch or entices a victim into a crooked gambling game (cf. SETTER n.¹).

take sheet and napkin, to phr. [17C–18C] to sleep and eat with someone.

take shit v. [1930s+] (orig. US) to suffer (and accept) humiliation or annoyance (cf. EAT SHIT v.). [SHIT n.⁴]

take sights v. [late 19C+] to watch, to survey. [obs. SE *sight*, a look or glance]

take snuff v. [late 16C–early 19C] to be offended. [SE *snuff*, the unpleasant smell of a snuffed candle, thus one fig. 'turns up one's nose']

take some doing see TAKE A BIT OF DOING.

take someone a buttonhole lower see TAKE SOMEONE DOWN A BUTTONHOLE.

take someone apart, to phr. [1950s+] **1** to beat someone severely. **2** to reprimand someone.

take someone down a buttonhole/a buttonhole lower, to phr. [late 16C–mid-17C] to humiliate someone, to deflate someone (cf. TAKE ONE DOWN A PEG). [the image of humiliating someone by undressing them in public]

take someone down a peg/peg or two, to phr. [mid-19C+] to reduce someone, usu. in their own excessive esteem. [the gradations of a SE *peg* tankard]

take someone for v. [1930s+] to trick, to deceive, to obtain from one who is unwilling otherwise to give, esp. in the extraction of money, e.g. *I took him for a tenner*.

take someone out of winding, to phr. [1920s+] (Aus.) to silence someone, to leave someone 'at a loss for words'. [SE *wind*, breath]

take someone's measure, to phr. [late 17C–early 19C] to assess someone's character (cf. GET SOMEONE'S MEASURE).

take someone's mind, to phr. [1940s–70s] (US Black) to manipulate someone's mind, usu. for neg. purposes.

take someone's pulse, to phr. [1970s] (gay) to fondle someone's genitals.

take/send someone to the cleaners, to phr. [1930s+] **1** to defraud, outwit and otherwise remove all of a victim's assets in a wager, by extortion or by similar legal or illegal means (cf. CLEAN SOMEONE'S CLOCK). **2** to defeat someone thoroughly, to trounce.

take someone up on something, to phr. [1910s+] to accept a proposal, an invitation.

take stock/large stock in/of, to phr. [mid-19C–1900s] (orig. US) to care about, to see as important, to take account of. [SE *stock*, a company share]

take stripes v. [late 19C] (US) to be sent to prison. [the old striped uniforms]

take tea with someone, to phr. [late 19C+] **1** (Und.) to outsmart a clever person or to defeat someone in authority. **2** (Aus.) to consort with someone, to associate with someone. [orig. colonial phr. *take tea with*, to associate with, esp. when the relations are mainly hostile]

take ten see TAKE FIVE.

take the air, to phr. [1910s–30s] (US) to leave, to escape, esp. as imper. (cf. AIR OUT).

take the bark off, to phr. [early–mid-19C] to reduce in value. [SE *bark*, the 'skin' of a tree]

take the bats, to *phr.* [1920s] to be eccentric or insane. [BATS adj.]

take the bayonet course, to *phr.* [1910s–40s] to be subjected to a cure of bismuth subcarbonate and neoarsphenamine for venereal disease; injections of the drugs continued weekly over a period of years (cf. RIDE THE SILVER STEED).

take the bent stick, to *phr.* [1910s–30s] of a woman who may no longer be easily marriageable, to abandon one's hopes of a perfect partner, substituting instead an elderly but constant admirer.

take the big dive, to *phr.* [1970s] to commit suicide.

take the big jump, to *phr.* [20C] (US, West.) to die.

take the biscuit, to *phr.* [late 19C+] to beat all rivals, esp. with the implication that the person, announcement, event etc is even more startling or appalling than might have been expected (cf. CAPTURE THE PICKLED BISCUIT; TAKE THE BUN; TAKE THE CAKE; TAKE THE CHEESE; TAKE THE COOKIE; TAKE THE FLOUR). [the fig. 'sweetness' or 'tastiness' of the *biscuit*]

take the bit of stiff *see* DO A BIT OF STIFF.

take the bun, to *phr.* [late 19C–1900s] (US) to surpass, to outdo, esp. in excessive or extreme behaviour (cf. TAKE THE BISCUIT). [var. on TAKE THE CAKE]

take the burnt chops, to *phr.* [1930s–40s] (N.Z.) to take up work as a musterer or drover. [the campfire meals musterers eat]

take the bus, to *phr.* [1970s+] (US teen) to go on the cheap, to bargain-hunt. [the price of bus fares, as opposed to airfares]

take the cake, to *phr.* [late 19C+] **1** to surpass, to outdo, esp. in excessive or extreme behaviour or of a near-intolerable situation or happening. **2** to be highly improbable (cf. TAKE THE BISCUIT). [the perceived 'tastiness' of the *cake*]

take the cheese, to *phr.* [late 19C] of a neg. circumstance or objectionable person, to surpass, to outdo (cf. TAKE THE BISCUIT). [CHEESE n.[1] (1)]

take the cookie, to *phr.* [late 19C] (US) of a neg. circumstance or objectionable person, to surpass, to outdo. [var. on TAKE THE BISCUIT]

take the corn, to *phr.* [mid-19C] (US) to become the focus of attention. [SE *corn whisky*, in the context of passing the bottle]

take the count, to *phr.* [late 19C–1900s] to die. [boxing imagery]

take the cure, to *phr.* [20C] (US) to give up something or refrain from doing something. [SE *take the cure*, to withdraw from alcohol/drug addiction]

take the dairy off, to *phr.*[1] [20C] to take the best of something. [i.e. to *skim the cream*]

take the dairy off, to *phr.*[2] [1970s] to divert suspicion. [corruption of SE *direction*, i.e. redirect attention]

take the day off to carry bricks, to *phr.* [1970s+] (N.Z.) to take a day off to do some of one's own work, e.g. do-it-yourself.

take the deep six *see* HIT THE DEEP SIX.

take the Dublin packet, to *phr.* [mid-19C–1900s] to run round the corner. [? SE *double*, to evade escape or the image of a literal escape from the UK to Ireland by the SE *packet-boat*, e.g. by a debtor or criminal]

take the dust, to *phr.* [late 19C] (US) to be overtaken. [the *dust* emanating from the passing vehicle]

take the Dutch route, to *phr.* [20C] (US prison) to commit suicide. [ext. of DUTCH ACT]

take the easy way out, to *phr.* [20C] to commit suicide. [ironic use of SE]

take the egg, to *phr.* [late 19C] (US) to win. [the perceived excellence of an *egg*]

take the fall, to *phr.* [1920s+] (US) to volunteer oneself as a victim, usu. as the alleged perpetrator of a crime, in the place of the real villain. [FALL n. (3)]

take the fatal step/the leap/the plunge, to *phr.* [20C] to get married.

take the flour, to *phr.* [late 19C] (US) of a neg. circumstance or objectionable person, to surpass, to outdo (cf. TAKE THE BISCUIT). [var. on TAKE THE CAKE]

take the gap, to *phr.* **1** [1950s+] to leave a party while it is still at its height. **2** [1960s+] (S.Afr.) to leave the country. [rugby jargon *take the gap*, to break past one's opponents]

take the gas, to *phr.* [20C] to endure punishment, esp. in a boxing ring. [the *gas* that knocks one out at the dentist's]

take the gas out of, to *phr.* [late 19C–1900s] to reduce (a person), usu. in their own excessive esteem (cf. TAKE ONE DOWN A PEG). [i.e. to deflate]

take the gilt off the gingerbread, to *phr.* [early 19C+] to disillusion, to remove one's fantasies, to downgrade. [according to Ware, 'the past-away annual fairs were made ghastly gay with flat gingerbread cakes, covered with Dutch metal (a zinc-copper mix that counterfeited gold leaf), which tried to look like gilt']

take the heat off, to *phr.* [1960s+] to relieve pressure on (a person). [HEAT n.[2]]

take the hot squat, to *phr.* [1920s+] (US) to be executed in the electric chair (cf. SIT IN THE HOT SEAT). [*hot squat* (*see* HOT SEAT)]

take the Huntley and Palmer, to *phr.* [late 19C–1910s] of a neg. circumstance or objectionable person, to surpass, to outdo. [play on TAKE THE BISCUIT, *Huntley and Palmer*, the well-known UK biscuit manufacturers]

take the inside out, to *phr.* [mid-19C] to finish, to empty, esp. of a glass of beer etc.

take the kettle, to *phr.* [late 19C] (Can.) to win, to take the prize.

take the kids to the pool, to *phr.* [1990s] to defecate. [coarse euph.]

take the knock, to *phr.*[1] [mid-19C+] (orig. US) **1** to accept the blame (cf. TAKE THE FALL). **2** to suffer an unpleasant surprise. [KNOCK v.[1] (4)]

take the knock *phr.*[2] *see* GET THE KNOCK.

take the last/long count, to *phr.* [1930s+] (US) to die (cf. HANG UP ONE'S BOOTS). [boxing imagery]

take the leap *see* TAKE THE FATAL STEP.

take the long count *see* TAKE THE LAST COUNT.

take the Michael *see* EXTRACT THE MICHAEL.

take the mickey/mike/mickey out of/mike out of, to *phr.* [1930s+] to tease; thus *mickey-take*, *mickey-taking* (cf. EXTRACT THE MICHAEL). [rhy. sl. *take the mickey bliss* = TAKE THE PISS]

take the monkey off your back! *excl.* [late 19C] calm down!

take the monster for a one-armed ride, to *phr.* [1990s] to masturbate.

take the needle, to *phr.* [20C] (Irish) to get angry. [var. on GET THE NEEDLE phr.[1]]

take the number off the door *phr.* [late 19C] a phr. used about a dwelling where the wife is seen as stronger than her husband. ['said of a domestic establishment where the wife is a shrew and by scolding draws attention to the domus. The removal of the number would make the cottage less discoverable' (Ware)]

take/thrash the pants off, to *phr.* [1930s+] to beat convincingly, to overwhelm.

take the pastry, to *phr.* [late 19C] (US) to lead. [ety. unknown]

take the pipe, to *phr.* [20C] (US) to fail to act or achieve under pressure, esp. in sports (cf. SWALLOW THE APPLE). [ety. unknown]

take the piss/piss out of, to *phr.* [20C] **1** to tease, esp. aggressively. **2** to attack verbally, to sneer or jeer at. [fig. use of PISS n.]

take the plunge *see* TAKE THE FATAL STEP.

take the rag off the bush/hedge, to *phr.* [19C] (US) to surpass, to excel, to outdo. [the image is of revealing one's abilities]

take the rap, to *phr.* [1950s+] **1** (US Und.) to take a punishment, often a prison sentence, that is actually due to someone else (cf. TAKE THE FALL). **2** (US) to take the blame when one is not the guilty party. [RAP n.³]

take the rust, to *phr.* [late 18C] of a horse, to become restive. [dial. *rust*, of a horse, restiveness]

take the scenic route, to *phr.* [1960s+] (orig. US teen) to concentrate on pleasure at the expense of efficiency or speed.

take the shine out of, to *phr.* [mid-19C] to beat, to surpass.

take the soles off someone's shoes, to *phr.* [late 19C] to surprise someone.

take the soup, to *phr.* [mid-19C+] to convert from Catholicism to Protestantism. [for ety. *see* SOUPER]

take the starch out of, to *phr.* [mid-19C+] of a woman, to have sexual intercourse with. [the wilted post-orgasmic penis]

take the tiles off, to *phr.* [late 19C] (society) to live in an extremely extravagant manner. [? one's fig. disposal of all one's assets, up to the house tiles]

take the tip, to *phr.* [early 19C+] to accept a bribe. [TIP n.² (2)]

take the track, to *phr.* [1910s+] (N.Z.) to be dismissed from a job.

take the weight, to *phr.* [1950s+] (US) to take the responsibility (cf. SHIFT THE WEIGHT).

take the weight off one's feet, to *phr.* [1930s+] to sit down, to relax.

take the wind, to *phr.* [1930s+] to leave. [sailing imagery]

take the wrinkles out of one's belly, to *phr.* [late 18C+] to assuage one's hunger (cf. KAFFIR'S TIGHTENER).

take the zero, to *phr.* [1980s+] (US campus) to pass something by, to turn down an offer, to reject. [ZERO n.]

take to *v.* [20C] (Aus./N.Z.) to attack, usu. with the fists. [abbr. SE *take one's fists to*]

take to one's scrapers, to *phr.* [late 18C–mid-19C] (Irish) to run off. [one's shoes 'scrape' the ground]

take to the fair, to *phr.* [20C] (Irish) to amaze, to astonish; thus *take things to the fair*, to exaggerate. [the excitements of a *fair*]

take to the hills, to *phr.* [1930s+] (orig. US) to run off. [Western or adventure film imagery]

take to lunch, to *phr.* [1980s+] (US) to surpass, to overcome. [i.e. *eat up*]

take to/hit the toe, to *phr.* [1950s+] (Aus./N.Z.) to leave quickly, to run off (cf. TOES LIVELY).

take two whiffs and a spit, to *phr.* [1910s–20s] to have a few puffs at a pipe. [SE *whiff*, a puff + *spit*]

take up *v.* [20C] (US) to arrest (cf. TAKE IN v.²).

take up one's foot and run *see* MAKE FOOT.

take water *v.* [20C] (Aus.) to leave a bar or public house after spending all one's cash on drink.

taking it easy *phr.* [19C] feeling slightly drunk (cf. ABOUT RIGHT adj.¹). [euph.]

Taki-Taki *n.* [20C] (W.I.) Sranan, the Surinamese Creole language. [i.e. 'talky-talky']

takkie/tackie *n.* [1910s+] (S.Afr.) a rubber-soled, laced canvas shoe. [SE *tacky*, sticky]

takkouri *n.* [1980s+] (drugs) marijuana. [ety. unknown]

talcum queen *n.* [1980s+] (US Black) a Black homosexual who prefers White partners. [SE *talcum* (powder, usu. white) + QUEEN n.¹]

tale *n.* [20C] any form of words designed to ensnare the listener for commercial purposes.

talent *n.* **1** [late 19C–1950s] (Aus.) a generic term for the criminal underworld. **2** [1940s+] attractive young women, esp. those standing around at a party, in a club or dance-hall etc.

tale of two cities *n.* [1950s] the female breasts (cf. BRISTOLS; CATS AND KITTIES). [rhy. sl. *tale of two cities* = titties (*see* TITTY n.²)]

tale-pitcher *n.* [late 19C] one who tells a good story, a romantic. [thus the popular nickname of the racing journalist, raconteur and bon viveur Arthur Binstead (1861–1914), 'The Pitcher', best known to the readers of the *Sporting Times*]

Taliano *n.* [20C] an Italian. [abbr. of Ital. *Italiano*]

talk *v.* [1920s+] (Und.) to confess or turn informer to the police or similar authority.

talk a blue streak, to *phr.* [early 19C+] (orig. US) to talk both fast and at great length. [SE *blue streak*, that which resembles a flash of lightning]

talk about ... *phr.* [mid-19C+] a phr. used to convey one's horror, surprise, amusement at a piece of information or action, often using a n. or phr. that is jokingly synon. with the subject of the phr., e.g. *Tall? Talk about Mount Everest ...* .

talk a good game/great ball game, to *phr.* [1970s+] (orig. US) to talk persuasively, but with the implication that nothing is ever actually done. [sporting imagery]

talk back to *v.* [mid-19C+] to make a rude response to, to be impudent.

talk big *v.* [late 17C+] to boast, to exaggerate.

talk bullock *v.* [mid-19C+] (N.Z.) to use a good deal of bad language. [the typical vocabulary of a *bullock*-driver + play on BALLOCKS n.² (2)]

talk business *v.* [1960s+] (US Black) to seduce, to charm.

talk by a bow, to *phr.* [late 19C] to argue, to quarrel. [ety. unknown; ? link to DRAW A LONG BOW]

talk church *v.* [mid-19C+] to talk solely of one's occupation, to TALK SHOP. [? orig. in clerical circles]

talk cock *v.* [mid-19C+] to talk nonsense. [COCK n.⁴; although the assumed link is to COCK n.² (1)]

talk cold turkey, to *phr.* [early 19C+] (orig. US) to speak frankly and without reserve, to talk hard facts, to get down to business. [ext. of TALK TURKEY v. (2)]

talk crisp *v.* [1910s–20s] to say unpleasant things. [note SE *talk sharply*]

talk double Dutch/Dutch, to *phr.* [late 18C+] to talk nonsense (cf. TALK DUTCH FUSTIAN; TALK HIGH DUTCH). [SE *double dutch*, incomprehensible language]

talk-down *n.* [1960s+] the comforting of someone who is having a bad experience, usu. through injudicious use of drugs, esp. a hallucinogen. [TALK SOMEONE DOWN v.]

talk Dutch *see* TALK DOUBLE DUTCH.

talk Dutch fustian, to *phr.* [late 16C–early 17C] to talk nonsense (cf. TALK DOUBLE DUTCH). [note late 16C *fustian*, Und. or thieves' jargon]

talkee-talkee house *n.* [late 19C] the Houses of Parliament. [fake pidgin, to underpin the image of empty chatter]

talker *n.¹* [mid-19C] a horse that is past its prime (cf. PIPER n.¹; ROARER n.²). [its heavy breathing]

talker *n.²* [1970s+] a prostitute's client who wishes only to talk, either of sex or merely of his life.

talkfest *see* BLABFEST.

talk forty to the dozen, to *phr.* [19C+] to talk enthusiastically and continually.

talk from the teeth out, to *phr.* [20C] (Ulster) to speak hypocritically. [i.e. such talk does not come 'from the heart']

talk fuck *v.* [1960s+] to murmur or shout obscenities during sexual intercourse for the gratification of one or both partners.

talk funny *v.* [1920s+] to speak in a manner other than that customary to the speaker (cf. TALK PROPER).

talk game v. [1970s+] (US) of a pimp, to chatter about pimping, whoring and those involved; thus *talk a good game*, to be persuasive. [GAME n.⁵]

talk goody v. [mid–late 19C] to talk in a vapid, sentimental manner. [GOODY n.¹]

talk head v. [1980s+] (US campus) to talk in a neg. manner. [? TV jargon *talking head*, a supposed expert brought onto TV who pontificates, often in a dry, didactic manner, on a topic of current interest]

talk High Dutch, to phr. [late 18C–mid-19C] to talk nonsense (cf. TALK DOUBLE DUTCH). [SE *high Dutch*, incomprehensible language, presumably fig. use not of 'Dutch' but *Hochdeutsch*, High German, the German spoken in the southern part of the country]

talk horse v. [late 19C] to boast, to 'talk big'.

talking n.¹ [1970s+] **1** (US campus) being involved in a relationship. **2** (lesbian) having a relationship with another woman while in prison. [euph.]

talking n.² [1980s+] a serious conversation.

talking n.³ [1980s+] a use of SE *talking* with the word 'about' unstated, implying not so much person-to-person communication, but as a way of emphasizing the importance and immediacy of the topic in hand, e.g. *we're talking telephone numbers*, this will be a very large sum of money. [originated in Hollywood where hyperbole is dominant, the implication is often one of slight reproof, i.e. don't forget, we are not discussing any old topic, sum of money etc but something quite exceptional or startling]

talking head/hairdo n. [1960s+] **1** a television presenter or interviewee (usu. in the role of 'expert') who is shot in head-and-shoulders close-up, the director eschewing any background or other movement. **2** (US Black) one who is in a bad temper and on the verge of fighting.

talking shit/trash phr.¹ [1930s+] (US Black) any verbal by-play, banter between men, flirtation between a man and a woman etc. [TALK SHIT v.¹/TALK TRASH]

talking shit phr.² [1930s+] (orig. US) talking nonsense. [TALK SHIT v.²]

talking-to n. [late 19C+] a scolding, a reprimand.

talking to jamie moore phr. [late 19C–1900s] (Scot.) drunk. [? anecdotal]

talking tommy n. [1930s] (juv.) a comb and paper used to make music.

talking trash see TALKING SHIT phr.¹.

talk like a book, to phr. [early 19C+] to appear well-educated and literate.

talk like a ha'penny book phr.¹ see TALK LIKE A PENNY BOOK.

talk like a ha'penny/halfpenny book, to phr.² [20C] (Irish) to talk nonsense. [SE *ha'penny book*, a comic, a cheap paperback]

talk like a man with a paper ass/asshole, to phr. [1940s+] (US) to talk nonsense. [ARSE n.¹/ARSEHOLE n.]

talk like an apothecary, to phr. [late 18C–early 19C] to talk nonsense. [the jargon-laden speech associated with apothecaries]

talk like a penny/halfpenny/ha'penny book, to phr. [late 19C–1900s] a phr. used by an illiterate person of one whose fluency is considered suspect and overly 'clever'. [any reading, however basic, is seen as 'clever']

talk like the back of a cigarette card, to phr. [20C] to pretend to greater knowledge than one has. [the cards that were once supplied in every pack of cigarettes and which carried a picture on one side and text (a description, a potted biography) on the other]

talk Miss Nancy, to phr. [19C] to speak in an effeminate manner. [SE *talk* + MISS NANCY]

talk off the top of one's head, to phr. [1960s+] to talk spontaneously, extempore, ad lib, with no factual backing.

talk of the devil! excl. [20C] an excl. used to greet someone who appears at the very moment one is talking, not necessarily antagonistically, about them. [17C pvb., 'talk of the devil and you'll see his horns and tail']

talk one's head off, to phr. [1950s+] (orig. US) to talk incessantly (cf. TALK SOMEONE'S EAR OFF).

talk on the great white telephone see SPEAK TO THE GREAT WHITE TELEPHONE.

talk out of one's head, to phr. [20C] (US Black) to talk nonsense (cf. TALK OUT OF THE BACK OF ONE'S NECK).

talk out of school, to phr. [20C] to tell tales, to talk unguardedly.

talk out of the back of one's neck, to phr. [1960s+] to talk nonsense.

talk out of the side of one's neck, to phr. [1970s+] (US Black) **1** to talk surreptitiously to ensure that one's conversation remains unheard by eavesdroppers. **2** to talk nonsense (cf. TALK THROUGH ONE'S ARSE).

talk out of turn, to phr. [20C] (US) to speak one's mind, to be frank.

talk packthread v. [late 18C–early 19C] to talk in double entendres. ['to use indecent language, well wrapt up' (Grose 1796). SE *packthread*, heavyweight cord or twine used for tying bundles]

talk poor mouth, to phr. [20C] (US) to deny one's assets or advantages. [POOR MOUTH]

talk pretty see SPEAK PRETTY.

talk proper v. [20C] to talk Standard English (cf. PROPER adv.; TALK FUNNY).

talk quietly to oneself, to phr. [1990s] to masturbate.

talk shit v.¹ [1930s+] (US Black) to seduce, to 'chat someone up' (cf. TALK TRASH). [SHIT n.³]

talk shit v.² [1930s+] (orig. US) **1** to talk nonsense. **2** (US campus) to criticize someone behind their back. **3** (US campus) to boast, to brag. [SHIT n.⁴]

talk shop v. [late 19C+] of people in the same trade or profession, to discuss one's job.

talk smack, to phr. [1990s] (US Black/teen) to gossip maliciously (cf. TALK SHIT v.²). [puns on SHIT n.⁵, heroin/SHIT n.⁴, nonsense, SMACK n.⁵, heroin and JUNK n.³, heroin/SE *junk*, rubbish]

talk someone down v. [1960s+] (drugs) to comfort a person who is having a bad experience, usu. after taking drugs, esp. LSD. [the comforter brings them down from the 'high' and back to normality]

talk someone's ear off, to phr. [1950s+] (orig. US) to talk incessantly (cf. TALK ONE'S HEAD OFF).

talk-talk n. [20C] (US) idle chatter (cf. TALKY-TALK).

talk talk and walk walk, to phr. [1960s+] (US Black) to do whatever is natural and comfortable (cf. TALK THAT TALK AND WALK THAT WALK).

talk that talk, to phr. [1930s+] (US Black) **1** to chatter inconsequentially. **2** to indulge in ritual name-calling, esp. based on insulting one's opponent's mother (cf. DOZENS).

talk that talk and walk that walk phr. [1960s+] (US Black) a phr. of encouragement for one's verbal skills.

talk the hind leg off a donkey/bird/cow/dog/horse/jackass, to phr. [early 19C+] to talk continually and obsessively, seemingly with no sign of ever stopping.

talk the leg off an iron pot, to phr. [20C] (N.Z.) to be overly talkative.

talk thirteen to the dozen, to phr. [19C+] to talk very fast and unintelligibly (cf. TALK FORTY TO THE DOZEN).

talk through one's arse/ass, to phr. [20C] to talk nonsense;

thus coarse *phr. be quiet/shut your mouth and give your ass a rest.* [ARSE n.[1]]

talk through one's braces, to *phr.* [1920s+] (Aus.) to talk nonsense, to talk rubbish. [var. on TALK THROUGH ONE'S HAT]

talk through one's fly-buttons, to *phr.* [1960s] **1** to talk nonsense, to talk rubbish (cf. TALK COCK). **2** to talk in a sexually provocative or sex-obsessed manner. [(1) var. on TALK THROUGH ONE'S HAT]

talk through one's hat, to *phr.* [late 19C+] (orig. US) **1** to talk nonsense. **2** to boast and exaggerate (cf. TALK THROUGH ONE'S ARSE/BRACES/FLY-BUTTONS).

talk through the back of one's neck, to *phr.* [late 19C+] to talk nonsense, to talk rubbish.

talk to *v.* [mid-19C+] (orig. US) to scold, to 'tell off'; thus *talking-to*, a 'telling-off', a reprimand.

talk to one's plate, to *phr.* [20C] (US) to say grace before a meal (cf. BRAG THE POTATOES).

talk to one's saddle, to *phr.* [late 19C+] to talk to oneself. [the loneliness of the solitary musterer]

talk to Ralph on the big white telephone, to *phr.* [1970s+] (orig. US campus) to vomit (cf. HUGHIE). [ext. of RALPH v.]

talk to the big white phone, to *phr.* [1970s+] (orig. US campus) to vomit. [the *big white phone* being the lavatory]

talk to the canoe-driver, to *phr.* [1960s] (US) to perform cunnilingus. [play on SE *canoe/cunnilingus*]

talk to the engineer, not the oily rag, to *phr.* [1950s+] to deal with the boss, not an assistant.

talk to the mike, to *phr.* [1980s+] (US teen) to perform fellatio. [SE *microphone*]

talk-trap *n.* [20C] (US) the mouth.

talk trash *v.* [1920s+] (US Black) to talk insincerely, to lie, esp. when pursuing sex (cf. TALK SHIT v.[1]).

talk turkey *v.* [early 19C+] (orig. US) **1** to talk agreeably or affably, to say pleasant things. **2** to speak frankly and without reserve, to talk hard facts, to get down to business (cf. TALK COLD TURKEY). **3** to use high-flown language. [the bird's central role in a trad. Christmas dinner]

talk under water/wet cement *phr.* [1970s+] (Aus.) a phr. used of a very talkative person, usu. as *they could talk under…* .

talk up a storm, to *phr.* [20C] (US) to talk loudly, at length and impressively. [SE *storm*]

talk wet *v.* [1910s+] to talk in a sentimental, 'soft' manner. [WET adj.[3]]

talky-talk *n.* [20C] idle, futile, empty talk (cf. TALK-TALK).

talky-talky boots *n.* [late 19C] (W.I.) squeaky shoes or boots.

tall *adj.*[1] **1** [mid-17C] of speech, boastful, high-flown. **2** [mid-19C] excellent in quality. **3** [mid-19C+] of speech, extravagant, untrue, esp. in phr. *tall story* (cf. TALLIE; TALL TALK). **4** [mid-19C+] (orig. US) very large (cf. TALL ORDER).

tall *adj.*[2] [mid-19C+] (orig. US) esp. of money, large in quantity.

tall *adj.*[3] [20C] (US) a general term of approbation, excellent, first-rate. [? the boastfulness of *tall stories*, in which everything appears to be marvellous, superlative etc]

tallawah *adj.* [1960s+] (W.I.) **1** honest, honourable, decent. **2** sturdy, fearless, physically capable. [synon. Ewe *talala*]

tall boy *n.* [late 17C–early 19C] **1** a large wineglass. **2** a 2.3-litre (2-quart) pot filled with wine.

tall cotton *see* HIGH COTTON.

tall habit *n.* [1950s–70s] (US Black) a serious drug addiction. [TALL adj.[2] + HABIT n.]

tallie *n.* [1930s+] (Aus.) a 'tall' story.

tall money *n.* [1940s–60s] (US Black) a large amount of money, substantial wealth. [TALL adj.[2]]

tall order *n.* [late 19C+] an excessive or extreme demand, also as *big order* (cf. LARGE ORDER). [TALL adj.[1]]

tallow *n.*[1] [19C] semen. [resemblance]

tallow *n.*[2] [mid–late 19C] (Aus.) one who has prospered as a grazier. [SE *tallow*, animal fat or dripping, thus they have enjoyed 'the fat of the land']

tallow-breeched *adj.* [18C–mid-19C] having fat buttocks. [SE *tallow*, fatness + *breech*, the posterior]

tallow-gutted *adj.* [18C–mid-19C] pot-bellied. [SE *tallow*, fatness + *guts*]

tall paper *see* BIG PAPER.

tall poppy *n.* [20C] (Aus.) a conspicuously high earner or other VIP.

tall talk *n.* [mid-19C+] (orig. US) boasting, bragging, the telling of far-fetched stories and anecdotes. [TALL adj.[1] + SE *talk*]

tall timbers *n.* [20C] (US) the rural areas, the backwoods (cf. RHUBARBS; STICKS n.[6]).

tall 'un *n.* [late 19C] a pint of coffee (cf. SHORT 'UN). [SE *tall one*]

tall weeping *n.* [late 19C] (US) intense grief. [TALL adj.[2] + SE *weeping*]

tally-ho *n.* [20C] (Irish) confusion, fuss. [SE excl. *tally-ho!*, esp. in foxhunting]

tally-husband/-man *n.* [late 19C] the man with whom a woman cohabits (cf. TALLY-WIFE). [LIVE TALLY]

tallywag/tallywhacker/tallywock *n.* [18C] the penis. [? SE *tally*, a notched stick or TAIL n.[1] (1)]

tallywagger *n.* **1** [18C] the penis (cf. TALLYWAG). **2** [20C] (Anglo-Irish) a thread dangling from the hem of a garment or from the edge of a rug, carpet etc (cf. TRALLYAGGER). [Devon/Cheshire dial. *tallywag*, penis]

tallywags/tarrywags *n.* [late 18C–early 19C] the testicles. [TALLYWAG]

tallywhacker *see* TALLYWAG.

tally-wife/-woman *n.* [late 19C] the woman with whom a man cohabits (cf. TALLY-HUSBAND). [LIVE TALLY]

tallywock *see* TALLYWAG.

tally-woman *see* TALLY-WIFE.

t.a.l.o.i.a. *phr.* [1950s+] *there's a lot of it about.* [abbr.]

talosk *n.* [late 19C] (tinker) weather. [Shelta]

tam *n.* [1950s+] (W.I. Rasta) the large woollen hat used by Rastafarians to cover their dreadlocks. [abbr. SE *tam o'shanter*]

tamale *n.* [1960s+] (gay) gaudy ceramic crockery typical of that sold to tourists in Mexico (cf. MEXICAN NIGHTMARE). [Mex. Sp. *tamale*, a delicacy, made of crushed Indian corn, flavoured with pieces of meat or chicken, red pepper etc, wrapped in corn husks and baked]

tamarboo *n.* [mid-19C] a coachman. [a contemporary song title]

Tambaroora *n.* [late 19C–1920s] (Aus.) a bar game in which the winner buys drinks for the players; thus *Tambaroora muster*, a group of drinkers pooling their money and buying one 'wholesale' round, since in this way more alcohol can be purchased. [*Tambaroora*, a town in New South Wales, home of the game]

tambourine man *n.* [1960s] (US drugs) a drug dealer. [? the Bob Dylan song *Mr Tambourine Man* (1964)]

tame the beef weasel, to *phr.* [1990s] to masturbate (cf. ACCOST THE OSCAR MEYER).

tampon braces *n.* [1930s–40s] (US Black) a derog. term for unattractive legs on a woman.

ta muchly! *excl.* [20C] thank you very much. [ext. of TA!]

tan *v.* [late 19C+] to attack, to hit; thus *tanning*, a beating, also used fig. e.g. *tan the bevvy*, to drink heavily. [abbr. TAN SOMEONE'S HIDE]

t.a.n. *adj.* [1980s+] (US campus) aggressively masculine. [abbr. *tough as nails*]

T & A *see* TITS AND ASS.

t & k *n.* [1980s+] (US drugs) the *t*orch and *k*nife used for smoking hashish on a blade. [abbr. *torch and knife*]

tandoori v. [1990s] to coat a man's penis with menstrual blood. [the red marinade that colours Ind. *tandoori* chicken]

tang n. [1970s] (US campus) someone who puts a damper on things. [SE *tang*, a flavour; such a person gives the situation an 'unpleasant flavour']

tangi n. [1930s+] (N.Z.) a gathering, a celebration, a 'beano'. [Maori *tangi*, a tribal gathering at a funeral]

Tangier n. [late 18C–early 19C] a room in Newgate gaol, dedicated to the imprisonment of debtors, who were known as *tangerines*. [the sufferings imposed on the victims of the contemporary Tangiers pirates]

tangle n. [late 19C–1900s] (Aus.) alcoholic liquor (cf. TANGLE-FOOT; TANGLE-LEG). [its effects]

tangle assholes, to phr. [1920s+] (US) to fight (cf. LOCK ASSHOLES). [SE *tangle* + ARSEHOLE n.]

tangled adj. [late 19C–1900s] (Aus.) drunk (cf. ADDLED). [TANGLE]

tangle-foot n. [mid-late 19C] whisky (cf. TANGLE-LEG); thus *tangle-footed*, drunk. [its effects]

tangle-leg n. [late 19C] whisky; thus *tangle-legged*, drunk (cf. TANGLE-FOOT). [its effects]

tangle-monger n. [late 19C] (society) a woman scandalmonger. [SE *tangle*, a knotted mess + sfx. -MONGER]

tangle with v. [1950s+] to become involved with, to fight with.

tango & cash n. [1980s+] (drugs) fentanyl. [film title *Tango & Cash*, 1989; ? rhy. sl. with APACHE n.²]

tango pirate n. [20C] (US) a gigolo. [such men took advantage of the tango craze of the early 20C to meet, seduce and even live off the affluent women they met at tea-dances]

tang out v. [1970s] (US campus) to abandon, to put an end to. [TANG n.]

tank n.¹ [1910s] a worn-out old prostitute. [the then newly invented SE *tank*, a bulky and misshapen form of weapon]

tank n.² **1** [1910s+] (Can./US prison) a prison. **2** [1910s+] (Can./US prison) a holding cell. **3** [1930s+] (N.Z. Und.) a safe; thus *tank artist, tankblower, tankman*, a safe-cracker. [SE *tank*, a storage receptacle]

tank n.³ [1930s–50s] (Aus.) a pint of beer. [? SE *tankard* or TANK V.¹]

tank v.¹ [late 19C+] (US campus) to drink heavily. [SE *tank*, a cistern]

tank v.² [20C] to abandon deliberately, to give up, possibly for illicit monetary gain, esp. in boxing; thus *tank fight, tank job*, a contest in which one fighter has been bribed to lose; *tanking*, the deliberate losing of matches (cf. TAKE A DIVE; GO IN THE TANK). [SE *tank*, a swimming pool, thus the boxer 'takes a dive']

tanka n. [1980s+] (US campus) a large container of soft drink. [? SE *tank of...*]

tanked/tanked up adj. [late 19C+] drunk; thus intensified in phr. *tanked to the wide*. [TANK V.¹]

tanker n.¹ [20C] a prize-fighter who has agreed to accept cash in return for losing a fight. [TANK V.²]

tanker n.² [1930s] a heavy drinker. [TANK V.¹]

tank time n. [1980s+] (US campus) time to start drinking. [TANK V.¹]

tank town n. [20C] (US) a small, insignificant town (cf. JERKWATER TOWN; WHISTLE STOP). [the positioning of water tanks at such railway stops, the only reason why a train might stop there]

tank up v. [1930s+] to drink heavily (cf. TANKED UP). [TANK V.¹]

tanky adj. [1930s+] (US) drunk. [TANK V.¹]

tanned adj. [1900s] thrashed, beaten. [TAN SOMEONE'S HIDE]

tanner n. [early 19C–1970s] sixpence, thus post-metrication 2½ pence (cf. GODDESS DIANA; LORD OF THE MANOR; SIMON; SUSY); thus [1900s–10s] *tannercab*, a sixpenny cab; [late 19C–1910s] *tannergram*, a sixpenny telegram. [Rom. *tawno*, small or f. a ponderous Bible joke about St Peter's supposed banking transaction when he 'lodged with one Simon a tanner']

tannery n. [late 19C] (US) a pair of outsize boots or shoes. [SE *tannery*, a leather-maker's]

tannie n. [1950s+] (S.Afr.) a narrow-minded, puritan, small-town woman. [Afk. *tante*, aunt; used affectionately or respectfully the word means simply 'auntie']

tan-pan-mi n. [1950s] (W.I.) ragged old work-clothes, esp. when very filthy. [lit. 'stand upon me', the clothing has become stiffened through the accretion of dirt]

tan pon it long phr. [1980s+] (W.I./UK Black teen) sexual stamina. [lit. 'stand up on it for a long time']

tan someone's hide/arse, to phr. [late 17C+] to beat someone severely, to spank someone severely. [SE *tan*, to process skins into leather + HIDE n.¹/ARSE n.]

tantadlin see TANTOBLIN.

tantaria n. [20C] (W.I.) an abusive, loud, shrewish woman. [? SE *tantara*, imitation word for the sound of a trumpet or drum]

tantivy/tantivy-boy n. **1** [late 17C–mid-18C] a nickname given to the post-Restoration High Churchmen and Tories, esp. in the reigns of Charles II (1660–85) and James II (1685–88). **2** [early 18C+] imitative of the sound of a hunting horn. [SE *tantivy*, a gallop at full tilt. The nickname use arose c.1680, when a caricature was published in which a number of High Church clergymen were represented as mounted upon the Church of England and 'riding tantivy' to Rome, behind the Duke of York]

tantoblin/tantoblin tart/tantadlin n. [mid-17C–late 18C] a piece of excrement. [SE *tantoblin*, a large, round sweet tart and dial. *tantablin tart*, cow dung]

tantony see ANTHONY.

tan track n. [late 19C+] the anus (cf. DIRT ROAD n.²; HERSHEY HIGHWAY).

tan-tracker/tan-track rider n. [1930s+] (orig. Aus.) a homosexual man. [TAN TRACK]

tantrems n. [mid-late 19C] pranks, games, jollification. [var. on TANTRUM n.² + dial. *tantrum*, a freak, a whimsy]

tantrum n.¹ [late 17C–late 18C] the penis. [northern dial. *tantril*, a wanderer]

tantrum n.² [early 18C–mid-19C] a burst of petulant ill-temper, seen as childish or actually produced by a child. [SE by 20C, ? Ital. *tarantella*, a whirling dance which may reduce the dancers to near- or apparent hysteria]

tanyok n. [18C+] a halfpenny. [Shelta]

taoc n. [mid-late 19C] a coat (cf. TOAC). [backsl.]

tap n. [early 17C–late 19C] a particular variety or type. [SE *tap*, the liquor drawn from a particular tap, a specific type of drink]

tap v.¹ [early 18C] to spend freely and generously. [the image is of 'turning on a *tap*' of gifts etc]

tap v.² [mid-late 19C] to arrest. [the *tap* on the shoulder]

tap v.³ [mid-late 19C] to hit and thus draw blood from a victim's nose. [SE *tap*, to hit + *tap*, a valve]

tap v.⁴ [1920s+] (US) to select for a college fraternity or society. [a *tap* on the shoulder]

tap v.⁵ [1960s–70s] (drugs) to inject oneself with a hypodermic syringe. [SE *tap*, to hit + *tap*, a valve]

tap a girl, to phr. [late 18C–early 19C] to deflower a woman. [SE *tap*, to open; added ref. to the release of blood]

tap a guinea, to phr. [late 18C–early 19C] to get change for a guinea. [SE *tap*, to open]

tap a house, to phr. [late 19C] to burgle a house. [SE *tap*, to open]

tap a judy, to phr.¹ [mid-late 19C] to deflower a girl. [SE *tap*, to hit + JUDY n.¹; there is a sub-ref. to TAP ONE'S CLARET, given the release of blood]

tap a judy, to phr.[2] [mid–late 19C] to cause one's nose to bleed with a blow. [ext. of TAP A JUDY phr.[1]]

tap a keg, to phr. [20C] (US) to urinate.

tap/tilt a kidney, to phr. [1970s+] (US) to urinate.

tap city n. [20C] **1** the state of being unable to raise a stake for further betting. **2** a state of poverty (cf. TAP SOMEONE FOR). [SE tap + sfx. -CITY, f. the tradition of tapping the table to signify one's situation]

tapdance, to phr. [1920s+] (orig. US) to wriggle out of trouble, to evade something cleverly.

tape n. [early 18C–mid-19C] a fiery drink, spirits, usu. gin (cf. BLUE TAPE; GLIM n.[2]; HOLLAND TAPE; RED TAPE; SATIN). [ety. unknown; ? link to SE taphouse]

taped adv. [1920s+] (US) for certain. [the use of a fig. tape measure]

taped-up adj. [1970s] (US Black) of a woman, already with a boyfriend, thus secured from other admirers.

tape off v. [1920s+] (Aus.) **1** to prepare, to get ready, to put into place. **2** to reprimand. **3** to measure out correctly. [SE tape measure]

taper adj. [mid-19C] of money or supplies, diminishing, running out.

tape the gerbil, to phr. [1990s] (US teen) to study hard. [ety. unknown]

tapioca n. [20C] (cards) a joker. [rhy. sl.]

tapioca adj. [1970s] (US campus) absolutely penniless (cf. TAP CITY). [TAPPED-OUT]

tap-lash n. **1** [early 17C–early 19C] inferior liquor, esp. its dregs. **2** [mid-17C–early 18C] a publican. [SE tap + lash, lit. 'beat the tap', i.e. thump it in order to extract the very last drips from the cask or barrel]

tap on the shoulder, to phr. [late 18C] to arrest.

tapped adj. [19C] insane, crazy. [DOOLALLY]

tapped-out adj. [1950s+] **1** out of money, having nothing to use for further betting (cf. TAP CITY). **2** (US) exhausted. [one's tap on the table, signifying that one has no more money; (2) is fig. use of (1)]

tapper n.[1] **1** [late 18C–early 19C] a bailiff (cf. SHOULDER-TAPPER). **2** [late 19C+] a cadger (cf. TAP SOMEONE FOR). [SE tap on the shoulder]

tapper n.[2] [1910s–20s] one who cuts into casks of wine or spirits and uses a straw to drink the contents. [SE tap, to broach a cask]

taps n. [mid-18C–mid-19C] the ears (cf. TAB n.[1]).

tap someone for v. [1930s+] to borrow, or attempt to borrow (money); thus on the tap, begging, scrounging (cf. PUT THE ARM ON; PUT THE BITE ON). [the lit. or fig. tap on the shoulder/arm]

tap someone's claret, to phr. [mid–late 19C] to cause one's nose to bleed with a blow.

tap the admiral, to phr. [mid-19C] to suck liquor through a straw from the ship's barrel which has been bored with a gimlet (cf. SUCK THE MONKEY). [according to Hotten (1864), the practice originated when sailors sucked out the liquor from the barrel in which Admiral Horatio Nelson's body had been preserved on the journey home after his death at the battle of Trafalgar, 'to such an extent as to leave the gallant Admiral high and dry']

tap-tub n. [mid-19C] the Morning Advertiser newspaper, also known as the Gin and Gospel Gazette. [SE tap, to broach a cask + tub (of liquor); the paper was the virtual house journal of the great and powerful brewing families]

tar n.[1] [mid-17C+] a sailor (cf. TARRY-BREEKS). [the use of tar on board ship]

tar n.[2] [20C] (drugs) opium, heroin. [colour and consistency of Mexican heroin]

ta-ra! excl. [1950s+] (mainly north) goodbye! (cf. TA-TA!).

taradiddle/tarradiddle n. [late 18C–late 19C] a petty lie; thus taradiddler, a petty liar. [DIDDLE]

Taranaki bullshit n. [1940s+] (N.Z.) excessive boasting. [BULLSHIT n. + ref. to the many Taranaki dairy herds]

Taranaki cow n. [1940s] (N.Z.) a nondescript, inferior cow.

Taranaki gate phr. [20C] (N.Z.) a gate made of strands of barbed wire interwoven with palings for strength. [Taranaki, an area of the South Island]

Taranaki sunshine n. [1990s] (N.Z.) rain or drizzle.

Taranaki top dressing phr. [20C] (N.Z.) cattle dung. [see TARANAKI GATE]

tar and feather n. [20C] leather, usu. a leather jacket. [rhy. sl.]

tarantula-juice n. [1930s] inferior whisky. [its alcoholic 'bite']

tar baby n. **1** [20C] (US) a 'sticky' problem. **2** [1940s+] (US) a Black person. **3** [1950s] (N.Z.) a derog. term for a Maori. [the Tar Baby, created by Joel Chandler Harris in 1881, when in one of his 'Uncle Remus' tales the scheming Br'er Fox, determined to catch Harris' lapine hero Brer Rabbit, 'got im some tar, en mix it wid some turkentime, en fix up a contrapshun what he call a Tar-Baby']

tar-boiler see TARHEEL.

tard n. [1970s+] (US) a fool. [abbr. RETARD]

tare an' ages! excl. [mid-19C] (Irish) a euph. oath. [SE tears and aches (of Christ)]

tare an' ouns! excl. [late 19C] (Irish) a euph. oath. [SE tears and wounds (of Christ)]

t.a.r.f.u. phr. [1940s+] (orig. US milit.) things are really fucked-up (cf. S.N.A.F.U. phr.). [abbr.]

target n.[1] [late 17C] the vagina (cf. BEST IN CHRISTENDOM). [coined by John Wilmot, Earl of Rochester (1642–80)]

target n.[2] [1970s–80s] (S.Afr. township) anything, esp. a motor vehicle owned by a White-run company, seen as symbolic of apartheid and as such liable to criminal and violent acts.

tarheel/tar-boiler n. [mid-19C+] a native of North Carolina. [SE tar, as a principal product of the state]

tarleather n. [17C] a general term of abuse directed at women. [SE tarleather, a strip of leather used in a flail. The women thus described are presumably seen as 'scolds' and, given that leather means vagina, the word is a distant precursor of PUSSY-WHIPPED]

tarnal adj. [late 18C+] (US) used as a neg. intensifier, cussed, damned (cf. TARNATION!). [SE eternal]

tarnation! excl. [late 18C+] (US) a euph. substitute for DAMNATION! (cf. TARNAL). [note 18C abbr. SE nation, damnation]

tar out v. [mid-19C–1900s] to punish, to beat (cf. WHALE THE TAR OUT OF). [i.e. to beat the tar out of]

tarp n. [20C] tarpaulin. [abbr.]

tarpaulin n. [mid-17C–1900s] a sailor, esp. (in the days when appointments were made as much on connections as on ability) a sailor with practical experience of seamanship. [use of SE tarpaulin on ships]

tarpaulin/blanket/calico/canvas muster n. [late 19C+] (Aus./N.Z.) a collection of money, either for a round of drinks or for donation to a third party or a cause. [naut. jargon tarpaulin muster, a collection or pooling of money among seamen]

tarpot n. [1940s] (N.Z.) a derog. term for a Maori. [SE tar is black]

tarradiddle see TARADIDDLE.

tarra-warra n. [1950s+] (W.I. Rasta) a polite way of expressing omitted bad words, a verbal asterisk. [? echoic of the hesitation over or mumbling of 'bad' words]

tarry-breeks n. [late 18C] a sailor (cf. TAR n.[1]). Similar nicknames include [early 19C–1910s] tarry-jacket; [late 18C–1910s] tarry-John. [lit. 'tarry breeches']

tarryin *n.* [18C+] (tinker) a rope. [Shelta]

tarry rope *n.* [1950s–60s] (Aus.) a woman, poss. a prostitute, who associates with sailors. [SE *tarry*, covered in tar + *rope*]

tarrywags *see* TALLYWAGS.

tart *n.* **1** [mid-19C+] a woman, a girlfriend (cf. BANANA *n.*²). **2** [late 19C+] a promiscuous woman, a prostitute. **3** [1930s+] (gay) an older man's young lover. **4** [1930s+] (gay) a gay prostitute. [although (1) can be found, usu. in dial., (2) has come to dominate since early 20C, apart from Aus./N.Z., where the term remains pos. or neutral]

tart *v.* [1940s] (Aus./N.Z.) to pursue women. [TART *n.* (1)]

tart about *v.* [1930s+] of a woman, to act in a promiscuous manner. [TART *n.* (2)]

tartan banner *n.* [1900s–70s] sixpence (2½p). [rhy. sl. *tartan banner* = TANNER]

tartar *n.* **1** [late 16C–late 17C] a strolling vagabond, a beggar, a criminal mendicant. **2** [late 16C–late 17C] a general derog. description. **3** [late 18C] a champion, an expert. **4** [20C] a domineering woman. [proper name *Tartar*, an inhabitant of the region of Central Asia extending east from the Caspian Sea, and formerly known as Independent and Chinese Tartary; ult. Persian *Tatar*, but linked in Western ears and superstitions with Lat. *tartarus*, hell]

tartarian *n.* [early–mid-17C] a thief. [ext. of TARTAR *n.* (1)]

tarted up *adj.* **1** [1920s+] usu. of women, flashily over-dressed (cf. DOLLED OUT; DOLLED UP; FLOSSED UP). **2** [1960s+] applied to anything overdecorated, e.g. a 'theme pub'. [TART *n.* (2)]

tart up *v.* [1920s+] to decorate, to ornament (cf. PONCE UP). [TART *n.* (2)]

tarty *adj.* [1910s+] cheap, gaudy, vulgar, thus fig. reminiscent of a prostitute. [TART *n.* (2)]

Tas/Tassie *n.* [late 19C+] (Aus.) **1** *Tas*mania. **2** an inhabitant of *Tas*mania. [abbr.]

Tas/Tassie *adj.* [late 19C+] (Aus.) *Tas*manian. [abbr.]

tash/tache *n.* [1940s+] mous*tache*. [abbr.]

Tassie *see* TAS.

taste *n.*¹ **1** [late 19C] (Und.) a share of e.g. a bribe, the proceeds of a robbery. **2** [late 19C] a very small amount, an almost imperceptible degree. **3** [1940s+] a sample of drugs.

taste *n.*² [1960s+] (US) alcohol, a drink.

taste *v.* [19C] to have sexual intercourse (cf. NIBBLE *v.*³).

taste bud *n.* [1960s+] the clitoris. [esp. in the context of cunnilingus]

taste the sun, to *phr.* [late 19C] of a Londoner, to spend a day in the country.

tastey *n.* [1990s] (US Black teen) an attractive woman. [SE *tasty*/TASTY *adj.* (2)]

tasty *adj.* **1** [late 19C] pleasant, attractive. **2** [late 19C+] sexu-ally alluring. **3** [1970s+] of a person, smart, sharp, prob. crim-inal; thus *tasty villain*, a known criminal. **4** [1970s+] of a thing (usu. some form of criminal plan), valuable, worthwhile.

tasty pastry/bit of pastry *phr.* [1940s+] a sexy woman. [TASTY *adj.* (2) + PASTRY]

Taswegian *n.* [1930s+] (Aus.) a person from Tasmania. [abbr. + play on SE *Glaswegian*]

tat *n.*¹ [late 18C–late 19C] (Anglo-Ind.) a pony. [Hind. *tatti*, a native-bred pony; Ind. army officers imported their own horses]

tat *n.*² **1** [mid-19C] an old rag; thus *milky tats*, linen or other-wise white cloth rags. **2** [1920s+] anything seen as mediocre, vulgar, rubbishy. [Hind. *tāt*, a strip of coarse canvas, used to make mats or screens; thus as SE, coarse canvas made esp. of jute and used for sacking]

tat *n.*³ [20C] (US) any confidence trick performed with dice. [TATS *n.*¹]

tat *n.*⁴ [1960s+] (orig. US prison) a tattoo.

tat *v.*¹ [early–mid-19C] to flog, to thrash. [Hampshire dial. *tat*, to pat]

tat *v.*² [mid-19C] to gather rags for a living. [TAT *n.*²]

tata *n.*¹ [1920s+] a foolish person. [such a person tends to use baby talk, e.g. *go for a tata*, go for a walk]

tata *n.*² [1950s+] (W.I. Rasta) father, an affectionate and respectful title for an old man. [infant mispron. but note its use in many African languages, e.g. Ewe, Ge, N'gombe]

ta-ta! *excl.* [late 19C+] goodbye! (cf. TA-RA!). [earlier use in nursery context]

tataram *n.* [1930s+] (W.I./Belz.) a foolish old man, esp. one with sex on his mind. [TATA *n.*² + RAM *n.*¹]

tatas *n.* [1980s+] (US) the female breasts. [TITTIES]

tat-box *n.* [mid-19C] a dice-box (cf. TATT-BOX). [TATS *n.*¹ + SE *box*]

Tate and Lyle *n.* [20C] style, i.e. cheek, audacity. [rhy. sl.; ult. a well-known brandname]

tater/'tatur *n.* [late 19C+] **1** a po*tato*. **2** a hole in one's sock (cf. SPUD). [(1) abbr.; (2) fig. use of (1), i.e. the exposed, dirty flesh resembles the vegetable]

tater and point *n.* [mid–late 19C] a meal made up almost entirely of potatoes. [dial. *taties and point*, potatoes plus a small piece of fish or meat, so tiny as only to be pointed at, rather than providing any nutrition]

tater-pillin' *n.* [20C] a shilling (5p). [rhy. sl.]

taters/taties *adj.* [20C] cold. [rhy. sl. *taters in the mould* = cold]

tater-trap *n.* [mid-19C–1910s] the mouth (cf. TATTIE-TRAP). [TATTER + SE *trap*]

tatey farmer *n.* [1990s] a fool, one who is socially un-acceptable. [TATIE + SE *farmer*; stereotyping of rural imagery]

tatie/tato *n.* [19C+] a po*tato*. [abbr.]

taties *see* TATERS.

tatler/tattler *n.* [17C–19C, 1940s] a watch, esp. a striking watch or a repeater. [SE *tattler*, one who tattles or gossips, use revived by US Blacks]

tat-monger *n.* [17C–early 19C] a professional dice-cheat (cf. TATT-MONGER). [TATS *n.*¹ + sfx. -MONGER]

tato *see* TATIE.

tats/tatts *n.*¹ **1** [16C+] dice, esp. crooked dice; thus [early 19C] *tat-shop*, a gambling den (cf. TAT-BOX). **2** [20C] (Aus./N.Z.) teeth. **3** [1900s–10s] (Aus./N.Z.) a set of false teeth. [ety. un-known; ? the rattle of dice as they hit the table; (2) refers to the ivory in dice and teeth]

tats *n.*² [mid-19C] rags. [SE *tatters*]

tats and all! *excl.* [early 19C] nonsense! rubbish! humbug! (cf. BENDER!; WALKER!). [fig. use of TATS *n.*¹]

tatt-box *n.* [early 19C] a dice-box (cf. TAT-BOX). [TATS *n.*¹ + SE *box*]

tatter *n.* [mid–late 19C] a rag-collector. [TAT *n.*²]

tatter *v.* [mid–late 19C] to collect rags. [TATTER *n.*]

tatter a kip, to *phr.* [mid-18C] to wreck a house. [SE *tatter*, to tear to pieces + KIP *n.*]

tatterdemallion *n.* [late 17C–18C] (Und.) a wandering beggar who deliberately adopts ragged, filthy clothes in the hope of extracting more money from the kind-hearted (cf. ABRAHAM-MAN). [SE *tatterdemallion*, a person in ragged clothing]

tattered *adj.* [1980s+] (US campus) drunk.

tattie-trap *n.* [late 19C] the mouth (cf. TATER-TRAP). [TATIE + TRAP *n.*³]

tatting *n.* [mid-19C] gathering old rags. [TAT *n.*²]

tattle-basket *n.* [18C] a gossip.

tattle-box *n.* [18C] a gossip (cf. PRATTLE-BOX).

tattlebudget *n.* [20C] (US) one who chatters on to excess (cf. FUSSBUDGET; SPUTTERBUDGET). [SE *tattle* + *budget*, one who has certain characteristics]

tattler *see* TATLER.

tattle-tale n. [18C] a gossip.

tatt-monger n. [late 17C] a cheat at dice (cf. TAT-MONGER). [TATS n.¹ + sfx. -MONGER].

tattogey n. [late 19C] **1** a dice-cloth, onto which one tosses the dice. **2** one who cheats by using loaded dice. [elision of TATTY TOG]

Tatt's n. **1** [mid–late 19C] *Tattersall's* horse market in London. **2** [late 19C] (Aus.) *Tatt's* sweep, a lottery established in 1881 on that year's Sydney Gold Cup by George Adams (1839–1904), licensee of Tattersall's Hotel, Sydney. [abbr.]

tatts see TATS n.¹.

tatty adj. [1920s+] **1** fussy, overdecorated. **2** (Aus.) inferior, cheap, badly-made. **3** unkempt, untidy, dishevelled. [TAT n.²]

tatty tog n. [early 19C] a gaming cloth. [TATS n.¹ + TOG n.]

'tatur see TATER.

taturs n. [19C+] pot*atoes*. [abbr.]

Taunton turkey n. [mid–late 19C] a salt herring (cf. ABERDEEN CUTLET). [the trade in such herrings in the town]

taunty n. [mid-19C+] human excrement. [Cheshire dial.]

tawny adj. [1980s+] (US teen) excellent, great.

taws n. [20C] (Irish) the testicles. [SE taws, marbles]

tax n. [1990s] (drugs) a charge paid to enter a building where crack cocaine is sold. The charge is based either on the race of the customer (Whites pay more) or on the frequency of their custom.

tax v. **1** [mid–late 19C] (US, esp. New England) to set a price on, to charge. **2** [1980s+] to extort, to demand money with menaces. **3** [1980s+] to rob.

tax bite n. [1950s+] (US) the amount of tax one has to pay on a sum of money or salary cheque.

tax break n. [1960s+] (orig. US) a way of legally minimizing one's taxes.

tax-collector n. [mid–late 19C] a highwayman.

taxes, the n. [late 19C] a tax-collector. [metonymy]

tax-fencer n. [late 19C] a disreputable shopkeeper, whose prices are set extortionately high. [SE *tax* + FENCER]

tax fiddle n. [1950s+] a way in which one can cheat or bypass the proper payment of one's taxes; thus *tax-fiddler*, one who cheats in this way.

taxi n.¹ [1910s–40s] a small passenger aeroplane; thus *taxi-driver*, the pilot of such an aeroplane.

taxi n.² [1930s+] (US) a sentence of 5 to 15 years. [New York cabs which displayed these figures, indicating their rates per mile, on the side]

taxicabs n. [20C] body lice. [rhy. sl. *taxicabs* = CRABS]

taxi eleven n. [1950s+] (W.I.) one's legs; thus *catch taxi eleven*, to walk (cf. LEGS ELEVEN). [the supposed similarity of shape]

taxing n. [1980s+] (drugs) the robbery by small-time dealers of their more successful peers. [TAX v. (2)]

taxi-rank v. [1970s] to masturbate. [rhy. sl. *taxi-rank* = WANK v.]

taxpaper n. [1920s–50s] (US) **1** a building on which the rents earned just about equal the taxes that one has to pay for owning it. **2** any small building. [SE *tax* + *paper*; play on SE *tar paper*, used to cover very poor housing]

taylor n. [20C] (Irish) a measure of spirits, equivalent to the UK 'double'. [? a brand of whisky]

taz n. [1920s+] **1** a beard. **2** light adolescent facial hair (cf. BUM-FLUFF). [var. on TASH]

taz/tazzie v. [1930s+] to go, to wander off, to leave. [ety. unknown; link to TODDLE, TOOTLE]

t.b. n.¹ [1920s+] (Aus.) a pair of large and shapely breasts. [abbr. *two beauts*]

t.b. n.² [1930s] (US) a confidence trickster. [abbr. *TB*, tuberculosis, consumption, *con* = abbr. *consumption*, also *confidence-man*]

t.b. adj. [1980s] (teen society) *très brill*, absolutely wonderful. [Fr. *très*, very + BRILL!]

t.b.a. n. [20C] (US society) a young man who is *to be avoided* (cf. N.S.I.T.). [abbr.]

t.b.h. n. [1980s+] (gay) a potential sexual conquest. [abbr. *to be had*]

T-bird n. [1960s+] **1** a Ford Thunder*bird*. **2** Thunder*bird* wine, a cheap wine drunk primarily by alcoholics. [abbr.]

T-bone n. [1950s+] (US Black) a common Black nickname. [? SE *T-bone* steak, thus implying virility; however, Major (1994) associates the def. with blues musician Aaron 'T-bone' Walker (1910–75), who took the name from his own middle name, Thibeaux, thus implying that the man, not the meat, was the paradigm]

T-buzz n. [1970s] (drugs) phencyclidine (cf. ACE n.³). [ety. unknown; ? link to T-ZONE]

tchotchke/tchatchka/tchotzke/tsatske n. [20C] (US) **1** any small decorative thing. **2** an adorable person, esp. a small child. **3** a woman considered as a plaything. [Yid. *tsatske*, Slav *shaleh*, a plaything]

t'd off see TEE'D OFF.

tea n.¹ **1** [late 17C–18C] brandy. **2** [early 18C] urine. [reflecting the colour of tea without milk]

tea n.² (drugs) **1** [1920s+] marijuana. **2** [1970s+] phencyclidine (cf. ACE n.³). [the OED citation from the *Boston Sunday Herald* (26 March 1967), 'Marijuana ... when brewed with hot water' is surely no more than a teasing hippie gulling a foolish journalist]

tea and cocoa n. [20C] say-so. [rhy. sl.]

tea and sugar burglar/bandit n. [20C] (Aus.) **1** a vagrant. **2** a petty thief. [(1) the fig. 'theft' of the commodities, which are more likely offered free; (2) the smallness of the objects that are stolen (cf. GAS-METER BANDIT; KNICKERS BANDIT)]

tea-and-tattle n. [1920s+] (Aus.) a formal afternoon tea for a number of guests, a minor social get-together.

tea-and-toast n. [20C] the post, the mail. [rhy. sl.]

tea-and-toast struggle n. [late 19C] a Wesleyan tea meeting, where the supply of tea rarely meets the demand.

tea and turn out phr. [late 19C] a phr. used to indicate that there is no tea; i.e. one is simply SE *turned out*]

tea-bagging n. [1990s] (US) sucking the testicles.

tea-bottle n. [late 19C] (middle-class) an unmarried woman; a spinster. [her supposedly preferred beverage]

tea-canister n. [mid-19C] a brandy flask. [TEA n.¹ (1)]

teach n. [1950s+] **1** (US) *teach*er. **2** (US Black) anyone considered intelligent or intellectual (cf. PROFESSOR). [abbr. SE *teacher*; (2) fig. use of (1)]

teach a pig to play the flute, to phr. [early 19C] to attempt the impossible.

teach one's dame/grandame to spin/grope a goose/grope ducks/sup sour milk, to phr. [17C] **1** foolishly to attempt to advise an expert on their own speciality. **2** to inform someone of the obvious. [vars. on TEACH ONE'S GRAND-MOTHER TO SUCK EGGS]

teach one's grandmother to suck eggs, to phr. [early 17C+] **1** foolishly to attempt to advise an expert on their own speciality. **2** to inform someone of the obvious (cf. SUCK EGGS!; TEACH ONE'S DAME TO SPIN).

teach one's dog to spit, to phr. [1990s] to masturbate. [DOG n.¹³ (1)]

tea'd up adj. [1930s+] (US drugs) intoxicated from marijuana. [TEA n.² (1)]

tea fight n. [mid-19C] **1** a tea party. **2** an evening party (cf. BUNFIGHT).

tea-for-two and a bloater n. [1900s–50s] a motorcar. [rhy. sl.]

tea grout n. [20C] a Boy Scout (cf. BRUSSELS SPROUT). [rhy. sl.]

Teague see TAIG.

Teagueland n. [late 17C–mid-19C] Ireland. [TEAGUE + SE *land*]

Teaguelander *n.* [late 17C–mid-19C] an Irishman. [TEAGUE + SE *lander*]

tea-head *n.* [1940s–60s] (drugs) a marijuana smoker. [TEA n.^{2} (1) + sfx. -HEAD (2)]

tea-hound *n.* [1920s] (US) **1** a man who frequents tea parties. **2** a womanizer.

teahouse *n.* [1930s+] (drugs) a house or apartment where people gather to buy and enjoy marijuana (cf. DOPE HOUSE; SPOT n.^{6}). [TEA n.^{2} (1)]

teaich gens *see* THEG GENS.

teaich-gir/teatchgir *adj.* [mid-19C] right (quality, not direction); thus *tadging*, first-rate, excellent. [backsl., pron. 'tadger']

teaich guy *n.* [mid-19C] 8 shillings (40p). [backsl.]

tea in a mug *phr.* [late 19C] (Anglo-Irish) a phr. that indicates bad breeding. [well brought-up tea-drinkers use a cup and saucer]

teakettle groom *n.* [late 19C] a groom who is forced to double as a member of the kitchen staff.

teakettle purger *n.* [mid–late 19C] a total abstainer (cf. TEA-POT). [? one who *purges*, i.e. cleans *teakettles* or uses tea to purge out alcohol]

tea leaf *n.* [late 19C+] a thief; thus *tea-leafing*, thieving. [rhy. sl.]

team *n.* [1950s+] **1** a squad of police. **2** a gang of criminals.

team *adv.* [1980s+] (US campus) wearing clothes or accessories that brand one as part of an identifiable subculture.

tea-man *n.* [1930s–50s] (US) a smoker of marijuana. [TEA n.^{2} (1) + sfx. -*man*]

team cream *n.* [1960s+] (gay) an orgy. [SE *team* + CREAM v.^{2}]

team-handed *adv.* [1950s+] (Und.) of working, in a group. [TEAM n.]

team Xerox *n.* [1980s+] (US campus) cheating. [TEAM XEROX v.]

team Xerox *v.* [1980s+] (US campus) to cheat. [*Xerox*, generic for 'to photocopy']

tea-oh! *excl.* [1940s+] (N.Z.) a call to indicate that it is time for a tea-break.

tea pad *n.* [1920s–50s] (drugs) a place for smoking marijuana. [TEA n.^{2} (1) + PAD n.^{2}]

tea party *n.^{1}* **1** [mid-19C–1900s] a lively disturbance. [the *Boston Tea Party* (1773), when a cargo of tea was thrown overboard from ships in Boston harbour as a protest against the taxation of the American colonies by the British government]

tea party *n.^{2}* [1920s–50s] (drugs) a gathering of people for the purpose of communal smoking of marijuana. [TEA n.^{2} (1) + SE *party*]

teapot *n.^{1}* [mid-19C] a Black person. [the colour of the typical brown/black *teapot*]

teapot *n.^{2}* **1** [late 19C] a total abstainer. **2** [20C] one who drinks an excessive amount of tea, often as *old teapot, regular teapot*.

teapot/teapot lid *n.^{3}* [20C] **1** a Jew. **2** a child. **3** £1 sterling. [rhy. sl. *teapot lid* = YID/KID/QUID]

teapot lid *v.* [late 19C+] to tease. [rhy. sl. *teapot lid* = KID v.]

tear *n.* [mid-19C+] (orig. US) a spree, a jollification, esp. in phrs. *go on a tear, go out on a tear* (cf. TEAR UP). [SE *tear*, to go at full tilt]

tear *v.* [late 16C+] to rush around excitedly, energetically.

tear and ages!/wounds! *excl.* [mid-19C] (Anglo-Irish) a general excl. of surprise, astonishment. [? dial. *tear*, a passion + *age*, aches]

tear-arse/-ass *n.^{1}* **1** [20C] cheese. **2** [1920s+] (Aus.) treacle, golden syrup. [their effect on the stomach]

tear-arse/-ass *n.^{2}* [1920s+] a very busy, energetic person. [TEAR ARSE v.]

tear arse *v.* [20C] to leave very quickly, to rush off (cf. TEAR ASS v.). [TEAR v. + ARSE n.^{1}]

tear arse about/around *v.* [20C] to rush hectically about. [TEAR v. + ARSE n.^{1}]

tear-ass *n. see* TEAR-ARSE n.^{1}, n.^{2}.

tear ass *v.* [1950s+] (US) to run or drive around fast and recklessly (cf. TEAR ARSE). [TEAR v. + ARSE n.^{1}]

tear a strip off *see* TEAR OFF A STRIP.

tearaway *n.* [late 19C+] a minor gangster, a small-time villain. [SE *tear away*, to leave at speed]

tearcat/tearer *n.* [16C] a thug, a bully. [SE *tear*, to rip apart]

tear down *v.* [1930s+] (US) to reprimand severely. [the victim's confidence is *torn down*]

teardrops *n.* [1980s+] (drugs) single dosage units of crack cocaine packaged in the cut-off corners of plastic bags. [resemblance]

tearer *see* TEARCAT.

tearing *adj.* **1** [mid-17C–late 19C] violent, rowdy or reckless in behaviour. **2** [late 17C–late 19C] impressive, splendid, first-rate. **3** [1920s] of work, exhausting. [TEAR v.]

tearing up the pea patch *phr.* [20C] (US) very energetic, boisterous.

tear into *v.* [20C] **1** to throw oneself enthusiastically into a task. **2** to attack physically (cf. GET STUCK IN; RIP INTO v.^{1}).

tear it *v.* [20C] to spoil one's chances, to put an end to one's plans etc., esp. in phr. *that tears it*, that puts an end to that.

tear-jerker *n.* [1920s+] (orig. US) a heavily romantic film, with either a sad or happy conclusion, either of which should guarantee a weeping audience. Similarly used to describe mawkish ballads and love-songs.

tear loose *v.* [1970s+] (US Black) to escape from a person or situation.

tear off *v.^{1}* [late 16C+] to rush away, to leave at speed. [TEAR v.]

tear off *v.^{2}* [20C] (US) to perform an action or activity. [SE *tear off*, to rip off a piece]

tear off a bit, to *phr.* [1970s+] of a man, to have sexual intercourse (cf. TEAR OFF A PIECE). [SE *tear off* + BIT n.^{5}]

tear off a chunk, to *phr.* [1970s+] (US) of a man, to have sexual intercourse (cf. TEAR OFF A BIT).

tear off a piece, to *phr.* [1940s+] (orig. Aus.) of a man, to have sexual intercourse (cf. KNOCK OFF A PIECE; SAW A CHUNK; TEAR OFF A BIT). [SE *tear off* + PIECE n.^{1}]

tear off a strip/a strip off, to *phr.* [1940s+] (orig. RAF/milit.) to criticize severely, to reprimand. [the fig. removal of a *strip(e)* of rank]

tear one's arse off, to *phr.* [1920s] to work furiously. [ARSE n.^{1}]

tear one's ass, to *phr.* [1930s+] to injure oneself, to get into trouble (cf. TEAR SOMEONE'S ASS). [SE *tear* + ARSE n.^{1}]

tearoom/t-room *n.* [1950s+] (US gay) a public lavatory popular for casual sex and assignations (cf. COTTAGE n.).

tearoom queen *n.* [1950s–70s] (US gay) a homosexual who hangs around public lavatories for sex. [TEAROOM + QUEEN n.^{1}]

tearoom/tea trade *n.* [1950s–70s] (US gay) the world of sexual assignations, pick-ups and consummation practised in public lavatories. [TEAROOM + TRADE n.^{1} (3)]

tear out *v.* [1900s–50s] (US Black) to rush away, to leave fast (cf. TEAR OFF v.^{1}).

tears *n.* [1940s] (US Black) pearls. [resemblance]

tears of the tankard *n.* [late 17C–mid-19C] drops of liquor that fall onto the careless drinker's clothing.

tear someone a new ass/asshole, to *phr.* [1930s+] (US) to attack someone savagely, either physically or verbally. [ARSE n.^{1}/ARSEHOLE]

tear someone's ass, to *phr.* [1930s+] **1** to criticize someone severely. **2** (W.I./Guyn.) to thrash severely, to flog (cf. CUT SOMEONE'S ARSE; TEAR ONE'S ASS). [SE *tear* + ARSE n.^{1}]

tear someone's meat-house down, to *phr.* [20C] (US) to defeat, to thrash. [SE *meat-house*, a larder, here meaning one's body]

tear someone up for arse-paper/dunny paper, to *phr.* [1910s+] (N.Z.) to scold, to reprimand, to attack and totally overcome in an argument; thus ext. as *well, I'll be torn up for arse-paper!*, an excl. of surprise or disbelief. [SE *tear up* + ARSE-PAPER/DUNNY + SE *paper*]

tear the doors off *see* BLOW THE DOORS OFF.

tear the end off, to *phr.* [1920s] to finish with a person or thing.

tear-up *n.* [mid-19C+] a commotion, esp. as adopted in [1950s+] US jazz use, a spell of wild, destructive behaviour, a mêlée.

tear up *v.* [1950s+] **1** (US) to distress, to upset. **2** (US Black) to enjoy oneself, to do something with relish; thus *tear up shit*.

tear up jack *see* CUT UP JACK.

tear up the pea patch, to *phr.* [1950s] (US) to go on a rampage.

tease *n.* **1** [mid-19C+] one who likes to tease. **2** [1970s+] a woman who provokes a man sexually but then resists intercourse (cf. COCKTEASE).

tease/teaze *v.*[1] [late 17C–late 19C] to flog, to whip. [SE *tease*, to 'thrash' out the fibres of wool, flax etc, before spinning]

tease *v.*[2] [mid-19C+] of a woman, to provoke a man sexually but to refuse him actual intercourse. [abbr. COCKTEASE]

teased-out *adj.* [1940s+] exhausted, worn-out.

tease one's crabs, to *phr.* [1990s] to masturbate (cf. PROMPT ONE'S PORPOISE).

teaser *n.*[1] [mid-18C–late 19C] **1** something that annoys or causes one annoyance. **2** something hard to deal with. [boxing jargon *teaser*, a tricky opponent, hard to beat]

teaser *n.*[2] [early–mid-19C] a flogging. [TEASE *v.*[2]]

teaser/teazer *n.*[3] [mid-19C] a sixpence (2½p). [? TIZZY]

teaser *n.*[4] [late 19C+] a woman who allows, even encourages some physical intimacies but, however daring, will always stop short of intercourse (cf. COCKCHAFER).

teaser *n.*[5] [1930s+] (orig. US) a sample of something to arouse or whet one's appetite, a taste.

tease the weasel, to *phr.* [1990s] to masturbate (cf. PROMPT ONE'S PORPOISE).

tease the weenie/wienie, to *phr.* [1990s] (US) to masturbate (cf. ACCOST THE OSCAR MEYER). [SE *tease* + WEENIE *n.*[1]]

tea shine *n.* [mid-19C] (US) a tea party (cf. TEA FIGHT).

teasing *n.* [early–mid-19C] a whipping, a flogging. [TEASE *v.*[1]]

teaspoon *n.* [1950s+] (drugs) a measure of narcotic drugs. [it is half a SPOON *n.*[2]]

teaspoons *n.* [late 19C] silver coins. [their potential for being melted down by counterfeiters]

tea squall *n.* [early 19C] a tea party (cf. TEA FIGHT).

tea-stick *n.* [1920s–50s] (US drugs) a marijuana cigarette. [TEA *n.*[2] (1) + STICK *n.*[11]]

tea strainers *n.* [1980s+] trainers. [rhy. sl.]

teatchgir *see* TEAICH-GIR.

tea trade *see* TEAROOM TRADE.

tea up *v.* [mid-19C] to make tea.

tea voider *n.* [late 18C–late 19C] a chamberpot. [TEA *n.*[1] (2) + SE *void*]

teaze *see* TEASE *v.*[1].

teazer *see* TEASER *n.*[3].

teazle *n.* [19C] the vagina (cf. BEAUTY SPOT *n.*[1]).

teazy-whacker *n.* [20C] (Irish) a slut, a promiscuous woman. [TEAZLE]

tec *n.* **1** [mid-19C+] a detective. **2** [1930s+] a detective story. [abbr.]

tec *v.* [mid-19C+] to survey or watch like a detective. [TEC *n.*]

tecata *n.* [1960s+] (US drugs) heroin. [Sp.]

tecato *n.* [1960s+] (US drugs) **1** a heavy user of marijuana. **2** a morphine or heroin addict. [TECATA]

tech *n.* [1940s+] (orig. US) a *technician*. [abbr.]

techie *n.* [1980s+] (US) a computer enthusiast or expert. [abbr. SE *technology* + sfx. *-ie*]

technicolour yawn/spit *n.* [1960s+] (orig. Aus.) the act of vomiting (cf. MULTICOLOURED YAWN). [the multicoloured effluvia so produced]

techno- *pfx.* [1980s+] (US) a comb. form used to indicate technological expertise or involvement, esp. as regards computing, e.g. *technofreak*.

ted *n.* [1950s+] a *teddy* boy. [abbr.; the youth cult orig. known as 'Edwardians' and named for their sartorial style, borrowed from the contemporary upper-class dandies who in turn had recreated the fashions of their own grandfathers]

ted *adj.* [1980s+] (US campus) drunk. [? abbr. WASTED *adj.* (4)]

teddy bear *n.*[1] [20C] a pear. [rhy. sl.]

teddy bear *n.*[2] [20C] (Irish) a large, brown shawl. [similarity to the covering of the child's toy]

teddy bear *n.*[3] [1950s+] (Aus.) a show-off, esp. a cricketer who jokes around on the field and plays to the crowd. [rhy. sl. *teddy bear* = LAIR *n.*]

teddy bear *n.*[4] [1950s+] (US Black) a plump, sexy woman.

teddy my godson *n.* [late 18C] (Anglo-Irish) a term of address used to a simpleton.

ted frazer *n.* [1960s+] a razor, always a cut-throat, 'open' model. [rhy. sl.]

Ted Heath *n.* [1970s] **1** a thief. **2** teeth. [rhy. sl. pron. 'heef', *Edward Heath* (b.1916), British prime minister 1970–74]

tedhi *see* THEDI.

teed/t'd off *adj.* [1950s+] (US) annoyed, irritated, upset. [? golfing *tee off* + PEE OFF]

teed up *adj.* [1920s+] drunk or intoxicated by drugs; ext. as *teed up to the tits* (cf. ABOUT RIGHT *adj.*[1]). [TEA *n.*[1] (1), TEA *n.*[2] (1), (2)]

teef *n.* [1980s+] (orig. Black) a thief. [W.I. pron.]

teefing *n.* [1980s+] (orig. Black) robbery, thieving. [TEEF]

teen- *pfx.* [1950s+] (orig. US) a comb. form for anything applicable to or enjoyed by teenagers, e.g. *teenflick*, *teenzine*, a magazine for teenagers.

teener/teenie/teeny *n.* [1950s+] (US) a teenager. [abbr.]

teenie weenie *n.* [1980s+] (US gay) a teenager available for being fellated. [*teenie* (*see* TEENER) + WEENIE *n.*[1]]

teensie-weensie *adj.* [late 19C+] (orig. US juv.) very small, minuscule. [infant pron. of SE *tiny*]

teenth *n.* [1990s] (drugs) a very small amount of cannabis. [abbr. SE a *sixteenth* of an ounce (2g)]

teeny *see* TEENER.

teenybopper/teenyrocker *n.* [1960s+] a young girl, usu. in very early teens, with a predilection for rock music and the boys who play it (cf. BOPPER *n.*[2]). [TEENY + BOP *v.* (3)]

tee off/on *v.*[1] [1950s+] (US) **1** to criticize, to reprimand, to attack verbally. **2** to hit very hard. [fig. use of golf jargon *tee off*]

tee off *v.*[2] [1950s+] (US) **1** to irritate or anger someone. **2** to feel anger or irritation. [euph. for PEE OFF; PISS OFF]

tee something up *see* TEE UP.

teeth *n.* **1** [1950s] (W.I. Rasta) bullets. **2** [1980s+] (drugs) cocaine, crack cocaine. [similarity in shape (1) and in colour/size (2)]

teetotal hotel *n.* [late 19C+] a workhouse. [where there would be absolutely no liquor]

teetottler *n.* [late 19C] a teetotaller, a total abstainer from alcohol.

tee up/something up *v.* [1930s+] to get (something) ready, to prepare (something). [golfing jargon]

tekelite *n.* [mid-19C] (debtors' prison) a defaulting debtor. Such figures were the lowest of the prison hierarchy and were forced to take on the most menial tasks. [the Bible, Dan. 5:25–7, 'Mene, mene, *tekel*, upharsin … Thou art weighed in the balances and art found wanting']

tek life *n.* [1980s+] (W.I./UK Black teen) a fashionable, popular person, a fashionable thing or place. [W.I. pron. of SE *take*, i.e. one who 'takes hold of' life]

tekram *n.* [mid-19C+] market, esp. Covent Garden; thus *ogging ot tekram*, going to market. [backsl.]

Tel *n.* [1970s+] the almost invariable nickname for working-class Londoners called Terry.

tele *n.* [1930s+] (orig. US) *tele*vision (cf. TELLY). [abbr.]

telegraph *n.* **1** [19C] a scout or spy. **2** [mid-19C–1900s] (Aus.) a member of a bushranging gang whose task is to keep the others informed of the whereabouts of potential victims or efforts to capture them. **3** [mid-19C+] a network of gossip and rumour that brings news (often inaccurate) before the official sources (cf. BUSH TELGRAPH). **4** [1960s+] (prison) a means of inter-cell communication in prison, by tapping mutually understood codes on the walls.

telegraph *v.* [1930s+] (US) to communicate one's intentions, usu. inadvertently.

telegraph one's punches, to *phr.* [1930s+] (orig. US) to reveal one's intentions to an opponent inadvertently. [boxing imagery]

telephone *n.* [1950s+] (Can.) a bilingual or multilingual Canadian who moves between the two national groups – Anglo*phone* and Franco*phone* – and is generally despised by both.

telephone j.o. *n.* [1960s+] (gay) masturbation while using the telephone, not necessarily while exchanging an erotic conversation. [SE *telephone* + abbr. JERK OFF]

telephone numbers *n.* [1960s+] extremely large sums of money. [the digits used in big city exchanges]

tell a bung, to *phr.* [late 19C] (juv.) to tell a lie. [BUNG *n.*⁵]

tell a French joke, to *phr.* [1960s–70s] (gay) to stimulate the anus orally. [FRENCH *adj.*]

tell a green man, to *phr.* [1900s–40s] (US Black) to impart information, esp. to a novice. [SE *green*]

tell a lie *phr.* [1920s+] a phr. used to reverse one's previous statement or emphasize that in speaking one has just made a mistake, e.g. *They were all blondes, tell a lie, there was one brunette.*

tell howdy to *see* SAY HOWDY TO.

telling-off *n.* [mid-19C+] a scolding, a reprimand.

tell it like it is, to *phr.* [1950s+] (orig. US Black/hippie) to be absolutely honest, to reject dissembling, also as *t.i.l.i.s.*

tell it to Sweeney! *excl.* [mid-19C+] (US) a dismissive excl. of disbelief in a previous far-fetched statement (cf. TELL IT TO THE MARINES). [? anecdotal or *Sweeney* as generic]

tell it to the marines!/horse marines! *excl.* [early 19C+] a dismissive excl. of disbelief in a previous far-fetched statement. [naut. use, sailors had a low opinion of Marine intelligence. The 'horse' was dropped *c.*1910]

tell me about it *phr.* [1990s] (US campus) an expression of agreement, usu. when the first speaker is recounting some tale of problems.

tell me another! *excl.* [1950s+] an excl. indicating disbelief and implying that the previous speaker is telling not facts but a string of jokes.

tell someone where to head in, to *phr.* [1910s–50s] (US) to scold, to reprimand.

tell someone what to do with something, to *phr.* [20C] (orig. US) to reject something vehemently; 'what they should do' is SHOVE IT UP (THEIR) ARSE!]

tell someone where they get off/to get off/to go, to *phr.* [20C] (orig. US) to scold someone for interfering, 'where they get off' or 'go to' is hell (cf. GO TO HELL!).

tell-tale *n.* [1950s+] (Aus.) a motor vehicle's indicator light. [it shows where one/the car is]

tell the players without a programme, to *phr.* [1960s+] (US gay) to identify the homosexuals in a crowd without being told. [sporting imagery; the increasingly blurred gender roles of the 1980s–90s have made this a more and more difficult task]

tell the tale, to *phr.*¹ [20C] **1** to tell a story designed to elicit a loan or a monetary gift. **2** to flirt with in the hope of seduction. **3** to tell any kind of unbelievable or pathetic story. **4** to be a confidence trickster; thus *teller of the tale*, one who talks in any of these ways.

tell the tale, to *phr.*² [1910s+] to deceive, to hoax, to cheat through verbal dexterity.

tell the truth! *excl.* [1950s+] (US Black) an excl. of general encouragement or affirmation.

tell the truth, snagger-tooth *phr.* [1930s–50s] (US Black) a joc. catchphrase, don't lie, be honest.

tell the works *see* GIVE THE WORKS.

tell what's what/what goes *phr.* [17C+] aware of the facts, abreast of a situation (cf. KNOW WHAT'S WHAT).

telly *n.* [1950s+] *tele*vision. [abbr.]

temmies/temazies/tems *n.* [1980s+] (drugs) *tem*azepam (a tranquillizer and short-acting hypnotic). [abbr.]

temp *n.* [20C] a *temp*orary worker; usu. a secretary. [abbr.]

temp *v.* [20C] to take on a job as a temporary worker, usu. a secretary. [TEMP *n.*]

temple *n.* [20C] the lavatory (cf. ALTAR).

temple balls *n.* [1960s+] (drugs) strong Nepalese hashish, sold in small balls and allegedly manufactured in Buddhist temples.

temple of low men *n.* [late 19C–1900s] a woman's genitals. [pun on *temple of Hymen*]

temple-pickling *n.* [late 17C–early 19C] (Und.) the ducking of court officials beneath a pump. [proper name *the Temple*, two of the Inns of Court (the Inner and Middle Temple) + SE *pickle*, i.e. to 'battle' in liquid. During 17C any bailiff caught within the limits of the temple was automatically thus punished]

tems *see* TEMMIES.

ten *n.*¹ [19C] Edinburgh prison (cf. PEN *n.*²; SMITH'S HOTEL). [ety. unknown]

Ten, the *n.*² [1930s+] (US Und.) the 10 Most Wanted Criminals List. [established as a publicity stunt in 1930s by J. Edgar Hoover (1895–1972), head of the FBI]

ten *n.*³ [1940s] (US Black) the human toes.

ten *n.*⁴ [1970s+] sexual intercourse. [the highest level on the petting scale of 1 to *10* used by some young people]

ten *n.*⁵ [1970s+] the ideal woman or man. [the 'perfect' score of *10* out of 10, reinforced by the film *10* (1979)]

tenant at will *n.* [late 18C–early 19C] one whose wife arrives at the alehouse to make him come home (cf. TENANT IN TAIL). [legal jargon, *tenant at will*, one whose tenancy only exists according to the will of the landlord]

tenant for life *n.* [19C] a married man (cf. TENANT AT WILL; TENANT IN TAIL). [pun on legal jargon]

tenant in tail *n.* **1** [mid-17C] one whose drunkenness promotes indiscriminate displays of affection; 'He that will be stil kissing all commers in' (*English Liberal Science*). **2** [late 18C–early 19C] one whose wife arrives at the alehouse to make him come home (cf. TENANT AT WILL). [legal jargon *tenant in tail*, a tenancy held under certain specific limitations + note TAIL *n.*¹ (2)]

ten-bob squats *n.* [late 19C] the stalls in a theatre. [the price (10 shillings/50p) of the seats]

ten bones *n.* [late 15C–early 16C; 1940s] the fingers of both hands; thus excl. *by these ten bones!* a mild oath. [20C use is US Black]

ten-carat *adj.* [1930s] (US) out-of-the-ordinary, remarkable, usu. in neg. contexts. [the SE *carat* scale of precious metals/stones]

ten-cent bag/ten cents *n.* [1950s+] (drugs) a $10 bag of marijuana or any other drug, e.g. crack cocaine (cf. DIME BAG).

tench *n.*¹ [19C] **1** (Aus.) the convict prison in Hobart, Tasmania; thus *tenchman*, an inmate of that prison. **2** the Clerkenwell House of Detention. [abbr. SE *penitentiary*]

tench *n.*² [mid-19C] the vagina. [? image of the vagina as a prison (cf. TENCH n.¹), or SE *tench*, and thus another term that equates the vagina with fish (cf. BEARDED CLAM)]

ten commandments *n.* **1** [mid-15C–mid-19C] a woman's fingers and thumbs. **2** [20C] (Irish) fingernails. [stereotyping of a domineering wife or an aggressive woman]

tendencies *n.* [1930s–60s] a propensity towards being a homosexual. [euph.]

tender *n.* [1970s+] (US Black) a young desirable man or woman (cf. TENDERONI).

tender box *n.* [1970s+] (gay) a young boy with alluring buttocks. [SE *tender* + BOX n.⁶ (5)]

tenderfoot *n.* [late 19C] (orig. US) a novice, an inexperienced person. [orig. used of the new arrivals in the mining or ranching areas of the West. US]

tenderloin *n.* [mid-19C+] the area of a city devoted to pleasure and entertainment, typically containing restaurants, theatres, gambling houses and brothels. [SE *tenderloin*, a tender cut of beef, pork etc. Coined for an area of New York City, the term was extended to cover similar areas of other major US cities, notably San Francisco, where it is still in use. The concept was linked to police corruption and so great were the bribes and pay-offs available to officers of the 29th Precinct, who administered the area, that they termed it 'the juicy part of the service'. First used in 1876 by a notably corrupt policeman, Alexander S. 'Clubber' Williams (nicknamed for his propensity for violence rather than any love of nightspots), who had just moved to the 29th Precinct. 'I will have been living on rump steak in the Fourth District,' he remarked, 'I will have some tenderloin now']

tenderoni *n.* [1990s] (US Black teen) a sweet young girl (cf. RONI). [cod Ital.]

tender parnel *n.* [late 17C–18C] **1** a squeamish, oversensitive person. **2** a prostitute who works in a brothel (cf. PANEL CRIB). [ironic uses of SE *tender parnel*, a tenderly educated and gently brought-up woman, but note 'Tender Parnell, who broke her finger in a posset drink' (Grose 1785)]

tenements to let *see* APARTMENT TO LET.

ten-four *phr.* [1970s+] message received and understood. [US police '10 codes', e.g. 10–15 civil disturbance, 10–31 crime in progress]

ten furlongs *n.* [20C] (Aus.) a daughter. [rhy. sl. *ten furlongs = a mile and a quarter*]

ten in the hundred *n.* [late 16C–late 18C] a usurer. [interest of 10% was considered extortionate]

tenip *n.* [mid–late 19C] a pint. [backsl.]

ten/five miles of bad road *n.* [20C] (US Black) bad luck, esp. if it persists.

tenner *n.* **1** [mid-19C+] £10, a £10 note (cf. AYRTON). **2** [late 19C+] (US) a $10 bill. **3** [20C] (US prison) a 10-year prison sentence.

tennies/tenny runners *n.* [1960s+] (US) tennis shoes or trainers. [abbr.]

tennis racket *n.* [20C] a jacket. [rhy. sl.]

tenny runners *see* TENNIES.

ten o'clock girl *n.* [1930s–50s] a London prostitute. [they had to surrender their bail at the Magistrates' Court at that time]

tenpence short of the full quid *phr.* [mid-19C+] not very intelligent, slightly eccentric, odd. One of a number of phrs. meaning stupid or eccentric (cf. NOT ALL THERE). [QUID n.; the pound sterling had 240 pence]

tenpence to the shilling *phr.* [mid-19C+] not very intelligent, slightly eccentric, odd. One of a number of phrs. meaning stupid or eccentric (cf. NOT ALL THERE). [a shilling had 12 pence]

tenpenny *n.*¹ [late 19C] **1** a blow, usu. as a *right tenpenny*. **2** a great success, a great surprise etc. [SE *tenpenny nail*, a large (7.5cm/3in) nail, and thus a pun on 'hitting the nail on the head'. (2) is fig. use of (1)]

tenpenny *n.*² [1940s] (W.I.) a bloated, fat stomach. [? size of tenpenny piece, an obsolete coin since 18C, or SE *tenpenny nail*, a large (7.5cm/3in) nail]

10%/ten per cent *see* FIVE PER CENT NATION.

ten-per-center *n.* [1920s+] (orig. US) an agent (cf. MR TEN PER CENT). [their cut]

tenpin *v.* [1990s] to insert the thumb into a woman's anus and the middle finger into her vagina simultaneously, doing a rhythmic swinging motion of the arm to provide sexual stimulation. [simulating the handling of a bowling ball]

ten pounds of shit in a five pound bag *phr.* [20C] (US) anything considered ugly, esp. someone obese or overweight.

tens and twos *n.* [20C] (Aus.) shoes. [rhy. sl.]

tense *adj.* [1990s] a general term of affirmation. [on bad = good pattern]

tension *n.* [1980s+] (drugs) crack cocaine. [its neg. effects]

tenski/tensky *n.* [1950s+] (US) **1** 10 per cent. **2** a $10 bill. [SE *ten* + 'Slav' sfx. *-ski*]

ten-spot *n.* [20C] **1** (US) a $10 bill or £10 note (cf. FIVE-SPOT; TWENTY-SPOT). **2** (US prison) a 10-year prison sentence. [SE *ten* + SPOT n.³]

ten stealers *see* STEALERS.

tent *n.* **1** [1900s] (Anglo-Irish) an umbrella. **2** [1970s] a fat woman dressed in a kaftan or similarly voluminous garment.

ten, ten, two-and-a-quarter *see* TEN, TWO-AND-A-QUARTER.

tenth part of a man *see* NINTH PART OF A MAN.

ten to four gentleman/toff *n.* [late 19C] a member of the upper ranks of the Civil Service. [his fig. elevation, during working hours, to the upper classes]

ten to two *n.* [1930s+] a Jew (cf. BOX OF GLUE). [rhy. sl.]

tent peg *n.*¹ [19C] the penis (cf. BAT n.⁷). [the shape, but note the Biblical story of Jael and Sisera, i.e. the penis as a weapon]

tent peg *n.*² [late 19C+] an egg. [rhy. sl.]

ten-two *n.* [1960s] (US) the traditional payment for sex, $10 for the woman, $2 for the room.

ten, two-and-a-quarter/ten, ten, two-and-a-quarter *n.* [mid-19C–1910s] (Aus.) the regular weekly ration of food, as issued to hands on a rural property. [10lb (4.54kg) of flour, 10lb of meat, 2lb (0.9kg) of sugar and ¼lb (113g) of tea]

tenuc *n.* [20C] the vagina. [backsl. *tenuc* = CUNT]

ten/10 wedding *n.* [late 19C] a wedding in which the wife, 1, is superior to the husband, 0.

teresa truncheon *n.* [1980s+] (camp gay) a policeman (cf. BRENDA n.²; LILY LAW).

termage *n.* [16C] (Und.) winnings at crooked gambling, esp. through cheating at bowls and later cards. [SE *term*, a limit, a full extent]

terminal *n.* [1990s] death, murder.

terminal *adj.* [1970s+] extreme, total. [SE *terminal*, used of disease that will kill the sufferer]

terminator *n.* [1980s+] a type of heroin (cf. PREDATOR). [from the *Terminator* films (1984, 1991)]

term of endearment among sailors *see* IT'S A TERM OF ENDEARMENT AMONG SAILORS.

terps *n.* [1980s+] (US drugs) elixir of *terp*in hydrate and codeine, a cough syrup with intoxicating qualities. [abbr.]

terr/terro *n.* (S.Afr.) **1** [1970s+] a *terr*orist. **2** [1980s+] a tourist, esp. from Transvaal (cf. TERRORIST). [abbr./pron.]

terrace *n.* [1940s+] (Aus.) trousers (cf. ROUND-THE-HOUSES). [rhy. sl. *terrace of houses* = trousers]

terra firma *n.* [late 17C–18C] a landed estate. [Lat. *terra firma*, land, as opposed to sea]

terri *n.* [early 18C+] coal. [Shelta]

terrible *adj.* **1** [mid-19C+] a general intensifier, usu. in neg. contexts, e.g. *terrible cold*. **2** [1950s–70s] (US Black/teen) wonderful, admirable, first-rate (cf. AWFUL *adj*.). [(2) on bad = good model]

terrible Turk *n.* [20C] work. [rhy. sl.]

terribly *adv.* [mid-19C+] a general intensifier, to a very great extent, extremely.

terrier crop *n.* [mid–late 19C] a bristly haircut, denoting a person's recent stay in prison, where hair is cropped short. [resemblance to a short-haired breed of dog]

terrific *adj.* **1** [19C] very much, excessive. **2** [1920s+] a general term of approval, wonderful, very good indeed, 'great'.

terrifically *adv.* [mid–late 19C] alarmingly, excessively, extremely. [note SE *awfully, dreadfully*]

terro *see* TERR.

terrorist *n.* [1980s+] (S.Afr., W. and S.W. Cape) a tourist, usu. from Transvaal (cf. TERR). [joc. mispron.]

terror to cats *n.* [late 19C] an ill-behaved small boy.

terry *n.* [early 18C+] an iron. [Shelta]

terry toon *n.* [1970s+] (Aus.) a pimp, one who lives off a prostitute. [rhy. sl. *terry toon* = HOON]

test/tess *n.* [20C] (W.I.) a person, a fellow. [? obs. SE *test*, a witness]

tester *n.* **1** [16C–mid-19C] sixpence (cf. TIZZY). **2** [mid-19C] (Aus.) 25 strokes of the lash (cf. BOB *n.*⁵). [Fr. *teston*, a silver coin struck at Milan by Duke Galeazzo Sforza (1468–76). It had his own head on it, as did similar testons coined by Louis XII (r.1498–1515) and his successor François I (r.1515–47) of France and by Henry VIII (r.1509–47) of England; (2) reflects the association of numbers of lashes with denominations of coins]

testicles to you! *excl.* [20C] a general excl. of dismissal or disdain (cf. BALLS!).

testicular elevation *n.* [20C] a somewhat ponderous synon. for the coarser BALLS-UP *n.*

testiculating *n.* [1970s] talking nonsense in an extremely animated manner. [SE *testicles* + *gesticulating*, the ref. is to 'talking balls']

testy *n.* [19C] a sixpence. [TESTER *n.* (1)]

test one's batteries, to *phr.* [1990s] to masturbate.

Tetbury portion *n.* [late 18C–early 19C] sexual intercourse that is followed by a does of venereal disease; 'A **** [CUNT] and a clap' (Grose 1796). [the poor image of the town of *Tetbury* in Gloucestershire]

tetched *adj.* [1930s+] (US) eccentric. [SE *touched*]

tete *n.* [20C] (W.I.) a bacterial skin disease, usu. attacking the feet. [? SE *tetter*, any pustule that erupts on the skin]

tetes *n.* [1960s] (W.I.) a large-breasted woman. [TITTY *n.*²]

tether one's nags on, to *phr.* [19C] (Scot.) to have sexual intercourse. [SE *tether*, tie up + NAG *n.*¹]

teuf-teuf *phr.* [1900s–20s] goodbye.

teviss *n.* [mid-19C] a shilling. [backsl. form of Du. *stiver*, a small coin]

tewel/tuel *n.* [late 14C] the anus. [SE *tewel*, a pipe]

texan rude *phr.* [mid-19C+] next door; thus *texan rude nam*, lit. 'next-door man', thus neighbour. [backsl.]

Texas mickey *n.* [1930s+] (Can.) a 3.84l (130fl oz) bottle of rye whisky. [proper name *Texas* + MICKEY *n.*⁴]

Texas steel *n.* [1970s+] (US prison) a prison.

Texas tea *n.* [1930s+] (drugs) marijuana. [proper name *Texas* + TEA *n.*² (1); the easy availability of wild marijuana in the state]

Texas turkey *n.* [20C] (US) an armadillo, as eaten *faute de mieux* during the Great Depression (cf. HOOVER HOG). [the armadillo is common in the state]

tex-mex *n.* [1980s+] (drugs) marijuana. [SE *Tex-Mex*, Texan-Mexican]

Tex Ritter *n.* [1990s] **1** bitter (beer). **2** the lavatory. [rhy. sl.; (2) *Tex Ritter* = SHITTER *n.*¹ (2); ult. Country and Western star *Tex Ritter* (1905–74)]

t.f.a. *adj.* [1980s+] (US campus) wonderful, exceptional, very good. [abbr. *too fucking awesome*]

t.f.m. *adj.* [1960s–70s] **1** wonderful, exceptional. **2** excessive. [abbr. *too fucking much*]

t.g. *n.*¹ [1920s+] an item of cutlery left unused after a meal. [abbr. *thank God*, a prayer uttered by the person who thus avoids washing it up]

t.g. *n.*² [1990s] (US Black gang) a junior member of a gang, under the age of 12. [abbr. *tiny gangsta*]

t.g.i.f. *phr* [1970s+] *thank God it's Friday* (cf. POET'S DAY). [abbr.]

t.h. *n.* [20C] *eight*. [backsl.]

Thai/Thai stick *n.* [1960s+] (drugs) a form of marijuana grown in Thailand, soaked in hashish oil and sold tied around a thin stick resembling a satay skewer (cf. BUDDHA STICKS).

thais *n.* [19C] a prostitute. [*Thaïs*, an Athenian courtesan among whose lovers were Alexander the Great and Ptolemy Lagus, king of Egypt]

Thai stick *see* THAI.

Thames butter *n.* [late 19C] totally rancid butter. [the 'South London Press ... published a paragraph to the effect that a Frenchman was making butter out of Thames mud at Battersea. In truth this chemist was extracting yellow grease from Thames mud-worms' (Ware)]

than a nigger in a —/than a nigger's — *phr.* [mid-19C+] (US) used in various phrs., usu. racist similes.

thang *n.* [1990s] (US Black teen) thing, esp. in phr. *do your own thang* etc. [pron.]

thanks a bunch *phr.* [1950s+] thank you very much, usu. ironic. [? ironic use of SE *bunch* as many, thus 'many thanks']

thanks a million *phr.* [1950s+] thank you very much, often ironic (cf. THANKS A BUNCH)

thanks, but no thanks *phr.* [1970s+] a phr. implying that a specific offer is very generous and/or alluring, but is ultimately not wanted.

thanks for nothing *phr.* [1950s+] a phr. of annoyance and contempt.

thanks for the buggy-ride *phr.* [1920s–30s] (US) thank you.

thank the mussies *phr.* [late 19C] a mild oath. [SE *thank the mercies!*]

thank you and good night *phr.* [1970s+] a dismissive, sarcastic phr., 'what a load of nonsense', 'is that the best you can offer?'.

thank-you-ma'am *n.* [20C] (US) a pothole. [abbr. WHAM BAM THANK YOU MA'AM, the image is of a sudden stumble or a bowing gesture]

thash on *v.* [1980s+] (US campus) to criticize, to attack verbally. [ety. unknown; SE *thrash*/TRASH *v.* (2)]

that *n.* [19C] the penis (cf. IT).

that *adj.* [mid-19C+] a mildly derog. use of 'that' to imply one's disapproval, e.g. *Are you seeing that Terry tonight?*

that accounts for the milk in the coconut *phr.* [mid-19C–1910s] a phr. used to respond to someone's explanation of an event or action.

that ain't/isn't hay/peanuts/chopped liver *phr.* [1930s+] (US) a phr. used to mean that something is a large and significant amount. [the perceived insignificance of the various items]

that all depends *see* IT ALL DEPENDS.

that and a dime/nickel/quarter will get you a cup of coffee *phr.* [1950s+] (US) used of something considered unimportant or worthless.

that and this *n.* [20C] urination. [rhy. sl. *that and this* = PISS n.]

that beats/licks creation *phr.* [early 19C+] (US) that is really amazing, that's beyond the bounds of possibility.

that bites/bites the big one *phr.* [1980s+] (US campus) an expression of commiseration. [i.e. that must hurt very much]

thatch *n.* **1** [mid-17C+] the human hair; thus *well-thatched*, having a good growth of hair. **2** [mid-19C] a woman's pubic hair.

thatched head *n.* [early 17C] an Irishman. [his stereotyped unkempt appearance]

thatched house/under the hill *n.* [19C] the vagina (cf. HOUSE UNDER THE HILL). [THATCH n. (2), but note *Thatched House* Lodge, Surrey, built for the keepers of Richmond Park in 1673 and subsequently owned by prime minister Sir Robert Walpole (1676–1745)]

thatch-gallows *n.* [late 18C–mid-19C] a worthless person. [all they are good for]

that cock won't fight *phr.* [19C] a phr. used to denigrate the previous statement, 'that won't do', 'you must be joking', 'I'm not having that'.

that'd be telling *see* THAT WOULD BE TELLING.

that does it *phr.* [1940s+] a phr. implying that something is the final straw, that one is at the end of one's patience.

that figures *phr.* [1940s+] (Aus.) that's right, that adds up as it should. [FIGURE v. (2)]

that gets me west *phr.* [1920s–30s] that worries me. [why 'west' should be seen as a neg. is undisclosed]

that guy *phr.* [1990s] (US teen) used to comment on one seen as acting inappropriately.

that how you living? *phr.* [1950s+] (US Black) why are you behaving in this (neg.) manner?

that is/was *phr.* [20C] a phr. used to give emphasis to what has just been said, e.g. *That's a nice bit of beef, that is.*

that isn't hay/peanuts/chopped liver *see* THAT AIN'T HAY.

that kills it *phr.* [1940s+] (US) that ruins everything.

that licks creation *see* THAT BEATS CREATION.

that licks me *see* IT LICKS ME.

that'll be frosty Friday *phr.* [1940s+] (Can.) never, that is very unlikely, 'that'll be the day'.

that'll be the day *phr.* [1930s+] (orig. N.Z.) **1** that will be a day or time worth waiting for. **2** an ironic and dismissive phr. used to pour scorn on a previous speaker's prophecy or promise.

that'll pin your ears back *phr.* [1930s+] (orig. US) that will surprise you (and poss. cause you trouble).

that'll put your back up *phr.* [1920s+] that will make you sexually excited. [the image of mating cats]

that'll tighten you *phr.* [20C] (Ulster) that's just what you deserve. [the physical tension that can accompany fear/anger]

that long *phr.* [20C] very long, usu. in neg. phrs., e.g. *I don't think it will take (all) that long.*

that makes the cheese more binding *phr.* [1940s–50s] (Can.) a general phr. of enthusiastic approval.

that makes two of us *phr.* [1950s+] a phr. used to underline one's emphatic agreement or the fact that the speaker too has had a similar (unfortunate) experience.

that moan's soon made *phr.* [late 19C] (orig. Scot.) that problem will soon go away, that grief will soon be forgotten.

that puts the tin hat on it *phr.* [20C] a phr. used to mean that something is finished or come to an end, usu. in a way the speaker dislikes; 'that's the end of that'. [play on BRASS HAT; i.e. the assumed incompetence/stupidity of senior officers]

that's a bit thick *phr.* [late 19C+] that is unpleasant, insufferable, distasteful. [SE *bit* adj. + THICK adj.³]

that's about it *see* THAT'S IT.

that's about the size of it *phr.* [1910s+] (orig. US) a phr. of agreement, yes, you pretty well understand what I'm saying, what is going on etc.

that's according *see* ACCORDING.

that's a cough lozenge for him *phr.* [late 19C] a phr. implying that someone is getting a due punishment. [a contemporary advertisement for 'cough no more lozenges', the implication being that they might kill the patient, for all that so drastic a remedy would certainly 'cure' their cough]

that's a good 'un *phr.* [19C–1920s] a phr. used ironically to characterize an esp. ludicrous, unlikely or mendacious story or statement.

that's a guild *phr.* [1990s] (US teen) a mocking phr. in response to someone's foolishness. [ety. unknown]

that's all *phr.* [mid-19C+] used as a general intensive, with either pos. implications e.g. *They only paid £500 for 50 words, that's all*; or neg. *I only lost every file on the drive, that's all.*

that's all gay *see* ALL GAY.

that's all one need *phr.* [1950s+] a phr. implying that whatever 'it' is, it is more than one can tolerate, usu. as *that's all I need.*

that's all I wanted to know *phr.* [1930s+] a phr. implying that the information received is exactly what one does *not* wish to hear.

that's all one needs *see* THAT'S ALL I NEED.

that's all she wrote *phr.* [1940s+] (orig. US milit.) a general term of finality, that's all there is (cf. GOOD NIGHT ALL). [? the unhappy man's remark on reaching the terminal statements of a DEAR JOHN letter]

that's an idea *see* IT'S AN IDEA.

that's another pair of shoes *see* QUITE A DIFFERENT PAIR OF SHOES.

that's another pair of sleeves *phr.* [1920s+] (Aus.) that's another matter.

that's Bible *phr.* [19C] that's excellent (cf. BIBLE).

that's big of you *phr.* [1930s+] that is very generous, magnanimous of you (usu. ironic).

that's chummy/dandy/ducky/great/lovely *phr.* [20C] an ironic phr. that implies that far from being *chummy*, *great* etc, the situation, information or whatever is just what the speaker does not desire.

that's close *phr.* [1970s] (US campus) an ironic comment implying that something is far from the truth.

that's cool *phr.* [1950s+] (orig. US) that's satisfactory, that's all right, don't worry. [COOL adj.³]

that's dandy/ducky *see* THAT'S CHUMMY.

that's fair *phr.* [1970s] (US campus) an ironic comment that something is not fair.

that's for sure *phr.* [1940s+] (orig. US) I agree unreservedly, you are absolutely right, often used as a comment on a relatively unpleasant/displeasing piece of information.

that's gear/the gear *phr.* [1920s+] (orig. milit.) a general term of approval, 'that's the stuff'. [SE *gear*]

that's gone to Pimlico *phr.* [late 19C] that's ruined, that's smashed beyond repair. [the contemporary reputation of Pimlico, London SW, as a home of 'fallen women']

that's great *see* THAT'S CHUMMY.

that shit don't fetch *phr.* [20C] (US) that doesn't add up. [SHIT n.³]

that's it/about it *phr.* [1960s+] a phr. used to state that there is nothing more to be said on or expected from a topic (cf. THAT'S THAT).

that's just too bad *phr.* 1930s+] (orig. US) a phr. used (often ironically) to acknowledge the inevitability of a situation, however unappealing.

that's love *phr.* [1990s] (US teen) a phr. of approval, encouragement, satisfaction. [popular phr. *ain't love wonderful*]

that's lovely *see* THAT'S CHUMMY.

that small thing *n.* [1950s+] the thing suggested, usu. in phr. '(Why don't) you do that small thing'.

that's my boy/girl *phr.* [20C] (US) an expression of approval and praise.

that's my eye *see* ALL MY EYE AND BETTY MARTIN.

that's my girl *see* THAT'S MY BOY.

that's my story and I'm sticking to it *phr.* [1930s+] usu. of an excuse or explanation, meaning 'like it or not, I have no intention of backing down'.

that's news *phr.* [1970s+] (US) a phr. used to acknowledge one's interest in whatever one has just been told.

that's news to me *see* IT'S NEWS TO ME.

that's persimmon/the ripe persimmon *phr.* [late 19C–1940s] (US) that's fine, that's satisfactory.

that's put the lid on *phr.* [1920s+] (orig. US) that's finished it, that's all one can do/say.

that's quacked! *excl.* [1980s+] (US campus) that's unfair! [play on SE *cracked*]

that's right enough *phr.* [late 19C+] that's satisfactory, within its limits, as far as you may be concerned (but not me).

that's round! *excl.* [late 16C–early 17C] an excl. of assertion, that's it! that's the way it is! [the completeness of a circle]

that's show business *phr.* [1940s+] (US) that's the unpredictable way of life.

that's so ill! *excl.* [1980s] (US teen) an all-purpose denunciation of an object or activity. [ILL adj., i.e. I want to be sick!]

that's telling ... *phr.* [1930s+] a phr. used to express approval or admiration for a statement, usu. an admonition of someone else, e.g. *that's telling her!*

that's tellings *see* THAT WOULD BE TELLING.

that's that *phr.* [early 19C+] a phr. used to declare the conclusion of a topic or discussion (cf. THAT'S IT).

that's/there goes the ball game *phr.* [1960s+] (US) that's it, no arguments accepted, forget it. [sporting imagery]

that's the barber *phr.* [mid-18C–early 19C] a general term of approbation. [ety. unknown; Grose (1785) describes it as 'a ridiculous and unmeaning phrase']

that's the gear *see* THAT'S GEAR.

that's the Limburger *phr.* [late 19C–1900s] that's the very best (cf. CHEESE n.¹). [proper name *Limburger*, a potently smelling, if not highly flavoursome cheese]

that's the man as married Hannah! *excl.* [mid–late 19C] excellent! that's the way! good for you! [generic/assonant use of proper name; i.e. pron. man a'/Hannah]

that's the ripe persimmon *see* THAT'S PERSIMMON.

that's the shot! *excl.* [1950s+] (Aus.) a general excl. of agreement or approval. [SHOT n.²]

that's the sort of clothes-pin I am *phr.* [mid-19C+] that's the sort of person I am, that's the way I am.

that's the story! *excl.* [1940s+] (N.Z.) a general excl. of encouragement.

that's the stuff to give the troops *phr.* [1910s+] (orig. milit.) a general phr. of enthusiastic approval.

that's the ticket *phr.* [mid-19C+] just what is wanted, the ideal thing; occas. as *that's the ticket for soup*. [the 'soup' ref. stems from the cards given out to beggars entitling them to a free meal at a soup kitchen]

that's the tip *phr.* [mid–late 19C] that's the way, that's the right thing (to do). [TIP n.⁴]

that's the tittup *phr.* [late 19C–1900s] that's the right thing. [SE *tittup*, a canter]

that's the tommy! *excl.* [late 19C] that's right! [? fig. use of TOMMY n.¹]

that's the way it goes *phr.* [20C+] that is the way things work out and one must accept the facts, like it or not (cf. THAT'S THE WAY THE COOKIE CRUMBLES).

that's the way the cookie crumbles/ball bounces *phr.* [1950s+] (orig. US) that is the way things work out and one must accept the facts, like it or not.

that's the way the mop flops *phr.* [1950s+] (US) that's the way things work out (cf. THAT'S THE WAY THE COOKIE CRUMBLES).

that's torn it *phr.* [20C] that has ruined it, spoiled it.

that's up against your shirt *phr.* [late 19C] said of an outstanding or comprehensive victory or success. [? the pinning on of a medal]

that's up your shirt *phr.* [mid-19C–1900s] that will prove a problem, a puzzler.

that's what *phr.* [late 18C] used to add emphasis to the preceding statement.

that's what's the matter *phr.* [mid–late 19C] (US) that's the truth.

that's where you spoil yourself *phr.* [late 19C] a phr. used of someone who is considered to be pushing themselves forward rather too keenly.

that's/that would be your best bet *phr.* [1930s+] a phr. advising the listener that their suggestion/decision is probably the optimum one.

that's your lot *phr.* [1920s+] a phr. of conclusion, that's all there is, you won't get any more.

that's your problem *phr.* [1960s+] (orig. US) I don't care, it's not my business, don't bother me, also as *that's his/her/my problem* etc. [the stress is on the personal pronoun, i.e. *your* problem as opposed to mine]

that's your sort *phr.* [late 18C–mid-19C] a general term of approval, agreement.

that takes it! *excl.* [late 19C+] an excl. meaning that is the absolute limit, that is simply too much to bear (cf. TAKE THE BISCUIT).

that there *n.* [20C] the vagina; thus *a bit of that there*, sexual intercourse (cf. DOWN BELOW). [euph.]

that thing *n.* [1900s–40s] (US Black) **1** sex. **2** the vagina (cf. DOWN BELOW). **3** the penis. [euph.]

that was *see* THAT IS.

that/this way *adj.*¹ [1910s+] engaged in crime. [euph.]

that way *adj.*² [1930s+] **1** in love. **2** (US) pregnant. **3** homosexual (cf. SO). [euphs.]

that will put hair on your chest *phr.* [1930s+] (orig. US) an invitation to drink. [the perceived masculinity of body hair + drinking]

that won't hoga *phr.* [mid-19C] (Anglo-Ind.) that won't do. [? link to Hind. *ho gya*, in trouble, confused, failed]

that won't pay the old woman her ninepence *phr.* [late 19C] used to describe an evasive act or statement. [coined at the Bow Street Police Court in London]

that would/that'd be telling/that's tellings *phr.* [late 19C+] a phr. used to avoid giving an honest, straightforward answer to a 'difficult' or probing question.

that would be your best bet *see* THAT'S YOUR BEST BET.

the *adj.* [mid-18C+] used before the names of certain well-known figures, esp. singers and actresses. [in imitation of a similar practice with the definite article in Fr. and Ital.]

theatre *n.* [mid-19C–1900s] a police court. [the accused, whether guilty or not, will 'act' their role, also the ironic acceptance that justice often depends more on image than facts]

thedi/theddy/tedhi *n.* [late 19C] fire. [Shelta]

the fuck I have!/you do! *excl.* [20C] absolutely not! [FUCK!]

theg/teaich gens *n.* [mid-19C] 8 shillings (40p). [backsl.]

theg yeneps *n.* [mid-19C] 8 pence. [backsl.]

Thelonius Monk *n.* [20C] semen. [rhy. sl. *Thelonius Monk* = SPUNK n.[1] (2); ult. jazz pianist *Thelonius Monk* (1917–82)]

them's my sentiments *phr.* [mid-19C–1940s] a general statement of agreement and approval.

them's the jockeys for me! *excl.* [mid-19C+] a general excl. of approval.

them things *n.* [20C] (drugs) marijuana cigarettes. [euph.]

then comes a pig to be killed *phr.* [late 19C] a phr. used to express disbelief. [according to Ware, the story of one Mrs Bond who allegedly called to her poultry, 'Come chicks, come! Come to Mrs. Bond and be killed!']

then the band began to play/played *phr.* [late 19C+] a phr. implying that that was the point at which the problems really began.

the ... of this world *phr.* [1950s+] used with a suitable personal or proper name to indicate a (usu. pej.) stereotype, e.g. *We all know how the Archers of this world get ahead.*

the rabbit died *phr.* [1950s+] I am pregnant. [the test formerly used to determine pregnancy]

there *adj.* **1** [20C] (US) of a person, well informed (cf. WITH IT). **2** [1930s] (US) drunk. **3** [1960s+] (drugs) intoxicated by drugs.

there first *n.* [late 19C] a thirst. [rhy. sl.]

there goes the ball game *see* THAT'S THE BALL GAME.

there is no great miss of *phr.* [19C] there is no great problem over the loss, absence, disadvantage etc of the person in question.

there is York Street concerned/York Street is concerned *phr.* [19C] someone is staring. [YORK v.]

there'll be blue murder if ... *phr.* [mid-19C+] a warning against performing any action with inevitably disastrous consequences (cf. THERE'LL BE HELL TO PAY). [BLUE MURDER]

there'll be hell to pay *phr.* [early 19C+] a warning against performing any action with inevitably disastrous consequences (cf. HELL TO PAY; THERE'LL BE BLUE MURDER).

thereoa *adj.* [1950s] other. [backsl.]

there's a dead nigger in the woodpile *phr.* [20C] (US) something is suspicious, something is not as it should be, someone is attempting to deceive the speaker (cf. DEAD CAT UP THE LINE). [note synon. US regional *monkey in the woodpile*; the phr. is now considered offensive]

there's a deal of glass about *phr.* [late 19C–1910s] a phr. used to indicate the presence of a showy, flashy person. [SE *glass*, i.e. paste rather than real jewels]

there's air!/'air! *excl.* [late 19C] there's a woman with a lot of hair. [ref. is to a hairstyle featuring the side hair being pulled up and then shaped]

there's a kangaroo loose in the top paddock *phr.* [1990s] (Aus.) a phr. describing a fool (cf. NOT ALL THERE). [SE *top paddock*, used fig. for the head]

there's a letter in the post office *phr.* **1** [mid-19C+] (US) a phr. used to warn a man his fly is undone or his shirt is out, also used to a woman when her slip is showing. **2** [late 19C–1910s] said of a woman who is menstruating.

there's a shape for you *phr.* [mid–late 19C] a remark used of a very thin person or animal.

there's been a fire *phr.* [late 19C] a phr. addressed to someone wearing a new suit. [the implication that it has been picked up cheap as salvage]

there's no ... about it *phr.* [1920s+] a phr. used as a rejoinder to another speaker's unequivocal statement, e.g. 'You must stay with your family.' 'There's no *must* about it.'

there's no intelligent life here *phr.* [1970s] (US campus) a

phr. denoting one's generally neg. reaction to a given situation (cf. BEAM ME UP SCOTTY!). [coined in the *Star Trek* TV series, usu. accompanying the phr. 'Beam me up, Scotty']

there's no work in Bourke/no lucre at Echuca *phr.* [1960s+] (Aus.) phrs. used to denote an unsatisfactory situation (cf. GIRLS ARE BANDY AT URANDANGIE). [assonant phr. based on Aus. place names]

there's one born every minute *phr.* [mid-19C+] a phr. referring to an absurd event or a person who has exhibited great foolishness. [the dictum of master showman P.T. Barnum (1810–91) to whom 'one' was a gullible victim]

there's slanging dues concerned *phr.* [early 19C] a phr. used to imply that one has been cheated. [SLANG v.[1]]

there with the goods *phr.* [20C] clever, intelligent, 'on the ball'. [GOODS n.[1]]

there you are *n.* [20C] **1** a bar. **2** tea. [rhy. sl.; (2) *there you are* = CHA n.[1]]

there you are *phr.* **1** [late 18C+] synon. for THERE YOU GO phr. (2). **2** [late 19C+] expressing or drawing attention to the simplicity or easy consummation of a process or action. **3** [late 19C+] synon. for *what did I tell you?*. **4** [20C] expressing resignation in the face of an unpleasant truth.

there you are then *phr.* [20C] a phr. used to bring an end to an argument, or to underpin the irreversibility of a situation or statement.

there you go *phr.* [1970s+] (orig. US) **1** a general phr. of agreement and approval. **2** a usu. neg. phr. implying that the person is acting in their own particular way (yet) again.

thery *v.* [19C] to speculate, to wonder. [? Rom. or SE *theory*]

these and those *n.* [20C] **1** clothes. **2** toes. [rhy. sl.]

thesp *n.* [1960s+] an actor. [abbr. SE *thespian*]

thespian *n.* [1970s] a lesbian. [pun on SE ? + alleged prevalence of homosexual men in theatre]

they *n.* [late 19C+] those in authority or power, the Establishment.

they're off, Mr Cutts! *excl.* [1940s+] (N.Z.) things have started! now we're getting down to business! [the racehorse trainer *Mr* E. *Cutts*, starter of the Auckland races, but note THEY'RE OFF, SAID THE MONKEY]

they're off, said the monkey *phr.* [late 19C] a phr. used to indicate that something has come loose. [image of castration, i.e. what is 'off' is the monkey's NUTS n.[2] (1)]

theydon bois *n.* [20C] noise. [rhy. sl., pron. 'boyze'; ult. *Theydon Bois*, a town in Essex]

thick *n.[1]* [mid-19C+] (orig./mainly juv.) a fool, an ignoramus. [THICK adj.[1]]

thick *n.[2]* **1** [late 19C] mud. **2** [late 19C–1940s] any drink having a dense consistency, e.g. porter, cocoa, coffee. **3** [1930s–60s] a thick fog. **4** [1990s] (US Black) one who has a muscular, well-developed physique. [SE *thick*]

thick *adj.[1]* [late 16C+] stupid, dull, foolish; often intensified as [1970s+] *thick as two* (*short*) *planks*. [abbr. SE *thick-headed*]

thick *adj.[2]* **1** [late 18C+] close, intimate; usu. in variety of *as thick as ...* phrs. **2** [20C] (US campus) emotionally involved, romantically attached.

thick *adj.[3]* [late 19C–1900s] unpleasant due to its excess, too much to handle.

thick *adj.[4]* [1970s+] (US Black/teen) deep, complex or meaningful.

thick *adj.[5]* [1990s] (US Black) of money, plentiful. [i.e. a thick roll of cash]

thick *adj.[6]* [1990s] (Black) **1** of a woman, physically attractive. **2** of a man, having a large penis.

thick *adv.* **1** [late 18C–mid-19C] heavily. **2** [late 19C+] intensely, severely. **3** [late 19C+] densely.

thick and thin *n.* [20C] **1** the chin. **2** gin. **3** (Aus.) the skin. [rhy. sl.]

thick as ... *phr.*[1] [late 17C+] very close, extremely intimate; used in a variety of combs, for the best-known of which see below. [THICK adj.[2]]

thick as ... *phr.*[2] [late 19C+] stupid; used in a variety of combs, for the best-known of which see below. [THICK adj.[1]]

thick as fiddlers in hell *phr.* [20C] (US) very plentiful.

thick as glue *phr.* [19C] very intimate (cf. THICK AS THIEVES). [THICK adj.[2]]

thick as peas in a pod/shell *phr.* [18C–19C] very close. [THICK adj.[2]]

thick as poundies *phr.* [late 19C–1900s] (Irish) very stupid. [THICK adj.[1] + Irish *poundies*, mashed potato mixed with onion and milk]

thick as thieves *phr.* [early 19C+] very intimate. [THICK adj.[2]]

thick as three in a bed *phr.* [early 19C] very intimate. [THICK adj.[2]]

thick as two inkle-weavers *phr.* [late 17C–early 19C] very close. [THICK adj.[2] + SE *inkle*, linen tape]

thick as two Jews on payday *phr.* [late 19C] very close. [THICK adj.[2] + racial stereotyping]

thick as two short planks *phr.* [1950s+] very stupid. [THICK adj.[1]]

thick dick *n.* [1980s] a fool (cf. DICKHEAD). [THICK adj.[1] + DICK n.[5] (1)]

thick ear *n.* [late 19C] an ear that has swollen up after a blow; usu. in phr. *give one a thick ear*.

thick end *n.* [mid-19C+] the larger portion.

thickening for something *phr.* [1950s+] pregnant. [pun on 'sickening for something']

thicker *n.* [mid–late 19C] £1 (cf. NICKER). [? THICK 'UN]

thick head *n.*[1] [20C] a hangover.

thickhead *n.*[2] [20C] a fool, a simpleton. [SE *thick* + sfx. -HEAD (1)]

thickie *n.* [1970s+] a fool (cf. THICKO). [THICK n.[1]]

thick in the clear *phr.* [mid-19C] confused, at a loss for coherence.

thick-legs *n.* [late 19C–1900s] navvies. [their physique]

thick 'n' thins *n.* [1950s–60s] (US Black) stylish nylon socks, usu. black or brown. [? the pattern which may include stripes of varying widths]

thicko *n.* [1970s+] a fool (cf. THICKIE). [THICK n.[1]]

thick one *see* THICK 'UN.

thick on the ground *phr.* [late 19C+] usu. of people, plentiful, in large (crowded) numbers.

thick starch double blue *n.* [late 19C] a holiday dress worn in the summer (such dresses were heavily laundered).

thick 'un/one *n.* [mid–late 19C] **1** a sovereign (£1). **2** 5 shillings, a crown (25p). **3** a slice of bread and butter (cf. DOOR-STEP). [the dimensions of the coin/foodstuff]

thief *n.* [late 19C] a horse that fails to run to form. [it 'steals' the bettors' money]

thief and robber *n.* [20C] (Aus.) a friend. [rhy. sl. *thief and robber* = COBBER n.[2]]

thieve *n.* [1960s] a theft, a burglary.

thieves' kitchen *n.* **1** [late 19C] the Law Courts in the Strand, London WC. **2** [1910s–20s] the Athenaeum Club, London. [ironic ref. to the supposed respectability and actual venality of such places]

thieving hooks *n.* [early 19C] the fingers. [HOOK n.[2]]

thieving irons *n.* [19C] scissors. [? their use in cutting purses]

thigh-opener *n.* [1950s+] (orig. Aus.) a drink given to a woman in the hope of getting her drunk enough for seduction (cf. COCK-OPENER).

thigh-slapper *n.* [1960s+] (often used ironically) a supposedly very amusing joke. [the exaggerated slapping of one's thighs to intimate the intensity of one's hilarity]

thimble *n.* [early 19C] (Und.) a watch. [naut. *thimble*, a thick ring of metal, through which a rope can be pushed; thus the similarity in shape]

thimble and bodkin army *n.* [mid-17C] the Parliamentary Army fighting during the English Civil War. [the meanness and paucity of the 'Roundheads' compared with the wealth of their royalist 'Cavalier' enemies]

thimble and thumb *n.* [1940s] rum. [rhy. sl.]

thimble and thumb, to *phr.* [1940s] to run. [rhy. sl.]

thimbled *adj.*[1] [early 19C] wearing a watch. [THIMBLE]

thimbled *adj.*[2] [early 19C] arrested. [pun on THIMBLED adj.[1] = watch = 'the watch', i.e. the police]

thimble-rig *n.* [mid-19C+] a version of the three-card trick, in which punters are asked to bet on which of three rapidly manipulated thimbles contains a pea; it is very rare that anyone other than the sharper's accomplice manages to bet correctly (cf. FIND THE LADY). [SE *thimble* + RIG n.[2] (2). Sante (1991) suggests this to be one of 'the only major gambling games actually invented in the United States'. However neither E.P. nor the *OED*'s first citation (*Hone's Every-day Book*, 1825) mentions this and Sante himself places its US appearance around 1860]

thimble-rigger/-screwer *n.* [mid-19C+] one who operates a game of THIMBLE-RIG. [SE *thimble* + RIG n.[2] (2)/SCREW v.[1]]

thimble-twister *n.* [mid-19C] (Und.) a thief who specializes in stealing watches from their wearers. [THIMBLE + TWISTER n.[2]]

thin *n.* [mid-19C–1910s] a *thin* slice of bread and butter (cf. THICK 'UN).

thin *adj.* [1920s+] (US tramp) without money, broke (cf. ONE THIN DIME).

thin *v.* [1920s] to swindle, to trick, to deceive. [one 'thins' the victim's wallet]

thin ale *n.* [late 19C] weak beer (cf. FAT ALE).

thin as a rasher of wind *phr.* [late 19C] very thin.

thing, the *n.*[1] [mid-18C+] whatever is correct or fashionable within the context.

Thing *n.*[2] [1910s+] used when one cannot remember a person's actual surname, e.g. *Mr Thing, Lady Thing.*

thing *n.*[3] **1** [1930s+] an obsession, e.g. *I have a thing about her*. **2** [1950s+] usu. as *one's own thing*, one's lifestyle, one's opinion etc.

thing *n.*[4] [1950s+] the penis. [euph.]

thing *n.*[5] [1960s] (drugs) heroin, cocaine, marijuana, whatever is one's current drug of choice. [euph. or ext. of THING n.[3] (2)]

thing *n.*[6] [1990s] (US) a non-specific descriptor, used when one either cannot or does not wish to use the correct term, e.g. *Shall we do the coffee shop thing? I have to do the work thing.*

thingamerry / thingamerrybob / thingumsmeribob *n.* [20C] (W.I.) anything otherwise unnamed, whether through choice or one's inability to recall the correct title (cf. THING-UMABOB).

thingo *n.* [20C] (Aus.) a nameless object. [abbr. THINGUMABOB]

things *n.*[1] **1** [early 17C+] one's possessions. **2** [mid-17C+] clothes in general, esp. those that women put on to go out, in addition to their indoor dress. **3** [late 17C] implements or equipment for some special use, utensils.

things *n.*[2] [1950s–60s] (drugs) capsules of illegal narcotic drugs (cf. THING n.[5]).

things are crook in Musclebrook/at Musellbrook/in Tallarook/weak at Julia Creek/things is weak in Werris Creek *phr.* [1960s+] (Aus.) various assonant/rhyming phrs. used to denote an unsatisfactory situation (cf. THERE'S NO WORK IN BOURKE).

thingstable *n.* [late 18C–early 19C] 'Mr Thingstable, Mr Constable, a ludicrous affectation of delicacy in avoiding the ... first syllable in the title of that officer, which in sound has some similarity to an indecent monosyllable' (Grose 1785).

thingum n. [late 17C–early 19C] an unnamed object or person (cf. THINGUMABOB; THINGUMAJIG; THINGUMMY).

thingumabob/thingumbob n. [mid-18C+] anything, often small, to which one cannot put a name (cf. DOHICKEY).

thingumabobs/thingumbobs n. [mid-18C+] the testicles. [euph. of THINGUMABOB]

thingumajig/thingamajigger/thingummijig n. [early 19C+] a nameless object (cf. DOHICKEY).

thingumbob see THINGUMABOB.

thingumbobs see THINGUMABOBS.

thingummies n. **1** [early 19C+] the testicles. **2** [1900s] trousers. [euph.]

thingummijig see THINGUMAJIG.

thingummy n. **1** [late 18C+] any nameless object (cf. DOHICKEY). **2** [early 19C+] the penis. [(2) is euph. use of (1)]

thingumsmeribob see THINGAMERRY.

thin-gut n. [late 19C] a very thin, starving person.

thingy n. [1930s+] **1** the penis. **2** an unnamed object or person (cf. DOHICKEY).

thin in the upper crust phr. [20C] (US) stupid. [cooking imagery]

think about breakfast, to phr. [late 19C–1910s] to be lost in thought. [one is lost in apparently important thought but it is more likely to be quite banal]

think and thank n. [late 19C] thanks, thank you. [Eng. translation of the Heb. morning prayer as used by Jewish Londoners]

thinkbox/thinkpad n. **1** [late 19C–1900s] (Aus.) the head. **2** [1930s+] (US) the brain.

thinker n. [19C] the mind, the brain.

think factory n. [1950s] (US) a research institution.

thinking box n. **1** [20C] a study. **2** [1930s+] (US) the brain (cf. THINKBOX).

thinking cap n. [mid-17C+] fig. use for the process of thought, esp. in phr. *don/put on one's thinking cap*, to ponder, to 'have a think'.

think one holds it, to phr. [late 19C] (orig. sporting) to think well of oneself, to be conceited. ['it' being some form of trophy]

think one is King Shit, to phr. [1950s+] (US) to be extremely conceited. [KING SHIT]

think oneself v. [1930s+] (Aus.) to be conceited, to admire oneself. [abbr. 'think well of oneself']

think one's penny silver, to phr. [late 16C–early 18C] to have a good opinion of oneself.

think one's shit doesn't stink, to phr. [late 19C+] (orig. US) to behave affectedly and in an arrogant manner (cf. ACT LIKE ONE'S SHIT DON'T SMELL).

thinkpad see THINKBOX.

think pumpkins of oneself, to phr. [late 19C–1900s] to admire oneself. [i.e. a fig. ref. to the size of the vegetable]

thinks it's just to pee through phr. [20C] a phr. denigrating an unsophisticated, inexperienced youth who supposedly has yet to appreciate the alternative function of his penis. [PEE v.]

think small beer/coals of, to phr. [19C] to have a low opinion of. [SE *small beer*, weak, inferior quality beer/SE *small coals*, slack, useless for a blazing fire]

think-tank n. [20C] the brain (cf. THINKBOX; THINKER).

think that the sun sets/shines in/out of someone's ass, to phr. [1930s+] (orig. US) to worship someone, to act extremely sycophantically. [ARSE n.[1]]

thin one n. [1930s–40s] (US Black) a dime, 10 cents (cf. ONE THIN DIME; THICK 'UN; THIN 'UN).

thin on the ground phr. [1910s+] (orig. milit.) sparse, well spread-out, in small number.

thin time n. [1920s+] a period of suffering or discomfiture.

thin 'un n. [mid-19C–1920s] a half-sovereign (50p) (cf. THICK 'UN; THIN ONE). [the coin's dimensions]

third base n. [1940s+] (US) the vagina, esp. in the context of sexual exploration (cf. FIRST BASE). [baseball imagery (a 'home run' would be intercourse)]

third degree n. [late 19C+] (orig. US Und.) the beating up and similar physical abuse of suspects by policemen in order to extract confessions. Although allegedly outlawed in the last couple of decades reality proves otherwise. [the *first* and *second* degrees of interrogation are never specified]

third eye n. [20C] (US) the anus (cf. ROUNDEYE).

third eyebrow n. [1990s] a moustache.

third leg n. [1970s+] the penis (cf. BEST LEG OF THREE; BLACKLEG n.[3]; BUCKINGER'S BOOT).

third-legger n. [1980s+] (US Black) a promiscuous woman. [THIRD LEG]

third rail n. [1910s–20s] (US) extremely strong liquor. [like the subway's electrified *third rail*, such liquor 'gives you a jolt']

third sexer n. [20C] (US) a homosexual. [SE *third sex*, homosexuality, coined by sexologist Magnus Hirschfeld]

third wheel n. [20C] (US) an unwanted or superfluous person. [the vehicle would be a bicycle]

third-world briefcase n. [1980s+] a large portable stereophonic tape deck/radio, particularly popular among Black youths in the US and UK (cf. GHETTOBLASTER). [SE *third-world*, i.e. non-White]

thirst n. [1980s+] (drugs) the need for crack cocaine; thus *thirst monster*, one who smokes crack cocaine to excess.

thirsty adj. [1980s+] (US drugs) in desperate need of drugs.

thirteen n. [1960s] (drugs) marijuana. [the initial letter *M*, 13th in the alphabet]

thirteence n. [1920s–40s] one shilling (5p). [there were 12 pence in a shilling; presumably a child could count 'elevenpence, twelvepence, one shilling', the 13th number]

thirteen clean shirts n. [19C–1950s] (prison) a 3-month sentence. [prisoners were allotted one clean shirt every week]

thirteenth juryman n. [late 19C] a biased judge, whether pro or con the defendant.

thirty n. [late 19C+] (US) the end. [the notation *–30–* used orig. by printers and telegraphers to indicate the end of a story or despatch]

thirty cents shy of a quarter phr. [1970s] (US Black) very poor. [a quarter is 35¢, thus lit. '–5¢']

thirty-eight n. [1950s+] (orig. US) a *.38* pistol. [abbr.]

38/thirty-eight hot adj. [1990s] (US Black) extremely angry. [THIRTY-EIGHT + HOT adj.[1] (2)]

thirty-first of May n. [1920s+] (Aus.) a fool, a simpleton. [rhy. sl. *thirty-first of May* = GAY n.[2]]

thirty-three-oh-five n. [1950s–60s] (US drugs/New York) an arrest for possession of drugs. [the statute number of the New York penal code]

…this! excl. [1980s+] (US campus) used in comb. with a n. to negate the previous speaker's suggestion, e.g. 'Let's play pool.' 'Pool this! I've got work to do.' [euph. for *fuck this*]

this and that n. [20C] **1** a hat. **2** a cricket bat. [rhy. sl.]

this child n. [mid-19C+] (orig. US Black) I, myself, e.g. *this child don't need no more trouble*.

thises and thats n. [1900s–10s] spats. [rhy. sl.]

this is all right phr. [late 19C] a phr. of disappointment or complaint that implies quite the opposite.

this is an A and B conversation, C yourself out phr. [1990s] (US Black) a phr. used to dismiss a third party who butts into a private conversation. [SE phr. *see yourself out*]

this is it phr. [1940s+] a phr. used when something unpleasant that has been expected happens.

this is my day out *phr.* [1930s+] a phr. used by someone standing treat for their friends.

this is protected by the red, the black, and the green – with a key *phr.* [1990s] (US Black teen) **1** keep out, this is none of your business. **2** this is for Blacks only, you couldn't understand, optionally ext. by *sisseeeee*. [the colours of Black nationalism; play on the minatory signs that indicate a building's security system]

this is the end *phr.* [20C] a phr. implying that 'this' is the very last straw in a situation.

this is the life *phr.* [20C] (orig. US) a general phr. of happiness, enthusiasm, pleasure etc.

this is where we came in *phr.* [1940s+] we've come full circle, we're back where we started. With ref. to conversation or discussion rather than physical movement. [the era of cinema's non-stop 'continuous performances', one could start watching at any point during the film]

thistledown *n.* [late 19C] (Anglo-Irish) children. [like blowing *thistledown*, they wander. Note Devon dial. *thistleseed*, gypsies]

this trip *n.* [mid-18C; 1900s] on this occasion.

this way see THAT WAY adj.[1].

this won't buy baby a new frock/dress *phr.* [20C] this is useless, this is pointless.

thomas *n.*[1] **1** [mid-19C] a liveried servant. **2** [mid-19C+] the penis. [abbr. JOHN THOMAS]

Thomas *n.*[2] [1950s] (W.I.) a stubborn, conceited man. [biblical figure Doubting *Thomas*]

thomas tilling *n.* [1920s–30s] a shilling (5p) (cf. ABRAHAM'S WILLING). [rhy. sl.; ult. 19C haulier *Thomas Tilling*]

thomyok/tomyok *n.* [early 18C+] a magistrate. [Shelta]

thornback *n.* [late 17C–early 18C] an old maid. [SE *thornback*, a ray or stickleback. The usage puns on the female child of a stickleback, a *maid* or (Scot.) *maiden-skate*]

thorny wire *n.* [20C] (Anglo-Irish) an ill-tempered, 'prickly' person.

thorough *adj.* **1** [1980s+] (US campus) of a person, admirable. **2** [1980s+] (US campus) used of one who is acting arrogantly or cheekily. **3** [1990s] (US teen) in absolute and complete control of a situation.

thoroughbred *n.* **1** [1950s+] (US Black) a dependable person, an admirable individual, a sophisticated hustler. **2** [1950s+] (drugs) a dealer who sells pure or high quality narcotics. **3** [1960s+] (Und.) a successful, trustworthy villain. **4** [1970s+] a prostitute with style, sophistication and knowledge, generally considered among the élite of her profession. [horse-racing imagery]

thoroughbred Black *n.* [1950s+] (US Black) the ideal Black woman.

thorough churchman *n.* [late 18C–early 19C] one who goes in at one door of a church and out of the other without stopping for prayer. [pun on SE *through*]

thorough cough *n.* [late 17C–mid-19C] a cough accompanied by a simultaneous breaking of wind. [the wind goes 'through' the body]

thoroughfare *n.* [1930s] (US Black) a promiscuous woman. [orig. W.I. use, many men have 'ridden' down her]

thorough-go-nimble *n.* [late 17C–early 19C] **1** sour or second-rate beer. **2** diarrhoea (cf. JERRY-GO-NIMBLE). [its effects on the stomach]

thorough good-natured wench *n.* [late 18C–early 19C] a promiscuous woman. ['one who being asked to sit down, will lie down' (Grose 1785)]

thorough-handed man *n.* [late 19C] (US) a generous person.

thorough passage *phr.* [late 17C–early 19C] going 'in one ear and out the other'.

thou *n.* [mid-19C+] (orig. US) 1000, esp. dollars. [abbr. SE *thousand*]

though *adv.* **1** [late 19C+] nonetheless, despite everything else, despite a statement to the contrary. **2** [20C] used as an intensifier, e.g. *doesn't she, though*.

though I say it as shouldn't *phr.* [early 17C+] a falsely self-deprecating phr. used after one has either praised one's own achievements or denigrated those of a rival.

thousand-eyes *n.* [1970s–80s] (US Black) a man's shoe with many perforations in the leather.

thousand-miler *n.* [1920s+] a dark shirt, made of black or navy twill, that does not show dirt. [orig. naut., its being washed after every 1000 miles of a voyage]

thousand-on-a-plate *n.* [1930s–40s] (US Black) a dish of peas or beans.

thousand pities *n.* [late 19C–1900s] a woman's breasts (cf. CATS AND KITTIES; LEWIS AND WITTIES; TALE OF TWO CITIES; TOWNS AND CITIES). [rhy. sl. *thousand pities = titties* (cf. TITTY n.[2])]

thrap/throp *v.* [1990s] to masturbate. [dial. *threap*, to beat, to flog]

thrash *n.* **1** [1950s+] a rumbustious, uninhibited party (cf. BASH n.[2]). **2** [1950s+] a drinking spree. **3** [1980s+] a form of fast, loud and harsh-sounding rock music.

thrash *v.* **1** [1960s+] (Aus./N.Z.) to overwork a piece of machinery, e.g. an automobile. **2** [1960s+] (Aus./N.Z.) to drive at great speeds. **3** [1980s+] (US campus) to wreck, to make a mess of.

thrashed *adj.* [1980s+] (US campus) **1** worn out, broken, exhausted. **2** drunk, intoxicated by a drug (cf. TRASHED).

thrasher *n.* [1990s] (US campus) **1** (orig. surfing use) a show-off. **2** a destructive person. **3** a skateboarder. **4** a wild party at which there are breakages. [THRASH v. (3)]

thrasher *adj.* [1990s] (US campus) of a party, wild, extreme. [THRASH v. (3)]

thrash or die! *excl.* [1980s+] (US campus) an ironic reversal of a clichéd slogan i.e. *march or die!*, to belittle those who are obsessed with skateboarding (cf. SURF OR DIE!). [THRASHER n. (3)]

thrash someone's jacket, to *phr.* [late 17C] to beat, to thrash (cf. TRIM SOMEONE'S JACKET).

thrash the daylights out of see BEAT THE DAYLIGHTS OUT OF.

thrash the pants off see TAKE THE PANTS OFF.

thray *n.* [1900s–60s] (N.Z.) a threepenny price. [TRAY n.[1]]

thread *v.* [1950s] to have sexual intercourse. [PLAY/PLAY AT ... (*thread the needle*)]

threads *n.* [1920s+] (orig. US) clothes. [metonymy]

threateners *n.* [1990s] breasts, usu. large.

three *n.* [1950s–70s] (drugs) a $3 bag of heroin (cf. TREY).

three acres and a cow *phr.* [late 19C] a phr. used to dismiss illogical optimism. [coined by a George Smith who suggested in a letter in the *Daily News* (27 August 1887) that an immediate renaissance could be achieved in British agriculture if every peasant could be guaranteed 'three acres and a cow'. He forbore to explain how such philanthropy might be funded]

three and sixpenny thoughtful *n.* [late 19C] (society) 'a feminine theory novel' (Ware), e.g. those of Mrs Craik (1826–87) or Mrs Humphry Ward (1851–1920), who wrote on social and religious themes, often dealing with women (but never suffragism). [play on PENNY DREADFUL; SHILLING SHOCKER]

three bags full *n.* [20C] (Aus.) a pack of lies. [rhy. sl. *three bags full* = a load of BULL n.[12]]

three balls *n.* **1** [mid-19C+] a pawnbroker's. **2** [1930s+] (US Black) a Jew. [traditional *three brass balls* that hang outside a pawnshop. The stereotypical pawnbroker was Jewish. The three balls themselves supposedly come from the arms of the Medicis (although these were 6 red balls, rather than the three gold ones of pawnbroking) and were imported to London by the Lombard bankers and thence to the US]

three blind mice n. [20C] (a sack of) rice. [rhy. sl.]

three blue beans in a/one blue bladder phr. [late 16C–early 18C] futile, pointless (if noisy) talk. [the image of a jester and his traditional bladder on a stick, made noisier by the dried beans it contains]

three bricks shy of a load phr. [20C] (US) not very intelligent, slightly eccentric, odd. One of a number of phrs. meaning stupid or eccentric (cf. FEW BRICKS SHORT OF A LOAD; NOT ALL THERE).

three Bs phr. **1** [late 19C] as used by churchmen, bright, brief and brotherly, three precepts for a good service, in all of which the younger clergy felt that the very conservative contemporary church was distinctly lacking. **2** [1920s+] (Aus.) burn, bash and bury, what should be done with rubbish that accumulates in the outback.

three-bullet joey n. [1960s–80s] (US Black) the police. [their being armed + generic use of proper name Joey]

three-card monte n. [late 19C] (orig. US) the three-card trick (cf. FIND THE LADY). [Sp. monte, a 19C game of chance, played with 45 cards. The modern game is played only by confidence tricksters. There is no gambling and unless the trickster desires otherwise – to entice a new victim – the house invariably wins]

three-cents adj. [20C] (W.I.) insignificant, unimportant, worthless. [the tiny sum]

three cheesing rows n. [20C] three rousing cheers. [joc. reversal]

three cold Irish see FENIAN n.[1].

three-cornered adj. [mid-19C+] (Aus.) of a horse, awkwardly shaped, scraggy, weak.

three-cornered scraper see SCRAPER n.[2].

three-cornered tree n. [mid-17C–late 18C] the gallows, esp. the great 'triple tree' at Tyburn (cf. DEADLY NEVERGREEN; THREE-LEGGED MARE; THREE-LEGGED STOOL; THREE TREES; TREE WITH THREE CORNERS; TRIPLE TREE).

three Cs n. [late 19C] the Central Criminal Court, London, i.e. the Old Bailey, technically the main court for the County of Middlesex, but acknowledged as the most important court in the UK]

three-d masher n. [late 19C] a young man who poses as a gentleman but lacks the savoir-faire, not to mention the funds. [SE three d, i.e. 3d or three old pence + MASHER n.]

three-dollar bill n. [1970s+] (US campus) anyone or anything eccentric or odd (cf. NINE-BOB NOTE). [no such currency exists]

three draws and a spit n. [late 19C–1900s] a cigarette. [SE draw, a puff]

three-ed up adj. [1960s+] (prison) living three to a cell.

three halfporth of gawdelpus n. [late 19C] a street urchin (cf. THREE PENNORTH OF GOD HELP US). [GAWDELPUS]

three hots and a cot n. [1970s+] (US) three meals a day plus a bed for the night, often used as a rate of payment (cf. THREE SQUARES).

three-hour tour n. [1970s+] (US teen) anything too tedious to be tolerated.

three is an awkward number phr. [late 19C] (society) synon. for 'two's company, three's a crowd'. [taken from evidence given in Lord Durham's divorce suit (1885)]

three jerks of a lamb's/dead lamb's/sheep's tail see TWO SHAKES OF A LAMB'S TAIL.

three-legged beaver n. [20C] a male homosexual (cf. OMEE-PALOME). [THIRD LEG + BEAVER n.[4]]

three-legged mare n. [late 17C–late 18C] the gallows, esp. the 'triple tree' at Tyburn (cf. THREE-CORNERED TREE).

three-legged stool n. [late 17C–18C] the Tyburn gallows (cf. THREE-CORNERED TREE). [for ety. see TYBURN]

three-letter man n. [1930s+] **1** (orig. RN) an unpleasant person. **2** (orig. US campus) euph. for a homosexual. [in (1) the letters were c-a-d; in (2) they were orig. f-a-g, now g-a-y]

three of the best n. [1920s+] (Aus.) a packet of condoms, usu. containing three (cf. THREE SCREWS).

three-out n. [mid-19C] a glass that holds 1.24l (one third of a quart) (of beer).

three pennorth of God help us n. [20C] (Aus.) a weakling, an insignificant person (cf. THREE HALFPORTH OF GAWDELPUS).

threepenny bits n. [late 19C+] **1** diarrhoea. **2** a woman's breasts (cf. FAINTING FITS; TREY-BITS). [rhy. sl. threepenny bits = SHITS/TITS n.[1] (1)]

threepenny dodger/Johnnie n. [1900s–10s] a silver threepenny bit. [SE dodge, i.e. one is hard to get hold of/generic use of proper name]

threepenny shot n. [late 19C] a round steak and kidney pudding, sold at threepence a portion.

threepenny/twopenny upright/uprighter n. [late 18C–early 19C] a cheap prostitute who has no room of her own and must stand against a wall for intercourse. [her fee of 3d/2d + SE upright]

three-piece set/suit/suite n. [1970s+] the male genitals (cf. ADJUST ONE'S SET; MEAT AND TWO VEG).

three planks n. [late 19C] a coffin.

three-point drinker n. [1920s–40s] one who drinks sixpennyworth of gin, with bitters, a shot of lime juice and soda. [the three additives]

three-pointer n. [1940s] (US Black) an urban street corner; thus three-pointer of the ace trill in the twirling top, any corner of 7th Avenue in Harlem.

three prices phr. [1920s] (Irish) expensive.

three quarters of a peck n. [mid-19C] the neck, usu. written as ¾. [rhy. sl.]

three-rounder n. [1950s–60s] a petty criminal. [junior or amateur boxing matches are restricted to three rounds, professional bouts run to 12 or (formerly) 15]

three screws n. [1920s+] (Can.) an aluminium container holding three condoms (cf. THREE OF THE BEST). [brandname, Three Screws, + pun SCREW n.[1] (2)]

three shakes of a lamb's/dead lamb's/sheep's tail see TWO SHAKES OF A LAMB'S TAIL.

three-sheet v. [20C] to advertise, thus to boast, to brag. [carnival/theatre use, a three-sheet poster is larger than usual]

three sheets in/to the wind adj. [mid-19C+] drunk, also as two/four/six sheets to the wind; abbr. as three sheets etc (cf. AFLOAT). [naval imagery, a ship carrying 'three sheets (sails) to the wind' is 'top-heavy']

three-six-nine/3-6-9 n. [1940s+] (US Black) anything unpleasant. [369, which in dream books (used to divine dreams for playing the NUMBERS or the lottery) represents shit; ult. f. Ralph Ellison's Invisible Man (1952), in which the hero finds a home in an underground sewer, with 1369 light bulbs]

365 n. [19C] ham and eggs or bacon and eggs. [the inevitable appearance of the dish on a café menu every day of the year]

three-sixty-five/365 adv. [1980s+] (orig. US Black) continually, lit. every day of the year (cf. TWENTY-FOUR-SEVEN).

threesome n. [1990s] group sex involving three people of the same or mixed sexes.

three-spot n. [1970s+] (N.Z. Und) a three-year prison sentence. [SE three + SPOT n.[3] (1)]

three squares n. [20C] three square meals, regular eating (cf. THREE HOTS AND A COT). [abbr.]

three star/stars n. [1950s+] a folding knife, made in Germany, that carries three stars on its handle (cf. OKAPI).

threeswins/treewins n. [late 17C–18C] threepence (cf. THREP; THRUMS). [SE three + WIN n.]

three-tap joint *n.* [late 19C] (US) an opium den (cf. HOP JOINT). [the *three taps* on the door that signalled one's wish to enter the den + JOINT n.³ (3)]

three tears and a bucket *phr.* [1970s] (US Black) a phr. of dismissal, disinterest (cf. BIG DEAL!). [the insignificant effect of *three tears* in *a bucket*]

three-time loser *n.* [1910s+] (US Und.) a prisoner who has been convicted of two crimes worthy of a prison sentence and faces a life sentence or execution if convicted a third time, thus general fig. use.

three times as queer as a three dollar bill *phr.* [1960s+] homosexual, in the eyes of the speaker, exceptionally or ostentatiously so (cf. BENT AS A NINE-BOB NOTE). [QUEER adj. + THREE-DOLLAR BILL]

three-times-seven *adj.* [late 19C–1950s] (US Black) of age, 21, i.e. legally adult.

three trees *n.* [late 16C–mid-17C] the gallows (cf. CLIMB THREE TREES WITH A LADDER; DEADLY NEVERGREEN; THREE-CORNERED TREE). [the early gallows was made of three vertical posts joined by a long horizontal bar]

three vowels *n.* [early 19C] an IOU.

three-way deal *n.* [1960s+] sex involving three partners at once; thus *four-way deal* etc (cf. THREESOME).

three-way girl *n.* [1960s+] a prostitute who will offer her vagina, anus and mouth to clients.

three-way woman *n.* [1990s] (US) a woman who permits simultaneous or sequential penetration by vagina, anus and mouth.

three weeks *n.* [1900s–10s] an intense but brief sexual relationship. [the title of the then 'sexy' novel by Elinor Glyn, *Three Weeks* (1907)]

three-wheel motion *n.* [1990s] (US Black teen) riding one's car on three wheels.

three-wheel skid *see* FOUR-WHEEL SKID.

three-year-old *n.* [early–mid-19C] (Anglo-Irish) a stone weighing approx. 1.36kg (3lb), used as a weapon. [the three-pound weight]

threp/threps/thrip/thrips/thrups *n.* [late 17C–20C] threepence. [colloq. pron.]

thresh/thresh-up *n.* [1930s+] (Aus.) a fight. [? SE *thrash/ thresh*]

thrifty *n.* [1930s–50s] a threepenny bit. [the 12-sided coin, minted only 1937–52, carried a picture of the plant *thrift* on its reverse + play on SE]

thrill *n.* **1** [late 19C] a sensational story, a 'thriller'. **2** [1910s+] an orgasm. **3** [1950s+] (Irish) a promiscuous woman. [ext. uses of SE]

thrill and chill *n.* [1970s+] (US Black) a sexual experience so wonderful it 'sends chills up one's spine'. [THRILL n. (2) + SE *chill*]

thrilled skinny *adj.* [20C] (Irish) very excited, very enthusiastic.

thriller *n.* [late 19C+] a sensational play, film or story (cf. SHILLING SHOCKER).

thriller-diller *see* KILLER-DILLER adj.

thrip/thrips *see* THREP.

throat *n.*¹ **1** [late 19C+] a sore throat, e.g. *I've got a terrible throat today* (cf. HEAD n.⁴). **2** [20C] (Irish) a thirst, usu. in phr. *have a throat on*, to want a drink.

throat *n.*² [20C] the frenum, the small ligament that links the head of the penis to the shaft. [SE *throat*, linking the head to the body]

throat *n.*³ [1940s+] (Aus.) the vulnerable point; thus *have it/ one by the throat*, to have a person or situation completely under one's control.

throat *n.*⁴ [1970s+] (US campus) someone who works harder than average, and enjoys it. [SE *cut-throat*]

throat latch *n.* [late 19C] (US) the Adam's apple.

throg *v.* [1980s+] (US campus) to drink. [? THROW DOWN v. ⁴ (1) + GROG n.]

throne *n.* [1920s+] a lavatory (cf. ALTAR).

throp *see* THRAP.

throttle *n.* [14C+] the throat. [northern UK dial.]

throttle-jockey *n.* [1940s] (US) a pilot. [SE *throttle* + JOCKEY n.²]

through *adj.* [1990s] (US Black/teen) drunk or intoxicated by drugs to the point of virtual collapse. [SE *through*, exhausted]

through and through *n.* [1970s+] (US Black) a wholly admirable (Black) person.

through it *see* THROUGH THE PIECE.

through oneself *adj.* [20C] (Ulster) confused.

through-shot *adj.* [late 19C–1920s] financially excessive, spendthrift. [one has 'shot through' one's funds]

through the piece/it *phr.* [early–mid-19C] (Und.) acquitted. [one has 'got through']

throw *n.*¹ [late 19C+] a go, each, usu. in comb. with a sum of money, e.g. *10 pence a throw.*

throw *n.*² [20C] an act of vomiting (cf. CHUCK n.⁴). [THROW v.³]

throw *v.*¹ [mid-19C+] (orig. US) to disconcert, to surprise, to worry.

throw *v.*² [mid-19C+] to lose deliberately, esp. in sports. [SE *throw away*]

throw *v.*³ **1** [20C] to vomit (cf. CHUCK v.²). **2** [1920s+] (US) to host a party or social event. **3** [1950s+] (US) to get rid of, to overcome. **4** [1970s] to have sexual intercourse.

throw *v.*⁴ [1980s+] (US) to sell, e.g. *throw joints*, to sell marijuana cigarettes (cf. SLANG v.³).

throw a boff/bop into *see* THROW A FUCK INTO.

throw a brick, to *phr.* **1** [1950s–60s] (US Black) to act violently, to kill someone, to commit a crime. **2** [1960s–70s] (US) to commit a minor crime. [the *throwing of a brick* through a shop window]

throw a buttonhole on, to *phr.* [1960s+] (US Black) to have anal intercourse. [pun on BUTT n.¹ (1) + SE *hole*]

throw a curve, to *phr.* [20C] (US) to act unpredictably. [baseball imagery]

throw a duck fit, to *phr.* [19C+] (US) to become hysterical, to lose one's temper, to become extremely excited. [one's resemblance to a furious duck]

throw a fit/forty fits, to *phr.* [20C] to lose all emotional control.

throw a fuck/boff/bop/screw into, to *phr.* [20C] (US) to have sexual intercourse with. [FUCK n.¹/BOFF n.¹/BOP n.¹/SCREW n.¹]

throw a leg over, to *phr.* [early 18C+] to have sexual intercourse (cf. LIFT A LEG ON).

throw a levant, to *phr.* [mid-19C–1900s] to leave, to run off. [SE *levant*, to 'steal away', esp. of a gambler, ult. Sp. *levantar la casa*, to break up housekeeping, *levantar el campo*, to break up the camp]

throw a lick, to *phr.*¹ [1940s] (W.I.) to strike, to beat. [SE *lick*, a blow]

throw a lick, to *phr.*² [1950s] (W.I.) to give someone a drink of liquor, esp. a 'shot' from a bottle. [abbr.]

throw a map, to *phr.* [1940s] (Aus.) to vomit (cf. MAP OF IRELAND). [the supposed similarity of a pool of vomit to a map of Australia]

throw a mickey, to *phr.* [1950s+] (Aus.) to lose one's temper, to have a tantrum. [var. on CHUCK A MICKEY]

throw/hurl a monkey wrench into the machinery, to *phr.* [1920s+] (orig. US) to obstruct something deliberately, to go out of one's way to wreck a plan or project (cf. THROW A SPANNER INTO THE WORKS); thus *monkey-wrenching*, this form of industrial sabotage, esp. performed by ecologists; *monkey-wrencher*, one who does this.

throw a moody, to *phr.* [1930s+] to become sulky, truculent, ill-tempered. [SE *moody*]

throw a punch, to *phr.* [20C] to defend oneself, verbally as well as physically. [boxing imagery]

throw a screw into *see* THROW A FUCK INTO.

throw a seven, to *phr.*[1] [late 19C+] **1** to die (cf. CASH IN ONE'S CHECKS). **2** to faint. **3** to vomit. [? craps dice, where 7, other than in one's initial pass, is a losing throw]

throw a seven *phr.*[2] *see* THROW A SIX.

throw a sickie/sicky, to *phr.* [1990s] (school) to miss a day's school on the grounds of illness (cf. TAKE A SICKIE). [SICKIE n.[1]]

throw a six/seven, to *phr.* [1940s+] (Aus.) to become hysterical, to lose one's temper (cf. CHUCK A SIXER). [? craps dice or play on SE *six/sick*]

throw a spanner in/into the works, to *phr.* [1930s+] to destroy or disable something that had hitherto been working perfectly, to ruin someone else's plans or system (cf. THROW A MONKEY WRENCH INTO THE MACHINERY).

throw ass/some ass, to *phr.* [1950s+] (US Black) **1** of a woman, to walk in an exaggeratedly or deliberately sexy manner. **2** to have sexual intercourse. [ARSE n.[1]]

throw a thing in someone's dish, to *phr.* [late 18C] to tease, to reproach. [? the image of tossing something other than money into a beggar's dish]

throw/give attitude/'tude *v.* [1980s+] (US campus) to act in an arrogant, surly, obnoxious manner. [ATTITUDE]

throwaway *n.* [1930s+] **1** any sort of leaflet or one-page document that can be discarded after reading. **2** a witty remark. [(2) abbr. *throwaway line*]

throwaway *adj.* [20C] (US) useless, hopeless, e.g. a *throwaway man*.

throw away belly/a baby/a child, to *phr.* [20C] (W.I.) to procure an abortion, to terminate a pregnancy.

throw a wing-ding, to *phr.* [1950s–60s] (drugs) to pretend to be suffering severe withdrawal pains in order to persuade a doctor to give one some heroin. [SE *throw* + WING-DING]

throw a wobbly/wobbler *see* CHUCK A WOBBLY *phr.*[1].

throw back *v.*[1] [late 19C–1910s] to revert to ancestral type. [SE *throwback*, a reversion (to type)]

throw back *v.*[2] [20C] (US) to eat or drink (cf. KNOCK BACK v.[2]).

throw bones, to *phr.* [1920s+] (US Black) to play dice (cf. ROLL THE BONES). [SE *throw* + BONES n.[1] (1)]

throw bouquets at, to *phr.* [20C] (US) to praise.

throw craps, to *phr.* [20C] (US) to fail (cf. CRAP OUT). [craps jargon *craps*, a losing throw]

throw-down *n.* [1900s] a defeat. [wrestling jargon *throw-down*, a fall]

throw down *v.*[1] [late 19C] to overcome, to prove too much for. [wrestling imagery]

throw down *v.*[2] [20C] (US) to discard, to abandon.

throw down *v.*[3] [1980s+] **1** (US) to challenge. **2** (US Black) to enjoy oneself vigorously. **3** (US Black) to start work on a major project. **4** (US Black) to get into a fight with. **5** (US teen) to challenge a rival break dancer. **6** (US campus) to engage in sex. [SE *throw down the gauntlet*]

throw down *v.*[4] [1980s+] (US campus) to eat or drink voraciously (cf. THROW BACK v.[2]).

throw down on *v.* **1** [1950s+] (US Und.) to hold a gun on. **2** [1960s+] to blame. [ext. THROW DOWN v.[3] (1)]

throw down/up one's cards, to *phr.* [late 17C+] to give up a project, a way of life.

throwed *adj.* [1990s] (US campus) defeated, humiliated. [SE *thrown*]

throw forty fits *see* THROW A FIT.

throw hands *v.* [1970s+] (orig. US Black) to punch, to hit.

throw-in *n.* [late 19C+] (Aus.) an unexpected piece of good luck. [SE *throw in*, to add (something) on for free, esp. in a transaction]

throw in one's alley, to *phr.* [1900s] (Aus.) to die, also as *chuck/pass/roll/sky/sling* (cf. TOSS IN ONE'S AGATE). [SE *throw in*, to toss + *alley*, a marble]

throw in one's cards, to *phr.* [20C] (US) to die (cf. CASH IN ONE'S CHECKS).

throw in one's hand, to *phr.* [1920s+] to give in, to surrender. [card use]

throw/toss in the air, to *phr.* [late 19C] (US) to jilt, to break off a relationship with.

throw/in/up/toss in the towel/sponge, to *phr.* [mid-19C+] **1** to give in, to capitulate. **2** to die (cf. END OF THE BALL-GAME). [boxing use, whereby a towel or sponge thrown into the ring indicates the retirement of a fighter who is losing badly]

throw iron *see* PUMP IRON.

throw it at someone/someone's face *see* THROW IT UP AGAINST SOMEONE.

throw it in *v.* [1910s+] (Aus.) to stop doing something (cf. CHUCK IT IN). [abbr. THROW IN THE TOWEL]

throw it up against/at/to someone/at someone's face, to *phr.* [early 19C+] (US) to criticize someone, to hold someone up as an object of reproach.

throw lead *v.* [20C] (US) to shoot a gun.

throw leather *v.* [1930s–50s] to box.

throw me in the dirt *n.* [mid-19C] a shirt (cf. DICKY DIRT). [rhy. sl.]

throw money around like a man with no hands, to *phr.* [1940s] (Aus.) to be very mean.

throw money at *v.* [1970s+] (US) to spend an extravagant amount of money on something, esp. in the hope of remedying a problem.

throw mud at the clock, to *phr.* [late 19C] **1** to be in utter despair. **2** to kill oneself. [the image is of stopping the clock and giving up on the passing of time]

thrown for a loss, to be *phr.* [20C] to die (cf. THROW IN ONE'S CHECKS).

throw-off *n.* [1910s–20s] a hostile or critical remark or allusion. [THROW OFF v.[1]]

throw off *v.*[1] **1** [early 19C+] (Und.) to boast of one's successful crimes. **2** [early 19C+] (orig. Und.) to deride, to ridicule (cf. SLING OFF v.[1]).

throw off/off upon *v.*[2] [1940s+] (W.I.) to give away things one no longer needs to a poorer person.

throw off upon *see* THROW OFF v.[2].

throw on/catch a face, to *phr.* [late 19C+] (US) to get drunk or intoxicated by drugs. [the face one 'throws on' is one's bleariness]

throw one's cookies, to *phr.* [1960s+] (US) to vomit.

throw one's feet, to *phr.* [late 19C–1950s] (US) to beg, to 'hustle' for money. [SE *throw the feet*, of a horse, to move its feet well, esp. when crossing rough ground]

throw one's voice, to *phr.* [1960s+] (Aus.) to vomit (cf. HURL; YELL n.[2]).

throw one's weight about, to *phr.* [1910s+] to act in an arrogant, aggressive manner.

throw out *v.* [1990s] to masturbate.

throw over the bridge, to *phr.* [19C] (Und.) **1** to double-cross, to betray (a confidence). **2** in gambling to deceive one's backer by deliberately losing the game (cf. BRIDGE v.[1]). [the image is of two confederates getting together to throw a third party from a (metaphorical) bridge]

throw over the perch, to *phr.* [late 16C] **1** to upset, to humiliate. **2** to overcome, to conquer. **3** to kill (cf. KNOCK OFF ONE'S PERCH; TURN OVER THE PERCH).

throw sets on *see* RUN SETS ON.

throw shade v. [1990s] (US campus) to humiliate (someone) exceedingly. [? to 'put in the shade']

throw sixes v. [20C] to die. [craps dice, a throw of 12 (double 6) is a losing throw]

throw sixers v. [20C] (Aus.) to vomit. [? craps dice or play on SE *sick*]

throw snot about v. [late 17C–1910s] to cry. [SNOT n. (1); i.e. one's running nose]

throw some ass *see* THROW ASS.

throw some dirt on, to phr. [1970s+] (US Black) to malign, to slander.

throw someone for v. [1940s–50s] (Aus.) **1** to cheat, to swindle. **2** to persuade someone to give up something.

throw someone for a loop, to phr. [1960s+] to disturb one, to worry one considerably, to put one off one's stride (cf. KNOCK FOR A LOOP).

throw someone into fits, to phr. [mid-19C+] **1** to worry one, to disturb one. **2** to reduce a person to anger or hysteria.

throw someone out on their ass/ear, to phr. [20C] (US) to eject someone forcibly.

throw something at v. [1970s+] (US) to attempt to solve or dismiss a problem with an excess of some resource.

throw the baby out with the bathwater, to phr. [1940s+] to be so keen on eliminating the large-scale errors that one simultaneously tosses out the less visible but highly valuable entities hidden among them.

throw the book at, to phr. [1930s+] (orig. US) to discipline heavily, to reprimand severely (cf. DO THE BOOK). [the 'book of rules' that one has contravened, orig. in legal context, to *throw the book at*, to give someone a maximum sentence]

throw the book away, to phr. [1940s+] (orig. US) to abandon the usual rules and regulations. [for ety. *see* THROW THE BOOK AT]

throw the boots to *see* GIVE THE BOOTS TO.

throw the D, to phr. [1980s+] (US Black) of a man, to have sexual intercourse (cf. THROW THE P). [abbr. DICK n.[5] (1)]

throw the dagger, to phr. [1980s+] (US campus) to have sexual intercourse. [SE *throw* + DAGGER n.[1]]

throw the feet, to phr. [20C] (orig. US) to beg. [i.e. the walking the streets, knocking on doors, in order to beg]

throw the gift, to phr. [1990s] (US Black) to banter, to chatter, to gossip (cf. SHOOT THE GIFT; SHOOT THE SHIT). [abbr. GIFT OF THE GAB]

throw the hammer, to phr. [late 19C] to obtain money under false pretences. [HAMMER n.[3] (1)]

throw the harpoon in/into, to phr. [1960s] (US) to have sexual intercourse (with).

throw/fling the hatchet, to phr. [mid-19C] to tell lies (cf. SHOOT WITH THE LONG BOW). [SLING THE HATCHET]

throw the hooks, to phr. [late 19C–1930s] (US Und.) to lure a victim. [fishing imagery]

throw the hooks into, to phr. (US) **1** [late 19C–1940s] to criticize viciously. **2** [1930s+] to cheat or swindle. [fishing imagery]

throw the house out of the windows, to phr. [mid-16C–mid-19C] to make a great deal of noise or disturbance in one's house.

throw the P, to phr. [1980s+] (US Black) of a woman, to have sexual intercourse (cf. THROW THE D). [abbr. PUSSY n.[1]]

throw 'tude *see* THROW ATTITUDE.

throw up v.[1] [late 19C+] to vomit. [THROW UP ONE'S ACCOUNTS]

throw up v.[2] [1920s+] to give up all hope. [? THROW IN THE TOWEL]

throw up v.[3] [1960s+] to produce, to provide.

throw up v.[4] [1990s] to place one's name on a piece of graffiti (cf. TAG v.).

throw up Jonah *see* HEAVE UP JONAH.

throw up one's accounts, to phr. [mid–late 18C] to vomit. [var. on CAST UP ONE'S ACCOUNTS]

throw up one's boots, to phr. [20C] (US) to vomit intensely. [a melodramatic ext. of THROW UP v.[1]]

throw up one's cards *see* THROW DOWN ONE'S CARDS.

throw up one's heels/toes, to phr. [20C] (US) to vomit copiously (cf. THROW UP ONE'S BOOTS; VOMIT UP ONE'S TOENAILS).

throw up the towel/sponge *see* THROW IN THE TOWEL.

throw words *see* DROP WORDS.

thrum v. [late 17C–early 19C] **1** to thrash (cf. THRUMSTER). **2** to have sexual intercourse (cf. BANG v.[1]). [SE *thrum*, to play on a stringed instrument]

thrumbuskins n. [mid-18C–19C] threepence (cf. THRUMS).

thrum-cap n. [19C] any form of roughly made or improvised headgear. [SE *thrum*, a short piece of waste thread or yarn]

thrums/thrummer/thrum-mop/thrumms/thrummup n. [late 17C–1960s] threepence.

thrumster n. [late 17C–early 19C] the penis. [THRUM]

thrups n.[1] *see* THREP.

thrups n.[2] [late 19C+] the breasts. [rhy. sl. *thrups* = THREEPENNY BITS n. (2)]

thrush n. [1920s–50s] (US) a woman singer (cf. CANARY n.[8]).

thrust n. [1970s–80s] (drugs) isobutyl nitrite. [the effects; it makes the heart beat faster]

thrusters n. [1960s] (drugs) amphetamine (cf. A n.[2]). [the effects; it makes the user 'go faster']

thud n. [1930s+] (Aus.) a bad fall (usu. in fig. contexts).

thud v. [1910s+] (Aus.) to hit someone. [SE *thud*, onomat. for an object hitting something hard]

thud and blunder n. [20C] any form of melodrama, usu. on film (cf. SKIET UND DONDER). [a play on SE *blood and thunder*, melodrama]

thugging n. [1990s] (US Black) relaxing, acting a cool manner (cf. CHILLING). [the image of the successful *thug* as a pos. role model]

thumb n.[1] [1960s+] (drugs) marijuana, a marijuana cigarette. [one sucks it]

thumb n.[2] [1970s] (US Black) a fight. [ety. unknown; ? thrusting a thumb into the opponent's eye]

thumb v.[1] [mid-18C–mid-19C] to drain a glass. [for ety. *see* SUPERNACULUM]

thumb v.[2] **1** [late 18C–late 19C] of a man, to have sexual intercourse; thus *well-thumbed girl*, a worn-out prostitute. **2** [20C] (Irish) of a woman, to masturbate. [SE *thumb*, to riffle through, to press or soil with the thumb]

thumb down v. [20C] (US) to reject, to veto. [abbr. SE *put one's thumb down*, the erroneous belief that in the Roman amphitheatre the emperor pointed his thumb down to signal his approval of a gladiatorial killing]

thumber n.[1] [19C] a sandwich. [one can hold it in the hand]

thumber n.[2] [1980s+] (US campus) a beggar, a borrower, someone constantly scrounging from their friends. [SE *thumb*, to put up one's thumb in the hope of getting a free ride]

thumb in bum and mind in neutral phr. [1950s+] (orig. Aus.) a phr. used of one who seems to have fallen into a vacant reverie. [BUM n.[2]]

thumb in one's eye n. [20C] (US) an irritation, an annoyance.

thumb of love n. [20C] the penis.

thumbs up/down n. [20C] a neg. or pos. response, usu. in phr. *give a thumbs up/down*, to approve, to disapprove. [for ety. *see* THUMB DOWN]

thump n. [1980s+] **1** (US Black) a street-fight, esp. with fists or knives. **2** (US teen) sexual intercourse.

thump v. **1** [late 16C+] to defeat heavily, esp. in battle or, more recently, in sport. **2** [1980s+] (US teen) of a man, to have sexual intercourse.

thump! *excl.* [1910s+] used to accentuate one's rejection of a statement or idea, synon. in this context with FUCK, e.g. *do I thump! is she thump!* etc. [euph.]

thumped over the head with Samson's jawbone *phr.* [19C] drunk. [the biblical Samson was supposedly drunk when he was stripped of his hair-engendered powers]

thumper *n.*[1] [early–mid-16C] a rank of villain. [the details are unknown, presumably the 16C equivalent of a mugger: 'Tynckers ... tryfullers, turners, and trumpers, Tempters, traytoures, trauaylers, and thumpers' (Anon., *A New Interlude called Thersites*, *c*.1537)]

thumper *n.*[2] [early 17C] a coin. [one thumps it on the counter or table]

thumper *n.*[3] **1** [mid-17C–mid-19C] anything notably large of its type (cf. BUMPER n.[1]). **2** [late 17C–mid-19C] a major lie. **3** [late 19C] (US) a dedicated liar.

thump hell out of *see* BEAT HELL OUT OF.

thumping *adj.* [late 16C+] enormous, very large; often as *thumping great* (cf. LICKING adj.).

thumpingly *adv.* [late 16C+] very, exceedingly. [THUMPING]

thump one's pumper, to *phr.* [20C] to masturbate.

thump seven kinds of shit out of, to *phr.* [1950s+] (orig. milit.) to beat up severely (cf. KICK THE SHIT OUT OF). [SHIT n.[1] (1)]

thump the hell out of *see* BEAT HELL OUT OF.

thump-up *n.* [1960s] a fight, usu. in the street or some public place (cf. PUNCH-UP). [SE *thump*]

thunder *v.* [1980s+] (US campus) to succeed, to do well. [i.e. to 'make a noise']

thunder! *excl.* [early 18C+] a euph. for FUCK or HELL in a variety of phrs., e.g. *for thunder's sake, like thunder, what in thunder, why in thunder, who the thunder* (cf. THUMP!).

thunder and lightning *n.* **1** [early 19C] gin and bitters. **2** [late 19C+] treacle and clotted cream. **3** [1900s] brandy sauce when ignited.

thunder and lightning! *excl.* [late 19C+] a general excl. of fury, surprise, indignation etc. [var. on synon. Ger. *Donner und Blitzen!*]

thunder and ouns! *excl.* [1910s] (Irish) a mild excl. [var. on Ger. *Donner und Blitzen!* thunder and lightning! + *ouns*, (Christ's) wounds]

thunder and rain *n.* [20C] (Aus.) a train. [rhy. sl.]

thunder and turf! *excl.* [mid-19C] a general excl. of fury, surprise, indignation etc.

thunderation! *excl.* [19C+] (orig. US) a mild expletive. [SE *thunder* + sfx. *-ation*]

thunderbags *n.* [20C] (Aus.) men's underpants (cf. THUNDERBOX n.[1]). [SE *thunder* + BAGS n.[1]; i.e. the noise of breaking wind]

thunderbox *n.*[1] **1** [20C] (US) the buttocks. **2** [1930s+] a lavatory. **3** [1930s+] a portable commode. [SE *thunder* + *box*; i.e. the noise of defecation]

thunderbox *n.*[2] [1980s+] (US) a portable tape deck or radio (cf. GHETTOBLASTER). [SE *thunder* + BOX n.[4]]

thunder chicken/chick *n.* [1970s+] (US Black) an unattractive or unpleasant woman.

thunderdom *n.* [1990s] (US Black) the act of suffering a beating by a prison guard.

Thunderer, the *n.* [early 19C+] the *Times* newspaper. [in its pre-Murdoch era the *Times*, then a newspaper of record, was seen as the effective voice of the British government and/or Establishment. The nickname is now used only ironically]

thundering *adj.* [late 16C+] a general intensifier, excessive, immense, also in phrs. e.g. *thundering cats!*

thundering *adv.* [late 16C+] a general intensifier, excessively, immensely, greatly.

thunderingly *adv.* [late 19C] excessively.

thundermug *n.* [1940s+] a chamberpot (cf. MEMBER MUG; THUNDERBOX). [SE *thunder* + MUG n.[2]; i.e. the noise of defecation/urination]

thunder-thighs *n.* [1980s+] an overweight person.

thunk *v.* [1960s] (US) I/you/he/she/we/they thought. [joc. past tense of SE *think*]

thusly *adv.* [mid-late 19C] (US) thus, to sum things up.

thuzzy-muzzy *n.* [late 19C–1910s] enthusiasm. [mispron. of SE]

tib *n.*[1] *see* TIB OF THE BUTTERY.

tib *n.*[2] [mid-19C] a bit, a piece. [backsl.]

tibby *n.*[1] [late 18C–mid-19C] a cat. [SE *tib*, a female cat]

tibby *n.*[2] [early 19C–1900s] the head. [Fr. *tête*, the head]

tibby *n.*[3] [1930s+] (Aus.) a tabloid newspaper. [? SE *tabloid*]

tibby drop *n.* [20C] hop. [rhy. sl.]

tib of the buttery/tib *n.* [16C–early 18C] a goose (cf. ROGER). [SE *tib*, a young woman or a cat, presumably the femininity is the point rather than the specific animal]

tib's eve *see* ST TIBB'S.

tic *n.* [20C] (drugs) phencyclidine (cf. ACE n.[3]; T n.[2]; TAC). [misreading of *THC*, i.e. tetrahydrocannabinol]

tical *n.* [1990s] (orig. US Black) marijuana. [? abbr. SE *practical*]

tich *n.* [1980s+] (US drugs) *tetra*hydro*c*annabinol (THC) in pill form.

tick *n.*[1] **1** [mid-17C+] an unpleasant, insignificant person. **2** [1970s+] (US campus) an overweight person. **3** [1970s+] (US campus) a greedy or selfish person. [SE *tick*, a parasitical mite]

tick *n.*[2] **1** [mid-17C+] credit; thus [1990s] *tick list*, a large number of debts; [1990s] *ticking*, obtaining goods on credit. **2** [mid-19C] a dunning letter, a bill. [abbr. SE *ticket*, the writing down of one's debt]

tick *n.*[3] **1** [late 18C–early 19C] a watch (cf. TICKER n.[2]). **2** [late 19C+] a second; thus [20C] *on the tick, to the tick*, precisely on time (cf. COUPLE OF TICKS; DEUCE OF TICKS; HALF A TICK; IN TWO TICKS; WAIT A TICK). **3** [20C] (US) a small degree or amount, usu. an increase. [the sound and thus its minimal duration]

tick *v.*[1] **1** [early 18C] to obtain on credit. **2** [mid-19C–1920s] to grant someone credit. [TICK n.[2]]

tick *v.*[2] [1980s+] (US campus) **1** to talk in class without having prepared the assignment. **2** to talk nonsense. [image of a clock which *ticks* mindlessly on]

tick being no-go *phr.* [mid-17C+] credit being unavailable. [TICK n.[2] + SE *no-go*]

ticked/ticked off *adj.* [1950s+] (orig. US) irritated, annoyed. [? euph. for PISSED OFF]

ticker *n.*[1] [mid-17C] one who obtains goods on credit but never pays for them. [TICK v.[1]]

ticker *n.*[2] **1** [19C] a watch (cf. TICK n.[3]). **2** [late 19C+] the human heart. **3** [1930s+] (Aus./US) courage. [the regular *ticking* or beating]

ticker *n.*[3] [late 19C] (Anglo-Ind.) one who is working on a job under contract. [Hind. *thika*, hire, fare, fixed price]

ticker *n.*[4] [1970s+] an accountant. [SE *tick off*, they tick off sums of money]

ticket *n.*[1] **1** [early 19C+] the right, proper or fashionable thing to do. **2** [mid-19C] the task in hand, the relevant procedure. [? SE *winning ticket* or Fr. *etiquette* (Hotten, 1867) or *ticket*, a bill or invoice]

ticket *n.*[2] **1** [20C] (US prison) a disciplinary record (cf. WRITE-UP). **2** [1960s–70s] a pass or passport, whether valid or counterfeit.

ticket *n.*[3] [1960s] (Aus. drugs) a single dose of LSD, dripped onto a small piece of absorbent paper. [resemblance to a SE *ticket* or abbr. THAT'S THE TICKET, i.e. its positive effects]

ticket *n.*[4] [1960s+] a person (used esp. by the mods of early 1960s). [abbr. THAT'S THE TICKET]

ticket *v.* [late 19C–1910s] to sentence to prison. [SE *ticket*, a written pass]

ticket-of-leaver *n.* [mid–late 19C] a general term of abuse. [SE *ticket-of-leave man*, a prisoner who has been released 'on licence']

ticket o' leave *n.* [late 19C] a holiday. [SE *ticket of leave*, a parole licence]

tickets *n.* [1960s+] (S.Afr.) the end, the finish. [? the tearing up of betting slips or tickets after one's choice has failed to win]

ticket-scalper *n.* [late 19C+] (orig. US) a ticket tout, who sells tickets to popular events at greatly inflated prices. [for ety. *see* SCALP *v.*[1]]

ticket-skinner *n.* [late 19C] (US) a ticket tout (cf. SCALPER). [play on SE *mule-skinner*, a mule-driver]

ticket tie *v.* [1980s] (drugs) to inject a drug. [ety. unknown]

ticketty-/tickety-/tiggerty-boo *adj.* [1920s+] (orig. services) fine, wonderful, all in order. [? THAT'S THE TICKET or Hind. *tikai babu*, it's all right, sir]

tickey/tickie/ticky *n.* [mid-19C+] (S.Afr.) **1** a threepenny piece (2½ cents post-decimalization). **2** anything or anyone very small; thus phrs. *half a brick/two bricks and a tickey high*, very small. [? dial. *ticky*, small, or Du. *stukje*, a little bit, or Hind. *taka*, a stamped silver coin]

tickey-box *n.* [1970s+] (S.Afr.) a public telephone. [TICKEY (1), the then charge for a call]

tickey-line *n.* [1960s+] (S.Afr.) a cheap prostitute (cf. PENNY-LINE); thus fig. *tickey-line*, cheap, second-rate. [TICKEY]

tickey-snatching *adj.* [mid-19C+] (S.Afr.) **1** making quick profits. **2** close-fisted, mean. [TICKEY + SE *snatch*]

tickey wire *see* LONG TICKEY.

tickie *see* TICKEY.

tickieman/tickman *n.* [1960s+] (Ulster) a doorstep salesman. [one gets the goods 'on tick']

tickle *n.* [1920s+] (Und.) **1** a robbery, esp. a successful and lucrative one (cf. GET A TICKLE). **2** a piece of information. [? it *tickles one's fancy* or the image of SE *tickling* trout]

tickle *v.* **1** [late 19C–1900s] to puzzle, to confuse. **2** [1920s+] to rob, to steal from. **3** [1920s+] (Aus.) to ask someone for a loan.

tickled *adj.* [1920s+] amused, pleased.

tickled to death *phr.* [1920s+] delighted, very happy, amused. [ext. of TICKLED]

tickle-faggot *n.* [19C] the penis. [SE *tickle* + *faggot*, a woman]

tickle-gizzard *n.* [19C] the penis.

tickle one's crack, to *phr.* [19C] of a woman, to masturbate. [CRACK *n.*[1] (1)]

tickle one's dick, to *phr.* [20C] to masturbate. [DICK *n.*[5] (1)]

tickle one's fancy, to *phr.* [20C] to masturbate. [play on SE]

tickle one's innards, to *phr.* [late 19C+] (US) to take a drink.

tickle one's pickle, to *phr.* [20C] to masturbate.

tickle pink *v.* [1920s+] to amuse enormously, to delight; esp. in phr. *tickled pink*, enormously amused or delighted.

tickle-pitcher *n.* **1** [late 17C–18C] a drunkard. **2** [mid-18C] a promiscuous person of either sex. [SE *pitcher*/PITCHER *n.*[2]]

tickler *n.*[1] [19C] a puzzle, something or someone that is hard to deal with or understand. [it *tickles* one's brain]

tickler *n.*[2] [early–mid-19C] (US) a small knife or pistol. [it 'tickles the ribs']

tickler *n.*[3] [late 19C–1920s] (US) a small measure of spirits (approx. 300ml/½ pint). [it *tickles* the palate]

tickler *n.*[4] **1** [late 19C] a short poker used to preserve the smarter, 'best' one. **2** [late 19C] a whip. **3** [late 19C+] the penis. **4** [1970s+] a junior official or assistant who is used by their superior(s) to pass on policies etc to still lower ranks, so that

the superiors don't have to make face-to-face contact themselves.

tickler *n.*[5] *see* FRENCH TICKLER.

tickler *n.*[6] [1960s+] (US) a pianist. [for ety. *see* TICKLE THE IVORIES]

ticklers *n.* [20C] the fingers.

tickle someone's ears, to *phr.* [1900s–20s] to flatter.

tickle someone's ribs *see* RIB TICKLE.

tickle someone's toby, to *phr.* [late 17C–mid-19C] to thrash, to beat. [TOBY *n.*[1]]

tickle someone's turnip, to *phr.* [late 16C–mid-17C] to thrash someone on the buttocks.

tickle-tail *n.* **1** [late 15C–late 18C] a prostitute, a promiscuous woman (cf. BANG-TAIL *n.*[1]). **2** [late 18C–early 19C] a cane. **3** [late 18C–early 19C] a schoolmaster. [SE *tickle* + TAIL *n.*[1] (2), (3)]

tickle-tail function *n.* [early 18C] a prostitute. [ext. of TICKLE-TAIL *n.* (1)]

tickle-text *n.* [late 18C–1900s] a parson.

tickle the ivories, to *phr.* [1940s+] to play the piano; thus *ivory-tickler*, a pianist. [the ivory keys]

tickle the ivory, to *phr.* [1990s] to masturbate. [play on TICKLE THE IVORIES]

tickle the minikin, to *phr.* [17C] to play the lute or fiddle. [usu. used with sexual innuendo; thus John Marston (?), *The Comedie of Pasquil & Katherine* (1601) 'When I was a yong man and could tickle the Minikin, I had the best stroke, the sweetest touch, but now I am falne from the Fidle, and betooke me to thee (the Pipe)']

tickle the peter, to *phr.* [1940s+] (mainly Aus./N.Z.) to rob a safe, till or cashbox. [SE *tickle* + PETER *n.*[3] (2)]

tickle the piss/shit out of, to *phr.* [1950s+] (US) to please or amuse someone. [fig. use of PISS *n.*/SHIT *n.*[1]]

tickle-thomas *n.* [19C] the vagina. [SE *tickle* + (JOHN) THOMAS]

tickle-toby *n.* **1** [late 17C–19C] the penis. **2** [late 17C–19C] a promiscuous woman. **3** [mid-19C] a rod or birch. [SE *tickle* + TOBY *n.*[1]]

tickle your fancy *n.* [20C] a homosexual. [rhy. sl. *tickle your fancy* = NANCY *n.*[2]]

tickman *see* TICKIEMAN.

tick off *v.*[1] **1** [late 19C+] to identify, to mark. **2** [1910s+] (orig. milit.) to scold, to reprimand; thus *ticking-off*, a scolding (cf. TELLING OFF).

tick off *v.*[2] [1950s+] (US) to irritate, to annoy. [? euph. PISS OFF]

tickrum *n.* [late 17C–early 19C] (Und.) a licence. [SE *ticket*]

tick someone off *v.* [1970s] (US campus) for a comment to prompt thoughts in the person at whom it is directed. [TICK OFF *v.*[1] (1)]

ticks walking *phr.* [1900s–30s] (US Black) clients are walking the streets in search of prostitutes. [TICK *n.*[1] (1) + SE *walking*]

tick-tack *n.*[1] [mid-16C+] sexual intercourse. [the rhythmical movements]

tick-tack *n.*[2] [late 19C+] a system of telegraphy used on racecourses to keep the bookmakers abreast of the changing odds; thus *tick-tack man*, one who performs such telegraphy (by using a 'vocabulary' of hand and arm movements and signals).

tick-tock *n.*[1] [1940s] (US Black) the heartbeat. [its regular beating]

tick-tock *n.*[2] [1950s] (Aus.) a clock or watch. [rhy. sl.]

ticky *see* TICKEY.

ticky-tacky *adj.* [1960s+] vulgar and banal, unsophisticated, corny. [ext. of TACKY *adj.*[1]]

tic-tac *n.*[1] [20C] a fact. [rhy. sl.]

tic-tac *n.*[2] [1970s] (drugs) phencyclidine (cf. ACE *n.*[3]). [misreading of SE *THC* (tetrahydrocannabinol)]

tid *n.* [1920s+] (Aus.) a drunkard. [abbr. TIDDLY *adj.*]

tidderly-push *see* TIDDLY-PUSH.

tiddivate *see* TITIVATE.

tiddle *n.* [20C] urine. [TIDDLE v.²]

tiddle *v.*¹ **1** [late 16C–late 19C] to fondle or indulge to excess, to tend carefully, to cherish. **2** [mid-19C–1920s] to fidget, to 'mess around'. **3** [mid-19C+] to move forward in slow stages. [? SE *tid*, to move forward in slow stages, Norfolk dial. *tid*, of a boat, to drift with the tide]

tiddle *v.*² [20C] to urinate. [var. on PIDDLE v. (1)]

tiddle a girl, to *phr.* [mid-19C+] to seduce a woman very slowly. [TIDDLE v.¹]

tiddle-a-wink *n.* [mid-19C] an unlicensed beerhouse. [var. on TIDDLEY-WINK n.¹]

tiddled *adj.* [1920s+] slightly drunk, tipsy. [TIDDLEY adj.]

tiddler *n.* **1** [19C+] anything small, esp. a small fish. **2** [19C+] a small boy's penis (cf. DIDDLER n.²). **3** [1920s–60s] (Aus.) £1 sterling (cf. TIDDLY n.²).

tiddler's bait *adj.* [20C] late. [rhy. sl.]

tiddley/tiddy *adj.* [mid-19C+] slightly drunk, tipsy. [rhy. sl. *tiddleywink* = drink]

tiddleypush/tiddley-hoy *n.* [1930s] (Irish) the genitals. [nonsense word + slight undertones of SE *fiddle* + the *push* of intercourse of the *hoy!* of encouragement]

tiddleywink *n.*¹ **1** [mid-19C] an unlicensed beerhouse (cf. KIDDLEYWINK). **2** [late 19C] a snack, a bite of food. [? TITLEY + (*on the*) *wink*, surreptitiously]

tiddleywink/tiddlywink *n.*² **1** [mid-19C] a drink, usu. a spirit rather than beer or wine. **2** [1970s+] a Chinese person. [rhy. sl.; (2) = CHINK n.³]

tiddleywink/tiddlywink *v.* [late 19C–1900s] to potter about, to fiddle. [? the relative triviality of the game of *tiddlywinks*]

tiddley-winky/tillywink *adj.* [late 19C–1900s] insignificant, trifling. [SE *tiddleywinks*]

tiddly *n.*¹ [20C] a drink. [rhy. sl. *tiddleywink* = drink]

tiddly *n.*² [1920s–60s] (Aus.) a threepenny bit. [the smallness of the coin]

tiddly *adj.* [20C] slightly drunk. [? TIDDLEYWINK n.¹ (1)]

tiddly-/tidderly-push *phr.* **1** [1920s–30s] a nonsense word used to say goodbye (cf. TINKERTY-TONK; TOODLE-PIP). **2** [1920s–60s] a nonsense phr. used when one cannot recall the proper name for a thing or person (cf. THINGUMMY; THINGUMABOB); thus *and tiddly-push*, and so on, and all that.

tiddlywink *n.*¹ [mid-19C–1920s] a slim person. [TIDDLYWINK adj.]

tiddlywink *n.*² *see* TIDDLEYWINK n.².

tiddlywink *adj.* [mid-19C–1920s] slim, thin, puny. [? the dimensions of a SE *tiddlywink*]

tiddlywink *v. see* TIDDLEYWINK v.

tiddlywinker *n.* [late 19C] a cheat, a swindler, a trifler. [TIDDLEYWINK v.]

tiddlywinking *n.* **1** [mid-19C] pottering around, wasting time on trifles. **2** [late 19C] (Aus.) spending money carelessly and to excess. [TIDDLEYWINK v.]

tiddlywinks *n.* [1960s–70s] twins. [? rhy. sl.]

tiddy/tiddy iddy *adj.*¹ [late 18C+] tiny, diminutive. [? SE *tiny*]

tiddy *adj.*² *see* TIDDLEY.

tiddy *adj.*³ [1930s] (society) of clothes, overfussy. [SE *titivated*]

tiddy iddy *see* TIDDY adj.¹.

tiddyvate *see* TITIVATE.

tidemark *see* HIGH-WATER MARK.

tidgen *n.* [1930s] night-time; thus *on tidgen*, on night-work. [backsl.]

tidy *adj.*¹ [mid-19C+] good, satisfactory, e.g. *a tidy few*, a good many.

tidy *adj.*² [20C] competent.

tidy *adv.* [mid-19C+] well, satisfactorily.

tidy! *excl.* [20C] a general excl. of agreement or admiration. [TIDY adj.²]

tidy and neat, to *phr.* [20C] to eat. [rhy. sl.]

tidy penny *n.* [mid–late 19C] a good deal of money, 'a pretty penny'. [TIDY adj.¹]

tie a bag on, to *phr.* [1940s+] (US) to get drunk. [TIE ONE ON + BAG n.⁶]

tie a can on *see* GET A CAN ON.

tie a can to, to *phr.* **1** [late 19C+] (US) to play an unpleasant trick on. **2** [1920s+] to reject or dismiss (a person). **3** [1920s+] to stop (an activity). [a child's tying of a can to an animal's tail]

tie a knot with the tongue that cannot be undone with the teeth, to *phr.* [late 16C–mid-19C] to get married.

tie a/the noose, to *phr.* [early 18C+] to marry.

tied to a woman's apron-strings *phr.* [18C+] dominated by one's wife.

tied up *adj.*¹ **1** [early 19C+] (orig. boxing jargon) finished, completed. **2** [mid-19C–1900s] married (cf. TIE THE KNOT). **3** [late 19C] constipated (cf. BUNGED UP adj.²). **4** [late 19C+] busy.

tied up *adj.*² [1920s] hanged.

tiefiness/tiefness *n.* [1950s+] (W.I.) theft, thieving. [pron. of SE *thief*]

tiefin tief *n.* [1950s] (W.I.) an absolute, uncompromising thief. [W.I. pron.; lit. 'a thieving thief']

tiefness *see* TIEFINESS.

tief-tief *v.* [1950s] (W.I.) to steal continually. [W.I. pron. of SE *thief* + redup.]

tie-head *n.* [20C] (W.I.) a member of the Spiritual Baptist Church. [they *tie* their *heads* in white scarves]

tie into *v.* (US) **1** [20C] to assault, to attack (cf. TIE ON). **2** [1940s+] to start working hard. **3** [1940s+] to start eating voraciously, to 'tuck into'.

tie off *v.* [1950s+] (drugs) to tie up a vein and isolate it before injecting narcotic drugs.

tie on *v.* [1930s+] (US Black) to fight (cf. TIE INTO).

tie one on *v.* [1950s+] **1** [UK/US] to be drunk (cf. BURN ONE ON). **2** (Aus.) to provoke a fight (cf. TIE ON). **3** (Ulster) to get dressed.

tie one's shoes, to *phr.* [20C] (US) to improve or correct one's behaviour (cf. PULL UP ONE'S SOCKS).

tiersman *n.* [1940s] (Aus.) one who lives in the mountains of Tasmania. [abbr. SE *frontiersman*]

tie-teeth *n.* [1910s+] (W.I.) a form of very tough toffee (cf. STAGGER-BACK). [chewing it 'ties up' one's teeth]

tie that bull outside/to another ashcan *phr.* [1920s+] (US) a derisive or dismissive phr. [BULL n.¹²]

tie the knot, to *phr.* [early 18C+] to get married.

tie the noose *see* TIE A NOOSE.

tie the rap on *see* HANG THE RAP ON.

tie to *v.* [late 19C] (US) to trust to, to seek support in (someone).

tie-tongue *adj.* [20C] (W.I.) suffering from any form of speech impediment.

tie-up *n.*¹ [early 19C] **1** a finish, a conclusion. **2** (boxing) a knock-out punch. [TIE UP v.³]

tie-up *n.*² [1950s+] (drugs) the rubber tube, handkerchief, string or other object used for tying off a vein before injecting narcotics. [TIE UP v.⁴]

tie up *v.*¹ **1** [19C+] to get a woman pregnant. **2** [late 19C] to perform a marriage ceremony, to join in marriage. **3** [late 19C–1910s] to get married (cf. TIE THE KNOT). **4** [20C] (W.I.) to secure a (usu. male) partner's affections, to make infatuated.

tie up *v.*² [early 19C] (Und.) to abandon, to give up, e.g. *tie up prigging*, to give up one's criminal life, to become honest. [the image of *tying up* one's villainy and putting it away]

tie up *v.*³ [early 19C–1900s] to defeat or disable in a contest, to finish.

tie up *v.*⁴ [1950s+] (US drugs) to inject a narcotic after tying a rubber tube around the arm to find a vein.

tie up a dog, to phr. [20C] (Aus.) to get credit at a public house or hotel. [DOG n.[9] (2)]

tie with St Mary's knot, to phr. [19C] to hamstring. [Scot.; ult. ety. unknown]

tiff n.[1] **1** [late 17C–early 19C] a drink, esp. a thin or diluted one. **2** [early 18C–early 19C] a sip. [? SE *tipple*]

tiff n.[2] [early 18C+] **1** a fit of temper. **2** a petty quarrel, esp. an argument between lovers. [? echoic of an exhalation of gas or breath, as in shouting]

tiff v.[1] [late 17C–early 19C] to have sexual intercourse. [? TIFFITY-TAFFETY or 15C SE *tiff*, to be busy with trifles]

tiff v.[2] [mid-18C–mid-19C] to drink, esp. in small sips. [TIFF n.[1]]

tiff v.[3] [mid-18C+] to have a petty argument. [TIFF n.[2]]

tiffed adj. [mid-18C+] angry, irritated; thus *tiffish*, prone to take offence. [TIFF n.[2]]

tiffin n. [late 18C–mid-19C] (orig. Anglo-Ind.) breakfast, a light midday meal, luncheon. [SE *tiff*, to take a small drink or sip, then redefined for Anglo-Ind. use).

tiffing n. [late 18C] snacking, eating other than at mealtimes. [TIFFIN]

tiffity-taffety n. [16C] a prostitute (cf. LOOSE-BODIED GOWN; WHITE APRON). [SE *tiffany* + *taffeta*, transparent silks used for dresses]

tiffle up v. [early 18C] to dress oneself up. [SE *tiff*, to adorn oneself, to dress up]

tiffter n. [1990s] an unwanted erection. [? dial. *tift*, a sudden gust of wind]

tiffy adj. [mid-19C] **1** quick to take offence. **2** overly particular, petty. **3** angry, irritated, 'tetchy'. [TIFF n.[2]]

tift n. [17C] a drink. [TIFF n.[1]]

tiger n.[1] **1** [19C] a smartly dressed manservant, esp. a boy who accompanies his master in his coach. **2** [19C] an overdressed, showy person. **3** [19C] (Aus.) a groom (often Black). **4** [19C] (Aus.) a menial outdoor worker. **5** [mid-19C] a parasite, a sponger, a rake. **6** [mid–late 19C] any male servant. **7** [late 19C] (US) a 'bouncer' in a casino. **8** [late 19C+] (Aus.) a worker in a shearing shed.

tiger n.[2] [mid-19C–1900s] (US) a form of college cheer, esp. in phr. *three cheers and a tiger*, the three usual 'hip-hip-hoorays' plus a long-drawn-out shriek, often of the word 'tiger'.

tiger n.[3] [mid-19C+] a faro table (cf. BUCK THE TIGER; FIGHT THE TIGER). [for ety. *see* TIGER DEN]

tiger n.[4] [late 19C] **1** (US) a prostitute. **2** a wife. [? she claws her partner + play on CAT n.[1]]

tiger n.[5] [late 19C–1900s] (juv.) bread with a tough crust. [its strength]

tiger n.[6] [late 19C+] (Und.) a convict who tears another convict's yellow prison suit to pieces.

tiger n.[7] [late 19C+] streaky bacon. [its stripes]

tiger n.[8] [20C] (Aus.) **1** alcoholic liquor. **2** a heavy drinker. [its 'bite']

tiger n.[9] *see* TIGER TIM.

tiger n.[10] [1920s+] an outstanding sportsman. [the reverse of RABBIT n.[5] (1)]

tiger n.[11] [1980s+] (drugs) heroin. [its 'bite']

tiger n.[12] [1980s+] (S.Afr. Black) a 10-rand note; thus *five tiger*, 50 rand, *half tiger*, 5 rand. [its design]

tiger v. [1950s+] (Aus.) to work hard, to labour. [TIGER n.[1]]

tiger bit him hard, the phr. [mid–late 19C] (US) said of one who loses heavily in a casino, esp. when playing faro. [for ety. *see* TIGER DEN]

tiger cage n. [20C] (US Und.) an underground high-security or punishment cell. [the tiny, cramped underground cells or pits used illegally by South Vietnamese and US forces c.1970. Such 'cages' were deemed to be instruments of torture]

tiger den n. [mid-19C–1900s] (US) a gambling house that

specializes in the game of faro (cf. BUCK THE TIGER). [the faro table was known as the *tiger* and playing the game was 'fighting' or 'bucking the tiger'. The card-game faro itself originated in mid-17C France, moving thence via Fr. immigrants to New Orleans and thus across the US. It takes its name f. the Egyptian *Pharaoh*, for unknown reasons, although it has been claimed that the early faro decks had a card with a picture of the Egyptian monarch]

tiger for n. [late 19C+] (Aus.) an enthusiast for a task. [one's 'tigerish' appetite for work]

tiger-hunter n. [late 19C] a gambler. [TIGER n.[3]]

tigering n. [1950s+] (Aus.) hard work. [TIGER v.]

tigerish adj. [19C] flashily dressed. [TIGER n.[1](2)]

tiger's milk n. [mid-19C+] (US/S.Afr.) **1** gin. **2** any form of strong liquor (cf. PANTHER PISS). [SE *tiger milk*/Afk. *tiermelk*, liquor]

tiger sweat n. [1930s] (US Black) cheap, homemade gin or whisky.

tiger tim/tiger n. [20C] (Aus.) a swim. [rhy. sl.]

tiggerty-boo *see* TICKETTY-BOO.

tiggy n. [late 19C–1900s] a detective. [? TEC or game of *tig*, a juv. catching game]

tight n.[1] [late 19C+] a difficult situation (cf. TIGHT CORNER). [TIGHT adj.[1]]

tight n.[2] [1990s] (US Black gang) one's intimate friend. [TIGHT adj.[5]]

tight adj.[1] [mid–late 18C] hard to deal with, difficult, tough. **2** [early 19C+] of a contest, one in which the contestants are evenly matched. **3** [mid-19C] of a sale, offering very little profit.

tight adj.[2] [early 19C+] impoverished, in financial difficulties.

tight adj.[3] [early 19C+] reasonably, not excessively drunk; ext. as [20C] *tight as a drum*; *tight as a fart*, very drunk.

tight adj.[4] **1** [mid-19C+] of an individual, mean, avaricious, ungenerous. **2** [mid-19C+] of money, hard to obtain. **3** [1920s+] (US) tough, unyielding, aggressive (cf. TIGHTWAD).

tight adj.[5] [1920s+] very close, friendly, intimate.

tight adj.[6] **1** [1970s+] (US campus) good-looking, well-built. **2** [1970s+] (US Black) well-dressed, fashionable. **3** [1990s] (US Black) of circumstances, secure, properly worked out, organized. **4** [1990s] (US teen) used of something that one likes very much.

tight-arse *see* TIGHT-ASS.

tight-arsed *see* TIGHT-ASSED.

tight as a boiled owl phr. [late 19C+] (US) extremely drunk. [TIGHT adj.[3]]

tight as/tighter than a fish's/crab's/duck's/ gnat's arse/ arsehole phr. [20C] extremely mean, very close-fisted. [TIGHT adj.[4] (1)]

tight as a mouse's earhole phr. [1950s+] of a vagina, very tight.

tight as/tighter than Dick's/Jimmy's hatband phr. [mid-19C+] (US) **1** extremely tight. **2** of one's finances, impoverished. [SE *tight*/TIGHT adj.[4] + DICK'S HATBAND]

tight as Kelsey's nuts phr. [20C] (US) very mean, stingy (cf. DEAD AS KELSEY'S NUTS). [TIGHT adj.[4] (1) + punning ref. to the US *Kelsey* Wheel Company, founded in 1910 to produce automobile wheels. The need for nuts and bolts to be exceptionally tight fitting to preclude wobbly wheels gave rise to the saying]

tight as O'Reilley's balls phr. [20C] (US) very mean, stingy (cf. TIGHT AS KELSEY'S NUTS). [TIGHT adj.[4]; unlike the original, for which this is merely synon., there is no brandname identification]

tight-ass/-arse n. [1980s+] (orig. US) **1** a mean person, a skinflint (cf. TIGHTWAD). **2** a puritan, a moral conservative. [SE *tight* + ARSE n.[1]]

tight-assed/-arsed *adj.* **1** [late 19C+] of a woman, chaste. **2** [1950s+] mean. **3** [1950s+] repressed, self-denying, puritanical. [TIGHT-ASS]

tightbuck *n.* [1950s+] (gay) the foetal position, popular for tying up participants in sado-masochistic sex. [the image of a dead *buck* deer tied for transport]

tight corner/spot/squeeze *n.* [mid-19C.+] a difficult situation. [TIGHT adj.¹ (1)]

tight cravat *n.* [late 17C–18C] a hangman's noose (cf. HEMPEN CRAVAT).

tight cunts and easy boots! *excl.* [late 19C–1910s] a general toast (cf. INSIDE AND OUTSIDE!).

tighten *v.*¹ **1** [mid-19C+] (Irish) to drink heavily (cf. TIGHTENER). **2** [late 19C] to wear a tight corset or stays.

tighten *v.*² [1990s] (US Black) to criticize, to urge someone to a better life (cf. BRACE v.).

tightener/tightner *n.* [mid-19C] a large, heavy meal (cf. KAFFIR'S TIGHTENER); thus *do the tightener*, to dine. [its effects on one's stomach]

tighten one's action, to *phr.* [1970s] (US) to begin behaving in a more effective or pos. manner (cf. TIGHTEN UP ONE'S GAME). [SE *tighten* + ACTION n.]

tighten one's wig, to *phr.* [1940s] to smoke marijuana. [SE *tighten* + WIG n.¹; the sensation of tightening of the skull that sometimes accompanies smoking]

tighten/grind someone's jaw, to *phr.* [1960s+] (US Black) to annoy someone.

tighten up one's game, to *phr.* [1950s+] (US Black) to take control of one's life or of a situation in which one is interested (cf. TIGHTEN ONE'S ACTION). [SE *tighten* + GAME n.⁴]

tighter than a fish's/crab's/duck's arse/arsehole *see* TIGHT AS A FISH'S ARSE.

tighter than a nun's cunt *see* TIGHTER THAN A WITCH'S CUNT.

tighter than a tick *phr.* [20C] (Can.) **1** very mean, grasping. **2** very secretive. [TIGHT adj.⁴(1)]

tighter than a witch's/nun's cunt *phr.* [20C] extremely tight-fitting. [CUNT n.¹]

tighter than Dick's/Jimmy's hatband *see* TIGHT AS DICK'S HATBAND.

tight eyes *n.* [1960s–70s] (US Black) an Asian (cf. SLANT n.³). [the shape]

tight hand *n.* [1950s] (W.I.) a miser.

tight head *n.* [1930s–40s] (US Black) a head of kinky black hair.

tighties *n.* [1930s] *tight*-fitting women's underwear. [abbr.]

tight jaws *n.* [1960s–70s] (US Black) intense anger (cf. HAVE TIGHT CHEEKS). [a grimace of fury]

tight-laced *adj.* [mid-19C] puritanical, censorious.

tightly wrapped *adj.* [1970s+] (US) sane and with full mental ability (cf. NOT WRAPPED TOO TIGHT).

tight money *n.* [mid-19C+] (US) money in times of scarcity or high inflation.

tightner *see* TIGHTENER.

tightness *n.* [mid-19C] the state of being tipsy. [TIGHT adj.³]

tights, the *n.* [20C] (US) impoverished or financially hard times. [TIGHT adj.⁴]

tight spot/squeeze *see* TIGHT CORNER.

tightwad *n.* [late 19C+] an ungenerous, mean person. [SE *tight* + WAD n.¹ (1)]

tightwad *adj.* [late 19C+] miserly. [TIGHTWAD n.]

tight with *phr.* [1920s+] very friendly with. [TIGHT adj.⁵]

tighty whites *n.* [1990s] (US campus) men's briefs (cf. TIGHTIES).

tigress *n.* [early–mid-19C] a flashily overdressed woman. [TIGER n.¹ (2)]

Tijuana bible *n.* [1940s+] a small, illustrated pornographic book (cf. EIGHT-PAGER). [named for the era when US citizens saw *Tijuana*, Mexico, as the vice capital of Central America]

Tijuana racetrack *n.* [1950s+] (US) stains on the underwear that result from an attack of diarrhoea (cf. MONTEZUMA'S REVENGE). [derog. ref. to *Tijuana*, Mexico, and thus Mexicans]

Tijuanero/Tijuanaera *n.* [1960s+] (US) a newly arrived immigrant from Mexico. [Sp., a citizen of *Tijuana*, the border town through which legal immigrants often pass]

tike-lurking *see* BUFFER-LURKING.

Tilbury *n.* [late 18C–mid-19C] sixpence (2½p). [the fare charged by the trans-Thames ferry from Gravesend to *Tilbury Fort*]

Tilbury docks *n.* [late 19C+] **1** socks (cf. ALMOND ROCKS). **2** venereal disease. [rhy. sl.; *Tilbury docks* (in East London) = (2) POX n.¹]

'tilda/tilder *n.* [late 19C] (Aus.) a vagrant's pack. [abbr. MATILDA]

tile *n.* [19C] a hat. [it sits on top of one's ROOF n. (2)]

tiled *adj.*¹ [early–mid-19C] **1** snug, comfortable. **2** arrested, locked up. [having a (*tiled*) roof over one's head]

tiled *adj.*² [late 19C] **1** wearing a hat. **2** possessing a good head of hair. [TILE]

tiler *n.* [mid-17C] a shoplifter. [ety. unknown]

till *n.* [19C] the vagina (cf. BANK n.¹). [its commercial potential/ one puts 'money', i.e. the penis, into it]

till *v.* [1970s+] (US Black) to have sexual intercourse (cf. PLOUGH v.²).

till all is blue *phr.* **1** [early 17C–mid-19C] to the extreme, esp. used of excessive drinking. **2** [19C] (US) to the very end, the 'bitter' end. [the effect of the alcohol on one's eyesight. According to Smyth, *Sailor's Wordbook* (1867) 'a phrase borrowed from the idea of a vessel making out of port, and getting into blue water']

till-boy *n.* [mid-19C] a shop assistant who steals from the shop till (cf. TILL-TAPPER).

tilley-vally *see* TILLY-VALLY.

till hell freezes/freeze over *phr.* [1910s+] for a very long or indefinite time, for ever; thus (W.I.) *from hell freeze* (cf. TILL THE COWS COME HOME).

till one is blue in the face *phr.* [mid-19C+] a phr. meaning one has tried one's hardest or done everything possible and one is unable to do more, e.g. *I have told him till I am blue in the face.*

till-tapper *n.* [1950s–60s] (US Und.) one who steals from a cash register, esp. when employed as the cashier (cf. TILL-BOY). [one gives the till a sharp *tap* to open it without ringing up an actual sale]

till the cows come home *phr.* [early 19C+] (orig. US) for an indefinite time, for ever.

till the last cat is hung *phr.* [mid-19C] (US) until the bitter end.

till the last dog is hung *phr.* [mid-19C+] to the very end, until everything is resolved.

tilly *n.*¹ [1900s–20s] (Aus./N.Z.) a vagrant's swag or pack. [abbr. MATILDA]

tilly *n.*² [1950s+] (Aus.) a utility vehicle (cf. UTE). [abbr. SE *utility*]

tilly *n.*³ [1950s+] (gay) the police. [the use of a woman's name to 'feminize' the force]

tilly-/tilley-/tully-vally *n.* [early 16C–late 19C] piffle, rubbish, nonsense. [ety. unknown]

tillywink *see* TIDDLEY-WINKY.

tilt *n.* [early 17C] an unspecified rank of villain. ['Base heapes tumbled together, ... high-way-standers, Foists, nips, and tylts, prinadoes, bawdes, pimpes, panders' (Thomas Dekker, *Dream*, 1620)]

tilt a kidney *see* TAP A KIDNEY.

tilter *n.* [late 17C–early 18C] a rapier, a sword. [SE *tilter*, one who takes part in a joust or tournament]

timber *n.* **1** [17C] the stocks. **2** [late 19C] a match, also as *small timber*. **3** [1930s–40s] (US Black) a toothpick. **4** [1970s] (drugs) stems and stalks found in a batch of marijuana.

timber! *excl.* [20C] (US) a cry of triumph. [lumberjack excl. warning of a falling tree]

timber-doodle *n.* [mid-19C] (US) any form of spirituous liquor. [ety. unknown]

timber-head *n.* [mid–late 17C] a fool (cf. BLOCKHEAD; LUNK-HEAD). [SE *timber* + sfx. -HEAD (1)]

timber-merchant *n.* [mid-19C–1900s] a match-seller (cf. SPUNK-FENCER; WOOD MERCHANT). [TIMBER *n.* (2) + sfx. -MERCHANT]

timbers *n.* [18C–mid-19C] the legs. [SE *timber*, a wooden foundation]

timber-stairs *n.* [mid-18C] the treadmill. [its wooden construction]

timber-toe *n.* [late 18C–1900s] **1** a wooden leg. **2** a person who has a wooden leg.

timber-toed *adj.* [early 19C+] having a wooden leg.

timber-truck *n.* [late 19C] an early model of bicycle, with solid rather than rubber tyres (cf. BONE-SHAKER).

time *n.*[1] [mid-19C+] a prison sentence; thus *do time*, to serve a sentence (cf. BIRD *n.*[7]).

time *n.*[2] [1980s+] (US) a monthly credit payment.

time *prep.* [1910s+] at the time, by the time, once, e.g. *Time the day be done*.

time of day/o'day *n.* [mid-17–late 19C] **1** a trick, a ruse. **2** the current situation, what is going on; thus *put one up to the time of day*, explain the situation to one (cf. KNOW WHAT TIME IT IS).

times *n.* [mid-19C] multiples of one shilling (5p), e.g. *nine times*, 9 shillings (45p).

timothy *n.*[1] [mid–late 19C] a measure or glassful of alcohol. [Scot., ? the name of a real brewer]

timothy *n.*[2] [1950s+] (Aus.) a brothel. [? rhy. sl. *timothy grass* = ARSE or *timothy titmouse* = house]

tim-tim *n.* [20C] (W.I.) an unreliable story, a fantasy. [Carib.E. excl. *tim-tim!* used by a story-teller to indicate that he/she is about to tell a folk-tale. ? ult. Fr. *tiens*, hello! look! or SE (*it's*) *time*]

tin *n.*[1] [mid–late 19C] **1** money, esp. silver (cf. TINMAN). **2** (US) a trifling amount of money.

tin, the *n.*[2] [20C] (Aus.) tin-mining country.

tin *n.*[3] [1930s+] (US) a policeman's or sheriff's badge (cf. POTSY); thus police jargon *tin wife*, an officer's wife. [its main component]

tin *n.*[4] [1960s–70s] (drugs) **1** 28g (1oz) of marijuana (cf. LID *n.*[4]). **2** (US) a few grains of cocaine. [the selling of marijuana in measures based on the size of a popular brand tobacco tin; the use for cocaine may be a misinterpretation]

tin *n.*[5] [1980s+] (US campus) beer. [the can that contains it]

tin-arse/-back/-bum *n.* [1940s+] (Aus./N.Z.) an extremely lucky person. [TIN *n.*[1] (1) + ARSE *n.*[1]/*back*/BUM *n.*[2]]

tin-arsed *adj.* [1940s+] (Aus./N.Z.) thick-skinned, impervious to pain, lucky (cf. ARSEY). [TIN-ARSE]

tin-back *see* TIN-ARSE.

tin bath *n.* [20C] scarf. [rhy. sl., pron. 'barf']

tin-bum *see* TIN-ARSE.

tin can *n.* [1950s+] a dilapidated old car; thus *Tin Can Alley*, Great Portland Street, London, once the city's centre for second-hand car sales. [pun on TIN PAN ALLEY]

tin can cop *n.* [20C] (US) a rural sheriff (cf. TOWN CLOWN).

tin-chapel *adj.* [late-19C+] Nonconformist, esp. Methodist. [the building materials used for a typical Nonconformist Chapel]

tin cow *n.* [1920s–40s] (US tramp) tinned milk. [SE *tin* + COW *n.*[4]]

tincture *n.*[1] [1910s+] a drink. [hugely popularized by the 'Dear Bill' column in the magazine *Private Eye*, lampooning Denis Thatcher, husband of prime minister Margaret Thatcher (b.1925)]

tincture *n.*[2] [1960s+] (drugs) *tincture* of cannabis. [abbr.]

tin/tinned dog *n.* [late 19C+] (Aus./N.Z.) canned meat.

tin ear *n.* (Aus.) **1** [20C] an eavesdropper. **2** [1920s+] a fool, simpleton.

tin flute *n.* [20C] a suit. [rhy. sl.]

ting-a-ling *n.* [1900s] (US Black) the penis (cf. DINGALING *n.*[3]). [like a bell-pull, it *rings* the testicles]

tingle *n.* [1940s+] (Aus.) a call on the telephone (cf. TINKLE *n.*[1]).

tin grin *n.* [1970s+] (US campus) a person wearing orthodontic braces (cf. LASER LIPS).

tin hare *n.* **1** [1920s+] (mainly Aus.) the electric hare used for greyhound racing. **2** [1930s+] a train, esp. a rail-motor, i.e. a small passenger train consisting of the engine and one coach.

tin hat *n.* **1** [20C] a helmet. **2** [1910s] a senior officer (cf. BRASS HAT).

tin hat *adj.* [late 19C] drunk; thus *two tin hats*, very drunk, *three tin hats*, incapably drunk. [? abbr. THAT PUTS THE TIN HAT ON IT]

tin hat *v.* [1910s+] (Aus.) **1** to indicate one's contempt. **2** to patronize, to talk down to. [TIN HAT *n.* (2)]

tinhorn *adj.* [late 19C+] second-rate, inferior, superficially flashy. [abbr. gambling use *tinhorn gambler*, a second-rate class of gambler: 'Chuck-a-luck operators shake their dice in a "small churn-like affair of metal" – hence the expression, "tinhorn gambler", for the game is rather looked down upon as one for "chubbers" and chuck-a-luck gamblers not admitted within the aristocratic circle of faro-dealers.' G.F. Willison, *Here They Dug Gold* (1931)]

tinies *n.* [1920s+] a small child (cf. SHORT *n.*[6]; SHORTY).

tink *n.* [mid-19C+] **1** a *tinker*. **2** a foul-mouthed, obstreperous person. [(1) abbr.; ? (2) the stereotype of (1)]

tinkard *n.* [16C] (Und.) a tinker who alternates legitimate work with begging. [SE *tinker*; '[He] leaveth his bag a sweating at the ale house ... and in the mean season goeth abroad begging' (Awdeley)]

tinker *n.*[1] [late 19C+] an affectionate term used to a child by an exasperated parent. [SE *tinker*, a pedlar]

tinker *n.*[2] [1950s–60s] (Can.) the penis. [var. on TINKLE *n.*[2]]

Tinker Bell *n.* [1950s–60s] (camp gay) a pleasingly plump person. [the character *Tinker Bell* the FAIRY in J.M. Barrie's *Peter Pan* (1904)]

tinker's budget/news *n.* [mid–late 19C] stale news. [SE *tinker* + *budget*, a long letter full of news/*news*; a tinker, being on the move, would catch up with news late]

tinker's cuss/damn/fart/fiddler's damn *n.* [19C+] nothing, esp. in phrs. *not care a tinker's cuss/damn/fart*, also abbr. as *tinker's*. [the lack of importance one gives a curse thrown over the shoulder of a departing tinker who has been unable to sell anything or find work]

tinker's news *see* TINKER'S BUDGET.

tinker's time *n.* [20C] (Irish) unpunctuality (cf. AFRICAN PEOPLE'S TIME). [the slow progress and unreliability of the SE *tinker*]

tinkerty-tonk *phr.* [1920s–30s] a nonsense term used for goodbye (cf. TIDDLY-PUSH).

tinkle *n.*[1] **1** [1930s+] a ring on the telephone, usu. in phr. *give one a tinkle*. **2** [1930s+] urination. **3** [1960s] money. [the sounds involved]

tinkle *n.*[2] [1930s+] the penis. [? var. on WINKLE]

tinkle *v.* [1930s+] (usu. juv.) to urinate. [TINKLE *n.*[1] (2)]

tinkler *n.*[1] [18C–19C] a mendicant tramp. [? his bell or SE *tinker*]

tinkler *n.*² [mid-19C; 1930s–40s] a bell. [20C use is US Black]

tin lid *n.* [20C] (Aus.) a child. [rhy. sl. *tin lid = kid*]

tin lizzie *n.* [1910s+] (orig. US) a Model T Ford. [affectionate nickname]

tinman *n.* [late 19C] (sporting) a very rich man, a millionaire. [TIN n.¹ + SE *man*]

tinned *adj.* [1940s+] drunk (cf. CANNED adj.²). [tin beer cans]

tinned dog *see* TIN DOG.

tinnie/tinny *n.*¹ [1960s+] **1** (Aus., orig. surfer) a can of beer. **2** (Aus.) a small aluminium boat.

tinnie *n.*² [1980s+] (N.Z. drugs) silver foil, as used in smoking heroin.

tinny *n.*¹ [early 19C] a fire. [? Gaelic/Erse *teine*, fire, Shelta *tini*, fire or SE *tinder*, use in lighting fires]

tinny *n.*² *see* TINNIE n.¹.

tinny *adj.*¹ **1** [mid–late 19C] wealthy, rich. **2** [1910s+] (Aus./N.Z.) lucky; thus [1910s] *on the tinny luck*, by a fortunate chance. **3** [1930s+] (Aus./N.Z.) mean, grasping (cf. TIN-ARSED). [TIN n.¹]

tinny *adj.*² [1920s+] cheap, second-rate. [SE *tin*]

tinny house *see* BULLET HOUSE.

tinny-hunter *n.* [late 18C–early 19C] a thief who robs people whose homes are burning down, while pretending to give assistance. [TINNY n.¹ + SE *hunter*: 'No beast of prey is so noxious to Society, or so destitute of feeling, as these wretches' (George Parker, *A View of Society*, 1781)]

tin of beans *n.* [1960s+] jeans. [rhy. sl.]

Tin Pan Alley *n.* [late 19C+] (orig. US) the centre of the music business, esp. that area where music writers, lyricists and song pluggers have their offices, in its inter-war heyday the Times Square area of New York City and Denmark Street, London W1. [musician's jargon *tin-pan*, a piano + derog. description of the music as sounding like *tin pans* being clashed together. The term probably evolved through popular use within the business, although journalist/songwriter Monroe Rosenfeld claimed its coinage *c*.1899.]

tin plate *n.* [20C] a friend (cf. CHINA n.²). [rhy. sl. *tin plate = *MATE n.]

tin-pot *adj.* [late 19C+] (N.Z.) of a place, small, insignificant. [note naut. jargon *tin-potter*, an idler, one who shirks their duties by claiming to be ill. The use of *tin-pot* as cheap, inferior is SE]

tinsel teeth *n.* [1970s+] (US campus) a person wearing orthodontic braces (cf. LASER LIPS).

Tinsel Town *n.* **1** [1970s+] Hollywood, California. **2** [1980s+] (Aus.) Sydney. [the towns' glittering images]

tin shin off *v.* [late 19C] (US) to abscond with money. [TIN n.¹ + SHIN OFF]

tin soldier *n.* [1970s+] a prostitute's client, usu. middle- or upper-class, who doesn't want sex but only to act as a servant or 'slave' to the prostitute.

tin star *n.* [20C] (US) a private detective. [his identification]

tint *n.* [20C] (Irish) a measure of liquor. [abbr. SE *tincture*]

tin tabernacle *n.* [late 19C+] any church with an iron or tin roof (cf. TIN-CHAPEL).

tin-tack *n.* [late 19C+] dismissal from a job. [rhy. sl. *tin-tack = *SACK n.³]

tin-tacks *n.* [20C] facts. [rhy. sl.]

tin tank *n.* [late 19C–1930s] a bank (cf. J. ARTHUR). [rhy. sl.]

tints *n.* [1950s+] (US Black) fashionable dark glasses. [they are SE *tinted*]

tiny tim *n.* [20C] a £5 note. [rhy. sl. *tiny tim = *FLIM n. (1)]

Tio Taco *n.* [20C] (US) a derog. term for a Mexican who is considered insufficiently nationalistic by others (cf. TACO-BENDER; TACO-HEAD; TACO TOWN; UNCLE TOM n.). [Mex. *tio*, uncle + *taco*, the foodstuff]

tip *n.*¹ [early 18C–mid-19C] **1** a draught of liquor. **2** drink in general (cf. HAVE A TIP ON). [SE *tip a glass*]

tip *n.*² **1** [early 19C] money as used in any form of contract (cf. DUES). **2** [early–mid-19C] a bribe. [SE *tip*, a gratuity]

tip *n.*³ [mid–late 19C] (Aus.) an Irishman, esp. a gold-miner. [proper name *Tipperary*]

tip *n.*⁴ **1** [mid-19C+] a piece of 'inside' information, esp. as regards a sporting contest, usu. racing or boxing. **2** [mid-19C+] the subject of the tip, usu. a horse. **3** [late 19C+] a special hint or trick, a 'wrinkle'. **4** [late 19C+] a tip-off, but used as any reason for an arrest, not simply information given to the police.

tip *n.*⁵ [20C] (US Und.) a prison gang. [ety. unknown]

tip *n.*⁶ [1950s–60s] (US Black) a young woman, a girlfriend. [ety. unknown]

tip *n.*⁷ [1960s+] a very untidy, messy place, e.g. a child's bedroom. [abbr. SE *rubbish tip*]

tip *n.*⁸ [1980s+] (US Black) the aspect, the point of view, the angle, e.g. *on the art tip*, from the artistic point of view; *on the sales tip*, from the aspect of sales (cf. GAME n.⁴; THING). [SE *tip*, advice, guidance]

tip *n.*⁹ [1990s] the end, the ultimate.

tip *v.*¹ [17C–18C] to earn money. [? TIP v.⁵]

tip *v.*² [early 17C–early 18C] to render unsteady, to make drunk. [abbr. SE *tip over*]

tip *v.*³ [late 17C–early 18C] to die. [abbr. TIP OFF v.¹]

tip *v.*⁴ [late 17C+] to do, to make, to perform, usu. in phrs. (cf. TIP A DADDLE; TIP A YARN).

tip *v.*⁵ **1** [late 17C+] to give, to hand over, to lend. **2** [early 18C+] to give a monetary gratuity. [? SE *tip*, to touch lightly, orig. Und., but sl. by mid-18C]

tip *v.*⁶ **1** [early 18C–mid-19C] to drink. **2** [1970s] (US campus) to drink heavily. [abbr. SE *tipple*]

tip *v.*⁷ **1** [mid-18C] to indicate surreptitiously by a wink or similar gesture. **2** [late 19C+] to give information, esp. secret, privileged, 'inside' information (cf. TIP OFF v.²). **3** [1950s+] (Aus.) to guess. **4** [1950s+] (US Black) to gain knowledge of, to understand.

tip *v.*⁸ [mid–late 18C] to pose, to take on a character; poss. deliberately mimicking another person (cf. TIP n.⁸).

tip *v.*⁹ [early–mid-19C] to bribe. [TIP n.² (2)]

tip *v.*¹⁰ [1950s–60s] (US Black) to leave. [SE *tip*, to move lightly or tiptoe]

tip *v.*¹¹ [1970s+] (US Black) **1** to cheat on one's lover or mate. **2** to perform an illicit act. **3** to be in a place where one should not be. [? SE *tip*, to knock over]

tip a/the daddle, to *phr.* [late 18C–19C] to shake hands. [TIP v.⁴ + DADDLE n.]

tip a nod, to *phr.* **1** [late 18C+] to warn, to signal (cf. TIP THE WINK). **2** [mid–late 19C] to recognize someone. [TIP v.⁴ + SE *nod*]

tip-an-pawn *n.* [1950s] (W.I.) one who limps. [dial. *tip*, to strike lightly + *pawn*, to grasp, to pick up. The image is of the jerky movement of the legs]

tip a rise, to *phr.* [late 19C] to fool, to deceive. [TIP v.⁴ + RISE n.¹ (2)]

tip a settler, to *phr.* [early 19C] to hit hard, to knock out. [TIP v.⁴ + SETTLE v.]

tip a sock, to *phr.* [late 17C–late 19C] to hit hard, to knock out. [TIP v.⁴ + SOCK n.³]

tip a wrong 'un, to *phr.* [late 19C] to make a foolish or erroneous prophecy. [TIP v.⁴ + WRONG 'UN]

tip a yarn, to *phr.* [late 19C] to tell a story. [TIP v.⁴ + YARN]

tip-book *n.* [mid-19C] a schoolchild's study aid, a literal translation. [TIP n.⁴]

tip in *v.* [1960s+] to inform against. [TIP v.⁷]

tip in the wind, to *phr.* [1970s+] (US Black) to depart, to go away. [ext. of TIP v.¹⁰]

tip into v. [1960s] (US) to visit briefly.

tip-merry adj. [18C] tipsy. [TIP n.¹ + sfx. -merry]

tip-off n. **1** [20C] a piece of information, esp. concerning criminal activity. **2** [1940s+] an informer, an 'inside man'. [TIP OFF v.²]

tip off v.¹ [late 17C–early 19C] to die.

tip off v.² [20C] to warn, to provide with information. [ext. of TIP v.²]

tip off the blarney, to phr. [early 19C] to deceive, to trick by verbal facility. [TIP OFF v.² + BLARNEY]

tip one's dirt, to phr. [20C] to ejaculate.

tip one's fin, to phr. [late 18C–late 19C] to shake hands. [TIP v.⁴ + FIN n.¹]

tip one's legs a gallop, to phr. [early 19C] to run off, to leave fast. [TIP v.⁴]

tip one's mitt, to phr. [20C] (US) to disclose one's plans inadvertently. [TIP v.⁴ + MITT n. (1), (2)]

tip one's/the rags a double, to phr. [19C] to run off. [for ety. see TIP ONE'S RAGS A GALLOP + SE double, speed]

tip one's/the rags a gallop, to phr. [17C] to leave, to depart. [TIP v.⁴ + SE rags as clothes; RAGS n.⁵ is a later development]

tip out/over v. [late 19C+] (US Black) to have sex with someone other than one's spouse or regular lover. [ext. of TIP v.¹¹]

tip over v. [1970s+] (US) to rob. [ext. of TIP v.¹¹]

tip over the perch, to phr. [late 16C–17C] to die (cf. DROP OFF THE PERCH; TURN OVER THE PERCH).

tipped adj. [early 18C] drunk. [TIP n.¹]

tipper n.¹ [mid-19C] a beer brewed in Brighton, with a nationwide reputation. [proper name of the brewer Thomas Tipper. It was brewed from notably brackish water from one specific well.]

tipper n.² [mid-19C] a racecourse tipster. [TIP v.⁷ (2)]

Tipperary adj. [late 18C] drunk, tipsy. [one 'tips' over]

Tipperary fortune n. [late 18C–early 19C] **1** an Irish woman with no fortune other than her body. **2** the breasts, vagina and anus (cf. BALLINOCACK). ['Two town lands [the breasts], stream's town [the pudend] and ballinocack [the anus]' (Grose 1785)]

Tipperary lawyer n. [mid–late 19C] a cudgel (cf. PENANG LAWYER). [racial stereotyping]

Tipper Gore n. [1990s] (US teen) one who is narrow-minded, puritanical, repressive. [Tipper Gore, wife of politician Al Gore (b.1948), apostrophised by her critics as a byword for narrow-minded stupidity]

tippery n. [mid-19C–1900s] payment, i.e. the 'world of tips'. [SE tip/TIP v.⁵]

tippet n. [mid–late 19C] a generous person, someone who treats their companions. [TIP v.⁵]

tippin' adj. [1970s+] (US Black) in full control, on top of one's game. [TIP-TOP adj.]

tipple n. [late 16C+] **1** any alcoholic drink. **2** any drink, esp. that which one prefers, i.e. one's tipple. [SE tipple, to drink]

tippling-ken/-office n. [late 18C–early 19C] a public house, a tavern. [SE tipple + KEN n.²/OFFICE n.¹]

tipply adj. **1** [1900s] unsteady. **2** [1910s–30s] drunk. [TIPPLE]

tippy n. [late 18C–mid-19C] a dandy. [TIP-TOP ? + TIP n.⁴ (1)]

tippy adj.¹ **1** [19C] in the height of fashion, smart, fine; note also [late 18C–early 19C] the tippy, the height of fashion, the smart thing. **2** [early 19C–1900s] highly ingenious or clever. **3** [early 19C–1900s] neat, smart. [TIPPY n.]

tippy adj.² [late 19C] unsteady, prone to falling over. [SE tip (over)]

tippybob n. **1** [19C] (US) a member of the social élite. **2** [early 19C] a dandy. [ext. of TIPPY n.]

tipslinger n. [1920s+] (Aus.) a racecourse tipster. [TIP n.⁴ + SE slinger, lit. 'thrower']

tip someone the office, to phr. [late 19C] to warn someone (cf. GIVE SOMEONE THE OFFICE). [TIP v.⁷ + OFFICE n.³]

tip someone the sligo, to phr. [late 18C] to warn someone, to TIP SOMEONE THE WINK. [TIP v.⁷ + ? SE sly + go, i.e. leave quietly and surreptitiously]

tip someone the token, to phr. [18C] to give a partner a venereal disease. [TIP v.⁴ + TOKEN]

tip someone the wink see TIP THE WINK.

tipster n. [19C] **1** one who gives out or sells advice on horse-racing. **2** one who gives monetary tips to servants, employees etc. [SE from 1900, TIP n.⁴]

tip street n. [early 19C] a state of wealth. [fig. use of TIP n.²]

tip the brads, to phr. [19C] **1** to be generous. **2** to be a gentleman. [TIP v.⁵ + BRADS]

tip the bucket on see DROP THE BUCKET ON.

tip the claws/claws for breakfast, to phr. [18C] to be whipped, as a judicial punishment (cf. TIP THE SCROBY). [TIP v.⁴ + SE claws, those of the cat-o'-nine-tails]

tip the daddle see TIP A DADDLE.

tip the double, to phr. [late 18C–mid-19C] to run off, from a creditor or from the authorities; thus tip the double to sherry, to elude the sheriff. [TIP v.⁴ + SE phr. at the double]

tip the Dublin packet, to phr. [early 19C] (Und.) to run off, to escape. [TIP v.⁴ + pun on Dublin/SE double, to run; the Dublin packet also being a boat on which one could escape to Ireland]

tip the finger/little finger, to phr. [late 19C+] (Aus.) to have a drink.

tip the fives, to phr. [late 18C–19C] to shake hands (cf. TIP A DADDLE). [TIP v.⁴ + (BUNCH OF) FIVES]

tip the garrotte, to phr. [mid-19C] to work as a garrotter, a form of robbery with violence that became esp. popular in London during the garrotting scare of 1862. [TIP v.⁴ + SE garrotte]

tip the go-by, to phr. [late 18C] **1** to avoid, to disregard deliberately. **2** to allow, to turn a blind eye to. **3** to dismiss, to get rid of. [TIP v.⁴ + (GIVE THE) GO-BY]

tip the gripes in a dangle/tangle, to phr. [late 18C–late 19C] to shake hands (cf. TIP A DADDLE). [TIP v.⁴ + SE gripe, to grasp]

tip the lion, to phr. [late 18C–mid-19C] to squeeze someone's nose flat against their face and either poke their eyes with one's extended fingers or place them in the person's mouth, thus extending it. [the expression this hostile gesture produces is supposedly similar to that of a lion]

tip the little finger phr.¹ see TIP THE MIDDLE FINGER.

tip the little finger phr.² see TIP THE FINGER.

tip the long finger see TIP THE MIDDLE FINGER.

tip the long 'un, to phr. [late 19C–1900s] of a man, to have sexual intercourse. [TIP v.⁴ + SE long one]

tip the middle/little/long finger, to phr. [19C] of a man, to fondle a woman's genitals. [TIP v.⁴]

tip the queer on, to phr. [early 19C–1900s] to pass a sentence of imprisonment on. [TIP v.⁴ + QUEER adj.¹ (1)]

tip the quids, to phr. [late 17C–early 19C] **1** to spend money. **2** to lend money. [TIP v.⁴ + QUID n.]

tip the rags a double see TIP ONE'S RAGS A DOUBLE.

tip the rags a gallop see TIP ONE'S RAGS A GALLOP.

tip the scroby/the scroby for breakfast, to phr. [18C–mid-19C] to be whipped, as a judicial punishment (cf. TIP THE CLAWS). [TIP v.⁴ + ? SE scrub]

tip/play the traveller, to phr. [late 18C–19C] to boast, to exaggerate, also as phr. tip the traveller upon, to fool, to deceive with tall tales. [TIP v.⁸, the association of gypsies with tall tales]

tip the velvet, to phr. **1** [late 17C–late 19C] to kiss with the tongue. **2** [early–mid-19C] to tell off, to scold. [TIP v.⁴ + VELVET]

tip the/someone the wink, to *phr.* [late 18C+] to warn, to signal, usu. with an actual wink, but also fig. (cf. TIP A NOD TO). [TIP v.⁴ + SE *wink*]

tip-top *n.* **1** [early 18C] the very best, the ultimate. **2** [mid-18C–mid-19C] a collective n. for the cream of society, the 'bon-ton'. [TIP-TOP adj.]

tip-top *adj.* [early 18C+] excellent, supreme, ultimate; thus the superlative *tippest-toppest*. [SE *tip* + *top*, i.e. the top of the top]

tip-top *adv.* [early 18C+] excellently, superbly. [TIP-TOP adj.]

tip-topmost *adj.* [1930s+] very good, excellent, the best. [TIP-TOP adj.]

tip-topper *n.* [mid-19C] a dandy, a fashionable man. [TIP-TOP adj.]

tip up *v.* [mid-19C] to hand over (money), usu. as imper. [TIP v.⁴]

tip up the tin, to *phr.* [mid-19C] to hand over money, usu. as imper. [TIP v.⁴ + TIN n.¹]

tip up your fist/fin *phr.* [late 19C] a phr. meaning give me your hand, shake hands. [TIP v.⁴ + SE *fist*/FIN n.¹]

tip us the monish *phr.* [mid-19C] a phr. meaning give me the money. [TIP v.⁴? + mockery of the immigrant Jewish pron. of SE *money*]

tip us your fin *phr.* [mid-19C] a phr. meaning let's shake hands. [TIP v.⁴ + FIN n.¹]

tired *adj.*¹ [late 19C] extremely lazy; thus *born a bit tired*, a sarcastic description of a congenitally lazy person, e.g. *you have to forgive him, he was born tired.*

tired *adj.*² [late 19C+] of people, things or events, tedious, dull, hackneyed.

tired *adj.*³ [1960s+] drunk (cf. TIRED AND EMOTIONAL). [euph.]

tired and emotional *phr.* [1960s+] a euph. for extremely drunk. [coined in the magazine *Private Eye* f. the popular euph. to mask the activities of the famous. The orig. citation read: 'Mr [George] Brown [MP] had been tired and overwrought on many occasions' (*Private Eye*, 29 September 1967)]

tired-ass *adj.* [1960s+] (US) tedious, clichéd. [TIRED adj.² + sfx. -ASS]

tired blood *n.* [1950s] (US) a condition of listlessness. [an advertising slogan for a tonic, which promised to combat the condition]

tired people *n.* [1930s+] (orig. US Black) weak or displeasing people. [TIRED adj.²]

tired woman *n.* [1970s+] (US Black) a woman who lacks sophistication. [TIRED adj.²]

tiresome *adj.* [late 18C–late 19C] irritating, wearisome.

tirly-whirly *n.* [late 18C] the vagina. [coined by Robert Burns (1759–96); SE *tirly-whirly*, a whirligig or, Scots *tirly-whirly*, winding, intricate]

tirret/tirrit *n.* [late 16C+] a fit of temper. [? SE *tirl*, St Vitus's Dance]

tish/titch *n.* [1970s] (drugs) phencyclidine (cf. ACE n.³). [var. on TIC n.]

tish *v.* [20C] (US) to pad or enhance something. [abbr. SE *tissue paper*, used as a protective wadding]

tishy *n. see* TISSUE n.¹.

tishy *adj.* [1910s–30s] drunk. ['drunken' mispron. of *tipsy*]

tisket *n.* [1940s] a bastard. [song lyric 'A tisket, a tasket, a little yellow basket', thus cf. BASKET n.²]

tissick *n.* [20C] (Irish) a cough; thus *tizicky*, fastidious about one's food, self-conscious. [SE *phthisis*]

tissied up *adj.* [1920s+] (Aus.) dressed up (cf. GUSSIED UP). [TIZZY v.]

tissing *n.* [1990s] (US teen) the sound made by a Walkman with the sound turned up, heard from a short distance away.

tissue/tishy *n.*¹ [1950s–60s] (Aus./N.Z.) a cigarette paper.

tissue *n.*² [1980s+] (drugs) crack cocaine. [? its packaging]

tit *n.*¹ **1** [17C+] a breast; thus [1930s+] (orig. milit.) anything

considered to resemble a breast or, more often, the nipple, e.g. a button or a small switch etc. **2** [20C] something extremely simple and usu. rewarding, esp. a criminal scheme. [SE *teat*; (2) suggests the simplicity of a child's finding its mother's breast]

tit *n.*² [early 18C–mid-19C] a small or half-grown horse. [for ety. *see* TIT n.³]

tit *n.*³ **1** [early 18C+] a girl or woman, esp. in derog. or generic use, e.g. *a tasty bit of tit*, but also as a term of affection, often as *little tit*. **2** [early 18C+] generic for a person of either sex (cf. JOLLY TIT). **3** [early 18C–1900s] the vagina (cf. TIT-BIT; TITMOUSE). [despite SE *teat*/TIT n.¹, ety. is onomat. term meaning anything small + Scand. dial. terms *titta*, a little girl, *tita*, a small fish etc; coined in 16C but SE until *c*.1700]

tit *n.*⁴ [19C+] a fool; thus *look an absolute tit*, *look a right tit*, to appear a total fool, thus the tired school 'witticism', *I feel a right tit.*

tit *adj.* [20C] (S.Afr.) a general term of approval meaning excellent, wonderful, good-looking. [ext. of TIT n.¹ (1)]

tit about/around *v.* [1930s+] to play around, to waste time, to act in a trivial, pointless manner. [TIT n.⁴]

tit art *n.* [1950s+] (US) pictures of attractive young women (cf. TIT MAG). [TIT n.¹ (1)]

tit-bag *n.* [1940s+] a brassiere. [TIT n.¹ (1) + SE *bag*. Note synon. naut. use *tit-hammock*]

tit-bit *n.* [mid-17C–late 18C] **1** the vagina (cf. TIT n.³). **2** the penis.

titch *see* TISH n.

titchy *adj.* [20C] (mainly juv.) small, tiny, undersized; thus *Tich* or *Titch*, popular nickname for a short person (and, with heavy humour, for an exceptionally tall one). [according to *OED* the nickname preceded the wider use: 'The stage name Little Tich of the dwarfish music-hall comedian Harry Relph (1868–1928), who was given the nickname as a child because of a resemblance to the Tichborne claimant.' The claimant was Arthur Orton (1834–98), who claimed in 1866 to be Roger Charles Tichborne (1829–54), the heir to an English baronetcy, who was lost at sea. Orton was finally discredited and imprisoned in 1874]

titfer/titfa/tit-for *n.* [1920s+] a hat. [abbr. TIT-FOR-TAT n. (1)]

tit-for-tat *n.* [late 19C+] **1** a hat (cf. TITFER). **2** (Aus.) a rat, i.e. a non-trade unionist. [rhy. sl.]

tit fuck *n.* [1980s+] (orig. US) intercourse in which the man rubs his penis between the woman's breasts (cf. FRENCH FUCK). [TIT n.¹ (1) + FUCK n.¹]

titire-tu *see* TITTERY-TU.

titivate/tiddivate/tiddyvate *v.* **1** [early 19C+] to smarten oneself up, to put the finishing touches to. **2** [1920s] to treat kindly or gently. [? SE *tidy*]

titlark *n.* [late 18C] one who watches cases at Bow Street Magistrates' Court. [the gregariousness of the bird]

title *n.* [1900s] a titled person, an aristocrat. [metonymy]

title page *n.* [mid-19C] the face (cf. FRONTISPIECE).

titless wonder *n.* [1930s+] (orig. RAF) a flat-chested woman (cf. CHINLESS WONDER). [TIT n.¹ (1)]

titley *n.* [mid-19C+] a drink; thus *titley and binder*, a glass of beer and a piece of bread and cheese. [? dial. *titley* tickle; i.e. one's palate or SE *tiddly*, small, i.e. a small portion]

titley *adj.* [mid-19C+] slightly drunk, tipsy. [var. on TIDDLY adj.]

tit mag *n.* [1970s+] a magazine which features scantily clad women. The pictures are interspersed with varying amounts of prose, reviews etc but despite all other pretensions, they are in the end an aid to masturbation. [TIT n.¹ (1) + MAG n.³]

tit man *n.* [1950s+] a man who finds a woman's breasts her most appealing feature (cf. ARSE MAN). [TIT n.¹ (1) + SE *man*]

titmouse *n.* [mid-17C–late 18C] the vagina (cf. MICKEY MOUSE n.²; TIT n.³).

tit-proud *adj.* [1950s] (N.Z.) used of a woman who is proud of her breasts. [TIT n.¹ (1)]

tits, the *n.* [1950s+] perfection, excellence, an ideal situation. [fig. use of TIT n.¹ (1)]

tits *adj.* [20C] **1** (US) wonderful, excellent. **2** (US campus) easy, simple. [TIT n.¹]

tits and ass/arse/t.a./T & A *n.* [1950s+] (orig. US) **1** a burlesque show, cheap sex-orientated entertainment which features strippers etc. **2** any soft-core pornography. [TIT n.¹ (1) + ASS/ARSE n.]

tits and ass/arse/t.a./T & A *adj.* [1950s+] (orig. US) relating to sex-orientated entertainment or soft-core pornography. [TITS AND ASS n.]

tits and bums *n.* [1970s+] a burlesque show, cheap sex-orientated entertainment which features strippers etc (cf. TITS AND ASS n.). [TIT n.¹ (1) + BUM n.²]

tits and zits *adj.* [1970s+] (US) pertaining to teenage love and sex. [TIT n.¹ (1) + ZIT]

tit show *n.* [1930s+] a burlesque or striptease show. [TIT n.¹ (1) + SE *show*]

tits off! *excl.* [1950s–70s] go away! (cf. BUGGER OFF; FUCK OFF!; SOD OFF!).

tits on a bull/boar/canary *phr.* [1940s+] used of something utterly useless, usu. in phr. *no more use than tits on a bull* etc.

tits on toast *n.* [1900s–10s] (N.Z.) belly-pickled pork on toast. [the belly-pork often has nipples still attached]

tits-up *adj.* [1960s+] (orig. Can. prison) dead, i.e. laid out on one's back.

titter *n.* [19C] a young woman (cf. TIT n.³). [SE *titter*, to giggle, or TITTY n.²]

tittery *n.* [early–mid-18C] gin. [dial. *tittery*, unstable, on the verge of falling, i.e. its effects]

tittery-/titire-/tityre-/tytere-tu *n.* [17C] a street gang, esp. of well-to-do roughs who infested the London streets, committing their crimes for amusement rather than gain (cf. HAWCUBITE). [the first words of Virgil's first eclogue, '*Tityre, tu patulae recubans sub tegmine fagi*'. The Lat. tag implied that these privileged rogues were men of leisure and fortune, who 'lay at ease under their patrimonial beech trees']

tittle *v.* [20C] (Ulster) to walk in a mincing manner. [? SE *teeter* or dial. *tittle*, very lightly]

tittle-tat *n.* [1960s+] (Aus.) a gossip. [abbr. SE *tittle-tattle*]

tittup *see* TITUP.

titty *n.¹* [19C] milk. [TIT n.¹ (1), in this case a cow's udder]

titty *n.²* [19C+] a woman's breast. [dimin. of TIT n.¹ (1) and orig. the nipple only]

titty fuck *n.* [1990s] (US) masturbation or intercourse in which the man inserts his penis between the woman's breasts (cf. TIT FUCK). [TITTY n.² + FUCK n.¹]

titup/tittup *n.* [late 19C–1900s] the correct or fashionable thing. [SE *tittup*, a horse's canter]

tit up *v.* [late 19C] to toss coins in order to reach a decision. [note naut. use *tittup*, to toss for drinks]

titwank *n.* [1990s] a general term of abuse. [TIT n.¹ (1) + WANK n.]

tit willow *n.* [late 19C+] a pillow. [rhy. sl.]

titwrench *n.* [1990s] an extremely foolish or misguided person, usu. male. [TIT n.¹ (1) + SE *wrench*]

tityre-tu *see* TITTERY-TU.

tius *n.* [late 19C] a suit of clothes. [backsl.]

Tiv, the *n.* [late 19C–1910s] the *Ti*voli Music Hall, London. [abbr.]

'tives *n.* [1970s] (US campus) one's rela*tives* (cf. RELLIE). [abbr.]

tivvy *n.* [19C] the vagina. [SE *activity*]

'Tizer, the *n.* [mid-19C] the *Morning Adver*tis*er* newspaper (cf. TAP-TUB).

tiz up *v.* [1930s+] (Aus.) to dress up. [TIZZY v.]

tizz *see* TIZZY n.².

tizzy *n.¹* [early 19C] a sixpence (2½p). [? TILBURY or TESTER]

tizzy/tizz *n.²* [1930s+] (orig. US) a panic, a 'state', a flap (cf. ALL OF A TISWAS). [ety. unknown; ? echoic of one's rushing around, whether lit. or fig.]

tizzy *adj.* [1930s+] (Aus.) **1** showily or flashily overdressed. **2** of a person, ostentatious, showy, vulgar. **3** of an object, flashy but cheaply manufactured. [TIZ UP v.]

tizzy *v.* [1960s+] (Aus.) to titivate, to dress up in one's finery. [? SE *titivate* + *dress*]

T.J. *n.* [20C] (US) *T*i*j*uana, Mexico. [abbr.]

tjeers! *excl.* [1950s+] (S.Afr.) goodbye! (cf. CHEERS!).

tjommie *see* CHOMMIE.

tjorie/tjorrie *see* CHORRIE.

t.k.o. *v.* [1950s+] (orig. US) to defeat in theory, if not in practice. [boxing jargon *t.k.o.*, a technical *k*nock-*o*ut]

t.l. *n.* [1950s+] (US) a toady, a sycophant. [abbr. Yid. *toches lecher*, arse-licker]

t.l.c. *n.* [1960s+] (orig. US) kindness, consideration etc. [abbr. *tender loving care*]

t.m. *n.* [1930s+] (Aus.) a factory-made cigarette. [abbr. TAILOR-MADE]

T-man *n.* [1930s+] (US) a law enforcement officer of the US Treasury Department (cf. G-MAN). [abbr. the lit. *Treasury-man*]

t.n.t. *n.¹* [1960s+] the female breasts. [abbr. *two nifty tits*]

t.n.t. *n.²* [1970s+] (US Black) anyone or anything that is metaphorically 'dynamite', wonderful, exceptional etc. [SE *TNT*, trinitrotoluene]

t.n.t. *n.³* [1980s+] (drugs) **1** heroin. **2** fentanyl (cf. APACHE n.²). [? SE *TNT*, trinitrotoluene; i.e. its 'explosive' effects]

T.O. *n.* [1950s+] (US) *T*oronto, *O*ntario. [abbr.]

toac *n.* [mid-19C] a coat. [backsl.]

to a cat's whisker *phr.* [20C] (US) very well, exactly, perfectly. [the fineness of a cat's whisker]

to a cow's thumb *phr.* [late 17C–18C] (done) to the finest detail. [dial. *cow's thumb*, a hair's-breadth, a small space]

toac-tisaw *n.* [mid-19C] a waistcoat. [backsl.]

toad *n.¹* [20C] **1** (US) a Black person. **2** (US gay) an unattractive middle-aged gay man.

toad *n.²* [1980s+] (US) the penis.

toad in the hole *n.* [mid–late 19C] a sandwich man who carries four, rather than the usual two boards. He is thus completely surrounded by advertising displays (cf. SANDWICH n.¹).

toadskin *n.* **1** [mid-19C] (US) a 5-cent stamp; thus *his purse is made of toadskin*, he is a mean, grasping person. **2** [1920s] (US/Aus.) a banknote. [play on FROG n.⁵]

toad-stabber *n.* [late 19C–1930s] (US) a large pocketknife or jackknife (cf. PIGSTICKER). [note synon. army jargon *cat-stabber*]

toad-sticker *n.* [mid-19C–1940s] (US) **1** a sword. **2** a large knife (cf. PIGSTICKER).

to a fare-thee-well *phr.* [20C] (US) thoroughly, completely.

to a frog's hair *phr.* [20C] to the very smallest degree.

to and fro *n.* [20C] snow. [rhy. sl.]

to-and-/to'ing-and-fro'ing *n.* [1940s+] moving around from place to place or moving continually within the same place.

to-and-from *n.¹* [1910s+] a concertina. [the movements of the player's arms]

to-and-from *n.²* [1940s+] (Aus.) a British immigrant to Australia. [rhy. sl. *to-and-from* = POM]

toast *n.¹* [late 17C–late 19C] **1** the Devil. **2** a lively old man. [abbr. OLD TOAST]

toast *n.²* [1950s+] (US Und.) a long and epic poem, often trad. in prisons. [SE *toast*, a dedicatory remark prefacing the taking of a drink]

toast *n.³* [1950s–70s] (US Black) the best, the finest, anything outstanding. [i.e. that which deserves a SE *toast*]

toast adj. [1950s–70s] (US Black/teen) excellent, wonderful. [TOAST n.³]

toast v. [1960s+] (W.I.) of a disc jockey, to perform one's own lyrics to the background of a reggae song, usu. in a dub (no lyrics, only bass and rhythm lines) version. [SE toast, to make a speech when drinking someone's health]

toast adv. [1980s+] (US campus) in big trouble, the victim of misfortune, esp. in phr. you're toast.

toasted adj.¹ [1970s+] **1** tipsy, slightly drunk (cf. FRIED). **2** (drugs) intensely intoxicated by a drug.

toasted adj.² [1980s+] (US) physically or mentally exhausted (cf. BURNT OUT).

toaster n. [1960s+] (US Black) a singer of reggae rap music. [TOAST v.]

toasting fork/iron n. [late 16C–early 19C] a sword.

toast rack n. **1** [20C] a horse-drawn tram as found at Douglas, Isle of Man. **2** [1920s–50s] (Aus.) a footboard tram in Sydney. [supposed resemblance]

toast your blooming eyebrows! excl. [late 19C–1910s] a general excl. of disdain or dismissal; 'a delicate way of telling a man to go to blazes' (Ware).

tobacco baron see BARON n.

tobacco pipes/tobacco-pipe curls n. [late 19C] a curled hairstyle popular among contemporary London costers. [the curve of a pipe stem]

Tobacco Road n. [20C] (US) any primitive rural area (cf. JEETER). [Erskine Caldwell's novel Tobacco Road (1932)]

to beat the band phr. [late 19C+] (US) to the utmost, very much. [one drowns out the band]

to beat the Dutch phr. [mid-18C] to the utmost, very much. [one even convinces a phlegmatic Dutchman]

tober omee n. [late 19C+] (Ling. Fr./Polari) a landlord. [Rom. tober, road + OMEE]

to be sure phr. [late 19C] a phr. used at the end of a sentence to underline one's certainty, absolutely, certainly, definitely.

toboggan n. [1910s+] (US) a rapid decline, usu. towards ultimate disaster, esp. in phr. on the toboggan.

to burn a wet dog/mule phr. [late 19C] (US) in very large quantities, e.g. money to burn a wet dog. [the size/dampness of the animal requires a large fire]

toby n.¹ **1** [late 17C–mid-19C] the posterior, the buttocks (cf. TICKLE SOMEONE'S TOBY). **2** [late 17C–1920s] a woman's genitals. [Toby, dimin. of proper name Tobias; thus euph.]

toby n.² [19C] the road, the highway, esp. as a place where robbers and highwaymen can find their victims. [Shelta tobar or Rom. tober, the road, ? ult. Irish bothar, road. Note police jargon toby, an area, a police division]

toby n.³ [late 19C] (society) a frilled collar worn by women. [the style of collar trad. worn in Punch and Judy shows by the dog Toby]

toby n.⁴ [late 19C–1900s] (US) a second-rate brand of cigar (cf. STOGIE). [abbr. brandname Conestoga]

toby n.⁵ [1920s+] (Aus.) a simple, foolish man, but one who is kind and amenable and thus popular. [proper name Tobias, + ref. to Toby, Mr Punch's dog]

toby v. [early 19C] to rob someone on the highway; thus done for a toby, arrested for highway robbery. [TOBY n.². Note toby refers spec. to robbing while on horseback, highway robbery in general is SPICE n.]

toby concern see TOBY LAY.

toby-gill n. [mid-19C] a highwayman (cf. HIGH-TOBY-GLOAK). [TOBY n.² + GILL n.¹]

toby-gloak/-man n. [early–mid-19C] a highwayman (cf. TOBY-GILL). [TOBY n.² + GLOAK/SE man]

toby jug n. [20C] **1** a fool. **2** an ear. [rhy. sl. toby jug = MUG n.⁴/LUG n.¹]

toby lay/concern n. [19C] highway robbery. [TOBY n.² + LAY n.⁴ (2)/SE concern]

toby-man see TOBY-GLOAK.

toby trot n. [19C] a rustic simpleton (cf. TOM TUG). [proper name/TOBY n.² + SE trot]

toch eno! excl. [mid-19C+] look out! take care! etc. [backsl. hot one!]

toches/tochus/tokis/tokus/tuches/tuchis/tuckus n. [20C] posterior, buttocks. [synon. Yid. toches]

toches/tokus-licker n. [20C] (orig. US) a toady, a sycophant (cf. ASS KISSER; ASS-LICKER; T.L.). [TOCHES + SE licker]

tochus see TOCHES.

tockley n. [1990s] (Aus.) the penis. [ety. unknown; ? link to SE tag]

toco/toko n. [early 19C–1920s] punishment; thus give one toco, to beat one, to thrash one. [? Gk. tokoz, interest (OED), Hind. tokna, to censure (Y&B), Maori toko, a rod (E.P.)]

today adj. [1960s+] (orig. US) fashionable, up-to-the-minute (cf. HAPPENING).

toddle/toddle off v. [20C] to leave. [Vaux (1812) cites toddle as 'Und.' in 1812, but OED says SE. E.P. suggests that 20C use is colloq.]

toddler n. [early–mid-19C] a walker. [TODDLE; 20C use refers exclusively to infants. Note toddler, 'one who toddles', e.g. a child or an infirm old person, is Und. in Vaux (1812) but is SE in the OED]

toddlers n. [mid-19C] the legs. [TODDLE]

toddy blossom n. [19C] a red face caused by the bursting of blood vessels through excessive long-term drinking (cf. GROG BLOSSOM). [SE toddy + blossom(-faced), having a red, bloated face]

toddy-stick n. [mid–late 19C] a muddler, one who 'messes (things) around'. [SE toddy-stick, a spatula, usu. of glass or metal, for stirring toddy]

todge v. [late 18C–early 19C] to beat, to thrash. [dial. todge, a very thick soup, spoon-meat, i.e. meat boiled almost to paste]

todger see TADGER.

to die/die for phr. [1980s+] (US) excellent, wonderful, perfect, e.g. that boy is to die pretty (cf. DROP-DEAD; TO KILL FOR). [note OED cites a single late 19C use, but then nothing until 1980s]

todoment n. [20C] (W.I./Bdos.) **1** noise, confusion. **2** open-air fun and excitement (cf. KADOOMENT). [SE to-do + sfx. -ment]

tod sloan phr. [20C] alone (cf. ON ONE'S TOD). [rhy. sl.; ult. the jockey Tod Sloan]

toe n. [late 19C+] (Aus./N.Z.) strength, speed. [the use of the toe, i.e. the foot, in running]

toe adj.¹ [1970s+] (S.Afr.) very stupid. [Afk. toe, closed]

toe/toe up/torn up adj.² [1990s] (US Black/campus) drunk. [US Black pron. of TORE UP]

toe cover n. [1980s+] a useless present or gift. [the pointlessness of such an object]

toeface n. [1910s–20s] an unpleasant or dirty person (cf. TOERAG n.¹).

toe-jam n. [1930s+] (US) dead skin and dirt found between unwashed toes.

toe-jam queen n. [1960s] (US gay) a male homosexual foot-fetishist. [TOE-JAM + QUEEN n.¹]

toe party n. [1920s–30s] (US Black) a party game whereby all the women present line up behind a sheet with nothing visible but their toes. The men then take turns to choose their preferred toes and pair off accordingly.

toe queen n. [1950s+] (gay) a foot fetishist. [SE toe + QUEEN n.¹]

toerag n.¹ [mid-19C+] **1** a tramp. **2** any unappetizing old person. **3** (prison) any highly unpopular person, young or old. [SE toerag, the foot-bindings used by tramps. Puxley suggests rhy. sl. toerag = SLAG n.¹]

toerag n.[2] [late 19C] (Aus.) a £1 note. [SE *toerag*, the foot-bindings used by tramps]

toerag n.[3] [late 19C] (N.Z.) a handkerchief. [SE *toerag*]

toe-ragger/-rigger n. [late 19C+] (Aus./N.Z.) **1** a down-and-out vagrant. **2** a general term of contemptuous abuse. **3** one who is given a short prison sentence. [TOERAG n.[1]]

toe's length n. [early 19C–1910s] a very short distance.

toes lively adv. [1970s+] very fast (cf. TAKE TO THE TOE).

toe/kick someone's bum, to phr. [late 19C–1920s] to throw someone out, lit. 'to kick someone's behind'. [SE *toe/kick* + BUM n.[2]]

toes up adj. [mid-19C] lying dead. [abbr. SE *turn one's toes up*]

toe up see TOE adj.[2].

toey n. (Aus./N.Z.) **1** [late 19C–1900s] a fashionable, smart person, a 'swell'. **2** [1970s+] an alert person; one who is 'on their toes'. [? fig. use of TOE n.]

toey adj. [1930s+] (Aus./N.Z.) **1** nervous, touchy. **2** of a horse, fast. [TOE n.]

toff/toft n. **1** [mid-19C+] an aristocrat. **2** [mid-19C+] anyone considered either to be or to be posing as a superior person. **3** [mid-19C+] one who acts bravely or 'nobly'. **4** [late 19C+] one who behaves kindly, generously; thus [late 19C+] *you're a toff*, you're very kind, thank you very much. [? SE *tuft* as in TUFT-HUNTER (any link to TOFFEE-NOSED is invalidated by chronology)]

toffee n.[1] **1** [1930s] tobacco. **2** [1970s] gelignite. [the colour or shape]

toffee n.[2] [1960s+] nonsense, flattery. [? the 'sweetness' of its content]

toffee-nose n. [1940s+] (orig. milit.) a snobbish or supercilious person. [TOFF + a nose fig. stuck in the air to avoid the noxious smells of everyday life]

toffee-nosed adj. [1940s+] snobbish, arrogant. [TOFFEE-NOSE]

toffee whizz n. [1980s+] (drugs) amphetamines (cf. A n.[2]; BILLY WHIZ). [SE *toffee* + WHIZZ n.[5]; ult. ? a brandname]

toffer n. [mid-19C] a well-dressed prostitute. [TOFF]

tofficky adj. [mid-19C] showily or ostentatiously dressed. [TOFF]

toffish/toffy adj. [late 19C+] aristocratic, stylish, 'swell'. [TOFF]

toff-ken n. [mid–late 19C] the house of prosperous owners. [TOFF + KEN n.[1]]

toff omee n. [late 19C] a very fine gentleman. [TOFF + OMEE]

toff-shoving n. [late 19C] (Und.) pushing about well-dressed gentlemen in a crowd, presumably to facilitate picking their pockets. [TOFF + SE *shove*]

toffy/taffy/taffee n. [20C] (US Black) a Black person. [the colour]

toffy adj. see TOFFISH.

toft see TOFF.

tog/togge n. [early 18C–1900s] **1** an outer garment, a coat; thus [late 18C] *long tog*; [early 19C] *upper tog* (cf. UPPER BENJAMIN); [1900s] *tog and kicks*, coat and trousers (cf. KICKS n.[1]). [abbr. TOGE/TOGEMANS/TOGS]

tog v. [early 19C] **1** to get dressed. **2** to supply someone with clothing. [TOG n.]

tog-bound adj. [late 19C] lacking decent or fashionable clothes. [TOG + sfx. *-bound*, limited]

toge n. [late 17C–18C] a coat. [TOGEMANS]

togemans/togeman/togman n. [16C–early 19C] a coat (cf. TOGS). [Fr. *toge* or Lat. *toga*, toga + sfx. -MANS]

together adj. [1960s+] **1** aware, in control, self-assured. **2** united. **3** happy. **4** au fait, sophisticated.

tog-fencer n. [late 19C–1910s] a tailor. [TOG n. + joc. use of FENCER; thus effectively derog.]

togge see TOG n.

togged down adj. [1930s–40s] (US Black) very well dressed (cf. DOLLED OUT). [TOG v.]

togged out adj. [early–mid-19C] dressed up in one's finest (cf. DOLLED OUT). [TOG v.]

togged to the bricks phr. [1930s–40s] (US Black) dressed in style. [TOG v.]

togged up adj. [late 18C+] dressed up (cf. DOLLED UP). [TOG v.]

toggery n. **1** [early–mid-19C] clothing, harness 'domestic paraphernalia of any kind' (Hotten). **2** [early 19C–1920s] any variety of official or vocational dress. [TOGS (1)]

toggy n. [early 18C–1900s] a cloak, a coat. [TOG n.]

tog it see TOG UP.

tog-maker n. [late 19C–1900s] a cheap tailor. [TOG n. + SE *maker*]

togman see TOGEMANS.

tog out see TOG UP.

togs n. **1** [14C+] clothes, often in combs., e.g. *long togs*, *sporting togs*, *Sunday togs* (cf. TOGEMANS). **2** [1930s+] (Aus./N.Z.) a swimming costume. [Lat. *toga*, a toga or cloak. One of the earliest sl. terms, it is found in the line 'Alle with taghte mene and towne in togers fulle ryche' (Sir Thomas Malory, *Morte d'Arthur*, ?1470)]

tog up/it/out v. [18C+] to get dressed up, esp. in preparation for a night out, a party or similar event. [TOG v.]

to heaven adv. [20C] (US) strongly, very much.

to hell and go phr. [1930s+] (W.I./Guyn.) a general intensifier. [abbr. TO HELL AND GONE]

to hell and gone phr. [1930s+] **1** very far away, a very long time. **2** (US) irretrievably, thoroughly.

to hell with it! excl. [1910s+] a milder form of the dismissive excl. FUCK IT!

to hell with you! excl. [1910s+] a milder version of the dismissive excls. FUCK OFF!, FUCK YOU!

to high heaven phr. [20C] (US) strongly, very much.

toilet n. [1950s+] (orig. US) anywhere considered disgusting, esp. (show business) a third-rate venue.

toilet roll n. [20C] the dole. [rhy. sl.]

toilet talk n. [1950s+] obscenities, coarse language.

toilet time n. [1990s] (US Black) any unpleasant situation.

toilet water n. **1** [1960s] (US) beer (cf. PISS n.). **2** [1980s] (drugs) amyl nitrite (cf. AIMIES n.[2]). [one 'inhales' them both]

toil like a tar on a horse/horseback, to phr. [late 18C–early 19C] to work clumsily. [the incongruity of a TAR (sailor) on a horse]

toil shop n. [19C] that section of a prison devoted to hard labour. [SE *toil* + SHOP]

to'ing-and-fro'ing see TO-AND-FRO'ING.

Tojo n. [1940s] (Aus.) the Japanese nation, esp. its armed forces; thus *Tojoland*, Japan. [proper name *Hideki Tojo* (1884–1948), Japanese general and milit. dictator during WW2]

toke n.[1] **1** [mid-19C] a lump, a chunk, a portion. **2** [mid–late 19C] dry bread, esp. in comb. *skilly and toke*, gruel and dry bread, as served in prisons and workhouses (cf. SKILLY). **3** [late 19C] bread. **4** [late 19C] food in general. [ety. unknown, ? link to Scot. *token*, a small quantity]

toke n.[2] [1950s+] (orig. US Black) **1** a puff or drag of any kind of cigarette. **2** a marijuana cigarette. [TOKE v.]

toke n.[3] [1970s+] **1** (US gambling) a gambling chip, esp. one given to a dealer as a gratuity. **2** (US) a tip given to a cabdriver for bringing clients to a gambling establishment, brothel etc. [abbr. SE *token*]

toke v. [1950s+] (drugs) to take a puff on a marijuana cigarette or a pipe of crack cocaine. [? ext. of TOKE n.[1] (1); i.e. a portion of the drug]

token n. [18C] venereal disease (cf. TIP SOMEONE THE TOKEN; TOKENS). [SE *token*, a sign, in this case of disease]

tokens n. [mid-17C–early 18C] the plague (cf. TOKEN). [SE *token*, a sign, in this case the gangrenous spots on the body that indicated the disease]

to kill for phr. [20C] perfect, wonderful, incomparable (cf. DROP-DEAD; TO DIE).

tokis see TOCHES.

toko n.[1] see TOCO.

toko n.[2] [1920s+] (Aus.) praise, esp. if 'laid on with a trowel'. [fig. use of TOCO]

tokus see TOCHES.

tokus-licker see TOCHES-LICKER.

Tokyo rose n. [1940s–50s] the nose. [rhy. sl., ult. WW2 pro-Japanese propagandist *Tokyo Rose* (Iva Toguri D'Aquino)]

tol n.[1] [late 17C–late 18C] (Und.) a sword (cf. BILBO; RUM DEGEN). [abbr. proper name *Toledo*, from where the best swords came]

tol n.[2] [mid-19C] a lot, a share. [backsl.]

told out phr. [mid-19C] exhausted, run down, 'finished'. [SE *tell*, to count, to enumerate; lit. counted out]

tolerable adv. [early–mid-19C] acceptably, not too bad. [SE adv. *tolerably*]

tolerably adv. [late 18C] moderately, reasonably, well.

toley see TOLY.

toliban/tolliban rig n. [late 18C–early 19C] a confidence trick carried out by a woman who poses as a deaf and dumb conjurer. [? TOLOBEN + RIG n.[2] (2), but note *toliban*, a turban, emphasizing the 'Oriental' exoticism of conjurers]

toll dish n. [17C] the vagina. [SE *toll dish*, a vessel used to measure the grain ground at a mill; thus added inferences of *grinding* etc]

toller/rifler n. [16C] (Und.) a horse-stealer. [SE *toller*, tax gatherer]

tolliban rig see TOLIBAN RIG.

tol-lol adj. 1 [mid-19C] tolerable, bearable. 2 [late 19C+] (Aus.) overbearing. 3 [late 19C+] (Aus.) foppish. [SE *tolerable*]

tol-lollish adv. [mid-19C] tolerably. [TOL-LOL]

tollywhacker n. [1920s+] a roll of paper used as a club in children's play. [juv. *tolly*, a candle + WHACK n.[1]; thus the similarity in shape]

toloben/tullibon n. [late 18C–19C] make-up, face-paint. [Rom. *tullipen*, lard, grease. F&H add 'the tongue', but E.P. rejects this on ety. grounds]

to look at phr. [mid-19C+] on the surface, as far as one can judge superficially, whether of people, objects, situations or ideas; e.g. *She's not much to look at* or *To look at him, you'd think pop star but really he's a banker*.

toly/toley n. [1960s+] a piece of excrement. [? Scot. *toalie*, a small round cake]

tom n.[1] [17C] 1 a generic term for a man. 2 a fool (cf. DICKHEAD). [abbr. SE *tom fool*]

tom n.[2] [17C] a donkey, an ass (cf. BALDWIN).

tom/tommy n.[3] [mid–late 19C] the penis (cf. ABRAHAM; JOHN THOMAS).

tom n.[4] [late 19C] (society) a lesbian. [the masculine name; euphemized by Ware as 'one who does not care for the society of others than of her own sex']

tom n.[5] see TOM THUMB.

tom n.[6] [20C] (Aus.) a woman. [abbr. TOM-TART]

tom n.[7] [1920s+] a tomato (cf. TOMMY n.[4]). [abbr.]

tom n.[8] see TOM MIX.

tom n.[9] [1930s+] a prostitute, esp. one working in Mayfair (cf. EDIE). [abbr. US Und. *tommy*, a girl/TOM n.[6]/TOM-TART]

tom n.[10] see TOMTIT.

tom/tommy n.[11] [1950s+] (orig. US Black) a subservient Black person, fitting willingly into the stereotyped and inferior image refined by generations of White supremacy. [abbr. UNCLE TOM]

tom n.[12] [1950s+] jewellery (cf. TOMFOOLERY). [rhy. sl. *tomfoolery*]

tom n.[13] [1980s+] a British soldier. [abbr. TOMMY ATKINS]

tom n.[14] [1990s] (US campus) a computer. [abbr. *totally obedient moron*]

tom v.[1] 1 [17C] of a man, to have sexual intercourse (cf. CAULK; CLICKET; MOUNT; RIFLE; SERVICE; TREAD). [SE *tom-cat*]

tom/tom it around v.[2] [1930s+] 1 to work as a prostitute. 2 of a woman, to act in a promiscuous way. [TOM n.[9]]

tom/tom it up/tom slick v.[3] [1950s+] (mainly US) of a Black person, to act in an inferior and obsequious manner to Whites, to act as a Black stereotype. [TOM n.[11]]

tomahawk n. [late 19C] a policeman's truncheon.

tomahawker/tommyhawker n. [20C] (Aus.) a rough, incompetent shearer.

tom-a-lee n. [1940s–60s] (US Black) a subservient Black (cf. UNCLE TOM). [a Black subservient enough to have worked for the Confederate general Robert E. Lee (1807–70)]

tom and dick phr. [1970s+] to be sick (cf. BOB, HARRY AND DICK; TOM, HARRY AND DICK). [rhy. sl.]

tom and funny n. [late 19C+] money. [rhy. sl., 20C use as *tom* in S.Afr. only, the rhy. sl. origin has presumably been forgotten]

tom and jerry n. 1 [19C] a hard round hat. 2 [early 19C–1930s] a highly spiced punch. [for ety. see TOM AND JERRY SHOP]

tom and jerry adj. [20C] merry. [rhy. sl.]

tom and jerry days n. [19C] the Regency, the reign of George IV. [for ety. see TOM AND JERRY SHOP]

tom and jerry gang n. [early–mid-19C] a gang of rowdy men, devoted to womanizing, drinking, gaming and other pleasures. [for ety. see TOM AND JERRY SHOP]

tom and jerry shop n. [early–mid-19C] a cheap tavern. [*Tom and Jerry*, two fictional men-about-town created by Pierce Egan in *Life in London, or Days and Nights of Jerry Hawthorne and his elegant friend Corinthian Tom* (1821), who lent their name to this low inn (note synon. JERRY SHOP, with no bearing on the book and found a year earlier), and to a drink (which is still being drunk in Damon Runyon's short stories more than a century later; and to Warner Bros. cartoon cat and mouse]

tom and sam n. [20C] (Aus.) jam. [rhy. sl.]

tom-and-try v. [1960s–70s] (US Black) to advance oneself professionally by conforming to White stereotypes of Black behaviour. [TOM v.[3] + SE *try*]

tomasso di rotto n. [late 19C] (middle-class youth) nonsense, rubbish. [cod Ital. 'translation' of TOMMYROT]

tomato n. [1920s+] (US) an attractive woman; thus [1950s–60s] *ripe tomato*, one who is ready for seduction or even marriage (cf. BANANA n.[2]). [the luscious ripeness of the fruit]

tomato can n. [1920s–30s] (US) the badge worn by a local or small-town policeman. [the cheapness of its manufacture]

tomato sauce n. [20C] a horse; thus *tomato sauces*, the horses, i.e. horse-races. [rhy. sl.]

tomb n. [20C] (US) the anus. [i.e. it is 'deep and dark']

tombhead n. [1960s] (W.I.) 1 a large head. 2 a person who has such a head. [the rounded top of the head supposedly resembles a tombstone]

tom bray's bilk n. [early–mid-19C] (gaming) laying out the ace and deuce when playing cribbage. [? anecdotal]

tom brown n. [early–mid-19C] in gaming, the game of 'twelve in hand', generally known as cribbage. [? anecdotal]

Tombs, the n. [mid-19C+] (US) New York City prison. [one is 'buried' there]

tombstone n.[1] [mid-19C] a pawn ticket. [the inscription 'in memory of' and the implication that once pawned, items are rarely possessed again]

tombstone *n.*[2] [mid-19C–1900s] a snaggle- or crooked tooth. [resemblance]

tomcat *n.*[1] [20C] a doormat. [rhy. sl.]

tomcat *n.*[2] [1920s+] (orig. US) a womanizer, a philanderer. [reverse anthropomorphism]

tom cat *v.* [1920s+] (orig. US) to strut around looking for sexual conquests (cf. BILLY-GOAT). [TOMCAT *n.*[2]]

tomcat house *n.* [1920s+] a male homosexual brothel (cf. ACCOMMODATION HOUSE). [SE *tomcat* + CAT-HOUSE]

tom coney/cony/conney *n.* [17C–early 19C] a fool, the victim of a confidence trick (cf. CONY-CATCHER). [TOM *n.*[1] + CONY *n.*[1]]

tom, dick and harry *n.* [early 19C] any men, young or old, irrespective of given names (cf. HABRA, DABRA AND THE CREW). [orig. sl. but SE by mid-19C]

tom doodle *n.* [18C] a fool. [TOM *n.*[1] + DOODLE *n.*[1]]

tom doolies *n.* [1950s] the testicles. [rhy. sl. *tom doolies* = GOOLIES; the popular song 'Hang Down Your Head, Tom Dooley' by the Kingston Trio, 1958]

tom double *n.* [late 18C–mid-19C] an equivocator, a cheat, a 'double-dealer'. [TOM *n.*[1] + DOUBLE *n.*[1]]

tom drum's entertainment *see* JACK DRUM'S ENTERTAINMENT.

tom essence *n.* [early 18C] a fop, a dandy. [TOM *n.*[1] + SE *essence*, a perfume]

tomette *n.* [1960s] (US Black) a Black woman criticized for being too fond of White society. [TOM *n.*[11] + fem. sfx. *-ette*]

tom-farthing *n.* [17C] a fool. [TOM *n.*[1] + FARTHING]

tomfoolery *n.* [1930s+] jewellery (cf. TOM *n.*[12]). [rhy. sl.]

tom fool's token *n.* [late 17C–mid-18C] money.

tom, harry and dick *phr.* [20C] sick. [rhy. sl.]

tom it around *see* TOM *v.*[2].

tom it up *see* TOM *v.*[3].

tomjohn *n.* [19C] (Anglo-Ind.) a form of sedan chair, properly a *tonjon*, carried by a single pole and 4 bearers. [? Hind. *tamjham*, support-thigh, but Y&B admit 'we cannot tell the origin' and that this ety. 'might' mean 'support-thigh']

tom long *n.* [late 17C–18C] a bore, a teller of long and tedious stories with neither end nor point (cf. SEND BY TOM LONG). [the proverbial figure, *John Long* (16C) or *Tom Long* (17C), 'the carrier who will never do his errand']

tomming *n.*[1] [1930s+] **1** working as a prostitute. **2** having sexual intercourse, acting in a promiscuous manner. [TOM *v.*[2]]

tomming *n.*[2] [1950s+] (US Black) acting subserviently. [TOM *v.*[3]]

Tom Mix/tom *n.* [1930s+] **1** a problem, a predicament, a fix. **2** the number six. **3** an injection of heroin. [rhy. sl.; (3) = FIX *n.*[1]; ult. US film cowboy *Tom Mix* (1880–1940)]

tommy *n.*[1] **1** [late 18C–19C] bread; thus *brown tommy*, brown bread (cf. SOFT TOMMY). **2** [late 18C–19C] solid food in general. **3** [20C] (Aus.) bread baked with sugar and currants. [orig. milit. jargon *tommy*, the bread supplied as part of rations. This in turn had evolved from orig. 18C *brown george* to *brown tommy* to *tommy brown* and thence to its abbr. Note that St Thomas' Day, on which bread was distributed by charities, preceded the milit. coinage]

tommy *n.*[2] *see* TOM *n.*[3]

tommy *n.*[3] [mid-19C–1960s] (Aus/N.Z.) an axe. [SE *tomahawk*]

tommy *n.*[4] [late 19C] a tomato (cf. TOM *n.*[7]). [abbr.]

tommy *n.*[5] [late 19C] used as a term of address to a young boy whose real name is unknown.

tommy *n.*[6] [late 19C+] menstruation. [euph.]

tommy *n.*[7] *see* TOMMYROT.

tommy *n.*[8] *see* TOMMY ATKINS.

tommy *n.*[9] [1910s–20s] a pimp. [? generic use of proper name]

tommy *n.*[10] [1920s+] (Aus/N.Z.) **1** a bookmaker. **2** a bookmaker's ledger. [ety. unknown; unless a derog. ref. to TOMMY *n.*[9]; *DNZE* suggests rhy. sl. on SE *book* or *Tommy Rook* (cf. ROOK *n.*[1])]

tommy *n.*[11] *see* TOM *n.*[11].

tommy *v.*[1] *see* TOMMY TRIPE.

tommy *v.*[2] [20C] (Aus.) to leave. [ety. unknown]

tommy and exes *n.* [late 19C] bread, beer and tobacco. [TOMMY *n.*[1] + abbr. SE *extras*]

tommy atkins/tommy *n.* [late 19C+] a generic for a typical private soldier in the British army, usu. in abbr. *tommy* or *tom*. ['arising out of the casual use of this name in the specimen forms given in the official regulations from 1815 onward ... In some of the specimen forms other names are used; but "Thomas Atkins" being that used in all the forms for privates in the Cavalry or Infantry, is by far the most frequent, and thus became the most familiar; thus 1815 (Aug. 31) War Office, Collection of Orders, Regulations etc 75 (Form of a Soldier's Book in the Cavalry when filled up). Description, Service, &c. of Thomas Atkins, Private, No. 6 Troop, 6th Regt. of Dragoons. Where Born ... Parish of Odiham, Hants ... Bounty, £6. Received, Thomas Atkins, his x mark' (*OED*)]

tommy brown *n.* [late 18C–19C] bread (cf. TOMMY *n.*[1]).

tommy dodd *n.*[1] [mid-19C] **1** in coin-tossing, the 'odd man' who goes out. **2** the game of coin-tossing itself. **3** the winner or loser in coin-tossing, the choice for the name allotted by previous agreement. [rhy. sl. *tommy dodd* = odd]

tommy dodd *n.*[2] **1** [late 19C] a sodomite. **2** [late 19C–1950s] God. **3** [1920s+] (US) a gun. [rhy. sl.; (1) = *sod*; (3) = ROD *n.*[1] (2)]

tommy dodd *n.*[3] [late 19C+] (Aus./N.Z.) a small glass of beer. [? anecdotal]

Tommy Farr *n.* [20C] a bar. [rhy. sl., ult. UK boxer *Tommy Farr*]

tommy gun *n.* [1920s+] (orig. US Und.) a sub-machine gun. [one of the earliest brands, the .45 calibre *Thomson*]

tommyhawker *see* TOMAHAWKER.

tommy man *n.* [1930s] (US Und.) an armed gangster. [TOMMY (GUN) + SE *man*]

Tommy O'Rann *n.* [mid-19C] food. [rhy. sl. *Tommy O'Rann* = SCRAN]

tommy rabbit *n.* [late 19C] a pomegranate (cf. NANNY *n.*[3]). [rhy. sl., if weak]

tommy roller *n.* [late 19C+] a collar. [rhy. sl.]

tommy rollocks *n.* [20C] the testicles (cf. JIMMY ROLLOCKS). [rhy. sl. *tommy rollocks* = BOLLOCKS]

tommyrot/tommy *n.* [late 19C+] absolute nonsense (cf. TOMASSO DI ROTTO). [? the red coat of a TOMMY ATKINS, thus euph. for BLOODY]

tommyrot *v.* [late 19C+] **1** to fool around. **2** to hoax, to deceive, to humbug. [TOMMYROT *n.*]

tommy steeles *n.* [20C] eels. [rhy. sl.; ult. UK pop star *Tommy Steele* (b.1936)]

tommy talker *n.* [1930s+] a kazoo. [generic/assonant use of proper name *tommy* + its sound]

tommy tana/tanna/tanner *n.* [1900s] (Aus.) a nickname for a Pacific Islander imported as a labourer (cf. KANAKA). [generic use of proper name *Tommy* + *Tanna*, an island near Vanuatu (the Near Hebrides)]

tommy tit *n.* [mid-18C–19C] a smart young fellow. [generic/assonant use of proper name *tommy* + SE *tit*, a person]

tommy tripe *n.* [20C] a (tobacco) pipe. [rhy. sl.]

tommy tripe/tommy *v.* [mid-19C] to examine, to survey, to keep a watch. [rhy. sl. *tommy tripe* = PIPE *v.*[2]]

tommy tucker *n.* [20C] a person. [rhy. sl., *tommy tucker* = FUCKER + ref. to the nursery rhyme]

tommy tupper *n.* [20C] supper. [rhy. sl.]

tom noddy *n.* [20C] (US) a body, i.e. a corpse. [rhy. sl.]

Tom of Bedlam *n.* [16C–early 19C] a genuine beggar (cf. ABRAM MAN; BEDLAM BEGGAR; BESS OF BEDLAM; MAD TOM). [proper name *Bedlam*, by the 16C a generic term for lunatic asylums, but originally applied spec. to the Hospital of St Mary of Bethlehem in London. A general hospital by 1330, in 1402 it became a hospital for the insane]

tomorrow v. [20C] to borrow; usu. in abbr. phr. *on the tommy, looking for a loan.* [rhy. sl.]

tom out v. [1950s–70s] (US Black) of a Black person, to inform against another Black person. [TOM v.[3]]

tom pat n.[1] [late 17C] a parson. [abbr. PATRICO]

tom pat n.[2] [19C] a shoe. [Rom. *tom pat*, a foot]

tom patrol/squad n. [1950s+] the vice squad, esp. as regards prostitution. [TOM n.[9] + SE *patrol/squad*]

tom pepper n. [early 19C+] a liar. [orig. naut., a mythical sailor ejected from Hell for lying]

tom pudding n. [20C] a chain of iron 'compartment boats' ferrying coal on canals. [ety. unknown]

tom rig n. [late 17C–18C] a promiscuous young woman. [TOM n.[1] + SE *rig*, a wanton woman]

tom right n. [mid-19C] the night. [rhy. sl.]

toms see TOMTITS.

t.o.m.s n. [1960s+] (Can.) the urban power élite of Canada, living and working in the three major cities of Toronto, Ottowa and Montreal.

tom sawyer n. [late 19C+] a lawyer. [rhy. sl.]

tom slick n. [1950s–70s] (US Black) a Black police informer. [TOM n.[11] + SLICK n.[1]; i.e. they charm their friends and inform on them to the police]

tom slick see TOM v.[3].

tom squad see TOM PATROL.

tom-tart n. [late 19C] (Aus.) a woman (cf. TART; TOM n.[6]). [? rhy. sl. *tom-tart* = sweetheart]

tom tell-troth n. [17C] an honest man. [ext. of 14C SE *Tom True-Tongue*]

tom tell-truth n. [early 17C–mid-19C] an honest man. [ext. of 14C SE *Tom True-Tongue*]

tom thacker n. [late 19C–1900s] tobacco. [rhy. sl., pron. 'tobacca']

tom thumb/tom n. **1** [late 19C–1900s] (orig. Aus.) rum. **2** [20C] the buttocks. **3** [1940s+] (Aus.) inside information. [rhy. sl.; (2) BUM n.[2]; (3) DRUM n.[6]]

tom tiddler's ground n. [mid-19C–1910s] **1** anywhere that money or other items can be obtained easily. **2** a no-man's-land, a debatable territory. [the children's game *Tom Tiddler's ground*, in which one player is 'Tom', who stands behind a 'land' which marks the 'ground'. The other players dash forward over the ground, singing 'We're on Tom Tiddler's ground, picking up gold and silver', and the first or sometimes last child caught becomes Tom]

tom tiler/tyler n. [late 16C–mid-17C] an ordinary man, 'Mr Average'. [TOM n.[1] + SE *tier*, used as generic for any ordinary job; assonant here]

tomtit/tom n. [1940s+] an act of defecation. [rhy. sl. *tomtit* = SHIT n.[1]]

tomtit v. [late 19C+] to defecate. [rhy. sl. *tomtit* = SHIT v.]

tomtits/toms n. [1960s+] (Aus.) diarrhoea. [rhy. sl. *tomtits* = SHITS]

tom topper/tug n. [mid-19C] a ferryman, a waterman. [popular song]

tom tripe n. [mid-19C] a pipe. [rhy. sl.]

tom tug n.[1] [19C] a fool, a victim. [rhy. sl. *tom tug* + MUG n.[5] (1)]

tom tug n.[2] see TOM TOPPER.

tom tug n.[3] [late 19C] a bedbug. [rhy. sl.]

tom turdman n. [early 18C–early 19C] a nightsoil cleaner; thus *tom turdman's fields, tom turdman's hole,* the dump where the nightsoil is deposited (cf. GOLD-FINDER). [TOM n.[1] (1) + TURD]

tom tyler see TOM TILER.

tomyok see THOMYOK.

ton n. **1** [mid-18C+] a very large (unspecified) amount. **2** [1940s+] £100; thus *half a ton*, £50. **3** [1950s+] 100 miles per hour. **4** [1960s+] any unit of 100, e.g. 100 miles per hour, 100 years, 100 runs (in cricket). [SE *ton*, 100 cubic feet]

toncho n. [1980s+] (US drugs) an octane booster which is inhaled. [ety. unknown]

tondalayo n. [1950s–60s] (camp gay) an ostentatious, flagrant homosexual. [proper name of any 'African queen']

toney see TONY adj.

tongue n. [20C] (US Und.) a public defender, a lawyer (cf. DUMPTRUCK; MOUTHPIECE). [metonymy]

tongue v.[1] **1** [mid-19C] to talk down. **2** [20C] (Ulster) to scold.

tongue v.[2] [1930s+] **1** (gay) to perform cunnilingus. **2** to kiss with each partner's tongue in the other's mouth.

tongue bath see AROUND THE WORLD.

tongued adj. [mid-19C] talkative. [TONGUE v.[1] (1)]

tongue is well hung phr. [mid-18C] a phr. used to describe one who is articulate (cf. ONE'S TONGUE IS WELL HUNG).

tongue job n. [1960s+] (orig. US) oral sex, whether fellatio or cunnilingus (cf. TONGUE v.[2]). [SE *tongue* + JOB n.[3]]

tongue lash v. [1930s+] (US gay) to perform fellatio or anilingus.

tongue pad n. **1** [late 17C–early 19C] a talkative person, esp. one who persuades one to act foolishly or against one's will (cf. TONGUE-PADDER). **2** [early 18C] a confidence trickster. [SE *tongue* + PAD n.[1], on model of FOOTPAD].

tongue pad v. [late 17C–early 19C] to scold, to tell off. [TONGUE PAD n. (1)]

tongue-padder n. [late 17C–early 19C] a lawyer. [TONGUE PAD n. (1)]

tongue pie n. [1910s–20s] a scolding, a telling off.

tongue sushi n. [1980s] (US 'preppie') deep kissing, 'French kissing'. [SE *tongue* + *sushi*, a form of Japanese snack, usu. based on rice and raw fish]

tongue tally n. [1950s] (W.I.) a gossip. [SE *tongue* + *tally*, to count up, to reckon; ? the image of someone tallying up the performances of their friends and acquaintances]

tonic n.[1] [early–mid-19C] a halfpenny. [ety. unknown; ? link to TANNER]

tonic n.[2] [late 19C+] alcohol (cf. TINCTURE n.[1]); thus (Aus.) *tonicked*, drunk.

tonight's the night! excl. [1910s+] an excl. underlining the speaker's expectation of something exciting or important, esp. of a possible seduction.

tonk n.[1] [1930s+] (US/N.Z.) a seedy, 'lowlife' bar. [abbr. HONKYTONK]

tonk n.[2] [1940s+] (Aus.) **1** a male homosexual, or an effeminate heterosexual man. **2** a fool. **3** someone whose speech appears to set them above their peers. [ety. unknown, ? link to TONKY]

tonk v. [1910s+] **1** to hit. **2** to have sexual intercourse (cf. BANG v.[1]). **3** (Aus.) to punish. **4** to masturbate. [echoic]

tonky adj. [1930s+] (N.Z.) smart, fashionable. [? TONY + SWANKY adj. or Fr. (*bon*) *ton*]

ton o' my rocks n. [20C] (Aus.) socks. [rhy. sl.]

tons adj. **1** [late 18C+] a very large amount, a great deal, e.g. *I feel tons better now.* **2** [late 19C+] (US campus) very, extremely, really etc.

tonsil polish n. [1950s+] alcohol.

tons of soil n. [1900s] a working man's club or similar institution. [joc. play on the title of many such places, which advertised themselves as open to 'Fellow Workers and Sons of Toil']

Tonto n. [20C] a Native American who is considered insufficiently nationalistic and overly subservient to the White man by other Native Americans. [the character *Tonto*, the 'Red Indian' sidekick, played by Jay Silverheels (1919–80), who rode with TV's *Lone Ranger* (1952–6)]

tonto *adj.* [1980s+] crazy.

Tonto no go to town *phr.* [1990s] (US Black teen) it wouldn't be prudent at this juncture. [for ety. *see* TONTO n., the line was a catchphrase of the *Lone Ranger* TV show]

ton-up boy *n.* [1950s+] a member of a motorcycle gang (cf. ROCKER). [TON n. (4)]

tony *n.* [early 17C–late 18C] a fool. [abbr. of proper name; coined in Middleton's play *The Changeling* (1623)]

tony/toney *adj.* [late 19C+] (orig. US) classy, sophisticated, chic. [SE *tone*, style]

tony *v.* [mid-17C] to swindle, to trick. [TONY n.]

tonygle *v.* [mid-16C] to niggle. [misprint in Harman (1566)]

too all-but *phr.* [late 19C] (society) a general term of approbation, stressing the inarticulacy that seems to overcome the speaker in the face of something or someone so admirable (cf. TOO-TOO).

too-a-roo *see* TOOROO.

took bad *see* TAKEN BAD.

too bloody stew!/Irish stew! *excl.* [20C] too true! [rhy. sl.]

too dead to skin *phr.* [late 19C] (US) absolutely worthless (cf. TOO FULL OF HOLES TO SKIN).

toodle-/tootle-oo *phr.* [20C] goodbye (cf. TOODLE-PIP; TOOROO). [? SE *toot*, the tooting of a horn, in this case as a coach moves off or Fr. *à tout à l'heure*, goodbye]

toodle-pip *phr.* [1920s–30s] a nonsense word used to say goodbye (cf. TOODLE-OO).

too drunk to see through a ladder *see* CAN'T SEE THROUGH A LADDER.

tooeys *see* TOOIES.

too far north *phr.* [mid–late 19C] too clever, too knowing; thus *a little more north*, stronger (as of an alcoholic drink).

toofer *n.* [1910s] an expensive cigar (cf. TWOFER). [the price, 'two for' whatever the cost]

too — for words *phr.* [1910s+] (orig. US) a phr. used to mean that somebody is something (and adj.) to an extent that defies proper description, e.g. *too stupid for words*.

too full of holes to skin *phr.* [mid–late 19C] (US) totally riddled with bullets (cf. TOO DEAD TO SKIN).

too hot for one's kettle *phr.* [1980s+] (US) too frightening or dangerous to be tolerated.

tooies/tooeys/tooles/toolies/tuies *n.* [1960s+] (drugs) barbiturates, esp. Tuinal.

tool *n.* **1** [late 17C–mid-19C] an unskilful workman; usu. as *dull tool*, *poor tool*. **2** [19C] a whip. **3** [mid-19C] a small boy who is put through a window that is too small for the adult members of that gang to enter and who then opens the door to admit them (cf. DARKMANS BUDGE; FAGGER). **4** [mid-19C+] the penis (cf. FORNICATING ENGINE). **5** [mid-19C+] a useless, socially inept person (cf. PRICK n.). **6** [20C] (US Und.) a pickpocket. **7** [1930s+] a weapon, usu. a gun or knife (cf. TOOLED UP). **8** [1930s+] a burglar's implement, spec. a jemmy. **9** [1970s+] (US campus) a very hard worker. [SE *tool*, an instrument of manual operation, ult. ON *tol*, to prepare or make; (4) (meaning any bodily organ, but primarily the penis) was SE mid-16C–mid-19C]

tool *v.*[1] [mid-18C–late 19C] of a man, to have sexual intercourse. [TOOL n. (4)]

tool *v.*[2] **1** [19C] to drive a mail coach or any other horse-drawn vehicle. **2** [mid-19C+] to proceed in a leisurely, aimless way. **3** [mid-19C+] to leave at speed. **4** [20C] (US) to drive a car or any other vehicle. [SE *tool*, i.e. the harness etc]

tool *v.*[3] [mid-19C] to pick pockets (cf. MOLL-TOOLER; TOOLER). [the use of implements of *tools* to enhance one's dexterity]

tool *v.*[4] **1** [mid–late 19C] to murder, usu. with a knife. **2** [1940s+] to stab; to slash with a razor. [coined by Thomas

De Quincey (1785–1859), punning on SE *tool*, a dagger + the decoration or 'tooling' of a blade; (2) underpinned by TOOL n. (7)]

tool about/around *v.*[1] [1930s+] to behave in an aimless, irresponsible manner. [TOOL n. (5)]

tool about/around *v.*[2] [1970s+] (US campus) to drive around at random in a car. [ext. TOOL v.[2]]

tool along *v.* [mid-19C+] to drive fast. [ext. of TOOL v.[2]]

tool around *see* TOOL ABOUT.

toolbox *n.* [19C+] the vagina. [TOOL n. (4) + SE *box*]

tool chest *n.* [19C] the vagina (cf. COCK-HOLDER; NEEDLECASE; PIN-CASE; PIN-CUSHION; PINTLE-CASE; POLE-HOLE; TOOLBOX). [TOOL n. (4) + SE *chest*]

tooled/tooled up *adj.* [1940s+] carrying a weapon. [TOOL n. (7)]

tooler *n.* [mid-19C] a pickpocket (cf. MOLL-TOOLER). [TOOL n. (5)]

Tooleries *n.* [late 19C] Toole's Theatre, sited in William IV Street, London WC (cf. COLINDERIES).

tooles *see* TOOIES.

Tooley Street tailor *n.* [late 19C] a braggart, a boaster. [the three tailors of Tooley St (SE1) who supposedly put together a petition to Parliament. It carried none but their own signatures but was headed grandiosely, 'We the people of England ...']

toolhead *n.* [1970s+] (US campus) a fool, an idiot (cf. DICK-HEAD). [TOOL n. (4) or (5) + sfx. -HEAD (1)]

toolie *n.* [1970s+] (US campus) an engineering student. [SE *tool*]

toolies *see* TOOIES.

tool in *v.* [1970s+] (US campus) to arrive, usu. at speed. [TOOL v.[2] (5)]

tooling *n.* [mid–late 19C] skilful pickpocketing. [TOOL v.[3]]

toolman *n.* [1940s+] **1** a lock-picker. **2** (US) a safe-breaker. [TOOL n. (8) + SE *man*]

tool off *v.* [late 19C–1920s] to leave, to go away. [TOOL v.[2] (5)]

tools *n.*[1] **1** [early 19C+] (Und.) any implements used in the commission of crime, e.g. housebreaking implements, guns, pistols or other weapons (cf. TOOL n.; TOOLED UP). **2** [mid-19C–1900s] the human hands. **3** [late 19C+] (US) eating utensils.

tools *n.*[2] [1960s] (drugs) equipment used for injecting drugs (cf. OUFIT n.[2]; WORKS).

tool the tits, to *phr.* [mid-19C] to drive a coach or similar conveyance. [TOOL v.[2] + TIT n.[2]]

tool up *v.*[1] [1920s+] of a man, to prepare oneself for sexual intercourse. [pun on SE *tool up*/TOOL n. (4)]

tool up *v.*[2] [1950s+] to arm oneself. [TOOL n. (7)]

too many *adj.* [mid-19C–1920s] (US) overwhelming (cf. TOO MUCH).

too many chiefs and not enough Indians *see* ALL CHIEFS AND NO INDIANS.

too many cloths in the wind *phr.* [late 19C] drunk. [var. on THREE SHEETS IN THE WIND]

too mean to give you the time of day/part with one's shit *phr.* [20C] (US) extremely greedy, avaricious.

too mean to raise *phr.* [late 19C] (US) utterly contemptible. [note *mean* here is in SAmE sense, unpleasant + play on SE *mean*, avaricious + poker *raise*, to challenge another player by topping their bet; one who is mean will simply surrender]

too much *adj.* [1930s+] (orig. US) **1** wonderful, excellent, the very best; sometimes ext. as *too fucking much*. **2** unpleasant, disgusting or overwhelming. [abbr. SE *too much to take*]

too much! *excl.* [1930s+] an excl. of surprise or shock. [TOO MUCH adj.]

too much information *phr.* [1990s] (US teen) a phr. indicating that one wishes to be told nothing more on a subject; abbr. as *t.m.i.*, pron. 'timmy'.

too much like right *phr.* [1900s–50s] (US Black) impossible, unacceptable, used of someone who persists in avoiding what others define as the 'right' course of action.

too much of a good thing *phr.* [early 19C+] a phr. used of something that, while undoubtedly alluring, can prove to have definite disadvantages.

too much with us *phr.* [late 19C] (society) used of a bore.

toon *n.* [1980s+] an animated cartoon, and the animations that 'populate' it. [abbr. SE *cartoon*, coined for the film *Who Killed Roger Rabbit?* (1987), which mixed animation and live action]

to one's name *phr.* [late 19C+] belonging to one.

to one's own cheek *phr.* [mid-19C] **1** to oneself, for one's own private use. **2** a share or portion. [metonymic use of SE *cheek*, the side of the face]

tooniopperty/tuniopperty *n.* [1920s] opportunity. [joc. reversal]

too numerous to mention *phr.* [late 19C] extremely and angrily drunk. [euph.]

toop *n.* [1960s+] hair. [Fr. *toupée*, a wig]

tooraloorals *n.* [late 19C] (orig. theatre) a woman's breasts, esp. as exposed by a notably decolleté dress. [SE *toora-looralay*, a popular, often ribald, song chorus]

too rich for one's blood *phr.* [mid-19C+] (US) excessive in any sense or context.

too right! *excl.* [1910s+] (orig. Aus.) a general excl. of agreement.

tooroo/too-a-roo *phr.* [1910s+] (Aus.) goodbye. [TOODLE-OO]

toosh *n.* [mid–late 19C] a sovereign. [? TOSHEROON]

tooshie *n.* [1930s+] (US) the buttocks. [TOCHES]

too slow to catch cold/the seven-year/itch, to be *phr.* [20C] (US) to be extremely slow.

toot *n.*[1] (orig. US) **1** [late 18C+] a drinking match. **2** [late 18C+] a drunken binge or spree. **3** [late 18C+] a tea party. **4** [1930s+] a swallow of a drink. **5** [1970s+] cocaine. **6** [1970s+] a device for inhaling cocaine. **7** [1970s+] a measure of cocaine, enough for a single inhalation. [Scot. *tout*, to drink copiously, to take a large draught, thus ext. to drug use]

toot *n.*[2] [1960s+] **1** excrement. **2** (Aus.) a lavatory. **3** breaking wind. [? dial. *tut*, a small seat]

toot *n.*[3] [1970s+] (S.Afr.) the whole thing, the lot. [Ital. *tutti*, Fr. *tout*, everything, all]

toot *v.*[1] [1970s+] to inhale cocaine. [TOOT n.[1] (5)]

toot *v.*[2] [1970s+] to break wind. [TOOT n.[2] (3)]

toothache *n.* [19C] an erection (cf. IRISH TOOTHACHE). [euph.]

tooth booth *n.* [1940s] (US Black) a dentist's surgery.

tooth carpenter *n.* [1930s–40s] (US) a dentist (cf. IVORY-CARPENTER).

toothful *n.* [1920s] a measure of alcohol, a dram. [Scot. *toothful*, to tipple]

toothman *n.* [1950s–60s] (Aus.) a hearty eater.

tooth music *n.* [late 18C–early 19C] chewing.

toothpick *n.*[1] **1** [19C] a heavy club, a shillelagh. **2** [mid-19C+] (US) a pocketknife (cf. ARKANSAS TOOTHPICK; HARLEM TOOTH-PICK). **3** [late 19C–1900s] a narrow, pointed boat. **4** [1970s+] (US Black) a thin marijuana cigarette.

toothpick *n.*[2] [late 19C] (US) a native of Arkansas. [generic use of ARKANSAS TOOTHPICK]

toothy-pegs *n.* [early 19C+] (juv.) the teeth. [SE *tooth*]

tooti-frooti *n.* [1960s+] (US Black) a homosexual man. [play on FRUIT n.[2] (2) + lit. Ital. *tutti-frutti*, 'all the fruits', a type of ice-cream filled with chopped preserved fruits, nuts etc]

Tooting/Tooting Bec *n.* [late 19C–1930s] **1** a light kiss. **2** food. [rhy. sl; *Tooting Bec* (a London suburb) = (1) SE *peck*; (2) PECK n.[1] (1)]

tooting/touting *n.*[1] [late 17C–early 18C] drinking. [Scot. *tout*, to drink a draught]

tooting *n.*[2] [early 18C] wind music. [SE *toot*, to make a noise]

tooting *adj.* [1920s+] (orig. US) a general intensifier, usu. in combs., e.g. *darn/durn tooting*, *plumb tooting*, *too damn tooting*. [SE *toot*, to make a noise (of e.g. a siren or horn). The image is the intensity of one's statement having a 'noisy' impact]

Tooting Bec *see* TOOTING.

tooting-/touting-ken *n.* [late 17C–early 19C] a tavern, an alehouse. [Scot. *tout*, the act of drinking a large draught, a large draught of liquor + KEN n.[1]]

tooting stomps *n.* [1940s] (US Black) a fashionable style of shoe. [SE *toot* + STOMP n.]

too tired to pull a greased stick out of a dog's arse *phr.* [1980s+] (Aus.) exhausted.

tootle/tootle around/along/off *v.* [20C] to wander aimlessly (about/around/away). [SE *toddle*]

tootledum-pattick *n.* [19C] a fool. [Cornish dial.]

tootle off *see* TOOTLE.

tootle one's flute, to *phr.* [1980s+] to masturbate. [SKIN FLUTE]

tootle-oo *see* TOODLE-OO.

tootmobile *n.* [1960s] (US Black) a car. [the 'toot-toot' of its horn]

toot one's horn, to *phr.* [1970s+] to experience the immediate post-inhalation high from cocaine. [TOOT v.[1]]

too-too *adj.* [18C+] a general term of approval, usu. regarded as somewhat affected (cf. TOO ALL-BUT). [redup. of SE *too*, which emphasizes the adj.]

toots *n.* [1930s+] **1** a girl or girlfriend. **2** a general form of address, usu. to a woman. [abbr. TOOTSIE]

tootsie/tootsey-wootsey/tootsie-wootsie *n.* (orig. US) **1** [mid-19C+] a playful or affectionate name for a foot, usu. a child's foot. **2** [late 19C+] an affectionate name, usu. for a woman or girl, occas. a male lover (cf. TOOTS). **3** [20C] (Aus.) a lesbian. [development of baby-talk that created (1)]

Tootsie Roll *n.*[1] (drugs) **1** [1960s+] a marijuana cigarette. **2** [1970s+] heroin (cf. CHOCOLATE n.[2]). **3** methadone. [brandname *Tootsie Roll*, a small chocolate cake. (1) plays on SE *roll*; (2) on the consistency and colour of Mexican heroin]

Tootsie Roll *n.*[2] [1970s+] (US Black) an attractive woman (cf. BANANA n.[2]). [brandname *Tootsie Roll*, a small chocolate cake + ref. to JELLYROLL]

Tootsie Roll *n.*[3] [1990s] (US Black teen) a dance in which the knees are moved inwards and outwards, supposedly showing off one's buttocks. [? TUSH + SE *roll*]

tootsies *n.* [mid-19C+] the feet. [babytalk; 'those of ladies and children in particular. In married life it is said that the husband uses this expression for the first six months, after that he terms them HOOFS' (Hotten, 1867)]

tooty *adj.* [1960s+] condescending, supercilious, arrogant. [? HOITY-TOITY adj. or SNOOTY]

too utterly too *adj.* [late 19C] a general term of approval, usu. regarded as somewhat affected (cf. TOO-TOO).

top *n.*[1] [mid–late 19C] a dying speech on the gallows (cf. CROAK n.). [TOP v.[3]]

top *n.*[2] [1950s+] (US Und.) a maximum prison sentence.

top *n.*[3] [1960s+] in a sado-masochistic relationship, the dominant partner (cf. BOTTOM n.[4]).

top *n.*[4] [1980s+] (US drugs) a vial of crack cocaine. [different varieties are indicated by the variously coloured plastic tops of the vial]

top *adj.* [1990s] excellent, first-rate.

top *v.*[1] **1** [mid-17C–early 19C] to insult. **2** [mid-17C–mid-18C] to impose upon, to intrude. **3** [mid-17C] to oppose. [i.e. one places oneself 'on top' of the other person]

top *v.*[2] [late 17C–early 19C] (Und.) to cheat, esp. at cards; thus [late 19C] *top the deck*, to use a mechanical device hidden beneath one's cuff to hold a card until it is required, when it is slipped surreptitiously onto the deck. [SE *top*, the required card is made to appear at the top of the deck]

top *v.*[3] [early 18C+] to kill, esp. to execute by hanging (cf. TOP ONESELF).

top a clout, to *phr.* [early 19C] (Und.) to position a hand-kerchief in a victim's pocket in readiness for removing it at an apposite moment. [SE *top* + CLOUT n.[1]]

top and tail, to *phr.* [1930s+] to wash a baby's face and bottom, rather than giving it a bath.

top ballocks/bollocks/buttocks *n.* [late 19C+] a woman's breasts (cf. FOREBUTTOCKS). [SE *top* + BALLOCKS n.[1]; the round-ness of both]

top banana *n.* [1950s+] (US) the chief, the boss, the president (cf. TOP DOG). [show business *top banana*, the leading comic in a burlesque show]

top bollocks see TOP BALLOCKS.

top brass *n.* [1930s+] (US) the highest of military officers (cf. BRASS HAT). **2** (US) the highest executive manager.

top buttocks see TOP BALLOCKS.

top cat *n.* [20C] (US Black) the leader of a group, esp. of a clique of down-and-outs (cf. GORILLA; TOP DOG). [SE *top* + CAT n.[9]]

top deck *n.* [1920s+] (Aus.) the head.

top-diver *n.* [late 17C–early 19C] a lecher, a womanizer. [SE *dive on top* (*of*)]

top dog *n.* [20C] the boss, a senior member of an organization, a leader (cf. TOP CAT).

top dollar *n.* [1970s+] (US) a high price.

top drawer *adj.* [20C] socially élite, aristocratic, upper-class.

top drawing room *n.* [late 19C] a garret.

top dressing *n.* [19C] the hair.

top end *n.* **1** [late 19C] the head (cf. ATTIC). **2** [1930s+] (Aus.) northern Australia; thus *top-ender*, one who lives there (cf. UP TOP n.).

toper *n.* [mid–late 19C] the road (cf. TOBY n.[2]). [Rom. *tober*, the road]

top-fencer/-seller *n.* [mid-19C] a seller of dying speeches and 'famous last words'. [TOP n.[1] + FENCER/SE *seller*]

top flat *n.* [late 19C] the head (cf. ATTIC; TOP PIECE).

top gob *n.* [mid-19C] a pot-boy. [backsl.]

top gun *n.* [1980s+] (drugs) crack cocaine. [film title *Top Gun* (1985); the importance of crack cocaine in the drug hierarchy; the film deals with élite fighter-pilots]

top hat *n.* [20C] a fool. [rhy. sl. *top hat* = PRAT n. (6)]

top-heavy *adj.* [mid-17C–mid-19C] drunk (cf. BRICKY adj.[2]; HAVE A BRICK IN ONE'S HAT; TOPPED UP).

top-hole *adj.* [late 19C] excellent, first-rate, the best. [synon. with TOPNOTCH, i.e. the *top hole* in any measure]

top-hole! *excl.* [20C] excellent, wonderful, perfect. [TOP-HOLE adj.]

topi/tops *n.* [1960s] (drugs) **1** peyote. **2** mescaline. [? the top of the peyote cactus]

top joint *n.* [mid-19C] a pint (590ml) of beer. [rhy. sl., *joint* pron. *jint*]

top kick/kicker *n.* [1920s+] (orig. US) the boss, the head of a group, whether legal or criminal. [US army jargon *top kick*, a first sergeant]

topknot *n.* [18C–late 19C] the head (cf. ATTIC). [SE *topknot*, a tuft of hair or ribbon on top of the head]

toplights *n.* [18C] the eyes (cf. DEADLIGHTS).

top-loftical *adj.* [early 19C–1920s] haughty, arrogant. [SE *top* + *lofty*]

top-lofty *adj.* [mid-19C–1920s] haughty, arrogant. [SE *top* + *lofty*]

topman *n.*[1] [early 17C] a hangman (cf. TOPPING COVE; TOPSMAN). [TOP v.[3] + SE *man*]

top man *n.*[2] **1** [late 19C+] a leading villain. **2** [late 19C+] a police superintendent. **3** [1960s+] the dominant partner in a homosexual sado-masochistic couple (cf. BOTTOM MAN).

topnobber *n.* [1900s–20s] (Anglo-Irish) an important person. [SE *top* + NOB n.[2]]

topnotch *adj.* [mid-19C+] excellent, first-class.

top-off/top-off man/merchant *n.* [1930s+] (Aus.) an informer. [TOP OFF v.[3]]

top off *v.*[1] **1** [late 19C+] to finish off, to put the finishing touch to. **2** [1930s+] to fill up, to complete a cargo. **3** [1940s+] to fill up a petrol tank.

top off/on *v.*[2] (Aus.) [1910s] to attack, to assault. [ext. of TOP v.[3] or knock the *top*, i.e. head off]

top off *v.*[3] [1930s–50s] (Aus./N.Z.) to inform against. [? TIP OFF v.[2]]

top-off man/merchant see TOP-OFF n.

top of/top o' Rome *n.* [mid-19C–1920s] home. [rhy. sl.]

top of the bill *phr.* [20C] the best, the ultimate. [theatrical imagery]

top of the house *phr.* [1940s+] (bingo) the number 99 or 100. [the highest numbers on a card]

top on see TOP OFF v.[2].

top oneself *v.* [1950s+] to commit suicide. [TOP v.[3] + SE *one-self*]

top o' reeb *n.* [mid-19C] a pot of beer. [backsl.]

top o' Rome see TOP OF ROME.

top out *v.* [1950s+] to reach a limit. [building trade jargon *top out*, to finish off a high building, to construct the very top floor]

top over tail see TAIL OVER TOP.

topped *adj.* [mid-19C+] hanged. [TOP v.[3]]

topped up *adj.* [1960s+] drunk.

topper *n.*[1] **1** [18C] the boss, the master. **2** [early 18C–late 19C] an outstanding person or thing of its kind. **3** [late 18C–late 19C] a blow on the head. **4** [early 19C+] a top hat. **5** [late 19C–1900s] a tall, thin person. **6** [1930s+] (usu. US) a loosely cut jacket or coat, generally worn by women and children. **7** [1950s+] a supposedly (but probably not very) funny story or joke, it 'tops' or surpasses all others.

topper *n.*[2] [mid-19C–1900s] **1** the stub of a cigar or cigarette. **2** the remains of burnt tobacco left in a pipe; thus *topper-hunter*, one who scavenges for cigar or cigarette stubs.

topper *n.*[3] [1920s] (tramp) a sovereign. [it is the *top*, i.e. the best coin]

topper *n.*[4] [1920s–30s] a hangman. [TOP v.[3]]

topper *n.*[5] [1940s+] (Aus.) an informer (cf. TOP-OFF n.). [TOP OFF v.[3]]

topper *v.* [early–mid-19C] to kill with a blow on the head. [TOPPER n.[1] (3)]

toppie *n.* [1960s+] (S.Afr.) an old person of either sex. [? Zulu *thopi*, growing sparsely (e.g. of hair) or Hind. *topi*, a hat]

top piece/storey *n.* [mid-19C] the head (cf. ATTIC; TOP FLAT).

topping *n.* [late 17C+] execution by hanging. [TOP v.[3]]

topping *adj.* [early 19C+] excellent, enjoyable, first-rate. [SE *top*, 20C use is either ironic or consciously archaic]

topping cheat *n.* [late 17C–early 19C] the gallows. [TOP v.[3] + CHEAT n. (1); lit. 'hanging thing']

topping cove *n.* [mid-17C–mid-19C] a hangman (cf. TOPMAN n.[1]; TOPSMAN). [TOP v.[3] + COVE]

topping fellow *n.* [mid-17C–mid-19C] a hangman (cf. TOPPER n.[3]; TOPPING COVE). [TOP v.[3] + pun on SE *topping fellow*, an admirable man]

topping man *n.* [late 18C–early 19C] a superior, rich man. [TOPPING adj. + SE *man*]

topping shed *n.* [mid-19C–1950s] that part of a prison in which the gallows is kept. [TOP v.[3] + SE *shed*]

topple up one's heels see KICK UP ONE'S HEELS phr.[1].

toppy *adj.* [late 19C–1910s] tipsy, slightly drunk. [? SE *top-heavy*]

tops *n.*[1] [mid-19C] pamphlets and broadsheets that purport to detail last words from the gallows, deathbed confessions etc. [TOP n.[1]]

tops *n.*[2] [1930s+] (gambling) doctored dice used for cheating purposes. [the predicted side rolls to the *top*]

tops *n.*[3] [1930s+] (orig. US) the best, the ultimate, the winner.

tops *n.*[4] *see* TOPI.

tops *adv.* [1960s+] at the most, at the top estimate, e.g. *five years tops, ten quid tops*. [SE *at a top estimate*]

tops and bottoms *n.* [20C] a roll of notes in which only those on the very top and bottom are genuine, the rest being paper trimmed to fit and to bulk out the roll (cf. CALIFORNIA BANK-ROLL).

top sawyer *n.* [mid-19C] **1** the leader in any profession, job, occupation. **2** the best of its kind. [timber trade: 'It is a piece of Norfolk slang and took its rise from Norfolk being a great timber country, where the top sawyers get double the wages of those beneath them' (Egan's Grose, 1823)]

top-seller *see* TOP-FENCER.

top sergeant *n.* [1940s] (gay) a masculine lesbian (cf. SER-GEANT).

top set *n.* [1980s] a woman's breasts.

top shelf *n.* [1950s+] (N.Z.) spirits (cf. UPSTAIRS n.[1]). [as stored in a bar]

top-shelf *adj.* [1970s+] (US Black) excellent, first-class, the best.

topside *adj.* [late 19C] in charge, in control. [? pidgin use]

topsider *n.*[1] [1910s+] (Aus.) a lazy dog. [? TOPSIDE; the image is that such a dog controls the master rather than vice versa]

topsider *n.*[2] [1960s+] (US) a top-ranking executive. [he is on the 'top side' of the firm]

topsman *n.* [late 18C–early 19C] a hangman (cf. TOPMAN n.[1]; TOPPING COVE). [TOP v.[3] + SE *man*]

top storey *see* TOP PIECE.

topsy boozy *adj.* [late 19C] tipsy, half-drunk. [TOPSY (FRIZY) + BOOZY adj.]

topsy frizy *adj.* [late 18C–late 19C] tipsy, drunk. [one's *top* is SE *frizy*, curled]

topsy-versy *adj.* [mid-18C–1910s] upside down. [SE *topsy-turvy* + ARSY-VERSY]

top 'uns *n.* [1940s–50s] a woman's breasts (cf. TOP BALLOCKS; TOP SET).

top up *v.* [mid-19C+] to end up, to conclude. [to place a fig. *top* on]

to put it mildly, to *phr.* [1930s+] to downplay one's feelings, usu. ironic, i.e. to put it very strongly.

top woman *n.* [1940s+] a senior or most favoured prostitute among a group working for a given pimp (cf. SISTER-IN-LAW).

top-yob *n.* [mid-19C] a pot-boy. [backsl.]

torch *n.* **1** [1930s+] (US) an arsonist. **2** [1960s] (US Black) an oversized cigarette lighter. **3** [1960s+] (US prison) the murder of a fellow inmate by tossing a Molotov cocktail or petrol bomb into the cell (cf. BARBECUE n.[1]). **4** [1970s] (drugs) a marijuana cigarette. **5** [1980s+] (drugs) a butane lighter used to ignite a crack cocaine pipe; thus *torch cooking*, using such a lighter and pipe.

torch *v.* [1930s+] (US) to commit arson.

torch-cul/torchecul *n.* [late 17C–18C] lavatory paper. [synon. Fr. sl. *torchecul*, lit. 'give one's arse a quick smack']

torch for *v.* [1940s+] (orig. US) to mourn a dead love-affair; to offer unrequited love. [CARRY A TORCH]

torch job *n.* [1930s+] (US) an act of arson. [TORCH v. + JOB n.[5]]

torch up *v.* [1960s+] (drugs) to smoke marijuana.

torchy *adj.* [1940s+] (US) suffering unrequited love. [CARRY A TORCH]

torcida, la *n.* [1980s+] (US teen gang) prison. [Sp.]

tore/torn down *adj.* **1** [1940s+] (US Black) depressed, miserable. **2** [1940s+] (US Black) unattractive, ugly (cf. TORE UP). **3** [1950s–60s] (drugs) drunk or intoxicated by a drug.

tore out of the frame *phr.* [1970s] (US campus) drunk.

tore up *adj.* [1950s+] (US Black/campus) **1** miserable, depressed. **2** drunk. **3** ugly (cf. TORE DOWN).

to rights *adj.* [mid-19C+] first-rate, excellent. [legal jargon *to be to rights*, to have a legal case against someone]

tormented *adj.* [early 19C–1930s] (US) a mild synon. for DAMNED.

tormentor *n.* [late 19C–1910s] **1** a back-scratcher. **2** a water-squirter.

tormentor of catgut *n.* [late 18C–early 19C] a fiddle player, a violinist (cf. GUT-SCRAPER).

tormentor of sheepskin *n.* [late 18C–early 19C] a drummer.

tormentors *n.* [mid-19C] riding spurs (cf. PERSUADER).

torment the trouser trout, to *phr.* [1990s] to masturbate. [SE *torment* + TROUSER TROUT]

tornado *n.* [1980s+] (drugs) crack cocaine. [play on advertising copy for a household cleaner billed as the 'white tornado']

tornado juice *n.* [mid-late 19C] (US) whisky (cf. TORPEDO JUICE).

torn down *see* TORE DOWN.

torn up *see* TOE adj.[2].

torp *see* TORPEDO JUICE.

torpedo *n.*[1] [1920s+] (US) a thug, a hoodlum, the 'weapon' used by a gang boss and sent out to destroy enemies.

torpedo *n.*[2] **1** [1940s] a fat marijuana cigarette. **2** [1950s–60s] a drink containing chloral hydrate (cf. MICKEY FINN). **3** [1970s+] (drugs) a tablet or capsule of a narcotic drug. **4** [1980s+] (drugs) a cigarette made of crack cocaine and marijuana. [the explosive imagery implicit in SE *torpedo*]

torpedo juice/torp *n.* [1940s+] (orig. milit.) extremely strong, home-distilled liquor (cf. TORNADO JUICE). ['a combination of [bush beer and toddy] and acquires its name from its lethal effect. The original torpedo juice was the neat alcohol extracted from torpedoes during the war by American servicemen and sometimes mixed with local bush beers' (*The Guardian*, 26 September 1961)]

torqued *adj.* [1980s+] **1** (US campus) drunk, intoxicated by a drug (cf. TWISTED). **2** (US) angry.

torrac *n.* [mid-19C] **1** a carrot. **2** the penis; thus *phr.* of dismissal *ekat a torrac*, take a carrot (presumably + and *shove it ...*) (cf. CARROT n.[2]). [backsl.]

torrid *adj.* [late 18C–mid-19C] drunk.

torril *n.* [19C] a general insult referring to a woman or a horse. [dial.]

torso-tosser *n.* [1920s–50s] an erotic dancer.

torture the tentacle, to *phr.* [1990s] to masturbate.

Tory *n.* **1** [late 17C] any of the dispossessed Irish who became outlaws, subsisting by plundering and killing the English settlers and soldiers. **2** [late 17C] any outlaw, including Rajput marauders and Highland rebels. **3** [late 17C–early 18C] the nickname given to one who opposed the exclusion of James, duke of York (a Roman Catholic) from the succession to the British crown. [Irish *tóraidhe*, pursuer, although some sources define a *tory* as the one pursued, and therefore an outlaw. The Bill of Exclusion 'led to a common Use of slighting and opprobrious Words; such as Yorkist. That did not scandalize or reflect enough. Then they came to Tantivy, which implied Riding Post to Rome ... Then, observing that the Duke favoured Irish Men, all his Friends, or those accounted such by appearing against the Exclusion, were straight become Irish, and so wild Irish, thence BOGTROTTER, and in the Copia of the factious Language, the Word Tory was entertained, which signified the most despicable Savages among the Wild Irish' (Roger North, *Examen*, 1740)]

tory rory *n.* [18C] one who wears their hat cocked distinctly to one side. [TORY + proper name *Rory*]

t.o.s. *n.*[1] [1960s+] (US) men picked up in the street, usu. used by hotel clerks in those hotels which let out rooms to working prostitutes. [abbr. *tricks off the street*]

t.o.s. *n.*[2] [1990s] (USPR) *termination on sight* (cf. B.O.S.). [abbr.]

tosh *n.*[1] [19C+] (Und.) a pocket. [Fr. *poche*, a pocket]

tosh *n.*[2] *see* TOSHEROON.

tosh *n.*[3] [late 19C] a hat. [backsl.]

tosh *n.*[4] [late 19C] the penis. [? dial. *tosh*, a tusk, i.e. 'a projecting or unseemly tooth' (*EDD*)]

tosh *n.*[5] [late 19C+] (orig. Oxford Univ.) nonsense, rubbish. [? BOSH n.[1] or dial. *toshy*, muddy]

tosh *n.*[6] [1940s+] a form of familiar address to someone whose name one does not know (cf. MOOSH; MUSH). [? Scot. *tosh*, smart, neat or dial. *toshy*, of masculine appearance, hairy-faced]

tosh and waddle *phr.* [late 19C+] (Aus.) absolute nonsense. [TOSH n.[5], but rhy. sl. *tosh and waddle* = TWADDLE]

tosher *n.* 1 [mid-19C] one who scavenges items from the Thames mud (cf. MUDLARK). 2 [1970s] a painter and decorator. [dial. *toshy*, muddy]

tosheroon/tosh/tush/tusheroon/tusseroon *n.* [mid-19C–1950s] (orig. Ling. Fr./Polari) half-a-crown, 2s 6d (12½p). [? mispron. of Polari MADZA CAROON]

toshy *adj.* [1900s] trashy, rubbishy. [TOSH n.[5]]

toss *n.*[1] [late 18C+] an act of masturbation. [TOSS v.[1]]

toss *n.*[2] *see* TOSSER n.[1].

toss *n.*[3] [1970s+] a search carried out by police. [TOSS v.[4]]

toss *v.*[1] [mid-18C+] to masturbate (cf. BEAT OFF; TOSS OFF).

toss *v.*[2] [1930s+] 1 to get rid of, to discard. 2 to give up, to abandon (a task). [SE *toss away*]

toss *v.*[3] [1970s+] (US campus) to vomit. [TOSS ONE'S COOKIES]

toss *v.*[4] [1970s+] (US police) to search an apartment, car or person, esp. for weapons etc.

toss/toss off *v.*[5] [1980s+] (US campus) to flirt for lack of anything better to do. [? TOSS OFF v.[1]; i.e. the image of wasting time]

toss a party, to *phr.* [1950s+] (Aus.) to 'throw' a party.

toss a reverse lunch, to *phr.* [1970s+] (N.Z.) to vomit. [the regurgitation of food]

toss-bags *n.* [20C] an unpleasant, worthless person. [TOSS v.[1] + sfx. -BAG]

tossed *adj.* [19C] drunk. [SE *tossed*, disordered, but note Scot. *tosie*, tipsy]

tossed salad *n.* [1990s] 1 (US Black teen) anilingus embellished by an application of jam or syrup. 2 (gay) anilingus and anal intercourse (cf. TOSS ONE'S SALAD). [ety. unknown; ? the general mixing of flesh and embellishments]

tosser/toss *n.*[1] 1 [late 19C+] (Aus.) an affectionate term of address (cf. BASTARD). 2 [1970s+] a masturbator. 3 [1970s+] a despicable, worthless person (cf. JERK-OFF; WANKER). [TOSS v.[1]; note the chronology of (1) suggests a much earlier if uncited use of (2) and (3)]

tosser *n.*[2] [1910s–30s] any coin, esp. a sovereign. [SE *toss*, to throw]

toss gapper, to *phr.* [1950s–70s] (US Black) to give something to someone, esp. to hand over drugs. [SE *toss* + GAPPER]

tossicate *v.* [20C] (Ulster) to disturb, to worry. [SE *intoxication* + *toss*]

tossication *n.* [20C] (Ulster) a disturbance, a disruption. [TOSSICATE]

toss in/it in *v.* [1950s] (Aus./N.Z./US) to give up, to finish.

toss in one's agate, to *phr.* [1900s] (Aus.) to die (cf. THROW IN ONE'S ALLEY). [SE *agate*, a type of marble]

toss in one's/the jock, to *phr.* [1950s] (US) to give up, to quit (cf. THROW IN THE TOWEL). [SE *toss* + JOCK n.[2] (2)]

toss in the air *see* THROW IN THE AIR.

toss in the bucket, to *phr.* [1940s+] to imprison (cf. CAN v.[3]).

toss in the jock *see* TOSS IN ONE'S JOCK.

toss in the sponge/towel *see* THROW IN THE TOWEL.

toss it *v.* [20C] to masturbate. [TOSS v.[1]]

toss it in *see* TOSS IN.

toss it up airy, to *phr.* [1920s] to put on airs.

toss-off *n.* 1 [mid-18C+] an act of masturbation. 2 [20C] a worthless, unpleasant person (cf. JERK-OFF; WANKER). [TOSS v.[1]]

toss off/toss oneself off *v.*[1] [late 18C+] to masturbate (someone or oneself) (cf. BEAT OFF; TOSS v.[1]).

toss off *v.*[2] *see* TOSS v.[5].

toss one's cookies/tacos, to *phr.* [1970s+] (US campus) to vomit.

toss oneself off *see* TOSS OFF v.[1].

toss one's lollies, to *phr.* [1980s+] (N.Z.) to vomit. [SE *lollipop*]

toss one's salad, to *phr.* [1990s] (US prison) to engage in anal intercourse, seen by otherwise heterosexual participants as a 'clean' non-homosexual form of quick and easy gratification; thus insulting excl. *Toss my salad!* (cf. TOSSED SALAD).

toss parlour *n.* [1990s] a brothel. [TOSS v.[1]]

tossplank *n.* [1990s] an extremely irritating, unpleasant person (cf. TOSSER n.[1]). [TOSS OFF v.[1] + SE *plank*; i.e. their insensitivity]

tosspot *n.* [late 19C+] a fool. [SE *tosspot*, a drunkard]

tossprick *n.* [20C] a general term of abuse (cf. JERK-OFF; TOSS-OFF; WANKER). [TOSS v.[1] + PRICK n. (1)]

toss someone across *v.* [1910s] (US) to deceive, to cheat (cf. PUT IT ACROSS).

toss the bull/bull around, to *phr.* [1920s] (US) to chatter, to gossip. [SE *toss* + BULLSHIT n.]

toss the ham javelin, to *phr.* [1990s] to masturbate (cf. ACCOST THE OSCAR MEYER). [ext. of TOSS v.[1]]

toss the squares, to *phr.* [1970s] (US Black) to pass a pack of cigarettes. [SE *toss* + SQUARE n.[6]]

toss the tiger, to *phr.* [1960s+] (N.Z.) to vomit. [SE *tiger*, echoic of vomiting]

toss-up *n.*[1] [early 19C+] a wager (esp. fig.) in which chances are even and either eventuality is equally likely. [SE *toss up coins*]

toss-up *n.*[2] [1980s+] (drugs) a woman who trades sex for crack cocaine or for money to buy crack cocaine. [SE *toss*, to throw; she throws herself 'up to' the man]

tossy *adj.* [1910s–20s] arrogant, supercilious, conceited. [SE *tossy*, contemptuous]

tost *adj.* [19C] drunk. [SE *tossed*]

tostada/tostado *n.* [1960s–70s] (US Black) a derog. term for a Mexican. [Mex. *tostado*, a popular toasted snack composed of a deep-fried cornmeal pancake topped with a seasoned mixture of beans, mincemeat and vegetables.]

tostificated *adj.* [19C] 1 drunk. 2 tossed about, distracted, perplexed. [mispron. of SE *intoxicated* but note TOSSED; TOST]

tot *n.*[1] 1 [early 18C+] a very small or tiny child, an infant. 2 [early 19C+] a small glass of alcohol, e.g. a *tot of rum*. 3 [early 19C+] a very small quantity of anything. 4 [early–mid-19C] a very small drinking vessel. [ety. unknown]

tot *n.*[2] [mid-18C–late 19C] the *total*, the sum. [abbr.]

tot/tote *n.*[3] [mid-19C] a very heavy drinker. [TOT n.[1] (2)]

tot *n.*[4] [mid-19C+] a bone (cf. TOTTER); thus *tot-picker, tot-raker*, a scavenger, a 'rag-and-bone man' (cf. TOT-HUNTER). [Ger. *tod*, dead]

tot *n.*[5] [late 19C] a *total* abstainer from alcohol. [abbr. + ? joc. ref. to TOT n.[1] (2)]

tot/tot up *v.*[1] [late 18C+] to add up. [TOT n.[2]]

tot *v.*² [mid-19C–1900s] to drink a dram. [TOT n.¹ (2)]

tot *v.*³ [late 19C+] to go rag-picking or scavenging. [TOT n.⁴]

totacho *n.* [1960s+] (US) the slang used in the barrio (cf. CALÓ). [Sp. 'our talk']

total *adj.* [1980s+] (orig. US teen) a general intensifier; absolute, complete (cf. TOTALLY).

total *v.* [1970s+] (orig. US) **1** to crash a car so badly as to render it beyond repair. **2** to destroy, kill or maim anything or anyone. [i.e. to destroy *totally*]

total blowchoice *phr.* [1980s] (US teen) appealing but essentially irrelevant. [TOTAL adj. + BLOW v.³ (1) + SE *choice*; i.e. it would be a wasted choice]

total lame-out *n.* [1990s] (US teen) really dumb or boring. [TOTAL adj. + LAME adj.]

totalled/totalled out *adj.* [1970s+] (orig. US) **1** unattractive. **2** wrecked (usu. of a car). **3** drunk or drugged.

totally *adv.* [1980s+] (orig. US teen) a general intensifier, utterly, absolutely, completely (cf. TOTAL adj.).

totally! *excl.* [1980s+] (orig. US campus) a general excl. of approval or enthusiasm, absolutely! exactly! really!

totally clueless *adj.* [1950s+] (orig. US teen) ignorant, unaware. [note orig. but poss. distinct 1930s RAF use]

totally penelope pitstop *phr.* [1990s] (US teen) admirable, excellent, fashionable. [the 1980s+ TV cartoon *Penelope Pitstop*]

total wreck *n.* [20C] a cheque. [rhy. sl.]

tot book *n.* [late 19C] a book in which complex sums can be written down. [TOT v.¹]

tote *n.*¹ *see* TOT n.³.

Tote *n.*² [late 19C+] (orig. Aus.) **1** the *Totalizator*, a machine that calculates the number of tickets sold to betters on each horse/greyhound in a race. **2** the system of betting based on these calculations. [abbr.]

tote *v.*¹ [late 17C+] (US) to carry, to haul a load; thus *tote fair*, carry one's fair share, *tote load*, as much as one can carry. [the *OED* dismisses either Black or Ind. origins, but Farmer (1889) suggests OE *totian*, to lift up, to elevate and legal jargon *tolt*, a writ by which a cause was removed from a court baron to the county court, itself f. Lat. *tolle*, to lift or remove]

tote *v.*² [1930s+] (US) to add up. [SE *total*]

tote the mail *see* HAUL THE MAIL.

to the bad *phr.* [mid-19C+] in debt, 'in the red' (cf. GO TO THE BAD).

to the balls *phr.* [1930s+] (US) completely, to the utmost (cf. BALLS AND ALL). [BALLS n.¹]

to the bone *phr.* [1930s+] (US Black) to the extreme, to the ultimate extent, usu. in combs. (cf. CLEAN TO THE BONE phr.; FONKY TO THE BONE; LAID TO THE BONE phr.²; SILKED TO THE BONE; TABBED TO THE BONE).

to the bricks *phr.* [1920s+] (US Black) to the limit, to the furthest extent. [the *bricks* are those of the walls]

to the ceiling *phr.* [1950s] (US) to the limit, to an extreme extent.

to the curb *phr.* [1980s+] (US Black/campus) **1** ugly, distasteful, unpleasant. **2** impoverished. [synon. of SE phr. *in the gutter*]

to the curb, to be *phr.* [1980s+] (US campus) to vomit. [the polite person steps off the pavement and carefully vomits into the gutter]

to the dot *phr.* [20C] prompt (cf. ON THE DOT). [the *dot* of the letter 'i'; note 18C SE *to the dot*, exactly, precisely]

to the ears *phr.* [late 19C–1950s] (US) completely, fully, absolutely. [abbr. SE *up to the ears*]

to the fullness *see* FULLNESS.

to the/up to the handle *phr.* [mid-19C+] (US) thoroughly, completely.

to the lips *phr.* [early 17C–late 19C] to the limit, full up (cf. TO THE BALLS).

to the max *phr.* [1960s+] the best, the most extreme. [SE *maximum*, orig. in the California youth cultures]

to the nines *phr.* [early–mid-19C] dressed up in one's finest. [ety. unknown; most feasibly the use of 9 (3 × 3) as a 'lucky' number]

tother side *n.* [mid-19C+] (Aus.) **1** used in West Australia to refer to the eastern states. **2** in Tasmania, the Australian mainland; thus *tothersider*, one who lives in an eastern state or (in Tasmania) one living in mainland Australia. [SE *the other side*]

t'other sider *n.* [19C] (Aus.) a transported felon. [he has come from 'the other side of the world']

to the ruffian *phr.* (Und.) **1** [16C] go to the Devil! **2** [late 18C] to the utmost perfection (cf. UP TO THE NINES). [RUFFIN]

tot-hunter *n.* [late 19C] a collector of bones, which were recycled in a variety of manufacturing processes. [TOT n.⁴ + SE *hunter*]

tot-hunting *n.* [late 19C] wandering the streets in search of pretty women. [TOTTIE + SE *hunting* + play on TOT-HUNTER]

totsie *n.* [1930s] a young woman, usu. one who is sexually available. [var. on TOTTIE n.²]

totter *n.* [late 19C+] a 'rag-and-bone' man, a scavenger. [TOT v.³]

tottie/totty *n.*¹ [early 19C–1930s] (S.Afr.) **1** a Khoikhoi. **2** any Black or esp. 'coloured' person. [abbr. (*Hotten*)*tot*, the orig. and derog. name for the Khoikhoi]

tottie/totty *n.*² **1** [late 19C] a high-class prostitute. **2** [late 19C+] a young woman, usu. one who is sexually available. [TOT n.¹ (1)]

tottie/totty *adj.* [early 19C–1930s] (S.Afr.) unpopular, vulgar, unfashionable. [TOTTIE n.¹; i.e. the vulgarity of such a woman]

tottie fie/fay/hardbake *n.* [late 19C+] a woman, usu. a prostitute or at least an 'enthusiastic amateur', who dominates her surroundings. [TOTTIE n.² (1) + SE *fie!*]

totty *see* TOTTIE.

totty all colours *n.* [late 19C] a woman whose dress resembles a 'coat of many colours'. [TOTTIE n.²]

totty-headed *adj.* [late 18C–early 19C] foolish, giddy. [SE *totter*]

totty one-lung *n.* [late 19C] an asthmatic or a sufferer from tuberculosis who still manages to muster some degree of style. [TOTTIE n.²]

tot up *see* TOT v.¹.

touch *n.*¹ **1** [early 18C–mid-19C] any item that will persuade purchasers to buy, albeit within certain price limits; thus *a sixpence touch, a guinea touch*. **2** [mid-19C–1910s] an act of stealing or theft, esp. of pocket-picking. **3** [mid-19C+] a loan, usu. small, and usu. cadged rather than freely offered.

touch *n.*² [20C] (Aus.) style, fashion, manner. [SE *touch*, ability, esp. of a performer]

touch *n.*³ [1910s+] (Aus.) a simpleton. [SE *touched*, eccentric, mad]

touch *n.*⁴ [1950s+] a woman who can be easily picked up. [? SOFT TOUCH]

touch *v.*¹ **1** [mid-17C–19C] to take money into one's own hands, to steal. **2** [mid-18C+] to borrow money from; often as *touch someone for* (a sum of money) (cf. TAP SOMEONE FOR). **3** [19C] to pick someone's pocket. **4** [1950s] (Aus.) to swindle, to cheat.

touch *v.*² [mid-19C–1900s] to equal, to rival, to compare with.

touch all bases, to *phr.* [20C] (US) to be very thorough, or adaptable and versatile. [baseball imagery]

touch and tap *n.* [20C] a cap. [rhy. sl.]

touch base/ground *v.* [1980s+] to communicate with, to make contact. [baseball imagery]

touch bone and whistle! *excl.* [late 18C–early 19C] usu. as an imper. ['Anyone having broken wind backwards, according to the vulgar law, may be pinched by any of the company till he has touched bone (i.e. his teeth) and whistled', Grose (1788)]

touch crib *n.* [19C] a brothel. [SE *touch* + CRIB n.³]

touched *adj.* [mid–late 19C] tipsy. [SE *touched*, mentally unstable]

touch 'em up *n.* [19C] the vagina.

toucher *n.*¹ **1** [mid-19C+] a very tight fit, an instance of very close contact. **2** [1980s+] (US Black/drugs) one who becomes physically affectionate after smoking crack cocaine (cf. NON-TOUCHER). [SE *touch*]

toucher *n.*² [mid-19C+] a cadger, one who solicits small loans. [TOUCH v.¹ (2)]

touch for *v.* [mid-18C+] to borrow money from. [TOUCH v.¹ (2)]

touch ground *see* TOUCH BASE.

touch-hole *n.* [17C–late 19C] the vagina (cf. BLACK HOLE n.¹). [SE *touch-hole*, the vent of a firearm, through which the charge is ignited]

touchie-feelie *adj.* [1970s+] (US) pertaining to therapies and sensitivity training which encourage people to touch, hug and support one another physically.

touching *n.* [early 18C–late 19C] **1** obtaining money through theft or pocket-picking. **2** bribery. [TOUCH v.¹ (2)]

touching cloth *phr.* [1990s] urgently in need of defecation. [the stool is already protruding]

touch ivory *v.* [early–mid-19C] to play dice (cf. RATTLE THE IVORIES). [IVORY n.¹ (2)]

touch lucky *v.* [late 19C–1910s] to experience good fortune.

touch-me *n.* [late 19C–1920s] one shilling (5p). [rhy. sl. *touch-me-on-the-nob* = BOB n.³]

touch-my-nob *n.* [late 19C] one shilling (5p). [var. on TOUCH-ME]

touch of 'em *n.* (Aus.) **1** [1900s] delirium tremens. **2** [1940s–60s] diarrhoea. [euph.]

touch/case of the ... *phr.* [1970s+] used with pl. (often proper) nouns to imply a condition that is seen as typical of the n., e.g. *touch of the New Labours*, *case of the Princess Di's* (cf. CASE n.⁸).

touch of the hairy heel *phr.* [late 19C] (society) betraying one's lower-class origins. [the image is of a carthorse as compared to a racehorse]

touch of the holy bone *phr.* [19C+] (orig. Irish, then US) sexual intercourse. [ironic ref. to the supposed power of holy 'relics', but note BONE n.⁶]

touch of the jim brits *phr.* [1950s] (Aus.) nerves, edginess. [JIMMY BRITTS]

touch of the seconds *phr.* [1970s] last minute hesitation. [abbr. SE *second thoughts*]

touch/dash/lick of the tarbrush *phr.* [mid–late 19C] a derog. term used to described someone who supposedly has a degree of Black ancestry. [SE f. 1900]

touch-on *n.* [1940s+] an erection (cf. HARD-ON; ROOT-ON).

touch one's kick/pants/strides/tweeds, to *phr.* [1950s+] (N.Z.) to pay for a round of drinks. [SE *touch* + KICK n.⁴/SE *pants*/STRIDES n. (1)/SE *tweeds*]

touch one's sky, to *phr.* [1950s+] (Aus.) to pay for a round of drinks (cf. HIT THE CAN). [SE *touch* + SKY(-ROCKET)]

touch someone for *v.* [mid-18C+] to cadge. [ext. of TOUCH v.¹ (2)]

touch someone off *v.* [late 19C–1930s] to cadge. [ext. of TOUCH v.¹ (2)]

touch someone up *v.* [mid-19C+] to urge someone into action. [SE *touch up*, to tap (a horse) with a whip]

touch the bun for luck, to *phr.* [late 18C] to touch one's wife's or girlfriend's pudendum for luck before leaving on a journey. [BUN n.², orig. a RN tradition]

touch the can, to *phr.* [1950s+] (Aus.) to pay for a round of drinks. [CAN n.⁵]

touch the monkey's head, to *phr.* [1990s] of a woman, to place one's fingers on a man's penis. [? joc./supposed similarity]

touch the spot, to *phr.* [late 19C] to suit the circumstances, to be absolutely satisfactory in the context (cf. HIT THE SPOT).

touch-trap *n.* [17C–late 19C] the penis (cf. TOUCH-HOLE). [SE *touch-trap*, a contrivance that operates when *touched*]

touch up *v.* **1** [late 19C] to jog the memory. **2** [late 19C+] to fondle or molest sexually.

tough *adj.* **1** [20C] (orig. US) resolute, vigorously uncompromising, severe. **2** [1920s+] unfair, 'mean'. **3** [1950s+] (US Black/campus) admirable, attractive. [(3) on bad = good model]

tough/tough it out *v.* [mid-19C+] to deal determinedly and courageously with a difficult situation. [TOUGH adj.]

tough act to follow *see* HARD ACT TO FOLLOW.

tough apples! *excl.* [1960s–70s] (US) response indicating a lack of sympathy with the speaker (cf. TOUGH SHIT!). [? euph. or abbr. ROAD APPLE]

tough as a jockey's tail-end *phr.* [20C] used of one who is considered 'hard' or 'tough'. [i.e. his TAIL n.¹ (3)]

tough as Old Nick *phr.* [late 19C+] used of one who is considered 'hard' or 'tough'. [OLD NICK]

tough as shoe leather *phr.* [mid-19C+] used of one who is considered 'hard' or 'tough'.

tough as tacker *phr.* [late 19C] extremely tough. [SE *tough* + *tacker*, a hob-nail, used to strengthen the soles of boots and shoes]

tough baby *n.* [1930s+] a thug, a violent, lawless person (cf. TOUGH GUY). [SE *tough* + BABY n.²]

tough beans! *excl.* [1960s+] (US) bad luck (not that I care) (cf. TOUGH SHIT; TOUGH TITTY).

tough bickkies/biccies/bickies *see* STIFF BICKKIES.

tough boy *n.* [1950s+] a thug, a violent, lawless person (cf. TOUGH BABY).

tough cat *n.* [1950s+] (US Black) a man who is a successful womanizer. [TOUGH adj. + CAT n.⁹]

tough cookie *n.* [1930s+] (US) a survivor, an emotionally strong person. [TOUGH adj. (1) + COOKIE n.³]

tough dancing *n.* [20C] physically close dancing, emphasizing (and offering an opportunity for) sexual intimacy (cf. BELLY RUB; RUB n.³; RUB JOINT). [the term and style originated in the brothels of San Francisco's BARBARY COAST and spread into the mainstream dance-halls, or their less salubrious counterparts]

tough darts! *excl.* [1970s+] (US) an excl. of dismissal, uninterest, that's your bad luck! (cf. TOUGH TITTY!). [euph. for TOUGH TITTY]

tough egg *n.* [1930s+] a thug, a violent person. [play on HARD-BOILED]

tough fit *n.* [1950s–60s] (US Black) a well-cut suit or other garment. [TOUGH adj. (3) + SE *fit*]

tough gut *n.* [1920s–30s] (Can.) a strong, hardy person. [lit. 'tough stomach']

tough guy *n.* [1930s+] (orig. US) **1** a thug. **2** someone who cannot easily be checked or thwarted. [TOUGH adj. (1) + GUY n.]

toughie *n.* **1** [1940s+] a 'hard', ruthless, callous person. **2** [1970s+] something that one finds 'tough' to do, understand, accept etc. [TOUGH adj. (1) + sfx. -*ie*]

tough it out *see* TOUGH v.

tough luck *n.* [1910s+] bad luck, esp. as excl. *tough luck!* (cf. TOUGH SHIT; TOUGH TITTY).

tough noogies! *excl.* [1950s+] (US) (that's) bad luck! [SE *tough* + fig. use of NOOGIE]

tough nut *n.* [mid-19C+] (orig. US) a person difficult, obstinate or dangerous to deal with. [TOUGH adj. (1) + NUT n.³]

tough on *adj.* [late 19C+] (orig. US) hostile towards, making life hard for someone. [TOUGH adj. (1)]

tough shit *n.* [1950s+] (orig. US) unfortunate or unpleasant circumstances (cf. TOUGH TITTY). [SHIT n.¹ (1)]

tough shit! *excl.* [1950s+] so what! see if I care! a response indicating little or no sympathy with the first speaker. [TOUGH SHIT n.]

tough stuff *n.* [1970s] (US Black) anything appealing or pleasing in the realms of sex or drugs. [on bad = good model]

tough takkie *n.* [1910s+] (S.Afr.) hard luck. [SE *tough* + fig. use of TAKKIE]

tough/hard titty/titties/tits *n.* [1950s+] bad luck; thus *tough tits, toots*, a phr. of dismissal (cf. BAD BONGOS). [SE *tough/hard* + TITTY n.²/TIT n.¹ (1)]

tough 'un *n.* **1** [late 19C] a very great lie. **2** [1910s+] a 'tough' person.

toup *n.* [1950s+] a wig. [abbr. SE *toupee*]

toupee *n.* [mid-18C–mid-19C] **1** a woman's pubic hair. **2** a pubic wig or merkin. [SE *toupee*, a wig]

tour/toure/towre *v.* [mid-16C–mid-17C] (Und.) to see, to survey, to spy on. [? SE *tower*, to stand high above (so as to look down on)]

tour guide *n.* [1960s+] (US drugs) a person who aids and supports someone having a psychedelic drug experience. [play on TRIP n.³ (1)]

touristas/turistas *n.* [1950s+] any form of stomach upset contracted on a foreign holiday (cf. APPLE-BLOSSOM TWO-STEP). [Sp., lit. 'tourists']

tour of the grand dukes *n.* [late 19C–1910s] (society) a euph. phr. to describe a trip to visit the smart *demi-monde* of Paris.

tousle *n.* [mid–late 19C] bushy whiskers.

tout *n.* **1** [early 18C] a thief's look-out; thus *strong tout*, a very observant eye. **2** [late 18C–early 19C] a 'look-out house' (Grose 1785). **3** [early 19C] the act of spying or surveying. **4** [20C] (US) a person who sells betting advice. **5** [1950s+] (Irish/Scot.) an informer. **6** [1980s+] (drugs) a runner for a drug dealer (they bring the drugs to the client). [TOUT v.]

tout *v.* **1** [late 17C–mid-18C] (Und.) to keep a careful look-out, to be on one's guard. **2** [late 17C–late 19C] to watch, to spy on. [SE *tout*, to peep, to peer]

touter *n.* [mid-19C] (Und.) a thief's look-out. [TOUT v. + sfx. *-er*]

touting *see* TOOTING n.¹.

touting-ken *see* TOOTING-KEN.

touzery/towzery gang *n.* [mid-19C] mock-auction swindlers. [? SE *touse*, to pull about, to abuse]

touzle *v.* [19C] of a man, to have sexual intercourse (cf. BANG v.¹). [Scot. *touzle*, to handle (esp. a woman) rudely or indelicately]

tow *n.* [late 19C] money. [SE *tow*, strands of flax used for a light (money, like tow, 'burns' fast)]

towel *n.* [late 18C–early 19C] a cudgel. [abbr. OAKEN TOWEL]

towel *v.* [18C+] to beat, to cudgel, to thrash (cf. RUB DOWN WITH AN OAKEN CUDGEL). [TOWEL n.]

towel-head *n.* [1980s+] a derog. term for an Arab from the Middle East (cf. HANKIE-HEAD; RAG-HEAD n.¹). [SE *towel* + sfx. -HEAD (3)/SE *head*; the term became particularly popular during and after the Gulf War of 1991]

towelling *n.* [mid-19C–1900s] a thrashing, a beating. [TOWEL n.]

towel up *v.* [1910s+] (Aus.) to beat, to thrash. [TOWEL v.]

tower *n.*¹ [late 18C–early 19C] clipped money. [*Tower Hill*, London, a centre of contemporary criminality]

tower *n.*² [19C] false hair. [SE *tower*, a very high head-dress worn by women late 17C–early 18C]

tower *v.* [late 18C–early 19C] to spy upon (cf. TOUR). [SE *tower*, to rise to a great height (and thus be able to spy on the surrounding area)]

tower bridge *n.* [20C] a fridge. [rhy. sl.]

Tower Hill play *n.* [late 17C–early 19C] 'A slap on the face and a kick on the breech' (Grose 1785). [the criminal environs of *Tower Hill* where such rough-housing would have been common]

Tower Hill vinegar *n.* [16C] the swordsman's block (cf. PREACH ON TOWER HILL). [the sword preceded the noose as a means of execution; criminals, esp. political ones, were executed at the Tower of London]

tower rook *n.* [early 18C] an official guide to the Tower of London. [the ravens, whose presence is an essential part of the Tower's history]

towie *n.* [1970s] (Aus.) the driver of a *tow*-truck. [abbr.]

towline *see* TOW OUT.

town *n.* [late 19C] a halfpenny. [rhy. sl. *town* = BROWN n.²]

town bicycle *n.* [1920s+] (orig. Aus.) a very promiscuous woman, who is constantly 'ridden' (cf. BARRACK HACK).

town bike *n.* [1940s+] a very promiscuous woman, always 'good for a ride' (cf. BARRACK HACK).

town bull *n.* **1** [late 17C–19C] a promiscuous man (cf. LAWLESS AS A TOWN BULL; VILLAGE RAM). **2** [1910s–20s] a pimp or procurer. [SE *town bull*, a bull housed in turn by the cow-keepers of a village]

town clown *n.* [1920s–40s] (US) a policeman working in a village or small town.

town crier *n.* [20C] a liar. [rhy. sl.]

townie/towny *n.* **1** [early 19C+] a *town*-dweller, esp. a Londoner. **2** [mid–late 19C] a fellow *towns*man. **3** [mid-19C+] (usu. campus) an inhabitant of the *town* rather than of the campus. [abbr.]

town lands *n.* [late 18C–early 19C] the female breasts (cf. STREAM'S TOWN). [for ety. *see* TIPPERARY FORTUNE]

town pump/punch *n.* [1970s+] a very promiscuous woman (cf. BARBER'S CHAIR). [SE *town* + PUMP n.¹ (2)/PUNCH n.]

town rake *n.* [18C] a womanizer, a lecher (cf. TOWN BULL; TOWN STALLION). [SE *town* + RAKE]

towns and cities *n.* [1900s–40s] a woman's breasts (cf. BRADFORD CITIES). [rhy. sl. *towns and cities* = *titties* (*see* TITTY n.²)]

town shift *n.* **1** [mid-17C–mid-18C] a scoundrel, esp. a card-sharp. **2** [early 18C] a male homosexual. [(1) and poss. (2) his constantly changing his address to keep ahead of the authorities and outraged victims]

town stallion *n.* [18C] a womanizer, a lecher (cf. TOWN BULL; VILLAGE RAM).

town tabby *n.* [mid-19C] a smart dowager. [colloq. *Town*, London + TABBY (1)]

town trap *n.* [early 18C] a police constable. [SE *town* + TRAP n.²]

town-went *adj.* [1990s] (US campus) used of something that is/has been done to excess. [play on GO TO TOWN (ON)]

towny *see* TOWNIE.

tow out/towline *v.* [early–mid-19C] (Und.) to decoy a potential victim away from the victim's premises so that one's accomplice can enter and rob them. [naut. imagery]

towre *see* TOUR.

tow row *adj.* [late 18C–early 19C] drunk (and disorderly). [SE *tow row*, a hubbub, a din. Note milit. jargon *tow row*, a grenadier]

tow-row *v.* [late 18C–early 19C] to make a noisy disturbance. [TOW ROW]

Tow Street *n.* [19C] a fig. 'street' in which one is decoyed; thus *be in Tow Street*, to be decoyed, to be persuaded (against one's will). [SE *tow*, to dray]

towze v. [early 17C–mid-18C] to have sexual intercourse (cf. BANG v.[1]). [Scot. *touse*, to pull (a woman) about rudely or indelicately]

towzery gang see TOUZERY GANG.

tox v. [mid-17C] to in*tox*icate; thus *toxed*, *toxt*, intoxicated, drunk. [abbr.]

toxic waste dump n. [1980s+] (US campus) a person who uses drugs.

toxy n. [1960s] (drugs) a small container of opium. [? misreading of TOY n.[3]]

toy n.[1] [19C] the penis.

toy n.[2] [19C] a watch; thus *toy and tackle*, a watch and chain (cf. RED TOY; WHITE TOY).

toy n.[3] (drugs) **1** [1930s–60s] a small container, approx. 2.54 cm (1in) diam., used to hold prepared opium (cf. HOP TOY). **2** [1930s–60s] a measure of opium, a small ball, approx. the size of a pea. **3** [1960s] a hypodermic syringe.

toy n.[4] [1980s] (US Black teen) a gullible person, a fool.

toy v.[1] [19C] to work as a prostitute. [16C–19C SE *toy*, to flirt, to play amorously]

toy v.[2] [1990s] (US Black/teen) to destroy another graffiti artist's work by drawing over it; thus *toy someone out*. [? SE *toy*, to play with, to tease + implication of acting childishly]

toy boy n. [1980s+] a young attractive boy popular among older, richer women (cf. BIMBO). [i.e. his role as a plaything]

toy-getter n. [late 19C] a thief specializing in stealing watches. [TOY n.[2] + SE *getter*]

toys n.[1] **1** [1960s+] (drugs) equipment for injecting narcotics (cf. BIZ n.[2] TOY n.[3]). **2** [1970s+] any appliances designed to increase sexual pleasure or fantasies.

toys n.[2] [1980s+] (US Black teen) a problem. [abbr. *trouble on your system*]

toy soldier n. [1940s] (US Black) an officer cadet. [derisive use of SE]

trac n. [1960s+] (Aus.) a prisoner who refuses to accept the rules. [abbr. SE *intractable*]

trace/trace off v. [1950s+] (W.I. Rasta) to curse or speak abusively to someone. [? link to UK dial. *trace*, to tell stories of old times or SE *trace*, to track, to pursue]

Tracey see SHARON.

track/trag n.[1] [mid-19C] 1 quart (757ml). [backsl.]

track n.[2] **1** [mid-19C+] the highway or street as the home of tramps, prostitutes, pickpockets etc. **2** [late 19C+] (Aus.) any outback road. **3** [1930s–40s] (US Black) a dance-hall, a ballroom, esp. the Savoy Ballroom in Harlem. **4** [1930s+] (US Black) the world of pimping, hustling, confidence tricks etc; the Eastern cities are the *fast track*, California and the West are the *slow track* or *soft track*.

track n.[3] see TURF n.[2].

Track, the n.[4] [1960s+] (Aus.) the Stuart Highway running from Darwin to the south, also known as *the Bitumen*.

track n.[5] [1990s] (US) a con*tract* to murder someone. [abbr./pron.]

track v.[1] [late 19C] (US) to wander aimlessly.

track v.[2] [1970s+] to maintain emotional or verbal stability, to 'keep on the right track'.

track v.[3] [1980s+] (drugs) to inject a drug. [TRACKS]

track dolie n. [1930s] (Aus.) an itinerant. [TRACK n.[2] (1) + DOLIE. During the Depression itinerants were issued with food ration cards, but were not allowed to remain in any one place]

tracking n. [1980s+] (drugs) injecting intravenously. [TRACK v.[3]]

track record n. [1960s+] (US) a reputation, of a person or thing, based on past performance.

tracks n. [1940s+] (drugs) punctures and scar tissue that accumulate along the veins of a regular drug addict (cf. HIT-MARK).

track square/straight v. [1910s+] (Aus.) to pursue a love affair with honourable intentions (i.e. eventual marriage rather than short-term sex) (cf. TRACK WITH). [SE *track* + SQUARE adj./STRAIGHT adj.[1]]

track up the dancers, to phr. [late 17C–late 19C] to rush quickly up the stairs. [SE *track*, to make one's way + DANCERS]

track with v. [1910s+] (Aus.) to associate with someone of the opposite sex (cf. TRACK SQUARE).

trade n.[1] **1** [late 17C+] prostitution. **2** [1930s+] a prostitute's client. **3** [1930s+] (gay) a man with whom one has (commercial) sex, a male prostitute (cf. ASS PEDDLER).

Trade, the n.[2] [1910s+] (orig. naut.) the Submarine Service. **2** [1960s+] the Secret Service.

trade adj. [1930s+] (gay) used of someone involved in commercial sex. [TRADE n.[1] (3)]

trade v. [1930s+] (US gay) to go looking for sexual partners (cf. CRUISE v.[1]). [TRADE n.[1] (3)]

trademark n. [late 19C] a scratch on the face.

trader n. [late 17C–mid-18C] a prostitute (cf. TRADE n.[1]; TRADING DAME). [TRADE n.[1] (1)]

tradesman n. [19C] a thief. [joc. euph.]

tradesman's/tradesman's entrance n. [1990s] the anus; thus *go in by/up the tradesman's*, to have anal intercourse. [a pun on *back passage*]

trading dame n. [late 17C] a prostitute (cf. TRADER). [TRADE n.[1] (1) + SE *dame*]

trading justices n. [late 18C–early 19C] 'Broken mechanics, discharged footmen, and other low fellows, smuggled into the commission of the peace, who subsist by fomenting disputes, granting warrants, and otherwise retailing justice' (Grose 1796).

traffic/traffique n. [16C] (Und.) a prostitute, esp. one working as a confidence trickster (cf. COMMODITY). [SE *traffic*, the buying and selling of goods or the goods themselves]

traffic cop n. [20C] (orig. US) a traffic policeman. [SE *traffic* + COP n.[1]]

traffique see TRAFFIC.

trag see TRACK n.[1].

tragic adj. [1970s+] an all-purpose neg. meaning disastrous, appalling, very bad.

tragic magic n. [1980s+] (US drugs) crack cocaine dipped in phencyclidine. [the potentially unpleasant, if exciting, effects]

trago n. [1960s+] (US) a drink. [Sp.]

trail n. [late 19C–1900s] a hoax. [TRAIL v.]

trail v. [late 19C–1900s] to hoax, to fool. [18C SE *trail*, to persuade, to seduce (non-sexually)]

trailer n. **1** [16C] a horse thief. **2** [late 16C] a footpad. [they *trail* their victims]

trailer trash/trash n. [1990s] (US) poor Whites living in trailers (large, static caravans), exhibiting a lack of sophistication and enjoying what is seen as a distasteful lifestyle. [SE *trailer* + (WHITE) TRASH]

trails n. [1980s+] (drugs) colourful incandescent paths in the air, 'seen' in the wake of moving objects by those who have taken hallucinogens such as LSD. [the SE *vapour trails* produced by jet aircraft]

trail the wing, to phr. [20C] (Ulster) to seek sympathy. [ornithological imagery]

traily adj. [mid-19C] weak, slovenly, languid. [orig. Cumbrian dial., such a person 'trails around']

train n.[1] [1960s+] (US Und.) transportation from one prison to another, the mode of transport is irrelevant (cf. BOAT n.[2]; DRAFT).

train n.[2] [1970s+] multiple orgasms; thus *toot one's train*, to achieve multiple orgasms. [one is 'riding along']

train *v.*[1] [late 19C] (US, mainly New England) to romp, to play around, to 'carry on'. [pun on CARRY ON (1)/SE *carry on*, to keep going]

train/train with *v.*[2] [late 19C–1940s] (US) to associate with, to cooperate with.

train *v.*[3] [1970s+] (Aus./US) of a woman, to have sex with several men in a single session. [(PULL A) TRAIN + an undertone of SE *train*, to teach (one) disciplined behaviour. This is not gang-rape as such, since the woman is ostensibly willing, but she may in reality have little option but to accede. Originated during a well-publicized incident at Ingham, N. Queensland in 1977]

train it *v.* [late 19C+] to travel by train.

trainspotter *n.* [1980s+] an obsessive, one who specializes in the collection of trivia, the knowledge of minutiae etc (cf. ANORAK). [generic use of SE]

train up *v.* [mid–late 19C+] to go fast, to hurry up.

train with *see* TRAIN *v.*[2].

traipse *see* TRAPES.

trake *n.* [1990s] (US Black teen) a general term of abuse, lit. somebody down whose throat you want to thrust your fingers. [SE *tracheostomy*, the operation of making an opening in the trachea (the windpipe) near its upper end, so that the patient can breathe through it]

trake- *pfx.* [1990s] (US Black teen) combined with a n. to create various terms of abuse, e.g. *trakeface, trakehead.* [TRAKE n.]

tra-la-la! *excl.* [late 19C] goodbye.

tra-la-las *n.* [late 19C] 'one of the wealthiest and most dissipated class of dissipated men' (B&L). [? his ability to say 'Tra-la-la!' to cares and problems that might cause trouble for less wealthy or dissipated people]

trallyagger *n.* [20C] (Irish) a loose thread hanging from the hemline of one's clothing (cf. TALLYWAGGER). [SE *trail*, to drag behind + *wag*]

tram fare *n.* [late 19C] twopence, esp. as a euph. used by the lowest ranks of prostitutes.

tramline *n.* [1940s+] a scar (cf. STRIPE).

tramlined *adj.* [1920s] of trousers, having a double crease due to poor ironing.

trammie/trammy *n.* [1910s+] (Aus./N.Z.) the driver or conductor of a *tram.* [abbr.]

tramp *n.* [1920s+] (orig. US) a promiscuous woman. [her 'wandering' from man to man]

tramp/tramp it *v.*[1] **1** [mid-19C+] to travel or wander, esp. as a beggar. **2** [mid–late 19C+] to cure one's feeling ill or 'out of sorts' by 'walking it off'. [SE *tramp*, to stride]

tramp/tramp it *v.*[2] [late 19C] to take a voyage on a tramp steamer.

tramp *v.*[3] [1940s+] (Aus.) to dismiss (from a job). [SE *tramp*, to stamp on, to crush]

tramped *adj.* [1920s+] (Aus.) dismissed from one's job. [TRAMP *v.*[3]]

trampers *n.* [19C] the feet. [SE *tramp*]

tramp it *see* TRAMP *v.*[1], *v.*[2].

trampler *n.* [early–mid-17C] a go-between, an intermediary, a lawyer. [they *trample* the path]

tramp's lagging *n.* [1940s–50s] (prison) a sentence of 90 days in imprisonment, commonly that meted out for vagrancy (cf. BEGGAR'S LAGGING). [SE *tramp* + LAGGING]

trams *n.* [20C] the legs. [rhy. sl. *tram* = GAM n.[1]]

tram troub/trube *see* TROUB.

trank/tranq *n.* (drugs) **1** [1960s+] any type of *tranquillizer*; thus *tranked, tranked out,* drugged by tranquillizers. **2** [1980s+] phencyclidine (cf. ACE n.[3]). [abbr.; (2) is used non-recreationally as an animal tranquillizer]

tranklement *n.* [19C] the stomach, the intestines (cf. TROLLOBUBS). [ety. unknown, logically SE *tracklement*, a jelly to accompany meat, but this was unknown until its coinage in 1954]

tranny/trannie *n.* **1** [1960s+] a transistor radio. **2** [1960s+] a Ford *Transit* van. **3** [1980s+] a transvestite. **4** [1980s+] a transsexual. [abbr.]

tranq *see* TRANK.

Trans, the *n.*[1] [1920s+] (Aus.) the train that runs from Adelaide to Perth across, i.e. *trans,* the Nullarbor Plain.

trans *n.*[2] [1970s+] (US Black/teen) a car. [abbr. SE *transport*]

transfer *v.* [late 19C] (society) to steal (cf. LIBERATE). [euph.]

transformer *n.* [1990s] (US Black gang) a spy. [the toy *Transformers,* popular in the 1980s, which appear to be one thing, e.g. a car, but can be changed into another, e.g. a robot]

translated *adj.* [late 19C] (society) very drunk, poss. to the extent of passing out. [satirical play on SE *translate,* to be taken to heaven]

translate the truth, to *phr.* [late 19C] (society) to lie. [euph.]

translators *n.* [late 17C–mid-19C] **1** second-hand shoes that have been rebuilt by the shoemaker and then resold. **2** the shoemakers specializing in this trade. [SE *translator,* a cobbler who renovates old shoes]

transmogrify / transmigrafy / transmogriphy / transmugrify *v.* [mid-16C–19C] **1** to metamorphose, to alter. **2** to astonish, to confound. [subseq. SE, *OED* suggests orig. version was *transmigrafy* and links it to illiterate corruption of SE *transmigure* or *transmigrate,* to move from one place to another]

transnear *v.* [late 17C–early 19C] to come up with or draw level with (a person). [? 17C SE *transnear,* to cross a street so as to meet]

tranx *n.* [1970s+] (drugs) *tranq*uillizers, any form of benzodiazepine (cf. TRANK). [abbr.]

trap *n.*[1] [late 17C–19C] **1** trickery, fraud; thus *understand trap,* to be aware, to know what is in one's interest, *up to trap,* aware, *trap is down,* the trick has failed (cf. SMELL TRAP).

trap *n.*[2] [early 18C+] (usu. in pl.) a policeman or similar agent of the law. [metonymy, by late 19C Aus. only]

trap *n.*[3] [late 18C+] the mouth, esp. in phrs. *keep your trap shut, shut your trap.*

trap *n.*[4] [19C] a small, sprung, two-wheeled carriage, a gig. [abbr. SE *rattletrap,* anything shaky or rickety]

trap *n.*[5] **1** [20C] a cubicle or stall in a public lavatory. **2** [1930s+] a place, esp. a nightclub. **3** [1960s] (drugs) a hiding place for drugs.

trap *n.*[6] [1940s] (US Black) the military draft during WW2.

trap *n.*[7] [1960s+] (US Black) the number of customers a prostitute is assigned as a daily tally by her pimp to reach a financial target; thus *trap money,* her daily earnings. [i.e. those whom she SE *traps*]

trap *n.*[8] [1980s+] (US campus) a woman who appears to be taking an interest in a man and then turns indifferent. [? *trap,* i.e. 'a snare and a delusion']

trap *v.* [1990s] (US Black teen) to sell drugs. [? link to TRAP n.[7]]

trapan/trepan *n.* [mid-17C–18C] (Und.) a person who benefits by ensnaring other people into actions that will harm them. [SE *trap*]

trapan/trepan *v.* [mid-17C–18C] (Und.) to ensnare, to deceive. [TRAPAN n.]

trapes/trapse/traipse *n.* [late 17C–mid-19C] **1** a slatternly woman. **2** a tedious, laborious task. [TRAPES v.]

trapes/traipse *v.* [late 16C+] to trudge about, to walk in a slovenly, aimless manner (with the image or actuality of one's clothes dragging on the ground). [? synon. SE *trape,* but chrono. is dubious (one citation 1440, then none until 1706, after coinage of *traipse*). ? OFr. *trapasser, trepasser,* to pass over or beyond]

trapeze artist n. [1930s+] **1** a sexual contortionist. **2** a woman who enjoys cunnilingus, esp. as part of sex exhibitions. [ARTIST n.²]

trapish adj. [18C] slovenly, aimless, dawdling. [TRAPES]

trap number two see TRAP TWO.

trap off v. [1990s] (US) to plea-bargain. [ety. unknown; ? the image of taking *off* a SE *trap*]

trapper n. [late 19C] a horse that draws a small two-wheeled carriage. [ext. of TRAP n.⁴]

traps n.¹ [early 19C+] **1** one's personal effects. **2** (Aus.) a pack. [SE *trappings*]

traps n.² [20C] drums or other percussion devices. [ety. unknown, ? fig. use of SE]

trapse see TRAPES.

trapstick n. **1** [late 17C–19C] the penis. **2** [early 18C–mid-19C] usu. in pl., legs, esp. thin legs. [SE *trapstick*, a stick used in the game of trap or trap-ball]

trap two/number two n. [1990s] the anus; thus *take it up trap two*, to submit to anal intercourse. [joc. use of greyhound terminology]

trash n.¹ [16C] money (cf. CRAP n.¹; DUST n.¹; MUCK n.¹). [the identification of money and dirt]

trash n.² see WHITE TRASH.

trash n.³ see TRAILER TRASH.

trash v. **1** [1960s+] to break windows, destroy appliances etc as part of a demonstration; thus *trasher*, a (political) vandal, *trashing*, the action of political vandalism. **2** [1960s+] to malign (cf. RUBBISH v.). **3** [1970s+] to beat up, to injure badly. **4** [1970s+] to criticize (a work of art or similar creative effort) so as to undermine its validity. **5** [1970s+] (US) to scavenge discarded goods, other people's rubbish. [SAmE *trash*, rubbish, garbage. (1) coined by the radical Weatherman movement. Note the 1960s 'underground' revolutionary cartoon hero 'Trashman', created by Spain Rodriguez]

trash an' ready adj. [1990s] (W.I./UK Black teen) attractive, fashionable, trendy. [ety. unknown]

trash around v. [1970s+] to slum, to pose as poorer than one is. [WHITE TRASH]

trash bag v. [1990s] to murder, dismember and dispose of in bin-liners or rubbish sacks. [SAmE *trash-bag*, a rubbish sack]

trashed adj. [1970s+] **1** very drunk. **2** very intoxicated by a drug. [fig. use of TRASH v. (3)]

trashmouth n. [1970s+] (US campus) one who regularly uses profanity or obscenity (cf. GARBAGE MOUTH). [SAmE *trash* + SE *mouth*]

trash talk v. [1960s+] (orig. US Black) to talk nonsense, to lie (cf. SELL A WOOF). [SAmE *trash*, rubbish]

trashy adj. **1** [mid-19C+] worthless, disreputable. **2** [1930s+] (US) characteristic of 'poor White trash' (cf. WHITE TRASH). **3** [1970s+] sluttish, tarty. [SAmE *trash*, rubbish]

trasseno see TROSSENO.

trat n.¹ [late 19C–1900s] a young and attractive prostitute. [backsl. *trat* = TART n. (2)]

trat/tratt n.² [1960s] a *trattoria* or small, Italianate restaurant, esp. fashionable in 1960s. [abbr.]

travel v. [late 19C+] to move quickly.

travel agent n. [1960s] (drugs) **1** LSD. **2** an LSD supplier. **3** an LSD guide. [play on TRIP n.³ (1)]

travel by Harry Pannell, to phr. [1920s+] (N.Z.) to go by foot, to walk. [*H(arry) Pannell* & Co; makers of stout walking boots]

travel by Mr Foot's horse see TAKE MR FOOT'S HORSE.

travel by rail, to phr. [1930s+] (Aus.) to be so drunk that one can only proceed by hanging onto things.

traveller n. **1** [18C–mid-19C] a highwayman. **2** [mid-18C–19C] a tramp. **3** [19C] an itinerant pedlar. **4** [19C] (Und.) a thief who moves from town to town. **5** [19C+] a gypsy. **6** [late 19C–1900s] a sermon which can be delivered by the same preacher on different occasions and in different places. **7** [1980s+] a young itinerant who travels the UK by car or caravan but has no Romany connections and is often from a hippie, punk or similar youth subculture and is often interested in a variety of 'green' or allied issues.

traveller at Her Majesty's Expense n. [mid-19C–1900s] a convict condemned to be transported.

traveller's tale/talent n. [early–mid-19C] a 'tall story', an exaggerated account (cf. TIP THE TRAVELLER).

travelling dandruff see GALLOPING DANDRUFF.

travel on one's thumb, to phr. [1920s+] to hitchhike. [the raising of one's thumb in hope of a lift]

travel on the slug, to phr. [mid-19C] (Aus.) to get credit on the basis of showing shopkeepers a large *slug* of silver, claiming that it is just part of a much larger strike.

trawler n. [1920s+] (Aus.) a police car or van. [it *trawls* the streets looking for suspects]

tray/trey n.¹ [late 19C+] **1** three, whether as a digit or a set of three. **2** a three-month prison sentence. **2** [1960s+] (US drugs) $3's worth of a given drug. [Ital. *tre*, three]

tray n.² see TREY-BIT.

trays n. [1980s+] (drugs) crack cocaine vials, in bundles of three.

tray saltee n. [mid-19C] threepence (cf. MADZA SALTEE). [Ital. *tre soldi*]

tray-trapper n. [1900s–50s] (Aus.) one who takes round a collection, 'passes round the hat'. [TREY-BIT + SE *trapper*]

treach adj. [1980s+] (teen) very good, excellent (cf. AWFUL adj.). [abbr. SE *treacherous*, on bad = good model]

treacle n. **1** [late 18C+] inferior port. **2** [early 19C] glutinously sentimental love-making.

treacle!/treacle-trousers! excl. [1920s] (Aus.) a jibe aimed at one whose trousers are too short. [? they stick to the wearer's legs]

treacle-arse n. [1940s–50s] (Aus.) a passive homosexual (cf. HONEY-BUM). [SE *treacle* + ARSE n.¹]

treacle-billy n. [20C] (Irish) a lodging house. [TREACLE (-MAN) n. (2)]

treacle-man n. [late 19C] **1** a good-looking man who works as a decoy for burglars by charming the housemaid while the gang slip in unnoticed. **2** a smooth-talking, good-looking travelling salesman, who 'sweet-talks' the 'lady of the house' into buying his wares. **3** a shop assistant, esp. in a draper's, who has the same effect on customers. [the stickiness and sweetness of SE *treacle*]

treacle sleep n. [mid-19C] deep, uninterrupted sleep. [the slow pouring of thick SE *treacle*]

Treacle Town n. [late 19C] **1** Bristol. **2** Macclesfield. [(1) its treacle refineries; (2) F&H posit an unlikely story of a treacle hogshead bursting and inundating the town's gutters]

treacle-trousers! see TREACLE!

tread v. [16C] of a man, to have sexual intercourse. [SE *tread*, of the male bird, to copulate with]

treaders n. [1940s] (US Black) shoes.

treadle/treddle n. [17C] a prostitute. [TREAD v.]

tread one's shoe awry, to phr. [mid-19C] to work as a prostitute.

tread one's shoe straight, to phr. [mid-19C] to be a respectable woman.

tread on someone's toes see STEP ON SOMEONE'S TOES.

treasure n.¹ [mid-16C+] **1** an admirable person. **2** an affectionate term of address, occas. abbr. as *treas*.

treasure n.² [19C] the vagina. [a relatively rare pos. image, also see TREASURE OF LOVE]

treasure of love n. [mid–late 18C] the vagina.

Treasure State n. [1930s] (US) Montana. [its reserves of precious metals]

treat *n.* **1** [late 18C+] anything (or occas. anyone) admirable, enjoyable or pleasurable, also used ironically. **2** [1980s+] (US campus) a good-looking woman.

treat, a *adv.* [late 19C+] wonderfully, extremely, excessively, e.g. *that'll go down a treat*.

treat like shit, to *phr.* [20C] to treat in a vile and unpleasant manner, deservedly or not. [SHIT n.[1] (1)]

treble cleft *n.* [19C] the vagina. [female physiology + pun on musical *treble clef*]

treble chance *n.* [20C] a dance. [rhy. sl.]

treddle *see* TREADLE.

tree *n.*[1] [1960s] (US Black, Los Angeles) a policeman who is susceptible to bribery. [play on SE *green* of a tree and GREEN n.[2]]

tree *n.*[2] [1980s+] (US campus) a very tall woman, 1.8m (6ft) or more (cf. TROLL n.[2]); thus *cherry tree*, a very tall virgin.

tree and sap *n.* [20C] (Aus.) a tap (faucet). [rhy. sl.]

treed *n.* [1980s+] (US drugs) extremely intoxicated by a drug.

tree-hugger/tree nymph *n.* [1990s] (US campus) an environmentalist.

tree-jumper *n.* [20C] (US prison) a rapist or sexual molester. [his jumping out of trees to attack a victim]

tree nymph *see* TREE-HUGGER.

tree of knowledge *n.* [1940s+] (S.Afr. drugs) marijuana.

trees *n.* [1990s] (drugs) marijuana.

tree suit *n.* [1940s–70s] (US Black) a coffin (cf. WOODEN OVERCOAT). [SE *tree*, i.e. wood]

tree that bears fruit all year round *n.* [late 18C–early 19C] the gallows (cf. DEADLY NEVERGREEN).

treewins *see* THREESWINS.

tree with three corners *n.* [late 18C–early 19C] the gallows (cf. DEADLY NEVERGREEN; THREE-CORNERED TREE).

tref/treff/trif/triff *n.* [1940s+] (US Und.) a clandestine meeting. [Ger. *Treffen*, meeting]

trembler *n.* [1960s+] (US prison) a young or new prisoner who is afraid of the other convicts.

tremblers *n.* **1** [19C] (Anglo-Irish) the stairs. **2** [1960s+] a woman's breasts, esp. when large, thus able to tremble.

trembles *n.* [19C] delirium tremens.

tremendous *adj.* [early 19C+] extraordinary, esp. admirable, remarkable.

trench *n.* [19C] the vagina (cf. GROTTO).

trenches *n.* [1990s] (US Black teen) any impoverished area.

trendinista *n.* (US campus) **1** [1980s] a political or social activist who combines heightened political consciousness with stylish clothing. **2** [1990s] someone who champions temporarily fashionable causes. [SE *trend* + a play on the Nicaraguan *Sandinistas*]

trendoid *n.* [1980s+] one who is slavishly devoted to following the latest trends (but never quite achieves the correct effect). [SE *trend*; on pattern of SF *android*, a human-like robot]

trendy *n.* [1960s+] a devoted, if not always wholly successful, trend-follower (cf. TRENDOID). [SE *trend*]

trepan *see* TRAPAN.

très *adj.* [1980s+] (US campus) very. [synon. Fr.]

trespassers *n.* [19C] the legs.

treswins *n.* [early 18C–19C] threepence. [var. on THREESWINS]

t. rex *n.* [1970s] sex. [rhy. sl., *T. Rex*, a pop group of the early 1970s]

trey *n.*[1] *see* TRAY.

trey *n.*[2] *see* TREY-BIT.

trey *n.*[3] [1940s–60s] (US Black/drugs) a $3 packet of heroin (cf. THREE). [TRAY n.[1]]

trey-bit/trey/tray *n.* [late 19C+] (orig. Aus./N.Z.) **1** a threepenny piece. **2** a term of contempt for an insignificant person.

trey-bits *n.* [1950s+] (Aus./N.Z.) **1** the female breasts (cf.

THREEPENNY BITS). **2** diarrhoea. [rhy. sl. *trey-bits* = TITS n.[1]/ SHITS]

trey eight *n.* [1980s+] (US Black) a .38 calibre gun. [TRAY n.[1] + SE *eight*]

treyning *see* TRINING.

treyning/trining cheat *n.* [mid–late 16C] the gallows. [? *trine to the gallows*, ult. 14C *trine*, to go or march, or *trine*, triple, and thus referring to the 'triple tree']

trey of sous *n.* [1940s] (US Black) three dimes, 30 cents; thus *trey of sous and a double ruff*, 4 nickels, 40 cents. [SE *trey*, three + Fr. *sou*, a coin of small value + RUFF n.]

trezzie *see* TRIZZIE.

tri *n.* [20C] a tricycle. [abbr.]

triangle *n.* [1930s+] a three-way relationship, in any combination of sexes and sexualities.

triangles *n.* [mid-19C] delirium tremens. [due to the hallucinations, nothing is 'on the square']

trib *n.* [late 17C–19C] **1** a prison. **2** a workhouse. [SE *tribulation*]

tribulation *n.* [mid-17C–mid-18C] the condition of being held in pawn or pledge. [SE *tribulation*, a condition of great affliction]

trichi *n.* [mid–late 19C] (Anglo-Ind.) a *Trichi*nopoly cigar. [abbr.]

trick *n.*[1] [mid-19C+] a robbery or theft (cf. TURN A TRICK).

trick *n.*[2] [late 19C+] (US/Aus.) a small or amusing adult, animal or child.

trick *n.*[3] **1** [late 19C+] a period of work, usu. one that is physically demanding or unpleasant. **2** [1930s+] (US) a term of service on a ship. **3** [1930s+] (US) a sentence in prison. [naut. use *trick*, a turn at the wheel]

trick *n.*[4] (orig. US) **1** [1910s+] sexual intercourse, esp. a prostitute's intercourse (or other activity) with a client. **2** [1910s+] a prostitute's client, whether hetero- or homosexual, the implication being of deceiving any such client into parting with money. **3** [1960s+] any casual sex partner. **4** [1960s+] (Black) one who can be easily manipulated. [? 17C *trick*, sexual intercourse (cf. PRANK; TOY) + TRICK n.[1]. Note TURN A TRICK phr. (1) and (2)]

trick *adj.*[1] [1960s+] relating to commercial or casual sex. [TRICK n.[4]]

trick *adj.*[2] [1980s+] (US campus) **1** interesting, pleasing. **2** technologically sophisticated. [SE *tricky, tricksy*]

trick *v.*[1] (US) **1** [1920s+] to work as a prostitute. **2** [1960s+] to have casual sex. **3** [1960s+] (gay) to pick up a partner for casual, unpaid sex. **4** [1960s+] (US Black) of a man, to spend money on a woman other than one's regular partner. [TRICK n.[4]]

trick *v.*[2] [1970s+] (US Und.) to inform.

trick-acting *n.* [20C] (Irish) showing off.

trick-ass *n.* [1980s+] (US Black) a general derog. term for a woman. [TRICK n.[4] (1) + sfx. -ASS]

trick baby *n.* [1930s+] (US Black) an illegitimate child born to a prostitute (cf. BACHELOR'S BABY). [TRICK n.[4] (2) + SE *baby*. Given no pos. evidence to the contrary, she assumes the father to have been one of the paying customers]

trick bag *n.* [1940s+] (US Black) an unpleasant and disadvantaged position, a no-win situation. [TRICK n.[4] (2) + BAG n.[6], the pimp assumption that only victims pay for sex and that such a victim deserves whatever happens to him]

trick cyclist *n.* [1940s+] (orig. milit.) a psychiatrist. [joc. derog. mispron.]

tricker *n.* [16C] (Und.) a burglar's tool, spec. a gadget used to force open a window. [SE *trick*, some form of pincers or expandable wedge; 'engines of Iron so cunningly wrought, that he wil cut a barre of Iron in two with them' (Greene, 1592)]

trickeration n. [1930s–40s] (US Black) **1** showing off, boasting, flaunting oneself or one's possessions. **2** the act of fooling, deceiving and otherwise manipulating someone. [SE *trick* + sfx. *-eration*]

trickett n. [late 19C–1900s] (Aus., New South Wales) a long drink of beer. [the New South Wales champion sculler *Trickett*, who stated, for advertising purposes, that 'beer's best for an A1 nation']

trick flick n. [1950s+] (gay) a pornographic film (cf. STAG MOVIE). [TRICK n.⁴ (1) + SE *flick*]

trick house n. [1940s+] (US Black) a brothel (cf. ACCOMMODATION HOUSE). [TRICK n.⁴ (1) + HOUSE n.¹]

trickie n. [20C] (Irish) an amusing, 'sharp' person. [TRICK n.²]

trickin'! excl. [1990s] (US teen) an excl. used when one makes a foolish mistake, whether verbal or physical, in the hope of pretending that it was all 'just a trick' or joke.

tricking n. [1970s+] (orig. US Black) having sex for money. [TRICK v.¹]

trickle v. [1910s+] to go, to make one's way, usu. in combs., e.g. *trickle down, trickle over, trickle down to, trickle over to.*

trick money n. [1940s+] (US Black) the money a prostitute earns and hands over to her pimp (cf. TRAP n.⁷). [TRICK n.⁴ (2) + SE *money*]

trick suit n. [1950s+] a prostitute's dress that can be removed easily and is thus suitable for business. [TRICK n.⁴ (2) + SE *suit*]

trick towel n. [1950s+] (gay) a towel for wiping oneself after intercourse. [TRICK n.⁴ (2) + SE *towel*]

trickum legis n. [late 18C–early 19C] a legal trick. [cod Lat.; 'trick of the law']

trick up v. [1920s+] (Aus.) to take advantage of, to confuse, to outwit.

trick willy n. [1950s+] (US Black) a gullible Black man (cf. BIG WILLIE). [TRICK n.⁴ (2) + generic *Willy*]

tried at Stafford Court, to be phr. [early 17C] to be beaten, to be thrashed (cf. STAFFORD LAW). [pun on SE *staff*]

trif see TREF.

trifecta n. [1970s+] (US) any chance situation involving three components. [gambling *trifecta*, a bet on the first three places in a horse-race]

triff n. see TREF.

triff adj. [1980s+] terrific, wonderful. [abbr. SE *terrific*]

trifle n. [19C] the penis (cf. TRINKET). [euph.]

triflin' n. [1970s+] (US Black) acting irresponsibly, esp. as a parasite, e.g. *Don't trust a word he says, that boy is just triflin'.* [SE *trifling*]

trig n.¹ [early 19C] (Und.) a piece of paper that is left to mark a door for the purpose of robbing an empty house. [TRIGGING THE JIGGER]

trig n.² [mid-19C+] *trig*onometry. [abbr.]

trig n.³ [late 19C] a trot, a hurried walk, a trip. [ety. unknown]

trigger/triggerman n. [1920s+] (US) **1** a gunman working for organized crime (cf. SOLDIER). **2** an armed bodyguard (cf. HIT MAN).

trigger v. [1930s+] (US Und.) to rob. [i.e. the use of a gun]

trigger happy adj. [1940s+] (orig. US) overemotional, keen to put action before thought. [SE *trigger happy*, over-eager to use a gun]

triggerman see TRIGGER n.

trigging the jigger phr. [early 19C] (Und.) placing a small piece of paper (the *trig*) in the frontdoor keyhole of a house that is presumed to be uninhabited. If the paper is still there a day later, the robber can presume that the house is empty and can be broken into safely. [TRIG n.¹ + JIGGER n.¹ (1)]

trig it v. [late 18C–early 19C] to play truant. [SE *trig*, to walk off quickly]

trig one's wig, to phr. [1940s] (US Black) to think fast. [SE *trig(ger)*, to set off, to launch + WIG n.¹]

trigry-mate n. [late 17C–1900s] **1** an idle woman companion. **2** an intimate friend. [SE *trig*, to walk briskly + SE *mate*; they are both people with whom one walks around]

trike n. [late 19C+] a *tric*ycle. [abbr.]

trilby n. [late 19C–1930s] (US) a foot. [the heroine of the novel *Trilby* (1894) by George du Maurier, whose feet were particularly attractive. Note SE *trilby*, a type of shoe fashionable in US *c*.1900]

trilby v. [1930s] (US Black) to leave, to depart. [TRILL v.]

trilby hat n. [20C] a fool. [rhy. sl. *trilby hat* = PRAT n. (6)]

trill n.¹ [18C] the anus. [? punning Lat. *ars musica*, the musical art]

trill n.² [1930s–40s] (US Black) **1** departure. **2** an affected way of walking. [TRILBY n.]

trill/trilly/trilly-walk v. [1930s–40s] (US Black) to leave, to walk off. [? SE *trill*, to trundle, to move on wheels]

trillbye n. [17C] a prostitute. [ety. unknown; ? SE *trill*, to whirl, to spin]

trill the bones, to phr. [mid-16C] to throw dice with a spinning motion. [SE *trill*, to whirl, to spin + BONES n.¹ (1).]

trilly/trilly-walk see TRILL v.

trim n. (orig. US Black) **1** [1930s+] a woman's genitalia. **2** [1930s+] a woman, always in a sexual context; thus *get some trim*, to seduce, to have sexual intercourse. **3** [1950s+] cunnilingus. [? SE *trim*, neat, attractive, pretty]

trim v. **1** [early 16C+] to beat, to trounce, to defeat. **2** [early 16C+] to reprimand, to scold. **3** [late 17C+] to cheat of money or possessions.

trimble adj. [20C] (W.I./Gren.) selfish, greedy, fearful of sharing what one has. [? SE *tremble*]

trimmer n.¹ **1** [mid-18C–late 19C] one who beats, scolds, reprimands etc. **2** [late 19C] a thieving prostitute. [TRIM v. (3)]

trimmer n.² [1950s+] (Aus./N.Z.) something that is excellent, wonderful, approved of. [SE *trimming*, excellent, first-rate]

trimming n. [16C] (Und.) sleight-of-hand used by a confidence trickster. [SE *trim*, to cut the hair, thus to 'fleece']

trimming adj. [late 18C–early 19C] excellent, first-rate, superlative. [SE *trim*, neat, smart]

trimmingly adv. [18C] excellently, very well, ideally. [TRIMMING adj.]

trimmings n. [late 19C] secretly drunk alcohol, usu. consumed by a woman. [a period when shops (as opposed to 'sinful' public houses) were allowed to sell alcohol. Shopkeepers, typically drapers and silk-merchants, thus itemized as 'trimmings' the drinks their female customers consumed, on the bills that were sent to their husbands]

trim one's horn, to phr. [1990s] to masturbate. [HORN n.² (1)]

trim one's wick, to phr. [1990s] to masturbate. [pun on SE phr./WICK n.]

trim/swinge someone's jacket, to phr. [mid-18C–early 19C] to beat, to thrash someone (cf. DUST SOMEONE'S JACKET; JACKETING; THRASH SOMEONE'S JACKET). [SE *trim*, to beat, cf. SE *dress*, *array*, to beat/*swinge*, to trash]

trim someone's lamps, to phr. [1940s–50s] to beat someone up. [? *lampblack*, thus to black one's eyes]

trim the buff, to phr. [late 18C] to deflower a woman. [SE *trim*, to clip + *buff*, bare skin]

trim-tram adj. [late 16C–late 19C] used by itself or more freq. in rhy. jingles to indicate equality; thus *trim-tram, like master like man.* [the 'balance' of the two words]

trine n. [mid-late 17C] Tyburn. [TRINE v.², Tyburn's 'occupation']

trine v.¹ [early 17C–mid-19C] to go, to step. [synon. 14C–16C SE *trine*, ult. OSwed. *trina*, to go]

trine v.² [late 17C–19C] (Und.) to hang (cf. TRINING). [? abbr. TRINE TO THE CHEATS but ? SE *trine*, to march (in this case, to the gallows)]

trine to the cheats, to phr. [mid-16C–18C] to go to the gallows, to be hanged. [TRINE v.¹ + CHEAT n. (2)]

tringham-trangham/tringum-trangum see TRINKUM-TRANKUM.

trining/treyning/tryning n. [16C] (Und.) hanging (cf. TRINE v.²). [prob. SE trine, threefold. The ref. is to the three-part Tyburn gallows. Alt. ety. is in TREYNING CHEAT, which gives the phr. trine to the gallows]

trining cheat see TREYNING CHEAT.

trinity kiss n. [late 19C] (society) a triple kiss given to children at bedtime by their parents.

trinket n. [mid-19C–1910s] a baby's or small boy's penis (cf. TRIFLE n.).

trinkets n. [19C] the male genitals (cf. FAMILY JEWELS).

trinkum-trankum / tringham-trangham / tringum-trangum n. 1 [late 17C–1900s] a whim or fancy. 2 [18C–20C] a trifle. [SE trinket]

trip n.¹ 1 [mid-19C–1930s] a prostitute or a thief's female companion, esp. one who decoys and then robs drunks. 2 [1920s+] (US Und.) an arrest. 3 [1920s+] (US Und.) a prison sentence (cf. FALL n.).

trip n.² [1910s–20s] an affectionate term of address. [neutral form of TRIP n.¹ (1)]

trip n.³ 1 [1950s+] the experience that follows the taking of LSD or another hallucinogenic (cf. ACID TRIP). 2 [1960s+] any form of experience, event, lifestyle or attitude, esp. when challenging, surprising or otherwise out of the ordinary. 3 [1970s+] (US campus) an odd, eccentric person. 4 [1980s+] (US campus) a cheering, pleasing event.

trip v.¹ [1960s+] (drugs) to take LSD. [TRIP n.³]

trip v.² [1980s+] 1 (US Black) to lose control, to go mad, to act under a misapprehension. 2 to be delighted, to be ecstatic, often as trip for, trip over. 3 to be passionately interested or involved in. [fig. non-drug uses of TRIP v.¹]

trip v.³ [1990s] (US Black gang) to make an error, to blunder.

trip down v. [1960s–70s] (US) to go, to leave. [SE trip, to walk lightly]

tripe/tripes n.¹ [mid-18C–mid-19C] usu. in pl., the guts, the intestines. [SE mid-15C–mid-18C]

tripe n.² [late 19C] nonsense, utter rubbish. [virtually SE by 20C]

tripe and trillibub n. [17C–18C] a fat person (cf. TRIPES AND TRILLIBUBS). [SE tripes and trillibubs, animal intestines]

tripe-hound n. 1 [1920s+] an unpleasant or contemptible person. 2 [1920s] a newspaper reporter or an informant. 3 [1930s] (Aus./N.Z. derog.) a dog, esp. a sheepdog.

triper adj. [late 19C] unclean. [Heb. treyfe, not kosher]

tripes see TRIPE n.¹.

tripes and trillibubs/trullibubs n. [late 18C–late 19C] a hostile nickname for a very fat person (cf. TRANKLEMENT; TROLLOBUBS). [SE tripes and trillibubs, the entrails of an animal]

tripewriter n. [20C] a typewriter. [joc. mispron.]

trip in v. [1960s–70s] (US) to arrive, to enter. [SE trip, to walk lightly]

triple burger with cheese see BURGER.

triple-clutcher n. [1950s+] euph. for MOTHERFUCKER.

triple-hip adj. [1940s–50s] (US Black) extra smart, very wise. [SE triple + HIP adj.]

triple master-blaster n. [1980s+] (drugs) a situation in which one smokes crack cocaine while simultaneously being fellated and sodomized. [SE triple + MASTER-BLASTER]

triple-treat queen n. [1960s+] (US gay) a gay man who is happy to put his penis into a mouth, an anus or an armpit. [SE + QUEEN n.¹]

triple tree n. [18C] the gallows, orig. that sited at Tyburn, London (cf. DEADLY NEVERGREEN; THREE-CORNERED TREE). [this

giant three-cornered gallows, capable of dispatching 21 villains at a time, stands menacingly in the background of Hogarth's 1747 engraving of a public hanging]

triple whammy n. [1950s+] (US) a three-part attack, threat or difficulty (cf. WHAMMY). [SE wham, to hit hard]

trip off/off of v. [1960s–70s] (orig. US) to enjoy. [TRIP v.¹; the image is of an experience so intense that it replicates the effects of LSD]

trip one out v. [1960s+] 1 to upset, to confuse, to disorientate. 2 to strike one as funny, crazy or extraordinary. 3 to be amazed or excited. [TRIP v.¹, such confusion is supposedly reminiscent of that experienced on LSD]

trip out v. [1960s+] to lose control, to leave normality. [TRIP v.¹]

tripped-out adj. [1960s+] 1 (drugs) under the influence of LSD or another hallucinogen. 2 disorientated, confused, upset. [TRIP n.³]

tripper n. [1960s+] (drugs) one who takes LSD or similar hallucinogens. [TRIP v.¹]

tripper-up n. [19C] a thief who robs innocent pedestrians who have been deliberately tripped up by a confederate. Often women, they preyed on drunken seamen. [SE trip]

tripping n.¹ 1 [1960s+] taking LSD. 2 [1960s+] fantasizing, acting in an irrational manner. 3 [1960s+] (US Black) doing something beyond the norm, in a pos. way. 4 [1990s] (US Black) responding to the effects of narcotics. 5 [1990s] (US Black) acting foolishly. [lit./fig. uses of TRIP v.¹]

tripping n.² [1980s+] (US campus) showing any form of extreme emotion, whether pos. or neg. [TRIP v.²]

-tripping sfx. [1960s+] a general sfx. denoting a style of action or opinion, power-tripping, asserting oneself over others, e.g. head-tripping, thinking. [TRIP v.¹]

trippy adj. [1960s+] 1 (orig. US) bizarre, strange, disturbing (fig. approximating the sensation of taking a hallucinogen). 2 (US teen) excellent, first-rate. [TRIP n.³]

trips n.¹ [1910s+] triplets. [abbr.]

trips n.² [1960s+] LSD.

trip to the moon n. [1970s+] (orig. gay) anal intercourse. [SE trip + MOON n.¹]

triss/trizz n.¹ [1920s+] (Aus.) a threepenny bit. [abbr. TRIZZIE]

triss/trizz n.² [1950s+] (Aus.) a male homosexual (cf. TRISSY). [TRISS ABOUT]

triss about v. [1940s+] (Aus.) to act in an effeminate manner. [synon. with SWISH v.²]

trissy/trizzy adj. [1950s+] (Aus.) homosexual, effeminate. [TRISS ABOUT]

trivet/trivit n. [1950s] 'a pound of shit stuffed into the toe of an old sock and used as a blackjack; ... a mashed potato turd stuffed down a sink' (G. Legman, Limerick, 1952) (cf. BLIVET).

trizz see TRISS.

trizzer n. [1920s+] (Aus.) a public lavatory. [a time when the charge for a 'wash-and-brush-up' was three pence, i.e. a TRIZZIE]

trizzie/trezzie n. [1920s–60s] (orig. Aus.) a threepenny piece. [TREY or SE three]

trizzy see TRISSY.

Troc, the n. [late 19C+] the Trocadero Music Hall, Piccadilly Circus, London. [abbr.; now recreated as a vast amusement arcade]

trods n. [1940s] (US Black) the feet. [SE tread]

troepie see TROOPIE.

trog n. [1950s+] (orig. naut.) a general term of disdain. [SE troglodyte, a prehistoric cave dweller, loosely defined in sl. contexts as 'the lowest form of human life']

Trojan/trusty Trojan n. 1 [late 17C–19C] an intimate companion, esp. as a fellow drinker and roisterer. 2 [late 17C–19C] a generally good fellow (cf. TRUSTY TROUT). 3 [early–mid-19C] a professional gambler. [proper name Trojan, a brave or plucky person, a person of great energy or endurance, ult. the Homeric legends]

Trojan horse *n.* [1960s+] (US gay) a gay man who poses as a 'straight' masculine person. [the Homeric myth of deception]

troll *n.*[1] [mid-19C+] a sluttish, idling woman. [abbr. SE *trollop* or TROLLING; 20C use is N.Z.]

troll *n.*[2] [1980s+] **1** (US campus) an ugly woman. **2** (US campus) a small girl or woman (cf. TREE *n.*[2]). **3** (US campus) a lecherous older man. **4** (US gay) an unattractive middle-aged gay man. [SE *troll*, a monster]

troll/troll about/around *v.* **1** [late 17C+] to wander around, to saunter. **2** [1950s–60s] of a prostitute, to look for clients. **3** [1960s+] (gay) to walk the streets in search of a sexual partner (cf. CRUISE *v.*[1]). [SE *troll*, to wander around aimlessly]

troll and troll by *n.* [mid-16C] (Und.) one who is esteemed by no one and esteems no one. [? SE *troll*, to wander]

troll around *see* TROLL *v.*

trolley/trolley and truck *n.* [1910s+] an act of sexual intercourse. [rhy. sl. *trolley and truck* = FUCK *n.*[1]. Note naval use *trolley-oggling*, acting as a voyeur]

trolley/trolley and truck *v.* [1910s+] to have sexual intercourse. [TROLLEY *n.*]

trolley and tram *n.* [20C] ham. [rhy. sl.]

trolley and truck *see* TROLLEY.

trolley/trolly dolly *n.* [1980s+] (gay) an air steward.

trolleyed *adj.* [1990s] drunk or under the influence of drugs. [OFF ONE'S TROLLEY]

trolleys *see* TROLLIES.

troll hazard of trace *n.* [mid-16C] (Und.) someone who follows their master as far as the master can be seen. [SE *troll*, to stroll, to saunter + *trace*, a track or line of footprints]

troll hazard of tritrace *n.* [mid-16C] (Und.) one who 'goeth gaping after his master' (*Awdeley*). [SE *troll*, to troll, to saunter + *tritrace*, an unknown word which ? linked to *trey-trace*, itself another mystery]

trollies/trolleys/trollys *n.* [20C] **1** underpants. **2** trousers (cf. TROLLY-WAGS). [Lancashire dial. *trollys*, a woman's drawers, itself linked to Scot. *trolly*, any object with its length disproportionate to its width, ? ult. SE *trail*]

trolling *n.* **1** [mid-19C+] idling, sauntering. **2** [1930s+] working as a prostitute. **3** [1960s+] (gay) strolling the streets looking for possible partners (cf. CRUISING). [SE *troll*, to saunter along; ult. OF *troller*, to search for game (without purpose) or Fr. *trôler*, to ramble]

trollobubs/trollybobs *n.* [19C] the stomach, the intestines (cf. TRANKLEMENT). [dial. *trollobubs*, entrails]

trollop *n.* [1960s] (US Black) an unattractive, ugly woman. [SE *trollop*, but without the sexual implications]

trollopee *n.* [mid-19C] a loose dress. [? pun on SE *trollop*, i.e. 'loose']

trollopping *adj.* [mid-late 18C] **1** like a trollop. **2** ungainly, gauche. [TROLLOP *n.*]

troll with *n.* [mid-16C] (Und.) a servant who walks alongside his master; 'he that no man shall know the seruaunt from ye Maister' (*Awdeley*). [SE *troll*, to stroll, to saunter]

trollybobs *see* TROLLOBUBS.

trolly lolly *n.* [late 17C–early 19C] a type of lace, coarsely made but once very fashionable. [Flem. *tralje/traalj*, trellis, lattice, mesh]

trollys *see* TROLLIES.

trolly-wags *n.* [19C] trousers (cf. TROLLIES). [? rhy. sl. *trolly-wags* = BAGS *n.*[1]]

trom *n.* [1990s] (drugs) marijuana. [ironic abbr. of SE *traumatize*, to damage psychologically]

trombone *n.* [1930s] a telephone. [partial rhy. sl., i.e. only one element rather than the usual two]

trompie *n.* [1970s+] (S.Afr. drugs) a long, conically-shaped marijuana cigarette. [Afk. *trompie*, a trumpet, a jew's harp]

tronk *n.* [late 18C+] (S.Afr.) prison. [Fr. *tronc*, box, Du. *tronk* or Buganese *tarunka*, a prison. The word could have been imported by Buganese and Balinese slaves]

t-room *see* TEAROOM.

troop *n.* [1980s+] (drugs) crack cocaine. [SE *troop*, a soldier; it gets users 'marching along']

troop/troop off *v.* [early 18C+] to leave. [late 20C use is mainly US campus]

trooper *n.*[1] [late 17C–18C] (Und.) half-a-crown, 2s 6d (12½p). [? its making up part of an SE *trooper's pay*]

trooper *n.*[2] **1** [mid-19C] a prostitute. **2** [1950s] a brave or stalwart person. [milit. *trooper*, but note theatrical/SE *trouper*, a veteran, stalwart actor]

troopie/troepie *n.* [1970s+] (S.Afr.) a soldier, esp. the lowest rank of national serviceman. [SE *trooper*]

troop off *see* TROOP *v.*

troops *n.* [1930s+] (US) a gang, a mob.

trophy *n.* [1970s] (US campus) 200ml (half a gallon) of alcohol.

tropical *adj.* **1** [1920s+] of language, obscene. **2** [1940s+] (Aus.) of stolen goods, illegal, dishonest. [fig. uses of HOT *adj.*[1], *adj.*[2]]

troppo *adj.* [1940s+] (Aus./N.Z.) mad, insane; thus *go troppo*, to go mad (cf. ASIATIC). [SE *tropical*, i.e. the effects of the heat]

tross *n.* [mid-19C] a sort (cf. DABTROS; SLING YOUR TROSS!; TROSSENO). [backsl.]

trosseno/trasseno *n.* [mid-19C] anything that is bad. [backsl., lit. 'one sort']

trossy *adj.* [late 19C] dirty, unkempt. [? dial. *make a trossle of oneself*, to be slatternly]

trot *n.*[1] **1** [18C–late 19C] the vagina (cf. TWAT). **2** [1920s+] (N.Z.) a woman. [SE *trot*, a prostitute]

trot *n.*[2] **1** [mid-19C–1920s] a child just learning to walk or run (cf. TROTTIE). **2** [late 19C] a baby animal. **3** [late 19C–1900s] a walk. **4** [1910s–30s] a fellow, esp. as *old trot*. **5** [1910s+] (Aus.) a sequence of consecutive events, a run of good or bad luck; thus phrs. *good/bad/lean/rough/tough trot*.

trot *n.*[3] [late 19C+] (US campus) a translation, a study aid (cf. ANIMAL *n.*[3]). [play on HORSE *n.*[7] or PONY *n.*[3]]

Trot *n.*[4] [1960s+] a *Trot*skyite, used indiscriminately for any hard-left group in the UK; thus media use *trot-slot*, a programme that concerns itself with, or apparently propagandizes for, such groups. [abbr.]

trot/trot out *v.* **1** [early 19C+] to leave, to move off. **2** [mid-19C+] to exhibit (someone), to put on display. **3** [mid-late 19C] to spend one's money; usu. as *trot out the pieces*. **4** [late 19C] to steal openly, in broad daylight. **5** [late 19C–1960s] to take out (a woman), to 'walk out with'.

trot away from the pole, to *phr.* [late 19C] (US) to wander off the subject. [sporting use, ref. to a racehorse wandering away from the starting line-up or failing to aim for the finishing post]

trot it out! *excl.* [late 19C+] confess! say your piece! start talking!

trot out *v.* [late 19C+] **1** to show (someone) around a place. **2** to produce, esp. of an excuse or a lie. [horse-racing jargon *trot out*, to exhibit, to display a horse]

trot out a song, to *phr.* [late 19C] to sing a song.

trot round *v.* [mid-19C+] to go round (to), to pay a call (on). [ext. TROT *v.* (1)]

trots *n.*[1] [early 19C+] diarrhoea (cf. BACK-DOOR TROT). [note synon. US Appalachian use *johnny trots*]

trots *n.*[2] [late 19C] **1** feet (cf. TROTTERS). **2** policemen. [(2) is fig. use of (1)]

trots, the n.³ [20C] (Aus.) a race meeting for *trotting* horses. [abbr.]

trot someone round v. [late 19C+] to show someone around a place.

trotter n. [1960s+] (Und.) a deserter from the armed forces. [TROT v. (1)]

trotter-boxes/-cases n. [early–mid-19C] shoes (cf. FEET-CASEMENTS; TROTTING-CASES). [TROTTERS + SE *box/case*]

trotters n. **1** [late 17C+] feet. **2** [20C] racehorses. [SE *trot*]

trottery n. [1940s–60s] (US) a dance-hall. [SE *trot*]

trot the udyju Pope o' Rome, to phr. [late 19C] to take one's wife home. [Pig Lat. *udyju*, JUDY + rhy. sl. *Pope o' Rome*, home]

trottie n. [late 19C–1900s] a toddler. [ext. of TROT n.² (1)]

trottie adj. see TROTTY.

trotting-cases n. [mid-19C] shoes (cf. TROTTER-BOXES). [TROT v.¹ (1)]

trot town n. [late 19C] a loafer, an idler, a wastrel. [SE *trot*, to walk + *town*]

trotty/trottie adj. [late 19C] of a person's figure, small, dainty. [TROT n.² (1)]

troub/tram trube/troub n. [1910s+] (Aus.) a tram conductor. [SE *troubador*, a wandering singer, i.e. the conductor 'sings out' the stops]

trouble n. [late 19C] (US) **1** a day of public festivity. **2** any interruption of ordinary work.

trouble v. [late 19C+] to bother, to worry (about).

trouble and fuss n. [20C] a bus. [rhy. sl.]

trouble and strife n. **1** [1900s] life. **2** [20C] one's wife (cf. ANCHOR n.²). [rhy. sl.]

trouble giblets v. [18C] to have sexual intercourse (cf. JOIN GIBLETS).

troubles and cares n. [20C] stairs. [rhy. sl.]

trough n. [20C] **1** eating. **2** the place at which one eats.

trough out v. [1980s+] (US campus) to eat voraciously.

trounce v. [19C] to have sexual intercourse (cf. BANG v.¹).

trouncer n. [19C] **1** a strong drink. **2** a highly capable or expert individual. **3** something amazing or astounding. **4** (Ulster) an attractive woman.

trouper n. [1950s+] a brave or stalwart person (cf. TROOPER n.²). [milit. *trooper*, but note theatrical/SE *trouper*, a veteran, stalwart actor]

trouser/trowser n. [late 19C] a jack of all trades. [? he will turn his hand to anything so long as he *trousers* his payment]

trouser v. [20C] to pocket.

trouser bandit n. [20C] a male homosexual (cf. ARSE BANDIT; BOOTY BANDIT).

trouser chuff n. [1980s+] a fart. [SE *trousers* + CHUFF n.² (1)]

trousered adj. [1990s] drunk.

trouser mauser n. [1990s] the penis (cf. BACON BAZOOKA). [SE *trouser* + *Mauser*, a type of pistol]

trouser trout n. [20C] (US) the penis (cf. TORMENT THE TROUSER TROUT).

trouser trumpet n. [1990s] the penis.

trout n.¹ [mid-17C–early 19C] a boon companion, a true friend (cf. TRUSTY TROUT). [? on pattern of FISH n.¹; note SE *trow*, faith, trust, belief]

trout n.² **1** [late 19C+] a woman (cf. OLD TROUT). **2** [1950s–60s] (US Black) the vagina (cf. BEARDED CLAM). [the identification of women and fish]

trout-fishing n.¹ [1960s+] (US gay) of a gay man, seeking out rich old women who offer money in return for companionship. [TROUT n.² (1) + SE *fishing*]

trout fishing n.² [1990s] urinating. [TROUSER TROUT]

trowser see TROUSER n.

troy/troy school n. [1940s–60s] (Aus.) a gambling game. [ety. unknown]

TR-6 n. [1980s+] (drugs) amphetamine (cf. A n.²). [? brand-name]

trucha v. [1960s+] (US) to be alert, to watch out. [Sp.]

truck n.¹ [mid-19C] a hat. [naut. jargon *truck*, the 'cap' on the very top of a mast]

truck n.² [1980s+] (US campus) someone who moves very slowly. [for ety. see TRUCK v.]

truck v. **1** [late 19C+] to move, to travel. **2** [1930s+] (US Black) to leave, to depart. **3** [1930s+] to dance the truck, a contemporary popular dance. **4** [1980s+] (US campus) to move slowly. [? 17C truck, to trudge, ult. synon. Ital. *truccare*; (3) 'that jerky yet rhythmic dance which combines a bend of the body, a tightening of the hand muscles and a slight strut with the legs' (Baltimore *Sun*, 15 November 1935)]

truck-driver n. [1950s+] (US Black) an ostentatiously 'masculine' homosexual, poss. dressed as a trucker or in similar macho clothes (cf. BUTCH; ROUGH TRADE n.³).

truck-drivers n. [1970s+] (drugs) amphetamines (cf. A n.²). [their use by *truck-drivers* and others in staying awake]

truck-end n. [1910s] the buttocks.

truckie n. [1950s+] (Aus./N.Z.) a long distance truck-driver. [var. on SAmE *trucker*]

trucking n.¹ **1** [late 19C+] (US Black) strutting, strolling. **2** [1960s+] moving, struggling along; esp. as in hippie slogan *keep on trucking*, an exhortation to continue with one's life. [TRUCK v. (1)]

trucking n.² **1** [1920s+] moving, walking, travelling. **2** [1930s+] dancing the truck. [TRUCK v.]

truck jewellery n. [1990s] (US Black teen) items of large, gold jewellery. [? one needs a SE *truck* to carry it or SE *truck*, miscellaneous articles suitable for barter]

trucks n. [mid-19C] trousers. [? TROLLY-WAGS or SE *trucks*, odds and ends]

true adj. [1990s] (US Black teen) loyal, faithful, dependable. [revival of 19C SE]

true blue adj. [mid–late 17C] used of a regular, dedicated drinker. [play on SE *true blue*, orig. the colour of 17C Scot. Covenanters (the reversal of the monarchy's red), subseq. of 19C+ Tories]

true dink/dinkum n. [1900s–30s] (Aus.) the absolute truth. [SE *true* + DINKUM adj.]

true marmalade n. [mid-19C] the best, the ultimate. [play on REAL JAM]

truepenny n. [late 16C–early 19C] a trusty, honest person. [the image of a sound coin]

true trout see TRUSTY TROUT.

truff n. [mid-19C] a purse. [SE *truffle*]

truff v. [mid-19C] (northern) to steal, to pilfer. [Scot. *truff*, to pilfer, to obtain by deceit]

trug n. [16C–early 18C] (Und.) **1** a prostitute. **2** a catamite or young homosexual boy. [It. *trucca*, 'a fustian or rogish word for a trull, a whore, or a wench' (Florio 1598). ? cognate with SE *truck*, to barter or exchange commodities]

trugging house/ken n. [16C] a brothel (cf. ACCOMMODATION HOUSE). [TRUG n. (1) + HOUSE n.¹/KEN n.¹]

trugging place n. [16C] a brothel. [TRUG n. (1) + SE *place*]

trugmoldy n. [early 18C] a prostitute. [? SE *trugmallion*, a prostitute]

trull n. [late 17C–18C] **1** a prostitute. **2** a tinker's companion (cf. DELL; DOXY; WALKING MORT). [Ger. *Trulle*, a prostitute]

trump n.¹ **1** [19C] an admirable person, an excellent fellow. **2** [1920s+] (Aus./N.Z.) a person in charge. [card-playing imagery]

trump n.² [late 19C–1900s] an act of breaking wind audibly. [TRUMP v.]

trump v. [early 15C+] to break wind loudly. [SE *trump*, to trumpet]

trumper *n.* [early–mid-19C] one who breaks wind loudly. [TRUMP v.]

trumpery *n.* [late 18C–early 19C] a worn-out old prostitute. [SE *trumpery*, valueless goods]

trumpet *n.* **1** [19C] the nose (cf. BUGLE n.¹). **2** [1970s+] the telephone. **3** [1990s] breaking wind. **4** [1990s] (US teen) one who has an extremely large ego.

trumpeter *n.* **1** [late 18C–early 19C] one who has bad breath. **2** [late 19C] a general term of affectionate address. [(1) to play the trumpet one needs 'strong', here 'bad' breath]

trumpeters *n.* [late 19C] (Aus. Und.) 'irons which connect ... ordinary leg-chains with a bazil [bezel] riveted around each leg immediately below the knees' (P. Warung, *Tales of the Early Days*, 1894). [? the noise of the chains]

trump the hump, to *phr.* [1930s–40s] (US Black) to climb a hill. [SE *tramp*]

trumpy *adj.* [1960s] dear in price. [it SE *trumps* cheaper prices]

truncheon *n.* [19C] the penis (cf. BAT n.⁷).

trundlers *n.* [late 17C–18C] peas. [SE *trundle*, to roll along (around one's plate)]

trundle-tail *n.* [17C] a derog. description of a person. [SE *trundle-tail*, a cur, a mongrel, lit. a dog with a curly tail]

trundling-cheat *n.* [mid–late 17C] any form of wheeled vehicle. [SE *trundle* + CHEAT n.]

trunk *n.*¹ [late 17C–1900s] the human nose; thus mocking phr. addressed to one who has a prominent nose, *how's your old trunk?* [an elephant's *trunk*]

trunk *n.*² [19C] a fool. [SE *trunk*, the body, bereft of the head]

trunkmaker-like *adj.* [late 18C–early 19C] used of someone who makes more noise than they do real work. [SE *trunkmaker*, one who makes trunks or boxes; thus the noise so created]

trunks *n.* [late 19C–1960s] an operator who, in the era before STD, dealt with 'trunk calls'.

trus mi *see* TRUS WI.

trust *v.* [mid-19C] used ironically or sarcastically to imply that a person is behaving in a totally predictable (and rarely admirable) manner; usu. in phrs. *trust him, trust you* etc.

trustafarian *n.* [1980s+] someone fortunate enough to have a trust fund to insulate them from work or 'real life'. [SE *trust (fund)* + joc. abbr. *(Rasta)farian*]

trust-buster *n.* [20C] (US) a campaigner against the power of monopolistic industrial or business trusts. [SE *trust* + BUST v.¹ (1)]

trusty *n.* [early 19C] (Anglo-Irish) an overcoat. [it can be trusted to keep one warm/dry]

trusty Trojan *see* TROJAN.

trusty/true trout *n.* [mid-17C–early 19C] a boon companion, a true friend (cf. TRUSTY TROJAN).

trus wi/mi *phr.* [1980s+] (W.I./UK Black teen) believe (in) us/ me, trust (in) us/me.

trut *n.* [1930s–60s] (Aus.) a threepenny bit. [SE *thruppence/ threepence*]

try a piece of sandpaper! *excl.* [20C] jeering cry offered to a young man who has adolescent down on his cheeks or is attempting to grow a moustache. [i.e. he has no need of an actual razor]

try for White, to *phr.* [1940s+] (S.Afr.) to attempt to pass oneself off as White (cf. CROSS THE LINE); less common are *try for Black, try for Coloured.*

try it on *v.* **1** [early 19C] to live by thieving. **2** [early 19C+] to attempt to get away with something, usu. that which one is not entitled to have.

try it on the dog, to *phr.* [late 19C+] usu. of a play or film, to experiment with, to try out. [the testing of possibly poisoned meat by giving it to an unfortunate dog or theatre jargon *try it*

on *the matinée dog*, the implication being that a matinée is less well-acted than an evening performance]

try it on with *v.* [early 19C+] to attempt to persuade someone who is otherwise unwilling. [ext. of TRY IT ON, 'it' being one's persuasive 'line']

tryning *see* TRINING.

try-on *n.* [early 19C+] **1** an attempt at imposition or deceit. **2** the subject of the attempt.

try on/something on for size, to *phr.* [1950s+] (orig. US) to try out, to see if something (often fig.) will work (cf. RUN UP THE FLAGPOLE).

try-out *n.* [1930s+] a trial run, a trial period, an experimental attempt.

try something on for size *see* TRY ON FOR SIZE.

try Taylor's best, to *phr.* [19C] to have a drink of port. [brand-name]

try the acid *see* PUT THE ACID ON.

try to front, to *phr.* [1980s+] (US campus) to denigrate, to make neg. comments. [FRONT v.⁴]

t/s *n.* [1970s+] a transsexual (cf. T.V.). [abbr.]

t.s. *phr.* [1940s+] (orig. US milit.) tough shit, often used ironically or mockingly as well as sympathetically. [abbr.]

t's! *excl.* [1990s] (US teen) no! [? SE *tease*, i.e. I didn't mean it, I was only teasing]

tsang *n.* [1960s–70s] (S.Afr. township) money. [ety. unknown; ? echoic of chinking coins]

tsatske *see* TCHOTCHKE.

t.s.h. *phr.* [1980s+] (US campus) an expression of commiseration. [abbr. *that shit happens*]

tsoris *see* TSURIS.

tsotsi *n.* [1940s+] (S.Afr.) **1** a flashily dressed township thug or gangster (cf. PANTSULA); thus *tsotsi taal*, the slang of the tsotsi world. **2** the tight trousers worn, in the 1950s, by such gangsters. [Sotho pron. of ZOOT SUIT]

tsuris/tsoris/tzuris *n.* [20C] troubles, worries, suffering. [Yid. *tsuris*, ult. Heb. *tsarah*, trouble]

t/t *abbr.* [1970s+] used in sex contact advertisements, *tit torture*. [abbr.]

T-tab *n.* [1960s–70s] (drugs) phencyclidine (cf. ACE n.³). [ety. unknown, but *see* T-ZONE]

t.t.f.n. *phr.* [1940s+] goodbye. [*ta-ta for now*, orig. created and popularized on comedian Tommy Handley's BBC Radio show *ITMA* (*It's That Man Again*, 1939–49). Dorothy Summers, as 'Mrs Mopp' (the comic charlady) actually used the phr., which was revived by BBC Radio 2 disc jockey Jimmy Young (b.1923)]

tub *n.*¹ **1** [mid-17C–mid-19C] a pulpit (cf. TUB-MAN). **2** [early 18C–early 19C] a coach, esp. a form of covered carriage known as a 'chariot'. **3** [mid-19C] a seatless carriage used on the early railways. **4** [mid–late 19C] (US) a fire engine. **5** [1920s–50s] (US) a boat (cf. TUBS n.²). [joc. uses of SE *tub*]

tub *n.*² [late 19C+] a fat person. [abbr. SE *tubby*]

tub *v.* [late 19C] to wash oneself (in a bath or tub).

tubbichon *n.* [mid–late 19C] a single curled lock of back hair, worn pulled forwards over the left shoulder (cf. REPENTANCE CURL; ZARNDRER). [Fr. *tirebuchon*, corkscrew, a term used to describe this hairstyle, popularized c.1860 by the Empress Eugénie]

tubbing *n.* [19C] (prison) a difficult sentence. [ety. unknown; ? link to SE *dubbing*]

tubby *n.* [late 19C+] (US) a fat person, often used as an affectionate nickname. [SE *tubby* adj.]

tub-drubber *see* TUB-THUMPER.

tube *n.*¹ **1** [late 19C–1950s] a telephone. **2** [1940s–50s] (prison) a prison officer who makes a habit of listening for information from prison informers (cf. BUBBLE n.⁴). **3** [1950s+] (Ulster) a general term of contempt. [the telephone's short-range predecessor, the SE *speaking tube*]

tube n.² **1** [late 19C+] the London Underground, orig. the *Twopenny Tube*. **2** [1920s] the penis. **3** [1930s–50s] (US) the New York Subway. **4** [1940s–70s] a cigarette. **5** [1950s+] (Aus.) a tall, thin beer glass. **6** [1960s+] (orig. Aus.) a bottle or can of beer. **7** [1980s+] (US drugs) a large water pipe.

tube n.³ [1950s+] (US) **1** television, as a media, the industry. **2** a television set. [abbr. cathode ray *tube*, a basic component of the TV]

tube n.⁴ [1980s+] (Scot.) a person. [ety. unknown]

tube/tube it v.¹ [20C] to travel on the London Underground. [TUBE n.² (1)]

tube v.² [1960s+] (US campus) to do badly at work. [GO DOWN THE TUBES]

tubed adj. [1960s+] very drunk. [GO DOWN THE TUBES + TUBE n.² (6)]

tube it v.¹ *see* TUBE v.¹.

tube it v.² [1950s+] to watch television. [TUBE n.³]

tubesteak n. [1960s+] (US) **1** a hot dog, a frankfurter. **2** the penis (cf. BACON n.¹).

tubesteak of love n. [1980s+] (US campus) the penis (cf. BACON n.¹). [ext. of TUBESTEAK n. (3)]

tubesteak tarzan n. [1990s] a homosexual. [TUBESTEAK + *Tarzan*]

tub-man/-preacher n. [mid-17C] a preacher, a parson (cf. TUB-POUNDER; TUB-THUMPER). [TUB n.¹ (1) + SE *man/preacher*]

tub of blood *see* BLOODY BUCKET.

tub of lard/guts n. [20C] a fat person (cf. BUCKET OF LARD; LARD-BUCKET).

tub-pounder n. [early 19C–1900s] a preacher, a parson (cf. TUB-MAN). [TUB n.¹ (1) + SE *pounder*]

tub-preacher *see* TUB-MAN.

tubs n.¹ [mid-19C] a butter seller. [the butter *tubs*]

tubs n.² [1920s–50s] transatlantic liners, esp. as venues for crime. [TUB n.¹]

tubs n.³ [1940s] (orig. US) drums. [the shape]

tubs n.⁴ [1980s+] (US gay) a gay bathhouse. [SE *tub*, a bath]

tubster n. [early 18C] a parson. [TUB n.¹ (1) + sfx. *-ster*]

tub-taster n. [mid-17C] a drinker. [SE *tub*, a container for liquid, i.e. alcohol]

tub-thumper/-drubber n. [late 18C+] a vehement preacher or orator, either clerical or secular (cf. PULPIT-THUMPER; TUB-MAN); thus *tub-thumping*, preaching or speechifying, whether or not of religious topics. [TUB n.¹ (1) + SE *thumper/drubber*]

tubular adj. [1980s] (US teen) the ultimate in perfection. [? surfer jargon *tube*, the inside curve of a good wave]

tuches/tuchis *see* TOCHES.

tuck n.¹ **1** [19C] a hearty meal, also as *tuck-in*, *tuck-out*. **2** [mid-19C+] (mainly juv.) food, esp. sweet cakes and pastries. **3** [mid-19C] a hearty appetite. [TUCK v.²; ? + ref. to the strain placed on the tucks in one's garments]

tuck n.² [late 19C] the head. [? play on SE *tuck box*, i.e. a container for food]

tuck v.¹ [late 17C–early 19C] to hang (cf. DANCE AT TUCK 'EM FAIR). [SE *tuck*, to tug or snatch]

tuck v.² [mid-18C–late 19C] **1** to eat, esp. heartily or greedily (cf. TUCK IN v.¹). **2** to overeat, to bloat oneself with excessive consumption.

tuck v.³ [1960s+] (transvestite) to tape the penis to the groin, (usu. in the context of transvestism). [one 'tucks it away']

tucked away adj. [20C] (Aus.) dead and buried.

tucked up adj. [20C] (Und.) captured without any chance of escape.

tuck 'em fair n. [18C] a judicial hanging (cf. PADDINGTON FAIR; SCRAG 'EM FAIR). [TUCK v.¹]

tucker n. [mid-19C+] (Aus./N.Z.) food; thus *hard tucker*,

meagre rations; *tucker job*, a poorly paid job (which just covers the cost of one's rations); *tucker money*, a pittance. [ext. of TUCK n.¹, orig. at 19C gold diggings]

tucker v. **1** [late 19C+] to eat a meal. **2** [1920s+] to provide someone with food. [TUCKER n.]

tuckerbox n. [1970s+] an informer. [Jack Moses poem (c.1920s) 'The dog sat on the tuckerbox/Nine miles from Gundagai', usu. recited as '*shat* on ...' thus the derog.]

tuckered out adj. [mid-19C] (Aus./US) exhausted, worn out. [9C–13C SE *tuck*, to punish, to ill-treat]

tuck-hunter n. [mid-19C] one who is keen to seek out sources of feasting. [TUCK n.¹ + SE *hunter*]

Tuckie/Tuk/Tukkie n. [1910s+] (S.Afr.) a student of the Transvaal University College, since 1930 renamed University of Pretoria (cf. UPPIE). [initials *T.U.C.* + dimin. *-kie*]

tuck in v.¹ [early 19C+] to eat heartily or greedily. [SE *tuck in*, in the sense of 'put away']

tuck in v.² [1990s] to beat up, to assault. [SE *tuck in*, but *see* ety. at TUCKERED OUT]

tucking in n. [early 19C+] eating heartily. [TUCK v.²]

tuck in your tuppeny phr. [late 19C] pull in your buttocks, don't slouch. [? rhy. sl. *twopenny bun* = BUM n.²]

tuck on a price, to phr. [late 19C] to put a price up to unacceptable heights.

tuck-out n. [mid-19C] (Aus.) a fight, a beating. [for ety. *see* TUCKERED OUT]

tucks of time n. [20C] (Irish) plenty of time.

tuck up v. **1** [mid-17C+] to hang. **2** [1940s–50s] to defraud, to steal from. [TUCK v.¹]

tuck up fair n. [mid-19C] the gallows (cf. DANCE AT TUCK 'EM FAIR; TUCK 'EM FAIR). [TUCK v.¹ + SE *fair*]

tuckus *see* TOCHES.

Tucson blanket *see* CALIFORNIA BLANKET.

'tude n. *see* ATTITUDE.

tuel *see* TEWEL.

Tuesday is longer than Monday *see* MONDAY COMES BEFORE SUNDAY.

tuff adj. [1990s] (US teen) good or cool. [mis-sp. SE *tough*]

tuft n.¹ [mid-18C–late 19C] a titled undergraduate. [for ety. *see* TUFT-HUNTER]

tuft n.² [1970s+] female pubic hair.

tuft-hunter n. [mid-18C–19C] a snob, a toady, a social climber (cf. TOFF). [university jargon *tuft-hunter*, one who pursued the acquaintance of rich or titled noblemen. The *tuft* was that adorning the mortarboards of titled students – of gold threads rather than the usual black, such aristocrats were themselves known as *tufts*]

tug n.¹ [late 19C–1900s] a dirty, uncouth, repellent person. [? generalized use of Etonian public school jargon *tug*, a scholar, a clever person, a (too) hard worker; itself abbr. SE *tug-mutton*, a ref. to their meals but ? also to masturbation. Such figures are disdained by their aristocratic peers]

tug n.² [late 19C–1930s] (Aus.) a card-sharp. [? they *tug* cards from the bottom of the pack]

tug n.³ [1950s+] masturbation; thus *have a tug* [1950s+] (Aus.) to masturbate. [SE *tug*]

tug n.⁴ [1960s+] an arrest (cf. GRAB; PULL).

tug-button Tuesday n. [mid-19C] the Tuesday before Advent (cf. CRIB-CRUST MONDAY; PAY-OFF WEDNESDAY; STIR-UP SUNDAY).

tugger n. [20C] (Irish) a woman who deals in old clothes. [the wicker boxcar in which she collects her stock and which she tugs around the streets]

tug-mutton n. [17C] a pimp. [SE *tug* + MUTTON n.²]

tug one's slug, to phr. [1990s] to masturbate.

tug one's taffy, to phr. [1990s] (US) to masturbate (cf. TAFFY-TUGGER). [SAmE *taffy*, toffee]

tug o' war n. [20C] a prostitute. [rhy. sl.]

tuies see TOOIES.

tuifu n. [1940s+] (US) a terrible blunder (cf. SNAFU phr.). [orig. usage, abbr. the ultimate in fuck ups]

Tuk/Tukkie see TUCKIE.

tulip n. [late 19C] a bishop's mitre. [resemblance]

tulip-sauce n. [1900s] a kiss, the act of kissing. [pun on 'two lips']

tulips of the goes n. [mid-19C] the cream of the fashionable world. [SE tulip + GO n.¹]

tullibon see TOLOBEN.

tully-vally see TILLY-VALLY.

tum/tum-tum n. [mid-19C+] (juv.) the stomach (cf. TUMMY). [abbr. + redup.]

tumble n.¹ [20C] an act of sexual intercourse (cf. BASH n.²). [TUMBLE v.¹]

tumble n.² [1900s–30s] a drink. [rhy. sl. tumble down the sink]

tumble n.³ [1920s+] (US) a sign of recognition, a response; usu. in phrs. (Aus.) give a tumble, take a tumble, to understand suddenly. [TUMBLE v.²]

tumble v.¹ 1 [early 17C+] to seduce, to have sexual intercourse (cf. BANG v.¹). 2 [1960s+] (Aus.) to confuse, to throw off balance. [SE tumble, to cause to fall]

tumble v.² 1 [mid-19C+] to realize, to notice; thus tumble to oneself, take a tumble to oneself, to wake up to a situation. 2 [late 19C] to agree (to), to take a liking (to). [fig. uses of SE tumble on, chance on]

tumble v.³ [20C] (US Und.) to be arrested (cf. FALL v.¹).

tumble v.⁴ [1930s+] to have a drink. [TUMBLE n.²]

tumble-a-bed n. [late 18C–19C] a chambermaid. [her stereotypical availability]

tumble and trip n. [20C] a whip-round. [rhy. sl.]

tumbledown n. 1 [early–mid-19C] grog. 2 [late 19C+] any form of alcohol. [rhy. sl. tumble down the sink = drink]

tumble down to grass, to phr. [late 19C] to go to rack and ruin. [the image of once cultivated fields returning to grass]

tumble-in n. [mid-19C] an act of sexual intercourse. [TUMBLE IN v.]

tumble in v. [mid-19C+] 1 to have sexual intercourse. 2 to go to bed. [ext. of TUMBLE v.¹]

tumble in the hay see ROLL IN THE HAY.

tumbler n.¹ [16C–early 19C] the member of a confidence tricking team who searches out and ensnares a suitable victim. [SE tumbler, a dog like a small greyhound, formerly used to catch rabbits (i.e. CONY n.¹)]

tumbler n.² [late 17C–early 19C] a cart (cf. SHOVE THE TUMBLER). [SE tumbler, a tumbril]

tumble to v. [mid–late 19C] 1 to involve oneself energetically or enthusiastically. 2 (US) to discover, to become aware of. [TUMBLE v.²]

tumble to pieces, to phr. [mid–late 19C] to go successfully through childbirth. [the pieces are the mother and the new-born child]

tumble-turd n. [1940s–50s] (W.I.) a short, stocky person. [18C US regional dial. tumble-turd, a large black beetle that rolls and buries pieces of dung]

tumble up v. [early–mid-19C] (orig. naut.) 1 to rush, to hurry. 2 to rise from bed. [SE tumble]

tum-jack n. [1940s–50s] the stomach. [corruption of SE stomach]

tummler n. [20C] 1 (US) the 'life and soul of the party', a person who talks a great deal but accomplishes little. 2 (US, show business) the MC of a (Jewish) hotel in Catskill Mts, NY (cf. BORSCHT BELT). [Yid./Ger. Tummel, disorder]

tummy n. [mid-19C+] (juv.) the stomach (cf. TUM). [abbr.]

tummy banana n. [1980s+] the penis (cf. LADIES' LOLLIPOP).

tummy mud n. [1990s] vomit.

tummy tickler n. [mid–late 19C] the penis.

tump n. [1930s+] rubbish, nonsense. [? dial. tump, a dump]

tump v. [17C] to have sexual intercourse. [SE tump, to pile a mound of earth round a root]

tumpa adj. [1950s+] (W.I. Rasta) a stump; thus tumpa-foot man, a one-footed man.

tump over v. [1970s] (US campus) to knock over. [SE tumble, to make fall]

tum-tum see TUM.

tun n. [mid-19C–1900s] a drunkard. [abbr. LUSHINGTON + pun on SE tun, a large barrel]

tuna/tuna fish n. [1950s+] 1 (US campus) a girlfriend, a woman. 2 (orig. US Black) the vagina (cf. BEARDED CLAM). [the identification of women with fish]

tunaface n. [1990s] a lesbian. [TUNA + sfx. -face]

tuna fish see TUNA.

tuna naan/taco n. [1990s] a woman's genitals. [TUNA (2) + naan, a variety of Ind. bread/taco, a Mexican cornmeal pancake]

tuna town n. [1990s] a woman's genitalia. [TUNA (2) + SE town]

tuna wagon n. [1970s+] (US) an old, decrepit car. [its only use would be to convey fish]

tune v. 1 [late 18C+] to beat, to thrash. 2 [1970s+] (S.Afr.) to speak, to tell. 3 [1980s] (S.Afr.) to enjoy life. 4 [1980s+] (S.Afr.) to tease, to hoax, to deceive. [? to get a fig. tune – pos. or otherwise – from one's target]

tuned adj.¹ [1920s+] (US) drunk. [SE tuned up]

tuned adj.² [1970s+] (Can. teen) having been used for sexual intercourse (cf. HAD). [? one has 'danced' to another's tune]

tuned in adj. [1950s+] aware of what is going on, at one with the nuances and niceties of a situation or conversation. [TUNE IN]

tuned out adj. [1950s+] 1 out of touch, unaware. 2 daydreaming, inattentive. [radio imagery]

tune in v. [1950s+] (US) to be aware, culturally sophisticated; thus 1960s hippie slogan 'turn on, tune in, drop out' (cf. TURN ON). [radio imagery]

tune off v. [1950s+] (US) to calm someone down, esp. when this will stop them from 'broadcasting' facts detrimental to one's own interest. [radio imagery]

tune one's pipes, to phr. [late 19C] to cry. [pun on SE pipe one's eye]

tune out v. [1970s+] to lose concentration, deliberately or otherwise. [radio imagery]

tunes n. [1980s+] (US campus) music.

tune someone grief/skeef, to phr. [1970s+] (S.Afr.) to abuse someone verbally, to give someone trouble. [TUNE v. + SE grief/S.Afr. skeef, disapprovingly, ult. Afk. skeef, askew, crooked]

tune the old cow died of n. 1 [mid-19C] a discordant or unpleasant piece of music. 2 [late 19C+] a lecture or homily delivered to a beggar instead of money; in Aus. as tune the old cow died on.

tune up v. [late 18C+] to beat, to thrash. [ext. of TUNE v. (1)]

tuniopperty see TOONIOPPERTY.

tunker n. [mid-19C–1900s] a street preacher (cf. DIPPER). [Penn Du. dunken, a Baptist, lit. 'dipped']

tunnel n. [19C] the vagina (cf. ALLEY n.¹).

tunnel v. [1960s+] (US Und.) to go into hiding.

tunnel-grunters n. [19C] potatoes. [dial.]

tunnel rat n. [20C] (US prison) one who escapes by digging their way out of prison (cf. MOLE n.²).

Tunnels n. [late 19C] the Opera Comique in the Strand. [the theatre, which was demolished in 1899 during the building of the Aldwych, was built largely underground and featured a number of subterranean passages, leading patrons from the street to the auditorium]

tunnel stiff *n.* [20C] (US) an underground tunnel worker. [SE *tunnel* + STIFF n.³]

tunti *n.* [1950s+] (W.I. Rasta) the vagina. [for ety. *see* TUN-TUN]

tun-tun *n.* [1950s+] (W.I./USVI) **1** the vagina. **2** a term of affection. [suggested links to DUNDUS or Carib.E. *tun-tun*, turned cornmeal, are unlikely; ? SE *turn* + redup., the movements of intercourse]

tup *n.¹* [late 16C+] a cuckold. [SE *tup*, a ram]

tup *n.²* [late 19C–1950s] (W.I.) **1** 1½ pence (post-1969 value 1.25 cents). **2** a very small amount. [abbr. SE *tuppence*]

tup *v.* [late 16C+] to have sexual intercourse. [SE *tup*, a ram; thus Shakespeare's *Othello* (1604), when Iago informs Brabantio that: 'An old Blacke Ram Is tupping your White Ewe']

tup *adj.* [late 19C] arrested. [pron. SE (*locke*)d *up*]

tup-an-gill *n.* [mid-19C+] (W.I.) 2½ pence (post-1969 value 2 cents). [TUP n.² + GILL n.²]

tuppence *n.* [1940s+] (Aus.) a fool, a halfwit (cf. NOT THE FULL QUID). [phr. '(only) *tuppence* in the quid']

tuppeny halfpenny *adj.* [late 19C+] cheap, second-rate, inferior. [the low value of the sum]

tupper *n.* [late 19C] (society) a bore. ['takes its rise from Mr Martin *Tupper* who wrote a phenomenally successful book called *Proverbial Philosophy* – composed entirely of self-evident propositions' (Ware)]

tuppy *adj.* [1910s] (Aus.) of an animal, worn out, thus worthless. [? SE *tupped*, used for breeding]

tu quoque *n.* [late 18C–early 19C] the vagina. [lit. Lat. 'you also', ? play on QUIM and similar terms for the vagina beginning with *q*]

turbo *n.* [1980s+] (drugs) crack cocaine and marijuana smoked together. [SE *turbo*-charged]

turbobitch/turboslut *n.* [1980s+] (US campus) an unpleasant, irritable, neg. woman (cf. HYPERDRIVE WHORE). [SE *turbo* + BITCH n.¹/SE *slut*]

turd *n.* [11C+] **1** a piece of excrement. **2** an unappealing person. [OE *tord*, ult. presumed Indo-Eur. root *der, tear or split. Orig. use, *c.*1000, was simply excrement, the additional pej. meaning was added mid-13C. Thus Harman's *Caveat* (1567) translates the Und. phrase 'Gerry gan the Ruffian cly thee' as 'A torde in thy mouth, the deuill take thee' (*Gerry*, JERE). As with many similar terms, vulgar rather than actual sl., *turd* was excluded from polite speech (and dictionaries) by late 18C. It has remained off-limits, although like many of the 'milder' obscenities, it has crept gradually into spoken, if not written English, esp. where, like its cognate SHIT, it refers not to excrement, but to a human object of derision or dislike]

turd-burglar *n.* [1960s+] (orig. Aus.) a homosexual man (cf. BUM-PUNCHER). [TURD + SE *burglar*, his predilection for anal intercourse]

turd for you! *excl.* [mid–late 19C] a general phr. of dismissal; i.e. *go to hell!* [TURD]

turd in the punchbowl *phr.* [1990s] (US) a general term of abuse. [TURD]

turd in your teeth! *excl.* [17C] go to hell! (and stay there). [TURD]

turd-packer *n.* [1930s+] (orig. US) a homosexual (cf. BUM-PUNCHER). [TURD + SE *packer*]

turd-puncher *n.* [1990s] a homosexual (cf. BUM-PUNCHER). [TURD + SE *puncher*]

turf *n.¹* **1** [mid-19C+] the highway or street as the home of the criminal underworld. **2** [1930s+] the area with which one is familiar and where one is recognized as a regular figure (cf. BEAT n.¹). **3** [1950s+] (US) the area controlled by a street gang. **4** [1970s+] that area of life, work or other activity in which a person's authority or influence is recognized.

turf/track, the *n.²* **1** [late 19C–1900s] the occupation of prostitution; thus *on the turf*, working as a prostitute.

turf *v.* [1940s–50s] (Aus.) to have sexual intercourse in the open air. [SE *turf*, the grass]

turfer *n.* [late 19C–1900s] a prostitute. [TURF n.²]

turf it *v.* [late 19C–1930s] to sleep outdoors, usu. under a tent.

turf it! *excl.* [1930s+] (Aus.) be quiet! shut up! [TURF OUT]

turf out/off *v.* [late 19C+] to eject, to throw out, supposedly on to some grass.

turf patrol *n.* [1980s+] (Irish) a session of smoking marijuana. [play on GRASS n.⁴]

turf up *v.* [1920s+] (Aus.) to abandon, to leave a job. [TURF (OUT)]

turistas *see* TOURISTAS.

turk *n.¹* **1** [late 17C+] a boorish, unpleasant person. **2** [mid-19C+] (US) an Irish immigrant. **3** [20C] a sexually active man. **4** [1930s+] (gay) one who enjoys anal intercourse. [racist stereotyping; (2) prob. underpinned by Irish *torc*, a boar or hog]

turk *n.²* [20C] (Aus.) a *turkey*. [abbr.]

turk *n.³* [1930s+] (US Black) the area with which one is familiar and where one is recognized as a regular figure. [TURF n.¹ (2)]

turk *v.* [20C] of a man, to have sexual intercourse, esp. with a degree of brutality. [racial stereotyping]

turkey *n.¹* [mid-19C+] (US) an Irish immigrant. [TURK n.¹ (2)]

turkey *n.²* [1910s] (Aus.) a vagrant's pack. [resemblance to the bulky bird]

turkey *n.³* **1** [1920s+] an appalling, unquestionable disaster, esp. in show business. **2** [1920s+] a failure, an incompetent. **3** [1930s+] (drugs) inferior quality or even fake drugs. **4** [1950s+] a dull, incompetent, unappealing person. **5** [1980s+] (US Und./teen) the victim of a mugging. [according to Cohen IV (1995) pp.100–19, originating in the theatrical *turkey show*, a touring show, usu. burlesque, mounted at a moment's notice and staffed by a third-rate cast, even stage-struck amateurs]

turkey *n.⁴* [1980s+] (drugs) **1** cocaine. **2** amphetamine (cf. A n.²). [ety. unknown]

turkey-buyer *n.* [late 19C] a rich person. [orig. use is Leadenhall Market; turkeys were beyond the pockets of the poor]

turkey merchant *n.* **1** [late 17C–18C] one who buys and sells turkeys. **2** [mid-18C–mid-19C] a poulterer. **3** [mid-19C] (Und.) a dealer in smuggled silk. [puns on SE *Turkey merchant*, one who trades with Turkey; in (3) the play was on *merchant*, i.e. a legitimate dealer]

turkey neck *n.* [1950s+] the penis (cf. BACON n.¹). [supposed resemblance]

turkey off *v.* [20C] (Aus./N.Z.) to leave in a hurry, to run off. [imitative of the farmyard bird]

turkey on a string *n.* [1970s+] (US Black) one who is infatuated and thus easily led and controlled. [ext. of TURKEY n.³ (4)]

turkey shoot *n.* [1940s+] (US) **1** a combat in which one's own side wins without any difficulty, killing and destroying on a large scale. **2** anything exceptionally easy. [the large SE *turkey* presents an easy target]

turking *n.* [20C] sexual intercourse, copulating. [TURK v.]

Turkish *n.* [late 19C–1900s] **1** *Turkish* tobacco. **2** *Turkish* delight. [abbr.]

Turkish delight *n.* [1960s+] (gay) pederasty. [racial stereotyping + pun]

Turkish rope *n.* [1990s] (US Black gang) a gold neck-chain, with large links, as worn by successful street thugs. [? the gold or chain comes from *Turkey*]

Turkish shore *n.* [late 17C–early 19C] Lambeth, Southark,

Rotherhithe, all areas south of the River Thames where the innocent visitor to London was liable to meet trouble. [the neg. image of *Turkey*]

turn *n.*[1] [late 16C–late 18C] a judicial hanging. [SE *turn off*, to kill]

turn *n.*[2] [19C] an act of sexual intercourse (cf. TAKE A TURN ON SHOOTER'S HILL). [SE *turn-up*, a prostitute + *turn*, an act, a performance]

turn *n.*[3] [mid-19C+] a shock, usu. unpleasant; often as *a nasty turn*.

turn *n.*[4] [1950s+] (Aus., usu. teen) a party. [TURN IT ON]

turn *v.*[1] [20C] (US Und.) to give state's evidence (cf. TURN STATE).

turn *v.*[2] [1980s+] (Black) to bribe. [i.e. to *turn* an innocent person into a villain; note espionage *turn*, to persuade an enemy agent to start working for one's own side]

turnabout *n.*[1] [20C] (Aus.) sodomy (cf. TURN OVER *v.*[3]). [the turning to present one's buttocks]

turnabout *n.*[2] [1980s+] (drugs) amphetamine (cf. A *n.*[2]). [the drug's effects]

turn and wind the penny, to *phr.* [late 17C–early 18C] to spend one's money judiciously.

turn an honest penny, to *phr.* [1910s–20s] to work as a pimp. [ironic reversal]

turn around *v.* [1960s+] (US) to change someone's attitude or behaviour.

turn a trick, to *phr.* (US) **1** [mid-19C+] to carry out a successful robbery or theft. **2** [1910s+] to be paid for sexual intercourse, either as a professional prostitute or on a one-off or occasional basis in between working as a student, actress or model. [TRICK *n.*[4] (1)]

turn blue! *excl.* [1950s–60s] euph. version of GO TO HELL!

turn charlie *v.* [1950s] to act in a cowardly manner, esp. when one thus lets down one's companions. [SE *turn* + CHARLEY (HOWARD)]

turn copper *v.* [late 19C+] (US) to become an informer (cf. COME COPPER). [SE *turn* + COPPER *n.*[3] (4)]

turn cur *v.* [late 19C] to turn informer (cf. DOG *n.*[8]).

turn dog *v.* [mid-19C+] (Aus.) to become an informer. [SE *turn* + DOG *n.*[8]]

turn down *v.*[1] [mid-18C–mid-19C] to drink down, to 'toss off' a drink. [the tilting of the glass or bottle]

turn down *v.*[2] [late 19C] (orig. US) to reject, to snub, to rebuke. [20C use is SE]

turn down one's cup, to *phr.* [late 19C] (society) to die. [the old habit of turning over one's tea or coffee cup as an indication that one no longer wished for it to be filled]

turned *adj.* [1930s+] (US) of a certain type, disposed, natured, always in combs., e.g. *nice-turned*, *mild-turned*.

turned around *adj.* [1960s–70s] (US) confused, disorientated.

turned off *adj.*[1] [late 19C–1910s] (society) married.

turned off *adj.*[2] [1950s+] **1** out of touch, unaware. **2** daydreaming, inattentive (cf. TUNED OUT). [electronics imagery]

turned on *adj.* **1** [1950s+] (US) intoxicated, esp. by drugs. **2** [1960s+] sexually stimulated. **3** [1960s+] aware, sophisticated, up-to-the-minute. [electrical imagery]

turned over *adj.* [mid-19C] remanded in custody pending one's trial. [? *turned over* to the authorities]

turned up *adj.* [early–mid-19C] **1** stopped and searched by the police. **2** acquitted of a crime in court, esp. through lack of evidence.

turner out *n.* [mid-19C] a counterfeiter. [SE *turn out*, to manufacture]

turn funny *see* GET FUNNY.

turn gay, to *phr.* [late 19C] to start working as a prostitute. [GAY *adj.*[1] (2)]

turn in *v.* **1** [late 17C+] to go to bed. **2** [20C] to stop doing something.

turn Indian *v.* [mid-19C] (US) to revert to nature, to abandon one's 'civilized' habits. [racist stereotyping]

turning-tree *n.* [mid-16C–mid-17C] the gallows. [SE *turn off*, to hang + (TRIPLE) TREE; also an image of the turning, hanging corpse]

turn in one's dinner pail *see* HAND IN ONE'S DINNER PAIL.

turn into fish food, to *phr.* [20C] to drown.

turnip *n.*[1] [mid–late 19C] an old-fashioned watch; thus *cut turnip-tops*, to steal a watch, chain and seals. [its rotundity and thickness]

turnip *n.*[2] **1** [mid-19C] a simpleton, a fool. **2** [mid-19C+] the head (cf. SWEDE *n.*[2]). **3** [1910s–20s] a term of affectionate address, usu. as *old turnip* (cf. OLD BEAN; OLD FRUIT).

turnip greens *n.* [1970s–80s] (US Black) marijuana. [play on the popular soul food]

turnip-pate *n.* [late 17C–18C] a very fair head of hair; thus *turnip-pated*, having white hair or very light blond hair.

turnip-snagger *n.* [20C] (Irish) a peasant, a country person. [SE *turnip* + *snag*, to snatch]

turn it down *v.* [1960s+] (gay) to moderate one's more flagrantly homosexual behaviour. [radio/TV imagery]

turn it on *v.* **1** [1940s+] (Aus.) to start a fight. **2** [1940s+] (Aus.) to provide food and drink. **3** [1940s+] (Aus.) to allow or offer sex, often with more than one partner. **4** [1980s+] to make things happen, to intensify things, to 'hot up' the atmosphere.

turn it up! *excl.* [17C+] stop doing that!

turn Japanese *v.* [1990s] to masturbate. [? one's eyes half-closed, supposedly resembling *Japanese* eyes, during orgasm; or play on PLAY CHOPSTICKS]

turn-off *n.* [1960s+] anything repellent, whether physical or emotional. [TURN OFF *v.*]

turn off *v.* [1960s+] **1** to alienate. **2** to repel sexually.

turn off the gas, to *phr.* [late 19C] to stop bragging or boasting (cf. TURN ON THE GAS). [GAS *n.*[1] (1)]

turn-on *n.* **1** [1950s–60s] (Can.) something done by an 'in-group' to provoke outsiders. **2** [1960s+] a thrill, sexual or otherwise. **3** [1960s+] (drugs) enough of a drug to produce its desired effects. [TURN ON *v.*]

turn on *v.* **1** [late 19C] to persuade someone to do something. **2** [1940s+] (Aus./N.Z.) to provide liquor, e.g. for a party. **3** [1950s+] to take drugs. **4** [1960s+] to offer drugs to another person. **5** [1960s+] to stimulate, usu. sexually, to appeal to someone. [(2), note exhortation by Timothy Leary (1920–96) to 'turn on, tune in and drop out']

turn on a cabbage-leaf, to *phr.* [20C] (N.Z.) of a horse, to react immediately to the rider's control. [the small dimensions of the leaf]

turn on a dime, to *phr.* [1960s+] (US) usu. of a vehicle, to turn in a very small space. [DIME *n.*]

turn one's damper down, to *phr.* [1900s–30s] (US Black) to calm down, to relax, esp. as imper.; *turn your damper down!* [SE *damper*, a device to slow down machinery]

turn oneself round *v.* [19C] to accustom oneself to a new job. [the image of a dog turning itself round when settling itself on the ground]

turn one's face to the wall, to *phr.* [1940s+] to die.

turn one's toes up/to the daisies, to *phr.* [mid-19C+] to die (cf. PUSH UP DAISIES).

turn on the fan, to *phr.* [20C] (US) to hurry, to move quickly. [FAN *v.*[2]]

turn on the gas, to *phr.* [late 19C] to start bragging or boasting (cf. TURN OFF THE GAS).

turn on/up the heat/on, to *phr.*[1] [1930s+] (US) to pressurize, to put pressure on.

turn on/up the heat/on, to phr.[2] [1930s+] (US) to cover with a gun. [HEAT n.[3]]

turn on the main see TURN ON THE WATERWORKS.

turn on the toe, to phr. [late 16C–early 17C] to push (the victim) off the ladder at the climax of a judicial hanging. [a ladder was employed before the early 19C development of the drop]

turn on the waterworks/main, to phr. [mid-19C+] to start crying (cf. TURN THE TAP ON).

turn-out n. [early 19C+] a fist-fight (cf. TURN-UP n.[1]). [the participants turn out to fight]

turn out v.[1] [19C] (Aus.) to leave home and become a bushranger. [SE turn out, to leave home and start work]

turn out v.[2] [early–mid-19C] to get out of bed. [SE turn-out, a getting up from one's bed]

turn out v.[3] [20C] to beat up. [? TURN-OUT n.[1]]

turn out v.[4] [1940s+] (orig. US Black) to initiate a newcomer in a variety of situations, e.g. (pimp) to run a prostitute on the streets; (Hell's Angels) to use a woman for multiple sex; (US Und.) to make a new inmate into a prison homosexual.

turn out crabs, to phr. [mid-18C–late 19C] to prove a disappointment. [gaming jargon crab, the lowest throw at the game of hazard (two aces)]

turn out one's lights/own lights, to phr. [20C] to commit suicide.

turn out the set/the set out/the shit out, to phr. [1970s+] (US Black) to disrupt a situation or occasion, esp. permanently. [SET n.[3] (1)/SHIT n.[6]]

turnover n. [1980s+] (US) one who is seen as betraying their race, usu. Black or Puerto Rican, by assimilating into or at least succeeding in the white society. [TURN OVER ON]

turn over v.[1] **1** [mid-19C+] (Und.) to search a house or apartment, usu. with the maximum of damage and mess. **2** [early 19C+] (Und.) to acquit for lack of evidence. **3** [1950s+] to beat up, to attack.

turn over v.[2] [mid-19C+] to distress, to make nauseous.

turn over v.[3] [1960s+] (gay) to allow anal intercourse (cf. TURN-ABOUT n.[1]). [the physical act that may precede the intercourse]

turn over on v. [1960s+] (US prison) to inform on (a fellow inmate) (cf. FLIP v.[3]).

turn over the perch, to phr. [late 16C] **1** to upset, to humiliate. **2** to overcome, to conquer. **3** to kill (cf. KNOCK OFF ONE'S PERCH).

turn paper collars, to phr. [late 19C] (US) to live in poverty. [SE paper collar, a symbolically 'poor' garment]

turnpike n. [19C] the vagina (cf. ALLEY n.[1]).

turnpike man n. [late 18C–early 19C] a parson. [from the fees or tolls the clergy collect for christenings and funerals: 'our entrance into and exit from the world' (Grose 1785)]

turnpike sailor n. [18C] a wandering beggar who poses as the victim of a shipwreck (cf. DRY-LAND SAILOR; FRESH WATER MARINER).

turn purple v. [20C] (US) to become very angry, livid. [one's lit. purple face]

turn red as a turkey-cock see GO RED AS A TURKEY-COCK.

turn roast to roast, to phr. [16C] to be reduced from arrogance to humility. [the turning of cooking meat]

turn-round pudding n. [late 19C] porridge or any form of pudding that requires stirring.

turn snitch v. [late 18C+] to become an informer. [SNITCH n.[1] (3)]

turn someone on/to v. [late 19C] to set someone to work.

turn someone's crank, to phr. [1970s] for something to give a person pleasure.

turn someone's mouth behind their back, to phr. [20C] (W.I.) to beat one up severely, to 'knock someone's face through the back of their neck'.

turn someone up v. [mid-19C+] (Und.) to inform against someone, to turn someone over to the police.

turn split v. [early 19C] to become an informer, to inform against someone. [SPLIT n.[5]]

turn square v. [mid-19C] of a criminal, to reform, to join the world of the law-abiding. [SQUARE adj.]

turn stag v. [late 18C–early 19C] to betray someone, to inform against someone. [STAG n.[2]]

turn state v. [20C] (US Und.) to give state's evidence. [abbr.]

turn the air blue see MAKE THE AIR BLUE.

turn the bucket on see DROP THE BUCKET ON.

turn the buckle of the girdle/belt, to phr. [late 16C–19C] to get oneself ready to fight. [the belt was pulled round so its buckle might not injure one's stomach]

turn the corner, to phr. [20C] of a man, to become homosexual or acknowledge one's homosexuality.

turn the hands on someone's dial, to phr. [mid-19C–1900s] to scar or otherwise disfigure someone's face, usu. in a fight. [DIAL]

turn the set/shit out see TURN OUT THE SET.

turn the tables, to phr. [1930s+] (gay) of a male homosexual prostitute, to blackmail a client. [SE turn the tables, to reverse the relations between two parties]

turn the tap on, to phr. [late 19C+] to weep. [the implication is of a lack of sincerity]

turn thumbs down, to phr. [20C] (US) to reject or refuse. [for ety. see THUMB DOWN]

turn ticks on v. [1950s] (W.I.) to beg from. [? TICK n.[2]]

turn to bag and wallet, to phr. [late 16C] to become a professional beggar. [SE bag + wallet, a pedlar's bag]

turn-tongue adj. [20C] (W.I.) duplicitous, hypocritical, lying.

turn tricks v. [20C] to engage in prostitution (cf. TURN A TRICK). [TRICK n.[4] (1)]

turn Turk v. [late 16C] to become a renegade, a rebel. [racial stereotyping, note TURK n.[1]]

turn turtle v. [1950s+] (orig. US) **1** to turn upside down. **2** to back down, to act in a cowardly manner.

turn-up n.[1] **1** [early–mid-19C] a boxing or wrestling match or contest. **2** [mid-19C–1900s] a sudden exit, a speedy departure. **3** [mid-19C+] a street fight. **4** [late 19C–1910s] (society) a minor quarrel, a tiff. [SE turn up, to throw into disorder]

turn-up n.[2] [mid-19C+] a surprise. [abbr. TURN-UP FOR THE BOOKS]

turn up v.[1] **1** [mid–late 17C] to prostitute oneself. **2** [19C] to have sexual intercourse. [OED cites sense (1) only as 'apparently'. Note TURN UP ONE'S TAIL]

turn up v.[2] **1** [early 18C+] to set free, to release (a prisoner). **2** [early–mid-19C] to run away. **3** [late 19C+] to alter, to change. **4** [late 19C+] to abandon, esp. in imper. turn it up, give up, stop what you are doing. [SE turn up, to turn a horse loose]

turn up v.[3] [mid–late 19C] to arrest, to search. [? SE turn upside down]

turn up a trump, to phr. [early 19C] to have a piece of financial good fortune. [card-playing imagery]

turn-up for the books phr. [mid-19C+] a pleasant surprise. [racing jargon turn-up, an unexpected piece of luck, ult. SE turn up, to arrive, to appear]

turn up jack see CUT UP JACK.

turn up one's heels see KICK UP ONE'S HEELS phr.[1].

turn up one's tail, to phr. [late 17C–early 18C] of a woman, to have sexual intercourse. [SE turn up + TAIL n.[1] (2)]

turn/curl up one's toes, to phr. [mid-19C] to die.

turn-ups n. [late 19C] the rejection of a suitor. [? ext. of TURN UP v.[2]]

turn up the heat/on see TURN ON THE HEAT.

turn up trumps, to *phr.* [mid-19C+] to turn out right in the end, esp. when this result comes as a surprise. [card-playing imagery]

turps *n.* [1930s+] (Aus.) **1** beer. **2** any form of alcohol; thus *on the turps*, drinking (heavily) (cf. METHO n.[1]). [abbr. SE *turpentine*]

turret-top *n.* [1940s] (US) a bald person. [SE *turret*, the conical steel cover for a large gun]

turtle *n.*[1] *see* TURTLEDOVE.

turtle *n.*[2] [20C] (orig. Aus.) a promiscuous woman. [i.e. 'once she's on her back, she's fucked']

turtledove/turtle *n.* [mid-19C+] usu. in pl., a glove, esp. those worn by housebreakers to hide fingerprints. [rhy. sl.]

turtle-frolic *n.* [mid-18C–late 19C] (orig. US) a feast, the centrepiece of which is a turtle.

turtleneck *n.* [1990s] (US gay) an uncircumcised penis. [resemblance]

turtles *n.* [1940s] (US Black) turning movements of the body when dancing, running or fighting.

turtle shit *n.* [1950s+] (US) nonsense, rubbish. Other less common combs. include *buzzard shit*, *cat shit*, *hen shit*, *owl shit*, *rat shit*, *whale shit* (cf. BULLSHIT n.). [SE *turtle* + SHIT n.[4]]

turtle soup *n.* [late 19C] sheep's head broth (cf. CLARE MARKET DUCK).

tush *n.*[1] *see* TOSHEROON.

tush/tushie *n.*[2] [late 19C+] the buttocks. [TOCHES]

tush *n.*[3] [1930s–50s] (US Black) a wealthy, light-skinned Black person. [ety. unknown; ? link to TUX; i.e. their use of a dinner jacket for social occasions]

tush *n.*[4] [1940s] (W.I.) human excrement. [Djerma *tosi*, excrement; but note TUSH n.[2]]

tush *adj.* [1930s–50s] (US Black) classy, well-mannered, sophisticated. [TUSH n.[3]]

tush *v.* [1910s] (W.I.) to excrete. [TUSH n.[4]]

tusheroon *see* TOSHEROON.

tushie *see* TUSH n.[2].

tushroon *n.* [1900s–50s] (US Black) money. [var. on TOSHEROON]

tush-teeth *n.* [20C] (W.I.) buckteeth, protruding teeth. [SE *tusk*]

tuskee/tuskie *n.* [1970s–80s] (US Black) a large marijuana cigarette. [? resemblance to an elephant's *tusk*]

tuskin *n.* [late 18C–early 19C] a country carter or ploughman. [? dial. *tush*, the broad part of a ploughshare, ult. *tusk*, tooth]

tusseroon *see* TOSHEROON.

tussle *v.* [mid–late 19C] to argue. [SE post-1890, Scot. *tousle*, to push around roughly, to struggle or contend with]

tussocker *n.* [late 19C] (Aus.) a tramp or vagrant pretending to seek work but actually keener on board and lodging (cf. SUNDOWNER). [Aus./N.Z. *tussock land*, uncultivated grassland used for sheep-grazing, across which he has travelled]

tussock-jumper *n.* [1960s+] (N.Z.) a musterer. [for ety. *see* TUSSOCKER]

tussy *n.* [19C] a drunkard (cf. TOSTIFICATED). [abbr. SE *intoxicated*]

tute *n.* [late 19C+] **1** a tutor. **2** a tutorial. [abbr.]

tutti-frutti *n.* [1980s+] (drugs) a variety of flavoured cocaine. [SE *tutti-frutti*, a multicoloured ice-cream]

Tuttle Nask *n.* [late 17C–late 18C] the Tothill house of correction in Tothill Fields, London. [*Tuttle*, i.e. Tothill + NASK]

tutus *n.* [1940s] (W.I.) the male genitals. [Carib.E. *tutu*, a conch shell]

tux *n.* [1920s+] (US) a dinner jacket. [abbr. SE *tuxedo*, a dinner jacket, named for Tuxedo Park, N.Y., where the jacket was first introduced at the country club in 1886]

tuzzy-muzzy/tuzimuzzy *n.* [early 18C–19C] the vagina. [dial. *tuzzy-muzzy*, dishevelled, ragged, rough]

t.v. *n.* [1970s+] a *t*ransvestite (cf. T/S).

TV style *n.* [1950s–60s] (gay) anal intercourse with one partner on his knees. [*TV*, television, which can optionally be watched when adopting this position for sex]

twack *n.* [1980s+] (US campus) a twelve-pack of beer. [*tw*elve + pack]

twaddle *n.* [late 18C] a bore. ['a fashionable term that for a while succeeded that of *bore*' (Grose 1796). SE *twaddle*, idle talk, nonsense, itself f. synon. *twattle*, ? ult. *tattle*]

twaddle *v.* [late 18C–mid-19C] to trifle, to 'mess around'. [SE *twaddle*]

twaddy *adj.* [late 18C] nonsensical. [SE *twaddle*]

twak *n.*[1] [mid-19C+] (S.Afr.) tobacco. [Afk. *tabak*]

twak *n.*[2] [1950s+] (S.Afr.) nonsense, rubbish. [Afk. *twak*, nonsense]

twam/twammy/twim *n.* [20C] the vagina. [? TWAT + QUIM or deliberate mispron. of TRIM n.]

twang *n.*[1] [late 17C–18C] a prostitute. [TWANG v.]

twang *n.*[2] [late 19C–1930s] (Aus.) opium. [Chinese or cod Chinese, ? f. *twankay*, green tea]

twang *v.* [17C+] to engage in spontaneous sexual intercourse. [? SE *twang*, to fire an arrow]

twange *n.* [1990s] the vagina. [? revival of TWANG n.[1] + MINGE]

twanger *n.* **1** [late 16C–late 19C] something very large or fine of its kind. **2** [20C] the penis (cf. BAT n.[7]). [fig. uses of SE *twang*, to reverberate]

twanging *adj.* [early 17C] excellent, first-rate (cf. RIPPING; STUNNING adj.). [SE *twang*, to give off a ringing note]

twangman *n.* [20C] (Irish) a pimp. [TWANG v. + sfx. -*man*]

twang one's/the wire, to *phr.* [1950s+] to masturbate.

twank *n.* [1960s+] **1** (gay) an older man. **2** in prostitute usage, an older man who enjoys watching young women at work but has no personal interest in sex. [? the pantomime 'dame' Widow *Twankey* or WANK n.]

twankay/twankey *n.* [1900s] gin. [tea trade jargon *twankey*, green tea, thus ? the root of the pantomime dame Widow *Twankey*]

twant *n.* [1980s+] (US drugs) a $20 bag of cannabis. [abbr. SE *twenty*]

twasted *n.* [1990s] an unpleasant person. [TWAT n. (2) + BASTARD]

twat/twot *n.* **1** [mid-17C+] the vagina. **2** [1920s+] a term of abuse. [? dial. *twitchel*, a narrow passage]

twatchel/twatchil/twatchylle *n.* [mid-17C–early 19C] the vagina. [dimin. of TWAT + dial. *twitchel*, a passage]

twat-faker *n.* [1900–20s] a pimp. [TWAT n. (1) + FAKER]

twat-hooks *see* CUNT-HOOKS.

twat-mag *n.* [1990s] a pornographic magazine. [TWAT n. (1) + SE *mag(azine)*]

twat-masher *n.* [1900–20s] a pimp, a procurer. [TWAT n. (1) + MASH v.[1] (1)]

twatmaster *n.* [1990s] a term of abuse or hostility. [TWAT n. (2) + sfx. -*master*]

twat-rug *n.* [late 19C–1900s] a woman's pubic hair. [TWAT n. (1) + SE *rug*]

twat-scourer *n.* **1** [late 17C] a general term of abuse. **2** [early 18C] a surgeon, a doctor. [TWAT n. (1) + *scourer*, a cleaner, a polisher]

twat-seller *n.* [20C] a prostitute. [TWAT n. (1) + SE *seller*]

twatted *n.* [1990s] assaulted, punched, beaten up. [thus rendered a TWAT n. (2)]

twattling-strings *n.* [early 17C–mid-18C] the anal sphincter, esp. in the context of breaking wind. [joc. use of dial. *twattle*, to chatter, to talk idly]

tweague *see* TWEAK n.[2].

tweak/tweake *n.*[1] **1** [late 17C–18C] a prostitute. **2** [early 18C–early 19C] a whoremonger. [? SE *tweak*, the act of tugging, thus fig. sexual intercourse]

tweak/tweague n.[2] [late 18C–early 19C] a state of excitement or agitation. [SE *tweak*, a wrench, a sharp tug]

tweak v.[1] [late 19C] to hit a target with a missile from a catapult. [TWEAKER n.[1]]

tweak v.[2] (drugs) **1** [1970s] to inject narcotics. **2** [1970s+] to suffer heroin or crack cocaine withdrawal. [SE *tweak*, to wrench, to pull sharply]

tweak/twig out v.[3] [1980s+] (US campus) **1** to hurt, to damage. **2** to lose control, to act eccentrically (cf. FREAK v.; FREAK OUT). [SE *tweak*, *twig* is mispron.]

tweake see TWEAK n.[1].

tweaked/tweeked adj. [1980s+] (US campus) **1** mad. **2** drunk or under the influence of a drug. **3** broken, out of order. **4** exhausted. **5** on edge, tense, nervous. [TWEAK v.[2]]

tweaker n.[1] [late 18C] a catapult. [SE *tweak*, to pinch]

tweaker n.[2] [1980s+] (drugs) a crack cocaine user searching desperately for drugs after a police raid. [TWEAK v.[2] (2)]

tweaking n. [1990s] (US Black) talking inappropriately or tactlessly. [SE *tweak*, i.e. to 'pinch' someone's sensibilities]

tweaking adj. [1990s] (US Black) intoxicated by drugs. [TWEAK v.[2]]

tweak mission n. [1980s+] (drugs) a search for crack cocaine. [TWEAK v. (2) + MISSION]

tweak one's twinkie, to phr. [20C] to masturbate.

twee adj. [20C] **1** 'sweet', dainty, chic. **2** 'affectedly dainty or quaint; over-nice, over-refined, precious, mawkish.' (*OED*). [juv. pron. of SE *sweet*]

tweeb see DWEEB.

tweed-capper n. [1910s] (Aus.) an immigrant from the UK. [the headgear worn]

tweedle, the n. [late 19C+] (Und.) **1** the selling of fraudulent diamonds, esp. in the form of a *tweedle*, a fake ring studded with paste diamonds. **2** the sale of any dubious goods. [SE *twiddle*, to twist]

tweedledum sir n. [late 19C] (society) usu. in pl., a baronet or knight who is given his honours for 'services to music', e.g. Sir Arthur Sullivan (1842–1900) (cf. GALLYPOT BARONET).

tweedler n. (Und.) **1** [1950s+] a small-time confidence trickster. **2** [1970s] a stolen vehicle which is passed off as perfectly legitimate. [TWEEDLE n.]

tweedling n. [1950s+] (Und.) selling stolen property or even non-existent property to innocent purchasers who assume the goods are legitimate. [TWEEDLE n.]

tweeds n. [1950s+] (Aus.) trousers; thus *drop one's tweeds*, of a woman, to have sexual intercourse.

tweegat jakkals n. [1990s] (S.Afr.) a term of extreme vilification. [Afk. *twee gat jakkals*, a jackal with two anuses]

tweek/tweeker n. [1980s] (drugs) methcathinone (cf. BATHTUB SPEED). [SE *tweak*; i.e. its effects]

tweeked see TWEAKED.

tweeker see TWEEK.

twelve godfathers n. [mid-19C] the jury; thus *you will be christened by twelve godfathers someday before long*. [they 'give a name' to one's crime]

1200 n. [1990s] in rap music, the Technics SL *1200* turntable, regarded as the best turntable for DJ'ing.

twelve-inch rule n. [20C] a fool. [rhy. sl.]

twelve o'clock! excl. [late 19C] time to be moving, time for action. [used by workmen with ref. to 12 o'clock midday, dinner time, when things are likely to speed up]

twelve o'clock high! excl. [1970s] (US Black) a cry of warning, the police are coming! [milit. jargon, the use of the clockface to indicate direction]

twelve o'clock high, check it out phr. [1980s+] (US campus) a phr. used to focus attention on someone in a group for the purpose of sex or romance. [for ety. *see* TWELVE O'CLOCK HIGH!]

twelver n. [late 17C–late 19C] one shilling (5p). [the twelve pennies it represented, use after 1730s mainly Aus.]

twenty n. [1980s+] (US drugs) $20 worth of crack cocaine.

twenty cents n. [1930s–70s] (US Black) **1** $20. **2** a $20 bag of marijuana.

twenty-five n.[1] [1960s+] (drugs) LSD. [its chemical name, *d-lysergic acid diethylamide-25*]

twenty-five n.[2] [1980s+] (US drugs) a $25 bag of cocaine.

25 boffos n. [20C] (US Und.) a 25-year sentence (cf. QUARTER n.[1]). [fig. use of BOFF n.[1]]

25 with an izl n. [1990s] (US) a prison sentence of 25 years to life. [SE *izl*, i.e. the * notation next to the years of one's sentence, denoting 'life']

twenty-four/twenty-two carat adj. [1930s+] totally reliable, wholly trustworthy. [fig. use of the SE descriptions of the purity of gold]

twenty-four-seven/seven-twenty-four/24-7/24-7-365 adv. [1980s+] every day, all the time. [lit. '24 hours a day, 7 days a week, (every day of the year)']

24/24 adv. [1980s+] (US prison) all day, continually (cf. TWENTY-FOUR-SEVEN). [24 hours out of the daily 24]

twenty in the pounder n. [late 19C] one who pays their debts in full rather than opting to pay in instalments. [i.e. twenty shillings to a (pre-decimal) pound]

twenty-nine and a wake-up n. [1960s+] (US prison) the period between receiving a notice of parole and one's actual release, i.e. one month (cf. WAKE-UP). [29 whole days and the WAKE-UP n.[3]; i.e. the last, on which one only wakes up in prison]

20 on the hype phr. [1950s] (drugs) a very heavy intake of heroin. [HYPE n.[2]]

twenty-sack n. [1990s] (US) $20 worth of drugs, usu. marijuana or crack cocaine.

twenty-spot n. [1960s+] a £20 note or $20 bill (cf. FIVE-SPOT; TEN-SPOT).

twenty-three skidoo/skiddoo phr. [1890–1910] (US) go away! get out! (cf. SKIDDOO); sometimes abbr. as *twenty-three!* [ety. unknown, theories include: downdraughts created by the Flatiron Building at the corner of Broadway and 23rd St, NYC, which would blow up women's skirts to the delight of male observers – the phr. developed f. the police who saw these men at *23* (the corner) and shooed them away with a shout of *skiddoo*; railway telegraph jargon *23*, a message of the greatest urgency; or a number signifying finality or completion; *skid* from SKID ROW, *23* from NYC's 23rd St which once had the ferries and depots for 80% of those – including the skid row tramps – who wished to leave the city]

twenty-twenty vision n. [20C] perfect vision, in a fig. sense; thus *twenty-twenty hindsight*, a fig. perfect understanding or appreciation of what has already been seen. [ophthalmic jargon *20/20*, perfect vision]

twenty-two carat see TWENTY-FOUR CARAT.

twerp n. [1930s–40s+] an idiot, a nincompoop. [ety. unknown, J.R.R. Tolkien (letter, 6 October 1944) suggests an early 20C Oxford contemporary *T.W. Earp*]

twibill n. [17C] a thug, a bully. [SE *twibill*, a two-edged axe]

twice v.[1] [late 19C] to double one's profit, efforts etc.

twice v.[2] [1940s] to cheat, to deceive. [TWO-TIME]

twice laid n. [20C] (US) a dish of minced meat on toast (cf. SHIT ON A SHINGLE).

twicer n. **1** [mid-19C] something very important, i.e. doubly valuable, relevant, forceful etc. **2** [mid-19C] (Aus. Und.) one who has twice been convicted of a criminal offence. **3** [late 19C–1900s] one who attends church twice on a Sunday. **4** [late 19C+] (orig. Aus.) a confidence trickster, one who engages in any form of 'double-dealing'. **5** [20C] a widow or widower who marries for the second time. **6** [1910s+] (Aus.)

a very demanding person, lit. one who asks for two helpings of food. **7** [1910s+] (Aus.) a greedy person, a sycophant. [SE *twice*]

twicers *n*. [late 19C] twins.

twiddle-diddles *n*. [late 18C–early 19C] the testicles. [SE *twiddle*, to play with + redup.]

twiddlepoop *n*. [late 18C–early 19C] an effeminate-looking man. [SE *twiddle*, to twirl around + POOP n.¹ (2)]

twig *n*.¹ **1** [mid-19C] style, fashion; thus *in twig*, handsome, fashionable, 'à la mode', often as *good/prime twig*. **2** [mid-19C] (orig. boxing) condition, fettle, spirits. [ety. unknown, ? TWIG v.²]

twig *n*.² **1** [1940s] (US Black) a tree. **2** [1960s–70s] a marijuana cigarette. **3** [1980s+] (US campus) a notably thin person.

twig *v*.¹ [early 18C] to disengage, to break off; thus (Und.) *twig the darbies*, knock off the handcuffs or irons. [? SE *tweak* or *twitch*]

twig *v*.² **1** [mid-18C–late 19C] to observe, to watch. **2** [late 18C–late 19C] to catch sight of, to become aware of. **3** [early 19C+] to understand. [? fig. uses of dial. *twick*, to jerk]

twig and berries *n*. [20C] a young boy's penis and testes.

twigged *adj*. [1980s+] (US drugs) intoxicated by drugs. [TWIG n.² (2)]

twigger *n*. [mid-16C–late 17C] a promiscuous woman, a prostitute. [SE *twigger*, a ewe that is a prolific breeder]

twiggy-vous the chose? *phr.* [late 19C] do you understand (what this is?/what's happening?) (cf. AH QUE JE CAN BE BÊTE). [a 'macaronic' or mixed-language phr. based on a Frenchified form of TWIG v.² (3) + Fr. *chose*, thing]

twig it *v*. [18C] to play truant. [HOP THE TWIG]

twig out *see* TWEAK v.³.

twigs *n*. [1930s–40s] (US Black) the human legs.

twilight time *n*. [1990s] (US Black teen) late nights, the time when people are out with criminal intent.

twim *see* TWAM.

twin-coat *n*. [1970s] (W.I.) a hypocrite (*see* TWO-MOUTH). [i.e. one who has two fig. *coats*]

twink *n*.¹ [20C] a moment, a very brief period of time. [SE *twinkling* (of a star)]

twink *n*.² [1970s+] (US gay) an available attractive young boy, whether working for money or not (cf. TWINKIE n.¹). [? the SE *twinkle* in his eye]

twink *n*.³ [1970s+] (US campus) someone unusual, crazy or stupid (cf. TWINKIE n.¹).

twinkie/twinky *n*.¹ [1970s+] **1** (US gay) a young, inexperienced homosexual man. **2** a young (underage) sex object, whether male or female and seen as suitable for exploitation (cf. CHICKEN n.⁵; KLEENEX; PRETTIES). **3** anyone considered odd or eccentric. [? fig. use of *Twinkie*, a variety of sweet biscuit]

Twinkie *n*.² [1990s] (US campus) an Asian who identifies with Caucasians (cf OREO). [a *Twinkie* biscuit, which is 'brown on the outside and White inside']

twinkie *n*.³ [1990s] (US Black) a $20 bag of marijuana (cf. TWENTY CENTS).

twinkle *n*. [1940s] (US Black) a doorbell. [the sound]

twinklers *n*. [19C+] the eyes. [SE *twinkle*, to sparkle]

twinkle teeth *n*. [1970s+] (US campus) a person with orthodontic braces (cf. LASER LIPS). [the supposed glinting of light on the metal braces]

twinky *see* TWINKIE n.¹.

twin-mouth *n*. [1970s] (W.I.) a hypocrite (cf. BACK-AND-BELLY n.²; TWO-MOUTH). [i.e. one who speaks with two fig. mouths]

twire *n*. [mid-17C] a glance, esp. a leer. [dial. *twire*, to look covertly, to peer, to peep]

twirl *n*.¹ **1** [late 19C+] (UK/US Und.) a key, esp. a skeleton or duplicate key. **2** [1930s+] (prison) a prison officer.

twirl/twist *n*.² [1950s–60s] a woman who loves dancing (cf. TWIST AND TWIRL).

twirler *n*. [1920s+] a key, esp. a skeleton or duplicate key. [TWIRL n.¹ (1)]

twirl the pearls, to *phr.* [1960s+] (US camp gay) to dance.

twiss *n*. [18C] (Irish) a chamberpot. [an attack on the English writer Richard *Twiss* (1747–1821), who had published the highly critical 'Tour in Ireland'. To take their revenge the Irish produced a chamberpot with a picture of Richard Twiss inside it, beneath which was inscribed the rhyme 'Let everyone piss/On lying Dick Twiss']

twist *n*.¹ [late 17C–mid-19C] **1** a drink of tea and coffee mixed together. **2** any mixed drink, typically brandy and eggs or brandy, beer and eggs, brandy and gin or a *gin twist*, gin and hot water.

twist *n*.² [late 18C–mid-19C] an appetite, a capacity for eating (cf. TWIST DOWN APACE). [TWIST v.¹]

twist *n*.³ **1** [mid-late 19C] the arm lock forced on a person who is being arrested. **2** [late 19C] (Und.) a hold on something or someone.

twist *n*.⁴ **1** [20C] (Irish) a quarrel, an argument; thus phrs. *in good twist*, on good terms; *in bad twist*, on bad terms. **2** [1930s+] cheating, dishonesty, treachery (cf. OLIVER n.²); thus *at the twist*, double-crossing. **3** [1970s+] (Irish) a turn.

twist *n*.⁵ **1** [20C] (US Und.) a girl, a woman. **2** [1950s+] the passive member of a lesbian relationship. [abbr. TWIST AND TWIRL]

twist *n*.⁶ [1910s+] (drugs) a marijuana cigarette. [it is *twisted* into shape]

twist *n*.⁷ [1910s+] (Aus.) a professional criminal. [abbr. TWISTER n.² or ? he not being 'straight']

twist *n*.⁸ *see* TWIRL n.²

twist/twist down *v*.¹ [late 17C–early 19C] to eat, esp. to eat heartily. [? the twisting of the wrist in eating or tearing pieces of bread from a loaf; note Worcestershire dial. *twist something down one*, to eat heartily]

twist *v*.² **1** [early 18C] to be hanged. **2** [20C] (Aus.) to be convicted of a crime. [lit./fig. twisting on the rope]

twist *v*.³ [1910s+] to cheat, to defraud. [i.e. 'twisting' the rules]

twist and twine, to *phr.* [20C] (Irish) to whine. [rhy. sl.]

twist and twirl *n*. [1900s] a girl (cf. TWIST n.⁵). [rhy. sl.]

twist down *see* TWIST v.¹.

twist down apace, to *phr.* [late 18C–early 19C] to eat heartily. [ext. of TWIST v.¹]

twisted *adj*.¹ [late 18C–early 19C] hanged. [TWIST v.² (1)]

twisted *adj*.² [1950s+] (orig. US) **1** extremely intoxicated by a drug, esp. the hallucinogens or cannabis. **2** annoyed, out of emotional control. **3** very drunk. **4** odd, bizarre, extraordinary.

twister *n*.¹ [late 17C] **1** a voracious eater. **2** (US) a spree (cf. BENDER n.¹). [TWIST v.¹]

twister *n*.² **1** [early 19C+] an untrustworthy person, a crook. **2** [1920s–30s] one who, through their own corruption, is impervious to the cheating and trickery of others.

twister *n*.³ [mid-late 19C] (US) something that causes a person to go into fig. contortions (cf. TWISTER n.⁵); thus *knock a twister*, to disconcert very much.

twister *n*.⁴ [late 19C+] (Aus./US) a cyclone, a tornado.

twister *n*.⁵ **1** [20C] (US prison) a prison warder (cf. KEY n.³). **2** [1930s–40s] (US Black) a frontdoor key; thus *twister to the slammer*, the door key. [the 'twisting' or turning of the key]

twister *n*.⁶ [1930s–50s] (drugs) **1** a user of marijuana. **2** an injection of mixed drugs (cf. SPEEDBALL n.¹; WHIZ BANG n.²). **3** violent retching or vomiting of blood or mucus during withdrawal sickness. **4** fake withdrawal symptoms. **5** a ration of narcotics. [one is SE *twisted* up by the drugs or their effects]

twistical adj. [19C] crooked, morally ambiguous. [SE twisted]

twisting n. **1** [early 19C] a scolding, a telling-off. **2** [1910s–20s] a cause of anxiety or unhappiness. [one's emotions are twisted]

twist one's crank, to phr. [20C] to masturbate.

twist someone's arm, to phr. [1950s+] to force someone to do something against their will (cf. PUT THE ARM ON).

twist the book on, to phr. [1920s–30s] to 'turn the tables' on (someone).

twistum n. [1930s–50s] (US drugs) a marijuana cigarette. [TWIST n.⁶ (1)]

twisty adj. [20C] (US) attractive, sexy. [TWIST n.⁵ + ? the 'twists' or curves of the body]

twit n. [1920s+] a fool, an idiot. [TWERP + TWAT (2)]

twit v. [late 17C–18C] to hit in the teeth. [SE twit in the teeth, to censure, to reproach]

twitch/twitches/twitchers, the n. [1980s+] (drugs) a nervous mannerism that afflicts regular users of crack cocaine.

twitched adj. [late 19C+] nervous, irritable. [SE twitch]

twitches/twitchers see TWITCH.

twitchety/twitchetty adj. [mid-19C] nervous, fidgety. [SE twitch]

twittoc n. [late 18C–mid-19C] two. [corruption of SE two]

twitty adj. [1980s+] (US campus) silly, foolish, ineffectual. [TWIT n.]

twixter n. [late 19C] a person of indeterminate sex. [SE betwixt and between]

twize n. [1970s] (US campus) Budweiser beer. [abbr./pron.]

twizzit n. [20C] a fool, usu. in phrs. of gentle reproof, e.g. you silly twizzit! [ext. of TWIT n.]

twizzle v. **1** [early 19C] to spin, to rotate fast. **2** [mid-19C] to shape by twisting or rotating, e.g. to twizzle a cigarette.

t.w.k. adj. [late 19C] (Anglo-Ind.) ? of a woman, too well known. [abbr.]

two n.¹ **1** [late 19C] two pennyworth (of spirits). **2** [20C] (Und.) a two-year sentence.

two n.² [1990s] (US) a Black person. [New York City police racial categorization on official reports (one = Caucasian, two = Afro-American, three = Hispanic]

two and eight n. [1930s+] a state, a panic. [rhy. sl.]

two-bagger see DOUBLE-BAGGER.

two-bit n. [mid-19C+] (W.I.) ninepence (post-1969 value 7.5 cents).

two-bit adj. [mid-19C+] (US) second-rate, inferior (cf. TWO-BITTY). [SE two + BIT n.¹, lit. worth 25 cents]

two-bit hustler n. [20C] **1** a low-priced prostitute. **2** a promiscuous woman. **3** a second-rate confidence trickster. [TWO-BIT adj. + HUSTLER]

two bits n. [1940s–60s] (US Black) $25. [ext. of two bits, 25 cents]

two-bitty adj. [1940s] (W.I.) feeling poorly, not up to much. [TWO-BIT adj.]

two-blink adj. [20C] (US) extremely small, insignificant. [the equivalent of blinking twice]

two-bob adj. [1940s+] (Aus.) inferior, useless, second-rate (cf. TWO-BIT adj.). [lit. worth 2s. (10p)]

two-bob bit/bits n. [20C] **1** an act of defecation. **2** diarrhoea. [rhy. sl. SHIT n.¹/SHITS]

two-bob each way phr. [1960s+] (Aus.) uncommitted. [the cheapness of such a bet]

two-bob hop n. [1920s+] (Aus.) a cheap dance. [SE two + BOB n.³ + HOP n.¹ (1)]

two bricks short of the load phr. [20C] not very intelligent, slightly eccentric, odd. One of a number of phrs. meanings stupid or eccentric (cf. FEW BRICKS SHORT OF A LOAD; NOT ALL THERE).

two by four/six to four n. [1950s–60s] a prostitute. [rhy. sl. = whore]

two-by-four adj. [late 19C+] (US) small, insignificant (cf. TWO-BIT adj.). [the minimal dimensions]

two camels n. [1940s] (US Black) ten minutes. [? the time needed to smoke two Camel cigarettes]

two can play at that game phr. [early 19C+] a phr. used to point out, when faced by unfairness or trickery, that such neg. actions can work in both directions.

two-cent adj. [mid–late 19C] inferior, second-rate. [var. on TWO-BIT adj.; worth only 2¢]

two-cent dosser n. [late 19C] a man who lives in stale-beer shops, which specialized in stale or old and strong beer. [SE two cents + DOSSER; note UK, despite US denomination]

two cents n. [1940s] (US Black) $2.

two cents' worth n. [mid-19C+] (US) **1** a little, a trivial amount. **2** one's personal opinion, a remark about a topic.

twocker n. [1990s] a youth who steals cars to use in a crime or for amusement (cf. HOTTING). [taking without owner's consent]

two dog night n. [1970s+] (Aus.) a very cold night. [orig. Abor. term, the need to sleep between a pair of dogs to batten onto their warmth]

two-dollar words n. [20C] (US) any language considered 'difficult' or 'intellectual' by its user, most likely a speaker who claims to despise such locutions.

two dots and a dash n. [1960s+] (US gay) the male genitals.

two ducks/little ducks phr. [late 19C+] (bingo) the number 22. [the supposedly similar shapes]

twoed-up adv. [1960s+] (prison) having two men in the same cell; thus threed-up etc (cf. DOUBLE-BUNKED).

211 n. [1990s] (US Black) an armed robbery (cf. 187). [California police code number]

two-ender n. [1930s] (tramp) a two-shilling piece (10p).

two ends and the middle of a bad lot phr. [late 19C] (middle class) a euph. phr. that describes a wholly 'bad lot'.

twoer n. **1** [late 19C] a two-wheeled cab. **2** [1940s+] £200.

two-eyed steak n. [late 19C] a kipper. [its flatness]

two eyes of blue! excl. [1920s+] too true! [rhy. sl.]

two-faced as a Methodist axe phr. [1960s+] (US) duplicitous, deceitful, untrustworthy. [US regional Methodist axe, a double-bladed axe]

two faces under one hood phr. [late 17C–18C] double-dealing, cheating, duplicity. [SE two-faced]

two fat cheeks/and ne'er a nose phr. [18C] the posterior, the buttocks (cf. BLIND CHEEKS; CHEEKS NEAR CUNNYBOROUGH).

two fat/old ladies phr. [1940s+] (bingo) the number 88. [the supposedly similar shapes]

twofer n. [20C] **1** a prostitute who is amenable to vaginal and/or anal intercourse (cf. TOOFER). **2** (US) a cheap cigar. **3** (US) a half-price theatre ticket. [? 'two for the price of one']

two-fisted adj. **1** [mid-19C] clumsy (cf. TWO-HANDED). **2** [mid-19C+] good at fist-fighting, thus tough, manly. [in 20C use of **3** extended to inanimate objects, e.g. two-fisted yarn, a tough, male-orientated story]

two-foot rule n. [mid-19C] a fool (cf. TWELVE-INCH RULE). [rhy. sl.]

two for nine n. [1980s+] (US drugs) two $5 vials or bags of crack cocaine for $9.

two Fs n. [late 19C] (middle class) fringe and followers. [abbr. (The supposed characteristics of a woman servant, whose hair was worn in a fringe and whose potential charms attracted a variety of suitors)]

two-handed adj. **1** [late 18C–mid-19C] usu. of people, large, strapping; thus two handed fellow, two-handed wench. **2** [mid-19C–1920s] clumsy, maladroit (cf. TWO-FISTED). **3** [1920s+] (US) generous.

two-handed put *n.* [late 18C–early 19C] sexual intercourse. [SE *two-handed*, whole-hearted + *put*, an act of thrusting or pushing]

two-headed *adj.* [20C] (US Black) very clever, exceptionally intelligent (cf. DOUBLE-HEADED; FOUR-HEADED). [the idea of having two brains; the orig. use comes f. hoodoo, a variant form of voodoo]

two hearts in a pond *n.* [late 19C] two baked hearts, cooked in a 'pond dish', i.e. a round dish divided in two halves by a 'wall'.

two-inched *adj.* [1990s] (US Black) of a woman, given insufficient sexual gratification. [the lit./fig. dimensions of the man's penis]

two inches beyond upright *n.* [late 19C] a hypocritical liar. [such a person cannot be considered as 'upright']

two jerks of a lamb's/dead lamb's/sheep's tail *see* TWO SHAKES OF A LAMB'S TAIL.

two-legged tree *n.* [19C] the gallows (cf. TRIPLE TREE).

two-legged tympany/tympany with two heels *n.* [late 16C–early 18C] a baby, esp. in embryonic stage; thus *have a two-legged tympany*, to be pregnant. [SE *tympany*, a morbid swelling or tumour]

two little crutches *n.* [1940s+] (bingo) the number 77. [the supposedly similar shapes]

two little ducks *see* TWO DUCKS.

two looking at you *n.* [20C] (US) two fried eggs 'sunny-side up'. [orig. short-order cooking jargon]

two-mac *n.* [1950s+] (W.I.) two shillings (post-1969 value 20 cents). [SE *two* + MAC]

two-minute brother *n.* [1990s] (US Black) a man who suffers from premature ejaculation. [SE *two minutes*, the length of the copulation + BROTHER n.]

two-mouth *n.* [1950s] (W.I.) a hypocrite (cf. BACK-AND-BELLY n.²; TWIN-MOUTH). [dial. *two-mouth*, a double-edged machete]

two old ladies *see* TWO FAT LADIES.

two-peg *n.* [1900s–60s] (Aus.) a florin, a two-shilling piece (10p). [SE *two* + PEG n.³]

two pence short of a bob *phr.* [20C] not very intelligent, slightly eccentric, odd (cf. NOT ALL THERE). [a BOB n.³ was composed of 12 *pence*]

twopenny *n.*¹ [mid-19C–1930s] the head. [rhy sl. *twopenny loaf* = *loaf of bread* = *head*]

twopenny *n.*² [late-19C–1910s] a pawnbroker's professional go-between, who charges twopence to take one's goods to the pawnshop and negotiate a deal.

twopenny *n.*³ [1910s–20s] a general term of affection.

twopenny burster *n.* [early 19C] a loaf of bread. [its price and its effect on the stomach]

twopenny-halfpenny *adj.* [early 19C+] virtually worthless, insignificant, paltry. [the value]

twopenny hop *n.* [mid-19C] cheap dance-halls and the dances held at them. [the 2d price of admission + HOP n.¹ (1): 'the clog hornpipe, the pipe dance, flash jigs, and horn pipes in fetters, à la Jack Sheppard, are the favourite movements' (Hotten 1867)]

twopenny rope *n.* [1920s–30s] (tramp) a hostel, a casual ward. [the rope strung across a room, on which bedless tramps could lean and fitfully sleep for a 2d payment]

twopenny tube *n.* [late 19C] the London Underground. [the original fare of 2d + TUBE n.² (1)]

twopenny upright/uprighter *see* THREEPENNY UPRIGHT.

two-pot screamer *see* ONE-POT SCREAMER.

two puppies fighting in a bag *phr.* [1970s+] very large, poorly contained and mobile breasts. [coined to describe the actress Elizabeth Taylor (b.1932)]

two sandwiches short of a picnic *phr.* [1980s+] not very intelligent, slightly eccentric, odd. One of a number of phrs.

meaning stupid or eccentric (cf. NOT ALL THERE; ONE SANDWICH SHORT OF A PICNIC).

two shakes of a donkey's tail *phr.* [1910s+] at once (cf. TWO SHAKES OF A LAMB'S TAIL).

two/three shakes/jerks of a lamb's/dead lamb's/sheep's tail *phr.* [mid-19C+] immediately, at once.

two-shoes *n.* [mid-19C+] a little girl. [the popular children's tale *The History of Little Goody Two-Shoes* (1765), supposedly written by Oliver Goldsmith (?1730–74) for the children's publisher John Newbury]

two snaps up *phr.* [1990s] (US campus) expression of approval. [referring to the snapping of one's fingers, and a play on the phr. 'two thumbs up' used by US TV film critics Roger Ebert and Gene Siskel]

two spaces *n.* [20C] (US Und.) a two-year prison sentence (cf. DEUCE n.²; TWO-SPOTTER). [i.e. two year-long spaces in one's life]

two-spot *n.* [mid-19C+] (US) a $2 bill. [SE *two* + sfx. -SPOT]

two-spotter *n.* [20C] (US Und.) a two-year prison sentence (cf. DEUCE n.²; TWO SPACES). [SE *two* + sfx. -SPOT]

two-stemmer *n.* [19C] (US) a small town. [on pattern of MAIN STEM; i.e. the two major streets that such a town could boast]

two stone underweight/wanting *adj.* [late 18C–1900s] castrated, thus a eunuch. [pun on STONES n.¹ (1)]

two-storey lorry *n.* [1940s] (US Black) a double-decker bus.

two's-up *phr.* [1990s] used of a woman who has two people simultaneously using her anus and vagina.

twot *see* TWAT.

two thieves beating a rogue *phr.* [late 18C–early 19C] a phr. said of a person beating their hands against their sides to get warm on a cold day (cf. BEAT THE BOOBY).

two-thirty *adj.* [late 19C+] dirty. [rhy. sl.]

two-time *v.* [1920s+] (orig. US) to cheat, esp. to double-cross.

two-time loser *n.* [1950s+] **1** (US Und.) a person who already has two convictions and so risks a higher sentence the third time. **2** (US) a person who has been divorced twice.

two-timer *n.* [1920s+] (orig. US) a cheat, a double-crosser. [TWO-TIME v.]

two-timing *adj.* [1920s+] (orig. US) duplicitous. [TWO-TIME v.]

two-to-one *n.* [mid-19C+] (US) a pawnbroker. [either the arrangement of the traditional three balls hanging outside the pawnbroker's (one above, two below) or the popular belief that it was two-to-one odds that one's pledge would never be redeemed]

two to one against you *phr.* [late 19C] you have no hope, the odds are stacked against you. [for ety. *see* TWO-TO-ONE]

two-to-one shop *n.* [late 18C–early 19C] a pawnbroker's shop. [for ety. *see* TWO-TO-ONE]

two/2 UEs *n.* [20C] (Aus.) fleas. [rhy. sl.]

two-upper *n.* [20C] (Aus.) a player of the gambling game of 'two-up'; thus *two-up school*, on the model of SE *card-school*, the place where the game is carried on.

two wafers short of a communion *phr.* [1960s+] not very intelligent, slightly eccentric, odd (cf. NOT ALL THERE).

two-way girl *n.* [20C] a woman who is amenable to vaginal and anal intercourse (cf. TWOFER).

two-way man *n.* [1930s+] a male prostitute who is willing to act as passive or active partner in sodomy or fellatio.

two-wheeler *n.* [20C] (Aus.) a woman. [rhy. sl. *two-wheeler* = SHEILA]

two white, two red, and after you with the blacking brush *phr.* [mid-19C] two dabs of white powder, two of red and a blacking brush for the eyebrows; often abbr. as *two white, two red and the brush* [a ref. to the excessive use of coloured cosmetics imported from Fr. *c.*1860–70.]

two with their eyes closed *phr.* [20C] (US) two fried eggs turned over in the pan (cf. OVER-EASY).

two with you *phr.* [late 19C] let's have a (twopenny) drink.

ty *n.* [1920s] (Aus.) *ty*phoid fever. [abbr.]

Tyburn *n.* [16C+] sited near what is now Marble Arch, the village of Paddington, the principal site of public executions in London between 1388–1783, when it was replaced by Newgate; not sl. as such but occurring in many combs. e.g. FETCH A TYBURN STRETCH; MAKE A TYBURN SHOW; PREACH AT TYBURN CROSS; TAKE A LEAP AT TYBURN.

Tyburn blossom *n.* [late 18C–early 19C] a young thief or pickpocket. ['who in time will ripen unto fruit born by the DEADLY NEVERGREEN.' (Grose 1796)]

Tyburn check *n.* [late 18C–early 19C] a hangman's noose (cf. TYBURN PICCADILL; TYBURN TIFFANY; TYBURN TIPPET).

Tyburn collar *n.* [mid-19C] a fringe of beard worn under the chin (cf. NEWGATE COLLAR).

Tyburn collop *n.* [16C] a miserable face (cf. TYBURN FACE).

Tyburn face *n.* [late 17C] a miserable, down-in-the-mouth look (cf. TYBURN COLLOP).

Tyburn foretop/top *n.* [late 18C–early 19C] a wig with its foretop combed forward over the eyes. Such wigs were esp. popular among the underworld.

Tyburn jig *n.* [late 18C–early 19C] a hanging (cf. DANCE THE TYBURN JIG).

Tyburn piccadill/piccadill *n.* [late 18C–early 19C] a hangman's noose (cf. TYBURN CHECK); thus *put on a Tyburn piccadill*, to be hanged. [*Tyburn*, generic for the execution ground + SE *piccadill*, an ornamented collar fashionable in the early 17C. The term comes from the Sp. *picadillo*, the dimin. of *picado*, meaning pricked, pierced, punctured, slashed or minced (thus *picada*, a puncture and *picadillo*, minced meat). The piccadill was brought to the UK either by Robert Baker (*The London Encyclopedia*, 1983) or by 'one Higgins' (*The Atheneum*, 1901). Whatever the name, the individual in question made a fortune from his import, sufficient to buy land around what is now Piccadilly Circus and to erect, *c.*1622, a large mansion which was promptly and irreverently christened Piccadilly Hall. The surrounding area soon became known as Piccadilly. However, the *OED* cites a source writing in 1656 who claimed that the house was thus named because, being at the furthest edge of the parish of St Martin in the Fields, in which it lay, it was therefore serving as a 'collar', or outer edge of the area]

Tyburn stretch *n.* [late 17C–early 19C] a hanging. [SE *stretch* one's neck]

Tyburn string *n.* [late 18C] a hangman's noose.

Tyburn tiffany *n.* [18C] a hangman's noose. [SE *tiffany*, a transparent gauze muslin, often used as a headcover]

Tyburn tippet *n.* [late 18C–early 19C] a hangman's noose (cf. TYBURN CHECK). [TYBURN + SE *tippet*, a scarf, a band of silk or fur worn around the neck]

Tyburn top *see* TYBURN FORETOP.

Tyburn tree *n.* [mid-18C–early 19C] the gallows sited at Tyburn (cf. DEADLY NEVERGREEN). [The *Tyburn tree*, a great triple gallows on which 21 malefactors could be 'turned off' simultaneously, was erected in June 1751. Its first victim was 'Romish Canonical Doctor' John Story]

tyee/tyhee *n.* [late 18C+] (US) an important person (cf. HIGH MUCKY-MUCK). [Chinook jargon *tyee*, a chief]

tyke *n.*[1] [18C+] a dog; thus *tiker*, *tyker*, a dog-handler. [Yorks. dial., also used [18C+] as a self-identification by 'professional' Yorkshiremen]

tyke *n.*[2] [1940s+] (Aus./N.Z.) a Roman Catholic. [TEAGUE]

tympany with two heels *see* TWO-LEGGED TYMPANY.

typ *adj.* [1940s] *typ*ical. [abbr.]

typer *n.* [1960s+] (orig. US) a *type*writer. [abbr.]

typewriter *n.*[1] [1910s+] a machinegun or sub-machinegun. [the tapping noise]

typewriter *n.*[2] [1920s+] a boxer, a fighter (lit. or fig.). [rhy. sl.]

tyrekicker *n.* [1980s+] (N.Z.) of a politician or other decision-maker, one who discusses and debates, but fails to act. [car sales use *tyrekicker*, one who examines a car at length, then does not buy it]

Tyrone Power *n.* [1940s+] (Aus.) a shower. [rhy. sl.; ult. real name US actor *Tyrone Power* (1914–58)]

tytere-tu *see* TITTERY-TU.

tzing-tzing *adj.* [late 19C] excellent, first-rate. [? CHIN-CHIN!]

T-zone *adj.* [1980s+] (US teen) lost in one's own world, in a state of transcendental bliss (cf. T-BUZZ *n.*[5]). [SE *transcendental* + zone]

tzuris *see* TSURIS.

U

u.a.w. *n.* [1950s+] (US Black) a nickname for the US union the *U*nited *A*utomobile *W*orkers (UAW), known for its racism and refusal to secure rights for such Black employees as it permitted. [abbr. *you a*in't *w*orking, *you a*in't *W*hite]

u.b.d.'d! *excl.* [1910s–20s] *you b*e *d*amned! [abbr.]

ubrown *n.* [1980s+] (S.Afr. township) brandy. [the colour]

u.b.s *n.* [1970s] (US campus) underwear, usu. female use. [abbr. *u*nder*b*odie*s*]

u.c. *adj.* [1990s] *u*pper *c*lass (cf. L.C.). [abbr.]

u/c *adj.* [1970s+] used in contact advertisements, *u*n*c*ircumcised. [abbr. *un*c*ut*]

ucky *see* YUCKY.

u-clever *see* CLEVER *n.*

udders *n.* [1930s+] the female breasts (cf. CREAM JUGS).

u.d.i. *phr.* [1990s] *u*nidentified *d*rinking *i*njury. [abbr.]

'ud's bobs/bodkins! *excl.* [early 18C] a mild oath, 'God's body!' (cf. CUD'S BOBS).

'ud's lidikins! *excl.* [early 18C] a mild oath, lit. 'God's little (eye)lids!'

'ud's my life! *excl.* [late 19C] a mild oath, lit. 'God's my life!'

'ud's niggers/noggers! *excl.* [early 18C] a mild oath, lit. 'God's fingers' or 'God's nose'.

'ud's wount-likins! *excl.* [early 18C] a mild, blasphemous oath, 'God's little wounds'.

U-ey *see* U-IE.

uff *see* OOF.

uggies *n.* [1990s] (Aus.) sheepskin boots or slippers. [SE *ugly*]

uglies, the *n.* **1** [mid-19C+] a fit of depression or bad temper. **2** [late 19C–1900s] delirium tremens. **3** [1970s] nitrogen narcosis, 'rapture of the deep'.

ugly *n.*[1] [mid-late 19C] (society) a bonnet shade. [what was generally seen as its lack of style or taste]

ugly *n.*[2] [mid-late 19C] a derog. term of address, also as *Mr Ugly*.

ugly *adj.* [late 19C] (coffee house) thick.

ugly as a hatful of arseholes *phr.* [1950s+] (Aus.) very ugly (cf. SILLY AS A HATFUL OF ARSEHOLES). [ARSEHOLE *n.*]

ugly as a hatful of bronzas *phr.* [1970s+] (Aus.) very ugly (cf. UGLY AS A HATFUL OF ARSEHOLES). [BRONZE *n.*]

ugly as bull-beef *phr.* [mid-19C] a general term of contempt; thus *go to the billy-fencer and sell yourself for bull-beef*.

ugly customer *n.* [early 19C+] an unpleasant, menacing individual. [SE *ugly* + *customer*; the format dates to 16C *lewd customer*]

uglyman *n.* [mid-late 19C] that member of the garrotting team who actually does the choking (cf. BACKSTALL).

ugly plug *n.* [19C] (US) an ugly face (cf. PLUG-UGLY).

ugly sister *n.* [20C] a blister. [rhy. sl.]

ugly ways *n.* [20C] (US Black) bad manners, bad behaviour.

ugsome *adj.* [1970s+] unpleasant, distasteful, unattractive. [so unpleasant etc that it makes one say *Ugh!*]

U-ie/U-ey/yewie/youee *n.* [1970s+] (orig. Aus.) a U-turn; thus *chuck a U-ie*, to make a U-turn (cf. HANG A U-IE).

uke *n.* [1910s+] (orig. US) *uke*lele. [abbr.]

ullage *n.* [late 19C] the dregs in the bottom of wine glasses or casks. [SE *ullage*, the amount of wine or other liquor by which a cask or bottle falls short of being quite full]

ultimate *n.* (drugs) **1** [1970s+] cocaine. **2** [1980s+] crack cocaine. [the potency and effects]

ultimate *adj.* [1970s+] referring to an occasion of organized group sex in which all those present have intercourse (cf. SOFT SWING).

ultimatum *n.* [early 19C] the buttocks, the posterior. [SE *ultimatum*, the final point, extreme limit]

ultra! *excl.* [1980s+] excellent! first-rate! wonderful!

ultracool *adj.* [1960s+] (orig. US) extremely sophisticated. [SE *ultra* + COOL *adj.*[3] (3)]

ultramarine *adj.* [late 19C–1910s] obscene, 'smutty'. [play on BLUE *adj.*[3]]

ultraswoopy *adj.* [1970s] (US) very stylish, streamlined.

umac *n.* [1960s+] (S.Afr. Black) a young man about town (cf. CLEVER *n.*). [pfx. *u*- + ? MACK *n.*[1]]

umberstick *n.* [20C] (Ulster) an umbrella. [SE *umbrella* + *stick*]

umble-cum-stumble *v.* [late 19C] to understand comprehensively (cf. UNDERCOMESTUMBLE).

umbrella *n.*[1] [1960s–70s] (US) police protection, obtained through bribery. [it keeps one from being RAINed ON]

umbrella *n.*[2] [1980s+] (drugs) a metal hanger or umbrella rod used to scrape residue in crack stems (cf. PUSHER *n.*[4]).

umbrella branch/brigade *n.* [1970s+] the Special Branch. [they may dress in the bowler hat and rolled umbrella uniform of their bureaucratic masters in Whitehall]

umlaut *n.* [1970s+] (US) half a bottle of *Löwenbräu* beer; thus *two umlauts*, a whole bottle. [the umlauts over the 'o' and 'a']

umpteen *n.* [1910s+] an unspecified large number or amount. [orig. WW1 milit. use, deliberately replacing a specific number with a noncommittal *um* for communications secrecy]

umpty/umpty-umph *adj.* (orig. milit.) **1** [1910s+] of an indefinite number, usu. a large one, in combs. e.g. *umpty-nine*, *umpty-eleven*; thus *umptieth*. **2** [1940s+] unpleasant, difficult.

umpty-doo *adj.* [1910s+] (Aus.) drunk. [the nursery rhyme *Humpty-Dumpty*, who 'fell off a wall']

u.m.s. *phr.* [1980s+] (US campus) a sudden, unpredictable change of mood. [abbr. *u*gly *m*ood *s*wing]

un *n.* [1990s] (US campus) an outsider, someone who does not fit in. [neg. SE pfx. *un*-]

una *n.* [mid-19C+] (Ling. Fr./Polari) the number one. [Ital. *uno*, one]

un-ass *v.* [1940s–60s] (US Black) hand over, give up. [SE pfx. *un*- + ASS *n.*]

unavoidable circumstances *n.* [late 19C] (US) formal dress breeches worn for Court appearances.

unbelt v. [late 19C] (US) to hand over money. [SE *unbelt*, to remove a sword]

unbenefit v. [1990s] (US teen) to disassociate oneself from someone after a disagreement or an unpleasant occurrence. [lit. 'to withdraw one's benefits from']

unbetty v. [early–mid-19C] to unlock. [BETTY n.[1]]

unbleached American n. [mid-19C] an African-American. [one of the earliest efforts to find a euph. for such derog. terms as NIGGER n.]

unbleached Australian n. [20C] a Native Australian, an Aboriginal. [*see* UNBLEACHED AMERICAN]

unboiled lobster n. [early 19C] a policeman (cf. BOILED LOBSTER; LOBSTER n.[1]; RAW LOBSTER). [the uncooked lobster is blue, like a police uniform. The cooked lobster has turned red/pink, like a soldier's]

unbridle v. [1920s–50s] to remove one's hat.

unbuttoned adj. [1920s+] unprepared, caught by surprise, taken unawares (cf. NAKED); thus *come unbuttoned*, to meet with disaster, to 'come to grief'.

unc n. [1950s+] (US) uncle (cf. UNK). [abbr.]

uncle n.[1] **1** [mid-18C+] a pawnbroker, usu. as *my uncle*. **2** [late 19C+] oneself. **3** [20C] (US) a receiver of stolen goods (cf. FENCE n.[1]). [SE *uncle*; thus the avuncular help he gives 'relatives' in temporary financial distress]

uncle n.[2] *see* DUTCH UNCLE.

Uncle n.[3] [mid-19C+] the USA, esp. the US armed forces or other federal/national authorities (FBI, CIA etc). [abbr. UNCLE SAM n.[1]]

uncle and aunt n. [20C] a plant. [rhy. sl.]

Uncle Arthur n. [20C] (Irish) generic for Guinness and the family who own it. [founder Arthur Guinness (1725–1803)]

Uncle-Ben Black n. [1960s] (US Black) a deep sense of one's Blackness. [*Uncle Ben's rice*, a staple Black food]

Uncle Bert n. [20C] a shirt (cf. DICKY DIRT). [rhy. sl.]

Uncle Bill n. [1930s–50s] a policeman, the police. [BILL n.[7]; OLD BILL n. (1)]

Uncle Bob n.[1] [20C] the penis. [rhy. sl. *uncle bob* = KNOB n.[1] (1)]

Uncle Bob n.[2] [1940s] a policeman. [BOBBY n. (1)]

Uncle Dick v. [1970s+] to be sick (cf. BOB, HARRY AND DICK; TOM AND DICK; TOM, HARRY AND DICK). [rhy. sl.]

Uncle Fred n. [20C] bread. [rhy. sl.]

Uncle Joe n. [1940s] (W.I.) a large, dense cake (cf. CREPE SOLE). [? anecdotal]

Uncle Lester n. [1990s] a child molester (cf. CHESTER MOLESTER). [rhy. sl.]

Uncle Mac n. [1980s+] (drugs) heroin. [rhy. sl., *Uncle Mac* = SMACK n.[5] (1)]

Uncle Melvin *see* MELVIN.

Uncle Milty n. [1950s+] (drugs) meprobamate, a mild tranquillizer. [brandname *Miltown* + ref. to the nickname of US comedian *Milton* Berle (b.1908)]

Uncle Nabs n. [1970s+] (US Black) the police. [NAB n.[2]]

Uncle Ned n. **1** [1920s+] a bed. **2** [1950s+] the head. **3** [1950s+] (Aus.) bread. [rhy. sl.]

Uncle Payther n. [20C] (Irish) a whinging complainer. [the characteristics of *Uncle Payther* (Peter Flynn) a character in *The Moon and the Stars* (1926) by Sean O'Casey]

Uncle Sam n.[1] [early 19C+] the USA, esp. the armed forces or federal agencies of the USA. [created during the War of 1812 as the equivalent symbol to UK's John Bull. 'He' is always pictured as a bewhiskered, high-hatted old gentleman, garbed in red, white and blue. The figure is supposed to have been based on a Samuel Wilson, an inspector of provisions based in Troy, NY. The symbol gained further currency during WW1 when he was painted by James Montgomery Flagg as a stern figure pointing a finger at passers-by, in a celebrated recruiting poster]

uncle sam n.[2] [20C] a cut of lamb. [rhy. sl.]

Uncle Samantha n. [1950s–60s] (camp gay) the United States government. [a camp feminization of UNCLE SAM n.[1]]

Uncle Sam's action n. [1940s] (US Black) the military draft. [UNCLE SAM n.[1] + ACTION n.[1]]

Uncle Sam's sheep n. [20C] (US) deer that has been illegally shot by poachers (cf. CAMP MEAT). [UNCLE SAM n.[1] + SE *meat*]

Uncle Sham n. [1960s–70s] (US Black) a derog. version of UNCLE SAM n.[1]. [SE *sham*, fake; coined by the US protest movement to ridicule the hollowness at the heart of the so-called 'American dream']

Uncle Thomas n. [1960s] (US Black) a subservient Black person, fitting willingly into the stereotyped and inferior image refined by generations of White supremacy; thus the nickname of US Supreme Court Justice Clarence Thomas (b.1948), elected amid much controversy (for alleged sexual harassment of a fellow lawyer) as a Black right-winger. [UNCLE TOM n.]

uncle three balls n. [late 19C] a pawnbroker. [UNCLE + the *three* golden *balls* that traditionally indicate a pawnshop]

Uncle Tom n. (orig. US Black) **1** [1920s+] a subservient Black person, fitting willingly into the stereotyped and inferior image refined by generations of White supremacy (cf. AUNT JANE n.[2]). **2** [1990s] a tattle-tale, a person who befriends another, usu. in the workplace, only to deceive them. [*Uncle Tom*, the hero of Harriet Beecher Stowe's anti-slavery novel *Uncle Tom's Cabin* (1852)]

Uncle Tom v. [1920s+] (US Black) to act in a subservient, obsequious manner to Whites (cf. TOM v.[3]). [UNCLE TOM n.]

Uncle Tomahawk n. [1960s+] (US) a Native American, who is condemned as insufficiently nationalistic (cf. APPLE n.[11]). [play on UNCLE TOM n. + SE *tomahawk*, the trad. 'Red Indian' weapon]

Uncle Whiskers n. [1920s+] (US Und.) a Federal agent or agency (cf. MISTER WHISKERS). [the facial hair trad. adorning images of UNCLE SAM n.[1]]

Uncle Wilf n. [20C] the police. [rhy. sl. *Uncle Wilf* = FILTH n.[2], pron. 'filf']

Uncle Willie adj. **1** [mid-19C+] silly. **2** [1920s+] chilly. [rhy. sl.]

unclog the drain/pipes, to phr. [20C] to masturbate.

unconscious n. [1920s–30s] a day-dreamer.

uncool adj. [1950s+] (orig. US) unpleasant, emotional, rude, tactless, unfair. Various neg. meanings as to a particular context. [pfx. *un-* + COOL adj.[3]]

uncut adj. **1** [1960s+] (drugs) pure, unadulterated. **2** [1980s+] (US gay) uncircumcised.

undeniable n. [19C] the vagina (cf. DOWN BELOW).

under n. [20C] sexual intercourse (cf. BIT OF UNDER). [i.e. the place of the genitals *under* the body]

under adj. [1940s+] drunk. [abbr. *under the influence*]

under a cloud phr. [early 16C+] in trouble, dubious (cf. CLOUDY).

under-arm adj. [1950s–60s] pornographic. [? UNDER THE ARM]

under-belongings n. [19C] the vagina (cf. DOWN BELOW; UNDERCARRIAGE; UNDER-DIMPLE; UNDER-ENTRANCE; UNDERTAKER; UNDERWORLD n.[1]).

under breeze adj. [20C] (W.I.) very fast. [sailing imagery]

undercarriage n. [1990s] the vagina (cf. UNDER-BELONGINGS).

undercomestumble/undercumestumble v. [mid-19C] to understand. [play on SE *stumble upon*]

undercover n.[1] [1950s+] (US Black) sexual intercourse.

undercover n.[2] [1960s+] a plain-clothes detective or *undercover* agent. [abbr.]

undercover man n. [20C] a male homosexual. [play on UNDERCOVER n.[2]]

undercumestumble *see* UNDERCOMESTUMBLE.

underdaks n. [1940s+] (Aus.) male underpants. [SE *under* + DAKS]

under-dimple n. [19C] the vagina (cf. UNDER-BELONGINGS).

underdone adj. [late 19C] said of one who has a pale complexion.

underdungers n. [1980s+] (N.Z.) underpants. [SE *under* + *dungarees* + play on *dung*]

under-entrance n. [19C] the vagina (cf. UNDER-BELONGINGS).

under glass adj. [1930s+] (orig. US) imprisoned, arrested. [the image of a show case]

undergraduate n. [19C] a horse in training.

underground mutton n. [1900s–30s] (Aus.) rabbit. [the animal's habitat and edibility]

under house adj. [1970s+] (US teen) in an uncontrollable state, emotionally unstable, furious. [SE *under house arrest*]

undermeat n. [1990s] the labia majora. [MEAT n. (3)]

under one's belt phr. **1** [mid-19C+] in one's stomach, swallowed. **2** [1950s+] personally achieved or experienced.

under one's hat phr. [1950s+] (US) secret.

under one's jacket phr. [19C] (US) in one's stomach.

under one's own steam phr. [1940s+] alone and unaided. [railway imagery]

under or over phr. [late 19C] (US) dead or divorced. [the phr. used of single women or widows and is an abbr. of *under the grass*, dead and buried, or *over the grass*, alive but separated]

underpinners n. [mid-19C] (US) the legs.

underpinnings n. [mid-19C+] the legs.

underput n. [early 17C] a mistress. [SE *put under*; i.e. the position of sexual intercourse]

under rations n. [1930s–40s] (US Black) sexual intercourse. [ext. of UNDER n.]

undershell n. [19C] a waistcoat.

understandings n.[1] **1** [late 18C–late 19C] boots or shoes. **2** [early–mid-19C] the legs. [puns]

understandings n.[2] [late 19C] of a woman, sexual conquests (cf. MAKE STANDING ROOM FOR). [pun + play on SE *understanding*, a relationship]

understand what's what see KNOW WHAT'S WHAT.

undertaker n. [19C] the vagina (cf. UNDER-BELONGINGS).

undertaker job n. [1930s+] (orig. US) **1** a hopeless proposition; thus 'dead'. **2** (gambling) a horse or greyhound which is deliberately – for the sake of the odds – not meant to win, whatever legitimate gamblers may presume. [SE *undertaker* + JOB n.[3]]

under the act phr. [late 19C–1910s] sentenced under the Habitual Criminals Act. [under this Act the police had the right to arrest without warrant a ticket-of-leave man (on license from jail) before the ending of their sentence, or anyone with two or more convictions. Magistrates could try and convict such men on suspicion only and it was up to the defendant to prove that he was living a law-abiding life. The Act was not repealed until 1967]

under the arm phr. [1930s–60s] second-rate, inferior, bad. [? the smell or the image of secrecy and hiding]

under the blinks phr. [late 19C] (US) asleep.

under the cosh phr. [1950s+] in trouble, at a disadvantage (cf. UNDER THE GUN); thus *have under the cosh*, to have one at a disadvantage. [fig. use of COSH n.]

under the daisies phr. [mid-19C+] dead and buried.

under the gun phr. [late 19C+] (orig. US) under great pressure, stress.

under the hammer phr.[1] [early 19C] for sale. [auctioneering use]

under the hammer phr.[2] [1950s+] in trouble, at a disadvantage (cf. UNDER THE GUN; UNDER THE COSH).

under the hatches phr. [late 17C–19C] in trouble, dead, in jail.

under the influence phr. [late 19C+] (orig. US) drunk. [the influence of alcohol]

under the lap phr. (Aus.) **1** [1930s+] confidentially. **2** [1940s+] clandestinely.

under the odds phr. [1920s+] easy, better than expected. [betting imagery]

under the rose see SUB ROSA adj.

under the screw phr. [mid-19C] in prison. [SCREW n.[2]]

under the sod phr. [mid-19C+] dead and buried (cf. SIX FEET UNDER). [SE *sod*, the earth]

under the table phr. [mid-19C+] **1** clandestine, secret, corrupt. **2** drunk, one has fallen there. [(2) allegedly coined by George Washington 'Chuck' Connors, a New York character known as 'the Bowery philosopher']

under the weather phr. [mid-19C+] **1** drunk. **2** not feeling perfectly well, miserable.

underwear n.[1] [1960s+] a underwear fetishist, esp. for soiled garments.

underwear n.[2] [1960s+] (US gay) an unshaven chin; thus *your underwear is showing*, you need a shave.

underworld n.[1] n. [19C] the vagina (cf. UNDER-BELONGINGS).

underworld n.[2] [1920s] (Und.) the jargon of the professional criminal.

under wraps adj. [1930s+] (orig. US) secret, hidden away.

undie adj. [1940s+] clandestine, secret. [abbr. SE *undercover*]

undies n. [20C] women's underwear. [abbr. SE *underwear*, *under-garments*]

undigested Ananias n. [late 19C] a triumphant liar. [the biblical figure *Ananias*, one who, 'with Sapphira his wife, sold a possession and kept back part of the price' (*Acts* v. 1, 2); used allusively for a liar]

undress v. [20C] (Aus.) of a sheep, to steal.

undub v. [early 19C] (Und.) to unlock. [DUB v.]

undue perversity n. [1980s+] (US campus) Purdue University, West Lafayette, Indiana. [joc. reversal]

unearthly adj. [mid-19C+] hyperbolic use of SE, usu. as *unearthly hour/time*, extremely early (cf. UNGODLY; UNHOLY).

unfair shake n. [1970s+] bad luck. [reverse of FAIR SHAKE]

unfledged adj. [1910s–20s] naked. [lit. 'featherless']

unfortunate n. [late 18C–1900s] **1** a prostitute, a 'fallen woman'. **2** (Irish) an idiot. [euph. SE *unfortunate woman*]

unglued adj. [1970s+] unstable, emotional, lacking control.

ungodly adj. [mid-19C+] appalling, awful, esp. as *ungodly hour*, very late (cf. UNEARTHLY).

ungrateful man n. [late 18C–early 19C] a parson, 'who at least once a week abuses his best benefactor, i.e. the devil' (Grose 1785).

unguentum aureum n. [late 18C–early 19C] a bribe. [Lat. 'golden ointment']

un-hip/un-hep adj. [1930s+] (orig. US) unaware, unsophisticated, ignorant. [HIP adj.]

unholy adj. [mid-19C+] appalling, intolerable, esp. as *unholy racket*, *unholy row*, intolerably loud noise (cf. UNEARTHLY). [hyperbolic use of SE]

uni n. [late 19C+] (orig. Aus.) university. [abbr.]

unicorn n. **1** [late 18C–early 19C] a coach drawn by three horses, two abreast and one in the lead (cf. SPIKE TEAM). **2** [late 19C] a woman and two men/two women and a man in league for criminal purposes. [the image of the *unicorn's* protruding horn]

uniform/uniforms n. [1950s+] (gay) a member/members of the armed or uniformed services. [metonymy]

Union, the n. [late 19C] the workhouse. [*Union House*]

union card n. [1970s] (US campus) a university degree certificate. [its use in gaining work]

union jack n. [20C] the human back. [rhy. sl.]

union wage n. [1970s+] (US Black) the police. [? the primary motivation for their activities]

units see PARENTAL UNITS.

universal staircase n. [19C] a prison treadmill (cf. EVER-LASTING STAIRCASE).

university of life n. [20C] the fig. 'college' attended by those who claim personal experience as infinitely superior to academic knowledge (cf. SCHOOL OF HARD KNOCKS).

unkie n. [1950s–60s] (drugs) morphine. [abbr. JUNKIE]

unkjay n. [1940s–50s] a heroin addict. [Pig Latin for JUNKIE]

unk/unkie n. [20C] uncle (cf. UNC). [abbr.]

unlaid adj. [1960s+] **1** a female virgin. **2** of a woman, one with whom no one, that one knows, has had sexual intercourse. [LAY n.¹]

unlax v. [1920s–30s] (US) to relax, unwind. [popularized by the 1930s–40s US radio series *Amos and Andy*]

unload v. [1960s+] (US gay) to ejaculate.

unloading n. [1990s] masturbation.

unload pewter v. [mid-19C] to drink from a quart pot.

unload the baby gravy, to phr. [1990s] to ejaculate. [SE un-load + BABY GRAVY]

unload the gun, to phr. [1990s] to masturbate.

unlucky for some n. [1940s+] (bingo) the number 13. [the number most prone to superstitious interpretation]

unmentionables/unspeakables/untalkaboutables/un-utterables / unwhisperables n. [mid-19C] trousers (cf. DON'T-NAME-'EMS). [the supposed 'obscenity' of the garment]

unmonkeyable adj. [1910s–20s] of a person, impervious to trickery. [MONKEY v.]

unnecessary adj.¹ [1900s–40s] (US Black) depressed, dejected, miserable.

unnecessary adj.² [1930s+] excited, usu. sexually.

unpalled adj. [early 19C] (Und.) of a thief, whose gang has been arrested and is thus forced to work solo. [PAL n.]

unparliamentary adj. [mid-19C] obscene. [SE unparliamentary language, as laid down in *Erskine May*, which covers all Parliamentary procedure]

unpaved adj. **1** [early 17C] castrated. **2** [late 19C] aggressively drunk. [(1) one has 'lost one's STONES']

unpick one's teeth see NOT PICK ONE'S TEETH.

unpin one's back hair, to phr. **1** [mid-19C+] (orig. US) to relax one's inhibitions. **2** [1930s+] to admit to being gay (cf. LET ONE'S HAIR DOWN).

unreal adj. [1960s+] **1** (orig. Aus. surfer) unbelievable, unacceptable, unpleasant, an all-purpose neg. that depends for precise meaning on context. **2** (Aus./N.Z./US campus) a term of all-encompassing approbation, esp. as used by teenage girls.

unrig v. [late 16C–19C] to strip off one's clothes. [RIGGING]

unrigged adj. [late 18C–early 19C] stripped. [UNRIG]

unruly member n. [19C] the tongue. [General Epistle of James, 3:5–8: 'Even so the tongue is a little member ... But the tongue can no man tame; it is an unruly evil, full of deadly poison']

unsheik v. [1920s] (US Black) to divorce. [brand-name *Sheik*, a popular US condom]

unshingle v. [early–mid-19C] (Aus.) to knock off someone's hat. [SE shingle, a roof tile]

unshop v. [1910s–20s] to dismiss a workman. [SE shop, a workshop, a place of work]

unsliced adj. [1980s+] (US gay) uncircumcised (cf. UNCUT).

unslour v. [early 19C] (Und.) to unlock. [pfx. un- + SLOUR]

unspeakables see UNMENTIONABLES.

unspit v. [late 19C] to vomit (cf. UNSWALLOW).

unstuck v. [1930s] to open up, to abandon secrecy, to tell tales.

unsus adj. [1950s+] unsuspicious, plausible. [SUS adj.]

unswallow v. [1930s] to vomit (cf. UNSPIT).

unsweetened n. [mid-19C–1910s] gin.

untalkaboutables see UNMENTIONABLES.

unthimble v. [early 19C] (Und.) to rob a man of his watch. [THIMBLE]

until the last dog is hung/dies phr. [20C] (US) till the very end. [note UK proverb 'give a dog a bad name and hang him']

untogether adj. [1960s+] **1** a general neg.; of a person, not in full possession of their faculties; of a situation, less than satisfactorily under control (cf. UNCOOL). **2** (US) unstylish, lacking social awareness. [antonym of TOGETHER]

untwisted adj. [late 17C–18C] ruined, 'undone'.

unutterables/unwhisperables see UNMENTIONABLES.

unzip v. [1970s+] (orig. US) **1** to sort out and solve a problem. **2** to open, to open up. In phr. unzip one's mouth, to talk.

u.p. phr. [late 19C] up, usu. in phr. it's all u.p. for him. [spelling out of SE up]

up n.¹ [late 19C–1920s] (US) bottled ale (cf. DOWN n.²). [? its fizziness]

up n.² [1940s+] a prospective purchaser in a store. [? they pick things up]

up n.³ [1960s+] (US) a blunder, mistake. [abbr. FUCK-UP]

up n.⁴ see UPPER n.².

up adj. [1940s+] (orig. US) **1** mentally stimulated, excited, hopeful; thus **2** intoxicated by a drug (cf. HIGH adj.¹).

up v.¹ **1** [mid-18C–late 19C] of mood or spirits, to raise, to pick up, to lift. **2** [1930s+] (orig. US) to raise, to increase prices, charges etc. **3** [1940s+] (orig. US) to promote. **4** [1960s+] (orig. US) to improve, to boost.

up v.² [late 19C] to have sexual intercourse with. [the man puts his penis up the vagina]

up v.³ [late 19C+] to begin, to push oneself forward, to say or do something, usu. in phr. ups and ... , e.g. he ups and starts saying ... .

up adv.¹ [mid-19C+] going on, happening, usu. in a neg. context, e.g. I think something is up.

up adv.² [1940s+] of food, ready, e.g. tea's up, grub's up.

up prep. [1950s+] at, e.g. up the market.

up against phr. [late 19C+] (orig. US) facing problems, in difficulties, esp. in phr. up against it.

up against one's duckhouse/fowlhouse phr. [1930s+] (Aus.) a setback, a problem, usu. in phr. that's one up against your duckhouse.

up against the stem phr. [1970s+] (drugs) addicted to smoking marijuana. [STEM n.¹]

up against the wall phr. **1** [1910s+] (orig. milit.) facing serious problems. **2** [1960s+] (US campus) foolish, stupid. [the putting of prisoners against a wall to face a firing squad, reinforced in (2) by the 1960s radical slogan, *Up against the wall, motherfucker!*]

up against you phr. [late 19C] it's up to you, what do you say to that?

up a gumtree phr. [late 19C+] (orig. Aus.) in trouble, facing a problem. [the chasing of an animal into such a tree where it is very hard to dislodge]

up-and-down n.¹ [20C] brown, usu. brown ale. [rhy. sl.]

up-and-down n.² [1920s+] a look, a scrutiny. [the movement of one's eyes]

up and down phr. [mid–late 19C+] (US) in a straightforward, open and honest manner.

up-and-downer n. [mid-19C+] a fight, a tussle. [the fluctuating fortunes of the fighters]

up and down like a fiddler's elbow phr. [late 19C+] very restless.

up and down like a yo-yo phr. [1930s+] used of one who is unable to keep still or whose emotions alternate continually between optimistic and pessimistic.

up and down like Tower Bridge phr. [late 19C] used in answer to the question, 'How are you?' [*Tower Bridge*, the only one of London's bridges across the Thames to be raised/lowered for the passage of ships]

up and dust v. [20C] (US Black) to leave in a hurry, to run away. [DUST v.³ (1)]

up and tear one's ass, to phr. [1930s] (US Black) to make a social error that is likely to bring retribution or bad luck on the perpetrator. [TEAR ONE'S ASS]

up and under v. [1950s+] (Aus.) to vomit [rhy. sl. *up and under* = CHUNDER v.]

up and up adj. [mid-19C+] (orig. US) fair, honest, straightforward (cf. ON THE UP AND UP; STRAIGHT UP).

up and up gee n. [20C] (US Und.) an inmate who has not properly learned prison survival. [UP AND UP + GEE n.⁴]

up arsehole street see IN ARSEHOLE STREET.

up a storm phr. [1950s+] intensely, enthusiastically, vehemently.

up a stump phr. [early 19C+] **1** in difficulties, perplexed (cf. UP A GUMTREE). **2** tipsy. [orig. UK but almost immediately taken over by US]

up a tree phr.¹ [early 19C+] in temporary difficulties. [the image of a cat perched, spitting down at an adversary, high in a tree]

up a tree phr.² [1970s+] (US campus) annoyed, emotionally unstable. [OUT OF ONE'S TREE]

up a tree for tenpence phr. [mid–late 19C] totally impoverished.

upbeat adj. [1940s+] (orig. US) optimistic, positive. [orig. jazz use]

up cack street phr. [1950s+] in trouble, in difficulties (cf. IN SHIT STREET). [CACK n.¹ (1)]

upchuck v. [1920s+] (orig. US) to vomit (cf. THROW UP v.¹). [CHUCK v.² (5)]

up each other phr. [1940s+] (Aus.) indulging in mutual flattery (cf. JERKING EACH OTHER OFF). [UP v.²; the image is of buggery]

up-foot v. [late 19C] to get to one's feet.

up for adj. [late 19C+] keen on, willing to do (cf. ALL FOR IT).

up for grabs phr. [1920s+] (orig. US) **1** available, on the market. **2** vulnerable.

up/in/out front adj. [1910s+] (orig. US Black) open, honest, outspoken, outgoing. [SE *front*]

up/in/out front adv. [1930s+] **1** (orig. US Black) first, at the start. **2** in advance, esp. of money paid for illegal activities, e.g. drug purchases. [FRONT v.³]

upful/uphill adj. [1950s+] (W.I. Rasta) positive, encouraging. [SE *hopeful*]

up goes the donkey phr. [mid-19C] a phr. used to extract as much money as possible before agreeing to perform any task. [the old showman's exhibition, as a finale to his act a donkey is hoisted into the air, but before he will do it, the crowd is exhorted to hand over some extra pennies to make it worth his while. The usu. phr. is *three more and up goes the donkey!* (the *OED* cites 'a penny more ...']

up her like a rat up a drain, to be phr. [1960s+] (orig. Aus.) used of a woman, a phr. outlining the assumption that she will be freely, easily and speedily sexually available to the speaker.

up her way phr. [late 19C+] of a man, having sexual intercourse (cf. UP v.²).

uphill see UPFUL.

uphill gardener n. [1990s] a male homosexual. [the ref. is to anal intercourse]

uphills n. [late 17C–18C] (Und.) fixed dice that will always show high numbers (cf. LOW MEN).

up in adj. [mid-19C+] well versed in, expert at.

up in/to G phr. [late 19C–1920s] (US) very best, superlative. [? play on the musical note G]

up in one's hat phr. [19C] drunk (cf. HAVE A BRICK IN ONE'S HAT).

up in the air phr. **1** [19C+] annoyed, irritated (cf. AERATED). **2** [19C+] happy, in a good mood. **3** [19C+] (US) cocky, self-opinionated. **4** [1930s–50s] doubting, speculative, hypothetical.

up in the boughs phr. [17C+] angry, irritated (cf. UP A TREE phr.²).

up in the bucks phr. [20C] (US) wealthy, prospering. [BUCK n.²]

up in the paints phr. [1930s+] (US) depending on context, old, high, superior, all meanings imply something more extreme. [gambling jargon *paints* = high (royal) cards]

up in the stirrups phr. [early 19C] prospering, doing well. [riding imagery]

up/away in the tea-tree phr. [20C] (N.Z.) in the deep countryside; in a very remote area. [SE *tea-tree*, the manuka or kanuka tree]

up in the tooth see OLD IN THE TOOTH.

upjump n. [1910s+] (Aus.) an upstart, a nouveau riche, a general term of abuse. [SE *jumped up*]

up jumps the devil phr. [1930s+] (US) used when an unexpected and unpleasant situation suddenly develops.

up King Street phr. [mid-19C–1950s] (Aus.) in financial difficulties; thus *go up King Street*, to become bankrupt. [*King Street*, Sydney, the site of the Supreme Court, which hears bankruptcy cases; note SE phr. *in carey street*]

up on adj. [20C] aware of what is happening, alert.

upon a squeeze see AT A SQUEEZE.

up one's arse/ass phr. [1970s+] (US) immediately behind and so irritating, bothering. [ARSE n.¹]

up one's back phr. [1980s+] (US) nagging, irritating.

up oneself phr. [1940s+] (Aus.) arrogant, self-satisfied, full of oneself. [image of auto-sodomy]

up one's petticoat phr. [late 18C–1900s] of a man, very familiar with a female.

up one's sleeve phr. [late 19C] drunk.

up one's street phr. [20C] suited to one's taste, often intensified as *right up one's street*.

up on it adj. [1980s+] (US Black) aware, knowledgeable (cf. HIP adj.).

upon my sam! excl. [late 19C+] a general excl. of emphasis. [? SALAMON]

upon/'pon my sivvy!/sivy!/sivey! excl. [mid–late 19C] a mild oath, on my soul!, on my oath! [? SE *asservation*, keeping one's word. E.P. rejects this, opting for *affidavit* (cf. DAVY) or SE *soul*]

upon my truly! see BY MY TRULY!

up on one's end phr. [20C] (Irish) antagonistic, spoiling for a fight.

up on the scoot see ON THE SCOOT.

up or down phr. [late 19C] heaven or hell.

upped adj. [1930s+] raped. [UP v.²]

upper n.¹ [1950s–60s] a member of the *upper* classes. [abbr.]

upper/up/ups/uppies n.² [1960s+] (drugs) amphetamine or a similar form of drug, e.g. methedrine (cf. A n.²; DOWNER n.⁴).

upper n.³ [1960s+] (US) a state of optimistic excitement. [fig. use of the effects of UPPER n.²]

upper and downer n. [late 19C] **1** a form of wrestling match in which the opponents attempt to throw each other, but do not use blows. **2** any form of physical fight.

upper apartment n. [19C] the head (cf. ATTIC; UPPER STOREY).

upper benjamin/ben n. **1** [late 18C–mid-19C] (Und.) an overcoat, a greatcoat (cf. BEN n.²). **2** [mid-19C] in pl., a pair of trousers. [according to Hotten (1874) an acknowledgement of the large number of (? Jewish) tailors called *Benjamin*]

upper-box jackadandy n. [late 18C] an apprentice or shop-assistant with aspirations to parading as a dandy. [SE *jackadandy* + upper box, the gallery of theatre, which was all such a person could afford]

upper crust *n.* **1** [early–mid-19C] the head, esp. in boxing use (cf. ATTIC). **2** [mid-19C] a hat. **3** [mid-19C+] the social élite, the aristocracy.

upper crust *adj.* [mid-19C+] conceited, snobbish. [UPPER CRUST n. (3)]

upper deck *n.* [1940s] (Aus.) the female breasts.

upper extremity/garret *see* UPPER STOREY.

upper Holloway *n.* [19C] the vagina (cf. BLACK HOLE n.¹). [SE *upper* + HOLLOWAY]

upper loft *see* UPPER STOREY.

upper roger *n.* [19C] (Anglo-Ind.) the heir apparent to a rajah's or other throne. [Hind. *yuva-raja*, a young king]

uppers and downers *n.* [1950s–60s] the teeth.

upper shell *n.* [19C] an overcoat (cf. UPPER BENJAMIN).

upper stock *n.* [late 18C–early 19C] breeches. [SE *upper stock*, the upper part of the stockings]

upper storey/extremity/garret/loft/works *n.* [late 18C–19C] the head, the brain, the mental capacity that resides within it; thus *his upper storey/garret is unfurnished*, he is a foolish or 'empty' person, he is 'not all there' (cf. ATTIC).

upper ten *n.* [mid-19C+] (orig. US) the social élite. [abbr. SE *upper ten thousand*, coined by the journalist Nathaniel Parker Willis (1806–67) in a piece entitled 'Necessity for a Promenade Drive' (1848) in which he stated 'At present there is no distinction among the upper ten thousand of the city.']

upper ten push *n.* [late 19C] (Aus. prison) upper-class prisoners. [UPPER TEN + PUSH n.² (2)]

upper ten set *n.* [late 19C] those servants who work for the 'upper ten thousand'. [UPPER TEN + SE *set*]

upper-tog/togger *n.* [early–mid-19C] a greatcoat, an overcoat (cf. UPPER BENJAMIN). [SE *upper* + TOGS]

upper works *see* UPPER STOREY.

uppie *n.* [1970s+] (S.Afr.) a student of the University of Port Elizabeth (cf. TUCKIE). [*U*niversity of *P*ort Elizabeth]

uppies *see* UPPER n.².

uppish *adj.* **1** [late 17C–early 18C] well-off, provided with sufficient money (cf. ON THE UP AND UP). **2** [18C] proud, arrogant (cf. UPPITY). [Johnson terms (2) a 'low word', thus its inclusion here, but *OED* lists as SE]

uppities *n.* [late 19C] (US) social climbers. [UPPITY]

uppity *adj.* [mid-19C+] (orig. US) cheeky, arrogant, one who refuses to 'know their place', esp. in phr. *uppity nigger*, a Black person who refuses to accept his or her second-class status (cf. DICTY adj.; HINCTY adj.¹; SEDDITY). [SE *up*]

upright *n.*¹ [late 18C–20C] sexual intercourse performed while standing up. (cf. UPRIGHT GRAND).

upright *n.*² [19C] a quart of beer mixed with a quarter pint of gin.

upright grand *n.* [1920s+] (Aus.) sexual intercourse while standing up. [UPRIGHT n.¹ + pun on SE *upright grand* piano]

upright grin *n.* [mid-19C] the vagina (cf. VERTICAL SMILE). [physiognomy]

upright man *n.* [16C–early 19C] (Und.) a senior criminal beggar, outranked, if at all, only by the RUFFLER. Such a villain held absolute power, demanding and receiving both cash and kind, including their women, from his inferiors and beating them without fear of revenge. 'He hath the chief place at any market walk ... and is not of any to be controlled.' (Awdeley) (cf. CANTING CREW). [his stance. He adopted no form of counterfeit physical deformity, as did many of his peers, in his pose as a solid citizen. As such he both gulled the public and commanded loyalty and financial dues from lesser thieves]

uprights *n.* [late 19C–1940s] (US Black) the legs.

upright sneak *n.* [late 18C–early 19C] (Und.) one who steals pewter pots from the boys employed by taverns to collect them (cf. EVENING SNEAK; MORNING SNEAK). [UPRIGHT n.² + SNEAK]

uproar *n.* [mid-18C–mid-19C] an opera. [a heavy pun]

ups *see* UPPERS n.².

upsadaisy!/upsidaisy!/oops-a-daisy! *excl.* [mid-19C+] a soothing excl. offered to a fallen child as one picks them up. [? the image of plucking a daisy from a lawn]

upsee *adj.* [17C] in the manner/style of, esp. as applied to drinking habits; thus *upsee-Dutch*, in the Dutch manner; *upsee-English*, in the English manner; *upsee-Freeze* (1) in the Friesian manner, or (2) strong drink; to drink *upsee-freeze cross*, to drink with arms intertwined. [Du. *op zijn*, on his. A second ety. suggests Du. *op zee*, overseas or imported, and thus refers to the drink itself, whether English, Dutch or whatever, rather than the manner of drinking]

upset Mrs Jones, to *phr.* [early–mid-19C] to empty the privy tub (cf. MRS JONES).

upset the lobster-cart, to *phr.* [early 19C+] (mainly US) to knock a person down.

up shit/shit's creek without a paddle *phr.* [1930s+] (orig. US) in deep trouble (cf. SHIT CREEK).

upshot *n.* [early 19C] a riotous frolic. [dial. *upshot*, a feast, a celebration]

upside *adj.* [1950s+] (US Black) next to, up against; thus *upside one's head*, of a blow, against the head.

upsides with *phr.* [mid-18C–late 19C] (Scot.) **1** on an equal footing. **2** level with.

up South *n.* [1950s–60s] (US Black) the Northern states. [the implication is that racism and prejudice is just as widespread as it is 'down South']

up stacks *see* UP STICKS.

upstage *adj.* [1920s+] (US) conceited, snobbish. [theatre jargon]

upstage *v.* [1920s+] (US) to outwit, to win or be superior to another person. [theatrical jargon]

upstairs *n.*¹ [late 19C] the best brands of spirits (cf. TOP SHELF n.). [kept on a special high shelf in the public house]

upstairs *n.*² **1** [1930s] (US) the mind, esp. as regards its intelligence. **2** [1930s+] (US) heaven (cf. MAN UPSTAIRS). **3** [1960s+] a higher authority, a senior position (cf. KICK UPSTAIRS).

upstakes *v.* [mid-19C+] (US) to leave, esp. abruptly (cf. UP STICKS). [SE *pick up one's stakes*, the boundary posts of a property]

upstate *n.* [1930s+] (New York Und.) prison. [the main New York state prisons are upstate]

up sticks/stacks *v.* [mid-19C+] to move, to pack up and leave (cf. AMPUTATE ONE'S MAHOGANY). [naut. jargon *up stick*, to ship the mast or *stick* before moving]

upta/upter *adj.* [20C] (Aus.) useless, no use whatsoever. [UP TO PUTTY]

up the ante, to *phr.* [20C] (US) to increase the amount, demand a higher price. [poker imagery]

up the ass *phr.* [1980s+] (US) thoroughly, very well. [ARSE n.¹]

up the butt *phr.* [1980s+] to an excess, to the extreme (cf. UP THE YING-YANG). [BUTT n.¹]

up the chute *phr.* [1920s+] (Aus.) useless, worthless, failed (cf. UP THE SPOUT).

up the creek *phr.* [1930s+] **1** (Aus.) pregnant (cf. UP THE DUFF; UP THE SPOUT). **2** in trouble, facing problems (cf. UP SHIT CREEK WITHOUT A PADDLE).

up the duff *phr.* [1940s+] (orig. Aus.) pregnant (cf. UP THE SPOUT). [SE *duff*, a pudding, thus cf. HAVE A BUN IN THE OVEN; IN THE PUDDING CLUB]

up the flue *see* IN THE FLUE.

up the gazoo/kazoo/wazoo *phr.* [1960s+] (orig. US) full up, as much as one can handle, to excess.

up the house-roof *see* AT THE HOUSE-ROOF.

up the housetop *see* AT THE HOUSETOP.

up the kazoo *see* UP THE GAZOO.

up the pole *phr.*[1] **1** [late 19C–1900s] drunk. **2** [late 19C+] wrong, in error, in trouble, facing difficulties. **3** [late 19C+] insane.

up the pole *phr.*[2] [1920s+] pregnant (cf. UP THE SPOUT).

up there *phr.* [1960s+] **1** on a level with, in the same league. **2** (US) in heaven.

up there Cazaly! *excl.* [1940s+] (Aus.) a cry of encouragement. [Australian rules football player Roy *Cazaly* (1893–1963), star of the South Melbourne team and noted for his leaps into the air for a 'mark']

up the river *phr.* [1930s+] (orig. US) in prison (cf. AWAY adj.; DOWN THE RIVER phr.[2]; SEND UP THE RIVER). [the penitentiary at Ossining ('Sing-Sing'), which is sited *up the river* from New York City]

up the spank *phr.* [late 19C] at the pawnbroker's (cf. UP THE SPOUT).

up the spout *phr.* **1** [early 19C–1920s] hospitalized, imprisoned. **2** [mid-19C] having problems, 'in a bad way'. **3** [mid-19C] bankrupt. **4** [mid-19C+] in the pawnshop. **5** [1930s+] pregnant (cf. UP THE DUFF; UP THE FLUE; KNOCKED UP). **6** [1930s+] dead. **7** [1930s+] (US) gone to waste, ruined. [SE *spout*, a lift formerly in use in pawnbrokers' shops, up which the articles pawned were taken for storage, thus the pawnshop itself]

up the stairs/steps *phr.* [1930+] on trial; thus *go up the stairs/steps*, to be tried at the Old Bailey, to be sent to the Old Bailey from a lower court. [the steps that lead from the cells beneath the Old Bailey up into the dock]

up the stick *phr.*[1] [1930s+] crazy, eccentric. [var. on UP THE POLE phr.[1] (3)]

up the stick *phr.*[2] [1930s+] (orig. Aus.) pregnant (cf. ON THE STICK adv.[2]; UP THE POLE phr.[2]; UP THE SPOUT).

up the wall *phr.* [1920s+] (US) crazy, eccentric or over-excited.

up the way *phr.* [20C] (Aus.) pregnant. [IN THE FAMILY WAY]

up the wazoo *see* UP THE GAZOO.

up the ying-yang *phr.* [1960s+] to an excess, to the extreme (cf. UP THE BUTT). [fig. use of YING-YANG]

up thine with turpentine *phr.* [20C] (US) a phr. of rejection, dismissal. [ext. of UP YOURS!]

uptight *adj.*[1] **1** [1950s+] close, friendly. **2** [1960s] satisfactory, good. [SE *tight*, faithful]

uptight *adj.*[2] [1960s] out of money, impoverished. [TIGHT adj.[2]]

uptight *adj.*[3] [1960s] (US Black) trapped, in a position from which there is no escape.

uptight *adj.*[4] [1960s+] **1** tense, nervous, annoyed. **2** formal, unbending, strait-laced. [SE *tight*, tense]

up to *adj.*[1] [19C] aware of, knowledgeable about. [20C use is SE]

up to *adj.*[2] [late 19C+] incumbent upon, obligatory (cf. DOWN TO).

up to a thing or two *phr.* [early 19C] aware, knowledgeable.

up to Dick/door *phr.* [mid–late 19C] up to standard, as required. [DICK n.[2]; *door* appears to be a corruption]

up to dictionary *phr.* [19C] intellectual, clever, learned. [the myth of the omniscient dictionary]

up to dolly's wax/pussy's bow *phr.* [1940s+] (Aus.) absolutely full of food. [nursery use, dolls used to have solid bodies surmounted with carefully modelled wax heads]

up to door *see* UP TO DICK.

up to G *see* UP IN G.

up to here *phr.* [1940s+] bored, disgusted, utterly intolerant of an event, someone's statements, actions etc. [HAVE HAD IT UP TO HERE]

up to mud *phr.* [1930s+] (Aus.) unsatisfactory (cf. UP TO PUTTY). [the innate worthlessness of mud]

up to no good *phr.* [1980s+] having sexual intercourse with someone (cf. DO THE NAUGHTY).

up to one's armpits *phr.* [1950s+] (orig. US) consumed by, overwhelmed by.

up to one's ass/ears in alligators/rattlesnakes *phr.* [1960s+] (US) in very serious troubles, facing overwhelming problems. [the saying *when you're up to one's ass ears in alligators, you don't worry about draining the swamp*, often used to imply that one has no time for (long-term liberal) social action, when faced by the immediate threat of criminality]

up to one's ears *phr.* [early 19C+] (orig. US) deeply involved, well supplied (cf. UP TO ONE'S ASS)

up to one's eyeballs/eyebrows *phr.* [1920s+] (US) completely full, as much as is bearable.

up to one's/the neck/neck in *phr.* [20C] (orig. US) deeply, totally involved or committed.

up top *n.* [1950s+] (Aus.) northern Australia; thus *uptoppers*, those who live there (cf. TOP END).

up top *phr.* [1960s+] in a position of authority or influence.

up to pussy's bow *see* UP TO DOLLY'S WAX.

up to putty *phr.* [1930s+] (Aus.) worthless, ineffectual (cf. UPTA; UP TO MUD). [the innate worthlessness of putty]

up to scratch *phr.* [late 19C+] as required, satisfactory; thus *come up to scratch*, to prepare oneself as well and efficiently as possible, to reach a particular standard (cf. UP TO SNUFF). [SE *scratch*, the starting line in a race + prize-fighting *scratch-line*, a line drawn across a boxing ring which an able contestant was required to touch with his toe.]

up to slum *phr.* [mid-19C] knowing, aware, on the look out for tricks. [UP TO adj.[1] + SLUM n.[1] (4)]

up to snuff *phr.* [early 19C+] efficient, capable, aware; extended as [late 18C–early 19C] *up to snuff and twopenny, up to snuff and a pinch above it* (cf. UP TO SCRATCH).

up to the arse/ass in *phr.* [mid-19C+] (orig. US) completely overwhelmed by. [ARSE n.[1]]

up to the cackle/gossip/try-on *phr.* [late 18C–mid-19C] aware of what is going on, shrewd, experienced. [UP TO adj.[1] + CACKLE n.[1]/SE *gossip*]

up to the chin *phr.* [mid-19C] totally involved, fully committed, overburdened (cf. UP TO ONE'S NECK).

up to the dodge *phr.* [mid-19C] (US) aware, shrewd, knowledgeable. [UP TO adv.[1] + DODGE n.]

up to the hammer *phr.* [late 19C] up to the standard, first-rate, excellent. [auction imagery]

up to the handle *see* TO THE HANDLE.

up to the high-water mark *phr.* [mid-19C–1920s] a general phr. of approval, in ideal condition.

up to the hub *phr.* [19C] (US) up to the very limit.

up to the knocker *phr.* [mid–late 19C] **1** fashionably dressed or over–dressed. **2** capable, up to a task. [KNOCKER n.[2] or fig. use of SE (*door*) *knocker*]

up to the neck *see* UP TO ONE'S NECK.

up to the nines *phr.* [late 18C+] to the highest perfection (cf. TO THE RUFFIAN). [? the numerologistic attribution of 9 as a mystic number or (according to Ware) a corruption of an older phr. *up to the eyen*, up to the eyes, i.e. the satisfaction of the eyes]

up the arse/ass *phr.* [1950s+] (US) to excess, in large amounts. [ARSE n.[1]]

up to trap *see* TRAP n.[1].

up to tripe *phr.* [1900s–10s] worthless, unpleasant, distasteful. [TRIPE n.[2]]

uptown *n.* **1** [1950s+] (W.I. Rasta) the upper classes. **2** [1970s] (US drugs) cocaine, always considered the drug of the more affluent. [UPTOWN adj.]

uptown *adj.* [1930s+] (US) sophisticated, worldly, rich. [SE *uptown*, the residential area of a US city]

up to your nuts-in-guts *phr.* [1990s] (orig. Aus.) of a man, engaged in an act of sexual intercourse. [NUTS n.² (1) + SE guts]

uptucker *n.* [mid-19C] the hangman (cf. TUCK 'EM FAIR). [TUCK v.¹]

upward drag *n.* [late 19C] a hairstyle for men in which the hair is brushed forward over the forehead and cut in a straight line from ear to ear (cf. PRETTY-BOY CLIP).

upways *n.* [1970s+] (US Black) a snobbish, stand-offish person. [SE *upways*, in an upward direction]

up West *adv.* [20C] the West End of London, as seen either from the East End or from the further western or suburban areas.

upya! *excl.* [1940s+] (Aus.) a dismissive, contemptuous excl., lit. *up you!*

up you! *excl.* [late 19C+] a dismissive, contemptuous excl. [*euph. of* FUCK YOU!, esp. when accompanied by the (orig. US) raised middle-finger gesture]

up you for the rent! *excl.* [1930s+] (Aus.) a dismissive, contemptuous excl. [ext. of UP YOU!]

up your alley! *phr.* [1970s+] a general phr. of rude dismissal (cf. UP YOUR ARSE!).

up your arse!/ass!/butt! *excl.* [1930s+] a dismissive, insulting excl. [ARSE n.¹; BUTT n.¹; a preceding 'stick it ...' is taken as read]

up your flue! *phr.* [1970s] a coarse phr. of dismissal (cf. UP YOUR ARSE!) [FLUE n.² (3)]

up your gig!/giggy! *phr.* [late 19C+] (US) a general phr. of contempt, dismissal. [GIG n.⁷]

up your gonga/gunga! *excl.* [20C] a euph. synon. of UP YOUR ARSE!

up your jacksie!/jack! *excl.* [late 19C+] an alternative version of UP YOUR ASS! [JACKSIE/JACK n.¹⁷]

up your jumper! *excl.* [1920s+] (Aus.) a euph. synon. of UP YOUR ARSE!

up your pipe! *excl.* [1930s+] a euph. synon. of UP YOUR ARSE!

up yours! *excl.* [1950s+] (orig. US) an excl. of contempt. [euph. abbr. of UP YOUR ARSE!]

urban surfing *n.* [1970s+] riding on the outside of moving vehicles.

urger *n.* [1910s–60s] (Aus.) **1** a man who obtains money illegally or dishonourably, esp. as a tipster at a racecourse. **2** a sponger or idler.

uriah heep *n.* [20C] an unpleasant person. [rhy. sl. *uriah heep* = CREEP n. (1); ult. *Uriah Heep*, a villain in Dickens' *David Copperfield* (1859–50)]

urinal of the planets *n.* [late 17C–mid-19C] Ireland. [a literary usage that reflects the country's high rainfall]

urky-purky *adj.* [1930s+] (Aus. juv.) disgusting, esp. of food (cf. UCKY). [echoic]

use *v.¹* [1930s+] (drugs) to take narcotic drugs, esp. heroin.

use *v.²* [1950s+] to need, to desire, 'do with', e.g. *I could use a decent meal.*

use at *v.* [late 19C] to frequent, to visit.

used-beer department *n.* [1920s+] (Can.) the lavatory in a bar.

used up *adj.* **1** [mid-18C–mid-19C] dead, killed in battle (cf. WASTED). **2** [mid-19C+] exhausted, whether of a person, a vehicle, a place. [a message sent by Gen. John Guise during his attack on Cartagena during the war with Spain *c.*1740 when he requested that he be sent more grenadiers because of the 1200 he already had, 50 per cent were killed or wounded, in other words 'used up']

useful *n.* [mid-19C+] (Aus.) a general helper, esp. in a public house. [SE *general/generally useful*]

useful/useless as an ashtray on a motorbike/a glass door on a dunny/a handbrake on a Holden/a hip pocket in a singlet/the Yarra *phr.* [1980s] (Aus.) various phrases to describe anything that is considered absolutely pointless. [DUNNY/proper name *Holden*, an Aus. make of car/*Yarra*, an Aus. river]

useless as a one-legged man at an ass-kicking contest *phr.* [1960s+] (US) absolutely worthless. [ARSE n.¹]

useless as a pork chop/a slice of bacon at a Jewish wedding *see* WENT DOWN LIKE A PORK CHOP AT A JEWISH WEDDING.

useless as a spare prick at a wedding/lesbian wedding *phr.* [1960s+] totally useless (cf. LIKE A SPARE PRICK AT A WEDDING). [PRICK n. (2)]

useless as monkey's grease *phr.* [18C] utterly useless. [monkeys are usu. very thin and thus render no 'grease']

useless smile *n.* [1980s+] one whose consumption of hallucinogens has rendered them incapable of rational thought or action, they have become little more than a happy, smiling vegetable.

use one's loaf/bean, to *phr.* [20C] to think, to work things out (cf. USE THE OLD BEAN). [LOAF n.²/BEAN n.⁴]

user *n.¹* [1930s+] a drug addict. [USE v.¹]

user *n.²* [1950s+] (orig. Aus.) one who habitually exploits others for their own gain. [SE *use*]

use the chump, to *phr.* [20C] to act intelligently [CHUMP n.¹]

use the English, to *phr.* [1930s+] (US gay) to wriggle one's buttocks while being penetrated anally. [snooker jargon *English*, a swerving shot]

use the five-fingered chequebook, to *phr.* [1980s+] (N.Z.) to shoplift.

use the glass, to *phr.* [late 19C+] to use a broken glass or bottle as a weapon in a fight, typically in a public house. [GLASS v.]

use the noggin, to *phr.* [early 19C+] (orig. US) to act intelligently, to be aware. [NOGGIN n.¹]

use the old bean/turnip, to *phr.* [20C] to act sensibly, intelligently, to think. [BEAN n.⁴/TURNIP n.² (2)]

use the windward passage, to *phr.* [late 18C–early 19C] to sodomize. [play on SE *windward* + (*breaking*) *wind*; but note naut jargon *use the windward passage*, to sail close to the wind]

u.s.g. *n.* [1990s] (US Black) the American Black community, i.e. the status of Blacks, governmental statements of equal rights notwithstanding, as regards the larger US world. [abbr. *United States ghettos*]

usher! *excl.* [late 19C–1920s] yes! [? Yid. *user*, it is so]

usher of the back door *n.* [late 18C–early 19C] a sodomite (cf. BACK-DOOR MAN n.²). [SE *usher* + BACK DOOR n.¹]

usher of the hall *n.* [late 19C] (society) the odd-job man in a great house.

usual *n.* [late 19C] **1** one's normal state of health. **2** one's habitual choice of drink or beverage.

ute *n.* [1940s+] (Aus.) a *ut*ility vehicle, a small truck. [abbr.]

UVs *n.* [1970s+] (US teen) sunshine; thus *soak up UVs*, to get a tan. [abbr. *u*ltra-*v*iolet *rays*]

uxter *n.* [late 19C] money. [dial. *uxter/oxter*, an armpit or armhole of a jacket, thus the wallet that is carried in an inside pocket; note dial. *come with a crooked oxter*, to bring a present, to come with a good dowry]

uzi *n.* [1980s+] (drugs) **1** crack. **2** crack pipe. [the *Uzi* automatic gun, a status symbol in the drug-dealing/consuming community]

V

V *n.* [1960s+] (drugs) the mild tranquillizer Valium. [abbr.]

v *adj.* [1960s+] (society) very. [abbr.]

Vaalie/Vaaljapie *n.* [1970s+] (S.Afr.) a native of the Transvaal, generally looked down upon by the citizens of Cape Town, esp. when they appear there on holiday. [*Transvaal* + JAAP]

vacation *n.* [1930s+] (US) time spent in prison.

vacuum *n.* **1** [19C] the vagina. **2** [1980s+] (US campus) a hearty eater.

vacuum cleaner *n.* [1940s–50s] a sports car. [it helps one 'pick up bits of fluff']

vacuum cleaners *n.* [1940s] (US Black) the human lungs.

vada *see* VARDA.

vade-mecum *n.* [19C] the vagina. [Lat. *vade mecum*, lit. 'come with me', fig. 'a useful thing']

vag *n.* **1** [mid-19C+] (Aus./N.Z./US) a *vagrant*. **2** [late 19C+] a charge of *vagrancy*; thus *on the vag, under the vag*, on a charge of vagrancy. [abbr.]

vag *v.* [20C] (Aus./US) to charge and/or arrest someone for vagrancy. [VAG n.]

vagabond *n.* [20C] (W.I.) **1** a lazy but inoffensive young man. **2** a lecherous old man.

vaggerie *v.* [mid-19C+] (Ling. Fr./Polari) to go, to leave. [Ital. *viaggiare*, to travel]

vagina little-finger *n.* [1950s–60s] (camp gay) a snob. [*vagina* puns on Virginia, seen as a typical upper-class name. *Little-finger* refers to the affected crooking of the little finger when drinking]

vakeel *n.* [mid-19C] (Anglo-Ind.) a barrister. [Urdu *vakil*, an attorney, an authorized representative]

valiant as an Essex lion *phr.* [17C–mid-19C] cowardly. [SE *valiant* + ESSEX LION]

vallie/vally/vals *n.* [1960s+] *Vali*um, a mild tranquillizer. [abbr.]

vamoose *v.* [mid-19C+] (orig. US) to go away, leave; esp. as imper. *vamoose!*, go away, be off! (cf. ADIOS). [Sp. *vamos!*, let's go!]

vamp *n.*¹ **1** [late 17C–18C] (Und.) a sock (cf. VAMPERS). **2** [mid-19C] an old stocking that has had the foot repaired. [SE *vamp*, that part of the stocking that covers the ankle and foot]

vamp *n.*² [mid–late 19C] a robbery. [VAMP v.]

vamp *v.* **1** [late 17C–19C] to pawn, to steal. [SE *vamp*, to repair, to patch up]

vamper *n.* [mid-19C] a thief, esp. one who deliberately starts fights between others in order to rob them in the confusion (cf. BULLY-BUCK; BULLY-COCK). [SE *vamp*, to improvise]

vampers *n.* [late 17C–18C] (Und.) stockings. [VAMP n.¹]

vampire *n.* [mid-19C] an intolerable bore. [they 'suck out' one's energy]

vampire's teabag *n.* [1980s+] (US Black) a sanitary napkin. [coarse use of SE]

vamp on *v.* [1960s–70s] (US Black) **1** to make an unjust attack, to arrest. **2** when aimed at the oppressor to correct; to force him to mend his ways. [? SE *vampire*, (2) was esp. popular with 1960s–70s radicals]

Van *see* VAN DER MERWE.

vancouver *n.* [20C] a vacuum cleaner, a hoover. [rhy. sl.]

vandemonianism *n.* [mid–late 19C] (Aus.) rowdyism, riotousness. [the one-time prison colony of *Van Dieman's* Land or Tasmania + ref. to SE *pandemonium*]

Vanderbilt *n.* [late 19C] (US) a very rich man. [New York's multi-millionaire *Vanderbilt* family]

Van der Merwe/Van *n.* [1960s+] (S.Afr.) the generic, stereotypical Afrikaner, the subject of a wide range of 'Van der Merwe' jokes characterizing him as loutish, bigoted and stupid; thus the *real Van der Merwe*, synon. with the REAL MCCOY, *meet one's Van der Merwe*, meet one's Waterloo. [the common Afrikaner surname]

van dragger *n.* [mid–late 19C] a thief who specializes in stealing goods from the back of vans and carts (cf. PETERER).

V and X store *n.* [1930s–40s] (US Black) a corner store. [Lat. *V*, five + *X*, ten, i.e. a 'five and ten cent' store]

van dyke *n.*¹ [1920s+] (Aus.) a lavatory. [pun on SE *dike*/Sir Anthony *Van Dyke*, portraitist (1599–1641)]

van dyke *n.*² [1960s+] (US gay) **1** a lesbian with a trace of a moustache on her upper lip. **2** a lesbian truck driver. [(1) puns on DYKE + portraitist Anthony *Van Dyke* (1599–1641) who was thus bearded; (2) puns on SE *van*, a truck + proper name Anthony *Van Dyke*]

vanilla *n.* **1** [1930s+] (US Black) a White person, esp. a female. **2** [1980s+] (US) a heterosexual who practises normal sexual behaviour. [for ety. see VANILLA adj.]

vanilla/plain vanilla *adj.* [1970s+] plain, simple, no frills. [the plainest ice-cream flavour. The phr. was popularized in the 1980s+ but ? coined by the saxophonist Lester Young *c*.1935]

vanilla queen *n.* [1980s+] (US Black) a gay Black male who prefers White partners. [VANILLA n. (1) + QUEEN n.¹]

vanilla sex *n.* [1980s+] (gay) a phr. for relatively conventional forms of sexual activity, usually in contrast to sado-masochistic sex. [VANILLA adj. + SE *sex*]

vanilla suburb *n.* [1970s+] (US) the White suburbs, as opposed to the Black inner city (cf. CHOCOLATE CITY). [VANILLA n. (1) + SE *suburb*]

vanity *n.* [late 19C] one's favourite liquor. [SE *vanity*, a thing of which one is vain]

vanity fair *n.* [20C] a chair. [rhy. sl.]

van John *n.* [mid-19C] in cards, the game of pontoon or 21. [Fr. *vingt-et-un*, (the game of) 21]

vantage loaf *n.* [19C] the 13th loaf in a 'baker's dozen'. [SE *vantage*, an advantage, in this case to the buyer]

vap *n.* [20C] (W.I.) **1** a bad mood. **2** an impulse (cf. CATCH A VAP). [? Fr. *vapeur*, dizziness, light-headedness + obs. SE *the vapours*]

vapors *n.*[1] [1980s+] (US drugs) the smoke issuing from a crack pipe.

vapors *n.*[2] [1990s] (US Black) **1** a newly realized desire for an individual who, once shunned, has now gained status/material possessions and is thus suddenly alluring. **2** jealousy. [? obs. SE *vapours*, a fantasy, a foolish boast]

varda/vada/vardi/vardo/vardy *v.* [mid-19C+] (Ling. Fr./Polari) to look at; thus *varda d'amour*, a loving look, esp. in imper., e.g. *varda the riah!* look at that hair! [Venetian *vardia*, a look]

vardo *n.* [early 19C+] a gypsy wagon; thus *vardo-gill*, a waggoner. [Rom. *vardo*; *wardo*, a cart]

vardo *v. see* VARDA.

vardy *n.* [late 18C–20C] an opinion, a viewpoint. [SE *verdit*, obs. form of *verdict*]

vardy *v. see* VARDA.

vark *n.* [1950s+] (S.Afr.) a general term of abuse, esp. of a policeman (cf. PIG n.). [Afk. *vark*, pig]

varment/varmint *n.* [early 19C] an amateur sportsman who has the skill of a professional. [? E.P. suggests dial. *varment/vermin*, any animal destructive of game but *OED* disputes this, rejecting any such link]

varmint *adj.* **1** [early 19C–mid-19C] fashionable, 'swell', dashing. **2** [19C] shrewd, knowing, 'au fait'. [VARMENT]

varnish *n.* [late 19C] **1** (society) second-rate champagne (cf. COFFIN VARNISH). **2** sauce offered with food sold from a coffeestall.

varnisher *n.* [mid-19C] a counterfeiter of fake sovereigns.

varnish one's pole, to *v.* [1980s+] to masturbate.

varnish remover *n.* [1950s] (US) cheap, inferior whisky (cf. PAINT REMOVER; VARNISH).

varnish the cane, to *phr.* [late 19C–1960s] (US) of a man, to have sexual intercourse (cf. CANDY CANE n.[1]).

varnish the flagpole, to *phr.* [1980s+] to masturbate.

vasbyt *v.* [1960s+] (S.Afr.) (orig. milit. use.) to keep going, to 'tough it out', 'bite the bullet'. [Afk. *vasbyt*, to bite hard, to seize with the jaws]

Vaseline heights *n.* [1970s+] (US gay) the gay centre of Portland, Oregon. [the lubricant uses of Vaseline]

Vaseline valley *n.* [1980s+] (Aus.) a stretch of Oxford Street, Sydney acknowledged as the city's gay centre. [the use of Vaseline to ease anal intercourse ? + pun on California's Silicon Valley]

Vaseline villa *n.* [1960s+] (US gay) a YMCA frequented by gay men. [for ety. *see* VASELINE VALLEY]

v.a.t. *n.* [1980s+] vodka *a*nd *t*onic (cf. B AND S). [abbr. from the TV series *Minder* (1979–81)]

vatch *v.* [mid-19C] to have. [backsl.]

vat en sit *n.* [1950s+] (S.Afr. township) a 'live-in lover', a common-law partner, an unsolemnized marriage, also as adj. [Afk. *vat en sit*, stay put, lit. take and sit]

vat hom Fluffie! *excl.* [1970s+] (S.Afr.) an exhortation, esp. in the context of sports events or business meetings when the subject(s) of the cry has to pull something special out of the hat. [Afk. lit. 'go get him Fluffie'; no record exists of the original Fluffie (a dog, presumably)]

vatican roulette *n.* [1920s+] the notoriously undependable rhythm method of contraception (cf. ROMAN ROULETTE). [the only form permitted by the Catholic Church]

vato *n.* [1950s+] a member of a Mexican teen gang; thus *vato loco*, a gang member with a reputation for extra violence, poise, courage and other attributes of street life.

vatterig *adj.* [1970s+] (S.Afr.) used of one who has 'wandering' hands. [Du. *vatten*, to take, to catch]

vault *v.* [16C] to have sexual intercourse (cf. JUMP v.[1]; VAULTING HOUSE). [SE *vault*, to jump, leap]

vaulting house/school *n.* [late 16C–late 18C] a brothel (cf. ACADEMY; ACCOMMODATION HOUSE). [VAULT + HOUSE n.[1]]

vay-ki-vay *adj.* [20C] (W.I.) unplanned, haphazard. [Fr. *vaille que vaille*, come what may, any old how]

vay-ki-vay *adv.* [20C] (W.I.) carelessly, shabbily. [VAY-KI-VAY adj.]

v.b.c. *phr.* [1980s+] (US campus) having the outline of one's buttocks showing through tight trousers; or revealing the top of one's buttocks due to wearing one's trousers lower than the waist (cf. V.P.L.). [abbr. *v*isible *b*utt *c*rack]

v.b.d. *n.* [1960s] (US Black) an unsatisfactory evening with a member of the opposite sex. [abbr. *v*ery *b*ad *d*ate]

v.c. *adj.* [late 19C] plucky, courageous. [abbr. *Victoria Cross*]

veal will be cheap – calves fall! *excl.* [late 17C] a mocking cry aimed at one who has very thin legs.

vee-dub *n.* [1970s+] (Aus.) a Volkswagen. [abbr. for *vee-double-you*]

veegle *n.* [1950s+] (Aus.) an automobile. [joc. mispron. of SE *vehicle*]

vee-in *n.* [1980s+] (US Black gang) an initiation ritual whereby the new member is beaten by other gang members for an allotted time, e.g. one minute (cf. COURT IN; JUMP IN). [? VAMP ON]

veeno *see* VINO.

veep *n.* [1940s+] (US) a *v*ice-*p*resident. [pron. of initial letters]

vee-wee *n.* [1960s+] a Volkswagen car. [pron. of initial letters]

veg/veggies *n.*[1] [1950s+] *veg*etables. [abbr.]

veg *n.*[2] [1980s+] a moron, a madman. [abbr. SE *vegetable*]

veg *v.* [1980s+] to do absolutely nothing, to lapse into semiconsciousness. [abbr. SE *vegetate*]

vega *n.* [1990s] (US Black teen) a marijuana cigarette rolled inside the outer leaves of a cigar (cf. BLUNT n.). [the cigar brand Garcia y *Vega*, the West Coast version of Phillies Blunts]

vegetable *n.* [1980s+] (US gay) a lesbian. [play on FRUIT n.[2] (2)]

vegetable *adj.* [1970s] (US campus) very drunk.

vegetable John *n.* [1920s] (Aus.) a Chinese greengrocer. [SE *vegetable* + JOHN CHINAMAN]

vegetarian *n.* [1960s+] (US) a female prostitute or male homosexual who will not perform fellatio, i.e. who 'won't eat meat'.

vegged *n.* [1980s+] (drugs) heavily intoxicated by drugs. [VEG v.]

veggie/veggy *n.*[1] [1960s+] a *veg*etarian. [abbr.]

veggie/veggy *n.*[2] [1980s+] (Irish) a derog. term for a physically or mentally disabled child. [abbr. SE *vegetable*]

veggies *see* VEG.

veg out *v.* [1970s+] (US campus) to let oneself slip into a totally apathetic and passive state. [SE *vegetate*]

V-8 *n.* [1940s] (US Black) a solitary woman who prefers her own company to that of others, esp. of men. [? abbr. SE *deviate*]

veiny bang-stick/love-stalk *n.* [1990s] a penis.

velcro head *n.* [1970s+] (US) a derog. term for a Black person. [*Velcro* + sfx. -HEAD (1), the supposed resemblance of the material to tightly curled hair]

velcro love triangle *n.* [1990s] the female genital area. [for ety. *see* VELCRO HEAD]

velveeta *adj.* [1980s+] (US campus) unappealing or unpleasant (cf. CHEESY). [*Velveeta*, a processed cheese spread]

velvet *n.*[1] [late 17C–19C] the tongue (cf. TIP THE VELVET).

velvet *n.*[2] [late 19C+] gain, profit, winnings; thus *to the velvet*, to the good.

velvet *n.*[3] [1950s] (Aus./N.Z.) any dark-skinned woman; thus *a bit of velvet*. [abbr. BLACK VELVET n. (1)]

velvet orbs *see* ORBS.

velvet room *n.* [late 19C] (US) the back room of a saloon where patrons might enjoy a slightly quieter and more salubrious atmosphere than in the rowdier front.

velvet tunnel *n.* [1990s] the vagina.

venerable monosyllable *see* MONOSYLLABLE.

venison out of Tup Park *n.* [late 17C–mid-18C] mutton. [SE *tup*, a ram]

ventilate *v.* [late 19C+] (orig. US) to shoot, to kill with a bullet. [i.e. to 'let air into']

vent man *n.* [20C] (US) a tramp, a street person. [their sleeping over warm subway air vents]

venture girl *n.* [mid-19C] a single woman sent out to India in the hope of winning herself a husband.

Venus *n.* [1990s] (drugs) 2-CB. [for ety. *see* NEXUS]

Venus's curse *n.* [19C] venereal disease.

Venus' highway/honeypot/mark/secret cell *n.* [19C] the vagina. [lit. euph.]

vXp *n.* [20C] (W.I.) a lift, a free ride. [Fr. *vXpres*, vespers, a service at which there is no collection and is thus 'free']

vera/victoria vice *n.* [1950s+] (gay) the police vice-squad. [joc. 'feminization' of the squad]

Vera Lynn *n.* [1940s+] **1** gin. **2** (Aus.) the chin. [rhy. sl.; ult. UK singer *Vera Lynn* (b.1917)]

verandah *n.* [late 19C] the gallery of the Old Vic Theatre, London.

verbal/verbals *n.* [1960s+] **1** (Und.) a statement, often self-incriminatory, to the police either voluntarily or during and after interrogation. **2** insults, abuse, 'backchat'; thus *give one the verbals*, to abuse. **3** a conversation.

verbal *v.* [1960s+] (Und.) of the police, to fake a confession by claiming that one's statement under interrogation admitted the crimes for which in court one is pleading not guilty. [VERBAL n.]

verbal diarrhoea *n.* [1940s+] excessive talk, esp. when meaningless, pointless and irritating to the hearer. [note late 17C–late 19C fig. use of SE *diarrhoea*, an excessive flow of words etc]

verb-grinder *n.* [early 19C–1920s] a nit-picking school master.

verdomde *adj.* [mid-19C+] (S.Afr.) damned, infernal. [Du. *verdoemd*, damned]

vermilion *v.* [early 19C] to cover or smear someone with blood.

Vermont charity *n.* [20C] (US tramp) sympathy. [? the kindliness of that state's authorities]

verneuk *v.* [late 19C+] (S.Afr.) to cheat, to swindle. [Du. sl. *verneuken*]

Veronica Lake *n.* [20C] a steak. [rhy. sl.; ult. the film star *Veronica Lake* (1919–73)]

versal *adj.* [early 18C] single. [abbr. SE *universal*]

versatile *adj.* [1950s–60s] bisexual. [euph.]

verse *v.* [16C] (Und.) to practise a fraud or deceit by verbal means (cf. CANT v.; VERSER; VERSING LAW). [SE *verse*, to pour out the voice]

verser/retriever *n.* [16C] (Und.) that member of a confidence trickster team who actually plays the game of chance through which a victim is defrauded and who would often claim to be a friend of one of the victim's friends (cf. BARNARD; SETTER n.¹). [VERSE]

versing law *n.* [16C] (Und.) those confidence tricks that focus on the use of counterfeit gold to entrap the victim (cf. BARNARD'S LAW; FIGGING LAW; HIGH LAW; SACKING LAW). [VERSE]

vertical bacon sandwich *n.* [1990s] (US) the labia majora.

vertical care-grinder *n.* [mid-late 19C] the prison treadmill (cf. EVERLASTING STAIRCASE).

vertical drinking *n.* [1950s+] (N.Z.) drinking while standing at the bar, esp. in a crowd.

vertical smile *n.* [20C] the vagina (cf. UPRIGHT GRIN).

very à la *phr.* [1940s–60s] very fashionable (cf. ALUM). [Fr. *à la (mode de)*, in the manner of, in the style of]

very dead spit *see* VERY SPIT.

very famillionaire *n.* [mid-19C] (society) typical of a nouveau riche. [play on SE *very familiar/millionaire*]

very froncey *adj.* [late 19C] (society) vulgar. [Fr. *trés français*, very French]

very how *phr.* [1950s+] (mainly Aus.) response to question, 'how are you?'

very idea! *see* IDEA!

very like *adv.* [late 19C] very likely, almost certainly.

very like a whale in a teacup *phr.* [mid-19C] utterly impossible, totally absurd. [note *Hamlet* (1601) III:ii, where Shakespeare uses a truncated version *very like a whale*]

very moral of *phr.* [mid-18C–late 19C] a likeness, a counterpart. [16C SE *moral*, a symbolic figure]

very spit *n.* [19C] of another person (often a relative), the exact image (cf. DEAD SPIT). [SPIT n.²]

very swift *adj.* [1970s+] (Und.) taking grossly unfair advantage. [SWIFT adj.]

very well *adj.* [mid-19C+] acceptable; thus *that's all very well … .* [lit. an intensifier of *well*]

vessel *n.* [early 19C] the nose. [when 'tapped' it 'overflows' with blood]

vestal *n.* [early 19C] a sexually unrestrained person. [SE *vestal virgin*, a Roman priestess supposedly dedicated to absolute chastity]

vestry *n.* [19C] the vagina (cf. PULPIT; VESTRYMAN).

vestryman *n.* [19C] the penis (cf. VESTRY).

vet, the *n.¹* [1930s+] (orig. milit.) a doctor, thus in (S.Afr.) a prison doctor. [SE *vet*, a veterinary surgeon]

vet *n.²* [1930s+] **1** an old-timer, an ageing or experienced person. **2** an ageing, experienced or worn-out prostitute. [abbr. SE *veteran*]

veterano *n.* [1960s+] (US) a veteran of gang life (cf. O.G. n.²). [Sp.]

vette *n.* [1960s+] a *Corvette* automobile. [abbr.]

vex *adj.* [1980s+] (orig. W.I.) annoyed, angry. [SE *vexed*]

vex-money *n.* [20C] (W.I./Trin.) money a woman carries with her on a date. If, for whatever reason (usu. the denial of sex) she is forced to make her own way home, she has some funds (cf. MAD-MONEY). [Carib.E. *vex*, irritating, annoying + SE *money*]

v.g. *adj.* [1960s+] very good. [abbr.]

V-girl *n.* [1940s] (US) a woman willing to have sex with servicemen for patriotic reasons. [abbr. *Victory-girl* + play on B-GIRL]

vibe/vibes *n.* [1960s+] atmosphere, feelings, intuition; thus *good vibes, bad vibes*. [abbr. SE *vibrations*]

vibe *v.* **1** [1960s+] (US) to experience, enjoy. **2** [1980s+] (US Black) to carry on a sexual relationship. [VIBE n.]

vibes *n.¹* [1930s+] a *vib*raphone or *vib*raharp. [abbr.]

vibes *n.²* *see* VIBE n.

vibe someone out, to *phr.* [1960s+] to produce emotional effects, usu. neg. and confusing, in someone. [VIBE n.]

Vic *n.¹* [mid-late 19C] **1** the *Vic*toria Theatre. **2** Queen *Vic*toria. **3** *Vic*toria railway station, London. [abbr.]

vic *n.²* [1930s+] **1** a *vic*tim of crime (cf. VICT). **2** (US Und.) a convict, i.e. a *vic*tim of justice. **3** (US) a *Vic*trola brand phonograph. [abbr.]

vic *v.* [1930s+] to *vic*timize, to make the subject of a crime. [abbr.]

vicar of bray *n.* [late 19C+] in cards, a three. [rhy. sl. *Vicar of Bray* = TRAY n.¹ (1)]

vice n. [1960s+] the *vice* squad. [abbr.]

vice v. [1960s+] (US Black) to do harm, to cheat, steal, to cause physical pain. [SE *vice*, to force, to strain, but note 15C *vice*, to treat arrogantly or oppressively]

vice-admiral of the narrow seas n. [mid-17C–early 19C] 'A drunken man that pisses under the table into his companions' shoes' (Grose 1796).

vicey-versey adv. [mid-19C+] vice versa. [deliberate joc. mispron.]

vicious adj. [1980s+] (US Black/teen) wonderful, excellent, admirable (cf. AWFUL adj.). [on bad = good model]

vicky-verky adv. [late 19C+] vice versa. [deliberate joc. mispron.]

vict n. [1930s–60s] (US Black) a crime *vict*im (cf. VIC). [abbr.]

victoria monk n. [late 19C–1900s] semen. [rhy. sl. *Victoria Monk* = SPUNK n.; ult. music hall star *Victoria Monks* (1884–1972), best known for her version of 'Won't you come home, Bill Bailey?']

victoria vice see VERA VICE.

Victor Trumper n. [20C] (Aus.) a dumper, a cigarette butt. [rhy. sl.; ult. Aus. cricketer *Victor Trumper* (1877–1915)]

victory n. [1940s–50s] (W.I.) a style of haircut that gave a man's hair a V-shape at the back. [the 'V for Victory' campaign of WW2]

victualler n. [late 16C–early 17C] a pimp; thus *victualling-house*, a brothel. [innkeepers who doubled as pimps]

victualling department/office n. [late 18C–19C] the stomach (cf. DUMPLING DEPOT).

vid n. [1980s+] **1** videotape. **2** an hallucination, presumably drug-induced. **3** a situation (cf. SCENE).

vidaholic n. [1980s+] (US) a TV/video addict. [SE *video* + sfx. -AHOLIC]

viddle-de-vop n. [1940s] (US Black) a low whistle. [? echoic]

vietas see FIETAS.

Vietnik n. [1960s–70s] (US) an active protester against the US involvement in the Vietnam War (1964–75). [*Viet(nam)* + sfx. -NIK]

viewy adj. [mid-19C] flashy, showy, attractive. [it/one becomes a SE *view*]

vigorish/vig/viggerish n. [1910s+] (US) interest on a loan, or debt; [? Yid./Rus. *vyigrysh*, profit, winnings]

vig ounce n. [1980s+] (US drugs) an ounce (28g) of narcotics. [ety. unknown]

viking n. [1990s] (drugs) marijuana. [? SE *Viking*, i.e. the strength]

Viking queen n. [1960s+] (gay) **1** a blond male. **2** one who prefers Nordic partners. [*Viking* + QUEEN n.[1]]

vile/ville/vyle n. [mid-16C+] a town or village. [before mid-19C only in combs., e.g. DAISYVILLE; ROMEVILLE]

Village, the n. [mid-19C] mainly hunting/horse-racing, London.

village butler n. [late 18C] 'old thieves, that would rather steal a dishclout than discontinue the practice of thieving' (Potter, *Dict. Cant*, 1795).

village ram n. [1930s+] (W.I.) a local philanderer and ladies' man (cf. TOWN BULL; TOWN STALLION). [SE *village* + RAM n.[1] (2)]

villain n. [1950s+] a professional criminal.

ville n.[1] see VILE.

Ville n.[2] [20C] Penton*ville* prison, London (cf. SCRUBS). [abbr.]

-ville sfx. [mid-19C+] (mainly US) used to emphasize a particular characteristic, e.g. *dragsville*, very boring; *sticksville*, very rural or suburban. [first use is UK, but popularized by 1950s US beatniks]

vin blong/vin blink/ving blong/vonblong n. [1910s+] (orig. milit.) cheap white wine; thus *vongrooge*, cheap red wine. [mispron. of Fr. *vin blanc/vin rouge*, white wine/red wine]

vincent n. [16C] (Und.) the victim of a crooked gambling game. [VINCENT'S LAW]

Vincent Price n. [20C] ice. [rhy. sl.; ult. film star *Vincent Price* (1911–93)]

vincent's law n. [16C–early 19C] (Und.) cheating for profit at bowls and later cards. [Lat. *vincens*, victorious; the use is ironic]

vine n.[1] [1930s+] (orig. US Black) a suit. [SE *vine*; i.e. a well-cut suit clings to the figure as does the plant to a tree]

vine n.[2] [1940s–50s] (Und.) any unofficial underground network of information. [(GRAPE)VINE n.[1] (1)]

vine, the n.[3] [1970s+] (US Black) wine.

vinegar n. [late 17C–18C] a cloak, an overcoat. [? its being worn in 'sharp' weather]

vinegar pisser n. [late 18C–early 19C] a miser, a mean person. [PISS v.]

vinegar strokes n. [1980s+] the final thrusts of sexual intercourse (cf. PARADISE STROKES). [? one 'puts a bit of vinegar' into them]

vines n. [1970s] (US Black) pubic hair.

vineyard n. [1970s+] (US Black) ironic ref. to anywhere that alcoholics congregate.

ving blong see VIN BLONG.

vingty n. [1930s–50s] the game of pontoon or *vingt-et-un*. [abbr./pron.]

vinnies n. [1980s+] (Aus./N.Z.) the Society of St *Vincent* de Paul. [abbr.]

vinny's n. [1980s] (Aus./N.Z.) the second-hand clothes shops run by the Society of St *Vincent* de Paul. [abbr.]

vino/veeno n. **1** [1910s+] cheap wine. **2** (Aus.) [1990s] a glass of wine. [Ital. *vino*, wine]

vintage n. [late 19C] (orig. US) the year of one's birth. [SE *vintage*, the year of a wine's creation]

vintner n. [mid-17C] a heavy drinker.

vinyl n. [1980s+] records, (as opposed to tapes or CDs); thus *vinyl junkie*, one who is obsessed by records, rejecting all other forms of recorded music.

violate v. [1970s+] (US) to forfeit one's parole for a violation of the rules and to be returned to prison.

violently adv. [late 18C] flashily, showily dressed.

violet/garden violet n. [late 19C–1940s] an onion, but in pl. spring onions or sage and onion stuffing. [although the terms are found in several dicts., none, incl. *OED*, provides an actual citation]

violet crumble v. [20C] (Aus.) to understand. [rhy. sl. *violet crumble* = TUMBLE v.[2]]

vip n. [1920s+] (Aus.) a miser. [? SE *viper*]

vipe v. [1930s–40s] (drugs) to smoke marijuana. [VIPER]

viper n. [1930s–50s] (drugs) a regular user of marijuana; thus *viper's drag/viper's weed*, marijuana, a marijuana cigarette. [ety. unknown; obviously f. SE *viper*, but which characteristics]

virgie n. [1930s–60s] a *virgin*. [abbr.]

virgin n.[1] [1910s–20s] **1** a cigarette made of *Virginia* tobacco. **2** (US) a martini, i.e. a mix of *vermouth* and *gin*. [abbr.]

virgin n.[2] [20C] (US Und.) a criminal with no convictions.

virgin bride n. [late 19C+] (Aus.) a ride. [rhy. sl.]

virginia n. [1990s] (US) the vagina. [mispron.]

virgin pullet n. [mid-19C] 'a young women who though often trod has never laid' (Jon Bee) (cf. TREAD).

virgins' bus n. [late 19C] the last bus to run westward from Piccadilly Circus. ['so named satirically in reference of the chief patronesses at that late hour' (Ware)]

virgin vault n. [1990s] (US campus) residence hall for females.

virtue rewarded n. [late 19C] prison. [the initials *V.R.*, i.e. *Victoria Regina*, on the side of the prison van]

virtuoso of the skin flute *n.* [20C] a masturbator. [SKIN FLUTE]

virus, the *n.* [1980s+] (US) HIV, the virus that causes AIDS. [euph.]

vishy *n.* [1950s–60s] (camp gay) a deliberately cruel insult. [SE *vicious*]

visitation *n.* [early 19C] an overly protracted social call or visit. [SE *visitation*, a visit of inspection made by an authority, usu. a senior clergyman]

visit from the stork *n.* [late 19C+] (society) the arrival of a new baby.

visiting fireman *n.* [1920s+] (orig. US) **1** a person or group who are especially well-looked after when visiting an organization of kindred spirits. **2** tourists who are expected to spend freely. [orig. 1855 when the Baltimore *Sun* reported that 'A company of firemen from Rochester, N.Y. ... continue to receive the attentions of their brother firemen of Baltimore ... This evening the visiting firemen will be the guests of the Washington Hose Company' (25 October 1855)]

visit Miss Murphy, to *phr.* [20C] to visit the lavatory. [euph.]

visit Mrs Jones *see* MRS JONES.

visit Niagara Falls, to *phr.* [20C] to masturbate. [NIAGARA FALLS]

visit one's Indian cousin, to *phr.* [1940s+] (W.I.) to have one's hair straightened. [Indian hair is straight]

visitor *n.* [1980s+] a menstrual period (cf. GEORGE CALLED). [euph.]

visitor to Vegemite valley *n.* [1990s] a male homosexual (cf. HERSHEY HIGHWAY; MARMITE DRILLER). [*Vegemite*, a popular spread, is brown, thus a ref. to anal intercourse]

visit rosy palm and her five daughters, to *phr.* [20C] to masturbate (cf. CONVERSE WITH HARRY PALM; MISS FIST).

visit Sir Harry, to *phr.* [mid-19C] to go to the lavatory. [euph.]

visit the sandbox, to *phr.* [20C] to go to the lavatory. [SE *sandbox*, a pet's litter tray]

vita *n.* [20C] (US) a curriculum *vita*e. [abbr.]

vitamin A *n.* [1980s+] **1** LSD. **2** MDMA. [ACID n.³]

vitamin C *n.* [1980s+] cocaine. [C n.²]

vitamin E *n.* [1980s+] MDMA. [ECSTASY]

vitamin K *n.*¹ [1980s+] (drugs) a synthetic hallucinogen, allegedly 5000 times stronger than LSD; according to researchers, it takes the user to subatomic reality and one can experience the consciousness of inanimate objects.

vitamin K *n.*² *see* SPECIAL K.

vitamins *n.* [1980s+] (drugs) any drugs available in pill or capsule form. [play on the supposedly health-giving properties of SE *vitamins*]

vitamin T *n.* [1980s+] (drugs) marijuana. [TEA n.² (1)]

vitamin X *n.* [1980s+] MDMA. [SE *vitamin* + pron. of ECSTASY]

vitamin XXX *n.* [1980s+] alcohol. [*XXX*, a mark of a beer's strength]

vitty *adj.* [18C] **1** fitting, proper, suitable. **2** nice, trim, neat. [synon. 16C–19C SE *fitty*]

viz *n.* [1990s] a face. [abbr. SE *visage*]

vj *n.* [1990s] (US) video jockey, a TV presenter of music videos. [abbr.; on pattern of DJ]

vlam *n.* [1970s+] (S.Afr.) methylated spirits (as drunk by alcoholics); thus *vlam-drinker* (cf. BLOUTREIN; JUICE n.³). [Afk. *vlam*, flame]

voce/votch/voche *n.* [mid-19C+] (Ling. Fr./Polari) the voice. [Ital. *voce*, a voice]

voddy *n.* [20C] vodka. [abbr.]

vodeodo *n.* [1930s] plunder, booty, cash. [play on musical *vo-do-deo-do*, a meaningless refrain used to produce rhythm + DOUGH]

voetjie-voetjie *n.* [1910s+] (S.Afr.) the surreptitious nudging

of someone's foot out of sight of anyone else, typically beneath a table; the contact is usu. a prelude to greater intimacy (cf. FOOTSIE-FOOTSIE). [Afk. *voet*, foot]

voetsak *n.* [1970s+] (S.Afr.) an infinite, non-specific number, e.g. *straight from the year voestek*, the equivalent of 'God knows when' or 'the year dot'. [Afk. *voertsek*, forward, more usu. found as a dismissive command, be off! go away!]

voetsak! *excl.* [mid-19C+] (S.Afr.) a general excl. of dismissal, go away! be off! get out! [Du *voort seg ik*, be off, I say!]

vogue *n.* [1980s+] (gay) a cigarette. [? its fashionability]

voit *n.* [1990s] (US teen) an annoying person; esp. one who attacks those more socially poised and popular than themselves. [ety. unknown; ? one who one should SE *avoid*]

voker *v.* [mid-19C+] **1** to speak. **2** to understand. [Lat. *vocare*, to speak]

volkie *n.* [1940s+] (S.Afr.) a derog. term for a coloured farm labourer. [Du. *volk*, people]

Volks *n.* [1940s+] a Volkswagen car. [abbr.]

Volksie *n.* [1960s+] (S.Afr.) a *Volks*wagen 'Beetle'. [abbr.]

volume *n.* [1960s+] (US) Valium, a mild tranquillizer. [deliberate mispron.]

voluntary knee drill *n.* [late 19C] abject adulation. [the subject throws themself to their knees]

vom *n.* [1960s+] bad, disgusting food. [VOM v.]

vom *v.* [1960s+] to be sick. [abbr. SE *vomit*]

vomatose *adj.* [1980s+] (US campus) disgusting. [SE *vomit* + *comatose*]

vomiting piper *n.* [1950s–60s] the penis.

vomiting viper *n.* [1950s+] the penis (cf. ONE-EYED TROUSER-SNAKE).

vomitrocious *see* VOMITY.

vomit up one's toenails, to *phr.* [20C] (US) to vomit copiously (cf. THROW UP ONE'S HEELS).

vomity/vomitrocious *adj.* [1970s+] (US) very disgusting. [SE *vomit*]

voompse/vumpse *v.* [20C] (W.I.) to pay attention to; usu. in neg., thus *not even voompse at/upon*, to ignore, to cut dead. [ety. unknown]

vooter *n.* [1990s] (US teen) an extremely tall person. [? corruption of SE *footer*, e.g. 'six-footer']

votch *see* VOCE.

vote for the alderman, to *phr.* [early–mid-19C] to take a drink. [joc. ref. to ALDERMAN LUSHINGTON]

vote khaki *v.* [1900s] to vote for the Liberal Unionists in the 'Khaki Election' of 1900, when they backed the prosecution of the Boer War.

voucher *n.* [late 17C–18C] (Und.) an accomplice who passes the counterfeit money produced by the coiner. [he *vouches* for its authenticity]

vowel *v.* [early 18C–early 19C] of a losing gamester, to pay off one's debts with an IOU (cf. THREE VOWELS). [the vowels IOU]

voy *n.* [1990s] a hooligan. [Fr. *voyou*, a 'lad']

v.p.l. *phr.* [1980s+] having the line of one's underwear visible through a tight outer garment. [abbr. visible *pantie line*]

v.r. *n.* [mid–late 19C] a prison van (cf. VIRTUE REWARDED). [the monarch's initials (for Victoria *R*egina, painted on its sides; also joc. abbr. vagabonds *r*emoved]

vreet *v.* [1970s+] (S.Afr.) to devour, to gobble up. [Du *vreten*, to eat; usu. of an animal and thus sl. when used of a person]

vrek *v.* [1910s+] (S.Afr.) to die; thus *gaan vrek*, drop dead. [Afk. *vrek*, to die, usu. of animals]

vrij *see* VRY.

vroe *see* FROE.

vroom *v.* [1960s+] (US) to go fast, esp. to drive a vehicle at speed. [echoic of the sound of an engine]

vrot *adj.* (S.Afr.) **1** [1910s+] rotten, lousy, esp. as a catch-all neg. **2** [1990s] drunk. [fig. use of Du. *verotten*, to rot]

vrow *see* FROE.

vrow-case *n.* [late 17C–mid-19C] a brothel (cf. CASE-FRO). [Du. *vrouw*, a woman + CASA; CASE]

vry/vrij/fraai/fray/frey *v.* [late 19C+] (S.Afr.) **1** to caress amorously, to pet. **2** to court, to woo. [synon. Afk. *vry*]

V-town *n.* [1990s] (US Black teen) Vallejo, California. [abbr.]

vuilgat/vuilgoed *n.* [1910s+] (S.Afr.) a general term of abuse, esp. to an extremely dirty person. [Afk. *vuil*, foul + GAT n.²]

vu jà dé *phr.* [1980s+] (US campus) I have never done anything of this sort before; this is a complete novelty. [inverse of Fr. *déjà vu*, already seen, the sense that one has been somewhere before, seen or done something previously]

vumpse *see* VOOMPSE.

v. w/e *adj.* [1960s+] used in sex contact advertisements, having notably large genitals. [abbr. very WELL-ENDOWED]

W

W *n.*[1] [1950s+] a lavatory. [abbr. W.C.]

W *n.*[2] [1950s+] (Und.) a warrant for arrest, search etc. [abbr.]

waai *v.* [1960s+] (S.Afr.) to leave (cf. BLOW v.[4]). [Afk. *waai*, to blow]

wab *n.* [1990s] the flaccid penis. [SE *wobble*]

wabbler/wobbler *n.* [19C] a boiled leg of mutton. [SE *wobble*]

wac/wack *n.* [1980s+] (drugs) a mixture of phencyclidine and marijuana. [? WACK adj.]

wack *n. see* WHACK n.

wack *adj.* [1980s+] (US Black) **1** second-rate, phoney, un-satisfactory; a general term of opprobrium; thus *wack-ass* (intensifier). **2** positive, extremely good. [orig. popularized in 1986 through the anti-CRACK n.[17] mural by Keith Haring (1958–90), which bore the slogan: 'Crack is wack.' Note W.I. *wacka-tac*, a disagreeable person]

wack *v. see* WHACK v.

wack!/wacker! *excl.* [1960s+] (orig./mainly Merseyside) a term of address to a male. [? dial. *wacker*, active, lively]

wack attack *see* WHACK ATTACK.

wack down *see* WHACK DOWN.

wacked out *see* WHACKED OUT.

wacked to the wide *see* WHACKED TO THE WIDE.

wacker *n. see* WHACKER n.[3].

wacker/whacker *adj.* [1940s+] (Aus.) excellent, wonderful. [WHACK v.[1]]

wack it *see* WHACK IT.

wack it in *see* WHACK IT IN.

wack it out *see* WHACK IT OUT.

wack it up *see* WHACK IT IN.

wack off *see* WHACK OFF.

wack out *see* WHACK OUT.

wack someone out *see* WHACK SOMEONE OUT.

wack the one-eyed worm/the weasel *see* WHACK THE ONE-EYED WORM.

wack willy *see* WHACK WILLY.

wacky *adj. see* WHACKY adj.

-wacky *sfx. see* -WHACKY.

wacky baccy/weed *see* WHACKY BACCY.

wad *n.*[1] **1** [early 19C+] money (cf. BUNDLE n.[2]). **2** [1920s+] (Aus.) a large quantity of a commodity. [repopularized *c.*1985 by comedian Harry Enfield's character 'Loadsamoney', with his Thatcherite credo, 'Wad is God']

wad *n.*[2] [mid–late 19C] straw used for bedding. [abbr. SE *wadding*]

wad *n.*[3] [20C] semen, esp. an ejaculation of semen (cf. SHOOT ONE'S WAD). [SE *wad*, a bundle]

wad *n.*[4] **1** [1910s–30s] a drink of alcohol. **2** [1910s+] (orig. milit.) food, esp. a bun, cake or sandwich. In all cases its filling qualities are more important than taste etc; thus *char and wads*, tea and buns. [SE *wad*, a bundle]

wad *n.*[5] [1980s+] (US campus) a fool, an idiot, an unpleasant person (cf. DICKHEAD). [abbr. DICKWAD]

-wad *sfx.* [1980s+] (US campus) an all-purpose usu. neg. sfx. that can be added freely to any word, e.g., *dickwad, asswad, stainwad*. [? WAD n.[5]]

waddie/waddy *n.* [19C] (US) a cowboy, esp. a temporary cowhand. [SE *wedding*, something that 'fills in']

waddle out of Change Alley as a lame duck *phr.* [late 18C–mid-19C] to default on one's debts at the Stock Exchange. [WADDLE OUT OF THE ALLEY + LAME DUCK]

waddle out of the alley *phr.* [late 18C–19C] to default on a debt or contract (cf. WADDLE OUT OF CHANGE ALLEY AS A LAME DUCK)

waddy *n.*[1] *see* WADDIE.

waddy *n.*[2] [late 19C+] (Aus.) a club or cudgel. [Dharuk *wadi*, a tree, a stick]

waddy *v.* (Aus.) **1** [late 19C] to beg, to implore. **2** [20C] to hit someone with a club or cudgel. [WADDY n.[2]]

wade *n.* [19C] a ford. [SE *wade*, to step through water]

wade in/into *v.* [late 19C+] (orig. US) to commit oneself whole-heartedly, esp. to a fight.

waders *n.* [1940s] (US Black) boots.

wadge/wodge *n.* [mid-19C+] a thick, chunky, dense lump. [orig. synon. dial.]

wad that would choke a wombat, a *n.* [20C] (Aus.) an exceptionally impressive roll of cash. [WAD n.[1]]

wafer-woman *n.* [early 17C–early 19C] a madame. [? her posing as a legitimate maker of *wafers*, i.e. filigree]

waffle *n.*[1] [1930s+] nonsense, rubbish. [orig. late 19C printers' jargon. 'Twaddle, gossip, or "jaw"' (*OED*)]

waffle *n.*[2] [1970s+] (US Und.) a male homosexual. [SE *waffle*, a form of batter-cake; ? play on SE *waffle iron* and IRON n.[4]]

waffle *v.*[1] [early 19C+] to dither, to talk nonsense. [orig. Scot./northern dial.; ult. *waff*, to yelp]

waffle *v.*[2] [1970s+] (US) to tread or trample. [play on WAFFLE STOMPERS]

waffle iron *n.* [20C] (US) a sidewalk or pavement grating. [resemblance]

waffles *n.* [mid-19C] an idler, a loafer. [WAFFLE v.[1]]

waffle stompers *n.* [1970s+] (US campus) heavy boots with thick cleated soles that resemble a waffle iron.

wag *n.*[1] [20C] (Ulster) **1** a general term of contempt. **2** anyone without firm opinions, a 'yes-man'. [their wagging head, whether through stupidity or the desire to affirm whatever has been said]

wag *n.*[2] [1970s+] (US police) a vagrant. [abbr./pron.]

wag *v.*[1] [19C+] **1** (US Black) to procrastinate, to find it hard to make any decisions. **2** to leave, to walk slowly. [SE *vagrant*]

wag/wag it/off *v.*[2] [mid-19C+] to play truant (cf. BUNK OFF; PLAY THE WAG). [HOP THE WAG]

wages n. [1920s+] any form of illicit earnings.

wagga/wagga blanket/rug n. [late 19C+] (Aus.) an improvised covering, made by stitching together a pair of chaff bags, sacks etc. [*Wagga Wagga*, a town in New South Wales; ult. Abor. phr. *many crows*]

wagga-wagga adj. [20C] (W.I.) plentiful, abundant. [Yoruba *waga-waga*, bundled together]

wagger n. [late 19C] a truant. [HOP THE WAG]

waggle v. [20C] **1** to wield, to put to use, esp. of sporting equipment. **2** (US) to overcome, to surpass.

waggon n. [1900s–40s] (S.Afr.) a cigarette. [? brandname]

waggon lay n. [late 18C–early 19C] (Und.) waiting in the street to waylay and rob waggons (cf. VAN DRAGGER). [SE *waggon* + LAY n.⁴ (2)]

wag hemp in the wind, to phr. [mid-16C–early 17C] to be hanged (cf. KICK THE CLOUDS; KICK THE WIND). [the hempen rope]

wag off see WAG v.¹.

wagon n.¹ [late 19C+] (US) a police patrol *wagon*.

wagon n.² [1990s] **1** (Irish) a derog. name for a woman. **2** a prostitute (cf. BARRACK HACK). [she gives you a 'ride']

wag one's bottom, to phr. [late 19C+] to work as a prostitute.

wag one's chin, to phr. [late 19C+] (US) to talk, to gossip.

wagon-hunter n. [mid-18C] a brothel-keeper's agent who solicited for customers at coaching inns.

wagoning n. [mid–late 19C] coach-driving.

wagon-load of monkeys see BARREL-LOAD OF MONKEYS.

wagons roll! excl. [1950s+] let's go! [the clichèd line of many Western films]

wagtail n. [late 17C–18C] a promiscuous woman, a prostitute (cf. BANG-TAIL n.¹). [SE *wag* + TAIL n.¹ (2)]

wag the red rag, to phr. [late 17C–18C] to chatter. [SE *wag* + RED RAG n.¹]

wail v. [1950s+] **1** (orig. US Black) to abandon one's inhibitions, to lose oneself in an activity, esp. of musicians during an improvised solo, or of sexual pleasure. **2** (orig. US Black) to sing. **3** (W.I.) to behave badly, aggressively; thus *wail down the place*, to dance and sing with utter abandon.

wailing/whaling adj. [1950s+] (US Black/campus) excellent, wonderful. [WAIL v.]

waistcoateer n. [17C] a prostitute. [the *waistcoat* that served as a 'badge of office']

waistcoat piece n. [late 19C] the breast and neck of mutton. [its supposed resemblance to that part of a suit]

waist tog n. [mid-19C–1900s] a waistcoat. [SE *waist* + TOG n. (1)]

wait v. [late 18C+] to postpone a meal.

wait about/around v. [late 19C+] to linger expectantly, to 'hang about'.

wait and linger n. [20C] a finger (cf. LEAN AND LINGER), [rhy. sl.]

wait a quarter of a sec! excl. [late 19C] intensifier of the more usual *wait half a sec!*

wait around see WAIT ABOUT.

wait a tick phr. [20C] wait just a very short time. [SE *wait* + TICK n.³ (2)]

waiters n. [1930s] (society) formal clothes, as *full waiters*, white tie and tails, *half waiters*, black tie and dinner jacket or tuxedo. [restaurant waiters' uniforms]

wait for a death, to phr. [late 19C–1910s] (Aus./N.Z.) to wait around in the hope of an employee being dismissed, which will give one the opportunity to apply immediately for their job.

wait for dead men's shoes, to phr. [late 17C–19C] to expect an inheritance, to hope to succeed to someone else's job.

wait for it phr. [1930s+] a phr. used to create a moment of suspense in the delivery of a joke or an amusing or ironic piece of information.

wait one! excl. [1950s+] (orig. milit.) wait a minute!

wajan/wajang/wajank n. [20C] (W.I./Trin.) **1** a prostitute, a promiscuous woman esp. from the slums. **2** an expert. [ety. unknown; ? pron. of SE *wait, John*]

wake-amine n. [1980s+] (drugs) amphetamine (cf. A n.²). [it 'wakes one up']

wake it! excl. [1980s+] (US campus) an exhortation to action, get with it!

wake it up! excl. [1950s+] (Aus.) hurry up! get on with it!

wake 'n' bake, to phr. [1980s+] (US drugs) to smoke marijuana upon waking.

wake snakes v. [mid–late 19C] (US) to drive to utmost fury.

wake the dead, to phr. [1990s] to masturbate. [the 'resurrection' of one's penis]

wake-up n.¹ [1910s+] (Aus.) an alert and resourceful person, always aware of the possibilities of a situation.

wake-up n.² [1960s+] (drugs) **1** a narcotics user's first injection of the day. **2** any form of stimulant and amphetamine, also as *wake-up pill*.

wake-up n.³ [1960s+] (US prison) the last day of one's sentence (cf. FLOP n.⁵; ROLLOVER). [the days left are calculated as 'X and a wake-up'; thus one 'wakes up' in an institution, but goes to bed in freedom; similarly used in US milit. for the final morning of one's service]

wake up v. see WISE UP.

wake up and smell the coffee, to phr. [1980s+] to come to one's senses.

wake-ups/full wake-up, to be phr. [1930s+] (Aus./N.Z.) to be fully aware of, to be alert. [WAKE-UP n.¹]

wakey, wakey! excl. [1940s+] **1** up you get! **2** get a move on! stop day-dreaming! [orig. milit. use; the *locus classicus* was as used in the 1950s radio show the *Billy Cotton Bandshow*, where the eponymous bandleader adopted it as a catch-phrase]

wal n. [1940s–60s] (Aus.) a policeman. [abbr. WALLOPER n.¹ (2)]

Waler n. [late 19C+] (Aus.) a native of New South *Wales*. [abbr.]

Wales, the n. [late 19C+] (Aus.) the Bank of New South *Wales*. [abbr.]

walk n. [20C] (US prison) the regular patrol route of a prison warder.

walk v.¹ [late 19C+] of objects, to go missing (presumed stolen).

walk v.² [20C] **1** (Und.) to be found not guilty. **2** (US prison) to be released from prison.

walk-about/-a-leg/-a-picky/walker-leg/walker-picky n. [20C] (W.I.) of a woman, a busybody, a gossip. [her tale-telling perambulations]

walk-about money n. [1930s+] daily expenses, petty cash rather than a large amount that needs investing or depositing.

walk a chalk-line see WALK THE CHALK.

walk-a-leg- see WALK-ABOUT.

walk against the wall see WALK UP THE WALL.

walk all over, to phr. [mid-19C+] **1** to treat someone with contempt. **2** to defeat someone comprehensively (cf. WALK AROUND).

walk and nyam n. [early 19C+] (W.I.) **1** a poor White (cf. WALKING BUCKRA). **2** a sponger of any race. [SE *walk* + NYAM n.]

walk-a-picky see WALK-ABOUT.

walk around v. [mid–late 19C] (orig. US) to defeat easily (cf. RUN RINGS AROUND; WALK ALL OVER).

walk away v. [mid-19C] to die.

walk-back n. [1930s–40s] (US Black) an apartment at the rear of the block (cf. WALK-UP).

walk/ride backwards up Holborn Hill, to *phr.* [late 18C] to go to the gallows (cf. THREE-CORNERED TREE). [the road to Tyburn led from Newgate jail along Holborn. Criminals traditionally stood in the cart facing backwards, possibly to increase their ignominy, but more likely to avoid seeing the approaching gallows until the last possible moment]

walkboy *n.* [1980s+] (US Black) a close male friend (cf. HOMEBOY). [they *walk* together]

walk by owl-light, to *phr.* [mid–late 17C] to fear an arrest.

walk cool *v.* [1960s] (US Black) to act in an unconcerned, relaxed manner, esp. in the face of problems or menaces. [SE *walk* + COOL adj.³]

walk dandy-dude *v.* [1940s] (W.I.) to kick out one's legs when walking, the result of a deformity. [SE *dandy* + DUDE]

walk-down *n.* [1940s] (US Black) a basement apartment (cf. WALK-BACK; WALK-UP).

walk down one's throat, to *phr.* [late 19C+] to tell off, to scold, to reprimand.

walked off *adj.* [1910s–20s] taken off to prison. [the condemned person is escorted from court]

walker *n.*¹ [mid–19C] a postman, a courier.

walker *n.*² [1980s+] a man, often rich, invariably personable and socially acceptable, who accompanies the wives of prominent men to parties, on shopping expeditions, to the theatre etc.

walker! *excl.* [19C] nonsense! humbug! rubbish! (cf. BENDER!). [abbr. HOOKEY WALKER]

Walker & Co. *n.* [20C] (W.I.) a notional place used fig. to mean a state of unemployment (cf. IDLE HALL). [one *walks* around searching for work]

walker-picky/walker-leg *see* WALK-ABOUT.

walkers *n.* [early 17C–early 19C] the feet.

walk-foot *n.* [1900s] (W.I.) **1** a poor White. **2** a beggar (cf. WALKING BUCKRA). [any White who walks rather than rides is assumed to be poor]

walk heavy *v.* [1900s–60s] (US Black) to impose oneself on the world, to walk about in a deliberately self-assured manner.

walkie-talkie *n.* [20C] (US Und.) a prisoner who is overly friendly towards the authorities. [he *walks* and *talks* to the guards]

walking buckra *n.* [early 19C] (W.I.) **1** a poor White. **2** a beggar. [SE *walking* + BUCKRA. A White man who had no horse and was thus forced to walk, was considered of the lowest rank]

walking dandruff *see* GALLOPING DANDRUFF.

walking distiller *n.* [early 19C] one who is easily annoyed, unable to take a joke (cf. DISTILLER). [CARRY THE KEG]

walking-go *n.* [late 19C–1900s] a walking contest. [SE *walking* + GO n.³ (5)]

walking mort *n.* [16C] (Und.) an unmarried female beggar, often accompanied by a child, who claimed to be widowed and begged for her and her offspring's keep (cf. CANTING CREW). [SE *walking* + MORT]

walking Moses! *excl.* [1910s–20s] a general excl. of surprise, excitement, alarm etc.

walking orders *n.* [early–mid-19C] a notice of dismissal (cf. WALKING PAPERS; WALKING TICKET).

walking papers *n.* **1** [early 19C+] (US) a notice of dismissal (cf. WALKING ORDERS). **2** [20C] divorce papers. **3** [1960s+] (US prison) an official notice to inform a prisoner that they have finished their sentence (cf. WALKING TICKET).

walking poulterer *n.* [18C] a rural thief who steals fowls, then hawks them from door to door.

walking stationer *n.* [late 18C–late 19C] a hawker of pamphlets, gallows confessions, popular songs and similar materials. [ext. of SE *walking* + *stationer*, a bookseller; cf.

early 17C SE *standing stationer*, one who has a stall in a market]

walking ticket *n.* **1** [early 19C+] (US) a notice of dismissal (cf. WALKING ORDERS). **2** [1960s+] (US prison) an official notice to inform a prisoner that they have finished their sentence (cf. WALKING PAPERS).

walking train *n.* [1920s+] (W.I.) a local train. [its lack of velocity]

walking wounded *n.* [1960s+] (US) anyone who, despite substantial problems in their life, is still able to function. [orig. WW1 milit.]

walk in Pimlico, to *phr.* [late 17C–early 18C] to be well-dressed. [*Pimlico* Paths, an area near the Globe Theatre, London, frequented by fashionable dandies]

walk into *v.* [mid-19C] **1** to attack, to overcome, to demolish. **2** to scold, to reprimand. **3** to eat or drink to excess. **4** to spend money freely. [all come from image of making a space or hole, whether in a meal, a purse or a person and *walking into it*]

walk into someone's affections, to *phr.* [mid-19C+] **1** to gain someone's love without any real effort. **2** to get into someone's debt.

walk it *v.* [1930s+] to win easily, usu. in a sporting context (cf. SNORE THROUGH; WIN IN A WALK). [the relative lack of effort put out]

walk like she can't mash ants *phr.* [20C] (W.I.) used of a woman, implying that she appears far more innocent than her behaviour would reveal. [note SE phr. *butter wouldn't melt in their mouth*]

walk old one-eye, to *phr.* [1990s] to masturbate.

walk on! *excl.* [1970s+] (US campus) a term of dismissal, disbelief, contempt (cf. STROLL ON!).

walk one's chalks, to *phr.* [mid-19C] to leave, to go away. [SE *walk* + CHALKS]

walk one's dog, to *phr.* [1960s] (US) to urinate. [the euph. excuse one makes when leaving the room]

walk on one's cap-badge, to *phr.* [1910s+] (orig. milit.) to be very drunk. [i.e. head-over-heels]

walk on rocky socks, to *phr.* [20C] (US) to walk unsteadily owing to an excess of drink.

walk out together/with, to *phr.* [1930s] (society) to have a clandestine affair. [ironical use of SE *walk out*, to go out with one's fiancé or boy- or girlfriend, usu. in the context of the middle or lower classes]

walk out with the bat, to *phr.* [late 19C] (society) to emerge a winner. [the cricketing image, although the usu. phr. is *carry one's bat*]

walk penniless in Mark Lane, to *phr.* [late 16C–early 17C] to have been cheated and to be aware of the fact. [pun on *mark*, the sum of 13s 4d/*mark*, to note, to appreciate]

walk round *v.* [late 19C–1900s] to prepare oneself to face an attack. [the image of a dog, circling warily on the look-out for enemies]

walk soft *v.* [20C] (US Black) to behave modestly (cf. WALK TALL).

walktalk *n.* [1910s+] (Aus.) a stroll on which the walkers chatter together.

walk tall *v.* [mid-19C+] (orig. US) to behave proudly, courageously and honestly (cf. WALK SOFT).

walk the barber, to *phr.* [mid-19C] to seduce a woman. [? ref. to the pubic hair]

walk the black dog on, to *phr.* [late 18C] to inflict a punishment on a new fellow-prisoner who refuses to pay the automatic fine that is levied on him as a new inmate.

walk the bricks, to *phr.* [20C] to wander around. [BRICKS]

walk the carpet, to *phr.* [19C] to receive a reprimand, esp. of household servants (cf. CARPET v.). [such errant servants were summoned into the carpeted parlour to be told off by the master or mistress]

walk the chalk/a chalk line, to phr. [early 19C+] **1** to walk along a chalked line in order to prove one's sobriety. **2** to behave in a sober, respectable manner. [(2) is fig. use of (1)]

walk the check, to phr. [1970s+] (US campus) to walk deliberately out of a restaurant without paying the bill. [abbr. SE walk away from the check]

walk the dog, to phr.[1] [1910s+] euph. for FUCK THE DOG.

walk the dog, to phr.[2] [20C] (US) to show off by driving or walking at speed (cf. PUT ON DOG).

walk the dog, to phr.[3] [20C] to masturbate (cf. PROMPT THE PORPOISE). [? the up and down hand movements are reminiscent of those used in making a yo-yo trick walk the dog]

walk the flats, to phr. [20C] (US prison) to clean the area outside the cells. [FLATS n.[4]]

walk the piazzas, to phr. [18C] to work as a prostitute. [the piazzas of Covent Garden were popular amongst prostitutes]

walk the plank, to phr. [20C] (US) to be dismissed from a job. [the trad. punishment of Caribbean pirates]

walk the way of a trollop, to phr. [1990s+] (US campus) of a woman, to signal sexual availability. [a play on the more usu. walk the way of the warrior, much loved by martial arts films etc]

walk turkey v. [late 19C] to walk around in a strutting manner. [such a promenade supposedly resembles a turkey's walk]

walk-up n. [20C] (US) an apartment on an upper floor that has to be reached by the stairs because no lift exists. That which lacks not only lifts but also proper plumbing is a coldwater walk-up. Less common terms are the walk-down, a basement apartment, and the walk-back, an apartment at the back of the block. [abbr. SE walk-up apartment]

walk up against the wall see WALK UP THE WALL.

walk-up fuck n. [20C] (Aus.) a woman who is readily available for sex. [SE walk up + FUCK n.[4]; one needs only to walk up and ask]

walk up Ladder Lane and down Hemp Street, to phr. [19C] to be hanged (cf. CLIMB THREE TREES WITH A LADDER; MOUNT THE LADDER). [orig. naut. jargon]

walk up the wall/up against the wall, to phr. [late 18C–mid-19C] to run up credit at a public house. [the landlord chalks one's running debts on the wall]

walk with me, talk with me phr. [1980s+] (US campus) a phr. use to express sympathy and invite confidences. What's the matter? what's the problem? tell me all about it.

walk with the hips, to phr. [late 19C] of a woman, to walk in an exaggeratedly 'sexy' manner.

wallaby n. [mid-19C+] (Aus.) a vagrant (cf. SWAGMAN; ON THE WALLABY). [his nomadic life]

wallaby track n. [mid-19C+] (Aus.) the route followed by an itinerant moving from station to station in search of work (cf. TRACK DOLIE). [WALLABY + SE track]

wallah n. **1** [late 18C+] a man, esp. in sense of a the man who is pertaining to or connected with something, usu. a job. **2** [1960s+] a bureaucrat, an administrator. [Hind. sfx. wala, pertaining to or connected with, and comes in turn from the Arabic wal, proximity. It is the equivalent, therefore, of the Latin -arius. Although found today as a single term, its 19C uses tended to be in combinations, such as Agra wallah, a native of Agra, banghy-wallah, a porter who carries loads with a banghy, or shoulder-yoke, howdah-wallah, an elephant accustomed to carry a howdah, and the Anglo-Indian competition wallah, those who entered the Civil Service competitive exams, established in 1856 to replace the old system of personal patronage]

wall-banger n. [1960s+] (US teen/drugs) **1** a Quaalude or methaqualone capsule. **2** anyone who is so intoxicated by drugs that they cannot walk straight. [the effect of methaqualone is to slow and 'soften' one's movements]

wallbanging n. [1980s+] (US gang) painting graffiti, esp. gang slogans or gang nicknames on walls (cf. GANGBANGING).

wall-eyed adj.[1] [mid–late 19C] **1** of any work badly done (cf. COCK-EYED). **2** of any odd or irregular action. [SE wall-eyed, squinting]

wall-eyed adj.[2] [1920s–30s] (US) drunk. [SE wall-eyed, squinting]

wall-falling adj. [1970s+] (Irish) exhausted, tired out.

wallflower n. **1** [early 19C+] a woman who does not join in dancing at a ball or dance, either through her inability to find a partner or through her desire to remain solo. **2** [1940s–50s] (prison) a prisoner obsessed with the possibility of escape. [(1) fig. use of SE; (2) fig. use of (1)]

wallflowers n. [early–mid-19C] old or second-hand clothes hanging up for sale.

wallflower week n. [20C] those days during which a woman is menstruating and is, traditionally, sexually inactive. [WALLFLOWER n. (1)]

wall fruit n. [mid-19C] kissing up against a wall.

wall it v. [mid-19C] to chalk up a debt on the wall of a public house (cf. MARK UP).

wallop n.[1] [early 19C+] **1** (orig. boxing) a resounding blow. **2** power, influence (cf. CLOUT n.[5]). [(1) WALLOP v.; (2) fig. use of (1)]

wallop n.[2] [mid-19C+] (orig. Aus.) beer, alcohol in general. [ext. of WALLOP n.[1], i.e. its strength; in WW2 beer only]

wallop v. **1** [early 18C–1910s] to make violent, noisy movements, to move clumsily or convulsively, to flounder. **2** [19C] to dangle, to flop about. **3** [early 19C+] to beat, to thrash, to hit hard. **4** [early 19C+] to overcome, to surpass. **5** [mid-19C+] (Ling. Fr./Polari) to dance on stage. [? Walloon waloper, to beat linen in water or Fr. galoper/Ital. gallopare, to gallop]

walloper n.[1] [early 19C+] anyone who beats up their victims with a cudgel or stick. **2** [1940s+] (Aus.) a policeman (cf. WAL). [WALLOP v. (3)]

walloper n.[2] [mid-19C+] (Ling. Fr./Polari) a dancer; thus wallops, choreography. [WALLOP v. (5)]

walloper n.[3] [1910s+] (US) anything or anyone exceptional in quality, size, character etc (cf. LOLLOPER). [WALLOPING]

walloper n.[4] [1930s] a hotel, a bar. [WALLOP n.[2]]

wallopies n. [1970s+] (US campus) female breasts, esp. large ones. [WALLOP v. (2)]

walloping adj. [mid-19C] a general intensifier, usu. as to size and often ext. as walloping great. [WALLOP v.]

wallop it in v. [20C] to penetrate sexually, therefore to have sexual intercourse. [WALLOP v.]

wallpaper n. **1** [20C] (US) worthless paper money such as counterfeit notes. **2** [1980s+] (drugs) money. [(1) it has no monetary use; (2) one has enough to use it as wallpaper]

wall-prop see MAKE WALLPAPER.

wall queen n. [1960s+] (US gay) **1** a man who leans against a wall while he has sex. **2** a gay man who enjoys reading the inscriptions on public lavatory walls. [SE wall + QUEEN n.[1]]

Wall Street didn't jump phr. [1970s+] (US teen) anything that fails to produce the anticipated and desired excitement from bystanders, let alone produce an effect on the US economy.

wall-to-wall adj. [1970s+] everywhere, all over. [ext. use of abbr. SE wall-to-wall carpet]

wally *n.*[1] **1** a pickled cucumber. **2** an olive.

wally/wolly *n.*[2] **1** [1970s+] an unfashionable, unintelligent, 'suburban' person, lacking in taste and sophistication. **2** [1970s+] (Aus.) a bungler. **3** [1980s+] (US campus) used of someone seen as acting like a big brother or sister. **4** [1990s] (US campus) an otherwise socially unacceptable person who is accepted into a social group because they are needed for their intelligence, athletic ability or good looks. [ety. unknown. ? abbr. Scot. *wally-drag*, a feeble, ill-grown or worthless person. The proper name *Walter* is sometimes categorized as a 'silly' name. In police jargon, a *wally* is a trainee and thus incompetent policeman: ext. of WALLY *n.*[1] (1)]

Wally-O *see* WALYO.

walnut-shell *n.* [early 19C] a very light carriage. [resemblance]

walrus *n.* **1** [1910s–50s] a large, bushy moustache, supposedly reminiscent of the animal. **2** [1920s+] (US) a short, fat person.

walter joyce *n.* [late 19C] the voice. [rhy. sl.]

waltz *n.* [1960s+] anything that can be accomplished with minimum effort, an easy success. [WALTZ *v.*[2]]

waltz/waltz around/off/into/up *v.*[1] **1** [mid-19C+] to move lightly, blithely, unconcernedly. **2** [20C] (US) to evade or deceive someone.

waltz *v.*[2] [1960s+] to achieve something easily, esp. in sporting use.

waltz into *v.*[1] *see* WALTZ *v.*[1].

waltz into *v.*[2] [1910s+] to attack.

waltz Matilda *v.* [late 19C+] (Aus.) to go on the tramp, carrying one's pack; thus *Matilda-waltzer*, a tramp (cf. CARRY MATILDA). [SE *waltz* + MATILDA]

waltz off *see* WALTZ *v.*[1].

waltz off on the ear, to *phr.* [late 19C] (US) to act precipitately, on the basis of hearing a statement but not considering its implications. [WALTZ *v.*[1] (1)]

waltz up *see* WALTZ *v.*[1].

walyo/Wally-O *n.* [20C] (US) **1** a young man, often used affectionately by an older man to a younger one. **2** an Italian man. [? Ital. dial. *uaglio*, a young one]

wamba *see* WONGA.

wamble *n.* **1** [late 17C–18C] a feeling of nausea, queasiness, often as *the wambles*; thus *wamble-cropped*, *wamble-stomached*, feeling nauseous, sick. **2** [mid-19C] a rolling, staggering style of walking; thus *on/upon the wamble*, staggering, wobbling. [SE *wamble*, to feel queasy, to walk unsteadily, ? ult. Dan. *vamle*, to feel nausea + Norw. *vamla*, to stagger]

wamblety-/womblety-cropped *adj.* [late 18C–19C] suffering from an upset stomach due to excessive drinking. [SE *wamble-cropped*, sick in the stomach]

wame *n.* [late 18C] the vagina. [Scot. *wame*, the womb]

wampo *n.* [1940s+] beer slops or overflow, recycled and served as fresh beer. [? RAF sl. *wampo*, intoxicating liquor]

wampum *n.* [late 19C] (orig. US) money. [Algonquin *wampumpeag*, beads made from quahog shells and used as money]

wampum and warpaint *n.* [late 19C] evening dress. [*wampum*, beads, worn as ornamental garments or jewellery + WARPAINT *n.* (2)]

wampus *n.* [1950s] (W.I.) a large man. [? abbr. CATAWAMPUS]

wampy *adj.* [1950s–70s] (N.Z.) mad, insane. [? WAMPO]

wana *n.* [1970s+] (drugs) marijuana. [abbr. and phonetic sp.]

wand *n.* [19C] the penis (cf. BAT *n.*[7]).

wanda wandwaver *n.* [1950s–60s] (camp gay) an exhibitionist. [WAND + SE *waver*]

wander *v.* [late 19C–1910s] to confuse, to lead astray, to make one's mind wander.

wander! *excl.* [late 19C] go away! (cf. BE MISSING!).

wang/wanger *n.* **1** [1930s+] (orig. US) the penis. **2** [20C] (S.Afr.) a cigarette. [WHANG *n.*[4]; (2) resembles the shape of (1)]

wanga *see* WONGA.

wanga/wonga gut *n.* [1980s+] (W.I./UK Black teen) greediness or jealousy (cf. LIKKI LIKKI). [? WONGAK + SE *gut*, i.e. one is 'hungry' for cash]

wangdoodle *see* WHANGDOODLE.

wanger *see* WANG.

wangle *n.* [late 19C–1910s] (Irish) a thin, tall, weak young man. [dial. *wangling*, sickly, weak, delicate]

wangle *v.* [late 19C+] to obtain what one wants, often through a degree of manipulation or cunning.

wangler *n.* [1910s–20s] one who uses a variety of irregular means to accomplish a purpose. [WANGLE *v.*]

wang-tang *n.* [1970s+] (US Black) anything on a sexual level, that is especially desirable. [? fig. use of WANG *n.* (1) + SE *tang*, a flavour]

wank *n.* [1940s+] masturbation. [WANK *v.*]

wank *v.* [late 19C+] to masturbate. [ety. unknown, but note the many 'beating' synons, the orig. sp. *whank* and late 18C Scot./dial. *whank*, to beat, to thrash]

wank! *excl.* [1970s+] (US campus) a general neg. retort. [WANK *v.*]

wanker *n.* [late 19C+] **1** spec. a masturbator. **2** a general derog. description of a lazy, incompetent, unpleasant person. [WANK *v.*, note late 19C Yorks./Norfolk dial. *wanker*, a simpleton]

wankered *adj.* [1990s] **1** exhausted, worn out (cf. KNACKERED). **2** to have consumed a large quantity of alcohol or drugs. [WANK *v.*]

wanker's doom *n.* [1920s+] (orig. RAF) a fig. unpleasant fate. [i.e. the insanity that awaits those who believe that masturbation is indeed a debilitating sin]

wanker the anchor, to *phr.* [1990s] to masturbate. [ext. of WANK *v.*]

wanking *n.* [late 19C+] masturbation. [WANK *v.*]

wanking spanners *n.* [1920s+] the hands. [WANKING + SE *spanners*]

wank mag *n.* [1960s+] a pornographic magazine. [WANK *v.* + MAG *n.*[3] (1)]

wank off *v.* [20C] to masturbate. [ext. of WANK *v.*]

wank on *v.* [20C] to bore, to talk nonsense for a long time. [fig. use of WANK *v.*]

wank pie *n.* [1990s] anything considered second-rate, unappealing etc. [WANK *v.* + SE *pie*]

wankstain *n.* [1970s+] an ineffectual person. [WANK *n.* + SE *stain*]

wank the crank, to *phr.* [1960s+] to masturbate. [WANK *v.* + CRANK *n.*[4]]

wanky *adj.* [1970s+] **1** inferior, second-rate. **2** sexually titillating, conducive to masturbation. [fig./lit. uses of WANK *v.*]

wannabe *n.* [1970s+] **1** an aspirant, one who yearns to be a certain individual, usu. more talented and famous than they are (cf. CARBON COPY). **2** (US prison) a young prisoner who poses as a prison-wise veteran. [SE *I want to be ...* , orig. US Black, where the term simply meant a fantasist and latterly a White person wishing to be Black + from surfing jargon a learner. Popularized with the rise of the pop star Madonna (Madonna Louise Veronica Ciccone, b.1958), whose fans declared, either verbally or in the way they dressed, *I wanna be like Madonna*]

wannabe raped look *n.* [1980s+] of a woman, a sluttish, provocative style of dressing (cf JUST-RAPED LOOK). [ext. of SE *want to be raped*]

wanna do a thing? *phr.* [1960s+] (US Black) asking a passing woman if she fancies intercourse.

wanna go out? *phr.* [1960s+] the ritual approach from a prostitute to a passing male (cf. DATE n.[4]).

wansteads *n.* [1920s–30s] spats. [rhy. sl. *Wanstead Flats* = spats; ult. East London area *Wanstead Flats*]

want *n.* [20C] (Irish) any form of mental deficiency; thus *wanting*, mentally deficient. [such a person is *in want* of some brains]

want a bet! *see* WANT TO BET ON IT!

want an apron, to *phr.* [late 19C] to be out of work. [an era when workmen wore some form of apron – before the modern overall – while at work]

want in *v.* [mid-19C+] to desire to make oneself part of (cf. WANT OUT).

wanting *adj.* [mid-19C] mentally unbalanced, insane. [SE *wanting* intelligence, brains etc]

wanton ace *n.* [19C] the vagina (cf. ACE OF SPADES). [SE *wanton* + RED ACE]

want one's hip buttons, to *phr.* [20C] (Ulster) to be less than wholly intelligent.

want out *v.* [mid-19C+] to wish to be disassociated from (cf. WANT IN).

want salt *v.* [late 19C] (US) to be a weakling; to need 'grit' of character.

want some *v.* [1980s+] (US campus) to search for sex (cf. GET SOME).

want/need something yesterday, to *phr.* [1970s+] to want something as quickly as possible.

want to bet on it!/want a bet! *excl.* [1940s+] a challenging refutation of the previous speaker's assertion.

want to do something about it? *see* WANT TO MAKE SOMETHING OF IT?

want to front *see* TRY TO FRONT.

want to make something of it?/do something about it? *phr.* [1930s+] (orig. US) a ritual request that may well herald a fight, but still gives the other person the chance to back down.

want to piss like a dressmaker, to *phr.* [late 19C] to be desperate to urinate. [? a dressmaker working in a sweatshop and not permitted to take a break]

wap *v.* [mid-16C–early 19C] to have sex, usu. used of a woman (cf. BANG v.[1]). [SE *wap*, to throw violently, to pull down]

wapi *n.* [1950s] (W.I.) sexual intercourse. [? WAP + familiarizing sfx. -*i*/-*y*]

wap-john *n.* [mid-19C] a gentleman's coachman. [SE *wap*, to hit + JOHN n.[1]]

wappen-bappen *n.* [1930s+] (W.I.) a tumbledown, slum shed or shanty made of old tins, bits of wood, discarded packaging and similar found objects. [echoic of hammering such a shack together]

wapper-eyed *adj.* [late 18C–early 19C] sore-eyed, squinting. [dial. *wapper*, to have sore eyes, to blink]

wapping *see* WHOPPING.

wapping-dell/-mort *n.* [17C] a prostitute. [WAP + DELL n./ MORT]

wappy *adj.* [1950s–60s] sentimental, idealistic, 'soft'. [? *wet* + *soppy*]

waps/wap-waps *n.* [1990s] the female breasts. [SE *wap*, to move, to shake]

warahoon *n.* [1960s+] (W.I.) a noisy ill-bred person. [? name of a tribe of (unidentified) S. American coastal Amerindians, poss. the Warrau of the Orinoco Delta and northwest Guyana]

war and strife *n.* [1920s–30s] one's wife (cf. TROUBLE AND STRIFE). [rhy. sl.]

warap *n.* [20C] (W.I.) **1** a cheap, tasteless meal, esp. a soup. **2** a cheap meal made of fish or meat and 'ground-provisions',

i.e. locally available starchy roots, all boiled up together. [Carib.E. *warap*, a drink made from fermented sugar cane, drunk by poor peasants]

wara-wara *n.* [20C] (W.I./Jam.) bits and pieces. [WARA-WARA adj.]

wara-wara *adj.* [20C] (W.I./Guyn.) cheap, of inferior quality, esp. of clothing. [Yoruba *wara-wara*, half done, in a hurry]

warb *n.* [1930s+] (Aus.) **1** a fool, a simpleton. **2** a dirty, unkempt person. **3** (Und.) a drunkard, a down-and-out (cf. WARBY). **4** a low-paid manual worker. [? SE *warble*, the maggot of a warble-fly]

war baby *n.* [1910s; 1940s] **1** an illegitimate child, conceived and born while the mother's husband is away on active service. **2** (US) a bond that is sold during wartime with the presumption that it will 'grow' in value.

warble *v.* [17C+] to talk in a pleasant manner.

warbler *n.* **1** [early 19C] '*Warblers*, singers who go about to 'free and easy' meetings, to chaunt for pay, for grog, or for the purpose of putting off benefit-tickets' (Jon Bee). **2** [1940s+] a female singer. **3** (US Und.) a public defender (cf. DUMP-TRUCK; MOUTHPIECE; TONGUE n.). **4** [1970s+] a telephone whose bell *warbles* rather than rings.

War Box *n.* [1940s+] the British War Office (cf. WAR HOUSE).

warby *adj.* [1920s+] (Aus.) unprepossessing in appearance or disposition, unkempt, disreputable, decrepit. [WARB n.]

war club *n.* [20C] (US) a baseball bat.

war cry *n.* [late 19C] a mixture of stout and mild ale. [a satire on the Salvation Army newspaper *The War Cry* and the belief that while the Army spoke 'stoutly' it used only 'mild' terms]

ware *n.* [late 18C–early 19C] the vagina (cf. BANK n.[1]). [SE *ware*, goods on sale]

warehouse *n.* **1** [1900s–20s] (society) a large, fashionable pawn shop. **2** [1960s+] a large and impersonal institution offering shelter to the mentally ill, the old or the poor.

warehouse *v.*[1] **1** [late 19C] to imprison (cf. SPRING ANKLE WAREHOUSE). **2** [1900s–20s] (society) to place in pawn. **3** [1970s+] (US) to place an individual, usu. a mental patient, in a large and impersonal institution, i.e. to 'put them away'.

warehouse *v.*[2] [1980s] to go to parties in abandoned warehouses, a popular youth amusement in the mid-1980s.

ware the hawk! *excl.* [16C–mid-19C] a warning cry, indicating that a bailiff or constable is approaching (cf. HAWK n.[1]). [hunting jargon *ware hawk!*, a warning cry either to or of animals. The *hawk* personifies any 'grasping' person, whether working for or against the law]

warhorse *n.* [late 19C+] (US) a veteran, an old-timer.

war-horse chaise *n.* [early 19C] a one-horse chaise. [the 'battle' is presumably that of the sexes]

War House *n.* [1910s+] the British War Office (cf. WAR BOX).

warlord *n.* [1950s+] (US Black/teen) a street-gang leader.

warm *adj.* **1** [late 18C–19C] rich, well-off. **2** [late 19C] of a large, possibly exorbitant bill. **3** [late 19C+] of a woman, sexy, provocative.

warm *v.* [mid-19C+] to thrash, to beat, esp. in descriptive combs., such as *warm one's arse*, *warm one's jacket*, to thrash.

warm *adv.* [20C] (W.I.) a great deal, much.

warm as they make them *phr.* [late 19C] of a woman, very sexy. [ext. of WARM adj. (3)]

warm beer *n.* [1960s+] urine. [its colour]

warm bit *n.* [late 19C] a promiscuous, sexy woman. [WARM adj. (3) + BIT n.[5]]

warm body *n.* [20C] (US) an insignificant person, someone who is present but does not participate (cf. CHAIR-WARMER).

warm corner *n.* [late 19C–1900s] anywhere frequented by prostitutes. [WARM adj. (3) + SE *corner*]

warmed over *adj.* [late 19C+] (US) derivative, unimaginative. [SE *warm over*, of food, to reheat, to warm up]

warm flannel *see* HOT FLANNEL.

warm fuzzy *n.* [20C] (US) a compliment, praise. [its effects on the listener]

warming pan *n.*[1] **1** [late 17C] a female bed companion (cf. SCOTCH WARMING PAN). **2** [mid-19C–1900s] a place-holder, a deputy, used orig. of clergy.

warming pan *n.*[2] [late 17C–19C] a large, gold pocket watch (cf. FRYING PAN). [the shape]

warm in one's gears *phr.* [late 17C–early 18C] settled down to one's work.

warm in the tail *see* HOT IN THE TAIL.

warm member *n.* [19C] a promiscuous man, a philanderer (cf. DEAREST MEMBER; HOT MEMBER; HOT 'UN). [WARM adj. (3) + SE *member*, a participant/euph. for the penis]

warm-mouth *n.* [1950s] (W.I.) the very first meal of the day, eaten between 4 and 6 a.m. and preceding a proper breakfast (cf. ALLEVIATOR).

warm shop/show *n.* [1910s–20s] a brothel. [WARM adj. (3)]

warm someone's ear, to *phr.* [20C] **1** (Ulster) to hit someone across the ear; usu. in unexecuted threat, *I'll warm your ear (for you!)* (cf. WARM v.). **2** (US) to chatter and gossip incessantly.

warm the cockles of the heart, to *phr.* [mid-19C+] to cheer up, to delight, also as *rejoice ... , tickle ...* . [? the resemblance of the heart to a *cockleshell* or the zoological name of the cockle, *cardium*, which in Gk. means heart]

warm the husband's dinner, to *phr.* [18C] to stand in front of the fire with lifted skirts.

warm the husband's/old man's supper, to *phr.* [19C] to stand in front of the fire with lifted skirts (cf. WARM THE HUSBAND'S DINNER).

warm the wax of someone's ear, to *phr.* [mid-19C–1910s] to box someone's ears. [WARM v.]

warm the whole of one's body, to *phr.* [20C] to stand with one's back to the fire. [pun on *whole/hole*, i.e. the anus]

warm 'un *n.* [19C] a prostitute. [WARM adj. (3) + SE *one*]

warm up *n.* [1970s+] **1** sexual foreplay. **2** a wash before intercourse.

warm with *n.* [late 19C] a drink of *warm* spirits *with* water.

warp *n.* [16C] (Und.) the look-out man for a team of thieves who steal by hooking objects from stalls or shop windows (cf. OAK n.[1]; STAND n.[1]). [? SE *ward*, to watch]

warpaint *n.* **1** [mid-19C] military uniform. **2** [mid-19C] court dress, formal dress. **3** [20C] cosmetics, make-up (cf. APACHE n.[1]).

warp out *v.* [1960s+] (US) to leave hastily. [the use of *warp speed* in the *Star Trek* TV series (from 1966) and films (from 1980)]

warrab *n.* [mid-19C] a barrow. [backsl.]

warra-warra *n.* [1950s+] (W.I. Rasta) euph. for politely omitted obscenities. [the mumbling that replaces the actual words]

warren *n.*[1] [late 17C–18C] 'He that is Security for Goods taken up, on Credit, by Extravagant young Gentlemen' (B.E.). [? SE *warrant*]

warren *n.*[2] [late 17C–early 19C] **1** a brothel. **2** a boarding school. [abbr. CUNNY WARREN]

warrior bold/warrior's hold *adj.* [20C] cold. [rhy. sl.]

warrocks! *excl.* [late 19C] (US) beware! look out! [SE *war hawks!* and presumably referring to an Indian attack]

warry *see* RUGGSY.

wart *n.* [late 19C+] (orig. US) an unpleasant, obnoxious person. [note milit. use *wart*, (RN) a junior midshipman, (Br. Army) a young subaltern]

warts and all *phr.* [1930s+] not excluding any deficiencies or neg. characteristics. [the story of Oliver Cromwell (1599–1658) ordering the painter Sir Peter Lely (1618–1680) to 'use

all your skill to paint my picture truly like me, and not flatter me at all; but remark all these roughnesses, pimples, warts and everything as you see me, otherwise I will never pay a farthing for it']

Warwick Farm *n.* [1940s–60s] (Aus.) an arm. [rhy. sl., *Warwick Farm*, a Sydney racecourse]

war zone *n.* [1980s+] (drugs) from a drug dealer's point of view, an area where a rival dealer operates.

was-bird *n.* [20C] a failure, a 'has-been' (cf. NEVER-WASER). [SE *was* + BIRD n.[3] (1)]

waser/wasser *n.* [1900s–10s] a young woman (cf. BIRD n.[4]). [Fr. *oiseau*, a bird]

wash *n.*[1] [early 17C] any worthless object. [SE *wash*, kitchen swill]

wash *n.*[2] **1** [late 19C–1900s] tea. **2** [1940s+] (US) a second drink, one to wash down the first.

wash *n.*[3] [1960s+] (W.I.) the mash of cheap grain and sugar that is distilled to produce the homemade spirit sold in illicit drinking clubs. [SE *wash*, malt, etc steeped in water to undergo fermentation]

wash *n.*[4] [1980s+] crack cocaine (cf. READYWASH). [the process of chemical purification, known as 'washing', that is used when making the drug]

wash *v.*[1] [mid-19C+] to stand a test, to face questioning, usu. in neg., *it/that won't wash*, the topic will not bear analysis or investigation.

wash *v.*[2] [1970s+] to 'de-criminalize' corruptly or illegally gained money by 'washing' it through a casino till or bank (cf. LAUNDER).

wash *v.*[3] [1980s+] (drugs) to alter the properties of cocaine base by a chemical process (cf. READYWASH; WASH n.[4]).

wash and go *n.* [1990s] (gay) one who leaves immediately after sex. [play on the brandname shampoo]

wash a Negro/the Ethiopian white *phr.* [late 16C–early 17C] to attempt the impossible. [racist fantasies]

wash away *v.* [1940s+] (US) to kill, to murder.

wash-belly *n.* [1950s] (W.I.) a woman's last child (cf. FIRST BELLY PAIN). [the image of finally 'cleaning out' the womb]

wash/put/wash it/put it down one's neck, to *phr.* [late 19C–1920s] to drink (cf. NECK v.).

washed *adj.* [1990s] (US teen) collapsed without warning, esp. of a computer on-line session. [SE *washed out*]

washed rock *n.* [1980s+] (drugs) crack cocaine. [WASH n.[4] + ROCK n.[3] (2)]

washed up/all washed up *adj.*[1] [1920s+] (orig. US) useless, exhausted, failed. [theatrical use *washed up*, finished for the night]

washed up *adj.*[2] [1980s+] (drugs) no longer using drugs. [i.e. one is CLEAN adj.[1] (3)]

washer *n.*[1] [20C] a flannel. [SE *wash*]

washer *n.*[2] [1940s] (US Black) a tavern, a bar, a fast-food restaurant. [? BELLY WASH]

washer *n.*[3] [1980s+] (US gay) a condom. [SE *washer*, anything placed between two surfaces to relieve friction]

washer-/water-dona *n.* [late 19C] a washerwoman. [SE *washer/water* + DONA]

washer-upper *n.* [1960s+] one who washes dishes, usu. in a restaurant, hotel etc.

washing *n.* [1980s+] (drugs) preparing crack cocaine (cf. READYWASH; WASH n.[4]). [WASH v.[3]]

washing powder *n.* [1970s+] (US Black) a douching solution.

washman *n.* [16C] (Und.) a criminal mendicant sporting fake sores and wounds. Their superior in the criminal hierarchy, the PALLIARD, saw them as inferior rivals and would treat them accordingly.

wash one's brain/head, to *phr.* [mid-19C] to drink wine.

wash one's dirty linen, to phr. [late 19C+] to discuss family matters, usu. as *wash one's dirty linen at home*, to keep family matters private, or *wash one's dirty linen in public*, to make such problems public (cf. AIR ONE'S DIRTY LINEN).

wash one's face in an ale clout, to phr. [16C–17C] to get drunk.

wash one's head see WASH ONE'S BRAIN.

wash one's head without soap, to phr. [late 16C–early 17C] to scold, to reprimand.

wash one's liver of milk, to phr. [late 17C–mid-18C] to stop behaving in a cowardly manner. [the idea that *milk* rather than blood is running through one's veins]

wash one's mouth upon, to phr. [1940s] (W.I.) to gossip about, to denigrate behind someone's back.

wash one's skin, to phr. [20C] (W.I.) to beat, to thrash, to defeat comprehensively.

wash one's tongue on, to phr. [20C] (W.I.) to malign.

wash-out n. **1** [20C] a disappointment, a failure. **2** [1910s+] a useless or unsuccessful person.

wash out v. **1** [1910s+] (orig. milit.) to remove, to cancel, to dismiss (e.g. from a course). **2** [20C] (US) to lose all one's money, esp. from gambling.

washpot see MOAB.

wash the Ethiopian white see WASH A NEGRO WHITE.

wash the ivories/sluice one's ivories, to phr. [mid-19C] to drink. [IVORY n.¹ (1)]

wash the meat, to phr. [20C] to masturbate (cf. ACCOST THE OSCAR MEYER). [MEAT n. (2)]

wash-up n. [1900s–50s] (Aus.) the final assessment, the outcome, the 'bottom line'.

wash up v. [1920s+] (US) to bring to a conclusion, to end. [supposedly coined thus: 'That guy might be all right if he washed up [washed, cleaned himself],' commented Buck ... Just then the stage manager called out, 'What will I do with this act, Mr. Ziegfeld?' 'Wash up him and the bird,' said Flo [Ziegfeld] and that was the last of the Italian and his trained canary ... Hype Igoe, the World's sporting writer, heard of the incident ... and in commenting ... upon Frank Moran, heavy weight pugilist, advised that matchmakers 'wash him up'. The phrase ... has become a colloquial fixture ... as a meaty synonym for finals and farewell' (N.Y. *World*, 25 October 1925); however note date of WASH-UP n.]

wash-your-foot-and-come n. [20C] (W.I.) an impromptu dance, with no special dressing-up required.

was my face red! excl. [1950s+] an excl. of embarrassed regret, usu. when recounting some shameful solecism.

wasp n.¹ [late 18C–mid-19C] a diseased prostitute (cf. STINGTAIL). ['she carries a sting in her tail']

WASP n.² [1960s+] White Anglo-Saxon Protestant, the predominant racial group in the USA; thus *wasp*, *waspish*, characteristic of this social grouping. [abbr. orig. Chicago sl./Ohio Valley social workers' jargon WASP, White Appalachian Southern Protestants]

wasp n.³ [1960s+] (Irish) a traffic warden. [the black and yellow colours of the uniform]

wasp and bee n. [20C] (Aus.) tea. [rhy. sl.]

wasser see WASER.

was she worth it?/seven and six n. [1940s+] (bingo) the number 76. [the then price of a UK marriage licence, 7s 6d (37.5 pence)]

waste v. [1950s+] **1** (orig. US milit.) to kill, to beat up. **2** (US teen/street gang) to defeat, to trounce.

waste-butt n. [early 19C] **1** a landlord, a publican. **2** an eating-house.

waste case n. [1980s+] (US campus) a drunkard. [WASTED adj. (4) + CASE n.⁶]

wasted adj. (orig. US) **1** [1950s+] killed. **2** [1950s+] (US) ruined, destroyed. **3** [1950s+] (US) penniless. **4** [1960s+] very drunk. **5** [1960s+] utterly overcome by a drug. [WASTE v.]

wastepipe n. [19C] the vagina.

waste product n. [1980s+] (US campus) a drunkard.

was there ever? phr. [early 19C+] who would believe it?

wasto n. [1990s] utterly overcome by drink or a drug. [WASTED adj. (4), (5) + sfx. -O]

wat n. [early 16C–late 17C] a hare. [dial.]

watch n. [16C] self, usu. as *my watch*, *his watch* etc. [perhaps the image is of the idea of a person being synonymous with one who is watching, i.e. is alive]

watch and chain n. [20C] the brain. [rhy. sl.]

watch and seals n. [mid-19C] **1** a sheep's head and pluck, i.e. heart, liver and lungs. **2** the male genitals (cf. MEAT AND TWO VEG).

watch clocks in a basket, to phr. [20C] (Irish) to do something virtually impossible. [dial. *clock*, a laying hen; ult. SE *cluck*]

watcher n. [1960s+] an expert, a specialist in, e.g. *Brusselswatcher*.

watchie/watchy n. [early–mid-19C] a *watch*man. [abbr.]

watch it v. [1910s+] to look out, to be careful, esp. in imper. *watch it!* used as a warning or a threat.

watch-maker n. [mid-19C] a thief specializing in stealing watches.

watch my dust! excl. [1960s+] (US) see me go! [the SE *dust* of departure; note DUST v.³]

watch my lips phr. [20C] (US) a euph. phr. that implies that one is actually being insulting.

watch my smoke phr. [1900s–40s] watch me go fast, watch what I am doing. [the *smoke* of a fig. departing ship/train]

watch one's ass, to phr. [1950s+] (orig. US) to take care, to take note, to be warned. [ARSE n.¹]

watch one's back, to phr. [1950s+] to take care of oneself (cf. WATCH SOMEONE'S BACK).

watch one's lip/mouth, to phr. [1940s+] to mind one's manners, to talk politely. [LIP n.¹/MOUTH n.¹ (3)]

watch/mind one's step, to phr. [1930s+] to be careful, lit. or fig.

watch one's waters, to phr. [late 18C–early 19C] to keep a close watch on one's actions (cf. HOLD ONE'S WATER; LOOK TO ONE'S WATER). [SE *hold one's water*, to delay urination]

watchpot n. [late 17C–1910s] (Irish) one who hangs around at mealtimes in the hope of being offered a meal. [they *watch* the cooking *pot*]

watch queen n. [1950s+] a male homosexual voyeur. [SE *watch* + QUEEN n.¹]

watch someone's back, to phr. [1950s+] to look after or protect someone else (cf. WATCH ONE'S BACK).

watch the ant races, to phr. [1970s+] to be excessively drunk. [the image of having collapsed on the floor]

watch the dickey-bird! excl. [20C] photographers' exhortation to their subjects to ensure smiling and alert faces for the picture (alt. 'say cheese').

watch the eyelid movies, to phr. [1960s+] to masturbate. [one's sexual fantasies]

watch the submarines, to phr. [1960s+] (US) to indulge in sexual by-play.

watch which way the cat jumps see SEE WHICH WAY THE CAT JUMPS.

watchy see WATCHIE.

watch your arse! excl. [1950s+] **1** look where you're going! take care of yourself! **2** behave yourself! mind your manners! (cf. WATCH YOUR HIP!). [ARSE n.¹]

watch your hip! excl. [1950s+] (W.I.) watch your manners! (cf. WATCH YOUR ARSE!). [euph. *hip*, the buttocks, the backside]

watch your vocab! *excl.* [1930s+] (Aus.) mind your bad language! (cf. LANGUAGE!). [abbr. SE *vocabulary*]

water, the *n.*[1] [20C] the River Thames; thus *over the water*, south of the Thames.

water *n.*[2] (drugs) **1** [1960s+] injectable amphetamine. **2** [1970s+] phencyclidine (cf. ACE n.[3]). [ety. unknown]

water *v.*[1] [mid-18C] to stand treat, to entertain. [SE *water*, to provide water for, usu., a horse]

water *v.*[2] [late 18C] (US) to 'pack' a jury with members who are likely to deliver a biased verdict. [SE *water*, to dilute]

waterbag *n.* [1920s+] (Aus.) a fanatical teetotaller.

water-barrel *see* WATER-BUTT.

water-bewitched *adj.* [late 17C–early 19C] **1** very weak. **2** of tea, punch or any other liquor, very weak.

water-bobby *n.* [late 19C] a river policeman. [SE *water* + BOBBY n. (1)]

water-bonse *n.* [late 19C–1910s] a 'cry-baby'. [SE *water* + BONCE, lit. *water-head*]

water-bottle *n.* [late 19C] a total abstainer, a teetotaller.

waterbox/watercourse/watergap *n.* [19C] the vagina (cf. DAMP n.).

waterboy *n.* [1930s+] (US) a useless boxer who accepts money to lose fights (cf. TANKER n.[1]). [i.e. he 'takes a dive']

water buffalo *v.* [1980s+] (US campus) to vomit. [? echoic]

waterbury watch *n.* [late 19C–1930s] Scotch whisky (cf. BOTTLE OF SCOTCH). [rhy. sl.; the popular watches made in *Waterbury*, Conn.]

water-butt/water-barrel *n.* [late 19C] the stomach.

water-cart *v.* [1920s] to weep, to cry.

watercourse *see* WATERBOX.

water-dog *n.* [mid-19C–1900s] a Norfolk dumpling, a plain dumpling made from bread dough. [the ref. is to *Norfolk Broads*; note a *Norfolk dumpling* also means a native of Norfolk]

water-dona *see* WASHER-DONA.

water-engine *n.* [late 19C] the urinary organs, irrespective of gender (cf. WATERWORKS).

waterfall *n.* [19C] **1** a handkerchief worn in the top pocket. **2** false hair. [resemblance]

water-funk *n.* [late 19C] one who is afraid to go into water. [SE *water* + FUNK n.[2] (2)]

watergap *see* WATERBOX.

water hen *n.* [1960s] the number 10. [rhy. sl.]

watering hole/water-hole *n.* [1960s+] **1** a restaurant, a bar, anywhere where alcoholic refreshment is available (cf. WATERING PLACE). **2** (gay) an area where one can wander in search of sexual partners, usually a park or a bar. [SE *water-hole*, a pool or reservoir, esp. as used by animals for drinking]

watering place *n.* [mid-19C] (US) a restaurant or similar place of entertainment for public drinking favoured by the rich (cf. WATERING HOLE).

waterlogged *adj.* [1910s–20s] very drunk.

waterloo *n.*[1] [late 19C] a halfpenny. [the halfpenny toll to cross *Waterloo* Bridge]

waterloo *n.*[2] [20C] stew. [rhy. sl.]

waterman *n.*[1] *see* WATER'S MAN.

waterman *n.*[2] [late 19C] an artist who uses watercolours.

waterman *n.*[3] [1950s] (W.I.) a heavy drinker, an alcoholic. [SE *water*, euph. for white rum]

watermelon man *n.* [1970s] (US Black) a drug seller. [euph.; stereotyped association of *watermelons* and US Blacks]

watermelons *n.* [1980s+] (US campus) large breasts (cf. APPLES n.[1]). [resemblance]

watermill *n.* [early 19C] the vagina (cf. DAMP n.; WINDMILL).

water of life *n.* **1** [mid-19C] whisky. **2** [mid-19C] gin. **3** [1950s+] (US Black) semen.

water one's cheeks, to *phr.* [1970s] (US Black) to cry.

water one's nag, to *phr.* [late 17C–mid-18C] to urinate (cf. WATER THE DRAGON). [SE *water* + play on SE *nag*, a horse/ NAG n.[2]]

water one's plants, to *phr.* [mid-16C–late 19C] to weep.

water one's pony, to *phr.* [20C] to urinate. [euph.]

water pad *n.* [late 17C–early 19C] a thief who specializes in robbing ships on the River Thames (cf. WATER SNEAK). [SE *water* + PAD n.[1] (3)]

water plant *n.* [early–mid-19C] an umbrella. [joc. resemblance]

water rat *n.* **1** [mid–late 19C] a sergeant in the Thames River Police (cf. BLACK BEETLE). **2** [1950s+] (Ulster) a customs officer. [the both check travellers/goods using 'the water']

waters *n.* [1940s] (US Black) wellington boots, galoshes. [their use on wet days]

water scriger *n.* [late 18C–early 19C] a doctor who diagnoses on the basis of a patient's urine (cf. PISS PROPHET). [SE *water*, urine ? + corruption of *scriver*, a scribe]

water's man/waterman *n.* [mid–late 19C] a costermonger's handkerchief, coloured light or dark blue (cf. BELCHER n.[1]; BILLY n.[4]; BIRD'S EYE FOGLE; BIRD'S EYE WIPE; BLOOD-RED FANCY; BLUE BILLY; CREAM FANCY; KINGSMAN; RANDAL'S MAN; YELLOW FANCY; YELLOW MAN). [the light and dark blue colours sported by Cambridge and Oxford university oarsmen]

water sneak *n.* [late 18C–early 19C] a thief who works on a river (cf. ARK-MAN; ARK-PIRATE; ARK RUFF; WATER PAD). [SE *water* + SNEAK n.[1]]

water sports *n.* [1960s+] urinating on a partner for sexual stimulation (cf. GOLDEN SHOWER).

water the dragon, to *phr.* [mid-19C] to urinate (cf. DRAIN THE DRAGON). [euph.]

water the flowers, to *phr.* [20C] to urinate. [euph.]

water the horses, to *phr.* [20C] to urinate (cf. LET MY HORSE OUT OF THE STABLE). [euph.]

water the mule, to *phr.* [1990s] (US) to urinate. [euph.]

water-wagon *n.* [20C] a fig. state of sobriety; usu. in phr. ON THE WAGON.

waterworks *n.* **1** [mid-19C+] the urinary organs. **2** [1930s] rain.

watery-headed *adj.* [late 18C–early 19C] tearful, prone to crying.

wattle *n.* [1940s–50s] (Aus.) a dirty, grubby person. [rhy. sl. *wattle and daub* = WARB n. (2)]

wattle *v.* [20C] to drink. [dial.]

wattles *n.* [late 18C–mid-19C] (orig. Und.) ears. [SE *wattles*, the 'ears' of a turkey or cock]

wave *n.* [1980s+] (drugs) crack cocaine. [ety. unknown]

wave a flag of defiance, to *phr.* [late 19C–1910s] to be drunk. [one's temporary boldness]

wave maker *n.* [1970s+] (US) a person who raises objections or difficult questions.

wave one's willy, to *phr.* [1960s+] of a man, to act in an exaggeratedly macho manner; thus *willy-waving*, acting in this manner (cf. BALL-CLANKER). [WILLIE n.[1] + SE *wave*]

wave the lily, to *phr.* [1970s+] (US) of an exhibitionist, to expose and wave one's penis.

wave the magic wand, to *phr.* [1990s] to masturbate.

Wavy Navy *n.* [1910s+] the Royal Naval Volunteer Reserve. [the *wavy* braid worn by its officers on their uniform sleeves until 1956]

wax *n.*[1] [mid–late 19C] a temper, state of anger; thus *waxy*, angry, *waxiness*, fury. [arch. SE *wax wrath*, to become angry]

wax *n.*[2] [1920s+] (orig. US) a gramophone record; thus *put on wax*, to record. [the *wax* master discs in which the recording stylus cuts its groove]

wax *n.*[3] [1950s–60s] (US Black) chewing gum.

wax *v.*[1] **1** [late 19C+] to defeat in competition. **2** [1960s+] to beat up, to thrash (cf. WAX SOMEONE'S ASS). **3** [1980s+] to have sexual intercourse. [SE *wax*, to grown in intensity + WHACK *v.*[1]]

wax *v.*[2] [1920s+] (orig. US) to make a record. [WAX n.[2]]

wax-borer *n.* [1930s+] (Aus.) a talkative bore. [i.e. they 'bore' through one's ear *wax*]

waxed *adj.* [late 19C+] having a personality and characteristics that are known well (cf. PEEP SOMEONE'S HOLE CARD). [20C use is US Black; ? SE *wax*, to polish, i.e. they 'shine' in a crowd]

waxed, buffed and simonized *phr.* [1980s+] (US Black) comprehensively defeated, beaten up. [WAX v.[1] (1) + car valeting imagery]

waxing *n.* [1930s+] a gramophone record or phonograph cylinder. [WAX v.[2]]

wax-pot *n.* [1910s–20s] an ill-tempered person. [WAX n.[1] + SE *fusspot*]

wax some ass, to *phr.* [1970s+] (US Black) to have sexual intercourse. [WAX v.[1] (3) + ARSE n.[1]]

wax someone's ass/tail, to *phr.* [1960s+] (US) to beat up, to thrash. [WAX v.[1] (1) + ARSE n.[1] (1)]

wax something up, to *v.* [late 19C] to ruin, to make a mess of. [WAX v.[1] (1)]

wax the buick / candle-stick / car / carrot / dolphin / surfboard/womb broom, to *phr.* [20C] to masturbate.

wax up *v.* [1970s+] (US Black) **1** to propitiate someone whom one has insulted or annoyed (cf. APPLE UP). **2** to hide evidence. [SE *wax*, to polish; (2) suggests making things look better]

waxworks *n.* [1980s+] (US gay) anywhere, e.g. a bar, mainly frequented by older, less attractive gay men (cf. WRINKLE ROOM).

waxy *n.* [mid-19C–1900s] a cobbler. [the *waxed* thread he uses]

waxy *adj.* [1940s+] (W.I.) **1** lively, exciting, enjoyable. **2** of a person, attractive. [SE *waxy*, i.e. an image of 'shininess']

way *adv.* [1970s+] (US) **1** very, extremely etc (cf. TOTAL adj.). **2** the affirmative response to the neg. *no way.* [WAY OUT or WAY TO GO, but note W.I. *waay, waay-ou*, an excl. of great amusement, excitement, exultation]

wayback *n.* [late 19C+] (Aus./N.Z.) **1** the outback. **2** a person or animal from the outback.

way back *adj.* [1930s–50s] (US Black) well-established, traditional, tried and tested (cf. OLD SCHOOL).

way-in *n.* [19C] the vagina (cf. BELLY ENTRANCE; ENTRANCE; FRONT GATE; GUT ENTRANCE; IVORY GATE).

way in *adj.* [1950s–60s] fashionable, chic.

way it plays *phr.* [1930s+] (US) as things go, the usual course of events. [PLAY v.[3]]

way of all flesh *phr.* [late 19C] dead. [var. on orig. Bible phr. *go the way of all the earth*; popularized in trans. of Douay Bible (1609)]

way of life *n.* [early 19C+] the profession of prostitution (cf. LIFE n.[1]). [euph.]

way-out *n.* [1960s+] (US) an unconventional or eccentric person; thus *way-outness*, unconventionality. [WAY-OUT adj.]

way-out *adj.*[1] [1950s+] (orig. US) bizarre, fantastic, exceptional. [orig. jazz use]

way-out *adj.*[2] [1950s+] (US) wholly wrong, greatly mistaken. [abbr. *way out of line*]

way past *adv.* [1980s+] (orig. US Black) a general intensifier, e.g. *way past bad, way past cool.* [lit. 'beyond']

way poo cow! *excl.* [20C] (W.I./Gren.) watch out for yourself! look out for the consequences! [Fr. *voir pour corps-vous*, lit. 'see for your body', hence look out for yourself]

ways *n.* [1950s+] the style and standards of the US Mafia.

wayside ditch/fountain *n.* [19C] the vagina (cf. DAMP n.).

way to go!/how to go! *excl.* [1940s+] of approval, i.e. *that's the right way to go … .* [allegedly coined for the 1940 film *Knute Rockne*]

waytoo *adj.* [1990s] (US teen) of anything that is bizarre or eccentric but still socially acceptable. [SE *way too much*]

way-up *adj.* [late 19C–1900s] (US) top-rank, first-class, socially and otherwise superior.

waz/wazz *n.* [1970s+] **1** urination. **2** masturbation. [WAZZ v.]

waz/wazz *v.* [1970s+] **1** of a man, to urinate. **2** of a woman, to masturbate. [dial. *wass*, to urinate]

wazoo *n.* [20C] (US) the buttocks, the anus. [? var. GAZOO/ KAZOO]

wazz *see* WAZ.

wazzock *n.* [1990s] a fool. [? WAZOO]

wazzocked *adj.* [1980s+] drunk or intoxicated by a drug. [var. on WAZZOOED]

wazzooed *adj.* [1970s+] (drugs) extremely intoxicated by a drug (cf. WASTED; WRECKED). [echoic or play on WAZ v. (1); i.e. PISSED]

w.c. *adj.* [1990s] working *class* (cf. L.C.). [abbr.]

w/e *adj.* [1960s+] used in sex contact advertisements, having notably large genitals (cf. V. W/E). [abbr. WELL-ENDOWED]

weak *n.* [late 19C] tea. [as opposed to coffee]

weak *adj.* [1940s+] **1** untrustworthy, unreliable. **2** poor, disappointing, ineffectual. **3** stupid.

weak *adv.* [1980s+] (US) badly, e.g. *paid weak*, badly paid, low paid.

weak as gin's piss *phr.* [1950s+] (Aus.) extremely weak (cf. CAT'S PISS; GNAT'S PISS; HORSE PISS; SHEEP WASH).

weak-ass *adj.* [1980s+] a derog. term for second-rate, unimpressive, powerless. [WEAK adj. + sfx. -ASS]

weak down *v.* [1900s–40s] (US Black) to become demoralized, to show a lack of courage, of determination. [WEAK adj.]

weakheart *n.* [1970s] (UK/W.I.) a derog. term for a policeman.

weakie *n.* [1940s+] (Aus.) an unreliable, untrustworthy person. [WEAK adj. + sfx. -*ie*]

weak in the arm *n.* [late 19C–1900s] a short measure of beer. [the publican has supposedly not pulled the beer tap to its fullest extent]

weak shit *n.* [1960s+] **1** second-rate, weak, inadequate words or actions. **2** (drugs) second-rate, relatively ineffective drugs. [WEAK adj. + SHIT n.[4], SHIT n.[5]]

weak sister *n.* [mid-19C+] (orig. US) the weakest member of a group, the sex is irrelevant. [a play on the earlier, biblical *weaker brethren*, a translation of the term Gk. *asthenes* 'applied by St Paul (esp. in Rom. 14 and 1 Cor. 8) to believers whose scruples, though unsound, should be treated with tenderness, lest they should be led by the example of the more enlightened into acts condemned by their conscience' (OED)]

weapon *n.* [early 11C+] the penis (cf. ARSE-OPENER; BAT n.[7]). [first cited in an 11C glossary and in Langland's *Piers Plowman* (1377), 'While thou art young and thy weapon keen …'. It was used more widely from the mid-18C]

wear *n.* [1950s+] (Irish) an open-mouthed kiss. [the echoic 'mwah!' of a kiss or the open mouth with which one says SE *wear*]

wear *v.* [1920s+] to tolerate, to stand, to believe.

wear a cut-glass veil, to *phr.* [1930s+] (US gay) to attempt unsuccessfully to hide one's homosexual preferences (cf. WEAR A MOURNING VEIL). [such a transparent 'veil' hides nothing]

wear a forker, to *phr.* [early 17C] to be cuckolded. [SE *fork*, i.e. the 'horns' that a cuckold wears]

wear a green bonnet, to *phr.* [19C] to be bankrupt. [the defunct tradition of a bankrupt wearing a green cap to denote his status]

wear a green sweater/tie *see* WEAR A RED SWEATER.

wear a head, to *phr.* [early 19C] to be intelligent.

wear a hempen necktie, to *phr.* [late 17C–18C] to be hanged (cf. HEMP CRAVAT). [the *hempen* rope]

wear a mourning veil, to *phr.* [1970s] to attempt to hide one's homosexual proclivities (cf. WEAR A CUT-GLASS VEIL). [such a 'veil' is black and thus impenetrable]

wear a red/green sweater/tie, to *phr.* [1960s+] (US gay) to act in an obviously homosexual manner. [? the brightness of the colours; i.e. one cannot hide one's sexuality; or the belief that such clothes denote a homosexual wearer]

wear a revolver-pocket, to *phr.* [late 19C–1900s] to carry a revolver.

wear-arse *n.* [late 18C–early 19C] a one-horse chaise or light, open carriage. [SE *wear out* + ARSE n.[1]; from the jolting]

wear a scarlet countenance, to *phr.* [late 19C–1910s] to be shameless, to act in a shameless manner. [SE *scarlet*, of an offender, 'deep-dyed', heinous]

wear a smile, to *phr.* [1900s–70s] (US Black) to be naked.

wear a straw in one's ear, to *phr.* [1910s–20s] of a woman, to seek a new husband. [? custom of standing with a straw in one's mouth, which indicates one's desire to find a new job; ? + dial. *draw a straw across*, to beguile]

we are the world *n.* [1980s] (US drugs) a brand of crack cocaine. [play on 'Feed the world', the chorus of 'Do they know it's Christmas?', the charity-based rock song, performed by a number of bands and singers in 1984]

wear face *v.* [1990s] (US Black) to wear make-up (cf. PUT ONE'S FACE ON).

wear Hector's cloak, to *phr.* [17C] to be punished for one's treacherous behaviour. [*Hector* Armstrong, who betrayed the Earl of Northumberland in 1569 and subseq. died in penury]

Wearie/Weary *n.* [20C] (Ulster) the Devil. [SE *weary* but note OE *wearg*, the accursed one]

wearies, the *n.* [20C] (US) tiredness, boredom, apathy.

wearing one's medals *phr.* [mid-19C+] walking around with one's fly open.

wear it *v.* **1** [early–mid-19C] (Und.) to be accused of becoming an informer. **2** [20C] (US Und.) to take the blame for a crime even when not actually guilty. [WEAR v.]

wear it upon *v.* [early 19C] (Und.) to inform against. ['it' is the nose, f. NOSE v.[3] (2)]

wear one's badge, to *phr.* [1960s] to wear an outward sign of being a homosexual. [formerly this was a red tie, now obs.]

wear one's business, to *phr.* [20C] (US Und.) to act in an obvious manner, to betray one's secrets. [BUSINESS n.[2] (1); var. on SE *to wear one's heart on one's sleeve*]

wear one's head large, to *phr.* [late 19C] to be suffering from a hangover.

wear one's sitting breeches *see* HAVE ONE'S SITTING BREECHES ON.

wear out one's soul-case *see* BURST OUT ONE'S SOUL-CASE.

wear someone out *v.* [1990s] (US Black) to have sex with someone.

wear someone's balls for necktie, to *phr.* [1920s+] used as a threat of violence, *try that again and I'll wear ...* (cf. GUTS FOR GARTERS).

wear the bands, to *phr.* [early 19C] (mainly Und.) to be hungry. [BANDED]

wear the barley cap, to *phr.* [late 16C–late 17C] **1** to be drunk. **2** to have a hangover. [SE *barley*, a main constituent of beer]

wear the beard, to *phr.* [1990s] usu. of a man, to perform cunnilingus. [BEARD n.[1]]

wear the bells, to *phr.* [20C] (US) to act the fool (cf. PLAY CAPS AND BELLS). [the traditional cap and bells worn by a jester]

wear the belt, to *phr.* [mid–late 19C] (US) to be the best, to surpass all rivals. [boxing imagery, a special *belt* is given to champions]

wear the blues, to *phr.* [1990s] (US) to be in prison (cf. WEAR THE BROAD ARROW). [the colour of prison uniforms]

wear the breeches, to *phr.* [16C+] of a wife, to assume authority over one's husband (cf. WEAR THE PANTS; WEAR THE TROUSERS).

wear the broad arrow, to *phr.* [late 19C] to be imprisoned (cf. WEAR THE BLUES). [the *arrows* that were printed onto prison clothing]

wear the dog, to *phr.* [1970s] (US Black) to go around looking deeply depressed (but cf. PUT ON THE DOG). [SE *hangdog* look]

wear the horns, to *phr.* [18C+] to be cuckolded. [HORNS]

wear the leek, to *phr.* [late 19C] to be Welsh. [SE *leek*, the national emblem]

wear the pants, to *phr.* [1930s+] (orig. US) to be the dominant member of a heterosexual partnership (cf. WEAR THE BREECHES). [coined in an era when only men were thought to wear pants (trousers)]

wear the ring, to *phr.* [1960s+] (US Black) to be in a regular relationship, whether actually married or not, and thus to reject any alternative entanglements. [the wedding *ring* + the image of a *ring* through a bull's nose]

wear the trousers, to *phr.* [1930s+] to dominate, usu. implying that the woman in a relationship is the one who dictates the rules (cf. WEAR THE BREECHES).

wear the willow, to *phr.* [late 16C–early 19C] to have been abandoned by one's mistress or lover. [abbr. SE *wear the willow garland*; the symbolic role of the weeping *willow*]

wear two hats, to *phr.* [20C] (US) to have two different jobs.

weary *n. see* WEARIE.

weary *adj.* [early 18C–1900s] drunk (cf. TIRED AND EMOTIONAL). [euph.]

wear yellow hose/stockings, to *phr.* [early 17C–19C] to be jealous. [thus the character of Malvolio in Shakespeare's *Twelfth Night* (1599)]

weary willie *n.* [20C] (US) a tramp, a migrant worker. [SE *weary* + assonant/generic *Willie*]

weary willie and tired tim *n.* [1930s–40s] a pair of idling, loafing individuals. [the cartoon tramps created in 1902 by Tom Browne (1870–1910)]

weasel *n.*[1] [mid-19C+] (US) a native of South Carolina. [the state has a large population of the animal]

weasel *n.*[2] [20C] an overcoat. [rhy. sl. *weasel and stoat* = coat]

weasel *n.*[3] [1920s+] (US) **1** an informer. **2** a policeman. [reverse anthropomorphism]

weasel *n.*[4] [1980s+] (orig. US) the penis. [it 'burrows']

weasel/weasel out *v.*[1] [late 19C+] (US) to evade, to equivocate. **2** to wriggle out of a promise or duty. [reverse anthropomorphism]

weasel *v.*[2] [1920s+] (US Und.) to inform. [WEASEL n.[3]]

weasel shit *n.* [1960s+] (N.Z.) a devious or cunning person. [SE *weasel* + SHIT n.[2]]

weathercock *n.* [late 19C] the head (cf. ATTIC).

weather gig *n.* [late 17C–early 18C] the vagina. [SE *wether*, a castrated ram + GIG n.[2]]

weatherhead *n.* [19C] a fool, a simpleton. [SE *weather* + sfx. -HEAD (1); the image is of the fool's head turning like that of a *weathercock*]

weather-sharp *n.* [1900s] (US) a weather-forecaster. [SE *weather* + SHARP n.[1] (2)]

weave *n.* [1950s–60s] (US Black) clothing (cf. BAD WEAVE; RAGS; THREADS).

weaver *n.* [1950s+] (US) a poor driver who *weaves* from lane to lane along the road.

weaving *n.* [mid-19C] in cards, cheating by secreting a number of cards on one's knee, or wedged between a knee and the underside of the table. These cards can be brought into the hand, swapping them for those one has been dealt, as and when required.

weaving leather aprons/dolls' eyes *phr.* [mid-19C] one of many responses used to defer a 'difficult' question as to 'what one has been doing?' (cf. MAKING A TRUNDLE FOR A GOOSE'S EYE; MAKING A WHIM-WHAM FOR A GOOSE'S EYE). [the absurdity of the task]

web-foot *n.* **1** [mid-19C–1910s] (US) an infantryman. **2** [late 19C] a native of Lincolnshire. **3** [1970s+] (US) an environmentalist. [they all encounter wet paths etc]

wedded to the Duke of Exeter's daughter *phr.* [15C] suffering the torture of the rack. [the rack had been introduced into England by John Holland, 4th *Duke of Exeter* in 1447]

wedding *n.*[1] [late 18C] the emptying of a privy. [? SE *weeding*]

wedding *n.*[2] *see* IRISH WEDDING.

wedding bells *n.* [1960s] (drugs) LSD. [ety. unknown; it 'rings' in one's skull]

wedding kit/tackle *n.* [1910s+] the male genitals (cf. ACCOUTREMENTS). [SE *wedding* + KIT n.[3]/TACKLE n.[1] (5)]

wedge *n.*[1] **1** [18C–19C] silver, money in general. **2** [18C–19C] silver plate. **3** [1970s+] a thick, chunky roll of banknotes, usu. folded in half (cf. BUNDLE n.[2]). [in (2) the silver plate was melted down into wedges by receivers]

wedge/wej *n.*[2] [mid-19C] a Jew. [backsl.]

wedge *n.*[3] [mid-19C] the penis (cf. ARSE-OPENER). [it SE *wedges* open the vagina]

wedge/wedges/wedgies *n.*[4] [1960s] (drugs) LSD. [? the shape of the capsule]

wedgeass *n.* [1970s+] a general term of abuse. [SE *wedge* + sfx. -ASS]

wedge feeder *n.* [mid-19C] a silver spoon. [WEDGE n.[1]]

wedge-hunter *n.* [mid-19C–1900s] (Und.) a thief specializing in silver plate and silver watches. [WEDGE n.[1]]

wedge-lobb *n.* [early 19C] a silver snuff-box. [WEDGE n.[1] + LOB n.[1] (1)]

wedges *see* WEDGE n.[4].

wedgie *n.* [1990s] a trick whereby one pulls an unsuspecting victim's underpants up between their buttocks. [SE *wedge*, to stick or thrust between]

wedgies *n.*[1] [1940s+] women's *wedge*-heeled shoes. [abbr.]

wedgies *n.*[2] *see* WEDGE n.[4].

wee/wee-wee *n.* [1920s+] (mainly juv.) urine, urination. [juv. mispron. of 'u-ween' or var. on PEE n.]

wee/wee-wee *v.* [1920s+] (mainly juv.) to urinate. [WEE n.]

weeb *n.* [1990s] (US teen) a lie.

wee buns!/bunions! *excl.* [20C] (Ulster) no problem!

weed *n.*[1] **1** [16C+] tobacco. **2** [mid-19C+] a cigar, esp. an inferior one. **3** [20C] a cigarette. **4** [1920s+] (drugs) marijuana. [ext. uses of SE]

weed *n.*[2] **1** [19C] an ill-conditioned, weak horse. **2** [mid-19C+] a weakling, a feeble and thus contemptible person (cf. DICK-WEED).

weed *n.*[3] [early 19C+] the practice of pocketing a certain amount of the cash that should be placed untouched into one's employer's tills; thus (Und.) *weed the swag*, to embezzle part of the booty before dividing what remains with one's gang.

weed *n.*[4] [mid-19C] a hatband. [SE *weed*, a mourning garment, often a black hatband]

weed *v.*[1] [late 19C] to take, to steal.

weed *v.*[2] [1940s] (US Black) to lend, esp. money; thus *weed a holler note until mother comes in*, to lend someone $100 until their gambling luck changes.

weedhead *n.* [1950s+] (drugs) a marijuana smoker. [WEED n.[1] (4) + sfx. -HEAD (2)]

weeding dues *n.* [early 19C] (Und.) 'Speaking of any person, place, or property, that has been weeded [i.e. robbed], it is said "weeding dues have been concerned"' (Vaux). [WEED v.[1]]

weed out *v.* [1950s+] (drugs) to smoke marijuana to excess (cf. AMPED-OUT). [WEED n.[1] (4) + pun on SE]

weeds, the *n.*[1] [1920s+] (US tramp) a hobo camp (cf. JUNGLE n.[1]). [its position on the edge of town]

weeds *n.*[2] [1950s+] (US) clothes.

weed tea *n.* [1920s–30s] (drugs) marijuana tea. [WEED n.[1] (4) + SE *tea*]

weedy *adj.* **1** [19C] of a horse, weak-legged, lacking strength. **2** [mid-19C+] of humans, weak, cowardly, spineless. [WEED n.[2]]

wee georgie wood *adj.* [20C] good. [rhy. sl.; the early 20C musical hall star]

weejee *n.* [mid-late 19C] **1** a chimneypot. **2** a chimneypot hat. **3** anything outstanding of its type, esp. an invention. [ety. unknown, ? (3) link to WHEEZE n.]

weejuns *n.* [1950s+] (US teen) moccasins, loafers. [brandname, *Weejuns*]

weekend *n.* [1940s–50s] (prison) a very short period of imprisonment.

weekender *n.* **1** [19C] a prostitute who only works at the weekend. **2** [1940s+] weekend cottage. **3** [1960s+] a suitcase suitable for packing those items needed for a weekend's trip or holiday.

weekend habit *n.* [1970s+] (drugs) an irregular drug user (cf. CHIPPIE n.[1]). [SE *weekend* + HABIT]

weekend ho/warrior *n.* [1960s+] a part-time prostitute, often without a pimp but poss. helping out her boyfriend with cash. [SE *weekend* + HO n.[1]/SE *warrior*]

weekend man *n.* [1970s+] (US Black) a family man who can only manage the street life at weekends.

weekend warrior *n.*[1] [1960s+] (US) members of the National Guard.

weekend warrior *n.*[2] *see* WEEKEND HO.

ween/weenie *n.* [1970s] (US campus) **1** a hard-working student (cf. GREASY GRIND; WEENIE BIN). **2** a boring, socially unappealing person. [WEENIE n.[1] (4)]

weenchy *adj.* [20C] (US) tiny, very little. [WEENY adj.]

weener *see* WEENIE n.[1].

weenie/weener/wiener/weeny/weeney/wienie *n.*[1] (US) **1** [1910s+] a frankfurter sausage. **2** [1910s+] (usu. juv.) the penis (cf. BACON n.[1]). **3** [1920s+] a young woman, an effeminate man. **4** [1960s+] a socially unacceptable person. [SAmE *wiener*, a Vienna sausage; ult. Ger. *Wienenwurst*]

weenie *n.*[2] *see* WEEN.

weenie bin *n.* [1970s] (US campus) a library carrel. [WEEN + SE *bin*]

weenie waver *n.* [1970s+] an exhibitionist. [WEENIE n.[1] (2) + SE *waver*]

weeny *n.*[1] [mid-19C+] a very young child. [WEENY adj.]

weeny *n.*[2] *see* WEENIE n.[1].

weeny *adj.* [late 18C+] tiny. [infant pron.]

weeny-bopper *n.* [1970s+] a very young pop fan (cf. TEENY-BOPPER). [WEENY n.[1] + BOP v. (3)]

weep and wail *n.* [late 19C–1950s] a tale, esp. a beggar's tale of woe. [rhy. sl.]

weeper *n.*[1] [late 19C] a long, sweeping moustache, long side-whiskers (cf. PICCADILLY WEEPERS). [? the trailing ends of crepe once worn at funerals – where mourners wept]

weeper *n.*[2] see WEEPIE.

weepers *n.* [1920s–40s] (US Black) one's best clothes and so those one wears to funerals.

Weepers! *excl.* [1950s+] (US teen) a mild exclamation of surprise or upset (cf. JEEPERS CREEPERS).

weepie/weeper *n.* [1920s+] (film) a film whose main effect is to reduce its audience to tears, usu. consciously romantic; thus *three-handkerchief weepie*, a very emotional film (cf. TEARJERKER).

weeping willow *n.* [late 19C–1940s] a pillow. [rhy. sl.]

weep Irish *v.* [late 19C+] to talk nonsense. [racial stereotyping]

weeps, the *n.* [20C] (US) tearfulness, crying.

wee small hours *n.* [mid-19C+] the very early morning.

wee-wee/wi-wi/wewi *n.*[1] [mid-19C] (orig. Aus./N.Z.) a French person. [the excl. *oui oui!*, yes, yes! + derog. pun on WEE]

wee-wee *n.*[2] see WEE.

wee-wee *v.* see WEE v.

we had one but the wheel came off *phr.* [1930s+] a phr. used to indicate that the speaker has not understood the subject of the conversation in which they had been involved.

we here *phr.* [1990s] (US campus) expression of support. [US Black var. of SE *we are here*]

weigh forty *v.* [early 19C] (Und.) for a thief to have moved into serious crimes, which will make it worth his arrest (cf. FORTY-POUNDER). [the £40 cash bonus awarded to any policeman who secured a 'Tyburn ticket', i.e. captured a murderer]

weigh in *v.* **1** [late 19C] (US) to assert oneself. **2** [20C] to join in, esp. in an argument. **3** [1920s+] to pay or give one's share, to play one's part. [horse-racing use, i.e. the pre-race *weigh-in*]

weigh into *v.* [1940s+] (orig. Aus.) to attack verbally or physically, to criticize.

weigh in with *v.* [late 19C+] to add, to include something extra. [ext. of WEIGH IN]

weigh-meat *n.* [late 19C+] (W.I.) bones that are weighed up by the butcher and charged for along with the meat that accompanies them.

weigh off *v.* **1** [1920s+] (Und.) to sentence a convicted prisoner; thus *weighed off*, sent off to prison. **2** [1930s+] to get one's own back, to take revenge on. [orig. milit.]

weigh one's thumb, to *phr.* [late 19C] to give short measure. [the age-old practice of a shopkeeper keeping his thumb pressing on the scales when weighing goods]

weigh out *v.* [late 19C] to apportion shares.

weight *n.*[1] (orig. US) **1** [1910s+] influence, importance (cf. THROW ONE'S WEIGHT AROUND). **2** [1950s–70s] responsibility, obligation, duty. **3** [1950s+] blame, emotional or psychological pressure.

weight *n.*[2] [1960s+] (drugs) **1** a large quantity of drugs (esp. pounds of hashish/marijuana, kilos of cocaine/heroin). **2** 1lb of marijuana, cannabis. **3** 1oz of heroin. [no article is required for (1) although it may be qualified by number, e.g. *five weight of hash*, 5lb of hashish]

weight *n.*[3] [1980s+] (US Black) a gun, a pistol. [its lit. + fig. SE *weight*]

weightless *adj.* [1980s+] (drugs) intoxicated by crack cocaine. [its effects]

weigh up *v.* [late 19C+] to appraise, to assess.

weird *adj.* [1920s+] (orig. society) wonderful, excellent.

weird and wonderful *phr.* [mid-19C+] odd, bizarre, often used ironically.

weirdie *n.* **1** [late 19C+] an eccentric person, esp. as *bearded weirdie*, a man with long hair and/or a beard and as such negatively stereotyped as an 'intellectual'. **2** [1940s+] anything, typically a book or film, that is considered fantastic, bizarre or grotesque. **3** [1960s] a male homosexual. [SE *weird* + sfx. *-ie*]

weirdo *n.* [1940s+] an eccentric, a peculiar person. [SE *weird* + sfx. *-o*]

weirdo *adj.* [1960s+] eccentric, odd, bizarre, out of the ordinary. [WEIRDO n.]

weird out *v.* [1960s+] **1** to horrify, to play mental games. **2** (drugs) to experience hallucinations from intoxication by narcotics. **3** to feel confused or at a loss because of someone's or something's strangeness.

weirdsville *n.* [1940s+] (US) anywhere considered off or out of the ordinary. [SE *weird* + sfx. -VILLE]

wej see WEDGE n.[2].

welch/welsh *v.* **1** [mid-19C+] to refuse to pay a gambling debt or other bill. **2** [1980s+] (US campus) to reject, to stand aside from, to turn down (all relate to a social engagement). [racist stereotyping, but note Ger. *Welsch*, foreigner]

Welch/Welsh comb *n.* [late 18C–mid-19C] the thumb and four fingers, used to smooth one's hair (cf. GERMAN COMB). [racial stereotyping]

welcher/welsher *n.* [mid-19C+] **1** anyone who refuses to pay their debts, gambling or otherwise. **2** an informer. [WELCH v.]

welcome, I'm sure! *excl.* [late 19C+] you're welcome to it. [an equivalent to the various European forms of acknowledgement that greet 'please', e.g. Ital. *prego*. In the UK, however, the form is strictly lower-/lower-middle-class]

welcome to the club *phr.* [1960s+] (US) a suggestion, often ironic, that someone else's (usu. adverse) situation or predicament is, whatever they may believe, by no means unique.

welfare mother *n.* [1960s+] (US Black) any woman, irrespective of status vis-à-vis welfare, who is poorly dressed and unkempt. [ironic use of SE]

welk! *excl.* [1980s+] (US campus) you're *welc*ome. [abbr.]

well *v.* (Und.) **1** [early 19C] to defraud one's criminal confederates, to divide booty unfairly. **2** [mid-19C] to pocket; thus *well it*, to be well-off, to make a good income. **3** [late 19C+] to conceal a proportion of one's income or estate from one's creditors.

well *adv.*[1] [late 19C] used as an intensifier in such combs. as *bloody well, damn well, jolly well* etc.

well *adv.*[2] [late 19C+] (orig. society, more recently cockney) a general intensifier, very, definitely, extremely etc; thus *well tasty, well sus* etc.

well away *adj.* [1920s+] **1** making headway in a seduction. **2** drunk or on one's way towards being so (cf. ABOUT RIGHT adj.[1]).

well-bushed *adj.* [20C] of a man, having notably large genitals, of a woman, having plentiful pubic hair.

well-cemented *adj.* [1940s] (Aus.) rich (cf. WELL-FIXED). [BUSH n.[4]]

well-covered see WELL-UPHOLSTERED.

well, duh *phr.* [1990s] (US teen) a phr. implying to the speaker that 'everyone knows what you're talking about'.

well-endowed *adj.* [1940s+] of a man, having notably large genitals (cf. WELL-FURNISHED; WELL-HUNG adj.[1]; WELL-LOADED). [euph.]

well-fixed *adj.* [early 19C+] (US) reasonably affluent, comfortable. [SE *fixed*, sorted out]

well-furnished *adj.* [1930s+] of a man, having notably large genitals (cf. WELL-ENDOWED). [euph.]

well-heeled *adj.*[1] [mid-19C+] (US) well-armed. [SE *heeled*, provided with a heel or heel-like extension, in this case a pistol]

well-heeled *adj.*[2] [late 19C+] rich. [the quality of a rich person's footwear]

well hove! *excl.* [1910s–20s] well done! well played! [SE *hove*, past tense of *heave*]

well-hung *adj.*[1] [early 19C+] of a man, having notably large genitals (cf. WELL-ENDOWED).

well-hung *adj.*[2] [20C] young. [rhy. sl.]

wellie/welly *n.* [1960s+] a *welli*ngton boot. [abbr.]

wellies *n.* [1980s+] the public-school educated, upper-middle and upper-class students, who are seen as playing rather than working their way through university. [SE *wealthy* + the green wellington boots (cf. WELLIE) such students wear for various rural pleasures]

well, I'll be dipped in shit! *excl.* [1960s+] (US) a general. excl. of surprise, amazement. [SHIT n.[1] (1)

well, I'm sure!/to be sure! *excl.* [mid-19C] a general excl. of surprise, I *am* surprised, who would have thought?

well-in *adj.* **1** [mid-19C+] (Aus.) well-off, affluent. **2** [late 19C+] popular, secure, entrenched. **3** [20C] successfully ingratiated, on the way to a successful seduction (cf. WELL AWAY)]

wellington *n.* [1960s+] (Aus.) sexual intercourse. [rhy. sl. *wellington boot* = ROOT n.[1]]

well-inlaid/-inlayed *see* INLAID.

well-lined *adj.* [20C] rich, prosperous. [one *lines one's pockets*]

well-loaded *adj.*[1] [early 19C+] of a man, having notably large genitals (cf. WELL-ENDOWED).

well-loaded *adj.*[2] [late 19C+] (orig. US) drunk (cf. LOADED adj.[1]).

well-mended *adj.* [20C] (Irish) of an ill person, improved in health.

well-oiled *adj.* [20C] very drunk (cf. NECK OIL). [OILED]

well put-on *adj.* [20C] (Ulster) well-dressed.

well set up *phr.* [late 19C] (US) possessing a substantial dowry. [SE *set up*, established]

well-shod *adj.* [late 19C] (US) rich (cf. WELL-HEELED adj.[2]). [fig., but also, no doubt, lit. 'wearing good shoes']

well-sinking *adj.* [late 18C–late 19C] (Anglo-Ind.) making money. [digging for buried treasure]

well-sprung *adj.* [1910s–30s] drunk. [one is 'bouncing up and down']

well-stacked *adj.* [1950s+] (US) of a woman, attractive, esp. having a good figure, spec. large breasts and buttocks. [ext. of STACKED adj. (2)]

well-thatched *adj.* [late 19C] possessing a good head of hair. [ext. of TILED adj.[2] (2)]

well, to be sure! *see* WELL, I'M SURE!

well to live *phr.* [17C] somewhat drunk.

well under *adj.* [1910s+] (Aus.) drunk (cf. WELL AWAY). [UNDER THE INFLUENCE]

well-upholstered/-covered *adj.* [1930s+] of a person, plump, fleshy, fat.

well, what do you know? *excl.* [1910s+] an excl. of surprise, revelation.

welly *n.*[1] *see* WELLIE.

welly *n.*[2] [1970s+] a kick, acceleration, usu. in phr. *give it some welly*, to make something go faster, to accelerate, to put some more energy into one's efforts. [SE *wellington boot*]

welly *v.* [1960s+] to kick, to trip up. [WELLY n.[2]]

welsh *see* WELCH.

Welsh bait *see* SCOTCH BAIT.

Welsh comb *see* WELCH COMB.

Welsh cricket *n.* [late 16C–early 17C] a louse. [neg. stereotyping]

Welsh ejectment *n.* [early–mid-19C] removing the roof of a tenant's house, with the purpose of making the house uninhabitable. [the stereotyped meanness of the Welsh]

welsher *see* WELCHER.

Welsh fiddle *see* SCOTCH FIDDLE.

Welsh goat *n.* [mid-18C–mid-19C] a Welshman.

Welshie/Welshy *n.* **1** [1920s] (Aus.) a native of New South Wales. **2** [1950s+] a Welshman.

Welsh parsley *n.* [early–mid-17C] hemp, as used in the hangman's rope.

Welshy *see* WELSHIE.

welter *n.* [late 19C] something exceptionally big or heavy of its kind. [northern dial.]

wen *n.* [mid-19C+] new; thus, *teg a wen eno*, get a new one. [backsl.]

wench *n.* [1980s+] (US campus) **1** an unpleasant woman (cf. BITCH n.[1]). **2** a promiscuous woman. **3** a woman. [SE use, coined c.1290, is archaic]

wench of the game *n.* [17C] a prostitute (cf. ON THE GAME). [SE *wench* + GAME n.[1]]

wendy *n.* [1980s+] (juv.) a school child (of either sex) who has been rejected by their fellows (cf. GOGGY). [? *Wendy*, the 'goody-goody' daughter in J.M. Barrie's *Peter Pan* (1904)]

went down like a/useless as a pork chop/slice of bacon at a Jewish wedding *phr.* [20C] failed utterly, usually in the way of making a gross social faux pas. [the prohibition on pork in orthodox Judaism]

went mad, and they shot him, he *phr.* [1940s+] (Aus.) a general phr. used in the reply to the question 'Where is X?' (cf. PADRE'S BIKE)]

wentworth falls/wentworth's balls *n.* [1920s+] (Aus.) the testicles. [rhy. sl. *Wentworth Falls* = BALLS n.[1] (1), ult. the *Wentworth Falls*, near Katoomba in the Blue Mountains of New South Wales]

were you born in a barn? *phr.* [mid-19C+] a phr. aimed at anyone who has failed to shut a door after entering a room.

were you born in a tent? *phr.* [1950s+] (Aus.) a phr. aimed at anyone who has failed to shut a door after entering a room. [var. on WERE YOU BORN IN A BARN?]

werris *n.* [1960s+] (Aus.) a Greek. [rhy. sl. *Werris Creek*]

Wessi *n.* [1990s] an occupant of the former West Germany (cf. OSSI). [Ger. sl.; ult. from *Westdeutsche*, West German]

west central *n.* [mid-19C] a water closet. [a pun on SE *WC*/the *W.C.* (west central) London postal district]

west coast turnarounds *n.* [1980s+] (drugs) amphetamines (cf. A n.[2]). [their use in keeping long distance drivers awake]

west hams *n.* [20C] nerves. [rhy. sl. *West Ham reserves*]

west hell *n.* [1900s–40s] (US) anywhere considered as far away, unpleasant and culturally alien (cf. BEE-LUTHER-HATCHEE).

westie *n.* [1970s+] (Aus.) one who lives in the *western* suburbs of Sydney (cf. PARRA).

Westminster abbey *n.* [20C] a cabbie. [rhy. sl.]

Westminster brougham *see* WHITECHAPEL BROUGHAM.

Westminster wedding *n.* [late 17C–18C] 'A Whore and a Rogue Married together' (B.E.) (cf. GO TO WESTMINSTER FOR A WIFE). [the contemporary neg. reputation of Westminster]

Westphalia *n.* [late 19C–1920s] the posterior, the buttocks. [pun on *Westphalia* ham/SE *ham*, the upper thigh]

Westralia *n.* [late 19C+] (Aus.) *Western Aus*tralia; thus *Westralian*, *Westralienne*, a Western Australian. [abbr.]

wet *n.*[1] [late 17C+] a drink.

wet *n.*[2] [late 19C+] (orig. juv.) an ineffectual, weak, foolish person.

wet, the *n.*[3] [late 19C+] (Aus.) the rainy season.

wet *n.*[4] [1920s+] the act of urination. [SE *wet*, to urinate]

wet *n.*[5] *see* WETBACK.

wet *adj.*[1] **1** [early 18C–mid-19C] drunk. **2** [mid-18C+] of a woman, sexually excited, 'secreting lech-water'. **3** [late 19C] (US) permitting the sale of alcohol; thus a *wet state*.

wet *adj.*[2] [early 18C–mid-19C] of a Quaker, lax in the observances of the sect (cf. WET QUAKER).

wet *adj.*[3] [late 19C+] (usu. upper-middle-/upper-class) weak, spineless; thus *wetness*, weakness, ineffectuality, spinelessness.

wet *adj.*[4] [1970s] (US Black) suspicious. [play on FISHY]

wet *v.*[1] [mid-19C] to drink; thus *wet the other eye*, have another drink.

wet *v.*[2] [1990s] (US Black) to excite a woman. [vaginal secretions; note WET adj.[1] (3)]

wet affairs *see* WET WORK.

wetback/wet *n.* [1940s+] a derog. term for an illegal Mexican immigrant to the USA; thus for Mexicans and so Hispanics in general. [the condition of the immigrants who traditionally swim the Rio Grande as the best means of beating border checks. Despite its reputation as a racist slur, Hispanics accept it; thus Mex.Am. self-description *los mojados*, the wet ones]

wet bargain *n.* [17C] a deal concluded over drinks (cf. DUTCH BARGAIN).

wet behind the ears *phr.* [1920s+] naïve, inexperienced, gauche (cf. DRY BEHIND THE EARS).

wet blanket *n.* [early 19C+] a dreary person, a spoilsport. [the use of a wet blanket to quench fires]

wetbrain *n.* [1970s+] a fool, a simpleton. [SE *water on the brain*, i.e. encephalitis]

wet deck *n.* [late 19C+] (Can./US) a woman or prostitute who performs serial sex acts (cf. BUTTERED BUN). [the accumulation of sexual fluids]

wet dream *n.* [1920s+] a fantasy, esp. a particularly optimistic one.

wet enough to bog a duck *phr.* [late 19C+] (Aus.) extremely wet.

wet foot *n.* [1960s+] a naïve, inexperienced, innocent person (cf. WET GOOSE).

wet goods *n.* [mid-19C] alcohol. [opp. of SE *dry goods*, groceries etc]

wet goose *n.* [20C] a foolish, naïve person. [WET adj.[3] + GOOSE n.[2] (1)]

wet hand/wet 'un *n.* [late 19C] a drunkard, a heavy drinker. [WET adj.[1] (1)]

wethead *n.* [1970s+] (US Black) a simpleton, an innocent, a novice (cf. WET BEHIND THE EARS). [SE *wet* + sfx. -HEAD (1)]

wet leg *n.* [1920s–30s] a self-pitying person. [? they are fig. urinating down their own leg]

wet nose *n.* [1940s+] (orig. US) a small child with a running nose.

wet one *n.* [late 19C+] a loose breaking of wind.

wet one's goozle, to *phr.* [19C] (US) to have a drink. [SE *wet* + GOOZLE n.[1]]

wet one's neck, to *phr.* [early 19C] to get drunk.

wet one's pants, to *phr.* [1970s+] to panic, to lose control. [the involuntary urination that may follow great fear]

wet one's whistle, to *phr.* [early 16C+] to take a drink (cf. DRENCH ONE'S GIZZARD). [14C + SE *whistle*, the throat]

wet parson *n.* [late 18C–early 19C] a parson with a taste for liquor (cf. WET QUAKER). [WET adj.[1] (1) + SE *parson*]

wet Quaker *n.* [late 17C–19C] one who pretends to be religious and abjure alcohol, but in fact drinks regularly in secret (cf. WET PARSON). [WET adj.[1] (1) + *Quaker*]

wet rag *n.* [1970s+] (US campus) an unpleasant, unpopular person.

wet smack *n.* [1920s+] (US) a weakling, an ineffectual person. [WET adj.[4] + fig use of SE *smack*]

wetter *n.* [late 19C] a soaking.

wet the baby's head, to *phr.* [late 19C+] to drink in celebration of a baby's birth.

wet the deal, to *phr.* [mid-19C+] to seal a deal with a drink.

wet-thee-through *n.* [mid-19C] gin.

wet the other/t'other eye, to *phr.* [mid-18C–mid-19C] to follow one drink immediately by another.

wet the tea leaves, to *phr.* [20C] to make tea.

wettie *n.* [1990s] (N.Z.) a wet suit. [abbr.]

wet t'other eye, to *see* WET THE OTHER EYE.

wet trance *n.* [late 19C–1900s] a daydream; thus *in a wet trance*, distracted, lost in thought.

wet 'un *n.*[1] [mid-19C] a diseased cow, technically unfit for human consumption, but often sold for conversion into sausages. [*wet 'un* presumably means 'wet brain' and the disease must have been the same as, or at least similar to, the late-20C BSE, 'mad cow disease']

wet 'un *n.*[2] *see* WET HAND.

wet 'uns *n.* [late 19C] tears.

wet-wash Baptist *n.* [20C] (US) a Baptist (cf. DRY-CLEAN METHODIST). [the method of baptism – Baptists use total immersion]

wet week *n.* [20C] (Irish) a short time. [? being *wet* it 'shrinks']

wet work/affairs *n.* [1970s+] assassination, esp. as carried out by secret services; thus *to get wet*, to be assassinated. [trans. KGB sl. *Mokryye Dela*, the department of wet affairs]

wewi *see* WEE-WEE n.[1].

we wuz robbed! *excl.* [1930s+] we were cheated! [coined by US boxing Manager Joe Jacobs, manager in 1932 of the German world heavyweight champion Max Schmeling. Defending his title in America, Schmeling systematically destroyed his opponent but was still declared the loser, outpointed by the challenger, local boy Jack Sharkey. Jacobs' phrase made his feelings plain]

w.g.f. *phr.* [1960s+] used by transsexuals to mean *whole girl fantasy*. [abbr.]

whack/wack *n.*[1] [mid-18C] a blow, usu. with some form of stick. [WHACK v.[1]]

whack/wack *n.*[2] **1** [late 18C+] a share, a portion. **2** [early 19C+] (US) a try, an attempt (cf. CRACK n.[14]; POP n.[5]). [fig. uses of WHACK v.[1]]

whack/wack *n.*[3] [late 19C–1920s] (Anglo-Irish.) food, sustenance. [Scot. *whack*, a slice, appetite]

whack/wack *n.*[4] [1920s–30s] a rage, a bad temper. [abbr. PADDYWHACK n.[2] (2)]

whack/wack *n.*[5] [1940s+] (US) a crazy or weird person. [abbr. WHACKO n.]

whack/wack *n.*[6] [1980s+] (US campus) a fool. [abbr. WHACKO]

whack/wack *v.*[1] [early 18C+] **1** to hit. **2** [late 19C+] to murder. **3** [late 19C+] to defeat in a competition. **4** [1940s+] (US) to cut or chop. **5** [1970s+] (US drugs) to dilute or 'cut' a narcotic.

whack/wack *v.*[2] [early 19C] to share or divide equally, thus *whack the blunt*, share out the money. **2** to charge money, usu. *whack for ...* . [WHACK n.[2] (1)]

whack-a-doo *n.* [20C] lunatic, eccentric (cf. WHACK n.[5]). [ext. of WHACKO n.]

whack/wack attack *n.*[1] [1980s+] (US Black) the onset of apparent insanity, usu. through the use of drugs. [WHACK n.[6] + SE *attack*]

whack/wack attack *n.*[2] [1980s+] masturbation. [WHACK n.[1] + SE *attack*]

whack/wack down *v.* [20C] to lay down money, to write down notes. [WHACK v.[1]]

whacked/wacked out *adj.*[1] (orig. US) **1** [late 19C+] murdered. **2** [late 19C+] exhausted. **3** [1950s+] having lost all one's money gambling. **4** [1970s+] under the influence of a drug or of alcohol. [WHACK v.[1]]

whacked/wacked out *adj.*[2] [20C] crazy, insane, eccentric. [WHACKO n.]

whacked/wacked to the wide *phr.* [late 19C+] absolutely exhausted. [WHACK v.[1]]

whacker *n.*[1] [19C] anything especially large or notable, e.g. a lie (cf. BUMPER n.[1]).

whacker *n.*[2] [1960s+] (Aus.) a fool. [WHACKY adj., but note WHACK OFF; thus the mythical links of masturbation and insanity]

whacker/wacker *n.*[3] [1980s+] (US) a masturbator. [WHACK OFF]

whacker *adj. see* WACKER adj.

whacking *n.* [mid-19C+] a blow, a beating. [WHACK v.[1]]

whacking *adj.* [early 19C+] a general intensifier usu. in *whacking great, whacking horrible* etc (cf. LICKING adj.).

whack/wack it *v.* [1960s+] to masturbate (cf. WHACK OFF). [fig. use of WHACK v.[1] (1)]

whack/wack it in/up *v.* [mid-19C+] of a man, to have sexual intercourse. [fig. use of WHACK v.[1] (1)]

whack/wack it out, to *phr.* [1910s–20s] to defend or support successfully. [WHACK v.[1] (1)]

whack it up *see* WHACK IT IN.

whacko *n.* [1970s+] an unstable or mentally ill person. [WHACKO adj.]

whacko *adj.* [1970s+] crazy, insane, eccentric. [WHACKY adj.]

whacko! *excl.* [1940s+] (Aus.) a general excl. of pleasure.

whack/wack off *v.* [1960s+] to masturbate (cf. BEAT OFF; WHACK IT). [fig. use of WHACK v.[1] (1)]

whacko the chook/goose *phr.* [1970s+] (Aus.) excellent, first-rate, absolutely wonderful. [WHACKO! + CHOOK/goose]

whacko the diddle-oh *phr.* [1960s+] (Aus.) excellent, splendid, first-rate. [WHACKO-THE-DIDDLE-OH!]

whacko the diddle-oh! *excl.* [1960s+] (Aus.) a general excl. of pleasure, esp. on seeing an attractive woman. [ext. WHACKO!]

whacko the goose *see* WHACKO THE CHOOK.

whack/wack out *v.* [1950s+] (US gambling) to lose all one's money. [ext. of WHACK v.[1] (3)]

whack/wack someone out *v.* [20C] to kill, to murder. [WHACK v.[1] (2)]

whack/wack the one-eyed worm/the weasel, to *phr.* [1960s+] to masturbate (cf. PROMPT ONE'S PORPOISE).

whack-up *n.* [early 19C+] a division of the spoils. [fig. use of WHACK v.[2]]

whack up *v.*[1] [late 19C] (US) to make a contribution, a donation.

whack up *v.*[2] [late 19C+] (US) to divide the loot. [WHACK-UP]

whack/wack willy *v.* [20C] to masturbate. [WHACK v.[1] + WILLIE n.[1]]

whacky/wacky *adj.* [1930s+] (orig. US) eccentric. [Yorks. dial. *whacky*, a fool, a simpleton, a blockhead; also Warwickshire dial. *whacky*, left-handed]

-whacky/-wacky *sfx.* [1930s+] (US) comb. adj. to describe an enthusiasm or habit e.g. *car-wacky*, car crazy. [WHACKY adj.]

whacky/wacky baccy/weed *n.* [1980s+] (drugs) marijuana. [WHACKY adj. + abbr. SE *tobacco/WEED* n.[1] (4)]

wha' gwaan *see* WHAT A GWAAN.

whail/whale *v.* [1940s–60s] (US Black) to do something especially well or efficiently (cf. WAIL).

whale *n.*[1] **1** [late 19C] (US campus) an exceptionally brilliant scholar. **2** [late 19C+] (US) an exceptionally large or fat person. [joc. uses of SE, the size of the creature]

whale *n.*[2] [20C] anchovies on toast.

whale *v.*[1] [early 19C+] (US) to hit, thrash or trounce. [? SE *wale*, to mark the flesh with wales (weals), or a *whale*bone whip]

whale *v.*[2] *see* WHAIL.

whale and whitewash *n.* [1920s–30s] (tramp) fish in white sauce.

whale away *v.* [mid-19C+] (US) to attack or work at something vigorously. [ext. of WHALE v.[1]]

whale in the bay *n.* [1960s+] (Aus.) someone who has money to spend and uses it on the assembled company (cf. CAPTAIN n.[4]).

whale into *v.* [20C] to attack physically. [ext. WHALE v.]

whale of a *phr.* [1910s+] (orig. US) a good deal of, a large amount of.

whale on, be a *v.* [late 19C] (US) to be very good at or keen on.

whaler *n.* [mid–late 19C] (US) anything considered large of its kind. [SE *whale*]

whaler's delight *n.* [1900s–20s] (Aus.) brown sugar mixed with cold tea to make a thick paste (cf. BULLOCKY'S DELIGHT). [WHALER n.[2] + SE *delight*]

whales on *adj.* [late 19C] (US) obsessed with, devoted to (cf. GO AHEAD LIKE A WHALE). [the size of a whale]

whale the shit/piss out of, to *phr.* [20C] to beat viciously. [WHALE v. (1) + SHIT n.[1]/PISS n.]

whale the tar out of, to *phr.* [late 19C] (US) to beat severely (cf. BEAT THE TAR OUT OF; TAR OUT).

whaling *see* WAILING.

w.h.a.m./w.h.a.m.s. *n.* [1980s+] (US campus) a woman who harms men physically or emotionally. [abbr. *women hate all men/women have all men scared*]

wham *n.* [1970s+] (US Black) a large, aggressive man. [WHAM v.]

wham *v.* [1920s+] (orig. US) to hit or strike. [echoic]

wham!/whammo! *excl.* [1940s+] (US) used to express surprise or convey the impact of a sudden violent attack or blow. [echoic]

wham-bam-thank-you-ma'am *phr.* [late 19C+] epitomizing brief sexual intercourse intended on the whole for male satisfaction only (cf. BIP-BAM-THANK-YOU-MA'AM). [echoic]

whambang *adj.* [1920s+] (US) loud, large and impressive.

whamdanglers *n.* [1990s] an extremely large pair of breasts. [WHAM n. + SE *dangle*]

whammer *n.* [20C] the penis (cf. ARSE-OPENER). [WHAM v.]

whammo! *see* WHAM!

whammy *n.* **1** [1950s+] a 'hex', an evil influence, the evil eye. **2** [1950s+] a punchline, anything devastating and beyond a similarly powerful response (cf. DOUBLE WHAMMY; TRIPLE WHAMMY). **3** [1980s+] (US campus) an extremely unattractive woman. [WHAM v. Note *Whammy*, a character who can paralyse with a stare in comic strip *Li'l Abner*]

whang *n.*[1] [early 19C+] a reverberating blow. [WHANG v.]

whang *n.*[2] [20C] (Irish) a thin, lanky person. [Scot. *whang*, a bootlace]

whang *n.*[3] [1910s+] a large piece, a portion, share (cf. WHANG n.[2]).

whang *n.*[4] [1930s+] (orig. US) the penis (cf. WANG n.).

whang *v.* **1** [early 19C+] to hit. **2** [early 19C+] to throw, drive, pull etc with force or with violent impact. **3** [1950s+] to shoot at. [SE *thong*, to flog or lash with a thong, ult. f. ON §*vengja*, to secure or fasten with a thong]

whangdoodle/wangdoodle/wingdoodle *n.*[1] (US) **1** [mid-19C] a mythical beast of uncertain character. **2** [20C] an unspecified object, something one does not know the name of. [nonsense word; (2) is fig. use of (1)]

whangdoodle/wangdoodle/wingdoodle *n.*[2] (US) [1970s+] the penis (cf. DOODLE n.[2]). [ext. of WHANG n.[4]]

whangee *n.* [late 18C+] a cane. [Chinese *huang*, bamboo sprouts that were too old for eating; thus the *whangee* was a cane made from the stem of one or other species of *Phyllostachys*, Chinese and Japanese plants allied to and resembling bamboos]

whanger *n.* [1930s+] the penis. [ext. WHANG n.[4]]

whap v. [mid-19C+] to hit. [? echoic]

wha'ppen phr. [1960s+] (W.I./UK Black teen) a form of greeting meaning what's happening?, what's going on?, how are you?

whapper see WHOPPER.

whapping see WHOPPING.

whap that thing! excl. [1960s–70s] (US Black) congratulatory remark to a passing woman, implying her supreme sexiness. [WHAP v.]

wharfie n. [1910s+] (Aus./N.Z.) docker. [SE wharf, the usu. Aus./N.Z. term for SE dock]

wharf-rat n. [mid–late 19C] (orig. US) anyone who hangs around wharfs, looking out for an opportunity to steal from a cargo. [SE wharf + RAT n.[3]]

what!/eh, what! excl.[1] [late 18C+] an expletive tacked on to the end of a sentence to give it greater emphasis but of no actual meaning.

what? excl.[2] [early 19C+] **1** short for What did you say? or What is it? **2** used as an affirmative at the end of a statement, isn't it/he/etc, e.g. That's a nasty fellow, what?

what a beanfeast! excl. [late 19C] a satirical remark intended to underline that the situation is in fact far from a 'beanfeast', but in fact second-rate, poor etc.

what a/wha' gwaan? phr. [1960s+] (W.I./UK Black teen) what is going on? what's happening? how are things?

what-all n. [20C] anything for which one has no proper name, often as I don't know what all.

what a/with a pox! excl. [late 16C+] a general excl. of annoyance, irritation (cf. POX!; POX ON!). [POX n.[1]]

what are you, new? phr. [1990s] (US teen) how could you not have realized that?

what are you pushing? phr. [1970s] (US Black) what sort of car do you drive?

what are you working out of? phr. [1990s] (US Black) an invitation to explain oneself, to justify one's actions or opinions.

what a trip! excl. [1960s+] how bizarre, how strange, what an odd experience. [TRIP n.[3] (2)]

what a turn-up! excl. [1970s+] what a surprise. [abbr. TURN-UP FOR THE BOOK]

what can I do you for? phr. [1920s+] a facetious reversal of SE what can I do for you?. [DO v.[4]]

whatchamacallit n. [mid-19C+] anything to which one cannot give a name when required (cf. THINGUMMIBOB).

what clock? see WHAT WATCH?

what did thought do? phr. [late 18C–19C] one of a variety of phr. that answer the excuse, 'I only thought ...', e.g. What did thought do? Lay in bed and beshit himself, What did thought do? Ran away with another man's wife.

what did you say? phr. [late 19C] a phr. used between two friends on viewing someone who appears to be either genuinely important, rich or otherwise self-regarding.

what does it look like? phr. [1970s] (US campus) hello (cf. WHAT'S HAPPENING?).

what dog is a-hanging? see WHOSE DOG IS DEAD?

what do I owe you? see DO I OWE YOU ANYTHING?

what-do-you-call-it n. [19C] the vagina (cf. DOWN BELOW). [euph.]

what do you know? phr. [1910s+] a greeting, 'hello and how are you', 'what are you/have you been doing?' (cf. WHAT'S HAPPENING?; WHAT'S SHAKING?).

what do you say? phr. [1920s+] (US) how are you?

what do you want, jam on it? see DO YOU WANT JAM ON IT?

what-d'you-call-it/-d'ye call 'em n. [mid-19C+] anything for which one has no precise name (cf. WHATCHAMACALLIT).

what else did you get for Christmas? phr. [1960s+] (US/Aus.) addressed to a driver who keeps honking their horn.

[the implication is that the horn is some kind of new and exciting toy]

what else is new? phr. [1960s+] (orig. US) deprecating comment on anything the previous speaker has said, esp. if that speaker had intended to make a big impression.

what-er?/what-y? n. [late 19C] a form of 'what' used when questioning the previous speaker's self-description, e.g. 'I'm a butcher.' 'A what-er?'

whatever adv. **1** [late 19C+] whatever happens, at all events. **2** [1990s] (US Black/teen) a general expression of dismissal, disinterest.

whatever floats your boat phr. [1980s+] (US campus) an expression of acceptance, I agree, you're right.

whatever turns you on phr. [1970s+] whatever you like, esp. as slightly sarcastic response to a revelation of an especially bizarre or distasteful pleasure (usu. sexual). [TURN ONE v. (4)]

what-for n. [late 19C+] a punishment, trouble, a fuss. [? abbr. of the question 'what are you doing this to me/is this happening for?']

what gives? phr. [1940s+] a general greeting; thus what gives with — ?, how is — ?, what is happening with — ? [Yid. vi geht's?, how goes it?]

what goes around comes around phr. [1970s+] (orig. US Black) fate determines what happens in life, esp. as regards one's treatment – good or bad – of others. [popular philosophizing]

what happen?/happening? excl. [1970s+] (W.I./UK Black) a general form of greeting, 'Hello, how are you?'

what Harry gave Doll n. [18C–19C] sexual intercourse. [generic use of proper names]

what has got — ? phr. [early 19C] what has happened to — ?

what ho! excl. [mid-19C+] a general excl., usu. of greeting.

what ho, she bumps! excl. [late 19C+] an excl. used on seeing a special display of energy, esp. by a woman. [orig. used of a boat moving through choppy seas]

what in blue blazes?/who the blazes?/why the blazes? excl. [early 19C+] a general excl. of extreme surprise, absolute confusion etc. [BLUE BLAZES, i.e. euph for HELL]

what/why in time? phr. [mid–late 19C] (US) a question, often deriving from one's incomprehension or surprise, 'what on earth', 'what in the world' etc.

what is it? phr. [1970s] (US campus) a greeting.

what is the matter with — ? phr. **1** [early 18C+] of people, what is your problem or trouble? **2** [late 19C+] of objects, ideas, what is the problem/difficulty?, what is the objection to?

what is this, Christmas? excl. [1980s+] a general excl. of pleasurable surprise.

what it B like? phr. [1980s+] (US Black gang) greeting used by the Bloods, one of the two leading Los Angeles gangs.

what it C like? phr. [1980s+] (US Black gang) greeting used by the Crips, one of the two leading Los Angeles gangs.

what it is! excl. [1980s+] (US Black) a friendly greeting, hello, how are you?

what it takes n. [1920s+] (orig. US) money (cf. NEEDFUL). [the centrality of money to daily life]

what makes one tick phr. [1930s+] the motives, personal characteristics etc that determine someone's behaviour.

what next – and next? phr. [late 19C] a phr. used to pour scorn on what is seen as an especially specious statement or claim.

what-nosed adj. [19C] drunk. [play on 'what do they know?', being so drunk + the swollen/red nose of drunkenness]

what odds?/what's the odds? phr. [mid-19C] what's the difference?

what-oh *n.* [1910s–20s] a 'fast' young woman. [the appreciative *what*, *oh* remark of a watching male]

what one is driving at *phr.* [1960s+] (US) the meaning or point of one's words or actions.

what Paddy gave the drum *phr.* [mid-19C+] (orig. milit.) a thrashing, a beating (cf. PADDYWHACK).

what price ... /what price the ... *phr.* [late 19C+] what do you think of (something/someone) now? [racing use *price*, the odds]

what say? *excl.* [1930s+] (orig. US) what did you say?, what was that?, what do you think?

what's biting you? *phr.* [1960s+] what's the matter? what's the problem?

what's buzzin' cousin? *phr.* [1930s+] (US) what's happening?, how have you been? [BUZ n.² + assonance]

what's cooking? *phr.* [1930s+] (orig. US) a phr. of greeting, what's going on? [jazz use]

what's crawling you? *phr.* [1910s+] what's the matter? [ref. is to lice]

what's going down? *see* WHAT'S HAPPENING?.

what's going on? *phr.* [1960s+] a common greeting (cf. WHAT'S HAPPENING?).

what shakes? *phr.* [mid-19C] (Und.) what chance is there of stealing something? [SE *shake*]

what-shall-call-um *n.* [early–mid-19C] a prostitute, a promiscuous woman. [euph.]

what's happening/what's going down *n.* [1960s+] (orig. US Black) the fashionable, chic, smart event, place, show etc; thus *not what's happening*, the opposite. [HAPPENING adj.]

what's happening? *phr.* [1960s+] a greeting, hello and how are you?, what are you/have you been doing? (cf. HOW'S TRICKS?; NOTHING HAPPENING; WHAT'S SHAKING?).

whatshisface/-herface/-hisass/-herass *n.* [20C] used for a name one has temporarily forgotten (cf. WHATSHISNAME).

whatshisname/-hername/-yourname/whatsname *n.* [late 17C+] any person or thing to which one cannot give a proper name.

whatsie *n.* [1950s+] (Aus.) any person or thing to which one cannot give a proper name. [abbr. WHATSHISNAME]

what's in it for me? *phr.* [20C] an honest statement of selfishness.

whatsit/whatsis/whatzis *n.* [late 19C+] (US) an unspecified or unspecifiable person or object.

what's it in aid of? *phr.* [1930s+] what exactly is the reason for all this?

what's its name *n.* [late 19C] the penis. [euph.]

what's it to you? *phr.* [20C] an aggressive reply to a questioner implying that whatever the answer may be, it is none of their business.

what's jumping *phr.* [1980s+] (US campus) a greeting (cf. WHAT'S BUZZIN' COUSIN?).

whatsname *see* WHATSHISNAME.

what's new? *phr.* [1960s+] a general greeting (cf. WHAT'S HAPPENING?).

what's on the rail for the lizard? *phr.* [1930s–40s] (US Black) what have you got to offer? esp. in context of money, sexual favours and other exciting, if unrespectable, pleasures.

what's shaking? *phr.* [1950s+] (US) a greeting, hello and how are you? (cf. NOTHING SHAKING; WHAT'S HAPPENING?). [SE *shake*]

what's that when it's at home?/who is he/she when he's/she's at home? *phr.* [late 19C+] deliberate misunderstanding of a word or statement, which the speaker is implying to be too 'clever' for them to understand.

what's the big idea? *phr.* [1910s+] (orig. US) more a threat than a question, usu. asked when someone is doing or saying something of which the speaker disapproves.

what's the deal? *phr.* [1940s+] (US) what's happening? what's going on?

what's the dynamite now? *phr.* [late 19C] (society) a phr. used when faced with a sudden burst of ill-temper. [the *dynamite* outrages of the period carried out by the Irish Republicans]

what's the good word? *phr.* [20C] (US) a cordial greeting, how are you?

what's the joke? *phr.* [1990s] (US teen) a phr. used when you can't believe something that just happened.

what's the lyddite now? *phr.* [1900s] a phr. used when faced with a sudden burst of ill-temper (cf. WHAT'S THE DYNAMITE NOW?). [SE *lyddite*, a high explosive, chiefly composed of picric acid, used in the manufacture of explosive shells]

what's the odds? *see* WHAT ODDS?

what's the percentage? *phr.* [mid-19C+] (orig. US) what's the point? what's the intention?; thus *no percentage*, no point, no advantage. [gambling use]

what's the scam? *phr.* [1960s+] (US) what's happening?, what's going on? [SCAM n.]

what's the story morning glory? *see* WHAT'S YOUR STORY MORNING GLORY?

what's the verdict? *phr.* [1990s] (US Black) what's happening?, what's going on?

what's the word! Thunderbird! *phr.* [1950s–60s] (US Black) a greeting. [assonance + ref. to *Thunderbird*, a sweet, fortified wine]

what's to pay? *phr.* [late 19C–1940s] what is the matter?

what suit did you give it up on? *phr.* [early 19C] how did it affect your intentions/actions? [card-playing imagery]

what's/what up? *excl.* [late 19C+] **1** a general enquiry or greeting. **2** what's the matter? esp. in *what's up with you/her/etc.*

what's up, G? *phr.* [1990s] (orig. US) a greeting. [WHAT'S UP + G n.⁷]

what's up with that? *phr.* [1990s] (US teen) what is going on or why is one doing something?

what's what/what goes *n.* [mid-16C+] the facts, the whole situation, usu. in phr. e.g. [17C+] *show what's what*, [18C+] *perceive what's what*, [19C+] *tell what's what*, [19C+] *understand what's what* (cf. KNOW WHAT'S WHAT).

what's with — ? *phr.* [1930s+] (US) what's the meaning of — ?, what's the matter with — ?

what's your dub? *phr.* [1990s] (US teen) what is your World-Wide Web location? [computer jargon *dub*, an Internet address]

what's your fighting weight? *phr.* [late 19C] a challenge to a fight.

what's your poison?/medicine? *phr.* [mid-19C+] a general invitation to have a drink (cf. NAME YOUR POISON; WHAT WILL YOU HAVE?). [POISON n.¹ (1)/MEDICINE n. (1)]

what's yours? *phr.* [1920s+] an invitation to take a drink.

what's your song, King Kong *phr.* [1940s] (US Black) how are you? how do you feel? [assonance]

what's your/the story morning glory? *phr.* **1** [1930s–50s] (US Black) explain yourself, what are you up to? **2** [1940s+] (orig. US) a general greeting: how are you? [(2) grew in popularity in the UK after the 1995 release of the album (*What's the Story*) *Morning Glory?* by Oasis]

whatter *see* WHATTY.

what the blazes *see* HOW THE BLAZES.

what the bloody letter! *see* WHAT THE LETTER!

what the cat dragged in *phr.* [20C] (US) something or someone unpleasant, nasty.

what the Connaught man shot at *n.* [late 19C] (Anglo-Irish) nothing (cf. FOOTLESS STOCKING WITHOUT A LEG).

what/who/why the devil! *excl.* [17C+] a general excl. indicative of annoyance or surprise. [all intensified forms of SE *why?*]

what the dickens? *excl.* [late 16C+] what the Devil? [euph.]

what the ding-dong! *excl.* [20C] a mild oath. [euph. for *Devil*]

what the fuck!/shit! *excl.* [20C] an excl. of shock, surprise (cf. WHAT THE HELL!; WHAT THE DEVIL!). [FUCK n.¹/SHIT n.¹ (1)]

what the Hanover! *excl.* [1900s–10s] an excl. of surprise, shock, alarm or resignation etc. [euph., via the initial 'h', for WHAT THE HELL!]

what the hell! *excl.* [early 19C+] a general excl. indicative of annoyance or surprise.

what the letter!/bloody letter! *excl.* [1910s–20s] semi-euph. oath, i.e. *what the bloody hell!* [pun on *hell/ell*]

what the Sam Hill! *excl.* [early 19C+] (US) an excl. of surprise, shock, alarm or resignation etc. [euph., via the initial 'h', for WHAT THE HELL!]

what the shit! *see* WHAT THE FUCK!

what the something-something! *excl.* [20C] a general euph. excl. (cf. BLANKETY-BLANK).

whatty/whatter *n.* [late 18C–early 19C; 20C] 'what did you say?', e.g. *You saw a whatter?*

what up? *see* WHAT'S UP?

what up dog? *phr.* [1990s] (US Black teen) a general greeting. [WHAT'S UP + DOG n.²⁴]

what watch?/clock? *phr.* [1950s+] (Aus.) what time is it?

what will you have? *phr.* [mid-19C+] a general invitation to have a drink (cf. WHAT'S YOUR MEDICINE?).

what will you liq? *phr.* [late 19C] (middle-class) what would you like to drink? [LIQ]

what would Mrs Boston say? *phr.* [late 19C] (US) a phr. mocking what might be seen as a risqué action or statement. [the equivalent of the UK *What will Mrs Grundy say?* In both cases the fictional lady is seen as a representative of prudish, censorious opinion]

what-y *see* WHAT-ER.

what you know? *phr.* [1980s+] (US campus) a greeting, hello.

what you see is what you get *phr.* [20C] (US) the situation, object or person is as it appears to be, nothing more, nothing less.

whatzis *see* WHATSIT.

whazood *adj.* [1970s+] (US campus) drunk. [var. on WAZZOCKED]

w.h.b. *phr.* [late 19C–1900s] men who take unwanted liberties with women, 'gropers'. [abbr. *wandering hand brigade*]

wheadle/wheedle *n.* [late 17C–early 19C] (Und.) a sharper, a confidence trickster; thus *cut a wheadle*, to ensnare a victim. [WHEADLE v.]

wheadle/wheedle *v.* [late 17C–early 19C] (Und.) to cheat. [SE *wheedle*, to flatter]

wheat *n.* [1960s+] (drugs) marijuana (cf. HAY n.³).

wheat belt *n.* [1920s+] (Aus.) a prostitute. [? pun on OATS n.¹]

wheedle *n. see* WHEADLE n.

wheedle *v.¹ see* WHEADLE v.

wheedle *v.² see* WHIDDLE.

wheedle *v.³* [early 18C] to inform on. [WHIDDLE]

wheedle the tire off a cart's wheel, can *phr.* [late 19C] (US) used of one who is supremely persuasive.

wheek *v.* [20C] (Ulster) to steal. [Antrim dial. *wheek*, to snatch away]

wheeker *n.* [20C] (Ulster) anything exceptionally good. [WHEEK, i.e. something worth stealing]

wheel *n.¹* **1** [19C] a 5-shilling coin (cf. HIND-COACH WHEEL). **2** [early 19C–1900s] (US) a $1 coin. [abbr. CARTWHEEL]

wheel *n.²* [20C] (W.I.) a bicycle (cf. WHEELS n.¹).

wheel *n.³ see* BIG WHEEL.

wheel/wheels/wheels of steel *n.⁴* [1980s+] the record turntable or turntables as used by HIP-HOP and RAP n.⁵ DJs. [the

circular shape of the turntable, usu. used in pl. The DJ manipulates two turntables (some even use three), simultaneously, selecting the portions of records and mixing them together]

wheel *v.* **1** [late 19C+] to ride a bicycle or similar pedal-powered vehicle; thus *wheeler*, one who rides such a vehicle. **2** [1930s+] (US Black) to drive an automobile.

wheel! *excl.* [1980s+] (W.I./UK Black teen) a demand that a DJ replay a favourite song; thus phr. *wheel and come again*.

wheel and deal, to *phr.* [1960s+] (US) to engage in many business arrangements expressly to make a profit (cf. WHEELER-DEALER). [abbr. BIG WHEEL + SE *deal*]

wheel-band in the nick *phr.* [late 17C–early 19C] drinking in the normal fashion, tilting the glass over the left thumb (cf. SUPERNACULUM). [SE *wheelband in the nick*, a tyre that runs along a regular groove]

wheelchair *n.* [1940s] (US Black) a motor vehicle.

wheeled *adj.* **1** [late 19C] conveyed in a cab. **2** [late 19C] successful, rich, important. [WHEEL v.; i.e. one who goes about in a *wheeled* cab]

wheeler *n.* [late 19C–1910s] a cyclist. [WHEEL v.]

wheeler-dealer *n.* [1960s+] an entrepreneur, an 'operator' (cf. WHEEL AND DEAL). [abbr. BIG WHEEL + SE *dealer*]

wheelie *n.¹* [1960s+] a trick riding on the back wheel only of a motorcycle or bicycle.

wheelie *n.²* [1990s] a *wheel*chair. [abbr.]

wheel in/out *v.* [1950s+] (orig. US) of a person or an object, to bring in to or remove from a meeting, an interview etc, esp. in *imper. wheel one in*, bring one in!

wheelman *n.¹* [late 19C] (US) a cyclist (cf. WHEELER).

wheelman *n.²* [1930s+] (Und.) an expert car driver, either for the police or for criminals.

wheel of life *n.* [19C] a prison treadmill (cf. EVERLASTING STAIRCASE). [pun on SE *life*, existence/*life sentence*]

wheel out *see* WHEEL IN.

wheels *n.¹* [1950s+] **1** a car (cf. WHEEL v.). **2** (US) the legs.

wheels *n.² see* WHEEL n.⁴.

wheels came off *phr.* [1960s] events went wrong, plans did not turn out as expected. [automobile imagery]

wheels of steel *see* WHEEL n.⁴.

whee up *v.* [1940s+] (US) to excite, to stimulate. [echoic excl. *whee!*, inferring speediness + GEE UP]

wheeze *n.* [mid-19C+] a trick or dodge frequently used, also, a piece of special information, a 'tip'. [orig. theatre use, a joke or comic gag introduced into the performance by a clown or comedian, esp. a constantly repeated catchphrase]

wheeze *v.* [late 19C–1900s] to pass on information, to betray.

wheezy anna *n.* [20C] a spanner. [rhy. sl.]

Whelan the Wrecker *n.* [1940s+] (Aus.) a vandal. [the name of a demolition firm, *Whelan the Wrecker*, Sydney Road, Coburg, Melbourne]

whelk *n.* [mid-late 19C] the vagina; thus the fake-threatening phr. *I'll have your whelk* (cf. BEARDED CLAM). [equation of the vagina with fish]

whelp *n.* [mid-19C+] a native of Tennessee (cf. BUCKSHINE; MUDHEAD).

whelp *v.* [late 19C–1900s] to give birth.

when Adam was an oakum boy in Brooklyn Navy Yard/ in Chatham Dockyard *phr.* [mid-19C+] a very long time ago (cf. SINCE ADAM NAMED THE ANIMALS).

when cock get/make teeth *phr.* [20C] (W.I.) absolutely never (cf. WHEN FOWL CUT TEETH).

when donkeys wore high hats *phr.* [1920s–30s] a very long time ago.

when ever/whenever *conj.* [mid-19C+] emphatic form of SE *when*. [SE early 18C–mid-19C]

when fowl cut/get teeth *phr.* [20C] (W.I.) never ever.

when hens make holy water *phr.* [17C] never.

when pigs fly *phr.* [early 17C+] never.

when push comes to shove *phr.* [1950s+] (orig. US) in the final assessment, when all other alternatives have been exhausted. [SE *push* is seen as less aggressive than *shove*]

when the balloon goes up *phr.* [1910s+] (orig. milit.) the start of proceedings, esp. when there is a potential for controversy or argument. [? raising of an observation *balloon* immediately before an attack]

when the band begins to play *phr.* [late 19C–1910s] when matters become serious.

when the chips are down *phr.* [1940s+] in the final event, at the denouement, when one has no option. [poker imagery]

when the crow/eagle shits/when the eagle's bowels move *phr.* [1970s+] (Aus.) payday. [a bird is engraved on the reverse of an Australian dollar coin]

when the devil is blind *phr.* [mid-17C–1900s] never.

when the eagle's bowels move *see* WHEN THE CROW SHITS.

when the eagle shits/flies/screams/walks *phr.*[1] [1940s+] (orig. US milit./ Aus.) payday. [the *eagle* engraved on the US silver dollar coin]

when the eagle shits *phr.*[2] *see* WHEN THE CROW SHITS.

when the goose pisses/pisseth *phr.* [early 18C–1900s] never.

when the jack takes the ace *phr.* [19C] sexual intercourse (cf. IRISH WHIST). [JACK n.[8] (1) + ACE OF SPADES]

when the maggot bites *phr.* [early 17C–late 19C] when one finally chooses, lit. when one is dead.

when the mark buss/bust/burst *phr.* [20C] (W.I.) when the truth comes out, when the facts are revealed. [Carib.E. *mark*, one of the 36 symbols – a centipede, a hog, an old lady – used in the gambling game of *Whe-Whe*. Each is identified by a number and players bet on which number will be found to reveal the winning symbol in a round]

when the morning comes *phr.* [1970s+] (US Black) when hard times finally disappear.

when the numbers are up/go up *phr.* [late 19C+] (Aus.) when the result is known. [the raising of a board carrying the numbers of the winning horses after a horse-race]

when the plate-fleet comes in *phr.* [late 17C–early 19C] when one finally makes a fortune, 'when one's ship comes in'. [SE *Plate fleet*, the fleet that brought home the annual yield of silver from the Indies to Spain]

when the red is over the pink, go for the brown *phr.* [1990s] when a woman is menstruating, opt for anal intercourse. [snooker imagery]

when the road runs red, hit the dirt track *phr.* [1990s] when a woman is menstruating, opt for anal intercourse.

when the shit hits the fan *phr.* [1940s+] difficulties start to happen, usu. such problems have been expected to occur sooner or later. Euph. alternatives include *the omelette hits the fan*, *the excrement hits the air conditioning*, *the solids hit the air conditioning*.

when the whips are cracking *phr.* [20C] (Aus.) when the action begins.

when two Sundays meet/come together *phr.* [mid–late 17C] never. [proverbial use]

when-we *n.* [1980s+] (S.Afr.) an immigrant from a country once part of the British Empire who maintains their old beliefs, including feelings of racial superiority. Such figures, who were often middle-ranking administrators, also despise the South Africans among whom they have been forced to live. The type, drawn to S. Africa by apartheid, have presumably all but died out since majority rule. [the common use of *when we were in* ... to start a bitterly nostalgic sentence]

when you were ... *phr.* [1920s+] a phr. based on one's childhood, or even earlier life, all of which mean a very long time ago: (Aus.) *... just a dirty look*, *... just a gleam/twinkle in your father's eye*, *... still in/wearing short pants*, *... running up and down your father's backbone*, (Aus.) *when your mother was cutting bread on you.*

whereabouts *n.* [1920s+] (Aus.) male underpants. [pun on SE *wear-abouts*]

where are you a-going to – can't you! *phr.* [late 19C] used when one is pushed rudely by a passer-by.

where did they dig him/her/that up from? *phr.* [mid-19C+] used of someone considered odd, ugly, eccentric, generally out of place.

where did you get that hat? *phr.* [late 19C–1910s] (orig. US) a general jeer or shout of derision.

where did you get the Rossa? *phr.* [late 19C] (orig. US) used when seeing someone in borrowed plumes. [the report of a New York trial in which the defendant was asked that question]

where did you get your licence? *phr.* [1970s+] (Aus.) a general excl. of annoyance aimed at a poor or allegedly poor driver, often with a suggestion such as 'Woolworths?' 'off a Weetabix packet?' etc.

where did you spring from? *phr.* [early 19C+] used to address someone who has appeared unexpectedly or suddenly.

where do we go from here/there? *phr.* [1920s+] what happens now/next?

where has it got to? *phr.* [late 19C+] what has happened to something?

where it's at/happening *phr.* [1960s+] the truth, the right place, the ideal situation, opinion, experience, an expression of approval/affirmation.

where one is at/coming from/one's head is at *phr.* [1960s+] (orig. US Black) one's lifestyle, attitudes, philosophy, mood or overall emotional state.

where one lives *phr.* [mid-19C+] (orig. US) at a vital or central point of one's emotions, e.g. *that gets me right where I live.*

where one's head is at *see* WHERE ONE IS AT.

where's it at? *phr.* [1970s] (US campus) hello (cf. WHAT'S HAPPENING?).

where's the beef? *phr.* [1980s+] (US) what's the real point, importance, inner meaning, content etc. [slogan for Wendy's hamburgers in 1984 + play on BEEF n.[2]]

where's the fire? *phr.* [1920s+] (orig. US) where are you running to? what's the hurry?

where's the war? *phr.* [1900s] a phr. used on encountering a street wrangle. ['from the Boer War after June 1890 – when both sides seemed to be distributed over creation, and never really appeared to get face to face' (Ware)]

where's your violin? *phr.* [1940s+] (Aus.) of someone whose hair is perceived as over-long. [the traditional identification of violin-playing with 'long-haired' intellectuals]

where the action is *phr.* [1960s+] (US) the place where exciting, important or fashionable events are happening.

where/out where the bull feeds/gets his bleeding breakfast *phr.* [20C] (Aus.) in the Outback.

where the crows fly backwards to keep the dust out of their eyes *phr.* [late 19C+] (Aus.) of anywhere that is considered beyond the bounds of civilization.

where the five'n'arf? *phr.* [1920s–30s] where in God's name? [rhy. sl. 5½ yards = one rod (unit of measurement) = God]

where the flies won't get it *phr.* [late 19C] (US) of the stomach after swallowing an alcoholic drink.

where the monkey shoves his nuts *n.* [late 19C+] the anus, usu. as *you can shove/ put it/ them where the monkey ... .*

where the monkey sleeps *phr.* [late 19C] a milder version of WHERE THE MONKEY SHOVES HIS NUTS.

where the queen goes on foot/sends nobody *phr.* [20C] the lavatory.

where the sun doesn't shine *phr.* [20C] (US) the anus.

where uncle's doodle goes *phr.* [mid–late 19C] the vagina. [DOODLE n.²]

wherever *adv.* [1910s+] at any place whatever, at some place or other, often preceded by 'or'.

wherewith/wherewithal *n.* [19C] money (cf. NECESSARY; NEEDFUL). [the role of money in sustaining life]

wherry-go-nimble *n.* [20C] 1 the lavatory. 2 diarrhoea. [? SE *where he go nimbly*]

whet one's knife on the threshold of the Fleet, to *phr.* [mid-17C–late 18C] to be free of debt. [*the Fleet* was a debtor's prison and *whetting one's knife* implies disrespect for its rules]

Whetstone Park deer/mutton *n.* [17C–18C] prostitutes (cf. BANKSIDE LADY). [proper name *Whetstone Park*, a lane between Holborn and Lincoln's Inn Fields, well known for its 'nest of wenches' (B.E.) + SE *deer*/MUTTON n.² (2)]

whetting corn *n.* [early 17C–mid-19C] the vagina (cf. GRINDSTONE). [lit. a 'grindstone']

whetting stone *n.* [17C] the vagina (cf. HONE). [lit. a 'grindstone']

whiblin *n.* [early–mid-17C] 1 anything for which one has no proper name (cf. THINGUMBOB; WHAT-D'YOU-CALL-IT). 2 the testicles. [ety. unknown]

whid/whidd *n.* [late 17C–19C] (Und.) 1 a word, usu. in pl. 2 a lie. [SE *word* and OE *cwide*, a statement]

whid *v.* [late 18C–early 19C] to talk criminal jargon, to lie. [WHID n.]

whiddle/wheedle *v.* [late 17C–19C] 1 to tell, to recount. 2 (Und.) to inform against, to raise a hue and cry. [? WHID v.]

whiddle beef *v.* [late 18C] to raise the alarm (cf. CRY BEEF). [WHIDDLE + HOT BEEF!]

whiddler *n.* [late 17C–18C] an informer. [WHIDDLE]

whiff/wif/wiff *n.* [1970s+] (US drugs) 1 cocaine. 2 an inhalation of cocaine. [WHIFF v.³]

whiff *v.¹* [late 19C+] to smell unpleasantly; thus *whiff out*, to 'stink out' a room. [ME *weffe*, an offensive odour or taste]

whiff *v.²* [1950s+] (US) to miss a ball; thus *whiff*, a miss. [SE *whiff*, to move as a puff of air, and so one hits air rather than the ball]

whiff *v.³* [1970s+] (US drugs) to inhale cocaine. [SE *whiff*, to inhale, to sniff]

whiffet *n.* [mid–late 19C] (US) an insignificant person, a whippersnapper. [SE *whiffet*, a small dog]

whiffle *n.* [early 19C] a blow. [SE *whiffle*, to blow on, as with a puff of air]

whiffle *v.* [20C] (Ulster) to make an evasive answer. [SE *whiffle*, to talk idly]

whiffled *adj.* [1930s] drunk. [? SE *whiffle*, to move lightly as if blown by a puff of air]

whifflegig *adj.* [mid-19C] 1 trivial, trifling. 2 a trifler, an insignificant or contemptible person. [SE *whiffle*, to talk idly + GIG n.¹]

whiffles *n.* [late 18C–early 19C] 'A relaxation of the scrotum' (Grose 1785). [SE *whiffle*]

whiffmagig *n.* [mid-17C–late 19C] a trifler, an insignificant or contemptible fellow (cf. WHIFFLEGIG). [SE *whiff*, a puff of wind]

whig *n.* [late 19C] an irresolute person, someone who constantly changes their mind. [the refusal of the parliamentary *Whig* party to stay firmly on one side or the other]

whiggish *adj.* [late 17C–early 18C] 'Factious, Seditious, Restless, Uneasy' (B.E.).

Whigland *n.* [late 17C–mid-19C] Scotland; thus *Whiglander*, a Scot. [its being a centre of *Whig* politics]

while one can/would say knife *see* BEFORE ONE CAN SAY KNIFE.

while the going is good *phr.* [1910s+] (orig. US) while the conditions are favourable.

whilk/giddy whilk *n.* [1910s–20s] a silly young woman. [var. on WELK]

whim-wham *n.* 1 [18C] the vagina. 2 [mid-19C] nonsense, rubbish (cf. FLIM-FLAM; MAKING A WHIM-WHAM FOR A GOOSE'S EYE). [SE *whim-wham*, a trifle, a trinket + link to QUIM]

whim-whams *n.* [late 19C+] (US) anxiety, nervousness (cf. JITTERS). [SE *whim-wham*, a trifle, a fantasy]

whin-bush *n.* [19C] the pubic hair (cf. BUSH n.⁴; DAMBER-BUSH; DILBERRY BUSH; FORT BUSHY; FURZE-BUSH; GOOSEBERRY-BUSH; QUIM-BUSH). [SE *whin-bush*, a furze-bush]

whiners *n.* [early 18C–mid-19C] prayers (cf. CHOP THE WINERS).

whingding *see* WING-DING.

whings *see* WINGS.

whip *n.¹* [late 19C+] (Aus.) an abundance. [play on SE *lashings*]

whip *n.²* [1920s+] (Aus.) rum. [its effects; i.e. one is 'whipped' into action]

whip *n.³* [1990s] a collection of money, an appeal for money. [abbr. WHIPROUND]

whip *v.¹* [US] 1 [mid-19C] to swindle. 2 [mid-19C+] to steal, to make off with (cf. FLOG v.³). [SE *whip*, to take briskly, suddenly]

whip *v.²* [1990s] (US campus) to fall asleep while sitting up. [? SE *whiplash*, the way in which one's head slumps suddenly onto one's shoulder]

whip a game on, to *phr.* [1940s+] (US Black) to hoax, to trick, to deceive, esp. when selling drugs. [WHIP v.¹ + GAME n.⁴]

whip and lash *n.* [20C] a moustache. [rhy. sl.]

whip and top, to *phr.* [20C] to masturbate. [rhy. sl. *whip and top* = SE *strop*]

whip-around *see* WHIPROUND.

whip-arse *n.* [early 17C] a schoolmaster. [SE *whip* + ARSE n.¹]

whip belly/whip-belly vengeance *n.* [19C] very thin beer (cf. PINCH-GUT VENGEANCE). [its unpleasant effects]

whip-cat *n.* [mid-19C] a tailor. [WHIP THE CAT phr.⁴ (4)]

whip-cat *adj.* [late 16C–early 17C] drunken. [WHIP THE CAT phr.¹ (1)]

whip-handle *n.* [17C] (Scot.) an unimportant little man.

whip her Ginny/whip-her-ginny *see* WHIPPERGINNIE.

whip it *v.* [20C] to masturbate (cf. WHIP AND TOP).

whip it on someone *phr.¹* (US) [1940s+] 1 to explain and inform someone of facts and events. 2 to give, to hand over.

whip it on someone *phr.²* (US) [1940s+] (drugs) to inject someone other than oneself with narcotics.

whip-jack *n.* [16C–late 19C] (Und.) a mendicant villain who poses as a discharged mariner, backed by a counterfeit licence, suitably adorned with fake seals, he also specialized in robbing stalls, fairground booths and similar open displays of goods (cf. CANTING CREW; FRESHWATER MARINER). [SE *whip*, to beat + *Jack*, a general nickname. An alt. ety., WHIP v.¹ + JACK n.⁵, requires a substantially later coinage]

whip off *v.¹* 1 [early 17C–early 19C] to drink greedily. 2 [late 17C–18C] (Und.) to steal (cf. WHIP v.¹). 3 [late 18C+] to run off. [SE *whip*, to move suddenly, to take briskly]

whip off *v.²* [20C] (US campus) to masturbate (cf. BEAT OFF; WHIP IT).

whip one's dripper, to *phr.* [1990s] to masturbate.

whip one's dummy *see* BEAT ONE'S DUMMY.

whip one's weight in wildcats/polecats/catamounts/bears, to *phr.* [early 19C+] (US) to be fit and strong, to fight hard.

whip one's wire, to phr. [1970s+] (US campus) to masturbate. [SE whip + WIRE n.³ (1)]

whip-out n. [20C] (US) money, esp. a first payment or investment. [one SE whips it out of one's pocket]

whip out v. [20C] (US) to shake hands. [orig. milit. whip out, to present arms]

whip o'will n. [1960s+] (Aus.) the act of vomiting. [? echoic of the noise]

whipped adj.¹ [mid-19C] (US) cheated of one's share. [WHIP v.¹]

whipped adj.² **1** [1940s] (US Black) hungover. **2** [1980s] (US campus) drunk.

whipped adj.³ [1970s+] (US campus/teen) **1** in love, infatuated. **2** dominated, subservient, meek. **3** willing to do anything one's partner demands. [fig. use of SE, underlined by abbr. PUSSY-WHIPPED]

whipped cream n. [1970s+] (US Black) semen (cf. BABY GRAVY). [resemblance]

whipped like a dog phr. [1980s+] absolutely defeated, trounced.

whipped out of one's boots phr. [late 19C] (US) absolutely defeated.

whipped to a custard phr. [late 19C] (US) overwhelmingly defeated, absolutely beaten.

whipped up adj. [1930s–50s] (US Black) exhausted, worn out, physically wrecked.

whipped with an ugly stick, to be phr. [1960s–70s] to be unattractive (cf. BEAT WITH AN UGLY STICK). [often cited as a supposed reason for the lack of good looks]

whipperginnie/whip her Ginny/whip-her-ginny n. [late 16C–early 17C] a term of abuse for a woman. [lit. whip her, Jenny.]

whippets n. [1970s] (drugs) nitrous oxide. [as dispensed from a can of whipped cream]

whipping n. [mid-19C+] (US) **1** a sound, comprehensive beating or defeat. **2** punishment, physical discipline. [SE whip, to vanquish, to beat]

whippy n. [1970s+] (Aus.) **1** a hiding place, esp. for money. **2** a wallet. **3** a pocket. [WHIP v.¹]

whipround/whip-around n. [mid-19C+] a collection, an appeal for money. [SE whip up, to enthuse a group of people towards a united action, also note naval jargon whip, 'after the usual allowance of wine is drunk at mess, those who wish for more put a shilling each into a glass handed round to procure a further supply' (Hotten, 1867)]

whips n. [1960s+] (US Black) **1** the White establishment. **2** the police. [the repressive imagery of their institutions]

whip saw v. [1950s+] (US) **1** to have at a complete disadvantage, to overcome completely. **2** to benefit or win by manipulating a situation so that one's rivals attack one another. **3** to attack, assault. [SE whip-saw, something that is disadvantageous in two ways]

whip-shack n. [1970s+] (US Black) anywhere one can have sexual intercourse (cf. KILLING FLOOR).

Whipshire n. [late 17C–18C] Yorkshire. [? the hunting gentry who live there]

whips of phr. [20C] (Aus.) a great deal, an abundance (cf. LASHINGS; WHIP n.¹). [dial. whips, plenty]

whip some skull on, to phr. [1970s+] to fellate (cf. GIVE HEAD). [SKULL n.⁵]

whip someone's arse/ass, to phr. [1950s+] (orig. US) to beat completely and comprehensively, whether or not with violence. [SE whip + ARSE n.¹]

whip someone's head to the red, to phr. [1930s–40s] (US Black) to threaten injury or retaliation (whether genuinely or as a bluff).

whipster n. **1** [late 17C–early 19C] a clever, cunning person.

2 [20C] (Irish) a forward, impudent woman. [they are 'sharp as a whip']

whip-stitch! excl. [late 17C–early 18C] an excl. used to indicate a sudden movement or action. [note SAmE phr. every whip-stitch, at short or frequent intervals]

whip that thing! excl. [1940s+] (US Black) a cry of pleasure and encouragement during sexual intercourse.

whip the baloney pony/dummy/lizard/pony/weasel/wire, to phr. [1990s] to masturbate (cf. ACCOST THE OSCAR MEYER). [SE whip + BALONEY n.²/DUMMY n.³/LIZARD n.³/SE pony/weasel/WIRE n.³ (1)]

whip-the-cat n. [mid–late 19C] an itinerant tailor. [synon. dial.]

whip the cat, to phr.¹ [17C] **1** to get drunk (cf. SHOOT THE CAT). **2** to vomit through excessive drinking (cf. FLAY THE FOX; JERK THE CAT).

whip the cat, to phr.² [17C+] to play a practical joke (cf. CATTING). ['A trick often practised on ignorant country fellows, by laying a wager with them that they may be pulled through a pond by a cat; the bet being made, a rope is fastened round the waist of the person to be catted and the end thrown across the pond, to which the cat is also fastened by a pack-thread, and three or four sturdy fellows are appointed to lead and whip the cat; these on a signal given, seize the end of the cord, and pretending to whip the cat, haul the astonished booby through the water' (Grose 1785)]

whip the cat, to phr.³ **1** [18C] to lay the blame of one's offences on someone else. **2** [mid-19C+] (Aus./N.Z.) to suffer guilt and remorse for past errors, to worry about something about which one can do nothing. **3** [mid-19C+] (Aus.) to complain ad nauseam, to whinge at length. [i.e. whip the cat that has spilt the milk over which one is crying]

whip the cat, to phr.⁴ **1** [19C] to be extremely mean as regards money. **2** [19C+] to shirk work on Mondays. **3** [early 19C] to idle on the job. **4** [early–mid-19C] to work as an itinerant tailor, carpenter, locksmith, knife-grinder etc. [19C dial. whip the cat, to go from house to house as an itinerant tailor, such a job was unlikely to reap very rich rewards]

whip the devil round a stump/the meeting-house, to phr. [late 18C–late 19C] (US) **1** to accomplish something by subterfuge. **2** to be evasive. **3** to be dilatory. [? proverbial]

whip the dog, to phr. [1910s+] (US) **1** to waste time and loaf on the job (cf. SCREW THE POOCH). **2** to bungle, to blunder. [euph. var. on FUCK THE DOG]

whip the dummy see WHIP THE BALONEY PONY.

whip the game, to phr. [1960s+] (US Black) to overcome difficulties, to succeed in life. [SE whip + GAME n.⁴]

whip the lizard/pony/weasel/wire see WHIP THE BALONEY PONY.

whip through the lungs, to phr. [late 17C–mid-19C] to pierce with a sword thrust through the chest. [note fencing jargon whip, to make a thrust in which the blade slides along the opponent's blade]

whip up v. [early 17C–early 19C] to drink greedily (cf. WHIP OFF).

whip up some sour cream, to phr. [1990s] to masturbate.

whirligig n. [1910s–20s] an otherwise unspecified gadget.

whirligigs n. [late 17C–early 19C] the testicles. [WHIRLIGIG; thus euph.]

whirling spray n. [1940s+] (Aus.) a talkative bore. [the words 'spray out']

whirlybird n. [1950s+] (US) a helicopter.

whisk n. [late 17C–mid-19C] an insignificant person, a whippersnapper (cf. PIMP WHISK). [they make no more impression on the world than does a quick whisk on dirt]

whiskbroom 'with' n. [late 19C] (US) drunkenness. [an anecdote of late-19C Prohibition (then restricted to certain states rather than the nationwide version of 1920–33), a temperance campaigner, on entering a haberdasher's to buy a whiskbroom was offered one 'with' and one 'without'. On asking what this meant she was shown that a broom 'with' had a small bottle of whisky hidden amid its bristles]

whisker n.[1] [late 17C–18C] anything excessive, esp. a great lie. [SE *whisk*, to move briskly]

whisker n.[2] [1910s+] (orig. US) a very small, infinitesimal amount or distance.

whisker n.[3] [1940s+] (Aus.) **1** the pubic hair (cf. BELLY WHISKERS; WHISKER-SPLITTER). **2** a young woman. [(2) is fig. use of (1)]

whiskerando n. [early 19C–1920s] a man who is heavily whiskered. [the character Don Ferolo *Whiskerandos* in R.B. Sheridan's play *The Critic* (1779)]

whisker-bed n. [mid-19C] **1** the face. **2** the jaw.

whiskeries/whiskyries n. [late 19C] the Irish Exhibition held in London in 1888 (cf. COLINDERIES). [Irish *whisky*]

whiskers n. [mid-19C+] (US) an old man.

whiskers! excl. [mid-19C+] a term of address to a noticeably bewhiskered man.

whisker-splitter n. [late 18C–early 19C] a womanizer (cf. BEARD-SPLITTER; RUMP-SPLITTER; WHISKER). [(NETHER) WHISKERS + SE *splitter*]

whiskin n. [mid-17C] a pimp. [abbr. *pimp-whiskin* (see PIMP WHISK)]

whisking adj. **1** [early 17C–early 19C] brisk, lively, smart. **2** [late 17C–late 18C] great, excessive. [SE *whisk*, to move briskly]

whisky-bottle n. [late 19C] a Scottish drunkard (cf. ALECAN). [stereotyping]

whisky-frisky adj. [late 18C] flighty. [SE *whisk* + *frisk*]

whiskyhead n. [1940s+] (US) **1** one who drinks a great deal of whisky. **2** delirium tremens. [SE *whisky* + sfx. -HEAD (2)/ HEAD n.[4]]

whiskyries see WHISKERIES.

whisky-skin n. [late 19C] (US) a mixed drink containing a large proportion of whisky.

whisky's talking see LIQUOR'S TALKING.

whisky-straight n. [mid-19C] (US) whisky without additional water.

whisper n.[1] **1** [19C] a criminal's look-out man. **2** [1950s+] a rumour, usu. of impending crimes.

whisper n.[2] [late 19C+] a walk. [rhy. sl. *whisper and talk* = walk]

whisper v. [late 19C–1920s] to borrow money from. [the hushed tone in which one requests the loan]

whispering dudder see DUDDER.

whispering gallery n. [late 19C] the bar of the Gaiety Theatre (cf. PROSSERS' AVENUE). [a play on the more respectable *Whispering Gallery* encircling the dome of St Paul's Cathedral, and from the less well-off patrons whispering 'Can you lend me ... ?']

whister-clister n. [late 18C–mid-19C] a blow on the ear. [dial. *whister*, whisper + SE *clyster*, an enema]

whister-snefet/-snivit n. [16C] a blow on the ear. [dial. *whister*, whisper + SE/dial. *snite*, to wipe/SE *snivel*, nasal mucus]

whisticaster n. [early 19C] a blow on the ear. [dial. *whister*, whisper + SE *cast*, to throw]

whistle n.[1] **1** [late 14C+] the mouth, the throat. **2** [late 19C] a flute. [? the sounds]

whistle n.[2] [late 19C] a child's penis. [resemblance]

whistle n.[3] [1930s+] a suit of clothes. [rhy. sl. *whistle and flute* = suit]

whistle v. [1930s] to smell unpleasantly. [it makes a 'noise']

whistle and flute n. [1930s+] a suit. [rhy. sl.]

whistle and toot n. [20C] money. [rhy. sl. *whistle and toot* = LOOT n.[1] (1)]

whistle-belly-vengeance n. [mid-19C] bad or thin beer (cf. WHIP-BELLY-VENGEANCE). [the rumbling it produces in the drinker's stomach]

whistle-blower n. [1960s+] **1** a scandalmonger, an investigator who reveals facts that disturb a hitherto satisfactory, though corrupt, status quo. **2** (US Und.) a police informer (cf. STOOL PIGEON; WHISTLER n.[2]).

whistlecock n. [late 19C+] (Aus.) a derog. name for a Native Australian, an Aborigine. [an initiation ritual-cum-prophylactic whereby the underside of the penis is slit to make a permanent incision in the urethra; the effect is to prevent the normal ejaculation of semen into one's partner]

whistled adj. [1930s+] (orig. milit.) drunk.

whistled drunk adj. [mid-18C] very drunk. [despite appearances, there seems to be no connection between this and WHISTLED adj.]

whistle Dixie v. [20C] (US) **1** to engage in wishful fantasies. **2** to boast, to brag without substance, usu. as *not just whistling Dixie*. [for ety. see DIXIE n.[1]]

whistle for v. [early 16C+] to hope vainly for something, often used in the dismissive phr. *you can go whistle for it* following someone's plea.

whistle for wind n. [late 19C] a fool.

whistle in the cage, to phr. [early–mid-19C] for a villain, on being arrested, to betray his accomplices (cf. SING; SING OUT). [SE *whistle* + CAGE n. (1)]

whistle in the dark, to phr.[1] [1930s+] **1** to hazard a guess, to speculate wildly. **2** to put on a brave front, to appear more confident than is true.

whistle in the dark, to phr.[2] [1960s+] (US) to perform cunnilingus (cf. YODEL IN THE CANYON).

whistle off v. [late 17C–late 18C] to run away, to leave at speed.

whistler n.[1] [early–mid-19C] the proprietor of an unlicensed spirit-shop in a prison (cf. WHISTLING SHOP). [his drinks are kept hidden so that when the police raid they can *whistle for them*]

whistler n.[2] **1** [19C] a broken-down horse, whose breath whistles in his lungs. **2** [1910s–20s] a revolver. **3** [1910s–20s] anything especially large. **4** [1940s] a female railway porter. **5** [1960s+] (US Und.) an informer (cf. WHISTLE-BLOWER).

whistler n.[3] [late 19C] a casual labourer at the docks. [he attempts to *whistle up* work]

whistlers n. [early 19C] (Und.) counterfeit farthings (cf. BROWNS). [the false ring when tapped]

whistle stop n. [20C] (US) a small town (cf. JERKWATER TOWN; TANK TOWN). [orig. railroad jargon *whistlestop town*, trains do not halt at such a town unless a passenger informs the conductor who then signals the fact by pulling on the signal cord and the engineer acknowledges the request by two whistles. The derog. sl. use led to the abandoning of the term by the railroads, who substituted *flag stop* or *flag station* to spare local feelings]

whistle up v. [1920s+] **1** to send for. **2** to arrange for the delivery or appearance of something or someone. [naut. *whistle up the wind*]

whistle up the breeze see RAISE THE WIND.

whistling-breeches n. [late 19C+] corduroy trousers. [the swishing noise the material makes as the legs brush together]

whistling shop n. [late 18C–mid-19C] **1** a room in the King's Bench (or any other) prison where one could buy drink illicitly (cf. BRACE). **2** any illicit drinking house. [WHISTLE n.[1] (1) + SHOP]

Whit/Whitt, the [17C–early 19C] Newgate prison. [abbr. WHITTINGTON COLLEGE]

white n.¹ **1** [mid-19C] gin (cf. WHITE SATIN). **2** [1930s+] (US) any form of alcohol.

white n.² **1** [1910s+] (drugs) morphine, heroin (cf. WHITE STUFF). **2** [1940s+] (US) cocaine. **3** [1960s+] (drugs) amphetamine (cf. A n.²). [the colour of the respective drugs]

white n.³ [1950s+] (orig. US) a white loaf. [abbr.]

white n.⁴ [1960s] (US Black) anyone, irrespective of colour, who is seen as immoral or unethical.

white adj.¹ [mid-18C–late 19C] silver (cf. RED adj.).

white adj.² [late 19C+] **1** honest, upright, fair-dealing. **2** (US Black) patronizing, exploitative (but not necessarily White-skinned). [coined without any consciously neg. overtones and representing a rare (if unsurprisingly) pos. racial stereotype, the term has been used in an increasingly ironic manner, esp. since 1960s; thus cf. WHITE n.⁴]

white adj.³ [1970s+] (S.Afr.) cheeky, insubordinate. [used of a Black person 'getting above themselves' and thus trespassing on White prerogatives]

white about the gills phr. [19C] frightened.

white-ant v. [1920s+] (Aus.) to sabotage, during a labour dispute; thus white-anter, a saboteur, white-anting, sabotage. [reverse anthropomorphism]

white ants n. [1900s–50s] (Aus.) eccentricity, insanity; thus have white ants, to be crazy. [the supposed eating away of one's brain by white ants]

white apron n. [16C] a prostitute. [the SE white apron that was recognized as a prostitute's 'uniform']

white-arsed adj. [1920s+] a general term of abuse. [SE white + ARSE n.¹]

white ash n. [mid-19C] (US) an oar; thus white-ash breeze, the oar's impetus through the water. [the white ash (Fraxinus americana), from which oars are made]

white as midnight's arsehole phr. [mid-16C–mid-17C] absolutely dark, totally black.

whiteball n. [1990s] (drugs) crack cocaine. [its colour]

white-belly rat n. [1920s–50s] (W.I.) a hypocrite (cf. BITE-AND-BLOW). [this variety of rat supposedly blows on the thing it bites to minimize the pain]

white bottle n. [late 19C] any white medicine.

white boy n.¹ [17C] an especial favourite, a 'mother's darling' (cf. WHITE-HAIRED BOY). [the image white to denote purity and innocence]

white boy n.² [1960s+] (drugs) heroin. [SE white/WHITE n.² + BOY n.⁵]

white brahmins n. [late 19C] (Ind.) the English, whose social exclusivity outdid even that of the Brahmins, the highest Hindu caste.

white bread adj. [1980s] **1** (US) used of anything pertaining to White, middle-class, mainstream styles, bland, unexciting, suburban (cf. WASP n.²; YANKEE WHITE). **2** (US campus) anything good, admirable.

white brick n. [1980s+] (drugs) cocaine. [its colour]

white/yellow callies n. [1980s+] (drugs) MDMA (cf. ECSTASY). [? SE white + California]

Whitechapel n.¹ [mid-19C] in coin-tossing, a score of two out of three wins. [presumably popular in this area of London's East End]

Whitechapel n.² [late 19C] a sex murder. [the 'Jack the Ripper killings', which took place in Whitechapel in 1888]

Whitechapel n.³ [20C] an apple. [rhy. sl.]

Whitechapel adj. [late 18C–late 19C] not sl. as such but used in the following combs. to denote poverty, roughness and criminality. [Whitechapel, the home of Cockney London and the heart of London's impoverished and thus often criminal East End]

Whitechapel beau n. [late 18C] one 'who dresses with a needle and thread, and undresses with a knife' (Grose, 1785). [ironic use of SE beau]

Whitechapel breed n. [late 18C] a woman who is 'fat, ragged and saucy' (Grose, 1785)

Whitechapel/Westminster brougham n. [mid-19C] a donkey. [the closed carriage known as a brougham was beyond the income of the average Whitechapel costermonger]

Whitechapel fortune see WHITECHAPEL PORTION.

Whitechapel oner n. [late 19C] a fashionable young man-about-Whitechapel, an East End dandy. [i.e. he is number one in local estimation]

Whitechapel play n. **1** [mid-18C+] in whist, the leading of all one's best cards, with no attempt to finesse the opponent. **2** [mid-19C+] in billiards, to pot an opponent's ball. [both uses stress the snobbish assumption that East Enders are unable to play ostensibly patrician games with the correct skill and subtlety]

Whitechapel portion/fortune n. **1** [late 17C–18C] the vagina, 'two torn smocks and what Nature gives' (B.E.). **2** [19C] 'a clean gown and a pair of pattens' (Hotten 1864) (cf. IRISH FORTUNE).

Whitechapel shave n. [mid-19C] whitening applied to the face to lighten the 'five o'clock shadow'. [the poor cannot afford a barber to shave them]

Whitechapel warriors n. [late 19C] the Aldgate militia. [Aldgate, in Whitechapel + SE warriors]

white-choker n. [late 19C–1910s] a clergyman. [the white bands that are part of his dress]

white-chokerism n. [mid-19C] (US) respectability. [WHITE-CHOKERY]

white-chokery n. [late 19C] the upper classes. [i.e. those who wear a white choker or large white neckerchief as part of their evening dress]

white cloud n. [1980s+] (drugs) crack cocaine smoke (cf. WHITE GHOST).

white corner/mouth n. [20C] (W.I.) an unpleasant, white discharge from the corner of one's mouth, usu. caused by vitamin deficiency.

white cow n. (US) **1** [1920s+] a vanilla milkshake (cf. BLACK COW). **2** [1940s+] a vanilla ice-cream soda. [COW n.⁴ (1)]

white cross n. (drugs) **1** [1900s–20s] cocaine. **2** [1970s] amphetamine pills with a white cross cut into one surface (cf. A n.²).

white dove n. [20C] a variety of MDMA (cf. ECSTASY). [SE white, i.e. the colour of the pill + DOVE n. (1)]

white dust n. [1970s] (drugs) phencyclidine (cf. ACE n.³). [the form in which the drug is sometimes sold]

white dynamite n. [1980s+] (drugs) heroin. [its colour and effects]

white ewe n. [late 17C–late 18C] a beautiful and important woman in a band of villains.

white eye n. [19C] cheap, rough whisky. [its alleged effect; one's eyes apparently roll up in their sockets, exposing the whites]

white-eyes n. **1** [20C] (Native American) White people. **2** [1970s+] (US Black) a White person. [the term paleface is generally fictional and invariably used by Whites rather than the 'Red Indians' to whom they attribute it]

white-faced calf n. [20C] (US) deer that has been illegally shot by poachers (cf. CAMP MEAT).

whitefish n. [20C] (US prison) a White inmate. [SE white + FISH n.⁵]

white flight n. [1960s+] (US) the movement of an older White population from the inner-cities, generated by a perceived fear of newer, non-White arrivals (cf. BROWN FLIGHT).

white friar n. [early 18C–mid-19C] a flake or particle of white scum or froth floating on liquid. [SE *white friars*, an order of monks distinguished by a white cloak and scapular]

white fustian n. [late 17C–early 19C] sherry (cf. RED FUSTIAN; WHITE WASH). [SE *white* + *fustian*, a coarse cloth, therefore note the contrast with 'smooth' SATIN, denoting gin]

white ghost n. [1980s+] (drugs) crack cocaine (cf. WHITE CLOUD). [the white smoke it exudes]

white girl n. [1960s+] (drugs) cocaine, heroin. [SE *white* + GIRL n.³]

white-haired boy n. [late 19C+] (orig. US) an especial favourite, one who can, in the right eyes, do no wrong (cf. FAIR-HAIRED BOY). [Share suggests the 'Celtic preference for fair hair']

white-haired lady n. [1980s+] (drugs) marijuana. [ety. unknown; only a very far-fetched resemblance, if any]

Whitehall warrior n. [1960s+] 1 a civil servant. 2 an officer in the services who has been seconded to administrative rather than active duties. [*Whitehall*, the home of the UK government]

white hat n. [1970s+] a hero, a 'good' character (as opposed to a 'bad' one) in any fictional medium. [*white hats* were worn by the heroes and black hats by the villains in the old, silent Western films]

Whitehaven docks n. [1970s] venereal disease. [rhy. sl. *Whitehaven docks* = POX]

white-headed boy n. [early 19C+] an especial favourite, one who can, in the right eyes, do no wrong (cf. FAIR-HAIRED BOY; WHITE-HAIRED BOY). [15–17C SE *white*, precious 'pet', 'darling']

white horizon n. [1970s+] (drugs) phencyclidine (cf. ACE n.³). [ety. unknown]

white horse n.¹ [late 19C] (Irish) cowardice. [tradition has it that King James II fled the battle of the Boyne riding a *white horse*]

white horse n.² [1910s] (US) pure alcohol, diluted for drinking. [its translucency and its effects]

white horse n.³ [1970s] (drugs) cocaine. [SE *white* + HORSE n.¹²; heroin is usu. brown, cocaine is white]

white house n. [1950s–70s] (US Black) the world of White society. [underpinned by a ref. to the *White House*, home of the US presidency]

white it out v. [mid-19C+] (Aus.) to serve a jail sentence. [? one SE *whites out*, i.e. erases, that period of one's life]

white jenny n. [18C–19C] a watch made of foreign silver (cf. WHITE LOT; WHITE 'UN). [? WHITE adj.¹ + SE *engine*]

white junk n. [1970s] (drugs) heroin. [SE *white* + JUNK n.³]

white kaffir n. (S.Afr.) 1 [mid-19C+] a derog. term for a White perceived as behaving badly by their peers. 2 [mid-19C+] a White who has become overly close to or assimilated into the Black community. 3 [1930s+] an albino (cf. FRECKLE-NATURE). [SE *white* + KAFFIR]

white-knuckle adj. [1970s+] (orig. US) terrifying, very frightening, often of a fairground ride or horror film. [the whitening of one's knuckles as one grips onto something to control one's emotions]

white-knuckler n. [1970s+] (US) 1 an aeroplane flight. 2 a tense, anxious person. [WHITE-KNUCKLE]

white lady n.¹ [1930s+] (Aus.) methylated spirits. [SE *white lady*, a cocktail made of two parts of dry gin, one of orange liqueur and one of lemon juice]

white lady n.² [1950s+] (drugs) 1 cocaine. 2 heroin (cf. BROWN SUGAR; WHITE GIRL; WHITE SHIT). [its colour, although the bulk of late-20C heroin is light brown]

white land n. [1960s–70s] land that is not designated or available for development or change of use. [its being printed in unadorned *white* on surveyors' maps]

white lightning n. 1 [1920s+] (US) illicit home-brewed whisky or poteen. 2 [1950s+] (S.Afr.) home-brewed liquor distilled from peaches or grapes. 3 [1960s–70s] (drugs) LSD. [the effects]

white lilies n. [1940s] (US Black) bed linen.

white line n. [1910s–20s] (US tramp) 1 alcohol that has been diluted. 2 a drinker. [ety. unknown]

white-line fever n.¹ [1970s+] the obsessive use of cocaine. [the white LINE n.⁴ (4) of the powdered drug that are inhaled by users]

white-line fever n.² [1970s+] (US) an obsessive driver. [the *white lines* that divide traffic lanes]

white list n. [20C] a list of people who are considered to be acceptable in a situation. [on the model of SE *black list*]

white liver n. [1930s+] a homosexual who has no interest whatsoever in women. [SE *white*, pure]

white-livered/liver-faced adj. [mid-16C+] cowardly. [the assumption that a coward has insufficient bile or 'choler' in his liver, so rendering it white and him weak]

white lot n. [19C] a silver watch (cf. RED TOY; WHITE STUFF; WHITE 'UN; WHITE WOOL n.¹). [SE *white*, silver + *lot*]

white magic n. [late 19C] (society) extremely beautiful women.

white man n.¹ [late 19C] (US) an honourable person (cf. WHITE adj.¹.). [Anglo-Saxon arrogance]

white man n.² [1950s] (W.I.) an albino (cf. FRECKLE-NATURE).

white man's burden n. [1940s–50s] work. [Kipling's poem 'The White Man's Burden', in which the task was the ruling of the 'new-caught sullen peoples/Half-devil and half-child']

white man's chance n. [mid-19C] (US) a fair chance (cf. CHINAMAN'S CHANCE). [as opposed to the treatment of non-Whites]

white man's disease n. [1980s+] (US Black) the relative inability of Caucasians to jump, a term of derision almost exclusively used in a basketball context.

white man's/whitey's out of jail phr. [1960s+] (US) a warning to a woman that her slip is showing.

white meat n. [1930s+] (US Black/W.I.) 1 a White person, usu. a woman and in a sexual context (cf. DARK MEAT). 2 a White penis (cf. BACON n.¹). [SE *white* + MEAT, pun on the genteel euph. for the 'breast' of a chicken. Note printers' jargon *white meat*, an actress]

white mice n. 1 [20C] (Aus.) lice. 2 [1940s–50s] dice. [rhy. sl.]

white money n. [20C] (US) an illegal political contribution. [it is 'invisible', unlike green dollars]

white Moor n. [mid-17C] a native of Genoa. [? the large population of Arab merchants]

white mosquitoes n. [1940s] (drugs) cocaine or any powdered drug. [the mosquito-bite-like mark left after an injection]

white mouth n. see WHITE CORNER.

white mouth v. [1930s] (US Black) to pretend servility in one's conversations with Whites. [one 'talks their language']

white mule n. [1920s–30s] (US) homemade whisky made from grain alcohol (cf. WHITE LIGHTNING). [it has a 'kick like a mule']

white-nayga n. [1960s] (W.I.) an albino (cf. FRECKLE-NATURE). [lit. 'white nigger']

white nigger n. 1 [mid–late 19C] a derog. term for a White person who does menial labour. 2 [late 19C] (Sierra Leone) a European. 3 [1950s+] (Can.) self-description by embittered French Canadians who see themselves as second-class citizens in a primarily British country. 4 [1950s–70s] beatniks, hippies and other counter-cultural groups who see their alienation from mainstream culture as analogous with the everyday role of any Black person (cf. WIGGA). **5** [1960s+] a Black person who is regarded as deferring to White people or accepting a role prescribed by them. [SE *White* + NIGGER n. In (4) note Norman Mailer *The White Negro* (1957): 'The hipster had absorbed the existentialist synapses of the Negro, and for practical purposes could be considered a White Negro']

white nurse *n.* [1930s–50s] (drugs) any form of powdered white drugs. [the 'health-giving' effects; note Rolling Stones' song 'Sister Morphine' (1969)]

white-on-white *n.* [1940s+] (US Black) a white Cadillac with white interior finish and white upholstery; thus *white-on-white-in-white*, a Black person who seeks the supposed status of association with White people, esp. through a White girlfriend and a white Cadillac (cf. BLACK-ON-BLACK).

whiteout *n.* [1980s+] (drugs) isobutyl nitrite. [its effect on the brain]

white owl *n.* [20C] a White penis.

white owsleys *see* OWSLEY.

white pipe *n.* [1980s] (S.Afr.) a mixture of marijuana, tobacco and a crushed tablet of Mandrax (the brandname of methaqualone) (cf. BUTTON n.⁶). [SE *white* + PIPE n.³]

white pointer *n.* [1990s] (Aus.) a highway patrolman. [? his uniform]

white powder *n.* [1930s+] any form of narcotic or other drug that comes in the form of white powder.

white prop *n.* [mid-19C] a diamond stickpin (cf. WHITE LOT). [SE *white* + PROP n.³]

white ribbon *n.* [19C] gin (cf. BLUE RIBBON; WHITE SATIN; WHITE TAPE). [SE *white* + RIBBON n.³ (1)]

white Russian *n.* [1960s+] (gay) the oral exchange of semen. [the similarity of white semen to the colour of a *white Russian* cocktail]

whites *n.*¹ [19C] venereal disease, spec. a vaginal discharge, gonorrhoea. [the colour of the discharge]

whites *n.*² [early 19C+] silver coins; thus in counterfeiters' jargon *large whites*, half-crowns, *small whites*, shillings.

whites *n.*³ [1960s] (W.I.) a drink of white rum.

whites *n.*⁴ [1960s+] (drugs) amphetamines (cf. A n.²; BLUES n.²).

white satin *n.* [mid-19C] gin (cf. SATIN; WHITE TAPE). [the term is still in use as a proprietory name for a brand of gin, *Sir Robert Burnett's White Satin Gin*]

white serjeant *n.* [late 18C–late 19C] a wife who dominates her husband (cf. ARRESTED BY THE WHITE SERJEANT).

white shirt *n.* [1950s+] (prison) a senior prison officer, who wears a white rather than the blue of the junior ranks.

white shit *n.* [1950s+] (drugs) **1** heroin (cf. WHITE BOY). **2** cocaine (cf. WHITE GIRL). [SE *white* + SHIT n.⁵]

white-shoe *n.* [20C] (US) a typical Ivy League student (cf. BLACK-SHOE). [their trad. footwear]

white-shoe *adj.* [1950s+] (US) **1** immature, effeminate. **2** of the US establishment, e.g. a *white-shoe law firm*. [WHITE-SHOE n.]

white soup *n.* [late 19C] (Und.) silver that has been melted down from the original, stolen plate.

white space *n.* [1980s+] free time. [the space in question is in the speaker's diary]

white stone *n.* [1940s–50s] (US Black) a fake diamond, esp. as used in a confidence trick.

white stuff *n.* **1** [mid–late 19C] anything made of silver (cf. WHITE LOT). **2** [1920s] (US) grain alcohol used for making illicit liquor. **3** [1930s+] (drugs) cocaine (cf. BROWN STUFF; GREEN STUFF).

white sugar *n.* [1990s] (drugs) crack cocaine. [var. on BROWN SUGAR]

white swallow *n.* [1990s] (US, mainly West Coast) semen, usu. in the context of fellatio.

white tape/wool *n.* [18C–early 19C] gin (cf. BIT OF TAPE; WHITE RIBBON; WHITE SATIN; WHITE WINE). [SE *white* + TAPE/SE *wool*]

white tornado *n.* [1980s+] (drugs) crack cocaine. [play on the slogan of a household cleaning liquid]

white toy *n.* [mid–late 19C] a silver watch. [WHITE adj.¹ + TOY n.²]

white trash/trash *n.* [late 18C+] (orig. US Black) a derog. term for the poor White population of the Southern states (cf. APPLE-KNOCKER n.²). [lit. 'White rubbish']

white 'un *n.* [mid–late 19C] a silver watch. [WHITE adj.¹ + SE *one*]

whitewash *n.*¹ [mid-19C–1900s] a glass of sherry taken as the finale after a meal spent drinking port and claret (cf. WHITEWASHER). [its relatively 'white' colour and its 'washing' away of the red wines]

whitewash *n.*² [mid-19C+] **1** in sport, the complete defeat of one team by another. **2** any crushing defeat.

whitewash *v.*¹ [mid-19C+] to have sexual intercourse (cf. WHITEWASH SOMEONE'S KIDNEYS; WHITEWASH SOMEONE'S TONSILS). [the whiteness of the semen]

whitewash *v.*² [mid-19C+] (US) to win decisively. [WHITEWASH n.²]

whitewashed *adj.* [mid-18C–19C] freed of one's debts by becoming a bankrupt.

whitewasher *n.* [mid-19C–1900s] a glass of white wine taken at the end of dinner (cf. WHITEWASH n.¹). [one 'cleans up' the palate]

whitewashing *n.* [mid-18C] (W.I.) insincerely accepting religious conversion when the alternative is to be killed. [the Black man or woman is 'washed white' through baptism]

whitewash someone's kidneys, to *phr.* [1950s+] (Aus.) to have anal intercourse. [WHITEWASH v.¹]

whitewash someone's tonsils, to *phr.* [1960s+] (US) to ejaculate in someone's mouth, following fellation. [WHITEWASH v.¹]

whitewater wristing *n.* [1990s] masturbation. [play on SE *whitewater rafting*]

white white *n.* [1990s] (US Black) **1** a White person without the slightest knowledge of or interest in Black culture. **2** a racist.

white widow *n.* [1990s] (drugs) a form of marijuana (i.e. super-compacted SUPERSKUNK) that is so dense as to exude white crystals.

white wine *n.* [mid-19C] gin (cf. WHITE SATIN; WHITE TAPE). [its translucence]

white wing *n.* [mid-19C+] (US) any wearer of a white uniform. [SE, the *locus classicus* was the nickname of the New York City street sweepers, who wore white uniforms after the reforms of the city's street cleaning by Col. George F. Waring in 1895]

white wool *n.*¹ [16C] (Und.) **1** the silver pieces that are left with the victim of a substitution fraud. **2** silver in general (cf. WHITE LOT; WHITE STUFF; WHITE TOY). [WHITE adj.¹ + SE *wool*]

white wool *n.*² *see* WHITE TAPE.

whitey *n.* [1940s+] **1** (Black) the White race in general. **2** any White individual (cf. BLANCO).

whitey's out of jail *see* WHITE MAN'S OUT OF JAIL.

whitey-whitey *n.* [1950s] (W.I.) an albino (cf. FRECKLE-NATURE).

whither-go-ye *n.* [late 17C–early 19C] a wife. [the question asked by a stereotypically nagging, over-inquisitive wife]

Whitt *see* WHIT.

Whittington/Whittington's college *n.* [17C–18C] (Und.) Newgate prison (cf. CITY COLLEGE). [the name of the Warden]

Whittington priory *n.* [late 19C] Holloway Prison. [its association with Dick *Whittington* (c.1358–1423), who 'turned again' at nearby Highgate]

Whittington's college *see* WHITTINGTON COLLEGE.

whittle *v.* **1** [16C] to confess on the gallows. **2** [20C] to talk emptily, aimlessly, to chatter. [WHIDDLE]

whittled as a penguin *phr.* [1960s] (Aus.) extremely drunk. [ety. unknown; ? link to WHITTLE *v.* (2); i.e. the drunkard's loquacity]

whittle the stick, to *phr.* [20C] to masturbate.

whiz *n.*[1] **1** [19C] noise, commotion, a 'buzz'. **2** [1910s+] (Aus.) energy, spirit. [echoic]

whiz *n.*[2] [mid–late 19C] (US) a deal, a bargain. [ety. unknown; ? the speed i.e. SE *whiz* of its conclusion]

whiz *n.*[3] [1910s+] a general term of approbation, esp. of a highly satisfying thing or event, or of a very skilful or talented person. [SE *wizard*]

whiz/whizz *n.*[4] [1920s+] a pickpocket; thus [1920s+] *whizz mob*, the world of pickpocketing, a gang of pickpockets, [1930s+] *whiz-boy, whizman*, a pickpocket. [SE *whiz*, to move fast]

whiz/whizz *n.*[5] [1960s+] amphetamine (cf. SPEED *n.*[2]). [SE *whiz*, to move fast]

whiz *n.*[6] [1970s] an act of urination. [WHIZ *v.*[2]]

whiz *n.*[7] [1980s+] (US campus) someone who is seen as socially unacceptable, unfashionable and thus unpopular. [abbr. CHEESE WHIZ]

whiz/whizz *v.*[1] [1920s+] (US Und.) to pickpocket (cf. WHIZ MOB; WHIZZER).

whiz/whizz *v.*[2] [1920s+] to urinate. [var. on WAZ + echoic of urine hitting the lavatory bowl]

whiz bang *n.*[1] [1910s+] (US) any person or thing that is impressive or successful. [WHIZ *n.*[3]]

whiz bang *n.*[2] [1930s–50s] (drugs) an injection of cocaine plus heroin or morphine. [the *whiz* of the cocaine + the *bang* of the opiate]

whiz jizzum *v.* [20C] to masturbate. [SE *whiz* + JISM]

whiz off *see* RACE OFF.

whiz mob *n.* [20C] the world of pickpockets. [WHIZ *n.*[4] + MOB *n.*[1] (4)]

whiz pop *n.* [1970s] (US campus) a stupid person. [they emulate a dud firework, which *whizzes* then sputters out with an anti-climatic *pop*]

whizz *n. see* WHIZ *n.*[4], *n.*[5].

whizz *v. see* WHIZ *v.*

whizz-bomb *n.* [1980s+] (drugs) MDMA (cf. ECSTASY).

whizzer *n.*[1] [late 19C+] something or someone extraordinary or wonderful. [WHIZ *n.*[3]]

whizzer *n.*[2] [1920s+] a pickpocket. [WHIZ *n.*[4]]

whizzer *n.*[3] [1960s] a spree, a drinking bout. [SE *whiz*]

whizzing *n.* [1920s–40s] working as a pickpocket. [WHIZ *v.*[1]]

whizzing *adj.* [1950s] (mainly juv.) wonderful, first-rate. [WHIZ *n.*[3]]

whizzo *adj.* [1940s+] (usu. juv., except when ironic) wonderful, brilliant, amazing. [WHIZ *n.*[3]]

whizzo! *excl.* [1940s+] (mainly juv.) wonderful!, marvellous!

whizz off *v. see* RACE OFF.

whizzy-whizzy *see* WIZZY-WIZZY.

whoaball/whoa-Ball/whoball/whow-ball *n.* [late 17C–early 19C] a milkmaid (cf. NONE OF JOHN WHOBALL'S CHILDREN). [SE *whoa*, stop + *Ball*, a common name for a cow]

whoa, bust me! *excl.* [19C] a general excl. of anger, amazement. [BUST *v.*[1] (1)]

whoa, carry me out *phr.* [late 19C] a phr. used to mock any statement or situation that is meant to be exciting, surprising, outstanding etc.

whoa, Emma! mind the paint *phr.* [late 19C] a phr. used to a woman who either looks odd or is behaving strangely or excessively in public. [an inquest on one *Emma* who had died

suddenly and whose husband had attempted to revive her with this phrase]

whoa, Jameson! *excl.* [late 19C] an excl. used, with a certain degree of admiration, to restrain one that the speaker feels is 'going too far'. [the audacious but politically disastrous *Jameson* Raid, 1896]

who am I to talk? *phr.* [1940s+] a phr. used to stress that one speaker is in no position to criticize another.

who are you? *phr.*[1] [late 19C] an aggressive phr. used in London streets, usu. greeted with the equally aggressive rejoinder 'Who are *you*?'

who are you? *phr.*[2] [1980s+] (US campus) **1** what's the matter, what's your problem? **2** shut up! be quiet!

whoball *see* WHOABALL.

who blew your trumpet? *phr.* [1960s–70s] what's making you so agitated?

who cares? *phr.* [mid-19C+] a dismissive phr. indicating one's lack of concern.

who cries stinking fish? *phr.* **1** [late 17C+] who would denigrate their own goods? **2** [early 18C+] who would denigrate themself?

who cut the cheese? *phr.* [1950s+] (usu. juv.) who broke wind? [the smell associated with some soft cheeses]

who'd ever *phr.* [mid-19C+] would you believe it?

whodunnit *n.* [1940s–50s] (prison) meat pie. [SE *whodunnit*, a murder mystery; the 'murder victim' is the prison cat]

who ever/whoever *prn.* [late 19C+] emphatic version of SE *who*.

who has any lands in Appleby *phr.* [late 17C–late 18C] a phr. addressed to 'the man at whose door the glass stands long, or who does not circulate it in due time' (Grose 1785).

who he/she when he's/she's at home? *see* WHAT'S THAT WHEN IT'S AT HOME?

who kicked your kennel/pigsty? *phr.* [1910s+] mind your own business.

whole apple, the *n.* [late 19C] (US) everything, 'the lot'.

whole bag of tricks, the *n.* [mid-19C+] everything necessary to deal with a situation.

whole ball of wax *n.* [1950s+] (US) absolutely everything (cf. WHOLE KIT AND CABOODLE).

whole bang shoot/bang shoot *n.* [late 19C+] everything relevant and involved.

whole bit *n.* [1960s+] everything.

whole boiling lot *n.* [19C+] absolutely everything (cf. WHOLE KIT AND CABOODLE).

whole box and dice *n.* [late 19C+] (Aus.) everything, the lot.

whole caboose *n.* [1930s+] (Aus.) everything, the lot (cf. WHOLE KIT AND CABOODLE).

whole cahoot *n.* [mid-19C] (US) everything. [SE *cahoot*, a company, a partnership]

whole cheese *n.* [late 19C+] (US) **1** everything. **2** an important person (cf. BIG CHEESE).

whole cooloo *n.* [1930s] everything, 'the lot'. [Arab. *cooloo*, all, or CABOODLE]

whole enchilada, the *n.* [20C] (US) everything, the lot.

whole famn damily, the *n.* [20C] (US) a euph. for the *whole damn family*.

whole-footed *adj.* [early–mid-18C] unreserved, frank, free and easy. [SE *whole-footed*, treading with one's whole foot, not just the toes]

whole gridiron, the *n.* [mid-19C+] everyone, the whole lot.

whole hog *adv.* [early 19C+] (orig. US) completely, without reservation (cf. ENTIRE ANIMAL).

whole hypothec, the *n.* [late 19C] (Scot.) the whole stock or lot, the whole 'concern' or 'business', the whole of anything. [SE *hypothecation*, an act of pledging as security]

whole jingbang, the *n.* [mid–late 19C] the whole thing, the whole affair, the whole lot (cf. WHOLE BANG SHOOT). [Scot., ? echoic of people moving]

whole kit *n.* [late 18C–mid-19C] the entire lot, the full collection (cf. WHOLE KIT AND CABOODLE).

whole kit and boiling *n.* [mid-19C–1920s] (US) absolutely everything and everyone, the lot (cf. WHOLE KIT AND CABOODLE).

whole kit and caboodle/kit and caboodle/boodle *n.* [mid-19C+] (orig. US) the lot, everything there is; an alt. version is *whole kit and boiling* (cf. WHOLE BOILING LOT). [KIT n.² + CABOODLE]

whole kit and cargo *n.* [mid–late 19C] (US) the lot (cf. WHOLE KIT AND CABOODLE).

whole lot of shit *n.* [1960s+] (US Black) a disturbance, a problem, confusion. [SHIT n.¹ (1)]

whole lot of yellow wasted *phr.* [1990s] (US Black) a derog. phr. used to refer to an unattractive light-coloured African American (cf. HIGH YELLOW; YELLOW GIRL). [the use of 'wasted' refers to the stereotype of light skin being a pos. commodity, but in this case, where the person is unattractive, it is of no use]

whole new ball game *n.* [1960s+] (US) a totally revised or new situation. [sporting imagery]

whole nine yards *n.* [1960s+] everything, the complete package (cf. UP TO THE NINES). [ety. unknown, but most of the many suggestions involve supposed standards of measurement, from the dimensions of a nun's habit to the capacity of a cement truck and the length of an ammunition clip to that of a hangman's rope. However, few, when checked, actually run to 9 yards. It is most likely to be the use of 9 as a form of 'mystic' number]

whole 'nother thing *n.* [1960s+] (US) a totally different situation; something else completely (cf. WHOLE NEW BALL GAME).

whole outfit, the *n.* [1910s+] the lot, everything.

whole schmear/schmeer/shmear/shmeer/shmier, the *n.* [1950s+] everything, the whole lot. [SE *whole* + fig. use of SCHMEER]

whole shebang *n.* [19C] absolutely everything. [US milit. jargon *shebang*, a soldier's tent, where his possessions were kept, ult. SE *shebang*, a hut, a dwelling]

whole shmear/shmeer/shmier *see* WHOLE SCHMEAR.

whole shooting gallery, the *n.* [1970s+] absolutely everything (cf. WHOLE BANG SHOOT; WHOLE SHOOTING MATCH).

whole shooting match, the *n.* [late 19C+] (orig. US) absolutely everything (cf. WHOLE BANG SHOOT; WHOLE SHOOTING GALLERY).

whole team/whole team and a little dog under the wagon/whole team and a horse to spare *n.* [19C–1920s] (US) a phr. used to indicate one's own self-importance, energy etc, usu. as *ain't I/he/she/they the whole team ... .*

who let you out? *phr.* [late 19C–1940s] a deliberately deflating response to someone who is behaving far too self-confidently. [one has been released from an asylum]

wholewheat bread *n.* [1970s+] (US Black) a light-skinned person (cf. BUCKWHEAT; WHITE BREAD adj.).

whole works, the *see* WORKS n.².

wholsies! *excl.* [1950s+] (US) a claim of first rights to something (cf. KEEPSIES!). [i.e. 'I want the whole thing']

whomp/whump *n.* (US) **1** [1920s+] a heavy, low sound. **2** [1970s+] a heavy blow. [echoic]

whomp/whump *v.* [1950s+] (US) **1** to defeat, trounce. **2** to hit. [WHOMP n.]

whomp on *see* WOMP ON.

whompy *see* WOMPY.

whomp up *v.* [1950s+] (US) **1** to create, devise or make up. **2** to stimulate, to stir up. [ext. of WHOMP v.]

who needs it? *phr.* [1950s+] (orig. US) a phr. implying that something is completely unnecessary or unwanted. [trans. of Yid. *ver darf es?*]

whoogie *n.* [20C] (US Black) a derog. term for a White person (cf. PINK WHOOGIE). [SE *white* + BOOGIE n.²]

whoop and a holler *n.* [early 19C+] (US) a short distance, also *two whoops and a holler*. [SE *whoop* + *holler*, both meaning shout, and so the distance such cries would carry]

whoop-de-do/-doodle *n.* [1920s+] (US) an uproar, noisy celebration.

whoop-de-do/-doodle *adj.* [1920s+] (US) uproarious, noisy.

whooped/whupped [1980s] (US campus) drunk (cf. WHIPPED adj.²). [WHOP v.]

whoopee *n.* [mid-19C+] (US) a wild party. [WHOOPEE!]

whoopee! *excl.* [mid-19C+] (orig. US) a cry of intense delight. [SE *whoop*, a cry + sfx. -*ee*]

whoopee mama *n.* [late 19C–1930s] a flighty young woman, usu. middle class, in her late teens or very early 20s, pursuing a lifestyle as far as possible removed from that desired by her parents (cf. FLAPPER). [WHOOPEE n.+ MAMA]

whooper-dooper *n.* [1920s+] (US) a wild celebration, a carouse. [SE *whoop* + redup.]

whooperup *n.* [late 19C] (US) a second-rate singer who produces noise rather than music. [SE *whoop*]

whooping *adj.* [mid-19C] very large of its type (cf. WHOPPING).

whoop it/things up *v.* [late 19C+] (orig. US) **1** to have a noisy, ostentatious good time. **2** to stir things up, to create excitement. [SE *whoop*, a cry]

whoops *v.* [1920s+] (US) to vomit. [SE *whoops!*, an excl. of apology]

whoop things up *see* WHOOP IT UP.

whoozis/whoozit *n.* [1920s+] (US) an unknown or unspecifiable thing or person. [SE *who's this/it*]

whop *n.* [1950s+] (US) an attempt, a try (cf. BASH n.²; CRACK n.¹⁴; POP n.⁵). [WHOP v.]

whop *v.* **1** [late 16C+] to hit, to beat, to flog. **2** [mid-19C+] to overcome, to surpass, to defeat; thus *whopping*, a severe beating or defeat. [? SE *quap*, to beat, to throb, ult. Ger. *quappen*, to flop, *quappeln*, to quiver]

who pawned her sister's ship? *phr.* [late 19C] a phr. directed at a passing woman. [? corruption of SE *shift* (an undergarment) and so a critique of the woman's clothing]

whopcacker/wopcacker *n.* [1920s+] (Aus.) anything notable, amazing etc (cf. HUMDINGER). [? WOOPKNACKER]

whop it up *v.* [1960s+] of a man, to have sexual intercourse, esp. in *I could whop it up her/that*, I would like to have sex with that woman (cf. WHACK IT UP). [fig. use of WHOP v. (1)]

whopper/whapper *n.* [late 18C+] **1** a notably large person (cf. BUMPER n.¹). **2** a particularly gross lie (cf. CAULKER). [fig. use of WHOP v.]

whopping/whapping *adj.* [mid-19C+] (mainly juv.) enormous, very large; esp. ext. as *whopping great* (cf. LICKING adj.). [fig. use of WHOP v.]

whop-straw/Johnny whop-straw *n.* [mid-19C] a countryman, a peasant. [his SE *whopping* or threshing straw]

who pulled your chain? *phr.* [1910s+] a derisive phr. to one who has 'butted in' to a private conversation, who asked you to make a comment? (cf. WHO BLEW YOUR TRUMPET?).

who put that monkey on horseback without tying his tail? *phr.* [late 18C] an antagonistic phr. aimed at a poor horse-rider.

who put the quarter in your slot? *phr.* [1980s+] (US campus) a sarcastic admonition to mind one's own business.

whore *n.* **1** [20C] a general derog. term of address, irrespective of sex. **2** [20C] in cards, the queen. **3** [1970s+] a promiscuous woman, but not necessarily, and not even usually, an actual prostitute. [rooted in SE *whore*, but carrying no commercial overtones]

-whore *sfx.* [1980s+] (US campus) used in a comb. with a noun to denote a fanatic, someone who is obsessed by the noun in question, e.g. *bookwhore, partywhore*.

whore-chaser *n.* [1950s–60s] (US Black) a womanizer, whether pursuing actual prostitutes or merely available women.

whoredog *n.* [1980s+] (US campus) **1** an unrespectable or criminal. **2** a promiscuous woman.

whore-hopper *n.* [1920s+] (US) a sexually voracious man who frequently visits prostitutes. [SE *whore* + HOP v. (2)]

whorehound *n.* [1950s+] a man who enjoys sex with prostitutes (cf. CUNTHOUND; PLEASURE HOUND; PUSSY HOUND). [SE *whore* + sfx. -HOUND]

whorehouse *adj.* [1940s+] (US) cheap, tawdry, in bad taste. [SE *whorehouse*]

whorehouse broad/chick/girl/woman *n.* [1940s+] (US Black) a prostitute who works in a brothel rather than on the streets. [SE *whorehouse* + BROAD n.²/CHICK n.⁴/SE *girl*/SE *woman*]

whore-pipe *n.* [late 18C–19C] the penis. [SE *whore* + fig. use of *pipe*]

whore's bird *n.* [late 18C–early 19C] a debauchee. [SE *whore* + BIRD n.³]

whore scars/scars *n.* [1940s–60s] (US Black) the scars left from continuous injections of narcotics (cf. TRACKS).

whore's curse *n.* [late 18C–early 19C] **1** 5s 3d. **2** the telling-off one received for offering 5s 3d. [the going rate for a prostitute's favours was half a guinea (10s 6d), the gold coin worth 5s 3d was substituted by mean customers who liked to be seen giving the woman gold, but saw no reason to be over-generous]

whore's ghost *n.* (Irish) **1** [1970s+] anything seen as intractable or obnoxious. **2** [1990s] a child of a prostitute.

whore shop *n.* [late 19C+] a brothel (cf. BUTTOCKING SHOP). [SE *whore* + SHOP n.¹ (2)]

whore's melt *n.* [20C] (Irish) a general term of abuse. [SE *whore*, i.e. woman + *melt*, spawn]

whore splash *n.* [1960s+] a brief, cursory shower, as taken by a prostitute between clients.

who ride *n.* [1990s] (US Black) any form of extreme activity, a shooting, a riot etc.

who robbed the barber? *phr.* [late 19C–1910s] a teasing phr. aimed at one who's hair is seen as over-long (cf. WHERE'S YOUR VIOLIN?).

whose dog is dead?/what dog is a-hanging? *phr.* [17C+] what is the matter?

whose mare is dead? *phr.* [late 16C–mid-18C] what is the matter?

whosermybob/whosermyjig *n.* [1930s+] (Aus.) anything or anyone that one has forgotten the name of. [vars. on THINGUM-MIBOB; THINGUMMIJIG]

who shot the dog? *phr.* [late 19C] a derisory phr. aimed at early members of the Volunteers, locally raised forces who served as auxiliaries to the regular army. [? an anecdote in which a Volunteer mistakenly shot a dog]

who slept in the knifebox? *phr.* [20C] a rhetorical question asked of a person, usu. a child, who is making cheeky or impertinent comments (cf. EAT RAZOR SOUP). [they are being too 'sharp']

who's milking this cow? *phr.* [late 19C+] mind your own business (cf. WHO'S ROBBING THIS COACH?).

who's robbing this coach? *phr.* [late 19C+] (Aus.) mind your own business. [an anecdote of the bush-ranging era, cited at length in *DSUE*, 1984, p.1336]

who stole the donkey? *phr.* [mid-19C] a phr. shouted after anyone wearing a white hat, and the reply is 'The man in the white hat'. [certainly anecdotal, but Hotten (1869) is 'unable to explain the phrase']

who stole the mutton? *phr.* [mid-19C] a mocking phr. aimed at a passing policeman. [an actual case of the theft of some mutton that baffled the police]

who struck Buckley? *phr.* [mid-19C] 'a common phrase used to irritate Irishmen' (Hotten 1864). [ety. unknown; presumably anecdotal, although poss. merely assonant]

who's your hatter? *phr.* [19C] a phr. aimed at one considered villainous or untrustworthy. [for ety. *see* BAD HAT]

who the blazes *see* HOW THE BLAZES.

who the devil! *see* WHAT THE DEVIL!

who took it out of you? *phr.* [late 19C–1900s] a phr. addressed to someone looking miserable or depressed. ['it' being the 'stuffing' or 'starch']

whow-ball *see* WHOA-BALL.

who you screwin'? *phr.* [1960s+] an aggressive question aimed at someone who is staring, or perhaps is not, but with whom the speaker wishes to challenge. [SCREW v.³]

whump *n.*¹ *see* WHOMP n.

whump *n.*² *see* WUMP.

whump *v. see* WHOMP v.

whup *v.* [20C] (US Black) to attack, to beat up (cf. WHAP; WHOP). [SE *whip*]

whup the game, to *phr.* [1970s+] (US Black) to succeed in life (cf. HAVE IT KNOCKED). [WHUP + GAME n.³]

whupped *see* WHOPPED.

why buy a cow when milk is so cheap? *phr.* [1930s+] (US) why get married when sexually permissive women are so available.

why don't you hire a hall? *phr.* [late 19C–1950s] (orig. US) a phr. used to reprove someone who has just informed one of bad news.

why ever/whyever *prn.* [late 19C+] (orig. US) emphatic form of SE *why*.

why in time *see* WHAT IN TIME?

why keep a dog and bark yourself? *phr.* [20C] urging one to use all available facilities if one is fortunate enough to have access to them.

whyms *n.* [late 19C] members of the Y.M.C.A. [a supposed 'telescoping' of the initials]

why the blazes *see* HOW THE BLAZES.

why the devil?/fuck?/hell?/shit? *phr.* [early 18C+] an exclamatory query of amazement, annoyance etc. [all intensified forms of SE *why?* + SE *devil*/FUCK/SE *hell*/SHIT n.¹]

wibble *n.* [late 18C–late 19C] any form of weak or bad drink. [it makes one's stomach *wibble*, i.e. wobble]

wibble-wobble/wibblety-wobblety/wibbly-wobbly *adv.* [mid-19C+] unsteadily.

wibling's witch/w.w. *n.* [late 18C–19C] the four of clubs. [the gambler James *Wibling* (*fl.* early 17C) who made a fortune from gambling and whose lucky card was supposedly the four of clubs]

wicher *see* WITCHER

wicher-cully *n.* [late 17C–18C] (Und.) a silversmith. [WITCHER + CULLY n. (2)]

Wichita *n.* [20C] (US prison) a betrayal. [? stereotyping of the town and its inhabitants]

wick *n.* [20C] the penis (cf. DIP THE WICK).

wicked *adj.* **1** [mid-17C+] unpleasant, terrible, awful. **2** [mid-17C+] very, really. **3** [1920s+] (orig. US) excellent, wonderful (cf. AWFUL adj.). [although modern 'bad = good' use properly dates f. 1970s US Black vocab. The *OED*'s first cited use is in F. Scott Fitzgerald's *This Side of Paradise* (1920): 'Phoebe and I are going to shake a wicked calf']

wicked awesome *adj.* [1990s] (US teen) anything especially excellent. [WICKED adj. (3) + AWESOME]

wicked lady *n.* [1940s–50s] (prison) the cat o' nine tails.

wicked loser *n.* [1980s+] (US campus) a failure, esp. one who could equally well have succeeded had they so decided. [SE *wicked* + LOSER n. (3)]

wicked pisser *n.* [1990s] (US, mainly northeast) something very good or very bad. When used without an article, e.g. *This food is wicked pisser*, it is taken to mean very good; when used with an article, e.g. *This job is a wicked pisser*, it is taken to mean something very bad. [WICKED + PISSER n.³]

wicked rumours *n.* [20C] bloomers. [rhy. sl.]

wicked thing *n.* [1970s+] (US Black) an extraordinary event or situation. [WICKED + SE *thing*]

wicked villainy *n.* [mid-19C] (Aus.) illicitly distilled whisky. [the 'Dickensian' cockney 'w' for 'v']

wicker *n.* [1980s+] (Black) a lesbian. [ety. unknown; ? SE *witch*]

wicket *n.* [19C] throat. [SE *wicket*, a gate]

widdle *n.* [1950s+] (mainly juv.) an act of urination. [WIDDLE v.]

widdle *v.* [1950s+] to urinate. [? WEE v. + PIDDLE v. (1)]

wide *adj.* [late 19C] **1** unrestrained, violent. **2** lax, loose, immoral. **3** 'sharp'. [prior use f. 16C is SE]

wide-awake *n.* [mid–late 19C] a soft felt hat with broad brim and low crown (cf. SLEEPY). [a pun on the material, which lacked a 'nap']

wide-awake *adj.* [19C] vigilant, aware, knowing.

wide boy *n.* [1930s+] a minor villain, often dabbling in 'get-rich-quick' schemes. [WIDE adj. (2) + SE *boy*]

wide load *n.* [1990s] (US campus) someone with large hips and buttocks.

wide-o *n.* [20C] a minor villain, a 'spiv' (cf. WIDE BOY). [on the pattern of RAPE-O]

wide-open *adj.*¹ [late 19C+] vulnerable, undefended. [boxing imagery]

wide-open *adj.*² [20C] (US) of driving, very fast. [the throttle is 'wide open']

wide-open *adj.*³ [1980s+] (US Black) sexually excited (cf. HAVE ONE'S NOSE OPEN).

wide open *adv.* [20C] (US) of driving, at full speed.

wide-open beaver *n.* [1970s+] a photograph or film of the inner labia (cf. SPLIT BEAVER). [SE *wide-open* + BEAVER n.⁴]

wide place in the road *phr.* [20C] (US) a derog. phr. for a small town or hamlet (cf. GREASY SPOT ON THE ROAD). [its unimportance in the eyes of those who drive through]

widgeon *n.* [early 17C–mid-18C] a fool (cf. PIG WIDGEON). [note Freddie *Widgeon*, one of P.G. Wodehouse's (1881–1975) foolish members of the Drones Club]

widgey *n.* [20C] (mainly Irish) the vagina (cf. WIGGER). [ety. unknown; ? link to SE *widgeon*, i.e. a BIRD n.⁵]

widgie *n.* [1950s+] (Aus.) the female counterpart of a BODGIE. [post-1960s use historical only; ? WIDGEY or RIDGIE-DIDGIE]

wido *n.* [mid-19C] an alert, aware person, one who is 'no fool' (cf. WIDE). [? earliest use of the -O sfx.; the cited chronology predates WIDE adj. but presumably is an offshoot thereof]

widow *n.*¹ **1** [early 18C] an expiring fire. **2** [late 19C] an extra hand dealt to the table in certain card-games.

Widow, the *n.*² [late 18C+] a nickname for Veuve Cliquot champagne, therefore champagne in general. [Fr. *veuve*, a widow]

Widow, the *n.*³ [late 19C] Queen Victoria. [widowed in 1861 on the death of her husband, Prince Albert, and ext. by the fiercely royalist Rudyard Kipling (1865–1936) as 'the widow at Windsor']

widow *n.*⁴ [1970s] (drugs) any black capsule that contains amphetamine. [abbr. BLACK WIDOW n.¹]

widow *n.*⁵ *see* BLACK WIDOW n.².

-widow *sfx.* [20C] of a woman who is left behind while her husband devotes himself to an obsession, usu. sport or a hobby; thus *golf-widow*, *cricket-widow* etc.

widow bewitched *n.* [early 18C–mid-19C] a woman whose husband is temporarily absent (cf. GRASS WIDOW).

-widower *sfx.* [1960s+] the male version of the more common -WIDOW sfx.

widower bewitched *n.* [early 18C] a husband separated from or deserted by his wife.

widow five-finger *n.* [20C] masturbation.

widow jones/widow jones's house *n.* [mid-19C] the lavatory. [var. on MRS JONES HOUSE]

widow-maker *n.* [1940s+] (Can./US) a dead branch caught high in a tree which may fall and kill or injure someone below.

widow's mite *n.* [late 19C–1920s] a light. [rhy. sl.]

widow's wink *n.* [1970s] a Chinese person. [rhy. sl. *widow's wink* = CHINK n.³ (1)]

widow twankey *n.* [20C] **1** a handkerchief, i.e. a *hankie*. **2** an American. [rhy. sl.; (2) = *yankee*]

wienie *see* WEENIE n.¹.

wif/wiff *n.*¹ [20C] (US) a wife.

wif *n.*² *see* WHIFF n.

wife *n.*¹ [mid-19C] (prison) **1** a key. **2** a fetter fixed to one leg. [she 'locks up' her husband]

wife *n.*² **1** [late 19C+] the supposedly subservient, 'female' partner in a gay couple. **2** [1980s+] (US campus) a regular girlfriend (cf. SPOUSE).

wife *n.*³ [1940s+] (US Black) a pimp's favoured prostitute.

wife-in-law *n.* [1940s+] (US Black) any woman in a pimp's group of prostitutes, other than his favourite and thus most privileged woman. [play on WIFE n.³]

wife in watercolours *n.* [late 18C–early 19C] a mistress. [the image of colours fading as do the passions of the newly married or the idea that the loving (if hired) prostitute was less strident than an intolerant harridan of a wife. Watercolours, suggests Grose 1785, are, like mistresses, 'easily effaced, or dissolved']

wife out of Westminster *n.* [18C–late 19C] a wife unconstrained by monogamy (cf. GO TO WESTMINSTER FOR A WIFE). [the then salacious image of *Westminster*]

wife's best friend *n.* [20C] the penis.

wife-starver *n.* [1960s+] (Aus.) a man who defaults on his maintenance payments.

wiff *n.*¹ *see* WIF n.¹.

wiff *n.*² *see* WHIFF n.

wiff, the *n.*³ [1990s] (US Black teen) **1** trying to do something and not getting any response. **2** missing an opportunity. [baseball jargon *whiff*, to miss the ball]

wiffle-woffle *n.* [1910s–20s] an arrogant person. [? WIFFLE-WOFFLES; i.e. a fig. stomach-ache renders them ill-humoured]

wiffle-woffles *n.* [mid-19C] stomach-ache.

wig *n.*¹ **1** [18C+] the head, the brain or its functions (cf. ATTIC). **2** [1930s+] (US Black) hair that has been artificially straightened. **3** [1950s] (W.I.) a male haircutting style that supposedly resembles a judge's wig. The hair is cut into a peak at the front and there is no sharp razor line at the back. Those requesting such a cut would tell the barber, 'Try me'.

wig *n.*² [late 18C–1900s] a severe scolding, a telling-off (cf. WIGGING). [? the BIGWIG, who might deliver one, or the wearing of SE *wigs* by admonitory judges]

wig *n.*³ **1** [19C] a dignitary, lit. one who wears a wig for professional reasons. **2** [1990s] a barrister.

wig *n.*⁴ [1950s+] (US) a jazz musician. [WIG v.² (4)]

wig *adj.* [1960s] (US teen) great, wonderful. [WIG v.² (5)]

wig *v.*¹ [early 19C+] to scold, to reprimand (cf. WIGGING). [the scolder uses quasi-judicial authority]

wig *v.*² **1** [1930s+] (US) to talk, chatter. **2** [1930s+] to annoy, to irritate. **3** [1950s+] (US) to become nervous, hysterical, overly stressed, mentally unbalanced (cf. WIG OUT). **4** [1950s+] (US) to play jazz music. **5** [1950s+] (US) to be in good spirits, to enjoy. [fig. uses of WIG n.¹ (1)]

wiganowns *n.* [late 18C–early 19C] a man wearing a notably large wig. [? ext. of SE *wig*]

wig-block *n.* [mid-19C–1920s] the head.

wig bust *n.* [1940s+] (US Black) the altering of a natural crinkly Black head of hair into a straight 'process' (qv) style. [WIG n.¹ (2) + BUST v.¹]

wig city *adj.* [1960s+] (US teen) eccentric, unbalanced (cf. WIGGY). [WIG v.² (3) + sfx. *-city*]

wigeon *n.* [1940s+] (Aus.) an affectionate term for a young woman (cf. WIDGIE). [SE *widgeon*; *wigeon*, a wild duck]

wig-faker *n.* [18C–late 19C] a wig-maker, a hairdresser. [SE *wig* + FAKER n.¹ (2)]

wigga/wigger *n.* [1990s] (orig. US) a White person who adopts a Black, specifically HIP-HOP/RAP n.⁵, lifestyle and is not merely a consumer of the records, but attempts to emulate what is otherwise an autonomous Black culture (cf. WANNABE; WHITE NIGGER). [SE *White* + NIGGA, invariably derog. term used by Blacks to sneer at those who ape their culture and by Whites in a generally racist sense]

wigga-wagga *n.* **1** [late 19C–1910s] a walking stick. **2** [1900s] the penis. [SE *wiggle/waggle*]

wigged out *adj.* (orig. US) **1** [1950s–60s] (drugs) intoxicated by a drug. **2** [1950s+] eccentric, insane, deluded, out of touch (cf. WIGGY). [WIG OUT]

wigger *n.*¹ [20C] (Irish) a derog. term for a woman. [WIDGEY]

wigger *n.*² *see* WIGGA.

wigging *n.* [mid-19C+] a reprimand, a telling off. [WIG v.¹, note Hotten (1860): 'If the head of a firm calls a clerk into the parlour, and rebukes him, it is an EAR-WIGGING; if done before the other clerks it is a WIGGING']

wigglers *n.* [1940s] (US Black) the fingers. [SE *wiggle*]

wiggy *adj.* [1960s+] **1** odd, bizarre, unpleasant, disturbing. **2** pleasing, enjoyable, exciting and up to date. **3** (US drugs) intoxicated with narcotics. [WIG v.² (3)]

wig hat *n.* [1950s+] (orig. US Black) a wig. [WIG n.¹ (1) + SE *hat*]

wig out *v.* [1950s+] (US) **1** to lose control, to have a breakdown; thus *wigged out*, eccentric, over-emotional. **2** (orig. jazz) to enjoy oneself, lose one's inhibitions. **3** to excite, to thrill. [WIG v.² (3), (5)]

wig-picker *n.* [1960s+] (US) a psychiatrist. [WIG n.¹ (1) + SE *picker*]

wigs! *see* MY WIG!

wigsby *see* MR WIGSBY.

wigs on the green *n.* [18C–mid-19C] (orig. Irish) an argument, a fight. [if one has not already removed it, one's wig is likely to fall or be knocked off in such a fight]

wigster *see* MR WIGSBY.

wig-wag *v.* [late 16C–1910s] to wave or move with a writhing movement; thus *wig-wagger*, one who *wig-wags*, *wig-waggy*, tortuous, winding. [SE *wiggle* + *wag*]

wigwam for a goose's bridle *phr.* [1930s+] (Aus.) an answer used to deflect an unwanted question, esp. as asked by a child.

wilbur *n.* [20C] a flight. [rhy. sl.; air pioneer *Wilbur* Wright (1867–1912)]

wild *n.* [mid-19C] (tramp) a village (cf. VILE).

wild *adj.* [1950s+] **1** eccentric, bizarre, weird, odd. **2** (US) exciting, wonderful. **3** (US Und.) consecutive, referring to a jail sentence (cf. BOWLEGGED).

wild *v.* [1980s+] (US Black) to go out looking for victims to mug and attack. [popularized through media reports of the savage rape and beating of New York's 'Central Park jogger' in 1989. According to the accused, 'wild', like its noun form 'wilding', is a nonce word, used by them alone and meaning simply going wild. It was elevated to a slang term after a report in the *New York Times* on 22 April 1989. However, the term is used, in the criminal sense, by the rapper Ice T on his album *Rhyme Pays* (1987); note also BUCKWILD]

wild and woolly *phr.* [late 19C+] (US) uncouth, raucous.

wild-ass/-assed *adj.* [1960s+] (US) crazy, insane, unbalanced. [WILD adj. + sfx. -ASS]

wild card *n.* [1960s+] (US) something or someone unknown or unpredictable, also as adj. [poker imagery]

wildcat *n.*¹ [19C] (US) **1** an unsound, dubious business, esp. a 'wildcat bank'. **2** the notes issued by a wildcat bank. [wildcat banks existed in the western US before the National Bank Act of 1863 and were virtually unregulated. The notes they issued were essentially worthless]

wildcat *n.*² **1** [late 19C–1940s] (US) illicitly distilled whisky. **3** [1980s+] (drugs) methcathinone (cf. BATHTUB SPEED). **4** [1980s+] (drugs) cocaine. [the effects]

wildcat *n.*³ [1970s+] (US Black) someone who participates intensely and also to his own advantage in street life. [SE *wildcat/wild* + CAT n.⁹ (3)]

Wild Cats and Tigers Union *n.* [1950s+] (N.Z.) the Women's Christian Temperance Union. [the initial letters + ref. to the predictable lack of Christian forbearance among such self-proclaimedly pious organizations]

wildfire *n.* [mid-18C] a fiery drink (cf. GLIM n.²). [its taste and effects]

wilding *n.* [1980s+] (US Black) going out in search of victims to mug and attack. [for ety. *see* WILD v.]

wild oats *n.* [mid-16C–early 17C] a dissolute young man, a rake. [SOW ONE'S WILD OATS]

wild rogue *n.* [16C–early 19C] (Und.) a dedicated professional villain (cf. CANTING CREW; ROGUE n.¹).

wild squirt *n.* [late 18C–1900s] diarrhoea (cf. HERSHEY SQUIRT).

wilds, the *n.* [late 19C–1900s] (Aus.) a fit of depression, a temper tantrum; thus *give one the wilds*, to depress, to 'bring down', to annoy. [WILD adj. (1)]

wild thing, the *n.* [1980s+] (orig. US Black/campus) **1** sexual intercourse. **2** rape. [cf. WILD v.].

wild west *n.* [20C] a vest or undershirt. [rhy. sl.]

Wilhelm II much *phr.* [late 19C] (society) too much, excessive. [a play on Kaiser *Wilhelm II* and SE *too much*; according to Ware, a ref. to the Kaiser's notoriously busy life]

wilkie bards *n.* [1920s–50s] playing cards. [rhy. sl.; ult. music-hall comedy star *Wilkie Bard* (1874–1944)]

willamakanka *see* BULLAMAKANKA.

will do *phr.* [1950s+] a general affirmative, OK, I'll do it.

willets *n.* [1990s] the female breasts. [ety. unknown]

william *n.*¹ **1** [mid-19C–1900s] a bill, esp. in phr. *meet sweet William*, to pay off a bill as soon as it is presented. **2** [mid-19C–1920s] (US) a dollar bill. [? rhy. sl.; abbr. of *William* = *will* = bill]

william *n.*² [mid-19C+] the penis (cf. ABRAHAM; WILLIE n.¹). [pun on abbr. of proper name]

william *n.*³ [1950s+] **1** excrement. **2** an act of defecation. [rhy. sl. *william pitt* = SHIT n.¹; ult. UK politician *William* Pitt the Younger (1759–1806)]

william hill *n.* [1990s] a pill. [rhy. sl.; the *William Hill* chain of bookmakers]

William Powell *n.* [20C] a towel. [rhy. sl.; ult. film star *William Powell* (1892–1984)]

William Tell *n.* [20C] a smell. [rhy. sl.; ult. the 15C Swiss hero *William Tell*]

william the third *n.* [1960s–70s] (Aus.) a piece of excrement, a stool. [rhy. sl., *William the Third* = TURD]

willie/willy n.[1] [20C] the penis. [orig. in northern but non-dial. use]

willie/willy n.[2] [20C] a male homosexual. [? proper name or WILLIE n.[1]]

willie/willy n.[3] [1940s+] (Aus.) **1** money, esp. as used in betting. **2** a wallet. [ety. unknown; ? given the context of betting, SE *will he … won't he* (and should I bet on it)]

willie n.[4] [1940s+] (orig. Aus.) a tantrum (cf. CHUCK A WILLIE). [? WILLIES]

willie lunchmeat/lump-lump n. [20C] (US Und.) a fool (cf. BEEF-HEAD; MEATHEAD). [generic use of proper name + the stolidity and density of SE *lunchmeat/lump*]

willies n. [late 19C+] nerves, worries, tension (cf. GEEWILLIES). [ety. unknown, ? link to fig. use of dial. *willy-wambles*, stomach-rumbling]

willie-/willy-waving n. [1970s+] acting, speaking or posing in an exaggeratedly macho fashion (cf. BALL CLANKER). [WILLIE n.[1] + SE *waving*]

willie, willie–wicked, wicked! excl. [late 19C] an excl. used when sighting an older woman chatting to a younger man. [from a case in which a middle-aged landlady sued her non-paying young lodger, whose defence was that not only would she come into his room, but she then proceeded to sit on his bed]

willing adj. [late 19C+] (Aus./N.Z.) pugnacious, aggressive, violent.

willing tit n. [late 18C–early 19C] a complaisant woman. [SE *willing* + TIT n.[3]]

will o'the wisps n. [20C] crisps. [rhy. sl.]

willow adj. [late 17C–18C] poor, of no reputation. [SE *willowy*, slim]

will's whiff n. [20C] syphilis. [rhy. sl. = abbr. *syph*; ult. brand-name of *Will's Whiff*, a small cigar]

willy see WILLIE n.

willy lees n. [1920s+] (Aus.) a flea, fleas. [rhy. sl.]

will you shoot? phr. [1900s–10s] (Aus.) will you pay for a drink? [SHOOT v.[4]]

will you short? phr. [late 19C] (Aus.) will you have a drink of spirits? [SHORT n.[1]]

will you tod? phr. [mid-19C] an invitation to drink. [SE *toddy*]

will you try a smile? phr. [19C] an invitation to drink. [SMILE n.[1]]

willy wacht n. [late 19C] a drink, esp. of whisky. [Scot.; *Willy* Arnot (a distiller? a landlord?), good whisky + *wacht/waught*, to drink deeply]

willy wag n. [20C] (Aus.) a pack. [rhy. sl. *willy wag* = SWAG n.[1] (7)]

willy-waving see WILLIE-WAVING.

wilma n. [1980s+] (US campus) an ugly, stupid woman (cf. BARNEY n.[5]). [the character *Wilma* in the cartoon (1960s) and film (1994) *The Flintstones*]

Wilson Pickett n. [1970s] a ticket. [rhy. sl.; ult. soul star *Wilson Pickett* (b.1941)]

Wilson's den n. [1960s] (bingo) the number 10. [10 Downing Street, then home to Prime Minister Harold *Wilson* (1916–95), presumably the name can be altered to fit the current incumbent]

wilt v. [late 19C] to fade, i.e. to run off, to bolt.

wimble n. [18C] the penis. [SE *wimble*, a gimlet, an instrument for boring into soft ground]

wimp n.[1] [1920s–40s] a woman. [note 1910s Oxford University sl. *go wimping*, for a male undergraduate to go out looking for women]

wimp n.[2] [1960s+] a weakling, an indecisive person. [? J. Wellington *Wimpy* a character in the cartoon film *Popeye*]

wimp dog n. [1980s+] (US campus) a male with little personality or assertiveness. [WIMP n.[2] + DOG n.[4]]

wimp-guts n. [1980s+] a coward, a weakling (cf. POSSUM-GUTS). [WIMP n.[2] + SE *guts*]

wimpo/wimpoid adj. [1980s+] (US) weak, ineffective, cowardly. [WIMP n.[2] + sfx. -*o*/-*oid*]

wimp out v. [1980s+] (orig. US) to act in a cowardly manner, to let someone down, to fail to live up to a commitment. [WIMP n.[2]]

wimpy n. [1980s+] (US) a hamburger. [the consumption of hamburgers by J. Wellington *Wimpy* in the *Popeye* cartoon; but note *Wimpy*, a chain of UK burger restaurants since 1960s]

wimpy adj. [1960s+] (US) weak, ineffective, cowardly. [WIMP n.[2]]

win/winn/wyn n. [mid-16C–1900s] a penny (cf. NOSE AND CHIN; TREEWINS; TRESWINS). [origin unknown, but Vaux (1812) suggests without further explanation an abbr. of *Winchester*]

win v. [late 17C–1910s] to steal (cf. ACQUIRE).

win a halo, to phr. [1970s] (US) to be killed in battle.

win a pair of gloves, to phr. [late 18C] to kiss a sleeping man. [the woman who does so was traditionally rewarded with a pair of gloves]

winchcombe carson n. [20C] (Aus.) a parson. [rhy. sl.]

winchester n. [early 19C] a penny. [WIN n.]

Winchester goose n. [16C] venereal disease. [the popular brothels of Southwark came under the jurisdiction of the Bishop of *Winchester*]

wind n.[1] [early–mid-18C] strong liquor, esp. gin. [it catches one's breath]

wind n.[2] [early 19C] life; thus (Und.) *lagged for one's wind*, transported for one's natural life. [SE *wind*, the breath of life]

wind v. [late 18C+] (W.I.) of a woman, to move in a provocative manner, with much swishing of the hips (cf. WINE n.[2]). [SE *wind*, to writhe, to wriggle]

windbag n. [19C+] a braggart, a boaster, a 'loudmouth' (cf. BAG OF WIND).

windbags/wind-pumps n. [mid-19C–1940s] (US Black) the lungs. [their role in one's body]

wind-cutter n. [19C] a cocked hat. [its shape]

wind do twirl n. [mid-19C] a woman. [rhy. sl. *wind do twirl* = girl]

wind down v. [1960s+] the process of reaching an end. [SE *wind down*, to come gradually to a close]

winded-settled see SETTLED.

winder n.[1] [early 19C] a sentence of transportation for life; thus *winded-settled*, transported for life. [WIND n.[2]]

winder n.[2] [mid-19C] something so astounding that it 'takes one's breath away'. [SE *wind*, to deprive of breath, usu. through a blow]

windgat n. [1980s+] (S.Afr.) a braggart, a boaster, a 'blow-hard'. [SE *wind* + Afk. *gat*; lit. 'windy-arse']

windgat adj. [1980s+] (S.Afr.) cocky, self-opinionated. [WINDGAT n.]

windie n. [1980s=] (N.Z.) a *wind*-surfer. [abbr.]

Windies n. [1960s+] (orig. Aus.) the West *Indies* cricket team. [elision]

winding boy n. [1920s–30s] (US Black) a sexual athlete. [he can 'wind up' his sexual 'machinery']

windjammer n.[1] [20C] (Aus.) a hammer [rhy. sl.]

windjammer n.[2] [20C] (Aus.) a male homosexual. [play on SE *jam*, to force + (the source of) *wind*, i.e. the anus]

windjammer n.[3] [1910s–40s] (orig. US) a talkative, loquacious person, thus a liar. [SE *wind*, i.e. 'hot air' + *jam*, to force]

windmill n. [early 19C] the anus; thus *she has no fortune but her mills*, i.e. the WINDMILL and WATERMILL. [SE *wind* + *mill*, i.e. the unpleasant odours]

windmill cocktail *n.* [20C] (US) rainwater. [the stream that runs by a mill]

wind one's ball of yarn, to *phr.* [1940s–60s] (US) of a man, to have sexual intercourse (cf. BALL OF YARN).

wind one's clock, to *phr.* [1970s] (US) of a woman, to have sexual intercourse.

wind one's/the horn, to *phr.* [17C–18C] to publicize the fact that one has been cuckolded. [HORNS + pun on SE *wind the horn*, of a huntsman, to blow the horn]

window/windowpane *n.* [mid-19C–1920s] a monocle (cf. BIT OF WINDOW).

window-blind *n.* [late 19C] a sanitary towel.

window glass *see* WINDOWPANE *n.*²

window man *n.* [1950s+] (S.Afr.) a coloured person who is trying to pass as White and thus cuts their darker friends or relatives when they see them in public (cf. PLAY-WHITE). [Afk. *vensterkies*, a little window or *vensterjies kyk*, to look at little windows, i.e. one who pretends to be gazing into shop windows when embarrassing friends appear]

windowpane *n.*¹ *see* WINDOW.

windowpane/window glass *n.*² [1960s+] a variety of LSD. [a small square of gelatine impregnated with LSD]

window-peeper *n.* [late 18C–early 19C] a collector of the window tax. [he 'peeps' at the number of windows a house has]

windows *n.* **1** [mid-19C] the eyes (cf. FRONT WINDOWS). **2** [1900s–10s] (US) spectacles.

window shop *v.* [1980s+] (US campus) to go out looking for desirable members of the opposite sex.

wind-pies/wind-pies and air sausages/nutten-chops/ wind-sandwich and breeze-pie *n.* [20C] (W.I./Bdos., Trin.) no food, nothing to eat.

wind pudding *see* AIR PUDDING.

wind-sandwich and breeze-pie *see* WIND-PIES.

wind-settled *see* SETTLED.

wind someone's clock, to *phr.* [1940s+] (US) to beat someone up (cf. CLEAN SOMEONE'S CLOCK).

wind someone's cotton, to *phr.* [mid-19C–1900s] to cause someone trouble, to create difficulties for someone.

windsor castle *n.* [20C] the anus. [rhy. sl. *Windsor castle* = ARSEHOLE *n.*¹ (1)]

wind-stopper *n.* [late 19C] a garrotter. [SE *wind*, breath + *stop*]

wind-sucker *n.* [mid-19C] a worn-out horse, fit only for slaughter (cf. KNACKER *n.*; ROARER *n.*²; WHISTLER *n.*²). [its heavy breathing]

wind the horn *see* WIND ONE'S HORN.

wind-trap *n.* [20C] a flap, esp. of hair. [rhy. sl.]

wind-up *n.* [1970s+] **1** a practical joke. **2** a deliberate attempt to worry or mislead. [WIND UP *v.*²]

wind up *adj.* [late 19C–1920s] taut. [rhy. sl. *wind up* = pinned up]

wind up *v.*¹ [1910s+] **1** to bring to a conclusion. **2** to end up, to find oneself somewhere. **3** to result. [SE *wind up*, i.e. the winding up something that has been extended while in use]

wind up *v.*² [1970s+] to tease, usu. maliciously. [SE *wind up*, i.e. winding up a clock to 'make it go']

wind-up artist/merchant *n.* [1980s+] someone who specializes in teasing, possibly to the point of at least verbal retaliation. [WIND-UP *n.* + ARTIST *n.*²/MERCHANT]

wind up the clock, to *phr.* [18C] to have sexual intercourse. [based on a mildly coarse scene in Laurence Sterne's novel *Tristram Shandy* (1759–67)]

windy *adj.*¹ **1** [17C–20C] conceited, boastful. **2** [late 18C–19C] foolish. [SE *wind*, i.e. 'hot air']

windy *adj.*² [1910s+] (usu. juv.) cowardly. [GET THE WIND UP]

Windy City *n.* **1** [late 19C+] (US) Chicago, Illinois. **2** [1980s+] (S.Afr.) Port Elizabeth. [the climate]

windy wallets *n.* [late 19C–1900s] a loquacious, talkative self-aggrandizing person. [i.e. a WINDBAG]

wine *n.*¹ [mid–late 19C] (orig. university) a party at which those assembled drink wine; thus *wine and dine*, to entertain others.

wine/wining *n.*² [20C] (W.I.) a form of highly erotic dancing, esp. as seen at carnivals; thus *wine*, to dance in this manner (cf. WIND *v.*). [W.I. pron. of SE *wind*; i.e. the partners would *wind* round each other]

wine *n.*³ [1930s–60s] (US Black) money. [? the turning of one into the other]

winebag *n.* [late 19C] a drunkard who prefers wine to beer or spirits (cf. ALECAN).

wine-dot *n.* [1950s+] (Aus.) a drinker of cheap wine. [a pun on SE *Wyandotte*, a breed of medium-sized domestic fowls, orig. found in US]

winehead *n.* [1960s+] (US) an alcoholic who opts for wine as their preferred intoxicant. [SE *wine* + sfx. -HEAD (2)]

winer *n.* [1900s] one who drinks wine.

winey *adj.* [mid-19C] tipsy, slightly drunk (cf. ALED UP).

wing *n.*¹ **1** [late 18C] an oar. **2** [early 19C+] an arm.

wing *n.*² [1920s+] a fit, esp. as suffered by a withdrawing narcotics user (cf. WING-DING).

wing *n.*³ [1900s–30s] (Aus./Irish) a pre-decimalization penny. [WIN *n.*]

wing *v.*¹ [mid-19C+] (US) to shoot but not kill; to wound. [lit. 'to hit in the SE *wing*']

wing *v.*² [1950s+] to improvise, to ad lib. [abbr. WING IT]

wing commander *n.* [1990s] a very unattractive woman. [punning ext. of R.A.F.]

wing'd *see* WINGED *adj.*¹.

wing-ding/whingding *n.* **1** [late 19C+] (orig. US) a boisterous, noisy party. **2** [1920s+] a fit, esp. as suffered by a withdrawing narcotics user, who may fake such a fit to convince a doctor of the need for a supply of drugs (cf. INGBING; THROW A WING-DING). **3** [1930s+] an outburst of emotion or temper. [WING *n.*² (2) + redup, the image of waving one's arms]

wing-dinger *n.* **1** [1940s] a fake fit. **2** [1970s] an outburst of emotion. [WING-DING]

wingdoodle *see* WHANGDOODLE.

winged/wing'd *adj.*¹ [mid-19C] tipsy, slightly drunk. [HIT UNDER THE WING]

winged *adj.*² [late 19C] (Aus.) wounded. [WING *v.*¹]

winged *adj.*² [late 19C] (Aus.) one-armed. [WING *n.*¹ (2)]

winger *n.* [mid-19C] long, bushy sideburns growing beyond the edge of the chin. [SE *wing*]

wing it *v.* [1950s+] to improvise, to ad lib, to play a situation by ear without practice or rehearsal. [one fig. 'takes wing']

wingman *n.* [1960s+] (Aus.) a drug dealer (cf. BAGMAN). [? they help one 'fly']

wing out *v.* [1990s] (Black) to leave, to go away. [SE *wing*, to fly]

wings/whings *n.* [1920s+] (US drugs) any powdered narcotic. [they make one 'fly']

wings and things *n.* [1990s] (US) a Chinese take-out, esp. chicken and vegetables.

wingy *n.* [late 19C+] (Aus./US) the 'automatic' nickname of any one-armed man. [WING *n.*¹ (2)]

wingy *adj.* [1920s+] (US drugs) intoxicated with narcotics. [WINGS]

win in a walk, to *phr.* [late 19C+] (orig. US) to win easily (cf. WALK IT).

wining see WINE n.[2].

winji *adj.* [1940s+] (W.I.) sickly, frail, weak, puny. [UK dial. *winge*, to shrivel, as in fruit that is drying out]

wink n.[1] [1920s–60s] (Aus.) a sixpence. [? WIN n.]

wink n.[2] [1980s+] (US gay) an uncircumcized penis. [the glans 'winks' from within the foreskin]

winker n. [1970s] the vagina. [its supposed resemblance to a vertical 'eye;]

winkers n.[1] **1** [late 19C] the eyes or eyelashes. **2** [20C] (Aus.) spectacles.

winkers n.[2] [mid–late 19C] long, flowing or wavy side-whiskers. [play on a horse's SE *blinkers*, positioned next to each eye]

winker-stinker n. [1960s+] (US prison) the anus. [the shape and the odour]

winkie n.[1] *see* WINKY.

winkie n.[2] [1970s+] (US) the buttocks.

winkie v. [20C] to masturbate. [WANK v.]

winkle n. [1940s+] (usu. juv.) the penis (cf. WINKIE n.[2]; WINNY-POPPER).

winklebag/winkle n. [1970s+] cigarette. [rhy. sl. *winklebag* = FAG n.[4]]

winkle-fishing n. [1910s–20s] picking one's nose.

winklepickers n. [1950s+] highly pointed boots or shoes (cf. BOIL-PRICKER; COCKROACH KILLERS). [orig. favoured by Teddy Boys in the 1950s, but latterly absorbed into the wide variety of teen fashions]

winkler n. [1970s] one who assists in the eviction of tenants, usu. by means of threats and pressure. [SE *winkle out*]

winks n.[1] *see* FORTY WINKS.

winks n.[2] [mid-19C] peri*winkles*. [abbr.]

wink the other eye, to *phr.* [19C] to disregard and dismiss what has just been said.

winky/winkie n. [late 19C+] a very small or a child's penis; thus excl. *my winky!* [WINKLE n. (1)]

winkybag n. [1990s] the scrotum. [WINKY + SE *bag*]

winn *see* WIN n.

winner n. [1910s+] a person or project that is a potential success.

winnick *adj.* [19C+] crazy, eccentric (cf. CALLAN PARK). [the asylum at *Winnick*, Lancashire]

winnings n. [late 17C–early 19C] (Und.) booty, plunder. [WIN v.]

winny-popper n. [1950s+] (Can. juv.) the penis (cf. WINKY). [WINKLE + POP v.[1]]

wino n. [1910s+] (orig. US) an alcoholic, usu. living in poverty. [SE *wine* + sfx. -o]

win or lose n. [20C] alcohol, liquor. [rhy. sl. *win or lose* = BOOZE n.]

win on v. [1940s+] (Aus.) to seduce a woman.

wino time n. [20C] (US Und.) a short sentence (cf. SLEEPING TIME). [WINO + TIME n.[1]; habitual drunkards generally receive short sentences, i.e. days rather than years in prison]

winter-campaign n. [late 19C] rioting, brawling drunkenly. [the contemporary Fenian bombing campaign]

winter cricket n. [late 18C–early 19C] a tailor. [the 'sewing' motions of the insect's legs]

winter Friday n. [20C] (Irish) a chilly looking, impoverished individual.

winter-hedge n. [late 19C–1920s] a clothes-horse. [the way a full clothes horse 'hedges off' a portion of the room; summer washing is dried out of doors]

winter palace n. [late 19C] a prison. [impoverished criminals or tramps deliberately have themselves jailed during the cold winter months]

winter rat n. [1970s+] (US) an old car.

win the porcelain hairnet / barbwire garter / cast-iron overcoat / fur-lined bathtub / hand-painted doormat / solid gold chamberpot, to *phr.* [20C] (US) to deserve a spectacularly useless reward, to perform a pointless action remarkably well.

win the shine/shiny rag, to *phr.* [mid–late 19C] to lose one's money by gambling. [? one is thus reduced to cleaning shoes for a living]

win the solid gold chamberpot *see* WIN THE PORCELAIN HAIRNET.

wipe n.[1] [late 16C–early 17C] the act of drinking. [? one 'wipes' the glass with one's lips]

wipe n.[2] [early 18C+] a handkerchief (cf. NOSE WIPER; PEN-WIPER; WIPER-DRAWER); thus *the wipe lay*, stealing handkerchiefs.

wipe n.[3] [late 19C+] (US) a killing, a murder. [abbr. SE *wipe out*]

wipe n.[4] [1950s+] lavatory paper. [abbr. ASSWIPE]

wipe v. **1** [mid–late 19C] to attack, whether physically or verbally. **2** [1920s+] (Aus./N.Z.) to refuse to grant a loan. **3** [1940s+] (Aus./N.Z.) to repudiate, to forget, to dismiss from one's mind. **4** [1950s+] (Aus./N.Z.) to make someone bankrupt. [SE *wipe out*]

wiped out *adj.* **1** [20C] exhausted. **2** [20C] (US) financially ruined. **3** [1940s+] drunk, intoxicated by drugs. [SE *wipe out*, to erase]

wipe down v. [mid-19C] to flatter, to pacify.

wipe-drawer *see* WIPER-DRAWER.

wipe-hauler *see* WIPER-DRAWER.

wipe it off v. [1940s+] (US) to stop smirking or grinning, usu. as imper. [abbr. SE *wipe that smile off your face*]

wipe-off n. [1930s+] (Aus.) a rejection, a dismissal. [SE *wipe*, to erase]

wipe off v. [1920s+] (Aus.) to bid a last farewell, esp. to a place. [SE *wipe*, to erase]

wipe off one's chin, to *phr.* [mid–late 19C] (US) **1** to take a drink. **2** to be quiet, to stop talking.

wipe oneself out v. [20C] to commit suicide.

wipe one's eye, to *phr.* [mid-19C] to take a drink, esp. to offer or to accept another drink (cf. SHED A TEAR). [WIPE n.[1]]

wipe-out n. [1960s+] **1** a failure. **2** a crushing defeat, annihilation, an overwhelming experience. **3** a killing. [orig. ski/surf jargon *wipe-out*, a spectacular fall]

wipe out v. [1920s+] **1** to beat up. **2** to kill. **3** to astonish. **4** (US) to defeat. [(1), (2) used by milit. mid-19C+]

wiper n.[1] [early 17C–late-18C] a handkerchief (cf. WIPE n.[2]; WIPER-DRAWER].

wiper n.[2] [late 19C] a severe physical blow, a harsh verbal attack, anything that will overwhelm an opponent. [WIPE v. (1)]

wiper-drawer/wipe-drawer/wipe-hauler n. [late 17C–18C] (Und.) a stealer of handkerchiefs; thus *wipe-drawing*, *wipe-hauling*. [WIPE n.[2]/WIPER n.[1] + SE *drawer*]

wipe round v. [late 19C+] to hit, usu. in phr. *wipe one round the face/mouth/head*. [ext. of WIPE v. (1)]

wipe someone's eye, to *phr.* **1** [early–mid-19C] to get the better of, to defeat. **2** [mid-19C+] to discomfit, to 'give someone a black eye'. [sporting use *wipe one's eye*, to shoot someone else's bird]

wipe someone's nose, to *phr.* [late 17C–18C] (Und.) to trick, to deceive. [note SE *wipe*, to cheat or defraud]

wipe that smile off someone's face *see* WIPE THE SMILE OFF SOMEONE'S FACE.

wipe the deck with, to *phr.* [1910s+] (orig. naut.) to beat heavily, to defeat totally.

wipe the floor/earth/ground with, to *phr.* [late 19C+] to beat decisively, to thrash (cf. MOP THE FLOOR WITH).

wipe the hell out of, to *phr.* [1920s+] to beat up, to thrash (cf. KNOCK THE HELL OUT OF).

wipe the/that smile off someone's face, to *phr.* [1930s+] to disappoint, to render a formerly cheerful person unhappy; the converse phr. is *wipe the/that scowl* … .

wipe your chin *phr.* [1900s+] (Aus.) a phr. used to upbraid one who is presumed to be lying. [? thus remove the 'shit' they are talking]

wire *n.*[1] **1** [mid–late 19C] a telegram. **2** [1920s+] a private warning; thus *give the wire*, give a warning or message. **3** [1930s+] (Aus.) a scolding, a reprimand. **4** [1940s+] (US Black) the gossip circuit, the 'grapevine'. **5** [1940s+] (US Black) a 'line' of talk. **6** [1950s+] any form of electronic eavesdropping device.

wire *n.*[2] [mid-19C–1920s] the pickpocket who actively steals from his victim, rather than the various accomplices on his team (cf. HOOK n.[2]). [the SE *wire* used as an adjunct to the fingers]

wire *n.*[3] **1** [20C] the penis; thus *pull one's wire*, to masturbate. **2** [1960s+] (drugs) a vein used for the injection of drugs.

wire *n.*[4] [1960s+] (US) a nervous or highly strung person. [back-form. f. WIRED adj.[1] (3)]

wire *v.* **1** [mid–late 19C] to send a telegram. **2** [1950s+] (US) to place an eavesdropping device in a room, 'to bug'. [WIRE n.[1] (1), (6)]

wired/wired up *adj.*[1] [1960s+] (orig. US) **1** (drugs) addicted to heroin. **2** using cocaine or some form of amphetamines or caffeine. **3** tense, nervous, irritable, full of 'electricity'. **4** drunk. **5** highly stimulated, excited, eager. [SE *wired*, carrying electricity]

wired *adj.*[2] [1960s+] (US) **1** important in political or business circles. **2** in control, secure and assured. [SE *wire*, a connection]

wired for sound *phr.*[1] [1950s+] (Aus.) wearing a hearing-aid or similar earpiece.

wired for sound *phr.*[2] [1960s+] (drugs) experiencing the most extreme effects of cocaine or amphetamines. [ext. of WIRED adj.[1] (2)]

wired into *adj.* [1960s+] (US) intimately involved in or with. [ext. of WIRED adj.[2]]

wire-draw *n.* [late 17C–mid-18C] (Und.) a trick that ensnares a victim; thus *wire-drawn*, tricked in this way. [SE *wire-draw*, to draw out, to persuade by subtle arguing]

wired up *see* WIRED adj.[1].

wire in/into *v.* [mid–late 19C] to set about one's work enthusiastically, to set about a meal and start eating heartily. [abbr. WIRE IN AND GET ONE'S NAME UP]

wire in and get one's name up, to *phr.* [mid–late 19C] **1** to seduce. **2** to attempt success. [orig. used as an invitation to enter a boxing ring and prepare for a contest]

wire-inspector *n.* [1900s–30s] (Aus.) a boundary rider. [SE *wire*, fencing]

wire into *see* WIRE IN.

wireless *n.* [1920s–30s] a baseless rumour. [WIRE n.[1] (2) + pun]

wire-puller *n.*[1] [late 19C+] a male masturbator. [WIRE n.[3] (1) + SE *pull*]

wire-puller *n.*[2] [1900s–20s] an electrician.

wirer *n.* [mid-19C] an expert pickpocket who uses a wire to remove objects from his victims. [WIRE n.[2]]

wire up *v.* [1970s+] (US Black) to explain the current situation, to tell what has been or is happening. [electronic imagery]

wiring *n.* [mid–late 19C] working as a professional pickpocket. [WIRE n.[2]]

Wisacres Hall *n.* [mid-18C–mid-19C] Gresham College, London, esp. as home of the Royal Society. [SE *wiseacre*, one who thinks himself, or wishes to be thought, wise]

wisdom-weed *n.* [1950s+] (W.I.) any herb that is seen as having the effect of making one wiser, esp. marijuana. [SE *wisdom* + *weed*/WEED n.[1] (4)]

wise *adj.* (orig. US) **1** [late 19C+] shrewd, cunning, aware. **2** [20C] stupid, foolish, in ironic use (cf. WISE GUY). **3** [1960s+] homosexually experienced.

-wise *sfx.* [1940s+] (orig. US) with reference to, as regards, e.g. *job-wise, success-wise.*

wise apple *n.* [20C] (US) one who is too clever for their own good (cf. WISE GUY).

wise-ass *n.* [1940s+] (US) one who sees themselves as cleverer than they really are (cf. SMART-ASS). [WISE adj. (2) + sfx. -ASS]

wise-ass *v.* [1940s+] (US) to act in a 'smart' manner. [WISE-ASS n.]

wise as waltham's calf, as *phr.* [early 16C–mid-19C] very stupid. [saying *as wise as Waltham's calf that ran 9 miles to suck a bull*]

wisecrack *n.* [1920s+] (orig. US) a witty retort, a smart comment, a joke at someone else's expense. [WISE adj. (1) + CRACK n.[13]]

wisecrack *v.* [1920s+] (orig. US) to make a witty retort or a smart comment, to make a joke at someone else's expense. [WISECRACK n.]

wised-up *adj.* [1920s+] (US) aware, knowledgeable. [WISE adj. (1)]

wise/smart guy *n.* (US) **1** [late 19C+] anyone who thinks they are particularly knowing or clever; thus a person too clever for their own good. **2** [late 19C+] (gambling) gamblers who are first to favour a particular line of betting, which influences the changing odds. **3** [20C] (US) a shrewd person. **4** [1970s+] a member of the US Mafia. [WISE adj. (1)]

wise guys *n.* [1970s+] (orig. US) the US Mafia. [both pos. and neg. senses of WISE adj.]

wise hombre *n.* [20C] (US) a shrewd, clever person (cf. WISE GUY). [WISE adj. (1) + HOMBRE n.[1]]

wiseman *n.* [1950s+] an expert advisor, e.g. on economics, used by a government, a business or other organization.

wise monkey *n.* [20C] a condom. [rhy. sl. *wise monkey* = FLUNKY n.[3]]

wisenheimer *n.* [20C] a know-it-all, a self-appointed smart fellow. [WISE adj. (1) + Ger./Jewish sfx. -*heimer*, usu. part of a surname]

wise off *v.* [1940s+] to make jokes at someone's expense. [WISE(CRACK) v.]

wise to *adj.* [late 19C+] aware of what is going on, 'in the know'. [WISE adj. (1)]

wise/wake up *v.* [20C] **1** to act sensibly, to cease from being stupid. **2** to explain, to pass on information. [WISE adj. (1)]

wish book *n.* [1920s+] (Can./US) a mail-order catalogue.

wish I had your job! *excl.* [20C] used to someone who appears to be having a very easy time.

wish/hope to hell, to *phr.* [late 19C+] (orig. US) to desire intensely.

wiskideon *n.* [1940s] a waistcoat. [SE *weskit*, note dial. *wisk*, a bulk wrapping for the neck]

wisty-castor/wistycastor *n.* [early 19C] a punch, a blow. [var. on WHISTER-CLISTER]

witblits *n.* [1930s+] (S.Afr.) home-distilled spirits, often sold as 'brandy' (cf. WHITE LIGHTNING). [Du. *wit*, white + *blits*, lightning]

witch, the *n.* [1940s–60s] (drugs) heroin, cocaine. [? it 'bewitches' the user]

witcher/wicher *n.* [late 17C–early 19C] (Und.) silver; thus *witcher bubber*, a silver bowl, *witcher cully*, a silversmith, *witcher tilter*, a silver-hilted sword. [? WHITE adj.[1] + SE *silver*]

witcher-bubber n. [late 17C–early 19C] (Und.) a silver bowl. [WITCHER + BUBBER n.[1] (2)]

witcher-cully n. [late 17C–early 19C] (Und.) a silversmith. [WITCHER + CULLY]

witcher-tilter n. [late 17C–early 19C] (Und.) a silver-hilted sword. [WITCHER + TILTER]

witchetty grub n. [20C] (Aus.) a boy scout. [rhy. sl., *witchetty grub* = *cub*]

witch-hazel n. [1980s+] (drugs) heroin. [ext. of WITCH + ref. to the light brown colour of much heroin]

witch-tit adj. [1960s+] of weather, very cold [phr. *cold as a witch's tit*]

with/without prep. [mid-19C] of a mix of warmed or chilled alcohol, i.e. *with/without sugar*.

with a bang phr. [20C] (US) used of something that goes well, successfully.

with a continuando phr. [late 17C–early 18C] for a very long time, usu. referring to a drinking bout and thus prefaced by 'drunk …'. [Sp.]

with a pox! see WHAT A POX!

with a purple passion phr. [20C] (US) very enthusiastically.

with a stick in it phr. [19C] (US) of tea or coffee, with a measure of brandy in it.

with bells on/tits on phr. **1** [late 19C+] in a joyous mood, enthusiastic. **2** [20C] with melodramatic, lurid and otherwise exciting embellishments (cf. ALL SINGING ALL DANCING, BELLS AND WHISTLES; WITH KNOBS ON). **3** [20C] (US) definitely, without doubt. [? the bells that adorned a jester's outfit or the practice in Old West of outfitting the lead animals of a freight-hauling team with bells, to announce their presence and thus minimize accidents]

with ears/earflaps/earlaps phr. [1930s+] (US) to an extreme and insufferable degree. [the creation of fig. 'noise']

within a cooee of/within cooee phr. [late 19C+] (Aus./N.Z.) within hailing distance, within easy reach, near. [Abor. *cooee*, a bush call later adopted by the colonists and thence by UK English-speakers]

within a gnat's phr. [1970s+] very near indeed. [abbr. GNAT'S EYEBROW]

within a mile of an oak phr. [late 16C–early 18C] a non-specific distance, a somewhat dismissive answer to 'how far is … ?', i.e. near enough, somewhere around.

within an ass's roar/roar of phr. [20C] (Irish) very near.

within cooee see WITHIN A COOEE OF.

with it adj. [1930s+] *au fait*, aware, knowledgeable, fashionable, up-to-date; thus *get with it*, to get oneself informed or up-to-date. [esp. popular during the 'Swinging London' period of the 1960s]

with knobs on phr. [1920s+] embellished, with 'add-ons', decorations. [i.e. with 'extras' but ? ref. to KNOB n.[1]]

with knobs on! excl. [1920s+] (usu. juv.) an excl. retort meaning the same to you and more so! [WITH KNOBS ON n.]

with long teeth phr. [1970s+] (S.Afr.) reluctantly, without enthusiasm. [Afk. *eet met lang tande*, to eat with long teeth, to eat with distaste or reluctance]

with one's hand in the till/cookie jar phr. [20C] (US) discovered or caught in the act, with no possibility of escape or evasion.

with one's hand tied behind one's back phr. [20C] (US) very easily, esp. in phr. *one could do that with one hand behind one's back*.

with one's tail on fire phr. [late 17C–early 18C] infected with venereal disease. [TAIL n.[1] (1), (2)]

without see WITH.

without a mintie phr. [1930s] (Aus.) penniless. [MINTIE n.[2]]

without any phr. [late 19C] abstaining from liquor, usu. for a stated period.

without a pot to pee/piss in see NOT HAVE A POT TO PEE IN.

without a rag phr. [late 16C+] impoverished.

with the bark on phr. [mid-19C–1900s] (US) of a statement, absolutely unvarnished, totally honest.

with the program phr. [1970s+] in tune with the prevailing situation in a pos. manner; thus (US Black teen) *get with the program*, pay attention. [PROGRAM n.; from the recovery techniques of Alcoholics Anonymous/Narcotics Anonymous and other groups that offer their variously habituated members a 12-point *program* of self-help]

with tits on see WITH BELLS ON.

with your two long hands phr. [20C] (W.I.) a phr. used of someone who is poor, empty-handed and lacking material possessions.

wit ou n. [1970s+] (S.Afr. Indian) a White person. [Afk. *wit*, white + OU]

witpyp v. [1960s+] (S.Afr.) to smoke a mixture of marijuana and powdered methaqualone (Mandiax). [Afk. 'white pipe'; the capsules of Mandrax are white]

witter v. [early 19C+] to chatter on pointlessly. [? SE *whitter*, to twitter]

wittol n. [15C] a complaisant husband who makes no effort to discourage his wife's adventuring. [SE *woodwale*, a bird that is often the target of a cuckoo, who lays its egg in the wood-wale's nest]

wi-wi see WEE-WEE n.[1].

wizard adj. [1920s+] (orig. US) a general term of approval, excellent, wonderful. [despite US origin, the main use has been UK society, esp. by those who attended prep schools]

wizzy-wizzy/whizzy-whizzy v. [20C] (W.I./Bdos.) to whisper together. [SE *whisper*]

wobbegong n. [1920s+] (Aus.) **1** anything excellent or outstanding. **2** any form of unnamed insect. [? Abor. *wobbegong*, a carpet-shark + play on SE *woebegone*]

wobble n.[1] [20C] (Irish) shaving lather. [the stirring of the lather before its use]

wobble/wobble-weed n.[2] [1970s+] (US drugs) phencyclidine (cf. ACE n.[3]). [its effects]

wobbler n.[1] see FOOT-WARBLER.

wobbler n.[2] see WABBLER.

wobbler n.[3] see WOBBLY n.[1].

wobbler n.[4] see WOBBLY n.[2].

wobble-shop n. [mid-19C] an unlicensed liquor store. [the effects of the liquor one buys there]

wobble-weed see WOBBLE n.[2].

wobbly/wobbler n.[1] [1960s+] a fit of nerves, of panic, of bad temper.

wobbly/wobbler n.[2] [1960s+] a dubious or untrustworthy story

wobbly adj. [1970s+] unlikely, 'shaky', e.g. of plans or prospects.

wobbly eggs n. [1990s] Temazepam. [the oval shape + the effect on the user]

wobbly pop n. [1990s] (US) beer. [SE *wobbly* + POP n.[2] (1); its fizziness + its impairing effects]

wodge see WADGE.

woe betide you phr. [early 19C+] a phr. of warning or threat, you'll get into trouble.

woema n. [1970s+] (S.Afr.) energy, power. [? Zulu *vuma*, to thrive]

woes adj. [1970s+] (S.Afr.) (usu. juv.) furious, ill-tempered. [Du. *woest*, fierce]

woffle v. [19C] to eat. [? dial. *woffle*, to chew]

woffle dust n. [20C] (Aus.) a fig. term for luck, esp. if gambling when one *puts a bit of woffle dust* on the cards/dice. [? nonce word]

wog *n.*[1] **1** [20C] (Aus. juv.) a very young child. **2** [1920s+] a derog. term for any non-White, esp. an Indian or Pakistani and latterly, in the UK, Bangladeshi. **3** [1920s+] any foreigner, esp. in the phr. *the wogs begin at Calais.* **4** [1960s] (US) an Irishman. **5** [1990s] an Indian meal, an Indian restaurant (cf. CHINESE n.; CHINK n.[3]; INDIAN n.[5]). [ety. unknown, suggestions include that of F.C. Bowen in *Sea Slang* (1929), who includes 'Wogs, lower class Babu shipping clerks on the Indian coast', but provides no further detail. Popular belief has always chosen the acronym *westernized oriental gentleman* or *wily oriental gentleman,* while E.P. opts for abbr. of SE *golliwog,* and certainly this once-popular doll, with its caricatured 'Black' features, has long since been marginalized as politically incorrect]

wog *n.*[2] [1930s–70s] (Aus.) **1** a germ or parasite, an insect. **2** an illness or disease, a 'bug'. [ety. unknown; ? link to dial. *wog,* to twitch, to move; (2) is fig. use of (1)]

wog box *n.* [1980s+] a large, portable stereo tape-recorder-cum-radio, particularly beloved of ghetto youths (cf. GHETTO-BLASTER; NIGGER BOX). [WOG n.[1] + BOX n.[4] (5)]

wog gut *n.* [1950s+] a stomach upset that assails a tourist in any exotic part of the world (cf. APPLE-BLOSSOM TWO-STEP). [WOG n.[1] + SE *gut*]

woler *n.* [1970s+] (society) a Rolls Royce motorcar (cf. ROLLER n.[4]). [deliberate mispron.]

wolf *n.*[1] **1** [mid-19C+] a male overtly pursuing women for sex. **2** [1910s+] (gay) the active partner in anal intercourse.

wolf *n.*[2] [1950s+] (W.I. Rasta) one who is not a Rastafarian but wears their hair in dreadlocks.

wolf *n.*[3] [1970s] (drugs) phencyclidine (cf. ACE n.[3]). [its non-recreational use as an animal tranquillizer]

wolf *v.* [1930s–40s] (US) to pursue women. [WOLF n.[1] (1)]

wolf-call *v.* [1940s–50s] to whistle at a passing woman in an admiring, lustful way (cf. WOLF-WHISTLE). [WOLF n.[1] (1) + SE *call*]

wolfess *n.* [1940s+] a sexually aggressive woman (cf. WOLVER-INE). [WOLF n.[1] (1) + sfx. *-ess*]

wolfing/wolfing it *n.* [1920s+] (US Black) talking grandi-loquently, but not always backing up one's words with action (cf. WOOFING). [WOOF v.[1]]

wolf in the breast *n.* [mid-18C–late 19C] (Und.) a trick practised by strolling beggar women, who ask for alms to obtain medicine to deal with a gnawing pain in their breast.

wolfish *adj.* [mid–late 19C] (US) extremely hungry. [SE *wolf,* to eat ravenously]

Wolfland *n.* [late 17C–early 18C] Ireland. [? Irish wolf-hounds]

wolf pack *see* RAT PACK n.[2].

wolf-pussy *n.* [1970s] (US Black) unpleasant vaginal odours. [? SE *whiff* + PUSSY n.[1] (1)]

wolf-whistle *n.* [1950s+] a two-note whistle aimed at a pass-ing woman by an admiring, lustful man (cf. WOLF-CALL). [WOLF n.[1] (1) + SE *whistle*]

wolf-whistle *v.* [1950s+] to whistle at a passing woman in an admiring, lustful way. [WOLF-WHISTLE n.]

wol house *n.* [19C] the workhouse. [? fig. use of dial. *wol,* a hole]

wollie/woola/woolah/woolie/woolies *n.* [1980s+] (drugs) a cigarette of crack or base cocaine, mixed with marijuana and wrapped in a cigar leaf (cf. WOOLLY BLUNT).

wollied *adj.* [1980s] drunk. [WALLY n.[2]; i.e. one is rendered stupid]

wollies *n.* [late 19C] olives. [? joc. excl. *oh olive!*]

wolly *see* WALLY n.[2].

wolverine *n.* [1930s–50s] (US Black) a sexually aggressive woman (cf. WOLFESS). [WOLF n.[1] (1)]

woman *n.* [early 19C] in coin-tossing, the reverse of a coin (cf. MAN n.[2]). [the engraving of Britannia; the face of the coin had the then male monarch's head]

woman about/of the town *n.* [late 17C–late 19C] a pros-titute. [as opposed to a *man about town* or *man of the town,* a generally congratulatory phr. These female counterparts were invariably condemnatory, however much a euph. the term might be]

woman and her husband *n.* [late 18C–early 19C] a married couple where the wife is larger than the husband. [reverse of usual order, SE *man and wife*]

woman-be-damned *n.* [1940s–50s] (W.I.) any form of cook-ing that is done by men only, e.g. a labouring gang.

woman-man *n.* [20C] (W.I./Gren.) an effeminate male homo-sexual (cf. HE-SHE; OMEE-POLONE).

woman of all work *n.* [late 18C–early 19C] a maidservant 'who refuses none of her master's commands' (Grose 1796), i.e. who not only waits upon but sleeps with her master. [pun on SE *maid of all work*]

woman of pleasure *n.* [18C] a prostitute. [euph.]

woman of the town *see* WOMAN ABOUT TOWN.

woman trouble *n.* **1** [1950s+] from a female point of view, gynaecological problems. **2** [1960s+] from a male point of view, problems in a relationship.

womba *see* WONGA.

wombat *n.*[1] [20C] (Aus./US) **1** a fool. **2** an eccentric. [SE *wombat,* a burrowing marsupial resembling a small bear]

wombat *n.*[2] [1980s+] an unappreciative male. [pun on he 'eats roots and leaves'/*eats,* ROOTS n.[1] (2) and leaves]

wombat *adj.* [20C] (Aus.) dead. [rhy. sl. *wombat = hors de combat*]

womble *n.* [1970s+] a fool, a socially unacceptable individual (cf. GONK; MUPPET). [the *Wombles,* puppet stars of a 1970s UK children's TV series]

womblety-cropped *see* WAMBLETY-CROPPED.

womlish/womnish *adj.* [mid-19C–1950s] (US Black) used of a young woman, cheeky, forward, acting unpopularly beyond her years. [fem. var. on MANNISH]

womp/whomp on *v.* [1980s+] (US campus) to have sexual intercourse with. [WHOMP v.]

wompy/whompy *n.* [1920s+] (Aus.) something that will make one ill. [? WHOMP, i.e. one is fig. 'hit']

won *adj.* [late 17C–19C] stolen. [WIN v.]

wonder, the *n.* [mid–late 19C] used in the phr. *why/how/when the wonder.* [abbr. of 17C–18C *the name of wonder*]

wonder star *n.* [1980s+] (drugs) methcathinone (cf. BATHTUB SPEED). [ety. unknown]

wonelly *adj.* [1980s] (US teen) admirable, very good etc. [i.e. *one* HELL OF A]

wong *n.*[1] [1980s+] (US gay) the penis. [var. on WANG]

wong *n.*[2] [1990s] (Black) money. [abbr. WONGA]

wonga/wamba/wanga/womba *n.* [20C] money. [Rom. *wanger,* coal, fig. money; thus Rom. *wongar-camming mush,* a miser, lit. 'one who loves coal' ? + pun on COLE]

wonga gut *see* WANGA GUT.

wonk *n.*[1] [1900s–60s] (Hong Kong) a scruffy mongrel. [Chinese pron. of letters 'y.d', i.e. yellow (mongrel) dog]

wonk *n.*[2] **1** [1930s–60s] (Aus.) a White person, usu. as an insult. **2** [1940s+] (Aus.) an effeminate or homosexual male. **3** [1980s] (US campus) anyone who works harder than the rest of the students see fit. [? WONKY adj.[1]; note political jargon *policy wonk,* an expert in the minutiae of policy]

wonk one's conker, to *phr.* [20C] to masturbate. [assonance, but note WANK v.]

wonky *adj.*[1] **1** [1910s+] of a person or object, unsteady, un-stable, out of kilter. **2** [1950s–70s] (Aus.) mad; thus *wonkite,* a mad person. [ety. unknown, note synon. Ger. *wankel*]

wonky adj.[2] [1980s+] (US campus) over-anxiously diligent in an academic context. [WONK n.[2] (3)]

won't eat you phr. [mid-18C+] a phr. used to encourage an individual who is reluctant to address or face an apparently threatening or unnerving person, e.g. *he won't eat you*.

won't quit/stop phr. [1960s+] (orig. US) outstanding, wonderful, beyond compare, e.g. *she's got legs that just won't quit*.

woo n. [1930s+] (N.Z.) a petting session. [SE *woo*, to court]

wood n.[1] [19C] money. [the barrels in which liquor is stored]

wood n.[2] **1** [19C+] the penis. **2** [1980s+] an erection; thus *get good wood*, to have a strong erection, *give wood*, to have sexual intercourse. [20C in W.I.; the solidity of the erection]

wood n.[3] [mid–late 19C] the pulpit. [its manufacture]

wood n.[4] [20C] (US Black) a derog. term for a White person (cf. WOOD HICK). [abbr. PECKERWOOD]

wood n.[5] [1960s–70s] (US Black) the Cadillac Fleet*wood* car. [abbr.]

wood-and-water joey n. [late 19C+] **1** (Aus.) a general labourer (cf. USEFUL). **2** a sycophant, a hanger-on. [JOEY n.[2] (2), they run for firewood, drinking water etc]

woodbine n. [1910s–30s] **1** (Aus.) an Englishman, esp. a soldier. **2** any cheap cigarette, irrespective of brand. [Wills' *Woodbine* cigarettes, a cheap UK brand]

wood-butcher n. [late 19C] a second-rate carpenter.

woodcock n. [late 18C–early 19C] a tailor who has presented a long bill (cf. SNIPE n.[1]). [pun on the bird's long *bill*]

woodcock's head n. [17C] a pipe. [the shape]

wooden/wooden out v. [20C] (Aus./N.Z.) to knock down, to knock out. [WOODENER n.[1]]

wooden aspro n. [1970s+] (N.Z. prison) a blow on the head with a truncheon. [SE *wooden* + *Aspro*, a painkiller]

wooden casemen/cravat n. [late 17C] the pillory.

wooden doublet n. [late 18C] a coffin (cf. DEAL SUIT).

wooden ears n. [1920s+] a general term of abuse, esp. to someone who at first seems to not have heard one's comment (cf. CLOTH EARS).

woodener n.[1] [late 19C–1920s] (Aus./N.Z.) a staggering blow; a knock-out punch. [it renders the recipient 'dead wood']

woodener n.[2] [1940s–50s] (prison) a one-month sentence. [the *wooden* spoon once issued + rhy. sl. *wooden spoon* = MOON n.[2] (2)]

woodener n.[3] [1940s–60s] (Irish) a cheap wooden seat at the cinema.

wooden fit n. [late 19C–1900s] a fainting fit. [one drops rigidly to the ground]

wooden habeas n. [late 18C–early 19C] a coffin; thus *go out with a wooden habeas*, to die in prison (cf. DEAL SUIT; HEMPEN HABEAS). [SE *wooden* + pun on *habeas corpus*, lit. 'thou shalt have the body', a writ whereby an accused and jailed person must be brought before the court and the reason for their imprisonment justified]

wooden horse n. [mid-16C–17C] the gallows (cf. RIDE THE HORSE FOALED BY AN ACORN).

wooden kimono n. [1920s–40s] a coffin (cf. DEAL SUIT).

wooden-legged mare n. [early 18C–mid-19C] the gallows.

wooden/copper nickel n. [20C] (orig. US) something worthless. [a non-existent and undoubtedly worthless coin]

wooden nutmeg n. [late 19C] (US) a native of Connecticut. [the use of such 'nutmegs' in confidence trickery; thus the neg. image of such individuals]

wooden out see WOODEN.

wooden overcoat n. [mid-19C+] a coffin, often used in fictional versions of organized crime (cf. CEMENT KIMONO; DEAL SUIT).

wooden parenthesis n. [early 19C] the pillory (cf. IRON PARENTHESIS; WOODEN RUFF). [the sides of the pillory supposedly resemble the curves of a *parenthesis*, i.e. ( )]

wooden pegs n. [20C] the legs (cf. SCOTCH PEGS). [rhy. sl.]

wooden plank n. [20C] an American. [rhy. sl. *wooden plank* = YANK n.]

wooden ruff n. [late 17C–early 19C] (Und.) a pillory; thus *wear the wooden ruff*, to stand in the pillory (cf. NORWAY NECKCLOTH; WOODEN PARENTHESIS). [like the SE *ruff* it encircles the neck]

wooden shoes n. [late 17C–mid-18C] **1** the supporters of the Old Pretender, James Stuart (1688–1766). **2** the French, France. **3** foreigners in general. [the wearing of wooden *sabots* by the French]

wooden spoon n.[1] **1** [late 19C] a fool (cf. DICKHEAD). **2** [20C] (orig. sports) a metaphorical prize for the competitor or team who comes last in a sporting contest (cf. LEATHER MEDAL). [the actual *wooden spoon* trad. awarded to that Cambridge undergraduate unfortunate enough to come bottom in the year's mathematical tripos. Note the synon. *wooden wedge*, named after the philologist Hensleigh Wedgwood, who took last place in the Cambridge classical tripos of 1824]

wooden spoon n.[2] [1920s+] an erect penis. [joc. use of WOODEN SPOON n.[1] + WOOD n.[2]]

wooden-stake v. [20C] (US) to postpone permanently, to file and thus forget about something. [the trad. use of a *wooden stake* to destroy a vampire]

wooden suit n. [1960s+] a coffin (cf. DEAL SUIT).

wooden surtout n. [late 18C–early 19C] a coffin (cf. DEAL SUIT). [SE *wooden* + *surtout*, an overcoat]

wooden swear n. [20C] slamming a door and leaving the room as the final punctuation of an argument. [the *wooden* door 'swears' as it slams shut]

woodentop n. [1980s] **1** a uniformed policeman. **2** a simpleton. [the UK children's TV series]

wooden ulster n. [late 19C] a coffin (cf. DEAL SUIT). [SE *ulster*, a long, loose overcoat]

woodhead n. [1990s] a stubborn fool. [SE *wooden-head*]

woodheap v. [1910s+] (Aus.) **1** to ostracize a fellow worker. **2** to force an itinerant to chop firewood in return for food and accommodation. [SE *woodheap*, a stack of firewood]

wood hick n. [19C] (US) a derog. term for a rustic, a peasant. [SE *wood(land)* + HICK n. (1)]

woodie/woody n.[1] [20C] **1** a Wills *Wood*bine cigarette. **2** any cheap cigarette. [abbr.; (2) is fig. use of (1)]

woodie/woody n.[2] [1960s+] (orig. surfer) a *wood*-panelled station wagon. [abbr.]

woodie/woody n.[3] [1990s] (US) the erect penis (cf. WOODEN SPOON n.[2]). [ext. of WOOD n.[3]]

wood merchant n. [late 19C–1910s] a street seller of matches.

woodpecker n.[1] **1** [16C–early 19C] in a crooked gambling game, the accomplice who urges on the victim, helping him by providing a succession of small stakes. **2** [1940s+] (US/Aus.) a machine-gun. [SE *woodpecker*, which takes repeated small pecks at a tree, gradually creating a substantial hole; (2) adds the tapping noise]

woodpecker n.[2] see PECKERWOOD.

woodpecker n.[3] [1950s] (W.I.) a district policeman. [the red stripes on his uniform, reminiscent of the bird's colouring]

woodpile n. [1930s] (US) a xylophone. [its manufacture]

woodpile cousin n. [20C] (US) a distant relation, e.g. a third or fourth cousin, a family friend (cf. BUTTONHOLE COUSIN). [the sharing of a common woodpile]

wood-pusher n. [1940s+] (US) a bad chess player. [they have no strategy and merely move the pieces]

woodrow n. [1990s] an erection. [ext. of WOOD n.[2]]

woods are full of ... *phr.* [20C] (US) there is an abundant supply of something.

woods colt *n.* [late 19C+] (US) an illegitimate child (cf. BRUSH COLT). [such a *colt* is conceived and/or reared in the *woods*, rather than in a stable]

woodser *see* JIMMY WOODSER.

wood-/woods-pussy *n.* [late 19C+] (Can./US) a skunk, a polecat. [lit. 'wood-cat']

Woodstock wannabe *n.* [1990s] (US campus) one whose behaviour is reminiscent of the 1960s. [the *Woodstock* Festival of 1969 was seen as the epitome of hippiedom]

woody *n. see* WOODIE n.

woof *n.* [1980s+] (US campus) an extremely unfashionable hairdo. [one resembles a DOG n.⁴ (6)]

woof *v.*¹ [1920s+] (US Black) to speak in a variety of ways, the meaning differs as to context: flirtatious, aggressive, meaningless, threatening, bullying, bluffing (cf. TRASH-TALK; YAP). [US Black pron. of SE *wolf* + SE *woof*, the sound of barking]

woof *v.*² [1970s+] (US campus) to vomit. [echoic]

woof! *excl.* [1990s] used by a male on seeing a passing attractive young woman. [? an imitation of the howl of a love-sick dog]

woofer *n.*¹ [1930s+] (US Black) a loud, loquacious talker who says a good deal, but with little actual meaning. [WOOF v.¹]

woofer *n.*² [1980s+] (US) a penis. [? play on DOG n.¹³ (1)]

woofer *n.*³ [1980s+] (drugs) a marijuana cigarette. [resemblance to a WOOFER n.² or the coughing or *woofing* it can cause]

woofing *adj.* [1920s+] (US Black) speaking in a variety of ways, the meaning differs as to context, e.g. flirtatiously, aggressively, meaninglessly, threateningly in a bullying or bluffing manner. [WOOF v.¹]

woof it *v.* [1980s+] (US gay) to perform fellatio energetically and voraciously. [SE *wolf*, to eat ravenously]

woofits *n.* [1910s–20s] nerves, tension; thus *get the woofits*, to become tense, nervous. [ety. unknown; ? link to SE *fit*, a seizure]

woofter *n.* [1980s+] a male homosexual. [var. on POOFTER]

woofterish *adj.* [1980s+] (Aus./N.Z.) of an argument, indecisive, unconvincing. [WOOFTER]

woo-hah! *excl.* [1990s] (US Black teen) an excl. implying one's domination of a situation.

woojang *n.* [1990s] a socially unacceptable individual. [ety. unknown]

wook *n.* [1980s+] an individual who is completely committed to an alternative lifestyle, living far outside mainstream society. [the *wookie*, the hair-covered quasi-ape who co-pilots the space ship *Millenium Falcon*, in the *Star Wars* films]

wool *n.*¹ [mid-19C] courage, fortitude, 'character' (cf. HAIR n.⁵). [orig. boxing jargon, note ALL WOOL AND A YARD WIDE]

wool *n.*² [20C] **1** hair, esp. female pubic hair. **2** a woman. [(2) is metonymic use of (1)]

wool *v.* [mid–late 19C] (US) **1** to pull someone's hair in play or anger. **2** to confuse, to discomfit. [(1) SE *wool*; (2) SE *pull the wool over someone's eyes*]

woola/woolah *see* WOLLIE.

woolas *n.* [1980s+] (US drugs) a smokeable mixture of crack cocaine and marijuana. [ety. unknown]

wool-barber *n.* [20C] (Aus.) a sheep-shearer.

wool/woolly bird *n.* [late 18C–mid-19C] a sheep. lamb; thus [mid-19C] *wing of a woodbird*, a shoulder of lamb.

wool-bug *n.* [late 19C–1930s] (N.Z.) a sheep-shearer. [SE *wool* + BUG n.¹ or n.⁵]

wool hat *n.* [early 19C+] (US) a rural person. [their stereotypical headgear]

wool-hawk *n.* [20C] (Aus.) a skilful shearer.

wool-hole *n.* [mid-19C–1900s] the workhouse. [orig. printers' jargon, an old or unemployed printer described himself as being *in the wool-hole*, a fig. use of wool-hole, defined in Savage's *Dictionary of Printing* (1841) as 'a place boxed off sometimes under a stair case, or in any situation where the dust will not affect the press room, in which the wool is carded wherewith to make the balls']

woolie *see* WOLLIE.

woolies *n.*¹ [late 19C+] long woollen underwear.

Woolies *n.*² [1930s+] a nickname for F.W. *Wool*worth's (1852–1919) department stores (cf. MARKS n.¹). [abbr.]

woolies *n.*³ *see* WOLLIE.

wool/woollen king *n.* [late 19C–1900s] (Aus./N.Z.) one who has made his fortune in sheep-farming.

woolloomooloo *adj.* [late 19C+] (Aus.) rough, unsophisticated, thuggish; thus *Woolloomooloo bushman*, one who rides a horse badly, *Woolloomooloo upper-cut*, kick to the groin. [*Woolloomooloo*, a waterside suburb in Sydney]

woolloomooloo Yank/Frenchman *n.* [1950s+] (Aus.) a relatively unsophisticated person who attempts to ape the supposedly more sophisticated style of an American or Frenchman (cf. PYRMONT YANK). [WOOLLOOMOOLOO adj.]

woolly *n.*¹ (Aus.) **1** [late 19C–1900s] a blanket. **2** [20C] a sheep. **3** [1960s+] a farmer.

woolly *n.*² [1960s+] a uniformed policeman. [var. on WALLY]

woolly *adv.* [mid-19C] in a bad temper. [given WOOL n., ? link to KEEP YOUR HAIR ON]

woolly-back *n.* [1960s+] an unsophisticated, country person. [the resemblance to their sheep]

woolly bird *see* WOOL BIRD.

woolly-blunt *n.* [1980s+] (drugs) a cigarette of crack or base cocaine, mixed with marijuana and wrapped in a cigar leaf. [WOLLIE + BLUNT n.²]

woolly crown *n.* [late 17C–mid-19C] a fool, i.e. a 'soft-headed fellow' (Grose 1785).

woolly woofter *n.* [1980s+] a male homosexual. [WOOFTER + assonance]

woolwich and greenwich *n.* [20C] spinach. [rhy. sl.]

woolwich ferry *n.* [20C] sherry. [rhy. sl.]

Woolworth marriage/wedding *n.* [1920s–60s] a 'marriage' that exists only in the cheap Woolworths' ring purchased for the occasion. [an era when hoteliers looked askance if a couple had no visible proof of their wedded status]

woop *n.* [1920s+] (Aus./N.Z.) a tough, but isolated and backward country-dweller. [WOOP-WOOP]

woopknacker *n.* [1920s+] (N.Z.) a very tough, recalcitrant person, a 'hard case'. [? WOOP + KNACKER n., lit. a country horse-butcher]

woop-woop *n.* [1910s+] (Aus.) an imaginary place that is a byword for backwardness and remoteness (cf. BULLAMAKANKA). [? redup. based on the style of Aborigine language]

woop-woop pigeon *n.* [1910s+] (Aus.) **1** a kookaburra. **2** a swamp pheasant. [WOOP-WOOP + SE *pigeon*]

woosey *see* WOOZY.

wooter *n.* [1960s] (US) the penis. [? WOOFER n.²]

woozily *adv.* [late 19C+] (orig. US) vaguely or unsteadily. [WOOZY]

woozled *adj.* [1900s–20s] tipsy, drunk (cf. WOOZY).

woozy/woosey *adj.* [late 19C+] (orig. US) **1** vague, befuddled, dizzy or unwell. **2** under the influence of drugs or drink, poss. of a blow on the head (cf. ADDLED). [? echoic of one's blurred mumblings]

wop *n.* [1910s+] a derog. term for an Italian. [Sp. *guapo*, a dandy, which was taken up in Sicily during an occupation by Spain and thus imported to the US by 19C immigrants; but note Latin *vappa*, sour wine, or fig. a worthless person]

wop *v.* [mid-19C] to hit. [var. on WHOP]

wopcacker *see* WHOPCACKER.

woppidown *n.* [1910s+] (Aus.) a damper. [? WHOP v. (1) *it down* on the plate]

wop town *n.* [1930s+] (US) that part of a town in which the Italian community lives (cf. BEAN TOWN n.²). [WOP n. + SE *town*]

wop-wop *n.* [1900s] (Aus.) a roustabout, a handyman, a casual labourer. [? WHOP v., i.e. the noise of the man running up and down the shearing shed carrying fleeces to the wool tables]

word, the *n.* [late 16C+] the summation, the *mot juste*, esp. in the phr. *... is not the word for it.*

word *adj.* [1980s+] (US campus) fashionable. [phr. *the last word in ...* ; ult. Fr. *le dernier cri*]

word *v.* [20C] (Aus.) **1** to speak to, accost, to tell, pass word to, to rebuke or tell off. **2** to tip off, to warn, to inform.

word! *excl.* (orig. US Black) **1** [1950s+] an excl. of approval, admiration, agreement etc. **2** [1980s+] an expression of farewell. **3** [1980s+] used to signify that one is having the final say in an argument. [abbr. SE *the last word in, that's my last word*]

-word *sfx.* [1980s+] a euph. sfx. used, with a single initial letter, to denote a variety of 'unsayable' synonyms, e.g. the *C-word*, CUNT n.¹; the *F-word*, FUCK; also, often in a newspaper context, to denote a topic of importance, which has become so over-used as to become tediously clichéd, e.g. the *M-word*, Maastricht etc.

word freak *n.* [1960s+] a client who wishes the prostitute to speak in obscenities for his sexual gratification. [SE *word* + sfx. -FREAK]

word-grubber *n.* [late 18C–mid-19C] one who deliberately uses hard words in their conversation (cf. WORD-PECKER). [SE *word + grub up*]

wordhole *n.* [1990s] (US) the mouth.

word in your ear, a *n.* [mid-19C+] a quick, confidential chat.

word is bond/born *phr.* [1980s+] (US Black) a general term of affirmation, I mean it, I promise (cf. WORD!). [SE phr. *my word is my bond*]

word-pecker *n.* [late 17C–mid-19C] a punster (cf. WORD-GRUBBER). [pun on SE *woodpecker*]

word to the mother! *excl.* [1990s+] (US Black) an excl. of approval, admiration etc. [ext. WORD!]

word up! *excl.* [1980s+] (orig. US Black) an excl. of approval, admiration, agreement etc. [ext. WORD!]

worf *n.* [1990s] (US teen) a bald man who combs his hair to hide the fact that he is bald. [ety. unknown]

work *n.* **1** [early 19C+] the criminal life or a criminal act. **2** [20C] (US Und.) the written records held by illegal bookmakers. [ext. uses of SE]

work *v.*¹ **1** [early 19C+] to do, to perform, to carry through a plan of action, usu. in combs. such as WORK THE BULLS, WORK THE ORACLE etc. **2** [mid-19C] to put to death, to hang. **3** [mid-19C] to work as a street seller. **4** [mid–late 19C] to deal with in some way, to get or to get rid of, esp. by artifice. **5** [mid-19C+] to practice one's occupation as a thief. **6** [20C] (US) to charm or enthral, esp. an audience (cf. WORK A CROWD).

work *v.*² **1** [20C] (orig. US Black) to have sexual intercourse. **2** [1960s–70s] (US Black) to exchange sexual favours for money. **3** [1980s+] (US campus) to beat up. **4** [1980s+] (US campus) to have energetic sex with.

work a crowd, to *phr.* [20C] to ply one's trade to an audience, begging, preaching, entertaining etc.

work a door, to *phr.* [1920s+] to work as a prostitute, standing or sitting in one's own doorway; thus *door*, a brothel.

work a ginger, to *phr.* [1930s+] (Aus.) for a prostitute and her accomplice to rob her customer (cf. MURPHY GAME). [WORK v.¹ + GINGER n.⁵]

workaholic/workoholic *n.* [1960s+] anyone who is obsessed by working and thus very rarely stops. [SE *work* + sfx. -AHOLIC/-OHOLIC]

work a point/work points, to *phr.* [late 19C+] (Aus.) to live by one's wits, to take advantage by trickery and deception.

work a ready, to *phr.* [late 19C+] (Aus.) to concoct a swindle or fraud. [WORK v.¹ + READY n.²]

work a spot, to *phr.* [1990s] (US Black) to sell drugs or sex from a specific location. [WORK v.¹ + SE *spot*]

work a street, to *phr.* [mid-19C] of a beggar or pedlar, to visit every house in a street, attempting to maximize one's sales and shouting as loudly as possible in order to alert every other person to one's presence. [WORK v.¹ + SE *street*]

workbench *n.* [early 19C] a bedstead. [WORK v.²]

work both sides of the street, to *phr.*¹ [20C] (US) to work exceptionally hard.

work/play both sides of the street, to *phr.*² [1930s+] to ally oneself to both sides in a dispute or division, to behave in an opportunistic manner.

worked *adj.* [1980s+] (US campus) exhausted, tired out. [abbr. SE *worked to death*]

worker *n.*¹ [mid-19C+] a criminal, usu. in combs. such as BADGER WORKER, CHARITY WORKER, DUNNIGAN WORKER, LUSH WORKER, SKIN WORKER, TAIL-WORKER. [WORK v.¹]

worker *n.*² [1960s+] (Aus.) a prostitute. [abbr. TAIL-WORKER]

work for one's living and do the naughty for one's clothes, to *phr.* [mid–late 19C] to be an amateur prostitute, who has a legitimate day-job but still goes out whoring to make extra money. [DO THE NAUGHTY]

work for Street and Walker, to *phr.* [1920s+] (Aus.) to be unemployed and walking the streets in search of a job. [puns]

work from a book, to *phr.* (US Black) **1** [1940s+] for a pimp to run his professional life by the recognized 'rules and regulations' of the pimping life, supposedly enshrined in an authoritative *Book*. **2** [1960s+] to conduct business through an address book, so eliminating many of the problems (esp. police interference) that are met in street prostitution.

workie. *n.* [1930s–40s] (US) the workhouse. [abbr.]

working *n.* [1980s+] (drugs) selling crack cocaine. [WORK v.¹]

working classes *n.* [20C] glasses. [rhy. sl.]

working girl/broad/chick/woman *n.* [1940s+] (US) a prostitute (cf. ASS-PEDDLER). [WORK v.¹ + SE *girl*/BROAD n.²/CHICK n.⁴/SE *woman*]

working half *n.* [1980s+] (drugs) a piece of crack cocaine weighing 0.5g or more. [ety. unknown; ? such a size is large enough to *work* effectively]

working-man's smile *n.* [1980s+] (US) the top of the crevice between a man's buttocks, visible when he bends over and the waist of his low-cut trousers is forced downwards (cf. BUILDER'S BUM).

working-over *n.* [1960s+] a beating. [WORK OVER]

working stiff *n.* [20C] an average, unexceptional working man (cf. BINDLE STIFF; MISSION STIFF). [SE *work* + STIFF n.⁴]

working the cuts *phr.* [20C] used of a prostitute who works on the street rather than in a brothel. [SE *cut*, a passage, a route]

work in the garden, to *phr.* [1990s] of a woman, to masturbate.

working woman *see* WORKING GIRL.

work it *v.* [late 19C+] to arrange, often by underhand or duplicitous methods. [WORK v.¹ (4)]

work it! *excl.* [20C] a general phr. of dismissal, lit. *work it up your arse!*

work like a kaffir, to *phr.* [1970s+] (S.Afr.) to work very hard. [SE *work* + KAFFIR]

workman *n.* [early–mid-19C] a card-sharp. [WORK v.¹ (1)]

workman's entrance *n.* [1990s] the anus. [i.e. 'the back door']

work off/oneself off *v.*[1] [16C+] to masturbate (cf. BEAT OFF).

work off *v.*[2] [mid-19C] to hang.

work one's arse/ass off, to *phr.* [1920s+] to work extremely hard (cf. WORK ONE'S TAIL OFF). [SE *work* + ARSE n.[1]]

work one's bot, to *phr.* [20C] to have sexual intercourse. [abbr. SE *bottom*]

work one's butt off, to *phr.* [1970s+] (orig. US) to work very hard. [BUTT n.[1] (1); var. on WORK ONE'S ASS OFF]

work oneself off *see* WORK OFF v.[1].

work one's last nerve *see* WORK ONE'S NERVES.

work one's mealie off, to *phr.* [1990s] (S.Afr.) to work very hard. [euph. var. on WORK ONE'S ARSE OFF]

work one's nerves/last nerve, to *phr.* [1990s] (US Black/campus) **1** to annoy, to irritate. **2** to exert emotional pressure upon someone.

work one's nut, to *phr.* [late 19C+] to scheme, to plot, to use one's brains to avoid work; thus synon. phrs. [20C] (Aus.) *to work one's head*, [1950s] (Aus.) *to work one's skull*, [1970s] *to work one's loaf*. [WORK v.[1] (4) + SE *head*/SE *skull*/LOAF n.[2]]

work/sweat one's tail off, to *phr.* [1930s+] (orig. US) to work very hard (cf. WORK ONE'S ARSE OFF). [fig. use of TAIL n.[1] (3)]

work one's ticket, to *phr.* [late 19C+] to malinger, to escape onerous duties by shamming illness or similar unsuitability. [orig. Br. Army use, obtaining a discharge through faking illness]

work-out *n.* [1900s–30s] the simultaneous sacking or dismissal of a large number of a firm's workers. [SE *work out*, to loosen, to get rid of]

work out *v.* [1940s–50s] (US Black) to have sexual intercourse. [SE *work out*, to exercise]

work out one's soul-case *see* BURST OUT ONE'S SOUL-CASE.

work over *v.* [1920s+] (orig. US) to beat up, to hurt to any extent short of murder; thus *work-over, working over*, a thrashing, a beating.

work points *see* WORK A POINT.

works *n.*[1] [late 19C–1900s] (US) the intestines of an animal. [SE *works*, the internal parts of a machine]

works/whole works, the *n.*[2] [late 19C+] everything, the lot.

works *n.*[3] [1950s+] (drugs) **1** the equipment used by a narcotics user for injecting themself. **2** the equipment used for smoking crack cocaine, heroin etc (cf. BIZ n.[2]; HARPOON n.). [SE *works*, machinery]

work the broads *see* FAKE THE BROADS.

work the bulls, to *phr.* [mid-19C] (Und.) to pass counterfeit crown coins. [SE *work* + BULL n.[3]]

work the dumb/hairy oracle, to *phr.* [late 18C–mid-19C] to have sexual intercourse. [SE *work* + DUMB/HAIRY ORACLE]

work the halo racket, to *phr.* [mid–late 19C] to complain, to be discontented, esp. without justification. [the image of a *halo*-ed saint complaining about heaven]

work the hole, to *phr.* [1950s+] (US Und.) to rob drunks who have passed out in the subway. [WORK v.[1] (5) + HOLE n.[2] (4)]

work the nails off, to *phr.* [1910s] (N.Z.) to work very hard; to make someone else work very hard.

work the oracle, to *phr.* [mid–late 19C] **1** to raise money. **2** to plan, to manoeuvre, to succeed through cunning. [WORK v.[1] + SE *oracle*, a prophet]

work the room, to *phr.* [1950s+] to chatter to people at a party or meeting. [show business use, for an entertainer to move through the audience, chatting to people and involving them in the act]

work the shallow, to *phr.* [mid–late 19C] to beg half-naked. [SHALLOW COVE]

work the shells, to *phr.* [late 19C] (US) to run a crooked gambling game in which the participants have to bet on the hiding place of a pea which is under one of three shells. [SHELL GAME]

work the stem, to *phr.* [1910s+] (US tramp) to beg on the streets. [WORK v.[1] + STEM n.[2]]

work the tear-pump, to *phr.* [late 19C–1900s] to burst, prob. insincerely, into tears.

work the tubs, to *phr.* [1920s–30s] (Und.) **1** to commit crimes, usu. card-sharping, on board transatlantic liners. **2** to pickpocket on the buses or at bus-stops. [WORK v.[1] + TUB n.[1] (5)]

work the well, to *phr.* [20C] (US Und.) for a pickpocket to use the crush getting on and off buses for stealing from travellers. [WORK v.[1] + SE *well*, the platform next to the bus doors]

work things *v.* [late 19C+] make things work out in the way one wishes, sometimes but not necessarily illicitly. [WORK v.[1] (4)]

work under the armpits, to *phr.* [early 19C] (Und.) to confine one's criminality to such activities that would be classed as petty larceny, bringing a maximum sentence of seven years transportation, rather than hanging; thus *work above the armpits*, to commit crimes that could lead to one's execution. [? a pickpocket's reaching under an armpit for the wallet]

work up *v.* [late 19C+] of a man, to have sexual intercourse.

work upon the prig and buzz, to *phr.* [late 18C] to work as a pickpocket. [WORK v.[1] (5) + PRIG n.[1] + BUZZ n.[1]]

workus *n.* [late 19C] **1** a workhouse. **2** a derog. term for a Methodist chapel. [(2) from its deliberate plainness]

work with the bogies, to *phr.* [late 19C+] to act as an informant. [SE *work* + BOGEY n.[2] (2)]

worky *n.* [20C] an employed person. [SE *work*]

world *n.* [late 18C] (society) a knowledge of the fashionable world, the *beau monde*.

worm *n.*[1] [mid-19C] a policeman. [? SE *worm*, an unpleasant, despicable person]

worm *n.*[2] [1970s+] (drugs) phencyclidine (cf. ACE n.[3]). [ety. unknown]

worm *n.*[3] [1980s+] the penis; thus *burp the worm*, to masturbate.

worm *v.*[1] [mid-19C] to remove the beard from an oyster or mussel. [SE *worm*, to remove intestinal worms from an animal]

worm *v.*[2] [1950s–70s] (US campus) to study hard. [abbr. SE *bookworm*]

wormbait *n.* [19C+] a corpse.

worm farm *n.* [1960s+] (orig. US) an eccentric, one whose mind is 'full of worms'; thus *living on a worm farm*, crazy, eccentric.

wormrod *n.* [1990s] a very unpleasant person. [SE *worm* + ROD n.[1]]

worms and snails *n.* [20C] fingernails. [rhy. sl.]

worrab *n.* [mid-19C+] (coster) a barrow. [backsl.]

worrit *n.* [mid-19C] **1** anxiety, worry. **2** a person suffering from such problems. [WORRIT v.]

worrit *v.* [early–mid-19C] **1** to worry someone, to nag. **2** to be worried, anxious. [orig. dial.]

worry and strife *n.* [1930s] one's wife. [rhy. sl., var. on TROUBLE AND STRIFE]

worryguts *n.* [1930s+] a pathological worrier, esp. as a term of address.

worry wart *n.* [1930s+] (US) a pathological worrier (cf. WORRYGUTS). [SE *worry* + WART]

worse for wear *phr.* [20C] drunk, intoxicated by drugs.

worse luck! *excl.* [mid-19C+] that's a shame, more's the pity.

worse than a fart/two-bob fart in a bottle *see* NOT WORTH A FART IN A BOTTLE.

worse things happen at sea *phr.* [1910s+] somewhat empty words of consolation when nothing deeper seems available to the speaker.

worship the porcelain god/goddess see KISS THE PORCELAIN GOD.

worst kind, the phr. [early 19C+] (US) to the greatest extent, extremely, very badly.

worst part n. [16C] the vagina (cf. BEST PART).

worth a bob or two phr. [20C] **1** of things, valuable. **2** of people, wealthy. [understatement]

worth a cent phr. [mid–late 19C] (US) to the least amount, e.g. you ain't helping your Mom worth a cent.

worth a guinea a box phr. [1920s–30s] used of any small item that while cheap is still very useful.

worth a jew's eye see JEW'S EYE.

worth a plum phr. [late 19C] wealthy. [PLUM n. (1)]

worth one's weight in burnt copper phr. [late 19C–1950s] worthless, worth very little. [copper has little value compared with gold]

wossname n. [20C] popular mis-sp. of WHATSHISNAME.

wotcher! excl. [late 19C+] a stereotypical cockney greeting. [elision of 16C+ SE what cheer]

wotchero! excl. [late 19C] hello! [ext. of WOTCHER]

would fuck up a wet dream see COULD FUCK UP A WET DREAM.

would I had Kemp's shoes to throw after you phr. [early 17C–early 19C] a phr. used to wish someone good luck. [William Kemp (fl. 1600), who had played the original Dogberry in the first performance of Much Ado About Nothing. In 1600 he was thrown out of Shakespeare's troupe at the Globe, and to restore his image and win some needed publicity, he danced his way from London to Norwich in nine days. The account he then printed and circulated was entitled Kemp's Nine Days Wonder]

would I shit you ... you're my favourite turd phr. [1950s+] (US) an assertion of one's sincerity, in answer to the previous speaker's 'Don't bullshit me ...'. [SHIT v.² + TURD]

would not take/want it as a gift phr. [mid-19C+] said of anything one would reject even when given free, also in fig. use.

wouldn't be seen/found dead in/with phr. [1910s+] to have absolutely nothing to do with. a person or place etc.

wouldn't be seen dead with someone in a 40-acre phr. [late 19C+] (orig. Aus.) an expression of extreme dislike.

wouldn't bust a fart in a ghost-town phr. [1990s] used of one who would never break the law or cause the least trouble. [BUST v.¹ + FART]

wouldn't give/tell one the time of day phr. [1950s+] said by one who ignores someone completely, spurning any and all advances, e.g. I wouldn't give them ...'.

wouldn't it! excl. [1940s+] (Aus./N.Z.) a general excl. of dismay, exasperation or disgust. [abbr. wouldn't it make you sick, wouldn't it root you? wouldn't it make you spit chips and similar phrs.]

wouldn't like to meet them in a dark alley phr. [20C] used of someone one finds repellent, frightening and generally unappealing; also as ... in the dark.

wouldn't tell one the time of day see WOULDN'T GIVE ONE THE TIME OF DAY.

wouldn't that freeze you? phr. [1930s] (US) isn't that amazing? [FREEZE v.³/SE freeze]

wouldn't that jar you? phr. [late 19C–1930s] (US) wouldn't that infuriate you? [SE jar, to shock]

wouldn't touch it with a 40-foot barge pole see WOULDN'T TOUCH IT WITH A 10-FOOT BARGE POLE.

wouldn't touch it with a red-hot poker phr. [20C] (Aus.) a phr. indicating one's absolute aversion.

wouldn't touch it with a pair of tongs see WOULDN'T TOUCH IT WITH YOURS.

wouldn't touch it with a 10-foot/40-foot barge pole phr.

[20C] used by one man to another to express his lack of interest in a woman they are observing.

wouldn't touch it with yours/with a pair of tongs phr. [late 19C+] a popular phrase between two men observing a woman when the speaker finds her unattractive – yours is the penis.

would ya do it for a Scooby Snack? phr. [1990s] (US Black teen) a phr. used in an effort to persuade someone to do something for you. [SCOOBY SNACK]

wounded soldier n. [1990s] (US campus) a partially empty beer container. [play on DEAD SOLDIER]

wounds! excl. [16C] a euph. excl., lit 'God's wounds!' (cf. BLOODY WOUNDS!; ZOUNDS!).

wow n.¹ [1920s+] an exciting, admirable or astonishing thing or person. [SE excl. wow!]

wow, the n.² [1940s+] (N.Z.) a psychiatric institution. [Whaw, a local nickname for an area of Avondale, Auckland, associated with such institutions since mid-19C]

wow v. [1920s+] to delight, to enthral, to please very much. [SE excl. wow!]

wowser n.¹ (Aus./N.Z.) **1** [late 19C+] a puritan, a self-appointed censor, a 'Mrs Grundy'; thus wowse, to act puritanically, wowserdom, the world of puritanism, wowserish, puritanical, wowseristic, prudish, wowserly, puritanically. **2** [late 19C+] a general term of abuse. **3** [1940s+] a blue-stocking. **4** [1940s+] a teetotaller. [UK dial. wow, to howl like a dog, to grumble, to complain. Claimed by John Norton (1858–1916), editor of the Sydney Truth, as his coinage. However, a correspondent (5 June 1910) cited him as the popularizer but not the coiner of a term that 'in the ordinary parlance of the proletariat ... signifies a "bald-headed, bad-breathed, bible-banging bummer, who ought to be banged with a bowser"']

wowser n.² [1920s+] (US) something impressive, sensational, successful. [ext. WOW n.]

wowser n.³ [1990s] the female pubic hair. [? WOWSER n.² + MOUSER n.⁶]

wowserland n. [1910s] (N.Z.) New Zealand. [WOWSER n.¹ + SE land]

wowzers! excl. [1990s] (US teen) a general excl. of approval. [WOWSER n.²]

w.p. n. [mid-19C–1900s] a place-holder, a deputy, used orig. of clergy. [abbr. WARMING PAN n.¹ (2)]

w.p.b. n. [late 19C] waste paper basket. [abbr.]

wrap n.¹ [1950s+] (Aus.) a boost, a commendation. [RAP n.³ (6)]

wrap n.² [1950s+] (drugs) a small quantity of powder-based drugs, e.g. heroin, cocaine, folded into a small square of paper.

wrap n.³ [1980s+] (US campus) a girlfriend. [? SE rapture; ? SE wrap around each other]

wrap v. see RAP v.⁵.

wrap around/round v. [1950s+] (orig. US) to crash one's car.

wrap it up/wrap up v. [1930s+] to bring to an end, to conclude, to stop doing something, esp. as imper. wrap it up!, stop!

wrap oneself around v. [late 19C+] (orig. US) to eat and drink, often as imper, wrap yourself around that.

wrapped adj. [1960s+] (orig. Aus./US campus) besotted with, infatuated by, in love with (cf. RAPT; WRAP n.³). [abbr. SE wrapped up in]

wrapped tight adj. [1970s+] **1** (US) sane, balanced, esp. in neg. uses, e.g. he's not wrapped too tight. **2** (US teen) feeling fine, happy. [the image of a neatly wrapped package]

wrapped up adj. **1** [18C–19C] ext. as all nicely wrapped up, masked by respectable language; thus not even wrapped up, expressed coarsely. **2** [1930s+] sorted out.

wrapper *n.* [early 19C] an overcoat (cf. WRAP-RASCAL). [note US *wrapper*, a woman's loose robe or gown]

wrapping *n.* [1970s+] (US teen) clothes, esp. female.

wrap-rascal *n.* [early 18C–late 19C] **1** a loose overcoat or greatcoat, worn mainly in the 18C. **2** a red great coat (cf. HAP-HARLOT; WRAPPER). [despite SE origin, not necessarily worn by criminals]

wrap round *see* WRAP AROUND.

wrap the sub, to *phr.* [1990s] (US campus) of a woman, to have sexual intercourse. [SE *wrap* + SUBMARINE *n.*² (1)]

wrapt up in the tail of his mother's smock *phr.* [late 18C–mid-19C] said of one who has notable success with women.

wrapt up in warm flannel *phr.* [late 18C–early 19C] drunk on spirits, esp. gin. [ref. to such terms as WHITE RIBBON; WHITE SATIN that, like flannel, are 'textiles' that describe gin]

wrap-up *n.*¹ [1940s+] (Aus.) a flattering account. [var. on RAP UP + image of SE *wrapping* the subject in fine words]

wrap-up *n.*² [1940s+] a sexually available young woman. [fig. use of WRAP IT UP; the easy conclusion of a seduction]

wrap-up *n.*³ [1960s] (Irish) a parcel of scraps from the butcher.

wrap-up *n.*⁴ [1960s+] the end, conclusion. [film jargon *wrap*, the end of a day's shooting]

wrap up *v.*¹ *see* WRAP IT UP.

wrap up *v.*² [1940s+] to stop talking, esp. as a command, *wrap up!*

wrap up *v.*³ *see* RAP *v.*⁵.

wrap up *v.*⁴ [1960s+] (Aus.) to praise, to flatter. [WRAP UP *n.*¹]

wrap up in clean linen, to *phr.* [18C–19C] to disguise distasteful or 'dirty' topics in respectable terminology.

wreath of roses *n.* [1900s–30s] a venereal ulcer. [the ring of ulcers that surround the diseased genitals]

wreck *v.* [1950s+] (gay) **1** to degrade a fellow homosexual when he is not expecting it. **2** to deliberately exaggerate one's effeminacy as a shock tactic (cf. RUIN *v.*).

wrecked *adj.* [1960s+] **1** (drugs) heavily affected by a drug. **2** very drunk.

wrecking crew *n.* [1980s+] (drugs) crack cocaine. [its destructive effects]

wren *n.* [1920s+] (US) an attractive woman.

wrester *n.* [16C] (Und.) a pick-lock. [SE *wrest*, to twist]

wrestle the bald-headed champion, to *phr.* [1990s] to masturbate.

wrestle the hash, to *phr.* [mid-19C+] (US) to dine.

wretch *n.* [1980s+] (US campus) an involuntary celibate, someone unable to find a sexual partner despite their best efforts. [SE *wretch*, a miserable, wretched person]

wriggle-diggle *n.* [1960s+] **1** petting, mutual fondling. **2** sexual intercourse. [the woman SE *wriggles*, the man SE *digs*]

wriggle like a cut snake, to *phr.* [20C] (Aus.) **1** to act the toady. **2** to be evasive.

wriggle navels/play/couple/wriggle one's navels *v.* [18C] to have sexual intercourse.

wriggle off *v.* [late 19C] to leave.

wriggler *n.* [18C] a prostitute. [her use of the WRIGGLING POLE]

wriggling pole/stick *n.* [18C] the penis (cf. WRIGGLER).

wringing and twisting *n.* [1930s–40s] (US Black) suffering racial discrimination and dealing with it either by rebellion or acquiescence. [i.e. the SE *wringing* and *twisting* is of other people's heads or one's own hands]

wring-jaw *n.* [late 18C–mid-19C] (US) rough cider. [its effects]

wring neck *see* RING NECK.

wring out one's sock, to *phr.* [20C] of a man, to urinate.

wring the dew off the branch, to *phr.* [20C] to urinate (cf. DRAIN THE DRAGON; SIPHON THE PYTHON; TAKE ONE'S SNAKE FOR A GALLOP; WRING THE RATTLESNAKE).

wring the dishrag, to *phr.* [1930s–50s] (US Black) to hold hands.

wring the rattlesnake, to *phr.* [20C] to urinate (cf. WRING THE DEW OFF THE BRANCH).

wrinkle *n.*¹ **1** [19C] a lie. **2** [early 19C+] an idea, device or trick, esp. a new one. **3** [early 19C+] a useful piece of information. [? 14–16C SE *wrinkle*, a tortuous, sinuous movement]

wrinkle *n.*² [1980s+] (US campus) an unpleasant, unsophisticated male. [abbr. PENIS WRINKLE]

wrinkle *v.* [early 19C] to lie; thus *wrinkler*, an habitual liar. [WRINKLE *n.*¹ (1)]

wrinkle-bellied *adj.* [late 18C–20C] having had a number of children, usu. used of a prostitute, i.e. *wrinkle-bellied whore*. [her stretch-marks]

wrinkle city *n.* [1960s+] (US) **1** lined, wrinkled skin as a result of old age. **2** a place mainly inhabited by old people. [SE *wrinkle* + sfx. -CITY]

wrinkle room *n.* [1960s+] (gay) that area of a club where older gay men gather (cf. WAXWORKS).

wrinkly/wrinklies *n.* [1970s+] (upper/upper-middle class youth) an old person, the old (cf. CRUMBLY).

wrist *n.* [1990s] an unpleasant person (cf. WANKER). [the movement of the wrist in masturbation, usually accompanied by using the forefinger of one hand to point to the wrist of the other]

wrist aerobics/marathon *n.* [1990s] masturbation.

wrist-slap *n.* [1950s+] a mild reprimand. [SE *slap on the wrist*]

writ bug *n.* [19C+] (US Und.) a prison inmate who has made themself into a self-taught lawyer, either to pursue their own case, combat prison corruption or help their fellow inmates (cf. JAILHOUSE LAWYER). [SE *writ* + BUG *n.*⁵]

write-off *n.* [1930s+] (orig. milit.) anything or anyone that is completely destroyed, beyond all hope of repair. [in orig. service use, it is *written off* the inventory]

write one's name across another's, to *phr.* [late 19C–1910s] (orig. sporting) to hit in the face.

write one's name on, to *phr.* [mid-19C+] to reserve for oneself, to have the first go at.

write one's own ticket, to *phr.* [1920s+] to be able to stipulate one's own conditions, to be in an advantageous position.

writer *n.*¹ [1930s+] (drugs) a doctor who will write prescriptions for narcotics and ask no questions about the user (cf. WRITING DOCTOR).

writer *n.*² [1980s+] (US) a graffiti artist.

write scrip/script *v.* [1940s+] (drugs) to give out prescriptions for narcotics. [SE *write* + SCRIP/SCRIPT]

write the book on, to *phr.* [20C] (orig. US) to be an expert on, an authority on, usu. in the phr. *one wrote the book on*, e.g. *Does he know about downloading? He wrote the book on downloading.*

write-up *n.* [20C] (US prison) a disciplinary record (cf. TICKET *n.*² (1)]

writing doctor *n.* [1930s+] (drugs) a doctor who will write prescriptions for narcotics and ask no questions about the user (cf. HUNGRY CROAKER; WRITER *n.*¹; WRITE SCRIP).

writing fool *n.* [20C] (drugs) a doctor who will write as many prescriptions for narcotics as there are people requesting them (cf. FOOL *n.*).

written all over it *phr.* [20C] fig. 'signed', i.e. bearing the obvious 'trade-marks' of the person who did it, usu. but not invariably of a crime.

wrokin *n.* [17C–late 19C] a Dutch woman. [? Du. *vrouw*, a woman + dimin. sfx *–kin*]

wrong *adj.* [20C] (US Und.) untrustworthy, too close to the authorities (cf. WRONG GUY).

wrong all round the corner *phr.* [late 19C–1920s] drunk.

wrong gee *n.* [1940s+] (US Und.) an untrustworthy man (cf. WRONG GUY). [WRONG + GEE n.⁴]

wrong guy *n.* [1940s+] (US Und.) **1** an incompetent, an untrustworthy person. **2** an informer. [WRONG + GUY n.²; (2) is spec. use of (1)]

wrong in one's garret *phr.* [late 18C] insane, eccentric. [SE *wrong* + GARRET n. (1)]

wrong in one's upper storey *phr.* [mid-19C] insane. [UPPER STOREY]

wrong number *n.* [1930s+] (US) **1** a mistaken idea. **2** a dangerous person. **3** a dishonest, untrustworthy person.

wrongo *n.* [1930s+] (US) **1** a criminal. **2** an undesirable person. **3** a mistake, error or lie. [SE *wrong* + sfx. -O]

wrongo *adj.* [1930s+] (US) mistaken, inept, prone to error. [WRONGO n.]

wrong riff *n.* [1940s] (US Black) a mistake, a blunder. [jazz use]

wrong side of the tracks *phr.* [mid-19C+] the poor, undesirable area of a town. [the building of many US towns athwart the railway tracks, although the term can exist even when an actual railroad does not]

wrong 'un *n.* [late 19C+] an untrustworthy, incompetent person, animal, action, circumstance, event. [racing jargon *wrong 'un*, a horse that had been deliberately pulled up during a race; ult. SE *wrong one*]

wrought *see* RORT n.

wrought iron! *excl.* [1970s] (US campus) an excl. of approval. [a play on the excl. RIGHT ON!]

wry mouth and a pissen pair of breeches *n.* [late 18C–early 19C] a hanging (cf. WRY NECK DAY). [SE *wry*, contorted, twisted + *pissen*, pissed upon; i.e. the effect on the victim's bodily functions]

wry neck day *n.* [late 18C–early 19C] the hanging day (cf. WRY MOUTH AND A PISSEN PAIR OF BREECHES). [for ety. *see* WRY MOUTH AND A PISSEN PAIR OF BREECHES]

w/s *n.* [1960s+] used in sex contact advertisements, urolagnia. [abbr. water *sports*]

W2 *n.* [late 19C] **1** the German Kaiser Wilhelm II (r.1888–1918). **2** any military-looking man. [the signature affixed to his telegram sent to Paul Kruger (1825–1904), president of the South African Republic and leader of the Boers, on New Year's day 1896]

wukka *n.* [1980s+] (US campus) a very good-looking man or woman. [? WICKED adj. (3) + PUKKA]

wump/whump *n.* [1920s+] a hard, slapping blow (cf. WHOMP n.). [echoic]

wuss *n.* [1970s+] (orig. US teen) a weakling, someone who cannot be depended on; thus *wussy*, indecisive, feeble. [WIMP n.² + PUSSY n.¹ (3)]

wusser *n.* [late 19C] a canal boat. [? play on Ger. *wasser*, water]

wu-tang *adj.* [1980s] (US Black) excellent, first-rate, admirable. [the martial arts film *Shao-Lin and Wu Tang* (1988)]

w.w. *see* WIBLING'S WITCH.

Wyatt Earp *n.*¹ [20C] a burp. [rhy. sl.; ult. US lawman *Wyatt Earp* (1848–1929)]

Wyatt Earp *n.*² [1970s] the penis. [backsl., *curp/kcirp* = PRICK n.¹ (1)]

wyn *see* WIN n.

2 [1980s+] (drugs) crack cocaine. [brandname of the syringe; (2) is a misreading of (1)]

yam *n.*[1] [early 18C+] food; 'this word is used by the lowest class all over the world; by the Wapping sailor, West India negro, or Chinese coolie' (Hotten, 1867). [West African words such as Hausa *nama*, flesh, meat, Swahili *nyama*, meat, Fulah *nyama*, to eat; all these in turn based on SE *yam*, a variety of edible tuber]

yam *n.*[2] [mid-19C–1920s] (US Black) a West Indian. [SE *yam*, an edible tuber; stereotyped as central to the W.I. diet]

yam *v.*[1] [early 18C+] to eat (cf. NYAM v.). [YAM n.[1]]

yam *v.*[2] [1980s+] (US campus) to have sex. [fig. use of YAM v.[1] + SE *yum*]

ya mamma! *see* YO' MAMA!

yang *n.* [20C] the penis (cf. YING-YANG). [var. on WANG n.]

yanga *see* NYANGA.

yang one's wang, to *phr.* [20C] to masturbate. [YANK v.[1] + WANG]

yang yang *n.* [1980s+] (US campus) nonsense, rubbish. [nonsense word + ? play on YANG on pattern of COCK n.[4] (2)]

Yank *n.* [late 18C+] a usu. derog. term for an American. [abbr. SE *Yankee*; ult. Du. *Janke*, a dimin. of Jan (John) and coined as a derisive nickname by either the Dutch or the English in the New England states. Substantial documentary evidence bears this out, with many late 18C–early 19C records of sailors, pirates and one Black slave nicknamed *yankey, yanky* or *yankee*. The term is most likely an elision of *Jan Kees* (Kees being a dimin. of Cornelius), the Dutch equivalent of 'Joe Doakes' or 'John Doe' and based in its turn on *Jan Kaas*, literally 'John Cheese'. It seems to have been coined as a nickname for the Dutch settlers, then, with the appearance of the English in Connecticut, turned on the newcomers by the Dutch and then extended to the whole of New England]

yank *v.*[1] [mid-19C+] **1** (orig. US) to drag, to pull. **2** (US) to victimize, to harass or to dupe (cf. JERK SOMEONE AROUND). [ety. unknown]

Yank *v.*[2] [1940s+] of British women, to pick up American servicemen during WW2. [YANK n.]

yankee *n.*[1] [mid-19C] (US) a glass of whisky sweetened with molasses. [a popular drink]

yankee *n.*[2] [1950s] (gay) masturbation. [YANK OFF]

yankee *v.* [mid-19C+] to cheat, to drive a hard bargain. [the neg. image of New England business people]

yankee dime *n.* [20C] (US) a kiss (cf. DUTCH KISS). [used in US South where *Yankee* is generic for thief; such a kiss has therefore been 'stolen']

yankee heaven/paradise *n.* [late 19C] Paris. [the dictum 'When good Americans die, they go to Paris', coined *c.*1860 by Thomas G. Appleton (1812–84)]

yankee one's wankee, to *phr.* [20C] to masturbate. [YANK v.[1] (1) + WANG; the substitution of 'k' is for assonance]

yankee particular *n.* [mid-19C] (Aus.) a glass of spirits (cf. YANKEE n.[1]).

yankeeries *n.* [late 19C] Buffalo Bill's Wild West Show, which arrived in London in 1887 (and was seen at Earl's Court by Queen Victoria) (cf. COLINDERIES). [SE *Yankee*]

yankee/Scotch shout *n.* [1950s–60s] (Aus./N.Z.) a round of drinks for which all present pay equally. [stereotyping of SE *Yankees* or *Scots* as mean + SHOUT n.[1]]

yankee's yawn *n.* [1950s–60s] (US gay) the open mouth of a climaxing male.

yank mags *see* YANKS.

yank off *v.* [20C] to masturbate (cf. BEAT OFF). [YANK v.[1] (1)]

yank one's crank, to *phr.* [20C] to masturbate (cf. CRANK ONE'S SHANK). [YANK v.[1] (1) + CRANK n.[4]]

yank one's wank, to *phr.* [20C] to masturbate. [YANK v.[1] (1) + WANK n.]

yank on/bite on/eat that! *excl.* [1980s+] (US campus) a general excl. of contempt, dismissal. [YANK v.[1]]

yanks/yank mags *n.* [1930s] American pulp magazines, as distributed in the UK. [YANK v.[1] (1) + MAG n.[3] (1)]

yank someone's chain, to *phr.* [1960s+] to irritate someone, to annoy someone, to remind or distract someone forcibly (cf. JERK SOMEONE'S CHAIN). [YANK v.[1]]

yank the plank, to *phr.* [1990s] to masturbate. [YANK v.[1] (1) + SE *plank*]

yank the yam, to *phr.* [20C] to masturbate. [YANK v.[1] (1) + SE *yam*]

yannups/yennups *n.* [late 19C] money. [backsl.]

yanta *n.* [20C] (US) a derog. term for a Black person. [ety. unknown; ? link to YENTA]

yantsy *adj.* [mid-19C+] (US) excited, aroused. [? var. on ANTSY]

y.a.p. *n.* [1980s] (US) a young American professional. [abbr.]

yap *n.*[1] **1** [late 19C+] (US) the mouth, usu. in derog. sense, *shut your yap!* etc. **2** [20C] (orig. US) idle, trivial chatter. **3** [1930s–50s] (orig. US) a chat, a conversation. [echoic]

yap *n.*[2] **1** [late 19C+] (US) a derog. term for a peasant, a rustic simpleton. **2** [late 19C+] (US) a contemptible person, irrespective of class or background. **3** [20C] (US Und.) a criminal's victim. [fig. uses of YAP n.[1]]

yap *n.*[3] [1950s] (W.I.) a Chinese person. [? Chinese surname]

yap *v.*[1] [mid-19C] to pay back; thus *yap-poo*, pay up. [backsl.]

yap *v.*[2] [late 19C+] to talk, esp. to shout at, like a dog. [dial. *yap*, to talk loudly, foolishly]

yappies, the *n.* [1940s+] (Aus.) 'the dogs', i.e. greyhound racing, coursing. [SE *yap*, to bark]

yappy *adj.*[1] [mid-19C+] foolish, soft. [YAP n.[2]]

yappy *adj.*[2] [mid-19C+] noisy, talkative. [YAP v.[2]; the imagery is of an irrepressible puppy]

yappy *adj.*[3] [20C] (Ulster) thin, hungry-looking. [YAP n.[1] (1); one's mouth is fig. open with hunger]

yapster *n.* [late 18C–late 19C] a dog. [SE *yap*, to bark + sfx. *-ster*]

yap-yap *n.* [1950s] obscenity, bad language. [YAP n.[1] (2) + redup.]

yap-yap *v.* [1950s] (W.I.) to open one's mouth wide through hunger. [YAP n.[1] (1) + redup.]

yarbles *n.* [1970s+] testicles (cf. YONGLES). [? link to dial. *yarb*, 'an opprobrious epithet' (*EDD*) + BALLS n.[1] (1); popularized by the film *A Clockwork Orange* (1971)]

yard *n.*[1] [19C] the penis (cf. CATSO; GADSO). [prior use SE f. late 14C; Old Teut. *gazdjo*, a thin pole ? + link to Lat. *hasta*, a spear + Ital. *cazzo*, penis]

yard *n.*[2] [1920s+] **1** (US) 100 or 1000, usu. of dollars (cf. CENTURY; HALF-A-YARD). **2** (US Und.) a sentence of 100 years.

yard *n.*[3] [1960s+] (US Black) the genitals, usu. female. [i.e. where the 'grass' or pubic hair grows]

yard *n.*[4] [1970s+] (UK Black) **1** one's home. **2** Jamaica.

yard *v.* [1950s+] (US Black) to be sexually unfaithful (cf. YARD ON). [abbr. fig. SE *play in someone's back-yard*]

yard-and-a-half *n.* [1960s+] (US) $150 (cf. BUCK-AND-A-HALF).

yardbird *n.* [1940s+] (US) **1** a civilian dock worker in a naval dockyard. **2** anyone confined by authority to a restricted area, usu. prison. [SE *yard* + BIRD n.[2] (14)]

yardbird lawyer *n.* [1940s+] (US Und.) a prison inmate who has become a self-taught lawyer, either to pursue his own case, to combat prison corruption or to help fellow inmates (cf. BARRACK-ROOM LAWYER). [YARDBIRD (2) + SE *lawyer*]

yard bull *n.* [20C] (US) **1** a railroad police officer, guard or detective. **2** a prison guard. [SE *yard* + BULL n.[10]]

yard dog *n.* [1930s–40s] (US Black) a fool, a gullible person.

yard hack *n.* [20C] (US) a prison guard. [SE *yard* + HACK n.[3]]

yardie *n.* [1980s+] (orig. W.I.) **1** a Jamaican (cf. YARDMAN).

XYZ

x *n.*[1] [mid-19C] a method of arrest whereby a policeman grasps the villain's collar and holds their arm in such a way that the more they struggle, the more likely it is for the arm to be broken. [the crossed position of the arm]

x *n.*[2] [20C] (US) a $10 bill, $10. [Roman numeral *X*, 10]

x/x-ing *n.*[3] (drugs) **1** [1950s] an injection. **2** [1980s+] MDMA, marijuana, amphetamine. [the use of *x* as a code, i.e. because drugs are prohibited]

x *n.*[4] [1950s+] (W.I.) the *acc*elerator on a car. [pron.]

x *adj.* [1950s+] angry. [*x* = lit. 'cross']

x *v.* [1980s+] (US campus) to stop, to eliminate. [*x*, a cross, thus cross out]

x-double-minus *adj.* [1970s+] (US) very bad, inferior, wretched. [play on academic marking]

x'ed out *adj.* [1970s] (US Black) used of something that, while once important, is no longer relevant. [X OUT]

Xerox *v.* [1990s] (US Black) to copy, to imitate, to mimic. [brandname of Rank *Xerox* Corp., leading photocopier manufacturers]

Xerox copy *n.* [1950s+] (Aus.) a Remembrance Day poppy. [rhy. sl.; see XEROX]

Xerox queen *n.* [1960s+] (US gay) a man who prefers all his sexual partners to resemble each other. [SE *Xerox* (see XEROX) + QUEEN *n.*[1]]

x-ing see X *n.*[3].

x out *v.* [1970s] (US Black) to discuss something as no longer important or relevant.

x-ray *v.* [1960s] (US Black) to watch closely, to stare at.

x-row *n.* [20C] (US Und.) the condemned cells (cf. C.C.; DEATH ROW). [fig. use of *x* as 'nameless']

x's/x.s. *n.* [late 19C+] expenses (cf. EXES). [abbr.]

X's hall *n.* [late 19C] the London session house. [*X*, one Hicks, a notoriously punitive judge]

XTC *n.* [1980s+] (drugs) MDMA. [pron. of ECSTASY]

x.x. *n.* [1930s–40s] (US) a betrayal, a 'double cross'.

Y *n.* [1910s+] (orig. US) the *Y*oung *M*en's *C*hristian *A*ssociation (*YMCA*). [abbr.]

-y *sfx.* [20C] (Aus.) a popular sfx. used both as a dimin. and as a mark of informality.

yabber *n.* [mid-19C+] (Aus.) talk, chatter. [? pidgin; ult. Wuywurung *yaba*, to speak, but note SE *jabber*]

yabber *v.* [mid-19C+] (Aus.) to talk, to chatter. [YABBER *n.*]

yabby *n.* [1980s+] (Aus.) in cricket, a wicket-keeper. [SAusE *yabby*, a crayfish; the crouching, padded and gauntleted keeper supposedly resembles one]

yachtie *n.* [1940s+] (Aus./N.Z.) a yachting enthusiast.

yack *n.*[1] [mid-19C] a watch (cf. CHURCH A YACK). [? Welsh gypsy *yakengeri*, a clock, lit 'a thing of the eyes']

yack/yak *n.*[2] [1950s+] **1** empty, tedious, trivial talk (cf. YACKETY-YACK). **2** an accent, a tone of voice. [echoic]

yack *v.*[1] [1950s+] to chatter tediously. [YACK *n.*]

yack *v.*[2] see YAK *v.*[2].

yacker/yakker *n.*[1] [late 19C+] (Aus.) **1** talk, chatter. **2** a gossip (cf. YACK *n.*[2]). [echoic]

yacker/yakker *n.*[2] [late 19C+] (Aus.) food. [YAKKA; i.e. the result of work is money to buy food]

yacker/yakker *v.* [late 19C+] (Aus.) to talk, to chatter, to gossip (cf. YACK *v.*[1]). [YACKER *n.*[1]]

yackety-/yakety-/yakkety-yak/-yack *n.* [1950s+] aimless chatter. [YACK *n.*[2] + redup.]

yackety-/yakety-/yakkety-yak/-yack *v.* [1950s+] to chatter aimlessly. [YACKETY-YAK *n.*]

yackum *n.* [late 19C] excrement. [var. on CACK *n.*[1]]

yacoo/yakoo *n.* [1960s+] (US Black) a White racist bigot. [*Yacub*, the white devil-figure of Black Muslim theology]

yad *n.* [mid-19C] a day. [backsl.]

yadnab *n.* [mid-19C] brandy. [backsl.]

yaffle *v.*[1] [late 18C–1930s] to eat or drink, esp. noisily or greedily. [echoic]

yaffle *v.*[2] [19C] to talk fast, to talk unintelligibly. [Yorks. dial. *yaffle*, to mumble or yelp]

yaffner *n.* [late 19C–1930s] (US Black) an untrustworthy person, a tell-tale. [ety. unknown]

yaga yaga *n.* [1980s+] (W.I. Rasta) a friend, an intimate (cf. RAGAMUFFIN). [YAGA-YAGA!]

yaga-yaga! *excl.* [1980s+] (W.I./UK Black teen) a greeting, a means of attracting attention to oneself (cf. YO!; YUSH!). [fig. use of RAGA-RAGA; the y/r substitution comes from the folktales of Anansi, the spider, whose 'Bungo' talk uses 'y' for 'r']

yahoo *n.*[1] [18C+] a person lacking cultivation or sensibility, a philistine, a hooligan. [Jonathan Swift's *Gulliver's Travels* (1727), in which *Yahoos* were an imaginary race of brutes having the form of men; note Aus. *yahoo*, a probably mythical creature resembling a large hairy man, said to haunt eastern Australia]

yahoo *n.*[2] see YEYO.

yak *n.*[1] see YACK *n.*[2].

yak *n.*[2] [1980s+] (US) a general term of abuse. [YACK *v.*[1]; i.e. one who talks rubbish all the time]

yak *v.*[1] see YACK *v.*[1].

yak/yack *v.*[2] [1990s] (US campus) to vomit (cf. BISON; WATER BUFFALO). [echoic]

yakety-yack/-yak see YACKETY-YAK.

yakka/yakker *n.* [late 19C+] (Aus.) exhausting work. [Jagara *yaga*, work; but note Ulster *yokkin*, a spell of work, lit. the 'yoking' of horses]

yakka/yakker *v.* [late 19C+] (Aus.) to work hard, to labour. [YAKKA *n.*]

yakker see YACKER.

yakkety-yack/-yak see YACKETY-YAK.

yakky *adj.* [1950s+] (US) talkative, garrulous. [YACK *v.*[1]]

yakoo see YACOO.

yale *n.* **1** [1960s–70s] (US drugs) a hypodermic syringe.

2 one of a gang of organized Jamaican criminals who specialize in purveying drugs and violence on an international level. [YARD n.⁴]

yardman n. [1970s+] (W.I./UK Black teen) a Jamaican. [YARD n.⁴]

yardnarb n. [late 19C] brandy. [backsl.]

yard nigger n. [20C] a subservient, acquiescent Black (cf. FIELD NIGGER n.¹; HOUSE NIGGER). [SE yard + NIGGER n.; the differentiation under slavery between the 'domesticated' Blacks who worked as house servants and those who, seen as more rebellious, merely toiled in the plantation fields]

yard of clay n. [mid–late 19C] a clay pipe with a notably long stem (cf. CHURCHWARDEN).

yard of pump water n. [late 19C] a tall, thin person (cf. LONG THIN; STREAK OF PISS).

yard of satin n. [early 19C–1920s] a glass of gin. [SE yard, a glass + SATIN n. (1)]

yard of tin n. [mid–late 19C] a horn, esp. in hunting or coaching.

yard of tripe n. [mid-19C] a pipe. [rhy. sl.]

yard on v. [1950s] (US Black) to be unfaithful sexually. [ext. of YARD v.]

yard patrol n. [20C] (US prison) **1** a group of convicts. **2** a prison guard.

yarker n. [late 19C–1900s] an ear. [SE hark + sfx. -er]

Yarmouth bloater n.¹ [mid-19C] an inhabitant of Yarmouth (cf. NORFOLK DUMPLING).

Yarmouth bloater n.² [1910s+] an automobile. [rhy. sl. Yarmouth bloater = motor]

Yarmouth/Norfolk capon n. [late 17C–19C] **1** a red herring. **2** a bloater (cf. ABERDEEN CUTLET). [the local fishing industry]

yarn n. **1** [mid-19C+] (orig. naut.) a story, esp. a long and possibly implausibly wonderful one. **2** [late 19C] a story, rather than a proper novel. [the stories told by sailors during the lengthy processes of making ropes; (2) implies the dichotomy between 'literary' and 'popular' writing]

yarn-chopper/-slinger/-spinner n. [late 19C–1920s] a story-teller, a chatterer. [YARN + SE chop/sling/spin]

yarpie n. [1980s+] (Aus.) a South African; thus Yarpieland, South Africa. [JAAP]

yar-poo v. [mid-19C] to pay up. [backsl.]

yarra adj. [late 19C+] (Aus.) insane (cf. CALLAN PARK). [the mental hospital at Yarra Bend, Victoria]

Yarra banker n. [late 19C+] (Aus.) **1** a soap-box orator. **2** an idler, a loafer found on the banks of Melbourne's Yarra River. [the banks of the Yarra are the equivalent of London's Hyde Park Corner]

yarrum/yarum n. [mid-16C–late 18C] (Und.) milk; thus poplars of yarrum, milk porridge. [? a corruption of SE yellow or yallow]

yasha n. [1950s–60s] (camp gay) an idiot, a fool. [Rus. yasha, a peasant]

yassas! see YISSUS!

yasser n. [1990s] (US) an erection. [abbr. Yasser CRACK A FAT, a pun on PLO leader Yasser Arafat (b.1929)]

yatata n. [1940s–50s] (US) talk, chatter. [YATATA v.]

yatata v. [1940s–50s] (US) to talk, to chatter. [YATTER n.]

yatter n. [early 19C+] talk, chatter, gabble. [Scot.]

yatter v. [early 19C+] to talk, to chatter, to gabble. [YATTER n.]

yaup see YAWP.

yaupy/yaupish adj. [19C] drunk. [YAWP]

yawn n. [late 19C+] anything considered tedious, boring and thus productive of yawns.

yawner n. [1940s+] (US) anything boring, yawn-producing. [YAWN + sfx. -er]

yawney n. [19C] a fool, a simpleton. [dial.; their mouth yawns open in stupidity]

yawp/yaup v. [late 19C+] (orig. US) to talk loudly or foolishly, to nag (cf. YAP v.²). [dial.]

yay-nay n. [mid-19C] a simpleton, an unsophisticated person (cf. YEA AND NAY MAN). [bereft of communicative powers, they can only answer 'yea' or 'nay' to any question]

y-bone steak n. [1990s] the female genitals. [the fork of the thighs + play on SE T-bone steak]

Y Dub n. [1950s] the YMCA (cf. Y.). [pron. 'wy double']

yea adj. [1950s+] (orig. US Black) this, e.g. yea big, this big; yea high, this high.

yea and nay man n. **1** [late 17C–18C] a Quaker. **2** [late 18C–mid-19C] a simpleton, capable of answering only 'yes' or 'no' (cf. YAY-NAY). **3** [mid–late 19C] a poor conversationalist, a monosyllabic person. [the Quakers' supposed predilection for simple, black and white answers]

yeah adv. [20C] (US) yes. [pron.]

yeah man n. [1980s+] (US campus) a boring person. [they chatter on; one intersperses their monologue by saying 'Yeah, man' occasionally]

yeaho see YEYO.

yeah, right! see RIGHT!

year n. [1940s–50s] (US Und.) $1; thus five years, $5 etc.

year dot n. [late 19C+] a very long time ago; usu. from the year dot, for ever.

yeasting n. [1940s–60s] (US Black) exaggerating, boasting. [the way in which yeast makes otherwise flat dough rise]

yecch see YUCK n.

yecch! see YUCK!

yecchy see YUCKY.

yech see YUCK n.

yech! see YUCK!

yegg n. [late 19C+] (US Und.) a thief, spec. a safe-cracker. [? John Yegg, a contemporary villain and the first safe-breaker to use nitroglycerine]

ye gods!/ye gods and little fishes! excl. [late 19C–1910s] a mild oath.

yeh n. [1980s+] (drugs) marijuana. [ety. unknown]

Yehudi n. [20C] (US) a Jew. [Heb. yehudi, a Jew]

yeknod n. [mid-19C] a donkey (cf. JERK-NOD). [backsl.]

yell n.¹ [mid–late 19C] beer. [its yellow colour]

yell n.² **1** [1920s+] a good time (cf. SCREAM n.¹). **2** [1960s+] an act of vomiting (cf. THROW ONE'S VOICE).

yeller feller see YELLOW FELLOW.

yellow n. [1910s] a sovereign, £1 sterling (cf. CANARY n.⁴). [the golden coin]

yellow adj.¹ [late 17C–mid-18C] jealous. [corruption of SE]

yellow adj.² **1** [mid-19C+] cowardly (cf. YELLOW-BACK n.¹, YELLOW BELLY n.³). **2** [late 19C] (US) unsatisfactory, second-rate, of dubious quality. [the neg. image of the colour]

yellow adj.³ [mid-19C+] (US) of a Black person, light-skinned (cf. YELLOW ASS).

yellow about the gills see BLUE ABOUT THE GILLS.

yellow agony n. [late 19C] (Aus.) Chinese immigrants to Australia. [generic use of SE yellow for Chinese; the agony was that of Aus. workers, esp. sailors, who saw their jobs threatened by such immigrants]

yellow around the gills see BLUE ABOUT THE GILLS.

yellow ass n. [1930s–50s] (US) a light-coloured Black girl. [YELLOW adj.³ + ARSE n.¹]

yellow back n.¹ [20C] a coward; thus yellow-backed, cowardly. [ext. YELLOW adj.² (1)]

yellow back n.² [1940s+] (Aus.) a gob of phlegm. [its colour]

yellow bam n. [1980s+] (drugs) methamphetamine. [SE yellow + BAM n.³ (2)]

yellow-bellied adj. [1920s+] used to describe a cowardly person. [ext. of YELLOW adj.² (1)]

yellow belly *n.*[1] [late 18C+] a native of Lincolnshire, esp. of the southern or fenland part of the county. [the yellow-stomached frog or the eels that abound there]

yellow belly *n.*[2] [early 19C] (US) a Mexican, esp. a soldier. [? the colour of their uniforms]

yellow belly/guts/heel *n.*[3] [1930s+] a coward. [YELLOW-BELLIED adj./SE *yellow* + *guts/heel*]

yellow belly *n.*[4] [1940s] (Aus.) a Japanese person. [the 'yellow' Oriental complexion]

yellow bird *n.* [mid–late 19C] (US) a dollar. [the eagle engraved upon it]

yellow boy *n.* [late 17C–19C] a golden guinea (cf. BOY *n.*[1]; CANARY *n.*[4]). [the colour of the golden coin]

yellow bullets *n.* [1940s+] (drugs) Nembutal, a barbiturate. [the colour of the tablets]

yellow callies *see* WHITE CALLIES.

yellow dimples *n.* [1970s] (drugs) LSD, esp. combined with another drug. [ety. unknown]

yellow dog *n.* [late 19C] (US) a general term of contempt.

yellow dog contract *n.* [20C] (US) an employee's work contract forbidding union membership. [YELLOW DOG + SE *contract*]

yellow fancy *n.* [mid-19C] a costermonger's handkerchief, yellow with white spots (cf. BELCHER *n.*[1]).

yellow fellow/yeller feller *n.* [20C] (Aus.) a mulatto, a half-White, half-Aborigine male. [YELLOW adj.[3] + SE *fellow*]

yellow fever *n.*[1] [1950s–60s] (camp gay) an obsession with Oriental lovers.

yellow fever *n.*[2] [1980s] (drugs) phencyclidine (cf. ACE *n.*[3]). [ety. unknown]

yellow fish *n.* [20C] (US) an illegal Chinese immigrant. [SE *yellow*, the Oriental complexion + FISH *n.*[1]]

yellow george *n.* [18C–19C] a guinea (cf. CANARY *n.*[4]). [SE *yellow*, its golden colour + GEORGE *n.*[1]]

yellow girl *n.* [mid-19C] a mulatto, a half-White, half-Aborigine woman. [YELLOW adj.[3] + SE *girl*]

yellow gloak *n.* [early–mid-19C] a jealous man, esp. a jealous husband. [YELLOW adj.[1] + GLOAK]

yellow guts *see* YELLOW BELLY *n.*[3].

yellowhammer *n.* [early–mid-17C] a golden guinea (cf. CANARY *n.*[4]). [the colour of the golden coin]

yellow heel *see* YELLOW BELLY *n.*[3].

yellow jack *n.* [early 19C] yellow fever (cf. BRONZE JOHN). [SE *yellow* + generic use of *jack*]

yellow jacket *n.* [mid–late 19C] (US) a wasp.

yellow jackets *n.* [1950s+] (US Black) Nembutal, a proprietary brand of pentobarbital sodium. [the yellow capsule]

yellow kelter *n.* [20C] (Irish) a gold coin. [SE *yellow* + KELTER]

yellow leg *n.* **1** [late 19C] (US) a US cavalryman. **2** [1940s+] (Can.) a member of the Royal Canadian Mounted Police. [the yellow stripe running down their uniform trousers]

yellow man *n.* [mid-19C] a costermonger's handkerchief, coloured plain yellow (cf. BELCHER *n.*[1]; YELLOW FANCY).

yellow mellow *see* MELLOW YELLOW *n.*[3].

yellow pack *n.* [1990s] (Irish) low-paid employment of young people and the concomitant dismissal of more expensive senior employees. [the yellow packaging of the 'own-brand' goods sold by the Quinnsworth chain of supermarkets]

yellow peril *n.* **1** [20C] a derog. term for any oriental person. **2** [20C] the Communist Chinese. **3** [1910s+] a Gold Flake cigarette.

yellow route *n.* [1980s] (S.Afr.) the departure of White South Africans in the face of the imminent take-over by a multi-racial government (cf. CHICKEN RUN). [YELLOW adj.[2]]

yellows *n.* [1940s+] (drugs) Nembutal, a depressant (cf. BLUES *n.*[2]). [the colour of the pills]

yellow sheet *n.* [20C] (US Und.) a criminal's record of arrests (cf. FORM *n.*[5]; RAP SHEET). [its colour]

yellow silk *n.* [late 19C–1900s] milk. [rhy. sl.]

yellow snake *n.* [late 18C] (W.I.) a mulatto.

yellow stuff *n.* [mid–late 19C] gold.

yellow submarine *n.* [1980s+] (drugs) **1** marijuana. **2** temazepam. [the poss. 'hallucinogenic' effects; ref. to Beatles' 'psychedelic' cartoon film *Yellow Submarine* (1967)]

yellow sunshine *n.* [1960s+] (drugs) a form of LSD. [var. on ORANGE SUNSHINE]

yells, nells and knells *n.* [20C] (Aus.) press announcements of births, marriages and deaths (cf. HATCHED, MATCHED AND DISPATCHED). [SE *yells*, *nuptials*, *knells*, the tolling of a bell]

yelper *n.* **1** [early 18C–early 19C] a town crier. **2** [late 18C] a wild beast. **3** [mid-19C] a whiner, a complainer. **4** [1950s+] (US) a police car or emergency vehicle siren.

yen *n.* **1** [late 19C+] (drugs) a desperate desire for a narcotic, usu. heroin. **2** [20C] a craving, an intense desire. [Beijing dial. Chinese *yen*, smoke, poss. reinforced by yearn]

yenams *see* YENEMS.

yen dong *n.* [late 19C–1930s] (US drugs) the lamp used to heat 'pills' of opium. [Chinese or mock-Chinese]

yenems/yenams/yenhams *n.* [1920s+] someone else's property, cigarettes etc. [synon. Yid. *yenams*, lit. 'his']

yenep *see* YENNEP.

yenhams *see* YENEMS.

yen hock/hok *n.* [late 19C–1960s] (US drugs) the needle used to prepare a pipe of opium. [Chinese or mock-Chinese]

yen hop *n.* [late 19C–1930s] (US drugs) the box that contains opium paraphernalia (cf. LAYOUT *n.*[3]). [Chinese or mock-Chinese]

yennep/yenep/yennap/yennop *n.* [mid-19C] a penny. [backsl.]

yennepatine *n.* [mid-19C] a penny a time. [backsl.]

yennep flatch *n.* [mid-19C] three halfpence. [backsl.]

yennups *see* YANNUPS.

yenork *n.* [mid-19C] a crown, 5 shillings (25p); thus *flatch yenork/enore*, half-a-crown, 2s 6d (12½p). [backsl.]

yen pok *n.* [late 19C–1930s] (US drugs) a pill of opium. [Chinese or mock-Chinese]

yen pop *n.* [1940s] (US drugs) marijuana. [Chinese or mock-Chinese]

yen-shee *n.* (US drugs) **1** [late 19C+] opium. **2** [late 19C+] opium residue; thus *yen-shee hop*, the box used to hold opium ashes, sold to impoverished users. **3** [1950s] heroin. [Chinese or mock-Chinese]

yen-shee baby *n.* [1930s+] (drugs) hard impacted faeces produced, often painfully, by a heroin addict during a period of withdrawal. [YEN-SHEE + SE *baby*; one effect of addiction is long-term constipation]

yen-shee suey *n.* [1930s–50s] (drugs) opium residue dissolved into wine. [YEN-SHEE + SE (*chop*) *suey*]

yen sleep *n.* [1960s+] (drugs) a restless, drowsy sleep that accompanies opiate withdrawal. [YEN + SE *sleep*]

yenta *n.* [1920s+] (orig. US) a nagging, whining person, usu. female (cf. KVETCH *n.*). [Ital. *gentile*, a lady; thence adopted by Yid. speakers and popularized through the fictional *Yenta Telebende*, created in the Jewish New York press by the humorist 'B. Kovner' (Jacob Adler)]

yen tsiang *n.* [late 19C–1930s] (US drugs) an opium pipe. [Chinese]

yentzer *n.* [20C] (US) a cheat, a deceiver, a liar. [Yid. *yenzter*, lit. 'FUCKER']

yen yen *n.* [late 19C–1930s] (US drugs) a craving for opium. [the term uses both the orig. Chinese and the derived SE term; however note Cantonese *yinyan*, craving for opium]

yep/yup *adv.* [early 19C+] (orig. US) yes. [pron.]

yer actual *see* YOUR ACTUAL.

yerba *n.* [1960s+] (drugs) marijuana; thus *yerba buena/mala*, good/bad marijuana. [Sp. *yerba*, herb]

yerknod/keynod/jirk-nod *n.* [mid-19C] a donkey. [backsl.]

yernt *n.* [1980s+] (US campus) a socially inept person. [? YENTA]

yerriso *n.* [20C] (W.I.) gossip, rumour. [pron. of SE *I hear so*]

yes! *excl.* [1980s+] a general excl. of approbation, pleasure, satisfaction; esp. on the completion of a task or triumph in a competition. [note slightly hissing pron., i.e. *yessss*]

yes-baas *n.* [1960s+] (S.Afr.) a servile, subservient Black (cf. JA-BAAS). [lit. 'yes, boss']

yesca *n.* [1940s+] (US drugs) marijuana. [Sp. *yesca*, tinder, fuel]

yes-girl *n.* [1960s] a sexually complaisant young woman. [play on YES-MAN]

yes-man *n.* [1910s+] (orig. US) an obsequious, subservient person, esp. in business, who always says 'yes' to superiors, in the belief that this is what they like to hear (cf. NO-MAN).

yes-sir-no-sir-three-bags-full-sir *phr.* [20C] a mocking jibe, aimed at someone who seems incapable of challenge any form of authority.

yes sir!/siree! *excl.* [late 18C+] (orig. US) an emphatic assertion.

yessus! *see* YISSUS!

yest *n.* [early 18C–late 19C] *yesterday.* [abbr.]

yet *adv.* [1930s+] (orig. US) an ironic intensive placed at the end of a sentence. [Yid. *noch*, another]

yet to be *adj.* [20C] free (both of behaviour and of cost). [rhy. sl.]

yewie *see* U-IE.

yeyo/yahoo/yeaho *n.* [1980s+] (drugs) **1** cocaine. **2** crack cocaine. [synon. Sp.]

Yid/Yit/Yitt *n.*[1] [mid-19C+] a Jew; both derog. and general use, depending on context. [Ger. *Jude*, Jew, ult. Yehuda or Judah, one of the biblical Jacob's sons. The term, as Rosten (1968) points out, is neutral if pronounced 'yeed' as it would be by Jews speaking the Judaeo-German language Yiddish, but unashamedly offensive if pronounced 'yid']

Yid/Yit/Yitt *n.*[2] [1900s–10s] (Aus.) a sovereign; thus *half a Yid*, a half sovereign, 10 shillings (50p). [rhy. sl. *Yid* = quid, but note stereotyped link of Jews and money]

Yiddified *adj.* [1930s] anti-Semitic. [YID n.[1]]

Yiddisher *adj.* [19C+] Jewish. [Yid. *yiddishe*, Jewish]

Yiddisher fiddle *n.* [20C] minor cheating or other illegality. [pun on *fiddle*/FIDDLE n.[2]]

Yiddisher piano *n.* [1910s+] a cash register (cf. JEWISH PIANO). [neg. stereotyping]

Yiddish highway *n.* [20C] (US) US30, the route from New York City to Miami. [New York Jews traditionally move to Miami for their retirement; the relatives use the highway for visits]

Yiddish Renaissance *n.* [1950s+] over-elaborate furniture in doubtful taste (cf. JEWY LOUIS). [racial stereotyping]

Yiddish screwdriver *see* JEWISH SCREWDRIVER.

Yiddle *n.* [20C] a Jew. [dimin. YID n.[1]]

Yidney *n.* [1970s+] (society) Sidney, Australia (cf. JEWBURG). [YID n.[1]; the city's Jewish population]

Yids, the *n.* [20C] Tottenham Hotspur Football Club. [YID n.[1]; the North London club's supposedly large number of Jewish supporters]

Yidsbury *n.* [1970s+] the London suburb of Finsbury (cf. ABRAHAMSTEAD). [YID; the large Jewish population in the district]

yield the crow a pudding *see* GIVE THE CROW A PUDDING.

yike *n.* [1930s+] (Aus.) an argument, a dispute, a fight, a brawl.

[ety. unknown; ? echoic or dial. *yike*, the call of the woodpecker]

yikes *n.* [1960s+] worries, nervousness. [? backform. of YIKES!]

yikes!/yipe!/yipes! *excl.* [1960s+] an excl. of surprise or shock. [? link to SE *yoicks!* or CRIKEY!]

Yim, Yoe and Yesus *n.* [1930s+] (Aus.) in cards, three knaves or jacks. [? an anecdote involving a Scandinavian]

yimyom *n.* [1980s+] (drugs) crack cocaine. [ety. unknown; var. on YEYO]

ying-yang *n.* [1960s+] **1** the anus, esp. in phr. *up the ying-yang*. **2** the penis. [? var. on WANG; *DAS*'s link to 'Hindu' *yin* and *yang* seems spurious]

yip *v.* [20C] (US) to talk in a petulant or irritating manner. [SE *yip*, to yelp]

yipe!/yipes! *see* YIKES!

yips *n.* [1960s+] nerves. [orig. golf use; according to a citation in P. Davies' *Dict. of Golfing Terms* (1980), coined by the golfer T.D. Armour]

yissus!/yassas!/yessus! *excl.* [1940s+] (S.Afr.) a general excl. (cf. GEE!; JEEPERS!). [JESUS!]

Yit/Yitt *see* YID n.[1].

Y.M./Y.W. *n.* [1910s+] (orig. US) the Young Men's Christian Association; or the Young Women's Christian Association. [abbr.]

Y.M.C.A. *adj.* [late 19C] priggish, puritan, 'goody-goody'. [the religiously based organization]

yo! *excl.* [1970s+] (US) a general term of address. [synon. Sp.]

yob *n.* **1** [mid-19C+] a boy. **2** [1920s+] an uncouth, vulgar youth. [backsl.; note WW1 milit. use, *yob*, a young, gullible officer]

yobbo *n.* [1930s+] a lout, a hooligan. [ext. of YOB n. (2)]

yo-boy *n.* [1980s+] (US Black) a White youth who apes his Black contemporaries (cf. YOYO n.[1]; YOM). [his use of the common Black greeting YO!]

yock/yok *n.* [20C] **1** a gentile. **2** a fool. [backsl. GOY]

yodel *v.* [1960s+] (Aus.) to vomit.

yodel/grin in the canyon/the canyon of love/up the valley, to *phr.* [1960s+] to perform cunnilingus (cf. BLOW SOME TUNES). [SE *yodel* + CANYON/SE *canyon*]

Yogi Bear *n.* [1960s+] (Aus.) a prison dandy. [rhy. sl. *Yogi Bear* = LAIR n.]

yok *see* YOCK.

yoke *n.* (Anglo-Irish) **1** [late 19C–1900s] a riding horse, as opposed to a racehorse. **2** [late 19C–1900s] a horse-drawn carriage. **3** [1920s–30s] any form of unspecified gadget. **4** [1980s+] the act of grabbing someone around the neck as part of a mugging. [SE *yoke*, a form of collar]

yoke *v.* [mid-19C+] (US) **1** to murder by strangulation or by cutting someone's throat from behind. **2** to rob while choking or strangling the victim, either with a rope or stick; one person does the *yoking*, the other rifles the victim's pockets (cf. MUG v.[2]). [SE *yoke*, a collar placed across the neck]

yoked *adj.* [1980s+] (US campus) muscular, well-built. [? one's shoulders resemble a SE *yoke*]

yoker *n.* [mid-19C+] (US) a mugger. [YOKE v. (2)]

yoks/yuks *n.* [1940s+] (US) laughs. [echoic]

yokuff *n.* [mid-19C] a large box, a chest. [SE *coffer*]

yola *n.* [1900s–40s] (US Black) a light-skinned young woman. [? Sp.]

yold *n.* [20C] (US) a gullible victim. [Heb. *yeled*, a boy]

yom/yomo *n* [1980s+] a Black street boy (cf. YO-BOY). [YO(UR) MOTHER]

yo'/your mama!/ya mamma!/your mammy! *excl.* [1940s] (US Black) a general excl. which, like MOTHERFUCKER, varies as to context, from the jovially teasing to the deliberately insulting. [US Black pron. of YOUR MOTHER!]

yomo *see* YOM.

yongles/yoongles *n.* [1990s] the testicles. [var. on YARBLES]

yonks *n.* [1960s+] a long time, esp. in phr. *for yonks.* [ety. unknown; ? DONKEY'S YEARS]

yonnie *n.* [1940s+] (Aus.) a small stone, a pebble. [ety. unknown; ? Abor. language]

yoof *adj.* [1980s+] used of anything, esp. TV programmes – high on pop gossip and fashion, low (in critical eyes) on intelligence, that are aimed at the young. [deliberate mispron. of SE *youth* + mimicry of the 'street-cred' London accents of presenters of such programmes and their doyenne, the TV executive Janet Street-Porter]

yoo-hoo boy *n.* [1930s+] (US) an effeminate homosexual. [his camp shrieks of *yoo-hoo!*]

yoongles *see* YONGLES.

york *n.* [19C] a stare, a glance. [YORK v.]

york *v.* [19C] to stare at. [? Cheshire dial. *york*, to pierce or the stereotyped Yorkshireman's shrewd appraisal]

Yorkie *n.* **1** [early 19C+] a *York*shireman. **2** [1950s+] a *York*shire terrier (cf. DACHS). [abbr.]

Yorkshire *n.* [mid-19C–1900s] sharp practice (cf. COME YORKSHIRE OVER). [Ware defines as 'fair and square payments', but this may be ironic]

Yorkshire *adj.* [mid-19C–1900s] mean, grasping. [stereotyping of Yorkshire people as mean, thus also in combs. that follow]

Yorkshire bite *n.* [19C] **1** over-reaching, greediness. **2** a grasping person.

Yorkshire compliment *n.* [mid-19C–1900s] a gift that means nothing to the donor and is useless to the recipient.

Yorkshire estate *n.* [mid-19C–1900s] money that is in prospect but not yet handed over; thus *when I come into my Yorkshire estates*, when I finally have some money. [neg. stereotyping of Yorks. business or legal methods]

Yorkshire hog *n.* [late 18C] a fat wether or castrated ram.

Yorkshire penny bank *n.* [20C] masturbation (cf. BARCLAY'S). [rhy. sl. *Yorkshire penny bank* = WANK]

Yorkshire reckoning *n.* [mid-19C] a situation where every member of the company pays for themselves. [COME YORKSHIRE ON]

Yorkshire rippers *n.* [1980s+] slippers. [rhy. sl.]

Yorkshire tyke *n.* [20C] microphone. [rhy. sl. = *mike*]

Yorkshire way-bit *n.* [mid-17C–mid-19C] a distance over a mile. [SE *Yorkshire* + *way-bit*, a short distance; ult. var. on SE *wee bit* and used in answering questions, 'How far is it?' 'A mile and a way bit']

yo thang *see* YOUR THING.

you ain't just whistling 'Dixie' *phr.* [20C] (US) you really mean what you're saying, you're not just being flippant? [for ety. *see* DIXIE]

you ain't saying nothing *phr.* [1960s] (US Black) a dismissive phr. meaning nothing you say is of the slightest importance.

you all set? *phr.* [1980s+] (US drugs) do you need to buy any drugs?; the response, if one requires nothing, is 'I'm set (for now)'. [SE *all set*, ready, prepared/*set up*, supplied with everything one needs]

you and me *n.* **1** [late 19C–1910s] a flea. **2** [20C] tea. **3** [20C] urination, urine. **4** [20C] (Aus.) a pea. **5** [1940s+] (bingo) the number three. [rhy. sl.; (3) *you and me* = PEE n.¹]

you and whose army? *phr.* [1930s+] (usu. teen) a phr. addressed to anyone who is threatening violence (cf. KILL WHO?).

you and your— *phr.* [early 17C] a contemptuous or teasing dismissal of a thing or person previously cited.

you are a one! *phr.* [late 19C] a phr. used in teasing or mockery (cf. AREN'T YOU THE ONE!). [ONE n.⁴ (1)]

you are a thief and a murderer and you have killed a baboon and stole his face *phr.* [late 18C] a general phr. of hostility and contempt.

you are Josephus rex *phr.* [late 18C] you are joking. [pun on SE abbr. *jo* + Lat. *rex*, king]

you are none of the Hotspurs *phr.* [early 18C–mid-19C] a phr. used to inform a person, esp. a braggart and boaster, that they are in fact more like a coward or weakling. [the famously brave *Hotspur* family]

you bet! *excl.* [mid-19C+] (orig. US) a general excl. of affirmation, agreement, certainly, I'll say so, indeed (cf. BETCHA!).

you better believe it *phr.* [mid-19C+] a phr. of affirmation, that's the truth!

you can/may gamble on that *phr.* [mid-19C+] (orig. US) you can be absolutely sure about that.

you can have/keep it *phr.* [late 19C+] no thanks, it's all yours, I don't want it.

you can kiss the Book on that *phr.* [late 19C] you can be absolutely sure about that. [i.e. the Bible]

you can never know your luck *phr.* [late 19C+] you never know when things may improve.

you can put a ring round that one *phr.* [1920s+] (N.Z.) you can be absolutely sure of that.

you can say that again *phr.* [1930s+] (orig. US) a phr. underlining the speaker's agreement with the previous statement (cf. YOU BETTER BELIEVE IT).

you can talk *see* YOU CAN'T TALK.

you can't fart against thunder *phr.* [late 19C+] don't try to do the impossible.

you can't fight city hall *phr.* [20C] (US) you can't win against the establishment.

you can't fly on one wing *phr.* [1940s+] (Can.) have another drink before you go.

you can't get there from here *phr.* [20C] (US) the situation or the problem is too hard to tackle or solve.

you can't take it with you *phr.* [mid-19C+] a phr. urging someone to spend their money, enjoy their possessions etc. [the unnamed journey is beyond the grave]

you can't/can talk *phr.* [mid-19C+] a phr. used to stress that one speaker is in no position to criticize another.

you can't think *phr.* [late 18C] a general phr., 'you cannot imagine ...'.

you can't win 'em all *phr.* [1950s+] a phr. used to say that one cannot be successful every time and to offer some slight comfort.

you could cut the atmosphere with a knife *phr.* [late 19C+] the atmosphere is so thick (whether lit. or fig.) that one could imagine slicing it with a sharp knife.

you could have fooled me *phr.* [1960s+] a phr. usu. in ironic use when one is actually commenting on something that is wholly predictable; I would never have thought so, what a surprise.

you could have knocked me down with a feather *phr.* [mid-19C+] a phr. implying one's utter surprise at a given circumstance or event.

you couldn't box kippers *phr.* [1920s+] a phr. used to decry a person as a physical weakling.

you couldn't see someone's arse/ass for dust *phr.* [late 19C+] said of someone who has run off very quickly. [ARSE n.¹]

you couldn't throw your hat over the workhouse wall *phr.* [1900s–30s] a phr. used to tease someone who has, or allegedly has, a number of illegitimate children. [such children were usually sent to the workhouse]

you could sow potatoes/scarlet runners on their neck *phr.* [late 19C] used of someone with a notably dirty neck.

you'd forget your head if it weren't screwed on/screwed on properly *phr.* [20C] a phr. used to an exceptionally forgetful person.

you don't get many of those to the pound *phr.* [20C] a phr. used by leering men observing a woman with large breasts.

you don't know the half of it! *excl.* [1930s+] (orig. US) an excl. used to say that someone doesn't know everything about a situation, with the assumption that the speaker does.

you don't know whether you want a shit or haircut/whether your arsehole's bored or punched/you're born *phr.* [20C] a phr. used to indicate that a person is very stupid. [SHIT n.[1] (2); ARSEHOLE]

you don't look at the mantelpiece when you're poking the fire *phr.* [20C] a phr. meaning that a woman's looks are irrelevant if she's sexually available.

you don't say/say so *phr.* [late 19C+] a heavily sarcastic response to a statement of the obvious.

you down with o.p.p.? *phr.* [1990s] (US Black teen) do you respect other people's property? [DOWN adj.[2] (2) + O.P.P. phr.]

youee *see* U-IE.

you got it! *excl.*[1] [1960s] a phr. implying that nothing new has happened, there is no information to pass on, usu. as response to the query *what's happening?*

you got it! *excl.*[2] [1970s+] (orig. US esp. Black) a general affirmative reply, usu. to a yes/no question.

you gotta let yer nutz hang *phr.* [1990s] (US Black teen) be yourself, don't let anybody dictate to you. [NUTS n.[2]]

you great beef *phr.* [late 19C–1900s] a general pej. form of address. [the image being of a brainless bull or cow]

you haven't got the brains you were born with *phr.* [20C] you are very stupid.

you heard! *excl.* [1940s+] (orig. US) used to someone who is pretending not to have heard an unpleasant statement or question; don't pretend you didn't hear what I said.

you know *phr.* [1960s+] a verbal punctuation, with no real meaning. [abbr. earlier *don't you know*]

you know it!/you know it is! *phr.* [late 19C; 1960s+] (orig. US) any form of emphatic agreement, yes indeed, you're right etc.

you know what *n.* [20C] **1** anything the speaker does not wish to name specifically. **2** sexual intercourse.

you know what you can do with ... *phr.* [1920s+] a dismissive phr. used to counter a suggestion, an unacceptable offer etc.

you know where *n.* [20C] a euph. depending on context; if sexual, ref. to the vagina or penis; if hostile, the anus or the testicles (cf. DOWN BELOW).

you'll be a long time dead *phr.* [late 19C+] a phr. addressed to anyone the speaker feels is wasting time, not putting their life to its best advantage etc.

you'll be sorry! *excl.* [1940s+] a semi-jocular cry of warning from those who have experienced a situation to those who are about to encounter it. [coined by WW2 troops; i.e. those leaving combat to those just entering]

you'll have to do the other thing *phr.* [late 19C+] a phr. meaning if you don't like it this way, then... (cf. LIKE IT OR LUMP IT).

you'll know me again, won't you? *see* DO YOU THINK YOU'LL KNOW ME AGAIN?

you lump of shit/piece of crap *phr.* [20C] a general term of abuse. [SHIT n.[1]/CRAP n.[3] (1)]

you make a better door than a window *phr.* [20C] a phr. used to someone who is blocking one's view (cf. YOUR FATHER'S A GLAZIER?).

you make me tired *phr.* [late 19C+] (orig. US) you bore me. [supposedly imported to UK by the contemporary Duchess of Marlborough, a fashion leader]

you make the place untidy *phr.* [1970s+] usu. said ungraciously, please stop standing around and sit down.

you may gamble on that *see* YOU CAN GAMBLE ON THAT.

you must be joking/you're joking/you've got to be joking *phr.* [1960s+] an excl. of disbelief.

you must have been drinking out of a damp glass/mug/pot *phr.* [20C] a phr. addressed to someone who has a cold or some form of muscular stiffness.

you must know Mrs Kelly *phr.* [late 19C–1900s] a phr. addressed to an especially voluble talker. [? the stereotyped loquacity of the Irish]

you never did! *excl.* [20C] I don't believe you! (except that, of course, I do).

young *adj.* [mid-19C+] diminutive, miniature, a small version of.

young and frisky *n.* [20C] (Aus.) whisky. [rhy. sl.]

young bantam *n.* [late 19C–1940s] (US Black) a very young girl. [SE *young* + BANTAM]

young blood *n.* [1970s+] (US Black) the up and coming youth who are learning the mores of street life.

young devil *n.* [17C+] a term of mildly reproving affection (cf. LITTLE DEVIL).

young, dumb and full of cum *phr.* [1970s+] (US) used of a teenager or young person whose enthusiasm for life (and esp. sex) outweighs their intelligence. [SE *young, dumb* + CUM n. (1)]

youngerly *adj.* [mid-19C] (US) reasonably young, youngish. [on pattern of SE *elderly*]

young fogey *n.* [1980s+] a young(ish) middle-class man of the 1980s who poses in dress, attitude and mannerisms as his middle-aged predecessor of the 1950s. [play on SE *old fogey*; Evelyn Waugh at his crustiest is supposedly the supreme avatar, the author A N Wilson was its perfect embodiment]

young hemp *n.* [late 18C–19C] an ill-behaved young man or boy. [? link to adj. *hempen*, e.g. HEMPEN CRAVAT, thus a candidate for the gallows]

youngie *n.* [1960s+] (Aus.) a young woman. [SE *young* + dimin./affectionate sfx. *-ie*]

young in the head *phr.* [mid-19C+] (US Black) childish, immature.

young kipper *n.* [20C] an inadequate meal. [a pun on the Jewish festival of *Yom Kippur*, the Day of Atonement, at which time it is customary to spend the day fasting]

youngs *n.* [late 19C] young people (cf. OLDS n.[1]).

young set-me-up *see* SET-ME-UP.

young shaver *n.* [late 16C+] a young man. [SE *young* + SHAVER n.[1]]

young suit *n.* [1930s–40s] (US Black) a badly fitting or too small suit.

young 'un *n.* [mid-19C+] a young person, often as a direct term of address.

younker *n.* [mid-19C] a lad, a boy. [Du. *jonker, jonkheer*, young master]

you pays your money and you takes your choice *phr.* [late 19C+] a phr. implying that those who put in something, whether or not actual money, have the right to demand certain privileges in return. [orig. showmen's patter]

you piece of crap *see* YOU LUMP OF SHIT.

your/yer actual *adj.* [1960s+] an emphatic intensifier of a person or object, e.g. *your actual Rolls Royce*. [coined by Barry Took and Marty Feldman for the 1950s–60s BBC radio show *Round the Horne*]

your arse!/ass! *excl.* [1920s+] a dismissive phr. meaning, 'I don't believe you' (cf. MY ARSE! excl.[2]).

your asshole's sucking wind *phr.* [1940s+] (orig. US) you are talking nonsense. [ARSEHOLE n.]

your ass is mine *phr.* [1950s+] a general threat, usu. following a conditional, e.g. *if you don't ... your ass is mine.* [ARSE n.[1]]

your bad self *phr.* [1950s+] (US Black) a compliment. [BAD adj.]

your barn door/gate is open/your barn door is open and the sheep will get out *phr.* [20C] (orig. US) advice to a man or boy that his trouser fly is open (cf. GARAGE DOOR IS OPEN).

your boyfriend's thinking of you *phr.* [20C] (US) a phr. used to indicate to a woman or girl that her slip is showing or her skirt hem is turned up (cf. CHARLIE'S DEAD).

your business is open *phr.* [20C] (US) advice to a man or boy that his trouser fly is open, a statement which elicits the reply, 'Is my salesman in or out?'.

your dog's dead *phr.* [1940s+] (W.I.) a phr. used to tell someone that they are in a hopeless situation or in irretrievable difficulties (cf. CRAPAUD SMOKE YOUR PIPE; DOG DEAD).

you're all about – like shit in a field *phr.* [20C] you're a useful, alert, efficient person – like hell you are! [SHIT n.[1] (1)]

you're another! *excl.* [mid-18C+] a meaningless or vaguely contemptuous and ultimately childish retort, responding to a speaker who has made the offensive comment, 'You're a ...'.

you reckon? *phr.* [1930s+] a semi-rhetorical response, is that what you really believe?

you're darn/durn tootin' *phr.* [20C] (orig. US) you're absolutely right. [DARN adj. (2) + TOOTING adj.; abbr. *you're darn tootin' right*]

you're joking *see* YOU MUST BE JOKING.

you're on my hook *phr.* [1940s–50s] (Aus.) you are getting in my way. [angling imagery]

you're singing my song *phr.* [20C] you and I agree in every way, you're my kind of person.

you're so sharp you'll cut yourself *phr.* [20C] a mocking phr. directed at someone who seems to think themselves exceptionally clever, well-informed etc. [SHARP adj.]

you're so tan I hate you *phr.* [1990s] (US campus) goodbye.

you're telling me *phr.* [1930s] that's absolutely right; I don't disagree at all, I know only too well. [? Gus Kahn song-title 'You're Telling Me' (1932): the first *OED* citation]

you're the boss *phr.* [1930s+] (Aus.) you make the decision, I'll just go along.

you're the doctor *phr.* [20C] a phr. implying 'you know best'.

your father's a glazier? *phr.* [late 18C] a phr. used to reprimand someone who is standing in the speaker's light (cf. YOU MAKE A BETTER DOOR THAN A WINDOW).

your friendly neighborhood/neighbourhood ... *phr.* [1950s+] (orig. US) a phr. used orig. in advertising, to promote local shops or services, latterly in relation to any well-known or popular person, thing or place; also in ironic use.

your funeral *phr.* [late 19C+] (orig. US) an unpleasant situation, used as a phr. of warning; usu. as *that's your funeral,* you have been warned, you are facing unpleasant consequences if you do that.

your gate is open *see* YOUR BARN DOOR IS OPEN.

your granny!/grandmother! *excl.* [early 19C+] (US) a general response of incredulity, disbelief, 'you must be joking!'.

your guess is as good as mine *phr.* [1930s+] don't ask me, I don't know either.

your horse is going to get out *phr.* [20C] (US) advice to a man or boy that his trouser fly is open; vars. include *the barn door's open, the horse will get out; lock the barn door before the horse gets out; King's horses; your horse is going to jump out of the stable; your horses are jumping out.*

your lunch bucket is open *phr.* [1970s+] (US) advice to a man or boy that his trouser fly is open.

your mal auntie! *excl.* [20C] (S.Afr.) a general excl. of dismissal, disbelief. [Afk. *mal,* mad, crazy]

your mama!/mammy *see* YO' MAMA!

your man *n.* [20C] (Irish) an unnamed, although quite possibly specified individual.

your mother *n.* [1940s+] (camp gay) oneself; thus *your mother needs a drink* etc. [the 'feminization' underpinning much camp gay sl.]

your mother! *excl.* [late 19C+] (US, mainly teen.) a rejoinder to an insult, implying that whatever that insult is, it applies most to the speaker's own mother (cf. DOZENS). [euph. for GO FUCK YOUR MOTHER!]

your mother wears army shoes! *excl.* [1940s+] (US, mainly juv.) a derisive taunt.

your mouth has got no cover *phr.* [20C] (W.I.) a phr. used of someone considered untrustworthy. Depending on the W.I. island, *cover* can be replaced by *backdoor, boundary, bridle, deep-freeze, hemming, licence, lining, padlock* and *stopper.*

your nibs *n.* [early 19C] yourself. [NIBS]

your nose is bleeding *phr.* [late 19C+] advice to a man or boy that his trouser fly is open.

your other eye! *excl.* [20C] (Irish) an excl. of disbelief, rubbish! nonsense!

your own best friend, to be *phr.* [1990s] to masturbate. [note Woody Allen's line in his film *Annie Hall* (1977) 'Hey, don't knock masturbation! It's sex with someone I love.']

yours and ours *n.* [20C] flowers. [rhy. sl.]

yourself *prn.* [late 19C+] used as a retort, mocking or rebutting what has just been said, e.g. *'Hello', 'Hello yourself!'.*

your slip is showing *phr.* [1940s+] you are giving yourself away.

yours truly *phr.* [mid-19C+] a jocular reference by a speaker to themself.

your thing/yo thang *n.* [1960s+] (orig. US Black) one's preference, one's own style, one's role within the group. [THING n.[3] (2)]

your Uncle Dudley *phr.* [1910s+] (US) oneself (cf. YOURS TRULY). [joc. use of proper name]

you said it! *phr.* [1920s+] (orig. US) a general excl. of emphasis and agreement.

you scratch my back and I'll scratch yours *phr.* [mid-19C+] (orig. US) an invitation to mutually reciprocate, let's do a favour for each other. [development of CLAW ME AND I'LL CLAW YOU]

you should be so lucky *phr.* [20C] usu. in ironic use, you should be so lucky – but there's almost no hope that you will be. [? a Yid. phr.; certainly orig. identified with Jewish use]

yout *n.* (W.I.) **1** [1950s+] a child, a young man, an immature man. **2** [1970s+] rebellious, politically active young people. [SE *youth*; in (3) the deliberate mispron. accentuates the oppositional stance of such young men]

you the man *phr.* [20C] (US Black) a phr. implying one's acceptance of another person's superiority. [MAN n.[3]]

yout'man *n.* [1980s+] (W.I./UK Black teen.) a young person, man or woman. [YOUT + sfx. *-man*]

you've got a nerve! *excl.* [late 19C+] how dare you! [? orig. US (the *OED* citation is three years before), although B&L credit Eton College sl. *nerve,* impudence, cheek]

you've got to be joking *see* YOU MUST BE JOKING.

you want a little memory powder *phr.* [late 19C] your memory is deficient. [obsolete SE *want,* require]

you want your head read *phr.* [1920s+] you're very stupid, you're very eccentric.

you what? *excl.* [1920s+] an excl. spoken as a challenge, say that again. [SE *what?,* the speaker pretends not to have heard what has been said]

you will in your shite! *excl.* [late 19C+] (Irish) no chance! no possible way! [fig. use of SHITE n.]

you wouldn't believe *phr.* [mid-19C+] a general intensifier, you can't imagine (how much/little/hard/soft etc).

you wouldn't give it to a Jap on ANZAC day *phr.* [1970s+] (Aus.) said of anything that is absolutely unacceptable. [*ANZAC day*, the Aus./N.Z. memorial to their joint forces landing at Gallipoli in 1995; then ext. to WW2]

you wouldn't read about it *phr.* [1950s+] (orig. Aus.) a phr. describing anything amazing or unbelievable and proving that nature is infinitely more bizarre than mere art.

you wouldn't want to know *phr.* [1950s+] 'ask no questions and you'll hear no lies'.

you wrote the book *phr.* [1950s+] a phr. used when offering what is appreciated as gratuitous advice to someone whose ideas are the same as, if not an improved version of, one's own.

yowsa! *excl.* [1990s] (US teen) a general excl., either of approval or of vaguely non-committal agreement. [SE *yes sir!*]

yoxter *n.* [mid-19C] a convict who has returned from transportation before the full expiry of their sentence. [ety. unknown; ? link to Scot./dial. *yox*, to vomit, to cough up, i.e. the convict has 'come up again']

yoyo *n.*[1] **1** [20C] the penis. **2** [1930s+] (US) a fool, an unpredictable person whose moods and actions go up and down (cf. DICKHEAD). [(2) is fig. use of (1)]

yoyo/yoyo boy *n.*[2] [1980s+] (US Black) a street youth (cf. YO-BOY). [YO!]

yuck/yecch/yech/yuk *n.* [1960s+] (US) anything or anyone seen as disgusting or repulsive. [YUCK!]

yuck *v.* [1960s+] (US campus/teen) to vomit. [echoic]

yuck!/yecch!/yech!/yuk! *excl.* [1960s+] an all-purpose usu. juv. excl. of distaste. [echoic]

yucko city *adj.* [1960s+] (US) disgusting, nasty. [YUCK! + sfx. -CITY]

yuck up *v.* [1960s+] (W.I.) **1** to annoy, to irritate. **2** to vomit. [ext. of YUCK v.]

yucky/yecchy/yukky/ucky *adj.* [1960s+] (usu. juv.) unpleasant, disgusting, with overtones of stickiness or smelliness (cf. OOKY). [YUCK!]

yuck your choad, to *phr.* [1960s+] to masturbate. [YUCK v. + CHOAD]

Yug/Yugo [1950s+] **1** a Yugoslav. **2** (Aus.) an immigrant from former Yugoslavia.

yuk see YUCK n.

yuk! see YUCK!

yuke *v.* [1990s] (US campus) to vomit (cf. YUCK v.). [echoic]

yukky see YUCKY.

Yukon mickey *n.* [20C] a large bottle of spirits. [fig. use of *Yukon* to imply macho masculinity and hard-drinking + MICKEY n.[5]]

yuks see YOKS.

Yuletide log *n.* [1970s] a dog (cf. CHRISTMAS LOG). [rhy. sl.]

yum!/yum-yum! *excl.* [late 19C+] an expression of praise for anything delightful, usu. delicious food. [echoic]

yummies *n.* [1980s+] (US gay) the male genitalia. [YUM!; i.e. 'good enough to eat']

yummy *n.* [1960s+] an attractive teenage girl (cf. BANANA n.[2]). [YUM!; 'good enough to eat']

yummy *adj.* [late 19C+] tasty, delicious, flavoursome. [YUM!]

yumpie *n.* [1980s] (US) a young, upwardly-mobile professional (cf. BUPPIE). [abbr.]

yum-yum *n.* [late 19C+] anything deliciously pleasurable, esp. love-making; thus *yum-yum girl*, a prostitute. [YUM!; note naut. jargon *yum-yum*, love letter]

yum-yum! *excl.* see YUM!

yum-yums *n.* [1970s+] (drugs) any drugs in pill or capsule form. [YUM!]

yunk *n.* [1910s+] (Aus.) a lump, a chunk; thus *yunk of dodger*, a slice of bread. [? SE *hunk*]

yup see YEP.

yuppie *n.* [1980s+] (orig. US) a young, upwardly-mobile professional (cf. BUPPIE). [abbr.]

yuppie flu *n.* [1980s+] ME, myalgic encephalomyelitis. [the condition, which appeared to become more prevalent during the 1980s and which resembled the most deleterious form of 'flu. It was often dismissed by doctors as no more than hypochondria, although its sufferers were able to demonstrate a variety of definite symptoms]

yuppie puppie *n.* [1990s] a child of the generation for whom children were seen as something of a fashion accessory in the early 1990s. [YUPPIE + SE *puppy*]

yush! *excl.* [1980s+] (W.I./UK Black teen) a general expression of greeting (cf. YO!).

yutz *n.* [20C] **1** a penis. **2** a fool, an idiot (cf. DICKHEAD; PUTZ). [US Yid. *yutz*, a penis]

Y.W. see Y.M.

y'what? *excl.* [1990s] (US teen) a general interrog. excl., as much punctuation as a question. [SE *you what?*]

z/zs/zee *n.*[1] [1960s+] (US) a nap, a sleep. [Z v.]

z/zee *n.*[2] [1980s+] (US drugs) **1** 1oz (28g) of cannabis. **2** 1oz (28g) of heroin. [abbr. *oz.*]

z/zee *v.* [1960s+] (US Black/teen) to sleep (cf. BAG ZS). [echoic of the sound of one's breathing]

za *n.* [1960s+] (US teen/campus) pizza; thus *do a za*, to buy or eat a pizza. [abbr.]

zac/zack/sac *n.* (Aus./N.Z.) **1** [late 19C+] a sixpence, a very small sum of money. **2** [1910s+] a 6-month prison sentence. [? SE *six* or Scot. *saxpence*]

Zacatecas purple *n.* [1970s+] (drugs) a variety of marijuana from Mexico. [the town of *Zacatecas*, Mexico, near which the marijuana is assumed to have been grown; the buds are coloured *purple*]

zachary scotts *n.* [1940s–50s] diarrhoea. [rhy. sl. *zachary scotts* = TROTS n.[1]; ult. film star Zachary Scott (1914–65)]

zack *n.* see ZAC.

'zack *n.* see BOZACK.

zad *n.* [late 18C–early 19C] a crooked person or thing. [the shape of the letter Z]

zaftig/zoftig *adj.* [20C] usu. of a woman, plump, buxom. [Ger. *zaftig*, juicy]

zak *n.* [1960s–70s] (S.Afr. township) money. [? ZAC]

zambi *n.* [1980s+] (drugs) marijuana. [? marijuana grown near the *Zambezi* river]

Zambuck/Zambuk *n.* [1910s–60s] (Aus.) a St John's Ambulance man. [name of *Zam-buk*, a proprietary antiseptic ointment]

zamie/zamie girl *n.* [1950s+] (W.I.) a lesbian; thus *make zamie*, to have a relationship with another woman. [? Fr. *les amies*, female friends]

zamietess *n.* [1950s+] (W.I.) a tough, brawling, noisy woman. [ZAMIE + sfx. *-ess*]

zandoli your hole! *excl.* [20C] (W.I.) an excl. used to tell someone to go away, 'push off!' (cf. FIND WHERE YOU LIVE!). [the Carib.E. *zandoli* lizard, which moves fast and lives in holes in the ground]

Zane Grey *n.* [20C] (Aus.) pay, wages. [rhy. sl.; ult. Western writer *Zane Grey* (1875–1939)]

zani *n.* [1980s+] (drugs) cannabis. [? SE *zany*]

zanzy *adj.* [1940s–50s] (US Black) attractive, first-rate. [*Zanzibar*, a part of Africa and thus good and authentic]

zap *n.* [1970s+] (orig. US) energy, enthusiasm. [ZAP!]

zap *v.* **1** [1930s+] (orig. US milit.) to kill. **2** [1930s+] (orig. street gang) to shock, to alarm. **3** [1950s+] (US Black) to move quickly. **4** [1960s+] to put an end to, to do away with. **5** [1960s+] (US campus) to fail someone in a test or examination. **6** [1960s+] to overwhelm emotionally. **7** [1960s+] to send, to put or to hit forcefully. **8** [1960s+] to engage in sexual relations. [ZAP!]

zap! *excl.* [1920s+] (US) used to describe the force of a sudden impact (cf. WHAM!). [? echoic of the noise of a speeding bullet]

zapped *adj.* [1930s+] killed, destroyed, exhausted. [ZAP v.]

zappy *adj.* [1960s+] (US) energetic, spirited, amusing (cf. ZINGY). [ZAP v.]

zar *n.* [1900s–50s] (US Black) anywhere considered as far away, unpleasant and culturally alien (cf. BEE-LUTHER-HATCHEE). [? SE *it's there*]

zarndrer *n.* [late 19C] a long, single curl brought from the back hair over the left shoulder and allowed to fall on the breast (cf. REPENTANCE CURL; TUBBICHON). [its originator, Princess, later Queen *Alexandra*, wife of King Edward VII]

zarp *n.* [late 19C] (S.Afr.) a policeman. [abbr. *Zuid Afrikaansche Republik Politie*, Republic of South Africa Police]

zasu pitts *n.* [1930s–50s] diarrhoea. [rhy. sl. *zasu pitts* = SHITS; ult. film star *Zasu Pitts* (1898–1963)]

zazz *adj.* [1940s+] (US) relating to the glamorous, fashionable world (cf. ZAZZ v.). [? abbr. PIZZAZZ]

zazz/zazz up *v.* [1940s+] (US) to make more glossy, decorative or stylish. [abbr. PIZZAZZ]

zazzle *n.* [1930s–60s] (US Black) sexual desire or sensuality. [? PIZZAZZ]

zazz up *see* ZAZZ v.

zazzy *adj.* [1930s–60s] (US Black) sexy, sensuous, erotic. [ZAZZLE]

Z-bird *n.* [1960s+] (US teen) a failure, a loser. [*Z*, the last letter of the alphabet + BIRD n.²]

'zblood!/'zbud! *see* 'SBLOOD!

Z car *n.* [1980s] (Aus.) an official limousine that ferries government members etc to and from houses, appointments and the like (cf. BLACK TAXI). [the privileged 'Z' number plates]

'zdeath! *see* 'SDEATH!

Z'd out *adj.* [1960s+] (US teen) unable to wake up properly, still sleepy. [z v.]

zeb *adj.* [mid–late 19C] best; thus *zeb taoc*, best coat. [backsl.]

zebra *n.* **1** [19C] (US) a striped prison uniform. **2** [20C] (US) a stripe-shirted sports umpire. **3** [1990s] (US Black teen) a White person who poses as Black (cf. WIGGA). [in all cases, the image is of a mixture of black and white]

zed *v.* [1980s+] (US Black) to sleep, to fall asleep (cf. COP ZS). [z v.]

zed about *v.* [late 19C] (UK society) to wander about in a zigzag manner. [the shape of the letter *Z*]

Zedland *n.* [late 18C–19C] the southwestern counties of England; Somerset, Devon, Cornwall, Dorset. [the local dials. in which 's' tends to be pronounced as 'z']

zee *see* z.

zeek/zoom out *v.* [1980s] (US teen) to act outrageously, to lose control, esp. through drugs or drink. [nonsense word *zeek* (the image is of going to extremes, in this case the last letter of the alphabet)/fig. use of SE *zoom*]

zelda *n.¹* [1950s+] (US teen) a dull, uninteresting girl. [? the 'old-fashioned' name, (*pace Zelda* Fitzgerald) or abbr. ZELDA GOOCH]

zelda *n.²* [1960s+] (S.Afr. gay) a pure blooded Zulu (cf. BETTY n.²). [initial letters]

zelda gooch *n.* [1950s] (camp gay) anyone considered unfashionable. [? anecdotal]

zen *n.* [1960s+] (drugs) LSD. [SE *Zen* Buddhism; i.e. its spiritual effects]

zep *n.* [1910s+] a *Zeppelin* airship. [abbr.]

zerked *adj.* [1970s+] (drugs) completely intoxicated on a drug. [? abbr. SE *berserk*]

zerking *adj.* [1970s+] (US teen) odd, bizarre. [ZERKED]

zero *n.¹* [1960s+] a nobody, a totally useless and insignificant person.

zero *n.²* [1980s+] (drugs) opium. [ety. unknown]

zero *adj.* [1970s+] none, not any.

zero cool *adj.* [1970s+] (US campus) extremely aware, sophisticated. [SE *zero* + COOL adj.³; i.e. 'no heat whatsoever']

zero minus *adj.* [1970s+] (US campus) utterly, completely impossible, unacceptable. [i.e. 'less than nothing']

zero out *v.* [1970s+] to run out of money. [one has SE *zero*, nothing]

zetz *n.* [20C] (US) a blow or punch (cf. ZOTZ v.). [synon. Yid.; ult. Ger. *Zurücksetzung*, a setting back]

zhlob/zhlub *see* SCHLUB.

zhlubby *adj.* [20C] (US) coarse, boorish. [SCHLUB]

zhoosh *v.* [mid-19C+] (Polari) to fix, to tidy. [echoic of one's rushing about]

zib *n.* [1930s–40s] (US) an eccentric person. [ety. unknown; ? ZIP n.¹]

ziff *n.¹* [mid-19C] a young thief. [? SE *thief*]

ziff *n.²* [20C] (Aus./N.Z.) a beard. [ety. unknown]

zig/zigaboo/ziggerboo *n.* [1920s+] (US) a derog. name for a Black person. [var. on JIGABOO n.¹]

ziggy *see* ZOOK.

zigzag *n.* [1950s+] (drugs) marijuana. [the *Zig-Zag* brand of rolling papers]

zigzagged *adj.* [1910s+] drunk or intoxicated by a drug. [one's unsteady gait]

zig-zig *n.* [1910s+] sexual intercourse; often found in pidgin slangs. [var. on JIG-A-JIG]

zilch *n.¹* (orig. US campus/teen) **1** [1930s+] an easy victim. **2** [1930s+] an ordinary person. **3** [1960s+] zero, nothing (cf. ZIP n.¹). [? US campus *Joe Zilsch*, an insignificant person, popularized in 1930s magazine *Ballyhoo* as Joe Zilch]

zilch *n.²* [1960s+] (US teen) a spot or skin blemish. [? var. on ZIT]

zimmer *n.* [1990s] (US teen) a girl. [? pun on *Zimmer* frame/ FRAME n.²; i.e. her attractive physique]

zim-zim *n.* [1980s] (S.Afr.) a member of a politically orientated Black youth gang. [SE *-ism*, i.e. shorthand for politico-ideological beliefs]

-zine *sfx.* [1960s+] (US) used to describe a type of maga*zine*, e.g. *fanzine*, *teenzine*. [abbr.]

zing *n.* [1910s+] (orig. US) **1** a high-pitched noise. **2** energy, enthusiasm. [echoic]

zing *v.* (orig. US) **1** [1920s+] to make a high-pitched noise. **2** [1960s+] to rush around energetically. **3** [1970s+] to insult, to tease (cf. ZINGER). **4** [1970s+] to make a snappy delivery of a witticism. [ZING n.]

zinger *n.* [1970s+] a witty line, a one-line joke or repartee. [ZING v. (4)]

zing up *v.* [1970s+] (orig. US) to enliven something, e.g. food. [ZING v. (2)]

zingy *adj.* [1960s+] (orig. US) enthusiastic, energetic (cf. ZIPPY). [ZING v. (2)]

zip/zippo *n.¹* **1** [late 19C+] (US campus) a grade or mark of zero. **2** [20C] (US) nothing. **3** [20C] an insignificant person. **4** [20C] an unpleasant person with no good qualities. [SE *zero*]

zip/zip gun *n.²* [20C] (US) a homemade firearm capable of firing single bullets. [SE *zip*, the noise of a fired bullet. One takes a short length of pipe, 4–10 ins. long with its inside diameter that of a bullet; a bullet is placed at one end and detonated by a sharp tap from a pointed steel rod which in turn is hit by the heel of one's hand or by a small object]

zip/zippo *n.*³ [1920s+] **1** a speedy, energetic, mobile person. **2** speed, enthusiasm, fervour, energy (cf. PIZZAZZ; ZING). [ZIP v.¹]

zip *n.*⁴ [1950ss+] (US) a derog. term for a Vietnamese (or other Indo-Chinese) person (cf. DINK n.³; GOOK n.³). [ZIP n.¹; i.e. their alleged lack of intelligence]

zip *n.*⁵ [1970s+] (drugs) cocaine. [ZIP v. (1)]

zip *n.*⁶ [1980s+] (US drugs) one ounce of a given drug. [ext. of Z n.²]

zip *v.*¹ (orig. US) [mid-19C+] to run around energetically, to be highly energetic. [echoic, esp. of a speeding bullet]

zip *v.*² (orig. US) [1970s+] to engage in sexual relations. [ZIP v.¹ but note SE zip(per)]

zip- *pfx.* [20C] (US prison) used in specifying the maximum length of a sentence; e.g. zip-five, from 0–5 years; zip-ten, 0–10 years etc. [ZIP n.¹]

zipalid/zipperhead/zipperlid *n.* [1970s+] a complete fool. [i.e. one whose head has been 'unzipped' and its brain removed]

zip coon *n.* [1980s] (US Black) a subservient Black person (cf. UNCLE TOM). [song 'Ole Zip Coon'; ult. COON n. (3)]

zip gun see ZIP n.².

zip it up! *excl.* [1930s+] be quiet! shut up! (cf. ZIP ONE'S LIP).

zip one's lip/mouth, to *phr.* [1930s+] (orig. US) to stop talking, esp. in imper.

zipper club *n.* [1980s+] (US gay) anywhere that plays host to repeated oral sex, e.g. a lavatory or bath-house (cf. CAFETERIA). [the lowering of the zipper of one's fly; one goes there to EAT v.³]

zipper dinner see ZIPPER SEX.

zippered *adj.* [1980s+] drunk. [ZIPALID]

zipperfish *n.* [1990s] the penis. [SE zip(per)]

zipperhead/zipperlid see ZIPALID.

zipper sex/dinner *n.* [1960s+] (US gay) quick, spontaneous fellatio without even dropping one's trousers, just pulling out the penis.

zippo *n.*¹ see ZIP n.¹; n.³.

zippo *n.*² [1990s] nothing. [ext. ZIP n.¹]

zippy *adj.* [1920s+] fast, speedy (cf. ZAPPY; ZINGY). [ZIP v. (1)]

zit *n.* [1950s+] (orig. US teen) **1** a spot, pimple or blackhead. **2** a skin blemish left by a lovebite (cf. HICKEY n.²). [ety. unknown]

zit doctor *n.* [1960s+] (US teen) a dermatologist. [ZIT + SE doctor]

zitsfleisch *n.* [20C] (US) patience, the ability to relax and do nothing, usu. used in neg. [Yid. zitsfleisch, flesh that is sat upon, i.e. the buttocks]

zizz *n.*¹ [1940s+] (US) gaiety, liveliness. [abbr. PIZZAZZ]

zizz *n.*² [1940s+] (orig. milit.) a nap, a snooze, a brief sleep (cf. SIGSTER; Z n.¹). [ZIZZ v.]

zizz *v.* [1940s+] to have a nap or snooze; thus zizzing, dozing, napping (cf. Z n.¹). [echoic]

zizzy *n.* [1940s+] US) a sleep or snooze. [ext. ZIZZ n.²]

'zlead!/'zleads!/'zlid! *excl.* [early 17C–late 18C] mildly blasphemous oaths, lit. 'God's lid(s)!'.

znees/znus/znuz *n.* [late 18C–19C] frost; thus zneesy, frosty (weather). [? SE sneeze, the product of such weather]

zod *n.* [1980s] (US teen) an eccentric, a strange person. [SE he's odd]

zod *adj.* [1980s] (US teen) bizarre, eccentric. [ZOD n.]

zoftig see ZAFTIG.

zoid *n.* [1980s] **1** a school child who has been rejected by their fellows (cf. GOGGY). **2** (US campus) a fan of punk rock and its attendant styles. [-ZOID]

-zoid *sfx.* [1980s+] (orig. US) used to invest a variety of terms,

usu. neg. and derog. descriptions of people, with a 'space-age', SF aura.

zol *n.* [1940s+] (S.Afr. drugs) **1** a hand-rolled cigarette. **2** a marijuana cigarette. **3** a measure of marijuana, enough to make a single cigarette. **4** cannabis. [ety. unknown; zol is recorded as 1950s US/Mex. border drug use, but no provable link exists; Branford (1993) notes the obs. trade name of miniature cheroots but gives no date; if it precedes drug use it would be an obvious root]

Zola Budd *n.* [1980s+] (S.Afr.) **1** a black taxi. **2** a slow armoured police vehicle (cf. MARY DECKER). [the S.Afr. runner Zola Budd Pieterse (b.1966) was permitted to represent England after a lengthy press campaign; she ran against the US champion Mary Decker Slaney and stepped on her foot; Decker was considered the superior athlete; thus Budd is equated with the slow vehicles]

zombie *n.*¹ **1** [1930s–50s] (US Black/campus) a bizarre-looking person. **2** [1930s+] a dullard, a slow-witted person. **3** [1940s–50s] (UK prison) a prison officer who looks permanently miserable and humourless. **4** [1970s+] (US Black) a very African-looking person, short of stature, with a dark complexion and broad features. [SE zombie, 'a soulless corpse said to have been revived by witchcraft; formerly, the name of a snake-deity in voodoo cults of or deriving from West Africa and Haiti' (OED); ult. Kongo nzambi, god, zumbi, fetish]

zombie/zombie weed *n.*² [1970s+] (drugs) phencyclidine (cf. ACE n.³). [its effects render one zombie-like]

zone/zoner *n.* [1980s+] (US drugs) a habitual drug user (cf. SPACE CADET). [ZONE v.]

zone/zone out *v.* [1980s+] **1** to lose consciousness or concentration. **2** to be intoxicated by a hallucinogenic drug (cf. SPACED OUT). [one is in one's own private SE zone]

zoned *adj.* [1980s+] (US) **1** intoxicated by a given drug. **2** exhausted, burned out. [ZONE v.]

zone out see ZONE v.

zoner see ZONE n.

zonk *n.* [1940s+] (S.Afr.) a sandwich. [ety. unknown]

zonk/zonk out *v.* **1** [1950s+] to hit or strike. **2** [1960s+] (US) to die, to lose consciousness, esp. from alcohol or drugs. **3** [1960s+] to fail. **4** [1960s+] to fall asleep. **5** [1960s+] to overcome, to knock out. [SE zonk, echoic of a blow or solid impact]

zonked/zonked out/zonkers *adj.* [1950s+] **1** intoxicated by a given drug. **2** (US) enthusiastic or excited. [ZONK v.]

zonker *n.* [1950s+] anyone who takes drugs to excess. [ZONK v.]

zonkers see ZONKED.

zonko *n.* [1970s+] (US campus) a boring, dull thus socially unacceptable person. [ZONK v. + sfx. -O]

zonk out see ZONK v.

zoo *n.* [1970s] (US campus) the lowest grade possible. [SE zero]

zoo daddy *n.* [1970s+] (US) a divorced father who rarely sees his children. [the inevitable trips to the zoo on 'visiting days']

zooed *adj.* [1980s+] (US drugs) highly intoxicated by a drug. [i.e. reduced to animal-like inarticulacy]

zooey *adj.* [1970s+] (US) **1** unpleasant, barbaric. **2** hectic, chaotic. [SE zoo]

zooie *n.* [1960s–70s] (drugs) implement that holds the butt of a marijuana cigarette. [ety. unknown]

zook/ziggy *n.* [1990s] (UK Black) a marijuana cigarette, esp. when laced with crack cocaine. [ety. unknown; ? ZOOM n.¹ + SE cigarette]

zoolooed *adj.* [1970s+] (US campus) drunk. [? Zulu; the image is of a charging warrior as portrayed in the 1964 film]

zoom *n.*[1] [1960s+] zest, vivacity, enthusiasm. [ZOOM v.[1]]

zoom *n.*[2] [1980s+] (drugs) **1** phencyclidine (cf. ACE n.[3]). **2** marijuana laced with phencyclidine. [its effects]

zoom/zoom around/off *v.*[1] [1920s+] to rush, to move fast. [SE *zoom*, echoic of moving at speed]

zoom *v.*[2] [1930s–40s] (US Black) to get something without paying for it (cf. WHIZ v.[1]). [i.e. one 'zooms off' with it/'zooms' it away]

zoom around *see* ZOOM v.[1].

zoom buggy *n.* [1950s–60s?] (US teen) a fast car. [ZOOM v.[1] (1) + BUGGY n. (1)]

zoomers *n.* [1980s+] (drugs) individuals who sell fake crack cocaine and then run off. [ZOOM v.[1] (1)]

zoom-in *n.* [1990s] (US) a sudden, unexpected and sometimes unwanted kiss (cf. CLOSE-UP). [ZOOM v.]

zoom off *see* ZOOM v.[1]

zoom out *see* ZEEK OUT.

zoom someone off, to *phr.* [1970s] (US Black) to deceive, to betray someone emotionally. [ZOOM v.[1]/v.[2]]

zoom someone out, to *phr.* **1** [1960s+] to amaze, to fascinate, to surprise (cf. BLOW ONE'S MIND). **2** [1970s–80s] (US Black) to overwhelm someone by the force of one's speech, to take over someone's mind. [ZOOM v.[1]]

zoom tube *n.* [1980s+] (drugs) a marijuana pipe. [ZOOM n.[2] + SE *tube*]

zoomy *adj.* [1970s+] (US) fast, stylish, high-flying. [ZOOM v.[1] (1)]

zoot *n.*[1] [1960s–70s] (US) a style of suit worn in the 1940s and 1950s. [abbr. ZOOT SUIT]

zoot/zootie/zut *n.*[2] [1990s] (UK Black) a cannabis cigarette. [ety. unknown]

zoot *v.* [1930s–40s] (US Black) to dress flashily or vulgarly. [ZOOT SUIT]

zooted/zooted up *adj.* [1980s+] (US campus) under the influence of drink or drugs. [ZOOT n.[2]]

zootie *see* ZOOT n.[2].

zoot suit *n.* [1930s–40s] (orig. US Black) a style of suit worn in the 1940s and 1950s, characterized by a long, draped jacket with padded shoulders and high-waisted tapering trousers; thus *zoot-shirt*, a brightly coloured shirt designed to be worn with a zoot suit; *zoot suit action*, a fashion competition in which a wearer of a zoot suit attempts to outdo their rivals. [? New Orleans patois *zoot*, cute]

zoot-suiter *n.* [1930s–40s] (US) a foolish, arrogant, vulgar young man, esp. when his image is boosted by flashy clothes. [ZOOT SUIT]

zooty *adj.* [1940s–60s] (US) flashily dressed. [ZOOT SUIT]

zorba *n.* [1980s] (Aus.) a Greek. [*Zorba the Greek* (1952) the novel and later film by Nikos Kazantakis]

zorba *v.* [1950s+] to urinate. [rhy. sl. *zorba the greek* = LEAK v.[1] (1)]

zorched *adj.* [1970s] experiencing the effects of an excess of drink or drugs. [? ZONKED + SE *torched*, set on fire]

zot/zotz *n.* [1960s+] (US campus) zero in an examination. [SE *zero* ? + SQUAT n.[2]]

zot *v.* [1960s+] (orig. US) to move quickly; thus *zot along*, *zot down* etc (cf. ZAP v.; ZIP v.). [ety. unknown; ? use of initial 'z' to denote speed]

zotz *n. see* ZOT n.

zotz *v.* [20C] to kill, to murder. [ZETZ]

zouch *n.* [18C] a slovenly, ungenteel man, one who walks with a slouch. [? SE *slouch*/SLOUCH]

zoucher *see* SYCHER.

'zoudikers! *excl.* [16C–17C] a mild oath, lit. 'God's hooks' (cf. GADZOOKS!).

zounds! *excl.* [17C] a euph. excl. sometimes intensified to *zounds and blood!*; lit. 'God's wounds!' (cf. 'SBORES!; GODSOOKERS!).

z out *v.* [1980s+] (US campus) to go to sleep (cf. COP ZS). [z v.]

zowie *n.* [1910s+] keenness, enthusiasm, energy. [ZOWIE!]

zowie! *excl.* [1910s+] (US) an excl. used to describe a sudden impact, or fig. amazement (cf. WHAM!; ZAP!). [echoic of speed]

Zs *see* Z n.[1].

zuch *n.* [20C] (US Und.) an informer. [? ZOUCH]

zug up *v.* [20C] (W.I./Gren.) to cut a man's or boy's hair in an amateurish, raggedy manner. [ety. unknown; ? the shape of the letter 'Z' implies raggedness]

zuke *v.* [1980s+] (US campus) to vomit. [echoic]

Zulu *n.* [20C] (US) a derog. term for a Black person. [SE *Zulu*, a member of a Bantu people inhabiting Zululand or Natal]

Zulu golf *n.* [20C] (US) pool (cf. ABYSSINIAN POLO). [ZULU + SE *golf*; racist stereotyping]

Zulu princess *n.* [1950s–60s] (US gay) a young, handsome Black man.

zurucker *n.* [20C] (Aus.) a police trooper. [Ger. *zurück*, backwards; thus ? detectives follow a line of clues *backwards* to the perpetrator, but note SAusE *blacktracker*, an Aboriginal tracker, seconded to police investigations]

zut *see* ZOOT n.[2].

zuuzuus and whamwhams *n.* [1960s+] (US prison) confectionery sold to the prisoners. [ety. unknown]

zweideener *n.* [late 19C] (Aus./N.Z.) a two-shilling (10p) piece. [Ger. *zwei*, two + DEENER]

Bibliography

Adams, Ramon F., *Western Words* (2nd rev. edn., Oklahoma, 1968)

Ade, George, *Fables in Slang* (1899) & *More Fables in Slang* (1900) (New York, 1960)

Algren, Nelson, *The Neon Wilderness* (New York, 1947)

Algren, Nelson, *The Man with the Golden Arm* (New York, 1949)

Algren, Nelson, *A Walk on the Wild Side* (New York, 1956)

Allen, Irving Lewis, *The City in Slang: New York Life and Popular Speech* (New York, 1993)

Allsopp, Richard, *Dictionary of Caribbean English Usage* (Oxford, 1996)

Alson, Peter, *Confessions of an Ivy League Bookie* (London, 1996)

Alvarez, A., *The Biggest Game in Town* (London, 1983)

Anonymous, *The English Liberal Science: or a new-found Art and Order of Drinking* (1650)

Anonymous, *The Sinks of London Laid Open* (London, 1848)

Armistead Maupin, *Further Tales of the City* (London, 1984)

Armistead Maupin, *More Tales of the City* (London, 1984)

Armistead Maupin, *Tales of the City* (London, 1984)

Ascham, Roger, *Toxophilus* (1545)

Austin, Max, *Out* (London, 1978)

Awdeley, John, *The Fraternitie of Vagabondes* (1561)

B., Jon (John Badcock), *Slang: A Dictionary of the Turf, the Ring, the Chase, the Pit, of Bon-Ton and the Varieties of Life* (London, 1823)

Bailey, Nathan, *A Universal Etymological English Dictionary* (London 1737; 1755)

Baker, Mark, *Nam* (New York, 1980)

Baker, Sidney J., *New Zealand Slang* (Christchurch, 1940)

Baker, Sidney J., *A Popular Dictionary of Australian Slang* (Melbourne, 1941)

Baker, Sidney J., *The Drum: Australian Character and Slang* (Sydney, 1960)

Baker, Sidney J., *The Australian Language* (Sydney, 1966)

Banner, Fiona, *The Nam* (London, 1997)

Barclay, Nick, *Curvy Lovebox* (London, 1997)

Barr, Ann, and York, Peter, *The Official Sloane Ranger Handbook* (London, 1982)

Barrère, Albert and Leland, Charles G., *A Dictionary of Slang Jargon and Cant* (1889)

Bartlett, John, *A Dictionary of Americanisms* (Boston, Mass., 1848)

Baumann, Heinrich, *Londonismen: Slang und Cant* (Berlin, 1887)

Beaumont, Francis & Fletcher, *John Beggar's Bush* (1622)

'Bede, Cuthbert' (Edward Bradley), *The Adventures of Mr Verdant Greene* (London, 1853–7)

Bentley, W.K. & Corbett, J.M., *Prison Slang* (New York, 1992)

Bergman, Andrew, *The Big Kiss-Off of 1944* (London, 1974)

Bergman, Andrew, *Hollywood and Le Vine* (London, 1976)

Bernbach, Lisa, *The Official Preppy Handbook* (New York, 1980)

Berrey, Lester V., and Van Den Bark, Melvin, *The American Thesaurus of Slang* (2nd edn.; London, 1954)

Bickerton, Anthea, *Australian/English; English/Australian* (Bristol, 1976)

Bing, Léon, *Do Or Die* (New York, 1991)

Binstead, Arthur, *Pitcher in Paradise* (London, 1903)

Blacker, Terence, *Blacker Fixx* (London, 1989)

Bleasdale, Alan, *Boys from the Blackstuff: Five Plays for Television* (London, 1983)

Bonfiglioli, Kyril, *All the Tea in China* (1978)

Booth, J.B., *Old Pink 'Un Days* (London, 1924)

The Boudoir, c.1880.

Bourgeois, Phillippe, *In Search of Respect: Selling Crack in El Barrio* (Cambridge, 1995)

Boycott, Rosie, *Batty, Bloomers and Boycott* (London, 1982)

Branford, Jean, with William Branford, *A Dictionary of South African English* (4th edn.; Cape Town, 1993)

Breslin, Jimmy, *The World of Jimmy Breslin* (New York, 1967)

Brown, Claude, *Manchild in the Promised Land* (New York, 1965)

Bruce, Lenny, *How to Talk Dirty and Influence People* (Chicago, 1965)

Bruce, Lenny, *The Essential Lenny Bruce*, ed. by John Cohen (New York, 1967)

Bukowski, Charles, *Post Office* (Santa Barbara, Calif., 1971)

Bukowski, Charles, *Erections, Ejaculations, Exhibitions and General Tales of Ordinary Madness* (San Francisco, Calif., 1972)

Bukowski, Charles, *Notes of a Dirty Old Man* (San Francisco, Calif., 1973)

Bukowski, Charles, *South of No North* (Santa Barbara, Calif., 1973)

Bukowski, Charles, *Factotum* (Santa Barbara, Calif., 1975)

Bukowski, Charles, *Women* (Santa Barbara, Calif., 1978)

Bukowski, Charles, *Ham on Rye* (Santa Barbara, Calif., 1982)

Bukowski, Charles, *Barfly* (Santa Barbara, Calif., 1984)

Bukowski, Charles, *Hollywood* (Santa Barbara, Calif., 1989)

Bukowski, Charles, *Screams from the Balcony: Selected Letters* (Santa Barbara, Calif., 1993)

Bukowski, Charles, *Pulp* (Santa Barbara, Calif., 1994)

Bukowski, Charles, *The Captain Is Out To Lunch* (Santa Barbara, Calif., 1998)

Bunker, Edward, *No Beast So Fierce* (London, 1973)

Bunker, Edward, *The Animal Factory* (London, 1977)

Bunker, Edward, *Little Boy Blue* (London, 1981)

Burke, David, *Street Talk 2* (Los Angeles, 1992)

Burroughs, William (as 'Lee, William'), *Junkie* (New York, 1953)

Burroughs, Jr., William, *Kentucky Ham* (New York, 1984)

Byrne, Josefa Heifetz, *Mrs. Byrne's Dictionary of Unusual, Obscure & Preposterous Words* (Boston, Mass., 1974)

Cameron, Jeremy, *Vinnie Got Blown Away* (London, 1995)

Cameron, Jeremy, *It Was an Accident ...* (London, 1996)

Carew, Bampfylde Moore, *The History of Bampfylde Moore Carew* (1750)

Caron, Roger, *Go-Boy* (London, 1979)

Carr, Rocky, *Brixton Bwoy* (London, 1998)

Carson, Tom, *Twisted Kicks* (Glen Ellen, Calif., 1981)

Caserta, Peggy, *Going Down With Janis* (New York, 1974)

Cassady, Neal, *The First Third* (San Francisco, Calif., 1971)

Cassidy, F.G. (ed.), *Dictionary of American Regional English*, (*DARE*), Vol. I (Boston Mass., 1985)

Cassidy, F.G., and Hall, J. (eds.), *Dictionary of American Regional English*, (*DARE*), Vol. II (Boston, Mass., 1991)

Cassidy, F.G., and Hall, J. (eds.), *Dictionary of American Regional English*, (*DARE*), Vol. III (Boston, Mass., 1996)

Cassidy, F.G. & LePage, R.B., *Dictionary of Jamaican English* (2nd edn., Cambridge, 1992)

Champion, Sarah (ed.), *Disco Biscuits* (London 1997)

Chandler, Raymond, *Farewell, My Lovely* (New York, 1940)

Chandler, Raymond, *The Long Good-Bye* (New York, 1953)

Chandler, Raymond, *The Notebooks of Raymond Chandler*, ed. by Frank MacShane (New York, 1976)

Chesney, Kellow, *The Victorian Underworld* (London, 1970)

Cock Lorell's Bote (c.1515) (London, 1970)

Cohen, G.L., *Studies in Slang Part 1* (Frankfurt-am-Main, 1985)

Cohen, G.L., *Studies in Slang Part 2* (Frankfurt-am-Main, 1989)

Cohen, G.L., *Studies in Slang Part 3* (Frankfurt-am-Main, 1993)

Cohen, G.L., *Studies in Slang Part 4* (Frankfurt-am-Main, 1995)

Cohen, G.L., *Studies in Slang Part 5* (Frankfurt-am-Main, 1997)

Cole, Nicholas, *Private Lists* (London, 1982/1983)

The Complete CB Slang Dictionary (Miami, Fla., 1980)

Cook, Robin, *The Crust on Its Uppers* (London, 1962)

Cooper, Jr., Clarence, *The Scene* (New York, 1960)

Cooper, Jr., Clarence, *The Syndicate* (New York, 1960)

Cooper, Jr., Clarence, *Weed* (New York, 1961)

Cooper, Jr., Clarence, *The Farm* (New York, 1967)

Copland, Robert, *The Hye Way to the Spytell House* (c.1540)

Cortez Cruz, Ricardo, *Straight Outta Compton* (Colorado, 1992)

Cox, Leslie J., and Fay, Richard J., 'Gayspeak, the Linguistic Fringe: Bona Polari, Camp, Queerspeak and Beyond' in *The Margins of the City: Gay Men's Urban Lives*, ed. by Stephen Whittle (Aldershot, Hants, 1994)

Dale, John, *Dark Angel* (1995)

Davies, Larry, *Candy* (Australia, 1998)

De Lannoy, William C., and Masterson, Elizabeth, 'Teenage Hophead Jargon', in *American Speech* magazine, 27: 1 (Alabama, 1954)

De Vries, Peter, *Tunnel of Love* (New York, 1949)

De Vries, Peter, *Comfort me With Apples* (New York, 1952)

Dekker, Thomas, *Shoemaker's Holiday* (1599)

Dekker, Thomas, *The Honest Whore* (1604)

Dekker, Thomas, *The Belman of London* (1608)

Dekker, Thomas, *Lanthorn and Candlelight* (1608)

Dekker, Thomas (?), *O Per Se O* (1612)

Del Vecchio, John M., *The Thirteenth Valley* (New York, 1982)

Dennis, C. J., *The Sentimental Bloke* (Sydney, 1957)

Dennison, Richard, Ogata, Michio, and Pwka, Mike, (eds.) *Rasta/Patois Dictionary* (1993–95)

Denton, William, *Twists, Slugs and Roscoes: A Glossary of Hardboiled Slang* (Miskatonic, US, 1993)

Diaz, Junot, *Drown* (London, 1996)

Dickson, Paul, *Words* (New York, 1983)

Doyle, Roddy, *The Woman Who Walked into Doors* (London, 1996)

Ducange, Anglicus, *The Vulgar Tongue* (London, 1857)

Dunne, John Gregory, *True Confessions* (New York, 1981)

Dury, Ian, *The Ian Dury Songbook* (London, 1979)

E., B., Gent, *A New Dictionary of the Terms ancient and modern of the Canting Crew* (c.1698)

Eble, Connie, *Slang and Sociability* (Chapel Hill, North Carolina, 1996)

Egan, Pierce, *Grose's Classical Dictionary of the Vulgar Tongue Revised and Corrected* (London, 1823)

Egan, Pierce, *Life in London* (1821) (London, 1859)

Ellroy, James, *Brown's Requiem* (New York, 1981)

Ellroy, James, *Clandestine* (New York, 1982)

Ellroy, James, *Because The Night* (New York, 1987)

Ellroy, James, *The Black Dahlia* (London, 1988)

Ellroy, James, *The Big Nowhere* (London, 1990)

Ellroy, James, *LA Confidential* (London, 1991)

Ellroy, James, *White Jazz* (London, 1992)

Ellroy, James, *Hollywood Nocturnes* (New York, 1994)

Ellroy, James, *American Tabloid* (London, 1995)

Ellroy, James, *My Dark Places* (London, 1996)

Farina, Richard, *Been Down So Long It Seems Like Up to Me*, (New York, 1983)

Farmer, John S., *Americanisms Old New* (London, 1889)

Farmer, John S., *Musa Pedestris* (London, 1896)

Farmer, John S. and Henley, W. E., *Slang and its Analogues* (1890)

Farrell, James T., *Studs Lonigan* (London, 1936)

Farren, Mick, *The Tale of Willy's Rats* (London, 1974)

Fennor, William, *The Counter's Commonwealth* (1617)

Fiction Illustrated, Vols. 1 & 3 (New York, 1976)

Folb, Edith A., *Runnin' Down Some Lines* (Cambridge, Mass., 1980)

Fowler, Christopher, *Rune* (London, 1990)

Fowler, Christopher, *Spanky* (London, 1994)

Fowler, Christopher, *Psychoville* (London, 1995)

Fowler, Christopher, *Disturbia* (London, 1997)

Fowler, Christopher, *Roofworld* (London, 1998)

Fowler, Christopher, *Soho Black* (London, 1998)

Fowler, Christopher, *Personal Demons* (London, 1998)

Franklyn, Julian, *A Dictionary of Rhyming Slang* (2nd edn., London, 1981)

George, Nelson, *Buppies, B-Boys, Baps and Bohos: Notes on Post-Soul Black Culture* (New York, 1992)

Goimes, Donald, *Dope Fiend* (New York, 1971)

Goldman, Albert, *From the Journalism of Lawrence Schiller: Ladies and Gentlemen, Lenny Bruce!* (London, 1975)

Goulart, Ron, *The Hard-Boiled Dicks* (London, 1967)

Green, Jonathon, *The Book of Drugs* (unpublished ms., London, 1974)

Green, Jonathon, *Newspeak: A Dictionary of Jargon* (London, 1984)

Green, Jonathon, *The Dictionary of Contemporary Slang* (London, 1984, 1992, 1995)

Green, Jonathon, *The Slang Thesaurus* (London, 1986)

Green, Jonathon, *Neologisms* (London, 1991)

Green, Jonathon, *Slang Down the Ages* (London, 1993)

Green, Jonathon, *Words Apart* (London, 1996)

Greene, Robert, *A Notable Discovery of Cozenage* (London, 1591)

Greene, Robert, *The Second Part of Cony-catching* (London, 1591)

Greene, Robert, *The Black Book's Messenger* (London, 1592)

Greene, Robert, *A Disputation between a He-cony-catcher and a She-cony-catcher* (London, 1592)

Greene, Robert, *The Third part of Cony catching* (London, 1592)

Greenlee, Sam, *The Spook Who Sat by the Door* (London, 1969)

Grogan, Emmett, *Ringolevio* (Boston, Mass., 1972)

Grose, Captain Francis, *A Classical Dictionary of the Vulgar Tongue* (London, 1785, 1788, 1796)

Gruber, Frank, *The Last Doorbell* (Manchester, 1951)

Hall, B.H., *College Words and Customs* (Cambridge, Mass., 1856)

Halliwell, J.O., *A Dictionary of Archaic and Provincial Words* (London, 1847)

Hancock, Ian, 'Shelta & Polari', in P. Trudgill, *Language in the British Isles* (Cambridge, 1984)

Hanklin, Nigel B., *Hanklyn-Janklin* (New Delhi, 1992, 1997)

Harman, Thomas, *A Caveat or Warning for Common Coursetors, Vulgarly Called Vagbonds* (1566)

Hawes, James, *A White Merc with Fins* (London, 1995)

Hawes, James, *Rancid Aluminium* (London, 1997)

Heard, Nathan, *Howard Street* (Los Angeles, 1968)

Heller, Peter, *In This Corner* (New York, 1973)

Herr, Michael, *Dispatches* (New York, 1977)

Hiaasen, Carl, *Tourist Season* (New York, 1986)

Hiaasen, Carl, *Double Whammy* (New York, 1988)

Hiaasen, Carl, *Skin Tight* (New York, 1989)

Hiaasen, Carl, *Native Tongue* (New York, 1991)

Hiaasen, Carl, *Strip Tease* (New York, 1993)

Hiaasen, Carl, *Stormy Weather* (New York, 1995)

Hiaasen, Carl, *Lucky You* (New York, 1997)

Higgins, George V., *The Digger's Game* (New York, 1973)

Higgins, George V., *A City on a Hill* (London, 1975)

Higgins, George V., *Cogan's Trade* (London, 1981)

Higgins, George V., *The Friends of Eddie Coyle* (New York, 1981)

Higgins, George V., *The Rat on Fire* (New York, 1981)

Higgins, George V., *Requiem for Jerry Kennedy* (New York, 1985)

Higgins, George V., *Defending Billy Ryan* (London, 1992)

Hilliard, David, *This Side of Glory* (Boston, Mass., 1993)

Himes, Chester, *Cotton Comes to Harlem* (New York, 1968)

Himes, Chester, *The Big Gold Dream* (Madison, N.J., 1973)

Hindley, Charles, *The True History of Tom and Jerry ... together with a Vocabulary and glossary of the Flash and Slang Terms* (London, ?1869)

Hoffman, Abbie, *Woodstock Nation* (New York, 1969)

Hoffman, Alice, *Property Of* (New York, 1978)

Hotten, John Camden, *A Dictionary of Modern Slang, Cant, and Vulgar Words ... by a London Antiquary* (1859, 1860, 1864, 1869, 1874)

Hotten, John Camden, (ed.), *Liber Vagatorum: The Book of Vagabonds* (1528) (London, 1860)

Howard, Kent, *Small Time Crooks* (London, n.d.)

Humphries, Barry, *A Nice Night's Entertainment: Sketches & Monologues 1956–1961* (London, 1981)

Huncke, Herbert, *A Herbert Huncke Reader* (London, 1998)

Irwin, Godfrey, *American Tramp and Underworld Slang* (London, 1931)

Jay, Karla, and Young, Allen, (eds.) *The Gay Report* (New York, 1979)

Jenkins, Dan, *Semi-Tough* (New York, 1972)

Jones, Jack, *Rhyming Cockney Slang* (Bristol, 1971)

Jones, LeRoi, (Baraka, Imamu Amiri), *Tales* (New York, 1968)

Jones, Lisa, *Bulletproof Diva* (New York, 1994)

Jonson, Ben, *Bartholemew Fair* (1614)

Judges, A.V., *The Elizabethan Underworld* (London, 1930)

Junker, Howard, 'The Fifties', in *Esquire* magazine (New York, 1969)

Keyes, Thom, *All Night Stand* (London, 1966)

Kidder, Tracy, *The Soul of a New Machine* (Boston, Mass., 1981)

King, Stephen, 'The Raft', in *Twilite Zone* magazine (New York, 1983)

Klein, Ronald, *Jailhouse Jargon & Street Slang* (unpublished ms., 1983)

Lambert, Eric, *Twenty Thousand Thieves* (London, 1955)

Land, Ed, *The Ghetto Slangs/Terms Dictionary* (n.p., 1995)

Landy, Eugene S., *The Underground Dictionary* (New York, 1967)

Lansdale, Joe R., *The Drive-In* (New York, 1981)

Lansdale, Joe R., *The Nightrunners* (New York, 1987)

Lansdale, Joe R., *The Drive-In* (New York, 1988)

Lansdale, Joe R., *Savage Season* (London, 1989)

Lansdale, Joe R., *Cold in July* (London, 1990)

Lansdale, Joe R., *Writer of the Purple Rage* (New York, 1994)

Lansdale, Joe R., *Mucho Mojo* (London, 1994)

Lansdale, Joe R., *Two-Bear Mambo* (London, 1995)

Lansdale, Joe R., *Bad Chili* (New York, 1997)

Lansdale, Joe R., *Rumble Tumble* (London, 1998)

Larner, Jeremy, and Tefferteller, Ralph, *The Addict in the Street* (New York, 1964)

Laurie, Peter, *Scotland Yard* (London, 1970)

Lawson, Henry, *Complete Prose Works* (Sydney, Australia, 1948)

Le Carre, John, *The Little Drummer Girl* (London, 1983)

Legman, G., 'The Language of Homosexuality: A Glossary', as Appendix VII in G. W. Henry, *Sex Variants: A Study of Homosexual Patterns* (New York, 1941)

Leonard, Elmore, *Maximum Bob* (London, 1991)

Leonard, Elmore, *Riding the Rap* (London, 1995)

Levitt, Jesse, *et al*, (eds.), *Geolinguistic Perspectives* (London, 1987)

Lewis, Nigel, *The Book of Babel* (London, 1994)

Lexicon Balatronicum by a Member of the Whip Club, (London, 1811)

Lighter, Jonathan, *Random House Historical Dictionary of American Slang* (Vol. 1 A–G) (New York, 1994), (Vol. 2 H-O) (New York, 1997)

Little, Eddie, *Another Day in Paradise* (London, 1997)

Lincoln, C. Eric, *The Avenue, Clayton City* (New York, 1988)

MacInnes, Colin, *City of Spades* (London, 1957)

MacInnes, Colin, *Absolute Beginners* (London, 1959)

MacInnes, Colin, *Mr Love & Justice* (London, 1960)

MacLachlan, Noel, (ed.), *The Memoirs of James Hardy Vaux* (London, 1964)

Major, Clarence, *Black Slang* (London, 1971)

Major, Clarence, *Juba to Jive: A Dictionary of Afro-American Slang* (New York, 1994)

Malcolm X, *The Autobiography of Malcolm X*, with the assistance of Alex Haley (New York, 1964)

Maledicta: The International Journal of Verbal Aggression, (1977–)

Manchon, J., *Le Slang·Lexique d'Anglais Familier et Vulgaire* (Paris, 1923)

Mandelkau, Jamie, *Buttons: The Making of a President* (London, 1971)

Manning, Frederic, *Her Privates We* (London, 1986 [1929])

Manser, Martin H., *A Dictionary of Contemporary Idioms* (London, 1983)

Matthews, William, *Cockney Past and Present* (London, 1938)

Maurer, David W., *Language of the Underworld* (Lexington, Ky., 1981)

Max, H., *Gay (S)language* (Austin, Tx., 1988)

May, Jonathan, *Confessions of a Gas-Man* (London, 1977)

Mayhew, Henry, *London Labour and the London Poor* (4 vols., 1861–62)

McBain, Ed, *Shotgun* (New York, 1982)

McFadden, Cyra, *The Serial: A Year in the Life Of Marin County* (New York,1977)

Meades, Jonathan, *Filthy English* (London, 1986)

Meades, Jonathan, *Peter Knows What Dick Likes* (London, 1989)

Meades, Jonathan, *Pompey* (London, 1993)

Michaels, Leonard, and Ricks, Christopher, (eds.), *The State of the Language* (Berkeley, Calif., 1980, 1990)

Middleton, Thomas & Dekker, Thomas, *The Roaring Girle, or Moll Cut-Purse* (1611)

Middleton, Thomas (?), *The Last Will and Testament of Lawrence Lucifer, The old Bachelor of Limbo ... being the Final Portion of the Black Book* (1604)

Milner, Christine and Richard, *Black Players: The World of Black Pimps* (London, 1972)

Moore, Charles, *CB Language in Great Britain* (London, 1981)

Moore, Susanne, *In the Cut* (New York, 1996)

Morgan, Seth, *Homeboy* (London, 1990)

Morrison, Arthur, *A Child of the Jago* (London, 1896)

Morrison, Arthur, *Tales of Mean Streets* (London, 1894)

Mortimer, John, *Rumpole and the Golden Thread* (New York, 1984)

Morton, James, *Lowspeak: A Dictionary of Criminal and Sexual Slang* (London, 1989)

Mowry, Jess, *Way Past Cool* (London, 1992)

Mowry, Jess, *Six Out Seven* (London, 1993)

Munro, Pamela, *Slang U: The Official Dictionary of College Slang* (New York, 1989)

Neaman, Judith S., and Silver, Carole G., *Kind Words: A Dictionary of Euphemisms* (New York, 1984)

Neville, Richard, *Hippie Hippie Shake* (London, 1996)

Newland, Courttia, *The Scholar* (London, 1997)

Newman, G. F., *A Detective's Tale* (London, 1977)

Newman, G. F., *A Prisoner's Tale* (London, 1977)

Newman, G. F., *A Villain's Tale* (London, 1977)

Norman, Frank, *Bang to Rights* (London, 1958)

Norman, Frank, *Stand On Me* (London, 1960)

Norman, Frank, *The Guntz* (London, 1962)

Norman, Frank, *Banana Boy* (London, 1969)

O'Brien, Tim, *If I Die in a Combat Zone* (New York, 1979)

O'Hagen, Andrew, *The Missing* (London, 1995)

Office of National Drug Control Policy, *Street Terms: Drugs and the Drug Trade* (Washington DC, 1995)

Orsman, H.W., (ed.), *The Dictionary of New Zealand English* (Auckland, 1998)

Owens, Tuppy, *Sex Maniacs' Diary* (London, 1991)

The Oxford English Dictionary, 2nd edn. on CD-ROM (Oxford, 1992)

Parker, George, *Life's Painter of Variegated Characters in Public and Private Life* (1789)

Partridge, Eric, *Dictionary of Slang and Unconventional English*, 8th edn., ed. Paul Beale (London, 1984)

Partridge, Eric, *Dictionary of Slang & Unconventional English*, 2 vols., (8th edn. London, 1984)

Partridge, Eric, *A Dictionary of Catch Phrases* (2nd edn., London, 1985)

Partridge, Eric, *A Dictionary of the Underworld* (London, 1949, 1968)

Partridge, Eric, *Origins* (London, 1966)

Partridge, Eric, *Slang Yesterday and Today* (4th edn., London, 1970)

Pearce, Donn, *Cool Hand Luke* (New York, 1965)

Perry, Charles, *Portrait of a Young Man Drowning* (New York, 1963)

Phillips, Gary, *Perditon USA* (London, 1998)

Pond, Mimi, *The Valley Girl's Guide to Life* (New York, 1982)

Poston, III, Lawrence, and Stillman, Francis J., 'Notes on Campus Vocabulary', in *American Speech* magazine 49 (Alabama, 1964)

Powis, David, *The Signs of Crime* (London, 1978)

The Presidential Transcripts: The Complete Transcripts of the Nixon Tapes (New York, 1974)

Price, Richard, *The Wanderers* (Boston, Mass., 1974)

Price, Richard, *Bloodbrothers* (Boston, Mass., 1976)

Price, Richard, *The Breaks* (New York, 1983)

Price, Richard, *Freedomland* (London, 1998)

Price, Richard, *Clockers* (London, 1992)

Proffitt, Michael, (ed.), *Oxford Dictionary Dictionary Additions Series* (Oxford, 1997)

Puxley, Ray, *Cockney Rabbit: A Dick 'n' Arry of Rhyming Slang* (London, 1992)

Pynchon, Thomas, *V* (Philadelphia, Pa., 1963)

Pynchon, Thomas, *Mason and Dixon* (London, 1997)

Q., *Deadmeat* (London, 1997)

Rawson, Hugh, *A Dictionary of Invective* (London, 1991)

Rawson, Hugh, *A Dictionary of Euphemisms and Other Doubletalk* (New York, 1981)

Ready, Susan, *Private Lists* (London, 1983)

Realistic Romances (New York, n.d.)

Rechy, John, *City of Night* (New York, 1962)

Rechy, John, *Numbers* (New York, 1967)

Rechy, John, *Rushes* (New York, 1979)

Rechy, John, *Bodies and Souls* (New York, 1983)

Rechy, John, *The Sexual Outlaw* (New York, 1984)

Robins, David, *Tarnished Vision* (London, 1992)

Robins, David, and Cohen, Philip, *Knuckle Sandwich* (Harmondsworth, 1978)

Robins, David, personal communication

Rodgers, Bruce, *The Queens' Vernacular* (San Francisco, Calif., 1972)

Rodriguez, Luis J., *Always Running: Gang Days in LA* (New York, 1993)

Roger's Profanisaurus (*Viz* comic no. 87, 12/1997)

Rosenthal, Jack, *The Knowledge* (TV play, 1979)

Rosten, Leo, *The Joys of Yiddish* (New York, 1968)

Rosten, Leo, *Hooray for Yiddish!* (New York, 1984)

Rowlands, Samuel (as S.R.), *Martin Markall Beadle of Bridewell His defence and Answers to the Bellman of London* (1610)

Runyon, Damon, *Runyon On Broadway* (London, 1950)

Rushkoff, Douglas, *The Ecstasy Club* (London, 1997)

Safire, William, *Safire's Political Dictionary* (2nd edn., New York, 1978)

Safire, William, *On Language* (New York, 1980)

Safire, William, *I Stand Corrected* (New York, 1984)

Salisbury, Harrison E., *The Shook-Up Generation* (New York, 1961)

Samuel, Raphael, *East End Underworld* (London, 1981)

Sanchez, Thomas, *Hollywoodland* (London, 1981)

Sanders, Ed., *The Family: The Story of Charles Manson's Dune Buggy Attack Battalion* (New York, 1972)

Sanders, Ed., *Tales of Beatnik Glory* (New York, 1978)

Sante, Luc, *Low Life* (New York, 1991)

Saunders, George, *CivilWarLand in Bad Decline* (London, 1996)

Schulberg, Budd, *What Makes Sammy Run?* (New York, 1941)

Schulberg, Budd, *On the Waterfront* (London, 1956)

Scott-Heron, Gil, *The Vulture* (New York, 1970)

Sculatti, Gene, *Cool: A Hipsters Dictionary* (London, 1983)

Seale, Bobby, *Seize the Time* (New York, 1970)

Selby, Jr. Hubert, *Last Exit to Brooklyn* (New York, 1964)

Shadwell, Thomas, *The Squire of Alsatia* (1688)

Shakur, Sanyika, *Monster: The Autobiography of an L.A. Gang Member* (New York, 1993)

Share, Bernard, *Slanguage: A Dictionary of Irish Slang* (Dublin, 1997)

Sharpe, Tom, *Wilt* (London, 1976)

Sharpe, Tom, *Vintage Stuff* (London, 1982)

Sheidlower, Jess, (ed.), *The F Word* (New York, 1995)

Shenk, David, and Silberman, Steve, *Skeleton Key: A Dictionary for Deadheads* (New York, 1994)

Shulman, Alix Kates, *On the Stroll* (New York, 1981)

Sillitoe, Alan, *The Loneliness of the Long-Distance Runner* (London, 1959)

Silva Penny, (ed.), *A Dictionary of South African English on Historical Principles* (Oxford, 1996)

Simes, Gary, *A Dictionary of Australian Underworld Slang* (Melbourne, 1993)

Simmons, Donald C., 'Some Special Terms Used in a U. of Connecticut Men's Dormitory', in *American Speech* magazine 49 (Alabama, 1969)

Simmons, Herbert, *Corner Boy* (New York, 1957)

Simpson, John, and Weiner, Edmund, (eds.), *Oxford English Dictionary Additions Series* vols. 1–2 (Oxford, 1993)

Skeat, W. W., *Etymological Dictionary of the English Language* (Oxford, 1879–82)

Slim, Iceberg, (Robert Beck), *Pimp* (New York, 1969)

Smitherman, Geneva, *Black Talk* (Boston, Mass., 1994)

Southern, Terry, and Hoffenberg, Mason, *Candy* (London, 1968)

Southern, Terry, *Red Dirt Marijuana & Other Tastes* (New York,1971)

Spears, Richard, *Slang & Euphemism* (New York, 1981)

Spears, Richard, *The Slang and Jargon of Drugs and Drink* (London, 1986)

Stanley, Julia P., 'Homosexual Slang', in *American Speech* magazine 45. (Alabama, 1970)

Stockley, David, *Drug Warning* (London, 1992)

Stone, Robert, *Dog Soldiers* (New York, 1975)

Tarantino, Quentin, *Reservoir Dogs* (film script, 1994)

Tarantino, Quentin, *Natural Born Killers* (film script, 1995)

Tempest, Paul, *The Lag's Lexicon* (London, 1950)

Teresa, Vincent, 'A Mafioso Cases the Mafia Craze', in *The Crime Society*, ed. by Francis Ianni and Elizabeth Rheuss-Ianni (New York, 1976)

Thelwell, Michael, *The Harder They Come* (London, 1980)

Thompson, Hunter S., *Hells Angels* (London, 1966)

Thompson, Jim, *Now and On Earth* (New York, 1942)

Thompson, Jim, *Heed the Thunder* (New York, 1946)

Thompson, Jim, *A Swell-Looking Babe* (New York, 1954)

Thompson, Jim, *Texas by the Tail* (New York, 1965)

Thompson, Jim, *South of Heaven* (New York, 1967)

Thompson, Jim, *Four Novels* (London, 1983)

Tosches, Nick, *Trinities* (New York, 1994)

Underwood, Gary, 'Razorback Slang', in *American Speech* magazine 51 (Alabama, 1976)

Uris, Leon, *Battle Cry* (New York, 1953)

Usborne, Richard, *Wodehouse at Work to the End* (London, 1977)

Vachss, Andrew, *Flood* (New York, 1985)

Vachss, Andrew, *Strega* (New York, 1987)

Vachss, Andrew, *Blue Belle* (New York, 1988)

Vachss, Andrew, *Hard Candy* (New York, 1989)

Vachss, Andrew, *Blossom* (New York, 1990)

Vachss, Andrew, *Sacrifice* (New York, 1991)

Vachss, Andrew, *Born Bad* (New York, 1994)

Vachss, Andrew, *Footsteps of the Hawk* (New York, 1995)

Vidal, Gore, *Duluth* (New York, 1983)

Vizinczey, Stephen, *An Innocent Millionaire* (London, 1983)

Walker, Gilbert (?), *A Manifest Detection of the most vile and detestable use of Dice-play, and other practices like the same ...* (1552)

Ward, Ned, *The London Spy* (1700) (London 1924)

Ware, J., *Redding Passing English of the Victorian Era* (London, 1909)

Waterhouse, Keith, *In the Mood* (London, 1983)

Webb, James, *Fields of Fire* (New York, 1979)

Webster's Third New International Dictionary (New York, 1966)

Weekley, Ernest, *Etymological Dictionary of Modern English* (London, 1921)

Weinreb, Ben and Hibbert, Christopher, (eds.) *The London Encyclopedia* (London, 1983)

Welsh, Irvine, *Trainspotting* (London, 1993)

Welsh, Irvine, *The Acid House* (London, 1994)

Welsh, Irvine, *Marabou Stork Nightmares* (London, 1995)

Welsh, Irvine, *Ecstasy* (London, 1996)

Welsh, Irvine, *Filth* (London, 1998)

Wentworth, Harold, and Flexner, Stuart Berg, *Dictionary of American Slang* (2nd Supplemental edn., New York, 1975)

Whitcomb, Ian, *Rock Odyssey: A Musician's Chronicle of the Sixties* (New York, 1983)

White, Edmund, *States of Desire* (New York, 1983)

Wilkes, G. A., *A Dictionary of Australian Colloquialisms* (London, 1978)

Wilkinson, Tony, *Down & Out* (London, 1981)

Willocks, Tim, *Bloodstained Kings* (London, 1995)

Willocks, Tim, *Green River Rising* (London, 1994)

Wodehouse, P. G., *The Pothunters* (London 1915)

Wodehouse, P. G., *My Man Jeeves* (London, 1919)

Wodehouse, P. G., *The Inimitable Jeeves* (London, 1923)

Wodehouse, P. G., *Very Good, Jeeves* (London, 1930)

Wodehouse, P. G., *Right Ho, Jeeves* (London, 1934)

Wodehouse, P. G., *Thank You, Jeeves* (London, 1934)

Wodehouse, P. G., *Young Men in Spats* (London, 1936)

Wodehouse, P. G., *The Code of the Woosters* (London, 1938)

Wodehouse, P. G., *Eggs, Beans & Crumpets* (London, 1940)

Wodehouse, P. G., *Joy in the Morning* (London, 1947)

Wodehouse, P. G., *The Mating Season* (London, 1949)

Wodehouse, P. G., *Jeeves in the Offing* (London, 1960)

Wodehouse, P. G., *Performing Flea* (London, 1961)

Wodehouse, P. G., *A Pelican at Blandings* (London, 1969)

Wodehouse, P. G., *The Girl in Blue* (London, 1970)

Wodehouse, P. G., *Much Obliged, Jeeves* (London, 1971)

Wodehouse, P. G., *Pearls, Girls & Monty Bodkin* (London, 1972)

Wodehouse, P. G., *Aunts Aren't Gentlemen* (London, 1974)

Wodehouse, P. G., *Carry On, Jeeves* (New York, 1975)

Wolfe, Tom, *The Kandy-Kolored Tangerine Flake Streamline Baby* (New York, 1965)

Wolfe, Tom, *The Pump House Gang* (New York, 1968)

Wolfe, Tom, *The Electric Kool-Aid Acid Test* (New York, 1969)

Wolfe, Tom, *Radical Chic & Mau-Mauing the Flak-Catchers* (New York, 1970)

Wolfe, Tom, *Mauve Gloves & Madmen, Clutter & Vine* (New York, 1976)

Wolfe, Tom, *The Right Stuff* (New York, 1979)

Wolfe, Tom, *In Our Time* (London, 1980)

Wolfe, Tom, *From Bauhaus to Our House* (New York, 1981)

Woods, Paula L., (ed.), *Spooks, Spies & Private Eyes* (London, 1996)

Wright, Peter, *Cockney Dialect & Slang* (London, 1981)

Comics and Cartoon Strips

Big Ass Comics (San Francisco, 1969)

Dreams of Love (New York, n.d.)

Greaser Comics (San Francisco, 1972)

Humphries, Barry, *Barry McKenzie*, cartoon strip in *Private Eye* (London, 1963–79)

Laugh in the Dark (Berkeley, Calif., 1971)

Motor City Comics (San Francisco, Calif., 1969)

The People's Comic (San Francisco, Calif., 1972)

San Francisco Comic Book 2 & 3 (San Francisco, Calif., 1970)

Tidy, Bill, *The Cloggies*, cartoon strip, in *Private Eye* (London, n.d.)

Tuff Shit Comics (Berkeley, 1972)

Newspapers and Magazines

American Speech magazine (University of Alabama Press)

Daily Express

Daily Mail

Daily Mirror

Daily Star

Daily Telegraph

Financial Times

Guardian

Hip Hop Connection

Independent on Sunday

Mail on Sunday

News of the World

Observer

RapPages magazine (1992–)

The Source

(Evening) Standard

Sun

Sunday Express

Sunday Mirror

Sunday People

Sunday Telegraph

Sunday Times

The Times

Trace

Twilite Zone magazine (New York, 1980)

Vibe

Records, Film, and Television

Coolio, *It Takes a Thief* (album, 1994)

Credit to the Nation, *Take Dis* (album, 1994)

Cypress Hill, *Black Sunday* (album, 1993)

Dr Dre and Snoop Doggy Dogg, *Murder Was the Case* (album, 1994)

Dread, Judge, 'Big Eight' (song)

Electro: Compilation Series 1–17 (1980+)

G., Warren, *Regulate ... G Funk Era* (album, 1994)

Griffiths, Leon, 'The Bengal Tiger', TV script (London, 1979)

House of Pain, *House of Pain* (album, 1993)

House of Pain, *Same As It Ever Was* (album, 1994)

Ice T, *Rhyme Pays* (album, 1987)

Ice T, *Power* (album, 1988)

Ice T, *OG: Original Gangster* (album, 1991)

Ice T, *VI* (album, 1996)

Kool G Rap, *4-5-6* (album, 1995)

Luniz, *Operation Stackola* (album, 1996)

Notorious Big, *Ready To Die* (album, 1995)

Payne, Andrew, *Dream House*, TV script (London, 1979)

Performance, film, directed by Nicholas Roeg; produced by Donald Cammell (London, 1970)

Snoop Doggy Dogg, *Pound Dogg Food* (album, 1995)

You Need Hands, TV script (London, 1981)

Waits, Tom, *Small Change* (album, London, 1976)

Wu Tang Clan, *Enter the Wu Tang* (album, 1993)

World Wide Web

The Alternative English Dictionary, http://www.notam.uio.no/~hcholm/altlang/ht/English.html

Aussie Strine & Kiwi Slang Guide, hhtp://www.heiniger.com/english/support_slang.html

The Book of Jive (January 1997), http://www-scf.usc.edu/~vanderpo/J.html

College Slang Dictionary (Jennifer Doyle: jmdoyle@phoenix.princeton.edu)

Cyberbraai: South African By Neil Lurssen, http://www.cyberbraai.com

College research slang project, http://www.intranet.csupomona.edu/~jasanders/slang/project.html

Dalzell, Tom, Flappers to Rappers, http://www.m-w.com/flappers/flaphome.htm

Denning, Chris, Polari Dictionary, http://www.cygnet.co.uk/~cdenning/

Dictionary of Gay Slang (1997), slang@gaymart.com

Drug Related Street Terms/Slang Words, http://www.addictions.org/slang.htm

Dunn, Jerry, Dictionary of Gambling Slang, jerryd@rain.org

Larry's Aussie Slang and Phrase Dictionary, http://www.qu.edu.aus/~zzlroid/slang.html

Maledicta Press, http://hermes.ucd.ie/~artspgs/mal/index.html

Mobspeak Glossary, http://www.gotti.com/glossary.html

Quinion, Michael B., World Wide Words, http:www.quinion.demon.co.uk/words

Sweary Marys Dictionary of Filth, http://www.viz.co.uk/swear/swear.htm

Twists, Slugs and Roscoes: a Glossary of Hardboiled Slang, by William Denton, http://www.vex.net/~buff/slang.html

Totally Unofficial Rap Dictionary, http://www.sci.kun.nl.thalia/rapdict/